I RECOMMEND LEONARD MALTIN'S GUIDE, WHICH HAS BECOME STANDARD.
—*Roger Ebert's Video Companion*

Summer blockbusters and independent sleepers; masterworks of Alfred Hitchcock, Billy Wilder, and Martin Scorsese; the timeless comedy of the Marx Brothers and Buster Keaton; animated classics from Walt Disney and Pixar; the finest foreign films ever made. This 2012 edition is loaded with the films you can't afford to miss—and those you can—from box-office smashes to cult classics to forgotten gems to forgettable bombs, listed alphabetically, and complete with all the essential information you could ask for.

"**THE BEST** of the bunch." —*San Francisco Examiner & Chronicle*

"**THE BEST** all-purpose video guide." —*New York Daily News*

"**THE BEST** organized . . . the most complete." —*Newsday*

- Date of release, running time, director, stars, MPAA ratings, color or black and white
- Concise summary, capsule review, and four-star-to-BOMB rating system
- Precise information on films shot in widescreen format
- Symbols for DVDs, videos, and laserdiscs
- Completely updated index of leading actors
- Up-to-date list of mail-order and online sources for buying and renting DVDs and videos

LEONARD MALTIN'S MOVIE GUIDE

"INDISPENSABLE."—*The New York Post*
"INCH FOR INCH, DOLLAR FOR DOLLAR, MALTIN'S BOOK GIVES YOU THE MOST."
—*Boston Sunday Herald*

"The mother of all video guides and **THE FIRST TO BUY**."
—*Louisville Courier Journal*

"The **DEFINITIVE** source of information."
—*The Cleveland Plain Dealer*

"Easily **THE MOST COMPREHENSIVE** book of its kind anywhere. It belongs next to every TV and VCR in every home." —*USA Today*

LEONARD MALTIN'S

MOVIE GUIDE

2012 Edition

Edited by Leonard Maltin

MANAGING EDITOR
Darwyn Carson

ASSOCIATE EDITOR
Luke Sader

CONTRIBUTING EDITORS
Mike Clark
Rob Edelman
Spencer Green
Pete Hammond
Joe Leydon
Michael Scheinfeld
Bill Warren

VIDEO EDITOR
Casey St. Charnez

CONTRIBUTORS
Jerry Beck
Jessie Maltin

A PLUME BOOK

791.43
MAL

PLUME
Published by the Penguin Group
Penguin Group (USA) Inc., 375 Hudson Street, New York, New York 10014, U.S.A. • Penguin Group (Canada), 90 Eglinton Avenue East, Suite 700, Toronto, Ontario, Canada M4P 2Y3 (a division of Pearson Penguin Canada Inc.) • Penguin Books Ltd., 80 Strand, London WC2R 0RL, England • Penguin Ireland, 25 St. Stephen's Green, Dublin 2, Ireland (a division of Penguin Books Ltd.) • Penguin Group (Australia), 250 Camberwell Road, Camberwell, Victoria 3124, Australia (a division of Pearson Australia Group Pty. Ltd.) • Penguin Books India Pvt. Ltd., 11 Community Centre, Panchsheel Park, New Delhi – 110 017, India • Penguin Group (NZ), 67 Apollo Drive, Rosedale, Auckland 0632, New Zealand (a division of Pearson New Zealand Ltd.) • Penguin Books (South Africa) (Pty.) Ltd., 24 Sturdee Avenue, Rosebank, Johannesburg 2196, South Africa

Penguin Books Ltd., Registered Offices: 80 Strand, London WC2R 0RL, England

First published by Plume, a member of Penguin Group (USA) Inc.

First Printing, September 2011
10 9 8 7 6 5 4 3 2 1

LEONARD MALTIN is one of the country's most respected film historians and critics. He presides over www.leonardmaltin.com, part of the indieWIRE blog network, and publishes a quarterly newsletter for old-movie buffs called *Leonard Maltin's Movie Crazy*. After establishing himself with a series of definitive books on topics ranging from cinematographers to the history of animated cartoons, he became known to an even wider audience on television's *Entertainment Tonight*, where he has worked since 1982. He also hosts the weekly program *Maltin on Movies* on ReelzChannel and introduces movies on Comcast. For three years he cohosted the movie review show *Hot Ticket*, and for six years served as film critic for *Playboy* magazine. His books include *Leonard Maltin's Classic Movie Guide*, *The Great American Broadcast*, *Leonard Maltin's Family Film Guide*, *Of Mice and Magic: A History of American Animated Cartoons*, *The Great Movie Comedians*, *The Disney Films*, *The Art of the Cinematographer*, *Movie Comedy Teams*, *Selected Short Subjects (The Great Movie Shorts)*, *The Whole Film Sourcebook*, *Leonard Maltin's Movie Encyclopedia*, and (as coauthor) *The Little Rascals: The Life and Times of Our Gang*. He teaches at the University of Southern California School of Cinematic Arts, and served for two years as president of the Los Angeles Film Critics Association. As a member of the National Film Preservation Board, he votes on the twenty-five films named each year to join the National Film Registry. In 2006 he was named by the Librarian of Congress to join the Board of Directors of the National Film Preservation Foundation. For nine years he was the editor and publisher of *Film Fan Monthly*; his articles have appeared in *The New York Times*, *The Los Angeles Times*, *The Times* (of London), *Premiere*, *Smithsonian*, *TV Guide*, *Variety*, *Esquire*, *Disney Magazine*, *Film Comment*, and *Cowboys & Indians*. He is also a contributor to Oxford University's *Dictionary of American Biography*. He has been a Guest Curator for the Department of Film at the Museum of Modern Art in New York City, and for nine years was a member of the faculty of the New School for Social Research. He has written a number of television specials, including *Added Attractions: The Hollywood Shorts Story*, and hosted and coproduced the popular DVD series *Walt Disney Treasures*. He has appeared on many other DVDs, and has produced, written, and hosted such cable TV and home-video programs as *Cartoon Madness: The Fantastic Max Fleischer Cartoons*, *Young Duke: The Making of a Movie Star* (which debuted on A&E's *Biography*), *Cliffhangers: Adventures from the Thrill Factory*, *The Making of "The Quiet Man,"* *The Making of "High Noon,"* *The Lost Stooges*, and *Cartoons for Big Kids*. He and his wife, Alice, are the proud parents of Jessica Bennett Maltin, who continues to solve riddles of popular culture and new media for both of them.

About the Editors

DARWYN CARSON has worked in the film industry for over fifteen years, as an actress (the prostitute who kills in *True Confessions*, the African mom with nothing to wear—literally—when meeting her adopted son in *North*, and her personal favorite, a conniving Romulan Tal Shiar Captain in a *Star Trek: DS9* episode), as an assistant to the justly esteemed Sidney Poitier, and as a professional print and online journalist/essayist (hi there, Zap2It.com readers!). She strove to bounce and weave her way through this—her third—year on *Leonard Maltin's Movie Guide*, with an acquired nimble agility and continues to view her fellow editors and Main Man Maltin (without whom she wouldn't be standing) with great respect and "not in Kansas, anymore" wonderment.

LUKE SADER was introduced to old movies by his father. He majored in English at Johns Hopkins University, then went backpacking abroad for a year, catching movies everywhere from Helsinki to Cairo. Since starting his television career at CBS News, he has held various producing positions at *Entertainment Tonight*, CNN, *Politically Incorrect with Bill Maher*, *The Wayne Brady Show*, and PBS' *Tavis Smiley*. He served as coeditor of *Leonard Maltin's Movie Encyclopedia*, and his film and book reviews appear in *The Hollywood Reporter* and *Quarterly Review of Film and Video*. Luke has also headed the jury at the Palm Beach International Film Festival.

MIKE CLARK writes the weekly "Mike's Picks" column/blog for *Home Media* magazine and before that spent twenty-five years at *USA Today* as both senior film critic and home viewing columnist for 1,275 consecutive weeks. After winning $16,000 at age ten in 1958 for his movie prowess on *The $64,000 Question*, he completed all course work at NYU's Graduate School of Cinema, was film critic for the *Detroit Free Press*, and director/program planner of the American Film Institute Theater in Washington, D.C. He has appeared on HBO, Cinemax, *Entertainment Tonight*, E! Entertainment, CNN's *Reliable Sources*, and Turner Classic Movies. He is a member of the National Society of Film Critics.

ROB EDELMAN has, for over the past decade, taught film history courses at the University at Albany (SUNY). He offers film commentary on WAMC (Northeast) Public Radio, and his work may be found on the WAMC Web site. He presents lectures in the Speakers in the Humanities program, sponsored by the New York State Council for the Humanities, and has coauthored (with his wife, Audrey Kupferberg) several books, including *Matthau: A Life*; *Meet the Mertzes*, a double biography of Vivian Vance and William Frawley; and *Angela Lansbury: A Life on Stage and Screen*. He also has written *Great Baseball Films*, *Baseball on the Web* (which Amazon.com cited as a Top 10 Internet book), and several children's books (on such subjects as Watergate and the Vietnam War), and is the editor of *Issues on Trial: Freedom of the Press* and a Contributing Editor of *Leonard Maltin's Classic Movie Guide*, *Leonard Maltin's Family Film Guide*, and *Leonard Maltin's Movie Encyclopedia*. His byline has appeared in many reference books (including *A Political*

Companion to American Film, Total Baseball, International Dictionary of Films and Filmmakers, The Total Baseball Catalog, Women Filmmakers and Their Films, Baseball and American Culture: Across the Diamond, and St. James Encyclopedia of Popular Culture) and dozens of periodicals (from American Film and Base Ball: A Journal of the Early Game to Variety and The Washington Post). He was director of programming for Home Film Festival and programmed film series at the American Film Institute; he authored an essay on early baseball films for the Kino International DVD Reel Baseball: Baseball Films from the Silent Era, 1899–1926; is an interviewee on several documentaries on the director's cut DVD of The Natural; and has been a juror at the National Baseball Hall of Fame and Museum's annual film festival.

SPENCER GREEN's latest biography is a pulse-pounding thrill-ride! Roger Ebert gives it four stars! And Armond White says, "Its binary transgressive morality rejects bourgeois meta-pastiche agitprop!" Mr. Green has written for In Living Color, AAAHH!!! Real Monsters, Duckman, Mad TV, The Fairly Oddparents, Denis Leary's Merry F#%$in' Christmas, and Americana for BBC Radio. He was a coeditor of Leonard Maltin's Movie Encyclopedia and also edited We'll Never Be Young Again: Remembering the Last Days of John F. Kennedy. Mr. Green performs at the Los Angeles comedic writers' salon Sit 'n Spin and is coauthor/colyricist of BUKOWSI-CAL! which won Outstanding Musical at the 2007 New York International Fringe Festival. He also writes for The Huffington Post and created the parody movie Web site The Parallel Universe Film Guide at www.parallel filmguide.com. Right now, Mr. Green is thinking of a number between one and ten. (No prizes for guessing; he just wanted you to know.)

PETE HAMMOND is currently film critic for Boxoffice magazine and Boxoffice.com, as well as Backstage magazine and Backstage.com. He is also now Awards Columnist for Deadline.com and Movieline (previously it was the Los Angeles Times/"The Envelope"). He served as film critic for Hollywood.com and for Maxim magazine for three years and was a frequent contributor to Variety. He is in his twelfth year as host of the KCET Cinema Series in Los Angeles, and has been a moderator for the Variety Screening Series and UCLA Extension's Sneak Preview. He has hosted panels at AFI Fest, the Santa Barbara Film Festival, Mill Valley Film Festival, CineVegas, San Francisco Film Festival, and Cannes Film Festival, and has interviewed top stars and filmmakers at screenings for such groups as SAG, DGA, BAFTA, and WGA. He has held talent producing positions at Entertainment Tonight, Access Hollywood, The Arsenio Hall Show, The Martin Short Show, and the AMC network. He is the recipient of five Emmy nominations for his TV writing and is the winner of the 1996 Publicists Guild of America's Press Award. He serves on the Board of Governors for the Academy of Television Arts & Sciences representing writers.

JOE LEYDON recently marked his twenty-first anniversary as a film critic for Variety and his eleventh as an adjunct professor at Houston Community College and the University of Houston's Jack J. Valenti School of Communication. He also is a blogger at MovingPictureBlog.blogspot.com, a contributing writer for Houston.CultureMap.com and *MovieMaker* and *Cowboys & Indians* magazines, a Q&A host at the Nashville and Denver film festivals and Cinema Arts Festival Houston, and author of the book *Joe Leydon's Guide to Essential Movies You Must See*. From 1982 until 1995, he was film critic for *The Houston Post*. More recently, he has reviewed films for *The San Francisco Examiner*, MSNBC.com, NBC affiliate KPRC-TV, and *The Houston Press*. Leydon also has written for *The New York Daily News*, *Los Angeles Times*, *Newsday*, *The Boston Globe*, *The Toronto Star*, *The (Nashville) Tennessean* and *The Shreveport Times*. He is the proud father of George Leydon (who is an upstanding young man because he takes after his mother, Anne Leydon) and the reluctant co-owner of three moody cats named Snowball, Little O, and Little Z.

MICHAEL SCHEINFELD is currently a writer for HBO GO and MAX GO. He served as Senior Writer for *TV Guide* for two decades, where he wrote the "Classic Movies" column and a DVD review column, as well as film reviews for both the magazine and the Web site. He also served as Contributing Editor of *Leonard Maltin's Classic Movie Guide* and *Leonard Maltin's Family Film Guide*. He wrote essays for the "City Secrets" book *Movies: The Ultimate Insider's Guide*, and has written for several other books and magazines, including *The Motion Picture Guide*, *The Virgin Film Guide*, *The 500 Best British and Foreign Films*, *Films in Review*, *Laserviews*, and *Trump World* magazine. He has also done work for American Movie Classics and MTV Films, and has produced and programmed film series for cable TV channels in Manhattan and Philadelphia.

BILL WARREN is the author of the two-volume *Keep Watching the Skies: Science Fiction Movies of the 1950s*, which was recently republished in an expanded edition; you can find it at Amazon.com. He also wrote *Set Visits*, comprised of interviews conducted on movie sets, and *The Evil Dead Companion*. He has written for such magazines as *Starlog*, *Fangoria*, *American Film*, *Video Watchdog*, and *Galaxy Online*. He contributed to *The New Encyclopedia of Science Fiction*, several books on Stephen King, and the annual Science Fiction Writers of America Nebula Award volumes. Without being able to speak much more French than *film noir* and *pommes frites*, for ten years he was the Hollywood correspondent for the French television show *Destination Series*. He is a frequent speaker at science-fiction conventions. He likes dogs, cats, monster movies, folk music, his wife, and Hawaii, not necessarily in that order.

CASEY ST. CHARNEZ is overeducated, with a Ph.D. from NYU, plus an M.A. in Cinema Studies, and an M.A. in English literature and comparative mythology. A former publicity associate with Paramount and Fox, he has written for *Film Fan Monthly* and *American Film*, and was a stringer for *The Hollywood Reporter*. A film critic for TV, radio, newspapers, and both print and online magazines, he is also the author of *The Complete Films of Steve McQueen*, and contributed an endword about Greer Garson to *100 Years: A Celebration of Filmmaking in New Mexico*. He continues to waltz with his favorite strawberry blonde, Lisa Suzonne Harris, and wonders if he'll ever have time to finish that kiss-and-tell about all the Maltin editors.

Introduction to 2012 Edition

We live in an age of contradictions. "Young people" don't care about movies anymore, especially in theaters, yet in its opening weekend this spring, *Fast Five* made $83 million in the U.S. and Canada alone. (I don't think there were many senior citizens standing in line to see it.) There is "no money" to fund independent films, we're told, yet hundreds of them still get made every year. "Nobody" is going to see them, yet distributors continue to bid against each other for rights to the cream of the crop.

The survival of this *Guide* in the Internet age is yet another contradiction. It says that some of us—including people like me who use a computer every day—still like the tactile experience of looking something up in a book. I feel impelled to add that I have nothing against the 'net. What's more, I'm proud of the electronic version of our book that exists as an app for iPhones and iPads. I see nothing wrong with loving books and using new media as well. Where is it written that we have to choose one over the other exclusively?

Yet that seems to be the mind-set of many people who stand to gain by giving technology the upper hand. Major movie studios are forcing theater owners to adopt digital projection and toss their sturdy 35mm projectors onto the scrap heap. We'll see if the new, expensive digital machines last a fraction as long as those iron horses, some of which have been in service for fifty to seventy-five years. The only sure thing about technology is that it is subject to change, if not outright obsolescence. (Does anybody still store their information on five-inch floppy discs?)

The only point old-media and new-media people seem to agree on is the ongoing need for content. That word has a broader definition than ever before: it can refer to a reference book like ours, a cutting-edge video game, or an old detective movie. The challenge is identifying worthwhile content and seeing that it reaches its intended audience.

That is one reason so many micro-indie film distributors have gone into business, including major festivals like Sundance, South by Southwest, and TriBeCa, which have launched outreach programs. They know they can reach a much wider audience by streaming films online than they can from a handful of screenings on their home turf. The next step is persuading potential viewers that their films are worth seeking out (and paying for).

The proliferation of small-scale features and documentaries from here and abroad has made our task that much more difficult. We can't track every single film that shows its face, however briefly, although we've added as many as possible this year. As it is, we've had to move a number of older titles from these pages to our companion volume, *Leonard Maltin's Classic Movie Guide.* After some forty years of maintaining old and new movies side by side, we have simply run out of room. Naturally, we have kept as many as possible—you'll never be without a write-up for *The Wizard of Oz* or *Roman Holiday*—but a great many others are now exclusively reviewed in the *Classic Guide.* We also had to sacrifice our Directors' Index, rather than slash another 150 titles from this edition. You just can't fit twenty pounds of potatoes into a ten-pound sack, although we did our best while bursting at the seams for a long, long time.

Based on feedback from our readers, we believe we still have a mission to fulfill for passionate movie lovers. If you go online to find out who costars with Matt Damon and Emily Blunt in *The Adjustment Bureau*, you'll be confronted with an avalanche of names like Florence Kastriner and Phyllis MacBryde. No offense to those actresses, but they probably aren't the ones you're looking for: they appear at the top of many cast lists because they're cited in order of appearance on-screen. You have to scroll way down to find Anthony Mackie, John Slattery, or Terence Stamp. Having seen these movies, we try to compile the most *useful* cast list possible, and we usually stick with "billing order."

And yes, we're still making corrections and changes to existing entries, even after some of them have sat undisturbed for decades. Alert readers who submit spelling corrections of actors' names or different running times or any number of other notes send us scurrying to confirm that information before we make the appropriate alterations. (What did we do before DVDs made so many films easily accessible?)

To us, the material in this book isn't merely "content." Each entry represents a movie, and we love movies. That's why cable or satellite channels that show older films in the wrong aspect ratio—or restaurants and bars that don't press the "format" button on their remote control and allow old movies to be stretched out to the wide proportions of their new TV sets—drive us crazy.

To work on this book you have to be a little crazy—crazy about films and crazy, period. Who else would spend hours checking the exact punctuation of a movie title or clocking a running time against the printed information on a DVD package? The first time I worked on this book I learned that the more people who check each entry, the better off I'd be. Over the years I've leaned on my stalwart team and they've never let me down. That's why I owe so much to Luke Sader, Spencer Green, Rob Edelman, Bill Warren, Mike Clark, Michael Scheinfeld, Joe Leydon, Pete Hammond, Casey St. Charnez, Jerry Beck, and Jessie Maltin. Their combined expertise and enthusiasm make this annual venture possible. No one works harder than Darwyn Carson, who juggles an infinite number of details and deadlines—not to mention a varied group of personalities in our ranks—with humor and aplomb.

In addition to faithful readers who send in corrections, I rely on such experts as Tom Weaver, Bruce Goldstein, and George Feltenstein to keep us as accurate as possible. They are all generous with their time and knowledge.

In this book's fifth decade of publication, I am especially grateful for the publishing professionals who oversee its journey to completion: Hugh Rawson, Bill Harris, Ken May, and Kathy Murray. I must add a special thank-you to my always-supportive boss at Penguin, Kara Welsh.

This year, and every year, I share my moviegoing adventures with my wife, Alice, and daughter, Jessie, without whom the process wouldn't be nearly as much fun. We love watching films together and debating them afterward, though we all agreed that seeing *Seven Brides for Seven Brothers* on a big screen at the 2011 TCM Classic Film Festival—following my conversation with its star, Jane Powell—was an experience we couldn't top this year.

When the going gets tough, as it always does at some point during our preparation for this *Movie Guide*, all it takes is running into someone who tells me that he or she relies on our book and consults it often. I always reply that a compliment like that has real meaning to me, and I'm not kidding. This book couldn't exist in a vacuum: it depends on an active partnership with you, our readers. Thanks so much for your loyalty.

—LEONARD MALTIN

Key to This Book

Alphabetization: Articles of speech—A, An, The—are eliminated (*The Dinner Game* is listed under *Dinner Game, The*). Aside from that, film titles are listed in strict letter-by-letter spelling sequence. Separation of words and punctuation are ignored; everything hinges on the letters. So, *Darker Than Amber* is listed before *Dark of the Sun* because "e" comes before "o." The exception to this rule is sequels, which we cluster in numerical order (*Scream, Scream 2,* etc.) for the reader's convenience. Titles that begin with *Mister* or *Doctor* will come before titles abbreviated *Mr.* or *Dr.* Let the alphabet be your guide, letter-by-letter, and you'll find the titles you're looking for.

Each entry lists title and year of theatrical release in a film's country of origin. (This doesn't include film festival exposure; a film may languish for one or more years before coming to theaters, by which time it might be trimmed and even bear a different name.) The letter "C" before a running time indicates that the film was made in color. "D:" indicates the name of the director. This is followed by a listing of the principal cast members. Alternate titles (if any) are noted at the end of the entry.

Ratings range from ✱✱✱✱, for the very best, down to ✱½. There is no ✱ rating; instead, for bottom-of-the-barrel movies, we use the citation BOMB.

▼ This symbol indicates the title is available on videocassette;
● indicates laserdisc availability;
◗ indicates DVD availability.

(These symbols indicate that a film has been released at one time; we cannot guarantee current availability.)

The MPAA rates with the following symbols:

G   General Audiences: All ages admitted.
PG   Parental Guidance Suggested: Some material may not be suit-
        able for children.
PG-13   Parents Strongly Cautioned: Some material may be inappro-
        priate for children under 13.
R   Restricted: Children under 17 require accompanying parent or
        adult guardian.
NC-17   No Children Under 17 Admitted (age may vary in certain
        areas).

The rating symbols GP, M, and X are no longer used to classify films.

Leonard Maltin's Favorite Films of the New Millennium

I'm not a great fan of lists, but I know people enjoy them—if only to argue with the list maker's choices. This particular list is arbitrary and highly personal; it's also incomplete, as there are many other good films I could cite. But these are the ones that resonate with me: an eclectic mixture of mainstream movies, Oscar winners, documentaries, and indie films. I think they're all worth watching and revisiting.

Amélie (2001)
Songcatcher (2001)
Startup.com (2001)
No Man's Land (2001)
Adaptation. (2002)
City of God (2002)
Talk to Her (2002)
About Schmidt (2002)
The Pianist (2002)
Road to Perdition (2002)
Lost in Translation (2003)
Finding Nemo (2003)
American Splendor (2003)
My Architect (2003)
The Barbarian Invasions (2003)
The Station Agent (2003)
Whale Rider (2003)
The Lord of the Rings: The
    Return of the King (2003)
Big Fish (2003)
The Fog of War (2003)
Spellbound (2003)
Born Into Brothels (2004)
The Motorcycle Diaries (2004)
Sideways (2004)
The Sea Inside (2004)
Million Dollar Baby (2004)
Downfall (2004)
Spider-Man 2 (2004)
Brothers (2004)
A History of Violence (2005)
Paradise Now (2005)
Syriana (2005)
The Squid and the Whale (2005)
Grizzly Man (2005)
The Queen (2006)
The Lives of Others (2006)
Little Children (2006)
Flags of Our Fathers (2006)
Children of Men (2006)
Pan's Labyrinth (2006)
Little Miss Sunshine (2006)

Juno (2007)
Waitress (2007)
No Country for Old Men (2007)
Into the Wild (2007)
Away From Her (2007)
Grindhouse (2007)
Once (2007)
Enchanted (2007)
The Diving Bell and the Butterfly
    (2007)
There Will Be Blood (2007)
The Curious Case of Benjamin
    Button (2008)
Slumdog Millionaire (2008)
Frost/Nixon (2008)
Milk (2008)
Frozen River (2008)
Man on Wire (2008)
Nowhere Boy (2009)
Up in the Air (2009)
The Hangover (2009)
Up (2009)
District 9 (2009)
Fantastic Mr. Fox (2009)
The King's Speech (2010)
The Town (2010)
The Ghost Writer (2010)
Another Year (2010)
The Social Network (2010)
Tangled (2010)
Carlos (2010)
The Kids Are All Right (2010)
Of Gods and Men (2010)
In a Better World (2010)
Incendies (2010)
The Tillman Story (2010)
Inside Job (2010)
Last Train Home (2010)
The Princess of Montpensier (2010)
Please Give (2010)
Win Win (2011)
Super 8 (2011)

Mail-Order and Online Sources
for Home Video

Welcome to this twenty-second installment of our movie hunters' guide.

Though cinema delivery systems have evolved from analog to digital over these decades, still it's the film itself that remains essential to our readers. Thus, we provide this list of assorted American video vendors that may help them find their must-have motion pictures.

Remember our bargaining advice: 1. Always be cautious. 2. Look around and compare prices. 3. Wait patiently for sales. 4. Check guarantees and return policies. 5. Investigate shipping. 6. Make a copy of your order.

We continue to notate our movies with a ◗ for DVD upon availability, along with a retro ▼ for tape and ● for laserdisc.

Note: Innumerable titles are now out of print; if they were ever released, we symboled them then, and encourage you still to look for them now.

And one major heads-up: Though many titles are obtainable exclusively in Canada and abroad, our video listings are strictly U.S.A., whether in public domain or under American copyright.

So with all that in mind, let's go movie shopping, everybody!

Absolute Beta Products, POB 130, Remington, VA 22734-0130 540-439-3259
www.absolutebeta.com; absolutebeta@earthlink.net Betamax repairs, Beta VCRs, Beta accessories, Beta-to-DVD transfers. Club dues: $9.95/yr., includes discounts and quarterly catalog. Sales to U.S. consumers only. Facebook. Established 1987. *Catalogs:* free sample with SASE.

Asymmetrical Entertainment Inc., 110 Remsen St., #3C, Brooklyn Heights, NY 11201-4215 info/fax 718-237-6031; asymmvideo@aol.com
Film fans tailor personalized purchases for other film fans. All films in circulation available. Est. 1995. *Catalog:* by mail.

BBC America Shop, POB 681, Holmes, PA 19043-0681
800-898-4921, fax 610-532-9001; www.bbcamericashop.com;
customerservice@bbcamericashop.com
An Anglophile's cloud nine, full of British Broadcasting Corp. program(me)s, plus movies, music, books, gifts, collectibles, even magazines. Facebook. Est. 2003. *Catalog:* paper and online.

Best Video, 1842 Whitney Ave., Hamden, CT 06517-1405
800-727-3843, 203-287-9286, fax 203-248-4910; www.bestvideo.com
info@bestvideo.com Comprehensive Blu-ray/DVD/VHS collection for sale or rent. Classics, foreign, cult, hits, more. Web site has personality plus. Facebook. Est. 1985. *Catalog:* online.

BitTorrent, Inc., 612 Howard St. #400, San Francisco, CA 94105-3905
www.bittorrent.com Free (meaning ad-supported) downloads work on Windows, Mac, Linux, etc. They're speedy, but some movies work only on certain systems, and some are only for U.S. customers. Check Web site for details. Facebook. Est. 2001. *Catalog:* online.

B-Movie, POB 2468, Liverpool, NY 13089-2468
315-652-3868, fax 315-622-2315; www.b-movie.com
Once again, the title says it all, with a choosy DVD/VHS catalog and more, including film fests and competitions, cult newsletter. Redesigned Web site. And, hey, it shoots its own indie productions, too. Facebook. Est. 2007. *Catalog:* online.

Captain Bijou, POB 7307, Houston, TX 77248-7307
713-864-8101, fax 713-837-1463; www.captainbijou.com;
info@captainbijou.com Monster collection of scary movies, serials, B pics, Westerns, Golden Age TV. Also buys and sells posters, autographs, photos. Updated Web site. U.S. sales only. Facebook. Est. 1984. *Catalog:* online.

CinemaNow; 310-314-3000; www.cinemanow.com; sales@cinemanow.com
Digital entertainment service instantly accesses rentals or purchases. Ancillary of Best Buy. Month/year memberships. Facebook. Est. 1999. *Catalog:* online.

ClassicFlix, 800-592-6149, 916-209-8520 www.classicflix.com; Strictly pre–1970 movie and TV titles, to buy or rent, from a mom-and-pop Internet storefront that's a little different. Est. 2007. *Catalog:* online.

Columbia Classics, www.sonypictures.com/homevideo/columbiaclassics
Another Golden Age studio invites fans to pick and choose on an on-demand basis. (See also **Fox Connect** and **Warner Archive**.) Facebook. Est. 2010. *Catalog:* online.

Criterion Collection, 215 Park Ave. So., 5th floor, New York, NY 10003-1614; www.criterion.com Top-of-the-line remastering and research of noteworthy films, domestic and foreign, is this distinguished merchant's hallmark. Loyalty program for repeat Web site buyers/renters. Facebook. Est. 1984. *Catalog:* online.

Critics' Choice, POB 642, Itasca, IL 60143-0642; 800-367-7765,
fax 815-431-1252; www.ccvideo.com; vcatalog@ccvideo.com A treasure trove of DVD/VHS movies, generally in stock, including bargains, exclusives. Daily specials. Est. 1987. *Catalog: Big Book of Movies*, $7.95; free monthly mailer.

Deal Oz, www.dealoz.com Impartial search service compares new, used, and auction prices at hundreds of online sites. Main thrust is books, but movie division is handy for cost-checking current titles. Intricate search options. Est. 2006. *Catalog:* none.

Eros Entertainment Inc., 550 County Ave., Secaucus, NJ 07094-2697
201-558-9001, fax 201-558-9026; www.erosentertainment.com;
customerservice1@erosintl.com
Devotees of cinema India may buy DVDs and Blu-Rays, download music, access on-demand entertainment, even sign up for mobile content, here at Bollywood central. Facebook. Est. 1977. *Catalog:* online.

Facets, 1517 W. Fullerton Ave., Chicago, IL 60614-2096
800-532-2387, 773-281-9075, fax 773-929-5437; www.facets.org; rentals@facets.org; members@facets.org Nonprofit DVD/VHS sales and rentals of international, classic, independent, animated and art titles. Many exclusives. Unlimited rental membership plan. Facebook. Est. 1975. *Catalog:* online.

Film Movement, 109 W. 27th St. #9B, New York, NY 10001-6208
866-937-3456, fax 212-941-7812
www.filmmovement.com; info@filmmovement.com Subscribers receive curated DVDs monthly, with unique movies and bonus shorts drawn from indie film, international releases, and film fest favorites. Facebook. Est. 2003. *Catalog:* online.

Fox Connect, www.foxconnect.com 877-369-7867 Another movie studio joins the happy trend of companies offering their film libraries straight from the source. DVD, Blu-Ray, digital. Facebook. Est. 2009. *Catalog:* online.

IArtHouse, 82 Industrial Dr. #3, Northampton, MA 01060-2389
800-811-4515, 413-529-0870; fax 425-969-8132; iarthouse.com,
support@eztakes.com International cinema ready to stream, burn, buy. EZTakes.com subsidiary is currently compatible with Windows and Mac OS X. Facebook. Est. 2008. *Catalog:* online.

International Film & Video Center, POB 1012, Washington Twp., NJ 07676-
1012 201-666-6772, fax 201-664-1426;
www.IFVC.com; IFVC@IFVC.com Around-the-world sales to individuals, corporations, schools. Accent on Iranian fare, but there's plenty more for everybody. Also produces its own features and documentaries. Est. 1985. *Catalog:* none.

LaserDisc Database, www.lddb.com Buyers and sellers unite at this exhaustive haven for '80s platter-heads who are still into large movies and old music. Est. 2002. *Catalog:* online.

A Million and One World-Wide Videos, 1239 Pine Creek Dr., Woodstock,
GA 30188-4010800-849-7309, 770-227-7309;
www.wwvideos.com; worldwidevideos@comcast.net Video detectives buy, sell, trade out-of-print and rare movie and TV titles, series. Free searches. VHS-to-DVD transfers from your tapes. Facebook. Est. 1989. *Catalog:* none.

Movies Unlimited, 3015 Darnell Rd., Philadelphia, PA 19154-3201
800-466-8437, 215-637-4444, fax 215-637-2350;
www.moviesunlimited.com; movies@moviesunlimited.com World's largest video dispenser by volume, including hard-to-finds and exclusives. Colorful Web site. New collector blog at www.moviefanfare.com. Facebook. Est. 1978. *Catalog:* $14.95 (816 pages!).

NetFlix Inc., www.netflix.com; 800-715-2135 Inventor of Internet-only DVD rental. Prepaid subscriptions. Downloads, streaming, etc. Facebook. Est. 1997. *Catalog:* on-site.

Oscilloscope Laboratories, POB 20090, New York, NY 10014-9992; 212-
219-4029; www.oscilloscope.net, info@oscilloscope.net
Nifty, kicky collection of the obscure and the known. Circle of Trust members get movies a week before street date. Fun perks. Company asserts it was est. 2008 B.C. Facebook. *Catalog:* online.

PBS Home Video, POB 609, Melbourne, FL 32902-0609
800-645-4727, fax 866-274-9043; www.shoppbs.org
Interesting assortment of exactly what one expects. Sidebar site
(http://teacher.shop.pbs.org) targets educators. All proceeds go to funding programs for the Public Broadcasting Service (est. 1969!). *Catalog:* free.

Right Stuf, Inc., POB 680, Grimes, IA 50111-0680
800-338-6827, fax 515-986-1129; www.rightstuf.com; info@rightstuf.com
Japanese animation DVDs, manga/graphic novels, related merchandise. Facebook. Est. 1987. *Catalog:* online; anime print catalog $4 (refundable with first order).

Robert's Videos, 107 Tucker Crescent, Saskatoon, SK S7H 3H7 CA
800-440-2960 (in North America), 306-955-3763 (outside N.A.)
www.robertsvideos.com, robertsvideos@shaw.ca Search service for hard-to-find DVD, VHS, PAL, etc. Est. 2002. *Catalog:* online.

Sinister Cinema, POB 4369, Medford, OR 97501-0168
541-773-6860, fax 541-779-8650;
www.sinistercinema.com; scinema@qwestoffice.net Offering a terrific selection of nostalgic sci-fi, horror, B Westerns, sword-and-sandal, etc., with offbeat tapes and wayout discs for $11.95–16.95. Est. 1984. *Catalog:* free.

Snag Films, www.snagfilms.com Freebie site streams documentaries only, organized by title and topic. Films may be watched on-site or "snagged" for mobile or Facebook use. Est. 2008. *Catalog:* online.

Something Weird Video, POB 33664, Seattle, WA 98133-0664
888-634-3320, 425-290-5830, fax 425-438-1832;
www.somethingweird.com; somethingweirdvideo@comcast.net An unparalleled collection of exquisite trash. Facebook. Est. 1990. *Catalog:* $5 (over 18 only).

Turner Classic Movies, 1050 Techwood Dr. NW, Atlanta, GA 30318-5604
404-885-5535 (message only); www.tcm.com An absolute must for anyone who's ever seen a movie. Check out the sales link for discounts and the vault for exclusives. Facebook. Est. 1994. *Catalog:* in print and online.

Video Discounters, POB 1448, Jensen Beach, FL 34958-1448
772-334-4386, fax 772-334-6296;
www.videodiscounters.net; videodiscounters@comcast.net Off-market titles, primarily VHS. U.S. only. Est. 1978. *Catalog:* title/price list on request.

Video Search of Miami, POB 492768, Lawrenceville, GA 30049-0047
678-836-5838; www.vsom.com; orders@vsom.com Contemporary and classic European and Asian imports in versions otherwise unavailable in U.S. Companion company deals in domestic cult DVD. Facebook. Est. 1988. *Catalogs:* VSoM (free print, online).

VideoWest, 1312 Stagecoach Rd. SE, Albuquerque, NM 87123-4321
505-292-0049; www.westernclippings.com; boyd@westernclippings.com
Provides VHS B Westerns, serials, and TV shows. Also publishes *Western Clippings* magazine (sample issue $1 ea.). Web site easy to get lost in. Est. 1977. *Catalog:* $5.

Warner Archive, www.warnerarchive.com Buffs may raid the pre-1986 Warner Bros., MGM, RKO, and Monogram vaults for hundreds of custom DVDs or digital downloads. Facebook. Est. 2009. *Catalog:* online.

Widescreen Glossary

An aspect ratio is the relationship between the width and height of a screen image. Virtually all sound films until 1953 were 1.37 to 1, that is, slightly wider than they were tall—a modest rectangle. Since television screen size is 1.33:1, little is lost when an older movie is shown on TV. (Even films in the later standard 1.66:1 don't suffer *too* badly.)

In the 1950s, however, Hollywood's attempt to lure people away from TV and back into theaters led to a battle of screen sizes, beginning with CinemaScope, more than twice as wide as it was high.

Today, most films are 1.85:1; since this has become the norm, they are no longer thought of as "widescreen." Our listings only cite films in special widescreen processes, such as the ones below:

Actionscope—2.35:1 (same as Toeiscope)

Agascope—2.35:1 (Sweden/Hungary)

Arriscope—2.35:1 (Arriflex cameras/lenses)

ArriVision—2.35:1 (in 3-D)

Cinepanormique—2.35:1 (France)

CinemaScope—2.35:1 (some early titles 2.66:1 and 2.55:1)

CinemaScope 55—2.35:1 (55mm)

Cinerama—2.6:1 to 2.8:1

Cinescope—2.35:1 (Italy)

Clairmont-Scope—2.35:1 (Clairmont cameras/lenses)

Colorscope—AIP studios' umbrella name for various ratios

Cromoscope—2.35:1 (same as Techniscope)

Daieiscope—2.35:1 (Japan)

Digital Video Widescreen—2.35:1 (digital video photography)

Digital Widescreen—2.35:1 (computer animated films)

Dimension 150—2.2:1 (70mm)

Dimensionscope—2.35:1 (in 3-D)

Duo-Vision—2.35:1 (split-screen)

Dyaliscope—2.35:1 (France)

Euroscope—2.35:1

Franscope—2.35:1 (France)

Grandeur—2:1 approx. (70mm)

Grandscope—2.35:1 (Japan)

Hammerscope—2.35:1 (England)

HD Widescreen (High Definition 24-frames-per-second Digital Video)

J-D-C Scope—2.35:1

Megascope—2.35:1 (England)

Metroscope—1.66:1 to 2:1 (hard-matted prints or negative)

MGM Camera 65—2.75:1 (70mm; same as Ultra Panavision)

Multi(ple)-Screen—2.35:1 (split screen)

Natural Vision—2:1 approx. (63.5mm)

Naturama—2.35:1 (Republic studios)

Nikkatsu Scope—2.35:1 (Japan)

Panascope—2:1

Panavision—2.35:1 (2.4:1 from 1971)

Panavision Super 70—2.2:1 (70mm); 2.35:1 (35mm)

Panoramic(a)—1.85:1 to 2.35:1 (Italy)

Part Widescreen—some scenes in 2.35:1 format

Realife—2:1 approx. (70mm)

Regalscope—2.35:1

RKO-Scope—2.35:1 (same as SuperScope 235)

Scanoscope—2.35:1

Shawscope—2.35:1 (Hong Kong)

Sovscope/Sovscope 70—2.35:1 (U.S.S.R.)

Space-Vision—2.35:1 (in 3-D)

Spectrascope—2.35:1

StereoScope—2.35:1 (in 3-D)

Superama—2.35:1 (same as Super 35)

SuperCinescope—2.35:1 (Italy)

Superpanorama 70—2.2:1 (70mm)

Super Panavision 70—2.2:1. (70mm); 2.35:1 (35mm)

SuperScope—2:1

SuperScope 235—2.35:1 (origin of Super 35)

Super Technirama 70—2.2:1 (70 mm)

Super Techniscope—1.85:1 to 2.35:1 (same as Super 35)

Super 35—1.85:1 to 2.35:1

SuperTotalscope—2.35:1 (Italy)

System 35—1.85:1 to 2.35:1 (same as Super 35)

Technirama—2.35:1

Techniscope—2.35:1

Technovision—2.35:1 (Italy)

Todd-AO—2.2:1 (70mm)

Todd-AO 35—2.35:1 (35mm)

Toeiscope—2.35:1 (Japan)

Tohoscope—2.35:1 (Japan)

Totalscope—2.35:1 (Italy/France)

Totalvision—2.35:1

2.35 Research PLC—2.35:1

Ultra Panavision 70—2.76:1 (70mm)

Ultrascope—2.35:1 (Germany)

Univision—2:1 (aka Uinivisium)

Vistarama—2.35:1

Vistascope—2.35:1

VistaVision—1.66:1 to 2:1 (1.85:1 recommended)

Vistascope—2:1 approx. (65mm)

WarnerScope—2.35:1

Warwickscope—2.35:1 (England)

"Widescreen" means uncredited or undetermined process

Aaron Loves Angela (1975) **C-98m.** *******
D: Gordon Parks, Jr. Kevin Hooks, Irene
Cara, Moses Gunn, Robert Hooks, Ernestine Jackson, José Feliciano. New York–
made variation on Romeo and Juliet set in
Harlem, with black boy (Kevin) in love with
Puerto Rican girl (Cara). OK combination
of comedy, drama, violence, and Feliciano's music. [R] ▼

Aaron Slick From Punkin Crick SEE:
Leonard Maltin's Classic Movie Guide

Abandon (2002) **C-99m.** ****** D: Stephen
Gaghan. Katie Holmes, Benjamin Bratt,
Charlie Hunnam, Zooey Deschanel, Gabrielle Union, Gabriel Mann, Mark Feuerstein,
Melanie Jayne Lynskey, Will McCormack,
Philip Bosco, Tony Goldwyn, Fred Ward.
Police detective with a checkered past is
assigned to investigate the disappearance
of a college boy but finds himself attracted
to the missing student's girlfriend. Murky
whodunit with paranormal ingredients that,
annoyingly, don't pay off. Directing debut for the Oscar-winning screenwriter of
TRAFFIC. Super 35. [PG-13] ▼ ▶

Abandoned, The (2007-Spanish-Bulgarian-
British) **C-96m.** ****½** D: Nacho Cerdà. Anastasia Hille, Karel Roden, Valentin Ganev,
Paraskeva Djukelova, Carlos Reig-Plaza.
American adoptee gets trapped in an endless labyrinth of horror when, after receiving a mysterious invitation, she returns to
Russia to learn more about her roots. In her
dank, oppressively creepy childhood home,
she must confront various evil forces, a
murderous clone, and the disturbing secrets
of her past. Anybody looking for a coherent
narrative will find this throwback to surreal
Euro-horror films of the '70s maddening.
Fails to build fear and tension, but Cerdà
fills the screen with enough gorgeous, chilling imagery to satisfy fans of nonlinear horror fare. Super 35. [R] ▶

Abandon Ship (1957-British) **100m.** *******
D: Richard Sale. Tyrone Power, Mai Zetterling, Lloyd Nolan, Stephen Boyd, Moira
Lister, James Hayter. Tyrone is officer
suddenly in command of lifeboat holding
survivors from sunken luxury liner. Tense,
exciting study of people fighting to stay alive
while exposed to savage seas and each other.
British title: SEVEN WAVES AWAY. ▼

Abbott and Costello Go to Mars (1953)
77m. ***½** D: Charles Lamont. Robert Paige,
Mari Blanchard, Martha Hyer, Horace Mc-
Mahon. Unimaginative vehicle has Bud and

Lou sailing through space with escaped gangsters, landing on Venus, a planet populated
with scantily clad women. Look quickly for
Anita Ekberg. ▼ ▶

Abbott and Costello in Hollywood (1945)
83m. ****** D: S. Sylvan Simon. Frances Rafferty, Robert Stanton, Jean Porter, Warner
Anderson, "Rags" Ragland. Uneven comedy
with A&C as barber and porter in Tinseltown.
A few peeks behind the scenes at MGM, with
several familiar faces appearing as themselves: Lucille Ball, Preston Foster, Jackie
"Butch" Jenkins, and director Robert Z. Leonard. Officially titled BUD ABBOTT LOU
COSTELLO IN HOLLYWOOD. ▼ ▶

Abbott and Costello in the Foreign Legion (1950) **80m.** ****** D: Charles Lamont.
Patricia Medina, Walter Slezak, Douglass
Dumbrille. Unexceptional vehicle pitting
A&C against nasty sergeant Slezak. Best
scene involves mirages in the desert. ▼ ▶

Abbott and Costello Meet Captain Kidd
(1952) **C-70m.** ****** D: Charles Lamont.
Charles Laughton, Hillary Brooke, Fran
Warren, Bill Shirley, Leif Erickson. Middling pirate spoof with too many lousy songs,
worth catching to see Laughton having the
time of his life in atypical low comedy. ▼ ▶

**Abbott and Costello Meet Dr. Jekyll
and Mr. Hyde** (1953) **77m.** ****** D: Charles
Lamont. Boris Karloff, Craig Stevens, Reginald Denny, Helen Westcott, John Dierkes.
Disappointing attempt to mix A&C with
Jekyll (Karloff) and Hyde (stuntman Eddie
Parker), with too few funny scenes. Special
effects are film's main asset. ▼ ▶ ●

Abbott and Costello Meet Frankenstein
(1948) **83m.** *****½** D: Charles Barton. Lon
Chaney, Jr., Bela Lugosi, Lenore Aubert,
Jane Randolph, Glenn Strange, Frank Ferguson. Dracula (Lugosi) plans to put Lou's
brain in Frankenstein's monster; werewolf
Larry Talbot (Chaney) has his paws full
convincing the boys they're in danger.
All-time great horror-comedy still works
beautifully, mainly because the monsters
play it straight. Yes, that *is* Vincent Price's
voice at the end. Officially titled BUD AB-
BOTT LOU COSTELLO MEET FRANK-
ENSTEIN. ▼ ▶ ●

**Abbott and Costello Meet the Invisible
Man** (1951) **82m.** ******* D: Charles Lamont.
Nancy Guild, Arthur Franz, Adele Jergens,
Sheldon Leonard. One of the team's best
vehicles, with Bud and Lou as detectives
helping boxer (Franz) who's been framed by

mobster Leonard, with aid of invisibility formula. The effects are top-notch.▼○●

Abbott and Costello Meet the Keystone Kops (1955) **79m.** ** D: Charles Lamont. Fred Clark, Lynn Bari, Mack Sennett, Maxie Rosenbloom, Frank Wilcox, Henry Kulky, Sam Flint. Low-budget comedy could have been better. Clark is fine as conniving producer in this synthetic period piece of silent-slapstick movie days.▼▶

Abbott and Costello Meet the Killer Boris Karloff (1949) **84m.** **½ D: Charles Barton. Lenore Aubert, Gar Moore, Donna Martell, Alan Mowbray. Pleasant blend of comedy and whodunit with bodies hanging in closets perplexing hotel dick Abbott, and phony mystic Karloff trying to do away with klutzy bellboy Costello.▼○●

Abbott and Costello Meet the Mummy (1955) **79m.** **½ D: Charles Lamont. Marie Windsor, Michael Ansara, Dan Seymour, Kurt Katch, Richard Deacon. Amusing adventure with A&C mixed up with villainess Windsor, a valuable tomb, and a mummy who's still alive. ▼○●

Abby (1974) **C-92m.** **½ D: William Girdler. Carol Speed, William Marshall, Terry Carter, Austin Stoker, Juanita Moore. Not-bad black variation on THE EXORCIST. Speed, wife of minister Carter and daughter-in-law of minister Marshall, is the possessed Abby. Out of circulation for years because of a lawsuit that claimed it was a ripoff of THE EXORCIST.▶

ABC Murders, The SEE: **Alphabet Murders, The**

Abdication, The (1974-British) **C-103m.** ** D: Anthony Harvey. Peter Finch, Liv Ullmann, Cyril Cusack, Paul Rogers, Michael Dunn. Plodding historical drama of what happened to Sweden's Queen Christina when she abdicated to convert to Catholicism. Finch is the cardinal who must test her sincerity and with whom she falls in love. [PG]▶

Aberdeen (2000-Norwegian-British) **C-106m.** *** D: Hans Petter Moland. Stellan Skarsgård, Lena Headey, Ian Hart, Charlotte Rampling. Raw, extremely well acted road movie in which two addictive personalities—a fast-and-loose-living cokehead (Headey) and her alcoholic wreck of a father (Skarsgård), from whom she has been long estranged—endure each other's company as she escorts him from Norway to Scotland. Sometimes tough to watch, as the characters wallow in their dysfunction, but they are vividly etched and their multilayered relationship is wholly believable.▼▶

Abigail: Wanted SEE: **Stingray** (1978)

Abominable Dr. Phibes, The (1971-British) **C-94m.** *** D: Robert Fuest. Vincent Price, Joseph Cotten, Peter Jeffrey, Hugh Griffith, Terry-Thomas, Virginia North. Above average camp horror film in which Price, disfigured in a car wreck, seeks revenge on those he believes responsible for the death of his wife. Sequel: DR. PHIBES RISES AGAIN!▼○●

About a Boy (2002) **C-101m.** *** D: Chris Weitz, Paul Weitz. Hugh Grant, Toni Collette, Rachel Weisz, Nicholas Hoult, Victoria Smurfit. Self-absorbed bachelor Grant, who happily lives a hedonistic existence, comes into the life of an isolated, misfit 12-year-old boy whose mom is chronically depressed. Out of this unlikely situation a friendship slowly develops in which the boy and the man fill voids in each other's lives. Bright, unpredictable, and refreshingly humanistic comedy-drama doesn't hew to any formula, and though it skirts credibility at times it comes up a winner. Based on the novel by Nick Hornby, coscripted by the directors. Super 35. [PG-13]▼▶

About Adam (2001-British-U.S.-Irish) **C-105m.** **½ D: Gerard Stembridge. Kate Hudson, Frances O'Connor, Stuart Townsend, Charlotte Bradley, Alan Maher, Rosaleen Linehan. Cute romantic comedy about a duplicitous charmer who woos all three sisters of an eccentric, close-knit Dublin family. Slight but charming fare has a refreshingly hedonistic attitude but never really convinces us why these robust Eves are so smitten by such a cipher of a man. Good showcase for its trio of leading ladies (Hudson, O'Connor, Bradley). [R]▼▶

About Last Night . . . (1986) **C-113m.** ** D: Edward Zwick. Rob Lowe, Demi Moore, James Belushi, Elizabeth Perkins, George DiCenzo, Michael Alldredge, Robin Thomas, Catherine Keener. True-to-life look at problems faced by a young couple fleeing the singles scene, biggest problem being his inability to make genuine emotional commitment to her. True-to-life doesn't make it terribly *interesting*, however. Expanded (and diluted) from David Mamet's one-act play *Sexual Perversity in Chicago*. Coscenarist Tim Kazurinsky appears briefly. [R]▼▶

About Mrs. Leslie (1954) **104m.** *** D: Daniel Mann. Shirley Booth, Robert Ryan, Marjie Millar, Alex Nicol, Sammy White, James Bell, Eileen Janssen, Henry (Harry) Morgan, Gale Page, Ellen Corby, Amanda Blake, Joan Shawlee, Benny Rubin, Jack Larson, Jerry Paris. Flashbacks reveal romance between chanteuse (Booth) and mysterious, lonely magnate (Ryan). Well-acted soaper; forgivable illogical coupling of stars.

About Schmidt (2002) **C-124m.** ***½ D: Alexander Payne. Jack Nicholson, Hope Davis, Dermot Mulroney, Kathy Bates, Len Cariou, Howard Hesseman, June Squibb. Superb human comedy about a newly retired insurance actuary in Nebraska who begins—for the first time—to question the choices he has made in life. Subtle, deliberately paced, and splendidly acted, with as many sad moments as funny ones. Nicholson's magnificently quiet, true performance may be the best of his career. Enhanced by Rolfe Kent's perfectly nuanced score. Payne and Jim Taylor (loosely) adapted Louis Begley's novel. [R] ▼❶

Above and Beyond (1952) **122m.** ******* D: Melvin Frank, Norman Panama. Robert Taylor, Eleanor Parker, James Whitmore, Larry Keating, Larry Gates, Marilyn Erskine, Jim Backus. Meaningful account of Paul Tibbets (Taylor), U.S. pilot who flew over Hiroshima with first atomic bomb; film focuses on his training and its effect on his personal life. Story also told in 1980 TV movie ENOLA GAY. ▼❶

Above Suspicion (1943) **90m.** ******* D: Richard Thorpe. Joan Crawford, Fred MacMurray, Conrad Veidt, Basil Rathbone, Reginald Owen, Richard Ainley. Crawford and MacMurray asked to do spy mission during European honeymoon on the eve of WW2. Pure escapism, with Joan more than a match for the Nazis. ▼❶

Above the Law (1988) **C-99m.** ****** D: Andrew Davis. Steven Seagal, Pam Grier, Sharon Stone, Henry Silva, Ron Dean, Daniel Faraldo, Thalmus Rasulala. Chicago cop doesn't hesitate to use his martial arts skills as he battles police corruption and drug dealing. Seagal's film debut reveals the real-life Aikido master to be more of the Chuck-norrisian than the Stanislavskian school of acting. Seagal also cowrote and coproduced; slick but stupid actioner. [R] ▼❶❶

Above the Rim (1994) **C-93m.** ****½** D: Jeff Pollack. Duane Martin, Leon, Tupac Shakur, David Bailey, Tonya Pinkins, Marlon Wayans, Bernie Mac. By-the-numbers tale of a promising high school basketball player (Martin) and his conflicting relationships with two very different brothers: one a drug dealer (Shakur), the other a troubled ex-scholastic hoop star (Leon) employed as a school security guard. Despite insightful moments, film wallows in clichés and plot contrivances. [R] ▼❶

Abre Los Ojos SEE: **Open Your Eyes**

Absence of Malice (1981) **C-116m.** ******* D: Sydney Pollack. Paul Newman, Sally Field, Bob Balaban, Melinda Dillon, Luther Adler, Barry Primus, Josef Sommer, John Harkins, Don Hood, Wilford Brimley. A reporter (Field) is duped by a scheming government investigator into printing a story that discredits innocent Newman; while she hides behind the privilege of the press, he determines to get even. Absorbing drama by former reporter Kurt Luedtke with two charismatic star performances. Filmed in Miami. [PG] ▼❶❶

Absent Minded Professor, The (1961) **97m.** ******* D: Robert Stevenson. Fred MacMurray, Nancy Olson, Keenan Wynn, Tommy Kirk, Ed Wynn, Leon Ames, Elliott Reid. MacMurray discovers flubber (flying rubber) in this Disney audience-pleaser, but no one will believe him except Keenan Wynn, who tries to steal the substance. Broad comedy and bright special effects make this a lot of fun. Also shown in computer-colored version. Sequel: SON OF FLUBBER. Remade in 1995 (as a TVM) and in 1997 as FLUBBER. ▼❶

Absolute Beginners (1986-British) **C-107m.** ****½** D: Julien Temple. Eddie O'Connell, Patsy Kensit, David Bowie, James Fox, Ray Davies, Eve Ferret, Anita Morris, Lionel Blair, Steven Berkoff, Mandy Rice-Davies, Sade Adu. Energetic, original musical set in London, 1958, when teenagers first came into their own. Highly stylized film (directed by music-video veteran Temple) suffers from two-dimensional characters and a misguided attempt to add substance by dealing with the rise of racism in England . . . but its virtues *almost* outweigh its shortcomings. Pulsating score supervised by jazz great Gil Evans; musical highlights from Sade ("Killer Blow") and jazz veteran Slim Gaillard ("Selling Out"). And don't miss that incredible opening shot! Adapted from Colin MacInnes' 1959 novel. Super Techniscope. [PG-13] ▼❶

Absolute Power (1997) **C-120m.** ****** D: Clint Eastwood. Clint Eastwood, Gene Hackman, Ed Harris, Laura Linney, Judy Davis, E. G. Marshall, Scott Glenn, Dennis Haysbert, Melora Hardin, Richard Jenkins. Aging thief pulls off one valedictory jewel heist, but along the way accidentally witnesses a sexual assault and murder involving none other than the President of the United States (Hackman). Barely credible (and fatally diluted) adaptation of David Baldacci's best-seller by William Goldman. Eastwood and Harris (as a wily cop) play a fun game of cat and mouse, but Hackman is over the top, and the whole thing runs aground in the second half. Panavision. [R] ▼❶

Absolution (1981-British) **C-105m.** ****½** D: Anthony Page. Richard Burton, Dominic Guard, Dai Bradley, Billy Connolly, Andrew Keir, Willoughby Gray. Burton gives a commanding performance as a humorless, by-the-book priest who teaches at a boys' school, and falls victim to a snowballing practical joke played upon him by his pet student. Straightforward melodrama loses credibility toward the end. Written by Anthony Shaffer. Filmed in 1978, unreleased in the U.S. until 1988, four years after Burton's death. [R] ▼❶

Absurdistan (2008-German-French) **C-84m.** ****½** D: Veit Helmer. Kristýna Malérová, Maximilian Mauff, Nino Chkheidze, Vano Ivantbelidze, Ani Amiridze, Ilko Stefanovski. Whimsical comic fable about a boy and girl from a remote Eastern European village who are destined to make love on a night when certain stars are in alignment. Their plans are threatened when the community's water supply runs dry, and the women stage a sex strike against their lazy menfolk, who refuse to fix the problem. Fanciful and lightly amusing, if not as good as the same filmmaker's TUVALU. **)**

Abyss, The (1989) **C-145m. ***** D: James Cameron. Ed Harris, Mary Elizabeth Mastrantonio, Michael Biehn, Leo Burmester, Todd Graff, John Bedford Lloyd, J.C. Quinn, Kimberly Scott, Jimmie Ray Weeks, Chris Elliott. Spectacular underwater saga about an oil-rig crew that gets involved in a perilous mission to rescue a sunken nuclear sub. Better as underwater adventure than futuristic sci-fi, with a couple of crises too many, but still a fascinating, one-of-a-kind experience. Great score by Alan Silvestri; Oscar winner for Visual Effects. Special edition includes 27m. of extra footage, some of it all-too-obviously cut from theatrical release. It fleshes out characters, amplifies plot points, and includes some spectacular special effects—but "literalizes" the other-worldly finale. Super 35. [PG-13] ▼●**)**

Accattone (1961-Italian) **120m. ***** D: Pier Paolo Pasolini. Franco Citti, Franca Pasut, Roberto Scaringella, Adele Cambria, Paolo Guidi, Silvana Corsini. Pasolini's first film is a vivid, unsentimental look at the desperate (and depressing) existence of pimps and petty thieves living in the slums of Rome. Bernardo Bertolucci was one of the assistant directors. Released in the U.S. in 1968. ▼●**)**

Accepted (2006) **C-93m. **** D: Steve Pink. Justin Long, Jonah Hill, Adam Herschman, Blake Lively, Columbus Short, Maria Thayer, Lewis Black, Anthony Heald. A group of teenagers who've been rejected by various colleges start their own in an abandoned mental institution. Premise is so far-fetched that it keeps you watching just to find out how it's going to resolve itself. Its message that a college education kills the creative genius that teenagers would otherwise cultivate on their own is hard to swallow after seeing the "self-made students" do nothing but drink and party. Soundtrack is full of cover songs paying homage to other, better teen-revolution movies. Super 35. [PG-13]**)**

Accident (1967-British) **C-105m. ***½** D: Joseph Losey. Dirk Bogarde, Stanley Baker, Jacqueline Sassard, Delphine Seyrig, Alexander Knox, Michael York, Vivien Merchant, Harold Pinter, Freddie Jones. Complex, thought-provoking script by Harold Pinter uses story (about Oxford professor who falls in love with a student) as just a foundation for examination of characters' thoughts and actions. A challenging film that operates on many levels; entire cast superb, including York in his first major film role. Based on a novel by Nicholas Mosley, who plays Don. Pinter is amusing as a TV producer. ▼**)**

Accidental Husband, The (2008) **C-91m.**
*½ D: Griffin Dunne. Uma Thurman, Jeffrey Dean Morgan, Colin Firth, Sam Shepard, Isabella Rossellini, Keir Dullea, Brooke Adams, Lindsay Sloane, Sarita Choudhury. Blue-collar guy (Morgan) sets out to get even with talk radio love expert (Thurman) after his fiancée dumps him due to the doc's glib on-the-air advice. Insipid, aching-to-be-romantic comedy is a waste of talent on all fronts. Released direct to DVD in the U.S. [PG-13] **)**

Accidental Tourist, The (1988) **C-121m. ***** D: Lawrence Kasdan. William Hurt, Kathleen Turner, Geena Davis, Amy Wright, Bill Pullman, Robert Gorman, David Ogden Stiers, Ed Begley, Jr. Hurt gives an exquisite performance as a man shattered by the death of his son, who comes out of his shell when he meets a kooky, aggressive young woman (Oscar winner Davis) who couldn't be less his type. Finely wrought, extremely faithful adaptation of Anne Tyler's novel dares to take its time; may be too slow and quiet for some viewers, but offers many rewards. Panavision. [PG] ▼●**)**

Accompanist, The (1992-French) **C-111m. **** D: Claude Miller. Richard Bohringer, Elena Safonova, Romane Bohringer, Samuel Labarthe, Bernard Verley. Somber drama of deceit (toward oneself and one's country) set during WW2. An unworldly young woman (Bohringer) is hired as accompanist to a famous Parisian singer who, with her husband, has been collaborating with the enemy. Potentially potent story but the result is too often bland and forgettable. ▼

Accused (1957) SEE: **Mark of the Hawk, The**

Accused, The (1988) **C-110m. ***** D: Jonathan Kaplan. Kelly McGillis, Jodie Foster, Bernie Coulson, Leo Rossi, Ann Hearn, Carmen Argenziano. Public prosecutor McGillis deals with a gang-rape case in cut-and-dried fashion, until the victim demands full retribution for what she has suffered. Compelling drama inspired by a notorious real-life case and propelled by Foster's powerhouse, Oscar-winning performance as the provocative, foul-mouthed woman who gets her day in court. Only quibble: Was the climactic reenactment really necessary? [R] ▼●**)**

Ace, The SEE: **Great Santini, The**

Ace Eli and Rodger of the Skies (1973) **C-92m. **** D: Bill Sampson (John Erman). Cliff Robertson, Pamela Franklin, Eric Shea, Rosemary Murphy, Bernadette Peters, Alice Ghostley. Tepid tale of 1920s stunt flyer and son who tags along. Muddled film sat on shelf a long time; doctoring didn't help. Story by Steven Spielberg. Peters' film debut. Panavision. [PG]

Ace High (1969-Italian) **C-123m. **** D: Giuseppe Colizzi. Eli Wallach, Terence Hill, Bud Spencer, Brock Peters, Kevin McCarthy, Steffen Zacharias. Awkwardly dubbed spaghetti Western tries to imitate Clint Eastwood–Sergio Leone epics, but director Colizzi lacks Leone's style. Hill plays a character named Cat Stevens, but there are no rock songs here. Techniscope. [M] ▼▶

Ace in the Hole (1951) 112m. *** D: Billy Wilder. Kirk Douglas, Jan Sterling, Bob Arthur, Porter Hall, Frank Cady, Richard Benedict, Ray Teal, Gene Evans. An embittered New Mexico reporter looking for the elusive brass ring finds it when he stumbles onto a story of a man trapped in an ancient Indian ruin. Unrelentingly cynical (yet mostly believable) tale of how the reporter exploits the "human interest story" for his own benefit—and how the potential tragedy turns into a three-ring circus—has a peculiarly contemporary ring to it. Biting and extremely well acted. Originally titled THE BIG CARNIVAL. Inspired by the actual 1925 Floyd Collins case; the real reporter won a Pulitzer Prize. ▶

Aces High (1976-British) C-104m. *** D: Jack Gold. Malcolm McDowell, Christopher Plummer, Simon Ward, Peter Firth. Strong antiwar statement focusing on indoctrination of WW1 pilot Firth and his disillusioned squadron leader (McDowell). Solid cast (with cameos by John Gielgud, Ray Milland, Trevor Howard, and Richard Johnson) and exciting aerial dogfights highlight this remake of R. C. Sherriff's JOURNEY'S END. [PG]

Aces: Iron Eagle III (1992) C-93m. *½ D: John Glen. Louis Gossett, Jr., Rachel McLish, Christopher Cazenove, Horst Buchholz, Sonny Chiba. This time, maverick pilot Gossett and a group of WW2 veteran pilots stage an air raid on a Peruvian cocaine factory (having run out of targets in the Middle East). Unsatisfying mélange of flyboy machismo, unintentional slapstick, and inane action—with novelty of female bodybuilder McLish in cast. [R] ▼▶

Ace Ventura: Pet Detective (1994) C-86m. ** D: Tom Shadyac. Jim Carrey, Courteney Cox, Sean Young, Tone Lōc, Dan Marino, Noble Willingham, Troy Evans, Randall "Tex" Cobb. Miami-based "pet detective" is hired to find the kidnapped mascot of the Dolphins football team. No-brainer comedy/whodunit was the breakout role for Carrey, who mugs nonstop (and we mean nonstop). Some good gags, but runs out of steam—which Carrey never does. Real-life members of the Miami Dolphins appear. A minute of new footage added for video. Followed by a sequel, an animated TV series, and a DVD sequel. [PG-13] ▼▶

Ace Ventura: When Nature Calls (1995) C-105m. ** D: Steve Oedekerk. Jim Carrey, Ian McNeice, Simon Callow, Maynard Eziashi, Bob Gunton, Sophie Okonedo, Tommy Davidson. Sloppy assemblage of gags (with most of the good ones near the beginning) ostensibly about Ace's anti-p.c. hijinks with battling African tribes while

trying to locate a rare white bat. Clever opening spoof of CLIFFHANGER and a funny sight gag involving asparagus; otherwise, more of the same. Super 35. [PG-13] ▼▶

Across 110th Street (1972) C-102m. *** D: Barry Shear. Anthony Quinn, Yaphet Kotto, Anthony Franciosa, Richard Ward, Paul Benjamin, Ed Bernard, Antonio Fargas, Norma Donaldson, Gilbert Lewis. N.Y.C. police race the mobs to catch three blacks who, disguised as cops, stole $300,000 from a Mafia-controlled bank; mutual distrust of both black and Italian hoods is mirrored by differences between cops Quinn and Kotto. Exciting, well paced, and extremely violent, with fine use of Harlem locations. Quinn was also coexecutive producer. [R] ▼▶

Across the Bridge (1957-British) 103m. *** D: Ken Annakin. Rod Steiger, David Knight, Marla Landi, Noel Willman, Bernard Lee, Bill Nagy, Eric Pohlmann. Smug German business magnate flees his home base in England when Scotland Yard investigates his corrupt dealings. His only hope is to get to Mexico through the U.S., but en route he switches identities with a fellow train passenger. Engrossing yarn based on a Graham Greene novella. Shot mostly in Spain. Later remade as DOUBLE TAKE. ▼▶

Across the Pacific (1942) 97m. **½ D: John Huston. Humphrey Bogart, Mary Astor, Sydney Greenstreet, Victor Sen Yung, Keye Luke, Richard Loo. Three MALTESE FALCON leads reteamed for enjoyable WW2 adventure. Bogart trails spies to Panama, has running battle of wits with Greenstreet, while romancing enticing Astor. Despite title, the movie never gets to the Pacific, much less across it. Also shown in computer-colored version. ▼▶

Across the Tracks (1991) C-101m. **½ D: Sandy Tung. Rick Schroder, Brad Pitt, Carrie Snodgress, David Anthony Marshall. Reasonably compelling teen sports drama with Schroder returning from reform school stint to compete on high school track team and outperforming straight-A track star brother (Pitt). Realistic portrayal of teen problems and aspirations make this best suited for young people, although the R rating (for normal raunchy high school language) may make this film inaccessible to its key audience. [R] ▼▶

Across the Universe (2007) C-131m. **½ D: Julie Taymor. Evan Rachel Wood, Jim Sturgess, Joe Anderson, Dana Fuchs, Martin Luther McCoy, T. V. Carpio, Spencer Liff, Lisa Hogg, Bill Irwin, James Urbaniak, Dylan Baker, Joe Cocker, Bono, Salma Hayek, Harry J, Lennix, Eddie Izzard. A young Brit comes to the U.S. in search of his father, and falls in love with an all-American girl, just as she (and her entire generation) experience the mind-bending changes of the Vietnam era. Routine story is just an excuse to pictorialize—and attempt to contextualize—more than 30 landmark Beatles songs. Imaginative at times but increasingly wearying as the song cues line up (yes, there are characters named Prudence, Maxwell, Jude, et al.), famous faces appear, and the plotline bogs down. Our favorite number: Joe Cocker singing "Come Together." Super 35. [PG-13]▶

Across the Wide Missouri (1951) **C-78m. **½** D: William Wellman. Clark Gable, Ricardo Montalban, John Hodiak, Adolphe Menjou, Maria Elena Marques, J. Carrol Naish, Jack Holt, Alan Napier, George Chandler, Richard Anderson. Location filming helps pedestrian frontier adventure about explorer Gable and other pathfinders moving westward in 19th century.▼

Action in the North Atlantic (1943) **127m. *** D: Lloyd Bacon. Humphrey Bogart, Raymond Massey, Alan Hale, Julie Bishop, Ruth Gordon, Sam Levene, Dane Clark. Rousing tribute to WW2 Merchant Marine, with officers Bogart and Massey, seamen Hale and Levene, usual hothead Clark, and Gordon as Massey's wife. Also shown in computer-colored version.▼▶

Action Jackson (1988) **C-95m. ** D: Craig R. Baxley. Carl Weathers, Craig T. Nelson, Vanity, Sharon Stone, Thomas F. Wilson, Bill Duke, Robert Davi, Jack Thibeau. Strictly standard B-movie fare pitting good guy Weathers (a cop) vs. bad guy Nelson. Plenty of explosions, car chases, corpses and noise. [R] ▼●▶

Act of Love (1953) **108m. **½** D: Anatole Litvak. Kirk Douglas, Dany Robin, Barbara Laage, Robert Strauss, Gabrielle Dorziat, Serge Reggiani, Brigitte Bardot. Entertaining if unremarkable chronicle of the romance between lonely American soldier and down-and-out French girl in Paris. Scripted by Irwin Shaw, based on Alfred Hayes' novel *The Girl on the Via Flaminia.*

Act of the Heart, The (1970-Canadian) **C-103m. *** D: Paul Almond. Genevieve Bujold, Donald Sutherland, Bill Mitchell, Monique Leyrac. Fascinating study of religious fanaticism manifesting itself in one young woman and her love for a Catholic priest. Beautifully atmospheric but ending deeply hurts film. [PG]

Act of Violence (1949) **92m. *** D: Fred Zinnemann. Van Heflin, Robert Ryan, Janet Leigh, Mary Astor, Phyllis Thaxter, Berry Kroeger, Taylor Holmes. Stark, well-acted drama, with crippled, embittered Ryan stalking former senior officer Heflin, who betrayed his men while a POW. Fine vignette by Astor as a sympathetic call girl.▶

Act One (1963) **110m. **½** D: Dore Schary. George Hamilton, Jason Robards, George Segal, Eli Wallach, Sam Levene, Ruth Ford, Jack Klugman. Interesting for

oddball cast, this fabrication of writer Moss Hart's autobiography lacks finesse or any sense of reality, but Robards is ideally cast as George S. Kaufman.

Actress, The (1953) **91m. **½** D: George Cukor. Spencer Tracy, Jean Simmons, Teresa Wright, Anthony Perkins, Mary Wickes. Flavorful account based on Ruth Gordon's experiences as a teenager in early 20th-century Massachusetts, determined to become an acting star; Tracy is the irascible father. Jackie Coogan appears in unbilled bit. Perkins' film debut.▶

Ada (1961) **C-109m. *** D: Daniel Mann. Susan Hayward, Dean Martin, Wilfrid Hyde-White, Martin Balsam. Rags-to-riches soaper of poor Hayward maneuvering easy-going Martin to governor's mansion, using hellbent stamina to overcome political corruption. Hayward vs. Hyde-White in state senate is highlight. CinemaScope.

Adalen 31 (1969-Swedish) **C-115m. *** D: Bo Widerberg. Peter Schildt, Kerstin Tidelius, Roland Hedlund, Stefan Feierbach. Strikers in a Swedish paper mill disagree over whether or not to make their case with violence; matters are further complicated when a striker's son falls in love with—and impregnates—the factory manager's daughter. Generally appealing mix of romance and history, though no one will ever mistake Widerberg (the director of EL-VIRA MADIGAN) for a gritty filmmaker of social realism. Technicscope. [X]

Adam (2009) **C-99m. *** D: Max Mayer. Hugh Dancy, Rose Byrne, Peter Gallagher, Amy Irving, Frankie Faison, Mark Linn-Baker. Sweet contemporary love story about a man with Asperger's syndrome who has little control over what he says or how he reacts to people; when his father dies he's left to face the world by himself for the first time. Then he meets a new neighbor in his N.Y.C. apartment building and a tentative relationship blossoms. Writer-director Mayer avoids cliché and formula in this winning, well-acted film. HD Widescreen. [PG-13]▼

Adam at 6 A.M. (1970) **C-100m. *** D: Robert Scheerer. Michael Douglas, Lee Purcell, Joe Don Baker, Grayson Hall, Charles Aidman, Meg Foster. Underrated film about young college professor from California who spends summer in Missouri working as a laborer. Authentic location footage and good performances by Purcell and Baker give rare, genuine feeling for the Midwest. [PG]▼

Adam Resurrected (2008-U.S.-German-Israeli) **C/B&W-106m. ** D: Paul Schrader. Jeff Goldblum, Willem Dafoe, Derek Jacobi, Ayelet Zurer, Hana Laszlo, Joachim Król. Take a dash of Kirk Douglas in THE JUGGLER, sprinkle in what you've heard about Jerry Lewis' THE DAY

THE CLOWN CRIED, then imagine what Schrader at his most left-field-ish could bring to a Holocaust story. Flashback film from Yoram Kaniuk's eponymous 1968 novel finds a once-popular prewar Berlin clown (Goldblum) in a postwar Israeli mental facility recalling concentration camp life—where he was forced to walk around on all fours like a dog by a commandant (Dafoe) who remembered him from his performing days. This merely scratches the weird surfaces of a brave, barely released movie (with a Goldblum performance tough to fault) that's at once flamboyant yet too chilly to engage many viewers. Super 35. [R] ◗

Adam Sandler's Eight Crazy Nights SEE: **Eight Crazy Nights**

Adam's Apples (2005-German-Danish) C-91m. ** D: Anders Thomas Jensen. Ulrich Thomsen, Mads Mikkelsen, Nicolas Bro, Paprika Steen, Ali Kazim, Ole Thestrup, Nikolaj Lie Kaas. Ineffectual black-comedy allegory about a clash of wills between Ivan (Mikkelsen), a hard-luck soul who embraces religion and is in denial about the existence of evil, and Adam (Thomsen), a hardened career criminal and neo-Nazi. Means to be profound, as it deals with the nature of good and evil, but it's merely overwrought. Super 35. [R] ◗

Adam's Rib (1949) 100m. **** D: George Cukor. Spencer Tracy, Katharine Hepburn, Judy Holliday, Tom Ewell, David Wayne, Jean Hagen, Hope Emerson, Polly Moran, Marvin Kaplan, Paula Raymond, Tommy Noonan. Smart, sophisticated comedy (by Ruth Gordon and Garson Kanin) about husband and wife lawyers on opposing sides of the same attempted-murder case. One of Hollywood's greatest comedies about the battle of the sexes, with peerless Tracy and Hepburn supported by movie newcomers Holliday, Ewell, Hagen, and Wayne. Cole Porter contributed the song "Farewell, Amanda." Remade in Bulgaria in 1956 (in this version the heroine rebels against tradition as a result of her conversion to Marxism-Leninism!). Later a TV series. Also shown in computer-colored version. ▼O◗

Adaptation. (2002) C-115m. ***½ D: Spike Jonze. Nicolas Cage, Meryl Streep, Chris Cooper, Tilda Swinton, Cara Seymour, Brian Cox, Judy Greer, Maggie Gyllenhaal, Ron Livingston, Stephen Tobolowsky. Super-neurotic screenwriter Charlie Kaufman (BEING JOHN MALKOVICH) is hired to adapt Susan Orlean's book *The Orchid Thief* as a movie, but finds it a torturous process. His carefree twin brother, Donald, has no such problems, and even tries his hand at writing. We also meet author Orlean (Streep) and her main subject, a colorful Southern character who knows everything there is to know about plants (Cooper, in an Oscar-winning performance). Surreal, dazzling, dizzying,

often perplexing but brilliant film about the creative process; Cage (in two distinct performances as the twin brothers), Streep, and Cooper are all great. Cameos by John Malkovich, Catherine Keener, John Cusack, David O. Russell, and Curtis Hanson (as Streep's husband). Screenplay is credited to Charlie and (the late) Donald Kaufman. [R] ▼◗

Addams Family, The (1991) C-101m. *** D: Barry Sonnenfeld. Anjelica Huston, Raul Julia, Christopher Lloyd, Dan Hedaya, Elizabeth Wilson, Judith Malina, Carel Struycken, Dana Ivey, Paul Benedict, Christina Ricci, Jimmy Workman. Piquant comedy based on Charles Addams' macabre cartoon family (later popularized on the same-named TV series), whose greedy lawyer tries to plunder their fortune by planting an impostor in the household who claims to be their long-lost Uncle Fester. Huston and Julia are absolutely perfect as Morticia and Gomez, and maintain a light touch while dispensing their gleefully ghoulish black humor. Impressive directorial debut for cinematographer Sonnenfeld. Followed by two sequels. [PG-13] ▼O◗

Addams Family Values (1993) C-93m. *** D: Barry Sonnenfeld. Anjelica Huston, Raul Julia, Christopher Lloyd, Joan Cusack, Christina Ricci, Carol Kane, Jimmy Workman, Carel Struycken, Dana Ivey, Peter MacNicol, Christine Baranski, Mercedes McNab, Nathan Lane, Peter Graves, Tony Shalhoub, David Hyde Pierce. Funny follow-up to the 1991 hit has scheming Cusack invading the Addams household, plotting to marry Fester for his money, then bump him off. Full of hilarious one-liners (delivered with gusto by Julia and Lloyd), but the real star is Ricci as the stone-faced Wednesday, who finally exacts her revenge for being sent to a summer camp run by a pair of giddy grown-ups (MacNicol and Baranski). Runs out of steam toward the end. Direct-to-video sequel: ADDAMS FAMILY REUNION. [PG-13] ▼◗

Addict SEE: **Born to Win**

Addicted to Love (1997) C-100m. ** D: Griffin Dunne. Meg Ryan, Matthew Broderick, Kelly Preston, Tcheky Karyo, Maureen Stapleton, Nesbitt Blaisdell, Remak Ramsay. Jilted lover Broderick settles in an abandoned N.Y.C. building across the street from his ex-girlfriend's apartment so he can watch her and her new lover. Then he's joined by the lover's ex-g.f., whose agenda is even more extreme: she wants revenge. Dark, twisted comedy has its moments, and a likable cast, but Ryan's seriously disturbed character makes it hard to "root" for her, and renders the inevitable fadeout scene less than ideal. Feature directing debut for actor-producer Dunne; his famous father, author Dominick Dunne, plays a restaurant critic. [R] ▼◗

Addiction, The (1995) 82m. *** D: Abel

Ferrara. Lili Taylor, Christopher Walken, Annabella Sciorra, Edie Falco, Paul Calderon, Kathryn Erbe, Michael Imperioli. Intelligent, allegorical vampire movie, shot in beautiful black-and-white, about an NYU philosophy student (well played by Taylor), a decent human being who is horrified by the atrocities of history. Her good intentions do not protect her from evil, as she is bitten by a vampiress and goes on to crave the blood of any- and everyone she meets. Not nearly as bloody and outrageous as some of Ferrara's earlier films; this one says the only hope for mankind is in spirituality. An interesting companion piece to Ferrara's KING OF NEW YORK and BAD LIEUTENANT. ▼●

Adding Machine, The (1969-U.S.-British) **C-100m.** **½ D: Jerome Epstein. Milo O'Shea, Phyllis Diller, Billie Whitelaw, Sydney Chaplin, Julian Glover. Accountant becomes desperate upon learning he's to be replaced by a computer. This Elmer Rice comedy-fantasy is flawed but interesting. Diller has unusual straight role as harridan. [M/PG]

Addio Kira SEE: **We the Living**

Adios Amigo (1975) **C-87m.** ** D: Fred Williamson. Fred Williamson, Richard Pryor, Thalmus Rasulala, James Brown, Robert Phillips, Mike Henry. Offbeat Western comedy, written, produced, and directed by Williamson, who plays perennial patsy to con man Pryor. No sex or violence in this innocuous film; too bad it doesn't pull together. Panavision. [PG] ▼◗

Adios, Sabata (1971-Italian-Spanish) **C-104m.** *½ D: Frank Kramer (Gianfranco Parolini). Yul Brynner, Dean Reed, Pedro Sanchez (Ignazio Spalla), Gerard Herter. Gunslinger gets involved with Mexican revolutionaries, helping himself to a cache of gold along the way. Ersatz sequel to SABATA (with Brynner instead of Lee Van Cleef) was titled INDIO BLACK until dubbed and retitled for U.S. release. Genuine sequel, THE RETURN OF SABATA, showed up in 1972. Techniscope. [PG]◗

Adjuster, The (1991-Canadian) **C-102m.** *** D: Atom Egoyan. Elias Koteas, Arsinee Khanjian, Maury Chaykin, Gabrielle Rose, Jennifer Dale, David Hemblen, Don McKellar. Audacious, provocative examination of voyeurism and the power of images. Among the characters are an insurance adjuster (Koteas) who plays peekaboo with the lives of those he deals with professionally and his wife (Khanjian), a censor who secretly tapes the pornographic material she's classifying. Panavision. [R]▼◗

Adjustment Bureau, The (2011) **C-106m.** **½ D: George Nolfi. Matt Damon, Emily Blunt, Anthony Mackie, John Slattery, Michael Kelly, Terence Stamp, Jennifer Ehle. Hotshot politician Damon, who has a self-destructive streak, chances to meet dancer Blunt one fateful evening and falls in love at first sight. But this was not part of "the plan," as he learns from the fedora-topped members of The Adjustment Bureau, who control such matters for the Big Boss. Undeterred, Damon struggles against fate in order to spend his life with Blunt. Unusual fantasy, based on a Philip K. Dick story, "Adjustment Team," is staged against the expansive backdrop of N.Y.C., but doesn't carry its momentum to a satisfying conclusion. Too bad; Damon and Blunt give it their best shot. Super 35. [PG-13] ◗

Adolescent, The SEE: **L'Adolescente**

Adoration (2009-Canadian) **C-101m.** ** D: Atom Egoyan. Arsinée Khanjian, Scott Speedman, Rachel Blanchard, Noam Jenkins, Devon Bostick, Kenneth Welsh, Maury Chaykin. After hearing his French teacher read an article about a man who sent his pregnant wife onto a plane with a bomb, a student writes an essay imagining the man and woman as his parents (who died some years ago) and presents it as the truth. This initiates a multilevel series of conversations, confrontations, and revelations about terrorism, personal responsibility, and family dynamics. Provocative at first, Egoyan's puzzlelike story actually becomes less interesting as the pieces fit together. [R] ◗

À Double Tour SEE: **Web of Passion**

Advance to the Rear (1964) **97m.** **½ D: George Marshall. Glenn Ford, Stella Stevens, Melvyn Douglas, Joan Blondell, Jim Backus, Andrew Prine. During Civil War, Northern soldier rejects are sent to Western territory. Stevens as Reb spy and Blondell as saucy worldly woman add only spice to predictable slapstick comedy. Panavision.◗

Adventure (1945) **125m.** ** D: Victor Fleming. Clark Gable, Greer Garson, Joan Blondell, Thomas Mitchell, Tom Tully, John Qualen, Richard Haydn. Gable's back, Garson's got him; they both sink in cumbersome comedy of seagoing roustabout and meek librarian. Not even breezy Blondell can save it.▼

Adventure, The SEE: **L'Avventura**

Adventureland (2009) **C-106m.** **½ D: Greg Mottola. Jesse Eisenberg, Kristen Stewart, Martin Starr, Bill Hader, Kristen Wiig, Ryan Reynolds, Margarita Levieva, Matt Bush, Jack Gilpin, Wendie Malick, Josh Pais, Mary Birdsong. In 1987, a brainy (and virginal) college graduate (Eisenberg) plans a trip to Europe before attending grad school, but a change in family finances forces him to take a menial summer job at a run-down amusement park in his hometown of Pittsburgh. Things take an interesting turn when he falls for a pretty coworker (Stewart). Seriocomic coming-of-age tale boasts strong acting and moments of insight, but covers familiar territory and drags in several spots. Mottola also wrote the semiautobiographical script. [R]◗

Adventure of Sherlock Holmes' Smarter

Brother, The (1975) **C-91m.** **½ D: Gene Wilder. Gene Wilder, Madeline Kahn, Marty Feldman, Dom DeLuise, Leo McKern, Roy Kinnear, John LeMesurier. Wilder's first film as writer-director-star is mild spoof of Sherlockian adventures, as Sigerson Holmes becomes involved with music-hall songstress Kahn, a damsel in distress. DeLuise, as hammy opera star, adds film's liveliest moments. Listen carefully for vocal cameo by Mel Brooks. Made in England. [PG]▼❙

Adventurers, The (1970) **C-171m.** BOMB D: Lewis Gilbert. Bekim Fehmiu, Candice Bergen, Ernest Borgnine, Olivia de Havilland, Leigh Taylor-Young, Thommy Berggren, Rossano Brazzi, Jaclyn Smith. Three-hour challenge to the kidneys based on Harold Robbins' best-seller about fictional South American republic that has a new revolution every two minutes. Incredible mess wastes attractive cast. Panavision. [PG—edited from original R rating]▼❙

Adventures in Babysitting (1987) **C-99m.** ** D: Chris Columbus. Elisabeth Shue, Maia Brewton, Keith Coogan, Anthony Rapp, Calvin Levels, Vincent Phillip D'Onofrio, Penelope Ann Miller, Albert Collins, George Newbern, John Ford Noonan, Lolita David (Davidovich). Shue, extremely winning in her first lead role, plays a teenager who takes her two babysitting charges into downtown Chicago to help get a friend out of a jam—and winds up in a snowballing series of wild adventures, à la FERRIS BUELLER'S DAY OFF. Young teens might go for it, but it's mediocre at best. Screenwriter Columbus' directing debut. [PG-13]▼❙

Adventures of a Young Man SEE: Hemingway's Adventures of a Young Man

Adventures of Baron Munchausen, The (1989) **C-126m.** *** D: Terry Gilliam. John Neville, Eric Idle, Sarah Polley, Oliver Reed, Charles McKeown, Winston Dennis, Jack Purvis, Valentina Cortese, Jonathan Pryce, Bill Paterson, Peter Jeffrey, Uma Thurman, Alison Steadman, Sting, Robin Williams. The legendary tale spinner returns in a new interpretation of his exploits by director-cowriter Gilliam. Breathtaking special effects go hand in hand with Gilliam's outlandishly funny and far-out ideas; a visual feast that's worth staying with through its occasional lulls. The Baron's exploits were previously filmed in 1943 and (as THE FABULOUS BARON MUNCHAUSEN) in 1961. [PG]▼❙

Adventures of Barry McKenzie, The (1972-Australian) **C-114m.** **½ D: Bruce Beresford. Barry Crocker, Barry Humphries, Peter Cook, Spike Milligan. Melbournian Crocker, not particularly fond of the British, finds himself displaced in England. Broad, gross comedy, overlong, and a bit much for American audiences. Beresford's first film, from a cartoon strip by Humphries and

Nicholas Garland. Sequel: BARRY McKENZIE HOLDS HIS OWN.

Adventures of Buckaroo Banzai Across the Eighth Dimension, The (1984) **C-103m.** ** D: W. D. Richter. Peter Weller, John Lithgow, Ellen Barkin, Jeff Goldblum, Christopher Lloyd. Off-the-wall pulp fiction by Earl Mac Rauch about a hero who's a neurosurgeon, physicist, rocket-car driver, rock singer, and government troubleshooter. Should be fun, but it's incoherent, like coming in at the *second* chapter of a Saturday matinee serial. Still, it has a fervent following. Aka BUCKAROO BANZAI. Panavision. [PG]▼❍❙

Adventures of Bullwhip Griffin, The (1967) **C-110m.** *** D: James Neilson. Roddy McDowall, Suzanne Pleshette, Karl Malden, Harry Guardino, Richard Haydn, Hermione Baddeley, Bryan Russell. Bright Disney spoof of gold-rush sagas, with McDowall as Bostonian butler who learns to fend for himself in the wild and woolly West. Clever comic ideas and visual gimmickry make this fun.▼❙

Adventures of Don Juan (1948) **C-110m.** *** D: Vincent Sherman. Errol Flynn, Viveca Lindfors, Robert Douglas, Alan Hale, Ann Rutherford, Raymond Burr. Handsome tongue-in-cheek swashbuckler has Errol stringing along countless maidens and even enticing the Queen (Lindfors); Oscar winner for Best Costumes. The lady at the end is Flynn's second wife, Nora Eddington. ▼❍❙

Adventures of Elmo in Grouchland, The (1999) **C-73m.** **½ D: Gary Halvorson. Mandy Patinkin, Vanessa L. Williams; voices of Kevin Clash, Fran Brill, Stephanie D'Abruzzo, Jerry Nelson, Caroll Spinney, Frank Oz, Steve Whitmire. TV's Elmo (the red, furry three-year-old monster from *Sesame Street*) loses his precious blanket and his search leads him to Grouchland, where he tangles with the villainous Huxley (Patinkin). Fine fare for young fans, but little else for older viewers. Elmo, Patinkin, and Williams seem to be having fun. [G]▼❙

Adventures of Felix (2000-French) **C-95m.** *** D: Jacques Martineau, Olivier Ducastel. Sami Bouajila, Patachou, Ariane Ascaride, Pierre-Loup Rajot, Charly Sergue. An HIV-positive young man travels to Marseilles to find the father he never knew, and along the way meets a variety of people whom he imagines as his ideal family. Tackles hard-hitting issues (AIDS, racism, homophobia) in the guise of a gentle social comedy. Beautifully photographed by Matthieu Poirot-Delpech. Soundtrack features sweet jazz vocals from Blossom Dearie. Super 35.▼❙

Adventures of Ford Fairlane, The (1990) **C-96m.** *½ D: Renny Harlin. Andrew Dice Clay, Wayne Newton, Priscilla Presley, Morris Day, Lauren Holly, Maddie Corman, Gilbert Gottfried, David Patrick Kelly, Brandon Call, Robert Englund, Ed O'Neill,

Tone Loc, Sheila E. Controversial standup comic Clay stars in an old-time private-eye yarn transplanted to the contemporary world of rock 'n' roll. Clay's got what it takes, but the film is clumsy, crude, and immature (just like his character). For rabid Clay fans only. Panavision. [R] ▼◑①

Adventures of Gerard, The (1970-British-Italian-Swiss) **C-91m.** BOMB D: Jerzy Skolimowski. Peter McEnery, Claudia Cardinale, Eli Wallach, Jack Hawkins, John Neville. Clumsy farce from Arthur Conan Doyle story about cocky but stupid officer who becomes fall guy for Napoleon's (Wallach) wartime strategy. Panavision.

Adventures of Hercules, The SEE: **Hercules II**

Adventures of Huck Finn, The (1993) **C-108m.** ** D: Stephen Sommers. Elijah -Wood, Courtney B. Vance, Robbie Coltrane, Jason Robards, Ron Perlman, Dana Ivey, Anne Heche, James Gammon, Paxton Whitehead, Tom Aldredge, Curtis Armstrong, Mary Louise Wilson, Frances Conroy. Utterly unimaginative rendering of Mark Twain's perennial, which should remain off-limits to Hollywood from this point on. As Huck, young Wood looks and acts too contemporary by decades, while Vance (as Jim) seems too young. Early scenes involving Huck's brutal father may be too intense for very young children . . . and this a Disney release! [PG] ▼◑①

Adventures of Huckleberry Finn, The (1960) **C-107m.** *** D: Michael Curtiz. Tony Randall, Eddie Hodges, Archie Moore, Patty McCormack, Neville Brand. Good version of Twain's story with an appealing Hodges (Huck) and excellent Archie Moore (Jim). Assorted characters played by veterans Buster Keaton, Andy Devine, Judy Canova, John Carradine, Mickey Shaughnessy, and Sterling Holloway. CinemaScope. ▼①

Adventures of Huckleberry Finn (1985) **C-105m.** *** D: Peter H. Hunt. Patrick Day, Jim Dale, Frederic Forrest, Lillian Gish, Barnard Hughes, Richard Kiley, Geraldine Page, Sada Thompson, Samm-Art Williams, Butterfly McQueen. Literate, enjoyable version of the Twain classic, with Day a smart, energetic Huck. Centers mostly on his relationship with Jim, the runaway slave (Williams); as richly rewarding for adults as for kids. Edited down from 240m. version, broadcast on PBS's *American Playhouse.* ▼

Adventures of Ichabod and Mr. Toad, The (1949) **C-68m.** *** D: Jack Kinney, Clyde Geronimi, James Algar. Voices of Eric Blore, Pat O'Malley, John Ployardt, Colin Campbell, Claude Allister, The Rhythmaires. Very entertaining animated doubleheader from Disney: a witty adaptation of Kenneth Grahame's *The Wind in the Willows,* about the puckish residents of Toad Hall centering on Toad's infatuation with motorcars, narrated by Basil Rathbone; and

a broad, cartoony version of Washington Irving's "The Legend of Sleepy Hollow," with a genuinely scary climax, narrated (and sung) by Bing Crosby. ▼◑①

Adventures of Mark Twain, The (1944) **130m.** *** D: Irving Rapper. Fredric March, Alexis Smith, Donald Crisp, Alan Hale, C. Aubrey Smith, John Carradine, Percy Kilbride. This Hollywoodized story of Samuel Clemens' colorful life may not be great biography, but it's consistently entertaining—despite some biopic clichés. March is fine in title role. Filmed in 1942. ▼①

Adventures of Mark Twain, The (1985) **C-90m.** ** D: Will Vinton. Voices of James Whitmore, Chris Ritchie, Gary Krug, Michele Mariana. Tom Sawyer, Huck Finn, and Becky Thatcher stow away on Mark Twain's amazing flying machine, heading for Halley's Comet in this clay-figure animated feature. Strangely disjointed and ineffectual, incorporating pieces of Twain stories with interesting (but unsettling) look at darker side of his personality. Still, impressive use of Claymation. [G] ▼◑①

Adventures of Milo and Otis, The (1989-Japanese) **C-76m.** **½ D: Masanori Hata. Narrated by Dudley Moore. Cute film for kids about a dog and a cat who venture away from their farm and experience a variety of adventures. Not very strong on story but buoyed (in the U.S. release version) by Moore's delightful narration. Original version, released in 1986, ran 90m. [G] ▼①

Adventures of Pinocchio, The (1996-British-French-German) **C-96m.** *** D: Steve Barron. Martin Landau, Jonathan Taylor Thomas, Genevieve Bujold, Udo Kier, Bebe Neuwirth, Rob Schneider, Corey Carrier, John Sessions; voice of David Doyle. Appealing live-action rendition of the Collodi fable about a wood-carver who creates the magical, mischievous marionette Pinocchio . . . who wants only to be a real boy. Some variations from the Disney version, but gentle of spirit and enjoyable throughout. Only adults are likely to question the variety of accents (American, British, German, Italian) in a story supposedly set in Italy. Followed by a direct-to-video sequel. Panavision. [G] ▼◑①

Adventures of Pluto Nash, The (2002) **C-95m.** *½ D: Ron Underwood. Eddie Murphy, Randy Quaid, Rosario Dawson, Joe Pantoliano, Jay Mohr, Luis Guzman, James Rebhorn, Peter Boyle, Pam Grier, John Cleese, Burt Young, Miguel A. Nunez, Jr., Illeana Douglas. Murphy sleepwalks through this dumb comedy as a nightclub owner on a moon colony in the year 2087 who tries to prevent a Mafia-type kingpin from turning his establishment into a gambling casino. Expensive misfire became Murphy's biggest box-office bomb, earning comparisons with HOWARD THE DUCK and ISHTAR. Alec Baldwin appears unbilled. [PG-13] ▼①

Adventures of Priscilla Queen of the Des-

ert, The (1994-Australian) **C-102m.** ✱✱✱ D: Stephan Elliott. Terence Stamp, Hugo Weaving, Guy Pearce, Bill Hunter, Sarah Chadwick, Mark Holmes. Cheerfully outrageous comedy about three flamboyant lip-sync performers—two drag queens and a transsexual—who journey to a remote desert gig on a converted schoolbus named Priscilla. Diverting, if you can get past the bitchy banter, and anchored by Stamp as the transsexual. A must for ABBA fans. Oscar winner for Costume Design. Later a stage musical. Arriscope (and Dragarama). [R]▼⊙)

Adventures of Robin Hood, The (1938) **C-102m.** ✱✱✱✱ D: Michael Curtiz, William Keighley. Errol Flynn, Olivia de Havilland, Basil Rathbone, Claude Rains, Patric Knowles, Eugene Pallette, Alan Hale, Herbert Mundin, Una O'Connor, Melville Cooper, Ian Hunter, Montagu Love. Dashing Flynn in the definitive swashbuckler, winning hand of de Havilland (never lovelier as Maid Marian), foiling evil prince Rains, dueling wicked Rathbone. Erich Wolfgang Korngold's outstanding score earned an Oscar, as did the art direction and editing. Scripted by Norman Reilly Raine and Seton I. Miller. Arguably Flynn's greatest role. ▼⊙)

Adventures of Robinson Crusoe (1952-Mexican) **C-90m.** ✱✱✱½ D: Luis Buñuel. Dan O'Herlihy, Jaime Fernandez. Colorful, entertaining adaptation of Daniel Defoe's classic story about a resourceful shipwreck victim, with some distinctive Buñuel touches; vivid performance by O'Herlihy. Screenplay by Philip Ansell Roll (Hugo Butler) and Buñuel. Excellent music score by Anthony Collins. Main title on film is ROBINSON CRUSOE.▼)

Adventures of Rocky and Bullwinkle, The (2000) **C-88m.** ✱✱½ D: Des McAnuff. Rene Russo, Jason Alexander, Robert De Niro, Piper Perabo, James Rebhorn, Randy Quaid, Taraji (P.) Henson; voices of Keith Scott, June Foray. FBI agent yanks Rocket J. Squirrel and Bullwinkle Moose out of cartoon reruns in order to foil world-domination plans of Fearless Leader (De Niro). Fans of Jay Ward's cartoons will probably cut this benign comedy more slack than others. De Niro (who also co-produced the film) has fun and even spoofs Travis Bickle! A number of stars appear in gag cameos. [PG]▼)

Adventures of Sebastian Cole, The (1999) **C-104m.** ✱✱✱ D: Tod Williams. Adrian Grenier, Clark Gregg, Aleska Palladino, Margaret Colin, John Shea, Marni Lustig, Joan Copeland, Tom Lacy, Rory Cochrane, Levon Helm, Famke Janssen. Compassionate coming-of-age story about an introverted adolescent and the impact on him and his family when his stepfather (Gregg) announces he is planning a sex-change operation. Despite this offbeat

premise, the film is more true to life than many other teen-angst tales. [R]▼)

Adventures of Sharkboy and Lavagirl 3-D, The (2005) **C-92m.** ✱✱½ D: Robert Rodriguez. Taylor Lautner, Taylor Dooley, Cayden Boyd, George Lopez, David Arquette, Kristin Davis, Jacob Davich. A daydreaming boy named Max is visited by two characters he created—Sharkboy and Lavagirl—who need his help to keep Planet Drool from being taken over by dark forces, including a nasty kid named Minus (who resembles Max's schoolyard tormentor) and his henchman Mr. Electric (who looks just like his teacher). Inspired by the drawings and dreams of his 7-year-old son Racer, Rodriguez uses computer wizardry to create an eye-popping world of wonder for young viewers . . . though his script and dialogue remain strictly earthbound. 3-D. [PG] ▼)

Adventures of Sherlock Holmes, The (1939) **85m.** ✱✱✱½ D: Alfred Werker. Basil Rathbone, Nigel Bruce, Ida Lupino, Alan Marshal, Terry Kilburn, George Zucco, E. E. Clive, Mary Gordon. The master sleuth faces one of his greatest challenges when the nefarious Professor Moriarty (Zucco) plots to steal the Crown Jewels. The second and last of Fox's excellent Rathbone-Bruce period pieces, which predated Universal's entertaining modern series.▼⊙)

Adventures of Sherlock Holmes' Smarter Brother, The SEE: **Adventure of Sherlock Holmes' Smarter Brother, The**

Adventures of the Great Mouse Detective, The SEE: **Great Mouse Detective, The**

Adventures of the Wilderness Family, The (1975) **C-100m.** ✱✱✱ D: Stewart Raffill. Robert F. Logan, Susan Damante Shaw, Hollye Holmes, Ham Larsen, Buck Flower, William Cornford. Good human-interest drama. Modern couple with two children forsake big city for life in magnificent but sometimes dangerous Rocky Mountain region. Followed by two look-alike sequels. [G]▼)

Advise & Consent (1962) **139m.** ✱✱✱ D: Otto Preminger. Henry Fonda, Don Murray, Charles Laughton, Walter Pidgeon, Peter Lawford, Gene Tierney, Franchot Tone, Lew Ayres, Burgess Meredith, Paul Ford, George Grizzard, Betty White. Long but engrossing drama of Washington wheeling and dealing, from Allen Drury novel. Cast is fine, with effective underplaying by Ayres and Tone standing out among more flamboyant performances by Laughton (his last film) and Grizzard. Also shown in computer-colored version. Panavision. ▼⊙)

Advocate, The (1994-British) **C-101m.** ✱✱✱ D: Leslie Megahey. Colin Firth, Amina Annabi, Jim Carter, Donald Pleasence, Ian Holm, Nicol Williamson, Lysette Anthony. Lawyer Firth abandons the bustle of 15th-century Paris for the supposedly more pastoral pace of rural France, only to get involved in a murder cover-up that culminates in his defending a pig—back when animals actually used to stand trial. Very offbeat but very accessible drama of courtroom intrigue with vivid characterizations. Aka HOUR OF THE PIG. [R]▼❶

Aeon Flux (2005) **C-93m.** *½ D: Karyn Kusama. Charlize Theron, Marton Csokas, Jonny Lee Miller, Sophie Okonedo, Frances McDormand, Pete Postlethwaite, Amelia Warner, Nikolai Kinski. Brainless sci-fi thriller in which a sexy rebel/assassin (Theron) battles to liberate a walled city from its dictatorial rulers. This nonsensical, sleep-inducing live-action cartoon is based on Peter Chung's animated MTV series; the material is far better served in its original format. Super 35. [PG-13]❶

Affair in Trinidad (1952) **98m.** **½ D: Vincent Sherman. Rita Hayworth, Glenn Ford, Alexander Scourby, Torin Thatcher, Juanita Moore, Steven Geray. Hayworth and Ford sparkle as cafe singer and brother-in-law seeking her husband's murderer. Hayworth is most enticing.▼❶

Affair of Love, An (1999-French-Belgian) **C-80m.** *** D: Frédéric Fonteyne. Nathalie Baye, Sergi Lopez. Provocative and interesting film about a woman who places an ad in a magazine to find a man who will participate in her sexual fantasy. Soon the couple is meeting on a weekly basis, but she is reluctant to take the next step and get to know him as a person. French title is UNE LIAISON PORNOGRAPHIQUE (A PORNOGRAPHIC AFFAIR), which refers to Baye's definition of their relationship; the film itself is fairly discreet. Super 35.▼❶

Affair of the Necklace, The (2001-U.S.-French) **C-120m.** ** D: Charles Shyer. Hilary Swank, Jonathan Pryce, Simon Baker, Adrien Brody, Brian Cox, Joely Richardson, Christopher Walken, Hayden Panettiere. Handsome but ponderous historical drama—based on real-life events—in which a young woman, seeking to restore her family name and reclaim her home, dares to scheme against Marie Antoinette and the power-hungry Cardinal Louis de Rohan. Swank's performance lacks fire and charisma, however, and the film itself never ignites. Narration, by King Louis' house minister (Cox), is heavy-handed and often unnecessary. Super 35. [R]▼❶

Affair to Remember, An (1957) **C-115m.** **½ D: Leo McCarey. Cary Grant, Deborah Kerr, Richard Denning, Neva Patterson, Cathleen Nesbitt, Robert Q. Lewis, Charles Watts, Fortunio Bonanova. Well-remembered but middling remake of McCarey's 1939 LOVE AFFAIR. Bubbling shipboard comedy in first half is overshadowed by draggy soap-opera clichés and unnecessary musical numbers in N.Y.C. finale. Still, Grant and Kerr make a wonderful couple.

Film is a major reference point in 1993 hit SLEEPLESS IN SEATTLE. Remade again as LOVE AFFAIR in 1994. Vic Damone croons the title song. CinemaScope.▼❶

Affliction (1998) **C-114m.** ** D: Paul Schrader. Nick Nolte, Sissy Spacek, James Coburn, Willem Dafoe, Mary Beth Hurt, Marian Seldes, Jim True. Portrait of a man whose screwed-up life—and mental imbalance—can be laid at the feet of his abusive father; the son (Nolte) tries to stay afloat, as traffic cop/jack-of-all-trades (and miserable part-time dad) in a small, wintry New Hampshire town. Bleak in the extreme, with no light or hope for any of its principal characters, but extremely well acted; Coburn won a Best Supporting Oscar. Schrader adapted Russell Banks' novel. [R]▼❶

Afghan Star (2009-British-Afghani) **C-88m.** *** D: Havana Marking. Interesting documentary about an *American Idol*–like TV show that's a sensation with the people of Afghanistan, although it rankles their fundamentalist rulers. We follow several finalists and learn the risks the female contestants face by flouting tradition, singing and dancing in public. Director Marking provides context by showing the modern culture of Afghanistan before the Taliban came to power in the 1980s. A thoughtful look at the conflict between a modern-thinking young population and its oppressive government.❶

Afraid of the Dark (1991-British-French) **C-92m.** **½ D: Mark Peploe. James Fox, Fanny Ardant, Paul McGann, Clare Holman, Robert Stephens, David Thewlis, Susan Wooldridge, Ben Keyworth. Offbeat psychological thriller, loaded with plot twists, about imaginative boy (Keyworth) whose father is a cop and whose mother is blind. The latter is at risk during a killing spree in which the victims are sightless females. Result is alternately gripping and ponderous. Feature directing debut for co-writer Peploe (THE LAST EMPEROR). [R]▼❶

African Cats (2011) **C-89m.** ** D: Alastair Fothergill, Keith Scholey. Narrated by Samuel L. Jackson. Third in Disney's contemporary "nature" series focuses on two mothers, a cheetah raising her cubs and an aging lioness tending to her offspring while trying to maintain her place in the pride. First-rate footage is undermined by Disney-fied narration that emphasizes the mothers' love and courage, while the images we see deal with the often-desperate struggle to survive in a kill-or-be-killed society. Although it's rated G, this is much too intense for younger children. Try Walt Disney's THE AFRICAN LION instead. [G]❶

African Lion, The (1955) **C-75m.** ***½ D: James Algar. Narrated by Winston Hibler. Outstanding True-Life documentary is perhaps Disney's best. Naturalists Alfred and

Elma Milotte filmed the African lion in his native habitat through a year's cycle of seasons. Filled with drama, excitement, color, humor. A gem.◗

African Queen, The (1951) **C-105m. ****** D: John Huston. Katharine Hepburn, Humphrey Bogart, Robert Morley, Peter Bull, Theodore Bikel, Walter Gotell. Superb combination of souse Bogart (who won an Oscar) and spinster Hepburn traveling downriver in Africa during WW1, combating the elements and the Germans, and each other. Script by James Agee and director Huston from C. S. Forester's novel; gorgeously filmed on location in the Belgian Congo by Jack Cardiff.▼◗

African Rage SEE: **Target of an Assassin**

Africa Screams (1949) **79m. *** D: Charles Barton. Bud Abbott, Lou Costello, Hillary Brooke, Max Baer, Clyde Beatty, Frank Buck, Shemp Howard, Joe Besser, Buddy Baer. A&C go on safari in this funny outing full of wheezy but often hilarious gags and routines. Also shown in computer-colored version.▼◗

Africa—Texas Style (1967) **C-106m. **½** D: Andrew Marton. Hugh O'Brian, John Mills, Nigel Green, Tom Nardini, Adrienne Corri. Feature (which later spun off a TV series, *Cowboy in Africa*) doesn't offer much excitement, with O'Brian helping Mills preserve wild game in the dark continent. Hayley Mills has a cameo.▼

After Dark, My Sweet (1990) **C-114m. **½** D: James Foley. Jason Patric, Rachel Ward, Bruce Dern, George Dickerson, James Cotton, Rocky Giordani, Corey Carrier. Piquant modern-day film noir based on a Jim Thompson novel, about a drifter who becomes involved with a beautiful but troubled woman and her criminally scheming friend. Interesting at first, but eventually you catch on that it's heading nowhere—10 miles per hour, at that. Both Patric and Dern are excellent. Super 35. [R]▼◗

Afterglow (1997-U.S.-Canadian) **C-113m. **½** D: Alan Rudolph. Nick Nolte, Julie Christie, Lara Flynn Boyle, Jonny Lee Miller, Jay Underwood, Domini Blythe, Yves Corbeil. Typically odd Rudolph fare, set in Montreal: longtime marrieds Nolte and Christie have hit an emotional roadblock; he's a handyman (named Lucky) who cats around while she seeks to relive her days as a movie actress. Meanwhile, businessman Miller has given his young, beautiful wife the cold shoulder—leaving her vulnerable to the charms of Nolte. Dense, slow, not entirely satisfying, but Christie is impressive as a woman who's drowning in sorrow. Written by Rudolph, produced by Robert Altman. [R]▼◗

After Hours (1985) **C-97m. **½** D: Martin Scorsese. Griffin Dunne, Rosanna Arquette, Verna Bloom, Thomas Chong, Linda Fiorentino, Teri Garr, John Heard, Cheech Marin, Catherine O'Hara, Dick Miller, Bronson Pinchot. Ordinary guy goes through a series of bizarre experiences during one incredible night in N.Y.C. How much you enjoy this comic nightmare will depend on how closely you identify with Dunne—the only normal person in the picture! [R]▼◗

After Life (1998-Japanese) **C-118m. ***½** D: Kore-eda Hirokazu. Aarata, Erika Oda, Susuma Terajima, Taketoshi Naito, Kyoko Kagawa, Kei Tani, Takashi Naito, Yusuke Iseya. Beautifully told story of caseworkers at a way station between heaven and earth, who help the recently deceased choose a single moment from their pasts to live inside for the rest of eternity. Quiet, poetic examination of life, death, and memory, filled with gentle humor and blessedly free of any feel-good bromides. A plea to Hollywood: *do not* remake this. Written by the director.▼◗

After.Life (2010) **C-103m. *½** D: Agnieszka Wojtowicz-Vosloo. Liam Neeson, Christina Ricci, Josh Charles, Justin Long, Chandler Canterbury, Celia Weston, Rosemary Murphy, Shuler Hensley. In this dreary psychological horror tale, a young woman seems to be hovering between life and death as she carries on conversations with a sinister undertaker who may have other plans for her. Or not. What Neeson is doing in this low-rent mumbo jumbo is a bigger mystery than anything in the script. Nothing here makes any sense, with a premise that wouldn't hold up as a half-hour *Twilight Zone* episode, much less an overlong, indulgent feature film that's as pretentious as its title. Super 35. [R]◗

After Midnight (1989) **C-90m. *½** D: Ken Wheat, Jim Wheat. Jillian McWhirter, Pamela Segall, Ramy Zade, Nadine Van Der Velde, Marc McClure, Marg Helgenberger, Billy Ray Sharkey. Four coeds take turns telling the scariest story they know in this weak and predictable horror anthology . . . with a high violence quotient. This got limited theatrical release before heading to videoland. [R]▼◗

After the Fox (1966-British-Italian) **C-103m. **½** D: Vittorio De Sica. Peter Sellers, Victor Mature, Britt Ekland, Martin Balsam. Not always successful comedy of Italian con man Sellers, who poses as a movie director. A must-see for Mature's performance as a fading romantic star with tremendous ego. Script by Neil Simon. Panavision.▼◗

After the Rehearsal (1984-Swedish) **C-72m. *** D: Ingmar Bergman. Erland Josephson, Ingrid Thulin, Lena Olin, Nadja Palmstjerna-Weiss, Bertil Guve. While staging the production of a Strindberg play a womanizing director is browbeaten by the actress daughter of an old lover, then a middle-aged actress/ex-lover who has fallen on tougher times. Short running time or not, you can exhaust yourself trying to figure out the relationships here. Small-screen viewing should make this original telefilm easier to take than it was in theatrical screenings. Fine acting. [R]▼

After the Sunset (2004) **C-93m.** ** D: Brett Ratner. Pierce Brosnan, Salma Hayek, Woody Harrelson, Don Cheadle, Naomie Harris, Chris Penn, Mykelti Williamson, Obba Babatundé. Master thief Brosnan and sexy accomplice Hayek escape to a sun-drenched paradise after pulling one final diamond heist, but FBI agent Harrelson (who's been thwarted by Brosnan before) tracks them down, seeking retribution—and hoping to prevent another theft. Aspires to be TO CATCH A THIEF but can't come close; attractive cast and scenery don't generate enough heat. Super 35. [PG-13] ▼▶

After the Thin Man (1936) **113m.** ***½ D: W. S. Van Dyke II. William Powell, Myrna Loy, James Stewart, Elissa Landi, Joseph Calleia, Jessie Ralph, Alan Marshal, Dorothy McNulty, William Law, Sam Levene, George Zucco. Delightful second entry in the series finds the urbane Charleses in San Francisco and, when not inordinately inebriated, investigating murder charges brought against Loy's unstable cousin (Landi). Slightly overlong but first rate, with a truly surprising culprit. Also shown in computer-colored version.

After the Wedding (2006-Danish-British) **C-124m.** *** D: Susanne Bier. Mads Mikkelsen, Rolf Lassgård, Sidse Babett Knudsen, Stine Fischer Christensen, Christian Tafdrup, Mona Malm. Dedicated social worker (Mikkelsen) who runs an orphanage in rural India is summoned home to Copenhagen to meet a wealthy man who may fund his projects. He arrives just as the industrialist's daughter is getting married, and at the wedding makes a shocking discovery. Bier (who cowrote this with Anders Thomas Jensen) explores her characters' moral dilemmas in ultra close-up. Stern, intense drama with superior performances. [R]▶

Afurika Monogatari (1981-Japanese) **C-120m.** BOMB D: Susumu Hani. James Stewart, Philip Sayer, Kathy, Eleanora Vallone, Heekura Simba. Pilot Sayer crashes plane in wilds of Africa, comes upon game preserve occupied by Stewart and granddaughter. Even old Jimmy is boring. Filmed in Kenya. Aka A TALE OF AFRICA and THE GREEN HORIZON. ▼

Against a Crooked Sky (1975) **C-89m.** ** D: Earl Bellamy. Richard Boone, Stewart Petersen, Geoffrey Land, Jewel Blanch, Henry Wilcoxon, Clint Ritchie. A boy searches for his sister, who's been kidnapped by Indians; simplistic, old-fashioned family Western. Todd-AO 35. [G] ▼▶

Against All Flags (1952) **C-83m.** **½ D: George Sherman. Errol Flynn, Maureen O'Hara, Anthony Quinn, Mildred Natwick. Flynn found his forte again as dashing 18th-century naval officer who maneuvers way into pirate fortress, while managing to flirt with O'Hara. Although not Flynn's final swashbuckler, this was his last *good* entry in that genre. Remade as THE KING'S PIRATE. ▼▶

Against All Odds (1968) SEE: **Blood of Fu Manchu, The**

Against All Odds (1984) **C-128m.** **½ D: Taylor Hackford. Rachel Ward, Jeff Bridges, James Woods, Alex Karras, Jane Greer, Richard Widmark, Dorian Harewood, Swoosie Kurtz, Saul Rubinek, Pat Corley, Bill McKinney, Kid Creole and the Coconuts. Unemployed jock accepts a job from a sleazy ex-teammate to find his girlfriend, who's run off to Mexico. The plot thickens, in several directions, in this loose remake of OUT OF THE PAST (with Greer playing the mother of her character in the original). Good stab at film noir feeling, but script is plot-heavy and unsatisfying. Best scene—a hair-raising race along Sunset Boulevard—is completely out of step with the rest of the film. An interesting misfire. Haunting title song by Phil Collins. [R] ▼▶

Against the Current (2009) **C-96m.** *** D: Peter Callahan. Joseph Fiennes, Justin Kirk, Elizabeth Reaser, Michelle Trachtenberg, Pell James, Constance Barron, Amy Hargreaves, Mary Tyler Moore. Thirty-something Fiennes, still grieving over the deaths of his wife and child five years before, decides to swim the Hudson River from upstate New York to N.Y.C. Leisurely paced, extremely downbeat film builds in intensity as it goes along and asks a provocative question: Is it possible to find meaning in life when fate has dealt you the cruelest of blows? Moore steals the film in her brief scenes as Reaser's royal pain of a mother. Callahan also scripted. Released direct to DVD in the U.S. [R] ▶

Against the Ropes (2004) **C-111m.** ** D: Charles S. Dutton. Meg Ryan, Omar Epps, Tony Shalhoub, Tim Daly, Charles S. Dutton, Kerry Washington, Joe Cortese. Jackie Kallen (Ryan), exposed to boxing since childhood, sets out to make a name for herself by promoting street brawler Epps as a potential champion. To do this, she has to buck some heavy-duty criminals and a pervasive prejudice against women in the business. Shaky script changes tone from one round to the next; surely the real-life Kallen's story wasn't this clichéd. Super 35. [PG-13] ▼▶

Agatha (1979) **C-98m.** *** D: Michael Apted. Dustin Hoffman, Vanessa Redgrave, Timothy Dalton, Helen Morse, Celia Gregory, Paul Brooke. Fictional speculation on writer Agatha Christie's famous 11-day disappearance in 1926; Redgrave is superb in this absorbing yarn, Hoffman oddly miscast as smooth American reporter who tracks her down. [PG] ▼▶

Agatha Christie's Endless Night SEE: **Endless Night**

Agency (1981-Canadian) **C-94m.** *½ D: George Kaczender. Robert Mitchum, Lee Majors, Valerie Perrine, Saul Rubinek, Alexandra Stewart. Shifty Mitchum plots to gain political clout via information transmitted subliminally in television ads. Fascinating idea, but result is dull and unconvincing. Aka MIND GAMES. [R] ▼▶

Agent Cody Banks (2003) **C-102m.** *** D: Harald Zwart. Frankie Muniz, Hilary Duff, Angie Harmon, Keith David, Ian McShane, Arnold Vosloo, Cynthia Stevenson, Daniel Roebuck, Darrell Hammond, Martin Donovan. A geeky, girl-shy 15-year-old (Muniz) who is secretly a junior agent for the CIA is assigned to befriend the cute daughter of a scientist developing a secret weapon for a sinister organization. This good-natured, broadly comic blend of Bond, SPY KIDS, and MEN IN BLACK is a teenage boy's dream come true, packed with hot babes, cool cars, extreme sports action, and high-tech gadgets galore. Followed by a sequel. Panavision. [PG] ▼▶

Agent Cody Banks 2: Destination London (2004) **C-99m.** ** D: Kevin Allen. Frankie Muniz, Anthony Anderson, Hannah Spearritt, Cynthia Stevenson, Daniel Roebuck, Anna Chancellor, Keith Allen, David Kelly, Keith David. That juvenile secret agent is back for a U.K. adventure, with Anderson all too obviously shoehorned into the proceedings for comedy relief as his watchdog. Muniz and perky Spearritt are ·game, but the characters and plotting are just plain dull. P.S. Madonna and Jason Alexander are among the executive producers! Panavision. [PG] ▼▶

Agent 8¾ (1964-British) **C-98m.** *** D: Ralph Thomas. Dirk Bogarde, Sylva Koscina, Leo McKern, Robert Morley, Roger Delgado, John LeMesurier. Released at height of James Bond craze, this spoof features Bogarde as a bumbling secret agent working in Czechoslovakia. Sometimes witty, bright comedy. Originally released in U.S. at 77m. Original British title: HOT ENOUGH FOR JUNE.

Age of Consent (1969-Australian) **C-103m.** **½ D: Michael Powell. James Mason, Helen Mirren, Jack MacGowran, Neva Carr-Glyn, Frank Thring. A put-upon artist escapes to the quietude of Australia's Great Barrier Reef, where he's inspired by a feisty young girl whom he persuades to pose (often nude) for him. General amiability and pretty scenery help make up for clumsy comedy relief and gaps in story and characterization. Based on life of Norman Lindsay, later the subject of SIRENS. [R] ▶

Age of Innocence, The (1934) **81m.** **½ D: Philip Moeller. Irene Dunne, John Boles, Lionel Atwill, Helen Westley, Laura Hope Crews, Julie Haydon. Modest but effective version of Edith Wharton's novel about a thwarted romance between an engaged attorney and a divorcée, in rigid 1870s Manhattan society. Starts off with a terrific Jazz Age montage prologue, then gets bogged down in static, stagy treatment as elderly Boles relates the story of his ill-fated affair to his grandson. Dunne gives a luminous and touching performance. Remade in 1993. ▶

Age of Innocence, The (1993) **C-133m.** **½ D: Martin Scorsese. Daniel Day-Lewis, Michelle Pfeiffer, Winona Ryder, Richard E. Grant, Alec McCowen, Geraldine Chaplin, Mary Beth Hurt, Miriam Margolyes, Sian Phillips, Michael Gough, Alexis Smith, Norman Lloyd, Jonathan Pryce, Robert Sean Leonard, Carolyn Farina; narrated by Joanne Woodward. In 1870s N.Y. society, well-bred young man (Day-Lewis), engaged to marry well-bred young woman (Ryder), is smitten by notorious beauty (Pfeiffer) with a somewhat scandalous background and an independent spirit. Sumptuous adaptation of Edith Wharton's Pulitzer Prize–winning novel about repressed emotions in a convention-bound society, but amidst the meticulous detail and opulent settings, it's hard to connect with these characters on an emotional level. Oscar winner for Costume Design. Filmed previously in 1924 and 1934. Super 35. [PG] ▼●▶

Agnes Browne (1999-U.S.-Irish) **C-92m.** **½ D: Anjelica Huston. Anjelica Huston, Marion O'Dwyer, Ray Winstone, Arno Chevrier, Gerard McSorley, Tom Jones. Good-natured film about a working-class stiff in late 1960s Dublin whose husband has just died, leaving her to raise seven children on her own. Fortunately, her best friend (O'Dwyer) is always there to lend a hand. Comedy is rich in atmosphere but pat, with a subplot involving singer Tom Jones pushing things a bit too far. [R] ▼▶

Agnes of God (1985) **C-98m.** ***½ D: Norman Jewison. Jane Fonda, Anne Bancroft, Meg Tilly, Anne Pitoniak, Winston Reckert, Gratien Gelinas. A young nun apparently became pregnant, then murdered the baby in the cloistered atmosphere of a convent, but court-appointed psychiatrist finds no easy explanations. Disturbing, not always satisfying, but electrified by three lead performances, and beautifully photographed by Sven Nykvist. Screenplay by John Pielmeier, from his play. [PG-13] ▼●▶

Agony and the Ecstasy, The (1965) **C-140m.** **½ D: Carol Reed. Charlton Heston, Rex Harrison, Diane Cilento, Harry Andrews, Adolfo Celi. Huge spectacle of Michelangelo's artistic conflicts with Pope Julius II has adequate acting overshadowed by meticulous production. Short documentary on artist's work precedes fragmentary drama based on bits of Irving Stone's novel. Todd-AO. ▼●▶

Agora (2009-Spanish) **C-127m.** ** D:

[15]

Alejandro Amenábar. Rachel Weisz, Max Minghella, Oscar Isaac, Ashraf Barhom, Rupert Evans, Homayoun Ershadi, Michael Lonsdale, Sami Samir, Richard Durden. It's pagans versus Christians in 4th-century Alexandria, Egypt, with beautiful, controversial teacher-philosopher-astronomer Hypatia (Weisz) at center stage. Potentially interesting tale of science and humanism in conflict with religious intolerance (with obvious parallels to the present day) is too simplistic and melodramatic to make an impression. [R] ▶

Agronomist, The (2004) **C-91m.** ***½ D: Jonathan Demme. Powerful, uncompromising documentary portrait of a fascinating individual: Jean Dominique, a leading Haitian radio personality and prominent figure in the country's struggle for human rights. While the film offers insight into the politics and history of (and U.S. influence in) Haiti during the latter 20th century, its primary purpose is to give us a vivid portrait of one man's fierce determination, deep-seated humanism, and passionate love of country. The finale is shattering. [PG-13]▶

Aguirre: The Wrath of God (1972-German) **C-94m.** ***½ D: Werner Herzog. Klaus Kinski, Ruy Guerra, Del Negro, Helena Rojo, Cecilia Rivera, Peter Berling. Powerful, hypnotic tale of deluded conquistador who leads a group of men away from Pizarro's 1560 South American expedition in search of seven cities of gold. Dreamlike film was shot on location in remote Amazon jungles; Kinski is perfect as the mad Aguirre. Filmed in both German- and English-language versions; try to avoid the latter.▶▮

Ah, Wilderness! (1935) **101m.** ***½ D: Clarence Brown. Wallace Beery, Lionel Barrymore, Aline MacMahon, Eric Linden, Cecilia Parker, Mickey Rooney, Frank Albertson, Bonita Granville. Rich Americana in this adaptation of Eugene O'Neill play about turn-of-the-century small-town life, focusing on boy facing problems of adolescence. Rooney, playing younger brother, took the lead in musical remake SUMMER HOLIDAY. Screenplay by Albert Hackett and Frances Goodrich.▶

AI Artificial Intelligence SEE: **Artificial Intelligence: AI**

Aimée & Jaguar (1999-German) **C-125m.** *** D: Max Färberböck. Maria Schrader, Juliane Köhler, Johanna Wokalek, Heike Makatsch, Elisabeth Degen, Detlev Buck. Felice (Schrader) is a Jewish lesbian who's employed, "underground" fashion, by the Germans in 1943 Berlin, while Lilly (Köhler) has four children by the Nazi husband on whom she cheats—with other Nazis. The two women fall in love, which would seem awfully contrived if it weren't based on a true story. Production values are surprisingly detailed and lush, and the acting is first-rate.

Title alludes to the affectionate nicknames the women have for each other.▶▮

Air America (1990) **C-112m.** ** D: Roger Spottiswoode. Mel Gibson, Robert Downey, Jr., Nancy Travis, David Marshall Grant, Lane Smith, Ken Jenkins, Burt Kwouk, Art La Fleur, Tim Thomerson. Pilots Mel and Bob are part of the C.I.A.'s smuggling operation in Laos during the Vietnam War. They crate anything and anyone anywhere—too bad they couldn't fly in a script doctor. Alleged action-comedy has few laughs and makes little sense. Even Gibson's patented swagger can't keep this one airborne. No relation to the 1998 TV series. Super 35. [R] ▶◐▮

Airborne (1993) **C-91m.** *½ D: Rob Bowman. Shane McDermott, Seth Green, Brittney Powell, Edie McClurg, Patrick O'Brien, Jack Black. Pedestrian teen film about a surfer who's shipped off to Cincinnati, where, away from the waves, he seeks to gain respect through his amazing skill on rollerblades. Tough skating for anyone but kids; some truly spectacular rollerblading stunts are the film's sole grace. [PG]▶◐▮

Air Bud (1997) **C-97m.** **½ D: Charles Martin Smith. Kevin Zegers, Michael Jeter, Wendy Makkena, Bill Cobbs, Eric Christmas. Innocuous Disney kiddie film about a new boy in town who befriends a lovable stray dog with the uncanny ability to shoot hoops. Jeter is malevolent fun as Bud's former owner, a terrible children's party clown who tries to cash in on the dog's celebrity. Mildly entertaining. Director Smith starred in NEVER CRY WOLF, a much superior Disney film about animals. Followed by a sequel. [PG]▶◐▮

Air Bud: Golden Receiver (1998) **C-90m.** **½ D: Richard Martin. Kevin Zegers, Gregory Harrison, Shayn Solberg, Cynthia Stevenson, Nora Dunn, Robert Costanzo, Tim Conway, Dick Martin. Title canine catches pigskins rather than shoots hoops. He and his young owner (Zegers, the lone cast member from the original) join the school football team—plus, a pair of Boris and Natasha–like villains plot to abduct the pooch for their traveling circus. Predictable but harmless fun. Followed by several direct-to-video sequels. [G]▶◐▮

Air Force (1943) **124m.** *** D: Howard Hawks. John Garfield, John Ridgely, Gig Young, Arthur Kennedy, Charles Drake, Harry Carey, George Tobias, Faye Emerson. Archetypal WW2 movie, focusing on archetypal bomber crew. Tough to stomach at times ("Fried Jap going down," chimes Tobias after scoring a hit), but generally exciting, well done.▶◐▮

Air Force One (1997) **C-124m.** *** D: Wolfgang Petersen. Harrison Ford, Gary Oldman, Glenn Close, Dean Stockwell, Wendy Crewson, Paul Guilfoyle, William H. Macy, Liesel Matthews, Xander Berkeley, Bill Smitrovich, Elya Baskin, Jürgen Prochnow. Supercharged thriller about brutal Kazakhstani terrorists taking over *Air Force One* and holding the President, his family, and his entourage hostage in midair. Intense, violent, edge-of-your-seat popcorn fodder, anchored by Ford as a two-fisted president who's not afraid to fight. Requires the usual suspension of disbelief, but pays back in spades. Thundering score by Jerry Goldsmith. Super 35. [R]▼●)

Airheads (1994) **C-91m.** ** D: Michael Lehmann. Brendan Fraser, Joe Mantegna, Steve Buscemi, Adam Sandler, Chris Farley, Michael McKean, Judd Nelson, Ernie Hudson, Amy Locane, Nina Siemaszko. Three metalheads with toy guns reluctantly take a rock radio station hostage, hoping to get play for their one existent demo tape. Not exactly the toughest subject to satirize, but the script is dull-witted anyway; fairly energetic direction and compact running time help a bit. [PG-13]▼●)

Air I Breathe, The (2008-U.S.-Mexican) **C-97m.** *½ D: Jieho Lee. Kevin Bacon, Julie Delpy, Brendan Fraser, Andy Garcia, Sarah Michelle Gellar, Clark Gregg, Emile Hirsch, Forest Whitaker, Kelly Hu, Evan Parke, Taylor Nichols, Victor Rivers, Jon Bernthal. Four overlapping, connect-the-dots storylines, based on a Chinese proverb and titled "Happiness," "Pleasure," "Sorrow," and "Love," comprise this mess of a movie. Starts out promisingly, as a disgruntled office drone (Whitaker) accidentally learns that a horse race has been fixed, then degenerates into a cartoonish train wreck. Pounding music score, jerky editing, and pretentious narration are no help. Super 35. [R]▶

Airplane! (1980) **C-86m.** *** D: Jim Abrahams, David Zucker, Jerry Zucker. Robert Hays, Julie Hagerty, Robert Stack, Lloyd Bridges, Peter Graves, Kareem Abdul-Jabbar, Leslie Nielsen, Lorna Patterson, Stephen Stucker. Very funny spoof of AIRPORT-type pictures (and Arthur Hailey's ZERO HOUR in particular), with a nonstop string of gags that holds up almost to the end (why carp?). Our favorite: the strange plight of Lt. Hurwitz. Stay tuned through final credits. Followed by a sequel. [PG]▼●)

Airplane II: The Sequel (1982) **C-85m.** **½ D: Ken Finkleman. Robert Hays, Julie Hagerty, Lloyd Bridges, Peter Graves, William Shatner, Chad Everett, David Paymer. Mildly funny rehash of AIRPLANE (by a new writer-director), but can't match the quantity, or quality, of laughs in the original. Many cameos include Raymond Burr, Chuck Connors, Sonny Bono, Rip Torn. [PG]▼●)

Airport (1970) **C-137m.** ***½ D: George Seaton. Burt Lancaster, Dean Martin, George Kennedy, Helen Hayes, Jean Seberg, Jacqueline Bisset, Van Heflin, Maureen Stapleton, Barry Nelson, Dana Wynter, Lloyd Nolan, Barbara Hale, Gary Collins. GRAND HOTEL plot formula reaches latter-day zenith in ultraslick, old-fashioned movie that entertains in spite of itself, detailing hectic winter night at metropolitan airport. Plastic performances dominate, with down-to-earth Kennedy, touching Stapleton, and nervous Heflin standing out. Helen Hayes won Oscar as impish stowaway. Based on the Arthur Hailey bestseller; followed by three sequels—so far. Todd-AO. [G]▼●)

Airport 1975 (1974) **C-106m.** *½ D: Jack Smight. Charlton Heston, Karen Black, George Kennedy, Efrem Zimbalist, Jr., Susan Clark, Helen Reddy, Gloria Swanson, Linda Blair, Dana Andrews, Sid Caesar, Myrna Loy, Nancy Olson, Roy Thinnes, Martha Scott. Yet another jetliner disaster epic, not worth your time unless you get your kicks watching a *Hollywood Squares*–type cast that includes Helen Reddy as a (singing) nun. Swanson plays herself in her final film. Look quickly for Sharon Gless. Panavision. [PG]▼●)

Airport '77 (1977) **C-113m.** **½ D: Jerry Jameson. Jack Lemmon, Lee Grant, Brenda Vaccaro, George Kennedy, James Stewart, Joseph Cotten, Olivia de Havilland, Darren McGavin, Christopher Lee, Robert Foxworth, Robert Hooks, Monte Markham, Kathleen Quinlan, Gil Gerard, Pamela Bellwood, Arlene Golonka, M. Emmet Walsh, Chris Lemmon. All the clichés and stock characters are trucked out for another made-to-order disaster epic, not bad as these things go: Stewart's private luxury jet is sabotaged and sinks in the ocean, forcing daring rescue attempt. Lemmon brings conviction to his role as dedicated pilot. Panavision. [PG]▼●)

Airport '79 SEE: **Concorde, The—Airport '79**

Air Up There, The (1994) **C-102m.** ** D: Paul M. Glaser. Kevin Bacon, Charles Gitonga Maina, Yolanda Vazquez, Winston Ntshona, Mabutho "Kid" Sithole, Sean McCann, Dennis Patrick. Brash ex-hoopster with college coaching aspirations journeys to Africa in search of the perfect prospect, leading to the standard culture-clashing situations one might expect. As affably minor as director Glaser's previous THE CUTTING EDGE, but not as deftly put together. [PG]▼●)

AKA (2002-British) **C-123m.** **½ D: Duncan Roy. Matthew Leitch, Diana Quick, George Asprey, Lindsey Coulson, Blake Ritson, Bill Nighy, Geoff Bell, Peter Youngblood Hills. Effective story of a young, gay, working-class boy who manages to infiltrate England's upper crust, posing as a lord and almost getting away with it. Shot on digital video, story is told via a triptych, simultaneously offering three views of each scene. Technique takes getting used to but ultimately the gimmick pays off. A mixed bag, but still worth checking out. Written by Roy, and based on his own experiences. ▼◗

A.K.A. Cassius Clay (1970) **C-85m.** **½ D: Jim Jacobs. Narrated by Richard Kiley. Interesting documentary about the controversial heavyweight champion. [PG]▼◗

Akeelah and the Bee (2006) **C-112m.** *** D: Doug Atchison. Laurence Fishburne, Angela Bassett, Keke Palmer, Curtis Armstrong, Tzi Ma, Lee Thompson Young, J. R. Villarreal. Irresistible story of an 11-year-old black girl from L.A. who's learned to suppress her intelligence in order to get along at school . . . until a teacher and the principal discover her talent for spelling. They introduce her to a demanding coach (Fishburne), who, it turns out, can learn a few things from her. A feel-good movie that actually makes you feel good, told with heart (and canny precision) by writer-director Atchison. Palmer is wonderful as Akeelah. Panavision. [PG]◗

Akira (1988-Japanese) **C-124m.** *** D: Katsuhiro Otomo. Voices of Jimmy Flanders, Drew Thomas, Lewis Lemay, Barbara Larsen, Stanley Gurd, Jr. Bloody and violent animated science-fiction feature based on Japanese comic-book novel. A group of motorcycle-riding teenagers living in post-apocalyptic Neo-Tokyo tries to stop one of the gang who has run amok after becoming empowered with telekinetic powers in a government experiment. Technically spectacular, with colorful animation somewhat derailed by confusing storytelling and a cryptic ending. A must-see for adult animation buffs. [R]▼◗◗

Akira Kurosawa's Dreams (1990-Japanese) **C-120m.** *** D: Akira Kurosawa. Akira Terao, Mitsuko Baisho, Mieko Harada, Chishu Ryu, Hisashi Igawa, Mitsunori Isaki, Toshihiko Nakano, Yoshitaka Zushi, Toshie Negishi, Martin Scorsese. Eight vignettes—increasingly apocalyptic—as "dreamt" by an 80-year-old widely regarded as the greatest living filmmaker of the era. Results vary in quality, though any three viewers are likely to rate the episodes in widely shuffled order. At least one—mountain climbers caught in an all-consuming blizzard—is vintage "K." Scorsese portrays Van Gogh in one segment. (Do you detect any Burt Lancaster in his speech patterns?) [PG]▼◗◗

Aladdin (1992) **C-90m.** *** D: John Musker, Ron Clements. Voices of Scott Weinger, Robin Williams, Linda Larkin, Jonathan Freeman, Frank Welker, Gilbert Gottfried, Douglas Seale; singing voices of Brad Kane, Lea Salonga. Disney's animated Arabian Nights tale is filtered through the sensibility of an old Warner Bros. cartoon, as Aladdin conjures up a Genie who's bursting with shtick. Williams' hilarious rapid-fire patter (with equally rapid-fire animation by Eric Goldberg) forms the centerpiece of this otherwise conventional story, colorfully (and tunefully) presented.

Music and lyrics by Alan Menken, Howard Ashman, and Tim Rice; Oscar winner for Best Music Score (Menken) and Best Song ("A Whole New World," by Menken and Rice). Followed by direct-to-video sequels and an animated TV series. [G]▼◗

Alambrista! (1977) **C-110m.** ***½ D: Robert M. Young. Domingo Ambriz, Trinidad Silva, Linda Gillin, Ned Beatty, Julius Harris, Paul Berrones, Edward James Olmos. Boyish, naive Ambriz illegally crosses the U.S.-Mexican border and is exploited as he seeks work to support his family. Touching, fresh, insightful; director Young's first feature.

Alamo, The (1960) **C-161m.** *** D: John Wayne. John Wayne, Richard Widmark, Laurence Harvey, Richard Boone, Carlos Arruza, Frankie Avalon, Pat Wayne, Linda Cristal, Chill Wills, Ken Curtis, Hank Worden, Denver Pyle, Olive Carey, Veda Ann Borg, John Dierkes, Guinn "Big Boy" Williams. Long, and long-winded, saga of the Alamo, with plenty of historical name-dropping and speechifying. Worthwhile for final attack, a truly memorable movie spectacle. Fine score by Dimitri Tiomkin includes popular "The Green Leaves of Summer." Filmed on location in Brackettville, Texas. Cut by 26m. after its L.A. premiere; restored on video. Todd-AO. ▼◗

Alamo, The (2004) **C-135m.** *** D: John Lee Hancock. Billy Bob Thornton, Dennis Quaid, Jason Patric, Patrick Wilson, Emilio Echeverría, Jordi Mollá, Leon Rippy, Marc Blucas, Rance Howard. Impassioned re-creation of events leading up to the legendary 1836 siege in San Antonio, Texas; more accurate than earlier renderings of the story, it still struggles to deal with the many facets of this historical event. Cowriter-director Hancock stresses the human element and captures the defenders' nobility in defeat. Thornton is the heart and soul of the film as Davy Crockett, who wasn't larger than life but became a hero just the same. Battle scenes are especially well photographed, staged, and edited—and frighteningly believable. Panavision. [PG-13]▼◗

Alamo Bay (1985) **C-98m.** **½ D: Louis Malle. Amy Madigan, Ed Harris, Ho Nguyen, Donald Moffat, Truyen V. Tran, Rudy Young. Well-made but strangely uninvolving film based on real-life conflict between Vietnamese immigrants and American fishermen on the Texas Gulf Coast. [R]▼◗

À la Mode (1994-French) **C-82m.** ** D: Remy Duchemin. Ken Higelin, Jean Yanne, Francois Hautesserre, Florence Darel. Lighthearted French comedy of a teenage orphan who becomes apprentice to a small village's tailor, only to break into the fashion world of the '60s. If the rest of the film were as witty as the clothing there might be more to recommend. Harmless fluff. Original French title: FAUSTO. [R]▼◗

[18]

Alan Smithee Film: Burn Hollywood Burn, An (1998) **C-86m.** BOMB D: Alan Smithee. Ryan O'Neal, Eric Idle, Coolio, Chuck D, Richard Jeni, Leslie Stefanson, Sandra Bernhard, Harvey Weinstein, Sylvester Stallone, Whoopi Goldberg, Jackie Chan. Any film with Robert Evans and Billy Barty in its cast can't be ignored—but this leaden, sophomoric Hollywood satire ought to be. Idle plays a filmmaker named Alan Smithee—but since that's also the pseudonym directors must use when they don't want screen credit, he's stuck when he wants to disown his latest movie. As one character says of the film-within-a-film, "It's worse than SHOWGIRLS." The ultimate irony: this film's director, Arthur Hiller, removed *his* name after squabbling with writer-producer Joe Eszterhas. [R]▼●❶

Alarmist, The (1998) **C-93m.** ** D: Evan Dunsky. David Arquette, Stanley Tucci, Kate Capshaw, Mary McCormack, Ryan Reynolds, Tricia Vessey, Michael Learned. Offbeat but uneven black comedy about a novice door-to-door security alarm salesman (Arquette) who discovers that his boss and self-styled mentor (Tucci) actually breaks into people's homes to stir up business. Then the young man falls in love with his first customer (Capshaw). Never the sharp satire on modern paranoia it strives to be, though Tucci is terrific. Arquette's father Lewis and brother Richmond appear as his on-screen family. [R]▼●❶

Alaska (1996) **C-110m.** **½ D: Fraser C. Heston. Thora Birch, Vincent Kartheiser, Dirk Benedict, Charlton Heston, Duncan Fraser, Gordon Tootoosis. Juvenile adventure yarn on a grand scale, as a brother and sister take off in search of their father and his downed airplane. Plotted like an old grade-B melodrama, but carried out with conviction against magnificent, snowy scenery . . . and featuring an irresistible polar bear who befriends the young people. Heston (whose son directed the picture) plays a mean, wily bad guy. Super 35. [PG]▼●❶

Albino Alligator (1997) **C-97m.** ** D: Kevin Spacey. Matt Dillon, Faye Dunaway, Gary Sinise, William Fichtner, Viggo Mortensen, John Spencer, Skeet Ulrich, M. Emmet Walsh, Joe Mantegna, Frankie Faison, Melinda McGraw. Disappointing chamber piece about a trio of dysfunctional criminals who hide out in a basement bar in New Orleans, inadvertently initiating a hostage siege. Meanwhile, the Feds gather outside, thinking a much more dangerous (and wanted) criminal is holed up inside. Spacey's directorial debut presents a good cast and gets off to a good start, but it sputters to a dramatic halt halfway through. Super 35. [R]▼●❶

Al Capone (1959) **105m.** **½ D: Richard Wilson. Rod Steiger, Fay Spain, James Gregory, Martin Balsam, Nehemiah Persoff, Murvyn Vye. Good latter-day gangster biography with Steiger tirading as scarfaced Capone; good supporting cast, bringing back memories of Cagney-Robinson-Bogart films of the '30s.▼❶

Alex & Emma (2003) **C-96m.** ** D: Rob Reiner. Kate Hudson, Luke Wilson, Sophie Marceau, David Paymer, Rob Reiner, François Giroday, Lobo Sebastian, Cloris Leachman, Rip Taylor. Anemic romantic comedy about a novelist who has 30 days to complete a manuscript and his budding relationship with the stenographer he hires to help him do the job. She also turns up, in various guises, as we see his fantasy vision of the story—set in the 1920s—unfold. The two leads are OK, but the big laughs never come. Inspired, believe it or not, by real-life experiences of Feodor Dostoyevsky while he was writing *The Gambler.* [PG-13]▼❶

Alexander (2004-French-British-Dutch) **C-175m.** *½ D: Oliver Stone. Colin Farrell, Angelina Jolie, Val Kilmer, Christopher Plummer, Jared Leto, Rosario Dawson, Anthony Hopkins, Jonathan Rhys Meyers, Brian Blessed, Tim Pigott-Smith. Lumbering historical epic about the life of Alexander the Great, as dictated some years after his demise by Ptolemy. Attempt to explore the many conflicts—from the moment of his birth onward—that shaped this fabled warrior sheds very little light and makes one wish the elephants who attack in a climactic scene would do their worst. Only Jolie, as Alexander's mother, Olympias, brings any spark to the film. Perhaps the first Oliver Stone movie one can honestly describe as boring. Director's cut runs 167m. Followed a year later by ALEXANDER REVISITED: THE FINAL CUT at 220m. Super 35. [R]▼❶

Alexander Nevsky (1938-Russian) **107m.** **** D: Sergei Eisenstein. Nikolai Cherkassov, Nikolai Okhlopkov, Alexander Abrikossov, Dmitri Orlov, Vassily Novikov. Epic tale of Cherkassov and Russian army repelling German invasion during the 13th century, a disturbing parallel to world situation at time of production. Magnificently visualized battle sequences, wonderful Prokofiev score. A masterpiece.▼❶

Alexander's Ragtime Band (1938) **105m.** *** D: Henry King. Tyrone Power, Alice Faye, Don Ameche, Ethel Merman, Jack Haley, Jean Hersholt, Helen Westley, John Carradine. Corny but entertaining musical chronicling the professional and romantic ups and downs of hot-headed aristocrat bandleader Power, nice-guy pianist-composer Ameche, and tough-but-vulnerable singer Faye (in one of her best performances). Sparked by Irving Berlin songs "Blue Skies," "Easter Parade," title tune.▼❶

Alexander the Great (1956) **C-141m.** *** D: Robert Rossen. Richard Burton, Fredric March, Claire Bloom, Danielle Darrieux, Harry Andrews, Stanley Baker, Peter Cushing, Michael Hordern, Helmut Dantine. Remarkable cast, intelligent acting, but a static

[19]

epic, lacking essential sweep to make tale of Greek conqueror moving. CinemaScope. ▼◐◖

Alex and the Gypsy (1976) **C-99m.** **½ D: John Korty. Jack Lemmon, Genevieve Bujold, James Woods, Gino Ardito, Robert Emhardt, Titos Vandis. Meandering story of romance between bailbondsman Lemmon and gypsy Bujold who's accused of attempted murder. Some interesting ideas lost in the muddle of an indecisive film. [PG—originally rated R]

Alex in Wonderland (1970) **C-109m.** ** D: Paul Mazursky. Donald Sutherland, Ellen Burstyn, Viola Spolin, Federico Fellini, Jeanne Moreau. Camera follows young film director Sutherland through tedium of his everyday life. Self-indulgent imitation of Fellini (who appears briefly) caused some wags to dub this film *1½*. Burstyn stands out as Sutherland's wife. [R]▼◖

Alex Rider: Operation Stormbreaker (2006-British-German) **C-93m.** *½ D: Geoffrey Sax. Alex Pettyfer, Robbie Coltrane, Stephen Fry, Damian Lewis, Bill Nighy, Ewan McGregor, Sophie Okonedo, Mickey Rourke, Andy Serkis, Alicia Silverstone, Ashley Walters, Sarah Bolger, Missi Pyle. When his superspy uncle dies under mysterious circumstances, young Alex is thrust into the world of the British Secret Service and must foil a plot to take over the world's supercomputers. Based on the first of Anthony Horowitz's best-selling books, this could have been a clever junior James Bond outing but gets caught up in its own cuteness. Takes off in unattractive directions and comes up a big double-zero. Original British title: STORMBREAKER. Super 35. [PG]◗

Alfie (1966-British) **C-114m.** ***½ D: Lewis Gilbert. Michael Caine, Shelley Winters, Millicent Martin, Julia Foster, Jane Asher, Shirley Anne Field, Vivien Merchant, Eleanor Bron, Denholm Elliott, Alfie Bass, Graham Stark, Murray Melvin. Well-turned version of Bill Naughton play (he also scripted). Caine is superb as philandering Cockney playboy who can't decide if bachelor life is so bloody marvelous. Cher sings title tune. Followed by ALFIE DARLING. Remade in 2004. Techniscope. ▼◐◖

Alfie (2004) **C-106m.** **½ D: Charles Shyer. Jude Law, Marisa Tomei, Omar Epps, Nia Long, Jane Krakowski, Sienna Miller, Susan Sarandon, Renee Taylor, Dick Latessa, Gedde Watanabe. N.Y.C. limo driver Alfie, an ex-Londoner, loves women but only on his own terms, meaning sex when he feels like it without any strings attached . . . but lately he's starting to think there may be something missing in his life. Law is saucy, the women are well cast, but it doesn't add up to much, especially compared to the 1966 original, which was darker and more misogynistic. [R] ▼◖

Alfie Darling (1975-British) **C-102m.** ** D: Ken Hughes. Alan Price, Jill Townsend, Joan Collins, Annie Ross, Sheila White, Rula Lenska. Forgettable sequel to ALFIE, with Price a most inadequate replacement for Michael Caine. This time around our hero falls for a chic magazine editor. Video title: OH, ALFIE.▼◖

Alfredo, Alfredo (1972-Italian) **C-98m.** *½ D: Pietro Germi. Dustin Hoffman, Stefania Sandrelli, Carla Gravina, Clara Colosimo, Daniele Patella, Duilio Del Prete. All-too-typical Italian comedy about a milquetoast who wins and weds a sexy woman, only to regret his conquest. Sole interest is observing Hoffman in this unusual setting (with a dubbed voice!). Originally 110m. [R]▼

Alfred the Great (1969-British) **C-122m.** ** D: Clive Donner. David Hemmings, Michael York, Prunella Ransome, Colin Blakely, Julian Glover, Ian McKellen. Story of young leader of 9th-century England can't decide if it's a serious historical chronicle or broad swashbuckler; succeeds in neither department. Only highlight is series of meticulously filmed battle scenes; otherwise, ambitious script is boring. McKellen's film debut. Panavision. [M/PG]

Algiers (1938) **95m.** *** D: John Cromwell. Charles Boyer, Sigrid Gurie, Hedy Lamarr, Joseph Calleia. Alan Hale, Gene Lockhart, Johnny Downs, Paul Harvey. Boyer as Pepe Le Moko falls in love with alluring Lamarr visiting Casbah district of Algiers: Calleia as police official, Lockhart as informer, stand out in well-cast romance. Remake of French PEPE LE MOKO, remade as CASBAH.▼◖

Ali (2001) **C-158m.** **½ D: Michael Mann. Will Smith, Jamie Foxx, Jon Voight, Mario Van Peebles, Ron Silver, Jeffrey Wright, Mykelti Williamson, Jada Pinkett Smith, Nona Gaye, Michael Michele, Joe Morton, Paul Rodriguez, Bruce McGill, Barry Shabaka Henley, Giancarlo Esposito, Laurence Mason, LeVar Burton. Disappointing bio of the extraordinary prizefighter, born Cassius Clay, covering the years 1964 to 1974. Despite its length, film is surprisingly sketchy; we learn very little about the man except his conversion to Islam and his determination to win in the ring. The "Rumble in the Jungle" finale, which ought to be triumphant, plays out as just one more fight, since we've seen so many others reenacted by then. Smith does a good job—but the real Ali was even more charismatic. Director's cut runs 165m. Super 35. [R] ▼◖

Alias Betty (2001-French-Canadian) **C-101m.** **½ D: Claude Miller. Sandrine Kiberlain, Nicole Garcia, Mathilde Seigner, Luck Mervil, Édouard Baer, Stéphane Freiss. So-so drama-thriller charting the spiraling events that occur when a little boy dies in an accident and his emotionally disconnected grandmother kidnaps another child to take his place. Opening scenes are riveting, but story bogs down as it gets involved with too many extraneous characters. Based on the Ruth Rendell novel *The Tree of Hands.* ▼◑

Alias Jesse James (1959) **C-92m.** *** D: Norman Z. McLeod. Bob Hope, Rhonda Fleming, Wendell Corey, Jim Davis, Gloria Talbott. One of Hope's funniest has him an insurance salesman out West, mistaken for sharpshooter. Fleming is a lovely Western belle; the two do a cute song together. Many guests appear at the climax. ▼◑

Alias Nick Beal (1949) **93m.** *** D: John Farrow. Ray Milland, Audrey Totter, Thomas Mitchell, George Macready, Fred Clark. Allegory of Devil (Milland) corrupting honest politician Mitchell with help of trollop Totter. Interesting drama with unusually sinister Milland.

Ali Baba and the Forty Thieves (1944) **C-87m.** *** D: Arthur Lubin. Maria Montez, Jon Hall, Turhan Bey, Andy Devine, Kurt Katch, Frank Puglia, Fortunio Bonanova, Scotty Beckett, Ramsay Ames. Straightforward retelling of classic *Arabian Nights* story, with young Ali (Beckett) pledging his love to young princess, then witnessing his father's betrayal and murder. He hides out with the Forty Thieves and returns years later (now played by Hall) to save the same princess from a forced marriage to Mongol plunderer Hulagu Khan (Katch). Lavish, exquisite production design and costumes in glorious Technicolor. The stars are beautiful, too! Remade (with stock footage) as THE SWORD OF ALI BABA (1965). ▼◑

Alice (1990) **C-106m.** ** D: Woody Allen. Mia Farrow, Alec Baldwin, Blythe Danner, Judy Davis, William Hurt, Keye Luke, Joe Mantegna, Bernadette Peters, Cybill Shepherd, Gwen Verdon, Patrick O'Neal, Julie Kavner, Caroline Aaron, Holland Taylor, Robin Bartlett, Bob Balaban, Elle Macpherson. One of Woody's "chamber films" with Farrow as the mousy, pampered wife of wealthy Hurt, trying to find herself, and contemplating the unthinkable—an extramarital affair. With that cast, it's certainly watchable, but the whimsy seems forced, the story overly familiar. Even Allen's usually infallible choice of soundtrack music is heavy-handed. Nice screen farewell for character actor Keye Luke, however. Judith Ivey has an unbilled cameo. [PG-13] ▼◑

Alice Adams (1935) **99m.** ***½ D: George Stevens. Katharine Hepburn, Fred MacMurray, Fred Stone, Evelyn Venable, Ann Shoemaker, Frank Albertson, Hattie McDaniel, Charley Grapewin, Grady Sutton, Hedda Hopper. Excellent small-town Americana with social-climbing girl finally finding love in person of unpretentious MacMurray. Booth Tarkington's Pulitzer Prize–winning novel becomes fine film, if

not altogether credible. The dinner-table scene is unforgettable. Screenplay by Dorothy Yost, Mortimer Offner, and Jane Murfin. Filmed before in 1923. ▼◑

Alice and Martin (1998-French-Spanish) **C-123m.** ** D: André Téchiné. Juliette Binoche, Alexis Loret, Mathieu Amalric, Carmen Maura, Jean-Pierre Lorit, Marthe Villalonga. A young man, tormented by his childhood, meets his half-brother's companion (Binoche), who is drawn to him in spite of his severe emotional wounds. His troubled past is gradually revealed in flashbacks, but it's difficult to care about him or his future in this off-putting film. [R] ▼

Alice Doesn't Live Here Anymore (1974) **C-113m.** ***½ D: Martin Scorsese. Ellen Burstyn, Kris Kristofferson, Billy Green Bush, Alfred Lutter, Diane Ladd, Jodie Foster, Harvey Keitel, Vic Tayback, Valerie Curtin. Excellent look at a woman's odyssey to find herself and some measure of happiness after her husband dies, leaving her and a young son penniless. Kristofferson is gentle, well-meaning man who tries to win her love. Burstyn won well-deserved Oscar for Best Actress. Rich screenplay by Robert Getchell. Look very carefully in the final diner scene for Ladd's daughter Laura Dern eating ice cream cone at counter. Later reworked into a long-running TV sitcom called *Alice.* [PG] ▼◑

Alice in the Cities (1974-German) **110m.** *** D: Wim Wenders. Rudiger Vogler, Yella Rottlander, Lisa Kreuzer, Chuck Berry. After wandering aimlessly across America, alienated journalist Vogler meets a woman—and finds himself saddled with her 9-year-old daughter when she mysteriously disappears. Intelligent, often hypnotic film reflects on the effect of American pop culture on postwar Europeans. The first in Wenders' "road movie" trilogy, followed by WRONG MOVE and KINGS OF THE ROAD. ▼

Alice in Wonderland (1951) **C-75m.** *** D: Clyde Geronimi, Hamilton Luske, Wilfred Jackson. Voices of Kathryn Beaumont, Ed Wynn, Richard Haydn, Sterling Holloway, Jerry Colonna, Verna Felton, Bill Thompson. Entertaining, if somewhat aloof, rendering of Lewis Carroll's classic, with the Walt Disney animation team at its best bringing the Cheshire Cat, the Queen of Hearts, and the Mad Hatter to life. Episodic film is given major boost by strong personalities of Wynn, Colonna, Holloway, et al., and such tunes as "I'm Late" and "The Unbirthday Song." ▼◑

Alice in Wonderland (2010) **C-108m.** *** D: Tim Burton. Johnny Depp, Mia Wasikowska, Helena Bonham Carter, Anne Hathaway, Crispin Glover, Matt Lucas, Marton Csokas, Tim Pigott-Smith; voices of Michael Sheen, Stephen Fry, Alan Rickman, Barbara Windsor, Paul Whitehouse, Timothy Spall, Christopher Lee, Imelda

Staunton, Michael Gough. Reinvention of Lewis Carroll's story (by Linda Woolverton, who wrote Disney's BEAUTY AND THE BEAST) has Alice as a willful 19-year-old who, faced with a loveless marriage, falls down a rabbit hole to "Underland," forgetting that she's been there before. Eventually she'll have to find both inner and outer strength to save the kingdom. Imaginative, if inconsistent, this ambitious visualization is anchored by Wasikowska's likable performance as Alice and sparked by a hilarious Bonham Carter as the Red Queen. Oscar winner for Colleen Atwood's costumes and for Art Direction (Robert Stromberg, Karen O'Hara). 3-D. [PG] ◗

Alice's Adventures in Wonderland (1972-British) **C-96m.** *½ D: William Sterling. Fiona Fullerton, Michael Crawford, Ralph Richardson, Flora Robson, Peter Sellers, Dudley Moore, Michael Jayston. Tedious British film version of Lewis Carroll's classic proves Americans don't have a monopoly on making bad children's musicals. Waste of a good cast. Todd-AO 35. [G]▼◗

Alice's Restaurant (1969) **C-111m.** *** D: Arthur Penn. Arlo Guthrie, Pat Quinn, James Broderick, Michael McClanathan, Geoff Outlaw, Tina Chen. Guthrie's popular record inspired this odd blend of satire, whimsy, melodrama, and social commentary. Generally fun, with quizzically downbeat ending, showing freeform lifestyle of group of friends headed by Broderick and Quinn (as Alice). Also shown in PG-rated version. [R]▼◗

Alice Sweet Alice SEE: **Holy Terror**

Alien (1979) **C-117m.** ***½ D: Ridley Scott. Tom Skerritt, Sigourney Weaver, John Hurt, Ian Holm, Harry Dean Stanton, Yaphet Kotto, Veronica Cartwright. Commercial spacecraft unwittingly takes on an alien being that wreaks merciless havoc on the crew. Space-age horror film reverts to 1950s formula, but unfolds at a deliberate pace, populates the story with interesting, colorful characters, and plants its (genuine) shock moments with exceptional skill. Imitated but seldom equaled. Screenplay by Dan O'Bannon, from his and Ronald Shusett's story; inspired by IT! THE TERROR FROM BEYOND SPACE. For 2003 reissue, Scott trimmed some material and added 4½m. of new footage, resulting in a 115m. movie. Followed by ALIENS. Panavision. [R] ▼◗

Alienator (1989) **C-92m.** ** D: Fred Olen Ray. Jan-Michael Vincent, John Phillip Law, Ross Hagen, Teagan, Dyann Ortelli, Jesse Dabson, Dawn Wildsmith, P. J. Soles, Robert Clarke, Richard Wiley, Leo V. Gordon, Robert Quarry. Gimlet-eyed Vincent, a cruel alien prison warden, sends unstoppable, Amazonian "hunter unit" Teagan after fugitive Hagen, who's crash-landed on Earth. OK sci-fi from the prolific Ray,

with a great B movie cast, but looks like two movies overlapping. [R]▼◗

Alien From L.A. (1987) **C-87m.** *½ D: Albert Pyun. Kathy Ireland, Thom Matthews, William R. Moses, Don Michael Paul, Richard Haines, Linda Kerridge, Janie du Plessis. California Valley Girl falls down hole, finds herself in the lost city of Atlantis. As silly as it sounds. [PG]▼◗

Alien Nation (1988) **C-94m.** **½ D: Graham Baker. James Caan, Mandy Patinkin, Terence Stamp, Kevin Major Howard, Leslie Bevins. In the near future, a race of odd-looking aliens is slowly (and grudgingly) being integrated into society. World-weary L.A. cop Caan agrees to take one on as his partner, so he can track down the alien who killed his former sidekick. A great concept that doesn't quite pay off, despite many clever touches and terrific performances by Caan and Patinkin. Followed by a TV series and three made-for-TV movies. Super 35. [R]▼◗

Alien Resurrection (1997) **C-108m.** ** D: Jean-Pierre Jeunet. Sigourney Weaver, Winona Ryder, Dominique Pinon, Ron Perlman, Gary Dourdan, Michael Wincott, Kim Flowers, Dan Hedaya, J. E. Freeman, Brad Dourif. Two hundred years after ALIEN [3], Ripley (Weaver) is cloned aboard a spaceship with a touch of alien in her makeup, and more aliens to battle with the help of a band of space pirates. Clumsy sequel with crummy logic, far too many wisecracks; a few good action scenes, but strictly for series fans. Special edition runs 116m. Followed by ALIEN VS. PREDATOR. Super 35. [R]▼◗

Aliens (1986) **C-137m.** ***½ D: James Cameron. Sigourney Weaver, Carrie Henn, Michael Biehn, Paul Reiser, Lance Henriksen, Bill Paxton, Jenette Goldstein. Weaver, the sole human survivor from ALIEN, returns to planet that spawned the yukky creatures with a Marine squadron that's ready to wipe them out. Intense, exciting sequel directed by Cameron the same way he did THE TERMINATOR—once it gets going there's just no letup! Weaver is sensational in compelling lead role. The special effects won an Oscar. "Director's cut" version runs 154m. Followed by ALIEN[3]. [R]▼◗

Aliens in the Attic (2009) **C-86m.** ** D: John Schultz. Carter Jenkins, Kevin Nealon, Robert Hoffman, Doris Roberts, Tim Meadows, Ashley Tisdale, Austin Butler, Andy Richter; voices of Thomas Haden Church, J. K. Simmons, Kari Wahlgren, Josh Peck. Close encounters of the frenetic kind ensue when youngsters vacationing with their parents find pint-sized extraterrestrials—advance scouts for a full-scale alien invasion—have taken over the upper floor of their summer home. Funniest scenes involve wild and crazy behavior by older vacationers, including a doting grandmother (Roberts) and a lecherous boyfriend (Hoffman). The aliens' resemblance to the critters from GREMLINS surely isn't coincidental. [PG] ◗

Alien's Return, The SEE: **Return, The**

Aliens vs. Predator: Requiem (2007) **C-94m. **** D: The Brothers Strause. Steven Pasquale, Reiko Aylesworth, John Ortiz, Robert Joy. Follow-up to 2004's monster matchup brings the iconic extraterrestrials together for an earthbound smackdown in a small Colorado town. More graphically violent, yet significantly less atmospheric, than ALIEN VS. PREDATOR, sequel offers undemanding, occasionally exciting B-movie thrills. Expectant mothers might do well to avert their eyes during an ingeniously creepy maternity-ward sequence. Full significance of the final scene will be lost on anyone not intimately familiar with arcane aspects of the ALIEN movie mythos. Unrated version runs 101m. Aka: AVPR: ALIENS VS. PREDATOR: RE-QUIEM. Followed by PREDATORS. Super 35. [R] ◗

Alien Terror SEE: **Sinister Invasion**

Alien³ (1992) **C-115m. **** D: David Fincher. Sigourney Weaver, Charles S. Dutton, Charles Dance, Paul McGann, Brian Glover, Ralph Brown, Danny Webb, Lance Henriksen, Pete Postlethwaite. More-of-the-same sequel has Weaver and other survivors of ALIENS on isolated prison planet where (you guessed it) the alien regenerates itself and runs amok. Good performances, some scares, but a definite feeling of déjà vu hangs over the proceedings. Special edition runs 144m. Followed by ALIEN RESURRECTION. Panavision. [R] ▼◗

Alien Thunder (1973-Canadian) **C-90m. **** D: Claude Fournier. Donald Sutherland, Kevin McCarthy, Chief Dan George, Jean Duceppe, Jack Creely, Francine Racette. Mountie Sutherland chases Cree Indian accused of a sergeant's murder in this handsome but tedious actioner. Video title: DAN CANDY'S LAW. [PG] ▼◗

Alien Trespass (2009-Canadian) **C-88m. **½** D: R. W. Goodwin. Eric McCormack, Jenni Baird, Robert Patrick, Jody Thompson, Dan Lauria, Aaron Brooks, Sarah Smyth. Amusing straight-faced spoof of 1950s sci-fi movies has a spacecraft crash-landing just outside a typical American town; before long an unseen force overtakes many of the residents, including pipe-smoking scientist McCormack. It's all been parodied before but this amiable film gets the look and feel just right. Opens with a faux newsreel that sets up the movie as a long-lost nugget of film history. [PG] ◗

Alien vs. Predator (2004-Czech-British-German-U.S.) **C-101m. *½** D: Paul W. S. Anderson. Sanaa Lathan, Raoul Bova, Lance Henriksen, Ewen Bremner, Colin Salmon, Tommy Flanagan, Joseph Rye, Agathe de la Boulaye, Carsten Norgaard. Lame attempt to attract fans of the ALIEN and PREDATOR films, with the scenario involving an archeological expedition to the ends of the earth, a bizarre underground world, and the presence of the deadly ALIEN and PREDATOR monsters. A waste. "Extended" version on DVD is one minute longer! Director's cut runs 115m. Aka AVP: ALIEN VS. PREDA-TOR. Followed by a sequel. Super 35. [PG-13] ▼◗

Ali—Fear Eats the Soul (1974-German) **C-94m. ***** D: Rainer Werner Fassbinder. Brigitte Mira, El Hedi Ben Salem, Barbara Valentin, Irm Hermann, Rainer Werner Fassbinder. Widow Mira, in her 60s, falls in love with and marries an Arab 30 years her junior. Interesting, quietly effective Fassbinder film, a remake of Douglas Sirk's ALL THAT HEAVEN ALLOWS. ▼◗

Ali G Indahouse (2002-British) **C-88m. **½** D: Mark Mylod. Sacha Baron Cohen, Michael Gambon, Charles Dance, Kellie Bright, Martin Freeman, Rhona Mitra, Barbara New, Emilio Rivera. Before he brought Borat to the big screen, Baron Cohen's other TV alter ego made his feature debut in this raunchy farce in which the white British gangsta-rapper wannabe searches for "realness" and "respek" while trying to thwart a plot to overthrow the Prime Minister. Silly, scatological, and tasteless, but also sometimes sharply satirical and quite funny. And keep an eye out for a quick cameo by Borat. Released direct to video in the U.S. [R] ◗

Alive (1993) **C-125m. ***** D: Frank Marshall. Ethan Hawke, Vincent Spano, Josh Hamilton, Bruce Ramsay, John Haymes Newton, David Kriegel, Kevin Breznahan, Sam Behrens, Illeana Douglas, Jack Noseworthy. Queasy movie about the rugby team that survived 72 days in the Andes Mountains when their plane crashed on its way from Uruguay to Chile. A half-good movie encumbered by clunky dialogue (or its delivery)—but physically impressive beyond the astonishing particulars of its story (which involves cannibalism). Unquestionably the most chilling portrayal of a plane crash in movie history. Scripted by John Patrick Shanley, from the book by Piers Paul Read. John Malkovich appears unbilled. Same story previously filmed as SURVIVE! [R] ▼◗

Alive and Kicking (1997-British) **C-98m. ***** D: Nancy Meckler. Jason Flemyng, Antony Sher, Dorothy Tutin, Anthony Higgins, Bill Nighy, Philip Voss, Diane Parish. Martin Sherman (author of the play *Bent*) scripted this touching drama about a self-involved gay dancer (Flemyng) who refuses to let the fact that he is afflicted with AIDS disrupt his career; he also becomes romantically involved with a therapist (Sher) who treats HIV-positive patients. The scenario may be familiar, but it's sincere and extremely well acted, and the world of dance is nicely rendered. Original British title: INDIAN SUMMER. [R]▼❶

All About Eve (1950) **138m. ****** D: Joseph L. Mankiewicz. Bette Davis, Anne Baxter, George Sanders, Celeste Holm, Gary Merrill, Thelma Ritter, Marilyn Monroe, Hugh Marlowe, Gregory Ratoff. Brilliantly sophisticated (and cynical) look at life in and around the theater, with a heaven-sent script by director Mankiewicz (based on the story "The Wisdom of Eve" by Mary Orr). Davis is absolutely perfect as an aging star who takes in an adoring fan (Baxter) and soon discovers that the young woman is taking over her life. Witty dialogue to spare, especially great when spoken by Sanders and Ritter. Six Oscars include Best Picture, Director, Screenplay, and Supporting Actor (Sanders). Later musicalized on Broadway as *Applause.*▼❶❷

All About My Mother (1999-Spanish-French) **C-101m. ***½** D: Pedro Almodóvar. Cecilia Roth, Marisa Paredes, Penélope Cruz, Antonia San Juan, Candela Peña, Rosa Maria Sardá, Eloy Azorin. When a woman loses her son, she returns to Barcelona, rekindles a dormant friendship with a transvestite pal, and becomes involved with a stage actress her son admired. Almodóvar's most moving film to date—more serious than most, but not without his trademark humor—and distinguished by exceptional performances all around. A paean to women, in real life and on stage and film. Oscar winner for Best Foreign Film. Panavision. [R]▼❶

All About Steve (2009) **C-98m. *½** D: Phil Traill. Sandra Bullock, Bradley Cooper, Thomas Haden Church, Ken Jeong, DJ Qualls, Keith David, Howard Hesseman, Beth Grant, Katy Mixon, M. C. Gainey, Jason Jones. Blond Bullock plays a relentlessly perky woman who creates crossword puzzles for a living and becomes obsessed with TV news cameraman Cooper. In fact, she stalks him around the country as he follows a variety of breaking news stories with his ego-driven lunkhead reporter (Church). Slim pickings for comedy in this script, which seems to advocate empowerment for loonies like Bullock's character! [PG-13]❶

All About the Benjamins (2002) **C-98m. *** D: Kevin Bray. Ice Cube, Mike Epps, Eva Mendes, Tommy Flanagan, Carmen Chaplin, Valarie Rae Miller, Roger Guenveur Smith, Anthony Michael Hall. Miami bounty hunter is determined to bring in petty con man Epps, but they both get caught in the cross fire of a diamond theft gone haywire. Attempt at an action-comedy in the 48HRS vein benefits from Epps' nonstop chatter, but doesn't sustain its thin, worn-out premise. Ice Cube cowrote the screenplay. Super 35. [R]▼❶

All American (1953) **83m. *** D: Jesse Hibbs. Tony Curtis, Lori Nelson, Richard Long, Mamie Van Doren, Gregg Palmer,

Stuart Whitman. Ordinary drama in which college football hero Curtis gives up the game after his parents' death and accepts an architecture scholarship at a snooty Ivy League–type school. Of note for appearances of several all-Americans (including Frank Gifford). Look fast for football great Tom Harmon in the announcing booth.

All-American Boy, The (1973) **C-118m. *** D: Charles Eastman. Jon Voight, E. J. Peaker, Ned Glass, Anne Archer, Carol Androsky. Muddled drama about Olympic hopeful Voight's attempt to succeed as a boxer; striking locations of northern California, but that's all. Panavision. [R]▼❶

All-American Murder (1992) **C-93m. *** D: Anson Williams. Christopher Walken, Charlie Schlatter, Josie Bissett, Joanna Cassidy, Richard Kind, Woody Watson, J. C. Quinn. Rebellious college student Schlatter is suspected of murdering the virginal girl he loved, but cop Walken's not so sure. Highly guessable plot studded with slasher-movie murders cheats viewers; frequent tilted camera angles may make you seasick. [R]▼❶❷

Allan Quatermain and the Lost City of Gold (1987) **C-99m.** BOMB D: Gary Nelson (additional scenes: Newt Arnold). Richard Chamberlain, Sharon Stone, James Earl Jones, Henry Silva, Robert Donner, Doghmi Larbi, Cassandra Peterson. Cheapjack followup to 1985 version of KING SOLOMON'S MINES with the same stars; Chamberlain returns to Africa in search of his brother, who's been tracking a lost white tribe. Post-production patchups are all too obvious. Remake of the 1977 KING SOLOMON'S TREASURE. J-D-C Scope. [PG]▼❶

All Dogs Go to Heaven (1989) **C-85m. *½** D: Don Bluth. Voices of Burt Reynolds, Loni Anderson, Judith Barsi, Dom DeLuise, Vic Tayback, Charles Nelson Reilly, Melba Moore. Bluth's colorful animation is only saving grace of this downbeat musical cartoon about an orphan "adopted" by an unlovable mutt (Reynolds) who has returned from heaven to do a good deed. Misguided film has some good moments (a musical sequence with a Cajun alligator), but hurt by unappealing characters, confused storytelling, and forgettable songs. Followed by three sequels and an animated TV series. [G]▼❶❷

All Dogs Go to Heaven 2 (1996-U.S.-British) **C-84m. **½** D: Paul Sebella, Larry Leker. Voices of Charlie Sheen, Sheena Easton, Dom DeLuise, Ernest Borgnine, George Hearn, Bebe Neuwirth, Adam Wylie, Dan Castellaneta, Wallace Shawn, Pat Corley, Bobby DiCicco, Jim Cummings, Maurice La Marche. Cartoon canine Charlie Barkin (Sheen), bored with life in heaven, volunteers a return to earth in an effort to retrieve Gabriel's horn, which was stolen by evil dog Carface (Borgnine). Big improvement over the first picture in terms of story and music, but fails to match the original's lush animation. Followed by two direct-to-video sequels. [G]▼●◗

Allegheny Uprising (1939) 81m. *** D: William Seiter. John Wayne, Claire Trevor, George Sanders, Brian Donlevy, Robert Barrat, Moroni Olsen, Chill Wills. Wayne leads band of brave men against crooked Donlevy, tyrannical British captain Sanders in pre-Revolutionary colonies. Fine, unpretentious film; Trevor appealing as girl who goes after Wayne. Also shown in computer-colored version.▼●◗

Allegro Non Troppo (1976-Italian) C-75m. *** D: Bruno Bozzetto. Animator Bozzetto's answer to Disney's FANTASIA is an uneven but imaginative collection of vignettes set to music by Debussy, Dvorak, Vivaldi, Stravinsky, and others, framed by heavy-handed live-action slapstick featuring an oafish orchestra-conductor. Best sequences: Sibelius' "Valse Triste," with a melancholy cat, and a chronicle of evolution set to Ravel's "Bolero."▼●◗

All Fall Down (1962) 110m. *** D: John Frankenheimer. Warren Beatty, Eva Marie Saint, Karl Malden, Angela Lansbury, Brandon de Wilde. Improbable but absorbing William Inge script about narcissistic young man (Beatty), his admiring younger brother (de Wilde), indulgent parents (Lansbury and Malden), and the older woman (Saint) with whom he becomes involved. Fine performances. Also shown in computer-colored version.▼◗

All Good Things (2010) C-101m. ** D: Andrew Jarecki. Ryan Gosling, Kirsten Dunst, Frank Langella, Philip Baker Hall, Kristen Wiig, Lily Rabe, John Cullum, Trini Alvarado, David Margulies, Michael Esper, Diane Venora, Nick Offerman, Stephen Kunken. Fictionalized account of real-life N.Y.C. Durst family and its headline-making scandals over several decades, beginning in 1971. Gosling, the son of real estate mogul Langella, falls in love with Dunst and marries her, hoping to avoid going into the family business, but his father forces the issue. That's when the dark side of his character comes out. Well made and well acted, but it's impossible to care much about the central character, an enigma from start to finish who perpetrates some truly nasty deeds. [R]◗

All I Desire (1953) 79m. **½ D: Douglas Sirk. Barbara Stanwyck, Richard Carlson, Lyle Bettger, Lori Nelson, Maureen O'Sullivan. Family togetherness and hometown approval is answer to title, in period piece uplifted by Stanwyck's valiant performance as erring mother of three who returns to her husband.▼◗

Alligator (1980) C-94m. *** D: Lewis Teague. Robert Forster, Robin Riker, Michael Gazzo, Perry Lang, Jack Carter, Henry Silva, Bart Braverman, Dean Jagger, Angel Tompkins, Sue Lyon, Pat Petersen. If

you've got to make a film about a giant alligator that's terrorizing Chicago, this is the way to do it—with a sense of fun to balance the expected violence and genuine scares. The knowing screenplay is by John Sayles; Silva does a hilarious self-parody as an egomaniacal Great White Hunter. Don't miss the graffiti in the final scene. Followed by a sequel. [R]▼◗

Alligator II: The Mutation (1991) C-92m. BOMB D: Jon Hess. Joseph Bologna, Dee Wallace Stone, Richard Lynch, Woody Brown, Holly Gagnier, Bill Dailey, Steve Railsback, Brock Peters, Julian Reyes. Another big alligator menaces another big city, with only cops Bologna and Brown, plus Cajun alligator hunter Lynch, to stop it from gobbling up the revelers at a lake. Lame-brained and dreary. [PG-13] ▼◗

All in a Night's Work (1961) C-94m. **½ D: Joseph Anthony. Dean Martin, Shirley MacLaine, Charlie Ruggles, Cliff Robertson. Featherweight (and often featherbrained) comedy about innocent office worker caught in compromising position with big-business exec, leading to a series of misunderstandings. Filled with familiar character actors (Gale Gordon, Jerome Cowan, Jack Weston, et al.).▼◗

All I Wanna Do (1998) C-97m. *** D: Sarah Kernochan. Kirsten Dunst, Gaby Hoffmann, Lynn Redgrave, Rachael Leigh Cook, Thomas Guiry, Vincent Kartheiser, Monica Keena, Matthew Lawrence, Heather Matarazzo, Hayden Christensen. Clever, funny comedy with serious undertones about a girls' boarding school in 1963—in the years just before women's lib—where newcomer Hoffmann bonds with a group of mischief-makers. Good showcase for its talented young cast, though somehow this never got a wide theatrical release. Written by the director. Originally screened as STRIKE! [PG-13]▼◗

All I Want (2002) C-92m. ** D: Jeffrey Porter. Elijah Wood, Franka Potente, Mandy Moore, Chris William Martin, Elizabeth Perkins, Deborah Harry, Aaron Pearl, Aloma Wright. Strictly derivative coming-of-age comedy about a quirky teenage boy who moves into a boardinghouse peopled exclusively by eccentrics—including two women who show more than casual interest in him. Attractive cast makes this watchable, but it has too many echoes of other, better movies. Never released theatrically. Aka TRY SEVENTEEN. [R]▼◗

All I Want for Christmas (1991) C-92m. *½ D: Robert Lieberman. Harley Jane Kozak, Jamey Sheridan, Ethan Randall (Embry), Kevin Nealon, Thora Birch, Leslie Nielsen, Lauren Bacall. Slapdash tale of kids' efforts to get their divorced parents back together for the title holiday. A feel-good movie whose emotion seems as authentic as a plastic Christmas tree. A waste of time for all concerned (including Bacall, as the children's grandmother). [G]▼●◗

All My Sons (1948) **94m.** *** D: Irving Reis. Edward G. Robinson, Burt Lancaster, Mady Christians, Louisa Horton, Howard Duff, Arlene Francis, Lloyd Gough, Henry (Harry) Morgan. Arthur Miller's compelling drama of returning soldier (Lancaster) discovering that his father (Robinson) cheated on a war matériel order, with tragic results. Post-WW2 drama is well acted, but verbose and preachy.▼

Allnighter, The (1987) **C-108m.** BOMB D: Tamar Simon Hoffs. Susanna Hoffs, Dedee Pfeiffer, Joan Cusack, Michael Ontkean, John Terlesky, James Anthony Shanta, Pam Grier, Meshach Taylor. Three female airheads stumble through assorted sexual hijinks during the final senior weekend at a Pacific party college. Grotesque in the AIDS era, though it would be a stinker anytime. Director Hoffs is the mother of the star, a member of The Bangles rock group. [PG-13]▼◗

All Night Long (1962-British) **95m.** **½ D: Basil Dearden. Patrick McGoohan, Marti Stevens, Betsy Blair, Keith Michell, Richard Attenborough, Paul Harris. Fair updating of *Othello,* about an interracial couple, a white singer and black bandleader, and their Iago, a drummer (amusingly played by McGoohan). Guest musicians include Dave Brubeck, Charlie Mingus, John Dankworth.◗

All Night Long (1981) **C-88m.** ***½ D: Jean-Claude Tramont. Gene Hackman, Barbra Streisand, Diane Ladd, Dennis Quaid, Kevin Dobson, William Daniels, Ann Doran. Married Hackman takes up with neighbor's wife Streisand after he's demoted to managing a downtown all-night drugstore, the clientele of which has torridly high weirdo quotient. Streisand is badly, if rather endearingly, miscast (she replaced Lisa Eichhorn after film was already in production), but Hackman is at the peak of his charm in this gentle, underrated comedy. [R]▼◗

All of Me (1984) **C-93m.** *** D: Carl Reiner. Steve Martin, Lily Tomlin, Victoria Tennant, Madolyn Smith, Richard Libertini, Dana Elcar, Jason Bernard, Selma Diamond. The soul and spirit of a crotchety millionairess (Tomlin) enter the body of a young, idealistic lawyer (Martin) with often hilarious results. Uneven comedy-fantasy actually gets better as it goes along, and characters become more endearing. Martin's performance is a comic tour-de force. [PG]▼◗

All or Nothing (2002-British) **C-128m.** ** D: Mike Leigh. Timothy Spall, Lesley Manville, Alison Garland, James Corden, Ruth Sheen, Marion Bailey, Paul Jesson, Sally Hawkins, Helen Coker, Daniel Mays.

Dim, drab slice of working-class life, with cabdriver Spall barely ekeing out a living, earning no thanks from his common-law wife (who gave up on him years ago), his hostile son, or his silent daughter. Neighbors in their housing project seem to be in similar doldrums, but for one doggedly optimistic soul (Sheen). Tough going, without the rich, rounded characterizations that have marked Leigh's better films. [R]▼◗

All Over Me (1997) **C-90m.** *** D: Alex Sichel. Alison Folland, Tara Subkoff, Wilson Cruz, Cole Hauser, Ann Dowd, Pat Briggs, Leisha Hailey, Shawn Hatosy. Dark, brooding but absorbing coming-of-age drama about two girls—one gay, one straight—whose friendship unravels after a fatal gay-bashing in their Hell's Kitchen neighborhood. The whole cast is excellent, but Folland as the shy budding lesbian is the emotional center. Powered by a terrific soundtrack featuring Patti Smith and Ani DiFranco, among others. Film's costars are also indie rockers: Briggs is the frontman of Psychotica, Hailey sings with The Murmurs. Written by director Sichel's sister, Sylvia. [R]▼●◗

All Over the Guy (2001) **C-92m.** *** D: Julie Davis. Dan Bucatinsky, Richard Ruccolo, Sasha Alexander, Adam Goldberg, Andrea Martin, Doris Roberts, Christina Ricci, Lisa Kudrow, Joanna Kerns. Likable comedy about two gay guys who survive a disastrous blind date and settle into friendship, not realizing true love is staring them right in the face. Loaded with smart one-liners and clever potshots at sexless gay studio movies like IN & OUT. Terrific supporting cast includes Martin as a touchy-feely therapist mom and THE OPPOSITE OF SEX costars Ricci and Kudrow. Written by Bucatinsky, based on his stage play. [R]▼◗

All Quiet on the Western Front (1930) **133m.** **** D: Lewis Milestone. Lewis (Lew) Ayres, Louis Wolheim, John Wray, Slim Summerville, Russell Gleason, Ben Alexander, Beryl Mercer. Vivid, moving adaptation of Erich Maria Remarque's eloquent pacifist novel about German boys' experiences as soldiers during WW1. Time hasn't dimmed its power, or its poignancy, one bit. Scripted by Milestone, Maxwell Anderson, Del Andrews, and George Abbott. Academy Award winner for Best Picture and Director. Originally shown at 140m., then cut many times over the years; restored in 1998. It's 130m. on video. Sequel: THE ROAD BACK. Remade for TV in 1979. ▼◗

All Screwed Up (1974-Italian) **C-105m.** *** D: Lina Wertmuller. Luigi Diberti, Nino Bignamini, Lina Polito, Sara Rapisarda. Appealing tragicomedy of various young working-class men and women, and what happens when they move into a Milan apartment. Released in the U.S. in 1976. [PG]▼

All That Heaven Allows (1955) **C-89m.** *** D: Douglas Sirk. Jane Wyman, Rock Hudson, Agnes Moorehead, Conrad Nagel, Virginia Grey, Gloria Talbott, William Reynolds, Charles Drake, Merry Anders. When middle-class widow Wyman allows gardener Hudson—a younger man—to romance her, she faces the ire of her children, friends, and society. Typically sleek Sirk soaper. Remade by Rainer Werner Fassbinder as ALI—FEAR EATS THE SOUL.▼❶

All That Jazz (1979) **C-123m.** **½ D: Bob Fosse. Roy Scheider, Jessica Lange, Ann Reinking, Leland Palmer, Cliff Gorman, Ben Vereen, Erzsebet Foldi, Sandahl Bergman, John Lithgow, Keith Gordon, Ben Masters, Nicole Fosse, Theresa Merritt, Wallace Shawn. Director-choreographer Fosse's own 8½ casts a self-indulgent and largely negative look at his life; great show biz moments and wonderful dancing are eventually buried in pretensions, and an interminable finale which leaves a bad taste for the whole film. But that opening number (set to George Benson's recording of "On Broadway") is a wow! [R]▼❶

All That Money Can Buy SEE: **Devil and Daniel Webster, The**

All the Boys Love Mandy Lane (2008) **C-90m.** *½ D: Jonathan Levine. Amber Heard, Anson Mount, Whitney Able, Michael Welch, Edwin Hodge, Aaron Himelstein, Luke Grimes, Melissa Price. Good-looking blonde high school girl attracts the wrong kind of attention from the wrong kind of boys. Then she heads off with some new "friends" for a weekend at one boy's parents' ranch and terrible things start to happen. Variation on a typical slasher film is boring and its characters obnoxious until a (sick) twist at the end, if you last that long. Mandy's character isn't explored or explained. Never released theatrically in the U.S. Super 35. [R]

All the Brothers Were Valiant (1953) **C-101m.** **½ D: Richard Thorpe. Robert Taylor, Stewart Granger, Ann Blyth, Keenan Wynn, James Whitmore, Lewis Stone. Waterlogged adventure based on Ben Ames Williams' novel. Taylor and Granger lack conviction as New Bedford whalers having career and romantic conflicts. Filmed before in 1923 and in 1928 (as ACROSS TO SINGAPORE). ▼❶

All the Fine Young Cannibals (1960) **C-112m.** *½ D: Michael Anderson. Robert Wagner, Natalie Wood, Susan - Kohner, George Hamilton, Pearl Bailey, Anne Seymour. Clichés abound in this romantic soap opera that was actually inspired by the life of jazz trumpeter Chet Baker (whose role is played here, somewhat improbably, by Wagner). British music group Fine Young Cannibals took its name from this film. CinemaScope.

All the King's Men (1949) **109m.** **** D: Robert Rossen. Broderick Crawford, Joanne Dru, John Ireland, Mercedes McCambridge, John Derek, Shepperd Strudwick, Anne Seymour. Brilliant adaptation (by director Rossen) of Robert Penn Warren's Pulitzer Prize–winning novel about the rise and fall of a Huey Long–like senator, played by Crawford in the performance of his career. He and McCambridge (in her first film) won well-deserved Oscars, as did the film, for Best Picture. Campaign montages directed by Don Siegel. Remade in 2006. ▼❶

All the King's Men (2006) **C-128m.** ** D: Steven Zaillian. Sean Penn, Jude Law, Kate Winslet, James Gandolfini, Mark Ruffalo, Patricia Clarkson, Kathy Baker, Jackie Earle Haley, Anthony Hopkins, Kevin Dunn, Tom McCarthy, Frederic Forrest, Tom Aldredge, Keb' Mo'. Remake of the 1949 classic traces the story of grassroots Southern politician Willie Stark (inspired by the real-life Louisiana governor Huey Long), his unlikely rise to power, and how it corrupts not only him but those around him. Penn's histrionics never ring true, and his talented costars are wasted in this disappointing production. Clarkson's role as Stark's savvy campaign strategist—and mistress—won Mercedes McCambridge an Oscar in the original film, but the character is barely sketched this time around. Zaillian wrote the ineffectual screenplay. [PG-13]❶

. . . All the Marbles (1981) **C-113m.** *** D: Robert Aldrich. Peter Falk, Vicki Frederick, Laurene Landon, Burt Young, Tracy Reed, Ursaline Bryant-King, Claudette Nevins, Richard Jaeckel. There's no reason why this sloppily constructed, shallowly written movie—about a pair of beautiful female wrestlers and their two-bit manager—should be so entertaining, but it is. The climactic championship bout is a real audience-rouser. Retitled THE CALIFORNIA DOLLS. Aldrich's final film. [R]▼❶

All the Mornings of the World SEE: **Tous les Matins du Monde**

All the President's Men (1976) **C-138m.** **** D: Alan J. Pakula. Robert Redford, Dustin Hoffman, Jason Robards, Jack Warden, Martin Balsam, Hal Holbrook, Jane Alexander, Stephen Collins, Meredith Baxter, Ned Beatty, Robert Walden, Polly Holliday, F. Murray Abraham, Lindsay Ann Crouse. Redford and Hoffman play real-life *Washington Post* reporters Bob Woodward and Carl Bernstein, who persevered in their investigation of Watergate break-in that led to earthshaking scandal. Best elements of newspaper pictures, detective stories, and thrillers rolled into one superb movie. Won Oscars for Supporting Actor (Robards), Screenplay (William Goldman), Art Direction, and Sound. [PG] ▼❶

All the Pretty Horses (2000) **C-117m.** **½ D: Billy Bob Thornton. Matt Damon, Henry

Thomas, Lucas Black, Penélope Cruz, Ruben Blades, Robert Patrick, Julio Oscar Mechoso, Miriam Colon, Bruce Dern, Sam Shepard. Ambitious but uneven adaptation (by Ted Tally) of Cormac McCarthy's prize-winning novel. A young man and his best friend, sensing no future in post-WW2 Texas, drift across the border in search of the cowboy life that's disappearing around them. Alternately leisurely and lurching in its storytelling, the film looks good, but never jells; signs of post-production cutting are painfully obvious. Damon and Thomas are quite good. Panavision. [R]▼❙

All the Queen's Men (2002-U.S.-Austrian-German-Hungarian) **C-105m.** BOMB D: Stefan Ruzowitzky. Matt LeBlanc, Eddie Izzard, James Cosmo, Nicolette Krebitz, Udo Kier, David Birkin, Edward Fox. Dreadful comedy, ostensibly based on the true story of a hotshot American undercover agent who's saddled with three ill-prepared British colleagues behind German lines—in drag—during WW2. Clunky film never finds the right tone, so it isn't funny or believable. Even Izzard doing a Dietrich turn isn't interesting. Widescreen. [PG-13]❙

All the Real Girls (2003) **C-108m.** **½ D: David Gordon Green. Paul Schneider, Zooey Deschanel, Patricia Clarkson, Maurice Compte, Danny McBride, Benjamin Mouton, Shea Whigham. Life in a small southern town is revealed in this slowly paced love story about a young man taking baby steps in a quest for his first meaningful relationship. Story complications disrupt the film's tone, and the film is never as satisfying as it promises to be. Good performances and evocative atmosphere overcome most obstacles, but this is no LAST PICTURE SHOW. Leading actor Schneider cowrote the story with Green. 2.35 Research PLC. [R]▼❙

All the Right Moves (1983) **C-91m.** **½ D: Michael Chapman. Tom Cruise, Craig T. Nelson, Lea Thompson, Charles Cioffi, Paul Carafotes, Christopher Penn. Amiable youth film about a goal-oriented high-school football player (Cruise) who runs afoul of his hotheaded—and equally ambitious—coach (Nelson). Location filming in Johnstown, Pa., adds flavor. [R]▼❍❙

All These Women (1964-Swedish) **C-80m.** **½ D: Ingmar Bergman. Jarl Kulle, Harriet Andersson, Bibi Andersson, Allan Edwall. Satirical frolic involving woman-chasing cellist. He bargains with music critic to have biography written by agreeing to play writer's composition. Notable only as Bergman's first film in color. Written by Bergman and Erland Josephson. Aka NOW ABOUT THESE WOMEN.

All the Vermeers in New York (1990) **C-87m.** *** D: Jon Jost. Emmanuelle Chaulet, Stephen Lack, Grace Phillips, Laurel Lee Kiefer, Gordon Joseph Weiss, Katherine Bean, Gracie Mansion, Roger Ruffin. Provocative drama with a singular cinematic sensibility, about a stressed-out Wall Street wheeler-dealer (Lack); while at the Metropolitan Museum, he meets a beautiful, mysterious French actress (Chaulet) who resembles a Vermeer portrait. Loaded with lingering shots, carefully composed images, and improvised dialogue; the scenario examines the relationship between art and commerce, and the hypocrisy beneath the surface of N.Y.C.'s high-powered art and financial worlds. "Conceived, photographed, directed, and edited" by avant-garde filmmaker Jost.▼❍❙

All the Way SEE: **Joker Is Wild, The**

All the Way Home (1963) **97m.** ***½ D: Alex Segal. Jean Simmons, Robert Preston, Aline MacMahon, Pat Hingle, Michael Kearney, John Cullum, Thomas Chalmers. Outstanding filmization of the Tad Mosel play, set in 1915 Tennessee, an adaptation of James Agee's *A Death in the Family*. Preston is subdued in the pivotal role of a father and husband who is accidentally killed, leaving his loved ones to interpret the meaning of their lives before and after his death. Beautifully done, with Simmons offering an award-caliber performance as Preston's wife. Fine script by Philip Reisman, Jr.

All the Way, Trinity SEE: **Trinity Is STILL My Name!**

All Things Bright and Beautiful (1979-British) **C-94m.** **½ D: Eric Till. John Alderton, Lisa Harrow, Colin Blakely, Bill Maynard, Richard Pearson, Paul Shelley. Pleasant, inoffensive film for kids who like animals and can appreciate an entertainment devoid of car crashes. Kind-hearted veterinarian James Herriot (Alderton) tends to under-the-weather animals in Yorkshire at the end of the '30s. Based on two of Herriot's books, *Let Sleeping Vets Lie* and *Vet in Harness*, published in the U.S. as *All Things Bright and Beautiful*. A sequel to ALL CREATURES GREAT AND SMALL, made for U.S. TV. Aka IT SHOULDN'T HAPPEN TO A VET. [G]

All Things Fair (1995-Swedish-Danish) **C-128m.** ***½ D: Bo Widerberg. Johan Widerberg, Marika Lagercrantz, Tomas Von Brömssen, Karin Huldt, Nina Gunke, Bjorn Kjellman, Kenneth Milldoff. In 1943 Sweden a recently transferred high school student falls for his attractive new teacher; their subsequent affair is both passionate and deceitful on many levels. Extremely well made film is exquisitely performed by the two leads (young Johan Widerberg is the director's son) and Swedish star Von Brömssen is equally adept in the role of an unorthodox cuckolded husband. Director Widerberg (of ELVIRA MADIGAN fame) also wrote the screenplay and edited this, his final film. This can stand alongside the best coming-of-age films.❙

All This, and Heaven Too (1940) **143m.**

★★★ D: Anatole Litvak. Bette Davis, Charles Boyer, Jeffrey Lynn, Barbara O'Neil, Virginia Weidler, Helen Westley, Walter Hampden, Henry Daniell, June Lockhart. Nobleman Boyer falls in love with governess Davis, causing scandal and death; stars do very well in elaborate filmization of Rachel Field book set in 19th-century France. ▼◗

All Through the Night (1942) 107m. ★★★ D: Vincent Sherman. Humphrey Bogart, Conrad Veidt, Kaaren Verne, Jane Darwell, Frank McHugh, Peter Lorre, Judith Anderson, William Demarest, Jackie Gleason, Phil Silvers, Barton MacLane, Martin Kosleck. Bogart's gang tracks down Fifth Columnists (Veidt, Lorre, Anderson) in WW2 N.Y.C. Interesting blend of spy, gangster, and comedy genres, with memorable double-talk and auction scenes. ▼◗

Almost a Bride SEE: **Kiss For Corliss, A**

Almost an Angel (1990) C-95m. ★★ D: John Cornell. Paul Hogan, Elias Koteas, Linda Kozlowski, Charlton Heston, Doreen Lang, Joe Dallesandro, David Alan Grier, Stephanie Hodge. Hokey, paper-thin afterlife fantasy with Hogan a thief who turns do-gooder after an otherworldly confrontation with God (Heston, naturally). Hogan's effortless charisma cannot salvage it. He also scripted and executive produced. Super 35. [PG] ▼◗

Almost Famous (2000) C-122m. ★★★½ D: Cameron Crowe. Billy Crudup, Frances McDormand, Kate Hudson, Jason Lee, Patrick Fugit, Anna Paquin, Fairuza Balk, Noah Taylor, Zooey Deschanel, Bijou Phillips, Philip Seymour Hoffman, Peter Frampton, Jimmy Fallon, Jay Baruchel, Rainn Wilson. Crowe won an Oscar for writing this appealing autobiographical story about a guileless 15-year-old boy who wants to write about rock music and goes on the road with a band for *Rolling Stone* magazine in the 1970s. Newcomer Fugit is perfect as the boy, McDormand a delight as his overprotective mother, Hudson adorable as the band follower who wins him over, and Crudup right on target as a charismatic musician. Layered with telling details; this one's from the heart. Alternate version (the so-called "bootleg cut") runs 159m. [R] ▼◗

Almost Heroes (1998) C-90m. ★½ D: Christopher Guest. Chris Farley, Matthew Perry, Eugene Levy, Kevin Dunn, Lisa Barbuscia, Bokeem Woodbine, Steve M. Porter, David Packer, Hamilton Camp, Lewis Arquette, Christian Clemenson; narrated by Harry Shearer. A would-be explorer hires a rowdy tracker in the hope of beating Lewis and Clark to the Pacific Ocean in 1804. Farley (in his last starring film, shot in 1996 and released six months after his death) is as bombastic as ever, but the gags are either flat or nonexistent in this misbegotten comedy. Levy and Dunn have all the best moments, in colorful supporting roles. [PG-13] ▼◗◗

Almost Perfect Affair, An (1979) C-93m. ★★½ D: Michael Ritchie. Keith Carradine, Monica Vitti, Raf Vallone, Christian De Sica, Dick Anthony Williams. Romantic comedy-drama about affair between naive American filmmaker and worldly wife of film producer; set against backdrop of Cannes Film Festival, it will appeal mostly to film buffs and insiders. [PG] ▼◗

Almost You (1984) C-96m. ★½ D: Adam Brooks. Brooke Adams, Griffin Dunne, Karen Young, Marty Watt, Christine Estabrook, Josh Mostel, Laura Dean, Dana Delany, Miguel Pinero, Joe Silver, Joe Leon, Spalding Gray. Muddled, overlong, self-satisfied "romantic comedy" about Dunne's attempts to break out of his plodding existence with wife Adams in N.Y.C. Originally shown at 110m, which only made matters worse. [R] ▼◗

aloha, bobby and rose (1975) C-88m. ★★ D: Floyd Mutrux. Paul LeMat, Dianne Hull, Tim McIntire, Leigh French, Martine Bartlett, Robert Carradine, Eddie (Edward James) Olmos. OK melodrama follows predictable pattern as auto mechanic LeMat and girlfriend Hull are inadvertently drawn into crime, causing them to take it on the lam with the law in pursuit. [PG] ▼◗

Aloha Summer (1988) C-98m. ★★ D: Tommy Lee Wallace. Chris Makepeace, Yuji Okumoto, Don Michael Paul, Tia Carrere, Andy Bumatai, Lorie Griffin, Sho Kosugi. Well-meaning but bland story about six young American, Japanese, and Hawaiian boys coming of age on surfboards in Waikiki during the summer of 1959. There's nothing fresh; the waves, however, are outtasight. [PG] ▼◗

Alone in the Dark (2005) C-96m. BOMB D: Uwe Boll. Christian Slater, Tara Reid, Stephen Dorff, Will Sanderson, Mark Acheson, Frank C. Turner. Paranormal investigator Slater tangles with a mad scientist in this unintelligible time-waster based on an Atari video game. The opening crawl is dopey and overlong; what follows is mind-numbingly awful. Casting Reid as an anthropologist is like assigning Curly Howard the role of a neurosurgeon. Unrated director's cut runs 99m. Super 35. [R] ▼◗

Along Came a Spider (2001) C-104m. ★½ D: Lee Tamahori. Morgan Freeman, Monica Potter, Michael Wincott, Mika Boorem, Dylan Baker, Michael Moriarty, Jay O. Sanders, Penelope Ann Miller. As if he were doing us any great favors, Freeman reprises his role from KISS THE GIRLS as psychologist/detective Dr. Alex Cross, from James Patterson's novels. Case here involves the day-school abduction of a U.S. senator's young daughter, and Freeman's sleuthing with guilt-ridden Secret Service agent Potter. Premise is unpleasant, its execution unspeakably dull, and a "big" plot twist just doesn't cut it. Panavision. [R] ▼▶

Along Came Polly (2003) **C-90m.** ** D: John Hamburg. Ben Stiller, Jennifer Aniston, Philip Seymour Hoffman, Debra Messing, Hank Azaria, Bryan Brown, Alec Baldwin, Jsu Garcia, Michele Lee, Bob Dishy, Missi Pyle, Judah Friedlander, Cheryl Hines, Caroline Aaron, Rabbi David Baron. An insurance risk manager gets married, only to have his wife cheat on him before their honeymoon is over. Back home in N.Y.C. he meets a cute but flaky woman and decides she's the right one for him—but she's the one who's scared of commitment. Yet another Ben Stiller comedy of embarrassment; if you're looking for a story about a man with irritable bowel syndrome, search no further! Azaria all but steals the film as a French stud who teaches scuba diving in St. Barts. [PG-13] ▼

Along the Great Divide (1951) **88m.** **½ D: Raoul Walsh. Kirk Douglas, Virginia Mayo, John Agar, Walter Brennan. Douglas is appropriately tight-lipped as lawman determined to bring in his man, despite desert storm; some spectacular scenery. ▼▶

Alpha and Omega (2010) **C-88m.** *½ D: Anthony Bell, Ben Gluck. Voices of Justin Long, Hayden Panettiere, Danny Glover, Dennis Hopper, Larry Miller, Vicki Lewis, Christina Ricci. Two wolves, a male and female with opposite personalities named Humphrey and Kate (get it?), are transported to Idaho to mate and expand the wolf population. Instead, they band together to trek back home to Canada, encountering numerous perils along the way; later, they work together to stop their packs from having a turf war. Animated film is aimed at the youngest members of the family, with slapstick antics and clichéd characters that will have parents squirming. Produced on a low budget and animated primarily in Mumbai, India. 3-D. [PG] ▶

Alphabet City (1984) **C-98m.** ** D: Amos Poe. Vincent Spano, Kate Vernon, Michael Winslow, Zohra Lampert, Jami Gertz, Raymond Serra. Slick, arty but shallow and almost plotless portrait of teenage hood Spano and his life on N.Y.C.'s Lower East Side. All imagery, no content. [R] ▼▶

Alphabet Killer, The (2008) **C-98m.** ** D: Rob Schmidt. Eliza Dushku, Cary Elwes, Timothy Hutton, Tom Malloy, Michael Ironside, Bill Moseley, Carl Lumbly, Brian Scannell, Larry Hankin, Jack McGee, Melissa Leo, Tom Noonan, Martin Donovan. A young girl is raped and strangled, and Rochester, N.Y., police detective Dushku, who has all sorts of psychological issues, becomes obsessed with solving the case. By-the-letters thriller poses one burning question: Who let this woman on the police force? Loosely based on a series of murders that took place in Rochester in the 1970s. Scripted by Malloy, who plays Officer Stephen Harper. [R] ▶

Alphabet Murders, The (1966-British) **90m.** **½ D: Frank Tashlin. Tony Randall, Anita Ekberg, Robert Morley, Guy Rolfe, James Villiers. Odd adaptation of Agatha Christie's *The ABC Murders* (the film's original British title), with Hercule Poirot after a killer who seems to be doing in his victims in alphabetical order. Strange casting of Randall as the Belgian sleuth and a little too much slapstick make this more a curiosity than anything else. Margaret Rutherford makes a gag appearance as Miss Marple. ▼

Alpha Dog (2007) **C-122m.** *½ D: Nick Cassavetes. Emile Hirsch, Ben Foster, Shawn Hatosy, Christopher Marquette, Justin Timberlake, Anton Yelchin, Bruce Willis, Sharon Stone, Lukas Haas, Alex Kingston, Harry Dean Stanton, Alex Solowitz, Dominique Swain, Alan Thicke, Vincent Kartheiser, Fernando Vargas, Amanda Seyfried. Two fun-filled hours about the cretins who orbit around amoral drug dealer Hirsch. The nihilistic fun and games turn serious when they snatch the kid brother of a "friend," then realize they've actually perpetrated a kidnapping. Cassavetes' screenplay is based on real-life events but the film is pointless . . . as is the framing device of a documentary about the case (using split-screen) which disappears after the opening scenes and returns abruptly at the end. J-D-C Scope. [R] ▶

Alphaville (1965-French) **95m.** ** D: Jean-Luc Godard. Eddie Constantine, Anna Karina, Akim Tamiroff, Howard Vernon. Constantine, as super private-eye Lemmy Caution, is sent to futuristic city run by electronic brain to rescue scientist trapped there. Jumbled Godard epic, recommended for New Wave disciples only. ▼▶

Alsino and the Condor (1982-Nicaraguan-Mexican-Cuban-Costa Rican) **C-89m.** *** D: Miguel Littin. Dean Stockwell, Alan Esquivel, Carmen Bunster, Alejandro Parodi, Delia Casanova. Idealistic young peasant (Esquivel) jumps out of a tree in the hope of flying; he becomes a hunchback, but learns to stand tall when he joins guerillas fighting in a Central American country. Certainly unsubtle, but far from uninteresting allegory, filmed in Nicaragua. [R] ▼●

Altered States (1980) **C-102m.** **½ D: Ken Russell. William Hurt, Blair Brown, Bob Balaban, Charles Haid, Thaao Penghlis, Dori Brenner, George Gaynes, Drew Barrymore. A scientist (Hurt, in his film debut) becomes involved with primal research, using himself as guinea pig with mind-bending results. Talky and cerebral at first, then turns into a cross between THE WOLF MAN and THE TIME MACHINE, using state-of-the-art special effects. More successful as an assault on the senses than as a film, with thoroughly unappealing protagonists and a ludicrous story resolution. Paddy Chayefsky disowned his adaptation of his novel, and the script is now credited to his given name, "Sidney Aaron." Barrymore's film debut. Look for John Larroquette as an X-ray technician. [R] ▼●▶

Alvarez Kelly (1966) **C-116m.** **½ D: Edward Dmytryk. William Holden, Richard Widmark, Janice Rule, Victoria Shaw, Patrick O'Neal. Slow-moving Civil War tale. Holden is cattle driver who sells herd to Yankees, then is kidnapped by Reb Widmark who wants him to steal cattle for the South; incongruous love scenes thrown in. Panavision. ▼●▶

Alvin and the Chipmunks (2007) **C-91m.** **½ D: Tim Hill. Jason Lee, David Cross, Cameron Richardson, Jane Lynch; voices of Justin Long, Matthew Gray Gubler, Jesse McCartney. The musical mythos of Ross Bagdasarian's singing chipmunks (Alvin, Simon, and Theodore) is amusingly re-imagined in this kid-friendly mix of cartoonish live-action and impressive CG animation. Lee is the nominal star, as David Seville (Bagdasarian's stage name), the critters' surrogate father, but Cross grabs every scene that isn't bolted to the floor as a snarky record producer. Followed by a sequel. [PG] ▶

Alvin and the Chipmunks: The Squeakquel (2009) **C-89m.** ** D: Betty Thomas. Zachary Levi, David Cross, Jason Lee, Wendie Malick, Anjelah Johnson, Kathryn Joosten; voices of Justin Long, Matthew Gray Gubler, Jesse McCartney, Amy Poehler, Anna Faris, Christina Applegate, Sean Astin. Follow-up to 2007 hit tracks the chipmunks' high school experiences after their antics put human authority figure David Seville (Lee) into the hospital. Harassing jocks treat the trio to men's room "swirlies," the chipmunks themselves prove adept at giving "wedgies," and hormonal considerations become an unexpected issue once a rival girl group (the Chipettes) arrives on the scene. Dubious material gets elevated a few inches by filmmakers keen on going with the flow, but the demographic for this film peaks around the age where one's thumb no longer has quite the succulent taste it did in previous years. [PG] ▶

Always (1985) **C-105m.** *** D: Henry Jaglom. Henry Jaglom, Patrice Townsend, Joanna Frank, Alan Rachins, Melissa Leo, Jonathan Kaufer, Bob Rafelson, Michael Emil, Andre Gregory. Often hilarious, but also insightful, comedy about what it means to be a couple. A trio of them—one about to get divorced, one about to get married, one solidly married—spend a July 4th weekend together. The first is played by the director and Townsend, his own ex-wife. Like all of Jaglom's stream-of-consciousness films, this one's not for all tastes. [R] ▼●▶

Always (1989) **C-121m.** **½ D: Steven Spielberg. Richard Dreyfuss, Holly Hunter, John Goodman, Brad Johnson, Audrey Hepburn, Roberts Blossom, Keith David, Marg Helgenberger. Slick remake of 1943's

A GUY NAMED JOE, with Dreyfuss as a cocky pilot who specializes in dousing forest fires from the air, and Hunter as the dispatcher who loves him—and fears for his life. When he does in fact die, he returns in spirit form to guide a young pilot (Johnson) who wants to pursue the same career and the same woman. Certainly entertaining but suffers from a serious case of The Cutes. Hepburn, in her final film appearance, plays an angel. [PG] ▼●▶

Always Leave Them Laughing (1949) **116m.** **½ D: Roy Del Ruth. Milton Berle, Virginia Mayo, Ruth Roman, Bert Lahr, Alan Hale. Berle is at home in tale of cocky comedian's ups and downs. Unfortunately, zesty opening leads into soggy drama. Lahr does his classic "stop in the name of the stationhouse" routine.

Amadeus (1984) **C-158m.** **½ D: Milos Forman. F. Murray Abraham, Tom Hulce, Elizabeth Berridge, Simon Callow, Roy Dotrice, Christine Ebersole, Jeffrey Jones, Cynthia Nixon. Abraham won well-deserved Oscar as composer Salieri, whose music never surpasses mediocrity, while a hedonistic young boor named Mozart expresses musical genius almost without trying! Literate, intelligent, exquisitely filmed (in Prague, by Miroslav Ondricek)... but fatally overlong and missing dramatic fire that distinguished Peter Shaffer's play (Shaffer rethought and rewrote it for the screen). Worth noting: Jones' wonderful performance as musical dilettante Emperor Joseph II. Winner of seven other Oscars, including Best Picture, Director, Screenplay, Art Direction. Reissued in 2002 with an additional 20m. Panavision. [PG] ▼●▶

Amal (2008-Canadian) **C-105m.** *** D: Richie Mehta. Rupinder Nagra, Naseeruddin Shah, Seema Biswas, Koel Purie, Vik Sahay, Roshan Seth, Tanisha Chatterjee, Amardeep Jha, Dr. Shiva. Heartwarming story of a poor rickshaw driver in New Delhi, India, whose humanity triumphs over tragedy and treachery. Amal's kindness to two strangers—a street beggar and a cantankerous passenger—has unusual repercussions. The story may be contrived, but its sincerity and the warmth of its actors make it difficult to resist. Debut feature for director Mehta, who expanded it from a 2004 short he wrote with his brother Shaun.

Amarcord (1974-Italian) **C-127m.** ***½ D: Federico Fellini. Magali Noel, Bruno Zanin, Pupella Maggio, Armando Brancia, Giuseppe Lanigro, Josiane Tanzilli. Fellini's nostalgia trip to the Italy of his youth in the 1930s; warm, funny, poignant, bawdy episodes about love, sex, politics, family life, and growing up. Academy Award winner as Best Foreign Film. [R] ▼●▶

Amateur, The (1982-Canadian) **C-111m.** BOMB D: Charles Jarrott. John Savage, Christopher Plummer, Marthe Keller, Arthur Hill, Ed Lauter, Nicholas Campbell, Graham Jarvis, John Marley. Savage is grossly miscast as a CIA computer whiz who hunts down the terrorists who seized the American Consulate in Munich and murdered his girlfriend. Complex and ultimately ridiculous spy thriller. [R]▼▶

Amateur (1994-U.S.-French) **C-105m. **½** D: Hal Hartley. Isabelle Huppert, Martin Donovan, Elina Lowensohn, Damian Young, Chuck Montgomery, David Simonds, Parker Posey. Typically quirky Hartley tale about an ex-nun (Huppert) who writes pornographic fiction (!) and hooks up with a seemingly harmless amnesiac (Donovan) with a disturbing past. As in all of the director's films, this one is filled with offbeat characters who do and say the weirdest things; among them are a pair of hit men who look like Wall Street yuppies. Interesting, but decidedly not for all tastes. An *American Playhouse* coproduction. [R]▼▶

Amateurs, The (2007) **C-99m. **½** D: Michael Traeger. Jeff Bridges, Tim Blake Nelson, Joe Pantoliano, William Fichtner, Ted Danson, Patrick Fugit, John Hawkes, Glenne Headly, Lauren Graham, Alex D. Linz, Jeanne Tripplehorn, Steven Weber, Isaiah Washington, Valerie Perrine, Judy Greer, Eileen Brennan, Brad Garrett, Elden Henson. Group of small-town losers decides to turn their lives around and make the world's first community-sponsored porno film. With Bridges' character leading the way they enlist an unlikely group of participants. Hilarious, if uneven, comedy delivers on its amusing premise with a sterling group of actors. Screened on the film festival circuit as THE MOGULS. [R]▮

Amati Girls, The (2001) **C-91m. **** D: Anne DeSalvo. Cloris Leachman, Mercedes Ruehl, Paul Sorvino, Sean Young, Dinah Manoff, Mark Harmon, Jamey Sheridan, Lily Knight, Lee Grant. Schmaltz-fest about a close-knit Italian-American family, focusing on a death-obsessed matriarch (Leachman) and her four daughters (Ruehl, Young, Manoff, Knight). In her directorial debut, actress DeSalvo juggles soapy stories, has a sense of humor and an unabashed reverence for Catholicism, but the results are not quite MOONSTRUCK. [PG]▼▶

Amator SEE: **Camera Buff**

Amazing Colossal Man, The (1957) **80m. **½** D: Bert I. Gordon. Glenn Langan, Cathy Downs, James Seay, Larry Thor. Army officer who survives an atomic explosion starts growing; at 60 feet he attacks Las Vegas! Starts well but ends up as your standard monster-on-the-loose flick. Sequel: WAR OF THE COLOSSAL BEAST.▼

Amazing Dobermans, The (1976) **C-94m. **½** D: David and Byron Chudnow. James Franciscus, Barbara Eden, Fred Astaire, Jack Carter, Billy Barty. Engaging action comedy that has Bible-quoting ex-con-man Astaire's five remarkable Doberman pinschers helping treasury agent Franciscus thwart a racketeer and his gang. Higher-budgeted sequel to THE DOBERMAN GANG and THE DARING DOBERMANS, aided by offbeat casting of Astaire. [PG—edited from original R rating]▼

Amazing Dr. Clitterhouse, The (1938) **87m. ***** D: Anatole Litvak. Edward G. Robinson, Claire Trevor, Humphrey Bogart, Allen Jenkins, Donald Crisp, Gale Page. Amusing film of "method doctor" Robinson trying to discover what makes a crook tick; he joins Bogart's gang and becomes addicted.▼▶

Amazing Grace (1974) **C-99m. **** D: Stan Lathan. Moms Mabley, Slappy White, Moses Gunn, Rosalind Cash, Dolph Sweet. A few laughs in Philadelphia-made comedy about an elderly busybody who disrupts corrupt Baltimore politics. Mabley's only starring film; cameos by Butterfly McQueen, unrecognizable Stepin Fetchit. [G]▼▶

Amazing Grace (2007-British) **C-116m. **½** D: Michael Apted. Ioan Gruffudd, Romola Garai, Benedict Cumberbatch, Albert Finney, Michael Gambon, Rufus Sewell, Youssou N'Dour, Ciarán Hinds, Toby Jones, Bill Paterson. Earnest and enlightening historical drama about William Wilberforce, who spent 20 exhausting years in the late 1700s trying to convince his fellow members of Parliament to ban slavery in the British Empire. Impressive roster of actors lends weight to this well-made film, but somehow it never reaches the dramatic heights it should, considering the passionate nature of its protagonist and the nobility of his cause. [PG]▮

Amazing Grace and Chuck (1987) **C-115m. *½** D: Mike Newell. Jamie Lee Curtis, Alex English, Gregory Peck, William L. Petersen, Joshua Zuehlke, Dennis Lipscomb, Lee Richardson. A 12-year-old Little League whiz decides to stop playing baseball until the world agrees to complete nuclear disarmament . . . and soon, other athletes around the world follow suit, as the protest escalates. Producer-writer David Field's Capraesque wish-fulfillment fantasy is one of those films you either swallow wholeheartedly, or don't. It's dripping with good intentions. [PG]▼●

Amazing Mr. Blunden, The (1972-British) **C-99m. ***** D: Lionel Jeffries. Laurence Naismith, Lynne Frederick, Garry Miller, Rosalyn Landor, Marc Granger, Diana Dors, James Villiers. Dickensian fantasy about a genial ghost who takes two children back in time to help two mistreated tots. Colorful family film whose only liability is somewhat muddled storyline. [G]▼

Amazing Panda Adventure, The (1995-U.S.-China) **C-85m. **½** D: Christopher Cain. Ryan Slater, Stephen Lang, Yi Ding, Huang Fei, Zhou Jiugou, Yao Erga. Time-honored "boy and his dog" story, except in this case it's a boy and his panda. Ten-year-old American boy and a Chinese girl trek through China in order to rescue the cub from poachers. Too predictable for adult viewers, but the spectacular Chinese scenery makes it worthwhile. Slater is Christian's younger brother. [PG]▼●)

Amazon Women on the Moon (1987) **C/B&W-85m.** *½ D: Joe Dante, Carl Gottlieb, Peter Horton, John Landis, Robert K. Weiss. Rosanna Arquette, Ralph Bellamy, Carrie Fisher, Griffin Dunne, Steve Guttenberg, Michelle Pfeiffer, Peter Horton, Sybil Danning, Ed Begley, Jr., Henny Youngman, Paul Bartel, Lou Jacobi, Howard Hesseman, B.B. King, Steve Allen, Steve Forrest, Russ Meyer, Arsenio (Hall), Phil Hartman, Joe Pantoliano, Rip Taylor, David Alan Grier, Angel Tompkins, Kelly Preston, Andrew Dice Clay, Mike Mazurki, Corinne Wahl, Bryan Cranston. Series of unrelated skits in the KENTUCKY FRIED MOVIE vein, most of them astonishingly unfunny. Parody of CAT WOMEN OF THE MOON that punctuates the film is so exact that you might as well watch the original—it's just as funny. Best of all is the 1930s sex-film spoof with Bartel and Fisher, but that comes at the very end. [R]▼●)

Ambassador, The (1984) **C-90m.** *** D: J. Lee Thompson. Robert Mitchum, Ellen Burstyn, Rock Hudson, Fabio Testi, Donald Pleasence, Michal Bat-Adam. Intelligent, entertaining thriller of American ambassador Mitchum, his adulterous wife Burstyn, and his attempts to peacefully mediate the Israeli-Palestinian crisis. Based on Elmore Leonard's novel *52 Pick-Up*, and remade just two years later under that name. Hudson's final theatrical film. [R]▼)

Ambassador's Daughter, The (1956) **C-102m.** **½ D: Norman Krasna. Olivia de Havilland, John Forsythe, Myrna Loy, Adolphe Menjou, Edward Arnold, Francis Lederer, Tommy Noonan, Minor Watson. Oomph is missing even though stars give all to uplift sagging comedy of de Havilland out for a fling in Paris, romanced by soldier Forsythe. CinemaScope.▼)

Ambition (1991) **C-100m.** BOMB D: Scott D. Goldstein. Lou Diamond Phillips, Clancy Brown, Cecilia Peck, Richard Bradford, Willard Pugh, Grace Zabriskie, Katherine Armstrong, J. D. Cullum, Haing S. Ngor. Awful thriller about a writer who becomes totally obsessed with his subject—a man who happens to be a convicted murderer. Phillips makes his screenwriting debut here but he's bitten off more than he can type. A bust! [R]▼●

Ambulance, The (1990) **C-95m.** ** D: Larry Cohen. Eric Roberts, James Earl Jones, Megan Gallagher, Richard Bright, Janine Turner, Eric Braeden, Red Buttons. Muddled thriller which tells the story of what happens when innocent people begin disappearing off the streets of N.Y. Routine stuff, but look for an especially fine performance by Buttons. Roberts plays a comic

book artist, and Marvel Comics editor Stan Lee appears as himself. [R]▼●)

Ambush Bay (1966) **C-109m.** **½ D: Ron Winston. Hugh O'Brian, Mickey Rooney, James Mitchum, Harry Lauter. Lackluster adventures of Marine group on Japanese-held island during WW2 trying to help partisans—good cast wasted.▶

Ambushers, The (1968) **C-102m.** BOMB D: Henry Levin. Dean Martin, Senta Berger, Janice Rule, James Gregory, Albert Salmi, Kurt Kasznar, Beverly Adams. Do you really care that the first U.S. flying saucer has been stolen right out of space? Third entry in the Matt Helm series may be the weakest, but few film scholars will want to take time making certain. Sequel: THE WRECKING CREW. ▼●)

Amelia (2009) **C-111m.** ** D: Mira Nair. Hilary Swank, Richard Gere, Ewan McGregor, Christopher Eccleston, Joe Anderson, Cherry Jones, Mia Wasikowska. Old-fashioned biopic traces the high-flying career of aviator Amelia Earhart, her relationship with publisher George Putnam (first her sponsor and booster, then her husband), and her lingering affair with fellow airman Gene Vidal. It all leads up to that fateful flight across the Pacific in 1937. While the facts may be true, they play like clichés from an old, not particularly inspired Hollywood movie, negating the film's good qualities and its handsome production. Hawk Scope. [PG]▶

Amélie (2001-French-German) **C-121m.** ***½ D: Jean-Pierre Jeunet. Audrey Tautou, Mathieu Kassovitz, Rufus, Yolande Moreau, Artus de Penguern, Urbain Cancelier, Dominique Pinon, Maurice Bénichou. Clever, charming comedy about a sheltered young woman who, in her first foray into "real life," decides to manipulate the people around her to make their lives happier. But when she encounters a man who is attracted to her, she can't figure out how to deal with the situation. Told with visual flair and originality, with a star-making performance by Tautou. Written by the director and Guillaume Laurant. Full title is LE FABULEUX DESTIN D'AMÉLIE POULAIN, or AMÉLIE FROM MONTMARTRE. Super 35. [R]▼)

AMEN. (2002-French-German) **C-130m.** *** D: Costa-Gavras. Ulrich Tukur, Mathieu Kassovitz, Ulrich Mühe, Michel Duchaussoy, Ion Caramitru, Marcel Iures. Compelling tale of an SS officer who discovers that the chemicals he's using to purify water for troops at the front are being used for Hitler's Final Solution. He turns to the Vatican for help and finds a willing priest but a reluctant hierarchy. Slow going at first, and not the biting indictment of the Roman Catholic Church you might expect from the director; instead, a tempered examination of self-preservation, sacrifice, and fear. Adapted by Costa-Gavras and Jean Claude Grumberg from Rolf Hochhuth's play *The Deputy*.▼❘

America (1986) **C-83m.** BOMB D: Robert Downey. Zack Norman, Tammy Grimes, Michael J. Pollard, Monroe Arnold, Richard Belzer, Liz Torres, Howard Thomashefsky, Laura Ashton. Downey lamely attempts to recapture the freewheeling satires of the 1960s (such as his classic PUTNEY SWOPE) with this amateurish tale of the loonies at a N.Y. cable TV station, whose signal is accidentally bounced off the moon, bringing them worldwide fame. Hopelessly dated; filmed in 1982. [R]▼

America, America (1963) **168m.** **** D: Elia Kazan. Stathis Giallelis, Frank Wolff, Elena Karam, Lou Antonio, John Marley, Estelle Hemsley. The dream of passage to America—as it unfolded for late 19th-century immigrants—is movingly captured by writer-director Kazan in this long, absorbing film, based on his uncle's experiences. Heartfelt and heart-rending, with impressive Oscar-winning art direction/set decoration by Gene Callahan.▼❘

American, The (2010-U.S.-British) **C-105m.** *** D: Anton Corbijn. George Clooney, Violante Placido, Thekla Reuten, Paolo Bonacelli, Johan Leysen. Intriguing mood piece features Clooney as a weapons expert (and assassin) who's forced to hide out temporarily in a small Italian town. He doesn't keep a low profile for long, interacting with a talkative priest and becoming seriously attracted to a beautiful prostitute. Provocative and satisfying adult yarn is European in its approach and leisurely pacing; in fact, Clooney is the only American ingredient. Super 35. [R] ❘

Americana (1981) **C-91m.** **½ D: David Carradine. David Carradine, Barbara Hershey, Michael Greene. Vietnam veteran Carradine attempts to rebuild a merry-go-round in rural Kansas town. Odd, thoughtful little drama, adequately directed by its star. Filmed in 1973. Panavision. [PG]▼❘

American Affair, An (2009) **C-92m.** *½ D: William Sten Olsson. Gretchen Mol, Cameron Bright, Noah Wyle, James Rebhorn, Mark Pellegrino, Perrey Reeves. Laughably bad drama about a 13-year-old boy (Bright) who develops a crush on the glamorous blond woman across the street in Washington, D.C.—little dreaming that she is the mistress of President John F. Kennedy. Mol is sexy but that's all one can say for this absurd mix of conspiracy yarn and teenage hormonal fantasy, which at one time carried the fanciful title BOY OF PIGS. [R]❘

American Anthem (1986) **C-100m.** *½ D: Albert Magnoli. Mitch Gaylord, Janet Jones, Michelle Phillips, R.J. Williams, Michael Pataki, Patrice Donnelly. Supremely corny, badly written tale of a gymnast with family problems which keep him from fulfilling his destiny. Inauspicious movie debut for Olympic gymnast Gaylord is strangely reminiscent of PURPLE RAIN, with the same music video approach to drama; Magnoli directed them both. [PG-13]▼❘

American Beauty (1999) **C-121m.** ***½ D: Sam Mendes. Kevin Spacey, Annette Bening, Thora Birch, Wes Bentley, Mena Suvari, Chris Cooper, Peter Gallagher, Allison Janney, Scott Bakula, Sam Robards, Jaret Winokur. Exceptional and original look at the American Dream gone sour. Spacey is having a midlife crisis, and decides to throw caution to the winds; his wife, Bening, who's forsaken him for her real estate career, seeks sexual fulfillment elsewhere. And their alienated teenage daughter is attracted to a strange young man next door. Amusing, bittersweet, and insightful script by Alan Ball is perfectly realized by a superb cast and first-time film director. Oscar winner for Best Picture, Director, Screenwriter, Actor (Spacey), and Cinematography (Conrad L. Hall). Super 35. [R] ▼❘

American Buffalo (1996) **C-87m.** *** D: Michael Corrente. Dustin Hoffman, Dennis Franz, Sean Nelson. Arresting film version of David Mamet's profane, provocative three-character play. Hoffman plays Teach, a self-enobled world expert who horns in on the plans of his friend, junk shop owner Don (Franz), to commit a robbery with the help of a teenaged protégé (Nelson). A simple character study, with perfectly cast actors bringing Mamet's own screen adaptation to life. One of the rare photographed stage plays that works. [R]▼❘

American Carol, An (2008) **C-83m.** *½ D: David Zucker. Kevin Farley, Kelsey Grammer, Trace Adkins, Robert Davi, Jon Voight, Chriss Anglin, Geoffrey Arend, Serdar Kalsin, Leslie Nielsen, Dennis Hopper, James Woods, Kevin Sorbo, Fred Travalena, Gary Coleman, David Alan Grier, Gail O'Grady. A slobbering, sarcastic "liberal" filmmaker (and Michael Moore clone) wants to abolish the Fourth of July. Several ghosts drop in to instill within him the true American spirit. Whatever your politics, this simpleminded, mean-spirited comedy deals in generalities—and has very few laughs to offer. Some familiar faces make cameo appearances. [PG-13]❘

American Dream, An (1966) **C-103m.** **½ D: Robert Gist. Stuart Whitman, Janet Leigh, Eleanor Parker, Barry Sullivan, Lloyd Nolan, Murray Hamilton, J. D. Cannon, Les Crane, Paul Mantee, Harold Gould, George Takei. Distorted, watered-down Norman Mailer novel, dealing superficially with TV commentator wanted by underworld and police for murdering his wife; nightmare sequences are sterile. ❘

American Dream (1989) **C-100m.** ***½ D: Barbara Kopple. Gripping, Academy Award–winning documentary about the hows, whats and whys of a labor strike at the Hormel meat plant in the small town of Austin, Minnesota. It's the story of a profitable company attempting to reduce wages and break a union just for the sake of doing so. This is the stuff of high drama. ▼●▶

American Dreamer (1984) **C-105m.** ★★ D: Rick Rosenthal. JoBeth Williams, Tom Conti, Giancarlo Giannini, Coral Browne, James Staley, Huckleberry Fox, C.B. Barnes. Misguided, miscast comedy-adventure yarn about a housewife who wins trip to Paris and (through circumstance) believes herself to be the daring heroine of a series of adventure thrillers. Cute idea (not dissimilar to ROMANCING THE STONE) that an otherwise able cast can't pull off. [PG] ▼▶

American Dreamz (2006) **C-107m.** ★★★ D: Paul Weitz. Hugh Grant, Dennis Quaid, Mandy Moore, Willem Dafoe, Chris Klein, Jennifer Coolidge, Sam Golzari, Marcia Gay Harden, Seth Meyers, John Cho, Judy Greer, Shohreh Aghdashloo, Tony Yalda, Marley Shelton. Self-loathing host of a hugely popular *American Idol*–like TV talent show meets a kindred spirit in deceptively sweet-faced contestant Moore. Then he's offered the President of the U.S. as a guest judge—little dreaming that the Chief Executive has been going through a near breakdown and crisis of confidence. Weitz's script veers between satire and farce but still treats its key characters as human beings. Entertaining and funny, with surprisingly dark, even subversive, elements. Contestant who sings "Rockin' Man" is *South Park*'s Trey Parker. [PG-13] ▶

American Flyers (1985) **C-114m.** ★★★ D: John Badham. Kevin Costner, David Grant, Rae Dawn Chong, Alexandra Paul, Janice Rule, Luca Bercovici, Robert Townsend, John Amos, Jennifer Grey. Two brothers—one of whom is dying—enter a grueling bicycle race marathon. Likable, sweet-natured, root-for-the-good-guys film, if a bit too pat and manipulative at times. Written by Steve Tesich, whose cycle theme fared even better in BREAKING AWAY. Panavision. [PG-13] ▼●▶

American Friend, The (1977-U.S.-French-German) **C-127m.** ★★★ D: Wim Wenders. Dennis Hopper, Bruno Ganz, Lisa Kreuzer, Gerard Blain, Jean Eustache, Sam Fuller, Nicholas Ray. Vague but suspenseful statement about American gangster films and the Americanization of European cinema and lifestyles, centering on a young German picture-framer (Ganz) hired to assassinate a mobster. Hopper is the title character, a mystery man; film directors Ray and Fuller appear as heavies. Based on Patricia Highsmith's *Ripley's Game*; remade under that title in 2003. Hopper's character, Tom Ripley, also appears in PURPLE NOON and its remake, THE TALENTED MR. RIPLEY. ▼●▶

American Friends (1991-British) **C-95m.** ★★½ D: Tristram Powell. Michael Palin,

Trini Alvarado, Connie Booth, Alfred Molina, David Calder, Simon Jones, Robert Eddison, Alun Armstrong. A very proper (and very repressed) senior tutor at Oxford chances to meet a young American girl during a holiday in the Swiss Alps and finds his outlook on life undergoing some dramatic changes. Slight, slowly paced, but diverting; Palin coscripted the film, based on journals left behind by his great-grandfather. ▼

American Gangster (2007) **C-157m.** ★★★ D: Ridley Scott. Denzel Washington, Russell Crowe, Chiwetel Ejiofor, Idris Elba, Ruby Dee, Cuba Gooding, Jr., Josh Brolin, RZA, John Ortiz, John Hawkes, Ted Levine, Yul Vazquez, Armand Assante, Joe Morton, Common, Tip Harris (T.I.), Carla Gugino, Roger Bart, KaDee Strickland, Jon Polito. Two parallel stories begin in the late 1960s. Washington is Frank Lucas, who figures the way to rule Harlem is to import heroin directly from Southeast Asia. But scrupulously honest cop Crowe can't bring down the man who's spreading pure heroin around the streets until he can identify him. Not the visceral gangland movie you might expect, but a methodical saga of two determined men who use their brains—and know when to bend the rules. Screenplay by Steven Zaillian, based on Mark Jacobson's article "The Return of Superfly." Clarence Williams III appears unbilled. Unrated version runs 176m. [R] ▶

American Gigolo (1980) **C-117m.** BOMB D: Paul Schrader. Richard Gere, Lauren Hutton, Hector Elizondo, Nina Van Pallandt, Frances Bergen, Bill Duke. Schrader presents his weakest variation yet on his favorite theme, the seamy side of American life. Feeble morality play, posing as a thriller, is further undermined by neurasthenic acting and some of the unsexiest sex scenes ever. [R] ▼●▶

American Gothic (1988) **C-90m.** BOMB D: John Hough. Rod Steiger, Yvonne De Carlo, Michael J. Pollard, Fiona Hutchison, Sarah Torgov, Mark Lindsay Chapman. Three couples off for an island weekend off the Seattle coast are forced to land at an unknown island dominated by murderous Ma and Pa (DeCarlo and Steiger) and their "kids" (grown-ups who've been kept mentally adolescent by their backward, backwoods parents). Populated exclusively by obnoxious characters; even Steiger can't help this one. [R] ▼●▶

American Graffiti (1973) **C-110m.** ★★★½ D: George Lucas. Richard Dreyfuss, Ronny Howard, Paul LeMat, Charlie Martin Smith, Cindy Williams, Candy Clark, Mackenzie Phillips, Wolfman Jack, Harrison Ford, Bo Hopkins, Kathy Quinlan, Suzanne Somers, Joe Spano, Debralee Scott. Highly entertaining, insightful mosaic about youngsters "coming of age" after high school graduation in 1962. Often hilarious, always on-target, this film made Dreyfuss a star and boosted many other careers. Reedited to 112m. for 1978 reissue to play up latter-day stars. Look fast for Kay Lenz at the dance. Sequel: MORE AMERICAN GRAFFITI. Techniscope. [PG]▼●◗

American Gun (2005) **C-95m.** ** D: Aric Avelino. Donald Sutherland, Forest Whitaker, Marcia Gay Harden, Linda Cardellini, Tony Goldwyn, Christopher Marquette, Nikki Reed, Arlen Escarpeta, Garcelle Beauvais-Nilon, Melissa Leo, Schuyler Fisk, Daniel Hugh Kelly, Amanda Seyfried, Michael Shannon. Ambitious but unsuccessful film offers multiple storylines about people in different states coming to grips with the effect of gun violence on their lives. Serious and well-intentioned treatise eschews melodrama where it can, but adds up to very little. Good cast tries hard. Fisk was one of the film's composers. Whitaker coexecutive-produced. [R]▼◗

American Haunting, An (2006-U.S.-British-Canadian-Rumanian) **C-90m.** *½ D: Courtney Solomon. Donald Sutherland, Sissy Spacek, Rachel Hurd-Wood, James D'Arcy, Matthew Marsh, Thom Fell, Sam Alexander. In early 19th-century rural Tennessee, the devout Bell family is driven increasingly batty by a spirit that takes over their house—and specifically targets their teenaged daughter in her bedroom. Based on a purportedly real incident, and briefly framed by a contemporary family's tale, the only real horror here is the film's meager story and one-note screenplay. Alternate version runs 91m. Super 35. [PG-13]◗

American Heart (1993) **C-113m.** *** D: Martin Bell. Jeff Bridges, Edward Furlong, Lucinda Jenney, Tracey Kapisky, Don Harvey, Maggie Welsh. Sobering, sometimes brilliant drama of gruff ex-con who is reunited with his son, an alienated teen in desperate need of a dad. Jarring, credible portrait of lost souls in urban America, with riveting performances by its stars. First fiction feature for Bell, who directed the documentary STREETWISE. Bridges also coproduced. [R]▼◗

American History X (1998) **C/B&W-118m.** *** D: Tony Kaye. Edward Norton, Edward Furlong, Fairuza Balk, Beverly D'Angelo, Avery Brooks, Stacy Keach, Jennifer Lien, Elliott Gould, William Russ, Joe Cortese. Hard-hitting drama of a young man who's seduced into a white supremacy movement in Venice, California, goes to prison after committing a heinous crime, and has his head straightened out. When he's released, his only thought is to steer his younger brother away from that same existence. Frighteningly powerful—and believable—performance by Norton sparks this intense drama of a family torn apart. [R] ▼●◗

American Hot Wax (1978) **C-91m.** *** D: Floyd Mutrux. Tim McIntire, Fran Drescher, Jay Leno, John Lehne, Laraine Newman, Jeff Altman, Chuck Berry, Jerry Lee Lewis, Screamin' Jay Hawkins. Rose-colored story of controversial 1950s disc jockey Alan Freed. Uneven dramatically, but McIntire is excellent, period flavor is strong, and the original rock 'n' roll acts are fun to see. Freed's life also is chronicled in MR. ROCK AND ROLL (in which the DJ plays himself) and the TVM MR. ROCK 'N' ROLL: THE ALAN FREED STORY. [PG]▼

American in Paris, An (1951) **C-115m.** ***½ D: Vincente Minnelli. Gene Kelly, Leslie Caron, Oscar Levant, Georges Guetary, Nina Foch. Joyous, original musical built around Gershwin score; dazzling in color. Plot of artist Kelly torn between gamine Caron and wealthy Foch is creaky, but the songs, dances, production are superb. Oscars include Best Picture, Story and Screenplay (Alan Jay Lerner), Cinematography (Alfred Gilks and John Alton), Scoring (Johnny Green and Saul Chaplin), Art Direction, Costume Design, and a special citation to Kelly. Look fast for Noel Neill as an art student. ▼●◗

Americanization of Emily, The (1964) **117m.** ***½ D: Arthur Hiller. James Garner, Julie Andrews, Melvyn Douglas, James Coburn, Joyce Grenfell, Keenan Wynn, Judy Carne, Liz Fraser, Edward Binns, William Windom, Alan Sues. Garner is fall guy for U.S. admiral's master plan to have American naval officer first Normandy invasion victim, with predictable results. Cynical Garner-Andrews romance blends well with realistic view of life among U.S. military brass. Script by Paddy Chayefsky, from William Bradford Huie's novel. Also shown in computer-colored version.▼●◗

American Justice SEE: **Jackals**

American Madness (1932) **81m.** *** D: Frank Capra. Walter Huston, Pat O'Brien, Kay Johnson, Constance Cummings, Gavin Gordon. Huston is dynamic as a put-upon bank president in the depths of the Great Depression; vivid, upbeat film marred only by idiotic romantic subplot.▼◗

American Me (1992) **C-126m.** **½ D: Edward James Olmos. Edward James Olmos, William Forsythe, Pepe Serna, Danny De La Paz, Evelina Fernandez, Sal Lopez, Daniel Villarreal, Cary Hiroyuki Tagawa. Ambitious look at the so-called "Mexican Mafia" reflected through the life of a crime lord (Olmos), and the cycle of gang violence which extends from prison to the Southwest's Hispanic barrio communities. Attempts to be epic in scope and subject, but is too unfocused to really score, despite many tough, powerful moments. Olmos—who made his directorial debut here—and Forsythe stand out in the large cast. The prison scenes at Folsom were actually shot there. [R] ▼●◗

American Movie (1999) **C-104m.** ***½ D: Chris Smith. Thoroughly engaging documentary about Mark Borchardt, an obsessive independent filmmaker whose aspirations clearly outweigh his talent. Unable to fund his most recent project, he sets out to complete the cheesy horror film he started but abandoned years earlier. Funny and revealing, but director Smith is never condescending toward his subject's dreams and desire for acknowledgment. [R]▼❍

American Ninja (1986) **C-95m.** *½ D: Sam Firstenberg. Michael Dudikoff, Steve James, Judie Aronson, Guich Koock, John Fujioka, Don Stewart, John LaMotta. Low-grade martial-arts entry series set at U.S. Army base in Philippines, with beefy Dudikoff as a soldier who finds ample reason to use his deadly skills. James comes off well as Dudikoff's equally proficient Army pal. Followed by four crummy sequels. [R]▼❍

Americano, The (1955) **C-85m.** **½ D: William Castle. Glenn Ford, Cesar Romero, Frank Lovejoy, Ursula Thiess, Abbe Lane. American cowboy Ford delivers a herd of cattle to Brazil, but stays on when he gets caught up in a quarrel between rancher Lovejoy and local peasants. He falls for Thiess and becomes friendly with bandit Romero (fun in a flamboyant role). Standard Western set in 1955 Brazil benefits from South American shooting and colorful characters.▼

American Outlaws (2001) **C-93m.** *½ D: Les Mayfield. Colin Farrell, Scott Caan, Ali Larter, Gabriel Macht, Gregory Smith, Harris Yulin, Will McCormack, Ronny Cox, Terry O'Quinn, Kathy Bates, Timothy Dalton. Awful oater, designed for brainless teens, which tells (yet again) the story of Jesse James (Farrell), Cole Younger (Caan), and their gang, who become Robin Hood–like outlaws while battling a greedy railroad tycoon. Plodding and predictable. [PG-13]▼❍

American Pie (1999) **C-95m.** *** D: Paul Weitz. Jason Biggs, Shannon Elizabeth, Alyson Hannigan, Chris Klein, Natasha Lyonne, Thomas Ian Nicholas, Tara Reid, Seann William Scott, Eugene Levy, Lawrence Pressman, Mena Suvari, Jennifer Coolidge. Good-natured teen comedy about four guys who vow to lose their virginity by the night of the high school prom. Raunchy gags gave this film its reputation, but they grow honestly out of its believable characters and situations. In fact, its values are old-fashioned, even if its sense of humor is not. Casey Affleck appears unbilled. Also available in unrated version. Followed by two theatrical sequels and four direct-to-video spin-offs. [R]▼❍

American Pie 2 (2001) **C-104m.** ** D: J.B. Rogers. Jason Biggs, Shannon Elizabeth, Alyson Hannigan, Chris Klein, Natasha Lyonne, Thomas Ian Nicholas, Tara Reid, Seann William Scott, Mena Suvari, Eddie Kaye Thomas, Eugene Levy, Chris Owen, Denise Faye, Lisa Arturo, Casey Affleck. Lazy sequel to comedy hit reunites the male friends for a summer at the beach after their first year of college; most of the female co-stars make only token appearances. Crude and obvious where the first film was clever and original, this squeezes all it can from echoes of the original movie and the likability of its cast. Jennifer Coolidge appears unbilled. Unrated version runs 111m. Followed by AMERICAN WEDDING. [R]▼❍

American Pimp (2000) **C-90m.** *** D: The Hughes Brothers. Hard-hitting documentary focuses on 30 real-life black male "entrepreneurs" and their experiences in "the life." The filmmakers wisely let their flashy subjects speak for themselves, and they do so with amazing candor, stripping away the Hollywood image and revealing them as misogynist capitalists. Makes witty use of classic blaxploitation movie images of pimps to juxtapose fantasy with cold, hard reality.▼❍

American Pop (1981) **C-97m.** **½ D: Ralph Bakshi. Voices of Ron Thompson, Marya Small, Jerry Holland, Lisa Jane Persky, Roz Kelly. Ambitious animated film, which follows 20th-century American music through pivotal characters in four generations. Bold graphics and a challenging narrative keep this interesting, if not always successful; animation buffs may wince at awkward rotoscoping (tracing from live action). Ultimate dilemma: the culmination of this heavily dramatic, multigenerational saga is the creation of punk rock! [R]▼❍

American President, The (1995) **C-113m.** *** D: Rob Reiner. Michael Douglas, Annette Bening, Martin Sheen, Michael J. Fox, Anna Deavere Smith, John Mahoney, Samantha Mathis, Shawna Waldron, David Paymer, Anne Haney, Richard Dreyfuss, Nina Siemaszko, Wendie Malick, Gail Strickland. Slick, entertaining Hollywood concoction about a widowed president who's attracted to a lobbyist and decides to pursue her—naively ignoring the political impact this liaison may have during an election year. Appealing performances and a bright screenplay (by Aaron Sorkin) help this likable movie glide along past its considerable gaps in credibility. This is the ultimate wish-fulfillment movie, with a president who's handsome, funny, forthright, decisive, and honest. If only! Panavision. [PG-13]▼❍

American Psycho (2000) **C-97m.** *½ D: Mary Harron. Christian Bale, Willem Dafoe, Jared Leto, Reese Witherspoon, Samantha Mathis, Chloë Sevigny, Justin Theroux, Guinevere Turner, Matt Ross. A 1980s Wall Street yuppie has all the trappings of success—and the need to fit in—but also has an uncontrollable drive to kill people. Intense adaptation of Bret Easton Ellis' 1991 novel makes its satiric points early on, then has nothing to add. Bale gives a dynamic performance in this turgid film. Unrated version also available. Followed in 2002 by a direct-to-video sequel. Super 35. [R]▼❍

American Rhapsody, An (2001) **C-106m.**
**½ D: Éva Gardos. Nastassja Kinski,
Tony Goldwyn, Scarlett Johansson, Kelly
Endrész Banláki, Ági Bánfalvy, Zsuzsa
Czinkóczi, Mae Whitman, Lisa Jane Persky, Larisa Oleynik. A couple fleeing from
Hungary in 1956 is forced to leave an infant
daughter behind. At age six she's torn from
the only mother and father she's ever known
to join her real parents in America. Heartfelt
film based on writer-director Gardos' own life
doesn't really gel until its heroine becomes a
teenager (Johansson) and rebels against her
overprotective mother. Coproducer Colleen
Camp appears briefly as a friendly neighbor.
[PG-13]▼❙
American Soldier, The (1970-German)
80m. **½ D: Rainer Werner Fassbinder.
Karl Scheydt, Elga Sorbas, Jan George,
Margarethe von Trotta, Hark Bohm, Ingrid
Caven, Kurt Raab. Fassbinder sacrifices
believability for mood in this dour film
noir about a Vietnam vet (Scheydt) who
becomes a hired assassin in the Munich
underworld. Not so much an ode to the celluloid American gangster or allegory about
the Vietnam war as a character study, loaded
with in-jokes and absurdist references (such
as the duplicitous moll named Rosa von
Praunheim). Fassbinder also scripted.▼❙
American Splendor (2003) **C-101m.** ***½
D: Shari Springer Berman, Robert Pulcini.
Paul Giamatti, Hope Davis, Judah Friedlander, James Urbaniak, Earl Billings,
Donal Logue, Molly Shannon. Innovative
film blends real life and dramatization in
telling the story of Cleveland, Ohio, cynic
Harvey Pekar, who becomes an unlikely
celebrity by chronicling his mundane life
in a series of comic books. The filmmakers
manage to fuse footage of Pekar, his family,
and friends with their movie alter egos in a
fresh and constantly surprising way. Giamatti is perfect as the unrepentant curmudgeon. Written by the directors. [R]▼❙
American Success SEE: **American Success Company, The**
American Success Company, The (1979)
C-94m. ** D: William Richert. Jeff Bridges,
Belinda Bauer, Ned Beatty, Steven Keats,
Bianca Jagger, John Glover. A contemporary fable about a young loser—in business
and marriage—who decides to change his
luck by emulating a macho prince. Offbeat
in the extreme, often funny, but decidedly
uneven. Filmed in Germany; based on a
story by Larry Cohen. Richert has twice
reedited and reissued the film: in 1981 as
AMERICAN SUCCESS, then in 1983 simply as SUCCESS. [PG]
American Tail, An (1986) **C-80m.** **½ D:
Don Bluth. Voices of Dom DeLuise, Christopher Plummer, Nehemiah Persoff, Madeline Kahn, Phillip Glasser, John Finnegan,
Cathianne Blore, Will Ryan. A young Russian mouse is separated from his family as

they're about to arrive at their new homeland, America, in the late 19th century.
Handsome, occasionally heart-tugging cartoon feature with a cute main character—
but serious story flaws (why are there *three*
climaxes?). Producer Steven Spielberg's
first foray into animation. Followed by
three sequels and an animated TV series,
Fievel's American Tails. [G]▼❙❙
American Tail: Fievel Goes West, An
(1991) **C-74m.** **½ D: Phil Nibbelink, Simon Wells. Voices of Philip Glasser, James
Stewart, Erica Yohn, Cathy Cavadini, Nehemiah Persoff, Dom DeLuise, Amy Irving,
John Cleese, Jon Lovitz. Pleasant enough
animated feature for small fry follows immigrant Fievel the mouse and his family
on a trek to the American West. Mediocre
songs and uninspired character animation
make it less than memorable—but Stewart's
performance as over-the-hill sheriff Wylie
Burp is a treat. Followed by two direct-to-
video sequels. [G]▼❙❙
American Teen (2008) **C-102m.** *** D:
Nanette Burstein. Enjoyable documentary
follows five prototypical teenagers during
their senior year of high school in Warsaw,
Indiana. Almost too conveniently they fit
into pigeonholes (a rich girl who's also the
most popular, a basketball star, an artsy
girl who doesn't fit in, a hunk, and a total
dweeb), but it's impossible to predict how
they will respond to various pressures that
arise during this crucial year in their lives.
Slickly packaged (and widely criticized
for that) but undeniably entertaining. [PG-
13]❙
American Violet (2009) **C-103m.** *** D:
Tim Disney. Nicole Beharie, Tim Blake
Nelson, Will Patton, Michael O'Keefe,
Xzibit, Charles S. Dutton, Alfre Woodard,
Malcolm Barrett, Tim Ware, Paul David
Story, David Warshofsky, Lucinda Jenney.
Forthright, emotion-packed account of Dee
Roberts (Beharie), an African-American
single mother living in Texas. After being
unjustly busted for drugs, she determinedly
fights the system rather than accept a plea
bargain for a crime she did not commit.
Fact-based story is both an eye-opener and
crowd-pleaser, with the 2000 presidential
election tellingly playing out in the back-
ground. Beharie is a real find. Super 35.
[PG-13]❙
American Way, The SEE: **Riders of the
Storm**
American Wedding (2003) **C-97m.** ** D:
Jesse Dylan. Jason Biggs, Alyson Hannigan, Thomas Ian Nicholas, Seann William
Scott, Eddie Kaye Thomas, Fred Willard,
Eugene Levy, January Jones, Deborah
Rush, Molly Cheek, Angela Paton, Jen-
nifer Coolidge, Nikki Ziering, Lawrence
Pressman. Biggs and Hannigan are getting
married, but things start to go wrong in this
second sequel to AMERICAN PIE . . . es-

pecially when Scott (as the ever-obnoxious Stifler) shows up. Some good farcical moments are offset by gross-out gags designed to see just how far one can go in search of laughs. Followed by two direct-to-video sequels. Super 35. [R] ▼▶

American Werewolf in London, An (1981) **C-97m.** *** D: John Landis. David Naughton, Jenny Agutter, Griffin Dunne, John Woodvine, Brian Glover. A young man is bitten by a wolf on the British moors, with terrifying results. Not a spoof, but a full-blooded horror film that happens to have a sharp sense of humor—as well as a reverence for horror films past. Dynamite direction and script by Landis, startling Oscar-winning makeup effects by Rick Baker. Followed by an in-name-only sequel. [R] ▼●▶

American Werewolf in Paris, An (1997-British-U.S.-Luxembourgian-Dutch-French) **C-97m.** *½ D: Anthony Waller. Tom Everett Scott, Julie Delpy, Vince Vieluf, Phil Buckman, Julie Bowen, Pierre Cosso, Tom Novembre, Thierry Lhermitte. Thrill-seeking American Scott falls for Parisienne Delpy, but she's a werewolf, and soon he's one, too, pitted against a group of leering lycanthropes bent on wiping out the unfit—such as American tourists. Begins well, but soon goes awry, with too much comedy and romance, and too much plot; the werewolf effects are plentiful but second-rate at best. No plot connections to the superior John Landis original. [R] ▼●▶

American Women SEE: **Closer You Get, The**

America's Heart & Soul (2004) **C-84m.** *** D: Louis Schwartzberg. An unsentimental portrait of America as seen through images, sounds, and the stories of some colorful people who represent individualism at its best—from a weaver carrying on a generations-old tradition to a disabled boy who competes in marathons in tandem with his father. This final story is so moving, nothing could follow it. [PG]▶

America's Sweethearts (2001) **C-102m.** **½ D: Joe Roth. Julia Roberts, Billy Crystal, Catherine Zeta-Jones, John Cusack, Hank Azaria, Stanley Tucci, Christopher Walken, Alan Arkin, Seth Green, Rainn Wilson, Emma Roberts. Slick if forgettable comedy about a much-loved Hollywood couple—now split—who agree to come together to promote their final film at a press junket. Crystal is the can-do publicist, Roberts is the sister and assistant to a very spoiled Zeta-Jones. No particular hilarity or insights here, but an easy-to-take mix of romantic comedy and farce, with some knowing jibes at the ritual of movie publicity. Crystal produced and cowrote with Peter Tolan. Panavision. [PG-13]▼▶

Americathon (1979) **C-86m.** BOMB D: Neil Israel. Harvey Korman, John Ritter, Nancy Morgan, Peter Riegert, Fred Willard, Zane Buzby, Richard Schaal, Elvis Costello, Chief Dan George, Tommy Lasorda, Jay Leno, Peter Marshall, Meat Loaf, Howard Hesseman. Unfunny comedy wastes great premise: in 1998, America must hold a telethon in order to raise money to save itself. Only spark is set by Buzby as Vietnamese punk-rocker. Narrated by George Carlin. [PG]▼▶

Amistad (1997) **C-152m.** *** D: Steven Spielberg. Morgan Freeman, Anthony Hopkins, Matthew McConaughey, Nigel Hawthorne, Djimon Hounsou, David Paymer, Pete Postlethwaite, Stellan Skarsgård, Anna Paquin, Tomas Milian, Austin Pendleton, Allan Rich, Paul Guilfoyle, Peter Firth, Xander Berkeley, Jeremy Northam, Arliss Howard, Chiwitel Ejiofor. Little-known saga of the Spanish slave ship *La Amistad,* whose "cargo" broke their chains in 1839—and wound up in a U.S. courtroom, ultimately attracting the attention of ex-president John Quincy Adams (Hopkins). A good film that's frustratingly uneven: the slave ship scenes are wrenching (and unavoidably reminiscent of Spielberg's SCHINDLER'S LIST), and Adams' final summation is a showcase speech. But the film is long, and the dramatic gaps too many. Hounsou offers a powerful presence as Cinque, the leader of the slave revolt. [R]▼●▶

Amityville Horror, The (1979) **C-117m.** *½ D: Stuart Rosenberg. James Brolin, Margot Kidder, Rod Steiger, Don Stroud, Murray Hamilton, Michael Sacks, Helen Shaver, Natasha Ryan, Val Avery, John Larch, Amy Wright, James Tolkan. Family moves into supposedly haunted Long Island home, finds that "supposedly" is inoperative. Based on Jay Anson's (supposedly) nonfiction best-seller, film is yawn-inducing rehash of old schticks; not even good for laughs, with Steiger mercilessly hamming it up as local priest. Followed by a prequel, AMITYVILLE II: THE POSSESSION, a TV movie, and several so-called sequels. Remade in 2005. [R] ▼●▶

Amityville Horror, The (2005) **C-89m.** ** D: Andrew Douglas. Ryan Reynolds, Melissa George, Jesse James, Jimmy Bennett, Chloë Grace Moretz, Rachel Nichols, Philip Baker Hall. Reynolds, his new wife, and stepchildren move into an old Long Island house where multiple murders occurred a year before. The youngest child is befriended by a ghost, while the husband is slowly driven into a homicidal rage. Professionally made, well-acted, but uninvolving tale is both familiar and overdone. Based on the same supposedly true story as the 1979 movie, but ends up resembling THE SHINING. Super 35. [R]▼▶

Amityville II: The Possession (1982) **C-104m.** BOMB D: Damiano Damiani. Burt Young, Rutanya Alda, James Olson, Jack Magner, Diane Franklin, Andrew Prine,

Ted Ross, Moses Gunn. Officially a prequel to THE AMITYVILLE HORROR, but actually just a ripoff. A loathsome lout (Young) moves into notorious Long Island house with his troubled family and all hell breaks loose. Alternately dull and disgusting. [R]▼●)

Amityville: The Demon SEE: **Amityville 3-D**

Amityville 3-D (1983) C-105m. **½ D: Richard Fleischer. Tony Roberts, Tess Harper, Robert Joy, Candy Clark, John Beal, Leora Dana, John Harkins, Lori Loughlin, Meg Ryan. Thoroughly familiar retread of spirit-in-the-house formula, with Roberts as a Doubting Thomas who buys the dreaded Amityville house (seen in two otherwise unrelated films). Competence at every level keeps this from being trash; excellent 3-D effects too. Shown on TV as AMITYVILLE: THE DEMON; followed by TV movie AMITYVILLE 4: THE EVIL ESCAPES and two direct-to-video sequels. 3-D ArriVision. [PG]▼●)

Among Giants (1998-British) C-96m. **½ D: Sam Miller. Pete Postlethwaite, Rachel Griffiths, James Thornton, Lennie James, Andy Serkis, Rob Jarvis, Alan Williams. A rough-hewn contractor hires a rowdy lot to paint the huge electric pylons that dot the British countryside. They become a sort of outlaw family, and are joined by an adventurous Aussie woman who likes heights. Good performances and rich atmosphere help, but it's a less successful dip into working-class life by the writer of THE FULL MONTY, Simon Beaufoy. [R]▼

Amongst Friends (1993) C-86m. **½ D: Rob Weiss. Joseph Lindsey, Patrick McGaw, Steve Parlavecchio, Mira Sorvino, Brett Lambson, Michael Artura. Superficial (and, by now, all-too-familiar) tale of young male punks coming of age on America's mean streets, only these are suburban rather than urban and the boys are wealthy instead of working-class. Well made and not uninteresting, but Martin Scorsese did it—and did it better—20 years earlier. [R]▼)

Amor Bandido (1979-Brazilian) C-95m. *** D: Bruno Barreto. Paulo Gracindo, Cristina Ache, Paulo Guarnieri, Lígia Diniz, Flavio Sao Thiago. Tough drama of 17-year-old dancer-hooker Ache, estranged from cop father Gracindo, who takes up with baby-faced killer Guarnieri. Uncompromising and, ultimately, sad; based on one of Brazil's most notorious criminal cases.▼●

Amores Perros (2000-Mexican) C-153m. *** D: Alejandro Gonzalez Inarritu. Emilio Echevarria, Gael Garcia Bernal, Goya Toledo, Alvaro Guerrero, Vanessa Bauche, Jorge Salinas, Marco Perez, Rodrigo Murray. Arresting look at divergent lives that intersect in a Mexico City car crash. Broken into three sections, film traces several different characters and their relationships, all connected in one way or another by their dogs, raising tough questions about the human condition in an unforgiving city. Brutally realistic (but judiciously edited) depiction of dogfights and their outcomes will make this tough for some viewers; for others there are considerable rewards here. Feature debut for TV commercial director Inarritu. English title: LOVE'S A BITCH. [R]▼)

Amorous Adventures of Moll Flanders, The (1965-British) C-126m. **½ D: Terence Young. Kim Novak, Richard Johnson, Angela Lansbury, George Sanders, Vittorio De Sica, Lilli Palmer, Leo McKern, Cecil Parker. Billed as female Tom Jones, Moll is far from thrilling. Fine cast romps through 18th-century England from bedroom to boudoir, but film needs more spice than Novak can muster. The two leads were married briefly in real life. Panavision. ▼●

Amorous Mis-adventures of Casanova, The SEE: **Casanova & Co.**

Amos & Andrew (1993) C-94m. BOMB D: E. Max Frye. Nicolas Cage, Samuel L. Jackson, Dabney Coleman, Brad Dourif, Michael Lerner, Margaret Colin, Chelcie Ross, I. M. Hobson, Jodi Long, Giancarlo Esposito, Loretta Devine, Bob Balaban, Tracey Walter. Agonizing comedy about a professionally distinguished black man who moves into a new home, only to be harassed by white neighbors who assume he's a prowler. Intended social satire is as broadly silly as a '60s Disney comedy; maybe they should have called this THAT DARN AFRO-AMERICAN. [PG-13]▼●)

Amreeka (2009-U.S.-Canadian) C-97m. **½ D: Cherien Dabis. Nisreen Faour, Hiam Abbass, Alia Shawkat, Melkar Muallem, Yussef Abu Warda, Joseph Ziegler, Amer Hlehel. Well-intentioned account of a Palestinian woman (Faour), reeling from the pressures of everyday life in the West Bank, who moves to Illinois (along with her teenage son) to live with relatives. Depiction of the struggles of immigrants in a new land is overly familiar and occasionally wallows in soap opera, but writer-director Dabis still manages to make you care about the characters. [PG-13]▶

Amsterdam Kill, The (1977) C-90m. **½ D: Robert Clouse. Robert Mitchum, Bradford Dillman, Richard Egan, Leslie Nielsen, Keye Luke. Tired drug bust movie gets a shot from Mitchum's presence as a retired narc who's lured back by a former colleague suspected of being part of an international dope ring. Panavision. [R]▼●

Amy (1981) C-100m. *** D: Vincent McEveety. Jenny Agutter, Barry Newman, Kathleen Nolan, Chris Robinson, Lou Fant, Margaret O'Brien, Nanette Fabray, Lance LeGault, Lucille Benson. Sincere, entertaining Disney tale of Agutter leaving her husband in the early 1900s, teaching at a school for the handicapped. Though the film is targeted at kids, parents won't be bored. Made for TV, released to theaters instead. [G]▼

Amy (1998-Australian) **C-103m.** **½ D: Nadia Tass. Alana De Roma, Rachel Griffiths, Ben Mendelsohn, Nick Barker, Kerry Armstrong, Jeremy Trigatti, William Zappa, Torquil Neilson. Unusual film about a little girl who's been traumatized into silence and her overprotective mother, the widow of a rock star. Some of the film's ingredients seem contrived, others endearing, as it shifts from quirky comedy to drama and back again. Written and photographed by Tass' partner and husband, David Parker. [PG-13]●

Amy's Orgasm (2001) **C-87m.** **½ D: Julie Davis. Julie Davis, Nick Chinlund, Caroline Aaron, Jeff Cesario, Mitchell Whitfield, Jennifer Bransford, Mark Brown. Writer-director Davis stars as an Ivy League–educated self-help author who somehow manages to fall for a shock jock with a reputation for dating bimbos. Although the romance between these two opposites develops a little too quickly, the actors make the budding relationship fun to watch anyway. Warning for those expecting a hot sex romp: the title is as steamy as it gets in this indie comedy. Aka AMY'S O. [R] ▼●

Anaconda (1997) **C-90m.** ** D: Luis Llosa. Jennifer Lopez, Ice Cube, Jon Voight, Eric Stoltz, Jonathan Hyde, Kari Wuhrer, Owen Wilson, Vincent Castellanos. Documentary film crew adrift on the Amazon is besieged by a giant killer snake. Hokey special effects and an expositionless script detract, but there's campy fun in the form of Voight's demonic snake poacher, who speaks with a bad Brandoesque drawl and strangles human victims between his knees. Film makes most of beautiful Brazilian rainforest locale, yet the big serpentine climax looks strangely like deepest, darkest Arcadia. (In fact, it's the Arboretum in L.A. County.) Followed by ANACONDAS: THE HUNT FOR THE BLOOD ORCHID and two TV sequels. Super 35. [PG-13]▼●

Anacondas: The Hunt for the Blood Orchid (2004) **C-96m.** ** D: Dwight H. Little. Morris Chestnut, Johnny Messner, KaDee Strickland, Matthew Marsden, Nicholas Gonzalez, Eugene Byrd, Salli Richardson-Whitfield. The original ANACONDA had Jennifer Lopez tied up to Ice Cube and a snake-regurgitated Jon Voight; in this sequel, we have Chestnut getting woozy after a rare spider gives him a 151-proof bite. Still, that's an apparent occupational hazard for anyone trekking the Borneo jungle seeking a fountain-of-youth plant right near the spot where snakes converge for mating season. There's a jolt or two to satisfy diehards. Super 35. [PG-13] ▼●

Analyze That (2002) **C-95m.** ** D: Harold Ramis. Robert De Niro, Billy Crystal, Lisa Kudrow, Joe Viterelli, Cathy Moriarty-Gentile, Reg Rogers, Callie Thorne, Pat Cooper. De Niro is sprung from Sing Sing into the custody of psychiatrist Crystal, who actually believes the mob boss is going to go straight. Another good argument for outlawing sequels; all the novelty and freshness of ANALYZE THIS is gone, replaced by contrived plotting and just a handful of laughs. Even watching De Niro sing tunes from *West Side Story* wears thin fast. Anthony LaPaglia appears unbilled. [R] ▼●

Analyze This (1999) **C-103m.** *** D: Harold Ramis. Robert De Niro, Billy Crystal, Lisa Kudrow, Joe Viterelli, Chazz Palminteri, Bill Macy, Leo Rossi, Max Casella, Molly Shannon, Pat Cooper, Elizabeth Bracco. Amusing comedy about a mob boss who's losing his grip and is persuaded to talk to a psychiatrist—which causes him great embarrassment. A small idea stretched out too far but made worthwhile by De Niro's wonderful comic performance as the foulmouthed mobster who feels "conflicted." Followed by ANALYZE THAT. [R]▼●

Anastasia (1956) **C-105m.** **** D: Anatole Litvak. Ingrid Bergman, Yul Brynner, Helen Hayes, Akim Tamiroff, Martita Hunt, Felix Aylmer, Natalie Schafer, Ivan Desny. Inspired casting makes this film exceptional. Bergman won Oscar as amnesiac refugee selected by Brynner to impersonate surviving daughter of Russia's last czar. High point: confrontation scene in which Hayes as grand duchess must determine if girl is her relative. Screenplay by Arthur Laurents based on Marcelle Maurette's play. CinemaScope.▼●

Anastasia (1997) **C-88m.** **½ D: Don Bluth, Gary Goldman. Voices of Meg Ryan, John Cusack, Kelsey Grammer, Angela Lansbury, Christopher Lloyd, Hank Azaria, Bernadette Peters, Kirsten Dunst, Andrea Martin, Jim Cummings, Liz Callaway, Lacey Chabert, Jonathan Dokuchitz. Elaborate but uneven cartoon musical about the daughter of Nicholas and Alexandra, who supposedly survived in Russia in 1917 only to reappear in Paris a decade later—where two schemers try to collect part of her inheritance from her grandmother, the Dowager Empress. Innocuous enough for kids, but adults may question the '90s American dialogue (and readings). Animation style is also inconsistent—some of it realistic, some of it wildly fanciful. Loosely based on the 1956 movie. Followed in 1999 by a direct-to-video sequel: BARTOK THE MAGNIFICENT. CinemaScope. [G]▼●

Anatomy of a Murder (1959) **160m.** **** D: Otto Preminger. James Stewart, Lee Remick, Ben Gazzara, Arthur O'Connell, Eve Arden, Kathryn Grant (Crosby), George C. Scott, Orson Bean, Murray Hamilton. Long, exciting courtroom drama; daring when released, tamer now. Sterling cast:

O'Connell as drunken lawyer inspired by Stewart, Scott as prosecuting attorney, Joseph Welch as judge (Welch was the famous Army-McCarthy hearings lawyer who later became a judge in real life). Stewart towers over all as witty, easygoing, but cagy defense lawyer. Script by Wendell Mayes, from novel by Robert Traver (Judge John D. Voelker). Duke Ellington composed the score and also appears on-screen. ▼●▶

Anatomy of a Syndicate SEE: **Big Operator, The**

Anatomy of Hell (2004-French) **C-80m.** BOMB D: Catherine Breillat. Amira Casar, Rocco Siffredi. After attempting suicide in the bathroom of a gay disco, a woman hires the man who rescues her to spend four nights in her company, challenging him to "watch me where I'm unwatchable." Meant to be provocative and controversial, but mostly it's pretentious and homophobic. There's plenty of XXX footage, which is alternately monotonous and unintentionally funny. The title is apt. ▼▶

Anchorman: The Legend of Ron Burgundy (2004) **C-95m.** ** D: Adam McKay. Will Ferrell, Christina Applegate, Paul Rudd, Steve Carell, David Koechner, Fred Willard, Danny Trejo, Missi Pyle, Holmes Osborne, Fred Armisen, Seth Rogen, Laura Kightlinger, Chris Parnell. In the 1970s, TV news anchor Ron Burgundy (Ferrell) "owns" San Diego, until an attractive and ambitious female reporter arrives on the scene. A sketch comedy inflated to feature length, with occasional laughs and a number of gag appearances that try to camouflage a threadbare, one-note script. Ferrell and director McKay coscripted. Unrated version runs 103m. [PG-13] ▼▶

Anchors Aweigh (1945) **C-140m.** **½ D: George Sidney. Frank Sinatra, Kathryn Grayson, Gene Kelly, Jose Iturbi, Dean Stockwell, Pamela Britton. Popular '40s musical of sailors on leave doesn't hold up storywise, but musical numbers still good: Sinatra's "I Fall in Love Too Easily," Kelly's irresistible dance with Jerry the cartoon mouse. ▼●▶

Anderson Platoon, The (1967-French) **65m.** ***½ D: Pierre Schoendorffer. Superior chronicle of soldiers in American Army platoon fighting, living, and dying in Vietnam. Vivid, striking images, photographed at the front line. A Best Documentary Academy Award winner. ▼

Anderson's Angels SEE: **Chesty Anderson, USN**

Anderson Tapes, The (1971) **C-98m.** *** D: Sidney Lumet. Sean Connery, Dyan Cannon, Martin Balsam, Ralph Meeker, Alan King, Margaret Hamilton, Christopher Walken, Garrett Morris. Fast-paced thriller of ex-con's master holdup plan, and strange electronic surveillances that have tracked him since he left prison. Climax

is particularly exciting. Fine Quincy Jones score; Walken's debut. [PG] ▼●▶

... And God Created Woman (1956-French) **C-92m.** **½ D: Roger Vadim. Brigitte Bardot, Curt Jurgens, Jean-Louis Trintignant, Christian Marquand, Georges Poujouly, Jean Tissier. Location shooting (at St. Tropez) and famous Bardot figure on display in simple tale of man-teaser finding it hard to resist temptation. Great cast clicks in Brigitte's best-known vehicle. Beware edited prints. Remade (in name only) by Vadim in the U.S. in 1988. CinemaScope. ▼●▶

And God Created Woman (1988) **C-100m.** *½ D: Roger Vadim. Rebecca De Mornay, Vincent Spano, Frank Langella, Donovan Leitch, Judith Chapman, Jaime McEnnan, Benjamin Mouton, David Shelley. Surprisingly tepid "variation" on director Vadim's one-time *scandale international* (see above). Luscious De Mornay marries carpenter Spano merely to secure her release from prison, then keeps him panting as she frolics with gubernatorial candidate Langella. Not all *that* different from Goldie Hawn's OVERBOARD; beware rock 'n' roll subplot. [R] ▼●▶

... And God Spoke (the making of...) (1993) **C-83m.** *** D: Arthur Borman. Michael Riley, Stephen Rappaport, Lou Ferrigno, Soupy Sales, Eve Plumb, Fred Kaz, Michael Medved. Occasionally clever satire in the THIS IS SPINAL TAP mold, only the subject here is the casting and production of a numbingly awful multi-million-dollar biblical epic. After one day the production is behind schedule. Lou (*The Incredible Hulk*) Ferrigno plays Cain; Eve (*The Brady Bunch*) Plumb is Mrs. Noah; and Soupy Sales is Moses! An amusing little sleeper. ▼▶

And Hope to Die (1972-French) **C-99m.** *** D: René Clement. Robert Ryan, Tisa Farrow, Jean-Louis Trintignant, Lea Massari, Aldo Ray. Above-average caper with offbeat touches; gang hired to kidnap girl goes through with scheme even though she's already dead. [PG] ▼

... And Justice for All (1979) **C-117m.** **½ D: Norman Jewison. Al Pacino, Jack Warden, John Forsythe, Lee Strasberg, Jeffrey Tambor, Christine Lahti, Sam Levene, Craig T. Nelson, Joe Morton. Lawyer Pacino single-handedly battles Maryland's judicial system. Outrageous satire mixes uncomfortably with painfully sad moments, in attempt to make biting statement on buying and selling of justice. Strong performances and good location photography cannot overcome weak script. Written by Barry Levinson and Valerie Curtin. Lahti's feature debut. [R] ▼●▶

And Nothing But the Truth (1982-British) **C-90m.** **½ D: Karl Francis. Glenda Jackson, Jon Finch, Kenneth Colley, James Donnelly, Emrys James, Karen Archer. An examination of the role and responsibility of the media, focusing on documentary filmmaker Jackson and reporter Finch at work on a TV magazine show. Earnest, not without merit, but ordinary; originally titled GIRO CITY, and released at 102m.▼

And Now For Something Completely Different (1971-British) **C-89m.** *** D: Ian McNaughton. Graham Chapman, John Cleese, Eric Idle, Terry Gilliam, Terry Jones, Michael Palin, Carol Cleveland, Connie Booth. First feature by the Monty Python troupe is a kind of "Greatest Hits" album, with some of the most popular sketches and animated bits from their long-running TV series. Fine introduction to their peculiar brand of humor includes Dead Parrot, The World's Deadliest Joke, Upper-Class Twit of the Year, and memorable Lumberjack Song. [PG]▼●▶

And Now ... Ladies and Gentlemen ... (2002-French) **C-129m.** ** D: Claude Lelouch. Jeremy Irons, Patricia Kaas, Thierry Lhermitte, Alessandra Martines, Claudia Cardinale, Ticky Holgado, Yvan Attal, Amidou. Thief Irons suffers from a memory disorder that complicates any recollection of having pulled off a robbery for which he's accused. Kaas (in real life a French recording star) has the same affliction and becomes a soul mate. Story seems to start in the middle but eventually straightens itself out; still longer than it needs to be. Large cast of characters rushes in and disappears as if they were merely showing up to plunk an extra quarter in a parking meter. The cinematography by Pierre-William Glenn (DAY FOR NIGHT and other Truffauts) is luscious. Super 35. [PG-13]▼▶

And Now Miguel (1966) **C-95m.** *** D: James Clark. Pat Cardi, Michael Ansara, Guy Stockwell, Joe De Santis. Flavorful, leisurely paced account of young boy who wants to join his father on his summer mountain trip to graze sheep; set in New Mexico. Techniscope.

And Now My Love (1975-French) **C-121m.** ***½ D: Claude Lelouch. Marthe Keller, Andre Dussollier, Charles Denner, Carla Gravina, Gilbert Becaud, Charles Gerard. A what'll-he-do-next kind of extravaganza, in which Lelouch salutes life, love and the 20th century, using comedy, drama, and music to bring wealthy Keller and ne'er-do-well Dussollier together for the fadeout. Opens in b&w. Originally 150m.; restored version runs 143m. [PG]▼▶

And Now the Screaming Starts! (1973-British) **C-87m.** ** D: Roy Ward Baker. Peter Cushing, Stephanie Beacham, Herbert Lom, Patrick Magee, Ian Ogilvy. Beacham weds Ogilvy and finds that she's living in a house that has been under a curse for years; OK horror drama. [R]▼▶

Andre (1994) **C-94m.** *** D: George Miller. Keith Carradine, Tina Majorino, Chelsea Field, Aidan Pendleton, Shane Meier,

Keith Szarabajka, Joshua Jackson. Agreeably old-fashioned family film, set in a coastal town in Maine in the early 1960s, about an animal-loving clan who adopts a baby seal that adopts them in return, and refuses to leave. Aimed at children, but amiable enough for parents, with a soundtrack full of 1960s pop music. Based on a true story; watch that vintage home-movie footage of Andre during the closing credits. Clairmont-Scope. [PG]▼●▶

Andrei Rublev (1966-Russian) **C/B&W-185m.** **** D: Andrei Tarkovsky. Anatoli Solonitzine, Ivan Lapikov, Nikolai Grinko, Nikolai Sergueiev. Brilliantly devised and directed account of famous 15th-century icon painter, focusing on an age-old conflict: should an artist participate in the political and social upheavals of the time, or should he simply record history with his brush? Magnificent film is worthy of comparison with the best of Eisenstein's historical dramas. Scripted by Tarkovsky and Andrei Milchakov-Konchalovsky; shelved by the Soviet authorities, and unseen until 1971. Restored version runs 20m. longer. Sovscope.▼●▶

Androcles and the Lion (1952) **98m.** *** D: Chester Erskine. Jean Simmons, Alan Young, Victor Mature, Maurice Evans, Elsa Lanchester, Robert Newton. Shaw's amusing satire of ancient Rome can't be dampened by dull production retelling fable of Christian and lion he befriends. ▼▶

Android (1982) **C-80m.** *** D: Aaron Lipstadt. Klaus Kinski, Don Opper, Brie Howard, Norbert Weisser, Crofton Hardester, Kendra Kirchner. Entertaining sci-fi story about an almost-human android who's been working as assistant to mad scientist Kinski on a remote space station and learns he is about to be put out of commission. Charming, quirky ultra-low-budget film made on leftover sets from Roger Corman's BATTLE BEYOND THE STARS. Opper, who plays Max 404, also cowrote screenplay. [PG]▼●▶

Andromeda Strain, The (1971) **C-130m.** **½ D: Robert Wise. Arthur Hill, David Wayne, James Olson, Kate Reid, Paula Kelly. Overlong sci-fi thriller in which small team of superscientists tries to isolate deadly strain of virus from outer space, racing against time and nuclear detonation. From Michael Crichton's novel. Remade as a TV miniseries in 2008. Panavision. [G]▼●▶

And Then There Were None (1945) **98m.** **** D: René Clair. Barry Fitzgerald, Walter Huston, Louis Hayward, Roland Young, June Duprez, C. Aubrey Smith, Judith Anderson, Mischa Auer, Richard Haydn. Highly suspenseful Agatha Christie yarn of ten people invited to lonely island where one by one they're murdered. Great script by Dudley Nichols complemented by superb visual ideas. Famous score by M.

Castelnuovo-Tedesco. Remade three times as TEN LITTLE INDIANS.**▼●❶**

And the Ship Sails On (1983-Italian) C-138m. *** D: Federico Fellini. Freddie Jones, Barbara Jefford, Victor Poletti, Peter Cellier, Janet Suzman, Elisa Mai Nardi, Norma West, Paolo Paoloni. Uniquely Felliniesque ocean voyage, circa 1914, with an earnest journalist (Jones) acting as our "host" and introducing us to a variety of celebrated guests who have gathered for funeral voyage of great opera star. Flagrantly unrealistic, deliciously absurd, and somewhat uneven, but full of striking images and those indelible Fellini faces . . . plus an opening sequence that's absolutely mesmerizing. [PG]**▼❶**

Andy Hardy series SEE: *Leonard Maltin's Classic Movie Guide*

Andy Warhol's Bad (1977) C-106m. **½ D: Jed Johnson. Carroll Baker, Perry King, Susan Tyrrell, Stefania Cassini, Cyrinda Foxe. Queens housewife supplements her facial-hair-removal business by running a murder-for-hire concern specializing in children and animals. Goes without saying that Warhol's most expensive film is in execrable taste, but it frequently succeeds as a sick joke; Baker, at least, seems to be having a good time. [R]**▼❶**

Andy Warhol's Dracula (1974-Italian-French) C-93m. ** D: Paul Morrissey. Udo Kier, Joe Dallesandro, Arno Juerging, Vittorio De Sica, Maxime McKendry, Roman Polanski. Dracula (Kier) learns he must have blood of virgins (pronounced "where-gins") in order to survive. Companion piece to ANDY WARHOL'S FRANKENSTEIN is far less bloody and has some amusing bits . . . but a long way from LOVE AT FIRST BITE. Originally released at 106m.; aka BLOOD FOR DRACULA and YOUNG DRACULA. [R—edited from original X rating] **▼❶**

Andy Warhol's Frankenstein (1974-Italian-German-French) C-94m. BOMB D: Paul Morrissey. Joe Dallesandro, Monique Van Vooren, Udo Kier, Srdjan Zelenovic, Dalila di Lazzaro. Mad baron Kier clones body-beautiful monsters out of bloody human innards. Campy and disgusting, with severed heads and hands galore. Aka FLESH FOR FRANKENSTEIN. [R—edited from original X rating.] 3-D Space-Vision. **▼❶**

Andy Warhol Superstar SEE: **Superstar**

Angel (1937) 91m. ** D: Ernst Lubitsch. Marlene Dietrich, Herbert Marshall, Melvyn Douglas, Edward Everett Horton, Laura Hope Crews. Disappointing film about Marlene leaving husband Marshall for vacation, falling in love with Douglas. Not worthy of star trio.**▼●**

Angel (1982) SEE: **Danny Boy**

Angel (1984) C-92m. *½ D: Robert Vincent O'Neil. Cliff Gorman, Susan Tyrrell, Dick Shawn, Rory Calhoun, John Diehl,

Donna Wilkes. Wilkes is a straight-A high school student by day, Hollywood hooker by night—but despite "colorful" characters like drag queen Shawn, film goes nowhere, and remains inexplicably tame in terms of what it shows. Sequel: AVENGING ANGEL. [R]**▼●❶**

Angela (1984-Canadian) C-100m. ** D: Boris Sagal. Sophia Loren, Steve Railsback, John Huston, John Vernon. Dreary story of the relationship between a woman and a younger man who turns out to be her son. Made in 1978.**▼**

Angel-A (2005-French) 91m. ** D: Luc Besson. Rie Rasmussen, Jamel Debbouze, Gilbert Melki, Serge Riaboukine, Akim Chir, Erik Balliet. Small-time swindler with endless debts and the mob on his tail decides to end it all by jumping off a bridge. A beautiful girl has the same idea and beats him to it, so he jumps in to rescue her; she returns the favor by turning his luck around. Besson's first time behind the camera since 1999 is a love letter to Paris, filmed in gorgeous widescreen black and white . . . but his foray into romantic comedy is a misstep, taking a sledgehammer approach to a very slight premise. Besson also wrote the screenplay. Super 35. [R]**❶**

Angel and the Badman (1947) 100m. *** D: James Edward Grant. John Wayne, Gail Russell, Harry Carey, Irene Rich, Bruce Cabot. First-rate Western with Russell humanizing gunfighter Wayne; predictable plot is extremely well handled. Remade for TV in 2009. Also shown in computer-colored version. **▼❶**

Angel, Angel, Down We Go (1969) C-103m. *½ D: Robert Thom. Jennifer Jones, Jordan Christopher, Holly Near, Roddy McDowall, Lou Rawls, Charles Aidman. Awesomely dated tale of corruption, sex, drugs, and fame. Overweight teenager (Near) is distraught when her rock 'n' roll lover (Christopher) begins an affair with her jewelry-obsessed mother (Jones). Reissued as CULT OF THE DAMNED. [R]

Angela's Ashes (1999) C-146m. **½ D: Alan Parker. Emily Watson, Robert Carlyle, Joe Breen, Ciaran Owens, Michael Legge, Ronnie Masterson, Pauline McLynn, Eanna Macliam, Gerard McSorley, Eamonn Owens; narrated by Andrew Bennett. Competent but uninspired adaptation of Frank McCourt's hugely popular, Pulitzer Prize–winning memoir about growing up in the dire poverty of Dublin in the 1930s and '40s, with a large family, a ne'er-do-well father, and an indomitable mother. Has the right look and feel, but lacks resonance and humor. [R]**▼❶**

Angel at My Table, An (1990-New Zealand) C-158m. ***½ D: Jane Campion. Kerry Fox, Alexia Keogh, Karen Fergusson, Iris Churn, K.J. Wilson, Martyn Sanderson. Stunning, biting autobiography of Janet Frame, a roly-poly, repressed little girl who grew up to become New Zealand's most famous novelist/poet—but not before being misdiagnosed a schizophrenic, spending eight years in a mental hospital. Campion beautifully portrays the various stages of Frame's life, and captures the writer's inner world. Fox is riveting as the adult Janet. Scripted by Laura Jones; adapted from a trio of Frame's autobiographies. Originally produced as a three-part television series. ▼○●

Angel Baby (1961) 97m. *** D: Paul Wendkos, Hubert Cornfield. George Hamilton, Salome Jens, Mercedes McCambridge, Joan Blondell, Henry Jones, Burt Reynolds. Penetrating exposé of evangelistic circuit plying backwood country; Jens in title role, Hamilton the promoter, McCambridge his shrewish wife—marvelous cameos by Blondell and Jones. Reynolds' film debut. ▼❍

Angel Baby (1995-Australian) C-105m. **½ D: Michael Rymer. John Lynch, Jacqueline MacKenzie, Colin Friels, Deborra Lee Furness. Lynch and MacKenzie play an emotionally fragile Melbourne couple who meet and fall in love in a rehabilitation center, throwing his family for a loop when she gets pregnant and can't subject the fetus to her medication. Well-acted but overelaborate treatment of the subject matter; won Australian Film Institute awards for Best Picture, Actor, Actress, Director, Screenplay, Cinematography, and Editing. ▼●

Angel Eyes (2001) C-103m. **½ D: Luis Mandoki. Jennifer Lopez, Jim Caviezel, Terrence Howard, Sonia Braga, Jeremy Sisto, Monet Mazur, Shirley Knight, Victor Argo. Lopez plays a Chicago cop who's cut off from her family; then a lost soul comes into her life, a man who's running from his past. Neither he nor she realizes that they share a special connection. Sincere performances by the two leads make this watchable, though the story is predictable and familiar. [R]▼❍

Angel Face (1952) 91m. **½ D: Otto Preminger. Robert Mitchum, Jean Simmons, Herbert Marshall, Mona Freeman, Leon Ames, Barbara O'Neil, Kenneth Tobey, Jim Backus. Slow-building but engrossing film noir provides uncharacteristic role for Simmons as wealthy Marshall's impulsive daughter, who lures Mitchum away from his job as an ambulance driver (and girlfriend Freeman) and into a job as a chauffeur. But as he falls for her, he's initially unaware that she's nuts and has dark plans for her hated stepmother (O'Neil). Preminger's best movie in this vein after LAURA; its reputation has steadily increased over the decades. ❍

Angel Heart (1987) C-113m. **½ D: Alan Parker. Mickey Rourke, Robert De Niro, Lisa Bonet, Charlotte Rampling, Stocker Fountelieu, Brownie McGhee, Michael Higgins, Charles Gordone, Kathleen Wilhoite, Pruitt Taylor Vince. Two-bit private eye Rourke is hired by mysterious De Niro to track down a missing man, which leads him into a serpentine investigation—and a kind of emotional quicksand. An American Gothic yarn, full of striking, sensual, and frightening images, though after a while it bogs down. Intriguing, if not terribly appealing. Script by director Parker, based on the novel *Falling Angel* by William Hjortsberg. A steamy sex scene was snipped (by seconds) to avoid an X-rating in the U.S.; it's restored on video. [R] ▼❍

Angel in My Pocket (1969) C-105m. ** D: Alan Rafkin. Andy Griffith, Lee Meriwether, Jerry Van Dyke, Kay Medford, Edgar Buchanan, Gary Collins. Griffith fans may enjoy homespun story of young minister trying to win confidence of new small-town parish. Predictable situations, cliché dialogue, with Van Dyke intolerable as obnoxious brother-in-law. Techniscope. [G]

Angel Levine, The (1970) C-104m. ***½ D: Jan Kadar. Zero Mostel, Harry Belafonte, Ida Kaminska, Milo O'Shea, Eli Wallach, Anne Jackson, Gloria Foster. Touching, humorous, and sad. Black angel named Levine, on the outs in Heaven, tries to help poor old Morris Mishkin. A tale often told—seldom this well. Based on a story by Bernard Malamud; script by Bill Gunn and Ronald Ribman. [PG]▼❍

Angel of Vengeance SEE: Ms. 45

Angelo, My Love (1983) C-115m. *** D: Robert Duvall. Angelo Evans, Michael Evans, Steve "Patalay" Tsigonoff, Millie Tsigonoff, Cathy Kitchen. Fascinating journey into world of modern-day gypsies, with "story" loosely wrapped around precocious Angelo Evans, a remarkable young street hustler. Surprisingly successful attempt by Duvall to weave fictional story into real settings with nonprofessional cast. Incidentally, the two men who sing "Golden Days" in a restaurant scene are Duvall's brothers. [R]▼❍

Angel on My Shoulder (1946) 101m. *** D: Archie Mayo. Paul Muni, Anne Baxter, Claude Rains, George Cleveland, Onslow Stevens. Entertaining fantasy of murdered convict Muni sent to earth by Devil as respected judge, and his efforts to outwit Satan while still in mortal form. Remade for TV in 1980 with Peter Strauss and Richard Kiley.▼❍

Angels SEE: **Angels Hard as They Come**

Angels & Demons (2009) C-138m. **½ D: Ron Howard. Tom Hanks, Ewan McGregor, Ayelet Zurer, Stellan Skarsgård, Pierfrancesco Favino, Nikolaj Lie Kaas, Armin Mueller-Stahl, Rance Howard, Gino Conforti. In this prequel to THE DA VINCI CODE (based on Dan Brown's best-selling novel), Harvard symbologist Hanks is recruited by the Vatican to help unravel a mystery with a ticking clock: four cardinals have been kidnapped and will die before midnight in ritualistic fashion before a stolen canister of powerfully explosive antimatter is detonated in St. Peter's Square. Is this the work of the ancient society known as the Illuminati? Or are the real enemies within the Vatican itself? Fast-paced thriller is engaging for a while, then turns repetitive, ponderous, and downright silly. As with THE DA VINCI CODE, this movie diminishes the power of the book. Extended edition runs 146m. Super 35. [PG-13] ▶

Angels and Insects (1995-U.S.-British) **C-116m.** *** D: Philip Haas. Mark Rylance, Kristin Scott Thomas, Patsy Kensit, Jeremy Kemp, Douglas Henshall, Saskia Wickham, Chris Larkin, Anna Massey. Fascinating, mature drama, set in Victorian England, with impoverished naturalist Rylance taken in by Kemp's wealthy family and falling for his lovely, soft-spoken daughter (Kensit). While the man of science studies the social order of the insect world, the humans around him appear increasingly eccentric. Film methodically builds to devastating conclusion; Scott Thomas (playing a poor relation assisting Rylance with his work) delivers an award-caliber performance. A. S. Byatt's novella *Morpho Eugenia* was adapted by the director and his wife, Belinda Haas. A PBS *American Playhouse* presentation. [R] ▼●▶

Angels Die Hard (1970) **C-86m.** ** D: Richard Compton. Tom Baker, William Smith, Connie Nelson, R. G. Armstrong, Beach Dickerson, Rita Murray, Dan Haggerty, Bambi Allen. Average biker picture has Angels turning out to be good guys for a change as they save people in a mine disaster. Boasts an impressive cast of regulars from this genre. [R] ▼

Angels Hard as They Come (1971) **C-90m.** *½ D: Joe Viola. James Iglehart, Gilda Texter, Gary Busey, Charles Dierkop, Gary Littlejohn, Larry Tucker, Sharon Peckinpah, Scott Glenn. Loosely structured road movie satirizes the format, but can't escape the clichés. Produced and cowritten by Jonathan Demme (who claims it's a biker version of RASHOMON); Busey's film debut. Aka ANGELS. [R] ▼▶

Angels in the Outfield (1951) **102m.** *** D: Clarence Brown. Paul Douglas, Janet Leigh, Keenan Wynn, Donna Corcoran, Spring Byington, Ellen Corby, Lewis Stone, Bruce Bennett; voice of James Whitmore. Cute comedy-fantasy with Douglas ideally cast as the Pittsburgh Pirates' hot-tempered, foul-mouthed manager, whose hard-luck team goes on a winning streak thanks to some heavenly intervention. Amusing cameos from the worlds of baseball and show business. Remade in 1994. ▼●▶

Angels in the Outfield (1994) **C-102m.** **½ D: William Dear. Danny Glover, Tony Danza, Brenda Fricker, Ben Johnson, Joseph Gordon-Levitt, Milton Davis, Jr., Christopher Lloyd, Jay O. Sanders, Taylor Negron, Matthew McConaughey, Dermot Mulroney, Adrien Brody. Inoffensive remake, with the last-place Pittsburgh Pirates of the original now the last-place California Angels. Glover is the team's scowling manager; the invisible angels of the original are now depicted with glitzy special effects; and the prayers of a boy (Gordon-Levitt), rather than a girl, result in the title miracle. OK for kids, but the original was better. Followed by two TV sequels. [PG] ▼●▶

Angels Over Broadway (1940) **80m.** **½ D: Ben Hecht, Lee Garmes. Douglas Fairbanks, Jr., Rita Hayworth, Thomas Mitchell, John Qualen, George Watts. Mordant, ahead-of-its-time black comedy in which hustler Fairbanks decides to do "one good deed"—rescuing suicidal embezzler Qualen—aided by chorus girl Hayworth and boozy Mitchell (who spouts reams of sardonic dialogue in a bravura performance). Hecht buffs will undoubtedly rate this higher, but despite impeccable production, it's just too offbeat (and pleased with itself about it) for most viewers. ▼●▶

Angel Street SEE: **Gaslight** (1940)

Angels Wash Their Faces, The (1939) **84m.** **½ D: Ray Enright. Ann Sheridan, Dead End Kids, Frankie Thomas, Bonita Granville, Ronald Reagan, Margaret Hamilton, Marjorie Main, Eduardo Ciannelli. Protective sister Sheridan tries to clear brother Thomas' police record, but he joins Dead End Kids for more trouble. OK juvenile delinquent drama, sequel to ANGELS WITH DIRTY FACES. ▶

Angels With Dirty Faces (1938) **97m.** ***½ D: Michael Curtiz. James Cagney, Pat O'Brien, Humphrey Bogart, Ann Sheridan, George Bancroft, Billy Halop, Leo Gorcey, Huntz Hall, Gabe Dell, Bobby Jordan, Bernard Punsley. Superior cast in archetypal tale of two playmates; one (Cagney) becomes a gangster, the other (O'Brien) a priest. The Dead End Kids idolize Cagney, much to O'Brien's chagrin. Rowland Brown's story was scripted by John Wexley and Warren Duff. Quintessential Warner Bros. melodrama, a favorite of parodists for decades. Followed by THE ANGELS WASH THEIR FACES. Also shown in computer-colored version. ▼●▶

Angel Unchained (1970) **C-92m.** ** D: Lee Madden. Don Stroud, Luke Askew, Larry Bishop, Tyne Daly, Aldo Ray, Bill McKinney. Biker Stroud joins a hippie commune. Dune buggy-riding cowboys don't like hippies, so it's Stroud's ex-buddies to the rescue. Anyway, the cast is interesting. [PG] ▼▶

Angel Wore Red, The (1960) **99m.** **½ D: Nunnally Johnson. Ava Gardner, Dirk Bogarde, Joseph Cotten, Vittorio De Sica. Sometimes engrossing tale of clergyman who joins the Spanish loyalist cause and his romance with a good-natured entertainer.

[46]

Anger Management (2003) **C-106m.** **
D: Peter Segal. Adam Sandler, Jack Nicholson, Marisa Tomei, John Turturro, Luis Guzman, Allen Covert, Lynne Thigpen, Kurt Fuller, Krista Allen, January Jones, Woody Harrelson, Kevin Nealon, Harry Dean Stanton. Sentenced to undergo therapy after an airline altercation that really wasn't his fault, Sandler is further bewildered when his therapist turns out to be the loosest cannon in New York (Nicholson with a Brillo beard). Comedy offers a dream cross-generational teaming but delivers nothing beyond it, with Nicholson giving a surprisingly one-note performance. Even surprise cameo appearances aren't as funny as they ought to be. Panavision. [PG-13] ▼●)

Angie (1994) **C-107m.** *** D: Martha Coolidge. Geena Davis, Stephen Rea, James Gandolfini, Aida Turturro, Philip Bosco, Jenny O'Hara, Michael Rispoli, Betty Miller, Charlaine Woodard, Bibi Osterwald. Davis shines in this star vehicle about an Italian-American from Brooklyn who's always marched to her own drum, and finds—when she's on the verge of marriage and motherhood—that something significant is missing from her life. Todd Graff's script runs the gamut from romantic comedy to melodrama, but Davis' character—both assertive and vulnerable—has the glue to keep it all together. She's surrounded by a fine supporting cast. Panavision. [R] ▼●)

Angry Harvest (1985-West German) **C-102m.** *** D: Agnieszka Holland. Armin Mueller-Stahl, Elisabeth Trissenaar, Kathe Jaenicke, Hans Beerhenke, Isa Haller, Margit Carstensen, Wojtech Pszoniak, Kurt Raab. Discerning drama, set during WW2, highlighting the intricacies in the relationship between a working-class Polish farmer (Stahl, who is outstanding) and the upper-class Viennese Jewish refugee (Trissenaar) he shelters. Scripted by director Holland. ▼)

Angry Hills, The (1959) **105m.** **½ D: Robert Aldrich. Robert Mitchum, Elisabeth Mueller, Stanley Baker, Gia Scala, Theodore Bikel, Sebastian Cabot. Mitchum shows vim in WW2 actioner as war correspondent plotting escape from Greece with valuable data for Allies.

Angry Red Planet, The (1959) **C-83m.** ** D: Ib Melchior. Gerald Mohr, Nora Hayden, Les Tremayne, Jack Kruschen, Paul Hahn. Martians sic incredible monsters on first Earth expedition to Mars. Lots of wild-eyed effects have given this film cult status. Filmed in odd "Cinemagic" process, which mostly turns everything pink. ▼●)

Angry Silence, The (1960-British) **95m.** *** D: Guy Green. Richard Attenborough, Pier Angeli, Michael Craig, Bernard Lee, Geoffrey Keen, Oliver Reed. Rewarding, unheralded film about brave stand by a simple British factory worker who refuses to join unofficial strike, the repercussions he and his family endure.

Anguish (1987-Spanish) **C-89m.** **½ D: Bigas Luna. Zelda Rubinstein, Michael Lerner, Talia Paul, Clara Pastor. Imaginative but overly violent horror film turns the action in on itself, as a mad-killer film unspools inside a theater where another mad killer is loose in the audience. Theatrical release carried warnings regarding use of subliminal effects on soundtrack. Well-recorded English dialogue. J-D-C Scope. [R] ▼●)

Angus (1995) **C-89m.** ** D: Patrick Read Johnson. Charlie Talbert, George C. Scott, Kathy Bates, Ariana Richards, Chris Owen, James Van Der Beek, Lawrence Pressman, Rita Moreno. Ostensibly well-meaning—but obvious and superficial—film about an overweight teenager with low self-esteem and a lifelong crush on a cute blond schoolmate. Amidst its upbeat, self-affirming messages, however, we get too many crude jokes and incompetently staged comic scenes that deflate film's impact. Scott's chess-playing partner is played by veteran director Irvin Kershner. [PG-13] ▼)

Animal, The (2001) **C-84m.** BOMB D: Luke Greenfield. Rob Schneider, Colleen Haskell, John C. McGinley, Edward Asner, Michael Caton, Louis Lombardi, Guy Torry, Adam Sandler, Norm Macdonald. A pathetic nobody awakens after a car accident to find that his body organs have been replaced by those of animals (a dog, a dolphin, a horse, etc.). Filled to the brim with bathroom humor, offensive dialogue, gratuitous nudity . . . everything but genuine comedy. Schneider cowrote. [PG-13] ▼)

Animal Behavior (1989) **C-88m.** BOMB D: H. Anne Riley. Karen Allen, Armand Assante, Holly Hunter, Josh Mostel, Richard Libertini, Alexa Kenin, Jon Matthews, Nan Martin. A man, a woman, a chimp, a campus—and let us all be thankful that Bonzo didn't live to see this. Allen, as a monkey researcher sweating out funding, delivers a most discomforting lemme-outa-here performance. Director's name is a pseudonym; Jenny Bowen started the picture in 1984; producer Kjehl Rasmussen finished it. [PG] ▼●

Animal Crackers (1930) **98m.** *** D: Victor Heerman. Groucho, Harpo, Chico, and Zeppo Marx, Margaret Dumont, Lillian Roth, Louis Sorin, Hal Thompson, Robert Greig. Marx Brothers' second movie, adapted from Broadway success, suffers from staginess and musical comedy plotting, but gives the zany foursome plenty of comic elbowroom. "Story" has to do with stolen painting, but never mind: Groucho performs "Hooray for Captain Spaulding," Chico and Harpo play bridge, Groucho shoots an elephant in his pajamas, etc. ▼●)

Animal Factory (2000) **C-95m.** *** D:

Steve Buscemi. Willem Dafoe, Edward Furlong, Mickey Rourke, Tom Arnold, Steve Buscemi, John Heard, Danny Trejo, Seymour Cassel. Compelling drama of prison life, with Furlong, locked up for marijuana dealing, becoming the protégé of Dafoe, who virtually runs the place. Dafoe is powerful, as always, but the film's distinction is the matter-of-fact way it deals with the horrors of life behind bars. Based on a novel by ex-con Edward Bunker, who coscripted. U.S. debut on cable TV. [R]▼◗

Animal Farm (1955-British) **C-75m.** ✱✱✱ D: John Halas, Joy Batchelor. Good straightforward animated-feature version of George Orwell's political satire. Ending changed from original to make it more upbeat, but trenchant views of government still hold fast. Not a kiddie film. Remade for cable TV in 1999. ▼◗

Animal House SEE: **National Lampoon's Animal House**

Animal Kingdom (2010-Australian) **C-113m.** ✱✱✱ D: David Michôd. Ben Mendelsohn, Joel Edgerton, Guy Pearce, Luke Ford, Jacki Weaver, Sullivan Stapleton, James Frecheville, Dan Wyllie, Anthony Hayes. When a 17-year-old boy's mother dies of a drug overdose, he (Frecheville) is taken in by his grandmother (Weaver), who mother-hens her three grown sons, who are all dangerous criminals. It's inevitable that the quiet boy will be dragged into this life, but first-time director Michôd's screenplay keeps us wondering when, and how he will respond, especially to his psychopathic uncle (Mendelsohn). Tough, uncompromising drama always has one more surprise up its sleeve than you expect. Super 35. [R] ◗

Animalympics (1979) **C-80m.** ✱✱ D: Steven Lisberger. Voices of Gilda Radner, Billy Crystal, Harry Shearer, Michael Fremer. Animated spoof of Olympics events and ubiquitous TV coverage by various anthropomorphic characters. Enough clever, funny material for a good short subject, but stretched to feature length. ▼

Anna (1951-Italian) **95m.** ✱✱½ D: Alberto Lattuada. Silvana Mangano, Raf Vallone, Vittorio Gassman, Gaby Morlay. Thoughtful study of confused young woman who enters convent to avoid deciding which man she really loves; fate forces her to decide. Look quick for Sophia Loren.▼

Anna (1987) **C-100m.** ✱✱½ D: Yurek Bogayevicz. Sally Kirkland, Paulina Porizkova, Robert Fields, Ruth Maleczech, Stefan Schnabel, Larry Pine. Middle-aged Czech actress, once a star in her native country but now struggling to survive in N.Y.C., takes in an impoverished young immigrant and teaches her the ropes—only to see her succeed where she has failed. Intriguing little film misses the bull's-eye but still has much to offer, especially a riveting and heart-rending

performance by Kirkland (who is *not* Czech). Supermodel Porizkova (who is) makes an impressive screen debut. [PG-13]▼◗

Anna and the King (1999) **C-147m.** ✱✱½ D: Andy Tennant. Jodie Foster, Chow Yun-Fat, Bai Ling, Tom Felton, Syed Alwi, Randall Duk Kim, Deanna Yusoff, Geoffrey Palmer. Lavish remake of the now-familiar story (memorably musicalized as THE KING AND I) about a young British widow who travels to Siam in 1862 to work as schoolteacher for the King's 58 children. Put off at first, she and the imperious monarch soon develop an understanding and an unspoken attraction. Unfortunately, film goes on too long, with at least one subplot too many and a terribly contrived action climax. Foster and Yun-Fat are fine. Panavision. [PG-13]▼◗

Anna and the King of Siam (1946) **128m.** ✱✱✱½ D: John Cromwell. Irene Dunne, Rex Harrison, Linda Darnell, Lee J. Cobb, Gale Sondergaard, Mikhail Rasumny. Sumptuous production chronicling the experiences of a British governess in 19th-century Thailand, and her battle of wits with strong-willed ruler. Based on Margaret Landon's book about real-life Anna Leonowens (renamed Anna L. Owens in the movie). Dunne and Harrison (in his Hollywood debut) are superb; won Oscars for Cinematography (Arthur Miller) and Art Direction/Set Decoration (then known as "Interior Decoration"). Screenplay by Talbot Jennings and Sally Benson. Later musicalized as THE KING AND I; remade as ANNA AND THE KING.▼◗

Anna Christie (1930) **90m.** ✱✱✱ D: Clarence Brown. Greta Garbo, Charles Bickford, Marie Dressler, Lee Phelps, George Marion. Garbo is effective in her first talkie as girl with shady past finding love with seaman Bickford. Film itself is rather static. From the play by Eugene O'Neill. Beware of 74m. prints. Filmed simultaneously in a German-language version, with Garbo and a different supporting cast. Filmed before in 1923, with Blanche Sweet. ▼◗

Anna Karenina (1935) **95m.** ✱✱✱✱ D: Clarence Brown. Greta Garbo, Fredric March, Freddie Bartholomew, Maureen O'Sullivan, May Robson, Basil Rathbone. Tolstoy's tragic love chronicle makes excellent Garbo vehicle, with fine support from March as her lover, Rathbone her husband, and Bartholomew, her adoring son. Filmed before with Garbo as LOVE; remade three times.▼◗

Anna Karenina (1948-British) **123m.** ✱✱½ D: Julien Duvivier. Vivien Leigh, Ralph Richardson, Kieron Moore, Sally Ann Howes, Niall MacGinnis, Martita Hunt, Marie Lohr, Michael Gough. Despite its stellar cast, this is a mostly turgid adaptation of the Tolstoy classic about a woman married to stodgy bureaucrat, who falls in love with a dashing army officer. Duvivier and Jean Anouilh were among the scriptwriters. ▼●◗

Anna Karenina (1997) SEE: **Leo Tolstoy's Anna Karenina**

Anna Lucasta (1949) **86m.** ** D: Irving Rapper. Paulette Goddard, William Bishop, Oscar Homolka, John Ireland, Broderick Crawford, Will Geer, Gale Page, Mary Wickes, Whit Bissell. Sluggish, watered-down version of Philip Yordan's Broadway play (which featured an all-black cast, as does the 1958 remake). Goddard plays the title role, a woman of the Brooklyn streets who was tossed out of her home by her alcoholic father; her oppressive brother-in-law tries to marry her off, in a money-making scheme. Scripted by Yordan (who also produced) and Arthur Laurents.

Anna Lucasta (1958) **97m.** ** D: Arnold Laven. Eartha Kitt, Sammy Davis, Jr., Frederick O'Neal, Henry Scott, Rex Ingram, Alvin Childress. Tepid remake of Philip Yordan's play about a prostitute who tries to leave her past behind. Kitt doesn't so much act as pose, but Ingram is excellent as her father.◗

Annapolis (2006) **C-103m.** ** D: Justin Lin. James Franco, Tyrese Gibson, Jordana Brewster, Donnie Wahlberg, Vicellous Reon Shannon, Chi McBride, Roger Fan, McCaleb Burnett, Wilmer Calderon, Charles Napier. Boilerplate service pic about blue-collar boxer Franco and his long-shot selection to the U.S. Naval Academy, where he rooms with a perfect ethnic mix of cohorts, who are only occasionally seen in class or cracking books. Co-cadet Brewster, seen at ringside during bouts or when Franco is punching the bag, takes on the equivalent of Burgess Meredith's role in ROCKY, though she looks cuter in khaki. A non-starter. Super 35. [PG-13] ◗

Anne Frank Remembered (1995-British) **C/B&W-117m.** ***½ D: Jon Blair. Narrated by Kenneth Branagh; diary read by Glenn Close. Deeply moving documentary on the young Jewish girl whose diary became an international best-seller. The filmmakers interview many who knew Anne and even turn up a brief home-movie scene of the girl herself. Perhaps the greatest impression is made by Miep Gies, the matter-of-fact Dutch woman who helped hide the Franks, and who found the diary. Oscar winner for Best Documentary. [PG] ▼◗

Anne of the Indies (1951) **C-81m.** **½ D: Jacques Tourneur. Jean Peters, Louis Jourdan, Debra Paget, Herbert Marshall. Peters isn't always believable as swaggering pirate, but surrounded by professionals and good production, actioner moves along. Built around stock footage from THE BLACK SWAN.

Anne of the Thousand Days (1969) **C-145m.** *** D: Charles Jarrott. Richard Burton, Genevieve Bujold, Irene Papas, Anthony Quayle, Peter Jeffrey. Often inaccurate but totally engrossing, well-acted historical drama centering on Anne Boleyn and King Henry VIII. Lovely scenery, brilliant performance by Bujold, and Oscar-winning costumes by Margaret Furse. Panavision. [M/PG] ▼●◗

Annie (1982) **C-128m.** **½ D: John Huston. Albert Finney, Carol Burnett, Aileen Quinn, Bernadette Peters, Tim Curry, Ann Reinking, Geoffrey Holder, Edward Herrmann. Overblown adaptation of the Broadway musical hit about the Depression's most famous foundling (based on Harold Gray's "Little Orphan Annie" comic strip). Appealing performances by Quinn, as Annie, and Finney, as Daddy Warbucks, help buoy an uninspired—and curiously claustrophobic—production. Followed by made-for-TV sequel. Remade for TV in 1999. Panavision. [PG] ▼●◗

Annie Get Your Gun (1950) **C-107m.** *** D: George Sidney. Betty Hutton, Howard Keel, Louis Calhern, Edward Arnold, Keenan Wynn, Benay Venuta, J. Carrol Naish. Lively filming of Irving Berlin's Wild West show musical about Annie Oakley getting her man—sharpshooter Frank Butler. Songs include "Anything You Can Do," "Doin' What Comes Naturally," "There's No Business Like Show Business." ▼◗

Annie Hall (1977) **C-94m.** **** D: Woody Allen. Woody Allen, Diane Keaton, Tony Roberts, Paul Simon, Shelley Duvall, Carol Kane, Colleen Dewhurst, Christopher Walken, Janet Margolin, John Glover. Woody's best film, an autobiographical love story with incisive Allenisms on romance, relationships, fame, N.Y.C. vs. L.A., and sundry other topics. Warm, witty, intelligent Oscar winner for Best Picture, Actress, Direction, Screenplay (Allen and Marshall Brickman). Look sharp and you'll spot future stars Jeff Goldblum (at the L.A. party), Shelley Hack (on the street), Beverly D'Angelo (on a TV monitor), and Sigourney Weaver (as Woody's date seen in extreme long-shot near the end of the picture). [PG] ▼●◗

Annie Oakley (1935) **88m.** *** D: George Stevens. Barbara Stanwyck, Preston Foster, Melvyn Douglas, Pert Kelton, Andy Clyde. Lively biography of female sharpshooter Stanwyck and her on-again off-again romance with fellow performer Foster. Tight direction within episodic scenes gives believable flavor of late 19th-century America. Moroni Olsen plays Buffalo Bill. Also shown in computer-colored version. ▼◗

Annie's Coming Out SEE: **Test of Love, A**

Annihilation of Fish, The (2001) **C-108m.** ** D: Charles Burnett. James Earl Jones, Lynn Redgrave, Margot Kidder. Fish (Jones), a former mental patient who is harassed by a demon named Hank, moves into a dingy L.A. boardinghouse and gradually befriends an alcoholic flake (Redgrave), who is obsessed by Puccini. Ambitious portrait of two nutty, lonely souls means to be poignant but doesn't really jell. Kidder—surprisingly—plays an elderly landlady. Shot in 1999. [R]

Anniversary, The (1968-British) **C-95m.** **½ D: Roy Ward Baker. Bette Davis, Sheila Hancock, Jack Hedley, James Cossins, Christian Roberts, Elaine Taylor. Human monster Davis uses date of wedding anniversary as excuse to reunite family, continue her stranglehold on them. Adapted from MacIlwraith stage play, black comedy emerges as vehicle for Davis' hammy performance. ▼▶

Anniversary Party, The (2001) **C-115m.** *** D: Jennifer Jason Leigh, Alan Cumming. Jennifer Jason Leigh, Alan Cumming, Jane Adams, Mina Badie, Jennifer Beals, Phoebe Cates, John Hickey, Parker Posey, Kevin Kline, Denis O'Hare, Gwyneth Paltrow, Michael Panes, John C. Reilly. Cumming and Leigh conceived, directed and star in this seriocomedy about an L.A. couple (he's a writer about to make his movie directing debut, she's an actress) who have an eventful and emotional anniversary party. Supporting parts were tailored for the filmmakers' actor friends, and they're all good, but the two children of real-life couple Kline and Cates almost steal the show. Beautifully shot on digital video by John Bailey. [R] ▼▶

À Nos Amours (1984-French) **C-102m.** *** D: Maurice Pialat. Sandrine Bonnaire, Dominique Besnehard, Maurice Pialat, Evelyne Ker, Anne-Sophie Maille, Christophe Odent. A 15-year-old's casual promiscuity runs her family through the ringer, but they've got problems of their own—Pop's moving out, Mom's a screaming neurotic, and Brother's embraces are too hearty to be healthy. Dramatically uneven and somewhat of a downer, but Bonnaire creates a full-blooded, memorable character. Winner of France's César. [R] ▼▶

Another Country (1984-British) **C-90m.** **½ D: Marek Kanievska. Rupert Everett, Colin Firth, Michael Jenn, Robert Addie, Cary Elwes, Anna Massey, Betsy Brantley. Faithful adaptation of Julian Mitchell's hit London play that speculates about the 1930s private-school experiences of Guy Burgess and Donald Maclean, who 20 years later were found to be spying for the Russians. Arguably more meaningful to British audiences, this examination of an oppressive existence that shuns any nonconformity makes for a pretty oppressive movie. [PG] ▼▶●

Another Dawn (1937) **73m.** **½ D: William Dieterle. Kay Francis, Errol Flynn, Ian Hunter, Frieda Inescort, Mary Forbes. Francis is torn between devotion to husband Hunter and officer Flynn in well-paced

adventure story set at British army post in African desert.

Another Day in Paradise (1998) **C-100m.** *** D: Larry Clark. James Woods, Melanie Griffith, Vincent Kartheiser, Natasha Gregson Wagner, James Otis, Paul Hipp, Brent Briscoe, Clarence Carter, Peter Sarsgaard. Arresting drama about a teenage junkie/thief who, with his girlfriend, goes on the road with a slick, experienced criminal and becomes part of his extended family. Woods is dynamite as the frighteningly intense, mood-swinging crime daddy, and Griffith is equally good as his nurturing girlfriend. Clark invests the film with a sense of immediacy and truth, even as its emotional peaks grow larger than life. Lou Diamond Phillips appears unbilled. [R] ▼▶●

Another 48HRS. (1990) **C-95m.** ** D: Walter Hill. Eddie Murphy, Nick Nolte, Brion James, Kevin Tighe, Ed O'Ross, David Anthony Marshall, Bernie Casey. Strictly by-the-numbers rehash of 48HRS., without its spontaneity, pizzazz, or humor: Nolte is forced to turn to Murphy (who's just being sprung from jail) to help him solve a case and save his police career. Watchable, but not terribly invigorating; must set some sort of record, however, for breaking more panes of glass than any movie in history. [R] ▼▶●

Another Gay Movie (2006) **C-92m.** ** D: Todd Stephens. Michael Carbonaro, Jonah Blechman, Jonathan Chase, Mitch Morris, Ashlie Atkinson, Scott Thompson. Four gay high school guys embark on a mission to lose their virginity before graduation, sending up every gay and teen comedy movie cliché along the way. Predictably dumb genre spoof, somewhat funnier and more engaging than many of its ilk. Hilariously meticulous reenactment of the prom scene from CARRIE makes one wish that the rest of the film were so clever. Features cameos by cult celebrities including Graham Norton, Lypsinka, and *Survivor*'s Richard Hatch (who reveals more than most would want to see). Followed by a DVD sequel. [R]▶

Another Man, Another Chance (1977-French-U.S.) **C-132m.** **½ D: Claude Lelouch. James Caan, Genevieve Bujold, Francis Huster, Jennifer Warren, Susan Tyrrell, Richard Farnsworth. Virtual remake of Lelouch's A MAN AND A WOMAN, with late-1800s Western setting; Bujold and Caan are widow and widower who fall in love after losing their spouses. Mild-mannered to the point of distraction, and much too long. [PG] ▼▶

Another Man's Poison (1951-British) **89m.** **½ D: Irving Rapper. Bette Davis, Gary Merrill, Emlyn Williams, Anthony Steel, Barbara Murray, Reginald Beckwith. Bette is feisty, man-hungry novelist on isolated Yorkshire farm who won't let her criminal husband, or his crony Merrill, get in her way. Well-paced melodrama can't hide its stage origins, but Davis wrings every drop out of a showy role. Coproduced by Douglas Fairbanks, Jr.▼●

Another Part of the Forest (1948) **107m.** *** D: Michael Gordon. Fredric March, Dan Duryea, Edmond O'Brien, Ann Blyth, Florence Eldridge, John Dall. Lillian Hellman's story predates THE LITTLE FOXES by tracing the Hubbard family's ruthlessness; unpleasant but well-acted movie.

Another Stakeout (1993) **C-109m.** **½ D: John Badham. Richard Dreyfuss, Emilio Estevez, Rosie O'Donnell, Dennis Farina, Marcia Strassman, Cathy Moriarty, John Rubinstein, Miguel Ferrer, Dan Lauria, Sharon Maughan. Lots of fun here for fans of the first STAKEOUT, but little for anyone seeking substance or Shavian wit. The inept cop partners return to track down no-good Moriarty, but are saddled with assistant D.A. O'Donnell and her dog, who are both along for the ride. Highlight: dinner party that goes from bad to worse to hysterical. Madeleine Stowe (costar of the original film) briefly re-creates her role but takes no billing. Panavision. [PG-13]▼●

Another Thin Man (1939) **105m.** *** D: W. S. Van Dyke II. William Powell, Myrna Loy, C. Aubrey Smith, Otto Kruger, Nat Pendleton, Virginia Grey, Tom Neal, Marjorie Main, Ruth Hussey, Sheldon Leonard. Murder strikes at a Long Island estate and the screen's favorite lush-detective couple (along with Asta and newborn son Nick, Jr.) move in to solve it, although motherhood has slowed down Nora's drinking a bit. Enjoyable third entry in the series and the last to be based on a Dashiell Hammett story.▼●

Another Time, Another Place (1958) **98m.** **½ D: Lewis Allen. Lana Turner, Barry Sullivan, Glynis Johns, Sean Connery. Unconvincing melodrama; Turner suffers nervous breakdown when her lover is killed during WW2. Filmed in England. VistaVision.▼●

Another Woman (1988) **C-84m.** ***½ D: Woody Allen. Gena Rowlands, Mia Farrow, Ian Holm, Blythe Danner, Gene Hackman, Betty Buckley, Martha Plimpton, John Houseman, Sandy Dennis, David Ogden Stiers, Philip Bosco, Harris Yulin, Frances Conroy. Woody ventures into Bergman territory again (with Ingmar's cameraman, Sven Nykvist, no less) with tremendous success. Rowlands plays a woman who has managed to live her life shielding herself from all emotions, until a series of incidents force her to take stock. Searing, adult drama with a magnificent cast and many memorable moments . . . though like Allen's other dramas, it's not to everyone's taste. [PG]▼●

Another Year (2010-British) **C-130m.** ***½ D: Mike Leigh. Jim Broadbent, Lesley Manville, Ruth Sheen, Peter Wight, Oliver Maltman, David Bradley, Karina Fernandez, Martin Savage, Imelda Staunton. Four seasons pass in the lives of a genial married couple (Sheen and Broadbent), who take life as it comes and who have passed on their sensibilities—and sense of humor—to their son (Maltman), who hasn't yet settled down. That's more than can be said of Sheen's desperately neurotic office-mate (Manville), who tests their friendship with her increasingly outlandish behavior. Not so much a story as a character portrait of "ordinary people," beautifully painted by writer-director Leigh and his superlative actors. Likable, funny, and ultimately quite moving. Super 35. [PG-13]▼

Another You (1991) **C-98m.** *½ D: Maurice Phillips. Richard Pryor, Gene Wilder, Mercedes Ruehl, Stephen Lang, Vanessa Williams, Phil Rubenstein, Peter Michael Goetz, Kevin Pollak, Vincent Schiavelli. Compulsive liar Wilder is released from a sanitarium into the care of parolee Pryor, a street hustler who's got to perform community service; together they become embroiled in an elaborate scam. Anemic comedy relies entirely on its stars to support third-rate material. Pryor's real-life health problems are all too apparent. [R]▼●

À Nous la Liberté (1931-French) **97m.** **** D: René Clair. Raymond Cordy, Henri Marchand, Rolla France, Paul Olivier, Jacques Shelly, Andre Michaud. Classic satire on machinery and industrialization centering on the adventures of escaped prisoner Cordy, who becomes owner of a phonograph factory, and his former jail friend (Marchand), now a vagrant. Predates and equals MODERN TIMES in poignancy, with groundbreaking use of music. Arguably, Clair's masterpiece. Clair recut film in 1950 to 83m.▼

Answer Man, The (2009) **C-96m.** *** D: John Hindman. Jeff Daniels, Lauren Graham, Lou Taylor Pucci, Olivia Thirlby, Kat Dennings, Nora Dunn, Tony Hale. Daniels plays an author who wrote about his conversations with God in a bestseller 20 years ago—but now lives as a recluse in his Philadelphia brownstone. As an attractive chiropractor (Graham) and a troubled used-book store owner (Pucci) come into his orbit, they discover that "the man with the answers" can't seem to get his own life in order. Likable, small-scale comedy written by the director; Daniels, Graham, and Pucci are a treat to watch. [R]●

Ant Bully, The (2006) **C-89m.** ** D: John A. Davis. Voices of Julia Roberts, Nicolas Cage, Meryl Streep, Paul Giamatti, Zach Tyler Eisen, Regina King, Bruce Campbell, Lily Tomlin, Cheri Oteri, Larry Miller, Ricardo Montalban, Allison Mack, Rob Paulsen. A boy who's always bullied by the neighborhood kids takes out his frustration on an ant colony in his front yard—until

[51]

he's shrunk to their size and put to work in their environment. Here he learns hard-won lessons about the value of teamwork and sacrifice. Uninspired morality tale has the novelty of human characters that are designed to look as grotesque as possible. From the book by John Nickle. [PG]❱

Anthony Adverse (1936) **141m.** *****½** D: Mervyn LeRoy. Fredric March, Olivia de Havilland, Donald Woods, Anita Louise, Edmund Gwenn, Claude Rains, Louis Hayward, Gale Sondergaard, Akim Tamiroff, Billy Mauch, Ralph Morgan, Henry O'Neill, Scotty Beckett, Luis Alberni. Blockbuster filmization of Hervey Allen bestseller (scripted by Sheridan Gibney) of young man gaining maturity through adventures in various parts of early 19th-century Europe, Cuba, and Africa. Sondergaard won Oscar as Best Supporting Actress in her film debut; rousing musical score by Erich Wolfgang Korngold and Tony Gaudio's cinematography also won. ❱❍

Antichrist, The (1974-Italian) SEE: **Tempter, The**

Antichrist (2009-Danish-German-French-Swedish-Italian-Polish) **C-105m.** ****** D: Lars von Trier. Willem Dafoe, Charlotte Gainsbourg. In grief because their infant son fell to his death while they were making love, a couple retreats to a remote cabin in a forest in order to work through their feelings. Intense, gorgeously designed drama becomes increasingly gruesome, with some scenes so brutally graphic they're nearly impossible to watch. This isn't SAW-type torture porn; it's grimly serious, but also very difficult to decipher, with touches of fantasy thrown in. To say it's not for all tastes is an understatement, but those interested in writer-director von Trier may well find something to their liking. HD Widescreen.❱

Antitrust (2001) **C-108m.** ******* D: Peter Howitt. Ryan Phillippe, Rachael Leigh Cook, Claire Forlani, Tim Robbins, Douglas McFerran, Richard Roundtree, Tygh Runyan, Yee Jee Tso, Nate Dushku, Ned Bellamy. Young computer whiz leaves his idealistic, computer-geek pals to work for the biggest software company in the world, after being recruited by its charismatic, highly persuasive chief (Robbins). He soon discovers that the company's take-no-prisoners approach to business hides many nefarious deeds. Cleverly plotted, mostly believable conspiracy yarn, a bit heavy-handed at times. David Clennon appears unbilled. Panavision. [PG-13]❱❱

Antonia & Jane (1991-British) **C-77m.** ******* D: Beeban Kidron. Saskia Reeves, Imelda Staunton, Brenda Bruce, Bill Nighy, Lila Kaye, Alfred Marks, Richard Hope. Pleasingly quirky, clever chronicle of the relationship between two friends from school. Antonia (Reeves) is attractive and arrogant; Jane (Staunton) is plump, but adventuresome.

They share mutual envy (as well as the same therapist) . . . and Antonia's husband is Jane's ex-boyfriend. Very funny little sleeper made for British television.❱

Antonia's Line (1995-Dutch-Belgian-British) **C-105m.** ******* D: Marleen Gorris. Willeke van Ammelrooy, Els Dottermans, Jan Decleir, Mil Seghers, Marina de Graaf, Jan Steen, Veerle Van Overloop, Elsie de Brauw, Thyrza Ravesteijn, Wimie Wilhelm. Spirited woman returns to her provincial Dutch village after WW2 and takes up residence there with her daughter. Then, over a span of years, she raises not only her own child but an extended family which comes under the shelter (and aura) of this unusual woman who defies convention. Disarmingly unpredictable comedy-drama is a treat from start to finish. Oscar winner as Best Foreign Film. [R]❱❍❱

Antony and Cleopatra (1972) **C-160m.** ***½** D: Charlton Heston. Charlton Heston, Hildegard Neil, Eric Porter, John Castle, Fernando Rey. Labor-of-love undertaking by Heston results in sluggish treatment of Shakespearean play, hampered by severe budgetary limitations. Todd-AO 35. ❱❱

Antwone Fisher (2002) **C-120m.** ******* D: Denzel Washington. Derek Luke, Denzel Washington, Joy Bryant, Salli Richardson, Earl Billings, Kevin Connolly, Viola Davis, Rainoldo Gooding, Novella Nelson. Newcomer Luke is excellent as the hero of this remarkable true-life memoir, a quick-tempered seaman who reaches a turning point when a Navy psychiatrist forces him to examine his life and confront his troubled childhood. A creditable directing debut for Washington, who also delivers a strong, compassionate performance as a doctor whose own life can use some healing. Cynics may find this sentimental or simplistic, but we bought into it one hundred percent. Screenplay by Antwone Fisher, based on his book. James Brolin appears unbilled. Panavision. [PG-13]❱❱

Antz (1998) **C-83m.** ******* D: Eric Darnell, Tim Johnson. Voices of Woody Allen, Sharon Stone, Sylvester Stallone, Gene Hackman, Christopher Walken, Anne Bancroft, Dan Aykroyd, Jane Curtin, Danny Glover, Jennifer Lopez, John Mahoney, Paul Mazursky. Entertaining computer-animated feature about an ant named Z (with the voice and personality of Woody Allen) who doesn't respond well to regimentation—especially after he's smitten with the queen ant's daughter, Princess Bala. Meanwhile, the colony is threatened, not only by termites but by a megalomaniacal general with his own agenda. Clever and enjoyable (all the more so for Woodyphiles), but too sophisticated and violent for young kids. [PG] ❱❍

Any Given Sunday (1999) **C-162m.** ****** D: Oliver Stone. Al Pacino, Cameron Diaz, Dennis Quaid, James Woods, Jamie Foxx, LL Cool J, Charlton Heston, Matthew Modine, Jim Brown, Ann-Margret, Aaron Eckhart, John C. McGinley, Lauren Holly, Lela Rochon, Lawrence Taylor, Bill Bellamy, James Karen, Elizabeth Berkley. Strident, one-note concoction about the world of pro football, on and off the field. Pacino is an aging coach who's given his all to the game, Diaz a demanding, mercurial team owner, Foxx an up-and-coming quarterback who gets a big head. Loud and obvious from the word go. Various sports figures play themselves; Stone appears as a booth announcer. Stone completely recut 157m. video version. Super 35. [R]▼●▶

Any Number Can Play (1949) **112m.** ** D: Mervyn LeRoy. Clark Gable, Alexis Smith, Wendell Corey, Audrey Totter, Mary Astor, Lewis Stone, Marjorie Rambeau, Darryl Hickman. Low-key drama of gambling-house owner Gable, estranged from wife Smith and son Hickman. Good character roles breathe life into film.▼

Anyone Can Play (1968-Italian-French) **C-88m.** ** D: Luigi Zampa. Ursula Andress, Virna Lisi, Claudine Auger, Marisa Mell, Brett Halsey, Jean-Pierre Cassel. Aside from obvious good looks of four leading actresses, tale of adultery in Italy is not one of that country's better farces. [R]

Anything But Love (2003) **C-99m.** *½ D: Robert Cary. Andrew McCarthy, Isabel Rose, Cameron Bancroft, Alix Korey, Ilana Levine, Sean Arbuckle, Victor Argo, Michael J. Burg, Eartha Kitt. Labored attempt to recall the charm of old MGM musicals, with a love triangle involving a lawyer, a cabaret singer, and a fledgling songwriter. Clearly a heartfelt, loving salute to those '50s films, but some soufflés just fall flat, despite the presence of Kitt. It shows just how skillful those old moviemakers were in making what they did seem effortless. Cary cowrote this with his leading lady. Aka STANDARD TIME. [PG-13]▼▶

Anything Else (2003) **C-108m.** BOMB D: Woody Allen. Woody Allen, Jason Biggs, Christina Ricci, Danny DeVito, Stockard Channing, KaDee Strickland, Jimmy Fallon, William Hill, Fisher Stevens, Diana Krall. Acerbic schoolteacher and would-be comedy writer Allen is mentor and advisor to a young man who's caught in an unfathomable relationship with the most obnoxious woman on earth (Ricci). Allen passes the torch to Biggs, who plays a younger version of Woody's archetypal character. The filmmaker's all-time worst movie; you know you're in trouble when it opens with Woody telling a couple of old jokes and even they aren't funny. Panavision. [R] ▼▶

Anything for Love SEE: **11 Harrowhouse**

Anything Goes (1936) **92m.** **½ D: Lewis Milestone. Bing Crosby, Ethel Merman, Charlie Ruggles, Ida Lupino, Grace Bradley, Arthur Treacher. Pleasant Crosby shipboard musical retains Merman from the cast of the Broadway show, but scuttles much of the plot and most of Cole Porter's songs (except "You're the Top" and "I Get a Kick Out of You"). Remade (again with Bing) in 1956.

Anything Goes (1956) **C-106m.** ** D: Robert Lewis. Bing Crosby, Jeanmaire, Donald O'Connor, Mitzi Gaynor, Phil Harris, Kurt Kasznar. Flat musical involving show business partners Crosby and O'Connor each signing a performer for the leading role in their next show. Sidney Sheldon's script bears little resemblance to the original Broadway show, though some Cole Porter songs remain. Crosby fared better in the 1936 film. VistaVision.▶

Any Wednesday (1966) **C-109m.** *** D: Robert Ellis Miller. Jane Fonda, Jason Robards, Dean Jones, Rosemary Murphy. Bedroom farce of N.Y.C. executive using his mistress' apartment for business deductions. Fonda is appropriately addled in unstagy sex comedy.▼▶

Anywhere But Here (1999) **C-114m.** ** D: Wayne Wang. Susan Sarandon, Natalie Portman, Hart Bochner, Shawn Hatosy, Bonnie Bedelia, John Diehl, Paul Guilfoyle, Caroline Aaron, Elizabeth Moss, Eva Amurri, Megan Mullally, Thora Birch. Optimistic single mom who can still turn heads and a wearily-seen-it-all adolescent daughter leave small-town Wisconsin to seek a new beginning in Beverly Hills, commencing a series of episodic adventures that never take emotional hold. Sizzleless adaptation of Mona Simpson's best-seller pales not only next to ALICE DOESN'T LIVE HERE ANYMORE and MEN DON'T LEAVE, but to the low-budget indie TUMBLEWEEDS. Super 35. [PG-13]▼▶

Any Which Way You Can (1980) **C-116m.** **½ D: Buddy Van Horn. Clint Eastwood, Sondra Locke, Geoffrey Lewis, William Smith, Harry Guardino, Ruth Gordon, Glen Campbell, Anne Ramsey, Logan Ramsey, Barry Corbin, James Gammon. This sequel to EVERY WHICH WAY BUT LOOSE is funnier, if no more intelligent. Clint's climactic bare-fisted fight with Smith is a highlight, but the filmmakers wisely gave most of the laughs to the star's orangutan friend, Clyde. [PG]▼●▶

Anzio (1968-French-Italian-Spanish) **C-117m.** ** D: Edward Dmytryk. Robert Mitchum, Peter Falk, Robert Ryan, Earl Holliman, Mark Damon, Arthur Kennedy, Reni Santoni, Patrick Magee. Undistinguished retelling of Allied invasion of Anzio; all-star cast, large-scale action, but nothing memorable. Aka THE BATTLE FOR ANZIO. Panavision. [M/PG]▼▶

Apache (1954) **C-91m.** ** D: Robert Aldrich. Burt Lancaster, Jean Peters, John McIntire, Charles (Bronson) Buchinsky. Pacifist Indian (Lancaster) learns might makes right from U.S. cavalry; turns to fighting one man crusade for his tribe's rights. Overacted and improbable (though based on fact).▼●)

Apache Massacre SEE: **Cry for Me Billy**

Apache Uprising (1966) **C-90m.** *½ D: R. G. Springsteen. Rory Calhoun, Corinne Calvet, John Russell, Lon Chaney (Jr.), Gene Evans, Richard Arlen, Arthur Hunnicutt, DeForest Kelley, Johnny Mack Brown, Jean Parker, Don "Red" Barry. No production values, but cast of familiar names may make it possible for some to sit through standard Western where Rory fights both Indians and outlaws. Techniscope.▼●

Aparajito (1956-Indian) **108m.** ***½ D: Satyajit Ray. Pinaki Sen Gupta, Smaran Ghosal, Karuna Banerji, Kanu Banerji, Ramani Sen Gupta. The second of Ray's Apu trilogy is a moving, beautifully filmed story of life and death in a poor Indian family, with the son, Apu (Ghosal), trekking off to college in Calcutta. Aka THE UNVANQUISHED.▼▌

Apartment, The (1960) **125m.** **** D: Billy Wilder. Jack Lemmon, Shirley MacLaine, Fred MacMurray, Ray Walston, Jack Kruschen, Edie Adams, David Lewis, Joan Shawlee. Superb comedy-drama that manages to embrace both sentiment and cynicism. Lemmon attempts to climb corporate ladder by loaning his apartment key to various executives for their extramarital trysts, but it backfires when he falls for his boss's latest girlfriend. Fine performances all around, including MacMurray as an uncharacteristic heel. Oscar winner for Best Picture, Director, Screenplay (Wilder and I.A.L. Diamond), Editing (Daniel Mandell), Art Direction–Set Decoration (Alexander Trauner, Edward G. Boyle). Later a Broadway musical, *Promises, Promises.* Panavision.▼●

Apartment Zero (1988-British) **C-124m.** *** D: Martin Donovan. Colin Firth, Hart Bochner, Dora Bryan, Liz Smith, Fabrizio Bentivoglio. Odd, intriguing psychological drama with political, moral, and sexual overtones. Fastidious film buff Firth's life is profoundly altered when he takes in freewheeling—and mysterious—Bochner as a boarder. Not for all tastes but extremely well acted and definitely worth a look. Set in Buenos Aires; scripted by Donovan and David Koepp. Shortened by 8m. for video by director; the full version is available on DVD. [R]▼●)

Apocalypse Now (1979) **C-153m.** ***½ D: Francis Coppola. Marlon Brando, Robert Duvall, Martin Sheen, Frederic Forrest, Albert Hall, Sam Bottoms, Larry Fishburne, Dennis Hopper, G. D. Spradlin, Harrison Ford, Scott Glenn, Tom Mason, Colleen Camp. Coppola's controversial Vietnam war epic, based on Joseph Conrad's *Heart of Darkness.* Special agent Sheen journeys upriver into Cambodia with orders to find and kill errant officer Brando, leading him (and viewer) on a mesmerizing odyssey of turbulent, often surreal encounters. Unfortunately, film's conclusion—when he does find Brando—is cerebral and murky. Still, a great movie experience most of the way, with staggering, Oscar-winning photography by Vittorio Storaro. Revised and reissued in 2001. The documentary HEARTS OF DARKNESS: A FILMMAKER'S APOCALYPSE chronicles the film's production. Technovision. [R]▼●)

Apocalypse Now Redux (2001) **C-197m.** ***½ Francis Coppola reedited his 1979 film and put back in footage he'd cut at the time, including a major sequence set at a plantation (featuring Christian Marquand). This is now the "official" version of his still-powerful film. Technovision. [R] ▼▌

Apocalypto (2006) **C-139m.** ***½ D: Mel Gibson. Rudy Youngblood, Dalia Hernandez, Raoul Trujillo, Jonathan Brewer, Morris Birdyellowhead, Carlos Emilio Baez. It's the early 16th century, Mayan culture is in decline, and hero Jaguar Paw (a terrific Youngblood) gets it from all directions from a rival raiding party. With his family imperiled and father assaulted, he's abducted to the city for intended slave labor. What follows is a huff-and-puff sprinter's marathon and transparent throwback to Cornel Wilde's THE NAKED PREY (to say nothing of THE MOST DANGEROUS GAME). Bolstered by today's state-of-the-art camerawork and sound technology, it's visceral and exciting despite a tendency to go over the top. Thanks to cutaways at crucial times, it's not *always* as violent as advertised or feared—but it's still pretty potent. Gibson coproduced and cowrote with Farhad Safinia. HD Widescreen. [R]▌

Apollo 13 (1995) **C-139m.** ***½ D: Ron Howard. Tom Hanks, Bill Paxton, Kevin Bacon, Gary Sinise, Ed Harris, Kathleen Quinlan, Miko Hughes, David Andrews, Chris Ellis, Joe Spano, Xander Berkeley, Marc McClure, Tracy Reiner, Brett Cullen, Christian Clemenson; opening narration by Walter Cronkite. Exhilarating story of ill-fated Apollo 13 moon mission, and how the heroic work of astronaut Jim Lovell and his crew, combined with the dogged persistence of the NASA team in Houston, averted tragedy. A rare instance where special effects actually serve the story and help make it completely credible; perfect 1970s period detail is another asset. Screenplay by William Broyles, Jr., and Al Reinert, from the book *Lost Moon* by Lovell and Jeffrey Kluger. Director Howard's brother Clint has a good role as one of the Houston eggheads; father, Rance, plays a priest; and mother, Jean, is a treat as Jim Lovell's mom. The real Lovell appears as an officer on the aircraft carrier in the final sequence. Winner of Oscars for Film Editing and Sound. Edited to 116m. for its 2002 release in IMAX. Super 35. [PG] ▼●❙

Apostle, The (1997) **C-134m.** *** D: Robert Duvall. Robert Duvall, Farrah Fawcett, Miranda Richardson, Billy Bob Thornton, June Carter Cash, Todd Allen, John Beasley, Billy Joe Shaver. Duvall—in an obvious labor of love as writer, director, producer, and star—is superb as a womanizing Pentecostal minister who is forced to leave his Texas home (and church) after committing a violent act. Fascinating study of a wayward man's journey to understand his life, and the many people who help him find his way. Wonderful small-town Southern atmosphere. Lags a bit, but the performances by Duvall and his supporting cast make up for it. James Gammon appears unbilled. [PG-13] ▼●❙

Appaloosa, The (1966) **C-98m.** **½ D: Sidney J. Furie. Marlon Brando, Anjanette Comer, John Saxon, Alex Montoya, Frank Silvera. Brooding Western set in 1870s with Brando trying to recover horse stolen from him by Mexican bandit; slowly paced, well photographed by Russell Metty. Techniscope. ▼●❙

Appaloosa (2008) **C-115m.** ** D: Ed Harris. Viggo Mortensen, Ed Harris, Renée Zellweger, Jeremy Irons, Timothy Spall, Lance Henriksen, James Gammon, Tom Bower, Ariadna Gil, Rex Linn. Western town under the thumb of a despotic ranch owner (Irons) brings in a hired gun (Harris) and his partner (Mortensen) to straighten things out—which they will only do on their own terms. Fairly simple story (from a novel by Robert B. Parker) takes an awfully long time to spin out. Harris and Mortensen make a great team, and their friendship is the most interesting aspect of this longwinded film. Harris coscripted and sings a Western song he cowrote over the closing credits . . . and that's his father Bob playing the judge. Panavision. [R]❙

Apple, The (1980) **C-90m.** BOMB D: Menahem Golan. Catherine Mary Stewart, Allan Love, George Gilmour, Grace Kennedy, Joss Ackland. Futuristic musical set in 1994, when a young couple's entry in songwriting contest is sabotaged by devilish Mr. Boogalow. As bad as it sounds—maybe worse—but now celebrated for its awfulness. Panavision. [PG] ▼❙

Apple Dumpling Gang, The (1975) **C-100m.** ** D: Norman Tokar. Bill Bixby, Susan Clark, Don Knotts, Tim Conway, David Wayne, Slim Pickens, Harry Morgan. Disney Western comedy with gambler Bixby inheriting three children. Predictable doings sparked by Knotts and Conway as bumbling crooks. [G] ▼●❙

Apple Dumpling Gang Rides Again, The (1979) **C-88m.** ** D: Vincent McEveety. Tim Conway, Don Knotts, Tim Matheson, Kenneth Mars, Elyssa Davalos, Jack Elam, Robert Pine, Harry Morgan, Ruth Buzzi.

More of the same, with Knotts and Conway as bumbling outlaws in the Old West; usual Disney slapstick, without much zip or originality. [G] ▼❙

Applegates, The SEE: **Meet the Applegates**

Appointment, The (1969) **C-100m.** **½ D: Sidney Lumet. Omar Sharif, Anouk Aimée, Lotte Lenya. Brilliant attorney falls in love with a girl who eventually ruins him. Soapy and long. [R]

Appointment With Death (1988) **C-108m.** *½ D: Michael Winner. Peter Ustinov, Lauren Bacall, Carrie Fisher, John Gielgud, Piper Laurie, Hayley Mills, Jenny Seagrove, David Soul. Ustinov returns yet again as Agatha Christie's detective Hercule Poirot in this obvious, depressingly unsuspenseful mystery. It seems that greedy Laurie wants her late husband's money all for herself. How soon will she be murdered? And how soon will Poirot name her killer? Another loser from Winner; scripted by Anthony Shaffer, Peter Buckman, and the director. [PG] ▼●

Apprenticeship of Duddy Kravitz, The (1974-Canadian) **C-121m.** ***½ D: Ted Kotcheff. Richard Dreyfuss, Micheline Lanctot, Jack Warden, Randy Quaid, Joseph Wiseman, Denholm Elliott, Joe Silver. Mordecai Richler's vivid comedy-drama of an ambitious kid from Montreal's Jewish ghetto in the 1940s, determined to make good no matter how many toes he steps on. Pretentious bar mitzvah movie made by Duddy's "client," artsy director Elliott, is just one comic highlight. Panavision. [PG] ▼

Apprentice to Murder (1988) **C-94m.** ** D: R. L. Thomas. Donald Sutherland, Chad Lowe, Mia Sara, Knut Husebo, Rutanya Alda. Odd, affected, fact-based account of a practitioner of medieval medicine (Sutherland, in a disappointing performance), and his complex relationship with young Lowe. Filmed in Norway. [PG-13] ▼●

Après Vous . . . (2003-French) **C-110m.** **½ D: Pierre Salvadori. Daniel Auteuil, José Garcia, Sandrine Kiberlain, Marilyne Canto, Michèle Moretti, Garancé Clavel, Fabio Zenoni. Agreeable French comedy about a good-hearted maitre d' who comes across a suicidal man one night and agrees to help him turn his life around by getting him a job as a wine steward in his restaurant. Of course, this act of kindness causes all sorts of complications in the lives of both men, but the farcical nature of the story is never overplayed. Auteuil is the perfect foil to Garcia, who is a total delight to watch. A minor but entertaining comedy. [R]❙

April Fools, The (1969) **C-95m.** ** D: Stuart Rosenberg. Jack Lemmon, Catherine Deneuve, Peter Lawford, Harvey Korman, Sally Kellerman, Myrna Loy, Charles Boyer, Melinda Dillon, Kenneth Mars, Jack Weston, David Doyle. Attempt at old-fashioned romantic comedy is forced, unbelievable, unfunny. Lemmon is married businessman who decides to chuck it all to run away with Deneuve, who's wasted, along with Loy and Boyer. Panavision. [M/PG]▼

April Fool's Day (1986) **C-88m.** ** D: Fred Walton. Deborah Foreman, Griffin O'Neal, Clayton Rohner, Thomas F. Wilson, Deborah Goodrich. Practical joker (Foreman) invites college pals to spend a weekend in her family's mansion on an off-coast island; one by one they're threatened and killed. Attempt to bring humor to FRIDAY THE 13TH formula isn't a total washout but doesn't quite click, either. Remade for DVD in 2008. Panavision. [R] ▼●◗

April in Paris (1952) **C-101m.** **½ D: David Butler. Doris Day, Ray Bolger, Claude Dauphin, Eve Miller, George Givot, Paul Harvey. Diplomatic corps bureaucrat tries to boost Franco-American relations and falls in love with a showgirl mistakenly chosen to appear in the "April in Paris" show he's staging. Mediocre Warner Bros. musical buoyed by the personalities of Day and Bolger—who make an unconvincing romantic couple.▼●◗

Apt Pupil (1998) **C-111m.** *½ D: Bryan Singer. Ian McKellen, Brad Renfro, Bruce Davison, Elias Koteas, Joe Morton, Jan Triska, Michael Byrne, Heather McComb, David Schwimmer, Joshua Jackson, James Karen. A student studying the Holocaust becomes overly absorbed in the subject. When he spots an old man on the bus and realizes that he's a former Nazi war criminal, he cultivates a curious "friendship" with the unrepentant elder. Fascinating premise, from a Stephen King novella, soon grows untenable—and doesn't know when to quit. Good performances by McKellen and Renfro can't save this extremely unpleasant film. Super 35. [R] ▼●◗

Aquamarine (2006) **C-103m.** ** D: Elizabeth Allen. Emma Roberts, Joanna "JoJo" Levesque, Sara Paxton, Jake McDorman, Arielle Kebbel. A mermaid escapes her overbearing father and arrives on land, where she needs to make a man fall in love with her or succumb to an arranged marriage to a merman back home. Meanwhile, her two new human girlfriends have to figure out how to stay together when one of their parents wants to move to another country. They all face the usual "fish out of water movie" calamities, but the infectiously sweet leads keep this from being a total bore. Based on a book by Alice Hoffman. [PG]◗

Aqua Teen Hunger Force Colon Movie Film for Theaters (2007) **C-79m.** BOMB D: Matt Maiellaro, Dave Willis. Voices of Dana Snyder, Dave Willis, Carey Means, Andy Merrill, C. Martin Croker, Chris Kattan, Bruce Campbell, Fred Armisen. Three fast-food icons, Master Shake (a milk-shake cup), Frylock (a large side of French fries), and Meatwad (a stupid meatball), tackle an immortal piece of exercise equipment, the Insanoflex, which threatens the balance of galactic peace. Feature version of *Adult Swim* cable TV cartoon series is strictly for stoners . . . and even they may demand a refund. Artless and unfunny, with a fart joke every ten minutes. Hanna Barbera's Space Ghost makes a cameo appearance. A complete waste of time. [R]◗

Arabesque (1966) **C-105m.** *** D: Stanley Donen. Sophia Loren, Gregory Peck, Alan Badel, Kieron Moore, George Coulouris. Modern secret-agent escapism as Peck is drawn into espionage with Sophia, who was never more beautiful. Exciting, beautifully photographed, minus any message or deep thought. Panavision. ▼◗

Arabian Adventure, An (1979-British) **C-98m.** **½ D: Kevin Connor. Christopher Lee, Milo O'Shea, Puneet Sira, Oliver Tobias, Emma Samms, Peter Cushing, Mickey Rooney, Capucine, John Ratzenberger. Just what the title says; colorful enough to entertain kids, with enough effects gimmicks and cameo performances to intrigue older viewers as well. [G]

Arabian Knight (1995) **C-72m.** ** D: Richard Williams. Voices of Vincent Price, Matthew Broderick, Jennifer Beals, Eric Bogosian, Toni Collette, Jonathan Winters, Bobbi Page, Clive Revill, Kevin Dorsey, Kenneth Williams. Colorful but disappointing (and ultimately, boring) yarn of a lowly cobbler who falls in love with a princess and does battle with a wily wizard named ZigZag. Some engaging and amusing scenes for kids, with exceptionally interesting graphics and color schemes, but the story is too fragmented to really take hold; the songs are instantly forgettable. This film shows the scars of major production woes; it was begun by Williams in 1968(!), then taken out of his hands in the early 1990s. Retitled THE THIEF AND THE COBBLER (the film's original name while in production) for video. Panavision. [G]▼●◗

Arabian Nights (1942) **C-86m.** **½ D: John Rawlins. Jon Hall, Maria Montez, Sabu, Leif Erickson, Turhan Bey, Billy Gilbert, Shemp Howard, John Qualen, Thomas Gomez. Colorful, corny escapist stuff—beautifully mounted in Technicolor—about a dashing hero, an enslaved Sherazade, and an evil caliph. Shemp also memorable as a retired Sinbad the Sailor. First teaming of Montez, Hall, and Sabu. ▼●◗

Arabian Nights (1974-Italian-French) **C-130m.** *** D: Pier Paolo Pasolini. Ninetto Davoli, Ines Pellegrini, Franco Citti, Tessa Bouche, Margarethe Clementi, Franco Merli. Several *Thousand and One Nights* tales are framed by the story of slave-girl Pellegrini, who becomes "king" of a great city. Dreamlike, exotic, and erotic; the last and best of Pasolini's medieval trilogy. Running time originally 155m. ▼●◗

Arachnophobia (1990) **C-109m.** ******* D: Frank Marshall. Jeff Daniels, Harley Jane Kozak, John Goodman, Julian Sands, Stuart Pankin, Brian McNamara, Mark L. Taylor, Henry Jones, Peter Jason, James Handy. Fear of spiders is taken to extremes in this slick comic thriller from Steven Spielberg and Co. Small-town doctor Daniels (who hates spiders) and family play host to a wayward tropical arachnid that promptly sets up web in the barn out back. Essentially Grade Z movie fodder is socked across here by a big budget and spirited performances. Directorial debut of longtime Spielberg producer Marshall. Not recommended for anyone who's *ever* covered their eyes during a movie. [PG-13]▼●❙

Ararat (2002-Canadian-U.S.) **C-126m.** ******½ D: Atom Egoyan. Bruce Greenwood, Arsinée Khanjian, Christopher Plummer, Elias Koteas, Charles Aznavour, Brent Carver, David Alpay, Marie-Josée Croze, Eric Bogosian, Simon Abkarian. Movie-within-a-movie about Turkey's 1915 genocide against Armenia has its moments, and as many subplots. Toronto filmmakers shoot a lame-looking historical epic about the incident, which is contrasted against a modern-day story dealing with sex between step-siblings, a disapproving dad with a gay son, and a lengthy incident involving a customs agent and a member of the film's crew. Heavy breathing, pedantic at times, but interesting and obviously heartfelt, given Egoyan's Armenian background. [R]▼❙

Architect, The (2006) **C-81m.** ******½ D: Matt Tauber. Anthony LaPaglia, Viola Davis, Isabella Rossellini, Hayden Panettiere, Sebastian Stan, Walton Goggins, Paul James. Chicago architect is unaware that the urban housing project he designed years ago is now a hellhole that one aggrieved mother (Davis) wants to tear down . . . or even that his wife and children aren't at peace in the modern-living space that is their home. Each character is in crisis here, and the brief screenplay (adapted by Tauber from David Greig's play) introduces more dilemmas than it resolves. Still, strong performances make this worth a look. LaPaglia also coexecutive-produced. [R]❙

Arch of Triumph (1948) **114m.** ******½ D: Lewis Milestone. Ingrid Bergman, Charles Boyer, Charles Laughton, Louis Calhern, Ruth Warrick, Roman Bohnen, J. Edward Bromberg, Ruth Nelson, Stephen Bekassy. Sluggish drama of doctor-refugee Boyer becoming involved with Bergman in pre-WW2 Paris. Based on Erich Maria Remarque's novel. William Conrad appears unbilled. Archivally restored to 131m. Remade for TV in 1985 with Anthony Hopkins and Lesley-Anne Down. ▼❙

archy and mehitabel SEE: **shinbone alley**

Arctic Tale (2007) **C-96m.** ****** D: Adam Ravetch, Sarah Robertson. Narrated by Queen Latifah. Quasi-documentary six years in the making follows the parallel stories of a walrus and her calf "pup" and a group of polar bears as they try to survive in the frozen arctic. While the footage itself is impressive, the "story" wrapped around it is strictly for very young kids. With cloying narration by Queen Latifah the film is clearly trying to emulate the success of a much more honest doc, MARCH OF THE PENGUINS. Too bad they didn't stick to the facts instead of trying to be BAMBI OF THE NORTH. [G]❙

Arena (1953) **C-83m.** ******½ D: Richard Fleischer. Gig Young, Jean Hagen, Polly Bergen, Henry (Harry) Morgan, Barbara Lawrence, Lee Aaker, Robert Horton, Lee Van Cleef. Colorful if utterly predictable story of rodeo star Young, on the verge of divorce from Bergen, falling under the spell of sexy Lawrence. Morgan is a standout as a onetime star reduced to taking a job as rodeo clown. Action scenes skillfully integrated. Filmed in Tucson, Arizona. 3-D.

Arena, The (1973) **C-83m.** ****** D: Steve Carver. Pam Grier, Margaret Markov, Lucretia Love, Paul Muller. Lavish (by Roger Corman standards) spectacle set in an ancient Rome in which all the gladiators are women. Rather surprisingly pro-feminist point of view, but Grier's and Markov's physiques remain the chief attractions. Retitled NAKED WARRIORS. Remade in 2001. Techniscope. [R]▼❙

Are We Done Yet? (2007) **C-92m.** *****½ D: Steve Carr. Ice Cube, Nia Long, John C. McGinley, Aleisha Allen, Philip Bolden, Jonathan Katz, Linda Kash, Alexander Kalugin, Dan Joffre, Pedro Miguel Arce, Tahj Mowry, Jacob Vargas. Inevitable sequel to ARE WE THERE YET? is also an official remake of the 1948 comedy MR. BLANDINGS BUILDS HIS DREAM HOUSE (complete with RKO Radio Pictures logo), but Ice Cube isn't Cary Grant and this script is much more bland than BLANDINGS. Premise is basically the same: a man moves his growing family out of the crowded city and into his "dream house" in the suburbs, where everything goes wrong. Endlessly unfunny slapstick antics may have you looking at your watch asking the *real* question: "Is it over yet?" [PG]❙

Are We There Yet? (2005) **C-95m.** *****½ D: Brian Levant. Ice Cube, Nia Long, Jay Mohr, Aleisha Allen, M. C. Gainey, Philip Daniel Bolden, Nichelle Nichols. If you wait long enough, just about anything can happen, including Ice Cube turning into Fred MacMurray. Actor Cube isn't the problem here, but a stale premise is: the child-hating owner of a sports memorabilia store transports two headstrong kids over a long, disaster-prone trip to Vancouver, all to help hottie-mama Long out of a scheduling jam while getting into her good graces. Before turning in this box-office success, director Levant did PROBLEM CHILD 2 and SNOW DOGS. Forewarned is forearmed. Followed by ARE WE DONE YET? [PG] ▼❶

Aria (1987-British) **C-90m.** BOMB D: Bill Bryden, Nicolas Roeg, Charles Sturridge, Jean-Luc Godard, Julien Temple, Bruce Beresford, Robert Altman, Franc Roddam, Ken Russell, Derek Jarman. John Hurt, Theresa Russell, Nicola Swain, Jack Kayle, Buck Henry, Anita Morris, Beverly D'Angelo, Elizabeth Hurley, Peter Birch, Julie Hagerty, Genevieve Page, Bridget Fonda, Tilda Swinton, Spencer Leigh, Amy Johnson. Godawful collection of short films, each one supposedly inspired by an operatic aria. Precious few make sense, or even seem to match the music; some are downright embarrassing. Roddam's bittersweet Las Vegas fable (set to *Tristan und Isolde*), Beresford's sweet and simple rendering of Erich Wolfgang Korngold's *Die Totestadt* are among the better segments—relatively speaking. A pitiful waste of talent. Fonda's first film. [R] ▼❶

Ariel (1988-Finnish) **C-74m.** *** D: Aki Kaurismaki. Turo Pajala, Susanna Haavisto, Matti Pellonpää. Surreal, dryly hilarious road movie from one of the most talented directors to emerge on the international film scene in the late 1980s. The scenario chronicles the plight of a mine worker (Pajala) who loses his job and sets out on a cross-country odyssey. ▼❶

Arise, My Love (1940) **110m.** **½ D: Mitchell Leisen. Claudette Colbert, Ray Milland, Walter Abel, Dennis O'Keefe, Dick Purcell. Reporter Colbert rescues flyer Milland from a Spanish firing squad in the days before WW2 breaks out in Europe. Bright stars make Billy Wilder–Charles Brackett script seem better than it is; Benjamin Glazer and John S. Toldy received Oscars for their original story.

Aristocats, The (1970) **C-78m.** *** D: Wolfgang Reitherman. Voices of Eva Gabor, Phil Harris, Sterling Holloway, Scatman Crothers, Paul Winchell, Lord Tim Hudson, Vito Scotti, Thurl Ravenscroft, Nancy Kulp, Pat Buttram, George Lindsey, Monica Evans, Carole Shelley. A cat and her offspring will inherit a fortune from their mistress, which makes them prime targets for her scheming butler, who'll collect the money if they're out of the picture. Enter Thomas O'Malley Cat (voiced by the inimitable Phil Harris) to the rescue. Derivative of earlier Disney animated features but entertaining just the same. [G] ▼❶❶

Aristocrats, The (2005) **C-89m.** **½ D: Paul Provenza. Stand-up comic Provenza and Penn Jillette (of Penn & Teller) set out to examine a notorious dirty joke that's become a touchstone for comedians of all ages. Comedy aficionados will find this irresistible, as a formidable parade of more than one hundred performers (Robin Williams, Phyllis Diller, George Carlin, Gilbert Gottfried, Larry Storch, to name just a few) cuts loose and dissects the appeal of the gag. Not surprisingly, some of the older comics get some of the biggest laughs . . . including an unannounced guest at the end of the credits. Not recommended for children or anyone easily offended. ▼❶

Arizona (1940) **127m.** **½ D: Wesley Ruggles. Jean Arthur, William Holden, Warren William, Porter Hall, Paul Harvey. Lively story of determined woman battling corruption and plundering while trying to settle in new Arizona territory. Well done, but seems to go on forever. ▼❶❶

Arizona Bushwhackers (1968) **C-86m.** *½ D: Lesley Selander. Howard Keel, Yvonne De Carlo, John Ireland, Marilyn Maxwell, Scott Brady, Brian Donlevy, Roy Rogers, Jr., James Craig; narrated by James Cagney. Confederate spy Keel takes job as sheriff in Arizona and routs Brady, who has been selling weapons to Apaches. Routine Western. Techniscope. ▼❶

Arizona Dream (1993-French-U.S.) **C-119m.** **½ D: Emir Kusturica. Johnny Depp, Jerry Lewis, Faye Dunaway, Lili Taylor, Paulina Porizkova, Vincent Gallo, Michael J. Pollard. Odd but intriguing film about a young dreamer (Depp) who's shanghaied into a trip to Arizona, where he catches up with a favorite uncle (Lewis) who wants him to settle down, and falls madly in love with an emotionally frail, childlike woman (Dunaway). European-styled film (from the Yugoslav director of WHEN FATHER WAS AWAY ON BUSINESS) boasts exceptionally good performances—one of Dunaway's best in years, one of Lewis' most impressive—though the often pathetic characters wear out their welcome after a while. Filmed in 1991; 142m. European version earned a brief U.S. theatrical release in 1995. [R] ▼❶

Arlington Road (1999) **C-119m.** ** D: Mark Pellington. Jeff Bridges, Tim Robbins, Joan Cusack, Hope Davis, Robert Gossett, Spencer Treat Clark, Mason Gamble. Labored conspiracy thriller about a history professor (Bridges) haunted by his wife's death, who becomes suspicious of his new neighbor (Robbins) and starts investigating his curious past. Obvious and overdone. Panavision. [R] ▼❶

Armageddon (1998) **C-151m.** ** D: Michael Bay. Bruce Willis, Billy Bob Thornton, Liv Tyler, Ben Affleck, Will Patton, Peter Stormare, Keith David, Steve Buscemi, Owen Wilson, William Fichtner, Udo Kier, Michael (Clarke) Duncan, Eddie Griffin, Christian Clemenson; narrated by Charlton Heston. Opens with a bang, and sets up an exciting (if improbable) story about NASA and the U.S. government turning to a veteran oil-well driller and his motley team to save humanity by flying to an asteroid and planting a nuclear bomb.

After a while it becomes so routine, so predictable, and so redundant that all the fun is drained away. Unrated director's cut runs 153m. Panavision. [PG-13] ▼●

Armed and Dangerous (1986) **C-88m.** *½ D: Mark L. Lester. John Candy, Eugene Levy, Robert Loggia, Kenneth McMillan, Meg Ryan, Brion James, Jonathan Banks, Don Stroud, Steve Railsback. Lame comedy sticks talented costars with unappealing script about two bozos who wind up working for an armed security company—and tangling with a gangland boss (Loggia, wasted in a stereotype role). Even the chase finale is weak. [PG-13] ▼●

Armed Response (1986) **C-85m.** ** D: Fred Olen Ray. David Carradine, Lee Van Cleef, Mako, Lois Hamilton, Ross Hagen, Brent Huff, Laurene Landon, Dick Miller, Michael Berryman. Modest actioner of Carradine and family becoming involved in a Chinatown war over a stolen jade art object. Cheapie benefits from a solid cast of both new and old B-movie favorites. [R] ▼●

Armored (2009) **C-88m.** ** D: Nimród Antal. Matt Dillon, Columbus Short, Jean Reno, Laurence Fishburne, Amaury Nolasco, Fred Ward, Milo Ventimiglia, Skeet Ulrich, Andre Jamal Kinney. Iraq War vet Short is trying to eke out a living and a life, serving as surrogate parent to his teenage younger brother and preventing the foreclosure of their house. When his colleagues in security at an armored-truck company band together for a large heist, he must decide whether to risk everything to join them. A throwback to low-budget B movies of yore, this OK actioner will neither overly impress nor greatly disappoint genre fans. Super 35. [PG-13] ●

Armored Attack SEE: **North Star, The**
Armour of God (1986-Hong Kong) **C-94m.** **½ D: Jackie Chan. Jackie Chan, Rosamund Kwan, Alan Tam, Lola Forna, Maria Dolores. Jackie plays an Indiana Jones–style adventurer who must find legendary suit of armor to rescue his girlfriend from a cult. Enjoyable film marred by slow spots and obviously cheated final stunt. Fight with four leather-clad women is a blast. Watch the outtakes at the end to see the mishap that nearly killed Chan. Followed by a sequel. ▼●

Armour of God 2: Operation Condor (1991-Hong Kong) **C-112m.** *** D: Jackie Chan. Jackie Chan, Carol (Dodo) Cheng, Eva Cobo de Garcia, Ikeda Shoko, Aldo Sanchez, Ken Lo. Lavish adventure epic sends Chan off to Europe and Africa in search of huge Nazi gold cache, with three female companions in tow. Crackerjack comedy-adventure filled with great fights, stunts, and slapstick; final battle in a wind tunnel is a knockout. One of Jackie's best. Recut, dubbed, and trimmed to 89m. for 1997 U.S. release as OPERATION CONDOR—

which isn't as good as the original. Technovision. [PG-13] ▼●

Army of Darkness (1993) **C-81m.** ** D: Sam Raimi. Bruce Campbell, Embeth Davidtz, Marcus Gilbert, Ian Abercrombie, Richard Grove, Michael Earl Reid, Timothy Patrick Quill, Bridget Fonda, Patricia Tallman, Theodore Raimi, Ivan Raimi. Mark Twain's Connecticut Yankee is crossed here with Bob Vila, as a hardware store employee is transported back (with his '73 Olds and a chainsaw) to King Arthur's 14th-century turf. Chiseled-grin Campbell's comic book features serve this movie well, as do a few witty bits and an army of skeletons obviously inspired by JASON AND THE ARGONAUTS. Doldrums set in when nifty special effects and verbal exchanges are out grabbing a smoke. Campbell also coproduced. Third in the EVIL DEAD series. Director's cut runs 96m. [R] ▼●

Army of Shadows (1969-French-Italian) **C-145m.** *** D: Jean-Pierre Melville. Lino Ventura, Simone Signoret, Paul Meurisse, Jean-Pierre Cassel, Claude Mann, Paul Crauchet, Christian Barbier, Serge Reggiani. Vivid period piece about the exploits of French Resistance agent Philippe Gerbier (Ventura) and the work he and his cohorts accomplish during WW2. Episodic but compelling, all the more so for Melville's matter-of-fact presentation of extraordinary feats. Signoret is featured as an especially ingenious and dedicated Parisian comrade. Based on Joseph Kessel's 1943 book, adapted by the director, who in real life worked for the Resistance. ●

Arnold (1973) **C-100m.** **½ D: Georg Fenady. Stella Stevens, Roddy McDowall, Elsa Lanchester, Shani Wallis, Farley Granger, Victor Buono, John McGiver, Patric Knowles. Bizarre horror comedy features novel deaths and offbeat humor, centering around luscious Stevens' marriage to corpse Norman Stuart. [PG] ▼

Around the Bend (2004) **C-83m.** **½ D: Jordan Roberts. Christopher Walken, Michael Caine, Josh Lucas, Glenne Headly, Jonah Bobo. Amiable-enough film about a man, separated from his wife, who takes care of his young son and his aged, eccentric grandfather when suddenly his own dad (who walked out when the boy was two) shows up on his doorstep. Culminates in a road trip through the Southwest. Generational story of forgiveness covers familiar emotional turf, but watching Walken is a treat. Written by the director. [R] ▼●

Around the World in Eighty Days (1956) **C-167m.** *** D: Michael Anderson. David Niven, Cantinflas, Shirley MacLaine, Robert Newton, Buster Keaton, Jose Greco, John Gielgud, Robert Morley, Marlene Dietrich, all-star cast. Oscar-winning favorite has lost much of its charm over the years, but even so, Mike Todd's version of the

Jules Verne tale offers plenty of entertainment, and more than 40 cameo appearances offer plenty of star-gazing for buffs. Great Victor Young score was also an Oscar winner, as was the screenplay (James Poe, John Farrow, S. J. Perelman), cinematography (Lionel Lindon), and editing (Gene Ruggiero, Paul Weatherwax). Remade in 1989 (as a TV miniseries) and in 2004. Todd-AO. ▼●▶

Around the World in 80 Days (2004-British-Irish-German) **C-119m.** *½ D: Frank Coraci. Jackie Chan, Steve Coogan, Cécile de France, Jim Broadbent, Ewen Bremner, Ian McNeice, Karen Joy Morris (Mok), Mark Addy, Will Forte, John Cleese, Macy Gray, Sammo Hung, Rob Schneider, Luke Wilson, Owen Wilson, Kathy Bates, Arnold Schwarzenegger. Absentminded Victorian inventor Phileas Fogg embarks on a global journey with a fugitive from justice (Chan) as his valet. Stumblebum remake of the Jules Verne saga is devoid of wit, and with so many CG effects shows no evidence of globetrotting in spite of having used several international locations. The 1956 movie had cameos by the likes of Sinatra and Dietrich; this one gives us Schwarzenegger in a funny wig. Super 35. [PG] ▼▶

Around the World in 80 Ways (1986-Australian) **C-90m.** **½ D: Stephen MacLean. Philip Quast, Allan Penney, Diana Davidson, Kelly Dingwall, Gosia Dobrowolska. Off-center Aussie farce about two brothers who contrive to spring their aging dad from his stultifying rest home and take him on an imaginary trip around the world. Wacky, and more than a bit crude at times, but likable throughout. [R] ▼●

Around the World Under the Sea (1966) **C-117m.** ** D: Andrew Marton. Lloyd Bridges, Shirley Eaton, David McCallum, Brian Kelly, Keenan Wynn, Marshall Thompson. Several TV personalities appear in this undistinguished underwater tour about testing earthquake warnings. Panavision. ▼

Arousers, The (1970) **C-90m.** *** D: Curtis Hanson. Tab Hunter, Nadyne Turney, Roberta Collins, Isabel Jewell. Little-known, case-history B movie with topnotch performance by Hunter as lonely Venice, California, psychopath who can't make love to women, so he ends up killing them. Unsung thriller packs a wallop; worth searching out. Originally released as SWEET KILL; aka A KISS FROM EDDIE. ▼

Arrangement, The (1969) **C-120m.** BOMB D: Elia Kazan. Kirk Douglas, Faye Dunaway, Deborah Kerr, Richard Boone, Hume Cronyn. Muddled, unpleasant film from Kazan's own novel about man fed up with Madison Avenue rat race who suddenly goes berserk, reevaluates his life, family, surroundings. Good cast down the drain; Kerr's role is particularly demeaning. Panavision. [R] ▼▶

Arrival, The (1996) **C-109m.** *** D: David

Twohy. Charlie Sheen, Ron Silver, Lindsay Crouse, Teri Polo, Richard Schiff, Tony T. Johnson, Leon Rippy, Buddy Joe Hooker. Radio astronomer is fired when he tells his boss that he's picked up signals proving there's intelligent life in space. Then he learns that the aliens are already here and up to no good. Clever, intelligent sci-fi thriller of the old school, with many bright ideas; suffers from flaccid pacing in the last third but remains fun throughout. Written by the director. Followed by a video sequel. [PG-13] ▼●

Arrivederci, Baby! (1966) **C-105m.** *½ D: Ken Hughes. Tony Curtis, Rosanna Schiaffino, Lionel Jeffries, Zsa Zsa Gabor, Nancy Kwan. Comic theme about Bluebeard type who murders his wives for their money has been handled more successfully by others. Not very funny. Panavision. ▼

Arrowhead (1953) **C-105m.** **½ D: Charles Marquis Warren. Charlton Heston, Jack Palance, Katy Jurado, Brian Keith, Milburn Stone. Well-paced account of cavalry scout Heston, who despises Indians, and his response when Apaches return to their reservation and Apache chief Palance arrives on the scene. Watch this, and you will understand why Native Americans have lambasted the manner in which they have been depicted by Hollywood. ▼●▶

Arrowsmith (1931) **99m.** **½ D: John Ford. Ronald Colman, Helen Hayes, Richard Bennett, A. E. Anson, Claude King, Russell Hopton, Myrna Loy, Beulah Bondi, John Qualen. Seriously flawed and illogical adaptation of Sinclair Lewis' novel about a dedicated young research doctor who spends most of his life facing the temptation of selling out. Worth seeing for some fine performances and stirring moments. Screenplay by Sidney Howard (who fared better with Lewis' *Dodsworth*). Originally 110m.; cut to 101m. for reissue, restored in recent years to 99m. ▼●▶

Arruza (1972) **C-75m.** **½ D: Budd Boetticher. Narrated by Anthony Quinn. Interesting documentary, many years in production, about bullfighter Carlos Arruza. Well made, but the impact is nowhere near that of Boetticher's own fictional BULLFIGHTER AND THE LADY. [M/PG] ▼

Arsenic and Old Lace (1944) **118m.** ***½ D: Frank Capra. Cary Grant, Priscilla Lane, Raymond Massey, Peter Lorre, Jack Carson, Josephine Hull, Jean Adair, James Gleason, Grant Mitchell, John Alexander, Edward Everett Horton. Hilarious adaptation of Joseph Kesselring's hit play (scripted by the Epstein Brothers) about two seemingly harmless old ladies who poison lonely gentleman callers. Frantic cast is excellent, especially Lorre and Massey as unsuspecting murderers holed up in Brooklyn household. Made in 1941. Hull, Adair, and Alexander repeat their Broadway roles. Also shown in computer-colored version. ▼●▶

Artemisia (1997-French-Italian-German) C-96m. **½ D: Agnès Merlet. Valentina Cervi, Michel Serrault, Miki Manojlovic, Luca Zingaretti, Emmannuelle Devos, Frederic Pierrot, Yahn Tregouet. Biopic of one of the earliest women painters in history, 17th-century Italian Artemisia Gentileschi. Her desire to express herself is tempered by her relationships with two strong men: her loving but rigid father (Serrault) and her mentor (Manojlovic), whose seduction and rape of his protégée leads to a notorious trial. An accomplished if uninspired depiction of this historical figure, whose fate is still debated by scholars and feminists. [R] ▼●)

Arthur (1981) C-97m. ***½ D: Steve Gordon. Dudley Moore, Liza Minnelli, John Gielgud, Geraldine Fitzgerald, Jill Eikenberry, Stephen Elliott, Ted Ross, Barney Martin. Winning 1930s-style comedy, written by first-timer Gordon, who died the following year. Spoiled millionaire must choose between continued wealth (in a planned marriage) and true love (with working-class waitress Minnelli). More genuine laughs than most recent comedies put together, and a memorable, Oscar-winning performance by Gielgud as a protective, acid-tongued valet; title song, "Arthur's Theme (Best That You Can Do)," also earned a statuette. Followed by ARTHUR 2: ON THE ROCKS. Remade in 2011. [PG] ▼●)

Arthur (2011) C-110m. **½ D: Jason Winer. Russell Brand, Helen Mirren, Greta Gerwig, Jennifer Garner, Geraldine James, Luis Guzmán, Nick Nolte, John Hodgman, Scott Adsit. Remake of the 1981 hit about a childlike N.Y.C. billionaire (Brand) who lives in a constant alcoholic stupor, tended to by his lifelong nanny (Mirren, taking on John Gielgud's butler role). His tycoon mother threatens to cut him off without a cent unless he marries her business-savvy associate (Garner, in a thankless role as a viper). That's when he meets Gerwig, a free spirit who doesn't care about money. Unattractively shot romantic comedy isn't terribly inspired but also isn't terrible, unless you compare it with the original. [PG-13] ●

Arthur 2: On the Rocks (1988) C-110m. ** D: Bud Yorkin. Dudley Moore, Liza Minnelli, John Gielgud, Geraldine Fitzgerald, Stephen Elliott, Paul Benedict, Cynthia Sikes, Kathy Bates, Jack Gilford, Ted Ross, Daniel Greene. Arthur goes broke and his wife wants to adopt a baby. The cast tries, and there are scattered laughs, but this schmaltzy sequel (executive produced by Moore) is a disappointment. Gielgud "appears" briefly as a ghost. That's Dudley's then-wife, Brogan Lane, as Liza's hash-slinging colleague. [PG] ▼●)

Arthur and the Invisibles (2006-French) C-94m. *½ D: Luc Besson. Freddie Highmore, Mia Farrow, Penny Balfour, Doug Rand, Adam LeFevre; voices of Madonna, Jimmy Fallon, Robert De Niro, Harvey Keitel, Chazz Palminteri, Emilio Estevez, Snoop Dogg, Anthony Anderson, Jason Bateman, David Bowie. Ten-year-old Arthur (Highmore) enters a fantasy world to find a hidden treasure. Rambling, confusing blend of live-action and below-par computer-generated animation. All-star cast of English-speaking actors dubbed the original French dialogue in the animated sequences. Besson co-scripted, based on his children's book. Super 35. [PG] ●

Article 99 (1992) C-99m. **½ D: Howard Deutch. Ray Liotta, Kiefer Sutherland, Forest Whitaker, Lea Thompson, John C. McGinley, John Mahoney, Keith David, Kathy Baker, Eli Wallach, Noble Willingham, Julie Bovasso, Troy Evans, Lynne Thigpen, Jeffrey Tambor, Rutanya Alda. Heartfelt but disappointingly one-dimensional, "lighthearted" exposé of Veterans' Administration hospital abuse, focusing on spunky surgeon Liotta and his compatriots, who try to thwart the bureaucracy; Sutherland is the new doc on the block. Hijinks are more reminiscent of DOCTOR IN THE HOUSE than THE HOSPITAL—and that's the problem. [R] ●

Artie Lange's Beer League SEE: **Beer League**

Artificial Intelligence: AI (2001) C-145m. ** D: Steven Spielberg. Haley Joel Osment, Jude Law, Frances O'Connor, Brendan Gleeson, Sam Robards, William Hurt, Jake Thomas, Ken Leung, Michael Mantell, Adrian Grenier; narrated by Ben Kingsley. In the near future, scientist Hurt and his team develop a highly sophisticated robot child who can experience emotions, including love, but his adoption by a loving couple who have lost a son is fraught with problems. Intriguing story draws us in, thanks in part to Osment's exceptional performance, but takes several wrong turns; ultimately, it just doesn't work. Spielberg rewrote the adaptation Stanley Kubrick commissioned of the Brian Aldiss short story "Super Toys Last All Summer Long"; result is a curious and uncomfortable hybrid of Kubrick and Spielberg sensibilities. Striking music score by John Williams. Robin Williams, Chris Rock, and Meryl Streep are unbilled for the use of their voices. [PG-13] ▼●

Artists and Models (1955) C-109m. *** D: Frank Tashlin. Dean Martin, Jerry Lewis, Shirley MacLaine, Dorothy Malone, Eva Gabor, Anita Ekberg. Cartoonist Martin uses Lewis's far-out dreams as inspiration for his comic strips in this deliciously garish Technicolor outing. VistaVision. ▼●)

Art of Getting By, The (2011) C-84m. **½ D: Gavin Wiesen. Freddie Highmore, Emma Roberts, Michael Angarano, Rita Wilson, Blair Underwood, Elizabeth Reaser, Sam Robards, Sasha Spielberg, Marcus Carl Franklin, Alicia Silverstone. Privileged

Manhattan high school student (Highmore) is paralyzed with fears about life and can't do any work, to the chagrin of his teachers and principal, who know he's smart. Then he's befriended by a girl (Roberts) who finds him interesting but is unaware that he's becoming infatuated with her. Quirky slice of life from debut writer-director Wiesen covers familiar ground but is given weight by his two youthful stars, who make up for the film's missteps. Super 35. [PG-13]

Art of Love, The (1965) **C-99m.** ** D: Norman Jewison. James Garner, Dick Van Dyke, Elke Sommer, Angie Dickinson, Ethel Merman, Carl Reiner. Ordinary comedy set in France, with a bemused cast headed by Van Dyke as a struggling artist who fakes death to increase the value of his work. Sommer is his virtuous girl, boisterous Merman a local madam with a yen for singing.

Art of War, The (2000) **C-117m.** **½ D: Christian Duguay. Wesley Snipes, Anne Archer, Maury Chaykin, Marie Matiko, Cary-Hiroyuki Tagawa, Michael Biehn, Donald Sutherland, James Hong. Unexceptional action thriller. Snipes is a secret agent for the U.N. who's framed for an assassination, so he tries to unsnarl a tangled plot centering on Chinese trade negotiations. Hong Kong–style fights and good cinematography (by Pierre Gill) help, but you've seen it all before. Title derives from Sun-Tzu's 2,500-year-old treatise on war. Followed by two DVD sequels. Super 35. [R]▼❶

Art School Confidential (2006) **C-102m.** *** D: Terry Zwigoff. Max Minghella, Sophia Myles, John Malkovich, Jim Broadbent, Anjelica Huston, Matt Keeslar, Ethan Suplee, Katherine Moennig, Dick Bakalyan. Freshman at an arts college wants desperately to be accepted, if not applauded, but no one will take his drawings or paintings seriously—while charlatans and showoffs thrive. More than anything he wants to impress a beautiful girl who models for his class. As darkly comic as GHOST WORLD (from the same director and writer, graphic novelist and comic book artist Daniel Clowes) but more human; we feel this young man's pain. Malkovich coproduced. Steve Buscemi and Michael Lerner appear unbilled. [R]❶

As Good As It Gets (1997) **C-138m.** ***½ D: James L. Brooks. Jack Nicholson, Helen Hunt, Greg Kinnear, Cuba Gooding, Jr., Skeet Ulrich, Shirley Knight, Yeardley Smith, Lupe Ontiveros, Bibi Osterwald, Randall Batinkoff, Brian Doyle-Murray. Professional malcontent (and full-time phobic) Nicholson is unavoidably drawn into the lives of his favorite waitress and his gay next-door neighbor. Gradually, and against his own judgment, he begins to show signs of humanity. Wonderful comedy-drama (written by Mark L. Andrus and Brooks) takes the viewer on an emotional journey, with laughs and tears along the way. Both

Nicholson and Hunt won Oscars for their roles. Writer-directors Harold Ramis, Lawrence Kasdan, Shane Black, and Todd Solondz all have small roles. [PG-13]▼❶

Ashanti (1979) **C-117m.** ** D: Richard Fleischer. Michael Caine, Peter Ustinov, Beverly Johnson, Kabir Bedi, Omar Sharif, Rex Harrison, William Holden. Beautiful wife Johnson of missionary-doctor Caine is kidnapped by slave trader Ustinov, prompting hot pursuit through the mideast. Tepid adventure yarn, despite great cast and promising story elements. Aka ASHANTI: LAND OF NO MERCY. Panavision. [R]▼❶

Ashes and Diamonds (1958-Polish) **96m.** ***½ D: Andrzej Wajda. Zbigniew Cybulski, Ewa Krzyzanowska, Adam Pawlikowski, Bogumil Kobiela, Waclaw Zastrzezynski. Stark, intelligent, perceptive account of the Resistance movement in Poland during the closing days of WW2. Cybulski, the Polish James Dean, came into his own with his portrayal of a young Resistance fighter. The last of Wajda's War trilogy, following A GENERATION and KANAL.▼

Ash Wednesday (1973) **C-99m.** BOMB D: Larry Peerce. Elizabeth Taylor, Henry Fonda, Helmut Berger, Keith Baxter, Margaret Blye. Liz undergoes a facelift to regain her youth, but she still looks older than Fonda. Sit through this one and you'll need surgery on your posterior. [R]▼

Ash Wednesday (2002) **C-98m.** *½ D: Edward Burns. Edward Burns, Elijah Wood, Rosario Dawson, Oliver Platt, Pat McNamara, James Handy, Michael Mulheren, Malachy McCourt, Julie Hale. Writer-director-star Burns tackles grimmer material than usual in this story of two brothers who reluctantly get mixed up with gangsters in early 1980s N.Y.C. Burns is good as the older sibling, but Wood fails to convince us that he is from the same family. Uninvolving story looks as if it was made on a shoestring. [R] ▼❶

Ask Any Girl (1959) **C-101m.** *** D: Charles Walters. David Niven, Shirley MacLaine, Gig Young, Rod Taylor, Jim Backus, Elisabeth Fraser. Effervescent gloss of naive MacLaine come to N.Y., discovering most men have lecherous designs on girls; she wants a husband, however. CinemaScope. ▼

Ask the Dust (2006) **C-117m.** ** D: Robert Towne. Colin Farrell, Salma Hayek, Donald Sutherland, Eileen Atkins, Idina Menzel, Justin Kirk, Jeremy Crutchley, William Mapother; narrated by Richard Schickel. Would-be novelist Arturo Bandini arrives in L.A. in the early 1930s full of ambition, but the reality of day-to-day living smothers his inner fire. He can't even give himself to a woman who might make him happy, a Mexican waitress. Intriguing, handsomely made, but unforgivably dreary adaptation of John Fante's 1939 novel, written by Towne as a kind of companion piece to CHINATOWN. [R]❶

Aspen Extreme (1993) **C-115m.** *½ D: Patrick Hasburgh. Paul Gross, Peter Berg, Finola Hughes, Teri Polo, William Russ, Trevor Eve, Martin Kemp, William Mc-Namara, Nicolette Scorsese. For two Detroit buddies, the Motown slopes are not enough—so it's off to the Colorado Rockies for sex, tragedy, and skiing success amid the lifestyles of the rich and banal. Satisfactory outdoor scenes, but little else beyond jarring lapses in plot continuity. Hollywood Pictures, which opened this a week after ALIVE, must have gotten a deal on some parkas. [PG-13]▼●❘

Asphalt Jungle, The (1950) **112m.** ***½ D: John Huston. Sterling Hayden, Louis Calhern, Jean Hagen, James Whitmore, Sam Jaffe, John McIntire, Marc Lawrence, Marilyn Monroe. The plotting of a crime, and the gathering of a gang to pull it off; a taut, realistic film full of fine characterizations (especially Jaffe, and Monroe in a memorable bit). A model of its kind, frequently copied, and remade no less than three times (as THE BADLANDERS, CAIRO, COOL BREEZE). Scripted by Ben Maddow and Huston, from a W. R. Burnett novel. Also shown in computer-colored version.▼●❘

Asphyx, The (1972-British) **C-99m.** *** D: Peter Newbrook. Robert Stephens, Robert Powell, Jane Lapotaire, Ralph Arliss, Alex Scott. Good fantasy plot has 19th-century scientist Stephens isolating the Asphyx, the spirit of death that appears around a person's body at times of imminent danger. In so doing, he becomes immortal. Lapotaire, who scored internationally on stage in *Piaf*, appears here as Stephens's daughter. Aka SPIRIT OF THE DEAD. Todd-AO 35. [PG]▼❘

Assam Garden, The (1985-British) **C-92m.** *** D: Mary McMurray. Deborah Kerr, Madhur Jaffrey, Alec McCowen, Zia Mohyeddin, Anton Lesser. Quietly rewarding drama with Kerr in her best role in years (and first theatrical release since 1969's THE ARRANGEMENT), as a stuffy, long-repressed, just-widowed woman. While tending her husband's garden and dealing with his memory, she strikes up a curious complex friendship with Indian neighbor Jaffrey.

Assassination (1987) **C-88m.** *½ D: Peter Hunt. Charles Bronson, Jill Ireland, Stephen Elliott, Jan Gan Boyd, Randy Brooks, Erik Stern, Michael Ansara, James Staley, Kathryn Leigh Scott. Bronson is a Secret Service bodyguard, Ireland the wife of the President, in this ridiculous, slapdash political thriller with more explosions than anything else. The First Lady is referred to here as One Mama! [PG-13]▼●❘

Assassination Bureau, The (1969-British) **C-110m.** *** D: Basil Dearden. Oliver Reed, Diana Rigg, Telly Savalas, Curt Jurgens, Clive Revill. Fun tale based on Jack London story of secret club that eliminates unworthy people, until greed more than dedication begins to cloud the operation. [M]▼●❘

Assassination of a High School President (2008) **C-99m.** *½ D: Brett Simon. Reece Thompson, Mischa Barton, Bruce Willis, Melonie Diaz, Zach Roerig, Josh Barclay Caras, Patrick James Taylor, Michael Rapaport, Josh Pais, Kathryn Morris, Luke Grimes. High school newspaper reporter's investigation of stolen SAT tests from the principal's safe has repercussions across the entire campus. Following in the same high school noir territory as the far more successful BRICK, this attempt to show the dark side of student affairs is a loud, jumbled mess. [R]❘

Assassination of Jesse James by the Coward Robert Ford, The (2007) **C-160m.** **½ D: Andrew Dominik. Brad Pitt, Casey Affleck, Sam Shepard, Mary-Louise Parker, Paul Schneider, Jeremy Renner, Garret Dillahunt, Zooey Deschanel, Michael Parks, Ted Levine, Sam Rockwell, Alison Elliott, James Carville, Tom Aldredge, Nick Cave. Retelling of the history leading up to the titular event and the strange relationship between the legendary—and moody—outlaw (Pitt) and his eventual killer (Affleck), who's consumed with hero worship. Well acted, beautifully made (with exquisite cinematography by Roger Deakins), but crippled by overlength—which is not matched by commensurate character development or the intended thematic insight into the nature (and effects) of myth and celebrity. Super 35. [R]❘

Assassination of Richard Nixon, The (2004-U.S.-Mexican) **C-95m.** *** D: Niels Mueller. Sean Penn, Don Cheadle, Jack Thompson, Michael Wincott, Mykelti Williamson, Naomi Watts, Nick Searcy, Brad Henke. Penn is brilliant as Sam Bicke (in real life Byck), who channeled his mounting frustrations with society into a doomed attempt to assassinate the President in 1974. The saga of a loser, made interesting by observational detail in the script (by Mueller and Kevin Kennedy) and Penn's incisive performance. Thompson is terrific as his bear of a boss; Watts is excellent in a low-key turn as Penn's estranged wife. Coproduced by Alfonso Cuarón and partly filmed in Mexico. Executive producers include Alexander Payne and Leonardo DiCaprio. [R]❘

Assassination of Trotsky, The (1972-French-Italian-British) **C-103m.** **½ D: Joseph Losey. Richard Burton, Alain Delon, Romy Schneider, Valentina Cortese. Last days of Russian rebel make for uneven melodrama of hunters and hunted. Burton's performance is strong but unconvincing. [R]▼●❘

Assassination Tango (2003) **C-114m.** **½ D: Robert Duvall. Robert Duvall, Ruben Blades, Kathy Baker, Luciana Pedraza,

[63]

Julio Oscar Mechoso, James Keane, Frank Gio, Frank Cassavetes, Michael Corrente. Hit man from Brooklyn is forced to disrupt his happy domestic life to travel to Argentina and carry out an assassination . . . but while he's waiting for the right moment, he takes up with a sexy tango dancer who introduces him to her world. Duvall is great to watch, and so are the tango sequences (some of them involving real-life masters of the art), but the results don't quite make a cohesive movie. Pedraza is Duvall's real-life companion. Duvall wrote and coproduced. [R] ▼🄳

Assassins (1995) C-132m. ** D: Richard Donner. Sylvester Stallone, Antonio Banderas, Julianne Moore, Anatoly Davydov. World's number one paid hit man is dogged at every turn by a young rival. Then he (inexplicably) falls in love with a female "mark." Stallone is in good form, but this big-scale action yarn/star vehicle suffers from rampant stupidity. [R] ▼🄾🄳

Assault (1971) SEE: **In the Devil's Garden**

Assault, The (1986-Dutch) C-149m. ***½ D: Fons Rademakers. Derek de Lint, Marc van Uchelen, Monique van de Ven, John Kraaykamp, Huub van der Lubbe, Elly Weller. A 12-year-old's family is liquidated in the final days of WW2, and he represses his memories and feelings while growing into manhood. Evocative performances and fine direction enhance a story that is both truthful and heartbreaking. Long, but suspenseful, with many thought-provoking moments. Screenplay by Gerard Soeteman based on a novel by Harry Mulisch. Winner of the Best Foreign Language Film Oscar. A film not easy to forget. [PG] ▼

Assault Force SEE: **ffolkes**

Assault of the Rebel Girls SEE: **Cuban Rebel Girls**

Assault on a Queen (1966) C-106m. **½ D: Jack Donohue. Frank Sinatra, Virna Lisi, Tony Franciosa, Richard Conte, Alf Kjellin, Errol John, Murray Matheson, Reginald Denny. Sloppy Sinatra vehicle about big heist of H.M.S. *Queen Mary*'s vault. Script by Rod Serling from novel by Jack Finney. Panavision. ▼

Assault on Precinct 13 (1976) C-90m. ***½ D: John Carpenter. Austin Stoker, Darwin Joston, Laurie Zimmer, Martin West, Tony Burton, Nancy Loomis, Kim Richards, Henry Brandon. A nearly deserted L.A. police station finds itself under a state of siege by a youth gang in this riveting thriller, a modern-day paraphrase of Howard Hawks' RIO BRAVO. Writer-director Carpenter also did the eerie music score for this knockout. Remade in 2005. Panavision. [R] ▼🄾🄳

Assault on Precinct 13 (2005) C-109m. ** D: Jean-François Richet. Ethan Hawke, Laurence Fishburne, John Leguizamo, Maria Bello, Jeffrey "Ja Rule" Atkins, Drea de Matteo, Gabriel Byrne, Brian Dennehy, Matt Craven, Dorian Harewood, Aisha Hinds, Kim Coates, Currie Graham. On a snowy New Year's Eve an old Detroit police station prepares to shut down, but the storm forces cops to deposit a handful of prisoners there, including a local crime boss who just killed an undercover officer. Violent remake of the lean, mean John Carpenter B movie adds a variety of plot complications—and with each one, another layer of disbelief. Well crafted but laughable at times. Super 35. [R] ▼🄳

Assignment, The (1977-Swedish) C-94m. **½ D: Mats Arehn. Christopher Plummer, Thomas Hellberg, Carolyn Seymour, Fernando Rey, Per Oscarsson, Walter Gotell. Modest drama of Swedish diplomat sent to mediate turbulent political situation in Latin American country. ▼

Assignment, The (1997) C-115m. **½ D: Christian Duguay. Aidan Quinn, Donald Sutherland, Ben Kingsley, Liliana Komorowska, Céline Bonnier, Claudia Ferri, Vlasta Vrana, Von Flores, Al Waxman. Well-directed, violent thriller with Quinn in a dual role as notorious terrorist Carlos the Jackal and a lookalike U.S. naval officer recruited to participate in an elaborate scheme to capture the terrorist. Sutherland is the CIA man who is obsessed with nabbing Carlos. [R] ▼🄾🄳

Assignment K (1968-British) C-97m. *½ D: Val Guest. Stephen Boyd, Camilla Sparv, Michael Redgrave, Leo McKern, Jeremy Kemp, Robert Hoffman. Still another spy drama—this one a dull story about secret agent's disillusionment upon discovering that his girl and seemingly everyone he knows is a double agent. Technicolor.

Assignment: Kill Castro SEE: **Cuba Crossing**

Assignment Terror (1970-Spanish-German-Italian) C-86m. BOMB D: Tulio Demicheli. Michael Rennie, Karin Dor, Craig Hill, Paul Naschy, Patty Shepard. Alien invader Rennie revives various earth monsters (including ersatz Frankenstein, Dracula, and Mummy) but socially conscious werewolf (Naschy) helps to combat his evil forces. Unwatchable stupidity. Aka DRACULA VS. FRANKENSTEIN. Techniscope. ▼🄳

Assignment to Kill (1968) C-102m. ** D: Sheldon Reynolds. Patrick O'Neal, Joan Hackett, John Gielgud, Herbert Lom, Eric Portman, Peter Van Eyck, Oscar Homolka. Private eye checks out shady corporation in Switzerland in this unrewarding thriller from the writer-director of TV's *Foreign Intrigue* series. Panavision. 🄳

Assisi Underground, The (1985) C-115m. ** D: Alexander Ramati. Ben Cross, James Mason, Irene Papas, Maximilian Schell, Edmund Purdom, Karl Heinz Hackl, Delia Boccardo, Riccardo Cucciolla. Good cast is wasted in this overblown thriller, with a based-on-fact scenario. Cross plays a courageous young minister in charge of disguising Jews in Assisi, Italy, during WW2. Mason's last film. Originally released at 178m. [PG]▼◗

Associate, The (1996) **C-114m.** **½ D: Donald Petrie. Whoopi Goldberg, Dianne Wiest, Eli Wallach, Tim Daly, Bebe Neuwirth, Austin Pendleton, Lainie Kazan, Colleen Camp Wilson, Allison Janney. Wall St. whiz Whoopi has hit the glass ceiling at her company, so she breaks off on her own, but can't make it without inventing a white male partner. Designed as a comedy, but laughs are few. Still, it's an interesting look at corporate America and the obstacles and slights that women and minorities endure. Wiest is terrific. Remake of the 1979 French film L'ASSOCIE; based on the novel *El Socio*. [PG-13]▼◗

Astro Boy (2009-Hong Kong-Japanese-Chinese) **C-94m.** ** D: David Bowers. Voices of Freddie Highmore, Nicolas Cage, Kristen Bell, Donald Sutherland, Nathan Lane, Eugene Levy, Bill Nighy, Samuel L. Jackson, Elle Fanning, Alan Tudyk, David Alan Grier, Charlize Theron. In the future, a brilliant scientist creates a super-powered robot duplicate of his son, who died in a lab accident. Falling short of his father's expectations, the boy robot leaves home and soon finds himself an object of desire for both a warmongering politician and a ruthless robot scavenger. Adapted from classic anime and manga by Osamu Tezuka, this iconic character has been homogenized here; result is a generic superhero story without humor, emotion, or heart. Action and explosions may keep 4-to-7-year-old boys enthralled, but fans of the original '60s TV cartoon series will be sorely disappointed. 3-D Digital Widescreen. [PG]◗

Astronaut Farmer, The (2007) **C-104m.** **½ D: Michael Polish. Billy Bob Thornton, Virginia Madsen, Bruce Dern, J. K. Simmons, Tim Blake Nelson, Max Thieriot, Jon Gries, Mark Polish, Richard Edson, Sal Lopez. Thornton is ideal as a proud, independent-thinking Texas farmer who's built a rocket in his barn and has convinced himself (and his loving family) that he's going to fly into outer space . . . until the U.S. government gets wind of his scheme. Capraesque story about a "little guy" who believes in a dream is beautifully rendered; only problem is that the guy in question is nuts! Written by Michael and Mark Polish; the latter plays one of the FBI agents, and their adorable daughters Jasper and Logan play two of Thornton's kids. Bruce Willis appears unbilled. Panavision. [PG]◗

Astronaut's Wife, The (1999) **C-109m.** *½ D: Rand Ravich. Johnny Depp, Charlize Theron, Joe Morton, Clea DuVall, Donna Murphy, Nick Cassavetes, Samantha Eggar, Gary Grubbs, Blair Brown, Tom Noonan. Happily married astronaut has a strange experience during a space mission. Has he changed somehow, or is it his young wife's imagination? ROSEMARY'S BABY–style thriller is just a big tease; sluggish and unsatisfying, with an especially stupid finale. [R]▼◗

Astro-Zombies, The (1967) **C-91m.** BOMB D: Ted V. Mikels. Wendell Corey, John Carradine, Tom Pace, Joan Patrick, Rafael Campos, Tura Satana. Demented Carradine creates title monsters in yet another nominee for worst picture of all time. Script by Mikels and Wayne Rogers (the same). Aka SPACE VAMPIRES. [PG]▼◗

Asylum (1972-British) **C-92m.** *** D: Roy Ward Baker. Barbara Parkins, Sylvia Syms, Richard Todd, Peter Cushing, Robert Powell, Barry Morse, Britt Ekland, Herbert Lom, Patrick Magee, Charlotte Rampling. Four fun chillers by Robert Bloch woven into puzzle that is solved at the conclusion of the fourth tale. Reissued in 1980 as HOUSE OF CRAZIES, trimmed to 86m. [PG]▼◗

Asylum (2005-British) **C-99m.** **½ D: David Mackenzie. Natasha Richardson, Hugh Bonneville, Marton Csokas, Gus Lewis, Ian McKellen, Joss Ackland, Judy Parfitt, Wanda Ventham. Psychiatrist's wife gets involved with one of her husband's patients, a prison inmate who was found guilty of the brutal murder of his wife. Uneven melodrama serves as a fine showcase for Richardson, playing a conflicted woman whose emotions begin to trump her logic. Csokas, as the object of her fatal attraction, does the best he can with a one-dimensional role. The sum of this film's parts don't add up to a satisfying whole. From a novel by Patrick McGrath. Arriscope. [R]◗

As You Desire Me (1932) **71m.** **½ D: George Fitzmaurice. Greta Garbo, Melvyn Douglas, Erich von Stroheim, Hedda Hopper, Owen Moore. OK version of Pirandello play about amnesiac (Garbo) returning to husband she doesn't really remember. Never as compelling as it should be.▼

As You Like It (1936-British) **96m.** *** D: Paul Czinner. Elisabeth Bergner, Laurence Olivier, Sophie Stewart, Henry Ainley, Leon Quartermaine, Felix Aylmer. Olivier is solid (and handsome) as Orlando in his first attempt at the Bard on celluloid, but Bergner's Rosalind is more a matter of taste. Overall, an enjoyable production of this Shakespeare comedy. ▼◗

As Young As You Feel (1951) **77m.** **½ D: Harmon Jones. Monty Woolley, Thelma Ritter, David Wayne, Jean Peters, Constance Bennett, Marilyn Monroe, Allyn Joslyn, Albert Dekker. Printing company employee Woolley is "retired" when he turns 65, and he just won't sit still for it. Amiable satire of corporate bureaucracy, with a first-rate cast, based on a story by Paddy Chayefsky.▼◗

Atanarjuat . . . (The Fast Runner) SEE: **Fast Runner, The**

At Close Range (1986) **C-115m.** **½ D:

James Foley. Sean Penn, Christopher Walken, Christopher Penn, Mary Stuart Masterson, Millie Perkins, Eileen Ryan, Alan Autry, Candy Clark, Tracey Walter, David Strathairn, Crispin Glover, Kiefer Sutherland. Brooding, but curiously unmoving, story about teenage half-brothers who first get to know their no-account father, and come to realize what a dangerous person he is. Downbeat drama is marked by good acting, thoughtful filmmaking, but emotional impact is muted. Based on a true incident. Super 35. [R]▼●)

A-Team, The (2010) C-119m. **½ D: Joe Carnahan. Liam Neeson, Bradley Cooper, Jessica Biel, Quinton "Rampage" Jackson, Sharlto Copley, Patrick Wilson, Gerald McRaney. A B movie tricked out with big-budget production values, inspired by the 1980s TV series about special-ops soldiers turned good-guy mercenaries. The original band of Vietnam vets are transformed here into Iraq War heroes, but the basic premise remains: convicted of a crime they didn't commit, four freewheeling, wisecracking antiheroes bust out of military prison to clear their names, smite some villains, and blow up a lot of stuff. As their commander, Neeson establishes the seriocomic tone with self-mocking sass and steely-eyed authority. Overdone, to be sure, but surprisingly entertaining. Jon Hamm appears unbilled. Unrated version runs 133m. Panavision. [PG-13]❿

At First Sight (1998) C-128m. **½ D: Irwin Winkler. Val Kilmer, Mira Sorvino, Kelly McGillis, Steven Weber, Bruce Davison, Nathan Lane, Ken Howard, Diana Krall. Driven N.Y.C. career woman falls in love with a self-reliant blind man. Then she finds a doctor who can restore his sight—but is this necessarily a good thing? Overtly soapy romantic drama doesn't pretend to be anything but what it is, and the stars are likable . . . but it goes on too long. Based on a true story chronicled by Dr. Oliver Sacks (AWAKENINGS). Having a George Shearing cut on the soundtrack is a nice touch. [PG-13]▼●)

ATL (2006) C-105m. ** D: Chris Robinson. Tip Harris, Lauren London, Antwan Andre Patton (Big Boi), Mykelti Williamson, Keith David, Lonette McKee, Evan Ross, Lauren Leah Mitchell. Another film about skatin' in the hood (after ROLL BOUNCE), featuring Harris, better known as recording star T.I. Pretends to be about young people trying to make it out of the ghetto, but takes itself way too seriously. When one girl tells a boy, "I've seen you skate and that's all I need to know about a man," we know we're in for a long sit. From a story by Antwone Fisher (yes, *that* Antwone Fisher). Coproduced by Will Smith. [PG-13]❿

Atlantic City (1980-Canadian-French) C-104m. **** D: Louis Malle. Burt Lancaster, Susan Sarandon, Kate Reid, Michel Piccoli, Hollis McLaren, Robert Joy, Al Waxman,

Wally Shawn. Rich character study of a city in transition, focusing on small-time losers who've stayed there too long and big-time dreamers who are just arriving. European in its ambience and storytelling approach, though its setting is an American resort. Lancaster gives one of his finest performances as an aging two-bit hood who's all style and no substance. Screenplay by John Guare. [R]▼●)

Atlantis: The Lost Empire (2001) C-95m. *** D: Kirk Wise, Gary Trousdale. Voices of Michael J. Fox, James Garner, Cree Summer, Leonard Nimoy, Don Novello, Claudia Christian, Jacqueline Obradors, John Mahoney, Corey Burton, David Ogden Stiers, Jim Varney. Good, old-fashioned animated-fantasy/adventure yarn about a young dreamer who tries to make good his father's attempts to find the lost underwater city of Atlantis and locate the key to its advanced civilization. Styled like a comic book, this Disney feature got a bum rap in theaters; it's good family entertainment. Followed by a direct-to-video sequel. Digital Widescreen. [PG]▼)

Atlas Shrugged (2011) C-97m. *½ D: Paul Johansson. Taylor Schilling, Grant Bowler, Matthew Marsden, Edi Gathegi, Graham Beckel, Jsu Garcia, Jon Polito, Michael Lerner, Rebecca Wisocky, Neill Barry, Christina Pickles, Geoff Pierson, Michael O'Keefe, Armin Shimerman, Paul Johansson. Dismal adaptation of Ayn Rand's influential novel (or, at least, the first ten chapters) sets events in 2016, when America is in economic turmoil and Big Government staunchly opposes efforts by railroad executive Schilling and steel magnate Bowler to build a railway with a revolutionary new metal alloy. Also, business leaders are mysteriously disappearing while our heroes ponder, "Who is John Galt?" Earnest enterprise is flattened by chunks of boring exposition, amateur soap opera, cardboard characters (with acting to match), and a lifetime's worth of railroad footage. First of a planned trilogy. Rand enthusiasts may rate this higher. [PG-13]

At Long Last Love (1975) C-118m. *½ D: Peter Bogdanovich. Burt Reynolds, Cybill Shepherd, Madeline Kahn, Duilio Del Prete, Eileen Brennan, John Hillerman, Mildred Natwick. Burt and Cybill are no Fred and Ginger. Bogdanovich's homage to 1930s Hollywood musicals has everything money can buy—including lavish sets and a Cole Porter score—but lacks the proper stars to put it over. Reedited (and ostensibly improved) for TV by the director; that version runs 115m. [G]

Atoll K SEE: **Utopia**

Atomic Cafe, The (1982) 88m. *** D: Kevin Rafferty, Jayne Loader, Pierce Rafferty. Consistently chilling, occasionally hilarious, arguably monotonal compilation of U.S. government and "educational" propaganda shows how Americans of the 1950s

Learned to Stop Worrying and Love the Bomb. One-of-a-kind is undeniably provocative, to say nothing of topical, but argues its point a little longer than necessary.▼▶

Atonement (2007-British-U.S.) **C-123m.** ** D: Joe Wright. James McAvoy, Keira Knightley, Romola Garai, Saoirse Ronan, Vanessa Redgrave, Brenda Blethyn, Juno Temple, Patrick Kennedy, Benedict Cumberbatch, Harriet Walter, Gina McKee. In the 1930s, spoiled young woman (Knightley) who has grown up in one of England's stately homes tries to deny her attraction to the housekeeper's son (McAvoy); when she finally gives in, it triggers great resentment in her younger sister (Ronan), who goes in for theatrics, and alters the course of McAvoy's life. Handsome but portentous adaptation of Ian McEwan's novel (by Christopher Hampton) never delivers the emotional impact it should, given its intriguing premise. Oscar winner for Dario Marianelli's score. The interviewer in the final scene is played by filmmaker Anthony Minghella. [R]▶

Ator, the Fighting Eagle (1983) **C-100m.** BOMB D: David Hills. Miles O'Keeffe, Sabrina Siani, Ritza Brown, Edmund Purdom, Laura Gemser. Ridiculous Italian-made imitation of CONAN THE BARBARIAN has muscular O'Keeffe as the mythical title warrior. Followed by two sequels: THE BLADE MASTER and ATOR III: THE FIGHTING EAGLE aka QUEST FOR THE MIGHTY SWORD. [PG]▼▶

Ator the Invincible SEE: **Blade Master, The**

At Play in the Fields of the Lord (1991) **C-187m.** *** D: Hector Babenco. Tom Berenger, Aidan Quinn, Kathy Bates, John Lithgow, Daryl Hannah, Tom Waits, Stenio Garcia, Nelson Xavier. Long, at first lumbering, but ultimately powerful rainforest epic of two Protestant missionaries (one a charlatan, one sincere) who end up doing about equal damage to the jungle Indians they are supposed to serve. Faithful, well-cast film of Peter Matthiessen's great (though admittedly difficult) novel; pace picks up a lot in the second half, leading to memorable finale. [R]▼▶

At Sword's Point (1952) **C-81m.** **½ D: Lewis Allen. Cornel Wilde, Maureen O'Hara, Robert Douglas, Dan O'Herlihy, Alan Hale, Jr., Blanche Yurka. Silly but likable variation on THE THREE MUSKETEERS, with Wilde, O'Herlihy, Hale, and O'Hara playing the sons and daughter of the original Musketeers. Energetic cast, vivid Technicolor settings.▼▶

Attack (1956) **107m.** *** D: Robert Aldrich. Jack Palance, Eddie Albert, Lee Marvin, Robert Strauss, Richard Jaeckel, Buddy Ebsen, William Smithers. Reenactment of the Battle of the Bulge, emphasizing a group of American soldiers "led" by cowardly captain Albert; tightly directed, avoids war movie clichés. ▼▶

Attack Force Z (1981-Australian-Taiwanese) **C-84m.** **½ D: Tim Burstall. John Phillip Law, Sam Neill, Mel Gibson, Chris Haywood, John Waters. Taut little war drama: commandos set out to rescue survivors of a plane crash on a Japanese-held island during WW2.▼▶

Attack of the 50 Foot Woman (1958) **66m.** BOMB D: Nathan Hertz (Juran). Allison Hayes, William Hudson, Yvette Vickers, Roy Gordon. A harridan with a philandering husband has an alien encounter and grows to mammoth proportions, seeks revenge on hubby. Hilariously awful sci-fi with some of the funniest special effects of all time. Remade for TV in 1993 with Daryl Hannah.▼▶

Attack of the Killer Tomatoes! (1980) **C-87m.** *½ D: John De Bello. David Miller, Sharon Taylor, George Wilson, Jack Riley, Rock Peace, The San Diego Chicken. Title and opening credits are the funniest things in this low-budget spoof of low-budget science-fiction, which cracks its one joke and then beats it to death for another 85 minutes. A staple at Worst Film Festivals, but nowhere nearly as hilarious as movies that aren't supposed to be. Followed by RETURN OF THE KILLER TOMATOES!, KILLER TOMATOES STRIKE BACK, KILLER TOMATOES EAT FRANCE!, and an animated TV series. [PG]▼▶

Attack of the Rebel Girls SEE: **Cuban Rebel Girls**

Attention Bandits SEE: **Bandits** (1986)

At the Circus (1939) **87m.** **½ D: Edward Buzzell. Groucho, Chico and Harpo Marx, Margaret Dumont, Eve Arden, Nat Pendleton, Kenny Baker, Fritz Feld, Florence Rice. Not top-grade Marx Brothers, but some good scenes as they save circus from bankruptcy. Highlight: Groucho singing "Lydia the Tattooed Lady."▼▶

At the Earth's Core (1976-British) **C-90m.** **½ D: Kevin Connor. Doug McClure, Peter Cushing, Caroline Munro, Cy Grant, Godfrey James, Sean Lynch. Colorful fantasy-adventure based on Edgar Rice Burroughs' novel. Inventor Cushing and protégé McClure bore their way from Victorian England to the center of the earth and encounter a lost world of prehistoric beasts and subhuman warriors. Competent special effects make this yarn palatable. [PG]▼▶

Attic, The (1979) **C-97m.** **½ D: George Edwards. Carrie Snodgress, Ray Milland, Rosemary Murphy, Ruth Cox, Francis Bay, Marjorie Eaton. Good cast helps this psychological thriller about a sheltered spinster's revolt against her tyrannical invalid father. A notch or two above routine. [PG] ▼▶

At War with the Army (1950) **93m.** **½ D: Hal Walker. Dean Martin, Jerry Lewis, Polly Bergen, Angela Greene, Mike Kellin. In their first starring feature, Dean and Jerry are in the service, with some funny sequences, including memorable soda machine gag. ▼◐)

Audrey Rose (1977) **C-113m.** **½ D: Robert Wise. Marsha Mason, John Beck, Anthony Hopkins, Susan Swift, Norman Lloyd, John Hillerman. Overlong, underplayed reincarnation thriller. Mason and Beck are happily married couple until a stranger (Hopkins) tells them that their 12-year-old girl is his dead daughter returned to life. Script by Frank DeFelitta, from his novel. [PG] ▼▶

Auggie Rose (2001) **C-108m.** ** D: Matthew Tabak. Jeff Goldblum, Anne Heche, Nancy Travis, Timothy Olyphant, Joe Santos, Richard T. Jones, Kim Coates. A slick yuppie insurance salesman (Goldblum) drops out of the game and assumes the identity of an ex-con he saw shot to death. He feels so obliged to pay the man tribute that he seeks out and falls in love with his sweet prison pen pal (Heche). Begins like a good short story, but becomes contrived and preachy about the nobility of the working class. Debuted in the U.S. on cable TV. Aka BEYOND SUSPICION. [R] ▼▶

August (1996-British) **C-90m.** *½ D: Anthony Hopkins. Anthony Hopkins, Kate Burton, Gawn Grainger, Rhian Morgan, Rhoda Lewis. *Uncle Vanya* comes to Wales in yet another version of the oft-adapted Chekhov play, with real-life Welshman Hopkins (in his directorial debut) misdirecting himself in the lead. Boring rendition with inaccessible characters about whom we do not care. Incidentally, Hopkins also composed the score. [PG] ▼●

August Rush (2007) **C-113m.** *½ D: Kirsten Sheridan. Freddie Highmore, Keri Russell, Jonathan Rhys Meyers, Terrence Howard, Robin Williams, William Sadler, Marian Seldes, Leon G. Thomas III, Mykelti Williamson, Alex O'Loughlin. Treacly fable of orphan Highmore's trek to find out where, and to whom, he may belong. Set mainly in N.Y.C., film is flooded with music of many types, since the boy is a prodigy. (It was a chance meeting between cellist Russell and Irish rocker Meyers that led to his birth—and his gift—in the first place.) The less said about Williams' new-millennium rendition of Dickens' Fagin the better. Super 35. [PG] ▶

Au Hasard Balthazar (1966-French-Swedish) **95m.** *** D: Robert Bresson. Anne Wiazemsky, François Lafarge, Philippe Asselin, Nathalie Joyaut, Walter Green. The sad, cruel life and death of a donkey that passes from owner to owner is used as a symbol for all the misery and inhumanity in the world in this stark and poetic allegory. Bresson also explores crime, adolescence, and family life with customary sensitivity and subtlety. ▶

Auntie Mame (1958) **C-143m.** ***½ D: Morton DaCosta. Rosalind Russell, Forrest Tucker, Coral Browne, Fred Clark, Roger Smith, Patric Knowles, Peggy Cass, Joanna Barnes, Pippa Scott, Lee Patrick, Willard Waterman, Connie Gilchrist, Robin Hughes, Jan Handzlik. Colorful film version of Patrick Dennis' novel about his eccentric aunt, who believes that "life is a banquet, and most poor suckers are starving to death." Episodic but highly entertaining, sparked by Russell's tour-de-force performance. Betty Comden–Adolph Green script was adapted from the Jerome Lawrence–Robert E. Lee Broadway play. Musicalized as MAME. Technirama. ▼◐)

Au Revoir, Les Enfants (1987-French) **C-103m.** ***½ D: Louis Malle. Gaspard Manesse, Raphael Fejto, Francine Racette, Stanislas Carre de Malberg, Philippe Morier- Genoud, Francois Berleand, Irène Jacob. Deeply felt film based on an incident from Malle's youth, during WW2, when the headmaster of his Catholic boarding school decided to shield several Jewish children in the midst of Nazi-occupied France. Filled with telling details, the story unfolds at a deliberate pace, leading up to an emotionally devastating finale. [PG] ▼◐)

Aurora Borealis (2006) **C-110m.** *** D: James Burke. Joshua Jackson, Donald Sutherland, Juliette Lewis, Louise Fletcher, Zack Ward, John Kapelos, Steven Pasquale, Tyler Labine. At 25, Jackson is still acting like an adolescent, hanging out with his old pals and screwing up one dead-end job after another . . . until his brother nudges him to visit their grandfather, who's suffering from Parkinson's disease. His fondness for the old man—and the cute visiting nurse (Lewis) who takes care of him—inspires him to get his act together, as best he can. Sutherland is terrific in a showy part, but Jackson and Lewis are also quite good in this sincere, well-written film set in snowy Minneapolis. Made in 2004. [R]▶

Austin Powers in Goldmember (2002) **C-94m.** ** D: Jay Roach. Mike Myers, Beyoncé Knowles, Michael Caine, Seth Green, Michael York, Robert Wagner, Mindy Sterling, Verne Troyer, Fred Savage. Third outing for the shagadelic spy opens with such a hilarious, surprising sequence that nothing can top it—and nothing does. No real story follows, as Austin travels to 1975 and hooks up with Foxxy Cleopatra (pop singer Knowles). The novelty of seeing Dr. Evil and Mini-Me is gone, Myers' new Goldmember character (sporting a Dutch accent) is more odd than funny; what's left are a lot of really crude jokes and missed opportunities. Worst of all, Caine is wasted as Austin's dad. Lots of stars appear in cameos. Super 35. [PG-13] ▼▶

Austin Powers: International Man of Mystery (1997) **C-89m.** ** D: Jay Roach. Mike Myers, Elizabeth Hurley, Michael York, Mimi Rogers, Robert Wagner, Seth Green, Fabiana Udenio, Charles Napier,

Will Ferrell. Swinging '60s spy is cryogenically frozen, then thawed out in the '90s to do battle with megalomaniac Dr. Evil—but he can't quite shake his mod '60s style or argot ("Groovy, baby!"). Myers (who also wrote and coproduced) is fun, especially as Dr. Evil, but this one-joke premise is stretched far beyond its limits. Carrie Fisher and Tom Arnold appear in unfunny cameos. Coproduced by Demi Moore. Followed by two sequels. Super 35. [PG-13]▼●]

Austin Powers: The Spy Who Shagged Me (1999) C-92m. **½ D: Jay Roach. Mike Myers, Heather Graham, Rob Lowe, Michael York, Elizabeth Hurley, Robert Wagner, Gia Carides, Seth Green, Verne Troyer, Mindy Sterling, Kristen Johnson, Will Ferrell, Fred Willard, Charles Napier. More swingin' '60s lunacy as Dr. Evil returns to Earth with a time-travel machine and goes back to 1969 to steal Austin's mojo. More laughs than the original—and more than enough gross-out gags—though it's still spotty. Several star cameos, though Troyer, as Mini-Me, steals the film. Myers cowrote and coproduced. Followed by AUSTIN POWERS IN GOLDMEMBER. Super 35. [PG-13]▼●]

Australia (2008-Australian-U.S.-British) C-165m. *** D: Baz Luhrmann. Nicole Kidman, Hugh Jackman, David Wenham, Jack Thompson, Bryan Brown, David Gulpilil, Brandon Walters, David Ngoombujarra, Ben Mendelsohn, Essie Davis, Barry Otto, Kerry Walker. Long, sprawling, deliberately old-fashioned romantic drama is also designed as a tribute to Australia. Britisher Kidman travels there in 1939 to settle her husband's estate and winds up staying, determined to make something of his barren ranch with the help of a cattle drover (Jackman) who refuses to settle down. She also adopts an aboriginal boy (Walters) to save him from being rounded up by the government. If you're looking for subtlety, look elsewhere—but it *is* entertaining. Cast is filled with Aussie icons, including Thompson, Brown, and Gulpilil. Super 35. [PG-13]▐

Author! Author! (1982) C-110m. *** D: Arthur Hiller. Al Pacino, Dyan Cannon, Tuesday Weld, Eric Gurry, Alan King, Bob Dishy, Bob Elliott, Ray Goulding, Andre Gregory, Ari Meyers. Pacino's flaky wife walks out on him and their kids (most from her previous marriages) just as his play is about to open on Broadway. Slight but winning little comedy; likable performances all around. Written by playwright Israel Horovitz. [PG]▼▐

Autobiography of a Princess (1975-British) C-60m. **½ D: James Ivory. James Mason, Madhur Jaffrey, Keith Varnier, Diane Fletcher, Timothy Bateson. Uneven (but not uninteresting) little film about an exiled Indian princess (Jaffrey) and an Englishman (Mason), who come together once a year to sip tea and watch home movies of their life in feudal India. Notable as a look at a time and place that no longer exist, but too often bogged down in talk. Scripted by Ruth Prawer Jhabvala.▼●]

Auto Focus (2002) C-104m. *** D: Paul Schrader. Greg Kinnear, Willem Dafoe, Rita Wilson, Maria Bello, Ron Leibman, Kurt Fuller, Ed Begley, Jr., Michael Rodgers, Michael McKean. Kinnear gives an excellent performance as clean-cut radio-host-turned-1960s-TV-star Bob Crane, of *Hogan's Heroes* fame, whose life, career, and happy marriage fall apart as he becomes literally addicted to sex. His pimp/partner in these escapades (Dafoe) also contributes to his decline by getting him hooked on the new technology of home video, which only fuels his obsession. A well-told story of one man's ruination, although it's not clear what the moral (if any) may be. [R]▼▐

Autumn Afternoon, An (1962-Japanese) C-115m. *** D: Yasujiro Ozu. Chishu Ryu, Shima Iwashita, Shinichiro Mikami, Keiji Sada, Mariko Okada. Contemplative study of loneliness and the fleeting nature of life, about a middle-class widower (Ryu) who dutifully arranges the marriage of his daughter. A series of subplots focus on various characters who are in some way connected to the nuptials. Ozu's final film.▼▐

Autumn Hearts: A New Beginning SEE: **Emotional Arithmetic**

Autumn in New York (2000) C-105m. ** D: Joan Chen. Richard Gere, Winona Ryder, Anthony LaPaglia, Elaine Stritch, Vera Farmiga, Sherry Stringfield, Jill Hennessy, Mary Beth Hurt, J. K. Simmons. Cornball May-December soaper in which a womanizing, 48-year-old restaurateur (Gere) falls for a gravely ill, Emily Dickinson–loving 21-year-old hat designer (Ryder). Some interesting supporting characters liven this up, and the cinematography (by Changwei Gu) is lovely, but Gere and Ryder lack chemistry; it's a wonder they could read some of their lines with a straight face. [PG-13]▼▐

Autumn Leaves (1956) 108m. **½ D: Robert Aldrich. Joan Crawford, Cliff Robertson, Vera Miles, Lorne Greene. Middle-aged typist marries younger man (Robertson), only to discover he is mentally disturbed and already married. Stalwart performance by Crawford as troubled woman.▼

Autumn Sonata (1978-Swedish) C-97m. *** D: Ingmar Bergman. Ingrid Bergman, Liv Ullmann, Lena Nyman, Halvar Bjork, Gunnar Bjornstrand. Ingrid, a famed concert pianist, locks horns with daughter Ullmann when they visit for the first time in seven years. Director Bergman's drama is full of déjà vu, but Ingrid (in her final theatrical film) keeps it on the track most of the time. Sven Nykvist's photography is peerless. [PG]▼●]

Autumn Tale (1998-French) C-112m.

***½ D: Eric Rohmer. Marie Rivière, Béatrice Romand, Alain Libolt, Didier Sandre, Alexia Portal, Stéphane Darmon. Delicious adult comedy dealing with two lifelong female friends, now in their 40s: one is happily married and would like to see her friend (a moody, independent vineyard owner) settle down, so she places a personals ad in the paper and "auditions" a proper suitor. Meanwhile, the younger generation gets involved producing comic complications. This is Rohmer at his best; glorious fun with a most appealing cast. [PG]▼

Avalanche (1978) C-91m. ** D: Corey Allen. Rock Hudson, Mia Farrow, Robert Forster, Jeanette Nolan, Rick Moses, Barry Primus. Disaster at the newly opened ski resort where hard-driving tycoon Hudson is determined to double his not insubstantial investment while his ex-wife Mia is making whoopee with one of the locals championing ecology. Stodgy performances almost outweighed by special effects. [PG]▼)

Avalanche Express (1979) C-88m. BOMB D: Mark Robson. Lee Marvin, Robert Shaw, Linda Evans, Maximilian Schell, Joe Namath, Mike Connors, Horst Buchholz. KGB head Shaw tries to defect on a Dutch train that's threatened by lots and lots of falling snow. Cast has enough stiffs in it to resemble audition time at the Hollywood Wax Museum. Sadly, final film for both Shaw and director Robson; in fact, most of Shaw's dialogue had to be dubbed by a mimic. Panavision. [PG]▼)

Avalon (1990) C-126m. *** D: Barry Levinson. Aidan Quinn, Elizabeth Perkins, Armin Mueller-Stahl, Joan Plowright, Lou Jacobi, Leo Fuchs, Eve Gordon, Kevin Pollak, Israel Rubinek, Elijah Wood, Grant Gelt, Bernard Hiller. Deeply felt, personal story by writer-director Levinson of an immigrant's life and times in Baltimore, and the changes the years bring to his large and boisterous family. Long, deliberately paced, and not always successful, but filled with telling moments and loving visual reminders of a way of life that's disappeared from our midst. The third of Levinson's Baltimore chronicles, following DINER and TIN MEN. Melancholy and evocative score by Randy Newman. [PG]▼)

Avalon (2001-Japanese-Polish) 106m. **½ D: Mamoru Oshii. Malgorzata Foremniak, Wladyslaw Kowalski, Jerzy Gudejko, Dariusz Biskupski, Bartek Swiderski, Katarzyna Bargielowska. Video gamers zap between vibrant illusion and grim reality as they earn their livings and risk true death to win entrance to a hallowed heroes' hall. Made by an Asian crew on the WW2-blasted terrain of Eastern Europe, this bleak techno-blitz—alternately mesmerizing and boring—unspools like Andrzej Wajda directing TRON. [R]▼)

Avanti! (1972) C-144m. ***½ D: Billy Wilder. Jack Lemmon, Juliet Mills, Clive Revill, Edward Andrews, Gianfranco Barra, Franco Angrisano. Sadly underrated comedy about stuffy Baltimore millionaire who falls in love with daughter of his late father's mistress when he comes to Italy to claim the old man's body. Closer to LOVE IN THE AFTERNOON than Wilder's satirical comedies; lovely scenery, wonderful performances by all, especially Revill as crafty hotel manager. [R]▼●)

Avatar (2009) C-161m. *** D: James Cameron. Sam Worthington, Zoë Saldana, Sigourney Weaver, Stephen Lang, Michelle Rodriguez, Giovanni Ribisi, Joel David Moore, CCH Pounder, Wes Studi, Laz Alonso. A disabled man takes the place of his late brother in a high-tech, high-stakes mining operation on the planet Pandora: he will climb into a chamber and control his twin's avatar, negotiating peaceful coexistence with the native Na'vi population. But he's torn between following the dictates of the scientists, led by Weaver, and the operation's paramilitary leader, zealous officer Lang. Innovative, futuristic fable, set in a rich, computer-generated environment and populated with strikingly designed creatures (performed by actors whose work was then enhanced by animators). Thrilling at times, with a cornucopia of wonders to behold. Cameron's parable about imperialism too often resorts to B-movie clichés and goes on too long, but the visual experience trumps most of its flaws. Oscar winner for Cinematography (Mauro Fiore), Art Direction, and Visual Effects. Also available in 170m. theatrical rerelease version and alternate 178m. edition. 3-D HD Widescreen. [PG-13]●)

Avengers, The (1998) C-89m. ** D: Jeremiah Chechik. Ralph Fiennes, Uma Thurman, Sean Connery, Jim Broadbent, Fiona Shaw, Eddie Izzard, Eileen Atkins, John Wood. Retread of the popular British TV show of the '60s about two saucy secret agents tries in vain to capture its stylishness and insouciance—but Fiennes is woefully miscast, Connery gives a one-note performance as a bad guy who wants to control the earth's weather, and a fine supporting cast is wasted. Thurman is likable enough, but the film is utterly flat. Patrick Macnee, star of the original series, has an amusing voice-only cameo. [PG-13]▼●)

Avenging Angel (1985) C-93m. BOMB D: Robert Vincent O'Neil. Betsy Russell, Rory Calhoun, Susan Tyrrell, Robert F. Lyons, Ossie Davis, Barry Pearl. Ex–teen prostitute, now college material, recruits pal Calhoun (still acting like the valedictorian at the Gabby Hayes Academy of Dramatic Arts) and takes to the street as an undercover cop. Follow-up to ANGEL proves conclusively that HEAVEN'S GATE is the only '80s film that can't rate a sequel. Followed by ANGEL III: THE FINAL CHAPTER. [R]▼●)

Avenging Force (1986) **C-103m.** **½ D: Sam Firstenberg. Michael Dudikoff, Steve James, John P. Ryan, James Booth, Bill Wallace, Karl Johnson. Dudikoff is retired secret agent Matt Hunter, who's forced into action when his one-time comrade (James), a black man running for office, is threatened by a right-wing terrorist group called Pentangle. A cut above the norm for the action/revenge genre, with exciting climax, and a truly heinous villain (well played by Ryan). Screenwriter James Booth also plays Dudikoff's former boss. [R]▼●

Avenging Spirit SEE: **Dominique**

Avenue Montaigne (2006-French) **C-106m.** *** D: Danièle Thompson. Cécile de France, Valérie Lemercier, Claude Brasseur, Dani, Albert Dupontel, Laura Morante, Sydney Pollack, Suzanne Flon. Sweet, naïve young woman (de France) comes to Paris and lands a job at a popular bar situated near a theater, concert hall, and auction house. Before long she finds herself involved with a famous actress, a classical pianist, and a wealthy man who's selling off his life's collection of art. These characters face very real crises—but somehow you know it's all going to turn out fine. Light and charming; Thompson's son Christopher cowrote the script with her and costars as the son of the art collector. Original French title FAUTEUILS D'ORCHESTRE. Super 35. [PG-13]▌

Aviator, The (1985) **C-98m.** ** D: George Miller. Christopher Reeve, Rosanna Arquette, Jack Warden, Sam Wanamaker, Scott Wilson, Tyne Daly, Marcia Strassman. Pioneer pilot Reeve crash-lands in the middle of some 1928 nowhere with whiny adolescent Arquette. Dull Ernest Gann story barely made it (and understandably so) to theaters; director is the MAN FROM SNOWY RIVER—not. MAD MAX—George Miller. [PG]▼▌

Aviator, The (2004) **C-170m.** ***½ D: Martin Scorsese. Leonardo DiCaprio, Cate Blanchett, Kate Beckinsale, John C. Reilly, Alec Baldwin, Alan Alda, Ian Holm, Danny Huston, Gwen Stefani, Jude Law, Adam Scott, Matt Ross, Kelli Garner, Brent Spiner, Edward Herrmann, Willem Dafoe. Audacious screen bio of Howard Hughes, the billionaire who sets out to conquer Hollywood (and as many of its glamorous actresses as possible) but makes his real mark in the world of aircraft. Along the way he is dogged by deafness, a belief that he's losing his mind, and hounding from a crooked senator. John Logan's script wisely focuses on a specific period of Hughes' life (the 1920s through the 1940s), and doesn't pretend to be literal. Scorsese stages it in grand fashion, replicating two-color, then three-strip, Technicolor, and using all forms of movie magic, with the help of cinematographer Robert Richardson, production designer Dante Ferretti, set decorator Francesca Lo

Schiavo, costume designer Sandy Powell, and editor Thelma Schoonmaker, who all won Oscars. DiCaprio is remarkably persuasive as the iron-willed aviator; Blanchett is great fun in an Oscar-winning turn as Katharine Hepburn. Super 35. [PG-13]▼▌

Aviator's Wife, The (1981-French) **C-104m.** ***½ D: Eric Rohmer. Philippe Marlaud, Marie Riviere, Anne-Laure Meury, Matthieu Carriere. Melancholy but charming story of young man's unhappy involvement with title character being interrupted by happy encounter with stranger in the park. Lovers of MAUD, CLAIRE, and CHLOE will be happy to find Rohmer in near-peak form after long layoff. [PG]▼▌

AVP: Alien vs. Predator SEE: **Alien vs. Predator**

AVPR: Aliens vs. Predator: Requiem SEE: **Aliens vs. Predator: Requiem**

Awake (2007) **C-84m.** *½ D: Joby Harold. Hayden Christensen, Jessica Alba, Terrence Howard, Lena Olin, Christopher McDonald, Sam Robards, Arliss Howard, Fisher Stevens, Denis O'Hare, Georgina Chapman. Real-life condition of "anesthetic awareness" is used to concoct a preposterous story in which a patient becomes alarmed at what he hears while undergoing open-heart surgery and must find a way to wake himself up. Bigger problem for the filmmakers is finding a way to keep the *audience* awake. Super 35. [R]▌

Awakening, The (1980) **C-102m.** *½ D: Mike Newell. Charlton Heston, Susannah York, Jill Townsend, Stephanie Zimbalist. Archeologist Heston enters the tomb of Egyptian Queen Kara, whose spirit enters the body of his newborn daughter. Need we continue? From a novel by Bram Stoker, filmed before as BLOOD FROM THE MUMMY'S TOMB. [R]▼●

Awakenings (1990) **C-121m.** ***½ D: Penny Marshall. Robert De Niro, Robin Williams, Julie Kavner, Ruth Nelson, John Heard, Penelope Ann Miller, Max von Sydow, Alice Drummond, Mary Alice, Anne Meara, Richard Libertini, Dexter Gordon. Powerfully affecting true-life story of a painfully shy research doctor who takes a job at a Bronx hospital's chronic care ward in 1969—and discovers that his comatose patients still have life inside them. Williams is superb as the doctor, and De Niro is his match as a patient who awakens from a 30-year coma to deal with life as an adult for the first time. Steven Zaillian's screenplay is based on the book by (and experiences of) Dr. Oliver Sacks. [PG-13] ▼●▌

Away All Boats (1956) **C-114m.** **½ D: Joseph Pevney. Jeff Chandler, George Nader, Julie Adams, Lex Barker, Keith Andes, Richard Boone, David Janssen. Strict, aloof captain Chandler must ignite spark of fighting spirit among inexperienced crew aboard WW2 attack transport *Belinda*. Exciting, inspiring story of battle action in Pacific Theater. Look fast for Clint Eastwood as a medical orderly near film's end. VistaVision. ▼▷

Away From Her (2007-Canadian) **C-110m.** *** D: Sarah Polley. Julie Christie, Gordon Pinsent, Olympia Dukakis, Wendy Crewson, Michael Murphy, Kristen Thomson, Alberta Watson. After 44 years of marriage, a couple recognizes that the wife is displaying early signs of Alzheimer's disease and makes plans to move her to an extended-care facility. As difficult as this is for her, it's devastating to him, especially when he sees her developing an attachment to another patient. Intelligent, empathetic film eschews sentimentality as the characters take this difficult journey. Remarkable first feature for actress Polley, who adapted Alice Munro's *New Yorker* short story "The Bear Came Over the Mountain." The cast couldn't be better, but Christie is especially good. [PG-13]▷

Away We Go (2009) **C-98m.** *** D: Sam Mendes. John Krasinski, Maya Rudolph, Catherine O'Hara, Jeff Daniels, Carmen Ejogo, Allison Janney, Jim Gaffigan, Maggie Gyllenhaal, Josh Hamilton, Chris Messina, Melanie Lynskey, Paul Schneider. Two modern-day flower children, about to have their first baby, feel the need to put down roots but can't figure out where, so they embark on a road trip to visit friends and family, hoping that one of their hometowns will strike them as the perfect spot. But each destination brings its own disaster as they discover old friends' eccentricities and failures. Laid-back road movie written by Dave Eggers and Vendela Vida won't be everyone's cup of tea, but has a gallery of rich performances, touching moments, and laughs. Super 35. [R]▷

Awfully Big Adventure, An (1995-British-Irish) **C-101m.** **½ D: Mike Newell. Hugh Grant, Alan Rickman, Georgina Cates, Rita Tushingham, Peter Firth, Alan Cox, Prunella Scales. Unfocused though rarely boring drama about a capriciously cruel stage director who browbeats a Liverpool rep company in the late 1940s. The screenplay, from Beryl Bainbridge's novel, is by Charles Wood, who cowrote HELP! for the Beatles. The photography—more stylized bleakness from NAKED's Dick Pope—is a plus. [R]▼●▷

Awful Truth, The (1937) **92m.** ***½ D: Leo McCarey. Irene Dunne, Cary Grant, Ralph Bellamy, Cecil Cunningham, Mary Forbes, Alex D'Arcy, Joyce Compton, Molly Lamont. Hilarious screwball comedy; Cary and Irene divorce, she to marry hayseed Bellamy, he to wed aristocratic Lamont. Each does his best to spoil the other's plans. McCarey won an Oscar for his inspired direction. Screenplay by Vina Delmar. Based on a play by Arthur Richman previously filmed in 1925 and 1929; remade in 1953 as the musical LET'S DO IT AGAIN.▼●▷

A.W.O.L. SEE: **Lionheart** (1991)

Ay, Carmela! (1990-Spanish) **C-103m.** ***½ D: Carlos Saura. Carmen Maura, Andres Pajares, Gabino Diego, Maurizio di Razza, Miguel A. Rellan. Maura shines in this clever, rapier-witted farce as a vaudevillian who entertains the partisans during the Spanish Civil War. Then she, her husband, and their mute assistant find themselves trapped behind enemy lines. Both funny and poignant. ▼●

Ayn Rand—A Sense of Life (1998) **C/B&W-145m.** **½ D: Michael Paxton. Narrated by Sharon Gless. Examination of the popular author, screenwriter, and philosopher, tracing her historic roots in the Soviet Union, her years in Hollywood, her talk show appearances expounding her controversial theories of Objectivism and individual rights, and her testimony before the House Un-American Activities Committee. Also incorporates dramatizations of her works and sequences illustrating her life. Too long—and pedantic—for some viewers, but a must for Rand enthusiasts. ▼▷

Baadasssss! (2004) **C-108m.** *** D: Mario Van Peebles. Mario Van Peebles, Joy Bryant, Terry Crews, Ossie Davis, David Alan Grier, Nia Long, Saul Rubinek, Rainn Wilson, T. K. Carter, Paul Rodriguez, Vincent Schiavelli, Khleo Thomas, Len Lesser, Sally Struthers, Adam West, Glenn Plummer. After his first taste of Hollywood success in the early 1970s, Melvin Van Peebles decides to make an uncompromising film from a black man's point of view (SWEET SWEETBACK'S BAAD ASSSSS SONG) and has to use guerrilla tactics to get the job done. He spares no one along the way, including his young son Mario. The younger Van Peebles gives a great performance as his father and makes us feel as if we're eyewitnesses to this incredible true story. Filmmaker John Singleton appears as a disc jockey; Troy Garity appears unbilled. [R] ▼▷

Baader Meinhof Complex, The (2008-German) **C-149m.** **½ D: Uli Edel. Martina Gedeck, Moritz Bleibtreu, Johanna Wokalek, Bruno Ganz, Nadja Uhl, Jan Josef Liefers, Stipe Erceg, Niels Bruno Schmidt. True story of the Red Army Faction, the radical German terrorist group of the 1970s that used extreme violent means—robberies, fire bombings, assassinations—to advance its revolutionary beliefs. Impeccably well-made historical drama (with echoes of THE BATTLE OF ALGIERS) faithfully re-creates the period and has many gripping moments, but covers way too much ground and becomes mired in details that shortchange character and fail to illuminate the political motivations behind the group's actions. Still, an often evocative look at an era and events rarely covered on the big screen. Based on the book by Stefan Aust. [R] ▷

Babar The Movie (1989-Canadian-French) **C-70m.** *** D: Alan Bunce. Voices of Gordon Pinsent, Gavin Magrath, Elizabeth Hanna, Sarah Polley, Chris Wiggins. Entertaining feature-length cartoon based on the classic children's books by Jean and Laurent de Brunhoff. Strictly serviceable (and uninspired) animation is made up for by an engaging storyline that's sure to appeal to young children. [G]▼○●

Babe, The (1992) **C-115m.** *** D: Arthur Hiller. John Goodman, Kelly McGillis, Trini Alvarado, Bruce Boxleitner, Peter Donat, James Cromwell, J. C. Quinn, Joe Ragno, Bernard Kates, Michael McGrady, Stephen Caffrey. Agreeably sentimental, old-fashioned bio of the great Babe Ruth is largely a vehicle for Goodman, who's terrific in the lead. Though facts are tampered with and often ignored, the essence of this larger-than-life character (and his genuine love of baseball) still comes through. [PG]▼○●

Babe (1995-U.S.-Australian) **C-92m.** ***½ D: Chris Noonan. James Cromwell, Magda Szubanski; voices of Christine Cavanaugh, Miriam Margolyes, Danny Mann, Hugo Weaving, Miriam Flynn, Russi Taylor, Evelyn Krape; narrated by Roscoe Lee Browne. Delightful, disarming family fodder about an orphaned pig taken in by a quietly eccentric farmer who develops a strong attachment to the little fellow. The farmyard animals all converse with one another in this endearing (and often very funny) tale, based on the book *The Sheep-Pig* by Dick King-Smith. The Oscar-winning special effects, combining real animals, animatronic doubles, and computer technology, are both seamless and convincing. This is one "family film" that adults can enjoy right along with their kids. Followed by a sequel. [G]▼○●

Babel (2006-Mexican-U.S.) **C-142m.** ***½ D: Alejandro González Iñárritu. Brad Pitt, Cate Blanchett, Gael García Bernal, Kōji Yakusho, Adriana Barraza, Rinko Kikuchi, Said Tarchaní, Boubker Ait El Caid, Elle Fanning, Nathan Gamble, Clifton Collins, Jr., Michael Peña. Bold, riveting drama combines stories from three continents: an American tourist (Pitt) in Morocco learns about fear and isolation when his wife (Blanchett) is wounded by a stray bullet. Meanwhile, their children in L.A. are cared for by housekeeper Barraza, who brings them along to her son's wedding in Mexico, little dreaming of the consequences. In Tokyo, a mute teenage girl (Kikuchi), traumatized by her mother's death, reaches out to a police detective. Maintains an extraordinary level of tension while pursuing its central theme about the need to communicate—and listen—in our post-9/11 world. Third of a trilogy written by Guillermo Arriaga, following AMORES PERROS and 21 GRAMS. Oscar winner for Gustavo Santaolalla's score. [R]○●

Babe: Pig in the City (1998-U.S.-Australian)

C-95m. **½ D: George Miller. Magda Szubanski, James Cromwell, Mickey Rooney; voices of E. G. Daily, Danny Mann, Glenne Headly, Steven Wright, Stanley Ralph Ross, Russi Taylor, Hugo Weaving, Naomi Watts; narrated by Roscoe Lee Browne. Disappointing (and superfluous) sequel puts Babe and everyone around him, human and animal, in almost continual peril, as the pig is taken to America by Mrs. Hoggett. Overblown, with unpleasant images unsuitable for the youngest children, but rescued somewhat by the indomitable Babe, who's as endearing as ever, and those three singing mice, whose choice of material is quite funny. [G]▼○●

Babes in Arms (1939) **96m.** **½ D: Busby Berkeley. Mickey Rooney, Judy Garland, Charles Winninger, Guy Kibbee, June Preisser, Douglas McPhail. Rodgers and Hart's musical, minus most of their songs, and one that's left, "Where or When," is trammeled to death. What remains is energetic but standard putting-on-a-show vehicle for Mickey and Judy. Dated fun. Original ending, "My Day," was a production number spoofing Mr. and Mrs. Franklin D. Roosevelt, which was removed for a 1948 reissue and later restored. Also shown in computer-colored version.○●

Babes in Toyland (1934) **73m.** ***½ D: Gus Meins, Charles R. Rogers. Stan Laurel, Oliver Hardy, Charlotte Henry, Henry Kleinbach (Brandon), Felix Knight, Jean Darling, Johnny Downs, Marie Wilson. L&H version of Victor Herbert operetta looks better all the time, compared to lumbering "family musicals" of recent years. Stan and Ollie are in fine form, and fantasy element of Toyland—especially attack by Bogeymen—is excellent. Video title: MARCH OF THE WOODEN SOLDIERS. Originally released at 79m. Remade in 1961. Also shown in computer-colored version.▼○●

Babes in Toyland (1961) **C-105m.** **½ D: Jack Donohue. Ray Bolger, Tommy Sands, Annette Funicello, Henry Calvin, Gene Sheldon, Tommy Kirk, Ed Wynn, Ann Jillian. Colorful but contrived Disneyfication of Victor Herbert operetta has no substance or heart; classic songs, visual gimmicks, clowning of Calvin and Sheldon keep it afloat. Remade for TV in 1986.▼○

Babes on Broadway (1941) **118m.** **½ D: Busby Berkeley. Mickey Rooney, Judy Garland, Fay Bainter, Virginia Weidler, Richard Quine, Ray McDonald, Donna Reed. Showcase for Mickey and Judy's talents, with duo doing everything from imitations of Carmen Miranda and Bernhardt to minstrel numbers. Standout is Judy's "F.D.R. Jones." Film debut of Margaret O'Brien. Look fast for Ava Gardner in the audience watching the final number.▼○●

Babette's Feast (1987-Danish) **C-102m.**

**** D: Gabriel Axel. Stephane Audran, Jean-Philippe Lafont, Gudmar Wivesson, Jarl Kulle, Bibi Andersson, Birgitte Federspiel, Bodil Kjer. Exquisite, delicately told tale of two beautiful young minister's daughters who pass up love and fame to remain in their small Danish village. They grow old, using religion as a substitute for living life . . . and then take in Parisian refugee Audran, a woman with a very special secret. Subtle, funny and deeply felt, with several wonderful surprises: an instant masterpiece that deservedly earned a Best Foreign Film Academy Award. Axel wrote the screenplay, from an Isak Dinesen short story. Don't miss this one. [G] ▼●)

Babies (2010-French-U.S.) **C-79m.** ****½** D: Thomas Balmès. Mildly diverting documentary tracing the birth and first two years of life of four babies around the world: in San Francisco, Tokyo, Mongolia, and a remote village in Namibia. Lack of narration is refreshing, allowing us to watch these infants discover the world around them. Despite many sweet, appealing moments, this doesn't add up to much. [PG]●

Baby, The (1973) **C-102m.** ****** D: Ted Post. Anjanette Comer, Ruth Roman, Marianna Hill. Social worker who gets in too deep with a man-child case, has to kill to keep "baby" at home with her. [PG] ▼)

Baby Blue Marine (1976) **C-90m.** ****½** D: John Hancock. Jan-Michael Vincent, Glynnis O'Connor, Katherine Helmond, Dana Elcar, Bert Remsen, Richard Gere, Art Lund. Norman Rockwell's America come to life, in bucolic tale of Marine dropout during WW2 who's mistaken for hero by residents of small town. Too bland to add up. [PG]

Baby Boom (1987) **C-110m.** ******* D: Charles Shyer. Diane Keaton, Harold Ramis, Sam Shepard, Sam Wanamaker, James Spader, Pat Hingle, Britt Leach, Mary Gross, Victoria Jackson, Paxton Whitehead, Annie Golden, Dori Brenner, Robin Bartlett, Christopher Noth. Keaton is in top comic form as a supercharged business exec whose life changes dramatically when she "inherits" a baby. Amiable comedy takes well-aimed potshots at '80s yuppie motherdom but remains agreeably sweet-natured start to finish, helping it over an occasional story lull. Written by Shyer and Nancy Meyers. Followed by a TV series. [PG] ▼●)

Baby Boy (2001) **C-129m.** ******* D: John Singleton. Tyrese Gibson, Taraji P. Henson, Omar Gooding, Tamara Bass, A. J. Johnson, Ving Rhames, Snoop Dogg, Candy Ann Brown, Mo'Nique. Ambitious, insightful portrait of an immature 20-year-old African American who lives off his mother and embraces irresponsibility, even though he has fathered two children by two

different women. Opens with a bang, but goes on too long, and offsets some strong characterizations—Gibson's straight-talking mother (Johnson) and her ex-con-gone-straight boyfriend (Rhames)—with sloppy storytelling. A companion piece to writer-director Singleton's BOYZ N THE HOOD, also set in South Central L.A. [R] ▼)

Baby Doll (1956) **114m.** *****½** D: Elia Kazan. Karl Malden, Carroll Baker, Eli Wallach, Mildred Dunnock, Lonny Chapman, Rip Torn. Starkly photographed on location in Mississippi, story revolves around a child bride, her witless and blustery husband, and a smarmy business rival bent on using both of them. Condemned by Legion of Decency when released, this Tennessee Williams story, although tame by today's standards, still sizzles. Film debuts of Wallach and Torn. ▼)

Baby Face (1933) **70m.** ****½** D: Alfred E. Green. Barbara Stanwyck, George Brent, Donald Cook, Margaret Lindsay, Douglass Dumbrille, John Wayne. Pre-Production Code item has Stanwyck bartending at a speakeasy, then literally sleeping her way floor by floor to the top of a N.Y.C. office building. Great first half gives way to sappily moralistic conclusion. Wayne's coat-and-tie bit—as one of the office help used by the heroine—is a hoot. Even harsher version discovered in 2004 runs about 5m. longer. ▼●)

Baby Face Nelson (1957) **85m.** ****** D: Don Siegel. Mickey Rooney, Carolyn Jones, Cedric Hardwicke, Jack Elam, Ted De Corsia. Rooney gives flavorful performance in title role of gun-happy gangster in Prohibition-Depression days; low-budget product, but action-filled.

Babyfever (1994) **C-110m.** ****½** D: Henry Jaglom. Victoria Foyt, Matt Salinger, Dinah Lenney, Eric Roberts, Frances Fisher, Elaine Kagan. An array of career-women at a Malibu baby shower examine, discuss, and discuss some more their own ticking biological clocks. Meanwhile, one of the guests (Foyt) is awaiting results of her own pregnancy test! Shot in Jaglom's usual vérité style, this is best appreciated by fans of the highly personal filmmaker. With the drubbing that men take here, this is definitely not a "first date" film. ▼)

Baby Geniuses (1999) **C-94m.** BOMB D: Bob Clark. Kathleen Turner, Christopher Lloyd, Peter MacNicol, Kim Cattrall, Dom DeLuise, Ruby Dee. Unless you want to see walking, talking toddlers hypnotizing DeLuise into picking his nose, steer clear of this almost history-making comedy clinker about power-mad child psychologist Turner, who's raising these bright babies in her lab. Technically shoddy and recipient of some of the decade's worst reviews (though people did go to see it). If these kids are such geniuses, why can't they spark even a single laugh? Followed by SUPERBABIES: BABY GENIUSES 2. Super 35. [PG] ▼●◗

Baby It's You (1983) **C-105m.** **½ D: John Sayles. Rosanna Arquette, Vincent Spano, Joanna Merlin, Jack Davidson, Nick Ferrari, Dolores Messina, Leora Dana, Sam McMurray, Tracy Pollan, Matthew Modine, Robert Downey, Jr., Caroline Aaron, Fisher Stevens. A middle-class Jewish girl is pursued by a working-class Italian Catholic boy who calls himself The Sheik in this slice-of-life set in 1960s New Jersey. Writer-director Sayles' eye for detail and ear for dialogue give his fine cast a solid foundation—but the script loses momentum after the characters graduate from high school. Story by coproducer Amy Robinson; Modine's film debut. [R] ▼●◗

Babylon A.D. (2008-U.S.-French-British) **C-90m.** BOMB D: Mathieu Kassovitz. Vin Diesel, Gérard Depardieu, Michelle Yeoh, Mélanie Thierry, Charlotte Rampling, Mark Strong, Lambert Wilson, Joel Kirby. Futuristic story in which a mercenary (played with one expression by Diesel) is hired to escort a girl from Eastern Europe to N.Y.C. With an evil high priestess hot on his tail, he soon learns the real purpose of his mission: his charge is carrying either a deadly disease or an organism that is the new messiah. Incoherent plotting makes this attempted sci-fi epic a complete fizzle. Based on the novel *Babylon Babies* by Maurice G. Dantec. Unrated version runs 101m. Super 35. [PG-13] ◗

Baby Maker, The (1970) **C-109m.** ** D: James Bridges. Barbara Hershey, Colin Wilcox-Horne, Sam Groom, Scott Glenn, Jeannie Berlin. Childless couple hires young semi-hippie to have a baby for the husband when wife discovers she is sterile. Made at a time when the notion of surrogate mothers was considered bizarre. [R] ▼◗

Baby Mama (2008) **C-99m.** **½ D: Michael McCullers. Tina Fey, Amy Poehler, Greg Kinnear, Dax Shepard, Romany Malco, Sigourney Weaver, Steve Martin, Maura Tierney, Holland Taylor, John Hodgman, Siobhan Fallon Hogan, Denis O'Hare, James Rebhorn. Career-minded Fey decides it's time to have a baby and signs up with an agency to match her with a surrogate mother: white-trash Poehler, who's running a scam. Given the comedic talent involved this is pretty bland, though certainly watchable. Martin has fun in a glorified cameo as Fey's boss, a New Age business mogul. [PG-13] ◗

Baby's Day Out (1994) **C-98m.** BOMB D: Patrick Read Johnson. Lara Flynn Boyle, Joe Mantegna, Jacob and Adam Worton, Joe Pantoliano, Brian Haley, Cynthia Nixon, Fred Dalton Thompson, John Neville, Eddie Bracken. In a "plot" reminiscent of several Swee Pea cartoons, a Chicago baby violently foils kidnappers as he embarks on a parentless Pampers odyssey to Marshall Field's, the zoo, and to the top of a skyscraper building site. A box office flop despite scripter/coproducer John Hughes' cynical HOME ALONE cloning; in standard Hughes fashion, it's full of kicked-and-torched gonads jokes, but all sweetness and light at the end. [PG] ▼●◗

Baby: Secret of the Lost Legend (1985) **C-95m.** ** D: B.W.L. Norton. William Katt, Sean Young, Patrick McGoohan, Julian Fellowes, Kyalo Mativo. Old-fashioned yarn about discovery of a dinosaur family follows basic KING KONG outline—and the baby dino is sure to charm kids—but elements of racism, sexism, and much-too-casual violence just about kill it. TV title: DINOSAUR . . . SECRET OF THE LOST LEGEND. Super Techniscope. [PG] ▼●◗

Babysitter, The (1969) **70m.** ** D: Don Henderson. Patricia Wymer, George E. Carey, Ann Bellamy, Cathy Williams, Robert Tessier, James McLarty. Low-budget drive-in fare is dated but still mildly enjoyable; young blonde babysitter seduces the district attorney and hilarity ensues. Carey produced, McLarty wrote the script. Followed by nonsequel, WEEKEND WITH THE BABYSITTER. [R]

Babysitter, The (1975-Italian-French-German) **C-111m.** BOMB D: René Clement. Maria Schneider, Sydne Rome, Vic Morrow, Robert Vaughn, Renato Pozzetto, Nadja Tiller. In misfired melodrama, Schneider is innocently duped into taking part in a kidnapping by roommate Rome. Schneider's nonacting is abysmal, as is miscasting of chubby Italian comedian Pozzetto as her boyfriend. Retitled: WANTED: BABYSITTER. Video title: THE RAW EDGE. ▼◗

Babysitter, The (1995) **C-90m.** ** D: Guy Ferland. Alicia Silverstone, Jeremy London, J. T. Walsh, Lee Garlington, Nicky Katt, Lois Chiles, George Segal, Ryan Slater. A beautiful teenager inspires sexual fantasies in the people around her as she babysits for Walsh and his wife. Unimaginative writing (by the director) and slow pace explain why this went straight to video, though it was released in theaters after Silverstone's great success in CLUELESS. [R] ▼●◗

Baby-Sitters Club, The (1995) **C-85m.** **½ D: Melanie Mayron. Schuyler Fisk, Bre Blair, Rachel Leigh Cook, Zelda Harris, Tricia Joe, Larisa Oleynik, Stacey Linn Ramsower, Austin O'Brien, Aaron Metchik, Christian Oliver, Brooke Adams, Peter Horton, Ellen Burstyn, Bruce Davison, Harris Yulin. Kristy (Fisk), founder and leader of the Baby-Sitter's Club, run by seven girls who are best friends, proposes starting a summer camp. Then her long-absent father shows up, and wants to spend time with her—but insists she keep his presence a secret. Good-hearted adaptation of Ann M. Martin's hugely popular books for preteen girls. Low-key, episodic, but agreeable entertainment. Director Mayron can be spotted briefly in the opening sequence. Fisk is the daughter of Sissy Spacek. [PG]▼●)

Baby Snakes (1979) **C-166m. BOMB** D: Frank Zappa. Frank Zappa, Ron Delsener, Joey Psychotic, Donna U. Wanna, Frenchy the Poodle, Ms. Pinky's Larger Sister, Angel, Janet the Planet, Diva, John, Chris, Nancy. Excruciatingly overlong ego trip for musical maverick Zappa. In every fifth shot, it seems, Frankie is in close-up or a fan rushes up to him, kisses him, and screeches for joy. Zappa finally cut it down to 91m. for 1984 reissue. Bruce Bickford's clay animation is film's sole virtue. [R]▼▮

Baby The Rain Must Fall (1965) **100m.** *** D: Robert Mulligan. Lee Remick, Steve McQueen, Don Murray, Paul Fix, Josephine Hutchinson, Ruth White. Much underrated account of ex-convict McQueen, returning to his wife and daughter, but unable to change his restless ways. Murray is sincere sheriff who tries to help. Screenplay by Horton Foote, from his play *The Traveling Lady*.▼●)

Bachelor, The (1991-Italian-Hungarian-British) **C-105m.** *** D: Roberto Faenza. Keith Carradine, Miranda Richardson, Kristin Scott Thomas, Sarah-Jane Fenton, Max von Sydow, Mario Adorf. Subtle, thoughtful story of repressed emotion, about a staid, middle-aged, unmarried doctor and self-described "nomad" (Carradine), and how he responds when his sister and long-time constant companion commits suicide. Richardson, in a dual role, plays the latter, as well as one of a trio of very different women with whom the doctor becomes involved. Based on a novel by Arthur Schnitzler.▼

Bachelor, The (1999) **C-101m.** *½ D: Gary Sinyor. Chris O'Donnell, Renée Zellweger, Hal Holbrook, James Cromwell, Peter Ustinov, Edward Asner, Brooke Shields, Mariah Carey, Artie Lange, Jennifer Esposito, Sarah Silverman. Hapless O'Donnell would do better aping Buster Brown than taking on the Buster Keaton role in a woeful update of the still uproarious 1925 classic SEVEN CHANCES, playing a misdirected 30-year-old youth who must find a wife immediately or forfeit a $100 million inheritance left him by his crotchety grandfather. A mistake from top to bottom. The view of women here might even offend the Rat Pack. Also available in PG version. [PG-13]▼●)

Bachelor and the Bobby-Soxer, The (1947) **95m.** *** D: Irving Reis. Cary Grant, Myrna Loy, Shirley Temple, Rudy Vallee, Ray Collins, Harry Davenport. Judge Loy orders playboy Grant to wine and dine her sister Temple, so the teenager will forget her infatuation for him. Breezy entertainment earned Sidney Sheldon an Oscar for

his original screenplay. Also shown in computer-colored version.▼●)

Bachelor Flat (1962) **C-91m.** ** D: Frank Tashlin. Tuesday Weld, Richard Beymer, Celeste Holm, Terry-Thomas. Weld visits her mother's beach house and finds scientist Thomas at work; she moves in anyway and creates eventual havoc. Thomas has had better material; film's entertainment is all in his lap. CinemaScope.

Bachelor in Paradise (1961) **C-109m.** ** D: Jack Arnold. Bob Hope, Lana Turner, Janis Paige, Jim Hutton, Paula Prentiss, Don Porter, Agnes Moorehead. Hope vehicle about the only bachelor in a community of married couples. Amusing, but not great. Hope has done better; Paige is fun as always. CinemaScope.▼▮

Bachelor Mother (1939) **81m.** ***½ D: Garson Kanin. Ginger Rogers, David Niven, Charles Coburn, Frank Albertson, Ernest Truex. Rogers unwittingly becomes guardian for abandoned baby in this delightful comedy by Norman Krasna. Remade as BUNDLE OF JOY (1956). Also shown in computer-colored version.▼●)

Bachelor Party, The (1957) **93m.** *** D: Delbert Mann. Don Murray, E. G. Marshall, Jack Warden, Patricia Smith, Carolyn Jones, Larry Blyden, Philip Abbott, Nancy Marchand. Perceptive Paddy Chayefsky drama (originally a TV play) about bachelor party for groom-to-be Abbott and its emotional effect on other married participants. Jones is exceptional as philosophical nympho. Film debuts of Smith, Blyden, Abbott, and Marchand. ▼

Bachelor Party (1984) **C-106m.** ** D: Neal Israel. Tom Hanks, Tawny Kitaen, Adrian Zmed, George Grizzard, Robert Prescott. Amiable comedy about preparations for a raunchy bachelor party has real laughs for a while, then gets increasingly desperate and tasteless. Followed by a direct-to-DVD sequel. [R]▼●)

Backbeat (1993-British) **C-100m.** **½ D: Iain Softley. Stephen Dorff, Sheryl Lee, Ian Hart, Gary Bakewell, Chris O'Neill, Scot Williams, Kai Weisinger, Paul Humpoletz. Stuart Sutcliffe (Dorff) goes along with his pal John Lennon when their rock 'n' roll band tries to establish itself in early '60s Hamburg—but his ambitions lie elsewhere. Initially intriguing true story of the man who deserted the about-to-be-Beatles grows tired after a while, especially when Lennon (as played by the dynamic Hart) seems so much more interesting. The period and its music are well captured, however. Later a stage musical. [R]▼●)

Back Door to Hell (1964) **68m.** **½ D: Monte Hellman. Jimmie Rodgers, Jack Nicholson, John Hackett, Annabelle Huggins, Conrad Maga. Mildly interesting film about WW2 reconnaissance mission in the Philippines; early collaboration of Nicholson and Hellman, who filmed FLIGHT TO FURY back to back with this.▶

Backdraft (1991) **C-135m.** ******* D: Ron Howard. Kurt Russell, William Baldwin, Robert De Niro, Donald Sutherland, Jennifer Jason Leigh, Scott Glenn, Rebecca De Mornay, Jason Gedrick, J. T. Walsh, Tony Mockus, Sr., Clint Howard. Two brothers whose father died fighting a fire now spend their time on the force battling each other. A hoary B-movie–type script fired up by square-jawed conviction, and stunning special effects; also the first film to ever explore a sheer fascination with fire. The gifted Leigh fails miserably playing a normal young woman. Super 35. [R]▼●◗

Backfire (1987-U.S.-Canadian) **C-92m.** ****½** D: Gilbert Cates. Karen Allen, Keith Carradine, Jeff Fahey, Bernie Casey, Dean Paul Martin, Dinah Manoff, Virginia Capers, Philip Sterling. Complicated plot with several surprises is best not revealed here, but it does involve wealthy, disturbed Vietnam vet Fahey, his wrong-side-of-the-tracks wife Allen, and mysterious drifter Carradine. Familiar story but well acted; builds up a fair amount of suspense. Good use of Canadian locations. [R]▼●◗

Backfire! (1994) **C-89m.** ***½** D: A. Dean Bell. Kathy Ireland, Robert Mitchum, Telly Savalas, Shelley Winters, Josh Mosby, Mary McCormack, Edie Falco. In the wake of AIRPLANE! and THE NAKED GUN comes this astoundingly unfunny comedy about an inept young man attempting to join an all-female fire department. Mitchum (as a semi-senile fire marshal) and Winters have come a long way since THE NIGHT OF THE HUNTER! [PG-13]▼

Back From Eternity (1956) **97m.** ****½** D: John Farrow. Robert Ryan, Anita Ekberg, Rod Steiger, Phyllis Kirk. Moderately engrossing account of victims of plane crash, stranded in South American jungle, and their various reactions to the situation. OK remake of FIVE CAME BACK.▼●

Background to Danger (1943) **80m.** ******* D: Raoul Walsh. George Raft, Brenda Marshall, Sydney Greenstreet, Peter Lorre, Osa Massen, Kurt Katch. Slam-bang WW2 story with Raft swept into Nazi intrigue in Turkey; terrific car chase caps fast-moving tale.▼◗

Back in the USSR (1991) **C-87m.** ***½** D: Deran Sarafian. Frank Whaley, Natalya Negoda, Roman Polanski, Ravil Issyanov, Dey Young, Andrew Divoff, Brian Blessed, Harry Ditson. American tourist Whaley gets involved in "the case of the disappearing icon" on a visit to Russia. It's almost impossible to follow this loophole-laden script where coincidences abound and the importance of the central object of desire—the icon—is never established.▼●

Backlash (1956) **C-84m.** ****½** D: John Sturges. Richard Widmark, Donna Reed, William Campbell, John McIntire, Barton MacLane, Henry (Harry) Morgan, Edward C. Platt. In the aftermath of an Apache ambush, Widmark (who believes his father was in the doomed party) and Reed (whose husband was killed in the massacre) become involved in a serpentine search for the lone survivor and some missing gold. Plotty Western written by Borden Chase.

Backlash (1986-Australian) **C-88m.** ****½** D: Bill Bennett. David Argue, Gia Carides, Lydia Miller, Brian Syron, Anne Smith. Well-meaning but muddled account of a young aborigine barmaid who's sodomized, then charged with the murder of her assailant, and finally treks across the outback in custody of two mindlessly jabbering cops. Bits of snappy dialogue and intriguing commentary on race relations, but far too much is left unexplained. [R]▼

Backroads (1977-Australian) **C-61m.** *****½** D: Phillip Noyce. Bill Hunter, Gary Foley, Zac Martin, Julie McGregor, Terry Camilleri. Aborigine Foley joins with loutish, self-centered white criminal Hunter, with tragic results. Superior drama is an incisive commentary on racism; in private life Foley is a radical black activist. Noyce's feature directorial debut.

Back Roads (1981) **C-94m.** ***½** D: Martin Ritt. Sally Field, Tommy Lee Jones, David Keith, Miriam Colon, Michael V. Gazzo, M. Emmet Walsh. Attractive leads are scant consolation for thoroughly unfunny comedy about a hooker and a drifter who find love on the road. Not as enjoyable as Hollywood's 10,000 previous derivations of the same script. Panavision. [R]▼

Backstage (2006-French) **C-115m.** ****½** D: Emmanuelle Bercot. Emmanuelle Seigner, Isild Le Besco, Noémie Lvovsky, Valéry Zeitoun, Samuel Benchetrit. Teenage girl is obsessed with a beautiful pop singer and manages to work her way into the star's inner circle . . . but their relationship takes many strange turns. Intriguing look at fandom gone amok and a tortured, mercurial, pampered star rings fairly true but goes on too long. Feature debut for writer-director Bercot.▶

Back Street (1932) **89m.** ******* D: John M. Stahl. Irene Dunne, John Boles, George Meeker, ZaSu Pitts, Arlette Duncan, June Clyde, William Bakewell, Doris Lloyd, Jane Darwell. Dunne shines in oft-filmed Fannie Hurst soaper of spirited young woman who becomes the mistress of Boles and must forever remain in the shadows. Dated, to be sure, but still entertaining. Remade in 1941 and 1961.

Back Street (1941) **89m.** ******* D: Robert Stevenson. Charles Boyer, Margaret Sullavan, Richard Carlson, Frank McHugh, Tim Holt. Fine team of Boyer and Sullavan breathes life into Fannie Hurst perennial soaper of woman whose love for man doesn't die when he marries another.

Back Street (1961) **C-107m.** ****½** D: David

Miller. Susan Hayward, John Gavin, Vera Miles, Charles Drake, Virginia Grey, Reginald Gardiner, Natalie Schafer. Lavish, unbelievable third version of Fannie Hurst's story of a woman's love for married man. Doesn't play as well as previous versions but a fashion show for Hayward in Jean Louis designs. Ross Hunter produced.▼

Back to Bataan (1945) 95m. *** D: Edward Dmytryk. John Wayne, Anthony Quinn, Beulah Bondi, Fely Franquelli, Richard Loo, Philip Ahn, Lawrence Tierney. Good, sturdy WW2 action film with officer Wayne leading Filipino guerrillas to victory in the South Pacific. Also shown in computer-colored version.▼●)

Back to God's Country (1953) C-78m. **½ D: Joseph Pevney. Rock Hudson, Marcia Henderson, Steve Cochran, Hugh O'Brian, Chubby Johnson. Sea captain Hudson and wife Henderson face rigors of nature and villainy of Cochran in the Canadian wilds. Competent programmer; from James Oliver Curwood's classic story, filmed before in 1919 and 1927.

Back to School (1986) C-96m. *** D: Alan Metter. Rodney Dangerfield, Sally Kellerman, Burt Young, Keith Gordon, Robert Downey, Jr., Paxton Whitehead, Terry Farrell, M. Emmet Walsh, Adrienne Barbeau, Ned Beatty, Severn Darden, Sam Kinison, Robert Picardo, Kurt Vonnegut, Jr., Edie McClurg, Jason Hervey. Bombastic, uneducated, self-made millionaire enrolls in college, in order to encourage his student son. Very entertaining comedy, full of hilarious Dangerfield one-liners, but key to the film's success is that Rodney's character is so likable. Kellerman shines, too, as English professor who becomes the apple of his eye. [PG-13]▼●)

Back to the Beach (1987) C-92m. ** D: Lyndall Hobbs. Frankie Avalon, Annette Funicello, Lori Loughlin, Tommy Hinckley, Connie Stevens, Demian Slade; guest appearances by Don Adams, Bob Denver, Alan Hale, Jerry Mathers, Tony Dow, Barbara Billingsley, Edd Byrnes, Pee-wee Herman (Paul Reubens), Dick Dale and The Del-Tones. Frankie and Annette return to the scene of their youth—older but no wiser—as the parents of teens. The fun wears thin pretty fast in this uninspired comedy—despite the efforts of *six writers* and the presence of 1950s and 60s TV sitcom stars in cameo roles. The songs are dull, too, though Annette's "Jamaica Ska" has its moments. [PG]▼●)

Back to the Future (1985) C-116m. *** D: Robert Zemeckis. Michael J. Fox, Christopher Lloyd, Crispin Glover, Lea Thompson, Wendie Jo Sperber, Marc McClure, Claudia Wells, Thomas F. Wilson, James Tolkan, Casey Siemaszko, Billy Zane, Jason Hervey. A teenager of the '80s travels back in time to the '50s, where he must arrange for his mismatched parents to meet—or else *he* won't exist! Wonderful, wacked-out time-travel comedy takes its time to get going, but once it does, it's a lot of fun, building to a frantic climax just like other Bob Gale–Robert Zemeckis scripts (USED CARS, I WANNA HOLD YOUR HAND, 1941). Lloyd is a standout as crazed scientist who sets story in motion. Huey Lewis, who sings film's hit song, "The Power of Love," has cameo as a high-school teacher. Produced by Steven Spielberg and company. Followed by two sequels and an animated TV series. [PG]▼●)

Back to the Future Part II (1989) C-107m. ** D: Robert Zemeckis. Michael J. Fox, Christopher Lloyd, Lea Thompson, Thomas F. Wilson, Harry Waters Jr., Charles Fleischer, Joe Flaherty, Elisabeth Shue, James Tolkan, Casey Siemaszko, Elijah Wood. Joyless, frenetic follow-up to Part 1 which sends mad inventor Lloyd and young Fox back into their time-traveling DeLorean. Considerable ingenuity, but hardly any laughs, and a surprising amount of unpleasantness. Works best toward the end when it creates a parallel existence to the climactic action in Part 1, but then it turns out to be a cliffhanger, advertising the upcoming Part III! Talk about a cheat . . . [PG]▼●)

Back to the Future Part III (1990) C-118m. ***½ D: Robert Zemeckis. Michael J. Fox, Christopher Lloyd, Mary Steenburgen, Thomas F. Wilson, Lea Thompson, Elisabeth Shue, Matt Clark, Richard Dysart, Pat Buttram, Harry Carey, Jr., Dub Taylor, James Tolkan, ZZ Top. Delightful conclusion to this time-travel trilogy sends Fox back to the Old West, circa 1885, in search of Lloyd—hoping to change history and keep him from being shot in the back by a bad guy. The dormant movie Western gets a major dose of adrenaline from this high-tech, high-powered comic adventure, which offers great fun, dazzling special effects, and imagination to spare. There's real movie magic at work here. [PG]▼●)

Backtrack (1989) C-98m. **½ D: Dennis Hopper. Dennis Hopper, Jodie Foster, Dean Stockwell, Vincent Price, John Turturro, Fred Ward, Charlie Sheen, G. Anthony (Tony) Sirico, Julie Adams, Sy Richardson, Frank Gio, Helena Kallianiotes, Bob Dylan, Catherine Keener. Contemporary melodrama about a hit man hired to rub out murder eyewitness Foster—but falling in love and taking it on the lam with her instead. Although film isn't particularly distinguished, it *is* entertaining—especially with that Who's Who cast. (Joe Pesci, despite a substantial role, appears unbilled.) Released first in Europe as CATCHFIRE; Hopper disowned that version. Restored to his cut (116m.) for U.S. release on cable and video in 1991. [R]▼●

Back-up Plan, The (2010) C-104m.

** D: Alan Poul. Jennifer Lopez, Alex O'Loughlin, Michaela Watkins, Eric Christian Olsen, Anthony Anderson, Noureen DeWulf, Linda Lavin, Tom Bosley, Robert Klein, Melissa McCarthy. Pedestrian comedy is buoyed by the engaging Lopez as a romantically frustrated woman and wannabe mother who decides to get artificially inseminated. Things get uber-complicated when she finally meets Mr. Right that same day. The sequence in which she joins a single moms' support group is disastrously unfunny and brings the whole film down several notches. At least Lopez and costar O'Loughlin have nice chemistry. Super 35. [PG-13] ▶

Backwoods Massacre SEE: **Midnight** (1981)

Bad and the Beautiful, The (1952) **118m.** ***½ D: Vincente Minnelli. Kirk Douglas, Lana Turner, Dick Powell, Gloria Grahame, Barry Sullivan, Walter Pidgeon, Gilbert Roland. Captivating Hollywood story of ambitious producer (Douglas) told via relationships with actress Turner, writer Powell, director Sullivan. Solid, insightful, witty, with Lana's best performance ever. Five Oscars include Supporting Actress (Grahame), Screenplay (Charles Schnee). David Raksin's wonderful score is another asset. Minnelli and Douglas followed this a decade later with TWO WEEKS IN ANOTHER TOWN. Also shown in computer-colored version. ▼●●

Bad Behavior (1993-British) **C-103m.** **½ D: Les Blair. Stephen Rea, Sinead Cusack, Philip Jackson, Clare Higgins, Phil Daniels, Mary Jo Randle, Saira Todd, Amanda Boxer. Amusing comedy with Rea and Cusack as a couple whose marital complacency is challenged by their friends, their jobs, and a bathroom renovation. A quietly quirky slant on domestic life in the Mike Leigh mold (the actors improvised from director Blair's story outline) which rambles along nicely without ever really catching fire. Rea and Cusack are charming in the lead roles. ▼▶

Bad Blood (1981-New Zealand-British) **C-104m.** *** D: Mike Newell. Jack Thompson, Carol Burns, Denis Lill, Donna Akersten, Martyn Sanderson, Marshall Napier. Set during WW2, this provocative drama is a fact-based account of a backwoods farmer (Thompson) who shoots several people and is hunted in the New Zealand bush. The incident ends up being exploited by Lord Haw-Haw, the notorious Nazi propagandist. ▼▶

Bad Blood (1986-French) **C-128m.** ** D: Léos Carax. Michel Piccoli, Juliette Binoche, Denis Lavant, Hans Meyer, Julie Delpy, Carroll Brooks, Hugo Pratt, Mireille Perrier, Serge Reggiani. Pretentious film noir takeoff about two-bit con artist Lavant, who finds himself in way over his head as he becomes involved in a plot to pilfer a serum that's an antidote for an AIDS-like disease; along the way, he falls for beautiful Binoche, the lover of one of his cohorts. Highly regarded by some, but the storytelling is fatally muddled and all the close-ups of faces and legs grow tiresome. Lavant plays the same character in Carax's BOY MEETS GIRL and THE LOVERS ON THE BRIDGE. Released in the U.S. in 2001. [R] ▼▶

Bad Boys (1983) **C-123m.** *** D: Rick Rosenthal. Sean Penn, Reni Santoni, Esai Morales, Eric Gurry, Jim Moody, Ally Sheedy, Clancy Brown, Alan Ruck. Tough urban melodrama about juvenile prison, and a personal vendetta that reaches its peak within prison walls. Criticized by some as being amoral—and not always credible—but certainly scores on an emotional level. Sheedy's feature film debut. [R] ▼●●

Bad Boys (1995) **C-126m.** **½ D: Michael Bay. Martin Lawrence, Will Smith, Téa Leoni, Theresa Randle, Tchéky Karyo, Marg Helgenberger, Anna Thomson, Joe Pantoliano. Highly formulaic but not altogether disposable Miami actioner about two cops—one married with kids, the other equipped with a bachelor apartment—who are forced to switch roles after they're mistaken for each other during a drug-murder case. A return by producers Don Simpson and Jerry Bruckheimer to the kind of corpse-littered escapism that established them in the '80s; wildly uneven comedy is aided by the spin Leoni puts on her role as a material witness who's hiding undercover with the heroes. A robust half hour padded into two hours. Followed by a sequel. [R] ▼●●

Bad Boys II (2003) **C-146m.** ** D: Michael Bay. Martin Lawrence, Will Smith, Jordi Mollà, Gabrielle Union, Peter Stormare, Theresa Randle, Joe Pantoliano, Michael Shannon, Jon Seda, Henry Rollins. Noisy, overlong sequel pits the Miami tactical team against a Cuban drug lord, while Lawrence's DEA sister (Union) goes undercover after the same prey. Film seemingly exists for the sole purpose of blowing things up, which it does well and often, but there's nothing else to recommend it. Plot is shopworn, and the banter between the two stars is forced and unfunny. Super 35. [R] ▼▶

Bad Company (1972) **C-93m.** ***½ D: Robert Benton. Jeff Bridges, Barry Brown, Jim Davis, David Huddleston, John Savage, Jerry Houser. Highly entertaining sleeper about two young drifters of wildly differing temperaments who rob their way West during the Civil War; aided immeasurably by Gordon Willis' subdued photography, Harvey Schmidt's piano score. Written by Benton and David Newman; Benton's directorial debut. [PG] ▼▶

Bad Company (1995) **C-108m.** *½ D: Damian Harris. Ellen Barkin, Laurence Fishburne, Frank Langella, Michael Beach, Gia Carides, David Ogden Stiers, Daniel Hugh Kelly, Spalding Gray, James Hong.

Ex-CIA staffer is recruited to join a private firm specializing in "covert operations"—like blackmail and murder—but there's more than meets the eye at every twist and turn. Never-ending series of double-crosses leads to a "who cares?" finale. Only some hot-and-heavy sex scenes stand out. Michael Murphy appears unbilled as Smitty. Panavision. [R]**▼●)**

Bad Company (1999-French) **C-93m. ***½** D: Jean-Pierre Améris. Maud Forget, Lou Doillon, Robinson Stévenin, Maxime Mansion, Cyril Cagnat, Delphine Rich, François Berléand, Micheline Presle. Incisive drama about Delphine (Forget), a bored, inexperienced 14-year-old who becomes fast friends with the new girl in school and falls in love (or so she thinks) with a manipulative young man. Sobering look at a young person who romanticizes everything from love and sex to depression and suicide, and who confuses sexual desire with emotional need. Not to be missed. Written by Alain Layrac. **▼●**

Bad Company (2002) **C-116m. *½** D: Joel Schumacher. Anthony Hopkins, Chris Rock, Gabriel Macht, Peter Stormare, John Slattery, Garcelle Beauvais-Nilon, Kerry Washington, Matthew Marsh, Brooke Smith, Irma P. Hall. Artificial hybrid of spy caper and Rock comedy that serves no one well, especially the audience. Contrived plot has CIA agent Hopkins training street hustler Rock to imitate his twin brother, who was a smooth operative on the verge of closing a deal for a nuclear weapon in Europe. Needlessly overlong, building to a suspense-free climax. Super 35. [PG-13] **▼●**

Bad Day at Black Rock (1955) **C-81m. ***½** D: John Sturges. Spencer Tracy, Robert Ryan, Anne Francis, Dean Jagger, Walter Brennan, John Ericson, Ernest Borgnine, Lee Marvin. Powerhouse cast in yarn of one-armed man (Tracy) uncovering skeleton in tiny desert town's closet. Borgnine memorable as slimy heavy. Millard Kaufman expertly adapted Howard Breslin's story "Bad Time at Hondo." Excellent use of CinemaScope. **▼●**

Bad Education (2004-Spanish) **C-109m. **½** D: Pedro Almodóvar. Gael García Bernal, Fele Martínez, Daniel Giménez Cacho, Lluís Homar, Javier Cámara, Petra Martínez, Nacho Pérez, Raúl García Forneiro. A struggling actor (Bernal) approaches a successful filmmaker (Fele Martínez) with an idea for a screenplay based on events that transpired at the Catholic school they both attended as boys. Complex, challenging, highly sexual story told in film noir style; clearly meaningful to Almodóvar, but somewhat distancing for the viewer, in spite of strong performances. R-rated version also available. Panavision. [NC-17]**▼●**

Bad for Each Other (1953) **83m. **½** D: Irving Rapper. Charlton Heston, Lizabeth

Scott, Dianne Foster, Ray Collins, Arthur Franz, Mildred Dunnock, Marjorie Rambeau. Doctor Heston has to choose between the needs of miners in his Pennsylvania hometown and big-city bluebloods. Predictable soap opera. **●**

Badge 373 (1973) **C-116m. *½** D: Howard W. Koch. Robert Duvall, Verna Bloom, Henry Darrow, Eddie Egan, Felipe Luciano, Tina Christiana. Very minor follow-up to THE FRENCH CONNECTION. Policeman Duvall tries to fight crime syndicate single-handedly in N.Y.C. Dull. [R]**▼●**

Bad Girls (1994) **C-99m. *½** D: Jonathan Kaplan. Madeleine Stowe, Mary Stuart Masterson, Andie MacDowell, Drew Barrymore, Dermot Mulroney, James Russo, Robert Loggia, Jim Beaver, Cooper Huckabee. Stowe and three other prostitutes go on the lam after a brothel shooting, eventually hooking up with a male outlaw from her past. Troubled production is an uneasy combination of feminist statement, homage to (or rip-off of) THE WILD BUNCH's finale, and an advertisement for good-looking Western duds. A collectible poster in search of a movie. Unrated version also available. [R]**▼●**

Bad Influence (1990) **C-99m. **½** D: Curtis Hanson. Rob Lowe, James Spader, Lisa Zane, Christian Clemenson, Kathleen Wilhoite, Tony Maggio, David Duchovny. Spader befriends Lowe after the latter gets him out of a tense barroom confrontation, then finds this psychopathic leech calling the shots in his romantic—and professional—life. Slick, high-tech variation on STRANGERS ON A TRAIN knows which buttons to push. Lowe is passable, but he's no Robert Walker. [R]**▼●**

Bad Jim (1990) **C-90m. ** D: Clyde Ware. James Brolin, Richard Roundtree, John Clark Gable, Harry Carey, Jr., Rory Calhoun, Ty Hardin, Pepe Serna, Bruce Kirby. Not-bad Western has three good/ bad men purchasing Billy the Kid's horse—and using it to pass themselves off as Billy's gang. Nice locations and welcome cast of veterans help make up for leisurely pace and lack of real action. Screen debut for Clark Gable's son, as the youngest of the bandit trio. [PG]**▼●**

Badlanders, The (1958) **C-83m. **½** D: Delmer Daves. Alan Ladd, Ernest Borgnine, Katy Jurado, Claire Kelly, Kent Smith, Nehemiah Persoff, Robert Emhardt. Nicely handled reworking of THE ASPHALT JUNGLE, set in 1898 Arizona, with ex-cons Ladd and Borgnine forming bond and becoming involved in gold robbery. CinemaScope. **▼●**

Badlands (1973) **C-95m. **½** D: Terrence Malick. Martin Sheen, Sissy Spacek, Warren Oates, Ramon Bieri, Alan Vint. Stark, moody, moderately successful thriller inspired by the Starkweather-Fugate killing spree in the '50s. Well-cast film has cult following. Malick's directorial debut; he also cameos as the visitor outside the rich man's house. [PG]▼●)

Bad Lieutenant (1992) **C-98m. ✱✱** D: Abel Ferrara. Harvey Keitel, Frankie Thorn, Paul Hipp, Victor Argo, Paul Calderone, Leonard Thomas. Also bad husband, bad substance abuser, all-around bad dude. Over-the-top Catholic guilt movie about a cop who starts to pull himself out of the abyss when he investigates the rape of a nun who refuses to press charges. More pretentious than Ferrara's earlier work, though film has substantial critical and cult following. Featured player Zoe Lund (who also coscripted with Ferrara) was formerly Zoe Tamerlis, star of Ferrara's MS. 45. At the very least, this is the first movie that offers full-frontal Keitel and a cameo by Jesus. [NC-17]▼●)

Bad Lieutenant: Port of Call: New Orleans, The (2009) **C-122m. ✱✱✱** D: Werner Herzog. Nicolas Cage, Eva Mendes, Val Kilmer, Alvin Xzibit Joiner, Fairuza Balk, Shawn Hatosy, Jennifer Coolidge, Tom Bower, Vondie Curtis Hall, Brad Dourif, Irma P. Hall, Denzel Whitaker, Michael Shannon, Shea Whigham, Lucius Baston. Wacky police procedural set in post-Katrina New Orleans, with Cage as a dedicated detective who winds up hopelessly addicted to drugs—which makes him more dangerous than most of the people he's hunting down. The slaughter of a family from Senegal that invaded a local drug lord's turf is the trigger for a long, tawdry, wide-ranging yarn in which the good guys and bad guys are hard to differentiate. Cage is terrific in a no-holds-barred performance. Bears no resemblance to the 1992 film BAD LIEUTENANT. [R]●)

Bad Love (1992) **C-94m.** BOMB D: Jill Goldman. Tom Sizemore, Pamela Gidley, Seymour Cassel, Richard Edson, Debi Mazar, Jennifer O'Neill, Margaux Hemingway, Joe Dallesandro. BAD MOVIE would be a more appropriate title. Perfectly dreadful drama about hot-tempered, two-bit hustler Sizemore and pretty loser Gidley who commence a hot-and-heavy, ill-fated romance. [R]▼)

Bad Manners (1998) **C-90m. ✱✱✱** D: Jonathan Kaufer. David Strathairn, Bonnie Bedelia, Saul Rubinek, Caroleen Feeney, Julie Harris. An egotistical musicologist and his companion spend the weekend with his ex-lover, who's now married to a college professor. Sparks fly from the start as the four flinty personalities collide; an exercise in sexual and psychological gamesmanship reminiscent of WHO'S AFRAID OF VIRGINIA WOOLF?, and splendidly acted all around. Adapted by David Gilman from his play *Ghost in the Machine*. [R]▼)

Bad Man's River (1972-Italian-Spanish) **C-89m. ✱✱** D: Gene (Eugenio) Martin.

Lee Van Cleef, James Mason, Gina Lollobrigida, Simon Andreu, Diana Lorys. Van Cleef is head of an outlaw gang repeatedly out-smarted by devilish Lollobrigida in this pallid comedy-Western made in Spain. Franscope. [PG]▼●)

Bad Medicine (1985) **C-96m.** BOMB D: Harvey Miller. Steve Guttenberg, Alan Arkin, Julie Hagerty, Bill Macy, Curtis Armstrong, Julie Kavner, Joe Grifasi, Robert Romanus, Taylor Negron, Gilbert Gottfried. Guttenberg can't get into any domestic medical schools, so he's forced to attend a dubious Central American institution run by Arkin. Cheap jokes and ethnic putdowns abound. Our prescription: skip it. [PG-13]▼

Bad Moon (1996) **C-79m. ✱✱** D: Eric Red. Mariel Hemingway, Michael Paré, Mason Gamble, Ken Pogue, Hrothgar Mathews. Hemingway is glad when her brother comes to live with her and her young son Gamble; only the family German shepherd knows that Paré is really the werewolf that has been killing locals in the Northwest woods. Good-looking horror movie with a strong performance from Paré is underpopulated and predictable, though the dog's great. From the novel *Thor* by Wayne Smith. Clairmont-Scope. [R]▼●)

Bad News Bears, The (1976) **C-102m. ✱✱✱** D: Michael Ritchie. Walter Matthau, Tatum O'Neal, Vic Morrow, Joyce Van Patten, Jackie Earle Haley, Alfred W. Lutter. Bright comedy about hopeless Little League baseball team that scores with an unlikely combination: a beer-guzzling coach (Matthau) and a female star pitcher (O'Neal). Some of film's major appeal—young kids spouting four-letter words—may be lost on TV. Clever use of Bizet's music from *Carmen*. Remade in 2005. Followed by two sequels and a TV series. [PG]▼●)

Bad News Bears (2005) **C-113m. ✱✱** D: Richard Linklater. Billy Bob Thornton, Greg Kinnear, Marcia Gay Harden, Sammi Kane Kraft, Jeffrey Davies, Timmy Deters, Brandon Craggs, Tyler Patrick Jones. Indolent, beer-guzzling exterminator (and ex-ball player) takes the job of coaching a woebegone Little League baseball team. Lackluster remake of the 1976 comedy goes through the motions, and uses foul language just as the first film did, but hasn't any zest or originality; even the reuse of themes from *Carmen* falls flat. Bill Lancaster's vintage script was adapted by the BAD SANTA team, Glenn Ficarra and John Requa. [PG-13] ▼)

Bad News Bears Go To Japan, The (1978) **C-91m. ✱✱** D: John Berry. Tony Curtis, Jackie Earle Haley, Tomisaburo Wakayama, George Wyner, Lonny Chapman. Curtis is good as a small-time hustler who sees money-making opportunity in the now-familiar baseball team. Third film was the kids' last, and it's easy to see why. [PG]▼●)

Bad News Bears in Breaking Training, The (1977) **C-100m.** **½ D: Michael Pressman. William Devane, Jackie Earle Haley, Jimmy Baio, Clifton James, Chris Barnes. Sentimental sequel to 1976 hit, with dirty talk largely absent. Star of the kids' baseball team, Haley heads for the Houston Astrodome and enlists the aid of estranged father Devane in coaching the misfits. Sporadically funny. [PG]▼●]

Bad Santa (2003) **C-91m.** *** D: Terry Zwigoff. Billy Bob Thornton, Tony Cox, Brett Kelly, Lauren Graham, Lauren Tom, Bernie Mac, John Ritter, Ajay Naidu. Outrageous, flagrantly foulmouthed black comedy about a self-loathing reprobate who works as a department store Santa with a conniving African-American "elf" who masterminds a series of robberies. Thornton's life reaches a crossroads when he encounters a hapless, isolated kid who truly believes in Santa. Provocative look at the seamiest Santa who ever lived is audaciously funny, but definitely not for all tastes. Dedicated to the late Ritter, who's very funny as an uptight store manager. Cloris Leachman appears unbilled. Unrated 98m. version available on DVD. Also available in R-rated 88m. director's cut. [R]▼●

Bad Seed, The (1956) **129m.** *** D: Mervyn LeRoy. Nancy Kelly, Patty McCormack, Henry Jones, Eileen Heckart, Evelyn Varden, William Hopper. Stagy but spellbinding account of malicious child McCormack whose inherited evil "causes" deaths of several people. Fine performances; Maxwell Anderson's Broadway play was adapted by John Lee Mahin, with Kelly, McCormack, Jones, and Heckart re-creating their stage roles. The corny "Hollywoodized" postscript is often cut but remains intact on video. Remade for TV in 1985. McCormack later played a bad seed grown up in MOMMY.▼●]

Bad Sleep Well, The (1960-Japanese) **150m.** *** D: Akira Kurosawa. Toshiro Mifune, Takeshi Kato, Masayuki Mori, Takashi Shimura, Akira Nishimura. Kurosawa effectively captures the spirit of 1940s Warner Bros. crime dramas in this engrossing tale of rising executive Mifune and corruption in the corporate world. Actually, it's a variation on *Hamlet.* Tohoscope. ▼●

Bad Taste (1988-New Zealand) **C-90m.** **½ D: Peter Jackson. Peter Jackson, Pete O'Herne, Mike Minett, Terry Potter, Craig Smith, Doug Wren, Dean Lawrie. Title is absolutely accurate in describing this gory comedy about callous alien fast-food entrepreneurs, here to harvest humanity, and battling it out with government hit squad. Quirky, fragmented direction matches subject matter and acting styles. Director Jackson also acted, wrote, edited, produced, and did the uneven but occasionally excellent makeup. A cult hit worldwide. ▼●]

Bad Teacher (2011) **C-92m.** ** D: Jake Kasdan. Cameron Diaz, Justin Timberlake, Jason Segel, Lucy Punch, John Michael Higgins, Phyllis Smith, Thomas Lennon, Molly Shannon, Eric Stonestreet, Dave (Gruber) Allen, Stephanie Faracy, David Paymer. Sleazy, unmotivated schoolteacher Diaz can't quit because her fiancé gets wise to her gold-digging ways and dumps her . . . so she faces another year at a job she has no use for. She sets her sights on a new substitute teacher (Timberlake) because he comes from a wealthy family, and she wants to buy herself a new pair of breasts. Heavy-handed, obvious (and crass) comedy paints every adult as a clueless idiot and has all the actors mug like crazy—except Diaz and gym teacher Segel—which would be OK if the film were funny. It isn't. [R]

Bad Timing: A Sensual Obsession (1980-British) **C-129m.** ***½ D: Nicolas Roeg. Art Garfunkel, Theresa Russell, Harvey Keitel, Denholm Elliott, Daniel Massey. Mesmerizing melodrama triumphs over badly miscast male leads and occasional pretentiousness. Roeg's kinetic style brings the necessary passion to oddball story of a psychiatrist sexually engulfed by a self-destructive tramp. Russell is simply great, as is knockout background music from The Who, Keith Jarrett, and Billie Holiday. Technovision. [R—originally rated X]▶

Bagdad Cafe (1988-West German) **C-108m.** **½ D: Percy Adlon. Marianne Sägebrecht, CCH Pounder, Jack Palance, Christine Kaufmann, Monica Calhoun, Darron Flagg. Nearly plotless charmer from the director and star of SUGARBABY has Sägebrecht stranded in the California desert, making friends with the kooky folks who hang out at Pounder's roadside cafe. Palance provides a special treat portraying an ex-Hollywood set decorator who becomes obsessed with painting Sägebrecht's portrait. German version runs 20m. longer. Later a TV series. [PG]▼●]

Bailiff, The SEE: **Sansho the Bailiff**

Bait (2000) **C-119m.** ** D: Antoine Fuqua. Jamie Foxx, David Morse, Kimberly Elise, Doug Hutchison, Robert Pastorelli, David Paymer, Jamie Kennedy, Mike Epps. Woefully overlong boilerplate urban comedy. A small-time crook is surgically implanted with a tracking device that the Feds think will lead them to hoods who've plundered $42 million in gold. A real mishmash, despite occasionally amusing comic shtick by Foxx, with an ugly climax involving a bomb-threatened baby. Drawing a cinematic-to-culinary correlation, film's title is extremely well chosen. Super 35. [R]▼●]

Baker's Hawk (1976) **C-98m.** *** D: Lyman D. Dayton. Clint Walker, Burl Ives, Diane Baker, Lee H. Montgomery, Alan Young, Taylor Lacher. Fine family drama about young boy (Montgomery) who befriends hermitlike Ives, and comes of age as he participates in parents' struggle against vigilante forces. Beautifully filmed on location in Utah. [G]▼●]

Baker's Wife, The (1938-French) **124m.**
***½ D: Marcel Pagnol. Raimu, Ginette
Leclerc, Charles Moulin, Robert Vattier,
Robert Brassac, Charpin. Abandoned by his
wife for a shepherd, baker Raimu is unable
to function; villagers, who love his bread as
much as he loves his wife, bring back the
wayward woman. Hilarious.▼

Balcony, The (1963) **84m.** ** D: Joseph
Strick. Shelley Winters, Peter Falk, Lee
Grant, Ruby Dee, Peter Brocco, Kent Smith,
Jeff Corey, Leonard Nimoy. Low-budget,
none-too-successful attempt to adapt Jean
Genet play to the screen, with Winters as
madam who maintains her brothel during
a revolution. Grant stands out as Winters'
lesbian confidante.▼◐

Ballad in Blue SEE: **Blues for Lovers**
Ballad of a Soldier (1959-Russian) **89m.**
*** D: Grigori Chukrai. Vladimir Ivashov,
Shanna Prokhorenko, Antonina Maximova,
Nikolai Kruchkov. Effectively simple, poetic love story chronicling the plight of Russian soldier who falls in love with country girl
while on leave during WW2. Works both as a
romantic drama and an allegory about the sadness and stupidity of war.▼◐

Ballad of Cable Hogue, The (1970)
C-121m. *** D: Sam Peckinpah. Jason
Robards, Stella Stevens, David Warner,
Strother Martin, Slim Pickens, L. Q. Jones,
R.G. Armstrong. Peckinpah's lyrical,
wholly enjoyable fable of loner who builds
a life for himself in remote part of the Old
West. Stevens has one of her best roles as
whore who joins Cable Hogue in quest for
the good life. Overlong. [R]▼◐

Ballad of Gregorio Cortez, The (1982)
C-99m. **½ D: Robert M. Young. Edward
James Olmos, James Gammon, Tom Bower,
Bruce McGill, Brion James, Alan Vint, Rosana DeSoto, Pepe Serna, William Sanderson, Barry Corbin, Tim Scott. True story, told
from several points of view, of 1901 incident
in which a young Mexican killed an American sheriff, then managed to elude a 600-man
posse for nearly two weeks! Authentic to the
core—almost like being in a time capsule, in
fact—but too subdued, especially in its portrayal of Cortez, whose plight isn't fully explained until the end of the film. [PG]▼◐

Ballad of Jack and Rose, The (2005) **C-
111m.** *½ D: Rebecca Miller. Daniel Day-
Lewis, Camilla Belle, Catherine Keener,
Paul Dano, Ryan McDonald, Jena Malone,
Jason Lee, Beau Bridges. Pretentious claptrap about an aging hippie environmental-
ist who lives in isolation on an island off
the East Coast of the U.S. with his teenage
daughter. He's dying of heart disease and
she's about to come of age, having lived
a sheltered, idyllic life; this prompts him
to ask his current companion (Keener) to
move in with them, her two teenage sons in
tow. Attempt at an ethereal fable is clunky
from the word go, despite the presence of

such solid actors as Day-Lewis, husband of
the film's writer-director. [R]▼▼

Ballad of Josie, The (1967) **C-102m.** **½
D: Andrew McLaglen. Doris Day, Peter
Graves, George Kennedy, Andy Devine,
William Talman, David Hartman, Don
Stroud. Uninspired Western spoof with
widow Day running a ranch and trying to
lead the good life. Techniscope.◐

Ballad of Little Jo, The (1993) **C-120m.**
*** D: Maggie Greenwald. Suzy Amis, Bo
Hopkins, Ian McKellen, David Chung, Carrie Snodgress, Rene Auberjonois, Heather
Graham, Sam Robards, Ruth Maleczech,
Anthony Heald, Melissa Leo. Fascinating
tale of a genteel young woman in 1866 who,
disgraced by having a child out of wedlock,
flees to the American West and quickly
learns that the only way to survive on her
own is to pretend that she's a man. Writer-
director Greenwald hits all the right notes
in this convincing and well-crafted piece of
fiction (inspired by a real-life woman), with
a first-rate cast making the most of every
incident. Amis is a revelation in the leading
role. Flavorful music score composed and
performed by David Mansfield. [R]▼◐

Ballad of Ramblin' Jack, The (2000) **C/
B&W-112m.** *** D: Aiyana Elliott. Son of
a Jewish doctor, Ramblin' Jack Elliott left
home to befriend and follow Woody Guthrie,
eventually becoming a folk music legend
himself. Engrossing documentary directed
by his somewhat estranged daughter in an
honest, unsentimental style. Ultimately,
the truth of the chronically footloose Elliott remains elusive. Among those appearing: Arlo Guthrie, Kris Kristofferson, Pete
Seeger, Odetta, and Alan Lomax.▼◐

Ballad of Tam Lin, The (1971) **C-107m.** **
D: Roddy McDowall. Ava Gardner, Ian Mc-
Shane, Stephanie Beacham, Cyril Cusack,
Richard Wattis, Sinead Cusack, Joanna
Lumley. A wealthy, beautiful woman gathers hedonistic young people around her—
and seeks to control their destinies. Based
(believe it or not) on a Robert Burns poem,
reset in England in the Swingin' Sixties.
McDowall's only directorial effort is ambitious and unusual, but unsatisfying. Shot in
1969, recut and released under various titles
including TAM LIN and THE DEVIL'S
WIDOW. Panavision. [PG]▼

Ballad of the Sad Cafe, The (1991) **C-
101m.** *½ D: Simon Callow. Vanessa Redgrave, Keith Carradine, Rod Steiger, Cork
Hubbert, Austin Pendleton, Beth Dixon,
Lanny Flaherty. Truly odd stab at filming
Depression-era tale of Southerner Redgrave,
a loner who rules rural hamlet like a despot—
until hunchback Hubbert and ex-con husband
Carradine appear. Far too theatrical in its
look, tone, and pacing; Redgrave's performance may interest drama students, but
nothing in film really works. Based on Carson
McCullers' novella (and its stage adaptation

by Edward Albee). Film directing debut of British actor/stage director Callow.▼▶

Ballast (2008) **C-94m.** *** D: Lance Hammer. Michael J. Smith, Sr., JimMyron Ross, Tarra Riggs, Johnny McPhail, Sam Dobbins, Albert Jay Levy, Dr. Sanjib Shrestha, Zachary Coleman, Anita R. Ballard. A man's sudden suicide numbs his morose twin brother (Smith), his soon-to-be-jobless widow (Riggs), and particularly his teenage druggie son (Ross). The bitter survivors reluctantly bond as a family to save their rural convenience store. Chilly, naturalistic indie doesn't have a single note of music or a smile in it, but it's got heart and a faint hope. Written and edited by the director, who shot it in Mississippi with a cast of mostly local non-pros. Super 35. ▶

Ballets Russes (2005) **C/B&W-118m.** ***½ D: Dan Geller, Dayna Goldfine. Irresistible documentary traces the rise and fall of a Russian-inspired troupe that introduced many Americans to dance in the 1930s, '40s, and '50s and launched a number of great careers. It also chronicles the creation of a rival company and the economic forces that eventually brought an end to these colorful enterprises. The dancers who appear on camera (most of them in their 80s and 90s) to recall their glory days are remarkably colorful and charismatic; a treat even if you have no particular interest in ballet.▶

Ballistic: Ecks vs. Sever (2002) **C-91m.** BOMB D: Kaos (Wych Kaosayananda). Antonio Banderas, Lucy Liu, Gregg Henry, Ray Park, Talisa Soto, Miguel Sandoval. Idiotic action film boasts what may be the worst movie title ever coined. Banderas plays an ex-FBI agent still mourning the death of his wife after seven years; his former boss recruits him for a kidnapping case by telling him his wife is still alive, and the kidnapper can lead him to her. But even that sliver of logic dissolves as the story unfolds. Only devotees of cars exploding into fireballs will find any value here. Super 35. [R] ▼▶

Ball of Fire (1941) **111m.** ***½ D: Howard Hawks. Gary Cooper, Barbara Stanwyck, Oscar Homolka, Dana Andrews, Dan Duryea, S. Z. Sakall, Richard Haydn, Henry Travers, Tully Marshall, Gene Krupa. Burlesque dancer moves in with eight prissy professors (led by Cooper) to explain "slang" for their new encyclopedia; delightful twist on *Snow White and the Seven Dwarfs* by screenwriters Billy Wilder and Charles Brackett. Remade (by same director) as A SONG IS BORN.▼▶

Balls of Fury (2007) **C-90m.** BOMB D: Robert Ben Garant. Dan Fogler, Christopher Walken, George Lopez, Maggie Q, James Hong, Terry Crews, Robert Patrick, Diedrich Bader, Aisha Tyler, Jason Scott Lee, Thomas Lennon, Patton Oswalt, Cary-Hiroyuki Tagawa, David Koechner, Kerri Kenney-Silver. Inane one-joke comedy about a has-been Ping-Pong champ enlisted for an undercover FBI mission in which his table-tennis skills are required to capture an Asian archvillain (Walken, in Fu Manchu mode). Every bit as stupid as it sounds. Fogler hams it up, while Hong, as the blind Mr. Miyagi–like mentor, steals every scene he's in, but, alas, it's petty theft. [PG-13]▶

Baltimore Bullet, The (1980) **C-103m.** **½ D: Robert Ellis Miller. James Coburn, Omar Sharif, Bruce Boxleitner, Ronee Blakley, Jack O'Halloran, Calvin Lockhart. Pleasant enough film about major-league pool hustlers Coburn and Boxleitner, and their buildup to a high noon showdown with smoothie Sharif. [PG]▼

Balto (1995) **C-77m.** **½ D: Simon Wells. Voices of Kevin Bacon, Bob Hoskins, Bridget Fonda, Jim Cummings, Phil Collins, Miriam Margolyes, Lola Bates-Campbell. Loosely based on a true story of the 1920s, Balto is a half-dog, half-wolf who overcomes his outcast past to guide a sled carrying urgent medical supplies to a town full of sick children in Alaska. Wholesome, lovingly told, and well animated, this offers humor, romance, villainy, warmth, and gives its young viewers something to think about. You could do a lot worse. Followed by two direct-to-video sequels. [G]▼●▶

Bambi (1942) **C-69m.** **** D: David Hand. Walt Disney's moving and exquisitely detailed animated feature about a deer, and how the phases of its life parallel the cycle of seasons in the forest. An extraordinary achievement, with the memorably endearing character of Thumper stealing every scene he's in. Followed by a direct-to-video sequel.▼●▶

Bamboo Saucer, The (1968) **C-100m.** **½ D: Frank Telford. Dan Duryea, John Ericson, Lois Nettleton, Nan Leslie, Bob Hastings. Better-than-average low-budget sci-fier about American and USSR teams investigating a UFO spotting in mainland China. Nettleton's tongue-in-cheek portrayal of a Russian scientist aids considerably. Duryea's last film. Aka COLLISION COURSE. [PG]▼

Bamboozled (2000) **C-135m.** ** D: Spike Lee. Damon Wayans, Savion Glover, Jada Pinkett-Smith, Tommy Davidson, Michael Rapaport, Thomas Jefferson Byrd, Paul Mooney, Sarah Jones, Mos Def, Tracy Morgan. Heavy-handed satire has eccentric TV producer Wayans pitching a deliberately offensive idea—a minstrel show for the millennium starring characters named Mantan and Sleep 'N Eat—hoping to be fired from his network. Instead, the idea takes on a life of its own. Only the vibrant performances of Glover and Davidson make this endless polemic endurable. Several celebrities appear in cameos. [R]▼

Banana Monster, The SEE: **Schlock**
Banana Peel (1964-French) **97m.** *** D:

Marcel Ophuls. Jeanne Moreau, Jean-Paul Belmondo, Gert Frobe. Rogues cheat millionaire out of a small fortune in this engaging comedy. Franscope.▶

Bananas (1971) **C-82m.** **** D: Woody Allen. Woody Allen, Louise Lasser, Carlos Montalban, Howard Cosell, Rene Enriquez, Charlotte Rae, Conrad Bain. Hilarious; the usual assortment of good jokes, bad jokes, bizarre ideas built around unlikely premise of Woody becoming involved in revolution south of the border. Funny score by Marvin Hamlisch; look for Sylvester Stallone as hoodlum, Allen Garfield as man on cross. [PG]▼●]

Bandidas (2006-U.S.-French-Mexican) **C-92m.** **½ D: Joachim Roenning, Espen Sandberg. Penélope Cruz, Salma Hayek, Steve Zahn, Dwight Yoakam, Denis Arndt, Audra Blaser, Sam Shepard. In old Mexico, farmhand Cruz and rich girl Hayek join forces as amateur outlaws when evil gringo Yoakam shoots their dads and grabs their lands. Light and full of action but not very funny; a pratfall-heavy EuroWestern, cowritten and coproduced by Luc Besson. Shepard cameos amusingly as the ladies' mentor in bank-robber protocol. Zahn, as the criminologist tracking the bosomy desperados, boasts the only nudity. Technovision. [PG-13]▶

Bandido (1956) **C-92m.** *** D: Richard Fleischer. Robert Mitchum, Zachary Scott, Ursula Thiess, Gilbert Roland, Rodolfo Acosta. Mitchum is gun supplier who tries to play both sides during 1916 Mexican rebellion; constant action, endless cat-and-mouse twists with rival Scott keep this one humming. CinemaScope.

Bandido (2004-Mexican-U.S.) **C-99m.** *½ D: Roger Christian. Carlos Gallardo, Angie Everhart, Matt Craven, Kim Coates, Ana La Salvia, Karyme Lozano. English-language film made in the spirit of EL MARIACHI by the coproducer and star of that 1992 film. Here, Gallardo plays Maximiliano Cruz (aka Bandido), a master thief coerced by the CIA to retrieve a classified computer disk from the lair of a Mexican underworld czar. Also along for the ride is tough ally Everhart; La Salvia is evil Coates' stunning wife, and prone to sumptuous milk baths. There's gunplay, stunts, music, and titillation, but little sense. Bandidon't. [R]

Bandit Queen (1994-Indian) **C-119m.** *** D: Shekhar Kapur. Seema Biswas, Nirmal Pandey, Manoj Bajpai, Rajesh Vivek, Raghuvir Yadav, Govind Namdeo. Action-packed, fact-based adventure/drama/character study of the notorious female Indian outlaw Phoolan Devi (Biswas), who emerged from a life of poverty and ritual brutalization to be charged with numerous kidnappings, robberies, and killings. Yet she remains beloved by many of her country's poor as a Robin Hood–like legend. The film

was as controversial as its subject; while based in part on diaries authored by Devi while in jail, she eventually repudiated the material.▼●]

Bandits, The (1967-Mexican) **C-89m.** ** D: Robert Conrad, Alfredo Zacharias. Robert Conrad, Jan-Michael Vincent, Roy Jenson, Pedro Armendariz, Jr., Manuel Lopez Ochoa. Ordinary Western about three cowboys, saved from the hangman's noose, who accompany their Mexican rescuer on various adventures south of the border. Unreleased here until 1979.▼

Bandits (1986-French) **C-98m.** ** D: Claude Lelouch. Jean Yanne, Marie-Sophie L. (Lelouch), Patrick Bruel, Corinne Marchand, Charles Gerard. Yanne is a criminal, just released from prison, who's out to revenge his wife's murder and become reunited with daughter Marie-Sophie L. (director Lelouch's real-life wife). Sentimental drama downplays the thrills in favor of a nostalgic approach similar to Lelouch's superior HAPPY NEW YEAR, in which Gerard played virtually an identical sidekick role. Striking widescreen photography. CinemaScope.▼

Bandits (2001) **C-123m.** **½ D: Barry Levinson. Bruce Willis, Billy Bob Thornton, Cate Blanchett, Troy Garity, Brian F. O'Byrne, Bobby Slayton, January Jones, Stacey Travis, Azura Skye. Film tells in flashback the story of two escaped convicts who become successful bank robbers, but have their lives complicated when a woman joins their roving band. Lighthearted comedy caper is a great vehicle for its three stars, and a fine showcase for Garity (son of Jane Fonda), but it becomes needlessly complicated and goes on far too long. Willis' real-life daughters play a bank manager's kids. Super 35. [PG-13]▼▶

Band of Angels (1957) **C-127m.** **½ D: Raoul Walsh. Clark Gable, Yvonne De Carlo, Sidney Poitier, Efrem Zimbalist, Jr., Patric Knowles. Flat costume epic from Robert Penn Warren's Civil War novel; Gable is Southern gentleman with shady past, in love with high-toned De Carlo who discovers she has Negro ancestors. Poitier is resolute educated slave. ▼●]

Band of Outsiders (1964-French) **97m.** *** D: Jean-Luc Godard. Anna Karina, Sami Frey, Claude Brasseur, Louisa Colpeyn. Karina enlists the aid of two male hoods to swipe her aunt's stash, but as usual the supposed plot is only a jumping-off point for Godard's commentary on Hollywood melodramas and other 20th-century artifacts. Among the more entertaining of the director's output; looks delightfully mellow today.▼▶

Band of the Hand (1986) **C-109m.** BOMB D: Paul Michael Glaser. Stephen Lang, Michael Carmine, Lauren Holly, John Cameron Mitchell, James Remar, Gerrit

Graham. Five Miami punks are whipped into shape by a Vietnam vet, then form a vigilante unit to wipe out drug dealers. Moronic, way overlong junk from the creators of *Miami Vice*; Bob Dylan (*why*, Bob?) sings the title tune. [R] ▼◐●

Bandolero! (1968) C-106m. **½ D: Andrew V. McLaglen. James Stewart, Dean Martin, Raquel Welch, George Kennedy, Andrew Prine, Will Geer. Jimmy and Dino play outlaw brothers whose gang flees across Mexican border with Raquel as hostage. Not exactly like real life, but nice outdoor photography makes it passable escapism. Panavision. [PG] ▼●

Bandslam (2009) C-111m. **½ D: Todd Graff. Aly Michalka, Vanessa Hudgens, Gaelan Connell, Scott Porter, Ryan Donowho, Lisa Kudrow, Charlie Saxton, Tim Jo. Bright teen comedy is better than you'd expect considering its generic title. Story revolves around a group of outcast kids putting together a rock group and entering a battle of the bands. Movie gets its zip and fresh-faced appeal from Connell, who plays the lead with a charming verve and originality missing from most formulaic teen movies. The music isn't half bad either. Writer-director Graff revealed his simpatico for offbeat kid culture in his debut film, CAMP. [PG]●

Band's Visit, The (2007-Israeli-French-U.S.) C-87m. *** D: Eran Kolirin. Sasson Gabai, Ronit Elkabetz, Saleh Bakri, Khalifa Natour, Imad Jabarin, Tarak Kopty. Imperial Egyptian police band arrives in Israel to perform at an Arab cultural center and promptly gets lost. Stranded overnight in a remote desert town, the band members and even their stiff, formal leader (Gabai) socialize with the locals. Disarming minimalist comedy brings to mind such Czech New Wave films as THE FIREMEN'S BALL as it explores cultural differences with deftness and charm. Feature debut for writer-director Kolirin. [PG-13]●

Band Wagon, The (1953) C-112m. **** D: Vincente Minnelli. Fred Astaire, Cyd Charisse, Oscar Levant, Nanette Fabray, Jack Buchanan. Sophisticated backstage musical improves with each viewing. Astaire plays a "washed-up" movie star who tries his luck on Broadway, under the direction of maniacal genius Buchanan. Musical highlights include "Dancing in the Dark," "Shine on Your Shoes," "That's Entertainment," and Astaire's Mickey Spillane spoof "The Girl Hunt." Written by Betty Comden and Adolph Green, based on the 1931 Broadway musical by Howard Dietz and Arthur Schwartz, incorporating many of their songs. ▼●

Bang (1997) C-98m. *** D: Ash. Darling Narita, Peter Greene, Michael Newland, Luis Guzar, Lucy Liu. A desperate, unemployed actress (Narita) finds personal meaning and

empowerment when she masquerades as a policewoman for a day. She also gets much more than she bargains for. Provocative look at L.A. on the brink. Film's shoestring budget and handheld camera work to brutally powerful effect despite uneven performances. ▼●

Bang, Bang, You're Dead! (1966-British) C-92m. **½ D: Don Sharp. Tony Randall, Senta Berger, Terry-Thomas, Herbert Lom, Wilfrid Hyde-White. Unsuspecting Randall gets involved with Moroccan gangsters in OK spoof; good location shooting. Shown on TV as BANG BANG!▼

Banger Sisters, The (2002) C-98m. **½ D: Bob Dolman. Goldie Hawn, Susan Sarandon, Geoffrey Rush, Robin Thomas, Erika Christensen, Eva Amurri. Onetime rock groupie who's never quite grown up goes to visit her friend and partner in crime, whom she hasn't seen in 20 years, only to find her transformed into a model wife, mother, and civic leader. Entertaining fluff is a good vehicle for Hawn and Sarandon, but can't stand up to any real scrutiny. Hawn's character makes an interesting bookend to daughter Kate Hudson's role in ALMOST FAMOUS. Amurri is Sarandon's real-life daughter. Written by the director. Panavision. [R] ▼●

Bangkok Dangerous (2008) C-99m. BOMB D: The Pang Brothers. Nicolas Cage, Shahkrit Yamnarm, Charlie Young, Panward Hemmanee, Nirattisai Kaljaruek, Dom Hetrakul. Unwisely choosing to remake their own 1999 Hong Kong success, the Pang Brothers drop the ball in this uninspired, incomprehensible rehash about an anonymous hit man sent to Thailand, where he teams up with an impressionable young man and falls for a local deaf girl. Typical lowbrow action merges uncomfortably with awkward romantic subplot. Cage is out of his element in this Pang-ful misfire. Call it BANGKOK BORING. [R]●

Bang the Drum Slowly (1973) C-97m. ***½ D: John Hancock. Michael Moriarty, Robert De Niro, Vincent Gardenia, Phil Foster, Ann Wedgeworth, Patrick McVey, Heather MacRae, Selma Diamond, Barbara Babcock, Tom Ligon, Nicolas Surovy, Danny Aiello. Touching study of two professional baseball players on fictional N.Y. team drawn to each other under unusual circumstances. Outstanding performances by two leads (Moriarty as hustling star pitcher, De Niro as simpleton catcher) in slightly longish, episodic script. Screenplay by Mark Harris, based on his 1956 novel; first dramatized on TV, with Paul Newman. Aiello's film debut. [PG] ▼●

Bank, The (2001-Australian-Italian) C-99m. **½ D: Robert Connolly. David Wenham, Anthony LaPaglia, Sibylla Budd, Steve Rodgers, Mitchell Butel, Kazuhiro Muroyama. Brilliant econometrist Wenham believes he's created a computer program that can predict stock-market crashes. LaPaglia is a ruthless bank executive ready to capitalize on anything (or anyone) to make a buck. Aims to be a slick intellectual financial thriller but never finds the right tone or pace, despite an interesting premise and good performances. ▼●)

Bank Dick, The (1940) 74m. **** D: Eddie Cline. W. C. Fields, Cora Witherspoon, Una Merkel, Evelyn Del Rio, Jessie Ralph, Grady Sutton, Franklin Pangborn, Shemp Howard, Russell Hicks, Reed Hadley. Classic of insane humor loosely wound about a no-account who becomes a bank guard; Sutton as nitwit prospective son-in-law, Pangborn as bank examiner match the shenanigans of Fields. Screenplay by "Mahatma Kane Jeeves." ▼●)

Bank Job, The (2008-British) C-111m. **½ D: Roger Donaldson. Jason Statham, Saffron Burrows, Richard Lintern, Stephen Campbell Moore, Daniel Mays, Peter Bowles, Keeley Hawes, Colin Salmon, Peter De Jersey, James Faulkner, David Suchet. Tired of just getting by on a series of dodgy schemes, Statham agrees to participate in a daring bank heist engineered by beautiful Burrows—but doesn't know she's acting on behalf of British Intelligence, which needs the contents of a particular safe-deposit box. Well-plotted caper inspired by a real-life 1971 incident known in London as the "Walkie-Talkie Robbery," but as it grows dark and violent it ceases to be fun. HD Widescreen. [R]❚

Bank Robber (1993) C-94m. BOMB D: Nick Mead. Patrick Dempsey, Lisa Bonet, Olivia d'Abo, Forest Whitaker, Judge Reinhold, Mariska Hargitay, Michael Jeter, Joe Alaskey. If you want to kill time, this film beats it to death . . . slowly and painfully. Dempsey plays a robber who pulls one last job and ends up hiding out in a seedy hotel where his anonymity comes at a price. Whitaker and Reinhold are "sensitive" officers looking for him; Bonet plays the good-hearted prostitute who falls for the robber. Video version trimmed for R rating. [NC-17]▼●

Bank Shot (1974) C-83m. *** D: Gower Champion. George C. Scott, Joanna Cassidy, Sorrell Booke, G. Wood, Clifton James, Bob Balaban, Bibi Osterwald. Fast-paced, engagingly nutty comedy with criminal mastermind Scott planning a literal bank robbery—making off with the entire building! Based on the novel by Donald Westlake, a sequel to THE HOT ROCK (with Scott in the role played by Robert Redford in the film version of that book). Panavision. [PG]▼

Banning (1967) C-102m. *** D: Ron Winston. Robert Wagner, Anjanette Comer, Jill St. John, Guy Stockwell, James Farentino, Susan Clark, Howard St. John, Mike Kel-

lin, Gene Hackman, Sean Garrison, Logan Ramsey. Entertaining soap opera about corruption and infidelity in and about a swank L.A. golf club. Wagner is the pro with a past, St. John a love-hungry young woman. Music score by Quincy Jones. Techniscope.

B*A*P*S (1997) C-91m. *½ D: Robert Townsend. Halle Berry, Natalie Desselle, Ian Richardson, Martin Landau, Luigi Amodeo, Jonathan Fried, Bernie Mac. With a dream of earning $10,000, waitresses Berry and Desselle (Black American Princesses) head for L.A. where, in contrived movie fashion, they wind up living in the mansion of fabulously wealthy Landau. This silly, fairy-tale-ish spin on the fish-out-of-water comedy formula falls flat on its face. Various sports and music personalities show up in cameos. [PG-13]▼●

Barabbas (1961) C-137m. *** D: Richard Fleischer. Anthony Quinn, Silvana Mangano, Arthur Kennedy, Jack Palance, Ernest Borgnine, Katy Jurado. Lavish production, coupled with good script (based on Lagerkvist's novel) and generally fine acting by large cast make for engrossing, literate experience. Overly long. Super Technirama 70. ▼

Baraka (1992) C-96m. *** D: Ron Fricke. Strikingly visual, insightful *National Geographic* issue come to life, which tells the story of the evolution of Earth and Mankind, and the manner in which man relates to his environment. Shot on location in 24 countries. There's no dialogue, only sounds and images; this will lose much of its effect on the small screen. Todd-AO 70mm. ▼

Baran (2001-Iranian) C-94m. ***½ D: Majid Majidi. Hossein Abedini, Zahra Bahrami. Terminal goof-off on a construction crew becomes a man when he experiences love from afar. Abedini is shocked to discover that the Afghanistan refugee he's been mocking is a woman in dire straits—and a pretty one at that. Crowd pleaser with strong, accessible characters also benefits from Majidi's credentials as a visual poet. [PG]▼)

Barbarella (1968-French-Italian) C-98m. **½ D. Roger Vadim. Jane Fonda, John Phillip Law, Anita Pallenberg, Milo O'Shea, David Hemmings, Marcel Marceau, Claude Dauphin, Ugo Tognazzi. Midnight-movie favorite based on popular French comic strip about sexy 41st-century space adventuress. Not especially funny, but watchable, with Fonda's strip-tease during opening credits the principal reason for its cult status. Trivia footnote: rock group Duran Duran took its name from O'Shea's character. Aka BARBARELLA, QUEEN OF THE GALAXY. Panavision. [PG]▼●)

Barbarian and the Geisha, The (1958)

C-105m. **½ D: John Huston. John Wayne, Eiko Ando, Sam Jaffe, So Yamamura. Twisting of 19th-century history allows Wayne as Ambassador Townsend Harris to romance Japanese beauty (Ando). Miscasting of Wayne is ludicrous, throwing costumer amuck. CinemaScope.▼

Barbarian Invasions, The (2003-Canadian-French) **C-99m. ***** D:** Denys Arcand. Rémy Girard, Stéphane Rousseau, Marie-Josée Croze, Marina Hands, Dorothée Berryman, Johanne-Marie Tremblay, Dominique Michel, Louise Portal, Yves Jacques, Pierre Curzi. Arcand reunites the characters from his 1986 film THE DECLINE OF THE AMERICAN EMPIRE as they gather to embrace one of their group who is dying. An estranged son flies to his bedside out of a sense of duty, but winds up using his smarts (and money) to help his father through the last phase of his life as peacefully and happily as he can. Arcand's extraordinary script deals with mortality, sexuality, dreams and hopes unfulfilled, the power of money, the erosion of intelligence, and much, much more. A rare film that is both cerebral and emotional; satiric, sophisticated, witty, and profoundly moving. Original Quebec release ran 18m. longer. Oscar winner for Best Foreign Language Film. Super 35. [R]▼◑

Barbarians, The (1987) **C-87m. *½ D:** Ruggero Deodato. David Paul, Peter Paul, Richard Lynch, Eva La Rue, Virginia Bryant, Sheeba Alahani, Michael Berryman. Staggeringly silly sword-and-sorcery saga starring two awesome-looking bodybuilders (brothers in real life), whose main achievement is keeping a straight face while mouthing their dialogue. [R]▼◑

Barbaric Beast of Boggy Creek, The, Part II (1985) **C-91m. ** D:** Charles B. Pierce. Charles B. Pierce, Cindy Butler, Serene Hedin, Chuck Pierce, Jimmy Clem. Slight, forgettable story of anthropology professor Pierce, who leads an expedition to find the Boggy Creek monster. Although titled "Part II," this is the third journey to Boggy Creek, following THE LEGEND OF . . . and RETURN TO . . . Filmed in 1983. Formerly titled BOGGY CREEK II. [PG]▼◑

Barbarosa (1982) **C-90m. *** D:** Fred Schepisi. Willie Nelson, Gary Busey, Isela Vega, Gilbert Roland, Danny De La Paz, George Voskovec. Nelson is fine as legendary, free-spirited outlaw constantly on the lam, with able support from Busey as country boy who becomes his protégé. Solid Western, flavorfully directed by Schepisi. Panavision. [PG]▼◑

Barbary Coast (1935) **90m. ***½ D:** Howard Hawks. Miriam Hopkins, Edward G. Robinson, Joel McCrea, Walter Brennan, Frank Craven, Brian Donlevy. Lusty tale of San Francisco in the late 19th century with dance-hall queen Hopkins running head-on

into big-shot Robinson. David Niven can be glimpsed as an extra.▼◑◑

Barbershop (2002) **C-102m. *** D:** Tim Story. Ice Cube, Anthony Anderson, Cedric the Entertainer, Sean Patrick Thomas, Eve, Troy Garity, Michael Ealy, Leonard Earl Howze, Keith David. Entertaining comedy about a neighborhood Chicago barbershop, which Ice Cube has inherited from his father; the burden of running this threadbare business puts a crimp in his dreams, but he begins to change his mind after one eventful day in the shop, which serves as a community gathering place. Canny screenplay manages to embrace many points of view, which counterbalances its sentimentality—and overlength. Followed by a sequel, and a spinoff, BEAUTY SHOP. [PG-13]▼◑

Barbershop 2: Back in Business (2004) **C-98m. **½ D:** Kevin Rodney Sullivan. Ice Cube, Cedric the Entertainer, Sean Patrick Thomas, Eve, Troy Garity, Michael Ealy, Leonard Earl Howze, Harry Lennix, Robert Wisdom, Jazsmin Lewis, Kenan Thompson, Garcelle Beauvais-Nilon, Queen Latifah. Neighborhood barbershop owner Ice Cube and his staff face the imminent arrival of a flashy, upscale haircutting salon right across the street. If you liked the first film, chances are you'll enjoy revisiting the characters, even in this contrived sequel. [PG-13]▼◑

Barb Wire (1996) **C-90m. ** D:** David Hogan. Pamela Anderson Lee, Temuera Morrison, Victoria Rowell, Jack Noseworthy, Steve Railsback. In 2017, the U.S. is run by a fascist dictatorship. Lee is a bounty hunter and nightclub owner living in a city on the fringe of freedom. Her former lover asks her to help him spirit his wife into Canada to help the rebellion. Lots of gaudy but uninvolving action; surly, pneumatic Lee is no actress, just a 15-year-old boy's fantasy figure. Actually rips off the plot of CASABLANCA! Also available in unrated video version. [R]▼◑

Barcelona (1994) **C-100m. **½ D:** Whit Stillman. Taylor Nichols, Chris Eigeman, Tushka Bergen, Mira Sorvino, Pep Munne, Nuria Badia, Hellena Schmied, Francis Creighton, Thomas Gibson, Jack Gilpin. Young, nerdy American businessman (Nichols) living in Spain is joined by his Naval officer cousin (Eigeman); the two woo a variety of women and debate anti-American attitudes and actions that prevail among the local populace. Set in the concluding months of the Cold War, film's theme is admirably original, and often amusing, if not always compelling. Writer-director Stillman's second offbeat talkfest (following METROPOLITAN) isn't quite as focused as the first, though reteaming of male costars is a plus.▼◑

Barefoot Contessa, The (1954) **C-128m.**

*** D: Joseph L. Mankiewicz. Humphrey Bogart, Ava Gardner, Edmond O'Brien, Marius Goring, Rossano Brazzi, Valentina Cortesa, Elizabeth Sellars, Warren Stevens. Cynical tale of beautiful Spanish dancer Gardner and how director Bogart makes her a Hollywood star. Mankiewicz's script is full of juicy dialogue, as usual. O'Brien won an Oscar as the press agent. ▼●)

Barefoot Executive, The (1971) C-96m. ****** D: Robert Butler. Kurt Russell, Joe Flynn, Harry Morgan, Wally Cox, Heather North, Alan Hewitt, John Ritter. Russell discovers chimp with ability to pick top-rated TV shows, and becomes vice-president of a network. Routine Disney slapstick. Remade for TV in 1995. [G] ▼▌

Barefoot in the Park (1967) C-105m. ******* D: Gene Saks. Robert Redford, Jane Fonda, Charles Boyer, Mildred Natwick, Herb Edelman, Mabel Albertson, Fritz Feld, Doris Roberts. Plotless, entertaining Neil Simon comedy finds Fonda and Redford newlyweds in five-story walkup apartment. Running gag about climbing stairs grows thin, but film doesn't. Redford and Natwick recreate their Broadway roles; Saks' screen directing debut. Later, briefly a TV series with an all-black cast. ▼●)

Barfly (1987) C-97m. ******* D: Barbet Schroeder. Mickey Rourke, Faye Dunaway, Alice Krige, Jack Nance, J.C. Quinn, Frank Stallone. Surprisingly enjoyable portrait of L.A. lowlife, and boozy, foolishly macho writer Henry Chinaski, played with comic bravado by Rourke. Dunaway is exceptional as his alcoholic soulmate. Based on the autobiographical writings of cult favorite Charles Bukowski, who can be glimpsed on one of the bar stools. Veteran character actor Fritz Feld has a lovely bit as a bum who gives Dunaway a light. Matt Dillon later played Chinaski in FACTOTUM. [R] ▼●)

Bar Girls (1994) C-95m. ****½** D: Marita Giovanni. Nancy Allison Wolfe, Liza D'Agostino, Camila Griggs, Justine Slater, Lisa Parker, Pam Raines. Amiable (if flawed) romantic comedy with a twist: all of its major characters are lesbians who congregate at L.A.'s Girl Bar. The main character is obsessive, wryly funny Loretta (Wolfe), a female Woody Allen who is forever seeking a perfect significant other while not quite understanding what it means to truly and completely love another person. The film's shortcomings are compensated for by clever dialogue and believable characters. Adapted for the screen by Lauran Hoffman from her play. [R] ▼●)

Barkleys of Broadway, The (1949) C-109m. ******* D: Charles Walters. Fred Astaire, Ginger Rogers, Oscar Levant, Billie Burke, Gale Robbins. Astaire and Rogers reteamed after ten years in this witty Comden-Green

script about show biz couple who split, then make up. Songs include "You'd Be Hard to Replace," "They Can't Take That Away from Me." Ginger reading "La Marseillaise" is a definite low point. ▼●)

Barney's Great Adventure (1997) C-75m. ****** D: Steve Gomer. George Hearn, Shirley Douglas, Trevor Morgan, Kyla Pratt, Diana Rice, David Joyner, Jeff Ayres. Preschoolers who cannot get enough of TV's Big Purple Dinosaur will take to this, Barney's first feature, in which he mixes with some kids on a farm; together, they set off on an adventure in search of a missing egg. Inoffensive, to be sure, but for anyone over five it's a real yawn. [G] ▼●)

Barney's Version (2010-Canadian-Italian) C-134m. ******* D: Richard J. Lewis. Paul Giamatti, Dustin Hoffman, Rosamund Pike, Minnie Driver, Rachelle Lefevre, Bruce Greenwood, Saul Rubinek, Scott Speedman, Mark Addy, Jake Hoffman, Maury Chaykin. Hack TV producer Barney Panofsky hasn't led an exemplary life, as we learn looking back at his Bohemian adventures in Rome and several marriages—not to mention the pursuit of a beautiful guest at his own (second) wedding. Colorful if free adaptation of Mordecai Richler's novel benefits from vivid performances by Giamatti and a perfectly matched Hoffman as his socially embarrassing father. Hoffman's real-life son Jake plays Giamatti's son Michael. Film buffs may enjoy spotting prominent Canadian directors David Cronenberg, Atom Egoyan, Denys Arcand, and Ted Kotcheff in cameo roles. [R] ▌

Barnyard (2006) C-90m. ****** D: Steve Oedekerk. Voices of Kevin James, Courteney Cox, Sam Elliott, Danny Glover, Wanda Sykes, Andie MacDowell, David Koechner, Jeff Garcia, Cam Clarke, Dom Irrera, Laraine Newman. Animated zaniness set on a farm where, after sundown, the animals turn the barn into a raucous nightclub. James is Otis, a cow who won't mature, much to the chagrin of his father, Ben (Elliott), who keeps watch for preying coyotes while the others party. Unspectacular, though there are commendable messages for kids regarding adoption and parenting. Irrera stands out as Duke the Dog. Written by the director. [PG] ▌

Baron Blood (1972-Italian) C-90m. ****½** D: Mario Bava. Joseph Cotten, Elke Sommer, Massimo Girotti, Rada Rassimov, Antonio Cantafora. Descendant of evil nobleman attempts "novel" rejuvenation principles. Standard plot livened by unusual settings and lighting. Aka THE TORTURE CHAMBER OF BARON BLOOD. Italian version runs longer. [PG] ▼●)

Baron Müenchhausen (1943-German) C-110m. ******* D: Josef von Baky. Hans Albers, Brigitte Horney, Wilhelm Bendow, Leo Slezak, Ferdinand Marian. Lavish, impressive curio which tells of the legendary, free-spirited Baron, his exploits in Russia, Turkey, Venice, and elsewhere, and his quest for beautiful princesses and empresses. While ostensibly an escapist entertainment, the Baron is an heroic German: noble, shrewd, and ever loyal to the Fatherland. Produced on the order of Goebbels, Hitler's Minister of Propaganda and Public Enlightenment, to mark the 25th anniversary of UFA, the German production studio. This would make a fascinating (if overlong) double bill with Terry Gilliam's THE ADVENTURES OF BARON MUNCHAUSEN. ▼▶

Baron of Arizona, The (1950) **96m.** **½ D: Samuel Fuller. Vincent Price, Ellen Drew, Beulah Bondi, Reed Hadley. Price has field day as landgrabbing scoundrel who almost gains control of Arizona in the 19th century. Based on a real-life historical incident. Fuller also scripted. ▼▶

Barquero (1970) **C-115m.** *½ D: Gordon Douglas. Lee Van Cleef, Warren Oates, Forrest Tucker, Kerwin Mathews, Mariette Hartley. Bad guy Oates, on the run after wiping out a town, has to deal with Van Cleef, a feisty ferry operator. [PG]

Barretts of Wimpole Street, The (1934) **110m.** *** D: Sidney Franklin. Norma Shearer, Fredric March, Charles Laughton, Maureen O'Sullivan, Katharine Alexander, Una O'Connor, Ian Wolfe. Handsome, well-acted, and most entertaining MGM production of classic romance between Elizabeth Barrett and Robert Browning in 19th-century England. Director Franklin remade this two decades later. Retitled for TV: FORBIDDEN ALLIANCE. ▼●

Barretts of Wimpole Street, The (1957-U.S.-British) **C-105m.** **½ D: Sidney Franklin. Jennifer Jones, John Gielgud, Bill Travers, Virginia McKenna. Tame interpretation of the lilting romance between poets Browning and Barrett, with actors bogged down in prettified fluff. Director Franklin fared better with this in 1934. CinemaScope. ▼●

Barrier (1966-Polish) **84m.** **½ D: Jerzy Skolimowski. Joanna Szczerbic, Jan Nowicki, Tadeusz Lomnicki, Maria Malicka. Interesting view of youthful attitudes in Poland, combining reportage with fantasy elements. Not a total success, but still intriguing.

Barry Lyndon (1975-British) **C-183m.** ***½ D: Stanley Kubrick. Ryan O'Neal, Marisa Berenson. Patrick Magee, Hardy Kruger, Steven Berkoff, Gay Hamilton, Murray Melvin, Frank Middlemass, Andre Morell, Leonard Rossiter, Marie Kean; narrated by Michael Hordern. Exquisite, meticulously detailed period piece stars O'Neal as Thackeray's 18th-century Irish rogue-hero who covets success but lets it go to his head. Long, deliberately paced but never boring. Won Oscars for John Alcott's photography, Leonard Rosenman's adaptation of period music, Art

Direction–Set Decoration, and Costume Design. Screenplay by Kubrick. [PG] ▼●

Barry McKenzie Holds His Own (1974-Australian) **C-93m.** *½ D: Bruce Beresford. Barry Crocker, Barry Humphries, Donald Pleasence, Dick Bentley, Louis Negin. Idiotic follow-up to THE ADVENTURES OF BARRY MCKENZIE, about oafish title character, his twin brother (both played by Crocker), and one Edna Everage (Humphries, in drag), who is kidnapped and taken to Transylvania. Panavision. ▼

Barry Munday (2010) **C-95m.** ** D: Chris D'Arienzo. Patrick Wilson, Judy Greer, Chloë Sevigny, Jean Smart, Cybill Shepherd, Malcolm McDowell, Billy Dee Williams, Shea Whigham, Missi Pyle, Christopher McDonald, Colin Hanks, Mae Whitman. Sexist slacker gets a shock when he's informed that he has impregnated a woman he doesn't even remember having sex with. Then, miraculously, he responds to the idea of being a father and tries to straighten himself out. Fine cast can only do so much with mediocre material; the film almost redeems itself toward the end, but the characters are so obnoxious and sketchily drawn that it's hardly worth the effort to get there. [R] ▶

Bartleby (1970-British) **C-78m.** **½ D: Anthony Friedmann. Paul Scofield, John McEnery, Thorley Walters, Colin Jeavons, Raymond Mason. Herman Melville's great short story about 19th-century auditing clerk who refuses to leave job after he is fired is admirably attempted in modern-day update, even though story doesn't really lend itself to filming; Scofield is fine as bewildered but sympathetic boss. Remade in 2002. ▼●

Bartleby (2002) **C-82m.** ** D: Jonathan Parker. Crispin Glover, David Paymer, Glenne Headly, Maury Chaykin, Joe Piscopo, Seymour Cassel, Carrie Snodgress, Dick Martin. Quiet Bartleby (Glover) is hired by Paymer to file public records. At first he's energetic, but in response to an innocuous request he replies, "I would prefer not to," and soon is saying it in response to all requests. Colorfully acted adaptation of the Herman Melville story, but cowriter-director Parker strains for effect and diminishes the already unfocused satire by making everyone loony. [PG-13] ▼▶

Barton Fink (1991) **C-117m.** **½ D: Joel Coen. John Turturro, John Goodman, Judy Davis, Michael Lerner, John Mahoney, Tony Shalhoub, Jon Polito, Steve Buscemi, David Warrilow, Richard Portnow, Christopher Murney. Self-important N.Y. playwright Turturro comes to Hollywood in 1941 to write a screenplay, and finds it a living hell—in more ways than one. Barbed look at vintage Hollywood, filled with incredible detail and amazing scenes; told in Joel and Ethan Coen's typically flamboyant visual style. BUT, at a crucial point the film takes a sharp left turn toward the bizarre, and never returns. Great performances all around. [R]▼◖◗

BASEketball (1998) **C-103m.** ** D: David Zucker. Trey Parker, Matt Stone, Yasmine Bleeth, Jenny McCarthy, Robert Vaughn, Ernest Borgnine, Dian Bachar, Trevor Einhorn, Bob Costas, Al Michaels, Robert Stack. Sporadically funny gross-out comedy about two goofballs who invent a driveway basketball game that soon sweeps the country—and turns them into professional athletes. Some funny gags, but a surprisingly pedestrian storyline makes it sag. Starring (but not written by) the creators of TV's *South Park.* Recommended for anyone eager to see Borgnine sing "I'm Too Sexy for My Shirt." [R]▼◖◗

Basic (2003) **C-95m.** ** D: John McTiernan. John Travolta, Connie Nielsen, Samuel L. Jackson, Giovanni Ribisi, Brian Van Holt, Taye Diggs, Cristián De La Fuente, Dash Mihok, Tim Daly, Roselyn Sanchez, Harry Connick, Jr. When things go awry during a military training exercise, base commander Daly calls in Travolta, the best interrogator he ever had, to question the remaining members of the group, whose stories don't add up. Essentially a whodunit, this film keeps adding layers of confusion so that it becomes less interesting as it goes along! The final "twist" seems to negate the entire story, like a bad shaggy-dog joke. Travolta is in great form, however. Panavision. [R]▼◖◗

Basic Instinct (1992) **C-127m.** *** D: Paul Verhoeven. Michael Douglas, Sharon Stone, George Dzundza, Jeanne Tripplehorn, Denis Arndt, Leilani Sarelle, Bruce A. Young, Chelcie Ross, Dorothy Malone, Wayne Knight, Stephen Tobolowsky. In-your-face sex thriller, with Douglas as a San Francisco cop who's fatally attracted to a key suspect in an ice-pick murder: brazenly sexy (and manipulative) Stone. Audacious, erotic, and larger-than-life—with an ending that falls short of real satisfaction. Released overseas in an unrated version that's even *more* sexually explicit! Both versions are available on video. The notorious eight shots of erotic grappling totaling 42 seconds were added for video. Followed by a sequel. Panavision. [R]▼◖◗

Basic Instinct 2 (2006-U.S.-German) **C-114m.** ** D: Michael Caton-Jones. Sharon Stone, David Morrissey, Charlotte Rampling, David Thewlis, Hugh Dancy, Iain Robertson, Stan Collymore. Long-gestating sequel to the notorious 1992 hit isn't the embarrassment you might have expected—or hoped for. What should have been high camp is instead a rather dull psychological-sexual thriller in which slippery novelist Catherine Tramell is up to her old tricks in London when a male companion turns up dead in her car. Did she or didn't she? Stone makes the best of this and looks sensational

while the impressive British cast tries hard to keep it afloat. Super 35. [R]◖◗

Basil (1998) **C-102m.** ** D: Radha Bharadwaj. Jared Leto, Christian Slater, Claire Forlani, Derek Jacobi, Rachel Pickup, David Ross. Turn-of-the-20th-century tale about a young aristocrat who (with the help of a mysterious friend) becomes entangled with a beautiful but selfish temptress. Murky slice of Gothic suffers from sluggish pacing and lack of passion. Leto struggles with his British accent and the lovely Forlani has one haughty facial expression for every emotion. Based on a Wilkie Collins novel. Never theatrically released. [R]▼◖◗

Basileus Quartet (1982-French-Italian) **C-118m.** *** D: Fabio Carpi. Pierre Malet, Hector Alterio, Omero Antonutti, Michel Vitold, Alain Cuny, Gabriele Ferzetti, Lisa Kreuzer. A violinist suddenly dies and his colleagues, who have lived only for music, must get on with their lives—which are profoundly altered by the young replacement for the deceased. Stark, quietly absorbing, beautifully realized.▼◖◗

Basketball Diaries, The (1995) **C-100m.** ** D: Scott Kalvert. Leonardo DiCaprio, Lorraine Bracco, Bruno Kirby, Marilyn Sokol, Mark Wahlberg, James Modio, Ernie Hudson. Drably downbeat and none-too-stylish rendering of poet-musician Jim Carroll's '60s recollections of heroin abuse and on-court prowess at a N.Y.C. Catholic school. DiCaprio is well cast in role intended for River Phoenix, but imprecise updating from Carroll's very specific time frame leads to a fuzzy point of view. [R]▼◖◗

Basket Case (1982) **C-91m.** **½ D: Frank Henenlotter. Kevin Van Hentenryck, Terri Susan Smith, Beverly Bonner, Robert Vogel, Diana Browne. Extremely self-conscious but intriguing tongue-in-cheek low-budget horror film about a twin who arrives in N.Y.C. from a small town carrying his deformed telepathic mutant brother in a basket. Some interesting animated sequences in this John Waters-ish film that boasts some effective horror moments. Followed by several sequels. [R]▼◖◗

Basket Case 2 (1990) **C-89m.** BOMB D: Frank Henenlotter. Kevin Van Hentenryck, Annie Ross, Jason Evers, Kathryn Meisle, Heather Rattray, Ted Sorel. Van Hentenryck and his monstrously deformed twin brother take refuge in a house of freaks, but are tracked down by tabloid reporter. Arch, pseudo-hip film totally lacks the conviction of the first; icy cold. [R]▼◖◗

Basket Case 3 (1992) **C-90m.** *½ D: Frank Henenlotter. Kevin Van Hentenryck, Annie Ross, Gil Roper, Tina Louise Hilbert, Dan Biggers, Jim O'Doherty. Van Hentenryck is separated from his deformed brother, who fathers a set of duodectuplets when the house of freaks from previous entry moves to Georgia. Flatly photographed, with a meandering, uninvolving plot. More serious than previous entry, but still strains for laughs. [R] ▼◐●

Basquiat (1996) **C-108m.** **½ D: Julian Schnabel. Jeffrey Wright, David Bowie, Dennis Hopper, Gary Oldman, Willem Dafoe, Michael Wincott, Benicio Del Toro, Claire Forlani, Parker Posey, Christopher Walken, Courtney Love, Tatum O'Neal, Paul Bartel, Sam Rockwell. Meandering though not uninteresting bio of controversial black artist Jean-Michel Basquiat, who went from unknown graffiti practitioner to spent comet between 1981 and 1987. The movie doesn't capture the presumed intensity of a rapid career ascent before death from heroin at 28. Yet the supporting cast is rich, topped by Bowie's portrayal of Andy Warhol, which is precise even down to the pasty skin. Look carefully at the chic party guests Basquiat spies through the gallery window, and you'll spot Isabella Rossellini. Directorial debut for artist Schnabel, who also scripted. [R] ▼◐●

Bat, The (1959) **80m.** **½ D: Crane Wilbur. Vincent Price, Agnes Moorehead, Gavin Gordon, John Sutton, Lenita Lane, Elaine Edwards, Darla Hood. Faithful filming of the Mary Roberts Rinehart–Avery Hopwood play, with mystery writer Moorehead renting an eerie mansion for the summer; she and her maid soon are plagued by the title fiend. Filmed before in 1915, 1926, and (as THE BAT WHISPERS) in 1930. ▼◐●

Bataan (1943) **114m.** *** D: Tay Garnett. Robert Taylor, George Murphy, Thomas Mitchell, Lloyd Nolan, Lee Bowman, Robert Walker, Desi Arnaz, Barry Nelson. Realistically made drama of famous WW2 incident on Pacific island; good combat scenes. Also shown in computer-colored version. ▼◐

Bathing Beauty (1944) **C-101m.** **½ D: George Sidney. Red Skelton, Esther Williams, Basil Rathbone, Ethel Smith, Xavier Cugat, Lina Romay, Harry James and His Orchestra. Esther's first starring vehicle gives Skelton and musical guest stars the spotlight most of the way, but does have a spectacular aquatic finale. Silly script, thankless role for Rathbone. ▼◐●

Batman (1966) **C-105m.** ** D: Leslie Martinson. Adam West, Burt Ward, Burgess Meredith, Cesar Romero, Frank Gorshin, Lee Meriwether, Neil Hamilton, Madge Blake, Reginald Denny. Quickly made feature to cash in on then-hot TV series pulls out all stops, features the Joker, Riddler, Penguin, and Catwoman trying to undo the caped crusader. Really misses the mark; the campy humor worked better in the TV series. ▼◐●

Batman (1989) **C-126m.** **½ D: Tim Burton. Jack Nicholson, Michael Keaton, Kim Basinger, Robert Wuhl, Pat Hingle, Billy Dee Williams, Michael Gough, Jack Palance, Jerry Hall, Tracey Walter, Lee Wallace. There's razzle-dazzle to spare in this dark, intense variation on Bob Kane's comic book creation—but there's also something askew when the villain (a particularly psychotic villain, played overboard by Nicholson) is so much more potent than the hero! Still, lots to grab your attention, including Anton Furst's Oscar-winning production design and Danny Elfman's terrific score. Prince contributes several songs. Followed by BATMAN RETURNS. [PG-13] ▼◐●

Batman & Robin (1997) **C-130m.** **½ D: Joel Schumacher. Arnold Schwarzenegger, George Clooney, Chris O'Donnell, Uma Thurman, Alicia Silverstone, Michael Gough, Pat Hingle, John Glover, Elle Macpherson, Vivica A. Fox, Vendela K. Thommessen, Coolio. Batman #4 spotlights two colorful villains, Schwarzenegger's lusty Mr. Freeze and Thurman's deliciously nasty Poison Ivy, who (for different reasons) want to destroy Gotham City, but even their antics can't sustain an overlong, episodic film in which the "story" often makes no sense. Clooney is OK but unremarkable as Bruce Wayne/Batman, ditto for Silverstone as the new Batgirl. The action and effects are loud, gargantuan, and ultimately numbing. End of this Batman cycle; followed in 2005 by BATMAN BEGINS. [PG-13] ▼◐●

Batman Begins (2005) **C-140m.** *** D: Christopher Nolan. Christian Bale, Michael Caine, Liam Neeson, Katie Holmes, Morgan Freeman, Gary Oldman, Cillian Murphy, Tom Wilkinson, Rutger Hauer, Ken Watanabe, Linus Roache, Rade Sherbedgia, Mark Boone Junior. Highly entertaining reinvention of the Batman legend traces the evolution of Bruce Wayne from privileged son of wealthy, generous parents to avenging crime-fighter hoping to save a corrupt Gotham City. Script (by David S. Goyer and director Nolan) also provides ingenious explanations of how the Caped Crusader came to adopt his various accoutrements. Impeccably cast (with the exception of Holmes, who seems lightweight in such heady company) and executed. Followed by THE DARK KNIGHT. Panavision. [PG-13] ▼◐

Batman Forever (1995) **C-121m.** *** D: Joel Schumacher. Val Kilmer, Tommy Lee Jones, Jim Carrey, Nicole Kidman, Chris O'Donnell, Michael Gough, Pat Hingle, Drew Barrymore, Debi Mazar, Rene Auberjonois, Joe Grifasi. Kilmer makes the role of Batman/Bruce Wayne his own in this well-written sequel in which the Caped Crusader battles Two-Face (Jones) and The Riddler (Carrey) while attempting— at least for a while—to resist the advances of a sexy psychologist (Kidman). He also acquires a partner in O'Donnell (as Robin), and it's this aspect of the film—the character relationships—that give it solidity. The loud, razzle-dazzle special effects are overkill. Ed Begley, Jr., appears unbilled.

Followed by BATMAN & ROBIN. [PG-13]▼●⦿

Batman: Mask of the Phantasm (1993) **C-76m.** **½ D: Eric Radomski, Bruce W. Timm. Voices of Kevin Conroy, Dana Delany, Hart Bochner, Mark Hamill, Stacy Keach, Jr., Efrem Zimbalist, Jr., Abe Vigoda, Dick Miller, John P. Ryan. Batman battles a mysterious figure who's killing the great gangsters of Gotham City, while, as Bruce Wayne, he romances his college sweetheart, just returned to town. Then the Joker turns up.... Excellent design (inspired by the 1940s Superman cartoons) is hampered by mediocre animation, but the story isn't bad, and the dialogue is better than you'd expect. Spinoff of animated *Batman* TV series was intended for video release, but went to theaters instead. [PG] ▼●⦿

Batman Returns (1992) **C-126m.** ** D: Tim Burton. Michael Keaton, Danny De-Vito, Michelle Pfeiffer, Christopher Walken, Michael Gough, Michael· Murphy, Cristi Conaway, Andrew Bryniarski, Pat Hingle, Vincent Schiavelli, Jan Hooks, Paul Reubens. Nasty, nihilistic nightmare movie about an abandoned freak baby who grows up to be The Penguin—a deadly threat to Gotham City, especially when he teams up with megalomaniac Max Shreck (Walken). Meanwhile, Batman finds a more personal enemy in Catwoman. Rich performances, dazzling production design, and occasional cleverness can't make up for a dark, mean-spirited (and often incoherent) screenplay. Followed by Keatonless BATMAN FOREVER. [PG-13]▼●⦿

Baton Rouge (1988-Spanish) **C-98m.** ** D: Rafael Moleon. Antonio Banderas, Victoria Abril, Carmen Maura, Andres Lopez, Laura Cepeda. Gigolo Banderas preys on a sexually dysfunctional wealthy woman, and winds up in a scam with her psychiatrist. Interesting sex scenes and suspense can't make up for utterly confusing plot twists. Another Banderas film taken off the shelf after he became known in the U.S. [R]▼

Bats (1999) **C-91m.** BOMB D: Louis Morneau. Lou Diamond Phillips, Dina Meyer, Bob Gunton, Leon, Carlos Jacott, David McConnell. Hordes of mutated killer bats attack a Southwestern community. That's all the plot the movie has, but it does feature a top-of-the-line motivation for its mad scientist (Gunton): he creates the bats, he says, because he *can*. Deplorable. DVD is rated R. Followed by a made-for-TV sequel. Clairmont-Scope. [PG-13] ▼⦿

*****batteries not included** (1987) **C-106m.** ** D: Matthew Robbins. Hume Cronyn, Jessica Tandy, Frank McRae, Elizabeth Pena, Michael Carmine, Dennis Boutsikaris. Steven Spielberg's Amblin Productions has gone to the same well once too often. Cloying sci-fi fantasy has a "family" of small alien spacecrafts arrive to assist New Yorkers whose tenement is about to be demol-

ished. Cronyn and Tandy do far more for the film than it does for them. [PG]▼●⦿

Battle Beneath the Earth (1967-British-U.S.) **C-91m.** **½ D: Montgomery Tully. Kerwin Mathews, Viviane Ventura, Robert Ayres, Peter Arne, Al Mulock, Martin Benson. Silly but enjoyable pulp fantasy about Chinese plan to invade U.S. through network of tunnels.▼

Battle Beyond the Stars (1980) **C-104m.** **½ D: Jimmy T. Murakami. Richard Thomas, John Saxon, Robert Vaughn, Darlanne Fleugel, George Peppard, Sybil Danning, Sam Jaffe, Morgan Woodward, Jeff Corey, Julia Duffy. Not-bad space saga from Roger Corman, with good special effects and a John Sayles script that uses the reliable SEVEN SAMURAI/ MAGNIFICENT SEVEN formula (with Vaughn from the SEVEN cast). Sets and special effects were reused for countless subsequent Corman cheapies. [PG]▼●⦿

Battle Circus (1953) **90m.** **½ D: Richard Brooks. Humphrey Bogart, June Allyson, Keenan Wynn, Robert Keith, Philip Ahn. OK tale of MASH unit during Korean War is well acted, and occasionally exciting, but hampered by too much emphasis on the romance between surgeon Bogart and nurse Allyson. Surprisingly ordinary, coming from writer-director Brooks.▼

Battle Creek Brawl SEE: **Big Brawl, The**

Battle Cry (1955) **C-149m.** *** D: Raoul Walsh. Van Heflin, Aldo Ray, Mona Freeman, Nancy Olson, James Whitmore, Raymond Massey, Tab Hunter, Dorothy Malone, Anne Francis, William Campbell, John Lupton, Fess Parker, Rhys Williams, Allyn (Ann) McLerie. Entertaining version of Leon Uris WW2 Marine novel, with much barracks profanity removed for film, focusing on servicemen in training, wartime romance, and frustrating battle assignments—with Heflin striving to get his men the tough combat action they yearn for. Hunter as wholesome soldier and Malone a love-hungry Navy wife stand out in episodic actioner. Ray gives good performance as rough-hewn gyrene who falls in love with "nice girl" Olson. Film debut of Justus McQueen, who thereafter acted under the name of his character, L.Q. Jones. Musical score by Max Steiner. Screenplay by Uris. CinemaScope. ▼●⦿

Battlefield Earth (2000) **C-117m.** BOMB D: Roger Christian. John Travolta, Barry Pepper, Forest Whitaker, Kim Coates, Richard Tyson, Sabine Karsenti, Michael MacRae, Kelly Preston. Psychlos (business-minded aliens) conquered Earth a century ago; what remains of humanity are slaves or ignorant savages. Gold-greedy Psychlo security chief Travolta educates bright human Pepper, hoping "man animals" can mine the metal for him. Big mistake.... So is the movie, based on the novel by L. Ron Hubbard. Clumsy plot, misplaced sat-

ire, unbelievable coincidences and a leaden pace trample Travolta's weird but amusing performance. Super 35. [PG-13]▼▶
Battle for Anzio, The SEE: **Anzio**
Battle Force SEE: **Great Battle, The**
Battle for Terra (2009) C-79m. ** D: Aristomenis Tsirbas. Voices of Evan Rachel Wood, Brian Cox, James Garner, Chris Evans, Danny Glover, Amanda Peet, David Cross, Justin Long, Dennis Quaid, Luke Wilson, Mark Hamill, Ron Perlman, Beverly D'Angelo, Danny Trejo, Rosanna Arquette, Laraine Newman. The last remains of the human race, in their quest to survive, threaten to annihilate the inhabitants of a peaceful planet. When a friendship forms between a downed Earthling invader and a Terranian princess, they plot together to drive the humans away. Environmentally conscious animated film with a strong antiwar message is a tolerable sit for adults. There are several spectacular aerial action sequences, but character designs are generic and personalities clichéd. 3-D Digital Widescreen. [PG]▶
Battle for the Planet of the Apes (1973) C-92m. ** D: J. Lee Thompson. Roddy McDowall, Natalie Trundy, Severn Darden, Paul Williams, Claude Akins, John Huston. Substandard; fifth (and last) apes installment attempts to bring entire series full-cycle. Good footage from earlier films helps, but not much. A TV series followed. Panavision. [G]▼●▶
Battleground (1949) 118m. *** D: William Wellman. Van Johnson, John Hodiak, Ricardo Montalban, George Murphy, Marshall Thompson, Denise Darcel, Don Taylor, Richard Jaeckel, James Whitmore, James Arness, Scotty Beckett. Star-studded replay of Battle of the Bulge: division of American troops, their problems and reactions to war. Robert Pirosh's slick script, which was awarded an Oscar, lacks genuine insight into the characters; Paul C. Vogel also earned a statuette for his cinematography. Also shown in computer-colored version.▼●▶
Battle Hymn (1957) C-108m. *** D: Douglas Sirk. Rock Hudson, Martha Hyer, Anna Kashfi, Dan Duryea, Don DeFore. Hudson gives convincing performance as real-life clergyman Dean Hess, who returns to military duty in Korean War to train fighter pilots; expansive production values. CinemaScope.▼▶
Battle in Seattle (2008) C-98m. *** D: Stuart Townsend. Charlize Theron, Woody Harrelson, Martin Henderson, André Benjamin, Michelle Rodriguez, Ray Liotta, Connie Nielsen, Channing Tatum, Joshua Jackson, Jennifer Carpenter, Isaach de Bankolé, Tzi Ma, Ivana Milicevic, Rade Sherbedzija. Compelling film about various people affected by the turbulent protests over the World Trade Organization conference in Seattle in 1999. Organizers Henderson, Rodriguez, and Benjamin are sincere in their goal of non-violent demonstrations, and mayor Liotta is counting on that, but nothing goes as planned. Not all of the personal stories are equally commanding, but first-time writer-director Townsend artfully blends dramatic re-creations with actual news footage to create visceral, immediate drama. [R]▶

Battle: Los Angeles (2011) C-116m. **½ D: Jonathan Liebesman. Aaron Eckhart, Michelle Rodriguez, Ramon Rodriguez, Lucas Till, Bridget Moynahan, Ne-Yo, Michael Peña, Will Rothhaar, Cory Hardrict. Sudden series of meteor showers turns out to be a full-scale alien invasion. A squadron of Marines—including a career staff sergeant (Eckhart) who's about to retire—is sent to Santa Monica to evacuate embattled residents, if they can. Adrenaline-charged mash-up of war, alien, and disaster-movie genres manages to weave personal stories about the intrepid Marines and the civilians they're trying to rescue into the bigger picture of Earth being invaded by hordes of aliens. Sometimes-cheesy dialogue reminds you that this is a popcorn/genre piece, but Eckhart is rock solid, the action is exciting, and the visual effects are potent. Super 35. [PG-13]▶
Battle of Algiers, The (1965-Italian-Algerian) 125m. ***½ D: Gillo Pontecorvo. Yacef Saadi, Jean Martin, Brahim Haggiag, Tommaso Neri, Samia Kerbash. Straightforward drama about revolt against the French by Algerians from 1954–1962. Its impressive pseudo-documentary style helped earn it many awards, and the searing imperialism vs. independence struggle it depicts still resonates today.▼●▶
Battle of Britain (1969-British) C-132m. ** D: Guy Hamilton. Harry Andrews, Michael Caine, Trevor Howard, Curt Jurgens, Kenneth More, Laurence Olivier, Christopher Plummer, Michael Redgrave, Ralph Richardson, Robert Shaw, Susannah York. Superb widescreen aerial sequences, which will suffer on TV, hardly redeem yet another "spot-the-star" WW2 epic, this time about British airmen who prevented threatened Nazi invasion. Panavision. [G]▼●▶
Battle of El Alamein (1968-Italian-French) C-105m. ** D: Calvin Jackson Padget (Giorgio Ferroni). Frederick Stafford, Ettore Manni, Robert Hossein, Michael Rennie, George Hilton, Ira Furstenberg. Plenty of action as Italians and Germans, partners in an uneasy alliance, fight the British in the North African desert in 1942. Hossein plays Rommel, and Rennie does an unsympathetic Field Marshal Montgomery (the British are the villains in this one). Cromoscope. [PG]▼▶
Battle of Mareth, The SEE: **Great Battle, The**
Battle of Neretva, The (1970-Yugoslavian-U.S.-Italian-German) C-102m. ** D: Veljko Bulajic. Yul Brynner, Sergei Bondarchuk, Curt Jurgens, Sylva Koscina, Hardy Kruger, Franco Nero, Orson Welles. Originally

an Oscar nominee for Best Foreign Film, but when this $12 million spectacle about Nazi invasion of Yugoslavia was cut down from nearly three hours, it lost most of its coherency. Too bad. Panavision. [G]▼

Battle of Shaker Heights, The (2003) C-79m. **½ D: Kyle Rankin, Efram Potelle. Shia LaBeouf, Elden Henson, Amy Smart, Billy Kay, Kathleen Quinlan, Shiri Appleby, William Sadler, Ray Wise, Anson Mount. Second of the prize-winning Project Greenlight screenplays executive produced by Matt Damon and Ben Affleck is a comedy-drama about a high school misfit (winningly played by LaBeouf) who glibly covers the hurt he feels inside from troubles at home. A weekend war reenactor, he teams up with a preppie pal to seek revenge on his high school nemesis . . . then develops a serious crush on his new friend's older sister. Nothing startling or new, but entertaining. [PG-13] ▼)

Battle of the Aces SEE: **Von Richthofen and Brown**

Battle of the Bulge (1965) C-163m. ** D: Ken Annakin. Henry Fonda, Robert Shaw, Robert Ryan, Telly Savalas, Dana Andrews, George Montgomery, Ty Hardin, Pier Angeli, Charles Bronson. Originally presented in Cinerama, this overinflated war drama about an important event cannot triumph over banal script. Read a good book on the subject instead. Ultra Panavision 70.▼O)

Battle of the River Plate, The SEE: **Pursuit of the Graf Spee**

Battle of the Sexes, The (1959-British) 84m. *** D: Charles Crichton. Peter Sellers, Robert Morley, Constance Cummings, Jameson Clark. Sparkling British comedy with macabre overtones; Sellers is elderly Scotsman contemplating murder. Supporting cast keeps this moving.▼

Battleship Potemkin (1925-Russian) 70m. **** D: Sergei Eisenstein. Alexander Antonov, Vladimir Barsky, Grigori Alexandrov, Mikhail Goronorov. Landmark film about 1905 Revolution. Unlike many staples of film history classes, this one has the power to grip any audience. Odessa Steps sequence is possibly the most famous movie scene of all time. Aka POTEMKIN.▼O)

Battlestar: Galactica (1979) C-125m. **½ D: Richard A. Colla. Richard Hatch, Dirk Benedict, Lorne Greene, Ray Milland, John Colicos, Patrick Macnee, Lew Ayres, Jane Seymour, Laurette Spang, Terry Carter. Feature adapted from first episode of short-lived TV series; Greene is commander of starship taking survivors of doomed planet in search of new home. Belongs on small screen, where it's moderately interesting and John Dykstra's special effects come off best. Premiere originally telecast at 148m. [PG]▼O)

Battle Stripe SEE: **Men, The**

Battletruck SEE: **Warlords of the 21st Century**

Battling Bellhop SEE: **Kid Galahad** (1937)

Battling Butler (1926) 71m. **½ D: Buster Keaton. Buster Keaton, Sally O'Neil, Snitz Edwards, Francis McDonald, Mary O'Brien, Tom Wilson, Eddie Borden. Pampered young millionaire falls in love with a girl during a camping trip, and then has to pretend he's actually a champion prizefighter. One of Buster's weaker silent features still has its share of funny moments. Based on a stage play. ▼O)

Bat*21 (1988) C-105m. *** D: Peter Markle. Gene Hackman, Danny Glover, Jerry Reed, David Marshall Grant, Clayton Rohner, Erich Anderson, Joe Dorsey. Air Force Colonel and strategist Hackman has only seen the war from 30,000 feet, until he's shot down behind enemy lines. Now it's up to Glover to get him out before the Viet Cong get him, and before his own forces carpet-bomb the area. Taut, compelling film, based on a true story, with fine acting all around. Costar Reed was executive producer and wrote some of the songs for the soundtrack. [R]▼O)

Bawdy Adventures of Tom Jones, The (1976-British) C-94m. ** D: Cliff Owen. Nicky Henson, Trevor Howard, Joan Collins, Terry-Thomas, Arthur Lowe, Georgia Brown. Mild doings, based on London stage musical, can't hold a candle to 1963 classic (TOM JONES). This time, Tom's amorous adventures are pat and predictable, with Collins, as highwaywoman Black Bess, adding only zing. [R]▼

Baxter (1973) C-100m. *** D: Lionel Jeffries. Patricia Neal, Scott Jacoby, Jean-Pierre Cassel, Lynn Carlin, Britt Ekland, Sally Thomsett. Well-acted drama about young Jacoby's emotional problems and his relationship with speech therapist Neal, who tries to correct his lisp. [PG]

Baxter (1991-French) C-82m. *** D: Jerome Boivin. Lise Delamare, Jean Mercure, Jacques Spiesser, Catherine Ferran, Jean-Paul Roussillon. Illuminating observation of the human condition as perceived through the unlikeliest of eyes: the title canine, a bull terrier who thinks and feels, and reveals what's on his mind. The most disturbing of his various masters: a seemingly average young boy who turns out to be a fascist-in-training. Boivin coscripted.▼O

Baxter, The (2005) C-91m. **½ D: Michael Showalter. Michael Showalter, Elizabeth Banks, Justin Theroux, Michelle Williams, Michael Ian Black, Zak Orth, Peter Dinklage, Catherine Lloyd Burns, Katharine Powell, Paul Rudd, Jack McBrayer. A Brooklyn CPA (Showalter) is standing at the altar when—boom!—the ex (Theroux) of his intended (Banks) crashes the wedding. This nice schlub is characterized as a "Baxter" who can't tell the difference between contentment and happiness. What else to do but turn to the ready advice and willing ministrations of his able temp (a cute Williams). Mild romantic comedy was written by the director, who would have benefited from a less cartoonish leading man. [PG-13]🅑

Bay Boy, The (1984-Canadian-French) C-107m. ** D: Daniel Petrie. Liv Ullmann, Kiefer Sutherland, Peter Donat, Mathieu Carriere, Isabelle Mejias, Alan Scarfe, Chris Wiggins, Leah Pinsent. Well-meaning but hopelessly predictable portrayal of a teenager (Sutherland, son of Donald), and his coming of age in rural Canadian community during 1930s. You've seen this one many times before; Ullmann in particular is one-dimensional as Sutherland's hardworking mother. [R]🅥●

Bay of Angels (1963-French) 79m. *** D: Jacques Demy. Jeanne Moreau, Claude Mann, Paul Guers, Henri Nassiet. Lesser-known but no less rewarding French New Wave drama tells the story of a young man whose chronic gambling leads him into a dangerous affair with a woman he meets in the casino. Their luck at the tables mirrors their own tumultuous relationship. A vividly blonde Moreau is sensational in one of her best, least-seen performances. Z master Costa-Gavras is credited as Assistant to Director. Shot in gorgeous b&w in the South of France; restored for 2002 U.S. reissue. Score by frequent Demy collaborator Michel Legrand is one of his best. CinemaScope.🅥🅑

Bay of Blood SEE: **Twitch of the Death Nerve**

Beach, The (2000) C-120m. **½ D: Danny Boyle. Leonardo DiCaprio, Tilda Swinton, Virginie Ledoyen, Guillaume Canet, Paterson Joseph, Robert Carlyle, Peter Youngblood Hills. Young American looking for "something different" goes to Bangkok, hooks up with a French couple, and together they follow a map to an elusive and secluded island beach . . . but paradise is not all it's cracked up to be. Consistently interesting if sometimes muddled adaptation of Alex Garland's novel is naive at times and leans toward purplish prose in DiCaprio's narration. Super 35. [R]🅥🅑

Beach Blanket Bingo (1965) C-98m. *** D: William Asher. Frankie Avalon, Annette Funicello, Paul Lynde, Harvey Lembeck, Don Rickles, Linda Evans, Jody McCrea, Marta Kristen, John Ashley, Deborah Walley, Buster Keaton, Bobbi Shaw, Timothy Carey. Fifth BEACH PARTY movie is the best; amid various plot entanglements (parachuting, kidnapped singing idol Evans, mermaid Kristen), Lynde sneers at everybody, Rickles insults everybody, and Lembeck gets to sing before being cut into two halves by Carey's buzzsaw. The ultimate wallow in '60s surfing nostalgia. Sequel: HOW TO STUFF A WILD BIKINI. Panavision.🅥●🅑

Beachcomber, The (1954-British) C-82m. *** D: Muriel Box. Glynis Johns, Robert Newton, Donald Sinden, Michael Hordern, Donald Pleasence. Remake of Somerset Maugham tale of South Sea island bum entangled with strait-laced sister of missionary is still flavorful.🔻

Beaches (1988) C-123m. **½ D: Garry Marshall. Bette Midler, Barbara Hershey, John Heard, Spalding Gray, Lainie Kazan, James Read, Grace Johnston, Mayim Bialik, Marcie Leeds. Bittersweet saga of a 30-year friendship that begins when two girls—one rich and pampered, the other poor and driven to show-biz success—meet on the beach at Atlantic City. OK as soap opera (not much depth to the characters and their motives, and at least two endings too many) but as a vehicle for Midler it's dynamite, and she even gets to sing. Based on a novel by Iris Rainer Dart; Midler coproduced. Director Marshall features his on-screen "regulars" in a variety of cameo roles, including Hector Elizondo as a justice of the peace. [PG-13]🅥●🅑

Beaches of Agnès, The (2008-French) C-112m. ***½ D: Agnès Varda. Deeply felt, strikingly original celluloid autobiography in which Varda, the legendary 80-something filmmaker, recalls moments and incidents from her life. Varda narrates and appears on-screen throughout, blending re-created images from her past (which have haunted her across the decades) with carefully chosen film clips that reflect her artistic vision. At its most poignant when Varda deals with her memories of, and feelings for, those who have passed on (including her late husband, filmmaker Jacques Demy). Not to be missed.🅑

Beachhead (1954) C-89m. *** D: Stuart Heisler. Tony Curtis, Frank Lovejoy, Mary Murphy, Eduard Franz, Skip Homeier, John Doucette. Tense WW2 drama in which a small group of Marines sets out to locate a French plantation owner, and a critical message, on a Japanese-held island. Filmed in Kauai, Hawaii.🅑

Beach Party (1963) C-101m. ** D: William Asher. Frankie Avalon, Annette Funicello, Bob Cummings, Dorothy Malone, Harvey Lembeck, Jody McCrea, John Ashley, Morey Amsterdam, Candy Johnson, Eva Six. Anthropologist Cummings studies teenagers' "wild" behavior, but comes to learn they aren't so bad after all. First in long-running series is typical blend of slapstick and forgettable songs, as well as introduction of Lembeck's dopey Brando-biker takeoff, Eric Von Zipper. Sequel: MUSCLE BEACH PARTY. Panavision.🅥🅑

Beach Red (1967) C-105m. *** D: Cornel Wilde. Cornel Wilde, Rip Torn, Burr De Benning, Patrick Wolfe, Jean Wallace. Hard look at military life in South Pacific attempts to show ugly side of war.🅑

Bean (1997-British) C-90m. *** D: Mel Smith. Rowan Atkinson, Peter MacNicol, Pamela Reed, Harris Yulin, Burt Reynolds, John Mills, Larry Drake, Johnny Galecki,

Tom McGowan, Sandra Oh. Mr. Bean, featured in a series of TV skits and specials, makes his feature-film debut as a guard at the National Gallery of Art in London who's sent to America, posing as a noted art expert, to accompany "Whistler's Mother" as it is unveiled at a California museum. Never quite as wonderful as you'd like it to be, but often very funny. Bean's misadventures are reminiscent of silent film comedy and largely dependent on the winning silliness of Atkinson himself. Followed by MR. BEAN'S HOLIDAY. [PG-13] ▼●)

Beans of Egypt, Maine, The (1994) C-100m. **½ D: Jennifer Warren. Martha Plimpton, Kelly Lynch, Rutger Hauer, Patrick McGaw, Richard Sanders, Michael MacRae. Episodic, mildly interesting account of the Beans, a large, rough-and-tumble backwoods clan, and the most notorious residents of Egypt, Maine (pop. 729). Film centers on the relationship, sexual and otherwise, between Beal Bean (McGaw), a hot, prideful young stud, and the Beans' neighbor (Plimpton). Based on the best-selling novel by Carolyn Chute. An *American Playhouse* coproduction. Retitled FORBIDDEN CHOICES for video. [R] ▼●

Bear, The (1984) C-112m. ** D: Richard Sarafian. Gary Busey, Cynthia Leake, Harry Dean Stanton, Jon-Erik Hexum, Carmen Thomas, Cary Guffey, D'Urville Martin. Incredibly corny, old-fashioned Hollywood bio of famed Alabama collegiate football coach Paul "Bear" Bryant. Busey's sincere, gravel-voiced portrayal can't compensate for episodic, repetitive, and undramatic script. [PG]

Bear, The (1989-French) C-93m. *** D: Jean-Jacques Annaud. Bart, Douce, Jack Wallace, Tchéky Karyo, Andre Lacombe. Captivating and unusual film about a bear cub who is orphaned and forced to fend for itself, until it finds a new protector in a giant Kodiak—the tempting target for a pair of hunters. Filmed with utmost respect for animals and a real sense of nature's magnificence, though manipulative, to be sure. Based on *The Grizzly King,* a 1917 novel by James Oliver Curwood. Panavision. [PG] ▼●)

Bear Island (1979-British-Canadian) C-118m. *½ D: Don Sharp. Donald Sutherland, Vanessa Redgrave, Richard Widmark, Christopher Lee, Barbara Parkins, Lloyd Bridges, Lawrence Dane. One of Alistair MacLean's best novels became one of his worst films, mixing murder, intrigue and stolen bullion near the top of the world. Strong cast, capable director and scenic locations come to naught. Barely released to theaters. Panavision. [PG] ▼

Bears and I, The (1974) C-89m. *½ D: Bernard McEveety. Patrick Wayne, Chief Dan George, Andrew Duggan, Michael Ansara. Vietnam vet Wayne tries to soothe relations in North Woods between Indians and white bigots. Mild Disney film. [G] ▼●

Beast, The (1971) SEE: **Equinox**
Beast, The (1988) C-109m. ** D: Kevin Reynolds. Jason Patric, Steven Bauer, George Dzundza, Stephen Baldwin, Don Harvey, Kabir Bedi. Soviet tank, cut off from its battalion in Afghan desert, tries to reach safety, while pursued by vengeful Afghan rebels. Eventually, a peace-minded Russian from the tank, left to die by his brutal commander, joins the rebels himself. Serviceable (if predictable) plot is undermined by ponderous pace and stereotyped characters. Filmed in Israel. [R] ▼▼

Beast From 20,000 Fathoms, The (1953) 80m. **½ D: Eugene Lourie. Paul Christian (Paul Hubschmid), Paula Raymond, Cecil Kellaway, Kenneth Tobey, Donald Woods, Lee Van Cleef, Ross Elliott. Prehistoric rhedosaurus wreaks havoc when thawed after an atom-bomb blast. Good Ray Harryhausen special effects, especially in amusement park finale. Suggested by the Ray Bradbury short story "The Fog Horn." ▼●

Beast in the Cellar, The (1970-British) C-87m. ** D: James Kelly. Beryl Reid, Flora Robson, John Hamill, T. P. McKenna, Tessa Wyatt. Two sisters hide their maniac brother in the cellar; performances of Reid and Robson bring movie to average level. British running time was 101m. ▼▼

Beastly (2011) C-86m. *½ D: Daniel Barnz. Alex Pettyfer, Vanessa Hudgens, Neil Patrick Harris, Dakota Johnson, Erik Knudsen, Mary-Kate Olsen, Peter Krause, LisaGay Hamilton. Egocentric teenager Pettyfer, who thinks beautiful people (like him) deserve success, annoys a classmate who has magic powers, so she makes him sort of ugly. To regain his good looks, he has to find someone who will love him as he is. Retelling of *Beauty and the Beast* from the Beast's viewpoint is uninvolving and unimaginative; best left to its target audience of undemanding teenage girls. Super 35. [PG-13] ▮

Beastmaster, The (1982) C-118m. ** D: Don Coscarelli. Marc Singer, Tanya Roberts, Rip Torn, John Amos, Rod Loomis. Yet another sword and sandal fantasy with Conan/Tarzan-clone hero who communicates with animals (including, believe it or not, some comedic ferrets), falls in love with slave girl Roberts and seeks revenge against evil priest (Torn) who killed his father. Cinematography by John Alcott (BARRY LYNDON). Followed by several sequels. [PG] ▼●

Beastmaster 2: Through the Portal of Time (1991) C-107m. *½ D: Sylvio Tabet. Marc Singer, Kari Wuhrer, Sarah Douglas, Wings Hauser, James Avery, Robert Fieldsteel, Arthur Malet, Robert Z'Dar, Michael Berryman, Larry Dobkin. Hero Dar returns (belatedly) to battle another evil wizard (Hauser)—this time, thanks to magician Douglas, in the streets of modern-day L.A.

Some cleverness, but cheaply made and contrived. *Nine* writers are credited. Followed by a TV sequel.▼●

Beast Must Die, The (1974-British) **C-93m.** *** D: Paul Annett. Calvin Lockhart, Peter Cushing, Charles Gray, Marlene Clark, Anton Diffring. New twists on the old werewolf theme make the difference. Millionaire sportsman Lockhart invites guests to his electronically bugged mansion, knowing one of them is a werewolf. Lockhart is overly mannered, while Cushing gains sympathy in his usual quiet but effective way. Like TEN LITTLE INDIANS, this movie gives audience a break to guess killer's identity. From story "There Shall Be No Darkness" by James Blish. Video title: BLACK WEREWOLF. [PG]▼●]

Beast of Blood SEE: **Beast of the Dead**
Beast of the Dead (1970) **C-90m.** BOMB D: Eddie Romero. John Ashley, Eddie Garcia, Beverly Miller, Celeste Yarnall. Sequel to MAD DOCTOR OF BLOOD ISLAND, with that film's headless monster stalking natives on Pacific island while mad doctor plans new head transplant. Filmed in the Philippines. Originally titled BEAST OF BLOOD. [PG]▼]

Beasts SEE: **Twilight People, The**
Beast with Five Fingers, The (1946) **88m.** **½ D: Robert Florey. Robert Alda, Andrea King, Peter Lorre, Victor Francen, J. Carrol Naish. Intriguing if not entirely successful mood-piece about aging pianist and strange doings in his household. Lorre's confrontation with disembodied hand a horror highlight.▼●

Beast Within, The (1982) **C-90m.** BOMB D: Philippe Mora. Ronny Cox, Bibi Besch, Paul Clemens, Don Gordon, R. G. Armstrong, L. Q. Jones, Meshach Taylor. Besch was raped by hairy-legged "thing" while on honeymoon; her son (Clemens), now a teenager, commences killing, and killing, and killing. Oh, yes, he changes into a monster at one point, if you care. Panavision. [R]▼]

Beat, The (1988) **C-98m.** *½ D: Paul Mones. John Savage, David Jacobson, Kara Glover, William McNamara, Jeffrey Horowitz. Well-meaning but painfully gauche drama of new kid Jacobson at a N.Y.C. high school dominated by gangs. He brings poetry and mystical fantasy into his classmates' lives. Earnest cast but treatment of generation gap issues is old hat. [R]▼●

Beat Generation, The (1959) **95m.** *½ D: Charles Haas. Steve Cochran, Mamie Van Doren, Ray Danton, Fay Spain, Louis Armstrong, Maggie Hayes, Jackie Coogan, Ray Anthony, Maxie Rosenbloom, Irish McCalla, Vampira. Exploitation-type story of detective Cochran tracking down insane sexual assaulter; vivid sequences marred by hokey script. Retitled THIS REBEL AGE. CinemaScope.●

Beat Girl SEE: **Wild for Kicks**
Beatrice (1988-French) **C-128m.** *** D: Bertrand Tavernier. Bernard Pierre Donnadieu, Julie Delpy, Nils Tavernier, Monique Chaumette, Robert Dhery, Michele Gleizer. Moody and well-mounted, if essentially ugly saga of the Hundred Years War; a father returns home from the front to bully his weakling son and engage his tougher (and beautiful) daughter in incest. Extremely violent and not for all tastes, but obviously the work of an outstanding filmmaker; try reconciling this with Tavernier's A SUNDAY IN THE COUNTRY. Video title: THE PASSION OF BEATRICE. [R]▼●

Beat Street (1984) **C-106m.** **½ D: Stan Lathan. Rae Dawn Chong, Guy Davis, Jon Chardiet, Leon W. Grant, Saundra Santiago, Robert Taylor. Urban ghetto kids find creative outlets in painting graffiti, breakdancing, rapping, and developing new disco d.j. routines. A slicker version of WILD STYLE that places the old Mickey & Judy "let's put on a show" formula into a more realistic contemporary setting. Innocuous trend piece, coproduced by Harry Belafonte. [PG]▼●

Beat That My Heart Skipped, The (2005-French) **C-108m.** *** D: Jacques Audiard. Romain Duris, Niels Arestrup, Jonathan Zaccaï, Gilles Cohen, Linh-Dan Pham, Aure Atika, Emmanuelle Devos. Entertaining reworking of James Toback's FINGERS, centering on a dour young man (Duris) who is unable to decide if he will embrace a life of classical music or lawbreaking. Not as gripping or provocative as the original, but still worthwhile.◗

Beat the Devil (1954) **89m.** *** D: John Huston. Humphrey Bogart, Jennifer Jones, Gina Lollobrigida, Robert Morley, Peter Lorre, Edward Underdown. Huston and Truman Capote concocted this offbeat, very funny satire of MALTESE FALCON-ish movies on location in Italy. Low-key nature of comedy eluded many people in 1954 and it immediately became a cult favorite, which it remains today.▼●

Beau Brummell (1954-U.S.-British) **C-113m.** **½ D: Curtis Bernhardt. Stewart Granger, Elizabeth Taylor, Peter Ustinov, Robert Morley. Handsome cast in lavish production from Granger's rash of costume epics. Here, he's the famous 19th-century British Casanova-fop (played by John Barrymore in the 1924 version).▼

Beaufort (2007-Israeli) **C-126m.** ***½ D: Joseph Cedar. Oshri Cohen, Itay Tiran, Eli Eltonyo, Ohad Knoller, Itay Turgeman, Alon Aboutboul. Beaufort Castle, a 12th-century Crusaders' fort, was captured by the Israeli army in 1982 on the first day of its war with Lebanon, though it was of no strategic importance. Israeli soldiers have been defending it against the bombs of a faceless enemy for almost two decades, and now they are ordered to abandon Beaufort as the Israelis plan their withdrawal from Lebanon. Subtly compelling drama offers an uncompromising portrait of men in combat and the pointlessness of war. Ron Leshem adapted his novel with Cedar. Super 35.█

Beau Geste (1939) **114m.** *** D: William Wellman. Gary Cooper, Ray Milland, Robert Preston, Brian Donlevy, Susan Hayward, J. Carrol Naish, Albert Dekker, Broderick Crawford, Donald O'Connor. Scene-for-scene remake of famous 1926 silent film (with Ronald Colman) isn't quite as good but faithfully retells story of three devoted brothers serving in the Foreign Legion and battling sadistic martinet commander (Donlevy). Nothing can top that opening sequence! Based on the novel by P.C. Wren. Remade in 1966.▼●)

Beau Geste (1966) **C-103m.** ** D: Douglas Heyes. Telly Savalas, Guy Stockwell, Doug McClure, Leslie Nielsen. The third version of Christopher Wren's adventure about honor in the French Foreign Legion is barely adequate, with brothers battling rampaging Arabs and sadistic commander Savalas. Techniscope.

Beau James (1957) **C-105m.** *** D: Melville Shavelson. Bob Hope, Vera Miles, Paul Douglas, Alexis Smith, Darren McGavin; narrated by Walter Winchell. Flavorful recreation of the political career of Mayor Jimmy Walker in 1920s N.Y.C., based on Gene Fowler's book. Hope is fine in basically noncomic performance. Guest appearances by Jimmy Durante, Jack Benny, George Jessel, Walter Catlett. VistaVision.

Beaumarchais the Scoundrel (1996-French) **C-100m.** *** D: Edouard Molinaro. Fabrice Luchini, Manuel Blanc, Sandrine Kiberlain, Jacques Weber, Florence Thomassin, Jean Yanne, Michel Piccoli, Michel Serrault, Jean-Claude Brialy. Luchini gives a marvelous performance as the 18th-century playwright, wit, and defender of human rights in this episodic biopic that encompasses everything from backstage theatrical drama and royal intrigue to gun-running for the American Revolution. As light and insubstantial as a soufflé, but beautifully crafted and always entertaining. Panavision.▼

Beau Père (1981-French) **C-120m.** ***½ D: Bertrand Blier. Patrick Dewaere, Ariel Besse, Maurice Ronet, Nicole Garcia, Nathalie Baye, Maurice Risch, Macha Meril. Piano player Dewaere is seduced by his determined stepdaughter, a 14-year-old childwoman (Besse), after the death of her mother. Thoughtful comedy-drama is sensitively, not exploitively, handled by director Blier. Panavision.▼)

Beautician and the Beast, The (1997) **C-105m.** *½ D: Ken Kwapis. Fran Drescher, Timothy Dalton, Ian McNeice, Patrick Malahide, Lisa Jakub, Michael Lerner, Phyllis Newman. Stuck in the salon with her TV aspirations going nowhere, a Queens beautician readily accepts when she's hired (on a blunder) to tutor the emotionally deprived children of Slovetzia's widowed dictator. No nun sings "Climb Ev'ry Mountain," but this comedy can be taken as a warped variation on THE SOUND OF MUSIC. Drescher's beguiling loopiness carries it for a while, but the already limited chuckles halt with a full half-hour to go. [PG]▼●)

Beauties of the Night (1954-French) **84m.** **½ D: René Clair. Gérard Philipe, Martine Carol, Gina Lollobrigida, Magali Vendeuil. Diverting fantasy involving aspiring composer Philipe with penchant for dreams wandering through various eras of history. ▼

Beautiful (2000) **C-112m.** *½ D: Sally Field. Minnie Driver, Joey Lauren Adams, Hallie Kate Eisenberg, Kathleen Turner, Leslie Stefanson, Michael McKean, Colleen Rennison, Bridgette Wilson. A young girl with the ambition of being a beauty pageant queen grows up to be a win-at-all-costs career contestant (Driver). When she accidentally becomes pregnant, she has her best friend raise the child. Good cast combats an uneven script filled with one-dimensional characters; a distant runner-up to SMILE. Field's feature-film directing debut. [PG-13]▼)

Beautiful Blonde From Bashful Bend, The (1949) **C-77m.** **½ D: Preston Sturges. Betty Grable, Cesar Romero, Rudy Vallee, Olga San Juan, Porter Hall, Sterling Holloway, El Brendel. Film was major flop in 1949, looks somewhat better today; broad Western farce has Grable a gun-toting saloon girl mistaken for schoolmarm in hick town. Hugh Herbert hilarious as nearsighted doctor.▼●

Beautiful but Deadly SEE: **Don Is Dead, The**

Beautiful Country, The (2005-U.S.-Norwegian) **C-125m.** *** D: Hans Petter Moland. Damien Nguyen, Nick Nolte, Bai Ling, Tim Roth, Be He, Xuan Phuc Dinh, Phat Trieu Hoang, Than Kien Nguyen. Boy who was the product of a Vietnamese mother and American G.I. who fought in the war becomes an outcast in his own village due to his mixed heritage. He sets off on a journey, eventually heading to Texas to find the father he never knew. Measured, well-made tale dramatizes the difficulties children of American servicemen encountered once the war was over and their biological fathers deserted them. Damien Nguyen is touching and genuine in his first major role, while Nolte does some of his finest work in what amounts to a cameo near the film's end. Super 35. [R]▼)

Beautiful Creatures (2001-British) **C-86m.** **½ D: Bill Eagles. Rachel Weisz, Susan Lynch, Iain Glen, Maurice Roëves, Alex Norton, Tom Mannion. Two women in Glasgow, each with lousy taste in men, unexpectedly meet and team up in a kidnapping/extortion scheme. Far-fetched variation on a familiar theme, laced with violence and humor. Norton is great as unconventional cop. [R]▼◐

Beautiful Dreamers (1990-Canadian) **C-107m.** ****½** D: John Kent Harrison. Colm Feore, Rip Torn, Wendel Meldrum, Sheila McCarthy. Free-spirited American poet Walt Whitman (Torn) befriends Dr. Maurice Bucke (Feore), intrigued by his progressive treatment of the mentally retarded. Their combined roguish idealism confounds their peers and sets Victorian sensibilities askew. Trite handling of interesting story, with outstanding performances by Torn and Feore. [PG-13]▼◐

Beautiful Girls (1996) **C-107m.** ******* D: Ted Demme. Timothy Hutton, Matt Dillon, Noah Emmerich, Annabeth Gish, Lauren Holly, Rosie O'Donnell, Max Perlich, Martha Plimpton, Natalie Portman, Michael Rapaport, Mira Sorvino, Uma Thurman, Pruitt Taylor Vince, Anne Bobby, Richard Bright, Sam Robards, David Arquette. Hutton, on the verge of marrying his girlfriend but unsure of himself, goes back to his Massachusetts hometown and hangs out with his pals from high school, whose lives—and relationships with women—haven't changed a bit. Well-observed and well-cast slice of life about the continuity of small-town working-class existence and the ruts both men and women can find themselves in. Some great moments for precocious Portman, smart-mouthed O'Donnell, and others in the ensemble. [R]▼◐●

Beautiful Joe (2000) **C-98m.** ****** D: Stephen Metcalfe. Sharon Stone, Billy Connolly, Gil Bellows, Ian Holm, Jurnee Smollett, Dann Florek. Good-hearted man, dumped by his wife, takes to the road in search of adventure, and finds it when he meets up with Stone, a woman with a knack for getting into trouble. Familiar and predictable. Connolly deserves a better vehicle. U.S. debut on cable TV. [R]▼◐

Beautiful Mind, A (2001) **C-135m.** ******* D: Ron Howard. Russell Crowe, Jennifer Connelly, Ed Harris, Paul Bettany, Christopher Plummer, Adam Goldberg, Judd Hirsch, Josh Lucas, Anthony Rapp, Austin Pendleton. Unusual story "inspired by incidents" in the life of John Nash, a brilliant West Virginia mathematician who flowers at Princeton in the late 1940s and then goes to work at M.I.T. But his marriage and sanity are put to a painful test. Central story twist is a doozy—and completely unexpected. Crowe is excellent as usual, and the film offers an overdue showcase for Connelly, as the student who becomes his wife. Oscar winner for Best Picture, Director, Supporting Actress (Connelly), and Adapted Screenplay (Akiva Goldsman). [PG-13]▼◐

Beautiful People (1999-British) **C-109m.** ******* D: Jasmin Dizdar. Charlotte Coleman, Charles Kay, Rosalind Ayres, Roger Sloman, Heather Tobias, Danny Nussbaum,

Siobhan Redmond, Gilbert Martin, Edin Dzandzanovic. Sharply observed film about various people—mostly Brits and Bosnians—caught in England's contemporary melting pot, but told with a sense of humor and hope in its heart instead of despair. A striking and believable film from writer-director Dizdar. [R]▼◐

Beautiful Thing (1996-British) **C-89m.** ******* D: Hettie Macdonald. Glen Berry, Linda Henry, Scott Neal, Tameka Empson, Ben Daniels, Martin Walsh. Amiable and insightful tale of two working-class adolescent boys (Berry and Neal), neighbors with very different home lives, who become sexually and romantically involved. Sharp bits of humor and the blue-collar setting add punch to the proceedings, resulting in a winning coming-out/coming-of-age story. Love that Mama Cass sound track! Scripted by Jonathan Harvey, based on his play. [R]▼◐

Beau Travail (2000-French) **C-93m.** ******* D: Claire Denis. Denis Lavant, Michel Subor, Gregoire Colin. Loose adaptation of Melville's *Billy Budd* is an austere tale of an ex–Foreign Legion officer (Lavant) who recalls his tenure in a dusty, impoverished East African locale, and his disdain for a young recruit (Colin). Denis expertly captures the boring existence of the legionnaires, and says something profound and deeply personal about the politics of male camaraderie.▼◐

Beauty and the Beast (1946-French) **95m.** ******** D: Jean Cocteau. Jean Marais, Josette Day, Marcel André. Cocteau's hauntingly beautiful, visually dazzling masterpiece, detailing what happens when, to save her father, Beauty (Day) gives herself to the Beast (Marais). Great fantasy, great filmmaking—beguiling on any level.▼◐●

Beauty and the Beast (1963) **C-77m.** ***½** D: Edward L. Cahn. Joyce Taylor, Mark Damon, Eduard Franz, Michael Pate, Merry Anders, Dayton Lummis, Walter Burke. Curse turns handsome prince into werewolf-like beast every night; princess defends him, while a usurper seeks his throne. Colorful but turgid. Makeup by the fabled Jack P. Pierce.▼

Beauty and the Beast (1991) **C-85m.** *****½** D: Gary Trousdale, Kirk Wise. Voices of Paige O'Hara, Robby Benson, Jerry Orbach, Angela Lansbury, Richard White, David Ogden Stiers, Jesse Corti, Rex Everhart, Bradley Michael Pierce, Jo Anne Worley, Kimmy Robertson. Classic Disney cartoon version of the classic tale, with bookish Belle and a ferocious Beast learning to love one another after he makes her prisoner in his desolate castle (where the only signs of life come from humanized household fixtures). Cannily presented in the style of a Broadway musical, with a fine-tuned script by Linda Woolverton, and a rousing, Oscar-winning score by Alan Menken (with another Oscar for Menken and Howard Ashman's title tune). The first animated feature to earn an Oscar nomination as Best Picture. Reissued at 89m. in 2002 with an additional musical sequence entitled "Human Again." Followed by a Broadway musical, a TV series, and two direct-to-video sequels. [G]▼●❶

Beauty and the Robot, The SEE: **Sex Kittens Go to College**

Beauty Shop (2005) C-105m. **½ D: Bille Woodruff. Queen Latifah, Alicia Silverstone, Andie MacDowell, Alfre Woodard, Mena Suvari, Kevin Bacon, Djimon Hounsou, Keshia Knight Pulliam, Bryce Wilson, Golden Brooks, Sherri Shepherd, Della Reese, Wilmer Valderrama, Dondre Whitfield, Paige Hurd. Latifah is back from BARBERSHOP 2 as Gina, now an Atlanta single mom/stylist. Fed up with boss Bacon (over-the-top and foreign), she all too predictably turns an eyesore into a salon of her very own, complete with attitude, plus upstairs neighbor Hounsou as a hunky handyman. The jokes fly, the tresses fall, and Silverstone plays the token role done by Troy Garity in BARBERSHOP. Panavision. [PG-13] ▼❶

Beaver, The (2011) C-91m. **½ D: Jodie Foster. Mel Gibson, Jodie Foster, Anton Yelchin, Jennifer Lawrence, Cherry Jones, Riley Thomas Stewart. A man suffering from severe depression tries to commit suicide and fails. Then he begins to put the pieces of his life back together, speaking only through the Cockney accent of a furry hand puppet, The Beaver. His wife is perplexed and appalled, while his young son blossoms under the newfound attention. Meanwhile, his older boy (Yelchin) fears that he has inherited all his father's worst traits. Intriguing, way-offbeat parable written by Kyle Killen gains traction through Gibson's fully committed performance, though it's hard to say what lessons are learned when it's all said and done. Panavision. [PG-13]❶

Beavis and Butt-head Do America (1996) C-80m. **½ D: Mike Judge. Voices of Mike Judge, Robert Stack, Cloris Leachman, Eric Bogosian, Richard Linklater. The unabashedly ignorant, flagrantly antisocial, hormonally charged duo from MTV's animated series find themselves on a cross-country odyssey that begins when someone steals their all-important TV set. Alternately stupid, gross, and hilarious, this modest cartoon feature is certainly true to itself and certain to please *B&B* fans. Bruce Willis, Demi Moore, and David Letterman contribute unbilled voices, but best of all is the casting of Stack as a hard-nosed Federal agent. Huh-huh-huh. [PG-13]▼●❶

Bebe's Kids (1992) C-74m. **½ D: Bruce Smith. Voices of Faizon Love, Nell Carter, Myra J., Vanessa Bell Calloway, Tone Loc, Wayne Collins, Jonell Green, Marques Houston. Raucous animated feature based on a routine by the late comedian Robin Harris (voiced here by Faizon Love) whose date with an attractive woman turns into a nightmare when she brings along her son—and three brats she's looking after. The first animated feature aimed squarely at a black audience is lively, often funny—but a bit protracted. [PG-13]▼●❶

Because I Said So (2007) C-102m. ** D: Michael Lehmann. Diane Keaton, Mandy Moore, Gabriel Macht, Tom Everett Scott, Lauren Graham, Piper Perabo, Stephen Collins, Ty Panitz, Tony Hale. Meddlesome mother has married off two of her girls but can't leave her remaining single daughter alone; she even takes out a personals ad in order to audition prospects, then steers the likeliest candidate (Scott) her way. But Moore is more attracted to a freewheeling musician (Macht) of whom her mom doesn't approve. Contrived romantic comedy is torpedoed by Keaton's character, who is unbelievably annoying. [PG-13]❶

Because of Winn-Dixie (2005) C-106m. ** D: Wayne Wang. AnnaSophia Robb, Jeff Daniels, Cicely Tyson, Eva Marie Saint, Dave Matthews, Courtney Jines, Elle Fanning, Harland Williams. Tepid adaptation of Kate DiCamillo's children's novel (and an offbeat choice for director Wang) about a 10-year-old girl and her minister father, whose wife has abandoned him . . . and a dog that changes a community. Genial to a fault, but packed with local eccentrics who seem more out of Central Casting than anyone's real life. Singer Matthews probably fares best as an ex-con who runs a pet shop, though young Robb at least has a winning smile. [PG]▼❶

Because You're Mine (1952) C-103m. ** D: Alexander Hall. Mario Lanza, James Whitmore, Doretta Morrow, Dean Miller, Paula Corday, Jeff Donnell, Spring Byington, Don Porter, Eduard Franz, Bobby Van. Opera star Lanza is drafted and falls in love with Morrow, the sister of his top sergeant (Whitmore). For Lanza fans only. ▼❶

Becket (1964) C-148m. **** D: Peter Glenville. Richard Burton, Peter O'Toole, John Gielgud, Donald Wolfit, Martita Hunt, Pamela Brown, Felix Aylmer. Stunning film, adapted by Edward Anhalt (who won an Oscar) from the Jean Anouilh play, centers on stormy friendship between Archbishop of Canterbury Thomas à Becket and his English King, Henry II. Superbly acted and magnificently photographed (by Geoffrey Unsworth) on location in England. Panavision. ▼●❶

Becky Sharp (1935) C-83m. **½ D: Rouben Mamoulian. Miriam Hopkins, Frances Dee, Cedric Hardwicke, Billie Burke, Alison Skipworth, Nigel Bruce. Witty but sometimes ponderous adaptation of Thackeray's *Vanity Fair* with Hopkins as self-reliant girl whose sole concern is herself. Historically important as first full-Technicolor (3-color) feature, designed by Robert

Edmond Jones (and photographed by Ray Rennahan). Long available only in inferior 67m. Cinecolor reissue prints; archivally restored in 1985. Previously filmed in 1923 and 1932, remade in 2004 (all as VANITY FAIR). ▼▶

Becoming Colette (1992-U.S.-German) **C-97m.** *½ D: Danny Huston. Klaus Maria Brandauer, Mathilda May, Virginia Madsen, Paul Rhys, John van Dreelen, Jean-Pierre Aumont. Ridiculous tale of the famed French writer Colette (May), depicted as an inexperienced country girl who weds publisher Brandauer. He prints her writing under his name, and sets up a threesome with Madsen (but becomes outraged when the women fall in love). The director is the son of John Huston, but may as well be the protégé of Zalman King. [R] ▼

Becoming Jane (2007-British) **C-113m.** *** D: Julian Jarrold. Anne Hathaway, James McAvoy, Julie Walters, James Cromwell, Maggie Smith, Joe Anderson, Lucy Cohu, Laurence Fox, Ian Richardson. Future novelist Jane Austen (Hathaway) is from humble Hampshire means and should be looking to secure an advantageous marriage. Instead, the headstrong young woman wants life on her own terms . . . but only after falling in love with a brash Irishman (McAvoy) does her writing mature and reveal "life experience." Entertaining film, based on Austen's letters, indicates that this episode in her life inspired *Pride and Prejudice*. Hathaway fares well in the midst of a mostly British cast. Super 35. [PG]🅓

Be Cool (2005) **C-114m.** **½ D: F. Gary Gray. John Travolta, Uma Thurman, Vince Vaughn, Cedric the Entertainer, André Benjamin (André 3000), Steven Tyleçcr, Christina Milian, Harvey Keitel, The Rock, Danny DeVito, Robert Pastorelli, Debi Mazar, Paul Adelstein. In this sequel to Elmore Leonard's GET SHORTY, Chili Palmer (Travolta) moves into the music business and chooses a promising young singer (Milian) as his protégée, despite the fact that she's already under contract to ruthless Keitel and his loose-cannon lieutenant, Vaughn. Amiable, good-looking film retains Leonard's story smarts but blunts the impact by allowing its comedic costars (Vaughn, Cedric) to riff to their heart's content. The Rock is especially funny as a bodyguard/Hollywood wannabe. James Woods appears unbilled; other music stars make cameo appearances. Super 35. [PG-13] ▼▶

Bed and Board (1970-French) **C-97m.** ***½ D: François Truffaut. Jean-Pierre Léaud, Claude Jade, Hiroko Berghauer, Daniel Ceccaldi, Claire Duhamel. Chapter Four of the Antoine Doinel story. Here, Doinel (Léaud) is married to Christine (Jade); he is confused, immature, becomes a father, and has an affair with Berghauer. Lovingly directed by Truffaut; Jacques Tati, in an amusing cameo,

impersonates M. Hulot. Followed by LOVE ON THE RUN. [PG] ▼▶

Bed & Breakfast (1992) **C-98m.** **½ D: Robert Ellis Miller. Roger Moore, Talia Shire, Colleen Dewhurst, Nina Siemaszko, Ford Rainey, Stephen Root, Jamie Walters, Victor Slezak. A debonair stranger makes his impact on a houseful of women, who span several generations. First-rate performances and a gorgeous setting on the Maine coast make this modest film worth seeing, especially on the small screen; filmed in 1989. [PG-13] ▼●

Bedazzled (1967-British) **C-107m.** *** D: Stanley Donen. Peter Cook, Dudley Moore, Eleanor Bron, Raquel Welch, Alba, Barry Humphries. Cult film updating Faust legend is as sacrilegious as THE SINGING NUN and usually funnier. The laughs aren't always consistent, but the Cook-Moore team is terrific and Donen's direction stylish. And remember the magic words: "Julie Andrews!" Remade in 2000. Panavision. ▼●▶

Bedazzled (2000) **C-93m.** **½ D: Harold Ramis. Brendan Fraser, Elizabeth Hurley, Frances O'Connor, Miriam Shor, Orlando Jones, Paul Adelstein, Toby Huss, Gabriele Casseus, Brian Doyle-Murray. Sweet-natured nerd sells his soul to a sexy Devil (Hurley) in exchange for seven wishes, but she manages to put a hitch into all of his dreams-come-true. All he really wants is for the coworker he worships from afar to fall in love with him. Funny in spots, with Fraser and Hurley hitting just the right note, but remake of 1967 film never catches fire. Panavision. [PG-13] ▼▶

Bedford Incident, The (1965) **102m.** *** D: James B. Harris. Richard Widmark, Sidney Poitier, James MacArthur, Martin Balsam, Wally Cox, Eric Portman, Donald Sutherland. Strong Cold War story of authoritarian Navy captain (Widmark) scouting Russian subs near Greenland and the mental conflicts that develop on his ship. Poitier is reporter too good to be true, Balsam a sympathetic doctor disliked by Widmark. Cast excels in intriguing battle of wits. ▼▶

Bedknobs and Broomsticks (1971) **C-117m.** *** D: Robert Stevenson. Angela Lansbury, David Tomlinson, Roddy McDowall, Sam Jaffe, Roy Snart, Cindy O'Callaghan, Ian Weighill. Elaborate Disney musical fantasy about amateur witch who helps British cause in WW2; no MARY POPPINS, but quite enjoyable, with Oscar-winning special effects and delightful animated cartoon sequences directed by Ward Kimball. Reissued at 98m. 141m. archival edition assembled in 1996, with more (and longer) songs, clearer plot, and more of a part for McDowall. [G] ▼●▶

Bedlam (1946) **79m.** *** D: Mark Robson. Boris Karloff, Anna Lee, Ian Wolfe, Richard Fraser, Billy House, Jason Robards, Sr. Atmospheric chiller of courageous Lee trying to expose shameful conditions at notorious 18th-century London insane asylum run by corrupt head Karloff. Producer Val Lewton also coscripted under pseudonym Carlos Keith. Robert Clarke appears unbilled.▼●▶

Bed of Roses (1996) **C-87m.** ** D: Michael Goldenberg. Christian Slater, Mary Stuart Masterson, Pamela Segall, Josh Brolin, Ally Walker, Debra Monk. Business exec Masterson is courted by florist Slater (a young widower), but her past troubled relationships prevent her from committing to him. Attempt at a serious romantic film is emotionally off the mark, though the performers try their best. [PG]▼●▶

Bedrooms & Hallways (1999-British) **C-95m.** ** D: Rose Troche. Kevin McKidd, Hugo Weaving, James Purefoy, Tom Hollander, Christopher Fulford, Julie Graham, Paul Higgins, Jennifer Ehle, Simon Callow. Ambitious but flat sex comedy about two gay roommates. One has a hot-and-heavy affair in which the emphasis is on sex; the other has a budding romance with a man who has just busted up with his longtime girlfriend. Good when it explores relationships, less successful in its silly parodies of men's groups and Jane Austen novels. ▼▶

Bedroom Window, The (1987) **C-112m.** *** D: Curtis Hanson. Steve Guttenberg, Elizabeth McGovern, Isabelle Huppert, Paul Shenar, Carl Lumbly, Wallace Shawn, Frederick Coffin, Brad Greenquist. An innocent man offers to alibi for his boss' sexy wife, who witnessed an assault from his bedroom window after they made love. This apparently simple gesture snowballs into a web of crime and duplicity, in this attractive, sexy, and suspenseful Hitchcock homage. Guttenberg is no Cary Grant (or James Stewart), but the film is consistently enjoyable—if not always absolutely believable. J-D-C Scope. [R]▼●▶

Bed Sitting Room, The (1969-British) **C-91m.** **½ D: Richard Lester. Rita Tushingham, Ralph Richardson, Peter Cook, Dudley Moore, Harry Secombe, Arthur Lowe, Roy Kinnear, Spike Milligan, Michael Hordern, Mona Washbourne. Moderately successful black-comedy look at distorted, devastated England three years after nuclear war. A few funny bits, great cast, but film doesn't click. Marty Feldman makes his film debut in a brief bit.

Bedtime for Bonzo (1951) **83m.** **½ D: Frederick de Cordova. Ronald Reagan, Diana Lynn, Walter Slezak, Jesse White, Lucille Barkley. Often cited as the pinnacle of absurdity in Reagan's career, but in fact it's a cute, harmless little comedy about a professor who treats a chimp as his child for a heredity experiment. Reagan did not appear in the sequel, BONZO GOES TO COLLEGE.▼▶

Bedtime Stories (2008) **C-99m.** ** D: Adam Shankman. Adam Sandler, Keri Russell, Guy Pearce, Courteney Cox, Russell Brand, Richard Griffiths, Jonathan Pryce, Carmen Electra, Lucy Lawless, Teresa Palmer, Aisha Tyler. Story of an underdog whose father's homespun motel has been transformed into a super-luxury hotel where he now works as a handyman. Then he discovers that telling bedtime tales to his niece and nephew has the potential to change his fortunes. Disney film had real potential, starting out as a fable about the power of storytelling . . . but it's been vulgarized (and needlessly cluttered) by Sandler and his writing cohorts. Young kids may still enjoy it but thoughtful parents will steer them elsewhere. Rob Schneider appears unbilled. Super 35. [PG]▶

Bedtime Story (1941) **85m.** *** D: Alexander Hall. Fredric March, Loretta Young, Robert Benchley, Allyn Joslyn, Eve Arden. Fine cast in sparkling comedy of playwright March trying to stop wife Young from retiring so she can star in his next play.

Bedtime Story (1964) **C-99m.** **½ D: Ralph Levy. Marlon Brando, David Niven, Shirley Jones, Dody Goodman, Marie Windsor. Offbeat casting of stars provides chief interest in lackluster comedy of con men Brando and Niven competing for Jones' affection. Remade as DIRTY ROTTEN SCOUNDRELS.▼

Bee Movie (2007) **C-90m.** *** D: Steve Hickner, Simon J. Smith. Voices of Jerry Seinfeld, Renée Zellweger, Matthew Broderick, Patrick Warburton, John Goodman, Chris Rock, Kathy Bates, Barry Levinson, Ray Liotta, Sting, Oprah Winfrey, Larry Miller, Megan Mullally, Rip Torn, Michael Richards. It's the ABCs of being a bee, as typified by the experiences of recent college grad Barry B. Benson (Seinfeld), who's disinclined to enter the trade of every family member and friend: keeping those honey coffers going. Brisk animation and a sardonically Seinfeld-ish tone keep this fun, though the relationship between the bee-boy protagonist and a female human he befriends (Zellweger) never really catches fire. More successful around the edges than down the middle, this gleans substantial chortles from its ragging of real-life celebrities. [PG]▶

Been Down So Long It Looks Like Up to Me (1971) **C-90m.** *½ D: Jeffrey Young. Barry Primus, Linda DeCoff, David Browning, Susan Tyrrell, Philip Shafer, Bruce Davison, Raul Julia. Bland, dated film version of Richard Fariña's novel about hip 1960s type trying to endure life on a 1958 campus. [R]

Been Rich All My Life (2006) **C-81m.** *** D: Heather Lyn MacDonald. Easy-to-take documentary about the Silver Belles, a troupe of indomitable tap-dancing octogenarians (Marion Coles, Elaine Ellis, Cleo Hayes, Fay Ray, Bertye Lou Wood) formed in the 1980s long after their prime showgirl days working at the Cotton Club and the Apollo. The movie's point, though, is to question how "prime" is defined; every woman here looks (and acts) about two decades younger than her given age. Racially inspired hardships are somewhat skimmed over, though it's intriguing to learn how just a few of these women shut down the Apollo during a strike for better wages.◗

Beer (1985) **C-82m.** *½ D: Patrick Kelly. Loretta Swit, Rip Torn, Kenneth Mars, David Alan Grier, William Russ, Saul Stein, Dick Shawn. Unimaginative, ultimately tasteless spoof of Madison Avenue hype, with Swit as an ad-agency executive who devises a highly successful commercial campaign to sell beer. Not so far from reality—and not terribly funny. [R]▼

Beerfest (2006) **C-110m.** ** D: Jay Chandrasekhar. Jay Chandrasekhar, Steve Lemme, Paul Soter, Erik Stolhanske, Kevin Heffernan, Jürgen Prochnow, M. C. Gainey, Cloris Leachman, Mo'Nique, Eric Christian Olsen. Two brothers travel to Munich for Oktoberfest and discover an underground "fight club" devoted to ancient beer-drinking games and other sports. They vow to recruit friends, train, and return to compete the next year. Gross-out concoction from the Broken Lizard comedy troupe goes for the most obvious, juvenile college humor, hitting an occasional bull's-eye, especially when Leachman starts in with beer and sausage jokes. Waaaaaay over the top, but harmless enough for the undemanding, possibly inebriated dudes likely to watch it. Donald Sutherland appears unbilled. Unrated version runs 112m. Super 35. [R]◗

Beer League (2006) **C-87m.** **½ D: Frank Sebastiano. Artie Lange, Ralph Macchio, Anthony De Sando, Cara Buono, Jimmy Palumbo, Joe Lo Truglio, Jerry Minor, Seymour Cassel, Michael Deeg, Laurie Metcalf. Motley group of thirtysomething losers on a slow-pitch New Jersey softball team have to shape up and beat their obnoxious rivals or get booted out of the league, but they spend most of their time boozing, brawling, and carousing. You don't have to be from Jersey to enjoy this affably lowbrow, gleefully politically incorrect update of THE BAD NEWS BEARS, although downing a six-pack will certainly help. Tina Fey makes a blink-and-you'll-miss-it cameo. Cowritten by Lange. Aka ARTIE LANGE'S BEER LEAGUE. [R]◗

Bees, The (1978) **C-83m.** *½ D: Alfredo Zacharias. John Saxon, Angel Tompkins, John Carradine, Claudio Brook, Alicia Encinias. After THE SWARM, if you sincerely want to see this low-budget disaster film about killer bees, you get what you deserve. Filmed in Mexico. [PG]▼

Bee Season (2005) **C-104m.** **½ D: Scott McGehee, David Siegel. Richard Gere, Juliette Binoche, Flora Cross, Max Minghella, Kate Bosworth. Ambitious but convoluted

drama about the power of words, the meaning of religion, and competition. Sixthgrader Cross almost mystically becomes a champion speller, and her success has a profound impact on the other members of her family. The filmmakers cleverly visualize the words and letters in the girl's mind, but Naomi Foner Gyllenhaal's script (adapted from Myla Goldberg's best-selling novel) lacks cohesion. Panavision. [PG-13]◗

Beethoven (1992) **C-87m.** **½ D: Brian Levant. Charles Grodin, Bonnie Hunt, Dean Jones, Oliver Platt, Stanley Tucci, Nicholle Tom, Christopher Castile, Sarah Rose Karr, David Duchovny, Patricia Heaton, Laurel Cronin, and Chris. Innocuous family comedy about an uptight Dad (Grodin) whose family talks him into keeping a runaway puppy that grows into a big, slobbering St. Bernard. It's fun to watch all-American, cleancut Jones playing a slimy, raspy-voiced villain. Followed by BEETHOVEN'S 2ND and five DVD sequels. [PG] ▼●

Beethoven's 2nd (1993) **C-86m.** **½ D: Rod Daniel. Charles Grodin, Bonnie Hunt, Nicholle Tom, Christopher Castile, Sarah Rose Karr, Debi Mazar, Chris Penn, Ashley Hamilton, Maury Chaykin, Jeff Corey, Virginia Capers, and Beethoven. Painless sequel, on par with its predecessor, which charts the various complications when Grodin's kids raise St. Bernard Beethoven's puppies on the sly. If you liked the original.... Followed by five DVD sequels. [PG] ▼●

Beetle Juice (1988) **C-92m.** *** D: Tim Burton. Michael Keaton, Alec Baldwin, Geena Davis, Jeffrey Jones, Catherine O'Hara, Winona Ryder, Sylvia Sidney, Robert Goulet, Glenn Shadix, Dick Cavett, Annie McEnroe. Newly deceased couple in need of help coping with the afterlife, and obnoxious family who's moved into their home, get it in the form of renegade spirit Betelgeuse (Keaton, who pulls out all the stops). Fantastic special effects make this a sort of live-action cartoon. Added treat: Sylvia Sidney as harried case worker in the hereafter. Great fun, and surprisingly good-natured. Music by Danny Elfman, with a strong assist from Harry Belafonte. Oscar winner for makeup. Followed by an animated TV series. [PG]▼●

Before and After (1996) **C-107m.** *** D: Barbet Schroeder. Meryl Streep, Liam Neeson, Edward Furlong, Alfred Molina, Julia Weldon, Daniel von Bargen, John Heard, Ann Magnuson, Larry Pine, Wesley Addy. Sober tale of a New England family torn apart—and ostracized—when the son is accused of murdering a teenage girl and then disappears. The father is willing to cover the boy's tracks, while mother and daughter want to tell the truth, in spite of the consequences. Absorbing and believable story (written by Ted Tally). Look for Paul Giamatti as a courtroom spectator. [PG-13] ▼●

Before Night Falls (2000) **C-125m.** **✱✱✱** D: Julian Schnabel. Javier Bardem, Olivier Martinez, Andrea Di Stefano, Sean Penn, Johnny Depp, Michael Wincott, Hector Babenco, Jerzy Skolimowski. Often compelling look at the life of Cuban writer Reinaldo Arenas, spanning several decades as he discovers his homosexuality, blossoms as a writer, then finds that in Castro's Cuba he's persecuted on both counts. Told in episodic fashion, the film has many great scenes, but goes on a bit too long. Bardem's performance is exceptional. Penn appears briefly as a Cuban peasant, Depp in two successive scenes as a transvestite prisoner and a warden. [R]**▼❶**

Before Sunrise (1995) **C-101m.** **✱✱½** D: Richard Linklater. Ethan Hawke, Julie Delpy. Young American strikes up a conversation with a fellow train passenger and persuades her to get off in Vienna and share his last night in Europe; they do, in fact, spend the entire night talking and falling in love. A somewhat daring idea for the '90s, buoyed by two engaging performers; it is (unavoidably) awfully talky, but it's also undeniably romantic. Followed by a sequel. [R]**▼❶❶**

Before Sunset (2004) **C-80m.** **✱✱✱½** D: Richard Linklater. Ethan Hawke, Julie Delpy. Disarming follow-up to BEFORE SUNRISE has the two characters meeting up nine years later as he passes through Paris on a book tour. They catch up in the short time he has before having to head for the airport, walking through various neighborhoods, gradually letting down their guards about their feelings toward one another. A beguiling look at chances lost and taken, the lasting effect of impulsive decisions, and how one meaningful encounter can resonate for years to come. Script is credited to the stars and director. [R]**▼❶**

Before the Devil Knows You're Dead (2007-U.S.-Irish) **C-117m.** **✱✱½** D: Sidney Lumet. Philip Seymour Hoffman, Ethan Hawke, Albert Finney, Marisa Tomei, Rosemary Harris, Aleksa Palladino, Brian F. O'Byrne, Amy Ryan, Michael Shannon, Leonardo Cimino. Pressured payroll manager (Hoffman) convinces his ne'er-do-well brother (Hawke) to rob a jewelry store for some quick (and easy) money. Naturally, things go wrong and the repercussions keep building and building. Tense, claustrophobic drama, told in time-splintered structure, is well acted and well staged by Lumet (in his final film), but the utter unpleasantness of the story and the characters becomes repetitious and wearying. [R]**❶**

Before the Rain (1994-Macedonian-British-French) **C-114m.** **✱✱✱** D: Milcho Manchevski. Katrin Cartlidge, Rade Serbedzija, Gregoire Colin, Labina Mitevska. Fascinating look at several intertwining lives in the newly independent, and strife-torn, Republic of Macedonia (formerly Yugoslavia), where rural poverty and violent rage

are prevalent. Story links a young monk, a globetrotting photojournalist, and a stylish young woman in London who is at a crossroads in her personal life. Film's structure resembles PULP FICTION, which debuted almost simultaneously. A strong statement that unfolds slowly; stick with this one. Technovision.**▼❶**

Before the Rains (2008-Indian-British-U.S.) **C-98m.** **✱✱✱** D: Santosh Sivan. Linus Roache, Jennifer Ehle, Rahul Bose, Nandita Das, Leo Benedict. Set in 1930s India at a time of emerging nationalism, ambitious young Indian man must choose between the past and his own future when he discovers an illicit affair is taking place between his English spice-baron boss and a village woman. First English-language film for Indian director Sivan captures the bustling soul of a community in transition, even if it surrenders to some soapy plotting sensibilities along the way. Based on *Red Roofs*, a segment in the 2001 film YELLOW ASPHALT: THREE DESERT STORIES. [PG-13]**❶**

Before the Revolution (1964-Italian) **115m.** **✱✱✱** D: Bernardo Bertolucci. Adriana Asti, Francisco Barilli, Alain Midgette, Morando Morandini, Domenico Alpi. Bertolucci's second feature (which he wrote when he was 22 years old) dramatizes the dilemma of young, middle-class Barilli. Will he embrace a life of social and political radicalism, or submit to the bourgeois status quo? Revealing 1960s time capsule, loaded with topical ideas, references, and fervor.**▼**

Before Winter Comes (1969-British) **C-102m.** **✱✱½** D: J. Lee Thompson. David Niven, Topol, Anna Karina, John Hurt, Anthony Quayle, Ori Levy. Topol is interpreter for British officer Niven in displaced persons' camp following WW2. Uneven comedy-drama with many touching moments, capturing plight of refugees. Topol's warmth shines in winning performance. [M/PG]

Beggar's Opera, The (1953-British) **C-94m.** **✱✱✱** D: Peter Brook. Laurence Olivier, Stanley Holloway, Dorothy Tutin, Daphne Anderson, Mary Clare, Hugh Griffith, Laurence Naismith. Celebrated stage director Brook made his film debut with this vivid, energetic version of John Gay's opera. Coproducer and star Olivier is somewhat miscast but more than makes up for it with his sly portrayal of a jailed highwayman who exaggerates his exploits into a musical revue.**❶**

Beginners (2011) **C-105m.** **✱✱½** D: Mike Mills. Ewan McGregor, Christopher Plummer, Mélanie Laurent, Goran Visnjic, Kai Lennox, Mary Page Keller, Lou Taylor Pucci. Highly personal story by writer-director Mills about a 38-year-old artist (McGregor) who's never had a successful relationship. After his father's death he reflects on his parents' lengthy but strained marriage, how his mother shaped his view of the world, and how his father came out of the closet at age 75. Plummer's warm embrace of his new lifestyle (shown in flashbacks) is contrasted with his son's inability to commit to a woman he's fallen in love with. Well acted all around, but how you respond to this quirky, nonlinear film may depend on how you relate to McGregor's locked-up character, who isn't nearly as interesting as his father. [R]

Beginning of the End (1957) **73m.** *½ D: Bert I. Gordon. Peggie Castle, Peter Graves, Morris Ankrum, Thomas Browne Henry. Awful sci-fi outing about giant grasshoppers (thanks to radiation) on the rampage; at the climax, they invade Chicago—but none too convincingly.▼❿

Beginning or the End, The (1947) **112m.** *** D: Norman Taurog. Brian Donlevy, Robert Walker, Beverly Tyler, Audrey Totter, Hume Cronyn. Engrossing account of atomic bomb development, depicting both human and spectacular aspects.

Beguiled, The (1971) **C-109m.** *** D: Don Siegel. Clint Eastwood, Geraldine Page, Elizabeth Hartman, Jo Ann Harris, Darleen Carr, Pamelyn Ferdin. Offbeat, methodically paced story set in Civil War South. Wounded Eastwood brought to girls' school to recuperate; he becomes catalyst for flurry of jealousy and hatred. Unusual Eastwood fare, but for patient viewers, a rich, rewarding film. [R]▼●❿

Behind Enemy Lines (1986) SEE: **P.O.W. The Escape**

Behind Enemy Lines (2001) **C-106m.** **½ D: John Moore. Owen Wilson, Gene Hackman, Gabriel Macht, Charles Malik Whitfield, Joaquim de Almeida, David Keith, Olek Krupa, Vladimir Mashkov. A cocky naval airman is shot down behind enemy lines in Bosnia and his commanding officer is unable to rescue him because of political constraints. Action yarn delivers a lot of excitement, but a hyperactive camera may produce motion sickness in some viewers. The corny finale seems to have come from a lesser-grade Hollywood movie of decades past. Followed by a direct-to-video sequel and a direct-to-DVD sequel. Super 35. [PG-13]▼❿

Behind Locked Doors (1948) **62m.** **½ D: Oscar (Budd) Boetticher. Richard Carlson, Lucille Bremer, Douglas Fowley, Thomas Browne Henry, Dickie Moore, Tor Johnson. Pretty good grade-B film noir about a private eye who checks into a sanitarium on a tip that a wanted judge is holed up there. Johnson is put to good use as a former prizefighter kept in solitary confinement. Aka THE HUMAN GORILLA. ▼❿

Behind the Iron Curtain SEE: **Iron Curtain, The**

Behind the Lines SEE: **Regeneration** (1997-British-Canadian)

Behind the Sun (2001-Brazilian-French-Swiss) **C-93m.** *** D: Walter Salles. José Dumont, Rodrigo Santoro, Rita Assemany, Luiz Carlos Vasconcelos, Flavia Marco Antonio, Ravi Ramos Lacerda. Lyrical, quietly absorbing fable set in rural Brazil in 1910 about two feuding families whose patriarchs dispatch their sons to kill each other's offspring in the name of honor. The unfolding events are seen through the eyes of a 10-year-old (Lacerda) who attempts to free himself and his brother from this ritual of violence. Extremely effective. Super 35. [PG-13]▼❿

Behold a Pale Horse (1964) **118m.** **½ D: Fred Zinnemann. Gregory Peck, Anthony Quinn, Omar Sharif, Mildred Dunnock, Christian Marquand, Raymond Pellegrin. Peck and Quinn wage an ideological battle in post–Spanish Civil War story of politics and violence that loses focus, becoming confused and talky. Valiant try by all.▼❿

Beijing Bicycle (2001-Taiwanese-Chinese) **C-113m.** ** D: Wang Xiaoshuai. Cui Lin, Li Bin, Zhou Xun, Gao Yuanyuan, Li Shuang, Zhao Yiwei, Pang Yan. Muddled account of a shy, naïve country boy (Lin), newly arrived in Beijing, who finds a job as a bicycle messenger; then, predictably, his bike is stolen. Potentially compelling allegory of the dreams and hopes of the young is done in by dullness and endless repetition. Obviously inspired by De Sica's BICYCLE THIEVES. [PG-13]▼❿

Being, The (1983) **C-79m.** *½ D: Jackie Kong. Martin Landau, Jose Ferrer, Dorothy Malone, Ruth Buzzi, Marianne Gordon Rogers, Murray Langston, Kinky Friedman, Johnny Dark. Creature spawned by nuclear waste terrorizes Idaho community. Humor is film's saving grace, but it isn't enough to overcome grade-Z script and production. Producer William Osco (Kong's then-husband) also costars under the name Rexx Coltrane. Filmed in 1980; briefly shown as EASTER SUNDAY. [R]▼❿

Being Human (1994-British-U.S.) **C-122m.** **½ D: Bill Forsyth. Robin Williams, John Turturro, Anna Galiena, Vincent D'Onofrio, Hector Elizondo, Lorraine Bracco, Lindsay Crouse, Grace Mahlaba, Dave Jones, Jonathan Hyde, Lizzy McInnerny, William H. Macy, Bill Nighy, Robert Carlyle; narrated by Theresa Russell. Queer duck of a movie with Williams as five different men—through five periods of time (spanning 10,000 years)—who are cosmically related. All of them are struggling and striving, without much success, to find happiness. If you can get past the off-putting narration, it's intermittently intriguing, a definite original from writer-director Forsyth. Williams makes this journey worthwhile. [PG-13]▼●❿

Being John Malkovich (1999) **C-112m.** ***½ D: Spike Jonze. John Cusack, John Malkovich, Cameron Diaz, Catherine Keener,

Orson Bean, Mary Kay Place, Charlie Sheen. Remarkable, audaciously original black comedy/fantasy about an iconoclastic puppeteer (Cusack) who discovers a portal into the mind of actor John Malkovich, and decides to exploit its possibilities. A far-out premise (by writer Charlie Kaufman) is ingeniously developed into a full-blown story and acted with pizzazz. Malkovich is a marvel in an especially sly, nuanced performance. Other stars make gag cameos. Feature debut for commercial and music video director Jonze. [R]▼●]

Being Julia (2004-Hungarian-Canadian-British) C-104m. **½ D: István Szabó. Annette Bening, Jeremy Irons, Bruce Greenwood, Miriam Margolyes, Juliet Stevenson, Shaun Evans, Lucy Punch, Maury Chaykin, Sheila McCarthy, Michael Gambon, Leigh Lawson, Rosemary Harris, Rita Tushingham, Thomas Sturridge. Married, middle-aged stage star in 1930s London is rejuvenated by a fling with a younger man but has other personal and professional obstacles to overcome. Bening is radiant and shines as her character blossoms, but the story sags until a deliciously funny finale. Budapest stands in for period London. Ronald Harwood adapted W. Somerset Maugham's novel *Theatre*. [R] ▼]

Being There (1979) C-130m. **½ D: Hal Ashby. Peter Sellers, Shirley MacLaine, Melvyn Douglas, Jack Warden, Richard Dysart, Richard Basehart, James Noble, David Clennon, Ruth Attaway, David Morrissey. A childlike man (Sellers) chances to meet important, powerful people who interpret his bewildered silence as brilliance. Low-keyed black humor, full of savagely witty comments on American life in the television age, but fatally overlong. Adapted by Jerzy Kosinski from his own story. Douglas won Oscar as political kingmaker. [PG]▼●]

Be Kind Rewind (2008) C-101m. *** D: Michel Gondry. Jack Black, Mos Def, Danny Glover, Mia Farrow, Melonie Diaz, Irv Gooch, Marcus Carl Franklin, Sigourney Weaver. Odd but endearing film set in Passaic, N.J., where Glover's dilapidated video-rental store—supposedly the birthplace of Fats Waller—is an anachronism, outside and in. When he leaves Def in charge, nutty pal Black (who's become magnetized) accidentally erases all the tapes in the store, forcing the duo to reinvent the missing films (GHOSTBUSTERS; 2001: A SPACE ODYSSEY; THE LION KING) with their old-fashioned video camera and the help of neighborhood allies. An eccentric ode to innocence, creativity, and community. Written by the director. J-D-C Scope. [PG-13]]

Bela Lugosi Meets a Brooklyn Gorilla (1952) 74m. BOMB D: William Beaudine. Bela Lugosi, Duke Mitchell, Sammy Petrillo, Charlita, Muriel Landers, Ramona the Chimp. One of the all-time greats. Mitchell and Petrillo (the very poor man's Martin and Lewis) are stranded on a jungle island, where Lugosi is conducting strange experiments. Proceed at your own risk. Aka THE BOYS FROM BROOKLYN. ▼]

Believe in Me (1971) C-90m. ** D: Stuart Hagmann. Michael Sarrazin, Jacqueline Bisset, Jon Cypher, Allen Garfield, Kurt Dodenhoff. Still another '70s film about drug addiction, and none too good; clean-cut career girl Bisset becomes addicted to speed in the East Village. Performers do their best. [R]

Believe in Me (2007) C-108m. *** D: Robert Collector. Jeffrey Donovan, Samantha Mathis, Bruce Dern, Bob Gunton, Heather Matarazzo, Alicia Lagano, Chris Ellis. Donovan moves to a small Oklahoma town in 1964 to take a coaching job, but when he arrives he learns he's been assigned to a girls' basketball team. What's more, the girls have no self-esteem and little support from the community. Sincere heartland story rises above its familiar sports-underdog formula. Donovan and Mathis (as his supportive wife) are first-rate. Based on the real-life experiences of Jim Keith. Written by the director. HD Widescreen. [PG]]

Believer, The (2002) C-98m. *** D: Henry Bean. Ryan Gosling, Summer Phoenix, Billy Zane, Theresa Russell, Glenn Fitzgerald, Ronald Guttman, Henry Bean. Ferocious examination of a yeshiva-educated young man in N.Y.C. who chooses to become a neo-Nazi skinhead. Gosling gives an award-caliber performance as a Jew (loosely based on fact) whose reasoning is questionable but whose passion is real. Veteran screenwriter Bean's directorial debut. Released overseas in 2001; U.S. debut on cable TV in 2002. [R]▼]

Believers, The (1987) C-114m. **½ D: John Schlesinger. Martin Sheen, Helen Shaver, Harley Cross, Robert Loggia, Elizabeth Wilson, Lee Richardson, Harris Yulin, Richard Masur, Carla Pinza, Jimmy Smits. Gripping, genuinely frightening story of widower and son who move to N.Y.C. and become involved (in more ways than one) with cultish religion of Santeria, which believes in the sacrifice of children. Well-crafted film knows how to manipulate its audience but shows no mercy, either: a boy sees his mother electrocuted in the very first scene! [R]▼●]

Belizaire the Cajun (1986) C-100m. **½ D: Glen Pitre. Armand Assante, Gail Youngs, Michael Schoeffling, Stephen McHattie, Will Patton, Nancy Barrett. Assante is well cast as a charismatic herbal dealer in love with the Cajun wife of a wealthy Anglo in this uneven and somewhat predictable drama about Anglo prejudice and violence against Cajuns in 19th-century Louisiana. Made with obvious enthusiasm on a low budget. Robert Duvall, credited as creative consultant, appears briefly as a preacher. [PG]▼●

Bella (2007-U.S.-Mexican) **C-92m.** *** D: Alejandro G. Monteverde. Eduardo Verástegui, Tammy Blanchard, Manny Perez, Ali Landry, Angélica Aragón, Jaime Tirelli, Ramon Rodriguez. Sweet, disarmingly simple heart-tugger about a once-promising soccer player (Verástegui), now a chef at a N.Y.C. restaurant, who comes to the emotional rescue of a pregnant waitress (Blanchard) when she's fired by his brother. First-time director (and cowriter) Monteverde shows admirable restraint in telling this story; a big-hearted film. [PG-13]●

Bell' Antonio (1960-Italian-French) **101m.** **½ D: Mauro Bolognini. Marcello Mastroianni, Claudia Cardinale, Pierre Brasseur, Rina Morelli. OK seriocomedy of what happens when Mastroianni is unable to consummate his marriage to Cardinale. Coscripted by Pier Paolo Pasolini. Video title: IL BELL' ANTONIO.▼

Bell Book and Candle (1958) **C-103m.** **½ D: Richard Quine. James Stewart, Kim Novak, Jack Lemmon, Janice Rule, Ernie Kovacs, Hermione Gingold, Elsa Lanchester. John Van Druten play becomes so-so vehicle to showcase Novak as fetching witch who charms about-to-be-married Manhattan publisher Stewart. Kovacs and Gingold supply their brands of humor.▼●

Bellboy, The (1960) **72m.** *** D: Jerry Lewis. Jerry Lewis, Alex Gerry, Bob Clayton, Sonny Sands. Amusing series of blackouts with Jerry as a bellboy at Fontainebleau in Miami Beach. No plot but a lot of funny gags. Milton Berle and Walter Winchell have guest appearances. Lewis's directorial debut.▼●

Belle de Jour (1967-French-Italian) **C-100m.** **** D: Luis Buñuel. Catherine Deneuve, Jean Sorel, Michel Piccoli, Genevieve Page, Francisco Rabal, Pierre Clementi, George Marchal, Françoise Fabian. Buñuel's wry and disturbing tale of a virginal newlywed who works the day shift in a high-class Parisian brothel, unbeknownst to her patient husband. Buñuel's straight-faced treatment of shocking subject matter belies the sharp wit of his script (cowritten with Jean-Claude Carrière). Deneuve's finest, most enigmatic performance. Almost 40 years later, Manoel de Oliveira directed a sequel, BELLE TOU-JOURS. [R]▼●

Belle Epoque (1992-Spanish) **C-108m.** *** D: Fernando Trueba. Fernando Fernan Gomez, Jorge Sanz, Maribel Verdu, Ariadna Gil, Miriam Diaz-Aroca, Penelope Cruz, Mary Carmen Ramirez, Michel Galabru, Gabino Diego. Set in 1931, a time of promise and optimism in pre-Franco Spain, this delightfully earthy, cheerful comedy tells of a hearty young army deserter (Sanz) who's befriended by an elderly recluse, and enchanted by his four beautiful daughters.

A multi-award winner in Spain; won Best Foreign Film Oscar. Panavision.▼●

Belle of New York, The (1952) **C-82m.** **½ D: Charles Walters. Fred Astaire, Vera-Ellen, Marjorie Main, Keenan Wynn, Alice Pearce. Uninspired musical set in Gay 90s N.Y.C. with Astaire a rich playboy chasing mission worker Vera-Ellen; Pearce adds comic touches. ▼●

Belle of the Nineties (1934) **73m.** *** D: Leo McCarey. Mae West, Roger Pryor, Johnny Mack Brown, Warren Hymer, Duke Ellington Orchestra. Mae struts, sings "My Old Flame," and heats up a gallery of admirers in amusing example of Western humor.▼●

Belles of St. Trinians, The (1954-British) **90m.** ***½ D: Frank Launder. Alastair Sim, Joyce Grenfell, George Cole, Hermione Baddeley, Beryl Reid. Hilarious filmization of Ronald Searle's cartoons about completely crazy school for girls, run by dotty headmistress whose brother, a bookie, wants to use school to his advantage. Sim plays dual role in delightful madcap farce which spawned several sequels. The series was then revived in 2007 with ST. TRINIAN'S. ▼

Belles on Their Toes (1952) **C-89m.** *** D: Henry Levin. Myrna Loy, Jeanne Crain, Debra Paget, Jeffrey Hunter, Edward Arnold, Hoagy Carmichael, Barbara Bates, Robert Arthur, Verna Felton, Martin Milner. Pleasing follow-up to CHEAPER BY THE DOZEN, with a potent feminist point of view. Here, widowed engineer Loy must struggle to support (as well as raise) her maturing brood. 20th Century-Fox backlot seen at its best in recapturing early 1900s America. Clifton Webb makes a brief appearance at the finale. Scripted by Henry and Phoebe Ephron.●

Belle Starr (1941) **C-87m.** **½ D: Irving Cummings. Randolph Scott, Gene Tierney, Dana Andrews, John Sheppard (Shepperd Strudwick), Elizabeth Patterson. Sophisticated Tierney miscast as notorious female outlaw in slowly paced account of her criminal career. Remade for TV in 1980 with Elizabeth Montgomery.

Belle Toujours (2006-Portuguese-French) **C-68m.** *** D: Manoel de Oliveira. Michel Piccoli, Bulle Ogier, Ricardo Trepa, Leonor Baldaque, Júlia Buisel. In this short, sweet follow-up to BELLE DE JOUR, almost four decades have passed and Henri Husson (Piccoli) spies Séverine (Ogier, replacing Catherine Deneuve) in an auditorium during a concert. He follows her, with the intention of revealing a secret. De Oliveira, who also scripted, was *97 years old* when he made this thoughtful meditation on aging and the diminishing of erotic desire as an homage to Luis Buñuel and Jean-Claude Carrière, the original's creators.●

Bell for Adano, A (1945) **103m.** ***½ D: Henry King. Gene Tierney, John Hodiak,

William Bendix, Glenn Langan, Richard Conte, Stanley Prager, Henry (Harry) Morgan, Hugo Haas, Fortunio Bonanova, Henry Armetta, Luis Alberni, Eduardo Ciannelli, Grady Sutton. John Hersey's moving narrative of American WW2 occupation of small Italian village; Hodiak is sincere commander, Bendix his aide, blonde Tierney the local girl he is attracted to. Scripted by Lamar Trotti (who also coproduced) and Norman Reilly Raine.

Bellissima (1951-Italian) **112m. ** D:** Luchino Visconti. Anna Magnani, Walter Chiari, Tina Apicella, Gastone Renzelli, Alessandro Blasetti. Obvious drama about pushy, patronizing stage mother Magnani, obsessed to the point of hysteria with getting her cute, obedient little daughter into the movies. Loud when it should be tender, and ultimately tiresome.▼

Bell Jar, The (1979) **C-107m. **½ D:** Larry Peerce. Marilyn Hassett, Julie Harris, Anne Jackson, Barbara Barrie, Robert Klein, Donna Mitchell, Jameson Parker, Thaao Penghlis. Sylvia Plath's virtually unfilmable novel about the crack-up of an overachiever in the '50s has a few powerful scenes and a good supporting performance by Barrie, but doesn't really come off. Hassett is well cast but fails to deliver the truly bravura performance this film needs. [R]▼

Bellman & True (1988-British) **C-112m. **½ D:** Richard Loncraine. Bernard Hill, Kieran O'Brien, Richard Hope, Frances Tomelty, Derek Newark, John Kavanagh, Ken Bones. Meek computer programmer is drawn into an elaborate bank heist scheme, without ever realizing just how dangerous the people he's associating with can be. More a character study than a caper film, very low key and very drawn out, but with a number of rewarding moments and vignettes. Original running time 122m. [R]▼

Bells SEE: **Murder by Phone**

Bells Are Ringing (1960) **C-127m. *** D:** Vincente Minnelli. Judy Holliday, Dean Martin, Fred Clark, Eddie Foy, Jr., Jean Stapleton, Ruth Storey, Frank Gorshin, Gerry Mulligan. Sprightly adaptation of Broadway musical hit by Betty Comden, Adolph Green, and Jule Styne, with Holliday recreating her starring role as an answering-service operator who falls in love with the man she's known only as a voice on the telephone. Songs include "Just in Time," "The Party's Over." Sadly, Holliday's last film. CinemaScope.▼◐

Bells of St. Mary's, The (1945) **126m. *** D:** Leo McCarey. Bing Crosby, Ingrid Bergman, Henry Travers, William Gargan, Ruth Donnelly, Joan Carroll, Martha Sleeper, Rhys Williams. Amiable if meandering sequel to GOING MY WAY, with Father O'Malley assigned to a run-down parish where Bergman is the Sister Superior. Bing introduces the song

"Aren't You Glad You're You?" Also shown in computer-colored version.▼◐

Belly (1998) **C-95m. *½ D:** Hype Williams. Nas, DMX, Taral Hicks, Tionne "T-Boz" Watkins, Method Man. Hyper-stylized, pretentious "gangsta" melodrama about two lifelong buddies (rappers Nas and DMX) whose friendship is violently tested when they get involved in dealing Jamaican heroin. Features some of hip-hop's finest; too bad they can't act. Clichéd script doesn't help. Followed by a DVD sequel. [R]▼◐

Belly of an Architect, The (1987-British-Italian) **C-108m. **½ D:** Peter Greenaway. Brian Dennehy, Chloe Webb, Lambert Wilson, Sergio Fantoni, Stephania Cassini, Vanni Corbellini. Highly personalized chronicle of an architect (Dennehy) and his wife (Webb), who arrive in Rome where he's to curate an exhibition. It's about architecture and art, obsession and omens, immortality and mortality; crammed with symbolism, striking visuals and beautiful cinematography by Sacha Vierny. Some will find it pretentious; others will be fascinated. [R]▼◐

Beloved (1998) **C-171m. ** D:** Jonathan Demme. Oprah Winfrey, Danny Glover, Kimberly Elise, Thandie Newton, Beah Richards, Lisa Gay Hamilton, Irma P. Hall, Albert Hall, Tracey Walter, Thelma Houston, Jason Robards, Wes Bentley. Excruciating (if well-crafted) adaptation of Toni Morrison's Pulitzer Prize–winning novel about a woman who's made her way from slavery to a free life in Ohio in 1873, and will do anything—anything—to protect her children. Filled with mysticism and mumbo jumbo, the story demands a leap of faith but doesn't reward the viewer in kind; its lead character isn't sympathetic enough to earn our empathy, even though we understand that she has suffered. Tough going, in more ways than one. Winfrey also produced with Demme. [R]▼◐

Beloved Infidel (1959) **C-123m. ** D:** Henry King. Gregory Peck, Deborah Kerr, Eddie Albert, Philip Ober, Herbert Rudley, John Sutton, Karin Booth, Ken Scott. Ill-conceived casting of Peck as F. Scott Fitzgerald makes romance with Hollywood columnist Sheilah Graham (Kerr) in late 1930s more ludicrous than real; lush photography is only virtue of blunt look at cinema capital. CinemaScope.▼

Below (2002) **C-105m. ** D:** David Twohy. Matt Davis, Bruce Greenwood, Olivia Williams, Holt McCallany, Scott Foley, Zach Galifianakis, Jason Flemyng, Dexter Fletcher, Nick Chinlund. Stultifyingly routine WW2 submarine movie that tries to incorporate elements of a whodunit, horror movie, and conspiracy thriller. Greenwood has recently taken command of his sub and buys trouble when he picks up three survivors from a torpedoed British hospital ship. One of them (Williams) soon discovers that her temporary home is awash in secrets

[109]

and unexplained events. Hard to believe this was cowritten (and coproduced) by cutting-edge filmmaker Darren Aronofsky. [R]▼●

Below the Belt (1980) **C-98m.** *** D: Robert Fowler. Regina Baff, Mildred Burke, John C. Becher, Annie McGreevey, Jane O'Brien, Shirley Stoler, Dolph Sweet. Waitress Baff seeks fortune and fame as a lady wrestler. Low-budget drama, filmed mostly in 1974; a sometimes fascinating portrait of people eking out existence on the edge of society. Based on a novel by Rosalyn Drexler. [R]▼

Ben (1972) **C-95m.** *½ D: Phil Karlson. Lee Harcourt Montgomery, Joseph Campanella, Arthur O'Connell, Rosemary Murphy, Meredith Baxter. WILLARD sequel finds sick youth befriended by Ben the rat. Title song (sung by young Michael Jackson) summed up situation but spared gory visuals that make this film so bad. [PG]▼

Benchwarmers, The (2006) **C-80m.** BOMB D: Dennis Dugan. Rob Schneider, David Spade, Jon Heder, Jon Lovitz, Craig Kilborn, Tim Meadows, Molly Sims, Nick Swardson, Norm MacDonald, Reggie Jackson, Bill Romanowski, Rachel Hunter; voice of James Earl Jones. Leaden comedy about nerds who try to reverse their grade school reputations by forming a three-man baseball team to compete against regular Little Leaguers. Adam Sandler–produced mess starring his aging *Saturday Night Live* costars has all the flatulence gags you'd expect. Only honest line is saved for last as Lovitz looks into the camera and says, "This was a complete waste of time, wasn't it?" Duh, dudes! [PG-13]▶

Bend It Like Beckham (2002-U.S.-British-German) **C-115m.** *** D: Gurinder Chadha. Parminder Nagra, Keira Knightley, Jonathan Rhys Meyers, Juliet Stevenson, Anupam Kher, Archie Panjabi, Shaznay Lewis. Winning comedy set in West London about a soccer-obsessed Anglo-Indian girl whose traditional-minded parents forbid her to play. No surprises (or subtlety) here, but the story is told with verve and filled with warm, amusing characters. A crowd pleaser in the best sense. Title refers to British soccer star David Beckham. [PG-13]▼●

Bend of the River (1952) **C-91m.** *** D: Anthony Mann. James Stewart, Arthur Kennedy, Julia (Julie) Adams, Rock Hudson, Jay C. Flippen, Lori Nelson, Stepin Fetchit, Henry (Harry) Morgan, Frances Bavier, Royal Dano. Compelling Western of 1840s Oregon, with bristling conflict between Stewart, outlaw turned wagon-train scout, and Kennedy, his one-time partner in crime who hijacks settlers' supplies for profit.▼●

Beneath the Planet of the Apes (1970) **C-95m.** **½ D: Ted Post. James Franciscus, Kim Hunter, Maurice Evans, Linda Harrison, Charlton Heston, Victor Buono, Thomas Gomez. Second APES film still has great sets, makeup and ideas, but somebody let it get away as Apes battle human mutants who survived a nuclear blast many years before. Followed by ESCAPE FROM . . . Panavision. [G]▼●

Beneath the 12-Mile Reef (1953) **C-102m.** **½ D: Robert Webb. Robert Wagner, Terry Moore, Gilbert Roland, J. Carrol Naish, Richard Boone, Peter Graves. Romeo-and-Juliet–ish tale of sponge-diving families on Key West, Florida. Scenery outshines all. One of the first CinemaScope films.▼●

Benefit of the Doubt (1993) **C-90m.** *½ D: Jonathan Heap. Donald Sutherland, Amy Irving, Rider Strong, Christopher McDonald, Graham Greene, Theodore Bikel, Gisele Kovach. Flat thriller in which ex-con Sutherland, jailed for murdering his wife, disrupts the life of daughter Irving (whose testimony helped convict him two decades earlier). With a bit of imagination, this could have been first rate. [R]▼

Bengal Brigade (1954) **C-87m.** ** D: Laslo Benedek. Rock Hudson, Arlene Dahl, Ursula Thiess, Torin Thatcher, Arnold Moss, Dan O'Herlihy, Michael Ansara. Low-level costumer with Hudson badly miscast as a British army officer working to thwart a Sepoy rebellion in India.

Ben-Hur (1925) **141m.** *** D: Fred Niblo. Ramon Novarro, Francis X. Bushman, May McAvoy, Betty Bronson, Claire McDowell, Carmel Myers, Nigel de Brulier. Biggest of all silent spectacles holds up quite well against talkie remake, particularly the exciting chariot race and sea battle (both directed by B. Reeves Eason); Novarro (as Judah) and Bushman (as Messala) give the performances of their careers. Trouble-plagued film was years in production, at a then-record cost of $4,000,000, but final result, despite a slow second half, is worth it. Some sequences filmed in two-color Technicolor. Filmed once before (in one reel!) in 1907.▼●

Ben-Hur (1959) **C-212m.** ***½ D: William Wyler. Charlton Heston, Jack Hawkins, Stephen Boyd, Haya Harareet, Hugh Griffith, Martha Scott, Sam Jaffe, Cathy O'Donnell, Finlay Currie. Epic-scale rendering of Gen. Lew Wallace's "tale of the Christ." Heston and Boyd are well matched as the proud Jew Ben-Hur and his boyhood friend Messala, whose blind allegiance to Rome turns him into a bitter enemy. Poky at times, but redeemed by the strength of its convictions. Some of the special effects show their age, though the galley-slave sequence and climactic chariot race (directed by Andrew Marton and staged by the legendary stunt expert Yakima Canutt) are still great. Won 11 Oscars for Best Picture, Director, Actor (Heston), Supporting Actor (Griffith), Cinematography (Robert L. Surtees), Music

Score (Miklos Rozsa), Art Direction, Film Editing, Sound, Costume Design, and Special Effects. MGM Camera 65. ▼●◗

Benjamin (1968-French) **C-100m.** BOMB D: Michel Deville. Catherine Deneuve, Michele Morgan, Pierre Clementi, Michel Piccoli, Francine Berge, Anna Gael. Beautiful Deneuve, Morgan, cinematography; otherwise, boring tale of country boy Clementi's initiation into upper-class immorality. Also shown at 105m. and 108m. [X]

Benji (1974) **C-86m.** ***½ D: Joe Camp. Peter Breck, Deborah Walley, Edgar Buchanan, Frances Bavier, Patsy Garrett. Instant classic of a remarkable dog (played by Higgins) who thwarts the kidnappers of two small children. Texas-made feature is ideal for family viewing. Sequel: FOR THE LOVE OF BENJI. [G] ▼◗

Benji Off the Leash! (2004) **C-99m.** **½ D: Joe Camp. Nick Whitaker, Nate Bynum, Chris Kendrick, Randall Newsome, Duane Stephens, Christy Summerhays, Carleton Bluford, Neal Barth. Minor but enjoyable film for kids about a boy who has to hide his mixed-breed puppy from an abusive stepfather who sells pups for a living. Whitaker is appealing, the grown-ups are fine (with broad comedy relief from a pair of bumbling dogcatchers), but it's the dogs who steal the show. Footage during closing credits reveals how they got these canines to perform so well. [PG] ▼◗

Benji the Hunted (1987) **C-88m.** *½ D: Joe Camp. Benji, Red Steagall, Frank Inn. Every dog has his day, but this talented canine deserves a better movie vehicle. Humans are incidental in this story of Benji surviving in the mountain wilds, and it looks as if they were incidental in making the film as well. Followed by BENJI OFF THE LEASH! [G] ▼●◗

Benny & Joon (1993) **C-98m.** *** D: Jeremiah Chechik. Johnny Depp, Mary Stuart Masterson, Aidan Quinn, Julianne Moore, Oliver Platt, CCH Pounder, Dan Hedaya, Joe Grifasi, William H. Macy, Eileen Ryan. Sweet-natured film about put-upon auto mechanic Quinn, who tries to look after his mentally ill sister. Almost accidentally he stumbles onto the perfect companion for her: a male misfit who sees himself as a reincarnation of Buster Keaton. Endearing performances put over this fable, which otherwise would strain all credibility. Depp is impressive as he recreates silent-comedy routines by Chaplin, Keaton, et al. [PG] ▼●◗

Benny Goodman Story, The (1955) **C-116m.** **½ D: Valentine Davies. Steve Allen, Donna Reed, Herbert Anderson, Hy Averback, Berta Gersten, Robert F. Simon, Sammy Davis, Sr., Gene Krupa, Lionel Hampton, Teddy Wilson. Typical Hollywood gloss about the bandleader's rise to fame and his romance with Reed; not 100%

factual, with cliché dialogue to spare, but the music is great. Additional guest performers include Harry James, Ziggy Elman, and Martha Tilton. Goodman himself dubbed Allen's clarinet playing. ▼◗

Benny's Video (1992-Austrian-Swiss) **C-105m.** *** D: Michael Haneke. Arno Frisch, Angela Winkler, Ulrich Mühe, Ingrid Stassner. Teenaged Benny (Frisch) is addicted to video, shooting images with his camera and endlessly watching ultra-violent tapes. While his parents are away he brings a young girl into his home and dispassionately kills her with a butcher's gun he stole from a farm. Obvious but potent allegory about the way young people can become desensitized. Second in a trilogy by writer-director Haneke, following THE SEVENTH CONTINENT and followed by 71 FRAGMENTS OF A CHRONOLOGY OF CHANCE. ◗

Bent (1997-British) **C-104m.** **½ D: Sean Mathias. Lothaire Bluteau, Clive Owen, Brian Webber, Ian McKellen, Mick Jagger, Nikolaj Waldau, Jude Law, Gresby Nash, Rupert Graves, Charlie Watts, Rachel Weisz. Raw drama following the plight of a brash, manipulative gay German (Owen) under Hitler, and his eventual internment in Dachau with fellow prisoner Bluteau. Stagy film, with undeniably powerful scenes, but not the formidable depiction of Nazi-era homosexuals it might have been. Scripted by Martin Sherman, from his groundbreaking 1979 play. [NC-17] ▼●◗

Beowulf (2007) **C-114m.** **½ D: Robert Zemeckis. Ray Winstone, Anthony Hopkins, Angelina Jolie, John Malkovich, Robin Wright Penn, Brendan Gleeson, Crispin Glover, Alison Lohman, Costas Mandylor. The ancient poem about a kingdom in need of a warrior to protect it from a monstrous attacker is reinterpreted by Neil Gaiman and Roger Avary and filmed in Zemeckis' "performance capture" medium. Hybrid of a superhero action movie and a graphic novel is fun to watch on a no-brainer level. The action scenes are visceral and effective, but the story bogs down and the faces of the female characters (except for Jolie, seen sparsely but memorably) are lifeless. Beowulf himself is a great character who looks nothing like the actor who voiced and acted his part (Winstone). A mixed bag, best appreciated in 3-D or IMAX. Also available in unrated version. 3-D Digital Widescreen. [PG-13] ◗

Beowulf & Grendel (2005-Canadian-British-Icelandic) **C-103m.** *½ D: Sturla Gunnarsson. Gerard Butler, Stellan Skarsgård, Ingvar Sigurdsson, Sarah Polley, Eddie Marsan, Tony Curran, Rory McCann, Ronan Vibert. In A.D. 500, a brave warrior named Beowulf goes into battle against Grendel, a barbaric troll who favors decapitating his victims. Ponderous adaptation of the famed Anglo-Saxon poem, with the 6th-century characters even getting to employ 21st-century profanity. Worth a look only for those stunning Icelandic panoramas. Super 35. [R]▶❍

Bequest to the Nation, A SEE: **Nelson Affair, The**

Berlin Affair, The (1985-Italian-West German) **C-96m.** BOMB D: Liliana Cavani. Gudrun Landgrebe, Kevin McNally, Mio Takaki, Massimo Girotti, Philippe Leroy, Hanns Zischler, William Berger. English-language misfire adapts Junichiro Tanizuki's novel *The Buddhist Cross.* Director Cavani (of THE NIGHT PORTER) is slumming in Nazi Germany again for a tale of a lesbian love affair between Landgrebe and ambassador's daughter Takaki. Lifeless film isn't even sexy, quite surprising in view of the casting of A WOMAN IN FLAMES star Landgrebe. Original European running time was 115m. [R]▼

Berlin Alexanderplatz (1980-German) **C-931m.** **** D: Rainer Werner Fassbinder. Gunter Lamprecht, Hanna Schygulla, Barbara Sukowa, Gottfried John, Elisabeth Trissenaar, Brigitte Mira, Karin Baal, Ivan Desny. Monumental adaptation of Alfred Doblin's novel about German life in the late 1920s, focusing on a simple Everyman (Lamprecht), who has just been released from prison. He yearns for respectability but is led like a sheep by forces beyond his control into criminality and insanity. An epic if there ever was one, with stunning performances, cinematography (by Xaver Schwarzenberger), and direction. Originally produced for television in 14 episodes. Filmed before in 1931.▼❙

Berlin Express (1948) **86m.** *** D: Jacques Tourneur. Merle Oberon, Robert Ryan, Charles Korvin, Paul Lukas, Robert Coote. Taut, suspenseful spy story set in post WW2 Europe. Members of several nations combine efforts to save German statesman kidnapped by Nazi underground.▼❍❙

Bernardine (1957) **C-95m.** ** D: Henry Levin. Pat Boone, Terry Moore, Janet Gaynor, Dean Jagger, Walter Abel. Very weak look at teen-age life (all different now) marked return of Janet Gaynor to films after 20 years. Wholesome Pat Boone (in his film debut) sings and sings and sings. Eh! CinemaScope.

Berserk (1967-British) **C-96m.** ** D: Jim O'Connolly. Joan Crawford, Ty Hardin, Diana Dors, Michael Gough, Judy Geeson. Sadistic shocker with Crawford the shapely owner of a British circus, haunted by series of brutal murders. Supporting cast lacks verve.▼❍

Bert Rigby, You're a Fool (1989) **C-94m.** ** D: Carl Reiner. Robert Lindsay, Robbie Coltrane, Anne Bancroft, Corbin Bernsen, Cathryn Bradshaw, Bruno Kirby, Jackie Gayle. Writer-director Reiner conceived this deliberately old-fashioned musical comedy as a showcase for Lindsay (who scored a smash on stage in *Me and My Girl*), and that's its only value. He's a delight—singing, dancing, and clowning as a jaunty British coal miner who wants to break into show business—but the well-meaning film is silly and contrived. [R]▼❍❙

Besieged (1998-Italian-British) **C-94m.** *** D: Bernardo Bertolucci. Thandie Newton, David Thewlis, Claudio Santamaria. Provocative film about an African immigrant who works as housemaid for a reclusive English pianist in Rome. She's intrigued by his mysterious ways, while he is infatuated with her and determines to find a way to prove his love. Sinuous and surprising, with fine performances by the two leads; written by Bertolucci and Clare Peploe, from a story by James Lasdun. Originally made for Italian TV. [R]▼❙

Best Boy (1979) **C-111m.** **** D: Ira Wohl. Poignant, beautifully filmed documentary about Wohl's 52-year-old mentally retarded cousin Philly and his family's struggle as he learns to relate to the outside world. Sequences related to his father's death and his visit backstage with Zero Mostel—together they sing "If I Were a Rich Man"—are especially moving. A Best Documentary Academy Award winner. Sequel: BEST MAN: 'BEST BOY' AND ALL OF US TWENTY YEARS LATER.▼❍❙

Best Defense (1984) **C-94m.** *½ D: Willard Huyck. Dudley Moore, Eddie Murphy, Kate Capshaw, George Dzundza, Helen Shaver, David Rasche. Unpleasant and unfunny comedy about defense-industry designer who inadvertently acquires blueprint sought by the KGB. "Strategic Guest Star" Murphy is no help. [R]▼❍❙

Best Foot Forward (1943) **C-95m.** *** D: Edward Buzzell. Lucille Ball, William Gaxton, Virginia Weidler, Tommy Dix, Nancy Walker, Gloria De Haven, June Allyson. Entertaining film of Broadway musical about movie star Ball visiting small-town school for a lark; score includes "Buckle Down Winsockie." Harry James and his band do definitive "Two O'Clock Jump." Walker, as dynamic plain-Jane, and Allyson make their feature film debuts re-creating their stage roles. Future filmmaker Stanley Donen can be glimpsed in "The Three B's" number, holding De Haven's legs.▼❍❙

Best Friends (1982) **C-116m.** ** D: Norman Jewison. Burt Reynolds, Goldie Hawn, Jessica Tandy, Barnard Hughes, Audra Lindley, Keenan Wynn, Ron Silver, Carol Locatell. Lackluster comedy vehicle for two top stars, as screenwriters who function better as lovers than as husband and wife. Some funny vignettes with fine supporting cast (including Richard Libertini as Mexican justice-of-the-peace), but the lead characters aren't terribly interesting. Indulgent script by real-life "best friends" Barry Levinson and Valerie Curtin. [PG] ▼●◗

Best House in London, The (1969-British) C-105m. BOMB D: Philip Saville. David Hemmings, Joanna Pettet, George Sanders, Dany Robin, Warren Mitchell. Boring comedy about group of government officials in London who sponsor official bawdy house. Film didn't deserve "X" rating it got at the time. Look for John Cleese in a bit part. [X]

Best in Show (2000) C-90m. *** D: Christopher Guest. Christopher Guest, Eugene Levy, Catherine O'Hara, Michael McKean, Parker Posey, Fred Willard, Larry Miller, Bob Balaban, Jennifer Coolidge, John Michael Higgins, Michael Hitchcock, Jane Lynch, Patrick Cranshaw, Don Lake, Ed Begley, Jr., Jim Piddock. Small-scale but entertaining mockumentary from the WAITING FOR GUFFMAN team about the various characters who enter their pets in a prestigious dog show. Largely improvised comedy (officially written by Guest and Levy) offers a lot of laughs, especially for fans of the filmmakers and cast. [PG-13] ▼◗

Best Intentions, The (1992-Swedish) C-182m. *** D: Bille August. Samuel Froler, Pernilla August, Max von Sydow, Ghita Norby, Lennart Hjulstrom, Mona Malm, Lena Endre, Anita Bjork. Ingmar Bergman scripted this ambitious epic tale of the courtship and subsequent marriage of his own parents. Henrik Bergman (Froler) starts out as a poor theology student, and wife Anna (August, the director's wife) comes from a wealthy, bourgeois family; their fundamental differences—and stormy relationship—form the crux of the film. A six-hour version was made for Swedish television. A follow-up to FANNY AND ALEXANDER; followed by SUNDAY'S CHILDREN and PRIVATE CONFESSIONS. ▼

Best Laid Plans (1999) C-93m. **½ D: Mike Barker. Alessandro Nivola, Reese Witherspoon, Josh Brolin, Rocky Carroll, Michael G. Hagerty, Terrence Dashon Howard. When an old pal comes back to town, a broke local and his girlfriend find themselves caught up in a web of blackmail and deceit. Convoluted film noir plays like a Gen-X USUAL SUSPECTS, but the problem is too many twists, and after a while this gimmicky thriller runs out of steam. Good acting, especially by Nivola in his first lead role. [R] ▼◗

Best Little Whorehouse in Texas, The (1982) C-114m. ** D: Colin Higgins. Burt Reynolds, Dolly Parton, Dom DeLuise, Charles Durning, Jim Nabors, Robert Mandan, Lois Nettleton, Theresa Merritt, Noah Beery, Jr., Barry Corbin. Flashy but unsatisfying musical (based on Broadway hit) about pressures brought to bear on sheriff (Reynolds) to close a popular establishment called The Chicken Ranch—run by his ladyfriend. Dolly's a delight, Durning has a showstopping number as the Governor, but occasionally film actually tries to get serious and screeches to a halt. Dolly's hit song "I Will Always Love You" (which she also wrote) had been #1 in 1974—and would be an even bigger hit for Whitney Houston in 1992's THE BODYGUARD. Panavision. [R] ▼●◗

Best Man, The (1964) 102m. *** D: Franklin Schaffner. Henry Fonda, Cliff Robertson, Edie Adams, Margaret Leighton, Kevin McCarthy, Shelley Berman, Lee Tracy, Ann Sothern, Gene Raymond, Richard Arlen, Mahalia Jackson. Sharp filmization of Gore Vidal's play about political conventioning with several determined presidential candidates seeking important endorsement at any cost; brittle, engrossing drama. Screenplay by Vidal. ▼●◗

Best Man, The (1998-Italian) C-106m. *** D: Pupi Avati. Diego Abatantuono, Inès Sastre, Dario Cantarelli, Cinzia Mascoli, Valeria D'Obici. Warm, wildly romantic comedy of manners set in a small Italian town on December 31, 1899, about a young woman who rebels against her arranged marriage to a wealthy businessman and falls in love with his best man during the wedding party. Slight but charming and evocative allegory, symbolically set on the eve of the 20th century. Written by the director. [PG] ▼◗

Best Man, The (1999) C-120m. **½ D: Malcolm D. Lee. Taye Diggs, Nia Long, Morris Chestnut, Harold Perrineau, Terrence Howard, Monica Calhoun. Galley proofs are circulating for a new novel full of thinly disguised characters, causing no shortage of problems for author Diggs, who has to contend with a slew of offended participants. Overlong feature debut for Spike Lee's writer/director cousin adds nothing new to the wedding-comedy genre, but attractive characters carry it for a while. The end-credits sequence, with spiffily dressed dancers, tries to convince you that you've had a better time than you've had. [R] ▼●◗

Best of Everything, The (1959) C-121m. *** D: Jean Negulesco. Hope Lange, Stephen Boyd, Suzy Parker, Diane Baker, Martha Hyer, Joan Crawford, Brian Aherne, Robert Evans, Louis Jourdan. Multifaceted fabrication about women seeking success and love in the publishing jungles of N.Y.C., highlighted by Crawford's performance as tough executive with empty heart of gold. Captures the zeitgeist of '50s N.Y.C.; adapted from Rona Jaffee's novel. CinemaScope. ▼◗

Best of the Best (1989) C-97m. BOMB D: Bob Radler. Eric Roberts, James Earl Jones, Sally Kirkland, Christopher Penn, Louise Fletcher, Phillip Rhee, John Dye. Yet another ROCKY-style rip-off in which five young men must overcome differences before they can unite as the U.S. Karate Team and compete in an international match. Top-drawer cast appallingly wasted. Followed by three sequels. [PG-13]▼●◗

Best of the Best II (1993) C-101m. ** D: Robert Radler. Eric Roberts, Phillip Rhee, Christopher Penn, Edan Gross, Ralph Moeller, Meg Foster, Sonny Landham, Wayne Newton. Sequel to the original flop bucks the odds and actually improves on its lame predecessor. Two former U.S. Karate Team members set out to avenge the death of their friend who was killed during a shady competition. Roberts has actually said he made this film to make up for the first one. What a considerate guy! [R]▼●◗

Best of Times, The (1986) C-104m. **½ D: Roger Spottiswoode. Robin Williams, Kurt Russell, Pamela Reed, Holly Palance, Donald Moffat, Margaret Whitton, M. Emmet Walsh, Donovan Scott, R. G. Armstrong, Kirk Cameron. Williams has never lived down the moment he dropped winning pass in a high-school football game—so, 20 years later he fires up former teammate (Russell), the rival team, and his entire home town for a rematch. Some quirky, offbeat touches highlight Ron Shelton's script, and the wives (Reed, Palance) are a treat but seemingly surefire film becomes too strident (and too exaggerated) to really score. [PG-13]▼●◗

Best of Youth, The (2003-Italian) C-363m. **** D: Marco Tullio Giordana. Luigi Lo Cascio, Alessio Boni, Adriana Asti, Sonia Bergamasco, Fabrizio Gifuni, Maya Sansa, Valentina Carnelutti. Majestically epic film, made for Italian television, deals with the loves, personal tragedies, and contrasting life choices of two brothers against a backdrop of social change in Italy from 1966 through the 1990s, involving Mafiosos, Red Brigades, and even a famed flood in Florence. Shown in two parts, this is one of the few films of which it can be said, "The early going is pretty good, but it really kicks in during the last three hours." A massive investment of time that amply rewards the viewer. Asti is positively luminous. Written by Sandro Petraglia and Stefano Rulli. [R]◗

Best Seller (1987) C-110m. ** D: John Flynn. James Woods, Brian Dennehy, Victoria Tennant, Allison Balson, Paul Shenar, George Coe, Anne Pitoniak. Dennehy, a cop-turned-author (à la Joseph Wambaugh), is approached by Woods to write the story of his former life as hit man for prominent businessman (Shenar) whose underworld tactics have long been covered up. Despite teaming of two terrific actors, film never quite cuts it, due to many holes in Larry Cohen's script—and Woods' largely unappealing character. [R]▼●◗

Best Things in Life Are Free, The (1956) C-104m. **½ D: Michael Curtiz. Gordon MacRae, Dan Dailey, Ernest Borgnine, Sheree North, Tommy Noonan, Murvyn Vye. Typical of the antiseptic 1950s musicals, this film "re-creates" the careers of Tin Pan Alley writers DeSylva, Brown, and Henderson. Highlight: North and Jacques D'Amboise dancing to "The Birth of the Blues." CinemaScope.

Best Years of Our Lives, The (1946) 168m. **** D: William Wyler. Myrna Loy, Fredric March, Dana Andrews, Teresa Wright, Virginia Mayo, Harold Russell, Hoagy Carmichael, Gladys George, Roman Bohnen, Steve Cochran. American classic of three veterans returning home after WW2, readjusting to civilian life. Robert Sherwood's script from MacKinlay Kantor's book perfectly captured mood of postwar U.S.; still powerful today. Seven Oscars include Best Picture, Wyler, March, Russell, Sherwood, Daniel Mandell's editing, Hugo Friedhofer's score. Russell, an actual veteran who lost his hands, also took home a second Oscar, a special award for bringing hope and courage to other veterans. Remade as 1975 TVM, RETURNING HOME, with Tom Selleck and Dabney Coleman.▼◗

Bethune (1977-Canadian) C-88m. *** D: Eric Till. Donald Sutherland, Kate Nelligan, David Gardner, James Hong. Thoughtful biography with Sutherland fine as Dr. Norman Bethune, the controversial, humanistic Canadian doctor who, most intriguingly, aided Mao Tse-tung's army during its famous march. Made for Canadian television; Sutherland also played the character in Phillip Borsos' BETHUNE: THE MAKING OF A HERO, a 1990 feature (which was released in the U.S. in 1993 as DR. BETHUNE).▼

Betrayal (1983-British) C-95m. *½ D: David Jones. Jeremy Irons, Ben Kingsley, Patricia Hodge. Harold Pinter's fascinating play about a triangle relationship—progressing *backward* in time—falls flat on screen, despite a powerhouse cast. [R]▼

Betrayal, The (2009) C-96m. *** D: Ellen Kuras. Arresting, highly emotional documentary about a large Laotian family whose lives are forever changed after the father is conscripted by the C.I.A. to help covert U.S. military operations there in the 1970s. The government's promises—both implicit and explicit—are forgotten after the Communists take over Laos in 1975; the father is removed and the family is ostracized. They manage to make their way to the U.S., where they start life anew in a squalid apartment in Brooklyn, N.Y. Amazing odyssey is told through footage shot over 23 years' time by cinematographer Kuras (in her directing debut). Her main character, the astonishingly resilient Thavisouk Phrasavath, is credited as editor, codirector, and cowriter. Aka NERAKHOON.

Betrayed (1954) C-108m. ** D: Gottfried Reinhardt. Clark Gable, Lana Turner, Victor Mature, Louis Calhern, O.E. Hasse, Wilfrid Hyde-White, Ian Carmichael. Colonel

Gable falls for Dutch Resistance member Turner, who's suspected of being in cahoots with the Nazis. Ho-hum WW2 melodrama, with some nice on-location filming in The Netherlands. Clark and Lana's fourth and final teaming.▼◐●

Betrayed (1988) **C-127m.** *½ D: Costa-Gavras. Debra Winger, Tom Berenger, John Heard, Betsy Blair, John Mahoney, Ted Levine, Jeffrey DeMunn, Albert Hall, David Clennon, Richard Libertini. Appalling botch of a film about the stupidest FBI undercover agent in movie history, who's sent to sniff out white supremacists in America's heartland—but falls in love with her target instead. Important and genuinely upsetting subject matter is dealt with in pedantic terms. Even the moments of straight suspense are muffed! Winger's performance is virtually the only saving grace. Timothy Hutton can be seen fleetingly at the fairgrounds. [R]▼◐●

Betsy, The (1978) **C-125m.** **½ D: Daniel Petrie. Laurence Olivier, Robert Duvall, Katharine Ross, Tommy Lee Jones, Jane Alexander, Lesley-Anne Down, Kathleen Beller, Edward Herrmann. Moderately enjoyable trash, adapted from Harold Robbins' novel about the multigenerational wheelings and dealings between an auto company patriarch and his family. Olivier's hamminess and Down's loveliness are the pluses here. [R] ▼◐●

Betsy's Wedding (1990) **C-94m.** *** D: Alan Alda. Alan Alda, Joey Bishop, Madeline Kahn, Anthony LaPaglia, Catherine O'Hara, Joe Pesci, Molly Ringwald, Ally Sheedy, Burt Young, Julie Bovasso, Nicolas Coster, Bibi Besch, Dylan Walsh, Samuel L. Jackson. Amusing social comedy about the plans, preparations, and events surrounding Ringwald's wedding—especially as they affect her father. One of writer-director-star Alda's better outings, a bit cluttered (and occasionally clumsy) but filled with enough truthful observations to strike a great many familiar chords. [R]▼◐●

Better Late Than Never (1982) **C-95m.** *½ D: Bryan Forbes. David Niven, Art Carney, Maggie Smith, Kimberly Partridge, Catherine Hicks, Melissa Prophet. Two ne'er-do-wells vie for acceptance by a 10-year-old heiress, who's a granddaughter to one of them. Nice locations in the South of France can't compensate for lightheaded script and waste of star talent. [PG]▼

Better Life, A (2011) **C-98m.** **½ D: Chris Weitz. Demián Bichir, José Julián, Delores Heredia, Joaquín Cosío, Carlos Linares. A hardworking Mexican gardener and single father, who only wants the best for his teenage son, makes a bold move by buying his former employer's truck and equipment to go into business for himself in L.A. An illegal immigrant, he knows the

risk he's taking, but as events unfold his son stands by his side and sees for the first time his father's strength of character. Modern variation on BICYCLE THIEVES is sincere, credible, and well acted, but follows an all-too-predictable path. [PG-13]

Better Luck Tomorrow (2003) **C-101m.** *** D: Justin Lin. Parry Shen, Jason Tobin, Sung Kang, Roger Fan, John Cho, Karin Anna Cheung, Jerry Mathers. Provocative, often disturbing look at suburban Southern California high school overachievers whose good grades buy them freedom from parental supervision . . . and the challenge of seeing just how much they can get away with. A fresh, serious-minded look at teenagers that cannily doesn't stress the fact that they are all Asian American. Flirts with melodrama toward the end, but never loses its focus. Exceptionally well filmed by editor, director and cowriter Lin. [R]▼◗

Better Off Dead . . . (1985) **C-98m.** **½ D: Savage Steve Holland. John Cusack, David Ogden Stiers, Kim Darby, Demian Slade, Scooter Stevens, Diane Franklin, Curtis Armstrong. Off-kilter comedy about teenage boy who's just lost the girl of his dreams. Frustrating film starts off with lots of funny, original gags—it even has a terrific "hamburger video" by clay-animation specialist Jimmy Picker—then it settles into much-too-conventional story and goes down the drain. Feature debut for writer-director Holland. [PG]▼◐●

Better Than Chocolate (1999-Canadian) **C-101m.** *** D: Anne Wheeler. Wendy Crewson, Karyn Dwyer, Christina Cox, Anne-Marie MacDonald, Peter Outerbridge, Marya Delver, Kevin Mundy. Engaging adult comedy about the evolving, hot-and-heavy relationship between college dropout/wannabe writer Dwyer and artist/drifter Cox. Loaded with wit, well-drawn characters, and perceptive commentary on such hot-button issues as censorship, and more personal ones, such as self-acceptance. Outerbridge is a standout as a transgendered lesbian. Unrated version runs 102m. [R]▼◗

Better Than Sex (2000-Australian-French) **C-84m.** *** D: Jonathan Teplitzky. David Wenham, Susie Porter, Catherine McClements, Kris McQuade, Simon Bossell, Imelda Corcoran. A man and woman meet at a party and agree to a one-night stand, since he's leaving the country in just a few days and there's no chance of entanglements. Or so they think. Eye-opening look at the mating game, exploring what men and women say and don't say before, during, and after sex. A fresh, frank and very sexy film with a delightful sense of humor.▼◗

Better Tomorrow, A (1986-Hong Kong) **C-95m.** *** D: John Woo. Chow Yun-Fat, Ti Lung, Leslie Cheung, Waise Lee. Exciting action thriller about a gangster (Lung) who wants to go straight and his brother

(Cheung), a dedicated police inspector who blames him for their father's death. Woo's breakthrough film (which became one of Hong Kong's highest grossers ever and gained international attention) is not as assured as his later work, but still has explosive set pieces and a terrific performance by Chow as a mob enforcer. Woo also coscripted. Followed by two sequels. ▼▶

Better Way to Die, A (2000) C-98m. *½ D: Scott Wiper. Andre Braugher, Joe Pantoliano, Natasha Henstridge, Lou Diamond Phillips, Scott Wiper, Mirjana Jokovic, Matt Gallini, Wayne Duvall, Carmen Argenziano, John Basinger, Jeanine Basinger. Young Chicago cop (Wiper) quits the force, intending to move to a small town to be with the one he loves, but there are predictable, violent complications. Not so much a story as a series of vignettes and set pieces that don't hold together. The result is half Eastwood, half Tarantino, and one total mess. Wiper also scripted. Released direct to video. [R] ▼▶

Betty (1992-French) C-100m. **½ D: Claude Chabrol. Marie Trintignant, Stephane Audran, Jean-Francois Garreaud, Yves Lambrecht, Christiane Minazolli. Boozy Betty, 28 and long since banished from home, is taken in by an older widow (who also enjoys the grape) in the posh hotel she owns. So-so character study is not one of Chabrol's stronger works; juggling of flashbacks will either keep you on your toes or zone you out into slumber. Adapted from a Georges Simenon novel. ▼▶

Betty Blue (1986-French) C-120m. **½ D: Jean-Jacques Beineix. Jean-Hugues Anglade, Beatrice Dalle, Gerard Darmon, Consuelo de Havilland, Clementine Celarie, Jaques Mathou, Vincent Lindon. Handyman and dangerously schizoid sexpot map-hop France practically waiting for her to crack up; when it finally happens, the grisly violence doesn't quite mesh with the light tone of what's come before. Well-photographed and sometimes quite funny, but ultimately much ado about nothing. If you're watching this for sex, don't miss the opening five minutes. Director's cut runs 185m. ▼▶●

Between Heaven and Hell (1956) C-94m. ** D: Richard Fleischer. Robert Wagner, Terry Moore, Broderick Crawford, Buddy Ebsen, Robert Keith, Brad Dexter, Mark Damon, Harvey Lembeck, Skip Homeier, L.Q. Jones, Carl Switzer, Frank Gorshin. Disjointed psychological drama about thoughtless Southerner Wagner, and how he is changed by his experiences in WW2 (especially while under the command of psycho Crawford). CinemaScope ▼▶

Between Strangers (2002-Canadian-Italian-U.S.) C-98m. ** D: Edoardo Ponti. Sophia Loren, Mira Sorvino, Deborah Kara Unger, Pete Postlethwaite, Julian Richings, Klaus Maria Brandauer, Malcolm McDowell, Gérard Depardieu, Robert Joy,

Wendy Crewson, John Neville. Stellar cast founders in this stale story of three women, strangers deeply in need of liberation from their fathers or husbands. Loren is laughably miscast as a haggard grocery store clerk weighed down by her obnoxious, disabled husband; Sorvino is a rising star photographer whose life is controlled by her famous father; Unger is an embittered cellist whose dad has just been released from prison. Ponti—the son of Loren and Carlo Ponti—also coscripted. [R] ▼▶

Between the Lines (1977) C-101m. ***½ D: Joan Micklin Silver. John Heard, Lindsay Crouse, Jeff Goldblum, Jill Eikenberry, Bruno Kirby, Gwen Welles, Stephen Collins, Michael J. Pollard, Lane Smith, Marilu Henner, Joe Morton, Southside Johnny & The Asbury Jukes. Thoroughly enjoyable sleeper about the emotional problems of the staff of a Boston underground newspaper which is about to be purchased by a print tycoon. The performances by a then-unknown cast are first rate all the way. Story by Fred Barron and David M. Helpern, Jr.; screenplay by Fred Barron. [R] ▼▶

Beverly Hillbillies, The (1993) C-93m. *½ D: Penelope Spheeris. Jim Varney, Diedrich Bader, Erika Eleniak, Cloris Leachman, Lily Tomlin, Dabney Coleman, Lea Thompson, Rob Schneider, Penny Fuller, Dolly Parton, Buddy Ebsen, Zsa Zsa Gabor. Big-screen rehash of the corny 1960s TV series, with the backwoods Clampett clan striking oil and moving to Beverly Hills, where they're prey for sharpie Schneider and his girlfriend (Thompson). The actors are earnest and enjoyable, but the script (by four writers—count 'em—four) is more lamebrained than the sitcom ever was, with smarmy sex jokes thrown in for good measure. Even worse, director Spheeris doesn't know how to stage a gag. [PG] ▼●▶

Beverly Hills Brats (1989) C-90m. *½ D: Dimitri Sotirakis. Peter Billingsley, Martin Sheen, Terry Moore, Burt Young, Ramon Estevez. Annoying, pretentious so-called satire, in which a wealthy but lonely boy arranges his own kidnapping so that parents will give him attention. This one was a family affair: associate producer is Janet (daughter of Martin) Sheen; Estevez is Sheen's son. Moore coproduced, and coauthored the original story. [PG-13] ▼●

Beverly Hills Chihuahua (2008) C-91m. **½ D: Raja Gosnell. Jamie Lee Curtis, Piper Perabo; voices of Drew Barrymore, Andy Garcia, George Lopez, Manolo Cardona, Cheech Marin, Paul Rodriguez, Edward James Olmos, Loretta Devine, Luis Guzmán, Plácido Domingo, Eddie "Piolin" Sotelo, Michael Urie, Marguerite Moreau, Nick Zano. Curtis has no idea what she's in for when she asks her impulsive, irresponsible niece (Perabo) to doggysit her beloved and spoiled Chihuahua, Chloe (Barrymore).

Perabo drags the pup along when she and her friends go on a Mexican vacation—and that's when the trouble starts. Sweet, likable family film with irresistible four-legged stars and good work by the human cast, too. Followed by DVD sequel, BEVERLY HILLS CHIHUAHUA 2. Super 35. [PG]🅭

Beverly Hills Cop (1984) C-105m. ***½ D: Martin Brest. Eddie Murphy, Judge Reinhold, John Ashton, Lisa Eilbacher, Ronny Cox, Steven Berkoff, James Russo, Jonathan Banks, Stephen Elliott, Paul Reiser, Damon Wayans. Smart-mouthed Detroit cop, who never plays by the rules, goes to L.A. to track down an old friend's killers. Sassy, tough, and very funny vehicle for Murphy, who's in peak form as a guy who's never caught off guard. Deft blend of comedy and violent action, extremely well cast, with terrific song score. Script by Daniel Petrie, Jr. Bronson Pinchot has hilarious scene-stealing role as gay art gallery worker. Followed by two sequels. [R] ▼●◑

Beverly Hills Cop II (1987) C-102m. ** D: Tony Scott. Eddie Murphy, Judge Reinhold, Jürgen Prochnow, Ronny Cox, John Ashton, Brigitte Nielsen, Allen Garfield, Dean Stockwell, Paul Reiser, Gil Hill, Robert Ridgley, Chris Rock. Contrived, cold-hearted (and misogynistic) sequel has few laughs, mediocre music, and a ridiculous story: it manages to coast as far as it does on the strength of Murphy alone. All credibility goes out the window at the start when B.H. Captain Cox is seen talking to Murphy about a fishing trip. Are these the same characters we saw in the first film? Super 35. [R] ▼●◑

Beverly Hills Cop III (1994) C-100m. **½ D: John Landis. Eddie Murphy, Judge Reinhold, Hector Elizondo, Theresa Randle, Bronson Pinchot, Timothy Carhart, John Saxon, Alan Young, Stephen McHattie, Al Green. Detroiter Murphy goes back to L.A., site of a theme park whose in-house security cops have hatched a counterfeiting ring—right under the nose of the sweet old gramps figure (Young) who's nominally in charge. Fast pace and inspired setting can't camouflage the bankruptcy of the concept. Gags are subordinate to action here—which, given the gags, may not have been such a bad idea. As usual, Landis features a number of prominent directors (including George Lucas, Joe Dante, Martha Coolidge, Arthur Hiller, Ray Harryhausen, Peter Medak, George Schaefer, Barbet Schroeder, and John Singleton) in cameo roles. Pinchot makes a welcome return from the original COP movie as Serge. [R] ▼●◑

Beverly Hills Ninja (1997) C-88m. *½ D: Dennis Dugan. Chris Farley, Nicollette Sheridan, Robin Shou, Nathaniel Parker, Soon-Tek Oh, Chris Rock. Baby Farley is washed ashore Moses style in Japan, whereupon he spends a klutzy lifetime being schooled in combat (and apparently, object breakage). Sheridan then hires him for an assignment back in Beverly Hills, where the two become (just as we know they would in real life) romantically involved. Subroutine comedy. [PG-13] ▼●◑

Beverly Hills Vamp (1989) C-89m. **½ D: Fred Olen Ray. Eddie Deezen, Britt Ekland, Tim Conway, Jr., Jay Richardson, Michelle Bauer, Robert Quarry, Dawn Wildsmith, Pat McCormick. Cheerfully cheap little film effectively spoofs itself while also being an entertaining vampire comedy. Jerry Lewis-oid Deezen is pitted against vampire madam Ekland and her three bloodsucking hookers. [R] ▼

Beware, My Lovely (1952) 77m. **½ D: Harry Horner. Ida Lupino, Robert Ryan, Taylor Holmes, O.Z. Whitehead, Barbara Whiting. Brooding, atmospheric psychological thriller with kindly WW1 widow Lupino hiring wanderer Ryan as a handyman and discovering he's a psychopath. ▼●

Beware of a Holy Whore (1970-German) C-103m. *** D: Rainer Werner Fassbinder. Lou Castel, Hanna Schygulla, Eddie Constantine, Marquard Bohm, Rainer Werner Fassbinder, Ulli Lommel, Margarethe von Trotta, Kurt Raab. Fascinating early Fassbinder film about filmmaking, as the cast and crew of a trouble-ridden German production spend most of their time drinking, talking, having sex, and hating each other while holed up in a Spanish hotel. Brutally funny and honest; reportedly based on Fassbinder's experiences filming WHITY in Spain. ▼◑

Beware! The Blob (1972) C-88m. *½ D: Larry Hagman. Robert Walker, Richard Stahl, Godfrey Cambridge, Carol Lynley, Larry Hagman, Cindy Williams, Shelley Berman, Marlene Clark, Gerrit Graham, Dick Van Patten. They should have left it frozen in the Arctic. Weak comedy-sequel finds the gooey mess doing its thing once again. Aka SON OF BLOB; reissued in 1982 with the tag line, "The Film That J.R. Shot!" [PG] ▼◑

Bewitched (2005) C-100m. ** D: Nora Ephron. Nicole Kidman, Will Ferrell, Shirley MacLaine, Michael Caine, Jason Schwartzman, Kristin Chenoweth, Heather Burns, Jim Turner, Stephen Colbert, David Alan Grier, Michael Badalucco, Steve Carell, Carole Shelley, Richard Kind, Amy Sedaris. Postmodern riff on the popular 1960s TV series, with Kidman as a real-life witch who decides she wants to live a "normal" life. Instead, egocentric actor Ferrell takes a shine to her and insists she be cast opposite him in a new version of . . . *Bewitched*. Inoffensive comedy allows Kidman to be cute, but has no genuine emotions or sentiments because its premise is so completely artificial. Carell channels the spirit of Paul Lynde and Shelley does the same for Marion Lorne in two of the film's brighter scenes. [PG-13] ▼◑

Beyond, The (1981-Italian) **C-87m.** ** D: Lucio Fulci. Katherine (Catriona) Mac-Coll, David Warbeck, Sarah Keller (Cinzia Monreale), Antoine Saint John (Antoine Domingo), Veronica Lazar. A woman inherits a hotel in Louisiana situated on one of the seven gates to Hell, where it's host to an army of zombies (definitely not good for tourism). Ultra-gory Italian splatter film has developed a cult, but it's just one bloody set piece after another, with outlandishly gruesome makeup effects (including crucifixions, acid poured onto faces, etc.). Aka SEVEN DOORS OF DEATH, which runs 82m. Techniscope.▼❶

Beyond a Reasonable Doubt (1956) **80m.** **½ D: Fritz Lang. Dana Andrews, Joan Fontaine, Sidney Blackmer, Philip Bourneuf, Barbara Nichols. Far-fetched tale of man who pretends to be guilty of murder to get firsthand view of justice system, unable to prove himself innocent later on. Pale production values. Intriguing idea doesn't hold up. Remade in 2009.▼❶

Beyond a Reasonable Doubt (2009) **C-105m.** ** D: Peter Hyams. Jesse Metcalfe, Amber Tamblyn, Michael Douglas, Orlando Jones, Lawrence Beron, Sewell Whitney, Joel David Moore. By-the-numbers remake of the 1956 noir: a low-energy courtroom thriller about an ambitious rookie reporter who sets himself up as a supposed murderer in order to expose the unethical practices of a corrupt district attorney who is running for the governor's seat. Actors do fine with predictable material, but it plays like TV fodder. Douglas' presence as the shady D.A. elevates it a little. Dina Merrill appears unbilled. [PG-13]❶

Beyond Atlantis (1973-U.S.-Filipino) **C-89m.** *½ D: Eddie Romero. Patrick Wayne, John Ashley, Leigh Christian, Lenore Stevens, George Nader, Sid Haig, Eddie Garcia, Vic Diaz. Low-budget fantasy about lost civilization, represented by amphibious humanoids; combines feminist subplot with philosophizing about modern extinction of cultures. [PG]▼❶

Beyond Borders (2003) **C-127m.** ** D: Martin Campbell. Angelina Jolie, Clive Owen, Teri Polo, Linus Roache, Yorick van Wageningen, Noah Emmerich, Kate Ashfield, Timothy West, Burt Kwouk. A married woman leaves her husband behind when she learns about rescue efforts in Africa and the dedication of one passionate doctor; their relationship continues over many years on several continents. Depiction of conditions in various trouble spots around the world is so vivid, and the urgency of helping victimized people so genuine, that it only heightens the absurdity of the love story that's been pasted onto it. Owen's solid presence helps. J-D-C Scope. [R] ▼❶

Beyond Evil (1980) **C-94m.** ** D: Herb Freed. John Saxon, Lynda Day George, Michael Dante, Mario Milano, Janice Lynde, David Opatoshu. Saxon and George move into an old house occupied by the spirit of a 100-year-old woman, who does not like this intrusion into her privacy. OK of its kind. [R]▼❶

Beyond Glory (1948) **82m.** **½ D: John Farrow. Alan Ladd, Donna Reed, George Macready, George Coulouris. Predictable account of West Point captain Ladd, a WW2 veteran, on trial for misconduct. Audie Murphy's first film.

Beyond Justice (1992) **C-113m.** *½ D: Duccio Tessari. Rutger Hauer, Carol Alt, Omar Sharif, Elliott Gould, Kabir Bedi, Brett Halsey, Peter Sands. Preposterous action-adventure story of Chairman of the Board Alt, who employs hired-gun Hauer to retrieve her kidnapped son from his Arab grandfather, Emir Omar. Amid the machine-gun fire we often don't know who is being shot at—nor do we care. [R]▼❶❶

Beyond Obsession SEE: **Beyond the Door** (1982)

Beyond Rangoon (1995) **C-99m.** **½ D: John Boorman. Patricia Arquette, Frances McDormand, Spalding Gray, U Aung Ko, Adele Lutz, Victor Slezak. Emotionally troubled American tourist puts herself at risk during a trip to Burma in 1988. She's soon fleeing from the military and heading to the Thai border with a former university professor who's now a wanted man. Hollow at times, and heavy-handed in its effort to promote awareness of the political situation in Burma (now Myanmar). Biggest problem is Arquette, who just doesn't register. Still, a fairly interesting story from an always-committed filmmaker. Panavision. [R]▼❶❶

Beyond Reasonable Doubt (1980-New Zealand) **C-127m.** **½ D: John Laing. David Hemmings, John Hargreaves, Martyn Sanderson, Grant Tilly, Diana Rowan. Adequate docudrama chronicling the conviction on trumped-up charges of innocent farmer Arthur Thomas (Hargreaves) for a double murder. Hemmings is good as the hard-boiled cop who plants evidence that leads to Thomas's downfall. Screenplay by David Yallop, from his book. Panavision. ▼

Beyond Silence (1996-German-Swiss) **C-105m.** *** D: Caroline Link. Sylvie Testud, Tatjana Trieb, Howie Seago, Emmanuelle Laborit, Sibylle Canonica. An eight-year-old German girl serves as the speaking voice (and a sometimes sly interpreter) for her deaf parents. When she matures and becomes a talented clarinetist, she considers heading for a Berlin conservatory, amid the repercussions of possibly leaving the nest. Nicely turned emotional tale of familial love and forgiveness, and a girl's growing pains. [PG-13]▼❶

Beyond Suspicion SEE: **Auggie Rose**

Beyond the Door (1974-U.S.-Italian) **C-**

94m. BOMB D: Oliver Hellman (Ovidio Assonitis). Juliet Mills, Richard Johnson, Elizabeth Turner, David Colin, Jr. Mills becomes pregnant with a fetus possessed by the Devil. Vulgar EXORCIST ripoff, complete with pea-green regurgitation, head spins, and Mercedes McCambridge–like voice. Warner Bros. even took legal action against the film. Followed by the inevitable BEYOND THE DOOR II. [R]▼▶

Beyond the Door II (1979-Italian) **C-92m.** *½ D: Mario Bava. Daria Nicolodi, John Steiner, David Colin, Jr., Ivan Rassimov. Corpse of dead man possesses his son, seeks vengeance on his wife. Nice directorial touches cannot save confusing, needlessly bloody EXORCIST clone; only resemblances to first film are actor Colin and "possession" plot line. [R]▼▶

Beyond the Door (1982-Italian) **C-116m.** ** D: Liliana Cavani. Marcello Mastroianni, Tom Berenger, Eleonora Giorgi, Michel Piccoli. Overbaked melodrama centering on complex relationship between jailed father Mastroianni and daughter Giorgi, complicated by arrival of American engineer Berenger. Also known as BEYOND OBSESSION.▼▶

Beyond the Fog SEE: **Horror on Snape Island**

Beyond the Forest (1949) **96m.** ** D: King Vidor. Bette Davis, Joseph Cotten, David Brian, Ruth Roman, Dona Drake, Regis Toomey. Muddled murder story of grasping Davis, her small-town doctor husband (Cotten), and wealthy neighbor (Brian). Davis' overly mannered performance doesn't help. This is the film in which she utters the immortal line, "What a dump!"▼

Beyond the Gates (2006-British-German) **C-115m.** **½ D: Michael Caton-Jones. John Hurt, Hugh Dancy, Dominique Horwitz, Louis Mahoney, Clare-Hope Ashitey, Nicola Walker, Steve Toussaint. Middling drama, based on the Rwandan experiences of BBC journalist David Belton, takes another screen look at the 1994 genocide against the Tutsis by the Hutu government. Unlike HOTEL RWANDA, this film traces the reactions of mostly white folks: devoted priest Hurt, teacher Dancy, and Belgian U.N. peacekeepers who remain strictly passive even under utmost provocation. Adequate in the day-to-day scenes but rises to the dramatic occasion in its most harrowing confrontations, which do carry power. Original British title: SHOOTING DOGS. Super 35. [R]▶

Beyond the Law (1968-Italian) **C-91m.** ** D: Giorgio Stegani. Lee Van Cleef, Antonio Sabato, Lionel Stander, Bud Spencer, Gordon Mitchell, Ann Smyrner. Formula Western with a whole lot of Van Cleef and almost as much humor. Bad guy turns good guy, becomes sheriff long enough to get his hands on a shipment of silver, and then splits. Aka

BLOODSILVER, THE GOOD DIE FIRST. Techniscope.▼▶

Beyond the Law (1992) **C-108m.** **½ D: Larry Ferguson. Charlie Sheen, Linda Fiorentino, Michael Madsen, Courtney B. Vance, Leon Rippy, Dennis Burkley, Rip Torn. Traumatized cop Sheen—he was abused as a child—has just been fired by his corrupt boss. Recruited to work undercover, he joins a band of scuzzy, drug-dealing bikers. Not bad of its type, with an unusually high level of character development, but the often illogical scenario eventually does it in. Based on a true story. [R]▼▶

Beyond the Limit (1983) **C-103m.** *½ D: John Mackenzie. Michael Caine, Richard Gere, Bob Hoskins, Elpidia Carrillo, Joaquim De Almeida, A Martinez. Muddled adaptation of Graham Greene's *The Honorary Consul* with Gere miscast as British doctor who becomes involved with revolutionaries in South American country—and sexually involved with the ex-prostitute wife of boozy diplomat (well played by Caine). Slow, murky, completely uninvolving. [R]▼

Beyond the Living (1978) **C-88m.** ** D: Al Adamson. Jill Jacobson, Geoffrey Land, Marilyn Joi, Mary Kay Pass. OK horrorpic in the CARRIE vein. Nurse is possessed by the spirit of a patient who died during surgery and begins killing the doctors who performed the operation. Best scene takes place in a foundry. Released to theaters as NURSE SHERRI. Video titles: HOSPITAL OF TERROR, HANDS OF DEATH, KILLER'S CURSE, BLACK VOODOO, THE POSSESSION OF NURSE SHERRI, and TERROR HOSPITAL.▼▶

Beyond the Mat (1999) **C-102m.** *** D: Barry Blaustein. Screenwriter Blaustein (best known for his work with Eddie Murphy) indulges his lifelong passion for professional wrestling in this absorbing documentary, which tries to put a human face on the often circuslike sport. Among his subjects: Mankind (aka Mick Foley), a WWF superstar who's nothing like his ring persona; an aging but still potent Terry Funk; and a very troubled Jake the Snake (Jake Roberts). Compelling viewing even for non–wrestling fans. [R]▼▶

Beyond the Poseidon Adventure (1979) **C-122m.** *½ D: Irwin Allen. Michael Caine, Sally Field, Telly Savalas, Peter Boyle, Jack Warden, Shirley Knight, Slim Pickens, Shirley Jones, Karl Malden, Mark Harmon, Veronica Hamel. Following THE SWARM, Caine teamed up with Irwin Allen for another career killer—a needless sequel about attempts to loot the vessel before it sinks. Panavision. [G]▼▶

Beyond Therapy (1987) **C-93m.** BOMB D: Robert Altman. Julie Hagerty, Jeff Goldblum, Glenda Jackson, Tom Conti, Christopher Guest, Genevieve Page, Cris Campion, Sandrine Dumas. Dreadful adaptation of

Christopher Durang's paper-thin comic play about neurotic singles and their psychiatrists. Given the director and cast, it's hard to believe how awful this is—until you see for yourself! Filmed in Paris, though set in N.Y.C. [R] ▼▶

Beyond the Reef (1981) C-91m. ** D: Frank C. Clark. Dayton Ka'ne, Maren Jensen, Kathleen Swan, Keahi Farden, Joseph Ka'ne. In the wake of THE HURRICANE, Dino De Laurentiis produced this innocuous South Seas romance with two attractive leads. Old-fashioned, to say the least. Completed in 1979. Aka SHARK BOY OF BORA BORA and SEA KILLER. [PG]

Beyond the Sea (2004-British-German) C-118m. **½ D: Kevin Spacey. Kevin Spacey, Kate Bosworth, John Goodman, Bob Hoskins, Brenda Blethyn, Greta Scacchi, Caroline Aaron, Peter Cincotti, William Ullrich. Biopic of singer-performer Bobby Darin covers his rise to success, marriage to movie star Sandra Dee, and the drive that came from knowing he didn't have long to live, after suffering rheumatic fever as a child. Takes a fanciful approach, with musical production numbers and a self-conscious device that enables grown-up Bobby to confront himself as a boy . . . all of which creates distance between the audience and the inherent emotion of the story. Spacey does his own singing, quite well, in this labor-of-love project, which he also cowrote and coproduced. Super 35. [PG-13] ▼▶

Beyond the Stars (1989) C-87m. *½ D: David Saperstein. Martin Sheen, Christian Slater, Robert Foxworth, Sharon Stone, Olivia d'Abo, F. Murray Abraham. Excruciatingly slow story of former astronaut Sheen who once walked on the moon. Would-be astronaut Slater idolizes him, to the consternation of his ex-NASA employee dad (Foxworth). Top cast cannot rise above a poor script. [PG] ▼▶

Beyond the Valley of the Dolls (1970) C-109m. *** D: Russ Meyer. Dolly Read, Cynthia Myers, Marcia McBroom, David Gurian, John LaZar, Michael Blodgett, Edy Williams, Erica Gavin, Phyllis Davis, Charles Napier, Strawberry Alarm Clock. Female rock trio attempts to make it (and make it and make it) in Hollywood. Time has been kind to raunchy in-name-only sequel to (and spoof of) VALLEY OF THE DOLLS. Screenplay by Roger Ebert, story by Meyer and Ebert, and picked by two prominent critics as one of the 10 best U.S. films 1968–78. Panavision. [NC-17—originally rated X] ▼▶

Beyond the Walls (1984-Israeli) C-103m. ** D: Uri Barbash. Arnon Zadok, Muhamad Bakri, Assi Dayan, Rami Danon, Boaz Sharambi. This potentially powerful drama about life in an Israeli prison, centering on the explosive relationship between Jewish and Arab convicts, is just a standard, predictable, noisy men-in-the-big-house yarn.

Incredibly, it earned a Best Foreign Film Oscar nomination. [R] ▼

B.F.'s Daughter (1948) 108m. *½ D: Robert Z. Leonard. Barbara Stanwyck, Van Heflin, Charles Coburn, Richard Hart, Keenan Wynn, Margaret Lindsay. Disastrous film of J. P. Marquand novel, with Stanwyck the domineering girl ruining marriage to professor Heflin. ▶

Bhowani Junction (1956-U.S.-British) C-110m. **½ D: George Cukor. Ava Gardner, Stewart Granger, Bill Travers, Abraham Sofaer. Set in post-WW2 India; Gardner is half-caste torn between love of country and love for a British colonel. Based on John Masters novel; strikingly shot on location. CinemaScope. ▼▶

Bible, The (1966-Italian) C-174m. BOMB D: John Huston. Michael Parks, Ulla Bergryd, Richard Harris, John Huston, Stephen Boyd, George C. Scott, Ava Gardner, Peter O'Toole, Franco Nero. Narrated by Huston. Unsuccessful epic dealing with Adam and Eve, Cain and Abel, Noah and the Flood, etc. (first 22 chapters of Genesis). Only Huston himself as Noah escapes heavy-handedness. Definitely one time you should read the Book instead. Dimension 150. ▼▶

Bicentennial Man (1999) C-131m. **½ D: Chris Columbus. Robin Williams, Sam Neill, Embeth Davidtz, Wendy Crewson, Hallie Kate Eisenberg, Stephen Root, Lynne Thigpen, Kiersten Warren, Oliver Platt. In the near future, a family buys an all-purpose robot, which turns out to have human emotions. His interactions with the family and their descendants are followed over the next 200 years. Sincere, sentimental, but goes for the jokes too often. Williams is good as the robot, too familiar when he becomes human. From a short story by Isaac Asimov and a novel by Asimov and Robert Silverberg. [PG] ▼▶

Bicycle Thieves (1948-Italian) 89m. **** D: Vittorio De Sica. Lamberto Maggiorani, Lianella Carell, Enzo Staiola, Vittorio Antonucci. A man whose livelihood depends on his bicycle spends a shattering week with his son searching for the men who stole it. Stunning in its simplicity, this was one of the cornerstones of the Italian neo-realist movement, filmed entirely on natural locations with nonprofessional actors. It also vividly captures life in post-WW2 Rome. Winner of a special Academy Award, given before there was a Foreign Language Film category. One of the all-time greats. Originally released in the U.S. as THE BICYCLE THIEF. ▼▶

Big (1988) C-102m. ***½ D: Penny Marshall. Tom Hanks, Elizabeth Perkins, John Heard, Jared Rushton, Robert Loggia, David Moscow, Jon Lovitz, Mercedes Ruehl, Josh Clark, Tracy Reiner. A 12-year-old boy wishes he were "big"—and gets his wish, waking up the next morning as a 30-year-old man! Charming fantasy tackles a rare modern-day subject—innocence—and pulls it off thanks to Hanks' superb, seemingly guileless performance, and Marshall's surefooted direction. A real treat. Written by coproducers Gary Ross and Anne Spielberg. Later a Broadway musical. [PG]▼●)

Bigamist, The (1953) **80m.** *** D: Ida Lupino. Edmond O'Brien, Joan Fontaine, Ida Lupino, Edmund Gwenn, Jane Darwell, Kenneth Tobey. Compassionate look at lonely man who finds himself married to (and in love with) two different women. Extremely well acted; one of Lupino's best directorial efforts and the only time she ever directed herself.▼●

Big Bad John (1990) **C-92m.** ** D: Burt Kennedy. Ned Beatty, Jack Elam, Bo Hopkins, Jimmy Dean, John Dennis Johnston, Jeff Osterhage, Ned Vaughn, Buck Taylor, Anne Lockhart. Dumb movie based on the long-ago hit song by costar Dean. Here, he plays a former Southern sheriff driving crosscountry to rescue his daughter—with the title character on his tail. The record was better. [PG-13]▼●●

Big Bad Love (2002) **C-111m.** *** D: Arliss Howard. Arliss Howard, Debra Winger, Paul LeMat, Rosanna Arquette, Angie Dickinson, Michael Parks, Alex Van, Zach Moody; voice of Sigourney Weaver. Offbeat but compelling tale of a frustrated writer who's trying to get his life in order—professionally and personally—having squandered his marriage and chance at fatherhood. Told in nonlinear spurts, combining reality with dreams and nightmares, the film manages to paint a rich picture of its main character, piece by piece. Not a perfect film, but emotionally true. Howard cowrote with his brother James, from Larry Brown's stories; Winger also produced. Super 35. [R]▼●

Big Bad Mama (1974) **C-83m.** *** D: Steve Carver. Angie Dickinson, Tom Skerritt, William Shatner, Susan Sennett,\Robbie Lee, Dick Miller, Joan Prather, Royal Dano, Sally Kirkland. Sexy knock-off of BONNIE AND CLYDE has Angie and her two teen daughters spending as much time fooling around with partners Shatner and Skerritt as they do robbing banks. Angie's nude scenes make this a cable-TV favorite (and led to a sequel 13 years later!). Flavorful score by David Grisman. [R]▼●

Big Bad Mama II (1987) **C-83m.** *½ D: Jim Wynorski. Angie Dickinson, Robert Culp, Danielle Brisebois, Julie McCullough, Bruce Glover. In this loosely linked sequel (more like a remake), Angie and her two daughters again shoot up rural, Depression-era America, robbing banks to avenge her husband's murder. Culp provides brief love interest. *Archie Bunker's Place* alumna Brisebois does a surprising topless scene. [R]▼●

Big Bang, The (1990) **C-81m.** *** D:

James Toback. Fascinating documentary in which Toback poses some basic philosophical questions—why were we born? who are we? and where are we going?—to a variety of people, from boxer/author José Torres to astronomer Fred Hess, basketball player Darryl Dawkins to film producer Don Simpson. Most amusing are the comments of an ex-mobster, and most sobering are those of an Auschwitz survivor. We even see Toback on camera, trying to finance the film. [R]▼

Big Bird Cage, The (1972) **C-88m.** **½ D: Jack Hill. Pam Grier, Anitra Ford, Sid Haig, Candice Roman, Vic Diaz, Carol Speed. Amusing spoof of Filipino prison films has pleasant team of Grier and Haig as thieving mercenaries who engineer a prison break from the outside. A follow-up to THE BIG DOLL HOUSE. Aka WOMEN'S PENITENTIARY II. [R]▼●

Big Blue, The (1988-U.S.-French) **C-119m.** ** D: Luc Besson. Rosanna Arquette, Jean-Marc Barr, Jean Reno, Paul Shenar, Sergio Castellito, Marc Duret, Griffin Dunne. Waterlogged chronicle of famed free diver Jacques Mayol (Barr), with Arquette redoing her DESPERATELY SEEKING SUSAN performance as a ditsy insurance investigator who falls for him. As much a psychological study as a drama of athletic competition—but who cares? Underwater photography is the main attraction here. Original French release (now on video in U.S.) runs 163m. CinemaScope. [PG]▼●

Big Boss, The SEE: **Fists of Fury**
Big Bounce, The (1969) **C-102m.** ** D: Alex March. Ryan O'Neal, Leigh Taylor-Young, James Daly, Robert Webber, Lee Grant, Van Heflin. Muddle-headed tale of drifter O'Neal becoming involved with vixenish Taylor-Young, who has strange ideas of what to do for kicks. Based on a novel by Elmore Leonard. Remade in 2004. Panavision. [PG—edited from original R rating]●

Big Bounce, The (2004) **C-89m.** ** D: George Armitage. Owen Wilson, Morgan Freeman, Gary Sinise, Sara Foster, Willie Nelson, Vinnie Jones, Bebe Neuwirth, Charlie Sheen, Harry Dean Stanton. Ne'er-do-well Wilson takes up with the sexy mistress of a wheeler-dealer on the North Shore of Oahu, despite friendly warnings from the local district judge (Freeman). Postcard views of Hawaii and George S. Clinton's evocative music are abetted by plentiful eye-candy shots of shapely Foster, but the movie's good vibes drain away as the caper grows more convoluted. Sinise, Nelson, Neuwirth, and Stanton are wasted in throwaway roles. Super 35. [PG-13]▼●

Big Brass Ring, The (1999) **C-104m.** ** D: George Hickenlooper. William Hurt, Miranda Richardson, Nigel Hawthorne, Irène Jacob, Ewan Stewart, Gregg Henry,

Ron Livingston. Independent politician running for governor of Missouri—with his wife's money—is unnerved when his former mentor threatens to unveil a skeleton in his closet, with an eager investigative reporter waiting to pounce. Strong cast and impressive pedigree (based on an unproduced screenplay by Orson Welles and Oja Kodar) can't change the fact that the film sinks under its own weight. After a while the characters are simply boring. Debuted on cable TV. [R]▼❶

Big Brawl, The (1980) **C-95m.** **½ D: Robert Clouse. Jackie Chan, Jose Ferrer, Kristine DeBell, Mako, Ron Max. The martial arts are applied to '30s gangster movie set in Chicago. Appealing cast, lots of comedy, along with director and some of the production staff from ENTER THE DRAGON, make this a moderately successful chop-socky. Aka BATTLE CREEK BRAWL. Panavision. [R]▼❶

Big Bully (1996) **C-97m.** *½ D: Steve Miner. Rick Moranis, Tom Arnold, Julianne Phillips, Carol Kane, Jeffrey Tambor, Curtis Armstrong, Faith Prince, Tony Pierce, Don Knotts, Stuart Pankin. Having parlayed his newly published book into an offer to teach a course at his old school, author Moranis is horrified to discover that his long unseen childhood tormentor is now the shop instructor. Comedy is so dull in the opening childhood flashbacks that it's already d.o.a. by the time Moranis and Arnold show up. Phillips disappears abruptly in the film's second half—lucky for her. [PG]▼❶

Big Bus, The (1976) **C-88m.** **½ D: James Frawley. Joseph Bologna, Stockard Channing, John Beck, Lynn Redgrave, Jose Ferrer, Ruth Gordon, Richard B. Shull, Sally Kellerman, Ned Beatty, Bob Dishy, Stuart Margolin, Richard Mulligan, Larry Hagman, Howard Hesseman, Harold Gould. Funny spoof of disaster films, using a superduper Trailways bus; all expected clichés come in for ribbing, but film doesn't sustain its promising idea. Murphy Dunne hilarious as inane cocktail pianist. Panavision. [PG]▼❶

Big Business (1988) **C-97m.** **½ D: Jim Abrahams. Bette Midler, Lily Tomlin, Fred Ward, Edward Herrmann, Michele Placido, Daniel Gerroll, Barry Primus, Michael Gross, Joe Grifasi, Mary Gross, Seth Green. Two sets of twins are mismatched and separated at birth; years later the girls who've grown up in the boonies come to N.Y.C. for a showdown with the conglomerate that's going to wipe out their little town, hardly dreaming that the corporation is run by their identical twins! Agreeable farce never really catches fire, though Bette is terrific and the effects are remarkable. [PG] ▼❶

Big Carnival, The SEE: **Ace in the Hole**
Big Chill, The (1983) **C-103m.** *** D: Lawrence Kasdan. Tom Berenger, Glenn Close, Jeff Goldblum, William Hurt, Kevin Kline, Mary Kay Place, Meg Tilly, JoBeth Williams, Don Galloway. Entertaining, surface-level look at a group of former college-radical friends who've dropped back into Society. Wonderful acting ensemble, irresistible soundtrack of '60s hits help camouflage weaknesses of script—which bears more than passing resemblance to John Sayles' RETURN OF THE SECAUCUS SEVEN. (Trivia note: the deceased friend was played by Kevin Costner, whose scenes were cut from the finished film. But that's still him being dressed for his funeral under the main titles!) [R]▼❶

Big Circus, The (1959) **C-108m.** **½ D: Joseph M. Newman. Victor Mature, Red Buttons, Rhonda Fleming, Kathryn Grant, Vincent Price, Peter Lorre, David Nelson, Gilbert Roland, Howard McNear, Steve Allen. Corny and predictable, but still entertaining hokum under the big top, with Lorre as a sardonic clown and Roland tightrope-walking over Niagara Falls. And what a cast! CinemaScope. ▼❶

Big City (1937) **80m.** **½ D: Frank Borzage. Spencer Tracy, Luise Rainer, Eddie Quillan, William Demarest, Regis Toomey, Charley Grapewin, Victor Varconi. Cabdriver Tracy and wife Rainer are pitted against crooked taxi bosses in well-acted but average film.❶

Big City (1948) **103m.** **½ D: Norman Taurog. Margaret O'Brien, Robert Preston, Danny Thomas, George Murphy, Karin Booth, Edward Arnold, Butch Jenkins, Betty Garrett, Lotte Lehmann. Syrupy Americana in which cantor Thomas, cop Murphy, and reverend Preston collectively adopt abandoned baby, who grows up to be precocious O'Brien. Irving Berlin's "God Bless America" is featured throughout.

Big City, The (1963-Indian) **131m.** *** D: Satyajit Ray. Madhabi Mukherjee, Anil Chatterjee, Vicky Redwood, Haren Chatterjee, Jaya Bhaduri, Haradhan Bannerjee. A proud Calcutta man is forced by financial circumstances to let his wife work; soon she is the only one with a job. Warm, humorous, and astutely observed portrait of domestic life and women's roles in Indian society. Long but rewarding. ▼

Big Clock, The (1948) **95m.** *** D: John Farrow. Ray Milland, Charles Laughton, Maureen O'Sullivan, George Macready, Rita Johnson, Dan Tobin, Henry (Harry) Morgan. Tyrannical publisher of crime magazine (Laughton) commits murder; his editor (Milland) tries to solve case and finds all the clues pointing to himself. Vibrant melodrama; taut script by Jonathan Latimer from Kenneth Fearing novel. Elsa Lanchester has hilarious vignette as eccentric artist. Remade as NO WAY OUT (1987). ▼

Big Combo, The (1955) **89m.** *** D: Joseph (H.) Lewis. Cornel Wilde, Jean Wallace, Brian Donlevy, Richard Conte, Lee Van

Cleef, Robert Middleton, Earl Holliman, Helen Walker. Raw, violent film noir about persistent cop Wilde going up against cunning, sadistic racketeer Conte. A cult item, stylishly directed; Donlevy's demise is a highlight.▼❍

Big Country, The (1958) **C-166m.** *** D: William Wyler. Gregory Peck, Burl Ives, Jean Simmons, Carroll Baker, Charlton Heston, Chuck Connors, Charles Bickford. Overblown Western has ex-sea captain Peck arrive to marry Baker, but forced to take sides in battle against Ives and sons over water rights. Heston as quick-tempered ranch foreman and Ives (who won an Oscar) as burly patriarch stand out in energetic cast. Jerome Moross's score has become a classic. Technirama.▼❍

Big Cube, The (1969) **C-98m.** *½ D: Tito Davison. Lana Turner, George Chakiris, Richard Egan, Dan O'Herlihy, Karin Mossberg. Absurd drama about relationship between beautiful young girl, her gigolo boyfriend, and her actress-mother at least offers some unintentional laughs. For camp followers only. [M/PG]❍

Big Daddy (1999) **C-95m.** **½ D: Dennis Dugan. Adam Sandler, Joey Lauren Adams, Rob Schneider, Jon Stewart, Leslie Mann, Josh Mostel, Joseph Bologna, Kristy Swanson, Steve Buscemi, Cole and Dylan Sprouse. An overgrown, irresponsible slacker tries to look after a young boy who's been dumped on his doorstep; naturally, he becomes attached to the youngster, and vice versa. Sandler vehicle is utterly contrived but delivers expected laughs; the courtroom climax is too silly for words. That's director Dugan as the man who won't cooperate on Halloween. [PG-13]▼❍

Big Day, The SEE: **Jour de Fete**

Big Deal on Madonna Street (1958-Italian) **106m.** ***½ D: Mario Monicelli. Vittorio Gassman, Marcello Mastroianni, Renato Salvatori, Rossana Rory, Carla Gravina, Totò. Classic account of misadventures of amateurish crooks attempting to rob a store; hilarious satire on all burglary capers. Retitled: BIG DEAL; remade as CRACKERS and in 2002 as WELCOME TO COLLINWOOD, and followed by a sequel, BIG DEAL ON MADONNA STREET ... 20 YEARS LATER, which was actually released 30 years later! Also adapted for Broadway—unsuccessfully.▼❍

Big Doll House, The (1971) **C-93m.** **½ D: Jack Hill. Judy Brown, Roberta Collins, Pam Grier, Brooke Mills, Pat Woodell, Sid Haig. Fast paced, tongue-in-cheek adventure shot in Philippines mixes sex, comedy, and violence in confrontation between sadistic warden and female prisoners. One of the earliest, most successful and influential of women-in-prison exploitation films. Followed by THE BIG BIRD CAGE. Aka WOMEN'S PENITENTIARY I. [R]▼❍

Big Easy, The (1987) **C-108m.** *** D: Jim McBride. Dennis Quaid, Ellen Barkin, Ned Beatty, John Goodman, Ebbe Roe Smith, Lisa Jane Persky, Charles Ludlam, Tom O'Brien, Grace Zabriskie, Marc Lawrence, Solomon Burke, Jim Garrison. Highly original crime yarn with steamy romance and unique New Orleans atmosphere. A stylish homicide detective (Quaid) runs afoul of the new, uptight assistant D.A. (Barkin) while investigating a local mob murder; soon they're romantically involved, even while they're at odds professionally. Sassy and sexy, with terrific Cajun music score. Written by Daniel Petrie, Jr. Later a cable TV series. [R]▼❍

Big Empty, The (2003) **C-92m.** ** D: Steve Anderson. Jon Favreau, Joey Lauren Adams, Bud Cort, Jon Gries, Daryl Hannah, Adam Beach, Gary Farmer, Rachael Leigh Cook, Kelsey Grammer, Sean Bean, Patti Smith, Danny Trejo, Melora Walters, Brent Briscoe. Favreau plays a loser actor who agrees to courier a suitcase to desert town peopled by loony hicks with more than a passing interest in alien visitors. Quirky, low-budget melodrama is ambitious but unsuccessful. The film is aptly titled. [R]▼❍

Big Fan (2009) **C-86m.** *** D: Robert Siegel. Patton Oswalt, Kevin Corrigan, Michael Rapaport, Marcia Jean Kurtz, Gino Cafarelli, Matt Servitto, Serafina Fiore, Polly Humphreys, Jonathan Hamm. Portrait of a loner (played to perfection by stand-up comic Oswalt) who lives with his mother, clocks in at a dead-end job, and lives only to cheer on the N.Y. Giants football team and badmouth its rival Philadelphia Eagles on a radio phone-in show. An unexpected turn of events shakes up his life but can't alter his obsession. Dark, well-observed (and perfectly cast) character study may remind some of TAXI DRIVER—without the blood. Written by Siegel (THE WRESTLER), making his directorial debut. [R]❍

Big Fat Liar (2002) **C-87m.** **½ D: Shawn Levy. Frankie Muniz, Paul Giamatti, Amanda Bynes, Amanda Detmer, Donald Faison, Lee Majors, Sandra Oh, Russell Hornsby, Dustin Diamond. Perpetual liar Muniz can't get his dad to believe that one of his school assignments was ripped off by a movie producer—so, with a friend (Bynes), he sets off for Hollywood to prove it's true. There, he's forced to exact revenge on the mean-spirited, egocentric film exec. Kids may enjoy this well-paced slapstick outing; adults will find few surprises. Jaleel White appears unbilled. [PG]▼❍

Big Fish (2003) **C-125m.** ***½ D: Tim Burton. Ewan McGregor, Albert Finney, Billy Crudup, Jessica Lange, Helena Bonham Carter, Alison Lohman, Robert Guillaume, Steve Buscemi, Danny DeVito, Missi Pyle, Marion Cotillard. Reporter Crudup ends a long estrangement with his father when he learns the old man is dying, and tries to penetrate his dad's hearty, tale-spinning façade. McGregor plays the younger Finney, whose life is made up of one amazing adventure after another. John August adapted Daniel Wallace's novel, which is perfect fodder for director Burton and his sense of heightened reality—but instead of the bizarre and baroque, we get a world of wonder and amazement. Maintains a consistent and disarming tone from start to finish, with pitch-perfect performances. [PG-13] ▼●

Big Fisherman, The (1959) **C-149m.** **½ D: Frank Borzage. Howard Keel, John Saxon, Susan Kohner, Herbert Lom, Martha Hyer, Ray Stricklyn, Alexander Scourby. Sprawling religious epic, from Lloyd Douglas' book about the life of St. Peter; seldom dull, but not terribly inspiring. Borzage's last film. Originally 184m., then cut to 164m. Super Panavision 70.

Big Fix, The (1978) **C-108m.** *** D: Jeremy Paul Kagan. Richard Dreyfuss, Susan Anspach, Bonnie Bedelia, John Lithgow, F. Murray Abraham, Ofelia Medina, Fritz Weaver. Good vehicle for now-familiar Dreyfuss personality as 1960s-campus-radical-turned-private-eye Moses Wine, who becomes involved in tangled whodunit in which a former hippie cult leader figures prominently. Screenplay by Roger L. Simon, based on his novel. Look fast for Mandy Patinkin as a pool cleaner. Leon Redbone's "I Want to Be Seduced" is not in video version. [PG]▼

Bigger Stronger Faster* (2008) **C-106m.** *** D: Christopher Bell. Compelling documentary investigates performance-enhancing drugs, presenting many points of view, which yield often-surprising results. First-time filmmaker Bell has personal involvement with the topic (and the film) since he and his brothers grew up idolizing wrestlers and movie musclemen who, in most cases, later turned out to be using steroids. An eye-opening look at a subject that usually provokes knee-jerk responses. Film's asterisked subtitle is THE SIDE EFFECTS OF BEING AMERICAN. [PG-13]▌

Bigger Than Life (1956) **C-95m.** *** D: Nicholas Ray. James Mason, Barbara Rush, Walter Matthau, Robert Simon, Roland Winters. Compelling drama of teacher Mason who becomes hooked on drugs, and its devastating effects on him and his family. Mason also produced the film. Quite bold for its time. CinemaScope. ▌

Biggest Battle, The SEE: **Great Battle, The**

Biggest Bundle of Them All, The (1968) **C-110m.** *½ D: Ken Annakin. Robert Wagner, Raquel Welch, Vittorio De Sica, Edward G. Robinson, Godfrey Cambridge. Supposedly a comedy, film is slapdash tale of amateur criminals who try to kidnap

American gangster. Filmed in France and Italy. Panavision.▼

Big Girls Don't Cry . . . They Get Even (1992) **C-96m.** ** D: Joan Micklin Silver. Hillary Wolf, David Strathairn, Margaret Whitton, Griffin Dunne, Patricia Kalember, Adrienne Shelly, Dan Futterman, Ben Savage. The product of a mélange of multiple divorces and remarriages, teenager Wolf, fed up with various stepparents and half-siblings, hightails it during her current family's vacation. Bittersweet comedy is too superficial (and predictable) to say anything meaningful on a subject relevant to many teens. [PG]▼●

Biggles: Adventures in Time (1986-British) **C-108m.** ** D: John Hough. Neil Dickson, Alex Hyde-White, Fiona Hutchinson, Peter Cushing, Marcus Gilbert. Curious, occasionally entertaining sci-fi adventure with Hyde-White inexplicably traveling through time from 1986 N.Y.C. to WW1 Europe . . . where he assists British flyboy Dickson. Based on characters created by Capt. W. E. Johns. Original British title: BIGGLES. [PG]▼●

Big Green, The (1995) **C-100m.** ** D: Holly Goldberg Sloan. Steve Guttenberg, Olivia d'Abo, Jay O. Sanders, John Terry, Chauncey Leopardi, Patrick Renna, Anthony Esquivel, Bug Hall. Slight Disney fare chronicling the plight of the "Bad News Bears" and the "Mighty Ducks" of soccer teams in a depressed Texas town. Overly familiar but inoffensive; OK for less discriminating children. [PG]▼●

Big Gundown, The (1966-Italian-Spanish) **C-90m.** *** D: Sergio Sollima. Lee Van Cleef, Tomas Milian, Walter Barnes, Fernando Sancho, Nieves Navarro, Luisa Rivelli. Ambitious lawman Van Cleef is hired by a railroad tycoon to track down Mexican bandito Milian, who's accused of raping and murdering a young white girl, but slowly realizes he's being manipulated for a more sinister purpose. Arguably the best non–Sergio Leone spaghetti Western; an exciting, ironic yarn boasting stylish widescreen photography, a great Ennio Morricone score, and an incisive political edge that's even more pronounced in the uncut 105m. foreign-release version. Followed by BIG GUNDOWN 2. Technicolor.

Big Hand for the Little Lady, A (1966) **C-95m.** *** D: Fielder Cook. Henry Fonda, Joanne Woodward, Jason Robards, Charles Bickford, Burgess Meredith. Excellent comedy centering on poker game in old West. Outstanding roster of character actors includes John Qualen, Paul Ford, and Robert Middleton. There's a neat surprise ending, too.▼▌

Big Hangover, The (1950) **82m.** ** D: Norman Krasna. Van Johnson, Elizabeth Taylor, Leon Ames, Edgar Buchanan, Rosemary DeCamp, Gene Lockhart. Ambitious but noble war veteran Johnson, whose allergy to alcohol makes him drunk at inopportune moments, joins a staid law firm. How long will he remain there? And will he hook up with wealthy Taylor? Predictable, as well as silly and boring. ▼

Big Heat, The (1953) **90m.** ******* D: Fritz Lang. Glenn Ford, Gloria Grahame, Jocelyn Brando, Alexander Scourby, Lee Marvin, Carolyn Jones, Jeanette Nolan. Time has taken the edge off once-searing story of cop determined to bust city crime ring; famous coffee-hurling scene still jolts, and Grahame is excellent as bad girl who helps Ford. ▼●)

Big Hit, The (1998) **C-99m.** ******* D: Che-Kirk Wong. Mark Wahlberg, Lou Diamond Phillips, Christina Applegate, China Chow, Avery Brooks, Bokeem Woodbine, Antonio Sabato, Jr., Lainie Kazan, Elliott Gould, Sab Shimono, Lela Rochon. Expert hit man Wahlberg is beset by insecurity, a confusing romantic life, and a treacherous partner (Phillips). The result is gunfire, car chases, explosions, and martial arts galore. Unique action comedy with Hong Kong flavors doesn't always work, but the cast is lively and the stunt work awesome, fueled by a blazing pace. [R] ▼●)

Big House, The (1930) **86m.** ******* D: George Hill. Wallace Beery, Chester Morris, Robert Montgomery, Lewis Stone, Karl Dane, Leila Hyams. The original prison drama, this set the pattern for all later copies; it's still good, hard-bitten stuff with one of Beery's best tough-guy roles. Won Oscars for Writing (Frances Marion) and Sound Recording. ▼)

Big Jake (1971) **C-110m.** ******* D: George Sherman. John Wayne, Richard Boone, Maureen O'Hara, Patrick Wayne, Chris Mitchum, Bobby Vinton, Bruce Cabot. Tough Westerner is called back by estranged wife to rescue their grandson from a gang of kidnappers headed by Boone (who's especially good). Underrated Western; well paced, handsomely shot. Wayne's fifth and final pairing with O'Hara; Chris Mitchum and the Duke's son Patrick play his sons. Panavision. [PG] ▼●)

Big Jim McLain (1952) **90m.** ****½** D: Edward Ludwig. John Wayne, Nancy Olson, James Arness, Alan Napier, Veda Ann Borg, Hans Conried. Wayne and Arness are HUAC investigators who go Commie-hunting in Hawaii. One of the Duke's few dull films, but fascinating as a relic of its era. ▼●)

Big Kahuna, The (2000) **C-90m.** ****½** D: John Swanbeck. Kevin Spacey, Danny DeVito, Peter Facinelli. Absorbing adaptation of Roger Rueff's play *Hospitality Suite*, essentially a three-character piece about two world-weary salesmen and a naive young colleague at an out-of-town convention. Their criticism clashes with the young man's religious fervor as they wait for an important customer to show up at their hotel suite. As photographed plays go this one is

pretty good, with top-notch performances, but it never quite becomes a movie. Co-produced by Spacey. [R] ▼)

Big Knife, The (1955) **111m.** ******* D: Robert Aldrich. Jack Palance, Ida Lupino, Wendell Corey, Jean Hagen, Rod Steiger, Shelley Winters, Ilka Chase, Everett Sloane, Wesley Addy, Paul Langton, Nick Dennis. Clifford Odets' cynical view of Hollywood comes across in this involving (albeit occasionally overheated) drama, chronicling a string of crises in the life of movie star Charlie Castle (Palance). Fine performances almost overcome stereotypes; Steiger chews the scenery as a despotic studio head. ▼●)

Big Lebowski, The (1998) **C-117m.** ****½** D: Joel Coen. Jeff Bridges, John Goodman, Julianne Moore, Steve Buscemi, Peter Stormare, David Huddleston, Philip Seymour Hoffman, Flea, Sam Elliott, John Turturro, David Thewlis, Ben Gazzara, Tara Reid, Christian Clemenson. One big shaggy-dog joke, courtesy of the Coen brothers, about a slacker who's mistaken for a crime bigwig of the same name—and then gets hired by the guy to pay off a ransom. Mostly an excuse for off-the-wall character vignettes, some of which are amusing, some of which are just . . . strange. Minor Coen concoction with a most agreeable cast. Turturro is a standout as Jesus the bowler, but Bridges' Dave the Dude has become a pop culture icon. [R] ▼●)

Big Lift, The (1950) **120m.** ****½** D: George Seaton. Montgomery Clift, Paul Douglas, Cornell Borchers, O. E. Hasse. GI flight technicians involved in post-WW2 Berlin airlift and romance with German women. More interesting for on-location photography than uneven storyline. ▼)

Big Lobby, The SEE: **Rosebud Beach Hotel, The**

Big Man, The SEE: **Crossing the Line**

Big Mo SEE: **Maurie**

Big Momma's House (2000) **C-98m.** ****** D: Raja Gosnell. Martin Lawrence, Nia Long, Paul Giamatti, Terrence Dashon Howard, Ella Mitchell, Jascha Washington, Anthony Anderson, Cedric the Entertainer. FBI agent (and disguise expert) Lawrence and partner Giamatti are sent to Georgia to stake out the home of a woman whose granddaughter may lead them to a dangerous criminal. Eventually, Lawrence pretends to be the aptly named Big Momma. Broad comedy is enthusiastically performed but thin as tissue paper. Followed by two sequels. [PG-13] ▼)

Big Momma's House 2 (2006) **C-99m.** ***½** D: John Whitesell. Martin Lawrence, Nia Long, Emily Procter, Zachary Levi, Mark Moses, Kat Dennings, Chloë Grace Moretz, Marisol Nichols, Sarah Joy Brown, Dan Lauria. FBI agent Lawrence again dons a fat suit and transforms himself into the title character; here, he poses as a nanny to spy on the alleged designer of a deadly computer worm. Gratuitous sequel is an uneasy mixture of stale humor and goopy sentiment. [PG-13]▶

Big Mommas: Like Father, Like Son (2011) **C-107m.** ** D: John Whitesell. Martin Lawrence, Brandon T. Jackson, Jessica Lucas, Michelle Ang, Portia Doubleday, Ana Ortiz, Ken Jeong, Max Casella, Susan Walters, Sherri Shepherd. Lawrence dons fat suit and female attire once again in second sequel to BIG MOMMA'S HOUSE. This time, Lawrence's cross-dressing FBI agent goes undercover with his similarly disguised teenaged son (Jackson) to find evidence incriminating a Russian mobster hidden somewhere on campus of an Atlanta girls' high school for performing arts. Frantic slapstick and action-comedy flourishes may please some fans, but a couple of spirited song-and-dance sequences indicate that this might have worked better as—no kidding!—a musical. Alternate unrated version runs 113m. Super 35. [PG-13]▶

Big Mouth, The (1967) **C-107m.** **½ D: Jerry Lewis. Jerry Lewis, Harold Stone, Susan Bay, Buddy Lester, Del Moore, Paul Lambert. Typical Lewis effort, with Jerry involved in murder and search for missing treasure in California.▼

Big Night, The (1951) **75m.** **½ D: Joseph Losey. John Barrymore, Jr., Preston Foster, Howland Chamberlain, Joan Lorring, Dorothy Comingore, Howard St. John. Brooding account of rebellious teenager Barrymore's emotional flare-up with humanity at large; well done.

Big Night (1996) **C-107m.** **½ D: Stanley Tucci, Campbell Scott. Stanley Tucci, Minnie Driver, Tony Shalhoub, Ian Holm, Isabella Rossellini, Campbell Scott, Allison Janney, Caroline Aaron, Marc Anthony. Endearing story of Italian immigrant brothers trying to survive as restaurateurs in 1950s America; one is an artist in the kitchen, the other a would-be businessman. Their bombastic rival (Holm) gives them a shot at the brass ring by inviting Louis Prima to be their guest one night. Finely tuned performances, amusing vignettes and observations make this small endeavor worthwhile, but it's too slow and quiet for its own good. Tucci also coscripted; codirector Scott has a small but funny part as a Cadillac salesman. The feast on-screen is mouthwatering! [R] ▼●)

Big One, The (1998-U.S.-British) **C-96m.** **½ D: Michael Moore. Puckish pest Moore chronicles the real-life events that occur (mostly at his own instigation) while on a book tour to promote his best-selling *Downsize This!* Self-aggrandizing documentary is sometimes smarmy, sometimes invasive . . . but it's also fast and consistently funny, as Moore routinely shows up at someone's corporate headquarters to launch some mischief. [PG-13]▼●)

Big Operator, The (1959) **91m.** ** D:

Charles Haas. Mickey Rooney, Steve Cochran, Mamie Van Doren, Mel Tormé, Ray Danton, Jim Backus. Ray Anthony, Jackie Coogan. Rooney tries to add vim and vigor to title role as tough hood who goes on violent rampage when federal agents investigate his business activities. Paul Gallico story filmed before as JOE SMITH, AMERICAN. Retitled: ANATOMY OF A SYNDICATE. CinemaScope.

Big Parade, The (1925) **141m.** **** D: King Vidor. John Gilbert, Renée Adorée, Hobart Bosworth, Claire McDowell, Claire Adams, Karl Dane, Tom O'Brien. One of the best war films ever, and a high-water mark for silent cinema. Clean-shaven Gilbert plays an all-American boy who's shipped off to France during WW1, where he becomes a man in every sense of the word. Adoree is unforgettable as the simple French girl with whom he falls in love. Filled with memorable vignettes and the most harrowingly realistic battle scenes ever put on film (until recent years). A triumph for Vidor and all concerned. Written by Harry Behn and Laurence Stallings.▼●

Big Parade of Comedy SEE: **MGM's The Big Parade of Comedy**

Big Payoff, The SEE: **Win, Place or Steal**

Big Picture, The (1989) **C-100m.** **½ D: Christopher Guest. Kevin Bacon, Emily Longstreth, J. T. Walsh, Jennifer Jason Leigh, Michael McKean, Kim Miyori, Teri Hatcher, Dan Schneider, Jason Gould, Tracy Brooks Swope. Slight but good-natured comedy about Hollywood wheeling and dealing. Bacon is a naive student filmmaker courted by a movie studio exec and swallowed whole into The System. Lots of inside jokes for Hollywood audiences. Very funny performance by Leigh as an arty dingbat, and many amusing cameos, including unbilled Martin Short as an agent. Guest's first feature directing (he also scripted with costar McKean and Michael Varhol). [PG-13]▼●

Big Red One, The (1980) **C-113m.** ***½ D: Samuel Fuller. Lee Marvin, Mark Hamill, Robert Carradine, Bobby Di Cicco, Kelly Ward, Siegfried Rauch, Stephane Audran. Fuller returned to filmmaking after a long hiatus with this vivid, autobiographical account of a special infantry squadron and its intrepid sergeant during WW2. Hard to believe one film could pack so much into its narrative; a rich, moving, realistic, and poetic film. Carradine narrates and plays Fuller's alter ego, complete with cigar. Reconstructed in 2004 to more closely resemble Fuller's intended cut, at 163m. [PG]▼●

Big Scam, The SEE: **Nightingale Sang in Berkeley Square, A**

Big Score, The (1983) **C-85m.** ** D: Fred Williamson. Fred Williamson, John Saxon, Richard Roundtree, Nancy Wilson, Ed Lauter, D'Urville Martin, Michael Dante, Joe Spinell. Barely adequate DIRTY

HARRY clone with narc Williamson ignoring the rules and taking on thug Spinell. (In fact, this script was originally commissioned by Clint Eastwood for a Dirty Harry vehicle that never got made.) [R]▼●

Big Shot, The (1942) **82m.** **½ D: Lewis Seiler. Humphrey Bogart, Irene Manning, Susan Peters, Minor Watson, Chick Chandler, Richard Travis, Stanley Ridges, Howard da Silva. OK grade-B gangster yarn with Bogey a three-time loser involved in robbery frameup and prison break.

Big Shots (1987) **C-90m.** **½ D: Robert Mandel. Ricky Busker, Darius McCrary, Robert Joy, Robert Prosky, Jerzy Skolimowski, Paul Winfield. So-so juvenile adventure about an inexperienced white boy and streetwise urban black who come together and become involved with dead bodies, hired killers, and other mayhem. Panavision. [PG-13]▼●

Big Sky, The (1952) **122m.** *** D: Howard Hawks. Kirk Douglas, Dewey Martin, Elizabeth Threatt, Arthur Hunnicutt, Buddy Baer, Steven Geray, Hank Worden, Jim Davis. Camaraderie and conflict as fur-trapper Douglas leads expedition up the Missouri River. Eventful, evocative film adapted from A. B. Guthrie, Jr. book by Dudley Nichols; well directed by Hawks. Originally released at 141m. Also shown in computer-colored version.▼

Big Sleep, The (1946) **114m.** **** D: Howard Hawks. Humphrey Bogart, Lauren Bacall, John Ridgely, Martha Vickers, Louis Jean Heydt, Regis Toomey, Peggy Knudsen, Dorothy Malone, Bob Steele, Elisha Cook, Jr. Classic mystery thriller from Raymond Chandler's first novel; detective Philip Marlowe (Bogart) becomes involved with wealthy Bacall and her uncontrollable little sister Vickers. So convoluted even Chandler didn't know who committed one murder, but so incredibly entertaining that no one has ever cared. Powerhouse direction, unforgettable dialogue; script by William Faulkner, Jules Furthman and Leigh Brackett. Prerelease version (shown to Armed Forces overseas in 1945) runs 116m., with 18m. of scenes reshot or unused in the official release. This version has less of Bogie and Bacall and a more linear plot, but is somehow less exotic and interesting. Also shown in computer-colored version.▼●

Big Sleep, The (1978-British) **C-100m.** ** D: Michael Winner. Robert Mitchum, Sarah Miles, Candy Clark, Oliver Reed, Richard Boone, James Stewart, Joan Collins, Edward Fox, John Mills, Harry Andrews, Richard Todd, Colin Blakely. Follow-up to FARE-WELL, MY LOVELY is less a remake of the Hawks classic than a more faithful rendering of the Chandler novel, albeit updated and set in London. If you can get by that, it's tolerable, with a strong cast, fresh locations, and thankful lack of camp. [R]▼●

Big Squeeze, The (1996) **C-98m.** *½ D: Marcus De Leon. Lara Flynn Boyle, Peter Dobson, Danny Nucci, Luca Bercovici, Teresa Despina, Michael Chieffo. Boyle works in a bar to support her injured ballplayer husband (Bercovici)—then learns he's neglected to inform her of a $130,000 settlement he's received, so she enlists a drifter-hustler (a miscast Dobson) to get the money. Pretty poor. Video version is 7m. longer, if you care. Aka BODY OF A WOMAN. [R]▼●

Big Steal, The (1949) **71m.** *** D: Don Siegel. Robert Mitchum, Jane Greer, William Bendix, Patric Knowles, Ramon Novarro. Mitchum is on the trail of Army payroll thief Knowles; he in turn is chased by Bendix, and becomes involved with enticing Greer. Well-made robbery caper, set in Mexico and shot on location, is full of terrific plot twists.▼●

Big Store, The (1941) **80m.** ** D: Charles Riesner. Groucho, Chico and Harpo Marx, Tony Martin, Virginia Grey, Margaret Dumont, Douglass Dumbrille, Henry Armetta. Big comedown for Marxes in weak film of detective Groucho investigating crooked Dumbrille's department store. Low spot is Martin's "The Tenement Symphony."▼●

Big Street, The (1942) **88m.** **½ D: Irving Reis. Henry Fonda, Lucille Ball, Barton Mac-Lane, Eugene Pallette, Agnes Moorehead, Sam Levene, Ray Collins, Hans Conried, Ozzie Nelson and Orchestra. Damon Runyon produced this treacly adaptation of his own *Collier's* magazine story "Little Pinks," about a timid busboy who devotes himself to a self-centered nightclub singer. Odd (and oddly watchable), with very unconventional roles for both Fonda and Ball.▼●

Big Tease, The (2000) **C-86m.** **½ D: Kevin Allen. Craig Ferguson, Frances Fisher, Mary McCormack, David Rasche, Chris Langham, Sara Gilbert, John Pankow, Donal Logue, Charles Napier, Larry Miller, Ted McGinley. Scottish hairdresser mistakenly thinks he's been invited to L.A. to take part in the World Freestyle Hairdressing Championship, but won't be deterred from competing for the Platinum Scissors award. Amusing if lightweight romp through the tresses of Tinseltown. Drew Carey (Ferguson's costar on TV's *The Drew Carey Show*) is among a handful of celebrity cameos. Cowritten by Ferguson. [R]▼●

Big Time (1988) **C-87m.** *** D: Chris Blum. Tom Waits. Concert footage filmed at L.A.'s Wiltern Theater is combined with scenes of the chameleonlike Waits as various and sundry characters: you'll see Waits the sleazy lounge lizard, Waits the gravel-voiced crooner, and Waits the truly amazing performer. For Tom Waits fans, this is the next best thing to seeing him live. [PG]▼

Big T.N.T. Show, The (1966) **93m.** ** D: Larry Peerce. David McCallum, Roger Miller, Joan Baez, Ike and Tina Turner,

Bo Diddley, The Ronettes, Ray Charles, The Lovin' Spoonful. Follow-up to THE T.A.M.I. SHOW casts a wider musical net, with lesser results, but Diddley, Tina Turner, and Ronnie Spector keep it pumping. Shot on tape, transferred to film; footage reused in THAT WAS ROCK.

Big Top Pee-wee (1988) **C-90m.** **½ D: Randal Kleiser. Pee-wee Herman, Penelope Ann Miller, Kris Kristofferson, Valeria Golino, Susan Tyrrell, Albert Henderson, Kevin Peter Hall, Kenneth Tobey, Stephanie Hodge, Benicio Del Toro; voice of Wayne White. Farmer Pee-wee allows a traveling circus to stay on his property, and quickly develops circus fever—as well as a romance with the pretty trapeze artist (Golino). Quirky if overly bland comedy (cowritten and produced by Pee-wee's alter ego, Paul Reubens) has many clever moments, along with some curious ones. Ought to please kids and family audiences. [PG] ▼●◗

Big Town, The (1987) **C-109m.** ** D: Ben Bolt. Matt Dillon, Diane Lane, Tommy Lee Jones, Tom Skerritt, Lee Grant, Bruce Dern, Suzy Amis, David Marshall Grant, Lolita David (Davidovich), Cherry Jones, Gary Farmer, Sarah Polley. Small-town crapshooter with a "golden arm" comes to Chicago in the 1950s to become a big-time gambler, but still has a lot to learn. With that cast (and Lane as a stripper) it's easy to watch . . . but just as easy to forget. [R] ▼●◗

Big Trail, The (1930) **110m.** *** D: Raoul Walsh. John Wayne, Marguerite Churchill, El Brendel, Tully Marshall, Tyrone Power, Sr., David Rollins, Ian Keith. Epic Western may seem creaky to some viewers, but remains one of the most impressive early talkies, with its grand sweep and naturalistic use of sound. John Wayne was "discovered" for starring role, and already shows easygoing charm. Also filmed in pioneer 70mm widescreen process called Grandeur, at 122m. ▼◗

Big Trees, The (1952) **C-89m.** ** D: Felix Feist. Kirk Douglas, Eve Miller, Patrice Wymore, Edgar Buchanan, John Archer, Alan Hale, Jr., Roy Roberts, Ellen Corby. Brutally ambitious lumberman Douglas runs afoul of a religious sect—and practically everybody else around him—in this cornball outdoor melodrama. A remake of VALLEY OF THE GIANTS with stock footage from that earlier color movie. ▼●◗

Big Trouble (1985) **C-93m.** ** D: John Cassavetes. Peter Falk, Alan Arkin, Beverly D'Angelo, Charles Durning, Robert Stack, Paul Dooley, Valerie Curtin, Richard Libertini. Harried insurance salesman Arkin needs money to put his three sons through Yale, so he becomes involved with ditsy D'Angelo in a plot to kill her loony husband (Falk). Pretty silly stuff, although the sardine-flavored liqueur does provide a couple of chuckles. Reteaming of tal-

ents from THE IN-LAWS (1979) had a troubled production and barely received theatrical release. Andrew Bergman wrote the script under the name Warren Bogle. [R] ▼●◗

Big Trouble (2002) **C-85m.** **½ D: Barry Sonnenfeld. Tim Allen, Rene Russo, Stanley Tucci, Tom Sizemore, Johnny Knoxville, Dennis Farina, Jack Kehler, Janeane Garofalo, Patrick Warburton, Ben Foster, Zooey Deschanel, Dwight Meyer (Heavy D), Omar Epps, Jason Lee, Sofía Vergara, Andy Richter. Farcical comedy set in Miami, where various characters' lives collide as two hit men from N.J. (Kehler and a very funny Farina) try to take out a local hotshot (Tucci), while his wife (Russo) falls in love with an ex-newspaperman (Allen). Meanwhile, a stolen nuclear device is being peddled by a couple of transplanted Russians. Lots of funny lines and situations, but goes flat somewhere along the way. Based on a novel by humorist Dave Barry. [PG-13] ▼◗

Big Trouble in Little China (1986) **C-99m.** *½ D: John Carpenter. Kurt Russell, Kim Cattrall, Dennis Dun, James Hong, Victor Wong, Kate Burton, Suzee Pai. Blowhard trucker Russell finds himself knee-deep in Chinatown intrigue (and mumbo-jumbo) when a friend's fiancée is kidnapped right in front of his eyes. High-tech INDIANA JONES–style adventure has heavy tongue-in-cheek attitude, but everything else about it is heavy, too . . . including Russell's John Wayne–ish swagger. Good electronic music score by director Carpenter. Panavision. [PG-13] ▼●◗

Big Wednesday (1978) **C-120m.** **½ D: John Milius. Jan-Michael Vincent, William Katt, Gary Busey, Lee Purcell, Patti D'Arbanville, Sam Melville, Robert Englund, Barbara Hale, Reb Brown, Steve Kanaly, Charlene Tilton. Half of a good flick on surfing, Pacific Coast–style, early '60s. Up to midway point, a ridiculous comedy about macho Vincent and his fun-loving, destructive ways. As he and buddies Katt and Busey get older and action is brought up to '70s, dramatic content improves. Hale (as Mrs. Barlow) and Katt are real-life mother and son. Milius later recut to 104m. Panavision. [PG] ▼●◗

Big White, The (2005-U.S.-German-Canadian-New Zealand) **C-94m.** **½ D: Mark Mylod. Robin Williams, Holly Hunter, Giovanni Ribisi, Alison Lohman, Tim Blake Nelson, Woody Harrelson, W. Earl Brown. Minor but amusing black comedy set in snowy Alaska, where desperate travel agent Williams concocts a scheme to collect insurance on his supposedly dead brother—and then stumbles onto a body just right for the purpose at hand. Ribisi is terrific as an insurance investigator who obsesses over the fraudulence of the case. [R] ◗

Biker Boyz (2003) **C-110m.** ** D: Reggie Rock Bythewood. Laurence Fishburne, Derek Luke, Orlando Jones, Djimon Hounsou, Lisa Bonet, Brendan Fehr, Larenz Tate, Kid Rock, Rick Gonzalez, Meagan Good, Salli Richardson-Whitfield, Vanessa Bell Calloway, Kadeem Hardison, Terrence Dashon Howard, Eriq La Salle, Tyson Beckford. By-the-numbers action drama about the subculture of California motorcycle clubs, spotlighting males of various ages who are addicted to fancy bikes and challenge each other in illegal road races. Fishburne is the longtime undefeated champ, Luke the ambitious young challenger. Attempts to focus on characters and relationships instead of just action, but the results are uninspired. [PG-13] ▼▶

Bikini Beach (1964) C-100m. **½ D: William Asher. Frankie Avalon, Annette Funicello, Keenan Wynn, Martha Hyer, Harvey Lembeck, Don Rickles, John Ashley, Jody McCrea, Meredith MacRae, Donna Loren, Candy Johnson, Timothy Carey, "Little" Stevie Wonder, Michael Nader. Third BEACH PARTY movie is second best, with Avalon in dual role as Frankie and a British singing rage called "The Potato Bug" (get it?). Relic of bygone era. Followed by PAJAMA PARTY. Panavision. ▼▶

Bill & Ted's Bogus Journey (1991) C-98m. **½ D: Peter Hewitt. Keanu Reeves, Alex Winter, William Sadler, Joss Ackland, George Carlin, Hal Landon, Jr., Pam Grier, Amy Stock-Poynton, Sarah Trigger. In this sequel, the dimwitted duo travel to Heaven, Hell, and points in between as they duel with an evil pair of robots who are posing as Bill and Ted. Along the way they meet (among others) Albert Einstein, the Easter Bunny, and the Grim Reaper! Special effects almost take over in this outing, but B&T are even dumber here than in the original film. One more sequel and they might have qualified as the Hope and Crosby of the '90s, dudes! [PG] ▼▶●

Bill & Ted's Excellent Adventure (1989) C-90m. ** D: Stephen Herek. Keanu Reeves, Alex Winter, George Carlin, Bernie Casey, Amy Stock-Poynton, Terry Camilleri, Dan Shor. Inseparable teenage airheads, who are about to flunk their history course, are given the opportunity to go traveling through time to meet (and round up) such historical figures as Napoleon, Joan of Arc, and Abraham Lincoln. Radical! Reeves and Winter are great fun as Bill and Ted, but this goofy comedy never takes off as it should. Followed by an animated TV series, a live-action TV series, and BILL & TED'S BOGUS JOURNEY. Panavision. [PG] ▼▶●

Bill Cosby: "Himself" (1982) C-105m. **½ D: Bill Cosby. Likable in-concert film, featuring Cosby on the subjects of child rearing, human nature, family life. Pleasant but hardly "an event." [PG] ▼▶●

Billion Dollar Brain (1967-British) C-111m. *** D: Ken Russell. Michael Caine, Karl Malden, Ed Begley, Oscar Homolka,

Françoise Dorleac. Third in series that began with THE IPCRESS FILE finds Harry Palmer (Caine) again up to his neck in exciting espionage, this time in Scandinavia. Look fast for a young Donald Sutherland. Based on Len Deighton's novel. Followed 30 years later by a pair of cable TV sequels. Panavision. ▶

Billion Dollar Hobo, The (1978) C-96m. *½ D: Stuart E. McGowan. Tim Conway, Will Geer, Eric Weston, Sydney Lassick, John Myhers, Frank Sivero. Dreary comedy about bumbling Conway becoming a hobo to qualify for inheritance. [G] ▼▶

Bill of Divorcement, A (1932) 69m. *** D: George Cukor. John Barrymore, Katharine Hepburn, Billie Burke, David Manners, Henry Stephenson. Barrymore gives sensitive performance as man released from mental institution who returns to wife Burke and gets to know his daughter for the first time. Dated but worth seeing; notable as Hepburn's screen debut. Originally released at 75m. Remade in 1940. ▼●

Bill of Divorcement, A (1940) 74m. **½ D: John Farrow. Maureen O'Hara, Adolphe Menjou, Fay Bainter, Herbert Marshall, Dame May Whitty, C. Aubrey Smith, Patric Knowles. Adequate remake with Menjou as mentally ill man who suddenly regains his sanity and returns home, with resulting dramatic fireworks. Scripted by Dalton Trumbo. Retitled NEVER TO LOVE.

Billy Bathgate (1991) C-106m. **½ D: Robert Benton. Dustin Hoffman, Nicole Kidman, Loren Dean, Bruce Willis, Steven Hill, Steve Buscemi, Billy Jaye, John Costelloe, Tim Jerome, Stanley Tucci, Mike Starr, Katharine Houghton, Rachel York, Moira Kelly. Absorbing, exceptionally good-looking adaptation of E. L. Doctorow's fanciful novel about young man who hooks up with gangster Dutch Schultz in the waning days of his crime career in the 1930s. Hoffman's commanding performance makes this flawed film worth watching, though the story's momentum erodes toward the end. Photographed by Nestor Almendros, with remarkable production design by Patrizia von Brandenstein. Screenplay by Tom Stoppard. [R] ▼●

Billy Budd (1962-U.S.-British) 122m. ***½ D: Peter Ustinov. Robert Ryan, Peter Ustinov, Melvyn Douglas, Terence Stamp, Paul Rogers, David McCallum. Melville's classic good vs. evil novella set in British Navy, 1797. Naive, incorruptible seaman is court-martialed for murder of sadistic master-at-arms. Film deals simply with heavier issues of morality. Sterling performances by all. Ustinov also produced and coscripted with DeWitt Bodeen. Stamp's film debut. CinemaScope. ▼●

Billy Elliot (2000-British) C-110m. ***½ D: Stephen Daldry. Julie Walters, Jamie Bell, Jamie Draven, Gary Lewis, Jean Heywood, Stuart Wells, Mike Elliot, Janine Burkett. Beautifully realized story, set in 1984, about an 11-year-old boy (Bell, in a glorious debut) growing up in a motherless household in a harsh English mining town where most of the workers are on strike. An inadvertent encounter with a dance class opens a new door in his life. A feel-good movie in the very best sense; Lee Hall's script dodges the formulaic ingredients you expect to find. Impressive film debut for theater director Daldry. Later a Broadway musical. [R]▼❚

Billy Galvin (1986) **C-95m.** **½ D: John Gray. Karl Malden, Lenny Von Dohlen, Joyce Van Patten, Toni Kalem, Keith Szarabajka, Alan North, Paul Guilfoyle, Barton Heyman. Well-meaning, fairly effective meat-and-potatos drama about title character (Von Dohlen), who wants to be a construction worker like his old man (Malden), a tough, obstinate codger who does everything to discourage him. Not without its share of moments, but also a bit too obvious. Good performances. An *American Playhouse* presentation. [PG]▼

Billy Jack (1971) **C-114m.** *½ D: T. C. Frank (Tom Laughlin). Tom Laughlin, Delores Taylor, Clark Howat, Kenneth Tobey, Bert Freed, Julie Webb. Half-breed karate expert protects a free school imperiled by reactionary townspeople in this grass-roots hit. Its politics are highly questionable, and its "message" of peace ridiculous, considering the amount of violence in the film. Memorable title sequence depicting slaughter of wild mustangs introduced hit song "One Tin Soldier" by Coven. Preceded by BORN LOSERS; followed by THE TRIAL OF BILLY JACK and BILLY JACK GOES TO WASHINGTON. [PG]▼❚❚

Billy Jack Goes to Washington (1977) **C-155m.** ** D: Tom Laughlin. Tom Laughlin, Delores Taylor, Sam Wanamaker, Lucie Arnaz, E. G. Marshall, Pat O'Brien. Contrived update of MR. SMITH GOES TO WASHINGTON, with writer-director-star Laughlin, a supposed "everyman," fighting big-time corruption in the Senate. Basic story is still good, but it goes on forever. Panavision.▼❚

Billy Liar (1963-British) **98m.** ***½ D: John Schlesinger. Tom Courtenay, Julie Christie, Wilfred Pickles, Mona Washbourne, Ethel Griffies, Finlay Currie, Leonard Rossiter. Cast excels in story of ambitious but lazy young man caught in dull job routine who escapes into fantasy world, offering some poignant vignettes of middle-class life. Based on Keith Waterhouse novel and play; scripted by Waterhouse and Willis Hall (who also cowrote stage version). Followed by a TV series and a musical. CinemaScope.▼❚

Billy Madison (1995) **C-89m.** *½ D: Tamra Davis. Adam Sandler, Darren McGavin, Bridgette Wilson, Bradley Whitford, Josh Mostel, Norm Macdonald, Mark Beltzman, Larry Hankin, Theresa Merritt. Another comic celebration of infantilism and crudity, as spoiled rich kid Sandler must repeat grades 1–12 in order to take over his millionaire father's business. A little of this goes a long way. Sandler (who can be funny and endearing when he wants to be) also cowrote the script. His *Saturday Night Live* castmate Chris Farley and Steve Buscemi appear unbilled. [PG-13]▼❚

Billy Rose's Diamond Horseshoe SEE: **Diamond Horseshoe**

Billy Rose's Jumbo (1962) **C-125m.** *** D: Charles Walters. Doris Day, Stephen Boyd, Jimmy Durante, Martha Raye, Dean Jagger. OK circus picture, at best during Rodgers and Hart songs, well staged by Busby Berkeley. Durante (who had starred in the 1935 Broadway production) and Raye are marvelous. Songs include "The Most Beautiful Girl in the World," "My Romance," "This Can't Be Love." Aka JUMBO. Panavision.▼❚

Billy's Hollywood Screen Kiss (1998) **C-92m.** **½ D: Tommy O'Haver. Sean P. Hayes, Brad Rowe, Richard Ganoung, Meredith Scott Lynn, Paul Bartel, Armando Valdes-Kennedy, Annabelle Gurwitch, Holly Woodlawn. Unemployed L.A. photographer Billy (Hayes) decides to recreate a series of classic movie kisses from Hollywood's golden age, utilizing drag queens and other gay pals. He immediately gets sidetracked upon meeting gorgeous Gabriel (Rowe). Flashy low-budget effort that manages to be both humorous and sensitive, though the writer-director isn't kidding when he calls it "A Tom O'Haver Trifle." He says his inspiration came from the ambiguity of the Clift–de Havilland romance in THE HEIRESS! Panavision. [R]▼❚

Billy the Kid (1930) **90m.** **½ D: King Vidor. Johnny Mack Brown, Wallace Beery, Kay Johnson, Karl Dane, Roscoe Ates. Realistic early talkie Western with marshal Beery trying to capture outlaw Brown; some performances seem badly dated today. Retitled: THE HIGHWAYMAN RIDES. Originally shown in early Realife 70 mm. widescreen process.

Billy the Kid (1941) **C-95m.** **½ D: David Miller. Robert Taylor, Brian Donlevy, Ian Hunter, Mary Howard, Gene Lockhart, Lon Chaney, Jr. Cast looks uncomfortable in remake of 1930 Western, but plot is sturdy enough for OK viewing, with Taylor in title role and Donlevy as marshal.▼❚

Billy the Kid vs. Dracula (1966) **C-74m.** ** D: William Beaudine. Chuck Courtney, John Carradine, Melinda Plowman, Virginia Christine, Walter Janovitz, Bing Russell, Olive Carey, Harry Carey, Jr. Famed outlaw decides it's time to get married—but doesn't realize that his bride's "uncle" is a vampire. Campy nonsense.▼❚

Billy Two Hats (1974) **C-99m.** **½ D: Ted Kotcheff. Gregory Peck, Desi Arnaz, Jr., Jack Warden, Sian Barbara Allen, David

Huddleston. Offbeat Western filmed in Israel, about a middle-aged Scot and a young half-Indian pursued by the law for bank robbery. Peck is appealing in unusual character role. Retitled THE LADY AND THE OUTLAW. [PG]▼●

Biloxi Blues (1988) **C-106m.** *** D: Mike Nichols. Matthew Broderick, Christopher Walken, Matt Mulhern, Corey Parker, Casey Siemaszko, Markus Flanagan, Michael Dolan, Penelope Ann Miller, Park Overall. The further adventures of Eugene Jerome, Neil Simon's youthful alter ego introduced in BRIGHTON BEACH MEMOIRS. Here, WW2 is winding down, and Eugene (Broderick) forsakes Brooklyn for Biloxi, Miss., and ten grueling weeks of army basic training, where he comes that much closer to manhood. Quite wonderful, in its best moments. Followed by TV movie BROADWAY BOUND. Super 35. [PG-13]▼●

Bingo (1991) **C-87m.** *½ D: Matthew Robbins. Cindy Williams, David Rasche, Robert J. Steinmiller, Jr., David French, Kurt Fuller, Joe Guzaldo, Glenn Shadix. Basic update of the "boy wants a dog, boy can't have a dog, boy finds a dog who has run away from the circus, boy hides the dog from his parents, boy must move out of town and leave the dog behind, boy finds dog again" genre. Kids might like it, but it's a real bow-wow. [PG]▼●

Bingo Long Traveling All-Stars & Motor Kings, The (1976) **C-110m.** *** D: John Badham. Billy Dee Williams, James Earl Jones, Richard Pryor, Ted Ross, DeWayne Jessie, Stan Shaw. Bright, original comedy about baseball player Williams trying to buck owners of Negro National League in 1939 by starting his own razzle-dazzle team. Williams' character is modeled after Satchel Paige, while Jones' is based on Josh Gibson. [PG]▼●

Bio-Dome (1996) **C-95m.** BOMB D: Jason Bloom. Pauly Shore, Stephen Baldwin, William Atherton, Joey (Lauren) Adams, Teresa Hill, Henry Gibson, Kevin West, Kylie Minogue, Patricia Hearst, Roger Clinton, Rose McGowan, Jack Black. Two layabouts from Tucson are sealed up for a year inside a Biosphere-like experimental habitat and drive the scientists in charge bonkers. A good comedy premise is trashed through crude writing, inept plotting, and having as heroes two worthless jerks we're supposed to find lovable. [PG-13]▼●

Birch Interval (1977) **C-104m.** *** D: Delbert Mann. Eddie Albert, Rip Torn, Ann Wedgeworth, Susan McClung, Brian Part. Eleven-year-old girl, sent to live with relatives in Amish country, finds out about life, love, suffering and compassion. Beautiful, sensitive film. [PG]▼

Bird (1988) **C-160m.** **½ D: Clint Eastwood. Forest Whitaker, Diane Venora, Michael Zelniker, Samuel E. Wright, Keith David, Michael McGuire, James Handy. Heartfelt but overlong biography of legendary saxophonist Charlie Parker, who revolutionized jazz music in the 1940s. While there's much music on hand, this is mostly the story of one man's drug addiction and self-destructive life. Fails to balance its story with any explanation of Parker's influence in the world of music. Excellent and believable performances help. Parker plays on the soundtrack, though all accompanying music was rerecorded in 1988. (The film won an Oscar for sound recording.) [R]▼●

birdcage, The (1996) **C-119m.** **½ D: Mike Nichols. Robin Williams, Gene Hackman, Nathan Lane, Dianne Wiest, Hank Azaria, Christine Baranski, Dan Futterman, Calista Flockhart, Tom McGowan, Grant Heslov, Kirby Mitchell. Polished if obvious remake of LA CAGE AUX FOLLES will please anyone who hasn't seen or doesn't remember the original: Williams is fairly subdued as a South Beach, Miami, nightclub owner who's forced to ask his highstrung, drag-queen performer/partner (Lane) to hide away while his son brings his prospective in-laws—an ultra-conservative couple— to dinner. Screenplay by Elaine May, who added fresh lines to the foolproof blueprint of the original. [R]▼●

Birdman of Alcatraz (1962) **143m.** *** D: John Frankenheimer. Burt Lancaster, Karl Malden, Thelma Ritter, Betty Field, Neville Brand, Edmond O'Brien, Hugh Marlowe, Telly Savalas. Pensive study of prisoner Robert Stroud who during his many years in jail became a world-renowned bird authority. Film becomes static despite imaginative sidelights to enlarge scope of action. 148m. version used for overseas release now turning up here.▼●

Bird of Paradise (1932) **80m.** ** D: King Vidor. Joel McCrea, Dolores Del Rio, John Halliday, Skeets Gallagher, Lon Chaney, Jr. Exotic but empty South Seas romance with McCrea as adventurer who falls in love with native-girl Del Rio. Handsome but unmoving; remade in 1951.▼▶

Bird of Prey (1996-U.S.-Bulgarian) **C-101m.** BOMB D: Temistocles Lopez. Jennifer Tilly, Boyan Milushev, Richard Chamberlain, Lenny Von Dohlen, Robert Carradine, Lesley Ann Warren. Preposterous thriller about a Bulgarian dissenter and an American photojournalist who unite to battle a slimy businessman. Tilly, playing Chamberlain's daughter (and Milushev's love interest), seems to be in another movie. It took four writers to concoct this clinker, which barely earned a theatrical release. [R]▼▶

Bird on a Wire (1990) **C-110m.** ** D: John Badham. Mel Gibson, Goldie Hawn, David Carradine, Bill Duke, Stephen Tobolowsky, Joan Severance, Jeff Corey. Star power is about all this lame action-comedy has going for it, as drug-running murderers force Mel, who's been hiding in the F.B.I. witness relocation program, and Goldie, his onetime sweetheart, to take it on the lam. Script on a shoestring. Super 35. [PG-13]▼●▶

Birds, The (1963) **C-120m.** ***½ D: Alfred Hitchcock. Rod Taylor, Tippi Hedren, Jessica Tandy, Suzanne Pleshette, Veronica Cartwright, Ethel Griffies, Charles McGraw, Joe Mantell, Elizabeth Wilson, Doodles Weaver, Richard Deacon, Suzanne Cupito (Morgan Brittany). Hitchcock's classic about a woman (Hedren) and mass bird attacks that follow her around isolated coastal California community. Not for the squeamish; a delight for those who are game. Hold on to something and watch. Script by Evan Hunter, loosely based on Daphne du Maurier's story. Followed by a terrible TV sequel in 1994. ▼●▶

Birds Do It (1966) **C-95m.** ** D: Andrew Marton. Soupy Sales, Tab Hunter, Arthur O'Connell, Edward Andrews, Beverly Adams, Frank Nastasi. Soupy's first starring vehicle has him under the spell of serum that enables him to fly. Fairly entertaining for kids.▶

Birds, The Bees and the Italians, The (1966-Italian-French) **115m.** *** D: Pietro Germi. Virna Lisi, Gastone Moschin, Nora Ricci, Alberto Lionello, Franco Fabrizi. Very funny bedroom farce chronicling the sexual and romantic exploits of various residents in a small Italian town.

Bird With the Crystal Plumage, The (1970-Italian-West German) **C-96m.** **½ D: Dario Argento. Tony Musante, Suzy Kendall, Eva Renzi, Enrico Maria Salerno, Mario Adorf, Renato Romano, Umberto Rano, Werner Peters. American writer living in Rome witnesses attempted murder in gallery; he and his mistress become involved in case. Uneven; best viewed on large screen. Reissued as THE PHANTOM OF TERROR. Cromoscope. [PG]▼●▶

Birdy (1984) **C-120m.** ***½ D: Alan Parker. Matthew Modine, Nicolas Cage, John Harkins, Sandy Baron, Karen Young, Bruno Kirby. Cage, reunited with schizophrenically silent Modine in an army hospital, flashes back to their adolescence in working-class Philadelphia and on Modine's lifelong desire to be a bird. William Wharton's allegorical novel, updated from WW2 to Vietnam, makes a surprisingly workable movie despite a weak "gag" ending. Terrific performances, with Modine a standout in a tricky, physically demanding role. Screenplay by Sandy Kroopf and Jack Behr. [R]▼●▶

Birgit Haas Must Be Killed (1981-French) **C-105m.** **½ D: Laurent Heynemann. Philippe Noiret, Jean Rochefort, Lisa Kreuzer, Bernard Le Coq. Unscrupulous police officer Noiret dupes innocent Rochefort into romancing former left-wing terrorist Kreuzer, intending to have her assassinated and hang the blame on Rochefort! Intriguing idea never

really catches fire, despite honorable efforts; might have worked better if the two male stars had switched roles.▼

Birth (2004) **C-100m.** *** D: Jonathan Glazer. Nicole Kidman, Cameron Bright, Danny Huston, Lauren Bacall, Alison Elliott, Arliss Howard, Anne Heche, Peter Stormare, Ted Levine, Cara Seymour, Zoe Caldwell. A man dies while jogging in Manhattan's Central Park, and a baby is born. Ten years later, as the man's widow is about to remarry, she is confronted by a 10-year-old boy who claims to be her husband. Eerie, riveting drama is remarkably effective in building and sustaining a mood of unease—and uncertainty. Striking score by Alexandre Desplat and cinematography by Harris Savides. Kidman is marvelous. Glazer wrote the screenplay with Jean-Claude Carrière and Milo Addica (who appears as a doorman). [R]▶

Birthday Girl (2002-British-U.S.) **C-93m.** ** D: Jez Butterworth. Nicole Kidman, Ben Chaplin, Vincent Cassel, Mathieu Kassovitz. Nerdy, sexually repressed British bank clerk (Chaplin) orders a Russian bride over the Internet; when she arrives he discovers (to his dismay) that she doesn't speak a word of English . . . but that turns out to be the least of his troubles. The woman's "cousin" and a friend soon show up and turn Chaplin's life inside out. Amusing at first, then unexpectedly dark: either way, the story is unbelievable—and unsatisfying. Super 35. [R]▼▶

Birthday Party, The (1968-British) **C-127m.** *** D: William Friedkin. Robert Shaw, Patrick Magee, Dandy Nichols, Sydney Tafler, Moultrie Kelsall, Helen Fraser. Uncinematic film version of Harold Pinter's play about boarding house and its mysterious tenant (Shaw) is helped by good acting and playwright's usual superior dialogue. [G]

Birth of a Nation, The (1915) **186m.** **** D: D. W. Griffith. Lillian Gish, Mae Marsh, Henry B. Walthall, Miriam Cooper, Robert Harron, Wallace Reid, Joseph Henabery. The landmark of American motion pictures. Griffith's epic story of two families during Civil War and Reconstruction is still fascinating. Sometimes the drama survives intact; other times, one must watch in a more historical perspective. Griffith's portrayal of Ku Klux Klan in heroic role has kept this film a center of controversy to the present day. Running time varies from print to print. ▼●▶

Biscuit Eater, The (1972) **C-90m.** **½ D: Vincent McEveety. Earl Holliman, Lew Ayres, Godfrey Cambridge, Patricia Crowley, Beah Richards, Johnny Whitaker, George Spell. Wholesome, uninspired Disney remake of 1940 film with Whitaker and Spell as the young friends who devote themselves to training a champion bird dog. [G]▼▶

Bishop's Wife, The (1947) **108m.** *** D: Henry Koster. Cary Grant, Loretta Young, David Niven, Monty Woolley, James

Gleason, Gladys Cooper, Elsa Lanchester. Christmas fantasy of suave angel (Grant) coming to earth to help Bishop Niven and wife Young raise money for new church. Engaging performances by all—and fun to see children from IT'S A WONDERFUL LIFE, Karolyn Grimes and Bobby Anderson, appearing together. Also shown in computer-colored version. Remade as THE PREACH-ER'S WIFE.▼●▶

Bitch, The (1979-British) **C-93m.** BOMB D: Gerry O'Hara. Joan Collins, Kenneth Haigh, Michael Coby, Ian Hendry, Carolyn Seymour, Sue Lloyd, John Ratzenberger. Weak entry in the Bimbo Chic genre, a follow-up to THE STUD, based on a book by Joan's sister, Jackie Collins. Joan gets involved in everything from smuggling to fixed horse racing in attempts to save her failing London disco, but who cares? And, yes, there is a title song. [R]▼▶

Bite the Bullet (1975) **C-131m. ★★★★** D: Richard Brooks. Gene Hackman, Candice Bergen, James Coburn, Ben Johnson, Ian Bannen, Jan-Michael Vincent, Robert Donner, Paul Stewart, Dabney Coleman, Sally Kirkland. Grand adventure in the classic tradition. Disparate types compete in a grueling, 700-mile horse race at the turn of the 20th century; the finalists develop a grudging—and growing—respect for each other. Script by director Brooks. Beautifully filmed on magnificent locations by Harry Stradling, Jr., in Panavision. [PG]▼●▶

Bitter Moon (1992-French-British) **C-139m. ★★½** D: Roman Polanski. Peter Coyote, Emmanuelle Seigner, Hugh Grant, Kristin Scott Thomas, Victor Banerjee, Sophie Patel. Deliciously trashy tale of wealthy, wheelchair-bound jerk Coyote, a failed American writer who's been living in Paris with voluptuous French wife Seigner. Once they were ecstatically in love, but their relationship has taken on a bizarre, sadistic bent; they go on an ocean voyage, and beguile a very proper British couple (Grant, Scott Thomas). Often overwrought, with laughable dialogue and not-to-be-believed sex scenes. A guilty pleasure, to be sure. Polanski also produced and coscripted. Stockard Channing appears unbilled. [R]▼●▶

Bitter Rice (1948-Italian) **107m. ★★★** D: Giuseppe De Santis. Silvana Mangano, Vittorio Gassman, Raf Vallone, Doris Dowling, Lia Corelli. Effective portrayal of the dreary, backbreaking existence of women toiling in the Po Valley rice fields, exploited by the rice growers and their go-betweens. The seductive Mangano, as a worker who betrays her comrades, became an international star.▼

Bitter Sweet (1940) **C-92m. ★★★** D: W.S. Van Dyke II. Jeanette MacDonald, Nelson Eddy, George Sanders, Felix Bressart, Lynne Carver, Ian Hunter, Sig Ruman. Ignore plot, enjoy Noel Coward's songs

in lavishly filmed operetta. Wonderful Herman Bing provides funniest scene as shopkeeper who hires Nelson and Jeanette to give his daughter music lessons. Filmed before in England in 1933. ▼

Bittersweet Love (1976) **C-92m. ★½** D: David Miller. Lana Turner, Robert Lansing, Celeste Holm, Robert Alda, Scott Hylands, Meredith Baxter Birney. Excellent cast wasted on improbable story of young married couple (expecting a baby) suddenly discovering they are half-brother and sister. Termination of pregnancy and marriage are then talked to death. [PG]▼

Bitter Tea of General Yen, The (1933) **89m. ★★★½** D: Frank Capra. Barbara Stanwyck, Nils Asther, Gavin Gordon, Toshia Mori, Richard Loo, Lucien Littlefield, Clara Blandick, Walter Connolly. May seem antiquated to modern audiences, but Capra's sensuous story of American woman's strange fascination with a Chinese warlord is still dazzling. A moody, beautifully atmospheric, sensitively performed film.▼

Bitter Tears of Petra Von Kant, The (1972-German) **C-119m. ★★** D: Rainer Werner Fassbinder. Margit Carstensen, Hanna Schygulla, Irm Hermann, Eva Mattes, Katrin Schaake, Gisela Fackeldey. Wealthy lesbian fashion designer Petra Von Kant (Carstensen) worries over habits of inconsistent lover Schygulla and unmercifully bosses secretary Hermann. The action is limited to Petra's apartment, and the pace is annoyingly slow. Based on a Fassbinder play; overrated by some.▼▶

Bitter Vengeance (1994) **C-90m. ★★** D: Stuart Cooper. Virginia Madsen, Bruce Greenwood, Kristen Hocking, Eddie Velez, Gordon Jump, Carlos Gomez, Tim Russ. Disappointing thriller about a self-pitying bank security guard (Greenwood) who takes out his anger on his supportive wife (Madsen). He eventually begins cheating on her, and concocts a robbery scheme in which his mate will take the fall. Holds your interest for a while, but eventually becomes much too implausible. [R]▼

Bitter Victory (1957-French) **82m. ★★★** D: Nicholas Ray. Richard Burton, Curt Jurgens, Ruth Roman, Raymond Pellegrin, Anthony Bushell, Christopher Lee. Strong WW2 story with Jurgens as unfit commander who leads mission against Rommel's desert headquarters; Roman is his wife who's had prior affair with officer Burton. 103m. versions now in circulation are from British release of this film. CinemaScope.▶

Biutiful (2010-Spanish-Mexican) **C-148m. ★★★** D: Alejandro González Iñárritu. Javier Bardem, Maricel Álvarez, Hanaa Bouchaib, Guillermo Estrella, Eduard Fernández, Cheikh Ndiaye, Diaryatou Daff, Taisheng Cheng, Luo Jin. Uxbal (Bardem) engages in shady business involving illegal immigrants in Barcelona, trying to stay one step ahead of the law while looking out for his two young children and his mercurial estranged wife. Then he learns he has terminal cancer. Again and again, Uxbal is tested, almost like Job, and just when it seems things couldn't get worse, they do. Personal, passionate film benefits from a heartfelt performance by Bardem, but it's extremely difficult to watch and unrelentingly downbeat. Some people found it uplifting; we didn't. The title reflects the way in which a young child might spell the word "beautiful." Based on a story by Iñárritu, who also coscripted. [R] ◗

Bix: An Interpretation of a Legend (1990-Italian) **C-100m.** ****½** D: Pupi Avati. Bryant Weeks, Emile Levisetti, Sally Groth, Mark Collver, Ray Edelstein, Julia Ewing, Barbara Wilder, Romano Luccio Orzari. Fragmented bio of 1920s jazz legend Bix Beiderbecke, who skyrocketed to fame—and burned out just as fast. Dramatically uneven, but enhanced by loving recreation of the period (using many authentic locations in and around Bix's home town of Davenport, Iowa) and great reproductions of his music by Bob Wilber and some first-class musicians. Originally 20m. longer.▼

Black and White (2000) **C-100m.** ******* D: James Toback. Bijou Phillips, Brooke Shields, Robert Downey, Jr., Allan Houston, Ben Stiller, Claudia Schiffer, Stacy Edwards, Gaby Hoffmann, Elijah Wood, Scott Caan, Jared Leto, Marla Maples, Method Man, Power, Raekwon, Joe Pantoliano, James Toback, Mike Tyson. Edgy N.Y.C. slice-of-life about social and sexual interaction between blacks and whites of various backgrounds, including a white teen hipster (Phillips) who hangs out in Harlem with an ambitious rap artist, a basketball player (real-life hoop star Houston) who's manipulated by his beautiful white girlfriend (Schiffer) and a documentary filmmaker (Shields) who's shooting a film on why white kids are so fascinated by hip-hop culture. Crammed with interesting ideas and observations. Toback also scripted. Super 35. [R]▼◗

Black and White in Color (1977-French-African) **C-90m.** *****½** D: Jean-Jacques Annaud. Jean Carmet, Jacques Dufilho, Catherine Rouvel, Jacques Spiesser, Dora Doll. Unusual and witty story of self-satisfied Frenchmen at remote African trading post who are fired by sudden patriotism at outbreak of WW1 and decide to attack nearby German fort. Oscar winner as Best Foreign Film. [PG]▼◗

Blackballed: The Bobby Dukes Story (2006) **C-91m.** ****½** D: Brant Sersen. Rob Corddry, Paul Scheer, Dannah Feinglass, Rob Riggle, Curtis Gwinn, Seth Morris, Jack McBrayer, Ed Helms. *Daily Show* correspondent Corddry stars as a paintball champion who fell from grace when he was caught cheating. Mockumentary follows his efforts to rescue his reputation by gathering a team of underdogs and attempting to win an important competition. Uneven but sweet, with a few laugh-out-loud moments and well-improvised characterizations. Made in 2004. ◗

Blackbeard's Ghost (1968) **C-107m.** ******* D: Robert Stevenson. Peter Ustinov, Dean Jones, Suzanne Pleshette, Elsa Lanchester, Joby Baker, Elliott Reid, Richard Deacon. Jones conjures up title character (Ustinov) who helps protect his descendants' home from being taken over by racketeers who want to make it a casino. Engaging slapstick comedy from Disney.▼◗

Blackbeard, the Pirate (1952) **C-99m.** ****** D: Raoul Walsh. Robert Newton, Linda Darnell, William Bendix, Keith Andes, Richard Egan, Irene Ryan. Newton is rambunctious as 17th-century buccaneer, with lovely Darnell his captive; fun for a while, but Newton's hamming soon grows tiresome.▼◗

Black Beauty (1971-British) **C-106m.** ****½** D: James Hill. Mark Lester, Walter Slezak, Peter Lee Lawrence, Ursula Glas. The story of a horse who passes from owner to owner; fails to capture the qualities that make Anna Sewell's novel a classic, but it's not bad. Filmed before in 1946. [G]▼◗

Black Beauty (1994) **C-85m.** ******* D: Caroline Thompson. Sean Bean, David Thewlis, Jim Carter, Peter Davison, Alun Armstrong, John McEnery, Eleanor Bron, Peter Cook, Andrew Knott; voice of Alan Cumming. Handsome remake of the Anna Sewell family classic about a horse's trials and tribulations as it passes from one owner to another in 19th-century England, experiencing everything from benevolent guardianship to ignorant abuse. Narrated, quite engagingly, by the horse itself. Evocative score by Danny Elfman. Screenwriter Thompson's directing debut. Made in England. [G]▼◗

Black Belly of the Tarantula (1972-Italian) **C-88m.** ***½** D: Paolo Cavara. Giancarlo Giannini, Stefania Sandrelli, Barbara Bouchet. Folks are being murdered in mysterious ways at health and beauty salon; none too exciting. [R]◗

Black Belt Jones (1974) **C-87m.** ****½** D: Robert Clouse. Jim Kelly, Gloria Hendry, Scatman Crothers, Alan Weeks, Nate Esformes. Black-oriented kung-fu mayhem from the team that made ENTER THE DRAGON. Kelly battles the Mafia to save his school of self-defense in Watts area of L.A. No gore, but lots of action and comedy. [R]▼

Black Bird, The (1975) **C-98m.** BOMB D: David Giler. George Segal, Stephane Audran, Lionel Stander, Lee Patrick, Elisha Cook Jr., Felix Silla, Signe Hasso. Horrendously bad, unfunny takeoff on THE MALTESE FALCON, with Segal as Sam Spade, Jr., not saved by the presence of Patrick and Cook from the '41 cast. [PG]▼

Blackboard Jungle (1955) **101m.** *****½** D:

Richard Brooks. Glenn Ford, Anne Francis, Vic Morrow, Louis Calhern, Sidney Poitier, Richard Kiley, Warner Anderson, Margaret Hayes, Emile Meyer, John Hoyt, Rafael Campos, Paul Mazursky. Excellent adaptation of Evan Hunter's novel (scripted by the director) of a teacher's harrowing experiences in N.Y.C. school system. Poitier memorable as a troubled youth. Hard-hitting entertainment. This was the first film to feature rock music—Bill Haley's "Rock Around the Clock" is played over the opening credits. Look for a young Jamie Farr (billed as Jameel Farah). Also shown in computer-colored version.▼●)

Black Book, The (1949) SEE: **Reign of Terror**

Black Book (2006-Dutch-British-German-Belgian) **C-145m. **½** D: Paul Verhoeven. Carice van Houten, Sebastian Koch, Thom Hoffman, Halina Reijn, Waldemar Kobus, Derek de Lint, Christian Berkel, Dolf de Vries, Peter Blok. Expansive saga of beautiful Jewish woman who goes to work for the Dutch resistance movement during WW2 and has to cozy up to a Nazi officer to carry out her most vital assignment. Fast-paced film, dotted with action, covers a lot of ground but quickly turns heavy-handed, punctuating its engrossing story with old-fashioned music cues and close-ups of sneering SS officers. Buoyed considerably by van Houten's charismatic and sexy performance. Verhoeven scripted with his longtime Dutch colleague Gerard Soeteman. Super 35. [R]❍

Black Bounty Killer, The SEE: **Boss Nigger**

Black Caesar (1973) **C-96m. **½** D: Larry Cohen. Fred Williamson, Art Lund, Julius W. Harris, Gloria Hendry, D'Urville Martin. Better-than-average gangster film follows rise to the top of shrewd, bloodthirsty black baddie. Sequel: HELL UP IN HARLEM. [R]▼●)

Black Castle, The (1952) **81m. *** D: Nathan Juran. Richard Greene, Boris Karloff, Stephen McNally, Paula Corday, Lon Chaney, Jr., John Hoyt. Uninspired gothic melodrama has Greene investigating disappearance of two friends who were guests of sinister Austrian count (McNally). Karloff reduced to colorless supporting role.▼)

Black Cat, The (1934) **65m. ***½** D: Edgar G. Ulmer. Karloff (Boris Karloff), Bela Lugosi, David Manners, Jacqueline Wells (Julie Bishop), Lucille Lund, Henry Armetta, Harry Cording. Polished horror film with bizarre sets, even more bizarre plot. Confrontation of architect/devil-worshiper Karloff and doctor Lugosi is still fascinating. The first of Boris and Bela's many teamings. Look fast for John Carradine as an organist at Satanic Mass. Film bears absolutely no resemblance to eponymous Edgar Allan Poe tale.▼●)

Black Cat, The (1941) **70m. **½** D: Albert S. Rogell. Basil Rathbone, Hugh Herbert,

Broderick Crawford, Bela Lugosi, Gale Sondergaard, Anne Gwynne, Gladys Cooper. Herbert and Crawford provide laughs, the others provide chills, in lively comedy-mystery not to be confused with earlier horror film. Look for Alan Ladd in a small role. Atmospheric photography by Stanley Cortez.▼)

Black Cat, White Cat (1998-Yugoslavian-French-German) **C-129m. **** D: Emir Kusturica. Bajram Severdzan (Doctor Kolja), Florijan Ajdini, Jas'ar Destani, Adnan Bekir, Zabit Mehmedovski, Sabri Sulejmani. Dizzying farce about gypsy families who live on the Danube and a bitter rivalry between two elders whose offspring cause them no end of headaches. Kusturica (who also coscripted) builds to a crescendo of slapstick action in this exuberant film that reminds us how much we all have in common, regardless of nationality. [R]▼

Black Cauldron, The (1985) **C-80m. **½** D: Ted Berman, Richard Rich. Voices of Grant Bardsley, Susan Sheridan, Freddie Jones, John Byner, John Hurt. Disney's expensive, ambitious animated feature is a pretty good but unmemorable sword-and-sorcery tale about a young boy who must find powerful black cauldron before it falls into the hands of evil Horned King. Good storytelling for kids, with impressive effects animation for buffs. Supporting characters Gurgi (a good guy) and Creeper (a baddie) have all the best moments. Super Technirama 70. [PG]▼●)

Black Christmas (1975-Canadian) **C-98m. **½** D: Bob Clark. Olivia Hussey, Keir Dullea, Margot Kidder, John Saxon, Art Hindle, Douglas McGrath, Andrea Martin. Bizarre horror thriller about warped murderer in sorority house on Christmas Eve and two days following. Not bad; Kidder steals it as a nasty, foul-mouthed sorority sister. Remade in 2006. Aka SILENT NIGHT, EVIL NIGHT and STRANGER IN THE HOUSE. [R]▼●)

Black Christmas (2006) **C-90m. BOMB** D: Glen Morgan. Katie Cassidy, Michelle Trachtenberg, Kristen Cloke, Crystal Lowe, Lacey Chabert, Mary Elizabeth Winstead, Andrea Martin, Oliver Hudson. Someone just *had* to remake the 1975 frightfest for the blood-and-gore generation. With no fresh ideas, this version sets up a group of sorority sisters as the next victims of a nutcase who's headed for his childhood home for a little merry slay time. Might have been bearable if we hadn't seen it all a hundred times before. At least the diabolical elf of terror makes clever use of ornaments. Look for Andrea Martin (who appeared in the 1975 version) as a soothing force of sanity for the girls. Unrated version runs 94m. Super 35. [R]❍

Black Dahlia, The (2006-U.S.-German) **C-121m. *½** D: Brian De Palma. Josh Hartnett, Scarlett Johansson, Aaron Eckhart, Hilary Swank, Mia Kirshner, Mike Starr, Fiona

Shaw, Patrick Fischler, James Otis, John Kavanagh, Pepe Serna, Rachel Miner, Gregg Henry, Rose McGowan, Anthony Russell. Torpid story of two L.A. cops in the 1940s whose partnership is strained by reverberations from the grisly murder of would-be starlet Elizabeth Short (Kirshner). Ostensibly based on James Ellroy's novel and the notorious real-life "Black Dahlia" killing, this boring, muddled film turns the case into a sidebar for a much duller tale of two damaged men and the women in their lives. Makes curious use of footage from the silent film THE MAN WHO LAUGHS. Kevin Dunn and k. d. lang appear unbilled. Super 35. [R]▶

Black Death (2010-British-German) C-102m. **½ D: Christopher Smith. Sean Bean, Eddie Redmayne, Carice van Houten, John Lynch, Kimberley Nixon, Andy Nyman, Tim McInnerny, David Warner. Mean-spirited tag-team match pits wandering 14th-century Christians against pagans when the latter villagers are suspected of using sorcery to rid their community of pervasive pestilence and disease. Minus point-of-view rooting interest or star power, plus a decidedly clinical approach to dismemberments and other brands of torture, it's a credit to the film's courage of its convictions that it maintains the mild interest it does. Pace picks up some when unseasoned monk Redmayne and brutal knight Bean finally meet up with a deceptively comely redhead (van Houten). [R]

Black Dog (1998) C-88m. *½ D: Kevin Hooks. Patrick Swayze, Randy Travis, Meat Loaf, Gabriel Casseus, Brian Vincent, Brenda Strong, Stephen Tobolowsky, Charles S. Dutton. An ex-con trucker with a suspended license makes one last run to avoid foreclosure, and his rig turns out to be full of concealed assault weapons that his corrupt boss is planning to sell. There's no dirty dancing for Swayze here but lots of dirty driving. Heavier on crashes than coherency. Super 35. [PG-13]▼●▶

Black Dragon SEE: **Miracles** (1989)

Black Dynamite (2009) C-84m. ** D: Scott Sanders. Michael Jai White, Kym Whitley, Tommy Davidson, Kevin Chapman, Byron Minns, Salli Richardson-Whitfield, Cedric Yarbrough, Mike Starr, Mykelti Williamson, Obba Babatundé, Nicole Sullivan, Bokeem Woodbine, Arsenio Hall, John Salley, Brian McKnight, Miguel Nuñez, Roger Yuan, Richard Edson. Good-natured parody of blaxploitation movies features White as a no-nonsense character named Black Dynamite who sets out to avenge his brother's death at the hands of drug pushers. Has the look, the feel, and the sound of a '70s genre piece, and offers some laughs, but they peter out after a while; the finale is a mess. You can get most of this film's amusement value out of the trailer. [R]▶

Black Eagle (1988) C-93m. **½ D: Eric Kar-

son. Sho Kosugi, Jean-Claude Van Damme, Vladimir Skontarovsky, Doran Clark, Bruce French, William H. Bassett. Standard martial arts adventure. Kosugi's the secret-agent hero, Van Damme's the Russian villain, and there's plenty of action. Kosugi's real-life children, Kane and Shane, appear in cameos as his screen character's kids. [R]▼▶

Black Evil SEE: **Demons of the Mind**

Black Eye (1974) C-98m. ** D: Jack Arnold. Fred Williamson, Rosemary Forsyth, Richard Anderson, Teresa Graves, Cyril Delevanti. Involved action-mystery has black private detective Williamson investigating murders connected with a dope ring in Venice, Cal. Bret Morrison, radio's "The Shadow," plays a porno movie-maker. Standard fare. [PG]▼

Black Fist (1976) C-105m. **½ D: Timothy Galfas, Richard Kaye. Richard Lawson, Philip Michael Thomas, Annazette Chase, Dabney Coleman, Robert Burr. Coleman's gritty performance as a crooked cop elevates this standard blaxploitation drama about tough Lawson, hired by a crime boss as a streetfighter. Aka THE BLACK STREETFIGHTER and HOMEBOY. [R]▼▶

Black Friday (1940) 70m. **½ D: Arthur Lubin. Boris Karloff, Bela Lugosi, Stanley Ridges, Anne Nagel, Anne Gwynne, Virginia Brissac. Well-made little chiller with Karloff putting gangster's brain into a professor's body. Jekyll-Hyde results are fascinating; Ridges excellent as victim. Lugosi has small, thankless role as gangster.▼▶

Black Fury (1935) 92m. *** D: Michael Curtiz. Paul Muni, Karen Morley, William Gargan, Barton MacLane, John Qualen, J. Carrol Naish, Vince Barnett. Hard-hitting melodrama about exploitation of coal miners, with Muni as robust "bohunk" who gets in over his head. Realistic, strikingly filmed, if a bit uneven dramatically. Muni's accent makes it tough to understand him at times. Based on a true story.▼▶

Black Girl (1972) C-97m. *** D: Ossie Davis. Brock Peters, Leslie Uggams, Claudia McNeil, Louise Stubbs, Gloria Edwards, Peggy Pettitt, Ruby Dee. One of the best black-oriented films of the 1970s spotlights the complex relationship between the title character (Pettitt), an aspiring dancer, and her emotionally clueless mother (Stubbs). Well acted by the entire cast; scripted by J. E. Franklin, and based on her play. [PG]

Black Gunn (1972) C-98m. ** D: Robert Hartford-Davis. Jim Brown, Martin Landau, Brenda Sykes, Luciana Paluzzi. Black nightclub owner goes after the Man when his brother is killed. Routine black actioner. [R]▼▶

Black Hand (1950) 93m. **½ D: Richard Thorpe. Gene Kelly, J. Carrol Naish, Teresa Celli, Marc Lawrence, Frank Puglia. If you can buy Kelly as an Italian immigrant in N.Y.C. (circa 1908), you'll probably go along with this naïve but entertaining story about a young man's attempt to avenge his father's murder by the infamous—and seemingly unstoppable—Italian crime syndicate known as the Black Hand. ▼

Black Hawk Down (2001) **C-143m.** **★★★** D: Ridley Scott. Josh Hartnett, Ewan McGregor, Tom Sizemore, Eric Bana, William Fichtner, Ewen Bremner, Sam Shepard, Gabriel Casseus, Kim Coates, Ron Eldard, Thomas Guiry, Danny Hoch, Željko Ivanek, Jeremy Piven, Orlando Bloom, Steven Ford, Hugh Dancy. Harrowing dramatization of the disastrous 1993 U.S. mission in Somalia, which resulted in the deaths of 18 American soldiers. Characters and political context take a backseat (intentionally) to the ferocious battle scenes, re-created in brutal detail by Scott, cinematographer Slawomir Idziak, and a team of technical wizards. Not for the faint of heart. Based on the book by Mark Bowden. Won Oscars for Film Editing (Pietro Scalia) and Sound. Alternate version runs 151m. Super 35. [R] ▼▶

Black Hole, The (1979) **C-97m.** **★★½** D: Gary Nelson. Maximilian Schell, Anthony Perkins, Robert Forster, Joseph Bottoms, Yvette Mimieux, Ernest Borgnine; uncredited voices of Roddy McDowall, Slim Pickens. U.S. expedition finds long-lost madman in space about to explore a "black hole." Disney studios' ambitious sci-fi effort is a throwback to 1957 Saturday matinee fodder, with thin story, cardboard characters. OK on that level—with great special effects—but should have been much better. Technovision. [PG—Disney's first] ▼▶

Black Ice (1992-Canadian) **C-90m.** **★★** D: Neill Fearnley. Michael Nouri, Michael Ironside, Joanna Pacula, Mickey Jones, Brent Neale, Arne Olsen, Rick Skene. Following the accidental death of her politician lover, Pacula has philosophical cabbie Nouri drive her from Detroit to Seattle during the winter; they're pursued by murderous Ironside. Good performances, and handsome wintry landscapes, can't overcome a complicated plot—and its unsatisfactory resolution. Unrated video version runs 92m. [R] ▼▶

Black Jack SEE: **Wild in the Sky**

Black Knight (2001) **C-95m.** **★★½** D: Gil Junger. Martin Lawrence, Marsha Thomason, Tom Wilkinson, Vincent Regan, Daryl Mitchell, Kevin Conway, Michael Burgess, Isabell Monk. A 21st-century homeboy who works at a run-down medieval theme park is magically transported back to 14th-century England, where he must use his wits to survive, and forms an alliance with a disgraced knight (Wilkinson) to help restore a deposed queen to the throne. Comedy vehicle for Lawrence gives you pretty much what you expect, though it would have meant a lot more if a better, more famous actress had played the queen. Super 35. [PG-13] ▼▶

Black Legion (1936) **83m.** **★★★** D: Archie Mayo. Humphrey Bogart, Erin O'Brien-Moore, Dick Foran, Ann Sheridan, Joe Sauers (Sawyer), Helen Flint, Dickie Jones, Henry Brandon. Factory worker Bogart, disappointed at losing a promotion to a coworker named Dombrowski (Brandon), becomes involved with a Ku Klux Klan–ish group. Powerful, still-relevant social drama, compactly told. ▼▶

Black Like Me (1964) **107m.** **★★★** D: Carl Lerner. James Whitmore, Roscoe Lee Browne, Lenka Petersen, Sorrell Booke, Will Geer, Al Freeman, Jr., Dan Priest, Raymond St. Jacques. Strong drama based on actual history of reporter who took drugs that allowed him to pass for black so he could experience racial prejudice firsthand. Some aspects of presentation are dated, but themes are still timely. ▼▶

Black Magic (1949) **105m.** **★★½** D: Gregory Ratoff. Orson Welles, Akim Tamiroff, Nancy Guild, Raymond Burr, Frank Latimore. Welles is predictably florid in chronicle of famous charlatan Cagliostro who seeks to rise to power in 18th-century Italy. (He codirected this handsome film, uncredited.) Filmed in Rome. ▼▶

Blackmail (1929-British) **86m.** **★★★** D: Alfred Hitchcock. Anny Ondra, Sara Allgood, John Longden, Charles Paton, Donald Calthrop, Cyril Ritchard. Young woman kills man who tries to rape her, then finds herself caught between investigating detective (who happens to be her boyfriend) and a blackmailer. Hitchcock's—and England's—first talking picture is still exciting, especially for fans and students of the director's work. Originally shot as a silent; that version, running 75m., also exists (and is significantly better). Leading lady Ondra had a heavy accent, so her voice was dubbed for the talkie by Joan Barry. ▼▶

Blackmail (1939) **81m.** **★★½** D: H. C. Potter. Edward G. Robinson, Ruth Hussey, Gene Lockhart, Bobs Watson, Guinn Williams, John Wray, Arthur Hohl. Well-respected Robinson, an expert at putting out oil fires, has a secret past: he escaped from jail after being falsely convicted of robbery. Slimy Lockhart shows up and threatens blackmail. Taut, clever drama-thriller, marred only by a pat finale.

Black Mama, White Mama (1972-U.S.-Filipino) **C-87m.** **★★** D: Eddie Romero. Pam Grier, Margaret Markov, Sid Haig, Lynn Borden. Clichéd, violent female rehash of THE DEFIANT ONES, as blonde Markov and black Grier escape chained together from a Filipino prison camp. Haig is hammy in cowboy costume. Story co-written by Jonathan Demme. [R] ▼▶

Black Marble, The (1980) **C-113m.** **★★½** D: Harold Becker. Robert Foxworth, Paula Prentiss, Harry Dean Stanton, Barbara Babcock, John Hancock, Raleigh Bond, Judy Landers, James Woods, Michael Dudikoff, Anne Ramsey, Christopher Lloyd. Insightful but curiously unmemorable love story about sexy cop Prentiss and her new partner (Foxworth), an alcoholic romantic drowning in the reality of his job. Misses much of the humor that marked Joseph Wambaugh's novel. Panavision. [PG]▼●]

Black Mask (1997-Hong Kong) **C-96m.** *** D: Danny Lee. Jet Li, Karen Mok, Françoise Yip, Lau Ching Wan, Patrick Lung Kang, Anthony Wong. Biologically engineered super-soldier Li gives up a peaceful life to battle his equally enhanced former comrades, who are trying to take over the Hong Kong drug rackets. Smart, stylish, lightning-paced thriller is an ideal showcase for the dazzling skills of Li (who, in his disguise, resembles the Green Hornet's Kato). Recut and revised from 106m. Hong Kong version. Followed by a direct-to-video sequel. [R]▼●]

Black Moon (1975-French-German) **C-101m.** **½ D: Louis Malle. Cathryn Harrison, Thérèse Giehse, Alexandra Stewart, Joe Dallesandro. Innocent young Harrison, adrift in a war-torn landscape in which the combatants are men and women, finds refuge in a country cottage that houses a bevy of bizarre characters. Surreal, futuristic *Alice in Wonderland*–like tale combines fantasy and reality and is very much of its time; ambitious and challenging, but decidedly not for all tastes. Malle coscripted. [R]❭

Black Moon Rising (1986) **C-100m.** BOMB D: Harley Cokliss. Tommy Lee Jones, Linda Hamilton, Robert Vaughn, Richard Jaeckel, Bubba Smith, Lee Ving, William Sanderson. Vaughn's hot-car ring steals the Black Moon, one of those zoom-across-the-salt-flats dream machines no taller than a munchkin's shin; high-tech thief Jones pursues. Punk-rocker-turned-actor Ving wears a coat and tie, but that's about it for novelty value; this one deserves to get a Big Moon Rising. From a story by John Carpenter. [R]▼●]

Black Narcissus (1947-British) **C-99m.** **** D: Michael Powell, Emeric Pressburger. Deborah Kerr, David Farrar, Sabu, Jean Simmons, Kathleen Byron, Flora Robson, Esmond Knight. Visually sumptuous, dramatically charged movie, from Rumer Godden novel, about nuns trying to establish a mission in a remote Himalayan mountaintop outpost amid formidable physical and emotional challenges. One of the most breathtaking color films ever made (winning Oscars for cinematographer Jack Cardiff and art director Alfred Junge). Scenes in which Sister Superior Kerr recalls her former life, a key plot element, were originally censored from American prints. ▼●]

Black Orchid, The (1959) **96m.** **½ D: Martin Ritt. Sophia Loren, Anthony Quinn, Ina Balin, Jimmie Baird, (Peter) Mark Richman, Naomi Stevens, Frank Puglia. Fabricated soaper of bumbling business-man (Quinn) romancing criminal's widow

(Loren) and the problem of convincing their children that marriage will make all their lives better. VistaVision. ▼●]

Black Orpheus (1959-French-Brazilian) **C-103m.** ***½ D: Marcel Camus. Breno Mello, Marpessa Dawn, Lea Garcia, Adhemar Da Silva, Lourdes De Oliveira. Street-car conductor Mello and country-girl Dawn fall in love in Rio de Janeiro during Carnival. Lyrical updating of the Orpheus and Eurydice legend is beautifully acted and directed. Oscar winner for Best Foreign Film; rhythmic score by Luis Bonfa and Antonio Carlos Jobim. Remade as ORFEU. ▼●]

Blackout (1978-Canadian-French) **C-89m.** ** D: Eddy Matalon. Jim Mitchum, Robert Carradine, Belinda Montgomery, June Allyson, Jean-Pierre Aumont, Ray Milland. Violent story of criminals who terrorize apartment dwellers during N.Y.'s 1977 power blackout. Balanced with black comedy for so-so results. [R]▼●]

Black Pirate, The (1926) **C-85m.** *** D: Albert Parker. Douglas Fairbanks, Sr., Billie Dove, Anders Randolf, Donald Crisp, Tempe Pigott, Sam De Grasse. Robust silent swashbuckler with Fairbanks a nobleman who turns pirate after being victimized by cutthroats. Filmed in early Technicolor process. ▼●]

Black Rain (1989) **C-126m.** **½ D: Ridley Scott. Michael Douglas, Andy Garcia, Ken Takakura, Kate Capshaw, Yusaku Matsuda, Shigeru Koyama, John Spencer. Tough, violent, foulmouthed action yarn about street-worn N.Y.C. cop and his partner who are supposed to deliver a Japanese mobster to cops in Osaka—then wind up pursuing him on his own turf. Too long, too predictable at times, but slick and entertaining. Super 35. [R]▼●]

Black Rain (1989-Japanese) **123m.** *** D: Shohei Imamura. Yoshiko Tanaka, Kazuo Kitamura, Etsuko Ichihara, Shoichi Ozawa, Norihei Miki, Keisuke Ishida. Somber, restrained, and very moving story detailing five years in the life of a family which survived Hiroshima, and the ways their bodies and souls are poisoned by the fallout—or "black rain." A quietly observant character study with a number of haunting black and white images. ▼●]

Black Rainbow (1991-British) **C-100m.** *** D: Mike Hodges. Rosanna Arquette, Jason Robards, Tom Hulce, Mark Joy, Ron Rosenthal, John Bennes, Linda Pierce. Offbeat, intriguing psychological drama-chiller with Arquette impressive as a medium who offers public exhibitions of her abilities. During one of them, she "sees" a murder and the killer—just before the crime is committed. Robards is her besotted father, a character worthy of Eugene O'Neill. Occasionally loses its way, but there's more than enough originality and good acting to compensate. Hodges also scripted; filmed in North Carolina. [R]▼▶

Black Rebels, The SEE: **This Rebel Breed**

Black Rider, The SEE: **Joshua** (1976)

Black Robe (1991-Canadian-Australian) C-101m. **½ D: Bruce Beresford. Lothaire Bluteau, August Schellenberg, Aden Young, Sandrine Holt, Tantoo Cardinal. Epic look at a 17th-century Jesuit priest who goes to Quebec to colonize the "Indian" tribes. Director Beresford travels much the same territory as DANCES WITH WOLVES, but paints a much bleaker picture. Beautifully photographed (by Peter James) but graphically violent, this flawed, fascinating film is for demanding viewers. [R] ▼●▶

Black Rodeo (1972) C-87m. **½ D: Jeff Kanew. Archie Wycoff, Clarence Gonzalez, Pete Knight, Marval Rogers, Reuben Heura. Offbeat, frequently interesting documentary about a rodeo that takes place largely in Harlem; background music is performed by such stars as B.B. King, Ray Charles, Dee Dee Sharpe. [G]

Black Room, The (1935) 67m. *** D: Roy William Neill. Boris Karloff, Marian Marsh, Robert Allen, Katherine DeMille, John Buckler, Thurston Hall. Excellent, understated thriller of twin brothers (Karloff) and the ancient curse that dominates their lives in 19th-century Hungary. Features one—no, *two*—of Karloff's best performances.▼●▶

Black Rose, The (1950) C-120m. ** D: Henry Hathaway. Tyrone Power, Cecile Aubry, Orson Welles, Jack Hawkins, Michael Rennie, Herbert Lom, James Robertson Justice, Finlay Currie, Bobby (Robert) Blake, Laurence Harvey. Sweeping pageantry follows Norman-hating Power on Oriental adventures during 1200s; plodding film only somewhat redeemed by dynamic action scenes. Filmed in England and North Africa by Jack Cardiff.▶

Black Sabbath (1963-Italian) C-99m. **½ D: Mario Bava. Boris Karloff, Mark Damon, Suzy Anderson, Jacqueline Pierreux. Italian three-part film hosted by Karloff, who appears in final episode about a vampire controlling an entire family. Other sequences are good, atmospheric.▼●▶

Black Sheep (1996) C-87m. BOMB D: Penelope Spheeris. Chris Farley, David Spade, Tim Matheson, Christine Ebersole, Gary Busey, Grant Heslov, Timothy Carhart, Bruce McGill. Gubernatorial candidate Matheson needs to keep his bumbling brother (Farley) out of the public eye, and Spade volunteers for the job. Insulting "comedy" reunites the stars of TOMMY BOY for virtually the same movie, which attempts to mine all the humor it can out of Farley's mugging and endless pratfalls, plus Spade's sarcasm. Pitiful and shameless. [PG-13]▼●▶

Black Sheep (2007-New Zealand) C-87m.

*** D: Jonathan King. Nathan Meister, Danielle Mason, Peter Feeney, Tammy Davis, Glenis Levestam, Tandi Wright, Oliver Driver, Nick Fenton. Young man (Meister) with a morbid fear of sheep returns to his sprawling family farm (naturally, a sheep ranch) to sell his portion of the estate to his tweedy, greedy older brother (Feeney). Everything and more goes wrong and bloody hell breaks out as ecoterrorists, evil scientists, visiting foreign investors, and our hero are attacked by genetically altered rampaging rams and ewes. Horrifically funny and gruesome *Monty Python*-esque horror comedy recalls early Peter Jackson. Written by the director. Super 35. ▶

Black Shield of Falworth, The (1954) C-99m. **½ D: Rudolph Maté. Tony Curtis, Janet Leigh, David Farrar, Barbara Rush, Herbert Marshall. Juvenile version of Howard Pyle novel *Men of Iron*; Curtis unconvincing as nobility rising through ranks to knighthood in medieval England. Settings, supporting cast bolster production. CinemaScope.▼▶

Black Sleep, The (1956) 81m. *½ D: Reginald LeBorg. Basil Rathbone, Akim Tamiroff, Lon Chaney (Jr.), John Carradine, Bela Lugosi, Tor Johnson, Herbert Rudley. Big horror cast cannot save dull, unatmospheric tale of doctor doing experimental brain surgery in remote English castle. Laughable. Reissued as DR. CADMAN'S SECRET.▼▶

Black Snake Moan (2007) C-115m. **½ D: Craig Brewer. Samuel L. Jackson, Christina Ricci, Justin Timberlake, S. Epatha Merkerson, John Cothran, David Banner, Kim Richards. Pent-up farmer and blues musician Jackson finds the town nympho (Ricci) beaten and unconscious, takes her in, and decides to heal her spiritually as well as physically—even if it means chaining her to his radiator. Honest. Steamy, sexy Southern Gothic tale benefits from robust, go-for-it performances, but the third act drags and the finale is somewhat ludicrous. Ricci's mother is played by former child actor Richards (ESCAPE TO WITCH MOUNTAIN). Exceptionally well shot by Amelia Vincent. Super 35. [R]▶

Black Stallion, The (1979) C-118m. *** D: Carroll Ballard. Kelly Reno, Mickey Rooney, Teri Garr, Clarence Muse, Hoyt Axton, Michael Higgins. Exquisitely filmed story of a young boy's adventures with a magnificent black stallion—from a dramatic shipwreck to a racing championship. Too slow at times, but still worthwhile, with many precious moments, stunning cinematography by Caleb Deschanel, Rooney's lovely performance as veteran horse trainer. Based on classic children's novel by Walter Farley. Followed by 1983 sequel, a TV series (with Rooney), and a prequel in 2003. [G] ▼●▶

Black Stallion Returns, The (1983) C-

**93m. **½ D: Robert Dalva. Kelly Reno, Vincent Spano, Allen Goorwitz (Garfield), Woody Strode, Ferdinand Mayne, Jodi Thelen, Teri Garr. Fair action sequel with Reno, now a teenager, searching the Sahara for his Arabian horse. Those expecting the magic of the original will be disappointed. First-time director Dalva edited the 1979 film. Followed by THE YOUNG BLACK STALLION. [PG]▼●)

Black Streetfighter, The SEE: Black Fist
Black Sunday (1961-Italian) **83m. **½ D: Mario Bava. Barbara Steele, John Richardson, Ivo Garrani, Andrea Checchi. Intriguing story of the one day each century when Satan roams the earth. Steele is a witch who swears vengeance on the descendants of those who killed her hundreds of years ago. Beautifully atmospheric.▼●)

Black Sunday (1977) **C-143m. *** D: John Frankenheimer. Robert Shaw, Bruce Dern, Marthe Keller, Fritz Weaver, Steven Keats, Bekim Fehmiu, Michael V. Gazzo, William Daniels. International terrorist organization plots to blow up the Super Bowl, enlists the aid of former Vietnam POW Dern, who pilots the TV blimp. Generally compelling adaptation (by Ernest Lehman, Kenneth Ross, Ivan Moffat) of the Thomas Harris best-seller, with Dern at his unhinged best. Splendid aerial photography. Panavision. [R]▼●)

Black Swan, The (1942) **C-85m. *** D: Henry King. Tyrone Power, Maureen O'Hara, Laird Cregar, Thomas Mitchell, George Sanders, Anthony Quinn, George Zucco. Power is at his dashing best in this lively swashbuckler from the Rafael Sabatini novel about rival pirate gangs in the Caribbean. Sanders seems to be having fun cast against type as a scurrilous brigand. Enhanced by Alfred Newman's music and Leon Shamroy's Oscar-winning Technicolor cinematography. ▼●)

Black Swan (2010) **C-108m. ** D: Darren Aronofsky. Natalie Portman, Mila Kunis, Vincent Cassel, Barbara Hershey, Winona Ryder, Benjamin Millepied, Sebastian Stan, Toby Hemingway, Marcia Jean Kurtz. Ballerina Portman, who lives a cloistered life with her overprotective mother (Hershey), is eager to win over her imperious, controlling ballet master (Cassel) and convince him to cast her in the leading role in *Swan Lake.* He doesn't think she has what it takes to play the black swan, which sends her spiraling into a hallucinatory world of paranoia, masturbation, sexual experimentation, and self-mutilation. Vividly realized fever-dream of a movie—with an Oscar-winning performance by Portman—gives new meaning to the word "overwrought," though some people found it brilliant. Matthew Libatique's cinematography is definitely worthy of praise. Super 16/HD Widescreen. [R]●)

Black Tights (1960-French) **C-120m. *** D: Terence Young. Cyd Charisse, Moira Shearer, Zizi Jeanmaire, Dirk Sanders, Roland Petit. Narrated by Maurice Chevalier. Ballet fans will feast on this quartet of stunning performances, featuring some of the era's top dance talent. Our favorite: the ballet of Rostand's *Cyrano de Bergerac,* with Shearer a lovely Roxanne. Super Technirama 70.▼)

Black Tuesday (1954) **80m. *** D: Hugo Fregonese. Edward G. Robinson, Peter Graves, Jean Parker, Milburn Stone. Throwback to 1930-ish gangster films, with Robinson and Graves as escaped convicts being hunted by cops. Nice gunplay, with Parker good as the moll.

Black Voodoo SEE: Beyond the Living
Black Werewolf (1974) SEE: Beast Must Die, The

Black Widow (1954) **C-95m. ** D: Nunnally Johnson. Ginger Rogers, Van Heflin, Gene Tierney, George Raft, Peggy Ann Garner, Reginald Gardiner, Virginia Leith, Otto Kruger, Cathleen Nesbitt, Skip Homeier. Broadway producer Heflin takes young writer Garner under his wing, is naturally suspected when she turns up dead in his apartment. Glossy but dull adaptation of Patrick Quentin mystery, with remarkably poor performances by Rogers as bitchy star and Raft as dogged detective. Johnson also produced and wrote the screenplay. CinemaScope.●)

Black Widow (1987) **C-103m. **½ D: Bob Rafelson. Debra Winger, Theresa Russell, Sami Frey, Dennis Hopper, Nicol Williamson, Terry O'Quinn, D. W. Moffett, Lois Smith, Mary Woronov, Rutanya Alda, James Hong, Diane Ladd, Christian Clemenson. Female investigator for the Justice Dept. becomes intrigued—then obsessed—by young woman who seduces, marries, and murders wealthy men. Handsome, stylishly crafted yarn, loaded with sexual tension, that stops just short of hitting the mark. Winger and Russell are both terrific. Photographed by Conrad Hall; effective music score by Michael Small. Amusing cameo by playwright David Mamet as one of Winger's poker-playing colleagues. [R] ▼●)

Black Windmill, The (1974-British) **C-106m. **½ D: Don Siegel. Michael Caine, Joseph O'Conor, Donald Pleasence, John Vernon, Janet Suzman, Delphine Seyrig. Slick, craftsmanlike but generally undistinguished thriller, as espionage agent Caine tries to locate his son's kidnappers. Siegel has done better. Panavision. [PG]▼

Blacula (1972) **C-92m. *** D: William Crain. William Marshall, Denise Nicholas, Vonetta McGee, Thalmus Rasulala, Ketty Lester, Elisha Cook, Jr., Gordon Pinsent. Dracula bit a Black Prince and now black vampire is stalking the streets of L.A. Some terrific shocks, and some very lively dialogue. Sequel: SCREAM, BLACULA, SCREAM. [PG] ▼●

Blade (1973) **C-90m.** **½ D: Ernest Pintoff. John Marley, Jon Cypher, Kathryn Walker, William Prince, John Schuck, Rue McClanahan, Morgan Freeman. N.Y.-made actioner about female-hating Cypher, who indulges in violent killings, and tough policeman Marley, who tracks him down. A bit pretentious and involved; fairly absorbing. [R] ▼

Blade (1998) **C-123m.** **½ D: Stephen Norrington. Wesley Snipes, Stephen Dorff, Kris Kristofferson, N'bushe Wright, Donal Logue, Udo Kier, Arly Jover, Traci Lords, Tim Guinee. If you think you've seen bloody urban-vigilante pics before... well, you haven't. Snipes is part human and part vampire, which means he's the perfect warrior to combat a megalomaniacal bloodsucker who's plotting world domination. A potentially rousing 90m. gorefest bloated by a half hour, film never tops its spectacularly gross opening set piece in a vampire disco. Based on the character created for Marvel Comics by Marv Wolfman. Followed by two sequels. Clairmont-Scope. [R] ▼●

Blade II (2002) **C-116m.** ** D: Guillermo del Toro. Wesley Snipes, Kris Kristofferson, Ron Perlman, Leonor Varela, Norman Reedus, Thomas Kretschmann, Luke Goss, Donnie Yen. Our half-human, half-vampire hero makes a highly unlikely move, joining forces with his vampiric enemies in order to wipe out a virulent band of mutants. Not much story here, and not much in the way of character; that leaves action and special effects, which are certainly slick, with lots of visceral violence, but the movie runs out of energy surprisingly early. Followed by BLADE: TRINITY. [R] ▼❚

Blade Master, The (1984-Italian) **C-92m.** *½ D: David Hills. Miles O'Keeffe, Lisa Foster (Lisa Raines), Charles Borromel, David Cain Haughton, Chen Wong. Silly sequel to ATOR THE FIGHTING EAGLE has O'Keeffe as the prehistoric warrior on a quest to protect the Earth from a primitive atomic bomb called the "Geometric Nucleus." As in TARZAN, THE APE MAN, O'Keeffe wrestles with an oversize rubber snake, but silliest scene has him hang-gliding to storm an enemy castle. Original title: ATOR THE INVINCIBLE. TV title: CAVE DWELLERS. [PG] ▼

Blade Runner (1982) **C-118m.** ·*½ D: Ridley Scott. Harrison Ford, Rutger Hauer, Sean Young, Edward James Olmos, William Sanderson, Daryl Hannah, Joe Turkel, Joanna Cassidy, Brion James. In 21st-century L.A., a former cop (Ford) is recruited to track down androids who have mutinied in space and made their way to Earth. A triumph of production design, defeated by a muddled script and main characters with no appeal whatsoever. However, the film has a fervent following. Loosely based on Philip K. Dick's novel *Do Androids Dream of Electric Sheep?* Futuristic stylings by Syd Mead and Lawrence G. Paull. At least two alternate versions have been released since the original, followed in 1993 by the "director's cut," which the film's champions hail as a vast improvement: Ford's voice-over has been dropped, footage has been added, and the ending has changed. In 2007 a 117m. "final cut" edition was released that clarifies at least one key plot point. Panavision. [R] ▼●

Blades of Glory (2007) **C-93m.** *** D: Josh Gordon, Will Speck. Will Ferrell, Jon Heder, Will Arnett, Amy Poehler, William Fichtner, Jenna Fischer, Craig T. Nelson, Andy Richter, Nick Swardson, Scott Hamilton, William Daniels, Rob Corddry, Tom Virtue, Rémy Girard. Two brawling superstar figure skaters are banned for life in the men's singles competitions after one fight too many. Years later these polar opposites reluctantly team up as the first male pairs skating team, much to the chagrin of a twisted brother-and-sister duo who consider them archrivals. Milking every moment on the ice and exhausting every crotch joke in their canon, Ferrell and Heder fill the rink with laughs. Look for a Luke Wilson cameo and a slew of real-life skating stars. [PG-13] ❚

Blade: Trinity (2004) **C-113m.** *½ D: David S. Goyer. Wesley Snipes, Kris Kristofferson, Dominic Purcell, Jessica Biel, Ryan Reynolds, Parker Posey, Mark Berry, John Michael Higgins, Callum Keith Rennie, Triple H (Paul Michael Levesque), James Remar, Natasha Lyonne, Eric Bogosian. Blade (Snipes) and the Night Stalkers, a band of vampire hunters, strain to save humanity from the grip of bloodsucking villains and a resurrected Dracula (Purcell). Poorly directed, lackadaisically plotted high-tech actioner may please BLADE fans, but it's pretty lame. Posey is campy fun as a scheming bloodsucker. Unrated DVD version runs 124m. Super 35. [R] ▼❚

Blair Witch Project, The (1999) **C/B&W-87m.** **½ D: Daniel Myrick, Eduardo Sanchez. Heather Donahue, Michael Williams, Joshua Leonard. Young woman hires a film crew to accompany her into the Maryland woods to chronicle local, age-old yarns and superstitions about witchcraft. Soon the threesome get lost, and with each day grow more desperate as spooky goings-on at night begin to frazzle their nerves. Largely ad-libbed, this comes off more as a student exercise than a movie, but by the end does create an atmosphere of fear and anxiety. Followed by BOOK OF SHADOWS: BLAIR WITCH 2. [R] ▼●

Blame It on Rio (1984) **C-100m.** **½ D: Stanley Donen. Michael Caine, Joseph Bologna, Valerie Harper, Michelle Johnson, Demi Moore, Jose Lewgoy. Caine has a fling with his best friend's sexy teenage daughter while vacationing in Rio de Janeiro. Caine's terrific, Johnson is voluptuous, Demi is obviously intimidated in topless beach scenes, and the script is kind of a sniggering TV sitcom, with a heavy-handed music score of too-familiar records. Written by Charlie Peters and Larry Gelbart. Remake of the French film ONE WILD MOMENT. [R]▼◉)

Blame It on the Bellboy (1992-British) **C-78m.** ** D: Mark Herman. Dudley Moore, Bryan Brown, Richard Griffiths, Penelope Wilton, Andreas Katsulas, Patsy Kensit, Alison Steadman, Bronson Pinchot, Lindsay Anderson. Behind the dynamic title lies an old-fashioned farce: three guys, named Orton, Lawton, and Horton, check into a Venice hotel, leading to the expected mix-ups after bellboy Pinchot confuses their messages. Brown (as a hit man) and the short running time keep this sometimes sleazy comedy from being a complete ordeal; even at 78m., though, you can feel the padding. [PG-13]▼◉)

Blame It on the Night (1984) **C-85m.** *½ D: Gene Taft. Nick Mancuso, Byron Thames, Leslie Ackerman, Dick Bakalyan, Merry Clayton, Billy Preston, Ollie E. Brown. Plodding tale of rock star Mancuso, who attempts to buy the love of his ultrastraight, illegitimate, military cadet son. Based on a story by Taft and Mick Jagger. [PG-13] ▼)

Blank Check (1994) **C-93m.** *½ D: Rupert Wainwright. Brian Bonsall, Karen Duffy, Miguel Ferrer, Michael Lerner, James Rebhorn, Jayne Atkinson, Michael Faustino, Chris Demetral, Tone Loc, Rick Ducommun, Debbie Allen, Lu Leonard. Comedy for blank minds shamelessly rips off HOME ALONE. 11-year-old manages to cash thug Ferrer's check for a million dollars, parlaying it into such life necessities as a dishy grownup girlfriend and a backyard water slide. Hard to swallow even on its own slumming-Disney level, but likely to hit very young children where they live. [PG]▼◉)

Blankman (1994) **C-92m.** *½ D: Mike Binder. Damon Wayans, David Alan Grier, Robin Givens, Christopher Lawford, Lynne Thigpen, Jon Polito, Jason Alexander. Shrill, witless comedy in which Wayans becomes a crimefighting superman in a crime-ridden metropolis. He has no super powers; he's aided instead by his own homemade contraptions. Might have some appeal to less-discriminating five-year-old boys. Wayans coscripted. [PG-13]▼◉)

Blast From the Past (1999) **C-111m.** **½ D: Hugh Wilson. Brendan Fraser, Alicia Silverstone, Christopher Walken, Sissy Spacek, Dave Foley, Jenifer Lewis, Rex Linn. Young man emerges after spending his entire 35 years in a fallout shelter with his loving parents, only to find that contemporary life in L.A. is not the way he pictured

it to be. Cute-enough comedy benefits from Fraser's enthusiasm, but Silverstone's character is fuzzily defined at best. Spacek and especially Walken are wonderful as the early '60s parents who remain in a time warp. Also available in PG version. Super 35. [PG-13]▼◉)

Blast-Off SEE: **Those Fantastic Flying Fools**

Blaze (1989) **C-119m.** **½ D: Ron Shelton. Paul Newman, Lolita Davidovich, Jerry Hardin, Gailard Sartain, Jeffrey DeMunn, Garland Bunting, Richard Jenkins, Robert Wuhl. Newman gives a flashy, uninhibited performance as Earl Long, the flamboyant governor of Louisiana in the 1950s who fell headlong in love with stripper Blaze Starr (Davidovich, in her first lead role). Seemingly surefire story, peppered with colorful characters and incidents, falls alarmingly flat after a while and never recovers. Real-life Blaze Starr appears fleetingly as Lily, the stripper whose shoulder Newman kisses backstage. [R]▼◉)

Blazing Magnums SEE: **Strange Shadows in an Empty Room**

Blazing Saddles (1974) **C-93m.** ***½ D: Mel Brooks. Cleavon Little, Gene Wilder, Harvey Korman, Madeline Kahn, Slim Pickens, David Huddleston, Alex Karras, Burton Gilliam, Mel Brooks, John Hillerman, Liam Dunn, Carol Arthur, Dom DeLuise, Robert Ridgely, George Furth. Brooks' first hit movie is a riotous Western spoof, with Little an unlikely sheriff, Korman as villainous Hedley Lamarr, and Kahn as a Dietrich-like chanteuse. None of Brooks' later films have topped this one for sheer belly laughs. Scripted by Brooks, Andrew Bergman, Richard Pryor, Norman Steinberg, and Alan Uger; story by Bergman. Title song sung by Frankie Laine. Panavision. [R]▼◉)

Bleak Moments (1971-British) **C-111m.** *** D: Mike Leigh. Anne Raitt, Sarah Stephenson, Eric Allan, Joolia Cappleman, Mike Bradwell, Liz Smith. Leigh's debut feature is a potent, deeply human drama, which charts the plight of a lonesome officeworker (Raitt) who looks after her mentally retarded sister and hopes that her relationship with a schoolteacher will lead to marriage. Leigh (who also scripted) offers knowing insight into his characters.▼)

Blessed Event (1932) **81m.** *** D: Roy Del Ruth. Lee Tracy, Mary Brian, Dick Powell, Emma Dunn, Frank McHugh, Allen Jenkins, Ned Sparks, Ruth Donnelly. Tracy's most famous role has him a Walter Winchell prototype whose spicy column makes him famous but also gets him in hot water; Powell makes film debut as crooner. Fast-moving, delightful.▼◉)

Bless the Beasts & Children (1972) **C-109m.** *** D: Stanley Kramer. Billy Mumy, Barry Robins, Miles Chapin, Ken Swofford, Jesse White, Vanessa Brown. Exciting and well-intentioned, if repetitious, story of six young misfit boys, campers at a ranch, who attempt to free a captive herd of buffalo scheduled for slaughter. The Barry DeVorzon–Perry Botkin music that later became known as "Nadia's Theme" and the *Young and the Restless* theme originated here. [PG]▼

Bless the Child (2000) **C-108m.** *½ D: Chuck Russell. Kim Basinger, Jimmy Smits, Holliston Coleman, Rufus Sewell, Angela Bettis, Christina Ricci, Michael Gaston, Ian Holm. Basinger has raised her addict sister's daughter (Coleman) to the age of six; when she shows signs of spiritual powers, the child is sought by millionaire Satanist Sewell, who's involved in a series of child killings. Smits is the detective on the case. Religious horror thriller veers wildly from the promising to the ludicrous, and is never remotely convincing. Based on the novel by Cathy Cash Spellman. Panavision. [R]▼

Blind Date (1984) **C-100m.** **½ D: Nico Mastorakis. Joseph Bottoms, Kirstie Alley, James Daughton, Lana Clarkson, Keir Dullea. Dr. Dullea tests a portable machine that stimulates vision on blind Bottoms, causing Bottoms to become obsessed with capturing a psycho killer who's on the loose. Solid cast perks up a contrived thriller, filmed in Greece. [R]▼

Blind Date (1987) **C-93m.** *½ D: Blake Edwards. Kim Basinger, Bruce Willis, John Larroquette, William Daniels, Phil Hartman, Stephanie Faracy, Joyce Van Patten, Alice Hirson, George Coe, Mark Blum, Graham Stark. Tiresome retread of all-too-familiar farcical material by Blake Edwards. Yuppie Willis takes Basinger out on a blind date, warned that she can't tolerate alcohol—and immediately gives her champagne. Alternately boring and grating. This was Willis' starring debut; guitarist Stanley Jordan makes a musical appearance. Panavision. [PG-13]▼●

Blind Date (2008-U.S.-Dutch) **C-80m.** *** D: Stanley Tucci. Patricia Clarkson, Stanley Tucci, Thijs Römer, Gerdy De Decker, Georgina Verbaan, Robin Holzhauer, Sarah Hyland, Peer Mascini. Small-time nightclub magician Tucci and retired dancer Clarkson respond to a personals ad and agree to meet in a bar. But in truth they're a married couple play-acting various roles (a blind man, a psychiatric patient, a reporter) for private, bittersweet reasons. Nine-chapter drama unfolds on a single set, melding deft acting with stabbing poignancy, in this only slightly Americanized remake of the 1996 Dutch original by Theo van Gogh. Tucci adapted the screenplay with David Schecter.▶

Blind Dating (2007) **C-99m.** **½ D: James Keach. Chris Pine, Eddie Kaye Thomas, Anjali Jay, Stephen Tobolowsky, Jane Seymour, Sendhil Ramamurthy, Frank Gerrish, Pooch Hall. Self-reliant young man (Pine) who's been blind all his life wants to find a woman to love who won't pity him. After endless dead-end dates he finds himself attracted to an Indian-American woman who works for his eye doctor . . . but she brings her own baggage to the relationship. Comedy-drama shifts tone from sweet sincerity to gross-out comedy, with mixed results. (Seymour, as Pine's psychiatrist, is so turned on during their sessions she feels impelled to shed her clothes!) [PG-13]▶

Blind Faith (1998) **C-107m.** **½ D: Ernest Dickerson. Courtney B. Vance, Charles S. Dutton, Kadeem Hardison, Lonette McKee, Garland Whitt. Two brothers, one a police captain and the other a defense attorney, find their relationship—and their own sense of self-worth as black men in 1950s America—turned upside down when the captain's son is accused of murder. Hard-hitting drama, which opens in the late '80s, focuses on the racial divide and unjust justice system. Solid performances, especially from the two leads. Released theatrically (at 118m.) after debut on U.S. cable TV. [R]▼●

Blindfold (1966) **C-102m.** **½ D: Philip Dunne. Rock Hudson, Claudia Cardinale, Jack Warden, Guy Stockwell, Anne Seymour. Attractive cast falters in film that wavers from comedy to mystery. Slapstick scenes seem incongruous as Hudson engages in international espionage with a noted scientist. Panavision.

Blind Fury (1990) **C-86m.** **½ D: Phillip Noyce. Rutger Hauer, Terrance (Terry) O'Quinn, Brandon Call, Lisa Blount, Randall "Tex" Cobb, Noble Willingham, Meg Foster, Sho Kosugi, Nick Cassavetes, Charles Cooper, Rick Overton. Smiling, sword-wielding, *blind* Vietnam vet Hauer carves up bad guys, saves a kid, and even duels with his mentor in this brash, lively (but failed) attempt to Americanize Japanese "Zatôichi" movies. Hauer is perfectly cast, and the film is amusingly tongue-in-cheek, but it doesn't altogether work. [R]▼●

Blindman (1972-Italian) **C-105m.** ** D: Ferdinando Baldi. Tony Anthony, Ringo Starr, Agneta Eckemyr, Lloyd Batista. Blindman (Anthony) seeks revenge on man who stole 50 mail-order brides. Mindless entertainment, though any movie with Ringo as a slimy Mexican bandit can't be *all* bad. Techniscope. [R]

Blind Man's Bluff SEE: **Cauldron of Blood**

Blindness (2008-Canadian-Brazilian-Japanese) **C-121m.** ** D: Fernando Meirelles. Julianne Moore, Mark Ruffalo, Danny Glover, Gael García Bernal, Alice Braga, Yusuke Iseya, Yoshino Kimura, Maury Chaykin, Don McKellar, Mitchell Nye, Sandra Oh. Dreary, pointless parable about people suddenly and randomly going blind including, ironically enough, an eye doctor (Ruffalo) but not his wife (Moore), who retains her sight. As they and other victims are herded into captivity by the government, all the worst elements of human nature rise to the surface in a bare-knuckle struggle for survival. Off-putting and ugly, to say the least. Based on a novel by José Saramago. [R]▶

Blind Side, The (2009) **C-129m.** ★★★ D: John Lee Hancock. Sandra Bullock, Tim McGraw, Quinton Aaron, Jae Head, Lily Collins, Ray McKinnon, Kim Dickens, Adriane Lenox, Kathy Bates. Remarkable story of a large, introverted black boy in Memphis who is taken in by a well-to-do white family and nurtured toward success and eventual fame as football star Michael Oher. Writer-director Hancock plays to the crowd and wrings every ounce of emotion out of a story that often seems too good to be true—but apparently is. Bullock is ideal in an Oscar-winning performance as the feisty woman who always gets her way. Based on Michael Lewis' book *The Blind Side: Evolution of a Game.* [PG-13]▶

Blind Spot: Hitler's Secretary (2002-Austrian) **C-87m.** ★★★½ D: André Heller, Othmar Schmiderer. Intense, fascinating documentary in which 81-year-old Traudl Junge recalls her life as Adolf Hitler's private secretary from 1942 until his death (later dramatized in DOWNFALL). There is no archival footage; the film consists of Junge talking, and what she says is so compelling that one can only watch, and listen, in stunned silence as she contrasts personal memories of her boss with the reality of who he was. She also reveals her subsequent guilt about working for him. Junge's recollections of Hitler's final days are especially gripping. She died just as the film debuted in Berlin. [PG]▼▶

Blind Swordsman, The SEE: **Zatôichi, the Blind Swordsman**

Blink (1994) **C-106m.** ★★½ D: Michael Apted. Madeleine Stowe, Aidan Quinn, Laurie Metcalf, James Remar, Peter Friedman, Bruce A. Young, Matt Roth, Paul Dillon. Did she or didn't she see a murderer leaving the scene of the crime? That's the central question when beautiful, strong-willed musician Stowe, blind since childhood, has her sight restored. Story relies on viewer's acceptance of screenwriter's gimmick of "retroactive vision," a post-surgery delayed reaction. Best thing in film is Stowe; otherwise this treads on too familiar blind-woman-in-jeopardy territory. Alternative Irish-American band The Drovers appear as themselves. Super 35. [R]▼▶

Bliss (1985-Australian) **C-111m.** ★½ D: Ray Lawrence. Barry Otto, Lynette Curran, Helen Jones, Miles Buchanan, Gia Carides, Tim Robertson. High-powered businessman has a major heart attack, sees himself dying, then revives—which changes his entire outlook on life. After a dynamic

opening this stylized satire slows to a snail's pace and loses its thrust. Nevertheless, it was an Australian Academy Award winner and an international film festival favorite, so judge for yourself. [R]▼▶

Bliss (1997) **C-103m.** ★★½ D: Lance Young. Craig Sheffer, Terence Stamp, Sheryl Lee, Spalding Gray, Casey Siemaszko, Ken Camroux, Pamela Perry, Leigh Taylor-Young, Lois Chiles, Theresa Saldana, Molly Parker. Unusual film about a young married couple's emotional journey into sexual awakening with the help of a sex therapist. Stamp excels as teacher and mentor to the husband, who unwittingly unlocks the door to his wife's forgotten past. Melodramatic story gets in the way of some genuinely interesting and even educational dialogue, though it's almost too clinical at times. Actress Taylor-Young is the sister of the writer-director. Filmed in 1995. [R] ▼▶

Bliss of Mrs. Blossom, The (1968-U.S.-British) **C-93m.** ★★★ D: Joe McGrath. Shirley MacLaine, Richard Attenborough, James Booth, Freddie Jones, Bob Monkhouse, John Cleese. Oddball, original comedy with delicious performances. Wife of brassiere manufacturer keeps a lover in their attic for five years. Bogs down toward the end, but for the most part a delight. [M/PG]▼▶

Blithe Spirit (1945-British) **C-96m.** ★★★½ D: David Lean. Rex Harrison, Constance Cummings, Kay Hammond, Margaret Rutherford, Hugh Wakefield, Joyce Carey. Delicious adaptation of Noel Coward's comedy-fantasy about a man whose long-dead first wife appears to haunt—and taunt—him in his newly married life. Rutherford is wonderful as Madame Arcati, the spiritual medium; this earned an Oscar for its special effects. Scripted by the director, the producer (Anthony Havelock-Allan), and the cinematographer (Ronald Neame).▼▶

Blob, The (1958) **C-86m.** ★★ D: Irvin S. Yeaworth, Jr. Steven McQueen, Aneta Corseaut (Corsaut), Earl Rowe, Olin Howlin. Endearingly campy classic of cheap '50s sci-fi has "Steven" (in his first starring role) leading teenagers into battle to save their small town from being swallowed up by giant glop of cherry Jell-O from outer space. Not really all that good, but how can you hate a film like this? (Especially when Burt Bacharach composed the title song.) Filmed in Valley Forge, PA. Later redubbed for comic effect as BLOBERMOUTH. Sequel: BEWARE! THE BLOB. Remade 30 years later.▼▶

Blob, The (1988) **C-95m.** ★★ D: Chuck Russell. Shawnee Smith, Donovan Leitch, Ricky Paull Goldin, Kevin Dillon, Billy Beck, Candy Clark, Joe Seneca. Needless, if undeniably gooey, remake about a man-made what's-it that wipes out the standard number of vagrants and oversexed teenagers on its way to enveloping a small town. Showstopper finds a restaurant employee getting pulled head first down a kitchen drain after foolishly attempting to "plunge" the Blob. [R] ▼●◗

Blockade (1938) 85m. *** D: William Dieterle. Madeleine Carroll, Henry Fonda, Leo Carrillo, John Halliday, Vladimir Sokoloff, Reginald Denny. Vivid romance drama of Spanish Civil War with globetrotting Carroll falling in love with fighting Fonda.◗

Block-Heads (1938) 55m. *** D: John G. Blystone. Stan Laurel, Oliver Hardy, Patricia Ellis, Minna Gombell, Billy Gilbert, James Finlayson. Stan's been marching in a trench for 20 years—nobody told him WW1 was over! Ollie brings him home to find he hasn't changed. Top L&H. Also shown in computer-colored version. ▼◗

Blockhouse, The (1973-British) C-90m. *½ D: Clive Rees. Peter Sellers, Charles Aznavour, Per Oscarsson, Peter Vaughan, Jeremy Kemp, Alfred Lynch. Dismal, downbeat story of laborers trapped in underground bunker when the Allies land at Normandy on D-Day. ▼◗

Blonde Ambition (2007) C-93m. ** D: Scott Marshall. Jessica Simpson, Luke Wilson, Rachael Leigh Cook, Penelope Ann Miller, Andy Dick, Larry Miller, Willie Nelson. Lightweight fluff about a small-town innocent (Simpson) who follows her unfaithful boyfriend to N.Y.C., where she lucks into a job as secretary for the president of a large construction company. Although obviously inspired by WORKING GIRL and LEGALLY BLONDE, this trifle actually plays more like some innocuous Gidget or Tammy comedy of yore. Simpson isn't half bad, and Larry Miller (as her boss) underplays amusingly. Look for a cameo by Penny Marshall, aunt of the movie's director. [PG-13]◗

Blonde Bait (1956-British) 70m. ** D: Elmo Williams. Beverly Michaels, Jim Davis, Joan Rice, Richard Travis, Paul Cavanagh, Thora Hird, Avril Angers, Gordon Jackson. Cheap, toothy blond bombshell Michaels excels as a Yank showgirl breaking out of a sedate British prison for women. British film, originally titled WOMEN WITHOUT MEN, was retitled, reedited, and reshot (with Davis, Travis, and Cavanagh added to cast) for U.S. release.

Blonde Bombshell SEE: **Bombshell**

Blonde Crazy (1931) 79m. **½ D: Roy Del Ruth. James Cagney, Joan Blondell, Louis Calhern, Ray Milland, Polly Walters, Nat Pendleton. Dated fun with Cagney as small-time con man who plays cat-and-mouse with big-time sharpie Calhern. Young Milland appears as businessman who marries Jimmy's girlfriend, Blondell. ▼●

Blonde Venus (1932) 97m. *** D: Josef von Sternberg. Marlene Dietrich, Herbert Marshall, Cary Grant, Dickie Moore, Sidney Toler, Hattie McDaniel. Episodic story of performer Dietrich returning to the stage while her chemist husband is off seeking a cure for his illness; plenty of complications ensue, including her evolving relationship with wealthy, powerful Grant. ▼●◗

Blondie series SEE: *Leonard Maltin's Classic Movie Guide*

Blood Alley (1955) C-115m. **½ D: William Wellman. John Wayne, Lauren Bacall, Paul Fix, Mike Mazurki, Anita Ekberg. Enjoyable escapism with Wayne, Bacall, and assorted Chinese escaping down river to Hong Kong pursued by Communists. CinemaScope. ▼●◗

Blood and Black Lace (1964-Italian-French-German) C-88m. *½ D: Mario Bava. Cameron Mitchell, Eva Bartok, Mary Arden. Gruesome thriller about a sex murderer doing in fashion models. Wooden script and performances don't help. Fans of the genre will at least enjoy Bava's imaginative direction. ▼●◗

Blood and Chocolate (2007-British-German-Romanian-U.S.) C-98m. ** D: Katja von Garnier. Agnes Bruckner, Olivier Martinez, Hugh Dancy, Bryan Dick, Katja Riemann, Chris Geere, Tom Harper, John Kerr, Jack Wilson. A teenage werewolf Juliet is torn between loyalty to her pack and love for a human Romeo, while clan leaders violently disapprove. Pallid adaptation of Annette Curtis Klause's 1997 palpably erotic young-adult novel inexplicably (and pointlessly) moves the drastically altered storyline from West Virginia to Romania! Results are thin and semisweet, albeit scenic. Super 35. [PG-13]◗

Blood & Concrete (1991) C-97m. **½ D: Jeffrey Reiner. Billy Zane, Jennifer Beals, Darren McGavin, James Le Gros, Nicholas Worth, William Bastiani, Harry Shearer. Offbeat but way overbaked comic thriller about third-rate car thief Zane and troubled singer Beals, who fall in love and become involved in murder and mayhem. Tries to be hip and stylish, and occasionally succeeds, but too self-conscious for its own good. The full title is BLOOD & CONCRETE: A LOVE STORY. [R] ▼●◗

Blood & Donuts (1995-Canadian) C-89m. *** D: Holly Dale. Gordon Currie, Justin Louis, Helene Clarkson, Fiona Reid, Frank Moore, David Cronenberg. Reluctant vampire Currie crawls into his bag when man first walks on the moon, reemerging in contemporary Toronto, where he holes up in a 24-hour donut shop. Characterful comedy/drama plays colloquially, like DINER, but at night and with fangs. Cronenberg plays a gangster. [R] ▼●

Blood and Roses (1961-Italian) C-74m. **½ D: Roger Vadim. Mel Ferrer, Elsa Martinelli, Annette Vadim, Marc Allegret. This story of a jealous girl's obsession with her family's history of vampirism was based on Sheridan Le Fanu's *Carmilla*. Despite effective moments, film does not succeed. Same story refilmed as THE VAMPIRE LOVERS and THE BLOOD-SPATTERED BRIDE. Technirama.▼

Blood and Sand (1922) **80m.** **½ D: Fred Niblo. Rudolph Valentino, Lila Lee, Nita Naldi, George Field, Walter Long, Leo White. Dated but still absorbing story of bullfighter Valentino torn between good girl Lee and vampish Naldi. Scènes of hero being seduced are laughable, but bullfight material holds up well. Remade in 1941 and 1989.▼○◖

Blood and Sand (1941) **C-123m.** *** D: Rouben Mamoulian. Tyrone Power, Linda Darnell, Rita Hayworth, Nazimova, Anthony Quinn, J. Carrol Naish, John Carradine, George Reeves, Laird Cregar. Pastel remake of Valentino's silent film about naive bullfighter who ignores true-love (Darnell) for temptress (Hayworth). Slow-paced romance uplifted by Nazimova's knowing performance as Power's mother; beautiful color production earned cinematographers Ernest Palmer and Ray Rennahan Oscars.▼◖

Blood and Sand (1989-Spanish) **C-95m.** ** D: Javier Elorrieta. Chris Rydell, Sharon Stone, Ana Torrent, Guillermo Montesinus, Albert Vidal, Simon Andreu, Antonio Glez Flores. Cocky young bullfighter achieves success in the arena and forsakes his loving wife for a sexy siren. Authentic Spanish locations and good bullfighting footage compensate for predictability of this drama; hot sex scenes are what distinguish it from the earlier versions.▼○◖

Blood and Wine (1997) **C-101m.** *** D: Bob Rafelson. Jack Nicholson, Michael Caine, Judy Davis, Stephen Dorff, Jennifer Lopez, Harold Perrineau, Jr. Juicy film noir about a Florida no-good with an embittered wife, a resentful stepson, and a sexy Cuban mistress, who takes on an unlikely partner (an oily, consumptive Caine) for a high-risk jewel robbery. Delicious detail fills this well-thought-out melodrama; only fault is that it goes on a bit too long. Nicholson and Caine make a marvelous team. [R]▼○◖

Blood Barrier (1979-British) **C-86m.** **½ D: Christopher Leitch. Telly Savalas, Danny De La Paz, Eddie Albert, Michael Gazzo, Cecilia Camacho. Savalas plays a maverick border-patrolman who hates slimy Gazzo's exploitation of poor Mexicans, illegally trucked by Gazzo to California to be day laborers. Interesting drama isn't fully developed and suffers from pointless finale. Exteriors filmed in Mexico. Originally titled THE BORDER. Aka BORDER COP. [R] ▼◖

Blood Bath (1966) **80m.** *½ D: Stephanie Rothman, Jack Hill. William Campbell, Jonathan Haze, Sid Haig, Marissa Mathes, Lori Saunders, Sandra Knight. Another AIP

paste-job, with half an hour from a Yugoslavian vampire film worked into tale of California artist who murders his models. Eerie atmosphere, some occasional frissons, but overall a mishmash. Shown on TV as TRACK OF THE VAMPIRE.▼◖

Bloodbrothers (1978) **C-116m.** **½ D: Robert Mulligan. Richard Gere, Paul Sorvino, Tony Lo Bianco, Lelia Goldoni, Yvonne Wilder, Kenneth McMillan, Marilu Henner, Danny Aiello. Interesting if somewhat overblown drama about big-city construction workers. Best when actors have opportunity to underplay, e.g., Sorvino's touching story of baby son's death, Gere's interplay with young hospital patients. Gere stands out as son who wants to break away from family tradition. Mulligan later recut this to 98m. [R]▼◖

Blood Demon, The SEE: **Torture Chamber of Dr. Sadism, The**

Blood Diamond (2006) **C-143m.** **½ D: Edward Zwick. Leonardo DiCaprio, Jennifer Connelly, Djimon Hounsou, Kagiso Kuypers, Arnold Vosloo, Michael Sheen, David Harewood, Basil Wallace, Ntare Mwine, Marius Weyers, Stephen Collins, Jimi Mistry. Loud, intense action drama with an Agenda: mercenary DiCaprio learns that a poor fisherman (Hounsou) who's been separated from his family in Sierra Leone has hidden a huge pink diamond ... and he means to find it, by any means necessary. Strong performances and well-staged action scenes would normally equal good entertainment, but extreme carnage and the heavily pounded message about "conflict diamonds" and their human toll make it difficult to take. Hounsou is outstanding as the simple man whose life is made a living hell in civil war–torn Sierra Leone, circa 1999. Hawk-Scope. [R]◖

Blood Evil SEE: **Demons of the Mind**

Blood Feud (1979-Italian) **C-112m.** ** D: Lina Wertmuller. Sophia Loren, Marcello Mastroianni, Giancarlo Giannini, Turi Ferro. Lawyer Mastroianni and hood Giannini both love Sicilian widow Loren, and she returns their favors. Loud, overblown, ineffective; set during the Fascist '20s. Also known as REVENGE, cut to 99m. [R]▼

Blood Fiend SEE: **Theatre of Death**

Blood for Dracula SEE: **Andy Warhol's Dracula**

Blood From the Mummy's Tomb (1971-British) **C-94m.** *** D: Seth Holt, Michael Carreras. Andrew Keir, Valerie Leon, James Villiers, Hugh Burden. Surprisingly satisfying chiller dealing with attempt at reincarnating ancient Egyptian high priestess. Based on Bram Stoker's *Jewel of the Seven Stars*. Remade as THE AWAKENING. [PG]▼◖

Bloodhounds of Broadway (1952) **C-90m.** **½ D: Harmon Jones. Mitzi Gaynor, Scott Brady, Mitzi Green, Marguerite Chapman,

Michael O'Shea, Wally Vernon, Henry Slate, George E. Stone, Sharon Baird, Charles Buchinski (Bronson). Lightweight musical inspired by Damon Runyon stories. Brady is "Numbers" Foster, a gambler on the lam who takes a shine to backwoods girl Gaynor and brings her to Manhattan, where she's a fish out of water but catches on fast. Green has too little to do, but future Mouseketeer Baird shines in a featured dance number.▶

Bloodhounds of Broadway (1989) **C-93m.** ** D: Howard Brookner. Matt Dillon, Madonna, Jennifer Grey, Rutger Hauer, Randy Quaid, Julie Hagerty, Esai Morales, Anita Morris, Madeleine Potter, Ethan Phillips, Steve Buscemi, Michael Wincott. Bland Damon Runyon tale chronicling the escapades of a gallery of gangsters, gamblers, and showgirl types on the Great White Way during New Year's Eve, 1928. The cast is game and there are some funny bits, but it's mostly a snooze. Documentary director Brookner's sole fiction feature; he died prior to its release. William Burroughs—the subject of one of his earlier films—appears in a small role as a butler. A PBS *American Playhouse* theatrical production. [PG]▼●▶

Blood Hunt SEE: **Thirsty Dead, The**
Blood In Blood Out SEE: **Bound by Honor**
Blood Island SEE: **Shuttered Room, The**
Blood Legacy (1971) **C-90m.** ** D: Carl Monson. John Carradine, Faith Domergue, John Russell, Merry Anders, Jeff Morrow, Richard Davalos. To claim inheritance, heirs to a fortune must spend a night in a "haunted" house. Awfully familiar stuff, helped by a few good scenes, and a familiar cast of veterans. Aka LEGACY OF BLOOD. [R]▼▶

Bloodline (1979) **C-116m.** BOMB D: Terence Young. Audrey Hepburn, Ben Gazzara, James Mason, Michelle Phillips, Omar Sharif, Romy Schneider, Irene Papas, Gert Frobe, Beatrice Straight, Maurice Ronet. Hepburn finds her life endangered after inheriting a Zurich-based pharmaceutical company. Unbearable adaptation of Sidney Sheldon's novel (one of those best-sellers California blondes read on the beach when no one wants to play volleyball). Nearly 40m. of footage added for network showing. Officially released as SIDNEY SHELDON'S BLOODLINE. [R]▼

Blood Oath SEE: **Prisoners of the Sun**
Blood of a Poet, The (1930-French) **52m.** *** D: Jean Cocteau. Lee Miller, Pauline Carton, Odette Talazac, Enrique Rivero, Jean Desbordes. Cocteau's first feature is a highly personal, poetic, symbolic fantasy, which supposedly transpires in a split second: the time it takes for a chimney to crumble and land. Imaginative, dreamlike, and still a visual delight. The commentary is spoken by Cocteau.▼▶

Blood of Dracula's Castle (1967) **C-84m.** BOMB D: Al Adamson. John Carradine,

Paula Raymond, Alex D'Arcy, Robert Dix, Barbara Bishop. Tacky low-budget mixture of vampirism and kinky sex, with Dracula and his bride "collecting" girls and chaining them up. [M]▼▶

Blood of Fu Manchu, The (1968) **C-91m.** ** D: Jesus Franco. Christopher Lee, Tsai Chin, Richard Greene, Gotz George, Howard Marion Crawford, Shirley Eaton, Maria Rohm. Fourth in Lee's FU MANCHU series, several pegs below its predecessors, finds him in the heart of the Amazon, injecting ten beautiful girls with a deadly potion and dispatching them to give the kiss of death to his enemies in various capitals. Aka KISS AND KILL and AGAINST ALL ODDS (1968). Sequel: THE CASTLE OF FU MANCHU. Released theatrically in the U.S. in b&w. Video title: KISS OF DEATH. [M/PG]▼▶

Blood of Ghastly Horror (1972) **C-87m.** BOMB D: Al Adamson. John Carradine, Kent Taylor, Tommy Kirk, Regina Carrol. Carradine stars as Dr. Van Ard, whose brain-transplant experiments lead to murder and mayhem. Ghastly indeed! Made in 1969; also known as THE FIEND WITH THE ATOMIC BRAIN, PSYCHO A GO-GO!, THE LOVE MANIAC, THE MAN WITH THE SYNTHETIC BRAIN, and THE FIEND WITH THE ELECTRONIC BRAIN. Techniscope. ▼▶

Blood of Heroes, The (1990-Australian-U.S.) **C-90m.** *½ D: David Peoples. Rutger Hauer, Joan Chen, Vincent Phillip D'Onofrio, Anna Katarina, Delroy Lindo. In the usual desolate post-nuclear war world one-eyed Hauer and apprentice Chen are specialists at "juggers"—a kind of futuristic rugby where the scorer places a dog's skull atop a vertical stick on the opposing team's goal line. Stick to *Home Run Derby* reruns on ESPN instead; this may be the grimiest movie since C.H.U.D., which did, after all, take place in a sewer. Australian title: SALUTE OF THE JUGGER. [R]▼●▶

Blood on Satan's Claw, The (1971-British) **C-93m.** *** D: Piers Haggard. Patrick Wymark, Linda Hayden, Barry Andrews, Michele Dotrice, Tamara Ustinov. In 17th-century Britain a demon is unearthed which a group of evil farm children begin worshipping, sacrificing other children to it. Richly atmospheric horror film with erotic undertones, somewhat gruesome at times. Original title: SATAN'S SKIN, running 100m. Retitled SATAN'S CLAW. [R]▼

Blood on the Moon (1948) **88m.** *** D: Robert Wise. Robert Mitchum, Barbara Bel Geddes, Robert Preston, Walter Brennan, Phyllis Thaxter, Frank Faylen, Tom Tully, Charles McGraw, Tom Tyler. Straightforward Western tale (from a novel by Luke Short) about a drifter who's hired by his former partner to help him bilk some naive landowners. Mitchum sizes up the situation and decides he doesn't like it; Preston is an unrepentant villain. Watch for that great confrontation scene in a darkened barroom. Also shown in computer-colored version.▼●

Blood on the Sun (1945) **98m.** ✱✱✱ D: Frank Lloyd. James Cagney, Sylvia Sidney, Wallace Ford, Rosemary DeCamp, Robert Armstrong. Newspaper editor Cagney, in Japan during the 1930s, smells trouble coming but is virtually helpless; good melodrama. Also shown in computer-colored version.▼●

Blood Red (1988) **C-91m.** BOMB D: Peter Masterson. Eric Roberts, Giancarlo Giannini, Dennis Hopper, Burt Young, Carlin Glynn, Lara Harris, Joseph Running Fox, Al Ruscio, Michael Madsen, Elias Koteas, Marc Lawrence, Frank Campanella, Aldo Ray, Susan Anspach, Horton Foote, Jr., Julia Roberts. Ruthless, Irish-born Hopper wants to build his railroad through the land of Sicilian immigrant Giannini and his fellow wine-growers in 1890s California. Dreadful film, with lots of explosions; huge, good cast can't save it. Julia Roberts, Eric's kid sister, makes her screen debut as his sibling (and Giannini's daughter). [R]▼

Blood Relatives (1978-French-Canadian) **C-100m.** ✱✱✱ D: Claude Chabrol. Donald Sutherland, Aude Landry, Lisa Langlois, Laurent Malet, Micheline Lanctot, Stephane Audran, Donald Pleasence, David Hemmings. Barely released thriller about a secret, incestuous relationship with deadly consequences. Interesting cast and Chabrol's cold, scientifically masterful direction make this less unpleasant and gory than it might have been. Not released until 1981 in U.S. [R]▼

Blood Salvage (1990) **C-98m.** ✱✱ D: Tucker Johnston. Danny Nelson, Lori Birdsong, John Saxon, Ray Walston, Evander Holyfield. Grisly gorefest (with humorous touches splattered throughout) has religious nutso Nelson running a body parts junkyard and preying on waylaid tourists. Not for the weak-stomached. Coexecutive producer of film, heavyweight boxer Evander Holyfield, challenged his pugilist peers to sit through this one without flinching; he reportedly had no takers. [R]▼●

Bloodsilver SEE: **Beyond the Law** (1968)

Blood Simple. (1984) **C-96m.** ✱✱✱ D: Joel Coen. John Getz, Frances McDormand, Dan Hedaya, Samm-Art Williams, M. Emmet Walsh. Flamboyant homage to film noir made on a shoestring by brothers Joel and Ethan Coen in Texas. A cuckolded husband hires slimy character to kill his wife and her boyfriend . . . but that's just the beginning of this serpentine story. A visual delight, full of show-offy stylistics; just a bit "cold around the heart," to quote an earlier noir classic. McDormand's film debut. Voice of Holly Hunter

can be heard on answering machine. Recut, remixed, restored, and reissued in 2000 with a new 5m. introduction. Remade by Zhang Yimou as A WOMAN, A GUN AND A NOODLE SHOP. [R]▼●|

Bloodsport (1987) **C-92m.** ✱✱ D: Newt Arnold. Jean-Claude Van Damme, Donald Gibb, Leah Ayres, Norman Burton, Forest Whitaker, Bolo Yeung. Belgian-born Van Damme joins the movie macho brigade in this story (based on true events) of American Ninja Frank Dux, the first westerner to win the Kumite, an international martial arts competition that tests its participants to their limits. Violent, low-budget action film has its moments. Followed by three direct-to-video sequels. [R]▼●|

Blood Suckers, The (1967) SEE: **Return from the Past**

Bloodsuckers (1970-British) **C-87m.** ✱½ D: Robert Hartford-Davis. Patrick Macnee, Peter Cushing, Alex Davion, Patrick Mower, Johnny Sekka, Medeline Hinde, Imogen Hassall, Edward Woodward. Confusing horror yarn about ancient vampire cult on Greek island of Hydra, somehow linked to sinister Oxford dons. Mishmash includes many narrated silent sequences and other evidence of considerable post-production tampering. Aka INCENSE FOR THE DAMNED and DOCTORS WEAR SCARLET. [R]▼●|

Blood Tide (1982) **C-82m.** ✱½ D: Richard Jeffries. James Earl Jones, José Ferrer, Lila Kedrova, Mary Louise Weller, Martin Kove, Deborah Shelton. Lovely Greek scenery is the only distinction of this substandard programmer in which a monster from the deep is unleashed, causing predictable mayhem. Good cast shamelessly wasted. Aka THE RED TIDE. [R]▼●|

Blood Ties (1986-Italian) **C-120m.** ✱✱✱ D: Giacomo Battiato. Brad Davis, Tony Lo Bianco, Vincent Spano, Barbara De Rossi, Delia Boccardo, Ricky Tognazzi, Maria Conchita Alonso, Michael Gazzo. Uncompromising crime actioner about an innocent American (Davis), coerced by the mob into assassinating his Sicilian cousin (Lo Bianco), who's been investigating Mafia activities. Good job all around. Originally a four-hour television movie; video version runs 98m.▼

Blood Wedding (1981-U.S.) SEE: **He Knows You're Alone**

Blood Wedding (1981-Spanish) **C-72m.** ✱✱✱ D: Carlos Saura. Antonio Gades, Cristina Hoyos, Juan Antonio Jimenez, Pilar Cardenas, Carmen Villena. Gades' adaptation for ballet of Federico Garcia Lorca's classic tragedy, performed in full costume in a bare rehearsal hall. Saura's direction is best described as intimate in this happy union of dance and film. ▼●|

Blood Work (2002) **C-111m.** ✱✱½ D: Clint Eastwood. Clint Eastwood, Jeff Daniels, Anjelica Huston, Wanda De Jesus, Tina Lifford,

Paul Rodriguez, Dylan Walsh. FBI profiler, who was forced to retire after heart transplant surgery, is persuaded to take on a murder case by the sister of the woman whose heart he inherited. Eastwood has never been more relaxed on-screen, and this movie fits him like a glove, but the buildup of the story is much better than the payoff, with a perfunctory finale and an all-too-obvious revelation about the bad guy. Adapted from the novel by Michael Connelly, which has a more satisfactory ending. Panavision. [R] ▼◗

Bloody Birthday (1986) C-85m. ** D: Ed Hunt. Susan Strasberg, Jose Ferrer, Lori Lethin, Melinda Cordell, Julie Brown, Joe Penny, Billy Jacoby, Michael Dudikoff. Three 10-year-old killer kids go on a rampage; they were born during a lunar eclipse. Formula horror fare "boasts" very tasteless premise but lapses into the usual killing spree. Filmed in 1980. [R] ▼◗

Bloody Dead, The SEE: **Creature With the Blue Hand**

Bloody Judge, The SEE: **Night of the Blood Monster**

Bloody Mama (1970) C-90m. *½ D: Roger Corman. Shelley Winters, Don Stroud, Pat Hingle, Robert De Niro, Clint Kimbrough, Robert Walden, Diane Varsi, Bruce Dern, Pamela Dunlap. Excellent performances cannot save sordid story of Ma Barker and her ugly brood. Film unsuccessfully mixes action narrative with psychological study. [R] ▼◗●

Bloody Sunday (2002-British-Irish) C-110m. *** D: Paul Greengrass. James Nesbitt, Tim Pigott-Smith, Nicholas Farrell, Gerard McSorley, Kathy Kiera Clarke. British soldiers and Irish civil rights workers clash in Derry, Northern Ireland, in 1972, with ramifications that extend to this day. Painstaking re-creation, on the cool side but cumulatively powerful, covers the preliminary events and awful aftermath of what was intended to be a peaceful protest. Documentary-like chronicle is obviously pro-Irish but shows faults on both sides of the conflict. U2's same-named anthem plays over the final credits. [R] ▼◗

Blow (2001) C-124m. ** D: Ted Demme. Johnny Depp, Penélope Cruz, Franka Potente, Paul Reubens, Ray Liotta, Rachel Griffiths, Jordi Molla, Max Perlich, Cliff Curtis, Ethan Suplee, Emma Roberts, Noah Emmerich, Bobcat Goldthwait. Episodic flashback saga of a working-class kid who, having seen his father struggle and his mother nag, vows never to be poor. When he moves to Southern California in the swingin' '60s, he quickly learns that selling drugs is an easy way to make money, and rapidly becomes America's leading cocaine dealer—in between prison terms. Well-acted film based on a real-life figure; only problem is finding a reason to care about him. Panavision. [R] ▼◗

Blow Dry (2001-British-U.S.) C-90m.

** D: Paddy Breathnach. Alan Rickman, Natasha Richardson, Rachel Griffiths, Josh Hartnett, Rachael Leigh Cook, Rosemary Harris, Bill Nighy, Heidi Klum. A small Yorkshire town hosts the National Hairdressing Championship, forcing an ex-husband-and-wife team to put aside their differences for the big wash and curl. The actors try their best but the material (by FULL MONTY writer Simon Beaufoy) is too contrived and calculated, veering wildly from wacky comedy to tearjerker. [R] ▼◗

Blowing Wild (1953) 90m. ** D: Hugo Fregonese. Gary Cooper, Barbara Stanwyck, Ruth Roman, Anthony Quinn, Ward Bond. Tempestuous Stanwyck is married to oil tycoon Quinn, but sets her sights on wildcatter Cooper, who's fully recovered from their one-time affair. Heated emotions can't warm up this plodding story, filmed in Mexico. ▼◗

Blown Away (1994) C-121m. ** D: Stephen Hopkins. Jeff Bridges, Tommy Lee Jones, Lloyd Bridges, Forest Whitaker, Suzy Amis, John Finn, Stephi Lineburg, Loyd Catlett, Caitlin Clarke, Chris De Oni, Ruben Santiago-Hudson. Dreary action thriller with Irish wacko Jones targeting Boston's bomb removal squad—and one member in particular (Bridges, a former IRA crony)—with his insidious explosions. Irish accents come and go, and so does story interest, which trods on all-too-familiar turf. Bridges Sr. is fun to watch as a wily old son of Eire. Cuba Gooding, Jr., appears unbilled. Super 35. [R] ▼◗●

Blow Out (1981) C-107m. **½ D: Brian De Palma. John Travolta, Nancy Allen, John Lithgow, Dennis Franz, Peter Boyden. Intriguing variation on Antonioni's BLOWUP (with a similar title, no less!) set in Philadelphia, about a sound-effects man who records a car accident that turns out to be a politically motivated murder. Absorbing most of the way, but weakened by show-off camerawork and logic loop-holes. Panavision. [R] ▼◗●

Blowup (1966-British-Italian) C-111m. ***½ D: Michelangelo Antonioni. Vanessa Redgrave, David Hemmings, Sarah Miles, Jill Kennington, Verushka, Peter Bowles, Jane Birkin, Gillian Hills, The Yardbirds. Writer-director Antonioni's hypnotic pop-culture parable of photographer caught in passive lifestyle during the swinging '60s. Arresting, provocative film, rich in color symbolism, many-layered meanings. Music by Herbie Hancock. ▼◗●

Blue (1968) C-113m. *½ D: Silvio Narizzano. Terence Stamp, Joanna Pettet, Karl Malden, Ricardo Montalban, Joe DeSantis, Sally Kirkland. Undistinguished, poorly written Western about American-born, Mexican-raised boy who trusts no one until bullet wounds force him to trust a woman. See also: FADE-IN. Panavision. ▼◗●

Blue (1993-French) **C-100m.** ****½** D: Krzysztof Kieslowski. Juliette Binoche, Benoit Regent, Florence Pernel, Charlotte Very, Helene Vincent, Philippe Volter, Hugues Quester, Emmanuelle Riva, Julie Delpy. Binoche loses her family in a tragic accident and decides to radically change her world; she leaves behind any memories of her husband, a renowned composer, and moves into a Paris flat to contemplate life. Slow-moving drama is borderline interesting but remains more a showcase for its leading lady than anything else. First of Polish director Kieslowski's "Three Colors" trilogy probing life in contemporary Europe: BLUE/"Liberty"; WHITE/"Equality"; RED/"Fraternity." ▼O◖

Blue Angel, The (1930-German) **106m.** *****½** D: Josef von Sternberg. Marlene Dietrich, Emil Jannings, Kurt Gerron, Rosa Valetti, Hans Albers. Ever-fascinating film classic with Jannings as stuffy professor who falls blindly in love with cabaret entertainer Lola-Lola (Dietrich), who ruins his life. Dietrich introduces "Falling in Love Again"; this role made her an international star. Robert Liebman scripted, from Heinrich Mann's novel *Professor Unrath*. Simultaneously shot in German and English versions; the former is obviously superior. Remade in 1959. ▼O◖

Blue Angel, The (1959) **C-107m.** ***½** D: Edward Dmytryk. Curt Jurgens, May Britt, Theodore Bikel, John Banner, Ludwig Stossel, Fabrizio Mioni. Disastrous remake of Josef von Sternberg–Marlene Dietrich classic, updated to 1950s Germany, from Heinrich Mann's novel of precise professor won over by tawdry nightclub singer. CinemaScope.

Bluebeard (1944) **73m.** ******* D: Edgar G. Ulmer. Jean Parker, John Carradine, Nils Asther, Ludwig Stossel, Iris Adrian, Emmett Lynn. Surprisingly effective story set in 19th-century Paris. Incurable strangler Carradine falls for smart girl Parker, who senses that something is wrong. ▼◖

Bluebeard (1962-French-Italian) **C-114m.** ****½** D: Claude Chabrol. Charles Denner, Michele Morgan, Danielle Darrieux, Hildegarde Neff, Stephane Audran, Catherine Rouvel, Françoise Lugagne. Retelling of life of French wife-killer, far less witty than Chaplin's MONSIEUR VERDOUX. Original French title: LANDRU. ▼

Bluebeard (1972) **C-125m.** ****** D: Edward Dmytryk. Richard Burton, Raquel Welch, Virna Lisi, Joey Heatherton, Nathalie Delon, Karin Schubert. Burton doesn't make much of an impression as world's most famous ladykiller. Women are all beautiful, but script gives them little to do. International production. [R] ▼◖

Bluebeard's Eighth Wife (1938) **80m.** ****** D: Ernst Lubitsch. Claudette Colbert, Gary Cooper, David Niven, Edward Everett Horton, Elizabeth Patterson, Herman Bing. Contrived comedy about a woman determined to gain the upper hand over an oft-married millionaire. One of Lubitsch's weakest films, notable mainly for the way its two stars "meet cute." Script by Billy Wilder and Charles Brackett. Previously filmed in 1923. ▼◖

Blue Bird, The (1940) **C-88m.** ****** D: Walter Lang. Shirley Temple, Spring Byington, Nigel Bruce, Gale Sondergaard, Eddie Collins, Sybil Jason. Released one year after THE WIZARD OF OZ, this lavish Technicolor fantasy (based on the famous play by Maurice Maeterlinck) has everything but charm. Even Shirley seems stiff. Filmed before in 1918, remade in 1976. ▼◖

Blue Bird, The (1976-Russian-U.S.) **C-99m.** ****** D: George Cukor. Todd Lookinland, Patsy Kensit, Elizabeth Taylor, Jane Fonda, Ava Gardner, Cicely Tyson George Cole, Will Geer, Robert Morley, Harry Andrews. Posh, star-studded but heavy-handed fantasy based on Maeterlinck's play about children seeking the bluebird of happiness. First coproduction between U.S. and Russia is unbelievably draggy. [G]

Blue Car (2003) **C-96m.** ******* D: Karen Moncrieff. David Strathairn, Agnes Bruckner, Margaret Colin, A. J. Buckley, Regan Arnold, Frances Fisher. Well-told story of an adolescent girl (Bruckner) who's never recovered from the blow of her father walking out on the family. She finds an outlet in writing poetry, encouraged by her English teacher (Strathairn), who also becomes a kind of father figure—for a while. Impressive feature debut for writer-director Moncrieff. [R] ▼◖

Blue Chips (1994) **C-101m.** ****½** D: William Friedkin. Nick Nolte, Mary McDonnell, J. T. Walsh, Ed O'Neill, Alfre Woodard, Bob Cousy, Shaquille O'Neal, Anfernee "Penny" Hardaway, Matt Nover, Anthony C. Hall, Robert Wuhl, Jerry Tarkanian, Bobby Knight, Richard Pitino, George Raveling. After his first losing season, hard-driving collegiate basketball coach Nolte agrees to look the other way while fat-cat recruiters bribe new talent to join his team. Reasonably compelling at first, then all too obvious and predictable. Written by Ron Shelton. Towering NBA superstar O'Neal is engaging as one of the recruits; other hoop stars like Larry Bird have small parts, while legendary champion Cousy plays the college athletic director. Louis Gossett, Jr., appears unbilled. [PG-13] ▼O◖

Blue City (1986) **C-83m.** BOMB D: Michelle Manning. Judd Nelson, Ally Sheedy, David Caruso, Paul Winfield, Scott Wilson, Anita Morris. Perfectly awful film about wiseguy kid who returns to Florida hometown after five years, discovers that his father was killed, and vows to avenge (and solve) his murder. Senseless and stupid; Nelson's unappealing character seems to possess a one-word vocabulary, and the word *isn't* fudge. Based on a good book by Ross Macdonald. [R]▼●)

Blue Collar (1978) **C-114m.** ***½ D: Paul Schrader. Richard Pryor, Harvey Keitel, Yaphet Kotto, Ed Begley, Jr., Harry Bellaver, George Memmoli. Punchy, muckraking exposé melodrama with Pryor, Keitel, and Kotto delivering strong performances as auto workers who find that it isn't just management ripping them off—it's their own union. Schrader's directing debut. [R]▼●)

Blue Crush (2002) **C-104m.** ** D: John Stockwell. Kate Bosworth, Matthew Davis, Michelle Rodriguez, Sanoe Lake, Mika Boorem, Chris Taloa, Kala Alexander, Faizon Love. Young woman dreams of winning a surfing championship in Hawaii—in spite of prejudice against females in the sport and other obstacles in her path, such as having to make a living and raise her kid sister. Then Mr. Right comes along (a handsome football star who's vacationing on the island) just in time to blur her focus. Bosworth is very watchable, but this sappy story never leaves shallow water. Several professional surfers appear as themselves. Followed by a direct-to-DVD sequel, BLUE CRUSH 2. [PG-13]▼)

Blue Dahlia, The (1946) **99m.** *** D: George Marshall. Alan Ladd, Veronica Lake, William Bendix, Howard da Silva, Hugh Beaumont, Doris Dowling. Exciting Raymond Chandler–scripted melodrama has Ladd returning from military service to find wife unfaithful. She's murdered, he's suspected in well-turned film. Produced by John Houseman. ▼

Blue Denim (1959) **89m.** *** D: Philip Dunne. Carol Lynley, Brandon de Wilde, Macdonald Carey, Marsha Hunt, Warren Berlinger, Roberta Shore. De Wilde and Lynley are striking as teenagers faced with Carol's pregnancy. Dated and naive, but well-acted adaptation of Broadway play. CinemaScope.

Blue Gardenia, The (1953) **90m.** *** D: Fritz Lang. Anne Baxter, Richard Conte, Ann Sothern, Raymond Burr, Jeff Donnell, George Reeves, Nat King Cole. Engaging murder caper with 1940s flavor. Baxter is accused of murdering wolfish Burr, decides to take columnist Conte's offer of help. Solid film with twist ending. ▼)

Blue Hawaii (1961) **C-101m.** **½ D: Norman Taurog. Elvis Presley, Joan Blackman, Angela Lansbury, Roland Winters, Iris Adrian. Agreeable Presley vehicle bolstered by Lansbury's presence as mother of ex-G.I. (Presley) returning to islands and working with tourist agency. Elvis performs one of his prettiest hits, "Can't Help Falling in Love." Panavision. ▼●)

Blue Ice (1992-British-U.S.) **C-105m.** **½ D: Russell Mulcahy. Michael Caine, Sean Young, Ian Holm, Alun Armstrong, Sam Kelly, Jack Shepherd. Retired British agent Caine is dragged out of his beloved jazz club and back into service to help crack an illegal arms ring. Cabaret legend Bobby Short has an acting role here, and unbilled Bob Hoskins turns up briefly as Caine's chum from the old days. U.S. debut on cable TV. ▼●)

Blue Iguana, The (1988) **C-88m.** BOMB D: John Lafia. Dylan McDermott, Jessica Harper, James Russo, Pamela Gidley, Tovah Feldshuh, Dean Stockwell, Yano Anaya, Flea, Michele Seipp. Amateurish spoof is a hybrid of B Western and film noir, with a down-and-out bounty hunter on a suicide mission to recover $20 million in contraband money from a gaggle of bad guys south of the border. This turkey barely made it to theaters; even an amusing cameo by Stockwell can't save it. [R]▼●)

Blue in the Face (1995) **C-84m.** *½ D: Wayne Wang, Paul Auster. Harvey Keitel, Lou Reed, Michael J. Fox, Roseanne, Mel Gorham, Jim Jarmusch, Lily Tomlin, Jared Harris, Giancarlo Esposito, Jose Zuniga, Victor Argo, Madonna, Mira Sorvino, Keith David, RuPaul. Meandering, overindulgent mess filmed immediately after SMOKE and improvised from sketches developed by Wang and Auster in collaboration with the actors. Set mostly in and around the Brooklyn cigar store managed by Keitel. In desperate need of a script. [R]▼●)

Blue Juice (1995-British) **C-99m.** ** D: Carl Prechezer. Sean Pertwee, Catherine Zeta-Jones, Steven Mackintosh, Peter Gunn, Ewan McGregor, Heathcote Williams, Colette Brown, Jenny Agutter. Low-octane tale of aging, self-absorbed surfer boy Pertwee, who's constantly putting off practical-minded (and increasingly flustered) girlfriend Zeta-Jones to hang with his mates. Superficial and predictable to an extreme; of note only for the early-career presence of Zeta-Jones and McGregor (as an obnoxious, pathetic slacker/drug dealer). [R]▼)

Blue Kite, The (1993-Chinese) **C-140m.** *** D: Tian Zhuangzhuang. Yi Tian, Zhang Wenyao, Chen Xiaoman, Lu Liping, Pu Quanxin, Li Xuejian. Absorbing, uncompromising saga of the life and times of—and emotional upheaval within—one Chinese family during the tumultuous 1950s and '60s, told from the point of view of a child. An unsubtle condemnation of blind revolution and the political system in Communist China. It was (unsurprisingly) highly controversial back home; at one point its filming was halted because of the scenario's "political leanings."▼●)

Blue Lagoon, The (1949-British) **C-101m.**

*** D: Frank Launder. Jean Simmons, Donald Houston, Noel Purcell, Cyril Cusack, Maurice Denham. Idyllic romance of Simmons and Houston, shipwrecked on tropic isle, falling in love as they grow to maturity; slowly paced but refreshing. Remade in 1980.

Blue Lagoon, The (1980) C-104m. *½ D: Randal Kleiser. Brooke Shields, Christopher Atkins, Leo McKern, William Daniels. Remake of the 1949 film is little more than softcore cinema for the heavy-petting set, as two children become sexually aware of each other after being shipwrecked on an island for several years. Nestor Almendros' photography can't save it. Followed over a decade later by RETURN TO THE BLUE LAGOON. [R]▼●)

Blue Lamp, The (1950-British) 84m. *** D: Basil Dearden. Jack Warner, Jimmy Hanley, Dirk Bogarde, Robert Flemyng, Bernard Lee, Peggy Evans, Patric Doonan, Gladys Henson, Meredith Edwards. Crackerjack manhunt thriller about Scotland Yard's search for murderer of policeman. Unpretentious and exciting—a key British postwar film. Music hall star Tessie O'Shea appears as herself.▼

Blue Manhattan SEE: **Hi, Mom!**

Blue Max, The (1966) C-156m. **½ D: John Guillermin. George Peppard, James Mason, Ursula Andress, Jeremy Kemp, Carl Schell. Fantastic aerial photography and memorable Jerry Goldsmith score are the assets of this silly drama, taken from German point of view, about dogfighting in WW1. Steamy Peppard-Andress love scenes aren't bad either. CinemaScope.▼●)

Blue Monkey (1987) C-98m. BOMB D: William Fruet. Steve Railsback, Gwynyth Walsh, Susan Anspach, John Vernon, Joe Flaherty, Robin Duke, Sarah Polley. Silly monster film set at hospital that's quarantined after a monster escapes. Poorly filmed in semi-darkness. Title is meaningless and randomly selected; it was originally called GREEN MONKEY! Video title: INSECT. [R]▼●

Blue Murder at St. Trinian's (1957-British) 86m. **½ D: Frank Launder. Terry-Thomas, George Cole, Joyce Grenfell, Lionel Jeffries, Eric Barker, Lisa Gastoni, Ferdy Mayne, Alastair Sim. OK entry in the series of farces set at the St. Trinian's School for Girls. Ever-mischievous students win a trip to the continent and become immersed in various hijinks. Sim appears too briefly (in drag) as Miss Amelia Fritton, the school's headmistress.▼

Blues Brothers, The (1980) C-130m. *** D: John Landis. John Belushi, Dan Aykroyd, The Blues Brothers Band, Cab Calloway, John Candy, Henry Gibson, Carrie Fisher, Charles Napier, Jeff Morris, Ray Charles, Aretha Franklin, James Brown, Kathleen Freeman. Engagingly nutty comedy about the title characters (deadpan musical performers introduced on TV's *Saturday Night Live*) trying to raise money to save their orphanage by reuniting their old band—and nearly destroying Chicago in the process. Off the wall from start to finish, with some fine music woven in, including wonderful numbers by Franklin and Calloway. Numerous cameos include Steven Spielberg, Frank Oz, Steve Lawrence, John Lee Hooker, Twiggy, and Paul Reubens (Pee-wee Herman). Special edition runs 147m. Followed by a sequel. [R]▼●)

Blues Brothers 2000 (1998) C-123m. **½ D: John Landis. Dan Aykroyd, John Goodman, Joe Morton, Nia Peeples, Kathleen Freeman, J. Evan Bonifant, Frank Oz, Steve Lawrence, Darrell Hammond, Erykah Badu. Just sprung from prison, Elwood Blues reunites his old band (minus brother Jake—the late John Belushi), with a young orphan (Bonifant) in tow. Silly "plot" goes on too long, but high spirits prevail, especially during infectious music numbers like "634-5789" and Aretha Franklin's "Respect." Incredible lineup of guest musicians includes B.B. King, James Brown, Junior Wells, Isaac Hayes, Eric Clapton, Dr. John, Wilson Pickett, Bo Diddley, Eddie Floyd, Jonny Lang, Billy Preston, Travis Tritt, and music supervisor Paul Shaffer. Aykroyd and Landis coproduced and scripted. [PG-13]▼●)

Blues for Lovers (1964-British) 89m. ** D: Paul Henreid. Ray Charles, Tom Bell, Mary Peach, Dawn Addams, Piers Bishop, Betty McDowall. Story of Charles (playing himself) and blind child is maudlin, but fans will like generous footage devoted to Ray's song hits, including "I Got a Woman" and "What'd I Say?" Aka BALLAD IN BLUE.▼)

Blues in the Night (1941) 88m. **½ D: Anatole Litvak. Priscilla Lane, Richard Whorf, Betty Field, Lloyd Nolan, Jack Carson, Elia Kazan, Wallace Ford, Billy Halop, Peter Whitney. Intriguing musical drama abandons early promise for soapy, silly melodramatics, in story of self-destructive musician (Whorf) and his band (young Kazan is featured as clarinetist). Good moments, wonderful Warner Bros. montages, but the great title song is never played once in its entirety!)

Blue Skies (1946) C-104m. *** D: Stuart Heisler. Fred Astaire, Bing Crosby, Joan Caulfield, Billy De Wolfe, Olga San Juan, Frank Faylen. Astaire and Crosby play onetime show-biz partners and rivals in this paper-thin vehicle kept aloft by lots and lots of Irving Berlin songs. Highlights: Astaire's terrific "Puttin' on the Ritz," star duo's "A Couple of Song and Dance Men."▼●)

Blue Skies Again (1983) C-90m. **½ D: Richard Michaels. Harry Hamlin, Robyn Barto, Mimi Rogers, Kenneth McMillan,

Dana Elcar, Andy Garcia, Marcos Gonzales. Friendly, well-meaning but ultimately minor-league chronicle of a young woman (Barto) attempting to play professional baseball. [PG]▼

Blue Sky (1994) **C-101m.** **½ D: Tony Richardson. Jessica Lange, Tommy Lee Jones, Powers Boothe, Carrie Snodgress, Amy Locane, Chris O'Donnell, Mitchell Ryan, Dale Dye, Tim Scott, Annie Ross, Anna Klemp. A dedicated military man endures continual embarrassment by his teasingly sexy (and emotionally unstable) wife, for one simple reason: he loves her. Intelligent and compassionate drama, set in the early 1960s, loses its way as it gets involved in a nuclear cover-up subplot, but rates as a must-see for anyone who admires its stars: both Jones and Lange (in an Oscar-winning performance) are extraordinarily good. Shot in 1990; director Richardson died the following year. Timothy Bottoms appears unbilled. [PG-13]▼●🅓

Blue Steel (1990) **C-102m.** *½ D: Kathryn Bigelow. Jamie Lee Curtis, Ron Silver, Clancy Brown, Elizabeth Pena, Louise Fletcher, Philip Bosco, Kevin Dunn, Richard Jenkins. Stupid thriller with Curtis as a rookie cop stalked by a slick psycho (Silver) in N.Y.C. Laughably ludicrous dialogue is matched by preposterous story turns. [R]▼●🅓

Blue Streak (1999) **C-94m.** ** D: Les Mayfield. Martin Lawrence, Luke Wilson, Dave Chappelle, William Forsythe, Nicole Ari Parker, Peter Greene. Loud boilerplate action comedy casts Lawrence as a so-called master thief who has socked away a stolen jewel in the innards of a construction site—only to discover, upon his release from jail, that the completed structure is a police precinct. The solution is to become a cop, just as the solution for Lawrence might be to stay away from moldy scripts like this. [PG-13]▼🅓

Blue Sunshine (1976) **C-97m.** **½ D: Jeff Lieberman. Zalman King, Deborah Winters, Mark Goddard, Robert Walden, Charles Siebert. Young man accused of murders eludes cops, discovers that apparently "random" killings derive from delayed drug reactions of 10-year-old college class. Offbeat psychological thriller, quite violent at times. [R]▼🅓

Blue Thunder (1983) **C-108m.** ** D: John Badham. Roy Scheider, Malcolm McDowell, Candy Clark, Daniel Stern, Warren Oates, Paul Roebling, Joe Santos. Slick action film built around L.A.'s police helicopter surveillance team. Fun at first, but gets stupider (and crueler) as film goes on—with villainous McDowell character especially ludicrous. Even escapist fare has to be believable on its own terms. Later a TV series. Panavision. [R]▼●🅓

Blue Valentine (2010) **C-112m.** *** D: Derek Cianfrance. Ryan Gosling, Michelle Williams, Faith Wladyka, John Doman, Mike Vogel, Ben Shenkman, Jen Jones, Maryann Plunkett. Compelling look at both the beginning and end of a relationship, from the first flush of attraction to the dissolution of a marriage. Film seamlessly hops back and forth in time, from the moment free-spirited, working-class Gosling woos med student Williams to the day they make their last attempt to reconnect as a couple—and as the parents of a sweet little girl. Sparked by striking, emotionally raw performances from its stars in a Cassavetes vein. Longish but well done. [R]🅓

Blue Veil, The (1951) **113m.** *** D: Curtis Bernhardt. Jane Wyman, Charles Laughton, Joan Blondell, Richard Carlson, Agnes Moorehead, Don Taylor, Audrey Totter, Everett Sloane, Cyril Cusack, Natalie Wood, Warner Anderson, Vivian Vance, Philip Ober. Wyman is self-sacrificing nursemaid whose life story is chronicled with intertwined episodes of her charges and their families. Well done.

Blue Velvet (1986) **C-120m.** ** D: David Lynch. Kyle MacLachlan, Isabella Rossellini, Dennis Hopper, Laura Dern, Hope Lange, Dean Stockwell, Jack Nance, Brad Dourif. Terminally weird, though flamboyantly original film about a young man's involvement in a small-town mystery involving a kinky nightclub singer, a sadistic kidnapper/drug dealer, and other swell folks. A highly individual look at the bizarre elements just behind the facade of a picture-perfect American town. Too audacious to be easily dismissed, but too strange to be easily enjoyed . . . yet this was one of the most critically praised movies of 1986! The director also wrote this one. J-D-C Scope. [R]▼●🅓

Blue Water, White Death (1971) **C-99m.** *** D: Peter Gimbel, James Lipscomb. Vivid documentary on one of the sea's most voracious and feared predators, the great white shark; terrifying underwater scenes but somewhat overstated. Techniscope. [G]🅓

Blume in Love (1973) **C-117m.** **½ D: Paul Mazursky. George Segal, Susan Anspach, Kris Kristofferson, Marsha Mason, Shelley Winters, Paul Mazursky. Self-indulgent film about divorce-lawyer Segal refusing to accept fact that his wife (Anspach) has walked out on him, determining to win her back. Good look at modern marriages, but overlong, rambling; Kristofferson delightful as man who moves in with Anspach. [R]▼🅓

B. Monkey (1999-British-U.S.) **C-90m.** ** D: Michael Radford. Asia Argento, Jared Harris, Jonathan Rhys Meyers, Rupert Everett, Tim Woodward, Ian Hart, Eddie Marsan. Superficial fluff about a mild-mannered British schoolteacher who falls for a sultry bank robber trying to leave her criminal past behind. Radford's first film since IL POSTINO is a disappointment, particularly since most of it reportedly ended up on the cutting room floor. Still watchable, with a smoldering central performance from Argento, daughter of horrormeister Dario Argento. Completed in 1996. [R] ▼❶

BMX Bandits (1983-Australian) **C-88m.** ** D: Brian Trenchard-Smith. David Argue, John Ley, Nicole Kidman, Angelo D'Angelo, James Lugton, Bryan Marshall. Two adolescent boys crash their BMX bikes. While trying to earn money to fix them, they and pal Kidman stumble onto a cache of stolen walkie-talkies. Harmless popcorn fodder, fashioned to appeal to young teens and preteens. One of Kidman's first film appearances. Panavision. ▼❶

Boarding Gate (2007-French) **C-105m.** *½ D: Olivier Assayas. Asia Argento, Michael Madsen, Carl Ng, Kelly Lin, Joana Preiss, Alex Descas, Kim Gordon. Argento plays an unscrupulous former hooker involved in corporate espionage and international drug smuggling in Paris and the Far East. She has little interest in her ex (shady businessman Madsen) but has the hots for her tough boss (Ng). Argento is rarely off-screen in this Eurotrashy thriller that had potential, but story of jet-set criminal lowlifes isn't as fascinating or meaningful (or coherent or intelligible) as intended, and this globe-trotting film goes nowhere. [R] ❶

Boarding School (1977-German) **C-98m.** *½ D: Andre Farwagi. Nastassja Kinski, Gerry Sundquist, Kurt Raab, Sean Chapman. Sex comedy with Kinski in one of her first starring roles, as an American girl in an exclusive Swiss boarding school, circa 1956. She devises a ruse of the girls pretending to be prostitutes in order to seduce cute guys at nearby boys' school. Original title: THE PASSION FLOWER HOTEL. ▼❶

Boardwalk (1979) **C-98m.** **½ D: Stephen Verona. Ruth Gordon, Lee Strasberg, Janet Leigh, Joe Silver, Eli Mintz, Eddie Barth. Poignant view of elderly couple struggling to survive in decaying neighborhood missteps into DEATH WISH melodramatics for its finale. Fine performances, including Leigh as duty-bound daughter.

Boat, The SEE: **Das Boot**

Boat People (1983-Hong Kong-Chinese) **C-106m.** ***½ D: Ann Hui. Lam Chi-Cheung, Cora Miao, Season Ma, Andy Lau, Paul Ching. Harrowing, heartbreaking, highly provocative account of Japanese photojournalist Chi-Cheung's experiences in Vietnam after Liberation, particularly his friendship with 14-year-old Ma and her family. [R]

Boat Trip (2003) **C-95m.** BOMB D: Mort Nathan. Cuba Gooding, Jr., Horatio Sanz, Roselyn Sanchez, Vivica A. Fox, Maurice Godin, Roger Moore, Lin Shaye, Victoria

Silvstedt, Richard Roundtree, Bob Gunton, Thomas Lennon. Appallingly bad comedy about two friends who book a cruise in order to meet women—unaware that they're heading out on a ship full of gay men. Gooding is as likable as ever, but the cumulative effect of this unfunny, tasteless, derivative film is deadening. Will Ferrell appears unbilled. [R] ▼❶

Bob & Carol & Ted & Alice (1969) **C-104m.** *** D: Paul Mazursky. Natalie Wood, Robert Culp, Elliott Gould, Dyan Cannon, Horst Ebersberg, Greg Mullavey, Lee Bergere. Glossy look at modern lifestyles; ultrasophisticated couple (Wood & Culp) try to modernize thinking of their best friends (Gould & Cannon) about sexual freedom. Sharp observations, fine performances, marred by silly, pretentious finale. Written by Mazursky and Larry Tucker; Mazursky's directorial debut. Later a short-lived TV series. [R] ▼❶

Bobbie Jo and the Outlaw (1976) **C-89m.** ** D: Mark L. Lester. Marjoe Gortner, Lynda Carter, Jesse Vint, Merrie Lynn Ross, Belinda Balaski, Peggy Stewart. Competent but excessively violent drive-in fare; bored carhop Carter hooks up with Marjoe and his gang for a robbing and killing spree. Noteworthy for a couple of glimpses of Lynda's left breast and the occasional film-buff in-joke (e.g., a tobacco-chewing deputy named Abel Gance), courtesy scripter Vernon Zimmerman. [R] ▼❶

Bobby (2006) **C-120m.** **½ D: Emilio Estevez. Harry Belafonte, Joy Bryant, Nick Cannon, Emilio Estevez, Laurence Fishburne, Brian Geraghty, Heather Graham, Anthony Hopkins, Helen Hunt, Joshua Jackson, David Krumholtz, Ashton Kutcher, Shia LaBeouf, Lindsay Lohan, William H. Macy, Svetlana Metkina, Demi Moore, Freddy Rodriguez, Martin Sheen, Christian Slater, Sharon Stone, Jacob Vargas, Mary Elizabeth Winstead, Elijah Wood. Twenty-two lives are interwoven during the course of one day—June 4, 1968—at L.A.'s fabled Ambassador Hotel, from kitchen workers to affluent guests to idealistic campaigners for Senator Robert F. Kennedy. The story ends tragically with the assassination of RFK, who has just won California's Democratic primary. Writer-director Estevez skillfully captures the period and the atmosphere of this grand hotel, but some of his characters' stories aren't terribly interesting or relevant. An emotional finale helps. Super 35. [R] ❶

Bobby Deerfield (1977) **C-124m.** BOMB D: Sydney Pollack. Al Pacino, Marthe Keller, Anny Duperey, Walter McGinn, Romolo Valli, Stephen Meldegg. Grand Prix race-car driver Pacino romances Florentine aristocrat Keller, who is dying of that unnamed disease that seems disproportionately to afflict movie heroines. Her suffering is nothing compared to the audience's; even

Pacino is deadening. Pollack later recut this to 99m. Panavision. [PG]▼◗

Bobby Jones: Stroke of Genius (2004) C-126m. ** D: Rowdy Herrington. Jim Caviezel, Claire Forlani, Jeremy Northam, Malcolm McDowell, Connie Ray, Brett Rice, Aidan Quinn. Overlong sports bio about the celebrated Southern gentleman golfer who was the idol of millions during the 1920s. Scenario lambastes athletes who dare to expect payment for their labors; Jones is depicted as a deity simply because he chose to maintain his amateur standing. Northam is well cast as Walter Hagen, Jones' links rival. Super 35. [PG]▼◗

Bob Le Flambeur (1955-French) 102m. *** D: Jean-Pierre Melville. Roger Duchesne, Isabel Corey, Daniel Cauchy, Guy Decomble, Andre Garet, Gerard Buhr, Howard Vernon. Witty inversion of THE ASPHALT JUNGLE: hard-luck gambler Duchesne enlists pals in intricate plan to knock over Deauville casino, but everything is so stacked against them that we almost hope he'll call it off. Clever and atmospheric, blessed with eerily sexy Corey and a great closing line. Unreleased in the U.S. until 1982. Remade as THE GOOD THIEF. [PG]▼◗

Bobo, The (1967) C-105m. ** D: Robert Parrish. Peter Sellers, Britt Ekland, Rossano Brazzi, Adolfo Celi, Ferdy Mayne. Misfire comedy casts Sellers as aspiring singing matador who's promised a booking if he can seduce Ekland, the most desirable woman in Barcelona, within three days. Filmed in Spain and Rome.▼◗

Bob Roberts (1992) C-101m. *** D: Tim Robbins. Tim Robbins, Giancarlo Esposito, Ray Wise, Rebecca Jenkins, Harry J. Lennix, John Ottavino, Robert Stanton, Alan Rickman, Gore Vidal, Brian Murray, Anita Gillette, David Strathairn, Jack Black, Jeremy Piven. Smart, funny political satire about a right-wing, folk-singing Senatorial candidate who knows how to manipulate an audience—and the media. Turns into a political polemic near the end, using speechifying instead of incident and dialogue to make its points. Still, a stimulating ride, and an impressive writing-directing debut for Robbins, who also composed the songs with his brother David. Funny cameos by a variety of famous actors as air-headed TV news anchors and reporters; Bob Balaban and John Cusack add verisimilitude to a pseudo-*Saturday Night Live* sequence. [R]▼◗

Boccaccio '70 (1962-Italian) C-165m. *** D: Vittorio De Sica, Luchino Visconti, Federico Fellini. Anita Ekberg, Sophia Loren, Romy Schneider, Peppino De Filippo, Dante Maggio, Tomas Milian. Trio of episodes: "The Raffle"—timid soul wins a liaison with a girl as prize; "The Job"—aristocrat's wife takes a job as her husband's mistress;

"The Temptation of Dr. Antonio"—fantasy of puritanical fanatic and a voluptuous poster picture which comes alive. A fourth episode, directed by Mario Monicelli, was dropped for U.S. release.▼◗

Bodies, Rest & Motion (1993) C-93m. **½ D: Michael Steinberg. Phoebe Cates, Bridget Fonda, Tim Roth, Eric Stoltz, Alicia Witt, Rich Wheeler. Low-key vignette about four young people trying to connect with each other—and with their own feelings—in a bleak Arizona town. Too obviously based on a stage play (by Roger Hedden), this laid-back film is often inert, but appealing performances—especially by Fonda and Stoltz—give it some spark. Amusing cameo by Bridget's father Peter Fonda. Stoltz also coproduced. [R]▼◗◗

Body, The (2001) C-100m. ** D: Jonas McCord. Antonio Banderas, Olivia Williams, Derek Jacobi, John Wood, John Shrapnel, Jason Flemyng, Muhamed Bakri. Vatican priest Banderas and Israeli archeologist Williams go head-to-head when they discover an ancient skeleton that just might be the body of Christ. Spiritual thriller isn't quite as hokey as it sounds but it isn't all that great either, especially with its cheesy shoot-out action climax. Shimmering cinematography from Vilmos Zsigmond helps. Shot on location in Jerusalem. Panavision. [PG-13]▼◗

Body and Soul (1947) 104m. **** D: Robert Rossen. John Garfield, Lilli Palmer, Hazel Brooks, Anne Revere, William Conrad, Joseph Pevney, Canada Lee. Most boxing films pale next to this classic (written by Abraham Polonsky) of Garfield working his way up by devious means, becoming famous champ. Superb photography by James Wong Howe, and Oscar-winning editing by Francis Lyon and Robert Parrish. Remade in 1981 and for TV in 1998.▼◗

Body and Soul (1981) C-100m. *½ D: George Bowers. Leon Isaac Kennedy, Jayne Kennedy, Peter Lawford, Michael V. Gazzo, Perry Lang, Kim Hamilton. Poor remake of the 1947 classic, with welterweight boxer Kennedy shunning corruption and becoming champion. Leon tries, but is defeated by his paper-thin screenplay. Muhammad Ali appears briefly as himself. [R]▼◗

Body Count (1998) C-80m. BOMB D: Robert Patton-Spruill. David Caruso, Ving Rhames, Linda Fiorentino, John Leguizamo, Donnie Wahlberg, Forest Whitaker. Good cast in an irredeemably awful film that (understandably) didn't make it to theaters in the U.S. A daring museum heist goes bad, leaving the volatile partners to drive to Miami to make their dropoff—if they can avoid killing each other along the way. A more despicable bunch of characters would be hard to imagine. [R]▼◗

Body Double (1984) C-109m. *½ D: Brian De Palma. Craig Wasson, Gregg Henry,

Melanie Griffith, Deborah Shelton, Guy Boyd, Dennis Franz. Gullible (and brainless) actor Wasson becomes obsessed with beautiful woman he's been eyeing through telescope and soon finds himself embroiled in labyrinthine murder plot. Another sleazy fetish film from De Palma, who not only rips off Hitchcock (again) but even himself (OBSESSION, DRESSED TO KILL, BLOW OUT). Some clever moments amid the sleaze, and a good performance by Griffith as porno actress. [R]▼●◗

Bodyguard, The (1992) **C-129m.** **½ D: Mick Jackson. Kevin Costner, Whitney Houston, Gary Kemp, Bill Cobbs, Ralph Waite, Tomas Arana, Michele Lamar Richards, Mike Starr, DeVaughn Nixon, Robert Wuhl, Bert Remsen, Stephen Shellen, Debbie Reynolds. Cold-as-steel professional bodyguard signs on to protect a music superstar (against his better judgment)—then falls in love with her. Overblown dual-star vehicle makes no sense, but has many crowd-pleasing ingredients—as well as moments of high kitsch. Solid film debut for Houston, who's most effective singing Dolly Parton's classic tune "I Will Always Love You." Lawrence Kasdan's screenplay was written years earlier—reportedly as a Steve McQueen vehicle. Remade in Hong Kong with Jet Li as THE DEFENDER (1994). [R]▼●◗

Body Heat (1981) **C-113m.** *** D: Lawrence Kasdan. William Hurt, Kathleen Turner, Richard Crenna, Ted Danson, J.A. Preston, Mickey Rourke. Hurt is a Florida lawyer whose brains work at half speed; Turner is a married socialite who turns on the heat and inspires him to bump off her husband. Overderivative of 1940s melodramas at first, then goes off on its own path and scores. Turner's first film; Kasdan's directorial debut. [R]▼●◗

Body of a Woman SEE: **Big Squeeze, The**
Body of Evidence (1993) **C-99m.** ** D: Uli Edel. Madonna, Willem Dafoe, Joe Mantegna, Anne Archer, Jürgen Prochnow, Julianne Moore, Frank Langella, Stan Shaw, Charles Hallahan, Lillian Lehman. Lawyer Dafoe—the kind of guy you don't want handling *your* case—falls under the spell of his client (Madonna), who's accused of killing her wealthy lover with too much rough sex. One-note melodrama with "hot" lovemaking scenes that inspire more discomfort than titillation. Also released in unrated version and an explicit NC-17 edition. [R]▼●◗

Body of Lies (2008) **C-129m.** **½ D: Ridley Scott. Leonardo DiCaprio, Russell Crowe, Mark Strong, Golshifteh Farahani, Oscar Isaac, Simon McBurney, Alon Aboutboul, Ali Suliman, Vince Colosimo. High-energy cloak-and-dagger yarn about hotshot CIA operative DiCaprio, who puts his life on the line every day in the Middle East. His cynical, emotionally detached superior in Langley (Crowe) surveys his every move but keeps valuable information from him that might affect his actions. Entertaining, but lets down and becomes all too conventional toward the climax. Strong makes a vivid impression as DiCaprio's high-level connection in Amman. William Monahan adapted David Ignatius' novel. Super 35. [R]◗

Body Parts (1991) **C-88m.** *½ D: Eric Red. Jeff Fahey, Lindsay Duncan, Kim Delaney, Brad Dourif, Zakes Mokae, John Walsh, Paul Benevictor. Attempt at a hyperkinetic sci-fi/horror shocker is just another variation on the same old "Hands of Orlac" plot: this time, *several* key body parts of a killer are grafted onto people, with violent results. Escalating plot also escalates viewer's disbelief. Panavision. [R]▼●◗

Body Rock (1984) **C-93m.** *½ D: Marcelo Epstein. Lorenzo Lamas, Vicki Frederick, Cameron Dye, Ray Sharkey, Michelle Nicastro. Formula break-dancing movie (shot by the great Robby Muller!) casts beefy Lamas as hero/heel who dumps his best friend, his bf's quietly voluptuous sis, and other pals when he's hired to emcee a chic uptown club. Watching L.L. clomp to the beat is like watching Victor Mature boogaloo. [PG-13]▼◗

Body Shots (1999) **C-105m.** BOMB D: Michael Cristofer. Sean Patrick Flanery, Jerry O'Connell, Amanda Peet, Tara Reid, Ron Livingston, Emily Procter, Brad Rowe, Sybil Temchen. Trying to shed light on the state of sex and dating in the 1990s, film follows eight twentysomethings as they explore the wild L.A. nightlife. Dark, dreary and derivative attempt to say something "important" about relationships. If this is truly where the world is heading, it's time to get off! Also available in 108m. unrated version. Super 35. [R]▼◗

Body Slam (1987) **C-89m.** **½ D: Hal Needham. Dirk Benedict, Tanya Roberts, Roddy Piper, Capt. Lou Albano, Barry Gordon, Charles Nelson Reilly, Billy Barty, John Astin. Barely released comedy, based on the successful rock 'n' roll/wrestling connection of the early 1980s, deserved better. Benedict is charming as an unscrupulous music promoter who latches onto wrestling as his meal ticket; "Rowdy" Roddy makes an engaging screen debut. Watch for cameos by many grapplers, including the Wild Samoans, Ric Flair, and Bruno Sammartino. [PG]▼◗

Body Snatcher, The (1945) **77m.** ***½ D: Robert Wise. Boris Karloff, Bela Lugosi, Henry Daniell, Edith Atwater, Russell Wade, Rita Corday. Fine, atmospheric tale from Robert Louis Stevenson short story of doctor (Daniell) who is forced to deal with scurrilous character (Karloff) in order to get cadavers for experiments in 19th-century

Edinburgh. Last film to team Karloff and Lugosi, their scenes together are eerie and compelling. Classic Val Lewton thriller. Screenplay by Philip MacDonald and Carlos Keith (Lewton).▼◕❸

Body Snatchers (1994) **C-87m.** **½ D: Abel Ferrara. Gabrielle Anwar, Meg Tilly, Forest Whitaker, Terry Kinney, Billy Wirth, Reilly Murphy, Christine Elise, R. Lee Ermey. Teenage Anwar moves to a military base with her family and soon discovers that pods from outer space are duplicating and replacing everyone there. Third version of Jack Finney's eerie novel is the least satisfactory; impatience, rather than tension, is aroused, and the horror is diminished because it's strangers who are being replaced. (Setting the story at a military base—where everyone is *supposed* to act alike—may not have been a good idea, either.) Both earlier versions titled INVASION OF THE BODY SNATCHERS. Arriscope. [R]▼◕❸

Body Stealers, The SEE: **Thin Air**

Boeing Boeing (1965) **C-102m.** *** D: John Rich. Jerry Lewis, Tony Curtis, Dany Saval, Christiane Schmidtmer, Suzanna Leigh, Thelma Ritter. A surprisingly subdued Lewis is paired with Curtis in story of American newspaperman who runs swinging pad in Paris, constantly stocked with stewardesses, to the chagrin of housekeeper Ritter. Amusing. Based on a play by Marc Camoletti. ▼●

Boesman & Lena (2000-French-South African) **C/B&W-88m.** **½ D: John Berry. Danny Glover, Angela Bassett, Willie Jonah. A once-happy, now-embittered couple is forced to survive on the road after the destruction of their shanty home. Rich performances (especially by Bassett) distinguish this faithful adaptation of Athol Fugard's play, filmed in South Africa, but it's all dialogue. Final film for director Berry, who died during postproduction. Super 35.▼▌

Bofors Gun, The (1968) **C-106m.** *** D: Jack Gold. Nicol Williamson, Ian Holm, David Warner, Peter Vaughn, John Thaw, Richard O'Callaghan, Barry Jackson, Donald Gee, Barbara Jefford. British soldier, on the eve of his return home in 1950s, comes tragically face-to-face with a rebellious Irish gunner. Engrossing, well acted.

Bog (1984) **C-87m.** BOMB D: Don Keeslar. Gloria De Haven, Aldo Ray, Marshall Thompson, Leo Gordon, Glen Voros, Rojay North, Ed Clark. Man in monster suit rises from bottom of lake and goes on rampage, sucking the blood from his victims. Ultra-cheap, ultra-bad time-killer. Filmed in Wisconsin in 1978. De Haven appears in a dual role.▼▌

Boggy Creek II SEE: **Barbaric Beast of Boggy Creek, The, Part II**

Bogus (1996) **C-111m.** ** D: Norman Jewison. Whoopi Goldberg, Gérard Depardieu, Haley Joel Osment, Nancy Travis,

Denis Mercier, Andrea Martin, Ute Lemper, Sheryl Lee Ralph, Al Waxman, Don Francks, Mo Gaffney. Curious fable about a boy whose single mom dies in an accident; his closest relative, a foster aunt (Goldberg), turns out to be an uptight businesswoman with no motherly instincts whatsoever. So he invents a friend, Bogus (Depardieu), who cheers him up and sticks by his side. Odd, melancholy, and vaguely unsatisfying—not to mention long and slow. [PG] ▼◕❸

Bogus Bandits SEE: **Devil's Brother, The**

Bohemian Girl, The (1936) **71m.** *** D: James Horne, Charles R. Rogers. Stan Laurel, Oliver Hardy, Thelma Todd, Antonio Moreno, Darla Hood, Jacqueline Wells (Julie Bishop), Mae Busch. Nifty comic opera with Stan and Ollie part of gypsy caravan. They adopt abandoned girl who turns out to be a princess. Todd's last feature, released posthumously. ▼●

Boiler Room (2000) **C-117m.** *** D: Ben Younger. Giovanni Ribisi, Nia Long, Vin Diesel, Ben Affleck, Ron Rifkin, Tom Everett Scott, Scott Caan, Jamie Kennedy, Nicky Katt, Taylor Nichols. Young man—like most of his generation, to hear him tell it—wants success without having to work for it. This puts him at odds with his judgmental father (who happens to be a judge) until he signs on at a maverick brokerage house where the money flows freely . . . *too* freely. Naive at times, but entertaining. Tyro writer-director Younger makes disarming reference to WALL STREET and GLENGARRY GLEN ROSS, which this movie echoes in certain ways. [R]▼▌

Boiling Point (1993) **C-92m.** ** D: James B. Harris. Wesley Snipes, Dennis Hopper, Lolita Davidovich, Viggo Mortensen, Dan Hedaya, Seymour Cassel, Jonathan Banks, Christine Elise, Tony LoBianco, Valerie Perrine, James Tolkan, Paul Gleason. Snipes plays a federal agent determined to nail the man responsible for killing his colleague and friend during a sting operation. Misnamed crime yarn is tepid at best, but well shot on L.A. locations, and filled with familiar faces. [R]▼◕❸

Bolero (1981-French) **C-173m.** *½ D: Claude Lelouch. James Caan, Geraldine Chaplin, Robert Hossein, Nicole Garcia, Daniel Olbrychski, Evelyne Bouix. Boring tale of various characters of different nationalities and their love of music, set during a 50-year time span. The actors play more than one character, and the result is confusion.▼▌

Bolero (1984) **C-104m.** BOMB D: John Derek. Bo Derek, George Kennedy, Andrea Occipinti, Ana Obregon, Olivia d'Abo. Colossally boring sexual drama, for Bo-peepers only . . . though even voyeurs will be yawning during long stretches between nude scenes. Bo also produced the picture. [R]▼◕❸

Bolt (2008) **C-96m.** *** D: Chris Williams, Byron Howard. Voices of John Travolta,

Miley Cyrus, Susie Essman, Mark Walton, Malcolm McDowell, Diedrich Bader, Nick Swardson, Chloe Moretz, Greg Germann, James Lipton. The canine star of a hit TV series knows no other world than the make-believe environment in which he plays a doggie superhero. Then he's accidentally shipped in a crate to N.Y.C. and gets his first taste of reality. At first the film threatens to choke on show-biz talk, but it develops a heart as it takes to the road. The character of Rhino, a hamster in a plastic ball (voiced by Disney artist Walton), is one of the all-time great Disney sidekicks. 3-D. [PG]🅓

Bomba the Jungle Boy series SEE: *Leonard Maltin's Classic Movie Guide*

Bombay Talkie (1970-Indian) **C-105m.** **½ D: James Ivory. Shashi Kapoor, Jennifer Kendal, Zia Mohyeddin, Aparna Sen, Utpal Dutt. A bored, pleasure-seeking British writer (Kendal) becomes romantically involved with an Indian movie actor (Kapoor). The subject—the interaction between different cultures—has been a staple in Ivory's films, but the presentation here is less than memorable. Scripted by Ivory and Ruth Prawer Jhabvala. [PG]🅥🅓

Bombers B-52 (1957) **C-106m.** **½ D: Gordon Douglas. Natalie Wood, Karl Malden, Marsha Hunt, Efrem Zimbalist, Jr., Dean Jagger. Ordinary love story between army pilot Zimbalist and Wood, with latter's sergeant father objecting, intertwined with good aerial footage of jet plane maneuvers. CinemaScope.🅥🅓

Bombshell (1933) **95m.** ***½ D: Victor Fleming. Jean Harlow, Lee Tracy, Frank Morgan, Franchot Tone, Una Merkel, Pat O'Brien, C. Aubrey Smith, Ted Healy, Isabel Jewell. Devastating satire of 1930s Hollywood, with Harlow a much-abused star, Tracy an incredibly unscrupulous publicity director making her life hell. No holds barred. Scripted by John Lee Mahin and Jules Furthman, from a play by Caroline Francke and Mack Crane. Retitled BLONDE BOMBSHELL.🅥🅞

Bone Collector, The (1999) **C-117m.** *** D: Phillip Noyce. Denzel Washington, Angelina Jolie, Queen Latifah, Michael Rooker, Mike McGlone, Luis Guzman, Leland Orser, John Benjamin Hickey, Ed O'Neill. The NYPD's leading forensics expert, now a bedridden quadriplegic, enlists the help of a reluctant cop (Jolie) to be his eyes and ears in tracking down a games-playing serial killer. First-rate suspense thriller/whodunit, based on a novel by Jeffery Deaver. Not for the squeamish. Super 35. [R]🅥🅞🅓

Bones (2001) **C-96m.** ** D: Ernest Dickerson. Snoop Dogg, Pam Grier, Clifton Powell, Bianca Lawson, Michael T. Weiss, Khalil Kain, Merwin Mondesir. Two young suburban brothers (in both senses) buy a dilapidated ghetto brownstone in hopes of turning it into a trendy nightspot . . .

but their entrepreneur father is panicked about the house's sinister history and his own participation in the 1979 slaying of its original owner (Dogg), who's now a ghost. If grossness makes you giggle, this speedy junk has a few grotesque jolts, plus the sight of still-shapely Grier to keep your own dad's heart beating adequately. Super 35. [R]🅥🅓

Bonfire of the Vanities, The (1990) **C-125m.** BOMB D: Brian De Palma. Tom Hanks, Bruce Willis, Melanie Griffith, Kim Cattrall, Saul Rubinek, Morgan Freeman, John Hancock, Kevin Dunn, Clifton James, Louis Giambalvo, Barton Heyman, Donald Moffat, Alan King, Mary Alice, Andre Gregory, Richard Libertini, Robert Stephens, Kirsten Dunst, Rita Wilson, Malachy McCourt, Camryn Manheim, Richard Belzer. Appallingly heavy-handed "comedy" about a cocky Wall Street wheeler-dealer whose well-insulated life begins to crumble when his wife learns he's fooling around, and he and his paramour are involved in a hit-and-run accident. With all the power—and nuance—of Tom Wolfe's novel removed, and all the characters turned into caricatures (racist and otherwise), what's left is a pointless charade, and a pitiful waste of money and talent. F. Murray Abraham appears unbilled as the Bronx D.A. Super 35. [R]🅥🅞🅓

Bonjour Tristesse (1958) **C/B&W-94m.** *** D: Otto Preminger. Deborah Kerr, David Niven, Jean Seberg, Geoffrey Horne, Mylene Demongeot. Teenager does her best to break up romance between playboy widowed father and his mistress, with tragic results. Francoise Sagan's philosophy seeps through glossy production; Kerr exceptionally fine in soaper set on French Riviera. CinemaScope.🅥🅓

Bonneville (2008) **C-93m.** **½ D: Christopher N. Rowley. Jessica Lange, Kathy Bates, Joan Allen, Tom Skerritt, Christine Baranski, Victor Rasuk, Tom Amandes, Tom Wopat. Recently widowed Lange finds herself at odds with her resentful stepdaughter over her husband's ashes. Feeling lost and confused, she winds up taking a road trip in his vintage convertible with two close friends. The presence of three skilled actresses elevates this pleasant but minor female-bonding tale. Panavision. [PG]🅓

Bonnie and Clyde (1967) **C-111m.** **** D: Arthur Penn. Warren Beatty, Faye Dunaway, Michael J. Pollard, Gene Hackman, Estelle Parsons, Denver Pyle, Gene Wilder, Dub Taylor. Trend-setting film about unlikely heroes of 1930s bank-robbing team has spawned many imitators but still leads the pack. Veering from comedy to melodrama and social commentary, it remains vivid, stylish throughout. When released, violent conclusion was extremely controversial. Screenplay by David Newman and Robert Benton. Parsons and cinematographer Burnett Guffey were Oscar winners. Wilder's first film.▼●◗

Bonnie Parker Story, The (1958) **81m.** **½ D: William Witney. Dorothy Provine, Jack Hogan, Richard Bakalyan, Joseph Turkel. With the success of BONNIE AND CLYDE, this film takes on added luster, recounting the lurid criminal life of the female crook (Provine)—though Clyde Barrow isn't even mentioned in this low-budget saga. Superama.

Bonnie Scotland (1935) **80m.** **½ D: James Horne. Stan Laurel, Oliver Hardy, June Lang, William Janney, Anne Grey, Vernon Steele, James Finlayson. Plot sometimes gets in the way of L&H, but their material is well up to par; Stan and Ollie inadvertently join a Scottish military regiment stationed in the desert.▼●◗

Bon Voyage! (1962) **C-130m.** *½ D: James Neilson. Fred MacMurray, Jane Wyman, Michael Callan, Deborah Walley, Tommy Kirk, Kevin Corcoran. Slow, drawn-out Disney comedy about "typical" American family's misadventures on trip to Europe. Aimed more at adults than kids, but too draggy and simple-minded for anyone.▼◗

Bon Voyage (2003-French) **C-114m.** **½ D: Jean-Paul Rappeneau. Isabelle Adjani, Gérard Depardieu, Virginie Ledoyen, Yvan Attal, Grégori Dérangère, Peter Coyote, Jean-Marc Stehlé. A self-centered film star (Adjani), a government minister (Depardieu), and a frail scientist and his determined protégée (Stehlé and Ledoyen) are a few of the disparate people who converge on Bordeaux on the eve of WW2. Film's real lead is the actress's bourgeois former lover (Dérangère), who is drawn into the story and finds himself playing the hero. Unusual blend of CASABLANCA-esque intrigue with farce doesn't quite come off as well as intended, but it's fast-paced, fairly broad fun. Panavision. [PG-13]▼◗

Bon Voyage Charlie Brown (and Don't Come Back!) (1980) **C-75m.** *** D: Bill Melendez. Voices of Daniel Anderson, Casey Carlson, Patricia Patts, Arrin Skelley. Charlie Brown and company travel to France as exchange students. Cute animated entertainment for Peanuts devotees. [G]▼◗

Bonzo Goes to College (1952) **80m.** ** D: Frederick de Cordova. Maureen O'Sullivan, Charles Drake, Edmund Gwenn, Gigi Perreau, Gene Lockhart, Irene Ryan, David Janssen. Follow-up to BEDTIME FOR BONZO has brainy chimp lead college football team to victory; good cast takes back seat to monkey-shines.

Boogeyman, The (1980) **C-86m.** *** D: Ulli Lommel. Suzanna Love, Ron James, Michael Love, John Carradine, Raymond Boyden. Shards of mirror that "witnessed" horrible murder cause gruesome deaths.

German art film actor-director Lommel lends unconventional angle to this combination of THE EXORCIST and HALLOWEEN. Effects are quite colorful, if somewhat hokey. Followed by BOOGEYMAN II. [R]▼◗

Boogeyman II (1983) **C-79m.** BOMB D: Bruce Starr. Suzanna Love, Shana Hall, Ulli Lommel. Survivor of BOOGEYMAN goes to Hollywood to live with producer who is going to turn her life story into a movie. Moronic slasher film depends mostly on footage from BOOGEYMAN, amply used in flashbacks. Almost laughable.▼◗

Boogeyman (2005-U.S.-New Zealand) **C-89m.** ** D: Stephen T. Kay. Barry Watson, Emily Deschanel, Skye McCole Bartusiak, Lucy Lawless, Tory Mussett. You already know the story: a young man returns to his childhood home, the setting of a traumatic experience where as a kid he either saw—or didn't see—a creepy guy/thing suck his loving father into eternal oblivion by way of the closet in his room. Now, years later, he must confront his fears alone . . . and you can guess the rest. Despite its predictable blueprint there are a couple of pretty decent scares to be had here. You might consider chapter-skipping on your DVD to get to the good stuff. Followed by two DVD sequels. [PG-13]▼◗

Boogie Man Will Get You, The (1942) **66m.** **½ D: Lew Landers. Boris Karloff, Peter Lorre, Jeff Donnell, Larry Parks, Slapsie Maxie Rosenbloom, Maude Eburne, Don Beddoe, Frank Puglia. Good cast in lightweight cash-in on ARSENIC AND OLD LACE. Karloff is dotty scientist attempting to make supermen out of traveling salesmen while Donnell tries to turn his home into Colonial tourist trap; Lorre is screwy doctor/sheriff/notary/loan shark. No great shakes, but pleasant.◗

Boogie Nights (1997) **C-152m.** ***½ D: Paul Thomas Anderson. Mark Wahlberg, Burt Reynolds, Julianne Moore, John C. Reilly, Don Cheadle, Heather Graham, Luis Guzman, Philip Seymour Hoffman, William H. Macy, Alfred Molina, Philip Baker Hall, Robert Ridgely, Ricky Jay, Jack Riley, Joanna Gleason, Thomas Jane. Extraordinary, intense re-creation of life among a "family" of pornographers in the San Fernando Valley, from the late 1970s through the early 1980s. Wahlberg plays a disaffected 17-year-old with no brains but a formidable sex organ who becomes a porn-movie sensation; Reynolds is perfect as the director/paterfamilias who makes him a star. Writer-director Anderson doesn't judge his characters, but makes them—and their actions—seem utterly real. Tough going at times, but gripping and funny as well. Panavision. [R]▼●◗

Boogie Woogie (2010-British) **C-94m.** **½ D: Duncan Ward. Gillian Anderson, Alan Cumming, Heather Graham, Danny Huston, Jack Huston, Christopher Lee, Joanna Lumley, Simon McBurney, Meredith Ostrom, Charlotte Rampling, Amanda Seyfried, Stellan Skarsgård, Jaime Winstone. Altman-like ensemble charbroils London's gallery scene, with high-class artists/buyers/sellers behaving classlessly. Title refers to a priceless Mondrian canvas owned by Lee and Lumley, coveted by Anderson and Skarsgård, and brokered by a dealer named Art. Mixed trysts sex up the venality, while real works by Brancusi, Hockney, et al. decorate the sets. Adapted by Danny Moynihan, only somewhat artfully, from his 2001 novel. [R] ▷

Book of Eli, The (2010) **C-118m.** **✱✱½** D: Albert Hughes, Allen Hughes. Denzel Washington, Gary Oldman, Mila Kunis, Ray Stevenson, Jennifer Beals, Frances de la Tour, Michael Gambon, Tom Waits, Chris Browning, Evan Jones, Malcolm McDowell. Washington does his best Clint Eastwood in this violent but entertaining postapocalyptic tale about a man of few words roaming the country, clutching a book that may hold all the answers for the future of mankind. As he makes his way across the desolate landscape, killing anyone who gets in his way, he must battle the evil forces of Oldman, who desperately wants this prized possession. Taking the "end of days" genre and wrapping it in the guise of a Sergio Leone spaghetti Western, the Hughes brothers create a lurid·guilty pleasure, with a "message" thrown in for good measure. HD Widescreen. [R] ▷

Book of Love (1990) **C-82m.** **✱½** D: Robert Shaye. Chris Young, Keith Coogan, Aeryk Egan, Josie Bissett, Tricia Leigh Fisher, Michael McKean, Danny Nucci, John Cameron Mitchell. Offensively inconsequential '50s teen romance about the usual clichés: James Dean, dilapidated cars, and greasy hair dressings. Standard anachronisms abound, starting with the use of the title oldie (a 1958 hit) in a film set in 1956. Inauspicious directorial debut for New Line Cinema's founder/CEO. Fisher (daughter of Connie Stevens and Eddie Fisher) is the sole standout as a tough girl with a soft heart. [PG-13] ▼ ●▷

Book of Numbers (1973) **C-80m.** **✱✱½** D: Raymond St. Jacques. Raymond St. Jacques, Phillip Thomas, Freda Payne, Hope Clarke, D'Urville Martin, Gilbert Green. Uneven but sometimes enjoyable story of a black numbers-racket operation in a rural town during the Depression. [R] ▼ ▷

Book of Shadows: Blair Witch 2 (2000) **C-90m.** **✱½** D: Joe Berlinger. Stephen Barker Turner, Tristen Skyler, Erica Leerhsen, Kim Director, Jeffrey Donovan. Student filmmakers visit Burkittsville, Maryland, hoping to find out what happened to the people who made THE BLAIR WITCH PROJECT. A straight melodrama, not a faux documentary like the first; clever at times, but plodding, gabby and highly uninvolving, with all the spooky stuff confined to the last couple of reels. Fictional filmmaking debut of documentarian Berlinger. [R] ▼ ▷

Book of Stars, The (2000) **C-98m.** **✱✱✱** D: Michael Miner. Mary Stuart Masterson, Jena Malone, Karl Geary, D. B. Sweeney, Delroy Lindo. Beautifully acted and directed drama about two parentless sisters, a sweet 15-year-old who is dying of cystic fibrosis and a vulnerable cynic who once published a book of poetry but now pops pills and toils as a hooker. This is no disease-of-the-week tearjerker, but a multileveled exploration of sisterly love and guilt. ▼ ▷

Boom (1968-U.S.-British) **C-113m.** **✱✱** D: Joseph Losey. Elizabeth Taylor, Richard Burton, Noel Coward, Joanna Shimkus, Michael Dunn. Thud: Only film buffs who admire Losey's very original directorial style are likely to appreciate fuzzy adaptation of Tennessee Williams' *The Milk Train Doesn't Stop Here Anymore.* Fine location photography in Sardinia and Rome; good performance by Shimkus can't save this. Panavision. [M/PG] ▼

Boomerang! (1947) **88m.** **✱✱✱½** D: Elia Kazan. Dana Andrews, Jane Wyatt, Lee J. Cobb, Arthur Kennedy, Sam Levene, Robert Keith, Taylor Holmes, Ed Begley, Karl Malden, Cara Williams, Barry Kelley; narrated by Reed Hadley. Minister's murder brings rapid arrest of an innocent man; prosecuting attorney determines to hunt out real facts. Brilliant drama in all respects. Richard Murphy's taut screenplay, from Anthony Abbott's article "The Perfect Case," is based on a factual incident. Playwright Arthur Miller appears as one of the line-up suspects. See if you can spot Brian Keith in the crowd outside the courthouse as Cobb escorts prisoner Kennedy. ▼ ▷

Boomerang (1992) **C-118m.** **✱✱** D: Reginald Hudlin. Eddie Murphy, Halle Berry, Robin Givens, David Alan Grier, Martin Lawrence, Grace Jones, Geoffrey Holder, Eartha Kitt, Chris Rock, Tisha Campbell, John Witherspoon, Melvin Van Peebles. Murphy makes a lumpy transition from comic to leading man, as a lifelong womanizer who finally meets his counterpart in his new boss (Givens). The women are fun to watch, but the humor is surprisingly crude at times, and the story is virtually nonexistent. A mixed bag at best, ridiculously padded out to two hours. [R] ▼ ●▷

Boom Town (1940) **118m.** **✱✱✱** D: Jack Conway. Clark Gable, Spencer Tracy, Claudette Colbert, Hedy Lamarr, Frank Morgan, Lionel Atwill, Chill Wills. No surprises in tale of get-rich-quick drilling for oil, but star-studded cast gives it life. Also shown in computer-colored version. ▼ ●▷

Boondock Saints, The (1999) **C-110m.** **✱✱** D: Troy Duffy. Willem Dafoe, Sean Patrick Flanery, Norman Reedus, David Della Rocco,

Billy Connolly, Ron Jeremy Hyatt, David Ferry. Ultra-violent, low-budget Tarantino wannabe focuses on two Irish-American brothers who decide to rub out what they perceive to be evil forces in Boston. With off-the-wall humor and Dafoe's loony, gay FBI agent thrown in for good measure, this ain't no Tea Party. A hit-or-miss affair. Duffy's trials in making this film were chronicled in the documentary OVERNIGHT. Followed by a sequel. Super 35. [R] ▼❶

Boondock Saints II: All Saints Day, The (2009) C/B&W-117m. *½ D: Troy Duffy. Sean Patrick Flanery, Norman Reedus, Clifton Collins, Jr., Julie Benz, Judd Nelson, Billy Connolly, Bob Marley, Brian Mahoney, David Ferry, David Della Rocco, Peter Fonda. Brainless sequel, with siblings Flanery and Reedus returning to Boston from Ireland to avenge the ritualistic murder of a priest. Loud, bloody . . . and bloody awful. Willem Dafoe appears unbilled, reprising his role from the first film. Super 35. [R] ❶

Boost, The (1988) C-95m. *½ D: Harold Becker. James Woods, Sean Young, John Kapelos, Steven Hill, Kelle Kerr, John Rothman, Amanda Blake, Grace Zabriskie. An anti-drug movie that's on the screen nearly an hour before you even realize it *is* an anti-drug movie. Woods is the hotshot salesman who goes to hell (and bankruptcy) via cocaine, with Young the sometime user who tries to stand by him. As with Jack Nicholson in THE SHINING, it's difficult to distinguish the "before" Woods from the "after" in this misfire. [R] ▼❶

Boot Hill (1969-Italian) C-87m. ** D: Giuseppe Colizzi. Terence Hill, Bud Spencer, Woody Strode, Victor Buono, Lionel Stander, Eduardo Ciannelli. Western ravioli representing another of the traditional teamings of blue-eyed, rock-jawed Hill and his bear of a sidekick Spencer. Uneven pasta of violence and comedy. Aka TRINITY RIDES AGAIN. Techniscope. [PG] ▼❶

Bootleggers (1974) C-101m. ** D: Charles B. Pierce. Paul Koslo, Dennis Fimple, Slim Pickens, Jaclyn Smith, Chuck Pierce, Jr. Typical yahoo action comedy set in 1930s Arkansas with Koslo and Fimple trying to outsmart and outdo rival moonshining family while running their supplies to Memphis. Retitled BOOTLEGGERS' ANGEL to capitalize on Smith's later TV stardom. Todd-AO 35. [PG] ❶

Bootmen (2000-Australian) C-93m. ** D: Dein Perry. Adam Garcia, Sam Worthington, Sophie Lee, Christopher Horsey, Lee McDonald, William Zappa, Richard Carter. Novice director Perry (of the dance group Tap Dogs) used his own steelworking background to create this toe-tapping look at a young man's escape into big-time show business—and then back again—as he rallies his blue-collar tap-dancing cronies to create his own contemporary dance show. Sort of a male FLASHDANCE, with a lame script but impressive footwork. [R] ▼❶

Booty Call (1997) C-77m. ** D: Jeff Pollack. Jamie Foxx, Tommy Davidson, Vivica A. Fox, Tamala Jones, Scott LaRose, Kam Ray Chan, Ric Young, Bernie Mac. Or, Two Guys in Search of Condoms. Raunchy comedy is definitely PC (politically correct and pro-condom) as these two hapless souls just can't seem to please their hot-to-trot girlfriends until they find the perfect latex helper. Just a couple of genuinely funny scenes in this broad, lowbrow comedy. [R] ▼❶

Bopha! (1993) C-120m. *** D: Morgan Freeman. Danny Glover, Malcolm McDowell, Alfre Woodard, Marius Weyers, Maynard Eziashi, Malick Bowens, Grace Mahlaba. Tense, involving drama with Glover and Woodard (who played Nelson and Winnie Mandela in the TV movie MANDELA) starring as a married couple residing in a peaceful South African township. He's a police officer who upholds the status quo; their world is sure to crumble when their son (Eziashi) takes part in a rebellion against the discipline and curriculum of the local white-run school. Freeman's directorial debut; Arsenio Hall executive produced. [PG-13] ▼❶

Borat: Cultural Learnings of America for Make Benefit Glorious Nation of Kazakhstan (2006) C-82m. ***½ D: Larry Charles. Sacha Baron Cohen, Ken Davitian, Pamela Anderson. Writer-producer-performer Baron Cohen adopts the alter ego of Borat Sagdiyev, well-meaning but clueless Kazakhstani television reporter who travels across the U.S. to learn about our country in this mockumentary. His bull-in-a-china-shop approach gets him into all kinds of trouble as he encounters a wide variety of Americans. Baron Cohen and company reveal elements of racism, sexism, homophobia, and xenophobia but envelop them in the context of an audaciously funny, gross-out, one-of-a-kind comedy. [R] ❶

Bordello of Blood (1996) C-87m. ** D: Gilbert Adler. Dennis Miller, Erika Eleniak, Angie Everhart, Chris Sarandon, Corey Feldman, William Sadler, Aubrey Morris. Private eye Miller tries to locate Eleniak's brother, who's wound up at a mortuary brothel staffed by gorgeous vampires and run by Everhart. Fitfully amusing juvenile horror comedy with a heavy t&a quotient; Miller created much of his wise-guy dialogue. Whoopi Goldberg has a cameo. On-screen title: *TALES FROM THE CRYPT PRESENTS BORDELLO OF BLOOD.* [R] ▼❶

Border, The (1982) C-107m. **½ D: Tony Richardson. Jack Nicholson, Harvey Keitel, Valerie Perrine, Warren Oates, Elpidia Carrillo. Border patrolman Nicholson, spurred on by money-hungry spouse Perrine, begins taking payoffs from illegal Mexican aliens he's supposed to be arresting, eventually becomes emotionally involved with young mother Carrillo. Cast and storyline beg for Sam Peckinpah in his prime; mildly interesting, but never really takes off. Nice music by Ry Cooder. Panavision. [R] ▼●▶

Border Cop SEE: **Blood Barrier**

Border Incident (1949) **92m.** ******* D: Anthony Mann. Ricardo Montalban, George Murphy, Howard da Silva, Teresa Celli, Charles McGraw. Tension-packed story of U.S. agents cracking down on smuggling of immigrants across Texas-Mexico border. Well directed, and uncompromisingly violent. ▶

Borderline (1950) **88m.** ****** D: William A. Seiter. Fred MacMurray, Claire Trevor, Raymond Burr, Jose Torvay, Morris Ankrum, Roy Roberts. Odd thriller-comedy in which L.A. cop Trevor attempts to gather evidence against wily drug smuggler Burr while mixing with tough guy MacMurray in Mexico. Starts out promisingly but soon bogs down in silliness. Burr makes a vivid villain. ▼●▶

Borderline (1980) **C-105m.** ****** D: Jerrold Freedman. Charles Bronson, Bruno Kirby, Bert Remsen, Michael Lerner, Kenneth McMillan, Ed Harris, Wilford Brimley. Bronson, minus Jill Ireland this time, is a Border Patrol officer searching for a killer. Undistinguished formula vehicle for Old Stone Face. [PG]▼

Border Shootout (1990) **C-110m.** ***½** D: C. J. McIntyre. Cody Glenn, Jeff Kaake, Glenn Ford, Lizabeth Rohovit, Michael Horse, Russell Todd, Michael Ansara, Michael Forrest. Naive rancher is made deputy in Arizona border town that's fed up with aging sheriff Ford, but the townspeople's lynching of alleged rustlers brings about immediate conflict. Good Western plot (from Elmore Leonard novel) ruined by amateurish production. Ford seems to be walking through his role. ▼▶

Bordertown (1935) **90m.** ******* D: Archie Mayo. Paul Muni, Bette Davis, Eugene Pallette, Margaret Lindsay. Fine drama of unusual triangle in bordertown cafe, with Davis as flirtatious wife of Pallette with designs on lawyer Muni; her overwrought scene on the witness stand is not easily forgotten. Used as basis for later THEY DRIVE BY NIGHT, but more serious in tone. Also shown in computer-colored version.◗

Bordertown (2006) **C-112m.** ***½** D: Gregory Nava. Jennifer Lopez, Martin Sheen, Maya Zapata, Juan Diego Botto, Sonia Braga, Antonio Banderas. In contemporary Ciudad Juárez, ambitious Chicago reporter Lopez tries to find out why thousands of female factory workers have disappeared over time. Befriending a survivor who crawled out of the grave places her in the gun sights of smarmy rich villains who casually rape and coldly murder. Director's script wants to be a bleak bilingual thriller, but is only brutal exploitation. Shot in Old and New Mexico. Released direct to DVD in the U.S. [R]◗

Boris and Natasha: The Movie (1992) **C-88m.** ****** D: Charles Martin Smith. Sally Kellerman, David Thomas, Paxton Whitehead, Andrea Martin, Alex Rocco, Larry Cedar, Arye Gross, Christopher Neame, Anthony Newley. Silly live-action version of the fondly remembered "Rocky and Bullwinkle" cartoon series with our dastardly (but dated) Russian spies up to no good as usual. Spirited, but not enough. John Candy, John Travolta, and director Smith pop up in cameos. Made as a theatrical feature in 1988 (when the Cold War was still topical). It debuted on cable TV instead. [PG]▼●▶

B.O.R.N. (1989) **C-92m.** ****** D: Ross Hagen. Ross Hagen, Hoke Howell, P. J. Soles, William Smith, Russ Tamblyn, Amanda Blake, Rance Howard, Clint Howard, Claire Hagen, Dawn Wildsmith. Someone is kidnapping young people from the streets of L.A. to cut up as involuntary organ donors, but they didn't reckon with hero Hagen and his ex-cop pal Howell. Wild-eyed, bizarre action thriller has too many characters and too much gunfire but has its moments too. Title refers to "Body Organ Replacement Network." Aka MERCHANTS OF DEATH. [R]▼▶

Born Again (1978) **C-110m.** ***½** D: Irving Rapper. Dean Jones, Anne Francis, Jay Robinson, Dana Andrews, Raymond St. Jacques, George Brent. If one is inspired by the religious rebirth of Pres. Nixon's Special Counsel (Charles Colson) after his Washington skullduggery, one might be absorbed by this one-dimensional film account. Others beware! [PG]▼

Born American (1986-U.S.-Finnish) **C-95m.** ****** D: Renny Harlin. Mike Norris, Steve Durham, David Coburn, Thalmus Rasulala, Albert Salmi. The Cold War lives on as three young Americans vacationing in Finland accidentally cross the border into Russia, where they fight it out with the local troops. OK action scenes and personable young cast sugarcoat the heavy-handed political overtones. [R]▼▶

Born Free (1966-British) **C-96m.** *****½** D: James Hill. Virginia McKenna, Bill Travers, Geoffrey Keen, Peter Lukoye. Exceptional adaptation of Joy Adamson's book about Elsa the lioness, who was raised as a pet by two Kenya game wardens (played by real-life couple McKenna and Travers). Sincere, engrossing film, a must for family viewing. Oscars for Best Original Score (John Barry) and Title Song (Barry and Don Black). Screenplay by Gerald L.C. Copley

(Lester Cole). Followed by a sequel (LIVING FREE) and a brief TV series. Remade for TV in 1996. Story is continued in TO WALK WITH LIONS (1999). Panavision. ▼●)

Born in East L.A. (1987) **C-87m.** *½ D: Cheech Marin. Cheech Marin, Daniel Stern, Paul Rodriguez, Jan-Michael Vincent, Kamala Lopez, Alma Martinez, Tony Plana. Third-generation American Hispanic gets caught in an immigration raid minus I.D. and is deported to Tijuana; it takes a tiresome hour and a half of screen time to get back. Nothing offensive but also nothing special; Rodriguez's dim-witted comedy relief is a particular drag. Based on Marin's popular Bruce Springsteen parody record. Alternate version runs 93m. [R] ▼●]
Born Into Brothels (2004-Indian-U.S.) **C-85m.** ***½ D: Zana Briski, Ross Kauffman. Photographer Briski, wanting to document Calcutta's red light district, gets the cold shoulder until she makes friends with the children of the prostitutes. Then inspiration strikes: she teaches these often-abused kids to take pictures. Oscar-winning documentary built on the foundation of a great idea; the results are unexpected and genuinely inspiring. [R] ▼●]
Born Losers, The (1967) **C-112m.** **½ D: T. C. Frank (Tom Laughlin). Tom Laughlin, Elizabeth James, Jeremy Slate, William Wellman, Jr., Robert Tessier. What seemed at the time just another biker film gained new interest in the '70s as the introduction of Billy Jack; he helps free young dropout James from the clutches of Slate's gang. Good action scenes, but Laughlin's use of violence as *an indictment of* violence is already present. Jane Russell makes a guest appearance as a mother. Followed by BILLY JACK. [PG] ▼]
Born on the Fourth of July (1989) **C-144m.** ***½ D: Oliver Stone. Tom Cruise, Willem Dafoe, Raymond J. Barry, Caroline Kava, Kyra Sedgwick, Bryan Larkin, Jerry Levine, Josh Evans, Frank Whaley, Stephen Baldwin, John Getz, Lili Taylor, Tom Berenger, Abbie Hoffman, Jason Gedrick, Ed Lauter, Michael Wincott, Tom Sizemore, Mike Starr, James Le Gros, John C. McGinley, Wayne Knight, Bob Gunton, Vivica A. Fox. Relentlessly realistic and powerful saga of real-life Vietnam vet Ron Kovic, who joined the Marines as a gung-ho recruit in the 1960s and came home paralyzed from the chest down—only to endure an even greater ordeal of physical and mental rehabilitation before emerging as an antiwar activist. Stone cowrote the screenplay with Kovic, and spares us nothing in re-creating some of America's most painful years. Stone's finest film to date. Cruise delivers a top-notch performance; enhanced by a great John Williams score. Kovic can be seen in opening parade scene;

Stone plays a TV reporter. Oscar winner for Best Director and Film Editing. Panavision. [R] ▼●]
Born Reckless (1959) **79m.** *½ D: Howard W. Koch. Mamie Van Doren, Jeff Richards, Arthur Hunnicutt, Carol Ohmart, Tom Duggan, Jeanne Carmen. Rodeo star Richards divides his time between busting broncos and busting heads of lecherous old cowpokes trying to paw Mamie. Not bad enough to be really funny, but it has its moments; Mamie sings five of film's eight songs, including unforgettable "I'm Just a Nice, Sweet, Home-Type of Girl."
Born Romantic (2001-U.S.-British) **C-96m.** **½ D: David Kane. Craig Ferguson, Olivia Williams, David Morrissey, Jane Horrocks, Jimi Mistry, Catherine McCormack, Adrian Lester, Ian Hart. Three lovelorn Londoner couples meet up at a local salsa dance club, but they're all left feet when it comes to matters of the heart. Enter Cupid-playing cabbie Lester. Slight, predictable romantic comedy works because of its terrific cast. It's especially fun to see the usually brazen McCormack and meek Horrocks playing against type. [R] ▼]
Born to Be Bad (1950) **94m.** **½ D: Nicholas Ray. Joan Fontaine, Robert Ryan, Zachary Scott, Joan Leslie, Mel Ferrer, Harold Vermilyea. "Little fake" Fontaine, despite attraction to writer Ryan, schemes to win wealthy Scott away from fiancée Leslie. And that's just for openers. Good cast in somewhat overwrought, predictable drama. ▼●]
Born to Be Wild (1995) **C-100m.** ** D: John Gray. Will Horneff, Helen Shaver, Peter Boyle, Jean Marie Barnwell, John C. McGinley, Marvin J. McIntyre. OK family film grafts a gorilla onto the FREE WILLY formula: a teenage boy forms a bond with an ape on the lam in Seattle, helping her in quest for freedom. Kids might go for it, even if they figure out that the lead "actor" is just an animatronic thespian passing for the real thing. [PG] ▼●]
Born to Dance (1936) **105m.** *** D: Roy Del Ruth. Eleanor Powell, James Stewart, Virginia Bruce, Una Merkel, Sid Silvers, Frances Langford, Raymond Walburn, Buddy Ebsen, Reginald Gardiner. Powell bears out title in good Cole Porter musical with sensational footwork and fine songs: "Easy To Love" (introduced by Stewart) and "I've Got You Under My Skin." ▼●]
Born to Kill (1947) **92m.** *** D: Robert Wise. Claire Trevor, Lawrence Tierney, Walter Slezak, Audrey Long, Elisha Cook, Jr., Phillip Terry. Murderer Tierney marries insecure Long, but can't stay away from her divorced sister Trevor. Super-tough film noir is uncharacteristically mean-spirited for director Wise, but is well put together nonetheless. A cult item. ▼]
Born to Kill (1974) SEE: **Cockfighter**

Born to Rock: The T.A.M.I. Show SEE: **That Was Rock**

Born to Win (1971) **C-90m.** **½ D: Ivan Passer. George Segal, Karen Black, Paula Prentiss, Jay Fletcher, Hector Elizondo, Robert De Niro. Unjustly neglected, but not altogether successful comedy-drama about ex-hairdresser in N.Y.C. and his $100-a-day heroin habit. Very well acted, particularly by Segal. Aka ADDICT. [R]▼●

Born Wild (1994) **C-98m.** ** D: Duncan McLachlan. Brooke Shields, John Varty, Martin Sheen, David Keith, Elmon Mhlongo, Norman Ansty, Thembe Ndaba, Renee Estevez. The story of real-life conservationist Varty, who plays himself, and his multiyear relationship with a family of leopards. When documentarian Shields wants to make a film of his experiences, her efforts are predictably sabotaged by jealous colleagues and corrupt game wardens. Set in South Africa, Kenya, and Zambia; extraordinary footage of animals in the wild is trivialized by the Hollywoodization of the movie within the movie. [PG]▼●

Born Yesterday (1950) **103m.** ***½ D: George Cukor. Judy Holliday, William Holden, Broderick Crawford, Howard St. John. Junk-dealer-made-good Crawford wants girlfriend (Holliday) culturefied, hires Holden to teach her in hilarious Garson Kanin comedy set in Washington, D.C. Priceless Judy repeated Broadway triumph and won Oscar for playing quintessential dumb blonde. Remade in 1993. ▼●)

Born Yesterday (1993) **C-101m.** **½ D: Luis Mandoki. Melanie Griffith, John Goodman, Don Johnson, Edward Herrmann, Max Perlich, Michael Ensign, Benjamin C. Bradlee, Sally Quinn, William Frankfather, Fred Dalton Thompson, Celeste Yarnall, Nora Dunn. Amiable remake of Garson Kanin comedy, set in Washington, D.C., about boorish tycoon who hires bookish reporter to give his mistress some education and couth. The three leads are well cast, but the movie sags after a while, losing its comic punch. [PG]▼●)

Borrower, The (1991) **C-97m.** **½ D: John McNaughton. Rae Dawn Chong, Don Gordon, Tom Towles, Antonio Fargas, Neil Giuntoli, Larry Pennell, Tony Amendola, Pam Gordon, Mädchen Amick, Stuart Cornfeld. An alien criminal is "devolved" to human shape and exiled on Earth; when his head explodes, he starts ripping the heads off human beings (and others) and donning them until they go bad, too. Understandably confused cops Chong and Gordon are on his trail. Gleefully outrageous horror premise supported by strong, stylish direction and a well-written script. [R]▼●

Borrowers, The (1997-British) **C-83m.** **½ D: Peter Hewitt. John Goodman, Jim Broadbent, Mark Williams, Hugh Laurie, Bradley Pierce, Flora Newbigin, Tom Felton, Celia Imrie, Ruby Wax. Just OK rendering of Mary Norton's children's novels about a household of tiny human pilferers who reduce baddie Goodman to rubble after he cheats a nice family out of their inherited house. Actors acting against oversized sets remains an irresistible concept, but the movie won't make anyone forget THE INCREDIBLE SHRINKING MAN or the wonderful fantasy scenes in Nicolas Roeg's THE WITCHES. A bit too much HOME ALONE–style slapstick violence, but the short running time helps. Filmed before as a TVM in 1973 and as a British miniseries in 1993. [PG]▼●

Borsalino (1970-French) **C-125m.** *** D: Jacques Deray. Jean-Paul Belmondo, Alain Delon, Michel Bouquet, Catherine Rouvel, Francoise Christophe. PUBLIC ENEMY, French-style; delightful seriocomic film of two likable hoods who become gangland chieftains in 1930s Marseilles. Stars in top form; Claude Bolling's infectious music helps. Sequel: BORSALINO & CO. [PG]▼

Borstal Boy (2000-Irish-British) **C-91m.** **½ D: Peter Sheridan. Shawn Hatosy, Danny Dyer, Lee Ingleby, Robin Laing, Eva Birthistle, Michael York. Nostalgia-soaked, revisionist coming-of-age portrait of an artist as a young man. Loosely based on the memoir of the same name by Brendan Behan, the fabled Irish writer-drunkard, the scenario depicts Behan (American actor Hatosy) as an idealistic 16-year-old I.R.A. member who lands in a British borstal (reform school). York has his best role in years as the borstal's warden. Debut feature for theater director Sheridan, who coscripted; he is the brother of Jim Sheridan, who co-executive produced.▼●

Boss SEE: **Boss Nigger**

Bossa Nova (1999-Brazilian-U.S.) **C-95m.** ** D: Bruno Barreto. Amy Irving, Antonio Fagundes, Alexandre Borges, Débora Bloch, Drica Moraes, Giovanna Antonelli, Alberto de Mendoza, Stephen Tobolowsky. Airy romantic comedy-of-errors involving Brazilian-based widow and English tutor (Irving), the successful older businessman who falls in love with her (Fagundes), and a variety of friends and family members whose love lives crisscross around them. Pleasant enough, with attractive scenery, but resolutely ordinary. Super 35. [R] ▼●

Boss Nigger (1975) **C-92m.** ** D: Jack Arnold. Fred Williamson, D'Urville Martin, R. G. Armstrong, William Smith, Barbara Leigh, Carmen Hayworth. Clichéd blaxploitation Western with Williamson as a bounty hunter who predictably outhustles every white man in sight! In spite of its title, not as offensive as others of the genre (mainly because there's no graphic violence). Williamson scripted; also known as BOSS and

THE BLACK BOUNTY KILLER. Todd-AO 35. [PG]▼

Boss Of It All, The (2006-Danish-Swedish-Italian-French) **C-99m.** *** D: Lars von Trier. Jens Albinus, Peter Gantzler, Fridrik Thor Fridriksson, Benedikt Erlingsson, Iben Hjejle, Henrik Prip, Mia Lyhne, Casper Christensen, Louise Mieritz, Jean-Marc Barr, Lars von Trier. Out-of-work actor (Albinus) signs on to impersonate a company CEO and becomes involved in a contentious negotiation. Insightful satire of corporate chicanery, employer-employee relations, and the psychology/egomania of actors. One of von Trier's more accessible films, but some may find his excessive use of jump cuts disconcerting. Filmed in Automavision, which allows a computer to determine camera angles and movement.▶

Boss' Son, The (1978) **C-97m.** *** D: Bobby Roth. Asher Brauner, Rudy Solari, Rita Moreno, Henry G. Sanders, James Darren, Richie Havens, Piper Laurie, Elena Verdugo. Good little independent feature by writer-director Roth about a young man reluctantly going into his father's carpet factory business. Credible, engaging.▼

Boss' Wife, The (1986) **C-83m.** *½ D: Ziggy Steinberg. Daniel Stern, Arielle Dombasle, Fisher Stevens, Melanie Mayron, Lou Jacobi, Martin Mull, Christopher Plummer, Thalmus Rasulala, Robert Costanzo. Interesting cast falters in this tepid will-he-or-won't-he comedy about an ambitious young stockbroker (Stern) and the title lady (Dombasle), who's out to seduce him. [R]▼

Boston Blackie series SEE: *Leonard Maltin's Classic Movie Guide*

Bostonians, The (1984) **C-120m.** ** D: James Ivory. Christopher Reeve, Vanessa Redgrave, Madeleine Potter, Jessica Tandy, Nancy Marchand, Wesley Addy, Linda Hunt, Wallace Shawn. Redgrave is perfectly cast as Henry James' 19th-century feminist heroine in this careful adaptation of his novel by Ruth Prawer Jhabvala . . . but the film itself, for all its period detail, is deadly slow and uninvolving. Reeve is in over his head as Redgrave's contrary cousin. ▼◖▶

Boston Strangler, The (1968) **C-116m.** *** D: Richard Fleischer. Tony Curtis, Henry Fonda, George Kennedy, Mike Kellin, Hurd Hatfield, Murray Hamilton, Jeff Corey, Sally Kellerman, William Marshall, George Voskovec, William Hickey, James Brolin. Absorbing drama, semidocumentary-style, detailing rise, manhunt, capture, prosecution of notorious criminal. Curtis gives startling performance as killer. Impact of complex multi-image technique may be lost on TV screen. Panavision. [R]▼▶

Botany Bay (1953) **C-94m.** **½ D: John Farrow. Alan Ladd, James Mason, Patricia Medina, Cedric Hardwicke. Based on

Charles Nordhoff novel set in 1790s, picturesque yarn tells of convict ship bound for Australia, focusing on conflict between prisoner Ladd and sadistic skipper Mason, with Medina as Ladd's love interest.▼

Bottle Rocket (1996) **C-95m.** **½ D: Wes Anderson. Owen C. Wilson, Luke Wilson, Robert Musgrave, Andrew Wilson, Lumi Cavazos, James Caan, Teddy Wilson, Jim Ponds. Original, low-key comedy about two young friends—and chronic screw-ups—who attempt to embark on a life of crime. Engaging performances by Owen C. Wilson (who cowrote the film), as Dignan, and his real-life brother Luke, as Anthony, stand out. (A third brother, Andrew, plays their friend's bullying older sibling.) Expanded from a 13m. short subject. [R]▼◖▶

Bottle Shock (2008) **C-108m.** **½ D: Randall Miller. Bill Pullman, Alan Rickman, Chris Pine, Freddy Rodriguez, Rachael Taylor, Dennis Farina, Miguel Sandoval, Eliza Dushku, Bradley Whitford. In 1976, Paris wine-shop owner Rickman travels to Napa Valley, California, to see if there is anything worth importing for a blind taste test he is planning. Meanwhile, struggling vineyard owner Pullman and his footloose son (Pine) may be on the verge of making their first really good wine. Great real-life story should have yielded a better film; there are good vignettes, and Rickman is a treat to watch, but subplot involving Pine's love life is a distraction. Super 35. [PG-13]▶

Boudu Saved From Drowning (1932-French) **87m.** *** D: Jean Renoir. Michel Simon, Charles Granval, Marcelle Hania, Severine Lerczynska. Title tramp is rescued from the Seine and taken home by well-meaning book dealer; he eventually takes over household, then seduces both the wife and maid. Classic attack on complacency still holds up, with ratty-bearded Simon giving the performance of a lifetime. U.S. remake: DOWN AND OUT IN BEVERLY HILLS.▼◖▶

Boulevard Nights (1979) **C-102m.** ** D: Michael Pressman. Richard Yniguez, Marta Du Bois, Danny De La Paz, Betty Carvalho, Carmen Zapata, James Victor, Victor Millan. Sincere but uninspiring story of Chicano youth who yearns to move away from street-gang life, but drawn back because of hot-blooded young brother. Filmed in the barrios of L.A. [R]▼

Bounce (2000) **C-106m.** **½ D: Don Roos. Gwyneth Paltrow, Ben Affleck, Joe Morton, Natasha Henstridge, Tony Goldwyn, Johnny Galecki, Alex D. Linz, Jennifer Grey, Caroline Aaron, Sam Robards. Hotshot ad exec gives his coveted airline ticket to a chance airport acquaintance who's eager to get home to his family . . . then the plane crashes. A year later, the guilt-ridden adman looks up the man's widow, and quickly finds himself attracted to her. So-so soap opera has appealing stars but suffers from a heavy air of contrivance, which is especially surprising from writer-director Roos. David Paymer appears unbilled. [PG-13]▼●

Bound (1996) **C-109m.** ******* D: The Wachowski Brothers (Larry, Andy). Jennifer Tilly, Gina Gershon, Joe Pantoliano, John Ryan, Christopher Meloni, Richard C. Sarafian. Sexy, stylishly violent noir with a Sapphic twist, about a handywoman (Gershon) and a gangster's moll (Tilly) who conspire to run off together with a suitcase containing two million bucks. The women have chemistry to burn, but Pantoliano steals the movie as the mobster caught in the middle. Impressive directorial debut from the screenwriting-brother duo. Lesbian-erotica author Susie Bright appears in the film, and served as technical adviser. [R]▼●

Bound and Gagged: A Love Story (1993) **C-101m.** ***½** D: Daniel Appleby. Ginger Lynn Allen, Karen Black, Chris Denton, Elizabeth Saltarrelli, Mary Ella Ross, Chris Mulkey. Yet another road movie; this one explores the sexual trials and tribulations of two bisexual women and a rather confused straight guy who's despondent over the breakup of his marriage. Quirky, rather than interesting. Was supposed to usher ex-porn queen Allen into a mainstream movie career. Better luck next time. [R]▼●

Bound by Honor (1993) **C-180m.** ****** D: Taylor Hackford. Damian Chapa, Jesse Borrego, Benjamin Bratt, Enrique Castillo, Victor Rivers, Delroy Lindo, Tom Towles, Carlos Carrasco, Teddy Wilson, Raymond Cruz, Lanny Flaherty, Billy Bob Thornton, Natalija Nogulich, Ving Rhames. Ambitious look at Chicano gang life concerns two half-brothers and a half-white cousin who evolve into a drug-addicted artist, a narcotics detective, and a repeat-offender prisoner. Despite lots of screen time (and a passable beginning), this violent film gives top-heavy emphasis to the cellblock portion of the saga. Script was predominantly written, with shared credit, by acclaimed poet Jimmy Santiago Baca. Video title: BLOOD IN BLOOD OUT. [R]▼●

Bound for Glory (1976) **C-147m.** *****½** D: Hal Ashby. David Carradine, Ronny Cox, Melinda Dillon, Gail Strickland, John Lehne, Ji-Tu Cumbuka, Randy Quaid, M. Emmet Walsh. Life of folk singer-composer Woody Guthrie, superbly played by Carradine, with great feeling for 1936–40 period as Guthrie travels the country fighting and singing for the underdogs, victims of the Great Depression. Haskell Wexler's Oscar-winning photography is tops throughout, as is Leonard Rosenman's score adaptation (also an Oscar winner). Beware of shorter prints. [PG]▼●

Bounty, The (1984) **C-130m.** ******* D: Roger Donaldson. Mel Gibson, Anthony Hopkins, Laurence Olivier, Edward Fox, Daniel Day-Lewis, Bernard Hill, Liam Neeson. Handsome, well made retelling of history's most famous mutiny (*not* based on the Nordhoff-Hall book) paints Bligh as repressed and stubborn, not mad, and Christian as a dilettante with no real substance. Interesting all the way, but emotionally aloof. Great use of widescreen. J-D-C Scope. [PG]▼●

Bounty Hunter, The (2010) **C-110m.** BOMB D: Andy Tennant. Gerard Butler, Jennifer Aniston, Jason Sudeikis, Jeff Garlin, Cathy Moriarty, Peter Greene, Siobhan Fallon Hogan, Carol Kane, Christine Baranski. Relentlessly charmless and frequently obnoxious romantic comedy about an investigative reporter (Aniston) who skips a court date to follow a story, only to be pursued by her bounty-hunting ex-husband (Butler). Even avid fans of the two leads will be disappointed, if not dismayed. Super 35. [PG-13]

Bourne Identity, The (2002) **C-121m.** *****½** D: Doug Liman. Matt Damon, Franka Potente, Chris Cooper, Brian Cox, Clive Owen, Julia Stiles. Crackling spy thriller, from the Robert Ludlum novel, about a CIA operative who's fished out of the ocean and has no memory of his identity or his mission. Soon, circumstances force him to take it on the lam, alongside a woman he chances to meet who happens to have a car. Kudos to Liman for keeping the action taut, the characters believable, and the excitement at a high pitch throughout. Filmed before as a TV miniseries in 1988. Alternate edition runs 119m. Followed by THE BOURNE SUPREMACY. Super 35. [PG-13]▼●

Bourne Supremacy, The (2004) **C-108m.** ****½** D: Paul Greengrass. Matt Damon, Franka Potente, Brian Cox, Joan Allen, Julia Stiles, Karl Urban, Gabriel Mann, Marton Csokas, Tom Gallop, John Bedford Lloyd, Michelle Monaghan, Karel Roden. When an assassin tracks down Jason Bourne and his girlfriend, who are living in exile in India, the CIA-trained killer is forced back into action to find out why he's being hunted. Filled with nail-biting car chases and fight scenes, edited in a rat-tat-tat manner, but lacks the humor and sexual spark that made THE BOURNE IDENTITY so good. Brutal and cold-blooded, like its leading character; we're rooting for Bourne not because he's a hero but simply by default. Chris Cooper appears unbilled, briefly reprising his role from the earlier film. Followed by THE BOURNE ULTIMATUM. Super 35. [PG-13]▼●

Bourne Ultimatum, The (2007) **C-115m.** ******* D: Paul Greengrass. Matt Damon, Julia Stiles, David Strathairn, Joan Allen, Scott Glenn, Paddy Considine, Édgar Ramírez, Albert Finney, Joey Ansah, Daniel Brühl. Third chapter in Robert Ludlum's *Bourne* series has the CIA-trained operative traversing the world as he continues to search for his identity and decide how to settle old scores. All you could ask from an action film, with well-chosen international locales, an intelligently wrought cat-and-mouse narrative, and one breathless action set piece after another. Damon, again, is right on target as Bourne, but his character's virtual indestructibility drains some of the humanity from the proceedings. Oscar winner for Sound Editing, Sound Mixing, and Film Editing (Christopher Rouse). Super 35. [PG-13]▊

The Bowery Boys series SEE: *Leonard Maltin's Classic Movie Guide*

Bowfinger (1999) **C-97m.** **½ D: Frank Oz. Steve Martin, Eddie Murphy, Heather Graham, Christine Baranski, Jamie Kennedy, Robert Downey, Jr., Terence Stamp, Adam Alexi-Malle, Barry Newman. Desperate, down-and-out filmmaker Bobby Bowfinger (Martin) schemes to make a movie with the top action star in Hollywood (Murphy)—without bothering to tell him that he's in the picture! Likable costars carry this comedy a long way; there are some good laughs throughout, but it's never as satisfying as you'd like it to be. Murphy has fun playing a doofus look-alike for the action hero. Written by Martin. [PG-13]▼●▎

Bowling for Columbine (2002) **C-123m.** *** D: Michael Moore. Onetime sharpshooting champion and lifelong NRA member Moore uses his confrontational, highly personal filmmaking style to examine America's love affair with guns. Depending on your point of view, you will find this wide-ranging film to be illuminating or infuriating. Our favorite segment is a condemnation of fear-mongering on TV newscasts . . . but a climactic interview with NRA president Charlton Heston isn't the showdown it should have been. Oscar winner for Best Documentary. [R] ▼▎

Box, The (2009) **C-116m.** ** D: Richard Kelly. Cameron Diaz, James Marsden, Frank Langella, James Rebhorn, Holmes Osborne, Sam Oz Stone. From the director of DONNIE DARKO, another fable percolating with apocalyptic portents. In '70s suburbia, an attractive, cash-strapped couple (Diaz, Marsden) can't resist temptation when a disfigured stranger (Langella) offers them a million dollars if they push a button that will trigger the death of a complete stranger. Not surprisingly, nothing good comes of this. Appreciably more coherent than Kelly's earlier efforts, but frustrating in its pretentiousness. Still, a few scenes have an undeniable power to unsettle, and the lead performances are spot-on. Freely adapted from "Button, Button," a Richard Matheson story that inspired a 1986 episode of the *Twilight Zone* TV series. HD Widescreen. [PG-13]▊

Boxcar Bertha (1972) **C-88m.** **½ D: Martin Scorsese. Barbara Hershey, David Carradine, Barry Primus, Bernie Casey, John Carradine. Scorsese's first studio film is yet another BONNIE AND CLYDE cash-in, with small-town girl Hershey falling in with Carradine and his band of train robbers. Good of its kind, but buffs looking for embryonic Scorsese stylistics may be a little let down . . . although there *are* two minor characters named Michael Powell and Emeric Pressburger! [R]▼●▎

Boxer, The (1971) SEE: **Ripped Off**

Boxer, The (1997-U.S.-Irish) **C-113m.** *** D: Jim Sheridan. Daniel Day-Lewis, Emily Watson, Brian Cox, Ken Stott, Gerard McSorley, Eleanor Methven, Ciaran Fitzgerald, Kenneth Cranham. Powerful, straightforward story of a boxer and former IRA member released from prison after 14 years, trying to rebuild his life in troubled Belfast and becoming involved with his old sweetheart, who's married to a political prisoner. Third teaming of Day-Lewis and director/cowriter Sheridan lacks the complexity and resonance of MY LEFT FOOT and IN THE NAME OF THE FATHER, but is still compelling human drama, anchored by Day-Lewis and the luminous Watson. Stunningly filmed by Chris Menges in Dublin. [R]▼●▎

Boxing Gym (2010) **C-91m.** *** D: Frederick Wiseman. Absorbing documentary about the title gymnasium—a facility in Austin, Texas, run by former professional-boxer-turned-trainer Richard Lord—and the diverse people who work, and work out, there. Director-editor Wiseman, one of the grand masters of cinéma vérité, employs his usual straightforward style—no talking heads, music, or narration—which allows the film (and viewers) to slowly, quietly build connections between the people on-screen and more meditative concerns about social interaction, physical and mental conditioning, and violence.

Boxing Helena (1993) **C-107m.** *½ D: Jennifer Chambers Lynch. Julian Sands, Sherilyn Fenn, Bill Paxton, Art Garfunkel, Kurtwood Smith, Betsy Clark, Nicolette Scorsese. Dreadful debut feature from the 24-year-old daughter of David Lynch, about an esteemed surgeon (Sands) whose obsession with sexpot Fenn leads to a bizarre set of circumstances. Tries to be provocative and shocking, but the result is unintentional laughter (when it's not boring). Originally NC-17, rerated after appeal. Super 35. [R]▼●▎

Box of Moon Light (1997) **C-107m.** **½ D: Tom DiCillo. John Turturro, Sam Rockwell, Catherine Keener, Lisa Blount, Annie Corley, Dermot Mulroney. A very slight slice of whimsy about an uptight engineer, supervising a construction project out of town, who quite by chance falls in with a free spirit who lives in the woods . . . and finds that he feels liberated as he spends time away from the precision of his normal life. Turturro is excellent, as always, and so is Rockwell as Kid, but the story has few surprises, and its charms are stretched pretty thin. DiCillo also scripted. [R] ▼●)

Boy A (2007-British) **C-106m.** **½ D: John Crowley. Andrew Garfield, Peter Mullan, Katie Lyons, Shaun Evans, Jeremy Swift, Alfie Owen, Taylor Doherty, Anthony Lewis. In northern England, a taciturn young man (Garfield) has been released from penitentiary and is starting life anew, guided by a dedicated, fatherly social worker (Mullan). While he attempts to build new personal and professional relationships we learn—via small flashback bits—how the former schoolboy got into trouble. Intentionally bleak and a bit contrived, grim film is still quite involving and well acted. Based on a novel by Jonathan Trigell. Debuted on British TV prior to theatrical release. [R]◗

Boy and His Dog, A (1975) **C-87m.** **½ D: L. Q. Jones. Don Johnson, Susanne Benton, Jason Robards, Alvy Moore, Helene Winston, Charles McGraw, Tiger; voice of Tim McIntire. Cult black comedy is definitely not a kiddie movie, despite its title. In the post-holocaust future, young punk Johnson, aided by his telepathic (and much smarter) dog, forages for food and women, then is lured into bizarre underground civilization. Faithful adaptation of Harlan Ellison's novella. Revised in 1982 to include a 1m. prologue. Techniscope. [R] ▼●)

Boy Cried Murder, The (1966-British) **C-86m.** **½ D: George Breakston. Veronica Hurst, Phil Brown, Beba Loncar, Frazer MacIntosh, Tim Barrett. A reworking of THE WINDOW set in Adriatic resort town. Youngster noted for his fabrications witnesses a murder; no one but the killer believes him.

Boy, Did I Get a Wrong Number! (1966) **C-99m.** BOMB D: George Marshall. Bob Hope, Elke Sommer, Phyllis Diller, Cesare Danova, Marjorie Lord. They sure did; result is worthless film that should be avoided. Absolutely painful.▼◗

Boy Friend, The (1971-British) **C-135m.** *** D: Ken Russell. Twiggy, Christopher Gable, Moyra Fraser, Max Adrian, Vladek Sheybal, Georgina Hale, Tommy Tune; cameo by Glenda Jackson. Director Russell's homage to Hollywood musicals works on several levels, from tacky matinee performance of a show to fantasy-world conception of same material, all loosely tied to Sandy Wilson's cunning spoof of 1920s musical shows. Busby Berkeley-ish numbers (choreographed by Gable) come amazingly close to spirit and execution of the Master himself. Originally released in U.S. at 110m. Panavision. [G]▼●)

Boyfriends and Girlfriends (1987-French) **C-102m.** *** D: Eric Rohmer. Emmanuelle Chaulet, Sophie Renoir, Anne-Laure Meury, Eric Viellard, Francois-Eric Gendron. The sixth of Rohmer's "Comedies and Proverbs" is a typically witty, perceptive, ironic account of two very different young women who strike up a friendship . . . and commence playing romantic musical chairs with a couple of men. Nobody can direct characters who are forever falling in and out of love quite like Eric Rohmer. Originally shown as MY GIRLFRIEND'S BOYFRIEND. [PG]▼●)

Boyfriend School, The SEE: **Don't Tell Her It's Me**

Boy in Blue, The (1986-Canadian) **C-98m.** ** D: Charles Jarrott. Nicolas Cage, Cynthia Dale, Christopher Plummer, David Naughton, Sean Sullivan, Melody Anderson. Humdrum tale of real-life 19th-century Canadian rowing champ Ned Hanlan; filled with stock characters, from faithful manager to "unattainable" love interest. Barely stays afloat. [R]▼◗

Boy in the Striped Pajamas, The (2008-U.S.-British) **C-94m.** *** D: Mark Herman. David Thewlis, Vera Farmiga, Rupert Friend, David Hayman, Asa Butterfield, Jack Scanlon, Amber Beattie, Sheila Hancock, Richard Johnson, Jim Norton. Unique Holocaust fable (from John Boyne's novel for young readers) about the 8-year-old son of an SS officer who moves with his family to a new home in the country. He can't help being curious about the "farm" nearby with a barbed-wire fence—and a boy about his age on the other side. Quietly powerful drama personalizes the qualms and contradictions facing German families during the Nazi era. Screenplay by the director. [PG-13]◗

Boy Meets Girl (1938) **86m.** **½ D: Lloyd Bacon. James Cagney, Pat O'Brien, Marie Wilson, Ralph Bellamy, Frank McHugh, Dick Foran, Penny Singleton, Ronald Reagan. Screwball spoof of Hollywood sometimes pushes too hard, but has enough sharp dialogue, good satire in tale of two sharpster screenwriters to make it worthwhile. Script by Samuel and Bella Spewack, from their Broadway play.▼

Boy Named Charlie Brown, A (1969) **C-85m.** *** D: Bill Melendez. Voices of Peter Robbins, Pamelyn Ferdin, Glenn Gilger, Andy Pforsich. *Peanuts* gang makes surprisingly successful feature-film debut, with ingenious visual ideas adding to usual fun. Only debit: Rod McKuen's absurd songs. [G]▼●)

Boynton Beach Club (2006) **C-105m.** *** D: Susan Seidelman. Dyan Cannon, Brenda Vaccaro, Sally Kellerman, Joseph Bologna, Len Cariou, Michael Nouri, Renee Taylor, Mal Z. Lawrence. Affecting, funny look at love among senior citizens in a Florida retirement community. Vaccaro is the newest (reluctant) recruit for the Boynton Beach Bereavement Club after her husband's sudden demise; in addition to companionship she needs to vent her anger over his needless death. Appealing performances by all the leading actors propel this minor but good-hearted film, one of the few to deal with older people without being coy or condescending. Inspired by Seidelman's mother Florence's experiences in one such community. [R]🄳

Boy on a Dolphin (1957) **C-111m.** **½ D: Jean Negulesco. Alan Ladd, Clifton Webb, Sophia Loren, Laurence Naismith, Alex Minotis, Jorge Mistral. Loren's Hollywood debut understandably caused a sensation for her initial appearance in a wet, clingy blouse; thereafter, it's an OK adventure about rival teams of divers racing to locate the titular statue, sunk centuries ago off the island of Hydra. Spectacular Greek locations are the real stars; Webb's droll villainy is another asset. CinemaScope.▼

Boys (1996) **C-88m.** ** D: Stacy Cochran. Winona Ryder, Lukas Haas, John C. Reilly, James LeGros, Skeet Ulrich, Wiley Wiggins, Russell Young, Chris Cooper, Jessica Harper, Catherine Keener. Moody but muddled coming-of-age story about a prep school boy (Haas) who helps a woman (Ryder) after an accident and then becomes entangled in her mysterious past. Frustrating plot takes time getting started, but has no real story to tell. Attractive New England locations and good performance by Haas can't make up for lapses in logic . . . and a tacked-on happy ending. [PG-13]▼●🄳

Boys and Girl From County Clare, The (2005-Irish) **C-90m.** *** D: John Irvin. Colm Meaney, Bernard Hill, Andrea Corr, Philip Barantini, Charlotte Bradley, Shaun Evans, Patrick Bergin. Two brothers (Meaney, Hill) who haven't seen each other in years revive a longtime rivalry when their bands compete in a traditional Ceili music festival. Entertaining comedy set in the 1960s stops just short of being too cute; sentimental, undemanding entertainment with canny performances by the leading actors. Corr, of the Irish pop group The Corrs, is an engaging love interest for Evans. Made in 2003. Panavision.▼🄳

Boys and Girls (2000) **C-94m.** BOMB D: Robert Iscove. Freddie Prinze, Jr., Claire Forlani, Jason Biggs, Amanda Detmer, Alyson Hannigan, Heather Donahue, Lisa Eichhorn. Two students (Prinze and Forlani) find their paths constantly crossing; then a friendship develops. Tiresome rehash of WHEN HARRY MET SALLY among the college set, with grating characters you just want to slap silly. [PG-13]▼🄳

Boys Are Back, The (2009-Australian-British) **C-104m.** **½ D: Scott Hicks. Clive Owen, Emma Booth, Laura Fraser,

George MacKay, Nicholas McAnulty, Julia Blake, Chris Haywood, Natasha Little, Erik Thomson. Busy sports reporter's wife suddenly dies, leaving him to raise their 6-year-old son . . . but he's never spent much time as a hands-on dad. Then an older son from an earlier marriage comes to visit from England, which further complicates the family dynamic. Well-intentioned drama never reaches the emotional peak it ought to—or might have had on the printed page. Based on a memoir by Simon Carr. [PG-13]🄳

Boys Don't Cry (1999) **C-119m.** **½ D: Kimberly Peirce. Hilary Swank, Chloë Sevigny, Peter Sarsgaard, Brendan Sexton III, Alison Folland, Alicia Goranson, Jeannetta Arnette. Searing drama based on the 1993 case of Brandon Teena (Swank, in an Oscar-winning performance), a girl who passes herself off as a boy in rural Nebraska. Moving to a new town, she/he finds a soul mate who deliberately doesn't ask too many questions . . . but infuriates the girl's trailer-trash friends and family. Well made in every respect, but fails to get inside the characters' heads; the violent conclusion is almost unbearable to watch. Same material explored in the documentary THE BRANDON TEENA STORY. [R]▼🄳

Boys From Brazil, The (1978) **C-123m.** **½ D: Franklin J. Schaffner. Gregory Peck, Laurence Olivier, James Mason, Lilli Palmer, Uta Hagen, John Dehner, Rosemary Harris, Anne Meara, John Rubinstein, Denholm Elliott, Steven Guttenberg, David Hurst, Jeremy Black, Bruno Ganz, Walter Gotell, Michael Gough, Prunella Scales. Former Nazi chieftain Dr. Josef Mengele (Peck) has insidious plan to breed new race of Hitlers. Interesting but ultimately silly and unbelievable; worth watching, though, for Olivier's brilliant, credible performance as aging Jewish Nazi-hunter. Based on Ira Levin novel. [R]▼●🄳

Boys From Brooklyn, The SEE: **Bela Lugosi Meets a Brooklyn Gorilla**

Boys in Company C, The (1978) **C-127m.** *** D: Sidney J. Furie. Stan Shaw, Andrew Stevens, James Canning, Michael Lembeck, Craig Wasson, Scott Hylands, James Whitmore, Jr., Lee Ermey. Shaw (in a standout performance) whips a bunch of green Marine recruits into shape for combat in Vietnam; good, tough film focuses on stupidity of military brass and demoralization of the soldiers. Panavision. [R]▼●🄳

Boys in the Band, The (1970) **C-119m.** ***½ D: William Friedkin. Kenneth Nelson, Peter White, Leonard Frey, Cliff Gorman, Frederick Combs, Laurence Luckinbill, Keith Prentice, Robert LaTourneaux, Reuben Greene. Excellent filmization of Mart Crowley's landmark play about nine men at a birthday party: eight are gay, the ninth insists he's not. Often hilarious, frequently sad, but always thought provoking, and sensationally acted by the original stage cast; a rare case where a single, claustrophobic set is actually an asset. [R] ▼●)

Boys Next Door, The (1985) C-88m. ** D: Penelope Spheeris. Maxwell Caulfield, Charlie Sheen, Christopher McDonald, Hank Garrett, Patti D'Arbanville, Moon Zappa. Alienated teens Caulfield and Sheen, just about to graduate high school, go on a murder spree. A not-uninteresting portrait of desperation and hopelessness that ultimately fails because there's no real insight into the boys' behavior. [R] ▼●)

Boys' Night Out (1962) C-115m. *** D: Michael Gordon. Kim Novak, James Garner, Tony Randall, Howard Duff, Janet Blair, Patti Page, Zsa Zsa Gabor, Howard Morris. Trio of married men and bachelor Garner decide to set up an apartment equipped with Novak. Some interesting innuendos, with comic relief from Blair, Page, and Gabor. CinemaScope. ▼)

Boys of Paul Street, The (1969-Hungarian-U.S.) C-108m. *** D: Zoltan Fabri. Anthony Kemp, Robert Efford, Gary O'Brien, Mark Colleano, John Moulder Brown. Allegory of children's battle for control of vacant lot in Budapest, from Ferenc Molnar's novel; eloquent statement on war. Filmed before in Hollywood as NO GREATER GLORY. Agascope. [G]

Boys on the Side (1995) C-117m. *** D: Herbert Ross. Whoopi Goldberg, Mary-Louise Parker, Drew Barrymore, Matthew McConaughey, James Remar, Billy Wirth, Anita Gillette, Estelle Parsons, Dennis Boutsikaris, Gedde Watanabe. Extremely likable film about three disparate women who travel cross-country and become involved in each other's lives. Any film incorporating physical abuse, premarital pregnancy, AIDS, and lesbianism has got its work cut out for it; three strong, appealing performances make up for story contrivances (and credibility gaps). Super 35. [R] ▼●)

Boys Town (1938) 96m. *** D: Norman Taurog. Spencer Tracy, Mickey Rooney, Henry Hull, Gene Reynolds, Leslie Fenton, Addison Richards, Edward Norris, Sidney Miller, Bobs Watson, Frankie Thomas. Tracy won Oscar as Father Flanagan, who develops school for juvenile delinquents; Rooney is his toughest enrolee. Syrupy but well done; Eleanore Griffin and Dore Schary also earned Oscars for their original story. Sequel: MEN OF BOYS TOWN (1941). Almost 60 years later, Rooney played Father Flanagan in the direct-to-video feature THE ROAD HOME. Also shown in computer-colored version. ▼●)

Boy Ten Feet Tall, A (1963-British) C-118m. *** D: Alexander Mackendrick. Edward G. Robinson, Fergus McClelland, Constance Cummings, Harry H. Corbett. Colorful, charming film about orphaned boy traveling through Africa alone to reach his aunt, who lives in Durban. Cut to 88m. for American release. Originally titled SAMMY GOING SOUTH. CinemaScope.

Boy Who Could Fly, The (1986) C-114m. **½ D: Nick Castle. Lucy Deakins, Jay Underwood, Bonnie Bedelia, Fred Savage, Colleen Dewhurst, Fred Gwynne, Louise Fletcher, Jason Priestley. Sensitive girl moves to a new neighborhood and befriends an autistic (and mysterious) boy next door. Warm, well-intentioned film moves very slowly and makes uncomfortable turn from believable drama to fantasy—undermining much of its effectiveness. Good feelings and good performances (especially Bedelia and newcomer Deakins) help keep it aloft. Written by director Castle. [PG] ▼●)

Boy Who Cried Bitch, The (1991) C-101m. *** D: Juan Jose Campanella. Harley Cross, Karen Young, Dennis Boutsikaris, Adrien Brody, Gene Canfield, Moira Kelly, Jesse Bradford, J. D. Daniels, Kario Salem, Samuel Wright. Thoughtful, unsettling drama about violent, psychotic 12-year-old Cross, whose mother hasn't given him proper parental attention, and whose psychiatric care is inadequate at best. Well made, extremely well acted, but be forewarned: it's unrelentingly grim and sad.

Boy Who Cried Werewolf, The (1973) C-93m. ** D: Nathan Juran. Kerwin Mathews, Elaine Devry, Scott Sealey, Robert J. Wilke, Susan Foster. Boy discovers his own father has become a werewolf and is on the prowl. More like an adventure thriller than a horror movie, but not much good as anything. Odd werewolf makeup. [PG]

Boy Who Had Everything, The (1984-Australian) C-94m. ** D: Stephen Wallace. Jason Connery, Diane Cilento, Laura Williams, Lewis Fitz-Gerald, Ian Gilmour. Uneven, inconsequential account of sensitive first-year university student Connery, his relationships with his mother and girlfriend, and his growing pains. Jason is the son of Sean Connery and Diane Cilento (who plays his mom here). [R]

Boy With Green Hair, The (1948) C-82m. *** D: Joseph Losey. Pat O'Brien, Robert Ryan, Barbara Hale, Dean Stockwell, Dwayne Hickman. Thought-provoking allegory of war orphan Stockwell, who becomes a social outcast when his hair changes color. Controversial on its release because of its pacifistic point of view. Dale Robertson and Russ Tamblyn appear uncredited. ▼●)

Boyz N the Hood (1991) C-107m. *** D: John Singleton. Larry Fishburne, Ice Cube, Cuba Gooding, Jr., Nia Long, Morris Chestnut, Tyra Ferrell, Angela Bassett, Whitman Mayo. Sober, thoughtful look at life in the black section of South Central L.A. A divorced father strives to raise his son with values—and steer him away from the ignorance and aimlessness that has led to an epidemic of senseless violence in the neighborhood. Impressive debut for 23-year-old writer-director Singleton; longish, and not always on-the-money, but overall quite potent and effective. Singleton has a bit part as a mailman. [R]▼●◗

Braddock: Missing in Action III (1988) C-101m. BOMB D: Aaron Norris. Chuck Norris, Aki Aleong, Roland Harrah III, Miki King. Dreary comic book sequel with Colonel Norris returning to Vietnam yet again, this time to look for his wife. Chuck even coscripted, with brother Aaron serving as director. [R]▼●◗

Brady Bunch Movie, The (1995) C-90m. **½ D: Betty Thomas. Shelley Long, Gary Cole, Michael McKean, Jean Smart, Henriette Mantel, Christopher Daniel Barnes, Christine Taylor, Paul Sutera, Jennifer Elise Cox, Jesse Lee, Olivia Hack, Reni Santoni. Dead-on parody of the enduringly popular early '70s TV sitcom, with America's favorite white-bread family unaware that values and mores have changed all around them. Long and Cole are a hoot as the parents, but if you're not a series devotee, many of the gags and story references will have no meaning whatsoever. Predictably, there are cameos by veterans of the original show. Followed by A VERY BRADY SEQUEL. [PG-13]▼●◗

Brain, The (1962-British-German) 85m. *** D: Freddie Francis. Anne Heywood, Peter Van Eyck, Cecil Parker, Bernard Lee, Maxine Audley, Jeremy Spenser, Jack MacGowran. Good remake of DONOVAN'S BRAIN, about scientist overtaken by the brain of a vengeance-seeking dead man that is being kept "alive" in his laboratory. Original British title: VENGEANCE.▼

Brain, The (1969-French) C-100m. ** D: Gerard Oury. David Niven, Jean-Paul Belmondo, Bourvil, Eli Wallach, Silvia Monti, Fernand Valois. Fine international cast in OK caper comedy about a train heist masterminded by Niven. Franscope. [G]▼

Brain Candy (1996) C-88m. **½ D: Kelly Makin. David Foley, Bruce McCulloch, Kevin McDonald, Mark McKinney, Scott Thompson, Kathryn Greenwood, Janeane Garofalo. New wonder drug that cures depression has devastating side effect on the population now addicted to the product. This premise intertwines the lives of over 30 characters played by Kids in the Hall, the Canadian TV sketch troupe in their feature-film debut. Funny sequences and bizarre characters don't add up to a satisfying whole, but the cast is energetic in many original and unusual guises, often in drag. Standout moment has Thompson "coming out" in splashy Hollywood musical production number. Brendan Fraser appears

unbilled. On-screen title is KIDS IN THE HALL BRAIN CANDY. [R]▼●◗

Brain Damage (1988) C-94m. *** D: Frank Henenlotter. Rick Herbst, Gordon MacDonald, Jennifer Lowry, Theo Barnes, Lucille Saint-Peter, Vicki Darnell. Extremely strange, oddly effective horror film about Herbst and a monster parasite that gives him psychedelic "highs" by injecting fluid into his brain. And that's not the half of it! Clever parable about drug addiction features a funny cameo by the star of Henenlotter's first film, BASKET CASE. [R]▼◗

Brain Donors (1992) C-80m. ** D: Dennis Dugan. John Turturro, Bob Nelson, Mel Smith, Nancy Marchand, John Savident, George De La Pena, Juli Donald, Spike Alexander, Teri Copley. Three social misfits team up to bilk a wealthy matron who wants to establish her own ballet company. Full-bore attempt to re-create an old-time movie comedy, officially "suggested" by A NIGHT AT THE OPERA, with Turturro as Groucho, Nelson as Harpo, Smith as Chico, and Marchand as Margaret Dumont. Scores high marks for good intentions but pretty much falls flat. Great Claymation title sequence by Will Vinton's studio. Written by Pat Proft. [PG]▼●◗

Brainscan (1994-U.S.-Canadian) C-95m. ** D: John Flynn. Edward Furlong, Frank Langella, T Rider-Smith, Amy Hargreaves, Jamie Marsh, David Hemblen. Teenaged Furlong has few friends, still grieves over the accident that killed his mother, and is obsessed by horror movies and computer games. All of which makes him ripe for the new game, Brainscan—which seems to be turning him into an unwitting murderer. A good cast and director do what they can with mediocre material. [R]▼●◗

Brain Smasher . . . A Love Story (1993) C-88m. *½ D: Albert Pyun. Andrew Dice Clay, Teri Hatcher, Yuji Okumoto, Deborah Van Valkenburgh, Brion James, Tim Thomerson, Charles Rocket, Nicholas Guest. One night in Portland, Oregon, nightclub bouncer Clay helps model Hatcher combat a mob of evil Chinese monks who are after the Red Lotus of Ultimate Power. Failed attempt to turn Clay into a Stallone-like action star is a slow, foggy bore. Hatcher is cute in hot pants, though. [PG-13]▼◗

Brainstorm (1983) C-106m. *** D: Douglas Trumbull. Christopher Walken, Natalie Wood, Louise Fletcher, Cliff Robertson, Joe Dorsey. Research scientists Walken and Fletcher perfect a sensory experience device—in the form of a headset—with explosive potential. Entertainingly old-fashioned "mad scientist" type tale brought up to date, though it's best not to examine story too closely. Fletcher gives film's standout performance, but Wood, in her last film (she died during production in

1981) has a basically thankless role. Sure to lose most of its impact on TV screens since Trumbull's state-of-the-art visual effects were designed for 70mm Super Panavision. [PG]▼●❍

Brainwash SEE: **Circle of Power**

BrainWaves (1982) **C-80m. ✻✻** D: Ulli Lommel. Keir Dullea, Suzanna Love, Tony Curtis, Vera Miles, Percy Rodrigues, Paul Willson. Young woman, injured in an accident, receives the brain (and brainwaves) of a murdered girl and then is stalked by her killer. A glum-looking Tony Curtis is the modern-day Dr. Frankenstein in this pedestrian thriller. [PG—edited from original R rating]▼●

Bramble Bush, The (1960) **C-105m. ✻✻½** D: Daniel Petrie. Richard Burton, Barbara Rush, Jack Carson, Angie Dickinson. Charles Mergendahl's potboiler becomes superficial gloss with Burton, totally ill at ease, playing New England doctor returning to Cape Cod, where he falls in love with his dying friend's wife.▼

Bram Stoker's Dracula (1992) **C-123m. ✻✻✻½** D: Francis Ford Coppola. Gary Oldman, Winona Ryder, Anthony Hopkins, Keanu Reeves, Richard E. Grant, Cary Elwes, Bill Campbell, Sadie Frost, Tom Waits, Jay Robinson, Monica Bellucci. Sumptuous retelling of the Dracula legend. Avenging the death of his beloved wife, a 15th-century Romanian warrior lives on through the ages . . . and sets his sights on Victorian London. Sexual, sinuous, exquisitely realized (using every movie artifice imaginable); occasionally let down by story lags . . . but always has one more goodie up its sleeve. Written by James Victor Hart. Kudos to Thomas Sanders' production design, Michael Ballhaus' cinematography, and Wojciech Kilar's powerful music. Won Oscars for makeup, sound effects editing, and costume design. [R]▼●❍

Branded (1950) **C-95m. ✻✻½** D: Rudolph Maté. Alan Ladd, Mona Freeman, Charles Bickford, Joseph Calleia, Milburn Stone. Outlaws use carefree Ladd to impersonate rancher Bickford's long-missing son, leading to much different outcome than anticipated; action and love scenes balanced OK.▼●❍

Branded to Kill (1967-Japanese) **91m. ✻✻✻** D: Seijun Suzuki. Jo Shishido, Koji Nambara, Annu Mari, Mariko Ogawa. Stylish and surreal deconstruction of the Yakuza genre, chronicling the bizarre exploits of "Number Three Killer," a hit man with a fetish for smelling boiled rice who finds himself being stalked by "Number One Killer" after he botches an assignment. Typically irreverent and subversive film from cult director Suzuki is also fairly incoherent but technically dazzling. Nikkatsu Scope.▼●

Brannigan (1975-British) **C-111m. ✻✻½** D: Douglas Hickox. John Wayne, Richard Attenborough, Judy Geeson, John Vernon, Mel Ferrer, Ralph Meeker, Lesley-Anne Down. A criminal flees to London to avoid extradition, and Chicago cop Wayne pursues him. Overlong, but change of locale serves Duke well; highlight is amusing brawl in pub. Panavision. [PG]▼●

Bran Nue Dae (2010-Australian) **C-81m. ✻✻✻** D: Rachel Perkins. Rocky McKenzie, Jessica Mauboy, Ernie Dingo, Missy Higgins, Geoffrey Rush, Deborah Mailman, Tom Budge, Magda Szubanski. Infectiously cheerful adaptation of the 1990 stage musical (by Jimmy Chi and Kuckles) set in 1969. Willie (McKenzie) is an aboriginal boy who's too shy to tell a girl he loves her, too weak to stand up to his mother, and too frightened to do anything but run away from the seminary school in Perth presided over by the exacting Father Benedictus (Rush). This sets him on a road trip that becomes a voyage of discovery. A knowing wink back at a not-so-distant time in Australia, with tuneful songs and an upbeat spirit. Super 35. [PG-13]❍

Brasher Doubloon, The (1947) **72m. ✻✻** D: John Brahm. George Montgomery, Nancy Guild, Conrad Janis, Roy Roberts, Fritz Kortner. Rare coin seems to be object of several murders in very uneven version of Philip Marlowe detective mystery. Filmed before as TIME TO KILL.

Brassed Off (1996-British-U.S.) **C-109m. ✻✻✻** D: Mark Herman. Pete Postlethwaite, Tara Fitzgerald, Ewan McGregor, Stephen Tompkinson, Jim Carter, Philip Jackson, Peter Martin, Sonue Johnston. Yorkshire mine workers eke out a living but find solace as members of an amateur, all-male brass band. They are threatened by the not unrelated factors of (a) the mining pit's possible closure and (b) a young woman invading their territory. Seriocomic drama provides an emotional tour de force for Postlethwaite as dogged bandleader, and also for Tompkinson as his beleaguered son. Those are the real-life musicians—members of the Grimethorpe Colliery Band—on the soundtrack. [R]▼●❍

Brass Target (1978) **C-111m. ✻✻** D: John Hough. John Cassavetes, Sophia Loren, George Kennedy, Max von Sydow, Robert Vaughn, Bruce Davison, Patrick McGoohan. Rambling thriller speculates that Gen. Patton (Kennedy) was assassinated just after WW2 because of major gold heist perpetrated by his subordinates. Unfocused storyline is major liability; von Sydow is major asset as the killer. Panavision. [PG]▼●

Bratz (2007) **C-102m. ✻½** D: Sean McNamara. Nathalia Ramos, Janel Parrish, Logan Browning, Skyler Shaye, Chelsea Staub, Lainie Kazan, Jon Voight, Kadeem Hardison. Silly live-action trifle, based on a popular line of fashion dolls, about four pretty, perky high schoolers whose friendships are strained by allegiances to rival cliques. May—repeat, *may*—appeal to preteen girls who treasure their Bratz collections. Super 35. [PG]🔴

Bravados, The (1958) **C-98m.** ******* D: Henry King. Gregory Peck, Joan Collins, Stephen Boyd, Albert Salmi. Compelling Western with embittered Peck showing up in a small town to witness a hanging—but there are complications. Joe De Rita (later Curly Joe of The Three Stooges) plays the hangman. CinemaScope. ▼🔴

Brave Bulls, The (1951) **108m.** ******* D: Robert Rossen. Mel Ferrer, Miroslava, Anthony Quinn, Eugene Iglesias. Flavorful account of public and private life of a matador, based on Tom Lea book. Film admirably captures atmosphere of bullfighting. Some prints now available run 114m., with bullfight footage originally deemed too gruesome for U.S. audiences.

Braveheart (1995) **C-177m.** *****½** D: Mel Gibson. Mel Gibson, Sophie Marceau, Patrick McGoohan, Catherine McCormack, Brendan Gleeson, James Cosmo, David O'Hara, Angus Macfadyen, Peter Henly, James Robinson, Alun Armstrong, Ian Bannen, Brian Cox. Big, booming, epic tale of 13th-century Scottish rebel warrior William Wallace, who builds a grassroots resistance to the tyranny of English King Edward I (McGoohan). Manages to tell a gripping personal story that grows in scale through a series of eye-popping (and bloody) battle scenes. Only the denouement starts to drag. A powerful, passionate film about a powerful, passionate man. Winner of Academy Awards for Best Picture, Director, Cinematography (John Toll), Makeup, and Sound Effects Editing. Panavision. [R] ▼🔴

Brave Little Toaster, The (1987) **C-90m.** ******* D: Jerry Rees. Voices of Jon Lovitz, Tim Stack, Timothy E. Day, Thurl Ravenscroft, Deanna Oliver, Phil Hartman. Entertaining animated feature about a group of humanized household appliances who embark on a perilous journey to find their young master. A welcome throwback to the cartoons of yore, with equal doses of heart and hip humor to please both kids and their parents. Some nice songs by Van Dyke Parks, too. Based on the novel by Thomas M. Disch. Followed by two direct-to-video sequels. ▼🔴

Brave One, The (1956) **C-100m.** ******* D: Irving Rapper. Michel Ray, Rodolfo Hoyos, Fermin Rivera, Elsa Cardenas, Carlos Navarro, Joi Lansing. Predictable but charming tale of peasant-boy Ray and his love for Gitano, a valiant bull destined to meet his fate in the arena. Filmed in Mexico. "Robert Rich" (a pseudonym for blacklisted Dalton Trumbo) received a Best Original Story Academy Award, which went unclaimed until 1975. CinemaScope. ▼🔴

Brave One, The (2007) **C-122m.** ****½** D:

Neil Jordan. Jodie Foster, Terrence Howard, Naveen Andrews, Carmen Ejogo, Nicky Katt, Mary Steenburgen, Jane Adams, Zoë Kravitz, Larry Fessenden. N.Y.C. radio host Foster turns troubled, gun-toting vigilante after she is attacked and her fiancé killed by hoods in Central Park. As the body count rises, she forms an unusual bond with the detective (Howard) who is investigating her handiwork. Serious attempt to examine a post-9/11 world of violence and paranoia becomes more unhinged (and more improbable) as it goes along and stubbornly remains a high-toned DEATH WISH, for better and worse. Typically strong work from Foster and Howard helps. Panavision. [R]🔴

Brazil (1985) **C-131m.** ******* D: Terry Gilliam. Jonathan Pryce, Kim Greist, Robert De Niro, Katherine Helmond, Ian Holm, Bob Hoskins, Michael Palin, Ian Richardson, Peter Vaughan. Dazzlingly different look at bleak future society (kind of a cross between 1984 and A CLOCKWORK ORANGE) where one hapless clerk (Pryce) clings to his ideals and dreams, including his Dream Girl (Greist). A triumph of imagination and production design, full of incredible black comedy . . . but also a relentless film that doesn't know when to quit: second half is often redundant and ineffectual. Gilliam cut film from 142m. for American release. Screenplay by Gilliam, Tom Stoppard, and Charles McKeown. [R] ▼🔴

Breach (2007) **C-110m.** ******* D: Billy Ray. Chris Cooper, Ryan Phillippe, Laura Linney, Dennis Haysbert, Caroline Dhavernas, Gary Cole, Bruce Davison, Kathleen Quinlan. Real-life espionage tale seen through the eyes of ambitious FBI man Eric O'Neill (Phillippe), who's given a thankless assignment. He must earn the confidence of agency veteran Robert Hanssen (Cooper), a devout Catholic and family man who's been selling high-level secrets to the Russians. Solid, straightforward drama with a superior performance by Cooper that reflects the many facets of Hanssen's personality . . . although we never really understand what makes him tick. [PG-13]🔴

Bread and Chocolate (1973-Italian) **C-107m.** *****½** D: Franco Brusati. Nino Manfredi, Anna Karina, Johnny Dorelli, Paolo Turco, Max Delys. Manfredi is marvelous as a Chaplinesque everyman, an optimistic lower-class worker who treks to Switzerland to make his fortune yet remains the eternal outsider. Memorable sequence in a chicken coop. Original running time: 111m. ▼🔴

Bread and Roses (2001-British-German-Spanish) **C-110m.** *****½** D: Ken Loach. Pilar Padilla, Adrien Brody, Elpidia Carrillo, George Lopez, Jack McGee, Alonso Chavez, Monica Rivas, Frank Davila. Gripping fictionalized account of the 2000 L.A. janitors' strike focuses on a Latina illegal immigrant (Padilla) who stands up to her corrupt employers and struggles to convince her coworkers to join the union. Plays a bit like an indie NORMA RAE (with Brody in the Ron Leibman role) but even more realistic. Loach's first American-based film stands among his best at capturing the plight of hard-working, disenfranchised people. Written by Paul Laverty. Features cameos from real-life Latino activists; actors William Atherton, Benicio Del Toro, Tim Roth, and Ron Perlman appear briefly as themselves. [R]▼▶

Bread and Tulips (2000-Italian-Swiss) C-114m. *** D: Silvio Soldini. Licia Maglietta, Bruno Ganz, Marina Massironi, Giuseppe Battiston, Felice Andreasi, Antonio Catania. Lighthearted drama of a woman's liberation, as a suburban housewife-mother, stranded while on vacation, finds a new, rewarding life in exotic Venice. Sweet-natured wish-fulfillment fantasy manages to convince thanks to the story's attention to detail and assured lead performance by Maglietta. [PG-13] ▼▶

Break, The (1998-British-Irish-German-Japanese) C-96m. **½ D: Robert Dornhelm. Stephen Rea, Alfred Molina, Rosana Pastor, Brendan Gleeson, Jorge Sanz, Pruitt Taylor Vince. Rea is excellent, as usual, as an IRA terrorist who unexpectedly becomes part of a Belfast prison break. Before long he's living in N.Y.C., where his long-ago training finds a new outlet as he becomes involved with Guatemalan immigrants. Engrossing if not terribly inspired film based on an idea by Rea. [R]

Breakdown (1997) C-93m. *** D: Jonathan Mostow. Kurt Russell, J.T. Walsh, Kathleen Quinlan, M. C. Gainey, Jack Noseworthy, Rex Linn, Ritch Brinkley. Married couple moving west have car trouble in the midst of the wide open spaces; a trucker picks up the wife so she can phone for help, but that's the last her husband sees of her . . . and no one seems willing or able to help. Superior thriller delivers the goods with airtight plot and all-too-believable situations. Hang on! Cowritten by director Mostow. Super 35. [R]▼▶

Breaker! Breaker! (1977) C-86m. BOMB D: Don Hulette. Chuck Norris, George Murdock, Terry O'Connor, Don Gentry. Cheap, stupid actioner with some (occasional) intentional comedy. Little made of the CB craze as trucker Norris searches for kid brother Michael Augenstein in corrupt judge Murdock's speedtrap town. [PG]▼▶

'Breaker' Morant (1979-Australian) C-107m. ***½ D: Bruce Beresford. Edward Woodward, Jack Thompson, John Waters, Bryan Brown, Charles Tingwell, Vincent Ball, Lewis Fitz-Gerald. Potent drama based on the true story of three soldiers whose actions during the Boer War are used as fodder for a trumped-up court martial—

in order to satisfy the political plans of the British Empire. Based on a play by Kenneth G. Ross. Winner of several Australian Academy Awards. [PG]▼▶

Breakfast at Tiffany's (1961) C-115m. ***½ D: Blake Edwards. Audrey Hepburn, George Peppard, Patricia Neal, Buddy Ebsen, Mickey Rooney, Martin Balsam, John McGiver. Charming film from Truman Capote's story, with Hepburn as Holly Golightly, backwoods girl who goes mod in N.Y.C. Dated trappings don't detract from high comedy and winning romance. Screenplay by George Axelrod. Oscar winner for Score (Henry Mancini) and Song, "Moon River" (Mancini and Johnny Mercer).▼▶

Breakfast Club, The (1985) C-97m. **½ D: John Hughes. Emilio Estevez, Judd Nelson, Molly Ringwald, Anthony Michael Hall, Ally Sheedy, Paul Gleason. A bold experiment in the era of teen raunch movies (written and directed by a man who's made more than his share): five kids sit and talk about themselves, during day-long detention. Alternately poignant, predictable, and self-important, but filled with moments of truth and perception. [R]▼▶

Breakfast of Champions (1999) C-110m. *½ D: Alan Rudolph. Bruce Willis, Albert Finney, Nick Nolte, Barbara Hershey, Glenne Headly, Lukas Haas, Omar Epps, Buck Henry, Vicki Lewis, Jake Johannsen, Will Patton, Owen Wilson, Chip Zien, Alison Eastwood. Lives in confusion: Car dealer Willis is suicidal, his salesman Nolte is a secret transvestite, and obscure sci-fi writer Kilgore Trout (Finney) is hitching cross-country to be honored for the first time. Rudolph's go-for-broke, in-your-face style does no favors to Kurt Vonnegut, Jr.'s already bizarre novel, which Rudolph adapted and Willis self-financed as a labor of love. Haas and Hershey are excellent. Vonnegut briefly appears. [R]▼▶

Breakfast on Pluto (2005-Irish-British) C-135m. **½ D: Neil Jordan. Cillian Murphy, Liam Neeson, Stephen Rea, Brendan Gleeson, Ruth Negga, Laurence Kinlan, Conor McEvoy, Gavin Friday, Ian Hart, Ruth McCabe, Steven Waddington, Eamonn Owens, Bryan Ferry. Episodic account of Murphy, who was abandoned as a baby in Ireland and taken in by a Catholic priest (Neeson). He grows up to be a flagrantly gay cross-dresser who calls himself Kitten, and sets off in search of his real mother. Jordan revisits themes he explored in THE CRYING GAME, including sexual identity and British-Irish politics, but the film is meandering and memorable only for Murphy's performance. Jordan scripted from Patrick McCabe's novel. [R]▶

Breakheart Pass (1976) C-95m. *** D: Tom Gries. Charles Bronson, Ben Johnson, Richard Crenna, Jill Ireland, Charles Durning, Ed Lauter, Roy Jenson, Bill McKinney,

Sally Kirkland, Casey Tibbs. Slambang action Western, with second unit work by Yakima Canutt. Based on Alistair MacLean novel and set mainly on a train, it has Bronson as an undercover agent seeking gun runners and confronting a false epidemic. Highlight: incredible fight between Bronson and former boxing champ Archie Moore. [PG]▼●)

Break In SEE: **Loophole**

Breakin' (1984) **C-90m.** ** D: Joel Silberg. Lucinda Dickey, Adolfo (Shabba-Doo) Quinones, Michael (Boogaloo Shrimp) Chambers, Ben Lokey, Christopher McDonald, Phineas Newborn 3rd, Ice-T. Harmless FLASHDANCE clone, but with the emphasis on break dancing. Here, heroine Dickey waitresses rather than welds. Look for Jean-Claude Van Damme and Lela Rochon as extras in the opening scenes. A sequel followed before the year was out. [PG] ▼●)

Breakin' 2: Electric Boogaloo (1984) **C-94m.** *½ D: Sam Firstenberg. Lucinda Dickey, Adolfo (Shabba-Doo) Quinones, Michael (Boogaloo Shrimp) Chambers, Susie Bono, Lela Rochon (Quinones). Two worthy adversaries—a toothy WASP developer who could rate a centerfold in *Forbes* and a young urban black whose earring is longer than a bola—clash when the former tries to bulldoze a community rec center. The 18 break dancing standards include "Do Your Thang" and "Oye Mamacita." [PG] ▼●)

Breakin' All the Rules (2004) **C-85m.** ** D: Daniel Taplitz. Jamie Foxx, Morris Chestnut, Gabrielle Union, Jennifer Esposito, Peter MacNicol, Bianca Lawson. Magazine editor gets dumped by his fiancée and writes a survival guide on the subject. Then his cousin, a self-styled player (Chestnut), asks for his help in losing a girlfriend (Union) who's getting too serious—and things start getting complicated. Slick comedy of errors has a lively, likable cast, but plays flat; the story is better told in the coming attractions trailer. Super 35. [PG-13]▼●

Breaking and Entering (2006-U.S.-British) **C-116m.** *** D: Anthony Minghella. Jude Law, Juliette Binoche, Robin Wright Penn, Martin Freeman, Ray Winstone, Vera Farmiga, Rafi Gavron, Poppy Rogers, Juliet Stevenson. Architect Law opens a new high-tech office with his partner in a dodgy London neighborhood, where they are repeatedly burglarized. He follows a teenage thief home one night, then finds an excuse to talk to his mother, an Eastern European immigrant (Binoche). This blossoms into a surprising relationship that reflects on the malaise of his marriage to Wright Penn. Writer-director Minghella explores issues of morality in a world where absolutes don't stand up anymore. Provocative and original. Super 35. [R]❙

Breaking Away (1979) **C-100m.** ***½

D: Peter Yates. Dennis Christopher, Dennis Quaid, Daniel Stern, Jackie Earle Haley, Barbara Barrie, Paul Dooley, Robyn Douglass, Hart Bochner, Amy Wright, John Ashton, Pamela Jayne (P.J.) Soles. Winning, unpretentious film about four college-age friends in Bloomington, Indiana, who don't know what to do with their lives; one of them (Christopher) has become obsessed with bicycle racing. Dooley stands out in first-rate cast as Christopher's bewildered father. This sleeper hit really comes to life with an audience. Steve Tesich's original screenplay won well-deserved Oscar; later spawned a brief TV series. [PG]▼●)

Breaking Glass (1980-British) **C-104m.** **½ D: Brian Gibson. Phil Daniels, Hazel O'Connor, Jon Finch, Jonathan Pryce, Peter-Hugo Daly, Mark Wingett. Rocker rises from playing small London clubs to superstardom, finds success isn't everything. Good performances by O'Connor, Daniels (as·her youthful manager), Pryce (as a junkie saxophone player) offset predictable storyline. Panavision. [PG]▼

Breaking In (1989) **C-91m.** **½ D: Bill Forsyth. Burt Reynolds, Casey Siemaszko, Sheila Kelley, Lorraine Toussaint, Albert Salmi, Harry Carey, Maury Chaykin, Steve Tobolowsky, David Frishberg. Low-key, off-center comedy about an aging safecracker who takes on a young protégé who's got a lot to learn about life, as well as his new profession. John Sayles' script, as interpreted by director Forsyth, is inventive and often quite funny . . . but not enough to keep this wispy film afloat. Reynolds is extremely good in his first character role. [R]▼●)

Breaking Point, The (1950) **97m.** ***½ D: Michael Curtiz. John Garfield, Patricia Neal, Phyllis Thaxter, Wallace Ford, Sherry Jackson. High-voltage refilming of Hemingway's TO HAVE AND HAVE NOT, with Garfield as skipper so desperate for money he takes on illegal cargo. Garfield and mate Juano Hernandez give superb interpretations. Screenplay by Ranald MacDougall. Remade again as THE GUN RUNNERS.

Breaking Point (1976-Canadian) **C-92m.** BOMB D: Bob Clark. Bo Svenson, Robert Culp, John Colicos, Belinda J. Montgomery, Stephen Young, Linda Sorenson. Svenson is pursued by Mafiosos after he testifies against them in court. Nothing new here. [R]▼▙

Breaking Point (1993-Canadian) **C-96m.** ** D: Paul Ziller. Gary Busey, Kim Cattrall, Darlanne Fluegel, Jeff Griggs. After a serial killer known as "The Surgeon" strikes close to home, haunted cop Busey is asked to capture him. This grisly and erotic thriller is titillating, mildly surprising at first, but ultimately predictable. [R]▼▙

Breaking the Rules (1992) **C-100m.** *½

D: Neal Israel. Jason Bateman, C. Thomas Howell, Jonathan Silverman, Annie Potts, Kent Bateman, Shawn Phelan. Yet another road movie in which two friends take their dying buddy on one last "journey of life." The story is meant to make you laugh and cry, but it's so manipulative it only induces yawns. Potts is the single standout, as a free-spirited waitress. Filmed in 1989. [PG-13]▼●

Breaking the Sound Barrier (1952-British) **116m. ***½** D: David Lean. Ralph Richardson, Ann Todd, Nigel Patrick, John Justin, Dinah Sheridan, Denholm Elliott. Grade-A documentary-style story of early days of jet planes, and men who tested them; Richardson particularly good. Written by Terence Rattigan. Oscar winner for Sound Recording. Originally shown in England as THE SOUND BARRIER at 118m.▶

Breaking the Waves (1996-Danish) **C-156m. ***½** D: Lars von Trier. Emily Watson, Stellan Skarsgård, Adrian Rawlins, Katrin Cartlidge, Jean-Marc Barr, Jonathan Hackett, Sandra Voe, Udo Kier. Extraordinary story of a young, simple-minded, God-fearing Scottish woman who willingly takes lovers in the belief that it will cure her paralyzed husband. A bold, often unsettling examination of love and faith, given immediacy and power by von Trier's documentarylike approach and cinematographer Robby Müller's faded visual scheme, which root the miraculous in the everyday world. Watson, in her film debut, is unforgettable in the lead role. Von Trier also wrote the screenplay. Super 35. [R] ▼●❍

Breaking Up (1997) **C-90m. *½** D: Robert Greenwald. Salma Hayek, Russell Crowe. Tiresome treatise on love in the '90s, showing how many times two self-centered adults can break up, reunite, and break up again. They can't stand each other, and we can't stand *them!* Screenplay by Michael Cristofer, from his play. Filmed in 1995. [R]▼●❍

Break of Hearts (1935) **80m. ** ** D: Philip Moeller. Katharine Hepburn, Charles Boyer, John Beal, Jean Hersholt, Sam Hardy, Susan Fleming, Jean Howard. Temperamental orchestra conductor Boyer, who has been spoiled by success, weds unknown composer Hepburn . . . then there are complications. Stars try hard but can do nothing with sappy, sub-par material. ▼●❍

Breakout (1975) **C-96m. *** ** D: Tom Gries. Charles Bronson, Robert Duvall, Jill Ireland, John Huston, Sheree North, Randy Quaid. Crisp action film generously laced with comedy touches has devil-may-care bush pilot Bronson taking on the job of spiriting Duvall, framed for murder, from a seedy Mexican prison. Awfully violent, though. Panavision. [PG]▼●❍

Breakthrough (1978-West German) **C-115m. *½** D: Andrew V. McLaglen. Rich-

ard Burton, Robert Mitchum, Rod Steiger, Curt Jurgens, Klaus Loewitsch, Helmut Griem, Michael Parks. Superficial sequel to CROSS OF IRON, with the focus on the western front during WW2. German sergeant Burton becomes entangled in anti-Hitler conspiracy, saves the life of U.S. colonel Mitchum. Particularly disappointing, considering cast. Also known as SERGEANT STEINER. [PG]▼

Break Up, The (2006) **C-106m. **½** D: Peyton Reed. Vince Vaughn, Jennifer Aniston, Joey Lauren Adams, Jon Favreau, Jason Bateman, Judy Davis, Justin Long, Ivan Sergei, John Michael Higgins, Cole Hauser, Vincent D'Onofrio, Ann-Margret, Peter Billingsley. Typical of what passes for romantic comedy these days: neither Vince nor Jen wants the other to end up with the condo they shared during happier times. Not without laughs, but this odd, unsatisfying film is mainly for viewers who find carping and bickering entertaining. Vince's real-life dad, Vernon Vaughn, plays Aniston's father. Stay for a rendition of "The Rainbow Connection" by Higgins' a cappella group, The Tone Rangers, during the end credits. Vaughn cowrote the story. [PG-13]▶

Breathing Room (1996) **C-90m. **½** D: Jon Sherman. Susan Floyd, Dan Futterman, Nadia Dajani, Edie Falco, Saverio Guerra, David Thornton, Paul Giamatti. Sweet film of contemporary N.Y.C. couple deciding on their future together by separating between Thanksgiving and Christmas. The issue of commitment is honestly explored and feels universal. A "date" movie with more food for thought than might be comfortable for unmarried couples.▼

Breathless (1960-French) **89m. ***½** D: Jean-Luc Godard. Jean Seberg, Jean-Paul Belmondo, Daniel Boulanger, Liliane David. Belmondo is ideally cast as a Parisian hood who, accompanied by American girl (Seberg), is chased by police after stealing a car and killing a cop. Groundbreaking, influential New Wave tale with a classic romanticized gangster-hero and great candid shots of Paris life. Dedicated to Monogram Pictures, with a story by François Truffaut. Remade in 1983. ▼●❍

Breathless (1983) **C-100m. ** ** D: Jim McBride. Richard Gere, Valerie Kaprisky, Art Metrano, John P. Ryan, William Tepper, Gary Goodrow. Remake of landmark 1959 Godard film follows basic outline of the original—an amoral punk on the lam from police—but lacks its sociological potency. Gere's kinetic performance is something to see, but his character, hooked on Jerry Lee Lewis music and "Silver Surfer" comics, soon grows tiresome. [R]▼●❍

Breath of Life (1992-Italian) **C-96m. ** ** D: Beppe Cino. Franco Nero, Vanessa

[176]

Redgrave, Fernando Rey, Lucrezia Rovere, Salvatore Cascio. Grim, episodic psychological study of the wounded lives of a group of Italians in a post-WW2 sanitarium. Nero gives a solid performance as a tubercular professor in love with a mentally troubled ballerina (Rovere). Unfortunately he has little to do with Redgrave here—his former CAMELOT costar and one-time real-life lover.

Breath of Scandal, A (1960) **C-98m.** ** D: Michael Curtiz. Sophia Loren, John Gavin, Maurice Chevalier, Isabel Jeans, Angela Lansbury. Molnar's play *Olympia* is limp costume vehicle for Loren, playing a princess romanced by American Gavin. Chevalier and Lansbury vainly try to pump some life into proceedings. Filmed in Vienna. Remake of John Gilbert's notorious HIS GLORIOUS NIGHT (1929). ▼▶

Breed Apart, A (1984) **C-101m.** ** D: Philippe Mora. Rutger Hauer, Powers Boothe, Kathleen Turner, Donald Pleasence, John Dennis Johnston, Brion James. Picturesque but illogical, uninvolving tale of famed mountain climber Boothe, hired to pilfer specimens of a new bald-eagle breed, and his entanglement with conservationist Hauer and fishing-supply store owner Turner. [R]▼

Breezy (1973) **C-108m.** ** D: Clint Eastwood. William Holden, Kay Lenz, Roger C. Carmel, Marj Dusay, Shelley Morrison, Joan Hotchkis. Jaded middle-ager finds Truth with a teenaged hippie in sappy romance. Fine performances by the leads only help up to a point. [R]▼▶

Brenda Starr (1992) **C-87m.** *½ D: Robert Ellis Miller. Brooke Shields, Tony Peck, Timothy Dalton, Diana Scarwid, Jeffrey Tambor, June Gable, Nestor Serrano, Kathleen Wilhoite, Charles Durning, Eddie Albert, Henry Gibson, Ed Nelson. This fiasco, based on Dale Messick's comic strip, sat on the shelf for years, and no wonder. Artist Peck enters the strip to talk Brenda out of quitting the paper, is drawn into her adventuresome life. Aimless and uninvolving. Filmed in 1986. [PG]▼▶

Brewster McCloud (1970) **C-101m.** *** D: Robert Altman. Bud Cort, Sally Kellerman, Michael Murphy, William Windom, Shelley Duvall, Rene Auberjonois, Stacy Keach, John Schuck, Margaret Hamilton. Patently indescribable movie following exploits of owlish boy (Cort) whose ambition is to take wing and fly inside Houston Astrodome. Extremely bizarre; for certain tastes, extremely funny. Altman fans have a head start. Panavision. [R]▼▶

Brewster's Millions (1985) **C-97m.** ** D: Walter Hill. Richard Pryor, John Candy, Lonette McKee, Stephen Collins, Jerry Orbach, Pat Hingle, Tovah Feldshuh, Joe Grifasi, Hume Cronyn. Seventh film version of venerable novel and play; here baseball player Pryor has one month to spend $30 million. Surefire premise squelched by unfunny script and wooden direction. When Pryor and Candy can't make it work, there's something wrong. [PG] ▼▶

Bribe, The (1949) **98m.** ** D: Robert Z. Leonard. Robert Taylor, Ava Gardner, Charles Laughton, Vincent Price, John Hodiak. Taylor looks uncomfortable playing federal man who almost sacrifices all for sultry singer Gardner.▶

Brick (2006) **C-117m.** *** D: Rian Johnson. Joseph Gordon-Levitt, Lukas Haas, Nora Zehetner, Noah Fleiss, Matt O'Leary, Noah Segan, Meagan Good, Emilie de Ravin, Brian White, Richard Roundtree. Teenaged Gordon-Levitt discovers the dead body of his ex-girlfriend and makes it his business to learn what happened to her. Clever, stylized film noir involving high school kids who speak in a hard-boiled 1930s argot (hard to understand at times though appealing just the same). A bit protracted but still an audacious, original piece of work. Haas turns up well into the story as a flamboyant drug kingpin and steals the show. Neat music score by Nathan Johnson is as offbeat as the film itself. Written by first-time director Rian Johnson. [R]▶

Brick Lane (2007-British) **C-101m.** *** D: Sarah Gavron. Tannishtha Chatterjee, Satish Kaushik, Christopher Simpson, Naeema Begum, Lana Rahman, Zafeen. Compassionate portrait of a Bangladeshi girl whose carefree life with her sister is curtailed after her mother dies and she is sent to London to enter into an arranged marriage. Now she's got a surly teenage daughter and suffers a daily existence with a pompous, ne'er-do-well husband. Then she chances to meet a young man who inspires her to assert herself for the first time in her life. Poignant and believable at every turn; even the husband is portrayed as a three-dimensional character. Abi Morgan and Laura Jones adapted Monica Ali's novel. Super 35. [PG-13]▶

Bridal Path, The (1959-Scottish) **C-95m.** ***½ D: Frank Launder. Bill Travers, Bernadette O'Farrell, Alex MacKenzie, Eric Woodburn, Jack Lambert, John Rae. Charming film of young islander who goes to Scottish mainland in search of a wife. Enhanced by beautiful scenery in color.

Bride, The (1985) **C-118m.** **½ D: Franc Roddam. Sting, Jennifer Beals, Clancy Brown, David Rappaport, Geraldine Page, Anthony Higgins, Veruschka, Quentin Crisp, Cary Elwes. Revisionist remake of BRIDE OF FRANKENSTEIN brilliantly captures look and feel of a great gothic horror film—but fails to deliver on its promise of enlightened psychological approach to the story. Both Sting and Beals give one-note performances. Film is easily stolen by Rappaport, as dwarf who befriends Dr.

Frankenstein's male monster (Brown); their sequences make film worth watching. [PG-13] ▼❒

Bride & Prejudice (2004-U.S.-British) C-111m. **½ D: Gurinder Chadha. Aishwarya Rai, Martin Henderson, Daniel Gillies, Naveen Andrews, Alexis Bledel, Namrata Shirodkar, Nitin Chandra Ganatra, Marsha Mason, Ashanti. Jane Austen goes ethnic in this cliché-laden but lightly entertaining update of *Pride and Prejudice* involving a desperate Indian mother's attempts to find husbands for her four daughters. Rai is a stunning presence as Lalita, the Elizabeth Bennet character, who becomes involved with an American hotel magnate named Darcy (Henderson). Interesting attempt to produce a Bollywood musical for Western audiences. Super 35. [PG-13] ▼❒

Bride Came C.O.D., The (1941) 92m. **½ D: William Keighley. James Cagney, Bette Davis, Stuart Erwin, Eugene Pallette, Jack Carson, George Tobias. Unlikely comedy team in vehicle made enjoyable only by their terrific personalities; he's a flier, she's an abducted bride. ▼❒

Bride of Chucky (1998) C-89m. ** D: Ronny Yu. Jennifer Tilly, Katherine Heigl, Nick Stabile, John Ritter, Alexis Arquette, Gordon Michael Woolvett, Kathy Najimy, voice of Brad Dourif. Wicked trailer trash Tilly works voodoo to revive Chucky (the killer doll from three earlier CHILD'S PLAY movies), and ends up a literal living doll herself. Better than you'd expect, with good lines and an impressively raunchy performance by Tilly, but it's let down by clumsy plotting. Followed by SEED OF CHUCKY. [R] ▼❒

Bride of Frankenstein (1935) 75m. **** D: James Whale. Karloff (Boris Karloff), Colin Clive, Valerie Hobson, Ernest Thesiger, Elsa Lanchester, Una O'Connor, E. E. Clive, Gavin Gordon, Douglas Walton, O. P. Heggie, Dwight Frye, John Carradine. Eye-filling sequel to FRANKENSTEIN is even better, with rich vein of dry wit running through the chills. Inimitable Thesiger plays weird doctor who compels Frankenstein into helping him make a mate for the Monster; Lanchester plays both the "bride" and, in amusing prologue, Mary Shelley. Pastoral interlude with blind hermit and final, riotous creation scene are highlights of this truly classic movie. Scripted by John L. Balderston and William Hurlbut. Marvelous Franz Waxman score, reused for many subsequent films. Followed by SON OF FRANKENSTEIN; reworked in 1985 as THE BRIDE. ▼❒

Bride of Re-Animator (1990) C-99m. ** D: Brian Yuzna. Jeffrey Combs, Bruce Abbott, Claude Earl Jones, Fabiana Udenio, David Gale, Kathleen Kinmont. Follow-up to RE-ANIMATOR with more gory fun

from that wacky pair of ·Dr. Frankenstein wannabes, Combs and Abbott. Strong stuff, with much splicing of bloodied body parts; wait till you see the crawling eyeball! This sort-of homage to BRIDE OF FRANKENSTEIN isn't nearly as successful as original RE-ANIMATOR. Nominally based on H. P. Lovecraft's *Herbert West—Re-Animator.* Unrated director's cut also available. Followed in 2003 by BEYOND RE-ANIMATOR. [R] ▼❒

Bride of the Gorilla (1951) 76m. ** D: Curt Siodmak. Raymond Burr, Barbara Payton, Lon Chaney, Jr., Tom Conway, Paul Cavanagh. Surprisingly watchable trash set on a South American jungle plantation, where hulking Burr marries sexy Payton—only to find himself the victim of a voodoo curse. Terrible but fun. ▼❒

Bride of the Monster (1955) 69m. BOMB D: Edward D. Wood, Jr. Bela Lugosi, Tor Johnson, Tony McCoy, Loretta King, Harvey B. Dunn, George Becwar, Don Nagel, Bud Osborne. A dissipated Lugosi creates giant rubber octopus that terrorizes woodland stream. Huge Swedish wrestler Johnson provides added laughs as hulking manservant Lobo. Another hilariously inept Grade Z movie from the king of bad cinema. Sequel: REVENGE OF THE DEAD (aka NIGHT OF THE GHOULS). ▼❒

Bride of the Wind (2001) C-99m. *½ D: Bruce Beresford. Sarah Wynter, Jonathan Pryce, Vincent Perez, Simon Verhoeven, Gregor Seberg. Passions run low in this drab period drama set in fin-de-siècle Vienna about Alma Schindler, the real-life muse for many celebrated men, including composer Gustav Mahler (played as a milquetoast by Pryce). Slow as a funeral dirge, the movie features a blur of a central performance from Wynter. All talk about art and obsession without anything to show for it. [R] ▼❒

Bride of Vengeance (1949) 91m. ** D: Mitchell Leisen. Paulette Goddard, John Lund, Macdonald Carey, Raymond Burr, Albert Dekker, Rose Hobart. Medium-warm costumer of medieval Italy with Goddard as a Borgia sent to do mischief but instead falling in love.

Brideshead Revisited (2008-British) C-133m. **½ D: Julian Jarrold. Matthew Goode, Ben Whishaw, Hayley Atwell, Emma Thompson, Michael Gambon, Greta Scacchi, Jonathan Cake, Patrick Malahide, Ed Stoppard, Felicity Jones, Joseph Beattie. Re-thinking of Evelyn Waugh's 1945 novel, dramatized so memorably in a 1981 British TV miniseries. An unworldly working-class boy (Goode) arrives at Oxford and is befriended by flamboyant Sebastian Flyte (Whishaw), who reluctantly introduces him to his sister (Atwell) and their imperious mother, who rules over their massive estate—and their lives. Ragged at times as it tries to compress many complexities into two hours' length, but impeccably performed. Thompson is subtly brilliant as Lady Marchmain. Screenplay by Andrew Davies and Jeremy Brock. Super 35. [PG-13]▶

Bridesmaid, The (2004-French) **C-111m.** *** D: Claude Chabrol. Benoit Magimel, Laura Smet, Aurore Clement, Bernard Le Coq, Solène Bouton, Anna Mihalcea, Michel Duchaussoy, Suzanne Flon, Thomas Chabrol. It's happened to almost everyone, and it happens to upwardly mobile career man Magimel: instant attraction to a stranger while attending a wedding. Premise is served with a typical Chabrol twist when the woman he meets turns out to be a sociopath . . . or even worse. The extent to which she (Smet) cajoles him to "prove his love" by committing a fateful act ratchets up suspense little by little. May not be up to the director's masterpieces of the '60s but it's engrossing all the way. Based on a novel by Ruth Rendell. ▶

Bridesmaids (2011) **C-125m.** ** D: Paul Feig. Kristen Wiig, Maya Rudolph, Rose Byrne, Wendi McLendon-Covey, Ellie Kemper, Melissa McCarthy, Chris O'Dowd, Matt Lucas, Jill Clayburgh, Rebel Wilson, Terry Crews, Franklyn Ajaye, Ben Falcone. Wiig has made a wreck of her love life and career, so when lifelong friend Rudolph asks her to be maid of honor at her upcoming nuptials, she wants to do a great job. Then she becomes insanely jealous of Rudolph's new gal-pal Byrne, a "Little Miss Perfect" who's used to getting her way. Raunchy, female-centric comedy (written by Wiig and Annie Mumolo, who plays one of the airplane passengers) is alternately funny, serious, heartfelt, dull, plodding, and out of control. Its best moments were apparently improvised, but that must also account for its slow stretches and detours. Jon Hamm appears unbilled. Produced by Judd Apatow. Clayburgh's final film. Super 35. [R] ▶

Brides of Dracula, The (1960-British) **C-85m.** *** D: Terence Fisher. Peter Cushing, Martita Hunt, Yvonne Monlaur, Freda Jackson, David Peel, Miles Malleson, Andree Melly. In the Carpathian Mountains, a young teacher (Monlaur) is attracted to a nobleman (Peel) held captive by his own mother (Hunt). When the young woman sets him free, he's revealed as a vampire—and a disciple of Count Dracula. Vampire hunter Van Helsing (Cushing) energetically comes to her aid. Exciting, colorful period horror, this first sequel to HORROR OF DRACULA is one of Hammer's best thrillers. Dracula never turns up—but you won't miss him. ▼●▶

Brides of Fu Manchu, The (1966-British) **C-94m.** **½ D: Don Sharp. Christopher Lee, Douglas Wilmer, Marie Versini, Tsai Chin. Fu doesn't give up easily, still bent on conquering the world by forcing scientists to develop powerful ray gun. Sequel to FACE OF FU MANCHU, not as good, still

diverting; followed by VENGEANCE OF FU MANCHU. ▼▶

Bride Wars (2009) **C-89m.** *½ D: Gary Winick. Kate Hudson, Anne Hathaway, Bryan Greenberg, Chris Pratt, Steve Howey, Candice Bergen, Kristen Johnston, Michael Arden, Victor Slezak. Dreadful comedy pits lifelong best friends against each other when their dream weddings at N.Y.C.'s Plaza Hotel are inadvertently double-booked for the same day and neither will budge. Both women scheme to destroy the other's golden day as they blame each other for the not-so-merry mix-up and act like 8-year-olds. Witless, contrived, and unfunny tale sets the women's movement back about four decades. It's a shame to see such attractive talents as Hudson and particularly Hathaway doing this kind of juvenile slapstick (and Hudson was one of the producers). Only Johnston manages to mine any laughs as Hathaway's desperate choice for her maid of honor. [PG]▶

Bride With White Hair, The (1993-Hong Kong) **C-89m.** *** D: Ronny Yu. Brigitte Lin, Leslie Cheung, Ng Chun-yu, Elaine Lui, Nam Kit-ying. Beautifully made tale based on a famous Chinese fable about rival Ming Dynasty clans and a forbidden love affair between a swordsman and a "wolf girl" who possesses supernatural powers. Highly effective blend of myth, romance and super-stylized violence, plus elegant use of color and widescreen, puts this a cut above the usual Hong Kong actioner. Followed by a sequel the same year. Panavision. ▼●▶

Bride Wore Black, The (1968-French) **C-107m.** ***½ D: François Truffaut. Jeanne Moreau, Claude Rich, Jean-Claude Brialy, Michel Bouquet, Michel Lonsdale, Charles Denner. Hitchcockian suspenser about Moreau tracking down and killing the quintet of men who accidentally killed her husband on their wedding day. Exciting, entertaining homage to The Master, right down to the Bernard Herrmann score (although Truffaut omitted the twist ending of the novel by William Irish, aka Cornell Woolrich). ▼●▶

Bride Wore Boots, The (1946) **86m.** ** D: Irving Pichel. Barbara Stanwyck, Robert Cummings, Diana Lynn, Peggy Wood, Robert Benchley, Natalie Wood, Willie Best. Witless comedy of horse-loving Stanwyck saddled by Cummings, who does his best to win her total affection; they all try but script is weak. ▶

Bride Wore Red, The (1937) **103m.** **½ D: Dorothy Arzner. Joan Crawford, Franchot Tone, Robert Young, Billie Burke, Reginald Owen, Lynne Carver, George Zucco, Dickie Moore. Lowly Crawford is thrust into society on the whim of a count and becomes the romantic object of aristocrat-playboy Young and soulful peasant Tone. Glossy soaper based on a play by Ferenc Molnár. ▼

Bridge, The (1999-French) **C-90m.** **½

D: Gérard Depardieu, Frederic Auburtin. Gérard Depardieu, Carole Bouquet, Charles Berling, Stanislas Crevillen, Dominique Reymond. Normandy, 1962. A housewife/mother (Bouquet, never lovelier) finds release from her working-class existence in the arms of a handsome engineer (Berling). Adultery is not exactly new subject material for French cinema, but this is a subtle treatment of the dissolution of a marriage. Co-director Depardieu shows a sure hand with his actors and acquits himself well as the meek husband. Film's biggest flaw is its lack of resolution. Original title: UN PONT ENTRE DEUX RIVES. ▼❶

Bridge at Remagen, The (1969) **C-115m.** **½ D: John Guillermin. George Segal, Robert Vaughn, Ben Gazzara, Bradford Dillman, E.G. Marshall, Peter Van Eyck. Well-acted film about group of Allies defending bridge toward the end of WW2 can't quite overcome familiar plot line; lots of good explosions for those who care. Panavision. [M/PG] ▼❶

Bridge of San Luis Rey, The (1944) **89m.** ** D: Rowland V. Lee. Lynn Bari, Nazimova, Louis Calhern, Akim Tamiroff, Francis Lederer, Blanche Yurka, Donald Woods. Thornton Wilder's moody, unusual story of five people meeting doom on a rickety bridge makes a slow-moving film. Previously filmed in 1929 and remade in 2004. ▼❶

Bridge of San Luis Rey, The (2004-British-French-Spanish) **C-120m.** ** D: Mary McGuckian. F. Murray Abraham, Kathy Bates, Gabriel Byrne, Geraldine Chaplin, Robert De Niro, Émilie Dequenne, Adriana Domínguez, Harvey Keitel, Samuel Le Bihan, Pilar López de Ayala, John Lynch, Dominique Pinon, Mark Polish, Michael Polish. Five people die when a rickety bridge collapses in 18th-century Peru; a priest investigates their lives to find out what brought them all together on that tragic day. Previously filmed in 1929 and 1944, this visually plush version of Thornton Wilder's Pulitzer Prize–winning novel exploring fate, reason, and religion is emotionally inert and overlong, with most of its illustrious cast giving surprisingly lifeless performances. [PG] ❶

Bridge on the River Kwai, The (1957-British) **C-161m.** **** D: David Lean. William Holden, Alec Guinness, Jack Hawkins, Sessue Hayakawa, Geoffrey Horne, James Donald, Andre Morell, Ann Sears. British soldiers in Japanese prison camp build a bridge as a morale exercise—under single-minded leadership of British colonel Guinness—as Holden and Hawkins plot to destroy it. Psychological battle of wills combined with high-powered action sequences make this a blockbuster. Seven Oscars include Picture, Director, Actor (Guinness), Cinematography (Jack Hildyard), Editing (Peter Taylor), Scoring (Malcolm Arnold—who

used the famous WW1 whistling tune "Colonel Bogey March"), and Screenplay (by Carl Foreman and Michael Wilson, based on Pierre Boulle's novel). The writers were blacklisted, so Boulle—who spoke no English—was credited with the script! Filmed in Ceylon. CinemaScope. ▼❶

Bridges at Toko-Ri, The (1954) **C-103m.** ***½ D: Mark Robson. William Holden, Grace Kelly, Fredric March, Mickey Rooney, Robert Strauss, Earl Holliman. Powerful, thoughtful drama, based on the James Michener best-seller, focusing on the conflicts and exploits of lawyer Holden after he is recalled by the Navy to fly jets in Korea. While the flying sequences are exciting—the special effects earned an Oscar—the ultimate futility of the Korean War is in no way deemphasized. ▼❶

Bridges of Madison County, The (1995) **C-135m.** *** D: Clint Eastwood. Clint Eastwood, Meryl Streep, Annie Corley, Victor Slezak, Jim Haynie. In the 1960s, an itinerant *National Geographic* photographer comes to Iowa to shoot covered bridges and chances to meet a woman who's vaguely dissatisfied with life as farm-bound wife and mother. Modern spin on BRIEF ENCOUNTER (based on Robert James Waller's hugely popular book) features a winning and vulnerable Eastwood and a wondrous Streep as an unlikely but convincing couple. A satisfying and romantic film, if a bit long and slow at times. That bass player in the blues band who gets a closeup is Eastwood's son, Kyle. [PG-13]▼❶

Bridget Jones's Diary (2001-U.S.-British-French) **C-94m.** *** D: Sharon Maguire. Renée Zellweger, Hugh Grant, Colin Firth, Gemma Jones, Jim Broadbent, Sally Phillips, Shirley Henderson, James Callis, Embeth Davidtz, Celia Imrie, Honor Blackman. Entertaining, often hilarious adaptation of Helen Fielding's book about a 32-year-old single woman and her misadventures with a pair of men—her scoundrel of a boss and a tight-lipped barrister who seems to be a snob. Zellweger, sporting a perfect British accent and extra pounds, is delightful as the self-deprecating title character. Followed by a sequel. Super 35. [R] ▼❶

Bridget Jones: The Edge of Reason (2004-U.S.-British-French-German-Irish) **C-108m.** ** D: Beeban Kidron. Renée Zellweger, Hugh Grant, Colin Firth, Jim Broadbent, Gemma Jones, Jacinda Barrett, Sally Phillips, James Callis, Shirley Henderson, James Faulkner, Celia Imrie. Pointless sequel to the hit romantic comedy, centering on the title character's involvement with boyfriend Firth and ex-suitor Grant, and her endless mishaps. Appeal of the original has largely evaporated, with likable, pleasingly chunky Bridget transformed into a charmless dunce. Only comes alive when Grant is on-screen, which isn't often enough.

Coscripted by Helen Fielding, based on her published sequel to BRIDGET JONES'S DIARY. Panavision. [R] ▼▶

Bridge to Nowhere (1986-New Zealand) **C-86m.** *½ D: Ian Mune. Bruno Lawrence, Alison Routledge, Philip Gordon, Margaret Umbers, Stephen Judd, Shelley Luxford, Matthew Hunter. Kiwi variation on a familiar theme: backpacking kids raise the ire of hermit Lawrence, causing a war for survival. Well made but trite; features a solid role for Lawrence, the ubiquitous star of New Zealand films. ▼

Bridge Too Far, A (1977-British) **C-175m.** ** D: Richard Attenborough. Dirk Bogarde, James Caan, Michael Caine, Sean Connery, Edward Fox, Elliott Gould, Gene Hackman, Anthony Hopkins, Hardy Kruger, Laurence Olivier, Ryan O'Neal, Robert Redford, Maximilian Schell, Liv Ullmann, Arthur Hill, John Ratzenberger. Lifeless, overproduced version of the fine Cornelius Ryan book about disastrous 1944 Allied airdrop behind German lines in Holland. Some prints run 158m. Panavision. [PG] ▼▶

Bridge to Terabithia (2007) **C-94m.** **½ D: Gabor Csupo. Josh Hutcherson, Anna-Sophia Robb, Robert Patrick, Zooey Deschanel, Bailey Madison, Lauren Clinton. Faithful adaptation of Katherine Paterson's much-admired juvenile novel depicts a young loner (Hutcherson) who finds a soul mate in a free-spirited girl who moves in next door (Robb). Her generous nature has a profound effect on Jess; together they fashion a hideaway in the nearby woods and imagine it to be a magic kingdom. Then reality intrudes. Captures the heightened emotions of sensitive young people, with fine performances, but by literally showing the world they envision, film undermines the book's celebration of imagination. [PG]▶

Brief Crossing (2003-French) **C-80m.** ** D: Catherine Breillat. Sarah Pratt, Gilles Guillain. A thirtysomething Englishwoman and a 16-year-old French boy meet, converse, and engage in a one-night stand on a ferry crossing the English Channel. Another of Breillat's cynical forays into male-female expectation and manipulation, offering her usual generalizations about male sexuality. Leaves a bitter aftertaste. ▼▶

Brief Encounter (1945-British) **85m.** **** D: David Lean. Celia Johnson, Trevor Howard, Stanley Holloway, Cyril Raymond, Joyce Carey. Two ordinary strangers, both married, meet at a train station and find themselves drawn into a short but poignant romance. Intense and unforgettable, underscored by perfect use of Rachmaninoff's *Second Piano Concerto*. Adapted by Noel Coward from his one-act play "Still Life" (from *Tonight at Eight-thirty*); screenplay by director Lean and Ronald Neame. A truly wonderful film. Remade as a TV movie in 1974 with

Richard Burton and Sophia Loren. Later a stage musical. ▼▶▶

Brief History of Time, A (1992-U.S.-British) **C-84m.** ***½ D: Errol Morris. Another outstanding documentary from Morris (GATES OF HEAVEN, THE THIN BLUE LINE), this one a portrait of cosmologist Stephen Hawking, who's afflicted with amyotrophic lateral sclerosis and communicates verbally with a voice synthesizer. In Hawking's best-selling book, for which the film is named, he explains the nature of the universe in layman's terms; even those who are bored or perplexed by science will enjoy this unique film. ▼

Brief Interviews With Hideous Men (2009) **C-80m.** *½ D: John Krasinski. Julianne Nicholson, Will Arnett, Bobby Cannavale, Michael Cerveris, Josh Charles, Dominic Cooper, Frankie Faison, Will Forte, Benjamin Gibbard, Malcolm Goodwin, Timothy Hutton, John Krasinski, Christopher Meloni, Chris Messina, Max Minghella, Denis O'Hare, Clarke Peters, Lou Taylor Pucci, Ben Shenkman, Joey Slotnick, Corey Stoll, Rashida Jones. Grad student Nicholson, studying the effects of the feminist movement, interviews (and listens in on the conversations of) a cross-section of men, most of whom are patronizing, pompous idiots. Dull, one-note film comes off as little more than an acting exercise. One sequence, involving a black man's feelings about his bathroom-attendant father, seems to be from an entirely different film. Krasinski's directing debut; he also adapted David Foster Wallace's collection of short stories. Panavision. ▶

Brief Vacation, A (1973-Italian) **C-106m.** *** D: Vittorio De Sica. Florinda Bolkan, Renato Salvatori, Daniel Quenaud, Jose Maria Prada, Teresa Gimpera. Poorly educated woman leaves terrible job, despicable in-laws, and callous husband for a comparatively pleasant stay in a TB sanitorium. De Sica's sure-handed direction and Bolkan's knowing performance make this worth watching. [PG]▶

Brigadoon (1954) **C-108m.** *** D: Vincente Minnelli. Gene Kelly, Van Johnson, Cyd Charisse, Elaine Stewart, Barry Jones, Hugh Laing. Americans Kelly and Johnson discover magical Scottish village in this entertaining filmization of Lerner & Loewe Broadway hit. Overlooked among 1950s musicals, it may lack innovations but has its own quiet charm, and lovely score, including "The Heather on the Hill." Cinema-Scope. ▼▶

Brigham Young (1940) **114m.** ** D: Henry Hathaway. Tyrone Power, Linda Darnell, Dean Jagger, Brian Donlevy, John Carradine, Jane Darwell, Jean Rogers, Mary Astor, Vincent Price. Well-intentioned but ineffectual depiction of Mormon leader with Jagger nominally in the lead, focus shifting to tepid romance between Power and Darnell; Astor all wrong as homespun wife. Advertised as BRIGHAM YOUNG, FRONTIERSMAN, in an attempt to widen its appeal. ▼◗

Bright Angel (1991) **C-94m.** **½ D: Michael Fields. Dermot Mulroney, Lili Taylor, Sam Shepard, Burt Young, Valerie Perrine, Bill Pullman, Mary Kay Place, Kevin Tighe, Sheila McCarthy, Delroy Lindo, Benjamin Bratt. Teenaged Montana boy, shaken by events at home, agrees to take a runaway girl to Wyoming so she can bail her brother out of jail. Uneven, sometimes affecting slice of life, with a very stylized script by novelist Richard Ford and a cast full of familiar faces. Mulroney is first-rate in the lead. [R]▼

Bright Eyes (1934) **83m.** **½ D: David Butler. Shirley Temple, James Dunn, Judith Allen, Jane Withers, Lois Wilson, Charles Sellon. Early Shirley, and pretty good, with juvenile villainy from Withers in tale of custody battle over recently orphaned Temple. Includes "On the Good Ship Lollipop." Also shown in computer-colored version. ▼◗

Bright Leaf (1950) **110m.** **½ D: Michael Curtiz. Gary Cooper, Lauren Bacall, Patricia Neal, Jack Carson, Donald Crisp. Loose chronicle of 19th-century tobacco farmer (Cooper) building successful cigarette empire, seeking revenge on old enemies and finding romance.◗

Bright Leaves (2004-U.S.-British) **C-107m.** *** D: Ross McElwee. Another filmic essay by McElwee, this one about investigating his family's roots in North Carolina. On the one hand, there is the intriguing discovery that his great-grandfather (supposedly portrayed, in fictional guise, by Gary Cooper in the 1950 movie BRIGHT LEAF) may have been an unsung hero of the tobacco industry. Then again, there is terrible guilt in pondering the damage that tobacco has wrought on the human race. Amusing, ironic, thoughtful, and highly personal. Patricia Neal, costar of BRIGHT LEAF, appears briefly. ◗

Bright Lights, Big City (1988) **C-110m.** **½ D: James Bridges. Michael J. Fox, Kiefer Sutherland, Phoebe Cates, Swoosie Kurtz, Frances Sternhagen, Tracy Pollan, John Houseman, Charlie Schlatter, Jason Robards, Dianne Wiest, William Hickey, Kelly Lynch, David Hyde Pierce. Everyone gets an A for effort on this adaptation of Jay McInerney's popular novel. Fox gives a good performance as the young Midwesterner whose life has started coming apart at the seams in N.Y.C., where he gets caught up in an endless cycle of drugs and nightlife. But the more cerebral aspects of the book (and some of its purple prose) don't translate to film . . . and it takes a long time to develop any real sympathy for Fox and his plight. Sutherland is convincingly smarmy as his druggie pal. [R] ▼◗

Brighton Beach Memoirs (1986) **C-110m.** **½ D: Gene Saks. Blythe Danner, Bob Dishy, Jonathan Silverman, Brian Drillinger, Stacey Glick, Judith Ivey, Lisa Waltz, Jason Alexander, Steven Hill, Fyvush Finkel. Pleasant, if mostly undistinguished, adaptation of Neil Simon's celebrated autobiographical play about two families living under the same roof in 1937 Brooklyn. Oddly cast—Danner and Ivey play Jewish sisters—with attractive production design; Dishy underplays nicely as narrator Silverman's father. Followed by BILOXI BLUES and (on TV) BROADWAY BOUND. [PG-13] ▼◗

Bright Road (1953) **69m.** ** D: Gerald Mayer. Dorothy Dandridge, Harry Belafonte, Robert Horton, Philip Hepburn. Well-intentioned but labored tale of black teacher in small Southern town trying to solve her young pupils' problems. Belafonte's film debut.

Bright Star (2009-French-Australian-British) **C-119m.** **½ D: Jane Campion. Abbie Cornish, Ben Whishaw, Paul Schneider, Kerry Fox, Edie Martin, Thomas Sangster, Antonia Campbell-Hughes. Romance poet John Keats falls in love with his muse, vivacious, clever Fanny Brawne, but since he is a poor man with no prospects, marriage is out of the question. Brawne's affections remain steadfast, while Keats wafts back and forth at once totally besotted, next distancing himself from her to make way for well-heeled suitors. Handsome production has lots of tears and reciting of verse, but somehow falls short. [PG] ◗

Bright Victory (1951) **97m.** *** D: Mark Robson. Arthur Kennedy, Peggy Dow, Julia (Julie) Adams, James Edwards, Will Geer, Nana Bryant, Jim Backus, Murray Hamilton, Richard Egan. Touching account of blinded ex-soldier who slowly readjusts to civilian life, even finding love. Potentially sticky subject handled well, with Kennedy excellent in lead role. Rock Hudson can be glimpsed as a soldier.

Brighty of the Grand Canyon (1967) **C-89m.** **½ D: Norman Foster. Joseph Cotten, Pat Conway, Karl Swenson, Dick Foran, Jason Clark. Harmless tale of a burro in the title locale; best for the kids.▼◗

Bright Young Things (2003-British) **C-105m.** ** D: Stephen Fry. Emily Mortimer, Stephen Campbell Moore, James McAvoy, Michael Sheen, David Tennant, Fenella Woolgar, Dan Aykroyd, Jim Broadbent, Simon Callow, Jim Carter, Stockard Channing, Richard E. Grant, Julia McKenzie, Peter O'Toole, Imelda Staunton, Margaret Tyzack, Bill Paterson, John Mills. Fry's adaptation of Evelyn Waugh's novel *Vile Bodies* tries to draw parallels between contemporary society and its obsession with celebrity and the hedonism of the 1930s. These "bright young things" live in a nonstop party atmosphere even while flames are igniting throughout Europe. Curiously annoying, despite a

strong cast (including 94-year-old Mills, in a silent cameo). Fry, making his directorial debut, appears briefly as a chauffeur. [R]●
Brilliant Lies (1996-Australian) **C-93m.** *** D: Richard Franklin. Anthony LaPaglia, Gia Carides, Zoe Carides, Ray Barrett, Michael Veitch, Catherine Wilkin, Neil Melville, Grant Tilly. As testimony is given in a woman's sexual harassment suit, her boss is shown to be a chauvinist pig . . . but she's revealed as promiscuous gold digger whose own sister doubts her. The ultimate truth proves to be more complicated than it appears. Absorbing, well-acted adaptation of David Williamson's play about the subjective nature of truth, which unfolds in fragmented flashbacks as each party gives their side of the story. LaPaglia and Gia Carides are a couple in real life. ▼
Brimstone & Treacle (1982-British) **C-85m.** **½ D: Richard Loncraine. Sting, Denholm Elliott, Joan Plowright, Suzanna Hamilton. Strange, intriguing (but often unpleasant) film about a young man who worms his way into the lives of a vulnerable middle-class couple, whose daughter lies in a coma. Good performance by Sting. [R]▼●
Bringing Down the House (2003) **C-105m.** ** D: Adam Shankman. Steve Martin, Queen Latifah, Eugene Levy, Joan Plowright, Jean Smart, Kimberly J. Brown, Angus T. Jones, Missi Pyle, Michael Rosenbaum, Betty White, Steve Harris. Martin is wasted in this crude collection of racial and sexual comic stereotypes as an uptight WASP tax attorney whose Internet chat-room mate turns out to be a black convict (Latifah) who wants him to clear her name. Naturally she loosens him up while straightening out his kids and helping him land a big deal at work. Strictly a routine big-screen sitcom, unless you find the prospect of Martin talking jive and bustin' a groove in hip-hop garb to be the height of hilarity. Latifah coexecutive-produced. Super 35. [PG-13] ▼●
Bringing Out the Dead (1999) **C-121m.** *** D: Martin Scorsese. Nicolas Cage, Patricia Arquette, John Goodman, Ving Rhames, Tom Sizemore, Marc Anthony, Mary Beth Hurt, Cliff Curtis, Aida Turturro. Life on the N.Y.C. streets from the point of view of a paramedic: a surreal, episodic film about a burntout case whose only hope for sanity and salvation is to save someone's life. Based on the book by former EMS driver Joe Connelly, told in harrowing and visually arresting fashion. Script by Paul Schrader; remarkable cinematography by Robert Richardson. Panavision. [R] ▼●
Bringing Up Baby (1938) **102m.** **** D: Howard Hawks. Cary Grant, Katharine Hepburn, Charlie Ruggles, May Robson, Barry Fitzgerald, Walter Catlett, Fritz Feld, Ward Bond. In her sole venture into slapstick, Hepburn plays a madcap heiress—"Baby" is her pet leopard—who sets her

sights on absentminded zoologist Grant and inadvertently (?) proceeds to make a shambles of his life. Not a hit when first released, this is now considered the definitive screwball comedy and one of the fastest, funniest films ever made; grand performances by all. Screenplay by Dudley Nichols and Hagar Wilde, from Wilde's original story. More or less remade as WHAT'S UP, DOC? Also shown in computer-colored version. ▼●
Bring It On (2000) **C-99m.** *** D: Peyton Reed. Kirsten Dunst, Eliza Dushku, Jesse Bradford, Gabrielle Union, Clare Kramer, Nicole Bilderback, Rini Bell, Lindsay Sloane, Richard Hillman, Ian Roberts, Holmes Randolph. High-spirited, high-energy movie about a championship high school cheerleading squad and its new captain (Dunst), who learns that their routines were stolen from a black, inner-city school. Sharp writing (by Jessica Bendinger), driving direction, and likable performances make this a winner. Followed by four DVD sequels. [PG-13]▼●
Bring Me the Head of Alfredo Garcia (1974) **C-112m.** ** D: Sam Peckinpah. Warren Oates, Isela Vega, Gig Young, Robert Webber, Helmut Dantine, Emilio Fernandez, Kris Kristofferson. American piano player in Mexico gets involved with a smorgasbord of psychos; sub-par bloodbath doesn't even have the usual Peckinpah fast pace. [R]▼●
Bring On the Night (1985-British) **C-97m.** *** D: Michael Apted. Sting, Omar Hakim, Darryl Jones, Kenny Kirkland, Branford Marsalis, Dolette McDonald, Janice Pendarvis, Trudie Styler, Miles Copeland. First-rate musical documentary about the formation of Sting's rock-jazz band, culminating in their first concert performance (performing the serious, often politically oriented material on the *Dream of the Blue Turtles* album). More than just a concert movie, thanks in large part to director Apted. Handsomely photographed by Ralf Bode. [PG-13]▼●
Brink of Life (1958-Swedish) **84m.** **½ D: Ingmar Bergman. Eva Dahlbeck, Ingrid Thulin, Bibi Andersson, Barbro Hiort af Ornas, Erland Josephson, Max von Sydow, Gunnar Sjoberg. Realistic, almost documentary-like chronicle of the lives of three women in a maternity ward. Meticulously filmed, but also gloomy and static; one of Bergman's lesser efforts. ▼
Brink's Job, The (1978) **C-103m.** *** D: William Friedkin. Peter Falk, Peter Boyle, Allen Goorwitz (Garfield), Warren Oates, Gena Rowlands, Paul Sorvino, Sheldon Leonard. Entertaining, comically oriented account of the infamous 1950 Boston heist, masterminded by Falk and motley gang of accomplices. Excellent period and location flavor. [PG]▼

Britannia Hospital (1982-British) **C-115m.** **½ D: Lindsay Anderson. Leonard·Rossiter, Graham Crowden, Malcolm McDowell, Joan Plowright, Jill Bennett, Marsha Hunt, Frank Grimes, Roland Culver, Fulton Mackay, Vivian Pickles, Mark Hamill, Liz Smith, Alan Bates, Arthur Lowe. Absurdist comedy about a hospital beleaguered by labor woes, protest groups, impatient patients, a resident mad doctor, and an impending visit by the Queen Mother. Heavy-handed satire, but entertaining nonetheless, with some actors in continuing roles from Anderson's IF . . . and O LUCKY MAN! Written by David Sherwin. [R]▼●)

Britannia Mews SEE: **Forbidden Street, The**

Broadcast News (1987) **C-131m.** *** D: James L. Brooks. William Hurt, Albert Brooks, Holly Hunter, Robert Prosky, Lois Chiles, Joan Cusack, Peter Hackes, Jack Nicholson, Christian Clemenson. Appealing and intelligent comedy about a highly charged, neurotic woman who's a successful TV news producer, and her attraction to a pretty-boy anchorman who joins her network—and represents everything she hates about TV news. All three stars are fine, but Brooks is a special standout as an ace reporter, and Hunter's best friend, who's really in love with her. Nicholson contributes a funny unbilled performance as the network's star anchorman. Written by the director; set and filmed in Washington, D.C. [R]▼●)

Broadway Bill (1934) **102m.** *** D: Frank Capra. Warner Baxter, Myrna Loy, Walter Connolly, Helen Vinson, Lynne Overman, Raymond Walburn, Clarence Muse, Douglass Dumbrille, Charles Lane, Ward Bond, Margaret Hamilton, Clara Blandick, Frankie Darro, Jason Robards (Sr.), and Broadway Bill. Baxter, who's "sold out" and married money, risks his marriage and his future on a racehorse; Loy, his wife's sister, seems to be the only one who believes in him. The unremitting good cheer of this Capra concoction overcomes its flaws. Script by Robert Riskin, from the Mark Hellinger story "On the Nose." Remade (by Capra) in 1950 as RIDING HIGH—using some of the same actors, and even some of the same footage. Look fast for a young, blonde Lucille Ball as a telephone operator.▼●)

Broadway Danny Rose (1984) **86m.** *** D: Woody Allen. Woody Allen, Mia Farrow, Nick Apollo Forte, Sandy Baron, Corbett Monica, Morty Gunty, Will Jordan, Milton Berle, Joe Franklin. Allen is wonderful as pathetic small-time manager who tries to boost career of over-the-hill singer Forte. Terrific casting, funny show-biz jokes but eventually wears a bit thin; a slight but amusing film. [PG]▼●)

Broadway Melody, The (1929) **100m.** **½

D: Harry Beaumont. Bessie Love, Anita Page, Charles King, Jed Prouty, Kenneth Thomson, Edward Dillon, Mary Doran. Early talkie musical curio about a pair of stage-struck sisters who seek fame on the Great White Way and fall for a charming song-and-dance man. This was the first musical to win a Best Picture Academy Award. Awfully dated today, but there's still a good score by Arthur Freed and Nacio Herb Brown: Title tune, "You Were Meant for Me," and "The Wedding of the Painted Doll." Some sequences originally in Technicolor; remade as TWO GIRLS ON BROADWAY.▼●)

Broadway Melody of 1936 (1935) **101m.** *** D: Roy Del Ruth. Jack Benny, Eleanor Powell, Robert Taylor, Una Merkel, Sid Silvers, Buddy Ebsen. Pleasant musi-comedy with Winchell-like columnist Benny trying to frame producer Taylor via dancer Powell, whose solo spots are pure delight. Arthur Freed–Nacio Herb Brown songs: "You Are My Lucky Star," "Broadway Rhythm," "I've Got a Feelin' You're Foolin' " (which earned an Oscar for Dave Gould's dance direction).▼●)

Broadway Melody of 1938 (1937) **110m.** **½ D: Roy Del Ruth. Robert Taylor, Eleanor Powell, George Murphy, Binnie Barnes, Buddy Ebsen, Judy Garland, Sophie Tucker, Charles Igor Gorin, Raymond Walburn, Robert Benchley, Willie Howard, Billy Gilbert. Not up to 1936 MELODY, with tuneful but forgettable songs, overbearing Tucker, and elephantine finale. Powell's dancing is great and Garland sings "Dear Mr. Gable."▼●)

Broadway Melody of 1940 (1940) **102m.** *** D: Norman Taurog. Fred Astaire, Eleanor Powell, George Murphy, Frank Morgan, Ian Hunter, Florence Rice, Lynne Carver, Ann Morriss. Friendship and rivalry between dance partners Astaire and Murphy spark delightful, underrated MGM musical, with hilarious vignettes, fine performance from Astaire, outstanding Cole Porter songs, and matchless Astaire-Powell numbers like "Begin the Beguine" (danced *twice* in the finale). If only they'd tie up the plot a bit sooner. Douglas McPhail (unbilled) introduces the Porter standard "I Concentrate On You."▼●)

Broadway: The Golden Age (2004) **C-109m.** ***½ D: Rick McKay. Combining interviews with more than one hundred veterans of Broadway during its heyday (roughly the 1930s through the 1960s), archival footage of N.Y.C., and rarely seen performance excerpts, this simple, straightforward film succeeds in capturing both an era and a way of life for a generation of performers and theatergoers. Highlights include a tribute to the revered Laurette Taylor and a television performance of John Raitt singing the "Soliloquy" from *Carousel*. A rich, deeply moving experience for anyone who loves Broadway theater or wants to introduce its wonders to a new generation. ◗

Brokeback Mountain (2005) **C-134m.** **★★★** D: Ang Lee. Heath Ledger, Jake Gyllenhaal, Randy Quaid, Michelle Williams, Anne Hathaway, Graham Beckel, Anna Faris, Linda Cardellini, Roberta Maxwell, Peter McRobbie. In 1963, two young cowboys meet while sheepherding in Wyoming and unexpectedly fall in love. Despite each subsequently marrying and raising a family, they continue their relationship through the years, always aware of the external limits placed on their true feelings. Bold subject matter (for mainstream audiences) is given sensitive if traditional treatment by director Lee; slow, stately, and often moving, but also a bit distant. Ledger is excellent in a complex, brooding role, and the whole cast matches him. Oscar winner for Director, Adapted Screenplay (by Larry McMurtry and Diana Ossana, from Annie Proulx's short story), and Original Score (Gustavo Santaolalla). [R] ◗

Brokedown Palace (1999) **C-100m.** **★★** D: Jonathan Kaplan. Claire Danes, Kate Beckinsale, Bill Pullman, Jacqueline Kim, Lou Diamond Phillips, Daniel Lapaine, Tom Amandes, Aimee Graham, John Doe. By-the-numbers cautionary melodrama in which naive best pals Danes and Beckinsale, on a trip to Thailand to celebrate their high school graduation, are set up by a drug smuggler and tossed into prison. Done in by its sheer predictability—and lack of chemistry between the stars. Super 35. [PG-13] ▼◗

Broken Arrow (1950) **C-93m.** **★★★** D: Delmer Daves. James Stewart, Jeff Chandler, Debra Paget, Will Geer, Jay Silverheels. Authentic study of 1870s Apache Chief Cochise (Chandler) and ex-Army man (Stewart) trying to seek accord between feuding Indians and settlers. Flavorful and effective; good action sequences. Screenplay, credited to Michael Blankfort, was actually written by Albert Maltz, then a blacklistee. Chandler played Cochise again in THE BATTLE AT APACHE PASS. Later a TV series. ▼◗

Broken Arrow (1996) **C-108m.** **★★** D: John Woo. John Travolta, Christian Slater, Samantha Mathis, Delroy Lindo, Bob Gunton, Frank Whaley, Howie Long, Vondie Curtis Hall, Jack Thompson, Kurtwood Smith, Daniel von Bargen. Extraordinarily stupid action movie about a high-security, high-tech Air Force pilot who deliberately crashes a U.S. plane in the midst of Utah and plans to hold its nuclear weapons for ransom. He doesn't reckon with his younger copilot (Slater) or the U.S. park ranger (Mathis) who join in a determined pursuit to thwart him. Packed with director Woo's expected action set pieces and stunts, but Travolta's over-the-top bad guy is fairly monotonous, and story continuity/credibil-

ity is almost nonexistent. Did it have to be *this* dumb? Super 35. [R] ▼◗

Broken Blossoms (1919) **95m.** **★★★** D: D. W. Griffith. Lillian Gish, Richard Barthelmess, Donald Crisp, Arthur Howard, Edward Piel. Dated but lovely film of Chinaman Barthelmess protecting frail Gish from clutches of brutal father Crisp; still creates a mood sustained by sensitive performances. One of Griffith's more modest, and more successful, films. Remade in England in 1936. Full title on-screen is BROKEN BLOSSOMS OR THE YELLOW MAN AND THE GIRL. ▼◖

Broken Bridges (2006) **C-105m.** **★½** D: Steven Goldmann. Toby Keith, Kelly Preston, Lindsey Haun, Tess Harper, Anna Maria Horsford, Katie Finneran, Josh Henderson, Willie Nelson, BeBe Winans, Burt Reynolds. The deaths in a training accident of five GIs from the same small Tennessee town set in motion a series of events involving two of the town's natives: Miami TV reporter Preston, who is long estranged from her family, and troubled, fading country-western singer Keith, the father of her adolescent daughter. Languid tale of regret and reconciliation offers a rose-colored view of small-town America. Country singer Keith's film debut; produced by Country Music Television. [PG-13] ◗

Broken Embraces (2009-Spanish) **C-127m.** **★★★½** D: Pedro Almodóvar. Penélope Cruz, Lluís Homar, Blanca Portillo, José Luis Gómez, Rubén Ochandiano, Tamar Novas, Ángela Molina. Blind writer (Homar) cares for his secretary's son after he's injured, and while nursing him reveals the true story of his life, up until the night he lost his sight 14 years ago. A movie director, he fell in love with a beautiful woman (Cruz) he cast in his latest film—unaware that she was in the grip of a powerful man who refused to share her affections. Sinuous, mesmerizing story plays out in two time frames; along the way Almodóvar pays homage to Audrey Hepburn, Roberto Rossellini, and film noir. He's also fashioned another perfect vehicle for Cruz's talent and beauty. Panavision. [R] ◗

Broken English (1996-New Zealand) **C-92m.** **★★★** D: Gregor Nicholas. Aleksandra Vujcic, Julian Arahanga, Rade Serbedzija, Marton Csokas, Madeline McNamara. A Croatian tyrant living in New Zealand goes ballistic when his daughter becomes romantically involved with a hunkish Maori cook. Consistently absorbing drama—and an interesting thematic companion piece to ONCE WERE WARRIORS—gets its surprising NC-17 rating from an exuberant bed-breaking scene of young lovers in love. Seconds were shaved for R version available on video. [NC-17] ▼

Broken English (2007-U.S.-French) **C-97m.** **★★½** D: Zoe Cassavetes. Parker Posey,

Melvil Poupaud, Drea de Matteo, Justin Theroux, Gena Rowlands, Peter Bogdanovich, Tim Guinee, James McCaffrey, Josh Hamilton, Phyllis Somerville, Dana Ivey, Bernadette Lafont, Roy Thinnes. N.Y.C. career woman Posey makes consistently bad choices in men, so when a genuinely nice, freewheeling Frenchman (Poupaud) is attracted to her she doesn't know how to respond. Uneven romantic comedy is salvaged by Posey's empathetic performance, in a rounded portrait of a woman who keeps screwing up her life because she has no self-esteem. Feature writing-directing debut for Cassavetes, whose mother (Rowlands) plays Posey's mom. [PG-13]▶)

Broken Flowers (2005) **C-106m.** ** D: Jim Jarmusch. Bill Murray, Jeffrey Wright, Sharon Stone, Jessica Lange, Tilda Swinton, Frances Conroy, Christopher McDonald, Julie Delpy, Chloë Sevigny, Heather Alicia Simms, Alexis Dziena, Mark Webber, Larry Fessenden. Deadpan Don Juan (Murray) receives an unsigned letter from a former lover telling him he has a 19-year-old son. His neighbor (Wright), an amateur sleuth, convinces him that he should look up all his old girlfriends to learn who sent the note, and, reluctantly, he does. Writer-director Jarmusch, the ultimate movie minimalist, is as inscrutable as ever, even with an A-list cast. Intriguing but not really satisfying. That's Murray's real-life son Homer near the end of the film. [R]▼)

Broken Hearts Club—A Romantic Comedy, The (2000) **C-94m.** **½ D: Greg Berlanti. Zach Braff, Dean Cain, Andrew Keegan, Nia Long, John Mahoney, Mary McCormack, Matt McGrath, Timothy Olyphant, Billy Porter, Justin Theroux, Jennifer Coolidge, Chris Weitz. Comedy-drama about gay friends in West Hollywood who harass each other as much as they support one another . . . and seemingly spend every waking moment talking about their troubled relationships. Veers from empathic and well observed to self-consciously clever and tiresome. Super 35. [R]▼)

Broken Lance (1954) **C-96m.** ***½ D: Edward Dmytryk. Spencer Tracy, Robert Wagner, Jean Peters, Richard Widmark, Katy Jurado, Hugh O'Brian, Eduard Franz, Earl Holliman, E. G. Marshall. Tracy is superlative in tight-knit script (by Richard Murphy, from an Oscar-winning Philip Yordan story) about patriarchal rancher who finds he's losing control of his cattle empire and his family is fragmenting into warring factions. Remake of HOUSE OF STRANGERS (although it owes more to *King Lear!*). CinemaScope.▼○)

Broken Lizard's Club Dread SEE: **Club Dread**

Broken Rainbow (1985) **C/B&W-70m.** *** D: Maria Florio, Victoria Mudd. Narrator: Martin Sheen. Historical voices: Burgess Meredith. Translator: Buffy Sainte-Marie. Touching, biting, appropriately one-sided, yet sometimes unnecessarily romanticized documentary about the relocation—and resistance—of Navajo Indians in Arizona. A Best Documentary Academy Award winner.▼)

Broken Sky (1982-Swedish) **C-96m.** **½ D: Ingrid Thulin. Susanna Kall, Thommy Berggren, Agneta Eckemyr, Margaretha Krook. Ambitious but uneven account of 13-year-old Kall, in the process of breaking free from her childhood, and her relationships with various family members. Thulin also wrote the script.

Bronco Billy (1980) **C-119m.** *** D: Clint Eastwood. Clint Eastwood, Sondra Locke, Geoffrey Lewis, Scatman Crothers, Bill McKinney, Sam Bottoms, Dan Vadis, Sierra Pecheur, Juliette Lewis. Enjoyable yarn about self-styled cowboy hero who runs a fly-by-night Wild West show and the spoiled heiress who joins his entourage of escapees from reality. Locke's rich-bitch character is a bit hard to take, but neither she nor some superfluous subplots can sour the charm of this film. Look fast for Hank Worden! [PG]▼○)

Bronco Buster (1952) **C-81m.** **½ D: Budd Boetticher. John Lund, Scott Brady, Joyce Holden, Chill Wills, Casey Tibbs. Minor story of rodeo star Lund helping Brady learn the ropes, forced to fight him for Holden's love. Good rodeo action.

Brontë (1983-Irish-U.S.) **C-88m.** *** D: Delbert Mann. Julie Harris. Engrossing performance by Harris portraying Charlotte Brontë in one-woman show recounting her life and family troubles via intimate, first-person monologues. Unusual, literate film benefits from all-location filming in Ireland. Script by William Luce from his radio play based on Brontë's own writings.

Brontë Sisters, The (1979-French) **C-115m.** **½ D: André Téchiné. Isabelle Adjani, Marie-France Pisier, Isabelle Huppert, Pascal Gregory, Patrick Magee. Well-mounted but slightly sluggish portrait of the famous literary sisters and their repressed lives. Worth a look mainly to see three of France's most appealing actresses in one film. Also shot in English-language version, which doesn't play as well.

Bronx Tale, A (1993) **C-122m.** ***½ D: Robert De Niro. Robert De Niro, Chazz Palminteri, Lillo Brancato, Francis Capra, Taral Hicks, Kathrine Narducci, Clem Caserta, Alfred Sauchelli, Jr., Frank Pietrangolare, Joe Pesci. Longish but well-observed slice of life, as a boy grows up with two heroes of conflicting nature and beliefs—his loving, hard-working father, and the neighborhood capo, who takes him as a personal protégé. Written by Palminteri, and based on his play; an impressive directorial debut for De Niro, who brings a keen eye and equally strong sensibility to this potent (but ultimately upbeat) material. Incidentally, to re-create the Bronx of the 1960s, De Niro had to shoot this in Brooklyn and Queens! [R]▼●]

Bronx War, The (1990) **C-91m.** ** D: Joseph B. Vasquez. Joseph, Fabio Urena, Charmaine Cruz, Andre Brown, Marlene Forte, Frances Colon, Miguel Sierra, Kim West. Ambitious, gritty but annoyingly uneven actioner chronicling the plight of Tito Sunshine (Joseph), a product of the mean streets of The Bronx, whose good intentions are obscured by the fact that he's a crack dealer. Dramatically overwrought, unrelentingly violent and profane, but not without its moments. Available on video in R and unrated versions. ▼)

Brood, The (1979-Canadian) **C-90m.** BOMB D: David Cronenberg. Oliver Reed, Samantha Eggar, Art Hindle, Cindy Hinds, Nuala Fitzgerald, Susan Hogan. Eggar eats her own afterbirth while midget clones beat grandparents and lovely young schoolteachers to death with mallets. It's a big, wide, wonderful world we live in! [R]▼●]

Brooklyn Rules (2007) **C-99m.** ** D: Michael Corrente. Freddie Prinze, Jr., Alec Baldwin, Scott Caan, Jerry Ferrara, Mena Suvari, Robert Turano, Phyllis Kay, Monica Keena. Coming-of-age story set in Brooklyn of 1985 about three friends and their relationship with the local Mafia figures who dominate their neighborhood. When tragedy strikes, their lives are irreversibly changed. Screenplay by Terence Winter, a key creative force of *The Sopranos*, but the movie is *Sopranos*-lite at best. Baldwin could play the local mob boss in his sleep; only Ferrara (of *Entourage*) stands out in the young cast. Panavision. [R]❙

Brooklyn's Finest (2010) **C-123m.** *** D: Antoine Fuqua. Richard Gere, Don Cheadle, Ethan Hawke, Wesley Snipes, Will Patton, Lili Taylor, Michael Kenneth Williams, Ellen Barkin, Brian F. O'Byrne, Shannon Kane, Vincent D'Onofrio. Impressively gritty, sometimes shockingly violent urban drama follows the largely separate but ultimately intertwined stories of three stressed-out N.Y.C. cops: a detective (Hawke) who robs drug dealers to provide for his ailing wife (Taylor) and children; an undercover vice cop (Cheadle) ordered to build a case against an old friend (Snipes); and a cynical uniformed officer (Gere) who gets a shot at redemption just a few days before retirement. Covers familiar ground, but strong performances (especially from Gere and Cheadle) and punchy direction breathe fresh life into clichés and conventions. Super 35. [R]❙

Brother (2000-U.S.-Japanese-French-British) **C-107m.** *** D: Takeshi Kitano. Beat Takeshi (Kitano), Omar Epps, Kuroudo Maki, Masaya Kato, Ren Osugi, Susumu Terajima, Ryo Ishibashi, James Shigeta.

Stoic Japanese gangster Takeshi becomes the Fastest Gun in the West as he arrives in L.A. and becomes immersed in gang rivalries while bonding with a young African American (Epps). Ultraviolent, to be sure, but this is no mindless actioner; rather, it is a meditation on the meaning of loyalty, and deftly contrasts the tough, anarchic urban-American subculture and the rituals of Japanese Yakuza. Signature bits of Kitano's wry humor are added to the mix; he also scripted and edited. [R]▼)

Brother Bear (2003) **C-81m.** *** D: Aaron Blaise, Bob Walker. Voices of Joaquin Phoenix, Jeremy Suarez, Jason Raize, Rick Moranis, Dave Thomas, D. B. Sweeney, Michael Clarke Duncan, Harold Gould, Estelle Harris. The life of a Native American boy takes an unexpected turn when the Great Spirits transform him into the creature he hates the most: a bear. As he sets out to regain his human form, he sees things from a different perspective (even befriending a bear cub) while trying to evade his brother, who's pursuing him on a mission of revenge. Absorbing, beautifully executed animated feature infuses a highly unusual tale with ingredients of traditional Disney storytelling. It's fun to have Moranis and Thomas do a variation on their McKenzie Brothers characters—as moose! Followed by a direct-to-DVD sequel. Digital Widescreen. [G] ▼)

Brother Can You Spare a Dime (1975) **103m.** **½ D: Philippe Mora. Documentary on 1930s has fuzzy point of view, and no narration to tie footage together; it also mixes newsreels and Hollywood clips. If you know and like the period, the footage will speak for itself and provide a certain measure of entertainment. [PG]▼)

Brother From Another Planet, The (1984) **C-104m.** *** D: John Sayles. Joe Morton, Darryl Edwards, Steve James, Leonard Jackson, Maggie Renzi, Rosetta Le Noire, David Strathairn, Bill Cobbs. Amiable, ingenious contemporary fantasy, filmed on a shoestring, about a black visitor from another planet who (like Chance in BEING THERE) impresses most of the people he meets because he doesn't say a word—and lets them do all the talking! Falls apart toward the end with a subplot about drug dealers, but still worthwhile. Fine dialogue by writer-director Sayles, who, as usual, gives himself a funny role (as one of the Brother's outer-space pursuers). ▼)

Brotherhood, The (1968) **C-98m.** *** D: Martin Ritt. Kirk Douglas, Alex Cord, Irene Papas, Luther Adler, Susan Strasberg, Murray Hamilton. Excellent story of Mafia in changing times; tradition-bound Douglas clashes with younger brother Cord who feels no ties to old-fashioned dictates. Pre-GODFATHER, but in the same league. [M]▼●]

Brotherhood (2011) **C-76m.** *½ D: Will Canon. Trevor Morgan, Jon Foster, Lou

[187]

Taylor Pucci, Arlen Escarpeta. All hell breaks loose when an initiation ritual for a college fraternity goes terribly wrong and the pledges must decide whether it's more important to save their friend or be loyal to their future brothers. While the acting isn't bad, it's hard to become genuinely involved in the story (which is quite complicated), and the nonstop barrage of expletives becomes tiresome. A clever twist at the end doesn't make up for the rest of the film's flaws. HD Widescreen. [R]▶

Brotherhood of Satan (1971) C-92m. **½ D: Bernard McEveety. Strother Martin, L. Q. Jones, Charles Bateman, Ahna Capri, Charles Robinson. Satanists take over town in this horrifying little terror tale. Techniscope. [PG]▼▶

Brotherhood of the Wolf (2001-French) C-142m. ** D: Christophe Gans. Samuel Le Bihan, Mark Dacascos, Vincent Cassel, Monica Bellucci, Émilie Dequenne, Jérémie Renier. Based on a famous legend, this *very* strange film chronicles the attempt to track down a mysterious wolflike creature that is terrorizing the French countryside in 1765. A scientist and his Iroquois "blood brother" take on the job for King Louis XV, but they meet resistance at every turn. Bizarre, unsatisfying mélange of costume piece, occult drama, sexual fantasy, and horror film! Super 35. [R]▼▶

Brotherhood of the Yakuza SEE: **Yakuza, The**

Brother John (1972) C-94m. *** D: James Goldstone. Sidney Poitier, Will Geer, Bradford Dillman, Beverly Todd, Ramon Bieri, Warren J. Kemmerling, Lincoln Kilpatrick, Paul Winfield. Highly entertaining tale of the Messiah's return—only no one knows that he's come, and that he's black. [PG]▼▶

Brotherly Love (1970-British) C-112m. *** D: J. Lee Thompson. Peter O'Toole, Susannah York, Michael Craig, Harry Andrews, Cyril Cusack, Judy Cornwell, Brian Blessed. Very funny study of relationships in upper-class British household. O'Toole and York are delightful. Original British title: COUNTRY DANCE. [R]

Brother Orchid (1940) 91m. *** D: Lloyd Bacon. Edward G. Robinson, Ann Sothern, Humphrey Bogart, Ralph Bellamy, Donald Crisp, Allen Jenkins. Farfetched but entertaining yarn of racketeer Robinson who seeks "the real class" in life. Double-crossed by his old mob, he winds up in a monastery, of all places. Sothern delightful as his ever-faithful girlfriend.▼▶

Brother Rat (1938) 90m. *** D: William Keighley. Priscilla Lane, Wayne Morris, Johnnie Davis, Jane Bryan, Eddie Albert, Ronald Reagan, Jane Wyman, William Tracy. Comedy of three pals at Virginia Military Institute isn't as fresh as it was in the 1930s, but still remains entertaining, with enthusiastic

performances by all. Albert stands out in his screen debut, in a role he played on the stage. Sequel: BROTHER RAT AND A BABY. Remade as ABOUT FACE.

Brothers (1977) C-104m. **½ D: Arthur Barron. Bernie Casey, Vonetta McGee, Ron O'Neal, Renny Roker, Stu Gilliam, John Lehne. Well-intentioned story based on relationship between militant professor Angela Davis and literate black convict George Jackson during 1960s. Sloppy filmmaking and awkward scripting diminish impact of film's better moments. [R]

Brothers, The (2001) C-106m. ** D: Gary Hardwick. Morris Chestnut, Shemar Moore, D.L. Hughley, Bill Bellamy, Gabrielle Union, Susan Dalian, Tamala Jones, Marla Gibbs, Jenifer Lewis, Clifton Powell, Tatyana Ali, Vanessa Bell Calloway. Four childhood friends are now successful doctors, lawyers, etc., all nearing 30, with three of the four still single. Film examines the tumultuous personal lives of these guys, who under the three-piece suits are just hoop-shooting overgrown kids. Overly melodramatic, though comedians Bellamy and Hughley spout some awfully funny, racy lines. Hardwick scripted and appears as T-Boy. [R]▶

Brothers (2004-Danish) C-110m. ***½ D: Susanne Bier. Connie Nielsen, Ulrich Thomsen, Nikolaj Lie Kaas, Bent Mejding, Solbørg Højfeldt, Paw Henriksen. A man leaves his wife and two daughters to fight in Afghanistan, just as his chronic screwup brother is released from prison. The family does its best, feeling the pain of the "good" brother's absence and the tension of the "bad" brother's presence. Subsequent events reveal the true nature of the leading characters. Searing, intense, adult drama; Nielsen (in her Danish feature debut) heads a superb cast. Intimately photographed by Morten Søborg on digital video. Screenplay by Anders Thomas Jensen from a story he cowrote with director Bier. Remade in the U.S. in 2009. [R]▶

Brothers (2009) C-104m. **½ D: Jim Sheridan. Tobey Maguire, Jake Gyllenhaal, Natalie Portman, Sam Shepard, Bailee Madison, Patrick Flueger, Clifton Collins, Jr., Mare Winningham, Taylor Geare, Carey Mulligan, Ethan Suplee. A loving husband and father (Maguire) is called to duty in Afghanistan; while he's away his screwup brother (Gyllenhaal), just released from prison, tries to look after the family and develops strong feelings for his sibling's wife (Portman). Remake of the powerful 2004 Danish film sticks pretty close to the original, but having movie stars in the leading roles seems to dull its impact. Super 35. [R]▶

Brothers Bloom, The (2009) C-109m. **½ D: Rian Johnson. Rachel Weisz, Mark Ruffalo, Adrien Brody, Rinko Kikuchi, Robbie Coltrane, Maximilian Schell; narrated by Ricky Jay. Picaresque fable of two orphaned brothers who find their way in the world as con artists, following scenarios devised by the inventive younger sibling. But during what is planned as their final caper, the older brother (Ruffalo) falls in love with their mark (Weisz), a beautiful recluse who treats the experience as a glorious adventure. Self-consciously clever, to be sure, but it's fun for a while until the air deflates from the balloon at a certain point. The Eastern European settings are colorful, and Weisz is delightful as a madcap. Enjoyably eclectic score by Nathan Johnson. Look fast for Joseph Gordon-Levitt (star of Johnson's debut film, BRICK). Super 35. [PG-13] ▶

Brothers Grimm, The (2005-U.S.-Czech) **C-118m. **** D: Terry Gilliam. Matt Damon, Heath Ledger, Peter Stormare, Lena Headey, Jonathan Pryce, Monica Bellucci, Petr Ratimec, Barbara Lukêsova, Anna Rust, Jeremy Robson. Fictionalized (and bloated) account of the brothers Wilhelm and Jacob Grimm, here called Will and Jake, depicted as con men who travel from village to village in Napoleonic-era Germany and exploit the superstitions of the townspeople. Eventually they are recruited to determine why the children of one hamlet are mysteriously disappearing. Extravagant sets, costumes, and imagery are pure Gilliam, but the film is hollow and disappointing. This had a long and troubled production history, and it shows. Grimm indeed. [PG-13] ▶

Brother's Justice, A SEE: **Gleaming the Cube**

Brothers Karamazov, The (1958) **C-146m. *** D: Richard Brooks. Yul Brynner, Maria Schell, Claire Bloom, Lee J. Cobb, Richard Basehart, William Shatner, Albert Salmi. Set in 19th-century Russia, film version of Dostoyevsky's tragedy revolving about death of a dominating father (Cobb) and effect on his sons: fun-seeking Brynner, scholarly Basehart, religious Shatner, and epileptic Salmi. Exceptionally well scripted by Brooks. William Shatner's first film. ▼

Brother's Keeper (1992) **C-104m. ***½** D: Joe Berlinger, Bruce Sinofsky. Exceptional documentary/slice-of-life which offers a portrait of backwoods America rarely seen in mainstream movies. It's the story of Delbert Ward, a reserved, uneducated upstate New York farmer who was thrown into jail after being accused of murdering his sickly brother. When he goes on trial, his neighbors, who barely know him, rally to his defense. An intriguing treatise on human nature and a telling look at how the media plays a role in a controversial case like this. ▼●

Brother's Kiss, A (1997) **C-92m. *** D: Seth Zvi Rosenfeld. Nick Chinlund, Michael Raynor, Talent Harris, John Leguizamo, Cathy Moriarty, Adrian Pasdar, Rosie Perez, Justin Pierce, Marisa Tomei, Michael Rapaport, Joshua Danowsky. Raw, riveting drama depicting the complex relationship between brothers, Lex (Chinlund)

and Mick (Raynor), who came of age on the mean streets of N.Y.'s East Harlem. Mick, the younger, has become a cop, while Lex, who's never been able to catch a break, is a drug addict. Flashbacks to the brothers' childhood are especially effective—and heartbreaking. Based on Rosenfeld's stage play. [R] ▼●

Brothers McMullen, The (1995) **C-97m. **½** D: Edward Burns. Jack Mulcahy, Mike McGlone, Edward Burns, Shari Albert, Maxine Bahns, Connie Britton, Jennifer Jostyn, Elizabeth P. McKay, Catherine Bolz. Three brothers are temporarily living together under one roof; the married one is tempted to stray, the one who's involved with a woman has Catholic guilt about sinning, and the third wears his cynicism about relationships on his sleeve—even after he falls in love. Made on a minuscule budget, this modest film grows more compelling as it goes along, with two assets missing from slicker Hollywood movies: The actors are appealing and their conversations are totally believable. First-time director Burns also wrote the script and costars. [R] ▼●

Brothers of the Head (2006-British) **C-93m. *** D: Keith Fulton, Louis Pepe. Harry Treadaway, Luke Treadaway, Bryan Dick, Sean Harris, Tania Emery, Diana Kent, Tom Bower, David Kennedy, Elizabeth Rider, Jane Horrocks, Jonathan Pryce, John Simm, Ken Russell, Ray Davies. Various talking heads look back on the lives and careers of conjoined twins who, in the mid-1970s, shined brightly but briefly as proto-punk rockers in this faux documentary. Flashy, potentially intriguing portrait of excess is longwinded and predictable; there's about a half hour's worth of material here. Based on a novel by Brian Aldiss. [R]●

Brothers O'Toole, The (1973) **C-90m. *** D: Richard Erdman. John Astin, Steve Carlson, Pat Carroll, Hans Conried, Lee Meriwether, Allyn Joslyn, Jesse White. Strictly for the kids is this comedy Western. Actor turned director Erdman has a bit. [G] ▼▶

Brothers Rico, The (1957) **92m. **½** D: Phil Karlson. Richard Conte, Dianne Foster, Kathryn Grant (Crosby), Larry Gates, James Darren. Incisive gangster yarn; Conte comes to N.Y.C. to counteract nationwide criminal gang's plot to eliminate his two brothers. Based on Georges Simenon novel; remade for TV as THE FAMILY RICO in 1972.●

Brothers Solomon, The (2007) **C-93m.** BOMB D: Bob Odenkirk. Will Arnett, Will Forte, Chi McBride, Kristen Wiig, Malin Akerman, Lee Majors, Michael Ormsby, Bill Hader, Jenna Fischer, Bob Odenkirk. Distant cousin of DUMB AND DUMBER in which Arnett and Forte play brothers who hatch a scheme to revive their comatose father by delivering him the grandchild he always wanted. Setting out to find a girl to do the deed, the two dopey siblings each try to impregnate her . . .

with predictable complications. Forte wrote this comatose script, which he and Arnett try to bring to life. [R]❚

Brother Sun Sister Moon (1973-Italian-British) **C-121m.** **½ D: Franco Zeffirelli. Graham Faulkner, Judi Bowker, Leigh Lawson, Alec Guinness, Valentina Cortese, Kenneth Cranham. Zeffirelli's wide-eyed youth-oriented slant on Francis of Assisi story runs hot and cold; some delicate, lovely scenes, but other ideas don't always come across. Songs by Donovan. [PG]❚▶

Brown Bunny, The (2004) **C-92m.** *½ D: Vincent Gallo. Vincent Gallo, Chloë Sevgny, Cheryl Tiegs, Elizabeth Blake, Anna Vareschi. Auteur antics from producer/writer/director/cinematographer/productiondesigner/editor/actor Gallo about a ponderous New Hampshire-to-California road odyssey taken by a motorcycle racer whose secret (divulged in the movie's final quarter) motivates his every move. Cut by almost a half hour from the version that played the 2003 Cannes Film Festival to wide derision and disbelief. A workable tale sunk by too many moments where the camera does little but grind . . . and a predilection toward the grotesquely weird (Tiegs' scene is mind-bending nonsense). Without the notorious finale, an on-the-level fellatio scene between Sevigny and Gallo, it's tough to imagine that the film would have ever been shown.❚

Browning Version, The (1951-British) **90m.** ***½ D: Anthony Asquith. Michael Redgrave, Jean Kent, Nigel Patrick, Brian Smith, Wilfrid Hyde-White, Ronald Howard, Bill Travers. Redgrave is superb as middle-aged boarding school teacher who realizes he's a failure, with an unfaithful wife and a new teaching position he doesn't want. Cast does full justice to the play by Terence Rattigan; he also scripted. Remade in 1994.❚

Browning Version, The (1994-U.S.-British) **C-97m.** **½ D: Mike Figgis. Albert Finney, Greta Scacchi, Matthew Modine, Julian Sands, Michael Gambon, Ben Silverstone, Maryam D'Abo, David Lever. Well-mounted, though stodgy, remake of Terence Rattigan's play of retiring schoolmaster whose dedication is unappreciated and whose marriage is unraveling. Finney is good as man out of step with the times, Scacchi is fine (if oddly cast). Touching and tragic, but it's hard to beat Michael Redgrave's performance in 1951 version. Panavision. [R]❚▶

Brown's Requiem (1998) **C-104m.** ** D: Jason Freeland. Michael Rooker, Tobin Bell, Selma Blair, Jack Conley, Kevin Corrigan, Brad Dourif, Harold Gould, Brion James, Barry Newman, William Newman, Valerie Perrine, William Sasso, Jack Wallace. Sluggish crime yarn, based on a James Ellroy novel, with alcoholic cop-turned-repo-man/P.I. Rooker hired by a corpulent caddie to watch over his sultry kid sister (Blair). Where are Bogie and Bacall when you really need them? 2.35 Research PLC. [R]❚▶

Brown Sugar (2002) **C-98m.** **½ D: Rick Famuyiwa. Taye Diggs, Sanaa Lathan, Mos Def, Nicole Ari Parker, Queen Latifah, Boris Kodjoe. Pleasant romantic comedy about two lifelong friends who love hip-hop music but can't admit they love each other. He's a record exec who marries the wrong woman; she's an eloquent and impassioned music journalist. A likable cast brightens this film, which goes on a bit longer than it has to, given the obvious conclusion of the story. Many recording artists appear as themselves. [PG-13]❚▶

Brubaker (1980) **C-132m.** **½ D: Stuart Rosenberg. Robert Redford, Yaphet Kotto, Jane Alexander, Murray Hamilton, David Keith, Morgan Freeman, Matt Clark, Tim McIntire, Linda Haynes, M. Emmet Walsh, Richard Ward, Albert Salmi, John McMartin, Wilford Brimley, Joe Spinell, Lee Richardson, Harry Groener, John Glover. Earnest but predictable prison drama based on true story of reform-minded warden who dares to uncover skeletons in corrupt Southern prison system. [R]❚◀▶

Bruce Almighty (2003) **C-101m.** *** D: Tom Shadyac. Jim Carrey, Morgan Freeman, Jennifer Aniston, Philip Baker Hall, Catherine Bell, Lisa Ann Walter, Steven (Steve) Carell, Nora Dunn, Sally Kirkland, Eddie Jemison, Tony Bennett. TV reporter who feels he keeps getting the short end of the stick winds up cursing God. As a result, he's summoned by the Almighty and given His powers, to do with as he pleases . . . but before long, the gift seems more like a curse. Entertaining fantasy-comedy stays rooted enough in reality to pull you in. Carrey is at his best, and Freeman is perfect as a down-to-earth Deity. Followed by EVAN ALMIGHTY. [PG-13]❚▶

Bruce Lee's Game of Death SEE: **Game of Death**

Bruno (2000) **C-108m.** **½ D: Shirley MacLaine. Alex D. Linz, Shirley MacLaine, Gary Sinise, Joey Lauren Adams, Kathy Bates, Kiami Davael, Stacey Halprin, Gwen Verdon, Jennifer Tilly, Brett Butler, Lainie Kazan. MacLaine made her feature directorial debut with this fable about a precocious 8-year-old Catholic schoolboy (and spelling-bee whiz) who likes to wear dresses. Quirky comedy-drama has poignant moments, and a gallery of stereotyped characters who are somewhat strident, but funny. Made for theaters, debuted on cable TV. Aka THE DRESS CODE. [PG-13]❚▶

Brüno (2009) **C-81m.** **½ D: Larry Charles. Sacha Baron Cohen, Gustaf Hammarsten, Bono, Chris Martin, Elton John, Slash, Snoop Dogg, Sting. Baron Cohen adopts the guise of flamboyantly gay Austrian fashionista Brüno, who will do (literally) anything to become famous. As in BORAT, the best sequences involve people being suckered into believing Brüno's outrageous words and actions: a TV talk show where he brings his adopted baby from Africa, a hunting trip with four good ol' boys, a macho wrestling arena. Some real laughs, but many hair-raising and painfully uncomfortable moments as well; a very mixed bag. [R]▶

Brute, The SEE: **El Bruto**

Brute Force (1947) 98m. ***½ D: Jules Dassin. Burt Lancaster, Hume Cronyn, Charles Bickford, Yvonne De Carlo, Ann Blyth, Ella Raines, Howard Duff, Whit Bissell, Jeff Corey, Sam Levene, Roman Bohnen, John Hoyt, Anita Colby. Tingling, hard-bitten prison film with its few clichés punched across solidly. Brutal captain Cronyn is utterly despicable, but you *know* he's going to get it in the end. Scripted by Richard Brooks, from Robert Patterson's story. Duff's film debut.▼●▶

Brylcreem Boys, The (1996-British) C-105m. ** D: Terence Ryan. Bill Campbell, William McNamara, Angus Macfadyen, Gabriel Byrne, Jean Butler, John Gordon Sinclair, Oliver Tobias. Allied airmen of WW2, shot down over Ireland, are astonished to learn that they are to be held in a POW camp, right alongside German prisoners—a quintessentially curious way for Ireland to maintain and enforce its official neutrality during the war. Intriguing premise gets mediocre treatment in this superficial and disappointing film.▼●▶

Bubba Ho-Tep (2003) C-92m. *** D: Don Coscarelli. Bruce Campbell, Ossie Davis, Ella Joyce, Bob Ivy, Heidi Marnhout. Engagingly silly film takes place in East Texas, where an elderly Elvis Presley shares the same nursing home as a man who claims to be JFK (even though he's black). When they discover that an ancient mummy is prowling their hallways at night, sucking the life out of fellow patients, they team up to save the day. Campbell and Davis play this so well that they manage to draw you in, in spite of yourself! Based on a short story by Joe R. Lansdale. [R]▼▶

Bubble, The (1966) SEE: **Fantastic Invasion of Planet Earth**

Bubble (2006) C-73m. **½ D: Steven Soderbergh. Debbie Doebereiner, Dustin James Ashley, Misty Dawn Wilkins, Kyle Smith, Decker Moody. In a drab Midwestern town, coworkers in a doll factory (a middle-aged woman and a younger man) have a pleasant-enough carpool relationship until a younger, prettier woman is hired. Everything about this film is muted, including the colors and the emotions, but Soderbergh creates a tangible and completely believable world with nonprofessional actors. More an experiment than an entertainment, and awfully dry, but well done. HD 24P Widescreen. [R]▶

Bubble Boy (2001) C-84m. BOMB D: Blair Hayes. Jake Gyllenhaal, Swoosie Kurtz, Marley Shelton, Danny Trejo, John Carroll Lynch, Verne Troyer, Stephen Spinella, Dave Sheridan, Patrick Cranshaw, Zach Galifianakis, Fabio. An infant, born without immunities, is raised in a plastic bubble by his overly cautious mother and passive father. As a young man he falls for the girl next door; when she moves away to marry another guy he creates a special suit so he can chase her across the country. An insipid attempt at a comedy; even the upbeat attitude of the lead character can't save this panoply of stupid stereotypes, gross-out gags, and inane situations. Super 35. [PG-13]▼▶

Buccaneer, The (1938) 124m. *** D: Cecil B. DeMille. Fredric March, Franciska Gaal, Margot Grahame, Akim Tamiroff, Walter Brennan, Anthony Quinn. Typically entertaining epic-scale saga from DeMille, with florid performance by March as pirate-hero Jean Lafitte, who aids American cause during Battle of New Orleans. Good storytelling and good fun. Remade in 1958.

Buccaneer, The (1958) C-121m. *** D: Anthony Quinn. Yul Brynner, Charlton Heston, Claire Bloom, Charles Boyer, Inger Stevens, Henry Hull, E. G. Marshall, Lorne Greene, Fran Jeffries, Woodrow (Woody) Strode. Starchy swashbuckler retelling events during Battle of New Orleans when Andrew Jackson (Heston) is forced to rely on buccaneer Lafitte (Brynner) to stem the British invasion; action is spotty but splashy. Quinn's only film as director; executive-produced by his then-father-in-law Cecil B. DeMille, who directed the 1938 original, and whose last film this was. VistaVision.▼●

Buchanan Rides Alone (1958) C-78m. *** D: Budd Boetticher. Randolph Scott, Craig Stevens, Barry Kelley, Tol Avery, Peter Whitney, Manuel Rojas, Jennifer Holden. Scott runs afoul of corrupt family in control of border town; taut B Western written by Charles Lang never runs out of plot twists.▶

Buck and the Preacher (1972) C-102m. **½ D: Sidney Poitier. Sidney Poitier, Harry Belafonte, Ruby Dee, Cameron Mitchell, Nita Talbot. Black-oriented Western of "hustler" preacher is long on getting to the action and short on staying with it. Good characterizations are major point of interest. Music by Benny Carter. Poitier's directorial debut. [PG]▼▶

Buckaroo Banzai SEE: **Adventures of Buckaroo Banzai Across the Eighth Dimension, The**

Bucket List, The (2007) C-97m. **½ D: Rob Reiner. Jack Nicholson, Morgan Freeman, Sean Hayes, Beverly Todd, Rob Morrow, Alfonso Freeman, Rowena King. Philosophical garage mechanic who's diagnosed with terminal cancer winds up sharing a hospital room with a self-centered tycoon who gets the same bill of health.

They decide to escape and live out their remaining days pursuing Freeman's list of things he's always wanted to do before kicking the bucket. Contrived, borderline-cute screenplay is validated by the presence of two great actors, though Nicholson resorts to mugging. [PG-13]❿

Bucket of Blood, A (1959) 66m. *** D: Roger Corman. Dick Miller, Barboura Morris, Antony Carbone, Julian Burton, Ed Nelson, Bert Convy. Wimpy busboy impresses his coffeehouse betters with amazingly lifelike "sculptures." Writer Charles Griffith's predecessor to THE LITTLE SHOP OF HORRORS is nifty semi-spoof of dead-bodies-in-the-wax-museum genre. Nicely captures spirit of beatnik era; cult actor Miller's finest hour (he's reused his character's name, Walter Paisley, several times since). Remade for TV as THE DEATH ARTIST in 1996. ▼❿

Buck Privates (1941) 84m. **½ D: Arthur Lubin. Bud Abbott, Lou Costello, Lee Bowman, Alan Curtis, The Andrews Sisters, Jane Frazee, Nat Pendleton, Shemp Howard. Dated but engaging Army opus with Bud and Lou accidentally enlisting. Brassy songs (including Andrews Sisters' "Boogie Woogie Bugle Boy") and subplots get in the way, but A&C's routines are among their best; their first starring film. ▼❿❿

Buck Privates Come Home (1947) 77m. *** D: Charles Barton. Bud Abbott, Lou Costello, Tom Brown, Joan Fulton (Shawlee), Nat Pendleton, Beverly Simmons, Don Beddoe. One of A&C's most enjoyable romps has boys returning to civilian life and trying to smuggle a young European orphan into this country. Climactic chase a highlight. ▼❿❿

Buck Rogers in the 25th Century (1979) C-89m. ** D: Daniel Haller. Gil Gerard, Pamela Hensley, Erin Gray, Tim O'Connor, Henry Silva, Joseph Wiseman, Felix Silla; voice of Mel Blanc. The legendary space hero returns, decked out in contemporary glibness, trying to prove he's not in league with intergalactic pirates. Much of the hardware and gadgetry (along with some footage) is from TV's expensive dud BATTLESTAR GALACTICA, turned out by the same producers. Pilot for the TV series; released theatrically first. [PG]▼❿

Buckskin (1968) C-97m. *½ D: Michael Moore. Barry Sullivan, Joan Caulfield, Wendell Corey, Lon Chaney, John Russell, Barbara Hale, Barton MacLane, Leo Gordon. Land-baron Corey tries to force homesteaders out of territory, but Marshal Sullivan is there to stop him. [G]▼❿

Bucktown (1975) C-94m. *½ D: Arthur Marks. Fred Williamson, Pam Grier, Thalmus Rasulala, Tony King, Bernie Hamilton, Art Lund. Repellent blaxploitation picture about war between whites and blacks in corruption-filled Southern town, which intensifies when blacks get into office and make things even worse. [R]▼❿

Bud Abbott Lou Costello in Hollywood SEE: Abbott and Costello in Hollywood
Bud Abbott Lou Costello Meet Frankenstein SEE: Abbott and Costello Meet Frankenstein

Buddy (1997) C-84m. **½ D: Caroline Thompson. Rene Russo, Robbie Coltrane, Alan Cumming, Irma P. Hall, Paul Reubens, John Aylward, Mimi Kennedy. Sweet-natured film about a most unusual woman, real-life Gertrude Lintz, who in the 1920s kept an incredible menagerie of animals on her Long Island estate. Her greatest challenge: raising a gorilla from infancy and treating him almost like a human child. Russo is excellent, and the film has much charm, but it's too leisurely and likely to make kids squirm in their seats. Based on William Joyce's book. Panavision. [PG]▼❿❿

Buddy Buddy (1981) C-96m. *** D: Billy Wilder. Jack Lemmon, Walter Matthau, Paula Prentiss, Klaus Kinski, Dana Elcar, Miles Chapin, Joan Shawlee. Modest black comedy about a hit man whose current job is mucked up by an intrusive stranger. A simple farce, played to perfection by Lemmon and Matthau, adapted by Wilder and I.A.L. Diamond from the French film A PAIN IN THE A—. Wilder's final film as director. Panavision. [R]▼

Buddy Holly Story, The (1978) C-113m. ***½ D: Steve Rash. Gary Busey, Charles Martin Smith, Don Stroud, Maria Richwine, Amy Johnston, Conrad Janis, Dick O'Neill, William Jordan, Will Jordan (they're different actors), Fred Travalena, "Stymie" Beard. Busey gives an electrifying performance as the rock 'n' roll legend in this long but very satisfying musical drama, not quite the usual glossy Hollywood biography. Busey, Smith and Stroud sing and play "live," giving an extra dimension to Holly's hit songs; Joe Renzetti won an Oscar for Score Adaptation. [PG]▼❿❿

Buddy System, The (1984) C-110m. **½ D: Glenn Jordan. Richard Dreyfuss, Susan Sarandon, Nancy Allen, Jean Stapleton, Wil Wheaton, Edward Winter, Keene Curtis. Lonely kid tries to play matchmaker between his single mom and a grown-up friend, would-be novelist and gadget inventor Dreyfuss, but there are emotional complications. Nicely played but overly familiar (and overlong) romantic comedy. [PG]▼

Buena Vista Social Club (1999-U.S.-German-French-Cuban) C-105m. *** D: Wim Wenders. Seductive documentary about the title group, composed of veteran Havana musicians and singers brought together by American guitarist Ry Cooder after years in obscurity. Two years after cutting a top-selling, award-winning record, they are filmed by Wenders at a recording session, in concert, and reminiscing about their music and their lives. Some are in their 80s (and even 90s), but their music is timeless and musicianship invigorating. [G] ▼▶

Buffalo Bill and the Indians or Sitting Bull's History Lesson (1976) **C-120m.** ** D: Robert Altman. Paul Newman, Joel Grey, Kevin McCarthy, Burt Lancaster, Geraldine Chaplin, Harvey Keitel, Frank Kaquitts, Will Sampson. Altman makes the point that Buffalo Bill was a flamboyant fraud, then belabors it for two hours. Not without interest, but still one of the director's duller movies. Panavision. [PG] ▼◉

Buffalo 66 (1998) **C-112m.** ** D: Vincent Gallo. Vincent Gallo, Christina Ricci, Anjelica Huston, Ben Gazzara, Kevin Corrigan, Mickey Rourke, Rosanna Arquette, Jan-Michael Vincent. Director-star Gallo plays a convict just released from prison who kidnaps a teenage girl (Ricci) and demands that she pose as his wife to impress his parents. Their evolving relationship makes up the bulk of this sincere, rambling film, which has its moments but confuses grittiness and endless repetition with integrity and truth, and fails to create much interest in the characters. Gallo, whose directing debut this is, also cowrote the screenplay and composed the music. ▼◉

Buffalo Soldiers (2003-British-German-U.S.) **C-98m.** ** D: Gregor Jordan. Joaquin Phoenix, Ed Harris, Scott Glenn, Anna Paquin, Elizabeth McGovern, Michael Peña, Leon Robinson, Gabriel Mann, Dean Stockwell. In 1989, the peacetime U.S. Army stationed in Germany is largely manned by guys who had a choice of prison or time in the service. One of them (Phoenix) is a clerk who wheels and deals, Bilko-like, under the nose of his ignorant CO (Harris) until a new top sergeant shows up (Glenn) who's determined to make a clean sweep. Not-bad black comedy grows increasingly unpleasant as its story develops. Based on a novel by Robert O'Connor. Completed in 2001. Super 35. [R] ▼▶

Buffet Froid (1979-French) **C-95m.** ***½ D: Bertrand Blier. Gérard Depardieu, Bernard Blier, Jean Carmet, Geneviève Page, Denise Gence, Carole Bouquet, Jean Benguigui, Michel Serrault. Strange, surreal, outrageously funny black comedy detailing the misadventures of hapless murderers Depardieu, Carmet, and Blier (the director's father). Brilliantly acted and directed; a treat. ▼◉

Buffy the Vampire Slayer (1992) **C-86m.** **½ D: Fran Rubel Kuzui. Kristy Swanson, Donald Sutherland, Paul Reubens, Rutger Hauer, Luke Perry, Michele Abrams, Hilary Swank, Paris Vaughan, David Arquette, Randall Batinkoff, Candy Clark, Natasha Gregson Wagner, Tom Janes (Thomas Jane). Cute variation on vampire sagas, with high school Valley Girl Swanson turning out to be "the chosen one" of her generation to kill roaming vampires. Sutherland is ideal as her mentor and guide, and Reubens (the former Pee-wee Herman) is fun as one of the fanged menaces . . . but Hauer is an utter disappointment as vampire Uno. Look for Ben Affleck as a basketball player. Ricki Lake appears unbilled. Later a TV series. [PG-13] ▼◉

Bug (1975) **C-100m.** ** D: Jeannot Szwarc. Bradford Dillman, Joanna Miles, Richard Gilliland, Jamie Smith Jackson, Alan Fudge, Patty McCormack, Jesse Vint. Earthquake releases a disgusting variety of beetle from the earth, capable of setting people, animals, and objects on fire. Spray your set with Raid after watching this one. Produced and cowritten by William Castle, whose last film this was. [PG] ▼▶

Bug (2007) **C-101m.** *** D: William Friedkin. Ashley Judd, Michael Shannon, Harry Connick, Jr., Lynn Collins, Brian F. O'Byrne. Film version of Tracy Letts' play is a challenge to take seriously but not without twisted dazzle if you can accept it as a stunt. Barmaid Judd's motel digs scream "flea-trap," but it's the title critters that are taking it over: the ones imagined by the bugged-out head case who becomes her latest live-in (Shannon, repeating his stage role). As Judd's hunky ex-con husband, Connick rounds out what is predominantly a three-character drama, with Judd giving it her all once her character finds herself too open to Shannon's power of suggestion. Claustrophobic setting is suited for home screens, but Friedkin gives it cinematic flair. Wild finale. [R] ▶

Bugs Bunny Road-Runner Movie, The (1979) **C-92m.** **½ D: Chuck Jones, Phil Monroe. New footage of Bugs Bunny surrounds this compilation of some of Chuck Jones' best Warner Bros. cartoon shorts. Not the best way to see these wonderful films, as the repetition grows tiresome, but still worthwhile. First shown in theaters as THE GREAT AMERICAN CHASE. Followed by THE LOONEY, LOONEY, LOONEY BUGS BUNNY MOVIE. [G] ▼◉

Bugs Bunny's 3rd Movie: 1001 Rabbit Tales (1982) **C-76m.** **½ D: David Detiege, Art Davis, Bill Perez. Yet another compilation of Warner Bros. cartoons, with better-than-average linking material. Some good episodes with Daffy Duck, Tweety and Sylvester, et al., plus Chuck Jones' classic "One Froggy Evening" (minus the punchline), but these are still better seen as individual shorts, and not as an ersatz feature film. Produced by Friz Freleng. Followed by DAFFY DUCK'S MOVIE: FANTASTIC ISLAND. [G] ▼▶

Bugs Bunny Superstar (1975) **C-91m.** *** D: Larry Jackson. Narrated by Orson Welles. Modestly produced compilation of 1940's Warner Bros. cartoons features interviews with the men who created some of the greatest animated films ever made—

Bob Clampett, Friz Freleng, and Tex Avery—along with priceless home movies and behind-the-scenes material, as well as nine complete shorts, including A WILD HARE (the first real Bugs Bunny cartoon), CORNY CONCERTO, THE OLD GREY HARE, MY FAVORITE DUCK, and WHAT'S COOKIN' DOC?▼●】

bug's life, a (1998) C-94m. ***½ D: John Lasseter, Andrew Stanton. Voices of Dave Foley, Julia Louis-Dreyfus, Kevin Spacey, Phyllis Diller, David Hyde Pierce, Denis Leary, Richard Kind, John Ratzenberger, Roddy McDowall, Madeline Kahn, Bonnie Hunt, Edie McClurg, Alex Rocco. Terrific computer-animated feature from Pixar studio (of TOY STORY fame), about a well-meaning ant named Flik who tries to help his beleaguered colony from the plundering of Hopper and his grasshopper cronies. Meaning to hire tough insects to fight them off, he unwittingly recruits a circus troupe instead! Consistently clever and funny; in fact, overflowing with gags and visual ideas. A treat for young and old alike. Screenplay by Stanton, Donald McEnery, and Bob Shaw, from a story by Lasseter, Stanton, and Joe Ranft. Music by Randy Newman. Digital Widescreen. [G] ▼●】

Bugsy (1991) C-135m. *** D: Barry Levinson. Warren Beatty, Annette Bening, Harvey Keitel, Ben Kingsley, Elliott Gould, Joe Mantegna, Richard Sarafian, Bebe Neuwirth, Wendy Phillips, Robert Beltran, Bill Graham, Lewis Van Bergen, Debrah Farentino. Beatty gives the most forceful performance of his career as Benjamin "Bugsy" Siegel, the fabled crackpot gangster who helped build Las Vegas. Long but well-told tale manages to dodge gangster clichés. Beatty and Bening set off sparks together (just as they did in real life), and a strong supporting cast fleshes out James Toback's intelligent script (though Mantegna, as George Raft, is wasted). Keitel, cast as Mickey Cohen, played Siegel in the TV movie THE VIRGINIA HILL STORY. Oscar winner for Art Direction–Set Decoration and Costume Design. Extended version runs 149m. [R] ▼●】

Bugsy Malone (1976-British) C-93m. **½ D: Alan Parker. Scott Baio, Florrie Dugger, Jodie Foster, John Cassisi, Martin Lev. Unique musical spoof of Prohibition-era gangster films with all-kiddie cast; script clichés are intact, but the machine-guns shoot whipped cream instead of bullets. Beautiful production cannot escape coyness and doesn't hold up; plastic rendition of Paul Williams' score doesn't help. [G] ▼●】

Bugville SEE: **Hoppity Goes to Town**
Bulldog Drummond series SEE: *Leonard Maltin's Classic Movie Guide*
Bulldog Drummond (1929) 89m. ***½

D: F. Richard Jones. Ronald Colman, Joan Bennett, Lilyan Tashman, Montagu Love, Lawrence Grant, Claud Allister. Colman is a delight (in his first talking picture) as the bored ex-British Army officer who comes to the rescue of an American girl (Bennett) whose uncle is being held captive in an asylum by a sadistic doctor. Sidney Howard's polished script, Gregg Toland and George Barnes' stylish photography, and William Cameron Menzies' stylish sets help make this a classy and sophisticated romp.▼●

Bull Durham (1988) C-108m. *** D: Ron Shelton. Kevin Costner, Susan Sarandon, Tim Robbins, Trey Wilson, Robert Wuhl, Jenny Robertson, Max Patkin. Smart, sassy film about minor-league North Carolina baseball team and its attentive, intelligent groupie (Sarandon) who feels it is her mission to live with one young player per season and help him mature. Costner is a hardened young veteran of the game whose job is to help one particular player—cocky, undisciplined, but talented pitcher Robbins. Literate and funny, if a bit sluggish at times, with some seriously sexy scenes near the end. [R] ▼●】

Bullet for Sandoval, A (1970-Italian-Spanish) C-91m. ** D: Julio Buchs. Ernest Borgnine, George Hilton, Alberto De Mendoza, Gustavo Rojo, Leo Anchoriz, Annabella Incontrera. Average foreign oater, with lots of action. Ex-Confederate Hilton plots revenge on don Borgnine, grandfather of Hilton's illegitimate son, for indirectly causing the baby's death. Cromoscope. [PG] ▼】

Bullet for the General, A (1967-Italian) C-115m. ** D: Damiano Damiani. Gian-Maria Volonté, Lou Castel, Klaus Kinski, Martine Beswick. Blond gringo joins marauding guerrillas and contributes to gory bloodletting. Not bad for the genre. Techniscope.▼】

Bullet in the Head (1990-Hong Kong) C-136m. *** D: John Woo. Tony Leung, Jacky Cheung, Waise Lee, Simon Yam, Fennie Yuen, Yolinda Yan. Intense, highly charged story of three friends who leave Hong Kong to reap profits in war-torn 1967 Saigon and get caught up in a whirlwind of troubles that tests their loyalty. An epic film, emotional and overwrought, with action footage and confrontations (particularly a long sequence in a POW camp) that are as bold as anything Woo has attempted on-screen. Woo cowrote the screenplay and also edited. Running time is the full-length director's cut; most American prints run 100m.▼●】

Bulletproof (1988) C-94m. BOMB D: Steve Carver. Gary Busey, Darlanne Fluegel, Henry Silva, L.Q. Jones, R.G. Armstrong, Juan Fernandez, Rene Enriquez. L.A. cop Busey, who keeps the 39 bullets his body has taken in a bathroom mason jar, kamikazes across the Mexican border to rescue kidnapped Army personnel (ex-love Fluegel included) from Silva's Soviet stooge. Preposterous, but you have to admire Silva for having kept the same act going for so many years; peroxided hair is simply not to Busey's advantage. [R]▼O●

Bulletproof (1996) **C-85m.** BOMB D: Ernest Dickerson. Adam Sandler, Damon Wayans, James Caan, Kristen Wilson, James Farentino, Bill Nunn, Jeep Swenson. A racial inversion of 48HRS. without the redeeming craft. Undercover cop Wayans teams up with Sandler, the crook he's trying to bust. Their fortunes and ambitions are unified—often acrimoniously—by a vindictive drug kingpin/car dealer played by a pitifully hammy Caan. Once great cinematographer Dickerson squanders his talent here directing a sociopathic mix of graphic violence and slapstick. A catastrophe of continuity to boot. Super 35. [R]▼O●

Bulletproof Heart (1994) **C-100m.** ** D: Mark Malone. Anthony LaPaglia, Mimi Rogers, Peter Boyle, Matt Craven, Joseph Maher. Prosperous hit man LaPaglia gets a gig he's not quite prepared for: rub out a well-connected knockout who actually *wants* to die. Four well-shaped, well-played characters—including Boyle's shady mobster and Craven's dimwit sidekick—don't add up to a satisfying whole. The slim story could have used some serious fleshing out. Two pluses: an intriguingly steamy sex scene, and another incisive performance from Rogers. Played the film festival circuit as KILLER. ▼O●

Bulletproof Monk (2003) **C-103m.** **½ D: Paul Hunter. Chow Yun-Fat, Seann William Scott, Jaime (James) King, Karel Roden, Victoria Smurfit, Mako. Chow plays a monk who never ages while he guards an ancient scroll that possesses the secret of infinite power . . . but now it's time to find a successor, and he thinks it may be young pickpocket Scott, of all people. Lively and amusing when it doesn't get too silly; alas, special effects take the place of genuine martial-arts action most of the time. Coproduced by John Woo, and based on a comic book of the same name. Super 35. [PG-13] ▼●

Bullets or Ballots (1936) **81m.** *** D: William Keighley. Edward G. Robinson, Joan Blondell, Barton MacLane, Humphrey Bogart, Frank McHugh. Cop Robinson pretends to leave police force to crack citywide mob ring run by MacLane. Good, tough gangster film.▼O●

Bullets Over Broadway (1994) **C-99m.** *** D: Woody Allen. John Cusack, Dianne Wiest, Jennifer Tilly, Chazz Palminteri, Mary-Louise Parker, Jack Warden, Joe Viterelli, Rob Reiner, Tracey Ullman, Jim Broadbent, Harvey Fierstein, Stacey Nelkin, Edie Falco, Tony Sirico. Delightful Woody Allen bauble about a self-serious 1920s playwright who quickly sells out when he's offered a chance to direct his latest work on Broadway—with a gangster's moll in a key role and an intoxicatingly seductive star in the lead. An actors' field day, with particularly juicy parts for Wiest (who won an Oscar) as the flamboyant actress, Palminteri, as a thug with an unexpected gift, and Tilly as the ditsy moll. The period detail is so rich and right it all seems stunningly real. Allen coscripted with Douglas McGrath. [R] ▼O●

Bullfighter and the Lady (1951) **87m.** ***½ D: Budd Boetticher. Robert Stack, Joy Page, Gilbert Roland, Katy Jurado, Virginia Grey, John Hubbard. Cocky American visiting Mexico decides that he wants to tackle bullfighting and enlists the aid of the country's leading matador with tragic results. The movies' best treatment of this subject, a fine, mature drama with unforgettable bullfighting scenes and an appealing love story as well. Roland has never been better; only the second leads (Grey, Hubbard) are a detriment. Produced by John Wayne. Boetticher's version, running 124m., has been restored, and it's even better than the shorter print. ▼●

Bullitt (1968) **C-113m.** ***½ D: Peter Yates. Steve McQueen, Robert Vaughn, Jacqueline Bisset, Don Gordon, Robert Duvall, Simon Oakland, Norman Fell, Victor (Vic) Tayback. Definitive McQueen antihero: police detective who senses something fishy behind assignment to guard criminal witness. Taut action-film makes great use of San Francisco locations, especially in now-classic car chase, one of the screen's all-time best; Oscar-winning editing by Frank Keller. Scripted by Alan R. Trustman and Harry Kleiner, from Robert L. Pike's novel *Mute Witness.* [M/PG] ▼O●

Bullseye! (1989) **C-89m.** BOMB D: Michael Winner. Michael Caine, Roger Moore, Sally Kirkland, Lee Patterson, Deborah Barrymore, Mark Burns, Debra Lang, Lynn Nesbitt, Steffanie Pitt, Patsy Kensit, Alexandra Pigg, Jenny Seagrove. Deadly nonsense which completely wastes Caine and Moore as criminals who are dead ringers for a couple of nuclear scientists (up to no good themselves). Confusing story complications and heavyhanded humor make this a dog. Barrymore is Moore's real-life daughter; John Cleese has an unbilled cameo near the end. Released direct to video. [PG-13]▼

Bullshot (1983-British) **C-85m.** **½ D: Dick Clement. Alan Shearman, Diz White, Ron House, Frances Tomelty, Michael Aldridge, Ron Pember, Billy Connolly. Occasionally funny Monty Python–ish parody, with Shearman cast as one Captain Hugh "Bullshot" Crummond, a Bulldog Drummond caricature. Plenty of one-liners and slapstick, some humorous and some silly. The screenplay was adapted by Shearman, White, and House, from their stage play. [PG]▼▶

Bully (2001) **C-106m.** ** D: Larry Clark. Brad Renfro, Nick Stahl, Rachel Miner, Bijou Phillips, Daniel Franzese, Michael Pitt, Kelli Garner, Leo Fitzpatrick. Scuzzy cinema verité dramatization of a true story. Impressionable teen (Renfro) is convinced by his girlfriend (Miner) to kill his best friend, a sadistic rapist (Stahl) who, ironically, is the golden boy of the group, the only one bound for college. Undeniably powerful at times but Clark mashes your face in so much bruised, sweaty pubescent flesh that the film feels exploitative.▼▶

Bulworth (1998) **C-107m.** ***½ D: Warren Beatty. Warren Beatty, Halle Berry, Don Cheadle, Oliver Platt, Paul Sorvino, Jack Warden, Isaiah Washington, Joshua Malina, Christine Baranski, Amiri Baraka, Sean Astin, Laurie Metcalf, Richard Sarafian, Nora Dunn, Jackie Gayle, Michael Clarke Duncan, Debra Monk, Sarah Silverman, Barry Shabaka Henley, Chris Mulkey. Audacious political satire about a California senator, running for reelection in 1996, who solves his crisis of conscience by telling the truth—and embracing the black community. Unsettling at times—as it's meant to be—with trenchant observations on the political process and the plight of the poor. One of Beatty's best films—as actor, director, cowriter (with Jeremy Pikser). William Baldwin and Paul Mazursky appear unbilled. [R]▼▶●

Bunny Lake Is Missing (1965) **107m.** *** D: Otto Preminger. Laurence Olivier, Carol Lynley, Keir Dullea, Noel Coward, Martita Hunt, Finlay Currie, The Zombies. American Lynley, newly arrived in London, reports the disappearance of her preschool daughter—but police detective Olivier can't help but notice that Lynley has no proof that the child ever existed at all. Well paced, expertly acted, with some interestingly offbeat characters in the margins. Made in England. Panavision.▶

Bunny O'Hare (1972) **C-91m.** *½ D: Gerd Oswald. Bette Davis, Ernest Borgnine, Jack Cassidy, Joan Delaney, Reva Rose, John Astin. Bizarre, totally inept tale of bank robbers who look like hippies but are actually Davis and Borgnine. Don't bother watching. [PG]

Buona Sera, Mrs. Campbell (1969) **C-113m.** *** D: Melvin Frank. Gina Lollobrigida, Peter Lawford, Shelley Winters, Phil Silvers, Telly Savalas, Lee Grant, Janet Margolin. Bright comedy about Italian woman who's accepted money from three American men who all think they fathered her child during WW2. Now they're all coming back to Italy for Army reunion and "Mrs. Campbell" is in a state of panic. Good fun with top cast. [M/PG]▼●

'burbs, The (1989) **C-103m.** ** D: Joe Dante. Tom Hanks, Bruce Dern, Carrie Fisher, Rick Ducommun, Corey Feldman, Wendy Schaal, Henry Gibson, Brother Theodore, Courtney Gains, Gale Gordon, Dick Miller. Strange new neighbors set a neighborhood abuzz, and lead several slightly cracked compadres to extreme measures so they can learn just what's going on behind closed doors. Comically warped view of suburban life takes far too much time to play out its paper-thin premise, and leads to (mostly) predictable results. [PG]▼●▶

Burden of Dreams (1982) **C-94m.** ***½ D: Les Blank. Werner Herzog, Klaus Kinski, Claudia Cardinale, Jason Robards, Mick Jagger. Extraordinary documentary of the filming of Herzog's FITZCARRALDO in the Peruvian Amazon. Despite the filmmaker's high technology, his dream of completing the film is constantly thwarted by nature and clashing cultures. Some find this more compelling than FITZCARRALDO itself.▼▶

Bureau of Missing Persons (1933) **75m.** **½ D: Roy Del Ruth. Bette Davis, Lewis S. Stone, Pat O'Brien, Allen Jenkins, Ruth Donnelly, Hugh Herbert, Glenda Farrell, Alan Dinehart, George Chandler. Typically fast-paced—but strange—Warner Bros. programmer about big-city bureau of missing persons, where benevolent Stone plays God with the losers and hard-luck cases that come before him. Hip-shooting cop O'Brien is transferred there in hopes he'll mellow out, and we'll bet you a dollar six bits he doesn't. Davis is a mystery woman with whom he gets involved.▼▶

Burglar (1987) **C-102m.** *½ D: Hugh Wilson. Whoopi Goldberg, Bob Goldthwait, G.W. Bailey, Lesley Ann Warren, James Handy, Anne DeSalvo, John Goodman. Whoopi plays a cat burglar who accidentally witnesses a murder—and then tries to solve the crime, in order to clear herself. Unfunny, unsuspenseful, and completely unappealing comedy/mystery, with a superfluous, built-up secondary role for Goldthwait (who has a few good moments). Another waste of Whoopi's talent. [R]▼●▶

Burglars, The (1972-French) **C-117m.** **½ D: Henri Verneuil. Jean-Paul Belmondo, Omar Sharif, Dyan Cannon, Robert Hossein. Routine crime film set against lush Greek backdrop, with good cast. One good chase and it's all over. Remake of THE BURGLAR. Panavision. [PG]

Buried (2010-U.S.-Spanish-French) **C-94m.** **½ D: Rodrigo Cortés. Ryan Reynolds; voices of Tess Harper, Samantha Mathis, Stephen Tobolowsky, Erik Palladino, José Luis García-Pérez, Robert Paterson, Warner Loughlin, Kali Rocha, Chris William Martin, Anne Lockhart. Reynolds is an American contractor working as a truck driver in 2006 Iraq who awakens to discover he has been kidnapped and buried alive. Claustrophobic but intriguing film is definitely not for all tastes, but does tell an unusual story that is equal parts ingenuity and terror. Reynolds acquits himself ably, but this might have worked better as a longish short subject. Bests Hitchcock's LIFE-BOAT in one sense: its minuscule setting. Super 35. [R] ▶

Buried Alive (1990) **C-91m.** *½ D: Gerard Kikoine. Robert Vaughn, Donald Pleasence, Karen Witter, John Carradine, Nia Long, Ginger Lynn Allen. Murky thriller about a mansion where "doctor" Vaughn imprisons young women. Story uses elements from several Edgar Allan Poe stories, but juices them up with sex and gore. Filmed in South Africa. Carradine's last feature film. [R] ▼●

Burke & Wills (1986-Australian) **C-140m.** *** D: Graeme Clifford. Jack Thompson, Nigel Havers, Greta Scacchi, Matthew Fargher, Ralph Cotterill, Drew Forsythe, Chris Haywood. Impressive, larger-than-life historical drama chronicling the title characters' expedition through 1860 Australia, the first two men to cross the continent. Thompson is especially fine as Burke; another version of the saga was made the same year, titled WILLS AND BURKE. Panavision. [PG-13] ▼●

Burlesque (2010) **C-119m.** ** D: Steven Antin. Cher, Christina Aguilera, Stanley Tucci, Eric Dane, Cam Gigandet, Julianne Hough, Alan Cumming, Peter Gallagher, Kristen Bell, Dianna Agron, Glynn Turman, James Brolin. Wide-eyed girl from Iowa comes to L.A. to follow her dream and winds up working in Cher's Hollywood burlesque club—first as a waitress, then as a star performer. Other plot threads are just as clichéd, yet this flashy, forgettable musical goes on for two hours. Cher still has star magnetism, and Tucci brightens every line he utters as her gay best friend (a part he's played before). Pop star Aguilera does her best, but the movie bogs down when it focuses on her, with a few too many solo features. Cumming, a true talent, is reduced to a bit part. Super 35. [PG-13] ▶

Burmese Harp, The (1956-Japanese) **116m.** ***½ D: Kon Ichikawa. Rentaro Mikuni, Shoji Yasui, Tatsuya Mihashi, Tanie Kitabayashi, Yunosuke Ito. Private Yasui volunteers to persuade a group of mountain fighters to surrender at the end of WW2 and undergoes a religious experience, becoming obsessed with desire to bury war casualties. Extraordinary antiwar drama is affecting and memorable if a bit overlong. Also known as HARP OF BURMA; remade by Ichikawa in 1985. ▼●

Burn! (1969-Italian-French) **C-132m.** *** D: Gillo Pontecorvo. Marlon Brando, Evaristo Marquez, Renato Salvatori, Tom Lyons, Norman Hill. Egomaniacal Sir William Walker (Brando) is sent by the British

to instigate a slave revolt on a Portuguese-controlled sugar-producing Caribbean island. This political drama is visually striking but muddled, with a strong Brando performance. Ed Harris plays the same role in WALKER. Originally released in the U.S. at 112m. Aka QUEMADA! [PG] ▼●

Burn After Reading (2008) **C-95m.** **½ D: Joel and Ethan Coen. George Clooney, Frances McDormand, Brad Pitt, John Malkovich, Tilda Swinton, Richard Jenkins, Dermot Mulroney, Elizabeth Marvel, David Rasche, J. K. Simmons, Jeffrey DeMunn. Black comedy of errors set in Washington, D.C., takes off when CIA analyst Malkovich is fired; he then learns that his wife (Swinton) is sleeping with treasury marshal Clooney. Meanwhile, health club employee McDormand has set her sights on some expensive plastic surgery. Mixing ingredients of a political thriller with satiric jibes at Americans' obsession with self-improvement, this never quite jells, though it's fun to watch these talented stars playing morons. Pitt is especially entertaining as a goofball who works at a gym. [R] ▶

Burning, The (1981) **C-90m.** BOMB D: Tony Maylam. Brian Matthews, Leah Ayres, Brian Backer, Larry Joshua, Lou David, Jason Alexander, Fisher Stevens. Awful FRIDAY THE 13TH ripoff (with Tom Savini's bloody makeup effects) about an old caretaker at a summer camp who takes his revenge in the usual way. Holly Hunter's screen debut. [R] ▼●

Burning Cross, The SEE: **Klansman, The**

Burning Hills, The (1956) **C-94m** ** D: Stuart Heisler. Tab Hunter, Natalie Wood, Skip Homeier, Eduard Franz, Earl Holliman, Claude Akins. Passive Hunter can't spark life into tired script based on a Louis L'Amour novel. Man on run from cattle thieves is sheltered by Wood, miscast as a half-breed Mexican girl. CinemaScope. ▼

Burning Man, The SEE: **Dangerous Summer, A**

Burning Plain, The (2009-U.S.-Argentinean) **C-107m.** ** D: Guillermo Arriaga. Charlize Theron, Kim Basinger, Joaquim de Almeida, John Corbett, Robin Tunney, Brett Cullen, Danny Pino, Jose Maria Yazpik, Jennifer Lawrence, J. D. Pardo, Tessa Ia, Rachel Ticotin. The promiscuity of a Portland restaurant owner (Theron) masks her inner turmoil, while a New Mexico woman (Basinger) carries on an affair, unaware that her oldest daughter has caught on to what's happening. Piecing this story puzzle together is moderately intriguing but the characters' fates are discouragingly bleak. Somber, well-acted drama marks screenwriter Arriaga's directing debut, and follows his signature style of presenting seemingly disconnected stories that ultimately coalesce (21 GRAMS, BABEL, et al.), but doesn't have the impact of his better scripts. [R]▶

Burning Secret (1988-U.S.-British-German) **C-106m.** **½ D: Andrew Birkin. Faye Dunaway, Klaus Maria Brandauer, David Eberts, Ian Richardson. Brandauer offers a splendid performance (as usual) as a charming, amoral baron, a WW1 vet who's nursing a bayonet wound at a sanitarium. In order to get to Dunaway, he initiates a friendship with her impressionable, asthmatic 12-year-old son (Eberts). Generally compelling, and lushly filmed in Prague and Marienbad; however, Dunaway is ·miscast, and there are several key moments that simply don't work. Based on a Stefan Zweig short story; originally made in Germany in 1933 by Robert Siodmak, as BRENNENDES GEHEIMNIS. [PG]▼●

Burnt by the Sun (1994-Russian-French) **C-135m.** *** D: Nikita Mikhalkov. Nikita Mikhalkov, Ingeborga Dapkounaite, Oleg Menchikov, Nadia Mikhalkov, Andre Oumansky. The year is 1936, and Sergei Kotov (played by director Mikhalkov) is an aging hero of the Bolshevik Revolution whose eyes are closed to the present-day tyranny of Josef Stalin. All of this is about to change upon the arrival of his wife's ex-lover, who is employed by Stalin's governmental police. Provocative, moving meditation on the political and social realities of life in Stalinist Russia deservedly earned a Best Foreign Film Oscar. Sergei's daughter, Nadia, who has a key role in the story, is played by Mikhalkov's real-life daughter. Followed by BURNT BY THE SUN 2. ▼●

Burnt Offerings (1976) **C-115m.** ** D: Dan Curtis. Karen Black, Oliver Reed, Burgess Meredith, Eileen Heckart, Lee Montgomery, Dub Taylor, Bette Davis, Anthony James. Ordinary couple, with young son and aunt in tow, rent an old mansion as summer home, unaware that it's haunted. Strange occurrences lead to totally predictable "surprise" ending. A big buildup to nothing. From Robert Marasco's novel. [PG]▼●

Burn, Witch, Burn! (1962-British) **90m.** *** D: Sidney Hayers. Janet Blair, Peter Wyngarde, Margaret Johnston, Anthony Nicholls. Story of witchcraft entering lives of schoolteacher and his wife builds to shattering suspense, genuinely frightening climax. Fritz Leiber's novel *Conjure Wife* was filmed before as WEIRD WOMAN; this version scripted by Charles Beaumont and Richard Matheson. Later spoofed in WITCHES' BREW. Original British title: NIGHT OF THE EAGLE. ▼●

Bush Christmas (1983-Australian) **C-91m.** **½ D: Henri Safran. John Ewart, John Howard, Mark Spain, James Wingrove, Peter Summer, Nicole Kidman, Manalpuy, Vineta O'Malley. Agreeable updating of the 1947 Australian classic in which a trio of kids (including Kidman, in her feature debut) head off into the bush—

in the company of an Aborigine—to find the thieves who stole their horse. Aka PRINCE AND THE GREAT RACE.▼

Bushido Blade, The (1979-Japanese) **C-104m.** **½ D: Tom Kotani. Richard Boone, Frank Converse, James Earl Jones, Toshiro Mifune, Mako, Sonny Chiba, Laura Gemser. 19th-century Kung Fu action in Japan as Cmdr. Matthew Perry (Boone) leads a band of his men in the recovery of a treasured sword. Of note: Boone's last role; Mifune plays the Shogun, as he did in later TV miniseries. Aka THE BLOODY BUSHIDO BLADE. [R]▼●

Bushwhacked (1995) **C-90m.** *½ D: Greg Beeman. Daniel Stern, Jon Polito, Brad Sullivan, Ann Dowd, Anthony Heald, Tom Wood, Blake Bashoff, Corey Carrier, Michael Galeota, Max Goldblatt. On the lam for a murder he didn't commit, a delivery man "hides out" by posing as the leader of a Ranger Scout troop that embarks on a wilderness adventure neither he nor they will ever forget. Unfortunately, all of us will. Stern is way over the top in this familiar fish-out-of-water premise that draws on two of his past triumphs, CITY SLICKERS and HOME ALONE. For younger kids only. Clairmont-Scope. [PG-13] ▼●

Business As Usual (1987-British) **C-89m.** **½ D: Lezli-An Barrett. Glenda Jackson, John Thaw, Cathy Tyson, Mark McGann, Eamon Boland, James Hazeldine, Buki Armstrong, Stephen McGann. Passionate but didactic pro-labor drama with Jackson as a Liverpool boutique manager whose arbitrary firing (after she's lodged a complaint about sexual harassment on behalf of an employee) escalates into a national cause celebre. One of the angry anti-Thatcher films of the late '80s; written by first-time feature director Barrett. Excellent performances help a one-sided script. [PG]▼

Business of Strangers, The (2001) **C-83m.** *** D: Patrick Stettner. Stockard Channing, Julia Stiles, Frederick Weller. Interesting chamber piece about a female executive who, at the end of a tumultuous, career-changing day, takes up with a young woman at an airport hotel. The younger woman is an expert at playing mind games, and the exec finds herself drawn in, almost to the point of madness. A tour de force for Channing and Stiles, who are terrific, though the story's credibility is debatable. Written by the director. [R] ▼▶

Bus Riley's Back in Town (1965) **C-93m.** **½ D: Harvey Hart. Ann-Margret, Michael Parks, Janet Margolin, Brad Dexter, Kim Darby, Jocelyn Brando, Larry Storch, David Carradine. Muddled William Inge script of folksy people in the Midwest. Parks, ex-sailor, returns home, torn by faltering ambitions and taunted by wealthy ex-girlfriend Ann-Margret. Character cameos make the film worthwhile.▼

Bus Stop (1956) **C-96m.** ***½ D: Joshua Logan. Marilyn Monroe, Don Murray, Arthur O'Connell, Betty Field, Eileen Heckart, Hope Lange, Hans Conried, Casey Adams (Max Showalter). The film that finally proved Monroe really could act; excellent comedy-drama about innocent cowboy (Murray) who falls for saloon singer and decides to marry her—without bothering to ask. Fine performances by all, with MM's famed rendition of "(That Old) Black Magic" a highlight; adapted by George Axelrod from the William Inge play. Film debuts of Murray and Lange (who subsequently married). Later a brief TV series. CinemaScope. ▼●◗

Buster (1988-British) **C-102m.** **½ D: David Green. Phil Collins, Julie Walters, Larry Lamb, Stephanie Lawrence, Ellen Beaven, Michael Atwell, Ralph Brown, Christopher Ellison, Sheila Hancock, Martin Jarvis, Anthony Quayle. Buster Edwards, one of the men behind Britain's all-time biggest robbery, turns out to have been just a working-class stiff with big dreams and a bad track record of success, who wanted the good life for his wife and child. Singer Collins' starring film debut is a diverting (if forgettable) yarn, with Walters a good match as his loving, long-suffering spouse. Great soundtrack includes Collins' performances of "Two Hearts (One Mind)" and "Groovy Kind of Love." [R]▼●◗

Buster and Billie (1974) **C-100m.** *½ D: Daniel Petrie. Jan-Michael Vincent, Joan Goodfellow, Pamela Sue Martin, Clifton James, Robert Englund: Blubbery account of high school romance in 1948 rural Georgia (the loosest girl in class is redeemed by love) can't overcome clichéd premise. [R]▼

Buster Keaton Story, The (1957) **91m.** *½ D: Sidney Sheldon. Donald O'Connor, Ann Blyth, Rhonda Fleming, Peter Lorre, Larry Keating, Jackie Coogan, Richard Anderson, Cecil B. DeMille. Weak fiction ignores the facts about silent-star Keaton, making up its own. More private life than on-screen moments are detailed with Blyth as his true love and Fleming as a siren. Little comedy in this tale of a great comedian. Keaton himself was film's technical advisor. VistaVision.

Busting (1974) **C-92m.** **½ D: Peter Hyams. Elliott Gould, Robert Blake, Allen Garfield, Antonio Fargas, Michael Lerner, Sid Haig, Cornelia Sharpe. Realistic if empty comedy-action-drama with Gould and Blake as unorthodox L.A. vice cops. Gay activists complained about film's few minutes of homosexual caricatures. Hyams, once a CBS-TV newsman, also did script. [R]▼

Bustin' Loose (1981) **C-94m.** *** D: Oz Scott. Richard Pryor, Cicely Tyson, Robert Christian, Alphonso Alexander, Janet Wong. Despite the (expected) street language, this is at heart a family picture about

an ex-convict who shepherds teacher Tyson and a busload of emotionally and physically handicapped youngsters to a new life. Best scene: a KKK band becomes putty in Pryor's hands. Filmed mostly in 1979, but not completed until 1981 because of Pryor's near fatal accident. Pryor coproduced and wrote the story. Later a TV series. [R]▼●◗

Busy Body, The (1967) **C-90m.** **½ D: William Castle. Sid Caesar, Robert Ryan, Anne Baxter, Kay Medford, Jan Murray, Richard Pryor, Dom DeLuise, Godfrey Cambridge, Marty Ingels, Bill Dana, George Jessel. Broad, forced comedy involving gangsters and corpses, with Caesar as the patsy for Ryan's underworld gang. Supporting comics give film its funniest moments. Pryor's film debut. Techniscope. ◗

Butch and Sundance: The Early Days (1979) **C-110m.** **½ D: Richard Lester. William Katt, Tom Berenger, Jeff Corey, John Schuck, Michael C. Gwynne, Brian Dennehy, Christopher Lloyd, Jill Eikenberry, Peter Weller, Arthur Hill. Prequel to BUTCH CASSIDY AND THE SUNDANCE KID has everything going for it—engaging performances, beautiful atmosphere and location photography—except a story. Pleasant enough but ultimately disappointing. [PG]▼◗

Butch Cassidy and the Sundance Kid (1969) **C-112m.** **** D: George Roy Hill. Paul Newman, Robert Redford, Katharine Ross, Strother Martin, Henry Jones, Jeff Corey, George Furth, Cloris Leachman, Ted Cassidy, Kenneth Mars. Delightful seriocomic character study masquerading as a Western; outlaws Newman and Redford are pursued by relentless but remote sheriff's posse. Many memorable vignettes. Won Oscars for Cinematography (Conrad Hall), Original Score (Burt Bacharach), Song, "Raindrops Keep Fallin' On My Head" (Bacharach and Hal David), and William Goldman's original screenplay, which brims over with sharp dialogue. Look for Sam Elliott as a card player. Followed a decade later by a prequel, BUTCH AND SUNDANCE: THE EARLY DAYS. Then in 1976 Ross returned as Etta Place in TVM WANTED: THE SUNDANCE WOMAN (aka MRS. SUNDANCE RIDES AGAIN). Panavision. [PG]▼●◗

Butcher, The SEE: Le Boucher
Butcher Baker Nightmare Maker SEE: Night Warning
Butcher Boy, The (1997-U.S.-Irish) **C-106m.** ***½ D: Neil Jordan. Stephen Rea, Fiona Shaw, Eamonn Owens, Alan Boyle, Andrew Fullerton, Aisling O'Sullivan, Ian Hart, Sinéad O'Connor, Milo O'Shea, Brendan Gleeson. Arresting film about an Irish boy who doesn't have a chance in life: his father is a perpetual drunk, his mother a mentally fragile soul. Yet he greets the world with bravado and the gift of gab; the only problem is, he's deranged. Bold,

darkly (even absurdly) comic, hallucinatory at times, hiding its heartrending truths behind a glib facade—just like its hero. A true original. Written by Jordan and Patrick McCabe, from the latter's novel; McCabe also appears as the town drunk, Jimmy the Skite. [R]▼●▶

Butcher's Wife, The (1991) C-105m. **
D: Terry Hughes. Demi Moore, Jeff Daniels, George Dzundza, Mary Steenburgen, Frances McDormand, Margaret Colin, Max Perlich, Miriam Margolyes, Christopher Durang, Diane Salinger. North Carolina clairvoyant marries a Greenwich Village butcher, then begins dispensing advice: to a lesbian boutique owner, a spinsterish choir director, a soap opera actress and more. So strange that it almost compels a glance. Only Steenburgen, though, seems thoroughly in the swing of this comedy's intended whimsy. [PG-13]▼●▶

But I'm a Cheerleader (2000) C-84m. **
D: Jamie Babbit. Natasha Lyonne, Clea DuVall, Cathy Moriarty, Bud Cort, Mink Stole, RuPaul Charles, Eddie Cibrian, Melanie Lynskey, Michelle Williams, Richard Moll, Julie Delpy. The parents of high school cheerleader Lyonne think she's a lesbian, and send her off to True Directions, a rehab camp that deprograms gay teens. This satire is a one-note John Waters wannabe, occasionally amusing but more often silly and contrived. [R]▼▶

Butley (1974-British) C-127m. **** D: Harold Pinter. Alan Bates, Jessica Tandy, Richard O'Callaghan, Susan Engel, Georgina Hale. Bates is superb in American Film Theatre presentation, re-creating his 1971 London stage role as a teacher with sexual and other problems. Playwright Pinter made his film directing debut with this outrageous comedy by Simon Gray. [R]▼▶

But Not for Me (1959) 105m. *** D: Walter Lang. Clark Gable, Carroll Baker, Lilli Palmer, Barry Coe, Lee J. Cobb, Thomas Gomez, Charles Lane. Chic remake of Samson Raphaelson's ACCENT ON YOUTH. 22-year-old secretary/aspiring actress Baker falls for her has-been theatrical-producer boss (Gable), who won't admit he's on the dark side of 50. Palmer is his wily ex-wife, Cobb a faded playwright. VistaVision.▼

BUtterfield 8 (1960) C-109m. **½ D: Daniel Mann. Elizabeth Taylor, Laurence Harvey, Eddie Fisher, Dina Merrill, Mildred Dunnock, Susan Oliver, Betty Field, Jeffrey Lynn, Kay Medford. Adaptation of O'Hara novel substitutes clichéd ending in tale of high-class prostitute wanting to go straight, convincing herself she's found Mr. Right. Film's major assets: great supporting cast and old-style performance by Taylor, who won Oscar. CinemaScope. ▼●▶

Butterflies Are Free (1972) C-109m. ***
D: Milton Katselas. Goldie Hawn, Edward Albert, Eileen Heckart, Mike Warren, Paul Michael Glaser. Filmization of Leonard Gershe's Broadway play detailing blind boy's romance with kookie next-door neighbor (Hawn) and inevitable showdown with his overpossessive mother. Good light entertainment; Heckart won Best Supporting Actress Oscar. [PG] ▼●▶

Butterfly (1981-U.S.-Canadian) C-107m.
** D: Matt Cimber. Stacy Keach, Pia Zadora, Orson Welles, Lois Nettleton, Edward Albert, James Franciscus, Stuart Whitman, Ed McMahon, June Lockhart, Paul Hampton. Trashy soap opera, based on James M. Cain's novel, with gold-digging sex-kitten Zadora seducing Keach, who is supposed to be her dad. Welles steals the film—not difficult—as a judge. [R]▼●▶

Butterfly (1999-Spanish) C-95m. *** D: José Luis Cuerda. Fernando Fernán Gómez, Manuel Lozano, Uxía Blanco, Gonzalo M. Uriarte, Alexis de los Santos, Jesús Castejón. Compelling coming-of-age story depicts the impact of the Spanish Civil War on a Galician village, spotlighting the evolving friendship between a sensitive young boy (Lozano) and his nurturing, humanistic teacher (beautifully played by Fernán Gómez). Delicately rendered tale of a nation and its people at a historic crossroads is based on several short stories by Manuel Rivas. Panavision. [R]▼▶

Butterfly Affair, The (1970-French-Italian) C-100m. ** D: Jean Herman. Claudia Cardinale, Stanley Baker, Henri Charriere, Georges Arminel, Leroy Haynes, Joannin Hansen. Charriere (PAPILLON) wrote this diamond heist double cross story; he also co-stars as the mastermind, but his performance, like the picture, is routine. Claudia, at her sexiest, adds some bright moments. Original title: POPSY POP. [PG]▼

Butterfly Effect, The (2004) C-113m. **
D: Eric Bress, J. Mackye Gruber. Ashton Kutcher, Amy Smart, Eric Stoltz, William Lee Scott, Elden Henson, Ethan Suplee, Melora Walters. A boy suffers from repeated blackouts, during which bad things happen around him. As a young man he tries to summon up these repressed memories, go back in time, and change things for the better. Interesting premise takes much too long to develop; in the meantime the film wallows in unpleasantness. Kutcher also coproduced. Followed by two DVD sequels. [R]▼▶

Buy & Cell (1989) C-95m. *½ D: Robert Boris. Robert Carradine, Michael Winslow, Malcolm McDowell, Lise Cutter, Randall "Tex" Cobb, Roddy Piper, Ben Vereen, Fred Travalena, Tony Plana, Michael Goodwin. Uninteresting would-be comedy set in prison, where a framed stockbroker secretly sets up a multi-million-dollar business with the help of stereotyped inmates. Shot in Italy, set in U.S. [R]▼●

Bwana Devil (1952) C-79m. *½ D: Arch

Oboler. Robert Stack, Barbara Britton, Nigel Bruce, Paul McVey. Stack is determined to protect his railroad workers in Kenya (not to mention his wife) from being attacked by man-eating lions. Cardboard drama, with lame lion attacks, was the first commercial 3-D feature, but it's laughably clumsy. In some shots actors are clearly standing in front of rear-projection footage! Complete prints include b&w introduction to 3-D by Lloyd Nolan and puppets Beany and Cecil. Same true-life story later inspired THE GHOST AND THE DARKNESS. 3-D.

By Design (1981-Canadian) **C-88m.** ** D: Claude Jutra. Patty Duke Astin, Sara Botsford, Saul Rubinek, Sonia Zimmer. Lesbian fashion designer Astin decides she wants to be a mother. Potentially interesting subject matter is awkwardly handled; one of Astin's few bad performances.▼

Bye Bye Birdie (1963) **C-112m.** *** D: George Sidney. Janet Leigh, Dick Van Dyke, Ann-Margret, Maureen Stapleton, Paul Lynde, Jesse Pearson, Bobby Rydell, Ed Sullivan. Entertaining version of Broadway musical about drafted rock 'n' roll idol coming to small town to give "one last kiss" to one of his adoring fans. Lynde stands out as Ann-Margret's father. Remade for TV in 1995 with Jason Alexander and Vanessa Williams. Panavision. ▼●)

Bye Bye Blues (1989-Canadian) **C-116m.** *** D: Anne Wheeler. Rebecca Jenkins, Luke Reilly, Stuart Margolin, Kate Reid, Michael Ontkean, Wayne Robson, Robyn Stevan. Affectionate WW2 drama of Jenkins, proper, protected, and pregnant, who's stationed with her doctor-husband in India. Intensely moving story of how war affects the lives of those on the home front; if this doesn't give your tear ducts a workout, nothing will. Loosely based on the life of Wheeler's mother and a nice companion piece to her short documentary-drama, A WAR STORY. [PG]▼

Bye Bye Braverman (1968) **C-94m.** **½ D: Sidney Lumet. George Segal, Jack Warden, Joseph Wiseman, Sorrell Booke, Jessica Walter, Phyllis Newman, Zohra Lampert, Godfrey Cambridge, Alan King. To paraphrase one of the characters, in the sum of its many parts this yields pleasure of a kind; but fuzzy, unresolved story of four Jewish intellectuals on their way to a friend's funeral is ultimately disappointing.❚

Bye Bye Brazil (1980-Brazil) **C-110m.** *** D: Carlos Diegues. Jose Wilker, Betty Faria, Fabio Junior, Zaira Zambelli. Bawdy comedy- drama about a troupe of traveling entertainers is really a travelogue of the country, from jungles to honky-tonk port towns. Not quite the total sensual pleasure of DONA FLOR AND HER TWO HUSBANDS, but still one of the best Brazilian imports. [R]▼●)

Bye Bye Love (1995) **C-106m.** ** D: Sam Weisman. Matthew Modine, Randy Quaid, Paul Reiser, Janeane Garofalo, Rob Reiner, Amy Brenneman, Eliza Dushku, Ed Flanders, Maria Pitillo, Lindsay Crouse, Johnny Whitworth, Ross Malinger, Pamela Dillman, Brad Hall, Jack Black. Mediocre seriocomedy about three dads, devoted to their kids, trying to make their way through divorcehood. Some sincere moments and occasional comic insights are washed away in a sea of sappiness. Garofalo, as Quaid's hilarious date from hell, almost makes the film worth watching. [PG-13]▼●)

Bye Bye Monkey (1978-French-Italian) **C-114m.** BOMB D: Marco Ferreri. Gérard Depardieu, Marcello Mastroianni, Gail Lawrence (Abigail Clayton), James Coco, Geraldine Fitzgerald, Mimsy Farmer, Clarence Muse. Sardonic, bleak comedy about a group of misfits in a decrepit area of Manhattan where rats seem about to displace humanity in all the buildings. Depardieu, irresistible to women as always, prefers the company of a chimpanzee he finds near the carcass of a giant ape, presumably left over from the remake of KING KONG. Good cast is wasted, including Fitzgerald, who also has a love scene with Depardieu. Filmed in English in N.Y.C.▼●)

By Love Possessed (1961) **C-115m.** **½ D: John Sturges. Lana Turner, Efrem Zimbalist, Jr., Jason Robards, Jr., George Hamilton, Thomas Mitchell, Susan Kohner, Barbara Bel Geddes, Everett Sloane, Carroll O'Connor. Ultraglossy, well-cast but empty soaper, in which neurotic Turner commences an affair with Zimbalist, the law partner of her impotent husband (Robards). Based on—but not true to—the James Gould Cozzens novel.▼●)

By the Book SEE: **Renaissance Man**

By the Light of the Silvery Moon (1953) **C-102m.** **½ D: David Butler. Doris Day, Gordon MacRae, Leon Ames, Rosemary DeCamp, Mary Wickes, Billy Gray. Set in post WW1, this Booth Tarkington story finds returning soldier MacRae and fiancée Day readjusting to life. Ames wonderful as father thought to be romancing French actress, and Wickes delightful as family maid. Merv Griffin pops up in the closing scene. This old-fashioned musical was a sequel to ON MOONLIGHT BAY. ▼●)

By the Sword (1993) **C-91m.** *½ D: Jeremy Kagan, John McDonald. F. Murray Abraham, Eric Roberts, Mia Sara, Chris Rydell, Elaine Kagan, Brett Cullen, Doug Wert, Stoney Jackson. By-the-numbers revenge story set in the world of competitive fencing. Roberts is intense as usual, but the story isn't. If it's fencing you want, rent an Errol Flynn movie. Super 35. [R]▼

Cabaret (1972) **C-124m.** ***½ D: Bob Fosse. Liza Minnelli, Michael York, Helmut

Griem, Joel Grey, Fritz Wepper, Marisa Berenson. Stylish film based on Fred Ebb–John Kander Broadway musical, from John van Druten's play *I Am a Camera* (filmed before in 1955), now more a vehicle for Minnelli in her Oscar-winning performance as Sally Bowles, American girl caught up in phony glitter of prewar Berlin. Song numbers counterpoint dramatic narrative, including newly written "The Money Song," great duet for Minnelli and Oscar winner Grey. Screenplay by Jay (Presson) Allen; the story's genesis was Christopher Isherwood's book *Goodbye to Berlin*. Won eight Academy Awards in all, including Director, Cinematography (Geoffrey Unsworth), and Score Adaptation (Ralph Burns). [PG] ▼●)

Cabaret Balkan (1998-Yugoslavian-French) **C-102m.** **½ D: Goran Paskaljevic. Miki Manojlovic, Sergei Trifunovic, Mirjana Jokovic, Lazar Ristovski. In the strife-torn city of Belgrade, all sense of logic and order has evaporated, leaving a society so desperate and stressed-out that even a casual encounter may lead to violence. Powerful series of vignettes—sometimes grim, sometimes absurdly funny—but the film goes on a while after it's made its point. Originally shown in Europe as THE POWDER KEG. ▼

Cabin Boy (1994) **C-80m.** **½ D: Adam Resnick. Chris Elliott, Ritch Brinkley, James Gammon, Brian Doyle-Murray, Brion James, Melora Walters, Ann Magnuson, Russ Tamblyn, Ricki Lake, Andy Richter. Strange, fitfully amusing comedy of snobby "Fancy Lad" Elliott who accidentally boards a fishing boat with hard-nosed seamen . . . and becomes a man. Film's success depends largely on your tolerance for Elliot's obnoxious comic persona, but there are many clever jokes and an endearingly (and intentionally) tacky visual approach. Several good cameos, particularly one from Elliott's former boss David Letterman—billed as Earl Hofert. Elliott cowrote the film's story. Produced by Tim Burton. [PG-13] ▼●)

Cabinet of Caligari, The (1962) **104m.** **½ D: Roger Kay. Dan O'Herlihy, Glynis Johns, Richard Davalos, Lawrence Dobkin, Estelle Winwood, J. Pat O'Malley. Unimaginative remake of the 1919 German classic, removing all the mystery-exotic appeal; Johns tries hard as lady in ornate modern home confronted by O'Herlihy's sinister Caligari; many bizarre scenes. Written by Robert Bloch. CinemaScope. ▶

Cabinet of Dr. Caligari, The (1920-German) **69m.** ***½ D: Robert Wiene. Werner Krauss, Conrad Veidt, Lil Dagover. Somewhat stiff but still fascinating German Expressionist film about "magician" Caligari and hypnotic victim who carries out his evil bidding. Landmark film still impresses audiences today. Remade in 1962. ▼●)

Cabin Fever (2003) **C-93m.** *½ D: Eli Roth. Rider Strong, Jordan Ladd, James DeBello, Cerina Vincent, Joey Kern, Giuseppe Andrews, Robert Harris, Hal Courtney. A group of friends celebrate college graduation by going to a mountain cabin together, but things go very bad very fast. Did someone say "flesh-eating virus"? Blood-drenched homage to slasher movies lacks wit or originality, but seems to have pleased some fans of the genre. Followed by a direct-to-DVD sequel. Super 35. [R] ▼▶

Cabin in the Cotton, The (1932) **77m.** **½ D: Michael Curtiz. Richard Barthelmess, Dorothy Jordan, Bette Davis, Hardie Albright, David Landau, Berton Churchill, Henry B. Walthall, Tully Marshall. Dated melodrama of sharecroppers, with earnest Barthelmess almost led to ruin by Southern belle Davis; exaggerated, but interesting. Bette's immortal line: "Ah'd like to kiss ya, but Ah jes' washed mah hair." ▼

Cabin in the Sky (1943) **100m.** *** D: Vincente Minnelli. Eddie "Rochester" Anderson, Lena Horne, Ethel Waters, Louis Armstrong, Rex Ingram, Duke Ellington and His Orchestra, The Hall Johnson Choir. Stellar black cast in winning (if somewhat racist) musical fable about forces of good and evil vying for the soul of Little Joe (Anderson). John Bubbles' dancing, Waters singing "Happiness Is a Thing Called Joe" (written for the film) among musical highlights. First feature for Minnelli (who, with Waters and Ingram, came from the Broadway production). ▼●)

Cable Guy, The (1996) **C-96m.** **½ D: Ben Stiller. Jim Carrey, Matthew Broderick, Leslie Mann, George Segal, Diane Baker, Jack Black, Eric Roberts, Janeane Garofalo, Andy Dick, Charles Napier, Owen Wilson, Kathy Griffin. Black comedy about a cable TV installer who forces his friendship onto a vulnerable customer who's just moved out of his girlfriend's apartment. Many clever, funny scenes, but film wavers between comedy and a darker, more serious tone, which—while also interesting—keeps us off-balance. Repeated digs at TV are among the brightest moments; director Stiller has a funny recurring cameo. Super 35. [PG-13] ▼●)

Caboblanco (1980) **C-87m.** ** D: J. Lee Thompson. Charles Bronson, Jason Robards, Dominique Sanda, Fernando Rey, Simon MacCorkindale, Camilla Sparv, Gilbert Roland, Denny Miller. Murky ripoff of CASABLANCA, with Bronson as a barkeeper in Peru. Robards plays a Nazi, Rey a police captain, Sanda a Frenchwoman searching for her lover. Panavision. [R] ▼▶

Caché (2005-French-Austrian-German-Italian) **C-118m.** *** D: Michael Haneke. Daniel Auteuil, Juliette Binoche, Annie Girardot, Lester Makedonsky, Maurice Bénichou, Bernard Le Coq, Daniel Duval,

Nathalie Richard, Walid Afkir. Parisian host of a book-chat TV show and his wife are baffled by a succession of surveillance videotapes of their home's exterior, each anonymously left on the doorstep. Eventually, other cryptic messages appear, sketches that may have some hidden meaning. Writer-director Haneke (THE PIANO TEACHER) has constructed another icily meticulous, if protracted, drama, framed by a realistic portrait of a marriage and augmented with references to recent French history. [R]▌

Cactus (1986-Australian) **C-93m. **½ D:** Paul Cox. Isabelle Huppert, Robert Menzies, Norman Kaye, Monica Maughan, Banduk Marika. Slow, deliberately paced story of Huppert's agony when her sight is impaired in an auto mishap and her growing relationship with blind Menzies. Of interest only when it sticks to the story, which isn't often enough.▼▶

Cactus Flower (1969) **C-103m. **½ D:** Gene Saks. Walter Matthau, Ingrid Bergman, Goldie Hawn, Jack Weston, Rick Lenz, Vito Scotti, Irene Hervey. Glossy comedy was pretty thin for Broadway, even thinner on film, with Bergman as prim nurse to dentist Matthau who blossoms when she realizes she's in love with him. Best moments belong to Hawn, who won Oscar for her first big role. Remade as JUST GO WITH IT in 2010. [M/PG]▼▶

Caddie (1976-Australian) **C-107m. **½ D:** Donald Crombie. Helen Morse, Takis Emmanuel, Jack Thompson, Jacki Weaver, Melissa Jaffer. Adaptation of a popular Australian autobiography set in the late '20s and early '30s, telling story of an independent-minded young woman determined to succeed on her own, despite the pressure of having two children to raise. Moments of insight and originality give way too often to cliché and overriding blandness. Morse is fine in lead. ▼

Caddy, The (1953) **95m. *½ D:** Norman Taurog. Dean Martin, Jerry Lewis, Donna Reed, Fred Clark, Barbara Bates, Joseph Calleia. Weak Martin & Lewis vehicle about golf-nut Jerry coaching Dean to be a champion player. Dean introduces "That's Amore." ▼▶

CaddyShack (1980) **C-98m. ** D:** Harold Ramis. Chevy Chase, Rodney Dangerfield, Ted Knight, Michael O'Keefe, Bill Murray, Cindy Morgan, Sarah Holcomb, Scott Colomby, Brian Doyle-Murray, Chuck E. Rodent. ANIMAL HOUSE-type hijinks at a posh country club; another comedy where irreverence and destruction are a substitute for humor. Saving grace is Dangerfield, whose opening scenes are sidesplittingly funny. Followed by a sequel. [R]▼▶

CaddyShack II (1988) **C-99m. ** D:** Allan Arkush. Jackie Mason, Dyan Cannon, Robert Stack, Dina Merrill, Chevy Chase,

Dan Aykroyd, Randy Quaid, Jessica Lundy, Jonathan Silverman, Chynna Phillips, Brian McNamara. In-name-only sequel to 1980 hit gets a big boost from Mason, extremely winning in the role of a plain-talking, self-made millionaire whose daughter wants acceptance by the snooty crowd at a local country club. Unfortunately, film runs out of script (and laughs) after a half hour. [PG]▼▶

Cadence (1991) **C-97m. *½ D:** Martin Sheen. Charlie Sheen, Martin Sheen, Larry Fishburne, Michael Beach, Ramon Estevez, John Toles-Bey, Blu Mankuma, Harry Stewart, James Marshall. U.S. soldier Charlie lands in a West German brig, the lone white among a group of black prisoners; conflict, however, centers on warden Martin, who's slowly coming apart at the seams. Sheen family enterprise is overwrought and insignificant, with just one compelling scene: the brigmates march in jivey cadence to their own rendition of Sam Cooke's "Chain Gang." Would Ernie Borgnine's Fatso Judson have allowed this in FROM HERE TO ETERNITY? [PG-13]▼▶

Cadillac Man (1990) **C-97m. **½ D:** Roger Donaldson. Robin Williams, Tim Robbins, Pamela Reed, Fran Drescher, Zack Norman, Annabella Sciorra, Lori Petty, Paul Guilfoyle, Bill Nelson, Eddie Jones, Judith Hoag. Williams is terrific, as usual, playing an aggressive car salesman who may lose his job, his mistress, his other girlfriend, his Mafioso protector, and his daughter all during one eventful weekend. Wildly uneven film swings from comedy to melodrama, dragging and then picking up again. Elaine Stritch appears unbilled as a grieving widow. [R]▼▶

Cadillac Ranch (1996) **C-95m. **½ D:** Lisa Gottlieb. Suzy Amis, Renee Humphrey, Caroleen Feeney, Linden Ashby, Christopher Lloyd, Jim Metzler. Amiable tale of three sisters who, despite some long-time friction, band together to find a cache of money left behind by their Daddy when they were just kids . . . tracked, all the while, by bad guy Lloyd. Likable performances by the female trio boost this modest Texas-made production. Panavision. [R]▼▶

Cadillac Records (2008) **C-108m. **½ D:** Darnell Martin. Adrien Brody, Jeffrey Wright, Beyoncé Knowles, Gabrielle Union, Cedric the Entertainer, Columbus Short, Eamonn Walker, Emmanuelle Chriqui, Mos Def, Tammy Blanchard, Jay O. Sanders, Norman Reedus, Eric Bogosian. Colorful look at the birth and flowering of Chicago's Chess Records label in the 1940s and '50s, where Polish immigrant Leonard Chess (Brody) brought blues artists like Muddy Waters (Wright), Little Walter (Short), Howlin' Wolf (Walker), and Etta James (Knowles) to prominence, amidst much personal turmoil. Bites off more than one

[203]

film can chew but still offers a rich tapestry; each of these personalities deserves a separate film. The actors mostly perform their own songs, quite credibly, and Mos Def is a hoot as Chuck Berry. Vincent D'Onofrio appears unbilled. Super 35. [R]▶

Caesar and Cleopatra (1946-British) **C-134m.** ** D: Gabriel Pascal. Claude Rains, Vivien Leigh, Stewart Granger, Flora Robson, Francis L. Sullivan, Cecil Parker. Two fine stars suffer through static, boring rendition of George Bernard Shaw's play, which seems to go on forever. Occasional wit and intrigue can't keep this afloat.▼▶

Cafe au Lait (1994-French) **C-94m.** *** D: Mathieu Kassovitz. Julie Mauduech, Hubert Kounde, Mathieu Kassovitz. Kassovitz' first feature is the SHE'S GOTTA HAVE IT/JULES AND JIM–like story of a young, pregnant Parisian (Mauduech) who is uncertain which of her boyfriends is the father. Is it the African Muslim law student (Kounde)? Or the Jewish bicycle messenger (played by the director)? Sweetly funny, and a heartening look at contemporary relations between the races. Kassovitz also scripted.▼▶

Cafe Express (1981-Italian) **C-89m.** **½ D: Nanni Loy. Nino Manfredi, Adolfo Celi, Vittorio Mezzogiorno, Luigi Basagaluppi, Silvio Spaccesi. Manfredi, virtually repeating his characterization in BREAD AND CHOCOLATE, is a Neapolitan working man illegally selling coffee on the Milan to Naples train. Sometimes funny and profound, more often trite. Manfredi, as usual, is fine. Originally ran 105m.▼▶

Cafe Society (1995) **C/B&W-107m.** *** D: Raymond De Felitta. Frank Whaley, Peter Gallagher, Lara Flynn Boyle, John Spencer, Anna Thomson, David Patrick Kelly, Christopher Murney, Richard B. Shull, Paul Guilfoyle, Alan North, Kelly Bishop, Zach Grenier. Atmospheric, fact-based account, set in 1952, about Mickey Jelke (Whaley), a poor little rich boy set to inherit $5 million. Jelke hobnobs with N.Y.C. cafe society, and thinks nothing of pimping, just for the fun of it. Gallagher is the vice cop who's determined to nail him; Boyle (who makes a great noir heroine) is the woman with whom Jelke becomes involved, on several levels. De Felitta, working with a low budget, creates an impressive and authentic period feel. [R]▼

Cage, The (1978) SEE: **Mafu Cage, The**

Cage (1989) **C-101m.** BOMB D: Lang Elliott. Lou Ferrigno, Reb Brown, Michael Dante, Mike Moroff, Marilyn Tokuda, James Shigeta, Al Ruscio. Pointless, violent film provides viewers with the human equivalent of a cockfight as Ferrigno and Brown go at it in the Asian "sport" of cage fighting. A better title might have been THE INCREDIBLE HOKUM. [R]▼▶

Caged (1950) **96m.** *** D: John Crom-

well. Eleanor Parker, Agnes Moorehead, Ellen Corby, Hope Emerson, Jan Sterling, Jane Darwell, Gertrude Michael. Remarkable performances in stark record of Parker going to prison and becoming hardened criminal after exposure to brutal jail life. Remade as HOUSE OF WOMEN (1962).▶

Caged Heat (1974) **C-84m.** **½ D: Jonathan Demme. Juanita Brown, Erica Gavin, Roberta Collins, Rainbeaux Smith, Barbara Steele, Toby Carr-Rafelson. Demme's first feature is tongue-in-cheek but otherwise typical women's prison flick, chiefly novel for being set in the U.S. instead of some banana republic, plus neat turn by Steele as wheelchair-bound warden. Has a sizable cult following. Aka RENEGADE GIRLS. [R]▼▶

Cahill United States Marshal (1973) **C-103m.** ** D: Andrew V. McLaglen. John Wayne, George Kennedy, Gary Grimes, Neville Brand, Marie Windsor, Harry Carey, Jr. Marshal Wayne's law enforcement duties are complicated as one of his sons threatens to enter a life of crime; routine, violent Western suffers from the same kind of sermonizing that plagued most of the Duke's later films. Panavision. [PG]▼●▶

Caine Mutiny, The (1954) **C-125m.** **** D: Edward Dmytryk. Humphrey Bogart, Jose Ferrer, Van Johnson, Robert Francis, May Wynn, Fred MacMurray, E. G. Marshall, Lee Marvin, Tom Tully, Claude Akins. WW2 Naval officers Johnson and Francis mutiny against paranoid, unpopular Capt. Queeg (Bogart) and are court-martialed in this exciting adaptation (by Stanley Roberts) of Herman Wouk's Pulitzer Prize novel. Wartime mutiny scene during typhoon still packs a wallop. Followed by a TVM in 1988.▼●▶

Cairo Time (2009-Canadian-Irish-Egyptian) **C-90m.** ** D: Ruba Nadda. Patricia Clarkson, Alexander Siddig, Elena Anaya, Amina Annabi, Tom McCamus. Magazine editor (Clarkson) arrives in Egypt to spend a much-longed-for vacation with her diplomat husband who, delayed in troubled Gaza, sends a former coworker and trusted friend (Siddig) to meet her plane. Uncomfortable touring the streets of Cairo on her own, Clarkson reaches out to Siddig once more to serve as guide until her husband can join her. The pace is so unhurried it will put most viewers to sleep. Scenery is lovely, but the plot—hidden somewhere in the hint of a budding romance—is dull, if mostly nonexistent. [PG]▶

Cake Eaters, The (2009) **C-86m.** ** D: Mary Stuart Masterson. Elizabeth Ashley, Jayce Bartok, Bruce Dern, Miriam Shor, Aaron Stanford, Kristen Stewart, Talia Balsam, Melissa Leo, Jesse L. Martin. In a quiet upstate N.Y. town, teen Stewart (who's afflicted with a neuromuscular disease) is obsessed with losing her virginity to Stanford.

His older brother (Bartok), a failed musician, wants to rekindle a romance, and their just-widowed father (Dern) is in a long-term relationship with Ashley, Stewart's grandmother. Potentially powerful kitchen-sink drama is surprisingly mild and inconsequential, but Ashley and especially Dern are a pleasure to watch. Bartok also scripted; feature directing debut for Masterson. [R]▶

Cal (1984-British) **C-102m.** *** D: Pat O'Connor. Helen Mirren, John Lynch, Donal McCann, John Kavanagh, Ray McAnally, Stevan Rimkus, Kitty Gibson. Intelligent drama of modern-day Northern Ireland, with Lynch, 19, falling for older widow Mirren—despite his IRA involvement with her husband's murder. Strong performances, especially by Mirren; produced by David Puttnam. [R]▼

Calamity Jane (1953) **C-101m.** *** D: David Butler. Doris Day, Howard Keel, Allyn (Ann) McLerie, Philip Carey, Gale Robbins, Dick Wesson, Paul Harvey. Doris is irresistible as the bombastic, rootin'-tootin' title character in this lively musical, with Keel as Wild Bill Hickok, who only begins to realize his feelings for her when she makes a stab at becoming more "feminine." Sammy Fain–Paul Francis Webster score includes the Oscar-winning "Secret Love." Jane Alexander later played Calamity in a 1984 TVM. ▼○▶

Calendar (1993-Canadian-Armenian) **C-75m.** ** D: Atom Egoyan. Arsinée Khanjian, Ashot Adamian, Atom Egoyan. A photographer (Egoyan) and his wife (Khanjian) travel from Canada to Armenia to shoot photos of historical churches for inclusion on a wall calendar; as he looks through his lens, his marriage falls apart before his eyes as his mate comes in touch with her roots and falls for their guide. Some intriguing ideas are at work here, but the film is much like an out-of-focus snapshot and too loosely structured to be effective. Egoyan and Khanjian are married off screen.▼▶

Calendar Girl (1993) **C-90m.** ** D: John Whitesell. Jason Priestley, Gabriel Olds, Jerry O'Connell, Joe Pantoliano, Steve Railsback, Kurt Fuller, Stephen Tobolowsky, Emily Warfield, Maxwell Caulfield, Stephanie Anderson, Chubby Checker. Pat, overly familiar coming-of-age tale of three high school grads who head off to L.A. in 1962 to seek out their idol, Marilyn Monroe. Ultimately harmless, but you've seen it a million times before. One of the executive producers was Penny Marshall. [PG-13] ▼○

Calendar Girls (2003-British) **C-107m.** **½ D: Nigel Cole. Helen Mirren, Julie Walters, John Alderton, Linda Bassett, Annette Crosbie, Ciarán Hinds, Celia Imrie, Penelope Wilton, Graham Crowden, Geraldine James. Amiable comedy based on the true story of middle-aged women in

a small English town who pose nude for a fund-raising calendar. Mirren and Walters are so delightful, and abetted by such an engaging cast, that it's a shame the script isn't more inspired. Later a stage play. Super 35. [PG-13] ▼▶

California (1946) **C-97m.** **½ D: John Farrow. Barbara Stanwyck, Ray Milland, Barry Fitzgerald, Albert Dekker, Anthony Quinn, Julia Faye, George Coulouris. Ray is a wagonmaster with a past, Stanwyck a shady gal who makes good in this elaborately ordinary Western.▶

California Dolls, The SEE: **. . . All the Marbles**

California Dreaming (1979) **C-92m.** **½ D: John Hancock. Dennis Christopher, Glynnis O'Connor, Seymour Cassel, Dorothy Tristan, John Calvin, Tanya Roberts, Todd Susman, Alice Playten, Ned Wynn, Jimmy Van Patten, Stacey Nelkin, Marshall Efron. Revisionist beach party movie finds nerd Christopher trying desperately to fit in with the surfing crowd, blind to the fact that their lives are even emptier than his. Strong drama sometimes bites off more than it can chew, but overall fairly compelling and surprisingly erotic; Wynn also wrote the screenplay. [R]▼

California Split (1974) **C-108m.** **½ D: Robert Altman. George Segal, Elliott Gould, Ann Prentiss, Gwen Welles, Joseph Walsh, Bert Remsen, Jeff Goldblum. Realistic but rambling look at two compulsive gamblers, their strange lifestyles, and the emptiness of winning. Altman's multi-channel soundtrack only adds to the muddle. DVD version is 3m. shorter, due to music rights issues. Panavision. [R]▶

California Suite (1978) **C-103m.** *** D: Herbert Ross. Jane Fonda, Alan Alda, Maggie Smith, Michael Caine, Walter Matthau, Elaine May, Richard Pryor, Bill Cosby, Gloria Gifford, Sheila Frazier, Herb Edelman, Denise Galik. Four Neil Simon skits set at the Beverly Hills Hotel (and adapted from his Broadway hit). Oscar-winning Smith and husband Caine as gently bickering Britishers in town for Academy Awards come off best; Pryor and Cosby as unfunnily combative "friends" are the worst. Pleasant time-filler, with nice jazz score by Claude Bolling. [PG] ▼○

Caligula (1979) **C-156m.** *½ D: Tinto Brass. Malcolm McDowell, Peter O'Toole, Teresa Ann Savoy, Helen Mirren, John Gielgud, Guido Mannari. Filmdom's first $15 million porno (to say nothing of home!) movie, produced by *Penthouse* and set in Rome in the 1st century A.G. (After Guccione), follows ruthless ruler through endless series of decapitations and disembowelings. Chutzpah and 6m. of not-bad hard-core footage earn this half a star for the faithful, but most viewers will be rightfully repelled. And besides, Jay Robinson does much better by the title character in THE ROBE and DEMETRIUS AND THE GLADIATORS. Reissued in 105m., R-rated version—which is considerably changed. [R—edited from original unrated version] ▼●❍

Callan (1974-British) **C-106m.** **½ D: Don Sharp. Edward Woodward, Eric Porter, Carl Mohner, Catherine Schell, Peter Egan. Adequate drama of aging secret agent Woodward, demoted because he cares too much about his adversaries, assigned to kill a German businessman. Woodward had previously played same role on British TV. Video title: THE NEUTRALIZER.▼

Callas Forever (2002-Italian-French-Spanish-British-Romanian) **C-111m.** *** D: Franco Zeffirelli. Fanny Ardant, Jeremy Irons, Joan Plowright, Jay Rodan, Gabriel Garko, Manuel de Blas, Justino Díaz. Fictional imagining of the great opera diva Maria Callas at the end of her storied career. Her former manager comes back into her life and convinces her to regain her passion by doing a film of *Carmen* in which she would lip-sync to her great recordings of the past. Sumptuous production values and fine acting make this worth seeing if you are a fan of opera, Callas, or Zeffirelli (who actually directed Callas onstage several times). Barely released theatrically in the U.S. ❍

Callaway Went Thataway (1951) **81m.** **½ D: Norman Panama, Melvin Frank. Fred MacMurray, Dorothy McGuire, Howard Keel, Jesse White, Fay Roope, Natalie Schafer, Stan Freberg. Gentle spoof of early-TV "Hopalong Cassidy" craze, with Keel as lookalike who impersonates veteran cowboy star for promotional purposes; good fun until it starts getting serious. Several MGM stars make cameo appearances.

Calle 54 (2000-French-Spanish) **C-105m.** *** D: Fernando Trueba. Chucho Valdes, Gato Barbieri, Jerry Gonzalez, Tito Puente, Eliane Elias, Chico O'Farrill, Bebo Valdes. Fans of Latin jazz will want to catch Oscar-winning director Trueba's valentine to the music he grew up loving. With cameras ready to catch every moment, the filmmaker invited several Latin musicians into an N.Y.C. recording studio, then traveled to their hometowns to provide glimpses into their lives. Particularly gratifying to see Tito Puente still cookin' toward the end of his life. [G] ▼❍

Caller, The (1989) **C-97m.** ** D: Arthur Allan Seidelman. Malcolm McDowell, Madoyn Smith. Strange two-character mystery set mostly in an isolated cabin in the woods; the verbal sparring partners are not what they seem to be. Partly effective, but goes on much too long; might have worked as a *Twilight Zone* episode. Shot in Italy in 1987. [R] ▼❍

Call Him Mr. Shatter (1974-British) **C-90m.** *½ D: Michael Carreras. Stuart Whitman, Ti Lung, Lily Li, Peter Cushing, Anton Diffring. Hammer's entry into the

Kung Fu market, begun by Monte Hellman, stars Whitman as a burned-out hit man on assignment in Hong Kong. Plenty of action, but nothing to hold it together; presence of three cinematographers is a tip-off to extensive production woes. Aka SHATTER. [R] ▼●❍

Calling Northside 777 SEE: **Call Northside 777**

Call Me (1988) **C-96m.** **½ D: Sollace Mitchell. Patricia Charbonneau, Patti D'Arbanville, Sam Freed, Boyd Gaines, Stephen McHattie, Steve Buscemi, John Seitz, David Strathairn. Horny reporter saddled with a lackluster boyfriend begins receiving obscene phone calls and almost finds herself enjoying the experience. Very well acted by Charbonneau, but too many of the supporting roles are weakly cast; excessive melodrama detracts from what could have been a more compelling psychological study. [R] ▼●

Call Me Bwana (1963) **C-103m.** ** D: Gordon Douglas. Bob Hope, Anita Ekberg, Edie Adams, Lionel Jeffries, Arnold Palmer. Hope and Adams on jungle safari encounter Ekberg and Jeffries and nothing much happens. The ladies are lovely. ▼●❍

Call Me Madam (1953) **C-114m.** *** D: Walter Lang. Ethel Merman, Donald O'Connor, George Sanders, Vera-Ellen, Billy DeWolfe, Walter Slezak, Lilia Skala. Often stagy musical from Irving Berlin tuner based on Perle Mesta's life as Washington, D.C., hostess and Liechtenstein ambassadress. Merman is blowsy delight. Songs include "The Best Thing for You," "It's a Lovely Day Today," "You're Just in Love." ❍

Call Me Mister (1951) **C-95m.** **½ D: Lloyd Bacon. Betty Grable, Dan Dailey, Danny Thomas, Dale Robertson, Benay Venuta, Richard Boone, Frank Fontaine, Jeffrey Hunter. Acceptable plot line helps buoy this musical. Soldier Dailey, based in Japan, goes AWOL to patch up marriage with Grable traveling with USO troupe. Bears little resemblance to the Broadway revue on which it's supposedly based. An unbilled Bobby Short sings "Going Home Train."

Call Northside 777 (1948) **111m.** ***½ D: Henry Hathaway. James Stewart, Richard Conte, Lee J. Cobb, Helen Walker, Moroni Olsen, E. G. Marshall. Absorbing drama of reporter Stewart convinced that convicted killer is innocent, trying to prove it; handled in semi-documentary style. Retitled: CALLING NORTHSIDE 777. ▼●❍

Call of the Wild, The (1935) **81m.** *** D: William Wellman. Clark Gable, Loretta Young, Jack Oakie, Reginald Owen, Frank Conroy. More Hollywood than Jack London, this Yukon adventure/romance is lots of fun, and Owen a fine snarling villain. Original release was 95m. Remade in 1972 and as a TV movie in 1976, 1993, 1997, and in 2009 in 3-D. ❍

Call of the Wild (1972-British-French-German-Italian-Spanish) **C-100m. **½ D:** Ken Annakin. Charlton Heston, Michele Mercier, Maria Rohm, Rik Battaglia. Lackluster version of the Jack London adventure classic, produced by a multinational film combine and wasting the talents of a diverse cast. One redeeming quality: the striking Finnish scenery. [PG]▼▶

Call the Cops! SEE: **Find the Lady**

Camelot (1967) **C-178m. *½ D:** Joshua Logan. Richard Harris, Vanessa Redgrave, Franco Nero, David Hemmings, Lionel Jeffries. Appalling film version of Lerner-Loewe musical has only good orchestrations and sporadically good acting to recommend it; no one can sing and production looks cheap, in spite of big budget. This did, however, win Oscars for Costumes, Scoring, and Art Direction–Set Decoration. Film's nonstop use of close-ups may help it on TV screens. Panavision. ▼▶

Camera Buff (1979-Polish) **C-107m. ***½ D:** Krzysztof Kieslowski. Jerzy Stuhr, Malgorzata Zabkowska, Ewa Pokas, Stefan Czyzewski, Jerzy Nowak. Kieslowski's first international success is a compelling story about an ordinary workingman who buys an 8mm camera so he can shoot home movies as soon as his wife gives birth. Instead, he becomes galvanized by the power and fascination of the camera and ignores his wife and daughter in the process. A somewhat autobiographical story of a man's artistic and political awakening, this is just as powerful as the day it was made. Aka AMATOR. ▼▶

Cameraman, The (1928) **69m. *** D:** Edward Sedgwick. Buster Keaton, Marceline Day, Harold Goodwin, Sidney Bracy, Harry Gribbon, Edward Brophy. Buster plays a lovesick would-be newsreel cameraman in this entertaining silent comedy, a cut below his masterpieces but still brimming with invention, ingenious set pieces, and big laughs. Remade with Red Skelton as WATCH THE BIRDIE.▼▶

Camila (1984-Argentine) **C-105m. **½ D:** Maria Luisa Bemberg. Susu Pecoraro, Imanol Arias, Hector Alterio. Shades of ELVIRA MADIGAN, in a story based on 19th-century Argentine fact, about a Jesuit priest and a young Catholic socialite who commit love on the lam as the authorities stalk them for 500 miles. Interesting, but never altogether compelling.▼▶

Camilla (1994-Canadian-British) **C-95m. **½ D:** Deepa Mehta. Jessica Tandy, Bridget Fonda, Hume Cronyn, Elias Koteas, Maury Chaykin, Graham Greene, Ranjit Chowdhry, Atom Egoyan, Don McKellar. Tandy, in her final film, is the sole reason to see this otherwise so-so road movie about the budding friendship between a young would-be singer-songwriter (Fonda) and an elderly, eccentric (and high-spirited) former con-

cert violinist. Cronyn plays Tandy's former lover, and their on-screen time together is something special. [PG-13]▼▶

Camille (1937) **108m. ***½ D:** George Cukor. Greta Garbo, Robert Taylor, Lionel Barrymore, Elizabeth Allan, Laura Hope Crews, Henry Daniell, Joan Brodel (Leslie). Beautiful MGM production; in one of her most famous roles, Garbo is Dumas' tragic heroine who must sacrifice her own happiness in order to prove her love. Taylor is a bit stiff as Armand, but Daniell is a superb villain. Filmed before in 1915 (with Clara Kimball Young), 1917 (Theda Bara), and 1921 (Nazimova, with Rudolph Valentino as Armand). Remade for TV in 1984 with Greta Scacchi. Also shown in computer-colored version.▼▶

Camille (2007-U.S.-Canadian) **C-91m. **½ D:** Gregory Mackenzie. Sienna Miller, James Franco, David Carradine, Scott Glenn, Ed Lauter, Mark Wilson, Patricia Yeatman. Kentucky newlyweds bound for Niagara Falls suffer a setback when the happy bride dies in a road mishap . . . but she doesn't know it and keeps going like a decomposing Energizer bunny. Affable fable about the sweet undead, unrelated to other movie Camilles, has plenty of heart, credible acting, plus pretty pastel horses. Far too genteel for those who prefer a gutsy zombie. [PG-13]▶

Camille Claudel (1988-French) **C-149m. ** D:** Bruno Nuytten. Isabelle Adjani, Gérard Depardieu, Laurent Grevill, Alain Cuny, Madeleine Robinson, Katrine Boorman. Overblown biography of the French sculptress (Adjani), who has a "madness of mud" and who single-mindedly pursues her art; Depardieu plays Auguste Rodin, with whom she has a complex, turbulent relationship. Potentially provocative story is emotionally uninvolving, with an astonishing lack of depth. Wonderful production values and period detail, but all for naught. Cinematographer Nuytten's directorial debut. Original French running time 173m. Panavision. [R]▼▶

Camorra (1986-Italian) **C-115m. **½ D:** Lina Wertmuller. Angela Molina, Harvey Keitel, Daniel Ezralow, Francisco Rabal, Paolo Bonacelli, Isa Danieli, Lorraine Bracco. Complex tale of drug traffic, murder, and mayhem, focusing on the trials of ex-prostitute Molina; well-meaning in its depiction of how preteens are used and abused by drug kingpins. Generally better than the director's later work, but miles below her gems of the 1970s. [R]▼

Camouflage (1977-Polish) **C-106m. ***½ D:** Krzysztof Zanussi. Piotr Garlicki, Zbigniew Zapasiewicz, Christine Paul, Mariusz Dmochowski. Arrogant tenured professor Zapasiewicz challenges the independence of idealistic teaching assistant Garlicki at a summer school-camp for linguists. Pungently funny satire about conformity, the Communist hierarchy.

Camp (2003) **C-114m.** **½ D: Todd Graff. Daniel Letterle, Joanna Chilcoat, Robin De Jesus, Tiffany Taylor, Sasha Allen, Anna Kendrick, Don Dixon. A straight skater boy at a performing arts camp gets caught in a love triangle with a lovelorn ingenue and a gay Puerto Rican drag queen. Clichéd scripting hampers entertaining, easy-to-like backstage teen musical, but there's no denying the talented young cast. Divas-in-training Allen and Taylor are standouts. Writer and first-time director Graff, a former theater camper himself, knows his milieu; there's even a funny cameo from Broadway god Stephen Sondheim. [PG-13] ▼❍

Camp Nowhere (1994) **C-96m.** *½ D: Jonathan Prince. Jonathan Jackson, Andrew Keegan, Marne Patterson, Melody Kay, Christopher Lloyd, M. Emmet Walsh, Wendy Makkena, Kate Mulgrew, Burgess Meredith, Peter Scolari, Jessica Marie Alba. Computer geeks, show biz wannabes, kid commandos, and other neighborhood cast-offs band together to form their own communal summer camp, supervised by token adult Lloyd, who has somehow managed to convince parents he's a responsible authority figure. Assembly-line, end-of-summer release occasionally has a wittier gag than expected. [PG] ▼❍

Campus Man (1987) **C-94m.** ** D: Ron Casden. John Dye, Steve Lyon, Morgan Fairchild, Kim Delaney, Kathleen Wilhoite, Miles O'Keeffe. Glossy but vacuous teen comedy of collegiate entrepreneur (*i.e.* hustler) who publishes a male beefcake calendar featuring his roommate, a hunky diver, and spawning all kinds of complications. Based on story of Arizona State University alumnus Todd Headlee (the film's associate producer), whose ASU calendar launched the nationwide craze. [PG] ▼❍

Canadian Bacon (1995) **C-91m.** **½ D: Michael Moore. Alan Alda, John Candy, Rhea Perlman, Kevin Pollak, Rip Torn, Kevin J. O'Connor, Bill Nunn, G. D. Spradlin, Steven Wright, James Belushi, Brad Sullivan. In order to gain a strong platform for re-election, the president of the United States does the unthinkable and declares war on our neighbor to the north, Canada. Moore stumbles with his second film after the terrific ROGER & ME. A top cast is wasted in this one-joke premise which lacks the satiric edge it needs. [PG] ▼❍

Can-Can (1960) **C-131m.** **½ D: Walter Lang. Frank Sinatra, Shirley MacLaine, Maurice Chevalier, Louis Jourdan, Juliet Prowse. Lackluster version of Cole Porter musical of 1890s Paris involving lawyer Sinatra defending MacLaine's right to perform "daring" dance in her nightclub. Chevalier and Jourdan try to inject charm, but

Sinatra is blasé and MacLaine shrill. Songs: "C'est Magnifique," "I Love Paris," "Let's Do It," "Just One of Those Things." Todd-AO. ▼❍

Cancel My Reservation (1972) **C-99m.** BOMB D: Paul Bogart. Bob Hope, Eva Marie Saint, Ralph Bellamy, Forrest Tucker, Anne Archer, Keenan Wynn, Ned Beatty, Chief Dan George. Hope should have canceled this movie, a time-wasting turkey about a troubled talk-show host who gets involved in a murder case in Arizona. Based on a Louis L'Amour novel! [G]

Candidate, The (1972) **C-109m.** *** D: Michael Ritchie. Robert Redford, Peter Boyle, Don Porter, Allen Garfield, Karen Carlson, Melvyn Douglas, Quinn Redeker, Michael Lerner, Kenneth Tobey. Keen-eyed political satire doesn't stray far from reality. Redford is idealist talked into running for Senate with promise of absolute integrity in campaign, since he's bound to lose—or is he? Oscar-winning screenplay by Jeremy Larner. [PG] ▼❍

Candleshoe (1978) **C-101m.** *** D: Norman Tokar. David Niven, Jodie Foster, Helen Hayes, Leo McKern, Veronica Quilligan, Ian Sharrock, Vivian Pickles. Con man McKern tries to pass off orphan Foster as Hayes' heiress in order to locate hidden family treasure. Entertaining Disney comedy filmed in England, with Niven as disguise-laden butler. [G] ▼❍

Candy (1968-U.S.-Italian-French) **C-124m.** ** D: Christian Marquand. Ewa Aulin, Richard Burton, Marlon Brando, Charles Aznavour, James Coburn, John Huston, Walter Matthau, Ringo Starr, John Astin. Strained sexual satire about a nubile blonde who is attacked by every man she meets. Fair share of funny moments and bright performances (particularly by Burton and Astin), but not enough to sustain 124m. Adapted from Terry Southern and Mason Hoffenberg's book by Buck Henry. [R] ▼❍

Candy (2006-Australian) **C-108m.** **½ D: Neil Armfield. Abbie Cornish, Heath Ledger, Geoffrey Rush, Tom Budge, Roberto Meza Mont, Tony Martin, Noni Hazlehurst. Murky account of the evolving relationship between two attractive young people, a poet (Ledger) and a painter (Cornish), both of whom are hooked on heroin. Well acted, but the scenario is overly familiar. Armfield and Luke Davies scripted, based on Davies' novel. [R]❍

Candyman (1992) **C-93m.** *** D: Bernard Rose. Virginia Madsen, Tony Todd, Xander Berkeley, Kasi Lemmons, Vanessa Williams, DeJuan Guy, Michael Culkin. Effectively eerie psychological chiller, filled with clever, unusual touches, about an academic (Madsen) who begins researching the legend of a mysterious serial killer named Candyman (Todd); this leads her to Chicago's crime-infested Cabrini-Green public housing project. Rose (who plays the role of "Archie Walsh") also scripted, from Clive Barker's novel *The Forbidden* (which is set in Liverpool). Followed by two sequels. [R]▼●◗

Candyman: Farewell to the Flesh (1995) **C-94m.** ** D: Bill Condon. Tony Todd, Kelly Rowan, Timothy Carhart, Veronica Cartwright, William O'Leary, Fay Hauser, Bill Nunn, Matt Clark. Title avenger is resurrected in mediocre sequel to terrorize an aristocratic New Orleans family just in time for Mardi Gras. Good production values, including some convincing local color, are undermined by obvious plotting and nondescript supporting cast. Bland but for the menacing Todd in the title role. Followed by a direct-to-video sequel. [R] ▼●◗

Candy Mountain (1987-Canadian-French-Swiss) **C-91m.** ** D: Robert Frank, Rudy Wurlitzer. Kevin J. O'Connor, Harris Yulin, Tom Waits, Bulle Ogier, Roberts Blossom, Leon Redbone, Dr. John, Joe Strummer, David Johansen (Buster Poindexter). Uneven account of has-been rocker O'Connor and his trip through America and Canada in search of elusive guitarmaker Yulin. Intriguing collaboration between photographer/filmmaker Frank, screenwriter Wurlitzer, and an eclectic cast . . . but the results are too often dull. [R]▼

Candy Stripe Nurses (1974) **C-80m.** *½ D: Allan Holleb. Candice Rialson, Robin Mattson, Maria Rojo, Kimberly Hyde, Dick Miller, Stanley Ralph Ross, Monte Landis, Tom Baker. Last of Roger Corman's five "nurse" pictures is tired sex comedy, focusing on antics of pretty volunteers; kept afloat by cast full of old hands at this sort of thing. Aka SWEET CANDY. [R]▼◗

Can Hieronymus Merkin Ever Forget Mercy Humppe and Find True Happiness? (1969-British) **C-106m.** *½ D: Anthony Newley. Anthony Newley, Joan Collins, Milton Berle, Connie Kreski, George Jessel, Stubby Kaye. Fellini-influenced mess about song-and-dance man who reviews his debauched past. Low-grade in all departments, though Connie reveals why she was "Playmate of the Year." Newley and Collins were then real-life husband and wife. [R—edited from original X rating]

Can I Do It . . . Til I Need Glasses? (1977) **C-72m.** BOMB D: I. Robert Levy. Victor Dunlap, Moose Carlson, Walter Olkewicz, Joey Camen, Ann Kellogg, Robin Williams. Sophomoric series of sex-related skits, most of which would bore immature 11-year-olds. Williams appears very briefly, in footage tacked on after the film's premiere (and after his *Mork and Mindy* stardom). [R]▼◗

Cannery Row (1982) **C-120m.** **½ D: David S. Ward. Nick Nolte, Debra Winger, Audra Lindley, Frank McRae, M. Emmet Walsh, Sunshine Parker, Santos Morales, narrated by John Huston. Entertaining tug-of-war romance between baseball-player-turned-marine-biologist Nolte and drifter-turned-floozie Winger is hampered by sloppy, self-conscious direction, awkward continuity. Attractive performances by Nolte and Winger; great set design by Richard MacDonald. Based on John Steinbeck's *Cannery Row* and *Sweet Thursday.* Ward's directorial debut. [PG]▼●◗

Cannibal Girls (1973-Canadian) **C-84m.** ** D: Ivan Reitman. Eugene Levy, Andrea Martin, Ronald Ulrich, Randall Carpenter, Bonnie Neison. Confused, convoluted low-budget Canadian import, an early effort by young talents Reitman, Levy, and Martin, has funny first half about a couple stranded in eerie town where there's a rather strange restaurant. Second half falls apart. Warning buzzer precedes gore scenes (which aren't much), and doorbell-like sound announces they're over. [R]◗

Cannibal! The Musical (1998) **C-92m.** **½ D: Trey Parker. Juan Schwartz (Trey Parker), Dian Bachar, Ian Hardin, John Hegel, Matt Stone, Toddy Walters. Wacky, low-budget musical based on real-life story of Alferd Packer, who led an expedition that degenerated into cannibalism in the Colorado Rockies, circa 1874. Gross-out gags alternate for screen time with some pretty good songs; our favorite is "Shpadoinkle." First feature for the SOUTH PARK team of Parker and Stone. Made in 1993. [R]▼◗

Cannonball (1976) **C-93m.** ** D: Paul Bartel. David Carradine, Veronica Hamel, Bill McKinney, Gerrit Graham, Robert Carradine, Belinda Balaski, Judy Canova, Carl Gottlieb. Comic account of cross-country road race first depicted in THE GUMBALL RALLY. Funny moments are muted by unpleasant characters and inept stuntwork. As usual, many of Bartel's pals and coworkers appear in bits, including Sylvester Stallone, Roger Corman, and directors Martin Scorsese, Jonathan Kaplan, and Joe Dante. [PG]▼◗

Cannonball Run, The (1981) **C-95m.** BOMB D: Hal Needham. Burt Reynolds, Roger Moore, Farrah Fawcett, Dom DeLuise, Dean Martin, Sammy Davis, Jr., Terry Bradshaw, Jackie Chan, Bert Convy, Jamie Farr, Peter Fonda, Bianca Jagger, Molly Picon, Jimmy "The Greek" Snyder, Mel Tillis. Just what civilization needs—more Reynolds car-chase silliness, inspired by the same cross-country road race depicted in THE GUMBALL RALLY and CANNONBALL. Pretty unendurable, despite unusual cast; rumor has it that the one responsible for casting Dino and Sammy as priests is still doing his Hail Marys. Followed by a sequel. [PG]▼●◗

Cannonball Run II (1984) **C-108m.**

BOMB D: Hal Needham. Burt Reynolds, Dom DeLuise, Shirley MacLaine, Marilu Henner, Dean Martin, Sammy Davis, Jr., Susan Anton, Catherine Bach, Ricardo Montalban, Jim Nabors, Charles Nelson Reilly, Telly Savalas, Jamie Farr, Jack Elam, Frank Sinatra, Sid Caesar, and many others. Sequel to 1981 box-office hit looks like someone's bad home movies. Amateurish action comedy with tons of tacky guest-star cameos. What a waste! Final film roles for Martin and Sinatra. [PG] ▼●》

Can She Bake a Cherry Pie? (1983) C-90m. *½ D: Henry Jaglom. Karen Black, Michael Emil, Michael Margotta, Frances Fisher, Martin Harvey Friedberg. Neurotic, unpredictable Black, whose husband has just left her, takes up with Emil, who never seems to stop talking. A couple of chuckles, but all the rest is rambling, superficial. [R] ▼●

Can't Buy Me Love (1987) C-94m. **½ D: Steve Rash. Patrick Dempsey, Amanda Peterson, Courtney Gains, Tina Caspary, Seth Green, Sharon Farrell. Known as BOY RENTS GIRL during production, story has nerdy Dempsey paying senior heartthrob Peterson a hard-earned grand to pose as his girlfriend, correctly surmising his own stock will rise. Sentimental rendering of a terrific high school comedy premise. Peterson is excellent, Dempsey just adequate. Remade as LOVE DON'T COST A THING. [PG-13] ▼●》

Canterbury Tale, A (1944-British) 124m. *** D: Michael Powell, Emeric Pressburger. Eric Portman, Sheila Sim, John Sweet, Dennis Price, Esmond Knight, Charles Hawtrey, Hay Petrie. Curious and disarming film from the Powell-Pressburger writing-and-directing team draws on British eccentricities—and provincial flavor—to flesh out its simple story about three people whose lives cross in a small English village during the war. There's only the slightest tangent with the Chaucer work from which it draws its title. American version with added footage of Kim Hunter runs 95m. and doesn't retain the charm of the original. ▼》

Canterbury Tales, The (1971-Italian-French) C-121m. BOMB D: Pier Paolo Pasolini. Laura Betti, Ninetto Davoli, Pier Paolo Pasolini, Hugh Griffith, Josephine Chaplin, Michael Balfour, Jenny Runacre. Travelers recount a number of Chaucer stories—which, unfortunately, are enacted for the viewer. Tiresome, offensive, graphically sadistic, with Pasolini appearing as Chaucer. Italian-English cast; the second of the director's medieval trilogy. Also shown in 109m. English-language version. ▼●》

Canterville Ghost, The (1944) 96m. *** D: Jules Dassin. Charles Laughton, Robert Young, Margaret O'Brien, William Gargan, Reginald Owen, "Rags" Ragland, Una O'Connor, Mike Mazurki, Peter Lawford.

Enjoyable fantasy, loosely adapted from Oscar Wilde's short story, of 17th-century ghost Laughton, spellbound until descendant, WW2 soldier Young, helps him perform heroic deed. Remade for TV in 1986 (with John Gielgud) and 1996 (with Patrick Stewart). ▼●》

Can't Hardly Wait (1998) C-98m. ** D: Deborah Kaplan, Harry Elfont. Jennifer Love Hewitt, Ethan Embry, Charlie Korsmo, Lauren Ambrose, Peter Facinelli, Seth Green, Michelle Brookhurst. On high school graduation night, Embry tries to work up the nerve to express his long-pent-up feelings for Hewitt—who's just broken up with the class jock. Set in and around a wild house party, this cheerful but predictable teen comedy comes off as a poor relation to AMERICAN GRAFFITI aimed at teens of the 1990s. Jenna Elfman, Melissa Joan Hart, Breckin Meyer, and Jerry O'Connell appear unbilled. [PG-13] ▼●》

Can't Help Singing (1944) C-89m. **½ D: Frank Ryan. Deanna Durbin, Robert Paige, Akim Tamiroff, Ray Collins, Thomas Gomez. Durbin goes West to find her roaming lover; despite good cast and Jerome Kern songs, it's nothing much. ▼●》

Can't Stop the Music (1980) C-118m. ** D: Nancy Walker. The Village People, Valerie Perrine, Bruce Jenner, Steve Guttenberg, Paul Sand, Tammy Grimes, June Havoc, Barbara Rush, Jack Weston, Leigh Taylor-Young. One or two catchy production numbers aren't enough to salvage otherwise stiff comedy about the music-publishing biz, though some will feel they *have* to see what V. People and Jenner are doing in same film. Gay subtext abounds, despite eye-boggling profile shots of Perrine. Panavision. [PG] ▼》

Canyon Passage (1946) C-92m. *** D: Jacques Tourneur. Dana Andrews, Brian Donlevy, Susan Hayward, Ward Bond, Andy Devine, Lloyd Bridges. Plotty, colorful Western mixing action, beautiful scenery, heated love relationships, and Hoagy Carmichael singing "Ole Buttermilk Sky." Well made and entertaining. ▼》

Cape Fear (1962) 105m. *** D: J. Lee Thompson. Gregory Peck, Robert Mitchum, Polly Bergen, Martin Balsam, Lori Martin, Jack Kruschen, Telly Savalas, Barrie Chase, Edward Platt. Mitchum is memorably (and believably) creepy as a wily Southern excon who blames lawyer Peck for his incarceration and plots an insidious revenge on his family. Dated only in its lack of explicitness, but still daring for its time. Based on John D. MacDonald's novel *The Executioners*. Musical score by Bernard Herrmann is reminiscent of his best work with Hitchcock. Remade in 1991. ▼●》

Cape Fear (1991) C-128m. **½ D: Martin Scorsese. Robert De Niro, Nick Nolte, Jessica Lange, Juliette Lewis, Joe Don Baker,

Robert Mitchum, Gregory Peck, Martin Balsam, Illeana Douglas, Fred Dalton Thompson. Released from prison after 14 years, a self-educated wacko vows to make a living hell for the lawyer who sent him up. Remake of the 1962 thriller fleshes out its characters and adds fascinating psychological layers—but turns a gripping, realistic story into an overblown, unbelievable horror film: CAPE FEAR for the Freddy Krueger generation. Scorsese's brilliant command of the medium is squandered on severely unpleasant material (with an A-list of collaborators, including cinematographer Freddie Francis and composer Elmer Bernstein, adapting Bernard Herrmann's original score). Major asset: exceptionally good performances (including amusingly cast cameos by Mitchum, Peck, and Balsam, who starred in the '62 movie). Panavision. [R]▼●❙

Caper of the Golden Bulls, The (1967) **C-104m.** BOMB D: Russell Rouse. Stephen Boyd, Yvette Mimieux, Giovanna Ralli, Walter Slezak, Vito Scotti. Lots of bull but not much gold in this unendurable "thriller" about bank heist in Pamplona.▼

Cape Town Affair, The (1967) **C-103m.** ** D: Robert D. Webb. Claire Trevor, James Brolin, Jacqueline Bisset, Bob Courtney, Jon Whiteley, Gordon Milholland. Pedestrian remake of PICKUP ON SOUTH STREET, made in South Africa. Interest here is seeing Bisset and Brolin at the beginnings of their careers and Trevor making something different of the old Thelma Ritter role. Story deals with a Communist spy ring in Cape Town and an elusive envelope containing top secret microfilm.▼❙

Capitaine Conan (1996-French) **C-132m.** *** D: Bertrand Tavernier. Philippe Torreton, Samuel Le Bihan, Bernard Le Coq, Catherine Rich, François Berleand, Pierre Val. Powerful indictment of militarism and false heroism, centering on reckless title character, who leads French troops in a secret war in the Balkans following the end of WW1, but pays a heavy price for his valor. Torreton won a French César award for his forceful performance, as did Tavernier for his virtuoso direction. Super 35.▼❙

Capitalism: A Love Story (2009) **C-127m.** *** D: Michael Moore. Moore tackles America's economic collapse, the chicanery of the banking industry, and the misdeeds of Wall Street in his usual colorful fashion. Even people who dislike the activist-filmmaker's point of view may find this wide-ranging survey to be persuasive. It opens with an old classroom film about ancient Rome that depicts frighteningly apt similarities to the way we live now . . . and ends with a poignant newsreel featuring President Franklin D. Roosevelt talking about his (unrealized) plan for the future security of Americans. [R]❙

Capone (1975) **C-101m.** BOMB D: Steve Carver. Ben Gazzara, Susan Blakely, Harry Guardino, John Cassavetes, Sylvester Stallone, Frank Campanella. Gazzara has cotton in his jowls and a cigar in his mouth, making most of the dialogue in this gangster saga incomprehensible—but that's OK, you've heard it all before. One big shootout is stock footage from THE ST. VALENTINE'S DAY MASSACRE. [R]

Capote (2005) **C-115m.** ***½ D: Bennett Miller. Philip Seymour Hoffman, Catherine Keener, Clifton Collins, Jr., Chris Cooper, Bruce Greenwood, Bob Balaban, Amy Ryan, Mark Pellegrino. First-rate film about author Truman Capote concentrates on his relentless (and often ruthless) efforts to research and write the seminal book *In Cold Blood*—and what it cost him. Hoffman won a Best Actor Oscar for his brilliantly nuanced performance, but entire cast is excellent, and director Miller and screenwriter Dan Futterman incisively convey the ambiguity in Capote's motives and methods. Based on Gerald Clarke's book. Miller's first fiction feature. Same story is recounted in INFAMOUS. Super 35. [R]❙

Caprice (1967) **C-98m.** BOMB D: Frank Tashlin. Doris Day, Richard Harris, Ray Walston, Jack Kruschen, Edward Mulhare, Lilia Skala, Irene Tsu, Michael J. Pollard. Terrible vehicle for Doris as industrial spy plunged into international intrigue with fellow agent Harris. Muddled, unfunny, straining to be "mod." CinemaScope.❙

Capricorn One (1978) **C-124m.** *** D: Peter Hyams. Elliott Gould, James Brolin, Hal Holbrook, Sam Waterston, Karen Black, O. J. Simpson, Telly Savalas, Brenda Vaccaro, Denise Nicholas, David Huddleston, Robert Walden, David Doyle. Whirlwind contemporary adventure plays like a condensed Republic serial. First manned flight to Mars turns out to be a hoax, and when capsule supposedly burns up in re-entry, the astronauts suddenly realize they're expendable. Lots of great chases punctuated by Hyams' witty dialogue; not always plausible, but who cares? Panavision. [PG]▼❙

Captain Abu Raed (2008-U.S.-Jordanian) **C-103m.** *** D: Amin Matalqa. Nadim Sawalha, Rana Sultan, Hussein Al-Sous, Udey Al-Qiddissi, Ghandi Saber, Dina Ra'ad-Yaghnám. Poignant tale of a kindly, lonely widower (Sawalha, in a towering performance) who toils as an airport janitor. The children in his neighborhood—with one notable exception—come to believe he's a pilot and has lived a life filled with adventure. Also key to the story is his friendship with Sultan, an independent-minded woman who really is a pilot and whose father is pressuring her to marry. Heartfelt sleeper from writer-director Matalqa is an endearing story of childhood dreams fulfilled and unfulfilled.❙

Captain America (1990) C-103m. *½ D: Albert Pyun. Matt Salinger, Ronny Cox, Ned Beatty, Darren McGavin, Scott Paulin, Michael Nouri, Kim Gillingham, Melinda Dillon, Billy Mumy. Dismayingly awful adaptation of the great Joe Simon–Jack Kirby comic book. Cap (Salinger) barely gets in one failed WW2 adventure pitted against Red Skull (Paulin), before being frozen in Alaska ice. Thawed out 50 years later, he spends too long in civvies before facing the Skull again. Clumsy, synthetic direction, actionless plot, boring opponents overwhelm the sincerity of Salinger's performance. Never released theatrically in the U.S. ▼❚

Captain Apache (1971) C-94m. ** D: Alexander Singer. Lee Van Cleef, Carroll Baker, Stuart Whitman, Percy Herbert. Violence in Old West laid on with a trowel. Filled with stereotypes. Franscope. [PG] ▼❚

Captain Blood (1935) 119m. ***½ D: Michael Curtiz. Errol Flynn, Olivia de Havilland, Lionel Atwill, Basil Rathbone, Ross Alexander, Guy Kibbee, Henry Stephenson, Robert Barrat, Donald Meek, J. Carrol Naish. Flynn's first swashbuckler, based on Rafael Sabatini's novel, scores a broadside. He plays Irish physician Peter Blood who is forced to become a pirate, teaming for short spell with French cutthroat Rathbone, but paying more attention to proper young lady de Havilland. Vivid combination of exciting sea battles, fencing duels, and tempestuous romance provides Flynn with a literally star-making vehicle. First original film score for Erich Wolfgang Korngold. Beware of 99m. reissue version. Also shown in computer-colored version. ▼●❚

Captain Corelli's Mandolin (2001-U.S.-British) C-127m. **½ D: John Madden. Nicolas Cage, Penélope Cruz, John Hurt, Christian Bale, David Morrissey, Irene Papas, Piero Maggio, Patrick Malahide. A peaceful, tradition-bound Greek island is invaded by Italian troops during WW2, but they are no more warlike than the residents. Madden beautifully captures a sense of time and place, but the pace lags, the characterizations are inconsistent, and the love story between fun-loving Italian Cage and serious-minded Cruz (Spanish accent intact) is never as gripping as it's meant to be. Based on the novel by Louis de Bernieres. Panavision. [R] ▼❚

Captain From Castile (1947) C-140m. *** D: Henry King. Tyrone Power, Jean Peters, Cesar Romero, Lee J. Cobb, John Sutton, Antonio Moreno, Thomas Gomez, Alan Mowbray, Barbara Lawrence, George Zucco, Roy Roberts, Marc Lawrence, Reed Hadley, Jay Silverheels. Power, driven to avenge the cruel treatment of his family by Spanish Inquisitor (Sutton), eventually serves with Cortez (Romero) during his conquest of Mexico. Color and romance; magnificent location photography by Charles Clarke and Arthur E. Arling; Alfred Newman's majestic score ranks with Hollywood's very best. Peters' film debut. ▼●❚

Captain Horatio Hornblower (1951-British) C-117m. *** D: Raoul Walsh. Gregory Peck, Virginia Mayo, Robert Beatty, Denis O'Dea, Christopher Lee, Stanley Baker, James Robertson Justice. Exciting, well-produced sea epic based on C. S. Forester's British naval hero of the Napoleonic wars. ▼●❚

Captain January (1936) 75m. **½ D: David Butler. Shirley Temple, Guy Kibbee, Slim Summerville, Buddy Ebsen, June Lang, Sara Haden. Straightforward, sentimental tale of orphaned Shirley, and the new truant officer who tries to separate her from her adoptive father, lighthouse keeper Kibbee. Short and sweet. Shirley and Ebsen sing and dance "At the Codfish Ball." Also shown in computer-colored version. ▼❚

Captain Kronos: Vampire Hunter (1974-British) C-91m. *** D: Brian Clemens. Horst Janson, John Carson, Caroline Munro, Shane Briant, John Cater, Lois Diane, Ian Hendry. Unique blend of horror and swashbuckler genres follows sword-wielding stranger as he stalks new breed of vampire across European countryside. Artsy, exciting, almost intoxicatingly atmospheric chiller has developed considerable following; one of the best (and least typical) Hammer productions. Also released as KRONOS. [R] ▼❚

Captain Lightfoot (1955) C-91m. *** D: Douglas Sirk. Rock Hudson, Barbara Rush, Jeff Morrow, Finlay Currie, Kathleen Ryan. Fine, flavorful costume adventure about 19th-century Irish rebellion and one of its dashing heroes. Beautifully filmed on location in Ireland in CinemaScope. ❚

Captain Nemo and the Underwater City (1970) C-105m. **½ D: James Hill. Robert Ryan, Chuck Connors, Nanette Newman, Luciana Paluzzi. Average undersea fantasy centered on Captain Nemo who lives in an underwater fortress. Panavision. [G] ❚

Captain Newman, M.D. (1963) C-126m. *** D: David Miller. Gregory Peck, Angie Dickinson, Tony Curtis, Eddie Albert, Jane Withers, Bobby Darin, Larry Storch, Bethel Leslie, Robert Duvall. Provocative, well-acted comedy-drama about dedicated Army psychiatrist Peck, battling bureaucracy and the macho military mentality on a stateside air base during WW2. Darin is particularly good as a troubled, ill-fated corporal. Based on Leo Rosten's best-selling novel. ▼❚

Captain Ron (1992) C-100m. BOMB D: Thom Eberhardt. Kurt Russell, Martin Short, Mary Kay Place, Benjamin Salisbury, Meadow Sisto, Emmanuel Logrono,

Jorge Luis Ramos, J. A. Preston, Tanya Soler, John Scott Clough. Yuppies Get Away From It All by taking an inherited sailboat into the Caribbean, with eye-patched Russell (the very poor man's Robert Newton) at the helm. Dreadful time-waster establishes its comic credentials by giving Russell the funny role and Short the straight one; pirates and multiple falls into the drink are a given. Paul Anka (you tell *us* why) plays a boat salesman. [PG-13]▼●◗

Captains Courageous (1937) **116m.** **** D: Victor Fleming. Freddie Bartholomew, Spencer Tracy, Lionel Barrymore, Melvyn Douglas, Charley Grapewin, John Carradine, Mickey Rooney, Walter Kingsford. Spoiled rich-boy Bartholomew falls off cruise ship, rescued by Portuguese fisherman Tracy (who won Oscar for role). Boy learns to love seafaring on crusty Barrymore's fishing vessel. Enthusiastic cast in this splendid production of Kipling's story. Scripted by John Lee Mahin, Marc Connelly, and Dale Van Every. Remade as a TV movie in 1977 (with Karl Malden and Ricardo Montalban) and 1996 (with Robert Urich). Also shown in computer-colored version.▼●◗

Captains of the Clouds (1942) **C-113m.** *** D: Michael Curtiz. James Cagney, Dennis Morgan, Brenda Marshall, Alan Hale, George Tobias, Reginald Gardiner. Atmospheric wartime drama charting the shenanigans of cocky bush pilot Cagney, who joins the Canadian air force but refuses to follow regulations.▼●◗

Captain's Paradise, The (1953-British) **77m.** *** D: Anthony Kimmins. Alec Guinness, Yvonne De Carlo, Celia Johnson, Bill Fraser. Guinness has field day as carefree skipper who shuttles back and forth between wives in opposite ports. De Carlo and Johnson make a good contrast as the two women. Original British running time: 86m. Later a Broadway musical, *Oh, Captain!*▼●◗

Captive City, The (1952) **90m.** *** D: Robert Wise. John Forsythe, Joan Camden, Harold J. Kennedy, Marjorie Crosland, Victor Sutherland, Ray Teal, Martin Milner. Small-city newspaper editor Forsythe gradually learns that the Mafia has taken over bookie operations formerly run by corrupt local businessmen. Based-on-fact drama is earnest and intelligent, with fine noir-style photography by Lee Garmes. Sen. Estes Kefauver provides an afterword.◗

Captive Heart, The (1946-British) **108m.** ***½ D: Basil Dearden. Michael Redgrave, Mervyn Johns, Basil Radford, Jack Warner, Jimmy Hanley, Gordon Jackson, Ralph Michael, Rachel Kempson. Compelling examination of British POWs during WW2 and their German captors, with controlled, flawless performance by Redgrave and excellent supporting cast. Patrick Kirwan's story was scripted by Angus MacPhail and

Guy Morgan. Original British running time: 98m.▼◗

Captive Hearts (1987) **C-97m.** ** D: Paul Almond. Noriyuki (Pat) Morita, Chris Makepeace, Mari Sato, Michael Sarrazin, Seth Sakai. American soldier shot down and taken prisoner in Japan during WW2 falls in love with a Japanese woman. If that sounds familiar, or simplistic, wait till you see the film! Easy to see why this barely made it to theaters. [PG]▼

Captives (1995-U.S.-British) **C-99m.** **½ D: Angela Pope. Tim Roth, Julia Ormond, Colin Salmon, Keith Allen, Siobhan Redmond, Peter Capaldi. Unusual drama set in a contemporary London prison where a lonely female dentist ends up in a deadly game of blackmail when she falls for one of her convict patients. Some melodramatic silliness aside (including scenes of dental foreplay), this is a showcase for two highly skilled actors, Roth and Ormond. [R]▼●◗

Captivity (2007-U.S.-Russian) **C-85m.** BOMB D: Roland Joffé. Elisha Cuthbert, Daniel Gillies, Pruitt Taylor Vince, Michael Harney, Laz Alonso, Maggie Damon, Chrysta Olson. A supermodel is stalked, drugged, kidnapped, and imprisoned by a mysterious, unseen assailant. Vulgar, repulsive thriller earned notoriety for its lurid advertising campaign. It's a long way from Joffé's THE KILLING FIELDS. Also available in unrated version. Super 35. [R]◗

Capture, The (1950) **91m.** **½ D: John Sturges. Lew Ayres, Teresa Wright, Victor Jory, Jacqueline White, Jimmy Hunt, Barry Kelley, Duncan Renaldo. Oil field supervisor Ayres begins to ponder whether the payroll robber he shot was really an innocent man. Straightforward, well acted, but slow at times.▼◗

Capturing the Friedmans (2003) **C-107m.** ***½ D: Andrew Jarecki. Fascinating and deeply disturbing documentary about a notorious 1980s child molestation case that rocks a seemingly normal, happy, middle-class family on Long Island, N.Y. Thought–provoking examination of the relativity of truth seen through the prism of a domestic breakdown and the surrounding media frenzy. Anchored by amazing home-movie footage the Friedmans shot themselves, almost obsessively, throughout the years, which charts the family's disintegration. What to make of all this is (wisely) left to the viewer.▼◗

Car, The (1977) **C-95m.** *½ D: Elliot Silverstein. James Brolin, Kathleen Lloyd, John Marley, Ronny Cox, R.G. Armstrong, John Rubinstein. Hokey thriller about a killer car demonically running down most of the cast. *Twilight Zone* once did a tidier, quite similar job in one third the time. Panavision. [PG]▼●◗

Caramel (2007-Lebanese-French) **C-95m.** **½ D: Nadine Labaki. Nadine Labaki, Yasmine Al Masri, Joanna Moukarzel, Gisèle Aouad, Adel Karam, Aziza Semaan, Siham Haddad. Lightly likable comedy-drama, reminiscent of such American fare as STEEL MAGNOLIAS and BEAUTY SHOP, about life, love, and leg waxing in and around a Lebanese beauty salon. Director Labaki is first among equals in fine ensemble cast as Layale, owner of the Si Belle beauty shop in downtown Beirut, who's so caught up in a humiliating affair with an inattentive married man that she's slow to note the handsome traffic cop who pines for her. Interesting look at lives of women in a society where men make most of the decisions and almost all of the rules. [PG]▶

Carandiru (2003-Brazilian) **C-148m.** **½ D: Hector Babenco. Luiz Carlos Vasconcelos, Milhem Cortaz, Milton Gonçalves, Ivan de Almeida, Ailton Graça, Maria Luisa Mendonça, Rodrigo Santoro. Master filmmaker Babenco came back from serious illness to direct this story of real-life doctor Dráuzio Varella, who took his cause for AIDS prevention inside the horrifying Brazilian state penitentiary Carandiru, becoming an eyewitness to degrading conditions that led to a deadly riot in 1992. Surprisingly conventional prison picture with standard-issue characters is rescued by the true nature of the tale and Babenco's smarts behind the camera. Based on Varella's book *Carandiru Station.* [R]▼▶

Caravans (1978-U.S.-Iranian) **C-123m.** **½ D: James Fargo. Anthony Quinn, Jennifer O'Neill, Michael Sarrazin, Christopher Lee, Joseph Cotten, Barry Sullivan. Expensive-looking version of James Michener's contemporary desert epic about a search through the Middle East for the daughter (O'Neill) of a U.S. senator. Won't fool those who recognize it as just another updated version of THE SEARCHERS. Panavision. [PG]▶

Carbine Williams (1952) **91m.** *** D: Richard Thorpe. James Stewart, Jean Hagen, Wendell Corey, Paul Stewart, James Arness. Sturdy history of the inventor of famed rifle, his problems with the law, and his simple family life. Stewart is most convincing in title role. Also shown in computer-colored version.▶

Carbon Copy (1981) **C-92m.** ** D: Michael Schultz. George Segal, Susan Saint James, Denzel Washington, Jack Warden, Paul Winfield, Dick Martin, Tom Poston. Segal has hidden his identity as a Jew and become a successful corporate executive—until the arrival of his illegitimate 17-year-old son (Washington, in film debut), who is black. Silly, uneven, but not uninteresting blend of comedy and social drama. Written by Stanley Shapiro. Panavision. [PG]▼▶

Card, The SEE: **Promoter, The**

Cardinal, The (1963) **C-175m.** **½ D: Otto Preminger. Tom Tryon, John Huston, Romy Schneider, Carol Lynley, Jill Haworth, Raf Vallone, Joseph Meinrad, Burgess Meredith, Ossie Davis, John Saxon, Robert Morse, Dorothy Gish, Tullio Carminati, Maggie McNamara, Bill Hayes, Cecil Kellaway, Murray Hamilton, Patrick O'Neal, Chill Wills, Arthur Hunnicutt. Long, long story of an Irish-American's rise from priesthood to the College of Cardinals. Has some outstanding vignettes by old pros like Meredith, but emerges as an uneven, occasionally worthwhile film. Panavision. ▼▶

Care Bears Adventure in Wonderland!, The (1987-Canadian) **C-75m.** ** D: Raymond Jafelice. Voices of Bob Dermer, Eva Almos, Dan Hennessy, Jim Henshaw, Colin Fox. The Care Bears follow Alice through the looking glass in this typically bland kiddie outing, with music by John Sebastian. [G]▼▶

Care Bears Movie, The (1985-Canadian) **C-75m.** ** D: Arna Selznick. Voices of Mickey Rooney, Georgia Engel. Songs by Carole King, John Sebastian. Animated feature based on heavily merchandised characters is strictly for toddlers, tough sledding for anyone older. Produced by Canadian Nelvana animation studio. Followed by two sequels and a TV series. [G]▼▶

Care Bears Movie II, A New Generation, The (1986-Canadian-U.S.) **C-77m.** BOMB D: Dale Schott. Voices of Maxine Miller, Pam Hyatt, Hadley Kay. Your kids deserve better entertainment than this treacly stuff about the Kingdom of Caring. Prefab animation from the era of toy merchandising tie-ins. [G]▼▶

Career (1959) **105m.** *** D: Joseph Anthony. Dean Martin, Anthony Franciosa, Shirley MacLaine, Carolyn Jones, Joan Blackman, Robert Middleton, Donna Douglas. Occasionally shrill, generally forceful presentation of an actor's (Franciosa's) tribulations in seeking Broadway fame; Jones is excellent as lonely talent agent.▼▶

Career Girls (1997-British) **C-87m.** ***½ D: Mike Leigh. Katrin Cartlidge, Lynda Steadman, Kate Byers, Mark Benton, Joe Tucker, Andy Serkis. Another satisfying (and unpredictable) slice of life from writer-director Leigh, about two former roommates reunited after six years. Flashbacks reveal how much they've changed and matured from their uncertain college years, when Cartlidge was a mass of tics and Steadman was, in her friend's words, "a walking open wound." Remarkable performances from both actresses. Music by Tony Remy and Marianne Jean-Baptiste (costar of Leigh's previous film, SECRETS & LIES). [R]▼▶

Career Opportunities (1991) **C-84m.** *½ D: Bryan Gordon. Frank Whaley, Jennifer Connelly, Dermot Mulroney, Kieran Mulroney, John M. Jackson, Jenny O'Hara, Noble Willingham, Barry Corbin, Denise Galik, William Forsythe. Otherwise unemployable teen gets the night watchman job at an all-purpose department store; his first night is an idyllic round-the-clocker with a girl who's hiding out inside, and who just happens to be the town's no. 1 rich dish. Typical ode to arrested development from writer-producer John Hughes, a 10m. idea stretched into a feature. Tolerable only for John Candy's unbilled cameo, and as a showcase for gorgeous Connelly. Panavision. [PG-13] ▼●)

Carefree (1938) **83m.** *** D: Mark Sandrich. Fred Astaire, Ginger Rogers, Ralph Bellamy, Luella Gear, Jack Carson, Franklin Pangborn, Hattie McDaniel. Madcap Rogers is sent to psychiatrist Astaire, and romance naturally blossoms; Fred and Ginger's most comic outing, wacky and offbeat, with good Irving Berlin score including "Change Partners," "I Used to Be Color Blind." ▼●)

Careful, He Might Hear You (1983-Australian) **C-116m.** ***½ D: Carl Schultz. Wendy Hughes, Robyn Nevin, Nicholas Gledhill, John Hargreaves, Geraldine Turner. Involving drama about Depression-era custody battle between wealthy Hughes and working-class sister Nevin for their nephew, whose mother is dead and father has abandoned him. Manages to be credible yet larger-than-life at the same time, with wonderful shadings and observations. Makes exceptional use of widescreen. Michael Jenkins scripted, from a novel by Sumner Locke Elliott. Panavision. [PG] ▼)

Caretaker, The SEE: **Guest, The**

Caretakers, The (1963) **97m.** *** D: Hall Bartlett. Robert Stack, Joan Crawford, Polly Bergen, Susan Oliver, Janis Paige, Constance Ford, Barbara Barrie, Herbert Marshall. At times incisive view of a West Coast mental hospital, marred by flimsy script and poor editing. Good characterizations by Crawford and Ford as nurses, Bergen and Paige as patients. ▼)

Carey Treatment, The (1972) **C-101m.** *** D: Blake Edwards. James Coburn, Jennifer O'Neill, Pat Hingle, Skye Aubrey, Elizabeth Allen, Alex Dreier. Good solid whodunit set in hospital, where doctor Coburn is determined to clear colleague of murder charge. O'Neill provides love interest in complicated but satisfying mystery, shot in Boston. Based on the novel *A Case of Need* by Michael Crichton. Panavision. [PG]

Car 54, Where Are You? (1994) **C-89m.** *½ D: Bill Fishman. David Johansen, John C. McGinley, Al Lewis, Fran Drescher, Nipsey Russell, Rosie O'Donnell, Daniel Baldwin, Jeremy Piven, Penn & Teller, Tone Loc. This retread of the hilarious 1960s TV show about N.Y.C. cops with a hefty Keystone quotient is a woefully embarrassing assemblage of gags that would bring up the rear in POLICE ACADEMY. O'Donnell (her screen debut), Drescher, and Piven acquit themselves well, under the circumstances. Despite presence of Al Lewis—reprising his Schnauzer role from

the original Nat Hiken series—this turkey sat on the shelf after completion in 1991. [PG-13] ▼●)

Carla's Song (1996-British-Spanish) **C-125m.** * D: Ken Loach. Robert Carlyle, Oyanka Cabezas, Scott Glenn, Salvador Espinoza, Louise Goodall. Unusual political drama/love story set in 1987 with Glasgow bus driver Carlyle becoming involved with beautiful but deeply troubled Nicaraguan refugee Cabezas. It's difficult to navigate the Scottish accents at first, but the final part of the story, set in the Nicaraguan war zone, is poignant and heartbreaking. ▼●)

Carlito's Way (1993) **C-144m.** *** D: Brian De Palma. Al Pacino, Sean Penn, Penelope Ann Miller, Luis Guzman, John Leguizamo, Ingrid Rogers, James Rebhorn, Joseph Siravo, Viggo Mortensen, Richard Foronjy, Jorge Porcel, Adrian Pasdar. Street-wise Puerto Rican Pacino winds up a five-year jail term and tries to go straight, but loyalty to his sleazy lawyer (Penn), and his inability to accept the fact that "the street" has changed, seal his doom. Flawed but still compelling; based on two Edwin Torres novels about a man with an outmoded code of honor. Pacino is arresting as always; so is an almost unrecognizable Penn. Director Paul Mazursky has a terrific cameo as a judge at the beginning of the story. Followed by a direct-to-video "prequel" in 2005. Panavision. [R] ▼●)

Carlos (2010-French-German) **C-340m.** ***½ D: Olivier Assayas. Édgar Ramírez, Alexander Scheer, Nora von Waldstätten, Christoph Bach, Ahmad Kaabour, Fadi Abi Samra, Rodney El-Haddad, Julia Hummer. Riveting three-part film about real-life Venezuelan terrorist Ilich Ramírez Sánchez, who made his reputation in the early 1970s working for the Popular Front for the Liberation of Palestine. As he helps stage (or, in some cases, upstage) many bloody, headline-making incidents around the world, for various revolutionary causes, he becomes both famous and infamous. Ultimately his integrity is corrupted, as political upheavals make him less useful and desirable. Ramírez is superb as the contradictory, ever-changing idealist-turned-egoist in this densely packed but consistently compelling, clear-eyed drama, which unfolds on a number of far-flung locations. Written by Assayas and Dan Franck, from an idea by Daniel Leconte. Part One is 104m., Part Two is 112m., Part Three is 124m. Alternate theatrical version runs 166m.)

Carlton-Browne of the F.O. SEE: **Man in a Cocked Hat**

Carman: The Champion (2001) **C-90m.** ** D: Lee Stanley. Carman, Michael Nouri, Patricia Manterola, Jeremy Williams, Jed Allan, Romeo Fabian, Betty Carvalho. Retired professional-fighter-turned-preacher reenters the ring to raise money to expand his and his late father's dream project: an inner-city youth ministry. Along the way to the championship match he battles local gangs, becomes a surrogate father, saves some souls, and falls in love. Feature film debut for recording artist Carman (who also coscripted). Well-intentioned, moralistic tale. [PG-13]▼●▶

Carmen (1983-Spanish) **C-102m.** *** D: Carlos Saura. Antonio Gades, Laura Del Sol, Paco de Lucia, Cristina Hoyos, Juan Antonio Jimenez, Sebastian Moreno. Choreographer prepares dance production of Bizet's opera, but falls under spell of real-life Carmen he casts in leading role. Choreographer/star Gades and sensual Del Sol are superb, though dramatic impact dissipates somewhat during second half. A must for dance buffs. [R]▼●▶

Carmen (1984-French-Italian) **C-152m.** ** D: Francesco Rosi. Julia Migenes-Johnson, Placido Domingo, Ruggero Raimondi, Faith Esham, Jean-Philippe Lafont, Gerard Garino. Disappointing filmization of the Bizet opera is overbaked and unbelievably inept. Still, opera buffs will enjoy the music—if they close their eyes. [PG]▼●▶

Carmen Jones (1954) **C-105m.** ***½ D: Otto Preminger. Dorothy Dandridge, Harry Belafonte, Pearl Bailey, Roy Glenn, Diahann Carroll, Brock Peters. Powerful melodrama adapted from Bizet's opera by Oscar Hammerstein II, with exciting music and equally exciting Dandridge as the ultimate femme fatale. Stars' singing voices are all dubbed—Dandridge's by opera star Marilyn Horne. Film debuts of Carroll and Peters. CinemaScope. ▼●▶

Carmen Miranda: Bananas Is My Business (1994-U.S.-Brazilian) **C/B&W-91m.** *** D: Helena Solberg. Savvy exploration of the Brazilian Bombshell's life and times, chronicling the sad transition from revered musical artist in her homeland to caricatured cliché in Hollywood. Filmmaker Solberg's lifelong fascination with Miranda is expressed through film clips, revealing interviews with Brazilian and American colleagues and family, and strikingly, re-creations of moments in her life using a female impersonator! ▼▶

Carnage SEE: **Twitch of the Death Nerve**

Carnal Knowledge (1971) **C-96m.** *** D: Mike Nichols. Jack Nicholson, Candice Bergen, Arthur Garfunkel, Ann-Margret, Rita Moreno, Cynthia O'Neal, Carol Kane. Thought-provoking (if depressing) look at the sexual attitudes and obsessions of two male friends, from college through middle age. Ann-Margret won acclaim for performance as Nicholson's kittenish mistress. Jules Feiffer originally wrote this as a play, then adapted it as a screenplay instead; in 1990 it was staged off-Broadway. Kane's film debut. Panavision. [R]▼●▶

Carnet de Bal SEE: **Un Carnet de Bal**

Carnival of Souls (1962) **83m.** **½ D: Herk Harvey. Candace Hilligoss, Sid-

ney Berger, Frances Feist, Herk Harvey, Stan Levitt, Art Ellison. Eerie little film of "phantom figure" pursuing Hilligoss after she has seemingly drowned. Imaginative low-budget effort. Filmed mostly in Lawrence, Kansas. Has developed a strong cult reputation in recent years. Original running time: 91m. Computer-colored version also available. Remade in 1998 and 2008 (as YELLA). ▼●▶

Carnival Story (1954) **C-95m.** ** D: Kurt Neumann. Anne Baxter, Steve Cochran, Lyle Bettger, George Nader, Jay C. Flippen. Hardened Baxter is involved with sleazy Cochran. "Nice guy" high diver Bettger takes her on as a protégée, and there are complications. When this romantic melodrama is not trashy, it's sluggish. Set in Germany (and filmed in Munich), and not unlike E.A. Dupont's classic, VARIETY. A German version was also filmed, with Eva Bartok, Bernhard Wicki, and Curt Jurgens. ▼▶

Carnosaur (1993) **C-82m.** ** D: Adam Simon. Diane Ladd, Raphael Sbarge, Jennifer Runyon, Harrison Page, Ned Bellamy, Clint Howard. Brilliant geneticist Ladd hatches man-eating dinosaurs from virus-infected chicken eggs and lets them run amok in an unsuspecting Midwestern city. Roger Corman produced this forgettable film, whose only notoriety will be its legacy as 1993's "other" dinosaur movie (which starred Ladd's daughter, Laura Dern). Followed by two sequels. [R]▼●▶

Carny (1980) **C-107m.** *** D: Robert Kaylor. Gary Busey, Jodie Foster, Robbie Robertson, Meg Foster, Bert Remsen, Kenneth McMillan, John Lehne, Elisha Cook, Craig Wasson. Striking, atmospheric film about a symbiotic pair of carnival hustlers and the teenage runaway who joins them on the road. Candid, intimate (and somewhat voyeuristic) look at seamy midway life, hurt by unsatisfying and abrupt conclusion. Rock star Robertson also produced and cowrote the film. Wonderful score by Alex North. [R]▼●▶

Caro Diario (1994-Italian-French) **C-100m.** *** D: Nanni Moretti. Nanni Moretti, Renato Carpentieri, Antonio Neiwiller, Carlo Mazzacurati, Claudia Della Seta, Jennifer Beals, Alexandre Rockwell. Witty, thoughtful, three-part feature from Moretti, one of the most acclaimed contemporary Italian film director–comedians. He appears in each as himself. First he romps around Rome on a Vespa. Next he goes island-hopping in southern Italy, where he wryly examines Europeans' obsession with American pop culture. Lastly, and most soberly, he recounts his own cancer treatment.▼●▶

Carolina (2005-U.S.-Dutch) **C-98m.** ** D: Marleen Gorris. Julia Stiles, Shirley MacLaine, Alessandro Nivola, Mika Boorem, Azura Skye, Randy Quaid, Jennifer Coolidge,

Alan Thicke, Barbara Eden. Good cast does its best with a pedestrian (and predictable) script about a young woman who keeps looking for Mr. Right even though her best friend—and next-door neighbor—is the perfect man for her. Did we mention that she was raised by a wacky, eccentric grandmother? Disappointing Hollywood debut for Dutch filmmaker Gorris (ANTONIA'S LINE). Opened in Europe in 2003; released direct to video in the U.S. [PG-13] ▶

Carousel (1956) **C-128m.** ***½ D: Henry King. Gordon MacRae, Shirley Jones, Cameron Mitchell, Barbara Ruick, Claramae Turner, Robert Rounseville, Gene Lockhart. Excellent filmization of Rodgers & Hammerstein's memorable adaptation of Ferenc Molnár's *Liliom*, with MacRae as rowdy carousel barker Billy Bigelow, who tries to change for the better when he falls in love with Jones. Excitement of wide-screen location filming will be minimized on TV screen, but moving characters, timeless songs remain. Script by Phoebe and Henry Ephron. Filmed before as LILIOM in 1930 and 1934. CinemaScope 55.▼●▶

Carpetbaggers, The (1964) **C-150m.** **½ D: Edward Dmytryk. George Peppard, Carroll Baker, Alan Ladd, Bob Cummings, Martha Hyer, Elizabeth Ashley, Lew Ayres, Martin Balsam, Ralph Taeger, Archie Moore, Leif Erickson, Tom Tully, Audrey Totter. Blowsy claptrap based on Harold Robbins novel of millionaire plane manufacturer (Peppard) dabbling in movies and lovemaking à la Howard Hughes. Set in 1920s–30s; sexploitational values are tame. Ladd's last film; followed by prequel, NEVADA SMITH. Panavision.▼●▶

Carpool (1996) **C-90m.** **½ D: Arthur Hiller. Tom Arnold, David Paymer, Rhea Perlman, Rachael Leigh Cook, Rod Steiger, Kim Coates, Micah Gardener, Mikey Kovar, Colleen Rennison, Jordan Warkov. A desperate down-on-his-luck carnival owner (Arnold) botches his first holdup attempt and takes a harried carpool dad (Paymer) and his young passengers hostage. Some laughs in this likable but uneven comedy. Perlman is wasted. [PG]▼●▶

Carrie (1952) **118m.** **½ D: William Wyler. Jennifer Jones, Laurence Olivier, Miriam Hopkins, Eddie Albert, Mary Murphy, William Reynolds. Jones passively plays the title role in this uneven turn-of-the-century soaper of poor farm girl who comes to Chicago, eventually links up with unhappily married restaurant manager Olivier (who is excellent). David Raksin's score is a plus. Based on Theodore Dreiser's *Sister Carrie*. DVD includes restored "flop house" scene, which runs almost 3m.▼●▶

Carrie (1976) **C-97m.** **½ D: Brian De Palma. Sissy Spacek, Piper Laurie, William Katt, John Travolta, Amy Irving, Nancy Allen, Betty Buckley, P.J. Soles, Priscilla Pointer. Evocative story of high school misfit degenerates into cheap, gory melodrama when Spacek unleashes telekinetic powers in revenge against those who have mocked her. De Palma borrows much from Hitchcock, but has little of The Master's wit or subtlety. Screenplay by Lawrence D. Cohen, from Stephen King's novel. Debut film for Irving, Buckley and Soles. Later a stage musical. Remade for TV in 2002. Followed by THE RAGE: CARRIE 2. [R]▼●▶

Carried Away (1996) **C-107m.** **½ D: Bruno Barreto. Dennis Hopper, Amy Irving, Amy Locane, Julie Harris, Gary Busey, Hal Holbrook, Priscilla Pointer. Hopper gives a thoughtful performance in an unusual role: a small-town Midwestern farmer/teacher who keeps putting off marrying his fiancée (Irving), and then is not unwillingly seduced by teen vamp Locane. Abundant nudity may grab attention. Based on a novel by Jim Harrison. Barreto is Irving's husband, and Pointer is her mother. [R]▼●▶

Carriers (2009) **C-85m.** ** D: Àlex Pastor, David Pastor. Lou Taylor Pucci, Chris Pine, Piper Perabo, Emily VanCamp, Chris(topher) Meloni, Mark Moses, Kiernan Shipka. A quartet of young people struggle for survival in a postapocalyptic world inhabited by "carriers" who are infected with a deadly virus. Well-intentioned horror chiller is done in by overbaked dramatics, superficially profound dialogue, and a fatal air of predictability. Pine's character is one-dimensional and obnoxious. Main asset: Benoît Debie's eye-opening cinematography. Super 35. [PG-13] ▶

Carrington (1995-British-French) **C-122m.** *** D: Christopher Hampton. Emma Thompson, Jonathan Pryce, Steven Waddington, Rufus Sewell, Samuel West, Penelope Wilton, Janet McTeer, Peter Blythe, Jeremy Northam. Gifted English painter Dora Carrington is afraid of her own sexuality, until she meets eccentric (and homosexual) writer Lytton Strachey and experiences love for the first time. What's more, he feels the same way . . . except they're never able to resolve their hesitancy about a full commitment. Compelling character study is slowly paced and perhaps redundant at times, but made fascinating by the leads' superb portrayals. Playwright/screenwriter Hampton's directing debut. [R]▼●▶

Carrington, V. C. SEE: **Court Martial**

Carry On Camping (1969-British) **C-89m.** ** D: Gerald Thomas. Sidney James, Kenneth Williams, Joan Sims, Barbara Windsor, Bernard Bresslaw, Terry Scott. The gang encounters hippie types at weekend campsite; usual double-entendre jokes in entry from never-ending series. [R]▼▶

Carry On Cleo (1964-British) **C-92m.** **½ D: Gerald Thomas. Amanda Barrie, Sidney James, Kenneth Williams, Joan Sims, Kenneth Connor, Charles Hawtrey. Diverting reworking of ancient history to serve as amusing satire on CLEOPATRA epic, sufficiently laced with hijinks by perennial misfits. Aka CALIGULA'S FUNNIEST HOME VIDEOS. ▼▶

Carry On Doctor (1968-British) **C-95m. **** D: Gerald Thomas. Frankie Howerd, Kenneth Williams, Jim Dale, Barbara Windsor. Madcap group takes on medical profession. As usual, interest wanes after an hour and the amount of laughter varies quite a bit. [PG] ▼▶

Carry On Henry VIII (1971-British) **C-90m. **** D: Gerald Thomas. Sidney James, Kenneth Williams, Joan Sims, Charles Hawtrey, Barbara Windsor. Lecherous king, ribald times perfect milieu for "Carry On" gang's brand of farce; for fans only. Original title: CARRY ON HENRY. [PG] ▼

Carry On Nurse (1959-British) **90m. **½** D: Gerald Thomas. Kenneth Connor, Shirley Eaton, Charles Hawtrey, Hattie Jacques, Terence Longdon, Leslie Phillips, Joan Sims, Kenneth Williams, Wilfrid Hyde-White, Joan Hickson, Jill Ireland, Michael Medwin. Occasionally funny but too often silly farce detailing the various hijinks in a hospital ward. Typical entry in the series is crammed with lowbrow humor. ▼▶

Carry On Sergeant (1958-British) **88m. **** D: Gerald Thomas. William Hartnell, Bob Monkhouse, Shirley Eaton, Eric Barker, Dora Bryan, Bill Owen, Kenneth Connor. This time around prankish misfits are the bane of Army officer's existence, who swears he'll make these recruits spiffy soldiers or bust. ▶

Carry On Spying (1964-British) **88m. **½** D: Gerald Thomas. Kenneth Williams, Barbara Windsor, Bernard Cribbins, Charles Hawtrey, Eric Barker, Victor Maddern. Acceptable James Bond spoof with daffy novice spy-catchers on the hunt for enemy agents who stole secret formula. ▶

Cars (2006) **C-116m. ***** D: John Lasseter. Voices of Paul Newman, Owen Wilson, Bonnie Hunt, Larry the Cable Guy, Cheech Marin, George Carlin, Richard Petty, Michael Keaton, Tony Shalhoub, John Ratzenberger, Michael Wallis, Paul Dooley, Jenifer Lewis, Jeremy Piven, Bob Costas. Hotshot race car gets stuck in a town out West that time (and interstate highways) forgot. He begins to see that there's more to life than hogging the spotlight and winning big-money races. Evoking America's car culture of the 1950s and '60s, this cleverly conceived and designed CG-animated film from Pixar is more wistful and less laugh-oriented than some, but still a winner. It may speak most eloquently to adults of a certain age. Followed by a sequel. Digital Widescreen. [G]▶

Cars 2 (2011) **C-113m. **** D: John Lasseter. Voices of Owen Wilson, Larry the Cable Guy, Michael Caine, Emily Mortimer, Eddie Izzard, John Turturro, Joe Mantegna, Thomas Kretschmann, Peter Jacobson, Bonnie Hunt, Franco Nero, Vanessa Redgrave, Tony Shalhoub, Jason Isaacs, Jeff Garlin, Cheech Marin, Jenifer Lewis, Paul Dooley, Edie McClurg, Richard Kind, Katherine Helmond, John Ratzenberger. Hometown race-car-made-good Lightning McQueen is goaded into participating in a series of Grand Prix races overseas by his well-meaning but obnoxious buddy Tow Mater. The tow truck is then drawn into international intrigue by two spy sports cars (voiced by Caine and Mortimer). Cluttered, confusing, overlong animated feature is actually hard to follow, though kids who simply enjoy watching cars race around (or think Mater is endearing) may be entertained. A real letdown for Pixar, a studio that usually plays to its strength in storytelling. 3-D Digital Widescreen. [G]

Cars That Ate Paris, The (1974-Australian) **C-91m. **½** D: Peter Weir. Terry Camilleri, John Meillon, Melissa Jaffa, Kevin Miles. The poor people of Paris (Paris, Australia, that is) keep the economy going by inducing traffic accidents and selling the spare parts/scrap metal. Iffy black comedy has its moments; must viewing for those who've followed Weir's directorial career step-by-step into the big leagues. Originally released in the U.S. at 74m, retitled THE CARS THAT EAT PEOPLE; full-length version finally made it here in 1984. Panavision. [PG] ▼▶

Cars That Eat People, The SEE: **Cars That Ate Paris, The**

Cartouche (1962-French-Italian) **C-115m. ***½** D: Philippe De Broca. Jean-Paul Belmondo, Claudia Cardinale, Odile Versois, Jess Hahn, Jean Rochefort, Philippe Lemaire, Marcel Dalio, Noel Roquevert. Colorful, exciting exploits of 18th-century French Robin Hood who takes over a Parisian crime syndicate. Belmondo is dashing as Cartouche and Cardinale is ravishing as Venus, his gypsy-mistress, in this rousing action-comedy. Dyaliscope. ▼▶

Car Trouble (1985-British) **C-93m. ***** D: David Green. Julie Walters, Ian Charleson, Vincenzo Ricotta, Stratford Johns, Hazel O'Connor, Dave Hill. Low-key farce about a hilariously hideous couple whose Bickerson-like marriage is put to the ultimate test when he buys his dream car, and she goes for a fateful spin. Walters and Charleson are ideal, and the film offers some genuine belly laughs. [R] ▼

Carve Her Name With Pride (1958-British) **119m. ***** D: Lewis Gilbert. Virginia McKenna, Paul Scofield, Jack Warner, Maurice Ronet, Bill Owen, Denise Grey, Billie Whitelaw, Michael Caine. McKenna, widowed during WW2, becomes a courageous British secret agent. Solid and inspiring; based on a true story. ▼▶

Car Wash (1976) **C-97m. **½** D: Michael Schultz. Richard Pryor, Franklin Ajaye,

Sully Boyar, Ivan Dixon, George Carlin, Irwin Corey, Melanie Mayron, The Pointer Sisters, Garrett Morris, Antonio Fargas, Brooke Adams. Boisterous look at L.A. car wash is light excuse for barely connected comedy set pieces, involving various and sundry characters, and pulsating soul music performed by Rose Royce. Often very funny, but no awards for good taste; written by Joel Schumacher. [PG]▼●)

Casablanca (1942) **102m.** **** D: Michael Curtiz. Humphrey Bogart, Ingrid Bergman, Paul Henreid, Claude Rains, Conrad Veidt, Peter Lorre, Sydney Greenstreet, Dooley Wilson, Marcel Dalio, S. Z. Sakall, Joy Page, Helmut Dantine, Curt Bois. Everything is right in this WW2 classic of war-torn Morocco with elusive nightclub owner Rick (Bogart) finding old flame (Bergman) and her husband, underground leader Henreid, among skeletons in his closet. Rains is marvelous as dapper police chief, and nobody sings "As Time Goes By" like Dooley Wilson. Three Oscars include Picture, Director, and Screenplay (Julius & Philip Epstein and Howard Koch). Our candidate for the best Hollywood movie of all time. Spawned short-lived TV series in the 1950s and the 1980s. Also shown in computer-colored version.▼●)

Casa de los Babys (2003) C-95m. **½ D: John Sayles. Maggie Gyllenhaal, Marcia Gay Harden, Daryl Hannah, Susan Lynch, Mary Steenburgen, Lili Taylor, Rita Moreno, Vanessa Martinez, Pedro Armendáriz. A group of American women spend time together in a South American town as they wait for their adoptions to come through. Sayles' script explores many characters and points of view, including the locals who resent the "yanquis" taking their babies away and the young women who give up their children because they have no choice. Despite a fine cast, and many good scenes, the film feels like a draft for a screenplay that still needs fleshing out. [R]▼●)

Casanova (2005) C-110m. ***½ D: Lasse Hallström. Heath Ledger, Sienna Miller, Jeremy Irons, Oliver Platt, Lena Olin, Omid Djalili, Stephen Greif, Ken Stott, Charlie Cox, Natalie Dormer, Tim McInnerny, Leigh Lawson. The amorous bed-hopping lover of 18th-century Venice meets his match in a beautiful, headstrong woman, a protofeminist who is determined to resist his advances. This is a rare bird known as a romp, and Hallström and company pull it off, maintaining a light touch from start to finish. Location filming in Venice doesn't hurt, either. Fresh, funny, sexy, and smart; everyone is good, but Miller is a standout in a showcase role. Screenplay by Jeffrey Hatcher and Kimberly Simi from a story by Simi and Michael Cristofer. Super 35. [R]▼)

Casanova & Co. (1976-Austrian-Italian-French-German) **C-88m.** *½ D: Franz

Antel. Tony Curtis, Marisa Berenson, Sylva Koscina, Hugh Griffith, Britt Ekland, Marisa Mell, Umberto Orsini, Andrea Ferreol, Victor Spinetti, Lillian Muller. Misfired slapstick romp debunks the legend with Curtis playing dual roles of Casanova and a lookalike commoner. Diverse female cast (including former *Playboy* Playmates) disrobes at will, while Tony in drag explicitly mocks his classic SOME LIKE IT HOT role. Video titles: SEX ON THE RUN, SOME LIKE IT COOL, and THE AMOROUS MIS-ADVENTURES OF CASANOVA.▼)

Casanova Brown (1944) **91m.** **½ D: Sam Wood. Gary Cooper, Teresa Wright, Frank Morgan, Anita Louise, Isobel Elsom. Cooper has divorced Wright, but now she's pregnant; entertaining little comedy with stars outshining material. Filmed in 1930 and 1939 as LITTLE ACCIDENT.▼)

Casanova's Big Night (1954) **C-86m.** *** D: Norman Z. McLeod. Bob Hope, Joan Fontaine, Audrey Dalton, Basil Rathbone, Raymond Burr. Lavish costumed fun with Bob masquerading as Casanova (Vincent Price in an unbilled cameo role) in Venice and wooing lovely Dalton.▼●)

Casanova '70 (1965-French-Italian) C-113m. **½ D: Mario Monicelli. Marcello Mastroianni, Virna Lisi, Michele Mercier, Marisa Mell, Marco Ferreri, Enrico Maria Salerno. Dashing Major Mastroianni is only interested in seducing women when there is an element of danger involved. Modest, though amusing.▼

Casbah (1948) **94m.** *** D: John Berry. Tony Martin, Yvonne De Carlo, Peter Lorre, Marta Toren, Hugo Haas, Thomas Gomez, Douglas Dick, Katherine Dunham, Herbert Rudley, Virginia Gregg. If you can accept singer Martin as slippery thief Pepe Le Moko (he's actually quite good) you'll enjoy this musical remake of ALGIERS. It's stylishly directed and designed, and features Lorre in one of his best performances as the crafty inspector determined to nail Le Moko. Fine score by Harold Arlen and Leo Robin includes "For Every Man There's a Woman" and "Hooray for Love." Look fast and you'll spot Eartha Kitt, then one of the Katherine Dunham dance troupe.▼

Case 39 (2010-Canadian-U.S.) **C-109m.** *½ D: Christian Alvart. Renée Zellweger, Jodelle Ferland, Ian McShane, Bradley Cooper, Callum Keith Rennie, Adrian Lester, Kerry O'Malley, Cynthia Stevenson. Children's social worker Zellweger takes on Case 39, a young girl whose parents tried to kill her, and eventually comes to suspect they had good reason for their attempt. Unthrilling horror movie with little suspense and no sense of location, although Zellweger and Ferland (as the child) are good. The explanation for all the mysterious activity is only barely coherent. Filmed in

2006, released overseas in 2009; the delay wasn't long enough. Hawk Scope. [R]🅳

Casey's Shadow (1978) **C-117m.** **½ D: Martin Ritt. Walter Matthau, Alexis Smith, Robert Webber, Murray Hamilton, Andrew A. Rubin, Stephan Burns, Michael Hershewe. Generally satisfactory drama about a ne'er-do-well Louisiana horse trainer (Matthau) and his three sons, as he raises a fleet but fragile quarterhorse that just may allow him his one shot at glory. Panavision. [PG]🅥🅳

Cash McCall (1959) **C-102m.** **½ D: Joseph Pevney. James Garner, Natalie Wood, Nina Foch, Dean Jagger, E.G. Marshall, Henry Jones, Otto Kruger, Roland Winters. Garner is just right as business tycoon who adopts new set of values as he romances daughter (Wood) of failing businessman Jagger. Superficial film from Cameron Hawley novel.🅥🅳

Casino (1995) **C-182m.** ** D: Martin Scorsese. Robert De Niro, Sharon Stone, Joe Pesci, James Woods, Don Rickles, Alan King, Kevin Pollak, L. Q. Jones, Dick Smothers, Frank Vincent, Melissa Prophet, John Bloom (Joe Bob Briggs). Long, tedious tale of a numbers-obsessed gambler sent to Las Vegas by the mob to run a casino in the 1970s. Problem is, neither he nor his loose-cannon pal, who follows him, nor the hustler he decides to marry has any idea how to hold on to what they've got. Disappointing reteaming of Scorsese and writer Nicholas Pileggi, who scored big with GOODFELLAS; this time, their story is overlong, repetitive, and aloof. Stone makes her mark amidst a heavyweight cast with a full-blown dramatic performance. Super 35. [R]🅥🅳

Casino Jack (2010-U.S.-Canadian) **C-108m.** **½ D: George Hickenlooper. Kevin Spacey, Barry Pepper, Kelly Preston, Jon Lovitz, Rachelle Lefevre, Maury Chaykin, Spencer Garrett, Eric Schweig, Graham Greene, Christian Campbell, Yannick Bisson. Lively if dramatically uneven film about notorious Washington, D.C., lobbyist Jack Abramoff, who lives well and rides high until he gets too greedy for his own good, resulting in a Capitol Hill scandal. The material is intrinsically interesting, but the movie tries to cover too much ground. Spacey's brash performance validates it; the role of his corrupt cohort (Pepper) is underwritten. Worth comparing to Alex Gibney's documentary film CASINO JACK AND THE UNITED STATES OF MONEY. Super 35. [R]🅳

Casino Jack and the United States of Money (2010) **C-118m.** ***½ D: Alex Gibney. Riveting documentary chronicling the rise and fall of D.C. uber-lobbyist Jack Abramoff (who also produced the 1989 Dolph Lundgren bomb RED SCORPION). Examines how he made millions ripping off casino-rich Indian tribes and through his connections with the religious right and several conservative lawmakers. The result: a congressional scandal that led to his conviction for tax evasion, fraud, and conspiracy to bribe public officials. Provocative and alarming look at the corruption of the political process and abuse of power plays like a real-life MR. SMITH GOES TO WASHINGTON, replete with clips from that film, albeit without the happy ending. [R]🅳

Casino Royale (1967-British) **C-130m.** **½ D: John Huston, Ken Hughes, Robert Parrish, Joe McGrath, Val Guest. Peter Sellers, Ursula Andress, David Niven, Orson Welles, Joanna Pettet, Woody Allen, Deborah Kerr, William Holden, Charles Boyer, John Huston, George Raft, Jean-Paul Belmondo, Jacky (Jacqueline) Bisset. Gigantic, overdone spoof of James Bond films with Niven as the aging secret agent who relinquishes his position to nephew Allen and host of others. Money, money everywhere, but film is terribly uneven—sometimes funny, often not. Good score by Burt Bacharach, including hit song "The Look of Love." Remade in 2006. Panavision. 🅥🅳

Casino Royale (2006-U.S.-British-Czech-German) **C-144m.** *** D: Martin Campbell. Daniel Craig, Eva Green, Mads Mikkelsen, Judi Dench, Jeffrey Wright, Giancarlo Giannini, Caterina Murino, Simon Abkarian, Isaach De Bankolé. The James Bond franchise goes back to its roots with this installment, which shows how the secret agent got his license to kill and pits him against a banker funding worldwide terrorist groups. A bit overextended, but also refreshingly tough-minded, with some terrific set pieces (including an adrenaline-pumping opening sequence) and a worthy love interest in Green. Best of all, Craig (in his debut as 007) makes for a lean, mean, surprisingly human Bond, so good as to rival even our memories of Sean Connery. Filmed before (as a spoof) in 1967. Followed by QUANTUM OF SOLACE. Super 35. [PG-13]🅳

Casper (1995) **C-100m.** BOMB D: Brad Silberling. Christina Ricci, Bill Pullman, Cathy Moriarty, Eric Idle, Amy Brenneman, Ben Stein, Don Novello, voices of Malachi Pearson, Joe Nipote, Joe Alaskey, Brad Garrett. High-tech Hollywood "product" takes the vintage cartoon character—a friendly ghost—and literalizes him in this story of *a dead boy* whose haunted house is invaded by a widowed paranormalist (and daughter) seeking the spirit of his dead wife. Talk about family *fun!* Absolutely dreadful, wrong-headed movie is strictly for families who are already dead from the neck up. A handful of surprise Hollywood cameos add a few fleeting laughs. Followed by two DVD sequels. [PG]🅥🅳

Cassandra Crossing, The (1977-British) **C-127m.** *** D: George Pan Cosmatos. Richard Harris, Sophia Loren, Burt Lancaster, Ava Gardner, Martin Sheen, Lee Strasberg, O.J. Simpson, John Phillip Law, Ingrid Thulin, Alida Valli, Lionel Stander.

Entertaining disaster epic as train carrying plague approaches a weakened bridge. Filmed in France and Italy. [R]▼▶

Cassandra's Dream (2008-U.S.-British-French) **C-108m.** ** D: Woody Allen. Ewan McGregor, Colin Farrell, Hayley Atwell, Sally Hawkins, Tom Wilkinson, John Benfield, Clare Higgins, Phil Davis, Jim Carter. Well-intentioned but flawed—and far too predictable—morality tale about British working-class brothers. Trouble simmers when Farrell's gambling gets him into debt and McGregor becomes smitten with a beautiful actress who is the definition of high-maintenance. Allen deals with issues similar to those he explored more successfully in CRIMES AND MISDEMEANORS. Released overseas in 2007. [PG-13]▶

Cass Timberlane (1947) **119m.** **½ D: George Sidney. Spencer Tracy, Lana Turner, Zachary Scott, Tom Drake, Mary Astor, Albert Dekker, Margaret Lindsay, John Litel, Mona Barrie, Josephine Hutchinson, Rose Hobart, Selena Royle, Cameron Mitchell. Ordinary adaptation of Sinclair Lewis novel of an upright, upper-crust Minnesota judge (Tracy) whose friends are either corrupt or elitist and his marriage to bright, working-class Turner (in one of her best performances). Walter Pidgeon appears as himself in a cocktail party scene.▼▶

Cast a Dark Shadow (1955-British) **84m.** *** D: Lewis Gilbert. Dirk Bogarde, Margaret Lockwood, Kathleen Harrison, Kay Walsh, Robert Flemyng, Mona Washbourne. Tense suspenser with Bogarde in fine form as a psychotic Bluebeard who murders rich, aging mate Washbourne. Lockwood and Walsh won't be such easy prey, however.▼

Cast a Giant Shadow (1966) **C-142m.** ** D: Melville Shavelson. Kirk Douglas, John Wayne, Frank Sinatra, Yul Brynner, Senta Berger, Angie Dickinson, James Donald, Luther Adler, (Chaim) Topol. Hokey bio of Arab-Israeli war hero Mickey Marcus has Kirk leaving Angie's bed to join Senta and several other less sexy freedom fighters. Guest roles by big names make film seem even sillier. Panavision.▼●▶

Castaway (1987) **C-117m.** **½ D: Nicolas Roeg. Oliver Reed, Amanda Donohoe, Tony Rickards, Todd Rippon, Georgina Hale, Frances Barber. Scruffy Reed advertises for a "wife" to join him for a year on a desert island; Donohoe is the incongruously vavavoomish adventure seeker who answers it. Visually splendid adaptation of Lucy Irvine's bestseller seems unlikely *as told*, though it remains a visceral experience, particularly for Roeg fans. Eventually overplays its hand. [R]▼

Cast Away (2000) **C-143m.** ***½ D: Robert Zemeckis. Tom Hanks, Helen Hunt, Nick Searcy, Lari White, Chris Noth, Jenifer Lewis, Wilson. A man whose job depends on organizational skills and awareness of time survives a plane crash and winds up on a deserted Pacific island. Only an actor with Hanks' good will (and acting chops) could make us care as much as we do about this survivor, who battles the elements and struggles to retain his sanity. No narration, little music, just great moviemaking. Screenplay by William F. Broyles, Jr. [PG-13]▼▶

Castaway Cowboy, The (1974) **C-91m.** ** D: Vincent McEveety. James Garner, Vera Miles, Robert Culp, Eric Shea, Elizabeth Smith, Gregory Sierra. Cowboy Garner is shipwrecked on Hawaiian island, runs into pretty widow and bad-guy Culp who wants her land. Old B-Western plot, Disney-fied on Hawaiian locations. [G]▼▶

Castle, The (1968-German-Swiss) **C-93m.** *** D: Rudolf Noelte. Maximilian Schell, Cordula Trantow, Trudik Daniel, Helmut Qualtinger. Appropriately vague filmization of Kafka's novel: "K" (Schell), a land surveyor, is called to a castle for work but is unable to gain admittance.▼

Castle, The (1997-Australian) **C-84m.** *** D: Rob Sitch. Michael Caton, Anne Tenney, Stephen Curry, Anthony Simcoe, Sophie Lee, Wayne Hope, Tiriel Mora, Eric Bana, Charles (Bud) Tingwell. Winning low-budget comedy of the unsophisticated Kerrigan family, whose home sits atop a toxic landfill—adjacent to an airport runway! When Dad (Caton) decides to fight the government to keep their ramshackle abode, watch out. Equal parts Capraesque, goofy, and heartfelt. Conceived by several Australian radio and TV comedy hands; a smash in its native country. [R]▼▶

Castle, The (1997-Austrian-German-French) **C-123m.** *** D: Michael Haneke. Ulrich Mühe, Susanne Lothar, Frank Giering, Felix Eitner, Nikolaus Paryla, André Eisermann, Dörte Lyssewski, Inga Busch. Faithful, compelling adaptation of Kafka's celebrated, unfinished novel, involving K. (Mühe), a land surveyor who arrives at an inn in an isolated village where he has been hired for a job; he encounters bureaucracy and contempt, not to mention an array of odd characters who have peculiar emotional connections. Story is told via narration and short, choppy sequences that end in blackouts; this jumpy directorial style seems entirely appropriate for the material. Haneke also scripted this challenging cinematic exploration of alienation.▶

Castle in the Sky SEE: **Laputa: Castle in the Sky**

Castle Keep (1969) **C-105m.** *½ D: Sydney Pollack. Burt Lancaster, Peter Falk, Patrick O'Neal, Jean-Pierre Aumont, Scott Wilson, Al Freeman, Jr., Tony Bill, Bruce Dern, Astrid Heeren, Michael Conrad. Pretentious adaptation of William Eastlake's novel about eight soldiers on French border in WW2. Good cast, but film has no coherency. Panavision. [R]▼▶

Castle of Cagliostro, The (1979-Japanese) C-102m. ***½ D: Hayao Miyazaki. Voices of David Hayter, John Snyder, Richard Epcar, Dorothy Elias-Fahn, Dougary Grant, Kirk Thornton. Master thief Lupin pursues the source of counterfeit money and its valuable printing plates to a European castle, where he becomes involved with rescuing a princess in distress. Exciting, thrill-packed animated feature marks the debut of director Miyazaki and remains one of his best films. The main character is a descendant of Arsène Lupin, of the well-known Maurice Leblanc detective novels. The actor who voices Lupin, David Hayter, later wrote screenplays for X-MEN and WATCHMEN. ▼❾

Castle of Fu Manchu, The (1970-British-Spanish-Italian-German) 92m. BOMB D: Jess Franco. Christopher Lee, Richard Greene, Maria Perschy, Gunther Stoll, Howard Marion Crawford. Lee buries Fu Manchu with this one—the pits—experimenting with more deadly potions in his castle near Istanbul and parrying with his perennial adversary, Nayland Smith (Greene) of Britain's Home Office. Originally released in the U.S. as ASSIGNMENT ISTANBUL. [PG] ▼❾

Castle of the Walking Dead SEE: **Torture Chamber of Dr. Sadism, The**

Castles in the Sky SEE: **Yidl Mitn Fidl**

Casual Sex? (1988) C-97m. **½ D: Genevieve Robert. Lea Thompson, Victoria Jackson, Stephen Shellen, Jerry Levine, Andrew (Dice) Clay, Mary Gross. Lightweight look at two young women who are looking for something more than a one-night stand—especially in these cautious times—and try their luck at a health and fitness spa. Slight but engaging contemporary comedy from young women's point of view, adapted from the play by Wendy Goldman and Judy Toll. [R] ▼❾❿

Casualties of War (1989) C-113m. ** D: Brian De Palma. Michael J. Fox, Sean Penn, Don Harvey, John C. Reilly, John Leguizamo, Thuy Thu Le, Erik King, Sam Robards, Ving Rhames. Vietnam War picture focusing on one patrol, led by off-the-wall Penn, and its inhumane treatment of an innocent Vietnamese girl. As the Voice of Reason, Fox is well cast, but his clean-cut decency gets to be a bit much; Penn and Thu Le (the victim) are more effective. For all its good intentions, film has a jumbled, detached feel to it (though it's scripted by playwright David Rabe, a Vietnam veteran and author of *Sticks and Bones* and *Streamers*). Based on a real incident detailed in Daniel Lang's *New Yorker* article, later published as a book. Extended edition also available. Panavision. [R] ▼❾❿

Catamount Killing, The (1974-German) C-93m. ** D: Krzysztof Zanussi. Horst Buchholz, Ann Wedgeworth, Chip Taylor, Louise Clark, Patricia Joyce, Polly Holliday. German film made in Vermont with Polish director. Passably interesting story of two small-town people who try to pull off bank heist and then come to grips with themselves as criminals. ▼

Cat and Mouse (1975-French) C-107m. ***½ D: Claude Lelouch. Michele Morgan, Serge Reggiani, Philippe Leotard, Jean-Pierre Aumont, Valerie Lagrange. Anyone could've killed wealthy Aumont, philandering husband of Morgan, and Inspector Reggiani finds out who and why. Denouement is only letdown in this delightful comedy mystery, written, directed, and produced by master Lelouch. Dazzling views of Paris and the countryside. Released here in 1978. [PG] ▼

Cat and the Canary, The (1927) 74m. *** D: Paul Leni. Laura LaPlante, Tully Marshall, Flora Finch, Creighton Hale, Gertrude Astor, Lucien Littlefield. Delightful silent classic, the forerunner of all "old dark house" mysteries, with nice touch of humor throughout as heiress LaPlante and nervous group spend night in haunted house. Remade several times. ▼❾❿

Cat and the Canary, The (1939) 74m. *** D: Elliott Nugent. Bob Hope, Paulette Goddard, Gale Sondergaard, John Beal, Douglass Montgomery, Nydia Westman, Elizabeth Patterson, George Zucco. Entertaining remake of the venerable "old dark house" chiller, spiced with Hope's brand of humor. This film cemented his movie stardom and led to the even more successful scare comedy THE GHOST BREAKERS. Remade again in 1978. ❶

Cat and the Canary, The (1978-British) C-90m. **½ D: Radley Metzger. Honor Blackman, Michael Callan, Edward Fox, Wendy Hiller, Olivia Hussey, Carol Lynley, Peter McEnery, Wilfrid Hyde-White. Entertaining remake of the old-dark-house staple, with a likable cast; reasonably faithful to the original, with the nicest twist being Hyde-White's method of communicating with his heirs. Alternate version runs 102m. [PG] ▼❾❿

Cat Ballou (1965) C-96m. ***½ D: Elliot Silverstein. Jane Fonda, Lee Marvin, Michael Callan, Dwayne Hickman, Tom Nardini, John Marley, Reginald Denny, Jay C. Flippen, Arthur Hunnicutt, Bruce Cabot. Funny Western comedy, with Fonda as Cat Ballou, notorious school-teacher-turned-outlaw. Marvin copped an Oscar for his dual role as a drunken gunman and his twin, a desperado with an artificial nose. Nat King Cole and Stubby Kaye appear as strolling minstrels. Roy Chanslor's novel was adapted by Walter Newman and Frank R. Pierson. ▼❾❿

Catch a Fire (2006-British-South African-U.S.) C-101m. **½ D: Phillip Noyce. Tim Robbins, Derek Luke, Bonnie Henna, Mncedisi Shabangu, Tumisho K. Masha, Sithembiso Khumalo, Terry Pheto, Marius

Weyers. A hardworking, happily married man in South Africa (still under apartheid rule in the early 1980s) is wrongly accused of terrorist activities and tortured by a single-minded government agent (Robbins). This pushes him over the edge and causes him to join the freedom fighters who want to overturn their government. Somewhat simplistic story benefits from an exceptionally strong performance by Luke as Patrick Chamusso; Robbins' character isn't nearly as fleshed out. Chamusso himself appears in the film's closing moments. Screenplay by Shawn Slovo, who also wrote A WORLD APART. Super 35. [PG-13]█

Catch and Release (2007) C-112m. ** D: Susannah Grant. Jennifer Garner, Timothy Olyphant, Kevin Smith, Sam Jaeger, Juliette Lewis, Joshua Friesen, Fiona Shaw, Tina Lifford, Georgia Craig. Generally uninvolving drama about a young woman whose fiancé dies suddenly, leaving behind a boatload of secrets. As each revelation makes her angrier, she begins to loosen up and accept new possibilities in her life, including romance. Garner valiantly tries to lift this lifeless material above the TV-movie level but the endless banter sinks it. Smith's character has a sitcom-style retort for any situation. Feature directing debut for writer Grant (ERIN BROCKOVICH, IN HER SHOES). Super 35. [PG-13]█

Cat Chaser (1989) C-90m. **½ D: Abel Ferrara. Kelly McGillis, Peter Weller, Frederic Forrest, Charles Durning, Tomas Milian, Juan Fernandez. Wordy political thriller based on Elmore Leonard's novel about an ex-soldier reuniting with old flame whose husband happens to be the head of the secret police in Santo Domingo. Some decent performances, but film is often confusing and dull. Never released theatrically. Alternate, unrated version runs 92m. [R]▼▶

Catch Me a Spy SEE: **To Catch a Spy**

Catch Me If You Can (2002) C-141m. *** D: Steven Spielberg. Leonardo DiCaprio, Tom Hanks, Christopher Walken, Martin Sheen, Nathalie Baye, Amy Adams, James Brolin, Brian Howe, Jennifer Garner, Ellen Pompeo, Elizabeth Banks. In the 1960s, Frank Abagnale, Jr., not unlike Ferdinand Demara in THE GREAT IMPOSTOR, manages to con his way into a variety of jobs (airline pilot, surgeon, lawyer) using glibness, smarts, and knowledge of forgery . . . while FBI agent Hanks spends years tracking him. Brightly told for a story with so many dark undertones, with charismatic star performances and a moving turn by Walken as DiCaprio's ne'er-do-well father. Yet when the long tale is over, it has no resonance. Striking animated titles and a wonderful jazzy score by John Williams. Based on Abagnale's book. [PG-13]▼▶

Catch My Soul (1974) C-95m. *½ D: Pat-

rick McGoohan. Richie Havens, Lance LeGault, Season Hubley, Tony Joe White, Susan Tyrrell, Delaney and Bonnie Bramlett. Jack Good's rock-opera adaptation of Shakespeare's *Othello*, with Havens as sanctimonious preacher and LeGault as his Iago, is uninvolving, heavy-handed stuff. Some good music, but if the play's the thing, this one doesn't make it. Retitled: SANTA FE SATAN. [PG]

Catch That Kid (2004) C-91m. ** D: Bart Freundlich. Kristen Stewart, Corbin Bleu, Max Thieriot, Jennifer Beals, Sam Robards, James Le Gros, John Carroll Lynch, Michael Des Barres. Twelve-year-old climbing enthusiast Stewart and her two male best friends (and preteen romantic rivals) break into a bank's high-security vault, 100 feet off the ground, hoping to steal enough money to pay for experimental surgery for her father. Kids will enjoy the story and visual effects, though result is more video game than feature film—and parents may question its dubious ethics. Remake of a 2002 Danish film hit, KLATRETØSEN. [PG]▼▶

Catch-22 (1970) C-121m. **½ D: Mike Nichols. Alan Arkin, Martin Balsam, Richard Benjamin, Arthur (Art) Garfunkel, Jack Gilford, Buck Henry, Bob Newhart, Anthony Perkins, Paula Prentiss, Martin Sheen, Jon Voight, Orson Welles, Bob Balaban, Marcel Dalio, Norman Fell, Charles Grodin, Austin Pendleton, Peter Bonerz, Elizabeth Wilson. Long, labored, expensive film of Joseph Heller's book halfway succeeds in capturing surrealist insanity of WW2 Army life. Heavy-handedness spoils potential; good cast tries its best. Script by costar Henry. Panavision. [R]▼▶●

Catch Us If You Can SEE: **Having a Wild Weekend**

Catered Affair, The (1956) 93m. *** D: Richard Brooks. Bette Davis, Ernest Borgnine, Debbie Reynolds, Barry Fitzgerald, Rod Taylor. Davis sheds all glamour as Bronx taxi driver's wife wanting to give daughter ritzy wedding. Gore Vidal's script based on Paddy Chayefsky TV play. Also shown in computer-colored version. Later a Broadway musical.▼

Catfish (2010) C-87m. *** D: Ariel Schulman, Henry Joost. Two filmmakers and a photographer who document each other's lives become intrigued when the photographer, Nev Schulman, receives a painting inspired by one of his pictures, painted by a precocious 8-year-old girl in Michigan. This leads to a series of e-mails, texts, Facebook posts, and phone calls with the girl, her mother, and her sexy older sister. Eventually the threesome decide to visit Nev's "girlfriend" at her home, where the story takes an unexpected turn. Fascinating documentary (and cautionary tale) about the way people build so-called relationships nowadays. What makes it worthwhile is the film-makers' reaction to what they find. And yes, it's all genuine, not made up. [PG-13] ▶

Cat From Outer Space, The (1978) C-104m. **½ D: Norman Tokar. Ken Berry, Sandy Duncan, McLean Stevenson, Harry Morgan, Roddy McDowall, Ronnie Schell. Kids will probably like this Disney fantasy-comedy, though it holds few surprises: cat from another world seeks help from U.S. scientists to repair his spaceship, but military protocol and enemy spying get in the way. Coincidentally, plot has many similarities to later E.T.! [G] ▼●

Catherine & Co. (1975-French-Italian) C-99m. ** D: Michel Boisrond. Jane Birkin, Patrick Dewaere, Jean-Pierre Aumont, Vittorio Caprioli, Jean-Claude Brialy. Slight sexual comedy about young girl who becomes prostitute and decides to incorporate herself. TV prints run 84m. [R] ▼

Cathy Tippel SEE: **Keetje Tippel**

Cat in the Hat, The (2003) C-82m. *½ D: Bo Welch. Mike Myers, Kelly Preston, Alec Baldwin, Dakota Fanning, Spencer Breslin, Sean Hayes, Amy Hill, Clint Howard, Paris Hilton. A brother and sister spend an eventful day in the company of a magical cat while their single mom is off at work. Brightly colored adaptation of the beloved rhyming book for young children is a betrayal of everything Dr. Seuss ever stood for, injecting potty humor and adult (wink-wink) jokes into its mixture of heavy-handed slapstick and silliness. Hayes also provides the voice of The Fish. Officially known as DR. SEUSS' THE CAT IN THE HAT, which is an official insult. Super 35. [PG] ▼●

Catlow (1971) C-103m. **½ D: Sam Wanamaker. Yul Brynner, Richard Crenna, Leonard Nimoy, Daliah Lavi, Jo Ann Pflug, Jeff Corey. Outlaw tries to avoid interference on his way to $2 million gold robbery. Basically a comedy, with a surprisingly ebullient Brynner. Based on a Louis L'Amour novel. [PG] ▼●

Cat on a Hot Tin Roof (1958) C-108m. ***½ D: Richard Brooks. Elizabeth Taylor, Paul Newman, Burl Ives, Jack Carson, Judith Anderson, Madeleine Sherwood, Larry Gates. Southern patriarch Ives learns he is dying; his greedy family, except for son Newman, falls all over itself sucking up to him. Tennessee Williams' classic study of "mendacity" comes to the screen somewhat laundered but still packing a wallop; entire cast is sensational. Adaptation by Brooks and James Poe. Remade in 1983 for TV. ▼●

Cat o' Nine Tails, The (1971-Italian-German-French) C-112m. ** D: Dario Argento. Karl Malden, James Franciscus, Catherine Spaak, Cinzia De Carolis, Carlo Alighiero. Early Argento horror hit has Malden as ex-reporter, now blind, who per-

suades newsman Franciscus to join him in hunt for a crazed killer. Good atmosphere in uneven story, hurt by terrible dubbing. Techniscope. [PG] ▼●

Cat People (1942) 73m. *** D: Jacques Tourneur. Simone Simon, Kent Smith, Tom Conway, Jack Holt, Jane Randolph. Storyline and plot elements don't hold up, but moments of shock and terror are undiminished in the first of producer Val Lewton's famous horror films. Smith falls in love with strange, shy woman (Simon) who fears ancient curse of the panther inside her. Followed by THE CURSE OF THE CAT PEOPLE. Remade in 1982. ▼●

Cat People (1982) C-118m. ** D: Paul Schrader. Nastassia Kinski, Malcolm McDowell, John Heard, Annette O'Toole, Ruby Dee, Ed Begley, Jr., Scott Paulin, John Larroquette. Virginal Kinski moves in with brother McDowell, a "cat man," and falls in love with zoo curator Heard as a black panther rampages through community. Sexy, bloody, technically well crafted, but uneven and ultimately unsatisfying; Schrader seems more concerned with camera angles and nudity than coherent storyline. Loosely based on the 1942 film. [R] ▼●

Cats & Dogs (2001) C-87m. ** D: Lawrence Guterman. Jeff Goldblum, Elizabeth Perkins, Alexander Pollock, Miriam Margolyes; voices of Tobey Maguire, Alec Baldwin, Sean Hayes, Susan Sarandon, Joe Pantoliano, Michael Clarke Duncan, Jon Lovitz, Charlton Heston, Salome Jens. Beagle puppy is adopted by the family of a scientist trying to invent something that will end humankind's allergies to dogs. The cats (led by Blofeld-like Mr. Tinkles) are out to stop this, opposed by a spy network of dogs. Good premise (executed with a variety of special effects) is undone by an uneven blend of silliness and heavy-handedness. Cat lovers be warned: top billing isn't everything. Followed by CATS & DOGS: THE REVENGE OF KITTY GALORE. [PG] ▼●

Cats & Dogs: The Revenge of Kitty Galore (2010) C-82m. ** D: Brad Peyton. Voices of Bette Midler, James Marsden, Nick Nolte, Christina Applegate, Sean Hayes, Wallace Shawn, Roger Moore, Joe Pantoliano, Michael Clarke Duncan, Chris O'Donnell, Neil Patrick Harris, Jack McBrayer, Fred Armisen, J. K. Simmons. Sequel to 2001 movie is a secret agent spoof with an all-star cast of computer-generated house pets. Kitty Galore (Midler) plots world domination and unites the normally adversarial cats and dogs, who use all manner of high-tech gadgets to thwart her plans. Sequences that parody spy films are clever; numerous butt-sniffing gags are not. Passable children's fare. 3-D. [PG] ▶

Cats Don't Dance (1997) C-75m. *½ D: Mark Dindal. Voices of Scott Bakula, Jasmine Guy, Natalie Cole, Ashley Peldon, Kathy Najimy, John Rhys-Davies, George Kennedy, Rene Auberjonois, Hal Holbrook, Don Knotts, Betty Lou Gerson. Fairly dreary cartoon feature about a wide-eyed cat from Kokomo who goes to Hollywood to star in musical movies, circa 1939. What he finds instead is a town full of cynics and broken dreams. The villain is a hyper-bratty child star who hates animals. That's entertainment? Unmemorable songs by Randy Newman. Gene Kelly served as a choreography consultant. [G] ▼●)

Cat's Eye (1985) C-93m. *½ D: Lewis Teague. Drew Barrymore, James Woods, Alan King, Kenneth McMillan, Robert Hays, Candy Clark, James Naughton, Patricia Kalember, Charles Dutton. Trio of heavy-handed Stephen King stories, short on irony, long on mean-spiritedness. J-D-C Scope. [PG-13] ▼●)

Cat's Meow, The (2001-German-British) C/B&W-112m. *** D: Peter Bogdanovich. Kirsten Dunst, Edward Herrmann, Cary Elwes, Eddie Izzard, Joanna Lumley, Victor Slezak, Jennifer Tilly, James Laurenson, Claudia Harrison. Entertaining speculation about the doings on William Randolph Hearst's yacht in November of 1924, including an unrequited love by Charlie Chaplin (Izzard) for Marion Davies (Dunst) and the murder of down-and-out producer Thomas Ince (Elwes). Well shot and well cast; Herrmann is an ideal Hearst, and Izzard is persuasive as Chaplin. Steven Peros' script (based on his play) captures the spirit of the time, but the events portrayed are strictly from his imagination. [R] ▼●)

Cattle Annie and Little Britches (1980) C-95m. *** D: Lamont Johnson. Burt Lancaster, Rod Steiger, Amanda Plummer, Diane Lane, John Savage, Scott Glenn, Michael Conrad. Very pleasant little Western, which was thrown away by its distributor, Universal. In 1893, Eastern girls Plummer (Annie) and Lane (Britches) join remnants of the Doolin-Dalton gang and inspire them to pull a few more jobs. Winning cast, including Plummer in film debut. Based on Robert Ward's novel. [PG]

Cattle Queen of Montana (1954) C-88m. **½ D: Allan Dwan. Barbara Stanwyck, Ronald Reagan, Gene Evans, Lance Fuller, Anthony Caruso, Jack Elam. Stanwyck battles to protect her livestock and property from plundering by Indians—and a ruthless villain (Evans). Reagan plays second fiddle to feisty Stanwyck here—but they're both done in by mediocre script. Beautiful scenery (filmed in Glacier National Park, Montana) helps. ▼●)

Catwoman (2004) C-104m. *½ D: Pitof. Halle Berry, Benjamin Bratt, Sharon Stone, Lambert Wilson, Frances Conroy, Alex Borstein, Michael Massee, Byron Mann. Meek employee of a big cosmetics firm is murdered when she overhears incriminating evidence about a new face cream with grue-

some side effects . . . but instead of dying she's resurrected as Catwoman and tries to bring the guilty parties to justice. Nonsensical story concept, illogical in the extreme, gives us a "heroine" who's scarcely worth rooting for. Berry does her best; Stone manages to be dull even while parodying herself as the lethal wife of the cosmetics manufacturer. Based on the D.C. comic book. Super 35. [PG-13] ▼)

Cat-Women of the Moon (1954) 64m. *½ D: Arthur Hilton. Sonny Tufts, Victor Jory, Marie Windsor, Bill Phipps, Douglas Fowley, Susan Morrow. All-star cast in tacky sci-fi entry about a moon expedition that discovers female civilization and its underground empire. Aka ROCKET TO THE MOON. Remade as MISSILE TO THE MOON. 3-D. ▼)

Caught (1949) 88m. *** D: Max Ophuls. James Mason, Barbara Bel Geddes, Robert Ryan, Frank Ferguson, Curt Bois, Natalie Schafer. Compelling, intelligent story of young girl who marries powerful millionaire, tries to escape her shallow existence with him. Fine performances, skilled direction by Ophuls. ▼

Caught (1996) C-109m. *** D: Robert M. Young. Edward James Olmos, Maria Conchita Alonso, Arie Verveen, Bitty Schram, Steven Schub. Tension-packed, if somewhat familiar, film noir about long-married couple whose relationship is disrupted when a drifter (Verveen) comes to live with the couple and work in their fish store; then their married son (Schub) arrives on the scene. This POSTMAN ALWAYS RINGS TWICE variation has atmosphere to spare; sharply acted and scripted (by Edward Pomerantz, based on his novel *Into It*). [R] ▼●)

Caught Up (1998) C-95m. BOMB D: Darin Scott. Bokeem Woodbine, Cynda Williams, Jeffrey Combs, Tony Todd, Snoop Doggy Dogg, LL Cool J, Michael (Clarke) Duncan. Witless blaxploitation/film noir about an ex-con (Woodbine) who falls back into L.A.'s underworld when he gets involved with a sexy psychic (Williams) who's a dead ringer for his ex-wife (also Williams). Marked by convoluted plotting, gross stereotypes, and cameos by star rappers (Snoop plays a drug courier named Cool Kitty Kat—get it?). That's CANDYMAN's Tony Todd as a malevolent parole officer and RE-ANIMATOR's Jeffrey Combs as a Shakespeare-quoting eunuch security guard. [R] ▼●)

Cauldron of Blood (1967-Spanish-U.S.) C-95m. *½ D: Edward Mann (Santos Alcocer). Boris Karloff, Viveca Lindfors, Jean-Pierre Aumont, Jacqui Speed, Rosenda Monteros. Sordid, sleep-inducing tale of blind sculptor (Karloff) whose skeletal models are actually victims of his murdering wife. Also known as BLIND MAN'S BLUFF. Filmed in widescreen Panoramica. [PG] ▼

Cause for Alarm! (1951) 74m. *** D: Tay

Garnett. Loretta Young, Barry Sullivan, Bruce Cowling, Margalo Gillmore, Carl Switzer, Richard Anderson. Simple, effective thriller with Young registering as the panic-stricken wife of psychotic Sullivan. Tension builds, and there's a neat plot twist.▼⊙❙

Cavalcade (1933) **110m. ****** D: Frank Lloyd. Diana Wynyard, Clive Brook, Herbert Mundin, Ursula Jeans, Margaret Lindsay, Beryl Mercer, Una O'Connor, Billy Bevan, Frank Lawton. Lavish Hollywood adaptation of Noel Coward's London stage success (which may remind many of TV's *Upstairs, Downstairs*) chronicling two English families from eve of the 20th century to early 1930s. Nostalgic, richly atmospheric, but also sharply critical of war and the aftershocks that brought an end to a wonderful way of life. Oscar winner for Best Picture, Best Director, and "Interior Decoration" (it *is* handsome).▼❙

Cavalry Charge SEE: **Last Outpost, The** (1951)

Cave, The (2005-U.S.-German) **C-97m. *½** D: Bruce Hunt. Cole Hauser, Morris Chestnut, Lena Headey, Piper Perabo, Eddie Cibrian, Rick Ravanello, Marcel Iures, Kieran Darcy-Smith, Daniel Dae Kim. Somewhere below Romania, a team of professional cave divers gets trapped underground, often underwater, stalked by a CGI band of flying people-eaters. Good-looking production tries to float a fully foreseeable plot and to buoy its endlessly bickering characters, but it's a pretty underwhelming cross between JAWS and ALIEN. Super 35. [PG-13]▼❙

Cave Dwellers SEE: **Blade Master, The**

Caveman (1981) **C-92m. **½** D: Carl Gottlieb. Ringo Starr, Barbara Bach, John Matuszak, Shelley Long, Dennis Quaid, Avery Schreiber, Jack Gilford. Stoned-age spoof follows prehistoric Starr's adventures in One Zillion B.C. as a misfit who forms his own tribe, which is composed of outcasts from other caves. Dum-dum comedy saved by fantastic (and funny) special-effects dinosaurs created by Jim Danforth and David Allen. [PG]▼⊙❙

Caveman's Valentine, The (2001) **C-105m. *½** D: Kasi Lemmons. Samuel L. Jackson, Colm Feore, Ann Magnuson, Aunjanue Ellis, Rodney Eastman, Tamara Tunie, Jay Rodan, Anthony Michael Hall. A once-brilliant piano student now lives as a delusional hermit in an N.Y.C. cave, but turns detective to help solve a murder that takes place in the park outside his dwelling. Strange, unappealing film has almost nothing to recommend it. Screenplay by George Dawes Green, based on his well-regarded novel. [R]▼❙

Cave of the Yellow Dog, The (2006-German-Mongolian) **C-89m. ***** D: Byambasuren Davaa. Urjindorj Batchuluun, Buyandulam D. Batchuluun, Nansal Batchuluun, Nansalmaa Batchuluun, Batbayar

Batchuluun. Poignant family drama about a little girl and her puppy who live in a yurt in the Mongolian valleys, where cowpies are her toys, wolves kill livestock, vultures circle, and the anonymous big city beckons. Nonprofessionals sincerely enact the ethnographic details of daily life—child care, making cheese, sheep skinning—in a simple, satisfying tale not unlike LITTLE HOUSE ON THE STEPPES. Written by the director. Cute pooch. [G]❙

Cavern, The (1964-U.S.-Italian-West German) **94m. **½** D: Edgar G. Ulmer. Rosanna Schiaffino, John Saxon, Brian Aherne, Peter L. Marshall, Larry Hagman, Hans Von Borsody. Six soldiers are trapped for over a year in a cavern with Schiaffino, but plot contrivance isn't handled badly in above-average programmer. The prolific director's swan song.

CB4 (1993) **C-88m. **** D: Tamra Davis. Chris Rock, Allen Payne, Deezer D, Chris Elliott, Phil Hartman, Charlie Murphy, Khandi Alexander, Arthur Evans, Theresa Randle, Willard E. Pugh, Stoney Jackson, La Wanda Page. Group of middle-class guys, led by Rock (who also cowrote the film), takes on a tough, prisonlike persona to form a rap group called Cell Block 4—which leads to complications when they get mistaken for the real thing. Mildly amusing satirical look at the world of Gangsta Rap—is no THIS IS SPINAL TAP. [R]▼⊙❙

C.C. and Company (1970) **C-88m. *½** D: Seymour Robbie. Joe Namath, Ann-Margret, William Smith, Jennifer Billingsley, Teda Bracci, Greg Mullavey, Sid Haig, Bruce Glover, Wayne Cochran & The C.C. Riders. Broadway Joe gets sacked in his first starring role as a motorcyclist who tangles with Smith's biker gang while trying (not very hard) to fight off Ann-Margret's advances. Bracci's comedy relief is principal virtue, but the big laughs are unintentional. Produced by Roger Smith (who also wrote the screenplay) and Allan Carr. Aka CHROME HEARTS. [PG—edited from original R rating]▼❙

Cease Fire (1985) **C-97m. **½** D: David Nutter. Don Johnson, Lisa Blount, Robert F. Lyons, Richard Chaves, Rick Richards, Chris Noel. Earnest drama about Vietnam vet who's still haunted by his experiences 15 years later and unwilling to acknowledge that he has a problem. Sincere, poignant at times, but dramatically uneven. George Fernandez adapted script from his one-act play. [R]▼

Cecil B. Demented (2000-U.S.-French) **C-88m. *½** D: John Waters. Stephen Dorff, Melanie Griffith, Adrian Grenier, Alicia Witt, Larry Gilliard, Jr., Maggie Gyllenhaal, Jack Noseworthy, Mike (Michael) Shannon, Harriet Dodge, Mink Stole, Patricia Hearst, Ricki Lake, Roseanne, Kevin Nealon, Eric

Roberts. Dorff is a guerrilla film director who masterminds the kidnapping of a prima donna movie star and uses her to conduct a war on the blandness of mainstream movies. Noisy, frenetic, unfunny effort from the usually amusing Waters. [R] ▼●)

Cedar Rapids (2011) **C-86m.** *** D: Miguel Arteta. Ed Helms, John C. Reilly, Anne Heche, Isiah Whitlock, Jr., Sigourney Weaver, Stephen Root, Kurtwood Smith, Alia Shawkat, Thomas Lennon, Rob Corddry, Mike O'Malley. Naïve, almost childlike insurance man from a small town in Wisconsin (Helms, in a breakout role) is sent to an industry convention in Iowa, charged with bringing home an important award for his boss. Instead he gets a series of accelerated life lessons from a flirtatious colleague (Heche) and a bombastic rival (Reilly), among others. At first the film seems to be making fun of its protagonist, but the tone shifts once we arrive in Cedar Rapids; the result is both funny and disarming, as you'd expect from director Arteta. [R] ▶

Ceiling Zero (1936) **95m.** *** D: Howard Hawks. James Cagney, Pat O'Brien, June Travis, Stuart Erwin, Barton MacLane, Isabel Jewell. Irresponsible mail flier Cagney causes no end of grief for old pal (and boss) O'Brien, especially when he sets his sights on young pilot Travis. Typically machine-gun–paced Hawks drama belies its stage origins; one of the best Cagney-O'Brien vehicles. Based on the play by Frank "Spig" Wead; remade as INTERNATIONAL SQUADRON (1941). ▼

Celebration, The (1998-Danish) **C-101m.** ***½ D: Thomas Vinterberg. Ulrich Thomsen, Henning Moritzen, Thomas Bo Larsen, Paprika Steen, Birthe Neumann, Trine Dyrholm. A prodigal son's return for his prosperous father's sixtieth birthday party sets the stage for a dysfunctional family reunion in the Danish countryside. Harsh, sardonically humorous look at the dark side of relationships—and hidden skeletons. Strongly scripted by the director (who also has a bit as a cab driver) and Mogens Rukov, under the "pure cinema" rules of Dogma 95. [R] ▼▶

Celebration at Big Sur (1971) **C-82m.** ** D: Baird Bryant, Johanna Demetrakas. Joan Baez, Crosby, Stills, Nash and Young, Joni Mitchell, John Sebastian, Mimi Fariña. Lesser folk-rock documentary, filmed at 1969 Big Sur Festival, suffers from poor production values. Baez is highlighted, singing "I Shall Be Released," "Song for David," etc. [PG]

Celebrity (1998) **114m.** ** D: Woody Allen. Kenneth Branagh, Judy Davis, Joe Mantegna, Leonardo DiCaprio, Winona Ryder, Charlize Theron, Hank Azaria, Melanie Griffith, Famke Janssen, Michael Lerner, Bebe Neuwirth, Larry Pine, Marian Seldes, Andre Gregory, Gretchen Mol, Dylan Baker, Sam Rockwell, Allison Janney,

Celia Weston, Aida Turturro, Kate Burton, Patti D'Arbanville, Debra Messing, Donna Hanover, Karen Duffy, Isaac Mizrahi, Jeffrey Wright. Branagh becomes Woody Allen in this rambling look at a neurotic N.Y. magazine writer, his messed-up love life and career. Allen is coasting here, with an attractive cast, some amusing moments, but nothing much to say. Davis is, as always, incredibly good. Shot in black-and-white by Sven Nykvist. [R] ▼●)

Celeste (1981-German) **C-107m.** *** D: Percy Adlon. Eva Mattes, Jurgen Arndt, Norbert Wartha, Wolf Euba, Leo Bardischewski. Slow-moving but stunningly photographed and detailed account of the relationship between Marcel Proust (Arndt) and his devoted housekeeper (Mattes). Based on the real Celeste's memoirs. ▼

Celine and Julie Go Boating (1974-French) **C-193m.** ***½ D: Jacques Rivette. Juliet Berto, Dominique Labourier, Bulle Ogier, Marie-France Pisier, Barbet Schroeder, Nathalie Ansar. Librarian Julie (Labourier) strikes up a friendship with magician Celine (Berto), who tells her of a mythical haunted house, which the two visit; they eventually become involved in the "lives" of the ghosts who reside there. Eerie, thoroughly entrancing (if a bit overlong) comedy-drama-fantasy. Scripted by Berto, Labourier, Ogier, Pisier, Rivette, and Eduardo de Gregorio, based on short stories by Henry James. ▼

Cell, The (2000) **C-107m.** *** D: Tarsem Singh. Jennifer Lopez, Vince Vaughn, Vincent D'Onofrio, Jake Weber, Dylan Baker, Marianne Jean-Baptiste, James Gammon, Patrick Bauchau. Genuinely creepy film about an experimental program in which psychologist Lopez is able to enter the minds of her catatonic patients. FBI agent Vaughn prevails upon her to help him catch sick serial killer D'Onofrio. Full of arresting—but often distressing—images; not for the squeamish. Followed by a direct-to-DVD sequel. Super 35. [R] ▼▶

Cellular (2004) **C-94m.** **½ D: David R. Ellis. Kim Basinger, Chris Evans, William H. Macy, Eric Christian Olsen, Jessica Biel, Jason Statham, Richard Burgi, Eddie Driscoll, Adam Taylor Gordon, Noah Emmerich. Not-bad thriller in which science teacher Basinger is kidnapped and imprisoned in an attic. A cell phone is her only link to the outside world, and when a stranger answers her call, she tries to convince the young surfer-slacker (Evans) to help her. Entertaining enough, as long as you ignore the many plot holes; Macy is a big plus as a cop. Based on a story by Larry Cohen, who also wrote PHONE BOOTH. Super 35. [PG-13] ▼▶

Celluloid Closet, The (1995) **C-102m.** *** D: Rob Epstein, Jeffrey Friedman. Narrated by Lily Tomlin. Entertaining, insightful look at homosexuality as reflected in movies. Well-chosen clips are sandwiched by interviews with many actors and filmmakers (Whoopi Goldberg, Tony Curtis, Harvey Fierstein, Arthur Laurents, Shirley MacLaine, Tom Hanks, Susan Sarandon, Mart Crowley, John Schlesinger). One highlight: Gore Vidal revealing the gay subtext in his screenplay for BEN-HUR. Tomlin coexecutive-produced. [R]▼◐●

Celtic Pride (1996) **C-91m.** BOMB D: Tom De Cerchio. Damon Wayans, Daniel Stern, Dan Aykroyd, Gail O'Grady, Adam Hendershott, Paul Guilfoyle, Deion Sanders, Christopher McDonald. Two obsessed Boston Celtics fans drunkenly kidnap the arrogant star of the rival basketball team to ensure that theirs wins the championship. Might have worked as a wild farce, but in this "realistic" comic mode, it's a disaster, with repellent characters, leaden pacing, and no laughs. [PG-13]▼◐●

Cement Garden, The (1992-German-British-French) **C-105m.** **½ D: Andrew Birkin. Charlotte Gainsbourg, Andrew Robertson, Sinead Cusack, Hanns Zischler, Alice Coulthard, Ned Birkin, Jochen Horst. Strange, complex account of the way four young siblings react to the death of their parents (and go about hiding the demise of their mom)—with youthful bewilderment, erotic anxiety, and clandestine yearning. Vivid, but also terribly affected. The director (who scripted, from Ian McEwan's novel) is Gainsbourg's uncle, and Ned Birkin's father.▼◐

Cemetery Club, The (1992) **C-106m.** **½ D: Bill Duke. Ellen Burstyn, Olympia Dukakis, Diane Ladd, Danny Aiello, Lainie Kazan, Jeff Howell, Christina Ricci, Bernie Casey, Robert Costanzo, Wallace Shawn, Louis Guss. The friendship of three women (all Jewish, all played—none too persuasively—by Gentiles) is underscored by the loss of their husbands, until one of them enters into a tentative relationship with a man. Burstyn is a joy to watch, but Dukakis' and Ladd's caricatured performances throw modestly entertaining film off-balance. Ivan Menchell adapted his own play, though comic writer Marshall Brickman has "production consultant" credit. Jerry Orbach and Lee Richardson appear unbilled as husbands. [PG-13]▼◐●

Cemetery Girls SEE: **Velvet Vampire, The**

Cemetery Junction (2010-U.S.-British) **C-95m.** **½ D: Ricky Gervais, Stephen Merchant. Christian Cooke, Felicity Jones, Tom Hughes, Jack Doolan, Ralph Fiennes, Emily Watson, Matthew Goode, Ricky Gervais, Julia Davis. Three pals in a working-class town still fool around like adolescents, but one of them (Cooke) has ambitions and goes to work for local tycoon Fiennes, selling insurance. Then he sees that Fiennes' wife and pretty daughter are as straitjacketed in their lives as his own humdrum family. Sincere coming-of-age saga

set in the 1970s hits mostly familiar notes but has good performances and some great moments. Written by Gervais (who plays Cooke's father) and Merchant (who appears briefly as a guest at a corporate dinner). Released direct to DVD in the U.S. [R]◐

Cemetery Man (1995-U.S.-Italian) **C-100m.** ** D: Michele Soavi. Rupert Everett, Francois Hadji-Lazaro, Anna Falchi, Stefano Masciarelli, Mickey Knox. Zombies rise from the dead a week after their demise, and it's "Cemetery Man's" job to kill them again, with the assistance of a grotesque mute companion. Based on an Italian comic book series, *Dylan Dog,* a promising concept becomes overwhelming and repetitive. At times outrageous, funny, sexy, and disgusting, with a startlingly enigmatic and fascinating ending. [R]▼◐

Centerfold Girls, The (1974) **C-93m.** *½ D: John Peyser. Andrew Prine, Tiffany Bolling, Aldo Ray, Ray Danton, Francine York, Jeremy Slate, Mike Mazurki, Dan Seymour. Fine cast of familiar faces helps routine tale of psycho Prine killing pinup girls. [R]▼

Center of the Web (1992) **C-88m.** ** D: David A. Prior. Robert Davi, Charlene Tilton, Ted Prior, Tony Curtis, Bo Hopkins, William Zipp, Graham Timbes, Eric Stenson, Charles Napier. Hired killer is murdered, and government agents force a man who looks just like him to pose as the dead bad guy. Or is that what's really going on? Complicated plot, smoothly directed, but of no real distinction. [R]▼◐

Center of the World, The (2001) **C-86m.** *** D: Wayne Wang. Peter Sarsgaard, Molly Parker, Carla Gugino, Balthazar Getty, Alisha Klass. Millionaire computer nerd hires a stripper to accompany him to Las Vegas for a weekend—after she sets strict ground rules, including no sex. But his fantasy vision of her, and her illusion of having control, collide with reality as they begin to have genuine feelings for each other. Intense and intimate drama about sexual relationships, with compelling performances by the two leads. Unrated version runs 88m. ▼◐

Center Stage (2000) **C-113m.** ** D: Nicholas Hytner. Amanda Schull, Zoë Saldana, Susan May Pratt, Peter Gallagher, Donna Murphy, Debra Monk, Ethan Stiefel, Sascha Radetsky, Shakiem Evans. Routine backstage soaper about young students at a prestigious N.Y.C. ballet company, focusing on a plucky starlet's infatuation with the company's cocky male lead (American Ballet Theater star Stiefel). Lots of Broadway pedigree behind the scenes, including choreography by Tony Award–winner Susan Stroman, but this plays like *Dawson's Creek* in Capezios. Only a couple of the dance set pieces really fly. Fun cameo from ex-*Chorus Line* hoofer Priscilla Lopez. Followed by a sequel. Super 35. [PG-13]▼◐

Central Park Drifter SEE: **Graveyard Shift** (1989)

Central Station (1998-Brazilian-French) **C-107m.** *** D: Walter Salles. Fernanda Montenegro, Vinicius de Oliveira, Marilia Pêra, Sôia Lira, Othon Bastos, Otávio Augusto, Stela Freitas. A woman who writes letters for the illiterate at Rio de Janeiro's central train station feels obliged to help a 9-year-old boy whose mother has just been killed. The two form an unlikely bond and journey to a remote area of Brazil to try to find his father. Predictable on one level, but extremely well done, with a shining performance by Montenegro (one of Brazil's leading actresses) and newcomer de Oliveira. Super 35. [R]▼●

Century (1993-British) **C-112m.** ** D: Stephen Poliakoff. Charles Dance, Miranda Richardson, Clive Owen, Robert Stephens, Lena Headey, Neil Stuke, Joan Hickson, Fiona Walker. Romantic drama set in turn-of-the-century London examines the relationships of three very different people as the Victorian era dissolves into the 20th century and the world becomes a different place. Mildly involving period piece, but top-notch cast can't breathe life into a premise that doesn't quite come off.▼

Ceremony (2011) **C-89m.** ** D: Max Winkler. Uma Thurman, Michael Angarano, Lee Pace, Reece Thompson, Jake M. Johnson, Rebecca Mader, Brooke Bloom. A hyper-verbal self-styled sophisticate, young Angarano dupes a naïve friend (Thompson) into driving him to Long Island, where he intends to crash the weekend wedding of an older woman (Thurman) he loves. Romantic comedy almost never recovers from its introduction of Angarano, who is so strident it's hard to root for him—or believe that Thurman ever cared for him. Debut feature for writer-director Winkler shows promise, but by the time his two-dimensional characters finally reveal more colors it's almost too late. HD Widescreen. [R] ◗

Certain Fury (1985) **C-87m.** BOMB D: Stephen Gyllenhaal. Tatum O'Neal, Irene Cara, Nicholas Campbell, George Murdock, Moses Gunn, Peter Fonda. Atrocious film about two girls on the lam, featuring a pair of Academy Award winners (as the ads proclaimed) giving two of the worst performances in recent memory. Made in Canada. [R]▼●

Certain Smile, A (1958) **C-106m.** **½ D: Jean Negulesco. Rossano Brazzi, Joan Fontaine, Bradford Dillman, Christine Carere. Françoise Sagan's novella becomes overblown soap opera. Romance between Parisian students Dillman (in film debut) and Carere interrupted when she is beguiled by roué Brazzi; chic Fontaine is wasted. CinemaScope.

Certified Copy (2010-French-Italian-Belgian) **C-106m.** ** D: Abbas Kiarostami. Juliette Binoche, William Shimell, Jean-Claude Carrière, Agathe Natanson, Gianna Giachetti, Adrian Moore. British writer (Shimell) whose latest book examines the meaning of certifying the authenticity of artworks attends a conference in Tuscany and spends a day with a woman (Binoche) who appears to be an adoring fan. Is their connection intellectual, spiritual, romantic, sexual—or something else altogether? Talky, demanding, and ultimately depressing two-character drama is not so much a movie as a mind game. Worth seeing primarily (or only) for Binoche's emotion-packed performance. Iranian filmmaker Kiarostami's first feature made outside his native country.

Cervantes SEE: **Young Rebel**

Cesar (1936-French) **117m.** ***½ D: Marcel Pagnol. Raimu, Pierre Fresnay, Orane Demazis, Charpin, Andre Fouche, Alida Rouffe. Fanny's son (Fouche), now grown, learns that his father is Marius (Fresnay), not Panisse (Charpin). Raimu steals the film in the title role, particularly when he gives a poignant discourse on death. Third of Pagnol's trilogy, preceded by MARIUS (1931) and FANNY (1932). All three were the basis of the play and movie FANNY (1961).▼●

César and Rosalie (1972-French-Italian-German) **C-104m.** *** D: Claude Sautet. Yves Montand, Romy Schneider, Sami Frey, Umberto Orsini, Eva Marie Meineke, Isabelle Huppert. Appealing stars in typically French story of a menage à trois relationship (a woman and her two lovers) and how it changes over the years. [R]▼●

C'est la Vie (1990-French) **C-97m.** *** D: Diane Kurys. Nathalie Baye, Julie Bataille, Candice Lefranc, Richard Berry, Jean-Pierre Bacri, Zabou. Autobiographical coming-of-age chronicle, strikingly similar to Kurys' PEPPERMINT SODA, about a 13-year-old girl (Bataille) and her experiences one long-ago summer at a beach resort. Despite the familiarity of theme, the film is provocative and charming. A sequel—or, more precisely, companion piece—to ENTRE NOUS, which must be seen to fully appreciate the character of the girl's mother (here Nathalie Baye, in ENTRE NOUS, Isabelle Huppert). Panavision.◗

Cet Amour-là (2002-French) **C-98m.** **½ D: Josée Dayan. Jeanne Moreau, Aymeric Demarigny, Christiane Rorato, Sophie Milleron, Justine Lévy, Stanislas Sauphanor, Didier Lesour, Tanya Lopert. Ambitious but uneven depiction of the multilayered relationship between writer-filmmaker Marguerite Duras (Moreau) and Yann Andréa (Demarigny), a student almost four decades her junior who becomes her assistant and lover. Moreau (who appeared in a number of Duras films in her career) is well cast and as fascinating as ever, but the film itself is disappointing. Based on Andréa's autobiographical novel. Panavision.▼●

Chained (1934) **76m.** **½ D: Clarence Brown. Joan Crawford, Clark Gable, Otto Kruger, Stuart Erwin, Una O'Connor, Akim

Tamiroff. Chic formula MGM love triangle with Crawford torn between love for Gable and married lover Kruger. Watch for Mickey Rooney splashing in a swimming pool.▼❸

Chained Heat (1983-U.S.-German) **C-95m.** BOMB D: Paul Nicolas. Linda Blair, John Vernon, Sybil Danning, Tamara Dobson, Stella Stevens, Louisa Moritz, Nita Talbot, Michael Callan, Henry Silva, Edy Williams. Innocent Blair finds herself in a prison where the warden has a hot tub in his office. Strictly for the grind-house crowd on 42nd Street. Followed by CHAINED HEAT 2. [R]▼❸❸

Chain Lightning (1950) **94m.** ** D: Stuart Heisler. Humphrey Bogart, Eleanor Parker, Raymond Massey, Richard Whorf. After WW2, bomber pilot Bogart becomes a test pilot for jet manufacturer Massey. Some romantic rivalry over Parker with inventor Whorf is as low-key as the rest of this bland, uninvolving movie.▼❸

Chain of Desire (1992) **C-107m.** *½ D: Temistocles Lopez. Malcolm McDowell, Linda Fiorentino, Kevin Conroy, Seymour Cassel, Assumpta Serna, Elias Koteas, Angel Aviles, Patrick Bauchau, Grace Zabriskie, Tim Guinee, Jamie Harrold. Pompous reworking of LA RONDE, set in the era of AIDS and chronicling various out-of-the-ordinary sexual encounters among a group of shallow, jaded Manhattanites. Almost unbearably bad at times.▼

Chain of Fools (2000) **C-96m.** BOMB D: Traktor. Steve Zahn, Salma Hayek, Jeff Goldblum, Elijah Wood, David Cross, Tom Wilkinson, Orlando Jones, Kevin Corrigan, David Hyde Pierce, Lara Flynn Boyle, Craig Ferguson, Michael Rapaport. Wimpy barber accidentally kills a hoodlum, then decides to purloin the valuable coins the guy has just stolen. Woeful, would-be farce might be better described as CHAIN OF OBNOXIOUS IDIOTS. At one point Wilkinson moans, "How did I ever get into this mess?" Indeed. Traktor is the name of a Swedish collective, so no one person can be blamed for this. Released direct to video in the U.S. [R]❸

Chain Reaction (1980-Australian) **C-87m.** **½ D: Ian Barry. Steve Bisley, Arna-Maria Winchester, Ross Thompson, Ralph Cotterill, Patrick Ward. OK thriller chronicling the repercussions of a nuclear plant accident on a contaminated employee (Thompson) and an innocent couple (Bisley, Winchester) forced to contend with Big Brother. Look quickly for Mel Gibson as a bearded car mechanic. Video title: NUCLEAR RUN. ▼❸

Chain Reaction (1996) **C-106m.** *½ D: Andrew Davis. Keanu Reeves, Morgan Freeman, Rachel Weisz, Fred Ward, Kevin Dunn, Brian Cox, Joanna Cassidy, Nicholas Rudall, Michael Shannon. Machinist working on hydrogen-energy project is blamed

for a devastating explosion and takes it on the lam along with a female physicist on the project. What's really behind all this skulduggery? Uninspired, ultimately ludicrous blend of action, chase, and political thriller genres has barely a believable moment. [PG-13]▼❸

Chains of Gold (1991) **C-95m.** ** D: Rod Holcomb. John Travolta, Marilu Henner, Joey Lawrence, Bernie Casey, Ramon Franco, Hector Elizondo, Benjamin Bratt, Conchata Ferrell, Tammy Lauren. A dedicated social worker (Travolta) transforms himself into a Stallone clone as he sets out to rescue a young friend caught up with a gang of crack dealers. Ludicrous actioner is yet another of Travolta's grade-D pre–PULP FICTION efforts (although he cowrote this one!). Made for theatrical release in 1989, but debuted on cable TV. [R]▼❸

Chairman, The (1969) **C-102m.** **½ D: J. Lee Thompson. Gregory Peck, Anne Heywood, Arthur Hill, Alan Dobie, Conrad Yama. Lots of talk but little action in story of American scientist sent to Communist China on super-secret espionage mission. Released in Britain as THE MOST DANGEROUS MAN IN THE WORLD. Panavision. [M/PG]❸

Chairman of the Board (1998) **C-95m.** BOMB D: Alex Zamm. Carrot Top, Courtney Thorne-Smith, Larry Miller, Raquel Welch, Jack Warden, M. Emmet Walsh, Estelle Harris, Bill Erwin, Little Richard, Taylor Negron, Butterbean. Excruciatingly stupid story of inventor/beach bum Carrot Top, who inherits a major corporation from a complete stranger, to the vexation of sleazy corporate nephew Miller. Harris hits the film's low point as his landlady, a woman with a laryngectomy who ceaselessly curses. Someone thought this was funny? [PG-13] ▼❸

Chalk (2007) **C-84m.** ** D: Mike Akel. Troy Schremmer, Janelle Schremmer, Shannon Haragan, Chris Mass, Jeff Guerrero, Jerry Jarmon. Low-budget mockumentary about malcontent teachers with a cause lacks structure and comedic drive, getting by (a little) on goodwill. The two Schremmers are married in real life; he's the movie's focus (a history-teaching newcomer named Troy), and she's the default standout as a gym teacher who would like to make Troy her boy. Affectionate enough and probably even true enough, but just passable. [PG-13]❸

Chalk Garden, The (1964-British) **C-106m.** *** D: Ronald Neame. Deborah Kerr, Hayley Mills, John Mills, Edith Evans, Felix Aylmer, Elizabeth Sellars. Very-high-class soap opera with good cast supporting story of teenager set on right path by governess Kerr; colorful production, quite entertaining. From Enid Bagnold play.▼

Challenge (1974) **C-84m.** BOMB D: Martin Beck. Earl Owensby, William Hicks, Katheryn Thompson, Johnny Popwell. North

Carolina-based Owensby's first film (which he also produced) amateurishly goes through the usual vengeance-for-killing-my-family paces. Opening printed crawl celebrates this as return of "clean, decent entertainment," followed by Owensby causing the deaths of various badguys. But don't worry—none of his victims is naked. Dreadful. [PG]▼

Challenge, The (1982) **C-112m.** **½ D: John Frankenheimer. Scott Glenn, Toshiro Mifune, Donna Kei Benz, Atsuo Nakamura, Calvin Young. Entertaining but sometimes pretentious actioner, with American boxer Glenn becoming involved in conflict between brothers Mifune and Nakamura over rights to family swords. Scripted by John Sayles and Richard Maxwell. Exteriors shot mostly in Kyoto. Completely recut for TV release as SWORD OF THE NINJA, running 97m. [R]▼

Challenge for Robin Hood, A (1967-British) **C-85m.** ** D: C. M. Pennington-Richards. Barrie Ingham, James Hayter, Leon Greene, Peter Blythe, Gay Hamilton, Alfie Bass. Hammer Films produced this inoffensive but undistinguished adventure yarn, which is of little interest except to children. Originally 96m. [G]▼

Challenge To Be Free (1976) **C-88m.** **½ D: Tay Garnett. Mike Mazurki, Vic Christy, Jimmy Kane, Fritz Ford. Fur trapper is pursued by the law in Arctic surroundings; simple and simple-minded, best for younger viewers. Made in 1972 as MAD TRAPPER OF THE YUKON, this marked last film for veteran director Garnett, who appears briefly as Marshal McGee. [G]▼▼

Challenge to Lassie (1949) **C-76m.** **½ D: Richard Thorpe. Edmund Gwenn, Donald Crisp, Geraldine Brooks, Reginald Owen, Alan Webb, Ross Ford, Henry Stephenson, Alan Napier, Sara Allgood, Arthur Shields. Based-on-fact story, set in 19th-century Edinburgh, about a dog (actually a Skye terrier but played here by Lassie) who keeps returning to a churchyard where its master (Crisp) is buried. Pleasant film, with a fine character-actor cast. Remade as GREYFRIARS BOBBY, which also features Crisp (as the cemetery caretaker). ▼

Chamber, The (1996) **C-110m.** ** D: James Foley. Chris O'Donnell, Gene Hackman, Faye Dunaway, Robert Prosky, Raymond Barry, Lela Rochon, Harve Presnell, Bo Jackson. Young lawyer feels impelled to defend a Mississippi death row inmate, convicted of a racist/terrorist bombing years ago, because the man is his grandfather. Reopening this volatile case causes pain and hardship for all involved. Curiously unmoving (and talky) adaptation of the John Grisham best-seller. O'Donnell is earnest but unconvincing; Hackman never successfully disappears into the role of a racist pig. Panavision. [R]▼●)

Chambermaid on the Titanic, The (1997-

French-Spanish-Italian) **C-96m.** *** D: Bigas Luna. Olivier Martinez, Romane Bohringer, Aitana Sánchez Gijón, Didier Bezace, Aldo Maccione. Utterly original and beautifully filmed fable about fantasy, desire and storytelling, centering on a French foundry worker who wins a trip to watch the launch of the *Titanic* in England and becomes obsessed with a woman he meets there. When he returns home, he becomes famous for spinning fantastical tales—which may or may not be true—about his wild night of passion with the woman. Unpredictable, unexpectedly moving film from the usually outrageous Luna (JAMÓN JAMÓN). Aka THE CHAMBERMAID. Cinecam-Scope.▼

Chamber of Horrors (1966) **C-99m.** *½ D: Hy Averback. Patrick O'Neal, Cesare Danova, Wilfrid Hyde-White, Patrice Wymore, Suzy Parker, Marie Windsor, Tony Curtis, Wayne Rogers. Wax museum provides setting for uneven mystery about mad killer on the loose. Intended for TV, it has mark of low-budget film plus two gimmicks: the "Horror Horn" and the "Fear Flasher."▼

Chameleon Street (1991) **C-95m.** *** D: Wendell B. Harris, Jr. Wendell B. Harris, Jr., Angela Leslie, Amina Fakir. Knowing sleeper based on true story of William Douglas Street, Jr. (played by Harris), a black man whose uncanny ability to intuit other people's needs enables him to successfully impersonate a reporter, a surgeon, an exchange student, and an attorney. Ingratiating film with a biting comic edge, and something to say. [R]▼▼

Champ, The (1931) **87m.** ***½ D: King Vidor. Wallace Beery, Jackie Cooper, Irene Rich, Roscoe Ates, Edward Brophy, Hale Hamilton. Superb tearjerker about a washed-up prizefighter and his adoring son, played to perfection by Beery and Cooper (in the first of their several teamings). Simple, sentimental in the extreme, but very effective. Beery won an Oscar for his performance, as did Frances Marion for her original story. Remade in 1953 (as THE CLOWN) and 1979.▼●)

Champ, The (1979) **C-121m.** *½ D: Franco Zeffirelli. Jon Voight, Faye Dunaway, Ricky Schroder, Jack Warden, Arthur Hill, Strother Martin, Joan Blondell, Elisha Cook. Voight is too intelligent to convince as a dumb pug, and Dunaway, as a loving mother, looks as if she wants to bed down with her kid in hopeless remake of the 1931 sudser. Young Schroder cries (and cries) convincingly. [PG]▼●)

Champagne for Caesar (1950) **99m.** *** D: Richard Whorf. Ronald Colman, Celeste Holm, Vincent Price, Barbara Britton, Art Linkletter. Genius Colman becomes national celebrity on TV quiz show; sponsor Price sends temptress Holm to distract big winner. Enjoyable spoof; Price hilarious as neurotic soap manufacturer. ▼●)

Champagne Murders, The (1967-French) **C-98m.** *** D: Claude Chabrol. Anthony Perkins, Maurice Ronet, Stephane Audran, Yvonne Furneaux, Suzanne Lloyd, Catherine Sola. Sale of champagne company to U.S. conglomerate manipulated by various weird, competing types, complicated by murders which point to playboy (Ronet). Murder-mystery narrative backdrop for odd psychological drama; one-of-a-kind film was shot in both English and French-language versions. Techniscope.

Champion (1949) **99m.** ***½ D: Mark Robson. Kirk Douglas, Marilyn Maxwell, Arthur Kennedy, Ruth Roman, Paul Stewart, Lola Albright. Unscrupulous boxer punches his way to the top, thrusting aside everybody and everything. Douglas perfectly cast in title role; gripping film, with Harry Gerstad's Oscar-winning editing. Also shown in computer-colored version. ▼○)

Champions (1983-British) **C-115m.** **½ D: John Irvin. John Hurt, Edward Woodward, Jan Francis, Ben Johnson, Kirstie Alley, Peter Barkworth, Ann Bell, Judy Parfitt. Formula drama of determined jockey Hurt battling cancer and hoping to make a comeback in the Grand National Steeplechase. The opening is reminiscent of CHARIOTS OF FIRE, the finale of ROCKY; however, the scenes with Hurt and his niece, and Hurt among children undergoing cancer treatment, are quite moving. Based on a true story. [PG] ▼○)

Champions Forever (1989) **C-87m.** *** D: Dimitri Logothetis. Fascinating, insightful look back at the careers of five modern heavyweight boxing legends: Muhammad Ali, Joe Frazier, George Foreman, Larry Holmes, and Ken Norton. Interviews with each fighter are juxtaposed with classic footage of their ring battles with Ali the dominant presence throughout. Candor and a subtle pathos make the interviews as poignant as the boxing scenes are exciting. ▼○)

Chances Are (1989) **C-108m.** *** D: Emile Ardolino. Cybill Shepherd, Robert Downey, Jr., Ryan O'Neal, Mary Stuart Masterson, Christopher McDonald, Josef Sommer, Joe Grifasi, Susan Ruttan, Fran Ryan, James Noble. A woman remains devoted to her husband years after his death . . . and then, one day, his spirit returns in the body of a much younger man. Surprisingly skillful blend of fantasy and romantic comedy manages to maintain its sweet-natured tone from start to finish. Appealing stars are supported by a gallery of top character actors. Written by Perry Howze and Randy Howze. [PG] ▼○)

Chandler (1972) **C-88m.** *½ D: Paul Magwood. Warren Oates, Leslie Caron, Alex Dreier, Gloria Grahame, Mitchell Ryan. Private eye falls in love with ex-mistress of racketeer. Substandard yarn. Panavision. [PG])

Chanel Solitaire (1981-U.S.-French) **C-120m.** ** D: George Kaczender. Marie-France Pisier, Timothy Dalton, Rutger Hauer, Karen Black, Brigitte Fossey. Stylish but cliché-ridden biography of designer Coco Chanel, covering her first 38 years and focusing on her love life. [R] ▼○

Changeling, The (1979-Canadian) **C-109m.** *** D: Peter Medak. George C. Scott, Trish Van Devere, Melvyn Douglas, John Colicos, Jean Marsh, Madeleine Thornton-Sherwood. Good, scary ghost story with Scott as recently widowed musician who moves into old house inhabited by spirit of a child who died there 70 years ago. [R] ▼○)

Changeling (2008) **C-141m.** *** D: Clint Eastwood. Angelina Jolie, John Malkovich, Jeffrey Donovan, Michael Kelly, Colm Feore, Jason Butler Harner, Amy Ryan, Geoff Pierson, Denis O'Hare, Frank Wood, Peter Gerety, Reed Birney, Eddie Alderson. The disappearance of a 9-year-old boy in 1928 L.A. pits his distraught mother (Jolie) against the crushingly corrupt police force, which can't afford more bad publicity. Her refusal to be hushed comes at a shocking price to her safety and sanity—but ultimately she finds powerful friends. Then the case expands with the discovery of a serial killer. Incredible story is all true, as documented by screenwriter J. Michael Straczynski. Jolie is superb as the long-suffering heroine of this remarkable tale. Intense, often tough to stomach, but scrupulously filmed by Eastwood. Panavision. [R])

Change of Habit (1969) **C-93m.** ** D: William Graham. Elvis Presley, Mary Tyler Moore, Barbara McNair, Jane Elliot, Leora Dana, Edward Asner, Doro Merande, Regis Toomey. Moore, a nun, is forced to choose between Dr. Presley and the church in substandard drama that at least represents slight change from typical Elvis fare. Presley's last screen role. [G] ▼)

Change of Mind (1969) **C-103m.** **½ D: Robert Stevens. Raymond St. Jacques, Susan Oliver, Janet MacLachlan, Leslie Nielsen, Donnelly Rhodes, David Bailey. In an emergency operation, the brain of a white district attorney is successfully transplanted into the body of a black man. Racial-protest sci-fi thriller is contrived, to say the least. [R]

Change of Seasons, A (1980) **C-102m.** **½ D: Richard Lang. Shirley MacLaine, Anthony Hopkins, Bo Derek, Michael Brandon, Mary Beth Hurt, Ed Winter. College professor Hopkins, drowning in male menopause, has an affair with student Derek, so wife MacLaine decides to take a lover of her own. One of the better midlife crisis films of this period, though many thought its major asset was opening sequence of Bo bouncing in a hot tub. Cowritten by Erich Segal. [R] ▼)

Changing Lanes (2002) **C-99m.** *** D: Roger Michell. Ben Affleck, Samuel L.

Jackson, Toni Collette, Sydney Pollack, William Hurt, Amanda Peet, Richard Jenkins, Kim Staunton, John Benjamin Hickey, Dylan Baker. Yuppie N.Y.C. lawyer Affleck, who's married to the boss's daughter, crashes into pent-up working-class Jackson's car one rainy morning as the latter is on his way to a custody hearing over his son. When Affleck blithely zips off, Jackson fumes, but the escalating battle of wits between the two only exposes their mutual vulnerability. A rare and compelling Hollywood movie about ethics and human nature. Written by Chap Taylor and Michael Tolkin. Super 35. [R]▼●

Changing Times (2004-French) **C-100m.** *** D: André Téchiné. Catherine Deneuve, Gérard Depardieu, Gilbert Melki, Malik Zidi, Lubna Azabal, Tanya Lopert, Nabila Baraka, Nadem Rachati. Single, middle-aged man (Depardieu) convinces himself that he must win the love of his long-ago girlfriend (Deneuve), who is unhappily married and is mired in family issues. This Tangier, Morocco–set drama is a provocative exploration of life's missed opportunities and the failure of individuals to connect and commit in meaningful ways; it also serves to mirror the differences in European and Muslim lifestyles. ▶

Chan Is Missing (1982) **80m.** *** D: Wayne Wang. Wood Moy, Marc Hayashi, Laureen Chew, Judy Mihei, Peter Wang, Presco Tabios. Wry, low-key comedy of cabdrivers Moy and Hayashi tracking down the mysterious Mr. Chan Hung, who absconded with their $4,000. Independently produced on shoestring budget and shot in San Francisco's Chinatown.▼●

Chant of Jimmie Blacksmith, The (1978-Australian) **C-124m.** ***½ D: Fred Schepisi. Tommy Lewis, Freddy Reynolds, Angela Punch, Ray Barrett, Jack Thompson, Peter Carroll, Bryan Brown. Half-white aborigine Lewis, brought up by Methodist pastor, is caught between two cultures and exploited, with tragic results. Harrowing indictment of racism, a problem certainly not unique to U.S. Based on fact. Director Schepisi's screenplay was adapted from a Thomas Keneally novel (Keneally also plays the role of Cook). Most U.S. prints run 108m. Panavision.▶

Chaos Theory (2007) **C-85m.** *½ D: Marcos Siega. Ryan Reynolds, Emily Mortimer, Stuart Townsend, Sarah Chalke, Mike Erwin, Constance Zimmer, Matreya Fedor. Labored comedy about an efficiency expert whose whole life starts to fall apart when a woman tries to seduce him, triggering a tidal wave of misunderstandings and revelations that threaten his once-happy marriage. Quietly dumped into a handful of theaters on its journey to the DVD bargain bin. Panavision. [PG-13]▶

Chaplin (1992-British-U.S.) **C-144m.** **½

D: Richard Attenborough. Robert Downey, Jr., Dan Aykroyd, Geraldine Chaplin, Kevin Dunn, Anthony Hopkins, Milla Jovovich, Moira Kelly, Kevin Kline, Diane Lane, Penelope Ann Miller, Paul Rhys, John Thaw, Marisa Tomei, Nancy Travis, James Woods, David Duchovny, Deborah Maria Moore, Bill Paterson, John Standing, Robert Stephens. Reverent, lovingly detailed bio of Charlie Chaplin—from his squalid childhood in London to early moviemaking days with Mack Sennett, to international stardom, celebrity, and scandal. Downey is astonishingly good as Charlie and the film starts out great, but flattens midway through and tries to cover too much ground. Geraldine Chaplin plays her own grandmother, Charlie's severely neurotic mom. [PG-13]▼●

Chaplin Revue, The (1959) **119m.** ***½ D: Charles Chaplin. Charlie Chaplin, Edna Purviance, Sydney Chaplin, Mack Swain. Three of Chaplin's best shorts strung together with his own music, narration, and behind-the-scenes footage: A DOG'S LIFE (1918), one of his loveliest films; SHOULDER ARMS (1918), a classic WW1 comedy; and THE PILGRIM (1923), his underrated gem about a convict who disguises himself as a minister.▼●

Chapman Report, The (1962) **C-125m.** **½ D: George Cukor. Efrem Zimbalist, Jr., Shelley Winters, Jane Fonda, Claire Bloom, Glynis Johns, Ray Danton, Ty Hardin, Andrew Duggan, John Dehner, Harold J. Stone, Corey Allen, Cloris Leachman, Chad Everett, Henry Daniell, Jack Cassidy. Slick, empty yarn about Kinsey-like sex researchers coming to suburban community to get statistical survey, with repercussions on assorted females. Potboiler material elevated by good performances and direction.

Chappaqua (1966) **C/B&W-92m.** ** D: Conrad Rooks. Jean-Louis Barrault, Conrad Rooks, William S. Burroughs, Allen Ginsberg, Ravi Shankar, Paula Pritchett, Ornette Coleman. Rooks, an alcoholic heroin addict, travels to Paris for a sleep cure and hallucinates while withdrawing. Autobiographical—and vague, surreal, phony. Prints of 82m. and 75m. also exist.▼●

Chapter 27 (2008-U.S.-Canadian) **C-84m.** ** D: J. P. Schaefer. Jared Leto, Lindsay Lohan, Judah Friedlander, Ursula Abbott, Jeane Fournier, Brian O'Neill. Creepy but ultimately pointless portrait of Mark David Chapman in the days leading up to his shooting of John Lennon outside his home at the Dakota apartment building in N.Y.C. in 1980. Leto is eerily convincing as the overweight loner who fancies himself to be Holden Caulfield, but when the film is over we don't know much more about Chapman than we did at the start. [R]▶

Chapter Two (1979) **C-124m.** ** D: Robert Moore. James Caan, Marsha Mason,

Valerie Harper, Joseph Bologna. Neil Simon's autobiographical comedy-drama—one of his best Broadway plays—gets lost in screen translation. Caan is miscast as sharp-minded writer who's drawn into new romance (with Mason) before he's really recovered from death of his wife. Long, plastic, and unmoving. [PG]▼●

Character (1997-Dutch) **C-125m.** *** D: Mike van Diem. Fedja van Huet, Jan Decleir, Betty Schuurman, Victor Low, Tamar van den Dop, Hans Kesting, Lou Landre, Bernhard Droog. Oscar-winning, powerful story of a virtuous young man (van Huet), in 1920s Rotterdam, caught in a web of financial entanglements with his estranged, malevolent father (Decleir). Assured feature directorial debut by van Diem feels Dickensian, but moves like wildfire. Strong performances by a cast of stage actors, save Belgian film stalwart Decleir; young lead van Huet is a dead ringer for Robert Downey, Jr. [R]▼▶

Charade (1963) **C-114m.** ***½ D: Stanley Donen. Cary Grant, Audrey Hepburn, Walter Matthau, James Coburn, George Kennedy, Ned Glass, Jacques Marin. Suave comedy-mystery in Hitchcock vein, with Grant aiding widow Hepburn to recover fortune secreted by husband, being sought by trio of sinister crooks; set in Paris. Excellent screenplay by Peter Stone, score by Henry Mancini. Remade in 2002 as THE TRUTH ABOUT CHARLIE.▼▶

Charge at Feather River, The (1953) **C-96m.** **½ D: Gordon Douglas. Guy Madison, Vera Miles, Frank Lovejoy, Dick Wesson, Helen Westcott, Onslow Stevens, Steve Brodie, Neville Brand, Henry Kulky. Pretty good saga of Madison leading ragtag "guardhouse brigade" toward an inevitable clash with the Cheyenne at title location. Subplots involve a SEARCHERS-like rescue of two white girls raised by Indians and a bit too much comedy relief from Wesson and Kulky. Listen for Lt. Wilhelm! Lovejoy even spits at the camera, in 3-D!

Charge of the Light Brigade, The (1936) **116m.** *** D: Michael Curtiz. Errol Flynn, Olivia de Havilland, Patric Knowles, Henry Stephenson, Nigel Bruce, Donald Crisp, David Niven, C. Henry Gordon, Robert Barrat, Spring Byington, J. Carrol Naish. Thundering action based on Tennyson's poem, with immortal charge into the valley of death by British 27th Lancers cavalry. Lavish production values accent romantic tale of Flynn and de Havilland at army post in India. Max Steiner's first musical score for Warner Brothers is superb. Balaklava Heights charge directed by action specialist B. Reeves Eason. Remade in 1968. Also shown in computer-colored version. ▼●▶

Charge of the Light Brigade, The (1968-British) **C-130m.** **½ D: Tony Richardson. David Hemmings, Vanessa Redgrave, John Gielgud, Harry Andrews, Trevor Howard, Jill Bennett, Mark Burns. Exquisitely made, but ultimately disappointing drama of events leading up to British involvement in Crimean War. Stunning battle sequence cannot make up for dramatic loopholes in this story of military minds gone mad. Clever animated segments by Richard Williams. Redgrave and Richardson's young daughters Natasha and Joely are members of the wedding party. Panavision. [M/PG]▼▶

Chariots of Fire (1981-British) **C-123m.** ***½ D: Hugh Hudson. Ben Cross, Ian Charleson, Nigel Havers, Nick Farrell, Alice Krige, Cheryl Campbell, Ian Holm, John Gielgud, Lindsay Anderson, Patrick Magee, Nigel Davenport, Dennis Christopher, Brad Davis. Absorbing and unusual drama based on true story of two men—devout Scottish missionary Eric Liddell, driven Jewish Cambridge student Harold Abrahams—who run in the 1924 Olympics. Fascinating probe of their motives, challenges, and problems, and a case study of repressed emotions even in the midst of exultation. Feature debut for director Hudson. Oscars for Best Picture, Colin Welland's script, Vangelis' excellent score, and Milena Canonero's costumes. [PG]▼●▶

Chariots of the Gods? (1970) **C-98m.** *** D: Harald Reinl. First of too many speculative documentaries about ancient visitors from outer space who helped advance mankind's knowledge centuries ago. Well made and filled with many natural beauties. Based on Erich Von Daniken's book. [G] ▼●▶

Charley and the Angel (1973) **C-93m.** **½ D: Vincent McEveety. Fred MacMurray, Cloris Leachman, Harry Morgan, Kurt Russell, Vincent Van Patten, Kathleen Cody. MacMurray learns he has only a short time left on earth from helpful angel (Morgan) and changes his hard ways with family. Lightly amusing Disney film, but the warmth and nostalgia seem artificial this time around. [G]▼

Charley One-Eye (1973) **C-107m.** ** D: Don Chaffey. Richard Roundtree, Roy Thinnes, Nigel Davenport, Jill Pearson. Basically two-man show. Black Union Army deserter (Roundtree) and outcast Indian (Thinnes) thrown together in desert wasteland; gradual tragic relationship develops when outside forces interfere. Far too long; should've been a TV movie. [R]

Charley's Aunt (1941) **81m.** **½ D: Archie Mayo. Jack Benny, Kay Francis, James Ellison, Anne Baxter, Edmund Gwenn, Reginald Owen. Broad but surefire filming of Brandon Thomas play about Oxford student posing as maiden aunt, joke getting out of hand. Previously filmed six other times! Remade as musical WHERE'S CHARLEY?▶

Charley Varrick (1973) **C-111m.** ***½ D: Don Siegel. Walter Matthau, Joe Don Baker, Felicia Farr, John Vernon, Andy Robinson,

Jacqueline Scott, Sheree North, Norman Fell, Woodrow Parfrey. Neatly contrived thriller with Matthau as a bank robber who discovers that his small-town take is actually laundered Mafia money. On target all the way, with a particularly satisfying wrap-up. [PG]▼●❍

Charlie and the Chocolate Factory (2005) C-115m. **½ D: Tim Burton. Johnny Depp, Freddie Highmore, David Kelly, Helena Bonham Carter, Noah Taylor, Missi Pyle, James Fox, Deep Roy, Christopher Lee, Julia Winter, AnnaSophia Robb, Jordon Fry, Philip Wiegratz; narrated by Geoffrey Holder. Roald Dahl's classic story (previously filmed as WILLY WONKA AND THE CHOCOLATE FACTORY) about five children—one good, four rotten—invited to tour a strange, reclusive inventor's candy empire. Dazzling production is everything you'd expect from director Burton, but the scenes at the factory are less compelling than those dealing with Charlie and his family. And Depp, though amusing, is no Gene Wilder. Music by Danny Elfman with lyrics from Dahl's text. Roy, through digital technology, plays all the Oompa-Loompas. [PG]▼❍

Charlie Bartlett (2008) C-97m. **½ D: Jon Poll. Anton Yelchin, Robert Downey, Jr., Hope Davis, Kat Dennings, Tyler Hilton, Mark Rendall. Charismatic Charlie has been kicked out of various educational institutions, when all he really wants is to be the most popular kid in school; he finally gets his wish by becoming an all-purpose shrink to his fellow students. He also falls in love with the daughter of the school principal (Downey), who's got plenty of problems of his own. Offbeat comedy with serious undertones wanders all over the map but benefits from Downey's offbeat characterization and Yelchin's appealing performance. [R]❍

Charlie Bubbles (1968-British) C-91m. **½ D: Albert Finney. Albert Finney, Colin Blakely, Billie Whitelaw, Liza Minnelli. Finney's first directing attempt concerns itself with married writer who begins affair with his secretary. Not especially moving, but Minnelli's screen debut adds quite a bit of sparkle to film.

Charlie Chan series SEE: *Leonard Maltin's Classic Movie Guide*

Charlie Chan and the Curse of the Dragon Queen (1981) C-97m. *½ D: Clive Donner. Peter Ustinov, Lee Grant, Angie Dickinson, Richard Hatch, Brian Keith, Michelle Pfeiffer, Roddy McDowall, Rachel Roberts, Paul Ryan, Johnny Sekka. Boring comedy wastes its talented cast. Ustinov is badly miscast, gives one of the worst performances of his career. Hatch is his clumsy half-Jewish, half-Oriental grandson. Paging Warner Oland. [PG]▼❍

Charlie's Angels (2000) C-98m. **½ D: McG (Joseph McGinty Nicol). Cameron Diaz, Drew Barrymore, Lucy Liu, Bill Murray, Tim Curry, Matt LeBlanc, Sam Rockwell, Kelly Lynch, Crispin Glover, LL Cool J, Luke Wilson, Tom Green; voice of John Forsythe. Frothy, high-energy popcorn movie based on the popular 1970s TV series about three smart, beautiful operatives who work for an unseen boss at a detective agency. Great showcase for the sexy stars, but with nothing at its core, the fun starts to pall halfway through. Followed by a sequel. Super 35. [PG-13]▼❍

Charlie's Angels: Full Throttle (2003) C-111m. ** D: McG. Drew Barrymore, Cameron Diaz, Lucy Liu, Demi Moore, Bernie Mac, Crispin Glover, Justin Theroux, Robert Patrick, Rodrigo Santoro, Shia LaBeouf, Matt LeBlanc, Luke Wilson, John Cleese, Ja'net DuBois, Robert Forster, Eric Bogosian, Carrie Fisher. The girls are back in action, trying to track down a pair of information-laden rings that could spell disaster in the wrong hands. So much for story! The rest of the movie consists of high-decibel but fragmented sequences of video-game–style action, music, and eye candy, with a couple of extra plot threads—one involving an Angel gone bad (Moore). Much ado about much ado, minus the freshness and martial-arts fun that made the first film entertaining. Many star cameos dot the already busy landscape. Super 35. [PG-13]▼❍

Charlie's Ghost Story (1994) C-88m. ** D: Anthony Edwards. Cheech Marin, Anthony Edwards, Linda Fiorentino, Trenton Knight, Charles Rocket, J. T. Walsh, Daphne Zuniga. Occasionally funny story of the ghost of explorer Coronado haunting people to get his bones properly buried so he can finally rest in peace. Actually, it's a rather sad story of child neglect. Archeologist/dad Edwards is so enthralled with his discovery of Coronado's cave, he completely ignores his son, who is the target of the "haunting." Fiorentino is wasted in the thankless role of the family maid. Based on a story by Mark Twain. Aka CHARLIE'S GHOST: THE SECRET OF CORONADO. [PG]▼❍

Charlie St. Cloud (2010) C-99m. ** D: Burr Steers. Zac Efron, Charlie Tahan, Amanda Crew, Augustus Prew, Donal Logue, Kim Basinger, Ray Liotta, Dave Franco. Ethereal but flawed drama about a young man so upset over his younger brother's untimely death that he takes a job at the cemetery where the young boy is buried. Complications arise when he meets a girl and is torn between living in the past or the present. Efron is earnest and the film has its heart in the right place, but it doesn't quite work. Scenes between Efron and the ghost of his brother don't resonate as they were intended to. Based on Ben Sherwood's novel *The Death and Life of Charlie St. Cloud*. Panavision. [PG-13]❍

Charlie, the Lonesome Cougar (1968) C-75m. **½ No director credited. Narrated by Rex Allen. Ron Brown, Brian Russell, Linda Wallace, Jim Wilson. Average Disney animal adventure-comedy about a friendly cougar who lives in a lumber camp. ▼❚

Charlie Wilson's War (2007) **C-97m.** ***½ D: Mike Nichols. Tom Hanks, Julia Roberts; Philip Seymour Hoffman, Amy Adams, Ned Beatty, Emily Blunt, Om Puri, Ken Stott, John Slattery, Denis O'Hare, Jud Tylor. Womanizer and high-living Texas Congressman Wilson (Hanks) is the least likely man in Washington, D.C., to champion the cause of the Afghan people versus the Soviet Army in the 1980s. But using the same bravado with which he lives his reckless life, he cobbles together an amazing alliance *sub rosa.* Geopolitics has never been so entertaining, thanks to Nichols' breezy pacing, Aaron Sorkin's witty script, and pearly performances. Hoffman is perfect as a scruffy but dedicated CIA op. The inevitable conclusion, however, is far from funny. Based on a true story and the best-selling book by George Crile. [R]❚

Charlotte Gray (2001-British-Australian) **C-121m.** **½ D: Gillian Armstrong. Cate Blanchett, Billy Crudup, Michael Gambon, Rupert Penry-Jones, Anton Lesser, Ron Cook, James Fleet. During WW2, a Scottish woman volunteers to work undercover in France—in part, so she can locate her lover, an airman who was shot down. Once situated, she begins to understand the Resistance fighters' feelings, especially after growing close to one fiery young man. Interesting, handsomely made film never finds its true focus—and asks us to accept English-speaking actors of all nationalities as French. Blanchett is as compulsively watchable as ever. Based on a novel by Sebastian Faulks. [PG-13] ▼❚

Charlotte's Web (1973) **C-93m.** *** D: Charles A. Nichols, Iwao Takamoto. Voices of Debbie Reynolds, Henry Gibson, Paul Lynde, Agnes Moorehead, Charles Nelson Reilly; narrated by Rex Allen. Charming animated feature based on E. B. White classic of barnyard spider who befriends shy piglet. Above average for Hanna-Barbera cartoon studio. Songs by Richard M. and Robert B. Sherman. Followed by a direct-to-video sequel in 2003. Remade in 2006. [G]▼❚

Charlotte's Web (2006) **C-97m.** *** D: Gary Winick. Dakota Fanning, Kevin Anderson, Beau Bridges, Gary Basaraba, Siobhan Fallon; voices of Julia Roberts, Dominic Scott Kay, Robert Redford, Steve Buscemi, John Cleese, Oprah Winfrey, Cedric the Entertainer, Kathy Bates, Reba McEntire, Thomas Haden Church, André Benjamin; narrated by Sam Shepard. Likable adaptation of E. B. White's novel, blending live actors with computer-animated creatures, about a runt pig and the animals he meets in a barn. Charlotte, a spider, sets out to save him from the butcher's block by weaving words into her web. Entertaining and well made, but it falls short when compared to the well-loved book. [G]❚

Charly (1968) **C-103m.** ***½ D: Ralph Nelson. Cliff Robertson, Claire Bloom, Lilia Skala, Leon Janney, Dick Van Patten. Robertson won Oscar for fine work as retarded man turned into super-brain in scientific experiment (a role he first tackled on TV's *U.S. Steel Hour* in 1961). Bloom is sympathetic caseworker who becomes attached to Charly. Based on Daniel Keyes' *Flowers for Algernon* (and remade for TV in 2000 under that title). First rate. Techniscope. [M/PG]▼❚

Charro! (1969) **C-98m.** BOMB D: Charles Marquis Warren. Elvis Presley, Ina Balin, Victor French, Lynn Kellogg, Barbara Werle, Paul Brinegar. Attempt to change Presley's image by casting him in straight Western is total failure. Elvis sings only one song. Panavision. [G]▼❚

Chase, The (1966) **C-135m.** **½ D: Arthur Penn. Marlon Brando, Jane Fonda, Robert Redford, Angie Dickinson, Janice Rule, James Fox, Robert Duvall, E. G. Marshall, Miriam Hopkins, Martha Hyer. Intriguing, unsubtle drama of how prison escape by local boy (Redford) affects worthless Texas town and its sheriff (Brando). Based on a novel by Horton Foote. Notorious for behind-the-scenes conflicts with director Penn, screenwriter Lillian Hellman, and producer Sam Spiegel, it's not surprising that finished product misses the mark. Panavision. ▼❚

Chase, The (1994) **C-94m.** *½ D: Adam Rifkin. Charlie Sheen, Kristy Swanson, Henry Rollins, Josh Mostel, Wayne Grace, Rocky Carroll, Miles Dougal, Ray Wise, Claudia Christian, Natalija Nogulich, Flea, Anthony Kiedis, Cary Elwes, Cassian Elwes. Falsely accused prison escapee is forced to kidnap the daughter of California's version of Donald Trump, setting off a movie-length pursuit by police and a TV news helicopter. Why bother? [PG-13]▼❚

Chase for the Golden Needles, The SEE: **Golden Needles**

Chasers (1994) **C-101m.** *½ D: Dennis Hopper. Tom Berenger, Erika Eleniak, William McNamara, Crispin Glover, Matthew Glave, Dean Stockwell, Gary Busey, Seymour Cassel, Frederic Forrest, Marilu Henner. Two Navy men are assigned to prisoner-escort duty only to discover that the dangerous criminal they are escorting is—gulp!—a beautiful sexpot. Lowbrow comedy is no LAST DETAIL, and has little to recommend it, even for fans of t&a. Many of Hopper's acting cronies appear in small roles, and Hopper himself turns up as a perverted underwear salesman. [R]▼❚

Chasing Amy (1997) **C-111m.** ***½ D: Kevin Smith. Ben Affleck, Joey Lauren Adams, Jason Lee, Dwight Ewell, Jason Mewes,

Kevin Smith, Matt Damon, Casey Affleck. Winning, original comedy-drama about a comic book artist who lives with his dour work partner—until he meets an attractive up-and-coming female artist with a dynamite personality. He's seriously smitten—and stays that way even after learning that she's gay. Writer-director Smith hits all the right notes in this honest and appealing film, which refuses to take the easy way out (just like its lead character) right to the end. Affleck and Adams are perfect. Smith and Mewes reprise their Silent Bob and Jay characters. [R] ▼●▌

Chasing Dreams (1982) **C-105m.** *½ D: Sean Roche, Therese Conte. David G. Brown, John Fife, Jim Shane, Matthew Clark, Lisa Kingston, Claudia Carroll, Kevin Costner. Hopelessly hokey soaper of insecure, self-conscious farmboy Brown, who "finds" himself by playing college baseball. Of interest solely for early, brief appearance of Costner as Brown's older, medical-student brother. [PG] ▼

Chasing Liberty (2004-U.S.-British) **C-110m.** ** D: Andy Cadiff. Mandy Moore, Matthew Goode, Jeremy Piven, Annabella Sciorra, Caroline Goodall, Mark Harmon. Teenage daughter of the President of the United States yearns to break loose, and does just that during a trip to Europe. Little does she know that the guy who helps her escape from the Secret Service is in fact an agent himself. Starts out as what it should have been, a cute romantic-comedy vehicle for Moore in the ROMAN HOLIDAY mode, but descends into tiresome predictability. Even location filming in Europe doesn't add much. Super 35. [PG-13] ▼▌

Chasing Papi (2003) **C-80m.** ** D: Linda Mendoza. Roselyn Sanchez, Sofía Vergara, Jaci Velasquez, Eduardo Verástegui, Lisa Vidal, D. L. Hughley, Freddy Rodriguez, Maria Conchita Alonso, Pete Escovedo, Peter Michael Escovedo, Sheila E. Innocuous Latin-flavored comedy about a handsome advertising exec who has three women—in three different cities—convinced they are his one and only. Then they all decide to drop in on him unannounced. Silly storyline is played with gusto, but there's scarcely a laugh in sight. Paul Rodriguez appears unbilled. Co-produced by Forest Whitaker. [PG] ▼▌

Chastity (1969) **C-83m.** ** D: Alessio de Paola. Cher, Barbara London, Tom Nolan, Stephen Whittaker. Interesting story of girl who takes to the highway to find life of her own. Cher in solo acting debut is surprisingly good. Sonny Bono wrote, produced, and composed the music. [PG—originally rated R] ▌

Chastity Belt, The SEE: **On My Way to the Crusades, I Met a Girl Who . . .**

Château, The (2002) **C-92m.** *½ D: Jesse Peretz. Paul Rudd, Romany Malco, Sylvie Testud, Philippe Nahon, Donal Logue, Didier Flamand. Threadbare comedy, shot on digital video, about two American brothers—one white, one black—who bumble their way to France to inspect a castle they've inherited. It turns out a household staff comes along with the residence, and they don't greet the new owners with open arms, for a variety of reasons. Rudd's obnoxious character goes a long way toward sinking this. [R] ▼▌

Chato's Land (1972-Spanish-British) **C-100m.** **½ D: Michael Winner. Charles Bronson, Jack Palance, Richard Basehart, Ralph Waite, Richard Jordan, Victor French. Posse seeks Indian Bronson in connection with marshal's murder; usual quota of blood in lengthy film. [PG] ▼▌

Chattahoochee (1990) **C-98m.** ** D: Mick Jackson. Gary Oldman, Dennis Hopper, Frances McDormand, Pamela Reed, Ned Beatty, M. Emmet Walsh, William De Acutis, Lee Wilkof, Matt Craven, Gary Klar. Enervatingly straightforward account of man (Oldman) whose mental breakdown (actually post-Korea combat stress) wrongfully landed him in a Karloff-caliber Florida institution. Standard "reform" drama—though based on fact—with Hopper's role (as a fellow patient) a glorified cameo; McDormand and Reed do all right as, respectively, Oldman's wife and crusading sister. [R] ▼●▌

Chattanooga Choo Choo (1984) **C-102m.** ** D: Bruce Bilson. Barbara Eden, George Kennedy, Melissa Sue Anderson, Joe Namath, Bridget Hanley, Clu Gulager, Christopher McDonald, Davis Roberts, Tony Azito, Parley Baer. In order to collect inheritance, goofball Kennedy must restore the famous train and make one final 24-hour run from Pennsylvania Station. Spirited cast in a sitcom-level script. Rubber-limbed Azito is amazing as waiter who's never dropped a tray. [PG] ▼

Chavez: Inside the Coup SEE: **Revolution Will Not Be Televised, The**

Che! (1969) **C-96m.** BOMB D: Richard Fleischer. Omar Sharif, Jack Palance, Cesare Danova, Robert Loggia, Woody Strode. Comic-book treatment of famed revolutionary became one of the biggest film jokes of 1960s. However, you haven't lived until you see Palance play Fidel Castro. Panavision. [PG] ▼

Che (2008-U.S.-Spanish-French) **C-269m.** ** D: Steven Soderbergh. Benicio Del Toro, Demián Bichir, Elvira Mínguez, Rodrigo Santoro, Santiago Cabrera, Jorge Perugorría, Julia Ormond, Yul Vázquez, Catalina Sandino Moreno, Joaquim de Almeida, Franka Potente, Sam Robards, Lou Diamond Phillips, Mark Umbers, Jsu García, Matt Damon. Impressively shot but dramatically inert epic is the most elaborate of Soderbergh's indie "experiments" (interspersed between his OCEANS movies). This dramatizes the significant contribution that Argentine Ernesto "Che" Guevara made to the late-'50s revolution in Cuba, and his participation in a failed

Bolivian replication during the mid-1960s, culminating in his death. Part One of this two-parter has a narrative advantage because it at least deals with political victory. Throughout, the smaller moments of camaraderie while battling outdoor elements ring truest, which isn't a whole lot to say for a movie running more than four hours. Despite Del Toro's apt casting in the lead, it's the kind of grinder where, when the words "Day 302" are flashed onscreen, you turn to your viewing companion and say, "That's for damned sure." Part One (CHE: THE ARGENTINE) runs 134m.; Part Two (CHE: THE GUERRILLA), 135m. HD Widescreen. [R]◗

Cheap Detective, The (1978) **C-92m.** ★★★ D: Robert Moore. Peter Falk, Ann-Margret, Eileen Brennan, Sid Caesar, Stockard Channing, James Coco, Dom DeLuise, Louise Fletcher, John Houseman, Madeline Kahn, Fernando Lamas, Marsha Mason, Phil Silvers, Vic Tayback, Abe Vigoda, Paul Williams, Nicol Williamson, David Ogden Stiers. For Neil Simon and Peter Falk to parody Bogart movies like MALTESE FALCON is an easy task, but it's still pretty funny when not resorting to the obvious. Panavision. [PG]▼●◗

Cheaper by the Dozen (1950) **C-85m.** ★★★ D: Walter Lang. Clifton Webb, Myrna Loy, Jeanne Crain, Mildred Natwick, Edgar Buchanan. Charming turn-of-the-century story of the Gilbreth children, 12 strong, their exacting father (well played by Webb) and mother (Loy). From the Gilbreth-Carey novel. Loosely remade in 2003. Sequel: BELLES ON THEIR TOES. ▼◗

Cheaper by the Dozen (2003) **C-98m.** ★★★ D: Shawn Levy. Steve Martin, Bonnie Hunt, Piper Perabo, Hilary Duff, Tom Welling, Richard Jenkins, Kevin G. Schmidt, Alyson Stoner, Jacob Smith, Liliana Mumy, Morgan York, Forrest Landis, Alan Ruck, Vanessa Bell Calloway. Martin and Hunt are happy, harried parents of 12 kids until a major move and career changes (a football coaching job at his alma mater for him, an extended book-promotion tour for her) throw the family asunder. Cute family comedy, with predictable slapstick moments, is strengthened by Martin and Hunt's performances as genuinely loving parents. Although officially a remake, it has nothing to do with the 1950 film or the book that inspired it. Ashton Kutcher appears unbilled. Followed by a sequel. [PG] ▼◗

Cheaper by the Dozen 2 (2005) **C-93m.** ★½ D: Adam Shankman. Steve Martin, Bonnie Hunt, Tom Welling, Eugene Levy, Carmen Electra, Piper Perabo, Jaime King, Hilary Duff, Taylor Lautner, Alyson Stoner. Depressing sequel to the box-office hit finds the Bakers returning to the vacation spot of their youth, where dad Martin gets into a competitive spat with wealthy Levy. Once again, a comic known for his rapier wit is reduced to Z-list slapstick (e.g., taking falls chasing rodents). A far more compelling if unexplored movie was right under the filmmakers' eyes: Levy's courtship of wife Electra (surprisingly, a leveling influence here). Panavision. [PG]◗

Cheaper to Keep Her (1980) **C-92m.** BOMB D: Ken Annakin. Mac Davis, Tovah Feldshuh, Art Metrano, Ian McShane, Priscilla Lopez, Rose Marie, Jack Gilford, J. Pat O'Malley. Detective Davis is hired by lawyer Feldshuh to check out McShane and Gilford, who have been lax in their alimony checks. Sexist, racist, and obnoxious. [R]▼

Cheatin' Hearts (1993) **C-90m.** ★★ D: Rod McCall. Sally Kirkland, James Brolin, Kris Kristofferson, Pamela Gidley, Laura Johnson, Michael Moore, Renee Estevez. Very ordinary love story set in New Mexico, involving romantic relationships in a sleepy little town. Stars are all attractive, but story is just too thin to hold much interest. Kirkland and Brolin executive produced. [R]▼◗

Checkered Flag or Crash (1977) **C-95m.** ★★ D: Alan Gibson. Joe Don Baker, Susan Sarandon, Larry Hagman, Alan Vint, Parnelli Jones, Logan Clark. A 1,000 mile off-road race in the Philippines is the focal point of this unmemorable programmer; for car-action fans only. Panavision. [PG]

Checking Out (1989-U.S.-British) **C-96m.** *½ D: David Leland. Jeff Daniels, Melanie Mayron, Michael Tucker, Kathleen York, Ann Magnuson, Allan Havey, Jo Harvey Allen, Felton Perry, Alan Wolfe. When Daniels' best friend dies of a heart attack he suddenly turns into a raging hypochondriac, convinced the same thing will happen to him. After 90m. of this overblown black comedy you pray that it will. Panavision. [R]▼◗

Check Is in the Mail, The (1986) **C-91m.** ★★ D: Joan Darling. Brian Dennehy, Anne Archer, Hallie Todd, Chris Herbert, Michael Bowen, Nita Talbot, Dick Shawn. Ineffectual comedy about a beleaguered family man who decides to beat the system by making his home self-sufficient. Episodic, slow-paced film wears out its sometimes likable ingredients. [R]▼

Cheech & Chong's Next Movie (1980) **C-99m.** *½ D: Thomas Chong. Cheech Marin, Thomas Chong, Evelyn Guerrero, Betty Kennedy, Sy Kramer, Rikki Marin. After an auspicious debut in UP IN SMOKE, the pothead, put-on comic duo go seriously awry in this crude, incoherent film, which offers only sporadic laughs. Look for Phil Hartman and Rita Wilson in bits. [R]▼●◗

Cheech & Chong's Nice Dreams (1981) **C-89m.** ★★ D: Thomas Chong. Cheech Marin, Thomas Chong, Evelyn Guerrero, Paul Reubens (Pee-wee Herman), Stacy Keach, Dr. Timothy Leary, Sandra Bernhard. Episodic, generally below par C&C

comedy finds them as owners of an ice-cream truck that fronts for more lucrative grass trade. Some hilarity involving a sexually jealous biker; Guerrero once again an apt comic foil. [R] ▼●◖

Cheech & Chong's The Corsican Brothers (1984) **C-90m.** BOMB D: Thomas Chong. Cheech Marin, Thomas Chong, Roy Dotrice, Shelby Fiddis, Rikki Marin, Edie McClurg, Rae Dawn Chong, Robbi Chong. The boys (in three roles each) and their families (in one role each) star in their first non-drug (but still tasteless) comedy, an inept parody which seems all the more empty because of its magnificent French locations. Staggeringly unfunny even by C&C standards; the *previews* for START THE REVOLUTION WITHOUT ME have more laughs. [PG] ▼●◖

Cheetah (1989) **C-84m.** *** D: Jeff Blyth. Keith Coogan, Lucy Deakins, Collin Mothupi, Timothy Landfield, Breon Gorman, Ka Vundia, Kuldeep Bhakoo. Two Southern California kids join their parents for several months in Kenya, make friends with a young Masai, and adopt an orphaned cheetah, which they raise as a pet. Simple storyline is aimed squarely at kids, but it's believable and entertaining and teaches good lessons about tolerance and respect for the wild. A Disney release. [G] ▼●◖

Chef in Love, A (1996-French-Russian) **C-100m.** **½ D: Nana Djordjadze. Pierre Richard, Nino Kirtadze, Micheline Presle, Timur Kamkhadze, Jean-Yves Gautier, Ramaz Chkhikvadze, Danielle Darrieux. Yet another film which equates food with love and sex. Richard, a fabled French chef, comes to live in Georgia just before the Russian Revolution, where he romances a princess (Kirtadze) and opens a restaurant; his life is irrevocably altered upon the arrival of the Red Army. Despite some mouth-watering scenery (and food), the result is annoyingly uneven. [PG-13] ▼

Chelsea Walls (2002) **C-112m.** ** D: Ethan Hawke. Kevin Corrigan, Rosario Dawson, Vincent D'Onofrio, Robert Sean Leonard, Kris Kristofferson, Natasha Richardson, Little Jimmy Scott, John Seitz, Uma Thurman, Mark Weber, Tuesday Weld, Steve Zahn, Harris Yulin, Guillermo Diaz, Frank Whaley, Marisa Tomei, Christopher Walken. Impressionistic ode to N.Y.C.'s fabled Chelsea Hotel and the ghosts of tortured artistic souls like Dylan Thomas who affect the current inhabitants—from a newly arrived Midwestern folksinger to a booze-ridden novelist who can't get his act together. Not uninteresting as a mood piece, with some good performances, but unenlightening and fatally slow moving. Hawke's feature directing debut. [R] ▼◖

Chéri (2009-British-French-German) **C-93m.** ** D: Stephen Frears. Michelle Pfeiffer, Rupert Friend, Kathy Bates, Felicity Jones, Bette Bourne, Nichola McAuliffe, Frances Tomelty, Anita Pallenberg, Harriet Walter, Iben Hjejle. Frears reunites with screenwriter Christopher Hampton, from DANGEROUS LIAISONS, but this costume drama (based on a pair of Colette novels from 1920) goes awry. As the title youth, Friend is a lump opposite Pfeiffer's courtesan, the woman who taught him sexual basics in late-19th-century Paris and is now trying to rekindle the flame. Bates stretches patience as Chéri's mother, but Pfeiffer still has enough aging luminosity to suggest what the movie might have been. Panavision. [R] ◖

Cherish (2002) **C-102m.** *** D: Finn Taylor. Robin Tunney, Tim Blake Nelson, Nora Dunn, Brad Hunt, Lindsay Crouse, Liz Phair, Jason Priestley. Offbeat story of a misfit who's victimized by a stalker and then involved in an accident that lands her in jail—but her "prison" is an apartment, where an electronic device chained to her ankle restricts her movement. In time, the deputy who maintains the device becomes her only friend. Fresh, original thriller set in San Francisco from writer-director Taylor, anchored by Tunney's strong, appealing performance. [R] ▼◖

Cherry Orchard, The (1999-Greek-French) **C-141m.** **½ D: Michael Cacoyannis. Charlotte Rampling, Alan Bates, Katrin Cartlidge, Owen Teale, Tushka Bergen, Xander Berkeley, Gerald (Gerard) Butler, Andrew Howard, Melanie Lynskey, Ian McNeice, Frances De La Tour, Michael Gough. Melancholy, muted adaptation of Chekhov classic about a once-prosperous Russian family's struggle to cope with the imminent sale of their estate and the beloved title orchard. Made with care and well acted, but not quite effective as either a film or as an "opened-up" play. Adapted by the director. Released in the U.S. in 2002. ▼◖

Cherry 2000 (1988) **C-93m.** **½ D: Steve DeJarnatt. Melanie Griffith, Ben Johnson, Harry Carey, Jr., David Andrews, Tim Thomerson, Pamela Gidley, Jennifer Mayo. Post-MAD MAX adventure about a female mercenary hired to bust into a 21st-century robot warehouse operated by psychos in what used to be the American Southwest. Derivative, but a bit more fun than its limited theatrical release might lead you to believe; Johnson and Carey are worth their combined weights in audience goodwill. Filmed in 1986. [PG-13] ▼●◖

Chesty Anderson, USN (1976) **C-88m.** ** D: Ed Forsyth. Shari Eubank, Rosanne Katon, Dorri Thomson, Marcie Barkin, Timothy Carey, Scatman Crothers, Frank Campanella, Fred Willard, Betty Thomas. Sexploitation comedy about female naval recruits is so timid that it keeps its lovely cast clothed even during physical exams! Retitled ANDERSON'S ANGELS for TV. [R] ▼◖

Chevy Van SEE: **Van, The** (1976)

Cheyenne (1947) **100m.** ** D: Raoul Walsh. Dennis Morgan, Jane Wyman, Janis Paige, Bruce Bennett, Alan Hale, Arthur Kennedy, Barton MacLane. Standard Western as gambler attempts to capture outlaw—instead spends time with outlaw's wife. Later a TV series. Retitled THE WYOMING KID.

Cheyenne Autumn (1964) **C-145m.** *** D: John Ford. Richard Widmark, Carroll Baker, Karl Malden, Dolores Del Rio, Sal Mineo, Edward G. Robinson, James Stewart, Ricardo Montalban, Gilbert Roland, Arthur Kennedy, Patrick Wayne, Elizabeth Allen, Victor Jory, John Carradine, Mike Mazurki, John Qualen, George O'Brien. Sprawling, uneven, but entertaining John Ford Western (his last) about Cheyenne Indian tribe and its eventful journey back to original settlement after being relocated by the government. Director Ford's last film in Monument Valley. Dodge City sequence (with Stewart as Wyatt Earp) was cut after premiere engagements; restored to 154m. on video. Super Panavision 70. ▼●▮

Cheyenne Social Club, The (1970) **C-103m.** **½ D: Gene Kelly. Henry Fonda, James Stewart, Shirley Jones, Sue Ane Langdon, Elaine Devry. Jimmy inherits and runs a bawdy house in the Old West. Lots of laughs, but clichés run throughout. Panavision. [PG]▼▮

Cheyenne Warrior (1994) **C-86m.** *** D: Mark Griffiths. Kelly Preston, Pato Hoffmann, Bo Hopkins, Rick Dean, Clint Howard, Charles Powell, Dan Clark, Winterhawk, Dan Haggerty. Modest but engrossing Western character study about the growing bond between a proud Indian warrior and a naive white woman who loses her husband while heading west in the 1800s. Well cast and well written (by Michael B. Druxman). [PG]▼▮

Chicago (2002) **C-113m.** *** D: Rob Marshall. Renée Zellweger, Catherine Zeta-Jones, Richard Gere, Queen Latifah, John C. Reilly, Christine Baranski, Lucy Liu, Taye Diggs, Colm Feore, Dominic West. Ditzy Roxie Hart (Zellweger) shoots a man, then hires the slickest lawyer in Chicago to represent her so she'll become a media star like her idol, nightclub performer Velma Kelly. Entertaining film version of the Bob Fosse–John Kander–Fred Ebb Broadway show treats the musical moments as figments of Roxie's imagination, contrasted against the dark reality of her life. Some quibbles: director Marshall hammers across every song as if it's the closing number and uses music-video–style cutting to the point of distraction. The stars are good, but Zeta-Jones reveals her experience as a musical performer and provides the knockout punch. Story filmed before in 1927 and as ROXIE HART. Chita Rivera, of the original Broadway cast, has a cameo. Oscar winner for Best Picture, Supporting Actress (Zeta-Jones), Costume Design (Colleen Atwood), Art Direction, Film Editing, and Sound. [PG-13]▼▮

Chicago Joe and the Showgirl (1990-British) **C-103m.** **½ D: Bernard Rose. Kiefer Sutherland, Emily Lloyd, Patsy Kensit, Keith Allen, Liz Fraser, Alexandra Pigg, Ralph Nossek, Colin Bruce, John Lahr. Yank soldier-hood Sutherland, stationed in London during WW2, joins a self-deluded British tart (Lloyd) in committing petty crimes that escalate into murder. Famed British tabloid fodder gets the low-budget "period" treatment. Mildly interesting account never quite jells, though some of the violence offers surprisingly stylized jolts. Lloyd is a lot more interesting than her costar here. [R]▼●▮

Chicago 10 (2008) **C-110m.** *** D: Brett Morgen. Voices of Hank Azaria, Dylan Baker, Mark Ruffalo, Roy Scheider, Nick Nolte, Liev Schreiber, Jeffrey Wright, James Urbaniak. Unique documentary approach to the tumultuous events of 1968 when radical groups amassed in Chicago to protest the status quo, and the war in Vietnam, during the Democratic National Convention . . . contrasted with animated renderings of the trial and its instigators (taken verbatim from court transcripts), which became theater of the absurd. Without narration, talking-head interviews, period music, or very much contextual material, this narrowly focused film provides an emotional, empathetic, and immediate portrait of a seminal event in American history. [R]▮

Chicken Chronicles, The (1977) **C-95m.** *½ D: Francis Simon. Steven Guttenberg, Ed Lauter, Lisa Reeves, Meridith Baer, Branscombe Richmond, Gino Baffa, Phil Silvers. Lowjinks of a high school senior, circa 1969, whose principal preoccupation is bedding the girl of his dreams. Guttenberg's film debut. [PG]▼

Chicken Little (2005) **C-82m.** **½ D: Mark Dindal. Voices of Zach Braff, Garry Marshall, Joan Cusack, Steve Zahn, Amy Sedaris, Don Knotts, Harry Shearer, Patrick Stewart, Wallace Shawn, Fred Willard, Catherine O'Hara, Adam West, Patrick Warburton. No one in the idyllic suburban town of Oakey Oaks will let plucky young Chicken Little forget the time he said the sky was falling; they're certainly not going to believe him when he sees it happening again. Irresistible underdog hero and an amusing ensemble (our favorite: Fish Out of Water) draw you in, but the story goes askew. Likely to please younger kids. This is the Disney studio's first completely computer-generated cartoon feature. 3-D theatrical version contains one additional scene after closing credits. 3-D. [G]▮

Chicken Run (2000-British-U.S.) **C-84m.** *** D: Peter Lord, Nick Park. Voices of Mel Gibson, Julia Sawalha, Miranda Richardson, Jane Horrocks, Lynn Ferguson, Imelda Staunton, Timothy Spall. Endearingly loopy stop-motion animated feature from the Oscar-winning creators of Wallace and Gromit. The setting is a British barnyard where the chickens are determined to escape their fate and literally fly the coop. Amusing for adults on one level (with a number of savvy references to old POW movies) and just plain fun for kids. [G]▼◗

Chikamatsu Monogatari SEE: **Crucified Lovers, The**

Child, The SEE: **L'Enfant**

Childish Things SEE: **Confessions of Tom Harris**

Child Is Waiting, A (1963) 102m. *** D: John Cassavetes. Burt Lancaster, Judy Garland, Gena Rowlands, Steven Hill, Bruce Ritchey. Poignant story of Lancaster's attempts to treat retarded children with the help of overly sympathetic Garland. Sensitive subject handled with honesty and candor.▼●

Child of Satan SEE: **To The Devil—A Daughter**

Children, The (1990-British-West German) C-115m. ** D: Tony Palmer. Ben Kingsley, Kim Novak, Siri Neal, Geraldine Chaplin, Joe Don Baker, Britt Ekland, Donald Sinden, Karen Black, Robert Stephens, Rupert Graves. Kingsley's plans to marry recently widowed Novak are thrown askew by his involvement with the ill-cared-for children of an old college friend . . . and his gradual infatuation with the eldest teenage daughter. Based on an Edith Wharton novel filmed in 1929 as THE MARRIAGE PLAYGROUND. Kingsley and Novak are excellent, but film is irritating and slow, with tiresome use of steadicam. Filmed in Venice and Switzerland.▼

Children of a Lesser God (1986) C-110m. *** D: Randa Haines. William Hurt, Marlee Matlin, Piper Laurie, Philip Bosco, Alison Gompf, John F. Cleary, John Basinger. New teacher at school for the deaf is intrigued by an obviously intelligent but isolated young woman who works there as a janitor. The warmth of Hurt's performance, and the credibility of Matlin's, shine through this moving and unusual love story . . . though it lacks the edge and bite of Mark Medoff's play, on which it's based. An impressive feature-film directing debut for Haines. Matlin, also making her film debut, won an Oscar. Filmed in New Brunswick. [R]▼●◗

Children of Heaven (1997-Iranian) C-88m. *** D: Majid Majidi. Amir Naji, Mir Farrokh Hashemian, Bahareh Seddigi, Nafiseh Jafar Mohammadi, Fereshteh Sarabandi. Poignant story of a young boy trying to replace his sister's newly repaired pink shoes. This became Iran's first Oscar contender for Best Foreign Language Film, and deservedly so. Simple tale shows the importance of family, perseverance and honor, as we follow an eight-year-old's seemingly impossible quest to make up for his single misdeed. Well worth watching for children and adults alike. [PG]▼◗

Children of Huang Shi, The (2008-U.S.-Chinese-Australian-German) C-125m. ** D: Roger Spottiswoode. Jonathan Rhys Meyers, Radha Mitchell, Chow Yun-Fat, David Wenham, Michelle Yeoh, Guang Li. Situated in Shanghai during Japan's invasion of China, a young Oxford-educated journalist (Rhys Meyers) manages to coerce his way into the forbidden area, the strife-ridden city of Nanjing, where he experiences the war up close. Reluctantly seeking refuge in an all-but-forgotten, dilapidated children's orphanage moves his life in an unexpected direction. Spotty recounting of British journalist George Hogg's true experiences. Even a good cast can't raise the temperature of what should have been a heartwarming tale. Super 35. [R]◗

Children of Men (2006-U.S.-British) C-108m. ***½ D: Alfonso Cuarón. Clive Owen, Julianne Moore, Michael Caine, Chiwetel Ejiofor, Charlie Hunnam, Clare-Hope Ashitey, Pam Ferris, Danny Huston, Peter Mullan. Riveting look at the year 2027: women are sterile, and England is a bleak, Fascistic society. Onetime political activist Owen finds himself involved in a resistance movement again because of a girl who has miraculously become pregnant. Visceral action and chase scenes (incredibly shot by Emmanuel Lubezki) give us a real sense of being hunted, as Owen becomes an Everyman hero on the run. Caine adds some light moments as an aging hippie who's managed to survive in his own hideaway compound. Based on a novel by P. D. James, adapted by Cuarón, Timothy J. Sexton, David Arata, Mark Fergus, Hawk Ostby. [R]◗

Children of Paradise (1945-French) 195m. **** D: Marcel Carné. Jean-Louis Barrault, Arletty, Pierre Brasseur, Albert Remy, Maria Casarés, Leon Larive, Marcel Herrand, Pierre Renoir. Timeless masterpiece of filmmaking (and storytelling), focusing on a rough-and-tumble theatrical troupe in 19th-century France. Barrault plays the mime whose unfulfilled passion for free-spirited Arletty dominates his life, even as he achieves great fame on stage. Wise, witty, and completely captivating. Written by Jacques Prévert. Filming began in 1943 in Nazi-occupied France, but wasn't completed until 1945.▼●◗

Children of Sanchez, The (1978-U.S.-Mexican) C-117m. *½ D: Hall Bartlett. Anthony Quinn, Dolores Del Rio, Melanie Farrar, Katy Jurado, Stathis Giallelis, Lucia Mendez, Duncan Quinn. Quinn is a widowed Mexico City worker who has several common-law wives, and refuses to show affection for his children. Well-meaning look at the folly of machismo, but it's leaden-paced and often excruciating. Chuck Mangione's popular pop-jazz score too often seems to belong to another film. [R]▼❶

Children of Theatre Street, The (1977) C-92m. ***½ D: Robert Dornhelm, Earle Mack. Narrated by Princess Grace (Grace Kelly). Outstanding documentary about Leningrad's famed Kirov Ballet School, among whose graduates are Baryshnikov, Nureyev, Balanchine, and Nijinsky. The focus is on a trio of students, and the rigorous training they undergo. A must for balletomanes, and especially recommended as an introduction to the art of ballet for children. [G]▼❶

Children of the Corn (1984) C-93m. *½ D: Fritz Kiersch. Peter Horton, Linda Hamilton, R. G. Armstrong, John Franklin, Courtney Gains, Robby Kiger. Laughable adaptation of Stephen King short-short story about young couple who stumble onto Iowa town that's been taken over by sinister juvenile cultists—and then, like all stupid couples in movies like this, fail to get out while the getting is good. Pretty tacky. Followed by six sequels. Remade for TV in 2009. [R]▼❶

Children of the Corn II: The Final Sacrifice (1993) C-94m. *½ D: David F. Price. Terence Knox, Paul Scherrer, Rosalind Allen, Christie Clark, Ned Romero. Barely based on the Stephen King story. Once again, the kids of an isolated Nebraska farming community are killing the adults and nobody knows why. Nobody knows the reason for this movie's existence either. Followed by five more "sequels"! [R]▼❶

Children of the Damned (1964-British) 90m. **½ D: Anton Leader. Ian Hendry, Alan Badel, Barbara Ferris, Patrick White, Bessie Love. Follow-up to VILLAGE OF THE DAMNED suffers from unimaginative account of precocious deadly children and their quest for power.▼❶

Children of the Night (1992) C-92m. *½ D: Tony Randel. Karen Black, Peter DeLuise, Ami Dolenz, Evan MacKenzie, Maya McLaughlin, Josette DiCarlo, David Sawyer, Garrett Morris. Vampires take over a small town in this low-rent variation on SALEM'S LOT. Peculiar deviation from vampire mythology—they sleep underwater with their lungs floating on the surface—is the only novelty, unless you count the highly variable acting. [R]▼

Children of the Revolution (1996-Australian) C-101m. **½ D: Peter Duncan. Judy Davis, Sam Neill, F. Murray Abraham, Geoffrey Rush, Richard Roxburgh, Rachel Griffiths, Russell Kiefel, John Gaden. Fervent Stalinist (Davis) ends up secretly pregnant with the famed leader's son, then watches as he grows up mirroring his father's revolutionary behavior. Australian black comedy tackles the collapse of communism blending humor and tragedy, fact and fiction, but the pacing is uneven and the satire often heavy-handed. Worth seeing for two knockout performances, from the always reliable Davis and from Griffiths, as her policewoman daughter-in-law. [R]▼❶

Children Shouldn't Play With Dead Things (1972) C-85m. *½ D: Benjamin (Bob) Clark. Alan Ormsby, Anya Ormsby, Valerie Mauches, Jane Daly, Jeffrey Gillen. Young, kinky movie-makers take over a rural graveyard and unwittingly resurrect the evil dead. Weird. [PG]▼❶

Children's Hour, The (1961) 107m. **½ D: William Wyler. Audrey Hepburn, Shirley MacLaine, James Garner, Miriam Hopkins, Fay Bainter, Karen Balkin, Veronica Cartwright. Updated version of Lillian Hellman's play is more explicit in its various themes, including lesbianism, than original THESE THREE (also made by Wyler), but not half as good. Impact is missing, despite MacLaine and Hepburn as two teachers, Hopkins as meddling aunt, Bainter as questioning grandmother.▼❶

Child's Play (1972) C-100m. **½ D: Sidney Lumet. James Mason, Robert Preston, Beau Bridges, Ronald Weyand, Charles White, David Rounds, Kate Harrington, Jamie Alexander. Well-acted but somber and confusing account of rivalry between Catholic school professors Mason and Preston, and the seemingly senseless acts of violence perpetrated by some of their students. From the Robert Marasco play. [PG]

Child's Play (1988) C-87m. *** D: Tom Holland. Catherine Hicks, Chris Sarandon, Alex Vincent, Brad Dourif, Dinah Manoff, Tommy Swerdlow, Jack Colvin. Scary and clever horror thriller in which only young Vincent knows his new Chucky doll is really a monster, possessed with the spirit of dead murderer Dourif. His mom (Hicks) and the cop on the case (Sarandon) finally believe him but not before two deaths. Sleeper hit packs a wallop, with excellent special effects bringing the doll to life. Followed by four sequels. [R]▼❶

Child's Play 2 (1990) C-84m. *½ D: John Lafia. Alex Vincent, Jenny Agutter, Gerrit Graham, Christine Elise, Grace Zabriskie, Peter Haskell, Beth Grant, voice of Brad Dourif. Traumatized by Chucky's 1988 antics, affected youngster begins boarding with foster parents. Agutter and Graham ought to be anyone's couple-of-the-month, but the film is utterly worthless until the finale: 15 minutes of doll-factory yuck (with a particular nod to conveyor belts); its unexpected stylishness saves this d.o.a. from a BOMB rating. [R]▼❶

Child's Play 3 (1991) C-90m. BOMB D: Jack Bender. Justin Whalin, Perrey Reeves, Jeremy Sylvers, Peter Haskell, Dakin Matthews, Andrew Robinson, voice of Brad Dourif. It's been eight years since Chucky first terrorized young Andy Barclay (Whalin), and now the kid is a screwed-up loner of 16 in a military school; to make things worse, the prez of the Play Pals Toy Company is about to put the "C" doll back into production. An amusement park finale is desperately contrived, even by the standards of this junk. Followed by BRIDE OF CHUCKY. [R]▼●◗

Chill Factor (1999) **C-101m.** ** D: Hugh Johnson. Cuba Gooding, Jr., Skeet Ulrich, Peter Firth, David Paymer, Hudson Leick, Daniel Hugh Kelly, Kevin J. O'Connor. Convenience store clerk Ulrich and ice cream truck driver Gooding reluctantly team up to keep an explosive, safe as long as it's cold, from falling into the hands of terrorist Firth. Routine, predictable action movie helped by the likable (if miscast) leads. Panavision. [R]▼●◗

Chilly Scenes of Winter SEE: **Head Over Heels** (1979)

Chimes at Midnight (1965-Spanish-Swiss) **115m.** *** D: Orson Welles. Orson Welles, Jeanne Moreau, Margaret Rutherford, John Gielgud, Marina Vlady, Keith Baxter; narrated by Ralph Richardson. Welles combined parts of five Shakespeare plays with mixed results, with his own portrayal of Falstaff the most interesting aspect. Well cast, but limited budget hurt the effort. Aka FALSTAFF.▼

China Gate (1957) **97m.** *** D: Samuel Fuller. Gene Barry, Angie Dickinson, Nat King Cole, Paul Dubov, Lee Van Cleef, George Givot, Marcel Dalio. International soldiers under French command attack Communist munitions dumps in Indochina. Interesting subplots flesh out Fuller's dynamic action story, with early view of Vietnam's internal strife. CinemaScope.▼

China Girl (1987) **C-88m.** **½ D: Abel Ferrara. James Russo, Richard Panebianco, Sari Chang, David Caruso, Russell Wong. Atmospheric romantic thriller about warring Chinese and Italian youth gangs in N.Y.C., with Panebianco and Chang as star-crossed lovers. Director Ferrara provides tremendous energy and some over-the-top violence. [R]▼●

China Moon (1994) **C-99m.** ** D: John Bailey. Ed Harris, Madeleine Stowe, Charles Dance, Benicio Del Toro, Pruitt Taylor Vince, Roger Aaron Brown, Patricia Healy. Small-town cop Harris lusts after unhappily married Stowe in this moody film noir. A couple of neat twists, but production is more than a bit reminiscent of (the superior) BODY HEAT—down to the Florida locale. Directorial debut for Bailey, better known as a top cinematographer (ORDINARY PEOPLE, IN THE LINE OF FIRE). Filmed in 1991. Panavision. [R]▼●◗

China 9, Liberty 37 (1978) **C-102m.** **½ D: Monte Hellman. Warren Oates, Fabio Testi, Jenny Agutter, Sam Peckinpah. Sluggish, mythicized Western in which railroad barons save a man from gallows in exchange for killing former gunfighter; gunfighter's wife falls for killer and helps do his dirty work. Title refers to signpost giving distance to two nearby towns. Video title: GUNFIRE. Technovision. [R]▼◗

China Seas (1935) **90m.** *** D: Tay Garnett. Clark Gable, Jean Harlow, Wallace Beery, Lewis Stone, Rosalind Russell, Dudley Digges, Robert Benchley, C. Aubrey Smith, Hattie McDaniel. Impossible to dislike film with that cast, even if the story—about mysterious goings-on and relationships on Gable's Singapore-bound ship—is ludicrous. Also shown in computer-colored version.▼●◗

China Syndrome, The (1979) **C-123m.** **** D: James Bridges. Jane Fonda, Jack Lemmon, Michael Douglas, Scott Brady, James Hampton, Peter Donat, Wilford Brimley, James Karen. Heartpounding drama about attempted cover-up of accident at California nuclear plant is as much a probe of television news as it is a story of nuclear power—and it scores bullseye on both fronts. There is no music score; story tension propels film by itself, along with solid performances by Fonda as TV reporter, Douglas (who also produced film) as radical cameraman, and especially Lemmon as dedicated plant exec. Screenplay by Mike Gray, T.S. Cook, and Bridges. [PG]▼●◗

Chinatown (1974) **C-131m.** **** D: Roman Polanski. Jack Nicholson, Faye Dunaway, John Huston, Perry Lopez, John Hillerman, Roy Jenson, Dick Bakalyan, Joe Mantell, Bruce Glover, James Hong, Noble Willingham, Burt Young. Bizarre, fascinating mystery in the Hammett-Chandler tradition (and set in the 1930s) with Nicholson as L.A. private eye led into a complex, volatile case by femme fatale Dunaway. Director Polanski appears briefly as the hood who knifes Nicholson. Oscar for Best Original Screenplay (Robert Towne). Sequel: THE TWO JAKES. Panavision. [R]▼●◗

Chinchero SEE: **Last Movie, The**

Chinese Box (1997-Japanese-French-U.S.) **C-100m.** ** D: Wayne Wang. Jeremy Irons, Gong Li, Maggie Cheung, Michael Hui, Ruben Blades. Murky drama set in the final six months of Great Britain's rule over Hong Kong, with the smell of change in the air as China prepares to take over. Irons plays a jaded journalist whose own life is at a crossroads. Li is not well showcased in her first English-language film, as a woman "with a past" whom Irons adores but cannot have. Heavy-handed allegory was conceived by Wang, Paul Theroux, and Jean-Claude Carrière. [R]▼●◗

Chinese Coffee (2001) **C-99m.** ** D: Al Pacino. Al Pacino, Jerry Orbach, Susan Floyd, Ellen McElduff. Chamber piece, clearly based on a play (by Ira Lewis) about a pair of N.Y.C. artists, losers with a symbiotic relationship who spend a long night talking over their failures and resentments. If you're a fan of the two actors, you'll savor their performances, but as a film it never takes off. Lewis adapted his play. Shot in 1997. [R]◗

Chinese Connection, The (1972-Hong Kong) **C-107m. *** D:** Lo Wei. Bruce Lee, Miao Ker Hsiu, James Tien, Robert Baker. Violent Kung Fu film has Lee in Shanghai in early 1900s seeking vengeance on the murderers of his teacher. Graceful, powerful, humorous, and charismatic; Lee at his best. Original title: FIST OF FURY. Aka THE IRON HAND. Shawscope. [R] ▼●◗

Chinese Roulette (1976-German) **C-86m. *** D:** Rainer Werner Fassbinder. Margit Carstensen, Ulli Lommel, Anna Karina, Macha Meril, Brigitte Mira, Andrea Schober, Volker Spengler. Intense, biting comedy about a disabled girl (Schober), who plots to have her parents and their lovers visit a country house on the same weekend. Perceptive—but potentially off-putting—film is recommended mainly for Fassbinder fans. ▼●◗

Chino (1973-Italian) **C-98m. **½ D:** John Sturges. Charles Bronson, Jill Ireland, Vincent Van Patten, Marcel Bozzuffi, Fausto Tozzi, Melissa Chimenti. Offbeat Western that barely received theatrical release here in 1976; Bronson plays halfbreed whose attempts to maintain his horse ranch in peace are short-lived. Aka THE VALDEZ HORSES. [PG]▼◗

Chisum (1970) **C-111m. **½ D:** Andrew V. McLaglen. John Wayne, Geoffrey Deuel, Forrest Tucker, Christopher George, Ben Johnson, Glenn Corbett, Bruce Cabot, Patric Knowles, Lynda Day, Richard Jaeckel. Wayne is the real-life cattle baron of the title, but takes a back seat to Billy the Kid (Deuel) in this routine but handsome Western. It's about the efforts of good ranchers like Wayne and Knowles to prevent the takeover of Lincoln County, New Mexico, by corrupt Tucker. One of very few Wayne Westerns based on historical events. Panavision. [G]▼●◗

Chitty Chitty Bang Bang (1968) **C-142m. *½ D:** Ken Hughes. Dick Van Dyke, Sally Ann Howes, Lionel Jeffries, Gert Frobe, Anna Quayle, Benny Hill. Children's musical about flying car is one big Edsel itself, with totally forgettable score and some of the shoddiest special effects ever. Loosely based on book by Ian Fleming. Later adapted for the stage. Super Panavision 70. [G]▼●◗

Chloe (2010-Canadian-U.S.-French) **C-96m. ** D:** Atom Egoyan. Julianne Moore, Liam Neeson, Amanda Seyfried, Max Thieriot, R. H. Thomson, Nina Dobrev. Long-married Moore still loves her husband (college prof Neeson) but can't seem to connect with him anymore, sexually or even conversationally. When she suspects him of having an affair, she hires a young

prostitute (Seyfried) to tempt him and report his behavior. Instead, Moore becomes unexpectedly entangled in a relationship with the younger woman. Remake of the French film NATHALIE . . . (2004), adapted by Erin Cressida Wilson (SECRETARY), is sexually provocative—with plenty of female nudity—but winds up being downright silly. [R] ◗

Chloe in the Afternoon (1972-French) **C-97m. ***½ D:** Eric Rohmer. Bernard Verley, Zouzou, Francoise Verley, Daniel Ceccaldi. No. 6 of Rohmer's "Six Moral Tales" depicts married man's fascination with kooky girl during daylight hours. As Chloe, Zouzou becomes more alluring as film unwinds. Remade in the U.S. in 2007 as I THINK I LOVE MY WIFE. [R]▼●◗

Chocolat (1988-French-German-Camaroon) **C-105m. *** D:** Claire Denis. Isaach de Bankolé, Giulia Boschi, François Cluzet, Cécile Ducasse, Jean-Claude Adelin, Jacques Denis, Mireille Perrier. Subtle, slowly paced slice-of-life about a young woman's memories of her childhood in French West Africa, where whites are masters and most blacks are servants. This very personal, autobiographical film (which first-time director Denis co-scripted) is quietly rewarding. [PG-13]▼●◗

Chocolat (2000) **C-121m. ** D:** Lasse Hallström. Juliette Binoche, Lena Olin, Johnny Depp, Judi Dench, Alfred Molina, Peter Stormare, Carrie-Anne Moss, Leslie Caron, John Wood, Hugh O'Conor, Victoire Thivisol. A French village is virtually frozen in time and kept that way by its conservative leading citizen (Molina). Into this rigid community come a chocolatier (Binoche) and her daughter, whose free-spirited ways and tempting delicacies turn the town on its ear. Meant to be charming but hopelessly contrived, in spite of a fine cast. [PG-13]▼◗

Chocolate War, The (1988) **C-103m. *** D:** Keith Gordon. John Glover, Ilan Mitchell-Smith, Wally Ward, Bud Cort, Adam Baldwin, Jenny Wright, Doug Hutchinson. A Catholic boys school is divided by a power struggle between an idealistic student and a dictatorial acting headmaster, as each tries to deal with The Vigils, a secret society of schoolboys out for control. Chilling and impressive, well directed on a low budget by actor Gordon, who also adapted Robert Cormier's novel. Glover is wonderfully wicked. [R]▼●◗

Choice of Arms (1981-French) **C-117m. *** D:** Alain Corneau. Yves Montand, Catherine Deneuve, Gérard Depardieu, Michel Galabru, Gerard Lanvin. Well-directed drama about retired gangster Montand forced into antagonistic relationship with young punk Depardieu, leading to reciprocal violence. Despite hostility, both men come to understand how similar they are. Good performances by excellent cast, especially Depardieu. Original French running time 135m. Panavision.▼

Choice of Weapons SEE: **Dirty Knight's Work**

Choices (1981) **C-90m. **½** D: Silvio Narizzano. Paul Carafotes, Victor French, Lelia Goldoni, Val Avery, Dennis Patrick, Demi Moore, Billy Moses, Pat Buttram. Partially deaf teenager Carafotes becomes alienated when prevented from playing football because of his handicap. Well-intentioned but obvious drama is helped by fine performances. Moore's film debut.▼▶

Choirboys, The (1977) **C-119m.** BOMB D: Robert Aldrich. Charles Durning, Louis Gossett, Jr., Perry King, Clyde Kusatsu, Stephen Macht, Tim McIntire, Randy Quaid, Chuck Sacci, Don Stroud, James Woods, Burt Young, Robert Webber, Jeanie Bell, Blair Brown, Michele Carey, Charles Haid, Joe Kapp, Barbara Rhoades, Jim Davis, Phyllis Davis, Jack DeLeon, David Spielberg, Vic Tayback, Michael Wills, George DiCenzo. Supposedly comic escapades of L.A. cops who relieve work pressures by raunchy doings. Foul-mouthed, foul-minded, heavy-handed film from book by Joseph Wambaugh, who disavowed this turkey. [R]▼

Choke (2008) **C-92m. **½** D: Clark Gregg. Sam Rockwell, Anjelica Huston, Kelly Macdonald, Brad William Henke, Clark Gregg, Bijou Phillips, Gillian Jacobs, Jonah Bobo, Paz de la Huerta, Viola Harris, Joel Grey. Rockwell is perfect as the protagonist of Chuck Palahniuk's novel, a lifelong con man trying to deal with sex addiction while caring for his mother, who's in a mental hospital. Disconnected from society, he desperately needs to know who his father was. Darkly funny, extreme but inconsistent, this may appeal most to Palahniuk's faithful readers. First-time director Gregg also adapted the book and appears as Rockwell's priggish boss. [R]▶

Choke Canyon (1986) **C-94m. **½** D: Chuck Bail. Stephen Collins, Janet Julian, Lance Henriksen, Bo Svenson, Victoria Racimo, Nicholas Pryor. Fun sci-fi about stubborn cowboy physicist (!) who fights off corrupt industrialist's henchmen, trying to protect the environment against nuclear waste dumping on the eve of Halley's Comet's visit near Earth. Terrific aerial stuntwork. Widescreen. [PG]▼

C.H.O.M.P.S. (1979) **C-89m. *½** D: Don Chaffey. Wesley Eure, Valerie Bertinelli, Conrad Bain, Chuck McCann, Red Buttons, Larry Bishop, Hermione Baddeley, Jim Backus. Cartoon-makers Hanna & Barbera struck out with this Disneyesque comedy about a young inventor (Eure) and his mechanical dog. Originally rated PG for mild profanities voiced by *another* dog in the film—then redubbed for kids' sake. Title is acronym for Canine HOMe Protection System. [G]▼

Choose Me (1984) **C-106m. ***½** D: Alan Rudolph. Genevieve Bujold, Keith Carradine, Lesley Ann Warren, Rae Dawn Chong, Patrick Bauchau, John Larroquette, John Considine. Outrageously inventive tale of the various relationships, truths, and lies that link radio sex-talk-show hostess Bujold, bar owner Warren, and mental hospital escapee Carradine, among others. This comedy-drama about the different roles that people play in life is a real kick, with a wonderful from-midnight-till-dawn feel and good performances by all. Evocative use of L.A. locations and Teddy Pendergrass songs. A companion piece to Rudolph's WELCOME TO L.A. and REMEMBER MY NAME. [R]▼●▶

Chopper (2000-Australian) **C-93m. **½** D: Andrew Dominik. Eric Bana, Simon Lyndon, Kenny Graham, Kate Beahan. Fictionalized bio of Australian criminal Mark "Chopper" Read, who kills at the slightest provocation and mutilates himself, yet somehow becomes a cult hero. Stomach-churning violence might make you steer clear, but there's no denying the chilling lead performance by Bana. Features the nastiest ear-slicing since RESERVOIR DOGS.▼▶

Chopping Mall (1986) **C-76m. *½** D: Jim Wynorski. Kelli Maroney, Tony O'Dell, John Terlesky, Russell Todd, Paul Bartel, Mary Woronov, Dick Miller, Karrie Emerson, Barbara Crampton, Suzee Slater, Gerrit Graham, Mel Welles. Eight teenagers are trapped overnight in a shopping mall where three malfunctioning guard robots go on a killing spree. Endless injokes and cameo roles (including Bartel and Woronov in their EATING RAOUL characters) fail to save a story that lapses into clichés. Originally titled: KILLBOTS. [R]▼▶

Chop Shop (2008) **C-84m. ***½** D: Ramin Bahrani. Alejandro Polanco, Isamar Gonzales, Carlos Zapata, Ahmad Razvi, Rob Sowulski. Remarkably naturalistic look at Alejandro (or "Ale"), a self-reliant, street-smart Latino boy who works at (and lives in) an auto-body repair shop in Queens, N.Y. He persuades his older sister to join him there, hoping to pry her away from the bad influence of her friends and give her a goal to reach for: the purchase of a food van they can operate together. Bahrani (MAN PUSH CART), cowriter Bahareh Azimi, and cinematographer Michael Simmonds create a modern-day equivalent of 1940s neorealist gems like OPEN CITY and BICYCLE THIEVES in this striking—and heartbreaking—film.▶

Chorus, The SEE: **Les Choristes**

Chorus Line, A (1985) **C-113m. ** D: Richard Attenborough. Michael Douglas, Terrence Mann, Alyson Reed, Cameron English, Vicki Frederick, Audrey Landers, Gregg Burge, Nicole Fosse, Janet Jones. Auditionees for Broadway chorus line reveal their innermost thoughts and emotions in song and dance before a hard-boiled director (Douglas). Thoroughly uninspired, unmemorable filming of the landmark Broadway musical; watchable, especially if you never saw the play, but what can you say about a musical in which all the singing and all the dancing is mediocre? And the show's biggest number, "What I Did for Love," is treated as a throwaway! Super 35. [PG-13]▼●)

Chorus of Disapproval, A (1988-British) C-100m. ** D: Michael Winner. Jeremy Irons, Anthony Hopkins, Prunella Scales, Sylvia Syms, Lionel Jeffries, Gareth Hunt, Patsy Kensit, Alexandra Pigg, Jenny Seagrove. Shy, simple-minded widower moves to a seaside town and joins an amateur theatrical troupe, in which romantic intrigues abound. Some pearly performances (especially Hopkins, as the director, and Scales, as his wife) can't overcome the slightness of the material and its faltering execution. Adapted from Alan Ayckbourn's play by the author and Winner. [PG]▼●

Chosen, The (1978-Italian-British) C-105m. BOMB D: Alberto De Martino. Kirk Douglas, Agostina Belli, Simon Ward, Anthony Quayle, Virginia McKenna, Alexander Knox. Nuclear power exec Douglas slowly realizes that his son (Ward) is the Antichrist, who plans to use nuclear power to bring on world destruction. There! We just saved you 105 minutes. Originally titled HOLOCAUST 2000. Aka RAIN OF FIRE. Technovision. [PG]▼

Chosen, The (1981) C-108m. ***½ D: Jeremy Paul Kagan. Maximilian Schell, Rod Steiger, Robby Benson, Barry Miller, Hildy Brooks, Ron Rifkin, Val Avery. Excellent adaptation of Chaim Potok's novel, centering on friendship between Americanized Jew Miller and Hassidic Benson. Steiger, as Benson's rabbi father, gives his best performance in years, and even Robby isn't bad. Set in 1940s Brooklyn; later made into a Broadway musical. [PG]●

Chosen Survivors (1974) C-99m. ** D: Sutton Roley. Jackie Cooper, Alex Cord, Richard Jaeckel, Bradford Dillman, Pedro Armendariz, Jr., Diana Muldaur, Barbara Babcock. Good cast in formula nonsense about group of people "selected" to survive future holocaust in underground shelter. Just one hitch: the shelter is invaded by vampire bats. Dialogue and characterizations from grade-Z movies of the past. [PG]●

Christiane F. (1981-German) C-124m. **½ D: Ulrich Edel. Nadja Brunkhorst, Thomas Haustein, Jens Kuphal, Reiner Wolk. Grim, gruesome account of bored teenager Brunkhorst falling in with crowd of junkie-hustler Haustein. Well meaning but uneven; based on a true story. Features unmemorable David Bowie concert sequence. [R]▼●

Christian Licorice Store, The (1971) C-90m. ** D: James Frawley. Beau Bridges, Maud Adams, Gilbert Roland, Anne Randall, Allen Arbus, McLean Stevenson.

Quirky, dated comic study of tennis player Bridges looking for meaning in life. Loads of cameos, including directors Jean Renoir, Monte Hellman, Theodore J. Flicker, and James B. Harris. Filmed in 1969. [PG]

Christian the Lion (1976-British) C-89m. **½ D: Bill Travers, James Hill. Bill Travers, Virginia McKenna, George Adamson, Anthony Bourke. Pleasant docudrama about the efforts of BORN FREE stars—and real-life wildlife expert George Adamson, whom Travers portrayed in earlier film—to return a lion born in London Zoo to its native habitat in Kenya. Expanded from 1971's THE LION AT WORLD'S END. [G]▼

Christine (1983) C-111m. ** D: John Carpenter. Keith Gordon, John Stockwell, Alexandra Paul, Robert Prosky, Harry Dean Stanton, Christine Belford, Roberts Blossom, Kelly Preston. Stephen King bestseller about a '58 Plymouth with demonic powers never hits bull's-eye, despite a promising start that captures teenage life quite nicely. Panavision. [R]▼●

Christine Jorgensen Story, The (1970) C-89m. BOMB D: Irving Rapper. John Hansen, Joan Tompkins, Quinn Redeker, John W. Hines, Ellen Clark. Ludicrous biography of famed 50s phenomenon is not exactly an in-depth study; one problem is that actor Hansen looks more masculine as female Christine and vice versa. [R]

Christmas Carol, A (1938) 69m. *** D: Edwin L. Marin. Reginald Owen, Gene Lockhart, Kathleen Lockhart, Terry Kilburn, Barry MacKay, Lynne Carver, Leo G. Carroll, Ann Rutherford. Nicely done adaptation of Dickens' classic with Owen a well-modulated Scrooge, surrounded by good MGM players and period settings. Young June Lockhart makes her screen debut. Also shown in computer-colored version. ▼●

Christmas Carol, A (1951-British) 86m. **** D: Brian Desmond-Hurst. Alastair Sim, Jack Warner, Kathleen Harrison, Mervyn Johns, Hermione Baddeley, Clifford Mollison, Michael Hordern, George Cole, Carol Marsh, Miles Malleson, Ernest Thesiger, Hattie Jacques, Peter Bull, Hugh Dempster. Superb film is too good to be shown only at Christmastime; always delightful Sim makes Scrooge a three-dimensional character in this faithful, heartwarming rendition of the Dickens classic. Screenplay by Noel Langley. Patrick Macnee plays young Marley. Original British title: SCROOGE. Also shown in computer-colored version. ▼●

Christmas Carol, A (2009) C-95m. **½ D: Robert Zemeckis. Jim Carrey, Gary Oldman, Colin Firth, Bob Hoskins, Robin Wright Penn, Cary Elwes, Fionnula Flanagan, Daryl Sabara. Retelling of the Charles Dickens classic through performance-capture technology enables Carrey to play Ebenezer Scrooge and all three ghosts who visit him one fateful Christmas Eve; other actors play multiple parts as well. Other than that, this hybrid of animation and live action serves no apparent purpose except to go flying over and around the streets of Victorian London. The story is still effective but it's been told much better before. Aka DISNEY'S A CHRISTMAS CAROL. 3-D Digital Widescreen. [PG] ▶

Christmas Eve (1947) 90m. *½ D: Edwin L. Marin. George Brent, George Raft, Randolph Scott, Joan Blondell, Virginia Field, Ann Harding, Reginald Denny, Joe Sawyer. Slow-moving mixture of comedy and drama as foster sons discover evil intentions of relations to victimize Harding. Retitled: SINNER'S HOLIDAY.

Christmas Evil SEE: **You Better Watch Out**

Christmas Holiday (1944) 92m. *** D: Robert Siodmak. Deanna Durbin, Gene Kelly, Gale Sondergaard, Gladys George, Richard Whorf. Somerset Maugham novel reset in America. Crime story with Durbin gone wrong to help killer-hubby Kelly; songs include "Spring Will Be a Little Late This Year."

Christmas in Connecticut (1945) 101m. **½ D: Peter Godfrey. Barbara Stanwyck, Dennis Morgan, Sydney Greenstreet, Reginald Gardiner, S. Z. Sakall, Robert Shayne, Una O'Connor. Airy fluff with Stanwyck, a chic magazine writer who's supposed to be an expert homemaker, forced to entertain a war veteran (Morgan) and her boss (Greenstreet) for the holidays. Standard studio corn it may be, but a wonderful treat for late-night viewing on Christmas Eve. Remade for cable TV in 1992. Also shown in computer-colored version. ▼●▶

Christmas in July (1940) 67m. ***½ D: Preston Sturges. Dick Powell, Ellen Drew, Raymond Walburn, William Demarest, Ernest Truex, Franklin Pangborn. Top Sturges comedy about Powell going on shopping spree after mistakenly believing he has won big contest. Walburn and Demarest are at their best. ▼●▶

Christmas Story, A (1983) C-93m. **** D: Bob Clark. Peter Billingsley, Darren McGavin, Melinda Dillon, Ian Petrella, Scott Schwartz, Tedde Moore. Humorist Jean Shepherd's delightful memoir of growing up in the 1940s and wanting nothing so much as a Red Ryder BB gun for Christmas. Shepherd narrates in the first person, and Billingsley portrays him (delightfully) as a boy. Truly funny for kids and grown-ups alike; wonderful period flavor. Based on a portion of *In God We Trust, All Others Pay Cash.* Shepherd appears unbilled as a department store customer. Followed by IT RUNS IN MY FAMILY. [PG] ▼●▶

Christmas Tale, A (2008-French) C-152m. ***½ D: Arnaud Desplechin. Catherine Deneuve, Jean-Paul Roussillon, Mathieu Amalric, Anne Consigny, Melvil Poupaud, Hippolyte Girardot, Emmanuelle Devos, Chiara Mastroianni. The matriarch of a large, rambunctious family has contracted a rare disease and needs a bone-marrow transplant; this lies heavily over the clan's Christmas reunion, the first one that black sheep Amalric has been permitted to attend in a long time, because he may be the likeliest donor. A celebration of our contradictions and complexities as human beings, and how they affect the family dynamic. Deneuve's real-life daughter Mastroianni plays her unwelcome daughter-in-law. Eclectic music score ranges from Mendelssohn to Mingus; it shouldn't work but somehow (like everything else in this film) it does. Written by Desplechin and Emmanuel Bourdieu. Super 35. ▶

Christmas That Almost Wasn't, The (1966-Italian-U.S.) C-92m. *½ D: Rossano Brazzi, Rossano Brazzi, Paul Tripp, Lidia Brazzi, Sonny Fox, Mischa Auer. Santa is threatened with eviction from the North Pole in this substandard kiddie film. [G] ▼▶

Christmas Tree, The (1969) 110m. *½ D: Terence Young. William Holden, Virna Lisi, Bourvil, Brook Fuller, Madeleine Damien. Sappy tearjerker about relationship between young boy and his wealthy father when the latter learns his son's death is imminent. Cast is divided between those who overact and those who don't seem to care. Aka WHEN WOLVES CRY. [G] ▼

Christmas with the Kranks (2004) C-98m. BOMB D: Joe Roth. Tim Allen, Jamie Lee Curtis, Dan Aykroyd, M. Emmet Walsh, Elizabeth Franz, Erik Per Sullivan, Cheech Marin, Jake Busey, Austin Pendleton, Tom Poston, Julie Gonzalo, Felicity Huffman. Noxious holiday movie in which suburbanites Luther and Nora Krank, whose daughter has joined the Peace Corps, decide to forgo celebrating Christmas and take a Caribbean cruise—which, according to their outraged neighbors, is positively un-American. Alleged comedy pays homage to mediocrity, crass cohsumerism, and love-it-or-leave-it conformity. Screenplay by Chris Columbus, based on John Grisham's novel *Skipping Christmas*. Panavision. [PG] ▶

Christopher Columbus: The Discovery (1992-U.S.-Spanish) C-120m. BOMB D: John Glen. Marlon Brando, Tom Selleck, George Corraface, Rachel Ward, Robert Davi, Benicio Del Toro, Catherine Zeta Jones, Oliver Cotton, Mathieu Carriere, Nigel Terry. "In nineteen-hundred-and-ninety-two, Columbus sailed two screen boo-boos." Corraface plays the explorer in this one, which beat 1492: CONQUEST OF PARADISE to the big screen, bringing an infectious smile and notably heavy beard follicles to an extremely complex historical character. Brando has a cameo as Spanish

Inquisitor Tomas de Torquemada (his dullest performance since DESIREE), while Selleck dresses up as King Ferdinand—the guy with three ships and a lady. Not ripe for *rediscovery*. Panavision. [PG-13]▼●

Christopher Strong (1933) 77m. **½ D: Dorothy Arzner. Katharine Hepburn, Colin Clive, Billie Burke, Helen Chandler, Jack LaRue. Hepburn's an aviatrix in love with married Clive. Dated film intriguing for star's performance as headstrong, individualistic woman—and dig that silver lamé costume. Margaret Lindsay appears unbilled. ▼●▶

Christ Stopped at Eboli SEE: Eboli

Chrome Hearts SEE: C.C. and Company

Chronicles of Narnia: Prince Caspian, The (2008) C-140m. *** D: Andrew Adamson. Georgie Henley, William Moseley, Anna Popplewell, Skandar Keynes, Ben Barnes, Peter Dinklage, Warwick Davis, Sergio Castellitto, Vincent Grass, Alicia Borrachero, Tilda Swinton; voices of Liam Neeson, Eddie Izzard. In the second installment of C. S. Lewis' series, the Pevensie children—uncomfortable at home in England—are transported once again to Narnia, but hundreds of years have passed there, and the kingdom has suffered. They readily assume their roles as saviors and strike an uneasy alliance with Prince Caspian (newcomer Barnes) of the Telmarines, whose uncle—a ruthless ruler—has tried to kill him. Solid storytelling, strong performances, and breathtaking scenery put this across, though it's a dark tale, and the climactic battle scenes go on at length. Followed by THE VOYAGE OF THE DAWN TREADER. Super 35. [PG]▶

Chronicles of Narnia: The Lion, The Witch and The Wardrobe, The (2005) C-139m. *** D: Andrew Adamson. Georgie Henley, Skandar Keynes, William Moseley, Anna Popplewell, Tilda Swinton, James McAvoy, Jim Broadbent, Kiran Shah, James Cosmo; voices of Liam Neeson, Ray Winstone, Dawn French, Rupert Everett. Faithful rendering of C. S. Lewis' beloved book with a newly invented prologue: four children are sent from London to a professor's home in the country during WW2. The youngest, Lucy, discovers a magic wardrobe that leads to a mystical land called Narnia. When she learns it has been taken over by a devious witch (Swinton), she recruits her siblings to help win the battle of good vs. evil. Much of this is truly wondrous, though it does go on a bit and the special effects are extremely variable. Still, an impressive and worthwhile family film. Oscar winner for Best Makeup (Howard Berger, Tami Lane). Alternate version runs 150m. Followed by PRINCE CASPIAN. Super 35. [PG]▶

Chronicles of Narnia: The Voyage of the Dawn Treader, The (2010) C-113m. *** D: Michael Apted. Georgie Henley, Skandar Keynes, Ben Barnes, Will Poulter, Tilda Swinton; voices of Liam Neeson, Simon Pegg. During WW2, Lucy and Edmund Pevensie are separated from their parents and siblings and forced to live with their obnoxious cousin Eustace, until all three children are swept back to the world of Narnia. They reunite with Prince Caspian on his ship *The Dawn Treader* and embark on a perilous voyage to track down seven lost lords of the kingdom and their magical swords. Third of C. S. Lewis' Narnia stories offers plenty of action and breathtaking visual effects. An entertaining journey, although some aspects of story and character are skimped on in favor of those visuals. The human actors are consistently upstaged by the brave and courtly mouse named Reepicheep (voiced by Pegg). 3-D HD Widescreen. [PG]▶

Chronicles of Riddick, The (2004) C-119m. *½ D: David Twohy. Vin Diesel, Colm Feore, Thandie Newton, Judi Dench, Karl Urban, Alexa Davalos, Linus Roache, Yorick van Wageningen, Nick Chinlund, Keith David. Follow-up to the lean, mean PITCH BLACK is a densely plotted, overproduced action/sci-fi extravaganza, with Diesel as the escaped convict who attempts to ward off an invasion of planet Helion Prime by the Necromongers, led by the evil Lord Marshal (Feore). Laden with a self-serious storyline and enormous computer-generated settings and effects, it sinks under its own weight. Unrated director's cut runs 134m. Animated DVD feature THE CHRONICLES OF RIDDICK: DARK FURY bridges story between PITCH BLACK and this film. Super 35. [PG-13]▼▶

Chrystal (2004) C-107m. *½ D: Ray McKinnon. Billy Bob Thornton, Lisa Blount, Ray McKinnon, Harry Lennix, Walton Goggins, Grace Zabriskie, Johnny Galecki, Colin Fickes, Max Kasch, Harry Dean Stanton. A car crash left a little boy dead and his mother physically and psychologically impaired. The father, who was responsible for the accident, returns home seeking salvation after many years in prison. Muddled, slow-as-molasses hogwash set in the Arkansas Ozarks. Written by the director. [R]▶

Chubasco (1968) C-100m. **½ D: Allen H. Miner. Richard Egan, Christopher Jones, Susan Strasberg, Ann Sothern, Simon Oakland, Audrey Totter, Preston Foster. Young man working on tuna boat gets along with the skipper until he learns the boy has married his daughter; overlong but likable programmer. Jones and Strasberg were then married in real life. Panavision. ▶

Chu Chu and the Philly Flash (1981) C-100m. BOMB D: David Lowell Rich. Alan Arkin, Carol Burnett, Jack Warden, Danny Aiello, Adam Arkin, Danny Glover, Sid Haig, Ruth Buzzi, Vito Scotti, Lou Jacobi. Maddeningly moronic comedy revolving around bum Arkin, show-biz failure Burnett, and a briefcase filled with secret government papers. A low point in the careers of its stars; Burnett isn't even funny in Carmen Miranda getup. Scripted by Barbara Dana (then Mrs. Arkin). [PG]▼

Chuck & Buck (2000) **C-96m.** ******* D: Miguel Arteta. Mike White, Chris Weitz, Lupe Ontiveros, Beth Colt, Paul Weitz, Maya Rudolph, Mary Wigmore, Paul Sand. Buck (White), a 27-year-old who's never matured, is reunited with boyhood friend Chuck (Chris Weitz), and decides that they're still best pals. But Chuck feels uneasy, especially with his onetime friend's near-stalker tactics. Extremely offbeat but fascinating portrait of a pest who simply won't be ignored . . . and the reasons for his attachment. White also wrote this perceptive film; costar Weitz and supporting actor Paul Weitz are better known as screenwriters (AMERICAN PIE). [R]▼▶

Chuck Berry Hail! Hail! Rock 'n' Roll (1987) **C-120m.** *****½** D: Taylor Hackford. Chuck Berry, Keith Richards, Eric Clapton, Robert Cray, Etta James, Julian Lennon, Linda Ronstadt. Two delights in one: an overview of rock legend Chuck Berry's career—sparked by interviews with Richards, Clapton, Bo Diddley, Little Richard, Roy Orbison, The Everly Brothers, Willie Dixon, Bruce Springsteen, and the subject himself—and a climactic 60th birthday Berry concert held in his hometown of St. Louis. Whitewashes Berry's womanizing and early 1960s jail term, but his hot temper is much in evidence during some amusing skirmishes with concert producer Richards. Worthy of its title . . . if slightly overlong. [PG]▼▶

Chuck Norris Vs. The Karate Cop SEE: **Slaughter in San Francisco**

C.H.U.D. (1984) **C-90m.** BOMB D: Douglas Cheek. John Heard, Daniel Stern, Kim Greist, Brenda Currin, Justin Hall, Christopher Curry, Michael O'Hare, Sam McMurray, Patricia Richardson, Raymond Baker, Peter Michael Goetz, John Bedford Lloyd, John Goodman, Jay Thomas. That's Cannibalistic Humanoid Underground Dwellers, folks—a band of ragtag derelicts who come up to street level at night to munch on human flesh. Grimy on all levels. Followed by a sequel. [R]▼▶

C.H.U.D. II—Bud the Chud (1989) **C-84m.** BOMB D: David Irving. Brian Robbins, Bill Calvert, Gerrit Graham, Tricia Leigh Fisher, Robert Vaughn, Larry Cedar, Bianca Jagger, Larry Linville, Jack Riley, Norman Fell, June Lockhart. Teenagers swipe a corpse (Graham), unaware that it is a cannibalistic CHUD that passes on its tendencies to anyone it bites. Comedy sequel to straight original is far worse, but Graham is genuinely funny. Script credited to "M. Kane Jeeves." [R]▼▶

Chuka (1967) **C-105m.** ****** D: Gordon Douglas. Rod Taylor, John Mills, Ernest Borgnine, Luciana Paluzzi, James Whitmore, Angela Dorian, Louis Hayward. Good cast is wasted in routine Western about grizzled gunfighter who tries to promote peace between Indians and some undisciplined soldiers guarding nearby fort.▼▶

Chump at Oxford, A (1940) **63m.** ****½** D: Alfred Goulding. Stan Laurel, Oliver Hardy, Wilfred Lucas, Forrester Harvey, James Finlayson, Anita Garvin. So-called feature is more like a series of barely related shorts; film is nearly half over before L&H even get to Oxford. Still quite funny, especially when they settle down in the Dean's quarters. Peter Cushing plays one of the boys' tormentors. Also shown in computer-colored version. ▼●

Chumscrubber, The (2005) **C-106m.** ****** D: Arie Posin. Jamie Bell, Camilla Belle, Justin Chatwin, Glenn Close, William Fichtner, Ralph Fiennes, Allison Janney, Carrie-Anne Moss, Rita Wilson, Lou Taylor Pucci, Rory Culkin, Caroline Goodall, John Heard, Jason Isaacs, Lauren Holly. Bell is excellent as a misfit who goes even further into his shell when his best friend commits suicide. One-note observation of life in the affluent suburban development from hell, where teens are alienated and overmedicated, parents self-absorbed and clueless. Fine work from the adult cast, with Fiennes a standout as Wilson's fiancé, who experiences an epiphany that no one can share or comprehend. Super 35. [R]▶

Chungking Express (1994-Hong Kong) **C-103m.** ****½** D: Wong Kar-Wai. Brigitte Lin, Takeshi Kaneshiro, Tony Leung, Faye Wang, Valerie Chow, "Piggy" Chan. Two tangentially related stories of lovesickness, obsession, and the peccadilloes of relationships in a modern world. The catalyst for both liaisons, involving young Hong Kong policemen, is the proprietor of a fast-food establishment. Light, funny, and offbeat, though the second tale goes on far too long. Quentin Tarantino's Rolling Thunder company acquired this for U.S. release, and many critics applauded its postmodern approach and stylistics. [PG-13]▼●

Chunhyang (2000-Korean) **C-122m.** ****** D: Im Kwon Taek. Lee Hae Eun, Lee Hae Ryong, Kim Hak Yong, Lee Hyo Jung, Cho Seung Woo, Choi Jin Young. Grandly old-fashioned romantic epic about the son of a wealthy governor who falls head over heels for the daughter of a courtesan and the reverberations of their secret marriage. Lush cinematography distracts from the soggy melodrama. Film also uses a traditional pansori (Korean opera singer) as narrator, which can grate heavily on Western ears. Proudly wears its heart on its sleeve but never engages our emotions. [R]▼▶

Chushingura (1962-Japanese) **C-108m.** *****½** D: Hiroshi Inagaki. Koshiro Matsumoto, Yuzo Kayama, Chusha Ichikawa, Toshiro Mifune, Yoko Tsukasa. Young lord Kayama is forced to commit hara kiri by corrupt feudal lord Ichikawa, and his 47 samurai retainers (or ronin) seek vengeance. A version of an oft-filmed story, based on a real-life event: sprawling, episodic, exquisitely beautiful, if a bit slow. Sometimes referred to as the GONE WITH THE WIND of Japanese cinema. Originally released in Japan in two parts, running 204m. Tohoscope.▼●)

Ciao! Manhattan (1972) **C/B&W-84m.** **½ D: John Palmer, David Weisman. Edie Sedgwick, Wesley Hayes, Isabel Jewell, Jeff Briggs, Viva, Paul America, Brigid Berlin, Baby Jane Holzer, Roger Vadim, Christian Marquand, Allen Ginsberg. Eerie, fascinating, muddled, and boring mishmash in which Sedgwick essentially plays herself, a strung-out ex-superstar model. Filming started and stopped in 1967, and resumed four years later; Sedgwick died of a drug overdose months after its completion. Aka EDIE IN CIAO! MANHATTAN. [R] ▼●)

Ciao, Professore! (1992-Italian) **C-91m.** ** D: Lina Wertmuller. Paolo Villaggio, Isa Danieli, Gigio Morra, Sergio Solli, Esterina Carloni, Paolo Bonacelli. A middle-aged elementary school teacher from an upper-class section of Italy is mistakenly transferred to a run-down school in a decaying town near Naples. Naturally, both he and his students wind up learning a lot from each other. Wertmuller's attempt to comment on her country's educational system, this Italian TO SIR, WITH LOVE is a mostly labored lesson. [R]▼●)

Cider House Rules, The (1999) **C-125m.** **** D: Lasse Hallström. Tobey Maguire, Charlize Theron, Michael Caine, Delroy Lindo, Paul Rudd, Kathy Baker, Jane Alexander, Kieran Culkin, Erykah Badu, Kate Nelligan, Heavy D., K. Todd Freeman. Loving adaptation of John Irving's novel (by the author), telescoped from the sprawling story about a boy raised in a Maine orphanage (and abortion clinic) by an eccentric doctor who treats him like his own son—and begrudges the boy's decision to go out and see the world once he comes of age in the 1940s. Well cast, beautifully crafted; filmed on perfect locations throughout New England. Beautiful score by Rachel Portman and cinematography by Oliver Stapleton. Oscar winner for Best Adapted Screenplay and Supporting Actor (Caine). Super 35. [PG-13]▼▶

Cimarron (1931) **124m.** **½ D: Wesley Ruggles. Richard Dix, Irene Dunne, Estelle Taylor, Nance O'Neil, William Collier, Jr., Roscoe Ates. Edna Ferber's saga about an American family and the effect of empire building on the American West, 1889–1929. Oscar winner for Best Picture and Best Screenplay (Howard Estabrook), it dates badly, particularly Dix's overripe performance—but it's still worth seeing. Remade in 1960. ▼▶

Cimarron (1960) **C-147m.** **½ D: Anthony Mann. Glenn Ford, Maria Schell, Anne Baxter, Arthur O'Connell, Russ Tamblyn, Mercedes McCambridge, Vic Morrow,

Charles McGraw, Henry (Harry) Morgan, Edgar Buchanan, Robert Keith, Aline MacMahon, David Opatoshu, Mary Wickes. Edna Ferber's chronicle of frontier life in Oklahoma between 1889 and 1929 becomes an indifferent sprawling soap opera unsalvaged by a few spectacular scenes. CinemaScope.▼●)

Cincinnati Kid, The (1965) **C-103m.** **½ D: Norman Jewison. Steve McQueen, Ann-Margret, Edward G. Robinson, Karl Malden, Tuesday Weld, Joan Blondell, Rip Torn, Jack Weston, Cab Calloway. Roving card-sharks get together in New Orleans for big poker game; side episodes of meaningless romance. Robinson, Blondell, and Malden come off best as vivid members of the playing profession. Script by Ring Lardner, Jr., and Terry Southern. Ray Charles sings the title song. ▼●)

Cinderella (1950) **C-74m.** ***½ D: Wilfred Jackson, Hamilton Luske, Clyde Geronimi. Voices of Ilene Woods, Eleanor Audley, Rhoda Williams, Lucille Bliss, Verna Felton, Mike Douglas. One of Walt Disney's best animated fairy tales spins the traditional story with some delightful comic embellishments, including a couple of mice named Gus and Jaq who befriend the put-upon heroine. Tuneful score includes "A Dream Is a Wish Your Heart Makes" and "Bibbidi Bobbidi Boo." Followed by two DVD sequels. ▼●)

Cinderella Liberty (1973) **C-117m.** ***½ D: Mark Rydell. James Caan, Marsha Mason, Eli Wallach, Kirk Calloway, Burt Young, Bruce Kirby, Jr. (Bruno Kirby), Allyn Ann McLerie, Dabney Coleman, Sally Kirkland. Sensitive, original story by Darryl Ponicsan (based on his novel) about romance between simple, good-hearted sailor and a hooker with an illegitimate black son. Artfully mixes romance and realism, with sterling performances by Caan and Mason. Panavision. [R]▼▶

Cinderella Man (2005) **C-144m.** *** D: Ron Howard. Russell Crowe, Renée Zellweger, Paul Giamatti, Craig Bierko, Paddy Considine, Bruce McGill, Ron Canada, Rosemarie DeWitt. Rousing true-life story of boxer James J. Braddock, reduced to working on loading docks to support his family during the Depression, then given a second shot in the ring. Familiar underdog material pushes all the expected buttons, but is handled with skill and compassion. Colorful period detail and dynamic handling of boxing scenes, crowned by fine work from Crowe as Braddock and, especially, Giamatti as his loyal trainer and manager. Super 35. [PG-13] ▼▶

Cinderella Story, A (2004) **C-95m.** ** D: Mark Rosman. Hilary Duff, Jennifer Coolidge, Chad Michael Murray, Dan Byrd, Regina King, Julie Gonzalo, Lin Shaye, Madeline Zima, Andrea Avery, Mary Pat Gleason, Paul Rodriguez, Whip Hubley, Art Le Fleur. Modern-day Cinderella story set in the San Fernando Valley. An orphaned girl who acts as slavey to her oafish stepmother finds a soul mate online but doesn't know his identity until the night of a high school dance. Unfortunately, the story goes on from there. Duff and Murray are likable, but the built-in predictability makes this piece of puff a bore. Followed by a DVD sequel. [PG] ▼⬗

Cinderfella (1960) **C-91m.** **½ D: Frank Tashlin. Jerry Lewis, Ed Wynn, Judith Anderson, Anna Maria Alberghetti, Henry Silva, Count Basie. Jerry is the poor stepson turned into a handsome prince for a night by fairy godfather Wynn. Fairy tale classic revamped as a pretentious Lewis vehicle, with talky interludes and ineffectual musical sequences. ▼⬗

Cinema Paradiso (1988-Italian-French) **C-123m.** ***½ D: Giuseppe Tornatore. Philippe Noiret, Jacques Perrin, Salvatore Cascio, Mario Leonardi, Agnese Nano, Leopoldo Trieste. A young boy is mesmerized by the movie theater in his small Italian town (in the years following WW2), and pursues a friendship with its crusty but warm-hearted projectionist. Captivating, bittersweet film, with a perfect finale; Noiret and the boy (Cascio) are wonderful. Written by the director. After abortive Italian release in 1988, film was shortened and awarded a Special Jury Prize at the 1989 Cannes Film Festival; it went on to win the Best Foreign Film Oscar. Reissued in 2002 at 174m. [PG] ▼●⬗

Circle of Deceit (1981-French-German) **C-108m.** **** D: Volker Schlöndorff. Bruno Ganz, Hanna Schygulla, Jean Carmet, Jerzy Skolimowski, Gila von Weitershausen. Thoughtful, chilling, unrelentingly sober account of German journalist Ganz covering a Lebanese civil war, focusing on how he is affected by his experiences and his relationship with widow Schygulla. Filmed in Beirut against a backdrop of political turmoil; superior in every respect. Originally shown as FALSE WITNESS. [R] ▼⬗

Circle of Friends (1995-U.S.-Irish) **C-96m.** *** D: Pat O'Connor. Chris O'Donnell, Minnie Driver, Geraldine O'Rawe, Saffron Burrows, Alan Cumming, Colin Firth, Aidan Gillen. Spirited and individualistic young woman leaves her Irish village to attend university in Dublin and falls madly in love with a handsome lad. He loves her, too, but their relationship is impeded by chance and circumstance. Perhaps more ado than necessary for such a simple tale, but still satisfying; anchored by Driver's irresistible performance as Benny. Adapted from Maeve Binchy's novel and set in the 1950s. [PG-13] ▼●⬗

Circle of Iron (1979) **C-102m.** **½ D: Richard Moore. David Carradine, Jeff Cooper, Roddy McDowall, Eli Wallach, Erica Creer, Christopher Lee. Strange, sometimes silly, but watchable blend of martial arts action and Zen philosophy; from an idea

concocted by James Coburn and Bruce Lee. Cooper (looking like a California surfer) must pass rites of trial to find secret book of knowledge. Carradine plays four roles in this Stirling Silliphant–scripted fantasy, filmed in Israel as THE SILENT FLUTE. [R] ▼⬗

Circle of Love (1964-French-Italian) **C-105m.** *½ D: Roger Vadim. Jane Fonda, Jean-Claude Brialy, Maurice Ronet, Jean Sorel, Catherine Spaak, Anna Karina, Marie Dubois, Claude Giraud, Françoise Dorléac. Undistinguished remake of Ophuls' classic LA RONDE: A seduces B, B makes love to C, C has an affair with D—circling all the way back to A. Screenplay by Jean Anouilh; original running time: 110m. Franscope. ▼⬗

Circle of Power (1983) **C-103m.** **½ D: Bobby Roth. Yvette Mimieux, Christopher Allport, Cindy Pickett, John Considine, Julius Harris, Scott Marlowe, Fran Ryan, Walter Olkewicz, Danny Dayton, Denny Miller, Terence Knox. Intriguing—and disquieting—tale of businessmen and their wives who undergo EDT (Executive Development Training), which, as administered by Mimieux, turns out to be a horrifying and humiliating series of rituals. Based on actual events, believe it or not. Originally released as MYSTIQUE; aka BRAINWASH and THE NAKED WEEKEND. [R] ▼

Circle of Two (1980-Canadian) **C-105m.** ** D: Jules Dassin. Richard Burton, Tatum O'Neal, Nuala FitzGerald, Robin Gammell, Patricia Collins, Kate Reid. Sixty-year-old artist has romantic but platonic relationship with 16-year-old student. Burton is OK, and Dassin does not go for the cheap thrill, but the result is slight and forgettable. [PG] ▼⬗

Circuit, The SEE: Pulse (2001)

Circus, The (1928) **72m.** ***½ D: Charles Chaplin. Charlie Chaplin, Merna Kennedy, Allan Garcia, Betty Morrissey, Harry Crocker. Not the "masterpiece" of THE GOLD RUSH or CITY LIGHTS, but still a gem; story has Charlie accidentally joining traveling circus, falling in love with bareback rider. Hilarious comedy, with memorable finale. Chaplin won a special Academy Award for "versatility and genius in writing, acting, directing and producing" this. ▼●⬗

Circus of Fear SEE: **Psycho-Circus**

Circus World (1964) **C-135m.** **½ D: Henry Hathaway. John Wayne, Rita Hayworth, Claudia Cardinale, John Smith, Lloyd Nolan, Richard Conte. Made in Spain, film has nothing new to offer, but rehashes usual circus formula quite nicely with the Duke as Big Top boss trying to pull his three-ring wild west show through various perils during European tour. Climactic fire sequence is truly spectacular. Super Technirama 70. ▼●

Cirque du Freak: The Vampire's Assistant (2009) **C-108m.** ** D: Paul Weitz. John C. Reilly, Ken Watanabe, Josh Hutcherson,

Chris Massoglia, Jessica Carlson, Ray Stevenson, Patrick Fugit, Willem Dafoe, Salma Hayek, Orlando Jones, Frankie Faison, Michael Cerveris, Colleen Camp, Jane Krakowski. A teen attends a traveling freak show, where he becomes a "half vampire" (and assistant to vampire Reilly). Needless to say, his life is altered considerably. Fitfully amusing comedy-horror film is done in by an incomprehensible storyline. Screenplay by Weitz and Brian Helgeland, based on the fantasy book series by Darren Shan. Super 35. [PG-13]▐

Cisco Pike (1972) **C-94m.** *** D: B. L. Norton. Kris Kristofferson, Karen Black, Gene Hackman, Viva!, Roscoe Lee Browne, Harry Dean Stanton. Surprisingly good drama about crooked cop Hackman getting mixed up with drug dealing, and blackmailing ex-rock star Kristofferson (among Kris's songs is "Lovin' Her Was Easier"). [R]▐

Citadel, The (1938-U.S.-British) **112m.** ***½ D: King Vidor. Robert Donat, Rosalind Russell, Ralph Richardson, Rex Harrison, Emlyn Williams, Penelope Dudley-Ward, Francis L. Sullivan. Superb adaptation of A. J. Cronin novel of impoverished doctor Donat eschewing ideals for wealthy life of treating rich hypochondriacs, neglecting wife and friends in the process; tragedy opens his eyes. Weak ending, but fine acting makes up for it. Frank "Spig" Wead, Emlyn Williams, Ian Dalrymple, Elizabeth Hill, and John Van Druten all contributed to the script. Remade in Britain as a TV miniseries.▼▐

Citizen Kane (1941) **119m.** **** D: Orson Welles. Orson Welles, Joseph Cotten, Everett Sloane, Agnes Moorehead, Dorothy Comingore, Ray Collins, George Coulouris, Ruth Warrick, William Alland, Paul Stewart, Erskine Sanford. Welles' first and best, a film that broke all the rules and invented some new ones, with fascinating story of Hearst-like publisher's rise to power. The cinematography (by Gregg Toland), music score (by Bernard Herrmann), and Oscar-winning screenplay (by Welles and Herman J. Mankiewicz) are all first-rate. A stunning film in every way . . . and Welles was only 25 when he made it! Incidentally, the reporter with a pipe is Alan Ladd; Arthur O'Connell is another one of the reporters.▼●▐

Citizen Ruth (1996) **C-109m.** *** D: Alexander Payne. Laura Dern, Swoosie Kurtz, Mary Kay Place, Kurtwood Smith, Kelly Preston, M. C. Gainey, Kenneth Mars, Burt Reynolds, Alicia Witt, Tippi Hedren, Kathleen Noone. Dern is a pregnant chemical-inhaling homeless woman who inadvertently becomes the center of a pro-life vs. pro-choice struggle over her unborn child. A stinging satire of fanaticism, with many funny scenes, though it peters out a bit toward the end; well played by a devoted cast. Diane Ladd has a raunchy unbilled cameo. [R]▼●▐

Citizens Band SEE: **Handle With Care**

City, The (1999) **88m.** ***½ D: David Riker. Fernando Reyes, Marcos Martinez García, Moises García, Anthony Rivera, Cipriano García. Striking neorealist-style film offers four vignettes about Latino immigrants and their struggle for survival in N.Y.C. Alternately poignant, amusing, and heartbreaking, these living portraits are enacted with a keen eye for detail and an overwhelming amount of empathy. Writer-director Riker and cinematographer Harlan Bosmajian shot their film (in black & white) with non-professional actors over six years' time. Aka LA CIUDAD.▼▐

City by the Sea (2002) **C-108m.** ** D: Michael Caton-Jones. Robert De Niro, Frances McDormand, James Franco, Eliza Dushku, William Forsythe, Patti LuPone, George Dzundza, Anson Mount, Drena De Niro, Leo Burmester. Dreary, derivative saga of a N.Y.C. cop who returns to his hometown, the once thriving, now desolate beachfront community of Long Beach, Long Island, where his long-estranged son may have committed murder. Tries to paint a tragic saga of fathers, sons, and lost opportunities, but too often rings hollow. Inspired by a true story. Super 35. [R]▼▐

City for Conquest (1940) **101m.** *** D: Anatole Litvak. James Cagney, Ann Sheridan, Frank Craven, Arthur Kennedy, Donald Crisp, Frank McHugh, George Tobias, Elia Kazan, Anthony Quinn. Cagney makes this a must as boxer devoted to younger brother Kennedy. Beautiful production overshadows film's pretentious faults. A rare chance to see young Kazan in an acting role, as a neighborhood pal turned gangster. Long-missing prologue was restored in 2006, bringing running time to 104m.▼●▐

City Girl, The (1984-U.S.-Canadian) **C-85m.** *** D: Martha Coolidge. Laura Harrington, Joe Mastroianni, Carole McGill, Peter Riegert, Colleen Camp, Jim Carrington, Geraldine Baron. Solid, uncompromising tale of a young woman (expertly played by Harrington) attempting to advance her career as a photographer, and her various, unsatisfactory relationships with men. Refreshingly realistic, and even funny; a winner.

City Hall (1996) **C-111m.** **½ D: Harold Becker. Al Pacino, John Cusack, Bridget Fonda, Danny Aiello, Martin Landau, David Paymer, Anthony Franciosa, Richard Schiff, Lindsay Duncan, Nestor Serrano, Mel Winkler, Roberta Peters, John Slattery. N.Y.C. deputy mayor Cusack selflessly serves his mayor, a superb politician who really cares about his constituents. When a shootout involving a cop, a drug dealer, and an innocent child escalates into a citywide scandal, however, Cusack finds that the pathway to the truth is a political minefield. Snappy behind-the-scenes-of-urban-politics story pulls you in, then veers toward melodrama, with a finale that's pretty hard to swallow. This was the work of a real-life deputy mayor, Ken Lipper, and no fewer than three top screenwriters (Bo Goldman, Paul Schrader, Nicholas Pileggi)! [R]▼●◗

City Heat (1984) **C-97m.** ** D: Richard Benjamin. Clint Eastwood, Burt Reynolds, Jane Alexander, Madeline Kahn, Rip Torn, Irene Cara, Richard Roundtree, Tony Lo Bianco, William Sanderson, Robert Davi. Two macho stars do caricatures of themselves in this 1930s gangster/detective yarn that takes turns trying to be funny and serious (when they pour gasoline on a guy and set him on fire we're apparently supposed to find it funny). For diehard fans of Clint and Burt only. [PG]▼●◗

City Island (2010) **C-103m.** *** D: Raymond De Felitta. Andy Garcia, Julianna Margulies, Steven Strait, Alan Arkin, Emily Mortimer, Dominik García-Lorido, Ezra Miller. Prison guard Garcia (in one of his best performances) lives with his boisterous, eccentric family in a house his grandfather built in the title N.Y.C. community, and harbors a secret: he wants to be an actor. His wife thinks he's playing around, and this drives a wedge between them. Then he brings home a paroled convict, without telling anyone (including the young man) that it's his son, from a long-ago relationship. Likable comedy-drama seems to be saying, "Life is messy; learn to deal with it." Garcia's real-life daughter plays his offspring here. Written by the director, who also made TWO FAMILY HOUSE. [PG-13] ◗

City Lights (1931) **86m.** **** D: Charles Chaplin. Charlie Chaplin, Virginia Cherrill, Harry Myers, Hank Mann. Chaplin's masterpiece tells story of his love for blind flower girl and his hot-and-cold friendship with a drunken millionaire. Eloquent, moving, and funny. One of the all-time greats.▼●◗

City Limits (1985) **C-85m.** BOMB D: Aaron Lipstadt. Darrell Larson, John Stockwell, Kim Cattrall, Rae Dawn Chong, John Diehl, Don Opper, James Earl Jones, Robby Benson, Danny De La Paz, Norbert Weisser. Disastrous sci-fi followup by the team that made ANDROID, an incoherent mess set 15 years in the future after a plague has devastated the planet, leaving roving youth gangs warring in MAD MAX fashion. Most of the plot is expressed in tacked-on narration by Jones. [PG-13]▼

City of Angels (1998) **C-117m.** **½ D: Brad Silberling. Nicolas Cage, Meg Ryan, Andre Braugher, Dennis Franz, Colm Feore, Robin Bartlett, Joanna Merlin, Sarah Dampf. An angel, who longs to know more about human beings and finds himself attracted to a hard-working female doctor, decides to sacrifice his heavenly status and fall to earth so he can experience love. Americanization of Wim Wenders' haunting WINGS OF DESIRE is—by the very nature of American movie conventions—less ethereal than the original film, but still intriguing and in its own way romantic. Only the climax seems routine and therefore disappointing. Panavision. [PG-13]▼●◗

City of Ember (2008) **C-94m.** ** D: Gil Kenan. Saoirse Ronan, Harry Treadaway, Tim Robbins, Bill Murray, Martin Landau, Mary Kay Place, Toby Jones, Marianne Jean-Baptiste, Mackenzie Crook. Citizens of an isolated underground city that's falling apart are afraid to venture beyond its boundaries, unaware that instructions were left behind by a group of wise men who sought to protect them from the demise of civilization aboveground. A plucky girl (Ronan) and her friend (Treadaway), not intimidated by their do-nothing mayor (Murray), start poking around and making interesting discoveries in the dilapidated city of Ember. Adaptation of Jeanne Duprau's novel never fires the emotional response it needs so badly. The real star of the film is production designer Martin Laing. Super 35. [PG]◗

City of Fear (1959) **75m.** *½ D: Irving Lerner. Vince Edwards, Lyle Talbot, John Archer, Steven Ritch, Patricia Blair. Programmer involving escaped convict Edwards sought by police and health officials; container he stole is filled with radioactive material, not heroin.◗

City of Ghosts (2003) **C-116m.** ** D: Matt Dillon. Matt Dillon, James Caan, Stellan Skarsgård, Natascha McElhone, Gérard Depardieu, Sereyvuth Kem, Rose Byrne. Dillon plays an American rogue—a con man with a conscience—involved in murky business dealings and general intrigue in present-day Phnom Penh. Joseph Conrad and Graham Greene can rest easy: this lightweight drama is never as credible or compelling as intended. However, it does get points for atmosphere, having been filmed throughout Cambodia. Dillon's feature directing debut; he also cowrote. [R]▼◗

City of God (2002-Brazilian) **C-131m.** ***½ D: Fernando Meirelles. Matheus Nachtergaele, Seu Jorge, Alexandre Rodrigues, Leandro Firmino da Hora, Phelipe Haagensen, Jonathan Haagensen, Douglas Silva. Extraordinary portrait of life in the slums of Rio de Janeiro, where young—often incredibly young—hoodlums rule, violence is commonplace, and a rivalry turns the district into a war zone. One boy finds a way out of this existence by learning to use a camera. An arresting, and brutal, mosaic of stories spanning three decades, told with tremendous skill and creativity by director Meirelles, who also adapted Paulo Lins' book, and cast of mostly nonprofessional actors. Kátia Lund is credited as codirector.

Followed by Brazilian TV series *City of Men* and a same-named feature in 2007. [R]▼◗

City of Hope (1991) **C-129m.** **½ D: John Sayles. Vincent Spano, Tony Lo Bianco, Joe Morton, John Sayles, Angela Bassett, David Strathairn, Maggie Renzi, Anthony John Denison, Kevin Tighe, Barbara Williams, Chris Cooper, Jace Alexander, Todd Graff, Frankie Faison, Gloria Foster, Tom Wright, Michael Mantell, Josh Mostel, Joe Grifasi, Louis Zorich, Gina Gershon, Rose Gregorio, Bill Raymond, Lawrence Tierney, Maeve Kinkead, Ray Aranha. Ambitious multi-character drama about a strife-torn inner city and the people whose lives intersect within it. Writer-director-editor Sayles (who wrote himself a good part, as the slimy Carl) brings vivid and believable characters to life, and makes some pungent comments about contemporary society, but loses his momentum somewhere along the way. Panavision. [R] ▼◗

City of Industry (1997) **C-97m.** *½ D: John Irvin. Harvey Keitel, Stephen Dorff, Famke Janssen, Timothy Hutton, Wade Dominguez, Michael Jai White, Reno Wilson, Lucy Alexis Liu. Depressing story of robbery, deceit, murder, and revenge, set in current-day L.A. Keitel seems like a caricature of himself and Hutton is unconvincing as a sleaze, even with that scruffy beard. Elliott Gould appears unbilled. [R]▼◗

City of Joy (1992-British-French) **C-134m.** **½ D: Roland Joffé. Patrick Swayze, Pauline Collins, Om Puri, Shabana Azmi, Ayesha Dharker, Santu Chowdury, Imran Badsah Khan, Art Malik, Shyamanand Jalan. Aimless, cynical American surgeon Swayze, living in Calcutta, "finds" himself after becoming involved with a health clinic for the poor, taking on the local mafia, and befriending hardworking but poverty-stricken Puri. Well-intentioned but pretentious film scripted by Mark Medoff from Dominique Lapierre's book. Swayze tries his best, but is outshone by supporting cast; similar territory is covered better in SALAAM BOMBAY! Sam Wanamaker appears unbilled as Swayze's father. [PG-13]▼◗

City of Lost Children, The (1995-French-Spanish-German) **C-112m.** *** D: Jean-Pierre Jeunet, Marc Caro. Ron Perlman, Joseph Lucien, Daniel Emilfork, Mireille Mosse, Judith Vittet, Dominique Pinon. Provocative fantasy about a wicked scientist (Emilfork) who is unable to dream, and who goes about purloining children—with the help of remarkable "cloned" henchmen—and invading their dreams. Although dramatically uneven, this mix of *Oliver Twist* and BRAZIL is a marvel of production design, with sumptuous visuals and painstaking invention. The voice of Irvin, the disembodied brain, is provided by Jean-Louis Trintignant. [R]▼◗

City of Men (2007-Brazilian) **C-110m.** *** D: Paulo Morelli. Douglas Silva, Dar-

lan Cunha, Jonathan Haagensen, Rodrigo dos Santos, Camila Monteiro, Naima Silva, Eduardo BR. Companion piece to CITY OF GOD focuses on two young friends who are about to turn 18—one who's never known his father, the other who's already a reluctant father of a baby boy—and how their friendship is put to the test as gang war breaks out in their mountainside community (or *favela*). More intimate than its predecessor; immediate and powerful, about young men dealing with responsibility—and the need to make choices—for the first time in their lives. Sprinkled with flashbacks of the boys from CITY OF GOD and the TV series it spawned. [R]◗

City of Women (1980-Italian) **C-139m.** *** D: Federico Fellini. Marcello Mastroianni, Anna Prucnal, Bernice Stegers, Iole Silvani, Donatella Damiani. Marcello falls asleep on a train, dreams he has stumbled into an all-female society. Lavish fantasy could only have been made by one filmmaker; a Fellini feast or déjà vu o.d., depending on your mood and stamina. [R]▼◗

City of Your Final Destination, The (2010-U.S.-British) **C-117m.** **½ D: James Ivory. Anthony Hopkins, Omar Metwally, Laura Linney, Charlotte Gainsbourg, Hiroyuki Sanada, Norma Aleandro, Alexandra Maria Lara. U.S. college professor needs a family's approval to write the biography of a late, elusive author in order to keep his job—and his strong-willed girlfriend. He goes to Uruguay, hoping to persuade the widow, mistress, and brother of the writer, who all live together on a remote estate, to say yes. Not consistently compelling, but creates an intriguing mood as the characters come alive, to varying degrees, when the stranger enters their isolated environment. Ruth Prawer Jhabvala adapted Peter Cameron's novel. Filmed in 2006–07, this made the festival circuit before finally getting a desultory theatrical release. Kate Burton appears unbilled. [PG-13]◗

City on Fire (1979-Canadian) **C-101m.** *½ D: Alvin Rakoff. Barry Newman, Henry Fonda, Ava Gardner, Shelley Winters, Susan Clark, Leslie Nielsen, James Franciscus, Jonathan Welsh. Dull, fill-in-the-blanks disaster film about citywide fire torched by a disgruntled ex-employee of local oil refinery. Good cast wasted. For pyromaniacs only. [R]▼

City Slickers (1991) **C-112m.** *** D: Ron Underwood. Billy Crystal, Daniel Stern, Bruno Kirby, Patricia Wettig, Helen Slater, Jack Palance, Noble Willingham, Tracey Walter, Josh Mostel, David Paymer, Bill Henderson, Jeffrey Tambor, Phill Lewis, Kyle Secor, Jayne Meadows, Jake Gyllenhaal. Three friends who are going through various degrees of mid-life crisis sign up for a two-week cattle drive, to clear their minds and set them back on-course. Enjoyable comedy, whose generous array of funny lines and good moments makes up for its "serious" pretensions and flaws. Palance won Best Supporting Actor Oscar for his role as the leathery trail boss. Followed by a sequel. [PG-13] ▼●】

City Slickers: The Legend of Curly's Gold (1994) **C-116m.** **½ D: Paul Weiland. Billy Crystal, Daniel Stern, Jon Lovitz, Jack Palance, Patricia Wettig, Pruitt Taylor Vince, Bill McKinney, Noble Willingham, David Paymer, Josh Mostel. A contrived sequel if there ever was one, with Crystal and Stern going back West (with Billy's screw-up brother Lovitz) to locate gold from a treasure map Palance (from the first film) left behind. Lack of plot and purpose are balanced by magnificent Moab, Utah, scenery—and a lot of genuine laughs, in the script by Crystal, Lowell Ganz, and Babaloo Mandel. [PG-13] ▼●】

Civic Duty (2007) **C-98m.** *** D: Jeff Renfroe. Peter Krause, Richard Schiff, Khaled Abol Naga, Kari Matchett, Ian Tracey. Accountant loses his job and begins spying on his new neighbor, an Islamic college student he suspects of being a terrorist. When no one else buys into his obsession, he takes matters into his own hands. Krause delivers a powerful portrait of a man caught in the grip of media-fueled fear and paranoia. Independently produced nail-biter has echoes of REAR WINDOW but is clearly born out of the events of 9/11. [R]】

Civil Action, A (1998) **C-115m.** ***½ D: Steven Zaillian. John Travolta, Robert Duvall, Tony Shalhoub, William H. Macy, Željko Ivanek, Bruce Norris, John Lithgow, Kathleen Quinlan, Peter Jacobson, Sydney Pollack, Dan Hedaya, James Gandolfini. Slick Boston injury lawyer gets in over his head when he takes a case against two industrial giants whose alleged pollution of a river caused the deaths of children in Woburn, Mass. Engrossing, literate, well-observed film (adapted by the director from Jonathan Harr's best-seller) explores the foibles of American justice—and how pride, human frailty, and emotions can affect a case. Based on a true story. Kathy Bates appears unbilled. [PG-13] ▼●】

Civil Brand (2003) **C-91m.** **½ D: Neema Barnette. LisaRaye, N'Bushe Wright, Mos Def, Da Brat, Monica Calhoun, Clifton Powell, Reed R. McCants, Tachina Arnold, Lark Voorhies, MC Lyte, Robert Lynn. Forceful story of women who are mistreated in prison by an abusive supervisor and by a corrupt system that turns them into sweatshop laborers. Eye-opening subject matter alternates with melodramatic prison fodder, while some contrived, underscripted characters weaken the overall film. Even with its faults, it's still potent stuff. [R] ▼】

CJ7 (2008-Hong Kong) **C-88m.** ** D: Stephen Chow. Stephen Chow, Jiao Xu, Chi Chung Lam, Kitty Zhang Yuqi, Shing-Cheung Lee, Min Hun Fung. Chow works overtime to send his son (Xu) to an impressive private school, hoping that he can grow up and make something of himself. But when he gives his son a toy he finds at the dump, both of their lives are changed forever. Like Chow's other films, the movie's manic zigzagging from wacky to sincere makes it almost impossible to enjoy the story and genuinely care about anyone. Although it has some redeeming moments (due to the animated toy that comes to life), they are few and far between. Super 35. [PG]】

Claim, The (2000-British-Canadian) **C-120m.** ** D: Michael Winterbottom. Wes Bentley, Peter Mullan, Milla Jovovich, Sarah Polley, Nastassja Kinski, Sean McGinley. Thomas Hardy's *The Mayor of Casterbridge* reset in snowy northern California in the aftermath of the gold rush, in 1867. Mullan runs the town of Kingdom Come with an iron fist, but melts somewhat when his ex-wife and daughter (whom he sold in exchange for a gold claim years ago) turn up. Vivid and well acted, but emotionally hollow. Super 35. [R] ▼】

Clair de Femme (1979-French) **C-103m.** ** D: Costa-Gavras. Yves Montand, Romy Schneider, Romolo Valli, Lila Kedrova, Heinz Bennent, Roberto Benigni, Jean Reno. Slow-moving chronicle of the relationship between traumatized widower Montand and Schneider, who has been scarred by the death of her young daughter in an auto accident. Characters are one-dimensional, and film is gloomy, gloomy, gloomy. Based on novel by Romain Gary.

Claire Dolan (1998-U.S.-French) **C-95m.** *** D: Lodge Kerrigan. Katrin Cartlidge, Vincent D'Onofrio, Colm Meaney, Patrick Husted, Muriel Maida. Intriguing portrait of an Irish-American woman who works as a prostitute, caught in a viselike grip by her menacing and manipulative pimp (Meaney), until she decides to break free—if she can. Quiet, well-observed film that doesn't spell everything out about its characters, forcing us to fill in the blanks. Strong performances by all three leads. ▼】

Claire's Knee (1971-French) **C-103m.** ***½ D: Eric Rohmer. Jean-Claude Brialy, Aurora Cornu, Beatrice Romand, Laurence De Monaghan, Michele Montel. No. 5 of Rohmer's "Six Moral Tales" has widest appeal. A man about to be married is obsessed with a girl he doesn't even like, his attention focusing on her knee. Full of delicious relationships, but too talky for some viewers. [PG]】

Clambake (1967) **C-97m.** *½ D: Arthur Nadel. Elvis Presley, Shelley Fabares, Will Hutchins, Bill Bixby, Gary Merrill, James Gregory. Elvis is a millionaire's son who wants to make it on his own, so he trades places with water-skiing instructor Hutchins in Miami. One of Presley's weakest. Techniscope. ▼】

Clan of the Cave Bear, The (1986) **C-98m.** *½ D: Michael Chapman. Daryl Hannah, Pamela Reed, James Remar, Thomas G. Waites, John Doolittle, Curtis Armstrong. World's first feminist caveman movie, minus the anthropological detail of Jean Auel's popular book. Hannah is perfectly cast as outsider who joins band of nomadic Neanderthals, but the story (such as it is) is alternately boring and unintentionally funny. Subtitles translate cave people's primitive tongue. Screenplay by John Sayles. Technovision. [R]▼●❍

Clara's Heart (1988) **C-108m.** *½ D: Robert Mulligan. Whoopi Goldberg, Michael Ontkean, Kathleen Quinlan, Neil Patrick Harris, Spalding Gray, Beverly Todd. Whoopi plays a Jamaican domestic (think of Shirley Booth's *Hazel* with a reggae bias), a soft-spoken know-it-all who works for insufferable Maryland yuppies and their young, impressionable son (well played by Harris). The kind of movie best described as "nice" by undiscriminating viewers in search of blandness—and seemingly edited with a chainsaw. [PG-13]▼●

Clarence and Angel (1980) **C-75m.** *** D: Robert Gardner. Darren Brown, Mark Cardova, Cynthia McPherson, Louis Mike, Leroy Smith, Lola Langley, Lolita Lewis. Aggressive, kung-fu-mad Angel (Cardova) befriends his new schoolmate, shy, illiterate Clarence (Brown), who has recently arrived in Harlem from South Carolina, and teaches him to read. Technically crude, but funny and touching; sequence in principal's office, in which Clarence's mother fakes reading a test score, is a gem.▼

Clash by Night (1952) **105m.** *** D: Fritz Lang. Barbara Stanwyck, Paul Douglas, Robert Ryan, Marilyn Monroe, Keith Andes, J. Carrol Naish. Moody, well-acted Clifford Odets story of drifter Stanwyck settling down, marrying good-natured fisherman Douglas. Cynical friend Ryan senses that she's not happy, tries to take advantage. Andes and Monroe provide secondary love interest.▼●❍

Clash of the Titans (1981-British) **C-118m.** **½ D: Desmond Davis. Laurence Olivier, Harry Hamlin, Judi Bowker, Burgess Meredith, Sian Phillips, Maggie Smith, Claire Bloom, Ursula Andress, Tim Pigott-Smith. Juvenile fantasy-adventure based on Greek mythology. Olivier is Zeus, and Hamlin is his mortal son Perseus, who must face a variety of awesome challenges in pursuit of his destiny. Long and episodic, with some fine elements (the taming of Pegasus, the threat of Medusa—who can turn men into stone with one glance), but not enough guts or vigor. As is, mainly for kids. Special effects by Ray Harryhausen. Remade in 2010. [PG]▼●❍

Clash of the Titans (2010) **C-106m.** **½ D: Louis Leterrier. Sam Worthington, Liam Neeson, Ralph Fiennes, Jason Flemyng,

Gemma Arterton, Alexa Davalos, Mads Mikkelsen, Nicholas Hoult, Polly Walker, Pete Postlethwaite, Elizabeth McGovern, Danny Huston, Luke Evans. Raised by a human family, Perseus (Worthington) is a young man when he learns that he is the son of Zeus (Neeson)—but refutes his Olympian heritage after a fateful attack by Hades (Fiennes). Remake largely follows the trajectory of the 1981 movie with new-generation CGI creatures and visual effects. Some of these scenes are genuinely exciting, but there are dull patches in between. Worthington is a stoical hero; the women around him are quite beautiful. 3-D Panavision. [PG-13]❍

Class (1983) **C-98m.** ** D: Lewis John Carlino. Rob Lowe, Jacqueline Bisset, Andrew McCarthy, Stuart Margolin, Cliff Robertson, John Cusack, Alan Ruck, Remak Ramsay, Virginia Madsen, Casey Siemaszko, Anna Maria Horsford, Joan Cusack. Naive prep-school boy stumbles (almost literally) into affair with beautiful older woman, unaware of her identity. Slick but uneven mix of romance, comedy, and drama with one-dimensional characters and a lack of credibility. Some good moments lost in the shuffle. [R]▼●❍

Class, The (2008-French) **C-124m.** ***½ D: Laurent Cantet. François Bégaudeau, Nassim Amrabt, Laura Baquela, Cherif Bounaïdja Rachedi, Juliette Demaille, Esméralda Ouertani, Rachel Régulier, Franck Keïta, Wei Haung. Dedicated teacher in a working-class Parisian school tries to instill a passion for learning in his multicultural classroom but the freedom of expression he encourages makes every day a challenge. Invigorating drama has the spark of spontaneity from start to finish. The leading actor is in fact a teacher who wrote a novel about his experiences and coauthored this screenplay with Cantet and Robin Campillo—with input from the nonprofessional actors playing the students. Original French title: ENTRE LES MURS. Super 35. [PG-13]❍

Class Act (1992) **C-98m.** **½ D: Randall Miller. Christopher Reid, Christopher Martin, Meshach Taylor, Karyn Parsons, Doug E. Doug, Rick Ducommun, Lamont Johnson, Rhea Perlman. Straight-A student (Reid) and street-wise juvenile delinquent (Martin) switch identities when they both transfer to a new high school; complications ensue when they find it tough sledding in their new environs. Broad, cartoony comedy is nothing special; neither is the obligatory anti-drug rap song at the end of the film. [PG-13]▼●

Class Action (1991) **C-109m.** *** D: Michael Apted. Gene Hackman, Mary Elizabeth Mastrantonio, Colin Friels, Joanna Merlin, Larry Fishburne, Donald Moffat, Jan Rubes, Matt Clark, Fred Dalton Thompson, Jonathan Silverman, Dan Hicks. Crusading lawyer takes on a class-action suit against a negligent auto company—while his feisty daughter represents the other side. Crackling performances by the two stars, as the long-embattled father and daughter, make this well worth seeing, even though the story becomes obvious at the climactic turn. [R] ▼●)

Classe Tous Risques (1960-French) **103m.** *** D: Claude Sautet. Lino Ventura, Jean-Paul Belmondo, Sandra Milo, Marcel Dalio, Stan Krol. Solid crime drama with Ventura as a murderer who's been living in exile in Milan but decides to return to Paris after pulling one last heist. His plans go awry, and while he expects his criminal pals to help him when he arrives in Nice, they send a young guy instead (Belmondo) to pick him up. Tough, ironic tale filled with interesting characters and vivid location work. Great showcase for the young Belmondo, made around the same time as BREATHLESS.▶

Class of '44 (1973) **C-95m.** **½ D: Paul Bogart. Gary Grimes, Jerry Houser, Oliver Conant, Deborah Winters, William Atherton, Sam Bottoms, John Candy. Sequel to SUMMER OF '42 is less ambitious, lightly entertaining story, with Grimes going to college, falling in love, growing up. Good period atmosphere. Panavision. [PG] ▼)

Class of Miss MacMichael, The (1978-British) **C-99m.** *½ D: Silvio Narizzano. Glenda Jackson, Oliver Reed, Michael Murphy, Rosalind Cash, John Standing, Riba Akabusi, Phil Daniels. Echoes of TO SIR, WITH LOVE don't flatter this shrill comedy-drama of a dedicated teacher with a class full of social misfits. [R] ▼

Class of 1984 (1982) **C-93m.** ** D: Mark L. Lester. Perry King, Merrie Lynn Ross, Roddy McDowall, Timothy Van Patten, Stefan Arngrim, Al Waxman, Michael J. Fox, Lisa Langlois. Unpleasant, calculatedly campy melodrama about the harassment of high school teacher King by psychotic student Van Patten—with more than a few echoes of BLACKBOARD JUNGLE. As revenge movies go, the buzzsaw finale is not bad. Followed by CLASS OF 1999. [R] ▼●)

Class of 1999 (1990) **C-98m.** *½ D: Mark L. Lester. Bradley Gregg, Traci Lind, Malcolm McDowell, Stacy Keach, Patrick Kilpatrick, Pam Grier, John P. Ryan, Darren E. Burrows, Joshua Miller. Followup to CLASS OF 1984 pictures high school of the near-future as Hell on Earth, with ultraviolent gang members meeting their match in a trio of robots recruited as teachers. Heavy-handed film wavers between high camp and taking itself seriously as a message movie! Keach goes overboard as a maniacal robot operator. Unrated video version also available. 1993 sequel: CLASS OF 1999 II: THE SUBSTITUTE. [R] ▼)

Class of Nuke 'Em High (1986) **C-81m.** BOMB D: Richard Haines, Samuel Weil.

Janelle Brady, Gilbert Brenton, Robert Prichard, R. L. Ryan. Obnoxious horror comedy about a New Jersey high school near a nuclear waste spill that creates monsters and disgustingly transforms model teens Brady and Brenton. Dehumanizing, sadistic gags masquerade as lowbrow entertainment. Followed by two sequels. [R] ▼●)

Claudine (1974) **C-92m.** **½ D: John Berry. Diahann Carroll, James Earl Jones, Lawrence Hilton-Jacobs, Tamu, David Kruger, Adam Wade. Slice-of-life comedy with a serious edge: Romance between garbageman Jones and young ghetto mother Carroll is charming and credible, but the problems of dealing with her six kids, and their collective poverty, can't be treated so lightly. "Upbeat" finale just doesn't ring true. [PG] ▼)

Clay Pigeon (1971) **C-97m.** *½ D: Tom Stern, Lane Slate. Tom Stern, Telly Savalas, Robert Vaughn, John Marley, Burgess Meredith, Ivan Dixon. Good cast in dull crime melodrama of Vietnam vet settling into drug scene who experiences change of heart and goes after big-league pusher. [R]

Clay Pigeons (1998) **C-104m.** **½ D: David Dobkin. Joaquin Phoenix, Vince Vaughn, Janeane Garofalo, Georgina Cates, Scott Wilson, Vince Vieluf, Phil Morris. Clever film noir set in a small town out west. A patsy falls prey first to his best friend, then the friend's slatternly wife, and finally to a mysterious stranger just passing through, whose actions bring a cynical big-city FBI agent (Garofalo) to town. Twisty black comedy has much to enjoy but leaves the viewer less than completely satisfied. Overemphatic use of source music is a debit, but the opening is a grabber. [R] ▼●)

Clean (2004-Canadian-French-British) **C-110m.** **½ D: Olivier Assayas. Maggie Cheung, Nick Nolte, Béatrice Dalle, Jeanne Balibar, Don McKellar, Martha Henry, James Johnston, James Dennis, Rémi Martin. Unremarkable account of Cheung, the spouse of a second-tier rocker, who goes through hell after he dies of an overdose. She, too, is a junkie, and struggles to get her life in order. It's difficult to invest emotion in such an unlikable character, though her story becomes more involving as it goes along. Nolte is the best thing in the film, offering a touching performance as the deceased rocker's emotionally generous father. Written by the director. Super 35. [R] ▼)

Clean and Sober (1988) **C-125m.** *** D: Glenn Gordon Caron. Michael Keaton, Kathy Baker, Morgan Freeman, M. Emmet Walsh, Tate Donovan, Henry Judd Baker, Luca Bercovici, Claudia Christian, Pat Quinn, Ben Piazza. A young hustler enrolls in a drug rehabilitation program in order to duck out of sight for a while—refusing to admit to himself that he's an addict, too.

Powerful drama showcases Keaton in an utterly believable performance, though the film's relentlessness makes it tough to watch. [R]▼●◗

Cleaner (2007) **C-89m.** ** D: Renny Harlin. Samuel L. Jackson, Eva Mendes, Ed Harris, Luis Guzmán, Keke Palmer, Robert Forster. Former cop (Jackson) runs a hazardous waste containment enterprise, which includes cleaning up gruesome crime scenes. All is well until he sanitizes a murder scene before the police are notified of the homicide. Jackson and Harris are fine, but there's little surprise beyond the intriguing setup. Humdrum film released direct to DVD in the U.S. Super 35. [R]◗

Clean, Shaven (1993) **C-80m.** *** D: Lodge Kerrigan. Peter Greene, Robert Albert, Jennifer MacDonald, Megan Owen. Unusual, subtly chilling psychological drama about Peter (Greene), a schizophrenic released from an institution who is grasping for a human connection. Meanwhile, his young daughter has been put up for adoption by her mother, a cop, who's investigating the brutal murder of another child and becomes convinced Peter is the culprit. A meditation on deep feelings of loss and alienation; not always easy to follow, but challenging, even haunting.▼◗

Clean Slate (1981) SEE: **Coup de Torchon**

Clean Slate (1994) **C-107m.** ** D: Mick Jackson. Dana Carvey, Valeria Golino, James Earl Jones, Kevin Pollak, Michael Gambon, Michael Murphy, Olivia d'Abo, Tim Scott, Angela Paton, Jayne Brook, Gailard Sartain, Phil Leeds, Bryan Cranston. Carvey plays a detective who awakens each morning with no memory whatsoever. Did somebody say GROUNDHOG DAY? It's D.O.A. all the way, though there are some mildly amusing gags involving a klutzy terrier named Barkley. [PG-13] ▼◗

Clear and Present Danger (1994) **C-141m.** **½ D: Phillip Noyce. Harrison Ford, Willem Dafoe, Anne Archer, Joaquim de Almeida, James Earl Jones, Henry Czerny, Harris Yulin, Donald Moffat, Miguel Sandoval, Benjamin Bratt, Raymond Cruz, Dean Jones, Thora Birch, Ann Magnuson, Hope Lange. CIA whiz Jack Ryan finds himself waist-deep in highest-level Washington politics when his ailing mentor (Jones) names him as his replacement. Soon he's caught in the middle of double-dealing with a Colombian druglord. The always watchable Ford plays more a symbol than a character here, and the action climax seems somehow pat. Still, it's an intelligent and entertaining sequel to PATRIOT GAMES. Followed by THE SUM OF ALL FEARS. Panavision. [PG-13] ▼●◗

Clearcut (1991-Canadian) **C-98m.** **½ D: Richard Bugajski. Ron Lea, Graham Greene, Michael Hogan, Floyd (Red Crow)

Westerman, Rebecca Jenkins. Multileveled drama about Indian activist Greene (who kidnaps the boss of a sawmill company responsible for cutting down forests) and natively liberal laywer Lea (who's failed to halt the destruction in the courts). Presence of graphic violence in the midst of a thought-provoking drama is jarring, to say the least, but the subject, and Greene's performance, make it worthwhile. [R]▼

Clearing, The (2004) **C-94m.** **½ D: Pieter Jan Brugge. Robert Redford, Helen Mirren, Willem Dafoe, Alessandro Nivola, Matt Craven, Melissa Sagemiller, Wendy Crewson, Larry Pine, Diana Scarwid, Elizabeth Ruscio. A successful, married businessman is kidnapped one morning. As his wife and children go through the ordeal of having their lives invaded by the FBI, while waiting for further word, the victim gets to know his captor as they make their way in the woods. More a character study than a conventional story, this interesting, elliptical film plays with chronology in challenging ways but doesn't lead to a satisfying conclusion. The three stars are excellent. [R] ▼◗

Cleo From 5 to 7 (1962-French) **C/B&W-90m.** *** D: Agnès Varda. Corinne Marchand, Antoine Bourseiller, Dorothée Blanck, Michel Legrand, Anna Karina, Eddie Constantine, Jean-Luc Godard. Intelligent, fluid account of Parisian songstress forced to reevaluate her life while awaiting vital medical report on her physical condition. First scene is in color. ▼●◗

Cleopatra (1934) **100m.** ***½ D: Cecil B. DeMille. Claudette Colbert, Warren William, Henry Wilcoxon, Gertrude Michael, Joseph Schildkraut, C. Aubrey Smith, Claudia Dell, Robert Warwick. Opulent DeMille version of Cleopatra doesn't date badly, stands out as one of his most intelligent films, thanks in large part to fine performances by all. Top entertainment, with Oscar-winning cinematography by Victor Milner.▼●◗

Cleopatra (1963) **C-243m.** ** D: Joseph L. Mankiewicz. Elizabeth Taylor, Richard Burton, Rex Harrison, Pamela Brown, George Cole, Hume Cronyn, Cesare Danova, Kenneth Haigh, Andrew Keir, Martin Landau, Roddy McDowall, Robert Stephens, Francesca Annis, Herbert Berghof, Michael Hordern, John Hoyt, Carroll O'Connor. Saga of the Nile goes on and on and on. Definitely a curiosity item, but you'll be satisfied after an hour. Good acting, especially by Harrison and McDowall, but it's lost in this flat, four-hour misfire. Nevertheless earned Oscars for cinematography, art direction–set decoration, costumes, special effects. Released to TV at 194m. Todd-AO.▼●◗

Cleopatra Jones (1973) **C-89m.** ** D: Jack Starrett. Tamara Dobson, Bernie Casey, Shelley Winters, Brenda Sykes, Antonio Fargas, Bill McKinney, Esther Rolle. Black bubblegum stuff with Dobson as karate-chopping government agent chasing drug kingpins. Lots of action and violence. Panavision. [PG]▼❶

Cleopatra Jones and the Casino of Gold (1975) **C-96m.** **½ D: Chuck Bail. Tamara Dobson, Stella Stevens, Tanny, Norman Fell, Albert Popwell, Caro Kenyatta, Christopher Hunt. Wild, woolly, sexy, violent sequel to CLEOPATRA JONES. Stevens plays "The Dragon Lady," a tip-off on what to expect. Panavision. [R]▼❶

Clerks (1994) **89m.** *** D: Kevin Smith. Brian O'Halloran, Jeff Anderson, Marilyn Ghigliotti, Lisa Spoonauer, Jason Mewes, Kevin Smith. Black and white, $27,000 wonder by first-time filmmaker Smith is a brash, foul-mouthed, often very funny look at a day in the lives of a New Jersey convenience-store clerk and his abrasive pal, who mans the video place next door—when he feels like it. Well written and well acted; more provocative and entertaining than many glossy Hollywood movies of the '90s. Unrated director's cut runs 92m. Later an animated series. Followed by a sequel in 2006. [R]▼❶❶

Clerks II (2006) **C-97m.** **½ D: Kevin Smith. Brian O'Halloran, Jeff Anderson, Rosario Dawson, Kevin Smith, Jason Mewes, Trevor Fehrman, Ethan Suplee, Ben Affleck, Jason Lee, Wanda Sykes. After the Quick Stop burns down, Dante and Randal go to work for a local fast-food joint, but Dante (O'Halloran) has found an escape: a good-looking girl has fallen in love with him, and they're going to move to Florida and get married. His last day at Mooby's is unexpectedly eventful, however. Writer-director Smith is still in touch with his inner imbecile, but this CLERKS has little of the intelligence that made his breakout film so special in 1994 . . . but no shortage of potty-mouthed humor. [R]❶

Click (2006) **C-106m.** *½ D: Frank Coraci. Adam Sandler, Kate Beckinsale, Christopher Walken, David Hasselhoff, Henry Winkler, Julie Kavner, Jennifer Coolidge, Sean Astin, Rachel Dratch, Jonah Hill. Stressed-out, workaholic architect who never seems to have enough time for his family comes upon a crazy inventor who gives him a remote control that can manipulate his life—and even help him skip the boring parts. Good comedy premise unexpectedly morphs into a self-serious examination of a life gone wrong (as if this was IT'S A WONDERFUL REMOTE) . . . yet Sandler doesn't want to sacrifice any of his trademark crudity. An odd, unsatisfying mishmash. Rob Schneider appears uncredited. [PG-13]❶

Client, The (1994) **C-122m.** *** D: Joel Schumacher. Susan Sarandon, Tommy Lee Jones, Brad Renfro, Mary-Louise Parker, Anthony LaPaglia, Ossie Davis, Bradley Whitford, Anthony Edwards, J.T. Walsh, Walter Olkewicz, Will Patton, Anthony Heald, William H. Macy. Top-flight adaptation of John Grisham's bestseller about an 11-year-old boy who finds himself in hot water with both the Feds (led by Jones) and the Mob when he learns too much from a Mafia lawyer who's about to kill himself. Sarandon is the lawyer who takes the kid's case. Suspense is neatly woven with character development; satisfying entertainment. Later a TV series. Panavision. [PG-13]▼❶

Client 9: The Rise and Fall of Eliot Spitzer (2010) **C-117m.** ***½ D: Alex Gibney. Oscar-winning documentarian Gibney, at the top of his game, gets a subject in his wheelhouse: N.Y. State's controversial attorney-general-turned-governor who was brought down by personal hubris, high-priced call girls, and transparently cruddy political enemies that anyone would be proud to have. Compounding a dreadful situation: Spitzer was the only person of real power combating—way early in the game—the Wall Street excesses that eventually took the nation's economy down. Gripping throughout and remarkable in its ability to get key parties to speak for attribution. This said, the doc is up front about the fact that the escort who was Spitzer's most frequent companion did not want to speak on camera. The transcript of her lengthy interview is delivered by a professional actress (Wrenn Schmidt) and she is fabulous. [R]❶

Cliffhanger (1993-U.S.-French) **C-118m.** *** D: Renny Harlin. Sylvester Stallone, John Lithgow, Michael Rooker, Janine Turner, Paul Winfield, Ralph Waite, Rex Linn, Caroline Goodall, Leon, Craig Fairbrass, Michelle Joyner, Max Perlich. Self-doubting mountain rescue expert Sly is pitted against really rotten Lithgow and his gang, who are after $100 million lost in the Rockies. Eye-popping photography (by Alex Thomson), white-knuckle stunts, a swift pace, and entertaining characters add up to what a well-made action film should be: tons of fun. Story is thin, though. Italy's Dolomites stand in for the Rockies. Panavision. [R]▼❶❶

Clifford (1994) **C-89m.** *½ D: Paul Flaherty. Martin Short, Charles Grodin, Mary Steenburgen, Dabney Coleman, G. D. Spradlin, Anne Jeffreys, Richard Kind, Jennifer Savidge, Ben Savage. Moronic comedy in the (unfortunate) mold of PROBLEM CHILD, with Short uninspiringly cast as a cloyingly obnoxious ten-year-old who makes life pure hell for his uncle (Grodin). Short's playing a child is a gimmick which quickly proves tiresome. Completed in 1991, this could have stayed on the shelf. [PG]▼❶

Clifford's Really Big Movie (2004) **C-73m.** **½ D: Robert C. Ramirez. Voices of John Ritter, Grey DeLisle, Cree Summer, Kel Mitchell, Wayne Brady, Jenna Elfman, Judge Reinhold, John Goodman, Wilmer Valderrama, Ernie Hudson, Teresa Ganzel, Jess Harnell, Kath Soucie. Norman Bridwell's Big Red Dog gets the feature film treatment in this benign cartoon aimed at the preschool set. Clifford, concerned about being a financial burden to his owners, joins a carnival in hopes of entering a contest where the prize is a lifetime supply of his favorite doggy treats. Pleasant, undemanding fare for tots. [G] ▼❶

Climate for Killing, A (1990) **C-103m.** *******
D: J. S. Cardone. John Beck, Steven Bauer, Mia Sara, Katharine Ross, John Diehl, Phil Brock, Dedee Pfeiffer, Lu Leonard, Jack Dodson, Eloy Casados. A grisly murder confronts, and confounds, small-time Arizona cop Beck; he's joined by big city evaluator Bauer, who questions his approach to law enforcement while becoming involved with his daughter (Sara). Solid, engrossing mystery-drama. [R] ▼❶

Climax, The (1944) **C-86m.** ****½** D: George Waggner. Boris Karloff, Susanna Foster, Turhan Bey, Gale Sondergaard, Thomas Gomez, Scotty Beckett, George Dolenz, Jane Farrar, June Vincent, Ludwig Stossel. Technicolor tale of suave but sinister physician to the Vienna Opera House who takes an unnatural interest in their newest soprano (Foster)—just as he did another singer who disappeared ten years ago. No surprises here, but slickly done. ▼❶

Clinic, The (1982-Australian) **C-92m.** ****½** D: David Stevens. Chris Haywood, Simon Burke, Rona McLeod, Gerda Nicolson, Suzanne Roylance, Veronica Lang, Pat Evison. Straightforward but much too obvious comedy-drama about the goings-on in a VD clinic operated by doctor Haywood. ▼

Cloak and Dagger (1946) **106m.** ****½** D: Fritz Lang. Gary Cooper, Lilli Palmer, Robert Alda, Vladimir Sokoloff, Ludwig Stossel. Professor Cooper becomes a secret agent on his trip to Germany; Lang intrigue is not among his best, but still slick. ▼❶

Cloak & Dagger (1984) **C-101m.** ******* D: Richard Franklin. Henry Thomas, Dabney Coleman, Michael Murphy, John McIntire, Jeanette Nolan, Christine Nigra. Young Thomas gets involved with murderous espionage—but no one will believe him. Flawed but enjoyable reworking of THE WINDOW. Coleman's a delight in dual role as his father and his make-believe hero. [PG] ▼❶

Clock, The (1945) **90m.** *****½** D: Vincente Minnelli. Judy Garland, Robert Walker, James Gleason, Keenan Wynn, Marshall Thompson, Lucille Gleason. Soldier Walker has two-day leave in N.Y.C., meets office worker Judy; they spend the day falling in love, encountering friendly milkman Gleason, drunk Wynn; charming little love story with beguiling Garland. Also shown in computer-colored version. ▼❶

Clockers (1995) **C-129m.** ******* D: Spike Lee. Harvey Keitel, John Turturro, Delroy Lindo, Mekhi Phifer, Isaiah Washington, Keith David, Pee Wee Love, Regina Taylor, Tom Byrd, Sticky Fingaz, Mike Starr, Spike Lee. The night manager of a fast-food restaurant is murdered, but a no-nonsense Brooklyn cop doesn't believe that the young man who confessed to the crime is really guilty. He's got his eye on the suspect's brother (Phifer), who works for the neighborhood drug czar. A penetrating, multilayered look at the reality of life on the street and in "the projects," and a challenging treatise on personal responsibility. It's tough to decipher the street lingo and dialect in the opening scenes, but once the story kicks in, it's dynamite. Richard Price adapted his novel with Lee; a fortuitous merging of two distinctive talents. [R] ▼❶

Clockmaker, The (1974-French) **C-100m.** *****½** D: Bertrand Tavernier. Philippe Noiret, Jean Rochefort, Jacques Denis, Julien Bertheau. Noiret is superb as a watchmaker who is forced to reevaluate his life after his son is arrested for murder. Meticulously directed; based on a novel by Georges Simenon. Tavernier's feature directing debut. Alternate title: THE CLOCKMAKER OF ST. PAUL. ▼❶

Clockstoppers (2002) **C-94m.** ****** D: Jonathan Frakes. Jesse Bradford, French Stewart, Paula Garces, Michael Biehn, Robin Thomas, Garikayi Mutambirwa, Julia Sweeney, Lindze Letherman. Teenage boy acquires an experimental watch that can stop time, more or less. This scores big points with his new girlfriend, but gets him into a mess of trouble with bad guys who have threatened the watch's inventor—and the boy's scientist dad. Starts as a high-energy, good-time film for young viewers (from Nickelodeon Movies), but begins to drag halfway through its needlessly complicated script. [PG] ▼❶

Clockwatchers (1997) **C-105m.** ****** D: Jill Sprecher. Toni Collette, Parker Posey, Lisa Kudrow, Alanna Ubach, Helen Fitzgerald, Stanley DeSantis, Jamie Kennedy, Kevin Cooney, Paul Dooley, Bob Balaban. Four office temps in corporate hell form a fast friendship that ultimately jeopardizes their attempts at careers. Indie spin on NINE TO FIVE captures working-week tedium hilariously for a while, then gets bogged down in tedious Kafkaesque second half. Posey's bitchy comic flair throughout gives the film its only real juice. [PG-13] ▼❶

Clockwise (1986-British) **C-96m.** ****½** D: Christopher Morahan. John Cleese, Penelope Wilton, Alison Steadman, Stephen Moore, Sharon Maiden, Joan Hickson. Cleese is a school headmaster, obsessed with punctuality, en route to make a speech at a convention and constantly getting into trouble. A tour de force role that is a must for Cleese fans; others will be disappointed with the thinness of playwright Michael Frayn's script. [PG] ▼❶

Clockwork Orange, A (1971) **C-137m.** *****½** D: Stanley Kubrick. Malcolm McDowell, Patrick Magee, Michael Bates, Adrienne Corri, Aubrey Morris, James Marcus, Steven Berkoff, David Prowse. A scathing satire on a society in the not so distant future, with an excellent performance by McDowell as a prime misfit. Kubrick's vivid adaptation of Anthony Burgess' novel was too strong for some to stomach in 1971, and it remains potent today. [R—edited from original X rating] ▼●▶

Clone Wars, The (2008) **C-98m.** ** D: Dave Filoni. Voices of Matt Lanter, James Arnold Taylor, Ashley Eckstein, Tom Kane, Ian Abercrombie, Corey Burton, Samuel L. Jackson, Anthony Daniels, Christopher Lee. First entirely computer-animated STAR WARS feature takes place between Episodes II and III in George Lucas' epic space fantasy. Anakin Skywalker, Obi-Wan Kenobi, and a young female apprentice fight the Republic to rescue Jabba the Hutt's infant son from a kidnapping plot. Created as the first three episodes of *The Clone Wars* TV series—and feels like it. Special effects, alien landscapes, and spaceships are visually dazzling, and the battle sequences are thrilling, but the characters are as wooden and stiff as they look. Much more juvenile than the original movies, which means that kids may enjoy it more than diehard fans. Aka STAR WARS: THE CLONE WARS. Followed by a TV series. Digital widescreen. [PG]▐

Clonus Horror, The SEE: **Parts: The Clonus Horror**

Close Encounters of the Third Kind (1977) **C-135m.** **** D: Steven Spielberg. Richard Dreyfuss, François Truffaut, Teri Garr, Melinda Dillon, Cary Guffey, Bob Balaban. Superb, intelligent sci-fi (written by Spielberg) about UFO mystery that leads to first contact with alien beings. Dreyfuss is perfect Everyman struggling with frustrating enigma that finally becomes clear. Powerhouse special effects throughout, plus John Williams' evocative score. Vilmos Zsigmond's impressive cinematography won an Oscar. Reedited by Spielberg to tighten midsection and add alien-encounter material to finale and reissued in 1980 at 132m. as THE SPECIAL EDITION. (Then, for network showings, *all* existing footage was used!) Reedited yet again by Spielberg in 1998 to 137m. for a Collector's Edition. Panavision. [PG]▼●▶

Closely Watched Trains (1966-Czech) **89m.** *** D: Jiri Menzel. Vaclav Neckar, Jitka Bendova, Vladimir Valenta, Libuse Havelkova, Josef Somr. Enjoyable but slightly overrated tragicomedy about naive apprentice train-dispatcher Neckar's attempts at sexual initiation during the German Occupation. Academy Award winner as Best Foreign Film.▼●▶

Close My Eyes (1991-British) **C-109m.** *** D: Stephen Poliakoff. Alan Rickman, Clive Owen, Saskia Reeves, Karl Johnson, Lesley Sharp, Kate Gartside. Vaguely unhappy woman makes sexual overtures to

her brother, which explode into full-fledged incest five years later when she's married and living in a mansion by the Thames. Film is a bit haphazard setting up the basic situation, but soon becomes a riveting view. Extremely well acted, with confident performances by Owen and Reeves (as the taboo-flaunting siblings) and Rickman, in a supporting role as the husband. [R]▼▶

Closer (2004) **C-104m.** **½ D: Mike Nichols. Julia Roberts, Jude Law, Natalie Portman, Clive Owen. Four people fall in and out of love as they fall in and out of bed. Extremely well acted and intimately staged for the camera (though it's still obvious this derived from a stage work); the question is whether we care enough about the characters to endure their endless and brutal playing of mind games. Super-charged performances, especially by Owen and Portman, help a lot. More sexually explicit dialogue than any mainstream Hollywood movie we can remember! Patrick Marber adapted his play. [R] ▼▶

Closer, The (1990) **C-86m.** *½ D: Dimitri Logothetis. Danny Aiello, Michael Paré, Joe Cortese, Justine Bateman, Diane Baker, James Karen, Michael Lerner. Highly successful businessman is forced to retire and creates a tension-filled night of competition in order to pick his successor. Aiello is compelling as always, but this would-be *Death of a Salesman* never gets out of the gate. Aiello originated the role on Broadway in 1976; Louis La Russo II's play was titled *Wheelbarrow Closers.* [R]▼▶

Closer You Get, The (2000-Irish-British) **C-90m.** **½ D: Aileen Ritchie. Ian Hart, Sean McGinley, Niamh Cusack, Ruth McCabe, Ewan Stewart, Pat Shortt, Cathleen Bradley, Sean McDonagh. Flyweight comedy about a remote Irish island village where the young men decide to do something about the lack of eligible, attractive females: they take a want ad in a Miami newspaper, inviting sexy, athletic, marriage-minded American women to come on over. Self-consciously cute and padded out, but still amusing. Aka AMERICAN WOMEN. [PG-13]▼▶

Closet, The (2001-French) **C-86m.** **½ D: Francis Veber. Daniel Auteuil, Gérard Depardieu, Thierry Lhermitte, Michèle Laroque, Jean Rochefort, Alexandra Vandernoot, Michel Aumont. Slight but amusing social comedy from writer-director Veber concerning a nonentity who's about to be fired from his company after 20 years. His new neighbor hatches a plan to save the job: pretend he's gay so the firm won't risk the accusation of sexual prejudice. Naturally the ruse snowballs, in more directions than one. Likable, if a bit low key. Technovision. [R] ▼▶

Closet Land (1991) **C-89m.** *½ D: Radha Bharadwaj. Madeleine Stowe, Alan Rickman. Among the oddest of early '90s films: a two-character drama about the political interrogation of an allegedly subversive children's author by one of a totalitarian society's finest. Like a bad play that never went beyond workshop status, though no one can accuse the filmmakers of taking the easy way out. Well performed, under the circumstances. Coproduced by Ron Howard! [R]▼

Close to Eden (1992-Russian) **C-106m.** *** D: Nikita Mikhalkov. Badema, Byaertu, Vladimir Gostukhin, Babushka, Larissa Kuznetsova, Jon Bochinski, Bao Yongyan. Russian truckdriver accidentally comes into the lives of a Mongol family, adroitly raising the question of who's "civilized" and who isn't. Beautifully filmed in the Mongolian steppe region of inner China by the acclaimed director of DARK EYES. Worth seeing.▼

Close Your Eyes (2003-British) **C-103m.** *** D: Nick Willing. Goran Visnjic, Shirley Henderson, Miranda Otto, Paddy Considine, Claire Rushbrook, Fiona Shaw, Corin Redgrave, Sophie Stuckey. Scotland Yard detective Henderson draws hypnotherapist Visnjic into a troubling case involving a serial killer and a little girl who's been traumatized since she was held captive by him. Mixing occult elements with a whodunit, this original, genuinely creepy thriller stays on track right to the end. Based on the novel *Doctor Sleep* by Madison Smartt Bell. Super 35. [R]▼❙

Cloud Dancer (1980) **C-108m.** **½ D: Barry Brown. David Carradine, Jennifer O'Neill, Joseph Bottoms, Colleen Camp, Albert Salmi, Salome Jens, Nina Van Pallandt. Uneven tale of aerobatic-obsessed Carradine and his relationship with O'Neill. Nice—if too many—flying sequences, hokey melodramatics. Filmed in 1978. [PG]▼

Clouded Yellow, The (1950-British) **85m.** *** D: Ralph Thomas. Jean Simmons, Trevor Howard, Sonia Dresdel, Barry Jones, Kenneth More, Geoffrey Keen, Andre Morell, Maxwell Reed. Entertaining psychological drama/mystery/chase film in which ex-secret serviceman Howard takes a job cataloguing butterflies, and becomes involved with a strange, fragile young girl (Simmons)—and murder.▼

Cloudy With a Chance of Meatballs (2009) **C-90m.** *** D: Phil Lord, Chris Miller. Voices of Bill Hader, Anna Faris, James Caan, Andy Samberg, Bruce Campbell, Mr. T, Bobb'e J. Thompson, Benjamin Bratt, Neil Patrick Harris, Lauren Graham, Will Forte. Lifelong science whiz-kid Flint Lockwood finally devises an invention that might be beneficial: he can turn water into food. Soon it begins *raining* food of all sorts, which could be a boon to the island community where he lives . . . if he could only control it. Lively, funny animated yarn inspired by a popular children's book, with amusing character design, good voice work, and solid sight gags. It does gets a bit frantic toward the end. 3-D Digital Widescreen. [PG]❙

Cloverfield (2008) **C-85m.** *** D: Matt Reeves. Lizzy Caplan, Jessica Lucas, T. J. Miller, Michael Stahl-David, Mike Vogel, Odette Yustman, Chris Mulkey. A monster invades N.Y.C. and creates incredible havoc. This 1950s B-movie premise is executed 2008-style through the lens of a video camera held by a guy who starts out shooting a friend's farewell party and then gets caught up in "documenting" everything that happens. Runs on pure adrenaline and never lets up, with some good shocks and a formidable creature. Some people find the shaky handheld camerawork difficult to stomach. Coproduced by J. J. Abrams. [PG-13]▼

Clown, The (1953) **91m.** **½ D: Robert Z. Leonard. Red Skelton, Tim Considine, Jane Greer, Loring Smith, Philip Ober. Sentimental remake of THE CHAMP about a washed-up, self-destructive comic with a devoted son who looks out for him. Skelton's not bad in rare dramatic role; Considine is so good he overcomes some of the hokiness of script. Charles Bronson has a bit role in dice game scene.▼

Clowns, The (1970-Italian) **C-90m.** ***½ D: Federico Fellini. Fellini's homage to circus clowns is itself a clownish spoof of documentaries, a funny, fully entertaining piece of fluff from this great director, even making fun of himself. Made for Italian TV. [G]▼❙

Club, The (1980-Australian) **C-99m.** *** D: Bruce Beresford. Jack Thompson, Graham Kennedy, Frank Wilson, Harold Hopkins, John Howard. Thompson is excellent as a football coach in this searing drama about off-the-field politics in a football club. Script by David Williamson, based on his play. Aka PLAYERS. Panavision. ▼❙

Club Dead SEE: **Terror House**

Club Dread (2004) **C-104m.** BOMB D: Jay Chandrasekhar. Bill Paxton, Jay Chandrasekhar, Kevin Heffernan, Steve Lemme, Paul Soter, Erik Stolhanske, Jordan Ladd, Brittany Daniel, M.C. Gainey, Lindsay Price. Yes, *dread*ful comedy/horror film about an island resort populated by college-age partyers and a serial murderer who's offing the staff. Written by and starring members of the comedy troupe Broken Lizard. It's not a good sign when the audience is rooting for the killer. Unrated version also available. On-screen title: BROKEN LIZARD'S CLUB DREAD. Super 35. [R]▼❙

Club Extinction (1990-German-Italian-French) **C-112m.** ** D: Claude Chabrol. Alan Bates, Jennifer Beals, Jan Niklas, Hans Zischler, Benoit Regent, Peter Fitz, Andrew McCarthy, Wolfgang Preiss, Isolde Barth. A wave of suicides shocks near-future Berlin; police investigator Niklas begins to suspect involvement of Beals, spokesperson for an Edenlike resort, who's linked to media baron Dr. Marsfeldt (Bates). Chabrol's attempt at updating Dr. Mabuse (film credits Norbert Jacques' original novel, *Mabuse der Spieler*) misfires; Bates is miscast, and film lacks any thematic resonances. Still, an interesting curiosity. European title: DR. M. Shot in English. [R]▼●

Clubland (1999) **C-94m. **** D: Mary Lambert. Jimmy Tuckett, Lori Petty, Brad Hunt, Heather Stephens, Rodney Eastman, Buddy Quaid, Terence Trent D'Arby, Alexis Arquette, Steven Tyler. Young man and his buddies are determined to make it big in the music world by performing at a trendy club on L.A.'s Sunset Strip, but they have to deal with sleazy promoters and personality problems within the band. Contemporary music and trappings can't disguise, or overcome, a soggy story that might have been made as a 1930s B movie. Written by successful music producer Glen Ballard. [R]▼●

Clubland SEE: **Introducing the Dwights**

Club Life (1985) **C-92m. **½** D: Norman Thaddeus Vane. Tony Curtis, Tom Parsekian, Dee Wallace, Michael Parks, Jamie Barrett, Ron Kuhlman, Yana Nirvana, Pat Ast. Hunk Parsekian arrives in Hollywood with stars in his eyes, hoping for a movie career; instead, he finds himself toiling as a bouncer in Curtis' bar. Nicely stylized and acted (if all-too-familiar) tale of Tinseltown decadence. How could you not like a film in which Ast appears as a lesbian bar owner named Butch? Vane also produced and scripted.▼

Club Paradise (1986) **C-104m. **** D: Harold Ramis. Robin Williams, Peter O'Toole, Rick Moranis, Jimmy Cliff, Twiggy, Adolph Caesar, Eugene Levy, Joanna Cassidy, Andrea Martin, Robin Duke, Mary Gross, Simon Jones, Carey Lowell. Pleasant cast in pleasant surroundings, lacking only a script and a few more laughs. Williams plays Chicago fireman who retires to West Indian island, goes halfies with native Cliff on turning ramshackle beachfront property into vacation resort. Writers even try to shoehorn a "serious" subplot about exploitation of the natives into the proceedings! Best of all is Cliff's almost nonstop music; his performance isn't bad, either. [PG-13]▼●▶

Clue (1985) **C-87m. **½** D: Jonathan Lynn. Eileen Brennan, Tim Curry, Madeline Kahn, Christopher Lloyd, Michael McKean, Martin Mull, Lesley Ann Warren, Colleen Camp, Lee Ving, Bill Henderson, Howard Hesseman. Silly comic whodunit based on the popular board game of the same name with all the familiar characters (Mrs. Peacock, Colonel Mustard, Miss Scarlet, et al.) gathered for a murderous night in a Victorian mansion. Everyone tries very hard—*too* hard, since the script, by first-time feature director Lynn, is so slim; addle-brained Brennan and puckish butler Curry come off best. When this played theatrically, audiences saw one of three alternate endings. Video has all three in a row to total 96m. [PG]▼●▶

Clueless (1995) **C-97m. ***** D: Amy Heckerling. Alicia Silverstone, Stacey Dash, Brittany Murphy, Paul Rudd, Donald Faison, Breckin Meyer, Jeremy Sisto, Justin Walker, Elisa Donovan, Dan Hedaya, Wallace Shawn, Twink Caplan, Julie Brown. Sharp, funny, original take on Beverly Hills high school teens of the '90s, by the director of FAST TIMES AT RIDGEMONT HIGH (and based—believe it or not—on Jane Austen's *Emma*). Silverstone is perfect as Cher, who with her best friend Dionne—they're both named after famous pop singers—knows everything about being gorgeous, popular, and always in vogue. This laugh-out-loud satire is never mean, which is a big part of its charm; it also introduces wonderfully funny vernacular, which we won't spoil by reciting here. As if! Heckerling also scripted. Later a TV series. [PG-13]▼●▶

Cluny Brown (1946) **100m. ***½** D: Ernst Lubitsch. Charles Boyer, Jennifer Jones, Peter Lawford, Helen Walker, Reginald Gardiner, C. Aubrey Smith, Reginald Owen, Richard Haydn, Sara Allgood, Ernest Cossart, Una O'Connor, Florence Bates, Christopher Severn. Delightful comedy which charts the evolving relationship between orphan Jones and penniless Czech refugee professor Boyer in pre–WW2 England. Takes hilarious pot-shots at the British class system, with the help of a sterling cast of character actors. Screenplay by Samuel Hoffenstein and Elizabeth Reinhardt, from Margery Sharp's novel.

C'mon, Let's Live a Little (1967) **C-85m.** BOMB D: David Butler. Bobby Vee, Jackie De Shannon, Eddie Hodges, John Ireland, Jr., Suzie Kaye, Bo Belinsky, Patsy Kelly, Kim Carnes. Folk singer Vee enrolls in college, romances De Shannon, is manipulated by student radical Ireland. Perfectly awful. Techniscope.

Coach (1978) **C-100m. **** D: Bud Townsend. Cathy Lee Crosby, Michael Biehn, Keenan Wynn, Steve Nevil, Channing Clarkson, Sydney Wicks. Olympic gold medal winner Crosby is accidentally hired as a high school basketball coach for boys. Exploitation film is disappointingly tame and predictable. [PG]▼▶

Coach Carter (2005) **C-137m. **½** D: Thomas Carter. Samuel L. Jackson, Rob Brown, Robert Ri'chard, Rick Gonzalez, Nana Gbewonyo, Antwon Tanner, Channing Tatum, Ashanti, Texas Battle, Denise Dowse, Vincent Laresca, Sidney Faison, Debbi Morgan, Ray Baker, Marc McClure. New high school basketball coach in a working-class California town is determined to teach his rowdy players discipline and respect. Even when they start winning, he pushes them further, insisting that they improve their grades to earn the title "student athletes" and win a chance of going on to college. A few climaxes too many are the main debit in this inspirational saga, with Jackson a perfect choice to play the real-life Ken Carter. Super 35. [PG-13]▼❶

Coal Miner's Daughter (1980) **C-125m.** ***½ D: Michael Apted. Sissy Spacek, Tommy Lee Jones, Beverly D'Angelo, Levon Helm, Phyllis Boyens, Ernest Tubb. Rags-to-riches story of country singer Loretta Lynn is among the best musical bios ever made, though final quarter does slide over some "down side" details. Spacek won well-deserved Oscar (and did her own singing), but Jones, D'Angelo, and Helm (drummer for The Band) are just as good. Screenplay by Tom Rickman. [PG]▼❶

Coast of Terror SEE: **Summer City**

Coast to Coast (1980) **C-95m.** ** D: Joseph Sargent. Dyan Cannon, Robert Blake, Quinn Redeker, Michael Lerner, Maxine Stuart, Bill Lucking. A nutty woman (who's been institutionalized by her divorce-seeking husband) escapes from a sanitarium and travels cross-country with trucker Blake, who's got problems of his own. Strained road comedy, often abrasive, with occasional laughs. [PG]▼❶

Cobb (1994) **C-128m.** **½ D: Ron Shelton. Tommy Lee Jones, Robert Wuhl, Lolita Davidovich, Lou Myers, Stephen Mendillo, William Utay, J. Kenneth Campbell. Portrait of Ty Cobb—widely regarded as the greatest baseball player of all time—as an old, eccentric, embittered man, determined to tell his sanitized life story to sportswriter Al Stump (Wuhl). Perhaps a Hollywood first: a biopic that reveals its subject as the meanest sonofabitch who ever lived, with no redeeming qualities whatever. Fascinating for a while, but gets redundant. Worth seeing for Jones' commanding performance. Panavision. [R]▼❶

Cobra (1986) **C-87m.** *½ D: George P. Cosmatos. Sylvester Stallone, Brigitte Nielsen, Reni Santoni, Andrew Robinson, Lee Garlington, John Herzfeld, Art Le Fleur, Brian Thompson, David Rasche, Val Avery. Once more, Stallone wraps himself in the American flag and fights for the greater glory of mankind by going after criminal vermin; this time, he's a cop. Typical low-grade action fare, where all the other cops are stubborn dummies, and all the bad guys are repellent creeps. Some good action sequences. [R]▼❶

Cobra Woman (1944) **C-70m.** *** D: Robert Siodmak. Maria Montez, Jon Hall, Sabu, Lon Chaney (Jr.), Edgar Barrier, Lois Collier, Mary Nash. Deliriously silly camp classic; island beauty Montez, set to wed Hall, is kidnapped and discovers she has an evil twin sister. Sabu plays Hall's faithful (and ever-so-goofy) companion Kado. Co-scripted by Richard Brooks!

Cobweb, The (1955) **C-124m.** ** D: Vincente Minnelli. Richard Widmark, Lauren Bacall, Gloria Grahame, Charles Boyer,

Lillian Gish, John Kerr, Susan Strasberg, Oscar Levant, Tommy Rettig, Paul Stewart, Adele Jergens. Good cast in static soaper detailing the goings-on in psychiatric clinic headed by Dr. Widmark; of course, some of the personnel are more unbalanced than the patients. Scripted by John Paxton, produced by John Houseman. Film debuts of Strasberg and Kerr. CinemaScope.❶

Coca-Cola Kid, The (1985-Australian) **C-94m.** **½ D: Dusan Makavejev. Eric Roberts, Greta Scacchi, Bill Kerr, Chris Haywood, Kris McQuade, Max Gillies, Rebecca Smart. Droll, sometimes wacky comedy about a hotshot Coca-Cola sales exec sent on mission to Australia, leading to various misadventures. Roberts' performance strictly a matter of taste, as is this offbeat, mildly satiric film. Sexy Scacchi is the best thing in the picture. [R]▼❶

Cocaine Cowboys (1979) **C-87m.** BOMB D: Ulli Lommel. Jack Palance, Tom Sullivan, Andy Warhol, Suzanna Love, Pete Huckabee. Dreadful film about rock group that supports itself "between engagements" by dope smuggling; filmed at Warhol's Montauk home, where this film should have remained. [R]▼❶

Cocaine Cowboys (2006) **C-118m.** *** D: Billy Corben. Pumped-up, gruesome documentary exposé about the Colombian drug lords' invasion of Miami in the 1970s–'80s, and how they turned it into the blood money capital of the U.S., or so the movie asserts. Like a prequel to SCARFACE (1983), but built of chilling, often contradictory interviews with charismatic criminals and determined police, it details the smugglers' elaborate strategies as they try to outsmart the DEA and outshoot rival Cuban gangs. Too flashy and too long, but graphically persuasive. Followed by a DVD sequel. Digital Video/Super 35. [R]❶

Cockfighter (1974) **C-83m.** *** D: Monte Hellman. Warren Oates, Richard B. Shull, Harry Dean Stanton, Troy Donahue, Millie Perkins. Offbeat, violent but interesting drama of a man who trains fighting cocks in Georgia. Oates is silent until the very end, his thoughts serving as narration. Filmed in Georgia. Aka BORN TO KILL, WILD DRIFTER, GAMBLIN' MAN. [R]▼❶

Cocktail (1988) **C-100m.** ** D: Roger Donaldson. Tom Cruise, Bryan Brown, Elisabeth Shue, Lisa Banes, Laurence Luckinbill, Kelly Lynch, Gina Gershon, Ron Dean, Paul Benedict. Young hotshot comes to N.Y.C. to make his fortune, but winds up becoming a "hot" bartender instead, under the tutelage of self-styled barman/philosopher Brown. Cruise flashes his smile, Shue is cute, but that can't redeem the junior-high-school–level dramatics. [R]▼❶

Cocktail Molotov (1980-French) **C-100m.** *** D: Diane Kurys. Elise Caron, Philippe Lebas, François Cluzet, Genevieve Fontanel, Henri Garcin, Michel Puterflam. Pleasant follow-up to PEPPERMINT SODA, with a trio of teenagers wandering through Europe at the time of the '68 student rebellion. Caron, Lebas, and Cluzet are attractive as the youngsters testing their wings. [R]▼

Cocoanuts, The (1929) **96m. *** D: Joseph Santley, Robert Florey. Groucho, Harpo, Chico, Zeppo Marx, Kay Francis, Oscar Shaw, Mary Eaton, Margaret Dumont. The Marxes' first film suffers from stagy filming and stale musical subplot, but when the brothers have scenes to themselves it's a riot; highlights include hilarious auction, classic "viaduct" routine.▼●◗

Coco Before Chanel (2009-French) **C-110m. *** D: Anne Fontaine. Audrey Tautou, Benoît Poelvoorde, Alessandro Nivola, Emmanuelle Devos, Marie Gillain. Vivid biographical portrait of the early life of 20th-century fashion icon Coco Chanel. At a young age she is deposited at an orphanage by her uncaring father and develops a defiantly independent streak that carries into adult life. Tautou is excellent as the young woman who learns to "use" men but manages to defy convention—in her approach to life and her ideas about clothing—until one lover sweeps her off her feet. Exquisite in every detail, including Alexandre Desplat's score. See also: COCO CHANEL & IGOR STRAVINSKY. Panavision. [PG-13]◗

Coco Chanel & Igor Stravinsky (2009-French) **C-119m. **½** D: Jan Kounen. Anna Mouglalis, Mads Mikkelsen, Elena Morozova, Natacha Lindinger, Grigori Manoukov, Rasha Bukvic, Anatole Taubman, Nicolas Vaude, Eric Desmarestz. The 1913 debut performance of Stravinsky's *Rite of Spring* in Paris is a debacle, but designer Chanel finds it fascinating. Seven years pass before the two iconoclasts cross paths again. She invites the impoverished Russian émigré, his wife, and children to live at her country estate, where Stravinsky's wife endures her husband's growing attraction to Chanel as long as she can. Fairly compelling fiction suffers from a weak denouement, but real-life Chanel model Mouglalis—and much real-life Chanel décor—make this a feast for the eyes. [R] ◗

Cocoon (1985) **C-117m. ***½** D: Ron Howard. Don Ameche, Wilford Brimley, Hume Cronyn, Brian Dennehy, Jack Gilford, Steve Guttenberg, Maureen Stapleton, Jessica Tandy, Gwen Verdon, Herta Ware, Tahnee Welch, Barret Oliver, Linda Harrison, Tyrone Power, Jr., Clint Howard. Florida senior citizens discover an actual fountain of youth in this warm, humanistic fantasy-drama, marred only by derivative and too literal science-fiction finale. What a pleasure to watch this cast at work! (Ameche won Best Supporting Actor Oscar.) Screenplay by Tom Benedek, from David Saperstein's novel; another impressive directing job by Howard. Followed by a sequel. [PG-13]▼●◗

Cocoon: The Return (1988) **C-116m. *** D: Daniel Petrie. Don Ameche, Jack Gilford, Gwen Verdon, Maureen Stapleton, Steve Guttenberg, Hume Cronyn, Jessica Tandy, Wilford Brimley, Elaine Stritch, Tahnee Welch, Courteney Cox. Disappointing follow-up in which the elderly earthlings return for a visit to their home planet. Most of the magic and warmth of the original are missing; while it's always a joy to see Ameche and company on-screen, the actors are unable to transcend their material. [PG]▼●◗

Code, The (1968) SEE: **Farewell, Friend**

Code, The (2002-French) **C-106m. *** D: Manuel Boursinhac. Samuel Le Bihan, Samy Naceri, Clotilde Courau, Marie Guillard, Michel Duchaussoy, Philippe Nahon, Francis Renaud. Routine, brutal gangster drama in which an ex-con who wants to leave his criminal life behind is sucked back in one more time. All the usual clichés of this film genre are trotted out with a French accent. Film never finds a tone that makes it any different from dozens of other GODFATHER wannabes. Aka LE MENTALE. Widescreen. [R] ▼◗

Code, The (2009) **C-104m. *½** D: Mimi Leder. Morgan Freeman, Antonio Banderas, Radha Mitchell, Robert Forster, Rade Serbedzija, Michael Hayden, Marcel Iures, Gary Werntz. Veteran master thief (Freeman) recruits a brash crook (Banderas) to help him pull off a daring robbery of two priceless Fabergé eggs from the Russian mob. But everything is not what it appears to be, as we learn in the inevitable and exasperating "big twist." Fine cast deserves better than this direct-to-DVD fodder, with a script that's a checklist of heist-movie clichés. Aka THICK AS THIEVES. Super 35. [R]◗

Code 46 (2003-British) **C-92m. *** D: Michael Winterbottom. Tim Robbins, Samantha Morton, Jeanne Balibar, Om Puri, Essie Davis, Shelley King, David Fahm, Togo Igawa. In the near future, government investigator Robbins is sent to Shanghai to uncover the source of forged identity passes, without which people of the world are locked outside the gates of major cities to fend for themselves amidst the mob. But the normally businesslike agent becomes emotionally entangled with the woman who is his chief suspect. Intriguing idea is terminally aloof and gives us no one to care about. Super 35. [R]◗

Code Name: Emerald (1985) **C-95m. *** D: Jonathan Sanger. Ed Harris, Max von Sydow, Horst Buchholz, Helmut Berger, Cyrielle Claire, Eric Stoltz, Patrick Stewart, Graham Crowden. Old-fashioned WW2 espionage tale has Harris as a double agent in plot to capture an Overlord (person with information on the plans for the D-Day invasion). Credibility is undermined by miscasting of Stoltz, who looks way too young to be an intelligence lieutenant and the target Overlord. [PG]▼●◗

Code Name: The Cleaner (2007) **C-84m.** *½ D: Les Mayfield. Cedric the Entertainer, Nicollette Sheridan, Lucy Liu, Mark Dacascos, Will Patton, Callum Keith Rennie, Niecy Nash, DeRay Davis. Call it THE BORED IDENTITY. Flat, witless enterprise casts Cedric as a janitor who is suddenly swept up into the world of spies and murder after he is hit in the head and thought to be an undercover agent caught up in a big government conspiracy. Given the kind of lame script Allen and Rossi might have made in the '60s, Cedric walks through the film like a guy lost in an old TV variety show. Liu and Sheridan provide eye candy. [PG-13]◗

Code Name: Trixie SEE: **Crazies, The**

Codename: Wildgeese (1986-German-Italian) **C-101m.** ** D: Anthony M. Dawson (Antonio Margheriti). Lewis Collins, Lee Van Cleef, Ernest Borgnine, Klaus Kinski, Mimsy Farmer. Action footage redeems this cornball commando film of Collins and mercenary troops sent to wipe out a Far East drug stronghold. No relation to THE WILD GEESE or its sequel. Widescreen. [R]▼

Code of Silence (1985) **C-101m.** **½ D: Andy Davis. Chuck Norris, Henry Silva, Bert Remsen, Molly Hagan, Joseph Guzaldo, Mike Genovese, Dennis Farina. Norris plays a loner on Chicago police force who makes his own rules in dealing with violent gang war. In other words, it's "Dirty Chuckie." Formula action film, and not bad. [R]▼●◗

Code Unknown (2000-French-German-Roumanian) **C-117m.** ***½ D: Michael Haneke. Juliette Binoche, Thierry Neuvic, Alexandre Hamidi, Luminita Gheorghiu, Ona Lu Yenke, Josef Bierbichler. Challenging, fascinating tale involving several characters, most of them strangers, whose lives become briefly intertwined on a Paris street corner. They include an actress (Binoche), the discontented brother of her photojournalist lover, a young teacher of African descent, and a Roumanian illegal immigrant. This trenchant look at racism and emotional disconnection also offers food for thought about the nature of cinematic reality. ▼◗

Coeurs (2006-French-Italian) **C-123m.** *** D: Alain Resnais. Sabine Azéma, Lambert Wilson, André Dussollier, Pierre Arditi, Laura Morante, Isabelle Carré. In snowy Paris, various characters who are loosely connected go about their lives and look for love in all the wrong places. Meditative exploration of the human condition astutely scrutinizes the way people present themselves to others. What are they looking for? What will they settle for? How well do they know the people around them, the people who pass through their lives? Aka PRIVATE FEARS IN PUBLIC PLACES, the title of the Alan Ayckbourn play on which this is based. Panavision.◗

Coffee and Cigarettes (2004) **96m.** **½ D: Jim Jarmusch. Roberto Benigni, Steven Wright, Joie Lee, Cinqué Lee, Steve Buscemi, Iggy Pop, Tom Waits, Cate Blanchett, Meg White, Jack White, Alfred Molina, Steve Coogan, Bill Murray, GZA, RZA, Taylor Mead. Seriocomic anthology of vignettes, filmed as a series of short films beginning in 1986, about actors and musicians partaking in the titular addictive substances. Quintessentially Jarmuschesque in its slow pacing and seemingly random chitchat about everything from tea to Tesla coils. Borderline boring at first, but improves greatly in its second half with amusing sketches involving Blanchett (as herself and her jealous cousin), and Murray meeting up with rappers GZA and RZA from the Wu-Tang Clan. Funniest bit: Brit thesps Molina and Coogan taking a very Hollywood meeting. [R]▼◗

Coffy (1973) **C-90m.** **½ D: Jack Hill. Pam Grier, Booker Bradshaw, Robert DoQui, William Elliott, Allan Arbus, Sid Haig. Fast-moving, generally agreeable trash about nurse who goes after junkies who turned her young sister into an addict; lots of nudity in Grier's biggest hit. [R]▼●◗

Cohen & Tate (1989) **C-85m.** *½ D: Eric Red. Roy Scheider, Adam Baldwin, Harley Cross, Cooper Huckabee. In this grim variation on O. Henry's "Ransom of Red Chief," Scheider and Baldwin, the hit men of title, murderously kidnap young Cross, sole witness to a gang killing; story takes place almost entirely in their car. Clumsy irony, theatrical style, leaden illogic sink the film early. Scheider tries hard. [R]▼●◗

Cold Around the Heart (1997) **C-96m.** ** D: John Ridley. David Caruso, Kelly Lynch, Stacey Dash, Chris Noth, John Spencer, Pruitt Taylor-Vince, Richard Kind. Barely released and highly derivative thieves-fall-out crime drama. Grungy-looking Caruso is out for revenge against ruthless femme fatale Lynch when she double-crosses him after a jewel heist. Decent cast helps, but it's nothing you haven't seen done better about a million times before. Super 35. [R]▼◗

Coldblooded (1995) **C-91m.** ** D: M. Wallace Wolodarsky. Jason Priestley, Peter Riegert, Kimberly Williams, Janeane Garofalo, Robert Loggia, Josh Charles. Black comedy about a nerdy young bookkeeper for the mob who finally gets a chance to become a full-fledged hit man—and adapts to the job better than he ever dreamed. Love soon complicates the picture, and also bogs down what could have been a clever, if twisted, story. This "hit" is a miss. Look for Michael J. Fox (who coproduced the film) in a cameo. [R]▼

Cold Comfort Farm (1995-British) **C-95m.** *** D: John Schlesinger. Eileen Atkins, Kate Beckinsale, Sheila Burrell, Stephen Fry, Freddie Jones, Joanna Lumley, Ian McKellen, Miriam Margolyes, Rufus

Sewell. Deliciously eccentric comedy about a well-bred young woman who goes to live with distant relatives at their spooky old farm, which is dominated by a dotty grandmother living in the attic. Our heroine then implacably sets about reordering their lives! Good fun, based on a 1932 novel by Stella Gibbons. Made for British TV. [PG] ▼●❶

Cold Creek Manor (2003) **C-119m. ** D:** Mike Figgis. Dennis Quaid, Sharon Stone, Stephen Dorff, Juliette Lewis, Kristen Stewart, Ryan Wilson, Dana Eskelson, Christopher Plummer. Something new in thrillers: a story devoid of suspense. Manhattanites Quaid and Stone decide to move out of the city and give their kids a better life. They buy a run-down mansion in a rural, insular community and soon encounter the resentful former owner (Dorff), who lost the house in a foreclosure just before he went to jail for manslaughter. Obvious at every turn, and overlong to boot; the supposed scare moments are pallid at best. [R] ▼❶

Cold Feet (1984) **C-96m. ** D:** Bruce van Dusen. Griffin Dunne, Marissa Chibas, Blanche Baker, Mark Cronogue, Joseph Leon, Marcia Jean Kurtz. A couple of chuckles are not enough to save this sluggish comedy about the courtship of Dunne and Chibas, who've been unlucky in love before. Baker steals the film as Dunne's flaky ex-wife. [PG] ▼

Cold Feet (1989) **C-94m. *½ D:** Robert Dornhelm. Keith Carradine, Sally Kirkland, Tom Waits, Rip Torn, Bill Pullman, Kathleen York, Vincent Schiavelli. Carradine and Waits (the latter near-psychotic) squabble for hundreds of miles over a horse; marriage-hungry Kirkland is the flake who rounds out the threesome. Reminiscent in tone of coscripter Thomas McGuane's RANCHO DELUXE (which pops up on a theater marquee here)—but without the laughs; RANCHO'S Jeff Bridges is unbilled as a smalltown bartender. [R] ▼●❶

Cold Fever (1995-U.S.-Iceland) **C-82m. *** D:** Fridrik Thor Fridriksson. Masatoshi Nagase, Lili Taylor, Fisher Stevens, Gisli Halldorsson, Laura Hughes, Seijun Suzuki. Amiable, Jarmusch-like comic road movie that charts the adventures of Atsushi (Nagase), a Japanese businessman who decides to go to Iceland and trek to the site where his parents died, so their souls can rest in peace. In Iceland, there is plenty of snow, ice, and cold, and Atsushi is most definitely a stranger in a strange land. Coscripted by the director and Jim Stark, the producer of several Jim Jarmusch films. Panavision.▼

Cold Heaven (1992) **C-105m. ** D:** Nicolas Roeg. Theresa Russell, Mark Harmon, James Russo, Talia Shire, Will Patton, Richard Bradford. Adulterous wife (Russell) is on the verge of telling her husband (Harmon) that she is dumping him when he is killed in a gruesome vacation boating

accident—or is he? Russell's guilt and paranoia bring on a host of ponderous *sturm und drang* encounters and experiences. Lifeless and confusing. [R] ▼●

Colditz Story, The (1955-British) **97m. ***½ D:** Guy Hamilton. John Mills, Eric Portman, Christopher Rhodes, Lionel Jeffries, Bryan Forbes, Ian Carmichael, Richard Wattis, Anton Diffring, Theodore Bikel. Super-solid POW saga set in Germany's Colditz Castle, supposedly "escape-proof" but challenged by various European prisoners, and a hardy British group in particular.▼❶

Cold Mountain (2003-British-Romanian-Italian-U.S.) **C-155m. ***½ D:** Anthony Minghella. Jude Law, Nicole Kidman, Renée Zellweger, Eileen Atkins, Brendan Gleeson, Philip Seymour Hoffman, Natalie Portman, Giovanni Ribisi, Donald Sutherland, Ray Winstone, Kathy Baker, James Gammon, Charlie Hunnam, Jack White, Ethan Suplee, Jena Malone, Melora Walters, Lucas Black, Taryn Manning, Tom Aldredge, James Rebhorn, Cillian Murphy, Emily Deschanel. A shy young man and a minister's daughter make a brief but passionate connection before he marches off to fight for the Confederacy in the Civil War . . . and the thought of each other sustains them through the hell they both endure. Minghella's adaptation of the Charles Frazier best-seller captures both the grimness of battle and the starkness of life on the home front in the South. Meticulously crafted by such outstanding talents as cinematographer John Seale, film editor Walter Murch, production designer Dante Ferretti, costume designer Ann Roth (with Carlo Poggioli), and composer Gabriel Yared, among others, with first-rate performances all around. Oscar winner for Best Supporting Actress (Zellweger). Super 35. [R] ▼❶

Cold Souls (2009-U.S.-French) **C-101m. **½ D:** Sophie Barthes. Paul Giamatti, David Strathairn, Emily Watson, Dina Korzun, Katheryn Winnick, Lauren Ambrose, Mimi Lieber, Michael Tucker, Michael Stuhlbarg. An actor named Paul Giamatti (played by same) is emotionally challenged by Chekhov's play *Uncle Vanya*, so he's susceptible when he hears about a service that removes your soul and keeps it in cold storage. Needless to say, the process becomes more complicated than he envisions. Clever, often amusing, but overlong, this cheeky film is at its best when Giamatti is "consulting" with soul-sucking entrepreneur Strathairn. Written by the director. [PG-13]❶

Cold Steel (1987) **C-90m. ** D:** Dorothy Ann Puzo. Brad Davis, Sharon Stone, Jonathan Banks, Jay Acovone, Adam Ant, Eddie Egan. Standard actioner about cop Davis, his father murdered by disfigured psychotic Banks; he seeks revenge, natch. [R] ▼❶

Cold Sweat (1971-French-Italian) **C-94m. ** D:** Terence Young. Charles Bronson, Liv Ullmann, James Mason, Jill Ireland, Michel Constantin, Gabriele Ferzetti. Richard Matheson's thriller *Ride the Nightmare* has been converted into a predictable action movie with Bronson as American expatriate in France forced into the drug trade by crime czar Mason. [PG]▼●◗

Cold Turkey (1971) **C-99m.** *** D: Norman Lear. Dick Van Dyke, Pippa Scott, Tom Poston, Bob Newhart, Vincent Gardenia, Barnard Hughes, Edward Everett Horton, Jean Stapleton, Graham Jarvis. Bittersweet satire of contemporary America; minister Van Dyke leads township crusade to stop smoking, in order to win mammoth contest. Trenchant finale doesn't entirely gibe with rest of film; still worthwhile, with Bob & Ray hilarious as newscasters. Fine score by Randy Newman; Horton's last film. Made in 1969. [PG]▼●◗

Colin Nutley's House of Angels SEE: **House of Angels**

Collateral (2004) **C-120m.** **½ D: Michael Mann. Tom Cruise, Jamie Foxx, Jada Pinkett Smith, Mark Ruffalo, Peter Berg, Bruce McGill, Javier Bardem, Irma P. Hall, Barry Shabaka Henley, Bodhi Elfman, Debi Mazar, Richard T. Jones, Jason Statham. L.A. cab driver Foxx, who dreams of running his own business, picks up the wrong passenger (visiting hit man Cruise) and becomes embroiled in a long night of mayhem. Crisp action thriller, well shot in a digital format on L.A. locations, builds interesting characterizations, then tosses credibility down the drain during the climax. Still quite watchable, with a strong supporting cast backing up the stars. Panavision/HD 24P Widescreen. [R]▼◗

Collateral Damage (2002) **C-109m.** ** D: Andrew Davis. Arnold Schwarzenegger, Elias Koteas, Francesca Neri, Cliff Curtis, Miguel Sandoval, Harry Lennix, John Leguizamo, John Turturro, Lindsay Frost, Jane Lynch. L.A. fireman sees his wife and son killed in a bombing—and vows revenge on the terrorist who made it happen, even if it means stalking him in the jungles of Colombia. No worse than any number of other Schwarzenegger action vehicles, with a high body count, a superhuman hero, and a couple of villains who simply refuse to die . . . but we've seen it all before, done better. Anachronistic (to say the least) in the wake of the Sept. 11, 2001, attack on America. [R]▼◗

Collector, The (1965) **C-119m.** *** D: William Wyler. Terence Stamp, Samantha Eggar, Maurice Dallimore, Mona Washbourne. Disturbing story of man who collects more than just butterflies, which is where Eggar fits in. Chilling, if not altogether believable. Based on the novel by John Fowles.▼●◗

College (1927) **65m.** *** D: James W. Horne. Buster Keaton, Anne Cornwall, Flora Bramley, Harold Goodwin, Grant Withers, Snitz Edwards. Highbrow student Buster has to become an all-star athlete to please his girlfriend; episodic gag structure makes this less impressive than other Keaton features, but it's awfully funny.▼●◗

College (2008) **C-94m.** BOMB D: Deb Hagan. Drake Bell, Andrew Caldwell, Andree Moss, Carolyn Moss, Kevin Covais, Ryan Pinkston, Haley Bennett, Nick Zano. Stop us if you've heard this one before: three high school seniors (a fat one, a geeky one, a hunky one) take a weekend trip to check out a university campus and get indoctrinated by a bunch of mean fraternity brothers. Chock-full of typical adolescent behavior, gross-out gags, sex, and nudity; you won't need a college degree to smell this turkey a mile away. Barely released to theaters. [R]◗

College Confidential (1960) **91m.** *½ D: Albert Zugsmith. Steve Allen, Jayne Meadows, Mamie Van Doren, Walter Winchell, Herbert Marshall, Cathy Crosby, Conway Twitty, Ziva Rodann, Mickey Shaughnessy. Idiocy involving sociology professor Allen and what happens when he surveys the sexual activities of his students. "Special Guests" include Rocky Marciano, Sheilah Graham, Pamela Mason, and Earl Wilson.

College Road Trip (2008) **C-83m.** **½ D: Roger Kumble. Martin Lawrence, Raven-Symoné, Donny Osmond, Brenda Song, Margo Harshman, Lucas Grabeel, Will Sasso, Josh Meyers, Molly Ephraim, Kym E. Whitley, Eshaya Draper, Arnetia Walker. Officer Porter (Lawrence) has planned out every single part of his daughter's life, even deciding what college she'll attend close to home. When she informs him that she'd like to apply to schools that are farther away, he organizes a road trip in hopes of changing her mind. Intertwining remarkable amounts of cheesiness with good-natured comedy, this film goes for all the obvious gags but suits the family audience for whom it was made. Super 35. [G]◗

Collision Course (1968) SEE: **Bamboo Saucer, The**

Collision Course (1987) **C-96m.** ** D: Lewis Teague. Jay Leno, Pat Morita, Chris Sarandon, Ernie Hudson, John Hancock, Al Waxman, Randall "Tex" Cobb, Soon-Teck Oh. Cops Morita (from Japan) and Leno (from Detroit) link up on a case. Harmless, occasionally funny, instantly forgettable buddy movie. Leno's only starring role to date. [PG]▼●◗

Colonel Blimp SEE: **Life and Death of Colonel Blimp, The**

Colonel Chabert (1994-French) **C-110m.** **½ D: Yves Angelou. Gérard Depardieu, Fanny Ardant, Andre Dussollier, Fabrice Luchini, Daniel Prevost, Olivier Saladin, Claude Rich, Albert Delpy, Romane Bohringer, Julie Depardieu. Respectable costumer, adapted from a Balzac novel, about the belated return of an officer supposedly killed in the Napoleonic wars and the effect it has on his so-called widow (who's using his inheritance to boost husband no. 2's career). Well acted and well mounted, but the laundry put in extra starch; debuting director Angelou is the esteemed cinematographer of TOUT LES MATINS DU MONDE and UN COEUR EN HIVER. Julie Depardieu is the actor's daughter. ▼

Colonel Redl (1985-German-Hungarian-Austrian) **C-149m.** *** D: Istvan Szabo. Klaus Maria Brandauer, Armin Muller-Stahl, Gudrun Landgrebe, Jan Niklas, Hans-Christian Blech, Laszlo Mensaros, Andras Balint. Complex, fascinating account—inspired by John Osborne's *A Patriot for Me* as well as by actual historical evidence—of an ambitious, homosexual career soldier, whose ordinary family background does not hinder his rise to a position of high military rank in the Austro-Hungarian Empire prior to WW1. An incisive examination of the politics of power, highlighted by a superb Brandauer performance. Second in a trilogy, after MEPHISTO and followed by HANUSSEN. [R] ▼ ●]

Colorado Territory (1949) **94m.** *** D: Raoul Walsh. Joel McCrea, Virginia Mayo, Dorothy Malone, Henry Hull, John Archer, Frank Puglia. Strong, fast-moving Western with McCrea an outlaw on the lam; remake of director Walsh's HIGH SIERRA, later remade as I DIED A THOUSAND TIMES. Also shown in computer-colored version. ▶

Color Me Dead (1969-U.S.-Australian) **C-97m.** ** D: Eddie Davis. Tom Tryon, Carolyn Jones, Rick Jason, Patricia Connolly, Tony Ward. Story of a slowly poisoned man spending his last days tracking down his own murderer was done better as D.O.A. in 1950. Aka D.O.A. II. [R] ▼

Color Me Kubrick (2007-French-British) **C-86m.** *** D: Brian Cook. John Malkovich, Jim Davidson, Richard E. Grant, Luke Mably, Marc Warren, Terence Rigby, James Dreyfus, Peter Bowles, Ayesha Dharker, Robert Powell, Leslie Phillips, Honor Blackman, William Hootkins, Marisa Berenson, Peter Sallis, Ken Russell. Sardonically witty, fact-based account of Alan Conway (Malkovich, in a richly textured performance), a flamboyantly gay con artist who convinces ambitious wannabes in London that he is Stanley Kubrick, squeezing them for money, sex, and other favors. A lucid portrait of a deeply troubled personality and a rumination on the power of fame. Soundtrack effectively borrows from 2001: A SPACE ODYSSEY and A CLOCKWORK ORANGE; the director and screenwriter (Anthony Frewin) are former Kubrick associates. Luc Besson coexecutive produced. Full title is COLOR ME KUBRICK: A TRUE . . . ISH STORY. ▶

Color of Money, The (1986) **C-119m.** *** D: Martin Scorsese. Paul Newman, Tom Cruise, Mary Elizabeth Mastranto-

nio, Helen Shaver, John Turturro, Bill Cobbs, Robert Agins, Forest Whitaker. Sharply made, nicely textured sequel to THE HUSTLER, with Newman's Fast Eddie Felson finding a younger, greener version of himself in small-time pool hotshot Cruise, whom he decides to promote for another shot at the big time. Hardboiled script by Richard Price, flashy direction by Scorsese, flamboyant camerawork by Michael Ballhaus, and top-notch performances by Cruise and especially Newman make this a must-see . . . though film's second half is protracted and disappointing, with a hoped-for climax that never occurs. Newman finally picked up an Academy Award for his fine work here. [R] ▼ ●]

Color of Night (1994) **C-125m.** BOMB D: Richard Rush. Bruce Willis, Jane March, Ruben Blades, Lesley Ann Warren, Scott Bakula, Brad Dourif, Lance Henriksen, Kevin J. O'Connor, Andrew Lowery, Eriq La Salle, Jeff Corey, Kathleen Wilhoite, Shirley Knight. Ludicrous thriller in which weirded-out therapist Willis (whose patient has just committed suicide before his eyes) heads to L.A. for a breather; he immediately finds himself immersed in a murder mystery, and involved with mysterious March. Much-publicized sex scenes aren't very sexy; this garnered hype for the editing of Willis' full frontal nudity to earn an R rating. Also on video in an "R-rated director's cut," with 17m. of extra footage, including more of Bruce-in-the-buff and some sexy scenes with Warren and March. Rush's first feature since THE STUNT MAN (1980). [R] ▼ ●]

Color of Paradise, The (1999-Iranian) **C-88m.** ***½ D: Majid Majidi. Hossein Mahjub, Salime Feizi, Mohsen Ramezani, Elham Sharim, Farahnaz Safari, Mohammad Rahmaney. A blind eight-year-old Iranian student, who is deeply sensitive to nature, returns to his home in the heights of Northern Iran, where he must cope with a father who considers him a burden. Simple story, beautifully told, with writer-director Majidi eloquently conveying the young boy's harmony with the world around him. [PG] ▼]

Color Purple, The (1985) **C-152m.** ***½ D: Steven Spielberg. Danny Glover, Whoopi Goldberg, Margaret Avery, Oprah Winfrey, Willard Pugh, Akosua Busia, Desreta Jackson, Adolph Caesar, Rae Dawn Chong, Dana Ivey, Larry Fishburne. A black girl's life and hard times in the South, spanning some 40 years: a sprawling saga of characters both frustrated and fulfilled, and at the center a Survivor. Spielberg's controversial interpretation of Alice Walker's Pulitzer Prize–winning book will either grab you emotionally (in which case you'll overlook its flaws) or leave you cold. Masterfully filmed from Menno Meyjes's script, with striking cinematography by Allen Daviau, moving music score by Quincy Jones (who also coproduced). Rich performances include screen debut for Winfrey. (Avery's singing was dubbed, by the way.) Later a Broadway musical. [PG-13]▼●〉

Colors (1988) **C-120m.** *** D: Dennis Hopper. Sean Penn, Robert Duvall, Maria Conchita Alonso, Randy Brooks, Grand Bush, Don Cheadle, Rudy Ramos, Trinidad Silva, Damon Wayans, Glenn Plummer. Penn and Duvall are well matched as street cops assigned to gang detail in L.A. Their conflicts and experiences play out against the backdrop of nihilistic gang life in this realistic if unexceptional slice of life. Only serious flaw: unbelievable and unnecessary subplot with female lead Alonso. Hopper's 127m. version, altered by the theatrical distributor, is available on video. [R]▼●〉

Colors Straight Up (1998) **C-95m.** *** D: Michele Ohayon. Heartfelt, powerful documentary about an L.A. inner-city after-school drama program that gives at-risk Black and Latino teens a chance to strut their stuff onstage. Simply and beautifully done, with some truly amazing young subjects at its center. One teacher tells the group they must learn to "function in disaster and finish with style," and they do exactly that. Guaranteed to move you to tears.▼

Colossus of Rhodes, The (1960-Italian) **C-128m.** **½ D: Sergio Leone. Rory Calhoun, Lea Massari, Georges Marchal, Conrado Sanmartin, Angel Aranda, Mabel Karr. Big-budget sword-and-sandal spectacular about a slave revolt against the corrupt leaders of ancient Rhodes. Though Calhoun looks mighty uncomfortable in a toga and the dubbing is poor, Leone's directorial debut is notable for some well-staged battle scenes and impressive sets, including the title edifice. SuperTotalscope.◗

Colossus: The Forbin Project (1970) **C-100m.** *** D: Joseph Sargent. Eric Braeden, Susan Clark, Gordon Pinsent, William Schallert. Well-directed suspense thriller. Computer runs amok and uses its superior intelligence to sabotage man at every turn. Chilling and believable. Aka THE FORBIN PROJECT. Panavision.▼●〉

Coma (1978) **C-113m.** *** D: Michael Crichton. Genevieve Bujold, Michael Douglas, Elizabeth Ashley, Rip Torn, Richard Widmark, Lance LeGault, Lois Chiles. Someone is killing and stealing patients from a big-city hospital, and a woman doctor bucks male superiors to pursue her suspicions. Bujold and Widmark are well-matched adversaries in original suspenser that combines best of hospital pictures and mystery thrillers; scripted by director Crichton from Robin Cook's novel. Look for Tom Selleck as Murphy, Ed Harris as a pathology resident. [PG]▼●〉

Comancheros, The (1961) **C-107m.** *** D: Michael Curtiz. John Wayne, Stuart Whitman, Lee Marvin, Ina Balin, Bruce Cabot, Nehemiah Persoff. Well-paced actioner with Duke a Texas Ranger out to bring in gang supplying liquor and firearms to the Comanches. Curtiz' last film. CinemaScope.▼●〉

Comanche Station (1960) **C-74m.** **½ D: Budd Boetticher. Randolph Scott, Nancy Gates, Claude Akins, Skip Homeier, Richard Rust, Rand Brooks. Scott rescues a woman from Indian capture, then runs into an old nemesis who wants to turn her in himself—for a fat reward. Typically interesting Boetticher/Scott Western, with a Burt Kennedy script. CinemaScope.▼◗

Combination Platter (1993) **C-84m.** *** D: Tony Chan. Jeff Lau, Colleen O'Brien, Lester (Chit-Man) Chan, Colin Mitchell, Kenneth Lu. A young illegal immigrant from Hong Kong (Lau) toils in a Queens, N.Y., Chinese restaurant, and covets U.S. citizenship—but learns that this may mean having to marry an American, the thought of which staggers him. Hong Kong–born director-cowriter Chan, himself an immigrant, knowingly captures the experience of the foreigner in America. This marks the 23-year-old's directing debut.▼◗

Come and Get It (1936) **99m.** *** D: Howard Hawks, William Wyler. Edward Arnold, Joel McCrea, Frances Farmer, Walter Brennan, Andrea Leeds, Frank Shields, Mady Christians, Mary Nash. Arnold plays a self-made empire-builder who fights his way to the top in Wisconsin lumber business, sacrificing the one love of his life. Farmer has best screen showcase of her career, in dual role, as a saloon entertainer and (years later) her own daughter; Brennan won his first Best Supporting Actor Oscar playing Arnold's simple Swedish pal. Typically plotty, two-generation Edna Ferber saga. Reissued as ROARING TIMBER. ▼●〉

Come and See (1985-Russian) **C-142m.** ***½ D: Elem Klimov. Alexei Kravchenko, Olga Mironova, Lubomiras Lauciavicus. Thoroughly mesmerizing chronicle of the initiation of a young teen (impressively played by Kravchenko) into the horror and insanity of war, as the Nazis maraud through northwestern Russia in 1943. An extraordinary film about the need to maintain one's humanity and dignity no matter what the situation. Don't miss this one.▼〉

Come Back, Charleston Blue (1972) **C-100m.** ** D: Mark Warren. Raymond St. Jacques, Godfrey Cambridge, Jonelle Allen, Adam Wade, Peter DeAnda. Further adventures of Gravedigger and Coffin on their Harlem police beat. Loads of violence, no comedy; not nearly as good as original, COTTON COMES TO HARLEM. Fine Donny Hathaway score. [PG]▼

Come Back, Little Sheba (1952) **99m.** ***½ D: Daniel Mann. Burt Lancaster, Shirley Booth, Terry Moore, Richard Jaeckel, Philip Ober. William Inge play is emotional tour de force for Booth (who won an Oscar recreating her Tony Award–winning stage role) as slovenly housewife coping with drunken ex-chiropractor husband (Lancaster) and boarder Moore, whose curiosity about her landlords sets drama in motion. Screenplay by Ketti Frings. ▼⊙●

Comebacks, The (2007) **C-88m.** BOMB D: Tom Brady. David Koechner, Carl Weathers, Melora Hardin, Matthew Lawrence, Brooke Nevin, Bradley Cooper. Lame genre satire takes aim at an easy target—inspirational sports dramas such as RUDY, REMEMBER THE TITANS, etc.—and repeatedly shoots itself in the foot. Slight plot involving a chronically unsuccessful coach (Koechner) and his hapless college football team exists only as an excuse for a fusillade of AIRPLANE!-style allusions to other movies. Really, there's no excuse for this fiasco. Various comics and sports figures appear in cameos. Unrated version runs 107m. [PG-13]●

Come Back to the 5 & Dime Jimmy Dean, Jimmy Dean (1982) **C-110m.** **½ D: Robert Altman. Sandy Dennis, Cher, Karen Black, Sudie Bond, Kathy Bates, Marta Heflin. Girlfriends hold 20-year reunion of a James Dean fan club they formed when he was filming GIANT in a nearby Texas town; the get-together becomes an occasion for personal and painful revelations. Strong performances, and Altman's lively approach to filming Ed Graczyk's Broadway play, can't completely hide the fact that this is second-rate material. Cher's first film since CHASTITY in 1969. [PG]▼●

Comeback Trail, The (1974) **C-80m.** *½ D: Harry Hurwitz. Chuck McCann, Buster Crabbe, Robert Staats, Ina Balin, Jara Kahout. Two-bit movie czar McCann stars faded cowboy hero Crabbe in a film, hoping the resulting disaster will salvage his studio. Dismal comedy, with occasional film buff in-jokes, and guest appearances by Henny Youngman, Irwin Corey, Hugh Hefner, Joe Franklin, and Monte Rock III. Never released theatrically.

Come Blow Your Horn (1963) **C-112m.** *** D: Bud Yorkin. Frank Sinatra, Lee J. Cobb, Molly Picon, Barbara Rush, Jill St. John, Tony Bill. Sinatra is good as a free-swinging bachelor with wall-to-wall girls and a nagging father (Cobb). He also sings the title song, and teaches kid brother (Bill) the ropes. From Neil Simon play. Panavision.▼

Comedian (2002) **C-81m.** ***½ D: Christian Charles. Jerry Seinfeld has a camera crew follow him during his return to comedy clubs as he tries to build an all-new act. His craftsmanship and confidence are contrasted with the desperation of an up-and-comer named Orny Adams. Seinfeld talks shop with Chris Rock, Ray Romano, Colin Quinn, Jay Leno, Garry Shandling, and Bill Cosby in this revealing look at the world of stand-up comedy. [R] ▼●

Comedians, The (1967) **C-148m.** **½ D: Peter Glenville. Elizabeth Taylor, Richard Burton, Alec Guinness, Peter Ustinov, Paul Ford, Lillian Gish, Raymond St. Jacques, Zakes Mokae, Roscoe Lee Browne, Gloria Foster, Georg Stanford Brown, James Earl Jones, Cicely Tyson. Excellent cast in uninspired adaptation of Graham Greene's novel about political intrigue in Haiti, although film is more interesting today, since the departure of Duvalier. Beware 130m. prints. Panavision.▼●

Comedy of Innocence, The (2001-French) **C-99m.** **½ D: Raoul Ruiz. Isabelle Huppert, Jeanne Balibar, Charles Berling, Edith Scob, Nils Hugon, Laure de Clermont-Tonnerre. How will Huppert respond when, on his birthday, her young son informs her that his mother is actually someone else, a woman whose little boy died two years earlier? Eerie psychological drama draws you in and keeps you guessing, but leaves too many questions unanswered.▼●

Comedy of Power (2006-German-French) **C-110m.** *** D: Claude Chabrol. Isabelle Huppert, François Berléand, Patrick Bruel, Maryline Canto, Thomas Chabrol, Jean-François Balmer, Pierre Vernier. Huppert shines as an obsessive, highly principled investigative magistrate (whose surname, appropriately, is "Killman") who is determined to topple a gaggle of crooked, high-living politicians and corporate executives. At once a subtle, incisive character study, and an exploration of women, men, and power and the pervasiveness of corruption in high places. Loosely based on one such magistrate's real-life investigation of a scandal-ridden French gas company in the 1990s.●

Comedy of Terrors, The (1963) **C-84m.** **½ D: Jacques Tourneur. Vincent Price, Peter Lorre, Boris Karloff, Basil Rathbone, Joe E. Brown, Joyce Jameson. Medium horror spoof with undertaker Price trying to hasten customers' demise, "helped" by bumbling assistant Lorre. Great cast; Richard Matheson wrote the screenplay. Panavision.▼●

Come Early Morning (2006) **C-97m.** *** D: Joey Lauren Adams. Ashley Judd, Jeffrey Donovan, Laura Prepon, Diane Ladd, Scott Wilson, Stacy Keach, Pat Corley, Ray McKinnon, Tim Blake Nelson. Judd shines as an established contractor who boozes it up and parties at night until she finally hooks up with a down-home Arkansas guy who sees her as more than a one-night stand. Perfectly cast star knowingly embodies this lost Southern woman. First feature written and directed by actress Adams is independent to its core and filled with character insight. [R]●

Come Next Spring (1956) **C-92m.** *** D: R. G. Springsteen. Ann Sheridan, Steve Cochran, Walter Brennan, Sherry Jackson, Richard Eyer, Edgar Buchanan, Sonny

Tufts, Mae Clarke, Roscoe Ates, James Best. Charming slice of Americana, set in 1920s Arkansas. Cochran walked out on his wife and kids nine years ago; now he returns, cold sober and determined to make good (and try to make up for his past transgressions). Appealing performances and a nice feel for the material distinguish this modest film, which Cochran also produced.

Come 'n' Get It SEE: **Lunch Wagon**

Comes a Horseman (1978) **C-118m. **½** D: Alan J. Pakula. Jane Fonda, James Caan, Jason Robards, George Grizzard, Richard Farnsworth, Jim Davis, Mark Harmon. Starkly simple Western story (set in 1940s) about rival ranch owners whose roots are in the land. Low-key to the point of catatonia, but offers some beautiful tableaux and moving scenes. Panavision. [PG]▼○●

Come See The Paradise (1990) **C-138m. **** D: Alan Parker. Dennis Quaid, Tamlyn Tomita, Sab Shimono, Shizuko Hoshi, Stan Egi, Ronald Yamamoto, Akemi Nishino, Naomi Nakano, Brady Tsurutani, Pruitt Taylor Vince. Hotheaded union organizer Quaid falls in love with Tomita in L.A.'s Little Tokyo in the late 1930s; after the bombing of Pearl Harbor, he is separated from his wife and family when they are sent to a Japanese internment camp. Curiously aloof and unmoving story fashioned around one of the bleaker chapters of American history; should have been much stronger. Written by director Parker. [R]▼○●

Come September (1961) **C-112m. *** D: Robert Mulligan. Rock Hudson, Gina Lollobrigida, Sandra Dee, Bobby Darin, Walter Slezak, Joel Grey. Frothy comedy about the younger generation (Darin and Dee) vs. the "older" folks (Hudson and Lollobrigida) at an Italian villa. Good fun, with some dated Darin vocals. CinemaScope.▼▷

Come Spy With Me (1967) **C-85m. *½** D: Marshall Stone. Troy Donahue, Andrea Dromm, Albert Dekker, Mart Hulswit, Valerie Allen, Dan Ferrone. Except for those who want to tell their friends they actually saw a film called COME SPY WITH ME starring Troy Donahue, this secret-agent film about blond Dromm's attempts to solve murders of two Americans in the Caribbean isn't worth anyone's time. Smokey Robinson sings the title song!

Come to the Stable (1949) **94m. *** D: Henry Koster. Loretta Young, Celeste Holm, Hugh Marlowe, Elsa Lanchester, Regis Toomey, Mike Mazurki. Young and Holm register well as French nuns living in New England, seeking aid from a variety of local characters in building a children's dispensary. Warm, sentimental comedy-drama. Story by Clare Boothe Luce. ▼

Comfort and Joy (1984-British) **C-105m. *** D: Bill Forsyth. Bill Paterson, Eleanor David, C. P. Grogan, Alex Norton, Patrick Malahide, Rikki Fulton, Roberto Bernardi. Another quirky comedy from writer-director Forsyth (GREGORY'S GIRL, LOCAL HERO), though this one isn't as potent or consistent. Paterson plays a popular Scottish disc jockey who's going through some difficult changes in his personal life, then finds himself caught between two underworld families fighting for territorial rights to ice-cream vans! Entertaining and offbeat, though never as on-target as one might like it to be; Paterson is a delight. [PG]▼

Comfort of Strangers, The (1991-Italian-U.S.) **C-105m. *½** D: Paul Schrader. Christopher Walken, Natasha Richardson, Rupert Everett, Helen Mirren. Unmarried couple is befriended by a mysterious local while vacationing in Venice. Shaggy-dog lead-up to an "oh, come on" finale. As murky as canal sewage, offering sharply contrasting male acting styles: Everett is a posturing male mannequin, while Walken is a titan of twitch. Screenplay by Harold Pinter, from Ian McEwan's novel. [R]▼○

Comic, The (1969) **C-94m. **½** D: Carl Reiner. Dick Van Dyke, Michele Lee, Mickey Rooney, Cornel Wilde, Nina Wayne, Pert Kelton, Steve Allen, Carl Reiner, Jeannine Riley. Sincere seriocomedy about a silent-movie clown with a destructive ego. Artificial trappings surround truthful portrait (a composite of several real comics) by Van Dyke. Best of all: vivid re-creations of silent comedies. Uneven; of interest mainly to film buffs. [M/PG]▼○

Comic Book Confidential (1989-U.S.-Canadian) **C-90m. *** D: Ron Mann. R. Crumb, Will Eisner, Jack Kirby, William M. Gaines, Harvey Kurtzman, Stan Lee, Harvey Pekar, Lynda Barry, Frank Miller. Good introduction to the genuine art to be found in comic books, featuring interviews with many of the top talents of yesterday and today. Marred by too much effort to be "cinematic"; also demonstrates a bias against standard commercial comics.▼○●

Comin At Ya! (1981-Italian) **C-91m.** BOMB D: Ferdinando Baldi. Tony Anthony, Gene Quintano, Victoria Abril, Ricardo Palacios, Gordon Lewis. 3-D spaghetti Western take-off features rats, bats, and blood, all hugged to death by the camera (and often in slow motion!). No redeeming sense of humor, either. It's films like this that killed 3-D the first time around. 3-D Dimensionscope. [R]▼▷

Coming Apart (1969) **110m. *½** D: Milton Moses Ginsberg. Rip Torn, Viveca Lindfors, Megan McCormick, Lois Markle, Sally Kirkland. Fascinatingly bad drama about psychiatrist who sets up concealed movie camera in his apartment to record the messed-up lives of himself and women who visit him. Kirkland's most substantial screen role prior to ANNA in 1987.▼

Coming Attractions SEE: **Loose Shoes**

Coming Home (1978) **C-127m. ***½** D:

Hal Ashby. Jane Fonda, Jon Voight, Bruce Dern, Robert Carradine, Robert Ginty, Penelope Milford, David Clennon. Powerful look at the effect of Vietnam war on people at home. Fonda falls in love with paraplegic Voight while her husband (Dern) is overseas. Mature, gripping film, marred only by lapses into melodrama. Academy Awards went to Fonda, Voight, and writers Waldo Salt, Robert C. Jones, and Nancy Dowd. [R]▼●◗

Coming Out Under Fire (1994) C/B&W-71m. *** D: Arthur Dong. Narrated by Salome Jens. A tough ex-Marine, a WAC, a black, a heavily Dixie-toned Southerner, and a N.Y. Jew are among those who recall what it was like to be very, very quietly gay during WW2 and, in the most abjectly humiliating cases, to be mustered out of the service upon detection. A fresh and contemporary documentary despite recalling events that took place half a century earlier; in a clip from one of the era's official army sex education films, 1950s song-and-dance man Keefe Brasselle plays a G.I. with condoms on his mind.▼◗

Coming Soon (2000) C-91m. BOMB D: Colette Burson. Tricia Vessey, Gaby Hoffmann, Mia Farrow, Ryan O'Neal, Yasmine Bleeth, Spalding Gray, Peter Bogdanovich, Ashton Kutcher. Seniors in an exclusive N.Y.C. high school go to extremes to achieve orgasms from their less-than-adequate boyfriends. Touted as a female version of AMERICAN PIE; only differences are that this film isn't funny, its characters are despicable, and its script is pointless. [R]▼◗

Coming Through (1985-British) C-80m. ** D: Peter Barber-Fleming. Kenneth Branagh, Helen Mirren, Alison Steadman, Philip Martin Brown, Norman Rodway. Static tale of young D. H. Lawrence (Branagh), and his relationship with Frieda von Richthofen (Mirren), awkwardly paralleled with present-day story of young man who completely misses the point of Lawrence's writing. Sorely lacking the author's own fire and intensity.▼◗

Coming to America (1988) C-116m. *** D: John Landis. Eddie Murphy, Arsenio Hall, James Earl Jones, John Amos, Madge Sinclair, Shari Headley, Paul Bates, Allison Dean, Eriq La Salle, Louie Anderson, Calvin Lockhart, Samuel L. Jackson, Cuba Gooding, Jr., Vanessa Bell (Calloway), Frankie Faison, Vondie Curtis Hall. Cute change-of-pace film for Murphy, as the genteel prince of an African royal family who wants to choose his own wife, and decides that he will find her in America. Old-fashioned romantic comedy peppered with director Landis' in-jokes (including an update of TRADING PLACES, in which Murphy starred) and some surprise cameos. Subsequent litigation awarded columnist Art Buchwald with original story credit. [R]▼●◗

Coming Up Roses (1986-British) C-93m. ** D: Stephen Bayly. Dafydd Hywel, Iola Gregory, Olive Michael, Mari Emlyn. Whimsical Welsh-language comedy concerns a group of townsfolk who band together to save a local cinema by growing mushrooms in the darkness of the empty theatre. Cute, but lacks the wit and sharp ensemble acting of the hilarious British comedies of the 1940s and 1950s. [PG]▼

Comin' Round the Mountain (1951) 77m. *½ D: Charles Lamont. Bud Abbott, Lou Costello, Dorothy Shay, Kirby Grant, Joe Sawyer, Glenn Strange. Bud and Lou invade hillbilly country in this substandard comedy, with far too much footage of singing Shay.▼◗

Command Decision (1948) 112m. ***½ D: Sam Wood. Clark Gable, Walter Pidgeon, Van Johnson, Brian Donlevy, Charles Bickford, John Hodiak, Edward Arnold, Marshall Thompson, Richard Quine, Cameron Mitchell, John McIntire. Taut, engrossing adaptation of the William Wister Haines stage hit, with Gable a flight commander who knows that, to win the war, he must send his men on suicide missions over Germany. Intriguing look at behind-the-scenes politics of the U.S. war effort. Screenplay by William Laidlaw and George Froeschel. Also shown in computer-colored version.▼●◗

Commandments (1997) C-86m. ** D: Daniel Taplitz. Aidan Quinn, Courteney Cox, Anthony LaPaglia, Louis Zorich, Pamela Gray, Pat McNamara, Tom Aldredge, Alice Drummond, Jack Gilpin. When a man's life hits rock bottom he decides to test the whole concept of spirituality by breaking each of the Ten Commandments. Uneven black comedy shifts in tone from light to dark, losing its meaning along the way. Quinn is effective, but this must have looked a lot better on paper. [R]▼◗

Commando (1985) C-88m. ** D: Mark L. Lester. Arnold Schwarzenegger, Rae Dawn Chong, Dan Hedaya, Vernon Wells, David Patrick Kelly, Alyssa Milano, James Olson, Bill Duke, Bill Paxton. Exceptionally noisy comic-book yarn about retired special agent Schwarzenegger, who's forced to go back into action when vengeful goons kidnap his daughter. Film's sense of humor (courtesy scripter Steven E. de Souza) is largely obliterated by all the noise and mindless violence. Director's cut runs 90m. [R]▼●◗

Commandos (1968-Italian-German) C-89m. ** D: Armando Crispino. Lee Van Cleef, Jack Kelly, Giampiero Albertini, Marino Masé, Pierre Paulo Capponi, Duilio Del Prete. Cliché-filled war drama with familiar plot; Italian commandos, led by a couple of stalwart Americans, must secure an important oasis in North African desert in advance of Allied landings. Cromoscope. [PG]▼◗

Commando Squad (1987) C-89m. BOMB D: Fred Olen Ray. Brian Thompson, Kathy Shower, William Smith, Sid Haig, Ross Hagen, Robert Quarry, Mel Welles. Thompson and Shower (former *Playboy* Playmate of the Year) are government agents sent to Mexico to wipe out Smith's cocaine factory. Tiresome film features numerous screen veterans, including Marie Windsor and Russ Tamblyn. [R]▼

Commitments, The (1991-British-Irish) **C-117m.** ***½ D: Alan Parker. Robert Arkins, Michael Aherne, Angeline Ball, Maria Doyle, Dave Finnegan, Bronagh Gallagher, Félim Gormley, Glen Hansard, Dick Massey, Johnny Murphy, Kenneth McCluskey, Andrew Strong, Colm Meaney. Enormously satisfying tale of an ambitious young Dubliner who takes on the challenge of assembling and managing a band made up of other working-class Dubliners who sing '60s-style soul music! Disarmingly engaging from the word go, with charismatic cast of unknowns; filled with irresistible music. A real treat. Written by Dick Clement, Ian La Frenais, and Roddy Doyle; the first of Doyle's Barrytown trilogy, followed by THE SNAPPER and THE VAN. [R]▼◑

Committed (2000) **C-98m.** ** D: Lisa Krueger. Heather Graham, Casey Affleck, Luke Wilson, Goran Visnjic, Alfonso Arau, Patricia Velazquez, Mark Ruffalo, Clea DuVall, Summer Phoenix, Mary Kay Place, Art Alexakis, Jon Stewart, Dylan Baker, Carlin Glynn. Young N.Y.C. club manager believes in commitment at work and in her marriage (though she's surrounded by slacker friends), so she's thrown for a loop when her husband (Wilson) bolts to "find himself." Graham is the whole show here, but she's stuck in a lightweight road-movie/culture-clash tale. If this is screwball romance for the new millennium, we're in trouble. [R]▼▌

Common Threads: Stories From the Quilt (1989) **C/B&W-79m.** *** D: Robert Epstein, Jeffrey Friedman. Narrated by Dustin Hoffman. Compassionate documentary focusing on five individuals afflicted with AIDS: a former Olympic athlete, a retired U.S. Navy commander, an 11-year-old hemophiliac, a N.Y. writer and gay activist, and an I.V. drug user. Title refers to AIDS Memorial Quilt, consisting of thousands of panels, each dedicated to an AIDS victim. Produced by HBO; a worthy Best Documentary Academy Award winner.▼◑

Communion (1977) SEE: **Holy Terror**

Communion (1989) **C-107m.** **½ D: Philippe Mora. Christopher Walken, Lindsay Crouse, Frances Sternhagen, Andreas Katsulas, Terri Hanauer, Joel Carlson, Basil Hoffman. Psychological thriller with Walken well cast as writer Whitley Strieber, who finds himself visited by strange creatures. Does he need a psychiatrist or an exorcist? A bit overlong, and the dramatic scenes between Walken and wife Crouse don't quite work, but still effectively scary while never gratuitously gory. Strieber

adapted his own best-selling book, which he claims is true. Super 35. [R]▼◑

Companeros! (1971-Italian-Spanish-German) **C-105m.** ** D: Sergio Corbucci. Franco Nero, Tomas Milian, Jack Palance, Fernando Rey, Iris Berben, Karin Schubert. Swedish mercenary (Nero) seeks his fortune by running guns in revolution-racked Mexico at the turn of the century. Violent western fare. Techniscope. [R]▼▌

Company, The (2003) **C-112m.** *** D: Robert Altman. Neve Campbell, Malcolm McDowell, James Franco, Barbara Robertson, William Dick, Susie Cusack. Life behind the scenes during a season with the Joffrey Ballet of Chicago, focusing on one dedicated dancer (Campbell). Not so much a story as a low-key series of vignettes about the innumerable factors that go into maintaining a company, salving bruised egos, and surviving both on and offstage. The dance numbers are exhilarating and beautifully filmed; Campbell shines in a pas de deux set to "My Funny Valentine." Campbell coproduced and cowrote the story. HD 24P Widescreen. [PG-13]▼▌

Company Business (1991) **C-98m.** *½ D: Nicholas Meyer. Gene Hackman, Mikhail Baryshnikov, Kurtwood Smith, Terry O'Quinn, Daniel Von Bargen, Oleg Rudnick, Geraldine Danon. When a planned spy swap comes unglued, two aging agents (one CIA, one KGB) become unlikely allies as the old cold-war espionage rules they once lived by melt away. Interesting premise goes awry in this dumb spy comedy. [PG-13]▼◑

Company Man (2001) **C-81m.** ** D: Peter Askin, Douglas McGrath. Sigourney Weaver, Steven Banks, Douglas McGrath, John Turturro, Anthony LaPaglia, Ryan Phillippe, Alan Cumming, Denis Leary, Heather Matarazzo, Jeffrey Jones. With wife Weaver hungering for social prestige, 1950s high school English teacher/driving instructor McGrath bogusly tells her he's working for the CIA. One thing leads to another, and he actually *is* recruited by the Agency, eventually landing in the middle of the Bay of Pigs and Castro assassination attempts. Too smart for multiplex dunderheads, but also too silly and mild for savvier folks; affability and good-sport performances are about all it offers. Woody Allen (with whom McGrath wrote BULLETS OVER BROADWAY) appears unbilled. [PG-13]▼▌

Company Men, The (2010-British-U.S.) **C-113m.** *** D: John Wells. Ben Affleck, Tommy Lee Jones, Chris Cooper, Kevin Costner, Maria Bello, Rosemarie DeWitt, Craig T. Nelson, John Doman, Eamonn Walker, Patricia Kalember, Maryann Plunkett. When a major Boston corporation starts downsizing, no one is safe. Hotshot sales exec Affleck, suddenly unemployed, can't deal with his new reality, though his wife (DeWitt) is a pragmatist. Top-tier

Jones, the CEO's best friend, hates what's happening around him, and may not be able to protect longtime colleague Cooper. Empathetic slice of modern American life from veteran TV producer-writer Wells, here making his feature directing debut; while it may not score an emotional bull's-eye, it still has something valid to say about self-worth and self-respect. Costner is good in a supporting role as Affleck's blue-collar brother-in-law. [R] ◗

Company of Killers (1970) C-88m. ** D: Jerry Thorpe. Van Johnson, Ray Milland, John Saxon, Brian Kelly, Fritz Weaver, Clu Gulager, Susan Oliver, Diana Lynn, Robert Middleton. Gunman (Saxon) working for Murder, Inc. becomes target for his employers and big city police department after patrolman is shot down. Bites off more than it can chew. Video title: THE HIT TEAM. [G]▼

Company of Wolves, The (1984-British) C-95m. ** D: Neil Jordan. Angela Lansbury, David Warner, Stephen Rea, Tusse Silberg, Sarah Patterson, Graham Crowden. Freudian, adult version of "Little Red Riding Hood," based on the premise that a wolf may not be what he seems. Intriguing idea mired in murky presentation, encompassing several different stories; strange, slow, and unsatisfying. [R] ▼◗

Company She Keeps, The (1950) 83m. **½ D: John Cromwell. Lizabeth Scott, Jane Greer, Dennis O'Keefe, Fay Baker, John Hoyt, Don Beddoe. Satisfactory tale of ex-con Greer, who's determined to go straight. She yearns for companionship and makes a play for O'Keefe, the boyfriend of her parole officer (Scott). Produced by John Houseman. Jeff Bridges' screen debut; he's the baby in Greer's arms.

Competition, The (1980) C-129m. *** D: Joel Oliansky. Richard Dreyfuss, Amy Irving, Lee Remick, Sam Wanamaker, Joseph Cali, Ty Henderson, Priscilla Pointer, James B. Sikking. Two young pianists, competing for the same prize, fall in love. Nothing much more than that, but smoothly done, with some excellent piano "faking." Screenwriter Oliansky's directing debut. [PG]▼◗

Compromising Positions (1985) C-98m. **½ D: Frank Perry. Susan Sarandon, Raul Julia, Edward Herrmann, Judith Ivey, Mary Beth Hurt, Joe Mantegna, Josh Mostel, Anne De Salvo, Joan Allen. Long Island housewife becomes fascinated with the murder of a local dentist who (it turns out) was also an incredible womanizer. When it sticks to black comedy, the film is sharp and funny, but its other elements (male chauvinism, mystery, romance) don't pan out. Ivey has scene-stealing role as Sarandon's acid-tongued best friend. Screenplay by Susan Isaacs, from her novel. [R]▼◗

Compulsion (1959) 99m. ***½ D: Rich-ard Fleischer. Orson Welles, Diane Varsi, Dean Stockwell, Bradford Dillman, E.G. Marshall, Martin Milner. Hard-hitting version of Leopold-Loeb thrill murder case of 1920s Chicago. Good characterizations, period decor, and well-edited courtroom scenes. Story also told in earlier ROPE and later SWOON. CinemaScope.▼◗

Computer Wore Tennis Shoes, The (1970) C-91m. ** D: Robert Butler. Kurt Russell, Cesar Romero, Joe Flynn, William Schallert, Alan Hewitt, Richard Bakalyan. The first of Disney's carbon-copy comedies with young Russell as the college whiz injected with a computer-brain, which poses threat to local gangster Romero. Standard slapstick. Followed by NOW YOU SEE HIM, NOW YOU DON'T. Remade as a TVM in 1995. [G]▼◗

Comrade X (1940) 90m. **½ D: King Vidor. Clark Gable, Hedy Lamarr, Felix Bressart, Oscar Homolka, Eve Arden, Sig Ruman. NINOTCHKA-esque plot with American Gable warming up icy Russian Lamarr (a streetcar conductor). Synthetic romance tale never convinces; Bressart has great closing line, though.▼◗

Con Air (1997) C-115m. ** D: Simon West. Nicolas Cage, John Cusack, John Malkovich, Steve Buscemi, Ving Rhames, Colm Meaney, Mykelti Williamson, Rachel Ticotin, Nick Chinlund, M. C. Gainey, Brendan Kelly, Danny Trejo, Dave Chappelle. Megastupid megamovie about a federal marshals' plane carrying a cargo of heinous criminals—and a handful of parolees, including Cage, who was unfairly imprisoned in the first place. Once the plane is aloft, the bad guys quickly foil security and take over. Good actors can only do so much with a script this dumb, and dozens of explosions and stunts don't make enough of a difference. Unrated version runs 122m. Panavision. [R]▼◗

Conan the Barbarian (1982) C-129m. **½ D: John Milius. Arnold Schwarzenegger, Sandahl Bergman, James Earl Jones, Gerry Lopez, Mako, Ben Davidson, Sven Ole Thorsen, Max von Sydow, Valerie Quennessen, Cassandra Gaviola, William Smith. The sword-wielding warrior seeks vengeance on the cult leader who enslaved him and massacred his village in this full-blooded (and bloody) adventure epic based on Robert E. Howard's pulp tales. Ron Cobb's spectacular production design and Basil Poledouris' vibrant score help make this superior to the many low-grade imitations it spawned. Written by Milius and Oliver Stone. Also shown at 115m. and 123m. Sequel: CONAN THE DESTROYER. Todd-AO 35. [R]▼◗

Conan the Destroyer (1984) C-103m. *½ D: Richard Fleischer. Arnold Schwarzenegger, Grace Jones, Wilt Chamberlain, Mako, Tracey Walter, Sarah Douglas, Olivia D'Abo.

Lumbering attempt to pit Robert E. Howard's Hyborian Age hero against very derivative special effects—leading to ridiculous climax. J-D-C Scope. [PG]▼●▶

Conceiving Ada (1999) **C-85m.** ** D: Lynn Hershman Leeson. Tilda Swinton, Timothy Leary, Karen Black, Francesca Faridany, John O'Keefe, J. D. Wolfe. Clichéd fantasy that contrasts the lives of Emmy (Faridany), a contemporary computer genius, and Ada Byron King (Swinton), the daughter of Lord Byron, who in the mid-19th century helped conceive the Analytic Engine, the forerunner of the computer. Using some digital instruments she has invented, Emmy reconstructs Ada's life and determines to communicate with her. Premise is intriguing, but result is obvious and far too preachy. ▼▶

Concert, The (2009-French-Romanian-Belgian-Italian) **C-119m.** **½ D: Radu Mihaileanu. Alexeï Guskov, Dmitri Nazarov, Mélanie Laurent, François Berléand, Miou-Miou, Valeri Barinov, Lionel Abelanski, Laurent Bateau. Entertaining, if shamelessly manipulative, story of a once-great, now-disgraced Russian orchestra conductor who gets a one-in-a-million chance to redeem himself and reunite his former musicians for a concert in Paris. Outlandish story veers toward farce but still pushes the right emotional buttons, especially when the music takes over. [PG-13]▶

Concorde . . . Airport '79, The (1979) **C-123m.** BOMB D: David Lowell Rich. Alain Delon, Susan Blakely, Robert Wagner, Sylvia Kristel, George Kennedy, Eddie Albert, Bibi Andersson, John Davidson, Andrea Marcovicci, Martha Raye, Cicely Tyson, Jimmie Walker, David Warner, Mercedes McCambridge. Wagner is a brilliant scientist, Kennedy and Andersson make love by the fire, Davidson's hair stays in place when the plane turns upside down, and McCambridge is a Russian gymnastics coach. Thank goodness Charo is around for credibility. Aka AIRPORT '79. [PG]▼▶

Concrete Jungle, The (1960-British) **86m.** *** D: Joseph Losey. Stanley Baker, Margit Saad, Sam Wanamaker, Gregoire Aslan, Jill Bennett, Laurence Naismith, Edward Judd, Patrick Magee. Baker shines in this intense, stunningly directed account of a criminal who must contend with jailer Magee and, most tellingly, hood Wanamaker (with whom he robs a racetrack). More than just a crime drama, it's a story of how greed and lust for money can result in alienation and the destruction of the spirit. Original title: THE CRIMINAL, released at 97m.▶

Concrete Jungle, The (1982) **C-99m.** *½ D: Tom DeSimone. Jill St. John, Tracy Bregman, Barbara Luna, Peter Brown, Aimee Eccles, Nita Talbot, Sondra Currie. Bregman's heel boyfriend gets her wrongly busted for drugs, leading to standard women's prison melodrama with St. John the kind of movie warden who is given glasses to show how uptight she is. Luna's performance as a hard-bitten prison vet is a cut above the others'. Followed by CHAINED HEAT. [R]▼

Condemned, The (2007) **C-113m.** BOMB D: Scott Wiper. Steve Austin, Vinnie Jones, Robert Mammone, Victoria Mussett, Rick Hoffman. Wealthy, ruthless producer creates an illegal Internet reality show in which ten death-row convicts are attached to bombs, put on an island, and ordered to kill each other. Reprehensible exploitation film disguised as a morality tale, it titillates its audience with a constant stream of brutal violence, then attacks people who find violence entertaining and turn it into a commodity. Sanctimonious moralizing is ironic coming from World Wrestling Entertainment, which produced the film as a vehicle for its star, Stone Cold Steve Austin. [R]▶

Condemned of Altona, The (1962-Italian) **114m.** **½ D: Vittorio De Sica. Sophia Loren, Fredric March, Robert Wagner, Maximilian Schell, Francoise Prevost. Sluggish pseudo-intellectual version of Jean-Paul Sartre play about post-WW2 Germany involving dying magnate (March), his two sons—one a playboy (Wagner) with an actress wife (Loren); the other an insane Nazi war criminal (Schell). CinemaScope.

Condition Red (1995-U.S.-Finnish) **C-86m.** ** D: Mika Kaurismaki. James Russo, Cynda Williams, Paul Calderon, Victor Argo, Dierdre Lewis. Grittily realistic but ever-so-obvious thriller in which alienated, deeply troubled prison guard Russo becomes involved in a volatile sexual relationship with tough convict Williams, a singer doing jail time to protect her slimy boyfriend. Too many lapses in logic, though the performances are fine. [R]▼

Condorman (1981-British) **C-90m.** ** D: Charles Jarrott. Michael Crawford, Oliver Reed, James Hampton, Barbara Carrera, Jean-Pierre Kalfon, Dana Elcar. Cartoonist Crawford is transformed into Condorman, a comic book superhero who assists Soviet spy Carrera in her efforts to defect. Silly Disney film for only the most undiscriminating children. Panavision. [PG]▼▶

Conductor, The SEE: **Orchestra Conductor, The**

Conduct Unbecoming (1975-British) **C-107m.** **½ D: Michael Anderson. Michael York, Richard Attenborough, Trevor Howard, Stacy Keach, Susannah York, Christopher Plummer. Quaintly old-fashioned drama of honor and outrage among the Bengal Lancers, where an officer's widow (York) is sexually attacked. Too stuffy to be fun, yet too modern in other ways to be an antique; star performances are saving grace. [PG]▼▶

Coneheads (1993) **C-88m.** *** D: Steve Barron. Dan Aykroyd, Jane Curtin, Michelle

Burke, Michael McKean, Jason Alexander, Lisa Jane Persky, Chris Farley, David Spade, Phil Hartman, Dave Thomas, Sinbad, Jan Hooks, Michael Richards, Jon Lovitz, Kevin Nealon, Adam Sandler, Garrett Morris, Laraine Newman, Tim Meadows, Julia Sweeney, Ellen DeGeneres, Parker Posey, Joey Lauren Adams. Unexpectedly benign (and good-natured) comedy based on the 1970s *Saturday Night Live* skits. The Coneheads (from the planet Remulak) land on earth in a botched mission and, to their own surprise, adapt to middle-class suburban life. A most enjoyable family film that combines silliness with some sly and unexpected gags. Amusing cameos by a gaggle of past and present *SNL* cast members. Watch for Drew Carey in a taxi. Aykroyd also cowrote the film. [PG]▼●◗

Coney Island (1943) **C-96m. *** D:** Walter Lang. Betty Grable, George Montgomery, Cesar Romero, Charles Winninger, Phil Silvers, Matt Briggs. Breezy, enjoyable turn-of-the-century musical of saloon entertainer Grable turned into famous musical star by hustling Montgomery. Remade with Grable seven years later as WABASH AVENUE.

Confession, The (1970) **C-138m. **½ D:** Costa-Gavras. Yves Montand, Simone Signoret, Gabriele Ferzetti, Michel Vitold, Jean Bouise. True story of Czechoslovakian Communist Arthur London and his unjustified 1951 purge trial for treason; interesting tale well acted by Montand, but film is as talky and overrated as many of Costa-Gavras' other efforts. [PG]

Confessions of a Dangerous Mind (2002) **C-113m. *** D:** George Clooney. Sam Rockwell, Drew Barrymore, George Clooney, Julia Roberts, Rutger Hauer, Maggie Gyllenhaal, Kristen Wilson, Jennifer Hall, Michael Cera. Odd but entertaining adaptation of game-show maven Chuck Barris' believe-it-or-don't autobiography in which he claims he was a CIA assassin. Bold mix of love story, period piece, black comedy, psychological drama, and thriller (by writer Charlie Kaufman) is not seamless, nor does it necessarily add up to anything of substance, but first-time helmer Clooney handles it with style, and Rockwell is terrific as Barris. Real-life Barris colleagues like Dick Clark and Gene the Dancing Machine appear, as do a couple of movie stars in funny cameos. Super 35. [R]▼◗

Confessions of a Nazi Spy (1939) **102m. **½ D:** Anatole Litvak. Edward G. Robinson, Francis Lederer, George Sanders, Paul Lukas, Henry O'Neill, James Stephenson, Sig Rumann, Dorothy Tree, Lya Lys, Joe Sawyer. Fast-paced but obvious drama of FBI agent Robinson investigating vast Nazi spy ring operating in the U.S. Of interest mainly as a reflection of its era; Lukas, as a German-American Bund leader, clearly

patterns his mannerisms and speeches on those of Hitler.◗

Confessions of a Peeping John SEE: **Hi, Mom!**

Confessions of a Shopaholic (2009) **C-104m. ** D:** P. J. Hogan. Isla Fisher, Hugh Dancy, Krysten Ritter, Joan Cusack, John Goodman, John Lithgow, Kristin Scott Thomas, Fred Armisen, Leslie Bibb, Lynn Redgrave, Robert Stanton, Julie Hagerty, Nick Cornish, Clea Lewis, Wendie Malick, John Salley, Christine Ebersole. Manhattanite Fisher is addicted to shopping in spite of her meager income, fending off creditors with a nonstop series of lies. Then she stumbles into a job working for—of all things—a financial magazine, edited by dishy Dancy. Fisher is cute but this frantic, poorly written film makes her such a scatterbrain that it's difficult to root for her. Based on two of the best-selling novels by Sophie Kinsella. Fleeting appearance by Redgrave implies that there was yet another subplot trimmed from the film. Panavision. [PG]◗

Confessions of a Teenage Drama Queen (2004) **C-96m. **½ D:** Sara Sugarman. Lindsay Lohan, Adam Garcia, Glenne Headly, Alison Pill, Carol Kane, Eli Marienthal, Megan Fox, Sheila McCarthy. Self-styled drama queen Lohan suffers the ignominy of moving with her mom and two sisters from Manhattan to New Jersey, where she immediately finds a soul mate (Pill) and also runs afoul of the class snob. The promise of seeing her rock idol in his farewell concert propels the rest of the story, based on Dyan Sheldon's popular book. Innocuous Disney teen comedy; parents will enjoy Kane's funny performance as a schoolteacher. [PG]▼

Confessions of a Window Cleaner (1974-British) **C-90m. ** D:** Val Guest. Robin Askwith, Anthony Booth, Linda Hayden, Bill Maynard, Dandy Nichols. British sex farce about voyeuristic window cleaner was dated when it came out; too obvious to be terribly funny. Followed by other CONFESSIONS films. [R]

Confessions of Tom Harris (1972) **C-98m. ** D:** John Derek, David Nelson. Don Murray, Linda Evans, David Brian, Gary Clarke, Logan Ramsey. Offbeat, gritty study of a corrupt, amoral prizefighter, played by Murray, who also produced and wrote the story. Derek also photographed it. Filmed in 1966. First released in 1969 as CHILDISH THINGS. [PG]▼

Confetti (2006-British) **C-100m. ** D:** Debbie Isitt. Jimmy Carr, Olivia Colman, Vincent Franklin, Martin Freeman, Felicity Montagu, Jessica Stevenson, Robert Webb, Jason Watkins, Sarah Hadland, Julia Davis. Reality TV morphs into a big-screen affair when three couples compete in a magazine contest for the wedding of the year. Mockumentary follows all three scenarios as pairs of nudists, tennis players, and musical-comedy enthusiasts express themselves just as you'd expect on their big day. Wants to be another BEST IN SHOW but doesn't have the comic chops, just elaborate setups and a few funny bits. Despite a talented cast it's as disposable as the product that inspired its title. [R]▶

Confidence (1979-Hungarian) **C-117m.** ***½ D: Istvan Szabo. Ildiko Bansagi, Peter Andorai, O. Gombik, Karoly Csaki, Ildiko Kishonti. Bansagi and Andorai, each separately married, fall in love while posing as husband and wife to elude the Germans during WW2. Striking, involving tale of trust and survival.

Confidence (2003) **C-98m.** ** D: James Foley. Edward Burns, Rachel Weisz, Paul Giamatti, Dustin Hoffman, Andy Garcia, Luis Guzman, Donal Logue, Morris Chestnut, Robert Forster, Brian Van Holt. A cocky con man and his team are obliged to work for slimy crime lord Hoffman, while federal agent Garcia tails them at every turn. Strong cast in a disappointing yarn that's never as suspenseful, surprising, or satisfying as it ought to be. What's more, Burns' character is utterly unlikable. Foley uses every visual trick he can to maintain interest. Super 35. [R]▼▶

Confidentially Yours (1983-French) **111m.** *** D: François Truffaut. Fanny Ardant, Jean-Louis Trintignant, Philippe Laudenbach, Caroline Sihol, Philippe Morier-Genoud, Xavier Saint Macary. Businessman is wanted for murder, and his secretary takes on job of finding real killer while he hides out from the cops. Truffaut's final feature is airy mystery-comedy in the Hitchcock mold, based on an American novel (*The Long Saturday Night* by Charles Williams); beautifully shot in black & white by Nestor Almendros. No depth whatsoever, but lightly entertaining; Ardant is delightful. French title: VIVEMENT DIMANCHE! [PG]▼▶

Confidential Report SEE: **Mr. Arkadin**
Conflagration SEE: **Enjo**
Conflict (1945) **86m.** **½ D: Curtis Bernhardt. Humphrey Bogart, Alexis Smith, Sydney Greenstreet, Rose Hobart, Charles Drake, Grant Mitchell. Far-fetched story of husband (Bogart) plotting to murder wife (Hobart) to marry her sister (Smith). Unconvincing plot not salvaged by good cast.▼

Conflict (1966) SEE: **Judith**
Conformist, The (1970-Italian-French-West German) **C-115m.** ***½ D: Bernardo Bertolucci. Jean-Louis Trintignant, Stefania Sandrelli, Dominique Sanda, Pierre Clementi, Pasquale Fortunato, Gastone Moschin. Disturbing blend of character study and historical context of 1930s. Repressing homosexual drives, Marcello Clerici strives for "acceptable" life as member of Italian Fascist secret service, and middle-class would-be wife chaser, until odd series of events make

him a willing murderer. Film's overall mood uniquely tense. Cut by 5m. for American release; the missing "Dance of the Blind" sequence was restored for 1994 reissue. [R]▼▶

Congo (1995) **C-108m.** ** D: Frank Marshall. Laura Linney, Ernie Hudson, Tim Curry, Grant Heslov, Dylan Walsh, Joe Don Baker, Stuart Pankin, Mary Ellen Trainor, James Karen. Clumsily written Saturday-matinee nonsense about a gorilla expert who goes on a trouble-laden expedition to Africa with a Roumanian fortune hunter and a high-tech communications expert who's searching for her ex-fiancé. Sort of watchable, but poky pacing, unappealing characters, and senseless script sink it. The big special-effects climax is as unconvincing as Amy, the costarring gorilla. Michael Crichton's novel was adapted by—of all people—John Patrick Shanley (MOONSTRUCK). Joe Pantoliano appears unbilled. [PG-13]▼▶

Connecticut Yankee in King Arthur's Court, A (1949) **C-107m.** **½ D: Tay Garnett. Bing Crosby, Rhonda Fleming, William Bendix, Cedric Hardwicke, Henry Wilcoxon, Murvyn Vye, Virginia Field. Mark Twain's story becomes carefree Crosby musical, with Bing transported into past, branded a wizard. No great songs, but colorful production. Previously filmed in 1921 and 1931 (with Will Rogers); remade in 1979 (as UNIDENTIFIED FLYING ODDBALL); TVMs in 1989 and 1995. ▼▶

Connecting Rooms (1969-British) **C-103m.** ** D: Franklin Gollings. Bette Davis, Michael Redgrave, Alexis Kanner, Kay Walsh, Olga Georges-Picot, Leo Genn. Muddled melodrama of relationships in a rooming house. Davis is a street musician, Redgrave a former schoolmaster, and Kanner the rebellious youth who disrupts their equilibrium.

Connection, The (1961) **103m.** ***½ D: Shirley Clarke. William Redfield, Warren Finnerty, Garry Goodrow, Jerome Raphael, James Anderson, Carl Lee, Roscoe Lee Browne, Jackie McLean. Searing, admirably acted drama of junkies awaiting arrival of their "connection" with heroin, and a documentary filmmaker (Redfield) filming them. Independently produced, based on Jack Gelber's stage play. Original running time 110m.; some prints run 93m.▼

Connie and Carla (2004) **C-98m.** *** D: Michael Lembeck. Nia Vardalos, Toni Collette, David Duchovny, Stephen Spinella, Dash Mihok, Alec Mapa, Debbie Reynolds. Brassy, sometimes silly crowd-pleaser puts a new spin on SOME LIKE IT HOT: lounge entertainers Vardalos and Collette witness a murder and take it on the lam. They find refuge in West Hollywood, where they perform as drag queens and acquire a new circle of gay male friends. Duchovny is charming as Vardalos' love interest, but the spotlight is on the two stars, who perform show tunes ranging from "Oklahoma" to "Don't Cry for Me Argentina." Written by Vardalos. [PG-13]▼❶

Conqueror, The (1956) **C-111m.** ** D: Dick Powell. John Wayne, Susan Hayward, Pedro Armendariz, Agnes Moorehead, Thomas Gomez, John Hoyt, William Conrad. Mongols vs. Tartars, and John Wayne vs. the silliest role of his career, Genghis Khan. Expensive epic has camp dialogue to spare. The film had a sobering real-life aftermath, however: it was shot on location in Utah near an atomic test site, and an alarming number of its cast and crew (including the stars) were later stricken by cancer. CinemaScope.▼❶

Conqueror Worm (1968-British) **C-98m.** *** D: Michael Reeves. Vincent Price, Ian Ogilvy, Hilary Dwyer, Rupert Davies, Robert Russell, Patrick Wymark, Wilfred Brambell. As Matthew Hopkins, real-life witch-hunter during era of Cromwell, Price gives excellent nonhammy performance in underrated low-budget (and bloody) period thriller. Literate, balanced script pits him against young sympathetic lovers Ogilvy and Dwyer. Original British title: THE WITCHFINDER GENERAL.▼❶

Conquest (1937) **112m.** *** D: Clarence Brown. Greta Garbo, Charles Boyer, Reginald Owen, Alan Marshal, Henry Stephenson, Leif Erickson, Dame May Whitty, Maria Ouspenskaya, Vladimir Sokoloff, Scotty Beckett. Boyer as Napoleon and Garbo as Polish countess Walewska in fairly interesting costumer with fine performances making up for not-always-thrilling script.▼❶

Conquest of Space (1955) **C-80m.** **½ D: Byron Haskin. Eric Fleming, William Hopper, Ross Martin, Walter Brooke, Joan Shawlee. Despite some good special effects, this George Pal production about the first trip to Mars is hampered by a pedestrian script and an inappropriate emphasis on religion. A disappointment.▼❶

Conquest of the Planet of the Apes (1972) **C-87m.** **½ D: J. Lee Thompson. Roddy McDowall, Don Murray, Ricardo Montalban, Natalie Trundy, Severn Darden. Fourth APES feature shows how apes came to rebel and subsequently vanquish man. Loosely acted and often trite, but still interesting. Followed by BATTLE FOR THE PLANET OF THE APES. Todd-AO 35. [PG]▼❶

Conrack (1974) **C-107m.** *** D: Martin Ritt. Jon Voight, Paul Winfield, Hume Cronyn, Madge Sinclair, Tina Andrews, Antonio Fargas, Ruth Attaway. Pleasant film based on Pat Conroy's *The Water Is Wide*, about his attempts to bring commonsense education to backward black school on island off South Carolina. Subplot with hermitlike Winfield doesn't work, unfortunately. Panavision. [PG]▼

Conseil de Famille SEE: **Family Business** (1986-French)

Consenting Adults (1992) **C-100m.** *½ D:

Alan J. Pakula. Kevin Kline, Mary Elizabeth Mastrantonio, Kevin Spacey, Rebecca Miller, Forest Whitaker, E. G. Marshall, Kimberly McCullough, Billie Neal. There's Hell in Suburbia when Kline becomes morally polluted by a leechy neighbor who proposes a wife-swapping pact. Incredible lapses in logic for a director of Pakula's caliber, though Spacey is creepily credible as the murderer-next-door. Unintentional laughs help. [R]▼❶

Conspiracy Theory (1997) **C-135m.** *** D: Richard Donner. Mel Gibson, Julia Roberts, Patrick Stewart, Cylk Cozart, Stephen Kahan, Terry Alexander, Troy Garity. Lumpy but entertaining story about a half-crazed N.Y.C. cabdriver who lives a life of paranoia, obsessed with a woman who works for the Justice Department. One day, however, he comes to her with a story that seems to make sense about a conspiracy and cover-up; soon, they're both embroiled in a situation bigger than they ever imagined. The script isn't airtight, but it's enjoyable, with Gibson's edgy performance right on target. Panavision. [R]▼❶

Conspirator, The (2011) **C-123m.** **½ D: Robert Redford. James McAvoy, Robin Wright, Kevin Kline, Evan Rachel Wood, Danny Huston, Justin Long, Tom Wilkinson, Alexis Bledel, Colm Meaney, James Badge Dale, Johnny Simmons, Jonathan Groff, Stephen Root, Toby Kebbell, Shea Whigham, John Cullum. In the aftermath of Abraham Lincoln's assassination, key members of his cabinet seek to punish those responsible and stabilize the fragile nation. Rules of law are put aside for a military trial, and a former captain in the Union Army (McAvoy) is given the thankless task of defending Mary Surratt (Wright), who ran a boardinghouse where her son and others conspired with John Wilkes Booth. Historical drama never achieves the urgency it should, but McAvoy's impassioned performance is worth seeing. Super 35. [PG-13]❶

Constans SEE: **Constant Factor, The**

Constant Factor, The (1980-Polish) **C-96m.** *** D: Krzysztof Zanussi. Tadeusz Bradecki, Zofia Mrozowska, Malgorzata Zajaczkowska, Cezary Morawska. Idealistic mountain climber Bradecki refuses to kowtow to a hypocritical bureaucracy and winds up a window cleaner. Incisive, but not top-drawer Zanussi; filmed simultaneously with the director's CONTRACT.▼

Constant Gardener, The (2005-British-German) **C-128m.** *** D: Fernando Meirelles. Ralph Fiennes, Rachel Weisz, Danny Huston, Bill Nighy, Pete Postlethwaite, Hubert Koundé, Juliet Aubrey, Gerard McSorley. When his young, idealistic wife is murdered in Kenya, a low-level British diplomat investigates, for the first time, the cause she was fighting for. He also learns how his own government tried to quash a scandal involving a large pharmaceutical company, while abusing Africans desperate for medical care. Impassioned filming of John le Carré's fact-based novel (adapted by Jeffrey Caine) manages to balance muckraking drama and a love story; Fiennes and Weisz (Oscar winner as Best Supporting Actress) have great chemistry. [R]▼❍

Constant Husband, The (1955-British) C-88m. *** D: Sidney Gilliat. Rex Harrison, Margaret Leighton, Kay Kendall, Cecil Parker, Nicole Maurey, George Cole, Raymond Huntley, Michael Hordern, Robert Coote, Eric Pohlmann. Harrison, recovering from amnesia, realizes he's wed to more than one woman. Entertaining comedy, with sexy Rexy ideally cast (opposite real-life wife Kendall).

Constantine (2005) C-120m. BOMB D: Francis Lawrence. Keanu Reeves, Rachel Weisz, Tilda Swinton, Shia LaBeouf, Djimon Hounsou, Max Baker, Pruitt Taylor Vince, Gavin Rossdale, Peter Stormare. When demons from hell wreak havoc on earth, who ya gonna call? John Constantine, an exorcist who's actually been to hell. After two hours of this laborious twaddle, we know how he must feel. Dreary, to put it mildly; elaborate special effects are no compensation. Based on the D.C. Comics/Vertigo Hellblazer graphic novels. Super 35. [R]▼❍

Consuming Passions (1988-U.S.-British) C-98m. *½ D: Giles Foster. Vanessa Redgrave, Jonathan Pryce, Tyler Butterworth, Freddie Jones, Sammi Davis, Prunella Scales, Thora Hird. Dumb dud of a satire about what happens when three men are accidentally shoved into a vat of chocolate in a candy factory . . . and chocolate lovers favor the resulting confections. Sounds a lot more promising than it plays; based on a play by Michael Palin and Terry Jones. [R]▼❍

Contact (1997) C-150m. *** D: Robert Zemeckis. Jodie Foster, Matthew McConaughey, James Woods, John Hurt, Tom Skerritt, William Fichtner, David Morse, Angela Bassett, Geoffrey Blake, Rob Lowe, Jake Busey. A woman who has devoted her life to studying the stars—believing there's life Out There—is ostracized by her superior at the National Science Foundation, and eventually cut off, until she actually receives a message from space. Intensely involving story in which we're drawn into Foster's obsession and share her odyssey into the unknown. Passionate and intelligent, this film manages to inspire a feeling of awe and wonder, which makes up for its overlength and false endings. Foster is simply sensational. Based on the novel by Carl Sagan. Panavision. [PG]▼❍●

Contempt (1963-French-Italian) C-103m. ***½ D: Jean-Luc Godard. Brigitte Bardot, Jack Palance, Michel Piccoli, Giorgia Moll, Fritz Lang. Perversely funny look at international moviemaking with Piccoli as a dramatist of integrity who gets mixed up with a vulgar producer (Palance) and director (Lang—playing himself) in a film version of *The Odyssey*. Producer Joseph E. Levine didn't seem to understand that Godard, who appears here as Lang's assistant, held *him* in contempt, making this film a highly amusing "in" joke. Bardot's appearance only adds to the fun. Franscope.▼❍●

Contender, The (2000-German-U.S.) C-127m. *** D: Rod Lurie. Joan Allen, Jeff Bridges, Gary Oldman, Christian Slater, Sam Elliott, William Petersen, Saul Rubinek, Philip Baker Hall, Mariel Hemingway. The death of the vice president enables U.S. president Bridges to appoint a female Ohio senator as his successor. But a small-minded congressman (Oldman) with an axe to grind decides to humiliate her during public hearings—and she refuses to stoop to his level. Timely, engrossing political drama written by the director, with strong performances. Oldman, a particular standout, also coexecutive-produced. [R]▼❍

Contest Girl (1964-British) C-82m. **½ D: Val Guest. Ian Hendry, Janette Scott, Ronald Fraser, Edmund Purdom, Linda Christian. Film well conveys glamorous and seamy sides of beauty-contest world. Purdom gives effective performance. Original British title: THE BEAUTY JUNGLE. CinemaScope.

Continental Divide (1981) C-103m. ** D: Michael Apted. John Belushi, Blair Brown, Allen Goorwitz (Garfield), Carlin Glynn, Tony Ganios, Val Avery, Tim Kazurinsky. One of those "concept" movies that's all premise, no payoff: Belushi's a hard-hitting Chicago newspaper columnist, Brown's a self-reliant naturalist at home observing eagles in the Rockies. Can this romance survive? Interesting mainly to see Belushi playing such a "normal" and likable character. Written by Lawrence Kasdan, who obviously couldn't come up with a finish. Steven Spielberg was executive producer. [PG]▼❍

Continental Twist, The SEE: **Twist All Night**

Contraband (1940-British) 92m. ***½ D: Michael Powell. Conrad Veidt, Valerie Hobson, Hay Petrie, Joss Ambler, Raymond Lovell, Esmond Knight, Peter Bull, Leo Genn. Superior spy yarn from Michael Powell and Emeric Pressburger, very much in the Hitchcock vein. Veidt is a Danish merchant sea captain, Hobson an enigmatic passenger—both get caught up with London spy ring. Though set in 1939, film hardly seems dated at all! That's Bernard Miles as a disgruntled smoker. Powell and Brock Williams adapted Pressburger's story. P&P had teamed up with Veidt and Hobson the previous year for THE SPY IN BLACK. Original U.S. title: BLACKOUT.▼❍

Contract (1980-Polish) C-114m. ***½ D: Krzysztof Zanussi. Leslie Caron, Maja

Komorowska, Tadeusz Lomnicki, Magda Jaroszowna. Superb laced-in-acid comedy-satire centering on a wedding between the career-oriented son of a wealthy doctor and his none-too-eager bride. Zanussi incisively chides corrupt politicians and businessmen; Caron is memorable as a kleptomaniacal ballerina. Filmed simultaneously with the director's CONSTANS (THE CONSTANT FACTOR).▼

Contract, The (2006-German-U.S.) C-96m. ** D: Bruce Beresford. Morgan Freeman, John Cusack, Jamie Anderson, Alice Krige, Megan Dodds, Corey Johnson, Jonathan Hyde, Bill Smitrovich, Anthony Warren, Thomas Lockyer, Ned Bellamy. Does high school gym teacher Cusack possess the stamina and smarts to thwart renegade contract killer Freeman? Untidy actioner leaves plenty of questions unanswered while offering the barest minimum of thrills. Released direct to DVD in the U.S. Super 35. [R]▶

Control (2007-British-Japanese-Australian) 121m. ***½ D: Anton Corbijn. Sam Riley, Samantha Morton, Alexandra Maria Lara, Joe Anderson, James Anthony Pearson, Harry Treadaway, Craig Parkinson, Toby Kebbell. Darkly fascinating character study of Manchester rocker Ian Curtis, the moody Joy Division lead singer who committed suicide at age 23 in 1980, just as his band was on the cusp of international success. Effectively filmed in often noir-like b&w, biopic unromantically renders Curtis—played with the perfect balance of vulnerability and volatility by Riley—as an artist undone by the inner demons that informed his art. Based on a memoir by Curtis' wife (played here by Morton). Super 35. [R]▶

Convent, The (1995-Portuguese-French) C-90m. ** D: Manoel de Oliveira. Catherine Deneuve, John Malkovich, Duarte D'Almeida, Luis Miguel Cintra, Heloisa Miranda, Leonor Silveira. A professor (Malkovich) is attempting to prove that Shakespeare is of Spanish descent. To further his research, he and his wife (Deneuve) travel to an ancient convent, where there are eerie and mysterious goings-on. Languid tale made by the well-respected Portuguese writer-director de Oliveira (who was 86 years old when this was released!).▼▶

Conversation, The (1974) C-113m. **** D: Francis Ford Coppola. Gene Hackman, John Cazale, Allen Garfield, Frederic Forrest, Cindy Williams, Michael Higgins, Elizabeth MacRae, Teri Garr, Harrison Ford, Robert Shields. Brilliant film about obsessive surveillance expert (Hackman) who makes professional mistake of becoming involved in a case, and finds himself entangled in murder and high-level power plays. Coppola's top-notch, disturbing script makes larger statements about privacy and personal responsibility. An un-

billed Robert Duvall has a cameo. One of the best films of the 1970s. [PG]▼●▶

Conversation Piece (1975-Italian) C-122m. ** D: Luchino Visconti. Burt Lancaster, Silvana Mangano, Helmut Berger, Claudia Marsani, Claudia Cardinale. Ponderous story of aging, aloof professor Lancaster who becomes involved with matron Mangano's hedonistic children and her young lover, Berger. All talk. Filmed in both English and Italian-language versions. Todd-AO 35. [R]▼

Conversations With Other Women (2005) C-84m. **½ D: Hans Canosa. Aaron Eckhart, Helena Bonham Carter, Nora Zehetner, Erik Eidem, Olivia Wilde, Tom Lennon, Cerina Vincent, Brianna Brown, Brian Geraghty. Two people hook up at a wedding reception: His sis is getting married; she's a bridesmaid. They may have met before. In fact, they might have been married and had a daughter. Determinedly ambiguous two-character drama is a one-trick pony in split-screen, a cinematic trope that tries to add visual flair to a heavily conversational script. HD Widescreen. [R]▶

Conviction (2010-British) C-107m. *** D: Tony Goldwyn. Hilary Swank, Sam Rockwell, Minnie Driver, Melissa Leo, Peter Gallagher, Ari Graynor, Juliette Lewis, Loren Dean, Conor Donovan, Bailee Madison, Clea DuVall, Karen Young, Talia Balsam. A lifelong hell-raiser, Rockwell is accused of a brutal murder in his Massachusetts hometown, convicted on dubious evidence, and sentenced to life in prison in 1983. His devoted younger sister spends the next 18 years working to get a high school diploma, attend college, and earn a law degree for the sole purpose of proving his innocence. Trumps many films based on true stories by avoiding clichés and spotlighting its two talented stars, who give sincere and solid performances. What's more, the saga turns out to have more surprises than you might expect. [R]▶

Convicts (1991) C-95m. *** D: Peter Masterson. Robert Duvall, Lukas Haas, James Earl Jones, Starletta DuPois. A young boy (Haas) comes of age observing the violent scenes on a Texas Gulf Coast canefield in 1902—even as life seems to be cycling to an end for imposing plantation boss (Duvall) who survives by using convict labor to work in his fields. A towering performance by Duvall and stark, authentic dialogue by Horton Foote (based on his nine-play cycle *The Orphan's Home*) are the strengths in this poignant elegy. ▼●▶

Convicts 4 (1962) 105m. *** D: Millard Kaufman. Ben Gazzara, Stuart Whitman, Ray Walston, Vincent Price, Rod Steiger, Broderick Crawford, Sammy Davis, Jr., Jack Kruschen. Gazzara gives sincere portrayal as long-term prisoner who becomes professional artist. Oddball supporting cast. Retitled: REPRIEVE. ▼▶

Convoy (1978) **C-110m.** ** D: Sam Peckinpah. Kris Kristofferson, Ali MacGraw, Ernest Borgnine, Burt Young, Madge Sinclair, Franklyn Ajaye, Cassie Yates. Amiable comic-book movie based on the hit song about an independent trucker who leads protesting colleagues on a trek through the Southwest. Stupid script and blah acting redeemed somewhat by Peckinpah's punchy directorial style. Panavision. [PG]▼❚

Coogan's Bluff (1968) **C-95m.** *** D: Don Siegel. Clint Eastwood, Lee J. Cobb, Susan Clark, Tisha Sterling, Don Stroud, Betty Field, Tom Tully. Arizona lawman Eastwood comes to N.Y.C. to show city cops a thing or two about tracking down a wanted man. Stylish action film, good location work. Sterling enjoyable as hippie. Later evolved into the *McCloud* TV series. [R]▼●❚

Cookie (1989) **C-93m.** *** D: Susan Seidelman. Peter Falk, Dianne Wiest, Emily Lloyd, Michael V. Gazzo, Brenda Vaccaro, Adrian Pasdar, Lionel Stander, Jerry Lewis, Bob Gunton, Ricki Lake. Droll comedy about a sassy teenager who gets to meet her mobster dad for the first time when he's sprung from prison after a long stretch. No fireworks here, but the performances are great fun to watch, especially Wiest as Falk's breathless mistress (and Lloyd's mother). Written by Nora Ephron and Alice Arlen. [R]▼●❚

Cookie's Fortune (1999) **C-118m.** *** D: Robert Altman. Glenn Close, Julianne Moore, Liv Tyler, Chris O'Donnell, Charles S. Dutton, Patricia Neal, Ned Beatty, Courtney B. Vance, Donald Moffat, Lyle Lovett, Danny Durst, Matt Malloy. Picaresque yarn spun in a small Southern town where an eccentric woman's death sets in motion a series of events revealing the true nature—both good-hearted and greedy—of various relatives and friends. Colorful characters abound in this easygoing, fanciful film, sparked by Dutton's wonderful performance. [PG-13]▼❚

Cookout, The (2004) **C-97m.** ** D: Lance Rivera. Ja Rule, Tim Meadows, Jenifer Lewis, Meagan Good, Storm P (Quran Pender), Jonathan Silverman, Farrah Fawcett, Frankie Faison, Vincent Pastore, Queen Latifah, Danny Glover, Eve. Hot basketball star signs a $30 million deal and moves from his parents' traditional neighborhood to an exclusive gated community, where he decides to have a cookout for his friends and family, just as he did in his old 'hood. Latifah coproduced and helped cook up what story there is in this frantic, stereotyped, and only sporadically amusing comedy that looks like it was made up as the cameras rolled. [PG-13]❚

Cook The Thief His Wife & Her Lover, The (1989-French-Dutch) **C-124m.** *** D: Peter Greenaway. Helen Mirren, Michael Gambon, Tim Roth, Richard Bohringer, Alan Howard. Another stylish, challenging piece of cinema from Greenaway that's set in a plush gourmet restaurant and details the various relationships between the title characters. This parable about love, revenge, and, most of all, greed is both funny and horrifying—and right on target. However, those who do not appreciate Greenaway's cinematic sensibility may be put off. Sacha Vierny's cinematography is an asset. Technovision. [NC-17 and R-rated versions are available]▼●❚

Cool as Ice (1991) **C-100m.** BOMB D: David Kellogg. Vanilla Ice, Kristin Minter, Michael Gross, Candy Clark, Sydney Lassick, Dody Goodman, Naomi Campbell, Bobby Brown. The Sealtest man's rap numbers frame seemingly unreleasable "wandering cyclist" yarn about a numbskull who manages to romance the town's SAT standard-bearer. Oh, did we mention that her father is in the government's witness relocation program? Ice's parlance ("Drop that zero/get with the hero") in his first starring film does not rekindle fond memories of Ronald Colman. [PG]▼●❚

Cool Breeze (1972) **C-101m.** *½ D: Barry Pollack. Thalmus Rasulala, Judy Pace, Jim Watkins, Lincoln Kilpatrick, Sam Laws, Margaret Avery, Raymond St. Jacques. Routine remake of THE ASPHALT JUNGLE with plot line updated so that diamond robbery proceeds will go to set up a black people's bank.[R]

Cool, Dry Place, A (1999) **C-97m.** **½ D: John N. Smith. Vince Vaughn, Joey Lauren Adams, Monica Potter, Devon Sawa, Bobby Moat, Todd Louiso. Hotshot lawyer is raising his 5-year-old son since his wife walked out on them. Having lost his job, he tries to build a new life in Texas and meets a woman he likes . . . then the plot thickens. Believable story, if predictable at times; benefits from good performances. [PG-13]▼❚

Cooler, The (2003) **C-102m.** *** D: Wayne Kramer. William H. Macy, Alec Baldwin, Maria Bello, Shawn Hatosy, Ron Livingston, Estella Warren, Paul Sorvino, Joey Fatone, M.C. Gainey, Ellen Greene. A lifelong loser makes his living spreading bad luck around an old-style Vegas casino. Then a beautiful cocktail waitress falls in love with him and his luck begins to change. Clever story is perfectly cast; Baldwin is terrific as the hard-edged casino boss who decries the transformation of Vegas into Disneyland. Everything clicks—until the final scene. Evocative jazz score by Mark Isham. Super 35. [R]▼❚

Cooley High (1975) **C-107m.** *** D: Michael Schultz. Glynn Turman, Lawrence Hilton-Jacobs, Garrett Morris, Cynthia Davis, Corin Rogers, Maurice Leon Havis. Inner-city rip-off of AMERICAN GRAFFITI (set in Chicago, 1964) is nonetheless pleasing on its own terms, though only on the level of a good TV show. Lots of laughs. Look fast for Robert Townsend. Later evolved into the *What's Happening!!* TV series. [PG]▼●❚

Cool Hand Luke (1967) **C-126m.** ***½ D: Stuart Rosenberg. Paul Newman, George Kennedy, J.D. Cannon, Lou Antonio, Robert Drivas, Strother Martin, Jo Van Fleet, Wayne Rogers, Anthony Zerbe, Ralph Waite, Harry Dean Stanton, Dennis Hopper, Richard Davalos, Warren Finnerty, Morgan Woodward, Clifton James, Joe Don Baker. Modern slant on prison camps shows little change since Paul Muni; more irreverent, however, with memorably funny egg-eating contest. Top-notch film with Kennedy's Oscar-winning supporting performance as prisoner. Panavision.▼●◗

Cool Ones, The (1967) **C-95m.** BOMB D: Gene Nelson. Roddy McDowall, Debbie Watson, Gil Peterson, Phil Harris, Robert Coote, Glen Campbell, Mrs. Miller. Inane "musical" comedy spoofing trendy music business. Embarrassing on all counts, with broad performances. If you turn up your volume, you might hear a faint laugh track. Panavision.

Cool Runnings (1993) **C-97m.** *** D: Jon Turteltaub. Leon, Doug E. Doug, John Candy, Rawle D. Lewis, Malik Yoba, Raymond J. Barry. Family-oriented feel-good movie from Disney—based on a true story—about the unlikely formation of a Jamaican bobsled team to compete in the 1988 Winter Olympics. (The participants have never even seen snow, let alone a bobsled!) Candy is well cast as a disgraced former Olympian who redeems himself. [PG]▼●◗

Cool World, The (1964) **105m.** *** D: Shirley Clarke. Hampton Clanton, Yolanda Rodríguez, Bostic Felton, Gary Bolling, Carl Lee, Clarence Williams (III), Gloria Foster, Georgia Burke, Antonio Fargas. The streets, rhythms, and populace of Harlem are the stars of this justifiably celebrated cinéma vérité film. While primarily a mood piece, it does feature a gritty, realistic—and very un-Hollywood—storyline, which involves a young black teen gang member (Clanton, in his only screen appearance). Based on a novel by Warren Miller and played by Miller and Robert Rossen. Clarke also coscripted (with Lee) and edited. Produced by Frederick Wiseman.

Cool World (1992) **C-101m.** *½ D: Ralph Bakshi. Gabriel Byrne, Kim Basinger, Brad Pitt, Frank Sinatra, Jr. Pointless live-action/animation feature from Bakshi, who's covered this ground before, much more successfully. Ex-con comic-book artist Byrne discovers his cartoon creations are real, and live in a parallel universe called Cool World. After sexy "doodle" Holli (Basinger) has sex with Byrne, she becomes human and escapes to real world, with detective Pitt in tow. Too serious to be fun, too goofy to take seriously; lead characters unlikable and unappealing. Looks like a Roger Corman version of ROGER RABBIT. [PG-13]▼●◗

Coonskin (1975) **C-83m.** **½ D: Ralph Bakshi. Barry White, Charles Gordone, Scatman Crothers, Philip (Michael) Thomas. Outrageous, original film about the status of blacks in America is told with live-action and animation vignettes, the best of which are sly parodies of the stories from Disney and Uncle Remus' SONG OF THE SOUTH. Very much in the Bakshi vein; uneven but worth a look. Video title: STREET FIGHT. [R]▼

Cop (1987) **C-110m.** **½ D: James B. Harris. James Woods, Lesley Ann Warren, Charles Durning, Charles Haid, Raymond J. Barry, Randi Brooks, Annie McEnroe, Vicki Wauchope. Woods is excellent as usual in this otherwise familiar drama about a dedicated cop, his troubled marriage, and the difficulties he encounters while on a murder case. Woods and Harris coproduced. [R]▼●◗

Copacabana (1947) **92m.** ** D: Alfred E. Green. Groucho Marx, Carmen Miranda, Andy Russell, Steve Cochran, Gloria Jean, Louis Sobol, Abel Green, Earl Wilson. Potentially intriguing Marx-Miranda casting can't save this unengrossing musical comedy. Groucho is a Broadway agent attempting to promote Carmen, his only client, resulting in her being hired for two jobs (in two different guises) at the same nightclub. This was Groucho's first film without his brothers. Also shown in computer-colored version. ▼●◗

Cop & ½ (1993) **C-93m.** BOMB D: Henry Winkler. Burt Reynolds, Norman D. Golden II, Ruby Dee, Holland Taylor, Ray Sharkey, Sammy Hernandez, Frank Sivero. And a hemorrhoid-and-a-half to anyone who sits all the way through it. Circumstances (read: scriptwriter's contrivance) dictate that a cop-addicted black kid become the new partner of a white detective who's trying to crack a drug punk. Abjectly painful comedy. Low point: a urination bonding scene with Reynolds in which the youngster wants to "make swords." [PG]▼●◗

Cop au Vin (1984-French) **C-110m.** ***½ D: Claude Chabrol. Jean Poiret, Stephane Audran, Michel Bouquet, Jean Topart, Lucas Belvaux, Pauline Lafont. Chabrol is in fine form in this diverting, neatly paced thriller about a young mail boy, his widowed, invalid mother, and a greedy trio who attempt to evict them from their home. Murder brings a shrewd cop on the scene to investigate. Followed by a sequel, INSPECTEUR LAVARDIN.◗

Cop Killers SEE: Corrupt

Cop Land (1997) **C-105m.** **½ D: James Mangold. Sylvester Stallone, Harvey Keitel, Ray Liotta, Robert De Niro, Peter Berg, Janeane Garofalo, Robert Patrick, Michael Rapaport, Annabella Sciorra, Noah Emmerich, Cathy Moriarty, John Spencer, Frank Vincent, Malik Yoba, Bruce Altman, Edie Falco, Tony Sirico, Deborah Harry. Stallone plays a sheriff who's eaten a few too many donuts and is responsible for looking the other way in a New Jersey town inhabited almost exclusively by N.Y.C. cops who exist, it seems, above the law. Keitel is their ringleader, De Niro an Internal Affairs officer on his trail. A solid premise, and a riveting start, give way to increasingly conventional (and predictable) plotting by writer-director Mangold. [R]▼●◗

Cop-Out (1967-British) **C-95m.** **½ D: Pierre Rouve. James Mason, Geraldine Chaplin, Bobby Darin, Paul Bertoya, Ian Ogilvy, Bryan Stanton. OK murder mystery with dated generation-gap overtones. Reclusive lawyer Mason comes out of retirement to defend his daughter's boyfriend on trumped-up murder charge. Remake of 1942 French film STRANGER IN THE HOUSE.

Cop Out (2010) **C-113m.** BOMB D: Kevin Smith. Bruce Willis, Tracy Morgan, Adam Brody, Kevin Pollak, Guillermo Díaz, Seann William Scott, Jason Lee, Rashida Jones, Michelle Trachtenberg, Ana de la Reguera, Cory Fernandez, Susie Essman, Fred Armisen, Francie Swift. Crude, needlessly overlong, thoroughly excruciating cop/buddy "comedy" about two Brooklyn officers who play by their own rules. While going after a local drug ring, Willis is trying to figure out how he's going to pay for his daughter's wedding, and Morgan is convinced that his wife is cheating on him. Annoying music score is icing on the cake. Super 35. [R] ◗

Copper Canyon (1950) **C-83m.** **½ D: John Farrow. Ray Milland, Hedy Lamarr, Macdonald Carey, Mona Freeman, Harry Carey, Jr., Frank Faylen, Hope Emerson, Percy Helton. OK Western of post-Civil War days, with Confederate vet Milland faced with decision to assist fellow Southerners who are being harassed as they attempt to mine copper. Lamarr plays the femme fatale.▼●◗

Cops and Robbers (1973) **C-89m.** *** D: Aram Avakian. Cliff Gorman, Joseph Bologna, Dick Ward, Shepperd Strudwick, John P. Ryan, Ellen Holly, Dolph Sweet, Joe Spinell. Enjoyable Donald Westlake tale about two policemen who pull a million-dollar caper on Wall Street. Funny and exciting, with good location photography by David L. Quaid. [PG]▼◗

Cops and Robbersons (1994) **C-93m.** ** D: Michael Ritchie. Chevy Chase, Jack Palance, Dianne Wiest, Robert Davi, David Barry Gray, Jason James Richter, Fay Masterson, Mike Hughes, Richard Romanus. Veteran cop Palance and a young cohort need to borrow Chase's house to stake out a lowlife who's living next door; this, it turns out, is a dream come true for Chevy, who's addicted to TV cop shows and fancies himself a hero. Premise of a baby boomer living out his pop-culture fantasies echoes CITY SLICKERS (Palance included) but isn't nearly as good. [PG]▼●◗

Copycat (1995) **C-125m.** *** D: Jon Amiel. Sigourney Weaver, Holly Hunter, Dermot Mulroney, Harry Connick, Jr., William McNamara, Will Patton, John Rothman, J. E. Freeman. Psychiatrist (Weaver) who's an expert on serial killers—and now traumatized into an agoraphobic existence—joins forces with dedicated cops Hunter and Mulroney to track down the latest (and smartest) murderer in San Francisco. Slickly made, tense and entertaining, although it, like the concurrent SE7EN, forces us to get to know a sick mind better than we might care to. And like many visceral thrillers, it will not stand up to intense scrutiny. Panavision. [R]▼●◗

Copying Beethoven (2006-British-Hungarian) **C-103m.** ** D: Agnieszka Holland. Ed Harris, Diane Kruger, Matthew Goode, Phyllida Law, Joe Anderson, Ralph Riach, Karl Johnson, Nicholas Jones. Fictionalized depiction of an aged, maniacal Ludwig van Beethoven and the female (!) copyist trying to transcribe his Ninth Symphony while suffering his tirades. Harris, in his third teaming with director Holland, manages to be at once solid and hammy as the deaf maestro; Kruger is fine. Best to forget the histrionic subplots and enjoy the climax: the 1824 premiere of the "Ode to Joy" as conducted by its composer. Super 35. [PG-13]◗

Coraline (2009) **C-100m.** ***½ D: Henry Selick. Voices of Dakota Fanning, Teri Hatcher, John Hodgman, Jennifer Saunders, Dawn French, Keith David, Ian McShane, Robert Bailey, Jr. Deliciously original stop-motion animated feature about a girl who's just moved into a rambling old house with her parents and is feeling neglected. She discovers a doorway to an alternate world, where her Other Mother offers everything she's missing in real life—but, as she learns, it all comes at a terrible price. Intriguingly creepy and constantly surprising. Director Selick adapted Neil Gaiman's best-selling book and also did the amazing production design, which looks especially striking in 3-D. [PG] ◗

Core, The (2003) **C-136m.** *** D: Jon Amiel. Aaron Eckhart, Hilary Swank, Delroy Lindo, Stanley Tucci, DJ Qualls, Richard Jenkins, Tchéky Karyo, Bruce Greenwood, Alfre Woodard. Strange, seemingly isolated events around the world portend a larger disaster as the earth's electromagnetic field is deteriorating. The only solution involves a perilous journey to the earth's core, which requires the efforts of a motley band of scientific specialists. Exciting, old-fashioned Saturday-matinee film, packed with vivid special effects sequences; transcends its obvious formula with ample humor, colorfully written characters, and a first-rate cast. Panavision. [PG-13]▼◗

Corky (1972) **C-88m.** **½ D: Leonard Horn. Robert Blake, Charlotte Rampling,

Patrick O'Neal, Christopher Connelly, Ben Johnson, Laurence Luckinbill. Blake's obsession for stock-car racing shuts out everything else in his life, including wife and friends. Good racing sequences, fairly absorbing character study. Originally titled LOOKIN' GOOD. Panavision. [PG]

Corky Romano (2001) C-85m. BOMB D: Rob Pritts. Chris Kattan, Vinessa Shaw, Peter Falk, Peter Berg, Chris Penn, Fred Ward, Zach Galifianakis, Richard Roundtree. Dreadful comedy from the "idiot as hero" genre. Hyperkinetic Kattan (funny only in small doses) plays the wayward son of a Mob family who's forced to infiltrate the FBI to destroy evidence that would convict his father, Pops Romano (Falk). Clumsy in every department. Super 35. [PG-13] ▼ ▶

Cornbread, Earl and Me (1975) C-95m. **½ D: Joe Manduke. Moses Gunn, Bernie Casey, Rosalind Cash, Madge Sinclair, Keith Wilkes, Tierre Turner, Larry Fishburne. Well-intentioned but overly melodramatic account of a black youth, on his way out of the ghetto on a basketball scholarship, who is mistakenly gunned down by police bullets. Fine performances and warm sense of black life evaporate in TV clichés. Fishburne's film debut. [PG] ▼ ▶

Cornered (1945) 102m. *** D: Edward Dmytryk. Dick Powell, Walter Slezak, Micheline Cheirel, Nina Vale, Morris Carnovsky, Luther Adler. High-tension drama with determined Canadian flyer Powell in Buenos Aires, tracking down the man responsible for the death of his French bride during WW2. Powell is in peak form. Also shown in computer-colored version. ▼ ▶

Corn Is Green, The (1945) 114m. ***½ D: Irving Rapper. Bette Davis, Nigel Bruce, John Dall, Joan Lorring, Rhys Williams, Rosalind Ivan, Mildred Dunnock. Thoughtful acting in this story of devoted middle-aged teacher Davis in Welsh mining town coming to terms with her prize pupil. Emlyn Williams' play was adapted by Casey Robinson and Frank Cavett. Remade, beautifully, for TV with Katharine Hepburn in 1979. ▼

Corporate Affairs (1990) C-82m. *½ D: Terence Winkless. Peter Scolari, Mary Crosby, Chris Lemmon, Ken Kercheval, Richard Herd, Lisa Moncure, Kim Gillingham, Bryan Cranston. Doomed attempt to cross-pollinate WEEKEND AT BERNIE'S with WORKING GIRL. Scolari takes advantage of former lover Crosby when she gives CEO Kercheval a heart attack during a tryst. But is he really dead? Somehow enormous amounts of t&a are shown to advantage in a concurrent office orgy. [R] ▼ ▶

Corporation, The (2004-Canada) C-145m. ***½ D: Jennifer Abbott, Mark Achbar. Fascinating documentary presents a history of corporations, from the time courts granted them great power during the industrial revolution up to the present day, when private industry seems to have more influence on the workings of the world than governments. Hardly unbiased, but well researched and persuasive, including interviews with everyone from Michael Moore and Noam Chomsky to a CEO who underwent a major change of heart and now tries to convince his fellow executives that they cannot destroy the environment in the name of profit. Ambitious, eye-opening film based on the book by Joel Bakan; written by Bakan and Achbar. ▶

Corpse Bride SEE: **Tim Burton's Corpse Bride**

Corridors of Blood (1962-British) 86m. **½ D: Robert Day. Boris Karloff, Betta St. John, Finlay Currie, Christopher Lee, Francis Matthews, Adrienne Corri, Nigel Green. Middling account of 19th-century British doctor who experiments with anesthetics, becomes addicted to the narcotics, and winds up consorting with grave-robbers to continue his experiments. Filmed in 1958. ▼ ▶

Corrina, Corrina (1994) C-114m. *** D: Jessie Nelson. Whoopi Goldberg, Ray Liotta, Tina Majorino, Don Ameche, Wendy Crewson, Larry Miller, Erica Yohn, Jenifer Lewis, Joan Cusack, Harold Sylvester, Steven Williams, Patrika Darbo, Lucy Webb. Sweet-natured film about a young widower who hires a housekeeper to help take care of his daughter—little dreaming how important she'll become to both of them. As a document of social mores in the late 1950s this has its ups and downs, but endearing performances and upbeat point of view make it good entertainment. Written by the director. [PG] ▼ ▶

Corrupt (1983-Italian) C-99m. *** D: Roberto Faenza. Harvey Keitel, Nicole Garcia, Leonard Mann, John Lydon, Sylvia Sidney. Intriguing, entertaining psychological thriller about N.Y.C. policeman Keitel, his victimization by mysterious Lydon, and a hunt for a cop killer. Lydon used to be known as Johnny Rotten (of the punk rock group, The Sex Pistols). Fine performances; originally titled ORDER OF DEATH, with a 113m. running time, and also known as COP KILLERS and CORRUPT LIEUTENANT. [R] ▼ ▶

Corruption (1968-British) C-91m. ** D: Robert Hartford-Davis. Peter Cushing, Sue Lloyd, Noel Trevarthen, David Lodge, Kate O'Mara. Famed surgeon Cushing slowly becomes insane as he stops at nothing, including murder, to restore the disfigured face of his fashion model fiancée (Lloyd). Predictable, formulaic horror opus. [R]

Corrupt Lieutenant SEE: **Corrupt**

Corrupt Ones, The (1966-French-Italian-West German) C-92m. **½ D: James Hill. Robert Stack, Elke Sommer, Nancy Kwan, Christian Marquand, Werner Peters. Knock-about photographer Stack is befriended by stranger who gives him key (literally!) to ancient Chinese emperor's treasure. With better dialogue for its many grotesque characters, film could've been a knockout. Techniscope.▼

Corruptor, The (1999) **C-110m.** ** D: James Foley. Chow Yun-Fat, Mark Wahlberg, Ric Young, Paul Ben-Victor, Jon Kit Lee, Andrew Pang, Brian Cox, Elizabeth Lindsey, Byron Mann, Kim Chan, Tovah Feldshuh. Wahlberg is assigned to the otherwise all-Chinese NYPD Asian gang unit and gradually wins the trust of Yun-Fat, leader of the task force. However, not everyone is as honest as they seem. Routine cop action film enlivened—but not enough—by Yun-Fat's sizzling star performance and Wahlberg's solid work. Lee is both silky and slimy in the title role. Super 35. [R]▼O❍

Corsican Brothers, The (1941) **112m.** *** D: Gregory Ratoff. Douglas Fairbanks, Jr., Ruth Warrick, Akim Tamiroff, J. Carrol Naish, H. B. Warner, Henry Wilcoxon. Entertaining swashbuckler from Dumas story of twins who are separated, but remain spiritually tied. Fairbanks excellent in the dual lead, with strong support, ingenious photographic effects. Remade for TV in 1985.▼

Corvette Summer (1978) **C-105m.** ** D: Matthew Robbins. Mark Hamill, Annie Potts, Eugene Roche, Kim Milford, Richard McKenzie, William Bryant. High schooler Hamill falls for aspiring hooker Potts while in Vegas tracking down the person who stole the sports car restored by his shop class. Bland comedy drama offers Potts' disarmingly off-the-wall performance to keep your attention. [PG]▼❒

Così (1996-Australian) **C-100m.** ** D: Mark Joffe. Ben Mendelsohn, Barry Otto, Toni Collette, Rachel Griffiths, Aden Young, Colin Friels. Professionally unfulfilled drifter with a stable law school girlfriend makes a desperate career move when he agrees to stage Mozart's *Così Fan Tutte* as part of a therapy session for Sydney mental inmates. Unusual but eventually tiresome comedy, from Louis Nowra's play, features lots of familiar faces (to fans of Australian cinema) in supporting roles. Greta Scacchi and Paul Mercurio appear unbilled. [R]▼O❍

Cosmic Eye, The (1985) **C-76m.** *** D: Faith Hubley. Voices of Maureen Stapleton, Dizzy Gillespie, Sam Hubley, Linda Atkinson. Wonderfully imaginative, life-affirming animated feature about the needs, rights, and struggles of mankind, most especially children, around the world. A tapestry that includes pieces of earlier animated shorts by John and Faith Hubley, with music by such notables as Dizzy Gillespie, Benny Carter, and Elizabeth Swados.▼O❍

Cote d'Azur (2005-French) **C-90m.** **½ D: Olivier Ducastel, Jacques Martineau.

Valéria Bruni-Tedeschi, Gilbert Melki, Jean-Marc Barr, Jacques Bonnaffé, Edouard Collin, Romain Torres, Sabrina Seyvecou. One randy summer in an old family house on the Riviera, where vacationing parents, progeny, tag-alongs, and old flames all collide in a simmering stew of middle-age lust and teenage hormones. Several overheated characters plus a lot of bedrooms and a shower stall . . . you do le math. Breezy but insubstantial scenario is wistfully unreal, a demi-musical (!) with singing, dancing, and experimental romancing. Written by the directors.❒

Cotter (1973) **C-94m.** **½ D: Paul Stanley. Don Murray, Carol Lynley, Rip Torn, Sherry Jackson. After tragic rodeo incident, unhappy Indian clown (Murray) struggles to reestablish himself in home town. Good cast in fair script that fares best in creating small-town atmosphere.▼❒

Cotton Club, The (1984) **C-127m.** **½ D: Francis Coppola. Richard Gere, Gregory Hines, Diane Lane, Lonette McKee, Bob Hoskins, James Remar, Nicolas Cage, Allen Garfield, Fred Gwynne, Gwen Verdon, Maurice Hines, Joe Dallesandro, Julian Beck, Jennifer Grey, Lisa Jane Persky, Tom Waits, Diane Venora, Woody Strode, Charles "Honi" Coles, Larry Fishburne, James Russo, Giancarlo Esposito. Homage to the days of colorful gangsters and Harlem nightlife has style to spare and a wonderful soundtrack full of Duke Ellington music (Gere plays his own cornet solos); all it needs is a story and characters whose relationships make some sense. Visually striking with good scenes scattered about. Not nearly as interesting as the published stories about its tumultuous production! [R]▼O❍

Cotton Comes to Harlem (1970) **C-97m.** *** D: Ossie Davis. Godfrey Cambridge, Raymond St. Jacques, Calvin Lockhart, Judy Pace, Redd Foxx, Emily Yancy, Cleavon Little. St. Jacques is Coffin Ed Johnson, Cambridge is Gravedigger Jones, black cops who suspect preacher Lockhart's back-to-Africa campaign is a swindle. Neatly combines action and comedy, with fine use of Harlem locales; from Chester Himes' novel. Sequel: COME BACK, CHARLESTON BLUE. [R]▼❒

Cotton Mary (1999-French-British-U.S.) **C-124m.** *½ D: Ismail Merchant. Greta Scacchi, Madhur Jaffrey, James Wilby, Sakina Jaffrey, Neena Gupta, Prayag Raaj, Laura Lumley, Gemma Jones, Sarah Badel. Stultifying drama, set in India in 1954, in which the Anglo-Indian title character manipulates her way into a British household and causes all sorts of tumult. Potentially interesting story of the clash between British and Indian cultures is full of obvious symbolism; a real snooze. Madhur Jaffrey (who plays Cotton Mary) is listed in the credits as "co-director." [R]▼❒

Couch in New York, A (1996-Belgian-

French-German) **C-105m.** *½ D: Chantal Akerman. Juliette Binoche, William Hurt, Stephanie Buttle, Barbara Garrick, Paul Guilfoyle, Richard Jenkins, Kent Broadhurst. N.Y.C. therapist Hurt, in desperate need of a change of scenery, switches apartments with Parisian dancer Binoche. Flat, uninspired romantic comedy. [R]▼●)

Couch Trip, The (1988) **C-97m.** **½ D: Michael Ritchie. Dan Aykroyd, Walter Matthau, Charles Grodin, Donna Dixon, Richard Romanus, Arye Gross, David Clennon, Mary Gross. Amusing, if somewhat lackluster, comedy about a mental institution escapee who masquerades as a successful Beverly Hills psychiatrist and radio adviser. Some good laughs, served by a solid cast, but the story is pretty thin. [R]▼●)

Countdown (1968) **C-101m.** ***½ D: Robert Altman. James Caan, Joanna Moore, Robert Duvall, Barbara Baxley, Charles Aidman, Steve Ihnat, Michael Murphy, Ted Knight. Near-flawless depiction of real-life trials and concerns of American astronauts, their wives, co-workers, leading to first flight to moon. Excellent ensemble performances, intelligent script by Loring Mandel, based on Hank Searls' novel. Dated technology only liability. An early gem from Altman. Look fast for Mike Farrell. Panavision.▼●)

Countdown at Kusini (1976-Nigerian) **C-101m.** ** D: Ossie Davis. Ruby Dee, Ossie Davis, Greg Morris, Tom Aldredge, Michael Ebert, Thomas Baptiste. Well-meaning treatment of liberation of fictional African country, "Fahari." Action and ideas are constantly swallowed up by romantic subplot. Financed by DST Telecommunications, subsidiary of Delta Sigma Theta, world's largest black sorority. [PG]▼

Count Dracula (1970-Italian-Spanish-German) **C-98m.** **½ D: Jess Franco. Christopher Lee, Herbert Lom, Klaus Kinski, Frederick Williams, Maria Rohm, Soledad Miranda. Flawed but interesting low-budget adaptation of Bram Stoker novel which sticks close to its source; Lee turns in remarkably low-key performance. [PG]▼)

Count Dracula and His Vampire Bride (1973-British) **C-84m.** *½ D: Alan Gibson. Christopher Lee, Peter Cushing, Michael Coles, William Franklyn, Freddie Jones, Joanna Lumley. Lee's last Hammer film as Dracula is awfully tired, despite modern-day setting; the Count gets hold of a plague virus that can destroy mankind. Cut for U.S. release from original 88m. version called THE SATANIC RITES OF DRACULA. Video title: THE RITES OF DRACULA. [R]▼●)

Counterfeiters, The (2007-Austrian-German) **C-98m.** ***½ D: Stefan Ruzowitzky. Karl Markovics, August Diehl, Devid Striesow, Martin Brambach, August Zirner, Veit Stübner. Cocky and talented Russian-Jewish counterfeiter is sent to the Sachsen-

hausen concentration camp to participate in Operation Bernhard, to help the Third Reich bring down the British and American economies by printing millions of phony pound notes and dollars. Chilling portrait of a man who pretends to care only about himself and the price he pays for survival. Based on an incredible true story; Ruzowitzky adapted the book by Adolf Burger, one of the protagonist's fellow prisoners (played here by Diehl). Oscar winner as Best Foreign Language Film. [R]▶)

Counterfeit Killer, The (1968) **C-95m.** ** D: Josef Leytes. Jack Lord, Shirley Knight, Jack Weston, Charles Drake, Joseph Wiseman, Don Hanmer. Adapted from TV film THE FACELESS MAN, meandering actioner has Lord a secret service man infiltrating a counterfeit syndicate, with predictable results. Video title: CRACKSHOT.▼

Counterfeit Traitor, The (1962) **C-140m.** ***½ D: George Seaton. William Holden, Lilli Palmer, Hugh Griffith, Erica Beer, Werner Peters, Eva Dahlbeck. Holden is a double agent during WW2, falls in love with Palmer between various dangerous missions. Authentic backgrounds and fine cast. Based on true story.▼●)

Counterpoint (1968) **C-107m.** *½ D: Ralph Nelson. Charlton Heston, Maximilian Schell, Kathryn Hays, Leslie Nielsen, Anton Diffring. Absurd WW2 melodrama about symphony conductor captured by Nazi general, forced to put on private concert; Heston looks comfortable because he doesn't have to change facial expressions while conducting. Techniscope.

Counter Punch SEE: **Ripped Off**

Counter Tenors, The SEE: **White Voices**

Countess Dracula (1970-British) **C-94m.** ** D: Peter Sasdy. Ingrid Pitt, Nigel Green, Peter Jeffrey, Lesley-Anne Down. Countess masquerades as her own daughter, needs blood to maintain facade of youth. OK shocker. Based on historical figure Elisabeth Bathory; has nothing to do with Dracula. ▼●)

Countess From Hong Kong, A (1967-British) **C-108m.** *½ D: Charles Chaplin. Marlon Brando, Sophia Loren, Sydney Chaplin, Tippi Hedren, Patrick Cargill, Margaret Rutherford. Director-writer-composer (and bit-part actor) Chaplin's attempt to make old-fashioned romantic comedy sinks fast, though everybody tries hard. Sophia stows away in shipboard stateroom of diplomat Brando. Badly shot, badly timed, badly scored. A pity, particularly because this is Chaplin's cinematic swan song.▼▶)

Count of Monte Cristo, The (2002-British-Irish-U.S.) **C-131m.** *** D: Kevin Reynolds. Jim Caviezel, Guy Pearce, Richard Harris, Dagmara Dominczyk, Michael Wincott, Luis Guzmán, James Frain, Alex Norton. Surprisingly good version of the Dumas evergreen, with Caviezel an impressive Edmond Dantes, who is unjustly imprisoned and vows revenge against those who wronged him. Final section of the story succumbs to the obvious, but overall a nice job. Harris is a standout as Dantes' fellow prisoner. Debut screenplay for veteran TV producer Jay Wolpert. Super 35. [PG-13] ▼⏺

Country (1984) **C-109m.** *** D: Richard Pearce. Jessica Lange, Sam Shepard, Wilford Brimley, Matt Clark, Therese Graham, Levi L. Knebel. Penetrating, believable look at modern farming family torn apart when government threatens to foreclose on loan and take their land away. It's the woman whose strength holds things together (and it's Lange who coproduced the film); all performances are first rate, and William D. Wittliff's script neatly avoids clichés. [PG] ▼⏺⏺

Country Bears, The (2002) **C-88m.** ** D: Peter Hastings. Christopher Walken, Stephen Tobolowsky, Daryl "Chill" Mitchell, M. C. Gainey, Diedrich Bader, Alex Rocco, Meagen Fay, Queen Latifah, Eli Marienthal; voices of Haley Joel Osment, James Gammon, Brad Garrett, Kevin Michael Richardson, Toby Huss, Stephen Root, Diedrich Bader. "Inspired by" a Disneyland attraction, this lazy excuse for a kid film has a young bear (who's been adopted by a human family) going back to his roots, and helping a legendary music group to stage a reunion and rescue their performance hall. If they spent more time on the script and less time setting up cameo appearances (Willie Nelson, Bonnie Raitt, Elton John, etc.) it might have been better. [G] ▼⏺

Country Dance SEE: **Brotherly Love**
Country Girl, The (1954) **104m.** ***½ D: George Seaton. Bing Crosby, Grace Kelly, William Holden, Anthony Ross. Kelly won an Oscar as wife of alcoholic singer (Crosby) trying for comeback via help of director (Holden). Crosby excels in one of his finest roles. Writer-director Seaton also won Academy Award for adaptation of Clifford Odets play. Remade for cable TV in 1982. ▼⏺

Country Life (1995-Australian) **C-107m.** *** D: Michael Blakemore. Sam Neill, Greta Scacchi, John Hargreaves, Kerry Fox, Michael Blakemore, Googie Withers, Maurie Fields, Robyn Cruze, Ron Blanchard. Chekhov's *Uncle Vanya* is transposed to an Australian sheep farm, circa WW1, and the result is absolutely delightful. Colonial Aussies simultaneously crave and clash with European sensibilities, especially when the enigmatic paterfamilias Alexander (a wickedly fun role, played by writer-director Blakemore) returns from London with the stunning Scacchi in tow. Subtle comedy, high drama, and a great deal of aroused passions ensue. And, yes, that's Britain's Googie Withers (longtime resident of Australia) as Hannah the maid—stealing every scene she's in. [PG-13] ▼⏺⏺

Country Strong (2010) **C-117m.** ** D: Shana Feste. Gwyneth Paltrow, Tim McGraw, Garrett Hedlund, Leighton Meester, Marshall Chapman. Labored soap opera about a country singer (Paltrow) whose husband (McGraw) springs her from rehab prematurely and puts her on the road—along with a talented singer-songwriter (Hedlund) who genuinely cares about her. Also on the tour is a pretty young thing (Meester) who catches everyone's eye, including Paltrow, who's jealous of her both personally and professionally. Characters' erratic behavior makes this a long slog, punctuated by a number of agreeable songs. Super 35. [PG-13] ▌

Count the Hours (1953) **76m.** ** D: Don Siegel. Teresa Wright, Macdonald Carey, Dolores Moran, Adele Mara, Jack Elam. Lawyer Carey takes case of migrant worker falsely accused of a double murder. Trim, well-directed (if implausible) story; Elam is at his slimiest as an alcoholic psycho.

Count Three and Pray (1955) **C-102m.** **½ D: George Sherman. Van Heflin, Joanne Woodward, Raymond Burr, Nancy Kulp. Atmospheric rural Americana in post-Civil War days, with Heflin exerting influence on townsfolk as new pastor with reckless past. Woodward (making film debut) as strongwilled orphan lass and Burr, the perennial villain, are fine. CinemaScope.

Count Yorga, Vampire (1970) **C-91m.** *** D: Bob Kelljan. Robert Quarry, Roger Perry, Donna Anders, Michael Murphy, Michael Macready. Sophisticated, clever vampire (Quarry) establishes coven in modern-day Southern California. Fast-paced and convincing. Alternate version, THE LOVES OF COUNT IORGA, VAMPIRE is rated PG-13. Sequel: THE RETURN OF COUNT YORGA. [PG] ▼⏺⏺

Count Your Blessings (1959) **C-102m.** ** D: Jean Negulesco. Deborah Kerr, Rossano Brazzi, Maurice Chevalier, Martin Stephens, Tom Helmore, Patricia Medina. Unfunny comedy that even Chevalier's smile can't help. Kerr marries French playboy Brazzi during WW2; he goes off philandering for years. Their child conspires to bring them together again. CinemaScope.

Count Your Bullets SEE: **Cry For Me, Billy**
Coup de Foudre SEE: **Entre Nous**
Coup de Grace (1976-French-German) **96m.** ** D: Volker Schlöndorff. Margarethe von Trotta, Matthias Habich, Rudiger Kirschstein, Valeska Gert. Disappointing tale of a self-destructive countess (von Trotta, wife of the director), who wastes her life because the officer she loves does not reciprocate her feelings. Bleak, sometimes confusing film, not as emotional or involving as it should be. ▼▌

Coup de Torchon (1981-French) **C-128m.** ***½ D: Bertrand Tavernier. Philippe Noiret, Isabelle Huppert, Stephane Audran, Irene Skobline, Eddy Mitchell, Jean-Pierre

Marielle, Guy Marchand. Strong, disturbing black comedy, based on a novel by American Jim Thompson that reset in 1936 Equatorial Africa. Easygoing police chief (Noiret) of small colonial town is a doormat for everyone in sight, especially his wife; he gradually realizes he can use his position to gain vengeance with impunity. Fascinating film eventually overplays its hand, but enthralling most of the way, with marvelously shaded performance by Noiret. Aka CLEAN SLATE. ▼●)

Coupe de Ville (1990) **C-99m.** ** ·D: Joe Roth. Patrick Dempsey, Arye Gross, Daniel Stern, Alan Arkin, Annabeth Gish, Rita Taggart, Joseph Bologna, James Gammon. Obvious, forgettable formula tale of three warring brothers forced to deal with their feelings as they drive dad Arkin's car from Detroit to Florida. Set in 1963 and—guess what?—there are oldies on the soundtrack. Still, the sequence in which the boys debate the origin of, and words to, "Louie, Louie" is almost worth the price of admission. Super 35. [PG-13] ▼●

Couples Retreat (2009) **C-113m.** **½ D: Peter Billingsley. Vince Vaughn, Jon Favreau, Jason Bateman, Faizon Love, Malin Akerman, Kristen Bell, Kristin Davis, Kali Hawk, Jean Reno, Tasha Smith, Carlos Ponce, Peter Serafinowicz, Temuera Morrison, John Michael Higgins, Ken Jeong. Bateman and Bell, trying to save their marriage, strong-arm three sets of friends to accompany them to a tropical resort for a week—unaware that rigorous therapy sessions are part of the regimen. The setting (French Polynesia) is beautiful, and so are the women, so this is pleasant enough to watch, but it's also surprisingly bland and predictable. Written by Vaughn, Favreau, and Dana Fox (who also plays a waitress). [PG-13]❙

Courage Mountain (1989-U.S.-French) **C-98m.** **½ D: Christopher Leitch. Juliette Caton, Charlie Sheen, Leslie Caron, Joanna Clarke, Nicola Stapleton, Jade Magri, Kathryn Ludlow, Jan Rubes, Yorgo Voyagis. Implausible though inoffensive updating of Johanna Spyri's *Heidi*, detailing what happens when the teenage girl is sent off to boarding school at the outset of WW1. Sheen is sorely miscast as Peter, her ever-loyal beau. [PG] ▼●)

Courage of Lassie (1946) **C-92m.** **½ D: Fred Wilcox. Elizabeth Taylor, Frank Morgan, Tom Drake, Selena Royle, George Cleveland, Carl (Alfalfa) Switzer. Third of the MGM Lassie movies has a radiant Taylor trying to rehabilitate the collie after his combat experiences during WW2. Despite title, the dog in question is called Bill, not Lassie, though played by the same collie who starred in the other studio films. Filmed on beautiful locations in Canada.▼❙

Courage Under Fire (1996) **C-115m.**

***½ D: Edward Zwick. Denzel Washington, Meg Ryan, Lou Diamond Phillips, Michael Moriarty, Sean Astin, Matt Damon, Seth Gilliam, Tim Guinee, Scott Glenn, Bronson Pinchot, Kathleen Widdoes, Diane Baker. Compelling tale of a career Army officer, troubled by Persian Gulf War incident in which he was involved in an accidental death. Now he's assigned to investigate the death of a female Captain (Ryan) nominated for the Medal of Honor. In RASHOMON-like flashbacks, we learn that there's more to her story than meets the eye. Intelligent, multilayered story (by Patrick Sheane Duncan) about integrity, personal honor, and public hypocrisy. [R] ▼●

Court Jester, The (1956) **C-101m.** ****
D: Norman Panama, Melvin Frank. Danny Kaye, Glynis Johns, Basil Rathbone, Angela Lansbury, Cecil Parker, Mildred Natwick, Robert Middleton, John Carradine. One of the best comedies ever made has Danny as phony jester who finds himself involved in romance, court intrigue, and a deadly joust. Delightfully complicated comic situations (scripted by the directors), superbly performed. And remember: the pellet with the poison's in the vessel with the pestle. VistaVision.▼●❙

Court Martial (1954-British) **105m.** ***
D: Anthony Asquith. David Niven, Margaret Leighton, Victor Maddern, Maurice Denham. Tense courtroom story of officer Niven accused of stealing military funds. The trial reveals provocations of grasping wife. A solid drama. Originally released as CARRINGTON, V.C.▼

Court-Martial of Billy Mitchell, The (1955) **C-100m.** *** D: Otto Preminger. Gary Cooper, Charles Bickford, Ralph Bellamy, Rod Steiger, Elizabeth Montgomery, Fred Clark, James Daly, Jack Lord, Peter Graves, Darren McGavin. Low-key drama about trial of military pioneer who in 1925 predicted Japanese attack on U.S. Steiger adds spark to slowly paced film as wily attorney; Montgomery made her movie debut here. CinemaScope.▼●

Courtship of Eddie's Father, The (1963) **C-117m.** *** D: Vincente Minnelli. Glenn Ford, Ronny Howard, Shirley Jones, Stella Stevens, Dina Merrill, Roberta Sherwood, Jerry Van Dyke. Cute family comedy with Howard trying to find wife for widower father Ford. Look sharp for Lee Meriwether as Glenn's assistant. Later a TV series. Panavision. ▼●

Cousin Bette (1998) **C-108m.** **½ D: Des McAnuff. Jessica Lange, Bob Hoskins, Elisabeth Shue, Hugh Laurie, Aden Young, Geraldine Chaplin, Laura Fraser, Toby Stephens, Kelly Macdonald, Janie Hargreaves, John Sessions, John Benfield. Lange sees her chance for revenge after a lifetime of mistreatment when her beautiful, pampered cousin dies and Lange becomes part of the cousin's household. But her plans go awry as each person in her scheme pursues his or her own selfish agenda. Venomously witty black comedy from the Balzac novel, set in 1840s Paris, dulls its impact by taking a few turns too many. Shue is ideal as a sexy, self-absorbed soubrette. Panavision. [R] ▼●]

Cousin Bobby (1991) C-70m. ***½ D: Jonathan Demme. Highly personal, intelligent documentary about director Demme looking up his cousin after many years, and learning about his work. The Reverend Robert Castle is a Harlem priest who is steadfastly devoted to his parishioners, and long committed to radical political activism. A fascinating portrait of a complex individual, and of his evolving relationship with his filmmaker cousin. ▼

Cousin, Cousine (1975-French) C-95m. *** D: Jean-Charles Tacchella. Marie-Christine Barrault, Victor Lanoux, Marie-France Pisier, Guy Marchand, Ginette Garcin, Sybil Maas. Barrault and Lanoux, married to others, become cousins by marriage and decide to go way beyond the kissing stage. Mild, easy-to-take comedy that became a surprise box-office sensation in U.S.—where it was later remade as COUSINS. [R] ▼●

Cousins, The (1959-French) 112m. ***½ D: Claude Chabrol. Jean-Claude Brialy, Gerard Blain, Juliette Mayniel, Claude Cerval, Genevieve Cluny. Complex, depressing, ultimately haunting tale of youthful disillusion, with decadent city boy Brialy and provincial cousin Blain competing for the affection of beauty Mayniel. Superbly directed by Chabrol. ▼]

Cousins (1989) C-110m. *** D: Joel Schumacher. Ted Danson, Isabella Rossellini, Sean Young, William Petersen, Lloyd Bridges, Norma Aleandro, Keith Coogan. A big family wedding sets the stage for romantic intrigues within two colorful clans. Highly enjoyable Americanization of the French hit COUSIN, COUSINE with charming performances by Danson, as a free-spirited soul, and Rossellini, as the married cousin to whom he's attracted. [PG-13] ▼●]

Cove, The (2009) C-94m. ***½ D: Louie Psihoyos. Disquieting, Oscar-winning documentary about fishermen who entice dolphins into an isolated cove off the coast of Taiji, Japan, then cruelly torture and kill them—all in the name of profit. Filmmaker (and *National Geographic* photographer) Psihoyos, *Flipper* dolphin trainer-turned-activist Richard O'Barry, and others endanger themselves as they set out to document the practice. As riveting as a Hollywood thriller, except its content is jarring, heartbreaking fact. [PG-13]]

Covenant, The (2006-U.S.-Canadian) C-97m. **½ D: Renny Harlin. Steven Strait, Sebastian Stan, Laura Ramsey, Taylor Kitsch, Toby Hemingway, Jessica Lucas, Chace Crawford, Wendy Crewson, Kyle Schmid, Kenneth Welsh. A quartet of teen-boy warlocks, descended from powerful Salem witches, admits a mysterious fifth member into their enchanted group, with the expected blast of repercussions. The dudes' misuse of debilitating magical powers is a heavy-handed allegory of drug addiction, but the theme still resonates. Something of a guys-in-Speedos movie, but darkly atmospheric. Super 35. [PG-13]]

Cover Girl (1944) C-107m. *** D: Charles Vidor. Rita Hayworth, Gene Kelly, Lee Bowman, Phil Silvers, Jinx Falkenburg, Eve Arden, Otto Kruger, Anita Colby. Incredibly clichéd plot is overcome by loveliness of Rita, fine Jerome Kern–Ira Gershwin musical score (including "Long Ago and Far Away"), and especially Kelly's solo numbers. Silvers adds some laughs, but Eve Arden steals the film as Kruger's wisecracking assistant. ▼●]

Cover Me Babe (1970) C-89m. BOMB D: Noel Black. Robert Forster, Sondra Locke, Susanne Benton, Robert S. Fields, Ken Kercheval, Sam Waterston, Regis Toomey. Depressingly bad movie about student filmmaker who lets nothing stand in the way of gaining a contract. [PG—edited from original R rating]

Cowards Bend the Knee (2003-Canadian) 64m. *** D: Guy Maddin. Darcy Fehr, Melissa Dionisio, Amy Stewart, Tara Birtwhistle, Louis Negin, Mike Bell. Delirious b&w silent melodrama that takes place in the catwalk of a hockey rink and at a seamy beauty parlor. Our hero abandons his girlfriend for a siren who insists that he cut off his hands and replace them with those of her dead father. If you're still reading this you may be ready to sample Maddin's unique semiautobiographical journey, originally presented as a series of ten Mutoscope shorts in an art installation. Plays like a hallucinatory silent film—a bad, splicy print with jump-cuts during titles that send them out of focus. Twisted, bizarre, and absolutely mesmerizing.]

Cowboy (1958) C-92m. *** D: Delmer Daves. Glenn Ford, Jack Lemmon, Anna Kashfi, Brian Donlevy, Dick York. Intelligent, atmospheric Western based on Frank Harris' reminiscences as a tenderfoot. Lemmon is Harris, with Ford as his stern boss on eventful cattle roundup. ▼]

Cowboy and the Lady, The (1938) 91m. **½ D: H. C. Potter. Gary Cooper, Merle Oberon, Patsy Kelly, Walter Brennan, Fuzzy Knight, Harry Davenport, Henry Kolker. Bored, aristocratic Oberon, whose father is a presidential aspirant, goes slumming at a rodeo and falls for reluctant cowpuncher Cooper. Slight (if sometimes overly cute) comedy. Leo McCarey cowrote the story; the script had contributions from Anita Loos and Dorothy Parker! ▼●]

Cowboy Bebop: The Movie (2002-Japanese)

C-114m. * D:** Shinichirô Watanabe. Voices of Beau Billingslea, Melissa Fahn, Nicholas Guest, Jennifer Hale. Delightfully stylish, refreshingly humorous animated tale about an eclectic team of space bounty hunters tracking down a bio-terrorist on Mars. Certain details will be lost on those unfamiliar with the TV show on which it's based, and there are a few of the plodding, pretentious moments that plague most anime, but the extremely dynamic action sequences and oddball charm of the characters make for an enjoyable romp. Original Japanese subtitle translates to COWBOY BEBOP: KNOCKIN' ON HEAVEN'S DOOR. [R]▼●)

Cowboys, The (1972) **C-128m. ** D:** Mark Rydell. John Wayne, Roscoe Lee Browne, Bruce Dern, Colleen Dewhurst, Slim Pickens, Lonny Chapman, A Martinez, Robert Carradine, Allyn Ann McLerie, Richard Farnsworth. Well-produced but sluggish Western about aging rancher forced to take 11 youngsters with him on cattle drive; disappointing film whose message seems to be that violent revenge is good. Carradine's first film. Later a short-lived TV series. Panavision. [PG] ▼●)

Cowboy Way, The (1994) **C-102m. ** D:** Gregg Champion. Woody Harrelson, Kiefer Sutherland, Ernie Hudson, Dylan McDermott, Tomas Milian, Marg Helgenberger, Luis Guzman, Travis Tritt, Allison Janney, Christopher Durang. Two rodeo pals from New Mexico come to N.Y.C. to see what's happened to a Cuban friend who disappeared there—and soon find themselves caught in underworld crossfire. Needlessly ugly, unrealistic; only the good-natured performances of the two leads carry it. [PG-13] ▼●)

Coyote Ugly (2000) **C-100m. **½ D:** David McNally. Piper Perabo, Adam Garcia, Maria Bello, John Goodman, Melanie Lynskey, Isabella Miko, Bridget Moynahan, Tyra Banks, Del Pentacost, Ellen Cleghorne, Bud Cort, LeAnn Rimes. Fairly innocuous fantasy/fluff about young woman who leaves New Jersey to make it as a songwriter in N.Y.C.—and winds up strutting alongside some hot-looking babes at a wild all-night bar. Elements of formula films (including producer Jerry Bruckheimer's FLASHDANCE) are cobbled together in routine but likable fashion. Director Michael Bay has a cameo as a photographer. Unrated version runs 107m. Super 35. [PG-13]▼●)

CQ (2002) **C-91m. **½ D:** Roman Coppola. Jeremy Davies, Angela Lindvall, Elodie Bouchez, Giancarlo Giannini, Gérard Depardieu, Billy Zane, Massimo Ghini, Jason Schwartzman, John Phillip Law, Dean Stockwell. Emotionally repressed film editor living in Paris in 1969 works on a BARBARELLA-like sci-fi film and becomes infatuated with its beautiful leading lady—while allowing a real-life relationship with a woman who loves him to evaporate. Nearly a good movie, but its

scattershot ideas have no dramatic momentum. Debut for writer-director Coppola (Francis' son), with a cameo by sister Sofia and a juicy role for cousin Schwartzman. Giannini is a standout as a bombastic Italian producer, and the movie within a movie is fun—with Law (from the real BARBARELLA) a welcome presence. [R]▼●

Crackers (1984) **C-92m. ** D:** Louis Malle. Donald Sutherland, Jack Warden, Sean Penn, Wallace Shawn, Trinidad Silva, Larry Riley, Christine Baranski, Charlaine Woodard, Irwin Corey. Remake of the classic caper comedy BIG DEAL ON MADONNA STREET, set in San Francisco, strives for the offbeat (in its motley collection of misfit characters) but forgets to go for the laughs, too. [PG]▼●

Cracking Up (1983) **C-83m. ** D:** Jerry Lewis. Jerry (Who Else?), Herb Edelman, Zane Buzby, Dick Butkus, Milton Berle, Sammy Davis, Jr., Foster Brooks, Buddy Lester. Jerry plays various characters in vignettes loosely tied to suicidal klutz seeking help from shrink Edelman. There are funny moments (some mildly risqué), but Jerry refuses to believe that Less Is More. Originally titled SMORGASBORD; shelved after test engagements. [PG]▼●

Crack in the Mirror (1960) **97m. *** D:** Richard Fleischer. Orson Welles, Juliette Greco, Bradford Dillman, Alexander Knox. Welles, Greco, and Dillman enact contrasting dual roles in intertwining love triangles set in contemporary Paris, involving murder, courtroom trial, and illicit love; novelty eventually wears thin, marring Grade-A effort. CinemaScope.

Crack in the World (1965-British) **C-96m. **½ D:** Andrew Marton. Dana Andrews, Janette Scott, Kieron Moore, Alexander Knox, Peter Damon. Believable sci-fi about scientists trying to harness earth's inner energy but almost causing destruction of the world; realistic special effects. ▶

Cracks (2009-U.S.-British-Irish) **C-104m. ** D:** Jordan Scott. Eva Green, Juno Temple, Maria Valverde, Imogen Poots, Ellie Nunn, Adele McCann, Zoe Carroll, Clemmie Dugdale, Sinéad Cusack. The arrival of a new student (who is "different," because she's from Spain) at a British girls boarding school in 1934 has a potent effect on her new classmates, as well as their manipulative, Miss Brodie–like teacher (Green). Potentially intriguing story of sexual awakening quickly becomes repetitive and sputters along to an unsatisfactory conclusion. Scott (who also coscripted, from Sheila Kohler's novel) is the daughter of Ridley Scott.▶

Crackshot SEE: Counterfeit Killer, The

Cradle 2 the Grave (2003) **C-99m. *½ D:** Andrzej Bartkowiak. Jet Li, DMX, Gabrielle Union, Anthony Anderson, Kelly Hu, Tom Arnold, Mark Dacascos, Michael Jace, Chi McBride. As an array of baddies and rival half-baddies pursue coveted black diamonds that look like oversized Chiclets, most of the actors playing these parts pursue their dramatically diverse audience demographics. Union is around for the demographic that enjoys seeing semi-unclad lookers, but even those viewers may have trouble with a script about diamonds with nuclear capabilities. DMX's neckwear looks as if it could pick up sandlot baseball games from Radio Havana. Super 35. [R] ▼▶

Cradle Will Rock (1999) **C-134m.** ***½ D: Tim Robbins. Hank Azaria, Ruben Blades, Joan Cusack, John Cusack, Cary Elwes, Philip Baker Hall, Cherry Jones, Angus Macfadyen, Bill Murray, Vanessa Redgrave, Susan Sarandon, Jamey Sheridan, John Turturro, Emily Watson, Bob Balaban, Paul Giamatti, Harris Yulin, Barnard Hughes, John Carpenter, Gretchen Mol, Audra McDonald, Stephen Spinella, Jack Black. Sprawling, invigorating concoction uses Orson Welles and John Houseman's legendary stage production of Marc Blitzstein's *The Cradle Will Rock* as a springboard for looking at 1930s art, culture, politics, and big business. Writer-director Robbins takes liberties with the facts but creates a fascinating patchwork of personalities, ideas, and ideals. Aims high and succeeds amazingly well. Super 35. [R] ▼▶

Craft, The (1996) **C-100m.** *** D: Andrew Fleming. Robin Tunney, Fairuza Balk, Neve Campbell, Rachel True, Christine Taylor, Skeet Ulrich, Assumpta Serna, Cliff De Young, Helen Shaver. Four teenage girls, students at a private L.A. school, dabble in witchcraft. At first, they're gleeful about their powers, but eventually things get out of hand. Surprisingly witty, intelligent movie handles this goofy premise better than you'd think but goes too far at the end. [R] ▼▶▶

Craig's Wife (1936) **75m.** *** D: Dorothy Arzner. Rosalind Russell, John Boles, Billie Burke, Jane Darwell, Dorothy Wilson, Alma Kruger, Thomas Mitchell. Russell scored first big success as domineering wife who thinks more of material objects than of her husband. Based on George Kelly play, remade as HARRIET CRAIG. ▼

Cranes Are Flying, The (1957-Russian) **94m.** ***½ D: Mikhail Kalatozov. Tatyana Samoilova, Alexei Batalov, Vasili Merkuriev, A. Shvorin. Lilting love story set in WW2 Russia. Doctor's son (Batalov) leaves his sweetheart (Samoilova) to join the army. She is seduced by his cousin, marries him, and from subsequent tragedies tries to rebuild her life. ▼▶▶

Crank (2006) **C-87m.** ** D: Mark Neveldine, Brian Taylor. Jason Statham, Amy Smart, Jose Pablo Cantillo, Efren Ramirez, Dwight Yoakam, Carlos Sanz, Reno Wilson. Professional assassin is injected with a dose of lethal poison that will become fatal the moment his heart rate drops. Knowing this, he embarks on a nonstop race against time in which he tries to foil the plot against him and find an antidote. Silly premise may entertain fans with the attention span of a beagle. The action doesn't let up, but forget about logic, good acting, and smart dialogue. It took two directors to make this non–thinking man's thriller. Try the original D.O.A. instead. Followed by a sequel. [R] ▶

Crank: High Voltage (2009) **C-96m.** *½ D: Mark Neveldine, Brian Taylor. Jason Statham, Amy Smart, Clifton Collins, Jr., Efren Ramirez, Bai Ling, David Carradine, Reno Wilson, Joseph Julian Soria, Dwight Yoakam, Corey Haim. Brainless, tasteless sequel picks up right where its predecessor ended. Thugs rob hit man Statham of his heart, which is implanted in the chest of an aged Chinese mobster (Carradine). The replacement is electrically powered and must be recharged on a regular basis. Ridiculous action thriller has no decipherable storyline and is crammed with gratuitous violence and sex. Strains to be hip, but comes off cheap and vulgar. HD Widescreen. [R] ▶

Crash! (1977) **C-85m.** *½ D: Charles Band. Jose Ferrer, Sue Lyon, John Ericson, Leslie Parrish, John Carradine. Strange, unbelievable mixture of occult and car chase. Jealous invalid husband Ferrer tries to kill wife Lyon, who uses demonic device to cause mayhem on her own. Panavision. [PG]

Crash (1996-Canadian) **C-100m.** *½ D: David Cronenberg. James Spader, Holly Hunter, Elias Koteas, Rosanna Arquette, Deborah Kara Unger, Peter MacNeil. Steely-cold look at alienated people who find sexual excitement in automobile crashes. Filled with explicit sex as well as fetishistic scenes involving car accidents. Curiosity seekers may find it intriguing for a while, but it's awfully hard to take. Cronenberg adapted this fatally unpleasant film from J. G. Ballard's novel. Creeps along at the pace of a Yugo. R-rated version cut by 10m. [NC-17] ▼▶

Crash (2005-U.S.-German) **C-112m.** ***½ D: Paul Haggis. Don Cheadle, Sandra Bullock, Matt Dillon, Thandie Newton, Brendan Fraser, Ryan Phillippe, Jennifer Esposito, Chris "Ludacris" Bridges, Terrence Howard, William Fichtner, Larenz Tate, Nona Gaye, Loretta Devine, Michael Pena, Shaun Toub, Beverly Todd, Keith David. Meditation on the clash of ethnic and racial cultures in L.A. as disparate lives intersect and ignite various characters' simmering anger. Provocative drama has powerful vignettes and performances, offering consistently disturbing (and believable) scenes of anger and bigotry, with tiny glimmers of hope in metaphoric moments. Directing debut for Haggis, who cowrote the screenplay with Bobby Moresco. Oscar winner for Best Picture, Original Screenplay, Film Editing (Hughes Winborne). Later a TV series. [R] ▼▶

Crash and Burn (1990) **C-85m.** ****** D: Charles Band. Paul Ganus, Megan Ward, Ralph Waite, Bill Moseley, Eva LaRue, Jack McGee, Elizabeth MacLellan. In the year 2030, a group isolated in a desert installation is menaced by one of them, secretly a killer android. A mix of ideas from THE THING, THE TERMINATOR, and ALIEN is occasionally effective, but too slow and familiar. Some good if brief David Allen effects involving a giant robot turn up at the end. From Full Moon. [R]▼◗

Crash Dive (1943) **C-105m.** ****½** D: Archie Mayo. Tyrone Power, Anne Baxter, Dana Andrews, James Gleason, Dame May Whitty, Henry (Harry) Morgan. Submarine battleground just backdrop for love story; Powers and Andrews both love young Baxter. Oscar winner for special effects, film's main asset. ▼◗

Crawlspace (1986) **C-82m.** BOMB D: David Schmoeller. Klaus Kinski, Talia Balsam, Sally Brown, Barbara Whinnery. Shameless imitation of PEEPING TOM, as Kinski spies on young women from his apartment's hidden crawlspace area and then kills them, the legacy of his father having been a Nazi war criminal. [R]▼◗

Craze (1974-British) **C-96m.** ***½** D: Freddie Francis. Jack Palance, Diana Dors, Julie Ege, Trevor Howard, Suzy Kendall, Michael Jayston, Dame Edith Evans. More laughs than horror as antique dealer Palance makes human sacrifices to African idol. Hugh Griffith and Howard wisely kid the material. British title: THE INFERNAL IDOL; aka THE DEMON MASTER. [R]▼◗

Crazies, The (1973) **C-103m.** ****** D: George Romero. Lane Carroll, W.G. McMillan, Harold Wayne Jones, Lloyd Hollar, Lynn Lowry. Biological plague hits small Pennsylvania town. The Army is called in to contain it; townspeople rebel, defy soldiers. Gory but exciting. Aka CODE NAME: TRIXIE. Remade in 2010. [R]▼◗

Crazies, The (2010-U.S.-United Arab Emirates) **C-101m.** ****** D: Breck Eisner. Timothy Olyphant, Radha Mitchell, Joe Anderson, Danielle Panabaker, Christie Lynn Smith, Brett Rickaby, Preston Bailey, Lynn Lowry. Olyphant, the sheriff of a small Iowa town, tries to deal with a growing plague of homicidal insanity to which no one seems immune. Remake of George A. Romero's 1973 thriller is intelligent and makes good use of real Midwestern locations, but the plotline is so familiar this is probably best left to genre diehards. Super 35. [R]◗

C.R.A.Z.Y. (2005-Canadian) **C-129m.** *****½** D: Jean-Marc Vallée. Michel Côté, Marc-André Grondin, Danielle Proulx, Émile Vallée, Pierre-Luc Brillant, Maxime Tremblay, Alex Gravel, Johanne Lebrun. From childhood, Zach is told he possesses a gift of healing granted to him by Jesus . . . but he's equally troubled by a suspicion that

he's gay. Already alienated from his older brothers, this puts him at risk of infuriating his proud, domineering (and homophobic) father. Absorbing comedy-drama covers many years in the life of a family, from 1960 to 1980, as it charts a young man's journey of self-awareness. Runs the emotional gamut but never strikes a false note. Written by Vallée and François Boulay. Winner of ten Genie awards, including Best Picture.◗

Crazy/Beautiful (2001) **C-99m.** ****** D: John Stockwell. Kirsten Dunst, Jay Hernandez, Bruce Davison, Lucinda Jenney, Taryn Manning, Rolando Molina. A wealthy white high school girl, whose hell-raising ways mask a troubled soul, falls in love with a Latino boy from the other side of the tracks. Story makes all the right moves at first, then ducks too many issues and whitewashes too many details to make sense, logically or emotionally. Too bad; this one had some potential. [PG-13]▼◗

Crazy Heart (2009) **C-111m.** ******* D: Scott Cooper. Jeff Bridges, Maggie Gyllenhaal, Robert Duvall, Colin Farrell, Beth Grant, Tom Bower. Aging, alcoholic country singer Bad Blake (Bridges) is reduced to playing bowling alleys, but life on the road takes an unexpected turn when he meets a woman he actually cares about. Then his protégé-turned-rival (Farrell) offers him a gig. Amiable film admirably flirts with clichés at every turn, but Bridges' true, empathetic performance (which earned him a Best Actor Oscar) makes this film worth seeing. He also does a fine job singing the songs created especially for this film, including Oscar-winning "The Weary Kind (Theme from Crazy Heart)" by T Bone Burnett and Ryan Bingham. Debuting director Cooper adapted Thomas Cobb's novel. HD Widescreen. [R]◗

Crazy House (1943) **80m.** ******* D: Edward F. Cline. Ole Olsen, Chic Johnson, Martha O'Driscoll, Patric Knowles, Cass Daley, Percy Kilbride. Olsen & Johnson take over film studio to make epic in frantic musicomedy with guests galore: Basil Rathbone, Count Basie, Allan Jones, Edgar Kennedy, Billy Gilbert, Andy Devine, etc.

Crazy House (1973-British) **C-90m.** ****** D: Peter Sykes. Ray Milland, Frankie Howerd, Rosalie Crutchley, Kenneth Griffith, Elizabeth McClennan. Horror spoof that fails as comedy but succeeds with the chills. Over-age entertainer Howerd finds he's related to Milland's greedy family, which is being killed off for an inheritance. U.S. title: NIGHT OF THE LAUGHING DEAD. Original title: THE HOUSE IN NIGHTMARE PARK. [PG]▼

Crazy in Alabama (1999) **C-104m.** ****½** D: Antonio Banderas. Melanie Griffith, David Morse, Lucas Black, Cathy Moriarty, Meat Loaf Aday, Rod Steiger, Richard Schiff,

John Beasley, Robert Wagner, Paul Mazursky, Elizabeth Perkins, Noah Emmerich, Fannie Flagg. Picaresque tale of the mid-1960s South: abused Griffith chops off her husband's head, leaves her seven kids, and goes to Hollywood seeking fame and fortune, toting hubby's head in a hatbox. Meanwhile, her nephew comes face-to-face with racism. Doesn't succeed in tying its parallel stories together but holds your interest. Creditable directing debut for Banderas, whose wife is well cast. Super 35. [PG-13]▼❙

Crazy Jack and the Boy SEE: **Silence**

Crazy Joe (1974-Italian-U.S.) **C-100m.** **½ D: Carlo Lizzani. Peter Boyle, Rip Torn, Fred Williamson, Eli Wallach, Paula Prentiss, Luther Adler. Crime drama based on the bloody career of New York racketeer Crazy Joe Gallo is tolerable, due to its cast. Henry Winkler can be seen as a mustached hoodlum. [R]▼

Crazy Love (2007) **C-92m.** *** D: Dan Klores, Fisher Stevens. Absorbing documentary about a woman who made headlines in 1959 when her suitor had acid thrown in her face. Today, the two of them are married! A wild, stranger-than-fiction, only-in-New-York yarn that reveals its story one layer at a time, through vintage news accounts and intimate new interviews. Fascinating and well told. [PG-13]❙

Crazy Mama (1975) **C-82m.** *** D: Jonathan Demme. Cloris Leachman, Stuart Whitman, Ann Sothern, Jim Backus, Donny Most, Linda Purl, Bryan Englund, Merie Earle, Sally Kirkland. Joyous, unrelentingly kitschy celebration of '50s America (opportunity, rock 'n' roll, and the road), made during Demme's exploitation days, follows three generations of women (Sothern, Leachman, Purl) and the men they pick up, on an absurdist crime spree from California to family homestead in Arkansas. Rough in places; overall a gem. Dennis Quaid and Bill Paxton have small parts in their film debuts. [PG]▼❙

Crazy Moon (1986-Canadian) **C-87m.** *** D: Allan Eastman. Kiefer Sutherland, Peter Spence, Vanessa Vaughan, Ken Pogue, Eve Napier. Occasionally clichéd, but still warm, winning little story of wealthy, alienated teen Sutherland and his romance with bright, independent—and deaf—salesgirl Vaughan. Originally titled HUGGERS. [PG-13]▼●

Crazy on the Outside (2010) **C-96m.** *½ D: Tim Allen. Tim Allen, Sigourney Weaver, Ray Liotta, Jeanne Tripplehorn, J. K. Simmons, Julie Bowen, Kelsey Grammer, Jon Gries. Blandly unremarkable comedy showcasing Allen as an affable ex-con eager to rebuild his life with help from a lovely single mom (Tripplehorn) who just happens to be his parole officer. For his debut effort as feature director, Allen evidently called in favors to assemble familiar

faces as supporting players, to little avail. [PG-13]❙

Crazy People (1990) **C-90m.** ** D: Tony Bill. Dudley Moore, Daryl Hannah, Paul Reiser, Mercedes Ruehl, J.T. Walsh, Bill Smitrovich, Alan North, David Paymer, Dick Cusack, Ben Hammer. Stressed-out ad exec Moore devises a series of brutally honest (and very funny) advertisements, which prompt his partner to place him in a mental institution. Then, to everyone's amazement, the ads are a sensational success. Though the mock ads are quite funny, film is bland, even dull. Ever likable Dudley chalks up a few extra points. [R]▼●❙

Crazy-Quilt, The (1966) **75m.** *** D: John Korty. Ina Mela, Tom Rosqui, David Winters, Ellen Frye. Korty's first feature is almost a home movie, featuring arresting images but diffuse, whimsical (ultimately pompous) story of girl's various romantic liaisons while her exterminator husband sits around and mopes. Filmed silent, with awkward post-synched dialogue; relies heavily upon Burgess Meredith's narration, unusual score by Peter Schickele.

Crazy Stranger SEE: **Gadjo Dilo**

Crazy Streets SEE: **Forever, Lulu**

Crazy World of Julius Vrooder, The (1974) **C-89m.** **½ D: Arthur Hiller. Timothy Bottoms, Barbara Hershey, George Marshall, Albert Salmi, Lawrence Pressman. Nobody likes this offbeat comedy of a confused Vietnam vet who acts insane to cope with a crazy world, but it has a certain charm. Veteran director Marshall returned to acting here shortly before his death. [PG]

Created to Kill SEE: **Embryo**

Creation (2009-British) **C-108m.** ** D: Jon Amiel. Paul Bettany, Jennifer Connelly, Jeremy Northam, Toby Jones, Benedict Cumberbatch, Jim Carter, Martha West, Teresa Churcher, Zak Davies, Harrison Sansostri. In mid-19th-century rural England, middle-aged, infirm Charles Darwin (Bettany) has lost his muse (his daughter Annie) and is wrestling with his groundbreaking treatise, *On the Origin of Species*, whilst his whole world, even his own household, remains rooted in religion. That household is the focus here, as his devout wife, Emma (Connelly—Bettany's real-life spouse), is at odds with her husband's scientific breakthroughs. As a result, both Darwins are wracked by guilt. Bettany does his best, but this melodrama is so narrow in scope that one aches for some sense of the excitement or controversy Darwin's work was to cause. Super 35. [PG-13]❙

Creator (1985) **C-107m.** ** D: Ivan Passer. Peter O'Toole, Mariel Hemingway, Vincent Spano, Virginia Madsen, David Ogden Stiers, John Dehner, Jeff Corey. O'Toole once again plays a Lovable Eccentric (which he does to perfection), this time a university-based scientist who's trying to revive his long-dead wife and who serves as mentor for impressionable student Spano. Amiable but aimless adaptation of Jeremy Leven's novel, redeemed only by O'Toole's magnetism. [R]▼●◗

Creature (1985) C-97m. ** D: William Malone. Stan Ivar, Wendy Schaal, Lyman Ward, Robert Jaffe, Diane Salinger, Annette McCarthy, Klaus Kinski. Imitation of ALIEN set on Saturn's moon Titan has nondescript cast investigating life forms discovered (fatally) by a previous mission. Guest star Kinski is funny, whether spouting gibberish or munching nonchalantly on a sandwich during otherwise tense scenes. Originally titled TITAN FIND. [R]▼●◗

Creature From the Black Lagoon (1954) 79m. *** D: Jack Arnold. Richard Carlson, Julia (Julie) Adams, Richard Denning, Antonio Moreno, Whit Bissell, Nestor Paiva, Ricou Browning, Ben Chapman. Archetypal '50s monster movie has been copied so often that some of the edge is gone, but story of Amazon expedition encountering deadly Gill Man is still entertaining, with juicy atmosphere, luminous underwater photography sequences directed by James C. Havens and Scotty Welbourne. Originally in 3-D, but just as good without it. Two sequels: REVENGE OF THE CREATURE and THE CREATURE WALKS AMONG US. 3-D. ▼●◗

Creature From the Haunted Sea (1961) 74m. *½ D: Roger Corman. Antony Carbone, Betsy Jones-Moreland, Edward Wain, E. R. Alvarez, Robert Bean. Gangster tries to cover crime wave by creating panic with story of sea monster . . . then real sea monster shows up. Roger Corman quickie comedy is not as freakish as his others. Costar Wain is actually Oscar-winning screenwriter Robert Towne. Remake of NAKED PARADISE. ▼◗

Creatures SEE: **From Beyond the Grave**
Creatures of the Prehistoric Planet SEE: **Vampire Men of the Lost Planet**
Creatures the World Forgot (1971-British) C-94m. *½ D: Don Chaffey. Julie Ege, Tony Bonner, Robert John, Sue Wilson, Rosalie Crutchley. Hammer Films gives us another prehistoric movie with no dinosaurs and little credibility. [PG]▼◗

Creature Walks Among Us, The (1956) 78m. ** D: John Sherwood. Jeff Morrow, Rex Reason, Leigh Snowden, Gregg Palmer. Sequel to REVENGE OF THE CREATURE has Gill Man (Ricou Browning in water, Don Megowan on land) captured by humans, subjected to surgery in hopes of humanizing him, returning to the ocean after a few mild tantrums.▼●◗

Creature Wasn't Nice, The (1981) C-88m. *½ D: Bruce Kimmel. Cindy Williams, Bruce Kimmel, Leslie Nielsen, Gerrit Graham, Patrick Macnee, Ron Kurowski. Silly monster-loose-in-spaceship parody:

Nielsen is the firm but obtuse commander, Macnee the loony scientist, Williams the only woman on board, etc. Believe it or not, this is a musical (one song is titled "I Want to Eat Your Face"). Aka SPACESHIP and NAKED SPACE. [PG]▼◗

Creature With the Blue Hand (1967-German) C-74m. ** D: Alfred Vohrer. Klaus Kinski, Diana Kerner, Carl Lang, Ilse Page, Harold Leopold. OK Edgar Wallace story has innocent man accused of murders perpetrated by title creature. Aka THE BLOODY DEAD. [PG]▼◗

Creeper, The SEE: **Rituals**
Creepers, The (1971) SEE: **In the Devil's Garden**
Creepers (1984-Italian) C-110m. *** D: Dario Argento. Jennifer Connelly, Donald Pleasence, Daria Nicolodi, Dalila Di Lazzaro, Patrick Bauchau, Fiore Argento. Typically stylish, bizarre Argento horror opus whose premise—a mad killer running amok at a Swiss girls' school—serves as a framework for some cleverly weird goings-on. For openers, Connelly plays a girl who has a most unusual relationship with insects. Don't say you weren't warned! Aka PHENOMENA. Also shown in 82m. version. [R]▼◗

Creeping Flesh, The (1973-British) C-94m. *** D: Freddie Francis. Peter Cushing, Christopher Lee, Lorna Heilbron, George Benson. Well-intentioned, old-fashioned monster film on reincarnation of ancient evil spirit. Cushing and Lee play rival brothers competing over ancient skeleton that slowly returns to life. Numerous subplots add to the fun. [PG]▼◗

Creeping Unknown, The SEE: **Quatermass Xperiment, The**
Creepshow (1982) C-120m. ** D: George Romero. Hal Holbrook, Adrienne Barbeau, Fritz Weaver, Leslie Nielsen, Carrie Nye, E. G. Marshall, Viveca Lindfors, Ed Harris, Ted Danson, Gaylen Ross. Romero nicely captures the look of a comic book in this homage to 1950s E.C. Comics, but Stephen King's five "fantastic tales" of revenge and just desserts are transparent and heavy-handed (King himself stars in the second episode, as an ill-fated rube). Finale has hundreds of cockroaches bursting through the stomach of a man with an insect phobia (Marshall). If that's your cup of tea, tune in. Followed by two sequels. [R]▼●◗

Creepshow 2 (1987) C-89m. *½ D: Michael Gornick. Lois Chiles, George Kennedy, Dorothy Lamour, Tom Savini, Domenick John, Frank S. Salsedo, Holt McCallany, David Holbrook, Page Hannah. George A. Romero scripted this trio of Stephen King short stories, but their combined reputations can't lift this cheap-looking movie out of the muck. As in the much slicker CREEPSHOW, all the stories are juvenile and heavy-handed (a wooden Indian comes to life, a hitchhiker run over by a motorist lives on to terrorize her, etc.). King appears briefly as a truck driver. Followed by a direct-to-video sequel. [R]▼●▶

Crest of the Wave (1954-British) **90m.** **½ D: John Boulting, Roy Boulting. Gene Kelly, John Justin, Bernard Lee, Jeff Richards. Static account of Navy officer Kelly joining British research group to supervise demolition experiments.

Crew, The (2000) **C-87m.** **½ D: Michael Dinner. Richard Dreyfuss, Burt Reynolds, Seymour Cassel, Dan Hedaya, Jennifer Tilly, Carrie-Anne Moss, Lainie Kazan, Jeremy Piven, Miguel Sandoval, Fyvush Finkel, Casey Siemaszko. Silly comedy about four Miami senior citizens who yearn to relive their glory days as mobsters . . . and unexpectedly get their chance when they run afoul of a Latino drug lord. Featherweight movie coasts on the good will of its cast. [PG-13]▼▶

Cries and Whispers (1972-Swedish) **C-106m.** *** D: Ingmar Bergman. Harriet Andersson, Liv Ullmann, Ingrid Thulin, Kari Sylwan, Erland Josephson, George Arlin, Henning Moritzen. Beautifully photographed and acted drama about lives of a dying woman, her sisters and a servant girl was tremendous critical success, but may be too talky for some. Cinematographer Sven Nykvist won an Oscar. [R]▼●▶

Cries in the Night SEE: **Funeral Home**

Crime and Passion (1976) **C-92m.** *½ D: Ivan Passer. Omar Sharif, Karen Black, Joseph Bottoms, Bernhard Wicki. Bizarre comedy-thriller set in Austrian Alps. Sharif is international financier who persuades secretary-mistress Black to wed industrialist Wicki for his money, then finds they are both marked for death by the husband. [R]▼

Crime & Punishment, USA (1959) **78m.** **½ D: Denis Sanders. George Hamilton, Mary Murphy, Frank Silvera, Marian Seldes, John Harding, Wayne Heffley. Trim, updated version of Dostoyevsky novel has Hamilton (film debut) a law student who becomes involved in robbery and murder.▶

Crime Busters (1980-Italian) **C-98m.** *½ D: E. B. Clucher (Enzo Barboni). Terence Hill, Bud Spencer, Laura Gemser, Luciana Catenacci. Filmed in Miami, this cop-movie parody is a hair better than other Hill-Spencer efforts, but not a patch on the Trinity films; chief novelty derives from watching them go through their paces in a contemporary American setting. Bad dubbing doesn't help. Filmed in 1976 as TWO SUPERCOPS. Originally 115m. [PG]▼▶

Crime Doctor series SEE: *Leonard Maltin's Classic Movie Guide*

Crime in the Streets (1956) **91m.** **½ D: Donald Siegel. James Whitmore, John Cassavetes, Sal Mineo, Mark Rydell, Virginia Gregg, Denise Alexander, Will Kuluva, Peter Votrian, Malcolm Atterbury. Incisive if overlong drama of angry, alienated teen Cas-

savetes, who conspires to commit murder. Good performance by Cassavetes, also Mineo and future director Rydell as his cronies and Whitmore as an idealistic social worker. Adapted by Reginald Rose from his 1955 teleplay; Cassavetes, Rydell, and Kuluva repeat their TV performances.▼▶

Crime of Father Amaro, The (2002-Mexican-Argentinean-Spanish-French) **C-120m.** *** D: Carlos Carrera. Gael García Bernal, Sancho Gracia, Ana Claudia Talancón, Damián Alcázar, Angélica Aragón, Pedro Armendáriz, Jr. Pointed melodrama about hypocrisy and corruption in the Catholic Church, centering on a handsome, newly ordained priest (Bernal) who becomes sexually involved with a beautiful 16-year-old parishioner. Controversial, to be sure, for its portrayal of desire and temptation (not to mention corruption) within the clergy. Based on a 19th-century Portuguese novel; a major box-office hit in Mexico. [R] ▼▶

Crime of Monsieur Lange, The (1936-French) **90m.** *** D: Jean Renoir. Rene Lefevre, Jules Berry, Florelle, Nadia Sibirskaia, Sylvia Bataille, Jean Daste. Clever (if a bit too talky) tale of an exploited publishing house clerk (Lefevre), who pens stories in his spare time, his evil, lecherous boss (Berry), and a host of complications. Scripted by Jacques Prévert, with a pointed anticapitalist message.▼●

Crimes and Misdemeanors (1989) **C-104m.** ***½ D: Woody Allen. Caroline Aaron, Alan Alda, Woody Allen, Claire Bloom, Mia Farrow, Joanna Gleason, Anjelica Huston, Martin Landau, Jenny Nichols, Jerry Orbach, Sam Waterston. Film's title indicates the themes of two separate stories, which are neatly tied up in the final scene. Landau plays a married man who is desperate to cut off an adulterous relationship in this somberly tragic tale. Allen is an unhappy documentary filmmaker who's wooing attractive Farrow while making a film about insufferably self-centered TV producer Alda, in a hilariously bittersweet story. Arguably Woody's most ambitious film, playing heavy drama against often uproarious comedy, and certainly one of his most passionately debated; a one-of-a-kind effort that only he could pull off. Daryl Hannah has an unbilled cameo as one of Alda's chippies. [PG-13]▼●▶

Crime School (1938) **86m.** **½ D: Lewis Seiler. Dead End Kids (Billy Halop, Bobby Jordan, Huntz Hall, Leo Gorcey, Bernard Punsley, Gabriel Dell), Humphrey Bogart, Gale Page. Bogart sets out to improve a reform school, but meets his match in the Dead End Kids. OK reworking of THE MAYOR OF HELL (1933), weakened by the Kids' disreputable personalities and Bogart's unlikely casting as a do-gooder. Story rehashed again as HELL'S KITCHEN.▶

Crimes of Dr. Mabuse, The SEE: **Testament of Dr. Mabuse, The**

Crimes of Passion (1984) **C-101m.** ** D: Ken Russell. Kathleen Turner, Anthony Perkins, John Laughlin, Annie Potts, Bruce Davison. Laughlin, trapped in a stale marriage, takes up with mysterious Turner—fashion designer by day, hooker by night. Watchable mess is, given the subject matter, less out of control than other Russell movies. Turner actually gives a performance; Perkins amuses in one of his standard nutso roles. One of the two homevideo versions has several minutes of kinky footage originally seen only in Europe. [R] ▼●

Crimes of the Heart (1986) **C-105m.** **½ D: Bruce Beresford. Diane Keaton, Jessica Lange, Sissy Spacek, Sam Shepard, Tess Harper, David Carpenter, Hurd Hatfield. Three Southern sisters, who are equally off-center, share their various woes and idiosyncrasies (along with pent-up jealousies and resentments) during a fateful reunion. Superior performances can't make a really good film out of Beth Henley's Pulitzer Prize–winning play, even though Henley wrote the screenplay herself. [PG-13] ▼●

Crime Spree (2003-U.S.-French-British-Canadian) **C-98m.** **½ D: Brad Mirman. Harvey Keitel, Gérard Depardieu, Johnny Hallyday, Renaud, Saïd Taghmaoui, Stéphane Freiss, Albert Dray, Abe Vigoda. Disparate group of thieves treks from Paris to Chicago to pull off a heist, but things don't go as planned. Tarantino-influenced comedy-crime film strives to be clever; innocuous fun, with some unnecessary flights into silliness. Depardieu is slumming here but Keitel, playing the underboss of the Chicago Mafia, deftly parodies his tough-guy image. [R] ▼)

Crime Wave (1954) **74m.** **½ D: Andre De Toth. Sterling Hayden, Gene Nelson, Phyllis Kirk, Ted de Corsia, Charles Buchinsky (Bronson), Jay Novello, James Bell, Dub Taylor, Timothy Carey. Neat little B picture about some escaped cons who try to involve a former prisonmate (who's now gone straight) in their latest heist. Actuality-style filming on L.A. locations gives this an extra boost.)

Crimewave (1985) **C-83m.** **½ D: Sam Raimi. Louise Lasser, Paul L. Smith, Brion James, Sheree J. Wilson, Bruce Campbell, Reed Birney, Edward R. Pressman, Julius Harris. After a successful debut with EVIL DEAD, director Raimi pays tribute to slapstick comedy with this weird, almost incoherent crime story set in Detroit. Smith and James are well cast as grotesque goons on a robbery/killing spree. This exercise in style was cowritten by Raimi's pals Joel and Ethan Coen. [PG-13] ▼

Crime Zone (1988) **C-93m.** **½ D: Luis Llosa. David Carradine, Peter Nelson, Sherilyn Fenn, Michael Shaner, Orlando Sacha. Moody sci-fi set in repressive, stratified future society. Upper-caste Carradine recruits young lovers to commit crimes for a surprising reason. Profane, satiric, well-crafted low-budgeter, but loses its way before the finish. Shot in Peru! [R] ▼

Criminal, The SEE: **Concrete Jungle, The** (1960)

Criminal (2004) **C-87m.** *** D: Gregory Jacobs. John C. Reilly, Diego Luna, Maggie Gyllenhaal, Peter Mullan, Jonathan Tucker, Enrico Colantoni, Zitto Kazann, Michael Shannon, Malik Yoba, Ellen Geer, Jack Conley. Cocky, small-time L.A. con artist (Reilly) takes on a protégé (Luna) who knows a trick or two himself. During the course of one eventful day they become involved in what could be the biggest deal of their lives. Entertaining yarn keeps you guessing to the very last minute. A remake of the Argentinian film NINE QUEENS. Jacobs' directing debut; he also cowrote the script with Sam Lowry (a pen name for co-producer Steven Soderbergh). [R] ▼)

Criminal Code, The (1931) **95m.** **½ D: Howard Hawks. Walter Huston, Phillips Holmes, Constance Cummings, Mary Doran, Boris Karloff, De Witt Jennings. Warden Huston—tough but essentially fair—faces a dilemma when his daughter falls in love with prisoner Holmes, who's shielding the killer of a squealer. Creaky in parts, lively in others, but cast and director make this a must for buffs. Remade as PENITENTIARY in 1938 and CONVICTED in 1950. ▼

Criminal Law (1989) **C-117m.** *½ D: Martin Campbell. Gary Oldman, Kevin Bacon, Karen Young, Joe Don Baker, Tess Harper, Elizabeth Sheppard. Weak suspense film, done in by an unsatisfying script and unbelievable story. Slick attorney Oldman (playing an American—and quite well) matches wits with wealthy psychopath Bacon in tale of serial murders in Boston. Unnecessarily pretentious, unintentionally funny, and filmed nowhere near Boston. [R] ▼●

Criminal Life of Archibaldo de la Cruz, The (1955-Mexican) **91m.** ** D: Luis Buñuel. Ernesto Alonso, Miroslava Stern, Rita Macedo, Ariadna Welter, Rodolfo Landa, Andrea Palma. Very minor psychological drama from Buñuel. As a boy, Archibaldo witnesses his governess' death and is fascinated by what he feels; as a man, he's obsessed with murder and dying. Much too talky; it sounds far more interesting than it plays. ▼

Crimson Altar, The SEE: **Crimson Cult, The**

Crimson Cult, The (1968-British) **C-87m.** ** D: Vernon Sewell. Mark Eden, Virginia Wetherell, Christopher Lee, Boris Karloff, Michael Gough, Barbara Steele. Lackluster script and pacing major flaws in standard witchcraft thriller featuring aging Karloff as expert on black magic, Steele (in green makeup) as 300-year-old witch. Original British titles: CURSE OF THE CRIMSON

ALTAR and THE CRIMSON ALTAR. [M/PG]▼●

Crimson Gold (2003-Iranian) **C-92m.** *** D: Jafar Panahi. Hossain Emadeddin, Kamyar Sheisi, Azita Rayeji, Shahram Vaziri, Ehsan Amani, Pourang Nakhaei, Kaveh Najmabadi, Saber Safaei. A pizza delivery man in Tehran · quietly endures a series of social indignities that eventually drive him to take desperate action. A subtle, pointed critique of class conflicts, told in slow, naturalistic style. Leading man Emadeddin was, in real life, a pizza delivery man. Written by (another) famed Iranian filmmaker, Abbas Kiarostami. This was banned in Iran.▼▌

Crimson Kimono, The (1959) **82m.** **½ D: Samuel Fuller. Victoria Shaw, Glenn Corbett, James Shigeta, Anna Lee, Paul Dubov, Gloria Pall. Two close-knit L.A. detectives investigate a stripper's murder and its ties to the city's Japanese community. Uniquely odd Fuller film explores racial identity and a seldom-seen facet of L.A.▌

Crimson Pirate, The (1952) **C-104m.** ***½ D: Robert Siodmak. Burt Lancaster, Nick Cravat, Eva Bartok, Torin Thatcher, Christopher Lee, James Hayter. Lancaster and Cravat swashbuckle their way across the Mediterranean in one of the great genre classics of all time. Well-loved film offers loads of thrills and laughs to both children and adults.▼●▌

Crimson Rivers, The (2000-French) **C-110m.** *** D: Mathieu Kassovitz. Jean Reno, Vincent Cassel, Nadia Farès, Dominique Sanda, Karim Belkhadra, Jean-Pierre Cassel. Compelling mystery-thriller about a police investigator called to a remote French valley where a grisly murder has occurred—the work of a deranged mind. Meanwhile, a detective from a small town miles away looks into the desecration of a young girl's tomb—which leads him onto the same path as his older, more famous colleague. Exciting, unpredictable film, adapted by Kassovitz and Jean-Christophe Grangé from the latter's novel. Followed by a direct-to-video sequel. Panavision. [R] ▼▌

Crimson Tide (1995) **C-115m.** *** D: Tony Scott. Denzel Washington, Gene Hackman, Matt Craven, George Dzundza, Viggo Mortensen, James Gandolfini, Rocky Carroll, Jaime P. Gómez, Michael Milhoan, Scott Burkholder, Danny Nucci, Lillo Brancato, Jr., Rick Schroder, Vanessa Bell Calloway, Steve Zahn, Ryan Phillippe. The producer-director team that brought you TOP GUN fashioned this macho power-play saga aboard a Navy nuclear submarine. Tensions run high when the U.S. is pushed to the brink of war with Russia, especially when veteran sub commander Hackman starts showing Capt. Queeg tendencies and his new lieutenant (Washington) tries to assert himself. Obvious, with a foregone

conclusion, but highly entertaining just the same. Jason Robards appears unbilled. Hip dialogue added (without credit) by Quentin Tarantino. Alternate unrated version is 123m. Panavision. [R] ▼●▌

Crisis (1950) **95m.** **½ D: Richard Brooks. Cary Grant, Jose Ferrer, Paula Raymond, Signe Hasso, Ramon Novarro, Antonio Moreno, Leon Ames, Gilbert Roland. Melodrama of American doctor (Grant) held in South American country to treat ailing dictator (Ferrer); intriguing but slow. Brooks's first film as director. Also shown in computer-colored version.▌

Criss Cross (1949) **87m.** *** D: Robert Siodmak. Burt Lancaster, Yvonne De Carlo, Dan Duryea, Stephen McNally. Lancaster returns to hometown, where he crosses path of ex-wife De Carlo, who's taken up with gangster Duryea. Potent film noir look (by cinematographer Franz Planer) and music (by Miklos Rozsa) help compensate for Lancaster's miscasting as an easily manipulated husband. Tony Curtis' screen debut; he's briefly seen as De Carlo's dance partner. Remade in 1995 as UNDERNEATH. ▼●▌

CrissCross (1992) **C-100m.** ** D: Chris Menges. Goldie Hawn, Arliss Howard, James Gammon, David Arnott, Keith Carradine, J. C. Quinn, Steve Buscemi, Paul Calderon. Good intentions abound in this low-key drama set in Key West, Florida, in 1969. A 12-year-old boy lives with his mom, trying to survive since his Dad (a messed-up Vietnam vet) deserted them three years ago. The boy's rootlessness and (eventual) moral dilemma are delineated in credible but much too leisurely fashion, making this potential sleeper a yawner instead. [R]▼●▌

Critical Care (1997) **C-109m.** **½ D: Sidney Lumet. James Spader, Helen Mirren, Kyra Sedgwick, Albert Brooks, Anne Bancroft, Wallace Shawn, Philip Bosco, Jeffrey Wright, Margo Martindale, Colm Feore, Edward Herrmann. A young resident, already cynical about the medical system and his career, is drawn into a controversy over a patient who's on a life support system, and whose two daughters disagree about his future. Satire of modern medicine (from the director of NETWORK) is heavy-handed and obvious at times, but redeems itself with a satisfying conclusion. Brooks is fun as the aged, once-brilliant doctor whose memory is now shot. And it's hard to dislike any film that begins with the Delta Rhythm Boys singing "Dry Bones." [R]▼●▌

Critical Condition (1987) **C-107m.** BOMB D: Michael Apted. Richard Pryor, Rachel Ticotin, Ruben Blades, Joe Mantegna, Bob Dishy, Sylvia Miles, Joe Dallesandro, Bob Saget, Randall "Tex" Cobb, Garrett Morris. Pryor is a con artist who takes charge at a prison hospital, with predictable results. He's in good form, but the material just isn't there; its semiserious and sentimental threads don't work at all, and the comedy is pretty anemic. [R]▼◐●

Critic's Choice (1963) C-100m. **½ D: Don Weis. Bob Hope, Lucille Ball, Marilyn Maxwell, Rip Torn, Jessie Royce Landis, Marie Windsor, John Dehner. An in-joke Broadway play diluted for movie audience consumption. Lucy as a novice playwright outshines Hope who plays her drama critic hubby. Film emerges as tired, predictable comedy, with best moments contributed by supporting players. Based on a play by Ira Levin. Panavision. ▼◑

Critters (1986) C-86m. **½ D: Stephen Herek. Dee Wallace Stone, M. Emmet Walsh, Billy Green Bush, Scott Grimes, Nadine Van Der Velde, Terrence Mann, Billy Zane. GREMLINS-inspired aliens roll along like tumbleweeds, gobbling everything in sight while chuckling to themselves—until they're menaced by critter-hunters from space. Pretty good little thriller with comic overtones. Followed by three sequels. [PG-13]▼◐●

Critters 2: The Main Course (1988) C-87m. ** D: Mick Garris. Scott Grimes, Liane Curtis, Don Opper, Barry Corbin, Tom Hodges, Sam Anderson, Lindsay Parker, Herta Ware, Terrence Mann, Roxanne Kernohan. The big-mouthed, quill-shooting nasties take on an entire town. Nothing special. Followed by two video sequels. [PG-13]▼◐●

"Crocodile" Dundee (1986-Australian) C-97m. *** D: Peter Faiman. Paul Hogan, Linda Kozlowski, John Meillon, David Gulpilil, Mark Blum, Michael Lombard, Irving Metzman. Amiable, laid-back Aussie comedy (that became an enormous worldwide hit) about an adventurer who shows a pretty American reporter around the bush country, then accompanies her to the equally strange terrain of N.Y.C. Irresistibly simple and old-fashioned, with a sweetness that's rare in modern comedies. Hogan, making his movie debut, also cowrote the screenplay (reportedly inspired by TARZAN'S NEW YORK ADVENTURE). For American release quotation marks were added around CROCODILE—lest anyone think it was about a reptile! Followed by two sequels. Panavision. [PG-13]▼◐●

"Crocodile" Dundee II (1988-U.S.-Australian) C-111m. **½ D: John Cornell. Paul Hogan, Linda Kozlowski, John Meillon, Ernie Dingo, Hechter Ubarry, Juan Fernandez, Charles Dutton, Kenneth Welsh, Luis Guzman, Stephen Root, Colin Quinn. Pleasant followup to the runaway hit reverses the original by opening in N.Y.C. and winding up in the bush country of Australia. This time the unflappable tracker runs afoul of an international drug kingpin. So leisurely that after a while you wish they'd get on with it—especially when all suspense about the outcome is eliminated. Hogan's charisma carries this almost singlehand-

edly. Written by Hogan and his son Brett. Panavision. [PG]▼◐●

Crocodile Dundee in Los Angeles (2001-U.S.-Australian) C-95m. *½ D: Simon Wincer. Paul Hogan, Linda Kozlowski, Serge Cockburn, Jere Burns, Jonathan Banks, Paul Rodriguez, Aida Turturro. Mick Dundee accompanies his '80s squeeze Sue (Kozlowski) to L.A. when she travels there to run the family newspaper and checks out the sights with their 9-year-old son. First *Croco*-pic in 13 years is as tired as it sounds, despite cameos by Mike Tyson and George Hamilton (touting coffee enemas. Decaf or regular?). Sue's investigative reporting attempts to discover why a Hollywood studio keeps producing unwanted sequels, which is more irony than this picture can handle. [PG]▼

Crocodile Hunter: Collision Course, The (2002-Australian-U.S.) C-90m. *½ D: John Stainton. Steve Irwin, Terri Irwin, Magda Szubanski, David Wenham, Lachy Hulme, Aden Young, Kenneth Ransom, Kate Beahan. Contrived movie vehicle for the popular Aussie TV host and animal lover Irwin features nail-biting footage of him confronting snakes, spiders, and crocodiles, but it's surrounded by a storyline so lame (enacted by an equally lame cast) that it hardly seems worth the trouble. For the record, a croc has swallowed a satellite capsule that the CIA needs to recover. Youthful fans are better off watching a rerun of the TV show instead. Super 35. [PG] ▼

Cromwell (1970-British) C-145m. ** D: Ken Hughes. Richard Harris, Alec Guinness, Robert Morley, Dorothy Tutin, Frank Finlay, Timothy Dalton, Patrick Wymark, Patrick Magee, Nigel Stock, Charles Gray, Michael Jayston, Geoffrey Keen. Turgid historical epic that has everything money can buy, but no human feeling underneath. Harris is coldly unsympathetic as 17th-century Briton determined to rid England of tyrannical rule; one feels more sympathy for King Charles I (Guinness), which is not the idea. Great battle scenes, great cinematography and Oscar-winning costume design, hampered by Harris and amateurish music score. Panavision. [G]▼◐●

Crónicas (2004-Mexican-Ecuadorian) C-98m. ** D: Sebastián Cordero. John Leguizamo, Leonor Watling, Damián Alcazár, José María Yazpik, Alfred Molina. Underdeveloped, repetitive story about a hotshot TV reporter who fancies himself a hero of the people. He intervenes in a lynching but learns that the man whose life he saved may have a connection to a serial killer. He keeps probing deeper, trying to get the elusive story while fending off his boss (Molina)—and carrying on an affair with the man's wife, who is also his producer. Leguizamo is good as usual, but the story doesn't add up. [R] ◐

Cronos (1992-Mexican) C-92m. *** D: Guillermo del Toro. Federico Luppi, Ron

Perlman, Claudio Brook, Margarita Isabel, Tamara Shanath, Daniel Cacho, Mario Martinez, Juan Colombo, Farnesio DeBernal. An elderly, kindly antique dealer accidentally activates the Cronos Device, an instrument that grants eternal life—but at a great price: it turns the person who uses it into a (nontraditional) vampire. Howard Hughes–like billionaire Brook sends his chuckling nephew Perlman after the gadget. Inventive, entertaining film blends wit, horror, tragedy, and suspense in about equal doses, adding lots of oddball character details.▼▶

Crook, The (1971-French) **C-120m.** *** D: Claude Lelouch. Jean-Louis Trintignant, Daniele Delorme, Charles Denner, Christine Lelouch. An elaborate kidnapping scheme takes surprising twists in this stylish and clever caper. [G]▶

Crooked Hearts (1991) **C-112m.** *** D: Michael Bortman. Vincent D'Onofrio, Jennifer Jason Leigh, Pete Berg, Cindy Pickett, Peter Coyote, Juliette Lewis, Noah Wyle, Marg Helgenberger, Wendy Gazelle. Engaging, multileveled domestic drama showing how husband/father Coyote's indiscretion affects the various members of his family. A thoughtful, well-acted sleeper. Bortman also scripted, from Robert Boswell's novel. [R]▼●▶

Crooklyn (1994) **C-132m.** **½ D: Spike Lee. Alfre Woodard, Delroy Lindo, David Patrick Kelly, Zelda Harris, Carlton Williams, Sharif Rashed, Tse-Mach Washington, Christopher Knowings, Jose Zuniga, Spike Lee, Frances Foster, Norman Matlock, Joie Susannah Lee, Vondie Curtis Hall, RuPaul. At times abrasive, at times embracing comedy-drama about a family's life and times in 1970s Brooklyn, focusing on young Troy (Harris), who has a special relationship with her fiery mother and warmhearted father—and little use for her four raucous brothers. Vivid, semi-autobiographical film, written by Lee with his brother and sister, has strong performances and many fine moments, but it seems aimless at first and goes on for quite some time. One long sequence is shot in a deliberately distorted format. [PG-13]▼●▶

Crooks and Coronets (1969-British) **C-106m.** ** D: Jim O'Connolly. Telly Savalas, Edith Evans, Warren Oates, Cesar Romero, Harry H. Corbett. Crooks Savalas and Oates are hired to rob Evans' estate, but can't bring themselves to do it once they get to know her. Amiable but ordinary heist comedy. Aka SOPHIE'S PLACE. [M/PG]▼

Cross and the Switchblade, The (1970) **C-106m.** *½ D: Don Murray. Pat Boone, Erik Estrada, Jackie Giroux, Jo-Ann Robinson. Crusading minister Boone winds up in New York street-gang rumbles. Uneven, uninteresting, though sincere attempt at uplifting, moralistic filmmaking. [PG]▼▶

Cross Creek (1983) **C-122m.** *** D: Mar-

tin Ritt. Mary Steenburgen, Rip Torn, Peter Coyote, Dana Hill, Alfre Woodard, Joanna Miles, Ike Eisenmann, Cary Guffey, Jay O. Sanders. Leisurely paced but rewarding drama of writer Marjorie Kinnan Rawlings' endeavor to "find herself" by moving to remote Florida backwoods home—and dealing with the simple people around her. Wonderful performances and regional flavor—though Dalene Young's script takes more than a few liberties with the facts. Steenburgen's then real-life husband Malcolm McDowell has cameo as famed editor Maxwell Perkins. [PG]▼▶

Crossed Swords (1954-Italian) **C-86m.** *½ D: Milton Krims. Errol Flynn, Gina Lollobrigida, Cesare Danova, Nadia Gray. Unsuccessful attempt to recapture flavor of swashbucklers of 1930s; set in 16th-century Italy with Flynn out to save Gina and her father's kingdom.

Crossed Swords (1978) **C-113m.** ** D: Richard Fleischer. Mark Lester, Oliver Reed, Raquel Welch, Ernest Borgnine, George C. Scott, Rex Harrison, Charlton Heston. Lester is too old for his dual role in well-acted but flat version of Mark Twain's *The Prince and the Pauper*. Lavish sets, costumes, and Jack Cardiff's photography are main assets. Aka THE PRINCE AND THE PAUPER. Panavision. [PG]▼

Crossfire (1947) **86m.** ***½ D: Edward Dmytryk. Robert Young, Robert Mitchum, Robert Ryan, Gloria Grahame, Paul Kelly, Richard Benedict, Sam Levene, Jacqueline White, Steve Brodie, Lex Barker. Engrossing film of insane ex-soldier leading city police in murderous chase. Anti-Semitic issue handled with taste, intelligence. Script by John Paxton, from Richard Brooks' novel *The Brick Foxhole*. Also shown in computer-colored version.▼●▶

Crossing Delancey (1988) **C-97m.** *** D: Joan Micklin Silver. Amy Irving, Reizl Bozyk, Peter Riegert, Jeroen Krabbé, Sylvia Miles, Suzzy Roche, George Martin, John Bedford Lloyd, Claudia Silver, Rosemary Harris, Amy Wright, David (Hyde) Pierce. Charming comedy about a self-reliant young N.Y.C. woman whose Jewish grandmother arranges for her to meet an eligible bachelor through the services of a marriage broker . . . much to her chagrin. Amusing, sometimes wistful look at the clash between old-world traditions and our modern way of life. Adapted by Susan Sandler, from her play. [PG]▼●▶

Crossing Guard, The (1995) **C-114m.** ** D: Sean Penn. Jack Nicholson, David Morse, Anjelica Huston, Robin Wright, Piper Laurie, Richard Bradford, Robbie Robertson, John Savage, Priscilla Barnes, Kari Wuhrer, Richard Sarafian, Joe Viterelli. Introspective mood piece about a man's inability to deal with the drunk-driving death of his young daughter six years earlier, and his pursuit of the killer, who's just been released from prison. Sober and somber, but heavy-handed and never terribly moving. Penn wrote the original screenplay; his mother, Eileen Ryan, plays a jewelry store customer, and his father, Leo Penn, plays the skipper of a fishing boat. [R] ▼●❙

Crossing Over (2009) **C-114m.** *½ D: Wayne Kramer. Harrison Ford, Ray Liotta, Ashley Judd, Jim Sturgess, Cliff Curtis, Summer Bishil, Alice Braga, Alice Eve, Jacqueline Obradors, Justin Chon, Melody Khazae, Lizzy Caplan. Police and border officials are confronted daily with the human drama of ethnic strife, urban violence, and fraud. Cross-section of L.A. intersects (à la CRASH) with the thread being illegal immigration and cultural assimilation. Ford and Curtis are fine as U.S. Immigration and Customs Enforcement agent-partners but, like the other leads, they are stranded in a jumbled film that oversimplifies everything. Exploitative hodgepodge involving multiple races and religions—as well as sleaze—just doesn't jell. Super 35. [R]❙

Crossing the Bridge (1992) **C-103m.** **½ D: Mike Binder. Josh Charles, Jason Gedrick, Stephen Baldwin, Cheryl Pollak, Jeffrey Tambor, Rita Taggart, Hy Anzell, Richard Edson, Ken Jenkins, David Schwimmer. Modest memory movie, set in the 1960s, about Detroit teens tempted to cross the bridge into Windsor, Canada—to transport hashish back into the States. Nothing special, but certainly nothing disgraceful, either. Stephen Baldwin gets a good showcase here. [R]▼❙

Crossing the Line (1991-U.S.-English-Scottish) **C-93m.** **½ D: David Leland. Liam Neeson, Joanne Whalley-Kilmer, Ian Bannen, Billy Connolly, Hugh Grant, Maurice Roeves, Rab Affleck. Two-fisted mine worker who's been blackballed out of work accepts an offer from a mysterious millionaire to fight bare-knuckled, but begins to worry that he's abandoned his principles for some quick cash. Serious-minded film has pretensions of eloquence and import, but doesn't really deliver; solid performances and canny filmmaking help. Connolly is a standout as Neeson's cheerfully sleazy friend. Based on William McIlvanney's novel *The Big Man* (also its video title). [R]▼❙

Cross My Heart (1987) **C-90m.** ** D: Armyan Bernstein. Martin Short, Annette O'Toole, Paul Reiser, Joanna Kerns. The story of a date where everything goes wrong, mainly because both the man and the woman refuse to act natural and be themselves. Winning costars bring out the truthful observations in this comic script (by director Bernstein and Gail Parent), but it's just too slight, and too slow. [R]▼❙

Cross of Iron (1977-British-West German) **C-119m.** *** D: Sam Peckinpah. James Coburn, Maximilian Schell, James Mason, David Warner, Senta Berger, Klaus Lowitsch. Peckinpah's only war film, told from

the viewpoint of Germans on the Russian front in 1943, is compelling without being particularly distinguished. The standard Peckinpah action scenes are excitingly done. European version runs 130m. Sequel: BREAKTHROUGH. [R]▼❙

Cross of Lorraine, The (1943) **90m.** ***½ D: Tay Garnett. Jean-Pierre Aumont, Gene Kelly, Cedric Hardwicke, Richard Whorf, Joseph Calleia, Peter Lorre, Hume Cronyn. High-grade propaganda of WW2 POW camp with hero Aumont rousing defeated Kelly to battle; Whorf is dedicated doctor, Lorre a despicable Nazi, Cronyn a fickle informer.

Crossover (1980) SEE: **Mr. Patman**

Crossover (2006) **C-95m.** ** D: Preston A. Whitmore II. Anthony Mackie, Wesley Jonathan, Wayne Brady, Kristen Wilson, Lil' JJ, Phillip "Hot Sauce" Champion, Eva Pigford, Alecia Fears. Onetime sports agent (Brady), now a hotshot gambler, tempts hoopster friends with an offer to escape Detroit and become L.A. superstars. Mackie hopes his underground streetballer skills can shoot him to the big time, while Jonathan aims to become a doctor on an athletic scholarship. So what's it gonna be: no go or go pro, M.D. or MVP? Faustian morality play has visual zip and the hop that's hip, but the director's script is less than a pip. [PG-13]❙

Crossover Dreams (1985) **C-86m.** ** D: Leon Ichaso. Ruben Blades, Shawn Elliot, Tom Signorelli, Elizabeth Pena, Frank Robles, Joel Diamond. Salsa performer Blades starts shafting his pals, enjoying the good life, when he thinks his upcoming album is going to make him a smash with mainstream audiences . . . then the record flops. Standard backstage drama offers nothing beyond novel ethnicity, though Blades has real presence on camera.▼❙

Crossroads (1942) **82m.** *** D: Jack Conway. William Powell, Hedy Lamarr, Claire Trevor, Basil Rathbone, Margaret Wycherly, Felix Bressart, Reginald Owen, Sig Ruman, H. B. Warner. Smooth, clever tale of respected diplomat Powell, who was once a victim of amnesia; he is accused by an extortionist of having a previous identity as a sly petty crook, causing much grief for him and his new wife (Lamarr). ❙

Crossroads (1986) **C-96m.** **½ D: Walter Hill. Ralph Macchio, Joe Seneca, Jami Gertz, Joe Morton, Robert Judd, Harry Carey, Jr. Cocky young musician tracks down legendary bluesman in a Harlem hospital and agrees to bring him back to his Mississippi home in return for some long-lost songs. Promising idea turns into contrived formula film (with undeveloped subplot about the old-timer having sold his soul to the devil). Gets a shot in the arm from Ry Cooder's music score and Seneca's flavorful performance as the cranky old bluesman. [R]▼●❙

Crossroads (2002) **C-94m.** **½ D: Tamra

Davis. Britney Spears, Anson Mount, Zoë Saldaña, Taryn Manning, Kim Cattrall, Dan Aykroyd, Justin Long, Beverly Johnson. Teenage girl who's always followed Daddy's wishes finally cuts loose by taking a cross-country road trip with two girlhood friends and a guy with a 1973 Cadil convertible. Her goal: to meet the mother who abandoned her when she was three. Debut vehicle for pop star Spears doesn't waste time showing her in her underwear—and also gives her a couple of songs. Innocuous, predictable teen fare with a few serious moments. [PG-13] ▼●

Crouching Tiger, Hidden Dragon (2000-Hong Kong-Taiwanese-U.S.) **C-119m.** **½ D: Ang Lee. Chow Yun-Fat, Michelle Yeoh, Zhang Ziyi, Chang Chen, Lung Sihung, Cheng Pei-Pei. Unusual hybrid of epic, romance, and martial arts, which follows the secret passions that a retiring warrior (Yun-Fat) and his longtime comrade (Yeoh) have for each other, and the dangerous young noblewoman (Ziyi) who affects their destiny. Beautifully filmed, with spectacular, gravity-defying fight sequences . . . but the characters and the (very protracted) story are never as compelling as one would like. Adapted from the novel by Wand Du Lu. The action was choreographed by Yuen Wo Ping, who performed similar chores on THE MATRIX. Oscar winner for Best Foreign Film, Cinematography (Peter Pau), Art Direction (Tim Yip), and Original Score (Tan Dun). Super 35. [PG-13] ▼●

Croupier (1999-British-German) **C-91m.** ***½ D: Mike Hodges. Clive Owen, Gina McKee, Alex Kingston, Alexander Morton, Kate Hardie, Paul Reynolds, Nick Reding, Nicholas Ball. Highly original film about a young man who, while pursuing his goal to become a published author, takes a job as croupier in a London casino—but never stops observing those around him, or remarking on his own behavior. Tough, smart script by Paul Mayersberg. ▼●

Crow, The (1994) **C-100m.** *** D: Alex Proyas. Brandon Lee, Ernie Hudson, Michael Wincott, David Patrick Kelly, Angel David, Rochelle Davis, Bai Ling, Tony Todd, Jon Polito. A year after his murder and that of his fiancée by inner-city hoodlums, a young rock musician rises from the grave, seeking vengeance; he's guided by a spectral crow. Dark, rainy, and violent, the film's familiar revenge plot is offset by a strong style and an aura of tragic melancholy. Great urban-hell production design, good performances. Lee died shortly before filming was complete; digital movie magic enabled him to appear in the rest of the picture. From James O'Barr's black and white comic book. Followed by a sequel, a TV movie, and TV series. [R] ▼●

Crow: City of Angels, The (1996) **C-84m.** BOMB D: Tim Pope. Vincent Perez, Mia Kirshner, Richard Brooks, Iggy Pop, Thomas Jane, Vincent Castellanos, Thuy Trang. Anemic follow-up to THE CROW, concerning a murdered man who returns to life in order to seek revenge on those who killed him and his cute young son. If you last to the end of the film, you'll be wishing he stayed six feet under. Perez is as grating as the nonstop soundtrack. [R] ▼●

Crowd, The (1928) **104m.** **** D: King Vidor. Eleanor Boardman, James Murray, Bert Roach, Daniel G. Tomlinson, Dell Henderson, Lucy Beaumont. Classic drama about a few happy and many not-so-happy days in the marriage of hard-luck couple. One of the greatest silent films; holds up beautifully. Written by Harry Behn, John V.A. Weaver, and director Vidor, from the latter's original story. ▼●

Crowd Roars, The (1932) **70m.** **½ D: Howard Hawks. James Cagney, Joan Blondell, Ann Dvorak, Eric Linden, Guy Kibbee, Frank McHugh. Exciting racing-driver tale with Cagney in typically cocky role, familiar plot devices, but well done by Warner Bros. stock company. Remade as INDIANAPOLIS SPEEDWAY.

Crucible, The (1956-French-East German) **140m.** *** D: Raymond Rouleau. Simone Signoret, Yves Montand, Mylene Demongeot, Jean Debucourt, Raymond Rouleau. Successful French translation of Arthur Miller's stirring play about the Salem witchcraft trials of the 17th century. Signoret and Montand are excellent, recreating their stage performances in the leading roles. Adaptation by Jean-Paul Sartre. Originally titled THE WITCHES OF SALEM. Remade in 1996. ▼

Crucible, The (1996) **C-123m.** *** D: Nicholas Hytner. Daniel Day-Lewis, Winona Ryder, Joan Allen, Paul Scofield, Bruce Davison, Rob Campbell, Jeffrey Jones, George Gaynes. Caught performing a "sinful" dance, a group of New England girls, led by Ryder, claim they were overtaken by the Devil; soon their village is caught in a frenzy of accusations, naming various citizens as witches without so much as a shred of evidence. First American film rendering of Arthur Miller's classic 1953 play about parallels between Salem witch-hunts of the 1600s and Communist witch-hunts of the 1940s and '50s. Gets off to a shaky start, but finds its voice as the story deepens, and hits its stride with the arrival of Scofield, who's brilliant as the judge and inquisitor. Miller himself wrote the screenplay. [PG-13] ▼●

Crucible of Horror (1971-British) **C-91m.** ** D: Viktors Ritelis. Michael Gough, Sharon Gurney, Yvonne Mitchell. Murdered man returns to haunt the living. Nothing new here. [PG] ▼●

Crucified Lovers, The (1954-Japanese) **100m.** ***½ D: Kenji Mizoguchi. Kazuo Hasegawa, Kyoko Kagawa, Yoko Minamida, Eitaro Shindo, Sakae Ozawa. Timid scroll-

[302]

maker Hasegawa loves his master's wife (Kagawa), with tragic results. Superior performances, stunning direction; originally a marionette play written in 1715. Better known by its original Japanese title, CHIKAMATSU MONOGATARI.▼

Cruel Intentions (1999) **C-97m.** ** D: Roger Kumble. Ryan Phillippe, Sarah Michelle Gellar, Reese Witherspoon, Selma Blair, Joshua Jackson, Eric Mabius, Christine Baranski, Swoosie Kurtz, Louise Fletcher, Tara Reid. Contemporary telling of Choderlos de Laclos' 18th-century novel *Les Liaisons Dangereuses* . . . with teenagers! Wealthy, jaded stepsiblings Phillippe and Gellar bet on whether he can seduce virgin Witherspoon. The cast is good, story is interesting, but sexual decadence among the young is sometimes hard to watch. Followed by video prequel (a failed TV pilot) and sequel. [R]▼●)

Cruel Sea, The (1953-British) **121m.** ***½ D: Charles Frend. Jack Hawkins, Donald Sinden, Denholm Elliott, Stanley Baker, John Stratton, Virginia McKenna, Alec McCowen. Well-conceived documentary-style account of British warship during WW2 and its crew. Original British running time 126m.▼)

Cruel Swamp SEE: **Swamp Women**

Cruising (1980) **C-106m.** *½ D: William Friedkin. Al Pacino, Paul Sorvino, Karen Allen, Richard Cox, Don Scardino, Ed O'Neil, voice of James Sutorius. Cop Pacino goes underground to ferret out bloody killer of homosexuals in this distasteful, badly scripted film. Gay world presented as sick, degrading, and ritualistic. Filmed on authentic N.Y.C. locations. [R]▼)

Crumb (1994) **C-119m.** ***½ D: Terry Zwigoff. Extraordinarily intimate portrait of underground comic artist (and cult hero) Robert Crumb, creator of "Keep on Truckin'" and Fritz the Cat. Zwigoff traces his career and celebrates his works while exploring the cultural influences that shaped him. By the time we meet Crumb's dysfunctional brothers, we realize that he survived a horrific upbringing and found a way to channel his own demons through his art. Perhaps this documentary's greatest achievement is enabling almost any viewer to feel better about his own family! [R] ▼●)

Crusades, The (1935) **123m.** *** D: Cecil B. DeMille. Loretta Young, Henry Wilcoxon, Ian Keith, C. Aubrey Smith, Katherine DeMille, Joseph Schildkraut, Alan Hale, C. Henry Gordon, J. Carrol Naish. Love, action, and great big siege machines in DeMille version of medieval era Holy Crusades spectacle that's good for fun, with Young a luminous queen who's kidnapped by infidels; Wilcoxon as Richard the Lion-Hearted must rescue her. Look fast for Ann Sheridan as a Christian girl.▼)

Crush (1992-New Zealand) **C-97m.** **½ D: Alison Maclean. Marcia Gay Harden, Donough Rees, Caitlin Bossley, William Zappa. Intriguing, multi-layered (if occasionally overbaked) tale of seduction, betrayal, jealousy and revenge, in which Harden impersonates her friend, literary critic Rees (who's just been injured in a car crash), and becomes involved in the lives of a writer and his teen daughter. Director-coscripter Maclean's feature debut is crammed with offbeat touches, hidden meanings, and agendas; at its best when exploring the complex relationship of the three female characters.▼)

Crush, The (1993) **C-89m.** *½ D: Alan Shapiro. Cary Elwes, Alicia Silverstone, Jennifer Rubin, Amber Benson, Kurtwood Smith, Gwynyth Walsh. Ridiculous thriller about a thick-witted, twentysomething journalist (Elwes) who becomes the target of a pretty, obsessive fourteen-year-old Lolita (Silverstone). A completely unnecessary FATAL ATTRACTION/HAND THAT ROCKS THE CRADLE/SINGLE WHITE FEMALE clone; for a perceptive, nonexploitive look at the same subject, see the 1981 French film BEAU PÈRE. [R]▼●)

Crush (2002-British) **C-115m.** *** D: John McKay. Andie MacDowell, Imelda Staunton, Anna Chancellor, Kenny Doughty, Bill Paterson, Caroline Holdaway. Headmistress of a British prep school shares secrets and gossip with two close female friends, but when she plunges into a passionate affair with a much younger man, they disapprove strongly and begin to meddle. Starts out light and funny and turns unexpectedly dark; not always believable, but consistently entertaining. Writer-director McKay wins us over on an emotional level in his debut feature. Panavision. [R]▼)

Crusoe (1988) **C-91m.** *** D: Caleb Deschanel. Aidan Quinn, Ade Sapara, Warren Clark, Hepburn Grahame, Jimmy Nail, Tim Spall, Michael Higgins, Shane Rimmer, Oliver Platt. Solid version of the oft-filmed Defoe classic, with Quinn cast as the title character, a slave trader who's shipwrecked on a deserted isle, where he must deal with loneliness, isolation, survival; most intriguing of all is his evolving relationship with black warrior Sapara. Strikingly photographed by Tom Pinter, mostly in the Seychelles. [PG-13]▼)

Cry-Baby (1990) **C-85m.** **½ D: John Waters. Johnny Depp, Amy Locane, Susan Tyrrell, Polly Bergen, Iggy Pop, Ricki Lake, Traci Lords, Kim McGuire, Troy Donahue, Mink Stole, Joe Dallesandro, Joey Heatherton, David Nelson, Patricia Hearst, Willem Dafoe. Baltimore, 1954, and good-girl Locane is torn between her pristine roots and kids in black leather—especially the Elvis type (Depp) who'd love her to mount his cycle. More polished than Waters' previous HAIRSPRAY, but not as well focused, though performed with gusto. Uneven and exhausting; a few set pieces really deliver.

Director's cut runs 95m. Later turned into a Broadway musical. [PG-13]▼●)

Cry Baby Killer, The (1958) **62m.** *½ D: Jus Addiss. Harry Lauter, Jack Nicholson, Carolyn Mitchell, Brett Halsey, Lynn Cartwright, Ed Nelson. Nicholson's film debut is a Roger Corman quickie about juvenile delinquent who panics when he thinks he's committed murder. A curio at best, with co-scripter Leo Gordon and Corman himself in bit parts. ▶

Cry Danger (1951) **79m.** *** D: Robert Parrish. Dick Powell, Rhonda Fleming, Richard Erdman, Regis Toomey, William Conrad. Effective revenge yarn; ex-con Powell hunts down those responsible for framing him.▼

Cry for Happy (1961) **C-110m.** **½ D: George Marshall. Glenn Ford, Donald O'Connor, Miiko Taka, Myoshi Umeki. Poor man's TEAHOUSE OF THE AUGUST MOON, involving Navy photography team in Tokyo using a geisha house for their home. CinemaScope.

Cry for Me, Billy (1972) **C-93m.** ** D: William A. Graham. Cliff Potts, Xochitl, Harry Dean Stanton, Don Wilbanks. Drifter falls in love with Indian girl, with tragic consequences, in this violent Western. Its title (and alleged year of release) keeps changing, but the film doesn't get any better. Aka FACE TO THE WIND, COUNT YOUR BULLETS, APACHE MASSACRE, and THE LONG TOMORROW. Panavision. [R]▼

Cry Freedom (1987-British) **C-157m.** *** D: Richard Attenborough. Kevin Kline, Penelope Wilton, Denzel Washington, Kevin McNally, John Thaw, Timothy West, Juanita Waterman, John Hargreaves, Alec McCowen, Zakes Mokae, Ian Richardson. Sweeping and compassionate film about South African activist Steve Biko (well played by Washington) and his friendship with crusading newspaper editor Donald Woods (Kline). Unfortunately second half of film, minus the Biko character, loses momentum as it spends too much time on Kline and his family's escape from South Africa, but cannily injects flashbacks of Biko to steer it back on course. Screenplay by John Briley. Super 35. [PG]▼●)

Cry "Havoc" (1943) **97m.** *** D: Richard Thorpe. Margaret Sullavan, Joan Blondell, Ann Sothern, Fay Bainter, Marsha Hunt, Ella Raines, Frances Gifford, Diana Lewis, Heather Angel. Female volunteers join some overworked American nurses on beleaguered island of Bataan during WW2. Reveals its stage origins and incorporates expected clichés, but also presents pretty honest picture of war. Robert Mitchum has a bit part as a dying soldier. ▶

Crying Game, The (1992-British) **C-112m.** ***½ D: Neil Jordan. Stephen Rea,

Miranda Richardson, Forest Whitaker, Jim Broadbent, Ralph Brown, Adrian Dunbar, Jaye Davidson. Strikingly original and adult story with Rea as an IRA volunteer who helps capture a British soldier (Whitaker) only to befriend him and later become involved with his lover. What begins as a thriller unexpectedly turns into a poignant and ironic love story, with plot twists that deepen the film's almost dreamlike power. Stunningly acted by Rea, Richardson, and Whitaker, with an amazing debut by Davidson, as Dil. A unique, seductive film that writer/director Jordan pulls off with poetic ease; he earned an Oscar for his screenplay. Panavision. [R]▼●)

Cry in the Dark, A (1988-U.S.-Australian) **C-121m.** ***½ D: Fred Schepisi. Meryl Streep, Sam Neill, Bruce Myles, Charles Tingwell, Nick Tate, Neil Fitzpatrick, Maurie Fields, Lewis Fitzgerald. Astonishing true story of Lindy Chamberlain, an Australian woman accused of murdering her baby, despite her claims that the child was carried off by a dingo (wild dog). Writer-director Schepisi tells his story with almost documentary-like reality, eloquently attacking the process of trial by rumor that made Chamberlain and her husband the most maligned couple in Australia. Streep and Neill are heartbreakingly good. Australian title: EVIL ANGELS. Panavision. [PG-13]▼●)

Cry in the Night, A (1956) **75m.** ** D: Frank Tuttle. Edmond O'Brien, Brian Donlevy, Natalie Wood, Raymond Burr, Richard Anderson. Why is mysterious, psychotic Burr spying on Wood and her boyfriend? And what happens after he kidnaps her? Overwrought drama, but fascinating as a time capsule of its era, and then prevalent attitudes toward cops and victims. Burr is quite good.

Cry of the Banshee (1970-British) **C-87m.** **½ D: Gordon Hessler. Vincent Price, Elisabeth Bergner, Essy Persson, Hugh Griffith, Hilary Dwyer, Sally Geeson, Patrick Mower. Witch Oona (Bergner) summons servant of Satan to avenge nobleman (Price)'s bloody reign of witch-hunting. Confusion sets in midway. [PG]▼●)

Cry of the City (1948) **95m.** **½ D: Robert Siodmak. Victor Mature, Richard Conte, Fred Clark, Shelley Winters, Betty Garde, Debra Paget, Hope Emerson. Rehash of MANHATTAN MELODRAMA about childhood pals, one who becomes a cop, the other a criminal—slick but predictable.

Cry of the Penguins (1971-British) **C-101m.** ** D: Al Viola. John Hurt, Hayley Mills, Dudley Sutton, Tony Britton, Thorley Walters, Judy Campbell. Can a womanizing young biologist find true happiness and redemption among an Antarctic colony of penguins? Do you care? Similar to later NEVER CRY WOLF—except in interest.

Famed documentary filmmaker Arne Sucksdorff shot the fascinating but horrifying scenes of life and death among a penguin colony; an uncredited Roy Boulting reportedly directed the scenes with Hayley Mills. Original British title: MR. FORBUSH AND THE PENGUINS.▶

Crystal Heart (1987) C-102m. ** D: Gil Bettman. Tawny Kitaen, Lee Curreri, Lloyd Bochner, Simon Andreu, May Heatherly, Marina Saura. Young man who must live his life like the "boy in a bubble," confined to a controlled environment, develops a relationship with a sexy rock singer with whom he's fallen in love long-distance. Mild, predictable outing with music video segments from Kitaen. [R]▼

Cry Terror! (1958) 96m. *** D: Andrew L. Stone. James Mason, Rod Steiger, Inger Stevens, Neville Brand, Angie Dickinson, Jack Klugman. Tight pacing conceals implausibilities in caper of psychopath Steiger forcing Mason to aid him in master extortion plot, filmed on N.Y.C. locations. Stevens good as Mason's frightened but resourceful wife. Also shown in computer-colored version.

Cry, the Beloved Country (1952-British) 111m. ***½ D: Zoltan Korda. Canada Lee, Charles Carson, Sidney Poitier, Geoffrey Keen, Reginald Ngeabo, Joyce Carey. Simple back-country minister journeys to Johannesburg in search of his son, while fate links his path with that of a wealthy, bigoted white landowner. Heartrending story chronicles racial divisiveness (and its roots) in South Africa without resorting to preachiness. Alan Paton's book was also basis for stage and film musical LOST IN THE STARS. Some prints run 96m. Remade in 1995.▼●

Cry, the Beloved Country (1995-U.S.-British-South African) C-106m. *** D: Darrell James Roodt. Richard Harris, James Earl Jones, Charles S. Dutton, Vusi Kunene, Leleti Khumalo, Ian Roberts, Dambisa Kente, Eric Miyeni. Moving remake of the 1951 film based on Alan Paton's celebrated novel, about a backwoods minister (Jones) who, in 1946, makes his first-ever trip to the city of Johannesburg in search of his errant son, while wealthy landowner Harris travels there to claim the body of *his* son, who has just been killed. Excellent performances by Jones, Harris, and a largely unfamiliar supporting cast. Not as understated as the original, but effective in its own way. Screenplay by Ronald Harwood. [PG-13]▼●

Cry Uncle! (1971) C-87m. **½ D: John G. Avildsen. Allen Garfield, Madeleine de la Roux, Devin Goldenberg, David Kirk, Sean Walsh, Nancy Salmon. Private detective gets involved with murder, sex and blackmail in spoof of questionable taste; frequently hilarious, however. [R]▼▶

Cry Wolf (1947) 83m. ** D: Peter Godfrey.

Barbara Stanwyck, Errol Flynn, Geraldine Brooks, Richard Basehart, Jerome Cowan. Static adventure-mystery of Stanwyck attempting to untangle family secrets at late husband's estate.▼▶

Cry_Wolf (2005) C-90m. BOMB D: Jeff Wadlow. Lindy Booth, Julian Morris, Jared Padalecki, Kristy Wu, Sandra McCoy, Paul James, Jon Bon Jovi, Jesse Janzen, Gary Cole, Anna Deavere Smith. A group of attractive, unlikable prep school students play a prank on their classmates by e-mailing a chain letter claiming that there's a masked murderer on the loose. Not surprisingly, a real killer shows up to murder the members of the clique one by one. First-time director won a contest that awarded him one million dollars to make a film; he wasted a great opportunity. Unrated version also available. Super 35. [PG-13]▶

Cuba (1979) C-121m. *** D: Richard Lester. Sean Connery, Brooke Adams, Jack Weston, Hector Elizondo, Denholm Elliott, Chris Sarandon, Lonette McKee. Entertaining adventure film/love story has mercenary Connery renewing an old affair with factory manager Adams, set against the fall of Batista in late '59. Director Lester is in pretty good form, with most scenes punctuated by memorable throwaway bits. [R]▼▶

Cuba Crossing (1980) C-90m. BOMB D: Chuck Workman. Stuart Whitman, Robert Vaughn, Caren Kaye, Raymond St. Jacques, Woody Strode, Sybil Danning, Albert Salmi, Michael Gazzo. Tough Whitman becomes embroiled in a plot to kill Fidel Castro. Filmed in Key West, Florida, and at least the scenery is pretty. Retitled KILL CASTRO and ASSIGNMENT: KILL CASTRO. Video titles: THE MERCENARIES and SWEET VIOLENT TONY. [R]▼▶

Cuban Rebel Girls (1959) 68m. BOMB D: Barry Mahon. Errol Flynn, Beverly Aadland, John McKay, Marie Edmund, Jackie Jackler. Flynn's last film is an embarrassment: playing himself, he aids Fidel Castro in his overthrow of Batista. Shot on location during the Castro revolution. Of interest only to see Flynn teamed with his final girlfriend, 16-year-old Aadland. Aka ASSAULT OF THE REBEL GIRLS and ATTACK OF THE REBEL GIRLS.▼

Cube (1998-Canadian) C-90m. ** D: Vincenzo Natali. Maurice Dean Wint, Nicole deBoer, Nicky Guadagni, David Hewlett, Andrew Miller, Julian Richings, Wayne Robson. Or, six characters in search of an exit, from a giant cube with countless compartments—many of them booby-trapped. How and why are they there—and how can they escape? Nerves start to wear thin, which may also apply to the audience, as this intriguing film becomes highly unpleasant . . . with an unsatisfying conclusion. Cowritten by the director. Followed by two direct-to-video sequels. [R]▼●

Cujo (1983) **C-91m.** ******* D: Lewis Teague. Dee Wallace, Danny Pintauro, Daniel Hugh-Kelly, Christopher Stone, Ed Lauter, Mills Watson. Genuinely frightening adaptation of Stephen King thriller about a woman and her son terrorized by a rabid St. Bernard dog. Builds slowly but surely to terrifying (but not gory) climax. Not for children. [R]▼●]

Cul-De-Sac (1966-British) **111m.** ******* D: Roman Polanski. Donald Pleasence, Françoise Dorléac, Lionel Stander, Jack MacGowran, Iain Quarrier, Jacqueline Bisset. Macabre comedy about two wounded gangsters who terrorize middle-aged milquetoast and his beautiful young wife. Not a total success, but good cast and stylish direction make it a winner. Some prints cut to 103m.▼]

Culpepper Cattle Co., The (1972) **C-92m.** ****½** D: Dick Richards. Gary Grimes, Billy "Green" Bush, Luke Askew, Bo Hopkins, Geoffrey Lewis, Wayne Sutherlin. A 16-year-old persuades trail boss to take him along on cattle drive, becomes a man in the process. Fair but excessively violent Western. [R]▼]

Cult of the Damned SEE: **Angel, Angel, Down We Go**

Cult of the Dead SEE: **Snake People**

Cup, The (1999-Bhutanese) **C-93m.** ******* D: Khyentse Norbu. Jamyang Lodro, Orgyen Tobgyal, Neten Chokling, Lama Chonjor, Godu Lama, Thinley Nudi. Sweet, funny comedy in which an adolescent, soccer-obsessed Tibetan monk-in-training (Lodro) schemes to win permission to watch the 1998 World Cup final between France and Brazil on television. Slowly paced but still winning, with an insightful subtext examining spirituality, modernity, consumerism, and Tibet's endless political struggle against China. Writer-director Norbu is himself a Bhutanese high lama. [G]▼]

Curdled (1996) **C-94m.** ***½** D: Reb Braddock. William Baldwin, Angela Jones, Bruce Ramsay, Lois Chiles, Barry Corbin, Mel Gorham, Daisy Fuentes, Kelly Preston, Carmen Lopez. Grisly black comedy about young woman obsessed with the how's and why's of violent crimes, who gets a job scrubbing up after them on the Post-Forensic Cleaning Service. Only for viewers with the darkest sense of humor. Executive-produced by none other than Quentin Tarantino. [R]▼●]

Cure, The (1995) **C-99m.** ****½** D: Peter Horton. Joseph Mazzello, Brad Renfro, Annabella Sciorra, Diana Scarwid, Bruce Davison, Nicky Katt, Aeryk Egan, Renee Humphrey. Imperfect but often moving story about two small-town, pre-teen outsiders who become fast friends: new-kid-in-town Renfro and AIDS-stricken Mazzello, who contracted the HIV virus during a blood transfusion. At its best when focusing on the boys' evolving relationship; the title

refers to a miracle AIDS cure which plays a key role in the story. [PG-13]▼●]

Curious Case of Benjamin Button, The (2008) **C-166m.** ******** D: David Fincher. Brad Pitt, Cate Blanchett, Taraji P. Henson, Julia Ormond, Tilda Swinton, Jason Flemyng, Mahershalalhashbaz Ali, Jared Harris, Elias Koteas, Phyllis Somerville, Rampai Mohadi, Elle Fanning. Fascinating premise, from F. Scott Fitzgerald's short story (which in turn was inspired by a remark by Mark Twain): a baby is born in 1918 New Orleans with all the qualities of a shriveled old man and grows younger with each passing year. The story is told in flashback as his soul mate (Blanchett) lies on her deathbed, just as Hurricane Katrina is heading to town. Exceptional, epic storytelling in a rare movie that's long but doesn't feel that way. Even more amazing: director Fincher and his writers (Eric Roth, who collaborated on the screen story with Robin Swicord) avoid sentimentalizing their saga. Kudos to the stars, Alexandre Desplat's beautiful score, and Oscar-winning visual effects, makeup (Greg Cannom), and production design (Donald Graham Burt and Victor J. Zolfo). HD Widescreen. [PG-13]

Curious George (2006) **C-86m.** ****½** D: Matthew O'Callaghan. Voices of Will Ferrell, Drew Barrymore, David Cross, Eugene Levy, Dick Van Dyke, Joan Plowright, Alexander Gould, Frank Welker. A mischievous monkey from the jungle stows away with a friendly man in a yellow hat when he returns to the Big City. Basic, straightforward—if uninspired—cartoon feature for kids. Thankfully this expansion of the beloved books by H. A. and Margret Rey doesn't sacrifice their simple sweetness. A dialogue-free opening sequence works best of all. Original songs by Jack Johnson. [G]▮

Curly Sue (1991) **C-101m.** ***½** D: John Hughes. James Belushi, Kelly Lynch, Alisan Porter, John Getz, Fred Dalton Thompson, Cameron Thor, Steven (Steve) Carell, Edie McClurg. Homeless con artist and his adopted waif leech onto a tightly wound dish of an attorney. She, in turn, determines that this four-flushing twosome is just what she needs to enrich her life. A John Hughes formula movie where the formula doesn't work, though if there's such a thing as "quintessential James Belushi" this is it. Lynch's obvious discomfort suggests she may have seen the rushes. [PG]▼●]

Curse, The (1987) **C-90m.** BOMB D: David Keith. Wil Wheaton, Claude Akins, Cooper Huckabee, John Schneider, Amy Wheaton. Actor Keith steps behind the camera to direct this down-home horror movie: a deadly meteorite lands on a Tennessee farm, literally driving the folks crazy after contaminating their food. Loosely based on H. P. Lovecraft's novella *The Color Out of Space*, previously filmed as DIE, MONSTER,

DIE! Aka THE FARM. Followed by three unrelated "sequels." [R] ▼●◑

Cursed (2005) **C-97m.** ** D: Wes Craven. Christina Ricci, Portia de Rossi, Mya, Shannon Elizabeth, Solar, Daniel Edward Mora, Jesse Eisenberg, Joshua Jackson. Contemporary werewolf-on-the-loose story is a rare miss in the thrills department from the SCREAM team of Craven and writer Kevin Williamson. Film starts out amusing but soon becomes ludicrous as the nubile young victims must fight back to become human again. Already dated picture is set at the now-defunct Craig Kilborn talk show, where Ricci is a producer spending what seems like days prepping an interview with Scott Baio. It's that kind of movie, folks. Unrated version runs 105m. Super 35. [PG-13] ▼▶

Curse of Frankenstein, The (1957-British) **C-83m.** **½ D: Terence Fisher. Peter Cushing, Christopher Lee, Hazel Court, Robert Urquhart, Valerie Gaunt, Noel Hood. OK retelling of original Shelley tale, with Cushing as Baron von Frankenstein, whose experimentation with creation of life becomes an obsession. First of Hammer Films' longrunning horror series, and itself followed by six sequels, starting with THE REVENGE OF FRANKENSTEIN. ▼●◑

Curse of the Cat People, The (1944) **70m.** *** D: Gunther von Fritsch, Robert Wise. Simone Simon, Kent Smith, Jane Randolph, Elizabeth Russell, Ann Carter, Julia Dean. Follow-up to CAT PEOPLE creates wonderful atmosphere in story of lonely little girl who conjures up vision of Simon, her father's mysterious first wife. Despite title, not a horror film but a fine, moody fantasy. Produced by Val Lewton, written by DeWitt Bodeen. Wise's directing debut. Also available in computer-colored version. ▼●◑

Curse of the Crimson Altar SEE: Crimson Cult, The

Curse of the Demon (1957-British) **95m.** ***½ D: Jacques Tourneur. Dana Andrews, Peggy Cummins, Niall MacGinnis, Athene Seyler, Liam Redmond, Reginald Beckwith, Maurice Denham. Andrews is a psychologist who doesn't believe that series of deaths have been caused by ancient curse, but film convinces audience right off the bat and never lets up. Charles Bennett and producer Hal E. Chester adapted Montague R. James' story "Casting the Runes." Exceptional shocker, originally called NIGHT OF THE DEMON. Beware of truncated 83m. version. ▼●◑

Curse of the Fly (1965-British) **86m.** *½ D: Don Sharp. Brian Donlevy, Carole Gray, George Baker, Michael Graham, Jeremy Wilkins, Charles Carson, Burt Kwouk. In the third and last of original THE FLY series, young escapee (Gray) from a mental institution winds up involved with the Delambre family, still doggedly trying to make their teleportation machine work. Highly

inadequate makeup, weak script, but very atmospheric direction produce oddly mixed results. CinemaScope. ▶

Curse of the Golden Flower, The (2006-Hong Kong-Chinese) **C-114m.** **½ D: Zhang Yimou. Chow Yun-Fat, Gong Li, Jay Chou, Liu Ye, Ni Dahong, Qin Junjie, Li Man, Chen Jin. During the Tang dynasty, Chinese emperor Ping (Yun-Fat) and his ailing empress (Li) try to outmaneuver one another during a festival of golden chrysanthemums. Palace intrigue, a mysterious invading army, and Shakespearean-style relationships play out amidst breathtakingly gorgeous sets and costumes. Not quite up to Yimou's other historical epics (HERO, HOUSE OF FLYING DAGGERS), this is still heady stuff, with ripe histrionics occasionally interrupted by martial arts scenes. From a 1930s play by Cao Yu, previously filmed in 1957 (with Bruce Lee!) and 1961 as LEI YU. Super 35. [R]▶

Curse of the Jade Scorpion, The (2001) **C-102m.** ** D: Woody Allen. Woody Allen, Helen Hunt, Dan Aykroyd, Charlize Theron, David Ogden Stiers, Elizabeth Berkley, Wallace Shawn, Brian Markinson, Irwin Corey, John Schuck. Sexist insurance investigator in 1940s N.Y.C. can't abide the fact that his new superior is a woman. The plot thickens when both of them are "put under" by a nightclub hypnotist. Great period flavor, as usual, in this Allen comedy, and Woody is in great form, but many of his one-liners fall surprisingly flat, and Hunt seems too contemporary for her Rosalind Russell–type role. [PG-13] ▼▶

Curse of the Living Dead SEE: Kill, Baby, Kill

Curse of the Mummy's Tomb, The (1964-British) **C-81m.** ** D: Michael Carreras. Terence Morgan, Ronald Howard, Fred Clark, Jeanne Roland, George Pastell, Jack Gwillim, Dickie Owen (as the Mummy). Handsomely photographed but routine Hammer thriller featuring vengeful mummy at large in Victorian London, killing the usual profaners of the tomb in foggy surroundings. Most unusual twist: The (human) villain is in fact the Mummy's brother. Follow-up, not sequel, to THE MUMMY (1959). Techniscope. ▶

Curse of the Pink Panther (1983) **C-109m.** *½ D: Blake Edwards. Ted Wass, David Niven, Robert Wagner, Herbert Lom, Joanna Lumley, Capucine, Robert Loggia, Harvey Korman, Burt Kwouk, Leslie Ash, André Maranne, Bill Nighy. Writer-director Edwards' pointless attempt to keep the Pink Panther series alive despite Peter Sellers' death—by putting Wass through Sellers' sight-gag paces, and surrounding him with costars of earlier Panther films, who (all too obviously) shot their cameos at the same time as TRAIL OF THE PINK PANTHER. What a waste! Niven's final film (with his voice dubbed by Rich Little). Panavision. [PG]▼◗

Curse of the Swamp Creature (1966) C-80m. BOMB D: Larry Buchanan. John Agar, Francine York, Shirley McLine, Bill Thurman, Jeff Alexander. A geological expedition stumbles onto a mad doctor who's trying to evolve a man-monster. Low-budget junk.▼◗

Curse of the Werewolf, The (1961-British) C-91m. **½ D: Terence Fisher. Clifford Evans, Oliver Reed, Yvonne Romain, Anthony Dawson. Reed has wolf's blood and struggles to control the monster within him; it finally erupts when he is denied his girl's love. Eerie atmosphere pervades this good chiller. Loosely based on novel *The Werewolf of Paris* by Guy Endore.▼◗

Curse III: Blood Sacrifice (1990) C-91m. *½ D: Sean Barton. Christopher Lee, Jennilee Harrison, Henry Cole, Andre Jacobs, Zoe Randall, Olivia Dyer. 1950, East Africa. Tribal magic produces murderous demonlike monster (unseen until the end) slaughtering mostly whites. Drearily routine; one would-be "tense" scene (with no payoff) after another. Lee looks very serious. Original title: PANGA. [R]▼◗

Curtain Call (1998) C-94m. ** D: Peter Yates. James Spader, Polly Walker, Maggie Smith, Michael Caine, Buck Henry, Sam Shepard, Marcia Gay Harden, Frances Sternhagen, Frank Whaley. Fine cast in fluffy fantasy about marriage-phobic book publisher Spader, who moves into a Manhattan brownstone that's haunted by the ghosts of a famous old theatrical couple who teach him about love and commitment. Curious, slowly paced blend of supernatural whimsy, romantic comedy and relationship drama never really jells. Made for theaters, this debuted on cable. Valerie Perrine appears unbilled. [PG-13]▼◗

Custer of the West (1968-U.S.-Spanish) C-140m. **½ D: Robert Siodmak. Robert Shaw, Mary Ure, Jeffrey Hunter, Robert Ryan, Ty Hardin, Charles Stalnaker, Robert Hall, Lawrence Tierney. Fairly ambitious bio of famed general suffers from script that doesn't quite know how to characterize him. Some prints run 120m. Super Technirama 70. [G]▼◗

Cutter and Bone SEE: **Cutter's Way**
Cutter's Way (1981) C-105m. **½ D: Ivan Passer. Jeff Bridges, John Heard, Lisa Eichhorn, Ann Dusenberry, Stephen Elliott, Nina Van Pallandt, Julia Duffy. Intriguing if not always satisfying film about a boozy, belligerent Vietnam vet (Heard) who prods his aimless friend (Bridges) into action after the latter has seen a man who may be a murderer. Low-key, sometimes enervating adaptation of Newton Thornburg's novel *Cutter and Bone* (this film's original title), enhanced by director Passer's eye for interesting detail. [R]▼◗

CutThroat Island (1995-U.S.-French) C-123m. ** D: Renny Harlin. Geena Davis, Matthew Modine, Frank Langella, Maury Chaykin, Patrick Malahide, Stan Shaw, Harris Yulin, Rex Linn, Paul Dillon, Chris Masterson, Jimmie F. Skaggs. Pirate Davis must join forces with roguish Modine to avenge her father's death, find a treasure map and battle her ferocious pirate uncle, Dawg (Langella). Or something like that. Hapless movie has special effects and stunts to spare, but nothing to get you involved. The actors do their best in cardboard roles. Where's Robert Newton when you really need him? Arrrr! Panavision and Technovision. [PG-13] ▼◗●

Cutting Class (1989) C-91m. *½ D: Rospo Pallenberg. Donovan Leitch, Jill Schoelen, Roddy McDowall, Brad Pitt, Martin Mull. A slasher is running amok at a high school. This one's only if your idea of a four-star movie is FRIDAY THE 13TH. [R]▼◗

Cutting Edge, The (1992) C-101m. **½ D: Paul M. Glaser. D. B. Sweeney, Moira Kelly, Roy Dotrice, Terry O'Quinn, Dwier Brown. Bitchy ice skater Kelly is paired with banged-up hockey player Sweeney in a last-ditch attempt to score an Olympic gold medal in paired figure skating. Cute, if predictable, comedy with Sweeney and Kelly building believable sexual tension as they're forced to work together, sniping all the way. Followed in 2006 by a direct-to-video sequel. [PG]▼◗

Cyborg (1989) C-86m. BOMB D: Albert Pyun. Jean-Claude Van Damme, Deborah Richter, Vincent Klyn, Alex Daniels, Dayle Haddon, Blaise Loong, Rolf Muller. Van Damme plays a savior battling evil gangs who seem to enjoy various plagues and finding gruesome ways to murder people. Even for a post-apocalyptic trash movie, this plumbs new depths. Repulsive. Followed by two unrelated sequels. [R]▼◗●

Cyborg 2087 (1966) C-86m. ** D: Franklin Adreon. Michael Rennie, Wendell Corey, Eduard Franz, Karen Steele, Warren Stevens. Future Earth civilization sends cyborg—part machine, part human—back in time to 1960s so future can be changed. Good idea all but ruined due to unconvincing script and TV-style production.

Cycle Savages, The (1969) C-82m. BOMB D: Bill Brame. Bruce Dern, Melody Patterson, Chris Robinson, Maray Ayres, Scott Brady. Psychotic biker/white slaver Dern is displeased when artist Robinson opens his sketch pad, so he plans to crush the budding Rembrandt's hands. Sadism and torture galore; coproduced by deejay Casey Kasem and record exec Mike Curb, later the lieutenant governor of California. [R]▼◗

Cyclone (1987) C-83m. ** D: Fred Olen Ray. Heather Thomas, Jeffrey Combs, Ashley Ferrare, Dar Robinson, Martine Beswicke, Robert Quarry, Martin Landau. TV star Thomas plays second fiddle to a high-tech motorcycle that's stolen by Landau's henchmen. Watch for numerous cameos including Huntz Hall, Troy Donahue, Russ Tamblyn, and Michael Reagan. [R]▼●◗

Cyclone Z SEE: **Dragons Forever**

Cyclops, The (1957) **66m.** **✶✶** D: Bert I. Gordon. James Craig, Gloria Talbott, Lon Chaney, Jr., Tom Drake. Expedition scours Mexico in search of Talbott's lost fiancé, discovers that radiation has transformed him into an enormous monster. Nothing much in this cheapie.▼◗

Cyrano de Bergerac (1950) **112m.** **✶✶✶½** D: Michael Gordon. Jose Ferrer, Mala Powers, William Prince, Morris Carnovsky, Elena Verdugo. Ferrer received an Oscar for portraying the tragic 17th-century wit, renowned for his nose but longing for love of a beautiful lady. From Edmond Rostand's play. Previously filmed in 1900, 1925, and 1945; later modernized as ROXANNE, and remade in 1990. Also shown in computer-colored version.▼●◗

Cyrano de Bergerac (1990-French) **C-138m.** **✶✶✶½** D: Jean-Paul Rappeneau. Gérard Depardieu, Anne Brochet, Vincent Perez, Jacques Weber, Roland Bertin, Philippe Morier-Genoud. Likely to remain the definitive screen version of the Edmond Rostand perennial (depending on your personal passion for Steve Martin's ROXANNE). Quite visceral, and frequently inspired (vide the decision to stage the balcony scene during a mild rainstorm), faltering only a little during the finale, which is overextended. Jean-Claude Carrière and director Rappeneau scripted; English subtitles by Anthony Burgess. [PG]▼●◗

Cyrus (2010) **C-91m.** **✶✶✶** D: Jay Duplass, Mark Duplass. John C. Reilly, Jonah Hill, Marisa Tomei, Catherine Keener, Matt Walsh, Tim Guinee. Disarming film about a divorced man whose life is a mess; he clings to his patient ex-wife, even as she's about to remarry, then meets a woman who genuinely likes him. But it turns out she has a grown son, Cyrus (Hill), who lives with her. The two are exceptionally close, so close that Cyrus is determined to sabotage his mom's budding relationship. Sincere where it might have been flip or crass, this unusual blend of comedy and drama is subtle, intimate, and quietly effective. The screenplay (by the directors) is perfectly realized by its talented stars. [R]◗

Da (1988) **C-102m.** **✶✶½** D: Matt Clark. Barnard Hughes, Martin Sheen, Karl Hayden, Doreen Hepburn, William Hickey, Hugh O'Conor, Ingrid Craigie. Sheen returns to his native Ireland for his father's funeral, which triggers a series of remembrances of his irascible "da." Hugh Leonard's adaptation of his autobiographical stage comedy doesn't work as well on the

screen, but remains a touching account of a father-son relationship that isn't interrupted by death. Hughes beautifully re-creates his Tony-winning performance, and Sheen is equally good. Hepburn is marvelous as Hughes' pesky wife; Leonard appears briefly as a pallbearer. Filmed mostly on location in Ireland. [PG]▼◗

Dad (1989) **C-117m.** **✶✶** D: Gary David Goldberg. Jack Lemmon, Ted Danson, Olympia Dukakis, Kathy Baker, Kevin Spacey, Ethan Hawke, Zakes Mokae, J. T. Walsh. Busy, distracted executive learns his father may be dying; he winds up becoming his dad's caretaker and companion, and they grow closer than they've ever been. Genuinely affecting tearjerker turns sappy and "cute" at the midway point, almost negating Lemmon's fine performance. Why couldn't they have quit while they were ahead? Feature directing debut for TV sitcom producer Goldberg. [PG]▼●◗

Daddy and Them (2001) **C-102m.** **✶✶** D: Billy Bob Thornton. Billy Bob Thornton, Laura Dern, Diane Ladd, Kelly Preston, Andy Griffith, Sandra Seacat, John Prine, Jeff Bailey, Jim Varney, Brenda Blethyn, Ben Affleck, Jamie Lee Curtis. Arkansas husband Thornton, his quarrelsome, jealous wife Dern, and her family drive to Little Rock to meet his kin, who are equally cantankerous. Populated with irritating characters; draggy pace picks up a lot by the second half, but it's a long haul getting there. Thornton also wrote this slice-of-life comedy-drama. Filmed in 1998. [R]▼◗

Daddy Day Camp (2007) **C-89m.** **✶½** D: Fred Savage. Cuba Gooding, Jr., Lochlyn Munro, Richard Gant, Tamala Jones, Paul Rae, Spencir Bridges, Brian Doyle-Murray. Frenetic but only fitfully funny sequel to DADDY DAY CARE, with Gooding filling in for Eddie Murphy as a day-care entrepreneur. This time, he takes over a ramshackle summer camp with a little help from his dad (Gant), a hard-boiled Marine colonel who whips (not literally, but almost) the campers into shape. Intended as a direct-to-video release, and it shows. [PG]◗

Daddy Day Care (2003) **C-92m.** **✶✶✶** D: Steve Carr. Eddie Murphy, Jeff Garlin, Steve Zahn, Regina King, Anjelica Huston, Lacey Chabert, Jonathan Katz, Kevin Nealon, Siobhan Fallon Hogan, Laura Kightlinger. When Murphy and his best friend Garlin lose their jobs, the boredom of being househusbands inspires them to start a business—a day-care center for kids—despite their almost complete ignorance of how to go about it. Surprisingly benign, non-cynical comedy with Murphy as a devoted dad who comes to realize what's really important in his life. A refreshing change from the usual run of so-called family entertainment. Followed by DADDY DAY CAMP. [PG]▼◗

Daddy Long Legs (1955) **C-126m.** **✶✶½** D: Jean Negulesco. Fred Astaire, Leslie

Caron, Thelma Ritter, Fred Clark, Terry Moore, Larry Keating. Overlong musical remake of oft-filmed story about playboy (Astaire) anonymously sponsoring waif's education—then she falls in love with him. Some good dance numbers, and Johnny Mercer score highlighted by "Something's Got to Give." Previously filmed in 1919, 1931, (as CURLY TOP) in 1935, and in the Netherlands in 1938. CinemaScope. ▼●❿

Daddy Longlegs (2010-U.S.-French) **C-99m. **½** D: Josh and Benny Safdie. Ronald Bronstein, Sean Williams, Eléonore Hendricks, Dakota Goldhor, Aren Topdjian, Leah Singer, Sage Ranaldo, Frey Ranaldo. Divorced N.Y.C. dad factors the annual two-week custody of his kids into his dreary daily mosaic of ex-wife woes, work worries, school confrontations, babysitting blues, and his world girlfriend. Rolling with the punches and trying to evolve from man-boy to adult, he always opts for the lesser of two evils. Homespun, handheld indie, the writer-directors' faintly fictionalized childhood memoir fitfully engages. Aka GO GET SOME ROSEMARY. [NR]

Daddy Nostalgia (1990-French) **C-105m. **½** D: Bertrand Tavernier. Dirk Bogarde, Jane Birkin, Odette Laure. Birkin rushes to the Cote d'Azur to be at the side of her father, who may be dying; during her extended stay she tries to sort out her relationship with him and understand the life he's led. Utterly believable, but not always compelling; Bogarde's charming (and commanding) screen presence makes it well worth seeing. Panavision. [PG]▼❿

Daddy's Dyin'... Who's Got the Will? (1990) **C-95m. **½** D: Jack Fisk. Beau Bridges, Keith Carradine, Beverly D'Angelo, Tess Harper, Judge Reinhold, Amy Wright, Patrika Darbo, Molly McClure, Bert Remsen. Affection, reminiscence, avarice, and hostility intermingle as a family of memorable oddballs gathers at the old Texas homestead to wait for their father to die and to find out what's in the will. Del Shores adapted his own stage play, and the results run from flat and predictable to sharp and funny; a terrific cast punches everything across. [PG-13]▼●❿

Daddy's Gone A-Hunting (1969) **C-108m. ***** D: Mark Robson. Carol White, Paul Burke, Scott Hylands, Rachel Ames, Mala Powers, James B. Sikking. Happily married and pregnant, White is horrified when her previous lover turns up, demanding she kill her baby to atone for having aborted his child. Though contrived, story becomes increasingly tense, with nail-biting climax; shot in San Francisco. [M/PG]▼❿

Daddy's Little Girls (2007) **C-95m. **½** D: Tyler Perry. Gabrielle Union, Idris Elba, Louis Gossett, Jr., Tracee Ellis Ross, Tasha Smith, Malinda Williams, Terri J. Vaughn, Gary Sturgis, China Anne McClain, Lauryn Alisa McClain, Sierra Aylina McClain.

Perry drops his drag act and stays behind the camera for this dramedy about a mechanic who gets romantically involved with the upscale attorney who is helping him win custody of his three daughters from his ne'er-do-well ex-wife and her thug boyfriend. Overly dramatic and predictable, but still a somewhat effective look at the difficulties involved when a relationship straddles both sides of the tracks. Perry wrote and coproduced. Aka TYLER PERRY'S DADDY'S LITTLE GIRLS. [PG-13]❿

Daffy Duck's Movie: Fantastic Island (1983) **C-78m. *½** D: Friz Freleng. Fourth and weakest of Warner Bros.' cartoon compilations. Linking material (spoofing TV's *Fantasy Island*) is flat, and few of the ten cartoon shorts included are better than average. Hardly Daffy's finest hour. [G]▼❿

Daffy Duck's Quackbusters (1989) **C-79m. ***** D: Greg Ford, Terry Lennon. Voice of Mel Blanc. Perhaps the most watchable of the Warner cartoon-compilation films, with a clever bridging story incorporating the studio's many vintage horror-movie spoofs. Daffy Duck inherits a fortune and sets up a "ghost-busting" service with pals Bugs Bunny and Porky Pig. Contains the new short THE DUXORCIST and a cameo appearance by Egghead. [G]▼●❿

Daggers of Blood SEE: **With Fire and Sword**

Dahmer (2002) **C-101m. **½** D: David Jacobson. Jeremy Renner, Bruce Davison, Artel Kayàru, Matt Newton, Dion Basco, Kate Williamson, Christina Payano. Rather than depicting the whole story of serial killer Jeffrey Dahmer, this unusual film dramatizes scenes from his life; it doesn't even include his arrest. The cast is uniformly good, it's well written (by Jacobson) and imaginatively directed, but it remains uninvolving, with an undefinable point of view. [R]▼❿

Daisy Kenyon (1947) **99m. **½** D: Otto Preminger. Joan Crawford, Dana Andrews, Henry Fonda, Ruth Warrick, Martha Stewart, Peggy Ann Garner, Connie Marshall. Love triangle starts intelligently, bogs down halfway into typical soapy histrionics (with a plot thread about child abuse surprising for its time). Good performances; handsomely filmed. Look sharp in the Stork Club scene for Walter Winchell, John Garfield, and Leonard Lyons.❿

Daisy Miller (1974) **C-91m. **½** D: Peter Bogdanovich. Cybill Shepherd, Barry Brown, Cloris Leachman, Mildred Natwick, Eileen Brennan, Duilio Del Prete. Handsome, intelligent adaptation of Henry James' story misses the mark; the tone is cold, and Shepherd's hollow performance as a naive American courting European society in the late 1800s nearly sinks the film. Screenplay by Frederic Raphael. Filmed in Italy. [G]▼❿

Dakota (1945) **82m. **** D: Joseph Kane.

John Wayne, Vera Ralston, Walter Brennan, Ward Bond, Ona Munson, Hugo Haas. Sprawling Wayne vehicle with Duke involved in pioneer railroad territory dispute; Vera is his lovely wife! ▼●)

Dakota (1988) C-97m. ** D: Fred Holmes. Lou Diamond Phillips, Eli Cummins, DeeDee Norton, Jordan Burton, Steve Ruge, John Hawkes. Well-meaning but slight, independently produced drama about a youth on the run (Phillips), who works on a Texas ranch and interrelates with various characters. Phillips, who served as associate producer, is the sole interest here; he made the film prior to attaining stardom in LA BAMBA. [PG] ▼●)

Daleks—Invasion Earth 2150 A.D. (1966-British) C-84m. **½ D: Gordon Flemyng. Peter Cushing, Bernard Cribbins, Andrew Keir, Ray Brooks, Jill Curzon, Roberta Tovey. Agreeable sequel to DR. WHO AND THE DALEKS, with the Earth threatened by Dalek aggressors. Retitled INVASION EARTH 2150 A.D. Techniscope. ▼●)

Dallas (1950) C-94m. **½ D: Stuart Heisler. Gary Cooper, Ruth Roman, Steve Cochran, Raymond Massey, Barbara Payton, Leif Erickson, Antonio Moreno. Action-packed post–Civil War Western, with Reb Cooper branded an outlaw, coming to Texas on a mission of revenge. ▼●)

Daltry Calhoun (2005) C-93m. BOMB D: Katrina Holden Bronson. Johnny Knoxville, Juliette Lewis, Elizabeth Banks, Kick Gurry, David Koechner, Sophie Traub, Andrew Prine, Beth Grant, James Parks, Matthew Sharp. Slovenly Knoxville morphs into a wildly successful sod seed manufacturer, but his plan to build a public golf course is disrupted by various complications, including the unexpected presence of his estranged, precocious 14-year-old daughter and her mother. Meandering Southern Fried mishmash aimlessly veers from stale comedy to half-baked sentiment. There's a parade of hit songs on the soundtrack to make you think you're being entertained. Writer-director is the daughter of Charles Bronson and Jill Ireland. Super 35. [PG-13] ▶

Damage (1992-British) C-111m. **½ D: Louis Malle. Jeremy Irons, Juliette Binoche, Miranda Richardson, Rupert Graves, Ian Bannen, Leslie Caron, Peter Stormare, Gemma Clark. Arch-to-a-fault adaptation of Josephine Hart's minimalist best-seller, about a middle-aged Brit politician who squanders his career and family by embarking on a hot-sex affair with his son's mysterious girlfriend. Binoche is frigidly one-note as the latter, sinking what in some ways is dispassionately accomplished filmmaking. Richardson is spectacularly good as Irons' spurned wife. Screenplay by David Hare. Fine score by Zbigniew Preisner. Unrated version available. [R] ▼●)

Dam Busters, The (1955-British) **119m.** ***½ D: Michael Anderson. Richard Todd, Michael Redgrave, Ursula Jeans, Basil Sydney. During WW2, British devise an ingenious plan to blow up Germans' Ruhr dam. Exciting and intelligent film. Look fast for a young Patrick McGoohan. ▼)

Dames (1934) **90m.** *** D: Ray Enright. Joan Blondell, Dick Powell, Ruby Keeler, ZaSu Pitts, Hugh Herbert, Guy Kibbee, Phil Regan. Short on plot (let's-back-a-Broadway-musical) but has top Busby Berkeley production ensembles like "I Only Have Eyes for You." Other songs include "When You Were a Smile on Your Mother's Lips and a Twinkle in Your Daddy's Eye," and classic title tune. ▼●)

Damien: Omen II (1978) C-107m. **½ D: Don Taylor. William Holden, Lee Grant, Lew Ayres, Sylvia Sidney, Robert Foxworth, Jonathan Scott-Taylor, Leo McKern, Meshach Taylor. Sequel to huge hit of 1976 is less effective, still has shock value from grisly murders, plus good work by Holden. Best scene is Ayres' death under an icy lake. Scott-Taylor is the demon child; Holden and Grant his stupidly unsuspecting kin. Taylor took over directing from Michael Hodges, who worked on screenplay. Followed by THE FINAL CONFLICT. Panavision. [R] ▼●)

Damnation Alley (1977) C-91m. *½ D: Jack Smight. Jan-Michael Vincent, George Peppard, Dominique Sanda, Paul Winfield, Jackie Earle Haley. Five survivors of nuclear wipeout travel cross-country in search of civilization. Futuristic van in which they travel is more interesting than story or characters in this uninspiring sci-fi saga. Distantly related to the Roger Zelazny novel. Panavision. [PG] ▼)

Damned, The (1962) SEE: **These Are the Damned**

Damned, The (1969-Italian-West German) C-155m. *** D: Luchino Visconti. Dirk Bogarde, Ingrid Thulin, Helmut Griem, Helmut Berger, Charlotte Rampling, Florinda Bolkan. Grim drama depicting the plight of a family of German industrialists during the 1930s; their decline parallels the rise of Hitler. Violent, melodramatic, and controversial, but undeniably illuminating. [X] ▼)

Damned Don't Cry, The (1950) **103m.** **½ D: Vincent Sherman. Joan Crawford, David Brian, Steve Cochran, Kent Smith, Richard Egan. Follow-up to FLAMINGO ROAD formula; Crawford is well cast as lower-class gal rising to wealth via wit and looks, discovering too late that a gangster's moll has no right to love and happiness. ▶

Damned United, The (2009-U.S.-British) C-97m. **½ D: Tom Hooper. Michael Sheen, Colm Meaney, Timothy Spall, Jim Broadbent, Henry Goodman, Maurice Roëves, Stephen Graham, Brian McCardie,

Peter McDonald. True story of how soccer manager Brian Clough (Sheen) takes his Derby County team to the top ranks—and then goes on to coach its principal rival, Leeds United, stepping into the big shoes of Don Revie (Meaney), but against the advice of his longtime assistant (Spall). Entertaining and credible, with a standout performance by Sheen in a sterling cast . . . but the finale lacks the punch one might like. Screenplay by Peter Morgan, based on a novel by David Peace. [R]◗

Damn the Defiant! (1962-British) **C-101m.** *** D: Lewis Gilbert. Alec Guinness, Dirk Bogarde, Maurice Denham, Nigel Stock, Richard Carpenter, Anthony Quayle. Bogarde vs. Guinness in stalwart tale of British warship during Napoleonic campaign. Production shows great attention to historic detail. CinemaScope.▼●◗

Damn Yankees (1958) **C-110m.** *** D: George Abbott, Stanley Donen. Tab Hunter, Gwen Verdon, Ray Walston, Russ Brown, Jimmie Komack, Jean Stapleton, Nathaniel Frey. Aging, frustrated Washington Senators baseball fan says he'd sell his soul to see the club get one good hitter; a devilish Mr. Applegate appears to fulfill his wish, and transforms *him* into the club's new star. Faithful translation of hit Broadway musical (with Walston, Verdon, and others repeating their original roles) loses something along the way, and has a particularly weak finale, but it's still quite entertaining. Songs include "(You Gotta Have) Heart," "Whatever Lola Wants," and a mambo memorably danced by Verdon and choreographer Bob Fosse.▼●◗

Damsel in Distress, A (1937) **101m.** *** D: George Stevens. Fred Astaire, George Burns, Gracie Allen, Joan Fontaine, Constance Collier, Reginald Gardiner, Montagu Love. Bright Gershwin musical set in London, with dancing star Astaire pursuing aristocratic heiress Fontaine. Burns and Allen have never been better—they even get to sing and dance. Songs include "Foggy Day in London Town," "Nice Work If You Can Get It." The clever "Fun House" sequence won an Oscar for Hermes Pan's dance direction. Based on a novel by P. G. Wodehouse, who cowrote the script.▼●◗

Dan Candy's Law SEE: **Alien Thunder**

Dance Flick (2009) **C-83m.** *½ D: Damien Dante Wayans. Damon Wayans, Jr., Shoshana Bush, Essence Atkins, Affion Crockett, Chris Elliott, David Alan Grier, Brennan Hillard, Amy Sedaris, Marlon Wayans, Shawn Wayans, Keenen Ivory Wayans. After her mother's tragic death, Bush enrolls at Musical High School and meets a group of kids from the wrong side of the tracks who want to teach her what life is really about. It isn't that hard to mock the dance movie genre, or for that matter musicals and pop culture. That's why this latest Wayans parody is so disappointing. While there are amusing mo-

ments and laughs, simply put, it should be funnier. Lochlyn Munro appears unbilled. [PG-13]

Dance Goes On, The (1991-Canadian) **C-103m.** ** D: Paul Almond. Matthew James Almond, James Keach, Genevieve Bujold, Bryan Hennessey, Louise Marleau, Leslie Hope, Cary Lawrence, Deborah Freeland. Young Almond, who's insensitive and money-hungry (because he has grown up in L.A.), arrives in Quebec where he's inherited his uncle's farm. Will he get in touch with his roots, and experience "real life"? Ever-so-predictable (not to mention boring) drama. Actor Almond is the son of Bujold and director Almond (who also produced and scripted).▼

Dancemaker (1999) **C-98m.** ***½ D: Matthew Diamond. Fascinating study of choreographer Paul Taylor and the endless difficulties managing his company and its dancers. Footage of his dance creations is artfully interspersed with preparations for the troupe's engagement in India. Film provides an insider's look at what it takes to be a dancer—and a dancemaker. A feast for dance buffs.◗

Dance of Death (1969-British) **C-138m.** *** D: David Giles. Laurence Olivier, Geraldine McEwan, Robert Lang, Malcolm Reynolds, Janina Faye, Carolyn Jones. Film version of National Theatre production of August Strindberg's angst-laden play about an aging sea captain, notable chiefly for Olivier's fiery performance. Unreleased in U.S. until 1979. [PG—originally rated G]

Dance of Death (1971) SEE: **House of Evil**

Dance of the Damned (1988) **C-83m.** **½ D: Katt Shea Ruben. Cyril O'Reilly, Starr Andreef, Deborah Ann Nassar, Maia Ford, Athena Worthy, Tom Ruben. Eerie, fascinating, very low-budget horror drama, in which a vampire selects an intelligent, troubled stripper as his next victim, but first insists she tell him what daylight is like. Slow to get started, but ambitious and mature, with good characterizations and acting. [R]▼●

Dance of the Dwarfs (1983) **C-93m.** *½ D: Gus Trikonis. Peter Fonda, Deborah Raffin, John Amos, Carlos Palomino. Female anthropologist (Raffin) searching for lost pygmy tribe in jungle hooks up with drunken helicopter pilot (Fonda) in this stupid AFRICAN QUEEN–ish adventure shot in Philippines. They encounter strange creatures, audience encounters boredom. Video title: JUNGLE HEAT. [PG]▼

Dance of the Vampires SEE: **Fearless Vampire Killers or: Pardon Me, But Your Teeth Are in My Neck, The**

Dancer in the Dark (2000-Danish-Swedish-French) **C-137m.** **½ D: Lars von Trier. Björk, Catherine Deneuve, David Morse, Peter Stormare, Joel Grey, Vincent Patterson, Vladica Kostic, Udo Kier, Željko Ivanek, Stellan Skarsgård. Ambitious, brazenly off-putting musical (!) about a Czech immigrant (Björk) who is going blind and must arrange an operation to save her son from the same fate. Writer-director von Trier's attempt to expand cinematic musical conventions is certainly thought provoking, but ultimately cold and very literal minded, and not helped by jagged song-and-dance numbers. Björk is impressive; she also composed the film's music. Super 35. [R]▼▷

Dancers (1987) C-99m. *½ D: Herbert Ross. Mikhail Baryshnikov, Alessandra Ferri, Leslie Browne, Thomas Rall, Lynn Seymour, Victor Barbee, Mariangela Melato, Julie Kent. Trite, inexplicably bad movie about a ballet star/lothario (Baryshnikov, ideally cast) who's rehearsing a screen version of *Giselle*, and becomes infatuated with an innocent young dancer. A waste of time. Baryshnikov, Browne, and Ross collaborated 10 years earlier on THE TURNING POINT. [PG]▼●

Dancer, Texas Pop. 81 (1998) C-95m. **½ D: Tim McCanlies. Ethan Embry, Breckin Meyer, Peter Facinelli, Eddie Mills, Ashley Johnson, Patricia Wettig, Michael O'Neill. Slight but pleasant LAST PICTURE SHOW–lite tale of four small-town teenage buddies facing life after high school and wondering whether they should make good on a childhood pact to move to L.A. Appealing performances by the male leads make up for their schematic roles. Promising debut for writer-director McCanlies. [PG]▼●▷

Dancer Upstairs, The (2002-U.S.-Spanish) C-124m. **½ D: John Malkovich. Javier Bardem, Laura Morante, Juan Diego Botto, Elvira Mínguez, Alexandra Lencastre, Oliver Cotton, Luis Miguel Cintra. Dedicated police detective Bardem is determined to identify and capture the leader of a volatile guerrilla movement in an unnamed Latin American country. Meanwhile, he finds himself attracted to his daughter's beautiful ballet teacher. Intriguing political drama, with a strong performance by Bardem, is weighed down by its slow pace and extended length. One might also question Bardem's naiveté at the story's conclusion. Nicholas Shakespeare adapted his own novel. Malkovich's feature directing debut. [R]▼▷

Dances With Wolves (1990) C-181m. **** D: Kevin Costner. Kevin Costner, Mary McDonnell, Graham Greene, Rodney A. Grant, Floyd Red Crow Westerman, Tantoo Cardinal, Robert Pastorelli, Charles Rocket, Maury Chaykin, Larry Joshua, Wes Studi. Altogether extraordinary film (all the more so for being Costner's directing debut) about an idealistic young Civil War soldier who makes friends with a Sioux Indian tribe and, eventually, becomes one of them. Simply and eloquently told, with every element falling into place (on breathtaking South Dakota locations). A triumph in every respect. Oscar winner for Best Picture, Direc-

tor, Screenplay (Michael Blake, from his novel), Original Score (John Barry), Cinematography (Dean Semler), Editing (Neil Travis), and Sound Recording. 237m. "special edition" expands the story and characterizations. Panavision. [PG-13]▼●▷

Dance With a Stranger (1985-British) C-101m. ***½ D: Mike Newell. Miranda Richardson, Rupert Everett, Ian Holm, Matthew Carroll, Tom Chadbon, Joanne Whalley, Jane Bertish. Stylish, trenchant study of romantic self-destruction based on the true story of Ruth Ellis, who in 1955 became the last woman ever executed in Britain. Peaks with about a half hour to go, but Richardson, her leading men, and a haunting atmosphere more than compensate. Ellis' story was earlier told in YIELD TO THE NIGHT (BLONDE SINNER), with Diana Dors. [R]▼●▷

Dance With Me (1998) C-126m. **½ D: Randa Haines. Vanessa L. Williams, Chayanne, Kris Kristofferson, Joan Plowright, Jane Krakowski, Beth Grant. Likable if formulaic (and overlong) film about a Houston dance instructor (Williams) who learns a thing or two from a Cuban émigré who's come to work at the dance studio. What the studio owner (Kristofferson) doesn't know is that the handsome young man is his son. Appealing cast and terrific dance sequences—including a knockout at a Latin dance club—give this life, and Plowright steals most of her scenes as a matronly but enthusiastic student. [PG]▼●▷

Dancing at Lughnasa (1998-U.S.-British-Irish) C-92m. *** D: Pat O'Connor. Meryl Streep, Michael Gambon, Catherine McCormack, Kathy Burke, Sophie Thompson, Brid Brennan, Rhys Ifans, Darrell Johnston; narrated by Gerard McSorley. Flavorful filmization of Brian Friel's play about a close-knit rural Irish family—five unmarried sisters—in the 1930s and the return of their brother, Jack (a priest), from his post in Africa. No strong story here but a rich feel for time, place, atmosphere, and character, with fine performances all around. [PG]▼●▷

Dancing at the Blue Iguana (2001-U.S.-British) C-123m. ** D: Michael Radford. Daryl Hannah, Jennifer Tilly, Sandra Oh, Sheila Kelley, Elias Koteas, Robert Wisdom, Vladimir Mashkov, W. Earl Brown, Chris Hogan, Charlotte Ayanna. The women who strip at a cheesy L.A. club gratify their customers but harbor longings and goals that they can't seem to realize. Developed by Radford and his cast through a series of improvisational workshops, which is all too apparent from the film's extenuated length and meandering nature. Strong performances from the leading actresses are the only compensation. [R]▼▷

Dancing Lady (1933) 94m. **½ D: Robert Z. Leonard. Joan Crawford, Clark Gable, Franchot Tone, May Robson, Nelson Eddy,

Fred Astaire, Robert Benchley, Ted Healy and His Stooges. Glossy backstage romance is best remembered for Astaire's film debut (he plays himself), dancing opposite a less-than-inspired Crawford. Show-biz story, three-cornered romance are strictly standard, but cast and MGM gloss add points. Funniest moments belong to The Three Stooges. Look fast for a young Eve Arden. ▼●)

Dandy in Aspic, A (1968-British) **C-107m.** ** D: Anthony Mann. Laurence Harvey, Tom Courtenay, Mia Farrow, Lionel Stander, Harry Andrews, Peter Cook. Wooden spy melodrama in which principals keep switching sides so rapidly it becomes impossible to follow. Mann died during filming; Harvey completed director's chores. Panavision. [R]▼●

Dandy, the All-American Girl SEE: **Sweet Revenge** (1977)

Danger: Diabolik (1968-Italian-French) **C-100m.** *** D: Mario Bava. John Phillip Law, Marisa Mell, Michel Piccoli, Adolfo Celi, Terry-Thomas, Claudio Gora. Entertaining, tongue-in-cheek exploits of super-criminal Diabolik (Law), with wonderfully outré sets and costumes, stylish photography, and a bizarre psychedelic score by Ennio Morricone. An indelible '60s time capsule based on the European comic-strip character. Originally released as DIABOLIK, at 105m. Panoramica.▼●

Danger in the Skies SEE: **Pilot, The**

Dangerous (1935) **78m.** **½ D: Alfred E. Green. Bette Davis, Franchot Tone, Margaret Lindsay, Alison Skipworth, John Eldredge, Dick Foran. Former stage star Davis, on the skids, is rehabilitated by Tone in good but syrupy tale, with sharp turn winning performance by Davis. Remade as SINGAPORE WOMAN.▼●

Dangerous Beauty (1998) **C-114m.** **½ D: Marshall Herskovitz. Catherine McCormack, Rufus Sewell, Jacqueline Bisset, Oliver Platt, Naomi Watts, Moira Kelly, Fred Ward, Jeroen Krabbé, Joanna Cassidy. Chronicle of a fascinating woman in 16th-century Venice, where women had no rights and no education—but courtesans did. Sacrificing her one true love, she becomes the most notorious, outspoken, and desired woman in Venice. McCormack is superb in the leading role, and Bisset is ideal as her mother, but the story takes a sharp turn toward the end (incorporating the plague and the Inquisition) and loses its dramatic grip. Still a good-looking and, for the most part, absorbing tale, based on a true story. Super 35. [R]▼●

Dangerous Break SEE: **Special Delivery**
Dangerous Friend, A SEE: **Todd Killings, The**

Dangerous Game (1993) **C-105m.** BOMB D: Abel Ferrara. Harvey Keitel, Madonna, James Russo, Nancy Ferrara, Reilly Murphy, Victor Argo, Leonard Thomas, Christina Futon. Humiliatingly banal Madonna

career-killer about filmmaker whose latest project begins to reflect his own life—or is it the other way around? Barely released and surprisingly tame, given Ferrara's previous movies and Madonna's inclination to hang it all out. Working title was SNAKE EYES, which is what the studio rolled when it bankrolled this one. [R]▼●)

Dangerous Ground (1997) **C-95m.** *½ D: Darrell James Roodt. Ice Cube, Elizabeth Hurley, Ving Rhames, Sechaba Morajele, Eric Miyeni. Dangerous, and silly, too. Back in rural South Africa for a funeral several years after his apartheid-imposed flight to the U.S., literature major Cube fulfills a promise to mom by tracking down his fugitive younger brother who's involved in a drug ring. Despite broad plot parallels, don't look for the solemn tone director Roodt brought to his remake of CRY, THE BELOVED COUNTRY. Hurley, in harsh makeup, is cast as the wayward brother's girlfriend. [R]▼●

Dangerous Liaisons (1988) **C-120m.** ***½ D: Stephen Frears. Glenn Close, John Malkovich, Michelle Pfeiffer, Swoosie Kurtz, Keanu Reeves, Mildred Natwick, Uma Thurman, Peter Capaldi. In 18th-century France, an unscrupulous woman manipulates the lives of those around her, just for amusement, with the help of a like-minded count. Excellent adaptation of Christopher Hampton's play *Les Liaisons Dangereuses,* based on the famous period novel. Close is magnificent, Malkovich good (though miscast). Hampton's screenplay won an Oscar, as did the art direction and costumes. Same story filmed in 1959 (as DANGEROUS LIAISONS 1960), 1976 (as UNE FEMME FIDÈLE, aka GAME OF SEDUCTION), 1989 (as VALMONT), 1999 (as CRUEL INTENTIONS), and 2003 (as UNTOLD SCANDAL). [R] ▼●

Dangerous Liaisons 1960 (1959-French) **106m.** *** D: Roger Vadim. Gérard Philipe, Jeanne Moreau, Jeanne Valérie, Annette (Stroyberg) Vadim, Simone Renant, Jean-Louis Trintignant. Modern-dress version of the 18th-century novel of sexcapades among the debauched . . . and who better to film it than Vadim? Faithful in spirit to its origins, though the leads here are a *married* couple, cavorting in Paris and the Alps. Lots of fun, with gorgeous actors and jazz soundtrack by Thelonious Monk, Art Blakey, and Duke Jordan, who also appear. Don't miss Vadim's priceless prologue, shot for 1961 American audiences. Vadim remade this in 1976 as UNE FEMME FIDÈLE (GAME OF SEDUCTION). French title: LES LIAISONS DANGEREUSES. ▼●

Dangerous Lives of Altar Boys, The (2002) **C-105m.** **½ D: Peter Care. Kieran Culkin, Jena Malone, Emile Hirsch, Vincent D'Onofrio, Jodie Foster, Jake Richardson, Tyler Long. Likable enough coming-of-age story about hell-raising teenage boys attending a Catholic school during the 1960s. They fantasize about their lives in the form of comic-book adventures (in which their unforgiving teacher, played by Foster, becomes Nunzilla). These animated sequences, produced by Todd McFarlane, give the familiar storyline considerable pizzazz. Foster also coproduced. [R]▼▶

Dangerous Minds (1995) **C-99m.** **½ D: John N. Smith. Michelle Pfeiffer, George Dzundza, Courtney B. Vance, Robin Bartlett, Bruklin Harris, Renoly Santiago, Wade Dominguez, Beatrice Winde, Lorraine Toussaint, John Neville. Wide-eyed, inexperienced teacher (and ex-Marine) takes over a class of "unteachable" inner-city kids. She learns that changing their attitude requires a deeper understanding of their hard-knock lives. What might seem like a superficial retread of BLACKBOARD JUNGLE or TO SIR, WITH LOVE is a well-meaning, well-acted film, although some of it just doesn't wash (Pfeiffer seems awfully mousy for an ex-Marine). Followed by a TV series. [R]▼▶●

Dangerous Moves (1984-Swiss) **C-100m.** *** D: Richard Dembo. Michel Piccoli, Alexandre Arbatt, Leslie Caron, Liv Ullmann, Daniel Olbrychski, Michel Aumont. Absorbing, thought-provoking film about international intrigue surrounding a world chess championship. Academy Award winner for Best Foreign Film.▼▶

Dangerous Summer, A (1981-Australian) **C-100m.** *½ D: Quentin Masters. Tom Skerritt, Ian Gilmour, James Mason, Wendy Hughes, Ray Barrett. Confusing, hilariously unsubtle drama of psychotic arsonist Gilmour trying to torch a summer resort. Good cast looks ill at ease. Originally titled THE BURNING MAN. Video title: FLASH FIRE. Panavision. ▼▶●

Dangerous When Wet (1953) **C-95m.** *** D: Charles Walters. Esther Williams, Fernando Lamas, Jack Carson, Charlotte Greenwood, Denise Darcel, William Demarest, Donna Corcoran, Barbara Whiting. Cute musical comedy, one of Esther's best, about a health-conscious family whose leading light tries to swim the English Channel. Williams cavorts underwater with the animated Tom and Jerry in one memorable scene. She later married leading-man Lamas in real life. ▼▶●

Dangerous Woman, A (1993) **C-99m.** ** D: Stephen Gyllenhaal. Debra Winger, Barbara Hershey, Gabriel Byrne, David Strathairn, Chloe Webb, John Terry, Laurie Metcalf, Jan Hooks, Paul Dooley. Muddled movie of Mary McGarry Morris' acclaimed novel, with Winger the unceasingly frank nebbish niece of wealthy widow Hershey (who's been having an affair with a married politician). Winger is memorable in an unattractive part; Hershey's role is impossible;

and Byrne (as the handyman who comes between them) comes off as the Great Stone Face. The director's children, Maggie and Jacob (Jake) Gyllenhaal, appear in small roles. [R]▼●

Daniel (1983) **C-130m.** *** D: Sidney Lumet. Timothy Hutton, Mandy Patinkin, Lindsay Crouse, Edward Asner, Ellen Barkin, Julie Bovasso, Tovah Feldshuh, Joseph Leon, Amanda Plummer, John Rubinstein. Excellent adaptation of E. L. Doctorow's *The Book of Daniel*, about the children of a couple patterned after Julius and Ethel Rosenberg who must confront their painful heritage in order to deal with their own lives in the protest-filled 1960s. Not without its flaws, but overall a provocative and extremely well-made film. [R]▼▶

Daniel Defoe's Robinson Crusoe SEE: **Robinson Crusoe** (1998)

Dan in Real Life (2007) **C-98m.** *** D: Peter Hedges. Steve Carell, Juliette Binoche, Dane Cook, Dianne Wiest, John Mahoney, Alison Pill, Emily Blunt, Amy Ryan, Norbert Leo Butz, Jessica Hecht, Matthew Morrison. Amiable comedy-drama of newspaper columnist Dan (Carell), the doting but harried single father of three daughters. When the family heads off to New England for a holiday at his parents' seaside home, this widowed dad unexpectedly meets someone (Binoche) who seems to be perfect for him. The family reunion is replete with sibling rivalries, secrets, and resentments. Manages to rise above familiar sitcom level to be an entertaining take on middle-aged affairs of the heart. [PG-13]▶

Danny Boy (1982-Irish-British) **C-92m.** ** D: Neil Jordan. Veronica Quilligan, Stephen Rea, Alan Devlin, Peter Caffrey, Honor Heffernan, Lise-Ann McLaughlin, Donal McCann, Ray McAnally, Marie Kean. Ambitious but pretentious, unrelentingly dreary melodrama of sax player Rea, who exchanges his instrument for a machine gun after witnessing a double murder. Jordan's directorial debut, which he also scripted; he and leading man Rea later reteamed for THE CRYING GAME. Original British title: ANGEL. [R]▼

Danny Deckchair (2003-Australian) **C-90m.** **½ D: Jeff Balsmeyer. Rhys Ifans, Miranda Otto, Justine Clarke, Rhys Muldoon, Frank Magree, Anthony Phelan, John Batchelor, Alan Flower. Mildly entertaining Capra-esque romantic fantasy of one of life's "little people," Danny Morgan (Ifans), a cement-truck driver who improbably escapes his everyday existence. On a lark, he ties some helium-filled balloons to a lawn chair and floats through the heavens, whisking him off to a new life and new set of values. Clarke is a find as Danny's calculating girlfriend. Based, apparently, on a true story. [PG-13]▼▶

Dante's Peak (1997) **C-108m.** *** D:

Roger Donaldson. Pierce Brosnan, Linda Hamilton, Jamie Renée Smith, Jeremy Foley, Elizabeth Hoffman, Charles Hallahan, Grant Heslov. Formulaic but entertaining disaster movie about a scientist from the U.S. Geological Survey who sniffs around a mountainside town in Washington just below a volcano that he feels is going to blow at any minute. Along the way he falls in love with the town's mayor. Critics dumped on the first of 1997's two volcano movies, but hey—it ain't supposed to be *Henry V*. The characters are likable and the effects are completely convincing. Super 35. [PG-13] ▼◐▶

Danton (1982-Polish-French) **C-136m.** **** D: Andrzej Wajda. Gérard Depardieu, Wojciech Pszoniak, Patrice Chereau, Angela Winkler, Boguslaw Linda. Literate, absorbing, knowing drama of Danton, Robespierre, and the Reign of Terror following the French Revolution. A brilliant film, with obvious parallels to contemporary political situation in Poland. Depardieu is magnificent in the title role. [PG] ▼◐▶

Danzón (1991-Mexican) **C-103m.** *** D: Maria Novaro. Maria Rojo, Carmen Salinas, Blanca Guerra, Margarita Isabel, Tito Vasconcelos. Arresting feminist tale about a dreary telephone operator (Rojo) who comes alive only when performing a ballroom dance known as the "danzón." Her life undergoes a transformation when her longtime partner mysteriously disappears, and she becomes obsessed with finding him. The scenes with Rojo and Vasconcelos (playing a transvestite nightclub performer) are especially effective. [PG-13] ▼▶

Darby O'Gill and the Little People (1959) **C-90m.** ***½ D: Robert Stevenson. Albert Sharpe, Janet Munro, Sean Connery, Jimmy O'Dea, Kieron Moore, Estelle Winwood. Outstanding Disney fantasy about an Irish caretaker (Sharpe) who spins so many tales that no one believes him when he says he's befriended the King of Leprechauns. An utter delight, with dazzling special effects—and some truly terrifying moments along with the whimsy. ▼◐▶

Darby's Rangers (1958) **121m.** **½ D: William Wellman. James Garner, Etchika Choureau, Jack Warden, Edward Byrnes, Venetia Stevenson, Torin Thatcher, Peter Brown, Corey Allen, Stuart Whitman, Murray Hamilton. Garner does well in WW2 actioner as leader of assault troops in North Africa and Italy, focusing on relationships among his command and their shore romances. ▼▶

Daredevil (2003) **C-104m.** *** D: Mark Steven Johnson. Ben Affleck, Jennifer Garner, Michael Clarke Duncan, Colin Farrell, Joe Pantoliano, Jon Favreau, David Keith, Erick Avari, Paul Ben-Victor, Leland Orser. Blinded as a boy in N.Y.C., Matt Murdock grows up to be a lawyer by day and crime fighter by night, using his heightened senses to punish bad guys . . . but he's a tortured hero. Colorful, entertaining comic-book fodder, played with conviction by Affleck and a crackerjack cast: Garner as the agile Elektra, Favreau as his comic-relief law partner, Duncan as the menacing Kingpin, and a wild-eyed Farrell as Bullseye. Mark Margolis appears unbilled as Fallon; amusing cameo by comics aficionado Kevin Smith. Based on the Marvel Comics character created by Stan Lee (who also cameos) and Bill Everett. Alternate version runs 120m. Followed by a spin-off: ELEKTRA. Super 35. [PG-13] ▼▶

Darfur Now (2007) **C-98m.** **½ D: Theodore Braun. Documentary about various people who are trying to make a difference in strife-ridden Darfur, including a man who operates the World Food Program, a lawyer who plans to prosecute government officials in the International Criminal Court, a local woman whose personal tragedy has led her to become an armed rebel, a young man from L.A. who tries to get the state of California to rid itself of Sudanese investments, and actor Don Cheadle, who uses his celebrity (and that of friends like George Clooney) to draw attention to the crisis. By trying to find the positive in all of this and appeal to a mainstream audience, this well-made film sacrifices deep emotional impact. Cheadle coproduced. [PG]▶

Daring Dobermans, The (1973) **C-90m.** **½ D: Bryon Chudnow. Charles Knox Robinson, Tim Considine, David Moses, Claudio Martinez, Joan Caulfield. Sequel to THE DOBERMAN GANG provides amiable family viewing as the canines are trained for another daring heist by a new gang of crooks. [G] ▼▶

Daring Game (1968) **C-100m.** **½ D: Laslo Benedek. Lloyd Bridges, Nico Minardos, Michael Ansara, Joan Blackman. Not bad adventure tale of underwater expert (guess who?) in search of husband and daughter of his former girlfriend.▼

Darjeeling Limited, The (2007) **C-91m.** **½ D: Wes Anderson. Owen Wilson, Jason Schwartzman, Adrien Brody, Anjelica Huston, Amara Karan, Wallace Wolodarsky, Waris Ahluwalia, Irfan Khan, Barbet Schroeder, Camilla Rutherford, Bill Murray. Three brothers who get on each other's nerves (including Wilson, in heavy bandages) take a stab at reconciling on an India train journey that includes a stop-off to see mom Huston, who's now in a Himalayan convent. Another visually inventive Anderson comedy, though its thin comic story has a melancholy air. For Anderson (and his cowriters Schwartzman and Roman Coppola) it's the journey, not the destination, that matters here. Natalie Portman, seen here in a passing bit, also stars with Schwartzman in the tangentially related short HOTEL CHEVALIER. Panavision. [R]▼▌

Dark, The (1979) **C-92m.** ✱✱ D: John (Bud) Cardos. William Devane, Cathy Lee Crosby, Richard Jaeckel, Keenan Wynn, Jacquelyn Hyde, Biff Elliott, Vivian Blaine. Fairly well made but predictable sci-fier; writer Devane and TV reporter Crosby take on a homicidal alien in a California town. Aka THE MUTILATOR. Panavision. [R]▼▌

Dark at the Top of the Stairs, The (1960) **C-123m.** ✱✱✱½ D: Delbert Mann. Robert Preston, Dorothy McGuire, Eve Arden, Angela Lansbury, Shirley Knight, Lee Kinsolving, Frank Overton, Robert Eyer. Simple, eloquent drama, set in 1920s Oklahoma, with Preston in top form as a traveling salesman caught in a passionless marriage. His relationships with wife McGuire, daughter Knight, and "friend" Lansbury are played out in a series of beautifully acted scenes. Poignant script by Irving Ravetch and Harriet Frank, Jr., from William Inge's play.

Dark Avenger, The SEE: **Warriors, The** (1955)

Dark Backward, The (1991) **C-104m.** ✱½ D: Adam Rifkin. Judd Nelson, Bill Paxton, Wayne Newton, Lara Flynn Boyle, James Caan, Rob Lowe, King Moody, Claudia Christian. Yes, that's a third arm growing out of Nelson's back—and it's putting the necessary edge on his wide professional reputation as the worst stand-up comic in showbiz history. Contrived in an attempt to be culty, but unsuccessful even on those terms. Still, film has a casting mix one could cherish. Lowe is fitted out with what appears to the untrained eye to be Mr. Hyde's dental work. Director Rifkin appears as Rufus Bing. [R]▼▌

Dark Blue (2003) **C-118m.** ✱✱ D: Ron Shelton. Kurt Russell, Brendan Gleeson, Scott Speedman, Michael Michele, Lolita Davidovich, Ving Rhames, Dash Mihok, Kurupt, Master P. Half-baked look at inbred corruption in the LAPD during the troubled days leading up to the riots of 1992. Russell (in a dynamic performance) plays a third-generation cop who no longer blinks at the methodology of his colleagues and superiors, but his young partner (Speedman) still has ideals. Awkward coincidences and a preposterous finale are just two major flaws in this narrative, which tries to be larger than life and realistic at the same time. Based on an original story by James Ellroy. Super 35. [R]▼▌

Dark Blue World (2001-Czech) **C-119m.** ✱✱½ D: Jan Sverák. Ondrej Vetchy©, Tara Fitzgerald, Krystof Hadek, Charles Dance, Oldrich Kaiser. From a 1950 Soviet-ruled Czech labor camp that's punishing a native pilot who flew for the R.A.F., we cut to a 1939 flashback to find the same guy (Vetchy©) involved with a Brit (Fitzgerald) whose husband is missing in action. The later story sounds more novel and interesting, but the dominant earlier one provides the flying scenes, which are surprisingly elaborate. Otherwise, there's not much to distinguish this capable but uninspired yarn from hundreds of other WW2 dramas. Arriscope. [R]▼▌

Dark City (1998) **C-100m.** ✱✱✱ D: Alex Proyas. Rufus Sewell, Kiefer Sutherland, Jennifer Connelly, Richard O'Brien, Ian Richardson, Colin Friels, Bruce Spence, William Hurt. In a city where it is always night, aliens conduct secret experiments to learn what makes us human. Meanwhile, his memory mostly gone, Sewell is suspected of being a serial killer, and finds he now has telekinetic powers. Richly plotted sci-fi has striking set design and excellent use of special effects; complex, with a new surprise every few minutes. Filmed in Australia. Cowritten by the director. Director's cut runs 111m. Super 35. [R]▼●▌

Dark Command (1940) **94m.** ✱✱✱ D: Raoul Walsh. Claire Trevor, John Wayne, Walter Pidgeon, Roy Rogers, George "Gabby" Hayes, Porter Hall, Marjorie Main. Pidgeon plays character based on 1860s renegade Quantrill, small-town despot who (in this story) launches his terror raids after clashing with new marshal Wayne. Dramatically uneven, but entertaining. Also shown in computer-colored version. ▼▌

Dark Corner, The (1946) **99m.** ✱✱✱ D: Henry Hathaway. Lucille Ball, Clifton Webb, William Bendix, Mark Stevens, Kurt Kreuger, Cathy Downs, Reed Hadley, Constance Collier. Top-notch mystery with secretary Ball helping moody boss Stevens escape from phony murder charge. Well-acted, exciting film noir. ▼▌

Dark Crystal, The (1982-British) **C-94m.** ✱✱✱ D: Jim Henson, Frank Oz. Performed by Jim Henson, Kathryn Mullen, Frank Oz, Dave Goelz, Brian Muehl, Jean Pierre Amiel, Kiran Shah. Elaborate fantasy—a cross between Tolkien and the Brothers Grimm—from the Muppets crew, with imaginative (and often grotesque) cast of characters enacting classic quest: a missing piece of the powerful Dark Crystal must be found or evil will take over the world. Takes time to warm up to, but worth the effort. Panavision. [PG]▼●▌

Dark Days (2000) **84m.** ✱✱✱½ D: Marc Singer. Exceptional documentary about a community of former street people who've created homes for themselves in railroad tunnels under the streets of Manhattan. First-time filmmaker Singer lived with his subjects for two years, and had them work as his crew, to fashion this compassionate and eye-opening film.▼▌

Dark End of the Street, The (1981) **C-90m.** ✱✱✱ D: Jan Egleson. Laura Harrington, Henry Tomaszewski, Michelle Green, Lance Henriksen, Pamela Payton-

Wright, Terence Grey, Ben Affleck. Low-budget independent feature, shot in and around Boston, about white teenagers who witness a black friend's accidental death. Realistic depiction of urban working-class lifestyle and problems. Fine performances, particularly by Harrington and Green (as her best friend).

Darker Than Amber (1970) **C-97m.** ****½** D: Robert Clouse. Rod Taylor, Suzy Kendall, Theodore Bikel, Jane Russell, James Booth, Janet MacLachlan. OK action melodrama casts Taylor as John D. MacDonald's detective Travis McGee; he's after thugs who beat up Kendall. Good location photography in Miami and Caribbean. [PG—edited from original R rating]▼

Dark Eyes (1987-Italian) **C-118m.** *****½** D: Nikita Mikhalkov. Marcello Mastroianni, Silvana Mangano, Marthe Keller, Elena Safonova, Pina Cei. Mastroianni gives a tour-de-force performance as a once-young, idealistic, aspiring architect, who settled for a life of wealth and ease after marrying a banker's daughter . . . and proved incapable of holding on to what's important to him. A rich, beautifully detailed, multileveled film that's at once sad, funny, and haunting. Based on short stories by Anton Chekhov (one of which was previously filmed as LADY WITH A DOG [1959]).▼●

Dark Forces SEE: **Harlequin**

Dark Habits (1984-Spanish) **C-116m.** ****½** D: Pedro Almodóvar. Cristina S. Pascual, Carmen Maura, Julieta Serrano, Marisa Paredes. Singer Pascual takes it on the lam after her lover ODs and finds herself in a convent crammed with wacky, free-spirited nuns. Funny, but not up to some of Almodóvar's later work.▼●

Dark Half, The (1993) **C-122m.** ****** D: George A. Romero. Timothy Hutton, Amy Madigan, Michael Rooker, Julie Harris, Robert Joy, Kent Broadhurst, Beth Grant, Rutanya Alda, Tom Mardirosian, Glenn Colerider, Chelsea Field, Royal Dano. Another Stephen King movie without a good half. Hutton plays a successful writer, under a pseudonym, who fails when he writes under his own name. When he's threatened with exposure, he announces the death of his alter ego—which causes the "pseudonym," to come to life and embark on a murderous rampage. (King himself published several novels under the pseudonym Richard Bachman before killing him off.) Scripted by Romero. [R]▼●

Dark Hazard (1934) **72m.** ****** D: Alfred E. Green. Edward G. Robinson, Genevieve Tobin, Glenda Farrell, Henry B. Walthall, Sidney Toler. Robinson is bright spot of programmer about his precarious married life to Tobin, endangered by girlfriend Farrell and urge to gamble.

Dark Knight, The (2008) **C-152m.** ****** D: Christopher Nolan. Christian Bale, Heath Ledger, Aaron Eckhart, Michael Caine, Maggie Gyllenhaal, Gary Oldman, Morgan Freeman, Monique Gabriela Curnen, Ron Dean, Cillian Murphy, Nestor Carbonell, Eric Roberts, Ritchie Coster, Anthony Michael Hall, Keith Szarabajka, William Fichtner. Gotham City (no longer futuristic, as it was depicted in BATMAN BEGINS) is brought to its knees by the evil machinations of The Joker. The new D.A. (Eckhart) wants to clean things up but Bruce Wayne isn't sure he can be trusted—especially since he's dating Rachel Dawes (Gyllenhaal, replacing Katie Holmes). A Batman story for the terrorist era, this is doomsday dark and palpably real. It's also incredibly long. Ledger is a vivid Joker but his character is so sick it's difficult to derive any pleasure from watching him. Oscar winner for Sound Editing and Best Supporting Actor, posthumously, for Ledger. Panavision and IMAX. [PG-13]❍

Darkman (1990) **C-95m.** ****½** D: Sam Raimi. Liam Neeson, Frances McDormand, Colin Friels, Larry Drake, Nelson Mashita, Jesse Lawrence Ferguson, Rafael H. Robledo, Danny Hicks, Bruce Campbell. Scientist hot on the trail of a formula for cloning body parts by computer is savagely attacked (and left for dead) by thugs who represent a crooked city developer. Retreating into a shadow world, and seeking revenge, the laboratory genius reinvents himself as Darkman. Grandiose melodramatics, and Raimi's over-the-top approach, are entertaining to a point, but there's a fundamental hollowness to this comic-book script. Old-fashioned laboratory montage and main titles by Pablo Ferro. Jenny Agutter and John Landis appear unbilled. Followed by two video sequels in 1995 and 1996. [R] ▼●

Dark Matter (2008) **C-86m.** ****½** D: Chen Shi-Zheng. Liu Ye, Meryl Streep, Aidan Quinn, Blair Brown, Bill Irwin, Joe Grifasi, Tsao Lei, Shan Jing. Brilliant Chinese student wins a scholarship to study for his Ph.D. in the U.S. in the early 1990s, working under famed cosmologist Quinn, but his tenacious interest in exploring "dark matter" threatens to outshine the work of his egocentric professor. Streep plays a college patron who helps newly arrived Chinese students acclimate to American life. Pointed observation of clashing cultures leads to a disturbing denouement that seems to come out of left field—even though it's inspired by a real-life incident. Film debut for noted stage and opera director Chen. [R]❍

Darkness (2002-Spanish) **C-88m.** ***½** D: Jaume Balagueró. Anna Paquin, Lena Olin, Iain Glen, Giancarlo Giannini, Fele Martínez, Stephan Enquist. Disjointed haunted-house story shot in Spain must have lost something in the translation. Paquin is a teenage girl whose family moves into a dreary home only to discover its terrifying past. U.S. distributor Miramax sat on this misfire for two years before cutting 14m. Original 102m. Spanish version is unrated. Super 35. [PG-13] ▼◗

Darkness Falls (2003) C-86m. BOMB D: Jonathan Liebesman. Chaney Kley, Emma Caulfield, Lee Cormie, Grant Piro, Sullivan Stapleton, Steve Mouzakis. Dreadful horror film about "The Tooth Fairy" gone amok. A man terrorized by the dentin pixie—that is, a local woman who appeared in that guise—since he lost his last baby tooth returns to his hometown of Darkness Falls to help a similarly plagued boy. Ridiculous premise spawns a film that gets worse as it goes along. Super 35. [PG-13] ▼◗

Dark Obsession (1989-British) C-87m. BOMB D: Nicholas Broomfield. Gabriel Byrne, Amanda Donohoe, Michael Hordern, Judy Parfitt, Douglas Hodge, Sadie Frost, Ian Carmichael. Byrne and his regiment buddies run over a chambermaid after a night of drinking—and the only one who feels guilt about the death is the only one who will suffer. Documentary director Broomfield's first fiction feature is an obvious, boring parable about the amorality of the rich and titled. Even Donohoe's frequent nudity quickly becomes dreary. Original British title: DIAMOND SKULLS. Released in U.S. in 1991. Available in both NC-17- (100m.) and R-rated versions. ▼◗

Dark of the Night (1985-New Zealand) C-89m. *** D: Gaylene Preston. Heather Bolton, David Letch, Gary Stalker, Danny Mulheron, Kate Harcourt, Michael Haigh. Bolton buys a used Jaguar that's seemingly haunted by its previous owner, a woman who was murdered. Entertainingly loopy psychological thriller that's also a keenly observed feminist fable about the frustrations and perils of a woman seeking independence in a "man's world." Original New Zealand title: MR. WRONG. ▼

Dark of the Sun (1968-British) C-101m. *** D: Jack Cardiff. Rod Taylor, Yvette Mimieux, Jim Brown, Kenneth More, Peter Carsten, Andre Morell, Calvin Lockhart. Excellent cast in nerve-wracking actioner with Rod the leader of mercenary expedition to retrieve uncut diamonds and besieged refugees in Congo. One of Taylor's best pictures. Original British title: THE MERCENARIES. Panavision. [PG] ▼◗

Dark Passage (1947) 106m. *** D: Delmer Daves. Humphrey Bogart, Lauren Bacall, Bruce Bennett, Agnes Moorehead. Engrossing caper of escaped convict (Bogart) undergoing plastic surgery, hiding out at Bacall's apartment till his face heals. Stars outshine far-fetched happenings. Also shown in computer-colored version. ▼◗◗

Dark Places (1975-British) C-91m. *½ D: Don Sharp. Christopher Lee, Joan Collins, Robert Hardy, Herbert Lom, Jane Birkin, Jean Marsh. Mild horror thriller. Hardy, heir

to an insane murderer's estate, is possessed by his spirit, kills those who try to do him out of it. [PG]

Dark Side of the Sun, The (1997-Canadian) C-101m. BOMB D: Bozidar Nikolic. Brad Pitt, Guy Boyd, Cheryl Pollak, Milena Dravic, Constantin Nitchoff. In MEET JOE BLACK, Pitt played Death; here he plays dying. Awful weepie about a young American exile who covers his body from head to toe in leather because of a fatal skin disease. He decides to chuck life for a few days of passion when he meets a traveling actress. Entire film takes place in the Slavic countryside and features an irritating polka score! Even diehard Pitt fans best beware. Made in 1990. ▼◗

Dark Star (1974) C-83m. **½ D: John Carpenter. Dan O'Bannon, Dre Pahich, Brian Narelle. Satiric, spaced-out comedy of weary astronauts whose mission is to blow up unstable planets; one of their sentient bombs gets its own ideas. Enjoyable for sci-fi fans and surfers; stretches its shoestring budget pretty well. Carpenter's first feature, expanded from a college short he wrote with O'Bannon. [G] ▼◗

Darktown Strutters (1975) C-85m. *½ D: William Witney. Trina Parks, Edna Richardson, Bettye Sweet, Shirley Washington, Roger E. Mosley, Stan Shaw, Christopher Joy. Poor spoof of black and white stereotypes. Story is about Parks attempting to find her kidnapped mother. Original running time: 90m. Retitled GET DOWN AND BOOGIE. [PG] ▼

Dark Tower (1987) C-91m. BOMB D: Ken Barnett. Michael Moriarty, Jenny Agutter, Carol Lynley, Anne Lockhart, Theodore Bikel, Kevin McCarthy, Patch Mackenzie. Appallingly bad supernatural thriller about architect Agutter's husband's ghost, which seems to be committing murder during the construction of her skyscraper. Barnett is a pseudonym for Freddie Francis (who's done far better). [R] ▼◗

Dark Victory (1939) 106m. ***½ D: Edmund Goulding. Bette Davis, George Brent, Humphrey Bogart, Geraldine Fitzgerald, Ronald Reagan, Cora Witherspoon, Henry Travers. Definitive Davis performance as spoiled socialite whose life is ending; Brent as brain surgeon husband, Fitzgerald as devoted friend register in good soaper. Bogart as Irish stable master seems out of place. Remade as STOLEN HOURS, and for TV in 1976 with Elizabeth Montgomery and Anthony Hopkins. Also shown in computer-colored version. ▼◗◗

Dark Water (2005) C-105m. *** D: Walter Salles. Jennifer Connelly, John C. Reilly, Tim Roth, Dougray Scott, Pete Postlethwaite, Camryn Manheim, Ariel Gade, Debra Monk. Newly separated Connelly takes an apartment in a seedy building on N.Y.C.'s isolated Roosevelt Island, hoping the change will do her and her 5-year-old daughter some good.

Instead, there are signs of dread and imminent danger everywhere, along with water dripping from the ceiling. Director Salles (in his American debut) milks every possibility for atmosphere in this creepy chiller, a remake of a 2002 Japanese film. Reilly adds a touch of humor as a hilariously sleazy rental agent. Unrated version also available. Panavision. [PG-13]▶

Dark Waters (1944) 90m. ** D: Andre de Toth. Merle Oberon, Franchot Tone, Thomas Mitchell, Fay Bainter, Rex Ingram, John Qualen, Elisha Cook, Jr. Cast sinks into the bog (some literally) in confused film of innocent girl staying with peculiar family.▼●▶

Dark Wind, The (1994) C-111m. *½ D: Errol Morris. Lou Diamond Phillips, Gary Farmer, Fred Ward, Guy Boyd, John Karlen. Disappointing feature from acclaimed documentarian Morris: a ponderously slow, muddled account of young Navajo cop Phillips, new to his district, who attempts to solve a mystery amid Navajo-Hopi differences. Script by Neal Jimenez and Eric Bergren, based on Tony Hillerman's novel. One of the executive producers was Robert Redford. Filmed in 1991. [R]▼▶

Darling (1965-British) 122m. ***½ D: John Schlesinger. Julie Christie, Dirk Bogarde, Laurence Harvey, Roland Curram, Jose Luis de Villalonga, Alex Scott, Basil Henson. Christie won Oscar as girl who rises from commonplace life to marry an Italian noble, with several unsatisfactory love affairs in between. Trendy, influential '60s film—in flashy form and cynical content. Frederic Raphael's script and costume designer Julie Harris also won Oscars.▼●▶

Darling Lili (1970) C-136m. *** D: Blake Edwards. Julie Andrews, Rock Hudson, Jeremy Kemp, Lance Percival, Jacques Marin, Michael Witney. Critically lambasted when first released, this entertaining spoof has Andrews and Hudson at their best, along with writer/director Edwards, keeping tongue-in-cheek but not becoming coy in telling story of German spy Julie posing as London entertainer during WW1, falling in love with squadron commander Hudson. Great fun, good music, including Johnny Mercer and Henry Mancini's lovely song "Whistling Away the Dark." Two decades after the fact, Edwards prepared an alternative "director's cut" of the film, more serious in tone, for cable TV; it runs 114m. Panavision. [G]▶

Darwin's Nightmare (2005-French-Austrian-Belgian) C-107m. *** D: Hubert Sauper. Sobering, stranger-than-fiction documentary about the effect one species of fish, the Nile Perch, has on the economy and ecology of Tanzania. Introduced to Lake Victoria years ago, the predatory fish now consumes all other species in the water, but its desirability as an export item single-handedly sustains the local economy. Following each thread of this story, the film deals with globalization, exploitation,

and other issues that affect all of us, not just the poor people of one African nation.▶

D.A.R.Y.L. (1985) C-99m. **½ D: Simon Wincer. Mary Beth Hurt, Michael McKean, Barret Oliver, Kathryn Walker, Colleen Camp, Josef Sommer, Steve Ryan, Danny Corkill. Childless couple adopts a little boy who's really a sophisticated robot. Good premise undermined by incredibly bland presentation; young kids might enjoy it. Panavision. [PG]▼●▶

Das Boot (1981-German) C-145m. ***½ D: Wolfgang Petersen. Jürgen Prochnow, Herbert Gronemeyer, Klaus Wennemann, Hubertus Bengsch, Martin Semmelrogge, Bernd Tauber, Erwin Leder, Martin May. Realistic, meticulously mounted nail-biter chronicling a German U-boat on a mission during WW2, with Prochnow solid as its commander. Manages to embrace an antiwar message, as well. Based on Lothar-Guenther Buchheim's autobiographical novel. Originally a five-hour German TV miniseries, which is available on DVD; later released in a 211m. Director's Cut. Well-dubbed American version is titled THE BOAT. [R]▼●▶

Das Experiment (2001-German) C-119m. *** D: Oliver Hirschbiegel. Moritz Bleibtreu, Christian Berkel, Justus von Dohnanyi, Oliver Stokowski, Maren Eggert, Andrea Sawatzki. Compelling drama about 20 men who sign up for a behavioral psychology experiment in which they pretend to be in prison for two weeks—some as inmates, some as guards. Needless to say, things go terribly wrong. A perfect story for the *Survivor/Big Brother* era, although it was inspired by a real-life incident from the 1970s. Aka THE EXPERIMENT. Remade in 2010. [R]▼▶

Date Movie (2006) C-82m. BOMB D: Aaron Seltzer. Alyson Hannigan, Adam Campbell, Jennifer Coolidge, Tony Cox, Fred Willard, Eddie Griffin, Sophie Monk, Meera Simhan, Carmen Electra, Lil Jon. Witless, brainless spoof of Hollywood romantic comedies involving an overweight young woman (Hannigan, in a fat suit) and the complications that arise when she finds her Mr. Right. Loaded with lame "comic" references to recent-vintage pop movies and tailored to people who think obesity and flatulence jokes are the height of hilarity. Unrated version also available. [PG-13]▶

Date Night (2010) C-88m. **½ D: Shawn Levy. Steve Carell, Tina Fey, Mark Wahlberg, Taraji P. Henson, Common, Jimmi Simpson, William Fichtner, Leighton Meester, J. B. Smoove, Kristen Wiig, Mark Ruffalo, James Franco, Mila Kunis, Jon Bernthal, Ari Graynor. Ordinary suburban N.J. couple treat themselves to a night out at a Manhattan restaurant, where they're mistaken for two other people who are involved in criminal activity and held at gunpoint. From there it's a nonstop series of chases, deceptions, and near misses. The two likable stars make a good couple; too bad the material isn't as good as they are. The film works awfully hard for laughs. Ray Liotta appears unbilled; other notable actors pop up in small parts. Alternate version runs 102m. HD Widescreen. [PG-13]

Date With an Angel (1987) **C-105m.** BOMB D: Tom McLoughlin. Michael E. Knight, Phoebe Cates, Emmanuelle Béart, David Dukes, Phil Brock, Albert Macklin. Aspiring musician Knight, about to be swallowed up by marriage and his future father-in-law's firm, finds salvation with the broken-winged angel who crashes into his pool on the night of his bachelor party. Unbearable comic fantasy despite Béart's appropriately ethereal beauty. J-D-C Scope. [PG] ▼●▶

Date With Death, A SEE: **McGuire, Go Home!**

Date With Judy, A (1948) **C-113m.** **½ D: Richard Thorpe. Wallace Beery, Jane Powell, Elizabeth Taylor, Carmen Miranda, Xavier Cugat, Robert Stack, Scotty Beckett. Musicomedy of two teenagers involved in family shenanigans; highlight is Beery dancing with Miranda. Songs include "It's a Most Unusual Day." ▼●▶

Daughters of Darkness (1971-Belgian-French) **C-87m.** **½ D: Harry Kumel. Delphine Seyrig, Daniele Ouimet, John Karlen, Andrea Rau, Paul Esser, George Jamin, Joris Collet, Fons Rademakers. Sophisticated, witty, but cold tale of honeymooning couple meeting lesbian vampire Elisabeth Bathory (a real historical figure), becoming enmeshed in her schemes. Elegant, but pretentious and slow. Highly regarded by many. Also shown at 96m. Director's cut runs 100m. ▼●▶

Daughters of Satan (1972) **C-96m.** ** D: Hollingsworth Morse. Tom Selleck, Barra Grant, Tani Phelps Guthrie, Paraluman. Witches' curses, mumbo jumbo, and a lot of hokum as young girl is lured into witches' coven. [R] ▼▶

Daughters of the Dust (1991) **C-114m.** **½ D: Julie Dash. Cora Lee Day, Alva Rodgers, Adisa Anderson, Kaycee Moore, Barbara O, Eartha D. Robinson, Bahni Turpin, Cheryl Lynn Bruce. Poetic, turn-of-the-20th-century tale of the Gullah, descendants of slaves who resided on islands near South Carolina and Georgia and maintained their West African heritage. The material is fascinating, and some of the imagery is stunning, but too much of the historical background remains unexplained, and the slow pace weighs it down. Dash also scripted this *American Playhouse* theatrical feature. ▼▶

Dave (1993) **C-110m.** *** D: Ivan Reitman. Kevin Kline, Sigourney Weaver, Frank Langella, Ben Kingsley, Kevin Dunn, Ving Rhames, Charles Grodin, Faith Prince, Laura Linney, Bonnie Hunt, Parley Baer, Stefan Gierasch, Anna Deavere Smith. Shades of PRISONER OF ZENDA! U.S. president,

incapacitated by stroke, is replaced by look-alike (and everyman) Kline, who proceeds to win over the press, public, and even the president's estranged wife (Weaver) in this amusing political comedy. Farfetched premise made believable by winning cast and cameos by celebrities, real reporters, and actual U.S. senators! [PG-13] ▼●▶

Dave Chappelle's Block Party (2006) **C-103m.** *** D: Michel Gondry. Freewheeling combination documentary–concert film in which stand-up comic Chappelle plans—and invites one and all to attend—a block party/outdoor concert on a street in rainy Bedford-Stuyvesant, Brooklyn, in 2004. Chappelle's interactions with everyday people are as fresh and funny as his onstage material. Kanye West, Mos Def, Erykah Badu, The Roots, The Fugees, Dead Prez, and others are seen in performance. Unrated edition is 126m. [R] ▶

David and Bathsheba (1951) **C-116m.** ** D: Henry King. Gregory Peck, Susan Hayward, Raymond Massey, Kieron Moore, James Robertson Justice, Jayne Meadows, John Sutton, George Zucco. Biblical epic with good production values but generally boring script; only fair performances. ▼●▶

David and Goliath (1960-Italian) **C-95m.** ** D: Richard Pottier, Ferdinando Baldi. Orson Welles, Ivo Payer, Edward Hilton, Eleonora Rossi-Drago, Massimo Serato. Juvenile spectacle based on biblical tale, with wooden script, bad acting, Welles as hefty King Saul. Totalscope. ▼▶

David and Lisa (1962) **94m.** *** D: Frank Perry. Keir Dullea, Janet Margolin, Howard da Silva, Neva Patterson, Clifton James. Independently made film about two disturbed teenagers is excellent, sensitively played by newcomers Dullea and Margolin. Da Silva is fine as an understanding doctor. Remade for TV in 1998. ▼●▶

David Copperfield (1935) **130m.** **** D: George Cukor. Freddie Bartholomew, Frank Lawton, W.C. Fields, Lionel Barrymore, Madge Evans, Roland Young, Basil Rathbone, Edna May Oliver, Maureen O'Sullivan, Lewis Stone, Lennox Pawle, Elsa Lanchester, Una O'Connor, Arthur Treacher. Hollywood does right by Dickens in this lavishly mounted, superbly cast production, following David's exploits from youth to young manhood, with such unforgettable characterizations as Fields' Micawber, Rathbone's Mr. Murdstone, Young's Uriah Heep, and Oliver's Aunt Betsey. A treat from start to finish. Screenplay by Howard Estabrook and Hugh Walpole; the latter also portrays the vicar. Also shown in computer-colored version. ▼●▶

David Holzman's Diary (1968) **74m.** ***½ D: Jim McBride. L. M. Kit Carson, Eileen Dietz, Louise Levine, Lorenzo Mans. Superior, perceptively funny cinéma vérité feature about a serious young filmmaker who seeks truth by making a movie of his life. A classic of its kind.**▼❙**

Da Vinci Code, The (2006) **C-148m.** ****** D: Ron Howard. Tom Hanks, Audrey Tautou, Ian McKellen, Jean Reno, Paul Bettany, Alfred Molina, Jürgen Prochnow, Jean-Yves Berteloot, Etienne Chicot, Jean-Pierre Marielle. While lecturing in Paris, Harvard symbologist Hanks is pulled into a murder case that has deep, dark implications involving a religious sect and links to the paintings of Leonardo da Vinci. Eagerly anticipated adaptation of Dan Brown's best-seller (which became a cultural phenomenon) is a letdown in every respect. Workmanlike at best, not especially well staged or shot, it lacks the electricity—and star chemistry—a thriller of this magnitude ought to have. Material still has pull, but Akiva Goldsman's script makes changes that aren't always an improvement on the book . . . and the movie plods as it heads down the stretch. Alternate version runs 28m. longer. Followed by ANGELS & DEMONS. Super 35. [PG-13]**❚**

Davy Crockett and the River Pirates (1956) **C-81m.** ****½** D: Norman Foster. Fess Parker, Buddy Ebsen, Jeff York, Kenneth Tobey, Clem Bevans, Irvin Ashkenazy. Second CROCKETT feature strung together from two Disney TV shows; first half is comic keelboat race with Mike Fink (York), self-proclaimed "King of the River," second half is more serious confrontation with Indians. Lightweight fun.**▼❙❙**

Davy Crockett, King of the Wild Frontier (1955) **C-93m.** ******* D: Norman Foster. Fess Parker, Buddy Ebsen, Basil Ruysdael, Hans Conried, William Bakewell, Kenneth Tobey. Originally filmed as three segments for Disney's TV show, this created a nationwide phenomenon in 1955; it's still fun today with Parker as famous Indian scout and Ebsen as his pal George Russel, whose adventures take them from Washington, D.C., to the Alamo.**▼❙**

Dawning, The (1988-British) **C-97m.** ****½** D: Robert Knights. Anthony Hopkins, Jean Simmons, Trevor Howard, Rebecca Pidgeon, Hugh Grant, Tara MacGowran. Set in Southern Ireland in 1920, this well-made but curiously ordinary drama chronicles the political turmoil of the time as perceived by a spirited, rapidly maturing 18-year-old girl (Pidgeon) who comes to the aid of a mysterious stranger (Hopkins). Howard's last film; he's cast as her wheelchair-bound grandfather. [PG]**▼❙❙**

Dawn of the Dead (1978) **C-126m.** *****½** D: George A. Romero. David Emge, Ken Foree, Scott Reiniger, Gaylen Ross, Tom Savini. Sequel-cum-remake of NIGHT OF THE LIVING DEAD is apocalyptic horror masterpiece; as zombie population increases, four people set up quasi-Utopian existence in barricaded shopping mall. Satiric, metaphori-cally rich adventure jerks viewers' emotions around with stunning ease, as zombies are, by turns, horrifying, heroic, made clownish, and even forgotten. Savini's hideously gory effects are mostly confined to the first and last half hours. Nontheatrical prints run 140m. Remade in 2004. Followed by DAY OF THE DEAD.**▼❙❙**

Dawn of the Dead (2004) **C-99m.** ******* D: Zack Snyder. Sarah Polley, Ving Rhames, Jake Weber, Mekhi Phifer, Ty Burrell, Michael Kelly, Kevin Zegers, Michael Barry, Lindy Booth, Jayne Eastwood, Matt Frewer. Exciting, fast-paced, bloodthirsty fun. The dead return to life and attack the living, constantly increasing their numbers. A group of uninfected survivors holes up in a shopping mall, where most of the story is set. An especially good cast flourishes under confident direction by Snyder, making his movie debut. Gruesome, yes, but also funny and even touching; compromised only by going too far in end-credits scenes. Super 35. [R] **▼❙**

Dawn Patrol, The (1930) **107m.** ****½** D: Howard Hawks. Richard Barthelmess, Douglas Fairbanks Jr., Neil Hamilton, William Janney, James Finlayson, Clyde Cook. John Monk Saunders' Oscar-winning story of a beleaguered aerial squadron in WW1 France. Devotees of director Hawks prefer this to 1938 remake, but it doesn't hold up as well, particularly the stiff, overdrawn performances.

Dawn Patrol, The (1938) **103m.** *****½** D: Edmund Goulding. Errol Flynn, Basil Rathbone, David Niven, Donald Crisp, Melville Cooper, Barry Fitzgerald. Remake of 1930 classic is fine actioner of WW1 flyers in France; Rathbone as stern officer forced to send up green recruits, Flynn and Niven as pilot buddies, all excellent. Insightful study of wartime camaraderie and grueling pressures of battlefront command.**▼❙**

Day After Tomorrow, The (2004) **C-124m.** ******* D: Roland Emmerich. Dennis Quaid, Jake Gyllenhaal, Ian Holm, Emmy Rossum, Sela Ward, Dash Mihok, Kenneth Welsh, Jay O. Sanders, Austin Nichols, Perry King. Quaid tries to convince his superiors in Washington, D.C. (including a Dick Cheney look-alike) that weather prognosticators are correct and worldwide calamity is imminent—with tidal waves, tornadoes, iceberg movement, etc.—due to global warming. Ultimately, he must make his way to a flooded Manhattan to rescue his son (Gyllenhaal). The characters are likable, the dialogue isn't dumb, and the effects are spectacular: in other words, a pretty good, old-fashioned disaster movie. Super 35. [PG-13] **▼❙**

Day at the Races, A (1937) **111m.** *****½** D: Sam Wood. Groucho, Harpo, Chico Marx, Allan Jones, Maureen O'Sullivan, Esther Muir, Margaret Dumont, Douglass Dumbrille, Sig Ruman, Dorothy Dandridge.

The Marxes wreak havoc at a sanitorium, where wealthy hypochondriac Dumont is the leading patient; often uproarious comedy features some of the trio's funniest set pieces (Chico selling race tips, the seduction scene, etc.). A perfunctory storyline and unmemorable songs keep it from topping its immediate predecessor, A NIGHT AT THE OPERA . . . but the comedy content is sensational.▼●▮

Daybreak (1939) SEE: **Le Jour Se Lève**

Daybreakers (2010-U.S.-Australian) **C-98m. **½** D: Michael and Peter Spierig. Ethan Hawke, Willem Dafoe, Sam Neill, Claudia Karvan, Michael Dorman, Vince Colosimo, Isabel Lucas. In the near future, vampires comprise the vast majority of the world's population, so human blood is in short supply and must be rationed. Enter humanistic vampire-hematologist Hawke, in the employ of greedy businessman Neill, who abandons his efforts to create synthetic blood after becoming convinced that there's a cure for vampirism. Provocative, well-made horror film is unrelentingly gory—and appropriately so—but also terminally predictable. HD Widescreen. [R] ▮

Daydreamer, The (1966) **C-98m. ***** D: Jules Bass. Ray Bolger, Jack Gilford, Margaret Hamilton, Paul O'Keefe; voices of Tallulah Bankhead, Boris Karloff, Burl Ives, Victor Borge, Terry-Thomas, Patty Duke. Partly animated story of Hans Christian Andersen as a 13-year-old who meets many of the fairy tale characters he later writes about. Surprisingly pleasant.▼▮

Day for Night (1973-French) **C-120m. ***½** D: François Truffaut. Jacqueline Bisset, Jean-Pierre Aumont, Valentina Cortese, François Truffaut, Jean-Pierre Léaud, Alexandra Stewart, Dani, Nathalie Baye. Enjoyable fluff about a motion picture director (Truffaut) and his problems in trying to film a silly love story; bright performances and a loving look into the intricacies of filmmaking. Oscar winner as Best Foreign Film. [PG]▼▮

Day in October, A (1990-Danish-U.S.) **C-97m. ***** D: Kenneth Madsen. D. B. Sweeney, Kelly Wolf, Daniel Benzali, Tovah Feldshuh, Ole Lemmeke. Gripping, fact-based drama set in WW2 Denmark chronicles the fate of young Jewish woman (Wolf); she brings a stranger—wounded resistance fighter Sweeney—into her home, disrupting the lives of her family. Knowing parable about the need to take sides (and take action) when confronted by evil. Don't miss this sleeper. [PG-13]▼▮

Day in the Country, A (1946-French) **40m. ****** D: Jean Renoir. Sylvia Bataille, Georges Saint-Saens (Georges Darnoux), Jacques Borel (Jacques Brunius), Jeanne Marken. At a picnic along a river, a bourgeois Parisian mother and daughter find romance while the menfolk try to fish. Nature plays a starring role in this cinematic tone poem about the emotional depth of spiritual love and the sexual high of a romp in the hay. Screenplay by Renoir, from a short story by Guy de Maupassant; among his assistants on this were Yves Allegret, Jacques Becker, Henri Cartier-Bresson, and Luchino Visconti! Renoir cast himself as Poulain the innkeeper. Shot in 1936, only partially completed, and edited in Renoir's absence. Original title: UNE PARTIE DE CAMPAGNE.▼

Day in the Death of Joe Egg, A (1972-British) **C-106m. ***½** D: Peter Medak. Alan Bates, Janet Suzman, Peter Bowles, Sheila Gish, Joan Hickson. Excellent black comedy about a couple with a diseased child who contemplate mercy-killing. Not a crowd-pleaser, but extremely well done. Peter Nichols adapted his own play. [R] ▼▮

Daylight (1996) **C-114m. ***** D: Rob Cohen. Sylvester Stallone, Amy Brenneman, Viggo Mortensen, Dan Hedaya, Jay O. Sanders, Karen Young, Claire Bloom, Vanessa Bell Calloway, Barry Newman, Stan Shaw, Colin Fox. Good old-fashioned disaster movie, built on a formulaic foundation. Stallone is a disgraced Emergency Medical Services worker who springs into action when a huge explosion cripples a tunnel under N.Y.C.'s Hudson River, with a handful of survivors inside. Great stunts and special effects. That's Sly's son Sage as a cocky young scam artist being taken to prison. [PG-13]▼●▮

Day Night Day Night (2007-U.S.-German) **C-94m. **½** D: Julia Loktev. Luisa Williams, Josh P. Weinstein, Gareth Saxe, Nyambi Nyambi, Frank Dattolo, Annemarie Lawless. Naïve 19-year-old girl arrives in the N.Y.C. area and is prepared for the task she's signed up for: to act as a suicide bomber in Times Square. Using a literal in-your-face approach, writer-director Loktev deliberately withholds information so we focus on the girl and the immediacy of her situation, not her motivation or her cause. Riveting at times, but peters out, although the filmmaker planned her surprising climax just that way.▮

Day of Anger (1969-Italian) **C-109m. *½** D: Tonino Valerii. Lee Van Cleef, Giuliano Gemma, Walter Rilla, Christa Linder, Ennio Balbo. Story of callous gunman and his relationship with young protégé is below par, even for an Italian Western; only for the Van Cleef cult. Aka DAY OF WRATH. Techniscope. [M/PG]▼▮

Day of the Animals (1977) **C-98m. **½** D: William Girdler. Christopher George, Lynda Day George, Leslie Nielsen, Richard Jaeckel, Michael Ansara, Ruth Roman. Fair action thriller in the nature-on-the rampage mold, with back packers in the High Sierras at the mercy of hostile creatures crazed by the sun's radiation after the earth's ozone layer has been destroyed. Final score: Beasts

7, Cast 0 (in acting as well as survival). Aka SOMETHING IS OUT THERE. Todd-AO 35. [PG]▼◗

Day of the Dead (1985) C-102m. ** D: George A. Romero. Lori Cardille, Terry Alexander, Joseph Pilato, Jarlath Conroy, Antone DiLeo, Jr., Richard Liberty, Howard Sherman. Romero's creatures trap a female scientist with some army sexists in an underground bunker; she wants to "study" them, but the army balks at being zombie brunch. Third DEAD entry is relentlessly talky for over an hour, but Tom Savini's effects do give this a show-stopping finale. Easily the least of the series. Remade in name only in 2007. ▼◗

Day of the Dolphin, The (1973) C-104m. ** D: Mike Nichols. George C. Scott, Trish Van Devere, Paul Sorvino, Fritz Weaver, Jon Korkes, Edward Herrmann, John Dehner. Big-budget misfire about scientist Scott using his trained (and talking!) dolphins to foil an assassination plot. A waste of many talents. Scripter Buck Henry also provides the voices for the dolphins. Panavision. [PG]▼◗

Day of the Evil Gun (1968) C-93m. ** D: Jerry Thorpe. Glenn Ford, Arthur Kennedy, Dean Jagger, John Anderson, Paul Fix, Nico Minardos, Royal Dano, (Harry) Dean Stanton. Very routine Western with Ford and Kennedy going after Indians who abducted the former's wife; Kennedy is smooth in likable-villain role he's played many times. Panavision. [G]

Day of the Jackal, The (1973-British-French) C-141m. ***½ D: Fred Zinnemann. Edward Fox, Alan Badel, Tony Britton, Cyril Cusack, Michel Lonsdale, Eric Porter, Delphine Seyrig, Derek Jacobi, Ronald Pickup. Exciting adaptation of Frederick Forsyth's best-seller about plot to assassinate De Gaulle and the painstaking preparations of the assassin. Beautifully filmed throughout Europe with a first-rate cast. Reworked in 1997 as THE JACKAL. [PG]▼◗

Day of the Locust, The (1975) C-144m. ***½ D: John Schlesinger. Donald Sutherland, Karen Black, Burgess Meredith, William Atherton, Geraldine Page, Richard A. Dysart, Bo Hopkins, Pepe Serna, Lelia Goldoni, Billy Barty, Madge Kennedy, Florence Lake, Natalie Schafer, Nita Talbot, Paul Stewart, John Hillerman, Robert Pine, Dennis Dugan, Jackie Earle Haley, David Ladd, Dick Powell, Jr. Excellent adaptation of Nathanael West's sweeping novel about Hollywood's netherworld in 1930s, seen mostly through eyes of a young artist (Atherton) who finds little glamor and a lot of broken-down people in Tinseltown. Disturbing, depressing . . . and absolutely fascinating. Script by Waldo Salt. [R]▼◗

Day of the Outlaw (1959) **91m.** *** D: Andre de Toth. Robert Ryan, Burl Ives, Tina Louise, Alan Marshal, Nehemiah Persoff, Venetia Stevenson, David Nelson, Jack Lambert, Elisha Cook. Stark Western melodrama of outlaw Ives and gang taking over isolated Western town.◗

Day of the Triffids, The (1963-British) C-95m. **½ D: Steve Sekely. Howard Keel, Nicole Maurey, Janette Scott, Kieron Moore, Mervyn Johns. Meteor display blinds everyone who watched, while mutating experimental plants into giant, walking maneaters. Based on John Wyndham's classic sci-fi novel. Variable special effects. Remade in 1981 as a British TV miniseries; and in 1997 as a cable TV movie. CinemaScope. ▼◗

Day of Wrath (1943-Danish) **110m.** ***½ D: Carl Theodor Dreyer. Thorkild Roose, Lisbeth Movin, Sigrid Neiiendam, Preben Lerdorff, Anna Svierker. Strikingly composed drama about an old woman accused of being a witch and the curse that she puts on the pastor who is responsible for her burning. Serious, stark cinema, peerlessly photographed by Carl Andersson. Some prints run 95m.▼◗

Days of Glory (2006-French-Moroccan-Belgian-Algerian) C-120m. ***½ D: Rachid Bouchareb. Jamel Debbouze, Samy Nacéri, Roschdy Zem, Sami Bouajila, Bernard Blancan, Mathieu Simonet, Benoit Giros, Mélanie Laurent, Antoine Chappey. Moving (and enlightening) saga of North African soldiers who joined their French brothers in combat during WW2—but were never accepted as equals. Built on a timeworn formula of following raw recruits as they become hardened combat veterans; by focusing on a handful of men and personalizing the story, this forgotten chapter of history comes to vivid life. Screenplay by the director and Olivier Lorelle. Original French title: INDIGÈNES. Hawk-Scope. [R]◗

Days of Heaven (1978) C-95m. ***½ D: Terrence Malick. Richard Gere, Brooke Adams, Sam Shepard, Linda Manz, Robert Wilke, Jackie Shultis, Stuart Margolin. Exquisite mood piece about a turbulent love triangle set against midwestern wheat harvests at the turn of the 20th century. Originally shown in 70mm, its visual beauty almost overwhelms the story—which is second priority here. Nestor Almendros won well-deserved Oscar for his cinematography. [PG]▼◗

Days of Thunder (1990) C-107m. ** D: Tony Scott. Tom Cruise, Robert Duvall, Randy Quaid, Nicole Kidman, Cary Elwes, Michael Rooker, Fred Dalton Thompson, John C. Reilly, Jerry Molen. Flashy, noisy race-car saga set in the South, by the filmmakers and star of TOP GUN. Viewer can a) savor crew chief Duvall's fine performance, b) revel in neurosurgeon/love interest Kidman's disdain for racing, c) sit back and soak up Cruise's charisma, or d) count the clichés (cooked up by coauthors Cruise and Robert Towne). Gives new meaning to the term Formula One. Panavision. [PG-13]▼●】

Days of Wine and Roses (1962) 117m. ***½ D: Blake Edwards. Jack Lemmon, Lee Remick, Charles Bickford, Jack Klugman, Alan Hewitt, Tom Palmer, Jack Albertson. Modern LOST WEEKEND set in San Francisco, with Lemmon marrying Remick and pulling her into state of alcoholism. Realistic direction and uncompromising writing combine for excellent results; poignant score by Henry Mancini, who also earned an Oscar for the title song with Johnny Mercer. Originally a television play, written by JP Miller.▼●】

Day That Shook the World, The (1977) C-111m. ** D: Veljko Bulajic. Christopher Plummer, Florinda Bolkan, Maximilian Schell. Plodding historical drama surrounding the events leading up to WW1 with the death of Archduke Ferdinand (Plummer) at Sarajevo. Yugoslavian-made with a humorless international cast, resulting in tedious though epic-sized chronicle. [R]▼

Day the Earth Caught Fire, The (1961-British) 99m. *** D: Val Guest. Edward Judd, Janet Munro, Leo McKern, Michael Goodliffe, Bernard Braden. Intelligent, absorbing sci-fi drama of gradual chaos that follows when atomic explosions start Earth spiraling toward the sun. Judd is the reporter who first breaks the story, with the assistance of Munro (whom he romances). Watch for Michael Caine as a policeman directing traffic! Dyaliscope.▼】

Day the Earth Stood Still, The (1951) 92m. **** D: Robert Wise. Michael Rennie, Patricia Neal, Hugh Marlowe, Sam Jaffe, Billy Gray, Frances Bavier, Lock Martin. Landmark science-fiction drama about dignified alien (Rennie) who comes to Earth to deliver anti-nuclear warning, stays to learn that his peaceful views are shared by most humans—but not all. Brilliantly acted, more timely than ever, with trenchant script by Edmund North, moody score by Bernard Herrmann. And remember: *Klaatu barada nikto!* Remade in 2008. ▼●】

Day the Earth Stood Still, The (2008) C-103m. ** D: Scott Derrickson. Keanu Reeves, Jennifer Connelly, Kathy Bates, Jaden Smith, Jon Hamm, John Cleese, Kyle Chandler, James Hong. Strange visitor from another planet arrives on Earth in a giant sphere and adopts human form. The government and the military respond with hostility and weapons but super-smart biologist Connelly makes a personal connection with the alien—though her young stepson (Smith) isn't as easily won over. Pallid remake of the 1951 classic turns Klaatu into a cipher and dissipates the impact of the story. Super 35. [PG-13]】

Day the Fish Came Out, The (1967-Greek-

British) C-109m. BOMB D: Michael Cacoyannis. Tom Courtenay, Candice Bergen, Colin Blakely, Sam Wanamaker, Ian Ogilvy. Plot about the loss of two atom bombs over the Aegean Sea provides framework for disastrous comedy about homosexuals; combo of Bergen plus whips, chains, and leather doesn't work.

Day the Hot Line Got Hot, The (1969-French-Spanish) C-92m. *½ D: Etienne Perier. Robert Taylor, Charles Boyer, George Chakiris, Dominique Fabre, Gerard Tichy. Hollow attempt at topicality as secret agents mess up Moscow-Washington hot line, causing international crisis. Taylor's final film. Video title: HOT LINE. [M/PG]▼

Day Time Ended, The (1980) C-79m. ** D: John (Bud) Cardos. Jim Davis, Dorothy Malone, Christopher Mitchum, Marcy Lafferty, Scott Kolden, Natasha Ryan. Sci-fi mishmash about a family living in the desert, who witness strange and terrifying phenomena. Badly scripted, and never really explained. Fine special effects by David Allen. Filmed in 1978 as TIME WARP. Panavision. [PG]▼●】

Dayton's Devils (1968) C-107m. ** D: Jack Shea. Rory Calhoun, Leslie Nielsen, Lainie Kazan, Hans Gudegast (Eric Braeden), Barry Sadler. Another heist film, this time about plot to rob an Air Force base of $2 million; Lainie's rendition of "Sunny" provides only special moment.▼

Daytrippers, The (1996) C-87m. *** D: Greg Mottola. Hope Davis, Stanley Tucci, Parker Posey, Liev Schreiber, Anne Meara, Pat McNamara, Campbell Scott, Marcia Gay Harden. Funny, touching first feature about Eliza, a Long Island wife who discovers what appears to be a clandestine love letter written to her husband; she and her family pile into a station wagon and set off on a road trip to (and through) Manhattan to confront him. Mottola also scripted this thoroughly likable, low-budget winner. [R] ▼】

Day Watch (2006-Russian) C-132m. *½ D: Timur Bekmambetov. Konstantin Khabensky, Mariya Poroshina, Vladimir Menshov, Galina Tyunina, Viktor Verzhbitsky. Weak, confusing, and endless sequel to NIGHT WATCH in which the forces of the "light" and the "dark" are at it again. After being framed, Anton (Khabensky) tries to save himself and his son from evil powers in post-apocalyptic Russia. Hollywood-style production proves that Russians can be just as corny as their American counterparts in turning out mindless supernatural drivel. At least the effects are good. Unrated version runs 146m. Super 35. [R]】

Day Without a Mexican, A (2004-Mexican-U.S.) C-100m. *½ D: Sergio Arau. Caroline Aaron, Tony Abatemarco, Melinda Allen, Fernando Arau, Frankie J. Allison,

Yareli Arizmendi, Maria Beck. Premise has Californians awakening to find there isn't a single Latino left in the state after they all mysteriously disappear. Let the comedy begin! Aiming for satire, the filmmakers miss the mark completely with this insipid, forgettable film, which has only a few amusing moments. Arau (son of Alfonso) and his wife, Arizmendi, originally made this as a short subject. [R] ▼▶

Day Zero (2008) C-93m. ** D: Bryan Gunnar Cole. Elijah Wood, Jon Bernthal, Chris Klein, Ginnifer Goodwin, Elisabeth Moss, Ally Sheedy, Sofia Vassilieva. The war in Iraq has escalated, the military draft has been reinstituted, and three young men—wishy-washy writer Wood, yuppie corporate lawyer Klein, and gung-ho cabdriver Bernthal—must decide how they will respond. Potentially fascinating subject matter is undermined by a simplistic, meandering storyline and disparate characters whose friendship lacks credibility. [R]▶

Dazed and Confused (1993) C-102m. *** D: Richard Linklater. Jason London, Wiley Wiggins, Sasha Jenson, Rory Cochrane, Milla Jovovich, Marissa Ribisi, Adam Goldberg, Anthony Rapp, Matthew McConaughey, Ben Affleck, Parker Posey, Joey Lauren Adams. Diverting, refreshingly unsentimental mid-1970s time capsule from director-screenwriter Linklater (SLACKER), following a varied group of suburban Texas teens on the last day of school in 1976. Characterization outweighs narrative here: Linklater accurately captures teen lifestyles and attitudes at a specific moment in time. Great soundtrack includes carefully selected period music. Look fast for Renée Zellweger. [R]▼●

D.C. Cab (1983) C-99m. **½ D: Joel Schumacher. Adam Baldwin, Charlie Barnett, Irene Cara, Anne DeSalvo, Max Gail, Gloria Gifford, DeWayne Jessie, Bill Maher, Whitman Mayo, Mr. T, Paul Rodriguez, Gary Busey, Marsha Warfield. Consistently likable, if loosely wound, comedy about a Washington taxi company staffed by misfits who get their act together when it really counts. [R]▼●

D-Day the Sixth of June (1956) C-106m. *** D: Henry Koster. Robert Taylor, Richard Todd, Dana Wynter, Edmond O'Brien. Well-executed study of WW2's Normandy invasion, with massive action shots; film focuses on American officer Taylor and British leader Todd, their professional and personal problems. You may like THE LONGEST DAY better. CinemaScope. ▼●

Dead, The (1987) C-83m. *** D: John Huston. Anjelica Huston, Donal McCann, Rachael Dowling, Cathleen Delany, Helena Carroll, Ingrid Craigie, Dan O'Herlihy, Frank Patterson, Donal Donnelly, Marie Kean, Maria McDernottroe, Sean McClory, Colm Meaney. All-Irish cast helps Huston bring James Joyce's short story (from *Dubliners*) to life, a vignette about a lively holiday dinner party in 1904, followed by a melancholy confrontation between a loveless husband and wife. Not for every taste, this finely embroidered film celebrates time, place, and atmosphere, without much discernible plot, but with a host of marvelous characterizations. Huston's last film as director scripted by his son Tony. [PG]▼●

Dead Again (1991) C-107m. **½ D: Kenneth Branagh. Kenneth Branagh, Andy Garcia, Derek Jacobi, Hanna Schygulla, Emma Thompson, Wayne Knight, Campbell Scott, Gregor Hesse, Christine Ebersole, Robin Williams. Unusually constructed film noir thriller about an L.A. gumshoe who tries to help a woman with amnesia, and finds they are both connected—in a strange twist of reincarnation—to a notorious 40-year-old murder. Intriguing, but ultimately the story is too dense, and too artificial, to really work. And talk about artificial—dig that aging makeup for Garcia! Williams appears as one of Branagh's sources. [R]▼●

Dead Alive (1992-New Zealand) C-97m. *** D: Peter Jackson. Timothy Balme, Diana Penalver, Liz Moody, Ian Watkin, Brenda Kendall. Pity poor Balme; not only is he in the thrall of his domineering mother, but when the bite of a rat monkey from Skull Island turns her into a hungry zombie, he still has to look after her—and all the other zombies that soon proliferate. Astonishing, vigorous, inventively gruesome comedy is—one hopes—the pinnacle of its kind. Warning: The rating above is *strictly* for those with a tolerance for extreme violence and gore. Original title: BRAIN DEAD. R-rated video version runs 85m. ▼●

Dead and Buried (1981) C-92m. **½ D: Gary A. Sherman. James Farentino, Melody Anderson, Jack Albertson, Dennis Redfield, Nancy Locke Hauser, Lisa Blount. Bizarre murders in a small New England town seem even stranger when the corpses come back to life. Gory but well-made chiller; from a Dan O'Bannon story. [R]▼▶

Dead Bang (1989) C-103m. *½ D: John Frankenheimer. Don Johnson, Penelope Ann Miller, William Forsythe, Bob Balaban, Tim Reid, Frank Military, Tate Donovan, Michael Higgins, Evans Evans. L.A. detective Johnson tries to forget about his dismal home life by chasing nasty white supremacists around the West. Unpleasant, fact-based action film offers nothing you haven't seen before, except for the hero vomiting on a suspect. [R]▼●

Dead Calm (1989-Australian) C-96m. *** D: Phillip Noyce. Sam Neill, Nicole Kidman, Billy Zane. A married couple, recovering from a family tragedy by spending some time on their yacht at sea, pick up a stranger who proceeds to terrorize them. Full-blooded thriller is so skillfully acted and directed that it enables you to gloss over its flaws—and forgive its slasher-movie–inspired finale. Based on a novel by Charles Williams. Panavision. [R]▼●◖

Dead Cert (1974-British) **C-92m.** ** D: Tony Richardson. Scott Antony, Judi Dench, Michael Williams, Nina Thomas, Julian Glover, Mark Digham, Ian Hogg. A horse is drugged before a race, and its owner-rider is killed. There's a massive cover-up, and jockey Antony investigates. Richardson coscripted this muddled mystery, based on a Dick Francis novel, with Dench wasted as the deceased's widow. That's Dench's real-life husband, Michael Williams, as Sandy.◖

Dead End (1937) **93m.** ***½ D: William Wyler. Sylvia Sidney, Joel McCrea, Humphrey Bogart, Wendy Barrie, Claire Trevor, Marjorie Main, Huntz Hall, Leo Gorcey, Gabriel Dell, Ward Bond, Billy Halop, Bernard Punsley, Allen Jenkins. Grim Sidney Kingsley play of slum life shows vignettes of humanity at breaking point in N.Y.C. tenements; extremely well directed, engrossing. Script by Lillian Hellman; magnificent sets by Richard Day. Introduced the Dead End Kids, who appeared in the original Broadway production.▼●◖

Deadfall (1968-British) **C-120m.** ** D: Bryan Forbes. Michael Caine, Giovanna Ralli, Eric Portman, Nanette Newman, David Buck. Jewel thief falls in love with beautiful woman who is married to her homosexual father. And you think you have problems? Overdirected film is not as interesting as it sounds. [R]◖

Deadfall (1993) **C-98m.** BOMB D: Christopher Coppola. Michael Biehn, Sarah Trigger, Nicolas Cage, James Coburn, Peter Fonda, Charlie Sheen, Talia Shire, Michael Constantine, Gigi Rice, Angus Scrimm, Micky Dolenz, Marc Coppola, Renee Estevez, Clarence Williams III. Bargain-basement, cliché-ridden vanity project about con man Biehn, who's always been a team with his dad; his world begins to unravel after he accidentally kills the old man. Almost unbearable at times, with an unrestrained Cage chewing and throwing up the scenery as a coke-snorting thug. Coppola is the nephew of Francis (and Cage's brother); he also coscripted. [R]▼●◖

Dead Girl, The (2006) **C-85m.** *** D: Karen Moncrieff. Toni Collette, Piper Laurie, Rose Byrne, Mary Beth Hurt, Marcia Gay Harden, Brittany Murphy, Kerry Washington, Giovanni Ribisi, James Franco, Mary Steenburgen, Bruce Davison, Nick Searcy, Josh Brolin. Five episodes about women dealing with crises in their lives, tied together by a dead girl (Murphy), whose body is discovered in the desert. Intriguing if downbeat vignettes are linked by an overall rumination about violence toward women

in our society. Writer-director Moncrieff offers her actors a superior showcase, and they're all terrific. [R]◖

Deadhead Miles (1972) **C-93m.** **½ D: Vernon Zimmerman. Alan Arkin, Paul Benedict, Hector Elizondo, Oliver Clark, Charles Durning, Larry Wolf, Barnard Hughes, Loretta Swit, Allen Garfield, Bruce Bennett, John Milius, Ida Lupino, George Raft. Plotless allegory about a trucker's experiences on the road, with unusual cast, loads of in-jokes. Unreleased and unseen for many years. A real curio, written by Zimmerman and Terrence Malick. [R]

Dead Heat (1988) **C-86m.** BOMB D: Mark Goldblatt. Treat Williams, Joe Piscopo, Lindsay Frost, Darren McGavin, Vincent Price, Keye Luke. Moronic, occasionally disgusting turkey with cops Williams and Piscopo confronted by criminals miraculously returning from the dead. [R]▼●◖

Dead Heat on a Merry-Go-Round (1966) **C-104m.** *** D: Bernard Girard. James Coburn, Camilla Sparv, Aldo Ray, Rose Marie, Severn Darden, Robert Webber. Involved but entertaining crime drama about an intricate plan to rob an airport bank, with a surprise ending. Look quickly for a barely recognizable Harrison Ford, in his film debut, playing a bellhop.◖

Dead Kids SEE: **Strange Behavior**

Deadlier Than the Male (1967-British) **C-101m.** **½ D: Ralph Thomas. Richard Johnson, Elke Sommer, Sylva Koscina, Nigel Green, Suzanna Leigh. Standard fare which half-heartedly resurrects Bulldog Drummond, trying to solve whodunit centering around two shapely suspects. Sequel: SOME GIRLS DO. Techniscope. ▼◖

Deadline (1987-German) **C-100m.** *½ D: Nathaniel Gutman. Christopher Walken, Hywel Bennett, Marita Marschall, Arnon Zadok, Amos Lavie. Convoluted political thriller with globe-trotting journalist Walken becoming enmeshed in various intrigues and lies in Lebanon. Strictly Grade-D stuff. [R]▼●◖

Deadline U.S.A. (1952) **87m.** *** D: Richard Brooks. Humphrey Bogart, Ethel Barrymore, Kim Hunter, Ed Begley, Warren Stevens, Paul Stewart, Martin Gabel, Joe De Santis, Audrey Christie, Jim Backus. Biting account of newspaper's struggle to survive and maintain civic duty. Bogey is tops as the crusading editor; taut, knowing script by director Brooks. Most enjoyable. Don't blink or you'll miss a young James Dean in a silent bit part during a newspaper production montage.

Deadly Affair, The (1967) **C-107m.** *** D: Sidney Lumet. James Mason, Simone Signoret, Maximilian Schell, Harriet Andersson, Harry Andrews, Lynn Redgrave, Kenneth Haigh, Roy Kinnear. Top-notch suspense tale with British agent Mason trying to unravel complicated mystery behind an agency official's suicide. Filmed in England and based on John le Carré's novel *Call for the Dead.*▶

Deadly Bees, The (1967-British) **C-85m.** ** D: Freddie Francis. Suzanna Leigh, Guy Doleman, Catherine Finn, Katy Wild, Frank Finlay. High-powered shock scenes involving swarming bees are only worthwhile attraction in dull horror film cowritten by Robert Bloch.▶

Deadly Blessing (1981) **C-102m.** ** D: Wes Craven. Maren Jensen, Susan Buckner, Sharon Stone, Lois Nettleton, Ernest Borgnine, Jeff East, Lisa Hartman. Following her husband's murder, widow and two friends are terrorized, apparently by nearby repressive sect, headed by the father (Borgnine) of the dead man. Rural horror thriller has some good shocks but becomes confused and ultimately silly, especially the ending. [R]▼

Deadly Companion SEE: **Double Negative**

Deadly Companions, The (1961) **C-90m.** **½ D: Sam Peckinpah. Maureen O'Hara, Brian Keith, Steve Cochran, Chill Wills. Ex-army officer accidentally kills O'Hara's son and he makes amends by escorting the funeral procession through Indian country. Peckinpah's first feature is decent if unspectacular Western. Panavision.▼●

Deadly Eyes (1982) **C-93m.** ** D: Robert Clouse. Sam Groom, Sara Botsford, Scatman Crothers, Lisa Langlois, Cec Linder. Overgrown rats on the warpath, with science teacher Groom and health official Botsford to the rescue. You've seen it all before. Originally titled, appropriately enough, THE RATS. [R]▼

Deadly Friend (1986) **C-92m.** **½ D: Wes Craven. Matthew Laborteaux, Kristy Swanson, Anne Twomey, Michael Sharrett, Richard Marcus, Anne Ramsey. Inventive teenager, in love with the girl next door, revives her (à la Frankenstein) after she's killed. More heart, and more actual entertainment, than you'd expect from a Wes Craven horror film . . . though it's probably the only movie ever made in which someone is beheaded by a basketball! [R]▼●

Deadly Games (1982) **C-95m.** **½ D: Scott Mansfield. Sam Groom, Jo Ann Harris, Steve Railsback, Dick Butkus, Alexandra Morgan, Colleen Camp, Christine Tudor, June Lockhart, Denise Galik. Groom is a cop, Harris a reporter in routine mystery about a slasher on the loose. In-jokes come fast and furious in this very knowing film, keyed to a horror board game played by the principals. Final plot explanation is really stupid. [R]▼

Deadly Hero (1976) **C-102m.** ** D: Ivan Nagy. Don Murray, Diahn Williams, James Earl Jones, Lilia Skala, George S. Irving, Conchata Ferrell, Charles Siebert, Dick A. Williams, Treat Williams, Joshua Mostel. Interesting premise: righteous cop (Mur-

ray) saves woman's life by killing her attacker (Jones) . . . but then woman begins to question the cop's motives. Performances outshine violent presentation. Treat Williams' film debut. Danny DeVito is also listed in the closing credits. [R]▼

Deadly Illusion (1987) **C-87m.** **½ D: William Tannen, Larry Cohen. Billy Dee Williams, Vanity, Morgan Fairchild, John Beck, Joseph Cortese, Dennis Hallahan, Joe Spinell. Fair programmer with Williams well cast as a detective framed in murder plot. Some humorous touches add to the proceedings. Cohen wrote the script; aka LOVE YOU TO DEATH. [R]▼●

Deadly Impact (1985-Italian) **C-91m.** *½ D: Larry Ludman (Fabrizio De Angelis). Bo Svenson, Fred Williamson, Marcia Clingan, John Morghen, Vincent Conte. Svenson and Williamson try to enliven unbelievable crime caper in which a computer is used to tap into Las Vegas casinos and predict when slot machines will pay off. Filmed in the U.S.A. in 1983.▼

Deadly Is the Female SEE: **Gun Crazy** (1949)

Deadly Strangers (1974-British) **C-93m.** *** D: Sidney Hayers. Hayley Mills, Simon Ward, Sterling Hayden, Ken Hutchison, Peter Jeffrey. Lurid, exciting thriller about Mills offering a ride to young man, unaware that a violent patient has escaped from a nearby mental hospital.▼

Deadly Thief SEE: **Shalimar**

Deadly Three, The SEE: **Enter the Dragon**

Deadly Trackers, The (1973) **C-110m.** BOMB D: Barry Shear. Richard Harris, Rod Taylor, Al Lettieri, Neville Brand, William Smith, Isela Vega. Dreadful, violent Western; Harris, an Irish sheriff of a small Texas town, trails bank robber Taylor and gang to Mexico to avenge the deaths of wife and son. Sam Fuller wrote story and was original director. [PG]▼●

Deadly Trap, The (1971-French-Italian) **C-96m.** BOMB D: René Clement. Faye Dunaway, Frank Langella, Barbara Parkins, Karen Blanguernon, Maurice Ronet. A deadly bore, about an industrious espionage organization that goes after one-time member Langella by harassing his emotionally fragile wife (Dunaway). Retitled DEATH SCREAM. [PG]▼

Deadly Treasure of the Piranha SEE: **Killer Fish**

Dead Man (1995-U.S.-German-Japanese) **120m.** *** D: Jim Jarmusch. Johnny Depp, Gary Farmer, Lance Henriksen, Michael Wincott, Mili Avital, Iggy Pop, Jared Harris, Billy Bob Thornton, Crispin Glover, Eugene Byrd, Gabriel Byrne, John Hurt, Alfred Molina, Robert Mitchum. In 1875, Cleveland accountant Depp heads west for a new job but ends up being pursued as a murderer by bounty hunters. Indian Farmer, who helps him, is convinced that he is the poet William Blake returned to life. One-of-a-kind Western, written by the director, is measured in its pace, full of unusual cameos, and occasionally quite funny though it's not a comedy. Steve Buscemi appears unbilled. [R]▼○》

Dead Man on Campus (1998) **C-94m.** BOMB D: Alan Cohn. Tom Everett Scott, Mark-Paul Gosselaar, Poppy Montgomery, Lochlyn Munro, Randy Pearlstein, Alyson Hannigan. Dead is right. This black comedy hinges on the urban myth that American universities will award 4.0 GPA's to any student whose roommate kills himself. Clean-cut straight arrow and his spoiled preppie pal team up to find a suicidal candidate. Laughless script aspires to be a teen ripoff of THE FORTUNE COOKIE, but these cocky kids are no Lemmon and Matthau. [R]▼○》

Dead Man Walking (1995) **C-122m.** ***½ D: Tim Robbins. Susan Sarandon, Sean Penn, Robert Prosky, Raymond J. Barry, R. Lee Ermey, Celia Weston, Lois Smith, Scott Wilson, Roberta Maxwell, Margo Martindale, Barton Heyman, Larry Pine, Peter Sarsgaard, Jack Black. Powerful drama based on the true story of a nun in Louisiana who becomes the spiritual advisor to a death row inmate, convicted of the murder of two young adults and awaiting execution. As she tries to redeem his soul, she must also reconcile his needs with the heinousness of the crime and the grief of the murdered children's parents. Strong performances by Sarandon (who won a Best Actress Oscar) and Penn anchor this sobering story which, despite the humanizing of its central character, is not a simple pro– or anti–death penalty treatise. [R]▼○》

Dead Men Don't Die (1991) **C-94m.** *½ D: Malcolm Marmorstein. Elliott Gould, Melissa (Sue) Anderson, Mark Moses, Mabel King, Jack Betts, Philip Bruns. Ten-cent rip-off of GHOST, with egotistical news anchor Gould murdered, then rising from the dead, with the assistance of medium/cleaning lady King (aping Whoopi Goldberg). A too-obvious parody of how TV news has become show biz. [PG-13]▼》

Dead Men Don't Wear Plaid (1982) **89m.** ** D: Carl Reiner. Steve Martin, Rachel Ward, Reni Santoni, Carl Reiner, George Gaynes, Frank McCarthy. A one-joke movie, based on 1940s film noir melodramas, has detective Martin interacting with clips from various vintage films, and a very live client (Ward). Fun at first, but with no story and cardboard characters, it wears thin fast; film buffs will enjoy it more than the average viewer. Dedicated to famed costume designer Edith Head, whose final film this was. [PG]▼》

Dead of Night (1945-British) **103m.** **** D: Cavalcanti, Basil Dearden, Robert Hamer, Charles Crichton. Mervyn Johns, Roland Culver, Antony Baird, Judy Kelly, Miles Malleson, Sally Ann Howes, Googie Withers, Ralph Michael, Michael Redgrave, Basil Radford, Naunton Wayne, Frederick Valk. Classic chiller of gathering at a country house, where guests trade supernatural stories. One of them (Johns) has been having a nightmare that now seems to be coming true; final sequence with Redgrave as a schizophrenic ventriloquist is a knockout. ▼○》

Dead of Night (1972) SEE: **Deathdream**

Dead of Winter (1987) **C-100m.** *** D: Arthur Penn. Mary Steenburgen, Roddy McDowall, Jan Rubes, William Russ, Ken Pogue, Wayne Robson. Down-on-her-luck actress is hired for a movie role by an eccentric man who lives in an eerie old mansion; eventually she realizes that she's being held prisoner. Somewhat predictable but extremely well-crafted thriller with crackerjack performances all around. Based, fairly transparently, on the 1940s B movie MY NAME IS JULIA ROSS: a key character name here is Julie Rose. [R]▼○》

Dead Pigeon on Beethoven Street (1972-German) **C-102m.** **½ D: Samuel Fuller. Glenn Corbett, Christa Lang, Stephane Audran, Anton Diffring, Alex D'Arcy. Fast-paced, tongue-in-cheek Fuller thriller (financed by German TV) has Corbett on a detective mission, aided by lovely Lang (Mrs. Fuller in real life). [PG]▼

Dead Poets Society (1989) **C-128m.** *** D: Peter Weir. Robin Williams, Robert Sean Leonard, Ethan Hawke, Josh Charles, Gale Hansen, Dylan Kussman, Allelon Ruggiero, James Waterston, Norman Lloyd, Kurtwood Smith, Lara Flynn Boyle. Williams is a charismatic English teacher at a staid New England prep school in 1959, whose infectious love of poetry—and insistence that each boy "seize the day" and make the most of life—inspires his impressionable students, not always in the right direction. Well made, extremely well acted, but also dramatically obvious and melodramatically one-sided. Nevertheless, Tom Schulman's screenplay won an Oscar. 13m. added for network showings. [PG] ▼○》

Dead Pool, The (1988) **C-91m.** **½ D: Buddy Van Horn. Clint Eastwood, Patricia Clarkson, Evan C. Kim, Liam Neeson, David Hunt, Michael Currie, James Carrey. Fifth (and final) DIRTY HARRY movie finds Callahan investigating a bizarre death-threat list, while becoming involved with a female TV reporter. The story's pretty straightforward—check out Carrey as a druggy rock star—the killing almost cartoonish, and the film surprisingly watchable (if not inspired). Eastwood's charisma makes all the difference. [R]▼○》

Dead Presidents (1995) **C-119m.** *** D:

The Hughes Brothers. Larenz Tate, Keith David, Chris Tucker, N'Bushe Wright, Freddy Rodriguez, Rose Jackson, Michael Imperioli, David Barry Gray, Jaimz Woolvett, Jenifer Lewis, James Pickens, Jr., Clifton Powell, Terrence Dashon Howard, Bokeem Woodbine. Absorbing and ambitious chronicle of a young black man's odyssey from the late 1960s Bronx, through a tour of duty in Vietnam, then back . . . to a dead-end existence. Tries to cover a broad landscape (with a passing nod to the Black Revolution movement), then winds up as a crime caper. Imperfect, but still a compelling tale of how the brutality of war spilled over onto America's urban streets. Warning: the violence is jarringly (and purposely) graphic. Scripted by Michael Henry Brown from Allen and Albert Hughes' story. Seymour Cassel and Martin Sheen appear unbilled. Super 35. [R]▼●]

Dead Reckoning (1947) **100m.** *** D: John Cromwell. Humphrey Bogart, Lizabeth Scott, Morris Carnovsky, William Prince, Wallace Ford. Bogart's fine as tough WW2 veteran solving soldier-buddy's murder. Well-acted drama.▼●]

Dead Right SEE: **If He Hollers, Let Him Go**

Dead Ringer (1964) **115m.** **½ D. Paul Henreid. Bette Davis, Karl Malden, Peter Lawford, Jean Hagen, George Macready, Estelle Winwood. A double dose of Davis, playing twin sisters (as she did earlier in A STOLEN LIFE) bearing a long-time grudge over a man, the sinister one trying to get even. Farfetched but fun; Bette's vehicle all the way, directed by her 1940s co-star Paul Henreid. Remade for TV as THE KILLER IN THE MIRROR (1986, with Ann Jillian).▼●]

Dead Ringers (1988-Canadian) **C-115m.** **½ D: David Cronenberg. Jeremy Irons, Genevieve Bujold, Heidi Von Palleske, Barbara Gordon, Shirley Douglas, Stephen Lack. Fascinating but extremely unpleasant story of twin gynecologists who share each other's lives—and lovers. Notable for a pair of superb performances by Irons, and the attendant trickery that makes us forget, at times, that we're watching one man play both roles. Based (believe it or not) on a true story! [R]▼●]

Dead Silence (1989) **C-98m.** **½ D: Harrison Ellenshaw. Clete Keith, Joseph Scott, Craig Fleming, Doris Anne Soyka, James Austin, Leslie Charles, Bruce R. Barrett. Young screenwriter and would-be director finds a backer for his newest movie—a mafioso type. But after taking his money, he learns that this road-company Godfather expects his stumblebum son to get the starring part in the picture! Amiable comedy about the perils of low-budget moviemaking, with a wonderful final twist. Written by Keith, who plays the filmmaker. Directing

debut for special effects whiz Ellenshaw. [R]▼

Dead Silence (2007) **C-90m.** ** D: James Wan. Ryan Kwanten, Amber Valletta, Donnie Wahlberg, Michael Fairman, Joan Heney, Bob Gunton, Laura Regan, Dmitry Chepovetsky, Judith Roberts. The creators of SAW fashioned this ho-hum horror chiller in which a young husband (Kwanten) sets out to decipher the reason for a brutal killing that occurs after he and his wife receive a mysterious package containing a ventriloquist's dummy. While not as gratuitously gory as many contemporary horror films, it's annoyingly illogical and overly familiar. Unrated version runs 91m. Super 35. [R]]

Dead Snow (2009-Norwegian) **C-91m.** **½ D: Tommy Wirkola. Vegar Hoel, Stig Frode Henriksen, Charlotte Frogner, Lasse Valdal, Evy Kasseth Røsten, Jeppe Laursen, Jenny Skavlan, Ane Dahl Torp, Ørjan Gamst. A group of 20-somethings head out into the snowy Norwegian wilderness for a weekend of whatever comes up. Unfortunately, what comes up is a legion of Nazi zombies, intent on devouring any live person they encounter. Handsomely made, mostly on dramatic daytime exteriors, with an intelligent script and well-drawn characters. But the familiarity of the setup (which even the characters mention) drains the film of most interest except for horror buffs, who'll gladly embrace it.]

Dead Tired SEE: **Grosse Fatigue**

Dead Zone, The (1983) **C-103m.** *** D: David Cronenberg. Christopher Walken, Brooke Adams, Tom Skerritt, Herbert Lom, Anthony Zerbe, Colleen Dewhurst, Martin Sheen, Nicholas Campbell, Jackie Burroughs. Absorbing Stephen King story of young man who emerges from near-fatal accident with the gift (or curse) of second sight—being able to tell a person's fate just by making physical contact. Walken's moving, heartfelt performance is the core of involving, if sometimes meandering movie where (despite reputations of King and Cronenberg) the emphasis is not on blood-and-guts horror. Later a TV series. [R]▼●]

Deaf Smith & Johnny Ears (1973-Italian) **C-91m.** *** D: Paolo Cavara. Anthony Quinn, Franco Nero, Pamela Tiffin, Ira Furstenberg. Well-made "buddy Western" teams deaf-mute Quinn with upstart Nero as two common-man bystanders during a time of social upheaval in Texas. Beautifully photographed by Tonino Delli Colli. Originally titled LOS AMIGOS. [PG]

Deal, The (2005-U.S.-Canadian) **C-107m.** **½ D: Harvey Kahn. Christian Slater, Selma Blair, Robert Loggia, Colm Feore, Angie Harmon, John Heard, Kevin Tighe, Françoise Yip. Low-budget suspense thriller had the misfortune to be released in the same year as the similar but far superior SYRIANA. Slater is an associate with a prestigious Wall Street investment firm who is brought in on a deal to complete a questionable merger between a giant American oil group and a Russian company that controls massive amounts of crude. Set during a nondescript future where gas is selling for $6 a gallon, the film is a bit too complicated, although its concerns couldn't be more relevant. Worth a look. [R] ▼◗

Deal (2008) **C-86m.** *½ D: Gil Cates, Jr. Burt Reynolds, Bret Harrison, Shannon Elizabeth, Charles Durning, Jennifer Tilly, Maria Mason, Gary Grubbs, Caroline McKinley, Michael Sexton, Vincent Van Patten. Former poker champ returns to the game 20 years after his last tournament to train a hotshot college kid, only to find himself lured back to the tables to compete against his protegé. Dull, derivative rehash of every gambling-movie cliché in the book—and THE COLOR OF MONEY in particular. Reynolds sleepwalks through his role. Several real-life poker champs play themselves. [PG-13]◗

Deal, The (2008-U.S.-Canadian) **C-100m.** *** D: Steven Schachter. William H. Macy, Meg Ryan, LL Cool J, Elliott Gould, Jason Ritter, Fiona Glascott, Sharon Reginiano, John Carson, David Hunt, Jeremy Crutchley. Suicidal Hollywood producer Macy takes his nephew's unfilmable script about Benjamin Disraeli and uses his considerable wiles to bamboozle a studio into funding its production—with an action star (LL Cool J) in the lead. Only studio exec Ryan seems aware of his chicanery, but watching the unflappable hustler stay one step ahead of seeing his scheme collapse is great fun. Macy and Schachter adapted Peter Lefcourt's knowing novel about the byzantine workings of the movie business. Released direct to DVD. [R]◗

Dealing: or The Berkeley-to-Boston Forty-Brick Lost-Bag Blues (1972) **C-99m.** **½ D: Paul Williams. Robert F. Lyons, Barbara Hershey, John Lithgow, Charles Durning, Joy Bang. Dated but still watchable adaptation of Robert and Michael Crichton's lighthearted novel about Harvard law student who runs pot on the side. Lyons is pretty blah, but compensation is provided by Hershey as his free-thinking girlfriend and Lithgow (in film debut) as the head dope. Panavision. [R]◗

Deal of the Century (1983) **C-99m.** ** D: William Friedkin. Chevy Chase, Sigourney Weaver, Gregory Hines, Vince Edwards, Richard Libertini, William Marquez, Eduardo Ricard, Wallace Shawn. Attempted satire of international weapons merchants. Its leading characters are so cold-blooded and unappealing, and its script (by Paul Brickman) so disjointed, that the results are a mishmash. [PG] ▼◗

Dean Koontz's Phantoms SEE: **Phantoms**
Dear Brigitte (1965) **C-100m.** **½ D: Henry Koster. James Stewart, Fabian, Glynis Johns, Cindy Carol, Billy Mumy, John Williams,

Jack Kruschen, Alice Pearce, Jesse White, Ed Wynn. Guest: Brigitte Bardot. Good cast in OK family farce about an 8-year-old genius (Stewart's son, Mumy) with a crush on Brigitte Bardot (who makes a brief appearance near the end). Tries to be whimsical but is contrived instead. Look fast for James Brolin as student spokesman. CinemaScope. ▼

Dear Detective (1977-French) **C-105m.** **½ D: Philippe De Broca. Annie Girardot, Philippe Noiret, Catherine Alric, Hubert Deschamps, Paulette Dubost. Girardot is fine as woman cop who becomes involved with old flame (pompous professor Noiret) as she hunts a killer. Sometimes funny, more often predictable and pointless. Remade in 1979 as a TV movie. Retitled DEAR INSPECTOR. Sequel: JUPITER'S THIGH. [PG]▼

Dear Frankie (2005-British-Scottish) **C-105m.** *** D: Shona Auerbach. Emily Mortimer, Jack McElhone, Gerard Butler, Sharon Small, Mary Riggans, Jayd Johnson. Sweet film set in Glasgow about a woman who lives with her mother and her deaf 9-year-old son. Constantly on the move, to avoid contact with her abusive ex-husband, she has invented a romantic father figure for her boy, telling him that his dad is away at sea; then she's forced to find someone to fill that role, just for one day. Warm, never mawkish, with fine performances all around. [PG-13]◗

Dear God (1996) **C-112m.** ** D: Garry Marshall. Greg Kinnear, Laurie Metcalf, Maria Pitillo, Tim Conway, Hector Elizondo, Jon Seda, Roscoe Lee Browne, Anna Maria Horsford, Nancy Marchand, Larry Miller, Rue McClanahan, Jack Sheldon, Coolio, Seth Mumy, Jack Klugman, Ellen Cleghorne. Con man Kinnear gets one last chance to go straight, with a job at the post office. There, in the dead-letter department, he and his motley colleagues make "miracles" happen for needy people who write to God. Whimsical comedy gets off to a good start but loses the one thing it needs most: conviction. Director Marshall has a cameo, along with various celebs (including stars of long-ago Marshall-produced TV series). [PG] ▼◗

Dear Heart (1964) **114m.** *** D: Delbert Mann. Glenn Ford, Geraldine Page, Michael Anderson, Jr., Barbara Nichols, Angela Lansbury, Patricia Barry, Charles Drake, Alice Pearce, Mary Wickes. Winning romance with gentlemanly traveling salesman Ford coming to N.Y.C., meeting up with sweetly wacky postmistress Page, who's in town for a convention. Excellent characterizations, with fine comic supporting players. ▼

Dear Inspector SEE: **Dear Detective**
Dear John (2010) **C-105m.** ** D: Lasse Hallström. Channing Tatum, Amanda Seyfried, Richard Jenkins, Henry Thomas, Scott Porter, David Andrews, D. J. Cotrona, Cullen Moss, Keith Robinson. A chance

meeting on a Charleston, South Carolina, beach leads to a pledge of love between student Seyfried and soldier Tatum. When he returns to active duty overseas they promise to write to one another, and do . . . but the long separation puts tremendous strain on their relationship. Innocuous love story, from Nicholas Sparks' novel, becomes dreary after a while and drags to an unsatisfying conclusion. Super 35. [PG-13] 🌓

Dear Mr. Wonderful (1982-German) C-115m. *** D: Peter Lilienthal. Joe Pesci, Karen Ludwig, Evan Handler, Ivy Ray Browning, Frank Vincent, Paul Herman, Tony Martin. Ruby Dennis (Pesci) owns a bowling alley-nightclub in Jersey City, thinks he's on the verge of crashing Las Vegas. The American Jewish working class experience, viewed with a European sensibility, doesn't ring true; still, a thoughtful portrait of a little man who must learn to take what life has to offer. The sequence with Martin is particularly memorable. Video title: RUBY'S DREAM. ▼🌓

Dear Wendy (2005-Danish-French-German-British) C-105m. **½ D: Thomas Vinterberg. Jamie Bell, Bill Pullman, Michael Angarano, Danso Gordon, Novella Nelson, Chris Owen, Alison Pill, Mark Webber. Thought-provoking allegory about America's fascination with firearms, centering on a band of alienated small-town teens who, despite their pacifistic nature, become obsessed with shooting guns. Provocative, albeit pretentious, film leads to an unsurprising finale. Audiences who are offended by foreign filmmakers who censure the U.S. may find this infuriating. Scripted (not surprisingly) by Lars von Trier. 🌓

Dear Zachary: A Letter to a Son About His Father (2008) C-95m. ***½ D: Kurt Kuenne. Riveting, emotionally charged documentary started out as a visual essay about Dr. Andrew Bagby, the filmmaker's oldest and best friend, who was murdered before the birth of his son. The fact that Zachary's mother became the prime suspect in the case is one of several twists in this chronicle of good and evil that illustrates how real life often is stranger than fiction. Kuenne also composed the film's score. 🌓

Death and the Maiden (1994) C-103m. *** D: Roman Polanski. Sigourney Weaver, Ben Kingsley, Stuart Wilson. Generally fluid filmization of Ariel Dorfman's three-character (and mostly one-room) play about an edgy onetime victim of torture and sexual abuse who gets a chance to exact at-home revenge. Though Weaver's occasionally over-the-top performance contributes to a wobbly midsection, Polanski is pretty much up to the tough claustrophobic challenge. Kingsley is exceptional as a physician who gets the surprise of his life when he drops in to a secluded beach house (presumably in Chile) for a nightcap. [R] ▼🌓

Death at a Funeral (2007-U.S.-British-German-Netherlands) C-91m. *** D: Frank Oz. Matthew Macfadyen, Keeley Hawes, Andy Nyman, Ewen Bremner, Daisy Donovan, Alan Tudyk, Jane Asher, Kris Marshall, Rupert Graves, Peter Egan, Peter Dinklage. Amiable comedy chronicling the mounting mishaps that occur as family and friends gather to attend the funeral of a British man at his country estate, including the arrival of the wrong corpse, the accidental ingestion of a hallucinogenic drug, and a mysterious mourner who threatens to unveil a shocking secret. Expert cast gets the most out of this material, which gathers momentum as it goes along in the fashion of a classic farce. Remade in 2010. [R] 🌓

Death at a Funeral (2010) C-92m. ** D: Neil LaBute. Chris Rock, Martin Lawrence, Tracy Morgan, Danny Glover, Zoë Saldana, James Marsden, Keith David, Loretta Devine, Ron Glass, Peter Dinklage, Luke Wilson, Regina Hall, Columbus Short. The 2007 British farce gets an instant replay in this African-Americanized version: A gathering for the funeral of a family patriarch goes very wrong when long-held secrets, bribes, sibling rivalries, hallucinogenic drugs, and a naked man on the roof all turn a somber event into a disaster. Virtually a shot-by-shot remake of the amusing original—with Dinklage reprising his role—this misguided reboot manages to make Rock and Lawrence straight men for the zany antics of supporting players Marsden and Morgan. This sort of thing seems to work better with British accents. Super 35. [R] 🌓

Death Becomes Her (1992) C-104m. ** D: Robert Zemeckis. Meryl Streep, Bruce Willis, Goldie Hawn, Isabella Rossellini, Ian Ogilvy, Adam Storke, Nancy Fish, Alaina Reed Hall, Michelle Johnson, Mimi Kennedy, Jonathan Silverman, Fabio. Black comedy about a glamorous, self-absorbed star (Streep) who's obsessed with staying young, and a woman scorned (Hawn) who vows revenge against her—at any price. Effects-laden comedy of absurd extremes is told with too heavy a hand, though Streep is a hoot as the egomaniacal actress. Film director Sydney Pollack is also funny in an unbilled bit as a Beverly Hills doctor. Won Visual Effects Oscar. [PG-13] ▼🌓

Deathbed SEE: **Terminal Choice**

Death Before Dishonor (1987) C-95m. ** D: Terry J. Leonard. Fred Dryer, Brian Keith, Paul Winfield, Joanna Pacula, Kasey Walker, Rockne Tarkington. Clichéd, by-the-numbers story of Marine gunnery sergeant Dryer (who keeps a picture of John Wayne from SANDS OF IWO JIMA on his wall), who singlehandedly battles Middle Eastern terrorists after they stage a massacre—and kidnap his superior (Keith). Lotsa stunts, little sense. [R] ▼🌓

Death Bite SEE: **Spasms**

Death Corps SEE: **Shock Waves**

Death Defying Acts (2008-U.S.-British-Australian) **C-97m. **** D: Gillian Armstrong. Guy Pearce, Catherine Zeta-Jones, Timothy Spall, Saoirse Ronan, Malcolm Shields, Leni Harper, Ralph Riach. After getting involved in a torrid affair with a beautiful psychic during his 1926 tour of Britain, Harry Houdini is lured into a sensationalized séance by the woman and her daughter in which they "attempt" to contact the magician's mother, from whose death he has never recovered. Disappointing period piece that fails to find the magic, or even any significant dramatic tension, in these colorful events. Pearce is sadly miscast and Zeta-Jones looks bored most of the time. Panavision. [PG]▶

Deathdream (1972-Canadian) **C-90m. **½** D: Bob Clark. John Marley, Richard Backus, Lynn Carlin, Henderson Forsythe. Backus is Vietnam vet, thought dead, who returns to his family a virtual stranger with a murderous lust for blood. Grim, fairly shocking. Aka DEAD OF NIGHT.▼▶

Death Drums Along the River SEE: **Sanders**

Death Game (1977) **C-89m. *½** D: Peter S. Traynor. Sondra Locke, Colleen Camp, Seymour Cassel, Beth Brickell. Unpleasant (and ultimately ludicrous) film about two maniacal lesbians who—for no apparent reason—tease, titillate, and torture a man in his own house. Filmed in 1974. Trivia fans: Sissy Spacek was one of the set decorators! Aka THE SEDUCERS. [R]▼▶

Death Hunt (1981) **C-97m. **** D: Peter R. Hunt. Charles Bronson, Lee Marvin, Andrew Stevens, Angie Dickinson, Carl Weathers, Ed Lauter. Tough Mountie Marvin pursues proud, self-reliant trapper Bronson, innocent of a murder charge, across icy Canada. Good action, but not enough of it. Angie is wasted. [R]▼●▶

Death in Granada SEE: **Disappearance of Garcia Lorca, The**

Death in the Garden (1956-French-Mexican) **C-92m. ***** D: Luis Buñuel. Simone Signoret, Georges Marchal, Charles Vanel, Michele Girardon, Michel Piccoli, Tito Junco. Fleeing an unspecified Fascist state, a ragged group—including a prostitute, a miner, and a priest—embark on a surreal trek through the jungles of South America. This may have merely been a "commercial chore" for the great Buñuel, but it's fascinating nonetheless. Originally titled LA MORT EN CE JARDIN at 97m. ▼▶

Death in Venice (1971-Italian) **C-130m. ***½** D: Luchino Visconti. Dirk Bogarde, Mark Burns, Marisa Berenson, Bjorn Andresen, Silvana Mangano, Luigi Battaglia. Study of an artist, his loves, his homosexuality, and continuous search for beauty. Thomas Mann's slow-moving classic is splendidly brought to the screen. Music by

Gustav Mahler (whom Bogarde is made up to resemble). Panavision. [PG]▼●▶

Deathline SEE: **Raw Meat**

Deathmask (1984) **C-87m. **** D: Richard Friedman. Farley Granger, Lee Bryant, John McCurry, Arch Johnson, Barbara Bingham, Danny Aiello, Ruth Warrick. Medical investigator Granger, haunted by the accidental drowning of his daughter, attempts to find the identity of a dead four-year-old boy. Done in by confusing direction, unnecessary exploitation elements. Video version is 103m.▼

Deathmaster, The (1972) **C-88m. **** D: Ray Danton. Robert Quarry, Bill Ewing, Brenda Dickson, John Fiedler, Betty Ann Rees, William Jordan. Spellbinding stranger (Quarry) leads on a group of unsuspecting hippies; their "guru" turns out to be a vampire in this bloody, run-of-the-mill outing. [PG]▶

Death of a Gunfighter (1969) **C-100m. **½** D: Allen Smithee. Richard Widmark, Lena Horne, John Saxon, Michael McGreevey, Darleen Carr, Carroll O'Connor, Kent Smith. Downbeat but interesting Western drama of unwanted sheriff who refuses to be fired. Horne wasted as Widmark's occasional love interest. Directed by Robert Totten and Don Siegel, credited to fictitious Smithee (his directorial "debut"). [M/PG]▼

Death of an Angel (1985) **C-95m. **** D: Petru Popescu. Bonnie Bedelia, Nick Mancuso, Pamela Ludwig, Alex Colon, Irma Garcia. Inspirational misfire about newly ordained female priest Bedelia getting involved with Mexican religious charlatan Mancuso after her crippled daughter (Ludwig) runs away to join his flock. Well-meaning, well-acted effort is extremely hokey, with a fantasy ending that is wholly unbelievable. [PG]▼●

Death of a President (2006-British) **C-93m. **** D: Gabriel Range. Hend Ayoub, Brian Boland, Becky Ann Baker, Robert Mangiardi, Jay Patterson, Jay Whittaker, Michael Reilly Burke, James Urbaniak. Politically loaded faux documentary depicts the future assassination of the then-current U.S. President, George W. Bush, while on a trip to Chicago in October 2007. The emphasis is not so much on the crime but its aftermath, and how the act is exploited by those who hold power in the U.S. Intriguing and frightening, depending on how much you buy into the premise. [R]▶

Death of a Prophet (1981) **C&B/W-60m. **½** D: Woodie King, Jr. Morgan Freeman, Yolanda King, Mansoor Najee-ullah, Sam Singleton, Tommie Hicks, Yusef Iman, Sonny Jim Gaines, Ossie Davis. Low-budget but involving drama (with some documentary scenes) about the last day in the life of a black American leader. He's clearly supposed to be Malcolm X, though that name is not mentioned. Freeman is excellent, and the film's documentary style is effective. Yolanda King is the daughter of Martin Luther King, Jr. ▼▶

Death of a Salesman (1951) 115m. ***½ D: Laslo Benedek. Fredric March, Mildred Dunnock, Kevin McCarthy, Cameron Mitchell, Howard Smith, Royal Beal, Jesse White. Arthur Miller's Pulitzer Prize–winning social drama of middle-aged man at end of emotional rope is transformed to the screen intact, with stagy flashbacks. March in title role can't fathom why business and family life failed; Dunnock is patient wife; McCarthy and Mitchell are disillusioned sons. Superb. Dunnock, Mitchell, and Smith re-create their Broadway roles; McCarthy repeats the role he played on the London stage.

Death of a Soldier (1986-Australian) C-93m. ** D: Philippe Mora. James Coburn, Reb Brown, Bill Hunter, Maurie Fields, Belinda Davey, Max Fairchild. Yank soldier in 1942 Melbourne is strangling Aussie women; the U.S. Army—which desperately needs Allied help just after MacArthur's arrival there from the Philippines—wants to hang the assailant instead of providing the professional help he really needs. Based on fact, but not as interesting as it sounds; Coburn is the American MP who gets caught in the middle. Panavision. [R] ▼

Death of Mr. Lazarescu, The (2005-Romanian) C-153m. ***½ D: Cristi Puiu. Ion Fiscuteanu, Luminita Gheorghiu, Gabriel Spahiu, Doru Ana, Dana Dogaru, Florin Zamfirescu. Bleak, fascinating, sadly funny film follows an older man, seized with stomach pain, who is shuffled from hospital to hospital as his condition deteriorates during the course of one long night . . . but a middle-aged ambulance attendant (Gheorghiu) refuses to abandon him. Potent meditation on bureaucracy and the inhumanity it breeds. Long but compelling; a humanistic look at the sorry state of health care, which is apparently a universal problem. Written by the director and Razvan Radulescu. [R] ▶

Death on the Nile (1978-British) C-140m. **½ D: John Guillermin. Peter Ustinov, Bette Davis, David Niven, Mia Farrow, Angela Lansbury, George Kennedy, Maggie Smith, Jack Warden, Lois Chiles, Olivia Hussey, Simon MacCorkindale, Jane Birkin, Jon Finch, Harry Andrews, I.S. Johar. Visually sumptuous but only marginally engrossing Agatha Christie mystery has Hercule Poirot (Ustinov) faced with a shipload of suspects after the murder of Chiles. A deserving Oscar winner for Anthony Powell's costume design; script by Anthony Shaffer. The first of Ustinov's portrayals of the Belgian detective. [PG] ▼▶

Death Proof SEE: **Grindhouse**

Death Race (2008) C-105m. *½ D: Paul W. S. Anderson. Jason Statham, Joan Allen, Ian McShane, Tyrese Gibson, Natalie Martinez, Max Ryan, Jacob Vargas, Jason Clarke. In the near future prisons are run like corporations that must make a profit. A tough-as-nails con, wrongly convicted of murdering his wife, is forced to enter a brutal car race (broadcast live on the Internet) in which inmates have to torture and kill one another before the sole survivor can claim victory and freedom. With mean warden Allen calling the shots from the sidelines, this ludicrous scenario exists only to showcase mayhem and violence at every turn. In-name-only remake of Roger Corman's exploitation favorite DEATH RACE 2000. David Carradine provides voice of Frankenstein. Unrated version runs 111m. Followed by DVD sequel, DEATH RACE 2. Super 35. [R] ▶

Death Race 2000 (1975) C-78m. **½ D: Paul Bartel. David Carradine, Simone Griffeth, Sylvester Stallone, Louisa Moritz, Mary Woronov, Don Steele, Joyce Jameson, Fred Grandy, Martin Kove, T. R. Sloane, John Landis. Outrageous tongue-in-cheek action film about futuristic society where no-holds-barred auto race is the national sport, and points scored by running down pedestrians. Fast-paced fun, marred by unnecessary gore. Remade, in name only, as DEATH RACE. Followed by DEATHSPORT. [R] ▼▶

Death Rage (1976-Italian) C-98m. *½ D: Anthony M. Dawson (Antonio Margheriti). Yul Brynner, Barbara Bouchet, Martin Balsam, Massimo Ranieri. Brynner plays American hit man duped into agreeing to kill underworld kingpin in Naples. All this film kills is time. [R] ▼▶

Death Rides a Horse (1967-Italian) C-114m. ** D: Giulio Petroni. Lee Van Cleef, John Phillip Law, Luigi Pistilli, Anthony Dawson. Long, drawn-out Italian revenge Western with Law seeking murderers of his family, unaware that his companion (Van Cleef) is one of them. Techniscope. [M] ▼▶

Death Sentence (2007) C-105m. *½ D: James Wan. Kevin Bacon, Garrett Hedlund, Kelly Preston, Aisha Tyler, John Goodman, Jordan Garrett, Stuart Lafferty, Leigh Whannell. Bacon is a picture-perfect family man whose life is thrown into a dangerous, downward spiral when a family member becomes an innocent victim in a gang robbery. He turns into a killing machine, and suddenly every B-movie cliché is dredged up. Exactly what you'd expect a pulp revenge film from the director of SAW to be. Almost worth watching for one unusually lengthy chase scene. Actually based on Brian Garfield's novel that was a sequel to his original *Death Wish*. Also shown in unrated version. Super 35. [R] ▶

Death Ship (1980-Canadian) C-91m. BOMB D: Alvin Rakoff. George Kennedy, Richard Crenna, Nick Mancuso, Sally Ann

Howes, Kate Reid, Saul Rubinek. Luxury liner collides with "death ship." Survivors board "death ship." "Death ship" tries to murder survivors. Forget it. [R]▼◗

Deathsport (1978) C-82m. ** D: Henry Suso, Allan Arkush. David Carradine, Claudia Jennings, Richard Lynch, David McLean, Jesse Vint. Follow-up to DEATH RACE 2000 again puts Carradine into future world where he and Jennings battle destructocycles to survive. Not as campy or enjoyable as earlier film, though Claudia unclothed is a visual asset. [R]▼◗

Deathstalker (1984) C-80m. BOMB D: John Watson. Richard Hill, Barbi Benton, Richard Brooker, Lana Clarkson, Victor Bo, Bernard Erhard. Tacky sword-and-sorcery opus, good only for unintended laughs and gratuitous female nudity. Filmed in Argentina. Followed by several sequels. [R]▼◗●

Deathstalker II (1987) C-77m. ** D: Jim Wynorski. John Terlesky, Monique Gabrielle, Toni La Zar, Toni Naples, Maria Socas. Princess in exile (Gabrielle) is trying to regain her throne, with the aid of soldier of fortune Terlesky, in a medieval fantasyland. Filmed on the cheap in Argentina. Voyeurs will appreciate topless scenes by former model Gabrielle (in a dual role, no less). Watch for funny outtakes at the end. Aka DEATHSTALKER II: DUEL OF THE TITANS. [R]▼◗●

Deathstalker III (1989) C-86m. BOMB D: Alfonso Corona. John Allen Nelson, Carla Herd, Terri Treas, Thom Christopher, Aaron Hernan, Roger Cudney, Claudia Inchaurregui. Cheap, boring time-waster, in which Nelson seeks a lost treasure and becomes involved with twin princesses (both played by Herd). Also known as DEATHSTALKER III: THE WARRIORS FROM HELL. Followed by DEATHSTALKER IV: MATCH OF TITANS. [R]▼●

Death Takes a Holiday (1934) 78m. ***½ D: Mitchell Leisen. Fredric March, Evelyn Venable, Guy Standing, Gail Patrick, Helen Westley, Kent Taylor, Henry Travers, Katherine Alexander. Fascinating allegory about Death (March) entering the human world to discover what makes us tick, and falling in love. Maxwell Anderson, Gladys Lehman, and Walter Ferris adapted Alberto Casella's play. Remade as a TVM in 1971 (with Melvyn Douglas, Myrna Loy, and Monte Markham), and as MEET JOE BLACK in 1998.▼◗

Death to Smoochy (2002) C-109m. ** D: Danny DeVito. Robin Williams, Edward Norton, Catherine Keener, Danny DeVito, Jon Stewart, Harvey Fierstein, Michael Rispoli, Pam Ferris, Danny Woodburn, Vincent Schiavelli. Sleazy TV kiddie show host (Williams) swears revenge on his replacement (Norton), who's ultra-sincere and doesn't realize that he's surrounded by greedy, self-promoting sharks. Satiric black comedy

revels in its own nastiness, but pummels all the fun out of the premise with its heavy-handed treatment. A major disappointment considering the talent involved. [R]▼◗

Death Trap (1976) SEE: **Eaten Alive**

Deathtrap (1982) C-116m. ** D: Sidney Lumet. Michael Caine, Christopher Reeve, Dyan Cannon, Irene Worth, Henry Jones, Joe Silver. Playwright Caine, suffering through a series of flops, might just kill to take credit for novice author Reeve's new work; Cannon is Caine's hysterical wife. An overlong, second-rate SLEUTH, adapted by Jay Presson Allen from Ira Levin's hit play. One sequence was added for original network showing. [PG]▼●◗

Death Valley (1982) C-87m. *½ D: Dick Richards. Paul Le Mat, Catherine Hicks, Stephen McHattie, A. Wilford Brimley, Peter Billingsley, Edward Herrmann. Young Billingsley, a city boy, visits mom in Arizona, becomes entangled with psychotic criminal McHattie. Pretty bad, with a fine cast wasted. [R]▼

Death Warrant (1990-Canadian) C-111m. **½ D: Deran Sarafian. Jean-Claude Van Damme, Robert Guillaume, Cynthia Gibb, George Dickerson, Art Le Fleur, Patrick Kilpatrick. Van Damme plays a Royal Canadian Mountie posing as a prisoner to find out who has been offing penitentiary inmates. You guessed it . . . his cover is threatened by incoming transfer of one of his old Mountie foes. Hard to say how Sgt. Preston would have handled this one. Slightly better than most of this genre. [R]▼●◗

Death Watch (1980-French-German) C-119m. *** D: Bertrand Tavernier. Romy Schneider, Harvey Keitel, Harry Dean Stanton, Max von Sydow. Intelligent sci-fi drama. In a future civilization, TV producer Stanton uses Keitel—who has a camera in his brain—to film a documentary on terminally ill Schneider. A biting commentary on media abuse and manipulation, with solid performances, direction. Panavision. [R]▼●

Death Weekend SEE: **House by the Lake**

Death Wheelers, The SEE: **Psychomania** (1971)

Death Wish (1974) C-93m. *** D: Michael Winner. Charles Bronson, Hope Lange, Vincent Gardenia, Steven Keats, William Redfield, Stuart Margolin, Stephen Elliott, Olympia Dukakis, Christopher Guest, Paul Dooley, Eric Laneuville. Audience manipulation at its zenith: Businessman Bronson's wife and daughter are savagely raped, and his wife dies, turning mild-mannered liberal Bronson into a vigilante on N.Y.C. streets. Chilling but irresistible; a bastardization of the Brian Garfield novel, in which vigilantism as a deterrent to crime is not a solution but another problem. Music by Herbie Hancock. One of the muggers is played by Jeff Goldblum, in his film debut. Followed by four sequels. [R]▼◗●

[335]

Death Wish II (1982) **C-93m.** BOMB D: Michael Winner. Charles Bronson, Jill Ireland, Vincent Gardenia, J. D. Cannon, Anthony Franciosa, Ben Frank, Robin Sherwood, Robert F. Lyons, Larry Fishburne. Bronson's back in action, this time bringing his one-man vigilante act to L.A. Made by profiteers, not filmmakers; poorly directed to boot, with Charlie giving a wooden-Indian performance. [R] ▼●)

Death Wish 3 (1985) **C-90m.** *½ D: Michael Winner. Charles Bronson, Deborah Raffin, Ed Lauter, Martin Balsam, Gavan O'Herlihy, Kirk Taylor, Alex Winter, Tony Spiridakis, John Gabriel, Marina Sirtis. Same old stuff, except that Bronson's "ordinary guy" vigilante is no longer convincing; his entire immediate family was wiped out in the first two movies! [R] ▼●)

Death Wish 4: The Crackdown (1987) **C-99m.** BOMB D: J. Lee Thompson. Charles Bronson, Kay Lenz, John P. Ryan, Perry Lopez, George Dickerson, Soon-Teck Oh, Dana Barron. Cheapie entry in this worn-out series has a different director and an L.A. setting. This time vigilante Bronson's mission includes wiping out the gangs supplying crack. [R] ▼●)

Death Wish V: The Face of Death (1994-Canadian) **C-96m.** BOMB D: Allan A. Goldstein. Charles Bronson, Lesley-Anne Down, Michael Parks, Chuck Shamata, Kevin Lund, Robert Joy, Saul Rubinek, Erica Lancaster. No plot, just a pretext: Bronson's fiancée is murdered on the orders of her mobster ex-husband (Parks), so (yawn) he turns vigilante yet again. Crude, stupid entry in weary series, very badly directed, with an emphasis on torture. [R] ▼●)

D.E.B.S. (2005) **C-91m.** ** D: Angela Robinson. Sara Foster, Jordana Brewster, Devon Aoki, Meagan Good, Michael Clarke Duncan, Jessica Cauffiel, Jill Ritchie, Holland Taylor. Leggy young women in short skirts are, in reality, spies. Their assignment: to carry, or at least sustain, a retro secret-agent spoof whose major story hook is lesbian puppy-love. Writer-director Robinson shows visual flair, but leads Foster and Brewster are fatally vapid as the spy and target who develop a yen for each other. Titillation aside, it plays no better than the spy comedies of the 1960s when James Bond was new. Allen and Rossi in THE LAST OF THE SECRET AGENTS?, anyone? Super 35. [PG-13] ▼)

Decameron, The (1970-Italian-French-West German) **C-111m.** **½ D: Pier Paolo Pasolini. Franco Citti, Ninetto Davoli, Angela Luce, Patrizia Capparelli, Jovan Jovanovic, Silvana Mangano, Pier Paolo Pasolini. An octet of tales from Boccaccio's *Decameron*, with Pasolini as Giotto, linking them up. Lively, earthy; the first of the director's medieval trilogy. [X] ▼●)

Deceived (1991) **C-103m.** ** D: Damian

Harris. Goldie Hawn, John Heard, Robin Bartlett, Ashley Peldon, Tom Irwin, Beatrice Straight, Kate Reid, Maia Filar, Jan Rubes, Amy Wright. In-name-only "thriller" about happily married N.Y.C. yuppie who discovers her husband's litany of duplicities after the guy is supposedly murdered. Hawn's attempt to play it straight is too derivative (to say nothing of incredible) to carry much clout. [PG-13] ▼●)

Deceiver (1998) **C-102m.** BOMB D: Jonas Pate, Joshua Pate. Tim Roth, Chris Penn, Michael Rooker, Renée Zellweger, Rosanna Arquette, Ellen Burstyn. Did Roth, a boozy rich kid with temporal lobe epilepsy, hack prostitute Zellweger in two? Pretentious, derivative groaner about Roth's subsequent police interrogation futilely tries to make us care. With its casting—Penn and Rooker as the grilling cops—it's a given that Roth isn't going to be the only one with personal demons. If you must watch, see if you can make sense of Arquette's role as Rooker's sex-starved wife. J-D-C Scope. [R] ▼●)

Deceivers, The (1988-British-Indian) **C-112m.** BOMB D: Nicholas Meyer. Pierce Brosnan, Saeed Jaffrey, Shashi Kapoor, Helena Mitchell, Keith Michell, David Robb. Limp adventure saga of British officer Brosnan going undercover in colonial India to infiltrate a murderous brotherhood. Intriguing premise, deadening result; Brosnan simply fails to register. Produced, oddly enough, by Ismail Merchant. [PG-13] ▼●)

December (1991) **C-92m.** ** D: Gabe Torres. Balthazar Getty, Jason London, Brian Krause, Wil Wheaton, Chris Young, Robert Miller, Ann Hartfield. In the wake of the Pearl Harbor bombing in 1941 five young men must decide what to do with their lives. Talky movie takes place mostly in dorm rooms; might have played better on a stage. [PG] ▼●)

December Boys (2007-Australian) **C-105m.** **½ D: Rod Hardy. Daniel Radcliffe, Lee Cormie, Christian Byers, James Fraser, Jack Thompson, Teresa Palmer, Sullivan Stapleton, Victoria Hill, Max Cullen. Four orphan boys spend the holidays with a friendly older couple who live on a beach cove. This break from day-to-day life at their orphanage brings out hopes, longings, and resentments as the boys experience puppy love, attachment to parental figures, and life among a group of genuine eccentrics. Adaptation of Michael Noonan's novel echoes other coming-of-age stories but is told with straightforward sincerity. Super 35. [PG-13] ▮)

December Bride (1991-British-Irish) **C-90m.** *** D: Thaddeus O'Sullivan. Donal McCann, Saskia Reeves, Ciarán Hinds, Patrick Malahide, Brenda Bruce. Austere but involving romantic drama set in a rural, conservative Irish farm community, in which an independent-minded servant (Reeves) becomes pregnant and refuses to reveal the identity of the father. A story of simple but deeply felt emotion, and an allegory about the constrictions of hell-and-damnation religion. Stunningly directed, and crammed with painterly images. ▼▶

Deception (1946) **112m.** ******* D: Irving Rapper. Bette Davis, Paul Henreid, Claude Rains, John Abbott. Talky but engrossing drama, set in the world of classical music, about a celebrated composer (a charismatic Rains) who seeks revenge when his lover (Davis) weds her old flame (Henreid). ▼▶

Deception (1993) **C-90m.** ****½** D: Graeme Clifford. Andie MacDowell, Liam Neeson, Viggo Mortensen, Jack Thompson, Paul Spencer, Chad Power, Monica Mikala, Jeff Corey, Miriam Reed. Better-than-average mystery follows a determined woman around the world as she sniffs out a trail of bank accounts left by her deceased husband. A pleasant diversion, enhanced by MacDowell and some nice scenery. Filmed as RUBY CAIRO, this languished on the shelf for a while. [PG-13]▼▶

Deception (2008) **C-108m.** ****** D: Marcel Langenegger. Hugh Jackman, Ewan McGregor, Michelle Williams, Lisa Gay Hamilton, Maggie Q, Natasha Henstridge, Charlotte Rampling, Margaret Colin, Paz de la Huerta, Rachael Taylor. Nerdy auditor (McGregor) warms to the friendly overtures of a slick lawyer (Jackman) who seems to have all the social skills he lacks. When he winds up with Jackman's cell phone he's drawn into a secret sex club—and enjoys it, until things turn sour. A suspense movie made by people who've apparently never seen a suspense movie; painfully obvious from the word go. Jackman coproduced. Super 35. [R]▶

Decision at Sundown (1957) **C-77m.** ****½** D: Budd Boetticher. Randolph Scott, John Carroll, Karen Steele, Noah Beery, Jr., John Litel. Scott tracks down man supposedly responsible for his wife's suicide in this odd but interesting Western. ▼▶

Decision Before Dawn (1951) **110m.** ******* D: Anatole Litvak. Richard Basehart, Gary Merrill, Oskar Werner, Hildegarde Neff, Dominique Blanchar, O. E. Hasse, Wilfried Seyfert. Top-notch WW2 espionage thriller, with Werner an idealistic German medic/POW who agrees to become a spy for his captors. Outstanding work by Werner, Neff (as a sympathetic bar-girl), and the supporting cast. Look quickly for Klaus Kinski as a whining soldier. Perceptive script by Peter Viertel; Litvak coproduced. ▶

Deck the Halls (2006) **C-95m.** ***½** D: John Whitesell. Danny DeVito, Matthew Broderick, Kristin Davis, Kristin Chenoweth, Fred Armisen, Alia Shawkat, Dylan Blue, Sabrina Aldridge, Kelly Aldridge, Jorge Garcia, Ryan Devlin, Jackie Burroughs. Two neighbors declare war after DeVito

decides to decorate his house with so many lights they can "be seen from space." When people start coming from all over town to see the display it causes great friction between him and Broderick, who feels he is being upstaged. Incredibly dumb holiday comedy that can't even meet the lowball standards set by JINGLE ALL THE WAY and CHRISTMAS WITH THE KRANKS. Deck the screenwriters instead. [PG]▶

Decline of the American Empire, The (1986-Canadian) **C-101m.** ******* D: Denys Arcand. Dominique Michel, Dorothée Berryman, Louise Portal, Geneviève Rioux, Pierre Curzi, Rémy Girard, Yves Jacques, Daniel Brière, Gabriel Arcand. Witty, on-target account of how men and women feel about each other, and use each other, in their quests for pleasure and happiness. Focus is on a group of friends: The men prepare a gourmet dinner, while the women exercise in a health club, then they come together. These characters gather again in THE BARBARIAN INVASIONS. [R]▼▶

Decline and Fall of a Bird Watcher (1968-British) **C-86m.** ****** D: John Krish. Robin Phillips, Colin Blakely, Leo McKern, Genevieve Page, Felix Aylmer, Robert Harris, Donald Wolfit, Patrick Magee. Uneven, often labored satirical farce about a young man who joins faculty of strange boys' school and becomes involved with manipulative older woman (Page). Adapted from an Evelyn Waugh novel. [PG]

Decline of Western Civilization, The (1981) **C-100m.** ******* D: Penelope Spheeris. Alice Bag Band, Black Flag, Catholic Discipline, Circle Jerks, Fear, Germs, X. Funny, revealing documentary record of the whos, whats, and whys of the L.A. punk rock scene at the end of the 1970s: the music, performers, dancing, clubs, violence, desperation. An aptly titled chronicle. Much of cast now dead. Followed by a sequel. [R]▼

Decline of Western Civilization Part II: The Metal Years, The (1988) **C-90m.** ******* D: Penelope Spheeris. Joe Perry, Steven Tyler, Gene Simmons, Paul Stanley, Chris Holmes, Lemmy, Ozzy Osbourne, Faster Pussycat, Lizzy Borden, London, Odin, Seduce, Megadeth. Follow-up to definitive punk rock documentary concentrates more heavily on interviews, juxtaposing thoughts of seen-it-all veterans (Osbourne, Simmons, Perry, and Tyler of Aerosmith) with young aspirants bucking odds for success. Sympathetic to its subjects without condoning lifestyle it depicts; probably only chance you'll ever get to see Osbourne cook breakfast. [R]▼

Deconstructing Harry (1997) **C-96m.** *****½** D: Woody Allen. Woody Allen, Richard Benjamin, Kirstie Alley, Billy Crystal, Judy Davis, Bob Balaban, Elisabeth Shue, Demi Moore, Robin Williams, Caroline Aaron, Eric Bogosian, Mariel Hemingway, Amy Irving, Julie Kavner, Eric Lloyd, Julia Louis-

Dreyfus, Tobey Maguire, Stanley Tucci, Hazelle Goodman, Gene Saks, Tony Sirico, Paul Giamatti, Jennifer Garner. A writer uses his life as fodder for his work—infuriating his friends, family, and lovers. Unusually candid (and foul-mouthed) self-examination by Allen, incorporating his various encounters as well as enactments of his fables and fancies; nonfans may think it overly indulgent, but Woodyphiles should find it fascinating and extremely funny. No one writes funnier dialogue—or keeps the spirit of Jewish humor alive so well. [R]▼●◗

Decoy (1946) **77m.** ✱✱✱ D: Jack Bernhard. Jean Gillie, Edward Norris, Herbert Rudley, Robert Armstrong, Sheldon Leonard, Marjorie Woodworth, Phil Van Zandt. Superior low-budget film noir about a gangster's ruthless moll (Gillie) who seduces a sap doctor as part of her outlandish scheme to find $400,000 in buried loot—by reviving her boyfriend after his execution in the gas chamber! Taut B movie, based on a story by Stanley Rubin, doesn't quite live up to its "lost classic" reputation, but the opening and closing scenes are knockouts, and the British Gillie makes an unforgettable femme fatale; Leonard has one of his finest hours as a jaded police detective.◗

Dedication (2007) **C-94m.** ✱½ D: Justin Theroux. Billy Crudup, Mandy Moore, Tom Wilkinson, Bob Balaban, Martin Freeman, Dianne Wiest, Bobby Cannavale, Peter Bogdanovich, Amy Sedaris, Christine Taylor. Children's book author Crudup is emotionally paralyzed by the death of his illustrator, who's also his only friend (Wilkinson). We soon find out why, as this off-putting movie asks us to show care and concern for a man who puts the funk in dysfunctional. When editor Balaban tries to force a female illustrator (Moore) on his reluctant author, you know romance is in the air—but the air in this movie is terminally foul. [R]◗

Deep, The (1977) **C-123m.** ✱✱ D: Peter Yates. Robert Shaw, Jacqueline Bisset, Nick Nolte, Louis Gossett, Eli Wallach, Robert Tessier. Endless film of Peter Benchley's novel about innocent couple who hit on treasure and drugs while scuba-diving off Bermuda coast. Gratuitous violence and titillation—not to mention unbelievable plot—sink this handsome production. NBC added 53m. for its first network showing. Panavision. [PG]▼●◗

Deep Blue Sea, The (1955-British) **C-99m.** ✱✱½ D: Anatole Litvak. Vivien Leigh, Kenneth More, Eric Portman, Emlyn Williams. Terence Rattigan play of marital infidelity and the repercussions on Leigh, frustrated well-married woman; slow moving, but interesting. CinemaScope.

Deep Blue Sea (1999) **C-105m.** ✱✱½ D: Renny Harlin. Thomas Jane, Saffron Burrows, Samuel L. Jackson, Jacqueline McKenzie, Michael Rapaport, Stellan Skarsgård,

LL Cool J, Aida Turturro. Floating scientific base is crippled by an unlikely accident, and the super-intelligent sharks developed by researchers ungratefully begin chasing down their creators as the base slowly sinks. Sometimes-exciting combination of JAWS and ALIEN has some surprises, but terrible dialogue and a preposterous premise. Ronny Cox appears unbilled. Super 35. [R]▼●◗

Deep Cover (1992) **C-112m.** ✱✱½ D: Bill Duke. Larry Fishburne, Jeff Goldblum, Victoria Dillard, Charles Martin Smith, Sydney Lassick, Clarence Williams III, Gregory Sierra, Roger Guenveur Smith, Def Jef, Glynn Turman. Fishburne, whose dad was killed during a holdup, grows up to be an undercover narc. Half standard urban action pic—but also half original. Goldblum puts a deliciously eccentric spin on his role as a lawyer who becomes Fishburne's unwitting "partner" in shady drug dealings. Better if taken purely as a genre picture, though there are indications the film wants to be something more; expert action scenes. [R]▼●◗

Deep Crimson (1996-Mexican-French-Spanish) **C-114m.** ✱✱✱ D: Arturo Ripstein. Regina Orozco, Daniel Gimenez-Cacho, Marisa Paredes, Veronica Merchant, Julieta Egurrola, Patricia Reyes Spindola. Spectacularly unpleasant and disturbing true-life crime story, based on the same "Lonely Hearts" case that inspired THE HONEYMOON KILLERS, about the murderous love affair between an obese nurse and a gigolo who swindle wealthy widows in 1940s Mexico. Extremely well acted and directed study of *l'amour fou* and the banality of evil. Packs a wallop, and pulls no punches in its horrific depiction of the couple's violent descent into madness.▼◗

Deep End (1970-U.S.-German) **C-88m.** ✱✱✱ D: Jerzy Skolimowski. Jane Asher, John Moulder-Brown, Diana Dors, Karl Michael Vogler. Innocent 15-year-old Moulder-Brown, an attendant in a dreary public bath, falls in love with his 20-ish female counterpart (Asher). Well-made tragedy of obsessive love; set in London, with music by Cat Stevens. [R]▼

Deep End, The (2001) **C-99m.** ✱✱✱ D: Scott McGehee, David Siegel. Tilda Swinton, Goran Visnjic, Jonathan Tucker, Josh Lucas, Peter Donat, Raymond Barry. A devoted mother of three thinks her teenage son may be accused of killing his gay lover, so she covers up the crime . . . but that's just the beginning of her problems. Intriguing thriller with surprising twists and nuanced character development, but a bit cold. Interestingly set and shot in Lake Tahoe, with a superb performance by Swinton. Based on the same novel by Elizabeth Sanxay Holding (*The Blank Wall*) that inspired THE RECKLESS MOMENT in 1949. Written by the directors. Panavision. [R]▼◗

Deep End of the Ocean, The (1999) **C-109m.** *** D: Ulu Grosbard. Michelle Pfeiffer, Treat Williams, Whoopi Goldberg, Jonathan Jackson, Ryan Merriman, John Kapelos, Michael Mcelroy. Persuasively acted adaptation of Jacquelyn Mitchard's best-seller about the disappearance of a three-year-old at his mother's high school reunion, and his chance return nine years later. Two-part story is admittedly a whopper, yet it's handled in credible fashion that makes one willing to accept it. Plays like a TV movie at times, but by and large, an exceptional one, with the dynamics between the two newfound brothers ringing true. [PG-13]▼●)

Deep Impact (1998) **C-120m.** *** D: Mimi Leder. Robert Duvall, Téa Leoni, Elijah Wood, Vanessa Redgrave, Morgan Freeman, Maximilian Schell, James Cromwell, Ron Eldard, Jon Favreau, Laura Innes, Mary McCormack, Richard Schiff, Blair Underwood, Bruce Weitz, Betsy Brantley, Charles Martin Smith, Leelee Sobieski. Exciting yarn about attempts to ward off a comet hurtling toward Earth—and preparations to save as many people as possible if it hits. Freeman is the rock-solid U.S. President, Duvall a veteran astronaut on a space mission to explode the comet; their authoritative presence adds weight to this saga, while Leoni seems a bit of a flyweight as the ambitious TV newswoman who breaks the story. Super 35. [PG-13]▼●)

Deep in My Heart (1954) **C-132m.** **½ D: Stanley Donen. Jose Ferrer, Merle Oberon, Helen Traubel, Doe Avedon, Tamara Toumanova, Paul Stewart, Douglas Fowley, Jim Backus; guest stars Walter Pidgeon, Paul Henreid, Rosemary Clooney, Gene and Fred Kelly, Jane Powell, Vic Damone, Ann Miller, Cyd Charisse, Howard Keel, Tony Martin. The life of composer Sigmund Romberg is not the stuff of high drama, but film sparkles in production numbers with MGM guest stars. Highlights include Kelly brothers' only film appearance together, Charisse's exquisite and sensual dance number with James Mitchell, and an incredible number featuring Ferrer performing an entire show himself.▼●)

Deep in the Heart (1983-British) **C-101m.** *** D: Tony Garnett. Karen Young, Clayton Day, Suzie Humphreys, Ben Jones. Thought-provoking, if occasionally simplistic, drama about the evolution of a young woman (nicely played by Young) from passivity to violence, resulting from her relationship with macho Texan Day. Originally titled HANDGUN. [R]▼)

Deep Red (1975-Italian) **C-98m.** **½ D: Dario Argento. David Hemmings, Daria Nicolodi, Gabriele Lavia, Macha Meril, Glauco Mauri. There's style to burn in senseless horror thriller with Hemmings on trail of sadistic psycho killer. Flashy, bizarre murders set to pounding rock soundtrack. Aka THE HATCHET MURDERS; original Italian version, PROFONDO ROSSO, is 28m. longer and much more violent. Cromoscope. [R]▼)

Deep Rising (1998) **C-106m.** ** D: Stephen Sommers. Treat Williams, Famke Janssen, Anthony Heald, Wes Studi, Kevin J. O'Connor, Djimon Hounsou, Derrick O'Connor. Skipper-for-hire Williams finds himself in over his head when his current clients (a scummy lot led by heavily armed Studi) attack a luxury liner, unaware that the ship has been under siege by some sort of horrific ocean creatures. High-tech scare movie with a hokey script; some fun on a no-brainer level. Super 35. [R]▼●)

Deep Six, The (1958) **C-105m.** **½ D: Rudolph Maté. Alan Ladd, Dianne Foster, William Bendix, Keenan Wynn, James Whitmore, Efrem Zimbalist, Jr., Joey Bishop, Ross Bagdasarian, Perry Lopez, Jerry Mathers. Commercial artist–Navy reserve officer Ladd (who was raised a Quaker) is called into the military during WW2 and must deal with his pacifism while in combat. One of Ladd's best late-career roles; Bendix offers solid support as "Frenchy" Shapiro of Brooklyn. ▼

Deep Space (1987) **C-90m.** **½ D: Fred Olen Ray. Charles Napier, Ann Turkel, Julie Newmar, James Booth, Ron Glass, Anthony Eisley, Bo Svenson, Peter Palmer. An ALIEN-like creature runs amok. Ultra-hokey sci-fi thriller with comic overtones. Napier is perfectly cast as a cop on its trail. Good fun for genre fans. Incidentally, title has nothing to do with the film! [R]▼

DeepStar Six (1989) **C-100m.** *½ D: Sean S. Cunningham. Greg Evigan, Nancy Everhard, Cindy Pickett, Miguel Ferrer, Taurean Blacque, Marius Weyers, Nia Peeples, Matt McCoy, Elya Baskin, Thom Bray. In the near future, an undersea research and missile-installation base is threatened by a carnivorous swimming crustacean. Plodding, familiar story and talky script (not to mention an elaborate but unconvincing monster) sink this. [R]▼●)

Deer Hunter, The (1978) **C-183m.** **** D: Michael Cimino. Robert De Niro, John Cazale, John Savage, Meryl Streep, Christopher Walken, George Dzundza, Chuck Aspegren. Stunning film about young Pennsylvania steelworkers, their lives before, during, and after wartime duty in Vietnam. Long but not overlong, this sensitive, painful, evocative work packs an emotional wallop. Story by Cimino, Deric Washburn, Louis Garfinkle and Quinn Redeker; scripted by Washburn. Five Oscars include Picture, Director, Supporting Actor (Walken), Editing (Peter Zinner). Panavision. [R] ▼●)

Def by Temptation (1990) **C-95m.** *** D: James Bond III. Cynthia Bond, Kadeem Hardison, James Bond III, Bill Nunn, Melba Moore, Samuel L. Jackson. Southern divinity student visits his older brother in N.Y.C., just in time for the latter to get involved with a seductive succubus who preys on men in bars. All-black sleeper is extremely stylish, aided no end by the photography of Spike Lee's longtime cameraman, Ernest Dickerson. [R]▼●)

Defcon-4 (1984) **C-89m.** BOMB D: Paul Donovan. Lenore Zann, Maury Chaykin, Kate Lynch, Tim Choate. It sounds like an industrial-strength roach killer, and it could use one. Three astronauts return to a post-holocaust earth run by some truly slimy punks. Next to C.H.U.D., the grimiest-looking movie of its time (at least *that* one took place underground). [R]▼●)

Defector, The (1966) **C-106m.** **½ D: Raoul Levy. Montgomery Clift, Hardy Kruger, Roddy McDowall, David Opatoshu. Hackneyed Cold War spy trivia filmed in Europe, interesting only as Clift's last film; good cameo by McDowall.▶

Defence of the Realm (1985-British) **C-96m.** ***½ D: David Drury. Gabriel Byrne, Greta Scacchi, Denholm Elliott, Ian Bannen, Bill Paterson, Fulton Mackay. Tough, obsessive journalist Byrne's investigative story causes a British MP to resign—but there's more to the case than he knows. A taut, extremely entertaining political thriller that also touches on the subject of journalistic responsibility and the public's right to know what its government is up to. [PG]▼●)

Defending Your Life (1991) **C-111m.** *** D: Albert Brooks. Albert Brooks, Meryl Streep, Rip Torn, Lee Grant, Buck Henry, George D. Wallace, Lillian Lehman, Peter Schuck, Ethan Randall (Embry). Brooks dies in a car crash and finds himself in Judgment City, where Torn is assigned to defend his life before a tribunal . . . and where he falls in love with fellow candidate Streep, who's too good to be true. Imperfect, like all of Brooks' movies, but full of funny ideas and hard to dislike. [PG]▼●)

Defendor (2010-Canadian) **C-95m.** **½ D: Peter Stebbings. Woody Harrelson, Kat Dennings, Elias Koteas, Sandra Oh, Lisa Ray, Charlotte Sullivan, Michael Kelly. Harrelson excels in a darkly comic twist on the standard comic book superhero. Taking on an evil drug lord, biker gangs, and corrupt cops while protecting a crack-addicted prostitute, Arthur (aka Defendor) is a powerless wannabe hero who comes alive only through a tacky outfit with a big "D" and a makeshift eye patch he wears to disguise his very ordinary life—and the childhood trauma that inspired his kitschy alter ego. The idea is better than its execution; Harrelson rises above the spotty script. Super 35. [R] ▶

Defenseless (1991) **C-104m.** **½ D: Martin Campbell. Barbara Hershey, Sam Shepard, Mary Beth Hurt, J. T. Walsh, Kellie Overbey, Jay O. Sanders, Randy Brooks,

John Kapelos, Sheree North. Suspense thriller in which attorney Hershey discovers her client (and lover) murdered—and finds herself not only suspected of the crime, but stalked by a mysterious killer. Not bad, and a good showcase for a first-rate cast, especially Hurt, who chews the scenery in a change-of-pace part. [R]▼●)

Defiance (1980) **C-102m.** **½ D: John Flynn. Jan-Michael Vincent, Art Carney, Theresa Saldana, Danny Aiello. Fernando Lopez, Rudy Ramos. Gritty little film about rootless blue-collar loner Vincent, who in an attempt to match up his dying youngster's bone marrow single-handedly tames a vicious N.Y.C. street gang. A synthesis of '30s Warner Bros. melodramas, B Westerns, ON THE WATERFRONT, and BOARDWALK, with atmospheric direction and colorful supporting performances. [PG]▼▶

Defiance (2008) **C-137m.** **½ D: Edward Zwick. Daniel Craig, Liev Schreiber, Jamie Bell, Alexa Davalos, Allan Corduner, Mark Feuerstein, Tomas Arana, Jodhi May, Kate Fahy, Iddo Goldberg, Iben Hjejle, Martin Hancock. After the Gestapo and its Russian surrogates have swept through their village in Belorussia in 1941, the three Bielski brothers head for the nearby woods and soon find themselves leading a growing band of Jewish refugees. Survival is the key, but so is leadership, and the two older siblings (Craig and Schreiber) have opposing points of view about how to deal with the enemy. Overlong and uneven, this is a great untold story of WW2 but not, alas, a great film. [R]▶

Defiant, The SEE: **Wild Pack, The**

Defiant Ones, The (1958) **97m.** **** D: Stanley Kramer. Tony Curtis, Sidney Poitier, Theodore Bikel, Charles McGraw, Cara Williams, Lon Chaney, Jr. Engrossing story of two escaped convicts—one black, one white—shackled together as they flee from police in the South. Fine performances by Williams and Chaney as people they meet along the way. Academy Award–winning screenplay by Harold Jacob Smith and Nathan E. Douglas (blacklisted actor-writer Nedrick Young) and cinematography by Sam Leavitt. Remade for TV in 1986 with Robert Urich and Carl Weathers.▼●)

Definitely, Maybe (2008-U.S.-British) **C-112m.** **½ D: Adam Brooks. Ryan Reynolds, Abigail Breslin, Elizabeth Banks, Isla Fisher, Rachel Weisz, Kevin Kline, Derek Luke, Kevin Corrigan, Adam Ferrara. Soon-to-be-divorced man recounts his romantic past to his 10-year-old daughter, who wants to know how he met her mother. Telling the tale of three separate romances, he weaves a story of how they affected his life and what led him to his current state of unwedded bliss. Attempt to do character comedy in the style of British films like LOVE ACTUALLY doesn't quite come off, though the cast is appealing. Robert Klein plays himself. Super 35. [PG-13]❤

Def Jam's How to Be a Player (1997) C-94m. *½ D: Lionel C. Martin. Bill Bellamy, Natalie Desselle, Lark Voorhies, Mari Morrow, Pierre, Jermaine "Big Hugg" Hopkins, A. J. Johnson, Beverly Johnson, Max Julien, Gilbert Gottfried, Bernie Mac, Elise Neal. Smooth-talking womanizer tries one-upping his sister and her friend after they invite all the "entries" in his little black book to the same party. Completely flat comedy is meant to capitalize on TV's no-holds-barred *Def Jam*, but the show seems a lot raunchier than this big-screen trifle. [R]❤O❶

Déjà Vu (1998-U.S.-British) C-116m. ***½ D: Henry Jaglom. Stephen Dillane, Victoria Foyt, Vanessa Redgrave, Glynis Barber, Michael Brandon, Noel Harrison, Rachel Kempson, Aviva Marks. Unusual romance about the inexplicable and profound attraction between an American woman abroad and a London painter. Though already attached to others, at every turn they receive "cosmic confirmation" of their belonging together. The acting is so good and story so satisfying that plot contrivances don't matter. Nepotism is a big plus, with Jaglom's wife Foyt in the lead and Redgrave's mother Kempson in their first joint screen appearance. Writer-director Jaglom's best; Foyt coscripted. [PG-13]❤❶

Deja Vu (2006) C-126m. **½ D: Tony Scott. Denzel Washington, Paula Patton, Val Kilmer, Jim Caviezel, Adam Goldberg, Elden Henson, Erika Alexander, Bruce Greenwood, Matt Craven, Elle Fanning. During Mardi Gras in New Orleans a sightseeing ferry explodes, killing hundreds. ATF agent Washington investigates a woman whose anomalous death attracts his interest. When he learns the FBI has a device that can view the past—and perhaps enter it—he goes back in time to find the killer and save the woman (Patton). Science fiction mixed with action and romance results in a shallow but entertaining thriller, though Washington, as always, is first-rate. Super 35/HD Widescreen. [PG-13]❶

Delgo (2008) C-90m. BOMB D: Marc F. Adler, Jason Maurer. Voices of Freddie Prinze, Jr., Jennifer Love Hewitt, Chris Kattan, Val Kilmer, Anne Bancroft, Kelly Ripa, Malcolm McDowell, Eric Idle, Burt Reynolds, Louis Gossett, Jr., Michael Clarke Duncan, Armin Shimerman; narrated by Sally Kellerman. In a fantasy universe, an alien teenager from one kingdom falls in love with the princess from a rival land, erupting hostilities between the two. Unappealing characters and confusing story combine to sink this animated fantasy, which tries too hard to combine every science-fiction/fantasy cliché into one messy concoction. A complete misfire. Final screen credit for Anne Bancroft, who portrays an evil Queen. [PG]❶

Delicate Balance, A (1973) C-132m. **

D: Tony Richardson. Katharine Hepburn, Paul Scofield, Lee Remick, Kate Reid, Joseph Cotten, Betsy Blair. Edward Albee's Pulitzer Prize–winning play about a neurotic Connecticut family and the old friends who decide to move in with them indefinitely makes for stagy, uninvolving film, extraordinary cast notwithstanding. An American Film Theater Production. [PG]❤❶

Delicate Delinquent, The (1957) 100m. *** D: Don McGuire. Jerry Lewis, Martha Hyer, Darren McGavin, Horace McMahon, Milton Frome. Jerry's first solo effort after splitting with Dean Martin has him as delinquent who becomes a cop with McGavin's help. Agreeable blend of sentiment and slapstick. VistaVision.❤❶

Delicatessen (1991-French) C-102m. ***½ D: Jean-Pierre Jeunet, Marc Caro. Marie-Laure Dougnac, Dominique Pinon, Karin Viard, Jean Claude Dreyfus, Ticky Holgado, Anne Marie Pisani, Edith Ker. Postapocalyptic comedy about a landlord who slices humans into cutlets for nonvegetarian tenants. At the very least, this is the most original and entertaining comedy about cannibalism made to date. Brown-and-white color schemes, which would ordinarily look like a lab mistake, contribute to the film's trenchant visual style. Codirector Caro plays Fox, one of the Cave Dwellers. "Presented" by Terry Gilliam.❤❶

Delinquents, The (1957) 75m. ** D: Robert Altman. Tom Laughlin, Peter Miller, Richard Bakalyan, Rosemary Howard, Helene Hawley. Intriguingly awful exploitation drama about nice boy who becomes involved with a street gang because girlfriend is too young to go steady. Altman's first film, made in Kansas City, with Julia Lee singing "Dirty Rock Boogie."

Delirious (1991) C-96m. *½ D: Tom Mankiewicz. John Candy, Mariel Hemingway, Emma Samms, David Rasche, Charles Rocket, Raymond Burr, Dylan Baker, Jerry Orbach, Renee Taylor. Astonishingly stupid comedy with a neat premise: a beleaguered soap-opera writer gets a conk on the head and dreams that he's stuck in his own story—in a heroic role that enables him to have his way with the woman he worships in real life. Bad writing and ham-handed direction foil a willing cast. [PG]❤❶

Delirious (2007) C-107m. **½ D: Tom DiCillo. Steve Buscemi, Michael Pitt, Alison Lohman, Gina Gershon, Kevin Corrigan, Callie Thorne, Richard Short, Tom Aldredge, Lynn Cohen, Elvis Costello. Thin but enjoyable satire of fame and celebrity as seen through the beady, bitter eyes of uncouth N.Y.C. paparazzo Buscemi. He grudgingly befriends a homeless actor-hopeful (Pitt) who, of course, may just become The Next Big Thing. DiCillo wrote this for Buscemi and together they have almost as much fun as in their first teaming, LIVING IN

OBLIVION. Should amuse anyone who has ever even dreamt of a show-biz career.▶

Deliverance (1972) **C-109m.** **** D: John Boorman. Jon Voight, Burt Reynolds, Ned Beatty, Ronny Cox, Billy McKinney, Herbert "Cowboy" Coward, James Dickey. Superlative re-creation of Dickey novel of four Atlanta businessmen who get more than they bargained for during a weekend canoe trip. McKinney and Coward are two of the most terrifying film villains in history; "Dueling Banjos" scene is equally memorable. Film debuts of Beatty and Cox. James Dickey adapted his own novel, and appears in the film as a sheriff; Ed O'Neill appears as a highway patrolman near end of film. The director's son Charley (later star of THE EMERALD FOREST) plays Voight's son here. Panavision. [R]▼●

Deliver Us from Eva (2003) **C-105m.** *** D: Gary Hardwick. James Todd Smith aka LL Cool J, Gabrielle Union, Duane Martin, Essence Atkins, Robinne Lee, Meagan Good, Mel Jackson, Dartanyan Edmonds, Kym Whitley, Terry Crews. Amusing film about a hostile, iron-willed woman who dominates the lives of her three younger sisters, inspiring their men to hire a "player" to distract her so they can carry on their relationships. Ingratiating performances by LL Cool J and Union spark this overlong but entertaining film. [R]▼▶

Deliver Us From Evil (2006) **C-101m.** *** D: Amy Berg. Potent documentary juxtaposes interviews with Father Oliver O'Grady (a pedophile whom leaders of the Catholic church repeatedly protected) with first-person stories of some of his victims. Timely film forgoes narration; instead, its interviewees paint a tawdry picture of corruption in a church that looked the other way while O'Grady was moved to several different parishes, where he continued committing his immoral acts. Fascinating and expertly made, but difficult to watch.▶

De-Lovely (2004) **C-125m.** ** D: Irwin Winkler. Kevin Kline, Ashley Judd, Jonathan Pryce, Kevin McNally, Allan Corduner, Sandra Nelson, Keith Allen, James Wilby, John Barrowman, Kevin McKidd, Peter Polycarpou, Richard Dillane. Handsome but awkward biopic of the great songwriter Cole Porter, whose love for his wife didn't preclude him from pursuing homosexual affairs. Using an awkward framing device (his life as a show), film incorporates many songs, sung by performers who are out of their element (Sheryl Crow, Elvis Costello, Alanis Morissette, Robbie Williams, et al.). Kline is much better than the film; the scene in which he teaches Barrowman how to sing "Night and Day" is a highlight. Oddest moment: Kline watching Cary Grant play Porter in NIGHT AND DAY. Super 35. [PG-13] ▼▶

Delta Factor, The (1970) **C-91m.** ** D: Tay Garnett. Christopher George, Yvette Mimieux, Diane McBain, Ralph Taeger. OK Mickey Spillane tale about a private eye on a CIA mission to rescue a scientist imprisoned on an island. [PG]

Delta Farce (2007) **C-90m.** *½ D: C. B. Harding. Larry The Cable Guy, Bill Engvall, DJ Qualls, Keith David, Danny Trejo, Marisol Nichols, Christina Moore, Lisa Lampanelli, Lance Smith, Glenn Morshower. Three moronic army reservists, told they are being sent to Iraq, are instead dropped into the Mexican desert, where Larry and his pals Everett and Bill (apparently Moe and Curly were unavailable) go into action against corrupt federales they mistake for Middle Eastern terrorists. Give this mind-numbingly dumb outing points for originality: it's probably the first (and hopefully last) lame-brained comedy to try milking laughs from repeated references to Shiites and Kurds! [PG-13]▶

Delta Force, The (1986) **C-129m.** **½ D: Menahem Golan. Chuck Norris, Lee Marvin, Martin Balsam, Joey Bishop, Robert Forster, Lainie Kazan, George Kennedy, Hanna Schygulla, Susan Strasberg, Bo Svenson, Robert Vaughn, Shelley Winters, Assaf Dayan, Kim Delaney. Surprisingly straightforward and straight-faced (considering that cast) account of terrorist plane hijack in the Middle East—until rescue climax when America's special squadron (led by Marvin and Norris) takes on bad guys in comic-book style. Uneven, to say the least, but never boring. Filmed in Israel. Followed by several sequels. [R]▼●

Delta Force 2 (1990) **C-110m.** *½ D: Aaron Norris. Chuck Norris, John P. Ryan, Paul Perri, Richard Jaeckel, Begonia Plaza, Mateo Gomez, Hector Mercardo, Billy Drago. Norris leads his Delta Force brigade into Latin America in an effort to snuff out an elusive drug lord. Strictly by-the-numbers. [R]▼●

Delta Fox (1977) **C-92m.** ** D: Beverly and Ferd Sebastian. Richard Lynch, Priscilla Barnes, Stuart Whitman, John Ireland, Richard Jaeckel. Unremarkable action-chase opus about a smuggler on the run from Miami to L.A.▼

Delusion (1990) **C-100m.** *** D: Carl Colpaert. Jim Metzler, Jennifer Rubin, Kyle Secor, Robert Costanzo, Tracey Walter, Jerry Orbach. Tough, taut thriller about a yuppie computer executive-embezzler and his plight after happening upon a Las Vegas showgirl and her killer-for-hire boyfriend (Secor, in an eye-opening performance) on a Death Valley highway. Thoroughly entertaining tale of desperation and isolation, with a point-of-view. Super 35. [R]▼

Dementia 13 (1963) **81m.** ** D: Francis Ford Coppola. William Campbell, Luana Anders, Bart Patton, Mary Mitchel, Patrick Magee. Gory horror film, set in Ireland, about a series of axe murders. Coppola's directorial debut—excluding his earlier nudie, TONITE FOR SURE—filmed for about 29¢ for Roger Corman; may be worth a look for curiosity's sake. ▼●]

Demetrius and the Gladiators (1954) C-101m. **½ D: Delmer Daves. Victor Mature, Susan Hayward, Michael Rennie, Debra Paget, Anne Bancroft, Richard Egan, Ernest Borgnine. Hokey sequel to THE ROBE has Emperor Caligula (Jay Robinson) searching for magic robe of Christ; Mature dallies with royal Hayward. CinemaScope. ▼●]

Demolition Man (1993) C-115m. **½ D: Marco Brambilla. Sylvester Stallone, Wesley Snipes, Sandra Bullock, Nigel Hawthorne, Benjamin Bratt, Bob Gunton, Glenn Shadix, Denis Leary, Jack Black, Jesse Ventura. Ex-cop Stallone is sprung after 36 years of deep-freeze imprisonment for manslaughter when blond Snipes (his long-ago psycho nemesis) escapes from his own government-imposed hibernation; the joke is that the "San Angeles" of 2032 is a pacifistic society that nixes violence and profanity (and where every restaurant is a Taco Bell). Fast, surprisingly funny, bloodletter is still only marginally brainier than Sly's TANGO & CASH. Panavision. [R] ▼●]

Demon (1977) C-95m. **½ D: Larry Cohen. Tony Lo Bianco, Sandy Dennis, Sylvia Sidney, Deborah Raffin, Sam Levene, Richard Lynch, Mike Kellin, Andy Kaufman. Weird, confusing shocker in which New York cop Lo Bianco investigates motiveless killings by ordinary people possessed by Christ-like demon. Some good scenes. Originally titled GOD TOLD ME TO. [R] ▼●]

Demon Barber of Fleet Street, The SEE: **Sweeney Todd, The Demon Barber of Fleet Street**

Demon Knight SEE: **Tales From The Crypt Presents Demon Knight**

Demonlover (2002-French) C-115m. **½ D: Olivier Assayas. Connie Nielsen, Charles Berling, Chloë Sevigny, Gina Gershon, Jean-Baptiste Malartre, Dominique Reymond. Ill-chosen moniker doesn't describe this dot-com thriller about a cold, calculating corporate spy who gets in over her head playing both sides of a business merger involving porno and torture Web sites. Slickly textured suspenser is seriously kinky and morally ambivalent, but its violence and voyeurism lead to an all-too-certain conclusion. Director's cut runs 117m. Original French version runs 128m. Super 35/Super 16. [R] ▼]

Demon Master, The SEE: **Craze**

Demonoid, Messenger of Death (1981) C-78m. *½ D: Alfred Zacharias. Samantha Eggar, Stuart Whitman, Roy Cameron Jenson, Erika Carlson, Lew Saunders. Eggar and husband, while working Mexican mine, unearth a hand, which possesses him,

wreaking terror and havoc. Insipid direction, a rotten script, and shoddy special effects get in the way of any suspense. Aka MACABRA. [R] ▼

Demon Planet, The SEE: **Planet of the Vampires**

Demons (1986-Italian) C-89m. *½ D: Lamberto Bava. Urbano Barberini, Natasha Hovey, Paolo Cozza, Karl Zinny, Fiore Argento, Fabiola Toledo, Nicoletta Elmi. A horror film transforms its audience one by one into drooling, fanged "demons" who attack the remaining humans. Extremely gruesome and violent; no characterization, no logic, no plot. Achieved critical fame in some quarters. Director, who shows some visual style, is son of horror maestro Mario Bava. Cowritten and produced by Dario Argento. Followed by several sequels. ▼●]

Demons 2 (1987-Italian) C-88m. ** D: Lamberto Bava. David Knight, Nancy Brilli, Coralina Cataldi Tassoni, Bobby Rhodes, Asia Argento, Virginia Bryant. Sequel is improvement on first film but highly derivative of NIGHT OF THE LIVING DEAD and THEY CAME FROM WITHIN. Demonic infection spreads among people in modern apartment building; they transform into fanged, clawed monsters and attack others. Like its predecessor, achieved great acclaim among gore fans. [R] ▼●]

Demon Seed (1977) C-94m. ***½ D: Donald Cammell. Julie Christie, Fritz Weaver, Gerrit Graham, Berry Kroeger, Lisa Lu. Intelligent futuristic thriller, provocatively written, stylishly directed, and well acted, especially by Christie, the beauty terrorized by an ultra-sophisticated computer (voice of Robert Vaughn) that's decided to take over the world. As riveting as it is bizarre. Adapted by Robert Jaffe and Roger O. Hirson from the Dean Koontz novel. Panavision. [R] ▼●]

Demons of the Mind (1971-British) C-89m. *** D: Peter Sykes. Paul Jones, Yvonne Mitchell, Gillian Hills, Robert Hardy, Patrick Magee, Michael Hordern, Shane Briant. A 19th-century baron imprisons his son and daughter, believing they are possessed. Enticingly eerie Hammer horror film. Aka BLACK EVIL and NIGHTMARE OF TERROR. [R] ▼]

Demon Within, The SEE: **Happiness Cage, The**

Denise Calls Up (1996) C-80m. *** D: Hal Salwen. Tim Daly, Caroleen Feeney, Dan Gunther, Dana Wheeler-Nicholson, Liev Schreiber, Aida Turturro, Alanna Ubach, Sylvia Miles. Nina tries to fix up a friend—no easy task—while Denise (Ubach) surprises Gunther with a phone call he never expected to get. Wickedly funny satire about New Yorkers who never seem to be able to get together and only talk on the phone. A one-joke premise, but writer-director Salwen keeps adding clever twists and touches. [PG-13]**▼●**

Dennis the Menace (1993) **C-94m. ** D:** Nick Castle. Walter Matthau, Mason Gamble, Joan Plowright, Christopher Lloyd, Lea Thompson, Robert Stanton, Paul Winfield, Amy Sakasitz, Arnold Stang, Ben Stein. Unconscionable, jerry-built ripoff of the HOME ALONEs from John Hughes, based on Hank Ketcham's comic strip, with the blond rascal's skirmishes with cantankerous neighbor Mr. Wilson (Matthau) a mere warmup to the more Culkin-ian climactic punch-out of a robber/ derelict (Lloyd). Fun for under-8's, but still a desperate collection of crotch and flatulence jokes. Followed by two direct-to-video sequels. [PG-13]**▼●**

Departed, The (2006) **C-151m. ***½ D:** Martin Scorsese. Leonardo DiCaprio, Matt Damon, Jack Nicholson, Mark Wahlberg, Martin Sheen, Ray Winstone, Vera Farmiga, Anthony Anderson, Alec Baldwin, James Badge Dale, David Patrick O'Hara, Mark Rolston, Kevin Corrigan, Dorothy Lyman. Potent, violent yarn about Irish crime bosses and cops in Boston, and how the lines cross, even over generations. Underworld bigwig Nicholson has raised and nurtured Damon, who's now his mole in the State Police and assigned to capture his mentor. DiCaprio tries to live down his shaky family history by joining the Boston police department, only to be sent undercover—to work with Nicholson. Tension mounts as the characters' paths intersect. Vibrant performances dominate the proceedings; the film's main fault is overlength. William Monahan's script was inspired by the 2002 Hong Kong police story INFERNAL AFFAIRS. Oscar winner for Best Picture, Director, Adapted Screenplay, and Editing (Thelma Schoonmaker). Super 35. [R]**●**

Departures (2008-Japanese) **C-131m. *** D:** Yojiro Takita. Masahiro Motoki, Tsutomu Yamazaki, Ryoko Hirosue, Kazuko Yoshiyuki, Kimiko Yo, Takashi Sasano. When a Tokyo orchestra is dissolved, cellist Motoki realizes he can't sustain a musical career, so he and his wife return to his hometown. There he answers a cryptic want ad and is hired as apprentice to a man who performs "encoffinnings," elaborately and ritualistically preparing dead people to be laid to rest. Offbeat, leisurely paced, and disarmingly funny at times, this likable film becomes highly emotional as loose ends in Motoki's life are tied up and he comes to embrace his unusual profession. Some will find this manipulative; others will succumb and tears will flow. Oscar winner for Best Foreign Language Film.**●**

Derailed (2005) **C-110m. ** D:** Mikael Håfström. Clive Owen, Jennifer Aniston, Vincent Cassel, Melissa George, Giancarlo Esposito, David Morrissey, Georgina Chapman, Tom Conti, Xzibit, RZA. Chicago businessman Owen misses his commuter train and strikes up a conversation with an attractive woman. This leads to a liaison, but that misstep quickly threatens to destroy everything in Owen's life: his family, his bank account, and his sanity. Modern spin on film noir starts well enough but descends into a state of incredulity and downright silliness. Good cast—including hip-hop stars Xzibit and RZA—is wasted here. Unrated version also available. Super 35. [R]**●**

Deranged (1974) **C-82m. **½ D:** Jeff Gillen, Alan Ormsby. Roberts Blossom, Cosette Lee, Leslie Carlson, Robert Warner, Marcia Diamond. Blossom's neat performance uplifts this predictable shocker of a mother-obsessed farmer who preserves the old lady's corpse, then kills and stuffs other women to keep her company. Based on the same real-life case that inspired PSYCHO and THE TEXAS CHAIN SAW MASSACRE. [R]**▼●**

Dersu Uzala (1975-Japanese-Russian) **C-140m. ***½ D:** Akira Kurosawa. Maxim Munzuk, Yuri Solomine. Simple, gentle Munzuk, a hunter of the Goldi tribe, teaches Russian explorer Solomine the rules of survival in Siberia; they develop mutual respect and friendship. A poignant, poetic examination of contrasting lives. Filmed in Russia; Best Foreign Film Oscar winner. Sovscope 70. [G]**▼●**

De Sade (1969-U.S.-West German) **C-92m. ** D:** Cy Endfield. Keir Dullea, Senta Berger, Lilli Palmer, Anna Massey, John Huston. Fictionalized biography of world's most celebrated sexual and physical pervert. If you're expecting something raunchy, forget it. Pretty tepid stuff. Original running time: 113m. [R]**●**

Descent, The (2005-British) **C-99m. ** D:** Neil Marshall. Shauna Macdonald, Natalie Mendoza, Alex Reid, Saskia Mulder, Nora-Jane Noone, MyAnna Buring, Oliver Milburn, Molly Kayll, Craig Conway. Six women bond every year during an "extreme" adventure. This time it's a journey into a cave in the Appalachian Mountains, but there are sparks flying between two of the participants . . . and the cave houses subhuman flesh-eating creatures! Standard horror outing with feisty all-female protagonists. Unapologetically gruesome. Written by the director. Ending altered for U.S. release; original unrated version available on DVD. Followed by a DVD sequel. Super 35. [R]**●**

Desert Attack (1960-British) **79m. *** D:** J. Lee Thompson. John Mills, Sylvia Syms, Anthony Quayle, Harry Andrews, Diane Clare. Well-handled psychological drama of British ambulance officer, two nurses, and a German soldier brought together in African desert. Original British version ICE COLD IN ALEX runs 132m.

Desert Bloom (1986) **C-106m. ***½ D:** Eugene Corr. Jon Voight, JoBeth Williams, Ellen Barkin, Annabeth Gish, Allen Garfield, Jay D. Underwood. Perceptive, exquisitely realized memoir, set in 1951 Nevada—the dawn of the Atomic Age. Heroine is 13-year-old Gish, whose mother (Williams) only sees what she wants to and whose stepfather (solidly acted by Voight) is an embittered, alcoholic WW2 hero reduced to running a gas station. Corr wrote the poignantly precise script from a story by Linda Remy and himself. [PG] ▼●〗

Desert Blue (1999) **C-93m.** *** D: Morgan J. Freeman. Brendan Sexton III, Kate Hudson, Christina Ricci, Daniel von Bargen, John Heard, Lucinda Jenney, Casey Affleck, Sara Gilbert, Peter Sarsgaard, Michael Ironside. A professor of American culture and his ambitious actress-daughter find themselves stuck in a remote western town, where the young woman bonds with the locals—especially Blue, who is fixated on realizing his late father's dream of building a water park in the desert! Well-drawn characters and a sharp sense of time and place help make this a winner. Written by the director. [R] ▼〗

Deserter, The (1971-Italian-Yugoslavian) **C-99m.** *½ D: Burt Kennedy. Bekim Fehmiu, John Huston, Richard Crenna, Chuck Connors, Ricardo Montalban, Ian Bannen, Brandon de Wilde, Slim Pickens, Woody Strode, Patrick Wayne. Dull cavalry pic about Indian fighting on Mexican border. Cast is capable, except for Fehmiu, who didn't improve after THE ADVENTURERS. Aka RIDE TO GLORY. Panavision. [PG] ▼

Desert Flower (2009-British-German) **C-120m.** ** D: Sherry Horman. Liya Kebede, Sally Hawkins, Craig Parkinson, Meera Syal, Anthony Mackie, Juliet Stevenson, Timothy Spall. Spotty biopic of fashion model Waris Dirie, born a Somalian nomad, who eventually became an international spokesperson against female circumcision, which she underwent at age 5 in a barbaric ritual that continues to this day. One can sympathize with director Horman for not quite finessing a consistent tone with which to tell this story, and sometimes the film is a little slick for its own good. Beyond some genuinely harrowing scenes, there are lots of familiar faces in the cast (which may be either a plus or a distraction) and an anchoring performance by real-life model Kebede, who is at least as stunning as the subject she portrays. [R] 〗

Desert Fox: The Story of Rommel, The (1951) **88m.** *** D: Henry Hathaway. James Mason, Cedric Hardwicke, Jessica Tandy, Luther Adler, Everett Sloane, Leo G. Carroll, George Macready, Richard Boone, Robert Coote. Mason standout as Field Marshal Rommel in sensitive account of his military defeat in WW2 Africa and disillusioned return to Hitler Germany. Mason repeated role in THE DESERT RATS. ▼●〗

Desert Hearts (1985) **C-93m.** **½ D: Donna Deitch. Helen Shaver, Patricia Charbonneau, Audra Lindley, Andra Akers, Dean Butler, Jeffrey Tambor. Uptight female professor comes to Reno to get a divorce in the 1950s and is pursued by a young woman who forces her to examine her own sexuality. Debut feature for writer-director Deitch (with a contemporary nod to THE WOMEN) has its moments, but characters are sketchily developed and story moves in fits and starts. [R] ▼●〗

Desert Patrol (1958-British) **78m.** **½ D: Guy Green. Richard Attenborough, John Gregson, Michael Craig, Vincent Ball. Staunch account of British patrol attempting to blow up Axis fuel dump before pending WW2 battle of El Alamein. Originally titled SEA OF SAND. ▼〗

Desert Rats, The (1953) **88m.** *** D: Robert Wise. Richard Burton, James Mason, Robert Newton, Chips Rafferty. Fine WW2 actioner with Mason convincing as Field Marshal Rommel (repeating his role from THE DESERT FOX); Burton is British commando trying to ward off Germans in North Africa. ▼〗

Desert Song, The (1953) **C-110m.** **½ D: H. Bruce Humberstone. Kathryn Grayson, Gordon MacRae, Steve Cochran, Raymond Massey, William Conrad, Dick Wesson. Third version of Sigmund Romberg operetta set in Africa creaks along on thin plot. American MacRae is secret leader of good natives (Riffs) in battle against evil Arabs. Songs: "The Riff Song," "One Alone." Previously filmed in 1929 and 1944. ▼

Designated Mourner, The (1997-British) **C-94m.** ** D: David Hare. Miranda Richardson, Mike Nichols, David de Keyser. Endlessly talky dissertation on the death of culture, set in an unnamed country in what could be the immediate future. Nichols marries into the intellectual upper crust of this mysterious society, which has cast off its artists and rendered them virtual prisoners. Shot in three days, the film (adapted by Wallace Shawn from his play) is a series of monologues and probably should have remained a theater piece. Nichols makes a long-awaited film acting debut, but perhaps he should have waited just a little while longer. [R] ▼〗

Design for Living (1933) **90m.** *** D: Ernst Lubitsch. Fredric March, Gary Cooper, Miriam Hopkins, Edward Everett Horton, Franklin Pangborn, Isabel Jewell, Jane Darwell. Ben Hecht adapted Noel Coward's stage comedy about artist Cooper and playwright March, best friends and Americans in Paris, and what happens when they both fall in love with Hopkins. Most of the witty innuendos are left intact (even if the pacing isn't quite right). ●〗

Designing Woman (1957) **C-118m.** *** D: Vincente Minnelli. Gregory Peck, Lauren Bacall, Dolores Gray, Sam Levene, Mickey Shaughnessy, Chuck Connors, Ed Platt, Jack Cole. Sportswriter and fashion designer marry and run head-on in this chic comedy reminiscent of the great Hepburn-Tracy vehicles. Bacall and Peck do their best; George Wells won an Oscar for Best Story and Screenplay. CinemaScope. ▼●◗

Desire and Hell at Sunset Motel (1992) **C-90m.** *½ D: Allen Castle. Sherilyn Fenn, Whip Hubley, David Hewlett, David Johansen, Paul Bartel. A paranoid salesman and his wife stay at a motel in Anaheim, California, on their way to Disneyland, but get involved in blackmail and murder instead. A "comedy noir" set in 1958, this *very* low-budget effort never quite escapes its stage origins. Fenn does look great, however. [PG-13] ▼●

Desiree (1954) **C-110m.** **½ D: Henry Koster. Marlon Brando, Jean Simmons, Merle Oberon, Michael Rennie, Cameron Mitchell, Elizabeth Sellars, Cathleen Nesbitt, Richard Deacon, Carolyn Jones. Tepid, elaborate costumer: Brando plays a confused Napoleon, Simmons his seamstress love who marries another man; Oberon is quite lovely as Empress Josephine. Fiction and fact are muddled backdrop for rise and fall of the Emperor; few action scenes. CinemaScope. ▼●

Desire Me (1947) **91m.** ** D: No director credited. Greer Garson, Robert Mitchum, Richard Hart, George Zucco, Morris Ankrum. Weak melodramatic romance with Garson caught between new love and old husband, presumed dead, who returns to make problems. Familiar story not helped by limp script. Directed mostly by George Cukor, who removed his name after studio tampering; Mervyn LeRoy and Jack Conway also had a hand in it.

Desire Under the Elms (1958) **114m.** **½ D: Delbert Mann. Sophia Loren, Anthony Perkins, Burl Ives, Frank Overton. Eugene O'Neill stage piece about family hatred and greed for land. Loren miscast as Ives' young wife in love with stepson Perkins, but she sparks some life into brooding account of 19th-century New England farm story. VistaVision. ▼●◗

Desk Set (1957) **C-103m.** ***½ D: Walter Lang. Spencer Tracy, Katharine Hepburn, Gig Young, Joan Blondell, Dina Merrill, Sue Randall, Neva Patterson, Diane Jergens, Merry Anders. Broadway play becomes a vehicle for Hepburn and Tracy, a guarantee for top entertainment. He's an efficiency expert automating her research department at a TV network; they clash, argue, and fall in love. Great fun. Scripted by Phoebe and Henry Ephron, from the stage play by William Marchant. Merrill's film debut. CinemaScope. ▼●◗

Despair (1978-West German) **C-119m.** *** D: Rainer Werner Fassbinder. Dirk Bogarde, Andrea Ferreol, Volker Spengler, Klaus Lowitsch. Playwright Tom Stoppard's adaptation of the Nabokov novel concentrates too many of its wittiest lines in the first third, but the film still has its moments. Bogarde is brilliant as the Russian émigré who runs a German chocolate factory as Nazis start to take power. ▼◗

Desperado (1995) **C-106m.** ** D: Robert Rodriguez. Antonio Banderas, Joaquim de Almeida, Salma Hayek, Steve Buscemi, Cheech Marin, Quentin Tarantino, Carlos Gomez, Angel Aviles, Danny Trejo, Tito Larriva. A mysterious stranger arrives in a Mexican town, seeking revenge on the local crime boss. Opens with an amusing shaggy-dog sequence featuring Buscemi and Marin and grabs your attention with its hyperkinetic scenes of gunplay, but soon it becomes clear that the film has no story—and no point. Physical attraction of Banderas and leading lady Hayek provides its only pizazz. This is Rodriguez's reworking of his inventive debut picture, EL MARIACHI. [R] ▼●◗

Desperados, The (1969) **C-91m.** **½ D: Henry Levin. Vince Edwards, Jack Palance, George Maharis, Neville Brand, Sylvia Syms. Civil War deserters ravage the West. Not bad. [M] ▼

Desperate (1947) **73m.** **½ D: Anthony Mann. Steve Brodie, Audrey Long, Raymond Burr, Douglas Fowley, William Challee, Jason Robards, Sr. An honest truck driver is victimized by racketeers and forced to flee with his wife. Well-made little film noir, if not as good as director Mann's follow-ups (RAW DEAL, T-MEN, etc.). Also shown in computer-colored version. ▼◗

Desperate Characters (1971) **C-88m.** *** D: Frank D. Gilroy. Shirley MacLaine, Kenneth Mars, Gerald O'Loughlin, Sada Thompson, Jack Somack, Rose Gregorio, Carol Kane. Story of the horrors of day-to-day living in N.Y.C. is a bit too theatrical but benefits from excellent acting; one of MacLaine's best performances. [R] ▼●◗

Desperate Hours, The (1955) **112m.** ***½ D: William Wyler. Humphrey Bogart, Fredric March, Arthur Kennedy, Martha Scott, Dewey Martin, Gig Young, Mary Murphy, Robert Middleton. Extremely well acted account of escaped convicts terrorizing family household. From Joseph Hayes' novel and Broadway play, inspired by actual events. Remade in 1990. VistaVision. ▼●◗

Desperate Hours (1990) **C-105m.** *½ D: Michael Cimino. Mickey Rourke, Anthony Hopkins, Mimi Rogers, Lindsay Crouse, Kelly Lynch, Elias Koteas, David Morse, Shawnee Smith, Danny Gerard, Matt McGrath. Ludicrous remake of the better-than-ever 1955 nailbiter, prison escapees Rourke et al. taking over the Hopkins-Rogers household. No suspense, at times laughable use of music, with daughter-victim you'll beg to see coldcocked. Cimino's unmotivated, kamikaze disrobings of attorney Lynch have already entered the realm of modern movie folklore. [R] ▼●◗

Desperately Seeking Susan (1985) **C-104m.**
*** D: Susan Seidelman. Rosanna Arquette, Madonna, Aidan Quinn, Mark Blum, Robert Joy, Laurie Metcalf, Steven Wright, Richard Hell, Ann Magnuson, Richard Edson, John Lurie, Anne Carlisle, John Turturro. Delightfully offbeat, original comedy about a bored suburban housewife whose fascination with a kooky character she's read about in the personal ads leads to her being mistaken for the woman herself. Sort of an upscale underground film, inventively directed by Seidelman, though it doesn't sustain its buoyancy straight to the end. [PG-13]▼●▶

Desperate Measures (1998) **C-105m.** *½ D: Barbet Schroeder. Michael Keaton, Andy Garcia, Marcia Gay Harden, Brian Cox; Joseph Cross. Offensively stupid thriller about San Francisco cop Garcia and the amount of physical damage he unintentionally causes when he finds a potential bone marrow donor for his dying son: hardened con Keaton. About as bad as a movie can get from a reputable filmmaker. Try to figure out how many charges Garcia would eventually be brought up on in real life! [R]▼●▶

Desperate Trail, The (1994) **C-93m.** *** D: P. J. Pesce. Sam Elliott, Craig Sheffer, Linda Fiorentino, Bradley Whitford, Frank Whaley, John Furlong, Robin Westphal, Boots Southerland. Tough, original Western saga released direct to video, with Elliott as an unforgiving marshal whose plan to deliver Fiorentino to the hangman goes awry when she flees with genteel outlaw Sheffer. Well-written (and well-acted) Western with interesting characters, some potent violence, and surprises in store to the very end of the trail. [R]▼●▶

Despicable Me (2010) **C-95m.** **½ D: Pierre Coffin, Chris Renaud. Voices of Steve Carell, Jason Segel, Russell Brand, Julie Andrews, Will Arnett, Kristen Wiig, Miranda Cosgrove, Jack McBrayer, Danny McBride, Mindy Kaling, Dana Gaier, Elsie Fisher. In order to pull off his latest nefarious scheme, world-class villain Gru adopts three little girls from a local orphanage, planning to use them to penetrate his rival's headquarters by selling him cookies. The last thing Gru expects is to actually become fond of the girls. Amiable if unmemorable animated feature is well designed and features engaging voice work. Kids will especially enjoy the antics of Gru's pint-sized minions, who are called—minions. 3-D. [PG]▶

Destination Gobi (1953) **C-89m.** **½ D: Robert Wise. Richard Widmark, Don Taylor, Casey Adams (Max Showalter), Murvyn Vye, Darryl Hickman, Martin Milner. Unusual WW2 actioner involving U.S. naval men joining forces with natives against Japanese assaults; nice action sequences.

Destination Mars! (2002) **80m.** *** D:

Richard Lowry. Blane Wheatley, Jessica Schroeder, Bobby Harwell, Henry Amitai, Sheila K, Blake Manion, Adrian Marinovich. Irresistible parody of tacky 1950s sci-fi movies—and Ed Wood's PLAN 9 FROM OUTER SPACE in particular—done in low-grade black & white, with dialogue, costumes, and so-called special effects to match. Trouble begins when Martians discover that earthlings have built an Atmos 4X Vaporizer that can wipe out whole planets. Everyone plays it straight, which is why this is such fun to watch. Even the names in the credits are a gag. Written by Tor Lowry. The same team later reunited for MONARCH OF THE MOON.▶

Destination Moon (1950) **C-91m.** **½ D: Irving Pichel. John Archer, Warner Anderson, Tom Powers, Dick Wesson, Erin O'Brien-Moore. One of the pioneer sci-fi films about the first manned expedition to the moon, modestly mounted but still effective. Striking lunar paintings by Chesley Bonestell. Won an Oscar for its special effects. Produced by George Pal; coscripted by Robert Heinlein. Woody Woodpecker makes a "guest appearance."▼●▶

Destination Tokyo (1943) **135m.** *** D: Delmer Daves. Cary Grant, John Garfield, Alan Hale, John Ridgely, Dane Clark, Warner Anderson, William Prince. Suspenseful WW2 account of U.S. submarine sent into Japanese waters and interaction among crew. Commander Grant, seamen Garfield and Clark ring true. John Forsythe makes his film debut. Also shown in computer-colored version.▼▶

Destiny Turns On the Radio (1995) **C-101m.** BOMB D: Jack Baran. Dylan McDermott, Nancy Travis, Quentin Tarantino, James Belushi, James LeGros, Janet Carroll, David Cross, Richard Edson, Bobcat Goldthwait, Barry "Shabaka" Henley, Lisa Jane Persky, Sarah Trigger, Tracey Walter, Allen Garfield. Escaped convict goes to Las Vegas to reclaim his girlfriend and a stash of loot he left with his partner at the Marilyn Motel. However, Fate—in the form of a mysterious dude named Destiny—has its own agenda. Pseudo-hip script, utterly bereft of wit, is directed with no energy. A complete waste of time. [R]▼▶

Destroy All Monsters! (1968-Japanese) **C-88m.** **½ D: Ishiro Honda. Akira Kubo, Jun Tazaki, Yukiko Kobayashi, Yoshio Tsuchiya, Kyoko Ai, Andrew Hughes. More Toho monsters than there are in heaven (including A-listers Godzilla, Mothra, and Rodan) are assembled for this good-natured monster's ball, as they initially threaten to destroy Earth under the control of female aliens, then are redirected by humans to do battle with an obstinate King Ghidorah. Ninth Godzilla movie, originally intended as a grand finale, is an enjoyable romp, with a rousing score by series mainstay Akira

Ifukube. More or less remade in 2004 as GODZILLA: FINAL WARS. Tohoscope. [G] ◗

Destructors, The (1974-British) **C-89m.** *** D: Robert Parrish. Anthony Quinn, Michael Caine, James Mason, Maureen Kerwin, Marcel Bozzufi, Maurice Ronet, Alexandra Stewart. Good Paris-located crime melodrama with Quinn a U.S. drug agent out to stop kingpin Mason. An animated Caine is fine as a likable assassin. Original title: THE MARSEILLE CONTRACT. [PG]▼◗

Destry (1954) **C-95m.** **½ D: George Marshall. Audie Murphy, Mari Blanchard, Lyle Bettger, Lori Nelson, Thomas Mitchell, Edgar Buchanan, Wallace Ford. Audie is gun-shy sheriff who tames town and dance-hall girl without violence. The 1939 version—DESTRY RIDES AGAIN—is still unsurpassed. Later a TV series.

Destry Rides Again (1939) **94m.** **** D: George Marshall. James Stewart, Marlene Dietrich, Charles Winninger, Brian Donlevy, Una Merkel, Mischa Auer, Allen Jenkins, Irene Hervey, Jack Carson, Billy Gilbert, Samuel S. Hinds. Slam-bang, action-filled Western satire, with Stewart taming rowdy town without violence and tangling with boisterous dance-hall girl Dietrich. Marlene sings "See What the Boys in the Back Room Will Have" in this sequel to Max Brand's story, filmed in 1932, then again in 1950 (as FRENCHIE), and in 1954 (as DESTRY). Screenplay by Felix Jackson, Gertrude Purcell, and Henry Myers. Simply wonderful.▼●◗

Detective, The (1954-British) **91m.** *** D: Robert Hamer. Alec Guinness, Joan Greenwood, Peter Finch, Cecil Parker, Bernard Lee, Sidney James, Ernest Thesiger. Guinness is in rare form as G. K. Chesterton's clerical sleuth after stolen art treasures; another British gem, superbly cast. British title: FATHER BROWN.▼

Detective, The (1968) **C-114m.** *** D: Gordon Douglas. Frank Sinatra, Lee Remick, Ralph Meeker, Jacqueline Bisset, William Windom, Al Freeman, Tony Musante, Jack Klugman, Robert Duvall. Trashy script, based on Roderick Thorpe's best-selling novel, pits cops against homosexuals; more than redeemed by fast, no-nonsense direction, good acting, particularly by Sinatra and Freeman. Panavision.▼◗

Detective (1985-French) **C-95m.** ** D: Jean-Luc Godard. Claude Brasseur, Nathalie Baye, Johnny Hallyday, Laurent Terzieff, Jean-Pierre Léaud, Alain Cuny, Stephane Ferrara, Julie Delpy. The scenario takes a backseat in this talky, contrived film noir homage about a variety of characters and their business and intrigues in an elegant Paris hotel. The look and feel are uniquely of the director, but it's ultimately annoying, more a concept than a movie.

Godard dedicated this to John Cassavetes, Edgar G. Ulmer, and Clint Eastwood!▼◗

Detective Story (1951) **103m.** ***½ D: William Wyler. Kirk Douglas, Eleanor Parker, Horace McMahon, William Bendix, Lee Grant, Craig Hill, Cathy O'Donnell, Bert Freed, George Macready, Joseph Wiseman, Gladys George, Frank Faylen, Luis van Rooten, Warner Anderson, Michael Strong, Gerald Mohr. Sidney Kingsley's once-forceful play about life at a N.Y.C. police precinct has lost much of its punch, but is still a fine film. Well cast, with Douglas a bitter detective, Parker his ignored wife, and Bendix, in one of his best roles, a sympathetic colleague. McMahon (the shrewd precinct head), Wiseman (an hysterical thief), Grant (unforgettable as a frightened shoplifter), and Strong (another thief) re-create their Broadway roles. This was Grant's first film—and also her last—before being blacklisted. Screenplay by Philip Yordan and Robert Wyler (the director's brother).◗

Deterrence (2000) **C-101m.** *** D: Rod Lurie. Kevin Pollak, Timothy Hutton, Sheryl Lee Ralph, Sean Astin, Badja Djola, Mark Thompson, Michael Mantell. Absorbing brinkmanship thriller in the vein of FAIL-SAFE, with Pollak (admittedly, an unlikely choice for President of the U.S.) stranded in a Colorado diner during a snowstorm, having to make a tough decision about firing a nuclear weapon, and involving the civilians who happen to be there in the mounting drama. Contrived but exciting; feature writing-directing debut for film critic Lurie. [R]▼◗

Detour (1945) **69m.** *** D: Edgar G. Ulmer. Tom Neal, Ann Savage, Claudia Drake, Edmund MacDonald, Tim Ryan, Esther Howard. Now-legendary B movie, filmed in less than a week, is the quintessence of film noir. Neal is a hitchhiking drifter who has the misfortune to become involved with a formidable femme fatale (Savage, in an unforgettable performance). Ulmer makes the most of his meager budget. Written by Martin Goldsmith. Remade in 1992 with Tom Neal, Jr.▼◗

Detroit Heat SEE: **Detroit 9000**

Detroit 9000 (1973) **C-106m.** *½ D: Arthur Marks. Alex Rocco, Hari Rhodes, Vonetta McGee, Ella Edwards, Scatman Crothers. Cops pursue jewel thieves. Bloody blaxploitation entry with an integrated cast. Aka DETROIT HEAT. [R]▼●◗

Detroit Rock City (1999) **C-94m.** **½ D: Adam Rifkin. Edward Furlong, Giuseppe Andrews, James De Bello, Sam Huntington, Lin Shaye, Natasha Lyonne, Shannon Tweed, Joe Flaherty, KISS. Ultra-dopey teen flick about four teenagers trying to scam tickets for a KISS concert, circa 1978. Lots of crude physical comedy and head-banging metal anthems, but that's the point. Plays like a cross between I WANNA HOLD YOUR HAND and an episode of *That '70s Show.* Shaye's a hoot as a bewigged mom on a crusade to stop rock 'n' roll. The original tongue-wagging glam rockers appear only briefly at the end. Super 35. [R] ▼▶

Deuce Bigalow: European Gigolo (2005) C-83m. BOMB D: Mike Mitchell. Rob Schneider, Eddie Griffin, Jeroen Krabbé, Til Schweiger, Douglas Sills, Carlos Ponce, Charles Keating, Hanna Verboom. Ads for this woefully unfunny sequel show Schneider sitting under a phallic Leaning Tower of Pisa that appears to be protruding from his groin area. This would have been the film's best joke—except it's not in the film; nor is any other form of humor. Deuce is sent to Holland to train as a high-end Euro man whore. When he discovers some of his fellow gigolos are being killed, he jumps undercover(s). Can we possibly prevent another sequel? Famous faces appear in cameos, if that matters to you. [R] ▼▶

Deuce Bigalow: Male Gigolo (1999) C-88m. **½ D: Mike Mitchell. Rob Schneider, William Forsythe, Eddie Griffin, Arija Bareikis, Oded Fehr, Gail O'Grady, Richard Riehle, Jacqueline Obradors, Amy Poehler, Big Boy. Professional fish-tank cleaner breaks an expensive tank, and in order to pay for it becomes a gigolo. (Why not?) Potty humor and outlandish situations abound, but Schneider's character is surprisingly likable in this silly comedy. Marlo Thomas appears unbilled. Followed by a sequel. [R] ▼▶

Deuces Wild (2002) C-97m. *½ D: Scott Kalvert. Stephen Dorff, Brad Renfro, Fairuza Balk, Norman Reedus, Frankie Muniz, Matt Dillon, Balthazar Getty, Max Perlich, Deborah Harry, Drea DeMatteo, Vincent Pastore, James Franco, Johnny Knoxville, Louis Lombardi. Empty-headed, clichéd dud, a WEST SIDE STORY wannabe set in Sunset Park, Brooklyn, in the late 1950s. The Deuces are a good-guy gang and the Vipers are a bad-guy gang; temperatures rise upon the release from prison of the Viper punk (Reedus) who sold a deadly dose of heroin to the brother of Deuces Dorff and Renfro. An interesting cast is wasted. Panavision. [R] ▼▶

Devil (2010) C-80m. ** D: John Erick Dowdle. Chris Messina, Logan Marshall-Green, Jenny O'Hara, Bojana Novakovic, Bokeem Woodbine, Geoffrey Arend, Matt Craven, Jacob Vargas. In a high-rise, an elevator carrying five strangers is stalled between floors. As mechanics and police struggle to free them, the passengers quarrel and gradually realize that one of them may be the Devil himself. There's about enough plot for a half-hour TV show, but the film is occasionally suspenseful and technically well made. First in a purported trilogy, THE NIGHT CHRONICLES, from stories by M.

Night Shyamalan, but written and directed by others. Full title: THE NIGHT CHRONICLES I: DEVIL. Super 35. [PG-13] ▶

Devil and Daniel Webster, The (1941) 85m. ***½ D: William Dieterle. Edward Arnold, Walter Huston, James Craig, Anne Shirley, Jane Darwell, Simone Simon, Gene Lockhart, John Qualen, H. B. Warner. Stephen Vincent Benet's story is a visual delight, with Huston's sparkling performance as Mr. Scratch (the Devil) matched by Arnold as the loquacious Webster. Oscar-winning score by Bernard Herrmann, cinematography by Joseph August, and special effects by Vernon L. Walker all superb. Screenplay by the author and Dan Totheroh. Cut for reissue in 1952; restored to 107m. for home video, adding interesting material missing from other extant prints. Remade as SHORTCUT TO HAPPINESS. Aka ALL THAT MONEY CAN BUY and DANIEL AND THE DEVIL. ▼●▶

Devil and Max Devlin, The (1981) C-96m. ** D: Steven Hilliard Stern. Elliott Gould, Bill Cosby, Bill Cosby, Susan Anspach, Adam Rich, Julie Budd, David Knell. Gould returns to life to recruit three innocent souls for devil Cosby. Undistinguished Disney fare. [PG] ▼▶

Devil and Miss Jones, The (1941) 92m. ***½ D: Sam Wood. Jean Arthur, Robert Cummings, Charles Coburn, Spring Byington, Edmund Gwenn, S.Z. Sakall, William Demarest. Delightful social comedy by Norman Krasna; millionaire Coburn masquerades as clerk in his own department store to investigate employee complaints. A must. ▼

Devil at 4 O'Clock, The (1961) C-126m. **½ D: Mervyn LeRoy. Spencer Tracy, Frank Sinatra, Jean-Pierre Aumont, Kerwin Mathews, Barbara Luna. Static production, not saved by volcanic eruption climax, involving priest Tracy helping to evacuate children's hospital in midst of lava flow. Stars are lost in weak film. ▼●▶

Devil Dogs of the Air (1935) 86m. ** D: Lloyd Bacon. James Cagney, Pat O'Brien, Margaret Lindsay, Frank McHugh. Tiresome potboiler with Marine Air Corps rivalry between Cagney and O'Brien. Their personalities, and good stunt-flying scenes, are only saving grace. ▼

Devil-Doll (1936) 79m. *** D: Tod Browning. Lionel Barrymore, Maureen O'Sullivan, Frank Lawton, Robert Greig, Lucy Beaumont, Henry B. Walthall, Grace Ford, Rafaela Ottiano. Very entertaining yarn of Devil's Island escapee Barrymore shrinking humans to doll size to carry out nefarious schemes. Coscripted by Erich von Stroheim. ▼●▶

Devil Doll (1964-British) 80m. *** D: Lindsay Shonteff. Bryant Haliday, William Sylvester, Yvonne Romain, Philip Ray.

Obscure, underrated mystery features an eerily effective Haliday as a hypnotist-ventriloquist trying to transfer Romain's soul into that of a dummy, as he had already done with his onetime assistant. An exquisitely tailored, sharply edited sleeper. ▼❶

Devil in a Blue Dress (1995) **C-102m.** **½ D: Carl Franklin. Denzel Washington, Tom Sizemore, Jennifer Beals, Don Cheadle, Maury Chaykin, Terry Kinney, Mel Winkler, Albert Hall, Lisa Nicole Carson, Jernard Burks, Barry Shabaka Henley. It's L.A., 1948; Washington is unemployed and thus easy prey for a hood who needs a favor done. All he has to do is find an elusive white woman, the former fiancée of a mayoral candidate. Oozing with atmosphere and period detail, but the look and feel overwhelm the convoluted (and not always compelling) story. Washington is terrific in a tailor-made part as Easy Rawlins; adapted from Walter Mosley's novel. Black point of view is the film's strong suit, making it unique in the film noir genre. [R] ▼❶❷

Devil in Love, The (1966-Italian) **97m.** *½ D: Ettore Scola. Vittorio Gassman, Mickey Rooney, Claudine Auger, Ettore Manni, Annabella Incontrera. Gassman comes up from Hell during the French Renaissance to botch up an impending peace between Rome and Florence, but loses his powers when he falls for Auger. Comedy is both heavy-handed and unfunny.

Devil in the Flesh (1946-French) **110m.** ***½ D: Claude Autant-Lara. Gérard Philipe, Micheline Presle, Denise Grey, Jacques Tati. Exquisitely filmed, compassionate story of WW1 love affair between married woman and sensitive high school student. Controversial in its day because of sensual love scenes and cuckolding of soldier husband. Remade in 1986. ▼

Devil in the Flesh (1986-Italian-French) **C-110m.** *** D: Marco Bellocchio. Maruschka Detmers, Federico Pitzalis, Anita Laurenzi, Riccardo De Torrebruna. Director Bellocchio remakes and updates the 1946 French classic as another of his studies of madness. Dutch actress Detmers burns up the screen as the going-nutty beauty torn between her terrorist boyfriend (De Torrebruna) and a handsome young boy (Pitzalis). Reportedly the first mainstream film in which a respected actress was involved in an explicitly pornographic sex scene. Available in both R- and X-rated versions. ▼❶❷

Devil in the House of Exorcism SEE: **Lisa and the Devil**

Devil Is a Woman, The (1935) **83m.** *** D: Josef von Sternberg. Marlene Dietrich, Lionel Atwill, Cesar Romero, Edward Everett Horton, Alison Skipworth. Sumptuous-looking film about alluring but heartless woman and the men who all but ruin their lives for her, set against backdrop of 19th-century Spanish revolution. Hypnotic, if dramatically shaky; Luis Buñuel used same source material for THAT OBSCURE OBJECT OF DESIRE. ▼❶

Devil Is a Woman, The (1975-Italian) **C-105m.** BOMB D: Damiano Damiani. Glenda Jackson, Adolfo Celi, Lisa Harrow, Claudio Cassinelli, Arnoldo Foa, Francisco Rabal. Ponderous, superficial melodrama: Jackson, the head of a religious hostel, casts spells over its "permanent residents." The convent is more like a psycho ward than a place for religious meditation. Indifferently acted, technically atrocious. Widescreen. [R] ▼

Devil Makes Three, The (1952) **96m.** ** D: Andrew Marton. Gene Kelly, Pier Angeli, Richard Egan, Claus Clausen. Kelly (none too convincing in one of his rare nonmusicals) plays a soldier returning to Munich to thank family who helped him during WW2; he becomes involved with daughter Angeli and black market gangs.

Devils, The (1971-British) **C-109m.** **½ D: Ken Russell. Oliver Reed, Vanessa Redgrave, Dudley Sutton, Max Adrian, Gemma Jones, Murray Melvin, Michael Gothard. Fine performances save confused mixture of history, comedy, and surrealism in wide-eyed adaptation of Whiting play and Huxley book dealing with witch-craft and politics in 17th-century France. A mad movie, with fiery finale not for the squeamish. Original British version is 12 minutes longer. Panavision. [R—edited from original X version] ▼

Devil's Advocate, The (1997) **C-144m.** *** D: Taylor Hackford. Al Pacino, Keanu Reeves, Charlize Theron, Jeffrey Jones, Judith Ivey, Connie Nielsen, Craig T. Nelson, Tamara Tunie, Debra Monk, Heather Matarazzo. Wild, over-the-top movie about a young hotshot lawyer from Florida who's recruited to join a sleek N.Y.C. firm run by a charming megalomaniac (Pacino) who earmarks the newcomer for Big Things. But there are devilish hints that all is not right. Reeves is completely believable, and Pacino gives a delicious, pull-out-the-stops performance as his manipulative mentor. The film goes on too long, but it's spiked with arresting scenes and fine performances. Great showcase, too, for Theron as Reeves' impressionable wife. Delroy Lindo appears unbilled. Panavision. [R] ▼❶

Devil's Angels (1967) **C-84m.** *½ D: Daniel Haller. John Cassavetes, Beverly Adams, Mimsy Farmer, Leo Gordon. Killer cyclists head for outlaw sanctuary breaking everything in their way. Lurid and cheap. Panavision. [PG] ▼

Devil's Backbone, The (2001-Spanish-Mexican) **C-106m.** ***½ D: Guillermo del Toro. Eduardo Noriega, Marisa Paredes, Federico Luppi, Iñigo Garcés, Fernando Tielve, Irene Visedo, Berta Ojea. A remote outpost serves as a school and shelter for displaced boys in the midst of the Spanish Civil War . . . and harbors the ghost of one youngster whose spirit cannot rest. A fascinating ghost story with multiple layers, strikingly shot and designed. Cowritten by the director, Antonio Trashorras, and David Muñoz. [R]▼❶

Devil's Bride, The (1968-British) **C-95m.** *** D: Terence Fisher. Christopher Lee, Charles Gray, Nike Arrighi, Patrick Mower, Sarah Lawson, Paul Eddington. Taut filming of Dennis Wheatley novel. Duc de Richleau (Lee) assists young friend under spell of Mocate, ultra-evil Satanist. Watch out for that climax! British title: THE DEVIL RIDES OUT. [G]▼❶

Devil's Brigade, The (1968) **C-130m. ** D: Andrew V. McLaglen. William Holden, Cliff Robertson, Vince Edwards, Michael Rennie, Dana Andrews, Carroll O'Connor, Gretchen Wyler, Andrew Prine, Claude Akins, Richard Jaeckel, Paul Hornung, Patric Knowles, James Craig, Richard Dawson. Standard WW2 fare about reckless recruits fashioned into creditable fighting unit; goes on far too long. Holden is wasted. Panavision.▼❶❶

Devil's Brother, The (1933) **88m.** *** D: Hal Roach, Charles R. Rogers. Stan Laurel, Oliver Hardy, Dennis King, Thelma Todd, James Finlayson, Henry Armetta. Destitute Stan and Ollie become bungling henchmen for notorious singing bandit Fra Diavolo (King) in this adaptation of Auber's 1830 operetta. One of the comedy team's best features. Aka FRA DIAVOLO. ▼❶❶

Devil's Disciple, The (1959-British) **82m.** ***½ D: Guy Hamilton. Burt Lancaster, Kirk Douglas, Laurence Olivier, Janette Scott, Eva LeGallienne, Harry Andrews, Basil Sydney, George Rose, Neil McCallum, David Horne, Mervyn Johns. Sparkling adaptation of George Bernard Shaw's satire, set during American Revolution, with standout performances by star trio (notably Olivier as General Burgoyne, who serves as Shaw's mouthpiece). Shows how, in Shaw's view, the bumbling British managed to lose their colonies. Screenplay by John Dighton and Roland Kibbee.▼

Devil's Doorway (1950) **84m.** *** D: Anthony Mann. Robert Taylor, Louis Calhern, Paula Raymond, Marshall Thompson, Edgar Buchanan. Well-turned Western with offbeat casting of Taylor as Indian who served in Civil War, returning home to find that he must fight to right the injustices done against his people. ❶

Devil's Eye, The (1960-Swedish) **90m.** *** D: Ingmar Bergman. Jarl Kulle, Bibi Andersson, Nils Poppe, Sture Lagerwall. A woman's chastity gives the Devil sty in his eye, so he sends Don Juan back to Earth from Hell to seduce her, but the modern-day woman finds his old-fashioned charm

amusing rather than irresistible. Droll Bergman comedy is a bit slow, but witty and playful.▼

Devil's Impostor, The SEE: **Pope Joan**
Devil's Men, The SEE: **Land of the Minotaur**

Devil's Own, The (1966-British) **C-90m.** *** D: Cyril Frankel. Joan Fontaine, Kay Walsh, Alec McCowen, Ann Bell, Ingrid Brett, Gwen ffrangcon-Davies. Good Hammer chiller with Fontaine as headmistress of private school who learns that a student is to be sacrificed by a local voodoo cult. British title: THE WITCHES.▼❶

Devil's Own, The (1997) **C-110m.** **½ D: Alan J. Pakula. Harrison Ford, Brad Pitt, Margaret Colin, Ruben Blades, Treat Williams, George Hearn, Mitchell Ryan, Natascha McElhone, Simon Jones, Julia Stiles. Young Irish terrorist comes to N.Y.C. to broker an arms deal, and gets room and board from a straight-arrow cop who has no idea who he is. Watchable film has two charismatic stars playing deeply committed characters; their separate stories build in intensity, but when their lives finally intersect the story peters out. Panavision. [R] ▼❶

Devil's Playground, The (1976-Australian) **C-107m.** *** D: Fred Schepisi. Arthur Dignam, Nick Tate, Simon Burke, Charles McCallum, John Frawley, Jonathan Hardy, Gerry Duggan. Young boys reaching puberty act out sexually while boarded at Roman Catholic school; meanwhile, their teachers have problems of their own. Pointed and well made, if a bit predictable.▼❶

Devil's Rain, The (1975) **C-85m.** **½ D: Robert Fuest. Ernest Borgnine, Ida Lupino, William Shatner, Tom Skerritt, Eddie Albert, Keenan Wynn, Joan Prather. Offbeat approach to story of Satanists provides some effective horror and also some unintentional humor. Most of the cast melts in a memorable finale. John Travolta makes his debut in a bit part. Todd-AO 35. [PG] ▼❶

Devil's Rejects, The (2005) **C-101m.** **½ D: Rob Zombie. Sid Haig, Bill Moseley, Sheri Moon Zombie, Ken Foree, William Forsythe, Geoffrey Lewis, Danny Trejo, Leslie Easterbrook, Priscilla Barnes. The three killers from Zombie's previous effort, HOUSE OF 1000 CORPSES, go on a violent road trip and find themselves stalked by a sheriff who shares their sadistic tendencies. Gripping horror film captures the mood and aesthetics of late '60s/early '70s exploitation films, but be warned: it's relentlessly violent, horrifying, and depressing. Filled with B-movie celebrity cameos and retro counterculture themes. Also available in unrated version. [R] ▼❶

Devil's Undead, The SEE: **Nothing but the Night**
Devil's Wanton, The (1949-Swedish) **72m.**

**½ D: Ingmar Bergman. Doris Svedlund, Birger Malmsten, Eva Henning, Hasse Ekman. Sober account of desperate girl finding romance with another equally unhappy soul, reaffirming their faith in humanity. Not released in U.S. until 1962.▼

Devil's Widow, The SEE: **Ballad of Tam Lin, The**

Devil Wears Prada, The (2006) C-109m. *** D: David Frankel. Meryl Streep, Anne Hathaway, Stanley Tucci, Simon Baker, Emily Blunt, Adrian Grenier, David Marshall Grant, James Naughton, Tracie Thoms, Rebecca Mader, Gisele Bündchen. Slick adaptation of Lauren Weisberger's bestselling roman à clef about working as personal assistant to the fashion magazine editor from hell. Streep dominates the proceedings with a wonderfully nuanced performance, never veering toward caricature; Hathaway is just right as the naïve college grad who gets a crash course in office politics and survival at the risk of losing her devoted boyfriend. Nice work, too, from Tucci (as one of Streep's loyal editors) and Blunt (as her long-suffering first assistant). Several fashionistas appear as themselves. Super 35. [PG-13]❍

Devil Within Her, The (1975-British) C-90m. *½ D: Peter Sasdy. Joan Collins, Eileen Atkins, Donald Pleasence, Ralph Bates, Caroline Munro, Hilary Mason, John Steiner. Collins' newborn baby is possessed. Another idiotic ROSEMARY'S BABY/EXORCIST rip-off. Aka I DON'T WANT TO BE BORN. [R]▼

Devonsville Terror, The (1983) C-82m. ** D: Ulli Lommel. Suzanna Love, Robert Walker, Donald Pleasence, Paul Wilson. Love (wife of German director Lommel) is the new teacher in the town of Devonsville, a burg haunted by a witch's curse from 300 years ago. Copycat horror film steals its climax directly from RAIDERS OF THE LOST ARK.▼❍

Devotion (1946) 107m. **½ D: Curtis Bernhardt. Olivia de Havilland, Ida Lupino, Paul Henreid, Sydney Greenstreet, Nancy Coleman, Arthur Kennedy, Dame May Whitty. Powerful real-life story of Brontë sisters becomes routine love triangle with Henreid in the middle; worthwhile for intense, dramatic performances. Made in 1943.❍

D. I., The (1957) 106m. **½ D: Jack Webb. Jack Webb, Don Dubbins, Lin McCarthy, Jackie Loughery, Monica Lewis, Virginia Gregg, Barbara Pepper. Ostensibly realistic account of Marine basic training is today a wonderful exercise in high camp. Webb is emotionally empty sergeant trying to whip his raw recruits (most of them played by actual soldiers) into shape; stubborn Dubbins is the chief thorn in his side. Sequence where soldiers search for a "murdered" sand flea is priceless. Story reused 13 years later (but with a different outcome) for a TVM, TRIBES.▼❍

Diabolical Dr. Mabuse, The SEE: **1,000 Eyes of Dr. Mabuse, The**

Diabolik SEE **Danger: Diabolik**

Diabolique (1955-French) 114m. ***½ D: Henri-Georges Clouzot. Simone Signoret, Vera Clouzot, Paul Meurisse, Charles Vanel, Michel Serrault. Tyrannical school-master (Meurisse) is bumped off by his long-suffering wife (Clouzot) and mistress (Signoret). Classic chiller builds slowly, surely to final quarter hour that will drive you right up the wall. A must. Older American prints run 107m. Aka LES DIABOLIQUES; remade for U.S. TV as REFLECTIONS OF MURDER (1974) and HOUSE OF SECRETS (1993), and for theaters in 1996. Rereleased theatrically in 1994 with 9m. of footage edited out of original U.S. theatrical version.▼❍

Diabolique (1996) C-107m. *½ D: Jeremiah Chechik. Sharon Stone, Isabelle Adjani, Chazz Palminteri, Kathy Bates, Spalding Gray, Shirley Knight, Allen Garfield, Adam Hann-Byrd, Clea Lewis. Top-notch cast founders in this amazingly monotonous (not to mention crude and embarrassing) redo of the 1955 classic, with Palminteri cast as the unmerciful school-master, Stone his icy, murderous mistress, and Adjani his more reserved wife. This dreary film thoroughly trashes the memory of the original—and even the made-for-TV remakes! [R]▼❍

Diagnosis: Murder (1975-British) C-95m. *** D: Sidney Hayers. Christopher Lee, Judy Geeson, Jon Finch, Tony Beckley, Dilys Hamlett, Jane Merrow. Psychiatrist is drawn into bizarre sequence of events when his wife disappears and he is accused of murdering her. Solid little suspenser.

Dial M for Murder (1954) C-105m. *** D: Alfred Hitchcock. Ray Milland, Grace Kelly, Robert Cummings, John Williams, Anthony Dawson. Frederick Knott's suspense play of man plotting wife's murder and subsequent police investigation: stagey at times but slick and entertaining. Remade for TV in 1981 with Angie Dickinson and Christopher Plummer, and in 1998 as A PERFECT MURDER. 3-D. ▼❍

Diamond Head (1963) C-107m. **½ D: Guy Green. Charlton Heston, Yvette Mimieux, George Chakiris, France Nuyen, James Darren, Aline MacMahon, Elizabeth Allen. Soap opera set in Hawaii with Heston the domineering head of his family, whose dictates almost ruin their lives. Panavision.▼❍

Diamond Horseshoe (1945) C-104m. **½ D: George Seaton. Betty Grable, Dick Haymes, Phil Silvers, William Gaxton, Beatrice Kay, Carmen Cavallaro, Margaret Dumont. Musical performer Grable has to choose between a long-cherished dream of luxury and life with struggling med student-cum-singer Haymes. Colorful escapism, with good Harry Warren–Mack Gordon songs: "The More I See You," "I Wish I Knew." Original title: BILLY ROSE'S DIAMOND HORSESHOE.

Diamond Lust SEE: **Kingfisher Caper, The**

Diamond Men (2001) **C-100m.** ******* D: Daniel M. Cohen. Robert Forster, Donnie Wahlberg, Jasmine Guy, Bess Armstrong, George Coe, Kristen Minter. A veteran diamond salesman, about to be put out to pasture, agrees to break in a "new guy" on his route in Pennsylvania. As the older man imparts his wisdom, the younger man tries to help his widowed mentor open himself up to female companionship. A small but irresistibly likable film, anchored by Forster's solid performance, which even makes an off-kilter denouement palatable. Written by the director. ▼❂

Diamonds (1975-Israeli) **C-101m.** ****** D: Menahem Golan. Robert Shaw, Richard Roundtree, Shelley Winters, Barbara (Hershey) Seagull, Shai K. Ophir. OK heist movie with Shaw in dual role, as diamond merchant who masterminds break-in at Tel Aviv diamond vault and twin brother who designed the security system there. Good location work in Tel Aviv and Jerusalem. [PG]▼❂

Diamonds (1999) **C-91m.** ******* D: John Asher. Kirk Douglas, Dan Aykroyd, Corbin Allred, Lauren Bacall, Kurt Fuller, Jenny McCarthy, Mariah O'Brien, John Landis. An elderly ex-boxer goes on a trip with his alienated son and loving grandson that winds up in Reno, where he searches for diamonds he stashed away decades ago. A tailor-made vehicle for Douglas makes excellent use of his macho image, his movie past (through clips from CHAMPION showing him in the ring), and even his real-life stroke in telling its likable, sentimental story. [PG-13]▼❂

Diamonds Are Forever (1971-British) **C-119m.** *****½** D: Guy Hamilton. Sean Connery, Jill St. John, Charles Gray, Lana Wood, Jimmy Dean, Bruce Cabot, Bruce Glover, Putter Smith, Bernard Lee, Lois Maxwell, Desmond Llewelyn, Leonard Barr, Laurence Naismith, Marc Lawrence. After a one-picture hiatus, Connery returned as James Bond in this colorful comic-book adventure set in Las Vegas; closer in spirit to Republic serials than Ian Fleming, but great fun. Panavision. [PG]▼❂❂

Diamond's Edge SEE: **Just Ask for Diamond**

Diamonds for Breakfast (1968-British) **C-102m.** ****** D: Christopher Morahan. Marcello Mastroianni, Rita Tushingham, Warren Mitchell, Elaine Taylor, Francisca Tu, Maggie Blye. Son of Russian nobleman tries to steal royal diamonds his father gambled away on the night of his birth. Offbeat comedy caper with fantasy elements just doesn't work, relies heavily on Mastroianni charm. [M/PG]

Diamond Skulls SEE: **Dark Obsession**

Diane (1956) **C-110m.** ****½** D: David Miller. Lana Turner, Pedro Armendariz, Roger Moore, Marisa Pavan, Sir Cedric Hardwicke, Henry Daniell. Although predictable, medieval romance has good cast, gorgeous sets and costumes, and comes off surprisingly well. Lana looks lovely, and Miklos Rozsa's score helps set the mood. CinemaScope. ▼❂

Diary of a Chambermaid (1946) **87m.** ****** D: Jean Renoir. Paulette Goddard, Hurd Hatfield, Francis Lederer, Burgess Meredith, Judith Anderson, Irene Ryan, Florence Bates, Reginald Owen. Uneasy attempt at Continental-style romantic melodrama, with blonde Goddard as outspoken maid who arouses all sorts of emotions in her snooty household. Tries hard, but never really sure of what it wants to be. Meredith as nutsy neighbor and Ryan as timid scullery maid do their best; Meredith also coproduced and wrote the screenplay. Remade in 1964. ▼

Diary of a Chambermaid (1964-French) **87m.** *****½** D: Luis Buñuel. Jeanne Moreau, Michel Piccoli, Georges Geret, Francoise Lugagne, Daniel Ivernel, Jean Ozenne. Remake of Jean Renoir's 1946 film concerns fascism in France in 1939 and how the bourgeoisie are viewed by maid Moreau. Sharp, unrelenting film from one of the great directors. Franscope. ▼❂❂

Diary of a Country Priest (1951-French) **120m.** *****½** D: Robert Bresson. Claude Laydu, Nicole Ladmiral, Jean Riveyre, Nicole Maurey, Andre Guibert, Martine Lemaire. The life and death of an unhappy young priest attempting to minister to his first parish in rural France. Slow moving but rewarding, with brilliantly stylized direction. Bresson also scripted. ▼❂❂

Diary of a Hitman (1992) **C-91m.** ******* D: Roy London. Forest Whitaker, John Bedford-Lloyd, James Belushi, Lois Chiles, Sharon Stone, Sherilyn Fenn, Seymour Cassel, Lewis Smith. Assassin-for-hire Whitaker plans to retire after one last job, but his intended victim (Fenn) tries to convince him to spare her. Riveting little thriller is well directed and extremely well acted by all (with kudos to Whitaker and especially Fenn). Scripted by Kenneth Pressman, based on his play *Insider's Price*. [R]▼❂

Diary of a Lost Girl (1929-German) **104m.** *****½** D: G. W. Pabst. Louise Brooks, Fritz Rasp, Josef Ravensky, Sybille Schmitz, Valeska Gert. Pabst and Brooks' followup to their PANDORA'S BOX is even more sordid, yet in some ways more intriguing: Louise is, in succession, raped, gives birth, is put in a detention home, then a brothel, inherits money, marries, is widowed . . . and writer Rudolf Leonhardt claims only the first half of his script was filmed. Fascinating nonetheless, with an explicitness that's still surprising. ▼○❶

Diary of a Mad Black Woman (2005) C-116m. *½ D: Darren Grant. Kimberly Elise, Steve Harris, Tyler Perry, Cicely Tyson, Shemar Moore, Tamara Taylor. Dumped by a hotshot lawyer husband with ties to unsavory characters, Elise reinvents herself by returning to her much humbler family, taking a modest job, and dating a romantically sincere hunk. If you've ever wondered what it would be like to have The Three Stooges show up in an otherwise straight production of *A Streetcar Named Desire*, this is probably the closest approximation. Perry, who wrote the play on which this is based, plays three characters, including a drag grandma named Madea. Elise strives mightily to keep her head above the water with an impassioned performance, but here comes the tide. Followed by MADEA'S FAMILY REUNION. Aka TYLER PERRY'S DIARY OF A MAD BLACK WOMAN. [PG-13]▼❶

Diary of a Mad Housewife (1970) C-103m. **½ D: Frank Perry. Richard Benjamin, Frank Langella, Carrie Snodgress, Lorraine Cullen, Frannie Michel, Katherine Meskill. Interesting but pointless story of harried N.Y.C. wife finding much needed release via affair with self-centered Langella. Asinine husband Benjamin would drive anyone mad. Peter Boyle has prominent bit in final scene. Script by Eleanor Perry from Sue Kaufman's novel. [R]▼

Diary of Anne Frank, The (1959) 170m. ***½ D: George Stevens. Millie Perkins, Joseph Schildkraut, Shelley Winters, Richard Beymer, Lou Jacobi, Diane Baker, Ed Wynn. Meticulously produced version of Broadway drama dealing with Jewish refugees hiding in WW2 Amsterdam. Unfortunately, Perkins never captures pivotal charm of title character, though Schildkraut is fine as father Frank. Winters won Supporting Actress Oscar as shrill Mrs. Van Daan, ever fearful of Nazi arrest, and the cinematography (William C. Mellor) and art direction-set decoration also earned Academy Awards. Frances Goodrich and Albert Hackett utilized Anne's diary for their stage play and its screen adaptation. Later cut to 156m. Remade several times. CinemaScope.▼○❶

Diary of a Wimpy Kid (2010) C-94m. **½ D: Thor Freudenthal. Zachary Gordon, Robert Capron, Rachael Harris, Steve Zahn, Devon Bostick, Chloë Grace Moretz, Grayson Russell, Laine MacNeil. In this adaptation of Jeff Kinney's best-selling illustrated kids' book, a middle school troublemaker rebels against parents, teachers, fellow students, and just about everyone else as he details his feelings in his daily journal. Full of the typical pranks and shenanigans you'd expect to find in this type of film, there will still be pangs of recognition for young viewers and nostalgic parents as well. Unfortunately,

the book's more intriguing subversive elements have been homogenized to the point that even DENNIS THE MENACE seems edgier. Followed by a sequel. [PG]❶

Diary of a Wimpy Kid: Rodrick Rules (2011) C-99m. **½ D: David Bowers. Zachary Gordon, Devon Bostick, Rachael Harris, Robert Capron, Steve Zahn, Peyton List, Laine MacNeil, Connor Fielding, Owen Fielding, Grayson Russell. Sequel to the 2010 hit comedy based on Jeff Kinney's best-selling series of kids' books is more of the same, with the emphasis this time on Wimpy Kid Greg Heffley's relationship with older brother Rodrick, who seems to enjoy torturing the poor guy. With their parents demanding a truce, the two siblings are left alone for a weekend and get into more trouble and slapstick situations than one could imagine. Capable cast makes this cartoonish, sitcom-style material work better than you might expect. Super 35. [PG]❶

Diary of Forbidden Dreams SEE: **What?**

Diary of Oharu SEE: **Life of Oharu, The**

Diary of the Dead (2008) C-95m. ** D: George A. Romero. Joshua Close, Scott Wentworth, Michelle Morgan, Joe Dinicol, Shawn Roberts, Amy Lalonde, Philip Riccio, Megan Park. When the dead revive and attack the living, a group of Pennsylvania college students try to flee to safety in a Winnebago, making a documentary as they go; this movie is supposedly that film. The scale of Romero's newest "living dead" outing is smaller than most of them. Unfortunately, pacing is erratic (at times boringly slow), and the characters are a mixed bag, including a highly unlikely college professor. Fans will embrace this; others beware. Listen for voice cameos by noted horror writers and actors. Aka GEORGE A. ROMERO'S DIARY OF THE DEAD. [R]❶

Dice Rules (1991) C-87m. **½ D: Jay Dubin. Andrew Dice Clay. Film opens with a series of curious and mostly embarrassing blackout skits with Clay imitating Jerry Lewis! Finally it moves on to the standup comic's sold-out Madison Square Garden concert, in which his audience communication is total, and his sex-oriented material is predictably crude, embarrassing, outrageous—and often very funny. [NC-17]▼❶

Dick (1999) C-95m. *** D: Andrew Fleming. Kirsten Dunst, Michelle Williams, Dan Hedaya, Dave Foley, Saul Rubinek, Harry Shearer, Jim Breuer, Will Ferrell, Teri Garr, Bruce McCulloch, Ted McGinley, G.D. Spradlin, Ana Gasteyer, Ryan Reynolds. Clever cross of CLUELESS and ALL THE PRESIDENT'S MEN has two likable teenage airheads (delightfully played by Dunst and Williams) stumbling into all the key players in the Watergate scandal—up to and including President Richard Nixon himself (Hedaya)—but never having an inkling of what is going on. Funny script by Fleming and Sheryl Longin is even more enjoyable if you remember the real-life events of the 1970s. [PG-13]▼)

Dickie Roberts: Former Child Star (2003) **C-98m.** ** D: Sam Weisman. David Spade, Mary McCormack, Jon Lovitz, Craig Bierko, Jenna Boyd, Scott Terra, Alyssa Milano, Doris Roberts, Rob Reiner, Leif Garrett, Barry Williams, Dustin Diamond, Danny Bonaduce, Edie McClurg. Washed-up former TV moppet Spade pays a family to allow him to move in and experience the childhood he never had in order for him to win a part in Reiner's new movie. Alternately smart-alecky and touchy-feely, this comedy (cowritten by Spade) isn't sure what it wants to be. Cast is peppered with real-life former child stars, many of whom appear in a music-video–style finale (including a few ringers like Jeff Conaway and Charlene Tilton). Panavision. [PG-13] ▼)

Dick Tracy series SEE: *Leonard Maltin's Classic Movie Guide*

Dick Tracy (1990) **C-104m.** *** D: Warren Beatty. Warren Beatty, Madonna, Al Pacino, Glenne Headly, Charlie Korsmo, Mandy Patinkin, Charles Durning, Paul Sorvino, William Forsythe, Seymour Cassel, Dustin Hoffman, Dick Van Dyke, Catherine O'Hara, James Caan, Michael J. Pollard, Estelle Parsons, James Tolkan, R.G. Armstrong, Kathy Bates. Colorful, high-style adaptation of the Chester Gould comic strip classic, with Beatty redefining the hawk-nosed, jut-jawed hero. Story is simple in the extreme, but there's so much to take in you really don't mind: a galaxy of guest stars as Gould's grotesque villains, eye-popping, Academy Award–winning makeup and art direction, and Madonna singing new Stephen Sondheim songs (if a few too many). One of them, "Sooner or Later (I Always Get My Man)," also won an Oscar. Standout: Pacino's hilarious, over-the-top performance as Big Boy Caprice. Super 35. [PG]▼●)

Did You Hear About the Morgans? (2009) **C-103m.** ** D: Marc Lawrence. Hugh Grant, Sarah Jessica Parker, Mary Steenburgen, Sam Elliott, Michael Kelly, Elisabeth Moss, Jesse Liebman, Dana Ivey, Wilford Brimley, Beth Fowler, Seth Gilliam. Separated N.Y.C. power couple witness a murder one night and are shuffled off to a witness relocation program in rural Wyoming. There they meet all the local yokels, awkwardly adjust to country living, and slowly rekindle the fires of their failing marriage. Mindless, predictable *Green Acres*–inspired hokum has appealing stars but little more to recommend it. Too bad Arnold the Pig wasn't available for a cameo. Hawk Scope. [PG-13] ▷)

Did You Hear the One About the Traveling Saleslady? (1968) **C-97m.** BOMB D: Don Weis. Phyllis Diller, Bob Denver, Joe Flynn, Eileen Wesson, Jeanette Nolan, Bob Hastings, David Hartman, Charles Lane, Kent McCord. You've all heard it, so why bother watching this dud. For only the most fervent Diller fans. Techniscope.

Die Another Day (2002) **C-132m.** *** D: Lee Tamahori. Pierce Brosnan, Halle Berry, Toby Stephens, Rosamund Pike, Rick Yune, Judi Dench, John Cleese, Michael Madsen, Samantha Bond. Entertaining James Bond outing, in the modern mode: less sophistication, more computer-generated effects. Bond is taken prisoner in Korea, ultimately freed to wage a battle of wits with a megalomaniacal industrialist (Stephens—the son of Maggie Smith and Robert Stephens). Along the way he joins forces with a sexy NSA agent named Jinx (Berry). Some of the effects are absurdly unrealistic (but then, so is Dench's renouncement of her top agent). Goes on one segment too long . . . but still fun to watch. Madonna sings (and cowrote) the title song, and appears unbilled. Panavision. [PG-13] ▼)

Die! Die! My Darling! (1965-British) **C-97m.** **½ D: Silvio Narizzano. Tallulah Bankhead, Stefanie Powers, Peter Vaughan, Donald Sutherland, Yootha Joyce. Tallulah, in her last film, has field day as weirdo who keeps Powers under lock and key for personal vengeance against the death of her son. Engaging fun, especially for Bankhead devotees. Script by Richard Matheson. Original British title: FANATIC.▼)

Die Hard (1988) **C-131m.** *** D: John McTiernan. Bruce Willis, Alan Rickman, Bonnie Bedelia, Alexander Godunov, Reginald VelJohnson, Paul Gleason, De'voreaux White, William Atherton, Hart Bochner, James Shigeta, Lorenzo Caccialanza, Robert Davi, Rick Ducommun, Rebecca Broussard. Dynamite action yarn about a N.Y.C. cop who just happens to be visiting an L.A. highrise when it's commandeered by terrorist thieves. Great action scenes and stunts, with Richard Edlund's special effects, and a perfect part for Willis, who plays cat-and-mouse with bad guy Rickman. Marred only by overlength and too many needlessly stupid supporting characters. Followed by three sequels. Panavision. [R]▼●)

Die Hard 2 (1990) **C-124m.** *** D: Renny Harlin. Bruce Willis, Bonnie Bedelia, William Atherton, Reginald VelJohnson, Franco Nero, William Sadler, John Amos, Dennis Franz, Art Evans, Fred Dalton Thompson, Sheila McCarthy, Robert Patrick, John Leguizamo, Don Harvey, Vondie Curtis Hall, Colm Meaney, Robert Costanzo. Stupendously unbelievable—but very entertaining—sequel to the action hit; while waiting for his wife to land at Washington's Dulles Airport, Willis dives head-first into trouble when he gets wind of an impending terrorist-type plot. Lots of violent, large-scale action, and lots of fun—just don't look for lots of logic. Based on Walter Wager's novel *58 Minutes.* Panavision. [R]▼●)

Die Hard With a Vengeance (1995) **C-**

128m. ******* D: John McTiernan. Bruce Willis, Jeremy Irons, Samuel L. Jackson, Graham Greene, Colleen Camp, Larry Bryggman, Anthony Peck, Nick Wyman, Sam Phillips. A madman (Irons) holds N.Y.C. hostage with bombings—and threats of more—targeting his demands at ousted cop John McClane (Willis), who inadvertently acquires a partner in hostile Harlem storekeeper Jackson. Logic and motivation take a backseat to big-scale action in this nonstop roller-coaster ride; it's like watching 12 chapters of a high-tech Saturday matinee serial all at once. Followed by LIVE FREE OR DIE HARD. Panavision. [R]▼●)

Die Laughing (1980) **C-108m.** BOMB D: Jeff Werner. Robby Benson, Linda Grovenor, Charles Durning, Elsa Lanchester, Bud Cort, Peter Coyote. Benson is star, coauthor, coproducer, and composer of this sophomoric black comedy and gives an excruciating performance as a cabbie who accidentally becomes implicated in the murder of a nuclear scientist. Cort is disgustingly oily as fascist villain. [PG]▼

Die Mommie Die! (2003) **C-90m.** ****½** D: Mark Rucker. Charles Busch, Philip Baker Hall, Jason Priestley, Frances Conroy, Natasha Lyonne, Stark Sands, Victor Raider-Wexler, Nora Dunn, Sara Gilbert. Fitfully amusing spoof of Ross Hunter–style Hollywood melodramas, with drag performer Busch cast as Angela Arden, a faded torch singer unhappily married to a domineering movie mogul and saddled with two twisted children. Based on Busch's play; despite some funny moments, this probably works better onstage. [R]▼

Die, Monster, Die! (1965) **C-80m.** ****** D: Daniel Haller. Boris Karloff, Nick Adams, Freda Jackson, Suzan Farmer, Terence de Marney, Patrick Magee. Based on H. P. Lovecraft story, this thriller has Karloff a recluse who discovers a meteor which gives him strange powers. Good premise is not carried out well. Filmed in England. Remade as THE CURSE (1987). Horrifying Colorscope.▼●)

Different for Girls (1997-British) **C-92m.** ******* D: Richard Spence. Steven Mackintosh, Rupert Graves, Neil Dudgeon, Saskia Reeves. A demure transsexual who writes greeting card verses takes up with a rowdy biker—the same long-ago schoolmate who protected her against adolescent persecutors before the operation that changed her life. One of the more distinctive odd-couple romantic comedies of our time; kept on track by the central performance of Mackintosh, who pulls off a difficult role. [R]▼●

Different Loyalty, A (2004-U.S.-Canadian-British) **C-96m.** ***½** D: Marek Kanievska. Sharon Stone, Rupert Everett, Julian Wadham, Michael Cochrane, Ann Lambton, Joss Ackland, Jim Piddock. Set during the Cold War, Stone plays an American wife

to Everett's British double agent. He's torn between her and his ideals, thus creating turmoil in the marriage. The two leads act their little hearts out, but the film is terminally dull. Loosely based on the life of Eleanor and Kim Philby. Actor Piddock also scripted and coproduced. [R]▼●

Different Story, A (1978) **C-108m.** ****½** D: Paul Aaron. Perry King, Meg Foster, Valerie Curtin, Peter Donat, Richard Bull, Barbara Collentine. Gays King and Foster get married to prevent his deportation, then fall in love. Sounds terrible, but first half is surprisingly good until film succumbs to conventionality. Foster is terrific. [PG—edited from original R rating]▼●

Digby—The Biggest Dog in the World (1973-British) **C-88m.** BOMB D: Joseph McGrath. Jim Dale, Spike Milligan, Milo O'Shea, Angela Douglas, Norman Rossington. Poor comedy-fantasy concerning liquid Project X, which causes sheepdog Digby to grow to huge proportions. Bad special effects, too. Written by Ted Key, creator of "Hazel"; strictly for kids. [G]▼

Digger (1994) **C-92m.** ****** D: Robert Turner. Adam Hann-Byrd, Joshua Jackson, Barbara Williams, Timothy Bottoms, Olympia Dukakis, Leslie Nielsen, P. Lynn Johnson, Lochlyn Munro. An attractive but depressing film of people dealing with losses in their lives: a couple who have buried a drowned child, a boy dying of leukemia therapy complications, and his friend whose parents are divorcing. Dukakis and Nielsen provide welcome relief as older couple in the throes of romance. [PG]▼●

Diggers (2007) **C-87m.** ****** D: Katherine Dieckmann. Paul Rudd, Lauren Ambrose, Ron Eldard, Josh Hamilton, Sarah Paulson, Ken Marino, Maura Tierney, Shannon Barry, Andrew Cherry. Set in 1970s Long Island, film focuses on two generations of clam diggers who are trying desperately to maintain their way of life (and loving) in a town that may be about to pass them by. Low-budget look at the changing ways of small-town America boasts an attractive cast but is less than compelling—unless you dig clams, of course. With its TV-friendly elements this might have been more suitable as a series pilot. Marino (who plays Lozo) wrote and coproduced. [R]●

Digging to China (1997) **C-98m.** ****** D: Timothy Hutton. Evan Rachel Wood, Kevin Bacon, Mary Stuart Masterson, Cathy Moriarty, Marian Seldes. Sincere but one-note film about the growing friendship between a troubled 10-year-old girl (Wood) and a mentally retarded young man (Bacon). Its offbeat qualities seem a bit too contrived, though the performances can't be faulted. Hutton's feature directing debut. [PG]▼●)

Diggstown (1992) **C-97m.** ****½** D: Michael Ritchie. James Woods, Louis Gossett, Jr.,

Bruce Dern, Oliver Platt, Heather Graham, Randall "Tex" Cobb, Thomas Wilson Brown, Duane Davis, Willie Green, George D. Wallace. Amiable yarn about a con artist just sprung from prison who sets his sights on a high-rolling meanie in a small Georgia town—with boxer Gossett as his lure for big-time bets. The two stars are very watchable, even if the script is contrived. Gossett's then-wife Cyndi plays his spouse on-screen. [R]▼●)

Digimon: The Movie (2000-Japanese) **C-82m. **** D: Takaaki Yamashita, Hisashi Nakayama, Masahiro Aizawa. Voices of Lara Jill Miller, Joshua Seth, Colleen O'Shaughnessy, Philece Sampler, Bob Glouberman, Mona Marshall. Three short stories (released as theatrical shorts in Japan) based on the animated TV series are strung together to form a "movie." A notch better than the POKÉMON movies, with a standout sequence in the middle section as digital monsters battle in a surreal internet world. Otherwise, strictly for wired small-fry. [PG]▼▼

Dilemma, The (2011) **C-118m. *½** D: Ron Howard. Vince Vaughn, Kevin James, Jennifer Connelly, Winona Ryder, Channing Tatum, Queen Latifah, Amy Morton, Chelcie Ross, Clint Howard, Rance Howard. Vaughn and James are best friends and business partners, so Vaughn is appalled when he sees James' wife (Ryder) making out with another guy . . . but can't figure out how to break the news to him. Purported comedy is awkward and unfunny. The actors are gung ho, but to no avail: this is a misfire. Super 35. [PG-13]❑

Dillinger (1973) **C-107m. ***** D: John Milius. Warren Oates, Ben Johnson, Cloris Leachman, Michelle Phillips, Richard Dreyfuss, Harry Dean Stanton, Steve Kanaly. Heavily romanticized gangster movie is aided by some rough, violent gun battles. Story follows Dillinger midway through his bank-robbing career up until his death outside the Biograph Theatre. [R]▼●)

Dillinger and Capone (1995) **C-94m. **** D: Jon Purdy. Martin Sheen, F. Murray Abraham, Stephen Davies, Catherine Hicks, Don Stroud, Sasha Jenson, Michael Oliver, Jeffrey Combs, Michael C. Gwynne, Anthony Crivello, Bert Remsen, Clint Howard. 1940: released from prison, Al Capone (Abraham) holds captive the family of John Dillinger (Sheen) who, here at least, wasn't gunned down at the Biograph. Big Al wants the famed bank robber to recover 15 million dollars of Capone's ill-gotten gains from a hotel in Chicago. The clever idea is boosted by slick acting, but it soon slides into a routine heist thriller. [R]▼❑

Diminished Capacity (2008) **C-89m. **½** D: Terry Kinney. Matthew Broderick, Alan Alda, Virginia Madsen, Lois Smith, Dylan Baker, Louis C.K., Jimmy Bennett, Bobby

Cannavale, Jim True-Frost, Tom Aldredge. First-rate cast in a desperately thin story about a Chicago newspaper columnist (Broderick) recovering from a head injury, who goes home to tend to his aging, memory-challenged uncle (Alda). Takes an odd turn as they return to Chicago to sell a rare baseball card.❑

Dimples (1936) **78m. **½** D: William Seiter. Shirley Temple, Frank Morgan, Helen Westley, Robert Kent, Stepin Fetchit, Astrid Allwyn. Prime Shirley, with our heroine doing her best to save her destitute father, played by marvelous Morgan. Songs: "Oh Mister Man Up in the Moon," "What Did the Bluebird Say." Also shown in computer-colored version.▼❑

Dim Sum: a little bit of heart (1984) **C-89m. ***** D: Wayne Wang. Laureen Chew, Kim Chew, Victor Wong, Ida F.O. Chung, Cora Miao. Occasionally slow—there are one too many shots of empty rooms—but mostly wise, endearing tale of Chinese-Americans in San Francisco, focusing on the dynamics of a mother-daughter relationship. Characters may be distinctively Chinese, but there's a refreshing, knowing universality to this comedy. [PG]▼●)

Diner (1982) **C-110m. ***** D: Barry Levinson. Steve Guttenberg, Daniel Stern, Mickey Rourke, Kevin Bacon, Timothy Daly, Ellen Barkin, Paul Reiser, Michael Tucker. Problems of growing up are nicely synthesized by writer-director Levinson in this look at a group of friends who hang out in a Baltimore diner in the 1950s. Obviously made with care and affection; a real sleeper. Levinson's directorial debut and first film of Barkin and Reiser. [R]▼●)

Dingaka (1965-South African) **C-98m. **½** D: Jamie Uys. Stanley Baker, Juliet Prowse, Ken Gampu, Siegfried Mynhardt, Bob Courtney. Film focuses on contrasting white-black ways of life and the clashes of the two cultures; production bogs down in stereotypes. CinemaScope.▼

Dingo (1991-Australian-French) **C-108m. **½** D: Rolf de Heer. Colin Friels, Miles Davis, Helen Buday, Joe Petruzzi, Bernadette Lafont, Bernard Fresson. A chance appearance by jazz trumpeter Billy Cross (Davis) in a boy's rural community inspires him to pursue music himself; now grown up, he still dreams of playing for a living—and winning the approval of his lifelong idol. Amiable but slow-paced story is sparked by Miles Davis' dynamic presence and ingratiating performance. Chuck Findley doubled Friels' trumpeting on the soundtrack. Invigorating score by Michel Legrand and Davis. Panavision.▼❑

Dinner at Eight (1933) **113m. ****** D: George Cukor. Marie Dressler, John Barrymore, Wallace Beery, Jean Harlow, Lionel Barrymore, Lee Tracy, Edmund Lowe, Billie Burke, Madge Evans, Jean Hersholt, Karen Morley, Phillips Holmes, May Robson. Vintage MGM constellation of stars portray various strata of society in N.Y.C., invited to dine and shine; Harlow in fine comedy form, but Dressler as dowager steals focus in filmization of George Kaufman–Edna Ferber play. Scripted by three top writers: Herman Mankiewicz, Frances Marion, and Donald Ogden Stewart. Don't miss this one. Remade for cable TV in 1989 with Lauren Bacall. ▼●❚

Dinner for Schmucks (2010) C-114m. ** D: Jay Roach. Steve Carell, Paul Rudd, Zach Galifianakis, Jemaine Clement, Stephanie Szostak, Lucy Punch, Bruce Greenwood, David Walliams, Ron Livingston, Larry Wilmore, Kristen Schaal, P. J. Byrne, Andrea Savage, Nick Kroll, Randall Park, Lucy Davenport, Jeff Dunham. Upwardly mobile business drone Rudd, in line for a possible promotion, reluctantly accepts his boss' invitation to a dinner where each guest brings the biggest idiot he can find. Then Rudd literally runs into Carell, a pathetic but well-meaning schlemiel, who immediately creates havoc for his newfound friend. Longer, cruder, clunkier, and much less funny than the film that inspired it, Francis Veber's hilarious THE DINNER GAME . . . though Carell is endearing. [PG-13] ❚

Dinner Game, The (1998-French) C-81m. ***½ D: Francis Veber. Thierry Lhermitte, Jacques Villeret, Francis Huster, Daniel Prévost, Alexandra Vandernoot, Catherine Frot. Laugh-out-loud farce (from the writer of LA CAGE AUX FOLLES) about a self-centered publisher who participates in a weekly ritual with his friends: to invite the stupidest person they can find to dinner. Lhermitte has found a doozy, civil servant Villeret (who created this part on stage), but the well-meaning oaf intrudes on his life in unexpected ways. Hilariously funny without being cruel—which is no mean feat. Remade as DINNER FOR SCHMUCKS. Technovision. [PG-13] ▼❚

Dinner Rush (2001) C-100m. *** D: Bob Giraldi. Danny Aiello, Edoardo Ballerini, Vivian Wu, Mike McGlone, Kirk Acevedo, John Corbett, Sandra Bernhard, Summer Phoenix, Polly Draper, Mark Margolis, Ajay Naidu. A tumultuous night in the life of a busy, newly chic N.Y.C. restaurant. Owner Aiello is thinking of giving up his bookmaking activities, his star chef is demanding part ownership of the eatery, two mobsters have come to pay an unfriendly visit, etc. Flavorful film has the ring of truth—inside the kitchen and out—and is brimming with life. Director (and real-life restaurateur) Giraldi is better known for his commercials and music videos. [R] ▼❚

Dino (1957) 94m. **½ D: Thomas Carr. Sal Mineo, Brian Keith, Susan Kohner, Joe De Santis, Penny Santon, Frank Faylen, Richard Bakalyan. Mineo at his rebellious best playing juvenile delinquent befriended by a girl (Kohner) and a social worker (Keith). Reginald Rose adapted his acclaimed TV play, and Mineo re-created his starring role.

Dinosaur (2000) C-82m. *** D: Ralph Zondag, Eric Leighton. Voices of D.B. Sweeney, Alfre Woodard, Ossie Davis, Max Casella, Hayden Panettiere, Samuel E. Wright, Julianna Margulies, Peter Siragusa, Joan Plowright, Della Reese. Disney story of a dinosaur raised by a family of lemurs; when a meteor shower destroys their island home, they flee to another island where they join a tribe of dinosaurs on a desperate trek to safety. On one level, a children's fable about survival and compassion; on another, a dazzling display of computer animation and technology that's almost overwhelming. But the use of modern dialogue for comedy relief ultimately brands the film as kid stuff. [PG] ▼❚

Dinosaur . . . Secret of the Lost Legend SEE: **Baby . . . Secret of the Lost Legend**

Dion Brothers, The SEE: **Gravy Train, The**

Diplomatic Courier (1952) 97m. *** D: Henry Hathaway. Tyrone Power, Patricia Neal, Stephen McNally, Hildegarde Neff, Karl Malden. Power seeks to avenge friend's death in Trieste, becomes involved in international espionage. Cold War film is exciting, well acted. Look for Lee Marvin, Charles Bronson, and Michael Ansara in small, unbilled roles. ▼

Dirigible (1931) 100m. **½ D: Frank Capra. Jack Holt, Ralph Graves, Fay Wray, Hobart Bosworth, Roscoe Karns. Frank "Spig" Wead story about Navy pilots' experimental use of dirigibles in the Antarctic has plenty of action and guts, but a sappy romantic story to weigh it down. On the whole, an interesting antique.

Dirt Bike Kid, The (1986) C-90m. **½ D: Hoite C. Caston. Peter Billingsley, Stuart Pankin, Anne Bloom, Patrick Collins, Sage Parker, Chad Sheets. Strictly formula teen melodrama, with young Billingsley taking on evil banker Pankin and some nasty bikers with the help of a very unusual Yamaha. Harmless and forgettable. [PG] ▼●❚

Dirty (2006) C-97m. *½ D: Chris Fisher. Cuba Gooding, Jr., Clifton Collins, Jr., Cole Hauser, Wyclef Jean, Keith David, Taboo, Wood Harris, Lobo Sebastian, Robert LaSardo, Aimee Garcia. Two battle-weary L.A. cops set out for a day's work, but Gooding doesn't know that his partner (Collins) has talked to Internal Affairs about their gang-busting unit's unethical tactics. Aggressively foulmouthed and foul-minded, this visually convulsive TRAINING DAY wannabe has ambitions, but offers neither its characters nor its audience any salvation. [R] ▼❚

Dirty Dancing (1987) C-97m. **½ D: Emile Ardolino. Jennifer Grey, Patrick Swayze, Jerry Orbach, Cynthia Rhodes,

Jack Weston, Jane Brucker, Kelly Bishop, Lonny Price, Charles "Honi" Coles, Wayne Knight. Superficial but audience-pleasing tale of spoiled teenage girl who learns something about real life—as well as a thing or two about dancing—during family vacation at a Catskills, N.Y., resort hotel in the early 1960s. Sparked by some hot dance numbers and charismatic leads. Most of the music is 1980s-style, not 1960s, but it seems to work. For a richer portrait of Catskills life see another 1987 release, SWEET LORRAINE. Oscar winner for best song: "(I've Had) The Time of My Life." Followed by a sequel in 2004, a TV series, and a stage musical. [PG-13]▼●〗

Dirty Dancing: Havana Nights (2004) C-86m. **½ D: Guy Ferland. Diego Luna, Romola Garai, Sela Ward, John Slattery, Jonathan Jackson, January Jones, Mika Boorem, Patrick Swayze, Mya Harrison, Rene Lavan, Heather Headley. Pleasant-enough fluff about a teenage girl whose family relocates to Cuba in 1958 as political tensions are growing. She loves the freedom of Latin dancing and finds a perfect partner, a boy who works as a waiter at her hotel. The two appealing leads make this fun to watch. Closing narration is clumsy and unnecessary. Swayze, who starred in the original DIRTY DANCING, plays a dance instructor here. [PG-13]▼〗

Dirty Dingus Magee (1970) C-90m. *** D: Burt Kennedy. Frank Sinatra, George Kennedy, Anne Jackson, Lois Nettleton, Michele Carey, Jack Elam, John Dehner, Henry Jones, Harry Carey, Jr., Paul Fix. Broad, bawdy spoof with Sinatra as $10 outlaw whose attempts to make it big are slightly hindered by equally bungling sheriff Kennedy (not to mention assorted whores, Indians, and the U.S. Cavalry). Subtle it's not, but fast paced and amusing, especially for Western buffs; Nettleton is a delight as Joanne Woodward–ish schoolmarm inappropriately named Prudence. Cowritten by Joseph Heller. Panavision. [PG]▼

Dirty Dishes (1978-French) C-92m. **½ D: Joyce Buñuel. Carole Laure, Pierre Santini, Catherine Lachens, Veronique Silver. Entertaining but obvious feminist comedy of Laure rebelling against her duties as a housewife. Director Buñuel is the late Luis Buñuel's daughter-in-law. [R]▼

Dirty Dozen, The (1967) C-150m. ***½ D: Robert Aldrich. Lee Marvin, Ernest Borgnine, Jim Brown, John Cassavetes, Robert Ryan, Charles Bronson, Donald Sutherland, George Kennedy, Telly Savalas, Ralph Meeker, Richard Jaeckel, Clint Walker, Trini Lopez. Box-office hit about 12 murderers, rapists, and other prisoners who get a chance to redeem themselves in WW2. Exciting, funny, and well acted, especially by Marvin and Cassavetes. Nunnally Johnson and Lukas Heller scripted from E. M.

Nathanson novel. Followed in 1985, 1987, 1988 by trio of inferior TV movies with such original cast members as Marvin, Jaeckel, Savalas, Borgnine; then a short-lived series. Metroscope.▼●〗

Dirty Hands (1976-French) C-102m. ** D: Claude Chabrol. Rod Steiger, Romy Schneider, Paolo Giusti, Jean Rochefort, Hans Christian Blech. Laughable wife-and-lover-conspire-to-murder-husband melodrama; corpses keep turning up alive with boring regularity. However, some striking camera work, eerie sequences. Aka INNOCENTS WITH DIRTY HANDS. [R]▼〗

Dirty Harry (1971) C-102m. ***½ D: Don Siegel. Clint Eastwood, Harry Guardino, Reni Santoni, John Larch, Andy Robinson, and John Vernon as "The Mayor." Riveting action film with Eastwood as iconoclastic cop determined to bring in psychotic serial killer Robinson, even if he has to break some rules. Brilliantly filmed and edited for maximum impact. Jazzy score by Lalo Schifrin. Filmed "in tribute to the police officers of San Francisco who gave their lives in the line of duty." Followed by MAGNUM FORCE, THE ENFORCER, SUDDEN IMPACT, and THE DEAD POOL. Panavision. [R]▼●〗

Dirty Knight's Work (1976-British) C-88m. ** D: Kevin Connor. John Mills, Donald Pleasence, Barbara Hershey, David Birney, Margaret Leighton, Peter Cushing. Birney enlists Mills' help in solving his father's murder, zeroes in on strange society of latter-day knights with vigilante tendencies. Offbeat and mildly diverting. Original title: TRIAL BY COMBAT. Video title: CHOICE OF WEAPONS. [PG]▼

Dirty Little Billy (1972) C-92m. *** D: Stan Dragoti. Michael J. Pollard, Lee Purcell, Charles Aidman, Richard Evans. Offbeat story based on early life of Billy the Kid. Grimy, muddy, adventurous; not a normal Western by any stretch of the imagination. Produced by Jack L. Warner! [R]〗

Dirty Mary Crazy Larry (1974) C-93m. *** D: John Hough. Peter Fonda, Susan George, Adam Roarke, Vic Morrow, Roddy McDowall. Very fast action as racing driver Fonda, pickup George and mechanic Roarke demolish every car in sight while escaping with supermarket loot. Hardly a letup, and marred only by downbeat finale. [PG]▼〗

Dirty Money (1972-French) C-98m. **½ D: Jean-Pierre Melville. Alain Delon, Richard Crenna, Catherine Deneuve, Ricardo Cucciolla, Michael Conrad. Pedestrian melodrama of bank robbery and drug trafficking. Delon and Crenna are muscular, Deneuve and the scenery gorgeous.〗

Dirty Pretty Things (2002-U.S.-British) C-97m. *** D: Stephen Frears. Audrey Tautou, Chiwetel Ejiofor, Sergi López, Sophie Okonedo, Benedict Wong, Zlatko Buric. Gripping story of a sober, hardworking Nigerian immigrant who's running from his past and juggling two jobs in London as a cab driver and hotel clerk. His innate sense of justice (and personal integrity) is affronted when he learns of grisly black-market transactions going on at the hotel, and he feels impelled to intervene. Tautou is his friend, a Turkish illegal who's been working as a hotel maid. Original and surprising at every turn; director Frears makes the most of Steven Knight's script. [R]▼❙

Dirty Rotten Scoundrels (1988) C-110m. **½ D: Frank Oz. Steve Martin, Michael Caine, Glenne Headly, Anton Rodgers, Barbara Harris, Ian McDiarmid, Dana Ivey. Career con artist Caine, who fleeces women with great elan in the south of France, must find a way to deal with crass new competition: American Martin. Eventually they decide to see who can dupe wide-eyed Headly first. Extremely pleasant but unremarkable comedy, a remake of the 1964 BEDTIME STORY, filmed on beautiful Riviera locations. Later a Broadway musical. [PG]▼❍❙

Dirty Shame, A (2004) C-89m. **½ D: John Waters. Tracey Ullman, Johnny Knoxville, Selma Blair, Chris Isaak, Suzanne Shepherd, Mink Stole, Patricia Hearst, Jackie Hoffman, Ricki Lake, David Hasselhoff. Ullman plays it to the hilt as a repressed, scowling convenience-store clerk who is conked on the head and awakens a sex addict. Waters' outlandish film depicts a cartoonish world that's gone sex-mad. Occasionally funny, mostly silly; plays like the concoction of a preteen boy who's just learned his first naughty word. R-rated version also available. [NC-17]❙

Dirty Work (1998) C-81m. *½ D: Bob Saget. Norm Macdonald, Jack Warden, Artie Lange, Traylor Howard, Don Rickles, Christopher McDonald, Chevy Chase, Chris Farley, Gary Coleman, Ken Norton, John Goodman, Rebecca Romijn. Crude, mean-spirited comedy vehicle for former *Saturday Night Live* star Macdonald about a shiftless loser who teams up with his best friend to start a "revenge business" for the common man. Potentially clever idea squandered by endless barrage of fat and gay jokes. Lots of comic talent wasted, although Rickles is good as an obnoxious movie theater manager. Adam Sandler appears unbilled. [PG-13]▼❍❙

Disappearance, The (1977-Canadian) C-88m. ** D: Stuart Cooper. Donald Sutherland, Francine Racette, David Hemmings, David Warner, Christopher Plummer, John Hurt, Virginia McKenna, Peter Bowles. Slow-moving account of a hit-man's preoccupation with the disappearance of his wife. Strong Sutherland performance is obliterated by confusing script, pretentiously arty direction. Originally 100m. [R]▼

Disappearance of Alice Creed, The (2010-British) C-100m. ** D: J Blakeson.

Gemma Arterton, Martin Compston, Eddie Marsan. Two seemingly hard-boiled criminals carefully plan the abduction of a young woman in order to soak her father for a fortune, but things don't go as planned. Writer-director Blakeson creates knotty tension from the start and takes us by surprise as the story unfolds, but the house of cards begins to fall when credulity is stretched—and you realize you don't care about *any* of the characters. [R]❙

Disappearance of Garcia Lorca, The (1997-U.S.-Spanish-Puerto Rican) C-108m. ** D: Marcos Zurinaga. Andy Garcia, Esai Morales, Edward James Olmos, Jeroen Krabbé, Marcela Wallerstein, Miguel Ferrer, Giancarlo Giannini. Dreary fictionalized account of the mysterious death of the radical Spanish poet-playwright Federico Garcia Lorca at the hands of Franco's Fascists in 1936. Film is good to look at, courtesy Juan Ruiz-Anchia's elegant widescreen photography, but script is hopelessly clichéd and contrived, and fails in its attempts to turn historical speculation into a political thriller. Original title: DEATH IN GRANADA. Panavision. [R]▼

Disaster in Time SEE: **Grand Tour, The**

Disaster Movie (2008) C-88m. BOMB D: Jason Friedberg, Aaron Seltzer. Matt Lanter, Vanessa Minnillo, Gary "G-Thang" Johnson, Nicole Parker, Crista Flanagan, Kim Kardashian, Carmen Electra, Ike Barinholtz, Tony Cox. A series of natural disasters are occurring—a massive earthquake has crippled the city and asteroids have struck Miley Cyrus—so a group of twenty-somethings decide to save the world. Spoofing ENCHANTED, HIGH SCHOOL MUSICAL, CLOVERFIELD, Indiana Jones, Amy Winehouse, et al., this ranks low on the parody charts. Amusing moments are few and far between. Also available in unrated version. [PG-13]❙

Disclosure (1994) C-127m. *** D: Barry Levinson. Michael Douglas, Demi Moore, Donald Sutherland, Caroline Goodall, Dylan Baker, Roma Maffia, Dennis Miller, Allan Rich, Nicholas Sadler, Rosemary Forsyth. Entertaining corporate thriller based on Michael Crichton's book about a not-so-bright exec (Douglas) in a highly competitive computer company who sues his new, sexy shark of a boss (Moore) for sexual harassment! Plotted like a mystery, with plenty of surprising twists and turns. Only complaint: hasn't Douglas played this same kind of role a bit too often? Panavision. [R]▼❍❙

Discreet Charm of the Bourgeoisie, The (1972-French) C-101m. **** D: Luis Buñuel. Fernando Rey, Delphine Seyrig, Stephane Audran, Bulle Ogier, Jean-Pierre Cassel, Michel Piccoli. A Buñuel joke on his audience, using friends' attempts to have dinner party as excuse for series of surrealistic sequences. Reality and illusion soon blur into one, with delicious comic results. Oscar winner as Best Foreign Film. Screenplay by Buñuel and Jean-Claude Carrière. [PG]▼●]

Disgrace (2008-Australian-U.S.-Dutch) **C-118m. **½** D: Steve Jacobs. John Malkovich, Jessica Haines, Eriq Ebouaney, Fiona Press, Antoinette Engel, David Dennis, Charles Tertiens. Provocative yet not entirely satisfying drama about a diffident poetry professor in Cape Town, South Africa, who takes advantage of an attractive student. He pays the price for his behavior, then moves in with his grown daughter, who's living on a farm in a remote part of the country where the challenges of getting along are even greater. Poses as many questions (about South African culture) as it answers. Based on a highly regarded novel by J. M. Coetzee. [R]▶

Dish, The (2000-Australian) **C-104m. **★** D: Rob Sitch. Sam Neill, Kevin Harrington, Tom Long, Patrick Warburton, Genevieve Mooy, Tayler Kane, Billie Brown, Roy Billing, John McMartin. Delightful comedy based on the true story of how an unlikely Australian community put itself on the map in 1969 by having the only satellite dish that could track the progress of Apollo 11 in the Southern Hemisphere as it made its way to the moon. Made by the same filmmaking collective responsible for THE CASTLE. [PG-13]▼]

Dishonored (1931) **91m. **★½** D: Josef von Sternberg. Marlene Dietrich, Victor McLaglen, Lew Cody, Warner Oland, Gustav von Seyffertitz. Alluring Dietrich makes the most of a creaky script starring her as secret agent X-27 during WW1. Worth seeing for her masquerade as peasant girl.▼

Disney's A Christmas Carol (2009) SEE: **Christmas Carol, A**

Disney's Teacher's Pet SEE: **Teacher's Pet** (2004)

Disney's The Kid (2000) **C-104m. **** D: Jon Turteltaub. Bruce Willis, Spencer Breslin, Emily Mortimer, Lily Tomlin, Jean Smart, Daniel von Bargen, Chi McBride, Dana Ivey, Juanita Moore. A cold-as-ice businessman who suppresses all memories of his childhood and shuns contact with his family is confronted with his 8-year-old self, and doesn't understand why. Well-meaning fable by Audrey Wells has its moments, but doesn't quite come off. Matthew Perry appears hirsute and unbilled. [PG]▼]

Disorderlies (1987) **C-86m. *½** D: Michael Schultz. The Fat Boys, Ralph Bellamy, Tony Plana, Anthony Geary, Marco Rodriguez, Troy Beyer. Get *down* with Bellamy, as a Palm Beach millionaire about to be murdered for his estate by a conniving nephew and the valet; the title chubs—kind of a rap version of The Three Stooges—come to the rescue. Pretty desperate, but the ultimate in casting curios. [PG]▼●]

Disorderly Orderly, The (1964) **C-90m. *** D: Frank Tashlin. Jerry Lewis, Glenda Farrell, Susan Oliver, Everett Sloane, Jack E. Leonard, Alice Pearce, Kathleen Freeman, Barbara Nichols, Milton Frome. First-rate slapstick and sight gags (including a wild chase finale) mix with cloying sentiment as Jerry runs amuck in a nursing home. Best scene: Jerry's suffering of "sympathy pains" as patient Pearce complains of her ills. Title tune sung by Sammy Davis, Jr.▼]

Disorganized Crime (1989) **C-101m. *½** D: Jim Kouf. Hoyt Axton, Corbin Bernsen, Ruben Blades, Fred Gwynne, Ed O'Neill, Lou Diamond Phillips, Daniel Roebuck, William Russ, Marie Butler Kouf. Witless crime-chase comedy about a quartet of crooks waiting for leader Bernsen, who's plotted the perfect bank heist but has managed to get himself arrested. [R]▼●]

Dispatch From Reuters, A (1940) **89m. **½** D: William Dieterle. Edward G. Robinson, Edna Best, Eddie Albert, Albert Basserman, Gene Lockhart, Nigel Bruce, Otto Kruger. Watchable (if not always inspired) Warner Bros. biography of the man who started famous worldwide news agency by using pigeons to transmit information across the European continent.

Distance (1975) **C-94m. **½** D: Anthony Lover. Paul Benjamin, Eija Pokkinen, James Woods, Bibi Besch, Hal Miller, Polly Holliday. Impressive, though flawed, independently made drama detailing the problems of two Army couples during the 1950s. Fine performances, particularly by Besch and Woods; Lover and producer George Coe were responsible for the classic short THE DOVE. [R]

Distant (2002-Turkish) **C-110m. *** D: Nuri Bilge Ceylan. Muzaffer Ozdemir, Mehmet Emin Toprak, Zuhal Gencer Erkaya, Nazan Kirilmis. Deliberately paced drama about a 40-year-old photographer in the city who is visited by his recently unemployed country cousin. We gradually recognize how the differences between them and their experiences cause problems in the relationship. Not for everyone, but patient viewers will find themselves rewarded by the simple truths of life the film explores. Toprak was tragically killed in an auto accident before the film's debut; he posthumously shared a Best Actor award with Ozdemir at the Cannes Film Festival. Turkish title: UZAK. ▼]

Distant Drums (1951) **C-101m. ** D: Raoul Walsh. Gary Cooper, Mari Aldon, Richard Webb, Ray Teal. Tame actioner of Seminole Indians on warpath in early 19th-century Florida, with Cooper as stalwart swamp fighter. A reworking of the central story idea from director Walsh's WW2 saga OBJECTIVE BURMA.▼●]

Distant Thunder (1973-Indian) **C-100m. *** D: Satyajit Ray. Soumitra Chatterji, Babita, Sandhya Roy, Gobinda Chakravarty, Romesh Mukerji. Famine strikes

Bengal in 1942 and affects the lives of various families in many different ways. Harsh, vividly filmed tale in which one can almost feel the sand and wind blowing across the screen.▼

Distant Thunder (1988-U.S.-Canadian) C-114m. ** D: Rick Rosenthal. John Lithgow, Ralph Macchio, Kerrie Keane, Reb Brown, Janet Margolin, Denis Arndt, Jamey Sheridan, Tom Bower. Well-intentioned but gooey soaper about yet one more emotionally troubled Vietnam vet (nicely played by the ever-reliable Lithgow), who lives alone in the wilderness, and whose long-abandoned son (Macchio) sets out to find him. [R]▼●◗

Distant Trumpet, A (1964) C-117m. **½ D: Raoul Walsh. Troy Donahue, Suzanne Pleshette, Kent Smith, Claude Akins, James Gregory. Paul Horgan's novel gets short-circuited in stock presentation of army men in the Old West combatting warring Indians while romancing women on the post; good supporting cast. Panavision.◗

Distant Voices, Still Lives (1988-British) C-85m. *** D: Terence Davies. Freda Dowie, Peter Postlethwaite, Angela Walsh, Diane McBain, Dean Williams, Lorraine Ashbourne. Strikingly visual evocation of England during the 1940s and '50s, a time when the corny, happy lyrics of popular songs can be contrasted to the drab, stultifying lives of the working class. Davies' autobiographical script mirrors the lives of his various family members, each of whom is brutalized by his irrationally cruel father. While there's little narrative structure and no depth to the characters, the haunting imagery makes this most worthwhile. Sequel: THE LONG DAY CLOSES. [PG-13]▼●

Distinguished Gentleman, The (1992) C-112m. *** D: Jonathan Lynn. Eddie Murphy, Lane Smith, Sheryl Lee Ralph, Joe Don Baker, Victoria Rowell, Grant Shaud, Kevin McCarthy, Charles S. Dutton, Victor Rivers, Noble Willingham, Gary Frank, Cynthia Harris, James Garner. Florida con artist Murphy realizes that the real con-game is the political scene in Washington, D.C.—and gets himself elected to the House of Representatives. Satirical barbs about the System blend neatly with Eddie's irresistible huckster persona for this ingratiating (if somewhat overlong) comedy, aided by a strong supporting cast. [R]▼●◗

District B13 (2004-French) C-84m. *** D: Pierre Morel. Cyril Raffaelli, David Belle, Tony D'Amario, Larbi (Bibi) Naceri, Dany Verissimo, François Chattot, Nicolas Woirion. Paris, year 2010: Undercover cop Raffaelli dives deep into a walled-off ghetto, guided by seasoned street rat Belle, to recover a bomb stolen by man-mountain drug lord D'Amario. Meanwhile, police headquarters launches a lethal plan of its own.

Politically pointed scenario is a jumping-off point—literally—for a way-cool display of the two leads' spring-loaded *parkour* stunt work, totally unaided by computer trickery. What you see is what they did. Produced and cowritten by Luc Besson, with a smashing kick-derriere hip-hop score by Da. Octopusss. Followed by DISTRICT 13: ULTIMATUM (2009). Super 35. [R]◗

District 9 (2009-U.S.-New Zealand) C-112m. ***½ D: Neill Blomkamp. Sharlto Copley, Jason Cope, David James, Vanessa Haywood, Mandla Gaduka, Kenneth Nkosi. A race of alien creatures who landed in Johannesburg, South Africa, 20 years ago are now treated as unwanted scum, and it's up to a can-do functionary (Copley) to serve eviction notices on the creepy, often violent subjects. Before long he's sucked into the bigger conflict surrounding these visitors, becoming both victim and hero. Told in documentary style, this canny, captivating science-fiction tale grabs you and never lets go. Exceptional visual effects are seamlessly woven into the storytelling. Written by director Blomkamp and Terri Tatchell, inspired in part by Blomkamp's 2005 short ALIVE IN JOBURG. Coproduced by Peter Jackson. [R]◗

Disturbed (1991) C-96m. *½ D: Charles Winkler. Malcolm McDowell, Geoffrey Lewis, Pamela Gidley, Priscilla Pointer, Irwin Keyes, Peter Murnik. Terrific, funny performance by McDowell can't save this florid thriller set in an insane asylum where what might have been a murder took place 10 years before. Flashy camerawork is merely distracting here; one shot is from the point of view of a penis! [R]▼●

Disturbia (2007) C-104m. **½ D: D. J. Caruso. Shia LaBeouf, David Morse, Sarah Roemer, Carrie-Anne Moss, Aaron Yoo, Jose Pablo Cantillo, Matt Craven, Viola Davis. Troubled teen LaBeouf is confined to his home by an electronic ankle bracelet and before long becomes a voyeur, keeping tabs on his neighbors—including a beautiful girl next door, and, more ominously, a man across the street whose behavior seems highly suspicious. Well-made film invites comparisons to REAR WINDOW but plays its cards right and builds considerable suspense, until it becomes obvious (and tedious) by the finale. Casting Morse as the neighbor also sends a transparent signal of what's to come. [PG-13]◗

Disturbing Behavior (1998-U.S.-Australian) C-83m. BOMB D: David Nutter. James Marsden, Katie Holmes, Nick Stahl, William Sadler, Bruce Greenwood, Steve Railsback, Tobias Mehler, Ethan Embry. Teenager Marsden, a newcomer in town, soon realizes there's a sinister plot by the high school guidance counselor to "reform" troubled kids: they become well groomed, love yogurt and freak out when horny. Predictable, coldly calculated and trendy, this is teen-targeted dreck. Give us SCREAM—or at least I WAS A TEEN-AGE WEREWOLF. Director's cut runs 94m. [R]▼●◗

Diva (1981-French) **C-118m.** ***½ D: Jean-Jacques Beineix. Wilhelmenia Wiggins Fernandez, Frederic Andrei, Richard Bohringer, Thuy An Luu, Jacques Fabbri. Music-loving mailman bootleg-tapes the concert of a superstar diva who's never made a recording, finds himself in even hotter water when his possession is mixed up with a second tape that will incriminate gangsters. High-tech melodrama occasionally rubs your nose in its technique, but still makes for whale of a directorial debut by Beineix. Subway motorcycle chase is an action classic. [R] ▼●◗

Dive Bomber (1941) **C-133m.** *** D: Michael Curtiz. Errol Flynn, Fred MacMurray, Ralph Bellamy, Alexis Smith, Robert Armstrong, Regis Toomey, Craig Stevens. Exciting, well-paced aviation film of experiments to eliminate pilot-blackout. Flynn, MacMurray, and Smith perform well in formula story.▼●◗

Divertimento SEE: **La Belle Noiseuse**

Divided We Fall (2000-Czech) **C-122m.** ***½ D: Jan Hrebejk. Boleslav Polívka, Csongor Kassai, Jaroslav · Dusek, Anna Sisková, Jirí Pecha, Martin Huba. To conceal from the local Nazi collaborators that they're hiding a Jew in their home, a reluctant hero uses his wife's so-called pregnancy as the excuse from having to house a Nazi clerk. Unfortunately, it's a matter of public record that husband Josef (Polívka) is sterile. Brilliant film shot in an edgy style that reflects its characters' growing neuroses; walks the tightrope between comedy and drama with Wallenda finesse. Screenwriter Petr Jarchovsky scripted from his novel. [PG-13] ▼◗

Divine Intervention (2002-French-Moroccan-German) **C-92m.** *** D: Elia Suleiman. Elia Suleiman, Manal Khader, Nayef Fahoum Daher, Amer Daher, George Ibrahim. Two Palestinian lovers try to carry on their relationship near the Israeli checkpoint that divides their respective cities, Jerusalem and Ramallah, in this funny, absurd, but ultimately sad look at the way some lives are lived in the Middle East. Original and inventively filmed, at times this movie seems as if it is something Jacques Tati might have made given a similar situation. Writer, director, and star Suleiman takes an almost impossible subject and puts a human face on it with insight and humor.◗

Divine Madness! (1980) **C-95m.** **½ D: Michael Ritchie. Bette Midler fanatics would probably up this rating a half-star or so, but unevenness and occasional oppressiveness of this concert film may even get to them. Some funny bits, but will someone tell her to quit desecrating rock'n'roll? Panavision. [R]▼●◗

Divine Nymph, The (1979-Italian) **C-90m.** *½ D: Giuseppe Patroni Griffi. Marcello Mastroianni, Laura Antonelli, Terence Stamp, Michele Placido, Duilio Del Prete, Ettore Manni, Marina Vlady. Poor melodrama chronicling beautiful Antonelli's involvements with marquis Mastroianni and baron Stamp. Of interest only when Laura doffs her duds.▼

Divine Secrets of the Ya-Ya Sisterhood (2002) **C-117m.** *** D: Callie Khouri. Sandra Bullock, Ellen Burstyn, Fionnula Flanagan, Ashley Judd, Maggie Smith, Shirley Knight, James Garner, Angus Macfadyen, Cherry Jones, Ron Eldard. Three lifelong female friends who made a blood pact of sisterhood as young girls in Louisiana try to reconcile the most eccentric and mercurial of their trio (Burstyn) with her grown-up daughter (Bullock). In flashbacks, we learn the reasons for the mother's erratic behavior, rooted in her childhood and beyond. (She's played as a young woman by Judd.) Begins as comedy, then grows much darker. A careful crafting of Rebecca Wells' title novel and *Little Altars Everywhere*, with strong performances all around. Feature directing debut for THELMA & LOUISE writer Khouri. Panavision. [PG-13]▼◗

Diving Bell and the Butterfly, The (2007-U.S.-French) **C-112m.** ***½ D: Julian Schnabel. Mathieu Amalric, Emmanuelle Seigner, Marie-Josée Croze, Anne Consigny, Patrick Chesnais, Niels Arestrup, Olatz López Garmendia, Jean-Pierre Cassel, Marina Hands, Isaach De Bankolé, Emma de Caunes, Agathe de la Fontaine, Max von Sydow. Remarkable portrait of Jean-Dominique Bauby, worldly editor of French *Elle* magazine, who suffered a stroke that paralyzed his entire body except for the left eyelid—and managed to dictate his bestselling memoir, one blink at a time. Potentially depressing subject becomes a visual and emotional tour de force that puts the viewer inside the protagonist's splintered consciousness. Schnabel's brilliant direction (aided no end by cinematographer Janusz Kaminski and editor Juliette Welfling) and Ronald Harwood's screen adaptation create a fascinating world of memory, fantasy, and self-reflection. The whole cast is exceptional, with von Sydow heartbreaking as Bauby's aged father. [PG-13]◗

Divorce American Style (1967) **C-109m.** *** D: Bud Yorkin. Dick Van Dyke, Debbie Reynolds, Jason Robards, Jean Simmons, Van Johnson, Joe Flynn, Shelley Berman, Martin Gabel, Lee Grant, Pat Collins, Tom Bosley, Eileen Brennan. Highly entertaining comedy of Van Dyke and Reynolds finding more problems than they expected when they get divorced. Stars are unusually good in offbeat roles. Written by Norman Lear.▼◗

[363]

Divorce—Italian Style (1961-Italian) **104m.** ***½ D: Pietro Germi. Marcello Mastroianni, Daniela Rocca, Stefania Sandrelli, Leopoldo Trieste. Marcello can't stomach wife Rocca, so he schemes to wed sexy young Sandrelli. Hilarious, flavorful comedy, which earned an Oscar for its story and screenplay. The twist ending adds a perfect—and most ironic—touch. ▼▶

Dixie Dynamite (1976) **C-89m.** *½ D: Lee Frost. Warren Oates, Christopher George, Jane Anne Johnstone, Kathy McHaley, Wes Bishop, Mark Miller, R. G. Armstrong, Stanley Adams. Johnstone and McHaley wreak havoc on town after they are dispossessed from their farm and their moonshiner father is killed by a trigger-happy deputy. Sound familiar? [PG] ▼▶

Django (1966-Italian-Spanish) **C-92m.** **½ D: Sergio Corbucci. Franco Nero, Loredano Nusciak, Eduardo Fajardo, Jose Bodalo, Angel Alvarez, Jimmy Douglas. Though not as good as the Leone-Eastwood spaghetti Westerns, this is an above-average example of the genre, with the gimmick of Nero as a ruthless gunfighter who drags around a coffin containing a machine gun wherever he goes. This became a cult film and inspired a slew of European oaters with the name "Django" in their titles. Followed by DJANGO STRIKES AGAIN. ▼▶

D.O.A. (1950) **83m.** ***½ D: Rudolph Maté. Edmond O'Brien, Pamela Britton, Luther Adler, Beverly Campbell (Garland), Lynn Baggett, William Ching, Henry Hart, Neville Brand. Gripping, original film noir with O'Brien desperately trying to find who has given him a slow-acting poison—and why. Inventively photographed (by Ernest Laszlo) on the streets of San Francisco and L.A. Written by Russell Rouse and Clarence Greene. Music by Dimitri Tiomkin. Remade in 1969 (as COLOR ME DEAD) and 1988. Also shown in computer-colored version. ▼▶●

D.O.A. (1981) **C-93m.** *½ D: Lech Kowalski. Sex Pistols, Dead Boys, Rich Kids, Generation X, Terry and the Idiots, X-Ray Spec, Nancy Spungen. Crummy documentary rip-off about the infamous punk rock band Sex Pistols. Of interest only for footage of the pathetic Sid Vicious and girlfriend Nancy Spungen. ▼

D.O.A. (1988) **C-100m.** BOMB D: Rocky Morton, Annabel Jankel. Dennis Quaid, Meg Ryan, Daniel Stern, Charlotte Rampling, Jane Kaczmarek, Christopher Neame. Noisy and needless remake of the film noir original, transplanted to academia. Quaid is a college professor fed a slow-acting toxin in a dispute over a prized fiction manuscript; Ryan is an innocent student helping him pursue his "killer." Badly overdirected by the *Max Headroom* creators; obvious red herrings abound. [R] ▼▶●

D.O.A. II SEE: **Color Me Dead**

DOA: Dead or Alive (2006-U.S.-German-British) **C-86m.** *½ D: Corey Yuen. Jaime Pressly, Holly Valance, Sarah Carter, Devon Aoki, Eric Roberts, Natassia Malthe, Matthew Marsden, Steve Howey, Kevin Nash, Brian White, Kane Kosugi. Three butt-kicking babes in various stages of undress are among the combatants invited to a remote island to compete in a $10 million fighting tournament hosted by a sinister scientist (a shamelessly hammy Roberts). Hong Kong action ace Yuen stages some slick martial-arts battles in this video-game adaptation, in reality a silly t&a jiggle-fest that looks like it was made by *Maxim* magazine. Super 35. [PG-13] ▶

Doberman Gang, The (1972) **C-87m.** **½ D: Byron Chudnow. Byron Mabe, Julie Parrish, Hal Reed, Simmy Bow, Jojo D'Amore. Trim low-budget heist movie about a crook's ingenious plan to use six dobermans to pull off bank job. Dogs steal not only the loot but the picture, and starred in two sequels. [G] ▼▶

Doc (1971) **C-96m.** ** D: Frank Perry. Stacy Keach, Harris Yulin, Faye Dunaway, Michael Witney, Denver John Collins, Dan Greenburg. Well-crafted but unpleasant anti-Western, telling the story of Wyatt Earp and Doc Holliday in revisionist terms. Script by Pete Hamill. [PG—edited from original R rating]

Doc Hollywood (1991) **C-104m.** **½ D: Michael Caton-Jones. Michael J. Fox, Julie Warner, Bridget Fonda, Barnard Hughes, Woody Harrelson, David Ogden Stiers, Frances Sternhagen, George Hamilton, Roberts Blossom, Barry Sobel. Fox is on his way to a career in L.A. plastic surgery when he crashes his car in South Carolina's podunk squash capital and is sentenced to perform much-needed medical community service. Agreeably played but nothing special. Warner has a memorable first scene, and there's an amusing star cameo near the end. Director Caton-Jones appears as a maître d'. [PG-13] ▼▶

Dock Brief, The (1962-British) **88m.** **½ D: James Hill. Peter Sellers, Richard Attenborough, Beryl Reid, David Lodge. Sellers is aging barrister who incompetently represents accused killer Attenborough with strange results; pleasant comic satire. John Mortimer adapted his own play. U.S. title: TRIAL AND ERROR. ▼▶

Docks of New York, The (1928) **76m.** **** D: Josef von Sternberg. George Bancroft, Betty Compson, Olga Baclanova, Mitchell Lewis, Clyde Cook, Gustav von Seyffertitz. Burly ship stoker Bancroft marries the suicidal girl he saved from the drink, first taking her for granted, then coming to love her. A rival to SUNRISE as the visual apogee of silent cinema, though the smoky hues of von Sternberg's waterfront dive can fully be appreciated only on the big screen. ▼▶

Doc Savage: The Man of Bronze (1975) C-100m. **½ D: Michael Anderson. Ron Ely, Darrell Zwerling, Michael Miller, Pamela Hensley, Paul Wexler, Robyn Hilton, William Lucking, Paul Gleason. Film debut of Kenneth Robeson's pulp hero was sold (and accepted) as camp; in reality, it's a straight-faced period adventure that just came out at the wrong time. Story has Doc (Ely) and his Fabulous Five heading to South America to investigate his father's death, tangling with evil Captain Seas (Wexler). Fun for kids and buffs, with amusing score built around Sousa marches; final film of producer George Pal. [G]▼●▶

Doctor, The (1991) C-125m. *** D: Randa Haines. William Hurt, Christine Lahti, Elizabeth Perkins, Mandy Patinkin, Adam Arkin, Charlie Korsmo, Wendy Crewson, Bill Macy. Successful surgeon is diagnosed with throat cancer—and for the first time in his career, learns what it's like to be a patient at the mercy of cold-blooded doctors and a bureaucratic hospital. Perkins stands out in a showy role as fellow cancer patient. Engrossing, well acted, and utterly believable; based on Dr. Ed Rosenbaum's own experiences, described in his book *A Taste of My Own Medicine*. [PG-13] ▼

Doctor and the Devils, The (1985) C-93m. ** D: Freddie Francis. Timothy Dalton, Jonathan Pryce, Twiggy, Julian Sands, Stephen Rea, Phyllis Logan, Beryl Reid, Patrick Stewart, Sian Phillips. Serious-minded but unsuccessful (and unappealing) Gothic tale of grave robbers who supply a dedicated doctor who's content not to ask too many questions. Based on a 1940s screenplay by Dylan Thomas, revised by Ronald Harwood. Reminiscent of vintage Hammer horror films; no coincidence, with veteran Francis directing. Made in England. J-D-C Scope. [R]▼

Doctor at Large (1957-British) C-98m. **½ D: Ralph Thomas. Dirk Bogarde, Muriel Pavlow, Donald Sinden, James Robertson Justice, Shirley Eaton, Derek Farr, Michael Medwin, George Coulouris, Anne Heywood, Lionel Jeffries, Mervyn Johns, Ernest Thesiger. Another entry in pleasing series, with novice doctor Bogarde seeking staff position in wealthy hospital. VistaVision.▼▶

Doctor at Sea (1955-British) C-93m. **½ D: Ralph Thomas. Dirk Bogarde, Brigitte Bardot, Brenda de Banzie, James Robertson Justice, Maurice Denham, Michael Medwin, Raymond Huntley. Preferring the bachelor life, Bogarde signs on as ship's doctor on passenger-carrying freighter, in second entry of this entertaining series. VistaVision.▼▶

Doctor Bull (1933) 75m. *** D: John Ford. Will Rogers, Marian Nixon, Ralph Morgan,

Rochelle Hudson, Berton Churchill, Louise Dresser, Andy Devine. Rogers in fine form as country doctor battling small-town pettiness as much as fighting illness. Stereotyped characters are perfect foils for Rogers' common-sense pronouncements; director Ford provides ideal atmosphere.▶

Doctor Death, Seeker of Souls (1973) C-73m. *½ D: Eddie Saeta. John Considine, Barry Coe, Cheryl Miller, Florence Marly, Jo Morrow. Cheap horror item about the transferring of souls by 1,000-year-old Considine. Few effective moments include The Three Stooges' Moe Howard in a gag bit. Aka DOCTOR DEATH. [R]▼

Doctor Detroit (1983) C-89m. ** D: Michael Pressman. Dan Aykroyd, Howard Hesseman, T. K. Carter, Donna Dixon, Lynn Whitfield, Lydia Lei, Fran Drescher, Kate Murtagh, George Furth, Andrew Duggan, Glenne Headly, James Brown. Wimpy college professor becomes embroiled with pimps, prostitutes, and underworld intrigue, but the results are surprisingly bland, and only sporadically funny. Story by Bruce Jay Friedman. Aykroyd later married costar Dixon. [R] ▼●▶

Doctor Dolittle (1967) C-144m. *½ D: Richard Fleischer. Rex Harrison, Samantha Eggar, Anthony Newley, Richard Attenborough, Peter Bull, Geoffrey Holder. Robert Surtees' photography is great, and that's it for this colossal musical dud that almost ruined 20th Century-Fox studios. The charm of Hugh Lofting's stories is gone. One merit: if you have unruly children, it may put them to sleep. Songs by Leslie Bricusse (including the Oscar-winning "Talk to the Animals") and choreography by Herbert Ross. Oscar winner for special visual effects. Originally 152m. Remade in 1998. Todd-AO.▼●▶

Doctor Dolittle (1998) C-85m. ** D: Betty Thomas. Eddie Murphy, Ossie Davis, Oliver Platt, Peter Boyle, Richard Schiff, Kristen Wilson, Kyla Pratt, Raven-Symoné, Jeffrey Tambor, Paul Giamatti; voices of Ellen DeGeneres, Norm Macdonald, Garry Shandling, Julie Kavner, Jenna Elfman, Albert Brooks, Chris Rock, Reni Santoni, John Leguizamo, Gilbert Gottfried, Jonathan Lipnicki, Paul Reubens, Brian Doyle-Murray. 1990s rethink of the Hugh Lofting character has Murphy as a busy, self-absorbed doctor who reacquires the gift he had as a child to understand animals' speech. Comic chaos ensues. Murphy is likable and energetic, but the film is awfully flat; bound to appeal to kids who don't mind that seemingly every other word in the script is "butt." Followed by DR. DOLITTLE 2 and four DVD sequels. [PG-13]▼●▶

Doctor Faustus (1967-British) C-93m. ** D: Richard Burton, Nevill Coghill. Richard Burton, Andreas Teuber, Ian Marter, Elizabeth Taylor. Burton's retelling of Faustus legend lacks everything but a buxom Mrs.

Burton (Elizabeth Taylor), who silently plays Faustus' devil wife, Alexander's paramour, and Helen of Troy. Strictly for their fans. ▼◗

Doctor In Clover (1965-British) **C-101m.** ** D: Ralph Thomas. Leslie Phillips, James Robertson Justice, Shirley Anne Field, John Fraser, Joan Sims. New doctor, same old zany situations in sixth entry of series. Doctor studies nurses more than medicine. Not up to the others' standard. ◗

Doctor In Distress (1963-British) **C-102m.** **½ D: Ralph Thomas. Dirk Bogarde, Samantha Eggar, James Robertson Justice, Mylene Demongeot, Donald Houston, Barbara Murray, Dennis Price, Leo McKern. Pompous chief surgeon falls in love for the first time, and his assistant tries to help the romance along while balancing his own love life. Another entertaining entry in comedy series. Bogarde's last appearance as Dr. Sparrow. ▼◗

Doctor in the House (1954-British) **C-92m.** ***½ D: Ralph Thomas. Dirk Bogarde, Muriel Pavlow, Kenneth More, Donald Sinden, Kay Kendall, James Robertson Justice, Donald Houston, Suzanne Cloutier, Geoffrey Keen, George Coulouris, Shirley Eaton, Joan Hickson, Richard Wattis. Hilarious comedy follows exploits of medical students intent on studying beautiful women and how to become wealthy physicians. This delightful film (from Richard Gordon's stories) spawned six other "Doctor" movies, plus a TV series. Justice memorable as Sir Lancelot Spratt. Scripted by Gordon, Ronald Wilkenson, and costar Nicholas Phipps. ▼◗

Doctor in Trouble (1970-British) **C-90m.** ** D: Ralph Thomas. Leslie Phillips, Harry Secombe, James Robertson Justice, Angela Scoular, Irene Handl, Robert Morley. Fair entry in the on-and-off British comedy series concerns Dr. Phillips' problems when he stows away on ocean liner; good supporting cast help a bit. [R] ▼◗

Doctor Mordrid (1992) **C-89m.** **½ D: Albert and Charles Band. Jeffrey Combs, Yvette Nipar, Brian Thompson, Jay Acovone, Keith Coulouris, Ritch Brinkley, Pearl Shear, Murray Rubin, Jeff Austin, John Apicella. A woman discovers her reclusive neighbor is a powerful sorcerer sworn to save the world from his evil counterpart. Satisfying little movie, confident of its intent, with a sensitive performance by Combs. From Full Moon. [R] ▼◗

Doctor's Dilemma (1958-British) **C-99m.** *** D: Anthony Asquith. Leslie Caron, Dirk Bogarde, Alastair Sim, Robert Morley. Bubbly Shaw period play of young wife Caron conniving to convince medical specialists that her scoundrel husband is worth saving.

Doctors Wear Scarlet SEE: **Bloodsuckers** (1970)

Doctors' Wives (1971) **C-100m.** *½ D: George Schaefer. Dyan Cannon, Richard Crenna, Gene Hackman, Rachel Roberts, Carroll O'Connor, Janice Rule, Diana Sands, Cara Williams, Ralph Bellamy. Super-sudsy soaper sparked by mysterious murder of cheating wife; glossy garbage. Scripted by a slumming Daniel Taradash. [R] ▼◗

Doctor X (1932) **C-80m.** ** D: Michael Curtiz. Lionel Atwill, Fay Wray, Lee Tracy, Preston Foster, Robert Warwick, Mae Busch. Police have tracked the "full-moon strangler" to Atwill's experimental N.Y.C. laboratory. Ludicrous Grand Guignol chiller (Wray's entrance has her screaming—for no reason at all) is a must for horror-film buffs because of its Anton Grot sets, special Max Factor makeup, and rich use of two-color Technicolor . . . but it creaks *badly* and seems much longer than it is. ▼◗●

Doctor, You've Got to Be Kidding (1967) **C-94m.** BOMB D: Peter Tewksbury. Sandra Dee, George Hamilton, Celeste Holm, Bill Bixby, Dick Kallman, Mort Sahl, Dwayne Hickman. Dee would rather marry the boss than pursue singing career. Even *her* singing might have helped this alleged comedy. Panavision.

Doctor Zhivago (1965) **C-197m.** ***½ D: David Lean. Omar Sharif, Julie Christie, Geraldine Chaplin, Tom Courtenay, Alec Guinness, Siobhan McKenna, Ralph Richardson, Rod Steiger, Rita Tushingham, Adrienne Corri, Geoffrey Keen, Jeffrey Rockland, Klaus Kinski, Jack MacGowran, Tarek Sharif. Sumptuous, sprawling epic from Boris Pasternak's acclaimed novel; Sharif is charismatic as Russian poet/doctor, an orphan who marries aristocratic Chaplin but falls in love with politicized nurse Christie. Spans several decades, including WW1 and Bolshevik Revolution, with stirring crowd scenes, gorgeous romantic vistas (set to Maurice Jarre's sweeping music) and a powerful exodus sequence on train. Overlong, but with top production values and superb acting in every role. Won Oscars for screenplay (Robert Bolt), cinematography (Freddie Young), art direction–set decoration (John Box and Terry Marsh; Dario Simoni), costume design (Phyllis Dalton), and score. Reissued at 180m. Remade as a cable miniseries in 2003. Panavision. ▼◗●

Dodes'ka-den (1970-Japanese) **C-140m.** **½ D: Akira Kurosawa. Yoshitaka Zushi, Tomoko Yamazaki, Hiroshi Akutagawa, Noboru Mitani. Episodic chronicle of life in a Tokyo slum; characters include a little boy who feeds himself and derelict dad by scrounging garbage—together, they visualize a dream house; a wan girl who makes artificial flowers to support her alcoholic stepfather; etc. Kurosawa's first film in color. Originally 244m. ▼◗●

Dodgeball: A True Underdog Story (2004) **C-92m.** **½ D: Rawson Marshall Thurber. Ben Stiller, Vince Vaughn, Christine Taylor, Rip Torn, Justin Long, Stephen Root, Gary Cole, Hank Azaria, Alan Tudyk, Missi Pyle, Jason Bateman. Vaughn's dilapidated gym is about to go belly-up and be taken over by snazzier rival Stiller, and it takes 17 minutes in a movie called DODGEBALL to establish that he's going to alleviate his debts by fielding a bunch of guys and a ringer babe who play . . . oh come on, venture a guess. Affable enough, with some funny surprise cameos and the seductive sight of Torn in shoulder-length hair . . . and an excess of gross-out gags. Stiller coproduced. Super 35. [PG-13] ▼●)

Dodge City (1939) **C-105m.** *** D: Michael Curtiz. Errol Flynn, Olivia de Havilland, Ann Sheridan, Bruce Cabot, Frank McHugh, Alan Hale, John Litel, Victor Jory, Ward Bond. Errol tames the West and de Havilland, in entertaining large-scale Western, with Warner Bros. stock company and the granddaddy of all barroom brawls. The principal inspiration for BLAZING SADDLES. ▼●)

Dodsworth (1936) **101m.** **** D: William Wyler. Walter Huston, Ruth Chatterton, Paul Lukas, Mary Astor, David Niven, Gregory Gaye, Maria Ouspenskaya, Spring Byington, Harlan Briggs. Superb adaptation of Sinclair Lewis novel about middle-aged American industrialist who retires, goes to Europe, where he and his wife find differing sets of values and new relationships. Intelligently written (by Sidney Howard), beautifully filmed, extremely well acted, with Huston recreating his Broadway role. John Payne (billed as John Howard Payne) makes screen debut in small role. Won Oscar for Interior Decoration (Richard Day). Unusually mature Hollywood film, not to be missed. ▼●)

Dog Day (1983-French) **C-101m.** **½ D: Yves Boisset. Miou Miou, Lee Marvin, Jean Carmet, Victor Lanoux, David Bennent, Bernadette Lafont, Jean-Pierre Kalfon, Pierre Clementi, Tina Louise. Intriguing if gratuitously violent thriller about a tough but doomed American gangster on the lam (Marvin, well cast) who hides out on the farm of a depraved French family. Fairly effective as an ode to the mythical image of the American screen hood. Panavision. ▼●

Dog Day Afternoon (1975) **C-124m.** ***½ D: Sidney Lumet. Al Pacino, John Cazale, Charles Durning, James Broderick, Chris Sarandon, Sully Boyar, Penny Allen, Carol Kane, Lance Henriksen, Dick Anthony Williams, Philip Charles Mackenzie. Incredible-but-true story of a loser who holds up a Brooklyn bank to raise money for his lover's sex-change operation, and sees simple heist snowball into a citywide incident. Pacino's performance and Lumet's flavor-

ful N.Y.C. atmosphere obscure the fact that this is much ado about nothing. Frank Pierson won an Oscar for his screenplay (based on an article by P. F. Kluge and Thomas Moore). [R] ▼●)

Dogfight (1991) **C-92m.** ***½ D: Nancy Savoca. River Phoenix, Lili Taylor, Richard Panebianco, Anthony Clark, Mitchell Whitfield, Holly Near, E. G. Daily, Brendan Fraser. Title refers to a cruel wager by Vietnam-bound Marines in 1963 San Francisco. Taylor (superb) is a physically plain folkie who becomes an unwitting partner in Phoenix's attempt to bring the ugliest "date" to a party. Original, barely released sleeper is surprisingly unmawkish, thanks to a good script by Bob Comfort and Savoca's tough direction. Unusually apt use of period music. [R] ▼●)

Dogma (1999) **C-135m.** **½ D: Kevin Smith. Matt Damon, Ben Affleck, Linda Fiorentino, Alan Rickman, Chris Rock, Salma Hayek, Jason Lee, Kevin Smith, Jason Mewes, George Carlin, Alanis Morissette, Janeane Garofalo, Bud Cort. Ambitious comic fantasy in which age-old battles between outcast angels, Lucifer, and God are played out in modern-day America, as a young woman who's lost her faith (Fiorentino) is chosen to save humanity. Irreverent, to say the least; challenging and clever at times, but also puerile and silly, not to mention long. Smith and Mewes reprise their characters from Smith's earlier films. Smith also scripted. Super 35. [R] ▼●)

Dog of Flanders, A (1999) **C-100m.** *½ D: Kevin Brodie. Jack Warden, Jeremy James Kissner, Jesse James, Jon Voight, Cheryl Ladd, Steven Hartley, Bruce McGill, Andrew Bicknell. A 19th-century Belgian boy rescues an abandoned dog and uses him to pull a milk-delivery cart for him and his grandfather . . . but the boy really longs to be a painter like the great Reubens. Despite excellent photography of Belgian locations, this adaptation of Ouida's classic children's novel is a joyless, anachronistic, moralistic snoozer. Previously made in 1935, 1959, and in 1975 as a Japanese animated feature. [PG] ▼●)

Dogora (2004-French) **C/B&W-78m.** ** D: Patrice Leconte. Documentary portrait of everyday life in Cambodia (accompanied by a thunderous orchestral score) is pleasant enough to watch, but has no structure, context, or momentum. Only Leconte's expert eye, which provides a series of attractive widescreen images, sets this apart from a routine travelogue. Original French title: DOGORA—OUVRONS LES YEUX. HD Widescreen. ●

Dog Park (1999-U.S.-Canadian) **C-91m.** *½ D: Bruce McCulloch. Natasha Henstridge, Luke Wilson, Kathleen Robertson, Janeane Garofalo, Bruce McCulloch,

Kristin Lehman, Harland Williams. Howlingly bad romantic comedy squanders cute premise about a group of Toronto singles whose lackluster love lives affect their pet pooches. Self-absorbed, unlikable lead characters and meandering subplots don't help. Inauspicious writing-directing debut from *Kids in the Hall* alum McCulloch; only laughs come from fellow *Kids* member Mark McKinney as a pet therapist. [R] ▼●

Dogpound Shuffle (1975) **C-95m.** *** D: Jeffrey Bloom. Ron Moody, David Soul, Pamela McMyler, Ray Stricklyn, Raymond Sutton. Unpretentious little fable about cynical ex-vaudevillian tap-dancer—now a bum—who must raise $30 to rescue his dog from the pound. Funny and wistful, with excellent character performance by Moody. Aka SPOT. [PG] ▼

Dogs of War, The (1980-British) **C-102m.** *** D: John Irvin. Christopher Walken, Tom Berenger, Colin Blakely, Hugh Millais, Paul Freeman, JoBeth Williams, Ed O'Neill. Appropriately mean if overly somber adaptation of the Frederick Forsyth best-seller about a mercenary who tangles with an Amin-like dictator in an African hellhole. Will not promote one-worldism, but Walken takes a screen beating nearly as impressively as Brando. British running time 118m. [R] ▼●

Dog Soldiers SEE: **Who'll Stop the Rain**

Dogtooth (2009-Greek) **C-97m.** *** D: Yorgos Lanthimos. Christos Stergioglou, Michelle Valley, Aggeliki Papoulia, Mary Tsoni, Hristos Passalis, Anna Kalaitzidou. A father and mother control the lives of their three young adult offspring, keeping them hidden away on an isolated estate and teaching them values that are, to say the least, extremely unconventional. Striking and offbeat do not begin to describe this challenging tragicomedy, which ponders the role of the parent within the family unit and the often irreversible consequences parental actions have on their children. If this film was rated, it surely would be NC-17. ▶

Dogtown and Z-Boys (2002) **C-90m.** ***½ D: Stacy Peralta. Narrated by Sean Penn. Exuberant, impassioned documentary of the pioneering Zephyr skateboarders, a group of misfit Venice, California, teens who revived the sport in the '70s and became overnight media sensations . . . and their bittersweet present-day reunion. Made by Peralta, one of the original thrasher stars of the group. Features candid interviews, a terrific classic rock soundtrack, and amazing footage of their killer moves gliding on the walls of drained swimming pools. Later transformed into a Hollywood feature, THE LORDS OF DOGTOWN. [PG-13] ▼●

Dogville (2003-Danish-Swedish-British-French-German-Dutch) **C-177m.** ***½ D: Lars von Trier. Nicole Kidman, Harriet Andersson, Lauren Bacall, Jean-Marc Barr, Paul Bettany, Blair Brown, James Caan, Patricia Clarkson, Jeremy Davies, Ben Gazzara, Philip Baker Hall, Siobhan Fallon Hogan, Željko Ivanek, Udo Kier, Cleo King, Chloë Sevigny, Stellan Skarsgård; narrated by John Hurt. Provocative and offbeat drama about enigmatic fugitive Kidman, who stumbles into an isolated 1930s Rocky Mountain hamlet and has a disturbing effect on the close-knit community. Dark, avant garde morality tale, with overtly theatrical staging (à la *Our Town*), fresh casting, and superior acting. Long, demanding, but fascinating and worthwhile. Written by the director. Followed by MANDERLAY. HD 24P Widescreen. [R] ▼●

Doing Time (1979-British) **C-95m.** **½ D: Dick Clement. Ronnie Barker, Richard Beckinsale, Fulton Mackay, Brian Wilde, Peter Vaughan. Barker is a delight as a habitual prison inmate who inadvertently escapes—and wants back in! Reportedly not as funny as the TV series on which it's based, but that's usually the case with feature spinoffs. (The show was tried on American TV as *On the Rocks*.) Original British title: PORRIDGE.

Doin' It SEE: **First Time, The** (1983)

Doin' Time (1985) **C-81m.** BOMB D: George Mendeluk. Jeff Altman, Dey Young, Richard Mulligan, John Vernon, Colleen Camp, Melanie Chartoff, Graham Jarvis, Pat McCormick, Eddie Velez, Jimmie Walker, Judy Landers, Mike Mazurki, Muhammad Ali. Shoddy, thoroughly obnoxious POLICE ACADEMY clone, set in the John Dillinger Memorial Penitentiary (yuk, yuk). [R] ▼

Doin' Time on Planet Earth (1988) **C-83m.** **½ D: Charles Matthau. Nicholas Strouse, Andrea Thompson, Hugh Gillin, Adam West, Candice Azzara, Hugh O'Brian, Matt Adler, Timothy Patrick Murphy, Roddy McDowall, Maureen Stapleton. Fresh-feeling but thin teen comedy about boy who feels *literally* alienated from his family and their Holiday Inn home: cheerful wackos West and Azzara convince him that he's really an alien born on Earth, destined to lead others back to the stars. Amusingly designed, inventively directed, but aimless. [PG] ▼

Dolemite (1975) **C-88m.** *½ D: D'Urville Martin. Rudy Ray Moore, Jerry Jones, Lady Reed. Occasionally funny but amateurish vehicle for standup comedian Moore (who also produced the film), a stout nonactor who combines the personality of Mr. T with a rhyming rap routine. Karate gangster spoof is set in the milieu of black nightclubs where Moore performs. [R] ▼●

$(Dollars) (1971) **C-119m.** ***½ D: Richard Brooks. Warren Beatty, Goldie Hawn, Gert Frobe, Robert Webber, Scott Brady.

[368]

Top-notch caper thriller (scripted by the director) set in Germany with unusual chase that goes on for more than a fifth of the film. Awfully similar to PERFECT FRIDAY. Bouncy Quincy Jones score. [R]▼●)

Dollman (1991) **C-86m.** BOMB D: Albert Pyun. Tim Thomerson, Jackie Earle Haley, Kamala Lopez, Humberto Ortiz, Nicholas Guest, Judd Omen. Tough alien cop (from a planet identical to a slightly futuristic Earth) chases a villainous flying head to our planet, but surprise! The cop is only 13 inches tall. Underproduced trifle with poor FX and a deadly slow pace. Followed by DOLLMAN VS. THE DEMONIC TOYS. [R]▼●)

Dolls (1987) **C-77m.** ** D: Stuart Gordon. Ian Patrick Williams, Carolyn Purdy-Gordon, Carrie Lorraine, Guy Rolfe, Hilary Mason, Bunty Bailey, Cassie Stuart, Stephen Lee. OK horror from the director of RE-ANIMATOR has unsuspecting people taking shelter from a storm in mansion owned by elderly couple who make murderous dolls. Nothing special here. [R]▼●)

Doll's House, A (1973-British) **C-105m.** **½ D: Patrick Garland. Claire Bloom, Anthony Hopkins, Ralph Richardson, Denholm Elliott, Anna Massey, Edith Evans. Bloom and Hopkins give thoughtful performances in this rather stagy filmization of Ibsen's play. Still, the words are there and the play is a strong statement about women's (and all people's) rights to be human beings. [G]▼)

Doll's House, A (1973-British) **C-106m.** **½ D: Joseph Losey. Jane Fonda, David Warner, Trevor Howard, Delphine Seyrig, Edward Fox. Moderately successful, cinematic version of Ibsen play, worth a look for Fonda's controversial interpretation of a 19th-century liberated woman. Howard shines as the dying Dr. Rank. [G]▼

Doll Squad, The (1973) **C-101m.** BOMB D: Ted V. Mikels. Michael Ansara, Francine York; Anthony Eisley, John Carter, Rafael Campos, Lisa Todd. Sexy York leads her all-female trio against ex-CIA agent Ansara, out to rule the world. Poorly made and boring, with very little action. Interesting only as a forerunner to *Charlie's Angels*; the smart one's even named Sabrina! Aka HUSTLER SQUAD. [PG]▼)

Dolly Sisters, The (1945) **C-114m.** **½ D: Irving Cummings. Betty Grable, John Payne, June Haver, S. Z. Sakall, Reginald Gardiner, Frank Latimore. Sassy hokum about popular vaudeville sister act with two lovely stars and a bevy of old song favorites, plus newly written "I Can't Begin to Tell You."▼●)

Dolores Claiborne (1995) **C-131m.** ***½ D: Taylor Hackford. Kathy Bates, Jennifer Jason Leigh, Judy Parfitt, Christopher Plummer, David Strathairn, Eric Bogosian, John C. Reilly, Ellen Muth, Bob Gunton. A Maine woman is accused of murdering her longtime employer, which brings her estranged daughter home for the first time in years. Now, the two women begin to sort out unanswered questions from the past. Gripping adaptation of Stephen King's novel (by Tony Gilroy) holds your interest from start to finish, as the real story unfolds. Bates' performance is a powerhouse, and the rest of the cast is equally fine. Kudos, too, to Hackford's arresting visual treatment. Panavision. [R]▼●)

Domestic Disturbance (2001) **C-89m.** **½ D: Harold Becker. John Travolta, Vince Vaughn, Teri Polo, Steve Buscemi, Ruben Santiago-Hudson, Susan Floyd. Divorced but devoted dad Travolta is wary of the man his ex is about to marry, all the more so after his son is eyewitness to a crime that no one will believe took place. Straightforward thriller where, for a change, everything adds up—but perhaps it's a little *too* neat. An ideal role for Travolta, with Buscemi a standout as Vaughn's sleazy friend. J-D-C Scope. [PG-13]▼)

Dominick and Eugene (1988) **C-111m.** *** D: Robert M. Young. Tom Hulce, Ray Liotta, Jamie Lee Curtis, Todd Graff, Mimi Cecchini, Robert Levine, Bill Cobbs, David Strathairn. Heartrending story of a bright young intern (Liotta) and his devotion to a childlike twin brother (Hulce) who needs looking after. An overtly sentimental, sometimes melodramatic, but completely affecting story of love, compassion and responsibility. Hulce's performance as the sweet-natured, slow-witted Dominick is superb. [PG-13]▼●)

Dominion: Prequel to The Exorcist (2005) **C-117m.** ** D: Paul Schrader. Stellan Skarsgård, Gabriel Mann, Clara Bellar, Billy Crawford, Ralph Brown. Years before exorcising Regan MacNeil in THE EXORCIST, Father Merrin battles internal and external demons during an archaeological dig in East Africa. This film became notorious when it was scrubbed and Renny Harlin was hired to remake it from scratch as EXORCIST: THE BEGINNING. Schrader's version (subsequently saved from movie limbo) is significantly more elegant, ambitious, and thoughtful and Skarsgård gives an effective performance. But in spite of all this, it's still pretty dull. Univision. [R]▶)

Dominique (1978-British) **C-100m.** ** D: Michael Anderson. Cliff Robertson, Jean Simmons, Jenny Agutter, Simon Ward, Ron Moody, Judy Geeson, Michael Jayston, Flora Robson, David Tomlinson, Jack Warner. Great cast tries its best in disappointing melodrama; crippled Simmons believes husband Robertson wants to drive her mad; she dies, but comes back to haunt him. Video titles: DOMINIQUE IS DEAD and AVENGING SPIRIT. [PG]▼)

Dominique Is Dead SEE: **Dominique**

Domino (2005-French-U.S.) **C-127m.** **✶✶½**
D: Tony Scott. Keira Knightley, Mickey Rourke, Édgar Ramírez, Rizwan Abbasi, Delroy Lindo, Mo'Nique, Lucy Liu, Christopher Walken, Mena Suvari, Macy Gray, Jacqueline Bisset, Dabney Coleman, T.K. Carter, Shondrella Avery, Tom Waits. Gritty but jumbled thriller inspired by the life of Domino Harvey (Knightley), an angry young woman who rebels against her background—she's the daughter of jet-setting actor Laurence Harvey—by becoming a bounty hunter. Potentially intriguing but dramatically convoluted, and fails to offer meaningful insight into its title character. Of note for Knightley's offbeat casting and the mass of familiar faces in supporting roles. Screenplay by Richard Kelly of DONNIE DARKO fame. Harvey died at age 35 of an apparent drug overdose after the film's completion but before its release. Super 35. [R] ▼❂

Domino Principle, The (1977) **C-97m.** BOMB D: Stanley Kramer. Gene Hackman, Candice Bergen, Richard Widmark, Mickey Rooney, Edward Albert, Eli Wallach. Muddled thriller about lunkhead Hackman's recruitment by a mysterious organization bent on political assassination. Bergen fails to convince as a lower-middle-class housewife. [R] ▼❶

Dona Flor and Her Two Husbands (1978-Brazilian) **C-116m.** **✶✶✶½** D: Bruno Barreto. Sonia Braga, José Wilker, Mauro Mendoca, Dinorah Brillanti. Braga is torn between giving body and soul to the dead, irresponsible husband who keeps returning to earth, or to the considerate dullard who's become her new mate. Original, very sexy fantasy. Remade as KISS ME GOODBYE. [R] ▼❂❶

Dona Herlinda and Her Son (1986-Mexican) **C-91m.** **✶✶✶** D: Jaime Humberto Hermosillo. Arturo Meza, Marco Antonio Trevino, Leticia Lupersio, Guadalupe del Toro, Angelica Guerrero. Amusing, cheerfully subversive comedy about a pair of gay men, one a surgeon and the other a student, who move in with the former's willful mother. Liberating in its depiction of the lovers; a film to be savored regardless of one's sexual preference. ▼❶

Don Is Dead, The (1973) **C-115m.** **✶½** D: Richard Fleischer. Anthony Quinn, Frederic Forrest, Robert Forster, Al Lettieri, Angel Tompkins, Ina Balin. Mafia wars form the convoluted plot of this trashy, derivative gangster saga. Retitled BEAUTIFUL BUT DEADLY. [R] ▼❶

Don Juan DeMarco (1995) **C-97m.** **✶✶✶** D: Jeremy Leven. Marlon Brando, Johnny Depp, Faye Dunaway, Geraldine Pailhas, Bob Dishy, Rachel Ticotin, Talisa Soto, Richard Sarafian, Tresa Hughes, Franc Luz. Psychotherapist on the verge of retirement becomes entranced with a new patient, a fervent young man who believes he is the world's greatest lover. Fanciful story (by director Leven) is made compulsively watchable by its stars: Brando, compelling as ever, Depp, hypnotically believeable, and Dunaway, a delightful match for Brando, as his wife. Ill-fated Tejano singer Selena appears in the opening scene. [PG-13] ▼❂❶

Donkey Skin (1971-French) **C-90m.** **✶✶✶** D: Jacques Demy. Catherine Deneuve, Jacques Perrin, Jean Marais, Delphine Seyrig. Charming adaptation of Charles Perrault's fairy tale about widowed King who vows that his new Queen must be as beautiful as his first. Sumptuous color production, witty script by Demy. ▼❶

Donnie Brasco (1997) **C-127m.** **✶✶✶½** D: Mike Newell. Al Pacino, Johnny Depp, Michael Madsen, Bruno Kirby, James Russo, Anne Heche, Željko Ivanek, Gerry Becker, Zach Grenier, Brian Tarantina, Val Avery, Gretchen Mol, Tim Blake Nelson, Paul Giamatti. Fresh, original take on life among the "wiseguys" in N.Y.C.'s Italian crime families, with rich characterizations by Pacino (as a low-level hood in the Mob food chain) and Depp (as an FBI undercover agent who becomes his protégé). Depp's assignment forces him to virtually abandon his wife and children, as he becomes more and more a part of his adoptive Mob family. Rings true start to finish; based on Joseph Pistone's memoir, scripted by Paul Attanasio. Also available in unrated 147m. version. Super 35. [R] ▼❂❶

Donnie Darko (2001) **C-113m.** **✶✶** D: Richard Kelly. Jake Gyllenhaal, Jena Malone, Drew Barrymore, James Duval, Maggie Gyllenhaal, Mary McDonnell, Holmes Osborne, Katharine Ross, Patrick Swayze, Noah Wyle, Seth Rogen. A tortured teen who attends a repressive high school in the 1980s has nightmarish visions. Are they premonitions or hallucinations? Writer-director Kelly has ambitious and interesting ideas, but the film builds to an unsatisfying conclusion. Barrymore executive-produced and has a relatively minor role as a schoolteacher. "Director's Cut," theatrically released in 2004, runs 133m. Followed by a DVD sequel, S. DARKO. Panavision. [R] ▼❶

Do Not Disturb (1965) **C-102m.** **✶✶½** D: Ralph Levy. Doris Day, Rod Taylor, Hermione Baddeley, Sergio Fantoni, Reginald Gardiner, Mike Romanoff, Leon Askin. Mild Day vehicle with Taylor as executive husband who brings her to suburban England. She meets suave Fantoni, enraging jealous hubby. Not up to her earlier fashion romps. CinemaScope. ❶

Donovan's Brain (1953) **83m.** **✶✶✶** D: Felix Feist. Lew Ayres, Gene Evans, Nancy Davis (Reagan), Steve Brodie. Scientist is dominated by brain of dead industrialist, which he's kept alive in his lab; intriguing story by Curt Siodmak; modest, capable production. Filmed before as THE LADY

AND THE MONSTER, again as THE BRAIN.▼○◑

Donovan's Reef (1963) **C-109m.** ✳✳✳ D: John Ford. John Wayne, Lee Marvin, Elizabeth Allen, Jack Warden, Cesar Romero, Dorothy Lamour, Mike Mazurki. Action-comedy bounces along with a good cast. Wayne and his freewheeling friends on a Pacific island are disrupted by Warden's grown daughter (Allen) who comes to visit. Lots of fun in Wayne's last feature film with John Ford. That's Ford's yacht *Araner* in several scenes.▼○◑

Don Quixote (1973) **C-107m.** ✳✳✳ D: Rudolf Nureyev, Robert Helpmann. Nureyev, Helpmann, Lucette Aldous, Australian Ballet. Fine ballet version of Cervantes' classic, choreographed by Nureyev, who plays barber Basilio; Helpmann is the wandering knight. Not just for ballet buffs. [G] ▼◐

Don's Party (1976-Australian) **C-91m.** ✳✳✳½ D: Bruce Beresford. John Hargreaves, Pat Bishop, Graham Kennedy, Veronica Lang, Candy Raymond, Harold Hopkins. Powerful black comedy chronicling the interaction—sexual and otherwise—among a group of young suburbanites who get together to watch election returns. (Important note: In Australia, the "liberals" are actually the conservative party.) Stunning direction, top performances by all; biting script by David Williamson, from his play. ▼◑

Don't Answer the Phone (1980) **C-94m.** BOMB D: Robert Hammer. James Westmoreland, Flo Gerrish, Ben Frank, Nicholas Worth, Stan Haze. Another sadistic killer who's a Vietnam veteran. Don't watch this movie. [R]▼◑

Don't Be a Menace to South Central While Drinking Your Juice in the Hood (1995) **C-88m.** ✳✳ D: Paris Barclay. Shawn Wayans, Marlon Wayans, Keenen Ivory Wayans, Chris Spencer, Suli McCullough, Darrell Heath, Helen Martin, Isaiah Barnes, Craig Wayans, Kim Wayans, Omar Epps, Faizon Love, Antonio Fargas, LaWanda Page, Damon Wayans, Bernie Mac. NAKED GUN–like spoof of coming-of-age "hood" pictures is only intermittently successful, despite the presence of more Wayanses than there are in Heaven. Thoroughly predictable. Marlon and Shawn (who also cowrote and coexecutive-produced) are amusing as homies. [R] ▼○◑

Don't Bother to Knock (1952) **76m.** ✳✳½ D: Roy (Ward) Baker. Richard Widmark, Marilyn Monroe, Anne Bancroft, Jeanne Cagney, Elisha Cook, Jr., Gloria Blondell. Title has more punch than improbable yarn of airline pilot Widmark getting involved with mentally disturbed Monroe hired as babysitter in large hotel. Bancroft's film debut. Remade for TV as THE SITTER.▼◑

Don't Come Knocking (2005-U.S.-German-French) **C-122m.** ✳✳½ D: Wim Wenders.

Sam Shepard, Jessica Lange, Tim Roth, Gabriel Mann, Sarah Polley, Eva Marie Saint, Fairuza Balk, George Kennedy, James Gammon, Marley Shelton, Julia Sweeney. Troubled Western movie star rides his horse off his current film set and journeys back to his roots—and the family he left behind decades earlier. Returning to the Southwest of PARIS, TEXAS, Wenders and Shepard (who collaborated on the story) seem to be slumming here, but screenwriter Shepard provides himself with a meaty role and makes the most of it, particularly in scenes with Saint (as his mother) and Lange. Franz Lustig's cinematography is a standout. Hawk-Scope. [R]◑

Don't Cry, It's Only Thunder (1982) **C-108m.** ✳✳✳ D: Peter Werner. Dennis Christopher, Susan Saint James, Roger Aaron Brown, Lisa Lu. Dramatically uneven, but moving account of G.I. Christopher and doctor Saint James' involvement with makeshift orphanage in Vietnam. Based on a true incident. [PG]▼

Don't Do It! (1994) **C-90m.** ✳½ D: Eugene Hess. Alexis Arquette, Balthazar Getty, Heather Graham, James Le Gros, Sheryl Lee, James Marshall, Esai Morales, Sarah Trigger. Talented cast flounders in this confusing, meandering Generation X drama of various couples whose love and sex lives are intertwined. Means to be insightful, but the result is a talky bore.▼◑

Don't Drink the Water (1969) **C-100m.** ✳✳ D: Howard Morris. Jackie Gleason, Estelle Parsons, Ted Bessell, Joan Delaney, Michael Constantine, Howard St. John, Avery Schreiber. Uninspired adaptation of Woody Allen play about American family held prisoner in Iron Curtain country of Vulgaria, and their desperate attempts to escape. Cast works hard, with sporadic results. Remade for TV in 1994. [G]▼◑

Don't Give Up the Ship (1959) **89m.** ✳✳✳ D: Norman Taurog. Jerry Lewis, Dina Merrill, Diana Spencer, Mickey Shaughnessy, Robert Middleton, Gale Gordon, Claude Akins. Top comedy with Jerry as U.S. Navy lieutenant who lost a destroyer escort during war and doesn't remember how. Shaughnessy is pal who helps look for it underwater. One of Lewis' all-time best. ▼

Don't Just Stand There (1968) **C-100m.** ✳✳½ D: Ron Winston. Robert Wagner, Mary Tyler Moore, Harvey Korman, Glynis Johns, Barbara Rhoades. Frantic comedy with perky stars; Wagner and Moore try to unravel mystery of disappearance of authoress Johns after writing the first half of a new book. Players' vivacity makes script seem better than it is. Techniscope.

Don't Knock the Twist (1962) **87m.** BOMB D: Oscar Rudolph. Chubby Checker, Gene Chandler, Vic Dana, Linda Scott, Mari Blanchard, Lang Jeffries. The Dovells. Television producer Jeffries, with

Checker's assistance, coordinates a twist show. Chandler, with cape, monocle and top hat, sings "Duke of Earl"; otherwise, you may want to twist your way to your TV set. ▶

Dont Look Back (1967) 96m. ***½ D: D. A. Pennebaker. Bob Dylan, Joan Baez, Donovan, Alan Price, Albert Grossman, Allen Ginsberg. Candid documentary about Dylan's '65 concert tour of England, highlighted by his pseudo-hip personality, appearances by Baez and Grossman (Dylan's manager). Dylan performs "The Times They Are a Changin'," "Don't Think Twice, It's All Right," "It's All Over Now, Baby Blue," and "Subterranean Homesick Blues." Pennebaker assembled a collection of never-before-seen outtakes and performances in 2007 and released it as 65 REVISITED.▼●)

Don't Look Now (1973-British) C-110m. *** D: Nicolas Roeg. Julie Christie, Donald Sutherland, Hilary Mason, Clelia Matania, Massimo Serato. Arty, over-indulgent but gripping Daphne du Maurier occult thriller about parents of drowned child and their horror-laden visit to Venice; highlighted by memorably steamy love scene and violent climax. [R]▼●)

Don't Make Waves (1967) C-97m. *** D: Alexander Mackendrick. Tony Curtis, Claudia Cardinale, Sharon Tate, Robert Webber, Mort Sahl, Jim Backus, Edgar Bergen, Joanna Barnes. The one gem out of nine million bad Tony Curtis comedy vehicles; satire on Southern California has good direction, funny performance by Sharon Tate, and a catchy title song sung by the Byrds. Good fun. Panavision.▼)

Don't Move (2004-Italian) C-125m. **½ D: Sergio Castellitto. Penélope Cruz, Sergio Castellitto, Claudia Gerini, Angela Finocchiaro, Pietro De Silva, Lina Berardi, Marco Giallini. Well-to-do Italian surgeon whose daughter lies on the brink of death after a motorcycle accident looks back on a torrid affair with a poor prostitute 15 years earlier, just before his child was conceived. Odd, very intense melodrama never quite comes together in the way it was intended. Offers an almost unrecognizable Cruz a showcase for her acting chops; she delivers with an effective portrayal that won her the Italian equivalent of the Oscar. Super 35. ▶

Don't Raise the Bridge, Lower the River (1968) C-99m. ** D: Jerry Paris. Jerry Lewis, Terry-Thomas, Jacqueline Pearce, Bernard Cribbins, Patricia Routledge. Jerry plays American in England whose get-rich-quick schemes have put him on verge of divorce; mild Lewis comedy scripted by Max Wilk, from his novel. [G]▼)

Don't Say a Word (2001) C-113m. *** D: Gary Fleder. Michael Douglas, Sean Bean, Brittany Murphy, Famke Janssen, Oliver Platt, Jennifer Esposito, Skye McCole Bartusiak, Victor Argo. In order to rescue his daughter from kidnappers, a successful N.Y.C. psychiatrist must unlock a secret guarded for ten years by a mental patient (Murphy)—on a one-day deadline. Entertaining thriller builds to a conventional Hollywood-style ending and a silly final scene, but the pace never flags and the cast is first-rate. Super 35. [R]▼)

Don't Tell (2005-Italian) C-120m. **½ D: Cristina Comencini. Giovanna Mezzogiorno, Alessio Boni, Stefania Rocca, Angela Finocchiaro, Giuseppe Battiston, Luigi Lo Cascio. A woman seemingly content in her marriage and career discovers she is pregnant at about the same time she starts having nightmares about her earlier life. She contacts her brother, a professor at a U.S. university, to help her uncover the secret in their family's past and unlock the answers that will enable her to move on. Melodrama is slow moving and hard to crack at times, but has fine performances and an intriguing story that grows on you. Comencini co-adapted her own novel. [R]▶

Don't Tell Her It's Me (1990) C-101m. *½ D: Malcolm Mowbray. Steve Guttenberg, Jami Gertz, Shelley Long, Kyle MacLachlan, Kevin Scannell, Madchen Amick, Beth Grant. If you can buy Guttenberg and Long as siblings, or Guttenberg in a skull cap and bloated facial makeup to convey Parkinson's disease radiation treatments, or Guttenberg masquerading as a scruffy New Zealand biker, then maybe you'll find something to like in this romantic comedy of mistaken identity . . . but don't tell her (or him) you did. Aka THE BOYFRIEND SCHOOL. [PG-13]▼●

Don't Tell Mom the Babysitter's Dead (1991) C-105m. ** D: Stephen Herek. Christina Applegate, Joanna Cassidy, John Getz, Keith Coogan, Josh Charles, David Duchovny, Kimmy Robertson, Eda Reiss Merin, Jayne Brook, Cathy Ladman, Christopher Plummer. Superficial comedy about kids whose babysitter dies, leaving them to get along without supervision or money. The core of the film is not as bad as the title might suggest—that is, if you can get past the first 15 minutes. Cassidy is a standout as Applegate's boss. [PG-13]▼●)

Don't Tempt Me (2001-Spanish-French-Italian) C/B&W-108m. *** D: Agustin Diaz Yanes. Penélope Cruz, Victoria Abril, Demián Bichir, Fanny Ardant, Gael García Bernal, Juan Echanove, Emilio Gutiérrez Caba, Cristina Marcos, Gemma Jones, Bruno Bichir, Elena Anaya, Peter McDonald. Heaven and Hell assign agents Abril and Cruz to vie for the soul of an embittered pro boxer. Gangsters, supermarket cashiers, and assorted otherworldly emissaries all figure into this oddball seriocomic fantasy. More than a little Almodóvaresque, with some truly weird soundtrack choices ("Kung Fu

Fighting"?!?). Original title: SIN NOTI-CIAS DE DIOS. Widescreen. [R] ▼〉

Don't Turn the Other Cheek (1973-Italian) **C-93m. **½** D: Duccio Tessari. Franco Nero, Lynn Redgrave, Eli Wallach, Marilu Tolo, Horst Janson. Slapstick spaghetti Western detailing exploits of unlikely trio: a fiery, revolution-fomenting Irish journalist (Redgrave), a bogus Russian prince (Nero), and a seedy Mexican bandit (Wallach) with proverbial heart of gold. Aka LONG LIVE YOUR DEATH. Techniscope. [PG]▼

Don't Worry, We'll Think of a Title (1966) **83m.** BOMB D: Harmon Jones. Morey Amsterdam, Rose Marie, Joey Adams, Danny Thomas, Milton Berle, Nick Adams. Grade-Z shambles, despite many guest cameos by big TV and movie stars. Start worrying when you turn it on.

Doogal (2005-British) **C-79m. *½** D: Dave Borthwick, Jean Duval, Frank Passingham. Voices of Daniel Tay, Jimmy Fallon, Whoopi Goldberg, Judi Dench, William H. Macy, Chevy Chase, Jon Stewart, Ian McKellen, Kevin Smith, Kylie Minogue, Bill Hader, John Krasinski. A group of pets takes on a quest to stop a power-mad wizard who has encased their village (and their human owners) in ice. Pedestrian computer-animated film is aimed strictly at kids. Based on a 1960s British children's TV series, *The Magic Roundabout*, and originally released in England under that title with an all-star British voice cast (including Tom Baker, Jim Broadbent, Joanna Lumley, and Robbie Williams). [G]〉

Doom (2005-British-Czech-German-U.S.) **C-100m.** BOMB D: Andrzej Bartkowiak. Karl Urban, The Rock, Rosamund Pike, DeObia Oparei, Ben Daniels, Raz Adoti, Richard Brake, Al Weaver, Dexter Fletcher, Brian Steele, Doug Jones. Brainless, high-testosterone sci-fi–horror drivel, with the ultra-macho Rapid Response Tactical Squad ordered into action when scientists are mysteriously locked down in a high-security lab located on Mars. Unimaginative ALIEN clone is all special effects, gore, and noise; a dumb script and leaden pacing don't help. Inspired by the controversial, wildly popular Doom video game. Unrated director's cut runs 113m. Super 35. [R]▼〉

Doom Generation, The (1995-U.S.-French) **85m. *½** D: Gregg Araki. Rose McGowan, James Duval, Johnathon Schaech, Margaret Cho, Lauren Tewes, Christopher Knight, Parker Posey, Amanda Bearse, Heidi Fleiss. Two young lovers turn their lives upside down when they pick up a dangerous drifter who involves them in murder and a sexual triangle. Bleak, bleak view of the younger generation makes KIDS look like THE LITTLE MERMAID. ▼〉

Doomsday (2008-British) **C-105m. **** D: Neil Marshall. Rhona Mitra, Bob Hoskins, Adrian Lester, Alexander Siddig, David O'Hara, Malcolm McDowell, Craig Con-way. Shamelessly derivative, ultraviolent postapocalyptic thriller in which the British authorities dispatch feisty action heroine Mitra and a band of mercenaries to sealed-off Scotland to find a cure for a deadly virus. Their foes include a standard-issue mad scientist (McDowell) and a Mohawk-coiffed zombie (Conway), who may as well be a refugee from a MAD MAX movie. Unrated DVD runs 113m. Super 35. [R]〉

Doomsday Machine, The (1972) **C-88m.** BOMB D: Lee Sholem, Harry Hope. Denny Miller, Mala Powers, Bobby Van, Ruta Lee, Grant Williams, Henry Wilcoxon. Tired cast in lumpy, stultifyingly boring melodrama about scientists on a space voyage who are constantly bickering. Aka ESCAPE FROM PLANET EARTH. ▼〉

Doomwatch (1972-British) **C-92m. ***** D: Peter Sasdy. Ian Bannen, Judy Geeson, George Sanders, John Paul, Simon Oates, Geoffrey Keen. Dr. Bannen investigates the effects of radioactivity on an island inhabited by a rather odd-acting population. Topical, thought-provoking mystery-thriller, not at all bad of its type. Based on the British TV series of the same name.▼〉

Door in the Floor, The (2004) **C-111m. ***** D: Tod Williams. Jeff Bridges, Kim Basinger, Jon Foster, Elle Fanning, Bijou Phillips, Mimi Rogers, Robert LuPone, Donna Murphy, Louis Arcella. Noted children's book writer/illustrator hires a college student as his assistant for the summer. The boy has no idea what he's in for, as the man and his wife are reeling from a family tragedy and acting out in entirely different ways. Their young daughter, meanwhile, has problems of her own. Williams adapted the first section of John Irving's best-selling novel *A Widow for One Year* to create this moving, multilayered drama. Despite superficial echoes of other stories, it has a feeling all its own. Fanning is Dakota Fanning's younger sister. Bridges is at the top of his form. Super 35. [R] ▼〉

Doors, The (1991) **C-135m. **½** D: Oliver Stone. Val Kilmer, Frank Whaley, Kevin Dillon, Meg Ryan, Kyle MacLachlan, Billy Idol, Dennis Burkley, Josh Evans, Michael Madsen, Michael Wincott, Kathleen Quinlan, John Densmore, Will Jordan, Mimi Rogers, Paul Williams, Crispin Glover, Bill Graham, Billy Vera, Bill Kunstler, Wes Studi, Costas Mandylor. Vivid impression of famed rocker Jim Morrison's rise to fame, and eventual undoing. Stone masterfully re-creates the late '60s/early '70s rock and drug scene, and Kilmer is perfect in the lead . . . but when it's all over you don't know very much more about Morrison than when the film began. The film's excesses also tend to parallel Morrison's. Stone appears briefly as a UCLA film professor. Panavision. [R]▼●〉

Door-to-Door Maniac (1961) **80m. *½** D: Bill Karn. Johnny Cash, Donald Woods,

Cay Forrester, Pamela Mason, Midge Ware, Victor Tayback, Ronny Howard, Merle Travis. Cash and Tayback plot a bank robbery. Of interest only for the cast; also known as FIVE MINUTES TO LIVE.▼🄳

Dopamine (2003) C-79m. **½ D: Mark Decena. John Livingston, Sabrina Lloyd, William Windom, Bruno Campos, Rueben Grundy, Kathleen Antonia, Nicole Wilder. Hit-and-miss "relationship" movie about a computer programmer (Livingston) who has difficulty interacting with women, and his connection to equally troubled kindergarten teacher Lloyd. Director-coscripter Decena attempts to offer a novel, perceptive take on modern romance; sincere, occasionally insightful, but static and talky. HD 24P Widescreen. [R] ▼🄳

Doppelganger SEE: **Journey to the Far Side of the Sun**

Doppelganger: The Evil Within (1992) C-104m. BOMB D: Avi Nesher. Drew Barrymore, George Newbern, Dennis Christopher, Leslie Hope, Sally Kellerman, George Maharis, Luana Anders. Screenwriter Newbern's roommate, heiress Barrymore, claims her doppelganger (ghostly double) is killing off her family in this sick, nonsensical, would-be slasher film. Loud (and corny) music renders the dialogue unintelligible, which is actually no loss. Drew's mother, Jaid Barrymore, plays her mom on-screen. [R] ▼🄳

Dorian Gray (1970-Italian-German-Lichtensteinian) C-93m. *½ D: Massimo Dallamano. Helmut Berger, Richard Todd, Herbert Lom, Marie Liljedahl, Margaret Lee. Trashy, slow-moving filmization of Oscar Wilde's novel, updated to the present: vain, immoral young man (Berger) ceases to grow older—his portrait ages instead. 1945's THE PICTURE OF DORIAN GRAY is vastly superior. Aka THE SECRET OF DORIAN GRAY. [R] ▼🄳

Dorian Gray (2009-British) C-112m. ** D: Oliver Parker. Ben Barnes, Colin Firth, Ben Chaplin, Rebecca Hall, Douglas Henshall, Rachel Hurd-Wood, Fiona Shaw, Maryam d'Abo, Michael Culkin, Caroline Goodall. Glum, often ghastly rendering of Oscar Wilde's novel about a handsome young man whose face never changes— while all of his sins are reflected in his portrait. Director Parker did well by Wilde in AN IDEAL HUSBAND, but this adaptation removes all the wit from the source material and substitutes gore and gloom. Released direct to DVD in the U.S. [R] 🄳

Do the Right Thing (1989) C-120m. *** D: Spike Lee. Danny Aiello, Ossie Davis, Ruby Dee, Richard Edson, Giancarlo Esposito, Spike Lee, Bill Nunn, John Turturro, Paul Benjamin, Frankie Faison, Robin Harris, John Savage, Sam (Samuel L.) Jackson, Rosie Perez, Martin Lawrence. Idealized, individualistic look at life in the black community of Bedford-Stuyvesant in Brooklyn, where a white-owned pizza parlor flourishes . . . and where circumstance leads to an outbreak of hostilities on a sweltering summer day. Entertaining and provocative, with a much-discussed (and troubling) finale. Writer-director Lee also stars as Mookie, the delivery boy; his real-life sister Joie plays his sister in the film. [R] ▼🄳🄳

dot the i (2003-British-Spanish) C-92m. **½ D: Matthew Parkhill. Gael García Bernal, Natalia Verbeke, James D'Arcy, Tom Hardy, Charlie Cox, Yves Aubert. Fiery Spanish woman is torn between her dull but devoted fiancé and a more attractive, passionate man she chances to meet one evening. Their relationship grows more fervent—and more dangerous—with each passing day, but all is not what it seems to be. Debut film for writer-director Parkhill is undeniably clever, but terribly self-conscious, and eventually runs out of steam. Bernal is charismatic and completely at ease in his first English-language film. Released in the U.S. in 2005. [R]🄳

Double Con SEE: **Trick Baby**

Double Dragon (1994) C-96m. *½ D: James Yukich. Robert Patrick, Mark Dacascos, Scott Wolf, Julia Nickson, Kristina Malandro Wagner, John Mallory Asher, Leon Russom, Alyssa Milano, Michael Berryman, Vanna White, George Hamilton. In the junky, gang-dominated post-earthquake "New Angeles" of 2007, martial artist brothers Dacascos and Wolf battle evil billionaire Patrick for the possession of a two-part Chinese medallion that grants mystical powers. Sometimes lively but mostly silly and tedious; based on an arcade game. [PG-13]▼🄳🄳

Double Dynamite (1951) 80m. ** D: Irving Cummings. Frank Sinatra, Jane Russell, Groucho Marx, Don McGuire. Sinatra plays a bank clerk falsely accused of robbery. Flat comedy marked a career low point for all three of its stars. Filmed in 1948.▼🄳

Double Edge (1992-U.S.-Israeli) C-86m. **½ D: Amos Kollek. Faye Dunaway, Amos Kollek, Mohammad Bakri, Makram Khouri, Anat Atzmon. Dunaway is well cast as an overly ambitious American reporter covering the Arab-Israeli conflict in this uneven drama about journalistic objectivity and responsibility. Never quite delivers as it should, but it does effectively mix fiction with fact, as Dunaway interviews Jerusalem mayor Teddy Kollek (the director-actor-screenwriter's father) and other real-life political figures. [PG-13]▼

Double Happiness (1994-Canadian) C-100m. *** D: Mina Shum. Sandra Oh, Stephen Chang, Allanah Ong, Frances You, Callum Rennie. Insightful, refreshingly unclichéd tale of a free-thinking young Chinese-Canadian woman (appealingly played by Oh), an aspiring actress whose

Old World parents are pressuring her to find a boyfriend and marry. Writer-director Shum does not paint the parents as stodgy villains; they just want what they feel is best for the daughter they love. Bright touches of humor enhance this charming film. [PG-13] ▼●❶

Double Impact (1991) C-118m. ** D: Sheldon Lettich. Jean-Claude Van Damme, Geoffrey Lewis, Alan Scarfe, Alonna Shaw, Cory Everson. Identical twins are separated at six months when Hong Kong thugs murder their parents, only to be reunited in revenge a quarter-century later. Van Damme's attempts to delineate two characters (one of them a gruff cigar-chomper) are nearly as goofy as one slow-motion love scene; studio press material, praising this Van Damme career stretch, extolled "the light, charming side of his persona that we haven't seen before." [R] ▼●❶

Double Indemnity (1944) 106m. **** D: Billy Wilder. Barbara Stanwyck, Fred MacMurray, Edward G. Robinson, Porter Hall, Tom Power, Fortunio Bonanova, Jean Heather, Bess Flowers. Wilder–Raymond Chandler script (from the James M. Cain novel) packs fireworks in account of insurance salesman MacMurray lured into murder plot by alluring Stanwyck and subsequent investigation by Fred's colleague Robinson. An American movie classic, with crackling dialogue throughout. Remade for TV in 1973 with Richard Crenna and Samantha Eggar, and the obvious inspiration for Lawrence Kasdan's BODY HEAT. ▼●❶

Double Jeopardy (1999) C-105m. *** D: Bruce Beresford. Ashley Judd, Tommy Lee Jones, Bruce Greenwood, Annabeth Gish, Roma Maffia, Davenia McFadden. Woman is framed for the murder of her husband; while serving the jail sentence she learns he's alive and vows revenge, especially since she can't be tried twice for the same crime. Slick entertainment gives you pretty much what you'd expect. Panavision. [R] ▼●❶

Double Life, A (1947) 104m. ***½ D: George Cukor. Ronald Colman, Signe Hasso, Edmond O'Brien, Shelley Winters, Ray Collins, Millard Mitchell. Colman gives a bravura, Oscar-winning performance as an actor whose stage roles spill over into his life—and now he's about to play Othello. Brilliant melodrama by Ruth Gordon and Garson Kanin, with wonderful New York theater flavor. Miklos Rozsa's fine score also won an Oscar. Watch for playwright Paddy Chayefsky as a crime-scene photographer. ▼❶

Double Life of Veronique, The (1991-Polish-French) C-97m. **½ D: Krzysztof Kieslowski. Irène Jacob, Wladyslaw Kowalski, Guillaume de Tonquedec, Philippe Volter. Two women (one Polish, one French, both played by Jacob) subtly affect each other's lives while remaining total strangers. Unfolds like a half-hour teleplay with a supernatural premise stretched to 1½ hours. Film, though, has enough going for it to pick up a cult, for which luminous lead Jacob deserves credit. ▼●❶

Double Man, The (1967-British) C-105m. **½ D: Franklin Schaffner. Yul Brynner, Britt Ekland, Clive Revill, Anton Diffring, Moira Lister, Lloyd Nolan. Unconvincing spy thriller with Brynner playing both unemotional C.I.A. agent *and* East German lookalike. Excellent photography by Denys Coop.❶

Double McGuffin, The (1979) C-89m. **½ D: Joe Camp. Ernest Borgnine, George Kennedy, Elke Sommer, Rod Browning, Dion Pride, Lisa Whelchel, Jeff Nicholson, Michael Gerard, Vincent Spano. Teenagers stumble onto clues leading to assassination plot, but no one will believe them. Family-oriented thriller from creator of BENJI. Orson Welles explains film's title at the outset, for non-Hitchcock devotees. [PG] ▼❶

Double Negative (1980-Canadian) C-96m. *½ D: George Bloomfield. Michael Sarrazin, Susan Clark, Anthony Perkins, Howard Duff, Kate Reid, Al Waxman, Elizabeth Shepherd, John Candy, Joe Flaherty. Confusing, annoying thriller with mentally tortured photojournalist Sarrazin attempting to track down his wife's murderer. Sarrazin is his usual bland self; Clark is wasted. Based on Ross Macdonald's *The Three Roads.* Aka DEADLY COMPANION. ▼

Double Take (2001) C-88m. BOMB D: George Gallo. Orlando Jones, Eddie Griffin, Edward Herrmann, Gary Grubbs, Shawn Elliott, Brent Briscoe, Daniel Roebuck, Garcelle Beauvais, Andrea Navedo. Slick, awful buddy pic about a buppie banker who swaps identities with a ghetto con artist when he's framed for laundering millions for a Mexican drug cartel. Full of car crashes and south-of-the-border caricatures . . . and perpetuates that old stereotype that all black people look alike. Inexplicably based on a Graham Greene short story, filmed before as ACROSS THE BRIDGE. Vivica A. Fox appears unbilled. Panavision. [PG-13] ▼❶

Double Team (1997) C-91m. *½ D: Tsui Hark. Jean-Claude Van Damme, Dennis Rodman, Mickey Rourke, Paul Freeman, Natacha Lindinger, Valeria Cavalli. Mismatched buddy film with Van Damme as a world-class counterterrorist who teams with weapons expert Rodman in a quest to stop Mickey Rourke (not a bad idea). Pointless action thriller from cult Hong Kong director Hark. Scenes in which the hero's baby is placed in constant jeopardy would be hard to stomach even in a coherent film—which this isn't. Super 35. [R] ▼●❶

Double Trouble (1962) SEE: **Swingin' Along**

Double Trouble (1967) **C-90m.** ** D: Norman Taurog. Elvis Presley, Annette Day, John Williams, Yvonne Romain, The Wiere Brothers, Chips Rafferty, Michael Murphy. Teen-age heiress falls for pop singer Presley when he's performing in England; usual Elvis fare, but he does sing "Long Legged Girl," one of his best post-Army tunes. Panavision.▼●》

Double Wedding (1937) **87m.** **½ D: Richard Thorpe. William Powell, Myrna Loy, Florence Rice, John Beal, Jessie Ralph, Edgar Kennedy, Sidney Toler, Mary Gordon, Donald Meek. Loy's orchestration of her sister's wedding is upset by the presence of free-spirited bohemian Powell. The stars are the whole show in this otherwise disappointing adaptation of Ferenc Molnár's play *Great Love.* ▼》

Doubt (2008) **C-104m.** *** D: John Patrick Shanley. Meryl Streep, Philip Seymour Hoffman, Amy Adams, Viola Davis, Alice Drummond, Audrie Neenan, Joseph Foster II, Paulie Litt. In a Bronx parish, circa 1964, a relentlessly stern nun who serves as high school principal suspects that her gregarious priest is showing unnatural interest in the school's first black student. She has certainty on her side; now she needs proof. Often-electrifying drama is played out by a peerless cast, though its power must have been even greater onstage, where it originated. Shanley adapted his own play. Davis shines as the student's mother in one extended, unforgettable scene. [PG-13]▐

Douchebag (2010) **C-81m.** *** D: Drake Doremus. Andrew Dickler, Ben York Jones, Marguerite Moreau, Nicole Vicius, Amy Ferguson, Wendi McLendon-Covey. Disarming micro-indie film about a nice young woman who takes it upon herself to bring her fiancé's impoverished brother to L.A. for their wedding, not realizing the friction that exists between the siblings. Story expands in unexpected ways, and the performances are spot-on. Intimate, real, and rewarding little film. Dickler, who plays Sam, cowrote the screenplay and edited the film.

Doughgirls, The (1944) **102m.** **½ D: James V. Kern. Ann Sheridan, Alexis Smith, Jane Wyman, Eve Arden, Jack Carson, Charlie Ruggles, Alan Mowbray, Craig Stevens, Regis Toomey. Brittle comedy, another tale of crowded wartime Washington, with newlyweds Carson and Wyman on hectic honeymoon. Arden stands out as Russian army officer.

Doug's 1st Movie (1999) **C-77m.** *½ D: Maurice Joyce. Voices of Thomas McHugh, Fred Newman, Chris Phillips, Constance Shulman, Doug Preis, Alice Playten. The star of TV's animated *Doug* is featured in this bland, formulaic story, strictly for kids. Mild-mannered preteen Doug Funnie's efforts to save a local endangered "monster"

conflict with his desire to take his girlfriend to the school dance. [G] ▼●

Doulos—The Finger Man SEE: **Le Doulos**

Dove, The (1974) **C-105m.** **½ D: Charles Jarrott. Joseph Bottoms, Deborah Raffin, John McLiam, Dabney Coleman. Pleasant round-the-world adventure based on true story of 16-year-old who sails to every imaginable port. Produced by Gregory Peck. Filmed on location. Panavision. [PG]▼

Down Among the Z Men (1952-British) **70m.** ** D: Maclean Rogers. Harry Secombe, Peter Sellers, Carole Carr, Spike Milligan, Clifford Stanton, Graham Stark, Miriam Karlin. Creaky vehicle for radio's The Goons in story of criminals who visit small town to steal a professor's secret scientific formula. Some good bits, especially Sellers doing impressions of Yank soldiers, but overloaded with dull song-and-dance numbers by a female chorus line.▼●》

Down and Out in Beverly Hills (1986) **C-103m.** **½ D: Paul Mazursky. Nick Nolte, Richard Dreyfuss, Bette Midler, Little Richard, Tracy Nelson, Elizabeth Pena, Evan Richards, Valerie Curtin, Barry Primus, Dorothy Tristan, Alexis Arquette, Mike the Dog. Bum moves in with neurotic, nouveau-riche Bev Hills family and takes over their lives. Slick, often funny, but unusually obvious satire for Mazursky (who also appears as one of Dreyfuss' fat-cat friends). Some good performances, though Mike the Dog easily steals the film. A remake of Renoir's BOUDU SAVED FROM DROWNING. Later a TV series. [R]▼●》

Down Argentine Way (1940) **C-90m.** *** D: Irving Cummings. Don Ameche, Betty Grable, Carmen Miranda, Charlotte Greenwood, J. Carrol Naish, Henry Stephenson, Leonid Kinskey. Enjoyable 20th Century–Fox musical with Grable (in the movie that boosted her to stardom) falling in love with smooth Argentinian horse breeder Ameche. Miranda is terrific in her first American movie, performing infectious Brazilian songs with her own band . . . and look out for the Nicholas Brothers, who do a dynamite specialty number. Picture-postcard color throughout.▼●》

Down by Law (1986) **107m.** **½ D: Jim Jarmusch. Tom Waits, John Lurie, Roberto Benigni, Ellen Barkin, Billie Neal, Rockets Redglare, Vernel Bagneris, Nicoletta Braschi. Third feature by writer-director Jarmusch is intriguing, amusing, and ever so slight, a look at three losers who wind up in jail together—and then make a break for it. Really comes alive when Italian comic Benigni turns up. Slow moving, strikingly photographed (in black & white) by Robby Müller on location in Louisiana. Costars Lurie and Waits also provide music on the soundtrack. [R]▼●

Downfall (2004-German) **C-155m.** ***½ D: Oliver Hirschbiegel. Bruno Ganz, Alexandra Maria Lara, Corinna Harfouch, Ulrich Matthes, Juliane Köhler, Heino Ferch, Christian Berkel, Matthias Habich, Thomas Kretschmann. Riveting dramatization of Hitler's final days in and around his Berlin bunker, as the Nazi leader descends into madness and paranoia and his adjutants respond in various ways, from jumping ship to standing firm alongside their Fuhrer. Inspired in part by the memories of his young secretary, Traudl Junge (interviewed on screen in BLIND SPOT), whose words bookend the film. Long but thoroughly engrossing; Ganz is outstanding. Screenplay by Bernd Eichinger. [R]◐

Downhill Racer (1969) **C-102m.** ******* D: Michael Ritchie. Robert Redford, Gene Hackman, Camilla Sparv, Karl Michael Vogler, Jim McMullan, Christian Doermer, Dabney Coleman. Vivid study of an empty life, with Redford as small-town egotist who joins U.S. Olympic ski team. Basically a character study; problem is an unappealing character. Dazzling ski scenes make lulls worth enduring. Ritchie's feature directorial debut. [M/PG]▼●◐

Down in the Delta (1998) **C-111m.** ****½** D: Maya Angelou. Alfre Woodard, Al Freeman, Jr., Wesley Snipes, Mary Alice, Esther Rolle, Loretta Devine. With her life a mess and virtually no hope of employment, single mom Woodard boards the bus with her two children to spend the summer in the Mississippi Delta, living with relatives and working in their chicken restaurant. Episodic drama recovers from clumsy exposition to win points for sheer likability, though it's put over almost exclusively by its cast. Woodard shines, and Freeman gives one of the best performances of his career. [PG-13]▼●

Down in the Valley (2006) **C-114m.** ****½** D: David Jacobson. Edward Norton, Evan Rachel Wood, David Morse, Rory Culkin, Bruce Dern, Geoffrey Lewis, Artel Kayàru, Ty Burrell. Interesting attempt to merge a classic Western motif into a contemporary story set in Southern California's San Fernando Valley, where a 30-something charmer rides into the life of an impressionable teenage girl. Their romance goes awry as he reveals his true personality. Norton, recalling a young Henry Fonda, is excellent, but writer-director Jacobson introduces and then drops too many story threads. Intriguing if violent character study seems like the bastard child of TAXI DRIVER and LONELY ARE THE BRAVE. Panavision. [R]◐

Down Periscope (1996) **C-92m.** ****½** D: David S. Ward. Kelsey Grammer, Lauren Holly, Bruce Dern, Rob Schneider, Rip Torn, Harry Dean Stanton, William H. Macy, Ken Hudson Campbell, Toby Huss, Duane Martin, Harland Williams. Maverick naval officer is finally given a submarine to command, but it turns out to be a mothballed wreck—with a crew that's not much better. But if he can prove his mettle (and

the ship's) in a war-game environment, he can graduate to a first-class nuclear sub. Mild comedy follows the misfits-make-good formula fairly well. [PG-13]▼●◐

Down the Drain (1990) **C-105m.** ****** D: Robert C. Hughes. Andrew Stevens, John Matuszak, Don Stroud, Teri Copley, Joseph Campanella, Stella Stevens, Jerry Mathers, Buck Flower, Pedro Gonzalez-Gonzalez, Benny (The Jet) Urquidez. Lawyer Stevens, with the help of his clients, pulls off a bank robbery. Strictly ho-hum. [R]▼●

Down to Earth (1947) **C-101m.** ****** D: Alexander Hall. Rita Hayworth, Larry Parks, Marc Platt, Roland Culver, James Gleason, Edward Everett Horton. Terpsichore, the Goddess of Dance (Hayworth), comes to Earth to help Parks with his mythological musical play. Rita's beauty is only asset of this hack musical, which appropriates Gleason, Horton, and Culver characters from HERE COMES MR. JORDAN. Remade as XANADU.▼●◐

Down to Earth (2001) **C-87m.** ***½** D: Chris Weitz, Paul Weitz. Chris Rock, Regina King, Chazz Palminteri, Eugene Levy, Frankie Faison, Mark Addy, Jennifer Coolidge, Greg Germann, Wanda Sykes, Greg Cho. A would-be standup comic is taken to heaven before his time, then returned to life in the body of a ruthless tycoon. Appallingly clumsy remake of HEAVEN CAN WAIT (and its source, HERE COMES MR. JORDAN), reshaped as a vehicle for Rock. He shines when he's doing a comedy riff, but his acting is monotonous. [PG-13]▼◐

Down to the Bone (2005) **C-105m.** ******* D: Debra Granik. Vera Farmiga, Hugh Dillon, Clint Jordan, Caridad "La Bruja" De La Luz, Jasper Moon Daniels, Taylor Foxhall. Working-class woman tries to keep her family and home intact while feeding a cocaine habit. Going through rehab helps her on a short-term basis but presents her with other challenges—and choices—after she comes to trust an addict-turned-counselor (Dillon). Superior fly-on-the-wall filmmaking is anchored by Farmiga's remarkably honest performance. Based on writer-director Granik's 1997 short SNAKE FEED, which won a prize at Sundance—as did this film.◐

Down to the Sea in Ships (1949) **120m.** ******* D: Henry Hathaway. Richard Widmark, Lionel Barrymore, Dean Stockwell, Cecil Kellaway, Gene Lockhart. Young Stockwell fulfills seafaring goal on crusty Barrymore's whaling ship, under guidance of sailor Widmark. Good atmospheric yarn.

Downtown (1990) **C-96m.** ****** D: Richard Benjamin. Anthony Edwards, Forest Whitaker, Joe Pantoliano, David Clennon, Penelope Ann Miller, Kimberly Scott, Art Evans, Rick Aiello. Naive white cop Edwards is transferred from easy suburban precinct to tough downtown area of Philadelphia and teamed with a sad, streetwise loner (Whitaker); together they go after a peculiar stolen-car ring. Uneasy mix of farce, melodrama, and buddy movie looks something like a pilot for a (bad) TV series. [R]▼●)

Down to You (2000) C-91m. BOMB D: Kris Isacsson. Freddie Prinze, Jr., Julia Stiles, Shawn Hatosy, Selma Blair, Zak Orth, Ashton Kutcher, Rosario Dawson, Henry Winkler, Lucie Arnaz. Prinze and Stiles futilely try chumming us up by speaking directly into the camera, explaining how their once-idyllic college romance went bust (though not as bust as the movie). Somehow, this manages to find room for subplots about a TV cooking show (hosted by Winkler, as Prinze's dad) and a buddy who dabbles as an adult-movie entrepreneur with a kind of bohemian/intellectual porn actress. Numbingly inept comedy. [PG-13]▼)

Down Twisted (1987) C-88m. *½ D: Albert Pyun. Carey Lowell, Charles Rocket, Trudi Dochtermann, Thom Matthews, Norbert Weisser, Linda Kerridge, Nicholas Guest. Unremittingly complicated, and unsatisfying, caper yarn with innocent young woman suddenly caught up in web of intrigue when she's thought to have a priceless artifact the bad guys are after. Echoes of other (better) movies abound.[R]▼

Down With Love (2003) C-94m. ** D: Peyton Reed. Renée Zellweger, Ewan McGregor, David Hyde Pierce, Sarah Paulson, Tony Randall, Jeri Ryan, Rachel Dratch. Spoof of 1960s Doris Day–Rock Hudson comedies has Zellweger as the author of a best-selling book on female independence in a battle of the sexes with playboy/magazine writer McGregor. Andrew Laws' lush, over-the-top Hollywood-fantasy production design is the real star here; everything else is heavy-handed and hollow, a self-consciously artificial parody of an already lightweight movie genre. Randall's final film. Panavision. [PG-13]▼)

Drabble SEE: **Black Windmill, The**
Dracula (1931) 75m. ***½ D: Tod Browning. Bela Lugosi, David Manners, Helen Chandler, Dwight Frye, Edward Van Sloan, Herbert Bunston, Frances Dade. Classic horror film of Transylvanian vampire working his evil spell on perplexed group of Londoners. Lugosi's most famous role with his definitive interpretation of the Count, ditto Frye as looney Renfield and Van Sloan as unflappable Professor Van Helsing. Reissued on video with a new score by Philip Glass. Sequel: DRACULA'S DAUGHTER.▼●)
Dracula (1931) 103m. *** D: George Melford. Carlos Villar (Villarias), Lupita Tovar, Pablo Alvarez Rubio, Barry Norton, Eduardo Arozamena, Carmen Guerrero, Manuel Arbo. Spanish-language adaptation of the horror classic was filmed simultaneously with the Hollywood version—at night, on the very same sets—but much of the staging

and camerawork is actually better! Other major difference: the women are dressed more provocatively. All that's missing is an actor with the charisma of Lugosi in the lead.▼)

Dracula (1958) SEE: **Horror of Dracula**
Dracula (1979) C-109m. *½ D: John Badham. Frank Langella, Laurence Olivier, Donald Pleasence, Kate Nelligan, Trevor Eve, Janine Duvitski, Tony Haygarth. Murky retelling of Bram Stoker classic, with Langella's acclaimed Broadway characterization lost amid trendy horror gimmicks and ill-conceived changes in original story. Filmed in England. Panavision. [R]▼●)
Dracula (1992) SEE: **Bram Stoker's Dracula**
Dracula A.D. 1972 (1972-British) C-100m. ** D: Alan Gibson. Peter Cushing, Christopher Lee, Stephanie Beacham, Michael Coles, Christopher Neame, Caroline Munro. Farfetched, confusing tale of modern-day descendant of Dr. Van Helsing (Cushing) battling recently revived vampire (Lee). Somewhat jarring to see Dracula amid 1970s youth setting. Aka DRACULA TODAY. Followed by THE SATANIC RITES OF DRACULA. [PG]▼)
Dracula and Son (1979-French) C-78m. *½ D: Eduard Molinaro. Christopher Lee, Bernard Menez, Marie-Helene Breillat, Catherine Breillat, Jack Boudet. Limp horror satire chronicling the comic misadventures of the title vampire (Lee) and his bumbling offspring (Menez); they become rivals for the pretty heroine. Virtually destroyed by grotesquely inappropriate English dubbing. Aka DRACULA, FATHER AND SON and DRACULA PERE ET FILS. [PG]▼
Dracula: Dead and Loving It (1995) C-90m. ** D: Mel Brooks. Leslie Nielsen, Peter MacNicol, Steven Weber, Amy Yasbeck, Lysette Anthony, Harvey Korman, Mel Brooks, Mark Blankfield, Megan Cavanagh, Clive Revill, Chuck McCann, Avery Schreiber, Charlie Callas, Anne Bancroft. Dracula gets the Mel Brooks treatment in this parody which spends so much time retelling the familiar Transylvanian's story it forgets to be funny. There are choice moments for Brooks fans . . . just not enough. The cast mugs its best, including MacNicol as Renfield, Brooks as Dr. Van Helsing, Korman in an amusing impression of Nigel Bruce, and Nielsen as the suavely sinister Count. Bancroft has a delightful cameo as "Madame Ouspenskaya." [PG-13]▼●)
Dracula, Father and Son SEE: **Dracula and Son**
Dracula Has Risen From The Grave (1968-British) C-92m. **½ D: Freddie Francis. Christopher Lee, Rupert Davies, Veronica Carlson, Barbara Ewing, Barry Andrews, Michael Ripper. Dracula runs afoul of small-town monsignor when he

pursues the churchman's beautiful blonde niece. Pretty good Hammer horror, third in the series. Sequel: TASTE THE BLOOD OF DRACULA. [G]▼●)

Dracula—Prince of Darkness(1966-British) **C-90m. ** D:** Terence Fisher. Christopher Lee, Barbara Shelley, Andrew Keir, Suzan Farmer. Sequel to HORROR OF DRACULA doesn't measure up. The vampiric Count (Lee) is revived by a servant and wreaks terror on a group of tourists in a secluded castle. Techniscope.▼●)

Dracula's Daughter (1936) **70m. *** D:** Lambert Hillyer. Gloria Holden, Otto Kruger, Marguerite Churchill, Irving Pichel, Edward Van Sloan, Nan Grey, Hedda Hopper. Sequel to the Lugosi classic depicts vampirish activities of Holden; Pichel adds imposing support as her sinister manservant. Hillyer, normally a B-Western director, manages to imbue this chiller with a moody, subtly sensual quality. ▼●)

Dracula's Dog (1978) **C-90m. ** D:** Albert Band. Jose Ferrer, Michael Pataki, Reggie Nalder, Jan Shutan, Libbie Chase, John Levin. Transylvanian vampire and bloodthirsty dog, endowed with vampirish traits by the original Count, go to L.A. to find Dracula's last living descendant. Horror cheapie with admittedly novel twist. Retitled ZOLTAN, HOUND OF DRACULA. [R]▼●)

Dracula 2000 SEE: **Wes Craven Presents: Dracula 2000**

Dracula's Widow (1989) **C-86m. *½ D:** Christopher Coppola. Josef Sommer, Sylvia Kristel, Lenny Von Dohlen, Stefan Schnabel, Marc Coppola, Rachel Jones. Kristel plays the title character, who comes to L.A. and takes up residence at a wax museum. Dull, minor fare. Twenty-five-year-old director Coppola is the nephew of Francis. Filmed in 1987. [R]▼

Dracula Today SEE: **Dracula A.D. 1972**
Dracula vs. Frankenstein (1970) SEE: **Assignment Terror**
Dracula vs. Frankenstein (1971) **C-90m. BOMB D:** Al Adamson. J. Carrol Naish, Lon Chaney, Jr., Zandor Vorkov, Russ Tamblyn, Jim Davis, Anthony Eisley. Self-conscious comedy masquerading as horror film wasting talents of old-timers Naish and Chaney; Dracula makes deal with aging Dr. Frankenstein so as to have steady supply of blood. Regrettably, both Naish and Chaney's final film. Aka THE REVENGE OF DRACULA. [PG]▼●)

Drag Me to Hell (2009) **C-99m. *** D:** Sam Raimi. Alison Lohman, Justin Long, Lorna Raver, Dileep Rao, David Paymer, Adriana Barraza. Raimi returns to his roots: Hoping to please her boss, bank employee Lohman turns down the loan extension sought by creepy old Gypsy woman Raver, who promptly curses her and sets off this vigorous, funny, and exciting horror thriller. Predictable ending is a letdown, but it's

fun until then, with a good performance by Lohman. Also available in unrated version. Super 35. [PG-13]●)

Dragnet (1954) **C-89m. *** D:** Jack Webb. Jack Webb, Ben Alexander, Richard Boone, Ann Robinson, Stacy Harris, Virginia Gregg, Dennis Weaver. "This is the city . . ." While investigating brutal murder, Sgt. Friday and Officer Frank Smith ignore 57 varieties of civil liberties; feature film version of classic TV show evokes its era better than almost anything. Highly recommended on a nonesthetic level.▼)

Dragnet (1987) **C-106m. **½ D:** Tom Mankiewicz. Dan Aykroyd, Tom Hanks, Christopher Plummer, Harry Morgan, Alexandra Paul, Jack O'Halloran, Elizabeth Ashley, Dabney Coleman, Kathleen Freeman. Aykroyd is a comic reincarnation of Jack Webb, playing Sgt. Joe Friday's dense but dedicated nephew in this parody. Hanks is fun as his freewheeling new partner, with Morgan, Webb's onetime sidekick, now promoted to captain of the L.A.P.D. Starts out quite funny, then goes flat . . . but the punchline is a howl. Aykroyd coscripted with Mankiewicz and Alan Zweibel. [PG-13]▼●)

Dragon and the Cobra SEE: **Fist of Fear, Touch of Death**

Dragonball: Evolution (2009-U.S.-Hong Kong) **C-85m. ** D:** James Wong. Justin Chatwin, Chow Yun-Fat, Emmy Rossum, Jamie Chung, James Marsters, Joon Park, Eriko Tamura, Randall Duk Kim, Ernie Hudson. Young man trained in mystic martial arts by his grandfather has to gather seven magical balls to make a wish that will save the world from the return of the supernatural villain Lord Piccolo. Based on the phenomenally popular Japanese *manga*, which spawned three *anime* TV series and *seventeen* animated feature films. Lively and colorful (with a mildly amusing turn by scruffy martial arts master Chow) and laden with extravagant special effects, this is, nonetheless, just colorful eyewash, barely comprehensible to non-initiates. Super 35. [PG]●)

Dragonfly (1976) SEE: **One Summer Love**
Dragonfly (2002) **C-103m. **½ D:** Tom Shadyac. Kevin Costner, Kathy Bates, Joe Morton, Ron Rifkin, Linda Hunt, Susanna Thompson, Jacob Vargas, Jay Thomas, Matt Craven. An emergency room physician, grieving for his dead wife, receives a series of signals from her—including messages from young patients who've had near-death experiences. But what do they mean? More drawn out than it needs to be, but an intriguing and unusual story of one man's spiritual—and physical—odyssey. Panavision. [PG-13]▼)

Dragonheart (1996) **C-103m. *** D:** Rob Cohen. Dennis Quaid, Sean Connery (voice only), David Thewlis, Dina Meyer, Julie Christie, Pete Postlethwaite, Jason Isaacs, Brian Thompson, Lee Oakes, Wolf

Christian, Terry O'Neill. Highly unusual fable about a knight "of the old school" (in the 10th century A.D.) whose youthful king turns evil after having his life saved by a dragon who gives him half of his heart. Years later, the knight befriends that same dragon and joins with him to vanquish the cruel king. Unlikely premise is made plausible by Quaid's persuasive performance and the commanding presence of Connery as Draco (matched by the creature's superior, state-of-the-art digital animation). Fine score by Randy Edelman. Followed by a direct-to-video sequel. Panavision. [PG-13] ▼●)

Dragon Seed (1944) 145m. **½ D: Jack Conway, Harold S. Bucquet. Katharine Hepburn, Walter Huston, Aline MacMahon, Turhan Bey, Hurd Hatfield, Agnes Moorehead, Frances Rafferty, J. Carrol Naish, Akim Tamiroff, Henry Travers; narrated by Lionel Barrymore. Well-meant but overlong film of Pearl Buck's tale of Chinese town torn asunder by Japanese occupation; fascinating attempts at Asian characterization. ▼)

Dragons Forever (1987-Hong Kong) C-94m. ***½ D: Samo Hung. Jackie Chan, Samo Hung, Yuen Biao, Yuen Wah, Benny Urquidez, Deannie Yip, Pauline Yeung. Simply delightful film has Chan playing a lawyer who enlists crook Hung and cracked friend Biao to help him spy on a woman involved with a case. Everything changes when love blossoms. Action, comedy, and romance blend together seamlessly under Hung's direction. All three stars shine in moments of incredible acrobatics and hilarious slapstick. Aka CYCLONE Z. ▼●)

Dragonslayer (1981) C-108m. *** D: Matthew Robbins. Peter MacNicol, Caitlin Clarke, Ralph Richardson, John Hallam, Peter Eyre, Albert Salmi. Enjoyable fantasy-adventure about a sorcerer's apprentice who takes on the challenge of slaying a dragon—and finds he is in over his head. A bit scary and graphic for some kids. Filmed in England, Scotland, and Wales with a mostly British cast but American MacNicol in the lead—somewhat incongruously. Fine Alex North score. Panavision. [PG] ▼●)

Dragon: The Bruce Lee Story (1993) C-119m. *** D: Rob Cohen. Jason Scott Lee, Lauren Holly, Robert Wagner, Michael Learned, Nancy Kwan, Kay Tong Lim, Sterling Macer, Ric Young, Sven-Ole Thorson. Corny but very likable biopic about legendary action-movie star who died at age 33 in 1973. Plenty of martial-arts mayhem, but also the story of a man who must overcome a variety of obstacles to find his place in the world. Adapted from a book by Lee's widow, Linda. The film's star is no relation to Bruce. Panavision. [PG-13] ▼●)

Dragon Wars (2007-South Korean) C-100m. ** D: Hyung-rae Shim. Robert For-

ster, Jason Behr, Amanda Brooks, Craig Robinson, Elizabeth Peña, Chris Mulkey, Aimee Garcia, John Ales, Cody Arens. With a reported budget of $70 million, South Korea's biggest production ever is a dopey B monster movie elevated (only slightly) by some impressive effects. What story there is revolves around a 500-year-old battle that is being reborn in contemporary L.A., where a young boy is imbued with the spirit of an ancient warrior in order to take on dreaded serpentlike creatures. There's some fun in watching a flying Korean zoo take hold of the town, but that's about it. Also known as D-WAR. Super 35. [PG-13] ▶)

Dragonworld (1994) C-84m. *** D: Ted Nicolaou. Sam Mackenzie, Brittney Powell, John Calvin, Lila Kaye, John Woodvine, Courtland Mead, Andrew Keir, Jim Dunk. Pleasant children's film about a young Scottish laird forced by taxes to put his big pet dragon on display in an amusement park. Entertaining, good-looking movie (one of the best from producer Charles Band), but did the plot have to be so similar to MIGHTY JOE YOUNG? Good effects by Mark Rappaport and David Allen. [PG] ▼●

Dragonwyck (1946) 103m. **½ D: Joseph L. Mankiewicz. Gene Tierney, Walter Huston, Vincent Price, Glenn Langan, Anne Revere, Spring Byington, Henry (Harry) Morgan, Jessica Tandy. Period chiller set at a gloomy mansion on the Hudson, with good cast but episodic presentation. Mankiewicz's directorial debut; he also scripted from the Anya Seton story. ▶)

Dr. Akagi (1998-Japanese) C-128m. *** D: Shohei Imamura. Akira Emoto, Kumiko Aso, Juro Kara, Masanori Sera, Jacques Gamblin, Keiko Matsuzaka. Pointed satiric drama set in the waning days of WW2 about a small-town doctor who fears that a hepatitis epidemic is about to sweep his country. Savagely lampoons Japanese military bureaucracy, but works best as a loving portrait of a dedicated man and those in his inner circle. ▼)

Dr. Alien (1988) C-87m. ** D: David DeCoteau. Judy Landers, Billy Jacoby, Olivia Barash, Stuart Fratkin, Raymond O'Connor, Arlene Golonka, Linnea Quigley, Troy Donahue, Ginger Lynn Allen, Edy Williams. Landers is an alien who disguises herself as a college professor and transforms freshman Jacoby from wimp to dreamboat. Silly stuff (with an all-star schlock movie supporting cast). [R] ▼●)

Drama of Jealousy, A SEE: **Pizza Triangle, The**

Draughtsman's Contract, The (1982-British) C-103m. ** D: Peter Greenaway. Anthony Higgins, Janet Suzman, Anne Louise Lambert, Hugh Fraser. Arrogant young artist takes commissions from the mistress of an estate in return for sexual favors; sumptuous-looking 17th-century tale, but cold and aloof. Will be of greater interest to fans of writer-director Greenaway. [R] ▼▶

Dr. Bethune (1990-Canadian-Chinese-French) **C-115m.** **½ D: Phillip Borsos. Donald Sutherland, Helen Mirren, Helen Shaver, Colm Feore, James Pax, Ronald Pickup, Guo Da, Anouk Aimée. Handsomely mounted but episodic account of controversial Canadian doctor Norman Bethune (well played by Sutherland), ardent anti-fascist and proponent of socialized medicine. Much terrain is covered, from his love life to his involvement in the Spanish Civil War and with Mao Tse-tung fighting the Japanese; unfortunately, you never really know what makes him tick. Original title: BETHUNE: THE MAKING OF A HERO. Released in the U.S. in 1993; Sutherland also starred in BETHUNE, a 1977 Canadian TV movie. ▼

Dr. Black and Mr. White SEE: **Dr. Black, Mr. Hyde**

Dr. Black, Mr. Hyde (1976) **C-87m.** **½ D: William Crain. Bernie Casey, Rosalind Cash, Marie O'Henry, Ji-Tu Cumbuka, Milt Kogan, Stu Gilliam. Black lab scientist Casey tests experimental serum on himself and turns into a white monster. No surprises, but not bad, either, with Casey doing first-rate job. Aka THE WATTS MONSTER and DR. BLACK AND MR. WHITE. [PG] ▼▶

Dr. Cadman's Secret SEE: **Black Sleep, The**

Dr. Christian series SEE: *Leonard Maltin's Classic Movie Guide*

Dr. Dolittle 2 (2001) **C-87m.** **½ D: Steve Carr. Eddie Murphy, Kevin Pollak, Kristen Wilson, Jeffrey Jones, Raven-Symoné, Kyla Pratt, Lil' Zane, Andy Richter. Amiable sequel to 1998 hit DOCTOR DOLITTLE has Murphy trying to save a forest by propagating an endangered species. In order to do so, a performing bear has to mate with his female counterpart in the wild. Meanwhile, Dolittle is trying to strengthen a shaky bond with his 16-year-old daughter. Considerably less raunchy than the earlier film, though there's no shortage of "mating" jokes. Many celebrities provide voices (Steve Zahn, Norm Macdonald, Lisa Kudrow, Michael Rapaport, Isaac Hayes, Andy Dick, Michael McKean, David L. Lander, Mandy Moore, Joey Lauren Adams, Frankie Muniz, Jamie Kennedy, John Leguizamo), not all of them credited. Followed by four DVD sequels. Super 35. [PG] ▼▶

Dream a Little Dream (1989) **C-99m.** *½ D: Marc Rocco. Corey Feldman, Meredith Salenger, Jason Robards, Piper Laurie, Harry Dean Stanton, William McNamara, Corey Haim, Susan Blakely, Victoria Jackson, Alex Rocco, Josh Evans. Yet another personality-exchange comedy—this one with Robards and Feldman switching bodies after a bike mishap. Perfectly dreadful. Director is son of costar Alex Rocco. Direct-to-video sequel: DREAM A LITTLE DREAM 2. [PG-13] ▼▶

Dreamboat (1952) **83m.** *** D: Claude Binyon. Ginger Rogers, Clifton Webb, Jeffrey Hunter, Anne Francis, Elsa Lanchester. Clever romp: silent-star Rogers cashes in on TV showings of her old movies, to chagrin of co-star Webb, now a distinguished professor. Scenes showing their old silent films are most enjoyable.

Dreamcatcher (2003) **C-131m.** ** D: Lawrence Kasdan. Morgan Freeman, Thomas Jane, Jason Lee, Damian Lewis, Timothy Olyphant, Tom Sizemore, Donnie Wahlberg, Michael O'Neill. This adaptation of a Stephen King novel seems like three or four different movies squashed into one. The initial story is the best, as four boyhood friends who share extrasensory powers meet for a weekend at their remote cabin in the woods, where things are definitely askew. Then we get a yucky-monster movie, a military paranoia film, a typical King childhood nostalgia vignette, and more. By the time we reach the climax, with the future of mankind at stake, it's difficult to muster any interest at all. Screenplay by Kasdan and William Goldman. Super 35. [R] ▼▶

DreamChild (1985-British) **C-94m.** **½ D: Gavin Millar. Coral Browne, Ian Holm, Peter Gallagher, Caris Corfman, Nicola Cowper, Jane Asher, Amelia Shankley, Shane Rimmer. Woman for whom Rev. Charles Dodgson (Lewis Carroll) invented his *Alice in Wonderland* stories comes to America at age 80 for the author's centenary, unable to understand the fuss, and fearful of her own repressed memories. Fascinating material seriously flawed by romantic subplot and ludicrous re-creation of N.Y.C. setting and characters of the 1930s. Browne's superb performance makes it all worthwhile. Jim Henson's Creature Shop provided Wonderland characters. Written by Dennis Potter. [PG] ▼▶

Dream Demon (1988-British-U.S.) **C-89m.** ** D: Harley Cokliss. Kathleen Wilhoite, Jemma Redgrave, Timothy Spall, Jimmy Nail, Susan Fleetwood, Mark Greenstreet, Annabelle Lanyon, Nickolas Grace. Soon-to-be-married Redgrave has horrifying dreams, unwillingly pulling into them Wilhoite, an American in London seeking secrets of her own past. Good special effects and performances undercut by who-cares story and many repetitive sequences. Released in the U.S. in 1993. [R] ▼

Dreamer (1979) **C-86m.** ** D: Noel Nosseck. Tim Matheson, Susan Blakely, Jack Warden, Richard B. Shull, Barbara Stuart, Pedro Gonzalez-Gonzalez. Bowling, a sport only slightly more cinematic than isometric exercises, gets the ROCKY treatment in this bland rags-to-riches story. Having Matheson's bowling ball made of Flubber might have helped pick up the pace. [PG] ▼

Dreamer: Inspired By a True Story (2005) C-102m. **½ D: John Gatins. Kurt Russell, Dakota Fanning, Kris Kristofferson, Elisabeth Shue, David Morse, Freddy Rodríguez, Luis Guzmán, Oded Fehr, Ken Howard, Dick Allen. Routine account of 10-year-old Fanning, who is convinced that a horse with a broken leg not only can be nursed back to health but will win the Big Race. Pleasant enough family film, although it's corny and awfully predictable. Super 35. [PG]▼▶

Dreamers, The (2003-British-Italian-French) C-115m. *** D: Bernardo Bertolucci. Michael Pitt, Eva Green, Louis Garrel, Robin Renucci, Anna Chancellor. Young American joins the die-hard film buffs at Paris' Cinematheque Française in 1968 and gets involved with an attractive brother and sister who draw him into a world of kinky sex and mind games. Any film that opens with footage of Parisians and filmmakers protesting the ouster of the Cinematheque's legendary Henri Langlois and goes on to "quote" movies ranging from FREAKS to QUEEN CHRISTINA is on the right track. Strongly reminiscent of films from the period it depicts: bold, excessive, daringly sexual, self-serious at times, but vibrantly alive. Screenplay by Gilbert Adair, from his novel *The Holy Innocents*. [NC-17]▼▶

Dream for an Insomniac (1998) C/B&W-88m. ** D: Tiffani DeBartolo. Ione Skye, Jennifer Aniston, Mackenzie Astin, Michael Landes, Seymour Cassel. Waitress/aspiring actress (Skye) falls for the new counter-boy/poet (Astin) just 48 hours before she's about to move to L.A. Cute but sitcom-ish romantic comedy set in a Sinatra-themed, family-owned coffeehouse in San Francisco. Charismatic casting helps, particularly Aniston as Skye's flaky best friend, but you wish they'd all stop their yapping. Written by the director. Filmed in 1995. [R]▼●▶

Dreamgirls (2006) C-130m. *** D: Bill Condon. Jamie Foxx, Beyoncé Knowles, Eddie Murphy, Danny Glover, Anika Noni Rose, Keith Robinson, Jennifer Hudson, Sharon Leal, Hinton Battle, Ken Page, Loretta Devine, John Lithgow, John Krasinski, Dawnn Lewis, Jaleel White, Eddie Mekka. Splashy, savvy adaptation of the 1981 Broadway musical by Tom Eyen and Henry Krieger inspired by the saga of The Supremes and Motown's Berry Gordy. Entrepreneur Foxx steers a female vocal trio to the top, no matter what it takes, and claims its glamorous star (Beyoncé) as his own. Hudson, as the forsaken member of the group, gives an extraordinary, emotion-charged performance. (This remarkable screen debut earned her a Best Supporting Actress Oscar.) Murphy is equally potent as a James Brown–ish singer who gives the girls their first break. There's so much pure entertainment here that quibbles (the energy

drops after Hudson's "first-act curtain" song, Beyoncé's star-solo number is too obviously shoehorned into the movie) don't stand up against the movie's virtues. Sharen Davis' costumes are a knockout. Also Oscar winner for Sound Mixing. Super 35. [PG-13]▶

Dreaming of Joseph Lees (1999-British-U.S.) C-92m. ** D: Eric Styles. Samantha Morton, Lee Ross, Rupert Graves, Frank Finlay, Miriam Margolyes, Nick Woodeson, Holly Aird, Lauren Richardson. Hackneyed soaper, set in rural England in 1958, in which a young woman (Morton) takes up with a self-absorbed pig farmer (Ross) despite her desire for her cousin, Joseph Lees (Graves), a gentle geologist who lost a leg while working in Italy. Morton rises above the trite material. [R]▼

Dreamland (2006) C-88m. *** D: Jason Matzner. Agnes Bruckner, Kelli Garner, Justin Long, John Corbett, Gina Gershon, Brian Klugman, Chris Mulkey. Teenaged Bruckner lives in a remote New Mexico trailer park called Dreamland with her father, who's never gotten over the death of her mother, and a best friend whose poor health has made her a chronic dreamer. Bruckner feels responsible for these needy people, putting her own life and dreams on hold. Well-acted mood piece went direct to DVD. [PG-13]▶

Dreamlife of Angels, The (1998-French) C-113m. ***½ D: Erick Zonca. Elodie Bouchez, Natacha Régnier, Grégoire Colin, Jo Prestia, Patrick Mercado. Evocative study of two young women—one generous and impulsive, the other sullen and despairing—who meet at a clothing factory in Lille, France, and become close friends, then drift apart as one becomes involved with a club owner. An elusive story, directed with quiet precision by coscreenwriter Zonca (his feature debut), which slowly, penetratingly reveals a wealth of detail about the bonds of friendship and the vagaries of destiny. Bouchez and Régnier are outstanding. [R] ▼▶

Dream Lover (1986) C-104m. *½ D: Alan J. Pakula. Kristy McNichol, Ben Masters, Paul Shenar, Justin Deas, John McMartin, Gayle Hunnicutt, Matthew Penn. Abysmal thriller about young woman's attempts to expunge recurring nightmare from her mind through "dream therapy." Intensely unsettling film with an interesting idea torpedoed by snail-like pacing and sterile atmosphere. What Hitchcock could have done with this! [R]▼▶

Dream Lover (1994) C-103m. **½ D: Nicholas Kazan. James Spader, Mädchen Amick, Bess Armstrong, Fredric Lehne, Larry Miller, Kathleen York, Blair Tefkin, Scott Coffey, Clyde Kusatsu, William Shockley. Handsome, wealthy architect Spader meets gorgeous, enigmatic Amick and the two become a passionate, perfect couple—until her cloudy past (eventually) raises his suspicions.

Fluid camerawork (by Jean-Yves Escoffier) and some smart dialogue go out the window as plausibility level declines alarmingly. Stars register well but can't overcome a noirish mystery that just misses. Feature directing debut for screenwriter Kazan. Also available in unrated version. [R]▼●]

Dream Machine, The (1990) C-86m. ** D: Lyman Dayton. Corey Haim, Evan Richards, Jeremy Slate, Randall England, Tracy Fraim, Brittney Lewis, Susan Seaforth Hayes. Super-wealthy Slate is murdered by an embezzler after cheating on his wife. She's just learned of his infidelity and, on an impulse, gives his new turbo-charged Porsche to immature college student Haim (who doesn't know the deceased's body is stuffed in the trunk). By-the-numbers action-thriller with an intriguing (if unlikely) premise. [PG]▼●

Dream of Kings, A (1969) C-107m. *** D: Daniel Mann. Anthony Quinn, Irene Papas, Inger Stevens, Sam Levene, Radames Pera, Val Avery. Emotional study of robust Quinn trying to find money to take ailing son to Greece. Vivid look at Greek community in Chicago; heart-rending story by Harry Alan Petrakis. Stevens exceptional as young widow attracted to Quinn. [R]▼]

Dream of Light (1990-Spanish) C-138m. ***½ D: Victor Erice. Unusual, understated documentary of renowned Spanish painter Antonio Lopez Garcia as he attempts to capture a backyard quince tree's beauty on canvas. A rare portrait of an artist at work as he deals with his inner voices—and the mundane details of life. Quiet, deliberate, and completely absorbing.▼

Dream of Passion, A (1978-Greek) C-106m. *½ D: Jules Dassin. Melina Mercouri, Ellen Burstyn, Andreas Voutsinas, Despo Diamantidou, Dimitris Papa-michael. Aside from Burstyn's powerhouse performance as an American jailed in Greece for killing her three children, this attempt to parallel her story with Medea's is the kind of idea that should never have left the story conference. Mercouri is typically hammy as the actress who takes up her cause. [R]▼

Dreams (1955-Swedish) 86m. ** D: Ingmar Bergman. Eva Dahlbeck, Harriet Andersson, Gunnar Bjornstrand, Ulf Palme, Inga Landgre. Sometimes fascinating but mostly vague—and, ultimately lesser—Bergman drama, about photo agency head Dahlbeck and model Andersson, and their dreams, torments, crises, oppression, relations with men. Aka JOURNEY INTO AUTUMN. ▼

Dreams (1990) SEE: **Akira Kurosawa's Dreams**

Dreamscape (1984) C-99m. *** D: Joseph Ruben. Dennis Quaid, Max von Sydow, Christopher Plummer, Eddie Albert, Kate Capshaw, George Wendt, David Patrick Kelly. Quaid finds he can physically enter other people's dreams in this entertaining

yarn; science-fantasy elements more successful than political intrigue subplot. [PG-13]▼●]

Dream Team, The (1989) C-113m. **½ D: Howard Zieff. Michael Keaton, Christopher Lloyd, Peter Boyle, Stephen Furst, Dennis Boutsikaris, Lorraine Bracco, Milo O'Shea, Philip Bosco, James Remar. Four mental-hospital patients become separated from their doctor while on a field trip to Yankee Stadium, and find themselves stranded in an even-larger looney bin: The Big Apple. Uneven farce seems inspired by ONE FLEW OVER THE CUCKOO'S NEST, and gets its mileage from the performances of its leading actors. [PG-13]▼●]

Dream Wife (1953) 101m. *½ D: Sidney Sheldon. Cary Grant, Deborah Kerr, Walter Pidgeon, Betta St. John, Buddy Baer, Movita, Steve Forrest. Silly bedroom farce about Grant's engagement to Middle Eastern princess and interference from his former fiancée, Kerr, a State Dept. official. Cast is wasted. Also shown in computer-colored version. ▼]

Dream With the Fishes (1997) C-96m. ** D: Finn Taylor. David Arquette, Brad Hunt, Cathy Moriarty, Kathryn Erbe, Allyce Beasley, Peter Gregory. Mismatched buddy tale about a suicidal voyeur and a terminally ill drug addict who decide to "go for it" when they take off on a memorable trip that involves, among other things, nude bowling and bank holdups. Small film has its charms but seems to be trying too hard to be quirky. [R]▼]

Dr. Ehrlich's Magic Bullet (1940) 103m. ***½ D: William Dieterle. Edward G. Robinson, Ruth Gordon, Otto Kruger, Donald Crisp, Maria Ouspenskaya, Montagu Love, Sig Ruman, Donald Meek. Outstanding chronicle of 19th-century German scientist who developed cure for venereal disease. Robinson earnest in superior script by John Huston, Heinz Herald, and Norman Burnside; surprisingly compelling.▼]

Dress Code, The SEE: **Bruno**

Dressed for Death SEE: **Straight on Till Morning**

Dressed to Kill (1946) 72m. **½ D: Roy William Neill. Basil Rathbone, Nigel Bruce, Patricia Morison, Edmond Breon, Carl Harbord, Patricia Cameron, Tom Dillon. Music boxes made in prison hold the key to the whereabouts of stolen bank plates in this lively final entry in the Rathbone *Sherlock Holmes* series. Also shown in computer-colored version. Aka PRELUDE TO MURDER. ▼●]

Dressed to Kill (1980) C-105m. ***½ D: Brian De Palma. Michael Caine, Angie Dickinson, Nancy Allen, Keith Gordon, Dennis Franz, David Margulies, Brandon Maggart. High-tension melodrama about a psycho-killer who stalks two women—one a frustrated suburban housewife, the other a street-smart hooker who teams up with the first woman's son to trap the murderer. Writer-director De Palma works on viewer's emotions, not logic, and maintains a fever pitch from start to finish. Chilling Pino Donaggio score. Unrated version also available. Panavision. [R]▼●

Dresser, The (1983-British) **C-118m.** ***½ D: Peter Yates. Albert Finney, Tom Courtenay, Edward Fox, Zena Walker, Eileen Atkins, Michael Gough, Cathryn Harrison. Excellent film adaptation of Ronald Harwood's play about an aging actor-manager (based on real-life Donald Wolfit) whose very survival depends on the constant pampering and prodding of his dresser–who lives vicariously through the old man's performances. Finney, as Sir, and Courtenay, as Norman the dresser, are simply superb. Yates captures the look and feel of wartime England and backstage atmosphere of a small touring company with uncanny ability. A must for anyone who loves acting and the theater. [PG]▼●

Dressmaker, The (1988-British) **C-89m.** **½ D: Jim O'Brien. Joan Plowright, Billie Whitelaw, Peter Postlethwaite, Jane Horrocks, Tim Ransom. Medium account of two Liverpool sisters, one repressed (Plowright) and the other spirited (Whitelaw), and what happens when their naive, fragile niece falls for an American GI during WW2. Well acted and starts off promisingly, but bogs down.▼●

Dr. Giggles (1992) **C-95m.** *½ D: Manny Cotto. Larry Drake, Holly Marie Combs, Cliff De Young, Glenn Quinn, Keith Diamond, Richard Bradford, Michelle Johnson. Gory, one-note horror drama in which crazed doctor, who giggles whenever nervous, goes on a murderous rampage after escaping from a looney-bin. Drake's fine performance is wasted. Super 35. [R]▼●

Dr. Goldfoot and the Bikini Machine (1965) **C-90m.** ** D: Norman Taurog. Vincent Price, Frankie Avalon, Dwayne Hickman, Susan Hart, Fred Clark. Mad scientist tries to make a fortune manufacturing lifelike lady robots to marry wealthy men. Good chase scene, but otherwise just silly. Panavision.▼●

Dr. Goldfoot and the Girl Bombs (1966-Italian) **C-85m.** *½ D: Mario Bava. Vincent Price, Fabian, Franco Franchi, Moana Tahi, Laura Antonelli. Dumb sequel to DR. GOLDFOOT AND THE BIKINI MACHINE finds Price now backed by Red China, dropping actual girl bombs into the laps of unsuspecting generals.▼●

Dr. Heckyl and Mr. Hype (1980) **C-99m.** **½ D: Charles B. Griffith. Oliver Reed, Sunny Johnson, Maia Danziger, Mel Welles, Virgil Frye, Jackie Coogan, Corinne Calvet. Reed is a grotesquely ugly podiatrist who

drinks a potion to commit suicide, instead turns into a handsome murderer. Moderately funny comedy, also written by Roger Corman veteran Griffith. [R]▼

Drifter, The (1988) **C-90m.** **½ D: Larry Brand. Kim Delaney, Timothy Bottoms, Al Shannon, Miles O'Keeffe, Loren Haines, Thomas Wagner. Interesting low-budget variation on the PLAY MISTY FOR ME/FATAL ATTRACTION formula as costume designer Delaney picks up virile O'Keeffe hitchhiking, has a one-night affair, and is then hounded by him. Director Brand (who also plays the cop on the case) shows promise but film suffers from lack of a coherent scenario. [R]▼●

Drifting Weeds SEE: **Floating Weeds**

Drillbit Taylor (2008) **C-102m.** **½ D: Steven Brill. Owen Wilson, Leslie Mann, Nate Hartley, Troy Gentile, David Dorfman, Alex Frost, Stephen Root, Josh Peck, Valerie Tian, David Koechner, Frank Whaley, Lisa Ann Walter, Danny McBride. Three awkward high school freshmen who've been targeted by a bully decide that they need professional protection and hire homeless goofball Wilson—who impresses them with his apparent street smarts. Amiable (if unremarkable) comedy coproduced by Judd Apatow plays like a prequel to SUPERBAD. Cowritten by Seth Rogen, based on a story idea by John Hughes (using his pseudonym Edmond Dantes). One of the protectors the boys interview is played by Adam Baldwin, star of 1980's MY BODYGUARD. Alternate version runs 109m. Super 35. [PG-13]●

Drive Angry (2011) **C-104m.** **½ D: Patrick Lussier. Nicolas Cage, Amber Heard, William Fichtner, Billy Burke, David Morse, Todd Farmer, Christa Campbell, Tom Atkins, Jack McGee, Pruitt Taylor Vince. Intense, black-clad John Milton (Cage) roars across the South in stolen cars with a loyal but puzzled partner (Heard), hoping to prevent his granddaughter's sacrifice by a Satanic cult. There's a bemused but determined emissary from Hell (Fichtner) on his trail. Wild, fast-paced yarn has exciting scenes and an effective Cage, but it misses its satirical mark by covering overly-familiar territory, and not being excessive enough to come off as a spoof. Exuberant use of 3-D. 3-D. [R]●

Drive, He Said (1971) **C-90m.** **½ D: Jack Nicholson. William Tepper, Karen Black, Michael Margotta, Bruce Dern, Robert Towne, Henry Jaglom, Michael Warren, Charles Robinson, David (Ogden) Stiers, Cindy Williams. Confusing tale of youth alienation contains fine performances but loses itself in its attempt to cover all the bases; Dern is fabulous as gung-ho college basketball coach. Nicholson's directorial debut; he also cowrote the screenplay with Jeremy Larner. [R]●

Drive-In (1976) **C-96m.** ** D: Rod Amateau. Lisa Lemole, Glen Morshower, Gary Cavagnaro, Billy Milliken, Lee Newsom, Regan Kee. Amiable low-budget trash about a night in the life of teenaged yahoos at a Texas drive-in during the unreeling of a campy disaster film (which takes up much of the screen time). Better after 20 beers. [PG]▼

Drive Me Crazy (1999) **C-91m.** ** D: John Schultz. Melissa Joan Hart, Adrian Grenier, Stephen Collins, Ali Larter, Mark Metcalf, William Converse-Roberts, Faye Grant. In order to win their dream prom dates, the most popular girl in school and a rebel outcast team up and pretend they're going steady. Predictable teen comedy could easily be called HE'S ALL THAT but is kept afloat by likable lead performances. Tries to have it both ways by featuring an on-screen number from punk girl band The Donnas and a title track by Britney Spears. [PG-13]▼●

Driven (2001) **C-117m.** BOMB D: Renny Harlin. Sylvester Stallone, Burt Reynolds, Kip Pardue, Til Schweiger, Stacy Edwards, Estella Warren, Gina Gershon, Brent Briscoe, Robert Sean Leonard. Embarrassing amalgam of racing-pic clichés finds has-been Sly (who scripted) hiring on as mentor to green Pardue, a member of Reynolds' Championship Auto Racing Team who's manipulated by his brother. This is the kind of movie in which two racers create nighttime havoc racing 195 mph through metropolitan streets, only to get off with just a $25,000 fine . . . the kind of movie whose contempt for its audience knocked both Stallone and Reynolds off their superstar thrones. Super 35. [PG-13]▼●

Driver, The (1978) **C-90m.** *** D: Walter Hill. Ryan O'Neal, Bruce Dern, Isabelle Adjani, Ronee Blakley, Matt Clark, Felice Orlandi. Tense throwback to the Hollywood film noir era pits getaway driver O'Neal against creepy cop Dern. Oddball melodrama doesn't seem like much at the time, but has a way of staying with you afterwards. Great car chase sequences. [PG— edited from original R rating]▼●

Driver's Seat, The (1974-Italian) **C-101m.** BOMB D: Giuseppe Patroni Griffi. Elizabeth Taylor, Ian Bannen, Mona Washbourne, Andy Warhol, Guido Mannari. Liz is a disturbed woman who comes to Rome in search of someone to do her in. You may wish to do the same after sitting through this turkey, maybe Taylor's all-time worst. Adapted from a Muriel Spark novel. Aka PSYCHOTIC. [R]▼●

Driving Lessons (2006-British) **C-98m.** *** D: Jeremy Brock. Julie Walters, Rupert Grint, Laura Linney, Nicholas Farrell, Michelle Duncan, Jim Norton, Tamsin Egerton. Adolescent Grint escapes from an enervating home life with his domineering, religious-fanatic mother (Linney) and his soft-spoken minister father (Farrell) by taking a job as companion and helper to an aged actress (Walters). Walters is great fun as a card-carrying eccentric and free spirit who has a

liberating effect on her young charge. Charming yet pointed film about youthful stumbling and adult hypocrisy. Directorial debut for screenwriter Brock (MRS. BROWN, CHARLOTTE GRAY), who drew on his own life for source material. [PG-13]▮

Driving Miss Daisy (1989) **C-99m.** *** D: Bruce Beresford. Morgan Freeman, Jessica Tandy, Dan Aykroyd, Patti LuPone, Esther Rolle. Genteel, entertaining adaptation of Alfred Uhry's stage play about a simple black man who's hired as chauffeur for a cantankerous old Southern woman, and winds up being her most faithful companion. A smooth and enjoyable ride, with fine performances by the two leads. Aykroyd is likable in an unusual "straight" role as Tandy's son, though you can never quite forget who's playing the part (especially with such obvious makeup). Oscar winner for Best Picture, Actress, Screenplay (by Uhry), and Makeup. [PG]▼●

Dr. Jekyll and Mr. Hyde (1920) **96m.** *** D: John S. Robertson. John Barrymore, Martha Mansfield, Brandon Hurst, Nita Naldi, Charles Lane, Louis Wolheim. One of several silent versions of famous tale, this one can hold its own next to the later March and Tracy filmings; Barrymore is superb as curious doctor who ventures into the unknown, emerging as evil Mr. Hyde. Bravura performance sparks well-made production.▼●

Dr. Jekyll and Mr. Hyde (1932) **97m.** *** D: Rouben Mamoulian. Fredric March, Miriam Hopkins, Rose Hobart, Holmes Herbert, Halliwell Hobbes. Exciting, floridly cinematic version of famous story with March in Oscar-winning portrayal of tormented doctor, Hopkins superb as tantalizing Ivy. Beware of 82m. re-issue version.▼●

Dr. Jekyll and Mr. Hyde (1941) **114m.** *** D: Victor Fleming. Spencer Tracy, Ingrid Bergman, Lana Turner, Donald Crisp, Ian Hunter, Barton MacLane, C. Aubrey Smith, Sara Allgood. Tracy and Bergman are excellent in thoughtful, lush remake of Robert Louis Stevenson's classic, which stresses Hyde's emotions rather than physical horror. Also shown in computer-colored version.▼●

Dr. Jekyll and Ms. Hyde (1995) **C-90m.** *½ D: David Price. Sean Young, Tim Daly, Lysette Anthony, Stephen Tobolowsky, Harvey Fierstein, Thea Vidale, Jeremy Piven, Polly Bergen, Stephen Shellen, Jane Connell, Julie Cobb, Robert Wuhl. Did we really need a comic retread of the classic Robert Louis Stevenson tale, with Jekyll's great-grandson (Daly) morphing into seductress Helen Hyde (Young)? If so, it should have been a lot better. [PG-13]▼●

Dr. Jekyll & Sister Hyde (1971-British) **C-94m.** **½ D: Roy Ward Baker. Ralph Bates, Martine Beswick, Gerald Sim, Lewis Fiander, Susan Broderick. Interesting twist to classic tale finds the good doctor discovering that his evil life is brought out in the form of a beautiful but dangerous woman. No thrills but fun; resemblance between Bates and Beswick is remarkable. Released in Britain at 97m. [PG]▼●)

Dr. Kildare series SEE: *Leonard Maltin's Classic Movie Guide*

Dr. M SEE: **Club Extinction**

Dr. No (1962-British) **C-111m.** ***½ D: Terence Young. Sean Connery, Ursula Andress, Joseph Wiseman, Jack Lord, Bernard Lee, Lois Maxwell. First James Bond film is least pretentious, with meaty story, fine all-round production of Ian Fleming caper. Bond investigates strange occurrences in Jamaica, encounters master-fiend Dr. No (Wiseman).▼●)

Drop Dead Fred (1991) **C-98m.** BOMB D: Ate De Jong. Phoebe Cates, Rik Mayall, Marsha Mason, Tim Matheson, Carrie Fisher, Keith Charles, Ron Eldard. Putrid fantasy-comedy about a repressed young woman who—as her life is crumbling around her—is revisited by her childhood make-believe "friend" Drop Dead Fred, a repulsive mischief-maker. Cates' appealing performance can't salvage this mess. Recommended only for people who think nose-picking is funny. [PG-13]▼●)

Drop Dead Gorgeous (1999) **C-98m.** *½ D: Michael Patrick Jann. Kirsten Dunst, Denise Richards, Kirstie Alley, Ellen Barkin, Allison Janney, Brittany Murphy, Sam McMurray, Amy Adams, Mindy Sterling, Mo Gaffney, Nora Dunn. Annoying pseudo-documentary satire about small-town Midwestern teen beauty pageants. Full of frantic mugging and outrageous gags about eating disorders, but most of them aren't funny. Only prize-winner here is Janney as good-hearted trailer trash. To see how it's done right, watch SMILE. [PG-13]▼)

Drop Squad (1994) **C-86m.** ** D: D. Clark Johnson. Eriq LaSalle, Vondie Curtis Hall, Ving Rhames, Kasi Lemmons, Leonard Thomas, Billy Williams, Eric A. Payne, Vanessa Williams, Nicole Powell, Paula Kelly. Unsatisfying tale of a black ad-agency employee (LaSalle) who conjures up idiotic advertising campaigns, thus forsaking his roots; he becomes the target of some vigilante deprogrammers who seek to make him aware of his ethnic and family loyalties. Well-intentioned satire of corporate racism, but neither as humorous nor as daring as it sets out to be. Executive producer is Spike Lee, who appears briefly in one of the commercials. [R]▼●)

Drop Zone (1994) **C-102m.** **½ D: John Badham. Wesley Snipes, Gary Busey, Yancy Butler, Michael Jeter, Corin Nemec, Kyle Secor, Luca Bercovici, Malcolm-Jamal Warner, Rex Linn, Grace Zabriskie, Claire Stansfield, Andy Romano. Solid if predictable actioner with U.S. marshal Snipes

going up against some sky-diving baddies out to pilfer data on undercover drug agents to sell to international narcotics dealers. The scenario is preposterous, but there are enough dazzling airborne stunts to keep you entertained. Panavision. [R]▼●)

Drowning by Numbers (1988-British) **C-118m.** ***½ D: Peter Greenaway. Joan Plowright, Bernard Hill, Juliet Stephenson, Joely Richardson. Another bizarre, fascinating celluloid put-on from Greenaway, about an obsessive coroner and his involvement with three generations of women from the same family. Stunningly filmed and very entertaining (but recommended most enthusiastically to Greenaway fans). Not released in U.S. until 1991.▼●

Drowning Mona (2000) **C-95m.** **½ D: Nick Gomez. Danny DeVito, Bette Midler, Jamie Lee Curtis, Neve Campbell, Casey Affleck, William Fichtner, Marcus Thomas, Peter Dobson, Kathleen Wilhoite, Tracey Walter, Will Ferrell. Fairly amusing black comedy about a small town shaken by the drowning of its most reviled citizen (Midler), and the repercussions felt by her idiot son and husband, the town sheriff (DeVito), and others who knew and loathed her. [PG-13]▼)

Drowning Pool, The (1975) **C-108m.** **½ D: Stuart Rosenberg. Paul Newman, Joanne Woodward, Anthony Franciosa, Murray Hamilton, Melanie Griffith, Richard Jaeckel, Gail Strickland, Linda Haynes. Newman returns as private eye Harper, (based on Ross Macdonald's Archer character) in slickly made but slow whodunit; here he is called to help former lover Woodward out of a jam. Screenplay by Tracy Keenan Wynn, Lorenzo Semple, and Walter Hill. Panavision. [PG]▼)

Dr. Phibes Rises Again! (1972-British) **C-89m.** **½ D: Robert Fuest. Vincent Price, Robert Quarry, Valli Kemp, Fiona Lewis, Peter Jeffrey, Peter Cushing, Beryl Reid, Terry-Thomas, Hugh Griffith. Campy sequel to THE ABOMINABLE DR. PHIBES finds Price looking for elixir to revive his dead wife, with Quarry hot on his trail throughout Egypt. [PG]▼●)

Dr. Popaul SEE: **High Heels**

Dr. Seuss' Horton Hears a Who! SEE: **Horton Hears a Who!**

Dr. Seuss' How the Grinch Stole Christmas SEE: **How the Grinch Stole Christmas**

Dr. Seuss' The Cat in the Hat SEE: **Cat in the Hat, The**

Dr. Strangelove or: How I Learned to Stop Worrying and Love the Bomb (1964-British) **93m.** **** D: Stanley Kubrick. Peter Sellers, George C. Scott, Sterling Hayden, Slim Pickens, Keenan Wynn, Peter Bull, James Earl Jones. U.S. President must contend with the Russians and his own political and military leaders when a fanatical general launches A-bomb attack on U.S.S.R.

Sellers plays the President, British captain, and mad inventor of the Bomb in this brilliant black comedy, which seems better with each passing year. Sellers' phone conversation with Soviet premier is classic. Outstanding cast, incredible sets by Ken Adam. Jones' film debut. ▼◖◗

Dr. Syn, Alias the Scarecrow (1962) C-98m. **½ D: James Neilson. Patrick McGoohan, George Cole, Michael Hordern, Tony Britton, Geoffrey Keen, Kay Walsh, Patrick Wymark. Agreeable Disney production made in England (and originally shown in three parts on the Disney TV show as *The Scarecrow of Romney Marsh*) about country vicar who in reality is a smuggler and pirate. McGoohan is well cast as the mysterious bandit-hero who conducts his nightly raids disguised as a scarecrow. Filmed before in 1937 with George Arliss; another 1962 version, NIGHT CREATURES, stars Peter Cushing. [G]▼◖

Dr. T & the Women (2000) C-122m. *½ D: Robert Altman. Richard Gere, Helen Hunt, Farrah Fawcett, Laura Dern, Shelley Long, Tara Reid, Kate Hudson, Liv Tyler, Robert Hays, Matt Malloy, Andy Richter, Lee Grant, Janine Turner. Dismal Altman misfire about a high-society Dallas gynecologist who reveres women, even though personally and professionally they are starting to shake up his world. Gere's fine, understated performance is almost buried under a pile of strident, unfunny female caricatures, pointless subplots, and an ending that seems rejected from MAGNOLIA. Super 35. [R] ▼◖

Dr. Terror's Gallery of Horrors SEE: Return from the Past

Dr. Terror's House of Horrors (1965-British) C-98m. **½ D: Freddie Francis. Peter Cushing, Christopher Lee, Roy Castle, Max Adrian, Michael Gough, Donald Sutherland, Neil McCallum, Edward Underdown, Ursula Howells, Jeremy Kemp, Bernard Lee. Don't let title steer you from this intelligent episodic thriller about a strange doctor (Cushing) who tells five men's fortunes on a train. Enjoyable horror-fantasy. Techniscope. ▼

Drugstore Cowboy (1989) C-100m. ***½ D: Gus Van Sant, Jr. Matt Dillon, Kelly Lynch, James Remar, James Le Gros, Heather Graham, Beah Richards, Grace Zabriskie, Max Perlich, William S. Burroughs. Fascinating, completely credible look at the world of a junkie and his "family," who rob drugstores to support their habit. No preaching or moralizing here, which is precisely what gives the film its impact. Standout performances, particularly from Dillon and Lynch. Based on prison inmate James Fogle's unpublished autobiographical novel of the 1970s. Screenplay by Van Sant and Daniel Yost. [R]▼◖◗

Drum, The (1938) SEE: **Drums**

Drum (1976) C-110m. BOMB D: Steve Carver. Warren Oates, Ken Norton, Isela Vega, Pam Grier, Yaphet Kotto, John Colicos, Brenda Sykes, Paula Kelly. Continuation of MANDINGO—a new and dreadful low in lurid characters and incidents. Norton in title role generates neither interest nor sympathy. [R]▼

Drumline (2002) C-118m. **½ D: Charles Stone III. Nick Cannon, Zoë Saldaña, Orlando Jones, Leonard Roberts, GQ, Jason Weaver, Earl C. Poitier, Candace Carey, J. Anthony Brown. Teenage drummer from N.Y.C. is accepted at a Georgia college where the marching band is all-important. But his cocky ways put him at odds with the unyielding band director, and his giant ego causes friction with fellow band members. Feel-good film covers fresh territory in a strictly formulaic way—and goes on a half hour too long—but the music is hard to resist. Alternate version runs 122m. Super 35. [PG-13] ▼◖

Drums Along the Mohawk (1939) C-103m. ***½ D: John Ford. Claudette Colbert, Henry Fonda, Edna May Oliver, John Carradine, Jessie Ralph, Arthur Shields, Robert Lowery, Ward Bond. John Ford richly captures flavor of Colonial life in this vigorous, courageous story of settlers in upstate New York during Revolutionary War. Action, drama, sentiment, humor deftly interwoven in beautiful Technicolor production. From Walter Edmonds' novel. ▼◖◗

Drunken Master (1978-Hong Kong) C-106m. **½ D: Yuen Wo Ping. Jackie Chan, Yuen Sui Tin, Wang Jang Lee, Hsu Hsia, Ling Yang, Dean Shek, Yuen Shun-Yee. Jackie plays Chinese folk hero Wong Fei Hung in this kung fu comedy, his first big hit. Almost plotless film has Wong studying under hard-drinking master played by Yuen Sui Tin, the director's father. Enjoyably silly, with some good stunt work and comic moments. Of note mostly for its importance to Chan's career. Aka DRUNKEN MONKEY IN THE TIGER'S EYE(!) Followed by a sequel in 1994. Widescreen. ▼◖

Drunken Master II (1994-Hong Kong) C-113m. *** D: Lau Kar Leung. Jackie Chan, Anita Mui, Ti Lung, Andy Lau, Gabriel Wong, Ken Lo, Chin Kar-Lok. Chan returns to the role that made him a star 16 years earlier, confronting art smugglers and a father who disapproves of his drunken fighting style. Some truly amazing fight sequences, especially the complex final battle in a steel mill—which may leave you as breathless as the performers! The fellow Jackie fights under the train is the film's director. Reissued in the U.S. as THE LEGEND OF DRUNKEN MASTER. Technovision. ▼◖

Drunks (1996) C-90m. **½ D: Peter Cohn. Richard Lewis, Faye Dunaway, Amanda Plummer, Spalding Gray, Parker Posey, Calista Flockhart, Howard Rollins, Lisa Gay Hamilton, Dianne Wiest, Sam

Rockwell, Kevin Corrigan. Potent, if stagy, character study about alcoholics (of varied backgrounds) who tell all at an Alcoholics Anonymous meeting. Comedian Lewis is effective as a particularly pained group leader. A fine actors' showcase with some strong moments. Debuted on cable TV before theatrical release. [R]▼❶

Dr. Who and the Daleks (1965-British) C-85m. **½ D: Gordon Flemyng. Peter Cushing, Roy Castle, Jennie Linden, Roberta Tovey, Barrie Ingham. Pleasing feature inspired by the long-running British TV serial, with the Doctor and his young friends transported to another world where humans are threatened by robotlike Daleks. Followed by DALEKS—INVASION EARTH 2150 A.D. Techniscope. ▼❶

Dry White Season, A (1989) C-107m. **½ D: Euzhan Palcy. Donald Sutherland, Janet Suzman, Zakes Mokae, Jürgen Prochnow, Susan Sarandon, Marlon Brando, Winston Ntshona, Thoko Ntshinga, Susannah Harker, Rowan Elmes. Disappointing film about South African apartheid, set in 1976, with Sutherland as a schoolteacher who slowly awakens to the appalling reality of how blacks are treated in his country. Crucially important subject matter is unfortunately presented in the context of a story that's contrived and dramatically hollow. Brando is magnetic (if somewhat askew) in a showy supporting role as an outspoken barrister. [R]▼❶●

D-TOX SEE: **Eye See You**

D2: The Mighty Ducks (1994) C-107m. ** D: Sam Weisman. Emilio Estevez, Kathryn Erbe, Michael Tucker, Jan Rubes, Carsten Norgaard, Maria Ellingsen, Joshua Jackson, Elden Ryan Ratliff (Hansen), Shaun Weiss, Matt Doherty. Having led his ragtag hockey team to surprise victory in THE MIGHTY DUCKS, Estevez now gets a chance to coach Team USA (incorporating his former Ducks) in the Junior Goodwill Games—and make a bundle of money as a potential celebrity. The kind of film that gives the word "contrivance" a bad name: a Disney movie with mixed messages about competition, commercialism, puberty, and sportsmanship. Kids may like it anyway. Sports stars ranging from Wayne Gretzky to Kareem Abdul Jabbar make cameo appearances. [PG]▼❶●

D3: The Mighty Ducks (1996) C-104m. ** D: Robert Lieberman. Emilio Estevez, Jeffrey Nordling, Joshua Jackson, David Selby, Heidi Kling, Joss Ackland, Elden Ryan Ratliff (Hansen), Shaun Weiss, Vincent A. Larusso, Matt Doherty, Colombe Jacobsen, Aaron Lohr. Those adolescent hockey players have won scholarships to a fancy private school, where they have a new, no-nonsense coach (Nordling) and find themselves outsiders in a snooty varsity league. Oh yes—and Charlie (Jackson) has

a girlfriend. The Ducks franchise has run out of steam. [PG]▼❶

Du Barry Was a Lady (1943) C-101m. *** D: Roy Del Ruth. Red Skelton, Lucille Ball, Gene Kelly, Virginia O'Brien, Rags Ragland, Zero Mostel, Donald Meek, George Givot, Louise Beavers, Tommy Dorsey and His Orchestra. Nightclub worker Skelton pines for beautiful singing star Ball; when he swallows a Mickey Finn, he dreams he's Louis XV, and has to contend with the prickly Madame Du Barry (Ball). Colorful nonsense, missing most of the songs from Cole Porter's Broadway score, though "Friendship" is used as the finale. Opens like a vaudeville show, with beautiful chorines and specialty acts, including young Mostel, and Dorsey's band—with Buddy Rich on drums—doing a sensational "Well, Git It." They turn up later in powdered wigs, as do The Pied Pipers, with Dick Haymes and Jo Stafford. Lana Turner has a bit part.▼❶

Dubious Patriots, The SEE: **You Can't Win 'Em All**

Duchess, The (2008-British) C-105m. **½ D: Saul Dibb. Keira Knightley, Ralph Fiennes, Charlotte Rampling, Dominic Cooper, Hayley Atwell, Simon McBurney, Aidan McArdle, Michael Medwin. Knightley is well cast as Georgiana Spencer, who marries well in the late 1700s and becomes the Duchess of Devonshire. However, she soon discovers that her husband has little interest in her beyond her ability to give him an heir. Vivid, well-appointed yet somewhat heavy-handed adaptation of Amanda Foreman's best-selling book *Georgiana: Duchess of Devonshire* about the real-life socialite whose plight bears some striking parallels to those that faced her descendant Princess Diana. Knightley and especially Fiennes are excellent but the film lacks a certain spark. Michael O'Connor earned an Oscar for Costume Design. Panavision. [PG-13]❶

Duchess and the Dirtwater Fox, The (1976) C-103m. *½ D: Melvin Frank. George Segal, Goldie Hawn, Conrad Janis, Thayer David, Roy Jenson, Bob Hoy, Richard Farnsworth. Dumb comedy about cardsharp Segal and dance-hall cutie Hawn teaming up in the Old West. Occasional laughs, inappropriate song interludes. Panavision. [PG]▼❶●

Duchess of Idaho (1950) C-98m. **½ D: Robert Z. Leonard. Esther Williams, Van Johnson, John Lund, Paula Raymond, Clinton Sundberg, Connie Haines, Mel Tormé, Amanda Blake. Williams vehicle has her going to Sun Valley to assist her lovesick roommate, attracting bandleader Johnson. Guest stars Lena Horne, Eleanor Powell (in her last film), and Red Skelton pep up formula production.▼

Duchess of Langeais, The (2007-French-Italian) C-138m. *** D: Jacques Rivette. Jeanne Balibar, Guillaume Depardieu, Michel Piccoli, Bulle Ogier, Barbet Schroeder. In post-Napoleonic France, an intense relationship unfolds as a glum, wounded general (Depardieu) is smitten with a flirtatious, married socialite (Balibar). What follows is like a moral chess match between love and religion, well played by the two leads. Master filmmaker Rivette uses occasional intertitles—some taken from the Honoré de Balzac source material—to play up the ironies and emotions. Even at this length, one of the more accessible Rivette films. Original title: NE TOUCHEZ PAS LA HACHE (DON'T TOUCH THE AXE).

Duck Season (2004-Mexican) **85m. *** D:** Fernando Eimbcke. Enrique Arreola, Diego Cataño, Daniel Miranda, Danny Perea. Disarmingly offbeat comedy set in a high-rise apartment building, where two 14-year-old boys spend a day together, joined by a girl from next door who borrows their oven and a pizza delivery guy, all of whom are affected by a power blackout. Deadpan vignettes and character observations make this a winner, so long as the viewer adjusts to its pace and sensibility. Screenplay by first-time director Eimbcke. [R]●

Duck Soup (1933) **70m. ****** D:** Leo McCarey. Groucho, Harpo, Chico, Zeppo Marx, Margaret Dumont, Louis Calhern, Raquel Torres, Edgar Kennedy, Leonid Kinskey, Charles Middleton. The Marx Brothers' most sustained bit of insanity, a flop when first released, but now considered a satiric masterpiece. In postage-stamp–sized Freedonia, Prime Minister Rufus T. Firefly (Groucho) declares war on neighboring Sylvania just for the hell of it. Enough gags for five movies, but our favorite is still the mirror sequence. Zeppo's swan song with his brothers. ▼●❶

DuckTales: The Movie—Treasure of the Lost Lamp (1990) **C-73m. **½ D:** Bob Hathcock. Voices of Alan Young, Christopher Lloyd, Rip Taylor, June Foray, Chuck McCann, Richard Libertini, Russi Taylor. Disney's premier "Movietoon" feature falls somewhere between traditional studio standards and Saturday morning gruel. Story centers on an archeological trek for a genie's lamp that can, among other things, make ice cream fall from the sky, pitting Uncle Scrooge McDuck against the evil Merlock. Mild vehicle for Huey, Dewey, Louie, and company. [G]▼●❶

Duck, You Sucker (1971-Italian) **C-158m. *** D:** Sergio Leone. Rod Steiger, James Coburn, Romolo Valli, Maria Monti. Big, sprawling story of Mexican revolution, and how peasant thief Steiger gets talked into taking sides by Irish explosives expert Coburn. Tremendous action sequences; Leone's wry touches and ultra-weird Ennio Morricone score make it worthwhile diversion. Aka A FISTFUL OF DYNAMITE; originally intended to be called ONCE UPON A TIME DURING THE REVOLUTION. Restored to complete Italian running time in 2006; other prints run 121m. and 138m. Techniscope. [PG]▼●❶

Dudes (1987) **C-90m.** BOMB D: Penelope Spheeris. Jon Cryer, Daniel Roebuck, Flea, Lee Ving, Catherine Mary Stewart. Incomprehensible, idiotic account of a trio of N.Y.C. punk rockers, and their fate when harassed by a gang of redneck killers in the Southwest. Thoroughly repugnant. [R]▼●

Dude, Where's My Car? (2000) **C-83m.** BOMB D: Danny Leiner. Ashton Kutcher, Seann William Scott, Kristy Swanson, Jennifer Garner, Marla Sokoloff, Charlie O'Connell, David Herman, Andy Dick. Witless comedy about two stoner pals (Kutcher, Scott) who attempt to piece together the events of the previous evening. Only for those who think of the title as the height of comic repartee. Brent Spiner appears unbilled. [PG-13]▼●

Dudley Do-Right (1999) **C-77m. *½ D:** Hugh Wilson. Brendan Fraser, Sarah Jessica Parker, Alfred Molina, Eric Idle, Robert Prosky, Alex Rocco, Jack Kehler, Louis Mustillo; narrated by Corey Burton. Poorly conceived live-action version of the delightful Jay Ward-produced TV cartoons of the 1960s about a stalwart (if thick-headed) Mountie, his sweetheart, Nell Fenwick, and the dastardly villain, Snidely Whiplash (played with gusto by Molina). A couple of laughs here and there can't make up for a desperate, everything-but-the-kitchen-sink script. Super 35. [PG]▼●❶

Due Date (2010) **C-100m. ** D:** Todd Phillips. Robert Downey, Jr., Zach Galifianakis, Michelle Monaghan, Jamie Foxx, Juliette Lewis, Danny McBride, RZA, Matt Walsh, Brody Stevens, Mimi Kennedy. Uptight businessman Downey has to get home to L.A. from Atlanta so he can see his wife give birth, but from the moment he runs into goofball Galifianakis at the airport, things go awry. They wind up driving cross-country together and having a series of wild misadventures. Shameless echo of PLANES, TRAINS & AUTOMOBILES follows its template pretty closely: Every time Downey is ready to strangle his bumbling road partner, he backs off because the guy is good-hearted—and clueless. Only the skill of the lead actors keeps this from being a total waste of time. Director and cowriter Phillips has a cameo as Lewis' boyfriend. Super 35. [R]❶

Duel at Diablo (1966) **C-103m. *** D:** Ralph Nelson. James Garner, Sidney Poitier, Bibi Andersson, Dennis Weaver, Bill Travers, William Redfield, John Crawford, John Hubbard, John Hoyt. Aging Indians vs. Cavalry formula comes alive in this exciting Western; offbeat casting with tight direction. Some may find it too violent, but a must for action and Western fans. Look for Richard Farnsworth as a wagon driver. ▼●❶

Duel at Silver Creek, The (1952) **C-77m.**

*½ D: Don Siegel. Audie Murphy, Stephen McNally, Faith Domergue, Susan Cabot, Gerald Mohr, Lee Marvin. Ponderous oater has Murphy as the "Silver Kid" helping marshal fight town criminals. ▼▶

Duel in the Sun (1946) **C-130m.** ******* D: King Vidor. Jennifer Jones, Joseph Cotten, Gregory Peck, Lionel Barrymore, Lillian Gish, Herbert Marshall, Walter Huston, Butterfly McQueen, Charles Bickford, Tilly Losch, Harry Carey. Producer-writer David O. Selznick's ambitious attempt to duplicate success of GONE WITH THE WIND: big, brawling, engrossing, often stupid sex-Western, with half-breed Jones caught between brothers Peck and Cotten. Great in Technicolor, with some memorable scenes and an unexpectedly bizarre finale. From the novel by Niven Busch. Superb score by Dimitri Tiomkin. ▼●

Duellists, The (1977-British) **C-101m.** ******* D: Ridley Scott. Keith Carradine, Harvey Keitel, Edward Fox, Cristina Raines, Robert Stephens, Diana Quick, Tom Conti, Albert Finney, Peter Postlethwaite. Competent screen version of Joseph Conrad's *The Duel* concerns long-running feud between French officers Carradine and Keitel during the Napoleonic wars. Supporting players are more convincing than two leads; film is among most staggeringly beautiful of its time. Scott's first feature. [PG] ▼●

Duet for Four (1982-Australian) **C-97m.** *½ D: Tim Burstall. Mike Preston, Wendy Hughes, Michael Pate, Diane Cilento, Gary Day, Arthur Dignam, Rod Mullinar. Middle-aged Preston's life is in turmoil: his wife has a lover, his mistress wants marriage, his daughter might be a drug addict, his business may be taken over. Weak drama does not delve beneath the surface of its characters. Panavision.

Duet for One (1986) **C-107m.** ****½** D: Andrei Konchalovsky. Julie Andrews, Alan Bates, Max von Sydow, Rupert Everett, Margaret Courtenay, Cathryn Harrison, Macha Meril, Liam Neeson. World-class violinist Andrews is stricken with multiple sclerosis, and her comfortable, rewarding life is shattered. Tom Kempinski based his two-character play (virtuoso and psychiatrist) on a real-life cellist, but for film it was opened up and, in the process, diluted. Husband Bates, therapist von Sydow, and rebellious protégé Everett are fine, but it's Andrews' gutsy performance that breathes life into the film. Made in England. [R] ▼

Duets (2000) **C-112m.** *½ D: Bruce Paltrow. Maria Bello, Andre Braugher, Paul Giamatti, Huey Lewis, Gwyneth Paltrow, Scott Speedman, Angie Dickinson, Marian Seldes, Lochlyn Munro. Three nobodies are paired with optimistic spiritual guides in this road-trip odyssey, culminating at an Omaha karaoke contest. Press notes claim "the funny, raucous world of karaoke bars and chain hotels" is revealed; we must have missed that part. Director Paltrow is Gwyneth's father. One of the karaoke performers is a young Michael Bublé. [R] ▼▶

Duffy (1968-U.S.-British) **C-101m.** *½ D: Robert Parrish. James Coburn, James Mason, James Fox, Susannah York, John Alderton. Scummy crime comedy about two half-brothers who decide to rob their father of bank notes he is transporting by ship. A waste of everyone's talents and lovely location photography. [M/PG] ▶

Duffy's Tavern (1945) **97m.** BOMB D: Hal Walker. Barry Sullivan, Marjorie Reynolds, Bing Crosby, Dorothy Lamour, Alan Ladd, Betty Hutton, Eddie Bracken, Veronica Lake, Robert Benchley, Paulette Goddard, Brian Donlevy. Disastrous "comedy" of radio character Ed Gardner trying to save Duffy's Tavern, Victor Moore trying to save his record company. No redeeming values despite guest appearances by several dozen Paramount stars.

Dukes of Hazzard, The (2005) **C-105m.** BOMB D: Jay Chandrasekhar. Johnny Knoxville, Seann William Scott, Jessica Simpson, Burt Reynolds, Willie Nelson, Lynda Carter, Joe Don Baker, M. C. Gainey, David Koechner, Kevin Heffernan, James Roday. Just as in the 1979–85 TV series, good ole boys drive and shoot, drink and deliver moonshine, spit and fight and chase women. A smutty, slutty, laughless, nearly plotless flat tire about a road race and a land grab in Georgia (though filmed in Louisiana). Kindly unfasten your seat belts. Unrated version is two minutes longer. Followed by a direct-to-video prequel. Also followed by an animated TV series. Super 35. [PG-13] ▼▶

Dulcima (1971-British) **C-93m.** ****½** D: Frank Nesbitt. Carol White, John Mills, Stuart Wilson, Bernard Lee, Sheila Raynor. Poor White moves in with and exploits wealthy old farmer Mills. OK melodrama benefits from solid work by the stars. Original running time: 98m. [PG] ▼

Duma (2005) **C-100m.** ******* D: Carroll Ballard. Alex Michaletos, Eamonn Walker, Campbell Scott, Hope Davis. Beautifully filmed story of a South African boy who raises an orphaned cheetah from the time it's a cub, then has to face the inevitable when it's time to return the animal to the wild. His chore becomes a journey of growth and self-discovery, with an unlikely adult ally at his side. First-rate family entertainment from the director of THE BLACK STALLION, inspired by a true story and a book that set it down in print. [PG] ▶

Dumb & Dumber (1994) **C-106m.** ****** D: Peter Farrelly. Jim Carrey, Jeff Daniels, Lauren Holly, Teri Garr, Karen Duffy, Mike Starr, Charles Rocket, Victoria Rowell, Cam Neely. No, dumb*est*: a self-proclaimed no-brainer about two idiot pals who drive cross-country to Aspen to return a briefcase which (unbeknownst to them) contains a fortune in ransom money. Cheesy, gross-out comedy has its moments here and there, and enthusiastic performances by the two stars, who deserve a better script than this. Followed by a prequel and an animated TV series. Unrated version runs 113m. [PG-13] ▼●)

Dumb and Dumberer: When Harry Met Lloyd (2003) **C-85m.** BOMB D: Troy Miller. Eric Christian Olsen, Derek Richardson, Rachel Nichols, Cheri Oteri, Luis Guzmán, Elden Henson, William Lee Scott, Mimi Rogers, Eugene Levy, Lin Shaye, Shia LaBeouf, Julia Duffy. Desperate prequel to the 1994 comedy hit shows the two oafish friends meeting up in high school and becoming pawns in their slimy principal's scheme to get funding for a special education class—and abscond with the funds. The actors playing younger versions of Jim Carrey and Jeff Daniels do a good job, but this movie is appallingly unfunny; a particular waste of Levy and Oteri's comedy talents. [PG-13] ▼)

Dumbo (1941) **C-64m.** ★★★★ D: Ben Sharpsteen. Voices of Sterling Holloway, Edward Brophy, Verna Felton, Herman Bing, Cliff Edwards. One of Walt Disney's most charming animated films, about pint-sized elephant with giant-sized ears, and how his friend Timothy the Mouse helps build his confidence. Never a dull moment, but pink-elephants dream sequence is special treat. Frank Churchill and Oliver Wallace's scoring earned them Oscars. ▼●)

Dummy (2003) **C-90m.** ★★½ D: Greg Pritikin. Adrien Brody, Milla Jovovich, Illeana Douglas, Vera Farmiga, Jessica Walter, Ron Leibman, Jared Harris, Mirabella Pisani. Slight though occasionally ingratiating comedy about a suburban schnook (Brody), the product of a stereotypically dysfunctional family, who decides to take up ventriloquism; his new wooden companion becomes his conscience and alter ego. The actors and their oddball characters give this film its thrust. Brody made this right before starring in THE PIANIST. [R] ▼)

Dune (1984) **C-140m.** ★½ D: David Lynch. Kyle MacLachlan, Francesca Annis, Brad Dourif, Jose Ferrer, Linda Hunt, Freddie Jones, Richard Jordan, Virginia Madsen, Silvana Mangano, Kenneth McMillan, Jack Nance, Sian Phillips, Jürgen Prochnow, Paul Smith, Sting, Dean Stockwell, Max von Sydow, Patrick Stewart, Sean Young, Alicia (Roanne) Witt. Elephantine adaptation of Frank Herbert's popular sci-fi novel set in the year 10,991. You know you're in trouble when film's opening narration (setting up the story) is completely incomprehensible! Visually imaginative, well cast, but joyless and oppressive—not to mention *long*. For devotees of Herbert's novel only. Alternate unrated version runs 177m. Remade in 2000 as a miniseries. Todd-AO 35. [PG-13] ▼●)

Dunera Boys, The (1985-Australian) **C-150m.** ★★½ D: Sam Lewin. Joseph Spano, Bob Hoskins, Joseph Furst, John Meillon, Warren Mitchell, Mary-Anne Fahey, Simon Chilvers, Steven Vidler, Moshe Kedem. Low-key, fact-based drama of Jewish refugees in England at the outset of WW2 who, because of their nationalities, are suspected of being Nazi spies and exiled to a POW camp in Australia. Hoskins plays a loutish fishmonger who's as English as Winston Churchill, but somehow is deported with the others. Fascinating subject matter, but film is overlong and uneven. Made for Australian television. ▼●

Dungeonmaster, The (1985) **C-73m.** ★½ D: Rosemarie Turko, John Buechler, Charles Band, David Allen, Steve Ford, Peter Manoogian, Ted Nicolaou. Jeffrey Byron, Richard Moll, Leslie Wing. It took seven—count 'em, seven—directors to make this short, sour chronicle of a girl held hostage by a villain. Her savior (atrociously played by Byron) must overcome seven challenges. You have only one: to sit through this. [PG-13] ▼●

Dungeons & Dragons (2000-U.S.-Czech) **C-107m.** ★½ D: Courtney Solomon. Jeremy Irons, Justin Whalin, Marlon Wayans, Zoe McLellan, Thora Birch, Bruce Payne, Kristen Wilson, Richard O'Brien, Tom Baker. In a sword-and-sorcery fantasy world, three young heroes opposed by evil sorcerer Irons and his henchman Payne try to obtain powerful talismans to help threatened princess Birch. Irons is spectacularly hammy, the effects highly variable, the writing and direction amateurish. Based on the game, whose fans are the most likely audience for this lavish but empty movie. Lots of dragons, though. Followed by two direct-to-video sequels. [PG-13] ▼)

Dunkirk (1958-British) **113m.** ★★★ D: Leslie Norman. John Mills, Richard Attenborough, Bernard Lee, Robert Urquhart, Ray Jackson, Lionel Jeffries. Near-epic dramatization of the rescue by the Royal Navy and small civilian craft of 300,000 British soldiers trapped on the French beach of the title in 1940. One of the last films of the famed Ealing studios. Very realistic, with a fine cast and good direction. Original British length: 135m. Metroscope.

Dunston Checks In (1996) **C-88m.** ★★½ D: Ken Kwapis. Jason Alexander, Faye Dunaway, Eric Lloyd, Rupert Everett, Graham Sack, Paul Reubens, Glenn Shadix, Nathan Davis, Jennifer Bassey. Easy-to-take kids' comedy about the sons of a hard-working hotel manager who discover that an orangutan has been sneaked into the establishment by a crafty thief. Alexander is excellent, the kids are appealing, the orangutan is just right, Everett does a Terry-Thomas homage, Dunaway goes slapstick, and everyone has a good time, including the audience. [PG] ▼●)

Dunwich Horror, The (1970) **C-90m.** ★★½

D: Daniel Haller. Sandra Dee, Dean Stockwell, Ed Begley, Sam Jaffe, Lloyd Bochner, Joanna Moore, Talia Coppola (Shire). Adaptation of H. P. Lovecraft's story about warlock Stockwell's sinister plans for girlfriend Dee. Often effective, but ending ruins the whole film. Remade as a TV movie with Stockwell in doctor's role. [M]▼●◗

Duplex (2003) **C-89m.** *½ D: Danny De-Vito. Ben Stiller, Drew Barrymore, Eileen Essell, Harvey Fierstein, Justin Theroux, James Remar, Robert Wisdom, Swoosie Kurtz, Wallace Shawn, Maya Rudolph, Amber Valletta, Tracey Walter. Young couple purchases a Brooklyn brownstone as their dream house, but the elderly tenant upstairs, who comes along as part of the deal, makes their life a living hell. A comedy about pain, destruction, and nastiness is standard De-Vito fare by now, but it's hard to watch such likable stars caught in this morass. Unbearable. [PG-13] ▼◗

Duplicity (2009) **C-125m.** **½ D: Tony Gilroy. Julia Roberts, Clive Owen, Tom Wilkinson, Paul Giamatti, Tom McCarthy, Denis O'Hare, Kathleen Chalfant, Wayne Duvall, Carrie Preston, Oleg Stefan, Ulrich Thomsen. High-toned hybrid of romantic comedy and espionage yarn with Roberts and Owen as sexually charged spies who wind up working for cutthroat rival industrialists Wilkinson and Giamatti in N.Y.C. It isn't hard to recognize this as the work of the same writer-director who brought us MICHAEL CLAYTON, though his complicated flashback/flash-forward structure will keep you on your toes. The stars' chemistry—and a strong supporting cast—trumps the realization that the movie is really one long shaggy-dog joke. Panavision. [PG-13]◗

Dust (1985-French-Belgian) **C-88m.** ***½ D: Marion Hansel. Jane Birkin, Trevor Howard, John Matshikiza, Nadine Uwampa, Lourdes Christina Sayo, Rene Diaz. Birkin gives a fine performance as an unmarried woman, in need of love and affection, who murders her arrogant father (Howard) after he seduces the wife of his farm's black foreman. An intense, rewarding portrayal of isolation, oppression, and degradation.

Dust Be My Destiny (1939) **88m.** **½ D: Lewis Seiler. John Garfield, Priscilla Lane, Alan Hale, Frank McHugh, John Litel, Billy Halop, Henry Armetta, Stanley Ridges, Bobby Jordan, Charley Grapewin. Garfield is ideally cast as an alienated drifter who finds himself in jail, where he falls for vicious prison foreman's stepdaughter (Lane). The stars rise above their less-than-original material.◗

Dust Devil (1993-British-French) **C-87m.** ** D: Richard Stanley. Robert Burke, Chelsea Field, Zakes Mokae, John Matshikiza, Rufus Swart, William Hootkins, Marianne Sägebrecht. In Africa's Namibia Desert,

evil spirit Burke, trapped in human form, must kill to enter a spiritual realm; he meets Field, fleeing an unhappy marriage, and is pursued by policeman Mokae. Interesting premise, good acting partly offset lethargic pace, pretentious approach. [R]▼●◗

Dusty (1982-Australian) **C-88m.** *** D: John Richardson. Bill Kerr, Noel Trevarthen, Carol Burns, Nicholas Holland, John Stanton, Kate Edwards. Subtle, touching little film about a dingo (wild dog of the bush), captured while a puppy and eventually raised by an old man (Kerr). Adults will enjoy it as much as kids.▼

Dusty and Sweets McGee (1971) **C-95m.** ***½ D: Floyd Mutrux. Unconventional, no-holds-barred docudrama detailing day-to-day life of various heroin addicts in Los Angeles area. [R]◗

Dutch (1991) **C-105m.** **½ D: Peter Faiman. Ed O'Neill, Ethan Randall (Embry), JoBeth Williams, Christopher McDonald, Ari Meyers, E. G. Daily, Kathleen Freeman. Yet another warm-hearted concoction from the John Hughes assembly line, in which a stuck-up rich kid learns all about life when he travels home for Thanksgiving with his mother's blue-collar boyfriend, Dutch. Some choice, almost Chaplinesque moments (particularly one terrific scene in a homeless shelter) and appealing performances by O'Neill and Randall can't make us forget that we've seen this formula many times before. [PG-13]▼●◗

Dutchman (1966-British) **55m.** **½ D: Anthony Harvey. Shirley Knight, Al Freeman, Jr. Two-character allegory, based on LeRoi Jones's play, of confrontation between sadistic white trollop Knight and naive black Freeman in a subway car. Tense and well acted, but contrived.▼◗

D-War SEE: **Dragon Wars**

Dying Gaul, The (2005) **C-101m.** **½ D: Craig Lucas. Patricia Clarkson, Campbell Scott, Peter Sarsgaard, Ryan Miller, Robin Bartlett, Linda Emond, Jason-Shane Scott. Grieving writer of an autobiographical screenplay becomes erotically entangled with a slick producer, who offers him one million dollars to produce the project as long as he makes the gay protagonists straight. Meanwhile, he becomes emotionally entangled with the producer's lonely wife, a former screenwriter turned stay-at-home mom. Twists, tragedies, and fine performances mark this intelligent but dense character study. Directorial debut for playwright Lucas (*Longtime Companion, Prelude to a Kiss*). [R]◗

Dying Young (1991) **C-105m.** **½ D: Joel Schumacher. Julia Roberts, Campbell Scott, Vincent D'Onofrio, Colleen Dewhurst, David Selby, Ellen Burstyn. Aimless young woman answers a classified ad and becomes nurse/companion to a 28-year-old poor-little-rich-boy who's suffering from leukemia; needless to say, they fall in love. As vehicle for Roberts' charms, it works; as love story it has its moments; but as a tearjerker it never really delivers, wandering toward an inconclusive (and unsatisfying) finale. Scott shares a few scenes with his real-life mother, Dewhurst. [R]▼●〗

Dylan Dog: Dead of Night (2010) C-107m. BOMB D: Kevin Munroe. Brandon Routh, Sam Huntington, Anita Briem, Peter Stormare, Taye Diggs, Kurt Angle. Dylan Dog (Routh) is a supernatural private eye, attempting to defend the Louisiana bayou from all of the monsters that lurk among the living. Now he must locate a dangerous artifact before the zombies and werewolves start a war. Huntington is entertaining as the loyal sidekick, but he can't salvage this unoriginal, dull, and lifeless (pun intended) film that tries to both take itself seriously and be funny. Based on an Italian comic book by Tiziano Sclavi. Super 35. [PG-13]〗

Dynamite Chicken (1971) C/B&W-76m. ** D: Ernie Pintoff. Richard Pryor, John Lennon, Yoko Ono, Sha Na Na, Ace Trucking Company, Joan Baez, Ron Carey, Andy Warhol, Paul Krassner, Leonard Cohen, Malcolm X, many others. Odd, dated pastiche of songs, skits, television commercial parodies and old movie clips, filmed when nudity and profanity on celluloid were still shocking. Worth a look alone for Pryor. [R]▼〗

DysFunKtional Family (2003) C-89m. ** D: George Gallo. Raucous, raunchy combination concert film–documentary spotlighting Eddie Griffin, actor/stand-up comic and wannabe Richard Pryor; he performs onstage and is seen in his Kansas City, Missouri, hometown, with his real-life family members. The humor is blunt and vulgar; some will find it racist, chauvinistic, and homophobic, while others will think it hilarious. Most interesting when Griffin recounts his childhood and his family members' impact on his life. [R]▼〗

Each Dawn I Die (1939) 92m. *** D: William Keighley. James Cagney, George Raft, George Bancroft, Jane Bryan, Maxie Rosenbloom, Stanley Ridges, Louis Jean Heydt, Abner Biberman, John Wray, Victor Jory, Thurston Hall. Reporter Cagney is framed, sent to prison, where he meets tough-guy Raft. Good performances all around—Cagney hits a white-hot peak as the embittered, stir-crazy fall guy—but last half of film becomes outrageously improbable. Music score by Max Steiner. ▼●〗

Eagle, The (2011) C-114m. *** D: Kevin Macdonald. Channing Tatum, Jamie Bell, Mark Strong, Donald Sutherland, Tahar Rahim, Denis O'Hare, Paul Ritter, Julian Lewis Jones. Old-fashioned sword-and-sandal adventure set in A.D. 140 about the journey of a centurion (Tatum) who, with his

slave (Bell), tries to restore his commander father's reputation and discover what happened to the Roman Ninth Legion and its symbol, the golden eagle. Characters are well developed, and the battles are nicely staged, against gorgeous Scottish scenery. Bell shines and Tatum at least looks the part. Director Macdonald certainly understands the genre but injects a classic western bravado that gives the enterprise an air of freshness. Based on a novel by Rosemary Sutcliff. Super 35. [PG-13]〗

Eagle and the Hawk, The (1933) 68m. ***½ D: Stuart Walker. Fredric March, Cary Grant, Jack Oakie, Carole Lombard, Guy Standing, Douglas Scott. Well-produced antiwar film with reluctant hero March, bullying gunner-observer Grant, everyone's friend Oakie, sympathetic society girl Lombard. Sobering John Monk Saunders story is still timely. Mitchell Leisen, credited as "associate director," reportedly directed most of the film. Originally 72m. ▼〗

Eagle and the Hawk, The (1950) C-104m. **½ D: Lewis R. Foster. John Payne, Rhonda Fleming, Dennis O'Keefe, Thomas Gomez, Fred Clark. Contrived actioner set in 1860s Mexico-Texas with O'Keefe and Payne U.S. law enforcers stifling coup to make Maximilian ruler of Mexico; Fleming is fetching love interest.

Eagle Eye (2008) C-117m. ** D: D. J. Caruso. Shia LaBeouf, Michelle Monaghan, Billy Bob Thornton, Rosario Dawson, Michael Chiklis, Anthony Mackie, Ethan Embry, Anthony Azizi, William Sadler, Lynn Cohen, Bill Smitrovich, Cameron Boyce, Marc Singer. LaBeouf is a college dropout mistaken for a terrorist by a U.S. government overly fond of surveillance. Forced to become a fugitive, he teams (on the run, natch) with earnest single mom Monaghan. Frequently preposterous action-thriller plays like DISTURBIA on steroids. Instead of an updated REAR WINDOW, film seems to have been inspired by numerous other Hitchcock plots (check out that climax), beefed up with gadgets galore. Tech-heads and LaBeouf buffs may enjoy it. Super 35. [PG-13]〗

Eagle Has Landed, The (1977) C-123m. *** D: John Sturges. Michael Caine, Donald Sutherland, Robert Duvall, Jenny Agutter, Donald Pleasence, Anthony Quayle, Jean Marsh, Sven-Bertil Taube, John Standing, Judy Geeson, Treat Williams, Larry Hagman, Jeff Conaway. Action-packed wartime adventure taken from fanciful Jack Higgins best-seller about Nazi plot to kidnap Winston Churchill. Hardly a dull moment, thanks to solid cast and lively, twist-laden story. Original running time in England was 134m. Panavision. [PG]▼〗

Eagle in a Cage (1971-British) C-98m. *** D: Fielder Cook. John Gielgud, Ralph Richardson, Billie Whitelaw, Kenneth

Haigh, Moses Gunn, Ferdy Mayne. Fine drama of Napoleon in exile on St. Helena. Haigh is quite impressive in the title role, and is surrounded by a top cast. Screenplay by Millard Lampell. [PG]▐

Eagle's Wing (1979-British) **C-111m.** *½ D: Anthony Harvey. Martin Sheen, Sam Waterston, Caroline Langrishe, Harvey Keitel, Stephane Audran, John Castle, Jorge Luke. God never intended penguins to fly or the British to make Westerns. Dreary, artsy glop entangling half a dozen plots cribbed from other, better oaters; principal one involves seesawing between renegade Indian Waterston and trapper Sheen for possession of magnificent white stallion. Billy Williams' lush cinematography doesn't help. Most U.S. prints run 98m. Panavision. [PG] ▼

Eagle vs. Shark (2007-New Zealand) **C-87m.** **½ D: Taika Waititi. Loren Horsley, Jemaine Clement, Brian Sergent, Rachel House, Craig Hall, Joel Tobeck. A celebration of life's oddballs, as mousy Lily (Horsley, who helped develop the story based on a character she created for the stage) sets her sights on self-styled macho man Jarrod (Clement), who lives only to exact revenge on the classmate who used to beat him up in high school. This likable absurdist comedy gives off the same vibe as NAPOLEON DYNAMITE, but seems overly self-conscious. [R]▐

Eagle With Two Heads, The (1948-French) **93m.** **½ D: Jean Cocteau. Edwige Feuillere, Jean Marais, Sylvia Monfort, Jacques Varennes, Jean Debucourt, Yvonne de Bray. Stuffy, slightly crazed Queen Feuillere's husband was assassinated a decade earlier, on their wedding day. Amid much court intrigue, a poet-anarchist (Marais) who bears a striking resemblance to the deceased monarch stumbles into her quarters. Static romantic drama is Cocteau's least successful film. He scripted, based on his play (which also starred Feuillere and Marais).▼

Early Summer (1951-Japanese) **125m.** *** D: Yasujiro Ozu. Setsuko Hara, Chishu Ryu, Kuniko Miyake, Chikage Awashima, Chiyeko Higashiyama. Stirring tale of a woman (Hara) who, at 28, is aging by her society's standards. She resides with her elderly parents and must deal with their pressure to marry the man of their choice. A sensitively rendered film about basic human emotions, made by a master filmmaker.▼O▐

Earrings of Madame de . . . , The (1953-French-Italian) **105m.** **** D: Max Ophuls. Charles Boyer, Danielle Darrieux, Vittorio De Sica, Jean Debucourt, Lia de Léa. Captivating classic detailing the events that unravel after fickle Darrieux pawns the earrings presented her by husband Boyer. A knowing look at the effect of living a shallow, meaningless life. Masterfully acted

and directed, with dazzling tracking shots. Screenplay by Marcel Achard, Ophuls, and Annette Wademant, from the novel by Louise de Vilmorin. ▼O▐

Earth (1930-Russian) **90m.** **** D: Alexander Dovzhenko. Semyon Svashenko, Stepan Shkurat, Mikola Nademsky, Yelena Maximova. Lyrical, deservedly famous classic about collective farming in the Ukraine, with peasants opposing a landowner and the arrival of a tractor symbolizing the transformation of Soviet society. This ode to the wonders of nature is loaded with beautiful imagery. Long a staple on all-time-best film lists.▼▐

Earth (2007-U.S.-British-German) **C-96m.** *** D: Alastair Fothergill, Mark Linfield. Narrated by James Earl Jones. Eye-filling look at the natural wonders of our planet, with a particular emphasis on the yearlong struggles of three species: a polar bear father trying to find food for his mate and her cubs, a great white whale and her calf making a 4,000-mile migration, and an elephant mother and child on an exhausting journey overland in search of water. Adapted from the acclaimed BBC/Discovery Channel TV series *Planet Earth*, with some footage never used in the show. U.S. version produced by Disney is aimed at family audiences with friendly, colloquial narration by Jones, a new score, and an upbeat ending. British version is narrated by Patrick Stewart. [G]▐

Earthbound (1981) **C-94m.** *½ D: James L. Conway. Burl Ives, Christopher Connelly, Meredith MacRae, Joseph Campanella, Todd Porter, Marc Gilpin, Elissa Leeds, John Schuck, Stuart Pankin. Average family from outer space lands in Middle America due to a faulty flying saucer. Will dastardly government official Campanella shoot them? Trite, dumb, idiotic. [PG]

Earth Girls Are Easy (1989) **C-100m.** **½ D: Julien Temple. Geena Davis, Jeff Goldblum, Jim Carrey, Damon Wayans, Julie Brown, Michael McKean, Charles Rocket, Larry Linville, Rick Overton, Angelyne. Infectiously goofy musical comedy about aliens landing in the San Fernando Valley and being ushered into materialistic Southern California life by a ditsy manicurist. Not enough substance to sustain a feature film, but there are some good laughs, and an endearing performance by Davis. Costar Brown (who sings airhead anthem " 'Cause I'm a Blonde") also cowrote the movie. Panavision. [PG]▼O▐

Earthling, The (1980-Australian) **C-102m.** **½ D: Peter Collinson. William Holden, Ricky Schroder, Jack Thompson, Olivia Hamnett, Alwyn Kurts. Holden, terminally ill, teaches Schroder, orphaned and lost, how to survive in the bush country. OK drama features much nature footage and will appeal mainly to kids. Originally released at 97m., later reedited and lengthened to 102m. Panavision. [PG]▼

Earthquake (1974) **C-129m.** BOMB D: Mark Robson. Charlton Heston, Ava Gardner, George Kennedy, Genevieve Bujold, Richard Roundtree, Lorne Greene, Barry Sullivan, Marjoe Gortner, Lloyd Nolan, Victoria Principal, Walter Matuschanskyasky (Walter Matthau), Gabriel Dell, Pedro Armendariz, Jr., Lloyd Gough, John Randolph, Donald Moffat. Title tells the story in hackneyed disaster epic originally released in Sensurround. Marjoe as a sex deviate and Gardner as Lorne Greene's *daughter* tie for film's top casting honors. Additional footage was shot for inclusion in network showings. Won Oscar for Sound, plus special achievement for Visual Effects and citations for the development of Sensurround. Panavision. [PG]▼●▶

Earth vs. the Flying Saucers (1956) **82m.** *** D: Fred F. Sears. Hugh Marlowe, Joan Taylor, Donald Curtis, Morris Ankrum, Tom Browne Henry; voice of Paul Frees. Matter-of-fact presentation gives tremendous boost to familiar storyline (alien invaders order us to surrender peaceably—or else). Literate dialogue, subdued performances, and solid Ray Harryhausen effects make this a winner that belies its B origins nearly every step of the way. Also available in computer-colored version. ▼●▶

Easiest Way, The (1931) **74m.** **½ D: Jack Conway. Constance Bennett, Adolphe Menjou, Robert Montgomery, Marjorie Rambeau, Anita Page, Clark Gable, Hedda Hopper. Bennett rises from dire poverty to a life of luxury after becoming the mistress of advertising mogul Menjou, but finds heartbreak when she falls for reporter Montgomery. Watered-down adaptation of notorious play about high-priced call girls starts out great, then turns into a standard romantic triangle melodrama to satisfy the Hays Office. Gable has a small but strong role in his first film as an MGM contract player.▶

Eastern Promises (2007-Canadian-British) **C-100m.** *** D: David Cronenberg. Viggo Mortensen, Naomi Watts, Armin Mueller-Stahl, Vincent Cassel, Sinéad Cusack, Jerzy Skolimowski, Sarah-Jeanne Labrosse, Mike Sarne. London hospital midwife Watts discovers the diary of an abandoned, pregnant teenager who dies in childbirth, and determines to locate the girl's family. This leads her into a shady, ruthless world of Russian mobsters operating out of Mueller-Stahl's restaurant, where she becomes intrigued by enigmatic chauffeur-enforcer Mortensen. Intelligent thriller set against a rich tableau, courtesy of screenwriter Steven Knight (DIRTY PRETTY THINGS). Mortensen is superb and has one unforgettable scene in a Turkish bathhouse. [R]▶

Easter Parade (1948) **C-103m.** ***½ D: Charles Walters. Judy Garland, Fred Astaire, Peter Lawford, Ann Miller, Jules Munshin. Delightful Irving Berlin musical about Astaire trying to forget ex-dance partner Miller while rising to stardom with Garland. Too good to watch just at Eastertime. Musical highlights include Astaire's solo "Steppin' Out With My Baby," Miller's "Shaking the Blues Away," Fred and Judy's "A Couple of Swells," and the Fifth Avenue finale with Berlin's title song. Oscar winner for musical scoring (Johnny Green and Roger Edens). Story by Frances Goodrich and Albert Hackett; they also scripted with Sidney Sheldon.▼●▶

Easter Sunday SEE: **Being, The**

East is East (1999-British) **C-96m.** *** D: Damien O'Donnell. Om Puri, Linda Bassett, Jordan Routledge, Archie Panjabi, Emil Marwa, Chris Bisson, Lesley Nicol, Gary Damer, Emma Rydal, Ruth Jones, John Bardon. Piquant look at a cross-cultural family in 1970s London. Pakistani immigrant George (Puri) has lived there for 25 years; his wife is English, and their seven children have been raised as Brits, but he clings to his old-world ways and (rather hypocritically) expects them to conform to Pakistani customs. Keenly observed social comedy-drama never betrays its stage origins; Ayub Khan-Din scripted from his play. [R]▼▶

East of Eden (1955) **C-115m.** **** D: Elia Kazan. James Dean, Julie Harris, Raymond Massey, Jo Van Fleet, Burl Ives, Richard Davalos, Albert Dekker. Emotionally overwhelming adaptation of the John Steinbeck novel about two brothers' rivalry for the love of their father; affects today's generation as much as those who witnessed Dean's starring debut. Van Fleet (in film debut) won Oscar as boys' mother. Screenplay by Paul Osborn. Remade as TV mini-series. CinemaScope.▼●▶

East of Elephant Rock (1977-British) **C-92m.** BOMB D: Don Boyd. Judi Bowker, John Hurt, Jeremy Kemp, Christopher Cazenove, Anton Rodgers. Inept period drama set in 1948 Malaya; final reel ripped off from W. Somerset Maugham's THE LETTER. Further sabotaged by campy songs on soundtrack as well as opening disclaimer, which invites viewers to "laugh and smile" at the film. Bowker is beautiful, as are Sri Lanka locations.▼

East of Shanghai SEE: **Rich and Strange**

East Side Story (1997-German-French) **C/B&W-87m.** ***½ D: Dana Ranga. "Soviet musicals" sounds like an oxymoron, but more than 40 were made behind the Iron Curtain from the early '30s until the late '60s. This documentary doesn't limit itself to clips from the films, but includes interviews with filmmakers, critics, and ordinary moviegoers. Some of the musicals are propaganda featuring deliriously happy workers, but others, especially those directed by Grigori Alexandrov, look so delightful you long to see titles like THE JOLLY FELLOWS and VOLGA VOLGA, Stalin's favorite movie. An absolute must for film buffs.▼▋

East Side, West Side (1949) **108m. **½** D: Mervyn LeRoy. Barbara Stanwyck, James Mason, Ava Gardner, Van Heflin, Cyd Charisse, Gale Sondergaard, William Frawley, Nancy Davis (Reagan). Stanwyck and Mason have pivotal roles as chic N.Y.C. society couple with abundant marital woes, stirred up by alluring Gardner and understanding Heflin. Static MGM version of Marcia Davenport's superficial novel.▼▋

East-West (1999-French-Russian-Spanish-Bulgarian) **C-121m. **** D: Régis Wargnier. Sandrine Bonnaire, Oleg Menchikov, Catherine Deneuve, Sergei Bodrov, Jr. A doctor and his French wife join other Russian émigrés who are invited back to their homeland following WW2, but once there, their lives become a nightmare. Fascinating historical subject matter is turned into a turgid soap opera. Deneuve has a small, thankless role as a politically active stage star, but Bonnaire is luminous. [PG-13]▼▋

Easy A (2010) **C-92m. **½** D: Will Gluck. Emma Stone, Penn Badgley, Amanda Bynes, Dan Byrd, Thomas Haden Church, Patricia Clarkson, Stanley Tucci, Cam Gigandet, Lisa Kudrow, Malcolm McDowell, Aly Michalka, Fred Armisen. Supersmart girl who's a nonentity at her high school tells her so-called best friend that she slept with an older guy, to earn a little notoriety, but her fib spirals way out of control. Postmodern spin on Hawthorne's *The Scarlet Letter* (complete with film clips featuring Lillian Gish and Colleen Moore) is sparked by Stone's bright presence and great actors in supporting roles, but its tone is wildly uneven, alternately funny and sour. It openly yearns to be as sweet and sincere as a John Hughes movie, but processes its feelings secondhand. [PG-13] ▋

Easy Come, Easy Go (1967) **C-95m. *½** D: John Rich. Elvis Presley, Dodie Marshall, Pat Priest, Elsa Lanchester, Frank McHugh, Pat Harrington. Presley's a frogman diving for buried treasure in this hackneyed comedy. Fortunately, he doesn't sing underwater. Yet he does get to perform such classics as "The Love Machine" and "Yoga Is As Yoga Does."▼▋

Easy Life, The (1962-Italian) **105m. ***** D: Dino Risi. Vittorio Gassman, Catherine Spaak, Jean-Louis Trintignant, Luciana Angiolillo. Gassman has proper joie de vivre for playing middle-aged playboy who introduces student Trintignant to life of frolic with tragic results; well played and haunting.▼

Easy Living (1937) **86m. ***** D: Mitchell Leisen. Jean Arthur, Edward Arnold, Ray Milland, Franklin Pangborn, William Demarest, Mary Nash, Luis Alberni. Millionaire Arnold throws spoiled wife's mink

out the window; it drops on unsuspecting working girl Arthur. Arnold's son Milland, off making his career, falls in love. The girl: Arthur. Highlight: a mêlée in an Automat. Delightful comedy written by Preston Sturges.▼▋

Easy Living (1949) **77m. ***** D: Jacques Tourneur. Victor Mature, Lizabeth Scott, Lucille Ball, Sonny Tufts, Lloyd Nolan, Paul Stewart, Jeff Donnell, Jack Paar, Art Baker. Mature is aging football star who can't adjust to impending retirement—especially under constant pressure from grasping wife Scott. Intelligent film from Irwin Shaw story, with good performance from Lucy as team secretary in love with Mature.▼●

Easy Money (1983) **C-95m. **½** D: James Signorelli. Rodney Dangerfield, Joe Pesci, Geraldine Fitzgerald, Candy Azzara, Taylor Negron, Jennifer Jason Leigh, Tom Ewell. Working-class slob has one year to give up all his bad habits—drinking, overeating, smoking, gambling—in order to collect big inheritance. Dangerfield's first starring comedy vehicle is pleasant enough—with a refreshing amount of restraint for an '80s comedy. Final gag is right out of W. C. Fields. [R]▼●▋

Easy Rider (1969) **C-94m. ***½** D: Dennis Hopper. Peter Fonda, Dennis Hopper, Jack Nicholson, Karen Black, Luke Askew, Luana Anders, Robert Walker, Phil Spector, Toni Basil. Low-budget film of alienated youth nearly ruined Hollywood when every studio tried to duplicate its success. Tale of two cyclists chucking it all and searching for "the real America," while inevitably dated, remains quite worthwhile, highlighted by fine Laszlo Kovacs photography, great rock soundtrack, and Nicholson's star-making performance as boozy lawyer who tags along. Written by Fonda, Hopper, and Terry Southern. [R]▼●▋

Easy to Love (1953) **C-96m. **½** D: Charles Walters. Esther Williams, Van Johnson, Tony Martin, John Bromfield, Carroll Baker. Pleasant Williams aquatic vehicle set at Florida's Cypress Gardens, with Johnson and Martin vying for her love. Spectacular production numbers by Busby Berkeley. Baker's first film.▼●▋

Easy Virtue (1927-British) **89m. **½** D: Alfred Hitchcock. Isabel Jeans, Franklin Dyall, Eric Bransby Williams, Ian Hunter, Robin Irvine, Violet Farebrother. Jeans suffers nobly as the wife of an alcoholic and the lover of a suicide in this melodramatic silent Hitchcock. Laughable dramatics but imaginatively shot, based on a Noel Coward play. Remade in 2008.▼▋

Easy Virtue (2008-U.S.-British) **C-96m. **½** D: Stephan Elliott. Jessica Biel, Colin Firth, Kristin Scott Thomas, Ben Barnes, Kris Marshall, Kimberley Nixon, Katherine Parkinson, Pip Torrens, Christian Brassington, Charlotte Riley. Lively if uneven adaptation of Noel Coward's play about a staid family that's shaken up when the prodigal son (Barnes) brings home a dashing American auto-racing champion (Biel) as his wife. Arch dialogue abounds in this deconstruction of the British class system, but director and coadapter Elliott tries to have it both ways, winking at the audience one moment and asking us to take things seriously the next. Great showcase for Biel, who holds her own amidst a top-notch British cast. Filmed before by Alfred Hitchcock in 1927. Super 35. [PG-13] ▶

Easy Wheels (1989) **C-94m.** ** D: David O'Malley. Paul Le Mat, Eileen Davidson, Marjorie Bransfield, Jon Menick, Barry Livingston, Mark Holton, Theresa Randle, Danny Hicks, George Plimpton, Ted Raimi, Ben Stein. A gang of good male bikers combats a baby-stealing gang of women bikers in the Midwest. Satirical action comedy is awkwardly directed, but has some good ideas. Writer "Celia Abrams" in the credits is really Sam Raimi. [R]▼

Eat a Bowl of Tea (1989) **C-104m.** *** D: Wayne Wang. Cora Miao, Russell Wong, Victor Wong, Lau Siu Ming, Eric Tsang Chi Wai. From 1924 until the end of WW2, most Chinese women were not allowed to accompany their menfolk who emigrated to the U.S. This charming but pointed ethnic comedy chronicles what happened when the ban was lifted, as American-born Russell Wong brings Chinese-born bride Miao to N.Y.C. A film that no one else but Wang could have made. [PG-13]▼●

Eat Drink Man Woman (1994-Taiwan) **C-124m.** *** D: Ang Lee. Sihung Lung, Kuei-Mei Yang, Chien-Lien Wu, Yu-Wen Wang, Winston Chao, Ah-Leh Gua, Sylvia Chang. Director Lee's follow-up to THE WEDDING BANQUET is another charming study of love, family, and tradition, which follows a Taipei master chef (Lung) who has lost his taste buds and has grown apart from his three daughters. The multiple stories and their resolutions are a bit too predictable, but Lee's handling of the action is dexterous and the entire cast is winning. The presentation of food onscreen is, in all senses of the word, delectable, ranking with the dishes of TAMPOPO, BABETTE'S FEAST, and LIKE WATER FOR CHOCOLATE. Lee coscripted as well. Remade in 2001 as TORTILLA SOUP. ▼●

Eaten Alive (1977) **C-91m.** **½ D: Tobe Hooper. Neville Brand, Mel Ferrer, Carolyn Jones, Marilyn Burns, William Finley, Stuart Whitman, Robert Englund. Ill-fated Hollywood debut feature by TEXAS CHAINSAW director Hooper is a garishly stylized, unrelentingly bizarre film about a psychopath (Brand) who has a crocodile living in the front yard of his hotel. Periodically guests who upset the management are fed to this pet. Originally titled DEATH TRAP; aka STARLIGHT

SLAUGHTER, LEGEND OF THE BAYOU, and HORROR HOTEL. ▼●▮

Eating (1990) **C-110m.** *** D: Henry Jaglom. Frances Bergen, Lisa Richards, Nelly Alard, Gwen Welles, Mary Crosby, Marlene Giovi, Marina Gregory, Daphna Kastner, Elizabeth Kemp, Toni Basil. A group of women, attending a birthday party, sit around talking about food and life—in that order. Typically idiosyncratic, low-budget Jaglom outing, but this one really works: the conversation is fascinating and often hilarious. Frances Bergen (Edgar's widow, Candice's mom) is a revelation. ▼▮

Eating Raoul (1982) **C-83m.** ***½ D: Paul Bartel. Paul Bartel, Mary Woronov, Robert Beltran, Susan Saiger, Buck Henry, Dick Blackburn, Edie McClurg, Ed Begley, Jr., John Paragon, Hamilton Camp. Delicious black comedy about the Blands, a super-square couple who lure wealthy swingers to their apartment and kill them, which both reduces the number of "perverts" and helps finance their dream restaurant. Sags a little here and there, but overall a bright, original, hilarious satire; Paragon has a super bit as a sexshop owner. Directors Joe Dante and John Landis also appear. [R] ▼▮

Eat My Dust! (1976) **C-90m.** *½ D: Charles Griffith. Ron Howard, Christopher Norris, Warren Kemmerling, Dave Madden, Rance Howard, Clint Howard, Corbin Bernsen. Nervewracking yarn about two young drivers unable to satisfy passion for speed. Hang on! [PG]▼▮

Eat Pray Love (2010) **C-140m.** **½ D: Ryan Murphy. Julia Roberts, James Franco, Javier Bardem, Richard Jenkins, Viola Davis, Billy Crudup, Hadi Subiyanto, Mike O'Malley, Tuva Novotny, Luca Argentero. N.Y.C. travel writer opts out of her marriage, rebounds with a love affair, but still feels a nagging sense of dissatisfaction, so she spends a year abroad. In Italy she makes friends and savors the wonderful food. In India she attempts to find spiritual enlightenment. And in Bali, she rekindles a friendship with a wise healer she met on an earlier trip and becomes attracted to a handsome, divorced Brazilian man. Roberts is ideally cast, but without having read Elizabeth Gilbert's best-selling memoir it's tough to understand her restlessness and angst. But as a travelogue and paean to Italian food, the film is easy on the eyes. Murphy and Jennifer Salt wrote the screenplay. Unrated version runs 143m. [PG-13] ▮

Eat the Peach (1986-Irish) **C-95m.** **½ D: Peter Ormrod. Stephen Brennan, Eamon Morrissey, Catherine Byrne, Niall Toibin, Joe Lynch, Tony Doyle. Two hard-luck friends in rural Ireland, suddenly unemployed, are inspired by a scene in Elvis Presley's movie ROUSTABOUT and decide to build a "wall of death" (a huge wooden cylinder in which they ride their motorcycles in a circuslike stunt). Can fame and fortune be far behind? Uniquely dour Irish sensibility permeates this uneven but engaging little film about hopes and dreams—even cock-eyed ones like these. Director Ormrod and producer John Kelleher based their script on a true story.▼

Eat the Rich (1987-British) **C-88m.** BOMB D: Peter Richardson. Nosher Powell, Lanah Pellay, Fiona Richmond, Ronald Allen, Sandra Dorne. Ironically tasteless black comedy about Pellay getting fired from his job in a restaurant, where he later returns leading a band of revolutionaries and begins serving human flesh on the menu. Weird point of view and noisy heavy metal music score by Motorhead. Many pointless cameos by the likes of Paul and Linda McCartney, Bill Wyman, Miranda Richardson, and Koo Stark. [R]▼❿

Ebirah, Horror of the Deep SEE: **Godzilla Vs. The Sea Monster**

Eboli (1979-Italian) **C-120m.** ***½ D: Francesco Rosi. Gian Maria Volonté, Irene Papas, Paolo Bonicelli, Alain Cuny, Lea Massari. Slow-moving but rewarding chronicle of anti-Facist writer/artist Carlo Levi's exile in a small, primitive southern Italian mountain village during the mid-1930s. Stunningly directed, with Volonté perfect as Levi. Video title: CHRIST STOPPED AT EBOLI; most prints with this title run 210m.▼❿

Echelon Conspiracy (2009) **C-105m.** **½ D: Greg Marcks. Shane West, Edward Burns, Ving Rhames, Martin Sheen, Yuriy Kutsenko, Sergey Gubanov, Steven Elder, Sandra De Sousa, Jonathan Pryce, Greg Donaldson. It may be BOURNE-lite but it's still an entertaining sci-fi spy thriller in which West's insanely smart cell phone sends him all over the world alerting him to big casino winnings, great stock tips, and all the beautiful women he can handle. Soon he is being chased around the globe by agents with high-tech gadgets of their own. This male fantasy is by-the-numbers filmmaking but it's a guilty pleasure with an attractive cast, good enough to pass the time between Bourne and Bond movies. Super 35. [PG-13]❿

Echoes (1983) **C-89m.** **½ D: Arthur Allan Seidelman. Richard Alfieri, Nathalie Nell, Mercedes McCambridge, Ruth Roman, Gale Sondergaard, Mike Kellin, John Spencer. Art student Alfieri becomes obsessed by a dream in which his twin brother, who died before birth, is out to kill him. Intriguing premise, just adequate result. [R]▼❿

Echoes of a Summer (1976) **C-99m.** ** D: Don Taylor. Richard Harris, Lois Nettleton, Jodie Foster, Geraldine Fitzgerald, William Windom, Brad Savage. Another film in the "disease" genre, as 12-year-old Foster's stolid reaction to impending death inspires those around her. Overwritten tearjerker, but Jodie is always worth a look. [PG]

Echoes of Paradise (1987-Australian)

C-92m. *½ D: Phillip Noyce. Wendy Hughes, John Lone, Steven Jacobs, Peta Toppano, Rod Mullinar, Gillian Jones. Frustrated Hughes' husband cheats on her, so while in Thailand she liberates herself by commencing an affair with Balinese dancer Lone. Boring (though attractive) soaper is an unfortunate misfire for talented stars and director. Australian title: SHADOWS OF THE PEACOCK. [R]▼❿

Echo Park (1986-Austrian-U.S.) **C-93m.** **½ D: Robert Dornhelm. Susan Dey, Thomas Hulce, Michael Bowen, Christopher Walker, Richard (Cheech) Marin, Cassandra Peterson, Timothy Carey. Small film set in older L.A. neighborhood, which follows the fortunes of three offbeat characters: a single mother/actress, a pizza delivery man/poet, and an Austrian weightlifter/TV hopeful. Bowen (as the latter) scores best in this mildly diverting film; first half is best. [R]▼❶❿

Eclipse (1962-French-Italian) **123m.** *** D: Michelangelo Antonioni. Alain Delon, Monica Vitti, Francisco Rabal, Lilla Brignone, Louis Seigner, Rossana Rory. Obvious but fascinating drama of alienation, Antonioni-style, about a translator (Vitti) who breaks up with her boyfriend and commences an affair with stockbroker Delon. Antonioni strikingly captures Vitti's isolation, and the world (and city of Rome) as filtered through her sensibilities. Third in a trilogy, following L'AVVENTURA and LA NOTTE. Original title: L'ECLISSE. ▼❿

Eclipse (2010) **C-124m.** **½ D: David Slade. Kristen Stewart, Robert Pattinson, Taylor Lautner, Xavier Samuel, Bryce Dallas Howard, Dakota Fanning, Anna Kendrick, Michael Welch, Christian Serratos, Jackson Rathbone, Ashley Greene, Sarah Clarke, Peter Facinelli, Elizabeth Reaser, Kellan Lutz, Nikki Reed, Justin Chon, Billy Burke, Cameron Bright, Jack Huston, Jodelle Ferland. Third installment in the *Twilight* series has Seattle plagued by a wave of brutal killings by wolflike creatures, and Bella being torn between her love for Edward and her friendship with Jacob. Seems to us the so-called fervent love affair with Edward pales alongside the tangible chemistry that exists between Bella and Jacob. But then, the CGI werewolves—and their bloody attacks—seem artificial as well. Just don't tell avid followers of the series.... Super 35. [PG-13] ❿

Ecstasy (1933-Czech) **88m.** **½ D: Gustav Machatý. Hedy Kiesler (Lamarr), Aribert Mog, Jaromir Rogoz, Leopold Kramer. A young bride discovers her husband is impotent and has an affair. Undistinguished romantic drama was once notorious for scenes of pre-Hollywood Hedy in the buff—and showing her in the throes of sexual passion.▼❿

Ed (1996) **C-94m.** *½ D: Bill Couturié.

Matt LeBlanc, Jayne Brook, Bill Cobbs, Jack Warden, Charlie Schlatter, Carl Anthony Payne II, Zacharias Ward, Tommy Lasorda. Nervous pitcher getting his big break on a minor-league baseball team becomes roommate with the club's new third baseman: a full-grown chimpanzee. Uninspired vehicle for *Friends* star LeBlanc (and Hollywood debut for award-winning documentary director Couturié). Strikes out as a warm family comedy, though younger viewers may be amused. [PG]▼●▮

Eddie (1996) C-100m. **½ D: Steve Rash. Whoopi Goldberg, Frank Langella, Dennis Farina, Richard Jenkins, Lisa Ann Walter, John Benjamin Hickey, Troy Beyer. Gimmicky star vehicle for Whoopi finds her going overnight from rabid N.Y. Knicks fan to being coach of the team—when the cynical new owner finds there's great publicity value in it. Despite the farfetched premise, Whoopi mines laughs—especially early on, before the film begins to take itself too seriously. Look for cameos by various N.Y. celebs and basketball stars. [PG-13]▼●▮

Eddie and the Cruisers (1983) C-92m. ** D: Martin Davidson. Tom Berenger, Michael Paré, Joe Pantoliano, Matthew Laurance, Helen Schneider, Ellen Barkin. Ideal premise—whatever happened to the members of a legendary, innovative rock 'n' roll band of the '60s—buried by terrible script. Paré plays band's iconoclastic leader, who ran his car off a pier; Barkin is TV reporter who tries to piece together story, a la CITIZEN KANE . . . but there's no Rosebud here. Good song score by John Cafferty. Followed by a sequel. [PG]▼●▮

Eddie and the Cruisers II: Eddie Lives! (1989) C-103m. BOMB D: Jean-Claude Lord. Michael Paré, Marina Orsini, Bernie Coulson, Matthew Laurance, Michael Rhoades, Anthony Sherwood, Bo Diddley. Now get this: Eddie Wilson did *not* die in a 1964 New Jersey car accident; he's living incognito in Montreal (where movies can be financed more cheaply) and is only surfacing now because the producers wanted a sequel. Eddie's life signs did not extend to the box office. [PG-13]▼●▮

Eddie Cantor Story, The (1953) C-116m. *½ D: Alfred E. Green. Keefe Brasselle, Marilyn Erskine, Aline MacMahon, Marie Windsor. If Brasselle doesn't turn you off as energetic entertainer Cantor, MacMahon's Grandma Esther or a putty-nosed young actor (Jackie Barnett) playing Jimmy Durante certainly will.▼▮

Eddie Macon's Run (1983) C-95m. **½ D: Jeff Kanew. Kirk Douglas, John Schneider, Lee Purcell, Leah Ayres, Lisa Dunsheath, Tom Noonan, John Goodman. Bumpy chase-and-car-crash picture that has wrongly convicted prison escapee Schneider (in his first starring role after attaining *Dukes*

of Hazzard fame) trying to elude his relentless pursuer (Douglas) and make it to Mexico. Based on the novel by James McLendon. Goodman's film debut. [PG]▼●

Eddie Murphy Raw (1987) C-93m. ** D: Robert Townsend. Occasionally uproarious but ultimately dispiriting Murphy concert film, shot at N.Y.C.'s Felt Forum. Best moments: the comic's imitations of Bill Cosby and Richard Pryor giving their opposing views on the crude tone of so much Murphy material. Worst: sexist slurs that too often predominate. Fades in the stretch; there's an amusing fictional prologue, "set" in the Murphys' home two decades ago. [R]▼●▮

Eddy Duchin Story, The (1956) C-123m. **½ D: George Sidney. Tyrone Power, Kim Novak, Victoria Shaw, James Whitmore, Shepperd Strudwick, Frieda Inescort, Rex Thompson, Larry Keating. Glossy, largely invented bio of popular pianist-bandleader of the 1930s and '40s (with Carmen Cavallero dubbing the keyboard tracks). You couldn't ask for two more attractive stars. CinemaScope. ▼●▮

Eden (1998) C-106m. *** D: Howard Goldberg. Joanna Going, Dylan Walsh, Sean Patrick Flanery, Sean Christensen, Edward O. Blenis, Jr. Original, provocative film set in 1965 about a young mother with MS, married to a prep school professor, who has an out-of-body experience that leads her away from her mundane life toward an exploration of her cosmic self. No mumbo jumbo here, but instead a gripping drama in which the main character forces the people closest to her to examine their own lives. Written by the director. Made in 1996. [R]▼▮

Edge, The (1997) C-117m. **½ D: Lee Tamahori. Anthony Hopkins, Alec Baldwin, Elle Macpherson, Harold Perrineau, L. Q. Jones, Bart the Bear. Quiet billionaire Hopkins accompanies his supermodel wife on a location shoot in Alaska, then finds himself stranded in the wilderness with photographer (Baldwin) and his assistant (Perrineau) when their plane crashes. The bookish rich guy turns out to be a pretty fair survivalist, but meets his match in killer Kodiak bear. Good acting, exciting action sequences, but a stretch of credibility (more in the relationships than in the survival mode) makes this an uneven outing. Written by David Mamet. Panavision. [R]▼●▮

Edge of Darkness (1943) 120m. ***½ D: Lewis Milestone. Errol Flynn, Ann Sheridan, Walter Huston, Nancy Coleman, Helmut Dantine, Judith Anderson, Ruth Gordon, John Beal, Roman Bohnen. Intense, compelling drama of underground movement in Norway during Nazi takeover in WW2. Eye-popping camerawork complements fine performances. Scripted by Robert Rossen, from William Woods' story. Also shown in computer-colored version.▼▮

Edge of Darkness (2010-U.S.-British) C-117m. *** D: Martin Campbell. Mel Gibson, Ray Winstone, Danny Huston, Bojana Novakovic, Shawn Roberts, David Aaron Baker, Jay O. Sanders, Damian Young, Denis O'Hare, Caterina Scorsone. Edgy indeed: a conspiracy thriller energized by violent action. Gibson plays a Boston detective whose grown daughter is murdered on his front doorstep. The cops think he may have been the target, but he learns that *she* was in hot water. As he investigates her recent activities he begins to unravel a huge web of corruption involving both government and industry. Visceral, rather than cerebral, this one delivers one punch after another right up to the finale. Based on Campbell's own 1985 BBC miniseries. [R] ▶

Edge of Doom (1950) 90m. ** D: Mark Robson. Dana Andrews, Farley Granger, Joan Evans, Mala Powers, Paul Stewart, Adele Jergens. Poor but hardworking Granger loses control when his mother dies; only parish priest Andrews understands his torment. Turgid drama.

Edge of Eternity (1959) C-80m. ** D: Don Siegel. Cornel Wilde, Victoria Shaw, Mickey Shaughnessy, Edgar Buchanan, Rian Garrick, Jack Elam. Deputy sheriff Wilde tracks killers to Grand Canyon, leading to shootout on mining buckets suspended on cables way above canyon. CinemaScope.

Edge of Heaven, The (2007-German-Turkish) C-116m. ***½ D: Fatih Akin. Nurgül Yesilçay, Baki Davrak, Tuncel Kurtiz, Hanna Schygulla, Patrycia Ziolkowska, Nursel Köse. Eloquent, insightful tale of several Turks and Germans who are displaced in foreign lands and how their lives intertwine. Characters include a middle-aged prostitute and her daughter, who is unaware of her profession; a brutally abusive older man and his quiet, unworldly college professor son; and an impulsive college student and her mother. As the lives of the characters mesh, the film veers off in surprising directions. Written by the director. ▶

Edge of Love, The (2008-British) C-111m. *½ D: John Maybury. Keira Knightley, Sienna Miller, Cillian Murphy, Matthew Rhys. Mawkish soaper, set during WW2, involving an egocentric poet (Rhys) and the two women in his life. One (Miller) is his high-spirited wife; the other (Knightley), a coolly beautiful singer, is a friend from childhood. Into their world comes an idealistic soldier (Murphy) who falls obsessively in love with Knightley. Means to be lyrical and insightful, but the characters are superficially rendered and the actors fail to rise above the material. It seems of minor importance that the poet is Dylan Thomas and the story is "inspired, in part, by actual events." Playwright Sharman Macdonald, Knightley's mother, penned the screenplay. ▶

Edge of Sanity (1989-British) C-90m.
*½ D: Gérard Kikoine. Anthony Perkins, Glynis Barber, Sarah Maur-Thorp, David Lodge, Ben Cole. Grotesque, overwrought travesty on *Dr. Jekyll and Mr. Hyde* (Robert Louis Stevenson is not even credited). Jekyll (Perkins) *accidentally* discovers the Hyde formula, transforms only very slightly, and becomes Jack the Ripper. Tasteless, pointless, and unpleasant. [R] ▼●

Edge of the City (1957) 85m. **** D: Martin Ritt. John Cassavetes, Sidney Poitier, Jack Warden, Ruby Dee, Kathleen Maguire, Ruth White. Somber, realistic account of N.Y.C. waterfront life and corruption. Friendship of army deserter Cassavetes and dock worker Poitier, both conflicting with union racketeer Warden, provides focus for reflections on integration and integrity in lower-class society. Masterfully acted by all. Ritt's first film as director. Robert Alan Aurthur adapted his own 1955 TV play, *A Man Is Ten Feet Tall* (which was also film's British title), in which Poitier originated his role. Also shown in computer-colored version. ●

Edie in Ciao! Manhattan SEE: **Ciao! Manhattan**

Edison Force (2006) C-99m. BOMB D: David J. Burke. Morgan Freeman, Kevin Spacey, Justin Timberlake, LL Cool J, Dylan McDermott, John Heard, Cary Elwes, Roselyn Sanchez, Damien Dante Wayans, Piper Perabo. Two Oscar winners topline this loud, violent direct-to-DVD clunker in which a menagerie of shady politicos, corrupt cops—and one intrepid reporter—clash in a crime-ridden metropolis. Indescribably bad film opens with a standard-issue shootout, and much of the dialogue that follows is unintentionally funny. Pop star Timberlake's acting debut. Originally screened at film festivals as EDISON. Super 35. [R] ●

Edison, the Man (1940) 107m. *** D: Clarence Brown. Spencer Tracy, Rita Johnson, Lynne Overman, Charles Coburn, Gene Lockhart, Henry Travers, Felix Bressart. Sequel to YOUNG TOM EDISON perfectly casts Tracy as earnest inventor with passion for mechanical ingenuity. Facts and MGM fantasy combine well in sentimental treatment. Also shown in computer-colored version. ▼●

Edith and Marcel (1983-French) C-104m. *½ D: Claude Lelouch. Evelyne Bouix, Marcel Cerdan, Jr., Jacques Villeret, Jean-Claude Brialy, Francis Huster, Jean Bouise, Charles Aznavour. Passionless retelling of the love affair between singer Edith Piaf and middleweight boxer Marcel Cerdan, who died in a 1949 plane crash. Bouix and Cerdan, Jr., are bland in the title roles. Originally 162m. Piaf and Cerdan's relationship is also dramatized in LA VIE EN ROSE. ▼

Edmond (2005) C-82m. ** D: Stuart Gordon. William H. Macy, Rebecca Pidgeon, Joe Mantegna, Julia Stiles, Jeffrey Combs,

Bai Ling, Debi Mazar, Denise Richards, Mena Suvari, George Wendt, Dylan Walsh, Dulé Hill, Bokeem Woodbine, Wren Brown. On his way home from work a middle-aged exec heeds a fateful tarot reading and leaves his wife to embark on an all-night odyssey through the city's underbelly. Adapted by David Mamet from his 1982 one-act play and episodic by design, this fable becomes more difficult to take as it goes on and Macy's character exorcises all of his sexist, racist paranoia. Something less than Homeric, made palatable only by Macy's commanding performance. [R]◗

Ed's Next Move (1996) **C-88m.** ✱✱✱ D: John Walsh. Matt Ross, Callie Thorne, Kevin Carroll, Ramsey Faragallah, Nina Sheveleva. Sweetly engaging romantic comedy; a sincere, knowing story of the difficulties of finding love in the Big City. The title character (Ross), a Wisconsin native who comes to N.Y.C. to make his fortune, is immediately attracted to a struggling musician (Thorne), who is already involved with someone. [R]▼●

Ed tv (1999) **C-122m.** ✱✱✱ D: Ron Howard. Matthew McConaughey, Jenna Elfman, Woody Harrelson, Sally Kirkland, Martin Landau, Ellen DeGeneres, Rob Reiner, Dennis Hopper, Elizabeth Hurley, Adam Goldberg, Viveka Davis, Clint Howard. Entertaining yarn about a desperate cable TV network that decides to broadcast an ordinary guy's life for every waking moment of the day—turning the poor sap into an overnight celebrity. Interesting twists in Lowell Ganz and Babaloo Mandel's script keep this from being a one-joke comedy. Well cast right down the line. Remake of a Canadian film, LOUIS XIX: ROI DES ONDES. [PG-13]▼●

Educating Rita (1983-British) **C-110m.** ✱✱✱ D: Lewis Gilbert. Michael Caine, Julie Walters, Michael Williams, Maureen Lipman, Jeananne Crowley, Malcolm Douglas. Entertaining adaptation of Willy Russell's stage play about a young working-class wife who wants to better herself, and selects boozy professor Caine as her tutor. Walters is excellent in her film debut (re-creating her stage role) and Caine has one of his best roles as her mentor. [PG-13]▼●◗

Education, An (2009-British) **C-99m.** ✱✱✱ D: Lone Scherfig. Peter Sarsgaard, Carey Mulligan, Alfred Molina, Dominic Cooper, Rosamund Pike, Olivia Williams, Emma Thompson, Cara Seymour, Matthew Beard, Sally Hawkins. Teenage girl from a working-class London family in the early 1960s is swept off her feet by a dashing older man who treats her like the woman she dreams of becoming. Keenly observed comedy about manners, mores, and social distinctions at a particular time and place. Mulligan is ideal in a star-making role, and she's surrounded by wonderful actors—

especially Molina as her class-climbing father. Nick Hornby adapted Lynn Barber's memoir. Super 35. [PG-13]◗

Education of Charlie Banks, The (2009) **C-101m.** ✱✱½ D: Fred Durst. Jesse Eisenberg, Jason Ritter, Eva Amurri, Christopher Marquette, Sebastian Stan, Gloria Votsis, Dennis Boutsikaris. Class-conscious coming-of-age story, set in the '70s and early '80s, about a well-bred Manhattan boy (Eisenberg) who thinks he's left a neighborhood tough guy (Ritter) behind when he goes to an Ivy League college. But Ritter shows up in his dorm one day, ostensibly for a visit, and finds the tony atmosphere (and Eisenberg's girlfriend, Amurri) to his liking. Highly uneven but interesting take on social mores and boundary lines; creditable feature directing debut for Durst, of the rock group Limp Bizkit (filmed before 2008's THE LONGSHOTS). Super 35. [R]◗

Education of Little Tree, The (1997) **C-114m.** ✱✱½ D: Richard Friedenberg. James Cromwell, Tantoo Cardinal, Joseph Ashton, Graham Greene, Mika Boorem, Christopher Heyerdahl. An 8-year-old boy, half-white/half-Cherokee, goes to live with his grandparents in the backwoods of Tennessee in 1935 and is taught the way of life and the land. Beautifully photographed family film never fully takes hold, but fine performances and solid values make it pleasant viewing. [G]▼●

Education of Sonny Carson, The (1974) **C-105m.** ✱✱½ D: Michael Campus. Rony Clanton, Don Gordon, Joyce Walker, Paul Benjamin, Ram John Holder. Interesting if overemotional drama of rebellious black youth in Brooklyn of the '50s and '60s. Based on Carson's autobiography; the film takes on additional meaning with regard to his latter-day notoriety on the N.Y.C. political scene. [R]▼●

Edukators, The (2004-German-Austrian) **C-127m.** ✱✱½ D: Hans Weingartner. Daniel Brühl, Julia Jentsch, Stipe Erceg, Burghart Klaussner, Hanns Zischler. Thoughtful, if verbose and overlong, satirical exploration of political idealism and hypocrisy in contemporary Germany. A pair of strident young radicals (Brühl, Erceg) see themselves as 21st-century Robin Hoods, which gives them an excuse to break into the homes of the well-heeled. Complications arise when Erceg's girlfriend (Jentsch) participates in one of their escapades. [R]◗

Edward, My Son (1949-British) **112m.** ✱✱½ D: George Cukor. Spencer Tracy, Deborah Kerr, Ian Hunter, James Donald, Mervyn Johns, Felix Aylmer, Leueen McGrath. Well-acted but talky, stagy drama in which brash, rags-to-riches Tracy pampers his son, failing to instill within him a sense of responsibility. Gimmicks of Tracy talking to viewer, title character never being shown, come off as forced. Based on a play by Robert Morley and Noel Langley.

Edward Scissorhands (1990) **C-100m.** *** D: Tim Burton. Johnny Depp, Winona Ryder, Dianne Wiest, Vincent Price, Alan Arkin, Anthony Michael Hall, Kathy Baker, Conchata Ferrell, Caroline Aaron, Dick Anthony Williams. Strikingly original fable (expanded from an idea Burton hatched as a child) about a man-made boy whose creator dies before attaching human hands to his body. Now he's adopted by a relentlessly cheery Avon Lady, and taken to live in American suburbia. Mixture of fairy tale elements and social satire loses its story momentum toward the end, but that can't erase its charm or good-natured humor. Depp is perfect as the fragile scissor-handed boy, and it's great fun to watch Price as his master. [PG-13] ▼●〗

Edward II (1991-British) **C-91m.** *** D: Derek Jarman. Steven Waddington, Kevin Collins, Andrew Tiernan, John Lynch, Dudley Sutton, Tilda Swinton, Jerome Flynn, Jody Graber, Nigel Terry, Annie Lennox. Trenchant (if unnecessarily violent) adaptation of the Christopher Marlowe play, written in 1592, about the downfall of the openly gay British monarch who rejects his queen for a male lover. Despite 14th-century setting, some characters wear contemporary clothing, and film works quite well as a condemnation of 20th-century gay-bashing. Not for all tastes—but never dull. Lennox, formerly of Eurythmics, appears in one scene singing Cole Porter's "Ev'ry Time We Say Goodbye." ▼●〗

Ed Wood (1994) **124m.** *** D: Tim Burton. Johnny Depp, Martin Landau, Sarah Jessica Parker, Patricia Arquette, Jeffrey Jones, G. D. Spradlin, Vincent D'Onofrio, Lisa Marie, Bill Murray, Mike Starr, Max Casella, Brent Hinkley, Juliet Landau, George "The Animal" Steele. A loving look at Edward D. Wood, Jr., a man of boundless enthusiasm and no talent who made some of the worst movies of all time (including GLEN OR GLENDA and PLAN 9 FROM OUTER SPACE). Cast to perfection, with Depp ideal in the title role. Landau—in Rick Baker makeup (both men won Oscars)—is positively astonishing as the aged and impoverished Bela Lugosi, whom Wood befriended. There isn't much story thrust here, but the vivid re-creation of time and place makes this a must for any old-movie buff. [R] ▼●〗

Eegah! (1962) **C-92m.** BOMB D: Nicholas Merriwether (Arch Hall, Sr.). Arch Hall, Jr., Marilyn Manning, Richard Kiel, William Watters (Arch Hall, Sr.). In the desert near Palm Springs, a prehistoric giant (Kiel) falls in love with teenage Manning. A staple at "All-Time Worst Film" festivals. Arch Hall, Jr., sings the memorable "I Love You, Vickie." ▼●〗

Eel, The (1997-Japanese) **C-117m.** *** D: Shohei Imamura. Koji Yakusho, Misa Shimizu, Fujio Tsuneta, Mitsuko Baisho, Akira Emoto, Sho Aikawa, Ken Kobayashi. A businessman brutally murders his wife upon discovering that she has been cheating on him. Eight years later, he is paroled from prison, and can only relate to his pet eel, because it will not disappoint or betray him. Then he saves a woman who has attempted suicide after a bad love affair. Pensive, poignant allegorical drama. ▼〗

Effect of Gamma Rays on Man-in-the-Moon Marigolds, The (1972) **C-100m.** *** D: Paul Newman. Joanne Woodward, Nell Potts, Roberta Wallach, Judith Lowry. Woodward gives superb performance in tale of secluded boor of a mother and her two strange daughters. Alvin Sargent adapted Paul Zindel's Pulitzer Prize–winning play. [PG]

Effi Briest (1974-German) **135m.** ***½ D: Rainer Werner Fassbinder. Hanna Schygulla, Wolfgang Schenck, Karl-Heinz Bohm, Ulli Lommel, Ursula Stratz, Irm Hermann. Sharply observed drama, set in 19th-century Germany, is one of Fassbinder's best. It's the story of the social and sexual victimization of the title character (Schygulla), an innocent teenager stifled by the conventions of society and lacking the resolve to challenge them. Fassbinder also scripted; based on a novel by Theodor Fontane, which was filmed three times before. ▼〗

Efficiency Expert, The (1992-Australian) **C-85m.** *** D: Mark Joffe. Anthony Hopkins, Alwyn Kurts, Rebecca Rigg, Russell Crowe, Angela Punch McGregor, Ben Mendelsohn, Bruno Lawrence, Toni Collette. Pleasant farce that follows the plight of Hopkins, an uncompromising management consultant whose attitude is ever-so-slightly altered by the various, humorously inefficient workers at a small factory. Hopkins offers a solid comic performance. Original title: SPOTSWOOD. [PG] ▼●〗

Egg and I, The (1947) **108m.** *** D: Chester Erskine. Claudette Colbert, Fred MacMurray, Marjorie Main, Louise Allbritton, Percy Kilbride, Richard Long, Donald MacBride, Samuel S. Hinds. Colbert is delightful as the city-girl wife of chicken farmer MacMurray, struggling to survive on his farm; first appearance of Ma and Pa Kettle. From Betty MacDonald's bestseller. Later a TV series. ▼●〗

Egyptian, The (1954) **C-140m.** ** D: Michael Curtiz. Jean Simmons, Victor Mature, Gene Tierney, Michael Wilding, Bella Darvi, Peter Ustinov, Edmund Purdom, Judith Evelyn, Henry Daniell, John Carradine, Tommy Rettig. Ponderous, often unintentionally funny biblical-era soaper with Purdom cast as the sensitive, truth-seeking title character, a physician in ancient Egypt. Darvi's performance as a femme fatale is hilariously awful; see how much of her dialogue you can understand. Loosely based on Mika Waltari's novel. CinemaScope.▼●)

Eiger Sanction, The (1975) **C-128m.** *½ D: Clint Eastwood. Clint Eastwood, George Kennedy, Vonetta McGee, Jack Cassidy, Thayer David, Heidi Bruhl, Reiner Schoene, Brenda Venus. Pseudo-James Bond misfire, often unintentionally funny. Thrilling mountain-climbing climax does not make up for film's many faults and ungodly length. Jack Cassidy as gay, treacherous spy contributes the only creative acting. Based on novel by Trevanian. Panavision. [R]▼●)

8½ (1963-Italian) **135m.** **** D: Federico Fellini. Marcello Mastroianni, Claudia Cardinale, Anouk Aimée, Sandra Milo, Barbara Steele, Rossella Falk, Madeleine LeBeau, Caterina Boratto, Edra Gale, Mark Herron. Fellini's unique self-analytical movie casts Mastroianni as a filmmaker trying to develop a new project, amid frequent visions and countless subplots. A long, difficult, but fascinating film, overflowing with creative and technical wizardry. Certainly one of the most intensely personal statements ever made on celluloid. Screenplay by Fellini, Tullio Pinelli, Ennio Flaiano, and Brunello Rondi. Oscar winner for Costume Design and as Best Foreign Language Film. Reworked as a Broadway musical, *Nine*, which was filmed in 2009. ▼●)

8½ Women (1999-British) **C-121m.** *½ D: Peter Greenaway. John Standing, Matthew Delamere, Vivian Wu, Shizuka Inoh, Barbara Sarafian, Kirina Mano, Toni Collette, Amanda Plummer, Natcha Amal, Manna Fujiwara, Polly Walker. When a successful businessman is widowed, his son tries to help him through his grief by taking him on a sexual odyssey. The women range from a former nun (Collette) to a horsewoman/pig fancier (Plummer) who wears a bizarre see-through harness. Copious male and female nudity can't keep this from being a colossal bore. A supposed homage to Fellini, this isn't in his league. [R]▼●)

Eight Below (2006) **C-120m.** **½ D: Frank Marshall. Paul Walker, Bruce Greenwood, Moon Bloodgood, Jason Biggs, Gerard Plunkett, August Schellenberg, Wendy Crewson. When the staff of a U.S. National Science Research team is ordered to abandon its Antarctic camp, wilderness guide Walker despairs about leaving his eight huskies behind. How the resourceful dogs struggle to survive, and how Walker refuses to give up on them, is the crux of this Disney film. Goes astray as story drags on much longer than it should, but the animal action and wintry location footage are first-rate. Loose remake of the fact-based 1983 Japanese movie NANKYOKU MONOGATARI (ANTARCTICA). Super 35. [PG]●

Eight Crazy Nights (2002) **C-75m.** BOMB D: Seth Kearsley. Voices of Adam Sandler, Rob Schneider, Jackie Titone, Kevin Nealon,

Norm Crosby, Jon Lovitz, Tyra Banks, Carl Weathers, Lainie Kazan, Alison Krauss. Adam Sandler fans and cartoon buffs beware! Raunchy animated musical comedy, about a small-town slacker given a second chance at redemption by aiding a pint-sized basketball coach. Scatological humor abounds at the expense of the handicapped, all religious groups and ethnicities. Story is set during the holiday season merely as an excuse for Sandler's popular comic "Hanukkah Song" to be sung over the end credits. Sandler provides voices for three characters and wrote the forgettable and numerous musical numbers. Not for kids, adults, or anyone. Full on-screen title is ADAM SANDLER'S EIGHT CRAZY NIGHTS. [PG-13]▼)

Eight Days a Week (1999) **C-92m.** **½ D: Michael Davis. Joshua Schaefer, Keri Russell, R. D. Robb, Mark L. Taylor, Marcia Shapiro, Catherine Hicks. A boy (Schaefer) in love with his beautiful next-door neighbor (Russell) decides to camp out on her front lawn until she agrees to go out with him. Sweet, well acted, a bit corny, but makes no excuses for what it is: a teenage romantic comedy. [R]▼)

18 Again! (1988) **C-100m.** **½ D: Paul Flaherty. George Burns, Charlie Schlatter, Tony Roberts, Anita Morris, Red Buttons, Miriam Flynn, Jennifer Runyon. 81-year-old Jack Watson (92-year-old Burns) becomes 18 again via his grandson's body and a bump on the head. Sound familiar? What it lacks in originality is made up in part by Schlatter's utterly charming performance as the young George, and that fountain of youth Burns (who, alas, we see precious little of). [PG]▼●)

Eighth Day, The (1996-French-Belgian) **C-118m.** **½ D: Jaco van Dormael. Daniel Auteuil, Pascal Duquenne, Miou-Miou, Isabelle Sadoyan, Henry Garcin, Michele Maes. Well-intentioned but overly familiar feel-good story of uptight, phony-baloney Belgian businessman Auteuil, who (predictably) undergoes a personality transformation after finding himself in the company of a Down's Syndrome victim (Duquenne, who actually suffers from the malady). If you've seen RAIN MAN . . . Super 35. ▼●

8 Heads in a Duffel Bag (1997-U.S.-British) **C-95m.** **½ D: Tom Schulman. Joe Pesci, Andy Comeau, Kristy Swanson, Todd Louiso, George Hamilton, Dyan Cannon, David Spade, Frank Roman, Ernestine Mercer. Mob hit man Pesci's bag of the title is accidentally swapped with that of a medical student on the way to a Mexican vacation. Many black-comedy complications ensue. Occasionally very funny, but not often enough, and debuting director Schulman's timing is limp; Spade and Louiso have the best moments. [R]▼●)

Eight Hundred Leagues Down the Ama-

zon (1993) **C-75m.** *½ D: Luis Llosa. Daphne Zuniga, Barry Bostwick, Adam Baldwin, Tom Verica, E. E. Bell, Ramsay Ross. In the 19th century, planter Bostwick, his daughter Zuniga, and others drift down the Amazon on a huge raft; scheming Baldwin causes complications. Underbudgeted but overplotted, this curio is as ponderous as its little-used raft. From a novel by Jules Verne. [PG-13]▼)

Eight Legged Freaks (2002) **C-99m.** **½ D: Ellory Elkayem. David Arquette, Kari Wuhrer, Scott Terra, Scarlett Johansson, Doug E. Doug, Rick Overton, Leon Rippy, Eileen Ryan. If you want to see a movie about giant marauding spiders, this one's for you: toxic waste turns the inhabitants of a spider farm into monsters that wreak havoc on an Arizona town. A female sheriff (Wuhrer) and her onetime boyfriend (Arquette) try to fend off the fearsome killers. A spirited, gooey, and amusing homage to 1950s films like TARANTULA and THEM! (which is glimpsed briefly on TV). Tom Noonan appears unbilled. Super 35. [PG-13]▼)

Eight Men Out (1988) **C-119m.** *** D: John Sayles. John Cusack, Clifton James, Michael Lerner, Christopher Lloyd, John Mahoney, Charlie Sheen, David Strathairn, D. B. Sweeney, Michael Rooker, Perry Lang, James Read, Bill Irwin, Kevin Tighe, Studs Terkel, John Anderson, Maggie Renzi. Exquisitely detailed period piece about the infamous 1919 "Black Sox" World Series, in which members of the Chicago White Sox agreed to throw the games in return for cash. Writer-director Sayles (who also appears as sportswriter Ring Lardner) touches all the bases, except perhaps in terms of emotion; the story doesn't have the impact it might have, though the actual baseball scenes are superb and the key performances (by Strathairn, Sweeney, and Cusack) are top-notch. Based on a book by Eliot Asinof. [PG]▼●)

8 Mile (2002) **C-110m.** *** D: Curtis Hanson. Eminem, Kim Basinger, Brittany Murphy, Mekhi Phifer, Evan Jones, Omar Benson Miller, Eugene Byrd, De'Angelo Wilson, Anthony Mackie, Taryn Manning, Michael Shannon. Angry young white rapper tries to use his music to escape the grimness of life in Detroit but freezes when forced to compete in a public forum with his glib black counterparts. Familiar underdog formula is given grit and resonance, and makes a convincing case for the power of self-expression. Real-life rapper Eminem is impressive in a tailor-made film that echoes his own life story. Oscar winner for Best Song, "Lose Yourself." Super 35. [R] ▼)

8 Million Ways to Die (1986) **C-115m.** BOMB D: Hal Ashby. Jeff Bridges, Rosanna Arquette, Alexandra Paul, Randy Brooks, Andy Garcia. Dreary tale of alcoholic ex-cop who gets involved with high-priced call girl and her "friends" (a powerful pimp and a sleazy drug dealer). Slow, arid film populated by unpleasant and uninteresting characters. Remarkably poor script (cowritten by Oliver Stone) has only faint resemblance to Lawrence Block's fine novel. [R]▼●

8MM (1999) **C-123m.** ** D: Joel Schumacher. Nicolas Cage, Joaquin Phoenix, James Gandolfini, Peter Stormare, Anthony Heald, Catherine Keener, Chris Bauer, Myra Carter. Private detective accepts an unusual assignment: to learn whether or not a "snuff" film in which a girl apparently dies is genuine. Despite himself, he becomes obsessed with the case and mired in a netherworld he cannot stand. An intensely grim, often unpleasant film, somewhat reminiscent of HARDCORE, is weakened by serious issues of credibility in Cage's character and motivation. Followed by a direct-to-video sequel in 2005. Super 35. [R] ▼●)

Eight on the Lam (1967) **C-106m.** BOMB D: George Marshall. Bob Hope, Phyllis Diller, Jonathan Winters, Jill St. John, Shirley Eaton. Another of Hope's horrible '60s comedies casts him as a widower with seven children who finds $10,000; even Winters can't help this dud.▼●

8 Seconds (1994) **C-104m.** **½ D: John G. Avildsen. Luke Perry, Stephen Baldwin, Cynthia Geary, James Rebhorn, Carrie Snodgress, Red Mitchell, Ronnie Claire Edwards, Linden Ashby, Renee Zellweger. OK bio of rodeo legend Lane Frost gets standard Avildsen ROCKY rah-rah treatment. Perry and Geary (as his wife) put the film over, up to a point, with natural, winning performances, but day-to-day rodeo life was captured with far more flavor in THE LUSTY MEN and JUNIOR BONNER. [PG-13]▼●

8 Women (2002-French) **C-113m.** **½ D: François Ozon. Danielle Darrieux, Catherine Deneuve, Isabelle Huppert, Fanny Ardant, Emmanuelle Béart, Virginie Ledoyen, Firmine Richard, Ludivine Sagnier. Wonderful opportunity to watch some of France's most formidable females in an odd whodunit-melodrama-musical set in the 1950s (and inspired, Ozon says, by the lush, artificial Technicolor films of Douglas Sirk and Vincente Minnelli). The story, a deliberate contrivance, involves a murder in an isolated mansion in winter, and the various secrets being hidden by the women of the household. Fun to a degree, especially when the actresses sing and dance, but awfully forced. [R]▼)

88 Minutes (2008) **C-108m.** BOMB D: Jon Avnet. Al Pacino, Alicia Witt, Leelee Sobieski, Amy Brenneman, Deborah Kara Unger, Benjamin McKenzie, Neal McDonough, William Forsythe, Victoria Tennant. Dread-

[404]

ful thriller about a forensic psychiatrist (and professor) who's received an all-too-palpable death threat from a man he helped send to Death Row (McDonough). Lumbering, heavy-handed theatrics and clumsy attempts at suspense make this a total waste of time. Super 35. [R]**)**

84 Charing Cross Road (1987) **C-97m.** ***½ D: David Jones. Anne Bancroft, Anthony Hopkins, Judi Dench, Jean De Baer, Maurice Denham, Eleanor David, Mercedes Ruehl, Daniel Gerroll. Loving, literate, and totally disarming film about the longtime correspondence, and growing friendship, between a feisty N.Y.C. woman and the British bookseller who provides her with the rare volumes she cherishes more than anything else in life. Affectionately detailed evocation of N.Y.C. and London over 20 years' time is capped by ideal performances. Based on the memoirs of Helene Hanff and the play adapted from her book. Screenplay by Hugh Whitemore. [PG]**▼○)**

84 Charlie Mopic (1989) **C-95m.** *** D: Patrick Duncan. Jonathan Emerson, Nicholas Cascone, Jason Tomlins, Christopher Burgard, Glenn Morshower, Richard Brooks, Byron Thomas. Imaginative low-budget film provides fresh approach to life on the front line in Vietnam. Writer-director Duncan tells his story completely from the point of view of a combat cameraman who's assigned to follow a special seven-man reconnaissance unit on a dangerous mission. Lulls in pace made up for by film's overall vitality, commanding performances by cast of unknowns. [R]**▼●**

80 Steps to Jonah (1969) **C-107m.** ** D: Gerd Oswald. Wayne Newton, Mickey Rooney, Jo Van Fleet, Keenan Wynn, Diana Ewing, Slim Pickens, Sal Mineo. A loner, running from the police, stumbles upon camp for blind children; new world changes his outlook on life. Major liability: casting of Newton in leading role. Music score by George Shearing. [G]

Eijanaika (1981-Japanese) **C-151m.** ***½ D: Shohei Imamura. Shigeru Izumiya, Kaori Momoi, Masao Kusakari, Ken Ogata, Shigeru Tsuyuguchi, Mitsuko Baisho. Fascinating, compelling saga of corruption, politics, greed, power, deceit, focusing on experiences of peasant who has just returned to Japan after being shipwrecked and sent to America during the 1860s. Fine performances, with a memorable finale. Some prints run 127m. **▼●**

El Bruto (1952-Mexican) **83m.** ** D: Luis Buñuel. Pedro Armendariz, Katy Jurado, Andres Soler, Rosita Arenas. Armendariz is conned by scheming boss into harassing tenants he unfairly wants to evict; seduced by the boss's lusty mistress (Jurado), he then falls in love with a girl whose father he accidentally murdered. Simplistic, quite unsubtle melodrama, a disappoint-

ment from a master filmmaker. Aka THE BRUTE. **▼)**

El Cantante (2007) **C-116m.** ** D: Leon Ichaso. Marc Anthony, Jennifer Lopez, John Ortiz, Manny Perez, Vincent Laresca, Federico Castelluccio, Nelson Vasquez. Puerto Rican–born Héctor Lavoe (Anthony) finds success in N.Y.C. introducing a new brand of Latin music called salsa in the 1970s. While he also finds the love of his life, drugs erode his success onstage and off. The two stars (married in real life) are extremely well cast in this biopic. Lopez looks gorgeous, and the music is great, but the story is a sad, one-note affair. Lopez also coproduced . . . and perhaps should have cut a few of those loving close-ups of herself. [R]**)**

El Cid (1961) **C-184m.** *** D: Anthony Mann. Charlton Heston, Sophia Loren, Raf Vallone, Genevieve Page, John Fraser, Gary Raymond, Hurd Hatfield, Massimo Serato, Herbert Lom, Michael Hordern. Mammoth Samuel Bronston spectacle, shot in Spain, celebrates that country's 11th-century warrior hero. When not clashing with Moors, Heston's Cid romances his equally statuesque wife (Loren). Uneven dramatics are sold by top-scale production values, including Miklos Rozsa's famed score. One of the better historical epics of its time. Super Technirama 70.**▼●**

El Condor (1970) **C-102m.** ** D: John Guillermin. Jim Brown, Lee Van Cleef, Patrick O'Neal, Mariana Hill, Iron Eyes Cody, Elisha Cook, Jr. Slow Western about two drifters in search of some gold supposedly buried in Mexican fortress; Hill looks good even with her clothes on. [R]**▼)**

El Crimen Perfecto (2004-Spanish-Italian) **C-105m.** **½ D: Álex de la Iglesia. Guillermo Toledo, Mónica Cervera, Luis Varela, Enrique Villén, Fernando Tejero, Javier Gutiérrez, Kira Miró. Top achiever in the women's department of a busy store is living the high life, bedding many of his customers, but when his quest to become floor manager fails, a nasty argument with his chief rival ends in murder. From here a darkly funny comedy takes incredible turns and loses the steam it has built up. Hitchcockian farce was a hit in its native Spain and takes a partially successful stab at pulling off the art of black comedy. Toledo is pretty much the whole show and delivers a sly performance. Super 35.**)**

El Dorado (1967) **C-126m.** *** D: Howard Hawks. John Wayne, Robert Mitchum, James Caan, Arthur Hunnicutt, Edward Asner, Michele Carey, Christopher George, Charlene Holt, Paul Fix, R. G. Armstrong, Johnny Crawford, Robert Donner. Followup to RIO BRAVO finds aging gunfighter Wayne helping drunken sheriff pal Mitchum quell a range war. Typically smooth Hawks mix of comedy and action, with zesty Leigh Brackett script and exemplary performances, especially by Mitchum, Caan as young gambler who can't shoot, and George as ultra-cool hired gun.▼●)

Election (1999) **C-103m.** ***½ D: Alexander Payne. Matthew Broderick, Reese Witherspoon, Chris Klein, Jessica Campbell, Mark Harelik, Phil Reeves, Molly Hagan, Delaney Driscoll, Colleen Camp, Matt Malloy. Audacious, wickedly funny satire about an earnest Nebraska schoolteacher's attempt to put a roadblock in the path of an overachiever who's running unopposed for class president. Highly original story also involves adultery, lust, and lesbianism; somehow manages to avoid mean-spiritedness while taking dead aim at its subjects. Written by Payne and Jim Taylor from the novel by Tom Perrotta. Broderick and Witherspoon are exceptionally good. Super 35. [R]▼●)

Electra Glide in Blue (1973) **C-113m.** *** D: James William Guercio. Robert Blake, Billy Green Bush, Mitchell Ryan, Jeannine Riley, Elisha Cook, Jr., Royal Dano. Violent film about highway cop Blake making up in brains what he lacks in height. Striking action sequences and good characterizations. Look, very fast, for Nick Nolte as a hippie at a commune. Panavision. [PG]▼●)

Electric Dreams (1984) **C-95m.** **½ D: Steve Barron. Lenny Von Dohlen, Virginia Madsen, Maxwell Caulfield, voice of Bud Cort. Old-fashioned boy meets girl story told in rock-video terms, with a third corner to the love triangle: a jealous computer. Good idea gets sillier as it goes along. [PG]▼●

Electric Horseman, The (1979) **C-120m.** **½ D: Sydney Pollack. Robert Redford, Jane Fonda, Valerie Perrine, Willie Nelson, John Saxon, Nicolas Coster, Wilford Brimley, James B. Sikking. Innocuous rip-off of LONELY ARE THE BRAVE tries to palm off Redford as a near-derelict who steals a $12 million thoroughbred from a Vegas hotel and heads for some grazing land. Pleasant, to be sure, but considering the people involved, a disappointment. Panavision. [PG]▼●)

Elegy (2008) **C-111m.** ***½ D: Isabel Coixet. Penélope Cruz, Ben Kingsley, Peter Sarsgaard, Patricia Clarkson, Dennis Hopper, Deborah Harry. Moving, adult drama about a self-possessed N.Y.C. college professor who is smitten with a beautiful ex-student, but consistent with his lifelong air of detachment, can't give her the emotional commitment she needs. Nicholas Meyer adapted Philip Roth's *The Dying Animal*, which is beautifully realized by Coixet and a superb cast. Cruz and Kingsley have never been better; the gifted Clarkson has an especially well-written part as Kingsley's longtime sex partner who's content with the boundary lines they've set for their relationship. [R]●

Elektra (2005) **C-96m.** *½ D: Rob Bowman. Jennifer Garner, Goran Visnjic, Kirsten Prout, Will Yun Lee, Terence Stamp, Cary-Hiroyuki Tagawa. Garner's Marvel character ended up dead in DAREDEVIL, but she's resurrected here, a fate not likely to happen to this movie's reputation. As an assassin, she's assigned by The Hand (another organization up to no good) to track a father and daughter on the lam. Lackluster fight scenes, Garner's sleepwalking, and a tendency toward the psychoanalytic (Elektra had a tough childhood) make this a groan . . . a far cry from the franchise it was intended to launch. Director's cut runs 104m. Panavision. [PG-13]▼)

Elektra Luxx (2011) **C-100m.** *½ D: Sebastian Gutierrez. Carla Gugino, Joseph Gordon-Levitt, Timothy Olyphant, Kathleen Quinlan, Malin Akerman, Marley Shelton, Adrianne Palicki, Emmanuelle Chriqui, Amy Rosoff, Vincent Kartheiser, Justin Kirk, Lucy Punch. Follow-up to WOMEN IN TROUBLE (with some of the same actors, recreating their roles) is a scattershot collection of vignettes built around the title character, a porn star who's now conducting a class for women who want professional sex advice. Don't look for more plot, coherence, or wit, except in Gordon-Levitt's lively video chats as Elektra's number-one fanboy. Julianne Moore appears unbilled. [R]❘

Element of Crime, The (1984-Danish) **C-104m.** *** D: Lars von Trier. Michael Elphick, Esmond Knight, Me Me Lei, Gerald Wells, Ahmed El-Shenawi, Astrid Henning Jensen, Lars von Trier. It's the post-holocaust future, and the world is suffering from an ecological imbalance; ragged cop Elphick undergoes hypnosis in order to properly investigate a series of horrible mutilation murders of young girls. Surreal, thought-provoking thriller is crammed with references to earlier films, from Hitchcock to film noir to BLADE RUNNER. Von Trier also scripted, in an impressive feature debut. Shot in English.▼)

Elena and Her Men (1956-French) **C-98m.** ** D: Jean Renoir. Ingrid Bergman, Jean Marais, Mel Ferrer, Jean Richard, Magali Noel, Juliette Greco, Pierre Bertin. Claude Renoir's exquisite cinematography highlights this otherwise so-so account of impoverished Polish princess Bergman's romantic intrigues with Marais and Ferrer. Overrated by some; far from Renoir's (or Bergman's) best. French-language version, called PARIS DOES STRANGE THINGS, is better and runs 95m.▼)

Eleni (1985) **C-117m.** **½ D: Peter Yates. Kate Nelligan, John Malkovich, Linda Hunt, Oliver Cotton, Ronald Pickup, Rosalie Crutchley, Dimitra Arliss, Glenne Headly. *N.Y. Times* reporter gets himself assigned to Athens bureau so he can resolve life-long obsession with finding truth about his mother's execution by communists in Greece following WW2. Steve Tesich's script is based on Nicholas Gage's book—and life—but coldness of the lead character is just one reason this film remains aloof and uninteresting. Nelligan plays Gage's mother in convincing flashback sequences. [PG]▼●

Elephant (2003) **C-81m.** ** D: Gus Van Sant. Alex Frost, Eric Deulen, John Robinson, Elias McConnell, Jordan Taylor, Carrie Finklea, Nicole George, Brittany Mountain, Timothy Bottoms, Matt Malloy. Dramatically inert yet sometimes queasily effective, this you-are-there mood piece takes a clinical rather than emotional approach to re-creating events leading up to a Columbine-type school massacre. Manages to create an under-your-skin sense of dreadful foreboding and offers a few telling details of high school life (like homogenized cafeteria food) but no insights whatsoever. Somehow this took the Palme d'Or award at Cannes. [R]▼●

Elephant Boy (1937-British) **80m.** *** D: Robert Flaherty, Zoltan Korda. Sabu, W. E. Holloway, Walter Hudd, Allan Jeayes, Bruce Gordon, D. J. Williams. Interesting early-day docudrama about native boy (Sabu, in film debut) who claims he knows location of mythic elephant herd.▼●

Elephant Man, The (1980) **125m.** ***½ D: David Lynch. Anthony Hopkins, John Hurt, Anne Bancroft, John Gielgud, Wendy Hiller, Freddie Jones, Michael Elphick, John Standing, Phoebe Nicholls, Kathleen Byron, Kenny Baker, Patricia Hodge. Moving dramatization of the story of John Merrick, a grotesquely deformed man shown compassion for the first time in his life by an eminent doctor in turn-of-the-century London. No relation to the Broadway play (in which one had to imagine how Merrick looked). Fine performances by all; rich Victorian atmosphere created by Lynch and veteran cameraman Freddie Francis—in beautiful black and white. Screenplay by Christopher DeVore, Eric Bergren, and the director. Panavision. [PG]▼●▐

Elephant Walk (1954) **C-103m.** ** D: William Dieterle. Elizabeth Taylor, Dana Andrews, Peter Finch, Abraham Sofaer. Overblown melodrama set on Ceylon tea plantation, with Taylor as Finch's new bride who must cope with environment and his father complex. Pachyderm-stampede climax comes none too soon. Vivien Leigh, replaced by Taylor, can be seen in long shots.▼▐

Elevator to the Gallows (1958-French) **91m.** ***½ D: Louis Malle. Jeanne Moreau, Maurice Ronet, Georges Poujouly, Yori Bertin, Jean Wall, Charles Denner, Jean-Claude Brialy, Lino Ventura. Malle's experience making documentaries informs his first fictional feature, as an amorous man and

woman attempt to pull off the perfect crime. Filmed by Henri Decaë on the streets of Paris in a bracing style that anticipates the New Wave. Famous score improvised by Miles Davis. Original U.S. title: FRANTIC. ▼▐

11:14 (2005-U.S.-Canadian) **C-86m.** **½ D: Greg Marcks. Henry Thomas, Blake Heron, Clark Gregg, Hilary Swank, Shawn Hatosy, Barbara Hershey, Stark Sands, Colin Hanks, Ben Foster, Patrick Swayze, Rachael Leigh Cook. At 11:14 p.m. a body lands on the windshield of a car and the tipsy driver tries to hide the corpse. Intersecting flashbacks reveal the mishaps immediately before and after the incident and how they converge to change the lives of several people one night in a small town. Despite the clever structure of the screenplay (by the director) and some amusing black comedy, it's hard to care about this collection of dumb, morally bankrupt characters. Without the time-juggling gimmick, the story would add up to very little. Filmed in 2002. [R]▐

11 Harrowhouse (1974-British) **C-98m.** *** D: Aram Avakian. Charles Grodin, Candice Bergen, James Mason, Trevor Howard, John Gielgud, Helen Cherry. Funny action spoof of heist films, as diamond merchant Grodin robs the world clearinghouse for gems. Grodin also adapted Gerald A. Browne's best-selling novel. Aka ANYTHING FOR LOVE and FAST FORTUNE. Panavision. [PG]▼▐

11th Hour, The (2007) **C-95m.** **½ D: Leila Conners Petersen, Nadia Conners. Coproducer Leonardo DiCaprio's intense sincerity serves him well as on- and off-screen narrator of this sprawling, frequently distressing documentary about the various ways mankind is despoiling our planet. In addition to footage of melting icecaps, widespread deforestation, overflowing landfills, etc., the directors include cogent testimony by disparate experts and activists, from Stephen Hawking to Mikhail Gorbachev, who suggest specific steps that can be taken to keep Earth inhabitable. [PG]▐

Elf (2003) **C-95m.** *** D: Jon Favreau. Will Ferrell, James Caan, Zooey Deschanel, Mary Steenburgen, Daniel Tay, Edward Asner, Bob Newhart, Faizon Love, Peter Dinklage, Amy Sedaris, Clint Howard, Michael Lerner, Andy Richter, Kyle Gass, Jon Favreau; voice of Leon Redbone. One of Santa's elves learns that he is actually a human being and sets off for N.Y.C. to meet his father—as un-Christmassy a character as ever lived. Ferrell is a delight as the elf who has a gift for spreading good cheer, even in a world of cynics, and ably carries this film (with a little help from old pros like Newhart and Asner, and the charming Deschanel), but Caan is miscast in an underwritten role as the father. Animated characters brought to life by the Chiodo Brothers recall Rankin-Bass TV specials of yore; the polar bear cub is voiced by stop-motion master Ray Harryhausen. [PG]▼▶

El Greco (1966-Italian-French) **C-95m.** ** D: Luciano Salce. Mel Ferrer, Rosanna Schiaffino, Franco Giacobini, Renzo Giovampietro, Adolfo Celi. Despite lavish trappings, story of painter reduced to soap-opera terms falls flat. Beautiful color, but no plot of any distinction. CinemaScope.

Eliminators (1986) **C-96m.** *½ D: Peter Manoogian. Andrew Prine, Denise Crosby, Patrick Reynolds, Conan Lee, Roy Dotrice. Woman scientist, white male guide, a ninja, and a cyborg team up to battle a mad-genius industrialist who wants to take over the world. Good to see an equal-opportunity adventure, but this RAIDERS clone has little to offer but low humor. Crosby is Bing's granddaughter. [PG]▼

Elizabeth (1998-British) **C-123m.** *** D: Shekhar Kapur. Cate Blanchett, Geoffrey Rush, Joseph Fiennes, Richard Attenborough, Christopher Eccleston, Vincent Cassel, Fanny Ardant, Kathy Burke, Eric Cantona, Emily Mortimer, John Gielgud, Edward Hardwicke, Daniel Craig. Queen Mary I dreads the prospect of her half-sister, a heathen Protestant, ascending to the throne, but upon Mary's death that's exactly what happens, leading to intrigues and divisiveness within the court. Elizabeth (Blanchett) tries to rule with common sense and sees no reason to abandon her lover simply to satisfy protocol. Interesting historical drama anchored by Blanchett's charismatic performance as a woman who was far ahead of her time. Oscar winner for Best Makeup. Followed by ELIZABETH: THE GOLDEN AGE. [R]▼◆▶

Elizabeth: The Golden Age (2007-British-French) **C-114m.** ** D: Shekhar Kapur. Cate Blanchett, Geoffrey Rush, Clive Owen, Rhys Ifans, Jordi Mollà, Abbie Cornish, Samantha Morton, Tom Hollander, Antony Carrick, David Threlfall, Eddie Redmayne, Susan Lynch. Blanchett re-creates the role that won her international acclaim almost a decade earlier (in ELIZABETH) with less-than-stellar results. In this seemingly fanciful sequel, the Queen becomes enamored of a dashing Sir Walter Raleigh (Owen) amid assorted intrigues. Ponderous and far from golden, although Blanchett always is worth watching. Oscar winner for Best Costume Design (Alexandra Byrne). [PG-13]▶

Elizabeth the Queen SEE: **Private Lives of Elizabeth and Essex, The**

Elizabethtown (2005) **C-123m.** ** D: Cameron Crowe. Orlando Bloom, Kirsten Dunst, Susan Sarandon, Alec Baldwin, Bruce McGill, Judy Greer, Jessica Biel, Paul Schneider, Loudon Wainwright III, Gailard Sartain. West Coast yuppie (Bloom) whose life is in disarray flies to Kentucky to attend to his father's funeral. A stranger in a strange land, he's given signposts by a worldly-wise flight attendant (Dunst), then finds himself immersed in the dynamics of his cheerfully oddball family. Writer-director Crowe casts his stars adrift in a pleasant but aimless comedy that seems to go on forever. [PG-13]▼▶

Ella Enchanted (2004) **C-101m.** *** D: Tommy O'Haver. Anne Hathaway, Hugh Dancy, Cary Elwes, Minnie Driver, Jimi Mistry, Eric Idle, Vivica Fox, Patrick Bergin, Parminder Nagra, Heidi Klum, Aidan McArdle, Joanna Lumley, Lucy Punch, Jennifer Higham; voice of Steve Coogan. Imaginative reinvention of the Cinderella story with Hathaway a delight as the plucky Ella, Dancy a charming Prince, and Elwes a sinister villain (in amusing contrast to his signature role in THE PRINCESS BRIDE). Visually inventive, with clever use of feel-good songs and contemporary humor; a family treat. Based on the award-winning book by Gail Carson Levine. [PG]▼▶

Ellery Queen series SEE: *Leonard Maltin's Classic Movie Guide*

Ellie Parker (2005) **C-95m.** **½ D: Scott Coffey. Naomi Watts, Rebecca Rigg, Scott Coffey, Mark Pellegrino, Chevy Chase, Blair Mastbaum, Keanu Reeves. Watts is the whole show in this digital video oddity about a struggling actress who treks off to auditions while breaking up with her boyfriend and questioning her existence. Inside look at life on the fringes of the L.A. "entertainment industry" will be of interest primarily to film-biz wannabes and Watts completists; it certainly showcases her range. Originally a 16m. short that premiered at the 2001 Sundance Film Festival, prior to Watts' stardom; expanded intermittently over four years' time. Watts coproduced with writer-director Coffey. [R]▶

Elling (2001-Norwegian) **C-89m.** *** D: Petter Naess. Per Christian Ellefsen, Sven Nordin, Marit Pia Jacobsen, Jorgen Langhelle, Per Christensen. Winning comedy about a middle-aged mama's boy (Ellefsen) who winds up in a mental institution after the death of his mother. Eventually, with his sex-obsessed hospital roommate, he moves into a state-provided apartment. This funny, charming film works so well because it never loses sight of who these characters are. This was Norway's all-time biggest box-office hit. [R] ▼▶

El Mariachi (1992) **C-81m.** *** D: Robert Rodriguez. Carlos Gallardo, Consuelo Gomez, Peter Marquardt, Jaime de Hoyos, Reinol Martinez, Ramiro Gomez. Energetic little film about a young singing guitarist (mariachi) who comes to a small town, where he's mistaken for a ferocious prison escapee. Arresting, original (and violent) film was shot in two weeks for just $7,000, but offers more entertainment than most of today's megabuck Hollywood movies. Director Rodriguez also photographed, edited, coproduced, and wrote the picture; Gallardo also served as coproducer. In

Spanish. Rodriguez later reworked this as DESPERADO. [R]▼●)

Elmer Gantry (1960) **C-145m.** ***½ D: Richard Brooks. Burt Lancaster, Jean Simmons, Dean Jagger, Arthur Kennedy, Shirley Jones, Patti Page, Edward Andrews, Hugh Marlowe, John McIntire, Rex Ingram. Lancaster gives a vibrant Oscar-winning performance as the salesman with the gift of gab who joins evangelist Simmons' barnstorming troupe in the 1920s Midwest. Jones won Academy Award as his jilted girlfriend turned prostitute; Brooks also won an Oscar for his sprawling screenplay from Sinclair Lewis' trenchant novel.▼●)

El Norte (1983) **C-139m.** **** D: Gregory Nava. Zaide Silvia Gutierrez, David Villalpando, Ernesto Gomez Cruz, Alicia del Lago, Heraclio Zepeda, Stella Quan, Lupe Ontiveros. Sweeping, emotional saga of a brother and sister who leave their violence-torn village in Guatemala to find a better life in The North—El Norte. Getting to America is half the story; making a life there is the other half. Writer-director Nava presents a heightened sense of reality that removes this from the realm of documentary; a compassionate, heart-rending, unforgettable film. Cowritten and produced by Anna Thomas, for *American Playhouse.* [R]▼)

El Super (1979) **C-90m.** *** D: Leon Ichaso, Orlando Jiminez-Leal. Raymundo Hidalgo-Gato, Zully Montero, Raynaldo Medina, Juan Granda, Hilda Lee, Elizabeth Pena. The trials of homesick exiled Cuban who labors as an apartment-house super in Manhattan. Hidalgo-Gato is excellent as a comically sad outsider, still in transit after a decade away from his homeland.▼)

El Topo (1970-Mexican) **C-125m.** ** D: Alejandro Jodorowsky. Alejandro Jodorowsky, Brontis Jodorowsky, Mara Lorenzio, David Silva, Paula Romo, Hector Martinez, Alfonso Arau. Clad in black leather, a gunslinger rides through the Old West with his naked 7-year-old son in tow and guns down everyone in sight, after which he sets himself on fire. Divided into sections, with such names as Genesis, Psalms, and Apocalypse, this pretentious head-trip cult film borrows from Fellini and Leone, while employing meaningless symbolism and lots of perverse sex and violence. Overlong and overrated, though it seemed pretty cool in its day. Rafael Corkidi's photography is striking.▼)

Elusive Corporal, The (1962-French) **108m.** **½ D: Jean Renoir. Jean-Pierre Cassel, Claude Brasseur, Claude Rich, O. E. Hasse, Jean Carmet. Pointed if predictable chronicle of French corporal who attempts to escape with his pals from a German prison camp during WW2. Sobering look at friendship and freedom, which Renoir explored more successfully in other, earlier films. The wry comic touches are an asset.▼●)

Elusive Pimpernel, The (1950-British) **C-109m.** *** D: Michael Powell, Emeric Pressburger. David Niven, Margaret Leighton, Cyril Cusack, Jack Hawkins, Arlette Marchal, Robert Coote, Patrick Macnee. Colorful remake of THE SCARLET PIMPERNEL. Niven is British fop who secretly aids victims of Reign of Terror; lively fun. This was filmed as a musical—you can tell where the numbers were cut! Released in U.S. in 1954 as THE FIGHTING PIMPERNEL. ▼

Elvira Madigan (1967-Swedish) **C-89m.** *** D: Bo Widerberg. Pia Degermark, Thommy Berggren, Lennart Malmer, Nina Widerberg, Cleo Jensen. Lovers on the run, in soft-focus photography: tightrope walker Degermark and married army officer Berggren run off together. Though based on a true story (and filmed before in 1943), stylistically this too often resembles a shampoo commercial. Still, it was a big hit, with attractive stars, lush photography, and canny use of Mozart music. [PG]▼●)

Elvira, Mistress of the Dark (1988) **C-96m.** BOMB D: James Signorelli. Elvira (Cassandra Peterson), W. Morgan Sheppard, Daniel Greene, Susan Kellermann, Jeff Conaway, Edie McClurg, William Duell. Peterson takes her TV horror host character to the screen in this flimsy story of a TV host shaking up a small New England town which she's visiting to pick up an inheritance. Unfunny, one-joke script (cowritten by Peterson) keeps its attention firmly riveted to the star's ample bosom. More yawns than yocks. [PG-13]▼●)

Elvis on Tour (1972) **C-93m.** ** D: Pierre Adidge, Robert Abel. Static study of rock 'n' roll's biggest super-star going through his paces at a series of U.S. concerts. Even the music is not up to standard. Multiple Screen. [G]▼●)

Elvis: That's the Way It Is (1970) **C-97m.** *** D: Denis Sanders. Engaging look at Elvis Presley offstage, preparing major nightclub act, culminating in opening-night performance in Las Vegas. Well-filmed if one-sided documentary paints vivid picture of Elvis as master showman. Reedited from original source material for cable and video release in 2001; that version runs 95m. Panavision.▼●)

Embassy (1972-British) **C-90m.** **½ D: Gordon Hessler. Richard Roundtree, Chuck Connors, Max von Sydow, Ray Milland, Broderick Crawford, Marie-Jose Nat. Spotty spy thriller about Russian defector von Sydow seeking asylum and the State Department's efforts to have agent Roundtree smuggle him out of the Mideast under KGB man Connors' nose. Good cast works valiantly with contrived plot, talky script. Aka TARGET: EMBASSY. [PG]▼)

Embryo (1976) **C-104m.** ** D: Ralph Nelson. Rock Hudson, Diane Ladd, Barbara Carrera, Roddy McDowall, Anne Schedeen. Sometimes interesting, sometimes repulsive horror sci-fi about woman and dog grown from fetuses outside the womb—with terrifying results. Retitled CREATED TO KILL. [PG]▼◗

Emerald Forest, The (1985) **C-113m.** ✱✱✱ D: John Boorman. Powers Boothe, Meg Foster, Charley Boorman, Dira Pass. American engineer spends ten years searching for his kidnapped son, who's been raised by primitive Amazon tribe. Fascinating look at a unique civilization, but lack of emotional empathy for the father and contrived storyline weaken overall impact. Still worthwhile. Script by Rospo Pallenberg; rich music score by Junior Homrich. And a completely convincing performance by young Boorman, son of the film's director. Panavision. [R]▼◗

Emigrants, The (1971-Swedish) **C-191m.** ✱✱✱ D: Jan Troell. Max von Sydow, Liv Ullmann, Eddie Axberg, Allan Edwall. Solid if rambling tale of peasant farmer von Sydow, wife Ullmann, and fellow Swedes who emigrate to America in the 19th century. Sequel, THE NEW LAND, is even better; both have been edited together for TV, dubbed in English, and presented as THE EMIGRANT SAGA. See also THE OX. [PG] ▼◗

Emigrant Saga, The SEE: **Emigrants, The** and **New Land, The**

Emily Brontë's Wuthering Heights SEE: **Wuthering Heights** (1992)

Eminent Domain (1991) **C-102m.** ✱✱½ D: John Irvin. Donald Sutherland, Anne Archer, Jodhi May, Paul Freeman, Bernard Hepton. Intriguing story of high political official (Sutherland) in pre-Solidarity Poland who wakes up one morning to discover his privileged Politburo position no longer exists and no one will give him a satisfactory reason for (or even acknowledge) the eerie snafu. Reminiscent of Kafka's *The Trial*; often disturbing, but confusing in spots. [PG-13]▼

Emma (1996) **C-111m.** ✱✱✱ D: Douglas McGrath. Gwyneth Paltrow, Jeremy Northam, Toni Collette, Greta Scacchi, Juliet Stevenson, Alan Cumming, Polly Walker, Ewan McGregor, James Cosmo, Sophie Thompson, Phyllida Law. Charming, witty adaptation of Jane Austen's comedy of manners about a headstrong young woman who makes a habit of playing matchmaker for others, but can't recognize her own true feelings—or those of the men who surround her. Paltrow is delightful and surrounded by an ideal (and highly attractive) cast. Thompson (sister of actress Emma T.) is wonderful as the talkative Miss Bates; that's her real-life mother, Law, playing Mrs. Bates. Script by McGrath, making his directorial debut. Oscar-winning score by Rachel Portman. [PG]▼◗

Emotional Arithmetic (2007-Canadian)

C-99m. ✱✱½ D: Paulo Barzman. Susan Sarandon, Christopher Plummer, Max von Sydow, Gabriel Byrne, Roy Dupuis, Dakota Goyo. Decades after the close of prewar Drancy Internment Camp on the outskirts of Paris, two survivors (von Sydow and Byrne) travel to the home of a third (Sarandon). This highly anticipated reunion leads to mental and emotional upheaval as unresolved issues are finally unearthed. Uneven drama (told partly in flashback) doesn't provide a fully satisfying experience. Still, it remains a sensitive and telling look at the way horrific events inform lives and how survivor guilt can bring down those who made it out . . . if they let it. Retitled AUTUMN HEARTS: A NEW BEGINNING. Super 35. [PG-13]◗

Emperor and the Assassin, The (1999-Chinese) **C-161m.** ✱✱✱ D: Chen Kaige. Gong Li, Zhang Fengyi, Li Xuejian, Wang Zhiwen, Chen Kaige, Lu Xiaohe. Sweeping, fact-based account of the ruler of a Chinese kingdom (Xuejian) in 320 B.C. who is determined to annex the country's other kingdoms and become its first emperor. For this purpose, he enlists the help of his concubine (Li, ravishing as ever); she, in turn, falls for an assassin (Fengyi). The story's predictability is outweighed by the beautifully staged spectacle; this is reportedly the most expensive Chinese film ever made. [R]▼◗

Emperor Jones, The (1933) **72m.** ✱✱½ D: Dudley Murphy. Paul Robeson, Dudley Digges, Frank Wilson, Fredi Washington, Ruby Elzy. Robeson plays Pullman porter who escapes from chain gang and improbably becomes king of a Caribbean island. Pretentious adaptation of Eugene O'Neill play derives its chief interest and value from Robeson himself. Look for Moms Mabley in bit part.▼◗

Emperor of the North (1973) **C-118m.** ✱✱✱½ D: Robert Aldrich. Lee Marvin, Ernest Borgnine, Keith Carradine, Charles Tyner, Harry Caesar, Malcolm Atterbury, Simon Oakland, Matt Clark, Elisha Cook. Unusual, exciting (and heavily symbolic) action film set during the Depression. Sadistic conductor Borgnine will kill any tramp who tries to cop a ride on his train; legendary hobo Marvin announces he will be the first to succeed. Beautifully filmed in Oregon by Joseph Biroc; taut script by Christopher Knopf and typically muscular Aldrich direction make this a unique entertainment. Initially released as EMPEROR OF THE NORTH POLE. [PG]◗

Emperor's Club, The (2002) **C-109m.** ✱✱✱ D: Michael Hoffman. Kevin Kline, Steven Culp, Embeth Davidtz, Patrick Dempsey, Joel Gretsch, Edward Herrmann, Emile Hirsch, Rob Morrow, Harris Yulin, Paul Dano, Roger Rees, Jesse Eisenberg. Absorbing story about a dedicated Classics professor at an exclusive prep school who puts his faith in a troublesome boy. This is not the film one might expect (in spite of renaming Ethan Canin's short story "The Palace Thief" to sound more like DEAD POETS SOCIETY), with interesting nuances and plot turns as it tackles issues of ethics and morality. Kline is perfectly cast, and so is young Hirsch. [PG-13] ▼●

Emperor's New Clothes, The (2002-British-Italian-German) **C-107m.** **½ D: Alan Taylor. Ian Holm, Iben Hjejle, Tim McInnerny, Nigel Terry, Hugh Bonneville, Murray Melvin, Clive Russell, Eddie Marsan. Slight but entertaining "what if" tale with Napoleon escaping forced exile on St. Helena in 1821 and heading to Paris to retake France. Unfortunately, his plan goes awry from the very beginning, starting with the hiring of a look-alike commoner to fool his captors. Holm seems to relish the dual roles (he played Bonaparte before, in TIME BANDITS and a 1974 British TV miniseries titled *Napoleon in Love*), but the story is thin and goes on too long. The return to Waterloo and sanitarium scenes are gems, however. [PG] ▼●

Emperor's New Groove, The (2000) **C-79m.** **½ D: Mark Dindal. Voices of David Spade, John Goodman, Eartha Kitt, Patrick Warburton, Wendie Malick, Kellyann Kelso, Tom Jones. An Incan emperor with an outsized ego is rousted by a scheming advisor and transformed into a llama—but that doesn't stop him from seeking revenge on those who wronged him. A most un-Disney-like Disney cartoon feature, this one has a fresh look and some funny moments, but relies too heavily on Spade's smart-alecky comic persona—a little of which can go a long, long way. Features two songs by Sting. Followed by a direct-to-video sequel. [G] ▼●

Emperor Waltz, The (1948) **C-106m.** **½ D: Billy Wilder. Bing Crosby, Joan Fontaine, Roland Culver, Lucile Watson, Richard Haydn, Sig Ruman. Lavish but lackluster musical set in Franz Joseph Austria with Bing selling record players to royalty. Awfully schmaltzy material for writer-director Wilder. Filmed in 1946. Jasper National Park in Alberta, Canada, fills in for Tyrolean Alps. ▼●

Empire (2002) **C-95m.** ** D: Franc. Reyes. John Leguizamo, Peter Sarsgaard, Denise Richards, Vincent Laresca, Nestor Serrano, Delilah Cotto, Sonia Braga, Isabella Rossellini, Treach, Fat Joe. South Bronx drug dealer Leguizamo is a success on his home turf, but is he out of his league when he becomes involved in a scheme with hotshot Wall Street financier Sarsgaard? Intriguing premise, but the plot holes are gaping and the Hispanic stereotypes are downright embarrassing at times. Rossellini is oddly cast as a Colombian drug lord. Super 35. [R] ▼●

Empire of Passion (1978-Japanese) **C-110m.** ** D: Nagisa Oshima. Kazuko Yoshiyuki, Tatsuya Fuji, Takahiro Tamura, Takuzo Kawatani. Peasant woman Yoshiyuki has affair with village good-for-nothing Fuji; they murder her husband, whose ghost returns to haunt them. Boring, despite interesting subject matter. A follow-up to IN THE REALM OF THE SENSES. Aka IN THE REALM OF PASSION. [R] ▼●

Empire of the Ants (1977) **C-90m.** *½ D: Bert I. Gordon. Joan Collins, Robert Lansing, Albert Salmi, John David Carson, Robert Pine, Jacqueline Scott. Laughable man-vs.-giant insects chiller from H. G. Wells' story. Vacationers on an isolated island find themselves at the mercy of voracious ants that have become monsters after feasting on a leaking barrel of radioactive waste. [PG] ▼●

Empire of the Sun (1987) **C-152m.** ** D: Steven Spielberg. Christian Bale, John Malkovich, Miranda Richardson, Nigel Havers, Joe Pantoliano, Leslie Phillips, Masato Ibu, Emily Richard, Rupert Frazer, Ben Stiller, Robert Stephens, Burt Kwouk. British boy, living a well-sheltered life in Shanghai, is separated from his parents and forced to fend for himself when Japan invades China at the outset of WW2. Sprawling, ambitious, but emotionally distant and loaded with cinematic crescendos (replete with crane camera shots and overbearing music by John Williams) that simply don't have the emotional content to warrant all that fuss. Tom Stoppard adapted J. G. Ballard's autobiographical novel (Ballard appears briefly in Beefeater costume in an early party scene). [PG] ▼●

Empire Records (1995) **C-91m.** *½ D: Allan Moyle. Anthony LaPaglia, Debi Mazar, Liv Tyler, Maxwell Caulfield, Rory Cochrane, Johnny Whitworth, Robin Tunney, Renée Zellweger, Ethan Randall (Embry). A day in the life of a record store, which the manager is desperately trying to save from a corporate takeover. A series of noisy vignettes which add up to nothing, despite attractive young cast. Disappointing outing from Moyle, who directed the more potent PUMP UP THE VOLUME. Alternate version runs 107m. Super 35. [PG-13] ▼●

Empire Strikes Back, The (1980) **C-124m.** **** D: Irvin Kershner. Mark Hamill, Harrison Ford, Carrie Fisher, Billy Dee Williams, Anthony Daniels, David Prowse, Peter Mayhew, Kenny Baker, Frank Oz, Alec Guinness, Clive Revill, Julian Glover, John Ratzenberger, voice of James Earl Jones. Smashing sequel to STAR WARS manages to top the original in its embellishment of leading characters' personalities, truly dazzling special effects (which earned a special Oscar) and nonstop spirit of adventure and excitement. Story threads include a blossoming romance between Han Solo and

Princess Leia, the cosmic education of Luke Skywalker (by the mystical Yoda), an uneasy alliance with opportunistic Lando Calrissian, and a startling revelation from Darth Vader. 1997 reissue included 3 minutes of additional footage. Full title onscreen is STAR WARS EPISODE V: THE EMPIRE STRIKES BACK. Sequel: RETURN OF THE JEDI. Panavision. [PG] ▼●)

Employee of the Month (2006) **C-108m.** *½ D: Greg Coolidge. Dane Cook, Jessica Simpson, Dax Shepard, Andy Dick, Tim Bagley, Brian George, Efren Ramirez, Harland Williams, Marcello Thedford, Danny Woodburn. At a warehouse store, slacker Cook and weasely Shepard compete and cheat for both knockout newbie Simpson and the title award. No laughs whatsoever in this CLERKS/OFFICE SPACE slapstick wannabe, and the performances are awful. Shot in New Mexico; too bad they didn't bury it there. [PG-13]▶

Empty Canvas, The (1963-French-Italian) **118m.** *½ D: Damiano Damiani. Bette Davis, Horst Buchholz, Catherine Spaak, Isa Miranda, Lea Padovani, Daniela Rocca, Georges Wilson. Artist Buchholz is obsessed with model Spaak, eventually decorates her naked body with bank notes. Davis is his wealthy mother; hopefully, she was well paid for her time. Based on an Alberto Moravia novel.▼

Empty Mirror, The (1999) **C-119m.** *½ D: Barry J. Hershey. Norman Rodway, Joel Grey, Peter Michael Goetz, Glenn Shadix, Camilla Soeberg, Doug McKeon. Ignorant of time and place, we're thrust into a strange environment where Adolf Hitler encounters key people from his past as he dictates his memoirs. Surreal, ambitious film, intercut with footage from TRIUMPH OF THE WILL and Eva Braun's home movies, pretty well lives up to its title: there's not much to reflect on. Grey's appearance as Joseph Goebbels is an interesting career counterpart to his m.c. from CABARET. [PG-13]▼▶

Enchanted (2007) **C-108m.** *** D: Kevin Lima. Amy Adams, Patrick Dempsey, James Marsden, Timothy Spall, Susan Sarandon, Idina Menzel, Rachel Covey; narrated by Julie Andrews. Wide-eyed Giselle (Adams) from Andalasia, about to marry a handsome prince, is hurled down a well by the evil queen and emerges in modern-day Manhattan. Divorce lawyer Dempsey and his 6-year-old daughter try to help her, though he can't believe she's for real. Adams' glowing performance buoys this delightful Disney fantasy, which opens with lush, hand-drawn animation (supervised by James Baxter) and segues into live-action. Terrific songs by Alan Menken and Stephen Schwartz include "That's How You Know," which inspires a dazzling production number in Central Park. Memorable costumes by Mona May. Affectionate spoof of clas-

sic Disney fairy tales features Jodi Benson (the voice of Ariel), Paige O'Hara (Belle), and Judy Kuhn (Pocahontas) in small parts. Only the finale seems anticlimactic—and unnecessary. Super 35. [PG]▶

Enchanted April (1991-British) **C-101m.** ***½ D: Mike Newell. Josie Lawrence, Miranda Richardson, Joan Plowright, Polly Walker, Alfred Molina, Jim Broadbent, Michael Kitchen, Adriana Fachetti. Utterly charming film about two repressed, married women who seize an impulse and rent an Italian villa for a month, taking on two very different women as housemates for this daring adventure. Ideally cast, nicely realized, and very romantic. Screenplay by Peter Barnes. Elizabeth von Arnim's 1921 novel was filmed before in 1935. Made for British television, released theatrically in the U.S. [PG]▼●)

Enchanted Cottage, The (1945) **92m.** **½ D: John Cromwell. Dorothy McGuire, Robert Young, Herbert Marshall, Mildred Natwick, Spring Byington, Hillary Brooke. Adaptation of Arthur Pinero play about two misfits, a homely woman and a disfigured man, who find each other beautiful in the enchanted cottage. Never quite as good as you'd like it to be. Previously filmed in 1924. Some prints run 78m.▼●)

Enchantment (1948) **102m.** *** D: Irving Reis. David Niven, Teresa Wright, Evelyn Keyes, Farley Granger, Jayne Meadows, Leo G. Carroll. Weepy romancer with elderly Niven recalling his tragic love as he watches great-niece Keyes' romance with Granger.▼●)

Encino Man (1992) **C-89m.** *½ D: Les Mayfield. Sean Astin, Brendan Fraser, Pauly Shore, Megan Ward, Robin Tunney, Rick Ducommun, Mariette Hartley, Richard Masur, Rose McGowan. Nerdy teenager Astin and his weirdo pal Shore dig up a frozen caveman in Astin's suburban L.A. backyard. The scant laughs come from plunging the affable Cro-Magnon into teenage life, circa 1992. Formulaic teen comedy; Shore's bogus slang irritates, but limber, good-natured Fraser (as the cavedude) has his moments. Followed by 1996 TV sequel, ENCINO WOMAN. [PG] ▼●)

Encore (1952-British) **85m.** *** D: Pat Jackson, Anthony Pelissier, Harold French. Nigel Patrick, Roland Culver, Kay Walsh, Glynis Johns, Terence Morgan. Entertaining trilogy of Somerset Maugham stories: brothers try to outdo one another over money; busybody matron almost ruins ship cruise; apprehensive circus performer faces a crisis.▼

Encounters at the End of the World (2008) **C-101m.** ***½ D: Werner Herzog. On assignment for the National Science Foundation, Herzog idiosyncratically profiles Antarctica, a land of no natives, no flora, no crime. Spiraling deeper into the continent's dreamy mysteries—among them, a tragically deranged penguin—the film dives far under an icy surface that might be no more than eight inches thick. It also profiles some of the brilliant misfits who have fallen to the bottom of the planet. This right-brain travelogue feeds the mind, the eye, and the mind's eye. Wryly, sometimes impatiently, narrated by the director, who dedicates the film to Roger Ebert. [G]◗

End, The (1978) C-100m. *** D: Burt Reynolds. Burt Reynolds, Sally Field, Dom DeLuise, Joanne Woodward, Kristy McNichol, Robby Benson, David Steinberg, Norman Fell, Carl Reiner, Pat O'Brien, Myrna Loy. Uneven but original black comedy by Jerry Belson about man who learns he's dying and decides to commit suicide. DeLuise is achingly funny as Burt's schizophrenic sanitarium pal, and Reynolds' final soliloquy is great (in uncensored version). [R]▼◗❶

Endangered Species (1982) C-97m. *½ D: Alan Rudolph. Robert Urich, JoBeth Williams, Paul Dooley, Hoyt Axton, Peter Coyote, Marin Kanter, Dan Hedaya, Harry Carey, Jr., John Considine. Self-important, preachy story—based on a serious real-life situation—about a N.Y. cop's investigation of cattle mutilations in the Western U.S. Tries to be a thriller, but telegraphs all its punches. [R]▼❶

Endless Love (1981) C-115m. BOMB D: Franco Zeffirelli. Brooke Shields, Martin Hewitt, Shirley Knight, Don Murray, Richard Kiley, Beatrice Straight, James Spader, Robert Moore, Penelope Milford, Jan Miner, Tom Cruise, Jami Gertz. Scott Spencer's deservedly praised novel about an obsessive romance between two teenagers is thoroughly trashed in textbook example of how to do everything wrong in a literary adaptation. Rightfully regarded as one of the worst films of its time. Cruise's and Spader's film debuts. [R]▼❶

Endless Night (1972-British) C-99m. *** D: Sidney Gilliat. Hayley Mills, Hywel Bennett, Britt Ekland, George Sanders, Per Oscarsson, Peter Bowles, Lois Maxwell. Gripping Agatha Christie thriller about chauffeur (Bennett) who marries rich American girl (Mills) and moves into "dream house" which turns out to be more a nightmare. Aka AGATHA CHRISTIE'S ENDLESS NIGHT.▼❶

Endless Summer, The (1966) C-95m. *** D: Bruce Brown. Mike Hynson, Robert August. Enjoyable documentary on surfing, filmed on location around the world, with a most diverting tongue-in-cheek narrative. Followed by a sequel—28 years later. Followed in 2000 by ENDLESS SUMMER REVISITED. ▼❶

Endless Summer II, The (1994) C-107m. *** D: Bruce Brown. Patrick O'Connell, Robert "Wingnut" Weaver. Superior sequel to Brown's 1966 surfing documentary,

enhanced this time by a bigger budget and sophisticated camera work. Exotic locales and eye-popping surfing footage will make this a must-see for hot-doggers; others will still enjoy the unspoiled beauty of big-wave beaches from Alaska to Java. Several of the veteran surfers from the original documentary turn up here as does some brief topless beachbunny nudity. Brown's son continued the surfing odyssey with STEP INTO LIQUID. [PG]▼❶

End of Days (1999) C-122m. *½ D: Peter Hyams. Arnold Schwarzenegger, Gabriel Byrne, Kevin Pollak, Robin Tunney, CCH Pounder, Rod Steiger, Derrick O'Connor, Miriam Margolyes, Udo Kier. The Devil takes the form of a wealthy New Yorker (Byrne) and sets out to find his pre-ordained bride; if he can impregnate her before midnight on New Year's Eve, 1999, he will bring about Hell on Earth, or Armageddon, or something. However, Satan never reckoned with Arnold, who's actually quite good as the burned-out cop/defender of humanity. Overproduced junk. Super 35. [R] ▼❶

End of Innocence, The (1991) C-102m. *½ D: Dyan Cannon. Dyan Cannon, John Heard, George Coe, Lola Mason, Rebecca Schaeffer, Steve Meadows, Billie Bird, Michael Madsen, Madge Sinclair, Renee Taylor, Eric Harrison. One woman's road to a breakdown, thanks to quarreling parents and a rich assortment of rotten men. Passionately acted by Cannon, who as a writer-director may have been in over her head. [R]▼

End of the Affair, The (1955-British) 106m. **½ D: Edward Dmytryk. Deborah Kerr, Van Johnson, John Mills, Peter Cushing, Michael Goodliffe. Graham Greene's mystic-religious novel about a wartime love affair in London loses much in screen version, especially from mismatched stars. Remade in 1999.▼❶

End of the Affair, The (1999-British-U.S.) C-109m. ***D: Neil Jordan. Ralph Fiennes, Julianne Moore, Stephen Rea, Ian Hart, Samuel Bould, Jason Isaacs. Finely wrought rendition of Graham Greene's (reportedly autobiographical) novel about a WW2 love affair that takes a surprising turn when the married woman (a radiant Moore) has an unexplained change of heart. Director-screenwriter Jordan captures the understatement and nuance of a vintage British drama with his keen eye and gifted stars. [R]▼❶

End of the Game (1976-German-Italian) C-103m. *** D: Maximilian Schell. Jon Voight, Jacqueline Bisset, Martin Ritt, Robert Shaw, Gabriele Ferzetti, Donald Sutherland. Complex thriller about dying police commissioner Ritt, who for three decades has been trying to nail omnipotent criminal Shaw. Director Ritt, in a rare acting role, is excellent; Voight plays his assistant, and

Sutherland appears as a dead man! Based on Friedrich Duerrenmatt's novel; aka GETTING AWAY WITH MURDER. [PG]

End of the Line (1987) C-105m. ** D: Jay Russell. Wilford Brimley, Levon Helm, Mary Steenburgen, Barbara Barrie, Kevin Bacon, Holly Hunter, Bob Balaban, Clint Howard, Rita Jenrette, Howard Morris, Bruce McGill, Trey Wilson. Two lifelong Southern railroad workers, suddenly unemployed when their parent company abandons the rails for air freight, take off for the Chicago corporate headquarters in a stolen engine. Labor of love for executive producer Steenburgen begins promisingly, quickly degenerates into silly Capra-esque fantasy. Cast makes it a curio. [PG]▼●]

End of the Road (1970) C-110m. ***½ D: Aram Avakian. Stacy Keach, Harris Yulin, Dorothy Tristan, James Earl Jones, Grayson Hall, Ray Brock, James Coco. Keach and Jones give stinging performances in solid filmization of bizarre John Barth novel about unstable college instructor who becomes involved with the wife of a professor. Tristan is superb in crucial and difficult role. Screenplay by Dennis McGuire, Terry Southern, and the director. [X]▼]

End of the World (1977) C-87m. ** D: John Hayes. Christopher Lee, Sue Lyon, Kirk Scott, Lew Ayres, Macdonald Carey, Dean Jagger, Liz Ross. Lee plays a priest and his sinister "double" in this strange sci-fi tale about imminent world destruction by alien invaders. Opens strong but drifts into dullness. [PG]▼]

End of the World in Our Usual Bed in a Night Full of Rain, The SEE: **Night Full of Rain, A**

End of Violence, The (1997) C-122m. ** D: Wim Wenders. Bill Pullman, Andie MacDowell, Gabriel Byrne, Traci Lind, Loren Dean, Daniel Benzali, Pruitt Taylor Vince, John Diehl, Peter Horton, Rosalind Chao, Frederic Forrest, Sam Fuller. Wenders' first American film since PARIS, TEXAS is gorgeous to look at but fuzzy and half-baked. Movie producer Pullman hides out with a Mexican family after surviving a professional "hit" that may have something to do with a high-tech project being run out of L.A.'s Griffith Park Observatory. Lind is appealing as a stuntwoman, MacDowell less so packing a rod while decked out in bikini nightwear. Ry Cooder's score sells the movie to a point, just as it did for UNTIL THE END OF THE WORLD. Super 35. [R]▼●]

Endurance (1999) C-82m. **½ D: Leslie Woodhead. Interesting, well-made docudrama about Ethiopian long-distance runner Haile Gebrselassie, who won a Gold Medal at the 1996 Atlanta Olympic Games. Dramatically recreates his difficult childhood and the decisions leading up to his extraordinary running career. (Haile is portrayed by his nephew

in flashback; his sister plays his mother.) Matter-of-fact, even sleepy at times, and missing the conclusive emotional punch you're waiting for. Olympic footage directed by Bud Greenspan. Coproduced by Terrence Malick and based on his idea. Super 35. [G]▼

Enduring Love (2004-British) C-100m. **½ D: Roger Michell. Daniel Craig, Rhys Ifans, Samantha Morton, Bill Nighy, Susan Lynch, Corin Redgrave. "Obsessive" love might be more apt. Professor Craig, picnicking in the countryside with girlfriend Morton, tries to assist balloonists in distress. Back in London, he not only can't shake the incident, he's puzzled by a visit from Ifans, a rural loner he met that fateful day. Contemporary psychological study of not just love but the fragility of relationships and the world around us; worth checking out. From a novel by Ian McEwan. Craig, director Michell, and producer Kevin Loader teamed the previous year on THE MOTHER. Super 35. [R]❙

Enemies: A Love Story (1989) C-119m. ***½ D: Paul Mazursky. Anjelica Huston, Ron Silver, Lena Olin, Margaret Sophie Stein, Alan King, Judith Malina, Rita Karlin, Phil Leeds, Elya Baskin, Paul Mazursky. Quietly haunting film about an aloof Jewish intellectual (Silver) who managed to hide from the Nazis during WW2 and now, in 1949, leads a double life in Coney Island, N.Y., married to his wartime protector (Stein) and fooling around with a sexy married woman (Olin). Things get even more complicated when his first wife (Huston), who was thought dead, turns up. Typically quixotic Isaac Bashevis Singer material—full of irony, wit, and heartbreak—is beautifully realized by Mazursky (who cowrote the screenplay with Roger L. Simon) and a perfect cast. Kudos also to Pato Guzman for his incredibly evocative production design. [R]▼●]

Enemy at the Gates (2001-German-British-Irish-U.S.) C-131m. **½ D: Jean-Jacques Annaud. Joseph Fiennes, Jude Law, Rachel Weisz, Ed Harris, Bob Hoskins, Ron Perlman, Eva Mattes, Gabriel Marshall-Thomson. A Russian sharpshooter is built up to be a hero to bolster his country's morale during the tense days surrounding the Battle of Stalingrad. As a result, the Germans send their top marksman (Harris) to pick him off, leading to a deadly battle of wits. Starts off strong but loses its way; interesting WW2 story is diminished by a silly romantic subplot. Super 35. [R]▼❙

Enemy Below, The (1957) C-98m. *** D: Dick Powell. Robert Mitchum, Curt Jurgens, Theodore Bikel, Doug McClure, Russell Collins, David Hedison. Fine submarine chase tale, which manages to garner interest from usual crew interaction of U.S. vs. Germany in underwater action; the special effects for this earned Walter Rossi an Academy Award. CinemaScope. ▼●]

Enemy From Space SEE: **Quatermass 2: Enemy from Space**

Enemy Mine (1985) **C-108m.** **½ D: Wolfgang Petersen. Dennis Quaid, Louis Gossett, Jr., Brion James, Richard Marcus. Mortal space enemies are stranded together on a barren planet, forced to become friends in order to survive. Warmhearted science-fiction tale gets a bit too cuddly at times, but it's entertaining. Gossett's lizardlike makeup (by Chris Walas) is incredible; so is Rolf Zehetbauer's production design. Super 35. [PG-13]▼●〗

Enemy of the People, An (1979) **C-103m.** **½ D: George Schaefer. Steve McQueen, Charles Durning, Bibi Andersson, Richard Bradford, Robin Pearson Rose, Richard A. Dysart. Bearded scientist McQueen defies community by taking stand against polluted water system in Arthur Miller's adaptation of the Ibsen play. Sincere, plodding effort was a labor of love for McQueen, but understandably sat on the shelf for years and received limited distribution. Still superior to other films from McQueen's final period. Filmed in 1977. [G]▌

Enemy of the People, An (1989-Indian) **C-100m.** **½ D: Satyajit Ray. Soumitra Chatterjee, Dhritiman Chatterjee, Ruma Guhathakurta, Mamata Shankar, Dipankar Dey. Adaptation of the Ibsen play, updated and set in Bengal. Its message, about the perils of greed, religious fanaticism, and environmental pollution may be topical, but the film is too static. Still, there are enough flashes of Ray's brilliance to make it worthwhile. The director also scripted.

Enemy of the State (1998) **C-132m.** *** D: Tony Scott. Will Smith, Gene Hackman, Jon Voight, Lisa Bonet, Regina King, Stuart Wilson, Tom Sizemore, Loren Dean, Barry Pepper, Ian Hart, Jake Busey, Scott Caan, Jason Lee, Gabriel Byrne, James LeGros, Dan Butler, Jamie Kennedy, Bodhi Pine Elfman, Jack Black. Crackerjack thriller about a successful D.C. lawyer who happens to get in the way of a ruthless executive at the National Security Agency (Voight). The NSA official finds it necessary to ruin the attorney's reputation and throw his life into disarray . . . but the lawyer finds help from an unlikely source. Never takes a breath! Jason Robards appears unbilled. Unrated version runs 140m. Panavision. [R]▼●〗

Enforcer, The (1951) **87m.** *** D: Bretaigne Windust. Humphrey Bogart, Zero Mostel, Ted de Corsia, Everett Sloane, Roy Roberts. When informer de Corsia dies, D.A. Bogart has to find another way to prove that Sloane is the head of a murder-for-hire ring. Loosely based on the true story of Murder, Inc., this is a generally effective, moody thriller. Mostel is particularly good as a frightened crook.▼●〗

Enforcer, The (1976) **C-96m.** *** D: James Fargo. Clint Eastwood, Tyne Daly,

Harry Guardino, Bradford Dillman, John Mitchum, DeVeren Bookwalter, John Crawford, Albert Popwell. Rule-breaking detective Dirty Harry Callahan (Eastwood) has to contend with a female partner (Daly) as he goes after an underground terrorist group in San Francisco. Violent, bubblegum-mentality script, but it's a formula that just seems to work. Followed by SUDDEN IMPACT. Panavision. [R]▼●〗

England Made Me (1973-British) **C-100m.** *** D: Peter Duffell. Peter Finch, Michael York, Hildegard Neil, Michael Hordern, Joss Ackland. Unappreciated in its initial release, drama of a powerful financier in Nazi Germany of 1935 is absorbing, thoughtful fare. Made in Yugoslavia. [PG]

Englishman Who Went Up a Hill but Came Down a Mountain, The (1995-British) **C-99m.** **½ D: Christopher Monger. Hugh Grant, Tara Fitzgerald, Colm Meaney, Ian McNeice, Ian Hart, Kenneth Griffith, Tudor Vaughn, Hugh Vaughn. Two British mapmakers raise the ire of a Welsh community during WW1 when they designate the village's prized landmark a hill and not a you-know-what. Woe be the one-joke movie when the joke isn't much of a grabber, despite being based on real Welsh legend. Agreeable cast and attractive physical trappings definitely help, though Grant's hemhaw acting style probably adds ten minutes to the running time. Panavision. [PG]▼●〗

English Patient, The (1996) **C-162m.** ***½ D: Anthony Minghella. Ralph Fiennes, Juliette Binoche, Willem Dafoe, Kristin Scott Thomas, Naveen Andrews, Colin Firth, Julian Wadham, Jürgen Prochnow, Kevin Whately. Mesmerizing adaptation (by Minghella) of Michael Ondaatje's novel about a man badly burned in a WW2 plane crash in the African desert; a Canadian nurse (Binoche) tends to him in an abandoned monastery in Italy, and slowly, bit by bit, his story emerges. Fiennes and Scott Thomas are perfectly matched in this intelligent, passionate romance about two people thrown together by chance during a tumultuous period. The story unfolds novelistically, layer by layer, drawing the viewer in with its sinuous, sensuous images and jarring depictions of wartime brutality. Strikingly photographed by John Seale. An exceptional achievement all around. Winner of nine Oscars: Best Picture, Director, Cinematography, Supporting Actress (Binoche), Art Direction, Sound, Score (Gabriel Yared), Costumes, and Editing. [R]▼●〗

Enid Is Sleeping (1990) **C-100m.** *** D: Maurice Phillips. Elizabeth Perkins, Judge Reinhold, Jeffrey Jones, Maureen Mueller, Rhea Perlman, Michael J. Pollard. Very black comedy about a woman who accidentally kills her much-hated sister—after being caught sleeping with her husband (who happens to be a police officer). Macabre humor may not be to everyone's taste, but slapstick antics with the "dead" body and genuine character development put this leagues ahead of the similar WEEKEND AT BERNIE'S. Severely cut by its studio, then reclaimed (and restored) by its star and director; a triumph for Perkins, who's never been better. Video title: OVER HER DEAD BODY. [R]▼❍

Enigma (1982-British-French) **C-101m.** **½ D: Jeannot Szwarc. Martin Sheen, Brigitte Fossey, Sam Neill, Derek Jacobi, Michel Lonsdale, Frank Finlay. The KGB sends out five crack assassins to eliminate five Soviet dissidents; CIA agent Sheen (who's apparently seen NOTORIOUS once too often) tries to stop them by having ex-lover Fossey cozy up to top Russian agent Neill. Fine cast does its best with so-so material; script by John Briley. [PG]▼❍

Enigma (2001-British-German-U.S.) **C-119m.** **½ D: Michael Apted. Dougray Scott, Kate Winslet, Jeremy Northam, Saffron Burrows, Tom Hollander, Corin Redgrave. A burned-out cryptographer is brought back to active duty at Bletchley Park where, during WW2, several hundred British operatives work day and night to crack the Nazi code—and understand the workings of their brilliantly designed "enigma" machine. Great material (adapted from Robert Harris' book by Tom Stoppard) and faultless re-creation of the period ought to make for a top-notch film, but this one peters out as it becomes unfocused and—yes—confusing. Coproduced by Mick Jagger, who appears briefly in a club scene. Panavision. [PG-13]▼❍

Enigma of Kaspar Hauser, The SEE: **Every Man for Himself and God Against All**

Enjo (1958-Japanese) **96m.** ***½ D: Kon Ichikawa. Raizo Ichikawa, Tatsuya Nakadai, Ganjiro Nakamura, Yoko Uraji, Tanie Kitabayashi. Troubled young novice priest Ichikawa cannot handle corruption around him and burns down a temple. Perceptive psychological study of a human being's destruction; based on a Yukio Mishima novel, fashioned around a true story. Aka CONFLAGRATION. Daieiscope.▼

Enormous Changes at the Last Minute (1983) **C-115m.** **½ D: Mirra Bank, Ellen Hovde. Maria Tucci, Lynn Milgrim, David Strathairn, Ellen Barkin, Ron McLarty, Zvee Scooler, Kevin Bacon, Jeffrey DeMunn, Sudie Bond. Three separate dramas about contemporary women living in N.Y.C., and their relationships with husbands, ex-husbands, lovers, parents, children. Ambitious but uneven, with some good performances and touching moments. Screenplay by John Sayles with Susan Rice, based on the stories of Grace Paley. "Faith's Story" was filmed in 1978; "Virginia's Story" and "Alexandra's Story" in 1982. Aka TRUMPS.▼❍

Enough (2002) **C-115m.** **½ D: Michael Apted. Jennifer Lopez, Billy Campbell, Juliette Lewis, Dan Futterman, Noah Wyle, Tessa Allen, Russell Milton, Chris Maher, Ruben Madera. Lopez plays a waitress who marries a customer and seems to be living happily ever after until she discovers what kind of man he really is and flees for her life, with her young daughter in tow. Lopez is well cast in this saga of domestic abuse (and revenge), but the ending is so set up and melodramatic that it robs us of real satisfaction. Panavision. [PG-13]▼❍

Enron: The Smartest Guys in the Room (2005) **C-113m.** *** D: Alex Gibney. Sharp documentary, based on the book by Bethany McLean and Peter Elkind, telescopes the Byzantine behind-the-scenes machinations that led to the collapse of the giant Houston energy company. Clean, understandable presentation of the events as they unfolded (with only an occasional nod to "wink-wink" filmmaking) and the larger implicit evils of corporate America. Some of the incriminating footage and facts involving bigwigs Kenneth Lay, Jeff Skilling, and Andy Fastow truly make the mind reel and the stomach turn. [R]❍

Ensign Pulver (1964) **C-104m.** ** D: Joshua Logan. Robert Walker, Jr., Burl Ives, Walter Matthau, Tommy Sands, Millie Perkins, Kay Medford. Flat sequel to MISTER ROBERTS has Walker sinking in Jack Lemmon role amid synthetic seaboard and coral-isle shenanigans. Worth noting for its large cast of future stars: Larry Hagman, Gerald O'Loughlin, Al Freeman, Jr., James Farentino, James Coco, Diana Sands, and Jack Nicholson. Panavision.▼❍

Enter Laughing (1967) **C-112m.** ** D: Carl Reiner. Reni Santoni, Jose Ferrer, Shelley Winters, Elaine May, Jack Gilford, Janet Margolin, David Opatoshu, Michael J. Pollard, Don Rickles, Nancy Kovack, Rob Reiner. Reiner's funny semi-autobiographical Broadway play becomes bland screen comedy as youngster struggles to make it as an actor, despite all manner of problems in his way.▼

Entertainer, The (1960-British) **104m.** ***½ D: Tony Richardson. Laurence Olivier, Brenda de Banzie, Roger Livesey, Joan Plowright, Daniel Massey, Alan Bates, Shirley Anne Field, Albert Finney, Thora Hird. Seedy vaudevillian (Olivier, recreating his stage role) ruins everyone's life and won't catch on. Film captures flavor of chintzy seaside resort, complementing Olivier's brilliance as egotistical song-and-dance man. Coscripted by John Osborne, from his play. Film debuts of Bates and Finney. Olivier and Plowright married the following year. Remade as a 1975 TVM starring Jack Lemmon.▼❍

Entertaining Angels: The Dorothy Day Story (1996) **C-110m.** ** D: Michael Ray Rhodes. Moira Kelly, Martin Sheen, Boyd Kestner, Lenny Von Dohlen, James

Lancaster, Heather Graham, Paul Lieber, Heather Camille. By-the-numbers biography, set in the 1920s and '30s, of Dorothy Day (Kelly), the fabled Roman Catholic activist. Scenario spotlights her spiritual evolution from journalist and suffragette in Greenwich Village to her conversion to Roman Catholicism and her devotion to helping the poor. Disappointingly superficial. [PG-13]▼◖

Entertaining Mr. Sloane (1970-British) **C-94m.** **½ D: Douglas Hickox. Beryl Reid, Harry Andrews, Peter McEnery, Alan Webb. Acting by McEnery, Reid, and Andrews is extraordinary in story of young man who becomes involved with both brother and sister. Uneven adaptation of Joe Orton play.▼

Enter the Dragon (1973) **C-97m.** ***½ D: Robert Clouse. Bruce Lee, John Saxon, Jim Kelly, Ahna Capri, Yang Tse, Angela Mao. Almost perfect Kung Fu film that forgets about plot and concentrates on mind-boggling action. Martial arts expert Lee (in last complete film role) infiltrates strange tournament on island fortress. This was filmed after (but released before) Lee's RETURN OF THE DRAGON. 3m. added on video in 1998. Aka THE DEADLY THREE. Panavision. [R]▼◖●

Enter the Ninja (1981) **C-94m.** *½ D: Menahem Golan. Franco Nero, Susan George, Sho Kosugi, Alex Courtney, Will Hare, Zachi Noy, Dale Ishimoto, Christopher George. Ninjitsu master Nero takes on greedy Christopher George and old rival Kosugi. Third-rate chop-socky actioner and certainly no ENTER THE DRAGON. Original running time: 99m. Followed by REVENGE OF THE NINJA. [R]▼

Entity, The (1983) **C-115m.** ** D: Sidney J. Furie. Barbara Hershey, Ron Silver, Jacqueline Brooks, David Lablosa, George Coe, Margaret Blye, Alex Rocco. Woman is raped repeatedly by giant invisible mass. Her psychiatrist thinks it's all in the mind, until parapsychologists set a trap for the critter. Effectively sensational but atrociously exploitive; supposedly based on actual incident. Panavision. [R]▼◖

Entrapment (1999) **C-112m.** **½ D: Jon Amiel. Sean Connery, Catherine Zeta-Jones, Will Patton, Ving Rhames, Maury Chaykin. American insurance investigator Zeta-Jones convinces her boss to let her set the bait to capture world-class art thief Connery, leading to a gigantic cat-and-mouse game played out in London and Kuala Lumpur. The two stars are easy to watch, and there are lots of gimmicky action scenes, but it's all rather flat. Connery coexecutive-produced. Panavision. [PG-13]▼◖●

Entre Nous (1983-French) **C-110m.** ***½ D: Diane Kurys. Miou Miou, Isabelle Huppert, Guy Marchand, Jean-Pierre Bacri, Robin Renucci, Patrick Bauchau. Moving,

multilayered story of two women who form a bond of friendship that lasts many years, takes many turns, and threatens their ineffectual husbands. Compassionate telling by Kurys of her own mother's story, with extraordinary performances all around. Original French title: COUP DE FOUDRE. Followed by C'EST LA VIE. Panavision. [PG]▼◖

Envy (2004) **C-99m.** *½ D: Barry Levinson. Ben Stiller, Jack Black, Rachel Weisz, Christopher Walken, Amy Poehler. The close relationship between two best friends who live across the street from each other changes drastically when one of them hits the jackpot with an invention that turns him into a multimillionaire. The cast can't be faulted for this wrongheaded comedy misfire, but the script can; it's unpleasant at best, mean at worst, a sketch idea drawn out to feature length. [PG-13]▼◖

Epic Movie (2007) **C-85m.** BOMB D: Jason Friedberg, Aaron Seltzer. Kal Penn, Adam Campbell, Jennifer Coolidge, Jayma Mays, Faune A. Chambers. Four siblings find themselves meandering through lame slapstick parodies of recent epic movies and other obvious pop-culture targets. Typically tedious, unfunny hack job, with an array of cameo appearances including Crispin Glover, who (as a perverted, sadistic Willy Wonka) provides the film with its only moments of admittedly sordid energy. Unrated version runs 93m. [PG-13]◖

Equilibrium (2002) **C-107m.** ** D: Kurt Wimmer. Christian Bale, Emily Watson, Taye Diggs, Angus Macfadyen, Sean Bean, David Hemmings, Matthew Harbour, William Fichtner. In the future, any display of emotion is against the law; citizens take a daily drug, and transgressors are punished by an elite corps of police. Writer-director Wimmer's warmed-over rehash of *1984, Brave New World,* and *Fahrenheit 451* doesn't make a lot of sense (some of the leading characters *do* show emotion), but it isn't worth the time or effort to figure out. Bale is so intense here it seems as if he might implode at any moment. Super 35. [R]▼◖

Equinox (1971) **C-80m.** ** D: Jack Woods. Edward Connell, Barbara Hewitt, Frank Boers, Jr. (Frank Bonner), Robin Christopher, Jack Woods, Fritz Leiber. Archaeology students confront Satanism—and mutantlike monsters—while searching for vanished professor. Late-1960s amateur film (directed by later special-effects Oscar winner Dennis Muren) was reworked for theatrical release, mixing movie clichés with good special effects. This film took several years to complete, and the young cast obviously ages in it. Aka THE BEAST. [M/PG]▼◖

Equinox (1993) **C-110m.** ** D: Alan Rudolph. Matthew Modine, Lara Flynn Boyle, Fred Ward, Tyra Ferrell, Marisa Tomei, Kevin J. O'Connor, Tate Donovan, Lori Singer, M. Emmet Walsh, Gailard Sartain,

Mark Modine. Slow-moving mystery with Modine playing two men—a weakling auto mechanic and an underworld tough guy—who live in the same city and lead parallel lives. Typically quirky Rudolph drama, but weaker than most; rife with commentary on contemporary mores and morals. [R] ▼●

Equus (1977) C-138m. **½ D: Sidney Lumet. Richard Burton, Peter Firth, Colin Blakely, Joan Plowright, Harry Andrews, Eileen Atkins, Jenny Agutter. Peter Shaffer's shattering play makes bumpy screen adaptation, its vivid theatricality lost on film; Burton, however, is superb as troubled psychiatrist trying to unlock deep-rooted problems of stable boy Firth. [R] ▼●)

Eragon (2006) C-104m. ** D: Stefen Fangmeier. Ed Speleers, Jeremy Irons, Sienna Guillory, Robert Carlyle, John Malkovich, Djimon Hounsou, Garrett Hedlund, Alun Armstrong, Joss Stone; voice of Rachel Weisz. Orphaned farm boy finds a mysterious egg that hatches the last of an extinct breed of magical dragons. The boy, the dragon, and his world-weary, wise old mentor travel across magical lands to save the oppressed people of his home kingdom from an evil king and his henchman wizard. Scenery is pretty and CGI effects are fine, but the movie is a patchwork quilt of conventions borrowed from other fantasy films and stories (with none of their entertainment value). Based on the first in a series of popular books by Christopher Paolini. Super 35. [PG]●

Eraser (1996) C-114m. *** D: Charles Russell. Arnold Schwarzenegger, James Caan, Vanessa Williams, James Coburn, Robert Pastorelli, James Cromwell, Danny Nucci, Joe Vittarelli, John Slattery, Roma Maffia, Camryn Manheim. High-octane, high-tech, violent and cartoonish action-thriller about a specialist in the Federal Witness Protection Program who vows to keep a female witness safe and sticks to his word even after he becomes as much a target as she. Explosive, cutting-edge action and special effects give fans their money's worth, and then some. Indefensible on any artistic level, but lots of fun. Panavision. [R] ▼●)

Eraserhead (1978) 90m. *** D: David Lynch. John (Jack) Nance, Charlotte Stewart, Allen Joseph, Jeanne Bates, Judith Anna Roberts, Laurel Near, V. Phipps-Wilson. Brooding experimental film full of repulsive imagery tells story of zombielike misfit, his spastic girlfriend, and their half-human offspring. Bona fide cult film is full of surreal, nightmarish tangents. Feature film debut of director Lynch. ▼●)

Erendira (1983-Mexican-French-German) C-103m. **½ D: Ruy Guerra. Irene Papas, Claudia Ohana, Michael Lonsdale, Oliver Wehe, Rufus. Strange does not begin to describe this fable of queenly Papas forcing beautiful, obedient granddaughter Ohana into prostitution in a vast, surreal desert. Ambitious and fluidly directed, but unmemorable; from a screenplay by Gabriel Garcia Marquez. Remade as ERENDIRA IKIKUNARI (2008). ▼

Erik the Conqueror (1961-Italian) C-81m. ** D: Mario Bava. Cameron Mitchell, Alice Kessler, Ellen Kessler, Françoise Christophe. Unexceptional account of 10th-century Viking life, with Mitchell fighting for virtue and love. Released on video as THE INVADERS at 88m. Dyaliscope. ▼)

Erik the Viking (1989-British) C-104m. BOMB D: Terry Jones. Tim Robbins, Mickey Rooney, Eartha Kitt, Terry Jones, Imogen Stubbs, John Cleese, Antony Sher, Gordon John Sinclair, Freddie Jones. Robbins is a revisionist Erik, but what's the Norse expression for "unwatchable satire"? Director's cut runs 79m. [PG-13] ▼●)

Erin Brockovich (2000) C-131m. *** D: Steven Soderbergh. Julia Roberts, Albert Finney, Aaron Eckhart, Marg Helgenberger, Cherry Jones, Conchata Ferrell, Tracey Walter, Mimi Kennedy, Peter Coyote. Roberts won a Best Actress Oscar for her performance as a brassy, divorced mother of three, at the end of her rope; she talks her way into a job in Finney's law office, then becomes obsessed with a pro bono case involving residents of a California desert town who have been exposed to poisonously polluted water. Energetic, engaging David vs. Goliath story never states—or overstates—the obvious, and travels far on Roberts' charisma and Finney's expertise. That's the real Erin Brockovich playing a waitress. [R] ▼)

Ernest Goes to Camp (1987) C-93m. *½ D: John R. Cherry 3rd. Jim Varney, Victoria Racimo, John Vernon, Iron Eyes Cody, Lyle Alzado, Gailard Sartain. Ernest, an obnoxious dimwit popularized in a spate of TV commercials, is the star of this clumsy and unfunny comedy about a dumb cluck who wants to be a summer camp counselor in the worst way—and gets his wish. Aimed at children who aren't very bright. Followed by ERNEST SAVES CHRISTMAS. [PG] ▼●)

Ernest Goes to Jail (1990) C-82m. ** D: John Cherry. Jim Varney, Gailard Sartain, Bill Byrge, Barbara Bush, Randall (Tex) Cobb, Barry Scott, Charles Napier. Third in the surprisingly successful series about Ernest P. Worrell finds our hero in prison as the result of a switch set up by an evil inmate lookalike (also played by Varney). Harmless, predictable, and hokey. Followed by ERNEST SCARED STUPID. [PG] ▼●)

Ernest Goes to School (1994) C-90m. BOMB D: Coke Sams. Jim Varney, Linda Kash, Bill Byrge, Corrine Koslo, Kevin McNulty, Jason Michas. Sub-atomic brain accelerator is used to make Chickasaw Falls High's school custodian, Ernest, a temporary genius in an attempt to undermine a plot to close the school. Completely predictable and unfunny;

only for die-hard Ernest fans. Followed by SLAM DUNK ERNEST. [PG]▼●

Ernest Saves Christmas (1988) **C-89m.** *½ D: John Cherry. Jim Varney, Douglas Seale, Oliver Clark, Noelle Parker, Robert Lesser, Gailard Sartain, Billie Bird. The title character, who makes Gomer Pyle seem like Albert Einstein, attempts to help Santa Claus on Christmas Eve. This is one Christmas present to be opened with extreme caution . . . unless you're a fan of Ernest P. Worrell. Followed by ERNEST GOES TO JAIL. [PG]▼●

Ernest Scared Stupid (1991) **C-91m.** *½ D: John Cherry. Jim Varney, Eartha Kitt, Austin Nagler, Jonas Moscartolo, Shay Astar. The fourth Ernest P. Worrell feature has a patently redundant title. Originally released at Halloween time, the story has dimwitted Ernest inadvertently releasing a villainous troll from its tomb. Pretty lame; Kitt is wasted as a witch. Followed by ERNEST GOES TO SCHOOL. [PG]▼●

Eros (2004-French-Italian-U.S.-Hong Kong) **C/B&W-108m.** *½ D: Wong Kar-wai, Steven Soderbergh, Michelangelo Antonioni. Gong Li, Chang Chen, Robert Downey, Jr., Alan Arkin, Christopher Buchholz, Regina Nemni, Luisa Ranieri. As if they were facing an overpowering baseball pitcher in the ninth inning, three internationally renowned directors strike out 1-2-3 in this anthology. Wong's episode is the meatiest, but seems twice as long as it is: A young tailor remains faithful to a courtesan (Gong) through her long professional slide. Shrink Arkin and patient Downey bandy in Soderbergh's shaggy dog joke, unworthy of the wait for a punch line. Antonioni's segment about an impaired relationship is the least substantive but most fun to watch; he still has his camera eye. [R]●

Erotique (1993-U.S.-German) **C-93m.** ** D: Lizzie Borden, Monika Treut, Clara Law. Kamela Lopez-Dawson, Bryan Cranston, Liane Curtis, Priscilla Barnes, Camilla Soeberg, Michael Carr, Peter Kern, Marianne Sägebrecht, Tim Lounibos, Hayley Man, Choi Hark-kin. Uneven feature in three parts, each a story with a female slant. Borden's piece, about a phone sex worker exacting revenge against one of her callers, is obvious and annoying; Treut tells the trite tale of a pair of lesbians who set out to seduce a man. By far the best of the lot is Law's perceptive study of the cultural differences between a Hong Kong woman and her Australian-Chinese boyfriend. A fourth episode, the muddled account of a teacher's erotic encounter while on a trip, was excluded from the final print but added to the video release. It is directed by Ana Maria Magalhaes and stars Claudia Ohana and Guilherme Leme. Video running time is 117m.▼●

Errand Boy, The (1961) **92m.** **½ D: Jerry Lewis. Jerry Lewis, Brian Donlevy,

Howard McNear, Sig Ruman, Fritz Feld, Iris Adrian, Kathleen Freeman, Doodles Weaver, Renee Taylor. Jerry on the loose in a movie studio has its moments. Long string of gags provide the laughter; veteran character actors produce the sparkle. ▼●

Escapade (1955-British) **87m.** *** D: Philip Leacock. John Mills, Yvonne Mitchell, Alastair Sim, Jeremy Spenser, Andrew Ray, Marie Lohr, Peter Asher. Mills is a professional pacifist whose life is anything but tranquil; his three sons, fearing that their parents are about to be divorced, react in a most unusual manner. Ambitious, insightful, solidly acted drama about the cynicism and hypocrisy of adults and the idealism of youth. Stick with this.▼

Escapade in Japan (1957) **C-93m.** ** D: Arthur Lubin. Cameron Mitchell, Teresa Wright, Jon Provost, Roger Nakagawa, Philip Ober, Kuniko Miyake, Susumu Fujita. Stunning location filming in Japan is the prime asset of this forgettable adventure about two young boys, one American and the other Japanese, and their search for the former's parents. Clint Eastwood appears briefly as a pilot. Technirama. ▼

Escape (1940) **104m.** *** D: Mervyn LeRoy. Norma Shearer, Robert Taylor, Conrad Veidt, Nazimova, Felix Bressart, Albert Basserman, Philip Dorn, Bonita Granville, Blanche Yurka. Countess Shearer, mistress of Nazi general Veidt, helps Taylor get his mother (Nazimova) out of German concentration camp before WW2; polished, with sterling cast. Based on Ethel Vance's 1939 best-seller. ❿

Escape (1948) **78m.** *** D: Joseph L. Mankiewicz. Rex Harrison, Peggy Cummins, William Hartnell, Norman Wooland, Jill Esmond, Frederick Piper, Marjorie Rhodes, Betty Ann Davies, Cyril Cusack. Intelligent, well-paced story of law-abiding man for whom a chance encounter leads to a prison sentence; morally outraged, he determines to escape. Harrison is excellent as the cerebral hero of this John Galsworthy story (which was filmed before in 1930). Shot on natural locations around England. Screenplay by Philip Dunne.

Escape (1970) SEE: **McKenzie Break, The**

Escape Artist, The (1982) **C-96m.** ** D: Caleb Deschanel. Griffin O'Neal, Raul Julia, Teri Garr, Joan Hackett, Gabriel Dell, Elizabeth Daily, Desiderio (Desi) Arnaz, Huntz Hall, Jackie Coogan, M. Emmet Walsh, David Clennon, Harry Anderson, Carlin Glynn, Margaret Ladd. Maddeningly muddled tale of teenager O'Neal, an amateur magician, and the adults who attempt to exploit him. Griffin, son of Ryan and brother of Tatum, has a pleasing screen presence. Directorial debut for cinematographer Deschanel. [PG]▼●

Escape From Alcatraz (1979) **C-112m.** *** D: Donald Siegel. Clint Eastwood,

Patrick McGoohan, Roberts Blossom, Jack Thibeau, Fred Ward, Paul Benjamin. Straightforward, methodical telling of true story about 1962 breakout from supposedly impregnable prison. Vivid and credible throughout. Watch for Danny Glover in his film debut. [PG]▼●❍

Escape From Fort Bravo (1953) **C-98m.** *** D: John Sturges. William Holden, Eleanor Parker, John Forsythe, Polly Bergen, William Demarest, William Campbell, Richard Anderson. Well-executed Civil War–era Western with Holden a hard-nosed cavalry captain at an Arizona fort where Confederate prisoners are held; both sides end up tangling with Indians.▼❍

Escape From L.A. (1996) **C-101m.** ** D: John Carpenter. Kurt Russell, Stacy Keach, Steve Buscemi, Cliff Robertson, Valeria Golino, Peter Fonda, Michelle Forbes, A. J. Langer, George Corraface, Pam Grier, Robert Carradine, Bruce Campbell, Paul Bartel. In the year 2013, the Island of L.A. is a penal colony for America's undesirables. Snake Plissken (Russell) is sent there to bring back a valuable destruction device that was smuggled away by the daughter of the U.S. President. Lackluster follow-up to ESCAPE FROM NEW YORK is tongue-in-cheek, but devoid of wit, and not likely to satisfy action fans, either. Russell coproduced and cowrote the script. On-screen title: JOHN CARPENTER'S ESCAPE FROM L.A. Panavision. [R]▼●❍

Escape From New York (1981) **C-99m.** ** D: John Carpenter. Kurt Russell, Lee Van Cleef, Ernest Borgnine, Donald Pleasence, Isaac Hayes, Adrienne Barbeau, Harry Dean Stanton, Season Hubley. For a "fun" film this is pretty bleak. The year is 1997, Manhattan is a maximum-security prison, and a character named Snake Plissken (Russell) must effect a daring rescue from within its borders. Reminiscent in some ways of Carpenter's ASSAULT ON PRECINCT 13, which was smaller—and better. Followed by ESCAPE FROM L.A. Panavision. [R]▼●❍

Escape From Planet Earth SEE: **Doomsday Machine, The**

Escape From the Dark SEE: **Littlest Horse Thieves, The**

Escape From the Planet of the Apes (1971) **C-98m.** *** D: Don Taylor. Roddy McDowall, Kim Hunter, Bradford Dillman, Natalie Trundy, Eric Braeden, William Windom, Sal Mineo, Ricardo Montalban. Third in series is best of the sequels, with the Apes in modern-day L.A.; ingeniously paves the way for 4th and 5th entries in series. Followed by CONQUEST OF THE PLANET OF THE APES. Panavision. [G]▼●❍

Escape Me Never (1947) **104m.** *½ D: Peter Godfrey. Errol Flynn, Ida Lupino, Eleanor Parker, Gig Young, Reginald Denny, Isobel Elsom. Sappy remake of 1935 Elisa-beth Bergner vehicle, with Lupino as an itinerant waif (!) and Flynn as struggling composer who marries her but takes up with his brother's aristocratic fiancée (Parker). Forget it.▼

Escape to Athena (1979-British) **C-101m.** **½ D: George Pan Cosmatos. Roger Moore, Telly Savalas, David Niven, Claudia Cardinale, Richard Roundtree, Stefanie Powers, Sonny Bono, Elliott Gould, William Holden. Agreeable time-filler, with all-star cast in outlandish adventure yarn about WW2 POWs planning escape and art heist at the same time. Released in England at 125m. Panavision. [PG]▼

Escape to Burma (1955) **C-87m.** ** D: Allan Dwan. Barbara Stanwyck, Robert Ryan, David Farrar, Murvyn Vye, Lisa Montell, Reginald Denny. Stanwyck rides herd over a tea plantation—and a pack of wild animals—but doesn't quite know how to deal with a wanted man who seeks refuge. Cast does what it can with pulp material. SuperScope.▼❍

Escape to the Sun (1972-British-Israeli) **105m.** *½ D: Menahem Golan. Laurence Harvey, Josephine Chaplin, John Ireland, Lila Kedrova, Jack Hawkins, Clive Revill. Suspense tale about aftermath of unsuccessful attempt by Soviet Jews to hijack a plane wastes a capable cast. [PG]▼

Escape to Witch Mountain (1975) **C-97m.** *** D: John Hough. Eddie Albert, Ray Milland, Kim Richards, Ike Eisenmann, Donald Pleasence. Excellent Disney mystery-fantasy: two children with mysterious powers try to discover their origins, while being pursued by evil Milland, who wants to use their powers for his own purposes. Remade for TV. Followed by sequel RETURN FROM WITCH MOUNTAIN. [G]▼●❍

Escape 2000 (1981-Australian) **C-92m.** BOMB D: Brian Trenchard-Smith. Steve Railsback, Olivia Hussey, Michael Craig, Carmen Duncan, Roger Ward. Repellently violent, unpleasant ripoff of THE MOST DANGEROUS GAME, set in future society where criminals are hunted in a controlled environment. Original title: TURKEY SHOOT. Beware of alternate 80m. version. Panavision. [R]▼❍

Especially on Sunday (1991-Italian-French-Belgian) **C-90m.** **½ D: Giuseppe Tornatore, Giuseppe Bertolucci, Marco Tullio Giordana. Philippe Noiret, Ornella Muti, Bruno Ganz, Maria Maddalena Fellini, Chiara Caselli, Andrea Prodan, Bruno Berdini, Nicoletta Braschi, Jean-Hugues Anglade. Trio of short films, each set in the Italian countryside, is a mixed bag. The first, by Tornatore (featuring Noiret as a barber who is comically harassed by a dog), is slight; the second, by Bertolucci (middle-aged Ganz picks up a pretty young woman and her mentally ill brother), is trite; the third, by Giordana (widow Fellini develops a most unusual unspoken bond with her new daughter-in-law), is the best of the lot, a thoughtful meditation on loneliness. Fellini is Federico's sister; this is her screen debut. European release version includes a fourth film, by Francesco Barilli. [R]

Esther and the King (1960-U.S.-Italian) C-109m. ** D: Raoul Walsh. Joan Collins, Richard Egan, Denis O'Dea, Sergio Fantoni. Cardboard biblical costumer pretends to re-create 4th-century B.C. Persia, with stony performances by Egan and Collins as the king and the Jewish maiden he wants to replace murdered queen. Filmed in Italy. CinemaScope.▼❙

Esther Kahn (2000-French-British) C-145m. *½ D: Arnaud Desplechin. Summer Phoenix, Ian Holm, Fabrice Desplechin, Frances Barber, Ian Bartholomew, Emmanuelle Devos. Overlong, overwrought drama about a single-minded young Jewess in late-19th-century London who struggles with her feelings and fears while setting out to become an actress. Potentially interesting subject matter is done in by boring stretches, laughably stilted dialogue, a maddeningly uneven lead performance by Phoenix, and unnecessary narration that telegraphs points and emotions. A plus: Eric Gautier's luminous cinematography.▼❙

Eternal Sunshine of the Spotless Mind (2004) C-108m. *** D: Michel Gondry. Jim Carrey, Kate Winslet, Kirsten Dunst, Mark Ruffalo, Elijah Wood, Tom Wilkinson, Jane Adams, David Cross, Deirdre O'Connell. A man learns his ex-girlfriend has had him literally erased from her memory and decides to get the same procedure done . . . but has second thoughts as his mind is being purged. Ingenious, Oscar-winning screenplay by Charlie Kaufman (from a story by Kaufman, Gondry, and Pierre Bismuth) is extremely well executed by director Gondry (and cinematographer Ellen Kuras), though the film tends to cleverly dance around the roots of emotional and romantic pain rather than fully engage them. Carrey has never been better; Winslet is (as always) exceptional. [R]▼❙

Ethan Frome (1993) C-107m. **½ D: John Madden. Liam Neeson, Patricia Arquette, Joan Allen, Tate Donovan, Katharine Houghton, Stephen Mendillo. Stately, just-adequate adaptation of Edith Wharton's famed 1911 novella of tragedy, irony, and repression, set in rural New England: the tale of a farmer who weds a domineering woman (Allen), then falls in love with her poor but pretty cousin (Arquette). Beautifully photographed (by Bobby Bukowski) and intelligently scripted (by Richard Nelson), but not as powerful and moving as it should be. An *American Playhouse* theatrical feature. [PG]▼❍❙

E.T. The Extra-Terrestrial (1982) C-115m. **** D: Steven Spielberg. Dee Wallace, Henry Thomas, Peter Coyote, Robert MacNaughton, Drew Barrymore, K.C. Martel, Sean Frye, Tom (C. Thomas) Howell. A 10-year-old boy (Thomas) befriends a creature from another planet that's been stranded on Earth. A warm, insightful story of childhood innocence, frustration, courage, and love . . . with a remarkable "performance" by E.T. An exhilarating experience for young and old alike. Screenplay by Melissa Mathison. John Williams won an Oscar for his soaring score, as did the sound and visual effects teams. Trivia note: Debra Winger contributed to E.T.'s voice. Reissued in a somewhat revised form in 2002, running 123m. [PG]▼❍❙

Eulogy (2004) C-91m. ** D: Michael Clancy. Hank Azaria, Jesse Bradford, Zooey Deschanel, Glenne Headly, Famke Janssen, Piper Laurie, Kelly Preston, Ray Romano, Rip Torn, Debra Winger, Curtis Garcia, Keith Garcia, Paget Brewster, Rene Auberjonois, Claudette Nevins, Micole Mercurio, Rance Howard. Dysfunctional family reunites over the death of the patriarch and standard sitcom shenanigans ensue, with frantic mugging and bad sex jokes. Hard to totally fail with this caliber of ensemble players, but still pretty weak. Laurie and Deschanel come off best as suicidal grandmother and her granddaughter (the only normal one in the pack). Winger uncharacteristically hits all the wrong notes as a homophobic, neurotic aunt. [R]▼❙

Eureka (1983) C-130m. ** D: Nicolas Roeg. Gene Hackman, Theresa Russell, Rutger Hauer, Jane Lapotaire, Ed Lauter, Mickey Rourke, Joe Pesci, Corin Redgrave. Klondike prospector becomes fabulously wealthy, watches his kingdom crumble 30 years later when his daughter's problems and Miami thugs converge on him at the same time. Odd drama, even for Roeg, that somehow climaxes with long, windy courtroom histrionics. Shelved by its studio, sporadically released in 1985. Aka RIVER OF DARKNESS. [R]▼❙

Eureka (2000-Japanese-French) 217m. **½ D: Shinji Aoyama. Koji Yakusho, Aoi Miyazaki, Masaru Miyazaki, Yoichiro Saito. A tragic and shattering event has life-changing consequences for both a bus driver and the two orphaned children who are the only survivors of the incident. Epic film deals with the aftermath of a traumatic moment as the characters search for meaning and redemption. Beautifully shot in black and white, this demanding film does have rewards for the adventurous filmgoer but is ultimately compromised by its indulgent overlength.

Europa Europa (1991-French-German) C-115m. ***½ D: Agnieszka Holland. Marco Hofschneider, Rene Hofschneider, Julie Delpy, Ashley Wanninger, Piotr Kozlowski, Halina Labornarska, Hanns Zischler. German-Jewish teenage boy flees the Nazis and conceals his identity—only to find himself drafted into Hitler's army! Eye-opening, fact-based WW2 Holocaust drama, from Solomon Perel's autobiography, is both harrowing and humorous; deftly blends horrific images with black comedy to depict the growing pains of a boy becoming a man in the midst of a world in chaos. Polish writer-director Holland has made a riveting and moving film. [R]▼●)

Europa '51 SEE: **Greatest Love, The**

Europeans, The (1979) **C-90m.** *** D: James Ivory. Lee Remick, Robin Ellis, Wesley Addy, Tim Choate, Lisa Eichhorn, Tim Woodward, Kristin Griffith. Meticulous film of Henry James novel vividly recreates 19th-century life in New England, as the arrival of two foreign cousins disrupts the stern-faced calm of a plain American family. Deliberately paced, but richly rewarding.▼●)

Eurotrip (2004) **C-92m.** ** D: Jeff Schaffer. Scott Mechlowicz, Jacob Pitts, Michelle Trachtenberg, Travis Wester, Jessica Boehrs, Vinnie Jones, Lucy Lawless, Fred Armisen, Diedrich Bader, Patrick Malahide, Matt Damon, Joanna Lumley. A high school grad who's just been dumped by his girlfriend goes to Europe to meet a German e-mail pen pal (who, he's just learned, is a hot babe); he and three hometown pals have a series of misadventures along the way. All too typical teen comedy should please adolescent boys with its female nudity and gross-out gags; others will take their cue from the fact that there is a vomit joke in the animated main titles! Jeffrey Tambor appears unbilled. Unrated version available on DVD. [R] ▼)

Eva (1962-British) **100m.** *** D: Joseph Losey. Jeanne Moreau, Stanley Baker, Virna Lisi, Nona Medici, Francesco Rissone, James Villiers. Brooding account of writer Baker whose continued attraction for Eva (Moreau) causes wife (Lisi) to have tragic death. Premise isn't always workable, but Moreau is well cast as personification of evil. Based on a novel by James Hadley Chase. Director's cut (titled EVE) runs 119m.▼)

Evan Almighty (2007) **C-96m.** *½ D: Tom Shadyac. Steve Carell, Morgan Freeman, Lauren Graham, John Goodman, Wanda Sykes, John Michael Higgins, Jonah Hill, Molly Shannon, Harve Presnell, Johnny Simmons, Graham Phillips, Jimmy Bennett. In this follow-up to BRUCE ALMIGHTY former newscaster Evan Baxter (Carell), a newly elected congressman, is told by God (Freeman) to build an enormous ark in preparation for a devastating flood. Wacky hijinks ensue. Wasting the likable and talented Carell, this shrill farce tries to sugarcoat its religious conservatism with a feel-good sitcom style, but possesses about as much genuine spirituality as a

velvet painting of Jesus. And is God really creating a flood to get back at a crooked Washington lawmaker? Super 35. [PG]❙

Evel Knievel (1972) **C-90m.** **½ D: Marvin Chomsky. George Hamilton, Sue Lyon, Bert Freed, Rod Cameron. Biography of daredevil motorcyclist contains some great action footage; modest but effective film. Shouldn't be confused with VIVA KNIEVEL! (in which Evel played himself). Remade for cable TV in 2004. [PG]▼)

Evelyn (2002-U.S.-Irish-British) **C-95m.** **½ D: Bruce Beresford. Pierce Brosnan, Aidan Quinn, Stephen Rea, Alan Bates, Julianna Margulies, Sophie Vavasseur. Brosnan's company produced this button-pushing, feelgood movie based on the true story of a working-class Irishman who has to battle the government to regain custody of his sons and daughter after his wife walks out on them. Set in 1953, the film doesn't seem to trust the inherent drama in its story, and plays everything broadly, with nudge-nudge wink-wink acting by its able cast. Could have, and should have, been much better. Panavision. [PG] ▼)

Even Cowgirls Get the Blues (1994) **C-97m.** BOMB D: Gus Van Sant. Uma Thurman, Lorraine Bracco, Angie Dickinson, Rain Phoenix, John Hurt, Roseanne Arnold, Keanu Reeves, Noriyuki "Pat" Morita, Sean Young, Crispin Glover, Ed Begley, Jr., Faye Dunaway, Steve Buscemi, Heather Graham, Victoria Williams, Carol Kane, Grace Zabriskie. Tom Robbins' hopelessly dated novel about a hitchhiker with oversized thumbs is a candidate for the decade's worst movie: there is not enough peyote in the entire American Southwest to render scenes set in the feminist-collective ranch comprehensible or possible to endure. Recut by the director after its stormy reception at the Toronto Film Festival knocked it off the '93 release schedule. The k.d. lang score is the movie's sole worthy component. William S. Burroughs is briefly seen at film's beginning on a N.Y.C. street. [R]▼)

Even Dwarfs Started Small (1970-German) **96m.** *** D: Werner Herzog. Helmut Doring, Gerd Gickel, Paul Glauer, Erna Gschwnedtner, Gisela Hartwig. Unusual, disturbing, truly unsettling parable about dwarfs and midgets confined to a barren correctional institution who literally take over the asylum. Reminiscent of Tod Browning's FREAKS.▼)

Evening (2007) **C-117m.** ** D: Lajos Koltai. Claire Danes, Toni Collette, Vanessa Redgrave, Patrick Wilson, Hugh Dancy, Natasha Richardson, Mamie Gummer, Eileen Atkins, Meryl Streep, Glenn Close, Barry Bostwick. Two sisters try to interpret their mother's ramblings while on her deathbed; they eventually learn about the unfulfilled love of her life in a series of extended flashbacks. Lugubrious translation of Susan Minot's time-skipping novel (by the author and Michael Cunningham), filmed on location in Newport, Rhode Island. Gummer is Streep's real-life daughter; they play the same character, young and old. Richardson is Redgrave's daughter, and they play mother and daughter on-screen. Super 35. [PG-13]▐

Evening Star, The (1996) **C-129m. ★★** D: Robert Harling. Shirley MacLaine, Bill Paxton, Juliette Lewis, Miranda Richardson, Ben Johnson, Scott Wolf, George Newbern, Marion Ross, Mackenzie Astin, Donald Moffat, China Kantner, Jack Nicholson, Jennifer Grant. The further adventures of feisty, eccentric Aurora Greenway, who's now raised three grandchildren (born to Debra Winger in TERMS OF ENDEARMENT). Trades on the memory of a much better movie; even Nicholson's brief appearance only reminds us of the earlier film. There's barely an honest moment in the picture. Ross stands out as MacLaine's loyal longtime housekeeper and friend. Based on Larry McMurtry's novel. Johnson's final film. [PG-13]▼○▐

Even Money (2007-U.S.-German) **C-113m. ★★** D: Mark Rydell. Forest Whitaker, Kim Basinger, Danny DeVito, Kelsey Grammer, Ray Liotta, Tim Roth, Jay Mohr, Nick Cannon, Carla Gugino, Grant Sullivan. Melancholy look at a handful of losers and dreamers—including compulsive gamblers Whitaker and Basinger, has-been magician DeVito, underworld boss Roth, and smalltime bookies Mohr and Sullivan. The resolutions to these stories are alternately squalid and improbable. Good performances pique your interest at first, but the movie runs out of gas. Director Rydell has a cameo near the end. [R]▐

Event, The (2003-Canadian) **C-110m. ★½** D: Thom Fitzgerald. Parker Posey, Don McKellar, Sarah Polley, Jane Leeves, Brent Carver, Olympia Dukakis, Joanna P. Adler, Dick Latessa, Christina Zorich. The investigation of an apparent suicide, one of a series of mysterious deaths in the gay community of N.Y.C.'s Chelsea neighborhood, leads to surprising revelations. Well intentioned but destroyed by a hopelessly muddled script, pedestrian direction, and a series of overdrawn stereotypes. Only Dukakis emerges with dignity intact, somehow managing to create yet another memorable screen mother. Cowritten by the director. [R]▼▐

Event Horizon (1997-U.S.-British) **C-95m. ★★** D: Paul Anderson. Laurence Fishburne, Sam Neill, Kathleen Quinlan, Joely Richardson, Richard T. Jones, Jack Noseworthy, Jason Isaacs, Sean Pertwee. In 2047, a rescue mission is launched to Neptune when the exploration ship *Event Horizon* reappears as mysteriously as it had vanished seven years before. The returned ship's crew is gone, but there's a disturbing presence aboard, perhaps connected to the black hole designed to warp space. Well-acted

movie begins promisingly but becomes increasingly unlikely; offers no explanation for the strange events. Some intense horror scenes. Panavision. [R]▼○▐

Eve of Destruction (1991) **C-98m. ★★** D: Duncan Gibbins. Gregory Hines, Renee Soutendijk, Michael Greene, Kurt Fuller, John M. Jackson, Kevin McCarthy. This muddled FRANKENSTEIN variation might have worked with a better script, and without a point of view that manages to at the same time be reverse-sexist and anti-feminist. Soutendijk gives her all in a dual role: Dr. Eve Simmons, a scientist, and Eve VIII, the android/robot bomb she's created in her own likeness—and which is running amok. Hines is the good guy who sets out to immobilize it. Dutch actress Soutendijk's U.S. film debut. [R]▼○▐

Ever After (1998) **C-122m. ★★★** D: Andy Tennant. Drew Barrymore, Anjelica Huston, Dougray Scott, Patrick Godfrey, Megan Dodds, Melanie Lynskey, Timothy West, Judy Parfitt, Jeroen Krabbé, Richard O'Brien, Jeanne Moreau, Toby Jones. The Queen of France (Moreau) summons the Brothers Grimm to her castle so she may tell them the true story of Cinderella: what unfolds is a charming rethinking of the classic fairy tale, with Barrymore as a feisty orphan (named Danielle) who puts her potential Prince Charming to shame with her bravery and regard for humankind. Long, but exquisitely filmed on location in France. Barrymore is a delight as a Cinderella for feminists. Alternate version is rated PG. Super 35. [PG-13] ▼○▐

Everlasting Moments (2008-Swedish) **C-131m. ★★★** D: Jan Troell. Maria Heiskanen, Mikael Persbrandt, Jesper Christensen, Callin Öhrvall, Ghita Nørby, Amanda Ooms, Emil Jensen. In early 20th-century Sweden a hardworking woman with many children—and a lusty, often abusive husband—finds purpose (and solace) by taking photographs with a camera she won in a lottery. Absorbing, evocative period piece is meticulously realized by Troell, who also shot the film (in collaboration with Mischa Gavrjusjov) and cowrote the story with his wife, Agneta Ulfsäter Troell, and Nikolas Rådström, based on a real-life woman's experiences. Title on-screen is MARIA LARSSON'S EVERLASTING MOMENTS. ▐

Everlasting Piece, An (2000) **C-105m. ★★½** D: Barry Levinson. Barry McEvoy, Brian F. O'Byrne, Anna Friel, Pauline McLynn, Ruth McCabe, Laurence Kinlan, Billy Connolly, Des McAleer. Intermittently funny, sometimes silly satire set in Belfast (rather than director Levinson's customary Baltimore), about a pair of inept barbers-turned-wig-salesmen; one (McEvoy) is insolent and Catholic, the other (O'Byrne) is more restrained and Protestant. McEvoy also scripted. [R]▼▐

Eversmile, New Jersey (1989-British-Argentinian) C-88m. *½ D: Carlos Sorin. Daniel Day-Lewis, Mirjana Jokovic, Gabriela Archer, Julio De Grazia, Ignacio Quiros, Miguel Ligero, Ana Maria Glunta. If you've waited all your life to see a film about a traveling missionary dentist, wait no more: Day-Lewis plays a fanatic who works for a "dental consciousness" foundation and travels the hinterlands to spread his noble message. Offbeat, to say the least, but grows wearisome after a while. Filmed in Argentina. [PG]▼●

Everybody Does It (1949) 98m. ***½ D: Edmund Goulding. Paul Douglas, Linda Darnell, Celeste Holm, Charles Coburn, Millard Mitchell, Lucile Watson, John Hoyt, George Tobias. Exceptionally amusing yarn of aspiring singer Holm, harried husband Douglas, and prima donna Darnell. Celeste wants vocal career, Douglas gets one instead. Remake of WIFE, HUSBAND, AND FRIEND; Nunnally Johnson adapted his earlier screenplay (based on a James M. Cain story).

Everybody Gets It in the End SEE: **Tag: The Assassination Game**

Everybody's All-American (1988) C-127m. *** D: Taylor Hackford. Jessica Lange, Dennis Quaid, Timothy Hutton, John Goodman, Carl Lumbly, Ray Baker, Savannah Smith Boucher, Patricia Clarkson. The 25-year saga of a college football hero and his homecoming queen, who find a rocky road living happily ever after. Quaid seems too aware of the caricature he is about to become, but Lange's bittersweet performance rings true throughout and makes this film worth seeing. Based on Frank Deford's novel. [R]▼●●

Everybody's Famous (2000-Belgian-French-Dutch) C-97m. *½ D: Dominique Deruddere. Josse De Pauw, Eva van der Gucht, Werner De Smedt, Thekla Reuten, Victor Löw, Gert Portael. Factory worker dreams of celebrity for his overweight daughter (a Madonna wannabe). He concocts an inane kidnapping scheme to that end, reveling in the notoriety it brings *him*. Odd, twisted comedy-drama struggles to entertain. Maybe you have to be Flemish. . . . [R]▼●

Everybody's Fine (1990-Italian) C-112m. **½ D: Giuseppe Tornatore. Marcello Mastroianni, Michele Morgan, Marino Cenna, Roberto Nobile, Valeria Cavali, Norma Martelli, Fabio Iellini, Salvatore Cascio. Mastroianni is elderly, slightly befuddled Sicilian patriarch who embarks on extended tour of Italy to visit his five grown children. Provocative idea of showing a parent's hopes and dreams dashed by reality; unfortunately, it becomes a lumbering Felliniesque travelogue. Creator of CINEMA PARADISO looks at flip side of nostalgia here with so-so success (and a typically

vital Mastroianni performance). Michele Morgan is lovely in small role of woman in tour group. Remade in 2009.▼●

Everybody's Fine (2009-U.S.-British) C-95m. *** D: Kirk Jones. Robert De Niro, Drew Barrymore, Kate Beckinsale, Sam Rockwell, Lucian Maisel, Damian Young, James Frain, Melissa Leo, Katherine Moennig, James Murtaugh. When his grown children all cancel their plans to visit him one weekend, retired widower De Niro decides to travel across the country to call on them, unannounced. As he does, he discovers they have been keeping secrets from him. Good cast makes the most of this likable, lightweight material, and writer-director Jones injects touching moments of De Niro interacting with ordinary people during his journey. Marcello Mastroianni originated this part in the 1990 Italian film. HD Widescreen. [PG-13]●

Everybody Sing (1938) 91m. ** D: Edwin L. Marin. Allan Jones, Judy Garland, Fanny Brice, Reginald Owen, Billie Burke, Reginald Gardiner. Shrill musical with stupid plot, unmemorable songs; good cast fighting weak material about nutty family involved in putting on a show. After loud finale you'll be waiting for a sequel called EVERYBODY SHUT UP.▼●●

Everybody Wins (1990) C-98m. BOMB D: Karel Reisz. Debra Winger, Nick Nolte, Will Patton, Jack Warden, Judith Ivey, Kathleen Wilhoite, Frank Converse, Frank Military. Private detective with an ax to grind ties his professional reputation to a schizoid small-town hooker who outbugs Bugs and Daffy. Arthur Miller's first screenplay since THE MISFITS (based on his one-act play "Some Kind of Love Story") gave fruit to this ironically titled fiasco; Winger flounders in a difficult—perhaps even unplayable—role. [R]▼●●

Every Day (2011) C-93m. **½ D: Richard Levine. Liev Schreiber, Helen Hunt, Brian Dennehy, Carla Gugino, Eddie Izzard, Ezra Miller, David Harbour, Tilky Jones. Well-cast film about a married couple facing various kinds of stress: her ailing (and demanding) father has just moved in with them, his producer at a TV show is impossibly mercurial and pairs him with a sexy writer on the staff, and their teenage son has declared that he is gay, which causes his father great discomfort. Director Levine's screenplay offers no revelations, but it's reasonably credible and the performances are solid. [R]●

Every Day's A Holiday (1937) 80m. *** D: A. Edward Sutherland. Mae West, Edmund Lowe, Charles Butterworth, Charles Winninger, Walter Catlett, Lloyd Nolan, Louis Armstrong. Mae sells Herman Bing the Brooklyn Bridge, so police detective Lowe orders her to leave N.Y.C. She returns to help expose crooked police chief Nolan.

Gay '90s setting for fast-moving West vehicle, written by the star herself. ▼

Every Girl Should Be Married (1948) 85m. **½ D: Don Hartman. Cary Grant, Franchot Tone, Diana Lynn, Betsy Drake, Alan Mowbray, Eddie Albert. Airy comedy of girl (Drake) setting out to trap bachelor (Grant) into marriage; Tone has thankless "other man" role. Drake also "captured" Grant in real life; they were married soon after this film came out. Also shown in computer-colored version. ▼●▶

Every Home Should Have One SEE: Think Dirty

Every Little Crook and Nanny (1972) C-91m. ** D: Cy Howard. Lynn Redgrave, Victor Mature, Paul Sand, Austin Pendleton, John Astin, Dom DeLuise, Pat Harrington, Severn Darden. Good idea—the kidnapping of a mobster's son by nanny Redgrave—gets away in this comic crime-and-caper film. One bright spot: Mature's gangster portrayal. [PG]

Every Man for Himself (1980-French-Swiss) C-87m. **½ D: Jean-Luc Godard. Isabelle Huppert, Jacques Dutronc, Nathalie Baye, Roland Amstutz, Anna Baldaccini. Self-conscious account of three characters whose lives are intertwined: Dutronc, who has left his wife for Baye; Baye, who is leaving Dutronc for life in the boondocks; and Huppert, country girl turned prostitute. Godard's "comeback" film was widely overrated, and certainly can't compare with his best work of the past.

Every Man for Himself and God Against All (1974-German) C-110m. **** D: Werner Herzog. Bruno S., Walter Ladengast, Brigitte Mira, Hans Musaus, Willy Semmelrogge, Michael Kroecher. Man kept in confinement from birth mysteriously appears in 1820s Nuremberg. Poignant tale based on real incident explores his alternate vision of the world and his attempts to adjust to society. Herzog's best film (from his own screenplay) features stunning performance by Bruno S. as Kaspar Hauser. Story also told in KASPAR HAUSER. Aka THE MYSTERY OF KASPAR HAUSER and THE ENIGMA OF KASPAR HAUSER. ▼▶

Everyone Says I Love You (1996) C-101m. *** D: Woody Allen. Woody Allen, Goldie Hawn, Alan Alda, Julia Roberts, Drew Barrymore, Edward Norton, Tim Roth, Natalie Portman, Gaby Hoffmann, Natasha Lyonne, Lukas Haas, Billy Crudup, David Ogden Stiers. The misadventures of an upper-class Manhattan family, at home, in Venice, and in Paris. A cheerful mess that's simply an excuse for Allen to make a musical. The sheer joy of watching the cast sing wonderful old songs (only Barrymore is dubbed) makes up for all the film's shortcomings (including a lack of story, and a curious habit of the camera's wandering away from whoever is singing, for no apparent reason). Everyone

seems to be having a good time, and Woody enthusiastically reprises his nebbish persona of yore. The score is brilliantly arranged by Dick Hyman. [R] ▼●▶

Everyone's Hero (2006) C-88m. **½ D: Christopher Reeve, Colin Brady, Dan St. Pierre. Voices of William H. Macy, Rob Reiner, Brian Dennehy, Raven-Symoné, Robert Wagner, Richard Kind, Jason Harris, Jake T. Austin, Joe Torre, Mandy Patinkin, Forest Whitaker, Whoopi Goldberg, Dana Reeve, Robin Williams. In this animated film aimed at kids, a boy sets out across country to "help" Babe Ruth and the 1932 N.Y. Yankees triumph in the World Series by finding and returning a stolen magical bat. Theme of persevering no matter what the odds can be traced to the spirit and guidance of initial director Reeve. A bit too obvious for any but the youngest viewers; still, there's heart and hope in the story and a stellar voice cast. Reeve's final film project; he died during production. [G]▶

Everything for Sale (1968-Polish) C-105m. *** D: Andrzej Wajda. Beata Tyszkiewicz, Elzbieta Czyzewska, Daniel Olbrychski, Andrzej Lapicki. Not top-drawer Wajda, but still an ambitious, fluidly directed examination of life on a movie set, the relationship between a director and his actors, and what happens when the leading man is accidentally killed. A very personal homage to Zbigniew Cybulski, Wajda's star of the '50s, who died in a freak mishap in 1967.▶

Everything Is Illuminated (2005) C-106m. *** D: Liev Schreiber. Elijah Wood, Eugene Hutz, Boris Leskin, Laryssa Lauret. Jonathan (Wood), a nerdy young Jewish American who is obsessed with the objects that link him to his family's past, travels to the Ukraine to explore his roots. Initially, his eccentric tour guides and their screwball antics are out of sync with the seriousness of the story, but once their journey begins—and especially when they discover an elderly woman who might have saved Jonathan's grandfather from the Nazis—the film becomes a poignant exploration of how objects allow us to hold on to memories. Scripted by first-time director Schreiber, from Jonathan Safran Foer's best-seller. [PG-13]▶

Everything Must Go (2011) C-97m. ** D: Dan Rush. Will Ferrell, Rebecca Hall, Laura Dern, Michael Peña, Christopher CJ Wallace, Stephen Root. Hotshot sales exec (and alcoholic) is fired after burning too many bridges, and goes home to find that his wife has left, changed the locks on their house, and thrown all his belongings onto the front lawn. He takes up residence there, befriending a lonely neighborhood kid (Wallace), who becomes an ally, and a woman (Hall) who's just moved in across the street. Adapted and perhaps foolishly expanded from a Raymond Carver short story by first-time director Rush, it runs out of steam too soon and introduces some characters and plot points too late. Saving grace is Ferrell, who's excellent in a skillful, serious performance. Panavision. [R] 🄳

Everything Put Together (2001) **C-88m.** ***½ D: Marc Forster. Radha Mitchell, Megan Mullally, Justin Louis, Catherine Lloyd Burns, Alan Ruck, Michele Hicks, Matt Malloy, Vince Vieluf. Probing look at a woman who's pregnant at the same time as her best friends . . . but when her newborn dies they abandon her and she goes through several stages of personal hell. Perceptive, mature, often uncomfortably real, with a superb performance by Mitchell. The director cowrote with costar Burns and Adam Forgash. Shot on digital video. [R] ▼🄳

Everything You Always Wanted to Know About Sex (But Were Afraid to Ask) (1972) **C-87m.** *** D: Woody Allen. Woody Allen, John Carradine, Lou Jacobi, Louise Lasser, Anthony Quayle, Tony Randall, Lynn Redgrave, Burt Reynolds, Gene Wilder, Jack Barry, Erin Fleming, Robert Q. Lewis, Heather MacRae, Pamela Mason, Sidney Miller, Regis Philbin, Geoffrey Holder, Jay Robinson, Robert Walden. One of Woody's most cinematic comedies, also most uneven, most tasteless. In multi-episode feature based very loosely on Dr. David Reuben's book, only a few segments stand out: final sequence inside male body during intercourse is a gem. [R] ▼🄳

Every Time We Say Goodbye (1986-Israeli) **C-95m.** **½ D: Moshe Mizrahi. Tom Hanks, Cristina Marsillach, Benedict Taylor, Anat Atzmon, Gila Almagor. Hanks' presence adds to this otherwise average soaper-romance, about an American flyer who falls for a Sephardic Jew (Marsillach) in WW2 Jerusalem. [PG-13] ▼🄳

Every Which Way but Loose (1978) **C-114m.** BOMB D: James Fargo. Clint Eastwood, Sondra Locke, Geoffrey Lewis, Beverly D'Angelo, Ruth Gordon. Clint takes the first pickup truck to Stupidsville, with an orangutan as his best friend, in this bizarre change of pace for the action star. The clumsiest comedy of its year. Sequel: ANY WHICH WAY YOU CAN. [PG] ▼🄳

Eve's Bayou (1997) **C-109m.** *** D: Kasi Lemmons. Jurnee Smollett, Meagan Good, Samuel L. Jackson, Lynn Whitfield, Debbi Morgan, Jake Smollett, Ethel Ayler, Diahann Carroll, Vondie Curtis Hall, Lisa Nicole Carson, Branford Marsalis, Victoria Rowell; narrated by Tamara Tunie. Absorbing tale of a privileged Creole family of the early 1960s, as seen through the eyes of a 10-year-old girl, who learns that her parents have very human frailties . . . and are still susceptible to age-old superstitions and even voodoo. Exceptional cast, led by young Smollett, give credence to the often fanciful story, which is drenched in Southern gothic atmosphere. Impressive writing and directing debut for Lemmons. Costar Jackson was one of the film's producers. [R] ▼🄳

Evictors, The (1979) **C-92m.** *½ D: Charles B. Pierce. Michael Parks, Jessica Harper, Vic Morrow, Sue Ane Langdon, Dennis Fimple, Bill Thurman. Couple moves into eerie house, unaware of its violent history. Tired rehash of an all too familiar formula. Panavision. [PG] ▼

Evil, The (1978) **C-90m.** **½ D: Gus Trikonis. Richard Crenna, Joanna Pettet, Andrew Prine, Cassie Yates, Lynne Moody, Victor Buono, George O'Hanlon, Jr. Doctor Crenna rents "haunted" house to use as clinic, but he and associates are violently victimized by powers within. Slow-moving film covers familiar ground; some chills. Video title: HOUSE OF EVIL. [R] ▼🄳

Evil (2003-Swedish) **C-113m.** **½ D: Mikael Håfström. Andreas Wilson, Henrik Lundström, Gustaf Skarsgård, Linda Zilliacus, Jesper Salén, Filip Berg, Fredrik af Trampe. Vivid and violent story of a troubled kid who's good with his fists; he's shipped to a boys' boarding school where the seniors rule and make life miserable for the younger ones. As he tries to change his ways and succeed academically he is sucked into the dark underworld of the campus. Although set in the '50s and featuring a tip of the hat to REBEL WITHOUT A CAUSE, this is closer in spirit to Lindsay Anderson's IF. . . . and FIGHT CLUB. Originally released in the U.S. unrated. [R] 🄳

Evil Dead, The (1983) **C-85m.** **½ D: Sam Raimi. Bruce Campbell, Ellen Sandweiss, Betsy Baker, Hal Delrich, Sarah York. Five kids at mountain cabin chop each other to pieces when demons possess everything. Wildly stylish, ultra-low-budget movie made by precocious college students is one of the grossest horror films ever. Borrowing inspiration from NIGHT OF THE LIVING DEAD, SUSPIRIA, THE EXORCIST and THE HOUSE ON HAUNTED HILL (just to name a few), it provides a deliriously imaginative roller coaster ride for those with strong stomachs. Video version rated R. Followed by two sequels. ▼🄳

Evil Dead II (1987) **C-85m.** *** D: Sam Raimi. Bruce Campbell, Sarah Berry, Dan Hicks, Kassie Wesley, Theodore Raimi, Denise Bixler, Richard Domeier. After recapping the first film, this inventive sequel takes off in a unique direction, blending horror and humor as no other movie ever has. In that same cabin, Campbell is again (or still) beset by demons, including, memorably, his own possessed hand. Vivid, fast paced, spectacularly gory, and highly original. Followed by ARMY OF DARKNESS. [R] ▼🄳

Evil Eye, The (1962-Italian) **92m.** **½ D: Mario Bava. Leticia Roman, John Saxon, Valentina Cortese, Dante Di Paolo. Incredible but enjoyable chiller set in Rome, with

Roman involved in a series of unsolved brutal murders. Aka THE GIRL WHO KNEW TOO MUCH.▼❍

Evil in the Deep SEE: **Treasure of Jamaica Reef, The**

Evil Mind, The SEE: **Clairvoyant, The**

Evil of Frankenstein, The (1964-British) **C-84m.** ** D: Freddie Francis. Peter Cushing, Duncan Lamont, Peter Woodthorpe, James Maxwell, Sandor Eles. Dr. F. thaws out his monster, with all-too-predictable consequences in this Hammer Films potboiler, a sequel to REVENGE OF FRANKENSTEIN. Followed by FRANKENSTEIN CREATED WOMAN.▼❍

Evil That Men Do, The (1984) **C-89m.** *½ D: J. Lee Thompson. Charles Bronson, Theresa Saldana, Joseph Maher, Jose Ferrer, Rene Enriquez, John Glover, Raymond St. Jacques, Antoinette Bower. Typical, violent Bronson entry, with Charlie a professional killer on the trail of a sadistic British doctor (Maher). For Bronson addicts only. [R]▼❍

Evil Under the Sun (1982-British) **C-117m.** ** D: Guy Hamilton. Peter Ustinov, Jane Birkin, Colin Blakely, Nicholas Clay, Roddy McDowall, James Mason, Sylvia Miles, Denis Quilley, Diana Rigg, Maggie Smith, Emily Hone. Murder at a resort hotel, with Hercule Poirot (Ustinov) to the rescue. An all-star cast and top production values, but still blah. Based on the Agatha Christie novel, with a script by Anthony Shaffer; exteriors filmed in Majorca. [PG] ▼❍

Evita (1996) **C-134m.** **½ D: Alan Parker. Madonna, Antonio Banderas, Jonathan Pryce, Jimmy Nail. The world's longest music video: a lavish adaptation of Andrew Lloyd Webber and Tim Rice's 1978 stage musical about the rise of Eva Peron, from her illegitimate childhood to near-deification as First Lady in 1940s Argentina. As pageant, it works, but there is no emotional center, leaving the viewer aloof from its leading character from start to finish. Madonna parades (and sings) well enough, but Pryce's strong presence as Juan Peron and Banderas's fiery singing commentary bring to life. Newly added song, "You Must Love Me," won an Oscar. 2.35 Research PLC. [PG]▼❍

Evolution (2001) **C-103m.** ** D: Ivan Reitman. David Duchovny, Orlando Jones, Julianne Moore, Seann William Scott, Ted Levine, Ethan Suplee, Michael Bower, Dan Aykroyd, Sarah Silverman, Richard Moll. Scattershot sci-fi-comedy/GHOSTBUSTERS throwback about a pair of Arizona community college science teachers (Duchovny, Jones) who investigate the crash of a meteor, which begins oozing aliens that quickly evolve. Loud, silly, and only occasionally funny. [PG-13]▼❍

Ex, The (2007) **C-89m.** **½ D: Jesse Peretz. Zach Braff, Amanda Peet, Mia Farrow, Charles Grodin, Jason Bateman, Donal Logue, Ian Hyland, Amy Adams, Fred Armisen, Amy Poehler, Paul Rudd. New York slacker must come to terms with career and family after his pregnant wife quits her high-paying law firm and forces him to move back to their Ohio hometown, where he goes to work for his father-in-law's ad company. Rarely lifts itself above the level of a TV sitcom but a likable cast does its best to make do with the material at hand. Grodin is an especially welcome presence in his first screen role in 13 years. Released briefly in 2006 as FAST TRACK. [PG-13]❍

Exam (2010-British) **C-101m.** ** D: Stuart Hazeldine. John Lloyd Fillingham, Gemma Chan, Adar Beck, Pollyanna McIntosh, Luke Mably, Jimi Mistry, Nathalie Cox, Chuk Iwuji, Colin Salmon. Dark times are brewing in this futuristic world. Jobs are scarce. An on-the-rise virus—while being managed—has no cure. Eight skilled individuals survive a harsh vetting process but have to do one last thing to snag the sole position available at a high-profile company: pass a test. Rules are strictly obeyed or they're out, and the winner must beat the other seven. First fifteen minutes of this slick psychological torture chamber are better than OK, but the story quickly plunges into pedestrian melodrama and unfortunately never crawls back out.❍

Excalibur (1981-British) **C-140m.** ***½ D: John Boorman. Nicol Williamson, Nigel Terry, Helen Mirren, Nicholas Clay, Cherie Lunghi, Corin Redgrave, Paul Geoffrey, Patrick Stewart, Gabriel Byrne, Liam Neeson. Eccentric but spellbinding, sexually aware rendition of the King Arthur legend by a stylish filmmaker working at the peak of his powers. Written by Rospo Pallenberg and Boorman. That's the director's son, Charley Boorman, as young Mordred. Magnificent production values. Later edited to 119m. and rated PG. [R]▼❍

Excess Baggage (1997) **C-101m.** *½ D: Marco Brambilla. Alicia Silverstone, Benicio Del Toro, Christopher Walken, Nicholas Turturro, Harry Connick, Jr., Sally Kirkland. Predictable story of rich, hostile brat Silverstone trying to get her neglectful father's attention by faking her own kidnapping. She smokes, drinks, and whines her way through this tedious "comedy" in which everybody involved in the convoluted plot is "clueless." [PG-13]▼❍

Excessive Force (1993) **C-90m.** *½ D: Jon Hess. Thomas Ian Griffith, James Earl Jones, Charlotte Lewis, Lance Henriksen, Burt Young, Tony Todd, W. Earl Brown. Martial arts whiz Griffith wrote this violent tale, and stars as a Chicago cop who's accused of stealing millions and setting up his partners for murder. Very familiar stuff for genre fans, with nothing much to set it apart from dozens of similar films. Followed by EXCESSIVE FORCE II: FORCE ON FORCE. [R]▼❍

Excuse My Dust (1951) **C-82m. **½ D:** Roy Rowland. Red Skelton, Sally Forrest, Macdonald Carey, Monica Lewis, William Demarest. Amiable Skelton musicomedy. Red invents automobile which almost costs him his sweetheart; her father owns town livery stable. ▶

Executioner, The (1970-British) **C-107m. ** D:** Sam Wanamaker. Joan Collins, George Peppard, Judy Geeson, Oscar Homolka, Charles Gray, Nigel Patrick, Keith Michell. Pedestrian thriller with British spy Peppard suspecting that colleague Michell is a double agent. Panavision. [PG] ▼▶

Executioner, Part II, The (1984) **C-85m.** BOMB D: James Bryant. Christopher Mitchum, Aldo Ray, Antoine John Mottet, Renee Harmon. Amateurish actioner, atrociously directed and acted, with homicide cop Mitchum hunting down a vigilante murderer. Has no connection to any other EXECUTIONER title. [R]▼

Executive Action (1973) **C-91m.** BOMB D: David Miller. Burt Lancaster, Robert Ryan, Will Geer, Gilbert Green, John Anderson, Ed Lauter, Sidney Clute, Lloyd Gough, Dick Miller. Excruciatingly dull thriller promised to clear the air about JFK's assassination but was more successful at clearing theaters. Scripted by Dalton Trumbo. Ryan's last film. [PG]▼

Executive Decision (1996) **C-132m. *** D:** Stuart Baird. Kurt Russell, Steven Seagal, Halle Berry, John Leguizamo, Oliver Platt, Joe Morton, David Suchet, Len Cariou, Mary Ellen Trainor, Marla Maples Trump, J. T. Walsh, Nicholas Pryor, B. D. Wong. The situation: Arab terrorists are in control of a 747. The solution: *Sneak an elite team aboard the plane, already in flight.* The problems: The team has to depend on inexperienced Russell, and there's a nerve gas bomb aboard that will wipe out Washington, D.C. Tense, inventive thriller that—until a misfired final reel—delivers the goods in high style. Directing debut for top editor Baird, who might have tightened the story a bit. Panavision. [R]▼▶

Executive Suite (1954) **104m. *** D:** Robert Wise. William Holden, June Allyson, Barbara Stanwyck, Fredric March, Walter Pidgeon, Louis Calhern, Shelley Winters, Paul Douglas, Nina Foch, Dean Jagger. Slick, multifaceted story of company power struggle with top cast, from Cameron Hawley novel . . . though similar film PATTERNS is much better. Later a TV series. ▼▶

Exile, The (1947) **95m. **½ D:** Max Ophuls. Douglas Fairbanks, Jr., Maria Montez, Paule Croset (Rita Corday), Henry Daniell, Nigel Bruce, Robert Coote. OK swashbuckler with exiled king Fairbanks falling in love with common girl; guest appearance by Montez.

Exiles, The (1961) **73m. ***½ D:** Kent Mackenzie. Yvonne Williams, Homer Nish, Tommy Reynolds, Rico Rodriguez, Clifford Ray Sam, Clydean Parker. Compelling, often harrowing documentary-style portrait of a community of American Indians in downtown Los Angeles during the late 1950s. Away from the reservation and their traditions, with drink as their only escape, these outsiders try the best they can to get through the night. A searing true-life drama, and an unforgettable b&w snapshot of L.A. before the area called Bunker Hill was torn down and rebuilt. Unreleased theatrically until 2009. ▶

eXistenZ (1999-Canadian-British) **C-97m. ** D:** David Cronenberg. Jennifer Jason Leigh, Jude Law, Willem Dafoe, Ian Holm, Don McKellar, Callum Keith Rennie, Sarah Polley, Christopher Eccleston. Preposterous film set in the near future about a virtual-reality game designer who gets trapped in one of her own games with a man who's supposed to be protecting her. At one point they wonder how to get out of the game; it's much easier to get out of the movie. Cronenberg also scripted this silly concoction. ▼▶

Exit to Eden (1994) **C-113m. *½ D:** Garry Marshall. Dana Delany, Paul Mercurio, Rosie O'Donnell, Dan Aykroyd, Hector Elizondo, Stuart Wilson, Iman, Sean O'Bryan, Stephanie Niznik, Rosemary Forsyth, Donna Dixon, John Schneider. Strange cinematic catastrophe, pried from an Anne Rice novel, attempts to jerry-build a standard cop sitcom (Aykroyd and O'Donnell investigate a murder) onto the sexual shenanigans at S&M island fantasy camp. O'Donnell's bright performance is the one justification for its existence. If anything, resembles a raunchier version of Marshall's old TV show *Love, American Style.* [R] ▼▶

Exit Wounds (2001) **C-101m. ** D:** Andrzej Bartkowiak. Steven Seagal, DMX, Tom Arnold, Isaiah Washington, Anthony Anderson, Michael Jai White, Bill Duke, Jill Hennessy, David Vadim. Blah actioner with aging, ever-wooden Seagal playing a tough loner cop who tangles with some on-the-take colleagues. Rapper DMX adds life to the proceedings as a mysterious drug entrepreneur. All too familiar, but the target audience might not mind. Super 35. [R] ▼▶

Ex-Lady (1933) **65m. **½ D:** Robert Florey. Bette Davis, Gene Raymond, Frank McHugh, Claire Dodd, Ferdinand Gottschalk. Davis, looking sensational, plays an independent-minded woman who loves Raymond but doesn't believe in marriage. Provocative and sexy, stylishly filmed, but begins to drag and become conventional by the second half. A remake of ILLICIT, filmed just two years earlier!▼

Ex-Mrs. Bradford, The (1936) **80m. *** D:** Stephen Roberts. William Powell, Jean Arthur, James Gleason, Eric Blore, Robert Armstrong. Chic à la THIN MAN comedy-mystery, with Powell teaming with ex-wife Arthur to crack a case. **▼O❍**

Exodus (1960) **C-213m.** ******* D: Otto Preminger. Paul Newman, Eva Marie Saint, Ralph Richardson, Peter Lawford, Lee J. Cobb, Sal Mineo, John Derek, Hugh Griffith, Gregory Ratoff, Felix Aylmer, Jill Haworth, David Opatoshu, Marius Goring, George Maharis. Leon Uris' sprawling history of Palestinian war for liberation becomes sporadic action epic. Newman as Israeli resistance leader, Saint as non-Jewish army nurse aren't a convincing duo; supporting roles offer stereotypes. Best scene shows refugees escaping Cyprus detention center, running British blockade into homeland. Ernest Gold won an Oscar for his score. Super Panavision 70. **▼O❍**

Exorcism of Emily Rose, The (2005) **C-119m.** ****** D: Scott Derrickson. Laura Linney, Tom Wilkinson, Campbell Scott, Jennifer Carpenter, Colm Feore, Joshua Close, Ken Welsh, Mary Beth Hurt, Shohreh Aghdashloo, Henry Czerny. An agnostic lawyer (Linney) is hired to defend a priest (Wilkinson) accused of negligent homicide in the death of a college student he attempted to exorcise. Peculiar mix of horror movie and courtroom melodrama is unconvincing on all levels, though handsomely produced and well acted. Loosely based on a real European incident, though the movie is set in the U.S. Unrated version runs 122m. Super 35. [PG-13]**▼❍**

Exorcist, The (1973) **C-121m.** *****½** D: William Friedkin. Ellen Burstyn, Max von Sydow, Linda Blair, Jason Miller, Lee J. Cobb, Kitty Winn, Jack MacGowran. Intense, well-mounted adaptation of William Peter Blatty's best-seller, calculated to keep your stomach in knots from start to finish. Blair is "normal" 12-year-old whose body is possessed by the Devil, Miller a troubled priest who attempts to confront the demon in her—and in himself. Oscar winner for Blatty's screenplay; vocal effects by Mercedes McCambridge. Followed by two sequels, a prequel, and countless imitations. Reissued in 2000 with 11m. of (mostly needless) additional footage. [R] **▼O❍**

Exorcist II: The Heretic (1977) **C-110m.** ***½** D: John Boorman. Richard Burton, Linda Blair, Loùise Fletcher, Kitty Winn, James Earl Jones, Ned Beatty, Max von Sydow. Preposterous sequel to 1973 hit. Special effects are only virtue in this turkey about priest (Burton) trying to unravel mystery of demon still living inside Blair. Boorman recut the film (from 117m.) the day after its premiere, and made numerous changes—to no avail. Restored to 117m. for homevideo. [R]**▼❍**

Exorcist III, The (1990) **C-110m.** ****** D: William Peter Blatty. George C. Scott, Ed Flanders, Brad Dourif, Jason Miller, Nicol Williamson, Scott Wilson, Nancy Fish,

George DiCenzo, Viveca Lindfors, Samuel L. Jackson. Police inspector Scott is confronted by a series of gruesome murders, unmistakably the work of a serial killer who was executed the same night as the exorcism of the original movie. Film begins well but grows more absurd and confusing until it self-destructs. Shows strong evidence of post-production tinkering. [R]**▼O❍**

Exorcist: The Beginning (2004) **C-114m.** ****** D: Renny Harlin. Stellan Skarsgård, Izabella Scorupco, James D'Arcy, Remy Sweeney, Ben Cross, Andrew French, Ralph Brown. Yet another in the endless line of EXORCIST follow-ups. This one attempts to explain Father Merrin's early years, in particular when he was in East Africa battling the demon Pazuzu, long before he exorcised demons from the body of Linda Blair. Competently made, shot by the great Vittorio Storaro, with many horrific images; all that's missing is a reason why we should care. Harlin replaced writer-director Paul Schrader, whose "scrapped" version is a separate film, DOMINION: PREQUEL TO THE EXORCIST. Univision. [R] **▼❍**

Exotica (1994-Canadian) **C-104m.** ****½** D: Atom Egoyan. Bruce Greenwood, Mia Kirshner, Don McKellar, Arsinee Khanjian, Elias Koteas, Sarah Polley, Victor Garber, David Hemblen. Five disparate characters become linked to each other's destinies, with a strip club called Exotica as the focal point. Only at the end of the film do we fully learn the "back story" that brought two key characters into each other's lives. Intriguing, like all of Egoyan's work, but not entirely satisfying. Winner of the Genie Award as Canada's Best Picture of 1994. [R]**▼O❍**

Expendables, The (2010) **C-103m.** ****** D: Sylvester Stallone. Sylvester Stallone, Jason Statham, Jet Li, Dolph Lundgren, Eric Roberts, Mickey Rourke, Terry Crews, Randy Couture, Steve Austin, David Zayas, Giselle Itié, Charisma Carpenter. Or, THE DIRTY HALF DOZEN: A group of mercenary pals accepts a job in a banana republic where a corrupt general has sold out his people to an ex-CIA sleazebag (Roberts) . . . but Stallone feels obliged to help the general's rebellious daughter (Itié). Inane action yarn has plenty of testosterone and explosions, but the script is weak. Not nearly as much fun as a gathering of veteran action stars ought to be—even with cameos from Arnold Schwarzenegger and Bruce Willis. Super 35. [R]**❍**

Experience Preferred ... but Not Essential (1982-British) **C-80m.** ******* D: Peter Duffell. Elizabeth Edmonds, Sue Wallace, Geraldine Griffith, Karen Meagher, Ron Bain, Alun Lewis, Robert Blythe. Simple, charming little film about a girl's experiences working as waitress for the summer at seaside resort hotel. June Roberts' script focuses on the blossoming of one young woman, while making humorous observations about the offbeat group of people around her. Short and sweet; made for British TV. [PG]▼

Experiment, The (2001) SEE: **Das Experiment**

Experiment, The (2010) **C-96m. ** D: Paul T. Scheuring. Adrien Brody, Forest Whitaker, Cam Gigandet, Clifton Collins, Jr., Ethan Cohn, Fisher Stevens, Travis Fimmel, Lavell "David Banner" Crump, Jason Lew, Damien Leake, Maggie Grace. Diverse group of men, including a humanist (Brody) and an introverted loser (Whitaker), are handsomely paid to participate in a behavioral experiment inside a makeshift prison. Little do they know what they'll be in for. At once fascinating and repellent film starts off strongly but degenerates into a melodramatic exercise in cruelty. Remake of the 2001 German film DAS EXPERIMENT is loosely based on the infamous 1971 Stanford Prison Experiment. Released direct to DVD in the U.S. [R]▶

Experiment in Terror (1962) **123m. *** ** D: Blake Edwards. Glenn Ford, Lee Remick, Stefanie Powers, Ross Martin, Roy Poole, Ned Glass. Taut suspense with bank clerk Remick terrorized by murderous extortionist Martin . . . but FBI agent Ford is on the case. Realistic, unsentimental, with convincing performances by Remick ·and Martin. Great Henry Mancini score, good use of San Francisco locations.▼◉▶

Experiment Perilous (1944) **91m. ** D: Jacques Tourneur. Hedy Lamarr, George Brent, Paul Lukas, Albert Dekker, Margaret Wycherly, Julia Dean. Static melodrama in the GASLIGHT tradition, with doctor Brent coming to the aid of—and falling in love with—fearful Lamarr, who's being terrorized by crazed husband Lukas.▼▶

Experts, The (1989) **C-83m. ** D: Dave Thomas. John Travolta, Arye Gross, Charles Martin Smith, Kelly Preston, Deborah Foreman, James Keach, Jan Rubes, Brian Doyle-Murray, Rick Ducommun. Fatally bland comedy about two Manhattan hipsters who are hired to open a nightclub in a small Nebraska town—which is really an exact replica of the hamlet built in the U.S.S.R. and used to train Russian spies. Weak in all respects and peculiarly sentimental about the 1950s. Barely released to theaters. Costars Travolta and Preston later married. [PG-13]▼◉

Explicit Ills (2009) **C-87m. ** D: Mark Webber. Paul Dano, Rosario Dawson, Naomie Harris, Lou Taylor Pucci, Frankie Shaw, Tariq Trotter, Francisco Burgos. Meandering, self-conscious account of the everyday travails of various low-income denizens of inner-city Philadelphia. They run the gamut from enterprising and clear-headed to drugged-out. The finale, involv-

ing a poor people's march for health care, seems tacked on. Webber's attempt to create a relaxed lyricism is reminiscent of the early works of his executive producer, Jim Jarmusch. Super 35. [R]◉

Exploding Girl, The (2010) **C-80m. *** D: Bradley Rust Gray. Zoe Kazan, Mark Rendall, Maryann Urbano. Flush with first love, college student Kazan arrives home, along with childhood friend Rendall, for spring break. When contacting her boyfriend— in this era of instant communication— becomes nearly impossible, her spirits soon sag. What's he doing and why? When will they connect? Is he withdrawn? Meanwhile, the implicit bond between the two old friends intensifies, though it's not clear she's aware of his unconditional constancy. Gray, who also scripted, skillfully interjects N.Y.C. sounds and locales throughout a contemplative, un-glitzy look at a young girl's budding foray into adulthood. Kazan's fragile characterization is wholly appealing—a good thing as she's in every scene. ◉

Explorers (1985) **C-109m. ** D: Joe Dante. Ethan Hawke, River Phoenix, Jason Presson, Amanda Peterson, Dick Miller, Robert Picardo, Dana Ivey, Meshach Taylor, Mary Kay Place. Youngster hooked on science fiction yearns to travel into space and gets his wish, with the help of a whiz-kid friend. Opens beautifully, takes its time developing story—then makes disastrous wrong turn in space that transforms film into a shaggy-dog joke! Director Dante has restructured film somewhat for video release. That version is 107m. [PG]▼◉▶

Explosive Generation, The (1961) **89m. ** D: Buzz Kulik. William Shatner, Patty McCormack, Billy Gray, Steve Dunne, Lee Kinsolving, Virginia Field, Phillip Terry, Edward Platt, Beau Bridges. High school teacher Shatner causes an uproar when he has his students write essays on their attitudes about sex. Based-on-fact account is an intriguing relic of its era (both for its subject and cast).◉

Exporting Raymond (2011) **C-86m. *** D: Phil Rosenthal. Rosenthal, creator of the wildly successful American TV comedy *Everybody Loves Raymond*, travels to Russia to supervise a Soviet version of the series. Rosenthal's realistic approach to comedy gets lost in translation, along with other speed bumps along the road to a successful collaboration, in this highly amusing documentary. Although the mood is lighthearted throughout, the film resonates with lessons about differences and similarities in our cultures—and the value of personal diplomacy. [PG]◉

Exposed (1983) **C-100m. *½** D: James Toback. Nastassia Kinski, Rudolf Nureyev, Harvey Keitel, Ian McShane, Bibi Andersson, Ron Randell, Pierre Clementi, James Russo. Girl from the Midwest quits school, comes to N.Y.C., hits it big as a fashion model, then gets involved with enigmatic Nureyev and his plan to kill terrorist Keitel in Paris. Seems like three different movies—all of them strange. Nureyev's performance might best be described as overripe. That's writer-director Toback in the role of Kinski's professor/lover. [R]▼

Exposure (1991-Brazilian) **C-100m.** ** D: Walter Salles, Jr. Peter Coyote, Tcheky Karyo, Amanda Pays, Raul Cortez, Giulia Gam, Cassia Kiss. Slick but corny, overbaked thriller about pompously poetic American photographer (Coyote), living in Rio de Janeiro, who becomes immersed in a seamy, violent underworld (and undergoes quite a personality change), searching for killer of young prostitute. [R]▼●

Express, The (2008) **C-129m.** *** D: Gary Fleder. Rob Brown, Dennis Quaid, Darrin Dewitt Henson, Omar Benson Miller, Nelsan Ellis, Charles S. Dutton, Justin Martin, Justin Jones, Nicole Beharie, Aunjanue Ellis, Clancy Brown, Saul Rubinek. Inspirational biography of Syracuse University football star Ernie Davis, the first African-American Heisman Trophy winner. Adapted from Robert Gallagher's book, this story of toughness and determination in the face of racism and tragedy may be formula stuff, but it's extremely well done. Super 35. [PG]●

Expresso Bongo (1959-British) **108m.** **½ D: Val Guest. Laurence Harvey, Sylvia Syms, Yolande Donlan, Cliff Richard, Ambrosine Phillpotts, Eric Pohlmann, Hermione Baddeley, Wilfrid Lawson, Kenneth Griffith, Susan Hampshire. Atmospheric but dated drama with Harvey shining as a high-energy, jive-spouting London hustler who thinks he's found his version of Elvis in poor young bongo-playing rocker Richard. Written by Wolf Mankowitz. DyaliScope.▼●

Exterminating Angel, The (1962-Mexican) **95m.** ***½ D: Luis Buñuel. Silvia Pinal, Enrique Rambal, Jacqueline Andere, Jose Baviera, Augusto Benedico. Guests at elegant dinner party cannot bring themselves to leave, begin to starve and die after several days. Wry assault on bourgeois manners by master surrealist Buñuel.▼●

Exterminator, The (1980) **C-101m.** BOMB D: James Glickenhaus. Christopher George, Samantha Eggar, Robert Ginty, Steve James, Tony Di Benedetto. Gore galore with Vietnam veteran Ginty aping Charles Bronson in DEATH WISH as he rubs out a gang who mugged and paralyzed a friend. If you love this film, good news—there's a sequel! Unrated director's cut runs 104m. [R]▼●●

Exterminator II (1984) **C-88m.** BOMB D: Mark Buntzman. Robert Ginty, Mario Van Peebles, Deborah Geffner, Frankie Faison, Scott Randolph, Arye Gross, John Turturro. Ginty and his blowtorch are back, hot after a

gang whose most sadistic member is named X. Obnoxious, grade Z garbage. [R]▼

Extract (2009) **C-92m.** **½ D: Mike Judge. Jason Bateman, Mila Kunis, Kristen Wiig, Ben Affleck, J. K. Simmons, Clifton Collins, Jr., Dustin Milligan, David Koechner, Beth Grant, Gene Simmons. Laid-back comedy about a manufacturer of food extract (Bateman) who's restless at home, where his wife is never "in the mood," and at work, where his oddball employees make life a constant surprise. Then one of his workers suffers an accident and is prodded to sue by a sexy woman (Kunis) who's also caught the eye of the boss. Funny observations and quirky characters abound, as you'd expect from writer-director Judge (who also appears as one of the workers), though the results are somewhat mild overall. [R]●

Extra Man, The (2010-U.S.-French) **C-108m.** *** D: Shari Springer Berman, Robert Pulcini. Kevin Kline, Paul Dano, Katie Holmes, John C. Reilly, Patti D'Arbanville, Alicia Goranson, Celia Weston, Marian Seldes, Dan Hedaya, John Pankow; narrated by Graeme Malcolm. Suddenly jobless academic (Dano) moves to Manhattan and rents a room from a world-class eccentric (Kline) who takes the younger man under his more-than-slightly-warped wing. A valentine to the oddballs who make N.Y.C. unique, focusing on two men who exist out of their time. Kline and Dano are simply perfect as a retrograde roué who lives off older society women and a young man who's still slightly unformed—though he does have a yen for cross-dressing. Jonathan Ames adapted his novel along with the directors, who make wonderful use of N.Y.C. locations. Super 35. [R]●

Extraordinary Measures (2010) **C-106m.** ** D: Tom Vaughan. Brendan Fraser, Harrison Ford, Keri Russell, Meredith Droeger, Diego Velazquez, Sam M. Hall, Jared Harris, Patrick Bauchau, Dee Wallace, Alan Ruck, David Clennon, Courtney B. Vance. Happily married family man's two younger children are afflicted with a rare form of muscular dystrophy known as Pompe disease. Upon learning that an iconoclastic research scientist (Ford) has some radical ideas that, with funding, could just possibly lead to new breakthroughs, the two strangers form an alliance. Fact-based film tells a decent story but is reminiscent of "disease-of-the-week" TV movies and prone to clichés. Fraser's performance is more hectic than impassioned. [PG]●

Extraordinary Seaman, The (1969) **C-80m.** BOMB D: John Frankenheimer. David Niven, Faye Dunaway, Alan Alda, Mickey Rooney, Juano Hernandez, Jack Carter, Manu Tupou, Barry Kelley. Extraordinarily muddled "comedy" of eccentric Niven piloting long-lost abandoned ship during WW2; shows signs of tampering from original conception of film. Barely received theatrical release. Only highpoints: clips from 1940s newsreels and Faye's eye makeup. Panavision. [G]

Extreme Adventures of Super Dave, The (2000) **C-91m.** ** D: Peter MacDonald. Super Dave Osborne (Bob Einstein), Dan Hedaya, Gia Carides, Steve Van Wormer, Art Irizawa, Don Lake, Carl Michael Lindner, Ray Charles. Daredevil ace Super Dave (a kind of live-action Wile E. Coyote) faces his ultimate challenge; heavy-handed feature-length extension of the cable TV series. Einstein also coscripted. Mike Connors appears unbilled as Super Dave's grandfather. Made for theaters in 1998, released on video instead. [PG]▼▶

Extreme Justice (1993) **C-105m.** ** D: Mark L. Lester. Lou Diamond Phillips, Scott Glenn, Chelsea Field, Yaphet Kotto, Ed Lauter, Andrew Divoff, William Lucking. Renegade cop finds himself caught in the crossfire after being recruited into a secret police unit that dispenses its own justice on the mean streets of L.A. Violence for violence's sake seems to be the theme of this theatrical film that premiered on cable. [R]▼●▶

Extreme Measures (1996) **C-118m.** ** D: Michael Apted. Hugh Grant, Gene Hackman, Sarah Jessica Parker, David Morse, Bill Nunn, John Toles-Bey, Paul Guilfoyle, Debra Monk, J. K. Simmons. Emergency room doctor senses something fishy going on after a man who dies mysteriously vanishes from the hospital's records. Medical conspiracy thriller starts out well enough but quickly becomes obvious and hollow. Grant has one of his best parts as a dedicated doctor; his girlfriend Elizabeth Hurley produced the film. Director David Cronenberg plays the head of a medical review board. Panavision. [R]▼●▶

Extreme Ops (2002-British-German-Luxembourgian) **C-93m.** ** D: Christian Duguay. Devon Sawa, Rupert Graves, Bridgette Wilson-Sampras, Rufus Sewell, Heino Ferch, Joe Absolom, Jana Pallaske. Ho-hum actioner in which a wild-and-crazy film crew, shooting a commercial in the Austrian Alps, tangles with a Serbian war criminal in hiding. The generic snowboarding/skiing/kayaking sequences look as if they've been lifted from a sports video. Super 35. [PG-13]▼▶

Extreme Prejudice (1987) **C-104m.** ** D: Walter Hill. Nick Nolte, Powers Boothe, Michael Ironside, Maria Conchita Alonso, Rip Torn, Clancy Brown, William Forsythe, Larry B. Scott. Boyhood friends Nolte and Boothe are now on opposite sides of the law, as Texas Ranger and drug kingpin on the Texas/Mexico border. Though its excesses (in characterization, music, and especially violence) are apparently deliberate, that doesn't make them any more entertaining,

though it helps if you accept it as tongue-in-cheek. [R]▼●▶

Extremities (1986) **C-89m.** *½ D: Robert M. Young. Farrah Fawcett, James Russo, Diana Scarwid, Alfre Woodard. A woman is victimized by a taunting rapist in her own home but manages to turn the tables and trap him. William Mastrosimone adapted his own play, but what worked in a theater doesn't translate to film; Fawcett's adequate but one-note performance is another liability. [R]▼●▶

Eye, The (2002-Hong Kong-Singaporean) **C-98m.** **½ D: Danny Pang, Oxide Pang. Lee Sin-Je, Lawrence Chou, Chuctcha Rujinanon, Candy Lo, Pierre Png, Ko Yin Ping, Edmund Chen. A young, blind violinist receives a cornea transplant . . . and is soon plagued by visions of dead people. Muted psychological horror piece is nicely atmospheric with some genuinely creepy moments but loses steam by the end. Followed by several sequels. Remade in India in 2005 (as NAINA) and in the U.S. in 2008. [R]▼▶

Eye, The (2008) **C-97m.** ** D: David Moreau, Xavier Palud. Jessica Alba, Alessandro Nivola, Parker Posey, Rade Serbedzija, Fernanda Romero, Rachel Ticotin, Obba Babatundé, Danny Mora, Chloe Moretz, Tamlyn Tomita. Violinist Alba, blind since childhood, has a successful cornea transplant. But there's a catch: she is now haunted by creepy visions and can see dead people. Slick but empty remake of the 2002 Asian horror film, with a wooden Alba appealing only as eye candy. Super 35. [PG-13]▶

Eye for an Eye, An (1966) **C-92m.** ** D: Michael Moore. Robert Lansing, Pat Wayne, Slim Pickens, Gloria Talbott. Oater with twist: two physically disabled men, who can function via teamwork as one sharpshooter, hunt down killers of older man's family. Video title: TALION.▼▶

Eye for an Eye, An (1981) **C-106m.** ** D: Steve Carver. Chuck Norris, Christopher Lee, Richard Roundtree, Matt Clark, Mako, Maggie Cooper, Terry Kiser. Cop Norris's partner is killed by drug traffickers; he has nightmares, becomes a one-man army seeking vengeance against villain Lee and his cronies. Silly and predictable, but delivers for formula fans. [R]▼▶

Eye for an Eye (1996) **C-101m.** ** D: John Schlesinger. Sally Field, Ed Harris, Kiefer Sutherland, Joe Mantegna, Beverly D'Angelo, Olivia Burnette, Alexandra Kyle, Darrell Larsen, Charlayne Woodard, Philip Baker Hall, Keith David, Natalija Nogulich, Armin Shimerman. When Field's teenage daughter is brutally raped and murdered, she seeks revenge on the creep who did it. Field is ideally cast as the mother driven to take the law into her own hands, but this is little more than DEATH WISH in drag, a manipulative movie that becomes awfully far-fetched. What's more, those attack scenes are very tough to take. [R] ▼○◗

Eye of the Beholder (1999-British-Canadian) **C-109m.** *½ D: Stephan Elliott. Ewan McGregor, Ashley Judd, Jason Priestley, k.d. lang, Patrick Bergin, Genevieve Bujold. Terrible but oddly watchable mess with high-tech private eye McGregor tailing sexy serial killer Judd around the U.S.—and falling in love with her in the process. Plays like a voyeuristic music video. U.S. release runs 101m. [R] ▼◗

Eye of the Cat (1969) **C-102m.** **½ D: David Lowell Rich. Michael Sarrazin, Gayle Hunnicutt, Eleanor Parker, Tim Henry, Laurence Naismith. Glossy but intriguing suspenser with seductive Hunnicutt teaming with Sarrazin to murder his aunt (Parker), who keeps a houseful of felines. Most terrifying scene has wheelchaired Parker tottering atop a San Francisco hill. [M/PG]

Eye of the Devil (1967-British) **92m.** **½ D: J. Lee Thompson. Deborah Kerr, David Niven, Donald Pleasence, Edward Mulhare, Flora Robson, Emlyn Williams, Sharon Tate, David Hemmings, John Le Mesurier. Excellent cast in odd, low-key thriller set in France. The Marquis de Bellac (Niven) abruptly leaves wife in Paris to "do what he must" at ancestral estate near Bordeaux. Strange continuity due to cuts before initial release. Also titled: 13. ◗

Eye of the Needle (1981) **C-112m.** *** D: Richard Marquand. Donald Sutherland, Kate Nelligan, Ian Bannen, Christopher Cazenove, Philip Martin Brown, Bill Nighy. Solid WW2 spy saga from Ken Follett's bestseller. Sutherland plays a super-cool German agent temporarily stranded on an island off the British coast, where he meets a lonely, sexually frustrated woman. [R] ▼○◗

Eye of the Storm (1991-German-U.S.) **C-94m.** *½ D: Yuri Zeltser. Craig Sheffer, Bradley Gregg, Lara Flynn Boyle, Leon Rippy, Dennis Hopper. After their parents are brutally murdered, and one of the boys is blinded, two brothers take over operation of the family's motel in a desolate location. When Boyle and Hopper rent a room, unsettling truths begin to emerge. Tedious until the last ten minutes. Super 35. [R] ▼○◗

Eye of the Tiger (1986) **C-90m.** *½ D: Richard Sarafian. Gary Busey, Yaphet Kotto, Seymour Cassel, Bert Remsen, William Smith, Kimberlin Ann Brown, Denise Galik, Judith Barsi. Ex-con Busey's town is invaded by Hells Angels types, who sadistically murder his wife . . . so he goes on a one-man crusade for revenge. Sound familiar? [R] ▼○◗

Eye See You (2002-U.S.-German) **C-96m.** *½ D: Jim Gillespie. Sylvester Stallone, Kris Kristofferson, Tom Berenger, Charles S. Dutton, Sean Patrick Flanery, Christopher

Fulford, Stephen Lang, Dina Meyer, Robert Patrick, Courtney B. Vance, Polly Walker, Jeffrey Wright, Rance Howard. Stallone is an FBI agent taunted by a serial killer. When his fiancée is murdered, our hero resorts to drink, attempts suicide, and winds up in rehab, conveniently located in the middle of nowhere. Guess who drops by for a visit? Stallone is actually good, but the story is ridiculous, and the slayings gruesome. This belongs in I.C.U. Debuted in U.S. on video. Aka D-TOX. Panavision. [R] ▼◗

Eyes in the Night (1942) **80m.** **½ D: Fred Zinnemann. Edward Arnold, Ann Harding, Donna Reed, Stephen McNally, Reginald Denny, Rosemary DeCamp, Mantan Moreland, Barry Nelson. Above-par mystery with Arnold as blind detective Duncan Maclain protecting Harding from Nazi agents. The dog steals the picture. Followed by THE HIDDEN EYE (1945). ▼◗

Eyes of an Angel (1994) **C-91m.** *½ D: Robert Harmon. John Travolta, Ellie Raab, Tito Larriva, Jeffrey DeMunn. When single parent Travolta and his daughter flee from the mobsters who threaten him, the fight dog she secretly nursed back to health makes a preposterous cross country trip to find her. Too violent for kids, too boring and absurd for adults. Sat on a shelf for four years; released after Travolta's PULP FICTION success. Original title: THE TENDER. Panavision. [PG-13] ▼○◗

Eyes of a Stranger (1981) **C-85m.** BOMB. D: Ken Wiederhorn. Lauren Tewes, Jennifer Jason Leigh, John DiSanti, Peter DuPre, Gwen Lewis. Overweight creep DiSanti rapes and kills women, and the blood flows like wine; Tewes tracks him down, while her deaf, dumb, and blind sister (Leigh) is established as a potential victim. Utter trash. Leigh's film debut. [R] ▼◗

Eyes of Laura Mars (1978) **C-103m.** **½ D: Irvin Kershner. Faye Dunaway, Tommy Lee Jones, Brad Dourif, Rene Auberjonois, Raul Julia, Frank Adonis, Darlanne Fluegel, Rose Gregorio, Michael Tucker. A high-fashion photographer has frightening premonitions of grisly murders; some genuine suspense, lots of red herrings, and a silly resolution add up to an OK thriller but Dunaway's kinky colleagues and their lifestyles are a real turnoff. John Carpenter cowrote. [R] ▼○◗

Eyes of Tammy Faye, The (2000) **C-79m.** *** D: Fenton Bailey, Randy Barbato. Narrated by RuPaul Charles. Eye-opening documentary about Tammy Faye Bakker-Messner, former wife of popular televangelist Jim Bakker, and her fall from grace. Interesting as a chronicle of money-driven TV ministries as well as an entertaining portrait of the movement's former First Lady. [PG-13] ▼◗

Eyes, the Mouth, The (1982-Italian-French) **C-100m.** ** D: Marco Bellocchio.

Lou Castel, Angela Molina, Emmanuele Riva, Michel Piccoli, Antonio Piovanelli. Dreary, pretentious pap about the effect of a man's suicide on his actor-brother (Castel), mother (Riva) and pregnant lover (Molina). At one point Castel and Molina see FIST IN HIS POCKET, also directed by Bellocchio and starring Castel. We suggest the viewer do the same. [R]▼

Eyes Wide Shut (1999) C-154m. *** D: Stanley Kubrick. Tom Cruise, Nicole Kidman, Sydney Pollack, Marie Richardson, Todd Field, Lisa Leone, Thomas Gibson, Vinessa Shaw, Rade Sherbedgia, Leelee Sobieski, Alan Cumming, Fay Masterson. Affluent, happily married N.Y.C. doctor starts to come apart after his wife admits to having had a potent sexual fantasy about a man she never met. This leads the husband to foray into a world of sexual adventure for the first time. Provocative film takes place in a distinctive Kubrick environment—contained, almost claustrophobic at times. Overlong, and flawed, but still compelling, with two megawatt star performances. Nudity is plentiful, but the European version (now available on DVD) is even more graphic and runs 158m. Screenplay by Kubrick and Frederic Raphael from a 1926 Arthur Schnitzler novel. Kubrick's final film. [R] ▼●

Eyes Without a Face (1960-French-Italian) 88m. *** D: Georges Franju. Pierre Brasseur, Alida Valli, Edith Scob. Moody horror film, a classic in some circles, about a brilliant but crazed scientist/surgeon/researcher (Brasseur) and his fate after disfiguring his daughter. Aka THE HORROR CHAMBER OF DR. FAUSTUS. ▼●

Eyewitness (1970) SEE: **Sudden Terror**

Eyewitness (1981) C-102m. ** D: Peter Yates. William Hurt, Sigourney Weaver, Christopher Plummer, James Woods, Irene Worth, Kenneth McMillan, Pamela Reed, Steven Hill, Morgan Freeman. Slick but unsatisfying thriller about a building janitor who uses his second-hand knowledge of an unsolved murder to get close to a female TV news reporter with whom he's been infatuated. Steve Tesich's script is needlessly cluttered with minor characters and story twists. [R]▼●

Fabulous Baker Boys, The (1989) C-113m. **½ D: Steve Kloves. Jeff Bridges, Michelle Pfeiffer, Beau Bridges, Ellie Raab, Jennifer Tilly. Two brothers' 15-year partnership as a twin-piano nightclub lounge act is shaken by the addition of a feisty (and sexy) singer, who sparks changes in their act—and their relationship. Writer Kloves' directing debut is stylish and self-assured, with some great scenes and set pieces, but it skimps on story—and never really fleshes out Jeff Bridges' sullen character. The real-life Bridges brothers are perfectly cast, Pfeiffer is ideal. Her steamy rendition of "Makin'

Whoopee" atop piano considered a minor classic. [R]▼●]

Fabulous Baron Munchausen, The (1961-Czech) C-84m. **½ D: Karel Zeman. Milos Kopecky, Jana Brejchova, Rudolph Jelinek, Jan Werich. Filmmaker Zeman (FABULOUS WORLD OF JULES VERNE) provides another visual delight here, but his episodic fantasy—which takes his hero from the inside of a whale to the surface of the moon—is stilted and uninvolving. Aka THE ORIGINAL FABULOUS ADVENTURES OF BARON MUNCHAUSEN. ▼●

Fabulous Dorseys, The (1947) 88m. ** D: Alfred E. Green. Tommy Dorsey, Jimmy Dorsey, Janet Blair, Paul Whiteman, William Lundigan. Limp "biography" of bandleading brothers, constantly arguing in between "Marie," "Green Eyes," and other hit songs. Musical highlight: a jam session with Art Tatum, Charlie Barnet, Ziggy Elman and Ray Bauduc. ▼●

Fabulous Journey to the Center of the Earth, The SEE: **Where Time Began**

Fabulous World of Jules Verne, The (1958-Czech) 83m. **½ D: Karel Zeman. Lubor Tokos, Arnost Navratil, Miroslav Holub, Jana Zatloukalova. Zeman's ingenious visual effects, reproducing the look of 19th-century engravings, outshine leaden enactment of fanciful sci-fi story by Verne. Released here in 1961 with Americanized names in credits and pointless introduction by Hugh Downs. ▼]

Face Behind the Mask, The (1941) 69m. *** D: Robert Florey. Peter Lorre, Evelyn Keyes, Don Beddoe, George E. Stone, John Tyrrell. Model B film of immigrant Lorre having face disfigured in fire, donning mask, bitterly turning to life of crime. Extremely well done on slim budget.

Face in the Crowd, A (1957) 125m. ***½ D: Elia Kazan. Andy Griffith, Patricia Neal, Anthony Franciosa, Walter Matthau, Lee Remick, Kay Medford. Perceptive script by Budd Schulberg about homespun hobo (Griffith) discovered by Neal and promoted into successful—and unscrupulous—TV star. Cast gives life to fascinating story. Film debuts of Griffith and Remick. Look for young Rip Torn and Lois Nettleton. Many celebrities also appear as themselves, including Burl Ives, Mike Wallace, Betty Furness, Bennett Cerf, Faye Emerson, and Walter Winchell. ▼]

Face/Off (1997) C-138m. *** D: John Woo. John Travolta, Nicolas Cage, Joan Allen, Alessandro Nivola, Gina Gershon, Dominique Swain, Nick Cassavetes, Harve Presnell, Colm Feore, John Carroll Lynch, CCH Pounder, Margaret Cho, Jamie Denton, Thomas Jane, Chris Baer. Two thirds of a terrific movie: Federal agent Travolta agrees to have a heinous criminal's face grafted onto his own, in order to fool the no-good's brother into spilling vital information. But the daring plan goes awry in more ways than one. Travolta and Cage are charismatically over the top, and Woo's staging of action scenes is powerfully good . . . but the film doesn't know when to stop. Silly plotting and dialogue might have been overlooked in a tighter film. Panavision. [R] ▼●▮

Face of Fu Manchu, The (1965-British) **C-96m.** *** D: Don Sharp. Christopher Lee, Nigel Green, James Robertson Justice, Howard Marion-Crawford, Tsai Chin, Walter Rilla. First of new series with Emperor Fu bent on conquering West. Great 1920s atmosphere, good international cast. Followed by THE BRIDES OF FU MANCHU. Techniscope. ▼

Faces (1968) **130m.** ***½ D: John Cassavetes. John Marley, Gena Rowlands, Lynn Carlin, Seymour Cassel, Fred Draper, Val Avery. Highly personal drama about assorted infidelities is one of the few Cassavetes films to make it with general public. Powerful film with great acting, especially by Carlin and Cassel. [R] ▼●▮

Face to Face (1976-Swedish) **C-136m.** *** D: Ingmar Bergman. Liv Ullmann, Erland Josephson, Gunnar Bjornstrand, Aino Taube-Henrikson, Kari Sylwan, Sif Ruud. Brilliant Ullmann performance and Sven Nykvist photography compensate somewhat for déjà vu feeling one gets from drama about woman psychiatrist who suffers severe nervous breakdown. As harrowing as they come; not for every taste or mood. Originally a four-part Swedish TV miniseries. [R] ▮

Face to the Wind SEE: **Cry for Me, Billy**

Facing the Giants (2006) **C-111m.** **½ D: Alex Kendrick. Alex Kendrick, Shannen Fields, Tracy Goode, Chris Willis, Bailey Cave, Steve Williams, Mark Richt, Jason McLeod. Faith-based family drama about a losing football coach whose Christian high school is about to fire him. He also faces a dying car, a deteriorating house, and a receding hairline. At his lowest ebb he pulls religion off the bench and the team begins to pray and play together as one. Sincere if familiar home-grown production was financed by the congregation of the Sherwood Baptist Church in Albany, GA, and cowritten and edited by the director, who also stars. The giants, incidentally, are failure and fear. [PG]▮

Factory Girl (2006) **C-90m.** ** D: George Hickenlooper. Sienna Miller, Guy Pearce, Hayden Christensen, Jimmy Fallon, Jack Huston, Armin Amiri, Tara Summers, Mena Suvari, Shawn Hatosy, Beth Grant, James Naughton, Edward Herrmann, Illeana Douglas, Sally Kirkland, Mary Kate Olsen, Don Novello, Grant James. Sad, true story of 1960s socialite Edie Sedgwick (Miller) and her self-destructive spiral into depravity and drug addiction after becoming one of Andy

Warhol's underground-movie "superstars." Christensen plays a famous musician who looks, acts, and sounds suspiciously like Bob Dylan, with whom she has a stormy affair. Miller gives a raw, passionate performance, while Pearce is uncanny, seemingly channeling Warhol's voice and mannerisms, but the script is repetitive and superficial, and last-minute reshoots and reediting are all too obvious. [R]▮

Factotum (2006-Norwegian-U.S.-German) **C-94m.** **½ D: Bent Hamer. Matt Dillon, Lili Taylor, Marisa Tomei, Fisher Stevens, Didier Flamand, Adrienne Shelly, Karen Young, Tom Lyons. Low-key adaptation of Charles Bukowski's 1975 novel, with Dillon excellent as the author's booze-soaked alter ego, Henry Chinaski, who floats through a series of jobs and women. Many well-observed moments, with solid performances, but as aimless as its source, and its protagonist's self-love becomes a bit wearying. Chinaski also is portrayed by Mickey Rourke in BARFLY. Full title on-screen is FACTOTUM (A MAN WHO PREFORMS MANY JOBS). [R]▮

Facts of Life, The (1960) **103m.** *** D: Melvin Frank. Bob Hope, Lucille Ball, Ruth Hussey, Don DeFore. Sophisticated comedy with Bob and Lucy leaving their spouses for an interlude together. The two stars make a team worth watching. ▼●▮

Faculty, The (1998) **C-104m.** **½ D: Robert Rodriguez. Josh Hartnett, Jordana Brewster, Elijah Wood, Salma Hayek, Piper Laurie, Famke Janssen, Chris McDonald, Robert Patrick, Bebe Neuwirth, Clea DuVall, Laura Harris, Shawn Hatosy, Usher Raymond, Jon Stewart, Daniel von Bargen. Ohio high school students who normally clash with one another band together when they discover that their teachers are being taken over by aliens. Self-referential horror film, with a healthy nod to INVASION OF THE BODY SNATCHERS, is a cut above usual teen gore fests and has a first-rate cast. Overlong but sharply written (by Kevin Williamson, from a story by David Wechter and Bruce Kimmel). [R] ▼●▮

Fade-In (1968) **C-93m.** ** D: Allen Smithee (Jud Taylor). Burt Reynolds, Barbara Loden, Noam Pitlik, Patricia Casey, James Hampton, Joseph Perry. Odd little film made concurrently with BLUE, about love affair between film editor Loden and man she meets while working on location. Not very good, but a definite curio; never released theatrically. BLUE actors Terence Stamp, Joanna Pettet, Ricardo Montalban, and Sally Kirkland can be glimpsed here. Video title: IRON COWBOY. ▼

Fade to Black (1980) **C-100m.** *½ D: Vernon Zimmerman. Dennis Christopher, Linda Kerridge, Tim Thomerson, Morgan Paull, Marya Small, Mickey Rourke. Weirdo film buff Christopher does in his

[435]

enemies while dressed up as his favorite cinema villains. Interesting idea ruined by excessive violence, poor performance by Christopher. Marilyn Monroe lookalike Kerridge, as Christopher's girlfriend, is like a rose in a cesspool. [R]▼❶

Fahrenheit 451 (1966) **C-111m.** ✳✳✳ D: François Truffaut. Julie Christie, Oskar Werner, Cyril Cusack, Anton Diffring, Jeremy Spenser, Bee Duffell, Alex Scott, Mark Lester. Odd and generally slow-going adaptation of Ray Bradbury sci-fi novel depicting future Earth civilization where all printed reading material is banned. Though viewer interest is held throughout, film has curiously reserved, unemotional feel to it. Truffaut's only film in English.▼❶❸

Fahrenheit 9/11 (2004) **C-122m.** ✳✳✳ D: Michael Moore. Moore's controversial, take-no-prisoners condemnation of George W. Bush, highlighting the Bush family's supposed ties to Saudi Arabia and Osama bin Laden and the manner in which the U.S. President allegedly exploited the tragedy of 9/11 to spearhead his own political agenda. At its best, the film pointedly undercuts Bush's justification for starting the Iraq war; it's less effective when spotlighting Moore and his patented, attention-getting theatrics. How you respond to this openly propagandistic film will depend on your political leanings and your tolerance for Moore's incendiary brand of filmmaking. [R]▼❶

Fail-Safe (1964) **111m.** ✳✳✳½ D: Sidney Lumet. Henry Fonda, Walter Matthau, Fritz Weaver, Dan O'Herlihy, Sorrell Booke, Larry Hagman, Frank Overton, Dom DeLuise. U.S. bomber is accidentally ordered to nuke Moscow, plunging heads of American and Russian governments into crisis of decision making as time runs out. High-tension drama done with taste and intelligence. Walter Bernstein adapted the Eugene Burdick–Harvey Wheeler best-seller. Remade in 2000 for TV. ▼❶❸

Failure to Launch (2006) **C-96m.** ✳✳½ D: Tom Dey. Matthew McConaughey, Sarah Jessica Parker, Zooey Deschanel, Justin Bartha, Bradley Cooper, Kathy Bates, Terry Bradshaw, Patton Oswalt, Stephen Tobolowsky, Rob Corddry. Bachelor McConaughey is content living at home with his folks, a fact that usually puts off any woman who's getting too serious about a relationship. Then his parents hire Parker, a so-called professional at motivating men like this to leave the nest. Pleasant-enough romantic comedy that heads exactly where you know it will. Super 35. [PG-13]❸

Fair Game (1995) **C-91m.** BOMB D: Andrew Sipes. William Baldwin, Cindy Crawford, Steven Berkoff, Christopher McDonald, Miguel Sandoval, Johann Carlo, Salma Hayek, John Bedford Lloyd. Totally pre-fab action thriller that almost looks as

if producer Joel Silver is trying to satirize himself. Miami lawyer Crawford survives the requisite amount of firepower and fireballs during her pursuit by former KGB operatives. Baldwin is the cop trying to keep them both alive. Arguably the worst movie of 1995. In her acting debut, supermodel Crawford makes a good jogger. [R]▼❶❸

Fair Game (2010-U.S.-United Arab Emirates) **C-107m.** ✳✳✳ D: Doug Liman. Naomi Watts, Sean Penn, Sam Shepard, Noah Emmerich, Bruce McGill, David Andrews, Tim Griffin, Liraz Charhi, Khaled Nabawy, Michael Kelly, Ty Burrell, Brooke Smith, Jessica Hecht, Tom McCarthy, Norbert Leo Butz, David Denman, Polly Holliday, Adam LeFevre. Washington, D.C., couple juggles dual careers while raising two young children, but only he knows that his wife is an agent with the CIA. His outspokenness against the Bush administration's claim of weapons of mass destruction in Iraq inspires an administration official to leak her name to the press. She is Valerie Plame and he is Joe Wilson; the year is 2003. Intimate, propulsive drama, based on their memoirs, reveals how these events affected their lives and threatened their marriage. Engrossing and credible; an especially fine showcase for Watts. Same story was fictionalized in NOTHING BUT THE TRUTH. HD Widescreen. [PG-13]❸

FairyTale: A True Story (1997-U.S.-British) **C-99m.** ✳✳✳ D: Charles Sturridge. Florence Hoath, Elizabeth Earl, Paul McGann, Phoebe Nicholls, Peter O'Toole, Harvey Keitel, Tim McInnerny, Bill Nighy. Charming film, rich in period flavor, spun around a real-life incident in 1917, when two girls photographed fairies in their garden—and no less a figure than Sir Arthur Conan Doyle declared them genuine. As it deals with death (one of the girls has lost her brother to pneumonia), the horrors of WW1, and real-life characters like Doyle and Houdini (Keitel), this may actually have greater appeal to grown-ups than to children. Mel Gibson, whose company produced the film, has a cameo role. [PG]▼❶

Faithful (1996) **C-88m.** ✳✳ D: Paul Mazursky. Cher, Chazz Palminteri, Ryan O'Neal, Paul Mazursky, Amber Smith, Elisa Leonetti, Stephen Spinella, Jeffrey Wright, Allison Janney. On her 20th anniversary, the unhappy, neglected wife of a wealthy businessman is seized by a hit man who ties her up and awaits a signal from her husband to murder her. Meanwhile, they engage in a lively and surprisingly revealing conversation. All too obviously derived from a stage play (by Palminteri, who also wrote the script), this interesting piece simply doesn't work on film, despite good performances. Filmed in 1994. [R]▼❶

Faithless (2000-Swedish-German) **C-155m.** ✳✳✳½ D: Liv Ullmann. Lena Endre, Erland

Josephson, Krister Henriksson, Thomas Hanzon, Michelle Gylemo, Juni Dahr. Ingmar Bergman scripted this forceful drama about the impact of an extramarital love affair. Sparks erupt when a successful, happily wed actress-mother (Endre) inexplicably becomes involved with her gloomy friend (Henriksson). Exquisitely played; a complex and provocative rumination on love, sex, desire, and betrayal. [R] ▼❶

Fakers, The SEE: **Hell's Bloody Devils**
The Falcon series SEE: *Leonard Maltin's Classic Movie Guide*

Falcon and the Snowman, The (1985) C-131m. **½ D: John Schlesinger. Timothy Hutton, Sean Penn, David Suchet, Lori Singer, Pat Hingle, Dorian Harewood, Mady Kaplan, Richard Dysart, Chris Makepeace, Michael Ironside. True story, based on Robert Lindsay's book about two young men from affluent families who decide to sell government secrets to the Russians. Much food for thought, but we never get to share Hutton's feelings, and that keeps this well-made film somewhat aloof. Standout: Penn's performance as a desperate, amoral, drugged-out kid. [R] ▼❶

Fall, The (2008-U.S.-Indian-British) C-118m. **½ D: Tarsem. Lee Pace, Catinca Untaru, Justine Waddell, Robin Smith, Julian Bleach, Jeetu Verma, Leo Bill, Daniel Caltagirone. In 1920s California, a young girl (Untaru) recuperating from a broken arm in a remote convalescent hospital befriends a suicidal patient (Pace), who spins an incredible yarn that holds her spellbound. In it, five heroic figures escape captivity on a desert island and go after the man who imprisoned them, a powerful governor. Visual opus by music video–commercial cult figure Tarsem is alternately whimsical and ponderous, but location filming in more than 20 countries provides a panorama of stunning locations for his showy, often imaginatively staged sequences. Based on a 1981 Bulgarian movie called YO HO HO. [R] ❶

Fallen (1998) C-124m. ** D: Gregory Hoblit. Denzel Washington, John Goodman, Donald Sutherland, Embeth Davidtz, James Gandolfini, Elias Koteas, Gabriel Casseus, Robert Joy, Aida Turturro, Barry Shabaka Henley. Philadelphia homicide cop investigates brutal copycat murders—but is slow to realize that there may be an explanation beyond the normal for how and why these deaths are being executed. Hybrid of supernatural and cop-thriller genres doesn't pay off, despite creepy atmosphere and solid performances. It takes much too long to get where it's going, and the finale subverts the film's own "ground rules." Panavision. [R] ▼❶

Fallen Angel (1945) 97m. **½ D: Otto Preminger. Alice Faye, Dana Andrews, Linda Darnell, Charles Bickford, Anne Re-vere, Bruce Cabot, John Carradine. Andrews, hard up and bitter, stops in a small California town and falls for sultry waitress Darnell. To get money to marry her, he plans to first wed mousy heiress Faye and fleece her. Slow-paced (if good-looking) film noir was an ill-fated change of pace for musical star Faye, in her last starring movie. ❶

Fallen Angels (1995-Hong Kong) C-95m. ** D: Wong Kar-Wai. Leon Lai, Michelle Reis, Takeshi Kaneshiro, Charlie Yeung, Karen Mok. Slickly made but emotionally uninvolving (and practically narrative-free) portrait of cultural alienation, which like its predecessor, CHUNGKING EXPRESS, focuses on two sets of characters: an assassin and the beautiful colleague who desires him; and a mute ex-con and the woman he covets. Dazzling cinematography, camera angles, and editing aside, this is mostly meandering and confusing—and as emotionally distant as the characters it portrays. ▼❶

Fallen Idol, The (1948-British) 94m. ***½ D: Carol Reed. Ralph Richardson, Michele Morgan, Bobby Henrey, Sonia Dresdel, Jack Hawkins, Bernard Lee. Young boy idolizes a household servant who is suspected of murdering his wife. Exceptional realization of Graham Greene story "The Basement Room," told in large part from the child's point of view. Scripted by Greene, Lesley Storm, and William Templeton. Also shown in computer-colored version. ▼❶

Fallen Sparrow, The (1943) 94m. **½ D: Richard Wallace. John Garfield, Maureen O'Hara, Walter Slezak, Patricia Morison, Martha O'Driscoll, Bruce Edwards, John Miljan, John Banner, Hugh Beaumont. Entertaining if somewhat vague WW2 thriller with Garfield returning to N.Y.C. after fighting in the Spanish Civil War, only to find himself hunted by undercover Nazis. Promising material never really pans out. ▼❶

Falling Down (1993) C-115m. **½ D: Joel Schumacher. Michael Douglas, Robert Duvall, Barbara Hershey, Frederic Forrest, Tuesday Weld, Rachel Ticotin, Lois Smith, Michael Paul Chan, Raymond J. Barry, D. W. Moffett, Brent Hinkley, Dedee Pfeiffer, Vondie Curtis Hall, Jack Kehoe, John Diehl. Nerdy Douglas blows his cool one morning, abandons his car in freeway traffic, and starts wandering L.A. on an increasingly violent odyssey—while Duvall, his last day before retiring from the police force, sniffs him out. Dead-on portrait of a disenfranchised, modern-day American who goes off the deep end. It's vivid, it's credible, it's extremely well acted . . . but what exactly is the point? Panavision. [R] ▼❶

Falling From Grace (1992) C-100m. BOMB D: John Mellencamp. John Mellencamp, Mariel Hemingway, Kay Lenz, Claude Akins, Dub Taylor, Larry Crane.

Warmed-over Larry McMurtry tripe about a country music star who returns to his hometown, opening old family wounds and reigniting a relationship with his onetime girlfriend, who's now married to his brother. Lenz's sexy character is the only one that avoids cliché; Mellencamp's performance is simply boring. This marked the singing star's directing debut. [PG-13] ▼●▮

Falling in Love (1984) **C-107m.** **½ D: Ulu Grosbard. Robert De Niro, Meryl Streep, Harvey Keitel, Jane Kaczmarek, George Martin, David Clennon, Dianne Wiest. Straightforward film about two married people who—against their better judgment—have an affair. BRIEF ENCOUNTER it's not, but De Niro and especially Streep lift it out of the ordinary. [PG-13] ▼●▮

Falling in Love Again (1980) **C-103m.** *½ D: Steven Paul. Elliott Gould, Susannah York, Stuart Paul, Michelle Pfeiffer, Kaye Ballard, Robert Hackman, Steven Paul. Amateurish slop wherein a frustrated Gould flashes back to his halcyon youth in the Bronx and his courtship of a WASP princess. Artificial, to say the least. Twenty-year-old producer-director-writer-actor Paul scores points for chutzpah, not talent, with this feature debut; also Pfeiffer's film debut. Aka IN LOVE. [PG] ▼●▮

Fall of the House of Usher (1960) SEE: **House of Usher**

Fall of the Roman Empire, The (1964) **C-180m.** ***½ D: Anthony Mann. Sophia Loren, Stephen Boyd, Alec Guinness, James Mason, Christopher Plummer, Anthony Quayle, John Ireland, Omar Sharif, Mel Ferrer, Eric Porter. Intelligent scripting, good direction, and fine acting place this far above the usual empty-headed spectacle. Mason and Guinness are superb; several action sequences are outstanding. A winner all the way. Screenplay by Philip Yordan, Ben Barzman, and Basilio Franchina. Ultra Panavision 70. ▼●▮

Falstaff SEE: **Chimes at Midnight**

Fame (1980) **C-133m.** **½ D: Alan Parker. Irene Cara, Lee Curreri, Eddie Barth, Laura Dean, Paul McCrane, Barry Miller, Boyd Gaines, Gene Anthony Ray, Maureen Teefy, Antonia Franceschi, Anne Meara, Albert Hague, Debbie Allen, Richard Belzer, Isaac Mizrahi, Meg Tilly. The dreams, aspirations, struggles, and failures of students at N.Y.C.'s High School for the Performing Arts should have made a great film, but this one just misses the mark, despite good ingredients and Oscar-winning music (by Michael Gore) and song (by Gore and Dean Pitchford). Moments of insight, excitement, and creativity eventually get lost in abrupt, disjointed continuity, which leaves a basket of loose ends and unresolved ideas. Later a TV series. Remade in 2009. [R] ▼●▮

Fame (2009) **C-107m.** *½ D: Kevin Tancharoen. Kay Panabaker, Naturi Naughton, Kherington Payne, Megan Mullally, Bebe Neuwirth, Debbie Allen, Kelsey Grammer, Charles S. Dutton, Asher Book, Kristy Flores, Paul Iacono, Paul McGill, Collins Pennie, Walter Perez, Anna Maria Perez de Tagle. Remake of the 1980 musical drama follows a group of students from N.Y.C.'s High School for the Performing Arts as they audition, perform, and learn about themselves at this difficult and competitive conservatory. Biggest problem with this unnecessary reprise is that most of the cast members aren't talented enough to make you believe they could be successful—and you never learn enough about any of them to care. Alternate version runs 123m. Super 35. [PG] ▮

Family, The (1970-Italian) **C-100m.** **½ D: Sergio Sollima. Charles Bronson, Jill Ireland, Telly Savalas, Michel Constantin, Umberto Orsini, George Savalas. Fast pacing fails to hide clichés in this action drama about an ex-con (Bronson) in single-minded hunt for the man who framed him and stole his girl. Lots of chefs involved in writing this brew, among them Lina Wertmuller. Also called VIOLENT CITY. Techniscope. [R] ▼▮

Family, The (1987-Italian) **C-127m.** *** D: Ettore Scola. Vittorio Gassman, Fanny Ardant, Stefania Sandrelli, Andrea Occhipinti, Jo Ciampa, Philippe Noiret. Episodic, revealing chronicle of 80 years in the life of an upper-middle-class Italian clan (with some characters portrayed through the decades by several different actors). An affectionate depiction, leisurely paced but well worth catching. Don't look for any sumptuous Roman exteriors: Scola never once strays from the family's apartment! [PG] ▮

Family Business (1986-French) **C-98m.** **½ D: Costa-Gavras. Johnny Hallyday, Fanny Ardant, Guy Marchand, Laurent Romor, Remi Martin, Juliette Rennes, Caroline Pochon. Well-made but inconsequential comedy of professional safecracker Hallyday, whose wife, daughter, and (most tellingly) son are involved in various ways with his "career." The motivations of his spouse (Ardant), particularly in relation to their son, are utterly confounding. Aka CONSEIL DE FAMILLE. ▼

Family Business (1989) **C-115m.** **½ D: Sidney Lumet. Sean Connery, Dustin Hoffman, Matthew Broderick, Rosana DeSoto, Janet Carroll, Victoria Jackson, Bill McCutcheon, Deborah Rush. Brainy Broderick, estranged from father Hoffman, enlists the aid of his grandfather Connery, a career criminal, to pull off a can't-miss heist. Worth seeing for three terrific performances by the charismatic leads, even though they're never quite believable as family—and the story lets them down. Further undermined by one of the most appalling music scores of recent memory, composed by Cy Coleman. Based on a novel by Vincent Patrick. [R]▼●◗

Family Game, The (1984-Japanese) **C-107m.** ✱✱✱ D: Yoshimitsu Morita. Yusaku Matsuda, Juzo Itami, Saori Yuki, Junichi Tsujita, Ichirota Miyagawa. Arrogant tutor is engaged to propel an indolent younger son into a classy school but ends up taking over entire household. Overlong, but original, satire of Japan's burgeoning middle class offers plenty of chuckles, insights into modern-day Japan.▼◗

Family Jewels, The (1965) **C-100m.** ✱✱½ D: Jerry Lewis. Jerry Lewis, Donna Butterworth, Sebastian Cabot, Robert Strauss, Milton Frome. Depending on your taste for Lewis, you'll either be in ecstasy or writhing on the floor in pain because he plays seven parts—all of them as potential guardians of little girl who is inheriting several million dollars.▼◗

Family Life (1971-British) **C-108m.** ✱✱✱ D: Kenneth Loach. Sandy Ratcliffe, Bill Dean, Grace Cave, Malcolm Tierney, Hilary Martyn, Alan MacNaughton. Forceful drama about a weak-willed and deeply troubled young woman (Ratcliffe) and her deepening psychological turmoil as her parents compel her to have an abortion. While Loach's left-of-center worldview makes this a politically loaded (and occasionally preachy) allegory, he and screenwriter David Mercer nonetheless paint a harrowing portrait of an uncaring medical bureaucracy. Originally titled WEDNESDAY'S CHILD.▼

Family Man, The (2000) **C-125m.** ✱✱✱½ D: Brett Ratner. Nicolas Cage, Téa Leoni, Jeremy Piven, Don Cheadle, Saul Rubinek, Josef Sommer, Harve Presnell, Mary Beth Hurt, Amber Valletta, Francine York. A ruthless financial exec with no emotional ties is magically transported into a life he's never known: the working-class suburban existence he might have had if he'd married his college girlfriend. Smart and sentimental: a rare contemporary holiday-themed comedy-fantasy that has the courage of its own convictions; this one scores a bull's-eye. Panavision. [PG-13] ▼◗

Family Plot (1976) **C-120m.** ✱✱½ D: Alfred Hitchcock. Karen Black, Bruce Dern, Barbara Harris, William Devane, Ed Lauter, Cathleen Nesbitt, Katherine Helmond. Hitchcock coasts along in this tongue-in-cheek thriller. Harris is phony psychic who gets involved in a murder plot hatched by sinister Devane. Mildly entertaining but never credible. Ernest Lehman scripted Hitch's final film. [PG]▼●◗

Family Prayers (1993) **C-108m.** ✱✱ D: Scott Rosenfelt. Joe Mantegna, Anne Archer, Patti LuPone, Julianne Michelle, Paul Reiser, Allen Garfield, Conchata Ferrell, David Margulies, Brittany Murphy, Tzvi Ratner-Stauber. Overlong drama of an adolescent Jewish boy struggling to prepare for his bar mitzvah, while suffering the ups and downs of life with a gambling-addicted father. Competent editing would have made this an excellent after-school special. This sat on the shelf after completion in 1991. [PG]▼◗

Family Stone, The (2005) **C-103m.** ✱✱✱ D: Thomas Bezucha. Diane Keaton, Sarah Jessica Parker, Dermot Mulroney, Luke Wilson, Claire Danes, Craig T. Nelson, Rachel McAdams, Ty Giordano, Brian White, Elizabeth Reaser, Paul Schneider. Warm-hearted comedy-drama about an eventful New England family gathering at Christmastime, where one of five siblings (Mulroney) brings his uptight girlfriend and potential fiancée (Parker) to meet his folks, who put her on the spot. Starts simply, then reveals a succession of layers that broaden and enrich the story. The cast couldn't be better. Written by the director. [PG-13]◗

Family That Preys, The (2008) **C-111m.** ✱✱½ D: Tyler Perry. Alfre Woodard, Sanaa Lathan, Rockmond Dunbar, KaDee Strickland, Cole Hauser, Taraji P. Henson, Robin Givens, Tyler Perry, Kathy Bates, Sebastian Siegel. Polished but over-the-top soaper involving the conflicts and interactions between two Southern families, one black and the other white, spotlighting the deep friendship of the matriarchs (Woodard and Bates, both well cast). Entertaining enough on a nonthink level, but don't look for subtlety or depth here. Aka TYLER PERRY'S THE FAMILY THAT PREYS. [PG-13]◗

Family Thing, A (1996) **C-109m.** ✱✱½ D: Richard Pearce. Robert Duvall, James Earl Jones, Michael Beach, Irma P. Hall, David Keith. When tractor salesman Duvall discovers his real mother was a black woman, he travels to Chicago to meet his half-brother, policeman Jones. Issues of race and family conflict are resolved a bit too easily in this rather contrived story, made sweet and believable by the efforts of a superior cast. Hall steals every scene as their blind aunt. Coscripted by Billy Bob Thornton. Super 35. [PG-13]▼◗

Family Viewing (1987-Canadian) **C-92m.** ✱✱✱ D: Atom Egoyan. David Hemblen, Aidan Tierney, Arsinée Khanjian, Gabrielle Rose, Selma Keklikian, Jeanne Sabourin, Rose Sarkisyan. Early Egoyan feature is a provocative, daring drama-cum-black comedy about a dysfunctional family and its members' fixation on television, video, and impersonal means of communication. On-target commentary on the way hollow imagery and technology have affected contemporary life. Written by the director.▼◗

Family Way, The (1966-British) **C-115m.** ✱✱✱ D: Roy Boulting. Hayley Mills, Hywel Bennett, John Mills, Marjorie Rhodes, Avril Angers, Murray Head. Winning comedy about young newlyweds' problems, including impotence, and difficulty of living in same house as his parents. This warm, gentle film was actually considered controversial in 1967 when released in U.S.! Music score by Paul McCartney.

Fan, The (1949) 80m. ** D: Otto Preminger. Jeanne Crain, Madeleine Carroll, George Sanders, Richard Greene. Oscar Wilde's comedy of manners *Lady Windermere's Fan*, involving marital indiscretion and social-climbing in Victorian England, loses much of its wit in this version. Madeleine Carroll's last film. Previously filmed in 1916, 1925, 1935 (in Germany), and 1944 (in Mexico), and remade in 2004 as A GOOD WOMAN.

Fan, The (1981) C-95m. *½ D: Edward Bianchi. Lauren Bacall, Michael Biehn, Maureen Stapleton, James Garner, Hector Elizondo, Anna Maria Horsford, Kurt Johnson, Dwight Schultz, Dana Delany, Griffin Dunne. Broadway actress Bacall is stalked by a psychotic admirer in this bloody, distasteful adaptation of the Bob Randall novel. Bacall's star appeal helps disguise the fact that this is just an exploitation cheapie in dress clothes. [R]▼●)

Fan, The (1996) C-117m. *½ D: Tony Scott. Robert De Niro, Wesley Snipes, Ellen Barkin, John Leguizamo, Benicio Del Toro, Patti D'Arbanville-Quinn, Chris Mulkey, Dan Butler, John Kruk, Jack Black. Ridiculous retread of all-too-familiar material, with De Niro cast as a '90s Travis Bickle, a loser on the edge, whose unhealthy passion is the S.F. Giants and their newest $40 million star, Snipes. This hollow melodrama is so overheated and overhyped by souped-up visuals and sound that the viewer feels he's been assaulted as much as the victimized baseball star. Worst of all, the film puts not one but two children in jeopardy and subjects them to psychological and verbal abuse. Ugh. Panavision. [R]▼●)

Fanatic SEE: **Die! Die! My Darling!**

Fanboys (2009) C-90m. *½ D: Kyle Newman. Jay Baruchel, Dan Fogler, Sam Huntington, Christopher Marquette, Kristen Bell, Ethan Suplee, Seth Rogen, Craig Robinson, Christopher McDonald, Danny Trejo. A long, long time ago (in 1998), an Ohio quartet of STAR WARS fanatics plots to sneak into George Lucas' Skywalker Ranch so their sick buddy can see the rough cut of Episode One before he dies. Overstuffed with pop-cult references, and too often obnoxious, sexist, and gross, this vision-quest road movie never once hits its emotional marks. Pretty much made for, well, fanboys, it's enlivened only by several in-joke cameos. [PG-13]●

Fancy Pants (1950) C-92m. *** D: George Marshall. Bob Hope (formerly Bob), Lucille Ball, Bruce Cabot, Jack Kirkwood, Lea Penman, Eric Blore. Amusing musical remake of RUGGLES OF RED GAP with Eng-

lish valet Hope accompanying nouveau riche wildcat Lucy to her Western home. ▼●)

Fandango (1985) C-91m. **½ D: Kevin Reynolds. Kevin Costner, Judd Nelson, Sam Robards, Chuck Bush, Brian Cesak, Marvin J. McIntyre, Suzy Amis, Glenne Headly. Five college pals have one last fling before moving on to face Real Life. Based on Reynolds' student film called PROOF, expanded to feature length under sponsorship of Steven Spielberg. Fresh and likable, if uneven. [PG]▼●)

Fanfan La Tulipe (1952-French) 99m. *** D: Christian-Jaque. Gérard Philipe, Gina Lollobrigida, Noel Roquevert, Olivier Hussenot, Marcel Herrand, Sylvie Pelayo, Genevieve Page. Delightful satire of swashbuckling epics; Philipe is ideal as sword-wielding, love-hungry 18th-century Frenchman joining Louis XV's army.●

Fanny (1932-French)120m. ***½ D: Marc Allegret. Raimu, Pierre Fresnay, Charpin, Orane Demazis, Alida Rouffe. Marius (Fresnay) abandons Fanny (Demazis) with his child; with Cesar (Raimu) playing Cupid, she marries Panisse (Charpin). Second of Marcel Pagnol's charming trilogy, preceded by MARIUS (1931) and followed by CESAR (1936). All three were the basis of the play and movie FANNY (1961).▼●)

Fanny (1961) C-133m. *** D: Joshua Logan. Leslie Caron, Maurice Chevalier, Charles Boyer, Horst Buchholz, Baccaloni, Lionel Jeffries. Gorgeously photographed and beautifully scored dramatic version of Marcel Pagnol's trilogy involving young girl left with child by adventure-seeking sailor. Chevalier and Boyer give flavorful performances.▼●)

Fanny and Alexander (1982-Swedish) C-197m. **** D: Ingmar Bergman. Pernilla Allwin, Bertil Guve, Gunn Wallgren, Allan Edwall, Ewa Froling, Jan Malmsjo, Erland Josephson, Harriet Andersson. Haunting, engrossing autobiographical family saga set in turn-of-the-century Sweden; a summing up of Bergman's career (announced as his final film). Scenes of joy, exuberance, pain, torment, exquisitely expressed, and largely seen through the eyes of a young boy. This earned Oscars as Best Foreign Film and for its costumes, art direction-set decoration, and Sven Nykvist's lovely cinematography. Edited from an even longer television miniseries, which ran 312m. Look for Lena Olin as a maid. Bergman's family history is further explored in THE BEST INTENTIONS, SUNDAY'S CHILDREN, and PRIVATE CONFESSIONS. [R]▼●)

Fan's Notes, A (1972-Canadian) C-100m. ** D: Eric Till. Jerry Orbach, Burgess Meredith, Patricia Collins, Julia Ann Robinson, Rosemary Murphy. Confused, football-obsessed writer becomes disillusioned with the Great American Dream of success and conformity, and ends up in mental hospital. Unfortunate misfire of Frederick Exley's highly regarded novel. [R]

Fantasia (1940) **C-120m.** ***½ D: Ben Sharpsteen (production supervisor). Leopold Stokowski and the Philadelphia Orchestra; narrated by Deems Taylor. Walt Disney's eight-part marriage of music and animated images remains an amazing achievement; Taylor's narration dates it more than the content. "The Sorcerer's Apprentice" (with Mickey Mouse), "The Dance of the Hours" (with dancing hippos and alligators), "Rite of Spring" (dinosaurs stalking the earth), and "A Night on Bald Mountain" (with Chernobog, the personification of evil) are so stunning that they make up for the less compelling sequences. Also notable for groundbreaking use of multichannel stereophonic sound. DVD (with newly filmed credits) runs 124m. Followed by FANTASIA 2000. ▼●▶

Fantasia 2000 (2000) **C-75m.** *** D: James Algar, Gaetan Brizzi, Paul Brizzi, Hendel Butoy, Francis Glebas, Eric Goldberg, Pixote Hunt, Don Hahn. Steve Martin, Bette Midler, James Earl Jones, Penn and Teller, Quincy Jones, Itzhak Perlman, Angela Lansbury, James Levine, Chicago Symphony Orchestra. Update of the 1940 Disney milestone suffers from the fact that marrying music and images is no longer a novel idea; TV-style host intros don't help. But there are a number of entertaining segments, including "The Pines of Rome," with its wondrous whales, "Rhapsody in Blue," a UPA-type cartoon set in N.Y.C., "Pomp and Circumstance," with Donald Duck as Noah's assistant, and the "Firebird Suite" finale. [G]▼▶

Fantasies (1981) **C-81m.** BOMB D: John Derek. Kathleen Collins (Bo Derek), Peter Hooten, Anna Alexiadis, Phaedon Gheorghitis, Therese Bohlin. Amateurish nonsense about Derek's and Hooten's efforts to renovate a Greek island into a tourist trap. Shot in 1973, when Bo was 16, as AND ONCE UPON A LOVE. [R]▼▶

Fantastic Four (2005) **C-106m.** ** D: Tim Story. Ioan Gruffudd, Jessica Alba, Chris Evans, Michael Chiklis, Julian McMahon, Hamish Linklater, Kerry Washington, Laurie Holden, Maria Menounos. Scientist Reed Richards (Gruffudd) tries to capture the power of a cosmic storm, with the backing of flamboyant billionaire Victor Von Doom (McMahon) . . . but something goes terribly wrong. This comic-book movie doesn't try to court an adult audience—and risks alienating hard-core fans by inventing a brand-new "origin" tale told in strictly two-dimensional terms. Best suited to 10-year-old boys. Based on the Marvel characters created by Stan Lee and Jack Kirby; Lee has a cameo as a mailman. Alternate unrated version runs 111m. Followed by 4: RISE OF THE SILVER SURFER. Super 35. [PG-13]▼▶

Fantastic Four: Rise of the Silver Surfer SEE: **4: Rise of the Silver Surfer**

Fantastic Invasion of Planet Earth (1966) **C-91m.** *½ D: Arch Oboler. Michael Cole, Deborah Walley, Johnny Desmond. Released theatrically in 3-D, this plays like a padded *Twilight Zone* episode; young couple find themselves trapped in seemingly deserted town enclosed in a giant Baggie. The original title, THE BUBBLE, was far less misleading: there are no aliens and no "invasion" in evidence, and not much excitement, either. Originally 112m. Filmed in widescreen Space-Vision. 3-D. ▼▶

Fantasticks, The (2000) **C-86m.** **½ D: Michael Ritchie. Brad Sullivan, Jean Louisa Kelly, Joe McIntyre, Joel Grey, Barnard Hughes, Jonathon Morris, Teller. Adaptation of the longest-running off-Broadway show in history (by Tom Jones and Harvey Schmidt) is sweet and slight; this musical fable of young lovers, their fathers and a mysterious showman is almost an anachronism. Beautifully shot (on some of the same Arizona locations used for OKLAHOMA!), it's a treat for musical devotees, even if it isn't perfect. Released after sitting on the shelf for five years, recut by Francis Ford Coppola; Ritchie's version, with additional songs, is on the DVD. Panavision. [PG]▼▶

Fantastic Mr. Fox (2009) **C-86m.** *** D: Wes Anderson. Voices of George Clooney, Meryl Streep, Jason Schwartzman, Bill Murray, Wally Wolodarsky, Eric Anderson, Michael Gambon, Willem Dafoe, Owen Wilson, Helen McCrory, Brian Cox, Adrien Brody. A sly fox promises his wife to mend his chicken-stealing ways and settle down—but he can't stifle his true nature, and makes elaborate plans to outwit three neighboring farmers. Amusing fable based on Roald Dahl's book, adapted and expanded by Anderson and Noah Baumbach, and brought to life through appealingly old-fashioned stop-motion animation. Fine voice work and a buoyant score by Alexandre Desplat complete the package. [PG]▶

Fantastic Planet, The (1973-French) **C-72m.** **½ D: Rene Laloux. Interesting animated feature about futuristic planet where men are dominated by superdeveloped mechanized race. Worthwhile, but static and aloof. [PG]▼▶

Fantastic Voyage (1966) **C-100m.** ***½ D: Richard Fleischer. Stephen Boyd, Raquel Welch, Edmond O'Brien, Donald Pleasence, Arthur O'Connell, William Redfield, Arthur Kennedy, James Brolin. Tremendously entertaining science fiction story of medical team reduced to microscopic size, injected inside human body. Film's then-state-of-the-art visual effects look great in widescreen. Screenplay by Harry Kleiner, based on a story by Otto Klement and Jay Lewis Bixby (Jerome Bixby). Won Oscars for art direction-set decoration and special visual effects. CinemaScope.▼●)

Fantômas Against Scotland Yard (1967-French-Italian) **C-104m.** **½ D: André Hunebelle. Jean Marais, Louis De Funès, Mylène Demongeot, Henri Serre. Third and final entry in series has super-criminal Marais setting his sights on a Scottish castle. Comedy trumps action this time around. Franscope.

Far and Away (1992) **C-140m.** **½ D: Ron Howard. Tom Cruise, Nicole Kidman, Thomas Gibson, Robert Prosky, Barbara Babcock, Colm Meaney, Eileen Pollock, Michelle Johnson, Cyril Cusack, Clint Howard, Rance Howard. Scrappy, dirt-poor Irish tenant farmer hooks up, in unlikely fashion, with the equally feisty daughter of a wealthy landowner, and together they sail for America to seek their ultimate destiny in the 1893 Oklahoma land rush. Ideal vehicle for Tom and Nicole, who are both beautiful and engaging; problem is a dire lack of story to fill the lulls between fight scenes. Filmed in Ireland and Montana. Climactic land rush really gallops in Panavision Super 70. [PG-13] ▼●)

Faraway, So Close! (1993-German) **C/B& W-140m.** **½ D: Wim Wenders. Otto Sander, Bruno Ganz, Solveig Dommartin, Peter Falk, Willem Dafoe, Nastassja Kinski, Horst Buchholz, Lou Reed, Mikhail Gorbachev. The perfect Wenders cast (if not the perfect Wenders movie) takes up where the more successful WINGS OF DESIRE left off; this time it is angel Sander who becomes mortal, joining old celestial pal Ganz—who's now married to circus performer Dommartin, with whom he's raising a daughter and running a pizza shop in unified Germany. Lighter going than its predecessor, but also more lightweight; it's still a borderline ordeal in the beginning and final segments, despite having been trimmed from 164m.▼●)

Far Country, The (1955) **C-97m.** *** D: Anthony Mann. James Stewart, Ruth Roman, Corinne Calvet, Walter Brennan, Jay C. Flippen, John McIntire, Harry Morgan, Jack Elam, Robert Wilkie, Connie Gilchrist, Kathleen Freeman. Cattleman Stewart, a confirmed loner, brings his herd to Alaska and finds nothing but trouble; solid Western set against colorful backdrop of mining camp towns. Story and screenplay by Borden Chase.▼●)

Farewell, Friend (1968-French-Italian) **C-115m.** ** D: Jean Herman. Alain Delon, Charles Bronson, Olga Georges-Picot, Brigitte Fossey, Bernard Fresson. Mercenaries return to Marseilles following service in Algeria, team up for robbery, and inevitably clash. Ordinary and overlong. Aka HONOR AMONG THIEVES and THE CODE (1968). [M/PG]▼)

Farewell, My Concubine (1993-Chinese) **C-155m.** ***½ D: Chen Kaige. Leslie Cheung, Zhang Fengyi, Gong Li, Lu Qi, Ying Da. Elaborate aria, no favorite at home

but cowinner of Cannes' top prize, about the contentious 52-year relationship of two male childhood apprentices in the Peking Opera, one a specialist in female roles with a lifelong atttraction to his heterosexual partner, who in turn marries a beauty from a brothel. A long but consistently absorbing drama spanning China's warlord era, the Cultural Revolution, and beyond. At its best in the first half; originally 170m. [R]▼●)

Farewell, My Lovely (1975-British) **C-97m.** *** D: Dick Richards. Robert Mitchum, Charlotte Rampling, John Ireland, Sylvia Miles, Jack O'Halloran, Anthony Zerbe, Harry Dean Stanton, Sylvester Stallone, Walter McGinn. Third film version of Raymond Chandler novel tries too hard to evoke its period, but Mitchum is appealing as a tired Philip Marlowe. Author Jim Thompson appears briefly. Filmed before as MURDER, MY SWEET and THE FALCON TAKES OVER; followed by THE BIG SLEEP (1978). [R]▼)

Farewell to Arms, A (1932) **89m.** *** D: Frank Borzage. Helen Hayes, Gary Cooper, Adolphe Menjou, Mary Philips, Jack LaRue, Blanche Frederici. Lushly romantic adaptation of Hemingway novel about ill-fated WW1 romance between American soldier and British nurse; dated but well done. Charles Lang's exquisite cinematography won an Oscar. Remade in 1951 (as FORCE OF ARMS) and 1957. Also shown in computer-colored version.▼●)

Farewell to Arms, A (1957) **C-152m.** **½ D: Charles Vidor. Rock Hudson, Jennifer Jones, Vittorio De Sica, Alberto Sordi, Mercedes McCambridge, Elaine Stritch, Oscar Homolka. Overblown, padded remake has unconvincing leads, static treatment of story so romantically told in Hemingway novel. Hudson is American ambulance driver wounded in WW1 Italy who falls in love with nurse Jones. Last film produced by David O. Selznick. CinemaScope.▼)

Farewell to the King (1989) **C-117m.** ** D: John Milius. Nick Nolte, Nigel Havers, James Fox, Marilyn Tokuda, Frank McRae, Aki Aleong, William Wise. Disappointing actioner with Nolte an army deserter who becomes the leader of a Borneo tribe during WW2. Goal: to protect his people from the atrocities of the Japanese and the lies of the British. Intriguing premise, but result sinks into cliché. Milius scripted, from Pierre Schoendoerffer's novel. [PG-13] ▼●)

Far From Heaven (2002) **C-107m.** *** D: Todd Haynes. Julianne Moore, Dennis Quaid, Dennis Haysbert, Patricia Clarkson, Viola Davis, James Rebhorn, Celia Weston. Fascinating filmmaking exercise in which writer-director Haynes replicates the look and feel of a 1950s Douglas Sirk Technicolor soap opera, while tackling issues that would have been taboo in that era. Moore is a picture-perfect suburban wife, Quaid her successful husband, but he has a dark secret, while she finds herself attracted to her Negro gardener (Haysbert). Not so much a parody as a re-creation, as if a 1957 movie were being made in 2002, with art direction, camerawork, costuming, music, and color that recall such films as ALL THAT HEAVEN ALLOWS. [PG-13]▼❶

Far From Home (1989) C-86m. *½ D: Meiert Avis. Matt Frewer, Drew Barrymore, Richard Masur, Karen Austin, Susan Tyrrell, Anthony Rapp, Jennifer Tilly, Andras Jones, Dick Miller. Dumb killer-on-the-loose programmer with sexy teen Barrymore being stalked while vacationing with her father. Of interest only for Drew's casting in her first adolescent movie role. [R]▼❶

Far From Home: The Adventures of Yellow Dog (1995) C-80m. **½ D: Phillip Borsos. Mimi Rogers, Bruce Davison, Jesse Bradford, Tom Bower, Joel Palmer, Josh Wannamaker, Margot Finley. Nicely done (if predictable) boy-and-his-dog tale, centering on young Bradford and his superbright Golden Labrador as they survive the capsizing of their boat, and must overcome assorted dangers. [PG]▼❶

Far From the Madding Crowd (1967-British) C-171m. ***½ D: John Schlesinger. Julie Christie, Peter Finch, Terence Stamp, Alan Bates, Prunella Ransome. Shamefully underrated adaptation of Thomas Hardy novel about beautiful woman and her profound effect on three men. Superb production, with brilliant photography by Nicolas Roeg, score by Richard Rodney Bennett, script by Frederic Raphael, and performances by Finch and Bates. Panavision.▼❶

Fargo (1996) C-97m. ***½ D: Joel Coen. Frances McDormand, William H. Macy, Steve Buscemi, Harve Presnell, Peter Stormare, Kirstin Rudrud, John Carroll Lynch, Larry Brandenburg, Steven Reevis, Jose Feliciano. The Coen brothers put a unique spin on a murder case, layering their story with droll observations about Minnesotans and winding up with a totally disarming comedy! McDormand is terrific as an efficient (and pregnant) police chief with multiple murders on her hands; Macy is equally good as a two-bit schemer who tries to stay cool when he finds himself way over his head in a quicksand of crime. Love that Muzak in the background! Oscar winner for Best Screenplay (Joel and Ethan Coen) and Actress (McDormand). [R]▼❶

Far Horizons, The (1955) C-108m. **½ D: Rudolph Maté. Fred MacMurray, Charlton Heston, Donna Reed, Barbara Hale, William Demarest. Movie fiction about Lewis and Clark expedition, beautifully photographed; sporadic action; implausible love interest. VistaVision.❶

Farinelli (1994-Belgian) C-110m. **½ D: Gerard Corbiau. Stefano Dionisi, Enrico Lo Verso, Jeroen Krabbé, Elsa Zylberstein,

Caroline Cellier, Marianne Basler. Sumptuously filmed saga of two brothers in 18th-century Europe, one a composer and the other a castrato opera singer (who, despite childhood castration, still woos women energetically, with the help of his brother). Rambling script has too many flashbacks and too little insight into the brothers' motivations; still, it's provocative and good-looking. Farinelli's castrato vocals were re-created by a digitally morphed mixture of a male and female opera singer. Original title: FARINELLI IL CASTRATO. [R]▼❶

Farm, The SEE: Curse, The

Farmer's Daughter, The (1947) 97m. ***½ D: H. C. Potter. Loretta Young, Joseph Cotten, Ethel Barrymore, Charles Bickford, Rose Hobart, Harry Davenport, Lex Barker, James Aurness (Arness), Keith Andes, Rhys Williams, Art Baker. Young won an Oscar for her irresistible performance as a naïve but straight-thinking farm girl who goes to work for a senator—and winds up running for a congressional seat against his party. Delightful comedy with an excellent cast. Allen Rivkin and Laura Kerr adapted Juhani Tervapää's play *Hulda, Daughter of Parliament*. Later a TV series. ▼

Farmer Takes a Wife, The (1953) C-81m. ** D: Henry Levin. Betty Grable, Dale Robertson, Thelma Ritter, John Carroll, Eddie Foy, Jr., Gwen Verdon. Musical remake of 1935 film is slow-paced account of life in 1800s along the Erie Canal.▼❶

Far North (1988) C-90m. *½ D: Sam Shepard. Jessica Lange, Charles Durning, Tess Harper, Donald Moffat, Ann Wedgeworth, Patricia Arquette, Nina Draxton. Shepard's directing debut, which he also scripted, is a pointless, artificial drama about the various members of a Minnesota family and what happens when patriarch Durning is almost killed by a wild horse. Good cast is wasted. [PG-13]▼❶

Far Off Place, A (1993) C-105m. *** D: Mikael Salomon. Reese Witherspoon, Ethan Randall (Embry), Maximilian Schell, Jack Thompson, Sarel Bok, Robert Burke, Patricia Kalember, Daniel Gerroll. Borderline-slow, but head-on-straight, Disney kids' adventure about a young Bushman guide, a game warden's daughter, and a visiting city boy who flee across the desert from murderous poachers. Frank treatment of death makes this iffy for young kids, but older children should find it rewarding. Based on the books *A Story Like the Wind* and *A Far Off Place* by Laurens van der Post. Juan Ruiz-Anchia's magnificent photography is a standout. Panavision. [PG]▼❶

Far Out Man (1990) C-81m. BOMB D: Tommy Chong. Tommy Chong, Shelby Chong, Paris Chong, C. Thomas Howell, Martin Mull, Rae Dawn Chong, Judd Nelson. Labeled "A Tommy Chong Attempt," this vanity production is high on nepotism but short on laughs—or coherence. Chong plays a burned-out, leftover 1960s druggie who's trying to find his ex-lady and their child (played by their real-life counterparts). Longtime partner Cheech Marin contributes a cameo, but is sorely missed throughout the rest of the grungy film. [R] ▼●❶

Fascination (2004–German-British) **C-95m.** BOMB D: Klaus Menzel. Jacqueline Bisset, Adam Garcia, Alice Evans, Stuart Wilson, James Naughton. Dad drowns despite being an excellent swimmer, and his son is irked when his mom immediately takes on a new squeeze with a grown daughter (who has her own checkered history). Elements are in place for a noir-ish mystery, but the only heat we get is solar from beach scenes shot in daylight. The real fascination comes from speculating how this even got made, let alone released (which it just barely was). Filmed in 2002. Super 35. [R] ▼❶

Fast & Furious (2009) **C-106m.** **½ D: Justin Lin. Vin Diesel, Paul Walker, Michelle Rodriguez, Jordana Brewster, John Ortiz, Laz Alonso, Gal Gadot, Jack Conley, Sung Kang. Fourth installment of the popular franchise reunites four stars of 2001's THE FAST AND THE FURIOUS for a mostly ridiculous but frequently exciting action-adventure set along the U.S.-Mexico border. Two reluctant allies (illegal street racer Diesel and maverick FBI agent Walker) team up for a vengeful campaign against a murderous drug cartel. Serviceable plot is merely an excuse for some spectacular high-speed car chases, but fans won't be disappointed by the thrills and spills of this demolition derby. Followed by FAST FIVE. Super 35. [PG-13]❶

Fast and the Furious, The (1954) **73m.** ** D: Edwards Sampson, John Ireland. John Ireland, Dorothy Malone, Iris Adrian, Bruce Carlisle, Jean Howell, Larry Thor. Ireland is fugitive on the lam from murder frameup who jockeys Malone's sports car, with uninspired romantic interludes and cops-on-the-chase sequences. Produced and written by Roger Corman, this was the first film for American Releasing Corporation—soon to be the fabled AIP (American-International Pictures). ▼❶

Fast and the Furious, The (2001) **C-107m.** **½ D: Rob Cohen. Paul Walker, Vin Diesel, Michelle Rodriguez, Jordana Brewster, Rick Yune, Chad Lindberg, Johnny Strong, Matt Schulze, Ted Levine, Ja Rule. A souped-up 21st-century version of a 1950s hot-rod movie. Newcomer Walker tries to ingratiate himself with the kingpin of Southern California street racing (Diesel), hoping to join his extended family. Rudimentary storyline frames some pulse-quickening action scenes . . . but this goes on longer than any drive-in movie really should. Followed by 2 FAST 2 FURIOUS. Super 35. [PG-13] ▼❶

Fast and the Furious: Tokyo Drift, The (2006) **C-104m.** **½ D: Justin Lin. Lucas Black, Brandon Brendel, Zachery Ty Bryan, Daniel Booko, David V. Thomas, Amber Stevens, Bow Wow, Lynda Boyd, Nikki Griffin, JJ Sonny Chiba. Third installment of the series travels to Japan when Black destroys his car in an illegal street race and is sent overseas to avoid jail or juvenile detention. But old habits die hard; while in Tokyo he gets involved in the dangerous underworld sport of "drifting" (racing cars around terrifying curves). Just as loud and frenetic as its predecessors, this benefits from a change of scenery and has a couple of ferocious pedal-to-the-metal sequences. Veteran martial arts star Chiba is fun to watch as an evil Yakuza boss. Followed by FAST & FURIOUS. Super 35. [PG-13]❶

Fast Break (1979) **C-107m.** *** D: Jack Smight. Gabriel Kaplan, Harold Sylvester, Mike Warren, Bernard King, Reb Brown, Mavis Washington, Bert Remsen, Richard Brestoff, Rhonda Bates, K. Callan. Basketball coach Kaplan accepts post at midwestern college, but brings his N.Y.C. street players along with him. Perfect, innocuous TV fare, with some good laughs and exciting game climax. [PG]▼

Fast Charlie, The Moonbeam Rider (1979) **C-99m.** **½ D: Steve Carver. David Carradine, Brenda Vaccaro, L. Q. Jones, R. G. Armstrong, Jesse Vint. Period action comedy-drama about a WW1 deserter who enters the first long-distance motorcycle race. Appealing performance by Vaccaro as an early-day bike groupie and picturesque recreations of post-WW1 America are definite pluses. Also known as FAST CHARLIE AND THE MOONBEAM. [PG]

Fast, Cheap & Out of Control (1997) **C/B&W-82m.** *** D: Errol Morris. Documentary filmmaker Morris delves into the lives of four disparate men: a topiary gardener, a lion tamer, a robot scientist, and a naked-mole-rat expert. Utilizing different film formats, Morris creates a fascinating examination of lifelong passions and occupations that touches on the nature of existence itself. A completely original film, enhanced by Caleb Sampson's music. [PG]▼❶

Faster (2010) **C-98m.** ** D: George Tillman, Jr. Dwayne Johnson, Billy Bob Thornton, Oliver Jackson-Cohen, Carla Gugino, Maggie Grace, Moon Bloodgood, Adewale Akinnuoye-Agbaje, Tom Berenger, Mike Epps, Xander Berkeley. Sanguinary revenger sets hulking ex-con Johnson ("Driver"), junkie Thornton ("Cop"), and conflicted hit man Jackson-Cohen ("Killer") on course to face off in a familiar three-sided showdown. Overpumped oil slick of a movie wallows in homage (clue: check out the assassin's ringtone), and looks as if it were edited with a strobe. Stirring performances, though, by Chevelle SS, GTO, and Ferrari. Super 35. [R] ❶

Fastest Guitar Alive, The (1967) **C-87m.** ** D: Michael Moore. Roy Orbison,

[444]

Sammy Jackson, Maggie Pierce, Joan Freeman. Doomed effort to turn recording star Orbison into a movie star—with the dumbest title imaginable for a Civil War espionage story! ▼▶

Fastest Gun Alive, The (1956) **92m.** ******* D: Russell Rouse. Glenn Ford, Jeanne Crain, Broderick Crawford, Russ Tamblyn. Sincere Western with a moral. Ford is a peace-loving storekeeper trying to live down renown as gunslinger, but there's always someone waiting to challenge him. Tamblyn has an impressive solo dance feature. Also shown in computer-colored version. ▼▶

Fast Five (2011) **C-130m.** ******* D: Justin Lin. Vin Diesel, Paul Walker, Jordana Brewster, Tyrese Gibson, Dwayne Johnson, Chris "Ludacris" Bridges, Sung Kang, Gal Gadot, Elsa Pataky, Tego Calderón, Don Omar, Matt Schulze, Joaquim de Almeida, Michael Irby. Larcenous street racer Diesel and ex-FBI agent Walker reunite in Rio de Janeiro to lead other alumni of THE FAST AND THE FURIOUS (2001) and subsequent sequels in a plot to pilfer millions from a powerful drug lord (de Almeida). Complicating matters: a hard-boiled federal agent (Johnson) has assembled his own hand-picked team to capture them. High-speed chases, slam-bang stunt work, and kinetically choreographed gunfights enhance the standard-issue caper-movie plot in this exceptionally exciting action-thriller. Easily the best (so far) of the franchise, with a teasingly clever coda during closing credits sure to please long-time fans. Super 35. [PG-13] ▶

Fast Food, Fast Women (2000-U.S.-French) **C-96m.** ****½** D: Amos Kollek. Anna Thomson, Jamie Harris, Louise Lasser, Robert Modica, Lonette McKee, Austin Argo, Angelica Torn, Austin Pendleton, Valerie Geffner, Mark Margolis. Breezy character-based comedy revolves around the ever-changing romantic lives of customers (and their dedicated waitress) in a downtown Manhattan coffee shop. Wonderful cast makes the most of the uneven but occasionally insightful script from writer/director Kollek. [R] ▼▶

Fast Food Nation (2006-U.S.-British) **C-114m.** ******* D: Richard Linklater. Greg Kinnear, Catalina Sandino Moreno, Wilmer Valderrama, Bobby Cannavale, Luis Guzman, Ashley Johnson, Avril Lavigne, Esai Morales, Patricia Arquette, Ethan Hawke, Lou Taylor Pucci, Paul Dano, Kris Kristofferson, Bruce Willis. Fast-food exec Kinnear is sent to a meat supplier in Colorado to check out ugly rumors about foreign content in their hamburgers. Valderrama and Sandino Moreno arrive in that same town with other illegal Mexican immigrants and get a harsh introduction to the American dream by working in the meatpacking plant. Potent, polemical (and disturbingly graphic) film about the fast-food mind-set of our society. Based on Eric Schlosser's nonfiction book; he and Linklater wrote the screenplay. [R] ▶

Fast Fortune SEE: **11 Harrowhouse**

Fast Forward (1985) **C-110m.** ***½** D: Sidney Poitier. John Scott Clough, Don Franklin, Tamara Mark, Tracy Silver, Cindy McGee, Gretchen F. Palmer, Irene Worth, Constance Towers. Eight squeaky-clean teens from Sandusky, Ohio, crash N.Y.C. in search of their Big Break in Show Biz. Despite the title, this film is stuck in the 1950s; break-dancing can't disguise such cornball stuff. [PG] ▼▶

Fast Runner, The (2002-Canadian) **C-161m.** ******** D: Zacharias Kunuk. Natar Ungalaaq, Sylvia Ivalu, Peter-Henry Arnatsiaq, Lucy Tulugarjuk, Madeline Ivalu, Paul (Pauloosie) Qulitalik. A sterling epic, perhaps the only Inuit-made film we'll ever see, about a young hunter (Ungalaaq) whose tribe has been cursed; he falls in love but must face the ire of a spiteful rival. The highlight is our hero's barefooted journey across the North Canadian wilderness. A privileged peek into Inuit culture and a stirring, deeply personal drama; based on an ancient Inuit folk tale. Beautifully filmed in wide-screen digital video. Aka ATANARJUAT . . . (THE FAST RUNNER). [R] ▼▶

Fast Times at Ridgemont High (1982) **C-92m.** ******* D: Amy Heckerling. Sean Penn, Jennifer Jason Leigh, Judge Reinhold, Robert Romanus, Brian Backer, Phoebe Cates, Ray Walston, Vincent Schiavelli, Forest Whitaker, James Russo, Pamela Springsteen, Martin Brest. Brashly entertaining look at Southern California high school kids, who hang out at the Mall and think mostly about sex. Funny, surprisingly honest, with a very appealing cast and a memorable performance by Penn as a doped-out goofball named Spicoli. High-energy feature debut for director Heckerling, based on Cameron Crowe's factual book. Film debuts of Forest Whitaker, Eric Stoltz, Anthony Edwards, and Nicolas Cage (billed under his real name, Nicholas Coppola). Some footage of Sean Penn was added for pay TV—but songs on soundtrack changed, altering running time to 90m. Later a TV series. [R] ▼●▶

Fast Track SEE: **Ex, The**

Fast-Walking (1982) **C-115m.** ****½** D: James B. Harris. James Woods, Tim McIntire, Kay Lenz, Robert Hooks, M. Emmet Walsh, Timothy Carey, Susan Tyrrell. Oddball prison picture, laced with black humor, stars Woods as Fast-Walking Miniver, mercenary prison guard who's hired to assassinate politico Hooks. McIntire gives a standout performance as a very cagey inmate in a film whose interesting but disparate elements never quite jell. [R] ▼▶

Fatal Assassin SEE: **Target of an Assassin**

Fatal Attraction (1987) **C-119m.** ****½** D: Adrian Lyne. Michael Douglas, Glenn Close, Anne Archer, Ellen Hamilton Latzen, Stuart Pankin, Ellen Foley, Fred Gwynne, Meg Mundy, Lois Smith, Jane Krakowski. Happily married man has a weekend fling with a sexy woman who turns out to be psychotic and proceeds to turn his (and his family's) life into a living hell. Audience-pleasing thriller telegraphs most of its suspense payoffs and features a finale that seems more appropriate to RAMBO. Still, it's extremely well acted and certainly holds your attention. The film's original ending, which was more subtle and intriguing (but dumped after an unsuccessful preview), is available on video. James Dearden based his screenplay on his own British short subject, "Diversion." [R] ▼●)

Fatal Beauty (1987) C-104m. BOMB D: Tom Holland. Whoopi Goldberg, Sam Elliott, Ruben Blades, Harris Yulin, John P. Ryan, Jennifer Warren, Brad Dourif, Neill Barry, Richard (Cheech) Marin. An inexcusably awful concoction with Goldberg as a narcotics cop. There's no shortage of gratuitous violence . . . and an antidrug message to rationalize its excesses. Some of the dialogue is mind-bogglingly awful. [R] ▼)

Fat Albert (2004) C-93m. ** D: Joel Zwick. Kenan Thompson, Kyla Pratt, Dania Ramirez, Shedrack Anderson III, Jermaine Williams, Keith D. Robinson. Late-adolescent Pratt is downtrodden because she has no friends, so Albert, Mushmouth, and the rest of the Philly-neighborhood Bill Cosby creations emerge from her TV set as live editions of their animated-cartoon selves. This solves her problem, but not before this mild but harmless family comedy throws in some blatant plugs for *Albert* DVDs. Cosby himself shows up; he also cowrote and co-executive produced with his wife, Camille. Other famous folk appear in cameos. Super 35. [PG] ▼)

Fatal Instinct (1993) C-88m. *½ D: Carl Reiner. Armand Assante, Sherilyn Fenn, Kate Nelligan, Sean Young, Christopher McDonald, James Remar, Tony Randall, Clarence Clemons, Michael Cumpsty, Blake Clark, Carl Reiner, Eartha Kitt, Bernard Hiller, Jane Lynch, George Lopez. Woeful, decades-belated spoof of vintage film noir, with contemporary references to BASIC INSTINCT, BODY HEAT, and FATAL ATTRACTION thrown in. Assante shows an unexpected flair for farce as a cop/lawyer targeted for murder by wife Nelligan and her lover (McDonald); Young fares best as a blonde sexpot named Lola. [PG-13] ▼●)

Fat City (1972) C-100m. *** D: John Huston. Stacy Keach, Jeff Bridges, Susan Tyrrell, Candy Clark, Nicholas Colasanto. Taut adaptation of Leonard Gardner's novel about tanktown boxer and his young protégé is one of Huston's best later films, with solid performances all around. [PG] ▼)

Fateless (2005-Hungarian-German-British) C-140m. *** D: Lajos Koltai. Marcell Nagy, Béla Dóra, Bálint Péntek, Áron Di-

mény, Péter Fancsikai, Zsolt Dér, Daniel Craig. During WW2 a Hungarian Jewish teen (Nagy) is picked off a bus and dispatched to the death camps of the Holocaust. Without analyzing his plight or anguishing over his wretched circumstances the boy settles into a pattern of life amid the horrors of Auschwitz and Buchenwald. Cinematographer Koltai's directorial debut is a powerful, sensitive rendering of Nobel Prize winner Imre Kertész's semiautobiographical novel, although at times the filmmaker's approach is a bit too operatic. Kertész also scripted. Panavision.▶)

Fat Girl (2001-French-Italian) C-86m. *** D: Catherine Breillat. Anaïs Reboux, Roxane Mesquida, Libero De Rienzo, Arsinée Khanjian, Romain Goupil, Laura Betti. Potent drama from the always-provocative Breillat explores the complex relationship between two sisters, aged 15 and 12, who (like all the director's heroines) are obsessed by sex. The older one (Mesquida) is pretty and desirable; the other (Reboux) may be plump and miserable, but has her own yearnings. Breillat offers a voice to the title character, a type who is usually the object of scorn or ridicule. Features graphic sex scenes and an unsettling finale.▶)

Father Brown SEE: **Detective, The** (1954)

Father Goose (1964) C-115m. *** D: Ralph Nelson. Cary Grant, Leslie Caron, Trevor Howard, Jack Good, Nicole Felsette. Grant goes native as shiftless bum on a South Seas island during WW2, who's persuaded to become a lookout for the Australian navy—and finds himself sheltering Caron and a gaggle of schoolgirls fleeing the Japanese. Lightweight and enjoyable. Oscar-winning script by Peter Stone and Frank Tarloff.▼)

Father Hood (1993) C-94m. *½ D: Darrell James Roodt. Patrick Swayze, Halle Berry, Sabrina Lloyd, Brian Bonsall, Michael Ironside, Diane Ladd, Bob Gunton, Adrienne Barbeau, Georgann Johnson. Embarrassingly bad action comedy about self-centered, two-bit hood Swayze, who inexplicably hooks up with his two kids (who've been ill treated while in foster care) and takes them on a less-than-enthralling odyssey. In desperate need of a coherent script and characters who are even slightly likable. [PG-13] ▼●)

Father of My Children, The (2009-French) C-110m. *** D: Mia Hansen-Løve. Chiara Caselli, Louis-Do de Lencquesaing, Alice de Lencquesaing, Alice Gautier, Manelle Driss, Eric Elmosnino, Sandrine Dumas, Dominique Frot. Thought-provoking look at a dedicated film producer who juggles many balls but always makes time for his wife and three daughters. An unexpected turn of events causes them to reexamine their lives and their future. Vividly captures the existence of a man who serves many masters and asks us to ponder the wisdom of his decisions. The actress who plays the oldest daughter is the real-life daughter of the film's leading man. Written by the director. Inspired by the life of French film producer Humbert Balsan.◗

Father of the Bride (1950) **93m. ****** D: Vincente Minnelli. Spencer Tracy, Elizabeth Taylor, Joan Bennett, Billie Burke, Leo G. Carroll, Don Taylor, Rusty (Russ) Tamblyn. Liz is marrying Don Taylor, but Dad (Tracy) has all the aggravation. Perceptive view of American life, witty script by Frances Goodrich and Albert Hackett (based on Edward Streeter's book), and peerless Tracy performance. Sequel: FATHER'S LITTLE DIVIDEND. Later a TV series. Remade in 1991. Also shown in computer-colored version.▼◗

Father of the Bride (1991) **C-105m. **½** D: Charles Shyer. Steve Martin, Diane Keaton, Martin Short, Kimberly Williams, Kieran Culkin, George Newbern, B. D. Wong, Peter Michael Goetz, Kate McGregor Stewart, Martha Gehman. Pleasant update of the 1950 comedy gem about a father unwilling to let go of his little girl. It's refreshing to find such "normal" characters in a '90s movie, but there are too many lulls (and a few too many sidesteps into silliness) for it to hit the bull's-eye as the original did. P.S.: Can we now arrange a moratorium on the song "My Girl"? Funny cameo by Eugene Levy. Followed by a sequel. [PG]▼◗

Father of the Bride Part II (1995) **C-106m. *** D: Charles Shyer. Steve Martin, Diane Keaton, Martin Short, Kimberly Williams, George Newbern, Kieran Culkin, B. D. Wong, Peter Michael Goetz, Kate McGregor Stewart, Jane Adams, Eugene Levy. Agreeable sequel has married daughter Williams announcing that she's pregnant, which impels Dad (Martin) to confront middle age. His midlife crisis includes a rash decision to sell their house and a renewed romanticism. Longish but fun. [PG]▼◗

Fathers and Sons (1992) **C-100m. *** D: Paul Mones. Jeff Goldblum, Rory Cochrane, Mitchell Marchand, Famke Janssen, Natasha Gregson Wagner, Paul Hipp, Ellen Greene, Samuel L. Jackson, Joie Lee, Rosanna Arquette. Odd, slow-paced drama about a movie director (Goldblum) now almost a recluse, who lives on the Jersey shore with his teenage son (Cochrane). Crowded plot involves drugs, a serial killer, a prophetic book, telepathy, mutated dolphins, and alcoholism. Tackles too much, but is occasionally effective; Goldblum is excellent, as usual. John C. McGinley appears unbilled. Written by the director. [R]▼

Fathers' Day (1997) **C-98m. *** D: Ivan Reitman. Robin Williams, Billy Crystal, Julia Louis-Dreyfus, Natassja Kinski, Charlie Hofheimer, Bruce Greenwood, Jared Harris, Louis Lombardi, Patti D'Arbanville, Charles Rocket, Meagen Fay. When her 16-year-old son runs away, a desperate Kinski tells each of two ex-lovers that he's the real father, hoping that this will spur one of them to find the boy. The two men—a genuine odd couple—wind up working together on this daunting task. Lackluster remake of Francis Veber's LES COMPÈRES gets whatever mileage it has from the two comic stars' personalities . . . but the boy is extremely dislikable, and a subplot with his stepfather (Greenwood) is a complete misfire. Panavision. [PG-13]▼◗

Father's Little Dividend (1951) **82m. *** D: Vincente Minnelli. Spencer Tracy, Joan Bennett, Elizabeth Taylor, Don Taylor, Billie Burke, Rusty (Russ) Tamblyn. Delightful sequel to FATHER OF THE BRIDE with same cast. Now Tracy is going to be a grandfather and he doesn't look forward to it. Also shown in computer-colored version.▼◗

Fathom (1967) **C-99m. *** D: Leslie H. Martinson. Tony Franciosa, Raquel Welch, Clive Revill, Greta Chi, Richard Briers, Ronald Fraser, Tony Adams. Fast-paced, tongue-in-cheek spy caper with sky-diver Welch getting mixed up with dubious good-guy Franciosa. Great fun, with Revill's performance as eccentric millionaire stealing the show. Music score by John Dankworth. CinemaScope.▼◖

Fat Man and Little Boy (1989) **C-126m. *** D: Roland Joffé. Paul Newman, Dwight Schultz, Bonnie Bedelia, John Cusack, Laura Dern, Ron Frazier, John C. McGinley, Natasha Richardson. Flawed but still arresting film about the development of the atomic bomb, personalizing the story by focusing on General Groves (Newman), the bullheaded Army officer who was handed the job, and the brilliant J. Robert Oppenheimer (Schultz), who organized the brain trust creating the bomb. One complaint: some decidedly non-1940s slang amid the dialogue. J-D-C Scope. [PG-13]▼◗

Fatso (1980) **C-94m. *** D: Anne Bancroft. Dom DeLuise, Anne Bancroft, Candice Azzara, Ron Carey, Michael Lombard, Sal Viscuso. Bancroft's only feature as writer-director is disappointing. Fat man DeLuise half-heartedly tries to reduce after the death of his obese cousin. Film veers unevenly between comedy and pathos, with a few too many excrement jokes, perhaps the uncredited contribution of Mel Brooks. [PG]▼◖

Fat Spy, The (1965) **C-75m. *½** D: Joseph Cates. Phyllis Diller, Jack E. Leonard, Brian Donlevy, Jayne Mansfield, Jordan Christopher, The Wild Ones, Johnny Tillotson. Once-in-a-lifetime cast makes this a must for camp followers—and a sure thing to avoid for most others. Fat Jack plays dual roles, in a story of a search for the Fountain of Youth. Shot in Florida.▼◖

Fauteuils d'Orchestre SEE: **Avenue Montaigne**

Favor, The (1994) **C-97m. *** D: Donald

Petrie. Harley Jane Kozak, Elizabeth McGovern, Bill Pullman, Brad Pitt, Ken Wahl, Larry Miller, Holland Taylor. "Happily" married Kozak asks best friend McGovern to look up—and sleep with—her high school hunk boyfriend, so she can vicariously experience the affair. Pleasant cast undone by comedy material that doesn't ring true for one minute. Sat on the shelf after completion in 1991; its latter-day release did no one any favors. [R]▼●

Favour, the Watch, and the Very Big Fish, The (1991-French-British) **C-89m.** ** D: Ben Lewin. Bob Hoskins, Jeff Goldblum, Natasha Richardson, Michel Blanc, Jacques Villeret, Angela Pleasence, Jean-Pierre Cassel, Samuel Chaimovitch. Pianist Goldblum agrees to pose as Christ on the cross for a photographer specializing in Biblical pictures—and then starts taking his role too seriously. Weak attempt at farce never quite connects, despite some amusing moments scattered about. This cast deserves better. [R]▼●

Fay Grim (2007-U.S.-German) **C-118m.** **½ D: Hal Hartley. Parker Posey, Jeff Goldblum, James Urbaniak, Saffron Burrows, Liam Aiken, Elina Löwensohn, Leo Fitzpatrick, Chuck Montgomery, Thomas Jay Ryan. Sequel to Hartley's HENRY FOOL picks up where that film left off, as Posey—abandoned by her husband, who may or may not be dead—struggles with her rebellious teenage son. She then becomes a pawn of CIA agent Goldblum and flies to Europe to carry out a strange bargain involving Henry Fool's unpublished manuscript, which supposedly contains volatile information. Highly committed performances by the cast invite you to go along on this screw-loose, convoluted, straight-faced but tongue-in-cheek journey, even though it doesn't make much sense. Hartley also edited and composed the score. [R]▶

FBI Story, The (1959) **C-149m.** *** D: Mervyn LeRoy. James Stewart, Vera Miles, Murray Hamilton, Larry Pennell, Nick Adams, Diane Jergens, Joyce Taylor. Well-mounted fabrication of history of F.B.I. as seen through career of agent Stewart, allowing for episodic sidelights into action-packed capers and view of his personal life. ▼●■

Fear (1996) **C-95m.** ** D: James Foley. Mark Wahlberg, Reese Witherspoon, William Petersen, Amy Brenneman, Alyssa Milano. Squeaky-clean teen falls for sexy psycho who locks horns with protective papa in a deadly battle. Passable slasher pic is somewhat redeemed by Foley's taut, stylish direction (the roller coaster scene is pretty steamy) and decent performances. Still, it's awfully derivative, especially the final showdown at the family nest. One of Wahlberg's earliest acting roles; he is menacing as the lovestruck hood. Executive producer Brian Grazer called this "FATAL ATTRACTION for teens." Panavision. [R]▼●■

Fear and Desire (1953) **68m.** ** D: Stanley Kubrick. Frank Silvera, Kenneth Harp, Paul Mazursky, Steve Coit, Virginia Leith; narrated by David Allen. Kubrick's elusive, shoestring-budget feature-film debut is an existential antiwar allegory centering on four G.I.s (including a very green Mazursky, in his film debut) stranded behind the lines of an unknown enemy and fighting a fictitious war in an unidentified country. Long suppressed by Kubrick himself—who also photographed, edited, and cowrote with poet/playwright Howard Sackler—the movie contains some striking imagery and shows the germs of budding talent, but generally comes off as an arty and pretentious student film.

Fear and Loathing in Las Vegas (1998) **C-119m.** BOMB D: Terry Gilliam. Johnny Depp, Benicio Del Toro, Tobey Maguire, Craig Bierko, Katherine Helmond, Mark Harmon, Tim Thomerson, Penn Jillette, Cameron Diaz, Lyle Lovett, Flea, Gary Busey, Christina Ricci, Michael Jeter, Harry Dean Stanton, Ellen Barkin. Excruciating adaptation of Hunter S. Thompson's 1971 book, which defined the counterculture of its day. The film, however, is simply one monotonous, painfully long drug trip—replete with closeups of vomit and swooping camera movements at any and every opportunity. Perhaps Thompson diehards will find some value here; others beware. Super 35. [R]▼●■

Fear Chamber, The (1971-Mexican-U.S) **C-80m.** *½ D: Juan Ibanez, Jack Hill. Boris Karloff, Julissa, Carlos East, Isela Vega, Yerye Beirute. Strange film about a semi-living stone from volcano caves that requires fluid from a terrified person in order to communicate with humans; dedicated scientist Karloff and his assistants are all too eager to help. Though faintly better than the other three Mexican-American productions Karloff worked on in 1968 (just before his death), this is still awful. Aka TORTURE ZONE.▼■

Fear City (1984) **C-96m.** *½ D: Abel Ferrara. Tom Berenger, Billy Dee Williams, Jack Scalia, Melanie Griffith, Rossano Brazzi, Rae Dawn Chong, Joe Santos, Michael V. Gazzo, Jan Murray, Ola Ray, Maria Conchita Alonso. Incredibly sleazy look at Manhattan lowlife—violent and repellent in the extreme. Remarkably good cast for this kind of exploitation fodder. [R]▼●■

FeardotCom (2002-British-Luxembourgian-German) **C-101m.** *½ D: William Malone. Stephen Dorff, Natascha McElhone, Stephen Rea, Udo Kier, Amelia Curtis, Jeffrey Combs, Nigel Terry, Michael Sarrazin. Cop Dorff and health worker McElhone link a series of strange deaths in N.Y.C. to a particular computer Web site. Dark, gloomy, and very gory, this urban nightmare is well visualized, but the story is confusing and hard to follow. Super 35. [R] ▼■

Fear Inside, The (1992) **C-115m.** *** D:

Leon Ichaso. Christine Lahti, Dylan McDermott, Jennifer Rubin, David Ackroyd, Thomas Ian Nicholas, Paul Linke. Lahti shines as an agoraphobic book artist held hostage at home by a pair of killers. David Birke's well-turned screenplay owes something, it seems, to LADY IN A CAGE. Theatrical film that premiered on cable television. [R]▼●

Fear in the Night (1947) **72m.** ******* D: Maxwell Shane. Paul Kelly, DeForest Kelley, Kay Scott, Ann Doran, Robert Emmett Keane. Nifty chiller in which bank teller Kelley dreams he has killed a man in a mirrored room—and wakes up to be confronted by evidence that his fantasy was in fact reality. Based on the story "Nightmare" by William Irish (Cornell Woolrich); remade under that title in 1956.▼●

Fear in the Night (1972-British) **C-94m.** ****** D: Jimmy Sangster. Judy Geeson, Joan Collins, Ralph Bates, Peter Cushing. Newlywed Geeson accompanies husband Bates to a private school where the only other inhabitants are a somewhat befuddled headmaster (Cushing) and his cool wife (Collins). Geeson can't get anyone to believe someone is trying to kill her. Minor Hammer thriller.▼●

Fear Is the Key (1972-British) **C-103m.** ***½** D: Michael Tuchner. Barry Newman, Suzy Kendall, John Vernon, Dolph Sweet, Ben Kingsley. Confused, unsatisfying Alistair MacLean thriller about a man driven to extremes in pursuit of stolen booty—and revenge for the murder of his wife and child. Kingsley's debut and only film work before GANDHI. Panavision. [PG]

Fearless (1993) **C-122m.** *****½** D: Peter Weir. Jeff Bridges, Isabella Rossellini, Rosie Perez, Tom Hulce, John Turturro, Benicio Del Toro, Deirdre O'Connell, John De Lancie, Spencer Vrooman, Daniel Cerny, Eve Roberts. A man feels his life, his outlook, his entire raison d'être changed after he survives a terrible plane crash; he can no longer deal with his own family, but is drawn to another survivor (Perez), who's unable to cope with the loss of her baby in the crash. Superior writing and acting, with Bridges (good as always) matched by Rossellini (in her best performance to date, as his wife) and Perez. Screenplay by Rafael Yglesias, based on his novel. [R]▼●▮

Fearless (2006) SEE: **Jet Li's Fearless**

Fearless Frank (1967) **C-83m.** BOMB D: Philip Kaufman. Jon Voight, Monique Van Vooren, Joan Darling, Severn Darden, Anthony Holland, Lou Gilbert, David Steinberg, Nelson Algren. Naive country boy Voight treks off to the Big City, is murdered by gangsters, and is reincarnated as a superhero and his monsterlike clone. Pretentious satire is of interest only as a curio—and as Voight's film debut. Filmed in Chicago in 1965. Aka FRANK'S GREATEST ADVENTURE and subsequently cut to 78m. Technicope.

Fearless Vampire Killers or: Pardon Me, But Your Teeth Are in My Neck, The (1967-British) **C-98m.** *****½** D: Roman Polanski. Jack MacGowran, Roman Polanski, Sharon Tate, Alfie Bass, Ferdy Mayne, Terry Downes, Ronald Lacey. Near-brilliant mixture of humor and horror: Professor Abronsius and assistant Alfred (great bumbling idiot team) attempt to destroy family of Slovonic vampires. Full 107m. version also available. Screenplay by Polanski and Gérard Brach. Later a Broadway musical called DANCE OF THE VAMPIRES (the film's alternate title). Panavision.▼●

Fear of a Black Hat (1993) **C-86m.** ******* D: Rusty Cundieff. Larry B. Scott, Mark Christopher Lawrence, Rusty Cundieff, Kasi Lemmons, Howie Gold, Eric Laneuville, Barry Heins, Shabaka (Barry Shabaka Henley). THIS IS SPINAL TAP goes rap in this nifty burlesque about those rude, crude gangsta rappers N.W.H. (Niggaz With Hats). Group members are Tasty Taste, Tone Def, and Ice Cold (the latter played by director Cundieff, who also scripted). Quite funny at times, with Cundieff cleverly chiding the self-serving "street politics" of Public Enemy and 2 Live Crew. [R]▼●

Fear Strikes Out (1957) **100m.** ******* D: Robert Mulligan. Anthony Perkins, Karl Malden, Norma Moore, Adam Williams, Perry Wilson. Stark account of baseball star Jimmy Piersall and his bout with mental illness; Perkins is properly intense, with Malden superb as his domineering father. VistaVision.▼●▮

Fear X (2003-Danish-Canadian-British) **C-91m.** BOMB D: Nicolas Winding Refn. John Turturro, Deborah Kara Unger, Stephen McIntyre, William Allen Young, Jacqueline Ramel, James Remar. Security guard Turturro is curious to find out who killed his wife and why. Slow, dull exercise in the emptiness of movies—uh, sorry, life . . . no, movies . . . life . . . *arggghhh!* The type of film where the viewer spends more time wondering at which yard sale the set decorator found the lamp than caring about the story or characters. Widescreen. [PG-13]▼●

Feast (2005) **C-87m.** BOMB D: John Gulager. Duane Whitaker, Balthazar Getty, Chauntae Davies, Diane Goldner, Josh Zuckerman, Henry Rollins, Eileen Ryan, Jason Mewes, Judah Friedlander, Krista Allen, Eric Dane. The filmmakers who starred on the reality TV show *Project Greenlight* came up with this noisy, tedious ordeal, in which a motley crew of strangers in a bar find themselves attacked by gooey, flesh-eating creatures. Doesn't have a shred of character development, plot, or suspense but offers copious amounts of gore, explosions, and incoherent, choppy editing. Director's father, Clu Gulager, plays a bartender. Unrated DVD also available. Followed by two DVD sequels. HD Widescreen. [R]▮

Feast of July (1995-U.S.-British) **C-113m.** **½ D: Christopher Menaul. Embeth Davidtz, Tom Bell, Gemma Jones, James Purefoy, Greg Wise, Kenneth Anderson, Ben Chaplin. A wandering, abandoned unwed mother finds shelter with three brothers and their parents, setting off sexual sparks in the formerly placid Victorian household. Poky prestige film, produced by Merchant-Ivory and based on the H. E. Bates novel, begins and ends satisfactorily, but the middle 90 minutes is slow going. Davidtz is almost *too* ambiguous in the lead. Super 35. [R] ▼●◗

Feast of Love (2007) **C-102m.** ** D: Robert Benton. Morgan Freeman, Greg Kinnear, Radha Mitchell, Selma Blair, Alexa Davalos, Billy Burke, Toby Hemingway, Fred Ward, Jane Alexander, Missi Pyle, Erika Marozsán. Love and heartache amidst a group of people whose lives interweave in Portland, Oregon, including a seemingly serene college professor (Freeman), an upbeat coffee shop owner (Kinnear) who can't ever see what's going on with the women in his life, and a young woman (Davalos) who promises to brighten things up. Genteel and attractive, but after a while you can feel the wheels turning . . . slowly. Based on a novel by Charles Baxter. Super 35. [R]◗

Federal Hill (1994) **100m.** *** D: Michael Corrente. Nicholas Turturro, Anthony DeSando, Libby Langdon, Michael Raynor, Jason Andrews, Robert Turano, Frank Vincent. Story of male camaraderie among young Italian-Americans "from the neighborhood" (Providence, R.I.) has an awfully familiar MEAN STREETS ring to it, but it's quite well done—extremely well acted and filled with unexpected twists. Turturro gives a star-making performance as the firecracker-tempered Ralphie, though the film concentrates on Nicky (DeSando), the local hunk infatuated with a pretty archeology student who's way out of his league. Director Corrente (who also scripted) plays Fredo. Available on video in original and computer-colored versions. [R]▼●◗

Fedora (1978-German) **C-114m.** **½ D: Billy Wilder. William Holden, Marthe Keller, Hildegarde Knef, Jose Ferrer, Frances Sternhagen, Henry Fonda, Michael York, Mario Adorf, Stephen Collins. Stylish but ponderous filmization of Thomas Tryon's short story about a producer's disastrous attempt to lure a Garbo-esque actress out of seclusion. Wilder's potshots at today's films and filmmakers might carry more weight if this film was better. [PG]▼●

Feds (1988) **C-82m.** *½ D: Dan Goldberg. Rebecca De Mornay, Mary Gross, Fred Dalton Thompson, Ken Marshall, Larry Cedar. Pert female cop and her bookish roommate conquer male-chauvinistic colleagues during their struggle to make "the cut" at the FBI Academy. Unlike the POLICE ACADEMY farces, this is played fairly straight, perhaps

in deference to Bureau cooperation; result is laughless—and thus, pointless—comedy. [PG-13]▼●◗

Feeling Minnesota (1996) **C-95m.** ** D: Steven Baigelman. Keanu Reeves, Vincent D'Onofrio, Cameron Diaz, Delroy Lindo, Courtney Love, Tuesday Weld, Dan Aykroyd, Levon Helm. Baigelman's highly touted writing and directing debut explores the explosive and unpredictable relationship between two brothers and the cagey young woman who comes between them. Watchable at times, but utterly disappointing; interesting cast is left high and dry, including the always welcome Weld as the boys' mother. Movie's title was suggested by a line in a song by Soundgarden. Super 35. [R]▼●◗

Feel the Noise (2007) **C-88m.** ** D: Alejandro Chomski. Omarion Grandberry, Giancarlo Esposito, Zulay Henao, James McCaffrey, Kellita Smith, Melonie Diaz. After running afoul of a Harlem gangster, a young would-be rapper (R&B singer Grandberry) seeks safe haven with his long-estranged father (Esposito) in Puerto Rico, where he develops a taste for *reggaetón*—a *muy caliente* mix of rap, hip-hop, reggae, and salsa. Stock characters abound in this formulaic music-fueled drama, but viewers may get in the groove while savoring energetic *reggaetón* performances and modestly steamy dance sequences. Look sharp, and you'll catch a glimpse of coproducer Jennifer Lopez (and husband Marc Anthony) during the movie's final minutes. [PG-13]◗

Felicia's Journey (1999-Canadian-British) **C-113m.** ** D: Atom Egoyan. Bob Hoskins, Arsinée Khanjian, Elaine Cassidy, Sheila Reid, Peter McDonald, Gerard McSorley, Brid Brennan. Mild-mannered catering manager at a British factory takes a kindly interest in a young pregnant woman who's come over from Ireland looking for the boyfriend who abandoned her . . . but the man's intentions are far from pure. A disappointment from Egoyan, from whom we expect more than just another story about a psycho—however layered it may be. Egoyan scripted from William Trevor's novel. Panavision. [PG-13]▼◗

Fellini Satyricon (1969-Italian) **C-129m.** *** D: Federico Fellini. Mârtin Potter, Hiram Keller, Max Born, Capucine, Salvo Randone. Opinions vary on merits of this visually stunning but overindulgent spectacle on ancient Rome, but if you love Fellini, you'll be more receptive than most viewers to his unique panorama of colorful and bizarre characters. Panavision. [R]▼●◗

Fellini's Casanova (1976-Italian) **C-158m.** **½ D: Federico Fellini. Donald Sutherland, Tina Aumont, Cicely Browne, John Karlsen, Daniel Emilfork Berenstein. Uninvolving if opulent version of 18th-century lover's life, made entirely at Rome's Cinecitta Studios. Sutherland is enigmatic, the film stylized to a sometimes absurd degree. Nino Rota's music helps. Danilo Donati won an Oscar for his costumes. [R]▼

Fellini's Roma (1972-Italian) **C-128m.** *** D: Federico Fellini. Peter Gonzales, Britta Barnes, Pia de Doses, Fiona Florence, Marne Maitland, Renato Giovannoli, Federico Fellini. Famed director's impressionistic ode to Eternal City of his youth, his adolescence, and the present—complete with fantasy sequence and usual carnival-of-life point of view. [R]▼●)

Fellow Traveler (1989-British) **C-97m.** *** D: Philip Saville. Ron Silver, Hart Bochner, Imogen Stubbs, Daniel J. Travanti, Katherine Borowitz. Excellent political thriller detailing the plight and fate of a pair of childhood pals, one (Bochner) a movie star and the other (Silver) a scriptwriter, who are both blacklisted during the McCarthy era. Especially on target as a reflection of the temper of the 1950s, with a perceptive script by Michael Eaton. ▼

Female on the Beach (1955) **97m.** ** D: Joseph Pevney. Joan Crawford, Jeff Chandler, Jan Sterling, Cecil Kellaway, Judith Evelyn, Natalie Schafer, Charles Drake. Hot, heavy—and very tacky—melodrama, in which fisherman-stud Chandler attempts to put the make on wealthy widow Crawford. Outrageously trashy script is crammed with sexual double entendres. A must for Crawford fans—but don't expect anything resembling a good movie.

Female Perversions (1997) **C-119m.** ** D: Susan Streitfeld. Tilda Swinton, Amy Madigan, Karen Sillas, Frances Fisher, Laila Robins, Clancy Brown, Paulina Porizkova, John Diehl, Lisa Jane Persky, Marcia Cross. Story of highly successful lawyer (Swinton), in line for a judgeship, who is consumed by self-doubt. She swings both ways sexually, and repeatedly puts her reputation at risk. That her Ph.D. candidate sister is a shoplifter is testimony to their highly dysfunctional upbringing. Disjointed, pretentious film with a title more titillating than the film itself. [R]▼)

Female Space Invaders SEE: **Starcrash**

Femme Fatale (1991) **C-90m.** BOMB D: André Guttfreund. Colin Firth, Lisa Zane, Billy Zane, Scott Wilson, Lisa Blount, Carmine Caridi. Firth is squeaky-clean newlywed whose mysterious bride vanishes on eve of their honeymoon; he then uncovers lurid underground lifestyle she came from and to which she may have returned. Lisa Zane isn't terribly enigmatic, just tedious. Psychological drama begs for a sensible screenplay. Lisa and Billy Zane are sister and brother. [Available in both R and PG versions]▼●

Femme Fatale (2002-French) **C-112m.** **½ D: Brian De Palma. Rebecca Romijn-Stamos, Antonio Banderas, Peter Coyote, Eriq Ebouaney, Edouard Montoute, Rie Rasmussen, Thierry Frémont, Gregg Henry. Giddy mix of ingredients from vintage De Palma

(and Hitchcock) thrillers with Romijn-Stamos in fine form—literally and otherwise—as a deadly blonde bombshell. She cheats her partners out of the loot from a daring theft and assumes a new identity, but she's been caught on film by photographer Banderas . . . and the twists just keep a-comin'. Story doesn't make much sense, but tries to intoxicate the viewer with its audacity and a swirl of stylish images and set pieces. Régis Wargnier and Sandrine Bonnaire appear in the Cannes Film Festival segment, screening their film EAST-WEST. Written by the director. [R] ▼)

FernGully . . . The Last Rainforest (1992) **C-76m.** *** D: Bill Kroyer. Voices of Tim Curry, Samantha Mathis, Christian Slater, Robin Williams, Grace Zabriskie, Cheech Marin, Thomas Chong, Tone Loc. Entertaining animated feature for kids, with an ecological message. Mystical miniature forest creatures are threatened when human invasion of their rainforest (with bulldozers) threatens to unleash an evil spirit who's been locked up in a tree for years. Lively and enjoyable, if not memorable, with plenty of laughs for grown-ups in the free-flowing dialogue of Batty Koda, a whacked-out bat voiced by Robin Williams. Followed by a video sequel, FERNGULLY 2: THE MAGICAL RESCUE. [G]▼●)

Ferris Bueller's Day Off (1986) **C-103m.** **½ D: John Hughes. Matthew Broderick, Alan Ruck, Mia Sara, Jeffrey Jones, Jennifer Grey, Cindy Pickett, Lyman Ward, Edie McClurg, Charlie Sheen, Ben Stein, Del Close, Virginia Capers, Louis Anderson, Max Perlich, T. Scott Coffey, Kristy Swanson. Saga of a cocky teenager's day of adventure while cutting classes. Starts off extremely funny, with on-target jabs at high school life, then wanders through heavy-handed slapstick and moody self-serious ruminations before regaining momentum for a bright finish. Typically uneven John Hughes script, but one of the pop-culture landmarks of its time. Later a TV series. Super 35. [PG-13]▼●)

Ferry to Hong Kong (1959-British) **C-103m.** **½ D: Lewis Gilbert. Orson Welles, Curt Jurgens, Sylvia Syms, Jeremy Spenser. Welles and Jurgens have field day as straight-faced ferry boat skipper and drunken Austrian on trip to Macao. Otherwise just routine. CinemaScope.▼)

Festival in Cannes (2002) **C-99m.** *** D: Henry Jaglom. Anouk Aimée, Maximilian Schell, Greta Scacchi, Zack Norman, Ron Silver, Jenny Gabrielle, Alex Craig Mann, Peter Bogdanovich. Slice-of-life drama set against the Cannes Film Festival, where everyone is after something: a deal, a script, a commitment, a comeback, a reconciliation. Told in Jaglom's loose, sometimes ragged improvisational style, with exceptional actors adding substance to the proceedings. Funny, observant, and especially recommended for movie buffs. Cameos include Faye Dunaway and William Shatner.▼)

Feud, The (1989) **C-96m.** ******* D: Bill D'Elia, Rene Auberjonois, Ron McLarty, Joe Grifasi, Scott Allegrucci, Gale Mayron, David Strathairn, Stanley Tucci, Lynne Killmeyer, Kathleen Doyle, Libby George. David Lynch meets Norman Rockwell in this oddly likable satire of 1950s small-town America, centering on a feud that erupts between two families in neighboring hamlets. Broadly played; has cult-status possibilities. Based on Thomas Berger's novel; coscripted by first-time director D'Elia. [R]▼

Fever (1989-Australian) **C-83m.** ******* D: Craig Lahiff. Bill Hunter, Mary Regan, Gary Sweet. Virtually silent film noir in the James M. Cain/Hitchcock vein. The ingredients are a tough cop, his younger wife, her shallow lover, and a suitcase full of money. Surprising throughout. [R]▼

Fever (2001) **C-93m.** ****½** D: Alex Winter. Henry Thomas, David O'Hara, Teri Hatcher, Bill Duke, Remak Ramsey, Marisol Padilla Sanchez, Irma St. Paule. Somber, pitch-black chiller about a struggling young artist/drawing instructor (Thomas) who lives in a dingy Brooklyn tenement. On the night a mysterious stranger moves in upstairs, his landlord is brutally murdered. Is his new neighbor real or imagined? Does the cop on the case think he's the killer? Occasional boring stretches are outweighed by genuinely creepy atmosphere and effectively understated performances; Winter (of BILL & TED fame) does a fine job of visualizing the artist's fears and growing paranoia. [R] ▼❂

Fever Pitch (1985) **C-96m.** BOMB D: Richard Brooks. Ryan O'Neal, Catherine Hicks, Giancarlo Giannini, Bridgette Andersen, Chad Everett, John Saxon, William Smith. Anachronistic look at gambling fever with newspaper columnist (and "fever" victim) O'Neal. Embarrassingly bad; overwritten by veteran Brooks with declamatory dialogue from the *Dragnet* school of scripts. [R]▼

Fever Pitch (1997-British) **C-102m.** ******* D: David Evans. Colin Firth, Ruth Gemmell, Neil Pearson, Lorraine Ashbourne, Mark Strong, Holly Aird, Ken Stott, Stephen Rea. Likable, often perceptive look at a soccer-obsessed schoolteacher and the colleague who falls in love with him but can't understand (or embrace) his obsession with a local team. Nick Hornby (HIGH FIDELITY) adapted his novel, which offers a fresh look at the differences between men and women. Remade in 2005. [R]▼❂

Fever Pitch (2005) **C-101m.** ******* D: Peter Farrelly, Bobby Farrelly. Drew Barrymore, Jimmy Fallon, James B. Sikking, JoBeth Williams, Willie Garson, Evan Helmuth, Ione Skye, KaDee Strickland, Marissa Jaret Winokur. Appealing comedy about a workaholic, just turning 30, who meets a nice-guy schoolteacher one winter, only to learn as spring arrives that he is a lifelong Boston Red Sox fanatic. Writers Lowell Ganz and Babaloo Mandel paint a believable picture of two people who love each other but have to overcome a major obstacle. A departure from gross-out absurdism for the Farrelly Brothers; the stars couldn't be more likable. Set against the backdrop of the Red Sox's amazing 2004 season. Based on Nick Hornby's novel, filmed before in 1997. Super 35. [PG-13]▼❂

Few Days in the Life of I. I. Oblomov, A SEE: **Oblomov**

Few Days With Me, A (1988-French) **C-131m.** ******* D: Claude Sautet. Daniel Auteuil, Sandrine Bonnaire, Jean-Pierre Marielle, Dominique Lavanant, Danielle Darrieux, Tanya Lopert. Intriguing chronicle of chameleonlike Auteuil, whose family owns a department-store chain, and the series of events that ensue upon his checking up on one outlet, located in a provincial town. Veers too much between comedy (some of which is hilarious) and drama.

Few Good Men, A (1992) **C-138m.** ******* D: Rob Reiner. Tom Cruise, Jack Nicholson, Demi Moore, Kevin Bacon, Kiefer Sutherland, Kevin Pollak, James Marshall, J.T. Walsh, Christopher Guest, J.A. Preston, Matt Craven, Wolfgang Bodison, Cuba Gooding, Jr., Noah Wyle. Aaron Sorkin's powerful one-set play is effectively expanded for movie retelling, as a slick young Navy lawyer (Cruise) is driven to investigate the case of two Marines who killed a compatriot. Nicholson bristles as the commanding officer of the base who doesn't want the whole story told. Smashing courtroom climax, top-grade performances all around, but a handful of contrivances keep this from scoring a direct hit. Panavision. [R]▼❂❂

ffolkes (1980) **C-99m.** ******* D: Andrew V. McLaglen. Roger Moore, James Mason, Anthony Perkins, Michael Parks, David Hedison, Jack Watson, Lea Brodie. Moore has fun playing an eccentric counterterrorist hired by the British government when a team of terrorists threaten to blow up two North Sea oil rigs. Surprisingly little action *per se,* but an entertaining yarn. Retitled ASSAULT FORCE for TV. Aka NORTH SEA HIJACK. [PG]▼❂

F for Fake (1974) **C-88m.** ****½** D: Orson Welles. Wellesian tomfoolery, which started out as a portrait of notorious art forger Elmyr de Hory. When one of the interviewees turned out to be Clifford Irving—who fooled the world with a bogus Howard Hughes autobiography—Welles was forced to alter his film. Now it's a free-form treatise on hoaxes, with Welles' on-camera charm compensating for some of the movie's rough edges. Joseph Cotten, Paul Stewart, and Laurence Harvey appear briefly as themselves, along with Welles' longtime companion, Oja Kodar.▼❂❂

Fickle Finger of Fate, The (1967-U.S.-

Spanish) **C-91m.** *½ D: Richard Rush. Tab Hunter, Luis Prendes, Patty Shepard, Gustavo Rojo, Fernando Hilbeck. Idiotic comedy with Hunter an American engineer falsely accused of smuggling a candlestick, known as The Finger of Fate, out of Spain. He goes undercover in an attempt to unmask the real culprit.▼

Fiddler on the Roof (1971) **C-181m.** *** D: Norman Jewison. (Chaim) Topol, Norma Crane, Leonard Frey, Molly Picon, Paul Mann, Rosalind Harris, Michele Marsh, Neva Small, Candice Bonstein, Paul (Michael) Glaser. Rousing, colorful location-filmed adaptation of Joseph Stein's hit play based on Sholem Aleichem stories of humble village of Anatevka. Topol is hearty as Tevye, trying to preserve Jewish heritage against growing odds. Sheldon Harnick–Jerry Bock score melodically performed; Isaac Stern's violin featured on soundtrack. Earned Oscars for Cinematography (Oswald Morris) and Scoring (John Williams). Reissued at 150m. For an interesting comparison, see the original Yiddish-language TEVYE. Panavision. [G]▼●]

Fido (2007-Canadian) **C-91m.** ** D: Andrew Currie. Carrie-Anne Moss, Billy Connolly, Dylan Baker, K'Sun Ray, Tim Blake Nelson, Henry Czerny, Sonja Bennett, Jennifer Clement, Rob LaBelle, Aaron Brown. Standard boy-and-his-dog formula is given a darkly amusing futuristic twist. A boy named Timmy (of course) adopts a domesticated six-foot-tall zombie that performs all the tasks a family pet might . . . until he starts sucking on the neighbors and terrorizing the tight-knit community. Smart premise could have been a contender in better hands; starts out great but quickly lapses into predictable silliness and gore. Connolly is fun to watch as Fido. Super 35. [R]❯

Field, The (1990-British) **C-107m.** ** D: Jim Sheridan. Richard Harris, John Hurt, Tom Berenger, Sean Bean, Brenda Fricker, Frances Tomelty, John Cowley, Sean McGinley, Jenny Conroy. Ireland, the 1930s: a bull of a man who's nurtured a rented field into a prime piece of land nearly goes crazy when the widow who owns it decides to sell it at auction. Grim tale of deep-rooted stubbornness (and provincial clannishness) plays out like a Greek tragedy, and despite Harris' towering performance, becomes aloof and largely unmoving. Based on a play by John B. Keane. [PG-13]▼●]

Field of Dreams (1989) **C-106m.** ***½ D: Phil Alden Robinson. Kevin Costner, Amy Madigan, Gaby Hoffmann, Ray Liotta, Timothy Busfield, James Earl Jones, Burt Lancaster, Frank Whaley, Dwier Brown. Costner plays a novice farmer in Iowa who hears "a voice" that inspires him to build a baseball diamond on his property, in the hope of bringing the legendary baseball star Shoeless Joe Jackson (whose career was cut short by the Black Sox scandal) back to life. A story of redemption and faith, in the tradition of the best Hollywood fantasies, with moments that are pure magic. Kudos to writer-director Robinson, who adapted W. P. Kinsella's book *Shoeless Joe*, for hitting (and maintaining) just the right note from start to finish. Lovely score by James Horner. [PG]▼●]

Fiendish Ghouls, The SEE: **Mania**

Fiendish Plot of Dr. Fu Manchu, The (1980-British) **C-108m.** BOMB D: Piers Haggard. Peter Sellers, Helen Mirren, Sid Caesar, David Tomlinson, Simon Williams, Steve Franken. Disastrous comedy features Sellers in a dual role, as the title character and as his archenemy, Scotland Yard detective Nayland Smith. Painfully unfunny and, sad to say, Sellers' last film. [PG]▼●]

Fiend Who Walked the West, The (1958) **101m.** **½ D: Gordon Douglas. Hugh O'Brian, Robert Evans, Dolores Michaels, Linda Cristal, Stephen McNally. Interesting if not altogether successful transposition of KISS OF DEATH to Western setting, with Evans ludicrous in the Widmark psycho role. CinemaScope.▼

Fiend Without a Face (1958-British) **74m.** *½ D: Arthur Crabtree. Marshall Thompson, Kim Parker, Terence Kilburn, Michael Balfour, Gil Winfield. Scientist materializes thoughts in form of invisible brain-shaped creatures which kill people for food. Horrific climax; good special effects.▼●]

Fiend With the Atomic Brain, The SEE: **Blood of Ghastly Horror**

Fiend with the Electronic Brain, The SEE: **Blood of Ghastly Horror**

Fierce Creatures (1997) **C-93m.** **½ D: Robert Young, Fred Schepisi. John Cleese, Jamie Lee Curtis, Kevin Kline, Michael Palin, Ronnie Corbett, Carey Lowell, Robert Lindsay. Heartless corporate mogul takes over a failing British zoo and insists it pay its own way, leaving the new zoo director (Cleese) to deal with a resentful staff and other complications. Pleasant enough farce cowritten by Cleese to reunite the cast of A FISH CALLED WANDA never quite pays off, but has its moments. Kline is fun in a dual role. Filmed in 1995, then largely rewritten and refilmed in 1996 with a new director (Schepisi); note how Lowell disappears from whole sections of the picture. Cynthia Cleese, one of the zookeepers, is John's daughter. Panavision. [PG-13]▼●]

Fierce People (2007) **C-112m.** ** D: Griffin Dunne. Diane Lane, Anton Yelchin, Donald Sutherland, Kristen Stewart, Elizabeth Perkins, Paz de la Huerta, Chris Evans. Sutherland's amusing performance as a reclusive billionaire dominates this wildly uneven adaptation of Dirk Wittenborn's novel, an '80s coming-of-age story about a substance-abusing masseuse (Lane), her codependent teenage son (Yelchin), and the eventful summer they spend as guests on the billionaire's New Jersey estate. Barely released two years after its film festival debut. [R]▶

Fiesta (1947) **C-104m.** **½ D: Richard Thorpe. Esther Williams, Akim Tamiroff, Ricardo Montalban, John Carroll, Mary Astor, Cyd Charisse. Williams trades in her bathing suit for a toreador outfit in this weak musical opus.▶

15 Minutes (2001) **C-120m.** *** D: John Herzfeld. Robert De Niro, Edward Burns, Kelsey Grammer, Avery Brooks, Melina Kanakaredes, Karel Roden, Oleg Taktarov, Vera Farmiga, John DiResta, Charlize Theron, Kim Cattrall, Darius McCrary, David Alan Grier. Headline-grabbing N.Y.C. detective finds himself with an unlikely partner—a young fire department arson investigator—as they track a series of grisly murders. The culprits are an immigrant duo who smugly seek to manipulate the American media/celebrity machine. Highly charged, in-your-face, sometimes over-the-top moviemaking with attitude to spare. Written by the director. Super 35. [R]▼▶

5th Ave. Girl (1939) **83m.** ** D: Gregory LaCava. Ginger Rogers, Walter Connolly, Verree Teasdale, James Ellison, Tim Holt, Kathryn Adams, Franklin Pangborn, Louis Calhern, Jack Carson. Tiresome social comedy with Rogers as homeless girl taken in by unhappy millionaire Connolly; even Ginger is lifeless in this film that purports to show that poor is better than rich if you've got a head on your shoulders.▼●▶

Fifth Day of Peace, The (1972-Italian) **C-100m.** ** D: Guilliano Montaldo. Richard Johnson, Franco Nero, Bud Spencer, Michael Goodliffe, Helmut Schneider. Episodic story of several disillusioned WW1 German soldiers aimlessly wandering war-ravaged Italian countryside following the armistice. [PG]▼●▶

Fifth Element, The (1997-French) **C-127m.** *** D: Luc Besson. Bruce Willis, Gary Oldman, Ian Holm, Milla Jovovich, Chris Tucker, Luke Perry, Brion James, Tommy "Tiny" Lister, Jr., Lee Evans, John Neville. Wildly imaginative tale set in the 23rd century, where a world-weary Brooklyn, N.Y., cab driver finds himself involved with a strange woman who may be responsible for saving the world from destruction. A visual candy store of futuristic images, but the film's strongest suit is its sense of humor. Unfortunately, it gets a bit tedious and formulaic toward the end, with Tucker's over-the-top radio host hogging the spotlight. Conceived by Besson when he was a teenager. Super 35. [PG-13]▼●▶

Fifth Floor, The (1980) **C-90m.** BOMB D: Howard Avedis. Bo Hopkins, Dianne Hull, Patti D'Arbanville, Sharon Farrell, Mel Ferrer, Julie Adams, John David Carson. A few laughs don't compensate for deriva-

tive story of college disco dancer who is wrongly committed to an insane asylum. Collectors of screen dementia should study Hopkins' performance. [R]▼

Fifth Monkey, The (1990) **C-93m.** *** D: Eric Rochat. Ben Kingsley, Mika Lins, Vera Fischer, Silvia De Carvalho. Straightforward, extremely enjoyable tale of snake and rare animal hunter Kingsley, and his escapades while attempting to sell chimps and earn enough money to wed the woman of his dreams. Rochat, who also scripted, movingly illustrates the necessity for mankind to respect the animal world. Beautifully filmed in Brazil. [PG-13]▼●

5th Musketeer, The (1979-Austrian) **C-103m.** **½ D: Ken Annakin. Beau Bridges, Sylvia Kristel, Ursula Andress, Cornel Wilde, Ian McShane, Lloyd Bridges, Alan Hale, Jr., Jose Ferrer, Helmut Dantine, Rex Harrison, Olivia de Havilland. Lavish, well-cast remake of THE MAN IN THE IRON MASK offers nothing new, but retells Dumas' story in capable fashion. Major points of interest: Austrian location, veteran cast. Filmed in 1977. [PG]▼●

Fifty Dead Men Walking (2009-British-Canadian) **C-117m.** *** D: Kari Skogland. Ben Kingsley, Jim Sturgess, Kevin Zegers, Natalie Press, Rose McGowan, Tom Collins, William Houston, Michael McElhatton. Taut, fact-based account, set in the late 1980s and early '90s, of Martin McGartland (Sturgess), a two-bit Belfast criminal who is recruited by British agent Kingsley to infiltrate the Irish Republican Army. Both a well-made thriller and a character study of McGartland and the impact his informing has on his life. Skogland scripted, based on a memoir penned by McGartland and Nicholas Davies. [R]▶

Fifty/Fifty (1992) **C-101m.** *½ D: Charles Martin Smith. Peter Weller, Robert Hays, Charles Martin Smith, Ramona Rahman, Kay Tong Lim, Dom Magwili. CIA mercenaries Weller and Hays bicker and bumble through the jungle in this silly action/ adventure, in which revolvers outshoot machine guns; takes a serious turn when the "heroes" finally take a stand. [R]▼▶

50 First Dates (2004) **C-96m.** ** D: Peter Segal. Adam Sandler, Drew Barrymore, Rob Schneider, Sean Astin, Lusia Strus, Blake Clark, Dan Aykroyd, Amy Hill, Allen Covert, Maya Rudolph, Nephi Pomaikai Brown. A veterinarian living in Hawaii who's known for quickie relationships falls in love with a woman who—it turns out—has short-term memory loss. That means he has to win her over every single day! Not-bad premise for an offbeat romantic comedy gets typical Sandler treatment, portraying him as a lovable guy while purveying a stream of crude jokes at the same time. Panavision. [PG-13] ▼▶

55 Days at Peking (1963) **C-150m.** ***

D: Nicholas Ray. Charlton Heston, Ava Gardner, David Niven, Flora Robson, John Ireland, Paul Lukas, Jacques Sernas. Stars provide most of the interest in confusing historical account of Boxer Rebellion in 1900s China. Super Technirama 70. ▼●

54 (1998) **C-93m.** ** D: Mark Christopher. Ryan Phillippe, Salma Hayek, Neve Campbell, Mike Myers, Sela Ward, Breckin Meyer, Sherry Stringfield, Ellen Albertini Dow, Heather Matarazzo, Lauren Hutton, Michael York, Daniel Lapaine, Mark Ruffalo, Ron Jeremy. Dreary drama attempts to capture the spirit of hedonistic nightclub Studio 54, which flourished in the 1970s and attracted naive young people like Phillippe, who thought entry meant a stepping-stone to success and self-esteem. Clichéd story takes focus off the most interesting person onscreen—Myers, in a canny performance as Steve Rubell, the ringmaster of this nightly drug-and-sex party. Various celebrities appear as themselves. [R] ▼●】

52 Miles to Midnight SEE: **Hot Rods to Hell**

52 Pick-Up (1986) **C-110m.** ** D: John Frankenheimer. Roy Scheider, Ann-Margret, Vanity, John Glover, Robert Trebor, Lonny Chapman, Kelly Preston, Clarence Williams III, Doug McClure. Self-made businessman is caught in web of blackmail and murder—and determines to break free by himself. Elmore Leonard's story is good, but the lead characters are cold, and film wallows too long in the sleazy, voyeuristic world of the bad guys. It also would have been better shorter. Same novel was adapted just two years earlier as THE AMBASSADOR. [R] ▼●】

Fight Club (1999) **C-139m.** ** D: David Fincher. Brad Pitt, Edward Norton, Helena Bonham Carter, Meat Loaf (Aday), Jared Leto. A disaffected office worker (Norton) whose life has turned gray finds unexpected release through violent fistfights, organized by a new "friend" (Pitt), who lives life on the edge. The impromptu battles evolve into an underground network of fight clubs where guys pummel each other . . . but the friend has an even more ambitious agenda. Draws you in with its intriguing story, black comedy, and flamboyant visuals, then shifts tone, turns heavy-handed, and heads toward an alarmingly senseless resolution. Nevertheless, it has a fervent following. Based on a novel by Chuck Palahniuk. Super 35. [R] ▼】

Fighter, The (2010) **C-115m.** *** D: David O. Russell. Mark Wahlberg, Christian Bale, Amy Adams, Melissa Leo, Jack McGee. Flavorful portrait of a wildly dysfunctional family in Lowell, Massachusetts, during the 1990s. "Irish" Micky Ward (Wahlberg) has the potential to be a boxing champ, but he's emotionally bound to his older half brother Dicky Eklund (Bale), a onetime contender who's hooked on crack but insists on remaining his trainer. Then there's his trash-talking mother (an amazing Leo), who mismanages his career but is certain she knows best. Based on a true story, this film has atmosphere to burn and showy performances—where did they find those women who play Micky's sisters?—though it peters out a bit in the final act. Mickey O'Keefe, a local cop who hangs out at the local gym, plays himself. Leo and Bale won Supporting Actress/Actor Oscars for their bravura work. Super 35. [R] 】

Fighting (2009) **C-105m.** *** D: Dito Montiel. Channing Tatum, Terrence Howard, Zulay Henao, Michael Rivera, Flaco Navaja, Peter Anthony Tambakis, Luis Guzmán, Anthony DeSando, Brian J. White, Roger Guenveur Smith, Altagracia Guzmán. Tightly written and directed melodrama about a small-town hustler who comes to N.Y.C. and is lured into the world of underground bare-knuckle fighting by a shady hood looking to make a quick buck. Vivid, action-packed fight sequences are supported by a solid storyline and strong performances from Tatum and Howard. Montiel proved with A GUIDE TO RECOGNIZING YOUR SAINTS (also with Tatum) that he knows his way around these particular mean streets; he impressively avoids turning this simple tale into a bad imitation of a grade-B '40s boxing movie. Alternate version runs 108m. [PG-13]】

Fighting Back (1982) **C-98m.** **½ D: Lewis Teague. Tom Skerritt, Patti LuPone, Michael Sarrazin, Yaphet Kotto, David Rasche, Ted Ross, Pat Cooper. A return visit to DEATH WISH territory; fed up with lackadaisical police, hotheaded South Philly deli owner (Skerritt, who's excellent) organizes Guardian Angels–like patrol to clean up criminal scum, but is unprepared for the complications which ensue. Unpleasant, but fast, slick, and convincing; these people know which buttons to push. [R] ▼

Fighting Back (1982-Australian) **C-100m.** **½ D: Michael Caulfield. Lewis FitzGerald, Paul Smith, Kris McQuade, Robyn Nevin, Caroline Gillmer. Ambitious if not entirely successful drama of teacher FitzGerald trying to tame unruly, illiterate 13-year-old (Smith, excellent in acting debut).

Fighting Kentuckian, The (1949) **100m.** **½ D: George Waggner. John Wayne, Vera Ralston, Philip Dorn, Oliver Hardy, Marie Windsor. Frontierland around 1810 is setting for two-fisted saga of Kentuckian (Wayne) combating land-grabbing criminals and courting Ralston, French general's daughter. Hardy makes rare solo appearance in character role. Also shown in computer-colored version. ▼】

Fighting Mad (1976) **C-90m.** **½ D: Jonathan Demme. Peter Fonda, Lynn Lowry, John Doucette, Philip Carey, Scott Glenn,

Kathleen Miller, Harry Northup. Typical revenge picture, with peaceable Fonda driven to violence by ruthless landowner who wants to take over his farm. On-target for this kind of entertainment. [R]▼◗

Fighting Pimpernel, The SEE: **Elusive Pimpernel, The**

Fighting Prince of Donegal, The (1966) **C-112m. *** D:** Michael O'Herlihy. Peter McEnery, Susan Hampshire, Tom Adams, Gordon Jackson, Andrew Keir, Donal McCann. Fine Disney swashbuckler made in England, with McEnery as new head of Irish clan who tries to unite his country but runs afoul of villainous Jackson. Vivid, colorful fun.▼◗

Fighting Seabees, The (1944) **100m. *** D:** Edward Ludwig. John Wayne, Susan Hayward, Dennis O'Keefe, William Frawley, Leonid Kinskey, J. M. Kerrigan, Ben Welden, Paul Fix, Grant Withers, Duncan Renaldo. Spirited WW2 saga of construction company boss Wayne and naval officer O'Keefe tangling professionally and personally, with journalist Hayward the love interest. The scenario charts the manner in which the "Seabees" (or battalion of construction worker–soldiers) came to be established. Screenplay by Borden Chase and Aeneas MacKenzie. Action-packed second unit direction by Howard Lydecker.▼◗

Fighting 69th, The (1940) **90m. **½ D:** William Keighley. James Cagney, Pat O'Brien, George Brent, Jeffrey Lynn, Alan Hale, Frank McHugh, Dennis Morgan, Dick Foran, John Litel, George Reeves, Frank Coghlan, Jr. Overripe (but tough to dislike) WW1 tale mixes roughneck comedy, exciting battle action, sloppy sentiment, incredible characterizations (especially Cagney's) detailing exploits of famed Irish regiment. Also shown in computer-colored version.▼◗

Fighting Sullivans, The SEE: **Sullivans, The**

Fighting Temptations, The (2003) **C-123m. **½ D:** Jonathan Lynn. Cuba Gooding, Jr., Beyoncé Knowles, Melba Moore, Mike Epps, Reverend Shirley Caesar, LaTanya Richardson, Steve Harvey, Montell Jordan, T-Bone, Faith Evans, The O'Jays, Angie Stone, Faizon Love, Rue McClanahan. A would-be mover and shaker who's talked his way out of a good job in N.Y.C. returns to Georgia and takes over his hometown church choir, aiming to win an annual gospel competition. He also has an eye for Knowles, who's something of an outcast in town but has a great voice. Obvious and overlong, but buoyed by heaping doses of great music. Super 35. [PG-13]▼◗

Figures in a Landscape (1970-British) **C-95m. *** D:** Joseph Losey. Robert Shaw, Malcolm McDowell, Henry Woolf, Christopher Malcolm, Pamela Brown. Capable leads and some amazing helicopter stunt work offer scant compensation for muddled allegory about two fugitives in an unnamed country pursued by an unnamed enemy. Barely released. Losey fans will want to give a look. Panavision. [PG]

File of the Golden Goose, The (1969-British) **C-105m. *** D:** Sam Wanamaker. Yul Brynner, Charles Gray, Edward Woodward, John Barrie, Adrienne Corri. Strictly formula effort with American agent and Scotland Yard man going undercover in London to get the goods on murderous counterfeiting gang. [M/PG]◗

File on Thelma Jordon, The (1949) **100m. **½ D:** Robert Siodmak. Barbara Stanwyck, Wendell Corey, Joan Tetzel, Stanley Ridges, Richard Rober. Paul Kelly. Tough little film noir focusing largely on romance between unhappily married assistant D.A. Corey and femme fatale Stanwyck. Handsomely photographed by George Barnes. Aka THELMA JORDON.

Fillmore (1972) **C-105m. *** D:** Richard T. Heffron. Bill Graham, The Grateful Dead, It's a Beautiful Day, Santana, Jefferson Airplane, Quicksilver Messenger Service. Good rock documentary about Fillmore West's final days is made even better by extensive footage of its magnetic owner, Bill Graham, on the phone and on stage; one of the better rock films. Multiscreen. [R]▼

Final Analysis (1992) **C-125m. **½ D:** Phil Joanou. Richard Gere, Kim Basinger, Uma Thurman, Eric Roberts, Paul Guilfoyle, Keith David, Robert Harper, Agustin Rodriguez. Stylish, sexy thriller about a San Francisco psychiatrist who becomes involved with a patient's unhappily married sister—only to find himself enmeshed in an elaborate Hitchcockian web of murder and duplicity. Basinger is surprisingly good, Gere distressingly low-key; but the film's plodding mid-section almost undermines a bravura finale. Written by Wesley Strick. Harris Yulin appears unbilled as the prosecuting attorney. [R]▼◗

Final Approach (1991) **C-100m. *½ D:** Eric Steven Stahl. James B. Sikking, Hector Elizondo, Madolyn Smith, Kevin McCarthy, Cameo Kneuer. Pilot Sikking, testing a stealth-type jet, apparently ejects—then awakens in the office of psychiatrist Elizondo, who wants to investigate the pilot's past. Weary, hackneyed plot treated as if it sparkles with originality. This was the first film recorded with digital technology; the sound is great, but the movie isn't. Panavision. [R]▼◗

Final Assignment (1980-Canadian) **C-92m. BOMB D:** Paul Almond. Genevieve Bujold, Michael York, Burgess Meredith, Colleen Dewhurst, Alexandra Stewart. Television reporter Bujold takes on the KGB when she discovers the Russians are conducting scientific experiments on children. Schlock production, with Montreal an unsatisfactory substitute for Moscow; poor script, embarrassing performances. [PG]▼

Final Chapter—Walking Tall (1977) **C-112m.** BOMB D: Jack Starrett. Bo Svenson, Margaret Blye, Forrest Tucker, Lurene Tuttle, Morgan Woodward. Yet another saga about true-life Tennessee sheriff Buford Pusser, and inferior to its predecessors. Despite title, this is not the final chapter; a TV movie (A REAL AMERICAN HERO) and series followed. Aka WALKING TALL—FINAL CHAPTER. [R]▼●❶

Final Conflict, The (1981) **C-108m.** *½ D: Graham Baker. Sam Neill, Rossano Brazzi, Don Gordon, Lisa Harrow, Mason Adams. The third OMEN movie has the anti-Christ Damien Thorn (Neill) 30ish and the U.S. Ambassador to England. For genre addicts only. Followed by a TVM, OMEN IV: THE AWAKENING. Panavision. [R]▼●❶

Final Countdown, The (1980) **C-104m.** *** D: Don Taylor. Kirk Douglas, Martin Sheen, Katharine Ross, James Farentino, Ron O'Neal, Charles Durning. An aircraft carrier (the real-life *U.S.S. Nimitz*) enters a time-warp and finds itself in the Pacific just before the attack on Pearl Harbor. Familiar but satisfying fantasy yarn; perfect TV fare although better viewed in widescreen. Panavision. [PG]▼●❶

Final Cut, The (2004-Canadian-German) **C-105m.** ** D: Omar Naim. Robin Williams, Mira Sorvino, Jim Caviezel, Mimi Kuzyk, Stephanie Romanov, Thom Bishops. Dour sci-fi piece set in a near future when humans have implanted memory chips that record their every moment. Williams is a digital whiz who is expert at editing his deceased wealthy clients' lives to give them a positive spin. Williams has played a repressed automaton before—but he does it well. Stylized mystery-thriller is funereal in more ways than one. Super 35. [PG-13] ▼❶

Final Destination (2000) **C-97m.** **½ D: James Wong. Devon Sawa, Ali Larter, Kerr Smith, Kristen Cloke, Daniel Roebuck, Roger Guenveur Smith, Chad E. Donella, Seann William Scott. Before the plane carrying him and his classmates to Paris takes off, teenager Sawa has a vision of it crashing. He and others leave the plane, which (of course) does explode—but the survivors soon start dying in mysterious accidents. Horror movie has an unusual and interesting premise, but paints itself into a corner; the ending is annoyingly unsatisfactory. Feature debut for *X-Files* vet Wong. Followed by three sequels. [R]▼❶

Final Destination, The (2009) **C-82m.** BOMB D: David R. Ellis. Bobby Campo, Shantel VanSanten, Krista Allen, Nick Zano, Mykelti Williamson, Haley Webb, Andrew Fiscella, Richard T. Jones. In the fourth and hopefully final installment of this series, we find yet another person who has horrific premonitions and attempts to alter

death's design. There's even less plot than usual and the CGI (and 3-D) effects make each death look so cartoonish that it's not frightening, just strange and silly. What's more, the characters don't seem to care that their friends are dying, so why should you? 3-D HD Widescreen. [R]❶

Final Destination 2 (2003) **C-90m.** *½ D: David R. Ellis. Ali Larter, A. J. Cook, Michael Landes, T. C. Carson, Jonathan Cherry, Keegan Connor Tracy, Sarah Carter, Lynda Boyd, David Paetkau. A girl has a premonition of death and learns (like the survivors of the plane crash in the first film) that by avoiding it she and others around her have cheated fate. Film exists for the sole purpose of killing its characters—through fire, car crash, crushing, decapitation, impalement, etc.—in horrifyingly realistic detail. But some people view this as comedy. If so, help yourself! [R] ▼❶

Final Destination 3 (2006) **C-92m.** *½ D: James Wong. Mary Elizabeth Winstead, Ryan Merriman, Kris Lemche, Texas Battle, Alexz Johnson, Jesse Moss, Gina Holden, Sam Easton, Crystal Lowe, Chelan Simmons, Amanda Crew. They used the word "Final" in the titles of two predecessors—but they lied. Winstead is a high school straight-arrow who gets a sense of deaths to come from a roller coaster ride. As expected, the survivors then suffer their own supernatural dispatching in TEN LITTLE INDIANS style. Most memorable demise comes after two senior-class slatterns who say "totally" a lot enter a tanning salon. Super 35. [R]❶

Final Fantasy: The Spirits Within (2001-Japanese-U.S.) **C-106m.** ** D: Hironobu Sakaguchi, Motonori Sakakibara. Voices of Ming-Na, Alec Baldwin, Ving Rhames, Steve Buscemi, Peri Gilpin, Donald Sutherland, James Woods, Keith David, Jean Simmons, Matt McKenzie. Dr. Aki Ross runs into trouble in the year 2065 when she and her mentor confront a power-hungry general over the best way to battle aliens in their midst. Notable as the first major feature to use computer-generated actors. Adaptation of popular computer game plays like a standard-issue sci-fi yarn with spiritual undertones. At their dullest, the actors who provide the voices would still be more interesting to watch than their hollow-eyed, computerized counterparts. [PG-13] ▼❶

Final Option, The (1982-British) **C-125m.** BOMB D: Ian Sharp. Lewis Collins, Judy Davis, Richard Widmark, Robert Webber, Edward Woodward, Tony Doyle, John Duttine, Kenneth Griffith, Ingrid Pitt. Laughably ridiculous account of Britain's Special Air Services team and how one officer (Collins) goes underground—more or less—to infiltrate a terrorist gang with plans to take over the American Embassy. Lots of violence, but no brains in sight. Third-billed Widmark has precious little screen time, as the U.S. Secretary of State. Original British title: WHO DARES WINS. [R]▼

Final Programme, The SEE: **Last Days of Man on Earth, The**

Final Season, The (2007) C-123m. ** D: David Mickey Evans. Sean Astin, Rachael Leigh Cook, Powers Boothe, Michael Angarano, Mackenzie Astin, Tom Arnold, Marshall Bell, Matthew W. Allen, James Gammon, Larry Miller. True story of Iowa baseball coach Kent Stock, who ditches his job (and wedding) to guide Norway High School to one final championship after their school is merged into a larger one. By-the-numbers sports story, with clichéd dialogue, doesn't really connect. Astin covered this turf much better in RUDY. Clairmont-Scope. [PG]▶

Final Terror, The (1981) C-82m. *½ D: Andrew Davis. John Friedrich, Adrian Zmed, Daryl Hannah, Rachel Ward, Mark Metcalf. Pretty bad dead-teenagers film set in the backwoods, of marginal interest for presence of latter-day stars in cast (though they don't get much of a showcase here). [R]▼▶

Finders Keepers (1984) C-96m. ** D: Richard Lester. Michael O'Keefe, Beverly D'Angelo, Louis Gossett, Jr., Ed Lauter, David Wayne, Pamela Stephenson, Brian Dennehy, John Schuck, Timothy Blake, Jim Carrey, Jack Riley. Wholehearted attempt at farce, involving stolen money, con artists in disguise, a bungling hit man, and other promising ingredients, remains disappointingly flat. Lester manages a few neat sight gags, and Wayne is genuinely funny as the world's oldest train conductor. [R]▼

Finding Amanda (2008) C-96m. **½ D: Peter Tolan. Matthew Broderick, Brittany Snow, Maura Tierney, Peter Facinelli, Daniel Roebuck, Bill Fagerbakke, Jennifer Hall, Steve Coogan, Ed Begley, Jr. Fading TV comedy writer and congenital liar Broderick heads to Las Vegas in search of his 20-year-old hooker niece. It's a bad place for him to be, given that he's addicted to gambling. Meanders at first but gets better as it goes along, particularly when it peels away the façade of the title character. One amusing bit: the pimp who's a wannabe screenwriter. Written by the director. [R]▶

Finding Forrester (2000) C-136m. **½ D: Gus Van Sant. Sean Connery, Rob Brown, F. Murray Abraham, Anna Paquin, Busta Rhymes, April Grace, Michael Nouri. Bronx high school student meets an odd neighborhood resident, a reclusive novelist who's been hiding from the world since his first burst of fame. The curmudgeon becomes his mentor as the boy moves to an upscale Manhattan private school, and has to examine his choices—and priorities. Slick entertainment, and a great vehicle for Connery (who also coproduced), but more than a bit pat—with heavy-handed "villainy" from jealous professor Abraham. Panavision. [PG-13]▼▶

Finding Nemo (2003) C-81m. ***½ D: Andrew Stanton. Voices of Albert Brooks, Ellen DeGeneres, Willem Dafoe, Geoffrey Rush, Allison Janney, Alexander Gould, Barry Humphries, Eric Bana, Brad Garrett, Stephen Root, Austin Pendleton, Vicki Lewis. Another delightful animated film from Pixar, set in a wondrous undersea environment. A timid clownfish named Marlin (voiced by a perfectly cast Brooks) tries to shield his only son from danger; when the little fish is captured and taken many miles away, Marlin embarks on a brave quest to rescue him. Full of great characters, animation, and design, and peppered with hilarious gags, many of them aimed at grown-ups rather than kids. Oscar winner for Best Animated Feature. [G]▼▶

Finding Neverland (2004-U.S.-British) C-101m. ***½ D: Marc Forster. Johnny Depp, Kate Winslet, Julie Christie, Radha Mitchell, Dustin Hoffman, Kelly Macdonald, Ian Hart, Freddie Highmore, Joe Prospero, Nick Roud, Luke Spill, Mackenzie Crook. Trapped in a loveless marriage, at a crossroads in his writing career, James M. Barrie is drawn to four young brothers who play at a nearby park—and their attractive, widowed mother—and becomes a surrogate member of their family. In time, they become the inspiration for his play *Peter Pan*. Beautifully crafted, nicely underplayed period piece set at the turn of the 20th century, anchored by an irresistible performance by Depp as the warmhearted but eccentric Scotsman. Oscar winner for Jan A. P. Kaczmarek's score. Super 35. [PG] ▼▶

Find Me Guilty (2006) C-124m. *** D: Sidney Lumet. Vin Diesel, Peter Dinklage, Linus Roache, Ron Silver, Alex Rocco, Annabella Sciorra, Raúl Esparza, Jerry Adler, Richard Portnow, Josh Pais. Diesel gives a wonderful, transformative performance as real-life N.J. gangster "Jackie Dee" DiNorscio, an outgoing character who decides to defend himself in a record-breaking Federal case against the Lucchese crime family in 1987–88. Better than most crime fiction, this lively courtroom–mob saga is impeccably cast and directed with brio by Lumet, who also cowrote the screenplay. Putting Louis Prima on the soundtrack doesn't hurt, either. [R]▶

Find the Lady (1976-Canadian-British) C-79m. *½ D: John Trent. Lawrence Dane, John Candy, Mickey Rooney, Peter Cook, Alexandra Bastedo, Dick Emery. Pre–POLICE ACADEMY comedy about inept cops Dane and Candy, on the trail of a kidnapped socialite. A couple of genuine laughs, but mostly silly—and occasionally offensive. Candy and Dane played same characters a year earlier in IT SEEMED LIKE A GOOD IDEA AT THE TIME. Aka CALL THE COPS! and KOPEK AND BROOM. ▼▶

Fine Madness, A (1966) C-104m. *** D: Irvin Kershner. Sean Connery, Joanne

Woodward, Jean Seberg, Patrick O'Neal, Colleen Dewhurst, Renee Taylor. It's stubborn, nonconformist poet Connery versus the rest of society in uneven but sometimes outrageously funny satire. Screenplay by Elliot Baker, from his novel.▼❶

Fine Mess, A (1986) C-88m. *½ D: Blake Edwards. Ted Danson, Howie Mandel, Richard Mulligan, Stuart Margolin, Maria Conchita Alonso, Jennifer Edwards, Paul Sorvino. A slapstick saga of two bumblers, with laughs few and far between. Familiar Blake Edwards trademarks, and the supposed inspiration of Laurel and Hardy's Oscar-winning short, THE MUSIC BOX, don't carry this very far. Panavision. [PG]▼❶

Fine Pair, A (1968) C-89m. BOMB D: Francesco Maselli. Rock Hudson, Claudia Cardinale, Thomas Milian, Leon Askin, Ellen Corby, Walter Giller. N.Y.C. policeman Hudson falls for Cardinale, daughter of an old pal, and helps her rob some jewels in terrible comedy-thriller minus laughs or suspense. Panavision. [M/PG]

Fine Romance, A (1992-U.S.-Italian) C-83m. ** D: Gene Saks. Julie Andrews, Marcello Mastroianni, Ian Fitzgibbon, Jean-Pierre Castaldi, Jean-Jacques Dulon, Maria Machado, Catherine Jarret. Andrews and Mastroianni try (but fail) to enliven this obvious, barely funny farce, cast as a pair whose mates have run off together, and who predictably become romantically involved themselves. Scripted by Ronald Harwood. [PG-13]▼❶

Finger of Guilt (1956-British) 85m. **½ D: Joseph Losey. Richard Basehart, Mary Murphy, Constance Cummings, Roger Livesey, Mervyn Johns, Faith Brook. Film director Basehart is blackmailed by woman claiming to be his mistress, which threatens his career and marriage. Intriguing film with disappointing resolution; good look inside British film studio, however. Directed by blacklistee Losey under pseudonyms Alec Snowden/Joseph Walton. Originally released in England as THE INTIMATE STRANGER at 95m.

Fingers (1978) C-91m. ***½ D: James Toback. Harvey Keitel, Jim Brown, Tisa Farrow, Michael V. Gazzo, Tanya Roberts, Marian Seldes, Danny Aiello, Ed Marinaro, Zack Norman. Crude but fascinating melodrama about an aspiring concert pianist who reluctantly "collects" on debts owed to his domineering father. Powerful, disturbing film is compellingly sensual and brilliantly acted, especially by Brown in a rare subdued role. Remade in 2005 as THE BEAT THAT MY HEART SKIPPED. Screenplay by the director. [R]▼❶

Finian's Rainbow (1968) C-145m. ***½ D: Francis Ford Coppola. Fred Astaire, Petula Clark, Tommy Steele, Keenan Wynn, Al Freeman, Jr., Don Francks, Barbara Hancock. Whimsical Burton Lane–E. Y. Harburg musical fantasy about racial injustice was ahead of its time in the late '40s on Broadway, embarrassingly dated 20 years later, but Coppola and an attractive cast work wonders with it in this imaginatively filmed, widescreen winner—perhaps the best movie musical of its era. Harburg's lyrics remain elegant and witty, and Astaire is fun as the transplanted Irishman whose leprechaun comes to life in the American South. Try to see it in a theater. Panavision. [G]▼❶

Finnegans Wake (1965) 97m. ***½ D: Mary Ellen Bute. Page Johnson, Martin J. Kelly, Jane Reilly, Peter Haskell. James Joyce's classic story of Irish tavern-keeper who dreams of attending his own wake is brought to the screen with great energy and control.

Fiorile (1993-Italian-French-German) C-118m. *** D: Paolo and Vittorio Taviani. Claudio Bigagli, Galatea Ranzi, Michael Vartan, Lino Capolicchio, Constanze Engelbrecht, Athina Cenci, Giovanni Guidelli, Chiara Caselli. While driving to visit his ailing, reclusive father, a man reveals to his two children the legend of their family's history, beginning with how their ancestors came into wealth dishonestly during the Napoleonic era. Complex, ironic tale of tarnished innocence, outside forces cruelly separating lovers, and how ill-gotten wealth will in one way or another taint the spirit. [PG-13]▼❶

Fire (1997-Canadian-Indian) C-104m. ** D: Deepa Mehta. Shabana Azmi, Nandita Das, Kulbushan Kharbanda, Jaaved Jaaferi, Ranjit Chowdhury, Kushal Rekhi. Ho-hum lesbian-feminist drama set in New Delhi, which charts the growing spiritual/sexual attraction between a long-married woman (Azmi) and her young, newlywed sister-in-law (Das). Without exception, every male character in the story is a simplistic chauvinist pig, and the result is a superficial drama that substitutes female outrage for thoughtful filmmaking.▼❶

Fire and Ice (1983) C-81m. **½ D: Ralph Bakshi. Voices of Susan Tyrrell, Maggie Roswell, William Ostrander, Stephen Mendel. Muscular hero and buxom heroine become involved in a power struggle between two warring world powers. Animated sword-and-sorcery saga is no worse (and arguably no better) than an average live-action entry, and benefits from graphic design by fabled illustrator Frank Frazetta, though the animation itself has been traced from live footage. Scripted by well-known comic book writers Roy Thomas and Gerry Conway. [PG]▼❶

Fireball 500 (1966) C-92m. BOMB D: William Asher. Frankie Avalon, Annette Funicello, Fabian, Chill Wills, Harvey Lembeck, Julie Parrish. Frankie is a stock-car racer who unknowingly transports moonshine whiskey. Desperately in need of a beach ball. Panavision.❶

Fire Birds (1990) C-85m. BOMB D:

David Green. Nicolas Cage, Tommy Lee Jones, Sean Young, Bryan Kestner, Dale Dye, Mary Ellen Trainor, J. A. Preston, Peter Onorati. High-tech Apache helicopters (with an assist from their pilots) take on South American drug cartels from the air. Standard military issue with a ruptured-duck script and no romantic chemistry between professional rivals Cage and Young. Jones doesn't evoke memories of Gregory Peck in TWELVE O'CLOCK HIGH when he pep-talks Cage into a "full-tilt boogie for freedom and justice." [PG-13]▼●)

Firechasers, The (1970-British) **C-101m.** ** D: Sidney Hayers. Chad Everett, Anjanette Comer, Keith Barron, Joanne Dainton, Rupert Davies, John Loder. Strong production values in familiar story of insurance investigator hunting for arsonist.

Firecreek (1968) **C-104m.** **½ D: Vincent McEveety. James Stewart, Henry Fonda, Inger Stevens, Gary Lockwood, Dean Jagger, Ed Begley, Jay C. Flippen, Jack Elam, Barbara Luna. Somber Western has makings of a classic at outset, but goes astray, and goes on too long. Stewart is mild-mannered part-time sheriff in small town terrorized by Fonda and fellow plunderers. Beautifully photographed (by William H. Clothier), but unrelentingly downbeat. Panavision. ▼)

Fired! (2007) **C-71m.** ** D: Chris Bradley, Kyle LaBrache. Writer-performer Annabelle Gurwitch uses her real-life dismissal from a play by Woody Allen as the basis for exploring what it means to be fired from a job. Scattershot, superficial first-person documentary tries to combine comedy, personal anecdotes, and social commentary with very mixed results; only former Labor Secretary Robert Reich's and Ben Stein's observations have any real impact. Other interviewees include Tim Allen, Fred Willard, Illeana Douglas, and Anne Meara.❱

Fire Down Below (1957-British) **C-116m.** **½ D: Robert Parrish. Rita Hayworth, Robert Mitchum, Jack Lemmon, Herbert Lom, Bernard Lee, Anthony Newley. Contrived but entertaining melodrama of Mitchum and Lemmon, owners of tramp boat, falling in love with shady Hayworth on voyage between islands. Title song composed by Lemmon. CinemaScope.▼❱

Fire Down Below (1997) **C-105m.** ** D: Felix Enriquez Alcalá. Steven Seagal, Marg Helgenberger, Kris Kristofferson, Stephen Lang, Harry Dean Stanton, Levon Helm, Richard Masur, John Diehl, Robert Ridgely, Randy Travis. You're looking for an E.P.A. agent to go work incognito avenging a murder in Appalachia—so who you gonna call? Well, how about Steve, with his standard haircut and man-in-black garb? Laughably bad action outing with a reasonable pace to match its outrageousness. Marty Stuart and Travis Tritt appear as themselves. [R] ▼●)

Fired Up! (2009) **C-90m.** **½ D: Will Gluck. Eric Christian Olsen, Nicholas D'Agosto, Sarah Roemer, Molly Sims, Danneel Harris, David Walton, Adhir Kalyan, AnnaLynne McCord, Philip Baker Hall, Juliette Goglia, John Michael Higgins, Margo Harshman, Amber Stevens, Francia Raisa, Masi Oka, Edie McClurg. As stars of the football team, D'Agosto and Olsen have conquered their school's entire female population and are in search of a new hunting ground. What better place than cheerleader camp? The two leads are funny but the story meanders; over-the-top supporting characters and bad acting detract from this otherwise entertaining comedy. Alternate version runs 91m. Super 35. [PG-13]❱

Firefly, The (1937) **129m.** **½ D: Robert Z. Leonard. Jeanette MacDonald, Allan Jones, Warren William, Billy Gilbert, Henry Daniell, Douglass Dumbrille, George Zucco. MacDonald plays a spy working in France on behalf of Spain during the Napoleonic wars in this rewrite of the Rudolf Friml–Otto Harbach operetta. Goes on much too long, but fans of Jeanette won't mind, and Jones introduces "The Donkey Serenade." ▼

Firefox (1982) **C-124m.** *½ D: Clint Eastwood. Clint Eastwood, Freddie Jones, David Huffman, Warren Clarke, Ronald Lacey, Stefan Schnabel, Nigel Hawthorne, John Ratzenberger. Lamentably dull, slow-moving espionage yarn, with Eastwood as burned-out U.S. pilot who goes behind Russian lines to steal the Soviets' latest aeronautic marvel: a supersonic fighting plane. Jones wins the Charles Laughton Award for Eccentric Performances. Originally released at 137m. Panavision. [PG]▼●)

Firehouse Dog (2007) **C-111m.** *** D: Todd Holland. Josh Hutcherson, Bruce Greenwood, Bill Nunn, Scotch Ellis Loring, Mayte Garcia, Teddy Sears, Steven Culp, Dash Mihok, Bree Turner, Hannah Lochner, Claudette Mink, Shane Daly. Clever variation of the boy-and-his-dog genre finds a pampered, spoiled superstar movie mutt named Rex (star of JURASSIC BARK and THE CANINE MUTINY) lost and alone in a small town when an airplane stunt goes wrong. He soon finds his way into the local fire station, which is about to be razed to make way for a new development, but can he save the day for the fire chief and his son? Predictable stuff, but executed with such skill it's hard to resist. Fun for kids and their parents, too. [PG]❱

Fire, Ice and Dynamite (1990-German) **C-102m.** BOMB D: Willy Bogner. Roger Moore, Shari Belafonte, Simon Shepherd, Uwe Ochsenknecht, Geoffrey Moore, Connie de Groot, Marjoe Gortner, Isaac Hayes. Obscenely wealthy Moore, whose empire is crumbling, fakes suicide to test the mettle of his children and creditors in an athletic competition. Loud, lame, occasionally offensive timewaster, redeemed (just barely) by the stuntwork. As inept as Bogner's earlier FIRE AND ICE. [PG] ▼

Fire in the Sky (1993) **C-107m.** ** D: Robert Lieberman. D. B. Sweeney, Robert Patrick, Craig Sheffer, Peter Berg, James Garner, Henry Thomas, Bradley Gregg, Noble Willingham, Kathleen Wilhoite. Failed sci-fi outing, allegedly based on fact, with Sweeney cast as Travis Wilson, a man who mysteriously disappeared for five days, during which time he supposedly was taken prisoner by extraterrestrials. Written by Tracy (son of Mel) Tormé, and based on Wilson's book *The Walton Experience.* Super 35. [PG-13] ▼●)

Firelight (1998-U.S.-British) **C-103m.** *** D: William Nicholson. Sophie Marceau, Stephen Dillane, Dominique Belcourt, Kevin Anderson, Lia Williams, Joss Ackland, Sally Dexter. Handsome 19th-century British aristocrat Dillane, in need of an heir, hires fiercely proud, beautiful Swiss governess Marceau to bear him a child. In dire circumstances beyond her control, Marceau, with few options open to her, reluctantly agrees. Well-made, old-fashioned Gothic soap in the MADAME X vein, with a touch of JANE EYRE thrown in. Written by the director. Panavision. [R] ▼●)

Firemen's Ball, The (1967-Czech) **C-73m.** ** D: Milos Forman. Jan Vostrcil, Josef Sebanek, Josef Valnoha, Josef Kolb, Vaclav Stockel. Acclaimed comedy of small-town firemen's ball which turns into sprawling disaster apparently has elusive charm that completely escaped us. ▼●)

Fire on the Amazon (1996) **C-81m.** ** D: Luis Llosa. Craig Sheffer, Sandra Bullock, Juan Fernandez, Judith Chapman, Ramsey Ross, David Elkin, Jorge Garcia Bustamante. Well-intentioned "save the rainforest" story, marred by appallingly reckless and hostile behavior of photojournalist Sheffer, whose stupidity should have had him blown away very early in the film. Contrived romance with activist Bullock is no more believable. Filmed in 1990. Executive-produced by Roger Corman. Unrated version also available. [R] ▼)

Firepower (1979-British) **C-104m.** **½ D: Michael Winner. Sophia Loren, James Coburn, O. J. Simpson, Eli Wallach, Anthony Franciosa, George Grizzard, Vincent Gardenia, Victor Mature. Another international all-star action thriller, with beautiful people in beautiful locations (this time, the Caribbean). Inane, complicated story has Loren seeking revenge for murder of her chemist husband. Passable time-filler, especially on TV. [R] ▼

Fire Sale (1977) **C-88m.** BOMB D: Alan Arkin. Alan Arkin, Rob Reiner, Vincent Gardenia, Anjanette Comer, Kay Medford, Sid Caesar, Barbara Dana, Alex Rocco, Richard Libertini, Augusta Dabney. Wretched black comedy about a department store owner

and his two sons gives bad taste a bad name. Truly unbearable. [PG]

Fires on the Plain (1959-Japanese) **105m.** ***½ D: Kon Ichikawa. Eiji Funakoshi, Mantaro Ushio, Yoshihiro Hamaguchi, Osamu Takizawa. Japanese soldiers struggle to survive at the finale of the Philippine campaign during WW2; focus is on travails of tubercular Funakoshi, separated from his unit. Graphically realistic, disturbing, and depressing vision of damnation on earth, with a sobering antiwar message. Daieiscope. ▼●)

Firestarter (1984) **C-115m.** ** D: Mark L. Lester. David Keith, Drew Barrymore, George C. Scott, Martin Sheen, Heather Locklear, Art Carney, Louise Fletcher, Moses Gunn, Freddie Jones. Silly, sometimes laughable yarn about little girl whose parents acquired unusual mental powers as a result of a government experiment and who herself can set anything on fire at will. Lumbering story wastes a lot of acting talent, though it certainly gave employment to a number of stunt people and special effects technicians. From Stephen King's best-seller. Followed in 2002 by a made-for-TV movie. J-D-C Scope. [R] ▼●)

Firestorm (1998) **C-89m.** *½ D: Dean Semler. Howie Long, William Forsythe, Scott Glenn, Suzy Amis, Christianne Hirt, Garwin Sanford. Wily con Forsythe and cohorts have pulled off a prison escape, incinerating a Canadian forest as their "cover." This makes the job of smoke jumpers (who parachute into difficult fires) all the more risky. By-the-numbers script is fashioned as an action vehicle for athlete Long, who suggests what Ed Harris might look like if he couldn't move his facial muscles. [R] ▼●)

Fires Within (1991) **C-86m.** ** D: Gillian Armstrong. Jimmy Smits, Greta Scacchi, Vincent D'Onofrio, Luis Avalos, Bertila Damas, Raul Davila, Bri Hathaway, Daniel Fern. Well-intentioned but underdeveloped story of anguish suffered by a Cuban political prisoner and his family when they're reunited in Miami after an eight-year separation. Smits and Scacchi certainly make a great-looking couple. [R] ▼)

Firewalker (1986) **C-104m.** BOMB D: J. Lee Thompson. Chuck Norris, Lou Gossett, Melody Anderson, Will Sampson, Sonny Landham, John Rhys-Davies, Ian Abercrombie. Anderson, hair perfectly intact throughout, hires Gossett and fellow mercenary Norris to find a hidden cache of loot she's imagined exists. Press releases described Norris' character as a "soldier-of-wacky-misfortune"; his light comedy skills recall a sportswriter's description of Yogi Berra playing third base—"like a man trying to put up a pup tent in a windstorm." Arguably Chuck's worst—but who wants to argue? [PG] ▼●)

Firewall (2006) **C-105m.** *½ D: Richard

Loncraine. Harrison Ford, Paul Bettany, Virginia Madsen, Robert Forster, Alan Arkin, Robert Patrick, Mary Lynn Rajskub, Carly Schroeder, Jimmy Bennett, Vince Vieluf. A security expert must break into his own bank in order to save his family; that's the premise of this muddled, often preposterous thriller. Ford seems an unlikely technophile, and while the action builds toward the end, by then the audience has been drained of all emotional investment. Super 35. [PG-13]▶

Fire With Fire (1986) **C-103m.** **½ D: Duncan Gibbins. Craig Sheffer, Virginia Madsen, Jon Polito, Jeffrey Jay Cohen, Kate Reid, Jean Smart, D. B. Sweeney. Story of a forbidden love affair between a boy imprisoned at a juvenile detention facility and girl who *feels* imprisoned at Catholic girls' school nearby. Pleasant enough to watch . . . until ludicrous finale. Film buffs should note Ann Savage in the small role of Sister Harriet. [PG-13]▼

Fire Within, The (1963-French) **108m.** ***½ D: Louis Malle. Maurice Ronet, Lena Skerla, Yvonne Clech, Hubert Deschamps, Jeanne Moreau, Alexandra Stewart. Shattering study of alcoholism, as wealthy Ronet, released from a sanitarium after a breakdown, visits his old friends in Paris one last time. Probably Malle's best early film—photographed, scored (with the music of Erik Satie), and acted to maximum effect—and with a minimum of self-pity.▼▶

Fireworks (1998-Japanese) **C-103m.** *** D: Takeshi Kitano. "Beat" Takeshi, Kayoko Kishimoto, Ren Osugi, Susumu Terajima, Tetsu Watanabe, Taro Itsumi. Tough cop's world crumbles around him: his wife is dying, his partner becomes confined to a wheelchair, and a young detective dies in a shootout because of his blunder, forcing him into a deal with the yakuza. Strongly directed film begins with clear but fragmentary flashbacks; melancholy, violent, sardonic, and romantic, it's an outstanding movie of its genre. The director, who also wrote and coedited, uses "Beat" Takeshi as an acting name. Original title: HANA-BI.▼▶

Firm, The (1993) **C-154m.** *** D: Sydney Pollack. Tom Cruise, Gene Hackman, Jeanne Tripplehorn, Holly Hunter, Ed Harris, Hal Holbrook, Terry Kinney, Wilford Brimley, David Strathairn, Gary Busey, Steven Hill, Tobin Bell, Barbara Garrick, Jerry Hardin, Paul Colderon, Jerry Weintraub, Karina Lombard, John Beal. Slick adaptation of John Grisham's bestseller about a Harvard law school grad who's wooed by a Memphis law firm and happily signs on, never suspecting the sinister truth behind its gracious facade. Good storytelling and good performances, but it goes on too long . . . and makes some unfortunate changes from Grisham's original. Still, it's attractive and entertaining. Paul Sorvino appears unbilled as a Mafioso. [R]▼●▶

First Blood (1982) **C-97m.** *½ D: Ted

Kotcheff. Sylvester Stallone, Richard Crenna, Brian Dennehy, David Caruso, Jack Starrett, Bill McKinney, Michael Talbott. Ex–Green Beret is falsely arrested by smalltown cops, escapes and leads his pursuers into all kinds of booby traps in the "jungles" of U.S. Northwest. Throws all credibility to the winds about the time he gets off with only a bad cut after jumping from a mountain into some jagged rocks. A kewpie doll to anyone who can understand more than three words of Sly's final monologue. Followed by RAMBO: FIRST BLOOD PART II. Panavision. [R]▼●▶

Firstborn (1984) **C-103m.** ** D: Michael Apted. Teri Garr, Peter Weller, Christopher Collet, Corey Haim, Sarah Jessica Parker, Robert Downey, Jr. Divorced mom is doing her best to raise two sons—until she lets her latest boyfriend (a real lout) move into the house and take over. Credible, if unappealing, drama leads to repellent conclusion, à la DEATH WISH, putting to waste the film's good qualities and performances. [PG-13]▼●

First Daughter (2004) **C-104m.** *½ D: Forest Whitaker. Katie Holmes, Marc Blucas, Amerie, Michael Keaton, Margaret Colin, Lela Rochon Fuqua, Michael Milhoan, Dwayne Adway. Fairy-tale romance for wholesome teens centers on the sheltered daughter of the U.S. President, who goes off to college to get away from her omnipresent Secret Service detail and falls for a hunky student whose true identity holds a big surprise (not really). CHASING LIBERTY was bad enough; did we really need another formulaic, juvenile variation of ROMAN HOLIDAY the same year? [PG] ▼▶

First Deadly Sin, The (1980) **C-112m.** *** D: Brian G. Hutton. Frank Sinatra, Faye Dunaway, David Dukes, Brenda Vaccaro, Martin Gabel, James Whitmore. Sinatra's first starring feature after 10-year absence finds him in good form in adaptation of Lawrence Sanders' best-seller about an N.Y.C. cop who stalks a psycho during his wife's illness. Dunaway's near-comatose role couldn't be more thankless, but good supporting cast and moody Gordon Jenkins score make this one of Frank's better serious vehicles. Look fast for Bruce Willis half-hidden under a cap in a bar scene. [R]▼●▶

First Family (1980) **C-104m.** ** D: Buck Henry. Bob Newhart, Gilda Radner, Madeline Kahn, Richard Benjamin, Bob Dishy, Harvey Korman, Rip Torn, Austin Pendleton, Fred Willard, Julius Harris, Buck Henry. Almost laughless political satire, written by Henry, with Newhart a bumbling U.S. President, Kahn his inebriated First Lady, Radner their horny First Daughter. However, Newhart's conversation with African Ambassador Harris is a gem. [R]▼

First Grader, The (2011-British-U.S.) **C-103m.** **½ D: Justin Chadwick. Naomie Harris, Oliver Litondo, Vusumuzi Michael

Kunene, Tony Kgoroge, Israel Sipho Makoe. In 2003, Kenya offers free primary-school education for the first time, and an 84-year-old villager (Litondo) shows up at Harris' overcrowded schoolroom. Bureaucrats and ignorant locals don't want him taking lessons alongside the children, but Harris is moved by his determination to learn to read. What seems like a feel-good movie, based on a true story, turns unexpectedly dark as we flash back to the elderly man's experiences as a Mau Mau freedom fighter. Simplistic storytelling brings a Hollywood touch to significant historical material, but the two leads' sincere performances compensate. [PG-13]

First Great Train Robbery, The SEE: **Great Train Robbery, The**

First Kid (1996) **C-101m.** *** D: David Mickey Evans. Sinbad, Brock Pierce, Blake Boyd, Timothy Busfield, Art La Fleur, Robert Guillaume, Lisa Eichhorn, James Naughton, Fawn Reed, Zachery Ty Bryan, Bill Cobbs. Very entertaining Disney comedy about a hang-loose Secret Service agent on the White House detail who gets the worst assignment in town: guarding the President's bratty son. Soon enough, however, he and the boy form a bond. Subplot about a disgruntled ex-agent gets a little intense for a family film, but otherwise this is bull's-eye stuff and a great comic vehicle for Sinbad. [PG]▼●)

First Knight (1995) **C-132m.** *** D: Jerry Zucker. Sean Connery, Richard Gere, Julia Ormond, Ben Cross, Liam Cunningham, Christopher Villiers, Valentine Pelka, Colin McCormack, Ralph Ineson, John Gielgud. Handsome, sweeping, romantic adventure saga that focuses on a love triangle involving King Arthur (Connery), Lady Guinevere (Ormond), and a restless, roving spirit, who lives by his wits, named Lancelot (Gere). Awkward narrative moments (and the casting of a contemporary-sounding American as Lancelot) outweighed by the overall intelligence of William Nicholson's script, John Box's breathtaking production design, Jerry Goldsmith's majestic score, and the splendid performances by Ormond and Connery. Camelot has never looked so magical. [PG-13] ▼●)

First Legion, The (1951) **86m.** *** D: Douglas Sirk. Charles Boyer, William Demarest, Lyle Bettger, Barbara Rush. Engrossing low-key account of Jesuit priest who is dubious about an alleged miracle occurring in his town. Boyer gives one of his best performances.▼

First Love (1970-British-French-Swiss) **C-90m.** *** D: Maximilian Schell. John Moulder-Brown, Dominique Sanda, Maximilian Schell, John Osborne. Original, often moving story of young lovers is total concept of Schell. While his direction often wanders, his script is extremely good. [R]▼

First Love (1977) **C-92m.** ** D: Joan Darling. William Katt, Susan Dey, John Heard, Beverly D'Angelo, Robert Loggia, Swoosie Kurtz. Youthful romance between right-thinking college boy and girl who's involved with older man; muddled film with unsatisfying conclusion. [R]▼

First Love, Last Rites (1998) **C-93m.** ** D: Jesse Peretz. Giovanni Ribisi, Natasha Gregson Wagner, Robert John Burke, Jeannetta Arnette, Donal Logue. Deadeningly slow story of two young lovers who shack up in a modest apartment on the Louisiana bayou. Feature directorial debut for music-video helmer Peretz has a sensual mood and attractive leads but is devoid of dramatic incident. Only plus: art-rockers Shudder to Think's score, which is meant to evoke old 45 singles. Based on a short story by Ian McEwan. [R]▼●

First Men in the Moon (1964-British) **C-103m.** *** D: Nathan Juran. Edward Judd, Martha Hyer, Lionel Jeffries, Erik Chitty. Lavish adaptation of H. G. Wells novel is heavy-handed at times, overloaded with comic relief, but still worthwhile; good Ray Harryhausen special effects. Cameo appearance by Peter Finch. Panavision.▼●)

First Monday in October (1981) **C-98m.** **½ D: Ronald Neame. Walter Matthau, Jill Clayburgh, Barnard Hughes, James Stephens, Jan Sterling, Joshua Bryant. Talky but OK adaptation of Jerome Lawrence–Robert E. Lee stage hit about Tracy-and-Hepburn-like clash of wills between first female member of the Supreme Court (a staunch conservative) and the most liberal of her brethren. Lost some of its novelty when it happened for real just before film was released, but still amusing. Panavision. [R]▼●)

First Name: Carmen (1983-French-Swiss) **C-85m.** *** D: Jean-Luc Godard. Maruschka Detmers, Jacques Bonnaffe, Myriem Roussel, Christophe Odent, Jean-Luc Godard. Title character is a femme fatale, terrorist, and aspiring filmmaker, and Godard plays her uncle, a famous but "sick" and "washed-up" director named Jean-Luc Godard. Funny and compelling, if you like Godard's later work; otherwise, it will seem like a waste of time and celluloid. ▼●)

First Nudie Musical, The (1976) **C-100m.** ** D: Mark Haggard, Bruce Kimmel. Stephen Nathan, Cindy Williams, Bruce Kimmel, Diana Canova, Alexandra Morgan, Leslie Ackerman. Basically a one-joke idea that wears thin despite an air of amiability: a desperate young filmmaker (Nathan) tries to rescue his studio by making a porno musical, complete with production numbers such as "Dancing Dildos." Best contributions come from those who keep their clothes on. Kimmel also scripted and wrote most of the songs. Ron Howard appears unbilled. [R]▼

First of the Few, The SEE: **Spitfire** (1942)
First Power, The (1990) **C-99m.** *½ D:

Robert Resnikoff. Lou Diamond Phillips, Tracy Griffith, Jeff Kober, Mykel T. Williamson, Elizabeth Arlen, Dennis Lipscomb. Cat-and-mouse battle between an L.A. cop and the spirit of an executed Devil's disciple who has the ability to pop in and out of other people's bodies. Very weak supernatural horror that fails to frighten, or offer anything fresh. Griffith is Melanie Griffith's half-sister. [R] **V O D**

First Snow (2007) **C-102m. **½ D: Mark Fergus. Guy Pearce, Piper Perabo, William Fichtner, J. K. Simmons, Shea Whigham, Rick Gonzalez, Luce Rains, Adam Scott, Jackie Burroughs. Slick salesman Pearce, who's always looking for the right angles and that elusive "big deal," consults a palm reader while his car is being repaired—and doesn't get good news about his future. What's more, a boyhood pal has just gotten out of jail and may be looking for him. Pretty good thriller bolstered by a first-rate cast. Written by Mark Fergus and Hawk Ostby, two of the writers of CHILDREN OF MEN; Fergus' directorial debut. Super 35. [R]❿

First Sunday (2008) **C-98m. ** D: David E. Talbert. Ice Cube, Katt Williams, Tracy Morgan, Loretta Devine, Michael Beach, Keith David, Regina Hall, Malinda Williams, Chi McBride, Clifton Powell, Nicholas Turturro, Olivia Cole. Two petty criminals scheme to rob their local church when they need quick cash in order to pay off a debt . . . but they get much more than they bargained for. Jokes mostly fall flat in this all-too-typical vehicle for Ice Cube and company. A couple of genuine laughs are provided by Williams and Morgan. [PG-13]❿

First Time, The (1969) **C-90m. *½ D: James Neilson. Jacqueline Bisset, Wes Stern, Rick Kelman, Wink Roberts, Gerald Parkes. Combination of *Ozzie and Harriet* and WALK ON THE WILD SIDE concerns a teenager's sexual initiation. Artificial look at adolescence. [M]▼

First Time, The (1983) **C-95m. *** D: Charlie Loventhal. Tim Choate, Krista Errickson, Marshall Efron, Wendy Fulton, Raymond Patterson, Wallace Shawn, Wendie Jo Sperber, Cathryn Damon. Surprisingly intelligent, funny portrait of virginal, movie-loving college freshman Choate. A cut above other films of its type, and a promising debut for young Loventhal, a protégé of Brian De Palma. Aka DOIN' IT. [R]▼

First to Fight (1967) **C-97m. **½ D: Christian Nyby. Chad Everett, Marilyn Devin, Dean Jagger, Bobby Troup, Claude Akins, Gene Hackman. Conventional WW2 yarn with Everett the one-time hero who almost loses his courage on the battlefield. Panavision.▼

First Traveling Saleslady, The (1956) **C-92m. ** D: Arthur Lubin. Ginger Rogers, Barry Nelson, Carol Channing, David Brian, James Arness, Clint Eastwood. Rogers and Channing try to elevate this plodding

comedy of girdle-sellers in the old West, but barely succeed. Carol and Clint make one of the oddest couples in screen history.

First Wives Club, The (1996) **C-102m. **½ D: Hugh Wilson. Goldie Hawn, Bette Midler, Diane Keaton, Maggie Smith, Dan Hedaya, Stockard Channing, Sarah Jessica Parker, Victor Garber, Stephen Collins, Elizabeth Berkley, Marcia Gay Harden, Bronson Pinchot, Jennifer Dundas, Eileen Heckart, Philip Bosco, Rob Reiner, James Naughton, Debra Monk, Kate Burton. Three college pals meet up years later at a mutual friend's funeral and discover they have something in common: husbands who've dumped (or dumped on) them. Predictable, but still pretty entertaining, thanks to three lively stars and an impressive supporting cast. Diluted from Olivia Goldsmith's novel. Heather Locklear appears unbilled. [PG]❿

Fish Called Wanda, A (1988) **C-108m. *** D: Charles Crichton. John Cleese, Jamie Lee Curtis, Kevin Kline, Michael Palin, Maria Aitken, Tom Georgeson, Patricia Hayes, Geoffrey Palmer. Funny farce about an uptight British barrister who becomes involved with a sexy con artist (Curtis), her mindlessly macho boyfriend (Kline), and their ambitious bank robbery and getaway scheme. Cleese's script includes enough bad-taste gags to either repel or delight his audience, depending on one's personal point of view. Kline won an Oscar for his flamboyant comic performance. The cast later reunited for FIERCE CREATURES. [R] ❿

Fisher King, The (1991) **C-137m. *** D: Terry Gilliam. Robin Williams, Jeff Bridges, Amanda Plummer, Mercedes Ruehl, Michael Jeter, Harry Shearer, John de Lancie, David (Hyde) Pierce, Christian Clemenson. Expansive, emotional fable of a smart-aleck, self-absorbed radio personality driven into a deep funk by an unexpected tragedy—and his unlikely rescue by a strange street vigilante who's in desperate need of rescue himself. Unusual and absorbing, both comic and tender, this takes the viewer on quite a journey. Ruehl won Best Supporting Actress Oscar as Bridges' girlfriend. Look fast for Kathy Najimy. Written by Richard LaGravenese. Super 35. [R]❿

Fish Hawk (1980-Canadian) **C-95m. ** D: Donald Shebib. Will Sampson, Charlie Fields, Geoffrey Bowes, Mary Pirle, Don Francks, Chris Wiggins. Bland family film about an alcoholic Indian who tries to mend his ways—and becomes a companion to an impressionable young farm boy. This is the kind of unchallenging, inoffensive fare that gives G-rated movies a bad reputation. [G]❿

Fish Tank (2009-British) **C-122m. ***½ D: Andrea Arnold. Katie Jarvis, Michael Fassbender, Kierston Wareing, Harry Treadaway, Rebecca Griffiths, Sydney Mary Nash. Testy teen Jarvis, prone to mood swings equally volatile and credible, wonders if a flair for hip-hop dancing can spring her from a nondescript Essex housing block. She's also in a subtle but escalating sexual competition with her eye-catching mom. Emotionally raw and gripping, even as it cracks the two-hour mark, this really kicks into gear with the appearance of mom's attractive lover (Fassbender), who genuinely cares for the girl but may also care in ways that will add to already hothouse living conditions. Jarvis, who'd never acted before, is quite remarkable. Written by the director.❿

Fish That Saved Pittsburgh, The (1979) **C-102m.** *½ D: Gilbert Moses. Julius Erving, James Bond III, Stockard Channing, Jonathan Winters, Margaret Avery, Jack Kehoe, Meadowlark Lemon, Nicholas Pryor, Flip Wilson, Kareem Abdul-Jabbar. Losing basketball team tries astrology to put them in winners' circle; low-grade comedy with disco soundtrack. Game hijinks are only saving grace. [PG] ▼❿

F.I.S.T. (1978) **C-145m.** **½ D: Norman Jewison. Sylvester Stallone, Rod Steiger, Peter Boyle, Melinda Dillon, David Huffman, Tony Lo Bianco, Kevin Conway, Cassie Yates, Henry Wilcoxon, Brian Dennehy. Stallone's one-dimensional performance prevents this well-produced epic about a Hoffa-like labor kingpin from sustaining a strong first half. Peter Boyle does well with a role inspired by former Teamster boss Dave Beck. Screenplay by Stallone and Joe Eszterhas. [PG] ▼●❿

Fistful of Chopsticks, A SEE: **They Call Me Bruce?**

Fistful of Dollars (1964-Italian) **C-100m.** *** D: Sergio Leone. Clint Eastwood, Gian Maria Volonté, Marianne Koch, Wolfgang Lukschy, Mario Brega, Carol Brown. Sagebrush remake of YOJIMBO single-handedly invented the "spaghetti Western," made an international superstar of Eastwood, and boosted the careers of Leone and composer Ennio Morricone as well. Clint plays the laconic Man With No Name, a tough gunslinger manipulating (and manipulated by!) two rival families warring over small frontier town. Amusing, violent, and very stylish. Released in the U.S. in 1967. Sequel: FOR A FEW DOLLARS MORE. Techniscope. ▼●❿

Fistful of Dynamite, A SEE: **Duck, You Sucker**

Fist in His Pocket (1965-Italian) **105m.** **** D: Marco Bellochio. Lou Castel, Paola Pitagora, Marino Mase, Liliana Gerace, Pier Luigi Troglio. Brilliant one-of-a-kind about a mad family of epileptics whose protagonist kills his mother and drowns his younger brother, while his sis merely settles for repressed incest. One of the great, if largely unheralded, foreign films of the '60s, with Castel more than up to the demands of the difficult role.❿

Fist of Fear, Touch of Death (1980) **C-90m.** *½ D: Matthew Mallinson. Fred Williamson, Ron Van Clief, Adolph Caesar, Aaron Banks, Bill Louis. Boring chopsocky film chronicling the happenings at a Madison Square Garden martial arts tournament. Highlighted are short clips of legendary Bruce Lee. Aka DRAGON AND THE COBRA. [R]▼❿

Fist of Fury SEE: **Chinese Connection, The**

Fist Right of Freedom SEE: **Fox and His Friends**

Fists of Fury (1971-Hong Kong) **C-103m.** ** D: Lo Wei. Bruce Lee, Maria Yi, Han Ying Chieh, Tony Liu, Miao Ker Hsiu. Lee, in his initial Kung Fu actioner, plays a young fellow who takes a job in an ice house, and discovers his boss is a drug smuggler. Feeble. Original title: THE BIG BOSS. Dyaliscope. [R]▼❿

Fitzcarraldo (1982) **C-157m.** **** D: Werner Herzog. Klaus Kinski, Claudia Cardinale, Jose Lewgoy, Miguel Angel Fuentes, Paul Hittscher. Vivid, fascinating portrait of a man obsessed (made by a man obsessed—see BURDEN OF DREAMS) who's determined to capture a shipping route on the Amazon, even though it means hauling a boat over a mountaintop, through hostile tribal territory. Then he's going to bring in grand opera! Astonishing and captivating movie, in spite of its length; admittedly not to everyone's taste. [PG]▼❿

Fitzwilly (1967) **C-102m.** **½ D: Delbert Mann. Dick Van Dyke, Barbara Feldon, Edith Evans, John McGiver, Harry Townes, John Fiedler, Norman Fell, Cecil Kellaway, Sam Waterston. Ordinary fluff about butler who has to rob Gimbel's on Christmas Eve to save his employer. Van Dyke's screen career was hurt by too many films like this one. This was Feldon's film debut. Panavision. ▼❿

Five (1951) **93m.** *** D: Arch Oboler. William Phipps, Susan Douglas, James Anderson, Charles Lampkin, Earl Lee. Intriguing, offbeat film by famed radio writer-director Oboler about the survivors of an atomic holocaust. Talky (and sometimes given to purple prose) but interesting. Filmed in and around Oboler's Frank Lloyd Wright house.❿

5 Against the House (1955) **84m.** **½ D: Phil Karlson. Guy Madison, Kim Novak, Brian Keith, Kerwin Mathews, Alvy Moore, William Conrad, Kathryn Grant. College buddies plan a "perfect crime" to rob a Reno, Nevada, casino. Dated film still has its moments. Stirling Silliphant and William Bowers adapted Jack Finney's story.❿

Five Angles on Murder SEE: **Woman in Question, The**

Five Ashore in Singapore SEE: **Singapore, Singapore**

Five Bloody Graves SEE: **Gun Riders**

5 Card Stud (1968) **C-103m.** *½ D: Henry

Hathaway. Dean Martin, Robert Mitchum, Inger Stevens, Roddy McDowall, Katherine Justice. Dino is a gambler and Mitchum virtually repeats his NIGHT OF THE HUNTER role in surprisingly disappointing Western; Maurice Jarre's Dr. Zhivago-on-the-range musical score doesn't help. Probably Hathaway's worst Western. [M/PG] ▼▶

Five Corners (1988) C-92m. *** D: Tony Bill. Jodie Foster, Tim Robbins, Todd Graff, John Turturro, Elizabeth Berridge, Rose Gregorio, Gregory Rozakis, John Seitz. Moody piece about young people whose lives converge in a Bronx neighborhood in 1964. One of them, just released from prison, stirs trouble for the others. Unexpectedly melodramatic but potent and believable . . . and seemingly the only 1960s period film not to use oldies to evoke the era. James Newton Howard's moody score is much more effective, anyway. Written by John Patrick Shanley. [R] ▶

Five Days from Home (1978) C-109m. ** D: George Peppard. George Peppard, Neville Brand, Savannah Smith, Sherry Boucher, Victor Campos, Robert Donner. Peppard breaks out of Louisiana prison, determined to reach L.A. and see his hospitalized son. Well-intentioned but improbable film. [PG]

Five Days One Summer (1982) C-108m. ** D: Fred Zinnemann. Sean Connery, Betsy Brantley, Lambert Wilson, Jennifer Hilary, Isabel Dean, Gerald Buhr, Anna Massey. Middle-aged man brings a young woman—ostensibly his wife—on Swiss vacation in the early 1930s where their hesitant relationship is explored against the natural drama of mountain climbing. Adaptation of a Kay Boyle story doesn't come off, despite impeccable production. Slow, ethereal, ultimately unsatisfying. Zinnemann's last film. [PG] ▼

$5 a Day (2009-U.S.-British) C-98m. ** D: Nigel Cole. Christopher Walken, Alessandro Nivola, Sharon Stone, Dean Cain, Peter Coyote, Amanda Peet. Minor-league road movie involving Nivola and his relationship with his irresponsible scam-artist father (Walken), who claims to be dying. Tries to be outrageous and endearing, with Walken gamely attempting to bring depth to his character, but the end result is inconsequential. [PG-13] ▶

Five Easy Pieces (1970) C-98m. **** D: Bob Rafelson. Jack Nicholson, Karen Black, Billy Green Bush, Fannie Flagg, Susan Anspach, Sally Struthers, Ralph Waite, Lois Smith. Brilliant character study of musician with great promise who gave up a career to work on an oil rig. Nicholson's performance is superb, but Black, Anspach, Smith, and Bush all contribute heavily. Helena Kallianiotes is hilarious as a malcontent hitchhiker; this is the film with Jack's famous "chicken salad sandwich" speech. Beautifully written by Adrien Joyce (Carole Eastman). [R] ▼▶

Five Finger Exercise (1962) 109m. **½ D: Daniel Mann. Rosalind Russell, Jack Hawkins, Maximilian Schell, Richard Beymer, Lana Wood, Annette Gorman. Peter Shaffer's play suffers from change of locale and alteration of original ideas; now it becomes embarrassing soap opera of possessive mother in love with daughter's tutor. Stars are miscast but try their best. ▶

5 Fingers (1952) 108m. *** D: Joseph L. Mankiewicz. James Mason, Danielle Darrieux, Michael Rennie, Walter Hampden, Oscar Karlweis, Herbert Berghof, John Wengraf, Michael Pate. Exceptionally intelligent spy thriller with Mason as a cool customer selling high-priced secrets right under the noses of his British government employers during WW2. Based on true-life events! Followed by a short-lived TV series. ▼

Five Fingers of Death (1973-Hong Kong) C-102m. *½ D: Cheng Chang Ho. Lo Lieh, Wang Ping, Wang Ching-Feng. Only interesting in that it is the Kung Fu film that began the craze in America. Family honor defended with every part of the body except the mouth, which is horrendously dubbed. Shawscope. [R] ▼▶

Five Golden Dragons (1967-British) C-93m. ** D: Jeremy Summers. Bob Cummings, Margaret Lee, Maria Perschy, Brian Donlevy, Christopher Lee, George Raft, Dan Duryea. Cummings is naive American caught up in international crime in Hong Kong; conventional actioner. Techniscope. ▼

Five Golden Hours (1961-British-Italian) 90m. ** D: Mario Zampi. Ernie Kovacs, Cyd Charisse, George Sanders, Kay Hammond, Dennis Price, Finlay Currie, Ron Moody. Con man Kovacs fleeces wealthy widows, but his luck is sure to change after falling for Charisse, whose husband has just died. Limp comedy wastes the talents of its cast. ▼

Five Graves To Cairo (1943) 96m. ***½ D: Billy Wilder. Franchot Tone, Anne Baxter, Akim Tamiroff, Erich von Stroheim, Peter Van Eyck, Fortunio Bonanova. WW2 intrigue situated in Sahara oasis hotel run by Tamiroff and Baxter; Tone attempts to obtain secrets from visiting Field Marshal Rommel (von Stroheim). Billy Wilder–Charles Brackett script manages to incorporate wit and humor into genuinely exciting wartime yarn. A remake of HOTEL IMPERIAL. ▼

Five Heartbeats, The (1991) C-120m. *** D: Robert Townsend. Robert Townsend, Michael Wright, Leon, Harry J. Lennix, Tico Wells, Diahann Carroll, Harold Nicholas, John Canada Terrell, Chuck Patterson, Hawthorne James, Paul Benjamin. Corny but entertaining saga of a 1960s singing group's rise to fame; loosely based on R&B group The Dells. Awfully predictable, but star/director/cowriter Townsend and his cast are so likable they make up for it. The scene in which a youthful belter named Tressa Thomas helps Townsend piece together a song on the spot is worth the price of admission. Coscripted by Keenen Ivory Wayans. [R]▼●▶

(500) Days of Summer (2009) **C-95m.** **½ D: Marc Webb. Joseph Gordon-Levitt, Zooey Deschanel, Geoffrey Arend, Chloë Grace Moretz, Matthew Gray Gubler, Clark Gregg, Rachel Boston, Minka Kelly. Unconventional boy-meets-girl story jumps back and forth in time to trace the relationship between two office workers: he's smitten with her, but she doesn't want to commit to a serious relationship, even though she likes him. Clever at times, with two very appealing stars, but heavy-handed narration and self-conscious gimmickry wear out their welcome. Makes wondrous use of downtown L.A. Super 35. [PG-13]▶

Five Million Years to Earth SEE: **Quatermass and the Pit: Five Million Years to Earth**

Five Minutes of Heaven (2009-Irish-British) **C-90m.** *** D: Oliver Hirschbiegel. Liam Neeson, James Nesbitt, Anamaria Marinca, Richard Dormer, Mark Davison, Kevin O'Neill. Television producers set up a "reconciliation meeting" between a one-time teenage IRA gunman and the younger brother of his victim, who witnessed the cold-blooded murder more than 30 years ago. It turns out both men have been haunted by that act of violence ever since. Thoughtful, unpredictable, and as potent as a punch in the gut, with great performances by Neeson and Nesbitt. Film also handily skewers the manipulative nature of reality television. Guy Hibbert's screenplay is based on real-life characters.▶

Five Minutes to Live SEE: **Door-to-Door Maniac**

Five Obstructions, The (2003-Danish-Swiss-Belgian-French) **C/B&W-88m.** *** D: Jørgen Leth, Lars von Trier. Unusual, stimulating semidocumentary in which von Trier mischievously dares his former teacher, Danish filmmaker Leth, to remake THE PERFECT HUMAN, a 12m. film he directed in 1967, with a proviso: Leth must create several versions, each with a different set of restrictions (or "obstructions") concocted by von Trier. Not for all tastes, but noteworthy as an exploration of the varying styles filmmakers employ and the artistic choices they make.▶

Five on the Black Hand Side (1973) **C-96m.** **½ D: Oscar Williams. Clarice Taylor, Leonard Jackson, Virginia Capers, D'Urville Martin, Glynn Turman, Godfrey Cambridge. Black family comedy about patriarchal barber was once refreshing amidst many black exploitation films, now seems foolish. [PG]▼▶

Five Pennies, The (1959) **C-117m.** **½ D: Melville Shavelson. Danny Kaye, Barbara Bel Geddes, Tuesday Weld, Louis Armstrong, Bob Crosby, Harry Guardino, Ray Anthony, Shelley Manne, Bobby Troup. Danny plays jazz trumpeter Red Nichols in this sentimental biography. Only bright spots are musical numbers, especially duets with Kaye and Armstrong. VistaVision. ▼●▶

Five Senses, The (1999-Canadian) **C-104m.** *** D: Jeremy Podeswa. Mary-Louise Parker, Pascale Bussieres, Richard Clarkin, Brendan Fletcher, Marco Leonardi, Nadia Litz, Daniel MacIvor. Intricately woven comedy-drama centers on the inhabitants of an office/apartment building in Toronto. Though the interconnected stories deal individually with the five senses, they're never tricky or schematic, but instead revealing, amusing, and moving. [R]▼▶

5,000 Fingers of Dr. T., The (1953) **C-88m.** *** D: Roy Rowland. Peter Lind Hayes, Mary Healy, Tommy Rettig, Hans Conried. A boy who hates to practice the piano has a vivid nightmare about a land where his officious teacher, Dr. Terwilliger (Conried), rules over hundreds of boys and a gigantic keyboard. Imaginative fantasy conceived by Dr. Seuss with clever songs by Seuss and Frederick Hollander. Major weakness: conventional "grown-up" leads played by then-popular performers Healy and Hayes. Look for George Chakiris among the dancers.▼●▶

5x2 (2004-French) **C-90m.** *** D: François Ozon. Valeria Bruni-Tedeschi, Stéphane Freiss, Géraldine Pailhas, Françoise Fabian, Michael Lonsdale, Antoine Chappey, Marc Ruchmann. Simple, effective drama charting the anatomy of a marriage; the gimmick is that the story is told in five episodes and in reverse chronological order, starting with the characters' divorce proceeding and ending with their initial meeting at a vacation resort. With a wisp of sadness, Ozon peels away the gradations of the relationship and the secrets and lies that tear it apart. [R] ▼▶

Five Weeks in a Balloon (1962) **C-101m.** **½ D: Irwin Allen. Red Buttons, Barbara Eden, Fabian, Cedric Hardwicke, Peter Lorre, Richard Haydn, Barbara Luna. Innocuous entertainment with formula script from Jules Verne tale of balloon expedition to Africa. Buoyed by fine cast, including veterans Billy Gilbert, Herbert Marshall, Reginald Owen, Henry Daniell. CinemaScope.▼●▶

Fixed Bayonets! (1951) **92m.** **½ D: Samuel Fuller. Richard Basehart, Gene Evans, Michael O'Shea, Richard Hylton, Craig Hill. Taut Korean War drama of platoon cut off from the rest of its outfit; typical tough

Fuller production. James Dean is one of the soldiers. ▶

Fixer, The (1968) **C-132m.** ** D: John Frankenheimer. Alan Bates, Dirk Bogarde, Georgia Brown, Hugh Griffith, Ian Holm, Jack Gilford, Elizabeth Hartman, David Warner, Carol White. Good acting helps, but Bernard Malamud's acclaimed novel fails on the screen; story of unjustly imprisoned Jewish handyman in turn-of-the-century Russia concerns itself too much with the thoughts of its main character to be effective as film. [M/PG]▼

Flags of Our Fathers (2006) **C-131m.** ***½ D: Clint Eastwood. Ryan Phillippe, Jesse Bradford, Adam Beach, John Benjamin Hickey, John Slattery, Barry Pepper, Jamie Bell, Paul Walker, Robert Patrick, Neal McDonough, Melanie Lynskey, Tom McCarthy, Chris Bauer, Judith Ivey, Joseph Cross, Scott Reeves, David Patrick Kelly, Beth Grant, Jon Polito, Gordon Clapp, Tom Verica, David Clennon, David Rasche, Jason Gray-Stanford, George Grizzard, Harve Presnell, George Hearn, Len Cariou. Intimate, involving portrait of the men who landed on Iwo Jima island in 1945, encountered death and unspeakable horrors, raised the U.S. flag, then were labeled heroes and put on display for a U.S. bond-selling tour. Told in flashback as the son of one such man—who came home and never spoke about his experiences—goes in search of his father's story. Stirring, sad, often profound in its simplicity and directness, with a hellish depiction of combat one didn't see in WW2 movies of the 1940s. Well cast and crafted on every level. Reeves, who has a small part as a Marine, is Eastwood's son. Screenplay by William Broyles, Jr., and Paul Haggis, from the book by James Bradley with Ron Powers. Followed by LETTERS FROM IWO JIMA. Panavision. [R]▶

Flame and the Arrow, The (1950) **C-88m.** *** D: Jacques Tourneur. Burt Lancaster, Virginia Mayo, Robert Douglas, Aline MacMahon, Nick Cravat. Bouncy, colorful action with Lancaster romping through his gymnastics as rebel leader in medieval Italy leading his people on to victory. Mayo is gorgeous heroine. ▼●▶

Flame and the Flesh, The (1954) **C-104m.** ** D: Richard Brooks. Lana Turner, Pier Angeli, Carlos Thompson, Bonar Colleano, Charles Goldner, Peter Illing. Pointless Turner vehicle filmed in Europe involving brunette Lana being romanced by continental Thompson, which causes a lot of misery.

Flamenco (1995-Spanish) **C-100m.** ***½ D: Carlos Saura. Saura's love of flamenco saturates this ecstatic, beautifully made performance film featuring flamenco singers, dancers, and guitarists of all ages, the best of whom are nothing short of dazzling. There are neither subtitles nor dialogue—and none are needed! ▼▶

Flame of New Orleans, The (1941) **78m.** *** D: René Clair. Marlene Dietrich, Bruce Cabot, Roland Young, Laura Hope Crews, Mischa Auer, Andy Devine. Dietrich can have her pick of any man in New Orleans, can't decide between wealthy Young or hard-working Cabot. Picturesque, entertaining. Clair's first American film.▼▶

Flame of the Barbary Coast (1945) **91m.** **½ D: Joseph Kane. John Wayne, Ann Dvorak, Joseph Schildkraut, William Frawley, Virginia Grey. Hick rancher Wayne competes with slick Schildkraut for savvy saloon singer Dvorak; undemanding fluff, with Republic Pictures' version of the San Francisco earthquake. Also shown in computer-colored version. ▼▶

Flame Over India (1959-British) **C-130m.** *** D: J. Lee Thompson. Lauren Bacall, Kenneth More, Herbert Lom, Wilfrid Hyde-White. Fast-paced actioner set on northern frontier of India as British soldiers and governess Bacall seek to speed an Indian prince to safety aboard a run-down train. Originally titled NORTH WEST FRONTIER. Cinema-Scope.▼

Flamingo Kid, The (1984) **C-100m.** *** D: Garry Marshall. Matt Dillon, Richard Crenna, Hector Elizondo, Jessica Walter, Fisher Stevens, Janet Jones, Bronson Pinchot, Martha Gehman, Brian McNamara, Steven Weber, Eric Douglas, Marisa Tomei, Tracy Reiner, John Turturro. Very likable film set in 1963, about a Brooklyn boy from a working-class family whose head is turned by a slick sharpie who holds court at the beach club where he works. Crenna scores a bull's-eye as the fat cat (and catches a glimpse of himself in *The Real McCoys* while testing his remote control TV in one scene). Nice coming-of-age story written by Neal Marshall (no relation to director). Tomei's film debut. [PG-13]▼▶●

Flamingo Road (1949) **94m.** *** D: Michael Curtiz. Joan Crawford, Zachary Scott, Sydney Greenstreet, David Brian, Gertrude Michael, Gladys George. Crawford is excellent as tough carnival dancer ditched in small town where she soon is loving Scott and Brian and matching wits with corrupt politician Greenstreet. Remade as TVM in 1980, which later spun off a TV series. ▼●▶

Flaming Star (1960) **C-91m.** *** D: Don Siegel. Elvis Presley, Barbara Eden, Steve Forrest, Dolores Del Rio, John McIntire. Elvis is excellent as a half-breed Indian who must choose sides when his mother's people go on the warpath. No songs after the first ten minutes but lots of action; along with JAILHOUSE ROCK, Presley's best film. CinemaScope.▼▶

Flanders (2006-French) **C-91m.** *** D: Bruno Dumont. Adélaïde Leroux, Samuel Boidin, Henri Cretel, Jean-Marie Bruveart, David Poulain. Pretty teen Leroux loves farmer Boidin, but he is unable to reciprocate her feelings, driving her into the arms of another. He goes off to war and she becomes pregnant. Compelling, vividly etched portrait of the cruelty of war and human existence, featuring inarticulate characters who are incapable of thinking or controlling their lives. Punctuated by jarring scenes of passionless, animalistic sex and senseless violence. Written by the director. Hawk-Scope.▶

Flannel Pajamas (2006) **C-124m.** ******* D: Jeff Lipsky. Justin Kirk, Julianne Nicholson, Rebecca Schull, Jamie Harrold, Chelsea Altman, Stephanie March. Two people meet, fall madly in love, get married, and almost immediately find that their diverging personalities are tearing the relationship apart. Intelligent, engaging character study with good performances and many moments that ring true, but the couple's transition from blissful to wildly dysfunctional seems implausibly quick. [R]▶

Flap (1970) **C-106m.** ****** D: Carol Reed. Anthony Quinn, Claude Akins, Tony Bill, Victor Jory, Shelley Winters. Uneven story of Indian outcast Quinn. You're supposed to pity Flapping Eagle, but script is so weak that the chances are you won't. At times funny, but supposedly tragic. Panavision. [PG]▶

Flareup (1969) **C-100m.** ****½** D: James Neilson. Raquel Welch, James Stacy, Luke Askew, Don Chastain, Ron Rifkin, Jean Byron. Go-go dancer gets stalked from Las Vegas to L.A. by psychopathic ex-husband of friend who blames her for breakup of the marriage. Fast melodrama is helped by good location footage. [M/PG]▼

Flashback (1990) **C-108m.** ***½** D: Franco Amurri. Dennis Hopper, Kiefer Sutherland, Carol Kane, Cliff De Young, Paul Dooley, Michael McKean, Richard Masur. Young straight-arrow FBI agent (Sutherland) is ordered to transport a recently captured "underground" political fugitive to the scene of his '60s crime—disruption of a Spiro Agnew rally. Enervatingly predictable until its (surprisingly) bloody climax. Masur and McKean, who seem to be winging it, amuse as onetime political activists now trapped in a middle-class environment. [R]▼●▶

Flashbacks of a Fool (2008-U.S.-British) **C-114m.** ****½** D: Baillie Walsh. Daniel Craig, Jodhi May, Claire Forlani, Harry Eden, Olivia Williams, Miriam Karlin, Mark Strong. Adult male's emotional age is stunted when, at 15, a traumatic event causes him to run away from home. Craig is on the mark as the now-successful Hollywood star who's boozing, womanizing, and drugging himself into oblivion. May stands out among a cast of top-notch actors. Scripted by Walsh, whose quiet, compelling direction helps give this soap-opera tale added dimension. Panavision. [R]▶

Flashdance (1983) **C-96m.** ****½** D: Adrian Lyne. Jennifer Beals, Michael Nouri, Lilia Skala, Sunny Johnson, Kyle T. Heffner, Lee Ving, Ron Karabatsos, Belinda Bauer, Cynthia Rhodes, Liz Sagal, Robert Wuhl. How to turn a rock video into a feature film—with glitzy images, high energy, an arresting music score (principally by Giorgio Moroder), and the stupidest story this side of Busby Berkeley. Still, this concoction about a girl with the perfect fantasy life (macho welder by day, sexy dancer by night, courted by the rich and handsome boss, watched over by a patron-saint ballerina) was a smash. Title song won an Oscar. [R]▼●▶.

Flash Fire SEE: **Dangerous Summer, A**

Flash Gordon (1980) **C-110m.** ******* D: Mike Hodges. Sam J. Jones, Melody Anderson, Topol, Max von Sydow, Ornella Muti, Brian Blessed, Timothy Dalton, Mariangela Melato. Updated version of comic strip is better than expected, thanks to eye-filling production/costume design by Danilo Donati, amusing rock score by Queen. Jones and Anderson are liabilities as Flash and Dale Arden, but Muti's evil Princess Aura (who would make any male stray from Right) leads a strong supporting cast. Todd-AO 35. [PG]▼●▶

Flash of Genius (2008) **C-120m.** ****½** D: Marc Abraham. Greg Kinnear, Lauren Graham, Dermot Mulroney, Jake Abel, Daniel Roebuck, Tim Kelleher, Bill Smitrovitch, Alan Alda, Mitch Pileggi. In the 1960s Detroit science teacher and inventor Robert Kearns (Kinnear) pitches his intermittent windshield washer to the Ford Motor Company. When they steal the invention he becomes obsessed with seeing justice done—and sacrifices everything (including his wife and six children) to that end. A true-life David and Goliath story with a twist: David isn't very likable. Interesting for a while, with good period flavor, but wears thin as we lose rooting interest. Super 35. [PG-13]▶

Flash of Green, A (1984) **C-131m.** ****** D: Victor Nunez. Ed Harris, Blair Brown, Richard Jordan, George Coe, Helen Stenborg, John Glover. Reporter in a small Florida coastal town gets in over his head when he plays footsie with a scheming county commissioner who's behind a shady land-fill development racket. Capable performances and refreshingly offbeat subject matter are eventually negated by overlength and plot redundancies. Made for *American Playhouse* and produced by costar Jordan. Based on John D. MacDonald's book.▼

Flashpoint (1984) **C-94m.** ****** D: William Tannen. Kris Kristofferson, Treat Williams, Rip Torn, Kevin Conway, Miguel Ferrer, Jean Smart, Roberts Blossom, Tess Harper. Two maverick Texas Border Patrol officers stumble into volatile territory when they discover a cache of money that figures in a long-dormant mystery. Intriguing overall premise (and good cast) defeated by uninteresting presentation. Bonus: the worst title song of 1984 (sung over closing credits). [R] ▼●)

Flatfoot SEE: **Knock Out Cop, The**

Flatliners (1990) C-105m. **½ D: Joel Schumacher. Kiefer Sutherland, Julia Roberts, Kevin Bacon, William Baldwin, Oliver Platt, Kimberly Scott, Hope Davis. Offbeat but sophomoric supernatural drama (with touches of horror and humor) about medical students experimenting with life after death. Slick camerawork and effects can't camouflage the superficiality of the script, which undermines an intriguing idea. Panavision. [R] ▼●)

Flawless (1999) C-110m. ** D: Joel Schumacher. Robert De Niro, Philip Seymour Hoffman, Barry Miller, Chris Bauer, Skipp Sudduth, Daphne Rubin-Vega. N.Y.C. cop suffers a stroke, and gets speech therapy lessons from the unlikeliest source imaginable, a drag queen he can't stand who happens to live in the same apartment house. Meanwhile, a local crimelord is searching for stolen money that's stashed somewhere in the building. Overlong, overplotted film (written by Schumacher) is kept afloat by the talent of its stars, De Niro and Hoffman. Panavision. [R] ▼●)

Flawless (2008-British) C-108m. **½ D: Michael Radford. Michael Caine, Demi Moore, Lambert Wilson, Nathaniel Parker, Shaughan Seymour, Nicholas Jones, David Barras, Joss Ackland. In the kind of film he could have made in the '60s (and did, only better), Caine's latest gambit finds him as a janitor who decides his retirement gift from the London Diamond Corp. should include some of their product. He enlists an underappreciated female exec at the office to help him with the heist. Caine could do this in his sleep but he's still fun to watch; Moore has learned a lot about acting since she played Caine's daughter in 1984's BLAME IT ON RIO. A pleasant enough diversion. Super 35. [PG-13] ▶

Flea in Her Ear, A (1968-U.S.-French) C-94m. ** D: Jacques Charon. Rex Harrison, Rosemary Harris, Louis Jourdan, Rachel Roberts. Unfunny farce about philandering barrister. Some of the slapstick gags go on interminably. Panavision. [M/PG]

Fled (1996) C-98m. *½ D: Kevin Hooks. Laurence Fishburne, Stephen Baldwin, Will Patton, Robert John Burke, Salma Hayek, Michael Nader, David Dukes, Brittney Powell, RuPaul, Taurean Blacque. Fishburne and Baldwin escape prison chained together in DEFIANT ONES style, leading to an extended chase that involves trains, trucks, cycles, cable cars, and the clichéd like. Self-conscious movie references abound

in a story dealing with a secret computer disk that has the goods on a Cuban mobster. Final gag isn't that great, but it's the best thing in the movie. [R] ▼●)

Fleet's In, The (1942) 93m. *** D: Victor Schertzinger. Dorothy Lamour, William Holden, Eddie Bracken, Betty Hutton, Betty Jane Rhodes, Leif Erickson, Cass Daley, Gil Lamb, Barbara Britton, Rod Cameron, Lorraine and Rognan, Jimmy Dorsey Orchestra with Bob Eberly and Helen O'Connell. Bouncy wartime musical with reputed romeo Holden trying to melt iceberg Lamour. Sensational score (composed by director Schertzinger and Johnny Mercer) includes "Tangerine," "I Remember You," and "Arthur Murray Taught Me Dancing in a Hurry." Feature debuts of Hutton (in a hilarious performance that made her an instant star) and Daley. Previously filmed as TRUE TO THE NAVY and LADY BE CAREFUL; remade as SAILOR BEWARE.

Flesh (1932) 95m. *** D: John Ford. Wallace Beery, Karen Morley, Ricardo Cortez, Jean Hersholt, Herman Bing, John Miljan. Unusual, melancholy drama with Beery as simple-minded German wrestler in love with Morley—who tries to hide her shady relationship with no-good Cortez. ▶

Flesh + Blood (1985) C-126m. ** D: Paul Verhoeven. Rutger Hauer, Jennifer Jason Leigh, Tom Burlinson, Jack Thompson, Susan Tyrrell, Ronald Lacey, Brion James, Bruno Kirby. Rowdy adventure set in 16th century: Leigh is betrothed to young Prince Burlinson but falls into clutches of Hauer and his motley band of warriors. Plenty of flesh *and* blood, but it's all rather foul and nasty; Verhoeven (in his first American English-language effort) *does* score points for sheer audaciousness. Aka THE ROSE AND THE SWORD. Technovision. [R] ▼▶

Flesh and Bone (1993) C-127m. **½ D: Steve Kloves. Dennis Quaid, Meg Ryan, James Caan, Gwyneth Paltrow, Scott Wilson, Christopher Rydell, Betsy Brantley, Julia Mueller. Moody but murky "sins of the father" drama, with Quaid well cast as a vending machine supplier who discovers that the tough-luck case he's been driving around Texas figured in the childhood tragedy that has dominated his life. Absolutely no dramatic payoff, but simply oozing in portent. Undeniable standouts are Philippe Rousselot's photography and the performance of Paltrow as a sexy con woman. [R] ▼●)

Flesh and the Devil (1927) 112m. *** D: Clarence Brown. John Gilbert, Greta Garbo, Lars Hanson, Barbara Kent, William Orlamond, George Fawcett, Eugenie Besserer. Garbo at her most seductive as temptress who comes between old friends Gilbert and Hanson. Pulsatingly romantic, beautifully filmed, probably the best Garbo-Gilbert love match. But talk about surprise endings! ▼▶

Flesh and the Fiends, The SEE: **Mania**

Flesh Feast (1970) **C-72m.** BOMB D: B. F. Grinter. Veronica Lake, Phil Philbin, Heather Hughes, Chris Martell, Martha Mischon. Lake's final film (which she coproduced) is embarrassing, amateurish gorefest. As a mad scientist working on rejuvenation, she tortures Hitler to death at film's climax (maggots eat at his face in close-up), then addresses us directly, shouting a patriotic, anti-Nazi diatribe! [R] ▼ ❿

Flesh for Frankenstein SEE: **Andy Warhol's Frankenstein**

Fletch (1985) **C-96m.** **½ D: Michael Ritchie. Chevy Chase, Dana Wheeler-Nicholson, Tim Matheson, Joe Don Baker, Richard Libertini, Geena Davis, M. Emmet Walsh, George Wendt, Kenneth Mars. Chase plays a smart-ass undercover reporter (with a penchant for disguises) who goes after major drug ring. Good mystery absolutely smothered in wisecracks, some funny, some tiresome; if you're not a fan of Chevy, stay clear! Watchable but never credible. Screenplay by Andrew Bergman from Gregory McDonald's novel. Followed by a sequel. [PG] ▼ ❿ ❿

Fletch Lives (1989) **C-95m.** ** D: Michael Ritchie. Chevy Chase, Hal Holbrook, Julianne Phillips, Cleavon Little, R. Lee Ermey, Richard Libertini, Randall (Tex) Cobb, George Wyner, Patricia Kalember, Geoffrey Lewis, Richard Belzer. Chase returns as Fletch, the multi-personality L.A. reporter, in silly sequel. He finds himself in Louisiana, dealing with a parade of stereotypical Southern morons. [PG] ▼ ❿ ❿

Flicka (2006) **C-95m.** ***D: Michael Mayer. Alison Lohman, Tim McGraw, Maria Bello, Ryan Kwanten, Dallas Roberts, Nick Searcy, Danny Pino, Dey Young. Teenage Lohman has no interest in school and only comes alive when she's home on her family's ranch. Then she encounters a wild horse and claims it as her own—in spite of her stern father's warnings to leave the animal alone. First-rate modern-day adaptation of Mary O'Hara's novel *My Friend Flicka* (filmed before in 1943) is ideal family fare. It's nice to see veteran Western actor Buck Taylor as the rodeo clerk. Followed by a DVD sequel. Super 35. [PG] ❿

Flight Command (1940) **116m.** ** D: Frank Borzage. Robert Taylor, Ruth Hussey, Walter Pidgeon, Paul Kelly, Nat Pendleton, Shepperd Strudwick, Red Skelton, Dick Purcell. Hackneyed story with good cast as upstart Taylor tries to make the grade in naval flight squadron. Look fast for John Raitt as a cadet. ❿

Flight of Rainbirds, A (1981-Dutch) **C-94m.** *** D: Ate de Jong. Jeroen Krabbé, Marijke Merckens, Henriette Tol, Huib Rooymans, Claire Wauthion. Thoughtful, whimsical tale of sex, death, and religion, with Krabbé in a dual role as an inept,

34-year-old biologist who's never had a date, let alone slept with a woman, and his Alter Ego, who informs him that he has seven days to seduce a woman; otherwise he'll die and end up in hell. ▼

Flight of the Doves (1971-British) **C-105m.** ** D: Ralph Nelson. Ron Moody, Jack Wild, Dorothy McGuire, Stanley Holloway, Helen Raye, William Rushton. Calculated cuteness mars tale of two Liverpool children who flee to Ireland to visit their grandmother; good cast isn't seen to best advantage. [G] ❿

Flight of the Eagle, The (1982-Swedish) **C-139m.** *** D: Jan Troell. Max von Sydow, Goran Stangertz, S. A. Ousdal, Eva von Hanno. Beautifully shot true story about a foolhardy but heroic balloon mission to the North Pole in 1897 strives to become its country's national film epic, but falls short of greatness. Stays in the memory, however, despite the fact that the second half of a lengthy running time deals only with three men freezing to death in the snow. Simultaneously filmed as a miniseries for Swedish TV. An Oscar nominee for Best Foreign Film. ▼ ❿

Flight of the Innocent (1992-Italian-French) **C-105m.** *** D: Carlo Carlei. Manuel Colao, Federico Pacifici, Sal Borgese, Giusi Cataldo, Lucio Zagaria, Massimo Lodolo, Francesa Neri, Jacques Perrin. Exciting, fast-paced thriller about a little Sicilian boy (well played by Colao) who finds himself immersed in Mafia warfare and is forced to flee for his life. Immensely entertaining, this film also observes the stranglehold that organized crime can have over a society. Excellent debut feature for director/coscripter Carlei. [R] ▼ ❿

Flight of the Intruder (1991) **C-113m.** *½ D: John Milius. Danny Glover, Willem Dafoe, Brad Johnson, Rosanna Arquette, Tom Sizemore, J. Kenneth Campbell, Dann Florek, Madison Mason, Ving Rhames, David Schwimmer. Dull adaptation of Stephen Coonts' novel, chronicling the exploits and frustrations of bombardiers in the Vietnam war. It plays like one of those 1950s service dramas that was "filmed in cooperation with the U.S. military," and this is incongruous given the story's setting. Super 35. [PG-13] ▼ ❿

Flight of the Navigator (1986) **C-90m.** **½ D: Randal Kleiser. Joey Cramer, Veronica Cartwright, Cliff De Young, Sarah Jessica Parker, Matt Adler, Howard Hesseman. 12-year-old boy is whisked away by an alien spaceship and returns home eight years later—still a 12-year-old boy. That's when the adventure really begins. Yet another film featuring a youthful hero and a cute robot; adequate entertainment for kids. The voice of the robot, billed as Paul Mall, is actually Paul Reubens, aka Pee-wee Herman. [PG] ▼ ❿ ❿

Flight of the Phoenix, The (1965) C-147m. ***½ D: Robert Aldrich. James Stewart, Richard Attenborough, Peter Finch, Hardy Kruger, Ernest Borgnine, Ian Bannen, Ronald Fraser, Christian Marquand, Dan Duryea, George Kennedy. A plane crash leaves a group of men stranded in the Sahara desert; film avoids clichés as tension mounts among the men. Stewart as the captain, Attenborough as the navigator stand out in uniformly fine cast. Remade in 2004. ▼●)

Flight of the Phoenix (2004) C-113m. ** D: John Moore. Dennis Quaid, Tyrese Gibson, Miranda Otto, Giovanni Ribisi, Tony Curran, Hugh Laurie, Kirk Jones (Sticky Fingaz), Jacob Vargas, Scott Michael Campbell, Jared Padalecki. Remake of the 1965 film has a plane crashing (this time) in the Gobi Desert, with captain Quaid and fellow passengers running out of water, patience, and hope. Solid but unspectacular and, unlike the original, clichéd. Panavision. [PG-13] ▼▶

Flight of the Red Balloon (2008-French) C-115m. *** D: Hou Hsiao-hsien. Juliette Binoche, Simon Iteanu, Song Fang, Hippolyte Girardot, Louise Margolin. Harried Parisian working mother tries to juggle her career in puppet theater while raising her young son, Simon. Bringing some calm into her life is a new nanny, a young Asian who tells Simon of the beloved 1956 short film by Albert Lamorisse, *The Red Balloon* (which features a boy Simon's age). Plot development is surrendered to exploration of character and the artistic temperament in this well-made if laid-back domestic drama. A red balloon plays a peripheral role here, appearing to be almost another hovering caregiver for the still-innocent boy. Emotionally powerful story, full of symbolic and cross-cultural touchstones, though not for all tastes. ▶

Flightplan (2005) C-98m. ** D: Robert Schwentke. Jodie Foster, Peter Sarsgaard, Erika Christensen, Sean Bean, Kate Beahan, Marlene Lawston, Greta Scacchi, Judith Scott, Michael Irby, Stephanie Faracy. Grieving mother (Foster, solid as always) takes her young daughter home on a jumbo plane that's also carrying her husband's coffin. When she wakes up from a nap, her little girl is missing and no one believes that the youngster ever boarded the plane! Suspenseful at first, this thriller becomes remote and uninvolving; by the climax it's just plain ridiculous. Too bad Miss Froy wasn't along. Super 35. [PG-13] ▶

Flight to Fury (1964) 76m. ** D: Monte Hellman. Dewey Martin, Fay Spain, Jack Nicholson, Jacqueline Hellman, Vic Diaz. Odd group of adventurers headed for Philippines location and hidden diamonds when plane crashes. Low-budgeter has its points, but never really comes across. Initially released at 62m., later reedited. ▼

Flim-Flam Man, The (1967) C-104m. *** D: Irvin Kershner. George C. Scott, Sue Lyon, Michael Sarrazin, Harry Morgan, Jack Albertson, Alice Ghostley, Albert Salmi, Slim Pickens. Scott is engaging as a veteran Southern con man who takes on Sarrazin as apprentice in his travels, but finds the novice a bit too honest. Entertaining comedy. Panavision. ▼

Flintstones, The (1994) C-92m. **½ D: Brian Levant. John Goodman, Elizabeth Perkins, Rick Moranis, Rosie O'Donnell, Kyle MacLachlan, Halle Berry, Elizabeth Taylor, Dann Florek, Richard Moll, Jonathan Winters; voices of Harvey Korman, Sheryl Lee Ralph, Laraine Newman, Jay Leno. If you're going to make a live-action feature from a one-note, two-dimensional TV cartoon series, this is about as good as you could hope for: a bouncy concoction with an enthusiastic cast, including a surprisingly funny Taylor as Fred Flintstone's nagging mother-in-law. Mainly for kids, who should understandably lap it up. Series creators Bill Hanna and Joe Barbera, and Wilma's original voice, Jean Vander Pyl, have cameos. Followed by a prequel. [PG] ▼●)

Flintstones in Viva Rock Vegas, The (2000) C-91m. ** D: Brian Levant. Mark Addy, Stephen Baldwin, Kristen Johnston, Jane Krakowski, Thomas Gibson, Joan Collins, Alan Cumming, Harvey Korman, Alex Meneses, John Taylor; voice of Rosie O'Donnell. Silly FLINTSTONES prequel featuring Fred and Barney as unmarried employees of the Bedrock Quarry; they court Wilma and Betty, while Wilma is pressured to wed snooty, slimy rich boy Chip Rockefeller. The cast is game, but this will appeal only to undiscriminating youngsters. Look for 10-year-old Kristen Stewart as ring toss girl. [PG] ▼▶

Flipped (2010) C-90m. *** D: Rob Reiner. Madeline Carroll, Callan McAuliffe, Rebecca De Mornay, Anthony Edwards, John Mahoney, Penelope Ann Miller, Aidan Quinn, Kevin Weisman. When a boy moving into a new neighborhood meets a girl who lives across the street, in the late 1950s, it's dislike at first sight. Six years later their prickly relationship continues unabated. Highly relatable story is told from both the boy's and girl's points of view, and its observations on the workings of young minds—and their parents'—make it honest and appealing. Reiner and Andrew Scheinman adapted Wendelin Van Draanen's popular juvenile novel and moved it to their favorite time period; naturally, the soundtrack is filled with familiar oldies. [PG] ▶

Flipper (1963) C-90m. **½ D: James Clark. Chuck Connors, Luke Halpin, Kathleen Maguire, Connie Scott. Typical wholesome family fare about a boy who befriends a dolphin. Spun off into a TV series in 1964 (with Halpin) and another in 1995. Remade in 1996. ▼▶

Flipper (1996) **C-96m.** **½ D: Alan Shapiro. Paul Hogan, Elijah Wood, Chelsea Field, Isaac Hayes, Jonathan Banks, Jason Fuchs, Jessica Wesson. Low-key but agreeable time-filler about a teenage boy who spends the summer with his unruly uncle in Coral Key, Florida, and is befriended by a supersmart dolphin. Simplistic storytelling aimed at a juvenile crowd. Luke Halpin, star of the earlier film and TV series, appears briefly. Super 35. [PG]▼●】

Flipper's New Adventure (1964) **C-103m.** ** D: Leon Benson. Luke Halpin, Pamela Franklin, Helen Cherry, Tom Helmore, Brian Kelly. Further exploits of everybody's favorite dolphin: Flipper and Halpin thwart escaped convicts' efforts to blackmail millionaire Helmore. Pleasant, inoffensive fare for kids, filmed in the Bahamas and Key Biscayne.▼】

Flirt (1995-U.S.-German-Japanese) **C-85m.** **½ D: Hal Hartley. Bill Sage, Parker Posey, Martin Donovan, Dwight Ewell, Geno Lechner, Peter Fitz, Miho Nikaidoh, Toshizo Fujisawa, Chikako Hara. Quirky three-part film in which the same minidrama is told three different ways: Flirt leaves lover to head off on a job, but the lover demands a commitment before the departure. The stories are set in N.Y.C., Berlin (with the characters gay), and Tokyo (with the male-female roles reversed). The point: male, female, gay, straight, and across the globe, people experience the same feelings and romantic crises. More interesting as an exercise than as entertainment.▼

Flirtation Walk (1934) **97m.** **½ D: Frank Borzage. Dick Powell, Ruby Keeler, Pat O'Brien, Ross Alexander, Guinn Williams, Henry O'Neill, Tyrone Power. West Point plot is clichéd and trivial as cadet Powell falls in love with officer's daughter Keeler; some fairly good numbers highlighted by "Mr. and Mrs. Is the Name."▼】

Flirting (1990-Australian) **C-100m.** *** D: John Duigan. Noah Taylor, Thandie Newton, Nicole Kidman, Bartholomew Rose, Felix Nobis, Josh Picker, Liri Paramore, Marc Gray, Greg Palmer, Joshua Marshall, David Wieland, Craig Black, Leslie Hill, Naomi Watts. Charming sequel to Duigan's THE YEAR MY VOICE BROKE, which finds shy Taylor at boarding school where he falls in love with a Ugandan girl (Newton) who goes to a nearby girls' school. Nothing particularly new but still a warm, perceptive look at the pains of adolescence, with winning performances from everyone in the cast. Director Duigan also wrote the screenplay.▼●】

Flirting With Disaster (1996) **C-92m.** **½ D: David O. Russell. Ben Stiller, Patricia Arquette, Téa Leoni, Alan Alda, Mary Tyler Moore, George Segal, Lily Tomlin, Josh Brolin, Richard Jenkins, Celia Weston, Glenn Fitzgerald, David Patrick Kelly, John Ford Noonan. Married and now a father, adopted Stiller decides to seek out his birth parents, with the help of a psychology grad student; taking his wife in tow, they embark on a cross-country trek that leads to calamity at every turn. Determinedly offbeat and full of comic twists, not all of which pay off; still, a cut above the norm for contemporary comedy. Moore and Segal make a great neurotic Jewish couple, matched by Tomlin and Alda as middle-aged flower children. [R] ▼●】

Floating Weeds (1959-Japanese) **C-119m.** ***½ D: Yasujiro Ozu. Ganjiro Nakamura, Machiko Kyo, Haruko Sugimura, Ayako Wakao. Struggling acting troupe visits remote island, where its leader (Nakamura) visits his illegitimate son and the boy's mother, with whom he had an affair years before. Powerful drama is meticulously directed, solidly acted. Ozu previously made this as A STORY OF FLOATING WEEDS (1934). Aka DRIFTING WEEDS.▼●】

Florentine, The (2000) **C-104m.** **½ D: Nick Stagliano. Michael Madsen, Chris Penn, Hal Holbrook, Mary Stuart Masterson, Virginia Madsen, Jeremy Davies, Tom Sizemore, Luke Perry, James Belushi, Burt Young, Maeve Quinlan, Lillo Brancato. Agreeable if unremarkable slice of working-class life involving love, money, crime, and morality. Set and shot in Pennsylvania; the Florentine is a neighborhood bar and meeting place. Based on a stage play. Released direct to video. [R]▼】

Floundering (1994) **C-97m.** *** D: Peter McCarthy. James LeGros, John Cusack, Ethan Hawke, Maritza Rivera, Kim Wayans, Ebbe Roe Smith, Steve Buscemi, Billy Bob Thornton, Alex Cox, Lisa Zane, Nelson Lyon, Olivia Barash, Sy Richardson, Jeremy Piven, Nina Siemaszko, Viggo Mortensen. Eye-opening sleeper with LeGros in a bravura performance as John Boyz, a sensitive and compassionate Southern Californian whose spirit is slowly being killed by the everyday injustices of modern urban life; through a series of bureaucratic blunders, he finds his own life in crisis. McCarthy's script is thoughtful and perceptive, and written with an acid pen. One of the most radical American films of the early 1990s.▼●】

Flower Drum Song (1961) **C-133m.** *** D: Henry Koster. Nancy Kwan, James Shigeta, Miyoshi Umeki, Benson Fong, Jack Soo, Juanita Hall, Reiko Sato, Patrick Adiarte, Victor Sen Yung. Rodgers and Hammerstein's Broadway musical becomes a bright Technicolor confection about life and love in San Francisco's Chinatown, where Old World traditions clash with modern American sensibilities. Songs include "I Enjoy Being a Girl." All-Asian cast was a rarity in Hollywood at that time. Opera singer Marilyn Horne dubs Sato's voice on "Love, Look Away."▼●】

Flower in His Mouth, The (1975-Italian) **C-113m.** *½ D: Luigi Zampa. Jennifer O'Neill, James Mason, Franco Nero, Orazio Orlando. O'Neill moves to small Italian town, finds its people paralyzed by fear but unwilling to tell why. Murky thriller isn't worth time it takes to figure out.

Flower of Evil, The (2003-French) **C-104m.** ** D: Claude Chabrol. Nathalie Baye, Benoît Magimel, Mélanie Doutey, Suzanne Flon, Bernard Le Coq, Thomas Chabrol. Low-key Chabrol melodrama, coscripted by the director, is set in contemporary Bordeaux, where a prosperous family harbors more twisted genealogical secrets than you can count. Film makes reference to France's murky WW2 history, but comes out flat; Baye's character, a local politician, is underwritten and her young, sexy costars' storyline doesn't add up to much. Longtime Chabrol devotées may boost rating of this cerebral film. ▼ ▶

Flower of My Secret, The (1995-Spanish-French) **C-100m.** **½ D: Pedro Almodóvar. Marisa Paredes, Juan Echanove, Imanol Arias, Carmen Elias, Rossy de Palma, Chus Lampreave, Joaquin Cortes, Manuela Vargas. A middle-aged woman (Paredes), who has been happy and a successful writer, seems to be suffering a breakdown. Her work and marriage (to an often absent military-strategist husband) are meaningless, and she must relearn the joys of living. A more focused, somber portrait than usual for Almodóvar—although not without farcical flare-ups—which seems strangely reminiscent of the Douglas Sirk–Jane Wyman collaborations of 1950s Hollywood. [R] ▼ ▶

Flowers in the Attic (1987) **C-95m.** ** D: Jeffrey Bloom. Louise Fletcher, Victoria Tennant, Kristy Swanson, Jeb Stuart Adams, Ben Granger, Lindsay Parker, Marshall Colt. Disappointing adaptation of the V.C. Andrews best-seller tones down the incest and sadomasochism of the story about four youngsters kept locked up by evil granny (Fletcher) in the family mansion. Material is strangely compelling nonetheless; benefits from effective casting. [PG-13] ▼ ▶

Flubber (1997) **C-93m.** ** D: Les Mayfield. Robin Williams, Marcia Gay Harden, Christopher McDonald, Raymond J. Barry, Clancy Brown, Ted Levine, Wil Wheaton, Edie McClurg, voice of Jodi Benson. Surprisingly dull remake of Disney's THE ABSENT MINDED PROFESSOR, with Williams as the fragile genius who accidentally invents flubber—flying rubber—but forgets to attend his own wedding. Needlessly complicated by John Hughes' heavily rewritten script, which manages to leave out most of the funny stuff from the original, except for the springy basketball game. Nancy Olson (the female lead in 1961) has a cameo as a secretary. [PG] ▼ ▶

Fluke (1995) **C-96m.** *** D: Carlo Carlei. Matthew Modine, Nancy Travis, Eric Stoltz,

Max Pomeranc, Ron Perlman, Jon Polito, Bill Cobbs, Collin Wilcox Paxton; voice of Samuel L. Jackson. Touching, beautifully filmed story of a young family man killed in a mysterious car accident and reincarnated as a dog named Fluke—while on his way to rejoin his wife and son. More appropriate for older audiences than for young kids, who might be disturbed by certain scenes and themes within the picture. Samuel L. Jackson provides the voice of Fluke's dog friend, Rumbo. Based on James Herbert's best-selling novel. [PG] ▼ ▶

Flushed Away (2006-U.S.-British) **C-84m.** *** D: David Bowers, Sam Fell. Voices of Hugh Jackman, Kate Winslet, Ian McKellen, Jean Reno, Bill Nighy, Andy Serkis, Shane Richie, Kathy Burke, David Suchet, Miriam Margolyes. A pampered pet mouse is flushed into the sewers of London by a rowdy rat. While struggling to find a way back home, he teams up with an intrepid garbage-scow captain (Winslet) and helps her evade the clutches of a menacing toad. Good fun with clever gags to please both grown-ups and kids, and an unlikely cast of heroes—including some very funny singing slugs. First computer-generated film from the clay-animation geniuses at Aardman studios. [PG] ▶

Fly, The (1958) **C-94m.** *** D: Kurt Neumann. Al (David) Hedison, Patricia Owens, Vincent Price, Herbert Marshall, Kathleen Freeman. Improbable but diverting sci-fi (screenplay by James Clavell!) about scientist who experiments with disintegration machine and has his atomic pattern mingled with that of a fly. "Help me! Help me!" Two sequels—RETURN OF THE FLY and CURSE OF THE FLY. Remade in 1986. CinemaScope. ▼ ▶

Fly, The (1986) **C-100m.** **½ D: David Cronenberg. Jeff Goldblum, Geena Davis, John Getz, Joy Boushel. Goldblum is just right as slightly crazed scientist who tests himself in a genetic transporter machine—and starts to evolve into a human fly. Extremely intense, sharply written remake of the 1958 movie that (unfortunately) goes over the line to be gross and disgusting. Written by Charles Edward Pogue and director Cronenberg. An Oscar winner for makeup (Chris Walas, Stephan Dupuis). Followed by a sequel. [R] ▼ ▶

Fly II, The (1989) **C-104m.** BOMB D: Chris Walas. Eric Stoltz, Daphne Zuniga, Lee Richardson, John Getz, Frank Turner, Ann Marie Lee, Gary Chalk, Saffron Henderson, Harley Cross, Matthew Moore. A case of "like father, like son"; too bad director Walas isn't like David Cronenberg. Stoltz, son of deceased Jeff Goldblum, has attained puberty at five with the intellect to match; now he's being unknowingly exploited by—here's a novel twist—the scientists in whose care he's entrusted. Alternately dull and messy but mostly dull. [R]▼●◗

Fly Away Home (1996) C-107m. *** D: Carroll Ballard. Jeff Daniels, Anna Paquin, Dana Delany, Terry Kinney, Holter Graham, Jeremy Ratchford. First-rate family film about a girl who goes to live with her estranged father in Canada after the death of her mom and only finds happiness when she adopts a flock of baby geese. Then father and daughter embark on the adventure of teaching the birds how to migrate! Credible, involving story (inspired by a real-life incident), sparked by Paquin's and Daniels' strong performances. Photographed by Caleb Deschanel, who previously collaborated with director Ballard on THE BLACK STALLION. [PG]▼●◗

Flyboys (2006) C-139m. **½ D: Tony Bill. James Franco, Martin Henderson, Jean Reno, David Ellison, Jennifer Decker, Tyler Labine, Abdul Salis, Philip Winchester, Daniel Rigby. Agreeably old-fashioned yarn about the diverse young Americans who went to France in 1916 to serve in the Lafayette Escadrille, long before the U.S. officially entered WW1. They bond, bicker, find love on the ground and danger in the air. No surprises here, but this modern update of films like THE DAWN PATROL still entertains, and offers cutting-edge CG imagery to make the aerial sequences more vivid than ever before. Despite a formulaic screenplay, the writers did their homework: most of the characters in this story really existed. HD Widescreen. [PG-13]▮

Flying (1986-Canadian) C-94m. ** D: Paul Lynch. Olivia d'Abo, Rita Tushingham, Keanu Reeves, Jessica Steen, Renee Murphy. Minor imitation of FLASHDANCE has statuesque d'Abo overcoming a leg injury to become a medal-winning gymnast; Tushingham (with shocking carrot-colored hair) is her tough coach. This formula has whiskers, but d'Abo is easy to watch, even though her full figure is unconvincing for a gymnast. Video title: TEENAGE DREAM. ▼

Flying Aces SEE: **Flying Deuces, The**

Flying Deuces, The (1939) 65m. *** D: A. Edward Sutherland. Stan Laurel, Oliver Hardy, Jean Parker, Reginald Gardiner, Charles Middleton, James Finlayson. Stan and Ollie join the Foreign Legion so Ollie can forget Parker; usual complications result. Good fun, faster paced than most L&H films, includes charming song and dance to "Shine On, Harvest Moon."▼●◗

Flying Down to Rio (1933) 89m. *** D: Thornton Freeland. Dolores Del Rio, Gene Raymond, Raul Roulien, Ginger Rogers, Fred Astaire, Blanche Frederici, Eric Blore, Franklin Pangborn. Slim Del Rio vehicle memorable for its scene of dancing girls cavorting on plane wings, plus Astaire and Rogers doing "The Carioca" in their first

screen teaming. Also shown in computer-colored version.▼●◗

Flying Leathernecks (1951) C-102m. *** D: Nicholas Ray. John Wayne, Robert Ryan, Jay C. Flippen, Janis Carter, Don Taylor, William Harrigan. Major Wayne is exceedingly tough on his Marines; executive officer Ryan thinks he should be a little nicer. Guess who wins this argument. Solid, if not especially original, WW2 actioner, with good aerial scenes and nice turn by Flippen as crafty sergeant.▼●◗

Flying Scotsman, The (2006-British-German) C-98m. ** D: Douglas Mackinnon. Jonny Lee Miller, Billy Boyd, Laura Fraser, Morven Christie, Steven Berkoff, Brian Cox. Based-on-fact triumph-of-the-underdog tale involving Graeme Obree (Miller), a young outsider for whom bicycling is an escape, a salvation. He is inspired to build a new kind of cycle, using homemade materials, which he hopes will allow him to set a world speed record . . . but there are complications and repercussions. Potentially rousing story is pleasant at best, but mostly episodic and uninspiring. [PG-13]▮

Flying Tigers (1942) 102m. **½ D: David Miller. John Wayne, John Carroll, Anna Lee, Paul Kelly, Mae Clarke, Gordon Jones, James "Jimmie" Dodd. Good war film in which Wayne commands the volunteer Flying Tigers in China prior to Pearl Harbor while contending with egotistical ace pilot Carroll. Exciting dog-fight scenes. Also shown in computer-colored version.▼●◗

FM (1978) C-104m. **½ D: John A. Alonzo. Michael Brandon, Martin Mull, Eileen Brennan, Cleavon Little, Cassie Yates, Alex Karras, Norman Lloyd, James Keach. Hip comedy (which could well have inspired TV's *WKRP*) about various conflicts at maverick radio station, chiefly against its profit-hungry parent company. More a series of sketches than a movie, but nicely captures feel of '70s L.A. and Mull is marvelous as the station's craziest dj. Good rock soundtrack, plus concert appearances by Linda Ronstadt, Jimmy Buffett, Tom Petty, and REO Speedwagon. Panavision. [PG]▼●◗

Focus (2001) C-106m. **½ D: Neal Slavin. William H. Macy, Laura Dern, David Paymer, Meat Loaf Aday, Kay Hewtrey, Michael Copeman. Gentile personnel director is demoted at work and shunned in his WW2-era Brooklyn neighborhood because his new glasses supposedly make him look Jewish. Well-acted relic, adapted from Arthur Miller's 1945 novel, establishes a concrete feel for its tight neighborhood milieu, even though it was shot in Toronto on a budget. Otherwise, it's heavy-handed and "small"—a lethal combination. [PG-13] ▼▮

Fog, The (1980) C-91m. **½ D: John Carpenter. Adrienne Barbeau, Jamie Lee Curtis, Hal Holbrook, Janet Leigh, John Houseman, Tommy Atkins, Nancy Loomis,

Charles Cyphers. Carpenter's follow-up to HALLOWEEN is a well-directed but obvious ghost story about a California coastal town cursed by a hundred-year-old shipwreck. Remade in 2005. Panavision. [R] ▼●]

Fog, The (2005-U.S.-British) **C-100m.** *½ D: Rupert Wainwright. Tom Welling, Maggie Grace, Selma Blair, DeRay Davis, Kenneth Welsh, Adrian Hough, Sara Botsford, Rade Sherbedgia. A dense fog from the Pacific creeps over a Northwest seaside village, bringing with it murderous, vengeful ghosts. Lame remake of John Carpenter's 1980 movie alters the plot slightly but is no improvement. Carpenter and longtime partner Debra Hill produced this. Alternate version also available. Super 35. [PG-13] ▼]

Fog of War, The (2003) **C-105m.** ***½ D: Errol Morris. Unique, memorable documentary about the life of Robert S. McNamara, the controversial former secretary of defense who played a pivotal role during the Vietnam War. Director Morris explores myriad political, social, and moral issues that resonate even more tellingly today, and McNamara—85 when the film was made—remains an outspoken and forceful personality who refuses to provide any easy answers about the history he helped to shape. An emotional powerhouse for anyone who lived through the era depicted here so vividly. Oscar winner for Best Documentary Feature. Film carries the subtitle ELEVEN LESSONS FROM THE LIFE OF ROBERT S. McNAMARA. [PG-13] ▼]

Fog Over Frisco (1934) **68m.** **½ D: William Dieterle. Bette Davis, Lyle Talbot, Margaret Lindsay, Donald Woods, Henry O'Neill, Arthur Byron, Hugh Herbert, Alan Hale, William Demarest. Snappy melodrama of deceitful, thrill-a-minute partygirl Davis involved in stolen-securities scheme; stepsister Lindsay tries to help.]

Folies Bourgeoises SEE: **Twist, The** (1976)

Folks! (1992) **C-107m.** BOMB D: Ted Kotcheff. Tom Selleck, Don Ameche, Anne Jackson, Christine Ebersole, Wendy Crewson, Robert Pastorelli, Michael Murphy. Excruciating comedic misfire about stockbroker Selleck trying to deal with aging dad Ameche's senility and death wish. An outrageous number of mishaps to Selleck give slapstick a bad name. [PG-13] ▼●]

Folks at Red Wolf Inn, The SEE: **Terror House**

Following (1999-British) **71m.** *** D: Christopher Nolan. Jeremy Theobald, Alex Haw, Lucy Russell, John Nolan. Interesting ultra-low-budget precursor to Nolan's MEMENTO: another nonlinear story about a young aimless man who decides to follow people, just for the hell of it . . . until one of his "subjects" turns the tables and lures

him into *his* world, where he robs empty apartments and invades his victims' lives. Provocative and original. [R] ▼]

Follow Me, Boys! (1966) **C-131m.** **½ D: Norman Tokar. Fred MacMurray, Vera Miles, Lillian Gish, Charlie Ruggles, Elliott Reid, Kurt Russell. Mile-high Disney corn about simple fellow who settles in small town during 1930s and starts Boy Scout troop, devoting his life to this inspiring pursuit. A little less syrup would have helped, but at least it's done with great conviction. ▼]

Follow Me Quietly (1949) **59m.** *** D: Richard O. Fleischer. William Lundigan, Dorothy Patrick, Jeff Corey, Nestor Paiva, Charles D. Brown, Paul Guilfoyle. Solid little film noir about police manhunt for self-righteous psychopathic killer called The Judge. Packs style and substance into just 59 minutes. ▼

Follow That Bird SEE: **Sesame Street Presents Follow That Bird**

Follow That Camel (1967-British) **C-95m.** **½ D: Gerald Thomas. Phil Silvers, Jim Dale, Peter Butterworth, Charles Hawtrey, Kenneth Williams, Anita Harris, Joan Sims. Silvers as conniving sergeant livens up otherwise standard CARRY ON outing with Foreign Legion setting. ▼

Follow That Dream (1962) **C-110m.** **½ D: Gordon Douglas. Elvis Presley, Arthur O'Connell, Anne Helm, Joanna Moore, Jack Kruschen, Simon Oakland. Presley and family move to southern Florida where they intend to homestead, despite all opposition. Easygoing comedy from Richard Powell's book *Pioneer Go Home.* Elvis sings "Home Is Where the Heart Is" and "On Top of Old Smokey"! Panavision. ▼●]

Follow the Boys (1944) **110m.** *** D: A. Edward Sutherland. Marlene Dietrich, George Raft, Orson Welles, Vera Zorina, Dinah Shore, W. C. Fields, Jeanette MacDonald, Maria Montez, Andrews Sisters, Sophie Tucker, Nigel Bruce, Gale Sondergaard. Universal Pictures' entry in all-star WW2 series has Raft organizing USO shows, Welles sawing Dietrich in half, MacDonald singing "Beyond the Blue Horizon," Fields doing classic pool-table routine, etc. Lots of fun. ▼

Follow the Boys (1963) **C-95m.** ** D: Richard Thorpe. Connie Francis, Paula Prentiss, Ron Randell, Janis Paige, Russ Tamblyn, Dany Robin. Dumb comedy unspiked by Francis' singing or antics as quartet of girls chase around the French Riviera seeking husbands. Panavision. ●

Follow the Fleet (1936) **110m.** **** D: Mark Sandrich. Fred Astaire, Ginger Rogers, Randolph Scott, Harriet Hilliard (Nelson), Astrid Allwyn, Betty Grable. Delightful musical with sailors Astaire and Scott romancing sisters Rogers and Hilliard. Irving Berlin songs include "Let's

Face the Music and Dance," "Let Yourself Go," "We Saw the Sea." A reworking of SHORE LEAVE, a 1925 Richard Barthelmess silent, and the 1930 musical HIT THE DECK. That's Lucille Ball as Kitty. ▼⦿◗

Follow the Sun (1951) **93m. **½ D:** Sidney Lanfield. Glenn Ford, Anne Baxter, Dennis O'Keefe, June Havoc. Fictionalized biopic of golfer Ben Hogan with hokey dramatics to fill in lean spots. ▼◗

Folly to Be Wise (1952-British) **91m. *** D:** Frank Launder. Alastair Sim, Elizabeth Allan, Roland Culver, Martita Hunt. Generally amusing nonsense with Sim an Army chaplain trying to enliven service life with various unique entertainment programs.

Fond Kiss, A (2004-British-Belgian-German-Italian-Spanish) **C-104m. *** D:** Kenneth Loach. Atta Yaqub, Eva Birthistle, Shabana Bakhsh, Shamshad Akhtar, Ahmad Riaz, Ghizala Avan, Pasha Bocarie. Provocative, refreshingly unformulaic drama about the ins and outs of a mixed-race relationship between a second-generation Pakistani (Yaqub) living with his Muslim family in Glasgow and a Catholic schoolteacher (Birthistle). All the characters are vividly etched, and Loach and screenwriter Paul Laverty offer no simple solutions to the problems their characters encounter. Original title is AE FOND KISS . . . [R] ▼◗

Food of the Gods (1976) **C-88m.** BOMB D: Bert I. Gordon. Marjoe Gortner, Pamela Franklin, Ida Lupino, Jon Cypher, Ralph Meeker. Dreadful adaptation of H. G. Wells' novel. Strange substance causes giant growth in wasps, worms, chickens, and rats. Not for the squeamish. Similar to VILLAGE OF THE GIANTS, filmed by Gordon 11 years earlier. [PG] ▼◗

Food of the Gods II (1989-Canadian) **C-91m.** BOMB D: Damian Lee. Paul Coufos, Lisa Schrage, Jackie Burroughs, Colin Fox, Frank Moore. This time, gigantic laboratory rats terrorize a college campus. No connection to the first film, or (goodness knows) H. G. Wells' novel. Ugh! Aka GNAW. ▼◗

Fool and His Money, A (1988) **C-84m.** BOMB D: Daniel Adams. Jonathan Penner, Sandra Bullock, Gerald Orange, George Plimpton, Jerzy Kosinski, Tama Janowitz, Jose Torres. Plimpton as "God" tells ex-musician/ex-ad man Penner to start his own business, so he founds the "Preferent Church," a religion whose main tenet is selfishness. Embarrassing attempt at satire features Bullock on the video box, but she only has about eight minutes on screen as a public defender who can't believe her boyfriend has turned into such a jerk. [R] ▼◗

Fool for Love (1985) **C-106m. ** D:** Robert Altman. Sam Shepard, Kim Basinger, Harry Dean Stanton, Randy Quaid. Altman's inventive direction tries to breathe life into what is ultimately a photographed play, Shepard's examination of two ex-lovers who find themselves inextricably bound together. Biggest problem is generating some interest in these characters. Very much of a piece with Shepard's other work; if you're a fan, you might adjust our rating upward. [R] ▼◗

Foolin' Around (1980) **C-111m. ** D:** Richard T. Heffron. Gary Busey, Annette O'Toole, Cloris Leachman, Eddie Albert, John Calvin, Tony Randall, W. (William) H. Macy. Dumb 1950s-style comedy about a good-hearted klutz who pursues a wealthy girl, although she's already engaged. Cardboard characters and clumsy slapstick. [PG] ▼

Foolish (1999) **C-96m.** BOMB D: Dave Meyers. Eddie Griffin, Master P, Amy Petersen, Frank Sivero, Daphnee Lynn Duplaix, Jonathan Banks, Andrew Dice Clay, Marla Gibbs, Bill Nunn, Bill Duke, Traci Bingham. Part drama, part comedy, part concert film, total disaster. Story centers around a comic who feels he is not using his talents wisely and throwing away his potential. Yeah, that's right; he coulda been a contender. Alas, nothing he says is even remotely funny. Film is also meant to capitalize on the success of hip hop star Master P, who also executive-produced. The title says it all. [R] ▼◗

Foolish Wives (1922) **107m. *** D:** Erich von Stroheim. Erich von Stroheim, Maud George, Mae Busch, Cesare Gravina, Malvine Polo. Von Stroheim's third film as director is a typically sophisticated, fascinating tale of seduction, fake counts, blackmail, suicide, lechery, and murder. Great photography by William Daniels and Ben Reynolds, and an incredible set depicting the Monte Carlo casino designed by von Stroheim and Richard Day. ▼⦿◗

Fools (1970) **C-97m.** BOMB D: Tom Gries. Jason Robards, Katharine Ross, Scott Hylands, Roy C. Jenson, Mark Bramhall. Wretchedly acted, written, and directed drama about love affair in San Francisco between horror movie star and beautiful, neglected wife of a lawyer. Storyline is vaguely similar to PETULIA but the execution certainly isn't. [PG] ▼◗

Fool's Gold (2008) **C-112m. **½ D:** Andy Tennant. Matthew McConaughey, Kate Hudson, Donald Sutherland, Alexis Dziena, Ewen Bremner, Ray Winstone, Kevin Hart, Malcolm-Jamal Warner, Brian Hooks, David Roberts. Newly divorced McConaughey and Hudson get back together when he gets a bead on some sunken treasure they've been trying to find for years . . . but they aren't the only ones after it. Needlessly plotty romantic comedy is notably unfunny at first but gets livelier and more engaging as the treasure hunt kicks in. Beautiful scenery helps. Panavision. [PG-13]◗

Fools of Fortune (1990-British) **C-109m.**

*½ D: Pat O'Connor. Mary Elizabeth Mastrantonio, Iain Glen, Julie Christie, Michael Kitchen, Sean McClory, Frankie McCafferty. Muddled, haphazardly organized family chronicle set against decades of fighting between the British army and the IRA, from 1920 on. Very difficult to sort out who's doing what to whom. Mastrantonio, who shows up quite late (despite her billing), is awkward as Glen's love interest. Based on William Trevor's novel. [PG-13]▼●

Fools' Parade (1971) **C-98m.** ** D: Andrew V. McLaglen. James Stewart, George Kennedy, Anne Baxter, Strother Martin, Kurt Russell, William Windom, Kathy Cannon. Another great Stewart performance can't save melodramatic treatment of Davis Grubb novel. Story of three ex-cons stalked by their former prison guard is unintentionally funny too many times to be taken seriously. [PG]

Fools Rush In (1997) **C-107m.** **½ D: Andy Tennant. Matthew Perry, Salma Hayek, Jon Tenney, Carlos Gomez, Tomas Milian, Siobhan Fallon, John Bennett Perry, Stanley DeSantis, Suzanne Snyder, Jill Clayburgh. Hard-working New Yorker Perry chances to meet self-reliant Mexican-American photographer Hayek in Las Vegas, and it's lust at first sight . . . but when she becomes pregnant, it's hard for either of them to know what course to take. Pleasant if unexceptional romantic comedy-drama with appealing and credible performances by the two stars. [PG-13]▼●)

Foot Fist Way, The (2008) **C-83m.** *½ D: Jody Hill. Danny McBride, Mary Jane Bostic, Ben Best, Spencer Moreno, Carlos Lopez IV, Jody Hill, Ken Aguilar, Collette Wolfe. Meandering, one-note account of self-deluded, painfully insufferable taekwondo instructor McBride. This crude, cringe-inducing comedy barely sustains interest and seems overlong even at 83m.! However, fans of JACKASS: THE MOVIE may feel otherwise. [R]●

Footlight Parade (1933) **104m.** ***½ D: Lloyd Bacon. James Cagney, Joan Blondell, Ruby Keeler, Dick Powell, Guy Kibbee, Ruth Donnelly, Hugh Herbert, Frank McHugh. Cagney plays a stage director who tries to outdo himself with spectacular musical numbers. Fast-paced Warner Bros. opus winds up with three incredible Busby Berkeley numbers back-to-back: "Honeymoon Hotel," "By a Waterfall," and "Shanghai Lil." ▼●)

Footlight Serenade (1942) **80m.** *** D: Gregory Ratoff. Betty Grable, Victor Mature, John Payne, Jane Wyman, Phil Silvers, James Gleason, Mantan Moreland, Cobina Wright, Jr. Cute backstage musical with cocky boxer Mature turning to Broadway and trying to woo Grable, who's secretly engaged to Payne. Good fun.▼

Footloose (1984) **C-107m.** **½ D: Herbert Ross. Kevin Bacon, Lori Singer, John Lithgow, Dianne Wiest, Christopher Penn, Sarah Jessica Parker, John Laughlin, Elizabeth Gorcey, Frances Lee McCain, Jim Young, Brian Wimmer. City kid moves to small town where dancing has been outlawed—and confronts hellfire minister (Lithgow) in effort to bring it back. Too much emphasis on hackneyed story in so-called musical (though the soundtrack did spawn a number of Top 10 hits). Bacon's charisma sparks innocuous film. Later a Broadway musical. [PG] ▼●)

Footsteps in the Dark (1941) **96m.** **½ D: Lloyd Bacon. Errol Flynn, Brenda Marshall, Ralph Bellamy, Alan Hale, Lee Patrick, Allen Jenkins. Flynn leads double life as happily married businessman and mystery writer. Silly but genial.▼)

Footsteps in the Fog (1955-British) **C-90m.** *** D: Arthur Lubin. Stewart Granger, Jean Simmons, Finlay Currie, Bill Travers, Ronald Squire. Cat-and-mouse battle involving servant girl who blackmails her employer for having murdered his wife. Fine acting, rich Victorian atmosphere.)

For a Few Dollars More (1965-Italian) **C-132m.** *** D: Sergio Leone. Clint Eastwood, Lee Van Cleef, Gian Maria Volonté, Josef Egger, Mara Krup, Rosemarie Dexter, Klaus Kinski, Mario Brega. Sequel to FISTFUL OF DOLLARS finds two gunslingers forming an uneasy alliance in their quest for outlaw Indio (Volonté) —although their reasons for chasing him are markedly different. Slightly draggy but still fun; don't miss the scene where Van Cleef strikes a match on the back of Kinski's neck! Trademark atmospheric score by Ennio Morricone. Released in the U.S. in 1967. Followed by THE GOOD, THE BAD, AND THE UGLY. Techniscope. [R—originally rated M]▼●)

For All Mankind (1989) **C-80m.** *** D: Al Reinert. Excellent documentary on the Apollo moon flights, culled from a zillion hours of NASA footage seamlessly edited into one representative journey. Impressive, if a bit on the cold side; end credits inform us film was shot "on location." Let us hope.▼●)

For Better, For Worse SEE: **Zandy's Bride**

Forbidden (1932) **81m.** ** D: Frank Capra. Barbara Stanwyck, Adolphe Menjou, Ralph Bellamy, Dorothy Peterson, Henry Armetta. A spinster librarian takes a cruise and falls in love with a man who can never marry her. Fine performances and stunning Joseph Walker photography buoy this BACK STREET soap opera until its ridiculous conclusion.

Forbidden (1953) **85m.** **½ D: Rudolph Maté. Tony Curtis, Joanne Dru, Lyle Bettger, Marvin Miller, Victor Sen Yung. OK suspenser in which two-fisted Curtis arrives in Macao, hired by a gangland chief to uncover the whereabouts of Dru (who just so happens to be Curtis' ex-girlfriend).

Forbidden Alliance SEE: **Barretts of Wimpole Street, The** (1934)

Forbidden Choices SEE: **Beans of Egypt, Maine, The**

Forbidden Dance, The (1990) **C-97m.** BOMB D: Greydon Clark. Laura Herring, Jeff James, Sid Haig, Richard Lynch, Barbara Brighton, Kid Creole. Brazilian jungle princess treks to America on behalf of her endangered rain forests, ends up on a TV special as . . . a lambada dancer?!? Marginally lesser of two " 'L'-word" quickies that opened the same week. Inability of ex-Miss USA Herring to dance is good for a few chuckles. [PG-13]▼●]

Forbidden Games (1952-French) **87m.** ***½ D: René Clement. Brigitte Fossey, Georges Poujouly, Louis Herbert. During WW2, young Parisian girl is orphaned and taken in by simple peasant family; she develops friendship with their youngest son, and shares with him a private world which the grown-ups cannot understand. Sad, intensely moving drama earned a Best Foreign Film Oscar.▼●]

Forbidden Kingdom, The (2008-U.S.-Chinese) **C-105m.** **½ D: Rob Minkoff. Jackie Chan, Jet Li, Michael Angarano, Collin Chou, Liu Yifei, Li Bing Bing. Boston boy is magically transported to a mystical kingdom, bearing a golden staff that must be returned to its rightful owner. He acquires a valuable ally in a seemingly drunken kung-fu master (Chan), and before long they encounter a silent monk (Li) who may or may not be on their side. Uninspired story unfolds against magnificent Chinese scenery and ornate sets, photographed by Peter Pau. Chan and Li square off for one great fight (choreographed by Woo-Ping Yuen) but the film as a whole is just lukewarm. Super 35. [PG-13]▶

Forbidden Planet (1956) **C-98m.** ***½ D: Fred McLeod Wilcox. Walter Pidgeon, Anne Francis, Leslie Nielsen, Warren Stevens, Jack Kelly, Richard Anderson, Earl Holliman, George Wallace, James Drury. Sci-fi version of Shakespeare's *The Tempest* remains one of the most ambitious and intelligent films of its genre; only slow, deliberate pacing works against it, as Nielsen and fellow space travelers visit planet where expatriate Pidgeon has built a one-man empire with daughter Francis and obedient Robby the Robot. Great effects, eerie electronic score. Beware 95m. reissue prints. CinemaScope. ▼●]

Forbidden Street, The (1949-British) **91m.** ** D: Jean Negulesco. Dana Andrews, Maureen O'Hara, Sybil Thorndike, Wilfrid Hyde-White, Fay Compton. Fanciful melodrama, set in Victorian England, of wealthy O'Hara defying her family by marrying beneath her class; Andrews has a dual role, as a down-and-out artist (with his voice dubbed) and an ex-barrister. Scripted by Ring Lardner, Jr. Originally titled BRITANNIA MEWS.

Forbidden World (1982) **C-86m.** *½ D: Allan Holzman. Jesse Vint, June Chadwick, Dawn Dunlap, Linden Chiles, Fox Harris. Roger Corman-produced ALIEN rip-off is followup to (and uses sets from) his GALAXY OF TERROR as well as battle scenes lifted from his BATTLE BEYOND THE STARS. Lots of gore, weak special effects. Aka MUTANT. [R]▼●]

Forbidden Zone (1980) **76m.** *½ D: Richard Elfman. Herve Villechaize, Susan Tyrrell, Marie-Pascale Elfman, Viva. Pastiche film set in the Sixth Dimension, an underground kingdom ruled by Villechaize and Tyrrell. Mostly a collection of bizarre, campy musical numbers, done in the style of 1930s Max Fleischer cartoons. If only everything about the film weren't so *ugly!* Has an inevitable cult following. [R]▼]

Forbin Project, The SEE: **Colossus: The Forbin Project**

Forced March (1989-U.S.-Hungarian) **C-104m.** **½ D: Rick King. Chris Sarandon, Renee Soutendijk, Josef Sommer, John Seitz. American actor Sarandon faces challenge after traveling to Budapest to star in a film about Miklos Radnoti, Hungarian-Jewish poet who fell victim to the Holocaust. Ambitious, potentially potent drama mostly falls flat; scenes of the actor are pointlessly interspersed with those of the film in which he is starring.▼●

Forced Vengeance (1982) **C-90m.** *½ D: James Fargo. Chuck Norris, Mary Louise Weller, Camilla Griggs, Michael Cavanaugh, David Opatoshu, Seiji Sakaguchi. Clichéd karate nonsense with Norris, badly in need of an acting lesson, taking on Hong Kong mobster Cavanaugh. [R]▼]

Force: Five (1981) **C-95m.** ** D: Robert Clouse. Joe Lewis, Pam Huntington, Master Bong Soo Han, Richard Norton, Benny "The Jet" Urquidez. Lewis and company attempt to rescue girl from the clutches of religious-cult-head Han. Retread of Clouse's much-used martial arts formula, with gimmick of disparate five-person "team" as the collective hero. Remake of HOT POTATO. [R]▼

Force of Arms (1951) **100m.** **½ D: Michael Curtiz. William Holden, Nancy Olson, Frank Lovejoy, Gene Evans, Dick Wesson. Updating of Hemingway's A FAREWELL TO ARMS to WW2 Italy, with unmemorable results. Reissued as A GIRL FOR JOE.▼]

Force of Evil (1948) **78m.** *** D: Abraham Polonsky. John Garfield, Beatrice Pearson, Thomas Gomez, Roy Roberts, Marie Windsor, Howland Chamberlin, Beau Bridges.

Rock-solid film noir about a racketeer's lawyer (Garfield, in a stunning performance), whose ideals have been obscured by his greed. Beautifully photographed (by George Barnes) and lit; this has become something of a cult item. Polonsky, who coscripted with Ira Wolfert, was blacklisted and didn't make another film until 1969's TELL THEM WILLIE BOY IS HERE.▼●🅓

Force of One, A (1979) **C-90m.** ****½** D: Paul Aaron. Chuck Norris, Jennifer O'Neill, Clu Gulager, Ron O'Neal, James Whitmore Jr., Clint Ritchie, Pepe Serna. Follow-up to GOOD GUYS WEAR BLACK has karate champ Norris using his expertise to help California town combat drug trafficking. OK action fare. [PG]▼🅓

Forces of Nature (1999) **C-104m.** ****** D: Bronwen Hughes. Sandra Bullock, Ben Affleck, Maura Tierney, Steve Zahn, Blythe Danner, Ronny Cox, Michael Fairman, Janet Carroll, David Strickland, Anne Haney, Bert Remsen. About-to-be-wed Affleck is stranded in N.Y. with fellow passenger Bullock when their plane crashes. The two strangers decide to travel together, by land, to their intended destination: Savannah, GA. What promises to be a standard road picture with two likable stars veers off-course early on thanks to Bullock's erratic character and a threadbare story; a disappointment. [PG-13]▼●🅓

Force 10 From Navarone (1978-British) **C-118m.** BOMB D: Guy Hamilton. Robert Shaw, Harrison Ford, Edward Fox, Franco Nero, Barbara Bach, Carl Weathers, Richard Kiel. Awful sequel to classic GUNS OF NAVARONE, poor in all departments, although Shaw, Ford, and Nero try to give it a lift. Mixed group (naturally), hindered by traitor Nero, attempt to blow a bridge vital to Nazis. They blew the film instead. Based on the Alistair MacLean novel. Restored to 128m. on laserdisc. Panavision. [PG]▼●🅓

For Colored Girls (2010) **C-134m.** ***½** D: Tyler Perry. Janet Jackson, Loretta Devine, Michael Ealy, Kimberly Elise, Omari Hardwick, Hill Harper, Thandie Newton, Phylicia Rashad, Anika Noni Rose, Tessa Thompson, Kerry Washington, Whoopi Goldberg, Macy Gray. And now for something completely different: director Perry, best known for adapting his own stage plays into raucous comedies (MADEA GOES TO JAIL, MADEA'S FAMILY REUNION, etc.), attempts a filmization of Ntozake Shange's award-winning stage drama. In the process, unfortunately, Shange's artfully stylized "choreopoem"—a series of monologues by African-American women driven to extremes of joy, anger, and despair—becomes a ham-handed, literal-minded melodrama in which soliloquies are sporadically cued like songs in a musical. Tonally discordant and wildly overwrought, despite game efforts by a first-rate cast. [R]🅓

Foreign Affair, A (1948) **116m.** *****½** D: Billy Wilder. Jean Arthur, Marlene Dietrich,

John Lund, Millard Mitchell, Peter Von Zerneck, Stanley Prager. Staid Arthur is sent to Berlin to investigate post-WW2 conditions, finds romance instead, with hot competition from Dietrich. Marlene sings "Black Market," "Ruins of Berlin," but Jean Arthur's Iowa State Song equally memorable in great Wilder comedy. Written by Charles Brackett, Billy Wilder, and Richard Breen.▼

Foreign Body (1986-British) **C-108m.** ****½** D: Ronald Neame. Victor Banerjee, Warren Mitchell, Trevor Howard, Geraldine McEwan, Amanda Donohoe, Denis Quilley, Eve Ferret, Anna Massey. In a real casting switch, a PASSAGE TO INDIA star Banerjee has a field day as an itinerant Indian in London who poses as a doctor and soon finds all the women dying to get him into bed. Throwback to the style of 1950s British sex comedies. [PG-13]▼

Foreign Correspondent (1940) **119m.** ******** D: Alfred Hitchcock. Joel McCrea, Laraine Day, Herbert Marshall, George Sanders, Albert Basserman, Robert Benchley, Edmund Gwenn, Eduardo Ciannelli, Harry Davenport, Martin Kosleck. McCrea in title role caught in middle of spy ring with reporters Sanders and Benchley, innocent Day, suspicious father Marshall. Tremendously entertaining film with several vintage Hitchcock showpieces. Scripted by Charles Bennett and Joan Harrison; dialogue by James Hilton and Benchley. ▼●🅓

Foreign Student (1994) **C-96m.** ****½** D: Eva Sereny. Robin Givens, Marco Hofschneider, Rick Johnson, Charlotte Ross, Edward Herrmann, Jack Coleman, Charles S. Dutton, Hinton Battle, Anthony Herrera. Mild, but fairly individualized, low-budget nostalgia piece about an 18-year-old Parisian's taboo romance with a beautiful black schoolteacher/domestic while attending a small college in Virginia's Shenandoah Valley in r&b 1956. Spotty little film mixes it up with subplots involving football, William Faulkner, and blues greats Howlin' Wolf and Sonny Boy Williamson; from wistful memoirs of filmmaker Philippe Labro, a huge bestseller in France. [R]▼●

Forever Amber (1947) **C-140m.** ******* D: Otto Preminger. Linda Darnell, Cornel Wilde, Richard Greene, George Sanders, Jessica Tandy, Anne Revere, Leo G. Carroll. "Musical beds" costumer, taken from Kathleen Winsor's once-scandalous novel, about blonde Darnell's ascension to the court of Charles II. Lengthy but colorful and entertaining, with David Raksin's outstanding score.▼●

Forever and a Day (1943) **104m.** ******* D: René Clair, Edmund Goulding, Cedric Hardwicke, Frank Lloyd, Victor Saville, Robert Stevenson, Herbert Wilcox. Brian Aherne, Robert Cummings, Ida Lupino, Charles Laughton, Herbert Marshall, Ray Milland, Anna Neagle, Merle Oberon, Claude Rains, Victor McLaglen, Buster Keaton, Jessie Matthews, Roland Young, C. Aubrey Smith,

Edward Everett Horton, Elsa Lanchester, Edmund Gwenn. Eighty-odd British (and American) stars contributed their services to this episodic film, about a house and its inhabitants over the years, to raise funds for British War Relief. Uneven result, but has many fine moments and star-gazing galore; once-in-a-lifetime cast. ▼❶

Forever, Darling (1956) **C-91m.** ****½** D: Alexander Hall. Lucille Ball, Desi Arnaz, James Mason, Louis Calhern. Ball's madcap antics nearly drive husband Arnaz to divorce, but guardian angel Mason saves the day. Contrived but enjoyable. ▼❶❶

Forever Female (1953) **93m.** *****½** D: Irving Rapper. Ginger Rogers, William Holden, Paul Douglas, Pat Crowley, James Gleason, Jesse White, Marjorie Rambeau, George Reeves, King Donovan, Marion Ross. Top-notch show-business satire with Rogers an aging Broadway star, Crowley an ambitious wannabe who can't settle on a stage name, Douglas an acerbic producer, Holden a talented but opinionated playwright. ▼❶

Forever, Lulu (1987) **C-85m.** BOMB D: Amos Kollek. Hanna Schygulla, Deborah Harry, Alec Baldwin, Annie Golden, Paul Gleason, Dr. Ruth Westheimer. Embarrassing, amateurish imitation of DESPERATELY SEEKING SUSAN has budding novelist Schygulla becoming embroiled in a real-life mystery in N.Y.C. involving drugs and killers. Despite having the title role, singing star Harry makes only a brief appearance. Israeli director Kollek also turns in a poor acting job as Schygulla's agent. Baldwin's first film. Aka CRAZY STREETS. [R] ▼❶❶

Forever Mine (2000-Canadian-British-U.S.) **C-115m.** ****½** D: Paul Schrader. Joseph Fiennes, Gretchen Mol, Ray Liotta, Vincent Laresca, Myk Watford, John Henry Canavan, Lindsey Connell. Florid, stylized romantic saga about a Florida cabana boy who falls deeply in love with a beautiful married guest and refuses to be deterred by her hot-tempered husband. An homage to the lush 1950s Douglas Sirk melodramas, this film isn't perfect, and demands a leap of faith, but offers the kind of passionate romance they don't make anymore. Written by the director. Made for theaters, U.S. debut on cable TV. Panavision. [R] ▼❶

For Ever Mozart (1996-French-Swiss) **C-84m.** ******* D: Jean-Luc Godard. Madeleine Assas, Frederic Pierrot, Ghalia Lacroix, Vicky Messica, Harry Cleven. One of Godard's better latter-career films is the complex, poetic account, set in four sections, of a director attempting to mount a movie. Here, Godard insightfully deals with one of his more prominent themes: how art (and, specifically, the art of cinema) relates to politics (in this case, the political implications of the war in Bosnia). ▼❶

Forever Young (1992) **C-102m.** ******* D: Steve Miner. Mel Gibson, Jamie Lee Curtis,

Elijah Wood, Isabel Glasser, George Wendt, Joe Morton, Nicolas Surovy, David Marshall Grant, Art LaFleur. The year is 1939, and test-pilot Gibson (whose girlfriend is comatose after being hit by a car) volunteers to be frozen as part of a cryogenics experiment. He's accidentally thawed out in 1992, and becomes involved in the lives of a young boy (Wood) and his mom (Curtis). This romantic comedy-fantasy may play out by the numbers as it tugs at your heartstrings, but it's hard to resist, thanks to a charismatic cast. [PG] ▼❶

Forget Paris (1995) **C-101m.** ******* D: Billy Crystal. Billy Crystal, Debra Winger, Joe Mantegna, Cynthia Stevenson, Richard Masur, Julie Kavner, William Hickey, Robert Costanzo, John Spencer, Cathy Moriarty, Tom Wright. Crystal plays a basketball referee who falls head over heels for Winger, while burying his father in Paris. Sharply written comedy (by Crystal and Lowell Ganz and Babaloo Mandel) about the trials and tribulations of making a marriage work—after falling in love. Many top basketball stars appear as themselves; Dan Castellaneta appears unbilled. [PG-13] ▼❶

Forgetting Sarah Marshall (2008) **C-112m.** ******* D: Nicholas Stoller. Jason Segel, Mila Kunis, Kristen Bell, Paul Rudd, Bill Hader, Russell Brand, Jonah Hill, Jack McBrayer, Maria Thayer, William Baldwin, Jason Bateman, Steve Landesberg, Gedde Watanabe, Kristen Wiig. After his TV-star girlfriend leaves him for another man, a self-pitying composer goes to Hawaii to mend his broken heart. Then his ex and her new boyfriend turn up at the same resort! Smart, funny comedy from Judd Apatow's comedy crew hits all the right notes, pushing the envelope for sexual content but never losing sight of real emotions. Segel wrote the screenplay and gives himself a great star vehicle, with plenty of room for other cast members to shine. Brand reprised his character in GET HIM TO THE GREEK. Unrated version runs 118m. [R] ❶

Forgotten, The (2004) **C-91m.** ****½** D: Joseph Ruben. Julianne Moore, Dominic West, Gary Sinise, Anthony Edwards, Alfre Woodard, Linus Roache, Robert Wisdom, Jessica Hecht. Woman still grieving for her son, who died more than a year ago, is told the boy never really existed! She refuses to believe this and doggedly seeks the truth, which leads her into unexplored territory. Thriller goes way off base for a while, testing our patience and credulity, before tying things up with an interesting payoff. A couple of real jolts along the way keep it from ever getting dull. Alternate version on DVD runs 94m. [PG-13] ▼❶

For Heaven's Sake (1926) **58m.** ******** D: Sam Taylor. Harold Lloyd, Jobyna Ralston, Noah Young, James Mason, Paul Weigel. Screamingly funny silent comedy has Lloyd a blase young millionaire whose crush on Ralston inspires him to help attract "customers" for her father's Bowery Mission. Even THE FRENCH CONNECTION hasn't dimmed the luster of Lloyd's chase climax on L.A. streets.◗

For Keeps (1988) **C-98m.** *½ D: John G. Avildsen. Molly Ringwald, Randall Batinkoff, Kenneth Mars, Miriam Flynn, Conchata Ferrell, Sharon Brown, Renee Estevez, Larry Drake. Studious teen Ringwald becomes pregnant, and must quickly face adult responsibilities. Subject matter is most worthwhile, but the result is predictable and phony. Tim Kazurinsky coauthored the screenplay. [PG-13]▼◗

For Love Alone (1986-Australian) **C-102m.** *** D: Stephen Wallace. Helen Buday, Sam Neill, Hugo Weaving, Hugh Keays-Byrne, Naomi Watts. Nicely filmed romantic drama, set in the 1930s, with Australian university student Buday falling in love with her professor (Weaving); even though he treats her poorly, she follows him to England. Neill does well as an altogether different man who enters her life. Based on the novel by Christina Stead. ▼

For Love of Ivy (1968) **C-102m.** ** D: Daniel Mann. Sidney Poitier, Abbey Lincoln, Beau Bridges, Leon Bibb, Nan Martin, Lauri Peters, Carroll O'Connor. Family wants to keep maid, so they find her a beau; ho-hum black romance. [G]▼◗

For Love of the Game (1999) **C-137m.** **½ D: Sam Raimi. Kevin Costner, Kelly Preston, John C. Reilly, Jena Malone, Brian Cox, J. K. Simmons, Vin Scully, Michael Emerson. Likable vehicle for Costner as a 20-year baseball veteran who looks back on the last five years of his life during an eventful end-of-season game. Effectively played for star value and sentiment, but goes into extra innings for no apparent reason, stretching out a conclusion that comes as no surprise. Panavision. [PG-13]▼◗

For Love or Money (1963) **C-108m.** **½ D: Michael Gordon. Kirk Douglas, Mitzi Gaynor, Gig Young, Thelma Ritter, William Bendix, Julie Newmar. Comedy strains to be funnier than it is. Widow Ritter hires lawyer Douglas to find spouses for her three daughters.

For Love or Money (1993) **C-95m.** ** D: Barry Sonnenfeld. Michael J. Fox, Gabrielle Anwar, Anthony Higgins, Michael Tucker, Bob Balaban, Isaac Mizrahi, Udo Kier, Simon Jones, Dianne Brill, Dan Hedaya, Fyvush Finkel, Bobby Short. Tepid APARTMENT variation about aggressive, ambitious Fox, concierge at an upscale N.Y.C. hotel, who'll do anything to please his guests. Trouble brews when he finds himself attracted to beautiful Anwar, the mistress of married Higgins (a Donald Trump clone). Fox and a fine cast try their best, but this comedy runs out of steam long before its predictable finale. [PG]▼◗

For Me and My Gal (1942) **104m.** **½ D: Busby Berkeley. Judy Garland, George Murphy, Gene Kelly, Marta Eggerth, Ben Blue, Horace (Stephen) McNally, Keenan Wynn, Richard Quine. Music sustains old-hat plot of vaudeville couple determined to play Palace, circa WW1. Kelly's film debut; he and Garland sing title tune and other old favorites. Also shown in computer-colored version. ▼◗

Formula, The (1980) **C-117m.** ** D: John G. Avildsen. George C. Scott, Marlon Brando, Marthe Keller, John Gielgud, G. D. Spradlin, Beatrice Straight, Richard Lynch, John Van Dreelen, Craig T. Nelson. Amazingly matter-of-fact thriller about a cop who investigates a friend's murder and finds him linked to a mysterious plot involving a formula for synthetic fuel. Scott and Brando are always worth watching, but writer-producer Steve Shagan telegraphs all his punches. [R]▼◗

Formula 51 (2001-British-Canadian) **C-91m.** **½ D: Ronny Yu. Samuel L. Jackson, Robert Carlyle, Emily Mortimer, Rhys Ifans, Meat Loaf, Sean Pertwee, Ricky Tomlinson, Paul Barber. Wild, tongue-in-cheek Hong Kong–style yarn loaded with action and violence. Jackson plays a pharmaceutical whiz who develops the ultimate narcotic, then double-crosses his L.A. connection (Meat Loaf) and flies to Liverpool to make a more lucrative deal there. Needless to say, things don't go smoothly. An indefensible guilty pleasure that offers no intellectual stimulus whatsoever. Mortimer is fun as a gun-toting, motorcycle-riding hit woman. Jackson also coexecutive-produced. Original British title: THE 51ST STATE. Super 35. [R] ▼◗

For Pete's Sake (1974) **C-90m.** **½ D: Peter Yates. Barbra Streisand, Michael Sarrazin, Estelle Parsons, William Redfield, Molly Picon, Louis Zorich, Vincent Schiavelli, Anne Ramsey. Amiable, featherweight comedy about devoted wife who tries to raise money for her ambitious cabdriver husband, and gets involved with assorted nuts and underworld types. Streisand is fine in forgettable film. [PG]▼◗

For Queen & Country (1988-British) **C-105m.** *** D: Martin Stellman. Denzel Washington, Dorian Healey, Amanda Redman, Sea Chapman, Bruce Payne. Striking, laced-in-acid contemporary thriller of life in Thatcherite England. Washington is well cast as a former paratrooper who struggles for survival in an atmosphere of racism, poverty, and corruption—and then loses his British citizenship because of an immigration-law technicality. The director also cowrote the screenplay. [R]◗

Forrest Gump (1994) **C-142m.** **½ D: Robert Zemeckis. Tom Hanks, Robin Wright, Gary Sinise, Sally Field, Mykelti Williamson, Michael Humphreys, Hanna

Hall, Haley Joel Osment. A slow-witted boy grows to adulthood, floating through life—like a feather—with only a vague understanding of the tumultuous times he's living through. (He manages to be on hand for virtually every socio-pop-political phenomenon of the formative Baby Boomer decades, from the rise of Elvis to the fall of Nixon.) Either you accept Hanks in this part and go with the movie's seriocomic sense of whimsy, or you don't (we didn't)—but either way it's a long journey, filled with digitized imagery that puts Forrest Gump into a wide variety of backdrops and real-life events. Based on the (more satiric) novel by Winston Groom. Oscar winner for Best Film, Best Actor (Hanks), Director, Film Editing, Visual Effects, and Adapted Screenplay. Panavision. [PG-13]▼●)

For Richer or Poorer (1997) **C-115m.** **½ D: Bryan Spicer. Tim Allen, Kirstie Alley, Jay O. Sanders, Michael Lerner, Wayne Knight, Larry Miller, Miguel A. Nunez, Jr., Megan Cavanagh, Carrie Preston, Katie Moore. Crass, filthy-rich New Yorkers Allen and Alley, whose marriage is on the rocks, are forced to take it on the lam when they're accused of tax fraud—and hide out on an Amish farm, where they pretend to be cousins of farmer Sanders. Spoiled and lazy, they're forced to do hard, honest work, and actually come to like it. Predictable in every way, but pleasant enough. Super 35. [PG-13]▼●)

For Roseanna (1997-British) **C-95m.** **½ D: Paul Weiland. Jean Reno, Mercedes Ruehl, Polly Walker, Mark Frankel, Giuseppe Cederna, Renato Scarpa. Sweet, well-intentioned film about a man who has promised his wife, who's terminally ill, that she will be buried in their village churchyard cemetery . . . but with only a few vacant plots left, he takes it upon himself to keep the other townspeople healthy! Winning performances and vivid Italian atmosphere help compensate for a script (by veteran TV comedy writer Saul Turteltaub) that strains credibility to the bursting point. Panavision. [PG-13] ▼●)

Forsaken, The (2001) **C-90m.** *½ D: J.S. Cardone. Kerr Smith, Brendan Fehr, Johnathon Schaech, Izabella Miko, Phina Oruche, Simon Rex, Carrie Snodgress. Straight-arrow Smith drives east from L.A., heading for Miami, but quickly discovers the Southwest has become infested with creepy nocturnal predators, led by Schaech. This vampire film offers no surprises. [R]▼)

Forsaking All Others (1934) **84m.** **½ D: W. S. Van Dyke II. Clark Gable, Joan Crawford, Robert Montgomery, Charles Butterworth, Billie Burke, Frances Drake, Rosalind Russell, Arthur Treacher. Gable, just back from Spain, is about to propose to Crawford but learns she's set to wed flaky Montgomery. Star trio sparkles in this so-

so romantic comedy, scripted by Joseph L. Mankiewicz. Butterworth is a treat, as always.▼●)

For Singles Only (1968) **C-91m.** BOMB D: Arthur Dreifuss. John Saxon, Mary Ann Mobley, Milton Berle, Lana Wood, Mark Richman, Chris Noel, The Nitty Gritty Dirt Band. Certainly not for those who like good movies. Two girls move into singles apartment where Berle is social director; result is a rape, an attempted suicide, and several songs.

Fort Apache (1948) **127m.** *** D: John Ford. John Wayne, Henry Fonda, Shirley Temple, Pedro Armendariz, John Agar, Ward Bond, George O'Brien, Victor McLaglen, Anna Lee, Irene Rich, Dick Foran, Guy Kibbee, Mae Marsh, Hank Worden. Fonda is effectively cast against type as stubborn martinet who rubs his own men—as well as neighboring Indians—the wrong way. First of Ford's cavalry trilogy tells its story slowly, deliberately, with time for comedy and telling characterizations. Followed by SHE WORE A YELLOW RIBBON. Also shown in computer-colored version.▼●)

Fort Apache The Bronx (1981) **C-125m.** *** D: Daniel Petrie. Paul Newman, Edward Asner, Ken Wahl, Danny Aiello, Rachel Ticotin, Pam Grier, Kathleen Beller. Taut urban drama about a policeman's life in a ravaged N.Y.C. neighborhood; credible and exciting, with a fine star performance from Newman. [R]▼●)

For the Boys (1991) **C-145m.** **½ D: Mark Rydell. Bette Midler, James Caan, George Segal, Patrick O'Neal, Christopher Rydell, Arye Gross, Norman Fell, Rosemary Murphy, Dori Brenner, Bud Yorkin, Jack Sheldon, Melissa Manchester, Brandon Call, Billy Bob Thornton, Xander Berkeley, Vince Vaughn. Midler is in top form as U.S.O. singer who becomes a star while performing during WW2 with Caan, a sexist, self-involved king of comedy; scenario follows their tumultuous relationship over the decades. Occasionally hokey but mostly entertaining. Arliss Howard appears unbilled as Bette's G.I. husband. [R] ▼●)

For the First Time (1959) **C-97m.** **½ D: Rudolph Maté. Mario Lanza, Johanna Von Koszian, Kurt Kasznar, Zsa Zsa Gabor, Hans Sohnker. Lanza is typecast as fiery opera singer who falls in love with beautiful deaf girl in Capri. Not bad, with plenty of music to satisfy Lanza fans; this was his last film. Technirama.▼●)

For the Love of Benji (1977) **C-84m.** *** D: Joe Camp. Benji, Patsy Garrett. Cynthia Smith, Allen Fiuzat, Ed Nelson, Peter Bowles, Bridget Armstrong. Moviedom's smartest pooch since Lassie in his second delightful screen adventure, scampering through the streets of Athens with secret agents in pursuit, trying to get the formula tattooed on his paw. Fine family entertain-

ment. Followed by OH, HEAVENLY DOG!
[G]▼▶

For Those Who Think Young (1964) C-96m. ** D: Leslie H. Martinson. James Darren, Pamela Tiffin, Paul Lynde, Tina Louise, Bob Denver, Robert Middleton, Nancy Sinatra, Claudia Martin, Ellen McRae (Burstyn), Woody Woodbury, Louis Quinn, Sammee Tong, Addison Richards, Mousie Garner, Benny Baker, Anna Lee, Jack La Rue, Allen Jenkins, Robert Armstrong, Lada Edmund, Jr. Great time-capsule cast in a silly time-waster about college high jinks. Notable for taking its title from a Pepsi slogan at the time—making this a milestone in the history of product placement! George Raft and Roger Smith appear unbilled. Technicolor.

Fortress (1993) C-91m. *½ D: Stuart Gordon. Christopher Lambert, Loryn Locklyn, Kurtwood Smith, Lincoln Kilpatrick, Clifton Gonzalez Gonzalez, Jeffrey Combs. Husband and wife flee futuristic society (which forbids them from having a second child) because she is pregnant again. They're captured and sent to a high-tech maximum security prison run by a sadistic warden. (Is there any other kind?) Intriguing premise is sabotaged by weak acting and a weaker script. Incredible international success resulted in a sequel. [R]▼▶●

Fort Saganne (1984-French) C-190m. **½ D: Alain Corneau. Gérard Depardieu, Philippe Noiret, Catherine Deneuve, Michel Duchaussoy, Roger Dumas, Sophie Marceau, Jean-Louis Richard. Handsomely mounted but clichéd and overlong epic detailing the exploits of Charles Saganne, a French officer of modest background who is posted to the Sahara in the years before WW1. Depardieu is quietly impressive, many of the desert sequences are well done, and Philippe Sarde's score adds to the atmosphere. Depiction of Depardieu's affair with journalist Deneuve is especially trite. Technovision.▼▶

Fort Ti (1953) C-73m. ** D: William Castle. George Montgomery, Joan Vohs, Irving Bacon, James Seay. Best facet of this oater set during French-Indian war of 1760s is its 3-D gimmickry; otherwise, standard stuff. 3-D.

Fortune, The (1975) C-88m. **½ D: Mike Nichols. Jack Nicholson, Warren Beatty, Stockard Channing, Scatman Crothers, Florence Stanley, Richard B. Shull. Nicholson and Beatty make like Laurel and Hardy in this uneven 1920s comedy about two bumblers who plan to murder a dizzy heiress to get her money. Worth seeing if only for Nicholson's wonderful comic performance. David Shire's period music is nice, too. Panavision. [PG]▼

Fortune and Men's Eyes (1971-Canadian) C-102m. **½ D: Harvey Hart. Wendell Burton, Michael Greer, Zooey (David) Hall, Danny Freedman. Homosexuality in prison is the theme; sincere but exploitative, unpleasant. [R]▼

Fortune Cookie, The (1966) 125m. *** D: Billy Wilder. Jack Lemmon, Walter Matthau, Ron Rich, Cliff Osmond, Judi West, Lurene Tuttle. Biting Wilder comedy about TV cameraman (Lemmon) injured during football game and shyster lawyer (Matthau) who exaggerates damages for insurance purposes. Matthau's Oscar-winning performance hits home. Scripted by Wilder and partner I.A.L. Diamond. Panavision.▼▶●

Fort Utah (1968) C-83m. *½ D: Lesley Selander. John Ireland, Virginia Mayo, Scott Brady, John Russell, Robert Strauss, James Craig, Richard Arlen, Jim Davis, Don "Red" Barry. Former gunfighter Ireland fights Brady, who is stirring up Indians around Fort Utah. See it only if you like the cast. Techniscope.

40 Carats (1973) C-110m. **½ D: Milton Katselas. Liv Ullmann, Gene Kelly, Edward Albert, Binnie Barnes, Deborah Raffin, Billy Green Bush, Nancy Walker, Don Porter, Rosemary Murphy, Natalie Schafer, Claudia Jennings, Brooke Palance. Bright Broadway comedy adapted from French farce suffers in transference to screen, mainly from miscasting of Ullmann as 40-ish New York divorcee, pursued by 20-ish Albert. Glossy, mildly amusing; pepped up by Barnes and Kelly. [PG]▼

40 Days and 40 Nights (2002) C-95m. *½ D: Michael Lehmann. Josh Hartnett, Shannyn Sossamon, Vinessa Shaw, Paulo Costanzo, Griffin Dunne, Maggie Gyllenhaal, Michael Maronna, Glenn Fitzgerald, Mary Gross, Adam Trese, Barry Newman. Young stud with an insatiable appetite for women—but no idea how to build a relationship—is so stung by his latest dumping that he decides to give up sex for Lent. Then he meets Miss Right—and can't explain to her why he's unable to consummate their relationship. Inane comedy, full of stupid, obnoxious characters. [R]▼▶

Forty Deuce (1982) C-89m. *½ D: Paul Morrissey. Orson Bean, Kevin Bacon, Mark Keyloun, Harris Laskaway, Tommy Citera. Heavyhanded, poorly directed drama of teenage hustler Bacon attempting to sell runaway to wealthy Bean; complications arise when the boy overdoses on heroin. From an off-Broadway play by Alan Bowne. Second half of film is in widescreen.▶

48HRS. (1982) C-97m. ***½ D: Walter Hill. Nick Nolte, Eddie Murphy, Annette O'Toole, James Remar, Frank McRae, David Patrick Kelly, Sonny Landham, Brion James, James Keane, Jonathan Banks, Denise Crosby, Olivia Brown, Jim Haynie, The Busboys. Slam-bang mix of action and comedy; weary cop Nolte springs Murphy out of the jug for two days to help him catch Murphy's escaped (and *really* disturbed) partner. Naturally, they hate each other's guts at first, but. . . . Murphy, in his screen debut, is sensational, but so is Nolte in his low-key, raspy way; scene where Murphy terrorizes a redneck bar is the standout. Written by Roger Spottiswoode, Larry Gross, Steven E. de Souza, and Hill. Sequel: ANOTHER 48HRS. [R]▼●◗

44 Inch Chest (2009-U.S.-British-Australian) **C-95m.** **½ D: Malcolm Venville. Ray Winstone, Ian McShane, John Hurt, Tom Wilkinson, Stephen Dillane, Joanne Whalley, Melvil Poupaud, Steven Berkoff. A cuckold's four sympathetic pals snatch his wife's lover so he can avenge his lost manhood any way he wants. Misogynistic exercise in male bravado launches a Mamet-esque blitz of F- and C-bombs over London, yet is, at its base, a love story (though a profane one) about a hard man with a soft heart. Some will find it gritty; others, simply vile. Clips from DeMille's SAMSON AND DELILAH form a curious interlude. [R] ◗

Forty Guns (1957) **80m.** **½ D: Samuel Fuller. Barbara Stanwyck, Barry Sullivan, Dean Jagger, John Ericson, Gene Barry. Florid, wildly dramatic Sam Fuller Western with Stanwyck as self-appointed land baroness of Tombstone Territory—until marshal Sullivan shows up. CinemaScope. ◗

49th Parallel (1941-British) **123m.** ***½ D: Michael Powell. Anton Walbrook, Eric Portman, Leslie Howard, Raymond Massey, Laurence Olivier, Glynis Johns, Niall MacGinnis, Finlay Currie. Taut, exciting WW2 yarn of Nazi servicemen whose U-boat is sunk off the Canadian coast. Topnotch cast, rich suspense and characterizations. Oscar winner for Best Story (Emeric Pressburger); screenplay by Pressburger and Rodney Ackland. U.S. title: THE INVADERS. ▼●◗

49 Up (2006-British) **C/B&W-135m.** *** D: Michael Apted. Seventh installment in the unique and remarkable series that began with the TV documentary *7 UP* in 1964. Apted revisits most of the young people who first participated in the series and brings us up to date on their lives, which in some cases have taken highly unexpected turns. Several of the interviewees talk about the impact these documentaries have had on their privacy and sense of self. Thoroughly absorbing.◗

40 Pounds of Trouble (1963) **C-106m.** **½ D: Norman Jewison. Tony Curtis, Phil Silvers, Suzanne Pleshette, Larry Storch, Howard Morris, Stubby Kaye, Claire Wilcox, Jack La Rue. "Cute" Curtis comedy of casino manager who "adopts" little girl with endless complications occurring. Disneyland locations and fine character actors pep it up. Carbon copy of LITTLE MISS MARKER. Panavision. ▼◗

42nd Street (1933) **89m.** ****D: Lloyd Bacon. Warner Baxter, Ruby Keeler, George Brent, Bebe Daniels, Dick Powell, Guy Kibbee, Una Merkel, Ginger Rogers, Ned Sparks, George E. Stone. The definitive backstage musical still has plenty of sass—along with its clichés. Ailing director Baxter puts everything into what may be his final show, then leading lady Daniels twists her ankle! Good thing Ruby Keeler's on hand. Harry Warren–Al Dubin songs include title tune, "Young and Healthy," "You're Getting to Be a Habit With Me," "Shuffle Off to Buffalo." Busby Berkeley's ground-breaking production numbers are sensational. Scripted by Rian James and James Seymour, from Bradford Ropes' story. Adapted for Broadway 50 years later. Also shown in computer-colored version. ▼●◗

47 Ronin, Part I, The (1941-Japanese) **112m.** ***½ D: Kenji Mizoguchi. Chojuro Kawarazaki, Yoshizaburo Arashi, Utaemon Ichikawa, Mieko Takamine. Legendary samurai warriors scheme to gain revenge for the death of their leader, who was tricked and forced to commit suicide. Based on a famous Japanese story, and fascinating as both cinema and as propaganda (remember, this was made during WW2). First of Mizoguchi's two-part epic, also known as THE LOYAL 47 RONIN. Several dozen versions of this same story have been filmed in Japan. ▼◗

47 Ronin, Part II, The (1942-Japanese) **113m.** ***½ D: Kenji Mizoguchi. Chojuro Kawarazaki, Yoshizaburo Arashi, Utaemon Ichikawa, Mieko Takamine. The 47 Ronin gain vengeance for their master's death. Together with its predecessor, this was the most impressive Japanese film produced during WW2; the finale is especially stirring and revealing. ▼◗

Forty Shades of Blue (2005) **C-108m.** ***½ D: Ira Sachs. Rip Torn, Dina Korzun, Darren Burrows, Paprika Steen, Red West. Longtime girlfriend of a famous but washed-up music producer finds her life shaken up by the arrival of the producer's estranged son. Torn and Korzun give knockout performances in this gem, which should have earned more attention than it got. Sachs' camera pays close attention to nuances of human behavior, and each shot and sequence adds another layer of emotional depth to the story. Almost painful to watch at times, but highly rewarding. ◗

43: The Petty Story SEE: Smash-Up Alley

42 Up (1999-British) **C/B&W-130m.** *** D: Michael Apted. Picking up where 35 UP left off, Apted revisits all but three of his lifelong subjects as they settle into middle age. As compelling as ever. Followed by 49 UP. ▼◗

40 Year Old Virgin, The (2005) **C-116m.** **½ D: Judd Apatow. Steve Carell, Catherine Keener, Paul Rudd, Romany Malco, Seth Rogen, Elizabeth Banks, Leslie Mann, Jane Lynch, Nancy Walls, Mo Collins, Cedric Yarbrough, David Koechner, Jonah Hill. When some rowdy, randy coworkers at an electronics store discover that the nerd in their midst is still a virgin, they make it their mission to coach him to manhood. Meanwhile, he awkwardly begins a relationship with a nice woman (who's got three kids) and doesn't want sex to be a stumbling block. Carell's first starring vehicle, which he cowrote with director Apatow, is funny, but its startlingly raunchy gags clash with the sweet romantic-comedy approach to its love story. Unrated version runs 133m. [R] ▼●❙

For Whom the Bell Tolls (1943) C-130m. ***½ D: Sam Wood. Gary Cooper, Ingrid Bergman, Akim Tamiroff, Arturo de Cordova, Joseph Calleia, Katina Paxinou, Vladimir Sokoloff, Mikhail Rasumny, Fortunio Bonanova. Hemingway story of U.S. mercenary Cooper fighting for Spain with motley crew of peasants, including Bergman; tense action, beautiful color, great love scenes, marvelous Victor Young score. Paxinou won Best Supporting Actress Oscar. Originally released at 170m.; archivally restored version runs 156m. ▼●❙

For Your Consideration (2006) C-86m. *** D: Christopher Guest. Catherine O'Hara, Harry Shearer, Parker Posey, Christopher Guest, Fred Willard, Jane Lynch, Bob Balaban, Michael McKean, Jennifer Coolidge, Eugene Levy, John Michael Higgins, Ed Begley, Jr., Ricky Gervais, Larry Miller, Paul Dooley, Don Lake, Michael Hitchcock, Christopher Moynihan, Sandra Oh, Richard Kind, John Krasinski, Jim Piddock, Carrie Aizley, Mary McCormack, Craig Bierko, Kevin Sussman, Rachael Harris, Deborah Theaker, Scott Williamson. While making a film called HOME FOR PURIM, aging actress O'Hara, veteran leading man Shearer, and costar Posey all buy into self-perpetuating "buzz" about their chances for Oscars. Uncanny in its dead-on parodies of TV and radio talk shows and other follies of show business, though not as resonant as Guest's other films, perhaps because Hollywood is just too easy a target. Guest's usual cohorts (and some talented newcomers) deliver the goods, but O'Hara takes the cake as a self-deluded star. Written by Guest and Levy. [PG-13]❙

For Your Eyes Only (1981-British) C-127m. *** D: John Glen. Roger Moore, Carole Bouquet, (Chaim) Topol, Lynn-Holly Johnson, Julian Glover, Jill Bennett, Cassandra Harris, Desmond Llewelyn, Lois Maxwell, Walter Gotell. After years of space-age gadgetry, cartoon villains, female mannequins, and giants with steel teeth came this one-shot return to Ian Fleming minimalism. No other James Bond film has provoked so much debate among 007 fans (even us); judge for yourself. The chases and stuntwork *are* spectacular; debuting helmer Glen directed 2nd-unit on some earlier Bonds. Look for Charles Dance as gunman. Panavision. [PG]▼●❙

For Your Love Only (1976-German) C-97m. ** D: Wolfgang Petersen. Nastassia Kinski, Christian Quadflieg, Judy Winter, Klaus Schwarzkopf. Young student Kinski has an affair with a teacher, then kills the man who tries to blackmail and seduce her. Turgid soap opera. Made for German TV; theatrical release in 1982. ▼

Foul Play (1978) C-116m. **½ D: Colin Higgins. Goldie Hawn, Chevy Chase, Burgess Meredith, Dudley Moore, Rachel Roberts, Eugene Roche, Marilyn Sokol, Billy Barty, Marc Lawrence, Brian Dennehy. Innocent woman (Hawn) gets caught in strange murder plot in San Francisco; no one believes her except detective Chase, who's falling in love with her. Likable stars, good fun, but protracted story, tasteless comedy, and Hitchcock plagiarism detract. Followed by a short-lived TV series. [PG] ▼●❙

Fountain, The (2006) C-95m. ** D: Darren Aronofsky. Hugh Jackman, Rachel Weisz, Ellen Burstyn, Cliff Curtis, Mark Margolis, Sean Patrick Thomas, Stephen McHattie, Donna Murphy, Ethan Suplee. Ambitious film about a man (Jackman) in three different time frames—16th-century Spain, the modern day, and the 26th century—who seeks to understand the essence of life. The contemporary research scientist is driven to cure his wife (Weisz), whose life is ebbing away from cancer. Sincere but overwrought new-age drama (mixing science fiction and soap opera) will elicit a wide range of opinion; the ultimate epiphany is the kind of thing that might work in a novel but doesn't play well on-screen. Written by the director. [PG-13]❙

Fountainhead, The (1949) 114m. **½ D: King Vidor. Gary Cooper, Patricia Neal, Raymond Massey, Kent Smith, Robert Douglas, Henry Hull, Ray Collins, Jerome Cowan. Ambitious but confused version of Ayn Rand philosophic novel, spotlighting an idealistic architect's clash with compromises of society; cast does what it can with the script. ▼●❙

Four Adventures of Reinette and Mirabelle (1987-French) C-99m. *** D: Eric Rohmer. Joelle Miquel, Jessica Forde, Philippe Laudenbach, Yasmine Haury, Marie Riviere, Beatrice Romand. Typically charming, perceptive Rohmeresque slice of life, chronicling the friendship between country girl Reinette (Miquel) and city girl Mirabelle (Forde), who become roommates in Paris. At its best when focusing on their contrasting viewpoints, and the manner in which their friendship evolves. ▼

Four Brothers (2005) C-108m. *** D: John Singleton. Mark Wahlberg, Tyrese Gibson, André Benjamin, Garrett Hedlund, Terrence Howard, Josh Charles, Sofia Vergara, Fionnula Flanagan, Chiwetel Ejiofor, Barry Shabaka Henley, Taraji P. Henson. Four incorrigible adopted brothers—two black, two white—reunite when their mother is murdered in Detroit and swear revenge, whatever the consequences. Violent, somewhat overlong action-thriller veers toward melodrama but maintains rooting interest for its rough-and-tumble "heroes" from start to finish. Flanagan is a standout in her few scenes as the boys' good-hearted mother. As widely noted, this plays like an updated urban version of THE SONS OF KATIE ELDER. Super 35. [R] ▼▶

Four Christmases (2008) C-88m. ** D: Seth Gordon. Vince Vaughn, Reese Witherspoon, Robert Duvall, Sissy Spacek, Jon Voight, Jon Favreau, Mary Steenburgen, Dwight Yoakam, Tim McGraw, Kristin Chenoweth, Katy Mixon, Colleen Camp, Peter Billingsley. Unsatisfying holiday comedy involving a couple (Vaughn, Witherspoon) forced to visit each of their divorced parents in one day. Main characters are unusual for this type of fare: they're unmarried, alienated from their families, and don't want kids. Even so, the film is predictable, the finale is illogical, and the stellar cast is wasted. Carol Kane appears unbilled. [PG-13] ▶

4 Clowns (1970) 97m. **** D: Robert Youngson. Laurel and Hardy, Buster Keaton, Charley Chase. A must for viewers of all ages: some of the best silent comedy ever. Interesting solo footage of Laurel and Hardy; Keaton's classic SEVEN CHANCES; hilarious sequences with underrated Chase including his best short, LIMOUSINE LOVE. One of compiler Youngson's very best efforts. [G]

Four Daughters (1938) 90m. ***½ D: Michael Curtiz. Claude Rains, Rosemary Lane, Lola Lane, Priscilla Lane, Gale Page, John Garfield, Jeffrey Lynn, Frank McHugh, May Robson, Dick Foran. Believable, beautifully acted soaper of small-town life; four young women with musical father Rains have lives altered by four young men. Garfield is superb in first film, matched by fine cast. Followed immediately by DAUGHTERS COURAGEOUS and sequels FOUR WIVES and FOUR MOTHERS. Remade as YOUNG AT HEART. ▼▶

Four Days in September (1997-Brazilian) C-106m. *** D: Bruno Barreto. Alan Arkin, Pedro Cardoso, Fernanda Torres, Luiz Fernando Guimaraes, Selton Mello, Claudia Abreu, Nelson Dantas, Fisher Stevens. Emotion-charged, based-on-fact account of the events surrounding 1969 kidnapping of American ambassador (Arkin) by an idealistic yet diverse group of young Brazilian revolutionaries. All sides are given a voice in this empathetic and well-detailed political drama. [R] ▼▶

Four Deuces, The (1975) C-87m. **½ D: William H. Bushnell, Jr. Jack Palance, Carol Lynley, Warren Berlinger, Adam Roarke, E. J. Peaker. Action comedy/drama involving Prohibition Era bootleg-

gers. Palance is a gang lord whose mob and casino bear the film's title; Lynley is the moll he loves and fights for. [R] ▼▶

Four Faces West (1948) 90m. **½ D: Alfred E. Green. Joel McCrea, Frances Dee, Charles Bickford, Joseph Calleia, William Conrad. Quiet, fact-based Western with McCrea a reluctant bank robber who becomes involved with nurse Dee while being pursued by sheriff Pat Garrett (Bickford). ▼▶

Four Feathers, The (1939-British) C-115m. **** D: Zoltan Korda. John Clements, Ralph Richardson, C. Aubrey Smith, June Duprez, Allan Jeayes, Jack Allen, Donald Gray, Clive Baxter. Grand adventure from A. E. W. Mason story of tradition-bound Britisher who must prove he's not a coward by helping army comrades quell Sudan uprising. Smith is just wonderful as tale-spinning army veteran. Screenplay by R. C. Sherriff, Lajos Biro, and Arthur Wimperis. Score by Miklos Rozsa. Original release ran 130m. Previously filmed in 1921 and 1929; remade as STORM OVER THE NILE (1955), as a TVM in 1978 with Beau Bridges, and in 2002. ▼●▶

Four Feathers, The (2002-U.S.-British) C-130m. **½ D: Shekhar Kapur. Heath Ledger, Kate Hudson, Wes Bentley, Djimon Hounsou, Michael Sheen, Lucy Gordon, Rupert Penry-Jones, Nick Holder, Alex Jennings, Tim Pigott-Smith. Well-crafted remake of the A.E.W. Mason story, set in the late 1800s, about a young British soldier who is branded a coward and then has to redeem himself. Ledger is excellent (and credible) in the leading role, and the battle scenes are impressive . . . but the story is confusing at times, the character motivations muddy, and a touch of humor (so memorably supplied in the 1939 version by C. Aubrey Smith) is sorely missed. Panavision. [PG-13] ▼▶

Four Flies on Grey Velvet (1971-Italian-French) C-101m. ** D: Dario Argento. Michael Brandon, Mimsy Farmer, Bud Spencer, Francine Racette. Unabsorbing psychological murder-mystery with performers who walk through their roles in a very disinterested fashion. Techniscope. [PG]

4 for Texas (1963) C-114m. *** D: Robert Aldrich. Frank Sinatra, Dean Martin, Anita Ekberg, Ursula Andress, Charles Bronson, Victor Buono, Richard Jaeckel, Mike Mazurki, Jack Elam, The Three Stooges, Yaphet Kotto. Nonsensical Sinatra-Martin romp set in the old West, with their antics only outdone by Buono as villainous banker. Ekberg and Andress both outstanding scenery attractions. ▼▶

Four Friends (1981) C-115m. *** D: Arthur Penn. Craig Wasson, Jodi Thelen, Jim Metzler, Michael Huddleston, Reed Birney, James Leo Herlihy, Glenne Headly, Mercedes Ruehl. A journey of self-discovery for an idealistic young Yugoslavian immigrant (Wasson), who lives through the turbulent American 1960s. Charming, coy, powerful, sentimental, and sometimes astonishingly old-fashioned—a real mixed bag, with many rewards and not a few flaws. Largely autobiographical script by Steve Tesich. [R]▼)

Four Horsemen of the Apocalypse, The (1921) **131m. *** D:** Rex Ingram. Rudolph Valentino, Alice Terry, Alan Hale, Jean Hersholt, Nigel de Brulier, Wallace Beery. Famous silent spectacle cemented Valentino's popularity via legendary tango scene, but aside from that it's a relentlessly grim antiwar story of cousins who end up fighting on opposite sides during WW1. Extremely well made, with imagery that still staggers and message that cannot be overlooked. Based on the Blasco Ibanez novel. Remade in 1962.▼●

Four Horsemen of the Apocalypse, The (1962) **C-153m. **½ D:** Vincente Minnelli. Glenn Ford, Ingrid Thulin, Charles Boyer, Lee J. Cobb, Paul Henreid, Paul Lukas, Yvette Mimieux, Karl Boehm. Glossy, padded trash, losing all sense of reality in its telling of a family whose members fight on opposite sides during WW2. Loose remake of the 1921 silent film based on a novel by Vincent Blasco Ibanez. Angela Lansbury dubbed in Thulin's lines. Great André Previn score. CinemaScope.▼●)

Four Hundred Blows, The (1959-French) **99m. **** D:** François Truffaut. Jean-Pierre Léaud, Patrick Auffay, Claire Maurier, Albert Remy, Jeanne Moreau, Jean-Claude Brialy, Jacques Demy, François Truffaut. Captivating study of Parisian youth who turns to life of small-time crime as a reaction to derelict parents. First of Truffaut's autobiographical Antoine Doinel series; followed by the "Antoine et Colette" episode in LOVE AT TWENTY. Dyaliscope.▼●)

4 Little Girls (1997) **C-102m. **** D:** Spike Lee. Shattering documentary about the fatal bombing of a black Birmingham, Alabama, church on September 15, 1963, which not only killed four innocent children but galvanized the entire nation and accelerated the civil rights movement. Remembering its young (ages 11 to 14) victims are families, now-grown-up friends, ministers, reporters, political activists, and the lawyer who, years later, helped convict the key perpetrator. One of filmmaker Lee's finest hours. Produced for HBO but also given theatrical release.▼)

Four Men and a Prayer (1938) **85m. *** D:** John Ford. Loretta Young, Richard Greene, George Sanders, David Niven, C. Aubrey Smith, William Henry, J. Edward Bromberg, Alan Hale, Reginald Denny, John Carradine. Compelling story of four

brothers determined to unravel mystery behind their father's murder; handsome, well-paced production. Remade as FURY AT FURNACE CREEK.▶

4 Months, 3 Weeks and 2 Days (2007-Romanian) **C-113m. ***½ D:** Cristian Mungiu. Anamaria Marinca, Laura Vasiliu, Vlad Ivanov, Alex Potocean, Ioan Sapdaru, Teo Corban, Tania Popa. In totalitarian Romania, 1987, a student agrees to help her roommate obtain an illegal abortion, never suspecting that it will turn into an emotional ordeal, as much for her as for her friend. Told in a series of long, unbroken takes with a fly-on-the-wall camera, this forceful film illustrates a society's moral decay, as well as one woman's awakening to reality. Its matter-of-fact tone makes it all the more devastating. Written by the director. Winner of the Palme d'Or at the Cannes Film Festival. Super 35.▶

Four Musketeers, The (1975) **C-108m. *** D:** Richard Lester. Oliver Reed, Raquel Welch, Richard Chamberlain, Frank Finlay, Michael York, Christopher Lee, Jean-Pierre Cassel, Geraldine Chaplin, Simon Ward, Faye Dunaway, Charlton Heston. Second half of Lester's irreverent but amusing approach to Dumas with less emphasis on slapstick this time around. Rich cast in top form. Filmed in 1973, at the same time as THE THREE MUSKETEERS. Followed by THE RETURN OF THE MUSKETEERS. [R]▼●

Four Nights of a Dreamer (1971-French) **C-83m. *** D:** Robert Bresson. Isabelle Weingarten, Guillaume des Forêts, Maurice Monnoyer, Jérôme Massart, Lidia Biondi. Slow-moving but beautifully filmed adaptation of Dostoyevsky's *White Nights*, updated to modern Paris. A painter meets a girl on a bridge as she's about to commit suicide and falls in love with her over the next few nights; then the lover who abandoned her returns. Possessed of Bresson's usual lyrical qualities, the film also contains an unexpected sense of humor and romance.

Four Poster, The (1952) **103m. ***½ D:** Irving Reis. Rex Harrison, Lilli Palmer. Jan de Hartog play is tour de force for stars who enact various phases of married couple's life; warm, witty script; superb performances enhanced by ingenious animated interludes by UPA studio. Later became the stage musical *I Do! I Do!*

4: Rise of the Silver Surfer (2007) **C-92m. ** D:** Tim Story. Ioan Gruffudd, Jessica Alba, Chris Evans, Michael Chiklis, Julian McMahon, Kerry Washington, Andre Braugher, Doug Jones, Brian Posehn, Kenneth Welsh, Vanessa Minnillo; voice of Laurence Fishburne. Sequel finds the earth imperiled by a mysterious force that is wreaking havoc with weather systems (and global landmarks), and making the impending N.Y.C. nuptials of Reed (Gruffudd) and Sue (Alba) difficult to plan. The culprit may be the Silver Surfer or possibly the returning Victor Von Doom (McMahon). A special-effectsapalooza masquerading as a feature film. Look for the comic's cocreator Stan Lee at a wedding. Super 35. [PG]🔲

Four Rooms (1995) **C-98m.** BOMB D: Allison Anders, Alexandre Rockwell, Robert Rodriguez, Quentin Tarantino. Tim Roth, Antonio Banderas, Jennifer Beals, Paul Calderon, Sammi Davis, Amanda de Cadenet, Valeria Golino, Kathy Griffin, Marc Lawrence, Madonna, David Proval, Ione Skye, Quentin Tarantino, Lili Taylor, Marisa Tomei, Tamlyn Tomita, Alicia Witt, Lana McKissack, Danny Verduzco, Salma Hayek. What a cast . . . what a waste! Embarrassingly awful compilation consisting of four short films, with the sole point of interest being which one is the worst. Set in an L.A. hotel on New Year's Eve, and linked by the participation of Ted the Bellhop (Roth). Bruce Willis appears unbilled in the final episode, by Tarantino. [R]▼●🔲

Four's a Crowd (1938) **91m.** **½ D: Michael Curtiz. Errol Flynn, Olivia de Havilland, Rosalind Russell, Patric Knowles, Hugh Herbert, Lana Turner. Lightheaded romance in which everyone loves another; straight comedy's a switch for Flynn. Pleasant.🔲

Four Seasons, The (1981) **C-107m.** *** D: Alan Alda. Alan Alda, Carol Burnett, Len Cariou, Sandy Dennis, Rita Moreno, Jack Weston, Bess Armstrong. Four stages of friendship among three middle-aged couples who vacation together. As comedy it scores, with warmly winning cast, but like its main character, it professes to discuss serious issues while pulling back after just touching the surface. Alda scripted, made feature directing debut; later a TV series. [PG]▼●🔲

Fourteen Hours (1951) **92m.** *** D: Henry Hathaway. Paul Douglas, Richard Basehart, Barbara Bel Geddes, Debra Paget, Agnes Moorehead, Robert Keith, Howard da Silva, Jeffrey Hunter, Martin Gabel, Grace Kelly, Jeff Corey. Well-made suspense drama about a man threatening to jump off the ledge of a building, told in semidocumentary fashion. Look for Harvey Lembeck and Ossie Davis as cabbies, Joyce Van Patten as Paget's girlfriend. Grace Kelly's film debut.🔲

1492: Conquest of Paradise (1992-U.S.-British-French-Spanish) **C-145m.** ** D: Ridley Scott. Gérard Depardieu, Sigourney Weaver, Armand Assante, Frank Langella, Loren Dean, Angela Molina, Fernando Rey, Michael Wincott, Tchéky Karyo. The second of 1992's Christopher Columbus epics, this effort is beautifully mounted, but a long haul in steerage. The burden falls on Depardieu as the famed explorer, a French actor cast as an Italian working for Spain in an English-language movie—and an actor who speaks English like Bela Lugosi reading from cue cards. Might have been better had the action aped director Scott's finale to THELMA & LOUISE, by having Columbus and crew sail off the edge of the world. Panavision. [PG-13]▼●🔲

1408 (2007) **C-104m.** *** D: Mikael Håfström. John Cusack, Samuel L. Jackson, Mary McCormack, Tony Shalhoub, Len Cariou, Isiah Whitlock, Jr., Jasmine Jessica Anthony, Kevin Dobson. There have been 56 deaths, natural and otherwise, in the title room, located in a Kafkaesque N.Y.C. hotel-from-hell. Intrepid occult writer Cusack is determined to spend the night there. Genuinely scary chiller, nicely paced with clever touches, brings new meaning to the Carpenters' song "We've Only Just Begun." Based on a Stephen King short story. Unrated director's cut runs 112m. Super 35. [PG-13]🔲

Fourth Kind, The (2009-U.S.-British) **C-98m.** *½ D: Olatunde Osunsanmi. Milla Jovovich, Will Patton, Elias Koteas, Hakeem Kae-Kazim, Corey Johnson, Enzo Cilenti, Olatunde Osunsanmi. Aliens are thought to be abducting people in Nome, Alaska; a psychiatrist interviews terrified victims on video. This claims to be based on facts, and footage of real people is split-screened with re-creations of the same interviews. The problem is that it's *all* fake; it's also unconvincing and more than a little boring. Title refers to J. Allen Hynek's categories describing the closeness of alien encounters, as does CLOSE ENCOUNTERS OF THE THIRD KIND. Super 35. [PG-13]🔲

Fourth Man, The (1983-Dutch) **C-104m.** ***½ D: Paul Verhoeven. Jeroen Krabbé, Renee Soutendijk, Thom Hoffman, Dolf De Vries, Geert De Jong. Sexy blonde hairdresser Soutendijk may or may not have murdered three husbands but definitely *does* screw up the mind of gay writer Krabbé when he tries to find out. Stylish dream-vs.-reality black comedy deserved its art-house success; flashy direction, eroticism to spare. ▼●🔲

Fourth Protocol, The (1987-British) **C-119m.** **½ D: John Mackenzie. Michael Caine, Pierce Brosnan, Joanna Cassidy, Ned Beatty, Betsy Brantley, Peter Cartwright, David Conville, Matt Frewer, Ray McAnally, Ian Richardson. Pretty good spy thriller adapted by Frederick Forsyth from his best-selling novel. Caine plays a British spy who's assigned to foil a Russian plot that would destroy relations between the U.S. and England by setting off a nuclear bomb near an American air base in the U.K. Brosnan does well as a Russian agent. J-D-C Scope. [R]▼●

Fourth War, The (1990) **C-91m.** **½ D: John Frankenheimer. Roy Scheider, Jürgen Prochnow, Tim Reid, Harry Dean Stanton, Lara Harris, Dale Dye. Well-done but ever-so-familiar Cold War thriller in which an American colonel (Scheider) and his Soviet counterpart (Prochnow) engage in a private, potentially disastrous war. Best for fans of the genre. Stanton looks very out of place as Scheider's commanding general. [R]▼●▶

Four Weddings and a Funeral (1994-British) **C-117m.** *** D: Mike Newell. Hugh Grant, Andie MacDowell, Kristin Scott Thomas, Simon Callow, Rowan Atkinson, James Fleet, John Hannah, Charlotte Coleman, David Bower, Corin Redgrave, Kenneth Griffiths, Jeremy Kemp, Rosalie Crutchley. Delightful contemporary comedy about a young man who can't sustain a relationship, while all his friends seem to be getting married. Then he hits it off with another wedding guest, and the plot thickens. Fine ensemble, headed by the engaging Grant, keep this buoyant under Newell's sure-handed direction. Richard Curtis' screenplay may not bear close scrutiny (that final conversation really seems out of place), but it's certainly fun. [R]▼●▶

Fox, The (1967) **C-110m.** *** D: Mark Rydell. Sandy Dennis, Keir Dullea, Anne Heywood, Glyn Morris. Nicely crafted tale of lesbians Dennis and Heywood, and what happens when intruder Dullea happens among them. Scripted by Lewis John Carlino and Howard Koch; based on a D. H. Lawrence novella. Filmed in Canada.▶

Fox and His Friends (1975-German) **C-123m.** **** D: Rainer Werner Fassbinder. Rainer Werner Fassbinder, Peter Chatel, Karlheinz Bohm, Adrian Hoven, Ulla Jacobsson. Compassionate, politically astute melodrama by German wunderkind Fassbinder about gay lower-class carnival performer winning lottery fortune only to have his upper-class lover exploit him. Fassbinder is brilliant in title role. Aka FIST RIGHT OF FREEDOM.▼▶

Fox and the Hound, The (1981) **C-83m.** *** D: Art Stevens, Ted Berman, Richard Rich. Voices of Mickey Rooney, Kurt Russell, Pearl Bailey, Jack Albertson, Sandy Duncan, Jeanette Nolan, Pat Buttram, John Fiedler, John McIntire, Paul Winchell, Corey Feldman. Charming Disney animated feature about the childhood friendship between two natural enemies, a fox cub and a hound pup; as they grow older their relationship is put to the test by their emerging instincts. Warm and brimming with personable characters, this one approaches the old Disney magic at times. Followed by a direct-to-video sequel. [G]▼▶

Foxes (1980) **C-106m.** **½ D: Adrian Lyne. Jodie Foster, Cherie Currie, Marilyn Kagan, Kandice Stroh, Scott Baio, Sally Kellerman, Randy Quaid, Lois Smith, Laura Dern. Four teenaged girls try coping with the standard non-*Our Town* problems brought by growing up in San Fernando Valley. Capable cast;

apparently sincere intentions undermined by choppy storyline that just isn't compelling enough. [R]▼●▶

Foxes of Harrow, The (1947) **117m.** **½ D: John M. Stahl. Rex Harrison, Maureen O'Hara, Richard Haydn, Victor McLaglen, Vanessa Brown, Patricia Medina, Gene Lockhart. Lavish but lumbering tale of philanderer breaking up his marriage to seek affluence and fame in New Orleans in 1820. Pretty stale despite the trimmings.

Foxfire (1996) **C-102m.** *½ D: Annette Haywood-Carter. Hedy Burress, Angelina Jolie, Jenny Lewis, Jenny Shimizu, Sarah Rosenberg, Peter Facinelli, Dash Mihok, Cathy Moriarty, Richard Beymer, John Diehl. Knee-deep adaptation of Joyce Carol Oates' novel about four high school girls who form a gang when an enigmatic female drifter comes to town. The cast tries hard but they're done in by a heavy-handed script; plays like an R-rated After School Special. Super 35. [R]▼●▶

Foxtrap (1986-U.S.-Italian) **C-88m.** *½ D: Fred Williamson. Fred Williamson, Chris Connelly, Arlene Golonka, Donna Owen, Beatrice Palme, Cleo Sebastian, Lela Rochon. Low-budget actioner of Williamson hired to bring runaway Owen back home from Europe to her family. Little more than a fashion show by director Williamson spotlighting his favorite actor: Williamson. [R]▼

Foxtrot (1976-Mexican-Swiss) **C-91m.** ** D: Arturo Ripstein. Peter O'Toole, Charlotte Rampling, Max von Sydow, Jorge Luke, Helen Rojo, Claudio Brook. O'Toole and his wife flee Rumania in the late 1930s and retreat to an island paradise to isolate themselves from a world about to erupt into war. Shallow, predictable drama; filmed in Mexico. Alternate version with additional sex footage titled THE OTHER SIDE OF PARADISE. [R]▼

Foxy Brown (1974) **C-94m.** *½ D: Jack Hill. Pam Grier, Peter Brown, Terry Carter, Kathryn Loder. Violence and little else in tale of nurse Grier and her vendetta against drug ring that killed her lover. [R]▼●▶

Fracture (2007) **C-112m.** **½ D: Gregory Hoblit. Anthony Hopkins, Ryan Gosling, David Strathairn, Rosamund Pike, Billy Burke, Fiona Shaw, Bob Gunton, Embeth Davidtz, Cliff Curtis, Xander Berkeley, Josh Stamberg, Joe Spano. Hopkins plays a cold, calculating man who shoots his wife after he discovers she's been sleeping with an L.A. police lieutenant. But there is no concrete evidence, which makes the case an unexpected challenge for assistant D.A. Gosling, who's just about to move on to a cushy job at a high-end law firm. Decent thriller has some surprises up its sleeve but takes a long time to lay them all out. Super 35. [R]▶

Fra Diavolo SEE: **Devil's Brother, The**
Fragment of Fear (1971-British) **C-96m.**

** D: Richard C. Sarafian. David Hemmings, Gayle Hunnicutt, Flora Robson, Wilfrid Hyde-White, Daniel Massey, Roland Culver, Adolfo Celi, Mona Washbourne. Hemmings is good in disappointing murder mystery that begins well, then falls apart. Photographed by the great Oswald Morris. [PG] ▶

Frailty (2002) **C-99m.** ** D: Bill Paxton. Bill Paxton, Matthew McConaughey, Powers Boothe, Matt O'Leary, Luke Askew, Jeremy Sumpter, Derk Cheetwood, Melissa Crider. A Texas widower tells his two young sons that he has had a vision: they have been chosen to destroy demons who are walking the earth in human form. His boys are then forced to witness—and participate in—a brutal series of axe murders. Story is told in flashback by Paxton's now grown-up son (McConaughey) to FBI agent Boothe. Twisty mood piece is well crafted by first-time director Paxton, but difficult to digest—especially for a parent. [R] ▼▶

Framed (1947) **82m.** ** D: Richard Wallace. Glenn Ford, Janis Carter, Barry Sullivan, Edgar Buchanan, Karen Morley. Rootless patsy Ford falls for scheming Carter but is kept in the dark as she hatches a robbery plan with banker Sullivan. Not especially stylish but efficient noir-ish melodrama.

Framed (1975) **C-106m.** **½ D: Phil Karlson. Joe Don Baker, Conny Van Dyke, Gabriel Dell, John Marley, Brock Peters, Roy Jenson. Railroaded to jail, Baker vows revenge on the corrupt cops who put him there. The writer, director, and star of WALKING TALL, old hands at this kind of action melodrama, make the most of the situation. [R] ▼

Frances (1982) **C-140m.** **½ D: Graeme Clifford. Jessica Lange, Kim Stanley, Sam Shepard, Bart Burns, Jeffrey DeMunn, Jordan Charney, Lane Smith, Anjelica Huston. Biography of 1930s movie star Frances Farmer—who wound up in a barbaric insane asylum—chronicles her tragic life in some detail, but doesn't help us understand the reasons for her self-destructive tendencies. Well crafted but cold and depressing, despite impressive performances by Lange and Stanley, as Frances' crazed mother. Her story is also told in the TVM, WILL THERE REALLY BE A MORNING? and in the independent feature COMMITTED. Look for Kevin Costner, who has one line in an alley. [R] ▼▶

Francesco (1989-Italian-German) **C-105m.** BOMB D: Liliana Cavani. Mickey Rourke, Helena Bonham Carter, Andrea Ferreol, Hans Zischler, Mario Adorf, Paolo Bonacelli. Laughably inept historical drama with a miscast Rourke muttering his way through his role as Francis of Assisi(!), son of a rich Italian merchant, who undergoes a spiritual rebirth. The narrative is often confusing, the direction is slipshod, and the result is a real snooze. [PG-13] ▼▶

Francis (The Talking Mule) series SEE: *Leonard Maltin's Classic Movie Guide*

Francis of Assisi (1961) **C-111m.** **½ D: Michael Curtiz. Bradford Dillman, Dolores Hart, Stuart Whitman, Cecil Kellaway, Finlay Currie, Pedro Armendariz. Lavish religious epic dealing with story of founder of school of monks with sympathetic performance by Dillman. Good cast and atmosphere. Script tends to sag at wrong moments. CinemaScope. ▼▶

Frank and Ollie (1995) **C-89m.** *** D: Theodore Thomas. Charming documentary about Frank Thomas and Ollie Johnston, friends since the early 1930s, next-door neighbors, and longtime animators at the Walt Disney studio, where they created some of the most memorable and expressive characters ever brought to life . . . from Thumper in BAMBI to Baloo and Mowgli in THE JUNGLE BOOK. Affectionate (and informative) portrait by Thomas's son and daughter-in-law, Kuniko Okubo. [PG] ▼▶

Frankenhooker (1990) **C-90m.** *½ D: Frank Henenlotter. James Lorinz, Patty Mullen, Charlotte Helmkamp, Shirley Stoler, Louise Lasser. Grim, gory, and seldom funny horror comedy about a novice mad scientist (Lorinz) who needs body parts to sew onto the severed head he has on ice back at the lab. When he sells N.Y.C. 42nd Street hookers a deadly "supercrack," they explode—giving him all the spare limbs and organs he desires. Offensive, cheap, and ugly—even by splatter genre standards. ▼▶

Frankenstein (1931) **70m.** ***½ D: James Whale. Colin Clive, Mae Clarke, Boris Karloff, John Boles, Edward Van Sloan, Dwight Frye, Frederick Kerr, Lionel Belmore. Definitive monster movie, with Clive as the ultimate mad scientist, creating a man-made being (Karloff) but inadvertently giving him a criminal brain. It's creaky at times, and cries for a music score, but it's still impressive . . . as is Karloff's performance in the role that made him a star. Long-censored footage, restored in 1987, enhances the impact of several key scenes, including the drowning of a little girl. Based on Mary Shelley's novel. Followed by BRIDE OF FRANKENSTEIN. ▼▶

Frankenstein (1994) SEE: **Mary Shelley's Frankenstein**

Frankenstein and the Monster From Hell (1974-British) **C-93m.** ** D: Terence Fisher. Peter Cushing, Shane Briant, Madeline Smith, Dave Prowse, John Stratton. Guess who runs a hospital for the criminally insane? Hammer's final entry in their Frankenstein cycle is amusing if you catch it in the right frame of mind. [R] ▼▶

Frankenstein Conquers the World (1965-Japanese) **C-87m.** ** D: Ishiro Honda. Nick Adams, Tadao Takashima, Kumi Mizuno.

Grade-C horror film, with Adams a scientist in Tokyo trying to combat giant, newly grown Frankenstein monster terrorizing the countryside; poor special effects. Tohoscope. ▼▶

Frankenstein Created Woman (1967-British) **C-92m.** ** D: Terence Fisher. Peter Cushing, Susan Denberg, Robert Morris, Barry Warren, Thorley Walters, Duncan Lamont. Sequel to THE EVIL OF FRANKENSTEIN finds Dr. Frankenstein (Cushing) trying to put the soul of recently (and wrongly) executed man into body of scarred lover (Denberg). Everything goes wrong, including script. Followed by FRANKENSTEIN MUST BE DESTROYED! ▼●▶

Frankenstein '88 SEE **Vindicator, The**

Frankenstein Island (1981) **C-89m.** BOMB D: Jerry Warren. John Carradine, Andrew Duggan, Cameron Mitchell, Steve Brodie, Robert Clarke, Katherine Victor. Low-budget filmmaker Warren's first feature in 15 years reunites some of his old hands (like Clarke and Victor) for a sort of remake of TEENAGE ZOMBIES, with a monster who only shows up at the end, and who may or may not be Frankenstein! [PG]

Frankenstein Meets the Space Monster (1965) **78m.** BOMB D: Robert Gaffney. James Karen, David Kerman, Nancy Marshall, Marilyn Hanold. Low-grade horror entry dealing with interplanetary robot that goes berserk. Bizarre, Flash Gordon–esque aliens also involved. Has gained a peculiar cult reputation. Aka MARS INVADES PUERTO RICO. ▼▶

Frankenstein Meets the Wolf Man (1943) **72m.** *** D: Roy William Neill. Lon Chaney, Jr., Patric Knowles, Ilona Massey, Bela Lugosi, Maria Ouspenskaya, Lionel Atwill, Dennis Hoey, Rex Evans, Dwight Frye. Sequel to both THE GHOST OF FRANKENSTEIN and THE WOLF MAN finds werewolf Chaney seeking Dr. Frankenstein, hoping to be put out of his misery. He finds the scientist is dead—but the Monster isn't. Slick, atmospheric, fast-paced fun; Lugosi's only stint as the Monster. Followed by HOUSE OF FRANKENSTEIN. ▼▶

Frankenstein Must Be Destroyed (1969-British) **C-101m.** **½ D: Terence Fisher. Peter Cushing, Simon Ward, Veronica Carlson, Freddie Jones. Cushing is more cold-blooded here than usual, as he forces young couple to help his brain transplant experiments. One of the best in Hammer series. Followed by THE HORROR OF FRANKENSTEIN. [M/PG]▼●▶

Frankenstein 1970 (1958) **83m.** BOMB D: Howard W. Koch. Boris Karloff, Tom Duggan, Jana Lund, Donald Barry. As last of the Frankenstein scientists, Karloff uses money from TV production shooting in his castle to revive original monster with atomic energy. Film is slow, monster unexciting, and Karloff hammy. CinemaScope. ▼▶

Frankenstein's Daughter (1959) **85m.** BOMB D: Richard Cunha. John Ashley, Sandra Knight, Donald Murphy, Sally Todd, Harold Lloyd, Jr. Low-grade descendant of famed monster series with a new female horror-robot being created with typical results; tinsel sets. ▼▶

Frankenstein Unbound (1990) **C-85m.** *½ D: Roger Corman. John Hurt, Raul Julia, Bridget Fonda, Nick Brimble, Catherine Rabett, Jason Patric, Michael Hutchence, Catherine Corman, Mickey Knox; voice of Terri Treas. Thoroughly expendable horror outing casts Hurt as a 21st-century scientist, not really mad, whose implosion experiments zap him back to the days of Doc Frankenstein (Julia) and Mary Shelley (Fonda). Capable cast goes slumming in schlockmeister Corman's first directorial effort in nearly 20 years. Hutchence, here Percy Shelley, was lead singer of Australian rock band INXS. ▼●▶

Frankie & Alice (2009-U.S.-Canadian) **C-101m.** ** D: Geoffrey Sax. Halle Berry, Stellan Skarsgård, Phylicia Rashad, Chandra Wilson, Rosalyn Coleman, Joanne Baron, Brian Markinson, Matt Frewer, Scott Lyster. Mistaken for a whack-job junkie, a stripper in 1973 L.A. roots out her hidden alter egos with the help of a shrink (Skarsgård, in an underwritten role) who doesn't mind bending the rules. Well-meaning but stale medical mystery rewrites THE THREE FACES OF EVE with a startling racial twist as it unearths one of those traumas that fracture psyches. Playing both title characters and then some, Halle is good, but this true-life study of repression become manifest is all thumbs, suffering from too many cooks (eight writers and nine producers, Berry among them). [R]

Frankie and Johnny (1966) **C-87m.** **½ D: Frederick de Cordova. Elvis Presley, Donna Douglas, Harry Morgan, Sue Ane Langdon, Nancy Kovack. Saloon song expanded into feature film story for Elvis. Riverboat setting, cohort Morgan, several pretty starlets, and tuneful songs make this a satisfactory time-filler. ▼●▶

Frankie and Johnny (1991) **C-118m.** *** D: Garry Marshall. Al Pacino, Michelle Pfeiffer, Hector Elizondo, Nathan Lane, Kate Nelligan, Jane Morris, Greg Lewis, Al Fann, K Callan, Phil Leeds. Winning (if overlong) Hollywoodization of Terrence McNally's Off-Broadway play *Frankie and Johnny in the Clair de Lune.* Pacino (never more appealing) plays a man recently released from prison who gets a job as a short-order cook and falls in love with a waitress who tries to keep all social contact at arm's length. Pfeiffer manages to overcome her miscasting with an equally affecting performance. A moving ode to loneliness. Screenplay by the playwright. [R]▼●▶

Frankie & Johnny Are Married (2004) **C-95m.** *** D: Michael Pressman. Michael

Pressman, Lisa Chess, Alan Rosenberg, Stephen Tobolowsky, Jillian Armenante. TV producer-director Pressman decides to direct his wife in a small-theater production of Terrence McNally's *Frankie and Johnny in the Clair de Lune* to help restore her self-esteem as an actress and possibly bring the two of them closer together. Forget reality TV: here's a winning, perceptive, truth-is-stranger-than-fiction story, filmed documentary-style, about people worth getting to know. A number of TV and show-business notables play themselves. [R]🄳

Frankie Starlight (1995-U.S.-Irish) **C-101m. ***** D: Michael Lindsay-Hogg. Matt Dillon, Anne Parillaud, Gabriel Byrne, Rudi Davies, Corban Walker, Alan Pentony, Georgina Cates. Engagingly offbeat drama, the tale of an Irish dwarf (a man imprisoned in a child's body) who writes a revealing, autobiographical novel in which he describes his youth; his mother (Parillaud), a WW2 refugee from France; and the two men (Byrne and Dillon) who love her and become his role models. A gentle, flavorful film that moves seamlessly from the past to the present. [R]▼●

Frank McKlusky, C.I. (2002) **C-82m.** BOMB D: Arlene Sanford. Dave Sheridan, Randy Quaid, Enrico Colantoni, Kevin Pollak, Orson Bean, Cameron Richardson, Andy Richter, Tracy Morgan, Joanie Laurer, Dolly Parton, George Lopez. Son of a daredevil grows up hyper-safety conscious, becoming a claims investigator for an insurance company. Crude, clumsy comedy barely got theatrical release. Many cameos include Scott Baio, Emmanuel Lewis, Gary Owens, Lou Ferrigno. [PG-13]▼●

Frank's Greatest Adventure SEE: **Fearless Frank**

Frantic (1958-French) SEE: **Elevator to the Gallows**

Frantic (1988) **C-120m. **½** D: Roman Polanski. Harrison Ford, Emmanuelle Seigner, Betty Buckley, John Mahoney, Jimmie Ray Weeks, Yorgo Voyagis, David Huddleston, Gerard Klein. American doctor is drawn into espionage, and the underworld, when his wife disappears on the first day of their trip to Paris. Carefully controlled suspense thriller never really cuts loose but keeps its grip thanks to Ford's believable performance. [R]▼●

Fraternity Row (1977) **C-101m. ***** D: Thomas J. Tobin. Peter Fox, Gregory Harrison, Scott Newman, Nancy Morgan, Robert Emhardt, Wendy Phillips. Well-done drama of campus life at exclusive Eastern college, 1954. Writer-producer Charles Gary Allison used USC students and crew, got professional Hollywood advice for polished look at tragic, fact-based, fraternity hazing. Cliff Robertson narrates, Don McLean did original score. Costar Newman is the late son of Paul Newman. [PG]

Fraternity Vacation (1985) **C-89m. *½** D: James Frawley. Stephen Geoffreys, Sheree J. Wilson, Cameron Dye, Leigh McCloskey, Tim Robbins, John Vernon, Britt Ekland, Nita Talbot, Max Wright, Amanda Bearse. Two frat animals, saddled with a nerdy "brother" on a pleasure trip to Palm Springs, bet a rival they can be the first to score with an aloof, beautiful blond. Less strident, and thus less offensive, than many of its ilk, but still nothing to enrich our moviegoing heritage. [R]▼●

Fraulein Doktor (1969-Italian-Yugoslavian) **C-102m. ***** D: Alberto Lattuada. Suzy Kendall, Kenneth More, Capucine, James Booth, Alexander Knox, Nigel Green, Giancarlo Giannini. Big cast and budget in rarely seen European antiwar film centering on career of real-life double-agent during WW1. Some of the battle sequences impressive. Same story has been filmed many times before, in Hollywood as STAMBOUL QUEST (1934) and in France as MADEMOISELLE DOCTEUR. [M]

Freaked (1993) **C-79m. **** D: Alex Winter, Tom Stern. Alex Winter, Megan Ward, Michael Stoyanov, Randy Quaid, Mr. T, Brooke Shields. Bratty movie star and entourage fall into the hands of mad circus owner who mutates them and adds them to his collection of freaks. Wildly inventive makeup and, well, freakish ideas are undercut by an in-your-face directorial style that hammers home every joke. It would make a terrific short. Winter's BILL & TED compatriot Keanu Reeves appears unbilled as Dog Boy. [R]▼●

Freakmaker SEE: **Mutations, The**

Freakonomics (2010) **C-93m. **** D: Seth Gordon, Morgan Spurlock, Alex Gibney, Eugene Jarecki, Heidi Ewing, Rachel Grady. Documentary adaptation of the best-selling book about the role of incentives on economics and human behavior by Steven Levitt and Stephen Dubner, with an all-star team of nonfiction filmmakers taking on different "chapters." Slickly made film offers some challenging ideas but just as many hollow ones that are surprisingly short on facts, resulting in conclusions that sometimes seem to contradict the authors' own thesis. Not helped by the widely varying tones of the individual directors' segments, which further diminish the material. The authors' brief segments on camera are among the film's strongest moments. [PG-13]🄳

Freaks (1932) **64m. ***½** D: Tod Browning. Wallace Ford, Olga Baclanova, Leila Hyams, Harry Earles, Roscoe Ates, Johnny Eck, Daisy and Violet Hilton, Prince Randian, Zip and Pip, Schlitze. A unique movie about a traveling sideshow and the camaraderie of its unusual performers, goaded to vengeance by cruel trapeze star Baclanova. Horror-film master Tod Browning gathered an incredible cast of real-life sideshow freaks for this bizarre and fascinating film. Severely cut in U.S. during release and banned in the U.K. for 30 years, some reissue prints are missing brief epilogue; aka NATURE'S MISTAKES. ▼●)

Freaky Friday (1977) **C-97m.** ******* D: Gary Nelson. Barbara Harris, Jodie Foster, John Astin, Patsy Kelly, Dick Van Patten, Sorrell Booke, Marie Windsor, Charlene Tilton. Harris and Foster shine as mother and daughter who magically switch personalities for a day; their performances make this exceptional Disney fare, even though Mary Rodgers' script winds up with formula slapstick chase. Same premise was the basis of the 1948 movie VICE VERSA and several later Hollywood comedies (including LIKE FATHER, LIKE SON and the 1988 VICE VERSA). Remade in 2003 and for TV in 1995. [G] ▼●)

Freaky Friday (2003) **C-97m.** ******* D: Mark Waters. Jamie Lee Curtis, Lindsay Lohan, Mark Harmon, Harold Gould, Chad Michael Murray, Stephen Tobolowsky, Christina Vidal, Rosalind Chao, Ryan Malgarini. Entertaining, souped-up remake of the 1977 Disney comedy about a stressed-out mother and her teenage daughter, who magically switch bodies and have to somehow cope with their new identities. Good fun, with top-notch performances by Curtis and Lohan as the mixed-up duo. Super 35. [PG] ▼●)

Fred Claus (2007) **C-115m.** ***½** D: David Dobkin. Vince Vaughn, Paul Giamatti, John Michael Higgins, Miranda Richardson, Rachel Weisz, Kathy Bates, Trevor Peacock, Chris "Ludacris" Bridges, Kevin Spacey, Elizabeth Banks, Allan Corduner. Ho, ho, ho? No, no, no. Tepid comedy about a motor-mouth Chicago hustler (Vaughn) who's forced to borrow a sizable sum from his much more successful younger brother—Santa Claus (Giamatti). Laughs aren't exactly plentiful as the ne'er-do-well older sibling pays off the loan (and, of course, becomes a much better person) while working alongside elves at the North Pole. It doesn't help that the special effects are strikingly shoddy. Super 35. [PG]●

Freddie as F.R.O.7 (1992-British) **C-90m.** ****** D: Jon Acevski. Voices of Ben Kingsley, Jenny Agutter, Brian Blessed, Nigel Hawthorne, Michael Hordern, Edmund Kingsley, Phyllis Logan, Victor Maddern, Jonathan Pryce, Prunella Scales, Billie Whitelaw. If James Bond was green, and animated, he might have turned out like Freddie. This toon saga of a secret agent frog is lively, but often difficult to follow. Reedited with James Earl Jones narration and retitled FREDDIE THE FROG. [PG]▼

Freddie the Frog SEE: Freddie as F.R.O.7

Freddy Got Fingered (2001) **C-87m.** BOMB D: Tom Green. Tom Green, Rip Torn, Marisa Coughlan, Eddie Kaye Thomas, Harland Williams, Stephen Tobolowsky, Anthony Michael Hall, Julie Hagerty, Drew Barrymore.

Instantly notorious word-of-mouth debacle became the poster child for all that's wrong with movie comedy. Next to unemployable at 28, but with vague hopes of becoming a cartoonist, live-at-home Green leaves for California to seek success and, hopefully, romance (which he finds with a wheelchair-bound simpleton who lives only to give him oral sex). Gags include the maiming of an innocent child and a newborn spun around in the air by its umbilical cord—compounded by the almost unimaginable ineptitude with which they're executed. [R]▼)

Freddy's Dead: The Final Nightmare (1991) **C-90m.** ***½** D: Rachel Talalay. Robert Englund, Lisa Zane, Shon Greenblatt, Lezlie Deane, Ricky Dean Logan, Breckin Meyer, Yaphet Kotto, Elinor Donahue. Don't believe the title. This NIGHTMARE ON ELM STREET entry has Freddy Krueger trying to break out of the town where he's been slaughtering teens in their dreams. Now the stage is set for the end-all Freddy showdown—a 10-minute 3-D finale that didn't even look good in theaters. A total yawner. Cameos by Alice Cooper, Roseanne and Tom Arnold, and Johnny Depp, whose film debut was the first NIGHTMARE. Followed by WES CRAVEN'S NEW NIGHTMARE. Part 3-D. [R]▼●)

Freddy Vs. Jason (2003) **C-97m.** ****** D: Ronny Yu. Robert Englund, Ken Kirzinger, Monica Keena, Jason Ritter, Kelly Rowland, Christopher George Marquette, Brendan Fletcher. Freddy Krueger (Englund), from the NIGHTMARE ON ELM STREET series, is stuck in Hell because the Elm Street kids don't believe in him anymore. So he uses hockey-masked, machete-wielding Jason Voorhees, from the FRIDAY THE 13TH series, to rouse the fear of Freddy. Tricky setup for a simple story that's basically a NIGHTMARE with Jason added. The fight promised by the title is a long time coming. OK at its sort, but mostly for fans (who were numerous, making this a major hit). Super 35. [R] ▼)

Freebie and the Bean (1974) **C-113m.** ***½** D: Richard Rush. James Caan, Alan Arkin, Loretta Swit, Jack Kruschen, Mike Kellin, Alex Rocco. Some good action, but mostly repellent humor as San Francisco cops Arkin and Caan nearly wreck the city trying to get the goods on a numbers racketeer. Valerie Harper has a nice cameo as Arkin's Latin wife. Later a short-lived TV series. Panavision. [R] ▼●)

Freedomland (2006) **C-112m.** ****** D: Joe Roth. Samuel L. Jackson, Julianne Moore, Edie Falco, Ron Eldard, William Forsythe, Aunjanue Ellis, Anthony Mackie, LaTanya Richardson Jackson, Philip Bosco. Affectionately regarded white teacher with a sad-sack personal history claims a black man abducted her young son. This exacerbates community-police testiness from vocal black neighborhood dwellers who say the cops are paying undue attention because the child is white; investigating cop Jackson is caught in the middle. Richard Price adapted his own praised novel in unwieldy fashion, while Roth's pedestrian direction undermines the story throughout. Moore's histrionics throw the film off balance and make it increasingly tough to watch. Super 35. [R]**D**

Freedom Writers (2007) **C-123m.** *** D: Richard LaGravenese. Hilary Swank, Patrick Dempsey, Scott Glenn, Imelda Staunton, April Lee Hernandez, Deance Wyatt, Mario, Vanetta Smith, John Benjamin Hickey, Pat Carroll. Idealistic young woman gets her first teaching job at a Long Beach, California, high school: she's to teach freshman English to the worst students on the campus, hardened by life and divided on racial lines. She turns their lives around by respecting and believing in them. Based on the real-life experiences of Erin Gruwell. LaGravenese's screenplay captures the raw emotions of its young characters and their indomitable teacher without condescension or phony Hollywood histrionics. Swank also coexecutive-produced. [PG-13]**D**

Free Enterprise (1999) **C-116m.** *** D: Robert Meyer Burnett. William Shatner, Rafer Weigel, Eric McCormack, Audie England, Patrick Van Horn, Jennifer Sommerfield, Phil LaMarr, Deborah Van Valkenburgh. Long-time friends and major sci-fi movie and TV buffs McCormack and Weigel are stunned to be befriended by William Shatner. But he has problems of his own, like his desire to stage *Julius Caesar* with himself in all the roles. Uneven but entertaining comedy gives Shatner a great, self-spoofing role. Written by director Burnett and Mark Altman, who based the lead characters on themselves. [R]**V●D**

Freejack (1992) **C-108m.** *½ D: Geoff Murphy. Emilio Estevez, Mick Jagger, Rene Russo, Anthony Hopkins, Jonathan Banks, David Johansen, Amanda Plummer, Grand L. Bush, Frankie Faison, Esai Morales, John Shea. Good cast is wasted in this mindless actioner, in which race car driver Estevez dies in 1991 and finds his body snatched into the year 2009 so that it may house the soul of ruthless tycoon Hopkins. Tiresome, superficial fare. Based on the novel *Immortality, Inc.* by Robert Sheckley. Jagger plays a bounty hunter; it's his first screen acting role since PERFORMANCE in 1970. Panavision. [R]**V●D**

Free Money (1999-Canadian) **C-94m.** *½ D: Yves Simoneau. Marlon Brando, Charlie Sheen, Thomas Haden Church, Donald Sutherland, Mira Sorvino, Martin Sheen, David Arquette, J. P. Bergeron, Christin Watson, Holly Watson. How does a movie with a cast like this get rejected for theatrical release and go straight to cable? By being a frantically unfunny "comedy" that's shrill and desperate from the word go. A

gargantuan, bald-headed, bushy-mustached Brando has his biggest role in years as a psychotic, small-town prison warden whose two idiot sons-in-law try to rob a train. Often embarrassing to watch. **V D**

Freeway (1988) **C-91m.** ** D: Francis Delia. Darlanne Fluegel, James Russo, Billy Drago, Richard Belzer, Michael Callan, Joey Palese, Steve Franken, Kenneth Tobey, Clint Howard. A nurse whose husband was the victim of a freeway shooting becomes obsessed with finding the Bible-quoting murderer, who habitually phones a radio psychiatrist from his car while cruising L.A. looking for new victims. Based on a novel but prompted by similar real-life crimes in L.A., this film is surprisingly nonexploitive, but slow and unconvincing. [R]**V●D**

Freeway (1996) **C-102m.** *** D: Matthew Bright. Reese Witherspoon, Kiefer Sutherland, Brooke Shields, Wolfgang Bodison, Dan Hedaya, Amanda Plummer, Michael T. Weiss, Bokeem Woodbine, Brittany Murphy, Conchata Ferrell. Corrosive modern version of *Little Red Riding Hood* in which a teenage girl, on her way to grandma's, hitchhikes a ride with a psychotic child psychiatrist (Sutherland). Extremely violent satire is bolstered by Witherspoon's one-of-a-kind lethal Lolita performance and a smart screenplay by debut director Bright. Not for the faint of heart. Deliciously oddball score by Danny Elfman. Followed by a direct-to-video sequel. [R]**V●D**

Free Willy (1993) **C-112m.** **½ D: Simon Wincer. Jason James Richter, Lori Petty, Michael Madsen, Jayne Atkinson, Michael Ironside, Richard Riehle, August Schellenberg, Mykelti Williamson. Wayward 12-year-old, ordered to remove paint from aquarium walls, befriends and helps train an orca whale, eventually exploited by his seedy owner. Aggressively marketed sleeper hit is perfectly OK children's fare, with an appealing performance by young Richter. Michael Jackson sings "Will You Be There" over closing credits. Followed by two sequels, an animated TV series, and a DVD sequel. Panavision. [PG]**V●D**

Free Willy 2: The Adventure Home (1995) **C-98m.** **½ D: Dwight Little. Jason James Richter, August Schellenberg, Jayne Atkinson, Jon Tenney, Elizabeth Pena, Michael Madsen, Francis Capra, Mary Kate Schellhardt, Mykelti Williamson, M. Emmet Walsh. Richter has younger half-brother Capra forced upon him, finds young love with Schellhardt, and helps his orca friend Willy (and Willy's relatives) when an oil spill endangers the cetaceans. Overplotted children's film lacks the spark of the first, but is still good entertainment of its kind. The killer whales are almost all miniatures or computer graphics. Panavision. [PG] **V●D**

Free Willy 3: The Rescue (1997) **C-85m.** ** D: Sam Pillsbury. Jason James Richter,

August Schellenberg, Annie Corley, Vincent Berry, Patrick Kilpatrick, Tasha Simms. Richter, now a teenager, gets a summer job on a marine biology research boat and clashes with a group of poachers who want to make whale sushi out of Willy and his pregnant girlfriend Nikki (or at least their animatronic/computer-graphic likenesses). Shortest entry in the series is easy to take, but utterly predictable and formulaic. [PG]▼●❙

Free Woman, A (1972-German) **C-100m.** **½ D: Volker Schlöndorff. Margarethe von Trotta, Friedhelm Ptok, Martin Luttge, Walter Sedlmayer. Von Trotta divorces Ptok, has trouble adjusting to life apart from husband and son as she tries to liberate herself from her traditional functions. Truthful but boring drama.

Free Zone (2005-Israeli-Belgian-French-Spanish) **C-90m.** **½ D: Amos Gitai. Natalie Portman, Hana Laszlo, Hiam Abbass, Carmen Maura, Makram Khoury, Aki Avni, Uri Klauzner. Young American woman living in Jerusalem breaks up with her Israeli boyfriend, jumps into a cab, and asks the female driver to take her "anywhere." Eventually they head to Jordan's Free Zone, where the cabbie (Laszlo) is to meet a mysterious person called The American, her husband's Palestinian business associate. A labor of love for Israeli-born Portman, the film turns out to be a showcase for Laszlo, who won a Best Actress prize at the Cannes Film Festival. Dialogue heavy and sometimes over the top, but worth it for the performances. Opening sequence in which the camera remains on a close-up of the anguished Portman is riveting. ❙

French Cancan (1955-French) **C-93m.** *** D: Jean Renoir. Jean Gabin, Françoise Arnoul, Maria Felix, Edith Piaf. Not top-drawer Renoir, but still an impressive, enjoyable fiction about beginnings of the Moulin Rouge and impresario Gabin's revival of the cancan. Originally released in the U.S. in 1956; a brilliantly beautiful restored version, with approximately 10m. of additional footage, opened theatrically in 1985. Originally released in France as ONLY THE FRENCH CAN at 102m. ▼●❙

French Connection, The (1971) **C-104m.** **** D: William Friedkin. Gene Hackman, Fernando Rey, Roy Scheider, Tony LoBianco, Marcel Bozzuffi. Landmark urban action film detailing attempted international heroin smuggle into N.Y.C. and maverick detective who stops it. Five Oscars include Best Picture, Actor, Director, Screenplay (Ernest Tidyman) and Editing (Jerry Greenberg), the latter particularly for one of the most exciting car chases ever filmed. Followed by a sequel and, in 1986, a TV movie, POPEYE DOYLE. [R]▼●❙

French Connection II (1975) **C-119m.** **½ D: John Frankenheimer. Gene Hack-

man, Fernando Rey, Bernard Fresson, Jean-Pierre Castaldi, Charles Millot, Philippe Leotard, Ed Lauter, Cathleen Nesbitt. Gruff N.Y. cop Popeye Doyle goes to Marseilles, determined to nail narcotics king (Rey) who eluded him in America. Enjoyable opening and riveting chase finale are separated by long, agonizing drug addiction segment that weighs whole film down. [R]▼●❙

French Conspiracy, The (1972-French-Italian-German) **C-124m.** ** D: Yves Boisset. Jean-Louis Trintignant, Jean Seberg, Gian Maria Volonté, Roy Scheider, Michel Piccoli. Realistic but unexciting political drama centering around left-wing reporter Trintignant, pawn in a plot to assassinate Third World leader Volonté. [PG]

French Detective, The (1975-French) **C-93m.** *** D: Pierre Granier-Deferre. Lino Ventura, Patrick Dewaere, Victor Lanoux. Neat, entertaining police story with Ventura a tough, independent, middle-aged cop who, with exuberant young partner Dewaere, determinedly pursues a hood working for politician Lanoux. ▼

French Kiss (1995) **C-111m.** ** D: Lawrence Kasdan. Meg Ryan, Kevin Kline, Timothy Hutton, Jean Reno, François Cluzet, Victor Garrivier, Susan Anbeh. Charmless contrivance about a jilted woman who follows her fiancé to Paris and hooks up with a French rogue. Will these opposites ultimately attract one another? Duh! The stars' comic savvy can only carry this so far . . . though they're good, and the French scenery is nice. Soundtrack harmonica by the great Toots Thielemans. Panavision. [PG-13]▼●❙

French Lieutenant's Woman, The (1981-British) **C-123m.** ***½ D: Karel Reisz. Meryl Streep, Jeremy Irons, Leo McKern, Hilton McRae, Emily Morgan, Charlotte Mitchell, Lynsey Baxter. A scandalous romance between a gentleman and a tainted woman in Victorian England is contrasted with a contemporary affair between the actor and actress who are playing those roles in a movie. The juxtaposition is jarring at first, but becomes more engaging as the film progresses. Beautifully visualized, with rich period detail, superb performances; script by Harold Pinter, from John Fowles' novel. [R]▼●❙

French Line, The (1954) **C-102m.** ** D: Lloyd Bacon. Jane Russell, Gilbert Roland, Arthur Hunnicutt, Mary McCarty, Craig Stevens, Steven Geray, Joyce McKenzie, Paula Corday, Scott Elliot. Russell's bust in 3-D was the gimmick to sell this dull musical. All that's left is flat tale of wealthy Texas girl in Paris being romanced by Parisian. McCarty's wisecracking is a blessing. If you blink, you'll miss Kim Novak modeling a gown. 3-D. ▼

French Postcards (1979) **C-92m.** ** D: Willard Huyck. Blanche Baker, Miles Chapin, Debra Winger, Mandy Patinkin,

Valerie Quennessen, David Marshall Grant, Marie-France Pisier, Jean Rochefort. Kind of follow-up to AMERICAN GRAFFITI from that film's authors (Huyck and Gloria Katz), detailing romantic misadventures of group of college students spending junior year abroad. Pleasant but forgettable comedy. [PG] ▼▶

French Provincial (1974-French) **C-91m.** ** D: André Téchiné. Jeanne Moreau, Michel Auclair, Marie-France Pisier, Claude Mann, Orane Demazis. Moreau, as a laundry woman who marries into a bourgeois family, shines in this otherwise flaky, superficially symbolic saga of economic change in France from the 1930s through 1970s.

French Quarter (1978) **C-101m.** *** D: Dennis Kane. Bruce Davison, Lindsay Bloom, Virginia Mayo, Alisha Fontaine, Lance LeGault, Laura Misch Owens, Ann Michelle, Becky Allen, Barry Sullivan, William Sims. Neglected drive-in treat is a genuine curiosity; tongue-in-cheek melodrama mixes PRETTY BABY plot with FRENCH LIEUTENANT'S WOMAN structure (but predates both!). Tale of young Fontaine, growing up in New Orleans as Storyville prostitute at the turn of the century, is paralleled by present-day story with same cast, linked by voodoo plot device. Ends bizarrely with narrator reminding us to "hang up your speakers and drive home safely." And Dick Hyman did the music! [R] ▼▶

French, They Are a Funny Race, The (1955-French) **83m.** ** D: Preston Sturges. Jack Buchanan, Noel-Noel, Martine Carol, Genevieve Brunet. Director-writer Sturges' last film is a misfire, with Buchanan as veddy-British major whose marriage to Frenchwoman sparks continuing nationalistic arguments. Original title: LES CARNETS DU MAJOR THOMPSON at 105m.

French Twist (1995-French) **C-100m.** **½ D: Josiane Balasko. Victoria Abril, Josiane Balasko, Alain Chabat, Ticky Holgado, Miguel Bosé, Catherine Hiegel, Catherine Samie. Bouncy comedy written and directed by French star Balasko (TOO BEAUTIFUL FOR YOU), who plays a gay van driver/drifter who accidentally meets a jolly housewife (Abril) and her philandering husband (Chabat). What follows is a *very* French twist on the old love triangle theme. Enjoyable farce is liberal to a fault but loses credibility as it unfolds. Still, Abril shines, as usual, in a terrific role. Original title: GAZON MAUDIT. ▼▶

French Way Is, The SEE: **Love at the Top**

Frenzy (1944) SEE: **Torment**

Frenzy (1972-British) **C-116m.** ***½ D: Alfred Hitchcock. Jon Finch, Barry Foster, Barbara Leigh-Hunt, Anna Massey, Alec McCowen, Vivien Merchant, Billie Whitelaw, Clive Swift, Jean Marsh. Hitchcock in high gear, telling story of suave London strangler (Foster) and innocent man

(Finch) suspected of murder spree. All classic Hitchcock elements are here, including delicious black humor, several astounding camera shots. Script by Anthony Shaffer. [R] ▼▶

Frequency (2000) **C-117m.** ** D: Gregory Hoblit. Dennis Quaid, Jim Caviezel, Andre Braugher, Elizabeth Mitchell, Noah Emmerich, Shawn Doyle, Jordan Bridges, Michael Cera. N.Y.C. cop whose fireman father died when he was six digs out his dad's old ham radio set, and by freakish fluke, finds he can communicate with his old man! Soon the father realizes he can help his son prevent crimes that are about to happen—and the son begins to wonder if he can keep his father from perishing in a flaming building. Entertaining at first but never quite convincing (like Quaid's unfortunate New York accent), this convoluted *Twilight Zone*–ish story misses the mark. Super 35. [PG-13] ▼▶

Fresh (1994-U.S.-French) **C-112m.** *** D: Boaz Yakin. Sean Nelson, Giancarlo Esposito, Samuel L. Jackson, N'Bushe Wright, Ron Brice, Jean LaMarre, Luis Lantigua. Disturbing, controversial chronicle of 12-year-old black youth who divides his time between school and his duties as a busy heroin courier. When he witnesses a playground killing, young Fresh (unforgettably played by Sean Nelson) must use his street smarts to fight for survival. An unflinching look at the urban narcotics nightmare; some may be disturbed by the ambivalent view of the bright young protagonist as drug dealer, victim, survivor, and hero. Impressive debut for writer-director Yakin. Music by Stewart Copeland. [R] ▼▶

Fresh Horses (1988) **C-105m.** **½ D: David Anspaugh. Molly Ringwald, Andrew McCarthy, Patti D'Arbanville, Molly Hagan, Viggo Mortensen, Doug Hutchison, Ben Stiller, Leon Russom. Collegian McCarthy, engaged to a wealthy dullard, falls for Ringwald's underage no-no, a semi-shantytramp who lives across the river from his Cincinnati campus. Slightly better than expected, thanks to fine Midwest location work from the director of HOOSIERS. Ringwald isn't totally convincing in the kind of role Gloria Grahame invented. [PG-13] ▼▶

Freshman, The (1925) **76m.** **** D: Sam Taylor, Fred Newmeyer. Harold Lloyd, Jobyna Ralston, Brooks Benedict, James Anderson, Hazel Keener. One of Lloyd's best-remembered films casts him as collegiate patsy who'll do anything to be popular on campus, unaware that everyone is making fun of him. Football game finale is one of several comic highlights. A real audience-rouser. ▼▶

Freshman, The (1990) **C-102m.** *** D: Andrew Bergman. Marlon Brando, Matthew Broderick, Maximilian Schell, Bruno Kirby, Penelope Ann Miller, Frank Whaley, Paul Benedict, B. D. Wong, Bert Parks. New

York University film student Broderick falls in with loony mob family headed by Brando in this infectious, off-center comedy. Not an outstanding film per se, but strong cast and New York flavor, plus Bergman's original and amusing screenplay, put it over. Best of all: Marlon's knockout performance (remind you of anyone?), and his rapport with Matthew. [PG]▼●◗

Freud (1962) **120m.** ***½ D: John Huston. Montgomery Clift, Susannah York, Larry Parks, David McCallum, Susan Kohner, Eileen Herlie. Intelligent, unglamorous account of Sigmund Freud as young doctor, focusing on his early psychiatric theories and treatments and his struggle for their acceptance among Viennese medical colleagues. Fascinating dream sequence. Originally released at 139m. Also known as FREUD: THE SECRET PASSION.

Frida (1984-Mexican) **C-108m.** *** D: Paul Leduc. Ofelia Medina, Juan Jose Gurrola, Max Kerlow, Salvador Sanchez, Claudio Brook. Solid biography effectively captures the spirit of an extraordinary woman: Frida Kahlo (Medina), Mexican artist and radical who dealt with various physical crises (resulting from polio and a paralyzing accident). Also central to her story are her relationships with Diego Rivera and Leon Trotsky. Visually captivating, with superior cinematography by Angel Goded and an unstructured narrative that not so much traces the incidents in its subject's life but paints a portrait of her.▼◗

Frida (2002) **C-123m.** **½ D: Julie Taymor. Salma Hayek, Alfred Molina, Geoffrey Rush, Ashley Judd, Antonio Banderas, Edward Norton, Valeria Golino, Mia Maestro, Roger Rees, Diego Luna, Patricia Reyes Spindola, Margarita Sanz, Saffron Burrows, Didi Conn. Ambitious biography of Mexican artist and activist Frida Kahlo, who fought both physical and emotional challenges throughout her life, while her work remained in the shadow of her husband, Diego Rivera. Hayek, who shepherded this project to fruition, does a good job; Molina is superb as the robust, womanizing Rivera, and Rush is equally good in a small part as Leon Trotsky. Despite the efforts of four credited writers, rich source material, and Taymor's visual embellishments, the movie never really soars . . . but it certainly covers a lot of ground. Oscar winner for Best Makeup and Score (Elliot Goldenthal). [R]▼◗

Friday (1995) **C-89m.** *½ D: F. Gary Gray. Ice Cube, Chris Tucker, Nia Long, Tiny "Zeus" Lister, Jr., John Witherspoon, Anna Maria Horsford, Regina King, Paul Jai Parker, Bernie Mac, Angela Means, Faizon Love, LaWanda Page. Rap star/actor Ice Cube coproduced, cowrote, and stars in this comedy, revealing the fun side he never showed in films like BOYZ N THE HOOD

and TRESPASS. Talented cast can't rescue this practically plotless film about youth trying to survive life in L.A.'s South Central 'hood. Followed by two sequels and an animated TV series. [R]▼●◗

Friday After Next (2002) **C-82m.** *½ D: Marcus Raboy. Ice Cube, Mike Epps, John Witherspoon, Don "D.C." Curry, Anna Maria Horsford, Clifton Powell, BeBe Drake, Terry Crews. Slipshod comedy from the 'hood follows FRIDAY and NEXT FRIDAY. After a scummy Santa Claus robs Cube and Epps, they're forced to get jobs as security guards in order to pay for a Christmas party. That's about it for story; the rest of the film is filled with notably foul language (including overuse of the "n" word), and enough stereotypes to set back civil rights a hundred years. Cube scripted and coproduced. [R]▼◗

Friday Foster (1975) **C-90m.** ** D: Arthur Marks. Pam Grier, Yaphet Kotto, Godfrey Cambridge, Thalmus Rasulala, Eartha Kitt, Jim Backus, Scatman Crothers, Ted Lange, Carl Weathers. Black bubble-gum nonsense based on comic strip about fashion photographer who gets involved in mystery and intrigue; here she tries to foil assassination/conspiracy plot against black politicians. [R]▼◗

Friday Night (2002-French) **C-90m.** *** D: Claire Denis. Valérie Lemercier, Vincent Lindon, Hélène de Saint-Père, Grégoire Colin. Seductive, dazzlingly visual account of a night in the life of a young Parisian (Lemercier) who is preparing to move out of her apartment and has an unusual encounter with a stranger. Using very little dialogue, Denis deftly employs the camera to tell her story, recording the minutest details of everyday life and creating a sense of intimacy that is purely cinematic. ▼◗

Friday Night Lights (2004) **C-117m.** *** D: Peter Berg. Billy Bob Thornton, Derek Luke, Jay Hernandez, Lucas Black, Garrett Hedlund, Tim McGraw, Connie Britton, Lee Thompson Young, Lee Jackson, Grover Coulson. Tough-minded sports movie about a real-life high school football team from Odessa, Texas, and the coach who drove them during their 1988 season. Expected clichés are surmounted by a hard look at small-town Church of Football mentality, exciting action, and a cast that scores (led by Thornton and country singer McGraw, impressive as a onetime player whose son is now on the team). Also nice to see Thornton reunited with his young SLING BLADE costar Black. Based on H. G. (Buzz) Bissinger's highly regarded book. Later a TV series. Super 35. [PG-13]▼◗

Friday the 13th (1980) **C-95m.** *½ D: Sean S. Cunningham. Betsy Palmer, Adrienne King, Harry Crosby, Laurie Bartram, Mark Nelson, Jeannine Taylor, Kevin Bacon. Palmer, who figures in an admittedly bravura finale, slaughters teens holed up in woodsy summer camp. Young folks unexpectedly made this gory, cardboard thriller a box-office smash—one more clue to why SAT scores continue to decline. Rates higher than BOMB simply because it's slightly better than part 2. Unrated DVD adds a few seconds of carnage. Followed by a seemingly never-ending series of sequels and a TV series. Remade in 2009. [R] ▼●)

Friday the 13th (2009) **C-97m.** *½ D: Marcus Nispel. Jared Padalecki, Danielle Panabaker, Amanda Righetti, Travis Van Winkle, Aaron Yoo, Derek Mears, Jonathan Sadowski. The 12th FRIDAY isn't a sequel but something like a remake of the 1st and 3rd. As before, some annoying teenagers encounter the silent, murderous Jason, who chops, stabs, and bludgeons his way through the cast, though without as much gore as in previous entries. Plodding, dull, and repetitive, this is only occasionally creepy and never scary. Yes, there's a setup for a sequel, if anyone cares. Panavision. [R]█

Friday the 13th, Part 2 (1981) **C-87m.** BOMB D: Steve Miner. Betsy Palmer, Amy Steel, John Furey, Adrienne King, Kirsten Baker, Stu Charno, Warrington Gillette. More nubile campers, more bloody executions. If you loved Part 1 . . . [R] ▼●)

Friday the 13th Part III (1982) **C-96m.** ** D: Steve Miner. Dana Kimmell, Paul Kratka, Tracie Savage, Jeffrey Rogers, Catherine Parks, Larry Zerner. Strictly amateur night in terms of acting and writing, but this entry deemphasizes explicit gore in favor of shocks, and delivers a few—especially in 3-D and widescreen 3-D. [R] ▼●)

Friday the 13th—The Final Chapter (1984) **C-91m.** BOMB D: Joseph Zito. Crispin Glover, Kimberly Beck, Barbara Howard, E. Erich Anderson, Corey Feldman, Ted White, Bruce Mahler, Lawrence Monoson. Why bother with a new script? Jason finally gets his—except that (title notwithstanding) the door is left open for yet another sequel! [R] ▼●)

Friday the 13th—A New Beginning (1985) **C-102m.** BOMB D: Danny Steinmann. John Shepard, Melanie Kinnaman, Shavar Ross, Richard Young, Carol Lacatell, Corey Parker, Corey Feldman. A clever title (after . . . THE FINAL CHAPTER) for more gore galore, as gruesome and disgusting as ever. Fifth in the series. [R] ▼●)

Friday the 13th, Part VI: Jason Lives (1986) **C-87m.** BOMB D: Tom McLoughlin. Thom Mathews, Jennifer Cooke, David Kagan, Renee Jones, Kerry Noonan, C. J. Graham, Tony Goldwyn, Ron Palillo. Jason's summer camp has enjoyed years of tranquility after changing its name, but watch out! If you really think there's something to gain from watching Jason rise from the grave again, good luck! The pits. [R] ▼●)

Friday the 13th Part VII—The New

Blood (1988) **C-88m.** *½ D: John Carl Buechler. Lar Park Lincoln, Terry Kiser, Susan Blu, Kevin Blair, Susan Jennifer Sullivan, Elizabeth Kaitan. Makeup expert Buechler fails to inject much life into this endless series. Pretty, blonde Lincoln foolishly travels to Crystal Lake (with her mom and her shrink) where her talent for telekinesis brings the monstrous Jason back up from his watery grave. [R] ▼●)

Friday the 13th Part VIII: Jason Takes Manhattan (1989) **C-100m.** ** D: Rob Hedden. Jensen Daggett, Kane Hodder, Peter Mark Richman, Scott Reeves, Barbara Bingham, V. C. Dupree. The best film in the "Friday" series, imaginatively directed and written by Hedden, is still just a slasher film, though less gruesome than most. Despite the title, most of the film takes place on a cruise ship. Too long and not really for fans of the series. Followed by JASON GOES TO HELL: THE FINAL FRIDAY. [R] ▼●)

Fried Green Tomatoes (1991) **C-130m.** *** D: Jon Avnet. Kathy Bates, Jessica Tandy, Mary Stuart Masterson, Mary-Louise Parker, Cicely Tyson, Chris O'Donnell, Stan Shaw, Gailard Sartain, Tim Scott, Gary Basaraba, Lois Smith, Grace Zabriskie. Enjoyable story-within-a-story film, in which repressed Southern wife Bates meets elderly Tandy at a nursing home and becomes captivated by her talespinning about two feisty female friends and their escapades in the 1920s and '30s. First-rate adaptation of Fannie Flagg's novel *Fried Green Tomatoes at the Whistle Stop Cafe* with just one problem: a couple of endings too many. Impressive feature directorial debut for producer Avnet. Flagg has an amusing cameo. Alternate unrated version runs 137m. [PG-13] ▼●)

Friendly Persuasion (1956) **C-140m.** **** D: William Wyler. Gary Cooper, Dorothy McGuire, Marjorie Main, Anthony Perkins, Richard Eyer, Robert Middleton, (Peter) Mark Richman, Walter Catlett, William Schallert. Charming account (from Jessamyn West novel) of Quaker family struggling to maintain its identity amid confusion and heartbreak of Civil War. Warm, winning performances in this beautifully made film. Music by Dimitri Tiomkin. Though no screenplay credit appears, film was written by blacklisted Michael Wilson; he received posthumous credit in 1996. Remade for TV in 1975 with Richard Kiley and Shirley Knight. ▼●)

Friends (1971-British) **C-102m.** BOMB D: Lewis Gilbert. Sean Bury, Anicee Alvina, Pascale Roberts, Sady Rebbot, Ronald Lewis. Yucky early-teen romance about French boy and girl who run off to the seashore, set up housekeeping, and have a baby . . . then Mommy and Daddy show up to take them home. Popular in its day, primarily due to Elton John song score. Buy the album instead. Sequel (!): PAUL AND MICHELLE. [R]▼

Friends & Lovers (1999) **C-104m.** *½ D: George Haas. Stephen Baldwin, Danny Nucci, George Newbern, Claudia Schiffer, Alison Eastwood, Suzanne Cryer, David Rasche, Neill Barry, Leon, Robert Downey, Jr., Ann Magnuson. Group of friends gather for a Christmas ski holiday that quickly finds them coupled in unlikely romantic pairings. Embarrassing on every level, a good group of actors is wasted in this would-be farce that sets its sights low and misses the mark anyway. In her first major film role, Schiffer proves that as an actress she's a mighty fine model.▼❶

Friends of Eddie Coyle, The (1973) **C-102m.** ***½ D: Peter Yates. Robert Mitchum, Peter Boyle, Richard Jordan, Steven Keats, Alex Rocco, Mitchell Ryan. Ultrarealistic depiction of criminals and police, as hardened con labors to supply guns and make deal with cops. Bleak nightmare picture of underworld enhanced by numerous Boston locations, flawless performances. Only liabilities: film's offbeat low-key narrative approach and finale. Adapted by Paul Monash from George V. Higgins' novel. [R]❶

Friends With Money (2006) **C-88m.** *** D: Nicole Holofcener. Catherine Keener, Jennifer Aniston, Frances McDormand, Joan Cusack, Simon McBurney, Jason Isaacs, Scott Caan, Ty Burrell, Bob Stephenson, Greg Germann. Wry slice of life examining the fault lines in the friendship of four women, three of whom are married and prosperous, one of whom (Aniston) is single, unhappy, and resentful. Good performances and sharp observations about marriage, money, and middle age make this a winner. Super 35. [R]❶

Fright (1971-British) **C-87m.** ** D: Peter Collinson. Susan George, Honor Blackman, Ian Bannen, John Gregson, George Cole, Dennis Waterman. Young babysitter (George) spends terror-filled evening at country house, menaced by mental hospital escapee. Contrived, mechanical direction and so-so script. [PG]▼❶

Frightened City, The (1961-British) **97m.** **½ D: John Lemont. Herbert Lom, John Gregson, Sean Connery, Alfred Marks, Yvonne Romain. Interesting inside look at a London racketeer amalgamating various city gangs for master plan syndicate. ▼❶

Frighteners, The (1996-New Zealand-U.S.) **C-109m.** **½ D: Peter Jackson. Michael J. Fox, Trini Alvarado, Peter Dobson, John Astin, Jeffrey Combs, Dee Wallace Stone, Jake Busey, Chi McBride, Jim Fyfe, Troy Evans, Julianna McCarthy, R. Lee Ermey. Overlong, but original blend of paranormal, horror, and black-comedy ingredients. Fox plays a psychic investigator/exterminator

on the trail of an otherworldly serial killer. Zigzags from grisly humor to slasher-movie horror. Combs (of RE-ANIMATOR fame) has a scenery-chewing role as a wacked-out FBI agent on the case. Definitely not for all tastes. Filmed in New Zealand, home of director/cowriter Jackson. Director's cut runs 123m. Super 35. [R] ▼❶

Fright Night (1985) **C-105m.** *** D: Tom Holland. Chris Sarandon, William Ragsdale, Amanda Bearse, Roddy McDowall, Stephen Geoffreys, Jonathan Stark. Teenage boy enlists the aid of TV horror-movie host (and erstwhile actor) to kill suave, cunning vampire who's moved in next door. Entertaining, old-fashioned horror outing energized by Richard Edlund's spectacular special effects and highlighted by two wonderful performances, by McDowall and Sarandon. Written by Holland. Followed by a sequel. Panavision. [R]▼❶

Fright Night Part 2 (1989) **C-104m.** ** D: Tommy Lee Wallace. Roddy McDowall, William Ragsdale, Traci Lin, Julie Carmen, Jonathan Gries, Russell Clark, Brian Thompson, Merritt Butrick, Ernie Sabella. Sister of the vampire who met a grisly end in FRIGHT NIGHT seeks revenge on the duo who destroyed him. More-of-the-same sequel is definitely a comedown from the earlier film, though well produced. Panavision. [R]▼❶

Fringe Dwellers, The (1986-Australian) **C-98m.** **½ D: Bruce Beresford. Kristina Nehm, Justine Saunders, Bob Maza, Kylie Belling, Denis Walker, Ernie Dingo. Ambitious young aborigine woman convinces her family to move out of their shantytown and into a prosperous, mostly white middle-class neighborhood in present-day Australia; the expected readjustment woes follow. Sincere, very well-acted drama (especially by Nehm) is undercut by sentimental, dramatically dishonest conclusion. Overall, worth a look. [PG]▼❶

Frisco Kid (1935) **77m.** ** D: Lloyd Bacon. James Cagney, Margaret Lindsay, Ricardo Cortez, Lili Damita, Fred Kohler, George E. Stone, Donald Woods. Routine drama of Barbary Coast with Cagney fighting his way to the top, almost dethroned by local gangs but saved by blueblood Lindsay.

Frisco Kid, The (1979) **C-122m.** **½ D: Robert Aldrich. Gene Wilder, Harrison Ford, Ramon Bieri, Val Bisoglio, George Ralph DiCenzo, Leo Fuchs, Penny Peyser. Offbeat story of Polish rabbi crossing U.S. in 1850 and developing friendship with young bank robber. Wilder's performance and some charming vignettes make up for many other shortcomings. [PG]▼❶

Fritz The Cat (1972) **C-78m.** *** D: Ralph Bakshi. X-rated animated feature somewhat based on Robert Crumb's underground comics character. Flawed but engaging, irreverent look at radical-hip lifestyles of the 1960s, geared for people who experienced that era. Imaginatively conceived cartoon. Sequel: THE NINE LIVES OF FRITZ THE CAT. [X]▼❶

Friz Freleng's Looney Looney Looney Bugs Bunny Movie SEE: **Looney Looney Looney Bugs Bunny Movie**

Frogmen, The (1951) **96m.** *** D: Lloyd Bacon. Richard Widmark, Dana Andrews, Gary Merrill, Jeffrey Hunter, Robert Wagner, Jack Warden. Intriguing look at underwater demolition squads in action in the Pacific during WW2.❶

Frogs (1972) **C-91m.** **½ D: George McCowan. Ray Milland, Sam Elliott, Joan Van Ark, Adam Roarke, Judy Pace. Patriarchal Milland has been destroying bayou wildlife and now all the swamp critters are out to destroy his whole family. Dumb but enjoyable thriller. [PG]▼❶

Frogs for Snakes (1999) **C-98m.** ** D: Amos Poe. Barbara Hershey, Robbie Coltrane, Harry Hamlin, Ian Hart, John Leguizamo, Lisa Marie, Debi Mazar, Ron Perlman, Clarence Williams III. Another Tarantino wannabe, this black comedy has a clever conceit: Struggling N.Y. actors who'll do anything for a good part make money on the side as hit men for a Russian racketeer (Coltrane). Story goes nowhere, despite a good cast. [R]▼

From a Whisper to a Scream SEE: **Offspring, The**

From Beyond (1986) **C-85m.** **½ D: Stuart Gordon. Jeffrey Combs, Barbara Crampton, Ted Sorel, Ken Foree, Carolyn Purdy-Gordon, Bunny Summers, Bruce McGuire. The RE-ANIMATOR team returns to H. P. Lovecraft territory for this similarly demented film based on a scientist's search for a sixth sense . . . which, in time, causes his associates to go berserk. Takes its time getting revved up, but then cuts loose in outrageous fashion. As before, this is not for the squeamish, but if you liked RE-ANIMATOR . . . [R]▼❶❶

From Beyond the Grave (1973-British) **C-97m.** *** D: Kevin Connor. Peter Cushing, Margaret Leighton, Ian Bannen, Donald Pleasence, David Warner, Diana Dors, Angela Pleasence, Nyree Dawn Porter, Lesley-Anne Down. Neat multi-storied horror pic. Visitors to Cushing's antique shop, Temptations Ltd., meet terrible fates. Leighton excels as wacky clairvoyant. Retitled: CREATURES. [PG]▼❶❶

From Dusk Till Dawn (1996) **C-108m.** ** D: Robert Rodriguez. Harvey Keitel, George Clooney, Quentin Tarantino, Juliette Lewis, Salma Hayek, Cheech Marin, Tom Savini, Fred Williamson, John Saxon, Kelly Preston, Marc Lawrence, Michael Parks, Ernest Lui, Danny Trejo, Tito Larriva. Two out-of-control criminal brothers mow their way through Texas, heading for a rendez-

vous in Mexico, and take a family (and their RV) hostage. But the rendezvous location turns out to be a hellish biker bar inhabited by vampires! Indefensible trash certainly works on a visceral level; how much you can take will depend on your G.Q. (grossout quotient). Rodriguez and screenwriter/actor Tarantino seem to be having fun, especially in their casting choices, but this is just a celebration of excess. In fact, it might be retitled NATURAL BORN VAMPIRES. Followed by two direct-to-video sequels. [R]▼❶❶

From Hell (2001) **C-122m.** *** D: The Hughes Brothers. Johnny Depp, Heather Graham, Ian Holm, Robbie Coltrane, Ian Richardson, Jason Flemyng, Katrin Cartlidge, Susan Lynch. Eccentric London police inspector Depp is determined to capture Jack the Ripper despite a growing sense that there is a cover-up at hand to protect some very important people. Gothic thriller treads familiar ground (for Ripperphiles) but is colorful and entertaining; an impressive showing for the Hughes Brothers. Only Graham seems out of place as a weathered Whitechapel prostitute. Based on a graphic novel by Alan Moore and Eddie Campbell. Panavision. [R]▼❶

From Hell to Victory (1979-French-Italian-Spanish) **C-100m.** ** D: Hank Milestone (Umberto Lenzi). George Peppard, George Hamilton, Horst Buchholz, Capucine, Sam Wanamaker, Jean-Pierre Cassel, Anny Duperey. Friends of various nationalities are torn apart by the coming of WW2. Undistinguished, superficial actioner. Technovision. [PG]▼❶

From Here to Eternity (1953) **118m.** **** D: Fred Zinnemann. Burt Lancaster, Montgomery Clift, Deborah Kerr, Donna Reed, Frank Sinatra, Philip Ober, Ernest Borgnine, Mickey Shaughnessy, Jack Warden, Claude Akins, George Reeves. Toned-down but still powerful adaptation of James Jones' novel of Army life in Hawaii just before Pearl Harbor. Depiction of Japanese sneak attack combines unforgettable action scenes with actual combat footage. Brilliantly acted by entire cast, including Sinatra in his "comeback" role as the ill-fated soldier Maggio. Eight Oscars include Best Picture, Director, Screenplay (Daniel Taradash), Cinematography (Burnett Guffey), and Supporting Actors Sinatra and Reed. Remade in 1979 as a TV mini-series, which in turn spun off a brief series.▼❶❶

From Justin to Kelly (2003) **C-81m.** *½ D: Rob Iscove. Kelly Clarkson, Justin Guarini, Katherine Bailess, Anika Noni Rose, Greg Siff, Brian Dietzen, Jason Yribar. Guzzle sunscreen instead of sitting through this insipid musical vehicle for TV's first *American Idol* stars, which finds them trying to make a love connection during Miami spring break. No one was expecting Shakespeare, but there's less heft here than in an *Archie* comic book. Justin and Kelly belt and gyrate through a series of forgettable numbers but generate no chemistry, even in a chaste Frankie-Annette sort of way. [PG] ▼▶

From Mao to Mozart: Isaac Stern in China (1980) **C-84m.** ***½ D: Murray Lerner. Isaac Stern, David Golub, Tan Shuzhen. Moving documentary about violinist Stern's '79 tour of China. Most memorably, he tutors talented Chinese students, encouraging them to *feel* their playing. Shuzhen, deputy director of the Shanghai Conservatory of Music, describes his incarceration during the Cultural Revolution. Deservedly won Best Documentary Academy Award. [G] ▼

From Mexico With Love (2009) **C-97m.** ** D: Jimmy Nickerson. Kuno Becker, Steven Bauer, Stephen Lang, Alex Nesic, Danay Garcia, Bruce McGill. Thoroughly predictable indie drama about a Mexican farm laborer (Becker) who trains as a boxer for a grudge match against the cocky son of a surly Texas landowner. Few boxing-movie clichés are left unrecycled before the final round, but three well-cast supporting players keep things mildly interesting: McGill as a grumpy trainer, Bauer as a smooth-talking wheeler-dealer, Lang as a farmer who exploits undocumented workers. [PG-13] ▶

From Nashville With Music (1969) **C-87m.** *½ D: Eddie Crandall. Marilyn Maxwell, Leo G. Carroll, (Pedro) Gonzalez-Gonzalez, Marty Robbins, Merle Haggard, Buck Owens. Some good C&W music, but one is better off buying one of the performers' albums instead of suffering through this story of a N.Y.C. couple who go to the Grand Ole Opry by mistake.

From Noon Till Three (1976) **C-99m.** **½ D: Frank D. Gilroy. Charles Bronson, Jill Ireland, Douglas Fowley, Stan Haze, Damon Douglas, Anne Ramsey. Likably offbeat story (adapted by Gilroy from his own novel) about a two-bit robber who enjoys a brief tryst with a woman who—after he is thought dead—fictionalizes their romance and turns him into a legendary hero. A kind of shaggy dog joke, which while pleasant, doesn't quite work. A nice change of pace for Bronson, though. [PG] ▼

From Paris With Love (2010-French) **C-92m.** **½ D: Pierre Morel. John Travolta, Jonathan Rhys Meyers, Kasia Smutniak, Richard Durden. Utterly preposterous action-adventure can be savored as an over-the-top guilty pleasure, thanks to TAKEN director Morel's pedal-to-metal pacing and Travolta's exuberantly gonzo-macho portrayal of a trigger-happy secret agent who teams with a straitlaced U.S. embassy functionary (Rhys Meyers) to exterminate Chinese drug dealers and Pakistani terrorists in Paris. Genuinely surprising plot twist at the two-thirds mark leads to an unexpectedly potent finale. Story by Luc Besson. Super 35. [R] ▶

From Prada to Nada (2011) **C-107m.** **½ D: Angel Gracia. Camilla Belle, Alexa Vega, Wilmer Valderrama, Nicholas D'Agosto, April Bowlby, Kuno Becker, Adriana Barraza. Lightweight comedy, very loosely based on Jane Austen's *Sense and Sensibility*, about two Mexican-American sisters—spoiled and sexy Vega, studious and bespectacled Belle—who must relocate from Beverly Hills to East L.A. after their free-spending father unexpectedly dies and leaves them penniless. Downward mobility forces both young women to reset their priorities and rediscover their roots, with sporadically amusing results. [PG-13] ▶

From Russia With Love (1963-British) **C-118m.** ***½ D: Terence Young. Sean Connery, Daniela Bianchi, Lotte Lenya, Pedro Armendariz, Robert Shaw, Bernard Lee, Lois Maxwell. Second James Bond film is one of the best; plenty of suspense and action, and one of the longest, most exciting fight scenes ever staged. Lenya makes a very sinister spy. ▼▶

From the Earth to the Moon (1958) **C-100m.** **½ D: Byron Haskin. Joseph Cotten, George Sanders, Debra Paget, Don Dubbins, Patric Knowles, Melville Cooper, Carl Esmond, Henry Daniell. Jules Verne's fiction doesn't float well in contrived sci-fi of early rocket flight to the moon. Veteran cast looks most uncomfortable. ▼▶

From the Hip (1987) **C-112m.** BOMB D: Bob Clark. Judd Nelson, Elizabeth Perkins, John Hurt, Darren McGavin, Ray Walston, Dan Monahan, David Alan Grier, Nancy Marchand, Allan Arbus, Edward Winter. Once again, Nelson plays a character only a mother could love: a lawyer who's made a name for himself by winning a hopeless case through outrageous courtroom tactics. Now he's given another challenge: defending Hurt, who's accused of murder. Hurt's flamboyant performance can't save this mongrel of a movie. J-D-C Scope. [PG] ▼▶

From the Life of the Marionettes (1980-German) **C/B&W-104m.** ***½ D: Ingmar Bergman. Robert Atzorn, Christine Buchegger, Martin Benrath, Rita Russek, Lola Muethel, Walter Schmidinger, Heinz Bennent. Powerful, provocative drama about a respectable, successful businessman (Atzorn), who ravishes and strangles a prostitute. He has also been obsessed with killing his wife (Buchegger), with whom he constantly quarrels. Not coincidentally, both were minor characters in SCENES FROM A MARRIAGE. [R] ▼▶

From the Mixed-Up Files of Mrs. Basil E. Frankweiler (1973) **C-105m.** **½ D: Fielder Cook. Ingrid Bergman, Sally Prager, Johnny Doran, George Rose, Georgann Johnson, Richard Mulligan, Madeline Kahn.

Fanciful tale of New Jersey kids Prager and Doran who hide out in N.Y.C.'s Metropolitan Museum, creating a dream world and befriending recluse Bergman, seen too briefly. Best for children. Blanche Hanalis adapted E. L. Konigsburg's novel. Reissued as THE HIDEAWAYS. Remade in 1995 for TV with Lauren Bacall. [G]▼▶

From the Terrace (1960) C-144m. *** D: Mark Robson. Paul Newman, Joanne Woodward, Myrna Loy, Ina Balin, Leon Ames, Elizabeth Allen, Barbara Eden, George Grizzard, Patrick O'Neal, Felix Aylmer, Mae Marsh. John O'Hara's ironic chronicle of young war veteran's rise to financial and social success is superficial film. Woodward is chic and Newman wooden; Loy is superb as drunken mother, Ames fine as bitter dad. CinemaScope.▼●▶

Front, The (1976) C-94m. **** D: Martin Ritt. Woody Allen, Zero Mostel, Herschel Bernardi, Michael Murphy, Andrea Marcovicci, Remak Ramsay, Joshua Shelley, Lloyd Gough, Danny Aiello, Charles Kimbrough, Josef Sommer. Bull's-eye comedy with serious theme. Allen is a schnook enlisted by blacklisted writers to put his name on their scripts during 1950s witchhunt era, leading to various complications. Allen's casting is perfect, and Mostel is standout as "tainted" comic fighting for survival. Original script by blacklisted Walter Bernstein; Ritt, Mostel, Bernardi, Shelley, and Gough were also blacklisted in real life. [PG]▼●▶

Frontier Hellcat (1966-German) C-98m. **½ D: Alfred Vohrer. Stewart Granger, Elke Sommer, Pierre Brice, Gotz George. Another Karl May *Winnetou* story, which captures flavor of Old West in adventure of pioneers passing through Rockies. Ultrascope.

Front Page, The (1931) 103m. ***½ D: Lewis Milestone. Adolphe Menjou, Pat O'Brien, Mary Brian, Edward Everett Horton, Walter Catlett, Mae Clarke, George E. Stone. First filming of Hecht-MacArthur play is forceful, funny, and flamboyantly directed, with Menjou and O'Brien a good pair as battling editor and reporter in Chicago. Stands up quite well alongside remake HIS GIRL FRIDAY. Remade again in 1974 and as SWITCHING CHANNELS (1988).▼▶

Front Page, The (1974) C-105m. *** D: Billy Wilder. Jack Lemmon, Walter Matthau, Carol Burnett, Susan Sarandon, Vincent Gardenia, David Wayne, Allen Garfield, Austin Pendleton, Charles Durning, Harold Gould, Herb Edelman, Dick O'Neill, Jon Korkes, Martin Gabel. Third filming of the Hecht-MacArthur play about wild and woolly Chicago newspapermen in the 1920s has hardly anything new to offer (except four-letter words) but remains an enjoyable vehicle for this fine cast. Only Burnett misses the boat as pathetic hooker

Molly Malloy. Remade again (!) in 1988 as SWITCHING CHANNELS. Panavision. [PG]▼●▶

Front Page Woman (1935) 82m. **½ D: Michael Curtiz. Bette Davis, George Brent, Winifred Shaw, Roscoe Karns, Joseph Crehan. Breezy yarn of rival reporters Davis and Brent trying to outdo each other covering unusual murder and trial. Prime ingenue Davis fare.

Frost/Nixon (2008) C-122m. **** D: Ron Howard. Frank Langella, Michael Sheen, Kevin Bacon, Rebecca Hall, Toby Jones, Matthew Macfadyen, Oliver Platt, Sam Rockwell, Patty McCormack, Joe Spano, Clint Howard, Andy Milder. Ebullient TV host David Frost, in a career lull, persuades disgraced former President Richard Nixon to agree to a series of television interviews. His backup team hopes to elicit a public apology for his misdeeds, while Nixon's loyalists intend to restore his tarnished reputation. Incredibly gripping drama conceived by Peter Morgan, who wrote THE QUEEN, and so effectively reinvented as a movie—by Morgan and director Howard—that you'd never know it originated on the stage. Langella and Sheen are superb and utterly believable, even if you remember the real-life figures they portray. Super 35. [R]▶

Frozen Assets (1992) C-96m. *½ D: George Miller. Shelley Long, Corbin Bernsen, Larry Miller, Dody Goodman, Matt Clark, Paul Sand, Teri Copley, Gloria Camden, Gerrit Graham. Low-octane comic trifle, in which Bernsen is transferred to a new bank—only to discover it's a sperm bank (get it?). He meets repressed biologist Long and after a lot of potency jokes they find themselves drawn to each other. Misguided movie vehicle for two proven TV stars. Corbin's mother, *The Young and the Restless*' Jeanne Cooper, has a small role. [PG-13]▼

Frozen Dead, The (1967-British) C-95m. ** D: Herbert J. Leder. Dana Andrews, Anna Palk, Philip Gilbert, Kathleen Breck, Karel Stepanek, Edward Fox. Bizarre account of scientist Andrews who froze group of top Nazis, now trying to revive them and the Third Reich; sloppy production values mar tale. Released theatrically in b&w.

Frozen River (2008) C-96m. *** D: Courtney Hunt. Melissa Leo, Misty Upham, Michael O'Keefe, Charlie McDermott, Mark Boone Junior, James Reilly, Jay Klaitz. The setting is upstate New York near the Canadian border. Working-class Leo, whose husband has run off with their money—leaving her with broken dreams and two kids to raise—gets an offer she can't refuse from a sullen young Mohawk woman (Upham) to make "easy" money transporting people across the border under perilous conditions. Low-key but utterly compelling drama with two finely etched performances. Based on writer-director Hunt's 2004 short subject of the same name. [R]▶

Fruit Machine, The (1988-British) **C-103m.** *** D: Philip Saville. Emile Charles, Tony Forsyth, Robert Stephens, Claire Higgins, Bruce Payne, Robbie Coltrane. Diverting contemporary thriller about two gay but very different Liverpool teens (Charles and Forsyth, in spirited performances) who witness a gangland murder and must flee for their lives. Scripted by Frank (LETTER TO BREZHNEV) Clarke. Video title: WONDERLAND.▼●

F.T.A. (1972) **C-94m.** ** D: Francine Parker. Jane Fonda, Donald Sutherland, Len Chandler, Holly Near, Pamela Donegan, Michael Alaimo. Unusual, rarely seen documentary of Fonda and Sutherland's *Free (or F***) the Army* revue, presented near Army bases and featuring antiwar skits and songs. Interesting only as a curio.▶

Fuel (2008) **C-112m.** *** D: Joshua Tickell. Documentary about activist-turned-filmmaker Tickell, a longtime exponent of biofuel as a source of clean energy. Revised after its 2008 Sundance debut (as FIELDS OF FUEL), when biofuel got a black eye in the media. Interviewees include scientists, cutting-edge innovators, and proactive celebrities (including Julia Roberts, Sheryl Crow, Woody Harrelson, Larry Hagman, and Neil Young). More interesting for its content than its fluidity as cinema, but undeniably educational and provocative.▶

Fugitive, The (1947) **104m.** ***½ D: John Ford. Henry Fonda, Dolores Del Rio, Pedro Armendariz, J. Carrol Naish, Leo Carrillo, Ward Bond. Brooding drama set in Mexico with revolutionist priest turned in by man who once sheltered him. Based on Graham Greene's novel *The Power and the Glory*. Superbly shot by Gabriel Figueroa. Also shown in computer-colored version.▼●

Fugitive, The (1993) **C-127m.** ***½ D: Andrew Davis. Harrison Ford, Tommy Lee Jones, Sela Ward, Julianne Moore, Joe Pantoliano, Jeroen Krabbé, Andreas Katsulas, Daniel Roebuck, L. Scott Caldwell, Jane Lynch. Slick, solid update of the 1960s TV series about a doctor wrongly convicted of murdering his wife; he takes it on the lam, with a dogged federal marshal (Jones, in an Oscar-winning performance) and his team on his trail. Great action and stunts, including an eye-popping bus crash/train wreck, but it's the cat-and-mouse game between two strong personalities—Ford and Jones—that makes this work. Scripted by Jeb Stuart and David Twohy from Twohy's story; based on coexecutive producer Roy Huggins' original TV premise. Followed by U.S. MARSHALS. [PG-13] ▼●▶

Fugitive Kind, The (1959) **121m.** **½ D: Sidney Lumet. Marlon Brando, Anna Magnani, Joanne Woodward, Maureen Stapleton, Victor Jory, R. G. Armstrong. Uneven filming of Tennessee Williams' *Orpheus Descending*, with strange casting. Wandering bum (Brando) arrives in Southern town, sparking romances with middle-aged married woman (Magnani) and spunky Woodward. Movie goes nowhere. Remade for cable TV in 1990 as ORPHEUS DESCENDING.▼▶

Fugitive Pieces (2008-Canadian-Greek) **C-106m.** **½ D: Jeremy Podeswa. Stephen Dillane, Rade Sherbedgia, Rosamund Pike, Ayelet Zurer, Robbie Kay, Ed Stoppard, Rachelle Lefevre, Themis Bazaka, Nina Dobrev. Jewish writer (Dillane) deals with his present-day demons while immersed in the memory of his boyhood during WW2: witnessing his parents' slaughter, wondering about the fate of his sister, being rescued by a kindly Greek archaeologist (Sherbedgia). Somber mood perfectly reflects the mindset of the main character, but the film is too drawn out and one-dimensionally downbeat. Podeswa scripted, based on Anne Michaels' acclaimed novel. [R]▶

Full Circle SEE: **Haunting of Julia, The**

Fuller Brush Girl, The (1950) **85m.** ** D: Lloyd Bacon. Lucille Ball, Eddie Albert, Jeff Donnell, Jerome Cowan, Lee Patrick. Low-grade slapstick with energetic Lucy as door-to-door salesgirl, mixed up with thieves.▼●

Fuller Brush Man, The (1948) **93m.** **½ D: S.Sylvan Simon. Red Skelton, Janet Blair, Don McGuire, Adele Jergens, Ross Ford, Hillary Brooke. Usual Skelton slapstick, with Red involved in murder while valiantly trying to succeed as a door-to-door salesman.▼●

Full Fathom Five (1990) **C-82m.** BOMB D: Carl Franklin. Michael Moriarty, Maria Rangel, Michael Cavanaugh, John LaFayette, Todd Field, Daniel Faraldo, Orlando Sacha. Roger Corman's "Red October" is a waterlogged mess: a group of renegades seize a Russian sub and threaten the nuclear annihilation of Houston, while the U.S. is preparing to invade Panama. Far too cheap for its ambitions. [PG]▼

Full Frontal (2002) **C-101m.** *½ D: Steven Soderbergh. Julia Roberts, David Duchovny, David Hyde Pierce, Catherine Keener, Nicky Katt, Mary McCormack, Blair Underwood, Brad Pitt, David Fincher, Terence Stamp, Enrico Colantoni, Erika Alexander, Brad Rowe, Cynthia Gibb, Jerry Weintraub, Sandra Oh, Rainn Wilson, January Jones. Self-indulgent, Hollywood-insider piffle offers a film within a film as we meet such L.A. denizens as a magazine writer and a movie star (both played by Roberts), an unhappily married couple (Pierce and Keener), and a movie producer (Duchovny) who's invited everyone to his 40th birthday party. Occasional moments of genuine emotion are undermined by showing us that it's "only a movie" after all. An unsatisfying mess. Shot on digital video. [R] ▼▶

Full Metal Jacket (1987) **C-116m.** ★★★ D: Stanley Kubrick. Matthew Modine, Adam Baldwin, Vincent D'Onofrio, Lee Ermey, Dorian Harewood, Arliss Howard, Kevyn Major Howard, Ed O'Ross. Adaptation of Gustav Hasford's *The Short-Timers* is divided into two sections: a harrowing look at Marine basic training on Parris Island; and combat experiences in Vietnam. The first half is so strong (thanks in part to real-life former D.I. Ermey) that the second half suffers in comparison, as it covers more familiar ground, while keeping emotions in check. Still, it's compelling, well acted, and supremely well crafted, certainly in keeping with Kubrick's recurring theme of dehumanization. Original music by Abigail Mead, aka Vivian Kubrick, the director's daughter. Filmed in England. [R] ▼●▶

Full Monty, The (1997-British-U.S.) **C-95m.** ★★★½ D: Peter Cattaneo. Robert Carlyle, Tom Wilkinson, Mark Addy, Lesley Sharp, Emily Woof, Steve Huison, Paul Barber, Hugo Speer, Deirdre Costello. Bull's-eye comedy about unemployed Sheffield steel-mill workers who, out of desperation, the need for money, and an equal need to have something to do, decide to become male strippers. Funny, well cast, and never mean spirited, this film earns its laughs honestly. Clever screenplay by Simon Beaufoy. Oscar-winning score by Anne Dudley. Later a Broadway musical. [R] ▼●▶

Full Moon High (1981) **C-94m.** ★★★ D: Larry Cohen. Adam Arkin, Ed McMahon, Elizabeth Hartman, Roz Kelly, Bill Kirchenbauer, Kenneth Mars, Joanne Nail, Alan Arkin. Infectiously silly teenage werewolf comedy, with Arkin as a high-school football star whose strange, right-wing father (McMahon) takes him to Transylvania and inadvertently changes his life. Lots of off-the-wall laughs and cameos by various comedy performers. [PG] ▼

Full Moon in Blue Water (1988) **C-93m.** ★★ D: Peter Masterson. Gene Hackman, Teri Garr, Burgess Meredith, Elias Koteas, Kevin Cooney, David Doty. Hackman is wallowing in self-pity over his drowned wife, as creditors duplicitously plot foreclosure on his coastal Texas bar. Also involved in the talky interchange are feisty bus driver Garr, Hackman's elderly father-in-law Meredith, and mentally shaky employee Koteas. This screen original by playwright Bill Bozzone feels like bad theater. [R] ▼●▶

Full Moon in Paris (1984-French) **C-102m.** ★★★ D: Eric Rohmer. Pascale Ogier, Fabrice Luchini, Tcheky Karyo, Christian Vadim, Virginie Thevenet. Neat little comedy from Rohmer about a headstrong young woman (Ogier), and her relationships with three men. Wonderful dialogue and characterizations, with a charming Ogier performance. [R] ▼▶

Full of It (2007) **C-93m.** ★★ D: Christian Charles. Ryan Pinkston, Kate Mara, Teri Polo, Craig Kilborn, John Carroll Lynch, Cynthia Stevenson, Amanda Walsh, Derek McGrath, Joshua Close, Matt Gordon, Carmen Electra. Passable teen comedy was probably pitched as LIAR, LIAR set in high school. Loser student with an active imagination suddenly finds all the whoppers he's been telling start coming true, making him the most popular guy on campus. Largely uninspired gags deal with every possible teenage fantasy. [PG-13] ▶

Full of Life (1956) **91m.** ★★★ D: Richard Quine. Judy Holliday, Richard Conte, Salvatore Baccaloni, Esther Minciotti. Holliday's pregnant wife antics almost matched by Baccaloni's as excitable father-in-law with his own way of running things. ▼

Fun (1993) **C-105m.** ★★★ D: Rafal Zielinski. Alicia Witt, Renee Humphrey, William R. Moses, Leslie Hope, Ania Suli. Jarring account of seemingly average young suburban teens who have just murdered a trusting elderly woman, for the "fun" of it! A thoughtful, disquieting film, every bit as impressive as HEAVENLY CREATURES, featuring riveting performances by its talented young leads. A biting commentary on "celebrity" in America. ▼▶

Funeral, The (1984-Japanese) **C-124m.** ★★★ D: Juzo Itami. Nobuko Miyamoto, Tsutomu Yamazaki, Kin Sugai, Ichiro Zaitsu, Nekohachi Edoya. Itami's debut feature is an on-target black comedy that chides solemn, traditional Japanese funeral rites. The scenario details what ensues when a modern family is compelled to hold a Buddhist funeral for its patriarch—who happened to own a brothel. ▼▶

Funeral, The (1996) **C-99m.** ★★½ D: Abel Ferrara. Christopher Walken, Chris Penn, Annabella Sciorra, Isabella Rossellini, Vincent Gallo, Benicio Del Toro, Gretchen Mol, John Ventimiglia, Paul Hipp, Victor Argo, Edie Falco. Moody 1930s gangster film which follows what happens as thug siblings Walken and Penn respond to the murder of their Communist kid brother (Gallo). Occasionally meanders, and the flashbacks are confusing, but there's atmosphere to spare, and Ferrara vividly depicts a macho world in which one must be unfeeling and conquer his fears in order to attain "manhood." He also deals with his familiar themes of God and religion in a world of brutality. [R] ▼●▶

Funeral Home (1982-Canadian) **C-93m.** ★★ D: William Fruet. Lesleh Donaldson, Kay Hawtrey, Barry Morse, Dean Garbett, Stephen Miller, Harvey Atkin. Teenager Donaldson investigates when guests begin disappearing from grandmother Hawtrey's summer motel. OK of its type; aka CRIES IN THE NIGHT. [R]▼❶

Funeral in Berlin (1966) C-102m. ** D: Guy Hamilton. Michael Caine, Eva Renzi, Paul Hubschmid, Oscar Homolka, Guy Doleman. Second of three Harry Palmer films (based on Len Deighton's novels) featuring Caine as the British spy arranging for defection of Russian officer in charge of Berlin war security. Caine and Homolka are good, Renzi attractive, but slowmoving tale just doesn't click. Followed by BILLION DOLLAR BRAIN. Panavision. ▼❶▶

Funhouse, The (1981) C-96m. **½ D: Tobe Hooper. Elizabeth Berridge, Cooper Huckabee, Miles Chapin, Largo Woodruff, Sylvia Miles, William Finley, Kevin Conway. Intense drama about four teenagers who decide to spend night in funhouse of a sleazy traveling carnival. Once inside, there is sex, violence, suspense and an increasing tension as they encounter the unknown. Stylish visuals help create an eerie atmosphere in this not entirely successful chiller. Panavision. [R]▼❶▶

Fun in Acapulco (1963) C-97m. **½ D: Richard Thorpe. Elvis Presley, Ursula Andress, Paul Lukas, Alejandro Rey. Scenery outshines story of Presley working as lifeguard and entertainer in Mexican resort city and performing the likes of "No Room to Rhumba in a Sports Car" and "You Can't Say No in Acapulco." Lukas is amusing as temperamental chef.▼▶

Fun Loving SEE: **Quackser Fortune Has a Cousin in the Bronx**

Funny About Love (1990) C-101m. *½ D: Leonard Nimoy. Gene Wilder, Christine Lahti, Mary Stuart Masterson, Robert Prosky, Stephen Tobolowsky, Anne Jackson, Susan Ruttan, Jean De Baer, David Margulies. Cartoonist Wilder and caterer Lahti can't conceive, despite the latest techniques of their laugh-a-minute fertility doctor; ensuing problems force Gene to take up with college sorority sister Masterson, obviously many years younger. Terminally mild comedy with odd, ham-handed flickers of black humor. [PG-13]▼❶▶

Funny Bones (1995-British-U.S.) C-126m. **½ D: Peter Chelsom. Oliver Platt, Lee Evans, Richard Griffiths, Leslie Caron, Jerry Lewis, Oliver Reed, Ian McNeice, George Carl, Freddie Davies, Ruta Lee, Harold Nicholas. Son of a famous and beloved comedian tries to make it on his own; when he fails, he goes back to Blackpool, England, to search for material—and his roots. Extraordinarily strange movie has many endearing moments (especially when it resurrects nuggets of show business past) but so many oddities that it never adds up— or figures out what it wants to be. Jerry is great, as Platt's father, and Caron is a delight as well. [R]▼❶▶

Funny Face (1957) C-103m. ***½ D: Stanley Donen. Audrey Hepburn, Fred Astaire, Kay Thompson, Michel Auclair, Suzy Parker, Ruta Lee. Stylish and highly stylized musical with Astaire as fashion photographer who turns Hepburn into chic Paris model. Top Gershwin score ("How Long Has This Been Going On," "He Loves and She Loves," "S'Wonderful," title tune), striking use of color, entertaining performance by Thompson as magazine editor. Cinematography by Ray June and John P. Fulton. Leonard Gershe based his screenplay on an unproduced stage musical—and Astaire's role was based on Richard Avedon, who's credited as visual consultant. VistaVision.▼❶▶

Funny Farm, The (1982-Canadian) C-95m. ** D: Ron Clark. Miles Chapin, Eileen Brennan, Jack Carter, Tracy Bregman, Howie Mandel, Marjorie Gross, Lou Dinos, Peter Aykroyd. Young man from Ohio comes to L.A. to make it as a stand-up comic. Slowmoving film introduces many unknown comics who do short bits at a "comedy store" owned by Brennan. Some funny moments, but overall is nothing much. [R]▼

Funny Farm (1988) C-101m. **½ D: George Roy Hill. Chevy Chase, Madolyn Smith, Joseph Maher, Jack Gilpin, Brad Sullivan, MacIntyre Dixon, Glenn Plummer, Mike Starr, Sarah Michelle Gellar. Oddly easygoing—and thus mildly endearing— Chase comedy about a N.Y. sportswriter who discovers, MR. BLANDINGS style, that country living isn't quite what it's cracked up to be. Has the look of quality (it was photographed by Miroslav Ondricek, designed by Henry Bumstead) but too many gags fizzle. Final episode is the best. [PG]▼❶▶

Funny Games (1997-Austrian) C-104m. ** D: Michael Haneke. Susanne Lothar, Ulrich Mühe, Arno Frisch, Frank Giering, Stefan Clapczynski, Doris Kunstmann, Christoph Bantzer, Wolfgang Glück. Two repugnant creeps bully their way into the country house of a middle-class family, who find themselves under siege physically and psychologically. Writer-director Haneke attempts to offer pungent commentary on the way contemporary society has been desensitized by violent images on TV and in movies, but this film is barely credible— and highly unpleasant. Remade by Haneke in 2008. ▼▶

Funny Games (2008-French-Italian-British) C-107m. ** D: Michael Haneke. Naomi Watts, Tim Roth, Michael Pitt, Brady Corbet, Devon Gearhart, Boyd Gaines, Siobhan Fallon Hogan, Robert LuPone. Suburban family is terrorized and systematically tortured by two seemingly normal young men who gain entry into their vacation home. Shot-by-shot remake of Haneke's 1997 Austrian thriller has been transported to a picturesque U.S. lakeside setting but still leaves a sickening aftertaste. With characters breaking the fourth wall and speaking directly to the audience, the filmmaker is trying to make a comment on extreme violence in movies in a story that provides plenty itself. Effectively made, but for strong stomachs only. [R]◗

Funny Girl (1968) **C-155m.** **★★★** D: William Wyler. Barbra Streisand, Omar Sharif, Kay Medford, Anne Francis, Walter Pidgeon, Lee Allen, Gerald Mohr. Streisand's Oscar-winning film debut as Fanny Brice, singer-comedienne whose unhappy private life contrasted comic antics onstage. Bad as biography, but first-rate as musical, including fine Bob Merrill–Jule Styne score ("People," title tune), memorable tugboat finale to "Don't Rain on My Parade," plus Brice standards "My Man" and "Second Hand Rose." Sequel: FUNNY LADY. Panavision. [G]▼◗

Funny Lady (1975) **C-137m.** **★★½** D: Herbert Ross. Barbra Streisand, James Caan, Omar Sharif, Roddy McDowall, Ben Vereen, Carole Wells, Colleen Camp. FUNNY GIRL sequel shows Fanny Brice at height of career, meeting and marrying ambitious showman Billy Rose (Caan). Disjointed film has fine moments of music and comedy, but a cliché-ridden script to contend with. Panavision. [PG]▼◗

Funnyman (1967) **C-98m.** **★★★** D: John Korty. Peter Bonerz, Sandra Archer, Carol Androsky, Larry Hankin, Barbara Hiken, Gerald Hiken. Winning little film about improvisational comic (Bonerz) who's nagged by the idea that he should be doing something more "important." Features great skits by The Committee and funny animated spoofs by director Korty.

Funny Money (2007-German) **C-98m.** **★½** D: Leslie Greif. Chevy Chase, Penelope Ann Miller, Armand Assante, Robert Loggia, Christopher McDonald, Alex Meneses, Kevin Sussman, Guy Torry, Rebecca Wisocky, Tim Stack. Droning worker bee at a wax-fruit factory (Chase) accidentally brings home the wrong briefcase one night—filled with 5 million dollars. Foreign crooks, a crooked cop, a horny boss, a randy art dealer, a comedic cabdriver, and assorted others descend upon Chase's home in the ruckus that follows. Ray Cooney's lowbrow British stage farce doesn't translate well to film. Made in 2005—mostly in Romania! [R]◗

Funny People (2009) **C-146m.** **★★½** D: Judd Apatow. Adam Sandler, Seth Rogen, Leslie Mann, Eric Bana, Jonah Hill, Jason Schwartzman, Aubrey Plaza, RZA, Aziz Ansari, Justin Long. Successful movie comedian learns he has a rare disease and may be dying. With no friends or family relationships, he impulsively hires a wannabe stand-up comic to be his assistant, companion, and nursemaid. Then he tries

to reconnect with the only woman he ever loved. Sprawling comedy-drama tackles everything from mortality to the emptiness of material success; gets an A for effort, though the results are extremely variable. And has the male sex organ ever been cited so many times—in so many ways—in one film? Rogen scores as the movie's one true mensch. Those cute girls are the real-life daughters of writer-director Apatow and leading lady Mann. Many comedians (and singer James Taylor) appear as themselves. Unrated version runs 153m. [R]◗

Funny Thing Happened on the Way to the Forum, A (1966) **C-99m.** **★★½** D: Richard Lester. Zero Mostel, Phil Silvers, Buster Keaton, Jack Gilford, Michael Crawford, Annette Andre, Michael Hordern. Frenzied adaptation of Broadway musical about conniving slave (Mostel) in ancient Rome; tries too hard, comes off forced. Still, with great comic cast, there's plenty worth seeing. Self-spoof on song "Lovely" is a highlight; score by Stephen Sondheim.▼◗

Fun With Dick and Jane (1977) **C-95m.** **★★½** D: Ted Kotcheff. Jane Fonda, George Segal, Ed McMahon, Dick Gautier, Allan Miller, John Dehner. Lightly amusing comedy about Segal losing his job, he and wife Fonda trying to cope with no income and finally turning to crime. Falls apart after promising start, becoming fragmented and pointless. Watch for Jay Leno in a bit. Remade in 2005. [PG]▼◗

Fun With Dick and Jane (2005) **C-90m.** **★★½** D: Dean Parisot. Jim Carrey, Téa Leoni, Alec Baldwin, Richard Jenkins, Angie Harmon, John Michael Higgins, Richard Burgi, Laurie Metcalf, Clint Howard. Not exactly a leader in the "crying need of remaking" department, this is obviously an Enron-influenced riff on the 1977 original about an upward middle-class couple who turn robbers after they're caught in an economic squeeze. Carrey gets promoted to VP in a company that barely exists, about a day before boss Baldwin helicopters away with the profits. Fitfully amusing comedy gets off to a fair start but loses its way into scattershot farce. Leoni makes a good fit with Carrey's manic persona. Super 35. [PG-13]◗

Fur: An Imaginary Portrait of Diane Arbus (2006) **C-120m.** **★★** D: Steven Shainberg. Nicole Kidman, Robert Downey, Jr., Ty Burrell, Harris Yulin, Jane Alexander. Attempting to explore famed photographer Arbus' artistic awakening in metaphoric terms, this film (set in 1958) follows her evolution from a stifled upper-class N.Y.C. wife and mother to an artist who's open to a world of society's outcasts that her parents taught her to shun. Downey plays a fugitive from a freak show with a furry body who moves in upstairs. He's a fictitious character in this "imaginary portrait" that tells us little about a very interesting woman. Ambitious and intriguing, with Kidman perfectly cast, but a strange, unsatisfying film. "Inspired by" Patricia Bosworth's biography of Arbus. [R]▶

Furies, The (1950) **109m.** ******* D: Anthony Mann. Barbara Stanwyck, Walter Huston, Wendell Corey, Gilbert Roland, Judith Anderson, Beulah Bondi, Thomas Gomez, Albert Dekker, Blanche Yurka, Wallace Ford. Fiery Stanwyck has always been able to sweet-talk her cattle-baron father, who presides over a vast New Mexico ranch called The Furies—but lately he isn't listening, and she locks horns with him. Operatic-style Western saga of love and hate, adapted by Charles Schnee from a Niven Busch novel and directed with flair by Mann. Striking cinematography by Victor Milner. This was Huston's final film.▶

Furry Vengeance (2010-U.S.-United Arab Emirates) **C-91m.** BOMB D: Roger Kumble. Brendan Fraser, Brooke Shields, Matt Prokop, Ken Jeong, Angela Kinsey, Wallace Shawn. Aggressively overplayed, desperately unfunny live-action comedy about wily forest creatures who battle a clueless land developer (Fraser). Recommended only for very small children who are easily amused by precocious animals and pratfalling grown-ups. [PG]▶

Further Adventures of Tennessee Buck, The (1988) **C-88m.** ****½** D: David Keith. David Keith, Kathy Shower, Brant van Hoffman, Sydney Lassick, Tiziana Stella, Patrizia Zanetti. Fun imitation of the INDIANA JONES films; big white hunter Keith goes on safari in Borneo with former *Playboy* Playmate of the Year Shower and her rich nerd husband van Hoffman. They meet up with a cannibal tribe whose women give Shower a vivid oil rubdown (the film's highlight). Actor-director Keith maintains a breezy tone. [R]▼●

Further Adventures of the Wilderness Family, The (1978) **C-105m.** ******* D: Frank Zuniga. Robert Logan, Susan D. Shaw, Heather Rattray, Ham Larsen, George (Buck) Flower, Brian Cutler. This clone of 1975's family hit ADVENTURES OF . . . has same cast, same elements, same magnificent Colorado scenery. So who's to argue with success? Aka THE WILDERNESS FAMILY, PART 2; followed by MOUNTAIN FAMILY ROBINSON.▼▶

Further Perils of Laurel and Hardy, The (1968) **99m.** ****½** D: Robert Youngson. Laurel and Hardy, Charley Chase, Max Davidson, James Finlayson. Repetitious format of "episodes" dulls edge of great material, but still fun, with rare L&H silent footage, pleasing interludes by Chase and Davidson.▼▶

Fury (1936) **94m.** *****½** D: Fritz Lang.

Sylvia Sidney, Spencer Tracy, Walter Abel, Bruce Cabot, Edward Ellis, Walter Brennan, Frank Albertson. Still timely drama of lynch mobs and mob rule in small town, making an embittered man of innocent Tracy, spoiling his love for sweetheart Sidney. Lang's first American film; he also scripted with Bartlett Cormack, from a Norman Krasna story. Also shown in computer-colored version.▼●▶

Fury, The (1978) **C-118m.** ******* D: Brian De Palma. Kirk Douglas, John Cassavetes, Carrie Snodgress, Amy Irving, Fiona Lewis, Andrew Stevens, Charles Durning, Gordon Jump, Dennis Franz. Stylish trash about young woman (Irving) with psychokinetic powers, and Douglas' desperate attempt to save his similarly gifted son from being used—or destroyed. Bloody and violent—the ultimate litmus test for those who prefer form over content. Film debut of Daryl Hannah; look fast for James Belushi as an extra. [R] ▼●▶

Future Cop SEE: **Trancers**

Future Shock (1994) **C-93m.** ****** D: Eric Parkinson, Francis "Oley" Sassone, Matt Reeves. Vivian Schilling, Scott Thompson, Martin Kove, Sam Clay, Bill Paxton, Brion James, Sidney Lassick, James Karen, Amanda Foreman, Tim Doyle. This three-story film's setup: Evil experimenters test virtual-reality scenarios on unsuspecting psychiatric patients. A frightened woman can't get her husband to understand her fears of urban violence and wolves in Malibu; a mild nerd is victimized by his punkish new roommate; a photographer becomes obsessed with guarding against accidental death. Only the final segment shows real imagination. Unrated version runs 97m. [PG-13]▼●▶

Futureworld (1976) **C-104m.** ******* D: Richard T. Heffron. Peter Fonda, Blythe Danner, Arthur Hill, Yul Brynner, Stuart Margolin, John Ryan. Suspenseful sequel to WESTWORLD has overtones of INVASION OF THE BODY SNATCHERS as robot duplicates try to take over. Short on action but intelligently done. [PG]▼●▶

Futz (1969) **C-92m.** ***½** D: Tom O'Horgan. Seth Allen, John Bakos, Mari-Claire Charba, Peter Craig, Sally Kirkland. Director O'Horgan, whose youthful touch made this a mild off-Broadway hit, brings bizarre tale to screen with disastrous results. No plot worth describing, except that there's a man in love with a pig.▼

Fuzz (1972) **C-92m.** ****** D: Richard A. Colla. Burt Reynolds, Raquel Welch, Yul Brynner, Jack Weston, Tom Skerritt, Peter Bonerz, Steve Ihnat, James McEachin, Bert Remsen. Oddball film tries to mix laughs and excitement, to be the MASH of police dramas, but doesn't have the style to pull it off; another disappointment for Reynolds fans. Script by Evan Hunter from one of his *87th Precinct* stories, written as "Ed McBain." [PG]▼❶

F/X (1986) **C-106m.** ******* D: Robert Mandel. Bryan Brown, Brian Dennehy, Diane Venora, Cliff De Young, Mason Adams, Jerry Orbach, Joe Grifasi, Josie DeGuzman, Martha Gehman. Movie special-effects man is hired to stage a phony "hit" with a Mafia man the target—but quickly learns that he's been double-crossed. Fast-moving, entertaining yarn that's a lot of fun, as long as you don't think about it for a moment afterward. Dennehy and Grifasi make a hilarious pair of Mutt and Jeff cops. Angela Bassett's film debut. Followed by a sequel and a TV series. [R]▼❶❶

F/X2 (1991) **C-109m.** ****½** D: Richard Franklin. Bryan Brown, Brian Dennehy, Rachel Ticotin, Joanna Gleason, Philip Bosco, Kevin J. O'Connor, Tom Mason, Dominic Zamprogna, Josie DeGuzman, John Walsh, James Stacy. Special-effects whiz Brown agrees to use his skills in a police case, but when things go wrong he finds himself embroiled in a deadly coverup—and calls on his ex-cop pal Dennehy to help. Amiable sequel has some engaging gimmickry, but the story gets too lumpy. [PG-13]▼❶❶

G (2005) **C-96m.** ****** D: Christopher Scott Cherot. Richard T. Jones, Blair Underwood, Andre Royo, Chenoa Maxwell, Laz Alonso, Nicoye Banks, Andrew Lauren, Jillian Lindsey. Shady character in the music industry rediscovers the great love from his past . . . but she's got a new man. Uncredited remake of THE GREAT GATSBY moves Fitzgerald's Jazz Age tragedy farther east on Long Island to the Hamptons, where the hip-hop–inflected romance remains faithful to its source in spirit if not in word (and that word would begin with F). Attractive, ultra-glam mounting with catchy music helps, but a bland Jones is no Redford—or Alan Ladd, for that matter. Written by the director. Shot in 2002. Super 35. [R]❶

Gabbeh (1996-Iranian-French) **C-75m.** *****½** D: Mohsen Makhmalbaf. Shaghayegh Djodat, Hossein Moharami, Roghieh Moharami, Abbas Sayahi. Simple, sweet allegory in which an elderly woman washes a *gabbeh* (carpet) by the side of a river. From the *gabbeh* emerges a young woman, a member of a nomadic tribe who recounts a series of related stories. This elegantly lyrical, stunningly visual fable allows a peek into a non-Western culture and the way it records its history.▼❶

Gable and Lombard (1976) **C-131m.** BOMB D: Sidney J. Furie. James Brolin, Jill Clayburgh, Allen Garfield, Red Buttons, Joanne Linville, Melanie Mayron. Pure tripe about offscreen romance of two great stars. Brolin and Clayburgh are game but one-dimensional; script and direction are hopeless. [R]❶

Gabriela (1983-Brazilian-Italian) **C-102m.** ****** D: Bruno Barreto. Marcello Mastroianni, Sonia Braga, Antonio Cantafora, Ricardo Petraglia. Obvious tale of barkeeper Mastroianni taking on luscious, free-spirited Braga as a cook and lover. Braga's body and smile are the main interests here. Based on Jorge Amado's novel, which was developed into a top soap opera on Brazilian television. [R]▼

Gabrielle (2005-French-Italian-German) **C-90m.** ****½** D: Patrice Chéreau. Isabelle Huppert, Pascal Greggory, Claudia Coli, Thierry Hancisse, Chantal Neuwirth, Thierry Fortineau. In fin-de-siècle France, a smug and wealthy publisher who thinks of his wife as his prized possession is shocked when she suddenly leaves him for another man. But she returns later that day, leading to an unexpected conclusion. Polished, penetrating, but cold and talky series of scenes from a marriage; expanded from Joseph Conrad's short story "The Return," changing the setting from London to Paris and shifting the dramatic focus from the pompous husband to the repressed wife. Chéreau coscripted. Panavision.❶

Gaby (1956) **C-97m.** ****½** D: Curtis Bernhardt. Leslie Caron, John Kerr, Sir Cedric Hardwicke, Taina Elg. Remake of WATERLOO BRIDGE, telling of ballerina Caron and her romance with soldier Kerr in WW2 England. Not bad but not up to original. CinemaScope.

Gaby—A True Story (1987) **C-110m.** ******* D: Luis Mandoki. Liv Ullmann, Norma Aleandro, Robert Loggia, Rachel Levin (Chagall), Lawrence Monoson, Robert Beltran, Tony Goldwyn. Incredible true story of Gaby Brimmer, born with cerebral palsy to wealthy European refugee parents in Mexico, leaving her body almost completely paralyzed—but not affecting her mind. Levin, who is not disabled in real life, gives a stunning performance in the lead (matched by Monoson as her boyfriend), with Aleandro a tower of strength as the woman who devotes her life to Gaby. An often painful but worthwhile film. Brimmer executive-produced. [R]▼❶

Gadjo Dilo (1998-French-Romanian) **C-97m.** ****** D: Tony Gatlif. Romain Duris, Rona Hartner, Izidor Serban, Ovidiu Balan, Angela Serban. During a bleak Romanian winter, a young Frenchman hoping to track down a legendary folk singer gets involved with a group of Gypsy villagers, becomes "adopted" by a loud old drunk, and falls in love with a peasant woman. Things get complicated when the drunk's real son, a Gypsy mafioso, arrives fresh from jail. Overdone and melodramatic, this story too often plays on one note. Aka CRAZY STRANGER.▼❶

Gaily, Gaily (1969) **C-107m.** ****** D: Norman Jewison. Beau Bridges, Melina Mercouri, Brian Keith, George Kennedy, Hume Cronyn, Margot Kidder, Wilfrid Hyde-White, Melodie Johnson. Ben Hecht's colorful memories of apprenticeship on Chicago newspaper are destroyed by silly, hollow script that even changes "Hecht" to "Harvey." Expensive sets, period flavor are only bright spots in contrived comedy. Kidder's film debut. [M]

Galaxina (1980) **C-95m.** *½ D: William Sachs. Stephen Macht, Dorothy R. Stratten, James David Hinton, Avery Schreiber. Cheap STAR WARS/STAR TREK spoof reeks of low production values, boring scenario, and non-acting. Definitely not a vehicle for the late Ms. Stratten, though the film is of interest for her appearance as a robot. Panavision. [R]▼●)

Galaxy of Terror (1981) **C-80m.** *½ D: B. D. Clark. Edward Albert, Erin Moran, Ray Walston, Robert Behrens, Zalman King, Sid Haig. Astronauts are killed off by monsters while on mission to aid spaceship marooned on another planet. A Grade D ALIEN clone. Aka MINDWARP: AN INFINITY OF TERROR and PLANET OF HORRORS. Followed by FORBIDDEN WORLD. [R]▼●)

Galaxy Quest (1999) **C-104m.** *** D: Dean Parisot. Tim Allen, Sigourney Weaver, Alan Rickman, Tony Shalhoub, Sam Rockwell, Daryl Mitchell, Enrico Colantoni, Robin Sachs, Patrick Breen, Missi Pyle, Justin Long, Rainn Wilson. Engaging comedy about the washed-up cast of a *Star Trek*–like TV show now reduced to making personal appearances at fan conventions; suddenly they're whisked off to a starship where an alien civilization (believing their television adventures to be real) seeks their help to save the aliens from oblivion. By Grabthar's hammer, it's clever, funny, and sweet. Panavision. [PG]▼)

Galileo (1975-British) **C-145m.** *** D: Joseph Losey. Topol, Edward Fox, Colin Blakely, Georgia Brown, Clive Revill, Margaret Leighton, John Gielgud, Michael Gough, Judy Parfitt, Patrick Magee, Tom Conti. Bertolt Brecht's play, whose 1947 U.S. premiere was staged by director Losey, turned into unremarkable but generally satisfactory film. Topol is a little much as the scientist whose theories of the universe confound the church, but supporting actors are excellent. An American Film Theatre Production. [PG]▼)

Gallant Hours, The (1960) **111m.** *** D: Robert Montgomery. James Cagney, Dennis Weaver, Ward Costello, Richard Jaeckel. Sincere, low-key biog of WW2 Admiral "Bull" Halsey played documentary-style. Cagney is reserved and effective, but production needs livening.▼)

Gallery of Horror SEE: **Return From the Past**

Gallipoli (1981-Australian) **C-110m.** ***½ D: Peter Weir. Mark Lee, Mel Gibson, Bill Kerr, Robert Grubb, David Argue, Tim McKenzie. Youthful idealists Lee and Gibson enlist in the military, meet their fate in title WW1 battle. Engrossing human drama with meticulous direction, striking feel for period detail. Final freeze-frame shot is reminiscent of Robert Capa's classic Spanish Civil War photo of soldier at the moment of death. Panavision. [PG]▼●)

Gal Young 'Un (1979) **C-105m.** ***½ D: Victor Nunez. Dana Preu, David Peck, J. Smith, Gene Densmore, Jenny Stringfellow, Tim McCormick. Low-budget gem about Prohibition-era widow Preu charmed and then exploited by foppish hustler Peck. Effective performances, use of locales (near Gainesville, Florida), depiction of the era. From Marjorie Kinnan Rawlings story.▼

Gambit (1966) **C-109m.** *** D: Ronald Neame. Michael Caine, Shirley MacLaine, Herbert Lom, Roger C. Carmel, John Abbott. Gimmicky robbery yarn with scoundrel Caine hiring Eurasian MacLaine to carry out perfect heist of invaluable piece of sculpture; great fun. Techniscope.▼

Gamble, The (1988-Italian) **C-105m.** **½ D: Carlo Vanzina. Matthew Modine, Faye Dunaway, Jennifer Beals, Corinne Clery, Federica Moro, Ana Obregon, Vernon Wells, Feodor Chaliapin, Ian Bannen. So-so adventure in the TOM JONES mold, in which roguish Modine gambles with sinister countess Dunaway. The stakes: his life, for the family fortune she won from his father. Hokey and irrational, and the ending doesn't work, but still amusing. [R]▼

Gambler, The (1974) **C-111m.** ** D: Karel Reisz. James Caan, Paul Sorvino, Lauren Hutton, Morris Carnovsky, Jacqueline Brookes, Burt Young, Carmine Caridi, Vic Tayback, Steven Keats, London Lee, M. Emmet Walsh, James Woods, Stuart Margolin. Misfire about college prof Caan's compulsion to gamble; much inferior to Altman's CALIFORNIA SPLIT. Written by James Toback. [R]▼●)

Gambler, The (1997-Hungarian-French) **C-97m.** ** D: Károly Makk. Michael Gambon, Jodhi May, Polly Walker, Dominic West, Luise Rainer, William Houston. An adaptation of Dostoevsky's 1866 novel, this is as much about the writing of that book as the story the author was trying to tell. Fiction and reality merge as Dostoevsky, with huge debts from his gambling habit, signs away rights to his life's work unless he can deliver a new novel in just 27 days. Lacks emotional power, despite fine performances by Gambon and Rainer (who's making her first big-screen appearance since 1943's HOSTAGES). [R]▼)

Gamblin' Man SEE: **Cockfighter**

Game, The (1997) **C-128m.** ** D: David Fincher. Michael Douglas, Sean Penn, Carroll Baker, Deborah Kara Unger, Armin Mueller-Stahl, Peter Donat, James Rebhorn. Coldhearted financial whiz (Douglas) gets an unusual birthday present from his brother (Penn)—a gift certificate for a sophisticated recreational company that stages a "game," the nature of which is never revealed. Before long, Douglas' entire existence is stripped away, on a roller-coaster ride heading straight down. Unusually mean-spirited film offers no letup—and has no sense of humor, either. Filmed in San Francisco. Super 35. [R]▼●◗

Game for Vultures (1979-British) **C-106m.** BOMB D: James Fargo. Joan Collins, Richard Harris, Richard Roundtree, Ray Milland, Jana Cilliers, Sven-Bertil Taube, Denholm Elliott, John Parsonson, Ken Gampu. Tired cast in a dreadful drama about racial strife in Rhodesia. The subject matter may be worthy, but the result couldn't be more ponderous. [R]▼

Game Is Over, The (1966-French) **C-96m.** **½ D: Roger Vadim. Jane Fonda, Peter McEnery, Michel Piccoli, Tina Marquand, Jacques Monod. Fonda marries wealthy Piccoli, falls in love with and seduces his son (McEnery). Handsome, updated version of Zola's *La Curée* is not bad; at the time, best performance of Jane's career. Panavision. [R]▼◗

Gamekeeper, The (1980-British) **C-84m.** *** D: Kenneth Loach. Phil Askham, Rita May, Andrew Grubb, Peter Steels, Michael Hinchcliffe. Simple, effectively subtle tale of conservative young gamekeeper Askham, who sublimates his anger at being unable to crack the British class system.

Game of Death, A (1946) **72m.** *½ D: Robert Wise. John Loder, Audrey Long, Edgar Barrier, Russell Wade, Russell Hicks, Jason Robards (Sr.), Noble Johnson. Second official version of THE MOST DANGEROUS GAME—madman Barrier hunts humans shipwrecked on his island. Moves well, but indifferently acted; nowhere nearly as exciting as the 1932 original. Next remake: RUN FOR THE SUN.

Game of Death (1978) **C-102m.** **½ D: Robert Clouse. Bruce Lee, Gig Young, Hugh O'Brian, Colleen Camp, Dean Jagger, Kareem Abdul-Jabbar, Chuck Norris. Lee died midway through production of this karate thriller. Six years later, Clouse reassembled the surviving actors and, with the use of doubles, completed the film. Standard fare until final, incredible half hour, when Lee goes one-on-one with each of the villains in some of the most explosive fight scenes ever filmed. Aka BRUCE LEE'S GAME OF DEATH. Panavision. [R]▼●◗

Game of Their Lives, The (2005) **C-96m.** ** D: David Anspaugh. Gerard Butler, Wes Bentley, Jay Rodan, Gavin Rossdale, Costas Mandylor, Louis Mandylor, Zachery Ty Bryan, Patrick Stewart, Terry Kinney, John Rhys-Davies, Freddy Adu. The director (Anspaugh) and screenwriter (Angelo Pizzo) of HOOSIERS and RUDY try for

the same results with this story of an Italian-American soccer team from St. Louis that becomes the core of an underdog U.S. squadron sent to Brazil for the 1950 World Cup games. Alas, all the emotions are told (in speeches) and heard (in the overbearing music) rather than felt. Widescreen. [PG]◗

Game Plan, The (2007) **C-110m.** **½ D: Andy Fickman. Dwayne "The Rock" Johnson, Madison Pettis, Kyra Sedgwick, Roselyn Sanchez, Morris Chestnut, Paige Turco, Gordon Clapp. Egocentric superstar quarterback (Johnson) becomes a better person—and a better player—after he spends quality time with the 8-year-old daughter (Pettis) he never knew he had. Predictable mix of rib-tickling and heart-tugging elements; this family-friendly comedy sticks close to the rulebook for movies about self-absorbed workaholics suddenly saddled with parental responsibilities. Johnson enlivens the tired material with megawatt charisma and first-rate comic timing. Super 35. [PG]◗

Gamer (2009) **C-95m.** **½ D: Mark Neveldine, Brian Taylor. Gerard Butler, Michael C. Hall, Kyra Sedgwick, Chris "Ludacris" Bridges, Amber Valletta, John Leguizamo, Keith David, Logan Lerman, Alison Lohman, Terry Crews, Zoë Bell, John de Lancie, Jonathan Chase, Aaron Yoo. Death row inmates volunteer to play a kill-or-be-killed game in an attempt to win their freedom. Neo-modern take on this premise is unexceptional in terms of plot but holds its own for techno-thriller devotees, upgraded by Hall and Butler's performances. [R]◗

Games (1967) **C-100m.** **½ D: Curtis Harrington. Simone Signoret, James Caan, Katharine Ross, Don Stroud, Estelle Winwood. After arrival of mysterious Signoret at kinky newlywed N.Y.C. apartment, borderline pranks become deadly conspiracy. The trick: guess who's double-crossing whom. Attempts at deeper meanings unfulfilling, despite good cast. Techniscope.▼

Games, The (1970-British) **C-97m.** *½ D: Michael Winner. Michael Crawford, Stanley Baker, Ryan O'Neal, Charles Aznavour, Jeremy Kemp, Elaine Taylor, Kent Smith, Sam Elliott, Mona Washbourne. Dull film on potentially interesting subject: preparation of four runners for grueling 26-mile marathon in the Olympics. Rafer Johnson plays one of the commentators. Panavision. [G]

Game 6 (2006) **C-83m.** **½ D: Michael Hoffman. Michael Keaton, Robert Downey, Jr., Ari Graynor, Bebe Neuwirth, Griffin Dunne, Shalom Harlow, Catherine O'Hara, Harris Yulin, Nadia Dajani, Tom Aldredge, Lillias White, Roger Rees. N.Y.C. in 1986: a playwright and rabid baseball fan whose newest show is about to open tries to deal with a variety of conflicts, including the daily struggle of existence in Manhattan and his beleaguered Red Sox's chance to win a World Series against the Mets. Consistently interesting, if not quite successful; a writer's film if there ever was one, marking the first screenplay by novelist Don DeLillo. Coproduced by Dunne. [R]▶

Gammera, The Invincible (1966-Japanese-U.S.) **88m.** *½ D: Noriaki Yuasi. Brian Donlevy, Albert Dekker, John Baragrey. A giant, jet-propelled fire-breathing space turtle terrorizes the earth following atomic explosion. First in a series of juvenile sci-fi films. Original Japanese version—without American actors and titled GAMERA—runs 82m. Daieiscope.▼●▶

Gandhi (1982-British-Indian) **C-188m.** ***½ D: Richard Attenborough. Ben Kingsley, Candice Bergen, Edward Fox, John Gielgud, Trevor Howard, John Mills, Martin Sheen, Rohini Hattangandy, Ian Charleson, Athol Fugard, Roshan Seth, Saeed Jaffrey, John Ratzenberger, Geraldine James, Michael Hordern, Marius Weyers, Om Puri. Sweeping account of the life and times of Mohandas K. Gandhi, who rose from a position of simple lawyer to become a nation's leader and a worldwide symbol of peace and understanding. Storytelling at its best, in the tradition of great Hollywood epics, though film's second half is less riveting than the first. Kingsley gives an unforgettable performance in the lead. Eight Oscars include Best Picture, Actor, Director, Screenplay (John Briley). Look for Daniel Day-Lewis as one of three youths who accost Gandhi in the street. Panavision. [PG]▼●▶

Gang Related (1997) **C-111m.** ** D: Jim Kouf. James Belushi, Tupac Shakur, Dennis Quaid, Lela Rochon, James Earl Jones, David Paymer, Wendy Crewson, Gary Cole, T. C. Carson, Brad Greenquist. Corrupt cops Belushi and Shakur sell coke to dealers, then kill them and recycle the drugs, but their scam starts to unravel when one of their victims turns out to be an undercover DEA agent. Sleazy crime thriller maintains some interest for a while, but falls apart due to its laughably contrived script and a schizophrenic tone that alternates faux-nihilism with shameless sentimentality. The late Shakur shows some talent in his last role, but Belushi gives an embarrassingly hammy performance. Super 35. [R]▼●▶

Gang's All Here, The (1943) **C-103m.** **½ D: Busby Berkeley. Alice Faye, Carmen Miranda, Phil Baker, Benny Goodman and Orchestra, Eugene Pallette, Charlotte Greenwood, Edward Everett Horton, Tony DeMarco, James Ellison, Sheila Ryan. Corny but visually dazzling wartime musical, with soldier Ellison going off to battle while both Faye and Ryan believe they're engaged to him. Two socko musical numbers courtesy of Berkeley: "The Lady with the Tutti-Frutti Hat" (featuring Miranda at her best) and the finale, "The Polka Dot Polka." Faye does "No Love, No Nothin'." And, as an added kitsch treat, Benny Goodman sings! Watch for June

Haver as a hat-check girl, Jeanne Crain by the swimming pool.●▶

Gangs of New York (2002) **C-168m.** ***½ D: Martin Scorsese. Leonardo DiCaprio, Daniel Day-Lewis, Cameron Diaz, Liam Neeson, Jim Broadbent, John C. Reilly, Henry Thomas, Brendan Gleeson, Gary Lewis, Eddie Marsan, David Hemmings, Alec McCowen, Cara Seymour, Barbara Bouchet. Epic-scale film about rivalries among warring factions of New Yorkers in the 1860s. A young man who's been away for 16 years returns to his home turf determined to avenge his father's death at the hands of Bill the Butcher (Day-Lewis), the self-appointed leader of the nationalistic "Native Americans." Visceral, cinematic storytelling, acted out on Dante Ferretti's extraordinary sets by a solid cast, led by a brilliant Day-Lewis as the eccentric—and ferocious—Bill. Introduction of the notorious draft riots toward the end seems abrupt, but the overall impact of the film is still formidable. Screenplay by Jay Cocks, Steven Zaillian, and Kenneth Lonergan, suggested by Herbert Asbury's 1928 book. Magnificently photographed by Michael Ballhaus. Super 35. [R] ▼▶

Gangster, The (1947) **84m.** *** D: Gordon Wiles. Barry Sullivan, Belita, Joan Lorring, Akim Tamiroff, Harry Morgan, John Ireland, Fifi D'Orsay, Shelley Winters. Sullivan gives strong performance as man who falls victim to his slum environment and ends up a vengeful crook. ▼▶

Gangster No. 1 (2000-British-German) **C-105m.** ** D: Paul McGuigan. Malcolm McDowell, David Thewlis, Paul Bettany, Saffron Burrows, Kenneth Cranham, Eddie Marsan. An aging mobster thinks back about his life, and how he went from being a street hood to a powerful racketeer. Stylish and interesting, with strong performances, but loses its story momentum and becomes repellently brutal. [R]▼▶

Gangster Story (1959) **65m.** *½ D: Walter Matthau. Walter Matthau, Carol Grace, Bruce McFarlan, Gerrett Wallberg. Matthau's lone film as director is a low-quality, ultra-low-budget chronicle of the plight of a bank robber and killer. Grace, as a librarian who falls for the thug, is real-life Mrs. Matthau.▼▶

Gang That Couldn't Shoot Straight, The (1971) **C-96m.** ** D: James Goldstone. Jerry Orbach, Leigh Taylor-Young, Jo Van Fleet, Lionel Stander, Robert De Niro, Herve Villechaize. Film version of Jimmy Breslin's best-seller about comical, twelfth-rate N.Y.C. crooks is well cast, but adapted in slapdash fashion and directed without much feeling for the material. [PG] ▼▶

Garbage Pail Kids Movie, The (1987) **C-100m.** BOMB D: Rod Amateau. Anthony Newley, MacKenzie Astin, Katie Barberi. Crude live-action kiddie film "inspired" by the popular and controversial bubble-gum cards which feature creatures with names like Greaser Greg and Valerie Vomit. They all live in a garbage pail, where they are destined to be joined by the negative of this movie. [PG]▼◗

Garbo Talks (1984) **C-103m.** **½ D: Sidney Lumet. Anne Bancroft, Ron Silver, Carrie Fisher, Catherine Hicks, Steven Hill, Howard da Silva, Dorothy Loudon, Harvey Fierstein, Hermione Gingold, Mary Mc-Donnell. Silver sets out to fulfill his dying mother's last request: to meet Greta Garbo. Bancroft is a treat as the feisty mom, but film is just a series of vignettes, occasionally poignant but overall self-conscious and contrived, further undermined by Cy Coleman's saccharine score. That's writer-performer Betty Comden as Garbo in the last scene. [PG-13]▼◗

Garde à Vue (1981-French) **C-87m.** *** D: Claude Miller. Lino Ventura, Michel Serrault, Romy Schneider, Guy Marchand. Prominent lawyer Serrault, suspected of raping and murdering two girls, is interrogated by police inspectors Ventura and Marchand. Tense, involving drama, with fine performances by all.

Garden, The (1990-British) **C/B&W-92m.** **½ D: Derek Jarman. Tilda Swinton, Johnny Mills, Philip MacDonald, Roger Cook, Kevin Collins, Pete Lee-Wilson, Spencer Lee, Jody Graber, Michael Gough. Surreal, deeply personal union of images and sound, which tells (in very abstract terms) the story of the Passion of Christ; however, the Christ figure is replaced by a pair of homosexual lovers, who are destined to experience suffering and humiliation. As with most of Jarman's work, some will find it thought provoking while others will be bored (if not offended). ▼

Garden of Allah, The (1936) **C-80m.** ** D: Richard Boleslawski. Marlene Dietrich, Charles Boyer, Tilly Losch, Basil Rathbone, Joseph Schildkraut, Henry Kleinbach (Henry Brandon), John Carradine. Flagrantly silly romance set in the Algerian desert; full of ripe dialogue, troubled glances, beauty shots of Marlene in a variety of gorgeous sheaths and flowing gowns, and some wonderful Technicolor scenery (which helped win its cameramen, W. Howard Greene and Harold Rosson, a special Oscar). It just isn't very good. ▼◗

Garden of Evil (1954) **C-100m.** **½ D: Henry Hathaway. Gary Cooper, Susan Hayward, Richard Widmark, Hugh Marlowe, Cameron Mitchell, Rita Moreno. Meandering adventure set in 1850s Mexico, with trio escorting Hayward through bandit territory to save her husband. CinemaScope.◗

Garden of the Finzi-Continis, The (1971-Italian) **C-95m.** **** D: Vittorio De Sica. Dominique Sanda, Lino Capolicchio, Helmut Berger, Fabio Testi, Romolo Valli. Exquisitely photographed drama about aristocratic Jewish family in WW2 Italy which conveniently ignores the spectre of the concentration camp until it's too late. Sad, haunting film boosted Sanda to stardom and won an Oscar as Best Foreign Film. Screenplay by Vittorio Bonicelli and Ugo Pirro; from novel by Giorgio Bassani. [R]▼◗

Gardens of Stone (1987) **C-111m.** **½ D: Francis Coppola. James Caan, Anjelica Huston, James Earl Jones, D. B. Sweeney, Dean Stockwell, Mary Stuart Masterson, Dick Anthony Williams, Lonette McKee, Sam Bottoms, Larry Fishburne. Well-acted story about life in Arlington National Cemetery's home guard during the thick of the Vietnam war—and one young soldier's determination to go into battle. Strong performances keep it going most of the way, but toward the end the dialogue sounds hollow, like the sentiment itself. Carmine Coppola's funereal music doesn't help. Jones steals the show in a warm-hearted role; young leading lady Masterson's real-life parents, Peter Masterson and Carlin Glynn, play her folks on-screen. [R]▼◗

Garden State (2004) **C-109m.** **½ D: Zach Braff. Zach Braff, Natalie Portman, Peter Sarsgaard, Ian Holm, Ron Leibman, Jean Smart, Method Man, Jim Parsons. After his mother's death, a wannabe actor returns to his New Jersey hometown and is slowly brought out of a numbed (and overmedicated) existence by a free-spirited young woman. Interesting debut feature from actor-writer-director Braff, who has an eye for original, quirky detail but slides into self-conscious whimsy a bit too often. Sarsgaard and, especially, Portman shine. Super 35. [R]▼◗

Garfield (2004) **C-80m.** ** D: Pete Hewitt. Breckin Meyer, Jennifer Love Hewitt, Stephen Tobolowsky; voices of Bill Murray, Nick Cannon, Alan Cumming, David Eigenberg, Brad Garrett, Jimmy Kimmel, Debra Messing. Murray is an ideal voice for the world's laziest (and hungriest) cat in this innocuous, uninspired comedy combining computer-generated animation and live action. Meyer is Garfield's hapless owner, who tries to woo attractive veterinarian Hewitt by adopting Odie, a homeless mutt, which spurs Garfield into defensive action. Based on Jim Davis' comic strip and animated TV series. Followed by a sequel. [PG]▼◗

Garfield 2 (2006) **C-78m.** **½ D: Tim Hill. Breckin Meyer, Jennifer Love Hewitt, Billy Connolly, Ian Abercrombie, Roger Rees, Lucy Davis, Jane Carr; voices of Bill Murray, Bob Hoskins, Sharon Osbourne, Tim Curry, Jane Leeves, Jane Horrocks, Richard E. Grant, Vinnie Jones, Rhys Ifans, Jim Piddock; narrated by Roscoe Lee Browne. While tagging along with Meyer on a trip to London, Garfield is mistaken for a lookalike cat who's come into a big inheritance. Minor but amusing. Alternate version runs

86m. Advertised as GARFIELD: A TAIL OF TWO KITTIES. [PG] ▶

Gas! (1970) **C-79m.** *** D: Roger Corman. Robert Corff, Elaine Giftos, Bud Cort, Tally Coppola (Talia Shire), Ben Vereen, Cindy Williams. Insane, often uproarious story focusing on reactions of youngsters in crisis: a gas kills everyone on Earth over 25. Reedited against Corman's wishes, causing much disjointedness, but stay with it. Aka GAS! OR IT BECAME NECESSARY TO DESTROY THE WORLD IN ORDER TO SAVE IT. Screenwriter Armitage plays Billy the Kid. [PG] ▼

Gas (1981-Canadian) **C-94m.** BOMB D: Les Rose. Donald Sutherland, Susan Anspach, Howie Mandel, Sterling Hayden, Sandee Currie, Peter Aykroyd, Helen Shaver. Noisy, moronic garbage about the effect of a phony gas shortage on an "average" American town. Car crashes *ad nauseam*, with Sutherland wasted as Nick the Noz, a hip disc jockey. [R] ▼

Gas Food Lodging (1992) **C-101m.** **½ D: Allison Anders. Brooke Adams, Ione Skye, Fairuza Balk, James Brolin, Robert Knepper, David Lansbury, Jacob Vargas, Donovan Leitch, Chris Mulkey, Tiffany Anders. Truck-stop waitress struggles to raise two daughters in a Laramie, N.M., trailer park, with the older one already jaded by men and the younger idealistic to the end. Overrated by some, but still fairly passionate despite a slender budget and minimalist cinematics. Good performances extend to Brolin's, as a wandering dad. Skye (Trudi) and Leitch (Darius) are real-life sister and brother. [R] ▼▶

Gaslight (1940-British) **84m.** ***½ D: Thorold Dickinson. Anton Walbrook, Diana Wynyard, Frank Pettingell, Cathleen Cordell, Robert Newton, Jimmy Hanley. First version of Patrick Hamilton's play about an insane criminal who drives his wife crazy in order to discover hidden jewels. Electrifying atmosphere, delicious performances, and a succinctly conveyed sense of madness and evil lurking beneath the surface of the ordinary. Screenplay by A. R. Rawlinson and Bridget Boland. U.S. title: ANGEL STREET. ▼▶

Gaslight (1944) **114m.** *** D: George Cukor. Ingrid Bergman, Charles Boyer, Joseph Cotten, Dame May Whitty, Angela Lansbury, Terry Moore. The bloom has worn off this classic chiller about a man trying to drive his wife insane, but lush production, Victorian flavor, and fine performances remain intact. Bergman won Oscar; Lansbury's film debut. Filmed before in 1940. Also shown in computer-colored version. ▼▶

Gate, The (1987) **C-92m.** ** D: Tibor Takacs. Stephen Dorff, Christa Denton, Louis Tripp, Kelly Rowan, Jennifer Irwin, Deborah Grove, Scot Denton. It's a boring weekend: Dorff is grounded, his sister is babysitting while the parents are away— then he and a pal discover the gate to hell in their suburban backyard. Worthless first half is somewhat redeemed by amusing/scary special effects in the second. Followed by a sequel. [PG-13] ▼▶

Gate II (1992) **C-95m.** *½ D: Tibor Takacs. Louis Tripp, Simon Reynolds, Pamela Segall, James Villemaire, Neil Munro. Demons of the underworld are resummoned by now-teenaged Tripp to grant his wishes. Though his intentions are on the naive side, it's safe to say that all hell breaks loose. None of THE GATE's goofy fright made its way into this unnecessary sequel. This spent three years on the shelf. [R] ▼▶

Gate of Hell (1953-Japanese) **C-86m.** ***½ D: Teinosuke Kinugasa. Machiko Kyo, Kazuo Hasegawa, Isao Yamagata, Koreya Senda. Stark, stunning historical drama, set in 12th-century Japan, about a Samurai who falls in love with—and then tragically shames—a married woman. This beautiful production earned Oscars for Costume Design and Best Foreign Film. ▼

Gates of Heaven (1978) **C-82m.** ***½ D: Errol Morris. Delightfully offbeat yet piercing documentary about a pet cemetery in—where else?—California. At once hilarious and an allegory about the absurdity of American priorities. Not to be confused with Michael Cimino's HEAVEN'S GATE, or Stephen King's PET SEMATARY, for that matter. ▼▶

Gathering of Eagles, A (1963) **C-115m.** *** D: Delbert Mann. Rock Hudson, Rod Taylor, Mary Peach, Barry Sullivan, Kevin McCarthy, Henry Silva, Leif Erickson. Crisp Strategic Air Command drama with novelty of peacetime setting; Hudson gives one of his best performances as less than likable colonel whose wife struggles to adjust to being a military spouse. Good script by Robert Pirosh. Look for Louise Fletcher as a patient's wife. ▼

Gatling Gun, The (1972) **C-93m.** *½ D: Robert Gordon. Guy Stockwell, Woody Strode, Patrick Wayne, Robert Fuller, Barbara Luna, John Carradine, Pat Buttram, Phil Harris. Cavalry, renegade soldiers, Apaches, fight over Gatling gun. Standard, forgettable Western. Aka KING GUN. Panavision. [PG] ▼▶

Gator (1976) **C-116m.** ** D: Burt Reynolds. Burt Reynolds, Jack Weston, Lauren Hutton, Jerry Reed, Alice Ghostley, Mike Douglas, Dub Taylor. Not-so-hot sequel to WHITE LIGHTNING, about Justice Dept. agent Weston and moonshiner ex-con Reynolds out to get the goods on corrupt Southern politicians. Some good action, but overlong and poorly constructed. Reynolds' directing debut. Todd-AO 35. [PG] ▼▶

Gator Bait (1976) **C-93m.** *½ D: Ferd and Beverly C. Sebastian. Claudia Jen-

[514]

nings, Sam Gilman, Doug Dirkson, Clyde Ventura, Bill Thurman. All the menfolk are after sexy swamp-girl (*Playboy* Playmate of the Year Jennings) but she has a surprise or two in store for them. A tedious tease of a film, with moments of truly repellent violence. Followed by a sequel. [R]▼

Gator Bait II: Cajun Justice (1988) **C-95m.** *½ D: Ferd and Beverly C. Sebastian. Jan MacKenzie, Tray Loren, Jerry Armstrong, Paul Muzzcat, Ben Sebastian. Just what you've been waiting for: a sequel, with Loren as the brother of the character played in the original by the late Claudia Jennings. City girl MacKenzie is his new wife; after being harassed by some stereotypically slobbering backwoods boors, she goes into action. [R]▼●

Gattaca (1997) **C-112m.** *** D: Andrew Niccol. Ethan Hawke, Uma Thurman, Jude Law, Gore Vidal, Loren Dean, Alan Arkin, Xander Berkeley, Blair Underwood, Ernest Borgnine, Tony Shalhoub, Jayne Brook, Elias Koteas. In the near future, parents can choose to have all genetic imperfections eliminated from their children prior to birth. This has given rise to a new form of discrimination: the genetically perfected "Valids" vs. the naturally born "In-Valids." In-Valid Hawke pays disabled Valid Law for the rights to his identity. Bracingly intelligent, wittily ironic, and very well acted. Given the premise, however, the dull, conformist society depicted seems unconvincing. Notable directing debut for Niccol, who also scripted. Super 35. [PG-13]▼●●

Gaudi Afternoon (2002-Spanish) **C-90m.** ** D: Susan Seidelman. Judy Davis, Marcia Gay Harden, Lili Taylor, Juliette Lewis, María Barranco, Christopher Bowen, Courtney Jines. Overbaked, gender-bending mishmash with oddball American Harden arriving in Barcelona, hiring translator Davis to help her find a missing person. Davis is shrill and Taylor doesn't so much act as yell, but Harden is a hoot in a most unusual role. Based on a book by Barbara Wilson. [R]▼▶

Gauntlet, The (1977) **C-109m.** **½ D: Clint Eastwood. Clint Eastwood, Sondra Locke, Pat Hingle, William Prince, Bill McKinney, Mara Corday. Eastwood stars as a none-too-clever cop escorting hooker Locke to trial; corrupt officials are determined to stop them, whatever the cost. Exciting at times, but not meant to be taken seriously. Panavision. [R]▼●▶

Gay Divorcee, The (1934) **107m.** ***½ D: Mark Sandrich. Fred Astaire, Ginger Rogers, Alice Brady, Edward Everett Horton, Erik Rhodes, Eric Blore, Betty Grable. Top Astaire-Rogers froth with usual needless plot and unusual musical numbers, including Oscar-winning "Continental" and Cole Porter's "Night and Day." Rhodes is memorable as would-be corespondent in divorce case. Incidentally, the Broadway hit on

which this was based was called *The Gay Divorce,* but the Hollywood Production Code disapproved. ▼●▶

Gay Purr-ee (1962) **C-86m.** **½ D: Abe Levitow. Voices of Judy Garland, Robert Goulet, Red Buttons, Hermione Gingold, Paul Frees, Morey Amsterdam. A naive cat's misadventures in Paris. Stylish cartoon from UPA studio, written by Chuck and Dorothy Jones, lacks storytelling oomph. Chief assets are Garland and Goulet performing original songs by Harold Arlen and E. Y. Harburg, who wrote THE WIZARD OF OZ score for Judy years earlier. ▼●▶

Gazebo, The (1959) **100m.** *** D: George Marshall. Glenn Ford, Debbie Reynolds, Carl Reiner, Doro Merande, John McGiver, Mabel Albertson. Offbeat comedy involving murder and a backyard gazebo that covers up crime. Character actors McGiver and Merande wrap this up, but stars are competent. Also shown in computer-colored version. CinemaScope.▼

Gazon Maudit SEE: **French Twist**

Geisha Boy, The (1958) **C-98m.** **½ D: Frank Tashlin. Jerry Lewis, Marie McDonald, Sessue Hayakawa, Nobu McCarthy, Suzanne Pleshette, Barton MacLane, Robert Hirano. Jerry, an inept magician, travels to Japan with disastrous consequences. Imaginative visual gags; there's a cute sequence featuring the Los Angeles Dodgers (and, in particular, Gil Hodges). Pleshette's film debut. VistaVision.▼

Gene Krupa Story, The (1959) **101m.** **½ D: Don Weis, Sal Mineo, Susan Kohner, James Darren, Susan Oliver, Yvonne Craig, Lawrence Dobkin, Red Nichols, Buddy Lester. Hackneyed version of great jazz drummer's life, his ups and downs, his siege of dope addiction.▼

Genealogies of a Crime (1997-French) **C-114m.** **½ D: Raul Ruiz. Catherine Deneuve, Michel Piccoli, Melvil Poupaud, Andrzej Seweryn, Bernadette LaFont. Deneuve is dazzling in a dual role as the lawyer for and victim of a strange young man who's accused of murdering his psychiatrist aunt after she allegedly subjected him to radical mind-control treatments. Well-acted but pretentious, intentionally confusing mixture of mystery, satire, and surrealism; tricked up with meaningless flashbacks within flashbacks and other narrative and visual gimmicks.▶

General, The (1927) **75m.** **** D: Buster Keaton, Clyde Bruckman. Buster Keaton, Marion Mack, Glen Cavender, Jim Farley, Joseph Keaton. One of Keaton's best silent features, setting comedy against true Civil War story of stolen train, Union spies. Not as fanciful as other Keaton films, but beautifully done; Disney did same story in 1956 as THE GREAT LOCOMOTIVE CHASE. ▼●▶

General, The (1998-Irish) **124m.** **½ D: John Boorman. Brendan Gleeson, Jon Voight, Adrian Dunbar, Sean McGinley,

Maria Doyle Kennedy, Angeline Ball, Eamonn Owens. Boorman scripted this character study of a true-life Dublin working-class criminal known as the General, who evaded police capture for years. Following his own skewed code of ethics, he masterminds robberies both large and small, extracts loyalty from his soldiers, loves two women simultaneously, and matches wits with a hard-nosed cop (Voight) who is determined to nail him. Interesting, well made, but overlong. Filmmaker Jim Sheridan has a bit part. Super 35. [R]▼●●

General Della Rovere (1959-Italian) **129m. ***½** D: Roberto Rossellini. Vittorio De Sica, Hannes Messemer, Sandra Milo, Giovanna Ralli, Anne Vernon. De Sica is brilliant as a con man forced by the Nazis to impersonate a just-deceased Italian general and find out the identity of a Resistance leader. Will this charade somehow transform a coward into a hero?▼▶

General Died at Dawn, The (1936) **97m. ***½** D: Lewis Milestone. Gary Cooper, Madeleine Carroll, Akim Tamiroff, Dudley Digges, Porter Hall, William Frawley. Fine, atmospheric drama of Oriental intrigue, with mercenary Cooper falling in love with spy Carroll while battling evil warlord Tamiroff. Author John O'Hara has cameo as reporter on train. Another celebrated writer, Clifford Odets, scripted from Charles Booth's novel.▼▶

General's Daughter, The (1999) **C-125m. **½** D: Simon West. John Travolta, Madeleine Stowe, James Cromwell, Timothy Hutton, Leslie Stefanson, Daniel von Bargen, Clarence Williams III, James Woods, John Frankenheimer. Army investigator Travolta uncovers more than he ever imagined when he looks into the murder of a popular general's daughter, herself a captain. As evidence of a major scandal grows, it becomes clear that the Army's only concern is keeping a lid on the matter. Slickly done, but this twisty tale (from Nelson DeMille's bestseller) has a heavy air of contrivance about it. Panavision. [R]▼●▶

Generation, A (1954-Polish) **88m. ***** D: Andrzej Wajda. Ursula Modrzinska, Tadevsz Lomnicki, Zbigniew Cybulski. Strong, necessarily downbeat drama about the Polish Resistance during World War 2 and what happens when a young man falls in love with the woman who leads the Resistance group. Wajda's first film and the first of a trilogy that includes the even better KANAL and ASHES AND DIAMONDS. Young Roman Polanski is featured in the cast.▼▶

Generation (1969) **C-104m. ***** D: George Schaefer. David Janssen, Kim Darby, Carl Reiner, Peter Duel, Andrew Prine, James Coco, Sam Waterston. Darby helps otherwise dreary comedy based on Broadway play about just-married couple who infuriate the girl's father when husband plans to

deliver their soon-to-arrive baby himself; plays like a TV sitcom. [M/PG]▼

Genevieve (1953-British) **C-86m. ***½** D: Henry Cornelius. Dinah Sheridan, John Gregson, Kay Kendall, Kenneth More, Geoffrey Keen, Joyce Grenfell, Michael Medwin. Lively, colorful comedy (by William Rose) pits two couples and their vintage roadsters against one another in a cross-country race. Uniquely British, brimming with charm and humor; a huge success in its day. Music score by harmonica virtuoso Larry Adler.▼

Genghis Khan (1965) **C-124m. *½** D: Henry Levin. Omar Sharif, Stephen Boyd, James Mason, Eli Wallach, Françoise Dorleac, Telly Savalas, Robert Morley, Yvonne Mitchell, Woody Strode. Laughable epic with gross miscasting and juvenile script, loosely based on legend of Mongol leader. No sweep or spectacle, but radiant Dorleac and earnest Sharif. Panavision.▶

Genova SEE: **Summer in Genoa, A**

Gentle Giant (1967) **C-93m. ***** D: James Neilson. Dennis Weaver, Vera Miles, Clint Howard, Ralph Meeker, Huntz Hall. Feature film which hatched TV series *Gentle Ben* is appealing children's story of boy and his pet bear.▼

Gentleman Jim (1942) **104m. ***½** D: Raoul Walsh. Errol Flynn, Alexis Smith, Jack Carson, Alan Hale, John Loder, William Frawley, Minor Watson, Ward Bond, Arthur Shields. Sassy biography of polished boxer Jim Corbett in fight game's early days. Flynn is dynamic in title role (reportedly his favorite), supported by colorful cast—especially Bond in larger-than-life role as legendary champ John L. Sullivan. Scripted by Vincent Lawrence and Horace McCoy. Also shown in computer-colored version. ▼●▶

Gentleman's Agreement (1947) **118m. ***** D: Elia Kazan. Gregory Peck, Dorothy McGuire, John Garfield, Celeste Holm, Anne Revere, June Havoc, Albert Dekker, Jane Wyatt, Dean Stockwell, Sam Jaffe. Sincere Oscar-winning adaptation of Laura Z. Hobson's novel of writer (Peck) pretending to be Jewish, discovering rampant anti-Semitism. Holm won Supporting Actress Oscar as chic but lonely fashion editor, as did Kazan for his direction. Then-daring approach to subject matter is tame now. Screenplay by Moss Hart. ▼●▶

Gentlemen Don't Eat Poets (1995-British) **C-97m. **** D: John-Paul Davidson. Alan Bates, Sting, Theresa Russell, Lena Headey, Steven Mackintosh, Anna Massey, Trudie Styler, Maria Aitken. An English butler, in cooperation with the mistress of the house, frames his master for murder in this blackest of black British comedies. Other than its clever (and somewhat prophetic) title, this lacks the necessary wit to succeed. Sting is understated as the butler; you get the feeling he's doing it only because his wife, Trudie

Styler, produced the film. Original title: THE GROTESQUE. Video title: GRAVE INDISCRETIONS. [R]▼●

Gentlemen Marry Brunettes (1955) **C-97m.** ** D: Richard Sale. Jane Russell, Jeanne Crain, Alan Young, Rudy Vallee, Scott Brady. Anita Loos' follow-up to GENTLEMEN PREFER BLONDES has Russell and Crain, two sisters in show biz in Paris, trying to avoid romances. Not up to original. CinemaScope.

Gentlemen Prefer Blondes (1953) **C-91m.** *** D: Howard Hawks. Jane Russell, Marilyn Monroe, Charles Coburn, Elliott Reid, Tommy Noonan, George "Foghorn" Winslow. Slick, colorful bauble of entertainment with two sassy leading ladies tantalizing the men of two continents; Marilyn is at her best as fortune-hunter Lorelei Lee, and Russell gives a sly, knowing comic performance as her pal. Based on the Broadway adaptation of Anita Loos' venerable story, with sprightly Leo Robin–Jule Styne songs including "Diamonds Are a Girl's Best Friend." Sequel: GENTLEMEN MARRY BRUNETTES.▼●

George A. Romero's Diary of the Dead SEE: **Diary of the Dead**

George Balanchine's The Nutcracker SEE: **Nutcracker, The** (1993)

George of the Jungle (1997) **C-91m.** **½ D: Sam Weisman. Brendan Fraser, Leslie Mann, Thomas Haden Church, Holland Taylor, John Bennett Perry, Abraham Benrubi, Greg Cruttwell, Richard Roundtree; voice of John Cleese; narrated by Keith Scott. Live-action Disney comedy feature based on Jay Ward's 1960s cartoon show about a clumsy king of the jungle. Aimed at kids, who should enjoy it thoroughly; for adults its one-note silliness wears thin, with a preponderance of story climaxes, but Fraser and Mann are immensely likable. Why couldn't they come up with at least a few funny lines for the Ape named Ape? Followed in 2003 by a direct-to-video sequel. [PG] ▼●

George's Island (1991-Canadian) **C-90m.** **½ D: Paul Donovan. Nathaniel Moreau, Ian Bannen, Sheila McCarthy, Maury Chaykin, Vicki Ridler, Brian Downcy. Young Nova Scotia boy is taken from his crusty grandpop—who has regaled him with tales of pirate ghosts and local buried treasure from Captain Kidd's raids—and must escape from a grim foster home to complete his treasure quest. Modest tale dwells too long on adult caricatures and too little on boyhood adventures.▼●

George Stevens: A Filmmaker's Journey (1984) **C/B&W-110m.** *** D: George Stevens, Jr. Katharine Hepburn, Cary Grant, Joel McCrea, Elizabeth Taylor, Fred Astaire, Ginger Rogers, and Warren Beatty are among those who help create vivid documentary portrait of director Stevens. Great clips from ALICE ADAMS, SWING TIME,

GUNGA DIN, THE MORE THE MERRIER, A PLACE IN THE SUN, SHANE, GIANT, etc. Stevens, Jr., supplies personal insights, plus fascinating home movies taken by his father on film sets—and color footage shot during WW2 in Europe.▼●

George Washington (2000) **C-89m.** *** D: David Gordon Green. Candace Evanofski, Donald Holden, Damian Jewan Lee, Curtis Cotton III, Rachael Handy, Paul Schneider, Eddie Rouse, Janet Taylor. Eye-opening debut feature from writer-director Green, spotlighting a small group of preteens in a lazy North Carolina town and how they individually and collectively react to a terrible accident. Strikingly original, dreamlike film is filled with beautiful imagery and naturalistic performances, hampered only by the constraints of its low budget. J-D-C Scope. ▼●

Georgia (1995) **C-117m.** ** D: Ulu Grosbard. Jennifer Jason Leigh, Mare Winningham, Ted Levine, Max Perlich, John Doe, John C. Reilly, Jimmy Witherspoon, Jason Carter, Tom Bower, Smokey Hormel. A strung-out, self-destructive young woman lives in the shadow of her older sister, a popular singer, and wants to *be* her—though the younger sister has no talent. Leigh is as brilliant as ever getting inside an intense and difficult character (she does her own vocals, too), but that doesn't mean we care about her much. She also coproduced the film with her mother, Barbara Turner (who wrote the screenplay). Winningham is excellent as the serene older sister and also does her own very appealing vocals. [R]▼●

Georgia, Georgia (1972) **C-91m.** **½ D: Stig Bjorkman. Diana Sands, Dirk Benedict, Minnie Gentry. Black singer's involvement with white photographer and American defectors. Interesting but uneven. [R]▼

Georgia Rule (2007) **C-113m.** *½ D: Garry Marshall. Jane Fonda, Lindsay Lohan, Felicity Huffman, Dermot Mulroney, Cary Elwes, Garrett Hedlund, Hector Elizondo, Laurie Metcalf, Rance Howard. Huffman takes her difficult, sexually precocious teenage daughter to live with her mother in Idaho for the summer. Grandma (Fonda) is a character in her own right whose own daughter can barely stand to be in the same room with her. What might seem like a multigenerational story of women clearing the clutter from their relationships turns into a strange story involving molestation, alcoholism, sexuality, and religion! Odd in the extreme, with a trio of characters who aren't easy to like, let alone understand. The polar opposite of a feel-good movie. Super 35. [R]●

Georgy Girl (1966-British) **100m.** ***½ D: Silvio Narizzano. James Mason, Alan Bates, Lynn Redgrave, Charlotte Rampling, Bill Owen, Claire Kelly, Rachel Kempson. Delightful, adult British comedy of modern-day morals, with Redgrave as ugly-duckling Georgy, Mason as the wealthy, aging married man who wants her for his mistress. Entire cast is excellent, with Rampling scoring as Georgy's bitchy roommate. Faithful adaptation of Margaret Forster novel; scripted by Forster and Peter Nichols. ▼◖◗

Germinal (1993-French) **C-158m.** ✱✱✱ D: Claude Berri. Renaud, Gérard Depardieu, Miou-Miou, Jean Carmet, Judith Henry, Jean-Roger Milo, Laurent Terzieff, Jean-Pierre Bisson, Bernard Fresson, Jacques Dacqmine, Anny Duperey. Sprawling adaptation of classic 1884 Emile Zola novel, this manages to tell both the epic tale of a bleak rural community and the personal story of coal miner Depardieu's impoverished family. The action begins when a young job-seeker (played by French singer Renaud, in his feature acting debut) stirs up the workforce in the mining village. Impressively re-creates the period, though the characters sometimes seem a bit hollow. Still, it's hard to come away unaffected. Previously filmed in France in 1963. Panavision. ▼◖

Geronimo: An American Legend (1993) **C-115m.** ✱✱½ D: Walter Hill. Jason Patric, Robert Duvall, Gene Hackman, Wes Studi, Matt Damon, Rodney A. Grant, Kevin Tighe, Steve Reevis, Carlos Palomino, Victor Aaron, Stuart Proud Eagle Grant, Stephen McHattie, Richard Martin, Jr., Roger Callard, Scott Wilson. Stately, intelligent—but dramatically slack—chronicle of the U.S. Army's attempts to subjugate the great Apache warrior. Strong performance by Studi in the lead, and rich characterizations by Hackman (as General Crook) and Duvall (as a veteran Indian scout), sustain interest for quite a while—along with magnificent Moab, Utah, scenery. Eventually, the film's point is made, and there's nothing left to maintain audience involvement. Screenplay by John Milius. Panavision. [R] ▼◖◗

Gerry (2003) **C-103m.** ✱✱ D: Gus Van Sant. Matt Damon, Casey Affleck. Two friends go for a hike and leave the marked path. Before long they realize they're lost and must adopt increasingly challenging tactics to survive and stay sane. The screenplay, such as it is, is credited to both stars and the director, although Van Sant devises clever and creative ways of staging and filming his characters' odyssey. Some may find this existential poppycock stimulating; others will run for the exits. Arriscope. [R] ▼◗

Getaway, The (1972) **C-122m.** ✱✱✱ D: Sam Peckinpah. Steve McQueen, Ali MacGraw, Ben Johnson, Sally Struthers, Al Lettieri, Slim Pickens, Dub Taylor, Bo Hopkins. Exciting, enjoyable film built around a chase. Bank robber McQueen and wife MacGraw take it on the lam when robbery goes haywire. Many fine vignettes, including hair-raising episode on garbage truck. Written by Walter Hill from a Jim Thompson novel. Music by Quincy Jones. Remade in 1994. Todd-AO 35. [PG] ▼◖◗

Getaway, The (1994) **C-115m.** ✱✱ D: Roger Donaldson. Alec Baldwin, Kim Basinger, Michael Madsen, James Woods, David Morse, Jennifer Tilly, James Stephens, Richard Farnsworth, Philip Seymour Hoffman, Burton Gilliam, Royce D. Applegate. He's nailed for robbery and thrown in prison; she frees him by playing up to a crime kingpin; he spends the rest of the movie resenting her. Or something like that. Action, violence, and sex by the numbers in this halfhearted remake of the 1972 hit; even the usually dynamic Woods seems to be just going through the motions. Watching real-life couple Baldwin and Basinger make love is uncomfortably voyeuristic. It takes Farnsworth, in the film's closing moments, to bring it to life. One sexy scene added for video. Panavision. [R] ▼◖◗

Get Back (1991) **C-89m.** ✱✱ D: Richard Lester. Adequate rockumentary of Paul McCartney's 1989–90 Get Back world tour. Recommended only for fans of McCartney's music, though there is also some vintage footage of The Beatles. Director Lester made more imaginative use of McCartney when he directed him and his compadres in A HARD DAY'S NIGHT and HELP! [PG] ▼◗

Get Bruce! (1999) **C-73m.** ✱✱½ D: Andrew J. Kuehn. Slight but very amusing look at Hollywood comedy writer and self-styled character Bruce Vilanch, whose credits range from the Academy Awards to *Hollywood Squares*. Not what you'd call a probing character profile (especially since it was done with its subject's complete cooperation), but the interviews with Robin Williams, Billy Crystal, Whoopi Goldberg, and others are often hysterically funny. [R] ▼◗

Get Carter (1971-British) **C-112m.** ✱✱✱ D: Mike Hodges. Michael Caine, Ian Hendry, Britt Ekland, John Osborne, Tony Beckley, George Sewell. Austere, brutal crime drama about a cheerless hit man who goes to Newcastle to investigate his brother's death. Caine perfectly embodies his amoral character, and the film's violence still packs a wallop. Based on a novel by Ted Lewis, adapted by Hodges. Remade a year later (as HIT MAN) and again in 2000. [R] ▼◗

Get Carter (2000) **C-104m.** ✱✱½ D: Stephen Kay. Sylvester Stallone, Miranda Richardson, Rachael Leigh Cook, Alan Cumming, Mickey Rourke, John C. McGinley, Michael Caine, Rhona Mitra, Johnny Strong. Las Vegas enforcer goes home to Seattle to investigate his brother's death and meets one sleazy character after another who may have been involved. Routine crime drama, enlivened by high-powered car chases but burdened by show-offy visual gimmicks. Remake of the far superior 1971 film that starred Caine, whose role here is thankless. Gretchen Mol appears unbilled. Super 35. [R] ▼◗

Get Crazy (1983) **C-92m.** ✱✱✱ D: Allan Arkush. Daniel Stern, Malcolm McDowell,

Gail Edwards, Allen Goorwitz (Garfield), Ed Begley, Jr., Miles Chapin, Lou Reed, Stacey Nelkin, Bill Henderson, Franklyn Ajaye, Bobby Sherman, Fabian Forte, Lori Eastside, Lee Ving. Arkush's years working at Fillmore East rock palace form the basis for wonderful cartoonlike comedy set at a trouble-plagued New Year's Eve concert. Gags fly at machine-gun pace, interspersed with delightful musical numbers; superb take-offs on Mick Jagger (McDowell), Bob Dylan (Reed), and Muddy Waters (Henderson), plus many familiar rock stars and character actors in bits. [R]▼

Get Him to the Greek (2010) C-109m. **½ D: Nicholas Stoller. Jonah Hill, Russell Brand, Rose Byrne, Elisabeth Moss, Sean Combs, Colm Meaney, Aziz Ansari. L.A. record company functionary Hill is charged with flying to London to see that bad-boy rocker Brand, whose career has been in free fall, makes it to his concert at the Greek Theatre 72 hours later. Hill comes to learn just how messed up (and insecure) Brand really is during a nonstop series of parties, flights, detours, TV appearances, and sexual escapades, with and without drugs. Likable stars buoy this scattershot comedy (with serious moments) that tries to pack way too much into one film. Brand's faux hit songs are surprisingly good and Combs is funny as a brutally candid music exec. Brand's character first appeared in FORGETTING SARAH MARSHALL. Many celebrities appear in cameos. [R]▶

Get Low (2010-U.S.-German-Polish) C-103m. *** D: Aaron Schneider. Robert Duvall, Sissy Spacek, Bill Murray, Lucas Black, Gerald McRaney, Bill Cobbs, Scott Cooper, Lori Beth Edgeman. A man who's lived as a hermit in the backwoods of Tennessee for 40 years suddenly comes to town to see if someone will throw him a funeral—while he's still alive. Murray plays the desperate, self-deprecating owner of a funeral home who's eager to accommodate Duvall, even though he is a uniquely thorny customer. Richly textured story set in the 1930s and inspired by a real-life incident, brought to life by a superb cast. Duvall is absolutely believable, and Murray has seldom been better. Feature directing debut for longtime cinematographer Schneider. Panavision. [PG-13]▶

Get on the Bus (1996) C-120m. *** D: Spike Lee. Ossie Davis, Charles S. Dutton, Andre Braugher, DeAundre Bonds, Albert Hall, Isaiah Washington, Thomas Jefferson Byrd, Hill Harper, Harry Lennix, Bernie Mac, Richard Belzer, Gabriel Casseus. Vibrant, highly energized film about a busload of black men heading from L.A. to the Million Man March in Washington, D.C., in October 1995. Not a polemic, but a series of character studies and vignettes; occasional speechifying and contrivances are forgivable because, overall, the film deals so well

with issues facing all Americans. Screenplay by Reggie Rock Bythewood. Kudos to Dutton as the bus company rep and Davis as the senior member of the brigade. This low-budget film was financed by 15 African-American men, including Danny Glover, Will Smith, and Wesley Snipes. Randy Quaid appears unbilled. [R]▼●▶

Get Out Your Handkerchiefs (1978-French-Belgian) C-109m. ***½ D: Bertrand Blier. Gérard Depardieu, Patrick Dewaere, Carole Laure, Riton, Michel Serrault, Eleonore Hirt. Disarming black comedy about a man who will do almost anything to keep his sexually frustrated wife happy; highly unconventional. Oscar winner for Best Foreign Film. [R]▼▶

Get Over It (2001) C-86m. ** D: Tommy O'Haver. Kirsten Dunst, Ben Foster, Melissa Sagemiller, Colin Hanks, Sisqó, Martin Short, Shane West, Swoosie Kurtz, Ed Begley, Jr., Carmen Electra, Kylie Bax, Zoë Saldaña, Mila Kunis. Teen variation of *A Midsummer Night's Dream*, with Foster unable to deal with being dumped by his girlfriend, ignoring the fact that his best friend's kid sister is in love with him. Cute film can't stay focused, which dampens the fun, but Short is hilarious as a high school drama coach. Opens with a dynamic musical number under the main titles. Super 35. [PG-13]▼▶

Get Real (1999-British) C-109m. **½ D: Simon Shore. Ben Silverstone, Charlotte Brittain, Brad Gorton, Louise J. Taylor, Tim Harris, Stacy Hart. Teenage schoolboy in England realizes he's gay but can't admit it to his parents, teachers, or schoolmates. Then he falls in love with the class jock. Sincere and well acted, but tends to plod at times. Scripted by Patrick Wilde from his play *What's Wrong With Angry?* Panavision. [R]▼▶

Get Rich or Die Tryin' (2005) C-117m. ** D: Jim Sheridan. Curtis "50 Cent" Jackson, Terrence Howard, Joy Bryant, Bill Duke, Adewale Akinnuoye-Agbaje, Omar Benson Miller, Viola Davis, Leon, Sullivan Walker, Russell Hornsby. The director of MY LEFT FOOT and IN AMERICA tackles a gangsta-rap saga, which isn't as jarring as it might seem given Sheridan's obvious affection for societal underdogs. Clichés and undeveloped story lines sink a promising beginning in which a fatherless youngster with musical inclinations tags along with a man-magnet mom as she deals drugs on the street. Jackson eventually takes over this autobiographical role and isn't commanding enough to carry a long movie. Super 35. [R]▶

Get Shorty (1995) C-105m. *** D: Barry Sonnenfeld. John Travolta, Gene Hackman, Rene Russo, Danny DeVito, Dennis Farina, Delroy Lindo, James Gandolfini, David Paymer, Martin Ferrero, Miguel Sandoval. Clever black comedy about a small-time, cool-as-ice Miami enforcer coming to L.A. on business, hooking up with a slick, grade-

Z producer who can fulfill his dream of being connected with the movies. Ingenious plotting, tip-top performances, and some delicious digs at Hollywood are offset by a certain aloofness. Scott Frank scripted from Elmore Leonard's novel. Bette Midler appears unbilled; other famous faces turn up in amusing cameos. Followed by BE COOL. [R]▼●▮

Get Smart (2008) **C-110m.** **½ D: Peter Segal. Steve Carell, Anne Hathaway, Dwayne Johnson, Alan Arkin, Terence Stamp, James Caan, Masi Oka, Nate Torrence, Ken Davitian, Terry Crews, David Koechner, Dalip Singh, Bill Murray, Larry Miller, Kevin Nealon, Blake Clark, Patrick Warburton, Bernie Kopell. Update of the much-loved 1960s spy-spoof TV series (created by Mel Brooks and Buck Henry) stars Carell as CONTROL Agent 86 Maxwell Smart, who's sent into "the field" for the first time alongside worldly Agent 99 (Hathaway) to expose a nuclear weapon plot hatched by KAOS. The stars' likability carries this overlong feature, which pays respect to the TV show but never equals it. Overblown action finale seems to belong in some other movie. Oka and Torrence's characters, Bruce and Lloyd, star in a companion DVD movie. [PG-13]▮

Getting Away With Murder (1976) SEE: End of the Game

Getting Away With Murder (1996) **C-92m.** BOMB D: Harvey Miller. Jack Lemmon, Dan Aykroyd, Lily Tomlin, Bonnie Hunt, Brian Kerwin, Jerry Adler, Andy Romano. Ethics professor Aykroyd discovers that his next-door neighbor (Lemmon) is a notorious Nazi war criminal who is plotting to leave the country. Strictly for those who found JUDGMENT AT NUREMBERG a laugh riot; a career nadir for the comic talents on both sides of the camera. [R]▼●▮

Getting Even With Dad (1994) **C-108m.** *½ D: Howard Deutch. Macaulay Culkin, Ted Danson, Glenne Headly, Saul Rubinek, Gailard Sartain, Hector Elizondo, Ron Canada. Ex-con cake decorator steals a rare coin collection with his two doofus pals, *just* as his 11-year-old son shows up for an extended visit. Touchy-feely comedy didn't touch many paying customers, despite Culkin's modified HOME ALONE-ing of comical villains Rubinek and Sartain; Danson's unlikely romance with policewoman Headly is as drab as the rest. [PG]▼●▮

Getting It Right (1989) **C-102m.** *** D: Randal Kleiser. Jesse Birdsall, Helena Bonham Carter, Peter Cook, Lynn Redgrave, Jane Horrocks, Richard Huw, John Gielgud, Shirley Anne Field, Pat Heywood, Judy Parfitt, Bryan Pringle. Sweetly comic story of a 31-year-old virgin and his attempts to cope with people—women in particular—seems mundane and meandering at first, and just gets better as it goes along. Some wonderful characterizations, especially Redgrave as a wealthy woman with a world-weary facade

who just wants to be loved. Screenplay by Elizabeth Jane Howard, from her novel. Made in England by an American director and producer. [R]▼●

Getting of Wisdom, The (1977-Australian) **C-100m.** **½ D: Bruce Beresford. Susannah Fowle, Hilary Ryan, Alix Longman, Sheila Helpmann, Patricia Kennedy, Barry Humphries, John Waters. A spirited, sensitive 13-year-old girl (Fowle) from the outback matures on her own terms at a snobbish Victorian ladies college. Fowle is miscast; however, the era is carefully recreated. Based on autobiographical novel by one Henry Handel Richardson.▼

Getting Straight (1970) **C-124m.** **½ D: Richard Rush. Elliott Gould, Candice Bergen, Jeff Corey, Max Julien, Cecil Kellaway, Robert F. Lyons, Jeannie Berlin, John Rubinstein, Brenda Sykes, Harrison Ford. A period piece, but central issue of graduate student Gould choosing between academic double-talk and his beliefs remains relevant. Gould's personality propels glossy film. Bob Kaufman adapted Ken Kolb's novel. [R]▼▮

Get to Know Your Rabbit (1972) **C-91m.** **½ D: Brian De Palma. Tom Smothers, John Astin, Suzanne Zenor, Samantha Jones, Allen Garfield, Katharine Ross, Orson Welles. Offbeat comedy was barely released, and heavily tampered with at that; starts with great premise of Smothers dropping out of establishment life to become tap-dancing magician, then loses itself. Still has some inventive moments, funny ideas. Filmed in 1970. [R]▼▮

Gettysburg (1993) **C-248m.** ***½ D: Ronald Maxwell. Tom Berenger, Jeff Daniels, Martin Sheen, Sam Elliott, Maxwell Caulfield, Kevin Conway, C. Thomas Howell, Richard Jordan, Royce D. Applegate, John Diehl, Patrick Gorman, Cooper Huckabee, James Lancaster, Brian Mallon, Andrew Prine, Stephen Lang, Richard Anderson, Bo Brinkman, Kieran Mulroney, George Lazenby, Dwier Brown, Buck Taylor. Ted Turner's answer to GONE WITH THE WIND, a magnificent re-creation of the Civil War's most famous battle. Based on Michael Shaara's Pulitzer Prize–winning novel, *The Killer Angels,* this long but engrossing slice of history was filmed on the battlefields of the Gettysburg National Military Park using over 5,000 Civil War "re-enactors" in the battle scenes. Look fast for filmmaker Ken Burns as General Hancock's aide and Turner as a Reb foot soldier during Pickett's Charge. Elliott, and especially Daniels, stand out in a cast full of great performances. Final film for Richard Jordan, who has the most poignant role in the picture as General Armistead. Superb score by Randy Edelman. Also available in 271m. director's cut. Followed by a prequel: GODS AND GENERALS. [PG] ▼●▮

G-Force (2009) **C-88m.** **½ D: Hoyt H.

[520]

Yeatman, Jr. Bill Nighy, Will Arnett, Zach Galifianakis, Kelli Garner, Niecy Nash; voices of Nicolas Cage, Sam Rockwell, Jon Favreau, Penélope Cruz, Steve Buscemi, Tracy Morgan. Government special ops squad of genetically enhanced guinea pigs (yes, guinea pigs) infiltrate bad guy Nighy's corporate empire to prevent the end of the world, and all that. Simplistic script and themes are typical of producer Jerry Bruckheimer, as is the noisy, pyrotechnical overproduction. But the nifty 3-D effects, several funny lines, and Cage's career high as star-nosed mole Speckles elevate this family fodder. 3-D Super 35. [PG]●

Ghidrah, The Three-Headed Monster (1964-Japanese) **C-85m.** **½ D: Ishiro Honda. Yosuke Natsuki, Yunko Hoshi, Hiroshi Koizumi, Akiko Wakabayashi, Takashi Shimura, Emi Ito, Yumi Ito. Beautiful princess, feared killed in a plane crash, reappears, claiming to be from Mars and warning that we're about to be attacked by a space dragon. Darned if she isn't right. Debut of King Ghidorah (whose name was misspelled by the original U.S. distributor) is one of the better Toho monster rallies, with Godzilla, Rodan, and Mothra calling a truce to battle this new foe. Akira Ifukube's dynamic score is a plus, as is the warm presence of the illustrious Shimura. Japanese running time is 92m. Tohoscope.▼❶

Ghost (1990) **C-122m.** *** D: Jerry Zucker. Patrick Swayze, Demi Moore, Whoopi Goldberg, Tony Goldwyn, Rick Aviles, Vincent Schiavelli, Gail Boggs, Armelia McQueen, Phil Leeds. Overlong but enjoyable mix of fantasy, thriller, and romance. Swayze is killed, and when he learns (in his ghostly state) that he was the victim of a botched hit, he tries to warn his grieving girlfriend (Moore) that she's in danger too. Storefront medium Whoopi (in an Oscar-winning role) turns out to be the only one who can convey his messages to her. Swayze runs the gamut of expressions from A to B, but the relationships are credible and as a result the fantasy works. Oscar winner for Best Original Screenplay (Bruce Joel Rubin). Later a stage musical. [PG-13]▼❶

Ghost and Mr. Chicken, The (1966) **C-90m.** **½ D: Alan Rafkin. Don Knotts, Joan Staley, Skip Homeier, Dick Sargent, Reta Shaw, James Millhollin, Phil Ober, Liam Redmond, Lurene Tuttle, Charles Lane. Featherweight comedy with Knotts a would-be reporter who seizes his big chance for a scoop by spending a night in a supposedly haunted house. Full of familiar character faces. Techniscope.▼❶

Ghost and Mrs. Muir, The (1947) **104m.** ***½ D: Joseph L. Mankiewicz. Gene Tierney, Rex Harrison, George Sanders, Edna Best, Vanessa Brown, Anna Lee, Robert Coote, Natalie Wood. A lonely widow is romanced by the ghost of a sea captain in her "haunted" English cottage. Charming, beautifully made fantasy, a distant cousin to later TV sitcom; lovely score by Bernard Herrmann. Philip Dunne scripted, from the R.A. Dick novel.▼❶

Ghost and the Darkness, The (1996) **C-109m.** **½ D: Stephen Hopkins. Michael Douglas, Val Kilmer, Tom Wilkinson, John Kani, Bernard Hill, Brian McCardie, Henry Cele, Emily Mortimer, Om Puri. In 1896, an Irish bridge builder heads to Africa for his latest project, but the campsite is soon cursed by violent and unexplainable attacks by a pair of man-eating lions. Eventually, renowned big-game hunter Douglas is called in. What begins as a rousing, old-fashioned adventure somehow loses its way—and its impact. Screenplay by William Goldman. Based on the same true story that inspired BWANA DEVIL. Panavision. [R]▼❶

Ghost Breakers, The (1940) **85m.** *** D: George Marshall. Bob Hope, Paulette Goddard, Richard Carlson, Paul Lukas, Anthony Quinn, Willie Best, Noble Johnson, Tom Dugan, Lloyd Corrigan. More plot than usual for a Hope film as Bob and Paulette investigate eerie Cuban castle that she's inherited. Some real chills as well as laughs in this first-rate film. Remade as SCARED STIFF (1953).▼❶

Ghost Brigade (1994) **C-80m.** **½ D: George Hickenlooper. Corbin Bernsen, Adrian Pasdar, Ray Wise, Martin Sheen, Cynda Williams, Billy Bob Thornton, David Arquette, Matt LeBlanc. Yankees and Rebs team up to confront supernatural brigade of evil soldiers that's been wreaking gruesome slaughter on both sides. Odd mix of Civil War and horror genres aspires to a Peckinpah–type brutality but generally opts for mere shock value. Putting APOCALYPSE NOW star Sheen and HEARTS OF DARKNESS documentary director Hickenlooper together gives viewer an unmistakable feeling of déjà vu, as if you're back up the delta in Cambodia looking for Col. Kurtz. Aka GREY NIGHT and THE KILLING BOX. [R]▼❶

Ghost Busters (1984) **C-107m.** *** D: Ivan Reitman. Bill Murray, Dan Aykroyd, Harold Ramis, Sigourney Weaver, Rick Moranis, Annie Potts, Ernie Hudson, William Atherton, Reginald VelJohnson. The first multimillion-dollar scare comedy, about a trio of flaky "paranormal investigators" who go into business flushing out ghosts and spirits in N.Y.C.—and find their business booming! Engagingly offbeat, even subdued at times, with Murray's flippant personality nicely contrasting Richard Edlund's eye-popping special effects. Great fun all the way; written by Aykroyd and Ramis. Followed by a sequel and an animated TV series. Panavision. [PG]▼❶

Ghostbusters II (1989) **C-102m.** *** D: Ivan Reitman. Bill Murray, Dan Aykroyd, Sigourney Weaver, Harold Ramis, Rick Moranis, Ernie Hudson, Peter MacNicol, David Margulies, Annie Potts, Ben Stein, Janet Margolin, Harris Yulin, Philip Baker Hall. Amiable, entertaining sequel has the ghost-busting boys reteaming five years after their last adventure to save N.Y.C. from a slime attack of gargantuan proportions, generated by all the "negative energy" in the air of the Big Apple. Longish but good-natured, with some solid laughs along the way. Chloe Webb has a funny unbilled cameo as a guest on Murray's cable TV show. Panavision. [PG]▼●◗

Ghost Dad (1990) C-84m. ** D: Sidney Poitier. Bill Cosby, Kimberly Russell, Denise Nicholas, Ian Bannen, Christine Ebersole, Barry Corbin, Salim Grant, Brooke Fontaine, Dakin Matthews, Dana Ashbrook, Arnold Stang. Overworked businessman (and widower) Cosby dies in a taxi accident, and learns he has only a few days to try to straighten out his finances so his three kids will be secure. Positive family message aside, this effects-laden fantasy plays like an extended sitcom. Younger kids may like it—others beware. [PG]▼●◗

Ghost Dog: The Way of the Samurai (1999-U.S.-French) C-116m. *** D: Jim Jarmusch. Forest Whitaker, John Tormey, Cliff Gorman, Henry Silva, Isaach de Bankolé, Tricia Vessey, Victor Argo. Ghost Dog (Whitaker), a solitary hit man who lives by the code of the Samurai, finds himself a target after a job gone wrong. Typically original (though sometimes pretentious) Jarmusch mix of mysticism, action, and even comedy, anchored by Whitaker's quiet, intense performance. Very bloody at times, and not for all tastes. Written by the director. [R]▼◗

Ghost in the Invisible Bikini, The (1966) C-82m. *½ D: Don Weis. Tommy Kirk, Deborah Walley, Aron Kincaid, Quinn O'Hara, Nancy Sinatra, Claudia Martin, Harvey Lembeck, Jesse White, Susan Hart, Basil Rathbone, Boris Karloff, Patsy Kelly, Francis X. Bushman, Benny Rubin. Seventh (and final) BEACH PARTY movie failed to provide a shot in the arm with entirely new set of characters (save Lembeck's Eric Von Zipper); larger-than-usual roster of veteran movie greats might attract masochistic film buffs. Panavision. ◗

Ghost in the Machine (1993) C-95m. *½ D: Rachel Talalay. Karen Allen, Chris Mulkey, Ted Marcoux, Wil Horneff, Jessica Walter, Brandon Quintin Adams, Rick Ducommun. The spirit of a dying serial killer is sucked into a computer mainframe in Cleveland, from which he continues to pursue his latest target, single mother Allen, by killing her friends and ruining her credit. Both obvious and ludicrous. [R]▼◗

Ghost in the Noonday Sun (1973-British) C-89m. BOMB D: Peter Medak. Peter Sellers, Anthony Franciosa, Spike Milligan, Clive Revill, Peter Boyle, Richard Willis. Absolutely atrocious pirate comedy which understand-ably never got full-fledged theatrical release. Milligan, who's credited with "additional dialogue," appears in one sequence with his *Goon Show* colleague Sellers, but even their chemistry can't save this turkey.▼

Ghost of Frankenstein, The (1942) 68m. **½ D: Erle C. Kenton. Cedric Hardwicke, Lon Chaney, Jr., Lionel Atwill, Ralph Bellamy, Bela Lugosi, Evelyn Ankers, Dwight Frye. Sequel to SON OF FRANKENSTEIN. Ygor (Lugosi) tries to convince Dr. Frankenstein (Hardwicke) to put his brain into the Monster. Good cast manages to save stale plot. Followed by FRANKENSTEIN MEETS THE WOLF MAN.▼●◗

Ghost Rider (2007) C-110m. ** D: Mark Steven Johnson. Nicolas Cage, Eva Mendes, Wes Bentley, Sam Elliott, Donal Logue, Matt Long, Peter Fonda, Brett Cullen. Daredevil motorcyclist makes a deal with the Devil (Fonda) in order to save his father's life, then tries to adjust to living a cursed existence. In time he finds his true identity as a cycle vigilante who rides engulfed in flames, his head a burning skull! Adaptation of the Marvel comic book set out West might have been better if it didn't take so long to spell out its premise and get up a head of steam. Unrated version runs 127m. Super 35. [PG-13]◗

Ghosts Can't Do It (1990) C-95m. BOMB D: John Derek. Bo Derek, Anthony Quinn, Leo Damian, Don Murray, Julie Newmar, Dee Krainz. And neither (at least on film) can John and Bo. Standard Derek atrocity involves Bo's international search for the perfect male body to house the spirit of her beloved but deceased husband (Quinn). Tony looks as if he's been photographed through the Lucille Ball MAME filter for the supernatural scenes. Just when you think it can't get any worse, Donald Trump shows up in a cameo. [R]▼◗

Ghost Ship, The (1943) 69m. *** D: Mark Robson. Richard Dix, Russell Wade, Edith Barrett, Ben Bard, Lawrence Tierney. Offbeat Val Lewton melodrama about young man who signs on merchant ship run by power-crazy captain (Dix) who's obsessed with "authority." Absorbing mood piece with unfortunately abrupt conclusion.▼●◗

Ghost Ship (2002) C-91m. ** D: Steve Beck. Julianna Margulies, Gabriel Byrne, Ron Eldard, Desmond Harrington, Isaiah Washington, Karl Urban. A salvage crew learns that a long-lost ocean liner is adrift in the vicinity, offering a potential windfall. Once aboard, they face a decidedly eerie environment and an alarming mortality rate. Flat, by-the-numbers horror fare, with some graphically gory scenes. [R]▼◗

Ghosts—Italian Style (1967-Italian) C-92m. ** D: Renato Castellani. Sophia Loren, Vittorio Gassman, Mario Adorf, Margaret Lee, Aldo Guiffre. Newlyweds Loren and Gassman move into haunted house. Weak vehicle for engaging stars. [G]

Ghosts of Girlfriends Past (2009) **C-100m.** ** D: Mark Waters. Matthew McConaughey, Jennifer Garner, Michael Douglas, Breckin Meyer, Lacey Chabert, Robert Forster, Anne Archer, Emma Stone, Daniel Sunjata. Tepid reimagining of *A Christmas Carol* as a romantic comedy, with McConaughey typecast as a roguish lothario who's encouraged to change his charming-wastrel ways while visited by various apparitions—including his late playboy uncle (scene stealer Douglas)—the night before his brother's wedding. Game actors aren't helped by flat cinematography (even Garner, as McConaughey's once and future sweetie, looks drab) and predictable writing. Super 35. [PG-13]▶

Ghosts of Mars (2001) **C-98m.** *½ D: John Carpenter. Natasha Henstridge, Ice Cube, Pam Grier, Clea DuVall, Jason Statham, Liam Waite, Joanna Cassidy, Wanda De Jesus, Duane Davis, Robert Carradine. In the near future, Mars has been colonized, but there's an outbreak of mass murder in some remote settlements. People are possessed by vengeful Martian ghosts; it's up to the team of a lady cop and a hardened criminal to battle them. Routine, predictable, and dull; unimaginatively, the Martian-possessed people adopt a punk/grunge look. Basically a remake of Carpenter's early ASSAULT ON PRECINCT 13. Panavision. [R]▼▶

Ghosts of Mississippi (1996) **C-130m.** *** D: Rob Reiner. Alec Baldwin, Whoopi Goldberg, James Woods, Craig T. Nelson, Susanna Thompson, Lucas Black, William H. Macy, Terry O'Quinn, Virginia Madsen, Bonnie Bartlett, Wayne Rogers, Diane Ladd. Straightforward drama about Mississippi assistant D.A. Bobby DeLaughter (Baldwin), who reopens the case against the murderer of civil rights leader Medgar Evers 30 years after the fact. Reminiscent of 1960s movies in its earnestness and sobriety, it still works, but lacks the edge and energy to make it soar. Goldberg is surprisingly good as Evers' widow, and Woods has a showy part (in heavy makeup) as the aged murderer, Byron De La Beckwith. [PG-13]▼▶

Ghost Story (1981) **C-110m.** **½ D: John Irvin. Fred Astaire, Melvyn Douglas, Douglas Fairbanks, Jr., John Houseman, Craig Wasson, Alice Krige, Patricia Neal, Ken Olin. Four elderly New Englanders are tormented by a 50-year-old secret, which now visits evil on one of their sons as well. Absorbing if not altogether satisfying simplification of Peter Straub's best-seller, which loses steam as it nears its resolution. Astaire's last film. [R]▼▶

Ghost Town (1988) **C-85m.** **½ D: Richard Governor. Franc Luz, Catherine Hickland, Jimmie F. Skaggs, Penelope Windust, Bruce Glover, Blake Conway, Laura Schaefer. Imaginative fantasy thriller has modern-day Western sheriff Luz chosen to rid a century-old town of its curse by avenging its dead sheriff in HIGH NOON fashion. Fine special effects distinguish this modest sleeper. [R]▼▶

Ghost Town (2008) **C-102m.** *** D: David Koepp. Ricky Gervais, Téa Leoni, Greg Kinnear, Billy Campbell, Kristen Wiig, Dana Ivey, Aasif Mandvi, Alan Ruck, Brian d'Arcy James. Acerbic, people-phobic N.Y.C. dentist Gervais is haunted by a ghost (Kinnear) who needs to resolve issues with his widow (Leoni) before he can rest in peace. Then the unexpected happens: the dentist falls in love with her. This is the kind of fantasy-comedy "they don't make anymore," buoyed by Gervais' distinctive comic persona and his hilarious mutterings. Funny and heartfelt; written by director Koepp and John Kamps. [PG-13]▶

Ghost World (2001) **C-111m.** **½ D: Terry Zwigoff. Thora Birch, Scarlett Johansson, Steve Buscemi, Brad Renfro, Illeana Douglas, Bob Balaban. A sour teenage iconoclast (Birch) finds her only friend (Johansson) drifting away after their high school graduation, so she attaches herself to geeky record collector Buscemi. A well-observed study of alienation, coscripted by Zwigoff and Daniel Clowes from the latter's comic book . . . but it's difficult to care about a character who refuses to be cared about. Zwigoff's first fictional feature, following CRUMB; in fact, R. Crumb contributed a drawing to this film. Teri Garr appears unbilled. [R]▼▶

Ghost Writer, The (2010-French-German-British) **C-128m.** *** D: Roman Polanski. Ewan McGregor, Kim Cattrall, Pierce Brosnan, Olivia Williams, Tom Wilkinson, Timothy Hutton, Jon Bernthal, Robert Pugh, Eli Wallach, James Belushi. Bristling paranoia thriller about a writer who's hired to "ghost" a former British Prime Minister's memoirs—because the last fellow on the job died, under mysterious circumstances. The more the ghost writer (McGregor) learns about his subject (Brosnan), the more he questions, which puts him at risk, like his predecessor. Masterfully orchestrated suspense drama with topical geopolitical references. Alexandre Desplat's score establishes a sense of dread from the opening scene; Polanski takes care of the rest. He and Robert Harris wrote the screenplay, from Harris' controversial novel *The Ghost.* HD Widescreen.[PG-13]▶

Ghoul, The (1975-British) **C-88m.** **½ D: Freddie Francis. Peter Cushing, John Hurt, Alexandra Bastedo, Gwen Watford, Veronica Carlson, Steward Bevan. Innocent people fall victim to a mysterious flesh-eating "monster" in Cushing's secluded home. Fairly interesting, nongory thriller, with Hurt as Cushing's crazed gardener.▼

Ghoulies (1985) **C-84m.** *½ D: Luca Bercovici. Peter Liapis, Lisa Pelikan, Michael Des Barres, Jack Nance, Peter Risch, Tamara de Treaux, Mariska Hargitay. Boring, ridiculous film about young man who invokes Satanic spirits in the form of gremlinlike creatures (who look like muppets dipped in shellac) at a creepy old mansion. Followed by three sequels. [PG-13]▼▼

Giant (1956) **C-201m.** **** D: George Stevens. Elizabeth Taylor, Rock Hudson, James Dean, Carroll Baker, Jane Withers, Chill Wills, Mercedes McCambridge, Dennis Hopper, Sal Mineo, Rodney (Rod) Taylor, Earl Holliman. Near-legendary epic based on Edna Ferber's novel about two generations of larger-than-life Texans holds up beautifully, although still very much of its time. Hudson's best performance, close to Taylor's best, and Dean's last film. Stevens won Oscar for direction. Screenplay by Fred Guiol and Ivan Moffat. ▼●❙

Giant Spider Invasion, The (1975) **C-82m.** BOMB D: Bill Rebane. Steve Brodie, Barbara Hale, Leslie Parrish, Alan Hale, Robert Easton, Bill Williams. Veteran cast can't do much for this tacky horror opus filmed in Wisconsin. [PG]▼▼

Giant Steps (1992-Canadian) **C-94m.** **½ D: Richard Rose. Billy Dee Williams, Michael Mahonen, Robyn Stevan, Ted Dykstra, Ranee Lee. Idealistic teen trumpeter Mahonen befriends his idol, Slate Thompson (Williams), a legendary, self-destructive jazz pianist attempting to remain true to his art. Well meaning but obvious and preachy.▼

G.I. Blues (1960) **C-104m.** **½ D: Norman Taurog. Elvis Presley, Juliet Prowse, Robert Ivers, Leticia Roman, Ludwig Stossel. Prowse's versatile performance as a cabaret dancer uplifts this standard Presley fare about a guitar-playing G.I. in West Germany. Elvis sings "Tonight Is So Right for Love," "Wooden Heart," "Blue Suede Shoes," and title song. ▼●❙

Gideon of Scotland Yard (1958-British) **C-91m.** *½ D: John Ford. Jack Hawkins, Dianne Foster, Cyril Cusack, Andrew Ray, James Hayter, Ronald Howard, Anna Massey, Anna Lee, Laurence Naismith. A typical day in the life of a Scotland Yard inspector; Hawkins is likable but the film is unbelievably dull. A surprising dud from director Ford. British version, titled GIDEON'S DAY, runs 118m. Originally released theatrically in the U.S. in b&w.

Gideon's Day SEE: **Gideon of Scotland Yard**

Gidget (1959) **C-95m.** **½ D: Paul Wendkos. Sandra Dee, James Darren, Cliff Robertson, Arthur O'Connell, Joby Baker, Yvonne Craig, Doug McClure, Tom Laughlin. California teenage girl hits the beach one summer and falls in love with two surfer boys. Dee is spirited in the title role of this hit movie (based on Frederick Kohner's novel about his daughter), which led

to a number of sequels and two different TV series! CinemaScope.▼●❙

Gidget Goes Hawaiian (1961) **C-102m.** ** D: Paul Wendkos. James Darren, Michael Callan, Deborah Walley, Carl Reiner, Peggy Cass, Eddie Foy, Jr. Inane follow-up has teenager off to the Islands, with embarrassing results for all.▼❙

Gidget Goes to Rome (1963) **C-101m.** ** D: Paul Wendkos. Cindy Carol, James Darren, Jessie Royce Landis, Cesare Danova, Jeff Donnell. Mild follow-up has fetching teenager off to Italy, involved in predictable romancing.▼❙

Gift, The (1982-French-Italian) **C-105m.** ** D: Michel Lang. Pierre Mondy, Claudia Cardinale, Clio Goldsmith, Jacques Francois, Cecile Magnet, Remi Laurent. Bank employees chip in to buy their colleague a surprise retirement gift: a beautiful prostitute. A "good clean sex farce," strained and silly, with no sex, very little nudity, and the improbable casting of beautiful Cardinale as Mondy's wife. [R]▼

Gift, The (2000) **C-111m.** **½ D: Sam Raimi. Cate Blanchett, Giovanni Ribisi, Keanu Reeves, Katie Holmes, Greg Kinnear, Hilary Swank, Michael Jeter, Kim Dickens, Gary Cole, Rosemary Harris, J. K. Simmons, Chelcie Ross. Young widow and mother Blanchett earns money doing psychic readings for her Georgia neighbors, but incurs the wrath of an abusive Reeves . . . and then becomes a key witness in a murder trial. Uneven blend of Southern gothic/psychic/courtroom/whodunit ingredients, made watchable by a strong ensemble. Written by Billy Bob Thornton and Tom Epperson. [R]▼❙

Gift From Heaven, A (1994) **C-102m.** *** D: Jack Lucarelli. Sharon Farrell, Gigi Rice, David Steen, Sarah Trigger, Gene Lythgow, Mark Ruffalo, Nicholas Worth, Molly McClure. Solid characterizations add immeasurably to this complex, impassioned drama about an emotionally scarred backwoods North Carolina mother (Farrell). She gave birth to the eldest of her two grown children (Steen) when she was twelve, after being seduced by her preacher uncle: the emotional sparks begin to fly upon the arrival of an orphaned cousin (Trigger). Actor Steen also scripted the film.

Gift Horse (1952-British) **100m.** *** D: Compton Bennett. Trevor Howard, Richard Attenborough, Sonny Tufts, James Donald, Joan Rice, Bernard Lee, Dora Bryan, Hugh Williams, Sidney James. Solid WW2 drama with Howard as a troublesome ship's captain, disliked by his crew, who comes into his own while battling a German U-boat. Also known as GLORY AT SEA.▼

Gift of Love, The (1958) **C-105m.** ** D: Jean Negulesco. Lauren Bacall, Robert Stack, Evelyn Rudie, Lorne Greene, Anne Seymour. If you could put up with SENTIMENTAL JOURNEY (1946) you might bear this remake, which isn't even as good. Bacall dies but returns to earth as guiding spirit for her husband and daughter. Remade again for TV as SENTIMENTAL JOURNEY (1984). CinemaScope.

Gig, The (1985) **C-92m.** ✳✳✳ D: Frank D. Gilroy. Wayne Rogers, Cleavon Little, Andrew Duncan, Jerry Matz, Daniel Nalbach, Warren Vache, Joe Silver, Jay Thomas. Perceptive, touching comedy-drama about dreams, compromises, disappointments— what it means to be alive. A group of middle-class, middle-aged men play jazz both to amuse themselves and to escape from the pressures of their lives; they are hired for their first professional engagement at a small resort, and the experience proves to be unexpectedly unsettling. Gilroy also wrote the script.▼

Gigantic (2009) **C-98m.** ✳✳✳ D: Matt Aselton. Paul Dano, Zooey Deschanel, John Goodman, Ed Asner, Jane Alexander, Ian Roberts, Robert Stanton, Clarke Peters, Susan Misner, Zach Galifianakis. Dano plays the son of older parents (Asner and Alexander) and baby brother of two robust siblings; his only goal in life is to adopt a baby from China. Then he meets Deschanel, who lives in the shadow of her bombastic father (Goodman). Quirky, hip, sexy New York–based comedy with a disarmingly oblique sense of humor. Feature directing debut for Aselton, who scripted with Adam Nagata. Super 35. [R]▶

Gigantis, the Fire Monster (1955-Japanese) **78m.** ✳✳ D: Motoyoshi Oda, Hugo Grimaldi. Hiroshi Koizumi, Setsuko Makayama. A new Godzilla, here called Gigantis, battles spiny Angorous, trashing another Japanese city. First sequel to GODZILLA, KING OF THE MONSTERS!, retitled: GODZILLA RAIDS AGAIN.▼

Gigi (1949-French) **83m.** ✳✳½ D: Jacqueline Audry. Daniele Delorme, Frank Villard, Yvonne de Bray, Gaby Morlay, Jean Tissier, Madeleine Rousset. Original version of Colette's novel is not a musical but a drolly amusing (if talky and uncinematic) comedy of manners. Delorme, who starred in two more films based on Colette stories, is delightful as Gigi, the girl trained to be a courtesan by her aunt and grandmother in fin de siècle Paris. Originally 109m.▶

Gigi (1958) **C-116m.** ✳✳✳✳ D: Vincente Minnelli. Leslie Caron, Maurice Chevalier, Louis Jourdan, Hermione Gingold, Jacques Bergerac, Eva Gabor. Joyous turn-of-the-20th-century musical based on Colette's story of a French girl who's groomed to be a courtesan. Exquisitely filmed, perfectly cast, with memorable Lerner & Loewe score: title tune, "Thank Heaven for Little Girls," "I Remember It Well." Winner of nine Academy Awards including Best Picture, Director, Writing (Alan Jay Lerner), Cinematography (Joseph Ruttenberg), Costumes (Cecil Beaton), Song ("Gigi"), and Scoring (Andre

Previn). Chevalier received an honorary Oscar. CinemaScope.▼●▶

Gigli (2003) **C-124m.** ✳½ D: Martin Brest. Jennifer Lopez, Ben Affleck, Justin Bartha, Lainie Kazan, Al Pacino, Christopher Walken, Missy Crider, Lenny Venito. Underworld functionary Affleck is hired to kidnap the brother of a federal prosecutor; then, inexplicably, Affleck's boss sends Lopez to keep an eye on him! Sorry excuse for a script (by Brest) lurches from one boring, silly, illogical, and/or unpleasant sequence to another, when in fact it exists merely to show off its sexy female star, who (in the film's most memorable scene) talks dirty while performing yoga. Super 35. [R]▼▶

Gigot (1962) **C-104m.** ✳✳✳ D: Gene Kelly. Jackie Gleason, Katherine Kath, Gabrielle Dorziat, Albert Remy, Yvonne Constant. Sentimental, well-acted tale of a deaf mute (Gleason) and a young girl in Paris. Simple film, well done; Gleason is excellent. Remade for TV as THE WOOL CAP MAN (2004).

G.I. Jane (1997) **C-124m.** ✳✳ D: Ridley Scott. Demi Moore, Viggo Mortensen, Anne Bancroft, Scott Wilson, Jason Beghe, Daniel Von Bargen. Contrived movie about a woman selected as a test case for admitting females into naval combat. She undergoes the unbelievable rigors of Navy SEALs training, determined not to be shown favored treatment. Pumped-up Moore is perfect for the part, though it's a toss-up as to which scenes are more off-putting—her body-building workouts or her physical abuse at the hands of her Master Chief (Mortensen). Typically dense Scott soundtrack renders much of the dialogue unintelligible—but it's no loss. Too bad they didn't lose the anticlimactic final action sequence. Panavision. [R]▼●

G.I. Joe: The Rise of Cobra (2009) **C-118m.** ✳✳½ D: Stephen Sommers. Channing Tatum, Sienna Miller, Marlon Wayans, Ray Park, Rachel Nichols, Byung-hun Lee, Joseph Gordon-Levitt, Jonathan Pryce, Christopher Eccleston, Kevin J. O'Connor, Saïd Taghmaoui, Dennis Quaid. Drawn from Hasbro's 1982 reboot of its iconic 1964 military toy for boys, this snazzy sci-fi actioner is dolled up with gadgetry galore and one astonishing set piece after another. But when the dazzle dims and the actors talk, they're action figures with unconvincing origin stories, in a standard-issue script about stolen warheads. Mercilessly violent but fairly bloodless, and sparked up by its wow effect. Brendan Fraser appears unbilled. Panavision. [PG-13]▶

Gilda (1946) **110m.** ✳✳✳ D: Charles Vidor. Rita Hayworth, Glenn Ford, George Macready, Joseph Calleia, Steven Geray. Highly charged story of emotional triangle— mysterious South American casino owner Macready, his new man-Friday Ford, and Macready's alluring wife (Hayworth)—

unfortunately cops out with silly resolutions. Rita has never been sexier, especially when singing "Put the Blame on Mame." ▼❍●

Gilda Live (1980) **C-90m.** **½ D: Mike Nichols. Gilda Radner, Father Guido Sarducci (Don Novello). Filmization of Radner's Broadway show, with the comedienne doing uncensored versions of her familiar *Saturday Night Live* TV characters. Best song: "Let's Talk Dirty to the Animals." [R] ▼●

Gilles' Wife (2004-French-Belgian-Swiss) **C-108m.** ***½ D: Frédéric Fonteyne. Emmanuelle Devos, Clovis Cornillac, Laura Smet, Colette Emmanuelle, Gil Lagay. A simple, happily married woman in a small Belgian village begins to suspect that her husband is seeing another woman—namely, her sister. Exquisite rendering of Madeleine Bourdouxhe's 1937 novel recalls French films of that period; much of the story is told through Devos' expressive face and the painterly images of cinematographer Virginie Saint-Martin. Deliberate in both its pacing and attention to detail. Fonteyne cowrote the screenplay with Philippe Blasband and Marion Hänsel. ❒

Gimme Shelter (1970) **C-91m.** **** D: David Maysles, Albert Maysles, Charlotte Zwerin. Rolling Stones, Jefferson Airplane, Tina Turner, Melvin Belli. Outstanding documentary of the Rolling Stones and the famous Altamont Speedway free concert that resulted in chaos and murder. Chilling, beautifully handled, with the Stones performing their best songs of the period ("Satisfaction," "Sympathy for the Devil," etc.). Reissued in PG form at 90m., then reedited for reissue in 2000 at 91m. [R] ▼●

Gina SEE: **Death in the Garden**

Ginger and Fred (1986-Italian) **C-126m.** *** D: Federico Fellini. Giulietta Masina, Marcello Mastroianni, Franco Fabrizi, Frederick Von Ledenberg, Martin Blau, Toto Mignone. Fellini satirizes TV, and the cult of instant celebrity, in this relaxed and amusing film. Ginger and Fred are, in fact, two small-time entertainers who used to *imitate* Rogers and Astaire and who are being reunited by an unctuous TV show. The targets are a bit obvious and the pace a bit leisurely, but the climactic sequence is fun, and the two stars are wonderful to watch, as always. [PG-13] ▼❒

Gingerbread Man, The (1998) **C-115m.** ** D: Robert Altman. Kenneth Branagh, Embeth Davidtz, Robert Downey, Jr., Daryl Hannah, Tom Berenger, Famke Janssen, Mae Whitman, Jesse James, Robert Duvall. Cocky Savannah lawyer (Branagh, with a terrific accent) sleeps with a woman he's just met (Davidtz, in a strong performance), then gets into hot water when he tries to protect her from her lunatic father. If he's so smart, how could he leave himself so vulnerable? Ask John Grisham, who wrote this thriller, which grows more implausible

with each new story twist. Final showdown is especially weak. Screenplay credited to a pseudonymous Al Hayes. [R] ▼●

Ginger in the Morning (1973) **C-89m.** **½ D: Gordon Wiles. Sissy Spacek, Monte Markham, Mark Miller, Susan Oliver, Slim Pickens. So-so romantic comedy about a lonely salesman who picks up a comely hitchhiker. He's attracted to her young, fresh independence; she's drawn to his old-fashioned romanticism. [PG] ▼❒

Girl by the Lake, The (2007-Italian) **C-96m.** *** D: Andrea Molaioli. Toni Servillo, Denis Fasolo, Nello Mascia, Giulia Michelini, Marco Baliani, Fabrizio Gifuni, Valeria Golino. The death of an attractive teenage girl, beloved by family and friends alike, brings an inspector (Servillo) to a mountainous village in northern Italy, where everyone knows each other and secrets are hard to keep hidden. Straightforward, well-crafted whodunit with a quietly commanding performance by Servillo. Based on the best-selling Inspector Sejer novels by Karin Fossum. ❒

Girl Can't Help It, The (1956) **C-99m.** **½ D: Frank Tashlin. Tom Ewell, Jayne Mansfield, Edmond O'Brien, Julie London. One-joke film about press agent Ewell trying to hype gangster's girlfriend (Mansfield) to stardom. Some good Tashlin sight gags; classic performances by Fats Domino ("Blue Monday"), The Platters ("You'll Never Know"), Gene Vincent and His Blue Caps ("BeBop A Lula"), Little Richard ("She's Got It," "Ready Teddy," and "The Girl Can't Help It"). CinemaScope. ▼❒

Girl Crazy (1943) **99m.** ***½ D: Norman Taurog. Mickey Rooney, Judy Garland, Gil Stratton, Robert E. Strickland, "Rags" Ragland, June Allyson, Nancy Walker, Guy Kibbee, Tommy Dorsey and His Orchestra. Rooney sent to small Southwestern school to forget girls, but meets Garland and that's that. Great Gershwin score includes "I Got Rhythm," "Embraceable You," "But Not For Me." Busby Berkeley (the original director) staged the finale. Filmed before in 1932; remade as WHEN THE BOYS MEET THE GIRLS (1965). ▼●

girlfight (2000) **C-113m.** *** D: Karyn Kusama. Michelle Rodriguez, Jaime Tirelli, Paul Calderon, Santiago Douglas, Ray Santiago, Elisa Bocanegra. A hotheaded Latina teenager who lives in Brooklyn finds a way to channel her anger—in the boxing ring. Making her way in a male-dominated sport is no easy matter, especially when she falls in love with a fellow boxer. Rodriguez is utterly believable in this entertaining debut feature for writer-director Kusama. John Sayles, who coexecutive-produced, has a small part as a science teacher. [R] ▼❒

Girl for Joe, A SEE: **Force of Arms**

Girlfriend Experience, The (2009) **C-77m.** **½ D: Steven Soderbergh. Sasha

Grey, Chris Santos, Philip Eytan, Timothy Davis, Mark Jacobson, David Levien, Alan Milstein, Dennis Shields, Glenn Kenny. Against the angst-ridden backdrop of the 2008 economic recession and the presidential election, a high-priced Manhattan escort (porn star Grey) struggles with her finances, her relationship with her live-in boyfriend (Santos), and her feelings for a new client. Fragmented, pseudo-Godardian study of prostitution as a metaphor for capitalism is generally engrossing but ultimately feels shallow and leaves little lasting impression. Stylishly shot and edited by Soderbergh using his usual pseudonyms (Peter Andrews and Mary Ann Bernard). Also available in unrated version. HD Widescreen. [R]◗

Girlfriends (1978) C-88m. *** D: Claudia Weill. Melanie Mayron, Anita Skinner, Eli Wallach, Christopher Guest, Bob Balaban, Amy Wright, Viveca Lindfors, Mike Kellin, Ken McMillan, Kathryn Walker, Kristoffer Tabori. A young woman tries to cope with love, a career, and personal independence after roommate/girlfriend leaves to get married. Mayron's warm, winning performance helps likable but uneven film over rough spots. [PG]▼◖

Girl From Jones Beach, The (1949) 78m. **½ D: Peter Godfrey. Ronald ·Reagan, Virginia Mayo, Eddie Bracken, Dona Drake, Henry Travers, Lois Wilson, Florence Bates. Breezy comedy about an artist trying to find living embodiment of the perfectly proportioned female in his illustrations. Capable romantic-comedy performance by Reagan.

Girl From Lorraine, The (1980-French-Swiss) C-107m. **½ D: Claude Goretta. Nathalie Baye, Bruno Ganz, Angela Winkler, Patrick Chesnais. Unemployed draughtswoman Baye, from the provinces, maintains her dignity in lonely, unfriendly Paris. Quietly rewarding drama with an extremely likable heroine; however, sometimes as dreary as some of the characters she meets. Originally titled LA PROVINCIALE.

Girl From Missouri, The (1934) 75m. *** D: Jack Conway. Jean Harlow, Lionel Barrymore, Franchot Tone, Lewis Stone, Patsy Kelly, Alan Mowbray. Delightful fluff about good girl Harlow trying to win a millionaire without sacrificing her integrity. Wise-cracking Kelly as her girlfriend is a treat.▼

Girl from Monaco, The (2008-French) C-95m. **½ D: Anne Fontaine. Fabrice Luchini, Roschdy Zem, Louise Bourgoin, Jeanne Balibar, Stéphane Audran, Gilles Cohen, Alexandre Steiger. High-powered lawyer·Luchini, defending an accused murderess in a controversial case, becomes the romantic and sexual object of a gorgeous, much younger free spirit (Bourgoin, in a striking debut) who happens to be the ex-girlfriend of his bodyguard. Ironic, multi-layered sex farce/thriller too often meanders;

works best as an exploration of the parameters of ambition and desire. Panavision. [R]◗

Girl From Petrovka, The (1974) C-104m. ** D: Robert Ellis Miller. Goldie Hawn, Hal Holbrook, Anthony Hopkins, Gregoire Aslan, Anton Dolin. Old-fashioned comedy-drama about a bittersweet affair between American correspondent Holbrook and Russian Hawn. Filmed in Vienna and Hollywood. Panavision. [PG]▼

Girl-Getters, The (1964-British) 79m. *** D: Michael Winner. Oliver Reed, Jane Merrow, Barbara Ferris, Julia Foster, David Hemmings. Realistic study of hoodlum youths at British seaside resort, their prankish games and romances; intelligently portrayed. Retitled: THE SYSTEM. ▼◖

Girl Happy (1965) C-96m. **½ D: Boris Sagal. Elvis Presley, Shelley Fabares, Harold J. Stone, Gary Crosby, Joby Baker, Nita Talbot, Mary Ann Mobley, Chris Noel, Jackie Coogan. Formula Presley musical with tiresome plot of Elvis in Fort Lauderdale chaperoning Fabares, daughter of Chicago mobster. Panavision.▼◖

Girl Hunters, The (1963-British) 103m. **½ D: Roy Rowland. Mickey Spillane, Lloyd Nolan, Shirley Eaton, Hy Gardner. Spillane plays his own fictional detective Mike Hammer in this rugged murder mystery. Since the disappearance of his devoted secretary, Hammer has been wallowing in alcohol; he sobers up, and goes into action, upon learning she might be alive. Panavision. ▼◖

Girl in a Swing, The (1989-U.S.-British) C-112m. BOMB D: Gordon Hessler. Meg Tilly, Rupert Frazer, Nicholas Le Prevost, Elspet Gray, Lorna Heilbron, Helen Cherry. Antique dealer marries a mysterious German woman after a whirlwind courtship and pays the consequences, surviving her hallucinations and related erratic behavior. Despite lots of simulated (and unrated) screen sex, this is absolutely unwatchable—though Frazer looks just enough like Regis Philbin to give this stinker some unexpected subtext. [R]▼◖

Girl in Every Port, A (1952) 86m. ** D: Chester Erskine.· Groucho Marx, Marie Wilson, William Bendix, Don DeFore, Gene Lockhart, George E. Stone. Nonsense of two gobs who become involved with a lame racehorse. Good cast is wasted.▼◖

Girl, Interrupted (1999) C-127m. *** D: James Mangold. Winona Ryder, Angelina Jolie, Clea DuVall, Brittany Murphy, Whoopi Goldberg, Vanessa Redgrave, Jared Leto, Jeffrey Tambor, Mary Kay Place, Joanna Kerns, Kurtwood Smith, Ray Baker, Elizabeth Moss. Vivid adaptation of Susanna Kaysen's autobiographical book (set in the late 1960s) about a girl who enters a mental institution at the age of 18, thinking she's normal compared to most of the others—though she did try to kill herself.

Jolie is incandescent in an Oscar-winning performance as the firebrand of the ward, who, like most of the others, hides her true emotions. [R]▼▶

Girl in the Red Velvet Swing, The (1955) C-109m. **½ D: Richard Fleischer. Ray Milland, Joan Collins, Farley Granger, Cornelia Otis Skinner, Glenda Farrell, Luther Adler. Glossy, fictionalized account of Evelyn Nesbit–Stanford White–Harry Thaw escapade of early 20th-century N.Y.C. Showgirl falls in love with prominent architect, which upsets mentally disturbed millionaire. CinemaScope.▶

Girl Next Door, The (1953) C-92m. *** D: Richard Sale. Dan Dailey, June Haver, Dennis Day, Billy Gray, Cara Williams, Natalie Schafer. Minor but cheerful musical about a chorus-girl-turned-star who moves next door to a widower and his son and threatens to break up their buddy relationship. Great set design, clever use of animation (by the UPA studio), bright Harry Warren–Josef Myrow songs, and eye-popping film noir production number "Nowhere Guy" spark this likable confection. Haver's last film before retiring.▶

Girl Next Door, The (2004) C-108m. **½ D: Luke Greenfield. Emile Hirsch, Elisha Cuthbert, Timothy Olyphant, James Remar, Chris Marquette, Paul Dano, Timothy Bottoms, Jacob Young. Straight-arrow high school senior breaks out of his nerdy routine when he falls head over heels for his new next-door neighbor, a blonde knockout who turns out to be a porn star trying to go straight. Excellent casting and some good laughs are mitigated by film's overreliance on ideas "borrowed" from RISKY BUSINESS, key scenes that don't ring true, and a storyline that's much more complicated than it has to be. [R]▼▶

Girl of the Golden West, The (1938) 120m. **½ D: Robert Z. Leonard. Jeanette MacDonald, Nelson Eddy, Walter Pidgeon, Leo Carrillo, Buddy Ebsen, Leonard Penn. Oft-produced tale of love affair of good girl MacDonald and bandit Eddy, with tuneful Gus Kahn–Sigmund Romberg score that didn't produce any hits.▼

Girl on a Motorcycle (1968-British-French) C-91m. ** D: Jack Cardiff. Marianne Faithfull, Alain Delon, Roger Mutton, Marius Goring, Catherine Jourdan. Cardiff also photographed this oddity: a mod, psychedelic, existential tale of a woman who leaves her husband and rides her motorcycle to visit her ex-lover. From André Pieyre De Mandiargues' novel. Trimmed from X-rated version titled NAKED UNDER LEATHER. [R]▼●▶

Girl on the Bridge, The (1999-French) 92m. *** D: Patrice Leconte. Daniel Auteuil, Vanessa Paradis, Demetre Georgalas, Bertie Cortez. A mysterious knife-thrower (Auteuil) saves a young woman from jumping off a bridge and recruits her for his death-defying act. Their success together is based not just on his skill, but on their almost telepathic (and sensual) sense of oneness. Stylish, provocative fable, shot in widescreen b&w, opens with real-life pop star Paradis delivering a mesmerizing monologue. Panavision. [R]▼▶

Girl on the Train, The (2009-French) C-97m. **½ D: André Téchiné. Émilie Dequenne, Catherine Deneuve, Michel Blanc, Ronit Elkabetz, Mathieu Demy, Nicolas Duvauchelle. Fictionalized version of a real-life incident about an unemployed 23-year-old woman who—after a horrendous ending to a heated romance, and for reasons never satisfactorily explained—invents a story, infused with anti-Semitic elements, about being attacked by youths on a train platform. A dramatic exercise in why good people do bad things, this treatise never makes any kind of point, even though the story strongly calls for one. First adapted for the stage by Jean-Marie Besset, who collaborated with Téchiné and Odile Barski on the film version. Super 35.▶

Girls, The (1968-Swedish) 90m. *** D: Mai Zetterling. Bibi Andersson, Harriet Andersson, Gunnel Lindblom, Gunnar Bjornstrand, Erland Josephson, Ulf Palme. Trenchant study of modern marriages and female roles, loaded with fantasy sequences. Fabulous cast drawn by actress-turned-director Zetterling from Ingmar Bergman's repertory company. Aka FLICKORNA.▶

Girls! Girls! Girls! (1962) C-106m. **½ D: Norman Taurog. Elvis Presley, Stella Stevens, Laurel Goodwin, Jeremy Slate, Benson Fong, Robert Strauss, Ginny Tiu. Presley is chased by a mass of girls and can't decide which one he prefers. Along the way, he sings "Return to Sender" and some other less memorable numbers (like "Song of the Shrimp").▶

Girl 6 (1996) C-105m. ** D: Spike Lee. Theresa Randle, Isaiah Washington, Spike Lee, Jenifer Lewis, Debi Mazar, Peter Berg, Michael Imperioli, Dina Pearlman, Maggie Rush, Kristen Wilson, Naomi Campbell, Desi Moreno, John Turturro, Madonna, Quentin Tarantino, Halle Berry, Richard Belzer, Ron Silver, Susan Batson, Gretchen Mol. A frustrated young actress takes (and becomes addicted to) a job as a phone-sex worker. Done in by its predictability and lack of insight into the character of Girl 6. Worth a look for Randle's appealing performance and Lee's vivid depiction of the phone-sex world. [R]▼●▶

Girls Just Want to Have Fun (1985) C-87m. **½ D: Alan Metter. Sarah Jessica Parker, Lee Montgomery, Morgan Woodward, Jonathan Silverman, Helen Hunt, Holly Gagnier, Ed Lauter, Shannen Doherty. Likable, upbeat teen comedy about girl with reactionary father who wants to enter dance contest. Clichés and contrivances are counterbalanced by believable portrayal of teenage girls, appealingly played by Parker and Hunt. [PG]▼●

Girls of Summer SEE: **Satisfaction**

Girls Town (1959) **92m.** *½ D: Charles Haas. Mamie Van Doren, Mel Tormé, Paul Anka, Ray Anthony, Maggie Hayes, Cathy Crosby, Gigi Perreau, Gloria Talbott, Jim Mitchum, Elinor Donahue, Sheilah Graham, The Platters, Harold Lloyd, Jr. Wisecracking bad girl is sent to title correctional institution, where she learns that she doesn't have all the answers. Absurd in the extreme, but has definite camp value just for the cast alone . . . plus, Anka sings "Ave Maria"! As Mamie says, it's "cool, crazy, fantabulous"! Aka INNOCENT AND THE DAMNED. ▼

Girls Town (1996) **C-90m.** **½ D: Jim McKay. Lili Taylor, Bruklin Harris, Anna Grace, Aunjanue Ellis, Guillermo Diaz, Ernestine Jackson, Tara Carnes, Michael Imperioli. Disparate clique of teenage girlfriends discover the depths of their individual secrets when one of their group inexplicably commits suicide. A largely improvised script results in realistic dialogue that considers the issues of teenage boredom, friendship, victimization of women, solidarity, and empowerment. A painfully unsentimental, sometimes humorous, coming-of-age in the '90s story. [R]▼●

Girl 27 (2007) **C-80m.** *** D: David Stenn. Fascinating, highly personal documentary by Hollywood historian-biographer Stenn about a forgotten woman named Patricia Douglas, who was raped during an MGM sales convention in 1937. Stenn does admirable detective work piecing this long-buried story together, and reveals his discoveries one by one. Use of 1930s movie scenes to parallel the true-life story told here doesn't always work, but the overall result is excellent.▌

Girl Who Couldn't Say No, The (1968-Italian) **C-83m.** ** D: Franco Brusati. Virna Lisi, George Segal, Lila Kedrova, Akim Tamiroff, Paola Pitagora, Felicity Mason. Square Segal and childhood friend Lisi fall for each other, but just can't maintain a permanent relationship; mild comedy. Technioscope. [M/PG]

Girl Who Had Everything, The (1953) **69m.** **½ D: Richard Thorpe. Elizabeth Taylor, Fernando Lamas, William Powell, Gig Young, James Whitmore, Robert Burton. Good cast uplifts murky remake of A FREE SOUL. Independent-minded Taylor is attracted to gambling kingpin Lamas, the client of her trial-lawyer father (Powell). Young has another of his thankless "other man" roles.▼●

Girl Who Kicked the Hornet's Nest, The (2009-Swedish) **C-148m.** **½ D: Daniel Alfredson. Michael Nyqvist, Noomi Rapace, Lena Endre, Annika Hallin, Jacob Ericksson, Sofia Ledarp, Anders Ahl-

bom Rosendahl, Mikael Spreitz, Georgi Staykov. Picking up where THE GIRL WHO PLAYED WITH FIRE left off, the film opens with Lisbeth Salander gamely recovering from her father's attempt to kill her, while reporter Mikael Blomkvist prepares to publish his explosive findings about the government conspiracy that harbored her father—and smeared her name. All the pieces gradually fall into place, and while that's satisfying to witness, it also gives this final installment of Stieg Larsson's *The Millennium Trilogy* a certain predictability. [R]▌

Girl Who Knew Too Much, The SEE: **Evil Eye, The**

Girl Who Knew Too Much (1969) **C-96m.** ** D: Francis D. Lyon. Adam West, Nancy Kwan, Nehemiah Persoff, Robert Alda. Adventurer who is hired to find the killer of a syndicate boss discovers Communist plot to infiltrate organized crime. [R]

Girl Who Played With Fire, The (2009-Swedish-Danish-German) **C-129m.** *** D: Daniel Alfredson. Noomi Rapace, Michael Nyqvist, Lena Endre, Peter Andersson, Yohan Kylén, Yasmine Garbi, Paolo Roberto, Georgi Staykov, Mikael Spreitz, Per Oscarsson, Hans-Christian Thulin. Lisbeth Salander returns to Sweden just as crusading journalist Mikael Blomkvist is helping a young freelancer complete his no-holds-barred investigation of a sex trafficking operation. Out of the blue Lisbeth is named as the leading suspect in a series of murders, so once more she has to go underground, while her few remaining friends become targets. Mikael, who knows she's innocent, ferrets out the truth, which is tied to the investigative piece his magazine is about to print. Second installment of Stieg Larsson's *The Millennium Trilogy* (following THE GIRL WITH THE DRAGON TATTOO) isn't as densely plotted as the first, but it's still brutally potent. Followed by THE GIRL WHO KICKED THE HORNET'S NEST. [R]▌

Girl With a Pearl Earring (2003-British-Luxembourgian) **C-99m.** ***½ D: Peter Webber. Colin Firth, Scarlett Johansson, Tom Wilkinson, Judy Parfitt, Cillian Murphy, Essie Davis, Joanna Scanlan, Alakina Mann. Exquisite rendering of Tracy Chevalier's best-selling novel about the circumstances that lead a scullery maid to pose for one of Johannes Vermeer's most famous portraits. First-time feature director Webber and his team create a breathtaking sense of time and place (Delft in the 17th century), and Johansson is perfect as the unassuming girl who seeks to find her place in the combustible Vermeer household. Screenplay by Olivia Hetreed. Super 35. [PG-13]▼●

Girl With a Suitcase (1960-Italian) **111m.** ***½ D: Valerio Zurlini. Claudia Cardinale, Jacques Perrin, Luciana Angelillo, Corrado Pani. Impressive film of devoted but shady girl Cardinale following her ex-lover to Parma, only to fall in love with his adolescent brother. Confusing at times, but extremely well acted. Original Italian running time 135m. ▼▶

Girl With Green Eyes (1964-British) **91m.** ★★★ D: Desmond Davis. Rita Tushingham, Peter Finch, Lynn Redgrave, T. P. McKenna, Marie Kean, Julian Glover. Moving drama of young farm girl falling in love with writer Finch, highlighted by winning Tushingham performance. Redgrave scores as her roommate. Filmed in Dublin. ▼▶

Girl With the Dragon Tattoo, The (2009 - Swedish - Danish - Norwegian) **C-147m.** ★★★ D: Niels Arden Oplev. Michael Nyqvist, Noomi Rapace, Lena Endre, Sven-Bertil Taube, Peter Haber, Peter Andersson, Ingvar Hirdwall, Marika Lagercrantz. Gripping adaptation of the first of Stieg Larsson's trilogy of best-selling books, about an investigative reporter from Stockholm who's hired by a wealthy man to look into the disappearance of his beloved niece some 40 years ago . . . and a punkish, embittered young female computer whiz who becomes his improbable ally in the complex search. Graphically brutal at times, but redeemed by its solid storytelling. Followed by THE GIRL WHO PLAYED WITH FIRE. Super 35. ▶

Girl With the Red Hair, The (1981-Dutch) **C-116m.** ★★½ D: Ben Verbong. Renee Soutendijk, Peter Tuinman, Loes Luca, Johan Leysen, Robert Delhez, Ada Bouwman. Determined student becomes a killer of Nazi informers during WW2. Tense, chilling, sober, but overlong and too often slow; good score by Nicola Piovani helps. Based on a true story. [PG]

Girly SEE: **Mumsy, Nanny, Sonny and Girly**

Giro City SEE: **And Nothing But the Truth**

Give a Girl a Break (1953) **C-82m.** ★★½ D: Stanley Donen. Marge and Gower Champion, Debbie Reynolds, Helen Wood, Bob Fosse, Kurt Kasznar, Richard Anderson, William Ching, Larry Keating. Innocuous musical fluff about three young women competing for the starring role in a Broadway musical. Watching Marge and Gower dance is always a treat, but the real highlight is seeing two of the greatest choreographers of all time (Champion and Fosse) dancing together. Undistinguished score by Ira Gershwin and Burton Lane. ▼▶

Give 'Em Hell, Harry! (1975) **C-102m.** ★★★ D: Steve Binder. James Whitmore. Straight reproduction of Whitmore's one-man stage triumph as Harry Truman, covering high points in both the political and personal life of our 33rd President. Videotaped and transferred to film for theatrical release, but original tape version used for TV. [PG]▼

Give My Regards to Broad Street (1984-British) **C-108m.** ★★ D: Peter Webb. Paul McCartney, Bryan Brown, Ringo Starr, Barbara Bach, Linda McCartney, Tracey Ullman, Ralph Richardson. Vanity film with silly "plot" about a missing album tape connecting a number of music video–type numbers ("Ballroom Dancing," "No More Lonely Nights"). Some of the music is good (and McCartney reprises a couple of Beatles songs) but mostly it's a big snooze. [PG] ▼▶

Gizmo (1977) **C/B&W-77m.** ★★½ D: Howard Smith. Entertaining compilation of film clips on 20th-century "inventors" and their often outlandish contraptions. Good fun, though it can't quite sustain feature length. [G]▼

Gladiator (1992) **C-98m.** ★½ D: Rowdy Herrington. Cuba Gooding, Jr., James Marshall, Robert Loggia, Ossie Davis, Brian Dennehy, Cara Buono, John Heard, Jon Seda, Lance Slaughter. Pubescent ROCKY wannabe about a tough Chicago teenager becoming involved in the tawdry underground boxing scene. Builds to ludicrous climax with crooked fight promoter Dennehy actually getting in the ring! [R]▼▶

Gladiator (2000) **C-154m.** ★★★ D: Ridley Scott. Russell Crowe, Joaquin Phoenix, Connie Nielsen, Oliver Reed, Derek Jacobi, Djimon Hounsou, Richard Harris, David Hemmings. Impressive tale from the days of the Roman Empire, with Crowe as a dedicated soldier who refuses to transfer his loyalty to the new emperor Commodus (Phoenix) and suffers the consequences, winding up a gladiator in the Roman Colosseum. Crowe is so good in his Academy Award–winning performance—and his character so compelling—that one is willing to forgive story lulls; the spectacle is grand, but the opening battle scene stresses chaos over coherence. Reed's last film; he died during production. Also won Oscars for Best Picture, Costume Design, Sound, and Visual Effects. Extended edition runs 171m. Super 35. [R]▼▶

Glass Bottom Boat, The (1966) **C-110m.** ★★★ D: Frank Tashlin. Doris Day, Rod Taylor, Arthur Godfrey, Paul Lynde, Eric Fleming, Alice Pearce, Ellen Corby, John McGiver, Edward Andrews, Dom De Luise, Dick Martin. Above-average Day nonsense, with widow Doris hired by research scientist Taylor as his biographer. He tries to seduce her; she's mistaken for a Russian spy. Lots of Tashlin's trademark slapstick. Panavision. ▼▶

Glass House, The (2001) **C-106m.** ★★½ D: Daniel Sackheim. Leelee Sobieski, Stellan Skarsgård, Diane Lane, Bruce Dern, Kathy Baker, Trevor Morgan, Chris Noth, Michael O'Keefe, Rita Wilson, Gavin O'Connor, Agnes Bruckner, January Jones. When their well-off parents are killed in an auto accident, late-teen Sobieski and her younger brother are adopted by family friends whose financial overextension makes the kids' trust fund look mighty attractive. Sobieski seems more sullen than vulnerable as the script degenerates into often-laughable chiller-melodrama clichés. As a drug-addicted mom, Lane's underdeveloped character compels more than the rest. Followed by a DVD sequel. Super 35. [PG-13]▼▶

Glass Houses (1972) C-90m. ** D: Alexander Singer. Jennifer O'Neill, Bernard Barrow, Deirdre Lenihan, Ann Summers, Phillip Pine, Lloyd Kino. Low-grade drama about infidelity and incestuous desire is mildly interesting in a lurid kind of way; O'Neill's first film, but released after RIO LOBO and SUMMER OF '42. [R]

Glass Key, The (1935) 80m. *** D: Frank Tuttle. George Raft, Claire Dodd, Edward Arnold, Rosalind Keith, Ray Milland, Guinn Williams. Solid Dashiell Hammett story about politician Arnold getting involved in mysterious murder, Raft trying to dig out the facts. Drags during second half, but still quite good. Remade in 1942.

Glass Key, The (1942) 85m. ***½ D: Stuart Heisler. Brian Donlevy, Veronica Lake, Alan Ladd, Joseph Calleia, William Bendix, Bonita Granville, Richard Denning. Fast-moving remake of 1935 film, with wardheeler Donlevy accused of murder, henchman Ladd bailing him out. Lake fine as mysterious love interest, Bendix effective as brutal bodyguard. Akira Kurosawa claims this was his inspiration for YOJIMBO. Dashiell Hammett novel neatly adapted by Jonathan Latimer.▼●

Glass Menagerie, The (1950) 107m. **½ D: Irving Rapper. Jane Wyman, Kirk Douglas, Gertrude Lawrence, Arthur Kennedy. More notable for its cast and intention than results. Slow-moving version of Tennessee Williams' drama of lame girl, her faded Southern belle mother, and idealistic brother, all living in their own fragile dream worlds. Remade twice.

Glass Menagerie, The (1987) C-134m. *** D: Paul Newman. Joanne Woodward, John Malkovich, Karen Allen, James Naughton. Respectable, well-made version of Tennessee Williams' now legendary play, with Woodward fine as Amanda Wingfield and Malkovich superb as son Tom. Woodward, Allen, and Naughton had appeared in two regional stage productions of Williams' play prior to making this film. [PG]▼●

Glass Shield, The (1995) C-108m. ** D: Charles Burnett. Michael Boatman, Lori Petty, Richard Anderson, Ice Cube, Bernie Casey, Elliott Gould, Michael Ironside, Don Harvey, Michael Gregory, M. Emmett Walsh, Sy Richardson, Natalija Nogulich, Wanda de Jesus, Victoria Dillard. Young, wide-eyed Boatman is the first black man assigned to a tight-knit office of the L.A.

Sheriff's Department; he soon discovers just how dirty this precinct really is. A polemic masquerading as a movie, with heavy-handed "villains" and a story that eventually loses its focus and its momentum. [PG-13]▼●▶

Glass Sphinx, The (1967-Italian-Spanish) C-91m. *½ D: Luigi Scattini. Robert Taylor, Anita Ekberg, Gianna Serra, Jack Stuart, Angel Del Pozo, Jose Truchado. World-famous archaeologist Taylor is on the trail of the tomb of a glass sphinx containing magic elixir; foreign agents have similar idea. Confusing and forgettable. Techniscope. ▼▶

Gleaming the Cube (1989) C-104m. ** D: Graeme Clifford. Christian Slater, Steven Bauer, Ed Lauter, Micole Mercurio, Richard Herd, Charles Cyphers, Le Tuan. Rebellious young skateboarder sets out to find his brother's murderers with the help of a street-smart detective. Skateboard stunts are sensational, but the story is by-the-numbers TV stuff. The title is skateboarding jargon for reaching the ultimate—which this movie never does. Retitled A BROTHER'S JUSTICE for TV. [PG-13]▼●▶

Gleaners and I, The (2001-French) C-82m. ***½ D: Agnès Varda. Outstanding documentary in which Varda offers a portrait of gleaners, or peasants who would "humbly stoop" while rummaging through fields for bits of food that remained after a harvest. The filmmaker contrasts the gleaners of yesteryear with those of today, many of whom are homeless street people who scrounge through garbage for food. Highly personal film explores a host of themes, including aging and the quest for survival. This is the work of a filmmaker who is keenly aware of her surroundings, and in complete command of cinematic language. Followed by THE GLEANERS AND I: TWO YEARS LATER. ▼▶

Glen and Randa (1971) C-94m. **½ D: Jim McBride. Steven Curry, Shelley Plimpton, Woodrow Chambliss, Garry Goodrow. Years after nuclear destruction of world, teenage lovers follow comic-book "clues" and look for Metropolis. [R—originally rated X]▼●▶

Glengarry Glen Ross (1992) C-100m. *** D: James Foley. Al Pacino, Jack Lemmon, Alec Baldwin, Ed Harris, Alan Arkin, Kevin Spacey, Jonathan Pryce, Bruce Altman, Jude Ciccolella. David Mamet's scorching, profane, Pulitzer Prize–winning play about an office full of desperate real-estate salesmen-cum-con-artists is faithfully reproduced (Mamet did the adaptation himself) with a gallery of stunning performances. Pacino is dynamic as the office hotshot, Lemmon totally credible as the loser, and Baldwin is dynamite (in a part created especially for the film) as an insulting "motivator." Never succeeds in being anything but a photographed play, but when the play and the actors are this good it's hard to complain. Super 35. [R] ▼◐●

Glenn Miller Story, The (1954) **C-116m.** *** D: Anthony Mann. James Stewart, June Allyson, Charles Drake, George Tobias, Harry Morgan, Frances Langford, Louis Armstrong, Gene Krupa. Stewart is convincingly cast as the popular bandleader in this extremely sentimental (and largely fictitious) account of his life. Music's the real star here, with most of Miller's hit records re-created. ▼◐●

Glen or Glenda (1953) **61m.** BOMB D: Edward D. Wood, Jr. Bela Lugosi, Dolores Fuller, Daniel Davis, Lyle Talbot, Timothy Farrell, "Tommy" Haynes, Charles Crafts, Conrad Brooks. Sensational but sincere "docu-fantasy" about transvestism could well be the worst movie ever made. Legendarily awful director Wood stars (under the name Daniel Davis) as Glen, who can't decide how to tell his fiancée he wants to wear her clothes. Dizzying hodgepodge of stock footage, demented dream sequences, and heartfelt plea for tolerance linked by campy Lugosi narrating from haunted house. "Bevare!" Even more inept and hilarious than Wood's infamous PLAN 9 FROM OUTER SPACE. Also released as I CHANGED MY SEX, I LED 2 LIVES, and HE OR SHE. Reissued at 67m. ▼◐●

Glimmer Man, The (1996) **C-92m.** *½ D: John Gray. Steven Seagal, Keenen Ivory Wayans, Michelle Johnson, Brian Cox, Bob Gunton, John Jackson, Stephen Tobolowsky. Seagal and Wayans team up to track down a serial killer who is terrorizing the L.A. area. Tired buddy/cop picture, even by Seagal's fairly low standards; he also coproduced. [R] ▼◐●

Glitter (2001) **C-104m.** *½ D: Vondie Curtis Hall. Mariah Carey, Max Beesley, Da Brat, Tia Texada, Valarie Pettiford, Ann Magnuson, Terrence Howard, Dorian Harewood, Grant Nickalls, Padma Lakshmi, Eric Benét. In 1980s N.Y.C. a backup singer is discovered by an ambitious club d.j. (Beesley) who vows to make her a star. That's fine with her, but if only she could reconcile with the mother who abandoned her when she was a child. . . . Vehicle for pop star Carey is tiresome at best and awash in clichés. Super 35. [PG-13] ▼●

Global Affair, A (1964) **84m.** **½ D: Jack Arnold. Bob Hope, Yvonne De Carlo, Robert Sterling, John McGiver, Lilo Pulver. Unwitty Hope vehicle has Bob in charge of a baby found at U.N., with female representative from each nation demanding the child. Also shown in computer-colored version. Metroscope. ▼

Global Heresy SEE: **Rock My World**
Gloomy Sunday (1999-German-Hungarian) **C-112m.** *** D: Rolf Schübel. Erika Marozsán, Joachim Król, Ben Becker, Stefano Dionisi, András Bálint, Géza Boros, Rolf Becker, Ilse Zielstorff. Old-fashioned love triangle set in Budapest during the 1930s and '40s, built around the title tune (made famous in the U.S. by Billie Holiday), which came to be known as "The Suicide Song." A genial restaurateur hires a moody young man to play piano in his establishment, little dreaming that the woman he loves will be torn between them. Romantic, sexy, and evocative of an earlier era (and its films). Based on a novel by Nick Barkow. ◗

Gloria (1980) **C-121m.** ** D: John Cassavetes. Gena Rowlands, Buck Henry, John Adames, Julie Carmen, Lupe Guarnica. Ex-mob mistress goes on the lam with a young neighbor-boy after gangland hit-men wipe out his parents. Good-looking but way overlong melodrama, which Cassavetes may or may not be playing for laughs. Remade in 1999. [PG] ▼◐●

Gloria (1999) **C-108m.** ** D: Sidney Lumet. Sharon Stone, Jean-Luke Figueroa, Jeremy Northam, George C. Scott, Cathy Moriarty, Bonnie Bedelia, Mike Starr. Unnecessary, sentimental remake of 1980 John Cassavetes melodrama with Stone stepping into Gena Rowlands' pumps as a tough ex–gun moll on the lam with an adorable Puerto Rican tyke (Figueroa) in tow. Still watchable, thanks to Stone's funny, full-bodied performance (once you get over her barely credible Noo Yawk accent) and her cuddly costar. Scott's final theatrical film. [R] ▼◐●

Glory (1989) **C-122m.** **** D: Edward Zwick. Matthew Broderick, Denzel Washington, Cary Elwes, Morgan Freeman, Jihmi Kennedy, Andre Braugher, John Finn, Donovan Leitch, John David Cullum, Bob Gunton, Cliff DeYoung. Exceptional story of America's first unit of black soldiers during the Civil War and the young, inexperienced Northerner (Broderick) who's given the job of training and leading them. Based in part on the letters of that young officer and brought to life with astonishing skill and believability. Grand, moving, breathtakingly filmed (by veteran cinematographer Freddie Francis) and faultlessly performed. One of the finest historical dramas ever made. Oscar winner for Cinematography, Sound, and Supporting Actor (Washington). Screenplay by Kevin Jarre. Jane Alexander (as Broderick's mother) and Raymond St. Jacques (as Frederick Douglass) appear unbilled. [R] ▼◐●

Glory Alley (1952) **79m.** **½ D: Raoul Walsh. Ralph Meeker, Leslie Caron, Gilbert Roland, Louis Armstrong, John McIntire. Just before the championship bout, boxer Meeker quits the fight game, then goes from skid row to war hero. New Orleans backgrounds allow for some good musical interludes.

Glory at Sea SEE: **Gift Horse, The**

Glory Boy SEE: **My Old Man's Place**

Glory Road (2006) **C-106m.** **½ D: James Gartner. Josh Lucas, Derek Luke, Austin Nichols, Jon Voight, Evan Jones, Schin A.S. Kerr, Alphonso McAuley, Mehcad Brooks, Sam Jones III, Damaine Radcliff, Emily Deschanel, Al Shearer, Tatyana Ali. Jerry Bruckheimer–produced feel-good movie about an obscure basketball coach named Don Haskins, who recruits raw but promising players—including a large number of blacks—for a community college in El Paso, Texas, and heads for the 1966 NCAA championship. Echoing REMEMBER THE TITANS, this film pushes the right buttons, and dramatizes the historic game in which an all-black team faced an all-white opponent . . . but glosses over some of the most interesting aspects of the real-life story. Super 35. [PG]▶

Glory Stompers, The (1967) **C-85m.** BOMB D: Anthony M. Lanza. Dennis Hopper, Jody McCrea, Chris Noel, Jock Mahoney, Lindsay Crosby. Hopper, pre-EASY RIDER, stars as motorcycle-gang leader who wears a swastika patch and mouths lines like, "Hey, like, ya know, I wanna dance with you, baby." And, from Noel: "I just want something better than being a Stompers girl." Hilariously bad; see if you can count how many times Hopper says "man." Colorscope.▼

Glove, The (1978) **C-91m.** ** D: Ross Hagen. John Saxon, Rosey Grier, Joanna Cassidy, Joan Blondell, Jack Carter, Aldo Ray, Keenan Wynn. Violent action flick (with episodic comic diversions by various "guest" veterans), pitting a world-weary bounty hunter against a vengeful ex-con who commits mayhem with a leather-laced steel riot glove. Also shown as THE GLOVE: LETHAL TERMINATOR and LETHAL TERMINATOR. [R] ▼▶

Glove: Lethal Terminator, The SEE: **Glove, The**

"G" Men (1935) **85m.** ***½ D: William Keighley. James Cagney, Ann Dvorak, Margaret Lindsay, Robert Armstrong, Barton MacLane, Lloyd Nolan, William Harrigan. Although raised by an underworld figure, Cagney joins F.B.I. when a pal is killed by gangsters, puts his first-hand knowledge to use. Exciting film, beautifully shot by Sol Polito; prologue with David Brian added for 1949 reissue. Also shown in computer-colored version.▼▶

Gnaw SEE: **Food of the Gods II**

Gnome-Mobile, The (1967) **C-90m.** *** D: Robert Stevenson. Walter Brennan, Matthew Garber, Karen Dotrice, Richard Deacon, Tom Lowell, Sean McClory, Ed Wynn. Crusty businessman Brennan, his niece, and nephew discover gnomes in redwood forest, try to protect them from freak-show entrepreneur and land-destroyers. Lively Disney fantasy outing with top special ef-

fects, broad comedy highlights. Based on Upton Sinclair novel.▼▶

Gnome Named Gnorm, A (1994) **C-84m.** ** D: Stan Winston. Anthony Michael Hall, Jerry Orbach, Claudia Christian, Eli Danker, Mark Harelik, Robert Z'Dar. An especially strange cop-and-partner action comedy teams eccentric young detective Hall with a gnome who's just burrowed up from his underground world. Short on action, whimsy, and wackiness. Special effects maestro Winston returned to what he did best after this sat on the shelf for five years. [PG]▼

Gnomeo & Juliet (2011-U.S.-British) **C-84m.** **½ D: Kelly Asbury. Voices of James McAvoy, Emily Blunt, Ashley Jensen, Michael Caine, Matt Lucas, Jim Cummings, Maggie Smith, Jason Statham, Ozzy Osbourne, Stephen Merchant, Patrick Stewart, Julie Walters, Hulk Hogan, Richard Wilson, Dolly Parton. CG-animated feature enacts a variation on Shakespeare's tragic love story with a cast of garden gnomes: the "reds" and "blues" live next door to one another but cannot overcome their owners' longtime feud, until Gnomeo falls in love with Juliet. Cute, sometimes clever, film for kids looks good but never develops its story and characters as fully as one might like. Songs (both old and new) by coexecutive producer Elton John and Bernie Taupin. 3-D. [G]▶

GO (1999) **C-103m.** ** D: Doug Liman. Sarah Polley, Katie Holmes, Desmond Askew, Taye Diggs, William Fichtner, J. E. Freeman, Jane Krakowski, Breckin Meyer, Jay Mohr, Timothy Olyphant, Scott Wolf, James Duval. A frenetic twenty-four hours in the lives of some hedonistic L.A. teens, as seen from several points of view. Energized, well cast, and cleverly contrived, this paean to a what-the-hell lifestyle is geared to appeal to like-minded young people . . . but others may find it too much like a junior PULP FICTION. Super 35. [R]▼●▶

Goalie's Anxiety at the Penalty Kick, The (1972-German) **C-101m.** ***½ D: Wim Wenders. Arthur Brauss, Erika Pluhar, Kai Fischer, Libgart Schwarz, Marie Bardischewski. Exceptionally knowing, haunting portrait of alienation, following a professional soccer goalie (Brauss), who abandons his team and sets out on an odyssey. Stunningly directed; a film you will not soon forget. Scripted by Peter Handke, based on his novel.▼

Goal! The Dream Begins (2006) **C-118m.** *** D: Danny Cannon. Kuno Becker, Alessandro Nivola, Stephen Dillane, Anna Friel, Marcel Iures, Sean Pertwee, Lee Ross, Cassandra Bell, Kieran O'Brien, Tony Plana, Miriam Colon. Since there have been "inspirational" sports movies on everything except contract bridge, another one about soccer (or football, as it's known internationally) was probably inevitable. Entertaining story of a poor Mexican-American player who travels from L.A. to England against his father's wishes for a chance to play in the big leagues. Less about the game than the young man's family and team relationships, providing plenty of heart and pluck. Real-life soccer superstars appear in cameos. Followed by two sequels. Super 35. [PG]🄳

Goat, The SEE: **La Chevre**

Go-Between, The (1971-British) C-116m. ***½ D: Joseph Losey. Julie Christie, Alan Bates, Dominic Guard, Margaret Leighton, Michael Gough, Michael Redgrave, Edward Fox. Beguiling film from L. P. Hartley story of boy who becomes messenger for love notes between aristocratic Christie and farmer Bates. Lushly filmed, full of nuances, fine performances. Script by Harold Pinter. A mood piece, not for all tastes. [PG]▼

GoBots: Battle of the Rock Lords (1986) C-75m. *½ D: Ray Patterson. Voices of Margot Kidder, Roddy McDowall, Michael Nouri, Telly Savalas. Hanna-Barbera and Tonka Toys present a 75-minute animated commercial about the war between good GoBots versus evil Renegades, and the struggle of innocent Rock people against wicked Rock Lords. Electronically altered soundtrack makes it difficult to hear big-name voice cast. [G]▼

Goddess, The (1958) 105m. *** D: John Cromwell. Kim Stanley, Lloyd Bridges, Steven Hill, Betty Lou Holland, Patty Duke. Absorbing biography of an ambitious girl seeking Hollywood fame. Author Paddy Chayefsky based his story on Marilyn Monroe; the film captures tragedy of the real-life Monroe with fine acting by Stanley and Bridges, among others. Film debuts of Stanley and Duke. ▼🄳🄾

Godfather, The (1972) C-175m. **** D: Francis Ford Coppola. Marlon Brando, Al Pacino, James Caan, Richard Castellano, John Cazale, Diane Keaton, Talia Shire, Robert Duvall, Sterling Hayden, John Marley, Richard Conte, Al Lettieri, Abe Vigoda, Al Martino, Morgana King, Alex Rocco. The 1970s' answer to GONE WITH THE WIND, from Mario Puzo's novel on the violent life and times of Mafia patriarch Don Corleone (Brando). Pulp fiction raised to the highest level; a film of epic proportions, masterfully done, and set to Nino Rota's memorable music. Absolutely irresistible. Academy Award winner for Best Picture, Actor (Brando), and Screenplay (Coppola and Puzo). Baby in baptism scene is actually Coppola's infant daughter Sofia—who later costarred in THE GODFATHER PART III. Followed by two sequels. [R]▼🄾🄳

Godfather Part II, The (1974) C-200m. **** D: Francis Ford Coppola. Al Pacino, Robert Duvall, Diane Keaton, Robert De Niro, John Cazale, Talia Shire, Lee Strasberg, Michael V. Gazzo, G.D. Spradlin, B. Kirby, Jr. (Bruno Kirby), John Aprea, Morgana King,

Mariana Hill, Troy Donahue, Joe Spinell, Abe Vigoda, Fay Spain, Harry Dean Stanton, Danny Aiello, Roger Corman, Dominic Chianese, James Caan. They said it couldn't be done, but cowriter-director Coppola made a sequel that's just as compelling. This one contrasts the life of melancholy "don" (Pacino) with early days of his father (De Niro) as an immigrant in N.Y.C. Winner of six Oscars including Best Picture, Director, Screenplay (Coppola, Mario Puzo), Supporting Actor (De Niro), Score (Nino Rota, Carmine Coppola), Art Direction/Set Decoration (Dean Tavoularis, Angelo Graham, George R. Nelson). [R]▼🄾🄳

Godfather Part III, The (1990) C-161m. *** D: Francis Ford Coppola. Al Pacino, Diane Keaton, Talia Shire, Andy Garcia, Eli Wallach, Joe Mantegna, George Hamilton, Bridget Fonda, Sofia Coppola, Raf Vallone, Franc D'Ambrosio, Donal Donnelly, Richard Bright, Helmut Berger, Don Novello, John Savage, Mario Donatone, Al Martino. Only a filmmaker like Coppola (teamed with writer Mario Puzo) could extend his history-making Mafioso saga and make it work so well. Absorbing story of Pacino's attempt to remove himself from the world of crime, and how fate and circumstance draw him back in, with his trigger-happy nephew (Garcia) and the rest of his family in tow. Longish, but masterfully told, with one almost-fatal flaw: the casting of Coppola's daughter Sofia (an amateur) in the pivotal role of Pacino's daughter. Video release is so-called "final director's cut," 9m. longer than theatrical version. Super 35. [R]▼🄾🄳

God Forgives, I Don't (1969-Italian-Spanish) C-101m. *½ D: Giuseppe Colizzi. Terence Hill, Bud Spencer, Frank Wolff, Gina Rovere, Jose Manuel Martin. In spite of colorful title, this spaghetti Western about an attempt to find some buried loot is like a thousand others. Hill's and Spencer's first film together. Techniscope. [M]🄳

God Grew Tired of Us: The Story of Lost Boys of Sudan (2006) C-89m. ***½ D: Christopher Dillon Quinn. Narrated by Nicole Kidman. The subject of 2003's THE LOST BOYS OF SUDAN is given a new, perhaps more human perspective in this documentary as we learn what happened when three survivors came to the U.S. after spending time in a Kenyan refugee camp. Scenes featuring the three are alternately touching and surprisingly funny and show the true meaning of life in America as seen through outsiders' eyes. [PG]🄳

God Is Great, I'm Not (2001-French) C-95m. **½ D: Pascale Bailly. Audrey Tautou, Edouard Baer, Julie Depardieu, Catherine Jacob, Philippe Laudenbach, Cathy Verney, Mathieu Demy. Tautou is winning as a flaky 20-year-old model who flits from relationship to relationship and religion to religion; she embraces Judaism, even though her newest boyfriend is a nonpracticing Jew. Ambitious attempt to reflect on how individuals search for meaning in their lives, but it's not as emotionally involving as it ought to be. Video title: GOD IS GREAT, AND I'M NOT. ▼)

God Said, "HA!" (1999) **C-83m.** **½ D: Julia Sweeney. Julia Sweeney. Faithful film record of Sweeney's one-woman show in which she describes, with disarming good humor, her experience caring for her brother as he died of cancer—then discovering that she had a rare form of cervical cancer herself. Quentin Tarantino coexecutive-produced. [PG-13] ▼)

Gods and Generals (2003) **C-223m.** **½ D: Ronald F. Maxwell. Jeff Daniels, Stephen Lang, Robert Duvall, Mira Sorvino, Kevin Conway, C. Thomas Howell, Frankie Faison, Matt Letscher, Jeremy London, William Sanderson, Kali Rocha, Bruce Boxleitner, Robert Easton. Writer-director Maxwell's prequel to GETTYSBURG is not in the same league but does manage to capture some of the sights, sounds, and personalities of the Civil War's early years, with an emphasis on the South. Lion's share of the story is devoted to Lang's pious "Stonewall" Jackson. Telling vignettes and vivid battle scenes make up for some ponderousness, speechiness, and overlength (it's even longer—231m.—on video). Film's backer, media mogul Ted Turner, has a cameo as a Confederate soldier. Based on the Jeff Shaara novel. Panavision. [PG-13] ▼)

Gods and Monsters (1998) **C-105m.** ***½ D: Bill Condon. Ian McKellen, Brendan Fraser, Lynn Redgrave, Lolita Davidovich, David Dukes, Kevin J. O'Connor. Exceptional (if entirely fictional) character study of film director James Whale (best remembered for FRANKENSTEIN and BRIDE OF FRANKENSTEIN), alone at the end of his life in the 1950s, and fearful of losing his mind. An exquisite rendering of time and place, with a superb performance by McKellen, matched by Fraser as a gardener who catches his fancy, and Redgrave as his hilariously severe but loving housekeeper. A quiet, deliberately paced film; beautifully rendered, with a unique blend of flashback and hallucination. Director Condon won an Oscar for adapting Christopher Bram's novel *Father of Frankenstein.* Super 35. ▼●)

God's Country (1985) **C-88m.** ***½ D: Louis Malle. Poignant, insightful, occasionally hilarious look at life in Glencoe, Minnesota, a small, conservative farming community. Mostly shot in 1979; Malle returned six years later to update the lives of his subjects.)

Godsend, The (1979-British) **C-93m.** ** D: Gabrielle Beaumont. Cyd Hayman, Malcolm Stoddard, Angela Pleasence, Patrick Barr. OMEN/EXORCIST-type horror film about an angelic little blonde girl who is left

at a family farm on a rainy night by a strange woman. In the years that follow, death, disaster, and hostility are visited upon the family in this medium thriller. [R]▼

Godsend (2004-U.S.-Canadian) **C-102m.** **½ D: Nick Hamm. Greg Kinnear, Rebecca Romijn-Stamos, Robert De Niro, Cameron Bright, Jenny Levine. A couple grieving over the loss of their 8-year-old son is approached by a medical researcher who promises that he can enable the woman to give birth to the identical child all over again—using a revolutionary (if illegal) cloning method he's perfected. Good performances and an interesting premise reel us in, but then the filmmakers string us along, teasing us about where the story is headed. It doesn't pay off. Filmed in Canada, which never looked more unlike the U.S. Super 35. [PG-13]▼)

God's Little Acre (1958) **117m.** *** D: Anthony Mann. Robert Ryan, Tina Louise, Aldo Ray, Buddy Hackett, Jack Lord, Fay Spain, Michael Landon, Vic Morrow, Rex Ingram. Picaresque Americana from Erskine Caldwell's best-selling book about a lusty, eccentric Georgia family. Amusing, passionate, and highly charged; quite sexy for its time. Some censored moments were restored years after its original release. Wonderful score by Elmer Bernstein. ▼)

Gods Must Be Crazy, The (1980-Botswana) **C-108m.** *** D: Jamie Uys. Marius Weyers, Sandra Prinsloo, N!xau, Louw Verwey, Michael Thys. Highly original, offbeat comedy about cultural clashes in Africa, involving a bushman who encounters civilization for the first time, a pretty schoolteacher whose new assignment is a remote village, and a bumbling scientist whose attempts to make her welcome result in slapstick catastrophes. Film itself is clumsy at times, but completely disarming. A U.S. sensation in 1984. Uys, who also wrote and produced, plays the reverend. Followed by a sequel. Techniscope. [PG] ▼●)

Gods Must Be Crazy II, The (1989-U.S.-Botswana) **C-97m.** *** D: Jamie Uys. N!xau, Lena Farugia, Hans Strydom, Eiros, Nadies, Erick Bowen. Follow-up to the surprise smash-hit farce is just as funny and endearing. N!xau returns as the bushman; here, his two young children are accidentally transported to "civilization" by a pair of poachers, and he follows them with the expected, comic result. This started shooting in 1985 and sat on the shelf for several years. [PG]▼●)

Gods of the Plague (1969-German) **91m.** *** D: Rainer Werner Fassbinder. Hanna Schygulla, Margarethe von Trotta, Harry Baer, Gunther Kaufmann, Ingrid Caven. A pair of pals plot a robbery, only to have their scheme disrupted by two women (both of whom love one of the men). Low-key, noirish gangster film is an ode to the Hollywood films of the genre, with a French New Wave sensibility. At the same time, it's a knowing portrait of an aimless, alienated postwar German generation. ▼◗

Godspell (1973) **C-103m.** **½ D: David Greene. Victor Garber, David Haskell, Jerry Sroka, Lynne Thigpen, Katie Hanley, Robin Lamont. Sophomoric updating of Jesus' life with young bouncy disciples following their leader around modern-day N.Y.C. Energetic adaptation of popular stage musical; brilliant use of N.Y.C. locations, good score by Stephen Schwartz including "Day by Day," but hollow and unmoving. [G]▼◗

God Told Me To SEE: **Demon**

Godzilla (1954-Japanese) SEE: **Godzilla, King of the Monsters!**

Godzilla (1998) **C-139m.** **½ D: Roland Emmerich. Matthew Broderick, Hank Azaria, Jean Reno, Maria Pitillo, Harry Shearer, Kevin Dunn, Michael Lerner, Vicki Lewis, Doug Savant, Arabella Field, Bodhi Elfman. Giant lizard monster moves swiftly from the Pacific to N.Y. harbor, and terrorizes the Big Apple. Biologist Broderick hooks up with mystery man Reno and his team to stop it. Giant-scale, fx-driven no-brainer doesn't make much sense, has shallow characters, and goes on too long— but still offers a surprising amount of fun. Super 35. [PG-13]▼◗

Godzilla, King of the Monsters! (1954-Japanese) **80m.** **½ D: Terry Morse, Ishiro Honda. Raymond Burr, Takashi Shimura, Momoko Kochi, Akira Takarada. A fire-breathing lizard threatens civilization: the special effects are the star in this, the original GODZILLA movie. Originally released in Japan in 1954 as GOJIRA (a far superior film), at 98m; over 20m. were eliminated, and inserts with Burr were added. Updated in 1985 and reworked in 1998. Original Japanese version restored in 2004. ▼◗

Godzilla Mothra King Ghidorah (2001-Japanese) **C-105m.** *** D: Shusuke Kaneko. Chiharu Nîyama, Ryudo Uzaki, Masahiro Kobayashi, Shirô Sano, Takashi Nishina. Writer-director Kaneko was brought in to "shake things up," and he certainly succeeded with this dark, very violent epic, which reverts Godzilla to a soulless, nuclear-created killing machine. Mothra, Baragon, and even King Ghidorah are now "guardian spirits" who are awakened to stop his wave of destruction. The 25th Godzilla movie is considered by many fans to be the apex of the series, with terrific special effects and a consistently adult tone; worth seeing even for nondevotees. Informally known as GMK. Full title on-screen is GODZILLA MOTHRA AND KING GHIDORAH MONSTERS ALL-OUT ATTACK. Super 35. [PG-13] ◗

Godzilla 1985 (1985-Japanese) **C-91m.** BOMB D: Kohji Hashimoto, R. J. Kizer. Raymond Burr, Keiju Kobayashi, Ken Tanaka, Yasuko Sawaguchi, Shin Takuma.

Supposed update of original GODZILLA is just a retread, with the atomic-fueled monster threatening Tokyo again. Burr is back in cheaply filmed insert sequences making like Greek chorus. Too straight to be funny; the Big Fella is just a Big Bore. [PG]▼◗

Godzilla on Monster Island (1972-Japanese) **C-89m.** ** D: Jun Fukuda. Hiroshi Ishikawa, Tomoko Umeda, Yuriko Hishimi, Minoru Takashima. Garbo talks? Ha! In this harmless, toylike movie, *Godzilla* talks, as he and spiny Angillus battle alien-summoned Ghidrah and new playmate Gigan, who has a buzz saw in his belly. Standard colorful Toho monster hijinks. Aka GODZILLA VS. GIGAN. Tohoscope. [G]▼◗

Godzilla Raids Again SEE: **Gigantis, the Fire Monster**

Godzilla's Revenge (1969-Japanese) **C-69m.** **½ D: Ishiro Honda. Kenji Sahara, Tomonori Yazaki, Machiko Naka, Sachio Sakai, Chotaro Togin, Yoshibumi Tujima. Fantasy of child daydreaming of adventures with Godzilla's son and other monsters. Battle scenes are mostly stock footage from GODZILLA VS. THE SEA MONSTER and SON OF GODZILLA. Good juvenile sci-fi. Tohoscope. [G]▼◗

Godzilla 2000 (1999-Japanese) **C-99m.** *** D: Takao Okawara. Takehiro Murata, Naomi Nishida, Mayu Suzuki, Hiroshi Abe, Shiro Sano, Tsutomu Kitagawa. Lively, well-made series entry centers on the discovery of a centuries-old alien craft designed to convert Earth's environment into one suitable for its creators. Godzilla is tricked into saving the planet again. Engaging film with fine effects and sharp script, weighed down only by a drawn-out monster-clash climax. Reworked, redubbed and rescored for U.S. release from the 107m. original. Super 35. [PG]▼◗

Godzilla vs. Gigan SEE: **Godzilla on Monster Island**

Godzilla vs. Hedorah SEE: **Godzilla vs. the Smog Monster**

Godzilla vs. Mechagodzilla SEE: **Godzilla vs. the Cosmic Monster**

Godzilla vs. Megalon (1976-Japanese) **C-80m.** *½ D: Jun Fukuda. Katsuhiko Sasaki, Hiroyuki Kawase, Yutaka Hayashi, Robert Dunham. Series sinks to new low as Godzilla teams up with robot superhero against Megalon and his pal Gigan. Incredibly cheap, with lots of unintended laughs. A hoho from Toho in Tohoscope. [G]▼◗

Godzilla vs. Monster Zero SEE: **Monster Zero**

Godzilla vs. Mothra SEE: **Godzilla vs. the Thing**

Godzilla vs. the Bionic Monster SEE: **Godzilla vs. the Cosmic Monster**

Godzilla vs. the Cosmic Monster (1974-Japanese) **C-80m.** ** D: Jun Fukuda. Masaaki Daimon, Kazuya Aoyama, Reiko

Tajima, Barbara Lynn, Akihiko Hirata. Godzilla battles robot duplicate of himself, built by alien apes intent on conquering the world. He's helped this time by ancient Okinawan monster Kingseesar. Pokey until zappity-pow climax. Aka GODZILLA VS. THE BIONIC MONSTER and GODZILLA VS. MECHAGODZILLA, and remade in 1993 under that title. Tohoscope. [G] ▼●◗

Godzilla Vs. The Sea Monster (1966-Japanese) **C-83m.** **½ D: Jun Fukuda. Akira Takarada, Kumi Mizuno, Chotaro Togin, Hideo Sunazuka, Toru Watanabe, Akihito Hirata, Toru Ibuki. Four people are shipwrecked on a South Seas island, where they not only have to avoid a terrorist organization called the Red Bamboo, but also Godzilla, Mothra, and a giant crablike creature called Ebirah. Seventh Godzilla movie (the first directed by Fukuda) is also the first to do away with trademark scenes of urban destruction. Splendid use of color and nice, change-of-pace jazzy score by Masaru Sato make this one of the more entertaining entries. Japanese running time is 87m. Aka EBIRAH, HORROR OF THE DEEP. Tohoscope. [PG] ▼◗

Godzilla vs. the Smog Monster (1972-Japanese) **C-87m.** **½ D: Yoshimitu Banno. Akira Yamauchi, Hiroyuki Kawase, Toshio Shibaki. Godzilla freelances as do-gooder in ridding Japan of monster born of waste, fed on factory fumes and smog. Dubbed and daffy. Aka GODZILLA VS. HEDORAH. [G—edited from original PG rating] ▼●◗

Godzilla vs. the Thing (1964-Japanese) **C-90m.** **½ D: Ishirô Honda. Okira Takarada, Yuriko Hoshi, Hiroshi Koizumi, Yu Fujiki. Vivid special effects highlight battle between reptile Godzilla and Mothra, giant moth. Aka GODZILLA VS. MOTHRA. Tohoscope. ▼●◗

Go Fish (1994) **87m.** *** D: Rose Troche. V. S. Brodie, Guinevere Turner, T. Wendy McMillan, Anastasia Sharp, Migdalia Melendez. A romantic tale about finding a soulmate; the difference here is that both partners are women. Funny, intelligent comedy about brash Turner forging a relationship with shy Brodie. Only quibble: the heavy-handed political correctness of the secondary characters. Made on a practically nonexistent budget; Troche (who coscripted with Turner) is a talent to watch. [R] ▼●◗

Go for Broke! (1951) **92m.** *** D: Robert Pirosh. Van Johnson, Lane Nakano, Henry Nakamura, George Miki, Henry Oyasato, Warner Anderson. Fine WW2 drama with Johnson, a bigoted Texan, assigned to train and lead the 442nd Regimental Combat Team, composed mostly of Japanese-Americans (Nisei). Crammed with ironic touches, and uncompromising in its point of view (reflecting the Nisei's collective heroic war record). Pirosh also scripted. ▼◗

Go Get Some Rosemary SEE: **Daddy Longlegs** (2010)

Go-Getter, The (2008) **C-93m.** ** D: Martin Hynes. Lou Taylor Pucci, Zooey Deschanel, Jena Malone, William Lee Scott, Maura Tierney, Judy Greer, Bill Duke, Julio Oscar Mechoso, Jsu Garcia. Recently orphaned teenager who can't get his act together impulsively steals a car and embarks on a road trip, hoping to find his elusive stepbrother (whom he hasn't seen in years) . . . but along the way he develops a relationship via cell phone with the owner of the car. Picaresque road movie benefits from strong lead performances, but its supposed spontaneity too often seems studied, and many fine actors appear in cameos that are frustratingly brief. Feature debut for writer-director Hynes. [R]◗

Gohatto SEE: **Taboo**

Goin' Cocoanuts (1978) **C-96m.** ** D: Howard Morris. Donny and Marie Osmond, Herbert Edelman, Kenneth Mars, Chrystin Sinclaire, Ted Cassidy, Marc Lawrence, Khigh Dhiegh, Harold Sakata. Bad guys go after Marie's necklace in Hawaii, but the villainy, like the story, is strictly kindergarten level. Of course, Donny and Marie get to sing. [PG]

Goin' Down the Road (1970-Canadian) **C-90m.** ***½ D: Donald Shebib. Doug McGrath, Paul Bradley, Jayne Eastwood, Cayle Chernin, Nicole Morin. Award-winning film made for less than $100,000 puts most Hollywood blockbusters to shame; modest tale of two unlucky Nova Scotians and their near-tragic finish packs a memorable punch. McGrath and Bradley are remarkably good. [PG—edited from original R rating]

Going All the Way (1997) **C-110m.** ** D: Mark Pellington. Jeremy Davies, Ben Affleck, Amy Locane, Jill Clayburgh, Lesley Ann Warren, Rose McGowan, Rachel Weisz. Listless screen version of Dan Wakefield's popular memory novel about two young army vets who become friends in 1950s Indianapolis despite having existed on wholly different social planes during their high school years. A good book but an indifferent (and familiar-seeming) coming-of-age movie, despite a Wakefield script. Set in 1954, film opens with a *huge* 1957 pop hit—never a good sign. [R] ▼●◗

Going Ape (1970) SEE: **Where's Poppa?**

Going Ape! (1981) **C-87m.** BOMB D: Jeremy Joe Kronsberg. Tony Danza, Jessica Walter, Stacey Nelkin, Danny De Vito, Art Metrano, Joseph Maher. Inept comedy, with Danza set to inherit $5 million if he cares for a trio of orangutans. Directorial debut for screenwriter Kronsberg, who also penned Clint Eastwood's EVERY WHICH WAY BUT LOOSE—with an orangutan prominently featured. [PG] ▼

Going Berserk (1983-Canadian) **C-85m.** BOMB D: David Steinberg. John Candy,

[537]

Joe Flaherty, Eugene Levy, Alley Mills, Pat Hingle, Richard Libertini, Paul Dooley, Murphy Dunne, Dixie Carter, Ernie Hudson. Awesomely inept comedy about the misadventures of a young dolt (Candy) who's set to marry the daughter of a pompous congressman. Only a performer as likable as Candy could survive such a debacle; his *SCTV* colleagues Flaherty and Levy have little to do. [R] ▼●➋

Going Home (1971) **C-97m.** *** D: Herbert B. Leonard. Robert Mitchum, Jan-Michael Vincent, Brenda Vaccaro, Jason Bernard, Sally Kirkland, Josh Mostel. Powerful, if downbeat, study of young man's troubled relationship with his father, who's just been released from prison after serving time for killing his wife. [PG] ▼●

Going in Style (1979) **C-96m.** ***½ D: Martin Brest. George Burns, Art Carney, Lee Strasberg, Charles Hallahan, Pamela Payton-Wright. Three retirees in Queens get more than they bargain for when they rob a bank in Manhattan to relieve their boredom. Unexpected gem from a 28-year-old writer-director is predictably funny but unpredictably moving, with Burns standing out in a terrific cast. [PG] ▼➋

Going My Way (1944) **126m.** **** D: Leo McCarey. Bing Crosby, Barry Fitzgerald, Rise Stevens, Frank McHugh, James Brown, Gene Lockhart, Jean Heather, Porter Hall, Fortunio Bonanova, Stanley Clements, Carl (Alfalfa) Switzer. Sentimental story of down-to-earth priest Father O'Malley (Crosby) winning over aging superior (Fitzgerald) and sidewalk gang of kids is hard to resist—thanks to the skills of writer-director McCarey, who won two Oscars. Academy Awards also went to Crosby, Fitzgerald, Best Picture, and Best Song: "Swinging on a Star." Sequel: THE BELLS OF ST. MARY'S. ▼●➋

Going Overboard (1989) **C-97m.** *½ D: Valerie Breiman. Adam Sandler, Tom Hodges, Liza Collins Zane, Pete Berg, Ricky Paull Goldin, Warren Selko, Billy Zane, Adam Rifkin, Steven Brill, Terry Moore, Scott LaRose, Billy Bob Thornton, Burt Young. Sandler, in his screen debut, plays a wannabe stand-up comedian toiling as a waiter on a cruise ship in this so-called farce. Inoffensive though painfully unfunny; a genuine curio, if only for its cast (and an unbilled appearance by Milton Berle, complete with laugh track). [R] ▼➋

Going Places (1974-French) **C-117m.** *** D: Bertrand Blier. Gérard Depardieu, Patrick Dewaere, Miou-Miou, Jeanne Moreau, Brigitte Fossey, Isabelle Huppert. Crude, overgrown juvenile delinquents Depardieu and Dewaere commit petty crimes, terrorize and share women. Funny, earthy, sometimes even lyrical examination of alienation; Moreau appears briefly as an ex-con who trysts with the boys. [R] ▼➋

Going Shopping (2005) **C-106m.** *½ D:

Henry Jaglom. Victoria Foyt, Rob Morrow, Lee Grant, Mae Whitman, Bruce Davison, Jennifer Grant, Cynthia Sikes, Martha Gehman, Juliet Landau, Pamela Bellwood, Robert Romanus. Santa Monica boutique is threatened with foreclosure unless its owner can come up with some quick cash. To do this she throws the mother of all Mother's Day sales. Means to explore women's obsession with shopping as EATING dealt with female food issues. This stitched-together film—indulgent even by Jaglom standards—stars the director's ex (Foyt, who also cowrote) and some of his usual troupe. At best a clearance-sale item. [PG-13]➋

Going the Distance (2010) **C-102m.** *** D: Nanette Burstein. Drew Barrymore, Justin Long, Charlie Day, Jason Sudeikis, Christina Applegate, Ron Livingston, Jim Gaffigan, Kristen Schaal. Would-be newspaper writer (Barrymore) and a record label functionary (Long) agree to a no-strings friendship with benefits during her last six weeks in N.Y.C. But when she moves to San Francisco they realize they're in love and struggle to maintain a cross-country relationship. By turns playfully raunchy and winningly romantic, this enjoyable comedy is surprisingly realistic while dealing with employment insecurities, steep air fares, and other recession-era impediments to happily-ever-aftering. Attractive leads are extremely engaging, backed by well-cast supporting players. Super 35. [R] ➋

Goin' South (1978) **C-109m.** *** D: Jack Nicholson. Jack Nicholson, Mary Steenburgen, Christopher Lloyd, John Belushi, Veronica Cartwright, Richard Bradford, Danny DeVito, Luana Anders, Ed Begley, Jr., Anne Ramsey. Amusing Western comedy, not for all tastes, with Nicholson saving himself from lynch mob by marrying a spinster. Steenburgen is refreshingly offbeat and Belushi's disappointingly small role is a real hoot. Film debuts of both. [PG] ▼●➋

Goin' to Town (1935) **74m.** *** D: Alexander Hall. Mae West, Paul Cavanagh, Ivan Lebedeff, Marjorie Gateson, Tito Coral, Gilbert Emery. Good West vehicle of dance-hall girl trying to crash society; highlight: Mae doing "Samson and Delilah" scenes. West wrote the screenplay. ▼➋

Go, Johnny, Go! (1958) **75m.** ** D: Paul Landres. Jimmy Clanton, Alan Freed, Sandy Stewart, Chuck Berry, Jo-Ann Campbell, The Cadillacs, Ritchie Valens, Eddie Cochran, Harvey (Fuqua), The Flamingos, Jackie Wilson. Orphan Clanton, booted out of church choir for playing rock 'n' roll, is transformed by Freed into "Johnny Melody," teen idol. ("He's dreamy. Oh wow, he's the living end.") Not very good, but an artifact of its era. Berry, who acts as well as sings, performs "Memphis, Tennessee," "Little Queenie," and "Johnny Be Good," Cochran performs "Teenage Heaven," and Wilson does "You'd Better Know It." ▼●

Gold (1974-British) **C-120m.** *** D: Peter Hunt. Roger Moore, Susannah York, Ray Milland, Bradford Dillman, John Gielgud. Grand-scale adventure action yarn about plot to control price of gold on world market by destroying South African mine. Moore is stalwart hero. Long but entertaining. Panavision. [PG]▼●

Gold Diggers of 1933 (1933) **96m.** ***½ D: Mervyn LeRoy. Joan Blondell, Ruby Keeler, Aline MacMahon, Dick Powell, Guy Kibbee, Warren William, Ned Sparks, Ginger Rogers, Sterling Holloway. Another spectacular Busby Berkeley dance outing with familiar let's-produce-a-Broadway-show plot. Highlights: Blondell's "Forgotten Man," Rogers' "We're In The Money" (with pig-Latin chorus), chorus girls' "Shadow Waltz."▼●▶

Gold Diggers of 1935 (1935) **95m.** *** D: Busby Berkeley. Dick Powell, Adolphe Menjou, Gloria Stuart, Alice Brady, Glenda Farrell, Frank McHugh, Winifred Shaw. Big-scale Berkeley musical with stereotypes providing plot line and laughs between fantastic precision production numbers, including "The Words Are In My Heart," and classic, Oscar-winning "Lullaby of Broadway," sung by Wini Shaw.▼●▶

Gold Diggers of 1937 (1936) **100m.** **½ D: Lloyd Bacon. Dick Powell, Joan Blondell, Glenda Farrell, Victor Moore, Lee Dixon, Osgood Perkins. Those gold-diggers won't give up; this time it's a group of insurance salesmen backing a show. Top song: "With Plenty of Money and You."▶

Gold Diggers: The Secret of Bear Mountain (1995) **C-94m.** ** D: Kevin James Dobson. Christina Ricci, Anna Chlumsky, Polly Draper, Brian Kerwin, Diana Scarwid, David Keith. New girl in town (Ricci) makes an unlikely friend—an aggressive, unpopular kid (Chlumsky) who's prone to telling lies. However, her tallest tale may not be bogus, and leads them on a search for long-buried treasure in a watery cave. Unsatisfying conclusion shortchanges this story; its strongest asset (sure to appeal to preteen girls) is the depiction of the girls' friendship. [PG]▼●▶

Golden Age of Comedy, The (1957) **78m.** **** D: Compiled by Robert Youngson. Laurel and Hardy, Carole Lombard, Ben Turpin, Will Rogers, Harry Langdon. Peerless grouping of some of silent comedy's greatest moments, including Rogers' classic spoofs of silent stars, and ending with Laurel and Hardy's legendary pie fight from BATTLE OF THE CENTURY.▼●▶

Golden Blade, The (1953) **C-81m.** **½ D: Nathan Juran. Rock Hudson, Piper Laurie, Gene Evans, George Macready, Kathleen Hughes, Steven Geray. Hudson, with the help of the magical Sword of Damascus, helps Baghdad princess Laurie battle her caliph father's grand vizier (Macready) and his strong-arm son (Evans). Typical but sprightly, entertaining Arabian Nights adventure; amusing and imaginative.▐

Golden Bowl, The (2001-British) **C-130m.** *** D: James Ivory. Uma Thurman, Nick Nolte, Kate Beckinsale, Jeremy Northam, Anjelica Huston, Madeleine Potter. Compelling adaptation of Henry James' novel about an Italian prince and an American woman, both impoverished, who must forsake their love in order to marry for money—but find themselves entangled just the same: he weds the sheltered daughter of an American billionaire, and she marries the father. Excellent performances amidst the beautiful settings one expects from a Merchant-Ivory period piece. Screenplay by Ruth Prawer Jhabvala. Panavision.▼▶

Golden Boy (1939) **99m.** *** D: Rouben Mamoulian. Barbara Stanwyck, Adolphe Menjou, William Holden, Lee J. Cobb, Joseph Calleia, Sam Levene, Don Beddoe. Italian immigrant's son is torn between his love of the violin—instilled by his insistent father—and his passion for prizefighting. Clifford Odets' story may seem like one giant cliché by now but it's played with gusto (perhaps too much gusto by Cobb as the Henry Armetta–ish father) and benefits from Stanwyck's heartfelt performance. This role propelled an unknown Holden to stardom.▼●▶

Golden Braid (1990-Australian) **C-88m.** *** D: Paul Cox. Chris Haywood, Gosia Dobrowolska, Paul Chubb, Norman Kaye, Robert Menzies, Jo Kennedy. Thoughtful, gentle film about a clockmaker (Haywood), obsessed with all things past, and what happens when he finds a braid of blonde hair in an 18th-century cabinet. A film with a refreshing point of view: clocks may stop ticking, and human hearts may stop beating, but time still goes on—and human beings must celebrate life.

Golden Child, The (1986) **C-96m.** BOMB D: Michael Ritchie. Eddie Murphy, Charlotte Lewis, Charles Dance, Victor Wong, Randall "Tex" Cobb, James Hong, J.L. Reate. Top candidate for the worst megahit of all time. A "perfect" child (Reate) is kidnapped despite his magical powers; as foretold by an ancient oracle, only Murphy can rescue him. Lewis is more wooden than most ex-models; entire reels go by with nary a chuckle. A box-office smash—but have you ever met anyone who liked it? [PG-13]▼●▶

Golden Coach, The (1952-Italian) **C-101m.** ***½ D: Jean Renoir. Anna Magnani, Odoardo Spadaro, Nada Fiorelli, Dante Rino, Duncan Lamont, Jean Debucourt. Delightful film about an acting troupe touring South America in the 18th century and the amorous adventures of its leading lady. Theatrical and stylized, this is one of the great films about acting—and a stunning achievement in the use of color. Ironically, it was a flop when first released, then critically rediscovered. Photographed by Claude Renoir; music by Vivaldi.▼●)

Golden Compass, The (2007) **C-118m.** *** D: Chris Weitz. Nicole Kidman, Dakota Blue Richards, Daniel Craig, Sam Elliott, Eva Green, Christopher Lee, Tom Courtenay, Derek Jacobi, Ben Walker, Simon McBurney, Jim Carter, Magda Szubanski; voices of Ian McKellen, Ian McShane, Freddie Highmore, Kathy Bates, Kristin Scott Thomas. Epic juvenile fantasy-adventure, based on the first book in Philip Pullman's *His Dark Materials* trilogy called *Northern Lights*. Richards is persuasive as a plucky 12-year-old who ventures to the Arctic Circle in search of a vanished friend—and evidence of a conspiracy to make children conform to the wishes of the all-powerful Magisterium. Does a good job of introducing us to an unfamiliar world (where every human has an animal companion), and its computer-generated creatures seem quite real, especially the great white bear voiced by McKellen. Oscar winner for Visual Effects. Super 35. [PG-13]▌

Golden Door (2006-Italian-German-French) **C-118m.** *** D: Emanuele Crialese. Charlotte Gainsbourg, Vincenzo Amato, Aurora Quattrocchi, Francesco Casisa, Filippo Pucillo, Isabella Ragonese, Vincent Schiavelli. Heartfelt, dreamlike account of a dirt-poor Italian family that treks from rural Old World Sicily to Ellis Island and the U.S., where they enter a new, modern world. Although it is set at the dawn of the 20th century, the film is a poetic ode to the aspirations of immigrants of all eras. Filled with stunning images, it begs for a sequel following these characters into the New World. Original Italian title: NUOVOMONDO. Super 35. [PG-13]▌

Golden Earrings (1947) **95m.** **½ D: Mitchell Leisen. Ray Milland, Marlene Dietrich, Murvyn Vye, Dennis Hoey, Quentin Reynolds. Incredible yet enjoyable escapism set in WW2 Europe has Milland joining gypsy Dietrich for espionage work; Dietrich most convincing. Gypsy Vye sings the title song.▼▌

GoldenEye (1995) **C-130m.** *** D: Martin Campbell. Pierce Brosnan, Sean Bean, Izabella Scorupco, Famke Janssen, Joe Don Baker, Judi Dench, Robbie Coltrane, Tchéky Karyo, Gottfried John, Alan Cumming, Desmond Llewelyn, Samantha Bond. Brosnan's debut as 007 is a slam-bang action adventure in the best Bond tradition, with eye-popping stunts, sexy women, and international intrigue. (There are also P.C. remarks about Bond being sexist and/or an anachronism.) The crux of the story is internal sabotage within Russia, and Bond's attempt to figure out who's behind it—and how to stop them before they use their stolen weapons to harm the free world. That's Minnie Driver as the Russian nightclub singer. Panavision. [PG-13]▼●)

Golden Gate (1993) **C-90m.** *½ D: John Madden. Matt Dillon, Joan Chen, Bruno Kirby, Teri Polo, Tzi Ma, Stan Egi, Jack Shearer. Young FBI agent Dillon pursues subversives in San Francisco during the McCarthy witchhunts, when guiltless Chinese were harassed simply for mailing money to their families back home. Potentially compelling film is hampered by listless direction and David Henry Hwang's meandering, melodramatic screenplay. An *American Playhouse* coproduction. [R] ▼●)

Goldengirl (1979) **C-104m.** ** D: Joseph Sargent. Susan Anton, Curt Jurgens, Robert Culp, Leslie Caron, Harry Guardino, Jessica Walter. Statuesque Anton is more or less turned into a robot so she can become a star in the Olympics. So-so. [PG]▼

Golden Heist, The SEE: **Inside Out** (1975)

Golden Needles (1974) **C-92m.** ** D: Robert Clouse. Joe Don Baker, Elizabeth Ashley, Jim Kelly, Burgess Meredith, Ann Sothern. Everyone seems out of place in this Hong Kong-L.A. filmed action pic about a scramble for golden statue containing youth-restoring acupuncture needles. Silly. Retitled THE CHASE FOR THE GOLDEN NEEDLES. Panavision. [PG]

Golden Rendezvous (1977) **C-103m.** ** D: Ashley Lazarus. Richard Harris, Ann Turkel, David Janssen, Burgess Meredith, John Vernon, Gordon Jackson, Keith Baxter, Dorothy Malone, John Carradine. Attractive cast in pointless adaptation of Alistair MacLean's novel about gambling ship held hostage by terrorists. Retitled NUCLEAR TERROR for television.▼

Golden Salamander (1950-British) **96m.** *** D: Ronald Neame. Trevor Howard, Anouk Aimée, Walter Rilla, Herbert Lom, Wilfrid Hyde-White. Courting a Tunisian girl, Howard becomes involved in gun smuggling; taut actioner.▼

Golden Seal, The (1983) **C-95m.** *** D: Frank Zuniga. Steve Railsback, Michael Beck, Penelope Milford, Torquil Campbell, Seth Sakai, Richard Narita, Sandra Seacat. Straightforward family film about a young couple and their son, living in the Aleutian islands, cut off from the world. Like the Aleut natives, the father (Railsback) has long pursued the golden seal, a near-mythical creature with an enormous bounty on its head, but it's the boy (Campbell) who finds him, and tries to protect him. Dialogue is stiff, but when the action picks up it's absorbing and enjoyable. [PG]▼▌

Golden Voyage of Sinbad, The (1974-British) **C-104m.** *** D: Gordon Hessler. John Phillip Law, Caroline Munro, Tom

Baker, Douglas Wilmer, Gregoire Aslan, John Garfield, Jr. Delightful rehash of earlier Sinbad adventures that evokes Saturday matinee fare of the 1950s, with Ray Harryhausen's finest "Dynamation" effects: a ship's figurehead comes to life, and a six-armed statue does sword battle with Sinbad in action highlights. Grand entertainment. [G]▼●❶

Goldfinger (1964-British) **C-111m.** ***½ D: Guy Hamilton. Sean Connery, Gert Frobe, Honor Blackman, Shirley Eaton, Bernard Lee, Lois Maxwell, Harold Sakata, Tania Mallet. Entertaining, exciting James Bond adventure, third in the series. Full of ingenious gadgets and nefarious villains, with hair-raising climax inside Fort Knox. Frobe (Goldfinger) and Sakata (Oddjob) are villains in the classic tradition. ▼●❶

Gold Is Where You Find It (1938) **C-90m.** **½ D: Michael Curtiz. George Brent, Olivia de Havilland, Claude Rains, Margaret Lindsay, John Litel, Barton MacLane. And gold-rush miners find it on California farmland, starting bitter feud in brisk film, perked by good cast.

Gold of Naples (1954-Italian) **107m.** *** D: Vittorio De Sica. Sophia Loren, Vittorio De Sica, Totò, Silvana Mangano, Paolo Stoppa. Four vignettes—poignant, perceptive, hilarious in turn: Loren as philandering wife of pizza baker; De Sica as avid cardplayer upstaged by 8-year-old; Toto as Milquetoast family man; Mangano as prostitute involved in unusual marriage. ▼❶

Gold Rush, The (1925) **82m.** **** D: Charlie Chaplin. Charlie Chaplin, Georgia Hale, Mack Swain, Tom Murray. Immortal Chaplin classic, pitting Little Tramp against Yukon, affections of dance-hall girl, whims of a burly prospector. Dance of the rolls, eating leather shoe, cabin tottering over cliff—all highlights of wonderful, timeless comedy. Chaplin reedited film in 1942; that version, with his narration and music, runs 72m. ▼●❶

Goldsmith's Shop, The SEE: **Jeweller's Shop, The**

Goldstein (1965) **85m.** **½ D: Benjamin Manaster, Philip Kaufman. Lou Gilbert, Ellen Madison, Thomas Erhart, Benito Carruthers, Severn Darden, Nelson Algren. The prophet Elijah (Gilbert) emerges from Lake Michigan, is pursued by sculptor Erhart. Quirky, inventive film made on a shoestring in Chicago. Based on a story by Martin Buber. Original running time: 115m. ❶

Golem, The (1920-German) **75m.** ***½ D: Paul Wegener, Carl Boese. Paul Wegener, Albert Steinruck, Ernst Deutsch, Lyda Salmonova. Chilling, visually dazzling story of the supernatural, based on a famous Jewish folktale of the 16th century. Rudolph of Hapsburg has exiled the Jews, blaming them for a plague; a rabbi conjures up a golem (a clay monster, played by Wegener) in order to convince the king to repeal the edict. This classic of German Expressionist cinema is also a forerunner of FRANKENSTEIN, from the way the golem is brought to life to his attraction to a child. The sets were designed by famed architect Hans Poelzig. The story has been filmed many times; Wegener also codirected versions in 1914 and 1917, and Julien Duvivier filmed it in 1938, with Harry Baur. Aka THE GOLEM: HOW HE CAME INTO THE WORLD. ▼❶

Go, Man, Go! (1954) **82m.** **½ D: James Wong Howe. Dane Clark, Pat Breslin, Sidney Poitier, Edmon Ryan. Imaginative telling of the formation of Harlem Globetrotters and their rise as famed basketball team. A rare directorial effort by celebrated cinematographer Howe.

Go Masters, The (1982-Chinese-Japanese) **C-123m.** *** D: Junya Sato, Duan Jishun. Rentaro Mikuni, Sun Dao-Lin, Shen Guan-Chu, Misako Honno, Tsu Kasa Itoh. Sprawling, involving romance-mystery-suspense, set between the 1920s and '50s and focusing on the relationships between two families, one Japanese and the other Chinese. Most fascinating is various characters' obsession with Go, a chesslike strategy game. The first Sino-Japanese co-production, and a smash hit in both countries.▼

Gomorrah (2008-Italian) **C-137m.** ***½ D: Matteo Garrone. Salvatore Abruzzese, Gianfelice Imparato, Maria Nazionale, Toni Servillo, Carmine Paternoster, Salvatore Cantalupo, Gigio Morra, Marco Macor, Ciro Petrone. Stark drama based on Roberto Saviano's best-selling exposé of the Neapolitan crime organization Camorra, which permeates every facet of life in the region. Separate stories follow a pair of SCARFACE-obsessed teenage thugs who want to be accepted as mobsters, an even younger boy who's heading in the same direction, a tailor whose moonlighting activities spell trouble, a bagman who tries to stay out of the line of fire, and a businessman's scheme to dump toxic waste quickly and cheaply. Absence of a music score helps achieve a level of authenticity in this film that feels like a punch to the gut. Italian title: GOMORRA. Super 35.❶

Gone Are the Days (1963) **97m.** *** D: Nicholas Webster. Ossie Davis, Ruby Dee, Sorrell Booke, Godfrey Cambridge, Alan Alda, Beah Richards. Davis' satiric fable *Purlie Victorious* survives cheap adaptation, thanks to buoyant performances and basic story: self-appointed preacher schemes to undo a despotic plantation owner, as a symbolic freeing of his people from ways of the Old South. Alda's film debut.▼❶

Gone Baby Gone (2007) **C-115m.** *** D: Ben Affleck. Casey Affleck, Michelle Monaghan, Morgan Freeman, Ed Harris, John Ashton, Amy Ryan, Titus Welliver, Amy

Madigan. Private detectives Affleck and Monaghan are asked to help investigate the disappearance of a 4-year-old girl from a working-class Boston neighborhood. They discover that the truth is elusive as they deal with police, drug dealers, and tangled community ties. Tense, gritty drama loses steam by the end, but an atmosphere of regional clannishness and thick moral rot is impressively conveyed by first-time director Affleck (who also has a great eye and ear for Boston "types"). His brother Casey stands tall in a terrific cast, with Ryan particularly good as the young girl's less-than-ideal mother. The director and Aaron Stockard adapted Dennis Lehane's novel. [R]🄳

Gone Fishin' (1997) **C-94m.** BOMB D: Christopher Cain. Joe Pesci, Danny Glover, Rosanna Arquette, Lynn Whitfield, Nick Brimble, Carol Kane, Willie Nelson. Annoyingly unfunny gambit of two bungling buddies off to the Florida Everglades where their dream fishing vacation is a catastrophe from beginning to end. This film really smells. [PG]🄵🄳

Gone in 60 Seconds (1974) **C-103m.** ** D: H. B. Halicki. H. B. Halicki, Marion Busia, Jerry Daugirda, James McIntire, George Cole, Parnelli Jones. Muddled drama about a car-theft ring is highlighted by a 40-minute-long chase sequence, which is well made—but so what? Remade (in name only) in 2000. [PG]🄵🄳

Gone in Sixty Seconds (2000) **C-117m.** *½ D: Dominic Sena. Nicolas Cage, Giovanni Ribisi, Angelina Jolie, Robert Duvall, Delroy Lindo, TJ Cross, William Lee Scott, Scott Caan, James Duval, Will Patton, Timothy Olyphant, Christopher Eccleston, Chi McBride, Jaime Bergman, Frances Fisher, Bodhi Elfman, Arye Gross. Relentlessly stupid remake of the 1974 drive-in hit about a reformed car thief who—to save his kid brother—agrees to marshal a mass theft in 48 hours' time, while cop Lindo is hot on his trail. Even for a no-brainer this is pretty poor, with low-octane action and a preposterous finale. Jolie is barely in it; Duvall and Lindo are wasted. Unrated version also available. Panavision. [PG-13]🄵🄳

Gone To Earth SEE: **Wild Heart, The**

Gone With the Wind (1939) **C-222m.** **** D: Victor Fleming. Clark Gable, Vivien Leigh, Leslie Howard, Olivia de Havilland, Thomas Mitchell, Barbara O'Neil, Victor Jory, Laura Hope Crews, Hattie McDaniel, Ona Munson, Harry Davenport, Ann Rutherford, Evelyn Keyes, Carroll Nye, Paul Hurst, Isabel Jewell, Cliff Edwards, Ward Bond, Butterfly McQueen, Rand Brooks, Eddie Anderson, Oscar Polk, Jane Darwell, William Bakewell, L. Kemble-Cooper, Eric Linden, George Reeves. If not the greatest movie ever made, certainly one of the greatest examples of storytelling on film, maintaining interest for nearly four hours. Margaret Mitchell's

story is, in effect, a Civil War soap opera, focusing on vixenish Southern belle Scarlett O'Hara, brilliantly played by Leigh; she won Oscar, as did the picture, McDaniel, director Fleming, screenwriter Sidney Howard (posthumously), many others. Memorable music by Max Steiner in this one-of-a-kind film meticulously produced by David O. Selznick. Followed over five decades later by a TV miniseries, *Scarlett.* 🅥🄾🄳

Gong Show Movie, The (1980) **C-89m.** BOMB D: Chuck Barris. Chuck Barris, Robin Altman, Mabel King, Murray Langston, Jaye P. Morgan, Jamie Farr, Rip Taylor, Phil Hartman. Barris created a bizarre TV show that belongs in a time capsule, but this movie (which dwells on Chuck's pressures and problems as host and producer of the show) belongs in the trash bin. [R]

Gonzo: The Life and Work of Dr. Hunter S. Thompson (2008) **C-120m.** ***½ D: Alex Gibney. Running the full political-commentary gamut from George McGovern to Patrick J. Buchanan, director Gibney's first outing following TAXI TO THE DARK SIDE examines the volatile career of celebrity journalism's most iconoclastic figure. Though it skimps on Thompson's formative years growing up as a Louisville outsider, this kinetic portrait is staggering on an "access" level, from both of Thompson's wives to writer Tom Wolfe to *Rolling Stone* publisher Jann Wenner to illustrator Ralph Steadman to Hells Angel Sonny Barger to Jimmy Carter. Johnny Depp reads passages from Thompson's classic *Fear and Loathing in Las Vegas* against clips from the screen version, in which he starred. [R]🄳

Good (2008-British-German) **C-96m.** ** D: Vicente Amorim. Viggo Mortensen, Jason Isaacs, Jodie Whittaker, Mark Strong, Gemma Jones, Steven Mackintosh, Rick Warden. German university professor (Mortensen) resists the rise of Nazism in the early 1930s but ultimately finds himself caught in its tide . . . to the astonishment of his best friend, a Jewish psychiatrist (Isaacs) whose life is made more hellish with each passing year. Ineffectual and unsatisfying, considering the dramatic ingredients. Based on a stage play by C. P. Taylor. Super 35. 🄳

Good Boy! (2003) **C-88m.** ** D: John Hoffman. Molly Shannon, Liam Aiken, Kevin Nealon, Brittany Moldowan, Hunter Elliot, Mikhael Speidel; voices of Matthew Broderick, Vanessa Redgrave, Delta Burke, Donald Faison, Cheech Marin, Carl Reiner, Brittany Murphy. Lonely boy finds a "best friend" in a dog from the neighborhood pound, but this canine is actually from another planet, fulfilling a mission on Earth. What's more, he enables the boy to hear what he and all his fellow dogs have to say. Mild fantasy-comedy may appeal to very young children. [PG]🅥🄳

Good Burger (1997) **C-95m.** ****** D: Brian Robbins. Kel Mitchell, Kenan Thompson, Sinbad, Abe Vigoda, Shar Jackson, Dan Schneider, Jan Schwieterman, Ron Lester, Carmen Electra, Shaquille O'Neal, Robert Wuhl. Broad, juvenile comedy aimed at fans of Kenan and Kel from their Nickelodeon TV series. The existence of a scruffy fast-food establishment ("Welcome to Good Burger, home of the good burger, may I take your order?") is threatened by the arrival of all-powerful Mondo Burger across the street. Like fast food itself, this film offers no real nourishment, but will appeal to kids just the same. [PG]▼●)

Goodbye Again (1961) **120m.** ******* D: Anatole Litvak. Ingrid Bergman, Tony Perkins, Yves Montand, Jessie Royce Landis, Diahann Carroll. Francoise Sagan's chic soaper becomes teary Bergman vehicle of middle-aged woman having affair with Perkins, still craving playboy Montand. Set in Paris.▼

Goodbye Charlie (1964) **C-117m.** ***½** D: Vincente Minnelli. Tony Curtis, Debbie Reynolds, Pat Boone, Walter Matthau, Martin Gabel, Ellen McRae (Burstyn). Tasteless, flat version of George Axelrod's play; crude gangster dies and comes back to earth as Reynolds. Even Matthau struggles for laughs. James Brolin is an extra in big party scene. CinemaScope.▼

Goodbye, Children SEE: **Au Revoir, les Enfants**

Goodbye, Columbus (1969) **C-101m.** ******* D: Larry Peerce. Richard Benjamin, Ali MacGraw, Jack Klugman, Nan Martin, Michael Meyers. Philip Roth's stinging portrait of successful suburban Jewish family as seen through eyes of young man (Benjamin, in his film debut) who falls in love with daughter (MacGraw, in her first starring role). Meyers steals the show as Ali's brother. Director's father Jan Peerce has a cameo role at a wedding; look for Jaclyn Smith as a model. Music composed and performed by The Association. [PG—originally rated R]▼●)

Goodbye Girl, The (1977) **C-110m.** *****½** D: Herbert Ross. Richard Dreyfuss, Marsha Mason, Quinn Cummings, Paul Benedict, Barbara Rhoades. Neil Simon's warmest comedy to date puts young actor Dreyfuss and dumped-on divorcée Mason together as unwilling tenants of the same N.Y.C. apartment, explores their growing relationship. High-caliber script and performances to match; Dreyfuss won Oscar. Nicol Williamson appears unbilled. Later a Broadway musical. Remade for TV in 2004. [PG] ▼●)

Good Bye Lenin! (2003-German-French) **C-119m.** ******* D: Wolfgang Becker. Daniel Brühl, Katrin Sass, Chulpan Khamatova, Maria Simon, Florian Lukas, Alexander Beyer, Burghart Klaussner. An East Berlin teenager (Brühl) feels liberated when the Wall comes down in 1989; his mother, a divorcée who has become an ardent Communist, falls into a coma just as Westernization is being welcomed. So the teen, with his older sister, decides to dupe his recuperating mother into believing German reunification never happened! Leisurely paced, lighthearted film deals with the transient nature of history as well as coming of age in a single-parent household. This was a box-office smash in Germany. [R]▼▼

Goodbye Lover (1999) **C-104m.** ***½** D: Roland Joffé. Patricia Arquette, Dermot Mulroney, Don Johnson, Ellen DeGeneres, Mary-Louise Parker, Ray McKinnon, Andre Gregory, John Neville, Lisa Eichhorn, Barry Newman. It's double-cross upon double-cross in this comic noir exercise of battling brothers Mulroney and Johnson—and the wacko femme fatale/realtor in their lives (Arquette), who takes her marriage vows loosely, to say the least. So bad it's almost fun, from a seriously slumming director. DeGeneres' sardonic detective seems to have wandered in from another movie altogether. Telltale trouble sign: Alex Rocco and Max Perlich are billed, but hard to spot. Super 35. [R]▼●)

Goodbye, Mr. Chips (1939-U.S.-British) **114m.** *****½** D: Sam Wood. Robert Donat, Greer Garson, Paul von Hernreid (Henreid), Terry Kilburn, John Mills. Donat won well-deserved Oscar for memorable portrayal of shy schoolmaster who devotes his life to "his boys," only coming out of his shell when he meets Garson. Extreme length works against film's honest sentiment, but Donat makes it all worthwhile. Garson's film debut made her a star overnight. Based on James Hilton's novel; scripted by R. C. Sherriff, Claudine West, and Eric Maschwitz. Remade as a musical in 1969. Also shown in computer-colored version. ▼●)

Goodbye, Mr. Chips (1969) **C-151m.** ****** D: Herbert Ross. Peter O'Toole, Petula Clark, Michael Redgrave, George Baker, Sian Phillips, Michael Bryant. Lumbering musical remake of 1939 classic. O'Toole is good as prim schoolteacher, but Clark's role as showgirl is shallow, ludicrous. Mediocre songs don't help; what emotion there is gets lost when film plods on to modern-day anticlimax. Ross' directorial debut. Some prints are 133m. Panavision. [G]▼●)

Goodbye, My Fancy (1951) **107m.** ******* D: Vincent Sherman. Joan Crawford, Robert Young, Frank Lovejoy, Eve Arden. Congresswoman Crawford returns to her old college, more to see former boyfriend Young than to receive honorary degree. Lovejoy is callous newsman. Film debut of Janice Rule.●)

Good-bye, My Lady (1956) **95m.** ****½** D: William Wellman. Walter Brennan, Phil Harris, Brandon de Wilde, Sidney Poitier. James Street novel of small boy (de Wilde), an elderly man (Brennan), and the basenji dog that brings joy into their lives is basis for easygoing, poignant film, set in the South.▼●)

Goodbye, New York (1985-U.S.-Israeli) **C-90m.** **½ D: Amos Kollek. Julie Hagerty, Amos Kollek, David Topaz, Aviva Ger, Shmuel Shiloh, Jennifer Babtist. Cute but slight, sometimes flat chronicle of New Yorker Hagerty, a Jewish American Princess of Irish extraction who finds herself penniless and stranded in Israel. She eventually adjusts to life on a kibbutz, getting to know part-time soldier Kollek. [R] ▼●

Goodbye, Norma Jean (1976) **C-95m.** BOMB D: Larry Buchanan. Misty Rowe, Terence Locke, Patch Mackenzie, Preston Hanson. Sleazy look at adolescent Marilyn Monroe and her rocky road to stardom. An utter piece of tripe. Techniscope. [R] ▼▶

Goodbye People, The (1984) **C-104m.** *½ D: Herb Gardner. Judd Hirsch, Martin Balsam, Pamela Reed, Ron Silver, Michael Tucker, Gene Saks. Absolute torture (adapted by Gardner from his play) about Balsam's begging-for-bankruptcy scheme to open a tropical drink stand on some ill-located beach property. Gardner's A THOUSAND CLOWNS may strike some as sentimental and dated, but this one doesn't even have comedy to carry it. A mawkish disaster, long on the shelf. [PG] ▼●

Goodbye Pork Pie (1981-New Zealand) **C-105m.** *** D: Geoff Murphy. Kelly Johnson, Tony Barry, Claire Oberman, Bruno Lawrence, John Beach, Frances Edmond. Amiable comedy/road movie about pair of alienated men, one (Johnson) in his teens and the other (Barry) about twice his age, who trek across New Zealand in a stolen car, the police on their trail. [R] ▼

Goodbye Solo (2009) **C-91m.** *** D: Ramin Bahrani. Souléymane Sy Savané, Red West, Carmen Leyva, Diana Franco Galindo, Lane "Roc" Williams, Mamadou Lam. Solo (Savané) is a garrulous cabdriver from Senegal who lives and works in Winston-Salem, North Carolina. A taciturn passenger named William (West) hires him for a future date for a trip far out of town to a spot where he plans to end his life. Solo refuses to mind his own business and insinuates himself into William's life. Vivid slice of life, with acute details of character and setting, from the director and cowriter of MAN PUSH CART and CHOP SHOP, and inspired by Abbas Kiarostami's A TASTE OF CHERRY. ▶

Good Companions, The (1957-British) **C-104m.** *** D: J. Lee Thompson. Eric Portman, Celia Johnson, Hugh Griffith, Janette Scott, John Fraser, Joyce Grenfell, Bobby Howes, Rachel Roberts, Thora Hird, Mona Washbourne, Alec McCowen, John Le Mesurier, Anthony Newley, Shirley Anne Field. Fabulous cast adds luster to this entertaining chronicle of a group of individuals who combine their resources to save a failing "concert party" (musical troupe).

Based on a novel by J. B. Priestley; first filmed in 1933. CinemaScope.

Good Die First, The SEE: **Beyond the Law** (1968)

Good Die Young, The (1954-British) **100m.** ** D: Lewis Gilbert. Laurence Harvey, Gloria Grahame, Richard Basehart, Stanley Baker, Margaret Leighton, John Ireland, Joan Collins. Solid cast fails to enhance standard robbery tale, with a quartet of strangers coming together to commit a holdup.

Good Earth, The (1937) **138m.** **** D: Sidney Franklin. Paul Muni, Luise Rainer, Walter Connolly, Charley Grapewin, Jessie Ralph, Tilly Losch, Keye Luke, Harold Huber. Mammoth Pearl Buck novel re-created in detail, telling story of greed ruining lives of simple Chinese farming couple. Rainer won Oscar as the ever-patient wife of Muni, as did Karl Freund for his cinematography. Screenplay by Talbot Jennings, Tess Slesinger, and Claudine West. The special effects are outstanding. ▼●▶

Good Fairy, The (1935) **97m.** ***½ D: William Wyler. Margaret Sullavan, Herbert Marshall, Frank Morgan, Reginald Owen, Alan Hale, Beulah Bondi, Cesar Romero. Sparkling romantic comedy, adapted from Molnar play by Preston Sturges; wide-eyed Sullavan tries to act as "good fairy" to struggling lawyer Marshall, while hotly pursued by wealthy Morgan. Hilarious, charming; movie spoof near beginning is priceless. Remade as I'LL BE YOURS. ▼▶

Good Father, The (1985-British) **C-90m.** **½ D: Mike Newell. Anthony Hopkins, Jim Broadbent, Harriet Walter, Fanny Viner, Simon Callow, Joanne Whalley, Michael Byrne. Hopkins is excellent in the role of a father who loses custody of his child and takes out his incredible anger by befriending Broadbent and funding latter's court case to regain *his* kid's custody. Callow is terrific as an unscrupulous lawyer. Dramatically uneven, but worth a look. Made for British TV. [R] ▼●▶

GoodFellas (1990) **C-146m.** ***½ D: Martin Scorsese. Robert De Niro, Ray Liotta, Joe Pesci, Lorraine Bracco, Paul Sorvino, Frank Sivero, Tony Darrow, Mike Starr, Frank Vincent, Chuck Low, Frank DiLeo, Christopher Serrone, Samuel L. Jackson, Henny Youngman, Jerry Vale, Debi Mazar, Kevin Corrigan, Michael Imperioli, Illeana Douglas. A boy grows up in an Italian-American neighborhood of Brooklyn and dreams of becoming part of the Mob. Fascinating look at the allure—and the reality—of day-to-day life in a Mafia family, based on experiences of Henry Hill (Liotta), who wound up in the Federal witness protection program. The violence is (necessarily) harsh and off-putting, like the film itself at times, but it's brilliantly realized by Scorsese and cinematographer Michael Ballhaus. Major criticism: It goes on too long.

Bracco and Oscar winner Pesci stand out in an exceptional cast; that's Scorsese's mother as Pesci's mom. Screenplay by the director and Nicholas Pileggi, based on the latter's book *Wiseguy*. [R]▼●)

Good Fight, The (1983) C/B&W-98m. ***½ D: Mary Dore, Sam Sills, Noel Buckner. Incisive, often moving documentary of the 3,200 American men and women who were among 40,000 volunteers battling Fascism in the Spanish Civil War. Franco may have won and they may have been harassed by their own government, but they are ultimately both authentic American patriots and survivors. Cut to 85m. for PBS showings.▼●)

Good German, The (2006) 107m. **½ D: Steven Soderbergh. George Clooney, Cate Blanchett, Tobey Maguire, Beau Bridges, Tony Curran, Leland Orser, Jack Thompson, Robin Weigert, Ravil Isaynov, Christian Oliver. War correspondent Clooney returns to Berlin in 1945 on the eve of the Potsdam conference and discovers a city in ruins, both physically and morally. His driver-escort (Maguire) has mastered the black market, and a woman Clooney knew before (Blanchett) has done God knows what in order to survive the war. Now Clooney finds himself knee-deep in international intrigue and murder—and still emotionally connected to Blanchett. Shot on the Warner Bros. back lot in order to invoke 1940s Hollywood movies, this is an interesting stylistic exercise for Soderbergh (who also shot and edited, under pseudonyms) and pretty entertaining, but it lacks, in Rick Blaine's words, a "wow finish." Paul Attanasio adapted Joseph Kanon's novel. [R]●)

Good Girl, The (2002) C-93m. ***½ D: Miguel Arteta. Jennifer Aniston, Jake Gyllenhaal, John C. Reilly, Zooey Deschanel, Tim Blake Nelson, Mike White, Deborah Rush, John Carroll Lynch. A 30-year-old woman who feels her life is at a dead end becomes intrigued with a 20-ish loner, and winds up putting her marriage at risk. A rare film that manages to make a transition from comedy to poignant drama, with a denouement that's nearly heartbreaking—thanks to good writing and wonderful acting by the leads. Screenplay by White, who costars as a security guard. [R] ▼●)

Good Guy, The (2010) C-91m. *½ D: Julio DePietro. Scott Porter, Alexis Bledel, Bryan Greenberg, Aaron Yoo, Anna Chlumsky, Jessalyn Wanlim, Andrew Stewart-Jones, Eric Thal, Trini Alvarado, Colin Egglesfield, Christine Evangelista, Andrew McCarthy, Adam LeFevre. Hackneyed account of the life and times of some young, contemporary, upscale New Yorkers. The males (with one exception) are hyperaggressive Wall Street players, the females are relationship-obsessed *Sex and the City* clones, and there's not a human being in

the bunch. The crux of the story involves the connection between pretty Bledel and her testosterone-laden boyfriend (Porter). [R]●)

Good Guys and the Bad Guys, The (1969) C-91m. **½ D: Burt Kennedy. Robert Mitchum, George Kennedy, David Carradine, Tina Louise, Douglas Fowley, Lois Nettleton, Martin Balsam, John Carradine. Mild Western comedy-drama has aging marshal Mitchum going after lifelong foe Kennedy, who has been abandoned by his outlaw gang for being over the hill. Panavision. [M/PG]▼)

Good Guys Wear Black (1979) C-96m. ** D: Ted Post. Chuck Norris, Anne Archer, James Franciscus, Lloyd Haynes, Dana Andrews, Jim Backus. Norris jumps feet first through a windshield and threatens to rearrange the face of bellman Backus—all in the name of national security. Silly political paranoia thriller kills time easily enough. Follow-up: A FORCE OF ONE. [PG]▼●)

Good Heart, The (2010-U.S.-Danish-Icelandic-French) C-98m. *** D: Dagur Kári. Brian Cox, Paul Dano, Isild Le Besco. After his fifth heart attack, a blunt-spoken, hot-tempered curmudgeon (Cox) reluctantly decides to train a mild-mannered young homeless man (Dano) as an apprentice to run, and eventually own, his seedy Manhattan tavern. Gruffly sentimental dramedy is amusing and affecting, with exceptionally fine performances and profanely funny dialogue. Cox has never been better. Written by the director. HD Widescreen. [R]●)

Good Humor Man, The (1950) 79m. **½ D: Lloyd Bacon. Jack Carson, Lola Albright, Jean Wallace, George Reeves, Richard Egan. Broad slapstick comedy about ice-cream vendor Carson, who stumbles into a crime ring. Written by Frank Tashlin.▼

Good Idea! SEE: **It Seemed Like a Good Idea at the Time**

Good Luck (1997) C-98m. **½ D: Richard LaBrie. Gregory Hines, Vincent D'Onofrio, James Earl Jones, Max Gail, Joe Theismann, Roy Firestone, Maria O'Brien, Sara Trigger. ROCKY-like story of a blind man and a paraplegic who decide to enter a white-water rafting race in order to prove their own self-worth. The theme of triumph over adversity is familiar, but the film's heart is in the right place. Some genuinely raucous and entertaining scenes. [R]▼●)

Good Luck Chuck (2007) C-96m. *½ D: Mark Helfrich. Dane Cook, Jessica Alba, Dan Fogler, Troy Gentile, Chelan Simmons. A lifelong curse is placed on playboy Cook that makes him the last man to sleep with a woman before she meets and marries her true love. When he falls head over heels for Alba he must keep from consummating the relationship or risk losing her. Really dumb premise is even worse than it sounds. Cook and Alba fumble every comic opportunity. Unrated version runs 101m. [R]▶

Good Luck, Miss Wyckoff (1979) C-105m. BOMB D: Marvin J. Chomsky. Anne Heywood, Donald Pleasence, Robert Vaughn, Carolyn Jones, Dorothy Malone, Ronee Blakley, John Lafayette, Earl Holliman. Repressed schoolteacher's first taste of sex comes via rape, in awkward adaptation of William Inge novel. Good cast generally wasted. Video titles: THE SIN, THE SHAMING, and SECRET YEARNINGS. [R]▼

Good Man in Africa, A (1994) C-93m. *½ D: Bruce Beresford. Colin Friels, Joanne Whalley-Kilmer, Sean Connery, John Lithgow, Louis Gossett, Jr., Diana Rigg, Sarah-Jane Fenton, Maynard Eziashi, Jackie Mofokeng. Crass, slapdash filming of William Boyd's novel about a weak-willed (and all-too-often insufferable) British diplomat (Friels) in a new African nation; the scenario accomplishes little more than to depict blacks as silly, unbelievable stereotypes. Connery is sorely wasted in the role of a sympathetic doctor. Boyd scripted and also coproduced with Beresford. [R]▼●

Good Marriage, The SEE: **Le Beau Mariage**

Good Morning Babylon (1987-Italian-French-U.S.) C-117m. *** D: Paolo and Vittorio Taviani. Vincent Spano, Joaquim De Almeida, Greta Scacchi, Desiree Becker, Charles Dance, Omero Antonutti, David Brandon. Two Italian brothers, whose artisan family has shaped and restored cathedrals for generations, come to America in 1915 and wind up working for D. W. Griffith on his epic film INTOLERANCE. A valentine to the early days of moviemaking, and a statement about the immortality of art, be it sculpture or film. Beguilingly naive, like the period (and the people) it depicts, with a surprising turn of events for its denouement. Dance is a standout as D.W. Griffith. [PG-13]▼●

Good Morning, Miss Dove (1955) C-107m. *** D: Henry Koster. Jennifer Jones, Robert Stack, Kipp Hamilton, Robert Douglas, Peggy Knudsen, Marshall Thompson, Chuck Connors, Biff Elliot, Jerry Paris, Mary Wickes, Richard Deacon. For several generations, small-town spinster schoolteacher has touched and helped shape lives of her students. Now hospitalized, her past is revealed through flashbacks. Sentimental, warm, and wonderful. CinemaScope.

Good Morning, Vietnam (1987) C-120m. *** D: Barry Levinson. Robin Williams, Forest Whitaker, Tung Thanh Tran, Chintara Sukapatana, Bruno Kirby, Robert Wuhl, J.T. Walsh, Noble Willingham, Floyd Vivino. Williams is the whole show here, playing an Army disc jockey who turns Armed Forces radio inside out when he's brought to Saigon in 1965. His manic monologues are so uproari-

ous that they carry the rest of the film, which has a weakly developed "story" and often irrelevant musical interludes. Apparently the real-life Adrian Cronauer, on whom story was based, wasn't nearly as funny or outrageous as Williams. [R]▼●▮

Good Mother, The (1988) C-103m. ** D: Leonard Nimoy. Diane Keaton, Liam Neeson, Jason Robards, Ralph Bellamy, Teresa Wright, James Naughton, Asia Vieira, Joe Morton, Katey Sagal, Tracy Griffith, Charles Kimbrough. Keaton is excellent as usual in the role of a divorced woman who finds sexual fulfillment for the first time in her life . . . but unwittingly jeopardizes her ability to raise her daughter in the process. Tedious adaptation of the Sue Miller novel. Film debut of Matt Damon (as an extra). [R]▼●

Good Neighbor Sam (1964) C-130m. *** D: David Swift. Jack Lemmon, Romy Schneider, Edward G. Robinson, Michael Connors, Dorothy Provine, Neil Hamilton, Joyce Jameson, Robert Q. Lewis. Good comedy of Lemmon's adventures pretending he's not married to his real wife but to luscious neighbor Schneider. Plenty of sight gags and chase scenes make this a lot of fun. Based on a novel by Jack Finney. ▼▮

Good News (1947) C-95m. *** D: Charles Walters. June Allyson, Peter Lawford, Patricia Marshall, Joan McCracken, Ray McDonald, Mel Tormé, Donald MacBride, Tom Dugan, Clinton Sundberg. Spirited remake of the 1920s collegiate musical (by DeSylva, Brown, and Henderson), given a new coat of varnish by screenwriters Betty Comden and Adolph Green. Lawford is Tait College's cocky football hero, and Allyson is the brainy girl who catches him on the rebound. Vintage songs include "The Best Things in Life are Free," "Just Imagine," "Varsity Drag"; new numbers include "The French Lesson" and "Pass That Peace Pipe." Filmed previously in 1930.▼●

Good Night, The (2007-U.S.-British-German) C-93m. **½ D: Jake Paltrow. Penélope Cruz, Martin Freeman, Michael Gambon, Gwyneth Paltrow, Simon Pegg, Danny DeVito, Keith Allen, Lucy DeVito. Pleasant enough Tylenol PM fantasy about a former pop star, now a bored composer for TV commercials, who yearns to find his (literal) dream girl. Then she becomes a tad too real. Somewhat like THE SCIENCE OF SLEEP without the metaphysics or VERTIGO without the murder. Easy to take but leaves you wanting more. A brunette Gwyneth dials down her glow to "dim" in this debut film from her brother, who also scripted. Third-billed Gambon barely appears. Lucy DeVito is Danny's daughter. [R]▮

Good Night, And Good Luck. (2005) 93m. ***½ D: George Clooney. David Strathairn, Patricia Clarkson, George Clooney, Jeff

Daniels, Robert Downey, Jr., Frank Langella, Ray Wise, Robert John Burke, Reed Diamond, Tate Donovan, Alex Borstein. Vivid dramatization of newscaster Edward R. Murrow's groundbreaking on-the-air confrontation with Commie-hunting Senator Joseph R. McCarthy in the 1950s. Skillful production design (by Jim Bissell), cinematography (Robert Elswit), and editing (Stephen Mirrione) combine with pitch-perfect performances to make us feel like a fly on the wall as CBS television journalists confer, converse, carouse, and put history-making television programs on the air. Strathairn is superb as Murrow; McCarthy "plays" himself in vintage kinescope footage. Written by Clooney and producer Grant Heslov. [PG]**❚**

Good Sam (1948) 113m. ** D: Leo McCarey. Gary Cooper, Ann Sheridan, Ray Collins, Edmund Lowe, Joan Lorring, Ruth Roman. Almost complete misfire, despite cast and director. Cooper is an incurable good Samaritan in this lifeless comedy. Some prints run 128m.**▼**

Good Shepherd, The (2006) C-167m. ***½ D: Robert De Niro. Matt Damon, Angelina Jolie, Alec Baldwin, Tammy Blanchard, Billy Crudup, Robert De Niro, Keir Dullea, Michael Gambon, Martina Gedeck, William Hurt, Timothy Hutton, Mark Ivanir, Gabriel Macht, Lee Pace, Joe Pesci, Eddie Redmayne, John Sessions, Oleg Stefan, John Turturro. Gripping story of an emotionally repressed young man who is recruited at Yale to do espionage work during WW2 and then to join the nascent Central Intelligence Agency, even though it means an enormous sacrifice to his family life. Eric Roth's fictional screenplay (based heavily on fact) covers a lot of ground and provides great insight into the nature of the "spy business." De Niro's treatment uses THE GODFATHER as its dramatic template, quite successfully. Damon is excellent and surrounded by well-chosen actors in every part, no matter how small. Exceptional cinematography by Robert Richardson. Super 35. [R]**❚**

Goods: Live Hard, Sell Hard, The (2009) C-89m. *½ D: Neal Brennan. Jeremy Piven, Ving Rhames, James Brolin, David Koechner, Kathryn Hahn, Ed Helms, Jordana Spiro, Tony Hale, Craig Robinson, Alan Thicke, Charles Napier, Ken Jeong. Ailing auto dealer Brolin hires sleazy hotshot Piven and his crew to recharge his slumping business by selling 211 dormant vehicles in four eventful days. Would-be comedy is burdened by a clumsy title and characters of appalling gall/stupidity; enthusiastically delivered, to no avail. Temecula, California, takes a lot of hits. Producer Will Ferrell has an unwarranted cameo. Gina Gershon appears unbilled. [R]**❚**

Good Son, The (1993) C-87m. ** D: Joseph Ruben. Macaulay Culkin, Elijah Wood, Wendy Crewson, David Morse, Daniel Hugh Kelly, Jacqueline Brookes, Quinn Culkin. Superficial BAD SEED–type thriller, which exploitively casts HOME ALONE star Culkin as an unremorseful, pre-teen sociopath who terrorizes his cousin (Wood), among many others. What's next: bringing back Shirley Temple and having her place high-tech explosives on the Good Ship Lollipop? Macaulay's sister Quinn plays his sibling, and his brother Rory can be glimpsed in a key photograph. [R]**▼❶**

Good, the Bad and the Ugly, The (1966-Italian-Spanish) C-161m. ***½ D: Sergio Leone. Clint Eastwood, Lee Van Cleef, Eli Wallach, Rada Rassimov, Mario Brega, Chelo Alonso. Third and best of Leone's "Dollars" trilogy, set during Civil War; three disparate low-lifes search for Confederate government treasure chest, each possessing only partial whereabouts. Long, funny, and flamboyant, with memorable Ennio Morricone score; the quintessential spaghetti Western. Followed by ONCE UPON A TIME IN THE WEST. Techniscope. Restored version (newly dubbed by Eastwood and Wallach) runs 180m. [R—originally rated M]**▼❶**

Good Thief, The (2003-British-Irish-French-Canadian) C-109m. ** D: Neil Jordan. Nick Nolte, Tchéky Karyo, Said Taghmaoui, Nutsa Kukhianidze, Gerard Darmon, Ouassini Embarek, Emir Kusturica, Marc Lavoine, Mark Polish, Mike Polish, Ralph Fiennes. Sleepy remake of Jean-Pierre Melville's BOB LE FLAMBEUR, with Nolte as a mumbling, heroin-addicted gambler and thief based in Nice who reluctantly takes part in a Riviera casino heist in order to replenish his finances. Colorfully cast and photographed (by Chris Menges), with Nolte making Robert Mitchum seem frenzied by comparison. Some regard this film as the ultimate in Cool; we find it lethargic. [R]**▼❶**

Good Times (1967) C-91m. **½ D: William Friedkin. Sonny and Cher, George Sanders, Norman Alden, Larry Duran. Back when the singing duo was considered kooky, they made this enjoyable little film, with Sonny fantasizing their potential movie roles and he and Cher singing "I Got You Babe." Friedkin's first film.**▼❶**

Good to Go (1986) C-87m. ** D: Blaine Novak. Art Garfunkel, Robert Doqui, Harris Yulin, Reginald Daughtry, Richard Brooks, Hattie Winston, Anjelica Huston. Forgettable fare about journalist Garfunkel, who's framed on a rape-murder charge. Of interest mainly for its go-go music, which came out of the Washington D.C. ghetto . . . and did *not* become the national music fad of its time. Highlighted are the performances of such go-go groups as Redds & the Boys, Trouble Funk, Chuck Brown &

the Soul Searchers, among others. Video title: SHORT FUSE. [R]▼

Good Wife, The (1986-Australian) **C-92m.** **½ D: Ken Cameron. Rachel Ward, Bryan Brown, Sam Neill, Steven Vidler, Jennifer Claire, Bruce Barry. Isolated, bored wife Ward becomes obsessed with the new man in town (Neill). Predictable and a bit slow but also well made and well acted. Overall, a very mixed bag. Original Australian title: THE UMBRELLA WOMAN. [R]▼●

Good Will Hunting (1997) **C-126m.** *** D: Gus Van Sant. Matt Damon, Robin Williams, Ben Affleck, Minnie Driver, Stellan Skarsgård, Casey Affleck, Cole Hauser. Four working-class friends hang out together in South Boston, but one of them, pugnacious Will Hunting (Damon), has an unusual gift: he's a genius. When M.I.T. math professor Skarsgård gets wind of this, he insists that the young man stop wasting his talents, and sends him to psychologist/ teacher Williams to try to crack his brittle shell. Well-acted fiction written by costars Damon and Ben Affleck doesn't bear close scrutiny but certainly entertains, with an array of good performances. Oscar nods for Best Original Screenplay and Best Supporting Actor (Williams). [R]▼●

Good Woman, A (2005-U.S.-Spanish-Italian-British-Luxembourg) **C-93m.** ** D: Mike Barker. Helen Hunt, Scarlett Johansson, Milena Vukotic, Stephen Campbell Moore, Mark Umbers, Roger Hammond, John Standing, Tom Wilkinson, Diana Hardcastle. Ill-conceived version of Oscar Wilde's *Lady Windermere's Fan* (filmed several times across the decades), set in Italy rather than England and updated from the 1890s to the 1930s. A number of Wilde's British characters now are Americans; one of them is Mrs. Erlynne (a sorely miscast Hunt), an insolvent adventuress who arrives in Amalfi and determines to seduce filthy-rich, newly married Robert Windermere (Umbers). Released in the U.S. in 2006. [PG]▮

Good Year, A (2006) **C-117m.** **½ D: Ridley Scott. Russell Crowe, Albert Finney, Marion Cotillard, Abbie Cornish, Didier Bourdon, Tom Hollander, Freddie Highmore, Isabelle Gardener, Archie Panjabi, Rafe Spall, Kenneth Cranham, Valeria Bruni Tedeschi. Ruthless London commodities trader learns that a beloved uncle has died and left him his property in Provence; when he goes back to this scene of happy childhood memories he slowly experiences a change in his outlook on life. Based on the book by Peter Mayle (who also wrote *A Year in Provence*), story takes a backseat to atmosphere, and while it's attractive, the film needs a light touch that neither Crowe nor director Scott can provide. Super 35. [PG-13]▮

Goofy Movie, A (1995) **C-78m.** **½ D: Kevin Lima. Voices of Bill Farmer, Jason Marsden, Jim Cummings, Kellie Martin, Rob Paulsen, Wallace Shawn, Jenna Von Oy, Frank Welker, Jo Anne Worley, Julie Brown, Joey Lawrence, Pat Buttram. Ever-lovable Goofy takes his son, Max, on a road-trip vacation, but it's a culture clash between the '90s boy and his old-fashioned father. Simple, straightforward Disney cartoon feature for kids with a handful of serviceable songs and a nice "message" about father-son relationships. No Disney classic, but pleasant enough. Followed by a direct-to-video sequel. [G]▼●

Goonies, The (1985) **C-114m.** **½ D: Richard Donner. Sean Astin, Josh Brolin, Jeff Cohen, Corey Feldman, Kerri Green, Martha Plimpton, Ke Huy Quan (Jonathan Ke Quan), John Matuszak, Anne Ramsey, Joe Pantoliano. A bunch of kids go in search of hidden treasure in this old-fashioned adventure yarn (from a story by Steven Spielberg, who may have recalled Our Gang's MAMA'S LITTLE PIRATE). Big, lively, and exceptionally noisy, aimed squarely at kids, with a likable bunch of kids onscreen. Also makes appropriate use of Max Steiner's swashbuckling theme from ADVENTURES OF DON JUAN. Panavision. [PG]▼●

Gor (1988) **C-95m.** *½ D: Fritz Kiersch. Urbano Barbarini, Oliver Reed, Rebecca Ferratti, Larry Taylor, Graham Clarke, Arnold Vosloo, Chris Du Plessis, Paul L. Smith, Jack Palance. Ordinary sword-and-sorcery adventure in which meek American professor is magically whisked off to "counter-Earth" Gor, where he becomes a hero and battles chuckling, tyrannical Reed. Based on the first in "John Norman's" series of Edgar Rice Burroughs-inspired adventure fantasies. Palance's role is just a cameo setting up the sequel, OUTLAW OF GOR. [PG]▼

Gordon's War (1973) **C-90m.** *** D: Ossie Davis. Paul Winfield, Carl Lee, David Downing, Tony King. When a Vietnam vet comes home to find his wife hooked on drugs, he trains four-man army to destroy the pushers. Good action, but gets lost toward the end. [R]▼●

Gordy (1995) **C-90m.** ** D: Mark Lewis. Doug Stone, Kristy Young, Michael Roescher, Tom Lester, Deborah Hobart, Ted Manson. Gordy is a talking pig who somehow becomes involved in big business— and a quest to save his family from the slaughterhouse. *Very* undemanding kids' film has its moments. Based on a story by *Green Acres* veterans Jay Sommers and Dick Chevillat. Besides top-billed Stone the film features such other country music stars as Roy Clark, Mickey Gilley, Jim Stafford, Box Car Willie, and Moe Bandy. [G]▼●

Gorgo (1961-British) **C-78m.** *** D: Eugene Lourie. Bill Travers, William Sylvester, Vincent Winter, Bruce Seton, Joseph O'Conor. Good sci-fi story of captured baby sea monster put into London circus and gigantic parent coming to rescue it. Exciting special effects. ▼●▮

Gorgon, The (1964-British) **C-83m.** **½ D: Terence Fisher. Peter Cushing, Christopher Lee, Richard Pasco, Barbara Shelley, Michael Goodliffe. In 19th-century Balkan village, one of the snake-headed Gorgons still survives, turning her victims to stone—but who is she by day? Good Hammer production. ▼●▮

Gorilla at Large (1954) **C-84m.** *** D: Harmon Jones. Cameron Mitchell, Anne Bancroft, Lee J. Cobb, Raymond Burr, Peter Whitney, Lee Marvin, Warren Stevens. Off-beat murder mystery at amusement park, with exceptionally able cast. 3-D. ▮

Gorillas in the Mist (1988) **C-129m.** *** D: Michael Apted. Sigourney Weaver, Bryan Brown, Julie Harris, John Omirah Miluwi, Iain Cuthbertson, Constantin Alexandrov, Waigwa Wachira. Absorbing drama based on the life of Dian Fossey, who journeyed to Africa in 1967 and, with no prior experience, set out to document the vanishing breed of mountain gorillas for *National Geographic*. Her transformation from diligent researcher to obsessive madwoman is a bit more abrupt than it ought to be, but it's still a good film, and Weaver is compelling in the lead. [PG-13] ▼●▮

Gorky Park (1983) **C-128m.** *** D: Michael Apted. William Hurt, Lee Marvin, Brian Dennehy, Ian Bannen, Joanna Pacula, Alexander Knox. Absorbing murder mystery set in Russia, where police investigator Hurt doggedly pursues the case of three bodies buried in Gorky Park. Lots of twists and turns, vivid atmosphere (with Helsinki doubling for Moscow)...marred somewhat by unconvincing romance and protracted finale. Dennis Potter adapted Martin Cruz Smith's novel. [R] ▼●▮

G.O.R.P. (1980) **C-90m.** BOMB D: Joseph Ruben. Michael Lembeck, Dennis Quaid, Philip Casnoff, Fran Drescher, David Huddleston, Robert Trebor, Julius Harris, Rosanna Arquette. Sophomoric, depressingly unfunny drug-oriented comedy set in a summer camp. Makes MEATBALLS seem like *Hamlet*; for people who think the word "Quaalude" is automatically funny. [R] ▼

Gosford Park (2001-U.S.-British) **C-137m.** **½ D: Robert Altman. Eileen Atkins, Bob Balaban, Alan Bates, Charles Dance, Stephen Fry, Michael Gambon, Richard E. Grant, Tom Hollander, Derek Jacobi, Kelly Macdonald, Helen Mirren, Jeremy Northam, Clive Owen, Ryan Phillippe, Maggie Smith, Geraldine Somerville, Kristin Scott Thomas, Sophie Thompson, Emily Watson, James Wilby. Another of Altman's multicharacter mosaics, painting a colorful picture of life upstairs and down during a weekend at an English country estate in 1932, where murder rears its head. Great

cast and telling details can't mask the film's superficiality, made worse by a poky pace and overlength. Balaban (who conceived the idea for the film with Altman) plays the producer of Charlie Chan mysteries; too bad no one remembered that those films run about an hour and a quarter. Nevertheless, Julian Fellowes' script won an Oscar for Best Original Screenplay. Super 35. [R] ▼▮

Gospel (1982) **C-92m.** ***½ D: David Leivick, Frederick A. Ritzenberg. James Cleveland and the Southern California Community Choir, Walter Hawkins and the Hawkins Family, Mighty Clouds of Joy, Shirley Caesar, Twinkie Clark and the Clark Sisters. Inspiring, tremendously entertaining concert film spotlighting top gospel performers. Each number is more rousing than the last. Followed in 2004 by OH HAPPY DAY (which is mostly a compilation of unused footage from this film). ▼▮

Gospel, The (2005) **C-105m.** *½ D: Rob Hardy. Boris Kodjoe, Idris Elba, Nona Gaye, Clifton Powell, Aloma Wright, Donnie McClurkin, Omar Gooding, Tamyra Gray, Keshia Knight Pulliam, Sean Nelson. Upon hearing that his preacher father has cancer, a rock star returns home to come to terms with his dad, his best-friend-turned-rival, and his mother's death. Surprisingly (or not) he still has time to begin a relationship with a single mother and stage a glitzy fund-raiser to help open a new church. Tedious, predictable, and composed entirely of clichés; at least the gospel numbers are well performed. [PG] ▼▮

Gospel According to St. Matthew, The (1964-Italian-French) **135m.** **** D: Pier Paolo Pasolini. Enrique Irazoqui, Margherita Caruso, Susanna Pasolini, Marcello Morante, Mario Socrate. Unconventional, austere film on life and teachings of Christ, based solely on writings of the Apostle, Matthew. Amateur cast (including director's mother) is expressive and moves with quiet dignity. Ironically, director of this masterpiece was a Marxist. ▼●▮

Gospel According to Vic, The (1985-British) **C-92m.** ** D: Charles Gormley. Tom Conti, Helen Mirren, David Hayman, Brian Pettifer, Jennifer Black. Very minor comedy of Catholic schoolteacher Conti and the series of miracles that befall him. Mirren is wasted as a music teacher/love interest. Aka HEAVENLY PURSUITS. [PG-13] ▼

Gospel of John, The (2003-Canadian-British) **C-180m.** **½ D: Philip Saville. Henry Ian Cusick, Stuart Bunce, Daniel Kash, Stephen Russell, Diana Berriman, Alan Van Sprang, Scott Handy; narrated by Christopher Plummer. Overlong but surprisingly compelling retelling of Jesus' life. Although the material is obviously familiar and well-worn movie fodder, Cusick's fresh and utterly believable performance as Jesus ranks favorably with any other cinematic interpretation. Effectively narrated by Plummer. 129m. version also available. [PG-13] ▼❶

Gospel Road, The (1973) C-83m. **½ D: Robert Elfstrom. Johnny Cash, June Carter, Robert Elfstrom. Musical ·journey through Holy Land follows story of Jesus from his birth to his death and resurrection. Sincere but not especially good. [G] ▼❶

Gossip (2000) C-91m. BOMB D: Davis Guggenheim. James Marsden, Lena Headey, Norman Reedus, Joshua Jackson, Kate Hudson, Marisa Coughlan, Eric Bogosian, Edward James Olmos, Sharon Lawrence. Inane tale of three college roomies who hatch a rumor as a class project that (naturally) gets way out of hand. Any dropout could guess these plot twists; viewer has an easier choice. Super 35. [R] ▼❶

Gotcha! (1985) C-101m. **½ D: Jeff Kanew. Anthony Edwards, Linda Fiorentino, Nick Corri, Alex Rocco, Marla Adams, Klaus Loewitsch, Christopher Rydell. Nerdy college kid goes to Paris on vacation, meets seductive older woman who involves him in espionage in East Berlin. Very nearly a good movie, with some sharp dialogue to start, but loses its appeal as it loses its credibility. [PG-13] ▼❶❶

Go Tell the Spartans (1978) C-114m. ***½ D: Ted Post. Burt Lancaster, Craig Wasson, Jonathan Goldsmith, Marc Singer, Joe Unger, David Clennon, Dolph Sweet, James Hong. Perceptive, moving Vietnam War picture, set in early 1964; Burt shines as "advisory group" commander who is already starting to have his doubts about the conflict. More realistic in dialogue and situation than other, more publicized, popular films on the subject. Wendell Mayes' cynically funny script is right on target. Based on Daniel Ford's novel *Incident at Muc Wa*. [R] ▼❶❶

Gothic (1986-British) C-90m. ** D: Ken Russell. Gabriel Byrne, Julian Sands, Natasha Richardson, Miriam Cyr, Timothy Spall. That night in 1816 when Mary Shelley (author of *Frankenstein*) and Dr. Polidori (*The Vampyre*) were inspired to write their Gothic classics—previously depicted in THE BRIDE OF FRANKENSTEIN—is given the wild Ken Russell treatment here. Too weird for some, too highbrow for many horror fans, but full of Russell's hallucinatory visuals. Same story was told two years later in HAUNTED SUMMER. [R] ▼❶❶

Gothika (2003) C-98m. *½ D: Mathieu Kassovitz. Halle Berry, Robert Downey, Jr., Penélope Cruz, Charles S. Dutton, John Carroll Lynch, Bernard Hill, Dorian Harewood. A mental health professional wakes up in the psychiatric ward of the prison where she works, accused of a brutal murder she doesn't remember committing. Take an earnest Berry, add a senseless script and misguided direction, and you get this horror/suspense/su-

pernatural thriller/murder mystery/SNAKE PIT hodgepodge. [R] ▼❶

Go Tigers! (2001) C-103m. *** D: Kenneth A. Carlson. Entertaining documentary about Massillon, Ohio, a working-class town where high school football has been a mania for 106 years. Now the team's very existence is at stake as a controversial school levy is put to the voters. An empathetic, close-up, cinéma vérité–style view of the star athletes, coaches, teachers, parents, boosters, and even naysayers over the course of one crucial season. P.S. The filmmaker grew up in Massillon. [R] ▼❶

Governess, The (1998-British) C-112m. **½ D: Sandra Goldbacher. Minnie Driver, Tom Wilkinson, Florence Hoath, Jonathan Rhys-Meyers, Harriet Walter, Arlene Cockburn, Emma Bird. Intriguing but somewhat unfocused film, set in the 1800s, about a spirited young Jewish woman who leaves her newly impoverished London family to take a job as governess on a remote Scottish island. There she develops an unusual relationship—both cerebral and passionate—with the master of the house. Slow-moving film has interesting passages but never jells. Written by the director. Super 35. [R] ▼❶

Go West (1940) 81m. ** D: Edward Buzzell. Groucho, Chico, and Harpo Marx, John Carroll, Diana Lewis, Walter Woolf King, Robert Barrat. Big letdown from Marxes, until hilarious train-ride climax. Occasional bits sparkle through humdrum script. ▼❶❶

Go West Young Man (1936) 82m. *** D: Henry Hathaway. Mae West, Randolph Scott, Warren William, Alice Brady, Elizabeth Patterson, Lyle Talbot, Isabel Jewell. Movie queen Mae is stuck in the Pennsylvania sticks, but passes time nicely with handsome mechanic. Not top-notch West, but still fun. Mae wrote the screenplay. ▼❶

Goya in Bordeaux (1999-Italian-Spanish) C-104m. **½ D: Carlos Saura. Francisco Rabal, José Coronado, Eulalia Ramón, Maribel Verdú, Dafne Fernández, Emilio Gutierrez Caba, Joaquin Climent, Manuel de Blas, Cristina Espinosa, José María Pou. Vivid, highly theatricalized vision of exiled Saragossan painter Francisco Goya's waning days in France, as he wanders through deathbed memories of the women and the wars that inspired his work. Sumptuously shot by Vittorio Storaro, but directed with a pervasive melancholy that makes for slow drama. Some nudity, but not nearly enough. Aka GOYA. Univision. [R] ▼❶

Goya's Ghosts (2007-U.S.-Spanish) C-113m. **½ D: Milos Forman. Javier Bardem, Natalie Portman, Stellan Skarsgård, Randy Quaid, José Luis Gómez, Michael Lonsdale. The kind of oddball movie only Forman can make. Two-part story begins during the Spanish Inquisition, as a Goya model

(Portman) is unjustly imprisoned and raped in her cell by a hypocritical Catholic Church Brother (Bardem). Returning 15 years later from Napoleonic France, the Brother is asked by Goya (Skarsgård) to help track down a daughter conceived by the rape. Cowritten by Forman and Jean-Claude Carrière, plot-heavy result is fairly zippy and not without entertainment value, but the tone is shaky and the wildly multinational casting distracts. Which isn't to say that Quaid as Spain's King Carlos IV isn't without its amusements. [R]◗

Grace Is Gone (2007) **C-85m.** ******* D: James C. Strouse. John Cusack, Shélan O'Keefe, Gracie Bednarczyk, Alessandro Nivola. Midwestern working-class father learns that his wife has died while serving in the U.S. Army in Iraq. Unable to confront his two young daughters with the news, he takes them on a road trip instead, trying to seize every opportunity for happiness. Touching film never goes overboard with sentiment; Cusack strikes just the right note, and the girls who play his daughters seem absolutely genuine. Marisa Tomei and Mary Kay Place make eyeblink-long appearances. Score by Clint Eastwood. Written by first-time director Strouse. [PG-13]◗

Grace of My Heart (1996) **C-115m.** ****½** D: Allison Anders. Illeana Douglas, John Turturro, Eric Stoltz, Matt Dillon, Patsy Kensit, Bruce Davison, David Clennon, Christina Pickles, Amanda De Cadenet, Chris Isaak, Bridget Fonda; voice of Peter Fonda. Disappointing film about a great subject: the pop music world centered around N.Y.C.'s Brill Building in the 1950s and '60s. Aspiring singer-songwriter Douglas finds doors closed to her as a performer but becomes a successful pop tunesmith instead; her destiny is then linked to a succession of men in the music business. Nice moments here and there but superficial at every turn—a real shame. Full of pleasant sound-alike songs from the period, plus one showstopper, "God Give Me Strength," written by Elvis Costello and pop veteran Burt Bacharach. [R]▼●◗

Grace Quigley (1985) **C-87m.** ***½** D: Anthony Harvey. Katharine Hepburn, Nick Nolte, Elizabeth Wilson, Chip Zien, Kit Le Fever, William Duell, Walter Abel, Denny Dillon. Abysmal misfire that manages to be both bland and tasteless, about lonely, elderly Hepburn, who hires hit man Nolte to kill her—and then others of her set who would all rather be dead. Filmed in 1983, first shown at 1984 Cannes Film Festival at 102m. However, another version of this exists, titled THE ULTIMATE SOLUTION OF GRACE QUIGLEY and put together by its scriptwriter, A. Martin Zweiback. Despite an uneven second half, it is a touching, funny, surreal black comedy about the problems of the elderly and the right of

choice. This cut runs 94m. and is rated ****½.** [PG]▼

Gracie (2007) **C-95m.** ****** D: Davis Guggenheim. Carly Schroeder, Elisabeth Shue, Dermot Mulroney, Andrew Shue, Jesse Lee Soffer, Joshua Caras, Julia Garro, Hunter Schroeder. Shue plays her mother in this sports biopic based on her own teenage years. Schroeder is adequately spunky as the future actress who wants nothing more than to play competitive soccer, circa 1978, just like her scrappy brothers. Extremely lightweight and predictable (and very loosely based on the facts), this should appeal to preteen girls. Elisabeth, her costar brother Andrew, and director Guggenheim (Elisabeth's husband) all coproduced. Super 35. [PG-13]◗

Graduate, The (1967) **C-105m.** ******** D: Mike Nichols. Anne Bancroft, Dustin Hoffman, Katharine Ross, Murray Hamilton, William Daniels, Elizabeth Wilson, Brian Avery, Norman Fell, Marion Lorne, Alice Ghostley. Landmark film of the late '60s that's still just as pungent—and funny—as ever. Hoffman, in his first major film role, plays ultra-naive college grad who's seduced by a middle-aged woman, then falls in love with her daughter. Perfect song score by Simon and Garfunkel. Script by Buck Henry (who plays the desk clerk) and Calder Willingham from Charles Webb's novel. Nichols won Best Director Oscar. Look fast for Mike Farrell in hotel lobby and Richard Dreyfuss in Berkeley rooming house. Later a Broadway play and a reference point for the 2005 movie RUMOR HAS IT . . . Panavision. [R]▼●◗

Graduation Day (1981) **C-96m.** BOMB D: Herb Freed. Christopher George, Patch Mackenzie, E. Danny Murphy, Michael Pataki, E. J. Peaker, Vanna White. A bloody FRIDAY THE 13TH clone, done with no talent or imagination. [R]▼◗

Graffiti Bridge (1990) **C-91m.** ***½** D: Prince. Prince, Morris Day, Jerome Benton & The Time, Jill Jones, Mavis Staples, George Clinton, Ingrid Chavez, Robin Power, T.C. Ellis, Tevin Campbell. Further auteur antics from the rocker-filmmaker (and nonactor), a sequel of sorts to PURPLE RAIN, but with murky religious overtones. Even the musical numbers, source of the film's socko CD soundtrack, are botched here. If you don't even like Prince's music, you'd better convert our rating to BOMB. Purple piffle. [PG-13]▼●◗

Grand Canyon (1991) **C-134m.** ****** D: Lawrence Kasdan. Danny Glover, Kevin Kline, Steve Martin, Mary McDonnell, Mary-Louise Parker, Alfre Woodard, Jeremy Sisto, Tina Lifford, Patrick Malone. Ruminations on why and how Life is Lousy, especially in L.A., as a handful of disparate lives intersect: a lawyer who feels distant from his wife, a wife who's discovered an abandoned baby, a tow-truck driver who's worried about his sister's survival in a violent neighborhood, etc. Give Kasdan (and cowriter Meg Kasdan) credit for attempting to make a serious film that deals with matters of importance . . . but the results are mushy, superficial, and unconvincing. Panavision. [R]▼●)

Grande Bouffe, The (1973-French-Italian) C-130m. **½ D: Marco Ferreri. Marcello Mastroianni, Ugo Tognazzi, Michel Piccoli, Philippe Noiret, Andrea Ferreol. Four bored middle-aged men decide to commit group suicide by eating themselves to death. Outrageous idea, but overbaked—no pun intended—and excessively, graphically gross. [X]▼)

Grand Highway, The (1987-French) C-104m. *** D: Jean-Loup Hubert. Anemone, Richard Bohringer, Antoine Hubert, Vanessa Guedj, Christine Pascal. Fine, subtle, slice-of-life tale of a fragile nine-year-old boy (Hubert, son of the director) and his experiences while spending three weeks in a rural village while his mother is off giving birth. Guedj is a delight as the tomboy who becomes his friend. Original title: LE GRAND CHEMIN. Remade in U.S. as PARADISE. [R]▼

Grand Hotel (1932) 113m. **** D: Edmund Goulding. Greta Garbo, John Barrymore, Joan Crawford, Wallace Beery, Lionel Barrymore, Lewis Stone, Jean Hersholt, Ferdinand Gottschalk, Tully Marshall, Mary Carlisle. Vicki Baum's novel and play of plush Berlin hotel where "nothing ever happens." Stars prove the contrary: Garbo as lonely ballerina, John B. her jewel-thief lover, Lionel B. a dying man, Crawford an ambitious stenographer, Beery a hardened businessman, Stone the observer. Scripted by William A. Drake. Best Picture Oscar winner; a must. Plot reworked many times (in HOTEL BERLIN, WEEK-END AT THE WALDORF, etc.). Later a Broadway musical. ▼●)

Grand Illusion (1937-French) 117m. **** D: Jean Renoir. Jean Gabin, Pierre Fresnay, Erich von Stroheim, (Marcel) Dalio, Dita Parlo, (Julien) Carette, Gaston Modot, Jean Dasté. Renoir's classic treatise on war, focusing on French prisoners during WW1 and their cultured German commandant. Beautiful performances enhance an eloquent script (by Renoir and Charles Spaak). Edited to 94m. for U.S. release in 1938. Beware of other versions with variant running times. ▼●)

Grandma's Boy (2006) C-96m. ** D: Nicholaus Goossen. Allen Covert, Linda Cardellini, Shirley Jones, Shirley Knight, Doris Roberts, Peter Dante, Kevin Nealon, Jonah Hill. Slacker accountant Covert moves in with granny Roberts and her golden-girl friends while taking a new job as a tester at a video game company supervised by babe Cardellini. Stoner comedy's crude humor (coscripted by Covert) occasionally engenders more chuckles than expected. As a veteran showbiz groupie whose liaisons included one with Don Knotts, Jones' raunchy role may color your future viewings of CAROUSEL or *The Partridge Family*. Coproduced by Covert and Adam Sandler; several comedy cronies appear unbilled. Super 35. [R]●)

Grand Prix (1966) C-175m. ** D: John Frankenheimer. James Garner, Eva Marie Saint, Yves Montand, Toshiro Mifune, Brian Bedford, Jessica Walter, Françoise Hardy. Big cast is saddled with rambling script about personal lives of auto racers and their loves; spectacular action scenes and use of split screen are best appreciated on the big screen. Deservedly won Oscars for the editing and sound effects people. Mifune's English dialogue is dubbed by Paul Frees. Super Panavision 70.▼●)

Grand Slam (1967-Italian-U.S.) C-120m. *** D: Giuliano Montaldo. Edward G. Robinson, Janet Leigh, Adolfo Celi, Klaus Kinski, Georges Rigaud, Robert Hoffman. International jewel-heist film, with all the trappings. Nothing new, but smoothly done, most enjoyable. Technicolor.

Grand Theft Auto (1977) C-85m. ** D: Ron Howard. Ron Howard, Nancy Morgan, Marion Ross, Pete Isacksen, Barry Cahill. Howard's directorial debut (he also co-scripted with his actor-father Rance) is typical unsophisticated car-crash action fare, no better or worse than many. [PG]▼●)

Grand Tour, The (1992) C-99m. **½ D: David N. Twohy. Jeff Daniels, Ariana Richards, Emilia Crow, Jim Haynie, David Wells, Nicholas Guest, Robert Colbert, Marilyn Lightstone. The proprietor of a small-town hotel fears that his unexpected guests are tourists from the future, visiting for a frightening reason. Intelligent, low-key sci-fi, well acted and consistently surprising, but too drawn-out. From the novella "Vintage Season" by Lawrence O'Donnell and C. L. Moore. Filmed for theatrical release but debuted on cable TV instead. Aka DISASTER IN TIME. [PG-13]▼●)

Grandview, U.S.A. (1984) C-97m. **½ D: Randal Kleiser. Jamie Lee Curtis, C. Thomas Howell, Patrick Swayze, Jennifer Jason Leigh, Ramon Bieri, Carole Cook, Troy Donahue, William Windom, Elizabeth Gorcey, M. Emmet Walsh, John Cusack, Joan Cusack, Michael Winslow. So-so slice of Americana, focusing on several characters in archetypal Midwestern town: a young boy coming of age, an independent young woman trying to make it on her own running her father's demolition-derby business, and a lovesick sap who's her ace driver. Passable time-filler but nothing more. [R]▼)

Gran Torino (2008) C-117m. *** D: Clint Eastwood. Clint Eastwood, Bee Vang, Ahney Her, Christopher Carley, Brian Haley, Geraldine Hughes, Brian Howe, Dreama Walker, John Carroll Lynch. With the death of his beloved wife, retired auto worker Walt Kowalski (Eastwood) is crankier than ever. Intolerant of the Asians who have taken over his Detroit neighborhood, he slowly develops a relationship with two youngsters who live next door and ultimately becomes protective of them. Eastwood channels Archie Bunker (and to some degree Dirty Harry) in this disarming fable about a man out of touch with a changing world who unexpectedly finds purpose to his life. Only Clint could have pulled this off—for an audience that's watched *him* grow and change over the years. Panavision. [R]◗

Grapes of Wrath, The (1940) 129m. **** D: John Ford. Henry Fonda, Jane Darwell, John Carradine, Charley Grapewin, Dorris Bowdon, Russell Simpson, John Qualen, O. Z. Whitehead, Eddie Quillan, Zeffie Tilbury, Darryl Hickman, Ward Bond, Charles Middleton, Tom Tyler, Mae Marsh, Jack Pennick. One of the great American films, an uncompromising adaptation of John Steinbeck's novel about impoverished Okie farmers making the trek to California during the Depression, where the good life they've hoped for is well out of reach. Fonda is great in his defining role as an ex-con whose social conscience is aroused; Darwell is unforgettable as the matriarch Ma Joad. She and Ford won well-deserved Oscars. Screenplay by Nunnally Johnson.▼◗●

Grass Harp, The (1996) C-107m. *** D: Charles Matthau. Piper Laurie, Sissy Spacek, Walter Matthau, Edward Furlong, Nell Carter, Jack Lemmon, Mary Steenburgen, Sean Patrick Flanery, Joe Don Baker, Charles Durning, Roddy McDowall, Doris Roberts, Scott Wilson; narrated by Boyd Gaines. Thoughtful drama based on Truman Capote's evocative memoir of his boyhood in the South, where he was raised by his wealthy aunt and her light-headed sister. Exquisite performance by Laurie as the boy's free-spirited soulmate, matched by Spacek as a woman who's been hardened by life. Director Matthau appears as a customer in McDowall's barbershop. [PG]▼◗●

Grasshopper, The (1970) C-95m. *** D: Jerry Paris. Jacqueline Bisset, Jim Brown, Joseph Cotten, Corbett Monica, Ramon Bieri. Episodic but fairly compelling chronicle of how a beautiful 19-year-old from British Columbia ends up as a burned-out Vegas call girl at age 22. Better than expected melodrama actually features Brown in a sympathetic role. Look fast for Penny Marshall. Aka THE PASSION OF EVIL and PASSIONS. [R]▼◗

Grass Is Greener, The (1960) C-105m. *** D: Stanley Donen. Cary Grant, Deborah Kerr, Robert Mitchum, Jean Simmons. Chic drawing-room fare that suffers from staginess. Grant-Kerr marriage is threatened by Simmons and Mitchum romancing the two, respectively. Technirama. ▼◗●

Grass Is Singing, The (1981-British-Swedish) C-108m. *** D: Michael Raeburn. Karen Black, John Thaw, John Kani, John Moulder Brown, Patrick Mynhardt. Black is excellent as a lonely woman who marries farmer Thaw and cannot adjust to life in the African woodland. Filmed in Zambia; based on a novel by Doris Lessing. Released in U.S. in 1984 as KILLING HEAT.▼◗

Grave Indiscretions SEE: **Gentlemen Don't Eat Poets**

Grave Robbers From Outer Space SEE: **Plan 9 From Outer Space**

Graveyard, The SEE: **Persecution**

Graveyard Shift (1989) C-89m. **½ D: Gerard Ciccoritti. Silvio Oliviero, Helen Papas, Cliff Stoker, Dorin Ferber, Dan Rose, Don Jones. Oliviero has the perfect occupation for a modern vampire: an all-night cabdriver. His only victims are those in "their cycle of death," but things get out of hand anyway. Intelligent, well-acted low-budgeter harmed only by not knowing when to quit. Filmed in 1985. Aka CENTRAL PARK DRIFTER. Followed by a sequel: THE UNDERSTUDY. [R] ▼◗●

Graveyard Shift (1990) C-87m. BOMB D: Ralph S. Singleton. David Andrews, Kelly Wolf, Stephen Macht, Brad Dourif, Andrew Divoff, Vic Polizos. Bottom-of-the-barrel, cliché-ridden shocker chronicling the goings-on in a mysterious mill, whose workers are disappearing within its rat-infested bowels. Poorly directed, with even worse special effects. Based on a short story by Stephen King. [R]▼◗●

Gravy Train, The (1974) C-96m. **½ D: Jack Starrett. Stacy Keach, Frederic Forrest, Margot Kidder, Barry Primus, Richard Romanus, Denny Miller. OK blend of fast-moving action and comedy as West Virginia brothers Keach and Forrest develop a liking for crime. Aka THE DION BROTHERS. [R]

Grayeagle (1978) C-104m. **½ D: Charles B. Pierce. Ben Johnson, Iron Eyes Cody, Lana Wood, Jack Elam, Paul Fix, Alex Cord. Interesting if flawed rehash of THE SEARCHERS with Johnson tracking the Indian (Cord) who kidnapped his daughter. Good classic Western style an asset, sluggish pacing a drawback. Produced, directed, written by Pierce, who also appears. Panavision. [PG]▼

Gray Lady Down (1978) C-111m. ** D: David Greene. Charlton Heston, David Carradine, Stacy Keach, Ned Beatty, Ronny Cox, Rosemary Forsyth. Tired drama about rescue of nuclear submarine, captained by Heston. Good special effects, and colorful performance by Carradine as designer of experimental diving craft. Look for Christopher Reeve as one of the officers. Panavision. [PG]▼▶

Gray Matters (2007) **C-96m.** ** D: Sue Kramer. Heather Graham, Tom Cavanagh, Bridget Moynahan, Alan Cumming, Molly Shannon, Sissy Spacek, Rachel Shelley, Gloria Gaynor. Gray—yes, that's her name—lives with her brother in Manhattan; they're inseparable, and most people think they're a "couple." Then he meets a beautiful woman and asks her to marry him. Gray is genuinely happy for her brother, then finds herself powerfully attracted to his fiancée. Artificial in the extreme, this attempt to emulate and update 1930s/'40s screwball comedies stays afloat only because its stars are so likable. Written by the director. [PG-13]▶

Gray's Anatomy (1996) **C/B&W-80m.** *** D: Steven Soderbergh. Spalding Gray. Gray's brilliance as a raconteur shines through in this witty, inventively directed monologue charting his experience of passing his 50th birthday and finding himself afflicted with a rare eye disease. His encounters with traditional and alternative medicine are both funny and frightening.▼▶

Grbavica: The Land of My Dreams (2006-Austrian-Herzegovinian-German-Croatian) **C-90m.** *** D: Jasmila Zbanic. Mirjana Karanovic, Luna Mijovic, Leon Lucev, Kenan Catic, Bogdan Diklic. Bosnian writer-director Zbanic (in her feature-film debut) provides a revealing look at life in postwar Sarajevo and the lingering impact it has on a struggling single mother and her rebellious 12-year-old daughter, who live in the city's Grbavica district (the site of a former prison camp where torture and rape were commonplace). An escalating rift between mother and daughter forces them to confront the harsh realities of their lives, and the war's continuing emotional toll. Impressive and powerful.▶

Grease (1978) **C-110m.** *** D: Randal Kleiser. John Travolta, Olivia Newton-John, Stockard Channing, Jeff Conaway, Didi Conn, Eve Arden, Sid Caesar, Joan Blondell, Edd Byrnes, Alice Ghostley, Dody Goodman, Lorenzo Lamas, Michael Tucci, Dinah Manoff, Barry Pearl. Energetic, imaginative filming of long-running Broadway show fantasizes 1950s life; spirited cast, clever ideas, and Patricia Birch's choreography make it fun. Hit songs (written for movie) include "You're the One That I Want," "Hopelessly Devoted To You," and title number, sung by Frankie Valli. Followed by a sequel. Panavision. [PG]▼▶

Grease 2 (1982) **C-114m.** BOMB D: Patricia Birch. Maxwell Caulfield, Michelle Pfeiffer, Adrian Zmed, Lorna Luft, Didi Conn, Eve Arden, Sid Caesar, Dody Goodman, Tab Hunter, Connie Stevens, Christopher McDonald. Mindless sequel to the musical hit; opens with a great back-to-school number, then goes downhill. Pedestrian music, clumsy comedy, uncharismatic leads; only the supporting players (like newcomer Luft and veteran Arden) shine through. Inauspicious directing debut for choreographer Birch. Panavision. [PG]▼●▶

Greased Lightning (1977) **C-94m.** ** D: Michael Schultz. Richard Pryor, Beau Bridges, Pam Grier, Cleavon Little, Vincent Gardenia, Richie Havens, Julian Bond. Spirited cast does little to enliven plodding, episodic bio of Wendell Scott, the first black racing car driver. A waste of Pryor, both dramatically and comically. [PG]▼▶

Greaser's Palace (1972) **C-91m.** *** D: Robert Downey. Allan Arbus, Albert Henderson, Luana Anders, George Morgan, Larry Moyer, Michael Sullivan, James Antonio, Ron Nealy. Super-offbeat Jesus Christ parody with Western setting. Drifter (Arbus) discovers "true identity" and heals "sick" cowboys in crazy, tiny town. Seven-year-old Robert Downey, Jr., appears as a mutilated child! Aka ZOOT SUIT JESUS.▼▶

Great Adventure, The (1975-Italian-Spanish) **C-87m.** ** D: Paul Elliotts (Gianfranco Baldanello). Jack Palance, Joan Collins, Fred Romer (Fernando Romero), Elisabetta Virgili, Manuel de Blas, Remo de Angelis. Middling Jack London tale of a boy and his dog trying to make it in the wilds of gold-rush Alaska—fighting the odds, marauding wolves, sinister town boss Palance, dancehall queen Collins.▼▶

Great American Broadcast, The (1941) **92m.** **½ D: Archie Mayo. Alice Faye, John Payne, Jack Oakie, Cesar Romero, The Four Ink Spots, James Newill, Mary Beth Hughes. Fictional fun of development of radio industry, with such musical guests as zany Wiere Brothers. Entertaining; bright cast.▶

Great American Cowboy, The (1974) **C-90m.** *** D: Kieth Merrill. Narrated by Joel McCrea. Exciting documentary on rodeo life focuses on rodeo superstar Larry Mahan and his competition with newcomer Phil Lyne. Oscar winner as Best Documentary Feature. [G]▼

Great Balloon Adventure, The SEE: Olly, Olly, Oxen Free

Great Balls of Fire! (1989) **C-102m.** **½ D: Jim McBride. Dennis Quaid, Winona Ryder, Alec Baldwin, Lisa Blount, Trey Wilson, John Doe, Steve Allen, Stephen Tobolowsky, Lisa Jane Persky, Michael St. Gerard, Peter Cook. Slick, highly stylized cartoon about the rise (and temporary fall) of '50s rocker Jerry Lee Lewis, a twice-married hellraiser whose doom was sealed when he took his 13-year-old second cousin as wife No. 3. Quaid's amusing but verrrry broad lead performance is balanced by Ryder's more even-keeled portrayal of cousin Myra. Reasonably entertaining but falls far short of its potential. [PG-13]▼●▶

Great Bank Robbery, The (1969) **C-98m.** *½ D: Hy Averback. Zero Mostel, Kim Novak, Clint Walker, Claude Akins, Akim Tamiroff, Larry Storch. Bogus preacher and company, Mexican gang led by Tamiroff, and local outlaws all compete for control of the town of Friendly. Spoof of Westerns is a total dud. Be warned. Panavision. [M/PG]▐

Great Battle, The (1978-German-Yugoslavian) **C-97m.** BOMB D: Humphrey Longan (Umberto Lenzi). Helmut Berger, Samantha Eggar, Giuliano Gemma, John Huston, Stacy Keach, Henry Fonda, Edwige Fenech. Amateurish muddle about WW2 combines tired vignettes with well-known stars, dubbed sequences with others, and newsreel footage narrated by Orson Welles. A waste of everybody's time. Aka THE GREATEST BATTLE, BATTLE FORCE, THE BATTLE OF MARETH, and THE BIGGEST BATTLE. [PG]▼

Great Buck Howard, The (2009) **C-90m.** *** D: Sean McGinly. John Malkovich, Colin Hanks, Emily Blunt, Ricky Jay, Tom Hanks, Debra Monk, Steve Zahn, Griffin Dunne, Wallace Langham, Matthew Gray Gubler, Adam Scott. Young man quits law school and stumbles into a job as road manager for a self-absorbed stage performer whose career peaked years ago on *The Tonight Show with Johnny Carson.* Small but entertaining film is worth seeing for Malkovich's endearing and persuasive performance as a "mentalist," inspired by The Amazing Kreskin. Tom Hanks coproduced the film and plays his real-life son Colin's dad. [PG]▐

Great Caruso, The (1951) **C-109m.** *** D: Richard Thorpe. Mario Lanza, Ann Blyth, Jarmila Novotna, Dorothy Kirsten. Biographical fiction about the legendary singer, entertainingly done. Fine music makes clichés endurable.▼●▐

Great Catherine (1968-British) **C-98m.** *½ D: Gordon Flemyng. Peter O'Toole, Jeanne Moreau, Zero Mostel, Jack Hawkins, Akim Tamiroff. Terrible adaptation of George Bernard Shaw's comedy about Catherine the Great wastes capable cast; wait for Dietrich's THE SCARLET EMPRESS.

Great Day in Harlem, A (1994) **C-60m.** ***½ D: Jean Bach. Dizzy Gillespie, Milt Hinton, Marian McPartland, Art Blakey, Gerry Mulligan, Sonny Rollins, Horace Silver, Bud Freeman, Art Farmer; narrated by Quincy Jones. Joyous celebration of a famous photo taken for *Esquire* magazine in 1958, which gathered dozens of jazz greats on a Harlem sidewalk. What could have been a prosaic "talking head" documentary becomes instead a lively collage of sights, sounds, and memories, with charming interviews, fascinating home movies of the event, and vintage performance footage of

these musicians at work. Film director Robert Benton—then *Esquire*'s art director—is one of the interviewees.▼●▐

Great Day in the Morning (1956) **C-92m.** **½ D: Jacques Tourneur. Virginia Mayo, Robert Stack, Ruth Roman, Alex Nicol, Raymond Burr. Good cast, beautiful color scenery help so-so story of pre–Civil War Colorado, when gold rush fever and separationist sentiments clashed. SuperScope.▼

Great Debaters, The (2007) **C-123m.** *** D: Denzel Washington. Denzel Washington, Nate Parker, Jurnee Smollett, Denzel Whitaker, Jermaine Williams, Forest Whitaker, Gina Ravera, John Heard, Kimberly Elise. At all-black Wiley College in rural Texas, circa 1935, radical professor Melvin B. Tolson (Washington) motivates his student debate team to work through their personal problems in order to excel. Eventually they travel to Harvard for a precedent-shattering debate. Inspiring true-life drama plays with the facts and succumbs to formulaic storytelling at times but never loses sight of its goal: to remind us that education—and determination—can help ordinary people surmount even the most formidable obstacles. Coproduced by Oprah Winfrey. Panavision. [PG-13]▐

Great Dictator, The (1940) **128m.** ***½ D: Charles Chaplin. Charles Chaplin, Paulette Goddard, Jack Oakie, Reginald Gardiner, Maurice Moscovich, Billy Gilbert, Henry Daniell. Chaplin's first full talkie; unusual comedy combines slapstick, satire, and social commentary, as he plays dual role of Jewish ghetto barber and dictator Adenoid Hynkel of Tomania. Unique, surprisingly effective film also features Oakie in unforgettable portrayal of Benzino Napaloni of rival country Bacteria.▼●▐

Great Escape, The (1963) **C-168m.** **** D: John Sturges. Steve McQueen, James Garner, Richard Attenborough, Charles Bronson, James Coburn, David McCallum, Donald Pleasence, James Donald, Gordon Jackson, John Leyton, Angus Lennie, Nigel Stock. Allied POWs plot massive escape from Nazi prison camp. Based on true story, this blockbuster was beautifully photographed by Daniel Fapp on location in Germany. Rip-roaring excitement with marvelous international cast; script by James Clavell and W. R. Burnett, from Paul Brickhill's book. Rousing score by Elmer Bernstein. Followed by a TV sequel 25 years later. Panavision.▼●▐

Greatest, The (1977) **C-101m.** *½ D: Tom Gries. Muhammad Ali, Ernest Borgnine, John Marley, Robert Duvall, James Earl Jones, Roger E. Mosley, Ben Johnson, Paul Winfield, Lloyd Haynes, Dina Merrill, David Clennon. Potentially exciting screen bio of the great heavyweight champ becomes an episodic mess suffering from a script devoid of dramatic focus and ham-handed direction. Ironically, Mosley (as Sonny Liston) has the charisma Ali lacks. Soundtrack features George Benson's "The Greatest Love of All." [PG] ▼▶

Greatest, The (2010) C-100m. *** D: Shana Feste. Pierce Brosnan, Susan Sarandon, Carey Mulligan, Johnny Simmons, Aaron Johnson, Zoe Kravitz, Jennifer Ehle, Amy Morton, Michael Shannon. Rigorously precise, emotionally powerful drama about grief and regeneration, with exceptional performances across the board. After a teenage boy dies in an auto mishap, his anguished mother (Sarandon), tightly controlled father (Brosnan), and vulnerable younger brother (Simmons) can't begin to overcome their trauma until the boy's pregnant girlfriend (Mulligan) unexpectedly enters their shattered lives. Panavision. [R] ▶

Greatest Battle, The SEE: **Great Battle, The**

Greatest Game Ever Played, The (2005) C-120m. *** D: Bill Paxton. Shia LaBeouf, Stephen Dillane, Josh Flitter, Peyton List, Elias Koteas, Marnie McPhail, Stephen Marcus, Luke Askew, Peter Firth, Len Cariou, Joe Jackson, Dawn Upshaw. Winning story of sportsmanship and class struggle surrounding the 1913 U.S. Open Tournament in Brookline, Massachusetts, where a caddy, Francis Ouimet (LaBeouf), is allowed to play opposite the much-admired British champion Harry Vardon (Dillane). Solid, old-fashioned storytelling with a modern eye; golf has never been portrayed like this before. Screenplay by Mark Frost, from his book. Eye-catching title sequence uses vintage photographs and footage to set the stage for this meticulously produced period picture. [PG] ▶

Greatest Love, The (1951-Italian) 110m. *½ D: Roberto Rossellini. Ingrid Bergman, Alexander Knox, Giulietta Masina, Teresa Pellati, Ettore Giannini. Bergman plays a wealthy American living in Rome, who feels compelled to help people in order to restore meaning to her own life after her son's suicide. Obvious, slow-moving story. Originally titled EUROPA '51. ▼

Greatest Movie Ever Sold, The (2011) C-90m. *** D: Morgan Spurlock. Clever, often very funny, yet thoughtful documentary about the ubiquitous nature of advertising in our lives, in particular the practice of product placement in movies and television shows. Spurlock transparently makes his own film a guinea pig and reveals the process of soliciting sponsors, while questioning the effect that commercialism has on our society. Most striking sequence: a visit to Sao Paolo, Brazil, where all outdoor advertising has been banned. Official title of the film is POM WONDERFUL PRESENTS: THE GREATEST MOVIE EVER SOLD. [PG-13] ▶

Greatest Show on Earth, The (1952) C-

153m. ***½ D: Cecil B. DeMille. Betty Hutton, Charlton Heston, Cornel Wilde, Dorothy Lamour, Gloria Grahame, James Stewart, Henry Wilcoxon, Lawrence Tierney, Lyle Bettger. Big package of fun from DeMille, complete with hokey performances, clichés, big-top excitement, and a swell train wreck. Stewart well cast as circus clown with mysterious past. Some funny surprise guests appear. Oscar winner for Best Picture and Story (Fredric M. Frank, Theodore St. John, Frank Cavett). ▼▶

Greatest Story Ever Told, The (1965) C-193m. **½ D: George Stevens. Max von Sydow, Charlton Heston, Carroll Baker, Angela Lansbury, Sidney Poitier, Shelley Winters, John Wayne, Ed Wynn, Jose Ferrer, Van Heflin, Claude Rains, Telly Savalas, many others. Some of the most spectacular scenes ever filmed lose all validity because of incessant cameos that run throughout film. Would *you* believe John Wayne as a Roman centurion supervising Christ's crucifixion? Carl Sandburg is listed in credits as a Creative Associate. Originally shown at 225m., then cut to 141m. Ultra Panavision 70. ▼▶

Great Expectations (1934) 102m. **½ D: Stuart Walker. Jane Wyatt, Phillips Holmes, George Breakston, Henry Hull, Florence Reed, Alan Hale, Francis L. Sullivan. Acceptable version of Dickens' story about a young boy and unknown benefactor is dwarfed by '46 classic. Sullivan plays Jaggers in both films. ▼

Great Expectations (1946-British) 118m. **** D: David Lean. John Mills, Valerie Hobson, Bernard Miles, Francis L. Sullivan, Finlay Currie, Martita Hunt, Anthony Wager, Jean Simmons, Alec Guinness, Ivor Barnard, Freda Jackson, Torin Thatcher, Eileen Erskine, Hay Petrie. One of the greatest films ever made, a vivid adaptation of Dickens' tale of a mysterious benefactor making poor young orphan a gentleman of means. Opening graveyard sequence is a gem. Oscars went to cinematographer Guy Green and art director John Bryan. Lean, Kay Walsh, Cecil McGivern, and producers Anthony Havelock-Allan and Ronald Neame all contributed to script. Filmed in 1934, 1974, and updated in 1998. Jean Simmons played Miss Havisham in a 1989 miniseries. ▼▶

Great Expectations (1998) C-111m. **½ D: Alfonso Cuarón. Ethan Hawke, Gwyneth Paltrow, Anne Bancroft, Chris Cooper, Hank Azaria, Robert De Niro, Josh Mostel, Kim Dickens, Nell Campbell, Stephen Spinella. Modern story based on the Dickens classic has Finn (né Pip) helping a convict on the Florida marshes, then being summoned to the decrepit mansion of equally decrepit Ms. Dinsmoor (née Havisham), where he meets the love of his life, the beautiful but heartless Estella. Eventually, he's whisked off to N.Y.C. to find fame and fortune as an artist. So stylishly crafted that it's a shame it doesn't add up to much of anything. The skeleton of Dickens is there, but no resonance. Panavision. [R]▼●)

Great Flamarion, The (1945) 78m. **½ D: Anthony Mann. Erich von Stroheim, Mary Beth Hughes, Dan Duryea, Stephen Barclay, Lester Allen, Esther Howard. Better than most von Stroheim cheapies, this one casts him as a vaudeville trick-shot artist who becomes romantically entangled with his scheming married assistant. ▼)

Great Gatsby, The (1949) 92m. **½ D: Elliott Nugent. Alan Ladd, Betty Field, Macdonald Carey, Barry Sullivan, Ruth Hussey, Shelley Winters, Howard da Silva. Misguided adaptation of F. Scott Fitzgerald's book about a mysterious young millionaire who crashes Long Island society in the 1920s. Too talky and much too literalminded. Ladd is pretty good, but Field (as Daisy Buchanan) gives a strangely petulant performance. Filmed before in 1926, again in 1974, and for TV in 2001.

Great Gatsby, The (1974) C-144m. **½ D: Jack Clayton. Robert Redford, Mia Farrow, Bruce Dern, Karen Black, Scott Wilson, Sam Waterston, Lois Chiles, Howard da Silva, Edward Herrmann, Patsy Kensit, Roberts Blossom. Bland adaptation of F. Scott Fitzgerald's jazz-age novel about a golden boy in Long Island society; faithful to the book, and visually opulent, but lacks substance and power. Script by Francis Ford Coppola; Theoni V. Aldredge's costumes and Nelson Riddle's score earned Oscars. [PG]▼●)

Great Georgia Bank Hoax, The SEE: **Great Bank Hoax, The**

Great Gilbert and Sullivan, The (1953-British) C-105m. *** D: Sidney Gilliat. Robert Morley, Maurice Evans, Eileen Herlie, Peter Finch, Martyn Green. Agreeable production is only a superficial biography of the legendary operetta composers, but does offer many highlights from their wonderful works. Their lives are probed more incisively in TOPSY-TURVY. Original British title: THE STORY OF GILBERT AND SULLIVAN.

Great Guy (1936) 75m. ** D: John G. Blystone. James Cagney, Mae Clarke, James Burke, Edward Brophy, Henry Kolker, Bernadene Hayes, Edward McNamara. Second-rate Cagney in low-budget production about inspector crusading against corruption in meat business. ▼)

Great Impostor, The (1961) 112m. **½ D: Robert Mulligan. Tony Curtis, Edmond O'Brien, Arthur O'Connell, Gary Merrill, Frank Gorshin. Incredible story of Ferdinand Demara, who succeeded in a variety of professional guises. Film is episodic and pat. ▼

Great Lie, The (1941) 107m. *** D: Edmund Goulding. Mary Astor, Bette Davis, George Brent, Lucile Watson, Hattie McDaniel, Grant Mitchell, Jerome Cowan. Brent marries Davis when alliance with Astor is annulled. He is lost in plane crash, leaving Davis and pregnant Astor to battle each other and the elements. Well-mounted soaper won Astor an Oscar as fiery concert pianist. ▼●)

Great Locomotive Chase, The (1956) C-85m. *** D: Francis D. Lyon. Fess Parker, Jeffrey Hunter, Jeff York, John Lupton, Eddie Firestone, Kenneth Tobey. True story of Andrews' Raiders (filmed before by Buster Keaton as THE GENERAL) comes to life in colorful Disney film; Parker is famous Union spy who leads a rowdy band in capturing and "kidnapping" a Confederate railroad train during Civil War. Retitled ANDREWS' RAIDERS. CinemaScope. ▼)

Great Lover, The (1949) 80m. *** D: Alexander Hall. Bob Hope, Rhonda Fleming, Roland Young, Roland Culver, George Reeves, Jim Backus. Vintage Hope; Bob's a boy scout leader on ship filled with his troop, luscious Fleming, and murderer Young. ▼)

Great Man, The (1956) 92m. ***½ D: Jose Ferrer. Jose Ferrer, Dean Jagger, Keenan Wynn, Julie London, Jim Backus, Ed Wynn. Well-loved TV star dies and Ferrer prepares memorial show, only to discover star was a despicable phony. Hard-bitten look at TV industry; top performances by senior and junior Wynns. Ferrer and Al Morgan adapted Morgan's thinly veiled novel about Arthur Godfrey.

Great Man's Lady, The (1942) 90m. **½ D: William Wellman. Barbara Stanwyck, Joel McCrea, Brian Donlevy, Thurston Hall, K. T. Stevens, Lucien Littlefield. Saga of the West is no great shakes as McCrea dreams of oil wells, Donlevy takes his girl. Stanwyck ages to 100 years to frame story. ▼)

Great Man Votes, The (1939) 72m. ***½ D: Garson Kanin. John Barrymore, Peter Holden, Virginia Weidler, Donald MacBride, William Demarest. Simple, sincere, delightful film of Barrymore, once a professor, now a souse, fighting for custody of his children, suddenly elevated to new stature when election time rolls around. MacBride fun as small-time politico, Demarest an energetic campaign promoter. ▼

Great McGinty, The (1940) 81m. *** D: Preston Sturges. Brian Donlevy, Muriel Angelus, Akim Tamiroff, Allyn Joslyn, William Demarest, Louis Jean Heydt, Arthur Hoyt. Sturges' directorial debut (and Oscar-winning screenplay) isn't up to his later comedy classics, but Donlevy is excellent as bum who is manipulated into governor's chair by crooked political machine—then blows it all when he tries to be honest. Typically sharp dialogue, plus fine work by Sturges' stock company of character actors. Donlevy and Tamiroff reprised their roles as a gag in Sturges' THE MIRACLE OF MORGAN'S CREEK. ▼●◗

Great Moment, The (1944) **83m.** **✶✶** D: Preston Sturges. Joel McCrea, Betty Field, Harry Carey, William Demarest, Franklin Pangborn, Grady Sutton, Louis Jean Heydt. Confused biography of anesthesia pioneer wavers from comedy to drama; ineffectual, filled with frustrating flashbacks. Very offbeat for writer-director Sturges, although film was taken out of his hands and reedited. Filmed in 1942. ▼●◗

Great Moments in Aviation SEE: **Shades of Fear**

Great Mouse Detective, The (1986) **C-80m.** **✶✶✶** D: John Musker, Ron Clements, Dave Michener, Burny Mattinson. Voices of Vincent Price, Barrie Ingham, Val Bettin, Susanne Pollatschek, Candy Candido, Eve Brenner, Alan Young, Melissa Manchester. Brisk animated adaptation of Eve Titus' book *Basil of Baker Street,* about a Sherlockian mouse who matches wits with the nefarious Prof. Ratigan (whose role is performed with gusto by Price). Not much depth to this Disney cartoon feature, but it *is* a lot of fun. Reissued in 1992 as THE ADVENTURES OF THE GREAT MOUSE DETECTIVE. [G] ▼●◗

Great Muppet Caper, The (1981-British) **C-95m.** **✶✶✶** D: Jim Henson. The Muppet Performers (Jim Henson, Frank Oz, Dave Goelz, Jerry Nelson, Richard Hunt), Charles Grodin, Diana Rigg, John Cleese, Robert Morley, Peter Ustinov, Jack Warden. The Muppets try to solve a London jewel robbery in their second feature film. Clever gags and ideas plus hilarious musical numbers with Miss Piggy make up for meandering script with more than its share of slow spots. [G] ▼●◗

Great New Wonderful, The (2006) **C-87m.** **✶✶✶** D: Danny Leiner. Olympia Dukakis, Jim Gaffigan, Judy Greer, Maggie Gyllenhaal, Tom McCarthy, Sharat Saxena, Naseeruddin Shah, Tony Shalhoub, Stephen Colbert, Dick Latessa, Will Arnett, Anita Gillette, Edie Falco, Jim Parsons. Striking drama, set one year after 9/11, focuses on an array of New Yorkers who are either struggling to deal with their feelings about that horrific day or going about their lives as if nothing had happened. They include a couple with a dysfunctional son, an elderly woman trapped in an unhappy marriage, a pair of security guards, and an outwardly affable accountant who worked at the World Trade Center and survived 9/11, unlike many of his coworkers. Subtle, incisive study of suppressed rage uses humor and insight to emphasize the importance of living a life that has meaning. [R] ◗

Great Northfield Minnesota Raid, The

(1972) **C-91m.** **✶✶✶** D: Philip Kaufman. Cliff Robertson, Robert Duvall, Luke Askew, R. G. Armstrong, Dana Elcar, Donald Moffat, Elisha Cook, Jr., Royal Dano, Mary-Robin Redd. Revisionist Western depicts the last major raid by the James gang, led by fanatic Jesse (Duvall) and easygoing Cole Younger (Robertson). Fictionalized, but more factual than most movie depictions of the famous raid. Robertson is genial in the leading role, Duvall amusingly intense as the brutal Jesse. Occasional comedic moments don't work terribly well. Written by the director. [PG] ▼◗

Great O'Malley, The (1937) **71m.** **✶½** D: William Dieterle. Pat O'Brien, Humphrey Bogart, Ann Sheridan, Donald Crisp, Mary Gordon, Frieda Inescort, Sybil Jason. Syrupy film of ruthless cop O'Brien and poor man Bogart who has lame daughter and turns to crime to support her. Pretty sticky.

Great Outdoors, The (1988) **C-90m.** **✶½** D: Howard Deutch. Dan Aykroyd, John Candy, Stephanie Faracy, Annette Bening, Chris Young, Ian Giatti, Hilary Gordon, Rebecca Gordon, Robert Prosky. Joyless scattershot comedy about disintegration of Candy clan's summer vacation by the uninvited appearance of boorish in-law Aykroyd and family. Written by John Hughes, apparently with something else on his mind. Bening's first film. [PG] ▼●◗

Great Race, The (1965) **C-150m.** **✶✶½** D: Blake Edwards. Tony Curtis, Natalie Wood, Jack Lemmon, Peter Falk, Keenan Wynn, Larry Storch, Dorothy Provine, Arthur O'Connell, Vivian Vance, Ross Martin, George Macready. Long, sometimes funny, often labored comedy, not the greatest ever made, as advertised. Duel sequence and barroom brawl are highlights, but pie fight falls flat, other gimmicks don't work. Definitely a mixed bag (although Natalie never looked better); one good song, "The Sweetheart Tree." Panavision. ▼●◗

Great Raid, The (2005) **C-132m.** **✶✶½** D: John Dahl. Benjamin Bratt, James Franco, Joseph Fiennes, Connie Nielsen, Marton Csokas, Motoki Kobayashi, Robert Mammone, Natalie Mendoza, Cesar Montano, Mark Consuelos, Sam Worthington, Dale Dye. Dramatization of a remarkable, little-known episode from WW2: the dramatic rescue of 500 Americans from a Japanese POW camp in the Philippines in 1945, involving an elite corps of freshly trained U.S. Rangers, Filipino guerrilla fighters, and members of the local resistance movement. Admirably old-fashioned in many ways, with impeccable staging of the climactic raid, but not nearly as good as the story it's re-creating. Completed in 2003. Super 35. [R] ◗

Great Rock 'n Roll Swindle, The (1980-British) **C-103m.** **✶✶✶** D: Julien Temple. Malcolm McLaren, Johnny Rotten (John

Lydon), Sid Vicious, Steve Jones, Paul Cook, Ronnie Biggs, Liz Fraser. Controversial, outrageously cynical free-form documentary about the infamous, groundbreaking punk-rock band Johnny Rotten and The Sex Pistols. Film also shows how Pistols' manager Malcolm McLaren cleverly marketed the group. One of the many highlights: the late Sid Vicious' version of "My Way."▼●◗

Great Santini, The (1979) C-116m. **½ D: Lewis John Carlino. Robert Duvall, Blythe Danner, Michael O'Keefe, Lisa Jane Persky, Stan Shaw, Theresa Merritt, David Keith. Character study of a career Marine who, in 1962, is "a warrior without a war," except for the one he wages with his adolescent son. Compelling performances give film its meat, but dramatic structure and resolutions are not nearly as strong. Adapted by Carlino from Pat Conroy's novel. Aka THE ACE. [PG]▼●◗

Great Scout & Cathouse Thursday, The (1976) C-102m. **½ D: Don Taylor. Lee Marvin, Oliver Reed, Robert Culp, Elizabeth Ashley, Howard Platt, Strother Martin, Sylvia Miles, Kay Lenz. Broad comedy set in Colorado of 1908 involves swindles, defanged snake, kidnapped prostitutes, and robbery of proceeds from big boxing match. Could have been funnier, but Reed is a delight as an Indian(!). [PG]▼◗

Great Sinner, The (1949) 110m. **½ D: Robert Siodmak. Gregory Peck, Ava Gardner, Melvyn Douglas, Walter Huston, Ethel Barrymore, Frank Morgan, Agnes Moorehead. Lavishly produced but murky, talky costumer of writer Peck falling for beautiful Gardner and becoming obsessed with gambling. Screenplay by Christopher Isherwood.

Great Smokey Roadblock, The (1976) C-84m. **½ D: John Leone. Henry Fonda, Eileen Brennan, John Byner, Dub Taylor, Susan Sarandon, Melanie Mayron, Austin Pendleton. Innocuous story of aging trucker (Fonda) attempting one perfect cross-country run before his truck is repossessed; his haul is a houseful of evicted prostitutes. Some nice vignettes. Originally titled THE LAST OF THE COWBOYS, running 106m. Co-produced by Sarandon. [PG]▼◗

Great Spy Mission, The SEE: **Operation Crossbow**

Great St. Trinian's Train Robbery, The (1966-British) C-94m. ** D: Frank Launder, Sidney Gilliat. Frankie Howerd, Reg Varney, Richard Wattis, Dora Bryan. Overly droll entry in popular series begins with the real Great Train Robbery, then injects political satire with usual hijinks as crooks' hiding place for loot becomes new site for infamous girls' school. Alastair Sim's presence is sorely missed.▼

Great Texas Dynamite Chase, The (1977) C-90m. *½ D: Michael Pressman. Claudia

Jennings, Jocelyn Jones, Johnny Crawford, Chris Pennock, Tara Strohmeier. A pair of sexy female bank robbers take to the roads in this all-too-typical low-budget outing. [R]▼◗

Great Train Robbery, The (1979-British) C-111m. *** D: Michael Crichton. Sean Connery, Donald Sutherland, Lesley-Anne Down, Alan Webb, Malcolm Terris, Wayne Sleep, Robert Lang. Stylish fun as an elegant trio conspire to pull off the greatest heist of all time, in the mid-1800s: stealing shipment of gold from a moving train! Crichton based his script on true incident, filmed it against beautiful Irish countryside. British title: THE FIRST GREAT TRAIN ROBBERY. [PG]▼●◗

Great Waldo Pepper, The (1975) C-107m. *** D: George Roy Hill. Robert Redford, Bo Svenson, Bo Brundin, Susan Sarandon, Geoffrey Lewis, Edward Herrmann, Margot Kidder, Scott Newman. Box-office disappointment from director of BUTCH CASSIDY and THE STING is a much more personal film, even though brilliantly photographed story of aviation pioneers wavers uncomfortably between slapstick and drama. Worth a look. Todd-AO 35. [PG]▼●◗

Great Wall, A (1986) C-100m. **½ D: Peter Wang. Peter Wang, Sharon Iwai, Kelvin Han Yee, Li Qinqin, Hy Xiaoguang. Good-natured story of culture clash that results when Chinese-American family makes its first trip to mainland China. Amiable but hardly inspired. First U.S.-Chinese coproduction is also Wang's first feature as co-writer, director, and star (he played the chef in CHAN IS MISSING by Wayne Wang—no relation). [PG]▼●◗

Great Waltz, The (1972) C-135m. BOMB D: Andrew L. Stone. Horst Buchholz, Mary Costa, Rossano Brazzi, Nigel Patrick, Yvonne Mitchell, James Faulkner. Bio of Johann Strauss is unintentionally funny in the way director Stone's SONG OF NORWAY was, but after 135 minutes, even the laughs begin to subside. Shot on location in Austria. Filmed before in 1938. Panavision. [G]

Great White Hope, The (1970) C-101m. *** D: Martin Ritt. James Earl Jones, Jane Alexander, Lou Gilbert, Joel Fluellen, Chester Morris, Robert Webber, R. G. Armstrong, Hal Holbrook, Beah Richards, Moses Gunn. Supercharged adaptation of Broadway success with Jones and Alexander (in her film debut) repeating stage roles as Jack Jefferson, famed heavyweight champion, and white mistress. Not a boxing film or social doctrine, but emotional character study. Holds up until final scene, which doesn't ring true. Howard Sackler adapted his own play. Panavision. [PG]▼◗

Great White Hype, The (1996) C-90m. **½ D: Reginald Hudlin. Samuel L. Jackson, Jeff Goldblum, Damon Wayans, Peter

Berg, Jon Lovitz, Corbin Bernsen, Cheech Marin, Jamie Foxx, Salli Richardson, John Rhys-Davies, Rocky Carroll. Flamboyant boxing promoter Jackson needs a new gimmick: his champ (Wayans) isn't drawing the big money anymore, so he realizes a *white* contender is required. Berg is amusing as the dumb-but-earnest rival. Occasionally very funny, often snidely cynical, but the satire is not as pointed as intended. Written by Ron Shelton and Tony Hendra. [R]▼●◗

Great World of Sound (2007) **C-106m.** *** D: Craig Zobel. Pat Healy, Kene Holliday, Robert Longstreet, Rebecca Mader, John Baker, Tricia Paoluccio. Two hucksters travel the country signing "undiscovered" singing talent to a bogus record label. Comedy mixes its fictional scenario with candid-camera–style real-life auditions, earning this clever independent film extra points as it merges originality and smart dialogue with believable situations. Holliday is a standout as a weathered salesman who has seen it all. [R]◗

Great Ziegfeld, The (1936) **176m.** ***½ D: Robert Z. Leonard. William Powell, Myrna Loy, Luise Rainer, Frank Morgan, Fanny Brice, Virginia Bruce, Reginald Owen, Ray Bolger, Stanley Morner (Dennis Morgan). Spectacular, immensely entertaining biography of flamboyant impresario Florenz Ziegfeld, with Powell quite dashing in the title role. However, Rainer (as Anna Held) is stunning, and won an Academy Award; her telephone scene is a classic. Also won Oscars for Best Picture and Dance Direction (the "A Pretty Girl Is Like a Melody" number, supervised by Seymour Felix). ▼●

Greed (1924) **140m.** **** D: Erich von Stroheim. Gibson Gowland, ZaSu Pitts, Jean Hersholt, Chester Conklin, Dale Fuller. Powerful adaptation of Frank Norris' novel *McTeague,* about a simple man whose wife's obsession with money eventually drives him to madness. Even though von Stroheim's version was taken from him and severely cut by the studio (it originally ran eight hours), this remains a stunning work, one of the greatest of all silent films. The final sequences in Death Valley are unforgettable. Reconstructed in 1999, using stills to cover long-lost footage; this version runs 242m.▼●

Greedy (1994) **C-113m.** ** D: Jonathan Lynn. Michael J. Fox, Kirk Douglas, Nancy Travis, Olivia d'Abo, Phil Hartman, Ed Begley, Jr., Jere Burns, Colleen Camp, Bob Balaban, Joyce Hyser, Mary Ellen Trainor, Siobhan Fallon, Kevin McCarthy, Tom Mason, Austin Pendleton, Kirsten Dunst. Venal family can't wait for a crotchety uncle to die, so they can get their hands on his money, but when he threatens to give it all to a sexy young companion, they dig up long-estranged nephew Fox. Naming the family McTeague (after von Stroheim's GREED) is the cleverest thing in Lowell Ganz and Ba-

baloo Mandel's wearisome script—which isn't helped by Lynn's slack-paced direction. (The director also appears as Kirk's put-upon butler.) Based, believe it or not, on Charles Dickens' *Martin Chuzzlewit.* [PG-13]▼●◗

Greek Tycoon, The (1978) **C-106m.** *½ D: J. Lee Thompson. Anthony Quinn, Jacqueline Bisset, Raf Vallone, Edward Albert, Charles Durning, Camilla Sparv, James Franciscus, Luciana Paluzzi, Kathryn Leigh Scott, Roland Culver, Linda Thorson, Lucy Gutteridge, Henderson Forsythe. Pointless fabrication about romance and marriage of Aristotle Onassis and a certain president's widow. Beautiful settings add only luster to tepid script that doesn't even rate as good trash. Alternate version runs 112m. Technovision. [R]▼◗

Green Berets, The (1968) **C-141m.** BOMB D: John Wayne, Ray Kellogg. John Wayne, David Janssen, Jim Hutton, Aldo Ray, Raymond St. Jacques, Bruce Cabot, George Takei, Jack Soo, Patrick Wayne, Mike Henry. Politics aside, this overlong, incredibly clichéd salute to the Special Forces has enough absurd situations and unfunny comedy relief to offend anyone; don't miss now-famous final scene, where the sun sets in the East. Panavision. [G]▼●◗

Greenberg (2010) **C-107m.** *** D: Noah Baumbach. Ben Stiller, Greta Gerwig, Rhys Ifans, Jennifer Jason Leigh, Brie Larson, Juno Temple, Chris Messina, Susan Traylor, Mark Duplass. Title character, who's just had a nervous breakdown, returns to L.A. from N.Y.C. to house-sit for his brother, and strikes up a tentative relationship with the aimless but likable young woman who works as an assistant to his brother's family. He also tries to rekindle old friendships from when he was an up-and-comer—quite some time ago. Baumbach and Leigh conceived this incisive, if laid-back, character study of a self-absorbed screwup (Stiller, in a finely tuned performance). Spending time with Greenberg may not be everyone's cup of tea, but the film has undeniable resonance, and paints a vivid portrait of everyday life in L.A. Super 35. [R] ◗

Green Card (1990-Australian-French) **C-108m.** **½ D: Peter Weir. Gérard Depardieu, Andie MacDowell, Bebe Neuwirth, Gregg Edelman, Ann Wedgeworth, Ethan Phillips, Mary Louise Wilson, Lois Smith, Simon Jones. Young woman agrees to marry Frenchman—in name only—so he may legally remain in this country . . . but when Immigration authorities begin to investigate, she's forced to spend time with the man. Thin, scarcely credible romantic comedy, written by the director; worth watching for Depardieu, who's charming in English-language debut. [PG-13] ▼●◗

Greendale (2004) **C-87m.** *** D: Bernard Shakey (Neil Young). Sarah White, Eric

Johnson, Ben Keith, Erik Markegard, Elizabeth Keith, Pegi Young, James Mazzeo. Provocative, free-flowing music video/rock opera about events that befall the Green family of Greendale, California. The script consists of lyrics from ten songs written and sung by Young, lip-synched by the actors; their content is deeply personal and political, tackling such issues as corporate corruption, ecological abuse, and media overkill. Those who caringly recall 1960s and '70s social activism (and Young's tenure with Buffalo Springfield) will likely find this most appealing. Filmed in Super 8, to look like a poorly shot home movie. Young appears in a cameo, as "Wayne Newton."▶

Green Dolphin Street (1947) **141m. **½** D: Victor Saville. Lana Turner, Van Heflin, Donna Reed, Richard Hart, Frank Morgan, Edmund Gwenn, Dame May Whitty, Reginald Owen, Gladys Cooper, Moyna MacGill, Linda Christian, Gigi Perreau. If only for its glossy production and Oscar-winning special effects (earthquake and resultant tidal wave), this plodding costumer has merit. Story of two sisters (Turner, Reed) after the same man in 19th-century New Zealand is tedious. ▼●

Greenfingers (2001-British-U.S.) **C-91m. **½** D: Joel Hershman. Clive Owen, Helen Mirren, David Kelly, Natasha Little, Warren Clarke, Danny Dyer, Adam Fogerty, Paterson Joseph. Minor but diverting film inspired by the real-life inmates at a progressive British prison who began gardening and wound up competing at England's leading flower show at Hampton Court. Owen plays a loner who's persuaded to try getting back to the soil by his aged, canny cellmate (Kelly). A bit too pat, but pleasant. [R] ▼▶

Green Fire (1954) **C-100m. **½** D: Andrew Marton. Grace Kelly, Stewart Granger, Paul Douglas, John Ericson, Murvyn Vye. Hokum about love and conflict between emerald prospector (Granger) and coffee-plantation owner (Kelly), set in Colombia, South America. Attractive stars, hot love scenes, slimy villain (Vye). CinemaScope.▼▶

Green for Danger (1946-British) **93m. ****** D: Sidney Gilliat. Alastair Sim, Sally Gray, Trevor Howard, Rosamund John, Leo Genn, Judy Campbell, Megs Jenkins. Exciting whodunit set in a rural English emergency hospital during WW2. Tension neatly counterbalanced by droll wit of Sim as implacable Scotland Yard inspector; a must-see classic. Written by Gilliat and Claude Guerney.▼●▶

Green Horizon, The SEE: **Afurika Monogatari**

Green Hornet, The (2011) **C-119m. *½** D: Michel Gondry. Seth Rogen, Jay Chou, Cameron Diaz, Tom Wilkinson, Christoph Waltz, David Harbour, Edward James Olmos, Jamie Harris, Chad Coleman, Edward Furlong. A dim bulb named Britt Reid inherits his father's fortune and L.A. newspaper when Dad mysteriously dies. Then he teams up with the old man's chauffeur, a wily would-be inventor named Kato, and decides to fight crime, using the paper to promote his new identity as The Green Hornet. Inane, nearly incoherent, attention-deficit mash-up of a superhero movie and a comedy. Written by Rogen and Evan Goldberg, who abandon all logic for the love of a cool car and plenty of explosions. James Franco appears unbilled. 3-D Panavision. [PG-13]▶

Green Ice (1981-British) **C-115m. ** ** D: Ernest Day. Ryan O'Neal, Anne Archer, Omar Sharif, Domingo Ambriz, John Larroquette. Emerald smuggling, with good guy O'Neal, bad guy Sharif, Archer the woman in between. Painless time-killer. [PG]▼●

Green Lantern (2011) **C-105m. **½** D: Martin Campbell. Ryan Reynolds, Blake Lively, Peter Sarsgaard, Mark Strong, Angela Bassett, Tim Robbins, Temuera Morrison, Jay O. Sanders, Jon Tenney, Taika Waititi; voices of Geoffrey Rush, Michael Clarke Duncan. Reckless test pilot Hal Jordan (Reynolds) is, curiously, chosen to join an intergalactic peacekeeping force known as the Green Lantern Corps. He likes being an overnight superhero but isn't really ready to take on the weight of responsibility that goes with it. Meanwhile, a nerdy scientist who's always been jealous of Jordan's relationship with flyer/aviation exec Carol Ferriss (Lively) is exposed to an alien corpse that begins to transform him into a kind of id monster who's out for revenge. Adaptation of DC comic book isn't innovative or deep, and doesn't necessarily make a lot of sense, but an attractive cast and spectacular visual effects make it fun to watch. 3-D Super 35. [PG-13]

Green Light (1937) **85m. **½** D: Frank Borzage. Errol Flynn, Anita Louise, Margaret Lindsay, Cedric Hardwicke, Henry O'Neill, Spring Byington, Erin O'Brien-Moore. Genuinely odd blend of melodrama, religion, purple prose, and medical drama with Flynn as an idealistic doctor who makes a career sacrifice and then tries to understand the larger meaning of his life. Adaptation of a Lloyd C. Douglas novel is entertaining enough but awfully hard to swallow seriously.▶

Green Man, The (1956-British) **80m. ***** D: Robert Day. Alastair Sim, George Cole, Terry-Thomas, Jill Adams, Avril Angers, Colin Gordon. Droll comedy of a seemingly timid clockmaker who prefers his part-time job as paid assassin.

Green Mansions (1959) **C-104m. **½** D: Mel Ferrer. Audrey Hepburn, Anthony Perkins, Lee J. Cobb, Sessue Hayakawa, Henry Silva, Nehemiah Persoff. W. H. Hudson's romance set in South America suffers from miscast Hepburn as Rima the Bird Girl, whom fate decrees shall not leave her sanctuary. Perkins properly puzzled as male lead. CinemaScope. ▼●◗

Green Mile, The (1999) **C-188m.** **½ D: Frank Darabont. Tom Hanks, David Morse, Bonnie Hunt, Michael Clarke Duncan, James Cromwell, Michael Jeter, Graham Greene, Doug Hutchison, Sam Rockwell, Barry Pepper, Jeffrey DeMunn, Patricia Clarkson, Harry Dean Stanton, Dabbs Greer, Eve Brent, Gary Sinise. An elderly man recalls the incident that changed his life, in 1935, when he supervised Death Row at a Louisiana state prison and encountered a gentle black behemoth (movingly played by Duncan) with an unusual gift. Well-made film has powerful moments, but they're needlessly stretched over three hours . . . and the central conceit isn't easy to buy. Repeated scenes of executions are tough to take. Based on Stephen King's best-seller. [R] ▼●◗

Green Room, The (1978-French) **C-95m.** ** D: François Truffaut. François Truffaut, Nathalie Baye, Jean Daste, Jean-Paul Moulin, Jeanne Lobre. Truffaut stars as a death-obsessed journalist who converts a rundown chapel into a memorial for his deceased WW1 comrades. Dreary, lifeless, disappointing, with Truffaut's character engulfed in his own rhetoric. Based on writings of Henry James; coscripted by Truffaut and Jean Gruault. [PG] ▼●◗

Green Slime, The (1969-Japanese-U.S.) **C-99m.** *½ D: Kinji Fukasaku. Robert Horton, Richard Jaeckel, Luciana Paluzzi, Bud Widom. On space station, title substance—which feeds on energy—grows into red-eyed, tentacled monsters that quickly multiply and threaten to spread to Earth. Not as much fun as it sounds. Toeiscope. [G] ▼◗

Green Street Hooligans (2005-U.S.-British) **C-106m.** ** D: Lexi Alexander. Elijah Wood, Charlie Hunnam, Claire Forlani, Marc Warren, Leo Gregory, Henry Goodman, Geoff Bell, Rafe Spall. American boy (Wood) who's unfairly expelled from Harvard flees to England, where his sister is living. He quickly falls in with his brother-in-law's rowdy sibling (Hunnam), the leader of a "firm" that regularly engages in bloody combat with rival gangs who support various football teams. To his surprise, the Yank finds that he likes living on the edge and engaging in mayhem. Intriguing film plays out badly, with story contrivances and changes in tone submerging some of its better qualities. Painfully violent at times. Followed by a DVD sequel. Super 35. [R]◗

Green Years, The (1946) **127m.** **½ D: Victor Saville. Charles Coburn, Tom Drake, Hume Cronyn, Gladys Cooper, Dean Stockwell, Jessica Tandy, Norman Lloyd, Wallace Ford. Sentimental A. J. Cronin weeper of orphaned Irish lad and his experiences growing up with his mother's family in Scotland. Coburn is wonderful as his great-

grandfather, an irascible teller of tall tales. Tandy plays Cronyn's *daughter* here.

Green Zone (2010) **C-115m.** ** D: Paul Greengrass. Matt Damon, Greg Kinnear, Brendan Gleeson, Amy Ryan, Khalid Abdalla, Jason Isaacs, Igal Naor. In 2003, U.S. Army officer Damon leads his squadron in a search for weapons of mass destruction in Baghdad, but after one too many blind alleys begins to question the intelligence reports he's receiving. Could his own government be lying? Retrospective look at the situation, "inspired by" Rajiv Chandrasekaran's nonfiction book *Imperial Life in the Emerald City*, asks us to be surprised at its discoveries—and the ultimate outcome of the story—when it's plain from the start to everyone but Damon's character. Vividly realized by Greengrass, a master of verisimilitude, but dramatically pointless. Super 35. [R]◗

Greetings (1968) **C-88m.** *** D: Brian De Palma. Jonathan Warden, Robert De Niro, Gerrit Graham, Richard Hamilton, Megan McCormick, Allen Garfield. Loose, informal, improvisational satire about the draft, sex, the counterculture. Exudes a late '60s N.Y.C.–Greenwich Village ambience not to be found in any Hollywood feature. Sequel: HI, MOM! [R—edited from original X rating] ▼●◗

Gregory's Girl (1981-Scottish) **C-91m.** *** D: Bill Forsyth. Gordon John Sinclair, Dee Hepburn, Chic Murray, Jake D'Arcy, Alex Norton, John Bett. Bright, winning comedy of wimpy teenager Sinclair's love for Hepburn, who takes his place on the school soccer team. Enjoyable, if perhaps a bit overrated. Followed in 1999 by GREGORY'S TWO GIRLS. [PG] ▼◗

Gremlins (1984) **C-106m.** ** D: Joe Dante. Zach Galligan, Phoebe Cates, Hoyt Axton, Frances Lee McCain, Polly Holliday, Glynn Turman, Dick Miller, Keye Luke, Scott Brady, Judge Reinhold, Jackie Joseph, Harry Carey, Jr., Corey Feldman. A teenager's unusual new pet spawns a legion of vicious, violent monsters who turn picture-postcard town into living hell. Comic nightmare is a cross between Capra's IT'S A WONDERFUL LIFE and THE BLOB; full of film-buff in-jokes but negated by too-vivid violence and mayhem. Cameos range from animator Chuck Jones to Robby the Robot—but you have to look fast for executive producer Steven Spielberg. Howie Mandel is the voice of Gizmo. Followed by a sequel. [PG] ▼●◗

Gremlins 2 The New Batch (1990) **C-106m.** *** D: Joe Dante. Zach Galligan, Phoebe Cates, John Glover, Robert Prosky, Robert Picardo, Christopher Lee, Haviland Morris, Dick Miller, Jackie Joseph, Gedde Watanabe, Keye Luke, Kathleen Freeman; voice of Tony Randall. Not so much a horror film as a goofy sendup of itself, this sequel turns the slimy creatures loose in

N.Y.C. Filled with gags, movie in-jokes, satiric barbs, and gratuitous cameo appearances. Glover is especially funny as a Donald Trump/Ted Turner type, and Lee is a delight as a genetic scientist. Be sure to stay with this through the closing credits. [PG-13]▼●■

Grendel, Grendel, Grendel (1980-Australian) **C-90m.** **½ D: Alexander Stitt. Voices of Peter Ustinov, Keith Michell, Arthur Dignam, Ed Rosser, Bobby Bright, Ric Stone. Crude but appealing animation highlights this fable about Grendel, a medieval monster only a mother could love, and his observations about the creatures he calls "man"—who murder and pillage. Based on a novel by John Gardner. Music by Bruce Smeaton.▼

Grey Fox, The (1982-Canadian) **C-92m.** *** D: Phillip Borsos. Richard Farnsworth, Jackie Burroughs, Wayne Robson, Ken Pogue, Timothy Webber. Low-key account of real-life robber Bill Miner, who switched from stagecoaches to trains after spending 33 years in jail. Director Borsos may be just a bit too laid back, but Farnsworth's charming and commanding performance makes up for that. The scene in which he watches THE GREAT TRAIN ROBBERY is a gem. [PG]▼●

Greyfriars Bobby (1961) **C-91m.** **½ D: Don Chaffey. Donald Crisp, Laurence Naismith, Alex Mackenzie, Kay Walsh, Duncan Macrae, Gordon Jackson. British Disney film based on true story of a Skye terrier who became "neighborhood pet" in Edinburgh during 19th century through unusual circumstances. Great charm, fine performances offset by slow pacing. A remake of CHALLENGE TO LASSIE, which also features Crisp (who played the dog's master in the earlier film). Remade in England in 2006.▼

Grey Gardens (1976) **C-95m.** *** D: David and Albert Maysles. Tasteless, suspect, but riveting documentary about Edith Bouvier Beale (79) and daughter Edie (57)—aunt and cousin of Jacqueline Onassis—filmed in their rotting, filthy 28-room mansion in East Hampton, N.Y., which was officially declared a health hazard. Fascinating for voyeurs, but film would have had more depth had we been given a better picture of mother and daughter in their youth. Later transformed into a stage musical and the basis for a 2009 cable TV movie. In 2006, Albert Maysles selected 90m. of outtakes of Edith and Edie to create entire new documentary, THE BEALES OF GREY GARDENS. [PG]▼

Grey Night SEE: **Ghost Brigade**

Grey Owl (1999-British-Canadian) **C-117m.** ** D: Richard Attenborough. Pierce Brosnan, Annie Galipeau, Nathaniel Arcand, Vlasta Vrana, David Fox, Charles Powell, Graham Greene. It's difficult to accept Brosnan as the title character, a celebrated North American Indian and conservationist whose true identity is discovered by a reporter in 1936; the rest of the story unfolds in flash-back. Sincere but ineffectual telling of this interesting tale went straight to video in the U.S. Panavision. [PG-13]▼■

Greystoke The Legend of Tarzan Lord of the Apes (1984) **C-129m.** *** D: Hugh Hudson. Christopher Lambert, Andie MacDowell, Ian Holm, Ralph Richardson, James Fox, Cheryl Campbell, Ian Charleson, Nigel Davenport. Retelling of Tarzan tale, liberally adapted from Edgar Rice Burroughs' original. Infant son of shipwrecked couple is raised by apes, discovered at manhood by a Belgian explorer, and returned to civilization—and his doting grandfather (Richardson, who's just wonderful in his final film performance). At its best in the jungle, with Rick Baker's incredible makeup effects; more sluggish back in Britain, and hampered by obvious signs of prerelease cutting. Leading lady MacDowell's voice was dubbed by Glenn Close. Alternate version runs 135m. Super Techniscope. [PG]▼●■

Grey Zone, The (2002) **C-108m.** *** D: Tim Blake Nelson. David Arquette, Steve Buscemi, Harvey Keitel, Mira Sorvino, Natasha Lyonne, Daniel Benzali, Allan Corduner, David Chandler, Lisa Benavides. Potent drama about day-to-day life at Auschwitz, based on the memoirs of Dr. Miklos Nyiszli, a Jewish doctor who carried out Josef Mengele's experiments in order to preserve his own life and his family's. Aiding him are the Sonderkommandos, Jewish prisoners who extend their lives by leading fellow Jews into the gas chambers. Episodic and stylized but still powerful, as it poses the question of how far someone will go in order to survive. Keitel coexecutive-produced. Adapted by Nelson from his stage play. [R] ▼■

Gridiron Gang (2006) **C-120m.** **½ D: Phil Joanou. Dwayne "The Rock" Johnson, Xzibit, L. Scott Caldwell, Leon Rippy, Kevin Dunn, Jade Yorker, David V. Thomas, Trever O'Brien, Setu Taase, Mo, Jurnee Smollett. The Rock, emoting more than usual, is a counselor at a detention facility for wayward kids who decides to form a football team. The program is threatened when bad outside influences take hold of some team members. Filled with sports-movie clichés and stereotypical characters, but has extra weight since it's based on a true story. Based on a documentary of the same name. Super 35. [PG-13]❚

Gridlock'd (1997) **C-91m.** **½ D: Vondie Curtis Hall. Tupac Shakur, Tim Roth, Thandie Newton, Charles Fleischer, Howard Hesseman, James Pickens, Jr., John Sayles, Eric Payne, Tom Towles, Vondie Curtis Hall, Kasi Lemmons, Lucy Alexis Liu. Occasionally spunky comedy (a poor cousin to TRAINSPOTTING) about drug-addicted musicians Shakur and Roth, who struggle (mostly against an uncaring bureaucracy) to kick their habits after their singer friend (Newton) overdoses. The two leads offer solid performances. Feature directorial debut for actor Curtis Hall (who also scripted). Elizabeth Peña appears unbilled. [R]📼🔘

Grifters, The (1990) C-114m. **★★★** D: Stephen Frears. Anjelica Huston, John Cusack, Annette Bening, Pat Hingle, Henry Jones, Michael Laskin, Eddie Jones, J.T. Walsh, Charles Napier, Stephen Tobolowsky, Sandy Baron, Gailard Sartain, Jeremy Piven. Icy cold adaptation of Jim Thompson's novel about con artists, with steely "working-woman" Huston coming back into the life of her grown son after many years of estrangement . . . and finding that he's taken up with a woman much like herself. Bleak and fascinating, with three first-rate performances. Screenplay by Donald E. Westlake. Coproduced and narrated by Martin Scorsese. [R]📼🔘

Grimm Brothers' Snow White, The SEE: **Snow White: A Tale of Terror**

Grim Prairie Tales (1990) C-94m. **★★** D: Wayne Coe. James Earl Jones, Brad Dourif, Will Hare, Marc McClure, Michelle Joyner, William Atherton, Lisa Eichhorn, Wendy Cooke. Lame, low-budget horror/Western anthology framed by Jones and Dourif spinning scary tales around a campfire. The four stories vary widely: a cowboy is buried alive by Indians; a traveling man is seduced by a pregnant, supernatural wanderer; a homesteader pursues a nocturnal hobby of lynching black men; and a gunslinger is haunted by one of his victims. [R]📼🔘

Grim Reaper, The (1981-Italian) C-81m. **★½** D: Joe D'Amato. Tisa Farrow, Saverio Vallone, Vanessa Steiger, George Eastman. Farrow and friends are stalked by killer on a Greek island. Trifling shocker. [R]📼🔘

Grind (1997) C-96m. **★★½** D: Chris Kentis. Billy Crudup, Adrienne Shelly, Paul Schulze, Frank Vincent, Saul Stein, Amanda Peet. Flawed but arresting drama about an ex-con/race car driver wannabe who moves in with his blue-collar brother and sister-in-law and becomes involved in an insurance scam. Predictable, but offers a thoughtful look at working-class lives, dreams and frustrations. Shot in 1994. 📼🔘

Grind (2003) C-105m. **BOMB** D: Casey La Scala. Mike Vogel, Vince Vieluf, Adam Brody, Joey Kern, Jennifer Morrison, Randy Quaid, Bam Margera, Summer Altice, Chad Fernandez, Christine Estabrook, Erin Murphy, Jason London, Christopher McDonald, Dave Foley. What should (and could) have been an innocuous teen movie about four skateboarding friends who want to go pro is torpedoed by a weak script that wallows in crass humor and sexism. Cameos by such comic luminaries as Tom Green and Bobcat Goldthwait can't compete with vomit jokes. [PG-13]📼🔘

Grindhouse (2007) C-192m. **★★★** D: Robert Rodriguez, Quentin Tarantino. "Planet Terror": Rose McGowan, Freddy Rodriguez, Josh Brolin, Marley Shelton, Michael Biehn, Jeff Fahey, Michael Parks, Naveen Andrews, Nicky Katt, Stacy Ferguson, Quentin Tarantino. "Death Proof": Kurt Russell, Rosario Dawson, Vanessa Ferlito, Jordan Ladd, Rose McGowan, Sydney Poitier, Tracie Thoms, Mary Elizabeth Winstead, Zoë Bell, Michael Parks, Eli Roth, Quentin Tarantino. Homage to exploitation double features of yore is long but a lot of fun. Rodriguez offers an unabashedly gory mutant-zombie yarn with plenty of action and a memorable prosthetic for victim-turned-heroine McGowan. Tarantino lingers on chick-power chatter before paying it off in his car-chase homage to VANISHING POINT, with real-life stunt woman Bell earning her paycheck. Faux trailers (by Rodriguez, Eli Roth, Rob Zombie, and Edgar Wright) are virtual replicas of '70s sleaze fare—more so than the features themselves. Bruce Willis appears unbilled; other familiar faces are in the trailers. Both features were expanded for separate release. One of the trailers was later expanded into the feature MACHETE. Super 35/HD Widescreen. [R]🔘

Grip of the Strangler SEE: **Haunted Strangler, The**

Grisbi SEE: **Touchez Pas au Grisbi**

Grissom Gang, The (1971) C-127m. **★★★** D: Robert Aldrich. Kim Darby, Scott Wilson, Irene Dailey, Tony Musante, Ralph Waite, Connie Stevens, Robert Lansing, Wesley Addy, Gary Grimes. Outlandish, extremely violent comic-book thriller set in the 1920s. Heiress Darby is kidnapped by family of drooling grotesques, whose leader (Wilson) starts to fall in love with her. Very funny if you appreciate the Aldrich sense of humor; otherwise, solid action fare. Remake of 1948 British film NO ORCHIDS FOR MISS BLANDISH. [R]📼🔘

Grizzly (1976) C-92m. **★★** D: William Girdler. Christopher George, Andrew Prine, Richard Jaeckel, Joan McCall, Joe Dorsey. OK rip-off of JAWS about an 18-foot, 2000-pound grizzly bear who launches series of attacks on campers in national park. Might be subtitled "Claws." Aka KILLER GRIZZLY. Todd-AO 35. [PG] 📼🔘

Grizzly Man (2005) C-103m. **★★★½** D: Werner Herzog. Amazing documentary about self-styled animal rights activist Timothy Treadwell, who spent thirteen summers filming his own exploits as he communed with bears in Alaska's Katmai National Park and Preserve before getting killed by one of them. Herzog (who also narrates) is the perfect director for this remarkable, empathetic study of obsession, identity, and the relationship between a filmmaker and his subject. Treadwell, whom we see in extensive footage from his own videos, is an amusing, confounding character. Footage of Treadwell on David Letterman's TV show is cut from the DVD. [R] 🔘

Grizzly Mountain (1997) C-96m. **★½** D: Jeremy Haft. Dan Haggerty, Dylan Haggerty, Nicole Lund, Kim Morgan Greene,

Perry Stephens, Martin Kove, Megan Haggerty. While camping in the Oregon mountains, two city kids go into a cave and are transported back to 1870, where they help a friendly mountain man (guess who) battle greedy developers who want to destroy sacred Indian land. Ultra-innocuous family film, but worthy message is lost amidst amateurish acting, cheesy production values, and lamebrained comedy relief. [G]▼●▶

Groomsmen, The (2006) C-98m. **½ D: Edward Burns. Edward Burns, Brittany Murphy, John Leguizamo, Jay Mohr, Matthew Lillard, Donal Logue, Shari Albert, Jessica Capshaw. Five lifelong pals reunite on the eve of Burns' nuptials to Murphy, stirring up a lot of unfinished business and reopening old wounds. The setup couldn't be more transparent, and the characters aren't very deep, but they do ring true for the most part and the cast is first-rate. Written by the director. [R]▶

Groove (2000) C-83m. *** D: Greg Harrison. Lola Glaudini, Hamish Linklater, Denny Kirkwood, Mackenzie Firgens, Rachel True, Steven Van Wormer, DJ John Digweed. Lively, ingratiating saga of a weekend rave in San Francisco, from start to finish, and the disparate characters whose lives crisscross there. Good spirits and vivid re-creation of the rave scene make up for the simplistic quality of director Harrison's script. [R]▼▶

Groove Tube, The (1974) C-75m. **½ D: Ken Shapiro. Ken Shapiro, Lane Sarasohn, Chevy Chase, Richard Belzer, Mary Mendham, Bill Kemmill. Sometimes funny, sometimes stupid collection of satirical episodes about television. Definitely has its heart in the right place, but a mixed bag. Originally X-rated, later trimmed; Chase's feature debut. [R]▼▶

Gross Anatomy (1989) C-109m. **½ D: Thom Eberhardt. Matthew Modine, Daphne Zuniga, Christine Lahti, Todd Field, John Scott Clough, Alice Carter, Robert Desiderio, Zakes Mokae. Doctor-in-training Modine doesn't take his studies as seriously as he should. Not bad, but not particularly distinguished; Lahti is wasted as the aspiring doctors' demanding instructor. Viewers who've attended medical school may appreciate this more. [PG-13]▼●▶

Grosse Fatigue (1994-French) C-87m. **½ D: Michel Blanc. Michel Blanc, Carole Bouquet, Philippe Noiret, Josiane Balasko, Christian Clavier, Charlotte Gainsbourg. French variation of STARDUST MEMORIES, with Blanc finding his celebrityhood turning into a bad dream after he is accused of defiling Balasko. Intriguing, self-involved, crammed with guest appearances by familiar faces from French cinema. Blanc, Balasko, and Bouquet all play "themselves." Video title: DEAD TIRED. [R]▼▶

Grosse Pointe Blank (1997) C-107m. **½ D: George Armitage. John Cusack, Minnie Driver, Alan Arkin, Dan Aykroyd, Joan Cusack, Hank Azaria, K. Todd Freeman, Mitchell Ryan, Jeremy Piven, Barbara Harris, Jenna Elfman. Professional hit man combines business with pleasure when he attends his 10-year high school reunion while on assignment . . . but the girl he dumped (and all his friends) want to know why and how he disappeared. Cusack cowrote and coproduced this sharp black comedy, brimming with hip dialogue and loaded with attitude. But the climactic violence leaves a bad taste and undermines the comedy. [R]▼●▶

Groundhog Day (1993) C-103m. ***½ D: Harold Ramis. Bill Murray, Andie MacDowell, Chris Elliott, Stephen Tobolowsky, Brian Doyle-Murray, Marita Geraghty, Angela Paton, Rick Ducommun, Rick Overton, Robin Duke, Michael Shannon. Smug TV weatherman Murray goes to Punxsutawney, Pa., to cover the Groundhog Day ceremony and finds himself trapped in a daily replay of the same 24 hours. Near classic comedy-fantasy improves on each viewing, with endless twists and turns that are funny, moving, and even profound. Murray, perfectly cast, provides just the right combination of edginess and incipient humanity. Director-cowriter Ramis has a brief scene as a local neurologist. [PG]▼●▶

Groundstar Conspiracy, The (1972-Canadian) C-96m. **½ D: Lamont Johnson. George Peppard, Michael Sarrazin, Christine Belford. When explosion smashes secret space project, espionage work first begins. Tightly made, but poor dialogue. Panavision. [PG]▼▶

Ground Truth, The (2006) C-77m. ***½ D: Patricia Foulkrod. A roster of the maimed, the burned, and the spiritually fried incisively describes life and death in the killing fields of Iraq. American youth, brainwashed by recruiters' lies and brutalized by boot camp sadists, morph into peer-approved mass murderers as they fight a war without armor, intel, or a clue. Using interviews strictly from the GIs' point of view, without input from generals or politicians, this film depicts a place where madness is the norm and the daily grind is worse than any horror movie. No sanctimony here. Unnerving soundtrack has contributions from Mos Def and Tom Waits. [R]▶

Ground Zero (1987-Australian) C-109m. *** D: Michael Pattinson, Bruce Myles. Colin Friels, Jack Thompson, Donald Pleasence, Natalie Bate, Simon Chilvers, Neil Fitzpatrick, Bob Maza, Peter Cummins. Cameraman learns that his father may have died because he saw—and photographed—too much during British A-bomb testing in Australia in the 1950s. Exciting political paranoia thriller, though sluggish in spots. Pleasence is excellent in supporting role as hermitlike survivor of those tests. A fictional story based on factual events. Panavision. [PG]▼●

[565]

Group, The (1966) **C-150m.** ******* D: Sidney Lumet. Candice Bergen, Joan Hackett, Elizabeth Hartman, Shirley Knight, Joanna Pettet, Mary-Robin Redd, Jessica Walter, Kathleen Widdoes, James Broderick, Larry Hagman, Richard Mulligan, Hal Holbrook, Carrie Nye, Leora Dana, George Gaynes. Uneven, but generally good adaptation of Mary McCarthy's high-class soap opera about eight graduates of Vassar-type college. Knight and Hackett stand out in excellent cast. Film debuts of Bergen, Hackett, Pettet, Widdoes, and Holbrook. ▼❶

Group Marriage (1972) **C-85m.** ****½** D: Stephanie Rothman. Victoria Vetri, Claudia Jennings, Aimee Eccles, Zack Taylor, Jeff Pomerantz, Jayne Kennedy, Milt Kamen. Engaging drive-in comedy with something to say. Group of young Californians sets up a communal housekeeping situation, gradually adding new members. Needless to say, the neighbors are less than thrilled. Nicely done, attractive cast. [R] ▼

Grown Ups (2010) **C-102m.** ***½** D: Dennis Dugan. Adam Sandler, Kevin James, Chris Rock, David Spade, Rob Schneider, Salma Hayek Pinault, Maria Bello, Maya Rudolph, Joyce Van Patten, Colin Quinn, Steve Buscemi, Tim Meadows, Norm Macdonald, Blake Clark. Their high school coach's death reunites a group of childhood friends 30 years later and inspires them to rent a lake house with their families for the 4th of July weekend. Sandler seems to be struggling to find a happy medium between the raunchy bathroom humor for which he's known and the family-friendly fare he'd like to create. Camaraderie among the lead actors is enjoyable to watch, but the touchy-feely moments feel forced and unnatural. [PG-13] ❶

Grudge, The (2004-U.S.-Japanese) **C-91m.** ****½** D: Takashi Shimizu. Sarah Michelle Gellar, Jason Behr, William Mapother, Clea DuVall, Grace Zabriskie, Bill Pullman, Ted Raimi, Ryo Ishibashi, Yuya Ozeki, Takako Fuji, KaDee Strickland. In Tokyo, a young American woman finds her life (and her friends' as well) in danger from ghosts haunting a modest home where murders took place. Remake of JU-ON: THE GRUDGE (2003) by same director (with some of the same cast) tells a more linear story than the original; it's a shade less effective, but still imaginative and intelligent. Alternate version runs 98m. Followed by THE GRUDGE 2 and a DVD sequel. [PG-13] ▼❶

Grudge 2, The (2006) **C-102m.** ***½** D: Takashi Shimizu. Amber Tamblyn, Arielle Kebbel, Jennifer Beals, Edison Chen, Christopher Cousins, Teresa Palmer, Misako Uno, Joanna Cassidy, Sarah Roemer, Matthew Knight, Takako Fuji, Shaun Sipos, Jenna Dewan, Sarah Michelle Gellar. The same creaking ghosts terrorize teenage girls (and others) in Japan and Chicago. Plodding, confusing mess, much inferior to the first, switching clumsily from Japan to the U.S. repeatedly. The two threads are unlinked until the last few minutes—that is, if anyone's still watching. Unrated version runs 108m. Followed by a DVD sequel. [PG-13] ❶

Grumpier Old Men (1995) **C-100m.** ****½** D: Howard Deutch. Jack Lemmon, Walter Matthau, Ann-Margret, Sophia Loren, Daryl Hannah, Kevin Pollak, Burgess Meredith, Ann Guilbert, Max Wright, James Andelin. Now reconciled, the longtime neighbors/nemeses argue over their offsprings' impending wedding, while a new arrival in town (Loren) turns their bait shop into a restaurant. Agreeable sequel, though it's discouraging to see two great comic actors reduced to getting cheap laughs by spouting epithets at one another. Loren is a breath of fresh air as Matthau's unlikely love interest. Meredith is back in form as Lemmon's horny dad. [PG-13] ▼❶

Grumpy Old Men (1993) **C-104m.** ****½** D: Donald Petrie. Jack Lemmon, Walter Matthau, Ann-Margret, Burgess Meredith, Daryl Hannah, Kevin Pollak, Ossie Davis, Buck Henry, Christopher McDonald. Engagingly performed but malnourished comedy about two mateless Minnesota retirees, rabid ice-fishermen, whose lifelong feud escalates when an attractive widow moves in across the street. Walter and Jack are fun as usual, but a few too many plot threads get wrapped up in the final 15 minutes. Compensations are a funny end-credit sequence and the singular chance to hear Meredith (as Lemmon's father) make endless salacious wordplays on the male organ of love. Followed by a sequel. [PG-13] ▼❶

Guadalcanal Diary (1943) **93m.** ****½** D: Lewis Seiler. Preston Foster, Lloyd Nolan, William Bendix, Richard Conte, Anthony Quinn, Richard Jaeckel, Lionel Stander. WW2 actioner based on Richard Tregaskis' best-selling account of the Marines taking a Pacific island stronghold. This hasn't aged especially well, with archetypes instead of characters, from Bendix's Brooklyn cabbie to Jaeckel (in his film debut) as the ultimate mama's boy. Still watchable, but for an overload of racial slurs. ▼❶

Guardian, The (1990) **C-93m.** ****** D: William Friedkin. Jenny Seagrove, Dwier Brown, Carey Lowell, Brad Hall, Miguel Ferrer, Natalia Nogulich. Yuppie couple hires a nanny for their newborn child, but we know there's something odd about her: she feeds babies to a tree in a nearby gully. Friedkin's first return to horror after THE EXORCIST has a few good scenes, but a ludicrous story and a humorless approach. Seagrove is very good in an almost unplayable role. Cowritten by the director from novel *The Nanny* by Dan Greenburg. [R] ▼❶

Guardian, The (2006) **C-139m.** ******* D:

Andrew Davis. Kevin Costner, Ashton Kutcher, Melissa Sagemiller, Bonnie Bramlett, Clancy Brown, Sela Ward, Neal McDonough, John Heard, Brian Geraghty, Dulé Hill, Omari Hardwick. After a tragic accident, veteran Coast Guard rescue swimmer Costner is reassigned to teach new recruits—and is especially hard on a young hotshot (Kutcher) with whom he has more in common than either one might suspect. Strictly formulaic military yarn is reminiscent of everything from AN OFFICER AND A GENTLEMAN to G.I. JANE, but goes through its paces with energy and conviction. Rescue scenes at sea are especially exciting. If only it didn't have three endings! [PG-13]▐

Guarding Tess (1994) **C-98m.** *** D: Hugh Wilson. Shirley MacLaine, Nicolas Cage, Austin Pendleton, Edward Albert, James Rebhorn, Richard Griffiths, John Roselius, David Graf, Dale Dye. Secret Service agent tries to get out of his demanding and frustrating assignment, protecting a former First Lady—but she won't let him go. Extremely satisfying comedy-drama buoyed by two perfect performances, by MacLaine and Cage. Incidentally, that's director/cowriter Wilson as the voice of the President on the phone. [PG-13]▼●▌

Guess Who (2005) **C-105m.** **½ D: Kevin Rodney Sullivan. Bernie Mac, Ashton Kutcher, Zoë Saldaña, Judith Scott, Hal Williams, Kellee Stewart, Robert Curtis Brown, RonReaco Lee, Sherri Shepherd, Richard Lawson, Jessica Cauffiel. Modern spin on GUESS WHO'S COMING TO DINNER, with Saldaña bringing fiancé Kutcher home to her mom and her demanding, overprotective dad—without telling them that he's white. Comedy quotient is fairly mild but it's all pleasant enough. [PG-13]▼▌

Guess Who's Coming to Dinner (1967) **C-108m.** *** D: Stanley Kramer. Spencer Tracy, Katharine Hepburn, Sidney Poitier, Katharine Houghton, Cecil Kellaway, Beah Richards, Roy E. Glenn, Sr., Virginia Christine, Isabel Sanford. Glossy tale of mixed marriage as Houghton (Hepburn's real-life niece) brings home fiancé Poitier to meet her perplexed parents. Fluff is given strength by Oscar-winning Hepburn and Tracy in his last film appearance. William Rose also took home an Oscar for his story and screenplay. Remade in 2005 as GUESS WHO. ▼●▌

Guest, The (1964-British) **105m.** *** D: Clive Donner. Alan Bates, Donald Pleasence, Robert Shaw. Derelict Pleasence invades the world of mentally ill Shaw and his sadistic brother Bates. Superior cast and superb performances, but claustrophobically directed by Donner. Screenplay by Harold Pinter, based on his play *The Caretaker,* which was also this film's title in Britain.

Guide for the Married Man, A (1967) **C-89m.** ***½ D: Gene Kelly. Walter Matthau, Inger Stevens, Robert Morse, Sue Ane Langdon, Claire Kelly, Elaine Devry; guest stars Lucille Ball, Jack Benny, Polly Bergen, Joey Bishop, Sid Caesar, Art Carney, Wally Cox, Jayne Mansfield, Hal March, Louis Nye, Carl Reiner, Phil Silvers, Terry-Thomas, Ben Blue, Ann Morgan Guilbert, Jeffrey Hunter, Marty Ingels, Sam Jaffe. Consistently funny, imaginative adult comedy of Morse trying to teach faithful husband Matthau the ABC's of adultery, with the aid of many guest stars who demonstrate Morse's theories. Joke of it all is that Matthau is married to gorgeous Inger Stevens! Panavision. ▼▌

Guide to Recognizing Your Saints, A (2006) **C-100m.** **½ D: Dito Montiel. Robert Downey, Jr., Shia LaBeouf, Chazz Palminteri, Dianne Wiest, Channing Tatum, Melonie Diaz, Martin Compston, Eric Roberts, Rosario Dawson, Adam Scarimbolo, Julia Garro, Peter Tambakis, Scott Michael Campbell. Montiel also scripted this autobiographical slice-of-life in which a successful L.A. writer (Downey, Jr.) returns to his Queens, N.Y., home for the first time in many years when he learns his father is seriously ill. Jumps between the present and past, when he's a rough-and-tumble teen who hangs out with his aimless friends and is inspired to escape into a better life. Ambitious film means to be cutting-edge, but often seems awkwardly improvisational and tends to ramble. [R]▌

Guilty as Charged (1992) **C-95m.** **½ D: Sam Irvin. Rod Steiger, Lauren Hutton, Heather Graham, Lyman Ward, Isaac Hayes, Zelda Rubinstein, Irwin Keyes, Michael Beach. Religious zealot turns out to be a self-made executioner who does away with criminals in his own homemade electric chair. Very black comedy seems a likely candidate for a cult following. Steiger's performance calls to mind his work in NO WAY TO TREAT A LADY; it's also fun to watch Isaac Hayes as one of his henchmen. Stylishly directed by first-timer Irvin. [R]▼▌

Guilty as Sin (1993) **C-107m.** ** D: Sidney Lumet. Rebecca De Mornay, Don Johnson, Stephen Lang, Jack Warden, Dana Ivey, Ron White, Norma Dell'Agnese, Sean McCann, Luis Guzman, Robert Kennedy. Clever lawyer De Mornay, obsessed with winning (whether or not her clients are guilty), takes the case of sleek womanizer Johnson, who's accused of murdering his wife. Then she learns she may have made a bargain with a killer—who now may have designs on *her*. The idea of intelligent opponents going head to head is intriguing, but Larry Cohen's script is underplotted and ordinary. [R]▼●▌

Guilty by Suspicion (1991) **C-105m.** ** D: Irwin Winkler. Robert De Niro, Annette

Bening, George Wendt, Patricia Wettig, Sam Wanamaker, Luke Edwards, Chris Cooper, Ben Piazza, Martin Scorsese, Barry Primus, Gailard Sartain, Stuart Margolin, Barry Tubb, Tom Sizemore, Illeana Douglas, Jon Tenney. Hollywood Blacklist drama, set in 1951, is earnest, superficial, and numbingly bland. De Niro is hotshot director who can't comprehend severity of Communist witch hunt; Bening is his sympathetic ex-wife, and Wettig (way over the top), an actress friend. Viewers unfamiliar with this dark chapter of history may find film as fascinating as intended. Wanamaker, who spent this era in exile in England, plays a villainous attorney. Veteran producer Winkler's (mediocre) writing and directing debut. [PG-13]▼●◖

Guinevere (1999-Canadian-U.S.) **C-104m.** **½ D: Audrey Wells. Stephen Rea, Sarah Polley, Jean Smart, Gina Gershon, Paul Dooley, Francis Guinan, Sandra Oh, Jasmine Guy, Gedde Watanabe. Well-played tale of a charming but iconoclastic photographer who acquires younger, female protégées, schooling them in the world of art as well as sex. His latest is a 20-year-old girl whose highly strung family doesn't understand her. Story sags at times, but is buoyed by Rea and Polley's enormously ingratiating performances. Written by the director. [R]▼◗

Gulliver's Travels (1939) **C-74m.** **½ D: Dave Fleischer. Singing voices of Lanny Ross, Jessica Dragonette. Max Fleischer's feature-length cartoon version of Jonathan Swift tale suffers from weak scripting, never getting audience involved in story. Town-crier Gabby is obnoxious, but he's got film's most memorable song, "All's Well."▼●◖

Gulliver's Travels (1977-British-Belgian) **C-80m.** *½ D: Peter R. Hunt. Richard Harris, Catherine Schell, Norman Shelley, Meredith Edwards; voices of Julian Glover, Murray Melvin, Bessie Love, others. Unimaginative retelling of the Jonathan Swift classic. Part live-action, part animation; the songs are the most forgettable since the 1973 LOST HORIZON. [G]▼

Gulliver's Travels (2010) **C-85m.** BOMB D: Rob Letterman. Jack Black, Emily Blunt, Jason Segel, Amanda Peet, Billy Connolly, Chris O'Dowd, James Corden, Catherine Tate, T. J. Miller. Gulliver (Black) is back in a contemporary reimagining of Jonathan Swift's classic tale, as a mailroom clerk who, in an attempt to impress a coworker (Peet), travels to the Bermuda Triangle to write an article on its mysteries. He finds himself washed up on the shores of Lilliput as a giant among its tiny people. Crude, meandering film barely focuses on the story and relies instead on terrible special effects, juvenile humor, and pop culture references. Not even this talented cast can save it. 3-D Super 35. [PG]◗

Gulliver's Travels Beyond the Moon (1966-Japanese) **C-78m.** ** D: Yoshio Kuroda. OK animated feature has Gulliver and companions going into outer space; acceptable kiddie fare.

Gumball Rally, The (1976) **C-107m.** *** D: Chuck Bail. Michael Sarrazin, Tim McIntire, Raul Julia, Normann Burton, Gary Busey, Nicholas Pryor, Susan Flannery, Steven Keats, J. Pat O'Malley, Tricia O'Neil, Med Flory. First of the cross-country road-race comedies is still the only good one, with genuinely funny characters, great cars, and loads of cartoon-like action. Julia steals the film as lecherous Italian who throws out his rear-view mirror because "what's behind me is not important." Definitely superior to CANNONBALL and the later CANNONBALL RUN movies, which were all inspired by the same real-life event. Panavision. [PG]▼●◖

Gumby the Movie (1995) **C-90m.** ** D: Art Clokey. Voices of Charles Farrington, Art Clokey, Gloria Clokey, Manny LaCarruba. Episodic clay-animated feature starring the popular character is slow going for all but the green guy's biggest fans. Convoluted story concerns Gumby's rock group, the Clayboys, and their benefit concert to help farmers thwarted by the Blockheads. Parodies of STAR WARS, TERMINATOR 2, and various swashbuckling epics do not help. Aka GUMBY 1.▼

Gummo (1997) **C-89m.** BOMB D: Harmony Korine. Jacob Reynolds, Nick Sutton, Jacob Sewell, Darby Dougherty, Chloë Sevigny, Carisa Bara, Linda Manz, Max Perlich. Plotless, clueless, mind-numbingly awful directorial debut for Korine (the 23-year-old scriptwriter of KIDS) about a circle of pathetic poor white trash in a small Ohio town. Tries to be shocking and outrageous—two of the characters kill cats and sell their corpses to a supermarket—but succeeds only in being trite, with scenes pointlessly dragging on . . . and on. [R]▼●◖

Gumshoe (1971-British) **C-88m.** **½ D: Stephen Frears. Albert Finney, Billie Whitelaw, Frank Finlay, Fulton Mackay, Janice Rule, Carolyn Seymour. Whimsical crime-comedy of small-time British vaudevillian who has seen too many Bogart films and decides to play private eye. Music score by Andrew Lloyd Webber. Finney also produced. [PG]▼◗

Gun Crazy (1949) **86m.** ***½ D: Joseph H. Lewis. Peggy Cummins, John Dall, Berry Kroeger, Morris Carnovsky, Anabel Shaw, Harry Lewis, Nedrick Young, Rusty (Russ) Tamblyn. Knockout of a sleeper in the BONNIE AND CLYDE tradition, stylishly (and sometimes startlingly) directed. Cummins is femme fatale who leads gun-crazy Dall into life of crime. Screenplay credited to MacKinlay Kantor and Millard Kaufman (who was "fronting" for then-blacklisted writer Dalton Trumbo), from Kantor's *Saturday Evening Post* story. Aka

DEADLY IS THE FEMALE. Loosely remade in 1992. ▼❚

Gun Crazy (1969) SEE: **Talent for Loving, A**

Guncrazy (1992) **C-96m.** ******* D: Tamra Davis. Drew Barrymore, James LeGros, Billy Drago, Rodney Harvey, Joe Dallesandro, Michael Ironside, Ione Skye. Noirish tale of an abused teenager from the wrong side of the tracks who falls for a born-again-Christian ex-con trying to go straight, ending up on a crime spree with him. Written by Matthew Bright but bearing a more than slight resemblance to a pair of 1949 favorites, the similarly titled GUN CRAZY and THEY LIVE BY NIGHT. Made for theaters, but debuted on cable. [R] ▼ ●❚

Gunfight, A (1971) **C-90m.** ****½** D: Lamont Johnson. Kirk Douglas, Johnny Cash, Jane Alexander, Raf Vallone, Karen Black, Keith Carradine. Off-beat Western about two aging gunfighters who meet and decide to sell tickets for a winner-take-all final shoot-out. Cash is good in his acting debut; also Carradine's first film. [PG] ▼❚

Gunfight at the O.K. Corral (1957) **C-122m.** ******* D: John Sturges. Burt Lancaster, Kirk Douglas, Rhonda Fleming, Jo Van Fleet, John Ireland, Lee Van Cleef, Frank Faylen, Kenneth Tobey, DeForest Kelley, Earl Holliman, Dennis Hopper, Martin Milner, Olive Carey. Stimulating Western filled with tense action sequences in recreation of Doc Holliday–Wyatt Earp battle in streets of Tombstone with Clanton gang. Written by Leon Uris. Frankie Laine sings title song. VistaVision. ▼ ●❚

Gunfighter, The (1950) **84m.** *****½** D: Henry King. Gregory Peck, Helen Westcott, Millard Mitchell, Jean Parker, Karl Malden, Skip Homeier, Verna Felton, Ellen Corby, Richard Jaeckel, Alan Hale, Jr. Peck is most impressive as gunslinger trying to overcome his bloody past. Classic psychological Western scripted by William Bowers and William Sellers; story by Bowers and Andre de Toth. Exteriors shot in Lone Pine, California. Catch this one! ▼ ●❚

Gunfight in Abilene (1967) **C-86m.** ****½** D: William Hale. Bobby Darin, Emily Banks, Leslie Nielsen, Michael Sarrazin. Undistinguished post-Civil War account of gun-shy Darin, town sheriff, taking up arms against outlaws. Techniscope. ▼

Gunfire (1978) SEE: **China 9, Liberty 37**

Gun Fury (1953) **C-83m.** ******* D: Raoul Walsh. Rock Hudson, Donna Reed, Phil Carey, Lee Marvin, Neville Brand, Leo Gordon. Hudson goes after men who have kidnapped his fiancée (Reed); formidable villainy, beautiful Arizona locations. 3-D. ▼ ●❚

Gunga Din (1939) **117m.** ******** D: George Stevens. Cary Grant, Victor McLaglen, Douglas Fairbanks, Jr., Joan Fontaine, Sam Jaffe, Eduardo Ciannelli, Montagu Love, Abner Biberman, Robert Coote, Lumsden Hare, Cecil Kellaway. *The* Hollywood action-adventure yarn, vaguely based on Rudyard Kipling's famous poem, about three soldier-comrades in 19th-century India battling the savage thuggee cult when they aren't busy carousing and getting into trouble. Water boy Jaffe saves the day in rousing climax. Splendid comic adventure whose story is credited to Ben Hecht and Charles MacArthur (who based the relationships of the central characters on the same marriage/rivalry device used in *The Front Page*); scripted by Joel Sayre and Fred Guiol. For years most prints ran 96m., until film was archivally restored. Shot on location in Lone Pine, California. Also shown in computer-colored version. Remade as SERGEANTS THREE. ▼ ●❚

Gung Ho! (1943) **88m.** ****½** D: Ray Enright. Randolph Scott, Grace McDonald, Alan Curtis, Noah Beery, Jr., J. Carrol Naish, David Bruce, Robert Mitchum, Sam Levene. Typical WW2 action film is marked by outrageous jingoism, celebrating the bloodthirsty misfits of the "gung ho" squadron as great American patriots. A jaw-dropping experience. Also shown in computer-colored version. ▼❚

Gung Ho (1986) **C-111m.** ******* D: Ron Howard. Michael Keaton, Gedde Watanabe, George Wendt, Mimi Rogers, John Turturro, Soh Yamamura, Sab Shimono, Clint Howard, Michelle Johnson. Cocky Keaton convinces Japanese company to reopen shuttered auto factory in his economically depressed hometown—but doesn't count on culture clash that follows. Extremely lightweight but entertaining comedy. Later a TV series. Panavision. [PG-13] ▼ ●❚

Gun in Betty Lou's Handbag, The (1992) **C-89m.** ***½** D: Allan Moyle. Penelope Ann Miller, Eric Thal, Alfre Woodard, William Forsythe, Cathy Moriarty, Julianne Moore, Andy Romano, Ray McKinnon, Xander Berkeley, Michael O'Neill, Billie Neal, Gale Mayron, Faye Grant, Marian Seldes, Meat Loaf, Catherine Keener, Cordell Jackson. Now *there's* a box-office title. Meek mouse Miller stumbles onto the title murder weapon, accidentally fires it in a public restroom, then capitalizes on her newfound attention by falsely confessing to the crime. Miller's considerable charm is tested and found wanting in this blandly trying comedy from Disney. [PG-13] ▼ ●❚

Gunman's Walk (1958) **C-97m.** ******* D: Phil Karlson. Van Heflin, Tab Hunter, Kathryn Grant (Crosby), James Darren. Rancher Heflin tries to train sons Hunter and Darren to be respectable citizens, but clashing personalities cause outburst of violence. Tight-knit Western. CinemaScope. ▼

Gunmen (1994) **C-90m.** ***½** D: Deran Sarafian. Christopher Lambert, Mario Van Peebles, Denis Leary, Patrick Stewart, Kadeem Hardison, Sally Kirkland, Richard Sarafian,

Robert Harper, Brenda Bakke, Deran Sarafian. U.S. agent Van Peebles and smuggler Lambert set out to recover the loot of drug lord Stewart (who's also responsible for the murder of Van Peebles' father). Strictly by-the-numbers actioner is often pointlessly violent; the in-your-face direction is no help. Real-life rappers (including Big Daddy Kane, Dr. Dre, and Ed Lover) appear as themselves. Panavision. [R]▼●◗

Gun Moll SEE: Jigsaw (1949)

Gunn (1967) C-94m. *½ D: Blake Edwards. Craig Stevens, Laura Devon, Edward Asner, Sherry Jackson, Helen Traubel, Albert Paulsen. Unsuccessful attempt to recapture flavor of *Peter Gunn* TV series; Herschel Bernardi, Lola Albright sorely missed, along with quiet understatement and wit that made it memorable. New story is tasteless, violent whodunit involving curious madam. Screenplay by Edwards and William Peter Blatty. Revived again for TV in 1989 as PETER GUNN.

Gunner Palace (2005-German-U.S.) C-85m. ***½ D: Michael Tucker, Petra Epperlein. Terrific documentary offers a firsthand, close-up look at daily life for a squadron of U.S. soldiers who are headquartered at Uday Hussein's former pleasure palace in Baghdad. Blending interviews, fly-on-the-wall footage taken during "routine" patrols and overtly dangerous assignments, and even inspired commentary in rap form, this film allows the soldiers' experiences to speak for themselves. Filmed in late 2003 and early 2004. [PG-13]◗

Gunpoint (1966) C-86m. ** D: Earl Bellamy. Audie Murphy, Joan Staley, Warren Stevens, Edgar Buchanan. Murphy as sheriff gathers a posse to catch outlaw gang who have kidnapped saloon girl.

Gun Riders (1970) C-98m. BOMB D: Al Adamson. Jim Davis, Scott Brady, Robert Dix, John Carradine. Ruthless gunman terrorizes settlers one more time, but his heroic counterpart is there to stop him. Cast is full of Western veterans, but they're not much help. Also known as FIVE BLOODY GRAVES and LONELY MAN. Techniscope. [PG—edited from original R rating]▼◗

Gun Runner (1984-Canadian) C-92m. *½ D: Nardo Castillo. Kevin Costner, Sara Botsford, Paul Soles, Gerard Parkes, Ron Lea, Mitch Martin, Larry Lewis, Aline Van Dine, Ruth Dahan. Murky gangster melodrama about idealistic Costner, seeking guns for Chinese rebellion during the 1920s, returning to native Canada and becoming involved with liquor smugglers. Tedious, to say the least, this film was (understandably) shelved until Costner's stardom prompted a 1989 video release . . . but he isn't very good in this one. [R] ▼●

Gun Runners, The (1958) 83m. ** D: Don Siegel. Audie Murphy, Eddie Albert, Patricia Owens, Everett Sloane, Jack Elam.

Murphy is involved with gun-smuggling to Cuba in this bland remake of TO HAVE AND HAVE NOT.◗

Guns at Batasi (1964-British) 103m. **½ D: John Guillermin. Richard Attenborough, Jack Hawkins, Mia Farrow, Flora Robson, John Leyton. Acting is all in this intelligent if predictable account of British military life in present-day Africa. CinemaScope.▼◗

Guns for San Sebastian (1968) C-111m. ** D: Henri Verneuil. Anthony Quinn, Anjanette Comer, Charles Bronson, Sam Jaffe, Silvia Pinal. Quinn plays a popular bandit who helps Mexican village defeat some Yaqui Indians after he is mistaken for a priest, but he can't conquer ridiculous script. Franscope.

Gun Shy (2000) C-102m. **½ D: Eric Blakeney. Liam Neeson, Oliver Platt, Sandra Bullock, Jose Zuniga, Richard Schiff, Andy Lauer, Mitch Pileggi, Paul Ben-Victor, Mary McCormack, Frank Vincent, Taylor Negron. Neeson gives a wonderful comic performance as an undercover DEA agent who's suffering from stress and goes to group therapy while working on a major sting operation. Platt is equally good as a not-too-bright hood, and Bullock (who produced the film) has a relatively minor role as Neeson's open-minded love interest. Plot-heavy but underdeveloped; written by the director. [R]▼◗

Guns of Darkness (1962-British) 95m. **½ D: Anthony Asquith. David Niven, Leslie Caron, David Opatoshu, James Robertson Justice, Eleanor Summerfield, Ian Hunter. Civilized drama of Niven searching for life's meaning, set in South America.

Guns of Navarone, The (1961) C-157m. ***½ D: J. Lee Thompson. Gregory Peck, David Niven, Anthony Quinn, Stanley Baker, Anthony Quayle, James Darren, Irene Papas, Gia Scala, James Robertson Justice, Richard Harris, Albert Lieven, Bryan Forbes, Walter Gotell. Explosive action film about Allied commandos during WW2 plotting to destroy German guns; high-powered adventure throughout this first-rate production, highlighted by Oscar-winning special effects. Script by Carl Foreman from the Alistair MacLean novel. Sequel: FORCE 10 FROM NAVARONE. CinemaScope.▼◗

Guns of the Magnificent Seven (1969) C-106m. **½ D: Paul Wendkos. George Kennedy, Monte Markham, James Whitmore, Reni Santoni, Bernie Casey, Joe Don Baker, Scott Thomas, Michael Ansara, Fernando Rey. Third time out, the "Seven" plot to free Mexican revolutionary leader from a well-guarded fortress. Nothing new, but well done, with plenty of action. Panavision. [G]▼◗

Guns of the Timberland (1960) C-91m. **½ D: Robert D. Webb. Alan Ladd, Jeanne Crain, Gilbert Roland, Frankie Avalon. Pat telling of loggers vs. townpeople.

Guns, Sin and Bathtub Gin SEE: **Lady in Red, The**

Gun the Man Down (1956) **78m. **** D: Andrew V. McLaglen. James Arness, Angie Dickinson, Robert Wilke, Emile Meyer, Harry Carey, Jr. Wounded Arness swears revenge on the cohorts (and his fiancée!) who abandoned him when a holdup went wrong. Sleepy Western drama produced by John Wayne's Batjac company.▶

Guru, The (1969) **C-112m. **** D: James Ivory. Michael York, Rita Tushingham, Utpal Dutt, Saeed Jaffrey, Madhur Jaffrey. Sincere but uninvolving story of rock star York who goes to India to learn sitar, meditation from guru Dutt. Director Ivory dwells on Indian lifestyle, settings; Tushingham provides welcome lighter moments in slow-moving film. [G]

Guru, The (2003-U.S.-British) **C-91m. **½** D: Daisy von Scherler Mayer. Heather Graham, Marisa Tomei, Jimi Mistry, Michael McKean, Christine Baranski, Rob Morrow, Emil Marwa, Malachy McCourt, Ajay Naidu, Anita Gillette. Innocuous comedy about an Indian dance teacher (Mistry) who comes to America seeking fame and fortune in the movies; instead, he lands a job in a porno film, is befriended by its beautiful star (who's actually a "good girl" leading a double life), then inadvertently becomes a celebrity as the "guru of sex." Some funny gags, a likable leading man, and good comic performances by Graham and Tomei enhance this uneven feel-good movie. The faux Bollywood number is fun. [R] ▼▶

Gus (1976) **C-96m. ***** D: Vincent McEveety. Edward Asner, Don Knotts, Gary Grimes, Tim Conway, Liberty Williams, Dick Van Patten, Dick Butkus. Football-kicking mule catapults a last-place team to victory; crooks try to kidnap Gus with usual results (like slapstick chase in a supermarket). Entertaining Disney comedy. [G] ▼●▶

Guyana: Cult of the Damned (1980-Mexican-Spanish-Panamanian) **C-90m. *½** D: Rene Cardona, Jr. Stuart Whitman, Gene Barry, John Ireland, Joseph Cotten, Bradford Dillman, Jennifer Ashley, Yvonne De Carlo. Not easy to turn the awesomeness of the Jonestown tragedy—where cult followers committed mass suicide—into lackluster drama, but that's what they've done here. [R]

Guy Named Joe, A (1943) **120m. **½** D: Victor Fleming. Spencer Tracy, Irene Dunne, Van Johnson, Ward Bond, James Gleason, Lionel Barrymore, Barry Nelson, Esther Williams, Don DeFore. Good cast flounders in meandering fantasy about WW2 pilot Tracy coming back to Earth to give young serviceman Johnson a hand in his romance with Tracy's girlfriend Dunne. Remade in 1989 as ALWAYS. ▼●

Guys, The (2003) **C-84m. ***** D: Jim Simpson. Sigourney Weaver, Anthony LaPaglia.

A N.Y.C. fire department captain who lost eight men in the 9/11 World Trade Center disaster gets help from a professional writer as he prepares to deliver eulogies for the deceased. Based on Anne Nelson's play, this works surprisingly well as a film, thanks to restrained emotions, honest performances by the two stars, and the nobility it finds in the lives of ordinary hardworking people. Director Simpson coscripted with Nelson; Weaver is his wife. [PG] ▼▶

Guys and Dolls (1955) **C-150m. ***** D: Joseph L. Mankiewicz. Marlon Brando, Jean Simmons, Frank Sinatra, Vivian Blaine, Stubby Kaye, B. S. Pully, Veda Ann Borg, Sheldon Leonard, Regis Toomey. Lavish Hollywoodization of classic Broadway musical based on Damon Runyon's colorful characters with Blaine, Kaye, Pully, and Johnny Silver reprising their stage performances and Brando making a not-bad musical debut as gambler Sky Masterson. Tuneful Frank Loesser score includes "Fugue for Tinhorns," "If I Were a Bell," "Luck Be a Lady," Blaine's memorable "Adelaide's Lament," and Stubby's show-stopping "Sit Down, You're Rockin' the Boat." CinemaScope. ▼●▶

Guy Thing, A (2003) **C-101m. *½** D: Chris Koch. Jason Lee, Julia Stiles, Selma Blair, James Brolin, Shawn Hatosy, Lochlyn Munro, Julie Hagerty, Diana Scarwid, Thomas Lennon, Jackie Burroughs. It took four writers to concoct this tiresome, derivative comedy of embarrassment about a guy who sleeps with a girl after his bachelor party—little dreaming she's his fiancée's cousin. Senseless from start to finish; even the likable leading ladies are wasted. Larry Miller appears unbilled. [PG-13] ▼▶

Guyver, The (1992-U.S.-Japanese) **C-92m. *½** D: Screaming Mad George, Steve Wang. Mark Hamill, Vivian Wu, Jack Armstrong, David Gale, Jimmie Walker, Michael Berryman, Peter Spollos, Spice Williams, Willard Pugh, Jeffrey Combs, David Wells, Linnea Quigley. All-American Armstrong, infected by an alien gadget, becomes an armored superhero; good thing, since almost everyone else in the movie can turn into a nightmarish monster. (CIA agent Hamill turns into a big cockroach.) Clumsy clumps of humor only make the contrived plot seem even more foolish. From a Japanese comic book. Followed by GUYVER: DARK HERO. [PG-13] ▼●▶

Guy With a Grin SEE: **No Time for Comedy**

Gymkata (1985) **C-90m. BOMB** D: Robert Clouse. Kurt Thomas, Tetchie Agbayani, Richard Norton, Edward Bell. Champion gymnast Thomas stars in this silly martial-arts potboiler, shot in Yugoslavia by the folks who brought you ENTER THE DRAGON. Amateurish stuff, based on Dan Tyler Moore's novel, *The Terrible Game*. [R] ▼◗

Gypsy (1962) **C-149m.** ******* D: Mervyn Le-Roy. Rosalind Russell, Natalie Wood, Karl Malden, Paul Wallace, Betty Bruce, Parley Baer, Harvey Korman. Entertaining screen version of bittersweet Broadway musical about the ultimate stage mother, Mama Rose, and her daughters Baby June (Havoc) and Gypsy Rose Lee. Can't lose with that Stephen Sondheim–Jule Styne score. Suzanne Cupito (Morgan Brittany) and Ann Jilliann (Jillian) both play young June. Remade as a TVM in 1993 with Bette Midler. Technirama. ▼◗▶

Gypsy Girl (1966-British) **C-102m.** ****½** D: John Mills. Hayley Mills, Ian McShane, Laurence Naismith, Geoffrey Bayldon. Brooding account of backward Hayley Mills finding her first romance with Mc-Shane; atmospheric but meandering. Originally titled SKY WEST AND CROOKED.

Gypsy Moths, The (1969) **C-110m.** ******* D: John Frankenheimer. Burt Lancaster, Deborah Kerr, Gene Hackman, Scott Wilson, Bonnie Bedelia, William Windom, Sheree North. Story of three skydivers in Kansas captures the Midwest well; Kerr, Wilson, and Bedelia help raise potential soap opera to a higher plane. [R] ▼◗▶

Hachi: A Dog's Tale (2010-U.S.-British) **C-93m.** ******* D: Lasse Hallström. Richard Gere, Joan Allen, Sarah Roemer, Jason Alexander, Cary-Hiroyuki Tagawa, Erick Avari. New England music professor, who commutes to work every day by train, finds an unclaimed Akita puppy at the station one night and takes him in. It doesn't take long for him to fall in love with the pooch, and Hachi becomes devoted to his master, so much so that he waits for him at the depot every afternoon—for years to come. Sweet, touching story, simply told, may bring tears to your eyes. Based on 1987 Japanese film HACHIKO MONOGATARI, which was inspired by a true story from the 1920s and '30s. Never released theatrically in the U.S.—for some strange reason. Aka HA-CHIKO: A DOG'S STORY. [G] ◗

Hackers (1995-U.S.-British) **C-105m.** ****½** D: Iain Softley. Jonny Lee Miller, Angelina Jolie, Fisher Stevens, Matthew Lillard, Laurence Mason, Jesse Bradford, Renoly Santiago, Alberta Watson, Lorraine Bracco, Wendell Pierce, Penn Jillette, Felicity Huffman, Marc Anthony. A group of young computer fanatics is framed for crimes committed by computer whiz and would-be master criminal Stevens, and have to use their own hacking skills to prove themselves innocent. No great shakes, but fast pace and vivid direction make it fun. Panavision. [PG-13] ▼◗◗

Hadley's Rebellion (1984) **C-96m.** ****** D: Fred Walton. Griffin O'Neal, William Dev-ane, Charles Durning, Adam Baldwin, Lisa Lucas. Another teenage-problem picture, this one centering on wrestling-obsessed O'Neal. Bland and superficial. [PG] ▼

Haiku Tunnel (2001) **C-90m.** ****½** D: Jacob Kornbluth, Josh Kornbluth. Josh Kornbluth, Warren Keith, Helen Shumaker, Amy Resnick, Brian Thorstenson, Sarah Overman, Harry Shearer. Small, fitfully amusing film about a temporary office worker and the struggle between "temps" and "perms." Leading actor/director Josh also cowrote the screenplay. [R] ▼◗

Hail Caesar (1993) **C-97m.** BOMB D: Anthony Michael Hall. Anthony Michael Hall, Robert Downey, Jr., Frank Gorshin, Samuel L. Jackson, Judd Nelson, Nicholas Pryor. Repulsive rock-star wannabe (Hall) is in love with an obnoxious debutante, whose father is involved in a plot to sabotage a peace conference. Astonishingly bad movie without a single likeable character; an inauspicious directing debut for Hall. Downey and Nelson, who get costar billing, have a total of six minutes' screen time. [PG] ▼◗

Hail! Hail! Rock 'n' Roll SEE: **Chuck Berry Hail! Hail! Rock 'n' Roll**

Hail, Hero! (1969) **C-97m.** ***½** D: David Miller. Michael Douglas, Arthur Kennedy, Teresa Wright, John Larch, Louise Latham, Charles Drake, Peter Strauss, Deborah Winters, Virginia Christine, John Qualen, Carmen Zapata. Talky, overblown drama about a well-scrubbed hippie (Douglas) who confronts his family as he sorts out his feelings about Vietnam war. Notable only as screen debuts for Douglas and Strauss, and a rare film contribution by musician Gordon Lightfoot, who composed and sings two songs. Originally 100m. [M/PG] ▼

Hail, Mafia (1965) **89m.** ****½** D: Raoul Levy. Henry Silva, Jack Klugman, Eddie Constantine, Elsa Martinelli, Micheline Presle. Fairly interesting melodrama about hired killers going after a witness to gangland mayhem; has some good European players and nice photography by Raoul Coutard. ▼◗

Hail Mary (1985-French-Swiss) **C-107m.** ***½** D: Jean-Luc Godard. Myriem Roussel, Thierry Rode, Philippe Lacoste, Manon Anderson, Juliette Binoche. Boring, overblown updating of the story of Christ's birth, with Mary a student/basketball player/ gas station attendant and Joseph her cabdriver boyfriend; although still a virgin, she finds herself pregnant. This film sparked much controversy and was even condemned by the Pope; however, all the fuss was much ado about very little. A variety of running times have been credited to this film, so beware; has been screened with THE BOOK OF MARY, an infinitely superior featurette about a girl and her bickering parents, directed by Godard associate Anne-Marie Mieville. ▼◗◗

Hail the Conquering Hero (1944) **101m.**
**** D: Preston Sturges. Eddie Bracken,
Ella Raines, Raymond Walburn, William
Demarest, Bill Edwards, Elizabeth Patterson,
Jimmy Conlin, Franklin Pangborn, Jack Nor-
ton, Paul Porcasi, Al Bridge, Freddie Steele.
Frail Bracken, rejected by Marine Corps, is
mistaken for war hero by home town. Satirical
Sturges at his best, with Demarest and Pang-
born stealing much of the crazed proceedings.
▼●◗

Hair (1979) **C-121m.** **½ D: Milos Forman. John Savage, Treat Williams, Beverly
D'Angelo, Annie Golden, Dorsey Wright,
Don Dacus, Cheryl Barnes, Nicholas Ray,
Charlotte Rae, Miles Chapin, Michael Jeter.
James Rado–Gerome Ragni–Galt MacDer-
mot's hit musical play celebrated the '60s as
the Age of Aquarius; unfortunately, it's now
a period piece and its impact considerably
muffled. Story of straitlaced midwesterner
who falls in with N.Y. hippies has exciting musical moments, but doesn't hang
together. Choreography by Twyla Tharp.
Among the singers: Nell Carter, Melba
Moore, Ellen Foley, Ronnie Dyson, Charlaine Woodard. [PG]▼●◗

Hairdresser's Husband, The (1990-French)
C-84m. *** D: Patrice Leconte. Jean Rochefort, Anna Galiena, Roland Bertin, Maurice
Chevit, Philippe Clevenot. Young boy with
a fixation on a bosomy haircutter grows up
to marry a woman who's practically a reincarnation of his childhood dream. Skillfully
assembled comedy-drama makes great use
of Rochefort's basset-hound face; slight but
charming. Definite U.S. remake possibilities. Panavision. [R]▼●

Hair High (2006) **C--75m.** **½ D: Bill
Plympton. Voices of Sarah Silverman,
Eric Gilliland, Dermot Mulroney, Beverly
D'Angelo, Zak Orth, Justin Long, Keith
Carradine, David Carradine, Martha Plimpton, Tom Noonan, Craig Bierko, Ed Begley, Jr., Matt Groening. The rose-colored
high school world of GREASE and *Happy
Days* is reimagined by animator Plympton,
though his fascination with anatomical grotesquerie doesn't seem an ideal fit for this
subject matter. Story tells of mismatched
high school classmates Spud, the bumbling
new kid in town, and Cherri, the pampered
cheerleader, and how they become sweethearts. A virtual one-man production, as
usual, for the talented animator-writer-
director-producer.

Hair Show (2004) **C-105m.** BOMB D:
Leslie Small. Mo'Nique, Kellita Smith,
Gina Torres, David Ramsey, Vivica A.
Fox, Tiny Lister, James Avery, John Salley, Roshumba Williams, Taraji P. Henson.
Insipid comedy finds loud, overbearing hair-
stylist (Mo'Nique) running to her sister's L.A.
salon to escape the I.R.S. Happy coincidence:
there's a hair design contest where the prize
money is the exact amount she owes. (Taxes

on winnings not included.) Yes, that's ten-
nis star Serena Williams in her film debut.
Coexecutive-produced by Earvin "Magic"
Johnson. [PG-13]◗

Hairspray (1988) **C-96m.** *** D: John Waters. Sonny Bono, Ruth Brown, Divine, Colleen Fitzpatrick, Michael St. Gerard, Debbie
Harry, Ricki Lake, Leslie Ann Powers, Jerry
Stiller, Shawn Thompson, Pia Zadora, Ric
Ocasek, John Waters. Shock/schlock merchant Waters goes PG, with irresistible
nostalgia satire about the integration of a
TV teen dance program in 1962 Baltimore.
"Name" performances include Harry as the
shellac-haired mother of a deposed local celebrity, Zadora as a pot-smoking Bohemian,
Brown as the owner of an r & b record store,
and director Waters as the deranged psychiatrist. Loses steam toward the end, but still
fun. Rich soundtrack mixes chestnuts and
deservedly unearthed oldies. Later a Broadway musical, which in turn was made into a
theatrical film in 2007. [PG]▼●◗

Hairspray (2007) **C-115m.** *** D: Adam
Shankman. John Travolta, Michelle Pfeiffer, Nikki Blonsky, Christopher Walken,
Queen Latifah, Amanda Bynes, Zac Efron,
Elijah Kelley, Brittany Snow, James Marsden, Allison Janney, Paul Dooley, Taylor
Parks, Jerry Stiller. Candy-colored musical
based on the Broadway adaptation of John
Waters' 1988 movie about Tracy Turnblad,
a perpetually cheerful teenage girl (newcomer Blonsky) in 1962 Baltimore whose
can-do attitude helps bring about change
all around her—even on the local teen-
dance TV show where whites and blacks
appear separately. Taking a cue from the
original film and show, Tracy's mother
Edna is played by a man in drag (Travolta).
Director-choreographer Shankman keeps
things moving; Waters and Ricki Lake (who
played Tracy in 1988) have cameos. Marc
Shaiman and Scott Wittman added new
songs to their Broadway score. Super 35.
[PG]◗

Half Angel (1951) **C-77m.** **½ D: Richard
Sale. Loretta Young, Joseph Cotten, Cecil
Kellaway, Basil Ruysdael, Jim Backus, Irene
Ryan, John Ridgely. Pleasant comedy of
Young blessed with sleepwalking troubles,
leading to romantic complications.

Half A Sixpence (1967) **C-148m.** *½ D:
George Sidney. Tommy Steele, Julia Foster, Penelope Horner, Cyril Ritchard, Grover
Dale. Boisterous but cardboard musical based
on show adapted from H. G. Wells' *Kipps*,
about draper's assistant who inherits fortune,
tries to crash society. Colorfully filmed in
England, but totally without charm. Story first
filmed in Britain (sans music) as KIPPS in
1941. Panavision.▼◗

Half Baked (1998) **C-85m.** *½ D: Tamra
Davis. Dave Chappelle, Jim Breuer, Har-
land Williams, Guillermo Diaz, Clarence
Williams III, Rachel True, Jon Stewart,

Tracy Morgan. Three potheads try to raise money for their buddy's release from jail by selling marijuana, without Chappelle's girlfriend finding out. Some surprisingly clever touches and attempts to moralize against drugs, completely overshadowed by Breuer's irritating character and general plot stupidity. Cameos include Steven Wright, Willie Nelson, Snoop Doggy Dogg, Tommy Chong, and Janeane Garofalo. [R]▼◐◗

Half-Breed, The (1952) C-81m. ** D: Stuart Gilmore. Robert Young, Janis Carter, Jack Buetel, Barton MacLane, Reed Hadley, Porter Hall. Unscrupulous profiteer incites Apaches to attack white settlers in this predictable Western.▼◗

Half Moon Street (1986) C-90m. BOMB D: Bob Swaim. Michael Caine, Sigourney Weaver, Keith Buckley, Patrick Kavanagh, Nadim Sawalha, Angus MacInnes. Intriguing premise has Weaver playing a Ph.D researcher by day and glorified call girl by night, Caine a British diplomat who becomes an extra special client. Sounds as if it can't miss, but is worthless on every level; perennially fresh Weaver gives the first stilted performance of her career. Adapted from *Doctor Slaughter,* the first half of Paul Theroux's two-part novella *Half Moon Street.* Look for Janet McTeer as a secretary. [R] ▼◐◗

Half Nelson (2006) C-106m. ***½ D: Ryan Fleck. Ryan Gosling, Shareeka Epps, Anthony Mackie, Deborah Rush, Jay O. Sanders, Tina Holmes, Denis O'Hare, Monique Curnen. Dedicated Brooklyn grade-school teacher tries to make a difference in the lives of his kids, and pays special attention to 13-year-old Drey (Epps), whom he fears is at risk of making the wrong choices. But she knows her teacher's darkest secret: he's a hopeless drug addict. Outstanding performances by Gosling and Epps anchor this riveting, intimate drama. Fleshed out from a short subject by director Fleck and cowriter Anna Boden. [R]◗

Half Past Dead (2002) C-99m. BOMB D: Don Michael Paul. Steven Seagal, Ja Rule, Morris Chestnut, Nia Peeples, Bruce Weitz, Tony Plana, Stephen J. Cannell, Claudia Christian, Mo'Nique. Seagal is an undercover FBI agent who arrives as an inmate at a prison on the same day a team of crooks—get this— break *into* the joint, to get a condemned man to tell them where there's a hidden stash of gold bars. To call this bad is an understatement . . . even by Seagal standards. Followed by a direct-to-video sequel. [PG-13]▼◗

Hallelujah (1929) 106m. ***½ D: King Vidor. Daniel L. Haynes, Nina Mae McKinney, William Fountaine, Everett McGarrity, Victoria Spivey. King Vidor's early talkie triumph, a stylized view of black life focusing on a Southern cotton-picker who becomes a preacher but retains all-too-human weaknesses. Dated in some aspects and unabashedly melodramatic, but still quite moving. Beautifully filmed on location, with outstanding musical sequences.▼◐◗

Hallelujah I'm a Bum (1933) 82m. ***½ D: Lewis Milestone. Al Jolson, Madge Evans, Frank Morgan, Harry Langdon, Chester Conklin, Tyler Brooke, Edgar Connor. Fascinating Depression curio about a hobo who tries to "reform" for the sake of a beautiful woman. Provocative, politically savvy script by Ben Hecht and S. N. Behrman, rhyming dialogue and lovely songs by Rodgers and Hart (who also make cameo appearances as a photographer and a bank clerk, respectively), and winning performances all around. Beware edited prints (reissue title: THE HEART OF NEW YORK) and the frequently screened British version, cut and redubbed as HALLELU-JAH I'M A TRAMP.▼◐◗

Hallelujah Trail, The (1965) C-165m. **½ D: John Sturges. Burt Lancaster, Lee Remick, Jim Hutton, Brian Keith, Martin Landau, Donald Pleasence, Pamela Tiffin; narrated by John Dehner. Remick is rambunctious temperance leader out to stop cavalry-guarded shipment of whiskey en route to thirsting Denver miners; amiable but lumbering western satire goes on and on. Ultra Panavision 70.▼◐◗

Halloween (1978) C-91m. *** D: John Carpenter. Donald Pleasence, Jamie Lee Curtis, Nancy Loomis, P. J. Soles, Charles Cyphers, Kyle Richards. Low-budget chiller about psychotic murderer who struck on Halloween as a child, and threatens to do so again 15 years later. Well made, with lots of scares, plus in-joke references for film buffs. Alternate 104m. version prepared for TV is available on video. Followed by several sequels and myriad clones. Curtis' feature film debut. Remade in 2007. Panavision. [R]▼◐◗

Halloween (2007) C-109m. ** D: Rob Zombie. Malcolm McDowell, Brad Dourif, Tyler Mane, Daeg Faerch, Sheri Moon Zombie, William Forsythe, Udo Kier, Richard Lynch, Clint Howard, Danny Trejo, Leslie Easterbrook, Bill Moseley, Sybil Danning, Dee Wallace, Micky Dolenz, Tom Towles, Sid Haig. Umpteenth rehash of the 1978 movie retells the story of Michael Myers, who kills his family and spends 17 years in a mental institution before escaping. As he searches for his younger sister he sets off on a rampage, treating the town of Haddonfield to his latest murderous tricks. Although horror fanatic Zombie remains faithful to the premise (with more backstory on Myers than ever before), it's clearly just an excuse to show off the latest advances in movie gore. Unrated version runs 121m. Zombie filmed a sequel, HALLOWEEN II, in 2009. Super 35. [R]◗

Halloween II (1981) C-92m. *½ D: Rick Rosenthal. Jamie Lee Curtis, Donald Pleasence, Charles Cyphers, Jeffrey Kramer,

Lance Guest, Pamela Susan Shoop, Dana Carvey. Explicitly bloody sequel is as bad as any of HALLOWEEN's countless clones, with maniac continuing to stalk Curtis on the same night on which the original ends. Scripted by John Carpenter and Debra Hill. Panavision. [R]▼●)

Halloween II (2009) **C-105m.** BOMB D: Rob Zombie. Malcolm McDowell, Tyler Mane, Sheri Moon Zombie, Brad Dourif, Danielle Harris, Brea Grant, Howard Hesseman, Scout Taylor-Compton, Angela Trimbur, Mary Birdsong, Daniel Roebuck, Bill Fagerbakke, Richard Brake, Dayton Callie, Margot Kidder, ("Weird") Al Yankovic. Michael Myers is back on the gory warpath in this lumbering sequel to Zombie's 2007 HALLOWEEN. There are pitifully few genuine scares . . . just a lot of blood and utterances of the "f" word. Unrated director's cut runs 119m. [R]❙

Halloween III: Season of the Witch (1982) **C-96m.** BOMB D: Tommy Lee Wallace. Tom Atkins, Stacey Nelkin, Dan O'Herlihy, Ralph Strait, Michael Currie. Genuinely repellent '80s-style horror film, with gore galore (after a slow start), about a maniacal plot to murder millions of children on Halloween. Nice, huh? No relation to either of the earlier HALLOWEEN films, but owes more than a bit to INVASION OF THE BODY SNATCHERS. Panavision. [R]▼●)

Halloween 4: The Return of Michael Myers (1988) **C-88m.** ** D: Dwight H. Little. Donald Pleasence, Ellie Cornell, Danielle Harris, George P. Wilbur, Michael Pataki, Beau Starr, Kathleen Kinmont. Unkillable monster is back, this time mindlessly headed for his hometown to murder his niece (young Harris). Standard horror thriller is technically well made but offers little novelty. [R]▼●)

Halloween 5 (1989) **C-96m.** *½ D: Dominique Othenin-Girard. Donald Pleasence, Danielle Harris, Donald L. Shanks, Wendy Kaplan, Ellie Cornell, Jeffrey Landman. Slightly more plot than before but still just a sequential slaughter of teenagers as Michael Myers (Shanks) again sets out to kill his young niece (Harris). Routine and plodding, with too many endings and unnecessary setup for sequel. [R]▼●)

Halloween H20: 20 Years Later (1998) **C-85m.** *** D: Steve Miner. Jamie Lee Curtis, Adam Arkin, Josh Hartnett, Michelle Williams, Adam Hann-Byrd, Jodi Lyn O'Keefe, Janet Leigh, LL Cool J, Chris Durand, Joseph Gordon-Levitt. Twenty years after the killings in HALLOWEEN, Laurie Strode (Curtis) has built a new life for herself and her son, but her psychotic brother Michael Myers is after her again with a big sharp knife. Surprisingly good belated sequel is plenty scary, and has a nice sense of humor (note Leigh's car), but the plot could

have used more complications. Curtis, who suggested this project, gives a terrific performance. Super 35. [R]▼●)

Halloween: Resurrection (2002) **C-89m.** *½ D: Rick Rosenthal. Jamie Lee Curtis, Brad Loree, Busta Rhymes, Bianca Kajlich, Sean Patrick Thomas, Daisy McCrackin, Thomas Ian Nicholas, Tyra Banks, Ryan Merriman. Six young people are chosen to spend a night in Michael Myers' childhood home, with Web cams watching their every move. Mayhem ensues. Forget logic, story construction, consistency of characterization—the filmmakers certainly did! This movie franchise shoulda stayed dead. Curtis is only here for her name value; the director appears as a college professor. Super 35. [R]▼)

Halloween: The Curse of Michael Myers (1995) **C-88m.** *½ D: Joe Chappelle. Donald Pleasence, Paul Stephen Rudd, Marianne Hagan, Mitchell Ryan, Kim Darby, Bradford English, Keith Bogart, Mariah O'Brien. Pursued by the masked killer, Michael's niece escapes from mysterious catacombs with her newborn baby. Then he starts killing a family which has the misfortune merely to live in his former home. Routine slash-fest, of interest only to the dedicated, even though this time it links Michael to the Druids! [R]▼●)

Halloween Party SEE: **Night of the Demons**

Hall Pass (2011) **C-105m.** *½ D: Bobby Farrelly, Peter Farrelly. Owen Wilson, Jason Sudeikis, Jenna Fischer, Christina Applegate, Stephen Merchant, Richard Jenkins, Larry Joe Campbell, Bruce Thomas, Derek Waters, Tyler Hoechlin, Rob Moran, Joy Behar, Alyssa Milano. On the advice of her mentor, a woman (Fischer) gives her husband (Wilson) a week off from marriage during which he may do whatever he wants with whomever he wants. A viable comedy concept, but the Farrellys always find a way to ruin a good moment with an unfunny and unnecessary dirty joke. Unattractive in every way. Alternate version runs 111m. Super 35. [R]❙

Halls of Anger (1970) **C-96m.** **½ D: Paul Bogart. Calvin Lockhart, Janet MacLachlan, James A. Watson, Jr., Rob Reiner, Jeff Bridges, Edward Asner. Standard violence-in-school story, but with a racial angle. No better or worse than a dozen other similar films. [M/PG]

Halls of Montezuma (1951) **C-113m.** *** D: Lewis Milestone. Richard Widmark, Karl Malden, Walter (Jack) Palance, Reginald Gardiner, Robert Wagner, Richard Hylton, Richard Boone, Skip Homeier, Jack Webb, Bert Freed, Neville Brand, Martin Milner, Philip Ahn. Gung-ho salute to the U.S. Marines as a squadron embarks on a typically rugged WW2 Pacific island invasion, with flashbacks to various men's civilian lives. Especially notable for a cast filled with future stars . . . including real-life ex-Marine Brand. ▼◗

Hambone and Hillie (1984) **C-89m.** **½ D: Roy Watts. Lillian Gish, Timothy Bottoms, Candy Clark, O. J. Simpson, Robert Walker, Jack Carter, Alan Hale, Anne Lockhart. Elderly Gish loses her devoted mutt at an airport and he races cross-country to find her. Sugar-coated soaper is no dog, but is also no BENJI. [PG] ▼

Hamburger Hill (1987) **C-110m.** ** D: John Irvin. Anthony Barrile, Michael Patrick Boatman, Don Cheadle, Michael Dolan, Don James, Dylan McDermott, M. A. Nickles, Tim Quill, Courtney B. Vance, Steven Weber. Cold, clinical, yet occasionally preachy re-creation of some true-life 1969 Vietnam carnage, with troops of the 101st Airborne Division encountering the enemy in mutual slaughter for the title reward. Authentic, with expertly staged battle scenes—but limited in its emotional power. Scripted by Jim Carabatsos. [R] ▼◗

Hamlet (1948-British) **153m.** **** D: Laurence Olivier. Laurence Olivier, Eileen Herlie, Basil Sydney, Felix Aylmer, Jean Simmons, Stanley Holloway, Peter Cushing. Brilliant adaptation of Shakespeare's play about Danish prince "who just couldn't make up his mind." Won Oscars for Best Picture, Best Actor (Olivier), Art Direction–Set Decoration, and Costumes. ▼

Hamlet (1969-British) **C-114m.** **½ D: Tony Richardson. Nicol Williamson, Gordon Jackson, Anthony Hopkins, Judy Parfitt, Mark Dignam, Marianne Faithfull. Richardson and Williamson moved their boisterous interpretation of the Shakespeare play from stage to screen with only fair results; perhaps the irritating overuse of close-ups will play better on TV. Interesting casting of Faithfull as Ophelia. [G] ▼

Hamlet (1990) **C-135m.** *** D: Franco Zeffirelli. Mel Gibson, Glenn Close, Alan Bates, Paul Scofield, Ian Holm, Helena Bonham Carter, Stephen Dillane, Nathaniel Parker, John McEnery. Agreeable re-do of the Shakespeare staple with Gibson giving an energetic interpretation of the Melancholy Dane. In fact, Mel comes off better than costar Close (Gertrude); Bates, as Claudius, is the standout in the stellar cast. Never as enthralling or perceptive as Kenneth Branagh's HENRY V, but still worthwhile. [PG] ▼◗

Hamlet (1996-U.S.-British) **C-242m.** *** D: Kenneth Branagh. Kenneth Branagh, Julie Christie, Derek Jacobi, Kate Winslet, Rufus Sewell, Richard Briers, Brian Blessed, Gérard Depardieu, Charlton Heston, Rosemary Harris, Jack Lemmon, Billy Crystal, Robin Williams, Richard Attenborough, Nicholas Farrell, John Gielgud, John Mills, Rowena King. Branagh's unexpurgated Bard workout is a movie of moments and mixed blessings, with the story's updating—to the second half of the 19th century—doing a lot to

defuse any criticism of its stunt casting. Jacobi (Claudius), Christie (Gertrude), and Winslet (Ophelia) come off extremely well, though Branagh essentially gives a stage performance that's nearly as cinematically over the top as some of his directorial touches. Guest star turns are extremely variable. Gorgeously shot in 70mm by Alex Thomson. Panavision Super 70. [PG-13] ▼◗

Hamlet (2000) **C-112m.** ** D: Michael Almereyda. Ethan Hawke, Kyle MacLachlan, Sam Shepard, Diane Venora, Bill Murray, Liev Schreiber, Julia Stiles, Karl Geary, Steve Zahn, Dechen Thurman, Jeffrey Wright, Paul Bartel, Casey Affleck. Transplant of Shakespeare's timeless play to modern-day N.Y.C., where the head of the Denmark Corporation has died, adds nothing to our understanding or appreciation of the story. Some clever gags and stunt casting score occasional points. Hawke, sporting a ski cap through much of the action, is easily outshone by Schreiber (as Laertes), MacLachlan (as Claudius), and Stiles (an impressive Ophelia). [R] ▼◗

Hamlet 2 (2008) **C-94m.** **½ D: Andrew Fleming. Steve Coogan, Catherine Keener, David Arquette, Amy Poehler, Melonie Diaz, Joseph Julian Soria, Skylar Astin, Phoebe Strole, Elisabeth Shue, Marshall Bell; narrated (uncredited) by Jeremy Irons. Twisted comedy about an overly earnest—but spectacularly untalented—high school drama teacher. When he's given notice, he decides to go out with a bang, and stirs up his unmotivated students to join him in a painfully autobiographical, and plainly blasphemous, concoction called *Hamlet 2.* Wildly inconsistent, this does have some very funny moments, with Coogan perfectly cast as the clueless hero. The film also offers a neat showcase for Shue, playing "herself." [R]◗

Hammer (1972) **C-92m.** *½ D: Bruce Clark. Fred Williamson, Bernie Hamilton, Vonetta McGee, William Smith, Charles Lampkin. Black boxer takes on the syndicate in fast, but mindless melodrama. Some violence may be cut. [R]◗

Hammer, The (2008) **C-90m.** **½ D: Charles Herman-Wurmfeld. Adam Carolla, Oswaldo Castillo, Heather Juergensen, Harold "House" Moore, Tom Quinn, Jonathan Hernandez. A once promising fighter, now 40 and aimlessly working at construction jobs, gets A Second Chance with a shot at making the Olympic boxing team. Modest, likable sports comedy trots out every cinematic underdog cliché, but comedian–radio host Carolla (who wrote the story and is a former Golden Gloves fighter) keeps things percolating with his sardonic working-class persona and scores some genuine laughs. Jane Lynch appears unbilled. [R]◗

Hammersmith Is Out (1972) **C-108m.** ** D: Peter Ustinov. Elizabeth Taylor, Richard

Burton, Peter Ustinov, Beau Bridges, Leon Askin, Leon Ames, John Schuck, George Raft. Grotesque comedy about mental patient, his male nurse, and a hash slinger proves once again that Liz and Dick would do anything for money; cast has more fun than viewers in this variation on the Faust legend. [R]▼

Hammers Over the Anvil (1994-Australian) **C-97m.** **½ D: Ann Turner. Charlotte Rampling, Russell Crowe, Alexander Outhred, Frankie J. Holden, Frank Gallacher. Too much narration hampers this heartfelt tale of a crippled boy coming of age in early-20th-century rural Australia. Crowe exudes charisma as a free-spirited but emotionally vulnerable horse breaker. Watch this and you'll see why he became an international star.▼▶

Hammett (1982) **C-97m.** *** D: Wim Wenders. Frederic Forrest, Peter Boyle, Marilu Henner, Elisha Cook, R. G. Armstrong, Richard Bradford, Roy Kinnear, Lydia Lei, Sylvia Sidney, Samuel Fuller, Royal Dano. Wenders' first American film is a real treat for detective buffs: an adaptation of Joe Gores' fiction about famed author Dashiell Hammett's involvement in a real-life mystery (elements of which would find their way into his later stories). You couldn't ask for a more faithful re-creation of 1930s studio look; a magnificent-looking (and sounding) film. [PG]▼▶

Hamster of Happiness, The SEE: **Second-Hand Hearts**

Hamsun (1996-Norwegian-Swedish-German) **C-152m.** ***½ D: Jan Troell. Max von Sydow, Ghita Nørby, Anette Hoff, Asa Soderling, Gard B. Eidsvold, Eindride Eidsvold. Famed Norwegian author Knut Hamsun (von Sydow), winner of the 1920 Nobel Prize, supported the Nazi takeover of his own country. This thoughtful film illuminates the combination of naïveté, arrogance, and nationalism that led to his sorry choice. Entire cast is excellent, but von Sydow and Nørby (as his ego-starved wife) are brilliant, and the movie deserves to be better known. Based on a book by Thorkild Hansen.▼▶

Hana-Bi SEE: **Fireworks**

Hancock (2008) **C-92m.** *½ D: Peter Berg. Will Smith, Charlize Theron, Jason Bateman, Eddie Marsan, Johnny Galecki, Thomas Lennon, Jae Head. Foul, wrongheaded "comedy" about a drunken, antisocial superhero and a struggling p.r. man (Bateman) who tries to rehabilitate him. It's bad enough that the material stinks, but director Berg shoots it in nausea-inducing handheld style, with pointless macro-close-ups of the actors. Woe to parents who share this with their kids in the misguided belief that it's going to be fun. Film's coproducers Michael Mann and Akiva Goldsman appear briefly. HD Widescreen. [PG-13]▶

Hand, The (1981) **C-104m.** *½ D: Oliver Stone. Michael Caine, Andrea Marcovicci, Annie McEnroe, Bruce McGill, Viveca Lindfors, Rosemary Murphy, Mara Hobel, Pat Corley, Charles Fleischer. Cartoonist Caine's drawing hand is severed in auto accident, which destroys his career and places additional strain on his shaky marriage. Life becomes even more nightmarish when the hand returns on a murderous spree; unfortunately it didn't get Caine or writer-director Stone. Stone plays a bum who gets killed. [R] ▼▶●

Handful of Dust, A (1988-British) **C-118m.** ***½ D: Charles Sturridge. James Wilby, Kristin Scott Thomas, Rupert Graves, Judi Dench, Anjelica Huston, Alec Guinness, Pip Torrens, Cathryn Harrison. Rich adaptation of Evelyn Waugh's ironic story about a doomed marriage among England's smart set in the early 1930s, and the unexpected results for both the stiflingly tradition-bound husband (brilliantly and movingly played by Wilby) and the nonchalantly selfish wife (perfectly essayed by Thomas). Superior script by Tim Sullivan, Derek Granger, and Sturridge is matched by an unerring eye for period detail. [PG]▼▶

Handgun SEE: **Deep in the Heart**

Handle With Care (1977) **C-98m.** *** D: Jonathan Demme. Paul LeMat, Candy Clark, Ann Wedgeworth, Marcia Rodd, Charles Napier, Alix Elias, Roberts Blossom, Ed Begley, Jr. Fine character studies and vignettes make up for shortcomings in bright, original film. Loosely revolves around LeMat and his obsession with C.B. radio; subplot with bigamist truckdriver is hilarious. Written by Paul Brickman. Originally released as CITIZENS BAND. [PG]▼

Handmaid's Tale, The (1990) **C-109m.** **½ D: Volker Schlöndorff. Natasha Richardson, Robert Duvall, Faye Dunaway, Aidan Quinn, Elizabeth McGovern, Victoria Tennant, Blanche Baker, Traci Lind. Intriguing story set in a near-future world in which young, healthy white women are brainwashed to become bearers of babies for a new, "pure" generation. Richardson must overcome the jealousy of an infertile wife (Dunaway) while fending off the advances of her high-powered husband (Duvall). Interesting but best described as sterile. Scripted by Harold Pinter from the novel by Margaret Atwood. David Dukes appears unbilled as a doctor. [R]▼▶●

Hands Across the Table (1935) **80m.** *** D: Mitchell Leisen. Carole Lombard, Fred MacMurray, Ralph Bellamy, Astrid Allwyn, Marie Prevost. Lombard sparkles as fortune-hunting manicurist who has to choose between glib gigolo MacMurray and wheelchair-bound Bellamy.▼▶

Hands of Death SEE: **Beyond the Living**

Hands of Orlac, The (1960-British-French) **95m.** ** D: Edmond T. Greville. Mel Ferrer, Lucile Saint-Simon, Christopher Lee, Dany Carrel, Felix Aylmer, Basil Sydney, Donald Wolfit, Donald Pleasence. Pianist gets hand transplant from a strange doctor—and finds he has the impulse to kill. Flat remake of Maurice Renard's famous story, filmed before in 1925 and (as MAD LOVE) in 1935. French-language version runs 105m. Also known as HANDS OF THE STRANGLER. ▼●

Hands of the Ripper (1971-British) **C-85m.** **½ D: Peter Sasdy. Eric Porter, Angharad Rees, Jane Merrow, Keith Bell, Derek Godfrey. Early believer in Freud tries to help young daughter of Jack the Ripper. Great atmosphere, solid performances, but after good start, dissolves into series of bloody murders. [R] ▼

Hands of the Strangler SEE: **Hands of Orlac, The**

Hands over the City (1963-Italian) **101m.** *** D: Francesco Rosi. Rod Steiger, Salvo Randone, Guido Alberti, Marcello Cannavale, Dante Di Pinto, Alberto Conocchia, Carlo Fermariello, Terenzio Cordova. The collapse of a building in a Naples slum triggers a series of shady political schemes and backroom deals, as a ruthless land developer (Steiger) uses his position as a city councilman to manipulate the investigation to his advantage. Fiery critique of civic corruption and capitalist greed in the name of "progress" is vividly filmed on location, using many real-life Neapolitan politicians in the cast.▶

Hand That Rocks the Cradle, The (1992) **C-110m.** ** D: Curtis Hanson. Annabella Sciorra, Rebecca De Mornay, Matt McCoy, Ernie Hudson, Julianne Moore, Madeline Zima, John de Lancie, Mitchell Laurance. Demented, revenge-seeking nanny De Mornay takes a job with unsuspecting married couple Sciorra and McCoy—guess what happens next. Some good performances (especially by De Mornay) boost this otherwise derivative shocker. Tension builds, but gruesome finale is fairly predictable. McCoy may be the most sensitive screen husband of the early '90s. [R] ▼●

Handyman, The (1980-Canadian) **C-99m.** ***½ D: Micheline Lanctot. Jocelyn Berube, Andree Pelletier, Jannette Bertrand, Paul Dion, Marcel Sabourin. Shy, boyish, romantic Berube—he's not exactly short, but other men seem to tower over him—has a love affair with a married woman. A sad, beautifully made little film about people who can never get what they want because they are unable to take stands.

Hangar 18 (1980) **C-93m.** *½ D: James L. Conway. Darren McGavin, Robert Vaughn, Gary Collins, James Hampton, Philip Abbott, Joseph Campanella, Pamela Bellwood, Steven Keats, Tom Hallick, William Schallert. This Sunn Classic Picture alleges that the U.S. government is concealing a captured UFO. Slickly made, but about as credible as THE THREE STOOGES IN ORBIT; shown on TV as INVASION FORCE with new ending that undermines entire film! [PG] ▼●

Hang 'em High (1968) **C-114m.** **½ D: Ted Post. Clint Eastwood, Inger Stevens, Ed Begley, Pat Hingle, Arlene Golonka, James MacArthur, Ruth White, Ben Johnson, Charles McGraw, Bruce Dern, Alan Hale Jr., Dennis Hopper, Bob Steele. Slick American attempt at spaghetti Western comes off fairly well. Eastwood survives his own hanging, swears vengeance on nine men who lynched him. Fine supporting cast; nice cameo by James Westerfield as a fellow dungeon prisoner. [M] ▼●

Hanging Garden, The (1997-Canadian) **C-91m.** *** D: Thom Fitzgerald. Chris Leavins, Kerry Fox, Seana McKenna, Peter McNeill, Christine Dunsworth, Troy Veinotte, Sarah Polley, Joel S. Keller, Joan Orenstein. Strikingly original, multi-layered psychological drama about Sweet William, the product of a dysfunctional family, who returns home after a ten-year absence to attend his sister's wedding. The film moves in and out of reality, and between present and past; a telling exploration of the complexities and emotional truths of family relationships. [R] ▼

Hanging Tree, The (1959) **C-106m.** *** D: Delmer Daves. Gary Cooper, Maria Schell, Karl Malden, George C. Scott, Karl Swenson, Ben Piazza, Virginia Gregg. Literate, low-key Western with outstanding performance by Schell as a blind girl nursed by Cooper, a frontier doctor with a past. Not for all tastes. Scott's first film. ▼

Hanging Up (2000) **C-94m.** BOMB D: Diane Keaton. Meg Ryan, Diane Keaton, Lisa Kudrow, Walter Matthau, Adam Arkin, Duke Moosekian, Ann Bortolotti, Cloris Leachman. Three sisters live most of their lives via cell phone, but Ryan finds herself the only one willing to bear responsibility for their father, who's hospitalized and senile. It's hard to think of a movie with more strident, obnoxious characters, or a script that makes so little sense from scene to scene. Three appealing stars are hung out to dry in this seriocomedy, written by Nora and Delia Ephron, from Delia's book. Matthau's final film. [PG-13] ▼▶

Hangin' With the Homeboys (1991) **C-88m.** *** D: Joseph P. Vasquez. Doug E. Doug, Mario Joyner, John Leguizamo, Nestor Serrano, Kimberly Russell, Mary B. Ward. Jarringly honest, energetically directed and acted account of a day in the lives of several young African-Americans and Puerto Ricans who've grown up on the mean streets of the South Bronx. Each is different, but all are linked in that they're traveling down a road to nowhere. [R] ▼●◗

Hangman, The (1959) **86m.** ** D: Michael Curtiz. Robert Taylor, Tina Louise, Fess Parker, Jack Lord, Mickey Shaughnessy, Shirley Harmer. Rugged Taylor is the lawman who must buck the entire Western town defending a man wanted for murder.

Hangmen Also Die! (1943) **134m.** **½ D: Fritz Lang. Brian Donlevy, Walter Brennan, Anna Lee, Gene Lockhart, Dennis O'Keefe, Lionel Stander. OK WW2 drama, loosely based on fact and spotlighting the resistance by Czech citizens against their Nazi occupiers and the plight of Donlevy after he assassinates Reinhard Heydrich, Nazi governor of Prague. Based on a story by Lang and Bertolt Brecht, which is also told in HITLER'S MADMAN. German version runs a minute longer. ▼◗

Hangover, The (2009) **C-100m.** *** D: Todd Phillips. Bradley Cooper, Ed Helms, Zach Galifianakis, Justin Bartha, Heather Graham, Sasha Barrese, Jeffrey Tambor, Ken Jeong, Rachael Harris, Mike Tyson, Mike Epps, Rob Riggle, Cleo King. Hilarious comedy about two pals—and a creepy brother-in-law-to-be—who accompany their friend to Las Vegas for a bachelor party. The morning after a wild night they wake up in a stupor, unable to remember anything that happened, and discover that the groom is gone. Occasionally raunchy but ingeniously plotted and well acted, this frantic farce never runs out of wild, funny ideas right through the closing credits. Screenplay by Jon Lucas and Scott Moore. Unrated version runs 108m. Followed by a sequel. Super 35. [R]◗

Hangover Part II, The (2011) **C-102m.** *½ D: Todd Phillips. Bradley Cooper, Ed Helms, Zach Galifianakis, Justin Bartha, Ken Jeong, Paul Giamatti, Jeffrey Tambor, Mason Lee, Jamie Chung, Sasha Barrese, Nirut Sirichanya, Nick Cassavetes, Mike Tyson. The "wolf pack" buddies travel to Thailand, where Helms is to be married, but the night before the wedding they go on a bender they cannot remember the next morning—and manage to lose the bride's 16-year-old brother altogether. Inevitable sequel to the box-office hit not only recycles its storyline, substituting Bangkok for Las Vegas, but forgets to include the most important ingredient: laughs. This could be the poster child for lame Hollywood sequels. Super 35. [R]

Hangover Square (1945) **77m.** *** D: John Brahm. Laird Cregar, Linda Darnell, George Sanders, Glenn Langan, Faye Marlowe, Alan Napier, Frederic Worlock. Cregar (in his final film) is delicious as unhinged composer who goes off his top and kills women whenever he hears loud, discordant noises. Barre Lyndon's script bears little relation to the Patrick Hamilton novel, but result is still entertaining, with superb Victorian London sets and evocative Bernard Herrmann score.◗

Hangup (1974) **C-94m.** ** D: Henry Hathaway. William Elliott, Marki Bey, Cliff Potts, Michael Lerner, Timothy Blake. Disappointing black-oriented actioner about a drug racket; Hathaway has done many fine films, but this, his last, isn't one. Bey is good as a doomed prostitute. Aka SUPER DUDE. [R]

Hanky Panky (1982) **C-110m.** *½ D: Sidney Poitier. Gene Wilder, Gilda Radner, Kathleen Quinlan, Richard Widmark, Robert Prosky, Josef Sommer, Johnny Sekka. Innocent architect Wilder is chased by spies, cops, etc. Predictable, barely funny comedy-thriller, with Radner miscast as the love interest. (The film was intended to be a follow-up to STIR CRAZY, but Richard Pryor's part was rewritten for Gilda.) You've seen it all before, and better. [PG]▼●◗

Hanna (2011-U.S.-German) **C-111m.** *** D: Joe Wright. Saoirse Ronan, Eric Bana, Cate Blanchett, Tom Hollander, Olivia Williams, Jason Flemyng, Jessica Barden. Teenage girl is raised in the wintry wilderness by her father, an ex-CIA operative who teaches her extreme survival skills. When she decides it's time to experience the real world for the first time, American agent Blanchett goes after her and her father, willing to kill either or both of them, for reasons that eventually become clear. Opens with a bang and barely ever lets up, with Ronan ably carrying much of the breathless action; she is also the heartbeat of the story, which becomes a bit conventional as the film wraps up. Super 35. [PG-13] ◗

Hannah and Her Sisters (1986) **C-106m.** ***½ D: Woody Allen. Woody Allen, Michael Caine, Mia Farrow, Carrie Fisher, Barbara Hershey, Lloyd Nolan, Maureen O'Sullivan, Daniel Stern, Max von Sydow, Dianne Wiest, J.T. Walsh, Richard Jenkins, Julie Kavner, Julia Louis-Dreyfus, John Turturro, Joanna Gleason, Bobby Short, Christian Clemenson. Allen strikes gold as he examines some typically interesting and neurotic New Yorkers whose lives intertwine. Superbly cast with Woody in peak form as Farrow's hypochondriac ex-husband; Wiest in a powerhouse performance as Mia's self-consumed, self-destructive sister. There's also an atypical Allen touch of warmth, even sentiment, as frosting on the cake—all of it set to some wonderful old songs. Academy Award winner for Best Supporting Actor (Caine), Best Supporting Actress (Wiest), and Woody's Original Screenplay. Tony Roberts and Sam Waterston appear unbilled. One of the children at the Thanksgiving celebrations is Soon-Yi Previn. [PG-13]▼●◗

Hannah Montana: The Movie (2009) **C-102m.** **½ D: Peter Chelsom. Miley Cyrus, Billy Ray Cyrus, Emily Osment, Jason Earles, Mitchel Musso, Moises Arias, Lucas Till, Vanessa Williams, Margo Martindale, Peter Gunn, Melora Hardin, Barry Bostwick, Jane Carr, Taylor Swift, Rascal Flatts. Feature version of popular Disney Channel TV series about a girl named Miley who leads a double life, as an average teen and (with blond wig) as pop star Hannah Montana. But when her dad (played by real-life dad Cyrus) takes her home to her grandmother's farm in Tennessee she finds it difficult to shed her alter ego and the trappings that go with it. Innocuous song-filled fare should please the show's young fans—but it's too bad the slapstick gags are staged so poorly. [G]◗

Hannah Takes the Stairs (2007) **C-83m.** BOMB D: Joe Swanberg. Greta Gerwig, Kent Osborne, Andrew Bujalski, Ry Russo-Young, Mark Duplass. Patience-testing time-waster is every bit as unfocused and self-indulgent as its eponymous heroine, a Chicago production company employee (gratingly played by Gerwig) who wanders through a series of short-lived relationships that aren't romances so much as crushes with benefits. If you're curious about the so-called Mumblecore genre of improvised indie films about aimless 20-somethings you're better off checking out Bujalski's MUTUAL APPRECIATION.◗

Hanna K. (1983-French) **C-108m.** ** D: Constantine Costa-Gavras. Jill Clayburgh, Jean Yanne, Gabriel Byrne, Mohammed Bakri, David Clennon. Intriguing but unsatisfying melodrama about flaky lawyer Clayburgh and her conflicting relationships with ex-husband Yanne, Israeli district attorney Byrne, and Palestinian Bakri, who's attempting to reclaim his ancestral home. Controversial because of its pro-Palestinian stand, but on artistic terms a major disappointment from Costa-Gavras. [R]▼

Hanna's War (1988) **C-148m.** *½ D: Menahem Golan. Ellen Burstyn, Maruschka Detmers, Anthony Andrews, Donald Pleasence, David Warner, Denholm Elliott, Vincenzo Ricotta, Ingrid Pitt. The true story of Hungarian freedom fighter Hanna Senesh (Detmers), based in part on her diaries, is a misguided mess. The young, Jewish WW2 martyr deserved a far better production than this overlong, uninspiring melodrama. Hanna's prison-issue designer blouses don't help matters. Panavision. [PG-13]▼●

Hannibal (1959-U.S.-Italian) **C-103m.** ** D: Edgar G. Ulmer. Victor Mature, Rita Gam, Gabriele Ferzetti, Milly Vitale. Cardboard costume saga follows Hannibal and his elephants across the Alps and into Rome . . . but *you* may not last that long. SuperCinescope.◗

Hannibal (2001) **C-132m.** ** D: Ridley Scott. Anthony Hopkins, Julianne Moore, Ray Liotta, Giancarlo Giannini, Gary Oldman, Frankie R. Faison, Francesca Neri, Željko Ivanek, Hazelle Goodman. A big, long tease of a movie, quite unlike its predecessor, SILENCE OF THE LAMBS, though mostly faithful to Thomas Harris' novel. Hannibal Lecter, now at large in Florence,

Italy, reenters the life of FBI agent Clarice Starling (Moore, taking over for Jodie Foster) at a troubled time in her career. A twisted, unfocused black comedy, stylish but slowly paced, with several key gross-out moments. Scripted by David Mamet and Steven Zaillian. Followed by a prequel: RED DRAGON. [R]▼◗

Hannibal Brooks (1969-British) **C-101m.** **½ D: Michael Winner. Oliver Reed, Michael J. Pollard, Wolfgang Preiss, Helmut Lohner, Karin Baal, Peter Karsten. Pleasant, forgettable film of British P.O.W. Reed assigned to evacuate valuable elephant from Munich zoo during WW2; forced to go on foot, he turns trip into escape plan. Wavers from comedy to melodrama, with Pollard major comic character; good action climax. [M/PG]

Hannibal Rising (2007-Italian-U.S.-French-Czech-Italian) **C-121m.** *½ D: Peter Webber. Gaspard Ulliel, Rhys Ifans, Gong Li, Helena Lia Tachovska, Dominic West, Aaron Thomas, Kevin McKidd, Richard Brake. The Secret Origin of Hannibal Lecter: as a child at the end of WW2 he had to watch while Nazi collaborators ate his younger sister! As a young adult (Ulliel), inspired by his Japanese aunt, he hunts down the killers and exacts brutal revenge. Handsome but ponderous, dull and self-important, though never as gory as might be expected. Scripted by Thomas Harris from his own novel. Ulliel never recalls Brian Cox, much less Anthony Hopkins. Super 35. [R]◗

Hannie Caulder (1971-British) **C-85m.** **½ D: Burt Kennedy. Raquel Welch, Robert Culp, Ernest Borgnine, Jack Elam, Strother Martin, Christopher Lee, Diana Dors. Bizarre, mystical Western about raped/widowed/homeless woman who begs bounty hunter Culp to teach her to shoot so she can seek vengeance. Neat idea to have bad guys Borgnine, Elam, and Martin play it a la The Three Stooges, but laughter is vitiated by their gory killings. Nice turn by Lee as sympathetic gunsmith. Panavision. [R]▼●◗

Hanoi Hilton, The (1987) **C-130m.** *½ D: Lionel Chetwynd. Michael Moriarty, Paul LeMat, Jeffrey Jones, Lawrence Pressman, Stephen Davies, David Soul, Rick Fitts. What may have been a sincere effort to dramatize the plight of American POWs in Vietnam becomes an unbearably dull, impossibly overlong, and embarrassingly clichéd drama, which does a real disservice to its subject . . . and throws in right-wing polemics and potshots at Jane Fonda to boot. [R]▼●◗

Hanover Street (1979) **C-109m.** ** D: Peter Hyams. Harrison Ford, Lesley-Anne Down, Christopher Plummer, Alec McCowen, Richard Masur, Michael Sacks. WW2 romance between married Englishwoman and American soldier who's sent on daring mission behind enemy lines is slick but contrived and unconvincing. Script by director Hyams. Panavision.[PG]▼●◗

Hans Christian Andersen (1952) **C-112m.** **½ D: Charles Vidor. Danny Kaye, Farley Granger, Jeanmaire, Roland Petit, John Qualen. Melodic Frank Loesser score ("Inchworm," "Ugly Duckling," "Thumbelina," etc.) can't save musical biography of vagabond tale-teller. Glossy and completely fabricated—has no relation to real Andersen's life story. ▼●◗

Hansel & Gretel (2002) **C-88m.** BOMB D: Gary J. Tunnicliffe. Jacob Smith, Taylor Momsen, Lynn Redgrave, Howie Mandel, Delta Burke, Gerald McRaney, Dakota Fanning; voices of Sinbad, Tom Arnold, Bobcat Goldthwait. Lame live-action rendition of the classic tale is not particularly faithful to the Brothers Grimm. It's also cheap-looking, lowbrow, and jokey. Arriscope. [PG] ▼◗

Hanussen (1988-German-Hungarian) **C-115m.** ***½ D: Istvan Szabo. Klaus Maria Brandauer, Erland Josephson, Ildiko Bansagi, Walter Schmidinger, Karoly Eperjes. Brandauer offers a compelling performance as the title character, a WW1 Austrian soldier who is shot in the head—and develops the ability to read minds and foretell the future. An intriguing, insightful, based-on-fact tale; third in a trilogy, following MEPHISTO and COLONEL REDL. [R]▼●

Happening, The (1967) **101m.** ** D: Elliot Silverstein. Anthony Quinn, George Maharis, Michael Parks, Robert Walker, Faye Dunaway, Milton Berle, Oscar Homolka, Jack Kruschen, Clifton James, Eugene Roche. Lighthearted and lightheaded caper story centering around kidnapping of a now respectable former gangster (Quinn). Turns unpleasantly serious towards end. Dunaway's film debut. The title song became a No. 1 hit for The Supremes.

Happening, The (2008) **C-89m.** ** D: M. Night Shyamalan. Mark Wahlberg, Zooey Deschanel, John Leguizamo, Betty Buckley, Frank Collison, Ashlyn Sanchez, Spencer Breslin, Robert Bailey, Jr., Alan Ruck. Philadelphia schoolteacher Wahlberg, his wife, and friends flee after a strange virus overtakes the city . . . but what's causing it and where can they be safe? Tense, even frightening at first, but then spins its wheels with nowhere to go. Shyamalan's signature portentousness is punctuated by moments so absurd they inspire unintended laughter; the director also appears in a small role. [R]◗

Happenstance (2000-French) **C-97m.** *** D: Laurent Firode. Audrey Tautou, Faudel, Eric Savin, Lysiane Meis, Irène Ismailoff, Eric Feldman. Sweet, thoughtful allegory in which a group of strangers become linked by a series of small, seemingly disconnected encounters, all of which lead to a "chance" meeting between two potential soul mates.

This winning exploration of destiny is sparked by a solid ensemble (including Tautou, as a wide-eyed salesgirl). [R] ▼◗

Happiest Days of Your Life, The (1950-British) **84m.** *** D: Frank Launder. Alastair Sim, Margaret Rutherford, Guy Middleton, Joyce Grenfell, Edward Rigby, Muriel Aked, John Bentley, Bernadette O'Farrell, Richard Wattis, Pat (Patricia) Owens. Funny comedy involving a boys' school sharing quarters with a displaced girls' academy, with frantic situations resulting. Launder and John Dighton scripted, from the latter's play. ▼

Happiest Millionaire, The (1967) **C-118m.** **½ D: Norman Tokar. Fred MacMurray, Tommy Steele, Greer Garson, Geraldine Page, Gladys Cooper, Hermione Baddeley, Lesley Ann Warren, John Davidson. Lively but overlong and uninvolving Disney musical (the last film he personally oversaw) about Philadelphia household of eccentric millionaire Anthony J. Drexel Biddle (MacMurray). Lightly entertaining. Originally tradescreened at 164m., then released at 141m.; reissued in 1984 at 159m.▼◗

Happily Ever After (1990) **C-74m.** ** D: John Howley. Voices of Irene Cara, Edward Asner, Carol Channing, Dom DeLuise, Phyllis Diller, Zsa Zsa Gabor, Linda Gary, Jonathan Harris, Michael Horton, Sally Kellerman, Malcolm McDowell, Tracey Ullman, Frank Welker. All-star voice cast gives major boost to this otherwise undistinguished sequel to the story of Snow White, who's surrounded here by dwarfelles. (Don't ask.) Produced by Filmation Studios with noticeably better animation than their Saturday morning product can boast. Aka SNOW WHITE IN THE LAND OF DOOM. [G]▼●◗

Happily Ever After (2005-French) **C-100m.** ** D: Yvan Attal. Charlotte Gainsbourg, Yvan Attal, Alain Chabat, Emmanuelle Seigner, Angie David, Alain Cohen, Aurore Clément, Anouk Aimée, Claude Berri, Johnny Depp. Gainsbourg and Attal are happily married, so why has he taken a lover? Well-intentioned exploration of long-term relationships offers too many coincidences; you never get to know the characters and what makes them tick. Thoroughly ordinary except for Depp's two striking, extended scenes. ◗

Happily N'Ever After (2006-German-U.S.) **C-87m.** *½ D: Paul J. Bolger, Yvette Kaplan. Voices of George Carlin, Andy Dick, Sarah Michelle Gellar, Jon Polito, Sigourney Weaver, Rob Paulsen, Freddie Prinze, Jr., Wallace Shawn, Phil Proctor, Patrick Warburton, Laraine Newman, Tom Kenny, Tress MacNeille, Kath Soucie. Not-so-clever storybook takeoff finds evil Frieda (Weaver) plotting to take over Fairy Tale Land, battling against stepdaughter Ella (Gellar), who fears she will be erased forever unless she takes matters into her own hands. Routine animation and a by-the-numbers script torpedo this low-budget 'toon that even kids will see right through. Followed by a DVD sequel. [PG]◗

Happiness (1965) SEE: **Le Bonheur**

Happiness (1998) **C-140m.** ***½ D: Todd Solondz. Jane Adams, Jon Lovitz, Philip Seymour Hoffman, Dylan Baker, Lara Flynn Boyle, Cynthia Stevenson, Molly Shannon, Louise Lasser, Ben Gazzara, Camryn Manheim, Jared Harris, Elizabeth Ashley, Marla Maples. Portrait of an unhappy family—three sisters, their mother and father—and others who come into their orbit, each dealing with personal demons. They range from a telephone stalker who can't confront women in person to an eternally hopeful young woman named Joy whose life is a perpetual mess. Any film that tackles such topics as masturbation and pederasts isn't going to appeal to everyone, but writer-director Solondz makes them real people and tempers everything with humor. A truly remarkable film. Followed by LIFE DURING WARTIME. ▼●◗

Happiness Cage, The (1972) **C-94m.** **½ D: Bernard Girard. Christopher Walken, Joss Ackland, Ralph Meeker, Ronny Cox, Marco St. John, Tom Aldredge. Uneven but thought-provoking drama about doctor in Germany who utilizes shock treatment on soldiers to stabilize aggressive behavior. Video titles: THE MIND SNATCHERS and THE DEMON WITHIN. [PG]▼◗

Happy Accidents (2001) **C-110m.** ** D: Brad Anderson. Marisa Tomei, Vincent D'Onofrio, Nadia Dajani, Holland Taylor, Tovah Feldshuh, Sean Gullette, Anthony Michael Hall. Fantasy-romance about a guy who tells a girl he is a time traveler from the future who fell in love with her old photo and just had to visit her era in order to meet her. Has some amusing moments, but somehow we just can't shake the feeling that we have seen this all before. [R]▼◗

Happy Birthday, Gemini (1980) **C-107m.** ** D: Richard Benner. Madeline Kahn, Rita Moreno, Robert Viharo, Alan Rosenberg, Sarah Holcomb, David Marshall Grant, Timothy Jenkins. Disappointing adaptation of Albert Innaurato's long-running Broadway play *Gemini*, centering on young man's sexual identity crisis. Colorful stage characters are lost on film. [R]▼

Happy Birthday to Me (1981-Canadian) **C-108m.** BOMB D: J. Lee Thompson. Melissa Sue Anderson, Glenn Ford, Tracy Bregman, Jack Blum, Matt Craven, Lawrence Dane. Is or is not Anderson killing off her classmates at Crawford Academy because they inadvertently caused her mother's death four years earlier? More killings, more blood, more exploitation; Ford, as Anderson's psychiatrist, hit rock bottom with this appearance. [R]▼●◗

Happy Birthday, Wanda June (1971) **C-**

105m. *** D: Mark Robson. Rod Steiger, Susannah York, George Grizzard, Don Murray, William Hickey, Pamelyn Ferdin, Steven Paul. Stagy but enjoyable film of Kurt Vonnegut, Jr., play. Male chauvinist explorer, returning home after eight years, finds his wife matured (and engaged), and his values now obsolete. Fine performances of Vonnegut's funny black-humor situations and dialogue; Hickey hilarious as Steiger's Jerry Lewis-esque buddy. [R]

Happy Ending, The (1969) **C-112m.** **½ D: Richard Brooks. Jean Simmons, John Forsythe, Lloyd Bridges, Shirley Jones, Teresa Wright, Dick Shawn, Nanette Fabray, Robert (Bobby) Darin, Tina Louise. Initially intriguing view of modern marriage drones on interminably, as Simmons walks out on husband and family trying to find herself. Michel Legrand score highlighted by "What Are You Doing the Rest of Your Life?" Panavision. [M/PG]▼

Happy Endings (2005) **C-130m.** *** D: Don Roos. Lisa Kudrow, Maggie Gyllenhaal, Tom Arnold, Jesse Bradford, Laura Dern, Steve Coogan, Jason Ritter, Bobby Cannavale, Sarah Clarke, David Sutcliffe. Kudrow has been living a lie for years, having given up a son for adoption; now a young would-be filmmaker essentially blackmails her into cooperating on a documentary. But everyone who has even tangential contact with these characters carries secrets around with them as well. Interesting mosaic-style comedy-drama wryly explores the nature (and consequences) of lies, half-truths, and hypocrisy in our contemporary culture. Peter Horton appears unbilled. Written by the director. Super 35. [R]▼◗

Happy Feet (2006-U.S.-Australian) **C-108m.** **½ D: George Miller. Voices of Elijah Wood, Robin Williams, Brittany Murphy, Hugh Jackman, Nicole Kidman, Hugo Weaving, Anthony LaPaglia, E. G. Daily, Magda Szubanski, Miriam Margolyes, Steve Irwin, Chrissie Hynde. An Antarctic penguin is ostracized from his tribe because he can't sing a mating call—but he sure can dance! Endearing characters, beautifully animated in a breathtaking landscape, make this an eyeful, and there's vintage pop music galore on the soundtrack . . . but the story becomes protracted as it tries to drive home an ecological message. Savion Glover's dancing and body language are successfully transposed to Mumble. Williams is very funny as the voice of Ramón. Oscar winner as Best Animated Feature. Digital Widescreen. [PG]◗

Happy Gilmore (1996) **C-92m.** ** D: Dennis Dugan. Adam Sandler, Christopher McDonald, Carl Weathers, Julie Bowen, Alan Covert, Bob Barker, Frances Bay, Joe Flaherty, Kevin Nealon, Richard Kiel, Dennis Dugan. Sporadically funny vehicle for Sandler, as a would-be hockey player whose inability to skate leads him to the pro golf tour, where he turns game on its ear with his unsportsmanlike antics. Highpoint: a brawl between Sandler and *The Price Is Right*'s Barker. Sandler cowrote the script. Ben Stiller appears unbilled. [PG-13] ▼●)

Happy-Go-Lucky (2008-British) **C-118m.** *** D: Mike Leigh. Sally Hawkins, Eddie Marsan, Alexis Zegerman, Andrea Riseborough, Sinéad Matthews, Kate O'Flynn, Sarah Niles, Sylvestra Le Touzel, Karina Fernandez. Schoolteacher Poppy (Hawkins) goes through life spreading good cheer—even where it isn't welcome—and refusing to dwell on the negative. Potentially annoying at first, we come to learn that Poppy isn't a fool; she's bright and compassionate and chooses to take an upbeat approach to life . . . unlike, say, her driving instructor (a memorable Marsan), who may explode at any moment. More a character study than a story, the film meanders a bit but Hawkins' genuine performance makes it worthwhile. Super 35. [R]●

Happy Hooker, The (1975) **C-96m.** ** D: Nicholas Sgarro. Lynn Redgrave, Jean-Pierre Aumont, Lovelady Powell, Nicholas Pryor, Elizabeth Wilson, Tom Poston, Conrad Janis, George Dzundza, Vincent Schiavelli, Mason Adams, Anita Morris. Xaviera Hollander's best-seller about her rise as N.Y.C.'s most prominent madam is so heavily sanitized that one wonders just what audience scripter William Richert had in mind; moderately amusing, and cast seems to be having a good time. Followed by two fictitious sequels. [R] ▼●)

Happy Hooker Goes Hollywood, The (1980) **C-85m.** *½ D: Alan Roberts. Martine Beswicke, Chris Lemmon, Adam West, Phil Silvers, Richard Deacon, Lindsay Bloom, Army Archerd, Edie Adams. Now Xaviera is a brunette; she and her girls rush to the aid of a corruption-riddled movie studio in this limp rehash of SILENT MOVIE. Fine comic cast is wasted, although film buffs might enjoy seeing cult actors Beswicke and Dick Miller in bed together. [R] ▼●)

Happy Hooker Goes to Washington, The (1977) **C-89m.** *½ D: William A. Levey. Joey Heatherton, George Hamilton, Ray Walston, Jack Carter, Phil Foster, Billy Barty, David White. Xaviera (a *blonde* this time) is called before Congress to answer charges that sex is ruining the country and subsequently gets involved in a CIA escapade. A few chuckles here and there, but overall, more silly than sexy; Hamilton and writer Bob Kaufman did considerably better with their next film, LOVE AT FIRST BITE. [R] ▼▶

Happy Hour (2004) **C-93m.** ** D: Mike Bencivenga. Anthony LaPaglia, Eric Stoltz, Caroleen Feeney, Robert Vaughn, Mario Cantone, Malachy McCourt. Uninspired novelist LaPaglia spends his days toiling at an ad agency and his nights in a bar. Then he befriends school teacher Feeney, who also loves to drink, and his life is no longer the same. Good performances save this often slow, dark film about relationships, emotional baggage, and mortality.▶

Happy Mother's Day Love, George (1973) **C-90m.** ** D: Darren McGavin. Patricia Neal, Cloris Leachman, Bobby Darin, Ron Howard, Simon Oakland. Unconvincing horror tale, despite some clever attempts by director McGavin to spice it up. Strange doings in seaside house include two great gory murders, but everything else is weak. Retitled: RUN, STRANGER, RUN. [PG]▼

Happy New Year (1973-French) **C-112m.** *** D: Claude Lelouch. Lino Ventura, Françoise Fabian, Charles Gerard, Andre Falcon. Two thieves plot a robbery, but one falls hard for the liberated charmer who runs the antique shop next to the target. Bright romantic caper film is easy to take. Remade in Hollywood in 1987. Retitled: THE HAPPY NEW YEAR CAPER.▼▶

Happy New Year (1987) **C-85m.** **½ D: John G. Avildsen. Peter Falk, Wendy Hughes, Charles Durning, Tom Courtenay, Joan Copeland. Falk is a treat to watch in this pleasant Americanization of Claude Lelouch's French comedy caper about a pair of sophisticated crooks and their plans to hit a jewelry store in West Palm Beach, Florida. Hughes is charming in her first American film; Lelouch has a cameo in the opening scene. [PG]▼

Happy New Year Caper, The SEE: **Happy New Year** (1973)

Happy Road, The (1957) **100m.** **½ D: Gene Kelly. Gene Kelly, Barbara Laage, Michael Redgrave, Bobby Clark, Brigitte Fossey. Two single parents—American Kelly and Frenchwoman Laage—are drawn together when their children run away from school together. Pleasant but minor family fare, enhanced by location filming in French countryside.

Happy Tears (2010) **C-95m.** *½ D: Mitchell Lichtenstein. Demi Moore, Parker Posey, Patti D'Arbanville, Rip Torn, Ellen Barkin, Roger Rees, Victor Slezak, Celia Weston, Christian Camargo, Billy Magnussen, Patti D'Arbanville. Two very different sisters return to their childhood home in order to deal with their rambunctious father's senility. With families of their own, they find taking care of a parent is even tougher, and discover that their upbringing wasn't always as idyllic as it once seemed. Moore and Posey do their best, but the script lets them down in this overwrought comedy that never gets off the ground. [R] ▶

Happy, Texas (1999) **C-99m.** *** D: Mark Illsley. Jeremy Northam, Steve Zahn, William H. Macy, Ally Walker, Illeana Douglas,

M.C. Gainey, Ron Perlman, Paul Dooley, Mo Gaffney. Engaging comedy about two prison escapees who steal a van and assume the identities of its owners, gay partners who stage kiddie talent contests. Holed up in a small Texas town, they're forced to assume those lives while getting more involved with the locals than they ever intended. Shot on a shoestring, but it doesn't show; Zahn is a comic standout in the first-rate cast. [PG-13]▼❶

happythankyoumoreplease (2011) **C-100m.** **½ D: Josh Radnor. Josh Radnor, Malin Akerman, Kate Mara, Zoe Kazan, Pablo Schreiber, Tony Hale, Michael Algieri. Would-be novelist takes in a boy who's been separated from his foster family on the subway, but he isn't as willing to commit to a woman he meets and likes. Two other couples grapple with different issues: whether or not to get married and whether a woman with low self-esteem (who has alopecia, making her hairless) will allow herself to be wooed by an office colleague who's crazy about her. Likable, if uneven, first feature for writer-director-star Radnor, with standout roles for Akerman and Hale as the latter duo. Richard Jenkins appears unbilled. HD Widescreen. [R]❶

Happy Time, The (1952) **94m.** ***½ D: Richard Fleischer. Charles Boyer, Louis Jourdan, Bobby Driscoll, Marsha Hunt, Kurt Kasznar, Linda Christian, Marcel Dalio, Jeanette Nolan, Richard Erdman. Charming film about a boy's coming of age in 1920s Ottawa, Canada, amidst a colorful and eccentric family. Driscoll is the adolescent who develops a crush on pretty magician's assistant Christian. Boyer is his understanding father, eternally forgiving of his two wayward brothers (Jourdan and Kasznar, re-creating his Broadway role). Earl Felton adapted Samuel A. Taylor's play, based on Robert Fontaine's autobiographical stories.

Happy Times (2000-Chinese) **C-102m.** *** D: Zhang Yimou. Zhao Benshan, Dong Jie, Dong Lihua. The director of RAISE THE RED LANTERN and TO LIVE indulges his sense of humor this time out. A 50-ish strikeout with women (Zhao) starts developing feelings for the blind stepdaughter (Dong Jie) of the emotional abuser she's been dating. With his equally ragtag buddies, he acquires an abandoned warehouse, tells the young woman it's part of a hotel he owns and "hires" her with fake paper money to be its masseuse, piping in street sounds through a boom box as she gives chaste, no-nonsense backrubs to cohorts posing as customers. Sentimental, but not overly so, movie holds its emotions in check until the affectingly wistful finale. [PG] ❶

Happy Together (1989) **C-102m.** ** D: Mel Damski. Patrick Dempsey, Helen Slater, Dan Schneider, Marius Weyers, Barbara Babcock, Brad Pitt. Slight, predictable romantic comedy in which college students

Dempsey and Slater are accidentally paired as roommates. You can just guess how this one turns out. [PG-13]▼●

Happy Together (1997-Hong Kong) **C/B&W-97m.** **½ D: Wong Kar-Wai. Leslie Cheung, Tony Leung Chiu-wai, Chang Chen. Polished production overshadows a predictable, paper-thin chronicle of a deeply troubled relationship between a constantly bickering Hong Kong gay couple in Buenos Aires. The filmmaker won a Best Director prize at Cannes for this, but pointedly the script did not.▼●❶

Happy Years, The (1950) **C-110m.** *** D: William Wellman. Dean Stockwell, Scotty Beckett, Darryl Hickman, Leo G. Carroll, Margalo Gillmore, Leon Ames. · High-spirited boy in turn-of-the-20th-century prep school finds he has trouble fitting in. Familiar comedy-drama, adapted from Owen Johnson's *Lawrenceville Stories*, is hardly typical Wellman fare, but well done. Robert Wagner makes his film debut.❶

Harakiri (1962-Japanese) **133m.** ***½ D: Masaki Kobayashi. Tatsuya Nakadai, Rentarô Mikuni, Akira Ishihama, Shima Iwashita, Tetsurô Tamba, Masao Mishima, Ichirô Nakaya. In 1630 Edo, an unemployed Hiroshima samurai begs the Iyi clan to permit his ritual suicide in their courtyard. But is this piteous ronin who he says he is, or just another poverty-stricken mercenary hoping for a handout during peacetime? Potent display of Asian machismo is a tale of desperation and a lesson in honor that plays like a gripping courtroom drama. Scalding, angry indictment of noble hypocrisy, rendered in monochromatic imagery, is far too bloody for color. Screenplay by Shinobu Hashimoto, from a story by Yasuhiko Takiguchi. Grandscope.❶

Hard Ball (2001) **C-106m.** **½ D: Brian Robbins. Keanu Reeves, Diane Lane, John Hawkes, Bryan Hearne, Julian Griffith, Michael B. Jordan, A. Delon Ellis, Jr., DeWayne Warren, Mike McGlone, D. B. Sweeney, Graham Beckel. Addictive gambler Reeves hits rock bottom and a friend agrees to bail him out *if* he will coach a kids' baseball team in the Chicago projects. Naturally, he regains his own self-esteem as he steers these emotionally needy kids onto the right path. Call it corny, but it works surprisingly well and emphasizes the fact that one person can make a difference in the world around him. Based on Daniel Coyle's experiences, as related in his book. [PG-13]▼❶

Hard-Boiled (1992-Hong Kong) **C-126m.** *** D: John Woo. Chow Yun-Fat, Tony Leung, Teresa Mo, Philip Chan, Anthony Wong, Kwan Hoi-Shan, A-Lung. Stylish, ultra-violent story of police inspector (Yun-Fat) who teams up with a mysterious hit man (Leung) to stop a gang of arms dealers. Standard plot of revenge and male bonding is springboard for unbelievable action sequences that are bloody, comic, and hypnotic. Yun-Fat is a perfectly assured hero, and director Woo (who wrote the original story) appears as a bartender. ▼●】

Hard Bounty (1995) **C-89m.** ** D: Jim Wynorski. Matt McCoy, Kelly LeBrock, John Terlesky, Felicity Waterman, Jay Richardson, Ross Hagen, Kimberly Kelley. Languid, corpse-laden Western, in which whore LeBrock and her entourage saddle up and seek revenge after tragedy strikes. McCoy is an Eastwood-esque bounty hunter known as The Holy Ghost. [R]▼】

Hard Candy (2006) **C-103m.** **½ D: David Slade. Patrick Wilson, Ellen Page, Sandra Oh, Jennifer Holmes. Essentially a two-character drama, supremely intense story has a 14-year-old girl meeting a 32-year-old photographer she has flirted with on the Internet. When they go back to his place, her real purpose is revealed as she traps him in a personal sting operation to extract a major price for what she believes is his criminal past. Watching her turn the tables on this sexual predator gives this tale a certain perverse fascination. While it has echoes of thrillers like FATAL ATTRACTION and MISERY, Page's brutal vengeance seeker makes Kathy Bates' character seem like Pippi Longstocking. Super 35. [R]】

Hard Contract (1969) **C-107m.** **½ D: S. Lee Pogostin. James Coburn, Lee Remick, Lilli Palmer, Burgess Meredith, Patrick Magee, Sterling Hayden, Karen Black. Hired killer Coburn starts to have self-doubts when a woman (Remick) humanizes him. Film is too concerned with making an "important statement" to become particularly entertaining or involving. Panavision. [PG]

Hardcore (1979) **C-108m.** **½ D: Paul Schrader. George C. Scott, Peter Boyle, Season Hubley, Dick Sargent, Leonard Gaines, David Nichols. Calvinistic Midwesterner Scott (in powerful performance) searches for teenage daughter who's inexplicably dropped out. He's heartsick after viewing porno film starring her, and his journey into netherworld of prostitution and porn is at times fascinating, sad, and repellent. Marred by unbelievable conclusion. [R]▼●】

Hard Country (1981) **C-104m.** **½ D: David Greene. Jan-Michael Vincent, Kim Basinger, Michael Parks, Gailard Sartain, Tanya Tucker, Ted Neeley, Daryl Hannah, Richard Moll. Good ole boy Vincent works all day, parties all night; his girlfriend (Basinger) wants to marry him, but also wants out of Texas. Overshadowed by URBAN COWBOY, but not bad and done with conviction. Music by Michael Martin Murphey. Film debuts of Basinger and Nashville star Tucker. [PG]▼●】

Hard Day's Night, A (1964-British) **85m.** **** D: Richard Lester. John Lennon, Paul McCartney, George Harrison, Ringo Starr,

Wilfrid Brambell, Norman Rossington, John Junkin, Victor Spinetti, Anna Quayle. First Beatles film is director Lester's idea of a typical day in the group's life. He lets his imagination run wild; result is a visual delight, with many Beatles songs on the soundtrack (including "Can't Buy Me Love," "And I Love Her," "I Should Have Known Better," and the title tune). Original screenplay by Alun Owen. Reissued in 1982 with a short prologue. ▼●】

Hard Driver SEE: **Last American Hero, The**

Hard Eight (1997) **C-101m.** *** D: Paul Thomas Anderson. Philip Baker Hall, John C. Reilly, Gwyneth Paltrow, Samuel L. Jackson, Phillip Seymour Hoffman. Spare but accomplished Nevada mood piece about a minor gambling pro who, for reasons that remain tantalizingly obscure for three-fourths of the movie's length, elects to tutor a much younger man in eking out a minimal living "working" casinos. Punctuated by sporadic and deftly timed spurts of violence; Paltrow is successfully cast against type as a cocktail waitress and sometime hooker with no brains at her disposal. Aka SYDNEY. Super 35. [R]▼●】

Harder They Come, The (1972-Jamaican) **C-103m.** *** D: Perry Henzell. Jimmy Cliff, Janet Barkley, Carl Bradshaw, Ras Daniel Hartman, Bobby Charlton. Country-boy Cliff comes to Kingston to make it as a singer; ironically, it isn't until he turns to a life of crime that his record starts to climb the charts. Crude but powerful film almost single-handedly launched reggae music's popularity in America; still a major cult favorite. Terrific song score includes "You Can Get It If You Really Want," "Many Rivers to Cross," title tune. [R]▼●】

Harder They Fall, The (1956) **109m.** ***½ D: Mark Robson. Humphrey Bogart, Rod Steiger, Jan Sterling, Mike Lane, Max Baer, Edward Andrews. Bogart's last feature casts him as cynical sportswriter-turned-press agent who realizes for the first time how badly prizefighters are manipulated by their unfeeling managers. Powerful drama by Budd Schulberg.

Hard, Fast and Beautiful (1951) **79m.** ** D: Ida Lupino. Claire Trevor, Sally Forrest, Carleton Young, Robert Clarke, Kenneth Patterson. Domineering mother pushes daughter into world of competitive tennis. Straightforward story, awkwardly filmed (and acted) at times. Director Lupino and Robert Ryan make cameo appearances.】

Hard Knocks (1980-Australian) **C-85m.** *** D: Don McLennan. Tracey Mann, John Arnold, Bill Hunter, Max Cullen, Tony Barry. Gritty, powerful drama centering on the efforts of ex-con Mann to straighten out her life, highlighted by a brilliant, multifaceted lead performance.▼

Hardly Working (1981) **C-91m.** ** D:

Jerry Lewis. Jerry Lewis, Susan Oliver, Roger C. Carmel, Deanna Lund, Harold J. Stone, Steve Franken, Buddy Lester. Jerry's "comeback" (filmed in Florida in 1979) is typical lamebrain comedy (about an unemployed circus clown who bumbles from one job to another), but an older Jerry wavers between playing the oafish kid of yore and a more "mature" character. Not a very good movie; the opening montage from earlier films is much funnier than anything that follows. Trimmed from European release length. [PG]▼

Hard Promises (1992) C-95m. *½ D: Martin Davidson. Sissy Spacek, William Petersen, Brian Kerwin, Mare Winningham, Jeff Perry, Olivia Burnette, Peter MacNicol, Ann Wedgeworth, Amy Wright, Lois Smith. Petersen gets the invitation to ex-wife Spacek's new marriage one day before the ceremony, and rushes home to small Texas town to disrupt the proceedings. Surprisingly unpleasant comedy, with Petersen's loutish behavior in the establishing scenes mitigating against any potential fun. Rip Torn (Spacek's cousin) appears unbilled. [PG] ▼O●

Hard Rain (1998) C-96m. **½ D: Mikael Salomon. Morgan Freeman, Christian Slater, Randy Quaid, Minnie Driver, Ed Asner, Michael Goorjian, Mark Rolston, Richard Dysart, Betty White. As a small Midwest town disappears under rising flood waters, a criminal gang headed by Freeman tries to catch armored car guard Slater, who's hidden the money they're after. The cast is above average, the effects are impressive, and the setting is unusual, but a routine script barely keeps this afloat. Super 35. [R]▼O●

Hard Ride, The (1971) C-93m. **½ D: Burt Topper. Robert Fuller, Sherry Bain, Tony Russel, Marshall Reed, Biff Elliot, William Bonner. Ex-sergeant Fuller accompanies the body of a black buddy home from Vietnam and tries to persuade the vet's white sweetheart and the Indian leader of his motorcycle gang to attend his funeral. Not just another cycle flick, and not bad. [PG]▼

Hard Target (1993) C-94m. **½ D: John Woo. Jean-Claude Van Damme, Lance Henriksen, Arnold Vosloo, Yancy Butler, Kasi Lemmons, Wilford Brimley, Chuck Pfarrer. Acclaimed action-director Woo's U.S. debut is a disappointing thriller featuring Van Damme as a sailor aiding hard-luck veterans being exploited by sadistic Henriksen (who by now can play this kind of role in his sleep). Not bad of its type, but doesn't match Woo's highly touted Hong Kong–made efforts. [R]▼O●

Hard Ticket to Hawaii (1987) C-96m. ** D: Andy Sidaris. Dona Speir, Hope Marie Carlton, Ronn Moss, Harold Diamond, Rodrigo Obregon, Cynthia Brimhill, Patty Duffek, Wolf Larson. Typical Andy Sidaris mix of action, beautiful scenery, and buxom bimbos baring their breasts. The story? Something about female undercover agents running a sting operation that gets them in hot water with drug lords. Does anyone *care* about the story? Followed by PICASSO TRIGGER. [R]▼O●

Hard Times (1975) C-97m. *** D: Walter Hill. Charles Bronson, James Coburn, Jill Ireland, Strother Martin, Maggie Blye, Michael McGuire. Bronson is a tight-lipped street-fighter and Coburn is the sharpster who arranges his bare-knuckled bouts in 1930s New Orleans. Colorful (but violent) entertainment. Hill's directorial debut. Panavision. [PG—edited from original R rating]▼O●

Hard to Hold (1984) C-93m. *½ D: Larry Peerce. Rick Springfield, Janet Eilber, Patti Hansen, Albert Salmi, Bill Mumy. Pampered rock star collides (literally) with spirited young woman who doesn't know—or care—who he is . . . so naturally he falls in love with her. Tiresome romance designed as star vehicle for teen idol Springfield, and retitled "Hard to Watch" by some wags. [PG—edited from original R rating]▼O●

Hard to Kill (1990) C-95m. ** D: Bruce Malmuth. Steven Seagal, Kelly LeBrock, Bill Sadler, Frederick Coffin, Bonnie Burroughs, Zachary Rosencrantz, Dean Norris. Police detective Seagal uncovers a major political corruption ring and is shot and left for dead; when he awakens from a seven-year coma, he's ripe for revenge. Full of the usual violence and chases for this genre, but Seagal is fun to watch. LeBrock, who nurses him back to health, was then the real-life Mrs. Seagal. [R]▼O●

Hard Traveling (1985) C-107m. **½ D: Dan Bessie. J. E. Freeman, Ellen Geer, Barry Corbin, James Gammon, Jim Haynie. Occasionally touching but ultimately disappointing drama about a gentle, decent, but uneducated and disadvantaged man (Freeman) who finds love and stability with widow Geer, but commits murder when unable to support her. Done in by too many flashbacks. Based on the novel *Bread and a Stone* by Alvah Bessie, father of the director. [PG]▼

Hardware (1990-British-U.S.) C-92m. ** D: Richard Stanley. Dylan McDermott, Stacy Travis, John Lynch, Iggy Pop, William Hootkins, Mark Northover. Somewhere in the post-nuke future, desert scavenger McDermott presents some android remains to Travis; eventually, the stuff rekindles what is apparently its life mission—to destroy all living things (and the Travis pad, besides). Surprisingly well made, but recalls many earlier (and better) films. Heavy violence nearly earned this an X rating, before it was trimmed. [R]▼O●

Hard Way, The (1942) 109m. *** D: Vincent Sherman. Ida Lupino, Dennis Morgan, Joan Leslie, Jack Carson, Gladys George, Julie Bishop. Intriguing but artificial story of strong-willed Lupino pushing younger sister Leslie into show business career. Holds up until improbable finale, although it seems unlikely that Broadway would cheer Leslie as the greatest discovery of the age. Morgan and Carson (in first of several teamings) match Lupino's fine performance. ▼●)

Hard Way, The (1991) **C-111m.** **½ D: John Badham. Michael J. Fox, James Woods, James Lang, Annabella Sciorra, Penny Marshall, John Capodice, Luis Guzman, LL Cool J, Delroy Lindo, Christina Ricci, Karen Lynn Gorney. Long, loud, loose cannon of a movie about a spoiled-brat Hollywood star who attaches himself to a reckless N.Y.C. street cop to prepare for his next movie role. Some laughs, lots of action, but it all goes out of control. Panavision. [R]▼●)

Hard Word, The (2002-Australian-British) **C-103m.** *** D: Scott Roberts. Guy Pearce, Rachel Griffiths, Robert Taylor, Joel Edgerton, Damien Richardson, Rhondda Findleton, Kate Atkinson, Vince Colosimo. Violent crime caper with a tough attitude, a sly sense of humor, and some neat story twists. Three convicts (led by Pearce, the brains of the outfit) commit a string of robberies with the help of their crooked warden and a slick lawyer—but a series of double-crosses leads to bitterness and a hunger for revenge, even if the score takes time to settle. Written by the director. Super 35. [R]▼●)

Harem (1985-French) **C-113m.** *½ D: Arthur Joffe. Nastassja Kinski, Ben Kingsley, Dennis Goldson, Zohra Segal, Michel Robin, Julette Simpson. Thin, boring drama about Arab prince Kingsley, who kidnaps Kinski and adds her to his harem. Solid production values can't take the place of a coherent scenario and fully fleshed-out characterizations. Panavision. ▼●)

Harlan County, U.S.A. (1977) **C-103m.** ***½ D: Barbara Kopple. Gripping, human documentary (an Academy Award winner) about the strike of Kentucky mine workers against the Eastover Mining Company, a subsidiary of Duke Power. Memorable scene of miner and Brooklyn cop having a "conversation." [PG]▼)

Harlem Globetrotters, The (1951) **80m.** ** D: Phil Brown. Thomas Gomez, Dorothy Dandridge, Bill Walker, Angela Clarke. Vehicle built around famed basketball team, with a few romantic interludes.

Harlem Nights (1989) **C-115m.** ** D: Eddie Murphy. Eddie Murphy, Richard Pryor, Redd Foxx, Danny Aiello, Michael Lerner, Della Reese, Berlinda Tolbert, Stan Shaw, Jasmine Guy, Lela Rochon, Arsenio Hall, Robin Harris. Proprietor of an after-hours club in 1930s Harlem (Pryor) and his adopted son (Murphy) try standing up to a white mobster determined to cut in on their take or put them out of business. Murphy's debut as writer-director is skimpily scripted

and completely devoid of energy. Even Pryor's effortless charisma can't breathe much life into this one. [R]▼●)

Harlequin (1980-Australian) **C-96m.** **½ D: Simon Wincer. Robert Powell, David Hemmings, Carmen Duncan, Broderick Crawford, Gus Mercurio, Alan Cassell. Faith-healer Powell helps politician Hemmings' son, who has leukemia; however, his wife (Duncan) is also attracted to the healer. Middling drama updating story of Rasputin, Nicholas, and Alexandra. Retitled DARK FORCES. Panavision. [PG]▼)

Harley Davidson & the Marlboro Man (1991) **C-99m.** *½ D: Simon Wincer. Mickey Rourke, Don Johnson, Chelsea Field, Daniel Baldwin, Giancarlo Esposito, Vanessa Williams, Tom Sizemore. Another title in search of a movie. Drifter Rourke and onetime rodeo cowboy Johnson rob a bank to help their pal, whose Rock 'n' Roll Bar and Grill is about to be closed by strong-armed creditors. Moderately futuristic comic-adventure moves fast enough, but even some unexpectedly silly encounters can't distinguish it. Touted in the studio press material as "the lighter side of Mickey Rourke." [R]▼●)

Harlow (1965) **C-125m.** **½ D: Gordon Douglas. Carroll Baker, Peter Lawford, Red Buttons, Michael Connors, Raf Vallone, Angela Lansbury, Martin Balsam, Leslie Nielsen. Slick, colorful garbage will hold your interest, but doesn't ring true. Baker could never match the real Harlow, but Vallone and Lansbury are good as her stepfather and mother. Rushed through production to compete with the slipshod Carol Lynley version. Panavision. ▼)

Harlow (1965) **109m.** ** D: Alex Segal. Carol Lynley, Efrem Zimbalist, Jr., Barry Sullivan, Hurd Hatfield, Ginger Rogers, Hermione Baddeley, Lloyd Bochner, Audrey Totter, John Williams, Robert Strauss. Amateurish off-the-cuff tedium loosely based on screen star of the 1930s. Rogers as Mama Harlow is best. This quickie production made news in 1965 because it was produced in an unusual manner: staged as a live television show and recorded as a kinescope.

Harmonists, The (1997-German-Austrian) **C-116m.** *** D: Joseph Vilsmaier. Ben Becker, Heino Ferch, Ulrich Noethen, Heinrich Schafmeister, Max Tidof, Kai Wiesinger, Meret Becker, Katja Riemann. Straightforward telling of a fascinating story about the formation of an innovative vocal group whose enormous popularity in late 1920s–early '30s Germany almost seems impervious to growing Nazi dictums—but inevitably runs afoul of the new government, as three of the singers are Jewish. The same story was chronicled in a German documentary, THE COMEDIAN HARMONISTS, which was this film's title in Europe. Super 35. [R]▼)

Harold & Kumar Escape from Guantan-

amo Bay (2008) **C-102m.** *½ D: Jon Hurwitz, Hayden Schlossberg. John Cho, Kal Penn, Rob Corddry, Jack Conley, Roger Bart, Neil Patrick Harris, Danneel Harris, Eric Winter, Paula Garcés, Jon Reep, Missi Pyle, Beverly D'Angelo, David Krumholtz, Christopher Meloni, Eddie Kaye Thomas, Ed Helms. Appalling follow-up to the 2004 comedy finds the pot-smoking slackers mistaken for terrorists. Corddry plays a Homeland Security Chief who's on their trail. The first film was benign and goofy, but this one is determined to be as raunchy as possible . . . to an astonishing degree. Harris again plays "himself," a drug-addled sexaholic. Alternate version runs 107m. [R]🔴

Harold & Kumar Go to White Castle (2004-U.S.-Canadian) **C-87m.** ** D: Danny Leiner. Kal Penn, John Cho, Paula Garcés, Neil Patrick Harris, David Krumholtz, Eddie Kaye Thomas, Christopher Meloni, Ryan Reynolds, Fred Willard, Ethan Embry, Jamie Kennedy, Malin Ackerman. Two friends try to satisfy a craving by driving to a White Castle hamburger stop in New Jersey but have a nightlong series of misadventures instead. Good actors in the leads and a distinctive goofball vibe are definite assets, but a spotty script too often fails to deliver on its promise. (We won't even mention the toilet scene.) Anthony Anderson appears unbilled; Harris plays himself. Unrated version runs 90m. Followed by a sequel. [R]▼🔴

Harold and Maude (1971) **C-90m.** ***½ D: Hal Ashby. Bud Cort, Ruth Gordon, Vivian Pickles, Cyril Cusack, Charles Tyner, Ellen Geer, Tom Skerritt. Black comedy focuses on loving relationship between 20-year-old Cort, who's obsessed with death, and 79-year-old swinger Gordon. Dismissed at time of release, this has become a cult favorite, and the cornerstone of writer Colin Higgins' reputation. Cort's phony suicides are hilarious. Music by Cat Stevens. [PG]▼🔴

Harold Lloyd's World of Comedy (1962) **94m.** *** Compiled by Harold Lloyd. Harold Lloyd, Bebe Daniels, Mildred Davis. Delightful comedy scenes show why Lloyd was so popular in the 1920s. Highlights include classic building-climbing episode and other great sight gags. A real gem.🔴

Harold Robbins' The Betsy SEE: **Betsy, The**

Harper (1966) **C-121m.** ***½ D: Jack Smight. Paul Newman, Lauren Bacall, Julie Harris, Shelley Winters, Robert Wagner, Janet Leigh, Arthur Hill, Pamela Tiffin, Robert Webber, Strother Martin, Harold Gould. High-grade action-mystery has Newman as private eye hired by Bacall to investigate disappearance of her husband; blowsy Winters, frustrated Harris are involved in fast-paced, sophisticated yarn. Screenplay by William Goldman, from Ross Macdonald's *The Moving Target.* Sequel: THE DROWNING POOL. Panavision.▼🔴

Harper Valley P.T.A. (1978) **C-102m.** ** D: Richard Bennett. Barbara Eden, Ronny Cox, Nanette Fabray, Susan Swift, Ron Masak, Louis Nye, Pat Paulsen, Audrey Christie, John Fiedler, Bob Hastings. Bubblegum comedy from hit Jeannie C. Riley song about small-town mother who arouses local wrath for her free-thinking ways, retaliates with series of elaborate revenges. Old pros eke some chuckles out of threadbare material. Later a TV series. [PG]▼🔴

Harp of Burma SEE: **Burmese Harp, The**

Harrad Experiment, The (1973) **C-88m.** **½ D: Ted Post. Don Johnson, James Whitmore, Tippi Hedren, B. Kirby, Jr. (Bruno Kirby), Laurie Walters, Robert Middleton, Victoria Thompson. Fair adaptation of offbeat best-seller by Robert Rimmer in which experimental coed college pushes policy of sexual freedom. Two pairs of relationships singled out as in book, but film actually should've been longer! Improvisational group Ace Trucking Co. appears as itself. Melanie Griffith (Hedren's daughter) was an extra in this—at age 14. Look for young Gregory Harrison. Sequel: HARRAD SUMMER. [R]▼🔴

Harrad Summer (1974) **C-103m.** **½ D: Steven H. Stern. Richard Doran, Victoria Thompson, Laurie Walters, Robert Reiser, Bill Dana, Marty Allen. Fair sequel to THE HARRAD EXPERIMENT, about sex-education school for young students that sends them home, where they can apply what they've learned. Aka STUDENT UNION. [R]▼

Harriet Craig (1950) **94m.** *** D: Vincent Sherman. Joan Crawford, Wendell Corey, Lucile Watson, Allyn Joslyn, Ellen Corby. Remake of CRAIG'S WIFE is well cast, with Crawford in title role of perfectionist wife who'll stop at nothing to have her house and life run as she wishes.▼

Harriet the Spy (1996) **C-101m.** **½ D: Bronwen Hughes. Michelle Trachtenberg, Vanessa Lee Chester, Gregory Smith, Rosie O'Donnell, J. Smith-Cameron, Robert Joy, Eartha Kitt. Young girl is encouraged by her eccentric nanny (O'Donnell) to keep a journal of everything she sees, which eventually gets her into trouble with friends and foes alike. Gets lost somewhere in the middle, but makes an impressive recovery in the final third, when an insightful look at childhood relationships comes to the fore. Based on the popular juvenile novel by Louise Fitzhugh. [PG]▼🔴

Harrison's Flowers (2002-French) **C-130m.** ** D: Elie Chouraqui. Andie MacDowell, David Strathairn, Elias Koteas, Adrien Brody, Brendan Gleeson, Alun Armstrong, Diane Baker, Marie Trintignant, Gerard Butler. When MacDowell is told that her photographer-husband has died in war-torn

Yugoslavia, she refuses to believe it and goes there to find him. Vivid look at life in the midst of a chaotic, seemingly senseless war, and the way photojournalists thrust themselves into the thick of that tumult . . . but surrounding story is woefully underwritten. Main character's odyssey is more grueling than inspiring. Super 35. [R]▼❶

Harry & Son (1984) **C-117m.** ** D: Paul Newman. Paul Newman, Robby Benson, Joanne Woodward, Ellen Barkin, Wilford Brimley, Judith Ivey, Ossie Davis, Morgan Freeman. Newman directed, coproduced and cowrote this contrived, meandering drama about the relationship between a widower father (who's just lost his job—and his self-respect) and son (who hasn't gotten his life in order yet). Newman isn't really convincing as the old man; Benson has played the younger role a bit too often. [PG]▼●

Harry and the Hendersons (1987) **C-110m.** **½ D: William Dear. John Lithgow, Melinda Dillon, Margaret Langrick, Joshua Rudoy, Kevin Peter Hall, David Suchet, Lainie Kazan, Don Ameche, M. Emmet Walsh. Family encounters a Bigfoot-type monster in the woods and takes it home, thinking it's dead. When it comes alive, the family finds itself becoming attached to the hairy fellow. Amusing but fatally overlong, this sweet-natured variation on E.T. THE EXTRA-TERRESTRIAL runs hot and cold; best recommended for kids. Lithgow is terrific as always. Rick Baker's makeup earned an Academy Award. Later a TV series. [PG]▼●●

Harry and Tonto (1974) **C-115m.** *** D: Paul Mazursky. Art Carney, Ellen Burstyn, Chief Dan George, Geraldine Fitzgerald, Larry Hagman, Arthur Hunnicutt, Joshua Mostel, Melanie Mayron, Herbert Berghof, Barbara Rhoades. An old man takes a cross-country trip with his cat as companion. Art Carney won an Oscar for his performance in this bittersweet, episodic comedy. [R]▼●

Harry and Walter Go to New York (1976) **C-123m.** ** D: Mark Rydell. James Caan, Elliott Gould, Diane Keaton, Michael Caine, Charles Durning, Lesley Ann Warren, Val Avery, Jack Gilford, Carol Kane. Lavish but lopsided period farce with Caan and Gould as low-grade vaudevillians in the 1890s who wind up trying their luck as safecrackers in N.Y. Spirited but strenuous comedy misses the mark. Nice art direction by Harry Horner. Panavision. [PG]▼●

Harry Brown (2009-British) **C-102m.** *** D: Daniel Barber. Michael Caine, Emily Mortimer, Charlie Creed-Miles, Ben Drew, Liam Cunningham, Iain Glen, David Bradley, Sean Harris. Caine's compelling performance in title role propels this gritty, gripping drama about an aged ex–Royal Marine driven to dole out vigilante justice after roving gangs take over his London public-housing complex and kill his best

friend. Interestingly, film was shot in gone-to-seed, crime-ridden neighborhood not far from where Caine grew up. Super 35. [R]❶

Harry in Your Pocket (1973) **C-103m.** *** D: Bruce Geller. James Coburn, Michael Sarrazin, Trish Van Devere, Walter Pidgeon. Engaging story of group of super-pickpockets and how they prey upon innocent victims. Pidgeon steals the film as sleazy professional crook.❶

Harry Potter and the Chamber of Secrets (2002) **C-161m.** **½ D: Chris Columbus. Daniel Radcliffe, Rupert Grint, Emma Watson, Kenneth Branagh, John Cleese, Robbie Coltrane, Warwick Davis, Richard Griffiths, Richard Harris, Jason Isaacs, Alan Rickman, Fiona Shaw, Maggie Smith, Julie Walters, Shirley Henderson, Miriam Margolyes, Mark Williams, Gemma Jones. J. K. Rowling's saga of witchcraft and wizardry continues in a darker vein as Harry, Ron, and Hermione enter their sophomore year at Hogwarts, where they battle a mysterious evil force that threatens the school's very existence. Second verse, pretty much the same as the first, with a plethora of engaging action set pieces (including another Quidditch match, a flying car, a CGI elf named Dobby, talking spiders, and a climactic battle with a formidable serpent), but the film suffers from overlength and uninspired transcription from page to screen. New cast members Branagh (as a pompous professor) and Isaacs (Draco Malfoy's malevolent father) add some spark. Super 35. [PG]▼❶

Harry Potter and the Deathly Hallows: Part 1 (2010-U.S.-British) **C-146m.** **½ D: David Yates. Daniel Radcliffe, Rupert Grint, Emma Watson, Helena Bonham Carter, Robbie Coltrane, Warwick Davis, Ralph Fiennes, Michael Gambon, Brendan Gleeson, Richard Griffiths, John Hurt, Jason Isaacs, Alan Rickman, Fiona Shaw, Timothy Spall, Imelda Staunton, David Thewlis, Julie Walters, Bill Nighy, Tom Felton, Helen McCrory, Clémence Poésy, Peter Mullan, Frances de la Tour, Rhys Ifans, Simon McBurney, Toby Jones, Rade Serbedzjia, Jamie Campbell Bower, Miranda Richardson. Following the death of Dumbledore, Harry is marked for death at the hands of Voldemort. His circle of friends vow to protect him, but most of them fall away as Harry, Hermione, and Ron are left to their own devices. Alternately hiding out in the woods and seeking help from possible allies, the trio experience a series of highs and lows—and so does the film. When the three pals are together it's enjoyable, even though their occasional squabbles have a repetitive ring to them. The moments of wizardry are vivid and exciting, but the film has an episodic feel, even more so than usual. Many of the familiar Potter characters are MIA or reduced to bit parts. The final scene leaves us in midair, and the result seems like more of a placeholder than a full-fledged movie. Super 35. [PG-13] ▶

Harry Potter and the Goblet of Fire (2005) C-157m. ***½ D: Mike Newell. Daniel Radcliffe, Rupert Grint, Emma Watson, Robbie Coltrane, Ralph Fiennes, Michael Gambon, Brendan Gleeson, Jason Isaacs, Gary Oldman, Miranda Richardson, Alan Rickman, Maggie Smith, Timothy Spall, Frances de la Tour, Pedja Bjelac, David Bradley, Warwick Davis, Robert Hardy, Robert Pattinson, Shirley Henderson. Harry's fourth year at Hogwarts is marked by the Quidditch World Cup and a Triwizard Tournament in which students from three schools compete in a series of increasingly challenging contests. By far the most intense installment in the series, dealing not only with the magical aspects of the characters' lives but also the trials of adolescence. Again, Steve Kloves tries to compress the contents of J. K. Rowling's hefty book into a cohesive screenplay, and while some avid fans of the novel may feel unfulfilled, the action, storytelling, and performances are excellent. The familiar players are joined here by several world-class newcomers. Super 35. [PG-13] ▶

Harry Potter and the Half-Blood Prince (2009) C-153m. *** D: David Yates. Daniel Radcliffe, Rupert Grint, Emma Watson, Helena Bonham Carter, Jim Broadbent, Robbie Coltrane, Michael Gambon, Alan Rickman, Maggie Smith, Timothy Spall, David Thewlis, David Bradley, Warwick Davis, Tom Felton, Julie Walters, Gemma Jones, Helen McCrory. Sixth in the series of J. K. Rowling adaptations. As Death Eaters fly around London, Professor Dumbledore asks Harry's help to persuade Horace Slughorn (Broadbent) to return to Hogwarts' teaching staff—but doesn't reveal why his presence is so important. This entry is unusually light and funny for much of the way as the three main characters deal with puppy love. Progressively more serious as the story develops; the film also loses some of its buoyancy around the two-hour mark. Still very entertaining, particularly for fans of the series. 3-D Super 35. [PG] ▶

Harry Potter and the Order of the Phoenix (2007) C-138m. *** D: David Yates. Daniel Radcliffe, Emma Watson, Rupert Grint, Gary Oldman, Imelda Staunton, Robert Hardy, Michael Gambon, Maggie Smith, Ralph Fiennes, Katie Leung, Helena Bonham Carter, Robbie Coltrane, Brendan Gleeson, Richard Griffiths, Jason Isaacs, Alan Rickman, Fiona Shaw, David Thewlis, Emma Thompson, David Bradley, Warwick Davis, Tom Felton, Julie Walters, Robert Pattinson. The longest Potter novel turned shortest Potter movie *begins* with Harry in trouble: standing in front of a tribunal for using his magical powers in front of a civilian. This sets a bum-luck tone for its protagonist in a

screenplay that seems in a rush to get on to the next entry; one senses some Harry midlife crisis in the wings. Acceptable slice of dank gloom-and-doom, minus some of the fun of earlier episodes. Highlighted by Staunton's outlandish but dead-on portrayal of the kind of shrew teacher everybody has had at least once. Production finesse and "event" aura made this entry one of the more watchable summer 2007 blockbusters. 3-D Super 35. [PG-13] ▶

Harry Potter and the Prisoner of Azkaban (2004) C-142m. *** D: Alfonso Cuarón. Daniel Radcliffe, Rupert Grint, Emma Watson, Robbie Coltrane, Michael Gambon, Richard Griffiths, Gary Oldman, Alan Rickman, Fiona Shaw, Maggie Smith, Timothy Spall, David Thewlis, Emma Thompson, Tom Felton, Julie Walters, David Bradley, Dawn French, Warwick Davis, Lenny Henry, Pam Ferris, Julie Christie. J. K. Rowling's much-loved characters Harry, Hermione, and Ron, now entering adolescence, begin their third year at Hogwarts School. Harry tangles with Sirius Black (Oldman), an evil wizard–escaped convict who was supposedly involved in the death of his parents. Episodic as ever, loaded with fantasy and special effects, but more foreboding and psychologically complex— and far more cinematic—than the first two offerings, a result of Cuarón taking over director's reins. Thompson and Thewlis add spunk as new Hogwarts professors. Screenplay by Steve Kloves. A mild-mannered Gambon replaces the late Richard Harris as Dumbledore. Super 35. [PG] ▼▶

Harry Potter and the Sorcerer's Stone (2001) C-152m. **½ D: Chris Columbus. Daniel Radcliffe, Rupert Grint, Emma Watson, Richard Harris, Robbie Coltrane, Maggie Smith, Ian Hart, Alan Rickman, John Hurt, John Cleese, Fiona Shaw, Richard Griffiths, Sean Biggerstaff, Tom Felton, Warwick Davis, Julie Walters, Zoe Wanamaker, David Bradley. At age 11, J. K. Rowling's bespectacled hero is freed from the custody of his miserable aunt and uncle to fulfill his destiny at Hogwarts School of Witchcraft and Wizardry, where he makes friends and enemies, learns dangerous secrets, and has many high-flying adventures. Begins with a real sense of wonder and magic, winds up an overlong, bombastic special-effects movie . . . but nothing can erase the charm of Rowling's characters and ideas, especially in the hands of a peerless British cast. Known outside U.S as HARRY POTTER AND THE PHILOSOPHER'S STONE. First of series. Super 35. [PG] ▼▶

Harry's Machine SEE: **Hollywood Harry**
Harry's War (1981) C-98m. **½ D: Kieth Merrill. Edward Herrmann, Geraldine Page, Karen Grassle, David Ogden Stiers, Salome Jens, Elisha Cook. Easygoing postman Herrmann battles the IRS after his aunt (Page) is unfairly billed for $190,000 in

back taxes. Capra-esque one-man-against-the-bureaucracy tale is sometimes touching but mostly over-baked. Herrmann performs earnestly; Merrill also wrote the screenplay. [PG]▼

Harry Tracy, Desperado (1982-Canadian) **C-100m.** **½ D: William A. Graham. Bruce Dern, Helen Shaver, Michael C. Gwynne, Gordon Lightfoot. Saga of outlaw who lives by his own moral code. Laid-back but worthwhile for Dern's fine performance and vivid re-creation of Western life at the turn of the 20th century. Original Canadian title: HARRY TRACY. [PG]▼●

Harsh Times (2006) **C-117m.** ** D: David Ayer. Christian Bale, Freddy Rodríguez, Eva Longoria, Terry Crews, Noel Gugliemi, Chaka Forman, Michael Monks, J. K. Simmons. Brutally intense drama about a former soldier, experienced in cold-blooded killing, who wants to join the L.A.P.D. but is much more interested in getting into trouble with his lifelong pal and keeping him from his responsibilities (including a promise to his girlfriend to go job-hunting). Bale makes yet another psychotic character utterly believable in this ugly, visceral portrait of society's underbelly. Gripping but emotionally draining. Directorial debut for TRAINING DAY writer Ayer. [R]▐

Hart's War (2002) **C-125m.** *** D: Gregory Hoblit. Bruce Willis, Colin Farrell, Terrence Howard, Cole Hauser, Marcel Iures, Linus Roache, Vicellous Shannon, Adrian Grenier, Joe Spano, Rory Cochrane, Sam Worthington. American soldier who's never seen action is taken prisoner during WW2 and wages a battle of wits with the ranking officer at his POW camp. The plot thickens when two black soldiers arrive on the scene and racism flares up. Entertaining yarn is a good showcase for Farrell and a perfect fit for Willis, though its message about honor is a bit muddy. There's still no villain quite like an urbane, educated Nazi. Based on a novel by John Katzenbach. Super 35. [R]▼●

Harum Scarum (1965) **C-86m.** **½ D: Gene Nelson. Elvis Presley, Mary Ann Mobley, Fran Jeffries, Michael Ansara, Jay Novello, Philip Reed, Theo Marcuse, Billy Barty. Visiting the Middle East gives usual Presley musical formula a change of scenery, via back-lot desert locations. ▼●

Harvard Man (2002) **C-100m.** *½ D: James Toback. Adrian Grenier, Sarah Michelle Gellar, Joey Lauren Adams, Eric Stoltz, Rebecca Gayheart, Gianni Russo, Ray Allen, John Neville. Harvard basketball player who's sleeping with his philosophy professor (Adams) as well as the daughter (Gellar) of a Mafioso borrows money from the don—mistake #1—then tries out a friend's new batch of LSD—mistakes #2, 3, and 4. Typically edgy, in-your-face Toback movie; arresting at first, but then goes com-

pletely haywire, with unbelievable and absurd story twists. Al Franken makes a very funny unbilled appearance. Super 35. [R]▼●

Harvest (1937-French) **127m.** **** D: Marcel Pagnol. Gabriel Gabrio, Orane Demazis, Fernandel, Edouard Delmont, Henri Poupon. Simple, stark tale of peasants Gabrio and Demazis struggling against all odds to till the land and give life to the earth. Magnificent, with Fernandel memorable as Demazis' comical husband.▼

Harvey (1950) **104m.** ***½ D: Henry Koster. James Stewart, Josephine Hull, Peggy Dow, Charles Drake, Cecil Kellaway, Victoria Horne, Jesse White, Wallace Ford, Ida Moore. Stewart gives one of his best performances as tippler Elwood P. Dowd, whose companion is a six-foot invisible rabbit named Harvey (actually, he's 6 feet, 3½ inches). Hull won Oscar as distraught sister. Mary Chase and Oscar Brodney adapted Chase's Pulitzer Prize–winning play. Hull and White re-create their Broadway roles. Remade for TV in 1998. ▼●

Harvey Girls, The (1946) **C-101m.** *** D: George Sidney. Judy Garland, Ray Bolger, John Hodiak, Angela Lansbury, Preston Foster, Virginia O'Brien, Marjorie Main, Kenny Baker, Cyd Charisse, Catherine McLeod. Westward expansion brings with it Fred Harvey's railroad station restaurants, and proper young waitresses who have civilizing influence on rowdy communities. Silly script made entertaining by good cast and a few musical highlights (like Oscar-winning "On the Atchison, Topeka, and the Santa Fe").▼●

Has Anybody Seen My Gal (1952) **C-89m.** **½ D: Douglas Sirk. Charles Coburn, Piper Laurie, Rock Hudson, Gigi Perreau, Lynn Bari, William Reynolds, Larry Gates, Skip Homeier. Pleasant, lightweight 1920s nostalgia about rich old Coburn planning to leave his fortune to the family of a woman who turned down his marriage proposal years earlier. Coburn's performance is the whole show; look fast for James Dean.▐

Hasty Heart, The (1949-British) **99m.** ***½ D: Vincent Sherman. Ronald Reagan, Patricia Neal, Richard Todd, Anthony Nicholls, Howard Crawford. Sensitive film version of John Patrick play, focusing on proud Scottish soldier who discovers he has short time to live and friendships he finally makes among his hospital mates. Remade in 1983 for cable TV.▼▐

Hatari! (1962) **C-159m.** ***½ D: Howard Hawks. John Wayne, Elsa Martinelli, Red Buttons, Hardy Kruger, Gerard Blain, Bruce Cabot. Marvelous lighthearted action film of wild-animal trappers in Africa, with just-right mixture of adventure and comedy. Wayne is at his best. Notable Henry Mancini score. Filmed in Tanganyika; title is Swahili for "Danger!"▼●

Hatchet (2007) **C-83m.** ** D: Adam

Green. Joel David Moore, Tamara Feldman, Deon Richmond, Kane Hodder, Tony Todd, Joel Murray, Patrika Darbo, Robert Englund. Horror fans might have a few guilty-pleasure giggles with this crude but knowing homage to '80s slasher movies. Mardi Gras revelers are methodically (and graphically) murdered by a misshapen psycho after they venture into a "haunted" Louisiana swamp. Also available in unrated version. Followed by a sequel. [R]●

Hatchet for the Honeymoon (1971-Italian-Spanish) **C-93m.** **½ D: Mario Bava. Stephen Forsyth, Dagmar Lassander, Laura Betti, Gerard Tichy, Femi Benussi. Characteristic Bava horror thriller: strong on vivid imagery, shot in fluid, cinematic style, with a screwy, hard-to-follow plot about a madman who murders brides, while haunted by the ghost of his own wife. [PG]▼●

Hatchet Murders, The SEE: **Deep Red**

Hate (1995-French) **95m.** *** D: Mathieu Kassovitz. Vincent Cassel, Hubert Kounde, Said Taghaoui, Karim Belkadra, Edouard Montoute. Two-fisted tale of three young hoods (an Arab, a Jew, and a black), living in the projects outside of Paris, who seek retribution when their best friend is beaten into a coma by the cops. Basically an antipolice polemic, this is short on subtlety but still powerfully effective. Bravura camerawork is reminiscent of Spike Lee, but Kassovitz's mise-en-scène is his own and aptly reflects the alienated world of lower-class kids without keys to their own city. Winner of Best Director award at Cannes. Original title: LA HAINE. [R]▼●

Hatful of Rain, A (1957) **109m.** *** D: Fred Zinnemann. Eva Marie Saint, Don Murray, Anthony Franciosa, Lloyd Nolan, Henry Silva, Gerald S. O'Loughlin, William Hickey. Realistic melodrama of the living hell dope addict Murray undergoes, and the effects on those around him; fine performances. Scripted by Michael V. Gazzo, Alfred Hayes, and Carl Foreman from Gazzo's play. CinemaScope.

Hatter's Ghost, The (1982-French) **C-120m.** *½ D: Claude Chabrol. Michel Serrault, Charles Aznavour, Monique Chaumette, Aurore Clement. Disappointing murder mystery from Chabrol, based on a Georges Simenon novel. Tailor Aznavour learns that nephew Serrault is a mass killer, but is too scared to inform the police. Potentially exciting thriller is badly handled.

Haunted Honeymoon (1986) **C-82m.** BOMB D: Gene Wilder. Gene Wilder, Gilda Radner, Dom DeLuise, Jonathan Pryce, Paul L. Smith, Peter Vaughan, Bryan Pringle. Tediously unfunny "scare movie" farce inspired by old Bob Hope/Red Skelton comedies; set in an old dark house full of creepy people (with one great gag lifted from Fred MacMurray's MURDER, HE SAYS). When you put Dom DeLuise in

drag and still can't get laughs, you know something's wrong. [PG]▼●●

Haunted House of Horror, The SEE: **Horror House**

Haunted Mansion, The (2003) **C-98m.** ** D: Rob Minkoff. Eddie Murphy, Terence Stamp, Wallace Shawn, Marsha Thomason, Jennifer Tilly, Nathaniel Parker, Dina Waters, Marc John Jefferies, Aree Davis. Workaholic real estate salesman Murphy brings his family along when his wife is summoned to a creepy old mansion. It seems the master of the house thinks she is his long-lost love. Flat, poky attempt at ghostly comedy, inspired by the great Disney theme park attraction; too scary for small children, too boring for adults, despite Murphy's trademark energy. Super 35. [PG] ▼●

Haunted Palace, The (1963) **C-85m.** **½ D: Roger Corman. Vincent Price, Debra Paget, Lon Chaney, Jr., Frank Maxwell, Leo Gordon, Elisha Cook, Jr., John Dierkes. When a man arrives in New England town to claim family castle, he discovers the town populated by mutants and the castle under an ancestor's evil spell, which soon possesses him. Good-looking but minor film from Corman's Edgar Allan Poe cycle, although based mainly on H. P. Lovecraft's *The Strange Case of Charles Dexter Ward*. Script by Charles Beaumont. Panavision.▼●

Haunted Strangler, The (1958-British) **81m.** **½ D: Robert Day. Boris Karloff, Anthony Dawson, Elizabeth Allan, Jean Kent, Derek Birch. Offbeat story set in 1880; socially conscious author Karloff investigates the case of a man who was executed 20 years earlier. Original British title: GRIP OF THE STRANGLER. ▼●

Haunted Summer (1988) **C-106m.** **½ D: Ivan Passer. Phillip Anglim, Laura Dern, Alice Krige, Eric Stoltz, Alex Winter. Flawed film version of Anne Edwards' novel about the fabled and emotional meeting between poets Lord Byron and Percy Shelley, novelist Mary Godwin, and Dr. John Polidori in Italy in 1816. The psychedelic '60s had nothing on *this* "summer of love" and experimentation. Beautifully filmed, and better than Ken Russell's similar GOTHIC, but it's still forced and unconvincing. [R]▼●

Haunting, The (1963) **112m.** ***½ D: Robert Wise. Julie Harris, Claire Bloom, Richard Johnson, Russ Tamblyn, Lois Maxwell, Fay Compton. 90-year-old New England haunted house is setting for chosen group being introduced to the supernatural, with hair-raising results. Don't see this one alone! Filmed in England; Nelson Gidding adapted Shirley Jackson's *The Haunting of Hill House*. Remade in 1999. Panavision. ▼●

Haunting, The (1999) **C-114m.** *½ D: Jan De Bont. Liam Neeson, Catherine Zeta-

Jones, Owen Wilson, Lili Taylor, Bruce Dern, Marian Seldes, Virginia Madsen. Three people are lured to a creepy mansion under false pretenses by a psychological researcher (Neeson). Incredibly dull chiller has all the special effects money can buy but no sense, no logic, and virtually no scares. Taylor's performance as a lonely woman who feels a kinship with the house is the only redeeming feature of this clunker, which has little in common with the 1963 movie or Shirley Jackson's novel, on which it's supposedly based. Panavision. [PG-13] **V●]**

Haunting Fear (1991) **C-88m.** *½ D: Fred Olen Ray. Brinke Stevens, Jay Richardson, Jan-Michael Vincent, Karen Black, Della Sheppard, Robert Clarke, Robert Quarry, Michael Berryman. Stevens fears being buried alive, her husband has a sexy mistress, and Vincent is lurking around in the street. Odd plot tries to bring it all together, but motivation is absent. Hasty, empty film allegedly based on Poe's "Premature Burial." **V●**

Haunting in Connecticut, The (2009) **C-92m.** *½ D: Peter Cornwell. Virginia Madsen, Kyle Gallner, Elias Koteas, Amanda Crew, Martin Donovan. Creaky horror picture show, purportedly based on fact, about a family that learns the hard way why they got such a great deal on a rental property with "a bit of a history." Long on spooky atmosphere, short on drama. There's nothing here you haven't seen done better, and scarier, in other haunted house dramas. Alternate version runs 102m. Super 35. [PG-13]**❚**

Haunting of Julia, The (1976-British-Canadian) **C-96m.** ** D: Richard Loncraine. Mia Farrow, Keir Dullea, Tom Conti, Jill Bennett, Robin Gammell, Cathleen Nesbitt. Occult thriller about a young woman who tries to start a new life after the death of her daughter and moves into a house inhabited by a troubled spirit. A good (if familiar) start, but soon lapses into unsatisfying contrivance. From a Peter Straub story. Originally titled FULL CIRCLE. Panavision. [R]**▼**

Haunting of Molly Hartley, The (2008) **C-87m.** *½ D: Mickey Liddell. Haley Bennett, Jake Weber, Chace Crawford, Shannon Marie Woodward, Shanna Collins, AnnaLynne McCord, Marin Hinkle, Nina Siemaszko. After being stabbed by her psycho mom, Bennett is dispatched to a hoity-toity prep school, where she comes to believe she may be demonic. Dull, clumsy horror thriller. [PG-13]**❚**

Haunts (1977) **C-98m.** *** D: Herb Freed. May Britt, Cameron Mitchell, Aldo Ray, William Gray Espy, Susan Nohr. You have to stay with it to appreciate this offbeat horror pic fully, but it's well worth the effort. Writers Anne Marisse and Herb Freed and a good cast have vividly captured small-town atmosphere when a series of murders grips the countryside. As a farm woman with demons of her own, Britt gives the best performance of her erratic career. [PG]**▼❚**

Havana (1990) **C-140m.** **½ D: Sydney Pollack. Robert Redford, Lena Olin, Alan Arkin, Tomas Milian, Daniel Davis, Tony Plana, Betsy Brantley, Lise Cutter, Richard Farnsworth, Mark Rydell. No masterpiece, overly reminiscent of CASABLANCA, and a huge box-office disaster, but still unjustly maligned as a stinker. Redford (aging, but marvelous) plays a professional gambler hoping to score in the waning hours of Batista's Cuba; Olin (surprisingly stiff) is the married Swede who takes his mind off the game. Production designer's dream is very entertaining for about 90 minutes, then tails off. Similar to the underrated Richard Lester film CUBA. Raul Julia appears unbilled. [R]**▼❚]**

Haven (2004-U.S.-British-German-Spanish) **C-98m.** ** D: Frank E. Flowers. Bill Paxton, Orlando Bloom, Stephen Dillane, Zoe Saldana, Razaaq Adoti, Agnes Bruckner, Victor Rasuk, Lee Ingleby, Anthony Mackie, Robert Wisdom, Joy Bryant, Bobby Cannavale, Serena Scott Thomas. Slickly directed but confusing, connect-the-dots story that opens with Paxton and his teen daughter fleeing to the Cayman Islands when the Feds show up on his doorstep. Who is he? Why is he on the run? More important, why should we care? Annoyingly fragmented narrative tries to be clever but succeeds only at being convoluted. Bloom coproduced. [R]**❚**

Have Rocket—Will Travel (1959) **76m.** **½ D: David Lowell Rich. The Three Stooges, Jerome Cowan, Anna Lisa, Bob Colbert. Good slapstick as the Stooges accidentally launch into space, meet a unicorn, and go on to become national heroes. This was the trio's first starring feature after being rediscovered on TV, though Joe DeRita had, by this time, filled the Curly/Shemp slot.**▼**

Having a Wild Weekend (1965-British) **91m.** **½ D: John Boorman. Dave Clark Five, Barbara Ferris, Lenny Davidson, Rick Huxley, Mike Smith, Denis Payton, David Lodge. Just as The Dave Clark Five tried to steal some of the Beatles' thunder, this fast-paced trifle tried to capture success of A HARD DAY'S NIGHT. The Five star as stuntmen who, along with a model (Ferris), search for a dream island. Songs include "Having a Wild Weekend," "Catch Us If You Can," "I Can't Stand It." Director Boorman's first film. Originally titled CATCH US IF YOU CAN.**▼**

Havoc (2005-U.S.-German) **C-85m.** ** D: Barbara Kopple. Anne Hathaway, Bijou Phillips, Shiri Appleby, Michael Biehn, Joseph Gordon-Levitt, Matt O'Leary, Freddy Rodriguez, Laura San Giacomo,

Mike Vogel, Cecilia Peck, Sam Bottoms. Well-meaning but overwrought chronicle of a bright, wealthy, bored teen who's sleepwalking through her life. She and her friends attempt to adopt a gangsta lifestyle but don't know what they're getting into when they mix with real inner-city Latinos. Potentially intriguing exploration of race, class, and teen lifestyles goes way over the top. Rare non-documentary effort by Kopple, scripted by another Oscar winner, Stephen Gaghan. Released direct to DVD in the U.S. Unrated version runs 93m. Followed by a direct-to-DVD sequel. [R] ◗

Hav Plenty (1998) C-92m. *½ D: Christopher Scott Cherot. Christopher Scott Cherot, Chenoa Maxwell, Hill Harper, Tammi Katherine Jones, Betty Vaughn. Smug, self-satisfied romantic comedy about down-and-out writer who finds unexpected sparks with his best friend when he spends New Year's weekend with her crazy friends and family. Maxwell gives a truly irritating performance as the inexplicable girl of Cherot's dreams, but the writer-director-editor-star has charisma; it's his filmmaking skills that need polishing. Dopey movie-within-a-movie ending features Shemar Moore, Nia Long, TLC's Chili, The Fugees' Lauryn Hill, and Mekhi Phifer. [R] ▼▶

Hawaii (1966) C-171m. *** D: George Roy Hill. Julie Andrews, Max von Sydow, Richard Harris, Torin Thatcher, Gene Hackman, Carroll O'Connor, Jocelyne LaGarde, John Cullum, George Rose, Michael Constantine. Sprawling filmization of James Michener's novel. Story (adapted by Dalton Trumbo and Daniel Taradash) follows growth of Hawaii in 1800s as fierce but well-intentioned missionary tries to bring religion to the undeveloped islands. Uneven but generally entertaining epic. Originally released at 189m.; some prints 151m. Look for Bette Midler as a passenger on the Hawaii-bound ship. Sequel: THE HAWAIIANS. Panavision. ▼▶◗

Hawaiians, The (1970) C-134m. *** D: Tom Gries. Charlton Heston, Geraldine Chaplin, John Phillip Law, Tina Chen, Alec McCowen, Keye Luke, Mako. Sequel to HAWAII is epic narrative of seafaring Heston returning home to a restless, changing Hawaii. Film follows several decades of relationships, conflict, hardship, progress, sex, leprosy—you name it. Compelling, colorful storytelling, with outstanding performance by Chen. Panavision.[PG] ◗

Hawk Is Dying, The (2006) C-107m. *½ D: Julian Goldberger. Paul Giamatti, Michelle Williams, Robert Wisdom, Rusty Schwimmer, Ann Wedgeworth, Michael Pitt. Amid much angst, a stressed-out man tries to find meaning in his life by capturing and attempting to train a red-tailed hawk. Unceasingly intense drama is done

in by pretension and confusion . . . and is an ordeal to sit through. Giamatti rises way above the material. Based on a novel by Harry Crews. ◗

Hawks (1988-British) C-107m. ** D: Robert Ellis Miller. Timothy Dalton, Anthony Edwards, Janet McTeer, Camille Coduri, Jill Bennett, Sheila Hancock, Connie Booth. Heavy-handed black comedy about British lawyer Dalton and American jock Edwards, both terminally ill with cancer but still equally red-blooded; they rip off an ambulance and head for the brothels of Amsterdam for one final fling. Uneasy mixture of humor and touchy-feely emotion does not work. Barry Gibb (of the Bee Gees, who did the music) is coauthor of the story upon which this is based. [R] ▼

Hawk the Slayer (1980-British) C-93m. *½ D: Terry Marcel. Jack Palance, John Terry, Bernard Bresslaw, Ray Charleson, Peter O'Farrell, Harry Andrews, Roy Kinnear, Ferdy Mayne. Brothers Palance and Terry vie for a magical family sword in this period costumer. Labored, with gimmicky direction. ▼◗

Hawmps! (1976) C-113m. ** D: Joe Camp. James Hampton, Christopher Connelly, Slim Pickens, Jack Elam, Denver Pyle. Amusing idea based on real life incident: camels trained as Army mounts in Texas desert. Some comedy results, but how far can you stretch one idea? Originally released at 126m. [G] ▼▶

Head (1968) C-86m. *** D: Bob Rafelson. The Monkees, Terry (Teri) Garr, Vito Scotti, Timothy Carey, Logan Ramsey, Frank Zappa, Jack Nicholson. Far-out film debut for TV rock group was written (or concocted) by Rafelson and Nicholson before they made big splash with FIVE EASY PIECES; this overlooked item is a delightful explosion of crazy ideas with no coherent plot, many old film clips, some good songs, and such unlikely guest stars as Sonny Liston and Victor Mature. Well worth seeing. [G] ▼◗

Head Above Water (1996-U.S.-British) C-92m. ** D: Jim Wilson. Harvey Keitel, Cameron Diaz, Craig Sheffer, Billy Zane, Shay Duffin. Black comedy–thriller about lovely substance abuser Diaz; she's married to judge Keitel, but her male friends still carry a torch for her, with disastrous consequences. Convoluted plot twists abound, but you don't really care what happens to any of these characters. Remake of same-named 1993 Norwegian film. U.S. debut on cable TV. Super 35. [PG-13] ▼◗

Heading South (2005-Canadian-French) C-108m. *** D: Laurent Cantet. Charlotte Rampling, Karen Young, Louise Portal, Ménothy Cesar, Lys Ambroise, Jackenson Pierre Olmo Diaz. Absorbing, politically loaded drama set in Haiti during the late 1970s, where pampered, sexually frustrated middle-aged female tourists have hunky young native boys service them, blissfully unaware of the pressures they face under the brutal dictatorship of "Baby Doc" Duvalier. The spotlight is on Rampling and Young, who vie for the attention of a handsome local (Cesar). Based on short stories by Dany Laferriere. ▶

Head in the Clouds (2004-Canadian-British) **C-133m.** ** D: John Duigan. Charlize Theron, Penélope Cruz, Stuart Townsend, Thomas Kretschmann, Steven Berkoff, David La Haye, Gabriel Hogan. Forthright young woman (Theron) lives a Bohemian life in 1930s Paris, some of it in a ménage à trois with a photographer's model (Cruz) and an uptight Irish beau (Townsend) who is drawn to the plight of the Spanish Republicans. Duigan's screenplay bites off more than it can chew, spanning 20 years, the evolution of two relationships, and a character's political awakening. WW2 section rings hollow; artificial backdrops don't help. Theron and Cruz are quite good, and very sexy. Super 35. [R] ▼▶

Headless Body in Topless Bar (1996) **C-101m.** *½ D: Ann Bruce. Raymond Barry, Jennifer MacDonald, Rustam Branaman, April Grace, Taylor Nichols, David Selby, Paul Williams, Biff Yeager. This "psychological dark comedy" based on the infamous 1983 *New York Post* headline is a talky character piece about an ex-con who takes the inhabitants of a topless bar hostage after killing the bartender. Might have worked better as a one-act play—or, better yet, left on the newsstand. ▼

Head Office (1986) **C-86m.** ** D: Ken Finkleman. Judge Reinhold, Eddie Albert, Jane Seymour, Danny DeVito, Rick Moranis, Don Novello, Michael O'Donoghue, Wallace Shawn, Lori-Nan Engler. Naive Reinhold is hired by world's most powerful multinational conglomerate after his father pulls strings, falls for board chairman's renegade daughter. Episodic, wildly uneven comedy wastes good cast, though Novello, Albert, and O'Donoghue have their funny moments, Seymour some sexy ones. Panavision. [PG-13] ▼▶

Head of State (2003) **C-95m.** **½ D: Chris Rock. Chris Rock, Bernie Mac, Dylan Baker, Nick Searcy, Lynn Whitfield, Robin Givens, Tamala Jones, James Rebhorn, Keith David, Stephanie March, Nate Dogg, Jude Ciccolella, Tracy Morgan, Chandra Wilson. A hardworking community activist and alderman from Washington, D.C., is drafted as a last-minute replacement candidate for president. He soon tires of following orders and begins to speak his mind. Rock is the whole show here, and he's on top of his game, spouting the kind of straight talk we'd all like to hear from candidates. The filmmaking is sloppy, as is the story development, but the direc-

tor, cowriter, and star deliver the laughs. [PG-13] ▼▶

Head-On (2004-German-Turkish-French) **C-121m.** *** D: Fatih Akin. Birol Ünel, Sibel Kekilli, Catrin Striebeck, Güven Kirac, Meltem Cumbul, Zarah McKenzie, Stefan Gebelhoff. Two Turks, one a late-30s alcoholic nightclub employee, the other a young but far-from-innocent woman determined to escape her traditional family, meet in a hospital in their adopted country of Germany. They embark on a paper marriage and live as roommates, but drugs and other influences cause their lives to intertwine in unexpected ways. Harsh, powerful drama of stubborn determination and immigrant culture provides a glimpse into a seedy milieu that never seems phony. ▶

Head Over Heels (1979) **C-97m.** **½ D: Joan Micklin Silver. John Heard, Mary Beth Hurt, Peter Riegert, Kenneth McMillan, Gloria Grahame, Nora Heflin, Griffin Dunne. Low-key story of Heard's obsession with winning back former girlfriend Hurt; the kind of film that engenders strictly personal reactions—it will either charm or annoy you. Based on Ann Beattie's novel CHILLY SCENES OF WINTER, and reissued under that name at 93m. Jazz harmonica great Toots Thielemans is prominently featured on the soundtrack. [PG] ▼

Head Over Heels (2001) **C-91m.** *½ D: Mark Waters. Monica Potter, Freddie Prinze, Jr., Shalom Harlow, Ivana Milicevic, Sarah O'Hare, Tomiko Fraser, China Chow, Timothy Olyphant. Klutzy, unlucky-in-love art restorer Potter falls for nice-guy fashion exec Prinze, whose apartment is next door to the one she's sharing with four fashion models. While peeping in on him, she thinks she sees him commit murder. Forget REAR WINDOW: this is an addlebrained, cliché-laden romantic comedy-farce-thriller. Super 35. [PG-13] ▼▶

Health (1979) **C-100m.** ** D: Robert Altman. Carol Burnett, Glenda Jackson, James Garner, Lauren Bacall, Diane Stilwell, Henry Gibson, Donald Moffat, Paul Dooley, Dick Cavett, Alfre Woodard. Offbeat political satire using health-food convention in Florida hotel as basis for various backroom shenanigans. Non-Altman buffs may like this more than devotees; Woodard steals the film—no easy feat considering that incredible cast—as hotel's ultra-patient manager. Shelved for two years. Title is acronym for Happiness, Energy, And Longevity Through Health. Panavision. [PG]

Hear My Song (1991-U.S.-British) **C-104m.** *** D: Peter Chelsom. Ned Beatty, Adrian Dunbar, Shirley Anne Field, Tara Fitzgerald, David McCallum, William Hootkins, Harold Berens, James Nesbitt. Wheeler-dealer nightclub owner must redeem himself with his girlfriend—and his community—by finding expatriate Irish tenor Josef Locke and bringing him back to England for an engagement. Charmingly offbeat, old-fashioned film written by its first-time feature director and leading man Dunbar, very loosely based on real-life story. If Beatty (as Locke) didn't pull off the climactic scene, it wouldn't work—but he does. [R]▼●

Hear No Evil (1993) **C-97m.** *½ D: Robert Greenwald. Marlee Matlin, D. B. Sweeney, Martin Sheen, John C. McGinley, Christina Carlisi, Greg Elam, Charley Lang, Marge Redmond. Plotline reminiscent of WAIT UNTIL DARK, except the terrorized young woman here is deaf, not blind. You can fill in the blanks. Grade-Z thriller, only partly redeemed by the presence of Matlin. [R]▼●

Hearse, The (1980) **C-100m.** ** D: George Bowers. Trish Van Devere, Joseph Cotten, David Gautreaux, Donald Hotton, Med Flory, Donald Petrie. Passably engrossing yarn right off the woman-in-distress/house-inhabited-by-spirits assembly line, with an unsatisfying conclusion. [PG]▼●

Heartaches (1981-Canadian) **C-93m.** **½ D: Donald Shebib. Margot Kidder, Annie Potts, Robert Carradine, Winston Rekert, George Touliatos, Guy Sanvido. Pregnant Potts abandons husband Carradine—who is not the baby's father—and becomes the unwilling buddy of man-hunting screwball Kidder. Fine lead performances spark this minor comedy. [R]▼●

Heart and Souls (1993) **C-104m.** *** D: Ron Underwood. Robert Downey, Jr., Charles Grodin, Alfre Woodard, Kyra Sedgwick, Tom Sizemore, David Paymer, Elisabeth Shue, Eric Lloyd, Bill Calvert, Lisa Lucas, Robert Portnow, B. B. King. Four disparate San Franciscans die in a bus accident in 1959, and find themselves inexorably linked with a baby who's been born at that same exact moment; what's more, only he can see and hear them. A great showcase for Downey—whose body is inhabited, at various times, by his heavenly friends—though Woodard is equally good, as usual. Fans of mushy, sentimental, old-fashioned Hollywood fantasies (like us) should enjoy this fable; others beware. Based on a 9m. short subject by the coauthors of this script. Look fast to see Bob Newhart's son, Robert William Newhart, impersonating his dad. Panavision. [PG-13]▼●

Heart Beat (1980) **C-105m.** *½ D: John Byrum. Nick Nolte, Sissy Spacek, John Heard, Ray Sharkey, Anne Dusenberry, Kent Williams, Tony Bill, Steve Allen. Hapless chronicle of the relationship between Jack Kerouac (Heard) and Carolyn (Spacek) and Neal (Nolte) Cassady. Byrum's flaky script (based more on fiction than on fact) has no continuity whatsoever. Sharkey stands out as the Allen Ginsberg-esque Ira;

good period score by Jack Nitzsche. Watch for John Larroquette. Cassady's life is also explored in NEAL CASSADY. [R]▼●

Heartbeeps (1981) **C-79m.** *½ D: Allan Arkush. Andy Kaufman, Bernadette Peters, Randy Quaid, Kenneth McMillan, Melanie Mayron, Christopher Guest; voice of Jack Carter. Two robots fall for each other in this misfired futuristic comedy. Students of makeup might want to take a peek at Stan Winston's work. Panavision. [PG]▼●

Heartbreaker (2010-French) **C-105m.** *** D: Pascal Chaumeil. Romain Duris, Vanessa Paradis, Julie Ferrier, François Damiens, Héléna Noguerra, Andrew Lincoln, Jacques Frantz, Jean-Yves Lafesse. Entertaining romantic comedy about a man whose business is breaking up relationships. He's usually hired by an angry parent, and he and his team are highly paid. But this time he may have met his Waterloo, trying to discourage a woman from marrying a wealthy man she genuinely loves—with only one week to accomplish the task. Avoids the pitfalls of predictability through inventive flourishes and an appealing pair of stars. Panavision. ●

Heartbreakers (1984) **C-98m.** **½ D: Bobby Roth. Peter Coyote, Nick Mancuso, Carole Laure, Max Gail, James Laurenson, Carol Wayne, Kathryn Harrold, Jamie Rose. Moody, provocative film about two male friends (avant-garde artist Coyote, second-generation businessman Mancuso) seeking creative and sexual fulfillment and trying to define their relationships with others. Highly personal, occasionally insightful film invites highly personal reactions. Bull's-eye performances, great use of L.A. locations. [R]▼

Heartbreakers (2001) **C-123m.** **½ D: David Mirkin. Sigourney Weaver, Jennifer Love Hewitt, Gene Hackman, Ray Liotta, Jason Lee, Anne Bancroft, Jeffrey Jones, Nora Dunn, Julio Oscar Mechoso, Carrie Fisher, Ricky Jay, Sarah Silverman, Zach Galifianakis, Shawn Colvin, Kevin Nealon, Elya Baskin. Sleazy but watchable comedy about mother-and-daughter con artists who marry men and then take them for everything they're worth in divorce settlements. Cast seems to be having a good time; wonderful performance by Hewitt's breasts. Panavision. [PG-13] ●

Heartbreak Hotel (1988) **C-93m.** **½ D: Chris Columbus. David Keith, Tuesday Weld, Charlie Schlatter, Jacque Lynn Colton, Angela Goethals, Chris Mulkey, Karen Landry. A reliable test of your whimsy threshold, as an Ohio teen (Schlatter) kidnaps Elvis in 1972, then transports him home to the divorced mom (Weld) who's carried a torch for the King since the mid-1950s. Keith's Presley, like the entire film, is fun, though the premise is so hard to swallow that you're likely to go with this—or reject it—all the way. Pair this with WILD IN THE COUNTRY or ROCK,

ROCK, ROCK for a compatible video double bill. [PG-13]▼●◗

Heartbreak Kid, The (1972) **C-104m.** ******* D: Elaine May. Charles Grodin, Cybill Shepherd, Jeannie Berlin, Eddie Albert, Audra Lindley. Neil Simon's supreme comedy of embarrassment, adapted from Bruce Jay Friedman's short story "A Change of Plan." Jewish boy (Grodin) gets married (to Berlin) but meets beautiful WASP blonde (Shepherd) on honeymoon, and determines to juggle plans. Either hilarious or horrifying, depending on your point of view; directed for maximum impact by May, whose daughter plays Grodin's bride. Remade in 2007. [PG]▼●◗

Heartbreak Kid, The (2007) **C-116m.** ****½** D: Bobby Farrelly, Peter Farrelly. Ben Stiller, Malin Akerman, Michelle Monaghan, Jerry Stiller, Rob Corddry, Carlos Mencia, Scott Wilson, Polly Holliday, Leslie Easterbrook, Eva Longoria. Eligible San Francisco bachelor Stiller chances to meet a beautiful blonde dream girl (Akerman) and in no time flat gets married. Only on their honeymoon to Mexico does he discover that she's the bride from hell . . . while striking up a warm relationship with an American tourist (Monaghan) staying at the same hotel. Reinvention of the 1972 hit plays surprisingly well, given the Farrellys' usual penchant for overlength and gross-out gags (though this one flopped). Super 35. [R]◗

Heartbreak Ridge (1986) **C-130m.** ****½** D: Clint Eastwood. Clint Eastwood, Marsha Mason, Everett McGill, Moses Gunn, Eileen Heckart, Bo Svenson, Boyd Gaines, Mario Van Peebles, Arlen Dean Snyder. Eastwood is so enjoyable to watch, as a hell-raising career marine sergeant who whips a squadron of young recruits into shape, that he makes this predictable and protracted film worthwhile. But it's still pretty thin stuff and takes longer to play out than the real-life invasion of Grenada it depicts. [R]▼●◗

Heartburn (1986) **C-108m.** ******* D: Mike Nichols. Meryl Streep, Jack Nicholson, Jeff Daniels, Maureen Stapleton, Stockard Channing, Richard Masur, Catherine O'Hara, Steven Hill, Milos Forman, Karen Akers, Anna Maria Horsford, Mercedes Ruehl, Joanna Gleason, Yakov Smirnoff, Kevin Spacey, Natasha Lyonne, Christian Clemenson. Nora Ephron adapted her own best-selling (and autobiographical) book about a sophisticated couple whose marriage seems just fine until she learns he's been having an affair—while she's pregnant! Lightweight, superficial story is supercharged by two charismatic stars, who make it a must-see. Director Forman's acting debut. [R]▼●◗

Heart Condition (1990) **C-95m.** ****½** D: James D. Parriott. Bob Hoskins, Denzel Washington, Chloe Webb, Roger E. Mosley, Ja'net DuBois, Alan Rachins, Ray Baker, Jeffrey Meek. Superficial but entertaining yarn about a crass, bigoted L.A. cop who gets a heart transplant and learns, to his dismay, that the donor was the slick black lawyer he'd been stalking. What's more, the deceased appears as a ghost/companion who wants the cop to help avenge his murder. Outlandish premise made palatable by its two dynamic leads. [R]▼●◗

Heart Is a Lonely Hunter, The (1968) **C-125m.** ******* D: Robert Ellis Miller. Alan Arkin, Sondra Locke, Laurinda Barrett, Stacy Keach, Jr., Chuck McCann, Biff McGuire, Percy Rodriguez, Cicely Tyson, Jackie Marlowe. Heart-rending drama of a deaf mute's lonely world, and how he helps an adolescent girl struggling to find herself. Sincere adaptation of Carson McCullers' novel, set in the Deep South, benefits from moving performances—including Arkin, Locke (whose debut film this was), and comic actor McCann, in a revelatory change-of-pace part as Arkin's simple-minded mute friend. Also marked film debut for Keach. [G]▼◗

Heart Is Deceitful Above All Things, The (2004-U.S.-British-French-Japanese) **C-97m.** ****** D: Asia Argento. Asia Argento, Jimmy Bennett, Cole Sprouse, Dylan Sprouse, Peter Fonda, Ben Foster, Ornella Muti, Kip Pardue, Michael Pitt, Marilyn Manson, Jeremy Sisto, Jeremy Renner. Pretentious drama about a woman who is ill equipped for parenthood but gains custody of her young son, who has been in foster care. He's justifiably angry; she callously toys with his feelings, with no regard for his safety. One-note film may be read as an outsider's warped view of an American heartland populated by abusive parents, perverts, and hypocritical Bible-thumping rednecks. Argento also scripted. Winona Ryder appears unbilled. [R]◗

Heartland (1979) **C-96m.** *****½** D: Richard Pearce. Rip Torn, Conchata Ferrell, Barry Primus, Lilia Skala, Megan Folson, Amy Wright. Simple, well-told story of hearty Americans surviving the rigors of frontier life, circa 1910. Ferrell plays a young widow who accepts a job as housekeeper for dour rancher Torn in the wilds of Wyoming. Well acted, well filmed, and beautifully understated; based on the actual diaries of a pioneer woman. [PG]▼◗

Heartland Reggae (1980-Canadian) **C-87m.** BOMB D: J. P. Lewis. Bob Marley and the Wailers, Peter Tosh, Jacob Miller and the Inner Circle Band, Althea and Donna. Shoddy documentary of '78 concert commemorating a visit to Jamaica by Haile Selassie. Even the music can't save it. ▼◗

Heart Like a Wheel (1983) **C-113m.** ****½** D: Jonathan Kaplan. Bonnie Bedelia, Beau Bridges, Leo Rossi, Hoyt Axton, Bill McKinney, Anthony Edwards, Dean Paul Martin, Paul Bartel, Dick Miller,

Terence Knox. Well-made but curiously uninspiring bio of race-car driver Shirley Muldowney, who had to fight sexism—and the conflict of career vs. marriage—to become a champion on the track. Bedelia's performance is outstanding, but disjointed narrative—particularly where her relationship with racer Connie Kalitta (Bridges) is concerned—is a handicap. [PG]▼●▶

Heart of Dixie (1989) **C-95m.** *½ D: Martin Davidson. Ally Sheedy, Virginia Madsen, Phoebe Cates, Treat Williams, Don Michael Paul, Kyle Secor, Francesca Roberts, Kurtwood Smith, Richard Bradford, Barbara Babcock. Forgettable story of Alabama college sorority in the late 1950s and one girl's awakening to larger realities of life—including the mistreatment of blacks in the South. Superficial and uninvolving, to say the least. [PG]▼●▶

Heart of Glass (1976-German) **C-93m.** *** D: Werner Herzog. Josef Bierbichler, Stefan Autter, Clemens Scheitz, Volker Prechtel, Sonia Skiba. A glassblower has died without revealing the secret formula of his craft, and this has a profound, disturbing effect on his fellow townspeople. Thematically muddled but visually stunning; crammed with stark, graphic, beautiful images. Based on a Bavarian legend; Herzog each day put his cast into a hypnotic trance, to attempt to achieve an effect of collective hysteria.▼▶

Heart of Me, The (2003-British) **C-96m.** **½ D: Thaddeus O'Sullivan. Helena Bonham Carter, Olivia Williams, Paul Bettany, Eleanor Bron, Luke Newberry, Tom Ward, Gillian Hanna, Andrew Havill, Alison Reid. A fine cast enlivens this earnest soap opera about an upper-class gent in 1930s London falling into an indiscreet affair with his wife's sister. Well made, with good period detail, this film works mainly as a showcase for its actors. Based on the novel by Rosamond Lehmann. [R] ▼▶

Heart of Midnight (1988) **C-93m.** *½ D: Matthew Chapman. Jennifer Jason Leigh, Peter Coyote, Gale Mayron, Sam Schacht, Denise Dummont, Frank Stallone, Brenda Vaccaro, Steve Buscemi. Psychological thriller about a young woman teetering on the edge of sanity, who inherits a seedy sex club which attracts a sick clientele. Good performance by Leigh and artsy approach to subject are minor diversions in this muddled and unpleasant film. Written by the director. [R]▼●

Heart of the Game, The (2006) **C-97m.** ***½ D: Ward Serrill. Narrated by Chris "Ludacris" Bridges. Filmmaker Serrill spent seven years filming a Seattle-area high school girls' basketball team, and his first gift was finding its unorthodox coach (college tax prof Bill Resler, moonlighting). Eventually, he was awarded a second (player Darnellia Russell, gifted but a

bundle of emotions) and the kind of unanticipated personal/legal plot twist that has to be the dream of all documentarians. HOOP DREAMS originated this kind of movie, but this is an extraordinary story and it gets the crowd-pleasing rendering it deserves. [PG-13]▶

Heart of the Stag (1984-New Zealand) **C-91m.** ** D: Michael Firth. Bruno Lawrence, Mary Regan, Terence Cooper, Anne Flannery. Lawrence is mysterious stranger who signs on as a farmhand and disrupts incestuous relationship of Cooper and his redheaded daughter Regan. Pretentious drama benefits from good acting, tense musical score by Leonard Rosenman. [R]▼▶

Hearts and Armour (1982-Italian) **C-101m.** ** D: Giacomo Battiato. Tanya Roberts, Barbara De Rossi, Zeudi Araya, Rick Edwards, Leigh McCloskey, Ron Moss. Well-mounted but confusing fantasy based on the 1516 classic *Orlando Furioso* by Ludovico Ariosto. De Rossi is a sexy female warrior in knight's armor fighting in the war between Christians and Moors. American stars such as Roberts and McCloskey add little to a film (also shot in TV miniseries form) aimed at an international audience. Technovision.▼

Hearts and Minds (1974) **C-110m.** ***½ D: Peter Davis. Oscar-winning documentary about our misguided involvement in Vietnam was political hot potato for a while, but may rate more frequent showings now that the country has caught up with it. Packs a wallop, regardless of one's political persuasion. [R]▼●▶

Hearts in Atlantis (2001) **C-101m.** ** D: Scott Hicks. Anthony Hopkins, Hope Davis, David Morse, Anton Yelchin, Mika Boorem, Alan Tudyk, Celia Weston, Tom Bower. An impressionable boy, being raised by his mother—who resents single parenthood—falls under the spell of a mysterious, charismatic stranger who comes to board with them. Mushy mumbo-jumbo, nostalgically set in 1960. Adapted by William Goldman from two short stories—Stephen King's—but not the one that bore this title! Super 35. [PG-13]▼▶

Hearts of Darkness: A Filmmaker's Apocalypse (1991) **C-96m.** ***½ D: Fax Bahr, George Hickenlooper. Top-notch documentary detailing the disaster-laden production of Francis Coppola's 1979 Vietnam epic, APOCALYPSE NOW. Expertly mixes footage shot by Eleanor Coppola (the director's wife) during the film's shooting in the Philippines and decade-later interviews with crew and cast (excluding Marlon Brando, who declined to participate). Revealing peek into the filmmaking process and a record of events during this particular film's chaotic shoot. [R]▼●▶

Hearts of Fire (1987) **C-95m.** BOMB D: Richard Marquand. Fiona (Flanagan),

Rupert Everett, Bob Dylan, Julian Glover, Suzanne Bertish, Ian Dury, Richie Havens, Larry Lamb, Maury Chaykin. Perfectly dreadful account of the rise of a rock singer (Fiona), and her relationships with her mentors: a British pop star (Everett) and a cynical, retired rock legend (who else but Dylan). Dylan's first screen appearance since 1978's RENALDO AND CLARA; Marquand's final credit as director. This turkey played briefly in England in 1987, and was released to video in 1990. There are 19 songs on the soundtrack (but none memorable enough to raise its rating). J-D-C Scope. [R]▼●

Hearts of the West (1975) **C-102m.** *** D: Howard Zieff. Jeff Bridges, Andy Griffith, Donald Pleasence, Blythe Danner, Alan Arkin, Richard B. Shull, Herb Edelman, Alex Rocco, Marie Windsor, Dub Taylor, William Christopher. Offbeat comedy. Starry-eyed Bridges comes to 1930s Hollywood hoping to be a Western writer, winds up starring in cheap cowboy films instead. Enjoyable but low-key. [PG]▼)

Heat (1972) **C-100m.** *** D: Paul Morrissey. Sylvia Miles, Joe Dallesandro, Andrea Feldman, Pat Ast, Ray Vestal. Andy Warhol meets SUNSET BOULEVARD in this hot and heavy tale of unemployed actor Dallesandro taking up with faded star Miles. Even nonfans of the Warhol group might like this. [R]▼)

Heat (1987) **C-101m.** BOMB D: R. M. Richards. Burt Reynolds, Karen Young, Peter MacNicol, Howard Hesseman, Neill Barry, Diana Scarwid, Joe Mascolo, Alfie Wise. Dim, dingy, scattershot film (written by William Goldman, of all people) about a Las Vegas tough, whose exact livelihood is never defined, but who knows how to handle the low-lifes—and teaches "protégé" MacNicol all he knows. So what? [R]▼●)

Heat (1995) **C-172m.** ***½ D: Michael Mann. Al Pacino, Robert De Niro, Val Kilmer, Jon Voight, Tom Sizemore, Diane Venora, Amy Brenneman, Ashley Judd, Mykelti Williamson, Wes Studi, Ted Levine, Dennis Haysbert, William Fichtner, Natalie Portman, Tom Noonan, Kevin Gage, Hank Azaria, Henry Rollins, Tone Loc, Jeremy Piven. Dynamite cops-and-robbers saga, with Pacino an obsessive, supersmart L.A. detective on the trail of high-tech, high-precision robber De Niro and his tight-knit gang. It turns out that the two have more in common than either one might think. A fascinating, multilayered character study studded with gripping (and often violent) action scenes, plus a chance to see two of the world's greatest actors working together—even though they share precious little screen time. Overlength is the only criticism of this crackerjack contemporary drama. Mann scripted, reworking his 1989 TV movie L.A. TAKEDOWN.

Bud Cort appears unbilled. Panavision. [R]▼●)

Heat and Dust (1983-British) **C-130m.** *** D: James Ivory. Julie Christie, Greta Scacchi, Christopher Cazenove, Julian Glover, Susan Fleetwood, Shashi Kapoor, Madhur Jaffrey, Barry Foster, Zakir Hussain, Patrick Godfrey. Englishwomen Scacchi and great-niece Christie, 60 years apart, fall in love with India and become pregnant by natives—yet still remain outsiders in a land they can never fully comprehend. Intelligent drama, lovely performances. Screenplay by Ruth Prawer Jhabvala, from her novel. [R]▼)

Heat and Sunlight (1988) **C-98m.** **½ D: Rob Nilsson. Rob Nilsson, Consuelo Faust, Don Bajema, Ernie Fosselius, Bill Bailey, Bill Ackridge. Photographer Nilsson must deal with his feelings and obsessions as his love affair with dancer Faust ends. Lively in its best moments, but also meanders and lacks structure. Characters are the most interesting element here. ▼●)

Heathers (1989) **C-102m.** **½ D: Michael Lehmann. Winona Ryder, Christian Slater, Shannen Doherty, Lisanne Falk, Kim Walker, Penelope Milford, Glenn Shadix, Lance Fenton. Sharp, somewhat smug satire of high school social strata, with Ryder in a terrific performance as a girl who hangs out with the school's bitch-queens but doesn't feel quite comfortable about their reign of terror. Outrageous black humor works at first, but isn't sustained; uneven script goes far astray. Slater is commanding in his Jack Nicholson-esque performance. Feature debut for director Lehmann and writer Daniel Waters, with many virtues as well as flaws. [R]▼●)

Heat of Desire (1980-French) **C-90m.** ** D: Luc Beraud. Patrick Dewaere, Clio Goldsmith, Jeanne Moreau, Guy Marchand, Pierre Dux, Jose-Luis Lopez Vasquez. Happily married university professor is whisked away for spontaneous sex by mysterious, loose-living free spirit, who soon destroys his marriage and scuttles his career. Silly but sometimes sexy heavy-breather; several screen-filling shots of Goldsmith's ample frame. U.S. release: 1984. [R]▼●

Heatwave (1982-Australian) **C-99m.** *** D: Phillip Noyce. Judy Davis, Richard Moir, Chris Haywood, Bill Hunter, John Gregg, Anna Jemison. Radical Davis protests destruction of neighborhood for $100 million redevelopment project by firm which might have mob connections. Situation further complicated by attraction between her and project architect Moir in this Aussie counterpart to CHINATOWN. From a real-life incident, which also inspired THE KILLING OF ANGEL STREET. [R]▼

Heaven (1987) **C-80m.** ** D: Diane Keaton. Nothing if not bizarre, this personal project of Keaton's intersperses oddly shot interviews with non sequitur clips from old movies on the subject of Heaven: how to get there, what it will be like, if it exists, etc. Clips range from METROPOLIS to THE HORN BLOWS AT MIDNIGHT—what's the point? [PG-13] ▼●)

Heaven (1998) C-103m. ** D: Scott Reynolds. Martin Donovan, Danny Edwards, Richard Schiff, Joanna Going, Patrick Malahide, Karl Urban. An intriguing premise goes unrealized in this muddled psychological thriller about a deeply troubled architect (Donovan) with a severe gambling problem who's been rejected by his wife. Endless, confusing plot twists are set in motion when he mixes with Heaven (Edwards), a transvestite stripper who is also clairvoyant. Super 35. [R] ▼)

Heaven (2002-U.S.-German) C-96m. *** D: Tom Tykwer. Cate Blanchett, Giovanni Ribisi, Mattia Sbragia, Alberto Di Stasio, Remo Girone, Alessandro Sperduti, Francesca Neri. English schoolteacher living in Italy, frustrated by a corrupt drug culture that's harming her students, plants a bomb in the office of a local bigwig and suffers the consequences. During her police interrogation, a young, naïve translator falls in love with her and helps her escape. Ethereal, existential drama takes us on a surprising journey—with the always-riveting Blanchett at its core. This was the final screenplay written by Krzysztof Kieslowski with his partner, Krzysztof Piesiewicz. [R] ▼)

Heaven and Earth (1990-Japanese) C-106m. **½ D: Haruki Kadokawa. Takaai Enoki, Masahiko Tsugawa, Atsuko Asano, Tsunehiko Watase, Naomi Zaizen, Binpachi Ito; narrated by Stuart Whitman. Physically impressive, large-scale Samurai epic, notable for budget (reportedly over $40 million) and because much of it was shot in Canada! Lacks the mastery of a Kurosawa at the helm, but fans of big battle scenes may enjoy it anyway. Released in Japan at 119m. ▼●)

Heaven & Earth (1993) C-140m. **½ D: Oliver Stone. Tommy Lee Jones, Hiep Thi Le, Joan Chen, Haing S. Ngor, Debbie Reynolds, Dustin Nguyen, Conchata Ferrell, Vivian Wu, Dale Dye, Liem Whatley. Vietnamese woman's painful odyssey from a peaceful childhood in a peasant village to a lifetime of upheaval both in Vietnam and the U.S. This true story (based on two published memoirs by Le Ly Hayslip) tells of a woman forever caught between forces of North and South in her native country; between the spiritual and the practical; between Vietnamese and American ways. A jumbled narrative, difficult to watch at times, but writer-director Stone lets us share the character's emotional catharsis at the conclusion. Hayslip can be seen briefly as a jewelry broker; Jeffrey Jones appears unbilled as a priest. Panavision. [R] ▼●)

Heaven Can Wait (1943) C-112m. ***½

D: Ernst Lubitsch. Gene Tierney, Don Ameche, Charles Coburn, Marjorie Main, Laird Cregar, Spring Byington, Allyn Joslyn, Eugene Pallette, Signe Hasso, Louis Calhern. Excellent comedy-fantasy told in flashback. Ameche, who believes he's lived a life of sin, recalls his past as he requests admission to Hades. Witty Samson Raphaelson script helps make this a delight. Based on the play *Birthdays* by Laszlo Bus-Fekete. ▼●)

Heaven Can Wait (1978) C-100m. *** D: Warren Beatty and Buck Henry. Warren Beatty, Julie Christie, Jack Warden, Dyan Cannon, Charles Grodin, James Mason, Buck Henry, Vincent Gardenia. Gentle, pleasing remake of HERE COMES MR. JORDAN with Beatty as good-natured football player who is taken to heaven ahead of schedule, and has to return to "life" in another man's body. Amiable but never moving, with Christie miscast as the woman who inspires Beatty. Scripted by Beatty and Elaine May. This was remade as DOWN TO EARTH (2001). [PG] ▼●)

Heaven Help Us (1985) C-104m. *** D: Michael Dinner. Donald Sutherland, John Heard, Andrew McCarthy, Mary Stuart Masterson, Kevin Dillon, Malcolm Danare, Jennie Dundas, Kate Reid, Wallace Shawn, Philip Bosco, Patrick Dempsey, Christopher Durang. Very funny evocation of Catholic high school life in Brooklyn, circa 1965, with solid ring of truth throughout. Shawn has hilarious cameo as priest who kicks off school dance with denunciation of lust. Impressive feature debuts for writer Charles Purpura and director Dinner. [R] ▼●)

Heaven Knows, Mr. Allison (1957) C-107m. *** D: John Huston. Deborah Kerr, Robert Mitchum. Marvelous, touching tale of nun Kerr and Marine Mitchum stranded together on a Japanese-infested Pacific island during WW2. Solid performances by the stars. CinemaScope. ▼)

Heavenly Creatures (1994-New Zealand) C-99m. ***½ D: Peter Jackson. Melanie Lynskey, Kate Winslet, Sarah Peirse, Diana Kent, Clive Merrison, Simon O'Connor. Dark, exhilarating story based on the true-life case of New Zealand teenagers Pauline Parker and Juliet Hulme, whose obsessive relationship drove them to murder. Very well acted, and stunningly directed by Jackson, who plunges us into the bizarre fantasy world that the girls create for themselves. The real-life Hulme, it was later discovered, has written best-selling murder mysteries for years under the pseudonym Anne Perry. Jackson also cowrote the screenplay with Frances Walsh. Director's cut runs 109m. Original New Zealand running time: 108m. Super 35. [R] ▼●)

Heavenly Kid, The (1985) C-89m. *½ D: Cary Medoway. Lewis Smith, Jason Gedrick, Jane Kaczmarek, Richard Mulligan, Mark Metcalf. Embarrassingly amateurish fantasy-comedy about a greasy teen of the early '60s who dies in a chicken race and can't get into heaven—until he helps out a young nerd in the 1980s. [PG-13]**▼)**

Heavenly Pursuits SEE: **Gospel According to Vic, The**

Heavens Above! (1963-British) **105m. ***** D: John Boulting. Peter Sellers, Cecil Parker, Isabel Jeans, Eric Sykes, Bernard Miles, Ian Carmichael, Irene Handl, Brock Peters, William Hartnell, Roy Kinnear, Joan Hickson. Wry satire on British clergy life; Sellers top-notch as the reverend who becomes bishop in outer space. Originally ran 118m. Produced by Roy Boulting.**▼)**

Heaven's Gate (1980) **C-149m. **** D: Michael Cimino. Kris Kristofferson, Christopher Walken, Isabelle Huppert, Jeff Bridges, John Hurt, Sam Waterston, Brad Dourif, Joseph Cotten, Geoffrey Lewis, Richard Masur, Terry O'Quinn, Mickey Rourke, Willem Dafoe. Writer-director Cimino's now-notorious spectacle is missing just one thing: a story. It deals, more or less, with the conflict between immigrant settlers of 19th-century Wyoming and the ruthless American empire-builders who want them eliminated. Stunningly photographed (by Vilmos Zsigmond) on magnificent locations, with incredible period detail—all to little effect, since the narrative, character motivations, and soundtrack are so hopelessly muddled. Originally shown at 219m. Panavision. [R]**▼●)**

Heaven's Prisoners (1996) **C-126m. **½** D: Phil Joanou. Alec Baldwin, Mary Stuart Masterson, Kelly Lynch, Eric Roberts, Teri Hatcher, Vondie Curtis Hall. Alcoholic former New Orleans cop Baldwin and his wife Lynch rescue a little girl from a wrecked aircraft, but this leads to involvement with drug runners and murder. Adaptation of James Lee Burke's popular novel about a Cajun detective is too long and slow, and captures little of the regional atmosphere; except for the miscast Baldwin, the cast is excellent, especially Masterson as a stripper and Roberts as a drug lord. Tommy Lee Jones later played detective Dave Robicheaux in IN THE ELECTRIC MIST. [R]**▼●)**

Heaven With a Gun (1969) **C-101m. **½** D: Lee H. Katzin. Glenn Ford, Carolyn Jones, Barbara Hershey, John Anderson, David Carradine. Peace-loving man is forced to return to world of violence in the Old West. Uneven. Panavision. [M]

Heavy (1996) **C-105m. **½** D: James Mangold. Pruitt Taylor Vince, Liv Tyler, Shelley Winters, Deborah Harry, Joe Grifasi, Evan Dando. Somber character study about Victor (Vince), a chubby, balding, hopelessly shy pizza chef who toils in a rural eatery run by his widowed mother (Winters). Enter a

pretty teen (Tyler), the new waitress; Victor fantasizes about becoming her boyfriend and savior. There is a sense of sadness and eloquence to Victor, but not quite enough. **▼●)**

Heavy Metal (1981-Canadian) **C-90m. ***** D: Gerald Potterton. Voices of Richard Romanus, John Candy, Joe Flaherty, Don Francks, Eugene Levy, Harold Ramis, John Vernon. Episodic animated feature is uneven, but great fun on a mindless, adolescent level. Sexy sci-fi stories and vignettes in a variety of graphic styles, many set to rock music. Our favorites: "Harry Canyon," about a N.Y.C. cabbie of the future, and "Den," a boy's macho fantasy. Film is actually the work of many animation studios, directors, and writers around the world. Followed in 2000 by an in-name-only direct-to-video sequel. [R] **▼●)**

Heavy Petting (1988) **C-80m. **½** D: Obie Benz. David Byrne, Sandra Bernhard, Allen Ginsberg, Ann Magnuson, Spalding Gray, Josh Mostel, Laurie Anderson, John Oates, Abbie Hoffman, Jacki Ochs. ATOMIC CAFE–style look at sexual mores in the 1950s, punctuated by celebrity interviews and highlighted by hysterical period film clips. Scattershot quasi-documentary lacks strong point of view, but it's tough to knock a film in which such "witnesses" as David Byrne, William S. Burroughs, and Zoe Tamerlis (of MS. 45 cultdom) offer their views on teen dating. [R]**▼●)**

Heavy Traffic (1973) **C-76m. ***½** D: Ralph Bakshi. Animated feature is somewhat pretentious and largely gross in telling of young New Yorker depressed by sights and sounds around him, finding refuge at drawing-board. Dazzling cinematic treatment, with often revolutionary combination of live-action and animation. Some brilliant set-pieces within loose story framework. [R—edited from original X rating]**▼)**

Heavyweights (1994) **C-97m. **** D: Steven Brill. Tom McGowan, Aaron Schwartz, Ben Stiller, Shaun Weiss, Tom Hodges, Leah Lail, Paul Feig, Max Goldblatt, Jeffrey Tambor, Jerry Stiller, Anne Meara. Yet another summer camp movie, this one about a haven for overweight kids where, as the press release said, "big is beautiful and thin isn't in." That is, until campers meet up with the fitness counselor of their nightmares. This heavy-handed comedy's intended "message" about self-esteem is undermined by a barrage of fat jokes! [PG] **▼●)**

Hedda (1975-British) **C-104m. **½** D: Trevor Nunn. Glenda Jackson, Peter Eyre, Timothy West, Jennie Linden, Patrick Stewart. Royal Shakespeare Company production of Ibsen's *Hedda Gabler* attains a modicum of vitality from Jackson's showy performance in the title role. So-so. [PG]**▼**

Hedwig and the Angry Inch (2001) **C-**

91m. * D:** John Cameron Mitchell. John Cameron Mitchell, Miriam Shor, Stephen Trask, Theodore Liscinski, Rob Campbell, Michael Aronov, Andrea Martin, Michael Pitt. Hedwig is an "internationally ignored" rock star, the survivor of a botched sex-change operation whose dumping by the boy-toy rock idol he helped nurture has left him dazed and embittered. *Very* offbeat off-Broadway musical is cleverly filmed by its author-star in an impressive directing debut. Even wary viewers might be pulled in by the terrific score (by costar Trask) and inventive musical numbers. Imaginative animation by Emily Hubley. [R]▼❍

He Got Game (1998) **C-136m. **½ D:** Spike Lee. Denzel Washington, Ray Allen, Milla Jovovich, Rosario Dawson, Hill Harper, Zelda Harris, Ned Beatty, Jim Brown, Joseph Lyle Taylor, Bill Nunn, John Turturro, Lonette McKee. A prisoner is freed for one week to convince his son—the country's hottest high school basketball player—to sign with the state governor's favorite college. Far-fetched premise is played out with conviction, but its points are obvious and hammered home redundantly. Redeemed by strong characterizations and powerful moments. Many basketball stars and coaches appear as themselves; young Allen is himself an NBA player. [R]▼❍

Heidi (1937) **88m. **½ D:** Allan Dwan. Shirley Temple, Jean Hersholt, Arthur Treacher, Helen Westley, Mady Christians, Sidney Blackmer, Sig Ruman, Marcia Mae Jones, Mary Nash. Classic children's story set in 19th-century Switzerland is good vehicle for Shirley, playing girl taken from grandfather (Hersholt) to live with cruel Nash. Nice tear-jerker for children. Also shown in computer-colored version.▼❍❍

Heidi (1965-Austrian-German) **C-95m. *** D:** Werner Jacobs. Eva Marie Singhammer, Gertraud Mittermayr, Gustav Knuth, Lotte Ledi. Fine retelling of classic children's story about young girl who leaves her cozy home in Swiss Alps for adventures in the world below.▼

Heidi's Song (1982) **C-94m. *½ D:** Robert Taylor. Voices of Lorne Greene, Sammy Davis, Jr., Margery Gray, Michael Bell, Peter Cullen. Animated feature from Hanna-Barbera studio reprises all-too familiar Heidi tale. Despite songs by Sammy Cahn and Burton Lane, awkward continuity, lifeless animation and an excess of cute animals leave this little better than most Saturday morning fare. [G]▼

Heights (2005) **C-93m. *** D:** Chris Terrio. Glenn Close, Elizabeth Banks, James Marsden, Jesse Bradford, Matt Davis, John Light, Andrew Howard, Eric Bogosian, George Segal, Isabella Rossellini, Rufus Wainwright, Tom (Thomas) Lennon, Jim Parsons. Compelling look at 24 hours in the life of hip, young Manhattanites, both gay and straight, and their tumultuous romantic relationships. Anchored by Close's bravura turn as an aging theater legend. Stylish feature debut for Terrio, adapted by Amy Fox from her one-act play. A Merchant-Ivory presentation. [R]❍

Heimat (1984-German) **C/B&W-940m. *** D:** Edgar Reitz. Marita Breuer, Dieter Schaad, Rudiger Weigang, Karin Rasenack, Willi Burger, Gertrud Bredel, Mathias Kniesbeck. No, that running time is not a typo! This is an ambitious epic, almost 16 hours in length, about life in a provincial German village between 1919 and 1982. First few hours are generally more compelling than the last. Has its boring stretches, and after a while it does seem like a glorified soap opera, but at its best, perceptive, comic, even poetic. Gernot Roll's cinematography is exquisite. Followed by two sequels. ▼❍

Heiress, The (1949) **115m. **** D:** William Wyler. Olivia de Havilland, Ralph Richardson, Montgomery Clift, Miriam Hopkins, Vanessa Brown, Mona Freeman, Ray Collins, Selena Royle. Henry James' novel *Washington Square* receives superlative screen treatment with Oscar-winning de Havilland as spinster wooed by fortune-hunter Clift in 19th-century N.Y.C., despite warnings from her cruel father, Richardson. Aaron Copland's music score also won an Oscar. Adapted by Ruth and Augustus Goetz from their stage play. Remade in 1997 as WASHINGTON SQUARE. ▼❍

Heist, The (1979-Italian) **C-85m. **½ D:** Sergio Gobbi. Charles Aznavour, Virna Lisi, Robert Hossein. Typical cop-chasing-gangster mishmash wastes its cast but is distinguished by some great stunt driving. Video version runs 92m.▼

Heist (2001) **C-107m. **½ D:** David Mamet. Gene Hackman, Danny DeVito, Delroy Lindo, Sam Rockwell, Rebecca Pidgeon, Ricky Jay, Patti LuPone, Jim Frangione. Career criminal is ready to retire with his girlfriend, but his backer insists on one more robbery—a daring heist of a Swiss cargo plane. Hackman and his crew aren't just thieves, they're master con artists, so the film is overloaded with cons, twists, twists on cons, etc. Mamet's script is sharp and funny but perhaps too clever for its own good; by the end it's no longer satisfying. [R]▼❍

He Knows You're Alone (1981) **C-94m. *½ D:** Armand Mastroianni. Don Scardino, Caitlin O'Heaney, Elizabeth Kemp, Tom Rolfing, Patsy Pease, Tom Hanks, Dana Barron, Paul Gleason. Yet another entry in slice-and-dice genre, this one with minor novelty of brides-to-be as victims. A bit less bloody than others of its ilk; otherwise, business as usual. Hanks' film debut. Aka BLOOD WEDDING. [R]▼❍

Hèlas Pour Moi (1993-French-Swiss) **C-84m.** ****½** D: Jean-Luc Godard. Gérard Depardieu, Laurence Masliah, Bernard Verley, Jean-Louis Loca. Pensive account of an average married couple (Depardieu and Masliah) who reside in a Swiss village, and what happens when the husband's body supposedly is borrowed by a "god." Of interest as an examination of the meaning of faith, but the narrative is much too fragmented and the film too cluttered with declarations and episode headings. Godard based his screenplay in part on Greek legend. Video title: OH, WOE IS ME. ▼▶

Held Up (2000) **C-91m.** ***½** D: Steve Rash. Jamie Foxx, Nia Long, Barry Corbin, John Cullum, Jake Busey, Michael Shamus Wiles, Eduardo Yanez, Sarah Paulson, Julie Hagerty. While vacationing in the Grand Canyon, Long dumps her fiancé (Foxx) upon learning that he's spent their nest egg on a vintage Studebaker. Then the car is stolen . . . and finally, Foxx is taken hostage. The real crime is that time-wasters like this make it to the screen. [PG-13] ▼▶

Helen (2010-German-Canadian) **C-119m.** ******* D: Sandra Nettelbeck. Ashley Judd, Goran Visnjic, Lauren Lee Smith, Alexia Fast, Alberta Watson, David Hewlett, Leah Cairns. Music professor Judd is blessed with a loving husband and daughter and oodles of friends. Only problem is, she suffers from suicidal depression. Appropriately somber, deliberately paced drama is quietly powerful, if a tad overlong. Smith is an eye-opening presence as a student grappling with her own psychological issues. Nettelbeck also scripted. [R] ▶

Helen Morgan Story, The (1957) **118m.** ****½** D: Michael Curtiz. Ann Blyth, Paul Newman, Richard Carlson, Gene Evans, Alan King, Cara Williams. Fiction about dynamic 1920s and '30s torch singer, dwelling on her romances and alcoholism; Blyth never captures the star's pathos or greatness. She's dubbed by Gogi Grant. CinemaScope. ▼▶

Helen of Troy (1956) **C-118m.** ****** D: Robert Wise. Stanley Baker, Rossana Podesta, Brigitte Bardot, Jacques Sernas, Cedric Hardwicke, Harry Andrews. Sweeping pageantry, but empty script spoils this version of story about the woman who caused the Trojan War. Filmed in Italy. CinemaScope. ▼▶

Hell and High Water (1954) **C-103m.** ****½** D: Samuel Fuller. Richard Widmark, Bella Darvi, Victor Francen, Cameron Mitchell, Gene Evans, David Wayne, Stephen Bekassy, Richard Loo. Uneven mixture of romance, espionage, and a demolition caper, stemming from submarine mission to Arctic. Tame film got a boost from being shot in CinemaScope. ▶

Hellbenders, The (1967-Italian-Spanish) **C-92m.** ***½** D: Sergio Corbucci. Joseph Cotten, Norma Bengell, Julian Mateos, Gino Pernice, Angel Aranda, Maria Martin. Dreary spaghetti Western in which crazed ex-Confederate officer Cotten schemes to rekindle the rebel cause, facing a variety of complications and crises. ▼▶

Hellbent (2005) **C-85m.** ****** D: Paul Etheredge-Ouzts. Dylan Fergus, Bryan Kirkwood, Hank Harris, Andrew Levitas, Matt Phillips, Wren T. Brown. A group of gay men find themselves stalked by a serial killer during West Hollywood's Halloween parade. This "first gay slasher film" (as its ads proclaimed) has moments that cleverly combine and send up slasher movie conventions and gay stereotypes, but it isn't much scarier or more entertaining than typical made-for-video horror fare. Still, after years of watching movies where straight people act stupid and get killed, gay horror fans may welcome a mediocre genre picture to call their own. [R] ▶

Hellbound (1993-U.S.-Canadian-Israeli) **C-95m.** ***½** D: Aaron Norris. Chuck Norris, Calvin Levels, Christopher Neame, Sheree J. Wilson, David Robb, Cherie Franklin, Jack Adalist, Erez Atar. After being imprisoned by Richard the Lion-Hearted in 1186, Satan's emissary (Neame) is freed in modern times to face a more formidable foe: Chuck Norris. Too much acting from Neame, not enough from Norris, and a silly story with little action. This sat on the shelf for two years before going direct to video. Some attractive Israeli settings. [R] ▼▶

Hellbound: Hellraiser II (1988-British) **C-97m.** ***½** D: Tony Randel. Ashley Laurence, Clare Higgins, Kenneth Cranham, Imogen Boorman, Sean Chapman, Doug Bradley, William Hope. Confusing, tedious sequel begins immediately after first film ends. Teenage heroine literally goes to Hell in effort to rescue ill-fated father, but encounters opposition from her revived stepmother and an occult-obsessed psychiatrist. But Hell is a boring, dusty labyrinth. Almost as gruesome as HELLRAISER (it's *not* a sequel to HELLBOUND), but nowhere near as entertaining. Followed by HELLRAISER III: HELL ON EARTH. [R] ▼▶

Hellboy (2004) **C-125m.** ******* D: Guillermo del Toro. Ron Perlman, John Hurt, Selma Blair, Rupert Evans, Karel Roden, Jeffrey Tambor, Doug Jones, Ladislav Beran, Bridget Hodson. Explosive adaptation of Mike Mignola's comic book about a powerful creature born during a (literally) hellish confrontation during WW2; nowadays he works as a "secret weapon" for the U.S. government. Only problem: he's a bit of a wiseguy. Enough effects and imaginative ideas for at least two movies stuffed into one, leavened by a disarming sense of humor. Perlman is terrific as the cigar-chomping, emotionally vulner-

able Hellboy. Del Toro also scripted. David Hyde Pierce provides the uncredited voice for Abe Sapien. Director's cut runs 145m. Followed by an animated series and a sequel. [PG-13] ▼❶
Hellboy II: The Golden Army (2008) C-110m. *** D: Guillermo del Toro. Ron Perlman, Selma Blair, Jeffrey Tambor, Doug Jones, John Alexander, James Dodd, Luke Goss, Anna Walton, John Hurt, Roy Dotrice; voice of Seth MacFarlane. Now married but just as ornery as ever, Hellboy (or Red, as his wife Liz calls him) and his paranormal partners battle a power-hungry "dark prince" who's determined to awaken a slumbering army of mechanical soldiers and take over the world. This one's all about the journey, not the destination; filled with wildly imaginative creatures, special effects set pieces, and the snarky sense of humor shared by del Toro and Mike Mignola, who created the *Hellboy* comic books. Only complaint: it goes on too long. [PG-13]❶
Hellcats of the Navy (1957) 82m. **½ D: Nathan Juran. Ronald Reagan, Nancy Davis (Reagan), Arthur Franz, Harry Lauter, Selmer Jackson. Satisfactory actioner of WW2 exploits of U.S. submarine and its crew. Ronald and Nancy Reagan's only screen appearance together. ▼❶
Hell Comes to Frogtown (1987) C-88m. *½ D: R. J. Kizer, Donald G. Jackson. Roddy Piper, Sandahl Bergman, Rory Calhoun, Cec Verrill, William Smith, Nicholas Worth, Kristi Sommers. Goofy post-holocaust tale with wrestler "Rowdy" Roddy as the only fertile male left on earth, who sets out to rescue women being held captive by froglike mutants. At least the frog masks are good. 1992 sequel: RETURN TO FROGTOWN. [R]▼❶
Hell Drivers (1957-British) 108m. *** D: C. Raker (Cy) Endfield. Stanley Baker, Herbert Lom, Peggy Cummins, Patrick McGoohan, William Hartnell, Wilfred Lawson, Sidney James, Jill Ireland, Alfie Bass, Gordon Jackson, David McCallum, Sean Connery. Taut account of ex-con joining trucking company that encourages reckless competition among the drivers making their daily rounds. What a cast! VistaVision.
Heller in Pink Tights (1960) C-100m. **½ D: George Cukor. Sophia Loren, Anthony Quinn, Margaret O'Brien, Steve Forrest, Edmund Lowe. Colorful tale of theatrical troupe that travels throughout the Old West—with the law often in pursuit. Based on a Louis L'Amour novel. ▼❶
Hellfighters (1968) C-121m. ** D: Andrew V. McLaglen. John Wayne, Katharine Ross, Jim Hutton, Vera Miles, Bruce Cabot, Jay C. Flippen. Broadly acted adventure about men who fight oil fires is made endurable by good cast. Wayne's character is based on real-life oil well firefighter Red Adair. Panavision. [R]▼❶

Hellfire Club, The (1961-British) C-93m. *** D: Robert S. Baker, Monty Berman. Keith Michell, Adrienne Corri, Peter Cushing, Peter Arne, Kai Fischer, David Lodge, Martin Stephens, Miles Malleson, Francis Matthews. Lively, entertaining 18th-century swashbuckler with familiar rightful-vs. wrongful-heir plot; acrobatic Michell makes a dashing hero. The depraved, powerful, real-life club of the title serves as backdrop. DyaliScope. ▼❶
Hell in the Pacific (1968) C-103m. *** D: John Boorman. Lee Marvin, Toshiro Mifune. Two men, one American, one Japanese, confront each other on deserted WW2 Pacific island. Gripping idea well executed, with two dynamic actors; only the finale disappoints. Panavision.▼❶
Hell Is for Heroes (1962) 90m. *** D: Donald Siegel. Steve McQueen, Bobby Darin, Fess Parker, Harry Guardino, James Coburn, Mike Kellin, Nick Adams, Bob Newhart. Tough, taut WW2 film about a small squadron forced to hold off a German attack by pretending they're larger—and more powerful—than they really are. Takes its time getting started but builds in intensity to a riveting climax. Only incongruous note: young Newhart, who even interpolates a variation on one of his telephone monologues into the story! Cowritten by WW2 specialist Robert Pirosh.▼❶
Hell Night (1981) C-101m. *½ D: Tom DeSimone. Linda Blair, Vincent Van Patten, Peter Barton, Jenny Neumann, Kevin Brophy, Suki Goodwin. How's this for originality? Four college fraternity/sorority pledges must spend a night in Garth Mansion, which is haunted by ghost of retarded killer. Unfortunately, reports of his death were greatly exaggerated. No nudity or explicit violence, which makes one wonder just what audience they had in mind. Extremely dull. [R]▼❶
Hello Again (1987) C-96m. ** D: Frank Perry. Shelley Long, Judith Ivey, Gabriel Byrne, Corbin Bernsen, Sela Ward, Austin Pendleton, Carrie Nye, Robert Lewis, Madeleine Potter, Illeana Douglas. Long Island housewife chokes to death but is brought back to life by her witchlike sister one year later . . . and soon discovers that she can't simply pick up her life where she left off. Contemporary comedy written by Susan Isaacs doesn't develop its premise with any logic or momentum, and quickly sags. Long tries her best. [PG]▼❶
Hello, Dolly! (1969) C-146m. **½ D: Gene Kelly. Barbra Streisand, Walter Matthau, Michael Crawford, E. J. Peaker, Marianne McAndrew, Tommy Tune, Louis Armstrong, Danny Lockin. Splashy treatment of smash Broadway play with Jerry Herman's popular score. Dolly Levi insists on playing matchmaker, even when she herself gets matched. Overblown and unmemorable, but colorful diversion. Based on Thornton Wilder's *The Matchmaker* (filmed in 1958). Oscar winner

for Sound, Art Direction, and Score (Lennie Hayton and Lionel Newman). Some prints run 118m. Todd-AO. [G] ▼●❿

Hello Down There (1969) C-98m. *½ D: Jack Arnold. Tony Randall, Janet Leigh, Jim Backus, Roddy McDowall, Ken Berry, Merv Griffin, Richard Dreyfuss. So-called comedy about family living in experimental underwater home might entertain children if you pay them to watch it. Reissued as SUB-A-DUB-DUB. [G]❿

Hello Frisco, Hello (1943) C-98m. ** D: H. Bruce Humberstone. Alice Faye, John Payne, Jack Oakie, Lynn Bari, Laird Cregar, June Havoc, Ward Bond. Hackneyed musicomedy of Payne getting too big for his britches as Barbary Coast entrepreneur; Oscar-winning song, "You'll Never Know." Big comedown from earlier musicals with star trio.▼❿

Hello-Goodbye (1970-British) C-107m. BOMB D: Jean Negulesco. Michael Crawford, Curt Jurgens, Genevieve Gilles, Ira Furstenberg, Lon Satton. Abysmal love triangle goes nowhere, makes no sense. Awful, loose, and annoying. [PG]

Hello Mary Lou: Prom Night II (1987-Canadian) C-96m. **½ D: Bruce Pittman. Lisa Schrage, Michael Ironside, Wendy Lyon, Justin Louis. No relation to PROM NIGHT. Lyon, who looks great in or out of costume, is possessed by the spirit of a murdered prom queen and becomes her instrument of revenge. [R] ▼●❿

Hellraiser (1987-British) C-94m. **½ D: Clive Barker. Andrew Robinson, Clare Higgins, Ashley Laurence, Sean Chapman, Oliver Smith, Robert Hines. Robinson and Higgins move into a roomy British dwelling, unaware that his half brother—and her former lover—is hiding upstairs in a kind of gelatinous/skeletal state; soon the beast is forcing her to lure stray men back to the house so he can replenish himself with their blood. Grisly but stylish directorial debut by famed horror novelist Barker; ugly all the way. Followed by HELLBOUND: HELLRAISER II. [R] ▼●❿

Hellraiser III: Hell on Earth (1992) C-93m. *½ D: Anthony Hickox. Terry Farrell, Doug Bradley, Paula Marshall, Kevin Bernhardt, Ken Carpenter, Ashley Laurence. Further adventures of the gross-out Pinhead goes for the jokes, not the jugular. This time Pinhead crosses paths with an ambitious TV newswoman who winds up with the grisliest (if not the biggest) story of her career. Freddy and Jason are starting to look good by comparison. [R] ▼●❿

Hellraiser: Bloodline (1996) C-85m. BOMB D: Alan Smithee. Bruce Ramsay, Valentina Vargas, Doug Bradley, Adam Scott, Charlotte Chatton. Pinhead matches wits with a demon lover/cohort, ironically named Angelique (Vargas). Dull and plot-heavy, even if you're a Clive Barker devotee.

Re-caulk your bathtub instead. Followed by five direct-to-video sequels. [R] ▼●❿

Hell Ride (2008) C-84m. *½ D: Larry Bishop. Larry Bishop, Michael Madsen, Eric Balfour, Vinnie Jones, Leonor Varela, David Carradine, Dennis Hopper, Julia Jones, Michael Beach, Laura Cayouette, Francesco Quinn. Generally dreadful Tarantino wannabe, charting the swagger and antics of a band of aging bikers. Oh yes, there's plenty of female nudity, with the babes collectively young enough to be the bikers' offspring. Bishop (the star of 1960s and '70s biker films) also scripted and produced. Quentin Tarantino, in fact, is one of the executive producers. Super 35. [R]❿

Hell's Angels (1930) 127m. ***½ D: Howard Hughes. Ben Lyon, James Hall, Jean Harlow, John Darrow, Lucien Prival, Roy Wilson. Hughes' expensive, indulgent WW1 aviation film is in a class by itself; slow-moving and sometimes corny storywise, but unmatched for aerial spectacle. Also the film that launched Harlow ("Would you be shocked if I put on something more comfortable?") to stardom. Two-color Technicolor party scene and tinted night sequences were restored in 1989. James Whale, credited as dialogue director, actually wrote and directed much of the film. Beware shorter prints.▼❿

Hell's Angels on Wheels (1967) C-95m. **½ D: Richard Rush. Adam Roarke, Jack Nicholson, Sabrina Scharf, Jana Taylor, John Garwood. Excellent photography by then-unknown Laszlo Kovacs, and Nicholson's characterization as gas station attendant named Poet, make this one tough to resist on a trash level. Famed Angel Sonny Barger was technical advisor.▼❿

Hell's Bloody Devils (1970) C-92m. ** D: Al Adamson. Broderick Crawford, Scott Brady, John Gabriel, Kent Taylor, John Carradine, Robert Dix, Keith Andes, Jack Starrett, Anne Randall, Vicki Volante. Traveling the low road to action with, believe it or not, a gang of sadistic bikers, a band of neo-Nazis, the Vegas mob, a sinister dude named Count von Delberg—all beating one another to a pulp. Add a cast of veteran actors and, incredibly, a score by Nelson Riddle! Aka THE FAKERS, SMASHING THE CRIME SYNDICATE, and SWASTIKA SAVAGES. [PG]❿

Hell's Long Road (1963-Italian) C-89m. **½ D: Charles Roberti. Elena Brazzi, Kay Nolandi, Berto Frankis, Bela Kaivi, Marcello Charli. Offbeat costume sudser set in ancient Rome during rule of Nero (Frankis), focusing on personal life of arch senator (Charli) and romance with splendiferous Brazzi; vivid settings.

Hellstrom Chronicle, The (1971) C-90m. **½ D: Walon Green. Lawrence Pressman. Documentary about man's impending struggle against insects somehow beat THE SORROW AND THE PITY for the Oscar, but sappy narration and repetitive structure lessen its effect. Still, microphotography is incredible; enjoyed brief vogue as a "head" movie. [G]▼

Hell to Eternity (1960) 132m. **½ D: Phil Karlson. Jeffrey Hunter, David Janssen, Vic Damone, Patricia Owens, Sessue Hayakawa. Straightforward drama based on true story of WW2 hero Guy Gabaldon, who was raised by Japanese foster parents; battle scenes galore.▼▶

Hell Up in Harlem (1973) C-96m. BOMB D: Larry Cohen. Fred Williamson, Julius W. Harris, Gloria Hendry, Margaret Avery, D'Urville Martin. Excessively violent, poorly filmed sequel to BLACK CAESAR as Fred makes N.Y.C. a decent place to live by annihilating all who stand in his way. [R]▼▶

Hell With Heroes, The (1968) C-95m. **½ D: Joseph Sargent. Rod Taylor, Claudia Cardinale, Harry Guardino, Kevin McCarthy, Peter Duel, William Marshall. OK pulp fiction about WW2 flyers Taylor and Duel who run air-cargo service, become involved with notorious smuggler Guardino and his mistress (Cardinale). Unprofound, but slickly done. Techniscope.

Hellzapoppin' (1941) 84m. *** D: H. C. Potter. Ole Olsen, Chic Johnson, Martha Raye, Mischa Auer, Jane Frazee, Hugh Herbert, Robert Paige, Shemp Howard, Elisha Cook, Jr. Famous madcap Broadway show is conventionalized by Hollywood, with romantic subplot and too many songs, but still has many inspired moments of lunacy, from a throwaway CITIZEN KANE gag to the mutterings of Hugh Herbert.

He Loves Me . . . He Loves Me Not (2002-French) C-96m. *** D: Laetitia Colombani. Audrey Tautou, Samuel Le Bihan, Isabelle Carré, Clément Sibony, Sophie Guillemin, Eric Savin. Evocative psychological thriller about a young art student (Tautou) who is obsessively in love with a married cardiologist (Le Bihan) and is convinced he's about to leave his wife for her. Then the story is told from his point of view. Most enjoyable, and an assured feature debut for director/coscreenwriter Colombani.▼▶

Help! (1965-British) C-90m. ***½ D: Richard Lester. John Lennon, Paul McCartney, George Harrison, Ringo Starr, Leo McKern, Eleanor Bron, Victor Spinetti, Roy Kinnear, Patrick Cargill. Crazy, funny film, the Beatles' second. Lots of wild gags, many songs (including "Ticket to Ride," "Another Girl," "You've Got to Hide Your Love Away," title tune). The story: a religious sect attempts to recover a sacrificial ring from Ringo. Written by Charles Wood and Marc Behm.▼▶

Help Me Dream (1981-Italian) C-112m. *** D: Pupi Avati. Mariangela Melato, Anthony Franciosa, Paola Pitagora, Jean-Pierre Léaud, Alexandra Stewart. Intriguing, original, winningly nostalgic musical romance centering on affable American flyer Franciosa hiding out with Italian Melato and children in a farmhouse during WW2. An ode to an idealized America, with period songs and choreography by Hermes Pan.

Hemingway's Adventures of a Young Man (1962) C-145m. ** D: Martin Ritt. Richard Beymer, Diane Baker, Paul Newman, Corinne Calvet, Fred Clark, Dan Dailey, James Dunn, Juano Hernandez, Arthur Kennedy, Ricardo Montalban, Susan Strasberg, Jessica Tandy, Eli Wallach, Simon Oakland, Michael (J.) Pollard. Loosely based on autobiographical data from his stories, this pretentious, drawn-out memory of the famed author is overblown, cornball, and embarrassing. Fine cast mostly wasted. Aka ADVENTURES OF A YOUNG MAN. CinemaScope.▶

Hennessy (1975-British) C-103m. **½ D: Don Sharp. Rod Steiger, Lee Remick, Richard Johnson, Trevor Howard, Peter Egan, Eric Porter. Interesting but unbelievable thriller about Irish man whose wife and child are killed in Belfast violence, stirring him to plan bombing of Parliament on opening day when the Royal Family attends. [PG]▼▶

Henry Aldrich series SEE: *Leonard Maltin's Classic Movie Guide*

Henry & June (1990) C-134m. ***½ D: Philip Kaufman. Fred Ward, Uma Thurman, Maria de Medeiros, Richard E. Grant, Kevin Spacey, Jean-Philippe Ecoffey, Bruce Myers, Jean-Louis Bunuel. Stylish, atmospheric, and surprisingly unerotic adaptation of the Anais Nin diaries dealing specifically—and in sexually explicit fashion—with her lover (author Henry Miller) and Henry's wife June. Performed with gusto (in Ward's case, broad gusto) and distinguished by brilliant production design of randy Paris, circa 1931. Screenplay by Philip and Rose Kaufman. Controversy over the adult material in this film finally caused the MPAA to create a new NC-17 rating. [NC-17]▼●▶

Henry Fool (1998) C-137m. **½ D: Hal Hartley. Thomas Jay Ryan, James Urbaniak, Parker Posey, Maria Porter, James Saito, Kevin Corrigan, Liam Aiken, Miho Nikaido, Gene Ruffini. Hartley just misses the mark with this characteristically offbeat tale of Simon Grim (Urbaniak), a bashful garbageman, and the title character (Ryan), a free spirit who encourages him to begin writing poetry. An allegory that, in its best moments, serves as an ode to nonconformity and risk-taking; but it's uneven and overlong. Scripted by Hartley. Followed a decade later by FAY GRIM. [R]▼▶

Henry VIII and His Six Wives (1972-British) C-125m. ***½ D: Waris Hussein. Keith Michell, Donald Pleasence, Charlotte Rampling, Jane Asher, Lynne Frederick. Adapted from BBC-TV series, historical pageant divides time evenly among the wives, Rampling and Frederick coming off best. Michell is exceptional as the King. [PG]▶

Henry V (1945-British) **C-137m.** ******** D: Laurence Olivier. Laurence Olivier, Robert Newton, Leslie Banks, Renee Asherson, Esmond Knight, Leo Genn, Ralph Truman, Harcourt Williams, Ivy St. Helier, Ernest Thesiger, Max Adrian, George Cole, Felix Aylmer, Robert Helpmann, Freda Jackson, Jimmy Hanley, John Laurie. Olivier's masterful rendition of Shakespeare play is a cinematic treat, filmed in rich color and framed by ingenious presentation of a typical performance at the Globe theater during 1500s. This earned Olivier a special Academy Award "for his outstanding achievement as actor, producer, and director in bringing HENRY V to the screen." ▼●)

Henry V (1989-British) **C-137m.** *****½** D: Kenneth Branagh. Kenneth Branagh, Derek Jacobi, Brian Blessed, Alec McCowen, Ian Holm, Richard Briers, Robert Stephens, Robbie Coltrane, Christian Bale, Judi Dench, Paul Scofield, Michael Maloney, Emma Thompson, Geraldine McEwan. Stunning revitalization of Shakespeare's play about the warrior-king, with Branagh (in an incredible directorial debut) breathing fire and meaning into the worthy text. A different reading from Olivier's but no less impressive; when he finishes his speech before leading his men into battle at Agincourt, you're ready to enlist! Superb music by Patrick Doyle. Supporting cast is peppered with familiar faces from the elite of British theater and film. Won Costume Design Oscar. ▼●)

Henry IV (1984-Italian) **C-95m.** ****** D: Marco Bellochio. Marcello Mastroianni, Claudia Cardinale, Luciano Bartoli, Latou Chardons, Leopoldo Trieste. Disappointing update of Pirandello's brilliant satirical play on the nature of madness and illusion. When a nobleman falls off his horse, he comes to believe he's Emperor Henry IV . . . or does he? The two stars do what they can to extract a few moments of lucidity from the confusion. [PG-13] ▼●

Henry Poole Is Here (2008) **C-99m.** ****** D: Mark Pellington. Luke Wilson, Radha Mitchell, Adriana Barraza, Cheryl Hines, George Lopez, Richard Benjamin, Morgan Lily, Rachel Seiferth, Beth Grant. Depressed man dumps his fiancée and business when he believes he is dying and moves back to the neighborhood where he grew up, wanting to be left alone. When neighbors think they see a stucco image of Christ on his property, his serenity is interrupted by constant visitors in search of a miracle. Wilson is dour and dreary throughout, but Barraza is wonderful as a gentle true believer. Simple story of a man's spiritual awakening is well told but not particularly compelling. Super 35. [PG] ●

Henry: Portrait of a Serial Killer (1990) **C-90m.** *****½** D: John McNaughton. Michael Rooker, Tracy Arnold, Tom Towles. Unpleasant, unexploitive, and brilliantly directed portrayal of diseased minds (not just Henry's), loosely based on the life of self-confessed Texas mass murderer Henry Lee Lucas. As disturbing as Michael Powell's PEEPING TOM, which it in many ways resembles. Definitely not for everyone, with some very graphic scenes; a powerful (if minimalist) movie experience. Screenplay by director McNaughton and Richard Fire. Filmed in 1986. Followed by a 1997 sequel. [X] ▼●)

Henry's Crime (2011) **C-108m.** ****½** D: Malcolm Venville. Keanu Reeves, Vera Farmiga, James Caan, Peter Stormare, Judy Greer, Danny Hoch, Fisher Stevens, Bill Duke, Currie Graham, David Costabile. Henry (Reeves) is in a prison of his own making. He lives a dull life in dreary Buffalo, N.Y. Then he's tossed into the pokey for real after being convicted of a crime he did not commit. Upon his release, he resolves to do the crime anyway, figuring that he's already done the time for it. Shaggy-dog story grows on you as it goes along and is generally amusing, despite some glaring plot holes and an inconclusive ending. Farmiga, as a high-strung actress, nails her character, as does Caan, in a showy role as a career con man who's happiest behind bars. There's also a most unusual performance of Chekhov's *The Cherry Orchard.* Super 35. [R] ●

Her Alibi (1989) **C-94m.** ****½** D: Bruce Beresford. Tom Selleck, Paulina Porizkova, William Daniels, James Farentino, Hurd Hatfield, Patrick Wayne, Tess Harper, Joan Copeland. Successful mystery writer hopes to cure his career slump by providing a fake alibi for accused murderer Porizkova (by putting her up in his dreamy country home and observing her behavior). Amiable but awkwardly directed comedy benefits from attractive leads and amusing supporting cast; would you believe Wayne in a ponytail and loud golf pants? [PG] ▼●)

He Ran All the Way (1951) **77m.** ****½** D: John Berry. John Garfield, Shelley Winters, Wallace Ford, Selena Royle, Gladys George, Norman Lloyd. Taut but predictable thriller with on-the-lam cop killer Garfield hiding out in Winters' home. Garfield's final film.

Herbie: Fully Loaded (2005) **C-101m.** ******* D: Angela Robinson. Lindsay Lohan, Michael Keaton, Matt Dillon, Justin Long, Breckin Meyer, Cheryl Hines, Jill Ritchie. Single father Keaton takes daughter Lohan to an auto junkyard so she can pick out a car as a college graduation present; instead, a car (Herbie) picks her. In fact, the Volkswagen Beetle steers her into a rivalry with cocky NASCAR driver Dillon. Family-friendly reprise of the Disney series that began with THE LOVE BUG, and a good vehicle for Lohan. Real-life racers and sportscasters appear as themselves; co-writer Thomas Lennon plays Dillon's hapless brother. [G] ●

Herbie Goes Bananas (1980) **C-100m.** *½ D: Vincent McEveety. Charlie Martin Smith, Steven W. Burns, Cloris Leachman, John Vernon, Elyssa Davalos, Harvey Korman, Richard Jaeckel, Alex Rocco, Fritz Feld. Fourth Disney LOVE BUG epic finds Smith and Burns driving ol' '53 toward a race in Brazil, but encountering all sorts of "hilarious" obstacles along the way. One amusing scene where the VW turns matador; otherwise, strictly scrap metal. A TV series followed. [G] ▼●)

Herbie Goes to Monte Carlo (1977) **C-91m.** ** D: Vincent McEveety. Dean Jones, Don Knotts, Julie Sommars, Roy Kinnear, Jacques Marin. Spy ring hides diamond in Herbie the Volkswagen's gas tank while Jones is racing in Europe. Disney's LOVE BUG formula is starting to run out of gas. [G] ▼●)

Herbie Rides Again (1974) **C-88m.** **½ D: Robert Stevenson. Helen Hayes, Ken Berry, Stefanie Powers, Keenan Wynn, John McIntire, Huntz Hall. OK sequel to THE LOVE BUG with similar special effects, as Herbie the Volkswagen tries to help Hayes and Berry steer clear of evil Alonzo Hawk (Wynn). Typical Disney slapstick. [G] ▼●)

Her Brother (1960-Japanese) **C-98m.** **½ D: Kon Ichikawa. Keiko Kishi, Hiroshi Kawaguchi, Kinuyo Tanaka, Masayuki Mori. Troublesome family is brought together when, immature brother-son Kawaguchi contracts tuberculosis; central to the scenario is his warm relationship with his older sister (Kishi). Sentimental drama. Daieiscope.

Hercules (1959-Italian) **C-107m.** **½ D: Pietro Francisci. Steve Reeves, Sylva Koscina, Gianna Maria Canale, Fabrizio Mioni, Ivo Garrani, Gina Rovere, Luciana Paoluzzi (Paluzzi). This Italian import became a surprise U.S. hit, and served as the prototype of all cloak-and-sandal pictures to come: Reeves is musclebound mythical hero in essentially a retelling of the story of Jason and the Golden Fleece. Sequel: HERCULES UNCHAINED. Dyaliscope. ▼●)

Hercules (1983-Italian) **C-98m.** *½ D: Lewis Coates (Luigi Cozzi). Lou Ferrigno, Mirella D'Angelo, Sybil Danning, Ingrid Anderson, William Berger, Brad Harris, Rossana Podesta. Silly, special-effects-laden epic with Hercules (Ferrigno) attempting to rescue kidnapped Princess Anderson. However, the ex-Incredible Hulk is undeniably well cast. Followed by a sequel. [PG] ▼●)

Hercules (1997) **C-93m.** *** D: John Musker, Ron Clements. Voices of Tate Donovan, Susan Egan, James Woods, Danny DeVito, Rip Torn, Samantha Eggar, Bobcat Goldthwait, Matt Frewer, Hal Holbrook, Barbara Barrie; opening narration by Charlton Heston. Entertaining Disney cartoon feature based on Greek mythology. Baby Hercules is stolen from Mount Olympus by the bungling henchmen of Hades; raised as a mortal with extraordinary strength, he must prove himself a real hero to regain entry to the home of the gods. Funny, well-paced story is peppered with gags and songs (by Alan Menken and David Zippel), and a standout characterization by Woods as the garrulous and glib villain. Followed by an animated TV series and a video sequel. [G] ▼●)

Hercules II (1985-Italian) **C-90m.** *½ D: Lewis Coates (Luigi Cozzi). Lou Ferrigno, Milly Carlucci, Sonia Viviani, William Berger, Carlotta Green, Claudio Cassinelli. Sequel to HERCULES (1983). Recommended for nondiscriminating viewers too young to read this. Video title: THE ADVENTURES OF HERCULES. [PG] ▼)

Hercules in New York (1970) **C-91m.** *½ D: Arthur Allan Seidelman. Arnold Stang, Arnold Strong (Schwarzenegger), Taina Elg, James Karen, Deborah Loomis, Ernest Graves, Tanny McDonald. Hercules journeys to Earth from Mt. Olympus and gets mixed up with wrestling promoters— and mobsters—in this lumbering comedy. Inept, but irresistible for the opportunity to watch a young, badly dubbed Schwarzenegger in his movie debut. (His original dialogue track was restored for the DVD.) Reissued as HERCULES—THE MOVIE at 82m., and HERCULES GOES BANANAS at 75m. [G] ▼●)

Hercules in the Haunted World (1961-Italian) **C-83m.** ** D: Mario Bava. Reg Park, Christopher Lee, Leonora Ruffo, Giorgio Ardisson, Ida Galli. Occasionally sparked by atmospheric settings, this sword-and-sandal epic narrates adventures of Park in the devil's kingdom. Totalscope Super/100. ▼)

Hercules Unchained (1959-Italian) **C-101m.** ** D: Pietro Francisci. Steve Reeves, Sylva Koscina, Primo Carnera, Sylvia Lopez. Par-for-the-course entry featuring the muscleman hero and his princess bride setting off for the city of Thebes; along the way he will bid to prevent a war and tangle with a sinister queen. Dyaliscope. ▼●)

Hereafter (2010) **C-129m.** **½ D: Clint Eastwood. Matt Damon, Cécile de France, Jay Mohr, Bryce Dallas Howard, George McLaren, Frankie McLaren, Thierry Neuvic, Marthe Keller, Derek Jacobi, Lyndsey Marshal, Richard Kind, Steven R. Schirripa, Jenifer Lewis. Three stories unfold and eventually converge: A troubled San Francisco man (Damon) shuns his "gift" of communicating with the deceased . . . a French TV host (de France) can't shake off her near-death experience during a vacation in the tropics . . . and a British boy is haunted by the demise of his twin brother and tries to contact him in the afterlife. Opens with a frighteningly realistic depiction of a tsunami, and Peter Morgan's script remains completely absorbing after that, but the all-important finale fails to provide us with the catharsis it seems to give the characters. Yet another example of daring and unconventional material for director Eastwood. Panavision. [PG-13] ▶

Here Comes Mr. Jordan (1941) **93m. ★★★★** D: Alexander Hall. Robert Montgomery, Evelyn Keyes, Claude Rains, Rita Johnson, Edward Everett Horton, James Gleason, John Emery. Excellent fantasy-comedy of prizefighter Montgomery accidentally sent to heaven before his time, forced to occupy a new body on earth. Hollywood moviemaking at its best, with first-rate cast and performances; Harry Segall won an Oscar for his original story, as did Sidney Buchman and Seton I. Miller for their screenplay. Characters used again in DOWN TO EARTH (1947); film remade as HEAVEN CAN WAIT in 1978 and DOWN TO EARTH (2001). Look fast for a young Lloyd Bridges. ▼●▶

Here Comes the Groom (1951) **113m. ★★★** D: Frank Capra. Bing Crosby, Jane Wyman, Franchot Tone, Alexis Smith, James Barton, Anna Maria Alberghetti. Crosby contrives to keep former fiancée Wyman from marrying millionaire Tone in this lightweight musical outing. Guest appearances by Louis Armstrong, Dorothy Lamour, Phil Harris, and Cass Daley, plus Oscar-winning song, "In the Cool, Cool, Cool of the Evening." ▼●▶

Here Comes the Navy (1934) **86m. ★★½** D: Lloyd Bacon. James Cagney, Pat O'Brien, Gloria Stuart, Dorothy Tree, Frank McHugh. Enjoyable but standard tale of cocky Cagney who becomes Navy hero; nothing new, but well done.

Here Come the Co-Eds (1945) **87m. ★★½** D: Jean Yarbrough. Bud Abbott, Lou Costello, Peggy Ryan, Martha O'Driscoll, June Vincent, Lon Chaney (Jr.), Donald Cook. Pretty zany Abbott and Costello comedy of two wacky caretakers turning formerly staid girls' school on its ear. ▼▶

Here Come the Girls (1953) **C-78m. ★★½** D: Claude Binyon. Bob Hope, Arlene Dahl, Rosemary Clooney, Tony Martin, Fred Clark, Robert Strauss, the Four Step Brothers. At times amusing romp with Hope a naive show biz-ite who becomes involved with killer on the loose. ▼●

Here Come the Nelsons (1952) **76m. ★★** D: Frederick de Cordova. Ozzie, Harriet, David, Ricky Nelson, Rock Hudson, Ann Doran, Jim Backus, Barbara Lawrence, Sheldon Leonard, Gale Gordon. Expanded version of radio's *Adventures of Ozzie & Harriet,* spotlighting a series of typical, comical situations. Light, predictable fare that paved the way for the long-running TV series. ▼

Here Come the Waves (1944) **99m. ★★★** D: Mark Sandrich. Bing Crosby, Betty Hutton, Sonny Tufts, Ann Doran, Gwen

Crawford, Noel Neill, Catherine Craig, Mae Clarke. Zippy wartime music-comedy with Crosby cleverly cast as a Sinatra-like crooner, the idol of bobby-soxers, who joins the Navy, and becomes involved with twin sisters (played by Hutton—and one's even demure!). Harold Arlen–Johnny Mercer score includes "Let's Take the Long Way Home," "(That Old) Black Magic" (reprised from STAR SPANGLED RHYTHM), and "Accent-u-ate the Positive," which is performed in blackface! Yvonne De Carlo and Mona Freeman have bit parts. ▼▶

Here on Earth (2000) **C-96m. ★★** D: Mark Piznarski. Chris Klein, Leelee Sobieski, Josh Hartnett, Michael Rooker, Bruce Greenwood, Annette O'Toole, Annie Corley, Elaine Hendrix, Stuart Wilson. Spoiled preppie Klein falls for small-town girl Sobieski while rooming with her boyfriend's family for the summer. Fateful teen romantic triangle is strictly by-the-numbers. Sobieski gets points for radiantly dangling two hunky guys along; if she were any more angelic she'd explode. [PG-13] ▼▶

Here We Go Round the Mulberry Bush (1968-British) **C-96m. ★★½** D: Clive Donner. Barry Evans, Judy Geeson, Angela Scoular, Sheila White, Vanessa Howard, Denholm Elliott. British teenager Evans is hung up on girls, but finds his pursuits a constant dead-end. Amusing, often clever adolescent romp; music by Stevie Winwood & Traffic, Spencer Davis Group.

Her Majesty Mrs. Brown SEE: **Mrs. Brown**

Hero, The (1970-British) **C-97m. ★★½** D: Richard Harris. Richard Harris, Romy Schneider, Kim Burfield, Maurice Kaufman, Yossi Yadin. Old-fashioned film about a soccer star and the young boy who idolizes him; partly filmed in Israel. Aka: BLOOMFIELD. [PG] ▼

Hero (1992) **C-112m. ★★½** D: Stephen Frears. Dustin Hoffman, Geena Davis, Andy Garcia, Joan Cusack, Kevin J. O'Connor, Maury Chaykin, Stephen Tobolowsky, Christian Clemenson, Tom Arnold, Warren Berlinger, Susie Cusack, James Madio, Darrell Larson. Seriocomic yarn about a ne'er-do-well (Hoffman) who saves lives after a plane crash, barely giving it a thought, until an impostor (Garcia) takes credit for the good deed, and becomes lionized by the public—and the media. Flawed but entertaining, with some glib, funny potshots at television. How many times did they watch MEET JOHN DOE before filming this? Chevy Chase, Edward Herrmann, Barney Martin, and Fisher Stevens appear unbilled. [PG-13] ▼●▶

Hero (2002-Hong Kong-Chinese) **C-96m. ★★★** D: Zhang Yimou. Jet Li, Tony Leung Chiu-wai, Maggie Cheung, Zhang Ziyi, Chen Dao Ming, Donnie Yen, Liu Zhong Yuan. A ruthless, ambitious king is attempting to merge the conflicting Chinese municipalities into a united empire in 3rd-century A.D., and the title character (Li, perfectly cast), a warrior called Nameless, relates how he overpowered the king's three most potent enemies. Different versions are offered in a RASHOMON-like manner, and each unfolds using a different color scheme. Action-packed, visually sumptuous saga also charts a love triangle between two of the enemy warriors (Cheung, Leung Chiu-wai) and a servant (Ziyi). A bit confusing at times, but visually dazzling. Aka JET LI'S HERO. Released in the U.S. in 2004. Super 35. [PG-13] ▼▶

Hero Ain't Nothin' But a Sandwich, A (1978) C-105m. **½ D: Ralph Nelson. Cicely Tyson, Paul Winfield, Larry B. Scott, Helen Martin, Glynn Turman, David Groh. Well-meaning drama (from Alice Childress' book) about intelligent but alienated black ghetto youth who takes up drugs. Moralistic film may get PTA recommendations, but doesn't really deliver; young Scott's performance is major asset. [PG] ▼ ●▶

Hero and the Terror (1988) C-96m. *½ D: William Tannen. Chuck Norris, Brynn Thayer, Steve W. James, Jack O'Halloran, Ron O'Neal, Billy Drago. Flat melodrama proves to be an unwise change of pace for action star Norris, here playing a "sensitive" police detective who must exorcise his personal demons by doing battle one last time with his larger-than-life maniac nemesis O'Halloran. Film's cowriter, former actor Michael Blodgett, has an endless cameo in a restaurant scene. [R] ▼ ●▶

Hero At Large (1980) C-98m. **½ D: Martin Davidson. John Ritter, Anne Archer, Bert Convy, Kevin McCarthy, Harry Bellaver, Anita Dangler. Unemployed actor Ritter is mistaken for do-gooding "Captain Avenger"; political hucksters Convy and McCarthy attempt to co-opt him. Winning if naive satire. Look fast for Kevin Bacon. [PG] ▼▶

Heroes, The (1972-Italian) C-99m. ** D: Duccio Tessari. Rod Steiger, Rod Taylor, Rosanna Schiaffino, Claude Brasseur, Terry-Thomas. A middling script sinks this forgettable actioner about a motley crew that bands together to pull off a heist of "lost" military money. Techniscope. ●

Heroes (1977) C-113m. **½ D: Jeremy Paul Kagan. Henry Winkler, Sally Field, Harrison Ford, Val Avery, Olivia Cole, Hector Elias. Innocuous film marked Winkler's first starring role, as crazy Vietnam vet who chases a dream of wealth and success cross-country; Field is appealing as the girl he meets and wins along the way. [PG] ▼▶

Heroes for Sale (1933) 73m. *** D: William A. Wellman. Richard Barthelmess, Loretta Young, Aline MacMahon, Robert Barrat, Grant Mitchell, Douglass Dumbrille, Charles Grapewin, Ward Bond. Potent melodrama with Barthelmess as an American Everyman who manages to survive one calamity

after another—from morphine addiction (as a result of a WW1 injury) to job-hunting during the Depression—and continues to endure, like the country itself. Ambitious script by Wilson Mizner and Robert Lord tackles everything from the hypocrisy of hero worship to Communism! A fascinating social document of the early 1930s. ▼▶

Heroes of Telemark, The (1965-British) C-131m. **½ D: Anthony Mann. Kirk Douglas, Richard Harris, Michael Redgrave, Mervyn Johns, Eric Porter. Douglas and Harris spend more time battling each other than the Nazis overrunning Norway in this pictorially striking (filmed on location), predictable blow-up-the-German-factory yarn. Panavision. ▼▶

He Said, She Said (1991) C-115m. ** D: Ken Kwapis, Marisa Silver. Kevin Bacon, Elizabeth Perkins, Sharon Stone, Nathan Lane, Anthony LaPaglia, Stanley Anderson, Charlaine Woodard, Danton Stone. We say, piffle. Gimmick comedy charts the dissolution of a romance between two Baltimore journalists who parlay their rival point/counterpoint columns into a popular local TV spot. Kwapis' half (marginally funnier) is shown from Bacon's point of view; Silver's (marginally better, thanks to Perkins) takes overlong story from the opposite perspective. About as contemporary as a '60s TV sitcom, with clumsy fantasy sequences. Panavision. [PG-13] ▼ ●▶

Hesher (2011) C-106m. *½ D: Spencer Susser. Joseph Gordon-Levitt, Natalie Portman, Rainn Wilson, Piper Laurie, Devin Brochu, John Carroll Lynch. A boy is reeling from the sudden death of his mother, while his father is seemingly shell-shocked and his grandmother tries to make the best of every day. Into their home comes a foulmouthed, antisocial hell-raiser named Hesher (Gordon-Levitt) who gooses them to life. Often vile, self-conscious "dark fairy tale" has little to offer in the way of enlightenment and seems to revel in its main character's sheer outrageousness. If that's your idea of fun, have at it. First-time director and cowriter Susser also drew the scatological illustrations for the closing titles, fyi. HD Widescreen. [R] ●

He's Just Not That Into You (2009) C-129m. *** D: Ken Kwapis. Ginnifer Goodwin, Jennifer Aniston, Jennifer Connelly, Scarlett Johansson, Drew Barrymore, Bradley Cooper, Ben Affleck, Kevin Connolly, Justin Long, Kris Kristofferson, Busy Philipps, Leonardo Nam, Sasha Alexander, Wilson Cruz. Men send signals to women—more than ever in the age of electronic devices—but some women don't know how to read them. That's what needy Goodwin tries to learn with help from self-styled master of communication Long. Other attractive couples face a variety of crises in this episodic comedy with unexpectedly serious undertones. Not another airheaded romantic comedy but a "battle of the sexes" for our times, based on the book by Greg Behrendt and Liz Tuccillo. Luis Guzmán appears unbilled. Panavision. [PG-13]🔴

He's My Girl (1987) **C-104m.** ** D: Gabrielle Beaumont. T.K. Carter, David Hallyday, Misha McK, Jennifer Tilly, David Clennon. A few amusing moments cannot save this silly comedy about Carter dressing in drag to accompany pal Hallyday on a free trip to Hollywood. Lots of energy, but it's mostly for naught. [PG-13]▼

Hester Street (1975) **92m.** ***½ D: Joan Micklin Silver. Steven Keats, Carol Kane, Mel Howard, Dorrie Kavanaugh, Doris Roberts, Stephen Strimpell. Young Jewish immigrant (Kane) joins her husband in N.Y.C. at turn of the century, only to find that he has forsaken his Old World ways and expects her to do the same. Disarmingly simple; outstanding period flavor. [PG]▼🔴

He Walked by Night (1948) **79m.** *** D: Alfred L. Werker. Richard Basehart, Scott Brady, Roy Roberts, Whit Bissell, Jack Webb. Grade-A drama of killer hunted by police; told in semi-documentary style (and partially directed by Anthony Mann). Great climax in L.A. storm drains; photographed by the great John Alton. This clearly inspired Webb's creation of *Dragnet*.▼🔴

Hex (1973) **C-92m.** *½ D: Leo Garen. Keith Carradine, Tina Herazo (Cristina Raines), Hilarie Thompson, Gary Busey, Robert Walker, Dan Haggerty, John Carradine, Scott Glenn. Off-the-wall bike movie that involves a motorcycle gang with occultism in post-WW1 Nebraska. You've been warned. Video title: THE SHRIEKING. [PG]▼🔴

Hexed (1993) **C-90m.** ** D: Alan Spencer. Arye Gross, Claudia Christian, Adrienne Shelly, Ray Baker, R. Lee Ermey, Michael Knight, Robin Curtis, Brandis Kemp, Norman Fell, Teresa Ganzel. Hotel clerk with delusions of grandeur gets involved with a once overweight fashion model whose long-ago act of arson killed 32 people. Very hit-and-miss—and at worst, terrible—but at least it isn't bland. Christian, as the model, is a stitch. [R]▼🔴

Hey Arnold! The Movie (2002) **C-76m.** ** D: Tuck Tucker. Voices of Spencer Klein, Francesca Marie Smith, Jamil Smith, Dan Castellaneta, Tress MacNeille, Paul Sorvino, Jennifer Jason Leigh, Christopher Lloyd, Vincent Schiavelli, Maurice LaMarche, Kath E. Soucie. Arnold leads his friends and neighbors in a protest when an industrialist threatens to tear down their neighborhood to build an elaborate mall. Adaptation of the popular animated TV series plays like an extended episode; OK for young children. [PG] ▼🔴

Hey Babu Riba (1986-Yugoslavian) **C-109m.** *** D: Jovan Acin. Gala Videnovic, Relja Basic, Nebojsa Bakocevic, Marko Todorovic, Dragan Bjelogrlic, Milos Zutic. Perceptive film combines nostalgia and political commentary in flashback story of four men recalling their pranks in the early 1950s when all were in love with dream girl Videnovic. Film buffs will appreciate picture being built around kids' fascination with Esther Williams in BATHING BEAUTY; also features vintage footage from the sexy Swedish classic SHE ONLY DANCED ONE SUMMER. [R]▼🔴

Hey Boy! Hey Girl! (1959) **81m.** *½ D: David Lowell Rich. Louis Prima, Keely Smith, James Gregory, Henry Slate, Asa Maynor, Sam Butera and The Witnesses. Minor low-budget musical about a singer (Smith) who will join Prima and The Witnesses only if they appear at a church bazaar. Louis sings the unforgettable "A Banana Split for My Baby (And a Glass of Water for Me)."

Hey Good Lookin' (1982) **C-86m.** *½ D: Ralph Bakshi. Voices of Richard Romanus, David Proval, Jesse Welles, Tina Bowman. Animated feature dips into "nostalgia" for street gangs in 1950s Brooklyn, and a sense of deja vu hangs over the proceedings. More interesting visually than Bakshi's other later films, because this one wasn't completely traced from live-action footage, but as entertainment it's vulgar and pointless. Originally made in 1975, then largely redone for 1982 release. [R]▼

Hey There It's Yogi Bear (1964) **C-89m.** ** D: William Hanna, Joseph Barbera. Voices of: Mel Blanc, J. Pat O'Malley, Julie Bennett, Daws Butler, Don Messick. First full-length cartoon from Hanna-Barbera studio stars Yogi Bear in amusing musical tale for younger folk.▼🔴

H.G. Wells' The War of the Worlds (2005) **C-179m.** BOMB D: Timothy Hines. Anthony Piana, Jack Clay, James Lathrop, Darlene Sellers, John Kaufmann, Jamie Lynn Sease, Susan Goforth, W. Bernard Bauman. One of *three* 2005 movies based on Wells' classic novel about a Martian invasion, this is easily the worst, though also the most ambitious in terms of fidelity to its source. The script essentially *is* the novel, retaining the 1890s setting, and proving conclusively that fidelity is not in itself a virtue. CGI effects are below video-game level. No tension, excitement, or interest, amateurish acting, and lousy, gold-toned color; what's more, it's three hours long. Shot in and around Seattle. Director's cut runs 135m.! [R] ▼🔴

H.G. Wells' War of the Worlds (2005) **C-90m.** *½ D: David Michael Latt. C. Thomas Howell, Rhett Giles, Andy Lauer, Tinarie Van Wyk-Loots, Jake Busey, Dash Howell, Peter Greene. Invading aliens in tanklike, multilegged fighting machines ravage the countryside. Scientist Howell struggles to reach Washington, D.C., in hopes of finding his wife and son. Direct-to-video adaptation of Wells' novel is respectable but dull with scant, mediocre effects. In this variation, it's our hero who finds a way to defeat the aliens. One of *three* 2005 movies based on the Wells novel. Followed by a cable TV sequel. [R]●

Hickey & Boggs (1972) **C-111m.** **½ D: Robert Culp. Robert Culp, Bill Cosby, Rosalind Cash, Sheila Sullivan, Isabel Sanford, Ta-Ronce Allen, Lou Frizzell. Tough melodrama by Walter Hill about two weary, hard-luck private eyes whose search for a missing girl brings death to almost everyone around them. Well made but extremely violent and downbeat; a sharp contrast to the stars' tongue-in-cheek antics on their *I Spy* TV series. Many now-familiar faces appear in bits: Robert Mandan, Michael Moriarty, Vincent Gardenia, James Woods, and Ed Lauter. [PG]●

Hidalgo (2004) **C-135m.** ***½ D: Joe Johnston. Viggo Mortensen, Omar Sharif, Louise Lombard, Saïd Taghmaoui, Peter Mensah, J.K. Simmons, Zuleikha Robinson, Silas Carson, Joshua Wolf Coleman, Adam Alexi-Malle, Floyd Red Crow Westerman, C. Thomas Howell. Mortensen is perfect as disenchanted real-life cowboy Frank T. Hopkins, who participates in the world's longest, most grueling horse race across the Arabian Desert with his trusty steed Hidalgo. An old-fashioned high adventure, set in 1890, with the added kick of desert veteran Sharif as the sheik who sponsors the race. There are doubts about the inspiration for this "true story," but there's no question about its entertainment value. Written by John Fusco. Malcolm McDowell appears unbilled. Panavision. [PG-13] ▼●

Hidden, The (1987) **C-96m.** *** D: Jack Sholder. Michael Nouri, Kyle MacLachlan, Ed O'Ross, Clu Gulager, Claudia Christian, Clarence Felder, William Boyett, Richard Brooks. L.A. cop Nouri pursues an alien criminal that loves violence, fast cars, and rock music—and can pass from one human body to another. FBI agent MacLachlan, helping out, is really an alien cop. Smart, fast-paced thriller effectively blends horror, sci-fi, and action with humor; good acting and savvy direction. Followed by a sequel. [R]▼●

Hidden II, The (1994) **C-95m.** BOMB D: Seth Pinsker. Raphael Sbarge, Kate Hodge, Jovin Montanaro, Christopher Murphy, Michael Weldon, Michael A. Nickles, Tony Di Benedetto, Tom Tayback. Fifteen years after the events in the original, the daughter of the L.A. cop who chased down the body-switching alien teams up with another alien cop, here to save us from more of the evil visitors. Cheap, slow-paced sequel distorts the premise of the original; result is stilted and routine, utterly devoid of the wit and energy that sparked the first. [R]▼●

Hidden Agenda (1990-British) **C-108m.** *** D: Ken Loach. Frances McDormand, Brian Cox, Brad Dourif, Mai Zetterling, Jim Norton, Maurice Roeves. American hu-

man rights activist McDormand and British police inspector Cox (both excellent) try to unravel mystery surrounding police ambush and cover-up in strife-ridden Belfast during the early 1980s. Effective political thriller set amidst the battleground of Northern Ireland. If not exactly unbiased (director Loach is known for films which are critical of the U.K.), it *is* believable. Many small roles played by Belfast non-actors. [R]▼●

Hidden Fortress, The (1958-Japanese) **126m.** ***½ D: Akira Kurosawa. Toshiro Mifune, Misa Uehara, Minoru Chiaki, Katamari Fujiwara, Susumu Fujita, Takashi Shimura. Autocratic young Princess Uehara and loyal general Mifune must make dangerous journey to their homeland with royal fortune, with only bare minimum of help from two bumbling misfits hoping to make off with a share of the gold. Solid comedy-adventure with great deadpan performance by Mifune; one of Kurosawa's personal favorites. Acknowledged by George Lucas as a primary inspiration for STAR WARS. Some U.S. prints cut to 90m.; released in Japan at 139m., and reissued in the U.S. in 1984 at that length. Tohoscope.▼●

Hidden Room, The (1949-British) **98m.** *** D: Edward Dmytryk. Robert Newton, Sally Gray, Naunton Wayne, Phil Brown, Michael Balfour, Olga Lindo. Very effective suspenser involving Newton's plan to eliminate a man threatening his marriage; nifty climax. Retitled: OBSESSION.▼●

Hide and Seek (2005) **C-101m.** ** D: John Polson. Robert De Niro, Dakota Fanning, Famke Janssen, Elisabeth Shue, Amy Irving, Dylan Baker, Melissa Leo. After psychologist De Niro's wife commits suicide, he and his traumatized daughter (Fanning) move to the country to start life anew; strange incidents begin occurring when the child befriends a noxious "imaginary" playmate. So-called thriller has a paper-thin script, limp pacing, and a less-than-inspired De Niro performance. Super 35. [R]▼●

Hideaway (1995) **C-112m.** BOMB D: Brett Leonard. Jeff Goldblum, Christine Lahti, Alfred Molina, Jeremy Sisto, Rae Dawn Chong, Kenneth Welsh, Alicia Silverstone. Horror film from best-selling novel by Dean R. Koontz about a man resuscitated after "dying," who returns psychically linked to a psychotic killer who's also back from the beyond—and intent on making the man's family his next victims. This goes nowhere for nearly two interminable hours; Koontz had the good sense to try and have his name taken off the picture. Super 35. [R]▼●

Hideaways, The SEE: **From the Mixed-Up Files of Mrs. Basil E. Frankweiler**

Hide in Plain Sight (1980) **C-98m.** *** D: James Caan. James Caan, Jill Eikenberry, Robert Viharo, Joe Grifasi, Barbra Rae, Kenneth McMillan, Josef Sommer, Danny

Aiello. Caan made a creditable directing debut with this true story about a divorced man whose children are swept away by the U.S. government when their new father is moved underground by the Justice Department's witness relocation program. Straightforward and well done. Panavision. [PG] ▼●

Hideous Kinky (1999-British-French) C-97m. *** D: Gillies MacKinnon. Kate Winslet, Saïd Taghmaoui, Bella Riza, Carrie Mullan, Pierre Clémenti, Sira Stampe. Interesting story about an immature young woman who's left her lover, and her life, in England to seek spiritual satisfaction in Morocco—with her two young daughters in tow. Well-observed study of selfishness, spontaneity, and social mores set in the early 1970s, anchored by Winslet's fine performance. Based on an autobiographical novel by Esther Freud. Super 35. [R] ▼▶

Hideous Sun Demon, The (1959) 74m. *½ D: Robert Clarke, Tom Boutross. Robert Clarke, Patricia Manning, Nan Peterson, Patrick Whyte, Fred La Porta. Doctor exposed to radiation discovers that sunlight turns him into ghastly lizard creature. Hideously low-budget production stars codirector Clarke himself as demon of title. ▼▶

Hider in the House (1991) C-109m. *½ D: Matthew Patrick. Gary Busey, Mimi Rogers, Michael McKean, Kurt Christopher Kinder, Candy Hutson, Elizabeth Ruscio, Bruce Glover. Disturbed Busey creates a secret living space in the home of a family he admires, but his efforts to try to ingratiate himself with them lead to violence. Routine thriller with a ludicrous premise; Busey is fine as the psycho. [R] ▼●

Hiding Out (1987) C-98m. ** D: Bob Giraldi. Jon Cryer, Keith Coogan, Annabeth Gish, Gretchen Cryer, Oliver Cotton, Tim Quill, Anne Pitoniak, John Spencer. Silly, thoroughly unbelievable teen comedy-thriller about stockbroker Cryer, who's on the lam from thugs. He hides out by dyeing his hair and becoming an instant high-school senior. Jon's real-life mother, actress/writer Gretchen Cryer, plays Aunt Lucy. [PG-13] ▼▶

Hiding Place, The (1975) C-145m. **½ D: James F. Collier. Julie Harris, Eileen Heckart, Arthur O'Connell, Jeanette Clift, Robert Rietty, Pamela Sholto. Well-meaning, sometimes effective, but draggy, predictable story of Dutch Christians aiding Jews in WW2. Produced by Billy Graham's Evangelistic Association. [PG] ▼▶

High and Low (1963-Japanese) 142m. *** D: Akira Kurosawa. Toshiro Mifune, Tatsuya Mihashi, Yutaka Sada, Tatsuya Nakadai, Kyoko Kagawa. Carefully paced study of business executive Mifune, who is financially ruined when he nobly pays ransom money to kidnappers who mistakenly stole his chauffeur's son. Based on

an Ed McBain story; one color sequence. Tohoscope. ▼●

High and the Mighty, The (1954) C-147m. *** D: William A. Wellman. John Wayne, Claire Trevor, Laraine Day, Robert Stack, Jan Sterling, Phil Harris, Robert Newton, David Brian, Paul Kelly, John Howard, Sidney Blackmer, Julie Bishop, Wally Brown, Doe Avedon, Karen Sharpe, John Smith, William Campbell, Douglas Fowley, (Pedro) Gonzales Gonzales, John Qualen, Ann Doran, Paul Fix, Joy Kim, Carl Switzer, William Hopper, Regis Toomey. Granddaddy of all airborne disaster films and more fun than most of them put together: a GRAND HOTEL cast of characters boards a flight from Honolulu to San Francisco, little dreaming of the trouble in store or the tensions in the cockpit. Corny at times, but still entertaining, bolstered by Dimitri Tiomkin's Oscar-winning music (including the title song, which became a big hit). Written by Ernest K. Gann, from his novel. CinemaScope. ▶

High Anxiety (1977) C-94m. **½ D: Mel Brooks. Mel Brooks, Madeline Kahn, Cloris Leachman, Harvey Korman, Dick Van Patten, Ron Carey, Howard Morris, Murphy Dunne, Jack Riley, Charlie Callas. Affectionate, well-made but uneven spoof of Hitchcock films with Brooks as psychiatrist who walks into trouble as new head of sanitarium. Isolated moments of great comedy bolster so-so film. Future RAIN MAN director Barry Levinson, who coscripted this film, appears as a hostile hotel bellman. Kahn's father is played by special effects maestro (and real-life Hitchcock collaborator) Albert J. Whitlock. [PG] ▼●

High Art (1998-Canadian) C-101m. *** D: Lisa Cholodenko. Ally Sheedy, Radha Mitchell, Patricia Clarkson, Tammy Grimes, Gabriel Mann, Bill Sage, David Thornton. Off-putting at first, but a clear-eyed character study of a naive young woman whose stock rises at a pretentious art magazine because of her budding relationship with a once brilliant photographer who had a breakdown years ago. The question is how deeply Mitchell is willing to immerse herself in Sheedy's hedonistic, heroin-infused, lesbian lifestyle. Sheedy is solid and understated; Clarkson is a hoot in a wonderfully showy performance as her companion, an eccentric, egomaniacal German actress. Sarita Choudhury appears unbilled. [R] ▼▶

High-Ballin' (1978-U.S.-Canadian) C-100m. **½ D: Peter Carter. Peter Fonda, Jerry Reed, Helen Shaver, Chris Wiggins, David Ferry, Chris Longevin. Good-buddy truckdrivers Fonda and Reed battle a rival kingpin's goons who want to force them off the road for good. Predictable action fare, with added spice from female trucker Shaver. [PG] ▼

High Barbaree (1947) 91m. ** D: Jack

Conway. Van Johnson, June Allyson, Thomas Mitchell, Marilyn Maxwell, Cameron Mitchell. Navy flier's life story told in flashback as he awaits rescue in plane in ocean. Good cast in inferior story.

High Bright Sun, The SEE: **McGuire, Go Home!**

High Commissioner, The (1968-British) **C-93m.** *½ D: Ralph Thomas. Christopher Plummer, Rod Taylor, Lilli Palmer, Camilla Sparv, Daliah Lavi, Clive Revill, Franchot Tone. Wonderful cast is wasted in tired spy thriller about diplomat involved in murder at height of Cold War negotiations. British title: NOBODY RUNS FOREVER.▶

High Crime (1973-Italian) **C-100m.** ** D: Enzo G. Castellari. Franco Nero, James Whitmore, Fernando Rey, Delia Boccardo. Energetic but superficial action drama. Narc Nero going up against Mafioso Rey. You've seen it all before. ▼

High Crimes (2002) **C-115m.** *** D: Carl Franklin. Ashley Judd, Morgan Freeman, Jim Caviezel, Amanda Peet, Adam Scott, Tom Bower, Bruce Davison, Juan Carlos Hernandez, Jude Ciccolella, Michael Shannon. Successful lawyer defends her husband when he's revealed to be a Marine who's been wanted for 15 years for a massacre he supposedly committed in El Salvador. Then she enlists the aid of a man who knows his way around a military courtroom, eccentric lawyer Freeman. Slick and entertaining, even though you can see some of the story twists coming around the corner. Panavision. [PG-13]▼▶

Higher and Higher (1943) **90m.** **½ D: Tim Whelan. Michele Morgan, Jack Haley, Frank Sinatra, Leon Errol, Marcy McGuire, Victor Borge, Mary Wickes, Mel Tormé. Bright, breezy, generally witless musical, with good cheer compensating for lack of material, as once-wealthy Errol schemes with his own servants to raise money. Sinatra's songs are fine: "The Music Stopped," "I Couldn't Sleep a Wink Last Night." This was his starring debut.▼▶

Higher Learning (1995) **C-127m.** **½ D: John Singleton. Omar Epps, Kristy Swanson, Laurence Fishburne, Michael Rapaport, Jennifer Connelly, Ice Cube, Jason Wiles, Tyra Banks, Cole Hauser, Bradford English, Regina King, Busta Rhymes, Jay Ferguson. Provocative drama of life at a big university where problems tend to break down along racial and sexual lines. Epps plays a young black athlete searching for direction and, sometimes blindly, raging at injustice. Fishburne is a political science professor who tries to help him see the world as it is. Credible, well-acted film goes awry when writer-director Singleton steers it toward melodrama and focuses on a group of extremist skinheads. [R]▼▶

High Fidelity (2000) **C-113m.** **½ D: Stephen Frears. John Cusack, Iben Hjejle, Todd Louiso, Jack Black, Lisa Bonet, Catherine Zeta-Jones, Joan Cusack, Tim Robbins, Lili Taylor, Joelle Carter, Natasha Gregson Wagner, Sara Gilbert, Bruce Springsteen. After his girlfriend leaves, a music-obsessed Chicago record store owner (Cusack) reflects on his failed relationships. Adaptation of Nick Hornby's novel (originally set in London) is alternately insightful and annoying, embodied by Cusack's direct-to-camera chats and the fanatically detailed depiction of the music scene and its inhabitants. Cusack coproduced and cowrote the screenplay. [R]▼

High Frequency (1988-Italian) **C-105m.** ** D: Faliero Rosati. Vincent Spano, Oliver Benny, Anne Canovas, Isabelle Pasco, David Brandon. Satellite relay station attendant Spano and young ham operator Benny see a murder on a satellite monitor and try to warn a woman they believe will be the killer's next victim. Ersatz REAR WINDOW lifts ideas—but not substance—from the Hitchcock classic. Italian production released with English-language soundtrack. [PG]▼●

High Heels (1972-French) **C-100m.** **½ D: Claude Chabrol. Jean-Paul Belmondo, Mia Farrow, Laura Antonelli, Daniel Ivernel. Well-acted but disappointing Chabrol comedy-mystery about a playboy doctor (Belmondo) attracted to women other men find unappealing. Originally titled DR. POPAUL. Aka SCOUNDREL IN WHITE. ▼

High Heels (1991-Spanish) **C-115m.** **½ D: Pedro Almodóvar. Victoria Abril, Marisa Paredes, Miguel Bosé, Feodor Atkine, Bibi Andersen, Rocio Munoz. So-so Almodóvar concoction about the conflicts and intricacies in the relationship between a famous, egocentric actress (Paredes) and her TV newscaster daughter (Abril). First half is vintage Almodóvar, but film becomes a bit more serious (than necessary) as it unfolds. Still, there are plenty of the director's outlandish touches—check out that women's prison—and also some interesting views on celebrity. Leading man Bosé (son of Italian actress Lucia Bosé and Spanish bullfighter Luis Miguel Dominguin) is a pop music star in Spain. [R]▼

High Heels and Low Lifes (2001-British-U.S.) **C-86m.** **½ D: Mel Smith. Minnie Driver, Mary McCormack, Michael Gambon, Danny Dyer, Kevin McNally, Mark Williams, Julian Wadham. Broad British import about a pair of down-on-their-luck best friends who accidentally discover a bank robbery in progress and decide to blackmail the burglars into giving up the money. Clever setup and appealing lead performances make this frisky fun, even though the violent climax puts a damper on things—and strains credulity. Enjoyable female buddy caper is more OUTRAGEOUS

FORTUNE than THELMA & LOUISE. [R]▼▶

High Hopes (1988-British) **C-112m.** ***½ D: Mike Leigh. Philip Davis, Ruth Sheen, Edna Dore, Philip Jackson, Heather Tobias, Lesley Manville, David Bamber. Extraordinary slice-of-life comedy-drama about love, alienation, and responsibility, centered on a young, laid-back working-class couple, his aged mother and manic sister. Writer-director Leigh offers a provocative, highly original view of life's misfits in modern-day England, and offers food for thought along with some very hearty laughs. ▼▶

Highlander (1986) **C-111m.** *½ D: Russell Mulcahy. Christopher Lambert, Roxanne Hart, Clancy Brown, Sean Connery, Beatie Edney, Alan North. Immortal being is tracked from 16th-century Scotland to modern-day America by his eternal archenemy. Interesting notion made silly and boring. Connery, at least, shows some style in smallish role as Lambert's survival tutor. Former rock video director Mulcahy's relentlessly showy camera moves may cause you to reach for the Dramamine. Ran 17m. longer outside U.S. (and reportedly made more sense). Director's Cut edition is 5m. longer. Followed by three sequels, a TV series, an animated TV series, and an anime feature. [R]▼▶

Highlander II: The Quickening (1991) **C-88m.** *½ D: Russell Mulcahy. Christopher Lambert, Virginia Madsen, Michael Ironside, Sean Connery, John C. McGinley, Allan Rich, Phil Brock, Rusty Schwimmer. Lambert has saved the world by a globe-encircling shield, but years later, the shield's the problem. At least, that seems to be the setup; hard to tell in a film so awesomely dull. Connery is dull, too, and in it very briefly. We learn new stuff about the immortals that contradicts the first film without adding anything interesting. Even those who liked the first one hated this. Some video versions run 108m. J-D-C Scope. [R]▼●▶

Highlander: Endgame (2000) **C-88m.** BOMB D: Douglas Aarniokoski. Adrian Paul, Christopher Lambert, Bruce Payne, Lisa Barbuscia, Donnie Yen, Ian Paul Cassidy, Sheila Gish. Tedious sequel in which 500-year-old Lambert goes up against fellow immortal Payne, a vengeance-seeking, power-hungry rogue. Also involved is Lambert's clan brother (Paul, from the TV series). Of interest only to die-hard series fans. Fifth in the series—HIGHLANDER: THE SOURCE. Video runs 101m. Super 35. [R]▼▶

Highlander: The Final Dimension (1994-U.S.-Canadian) **C-99m.** BOMB D: Andy Morahan. Christopher Lambert, Mario Van Peebles, Deborah Unger, Mako, Raoul Trujillo, Martin Neufeld, Michael Jayston. Conor McCloud, the wanderer from medieval Scotland, does battle in today's N.Y. with evil fellow immortal from the past, the

Mongol magician Cane (Van Peebles). Foolish, badly written piffle is a sequel only to the first film, ignoring the second and the TV series. Lambert is glum, Van Peebles shamelessly hammy. Dozens of unexplained elements, starting with Cane's perfect English. Video version rated R. Super 35. [PG-13] ▼●▶

High Noon (1952) **84m.** **** D: Fred Zinnemann. Gary Cooper, Thomas Mitchell, Lloyd Bridges, Katy Jurado, Grace Kelly, Otto Kruger, Lon Chaney (Jr.), Henry (Harry) Morgan, Lee Van Cleef, Robert Wilke, Sheb Wooley. On his wedding—and retirement—day, marshal Cooper learns that a gunman is coming seeking revenge. Though he has good excuses for leaving, he feels a responsibility to stay and face the gunman—but no one in town is willing to help. The story appears to unfold in "real time," as the many on-screen clocks will verify. Legendary Western drama about a crisis of conscience, written by Carl Foreman, underscored by Tex Ritter's performance of Oscar-winning Dimitri Tiomkin–Ned Washington song, "Do Not Forsake Me, Oh My Darlin'." Oscars also went to Cooper, Tiomkin's score, and Elmo Williams' and Harry Gerstad's editing. Followed by 1980 TV sequel with Lee Majors; remade for TV in 2000. Also shown in computer-colored version. ▼●▶

High Plains Drifter (1973) **C-105m.** *** D: Clint Eastwood. Clint Eastwood, Verna Bloom, Marianna Hill, Mitchell Ryan, Jack Ging, Stefan Gierasch. Moody, self-conscious but compelling story of drifter hired by townspeople to protect them from vengeful outlaws who have just been released from prison. Half-serious, half tongue-in-cheek, with great role for midget Billy Curtis. Panavision. [R]▼●▶

Highpoint (1980-Canadian) **C-88m.** BOMB D: Peter Carter. Richard Harris, Christopher Plummer, Beverly D'Angelo, Kate Reid, Peter Donat, Saul Rubinek. Confused and sloppy comedy thriller (reedited by a film doctor) has Harris as an accountant mixed up in a CIA plot and international intrigue. An excuse for frequent chases culminating in a poorly photographed stunt fall off Toronto's CN tower. ▼●

High Risk (1981) **C-94m.** **½ D: Stewart Raffill. James Brolin, Cleavon Little, Bruce Davison, Chick Vennera, Anthony Quinn, Lindsay Wagner, James Coburn, Ernest Borgnine. Preposterous movie about group of normal Americans becoming mercenaries, flying to South America, parachuting into jungle to rip off dope dealers . . . and that's just the beginning, because they soon run into bandidos. Ridiculous story, but good fun. [R]▼●▶

High Road to China (1983) **C-120m.** ** D: Brian G. Hutton. Tom Selleck, Bess Armstrong, Jack Weston, Wilford Brimley, Robert Morley, Brian Blessed. Low road to escapism, with Selleck (in his first starring feature) as a boozy ex-WW1 aerial ace hired by heiress Armstrong to find her father. Strictly mediocre, with substandard action scenes, and the flattest dialogue this side of the Great Wall. [PG]▼●◗

High School Confidential! (1958) **85m.** *½ D: Jack Arnold. Russ Tamblyn, Jan Sterling, John Drew Barrymore, Mamie Van Doren, Diane Jergens, Ray Anthony, Jerry Lee Lewis, Jackie Coogan, Charles Chaplin, Jr., Lyle Talbot, William Wellman, Jr., Michael Landon. Amateurish, hilariously awful marijuana exposé, with young undercover agent Tamblyn obtaining evidence against dope pushers. A most fascinating cast. Retitled YOUNG HELLIONS; followed by COLLEGE CON-FIDENTIAL! CinemaScope.▼●◗

High School High (1996) **C-86m.** ** D: Hart Bochner. Jon Lovitz, Tia Carrere, Louise Fletcher, Mekhi Phifer, Malinda Williams, John Neville. Lovitz plays an idealistic teacher who finds himself in an urban high school so mean it even has its own cemetery! Farcical at times, uncomfortably realistic at other moments, this film suffers from a severe identity crisis. AIRPLANE/ NAKED GUN veterans David Zucker and Pat Proft were among the writers. [PG-13]▼●◗

High School Musical 3: Senior Year (2008) **C-109m.** *** D: Kenny Ortega. Zac Efron, Vanessa Hudgens, Ashley Tisdale, Lucas Grabeel, Corbin Bleu, Monique Coleman, Olesya Rulin, Alyson Reed, Jemma McKenzie-Brown, Matt Prokop. Senior year at East High brings new challenges as basketball star Efron is persuaded to participate in the school musical and girlfriend Hudgens has to decide whether to pursue early admission to college, among other story threads. All the stars of the first two wildly successful Disney Channel TV movies are reunited for this lively, energetic teen musical, executed on a larger scale than its predecessors. Story-wise, this hearkens back to Archie and Veronica, but it's cheerful and upbeat throughout. Extended version runs 117m. [G]◗

High Season (1987-British) **C-92m.** ** D: Clare Peploe. Jacqueline Bisset, James Fox, Irene Papas, Sebastian Shaw, Kenneth Branagh, Lesley Manville, Robert Stephens. Romantic misfire has Bisset (stunningly lovely as always) as a photographer residing in Rhodes who becomes involved with obnoxious tourists, a spy, and her egotistical ex-hubbie Fox. Fluff offers little more than luscious views of Bisset and the Greek island setting. [R]▼●◗

High Sierra (1941) **100m.** *** D: Raoul Walsh. Ida Lupino, Humphrey Bogart, Alan Curtis, Arthur Kennedy, Joan Leslie, Henry Hull, Henry Travers, Barton MacLane, Jerome Cowan, Cornel Wilde, Donald MacBride,

John Eldredge, Isabel Jewell, Willie Best. Bogey is Mad Dog Earle, killer with a soft heart on the lam from police, in rousing (if not exactly credible) gangster caper. Lupino as the moll and Leslie as the lame innocent Bogart befriends offer interesting contrast. Screenplay by John Huston and W. R. Burnett based on Burnett's novel. Remade as I DIED A THOUSAND TIMES, and in Western garb as COLORADO TERRITORY. Also shown in computer-colored version.▼●◗

High Society (1956) **C-107m.** *** D: Charles Walters. Bing Crosby, Grace Kelly, Frank Sinatra, Celeste Holm, John Lund, Louis Calhern, Louis Armstrong, Sidney Blackmer. Fluffy remake of THE PHILA-DELPHIA STORY is enjoyable, but has lost all the bite of the original. Kelly is about to marry Lund when ex-hubby Crosby arrives, along with reporters Sinatra and Holm. Cole Porter songs include "True Love," "Did You Evah?," "You're Sensational," plus Bing and Satchmo's "Now You Has Jazz." Grace Kelly's last acting role. VistaVision.▼●◗

High Spirits (1988) **C-97m.** BOMB D: Neil Jordan. Peter O'Toole, Daryl Hannah, Steve Guttenberg, Beverly D'Angelo, Liam Neeson, Peter Gallagher, Jennifer Tilly, Ray McAnally, Donal McCann, Connie Booth, Liz Smith. Two yuppie stereotypes and a pair of 200-year-old ghosts romp around in an Irish castle threatened with foreclosure, with O'Toole—looking a bit ghostly here himself—playing ring master. Head-splitting farce full of collapsing sets and lots of wind-machine action; cast members complained that film's producers crudely altered the original whimsical intentions of writer-director Jordan. Unbearable. [PG-13]▼●◗

High Strung (1991) **C-93m.** *½ D: Roger Nygard. Steve Oedekerk, Denise Crosby, Fred Willard, Thomas F. Wilson, Ed Williams, Jani Lane, Kirsten Dunst, Tony Sawyer. A day in the life of chronic whiner Oedekerk (who cowrote film with Robert Kuhn). Grating comedy was rereleased in 1994 to capitalize on the success of Jim Carrey, who has a very small (about 5m.), unbilled role. [PG]▼●◗

High Tension (2003-French) **C-91m.** **½ D: Alexandre Aja. Cécile de France, Maïwenn (Maïwenn Le Besco), Philippe Nahon, Franck Khalfoun, Andrei Finti, Oana Pellea. French import about two girls trying to escape from a perverted serial killer in the isolated countryside was one of the most acclaimed entries in a seemingly endless series of '70s slasher-film revivals. While many of its frightening images and suspenseful, cleverly orchestrated sequences live up to its title, an unsatisfying final twist makes it seem even more dated than the movies it emulates. Cut for U.S. theatrical release. Super 35. [R]▼◗

High Tide (1987-Australian) **C-101m. **½**
D: Gillian Armstrong. Judy Davis, Jan
Adele, Claudia Karvan, Colin Friels, John
Clayton, Frankie J. Holden, Monica Tra-
paga, Mark Hembrow. Quietly emotional
story of a woman who inadvertently encounters the teenage daughter she abandoned years ago. Truthfully told, well acted,
and set against bleakness of an Australian
coastal town, but hampered by a leading
character we don't necessarily care about.
It's fun to see Davis in the opening scenes
playing a backup singer for a crummy Elvis
impersonator! [PG-13]▼●
High Time (1960) **C-103m. **½** D: Blake
Edwards. Bing Crosby, Fabian, Tuesday
Weld, Nicole Maurey. Middling Crosby
vehicle has Bing a widower resuming college career and trying to be one of the boys;
forced comedy. CinemaScope.
Highwayman Rides, The SEE: **Billy the
Kid** (1930)
Highway Patrolman(1991-U.S.-Mexican)
C-105m. **½ D: Alex Cox. Roberto Sosa,
Bruno Bichir, Vanessa Bauche, Zaide Silvia
Gutierrez, Pedro Armendariz, Jr., Malena
Doria. Portrait of an idealistic young highway patrolman (Sosa), who is committed
to upholding the law but gradually allows
himself to be corrupted. Mildly entertaining
and more straightforward than one might
expect from filmmaker Cox; if anything,
the problem is the story's lack of dramatic
tension.▼
Highway 61 (1991-Canadian-British) **C-
102m. **½** D: Bruce McDonald. Don
McKellar, Valerie Buhagiar, Earl Pastko,
Peter Breck, Jello Biafra. An odd couple—
introverted, inexperienced small-town
barber McKellar and eccentric, on-the-lam
roadie Buhagiar—find themselves traveling from Ontario to New Orleans, along the
highway immortalized by Bob Dylan, with
a coffin strapped to the roof of their car.
Quirky rock 'n roll road movie is strangely
likable, depending on your taste and tolerance for the material. McKellar also wrote
the script. [R]▼●
Highway to Hell (1992) **C-93m. *½** D:
Ate de Jong. Patrick Bergin, Chad Lowe,
Kristy Swanson, Richard Farnsworth, C. J.
Graham, Lita Ford, Kevin Peter Hall. Newlyweds Lowe and Swanson have their honeymoon ruined when she's abducted by a
cop from hell . . . literally! Lowe then learns
that local legend gives him 24 hours to rescue his bride. Oddball yarn is unexciting
and unfunny; even comic Gilbert Gottfried
in a cameo as Hitler can't salvage this one.
Filmed in 1989. [R] ▼●
High Wind in Jamaica, A (1965-British)
C-104m. * ** D: Alexander Mackendrick.
Anthony Quinn, James Coburn, Dennis
Price, Gert Frobe, Lila Kedrova, Nigel Davenport, Kenneth J. Warren, Deborah Baxter.
Excellent cast and intelligent script about

group of children who reveal their basic
natures when left adrift aboard a pirate vessel. Score composed by harmonica virtuoso
Larry Adler. CinemaScope.●
Hilary and Jackie (1998-British) **C-120m.
**** D: Anand Tucker. Emily Watson, Rachel Griffiths, James Frain, David Morrissey, Charles Dance, Celia Imrie, Rupert
Penry-Jones, Bill Paterson. Highly charged
portrait of British cellist Jacqueline du Pré
(Watson) and her complex relationship with
her sister, Hilary (Griffiths), which grows
more troubled as Jackie becomes a star in
the classical music world. Told in nonlinear fashion, with arresting performances by
both women; Watson's cello work is extraordinarily convincing. The facts (disputed by
some relatives and colleagues) come from
Hilary's memoir. Super 35. [R] ▼●
Hilda Crane (1956) **C-87m. ** D: Philip
Dunne. Jean Simmons, Guy Madison,
Jean-Pierre Aumont, Judith Evelyn, Evelyn
Varden. Twice-divorced Simmons returns
to the college town that used to be her home,
starts the local gossips to fluttering with her
behavior. Not much overall, but title character is surprisingly liberated for her time, making her one of the '50s' more interesting screen
heroines. Based on a play by Samuel Raphaelson. CinemaScope.
Hildegarde Withers series SEE: *Leonard
Maltin's Classic Movie Guide*
Hi-Life (1998) **C-82m. ** D: Roger Hedden. Katrin Cartlidge, Charles Durning,
Daryl Hannah, Moira Kelly, Peter Riegert, Campbell Scott, Eric Stoltz, Anne De
Salvo, Saundra Santiago, Bruce McVittie,
Carlos Alban. Characters and complications
abound in this contrived Christmastime tale
about a N.Y.C. bartender (Scott) and his
attempt to raise sufficient funds to pay for
what he has been led to believe is his sister's
abortion. MIRACLE ON 34TH STREET it
ain't, but the talented cast makes it watchable. [R]▼●
Hill, The (1965) **122m. ***½** D: Sidney
Lumet. Sean Connery, Harry Andrews, Ian
Hendry, Michael Redgrave, Ian Bannen,
Alfred Lynch, Ossie Davis, Roy Kinnear,
Jack Watson. Powerful drama of military
prison camp, with superb performances by
all. One problem: British actors bark at each
other and much dialogue is unintelligible
to American ears (though if you can make
it through the first reel, hang on). Written
by Ray Rigby. Also shown in computer-
colored version.▼●
Hillbillys in a Haunted House (1967) **C-
88m. *½** D: Jean Yarbrough. Ferlin Husky,
Joi Lansing, Don Bowman, John Carradine, Lon Chaney, Jr., Basil Rathbone,
Molly Bee, Merle Haggard, Sonny James.
Country singers Husky and Lansing spend
a night in an old mansion, become involved
with an espionage ring. Moronic comedy
with an elderly, tired cast; a follow-up to

LAS VEGAS HILLBILLYS. Sorry to say, Rathbone's last film.▼❶

Hills Have Eyes, The (1977) C-89m. **½ D: Wes Craven. Susan Lanier, Robert Houston, Virginia Vincent, Russ Grieve, Dee Wallace, Martin Speer, Michael Berryman. Typical American family on camping trip is harassed by savage, cannibalistic mutants. Above average of its type, with compact direction and plenty of amusing plot twists. Extremely gory film has acquired a cult following. Followed by a sequel. Remade in 2006. [R]▼❶

Hills Have Eyes Part II, The (1985-U.S.-British) C-88m. BOMB D: Wes Craven. Michael Berryman, John Laughlin, Tamara Stafford, Kevin Blair, John Bloom. Lame sequel has a group of young motocross enthusiasts stranded in the desert, preyed upon by primitive family. Loaded with flashback footage from 1977 film, including one sequence ludicrously purporting to be a recollection by a dog! Filmed in 1983. [R]▼❶

Hills Have Eyes, The (2006) C-107m. **½ D: Alexandre Aja. Michael Bailey Smith, Tom Bower, Ted Levine, Kathleen Quinlan, Dan Byrd, Aaron Stanford, Vinessa Shaw, Emilie de Ravin, Robert Joy, Billy Drago. A family follows a creepy gas station attendant's shortcut and gets stranded in the desert, surrounded by a community of deformed killers who inevitably attack. Remaining family members must fend for themselves and avenge their loved ones. Certainly not for all (or even most) audiences; gruesome, disturbing, and finally sort of hokey. Still, Aja deserves credit for a horror remake that—for once—manages to retain much of the original's intensity. Unrated version also available. Followed by a sequel. Super 35. [R]❶

Hills Have Eyes II, The (2007) C-89m. *½ D: Martin Weisz. Michael McMillian, Jessica Stroup, Daniella Alonso, Jacob Vargas, Lee Thompson Young, Ben Crowley, Eric Edelstein, Flex Alexander, Reshad Strik, Michael Bailey Smith. A National Guard troop training in the Southwestern desert comes up against that tribe of radioactively mutated cannibals from the previous film. Begins well but becomes predictable and routine, especially when everyone ends up in mine tunnels favored by the mutants. Good if grisly makeup effects. Written by Wes Craven and his son Jonathan. Not a remake of THE HILLS HAVE EYES PART II. Filmed in Morocco. Unrated version also available. Super 35. [R]❶

Hills of Home (1948) C-97m. *** D: Fred M. Wilcox. Edmund Gwenn, Donald Crisp, Tom Drake, Rhys Williams, Janet Leigh. Fine Lassie movie about doctor convincing Scottish father to urge son to study medicine.▼

Hills Run Red, The (1966-Italian) C-89m. ** D: Carlo Lizzani. Thomas Hunter, Henry Silva, Dan Duryea, Nando Gazzola. Civil War Western of stolen payrolls; poorly dubbed and loosely acted. Techniscope.❶

Hi-Lo Country, The (1998) C-114m. **½ D: Stephen Frears. Woody Harrelson, Billy Crudup, Patricia Arquette, Sam Elliott, Cole Hauser, Penelope Cruz, Darren Burrows, Jacob Vargas, James Gammon, Lane Smith, Katy Jurado. Story of two cowboy friends in post-WW2 New Mexico who happen to fall in love with the same woman—though she's already married. A paean to the cowboy way of life and the joys of true friendship, this film has so much going for it (including Harrelson's terrific performance as a hell-raiser and Oliver Stapleton's cinematography) that it's a shame it doesn't hit the bull's-eye . . . and Arquette is so dull. Screenplay by Walon Green from the novel by Max Evans. 2.35 Research PLC. [R] ▼❶

Hi, Mom! (1970) C/B&W-87m. ***½ D: Brian De Palma. Robert De Niro, Allen Garfield, Lara Parker, Jennifer Salt, Gerrit Graham, Charles Durning. Sequel to GREETINGS! is funny satire of the late '60s, with Vietnam veteran De Niro making dirty movies and bombing apartment houses. Aka CONFESSIONS OF A PEEPING JOHN and BLUE MANHATTAN. [R]▼❶

Hindenburg, The (1975) C-125m. ** D: Robert Wise. George C. Scott, Anne Bancroft, William Atherton, Roy Thinnes, Gig Young, Burgess Meredith, Charles Durning, Richard A. Dysart, Robert Clary, Rene Auberjonois, Katherine Helmond. Intriguing premise, that 1937 airship disaster was an act of sabotage, undermined by silly Grand Hotel–type characters and unexciting denouement combining original newsreel footage and newly shot material. This earned special Oscars for its visual and sound effects. 5m. were added to film for network showing. Panavision. [PG] ▼❶

Hired Hand, The (1971) C-93m. *** D: Peter Fonda. Peter Fonda, Warren Oates, Verna Bloom, Robert Pratt, Severn Darden. First-rate photography by Vilmos Zsigmond and good performances by Oates and Bloom aid this offbeat, sometimes pretentious Western about cowboy who goes to work for the wife he deserted seven years before. [PG] ▼❶

Hired to Kill (1990) C-91m. *½ D: Nico Mastorakis, Peter Rader. Brian Thompson, Oliver Reed, George Kennedy, Jose Ferrer, Michelle Moffett, Barbara Lee Alexander, Jordana Capra, Kendall Conrad, Kim Lonsdale, Jude Mussetter, Penelope Reed. Mercenary Thompson poses as a gay fashion designer to spring rebel leader Ferrer from Latin American prison. His commando squad: six gorgeous women posing as fashion models! Well produced, but awesomely silly. [R]▼

Hireling, The (1973-British) **C-108m.**
***½ D: Alan Bridges. Robert Shaw, Sarah
Miles, Peter Egan, Elizabeth Sellars, Caroline Mortimer, Patricia Lawrence. Artistic
adaptation of L. P. Hartley novel of stifling
class system of England. Chauffeur (Shaw)
helps upper-class woman (Miles) out of
mental depression, mistakenly assumes
she's interested in him. Ensemble British
cast, good direction. Screenplay by Wolf
Mankowitz. [PG]

Hiroshima, Mon Amour (1959-French-
Japanese) **91m.** ***½ D: Alain Resnais.
Emmanuele Riva, Eiji Okada, Stella Dassas, Pierre Barbaud, Bernard Fresson.
Resnais' first feature is a thoughtful, complex study of a French film actress (Riva)
and Japanese architect (Okada), each with
a troubled past, who have a brief affair in
postwar Hiroshima. Scripted by Marguerite
Duras.▼●

His Brother's Wife (1936) **90m.** ** D: W.
S. Van Dyke, II. Barbara Stanwyck, Robert
Taylor, Jean Hersholt, Joseph Calleia, John
Eldredge, Samuel S. Hinds. Glossy soaper
of dedicated scientist Taylor scorning Stanwyck, who marries his brother (Eldredge)
for spite. Stanwyck and Taylor married in
real life three years later.

His Girl Friday (1940) **92m.** **** D: Howard Hawks. Cary Grant, Rosalind Russell,
Ralph Bellamy, Gene Lockhart, Helen
Mack, Ernest Truex, Clarence Kolb, Porter Hall, Roscoe Karns, Abner Biberman,
Cliff Edwards, John Qualen, Frank Jenks,
Billy Gilbert. Splendid comedy remake of
THE FRONT PAGE with Grant as conniving editor, Russell as star reporter (and
his ex-wife), Bellamy as mama's boy she's
trying to marry amid hot murder story.
Terrific character actors add sparkle to
must-see film, scripted by Ben Hecht and
Charles Lederer. Remade (with the same
gender twist) in 1988 as SWITCHING
CHANNELS.▼●

His Kind of Woman (1951) **120m.** *** D:
John Farrow. Robert Mitchum, Jane Russell, Vincent Price, Tim Holt, Raymond
Burr, Charles McGraw, Marjorie Reynolds, Jim Backus. Mitchum blindly goes
to Mexico for a payoff of 50 grand, discovers he's the soon-to-be-dead chump whose
identity will help deported gangster Burr
re-enter the country. Cult film is overlong,
but its spoofing of he-man heroics predates
the more celebrated BEAT THE DEVIL
by three years; Price is hilarious as a ham
actor.▼●

His Majesty O'Keefe (1953) **C-92m.** **½
D: Byron Haskin. Burt Lancaster, Joan
Rice, Benson Fong, Philip Ahn, Grant Taylor. Another athletic Lancaster buccaneer
romp, set in the South Seas.▼▷

History Boys, The (2006-British-U.S.) **C-
109m.** *** D: Nicholas Hytner. Richard
Griffiths, Stephen Campbell Moore, Frances de la Tour, Samuel Barnett, Dominic
Cooper, Samuel Anderson, James Corden,
Andrew Knott, Sacha Dhawan, Jamie Parker,
Russell Tovey, Clive Merrison, Penelope
Wilton, Georgia Taylor. Screen adaptation of
riveting, Tony Award–winning Alan Bennett
play arrives with director and its London/
Broadway cast intact. Eight gifted goof-offs
face university exam prep with two contrasting profs: a wildly idiosyncratic veteran
who gives them life lessons (Griffiths) and a
humorless younger man hired to drill them
on test-taking tactics. Hardly cinematic, but
anyone who has ever loved GOODBYE,
MR. CHIPS won't mind. [R]▷

History Is Made at Night (1937) **97m.**
***½ D: Frank Borzage. Charles Boyer,
Jean Arthur, Leo Carrillo, Colin Clive, Ivan
Lebedeff, George Meeker, Lucien Prival,
George Davis. Arthur, fleeing from a jealous husband she doesn't love, falls in love
with Parisian headwaiter Boyer. Elegant,
adult romantic drama, seamlessly directed
by Borzage, with incredible shipboard climax and flawless performances by the two
leads.▼●

History of the World—Part 1 (1981)
C-92m. *½ D: Mel Brooks. Mel Brooks,
Gregory Hines, Dom DeLuise, Madeline
Kahn, Harvey Korman, Cloris Leachman,
Ron Carey, Sid Caesar, Pamela Stephenson, Mary-Margaret Humes, Howard Morris, Spike Milligan, Barry Levinson, many
guest stars; narrated by Orson Welles. Scattershot comedy wanders from the Stone
Age to Roman Empire to French Revolution, dispensing gags ranging from hilarious to hideous. After a while momentum's
gone, and it all just lies there, despite efforts of
a large comic cast. Caesar scores highest as a
caveman in opening scenes. Hines' film debut.
Panavision. [R]▼●

History of Violence, A (2005-U.S.-Canadian) **C-95m.** *** D: David Cronenberg.
Viggo Mortensen, Maria Bello, William
Hurt, Ed Harris, Ashton Holmes, Stephen
McHattie, Peter MacNeill. Soft-spoken
man who runs a small-town luncheonette
is suddenly confronted by two violent
strangers—and is more than ready to respond. His actions lead to questions and
repercussions. Sexually potent, harshly
violent story based on the graphic novel by
John Wagner and Vince Locke is arresting
entertainment that means to hit us right between the eyes, and does. [R]▼▷

Hit! (1973) **C-134m.** *** D: Sidney J.
Furie. Billy Dee Williams, Paul Hampton,
Richard Pryor, Gwen Welles. Detailed
and overlong, but exciting story of black
U.S. agent who seeks revenge on top drug
importers in Marseilles who are indirectly
responsible for his daughter's death. Panavision. [R]▼

Hit, The (1984-British) **C-98m.** *** D:
Stephen Frears. Terence Stamp, John Hurt,

Tim Roth, Laura Del Sol, Bill Hunter, Fernando Rey, Jim Broadbent. Sly, offbeat film about a criminal stool pigeon (Stamp) who's been in hiding for ten years but whose time has just run out: two hit men have tracked him down. Sharp, often very funny, and doggedly unpredictable. Written by Peter Prince; memorable theme music by Eric Clapton. Film debut of Tim Roth. [R]▼●◗

Hitch (2005) **C-117m.** ** D: Andy Tennant. Will Smith, Eva Mendes, Kevin James, Amber Valletta, Michael Rapaport, Adam Arkin, Julie Ann Emery, Kevin Sussman, Robinne Lee, Philip Bosco, Matt Malloy. Smith is a date doctor who coaches timid, nerdy New York guys on how to woo women, using several "basic principles." His latest client (James) is madly in love with a celebrated heiress (Valletta), but Smith doesn't see her as unattainable. Then he sets his own sights on gossip columnist Mendes. Likable at first, this romantic comedy becomes needlessly complicated and overlong. Smith also coproduced. Super 35. [PG-13]▼◗

Hitcher, The (1986) **C-97m.** **½ D: Robert Harmon. Rutger Hauer, C. Thomas Howell, Jennifer Jason Leigh, Jeffrey DeMunn, John Jackson. Hitchhiker Hauer keeps reappearing in Howell's life—is he real, or an hallucination? Reminiscent of other movies, except all those other movies (DUEL, NIGHT OF THE HUNTER) are better. Not without interest, but some of the violence is genuinely grisly and unappealing. Followed in 2002 by a direct-to-video sequel. Remade in 2007. Panavision. [R]▼●◗

Hitcher, The (2007) **C-83m.** *½ D: Dave Meyers. Sophia Bush, Sean Bean, Zachary Knighton, Neal McDonough. Unnecessary remake of the 1986 horror film in which a hitchhiker terrorizes a young couple who wish they'd never picked him up in the first place. Some good car stunts and a credible performance from Bean as the evildoer aren't enough to justify revisiting this material. Apparently the most original change filmmakers could think of was switching the gender in the notorious body "stretching" scene we first saw 20 years earlier. Super 35. [R]◗

Hitch-Hiker, The (1953) **71m.** **½ D: Ida Lupino. Edmond O'Brien, Frank Lovejoy, William Talman, Jose Torvay. Well-made suspense yarn about two men on a hunting trip whose car is commandeered by a murderous fugitive. Good performances, especially by a venal Talman in the title role, but the film's once-powerful impact has been muted by decades of more graphic and imaginative films. ▼●◗

Hitchhiker's Guide to the Galaxy, The (2005) **C-110m.** *** D: Garth Jennings. Martin Freeman, Sam Rockwell, Mos Def,

Zooey Deschanel, Bill Nighy, Anna Chancellor, John Malkovich, Simon Jones, David Leamer; voices of Alan Rickman, Helen Mirren, Richard Griffiths, Ian McNeice, Thomas Lennon; narrated by Stephen Fry. Clever if low-key screen adaptation of Douglas Adams' much-loved book (which began as a BBC radio serial) about an ordinary bloke who finds himself having an intergalactic adventure after earth is destroyed . . . and encountering other species in search of the Big Answers. Visually and verbally witty, though the energy lags at times. Filmed as a miniseries in 1981. Super 35. [PG]◗

Hitler's Children (1943) **83m.** *** D: Edward Dmytryk, Irving Reis. Tim Holt, Bonita Granville, Kent Smith, Otto Kruger, H. B. Warner, Lloyd Corrigan. Engrossing exploitation film of young people forced to live life of horror in Nazi Germany. Quite sensational in its day.▼

Hitler's Gold SEE: **Inside Out** (1975)

Hitler's Madman (1943) **84m.** **½ D: Douglas Sirk. Patricia Morison, John Carradine, Alan Curtis, Ralph Morgan, Howard Freeman, Ludwig Stossel, Edgar Kennedy. Vintage WW2 propaganda of citizens in small Czech village and their fate against their Nazi tormentors. Carradine is appropriately depraved as Reinhard Heydrich, Nazi governor of Prague. Coscripted by Yiddish playwright Peretz Hirchbein; look for Ava Gardner in a small part. Loosely based on fact; the story is also told in HANGMEN ALSO DIE!

Hitler: The Last Ten Days (1973-British-Italian) **C-108m.** ** D: Ennio de Concini. Alec Guinness, Simon Ward, Adolfo Celi, Diane Cilento, Gabriele Ferzetti, Eric Porter, Doris Kunstmann. Strange treatment of Hitler's final tyrannies is grimly amusing at times; muddled film doesn't really work. [PG]▼◗

Hit List (1989) **C-87m.** ** D: William Lustig. Jan-Michael Vincent, Lance Henriksen, Rip Torn, Leo Rossi, Jere Burns, Ken Lerner. Familiar urban thriller of ordinary guy whose child is mistakenly kidnapped by cold-eyed hit man working for flamboyant mobster Torn. Hero teams up with the real target, an informer. Lots of violent action. Torn and Henriksen are good, but you've seen it all before. [R]▼●

Hit Man (1972) **C-90m.** ** D: George Armitage. Bernie Casey, Pamela Grier, Lisa Moore, Don Diamond, Roger E. Mosley. Reworking of GET CARTER in black mold. Big rubout is key to crime story, and it loses steam before long. [R]◗

Hitman (2007) **C-93m.** ** D: Xavier Gens. Timothy Olyphant, Dougray Scott, Olga Kurylenko, Robert Knepper, Ulrich Thomsen, Henry Ian Cusick. Every bit as visually flashy and dramatically sketchy as you would expect a video-game–inspired action-adventure to be. Still, some genuinely rousing run-and-gun sequences—enhanced with rapid-fire editing, slo-mo flourishes, and very loud music—generate interest as prolifically lethal but increasingly self-doubting Agent 47 (Olyphant), a bald-pated, bar-code–tattooed assassin, dashes about Russia after being betrayed by his employers. Unrated version also available. Super 35. [R]🄳

Hitman, The (1991) **C-95m.** *½ D: Aaron Norris. Chuck Norris, Michael Parks, Al Waxman, Alberta Watson, Salim Grant, Ken Pogue, Marcel Sabourin. Fairly awful Chuck Norris vehicle in which the star goes undercover to infiltrate an organized crime ring. Norris gets to play a heavy—even though we know all along it's a ruse. This acting "stretch" still isn't enough to distinguish the film. Stuntwork remains the only redeeming quality. [R]▼○🄳

Hit Team, The SEE: **Company of Killers**

Hit the Deck (1955) **C-112m.** **½ D: Roy Rowland. Jane Powell, Tony Martin, Debbie Reynolds, Ann Miller, Vic Damone, Russ Tamblyn, Walter Pidgeon, Kay Armen, Gene Raymond. Second-string MGM musical of sailors on shore leave is pleasant timefiller, no more, with nice Vincent Youmans songs like "Hallelujah," "Sometimes I'm Happy," "More Than You Know." Filmed before in 1930. CinemaScope. ▼○🄳

Hit the Ice (1943) **82m.** **½ D: Charles Lamont. Bud Abbott, Lou Costello, Ginny Simms, Patric Knowles, Elyse Knox, Sheldon Leonard, Marc Lawrence, Joseph Sawyer. Bud and Lou are newspaper photographers involved with gang of thugs in zany comedy with good gags on skating rink. ▼○🄳

H. M. Pulham, Esq. (1941) **120m.** ***½ D: King Vidor. Hedy Lamarr, Robert Young, Ruth Hussey, Charles Coburn, Van Heflin, Fay Holden, Bonita Granville, Leif Erickson, Sara Haden. Intelligent, mature, and witty film (based on John P. Marquand story) about a man who's lived his life as he was supposed to—not as he chose to. Lamarr is excellent as the spirited career woman who coaxes proper Bostonian Young out of his shell, ever so briefly. Scripted by Elizabeth Hill and director Vidor. Anne Revere has unbilled bit as a secretary in flashback scenes. Look fast for Ava Gardner on the dance floor behind Lamarr and Young.🄳

Hoax, The (2007) **C-115m.** *** D: Lasse Hallström. Richard Gere, Alfred Molina, Hope Davis, Marcia Gay Harden, Stanley Tucci, Julie Delpy, Eli Wallach, Zeljko Ivanek, John Bedford Lloyd, Mamie Gummer. Entertaining look at one of the greatest frauds of the 20th century, when, in 1971, failed author Clifford Irving convinced a major publisher that he was the conduit to an autobiography of eccentric, elusive billionaire Howard Hughes. Gere brilliantly captures Irving's bravado, and his anxieties; Molina

is funny as his hapless partner in crime. Hallström and screenwriter William Wheeler's treatment of the material is unexpectedly complex and challenging, presenting a mental puzzle in cinematic form. [R]🄳

Hobson's Choice (1954-British) **107m.** *** D: David Lean. Charles Laughton, John Mills, Brenda de Banzie, Daphne Anderson, Prunella Scales, Richard Wattis, Helen Haye. Laughton is selfish, overbearing owner of bootshop in 1890s who's used to being tended to by his three subservient daughters; then his eldest (De Banzie) decides to take matters into her own hands. Beautifully staged and photographed (by Jack Hildyard), with Laughton having a field day in the lead. Loses momentum along the way, but still entertaining. Filmed before in 1920 and 1931; remade as a TVM in 1983. ▼○🄳

Hockey Night (1984-Canadian) **C-77m.** **½ D: Paul Shapiro. Megan Follows, Rick Moranis, Gail Youngs, Yannick Bisson, Henry Ramer, Sean McCann. A girl goalie makes the boys' hockey team in a small Canadian town. Unexceptional but still likable, and ideal nonexploitation fare for preand early teens. ▼🄳

Hocus Pocus (1993) **C-95m.** *½ D: Kenny Ortega. Bette Midler, Sarah Jessica Parker, Kathy Najimy, Omri Katz, Thora Birch, Vinessa Shaw, Amanda Shepherd, Larry Bagby III, Tobias Jelinek, Stephanie Faracy, Charlie Rocket, Kathleen Freeman, Don Yesso. Lonely male teen in Salem, Mass., conjures up three long-deceased witches who can only sustain themselves by sucking the life out of children. Someone certainly sucked the humor out of this ghoulish, effects-laden concoction. Hammy to the extreme, and a discredit to Disney "family entertainment." [PG]▼○🄳

Hoffa (1992) **C-140m.** **½ D: Danny DeVito. Jack Nicholson, Danny DeVito, Armand Assante, J. T. Walsh, John C. Reilly, Frank Whaley, Kevin Anderson, John P. Ryan, Robert Prosky, Natalija Nogulich, Nicholas Pryor, Karen Young, Cliff Gorman. Scattershot (and sanitized) biography of legendary Teamster boss Jimmy Hoffa, transformed into a must-see by the galvanizing performance of Nicholson. DeVito indulges in visual flourishes but seldom engages our emotions; nor does David Mamet's script, which never gives us much insight into the man or his motivations. Nicholson's daughter, Jennifer Nicholson, has a bit as a nursing nun in white. Bruno Kirby appears unbilled as a nightclub comic. Panavision. [R]▼○🄳

Hoffman (1970-British) **C-116m.** *** D: Alvin Rakoff. Peter Sellers, Sinead Cusack, Jeremy Bulloch, Ruth Dunning. Very odd, low-key dual character study with Sellers blackmailing attractive young bride-to-be to spend week with him. Slightly overlong; great performances. [PG]🄳

Holcroft Covenant, The (1985-British) C-112m. ** D: John Frankenheimer. Michael Caine, Anthony Andrews, Victoria Tennant, Lilli Palmer, Mario Adorf, Michael Lonsdale. Muddy, twisty, unbelievable tale from Robert Ludlum novel. Caine's late father (a comrade-in-arms of Adolf Hitler) has left a fortune behind, supposedly to make amends for his wrongdoing—and leading Caine on a globe-trotting series of adventures. Just old-fashioned enough to be watchable—but not very good. [R]▼●)

Hold Back the Dawn (1941) 115m. ***½ D: Mitchell Leisen. Charles Boyer, Olivia de Havilland, Paulette Goddard, Victor Francen, Walter Abel, Rosemary DeCamp. First-rate soaper with Billy Wilder–Charles Brackett script of gigolo Boyer marrying spinsterish Olivia to get into U.S. That's director Leisen in the Hollywood soundstage sequence, directing Veronica Lake and Brian Donlevy in I WANTED WINGS. Catch this one.

Hold Me Thrill Me Kiss Me (1992) C-92m. *** D: Joel Hershman. Max Parrish, Adrienne Shelly, Sean Young, Diane Ladd, Timothy Leary, Andrea Naschak, Bela Lehoczky. Parrish goes on the lam after shooting his fiancée (Young), a wealthy weirdo, and becomes involved with an oversexed, abusive stripper and her virginal kid sister, who live in a trailer park inhabited by assorted oddballs. Funky, extremely entertaining comedy. Fans of Pedro Almodóvar, John Waters, and early David Lynch will really go for this. Also available in unrated version. [R]▼●

Hold On! (1966) C-85m. *½ D: Arthur Lubin. Peter Noone, Herman's Hermits, Sue Ane Langdon, Karl Green, Shelley Fabares. Will NASA name a spaceship after Herman's Hermits? That's the burning question in this awful musical, set while the group is on a U.S. tour. One of their songs is titled "A Must to Avoid," which sums up this loser. Panavision.❿

Hold That Ghost (1941) 86m. *** D: Arthur Lubin. Bud Abbott, Lou Costello, Richard Carlson, Joan Davis, Mischa Auer, Evelyn Ankers, Marc Lawrence, Shemp Howard, Ted Lewis, The Andrews Sisters. Prime A&C, with the boys inheriting a haunted house. Fine cast includes hilarious Davis as professional radio screamer. Highlight: the moving candle.▼●)

Hold Your Man (1933) 86m. *** D: Sam Wood. Jean Harlow, Clark Gable, Stuart Erwin, Elizabeth Patterson, Blanche Friderici. Delightful film that effectively makes the transition from comedy to drama with Harlow falling for jailbound Gable. The stars are at their best here.▼

Hole, The (2001-British) C-102m. ** D: Nick Hamm. Thora Birch, Desmond Harrington, Daniel Brocklebank, Laurence Fox, Keira Knightley, Embeth Davidtz. Private school student Birch stumbles onto campus after she and fellow classmates have been missing for over two weeks. She tells a tale of how she and three teens ditched a weekend field trip to hang out in an underground bunker, only to find themselves trapped and at the mercy of a troubled soul. Birch's complex performance is the best part of this lackluster psychological horror film. Released direct to video in the U.S. in 2004. Super 35. [R]▼)

Hole in the Head, A (1959) C-120m. ** D: Frank Capra. Frank Sinatra, Edward G. Robinson, Eleanor Parker, Carolyn Jones, Thelma Ritter, Eddie Hodges, Keenan Wynn, Joi Lansing. Sticky story of a ne'er-do-well (Sinatra) and his son (Hodges) doesn't seem sincere. Only distinction is Oscar-winning song, "High Hopes." CinemaScope.▼●)

Holes (2003) C-118m. **½ D: Andrew Davis. Sigourney Weaver, Jon Voight, Shia LaBeouf, Khleo Thomas, Patricia Arquette, Tim Blake Nelson, Dulé Hill, Henry Winkler, Nate Davis, Rick Fox, Scott Plank, Eartha Kitt, Siobhan Fallon Hogan, Brenden Jefferson, Jake M. Smith. Boy from an eccentric family is sent to a strange desert detention camp where it's believed that digging holes builds character. As he gets to know the other misfits—among the kids and staff—pieces of his life begin to come together and make sense. Louis Sachar's adaptation of his popular, award-winning novel should please his juvenile audience, but adults may grow impatient as the artificial, incident-laden story plays out over two hours' time. Super 35. [PG] ▼)

Holiday (1930) 96m. *** D: Edward H. Griffith. Ann Harding, Robert Ames, Mary Astor, Edward Everett Horton, Hedda Hopper, Monroe Owsley. First version of Philip Barry's play about nonconformity is a pleasant surprise; an unstodgy early talkie with casting that in some cases (Astor, Owsley) even tops the more famous 1938 version (Horton plays the same role in both movies).

Holiday (1938) 93m. ***½ D: George Cukor. Katharine Hepburn, Cary Grant, Doris Nolan, Lew Ayres, Edward Everett Horton, Henry Kolker, Binnie Barnes, Jean Dixon, Henry Daniell. Fine, literate adaptation of Philip Barry's play (filmed before in 1930) about nonconformist Grant confronting stuffy N.Y.C. society family, finding his match in Hepburn (who had under-studied the role in the original Broadway company a decade earlier). Screenplay by Donald Ogden Stewart and Sidney Buchman. Delightful film.▼●)

Holiday, The (2006) C-135m. **½ D: Nancy Meyers. Cameron Diaz, Kate Winslet, Jude Law, Jack Black, Eli Wallach, Edward Burns, Rufus Sewell, Miffy Englefield, Emma Pritchard, Shannyn Sossamon, Bill Macy, Shelley Berman, Kathryn Hahn, John Krasinski. Stressed-out L.A. workaholic Diaz, who's just split with her long-time boyfriend, impulsively decides to swap houses for Christmas with Winslet, a Brit who's trying to get over her hopeless infatuation with Sewell. Each woman moves into a dream house and meets a dream guy in this highly attractive—but needlessly overlong—piece of fluff. Not without its charms, but awfully contrived. Written by the director. [PG-13]▶

Holiday Affair (1949) 87m. *** D: Don Hartman. Robert Mitchum, Janet Leigh, Wendell Corey, Gordon Gebert, Griff Barnett, Esther Dale, Henry O'Neill, Henry (Harry) Morgan. Well-done Christmastime story of war widow Leigh, with a young son, who's courted by nice guy Corey. Fate intervenes when she meets articulate, kindly rolling stone Mitchum. Remade for TV in 1997.▼▶

Holiday for Lovers (1959) C-103m. **½ D: Henry Levin. Clifton Webb, Jane Wyman, Jill St. John, Carol Lynley, Paul Henreid, Gary Crosby, Jose Greco. Arch Dr. Webb and Wyman escort attractive daughters on South American vacation, with predictable mating. CinemaScope.

Holiday in Mexico (1946) C-127m. *** D: George Sidney. Walter Pidgeon, Ilona Massey, Roddy McDowall, Jose Iturbi, Xavier Cugat, Jane Powell. Engaging, well-cast musical comedy of daughter of ambassador falling for noted musician.▼▶

Holiday Inn (1942) 101m. ***½ D: Mark Sandrich. Bing Crosby, Fred Astaire, Marjorie Reynolds, Virginia Dale, Walter Abel, Louise Beavers. Entertaining musical built on paper-thin plot about a romantic triangle, and the establishment of a country inn that's open only on holidays. That's the cue for a raft of Irving Berlin holiday songs (there's even one for George Washington's birthday!) including the timeless Oscar winner "White Christmas." Good fun, and snappier than partial remake WHITE CHRISTMAS. Bing's original Rhythm Boys partner, Harry Barris, plays the orchestra leader. Also available in computer-colored version.▼▶

Hollow Man (2000) C-114m. ** D: Paul Verhoeven. Kevin Bacon, Elisabeth Shue, Josh Brolin, William Devane, Greg Grunberg, Mary Jo Randle, Joey Slotnick, Steve Altes, Kim Dickens. New twist on *The Invisible Man* has cocky research lab genius Bacon deciding to try his revolutionary formula on himself, with incendiary results. Starts out fun, then turns nasty (in true Verhoeven style) and stupid. A shame, considering how great the special effects are. Fine score by Jerry Goldsmith. Alternate version runs 122m. Followed in 2006 by a direct-to-video sequel. [R]▼▶

Hollow Point SEE: **Wild Pair, The**
Hollow Reed (1996-British-German) C-104m. *** D: Angela Pope. Martin Donovan, Joely Richardson, Jason Flemyng, Ian

Hart, Sam Bould. Doctor Donovan, who is divorced, senses that his young son is being abused by his ex-wife's live-in boyfriend. He decides to petition for custody, but knows his concern for his son's safety will be obscured by the fact that he is gay. Intensely dramatic, extremely well-acted psychological drama works on two levels: as a top-notch suspense thriller and a no-holds-barred indictment of homophobia. [R]▼

Holly and the Ivy, The (1952-British) 80m. *** D: George More O'Ferrall. Ralph Richardson, Celia Johnson, Margaret Leighton, Denholm Elliott, Hugh Williams, Roland Culver. Straightforward adaptation of Wynyard Browne play revolving around Christmas holiday with Richardson, the small-town cleric, learning about his three grown-up children; nicely acted.

Hollywood Boulevard (1976) C-83m. **½ D: Joe Dante, Allan Arkush. Candice Rialson, Mary Woronov, Rita George, Jeffrey Kramer, Dick Miller, Paul Bartel. Shameless low-budgeter splices shots from various Roger Corman films into the "story" of a would-be actress who goes to work for some schlock moviemakers. Engaging nonsense and some funny gags (especially for film buffs and Corman devotees)—though not enough to completely hide the fact that this *is* a schlock movie. Miller and Bartel are great fun as an agent and a motivation-minded director. Don't miss gag after closing credits. [R]▼▶

Hollywood Canteen (1944) 124m. **½ D: Delmer Daves. Bette Davis, John Garfield, Joan Leslie, Robert Hutton, Dane Clark, Janis Paige; many guest stars including Joan Crawford, Ida Lupino, Barbara Stanwyck, Eddie Cantor, Jack Carson, Eleanor Parker, Alexis Smith, S. Z. Sakall. Amiable all-star silliness set in Hollywood's real-life haven for WW2 servicemen, featuring cofounders Davis and Garfield. Hutton plays G.I. with a crush on lovely Leslie. Best bits: Peter Lorre and Sydney Greenstreet; Jack Benny and violinist Joseph Szigeti. Roy Rogers introduces "Don't Fence Me In," later reprised by the Andrews Sisters.▼▶

Hollywood Cavalcade (1939) C-96m. **½ D: Irving Cummings. Alice Faye, Don Ameche, J. Edward Bromberg, Al Jolson, Mack Sennett, Stuart Erwin, Buster Keaton, Rin-Tin-Tin, Jr., Alan Curtis. Colorful saga of pioneering days in Hollywood (based, very loosely, on Mack Sennett and Mabel Normand) starts out fun, with some lively re-creations of silent slapstick comedies, but gets bogged down in clichéd dramatics later on.▶

Hollywood Dreams (2007) C-100m. *½ D: Henry Jaglom. Tanna Frederick, Justin Kirk, Zack Norman, Karen Black, David Proval, Melissa Leo, Jon Robin Baitz, Seymour Cassel, Sally Kirkland, Eric Roberts. Jaglom hits rock bottom with this familiar tale of a young midwestern wannabe star who comes to Hollywood and hooks up with a couple of producers who promise to put her in a movie. Dialogue is so corny and contrived, the whole film sinks under its weight. [R]█

Hollywood Ending (2002) **C-112m.** *** D: Woody Allen. Woody Allen, Téa Leoni, Debra Messing, Treat Williams, Mark Rydell, George Hamilton, Tiffany Thiessen, Marian Seldes, Isaac Mizrahi, Doug McGrath. Often hilarious comedy about a highly neurotic, washed-up movie director who gets a shot at making a comeback thanks to his ex-wife (Leoni) . . . but can't get over the fact that he now has to work for her fiancé, studio head Williams. Woody is in fine fettle here as writer, director, and star, and offers many laugh-out-loud moments as well as a fine showcase for leading ladies Leoni and Messing. [PG-13]▼▼

Hollywood Harry (1985) **C-99m.** ** D: Robert Forster. Robert Forster, Joe Spinell, Shannon Wilcox, Marji Martin, Katherine Forster, Mallie Jackson. Down-the-tubes private eye Forster hires on to find a young girl who's turned up in an X-rated movie. Strictly standard fare. Forster also produced and scripted; his 14-year-old daughter Kathrine plays Harry's niece. Aka HARRY'S MACHINE. [PG-13]▼

Hollywood Homicide (2003) **C-115m.** *½ D: Ron Shelton. Harrison Ford, Josh Hartnett, Lena Olin, Bruce Greenwood, Isaiah Washington, Lolita Davidovich, Keith David, Martin Landau, Master P, Gladys Knight, Lou Diamond Phillips, Dwight Yoakam, Eric Idle. Odd-couple L.A. cops (one a part-time realtor, the other an aspiring actor) are obliged to concentrate on a case when there's a bloody shoot-out at a prominent hip-hop club. The stars are good, but if director-cowriter Shelton set out to make a Big Dumb Hollywood Movie, he succeeded all too well. Trying to have us care about the story and turning it into a farce at the same time was not a good plan. Several stars and celebrities appear in cameos. Panavision. [PG-13]▼▼

Hollywood Hotel (1937) **109m.** **½ D: Busby Berkeley. Dick Powell, Rosemary Lane, Lola Lane, Ted Healy, Johnnie "Scat" Davis, Alan Mowbray, Frances Langford, Louella Parsons, Hugh Herbert, Glenda Farrell, Edgar Kennedy. Silly, paper-thin plot about Powell winning Hollywood talent contest but finding stardom elusive, buoyed by bright Johnny Mercer–Richard Whiting score, including "Hooray for Hollywood" and historic numbers by the Benny Goodman band ("Sing Sing Sing") and quartet (with Gene Krupa, Lionel Hampton, Teddy Wilson). Ronald Reagan has brief bit as radio announcer.█

Hollywood Knights, The (1980) **C-95m.** *½ D: Floyd Mutrux. Tony Danza, Michelle

Pfeiffer, Fran Drescher, Leigh French, Randy Gornel, Robert Wuhl, Stuart Pankin, P. R. Paul, Richard Schaal, Debra Feuer. A punk answer to AMERICAN GRAFFITI, which follows a band of high-school hell-raisers on Halloween Night, 1965, when their favorite drive-in hangout is about to close. Sophomoric humor to spare, only a small part of it funny. Danza's feature debut. [R]▼▶

Hollywoodland (2006) **C-127m.** ***½ D: Allen Coulter. Adrien Brody, Diane Lane, Ben Affleck, Bob Hoskins, Lois Smith, Robin Tunney, Larry Cedar, Jeffrey De-Munn, Caroline Dhavernas, Brad William Henke, Dash Mihok, Molly Parker, Kathleen Robertson, Joe Spano. Seedy, small-time private eye (Brody) whose life is a mess takes on a significant case when George Reeves' mother claims her son's death wasn't a suicide. As he pieces together the actor's story—from the time he met his longtime lover Toni Mannix, wife of a powerful MGM executive, to his sudden fame as TV's Superman, to his mysterious demise—he does some soul-searching of his own. Nuanced, well-written and -realized period piece, with Brody, Lane, Hoskins, and especially Affleck turning in flawless performances. Feature directing debut for Coulter. Screenplay by Paul Bernbaum. [R]█

Hollywood or Bust (1956) **C-95m.** **½ D: Frank Tashlin. Dean Martin, Jerry Lewis, Anita Ekberg, Pat Crowley. Starstruck Lewis teams up with gambler Martin on trek to crash the movie capital; typical comedy by the frantic team. Dean and Jerry's last film together opens with Jerry's "tribute" to movie fans around the world. VistaVision.▼▶

Hollywood Party (1934) **68m.** **½ No director credited. Jimmy Durante, Laurel and Hardy, Lupe Velez, Polly Moran, Charles Butterworth, Eddie Quillan, June Clyde, George Givot, Jack Pearl, Ted Healy and The Three Stooges, many others. Musical comedy hodgepodge built around screen star Durante throwing a gala party. Romantic subplot is for the birds, but Stan and Ollie battling fiery Velez, Durante as Schnarzan, befuddled Butterworth and opening title tune make it worthwhile. Richard Boleslawski, Allan Dwan, Roy Rowland directed various scenes without credit; some prints run 63m. and are missing appearance by Mickey Mouse and color Disney cartoon HOT CHOC-LATE SOLDIERS.▼●

Hollywood Revue of 1929, The (1929) **130m.** ** D: Charles Riesner. Conrad Nagel, Jack Benny, John Gilbert, Norma Shearer, Joan Crawford, Laurel and Hardy, Bessie Love, Lionel Barrymore, Marion Davies, Buster Keaton, Marie Dressler, Polly Moran, many others. MGM's all-star revue introducing its silent-film stars as talkie personalities, cohosted by Benny and Nagel. Definitely a curio for film buffs, rough sledding for others. Surviving 116m. print is missing some material; several scenes originally filmed in color. ◐

Hollywood Shuffle (1987) **C-82m.** **½ D: Robert Townsend. Robert Townsend, Anne-Marie Johnson, Starletta Dupois, Helen Martin, Craigus R. Johnson. Uneven but enjoyable comedy about young black actor trying to get a foothold in Hollywood, but running into problems of stereotyping at every turn. Townsend (who also directed and cowrote, with Keenen Ivory Wayans) is so appealing, and his message is so dead on-target, that it's hard to dislike this film, even though it's strictly hit-or-miss. [R] ▼●◐

Hollywood Vice Squad (1986) **C-100m.** BOMB D: Penelope Spheeris. Trish Van Devere, Ronny Cox, Frank Gorshin, Leon Isaac Kennedy, Carrie Fisher, Ben Frank, Robin Wright, Joey Travolta. Stupid comic variation on VICE SQUAD with Van Devere asking help of the cops to find her runaway daughter, who's now a hooker and heroin addict. Wright's film debut. [R] ▼●◐

Holocaust 2000 SEE: **Chosen, The** (1978)

Holy Lola (2004-French) **C-128m.** *** D: Bertrand Tavernier. Jacques Gamblin, Isabelle Carré, Bruno Putzulu, Lara Guirao, Frédéric Pierrot, Maria Pitarresi, Jean-Yves Roan. A French couple travels to Cambodia to adopt a baby; there they join a community of temporary expatriates, all desperately trying to deal with the bureaucracy, corruption, endless waiting, and turbulent emotions that are all part of the process. Heartrending and utterly credible at every turn; in fact, it's difficult to endure at times for just those reasons. Tavernier cowrote with his daughter Tiffany and son-in-law Dominique Sampiero.

Holy Man (1998) **C-114m.** ** D: Stephen Herek. Eddie Murphy, Jeff Goldblum, Kelly Preston, Robert Loggia, Jon Cryer, Eric McCormack, Sam Kitchin. Slick producer for a home shopping TV network stumbles onto a spiritual man named G who says he's on a pilgrimage. Before long, G has affected every part of the man's life and become a sensation on the air. Promising movie wanders all over the place and squanders Murphy's likable performance. It's still watchable, thanks to him, Goldblum, and Preston. Various celebrities appear in cameos, including, most curiously, designer Nino Cerutti. Panavision. [PG] ▼●◐

Holy Matrimony (1994) **C-92m.** *½ D: Leonard Nimoy. Patricia Arquette, Joseph Gordon-Levitt, Armin Mueller-Stahl, Tate Donovan, John Schuck, Lois Smith, Courtney B. Vance, Jeffrey Nordling. Arquette, on the lam for robbery, hides out in a Hutterite community and (through contrived circumstances) ends up married to 12-year-old Gordon-Levitt. Bland, juvenile, comedic variation on WITNESS, but Gordon-Levitt is charming. [PG-13] ▼●◐

Holy Rollers (2010) **C-89m.** *** D: Kevin Asch. Jesse Eisenberg, Justin Bartha, Danny A. Abeckaser, Ari Graynor, Jason Fuchs, Q-Tip, Bern Cohen, Hallie Kate Eisenberg. In the late 1990s, a young Hasidic man from Brooklyn, frustrated by his family's constant struggle to get by, succumbs to the lure of easy money when his neighbor tells him about a "job." He winds up smuggling Ecstasy pills into the U.S. from Israel, while maintaining some degree of denial (or self-delusion) about what he's gotten himself into. Modest but intriguing indie film inspired by a real-life news item. [R] ◐

Holy Smoke (1999-U.S.-Australian) **C-114m.** ** D: Jane Campion. Kate Winslet, Harvey Keitel, Julie Hamilton, Tim Robertson, Daniel Wyllie, Sophie Lee, Kerry Walker, Pam Grier. When a young Australian woman falls under the spell of an Indian guru, her family hires an expert American cult deprogrammer to bring her back to her senses. She turns the tables and finds him surprisingly susceptible to her mind games and sexual teasing. Naked performances—in every sense of the word—by the two leads and a layered script rife with quirky humor and sexual politics can't bring credibility to Keitel's character. This is supposed to be his 190th case; what were the other 189 like? [R] ▼

Holy Terror (1977) **C-96m.** ** D: Alfred Sole. Brooke Shields, Tom Signorelli, Louisa Horton, Paula Sheppard, Mildred Clinton, Linda Miller, Lillian Roth. Does 12-year-old Alice (Sheppard) kill her sister, parents, aunt, etc.? OK murder mystery is noteworthy mainly as Shields' feature debut—and she's bumped off in the first reel. Filmed in Paterson, N.J.; cameo appearance by Roth as a pathologist. Originally 108m. Aka ALICE, SWEET ALICE and COMMUNION. [R] ▼●◐

Hombre (1967) **C-111m.** *** D: Martin Ritt. Paul Newman, Fredric March, Richard Boone, Diane Cilento, Cameron Mitchell, Barbara Rush, Martin Balsam. Interesting Western (from an Elmore Leonard story) of Indian-raised Newman trying to survive in white man's world in Arizona circa 1880. Encounters with various characters on a stagecoach provide basis for film's action and drama; well acted, entertaining. Panavision. ▼●◐

Home (2008-Swiss-French-Belgian) **C-98m.** **½ D: Ursula Meier. Isabelle Huppert, Olivier Gourmet, Adélaïde Leroux, Madeleine Budd, Kacey Mottet Klein. Family of five resides happily alongside an uncompleted highway. Then one day, workmen arrive to finish paving the road, which soon opens to traffic, and the family's lives are irrevocably altered. Well-intentioned allegorical exploration of the impact of "progress" on the nuclear family is provocative but oh, so obvious. This has the feel of a short film stretched out to feature length; it's Meier's debut feature. ▶

Home Alone (1990) C-102m. **½ D: Chris Columbus. Macaulay Culkin, Joe Pesci, Daniel Stern, John Heard, Roberts Blossom, Catherine O'Hara, John Candy, Billie Bird, Angela Goethals, Devin Ratray, Hope Davis. Wildly successful comedy about an eight-year-old boy whose family inadvertently leaves him behind when they go to Paris for Christmas vacation. The plucky kid then proceeds to fend off two bumbling burglars with a variety of elaborate booby-traps. Culkin is terrific, but the film has its ups and downs; the violence, even for a cartoonish farce, is a bit extreme. Climactic scene with forbidding neighbor Blossom is certainly the film's high point. Macaulay's brother Kieran plays his cousin Fuller. Followed by two sequels and a made-for-TV movie. [PG] ▼●▶

Home Alone 2: Lost in New York (1992) C-120m. ** D: Chris Columbus. Macaulay Culkin, Joe Pesci, Daniel Stern, Catherine O'Hara, John Heard, Tim Curry, Brenda Fricker, Devin Ratray, Hillary Wolf, Eddie Bracken, Dana Ivey, Rob Schneider, Kieran Culkin, Gerry Bamman. Culkin boards the wrong plane at Christmastime, is separated from his family, and ends up in N.Y.C., where he befriends pigeon-lady Fricker and contends with nitwits Pesci and Stern, more than ever a pair of cartoon characters come to life. Essentially a reworking of its smash-hit predecessor, but it manages to be even more violent. There are also shameless plugs for the Plaza Hotel, replete with a walk-on by owner Donald Trump. Written and produced by John Hughes. [PG] ▼●▶

Home Alone 3 (1997) C-102m. **½ D: Raja Gosnell. Alex D. Linz, Olek Krupa, Rya Kihlstedt, Lenny von Dohlen, David Thornton, Haviland Morris, Kevin Kilner, Marian Seldes, Scarlett Johansson. Another little boy left home alone battles another gang of crooks, but this time they're high-tech industrial thieves after an important computer chip. Unexpectedly funny follow-up (rather than sequel), helped by an appealing little boy (Linz), smarter crooks, and a less sappily sentimental subplot. Written by John Hughes. [PG] ▼●▶

Home and the World, The (1984-Indian) C-130m. ***½ D: Satyajit Ray. Soumitra Chatterjee, Victor Banerjee, Swatilekha Chatterjee, Gopa Aich, Jennifer Kapoor. Wealthy, liberated estate owner allows his wife to break with the tradition of female seclusion—and she falls in love with his best friend, a nationalist leader. Set in early 20th-century Bengal, and based on a novel by Rabindranath Tagore; a masterful

and poignant film, made by a world-class filmmaker. ▼

Home at Seven (1952-British) 85m. *** D: Ralph Richardson. Ralph Richardson, Margaret Leighton, Jack Hawkins, Campbell Singer. Taut thriller of club treasurer who can't account for a day in his life when a murder and a robbery occurred. Aka MURDER ON MONDAY. ▼

Home at the End of the World, A (2004) C-93m. *** D: Michael Mayer. Colin Farrell, Robin Wright Penn, Dallas Roberts, Sissy Spacek, Matt Frewer, Erik Smith, Harris Allan, Andrew Chalmers. Two male friends explore their sexuality during an event-filled adolescence in late 1960s Cleveland. After years apart, they wind up living in a Greenwich Village apartment in the early 1980s with a free-spirited older woman. Michael Cunningham adapted his novel about unconventional relationships that redefine the notion of family. Impressive debut film for stage director Mayer. Farrell is excellent, playing an uncharacteristically gentle soul. Tom Hulce coproduced. Wendy Crewson appears unbilled. Super 35. [R] ▼▶

Home Before Dark (1958) 136m. *** D: Mervyn LeRoy. Jean Simmons, Dan O'Herlihy, Rhonda Fleming, Efrem Zimbalist, Jr. Shiny but poignant telling of Simmons' readjustment to life after nervous breakdown; on-location shooting in Massachusetts. ▶

Homebodies (1974) C-96m. **½ D: Larry Yust. Frances Fuller, Ian Wolfe, Ruth McDevitt, Paula Trueman, Peter Brocco, William Hansen. Bizarre horror-comedy will depend on one's taste for scenario. Elderly tenants of condemned building resort to murder to keep their home. Good cast, including Douglas Fowley as the builder. Made in Cincinnati. ▼

Homeboy (1976) SEE: Black Fist

Homeboy (1988) C-118m. **½ D: Michael Seresin. Mickey Rourke, Christopher Walken, Debra Feuer, Thomas Quinn, Kevin Conway, Antony Alda, Ruben Blades. Downbeat, rainy tale of aging, alcoholic boxer Rourke, his relationship with flashy, philosophical crook Walken, and his romance with a carousel owner. Very well made, with fine, quirky performances by the leads, but so unrelentingly grim it can scarcely be called entertainment. [R] ▼●▶

Homecoming (1948) 113m. ** D: Mervyn LeRoy. Clark Gable, Lana Turner, Anne Baxter, John Hodiak, Ray Collins, Cameron Mitchell. Gable and Turner have exciting WW2 romance in the trenches, but that can't support 113 minutes of dreary drama; one of Gable's lesser efforts. ▼▶

Homecoming, The (1973) C-111m. ***½ D: Peter Hall. Cyril Cusack, Ian Holm, Michael Jayston, Vivien Merchant, Terence Rigby, Paul Rogers. Jayston, long separated from his London family, brings wife Merchant home to meet his father and two brothers. Film version of the Harold Pinter play is among the most satisfactory of all stage-to-screen adaptations. An American Film Theater Production. [PG]▼▶

Home for the Holidays (1995) **C-103m.** ** D: Jodie Foster. Holly Hunter, Robert Downey, Jr., Anne Bancroft, Charles Durning, Dylan McDermott, Geraldine Chaplin, Cynthia Stevenson, Steve Guttenberg, Claire Danes, Austin Pendleton, David Strathairn, Amy Yasbeck, Shawn Hatosy. Dreary "comedy" about a woman at loose ends who flies home to spend Thanksgiving with her wildly dysfunctional family. Filled with unpleasant (and in some cases unfathomable) characters who are neither funny nor interesting. Why would *anybody* want to spend time with these people? [PG-13] ▼▶

Home Fries (1998) **C-93m.** *½ D: Dean Parisot. Drew Barrymore, Luke Wilson, Catherine O'Hara, Jake Busey, Shelley Duvall, Kim Robillard, Daryl "Chill" Mitchell. Black-comedy misfire has two brothers giving their stepfather a unique scare at the behest of Mom. As a result, his pregnant mistress (Barrymore) is left without a father for her child; matters grow complicated when one of the brothers shows interest. She's a Podunk fast-food waitress, which explains the title, but not why this farce is so poky—and laughless. [PG-13] ▼▶

Home From the Hill (1960) **C-150m.** *** D: Vincente Minnelli. Robert Mitchum, Eleanor Parker, George Peppard, George Hamilton, Luana Patten, Everett Sloane, Constance Ford. Strong drama, set in Southeastern Texas, centering on most prominent family in a small town. Patriarch Mitchum is estranged from wife, Parker, and takes over raising their son, Hamilton, when he comes of age. Peppard is a likable, fatherless local important to both the older man and his son. Low-key, involving, and intelligent; well directed by Minnelli, handling uncharacteristic material. Cast is very good, including Peppard and Hamilton in what may be career-best performances for both. From the best-selling novel by William Humphrey. ▼▶

Homegrown (1998) **C-103m.** **½ D: Stephen Gyllenhaal. Billy Bob Thornton, Hank Azaria, Kelly Lynch, Jon Bon Jovi, Ryan Phillippe, Judge Reinhold, Jon Tenney, Jamie Lee Curtis, John Lithgow, Ted Danson. When a big-time drug dealer is assassinated, three of his worker bees try to cover up the death so they can cash in on his latest marijuana crop. Needless to say, they find themselves in way over their heads. Alternately funny and serious, this unfocused film has a strong cast and interesting, often amusing vignettes, but never quite comes together. The director's children, Maggie and Jacob (Jake) Gyllenhaal, appear in small roles. [R] ▼▶

Home Is Where the Heart Is SEE: **Square Dance**

Home Movies (1979) **C-90m.** *½ D: Brian De Palma. Keith Gordon, Nancy Allen, Kirk Douglas, Gerrit Graham, Vincent Gardenia, Mary Davenport. Flaky farce reminiscent of De Palma's early work. Nebbish Gordon, an "extra in his own life," is given Star Therapy treatment by egomaniacal director Douglas (who has his own life filmed constantly), and sets out to woo Allen away from his nutsy older brother (Graham). Original in concept but tiresome in execution, although nobody eats a hamburger like Allen. Most of the production crew was made up of De Palma's filmmaking students from Sarah Lawrence College. Aka THE MAESTRO. [PG] ▼▶

Home of Our Own, A (1993) **C-104m.** **½ D: Tony Bill. Kathy Bates, Edward Furlong, Soon-Teck Oh, Tony Campisi, Clarissa Lassig, Sarah Schaub, Miles Feulner, Amy Sakasitz, T. J. Lowther. Bates is a determined single mother in 1962 L.A. who uproots her six children and settles in a desolate Idaho town; she has almost no money but a lot of energy and a fierce fighting spirit. Young Furlong is the reluctant "man of the family." Avoids becoming overly sentimental, but film is still basically Disney fare with an edge. Campisi—Bates' persistent boyfriend—is the actress' real-life husband. Director Bill has an unbilled cameo as a doctor. [PG] ▼▶

Home of the Brave (1949) **85m.** *** D: Mark Robson. James Edwards, Douglas Dick, Steve Brodie, Jeff Corey, Lloyd Bridges, Frank Lovejoy. More daring when made than now, but still hard-hitting account of black soldier Edwards suffering more abuse from fellow G.I.'s than the enemy while on a mission during WW2. From an Arthur Laurents play. ▼●

Home of the Brave (1986) **C-90m.** *** D: Laurie Anderson. Laurie Anderson, Adrian Belew, Richard Landry, Joy Askew, Dolette McDonald, Janice Pendarvis, William S. Burroughs. Concert film pretty well duplicates what fans of performance artist Anderson have been seeing for years; mix of music and provocative visuals doesn't quite add up to another STOP MAKING SENSE, but it's a generally rewarding introduction for the uninitiated. Mostly accessible, but the middle section will test your openness to unconventional music. ▼

Home of the Brave (2006) **C-105m.** **½ D: Irwin Winkler. Samuel L. Jackson, Jessica Biel, Brian Presley, Curtis "50 Cent" Jackson, Christina Ricci, Chad Michael Murray, Victoria Rowell, Joyce M. Cameron, Jeffrey Nordling. Story of returning Iraq war vets visits the same territory as such films as THE BEST YEARS OF OUR LIVES and COMING HOME but fails to pack their emotional punch. Focusing primarily on three vets as they readjust to life in Seattle, film has an episodic and sudsy feel, particularly in a scene where a drunken Samuel Jackson disrupts his family's Thanksgiving dinner. Biel is touching as a wounded soldier struggling to establish new relationships. HD Widescreen. [R]▶

Home on the Range (2004) C-76m. *** D: Will Finn, John Sanford. Voices of Roseanne Barr, Randy Quaid, Judi Dench, Jennifer Tilly, Cuba Gooding, Jr., Steve Buscemi, Estelle Harris, Charles Dennis, Charles Haid, Carole Cook, Joe Flaherty, G.W. Bailey, Ja'net DuBois. Three cows set out to capture an elusive rustler and use the reward money to save their beloved farm from foreclosure. A refreshingly "cartoony" Disney animated feature set in the Old West. Filled with colorful characters, funny gags, and lively songs by Alan Menken and Glenn Slater. Good fun for kids and grown-ups alike. Digital Widescreen. [PG]▼▶

Homer and Eddie (1990) C-99m. BOMB D: Andrei Konchalovsky. James Belushi, Whoopi Goldberg, Karen Black, Ernestine McClendon, Nancy Parsons, Anne Ramsey, Beah Richards. He's been mentally impaired since getting smacked in childhood by a flying baseball; she's dying of brain cancer; theirs is an odyssey-by-auto punctuated by service-station knock-offs and a musical interlude where they dance with paper bags on their heads. Not to be confused with Homer & Jethro or Flo & Eddie, though you may be praying for any and all to show up. [R] ▼▶

Home Room (2003) C-132m. *** D: Paul F. Ryan. Busy Philipps, Erika Christensen, Victor Garber, Holland Taylor, Ken Jenkins, Raphael Sbarge, James Pickens, Jr., Richard Gilliland, Rick Lenz. Thoughtful drama about the aftermath of a high school shooting rampage, focusing on three characters: an antisocial eyewitness (Philipps), who apparently had some relationship with the shooter; a straight-arrow classmate (Christensen), who survived with physical injuries and major emotional scars; and a compassionate cop (Garber), who's trying to make sense of the incident. Writer-director-editor Ryan wisely concentrates on his specific characters and doesn't try to drive home too many universal truths. [R] ▼▶

Hometown USA (1979) C-93m. BOMB D: Max Baer. Gary Springer, David Wilson, Brian Kerwin, Pat Delaney, Julie Parsons, Sally Kirkland. Yet another nostalgic look at teenagers in the late 1950s is just a sloppy, sleazy, unfunny AMERICAN GRAFFITI rip-off.▼▶

Homeward Bound: The Incredible Journey (1993) C-84m. *** D: DuWayne Dun-

ham. Robert Hays, Kim Greist, Jean Smart, Benj Thall, Veronica Lauren, Kevin Chevalia; voices of Michael J. Fox, Sally Field, Don Ameche. Three beloved household pets, separated from their youthful masters, embark on an almost impossible trek over mountainous terrain to rejoin them. Remake of 1963's THE INCREDIBLE JOURNEY enables us to hear the animals talking, and in true '90s fashion, their dialogue is overstuffed with lowbrow wisecracks. Still, the story is compelling, and the vocal performances excellent, especially Ameche, as the older, more faithful canine. Sure-fire Disney family entertainment. Followed by a sequel. [G]▼▶

Homeward Bound II: Lost in San Francisco (1996) C-88m. **½ D: David R. Ellis. Robert Hays, Kim Greist, Veronica Lauren, Kevin Chevalia, Benj Thall, Michael Rispoli, Max Perlich; voices of Michael J. Fox, Sally Field, Ralph Waite, Sinbad, Jon Polito. Congenial sequel has the three household pets forced to fend for themselves in the City by the Bay, where Chance, Sassy, and Shadow find themselves dodging both canine and human adversaries on the city streets. Enough snappy dialogue to amuse parents as well as their kids. [G]▼▶

Homework (1982) C-90m. *½ D: James Beshears. Joan Collins, Michael Morgan, Shell Kepler, Lanny Horn, Lee Purcell, Carrie Snodgress, Wings Hauser, Mel Welles, Beverly Todd, Betty Thomas. Atrocious, wildly inconsistent "comedy" about a teenage boy's sexual awakening—and embarrassment. Filmed mostly in 1979, it underwent major surgery, including attempt to simulate nude scenes with Joan Collins (using an alleged double) so it could be promoted as a young boy–older woman sex comedy à la PRIVATE LESSONS and MY TUTOR. [R] ▼▶

Homicidal (1961) 87m. **½ D: William Castle. Jean Arless, Joan Marshall, Patricia Breslin, Glenn Corbett, Eugenie Leontovitch, Alan Bunce, Richard Rust. One of Castle's less gimmicky shockers, about pretty but rather strange young nurse who presides over creepy household consisting of mute stroke victim and decidedly meek young man. Shamelessly steals a great deal from PSYCHO, and much of the dialogue is ludicrous, but still manages to deliver some shudders.▶

Homicide (1991) C-102m. **½ D: David Mamet. Joe Mantegna, William H. Macy, Natalija Nogulich, Ving Rhames, Rebecca Pidgeon, Vincent Guastaferro, Lionel Mark Smith, Jack Wallace, J. J. Johnston. Urban homicide detective is pulled off a major case to take care of a seemingly routine murder of an elderly shopkeeper, but soon finds himself embroiled in a strange, conspiracy-like situation that causes him to question his own motives and his identity as a Jew. Provocative material is underdeveloped by writer-director Mamet, and laid on with too heavy a hand . . . but the "Mametspeak" and lead performance are still quite commanding. [R] ▼●◗

Hondo (1953) **C-84m.** *** D: John Farrow. John Wayne, Geraldine Page, Ward Bond, Michael Pate, James Arness, Rodolfo Acosta, Leo Gordon, Lee Aaker, Lassie. Rousing, well-done Western with Wayne the tough, wily cavalry scout who comes upon Page and her young son living in the wilderness, unalarmed about a pending Apache uprising. Wayne is in top form here. Good script by James Edward Grant, from a story by Louis L'Amour. Later a short-lived TV series. 3-D. ▼◗

Honey (2003) **C-98m.** **½ D: Bille Woodruff. Jessica Alba, Mekhi Phifer, Lil' Romeo, Joy Bryant, David Moscow, Lonette McKee, Zachary Isaiah Williams, Laurie Ann Gibson, Anthony Sherwood, Missy Elliott, Shawn Desman, Ginuwine. Sweet story of a good-hearted girl who dreams of being a dancer and teaches inner-city kids at a community center. A music video director spots her and opens a door to her dream job—but also wants to own her. Alba is sincere and charismatic, which gives a big boost to an all-too-predictable story. [PG-13] ▼◗

Honeydripper (2007) **C-122m.** *** D: John Sayles. Danny Glover, Lisa Gay Hamilton, Yaya DaCosta, Charles S. Dutton, Vondie Curtis Hall, Gary Clark, Jr., Dr. Mable John, Stacy Keach, Mary Steenburgen, Sean Patrick Thomas, Keb' Mo', Kel Mitchell. Leisurely, entertaining slice of Southern life, circa 1950. Hard-luck Glover runs a threadbare bar and restaurant in a small Alabama town, and seizes his last chance to make good by hiring a popular bluesman to play his establishment. Less concerned with story than with character and atmosphere, this picaresque film is brimming with juicy performances and good music. Writer-director Sayles has a cameo as a liquor delivery man. [PG-13]◗

Honey, I Blew Up the Kid (1992) **C-89m.** *** D: Randal Kleiser. Rick Moranis, Marcia Strassman, Robert Oliveri, Daniel and Joshua Shalikar, Lloyd Bridges, John Shea, Keri Russell, Ron Canada, Gregory Sierra, Julia Sweeney, Ken Tobey. Bull's-eye sequel to the surprise Disney hit HONEY, I SHRUNK THE KIDS. This time, absentminded scientist Moranis accidentally enlarges his two-year-old son, who grows to gargantuan proportions and stalks the streets of Las Vegas! Good, clean fun with terrific special effects and a lot of genuine laughs; wears a bit thin after a while, but its upbeat spirit makes up for that. Video sequel: HONEY, WE SHRUNK OURSELVES. [PG] ▼●◗

Honey, I Shrunk the Kids (1989) **C-93m.** *** D: Joe Johnston. Rick Moranis, Matt Frewer, Marcia Strassman, Kristine Sutherland, Thomas Brown, Jared Rushton, Amy O'Neill, Robert Oliveri. Cute comedy-fantasy about a quartet of kids who accidentally trigger Moranis' experimental ray gun and find themselves reduced to microscopic size—and stranded across the yard from their home. Enjoyable family fare, with engaging special effects (by such whizzes as Phil Tippett and David Allen). Followed by HONEY, I BLEW UP THE KID and later a TV series. [PG] ▼●◗

Honeymoon Academy (1990) **C-94m.** *½ D: Gene Quintano. Kim Cattrall, Robert Hays, Leigh Taylor-Young, Charles Rocket, Lance Kinney, Christopher Lee. Time waster about a secret agent (Cattrall) who tries to take time off for a honeymoon in Madrid, but finds herself involved in espionage business all the same. Attempt at lighthearted chase comedy/romance doesn't come off . . . and incidentally, the film's title has nothing to do with the story. [PG-13] ▼●

Honeymooners, The (2005) **C-90m.** *½ D: John Schultz. Cedric the Entertainer, Mike Epps, Gabrielle Union, Regina Hall, Eric Stoltz, Jon Polito, John Leguizamo. Recasting the classic Jackie Gleason–Art Carney TV hit as an urban comedy might have looked good on paper, but what lands on-screen is a pale version of the original. Ralph Kramden is still a bus driver with big get-rich-quick schemes, but things never go as he plans. The jokes are lame and the actors try awfully hard to wring what life they can out of them. At least there's a cute dog. PG version also available. [PG-13] ▼◗

Honeymoon in Vegas (1992) **C-95m.** *** D: Andrew Bergman. James Caan, Nicolas Cage, Sarah Jessica Parker, Pat Morita, Johnny Williams, John Capodice, Robert Costanzo, Anne Bancroft, Peter Boyle, Burton Gilliam, Seymour Cassel, Jerry Tarkanian, Tony Shalhoub, Natasha Lyonne, Ben Stein. Cage and Parker finally decide to tie the knot—in Las Vegas—but he loses her in a rigged poker game to mobster Caan! Engaging farce from writer-director Bergman has enough twists, turns, and cockeyed humor to keep things lively from start to finish . . . including a corps of "flying Elvises." Presley music (performed by everyone from Billy Joel to Bono) fills the soundtrack. [PG-13] ▼●◗

Honeymoon Killers, The (1970) **108m.** *** D: Leonard Kastle. Shirley Stoler, Tony LoBianco, Mary Jane Higby, Doris Roberts. Taut, based-on-fact account of the Lonely Hearts Killers: Martha Beck (Stoler), a rotund nurse, and Ray Fernandez (LoBianco), a gigolo. Together, they scheme to swindle and murder wealthy, lonely women. Low-budget item has deservedly developed a cult reputation over the years. Martin Scorsese was the original director; he was replaced by Donald Volkman, who in turn was replaced by Kastle (who also scripted). Same story retold in Arturo Ripstein's DEEP CRIMSON and LONELY HEARTS (2006). [R]▼●❙

Honeymoon Machine, The (1961) C-87m. **½ D: Richard Thorpe. Steve McQueen, Jim Hutton, Paula Prentiss, Brigid Bazlen, Dean Jagger, Jack Weston. Pleasant comedy with a spirited cast about two sailors who find a way to beat the roulette table in Venice. Easy to take, easy to forget. CinemaScope.▼❙

Honey Pot, The (1967) C-131m. **½ D: Joseph L. Mankiewicz. Rex Harrison, Susan Hayward, Cliff Robertson, Capucine, Edie Adams, Maggie Smith, Adolfo Celi. Director/writer Mankiewicz updates *Volpone* in sly blend of high comedy and whodunit. Harrison pretends to be dying, sends for former mistresses to see their reactions; hoax evolves into elaborate murder scheme. Never as amusing as one would like it to be. Aka IT COMES UP MURDER.▼❙

Honeysuckle Rose (1980) C-119m. *** D: Jerry Schatzberg. Willie Nelson, Dyan Cannon, Amy Irving, Slim Pickens, Joey Floyd, Charles Levin, Priscilla Pointer, Mickey Rooney, Jr., Diana Scarwid. Appealing, low-key film about a country music star and his lifestyle at home in Texas and on the road, which begins to come apart when he starts fooling around with the young daughter of his longtime musical sidekick. Lots of good music by Willie, fiddler Johnny Gimble, and guest star Emmylou Harris. Officially based on INTERMEZZO, believe it or not! Retitled ON THE ROAD AGAIN. Panavision. [PG] ▼●❙

Hong Kong (1951) C-92m. ** D: Lewis R. Foster. Ronald Reagan, Rhonda Fleming, Nigel Bruce, Marvin Miller, Lee Marvin. Mediocre account of Reagan trying to heist a valuable antique from orphaned boy but going straight before finale. Strictly backlot Hong Kong.

Honkers, The (1972) C-102m. **½ D: Steve Ihnat. James Coburn, Lois Nettleton, Slim Pickens, Anne Archer, Richard Anderson, Joan Huntington, Jim Davis. Theme about aging rodeo performer was handled better in J. W. COOP and JUNIOR BONNER (all made same year!); actor Ihnat died shortly after directing this film. [PG]

Honky (1971) C-89m. **½ D: William A. Graham. Brenda Sykes, John Nielson, William Marshall, Maia Danziger, Marion Ross, Lincoln Kilpatrick. Not-bad drama of budding romance between black Sykes and white Nielson, and the problems they encounter. Score by Quincy Jones. Panavision. [R]▼

Honky Tonk (1941) 105m. **½ D: Jack Conway. Clark Gable, Lana Turner, Frank Morgan, Claire Trevor, Marjorie Main, Albert Dekker, Chill Wills, Veda Ann Borg. Good-gal Lana loves gambler Gable in romantic Western that's fun for a spell, then drags into talky marathon. Morgan and Wills offer fine character performances. Remade for TV in 1974. Also shown in computer-colored version.▼●❙

Honky Tonk Freeway (1981) C-107m. ** D: John Schlesinger. William Devane, Beverly D'Angelo, Beau Bridges, Jessica Tandy, Hume Cronyn, Geraldine Page, George Dzundza, Teri Garr, Joe Grifasi, Howard Hesseman, Paul Jabara, Frances Lee McCain, John Astin, David Rasche, Daniel Stern. An absurdist view of contemporary America, in fragmented vignettes of various oddballs whose lives converge in Ticlaw, Florida, a tiny town determined to attract tourists despite the lack of an exit ramp from the new freeway. As a statement on life, it's a failure; as a silly comedy, it sometimes succeeds. Reminiscent (in its narrative style) of NASHVILLE. [PG]▼❙

Honkytonk Man (1982) C-122m. *½ D: Clint Eastwood. Clint Eastwood, Kyle Eastwood, John McIntire, Alexa Kenin, Verna Bloom, Matt Clark, Barry Corbin. The kind of film that gives "change-of-pace" a bad name. Clint is Depression-era country singer hoping to make it to the Grand Old Opry before he dies of tuberculosis; son Kyle plays his nephew, who tags along. Artificial and overlong; many music greats appear in bits, including Marty Robbins, who provides film's sole touching moment and, ironically, died himself only days before the picture opened. [PG]▼●❙

Honor Among Thieves SEE: **Farewell, Friend**

Honor Guard, The SEE: **Wolf Lake**

Hoodlum (1997) C-130m. **½ D: Bill Duke. Laurence Fishburne, Tim Roth, Vanessa L. Williams, Andy Garcia, Cicely Tyson, Chi McBride, Clarence Williams III, Richard Bradford, William Atherton, Loretta Devine, Queen Latifah. GODFATHER wannabe about 1930s Harlem racketeer Ellsworth "Bumpy" Johnson, who locks horns with Dutch Schultz (Roth) and Lucky Luciano (Garcia), and tries to carve his own niche in the numbers game. Well-crafted, multi-character gangster saga has its moments, but takes a long time to tell its story and never builds the emotional punch it seeks. One welcome novelty: a '30s-style montage illustrating Bumpy's rise to power. [R]▼●❙

Hoodlum Priest, The (1961) 101m. *** D: Irvin Kershner. Don Murray, Larry Gates, Keir Dullea, Logan Ramsey, Cindi Wood. Based on real-life clergyman who devoted himself to trying to help would-be criminals, focusing on Murray's efforts to rehabilitate delinquent Dullea (in film debut); splendidly acted. Murray coproduced and cowrote (latter under pseudonym Don Deer).▼❙

Hoodlum Saint, The (1946) **91m.** ** D: Norman Taurog. William Powell, Esther Williams, Angela Lansbury, James Gleason, Lewis Stone, "Rags" Ragland, Frank McHugh, Slim Summerville. Confusing mishmash with Powell a cynical, money-obsessed WW1 vet who, between schemes, falls for pretty Williams. This one squeaks by solely on Powell's charm.

Hoods (1999) **C-92m.** **½ D: Mark Malone. Joe Mantegna, Kevin Pollak, Joe Pantoliano, Vincent Berry, Jennifer Tilly, Robert Costanzo, Richard Foronjy, John Capodice, Joseph Maher. Wry look at N.Y.C. mobsters and a hapless functionary who's stuck carrying out orders for his mentally incompetent father. Some genuinely funny scenes and ingratiating performances by an A-1 ensemble make this worth a look, even though the payoff is weak. Seymour Cassel and Charles Martin Smith appear unbilled. Made for theaters, debuted on cable. [R]▼❙

Hoodwinked (2005) **C-80m.** **½ D: Cory Edwards, Todd Edwards, Tony Leech. Voices of Anne Hathaway, Patrick Warburton, Glenn Close, Jim Belushi, David Ogden Stiers, Chazz Palminteri, Anthony Anderson, Andy Dick, Xzibit. In a storybook forest a froggy police detective tries to get the real story behind a well-known fairy-tale plot, told RASHOMON-style by its leading characters: Red Riding Hood, The Wolf, Granny, and the Woodsman. Each character breaks stereotypes with updated backstories and modern pop-culture references. Low-budget computer-animated feature makes up for artistic shortcomings with witty script and clever vocal performances. Several songs by cowriter-director Todd Edwards are funny and unobtrusive. Followed by a sequel. [PG]❙

Hoodwinked Too! Hood vs. Evil (2011) **C-86m.** ** D: Mike Disa. Voices of Hayden Panettiere, Glenn Close, Patrick Warburton, Joan Cusack, David Ogden Stiers, Bill Hader, Amy Poehler, Cory Edwards, Martin Short, Brad Garrett, Andy Dick, David Alan Grier, Cheech Marin, Tommy Chong, Phil LaMarr, Wayne Newton, Heidi Klum. Frenetic sequel to fresher and funnier HOODWINKED reunites characters from previous computer-animated comedy (including the martial arts–trained Little Red Riding Hood, her spunky Granny, and the misguidedly cocksure Wolf) to foil villains bent on exploiting Granny's secret recipe for magically enhanced truffles. Best suited for small children with short attention spans, though many of the undeniably funny pop-culture references likely will sail over their heads. 3-D. [PG]❙

Hook, The (1963) **98m.** *** D: George Seaton. Kirk Douglas, Robert Walker, Jr., Nick Adams, Nehemiah Persoff. Film ex-

amines men at war (Korean) and the taking of one life, face-to-face, as opposed to killing many in battle. Earnest, thought-provoking. Music by harmonica virtuoso Larry Adler. Panavision.

Hook (1991) **C-144m.** ** D: Steven Spielberg. Dustin Hoffman, Robin Williams, Julia Roberts, Bob Hoskins, Maggie Smith, Caroline Goodall, Charlie Korsmo, Amber Scott, Phil Collins, Arthur Malet, Dante Basco, Gwyneth Paltrow. Unfortunate cheapening of the beloved James Barrie tale of Peter Pan, with Williams as a heartless corporate takeover honcho who must rediscover his true identity—as Pan—in order to save his children, who've been kidnapped by Captain Hook. Great casting in key roles is dissipated by a script that offers no joy, and very little magic—with a troupe of TV-generation Lost Boys who'd be more at home in a McDonald's commercial. (Musician David Crosby and an unrecognizable Glenn Close have bit parts as pirates.) If this is Peter Pan for the '90s, give us the '50s instead. Panavision. [PG]▼●❙

Hooked Generation (1969) **C-92m.** BOMB D: William Grefe. Jeremy Slate, Willie Pastrano, Steve Alaimo, John Davis Chandler, Socrates Ballis. Narcotics peddlers slaughter Cuban contacts, kidnap innocent victims; poor excuse for a film. [R]▼

Hook, Line & Sinker (1969) **C-91m.** BOMB D: George Marshall. Jerry Lewis, Peter Lawford, Anne Francis, Pedro Gonzalez-Gonzalez, Jimmy Miller, Kathleen Freeman. Potentially funny premise about supposedly dying man who runs up $100,000 in credit card debts, only to discover he's healthy, is totally botched; even Lewis fans will be bored. [G]

Hooker Cult Murders, The SEE: **Pyx, The**

Hoop Dreams (1994) **C-169m.** ***½ D: Steve James. Exceptional documentary follows two Chicago inner-city kids (Arthur Agee and William Gates), who have dreams of basketball stardom, over four years' time. This intimate and engrossing film plays like drama, not documentary, except that it takes unexpected twists and turns no writer could invent. A searing commentary on our social system, the indomitable strength of the family unit, and the unpredictability of life. Overlong, perhaps, but fascinating most of the way. Produced by Steve James, Frederick Marx, and Peter Gilbert. [PG-13]▼●❙

Hooper (1978) **C-100m.** *** D: Hal Needham. Burt Reynolds, Jan-Michael Vincent, Sally Field, Brian Keith, John Marley, James Best, Adam West, Robert Klein. Lighthearted look at aging ace Hollywood stunt man Reynolds, his freewheeling lifestyle, and the young tyro who gets him to try the biggest stunt of all. [PG] ▼●❙

Hoosiers (1986) **C-114m.** *** D: David Anspaugh. Gene Hackman, Barbara Hershey,

Dennis Hopper, Sheb Wooley, Fern Parsons, Brad Boyle, Steve Hollar, Brad Long, David Neidorf. Hackman gets a last-chance job coaching a small-town Indiana high school basketball team in the 1950s, and faces the dual challenge of bringing the team to the state championship—and redeeming himself. Thoroughly ingratiating (and just as thoroughly calculated), this well-made slice of Americana is hard to resist. Hackman is terrific as usual; Hopper is fine in a showy role as an alcoholic basketball nut. Written by Angelo Pizzo. [PG]▼●▶

Hoot (2006) **C-93m.** **½ D: Wil Shriner. Logan Lerman, Brie Larson, Cody Linley, Luke Wilson, Tim Blake Nelson, Jessica Cauffiel, Jimmy Buffett, Neil Flynn, Eric Phillips, Clark Gregg, Robert Wagner, Kin Shriner. Well-meaning but strictly formulaic family comedy-drama in which Lerman, the new kid in middle school, copes with everything from a class bully to the vandalizing of a construction site that is home to endangered owls. Preteens may overlook plot holes and be amused by the innocuous lowbrow humor and the worthy pro-ecology message. Shriner adapted the novel by Carl Hiaasen, who coproduced, as did Buffett (who composed the score and plays a marine science teacher). [PG]▶

Hop (2011) **C-95m.** **½ D: Tim Hill. James Marsden, Gary Cole, Kaley Cuoco, Elizabeth Perkins, Chelsea Handler, David Hasselhoff, Tiffany Espensen; voices of Russell Brand, Hugh Laurie, Hank Azaria. Live action/animation hybrid is no WHO FRAMED ROGER RABBIT but has some charms of its own. The Easter Bunny's teenage son E.B., heir (or hare) to the family business, heads instead to Hollywood to pursue his dream of becoming a drummer in a rock band. Great voice work by Brand as E.B., and a goofy, likable performance from Marsden as the 20-something slacker he hooks up with. Azaria is also hilarious as the power-hungry chick Carlos and almost steals the show. Although kids are the primary audience, there are enough hip references and funny setups to make this bearable for parents. [PG]▶

Hope and Glory (1987-British) **C-113m.** ***½ D: John Boorman. Sarah Miles, David Hayman, Derrick O'Connor, Susan Wooldridge, Sammi Davis, Ian Bannen, Sebastian Rice-Edwards, Jean-Marc Barr, Annie Leon. A loving look back at British family life during the first years of WW2, as seen through the eyes of a young boy to whom the whole thing is a great adventure. Boorman's autobiographical tale (he scripted and produced, as well) is funny, moving and richly detailed; no one has captured the experience of living through the London air raids and bombings so well. Charley Boorman (the director's son, who starred in THE EMERALD FOREST) appears briefly as a German pilot who's been shot down. [PG-13]▼●▶

Hope Floats (1998) **C-114m.** *** D: Forest Whitaker. Sandra Bullock, Harry Connick, Jr., Gena Rowlands, Mae Whitman, Michael Paré, Cameron Finley, Kathy Najimy, Bill Cobbs. Learning her husband has been unfaithful, Bullock moves back to her Texas hometown, taking along her lonely daughter, Whitman. Her mother immediately tries to set her up with Connick, but Bullock is having a hard time just learning about herself. Well acted, particularly by Whitman, with inventive direction, the movie is entertaining throughout, but as shapeless as soup. Excellent song score. Rosanna Arquette appears unbilled. [PG-13]▼●▶

Hope Springs (2003-U.S.-British) **C-92m.** ** D: Mark Herman. Colin Firth, Heather Graham, Minnie Driver, Mary Steenburgen, Oliver Platt, Frank Collison. Having just been dumped by his fiancée (Driver), British artist Firth heads to the U.S. and falls for Graham. Then, wouldn't you know it, Minnie shows up. Spirited performances from everyone, but not enough laughs for a romantic comedy. Based on the novel *New Cardiff* by Charles (*The Graduate*) Webb. Super 35. [PG-13]▼▶

Hoppity Goes to Town (1941) **C-77m.** **½ D: Dave Fleischer. Pleasant animated feature about residents of bug-ville and their various problems—living in a human world, and threatened by villainous C. Bagley Beetle. Good-looking but uncompelling story-wise, with unmemorable Frank Loesser–Hoagy Carmichael score. Originally titled MR. BUG GOES TO TOWN. Aka BUGVILLE. ▼●▶

Hopscotch (1980) **C-104m.** *** D: Ronald Neame. Walter Matthau, Glenda Jackson, Sam Waterston, Ned Beatty, Herbert Lom. Entertaining contrivance about a maverick CIA operative who's fed up with his idiotic boss (Beatty) and decides to teach him a lesson by publishing his volatile memoirs. Barely believable, but fun to watch, thanks largely to Matthau. From the novel by Brian Garfield, who coproduced and coscripted the film. Panavision. [R]▼●▶

Horizons West (1952) **C-81m.** **½ D: Budd Boetticher. Robert Ryan, Julia (Julie) Adams, Rock Hudson, Raymond Burr, James Arness, John McIntire, Dennis Weaver. Standard Western of brothers Ryan and Hudson on opposite sides of the law; the latter attempts to block the former's efforts to ruthlessly acquire power in post–Civil War Texas.▼

Horizontal Lieutenant, The (1962) **C-90m.** ** D: Richard Thorpe. Jim Hutton, Paula Prentiss, Miyoshi Umeki, Jim Backus, Jack Carter, Marty Ingels, Charles McGraw. Artificial service comedy about inept army intelligence officer Hutton and his misadventures in the Pacific during WW2. CinemaScope.▼▶

Horn Blows at Midnight, The (1945)

78m. *** D: Raoul Walsh. Jack Benny, Alexis Smith, Dolores Moran, Allyn Joslyn, Reginald Gardiner, Guy Kibbee, John Alexander, Margaret Dumont, Franklin Pangborn, Bobby (Robert) Blake. Enjoyable, original comedy-fantasy about an angel (Benny) sent to destroy earth with a blast from Gabriel's horn. Broad, funny, no classic, but not the turkey Benny so often joked about either. Franklin Pangborn is especially funny as a flustered hotel detective. ▼●

Hornets' Nest (1970) **C-110m.** **½ D: Phil Karlson. Rock Hudson, Sylva Koscina, Sergio Fantoni, Jacques Sernas, Giacomo Rossi-Stuart, Tom Felleghi. Hudson and group of Italian children plot to blow up Nazi-controlled dam. Reasonably well done and exciting. [M] ▼

Horrible Dr. Hichcock, The (1962-Italian) **C-76m.** **½ D: Robert Hampton (Riccardo Freda). Robert Flemyng, Barbara Steele, Teresa Fitzgerald, Maria Teresa Vianello. Unaware her doctor husband is a (gulp!) necrophiliac, woman accompanies him to the mansion where his first wife apparently died 12 years earlier during sexual games. Eerie, handsome horror, with undertones of Poe. British version, TERROR OF DR. HICHCOCK, runs 88m. and is also available on tape. Followed by THE GHOST (1963). Panoramic. ▼

Horror Castle (1963-Italian) **C-83m.** *½ D: Anthony Dawson (Antonio Margheriti). Christopher Lee, Rossana Podesta, George Riviere, Jim Nolan, Anny Belli Uberti. Chiller about a demented WW2 victim running rampant in a Rhine castle, using assorted torture chamber devices on unsuspecting people. Effect is numbing. Aka THE VIRGIN OF NUREMBERG and TERROR CASTLE. British title: THE CASTLE OF TERROR. ▼)

Horror Chamber of Dr. Faustus, The SEE: **Eyes Without a Face**

Horror Creatures of the Prehistoric Planet SEE: **Vampire Men of the Lost Planet**

Horror Express (1972-Spanish-British) **C-88m.** *** D: Eugenio Martin. Christopher Lee, Peter Cushing, Telly Savalas, Silvia Tortosa, Jorge Rigaud. Crackerjack horror movie, ingeniously staged and well acted by the genre's superstars. Turn-of-the-century chiller has a long-frozen monster coming to life while being transported from Asia to the West. Lee and Cushing are rival anthropologists aboard the train and Savalas is a power-crazed Cossack officer. Aka PANIC ON THE TRANS-SIBERIAN EXPRESS. [R] ▼)

Horror House (1969-British) **C-79m.** *½ D: Michael Armstrong. Frankie Avalon, Jill Haworth, Dennis Price, George Sewell, Gina Warwick, Richard O'Sullivan. Below-standard thriller using dog-eared "let's-spend-a-night-in-a-haunted-house" script.

Frankie should have stayed on the beach with Annette. Original British title: THE HAUNTED HOUSE OF HORROR. [M/PG]

Horror of Dracula (1958-British) **C-82m.** *** D: Terence Fisher. Peter Cushing, Christopher Lee, Melissa Stribling, Michael Gough, Carol Marsh, John Van Eyssen, Valerie Gaunt, Miles Malleson. Probably Hammer Films' best shocker, a handsomely mounted retelling of the Stoker tale, with fantasy elements deemphasized. Lee is smooth as the Count, and Cushing perfect as tireless Professor Van Helsing. Script by Jimmy Sangster; full-blooded score by James Bernard. Released in Britain as DRACULA; followed by six sequels, the first of which was THE BRIDES OF DRACULA. ▼●)

Horror of Frankenstein, The (1970-British) **C-95m.** ** D: Jimmy Sangster. Ralph Bates, Kate O'Mara, Graham Jones, Veronica Carlson, Bernard Archard, Dennis Price, Joan Rice. New kind of Dr. Frankenstein: he arranges murder of father, cheats on his lover, kills his best friend, while creating new, laughable monster. Semi-spoof remake of CURSE OF FRANKENSTEIN. For aficionados only. Followed by FRANKENSTEIN AND THE MONSTER FROM HELL. [R] ▼●)

Horror of the Blood Monsters SEE: **Vampire Men of the Lost Planet**

Horror on Snape Island SEE: **Tower of Evil**

Horror Planet (1981-British) **C-86m.** BOMB D: Norman J. Warren. Robin Clark, Jennifer Ashley, Stephanie Beacham, Steven Grives, Barry Houghton, Victoria Tennant, Judy Geeson. Obnoxious, gory garbage about male and female space travelers and their discovery of a crawling terror. Interesting cast wasted in this awful ALIEN clone. Cut for U.S. release. Original title: INSEMINOID. J-D-C Scope. [R] ▼●)

Horror Show, The (1989) **C-95m.** BOMB D: James Isaac. Lance Henriksen, Brion James, Rita Taggart, Thom Bray, Matt Clark, Dedee Pfeiffer, Lewis Arquette, Lawrence Tierney, Alvy Moore. Henriksen gives typically strong performance as cop pursued by murderous—and already executed—maniac James, who's intent on wiping out the cop's family by turning nightmares into reality. Confused, silly and boring. Known outside U.S. as HOUSE III. [R] ▼

Horse Feathers (1932) **68m.** ***½ D: Norman Z. McLeod. Groucho, Harpo, Chico, and Zeppo Marx, Thelma Todd, David Landau, Robert Greig, Nat Pendleton. Groucho is head of Huxley College, building up football team to play rival Darwin U. in crazy Marx nonsense. The password is "swordfish." Originally released at 70m. ▼●)

Horse in the Gray Flannel Suit, The (1968) **C-113m.** *** D: Norman Tokar. Dean Jones, Diane Baker, Lloyd Bochner, Fred Clark,

Ellen Janov, Kurt Russell. Cheerful Disney comedy about advertising man (Jones) who finds a way to link his daughter's devotion to horses with an ad campaign. [G]▼❚

Horseman on the Roof, The (1995-French) C-122m. **½ D: Jean-Paul Rappenau. Juliette Binoche, Olivier Martinez, Pierre Arditi, François Cluzet, Jean Yanne, Gérard Depardieu. Gorgeous but rather leisurely spectacle, set in 1832, of Italian cavalry officer (Martinez), part of an underground network spread throughout southern France, who is trying to force Austrian overlords out of Italy. On top of everything else, a cholera epidemic is ravaging the French countryside. Binoche is noblewoman who becomes the horseman's traveling companion. Exquisite Provence locations help boost this adventure saga, based on Jean Giono's 1951 novel—a literary classic in France. Depardieu has a humorous cameo as an unorthodox police superintendent. Technovision. [R]▼❚

Horsemen, The (1971) C-109m. **½ D: John Frankenheimer. Omar Sharif, Leigh Taylor-Young, Jack Palance, David De Keyser, Peter Jeffrey. Sharif enters grueling buzkashi tournament to please his demanding father (Palance) and prove his machismo. Old-fashioned action-adventure mixes uncomfortably with soul-searching in Dalton Trumbo's script. Filmed in Afghanistan and Spain. Beautiful photography by Claude Renoir in Panavision. [PG]▼❚

Horsemen (2009-U.S.-Canadian) C-91m. BOMB D: Jonas Åkerlund. Dennis Quaid, Ziyi Zhang, Lou Taylor Pucci, Clifton Collins, Jr., Patrick Fugit, Paul Dooley, Barry Shabaka Henley, Eric Balfour, Chelcie Ross, Peter Stormare, Liam James. Overworked, recently widowed detective Quaid investigates a series of gruesome murders that are linked to the Book of Revelations and the Four Horsemen of the Apocalypse. Preposterous, sickening mystery-thriller is only for those who are entertained by graphic images of torture. [R]❚

Horse Named Comanche, A SEE: **Tonka**

Horseplayer, The (1990) C-89m. *½ D: Kurt Voss. Brad Dourif, Sammi Davis, M. K. Harris, Vic Tayback. Extremely odd story of an artist and his seductive sister who interrupt the life of a recluse when they move into his apartment building. No one is quite what they seem—but who cares? [R]▼❚

Horse's Mouth, The (1958-British) C-93m. ***½ D: Ronald Neame. Alec Guinness, Kay Walsh, Renee Houston, Mike Morgan, Michael Gough, Ernest Thesiger. Guinness adapted Joyce Cary's story into this droll screenplay about a brilliant, eccentric, egocentric—and perpetually starving—artist whom some consider a genius. Many others, who know him more intimately, think of him as a major irri-

tant. Score makes ideal use of Prokofiev's "Lieutenant Kije" suite.▼❚

Horse Soldiers, The (1959) C-119m. **½ D: John Ford. John Wayne, William Holden, Constance Towers, Althea Gibson, Hoot Gibson, Anna Lee, Russell Simpson, Ken Curtis, Denver Pyle, Strother Martin, Hank Worden. Ford's only feature set during the Civil War, based on actual incidents. Union Colonel Wayne leads sabotage party deep into Rebel territory, accompanied by somewhat pacifistic doctor Holden. Large-scale actioner rates only a "medium" by Ford buffs; others may like it better.▼❚

Horse Whisperer, The (1998) C-169m. ***½ D: Robert Redford. Robert Redford, Kristin Scott Thomas, Sam Neill, Dianne Wiest, Scarlett Johansson, Chris Cooper, Cherry Jones, Ty Hillman, Jeanette Nolan, Don Edwards. Exquisite rendering of Nicholas Evans' novel about a teenaged girl, traumatized in a horse-riding accident, whose domineering mother drives them both (and the horse) to Montana, where a renowned horse trainer tries to rehabilitate the animal—and simultaneously, the girl. Story offers a tailor-made part for Redford and an opportunity for mature romance, but like his character, Redford the filmmaker takes his time telling the story. It's risky, but it works. Screenplay by Eric Roth and Richard LaGravenese. Panavision. [PG-13]▼❚

Horton Hears a Who! (2008) C-88m. **½ D: Jimmy Hayward, Steve Martino. Voices of Jim Carrey, Steve Carell, Carol Burnett, Will Arnett, Seth Rogen, Dan Fogler, Isla Fisher, Jonah Hill, Amy Poehler, Jaime Pressly, Jesse McCartney; narrated by Charles Osgood. Another bloated movie based on a classic Dr. Seuss book—in this case, the beloved story of good-hearted Horton the elephant, who hears the teeny-tiny citizens of Whoville, while no one else believes they exist. Seuss' gentle tale is expanded and vulgarized, though it has its moments, and the CG animation from Blue Sky Studios is first-rate. Stick with Chuck Jones' 1970 half-hour TV adaptation. Aka DR. SEUSS' HORTON HEARS A WHO! [G]❚

Hospital, The (1971) C-103m. ***½ D: Arthur Hiller. George C. Scott, Diana Rigg, Barnard Hughes, Nancy Marchand, Richard A. Dysart, Stephen Elliott, Jordan Charney, Roberts Blossom, Robert Walden, Lenny Baker, Frances Sternhagen, Stockard Channing, Katherine Helmond. Sardonically funny view of modern city hospital where bitterly discouraged doctor (Scott) is drawn into chaos by crazy girl (Rigg) and her scheming father. Paddy Chayefsky's Oscar-winning script makes fun of serious situation by turning it into Marx Brothers-ish lunacy; ultimate truth in what's being said leaves viewer somewhat sad. That's

Chayefsky reading the opening narration. [PG]▼●

Hospital of Terror SEE: **Beyond the Living**

Host, The (2006-South Korean-Japanese) **C-119m.** ******* D: Bong Joon-ho. Song Kang-ho, Byeon Hie-bong, Park Hae-il, Bae Du-na, Ko Ah-sung, Scott Wilson. An American callously dumps toxic waste down a drain that leads to the Han River. Years later, a huge monster gallops out of the river and wreaks havoc on the populace; what's more, it may be hosting a new plague. When it carries away a little girl (Ah-sung), her somewhat dysfunctional family unites to get her back. Effective monster thrills and great CGI effects blend with satire, comedy, tragedy, and family values, sometimes all at once. A monster movie for the 21st century, this owes a lot to previous films, yet isn't like anything else. Korea's biggest-grossing home-grown movie to date. [R]▶

Hostage, The (1967) **C-84m.** ****½** D: Russell S. Doughton, Jr. Don O'Kelly, (Harry) Dean Stanton, John Carradine, Ron Hagerthy, Ann Doran. Well-done low-budget film about a six-year-old who stows away on moving van driven by two killers. Shot on location in Iowa. ▼▶

Hostage (1983-Australian-German) **C-90m.** ***½** D: Frank Shields. Kerry Mack, Ralph Schicha, Judy Nunn, Clare Binney. Young, carefree Mack is blackmailed into marriage by Nazi Schicha, and her life becomes hell on earth. Intriguing scenario, based on a true story and set in the '70s, but the result is disjointed, repetitive, boring. Original title: HOSTAGE: THE CHRISTINE MARESCH STORY. Video title: SAVAGE ATTRACTION.▼

Hostage (1992-British) **C-101m.** ****** D: Robert Young. Sam Neill, Talisa Soto, James Fox, Michael Kitchen, Art Malik, Cristina Higueras, Jean Pierre Reguerraz. British secret agent Neill wants out of the Service, but his slimy superiors won't let him go. Mildly interesting morality tale of kidnapping and ethical considerations in the world of international politics. [R]▼

Hostage (2005-U.S.-German) **C-113m.** ****½** D: Florent Emilio Siri. Bruce Willis, Kevin Pollak, Ben Foster, Jonathan Tucker, Marshall Allman, Michelle Horn, Jimmy Bennett, Kim Coates, Serena Scott Thomas. After fatally miscalculating an assignment as the LAPD's hostage negotiator, Willis relocates with estranged wife and daughter to what he thinks is a sleepier burg. Instead, he gets himself involved with *two* abductions (one an offshoot of the other), the first a household takeover by three teen carjackers, one of whom turns out to be a psycho. Filmed with style and a genuine camera eye, picture goes over the top even on a melodramatic level, though the central house provides the coolest movie digs in a while.

Willis' real-life daughter Rumer plays his daughter here. Super 35. [R] ▼▶

Hostage: The Christine Maresch Story SEE: **Hostage** (1983)

Hostel (2006) **C-95m.** ***½** D: Eli Roth. Jay Hernandez, Derek Richardson, Eythor Gudjonsson, Barbara Nedeljáková, Jan Vlasák. Three buddies on a European vacation backpack to a small Slovakian village lured by the promise of sex and drugs. Instead (of course) they encounter violence and bloodshed. Starts out promisingly as an atmospheric, ominously suggestive horror-mystery that pokes fun at a certain kind of dense, young American tourist, but quickly descends into seemingly endless sequences of torture that are as boring as they are gruesome and painful to watch. Quentin Tarantino coexecutive produced. A slightly gorier unrated version is available on DVD. Followed by a sequel. Super 35. [R]▶

Hostel: Part II (2007) **C-93m.** BOMB D: Eli Roth. Lauren German, Heather Matarazzo, Roger Bart, Bijou Phillips, Richard Burgi, Jay Hernandez, Jordan Ladd, Vera Jordanova. Dreary, pointless sequel to Roth's original "torture porn" bloodbath. In this variation, it's three beautiful young girls on vacation in Europe who come upon a chamber of horrors when they meet the wrong guys. Once inside they manage to turn the tables on their captors, American businessmen who pay big bucks to engage in sadomasochistic activities. Here's hoping there won't be a PART III. Unrated version also available. Super 35. [R]▶

Hostile Guns (1967) **C-91m.** ****½** D: R. G. Springsteen. George Montgomery, Yvonne De Carlo, Tab Hunter, Brian Donlevy, John Russell. U.S. marshal, transporting prisoners to penitentiary, discovers that female prisoner is a woman he once loved. Typical. Techniscope. ▼●

Hot Blood (1956) **C-85m.** ***½** D: Nicholas Ray. Jane Russell, Cornel Wilde, Luther Adler, Joseph Calleia. Jane Russell shakes her tambourines and drives Cornel Wilde, in this supremely silly (not to mention unbelievable) gypsy yarn. CinemaScope.▼

Hot Box, The (1972) **C-85m.** ****** D: Joe Viola. Margaret Markov, Andrea Cagan, Ricky Richardson, Laurie Rose, Charles Dierkop. Filipino-shot women's prison film adequately runs through the standard changes, as heroines break out and foment a local revolution. Cowritten and produced by Jonathan Demme. [R]▼

Hot Car Girl SEE: **Hot Rod Girl**

Hot Chick, The (2002) **C-104m.** ****** D: Tom Brady. Rob Schneider, Anna Faris, Matthew Lawrence, Eric Christian Olsen, Robert Davi, Melora Hardin, Alexandra Holden, Rachel McAdams, Maritza Murray, Tia Mowry, Tamera Mowry, Michael O'Keefe. Ancient earrings cast a magical spell and put spoiled high school girl Mc-

Adams into scuzzy Schneider's body—and vice versa. Schneider is surprisingly good in this very broad comedy, with the now-usual dose of crudities, but when it tries to get warm and fuzzy that's asking too much. Recognize that bathroom attendant? It's '60s comic icon Dick Gregory. Schneider coscripted. Adam Sandler, who coexecutive-produced the film, appears unbilled. Super 35. [PG-13] ▼❒

Hot Dog . . . The Movie (1984) **C-96m.** *½ D: Peter Markle. David Naughton, Patrick Houser, Tracy N. Smith, John Patrick Reger, Frank Koppola, Shannon Tweed. Hijinks at a ski resort: an updating of '60s Beach Party–type movies, just as dumb, but now much raunchier. Good ski sequences, but that's about it. Film is so titled to avoid confusion with HOT DOG . . . THE OPERA. [R]▼❒

Hotel (1967) **C-124m.** ** D: Richard Quine. Rod Taylor, Catherine Spaak, Karl Malden, Melvyn Douglas, Richard Conte, Michael Rennie, Merle Oberon, Kevin McCarthy. Adaptation of still another Arthur Hailey multicharactered novel is not all that inferior to AIRPORT, but that's faint praise; Douglas has some good scenes. Later a TV series.▼❒

Hotel (2002-British-Italian) **C-109m.** BOMB D: Mike Figgis. Rhys Ifans, David Schwimmer, Salma Hayek, Max Beesley, John Malkovich, Saffron Burrows, George DiCenzo, Valeria Golino, Danny Huston, Jason Isaacs, Lucy Liu, Mía Maestro, Chiara Mastroianni, Ornella Muti, Burt Reynolds, Julian Sands. Figgis returns to TIMECODE territory (with new, much-touted handheld riggings for picture, sound, and even night-vision photography, which is pointlessly exploited throughout) for another largely improvised story about a foredoomed film troupe attempting to shoot a version of *The Duchess of Malfi* in Venice. Only Ifans, as the egomaniacal director, has any real spark. This astonishing indulgence prompts two repeated questions from the viewer: "Is it over yet?" and "Why not?"▼❒

Hotel Colonial (1983-Italian-U.S.) **C-104m.** BOMB D: Cinzia Torrini. John Savage, Rachel Ward, Robert Duvall, Massimo Troisi. International mishmash wastes a good cast in downbeat tale of Savage going to Colombia to investigate the death of his brother, aided by embassy attaché Ward and thwarted by evil Duvall. Pretty Mexican scenery is film's only merit. [R]▼●

Hotel for Dogs (2009) **C-100m.** **½ D: Thor Freudenthal. Emma Roberts, Jake T. Austin, Kyla Pratt, Lisa Kudrow, Kevin Dillon, Don Cheadle, Johnny Simmons, Troy Gentile, Ajay Naidu. Cute film for kids about an orphaned brother and sister, now living with flaky, irresponsible foster parents, who manage to keep the existence of their pet dog a secret. Then they discover an abandoned hotel that becomes a refuge not only for their pooch but for every stray in the city. Likable bit of make-believe with appealing canine costars and some nifty Rube Goldberg–like devices. [PG]❒

Hotel New Hampshire, The (1984) **C-110m.** *** D: Tony Richardson. Rob Lowe, Jodie Foster, Beau Bridges, Nastassja Kinski, Paul McCrane, Jennie Dundas, Dorsey Wright, Matthew Modine, Wilford Brimley, Amanda Plummer, Wallace Shawn, Anita Morris, Joely Richardson. Faithful adaptation of John Irving's sprawling seriocomic novel about an unconventional family and its bizarre adventures—social, sexual, and political—on both sides of the Atlantic. Some fine vignettes and good performances make this worth watching, though characters eventually wear out their welcome. [R]▼●❒

Hotel Paradiso (1966-British) **C-96m.** **½ D: Peter Glenville. Alec Guinness, Gina Lollobrigida, Robert Morley, Akim Tamiroff. Pretentious farce of manners is only fitfully amusing; meek Guinness tries to carry on his rendezvous with gorgeous neighbor Gina, but everything interferes. Based on the Georges Feydeau play. Panavision.▼

Hotel Rwanda (2004-South African-British-Italian) **C-123m.** ***½ D: Terry George. Don Cheadle, Sophie Okonedo, Joaquin Phoenix, Nick Nolte, Desmond Dube, David O'Hara, Cara Seymour, Fana Mokoena, Hakeem Kae-Kazim. The slaughter of nearly one million Tutsis in the African nation of Rwanda in 1994 is dramatized through the experiences of Paul Rusesabagina, a career-minded hotel manager who becomes a hero, sheltering innocent people within the walls of his establishment. Powerful film avoids being overly didactic by focusing on one compelling character, believably brought to life by Cheadle. Written by director George and Keir Pearson. Jean Reno appears unbilled. Super 35. [PG-13] ▼❒

Hotel Sahara (1951-British) **96m.** **½ D: Ken Annakin. Yvonne De Carlo, Peter Ustinov, David Tomlinson, Roland Culver. Pleasant fluff about North African hotel owner and beautiful fiancée who must shift "loyalties" every time new army marches into town during WW2.

Hotel Sorrento (1995-Australian) **C-112m.** *** D: Richard Franklin. Caroline Goodall, Caroline Gillmer, Tara Morice, Joan Plowright, John Hargreaves, Ben Thomas, Ray Barrett. Atmospheric, well-acted drama, set in a small seaside Australian town, focusing on the reunion of a trio of very different sisters, one of whom has just published a highly successful autobiographical novel. What follows may be predictable, but the result is compelling nonetheless. Also known as SORRENTO BEACH. [R] ▼

Hotel Terminus: The Life and Times of Klaus Barbie (1987) **C-267m.** ***½ D:

Marcel Ophuls. Sobering, Oscar-winning documentary about the infamous Nazi war criminal who, decades after WW2, was expelled from Bolivia and returned to France for trial. Filled with incisive interviews with key individuals in his life. A fine companion piece to Ophuls' THE SORROW AND THE PITY.▼◑❶

Hot Enough for June SEE: **Agent 8¾**

Hot Fuzz (2007-British-U.S.) **C-120m.** ** D: Edgar Wright. Simon Pegg, Nick Frost, Jim Broadbent, Paddy Considine, Timothy Dalton, Billie Whitelaw, Edward Woodward, Rafe Spall, Olivia Colman, Paul Freeman, Martin Freeman, Bill Nighy, Kenneth Cranham, Stuart Wilson, Lucy Punch, David Threlfall. SHAUN OF THE DEAD team reunites for a protracted, disappointing spoof of crime/buddy movies. Pegg (who cowrote with director Wright) plays a by-the-book London cop who's so outstanding he makes everyone else look bad, so his superiors transfer him to a quiet country village. It seems resolutely dull, but Pegg soon discovers otherwise. Some funny gags scattered about can't compensate for unevenness and extreme overlength. Cate Blanchett and Steve Coogan appear unbilled. Super 35. [R]❶

Hot Lead SEE: **Run of the Arrow**

Hot Lead and Cold Feet (1978) **C-90m.** *** D: Robert Butler. Jim Dale, Darren McGavin, Karen Valentine, Jack Elam, Don Knotts, John Williams. Amiable Disney Western spoof with lots of slapstick features British comic Dale in three roles: tough patriarch, tougher gunfighter son, and meek twin, a Salvation Army lad. The brothers participate in a wild obstacle race to gain possession of the town, then to defeat villainous Mayor McGavin. Good Oregon location filming. [G]▼❶

Hot Line SEE: **Day the Hot Line Got Hot, The**

Hot Millions (1968-British) **C-105m.** *** D: Eric Till. Peter Ustinov, Maggie Smith, Karl Malden, Bob Newhart, Robert Morley, Cesar Romero. Wry piece of fluff about Ustinov using a computer to siphon off big bucks from huge American conglomerate. Good performers aid pleasant romp, which became one of the biggest sleepers of its year. Ustinov cowrote script. [G]▼❶

Hot Potato (1976) **C-87m.** *½ D: Oscar Williams. Jim Kelly, George Memmoli, Geoffrey Binney, Irene Tsu, Judith Brown. Idiotic action film in which karate expert Kelly and two cohorts try to rescue kidnapped Senator's daughter from Oriental villain. Comic-book stuff. Filmed in Thailand. Remade as FORCE: FIVE. [PG]▼

Hot Pursuit (1987) **C-93m.** *½ D: Steven Lisberger. John Cusack, Robert Loggia, Wendy Gazelle, Jerry Stiller, Monte Markham, Shelley Fabares, Ben Stiller. Student Cusack, grounded by bad grades, has been prevented from taking a dream

vacation with the family of his wealthy girlfriend. Then he gets last-minute reprieve from a kindly prof, and tries to catch up with them on the road. Silly comedy will probably remind you of Cusack's earlier THE SURE THING—and the comparison isn't favorable. [PG-13]▼◑❶

Hot Rock, The (1972) **C-105m.** *** D: Peter Yates. Robert Redford, George Segal, Ron Leibman, Paul Sand, Zero Mostel, Moses Gunn, William Redfield, Charlotte Rae, Topo Swope. Light, funny caper comedy where inept robbers blunder every step of carefully planned jewel heist. Best bit: the raid on the police station. Screenplay by William Goldman from Donald Westlake's novel; followed by BANK SHOT. Panavision. [PG]▼◑❶

Hot Rod (2007) **C-88m.** *½ D: Akiva Schaffer. Andy Samberg, Bill Hader, Isla Fisher, Jorma Taccone, Will Arnett, Chris Parnell, Chester Tam, Sissy Spacek, Ian McShane. In order to raise money for his abusive father's heart operation, a young Evel Knievel–style daredevil plans a major stunt in which he must jump over 15 buses. Smart-aleck humor and thin script short on laughs make this an ordeal to sit through, even though it's under 90 minutes. *Saturday Night Live*'s digital shorts star Samberg proves he is not quite ready for feature films. Super 35. [PG-13]❶

Hot Rod Gang (1958) **72m.** *½ D: Lew Landers. John Ashley, Gene Vincent, Jody Fair, Steve Drexel. Low-budget relic of its era, about hot-rod-happy Ashley joining Vincent's band to earn money to enter big race.

Hot Rod Girl (1956) **75m.** BOMB D: Leslie H. Martinson. Lori Nelson, Chuck Connors, John Smith, Frank Gorshin, Roxanne Arlen, Dabbs Greer. Blah juvenile delinquency potboiler, with sympathetic cop Connors establishing drag strip to keep hot-rodding teens off the streets. Aka HOT CAR GIRL.▼❶

Hot Rod Rumble (1957) **79m.** *½ D: Leslie Martinson. Brett Halsey, Richard Hartunian, Joey Forman, Leigh Snowden. Title tells all in this formula programmer of juvenile delinquents.

Hot Rods to Hell (1967) **C-92m.** **½ D: John Brahm. Dana Andrews, Jeanne Crain, Mimsy Farmer, Laurie Mock. Fast-paced actioner has Andrews and family tormented by hot-rod-happy juvenile delinquents. Original title: 52 MILES TO MIDNIGHT.❶

H.O.T.S. (1979) **C-95m.** *½ D: Gerald Seth Sindell. Susan Kiger, Lisa London, Pamela Jean Bryant, Kimberly Cameron, Lindsay Bloom, Mary Steelsmith, Angela Aames, Danny Bonaduce, Ken Olfson. Lame-brained knock-off of ANIMAL HOUSE with two sororities at each other's throats until they settle their differences with a strip football game. Leering sexploitation fare at least has gorgeous girls (including several *Playboy* playmates) and decent production, making this best watched with the sound off. Written by two women, believe it or not, one of them actress Cheri Caffaro (whose husband produced the film). Aka T&A ACADEMY. [R]▼▶

Hot Shots! (1991) **C-85m.** **✱✱✱** D: Jim Abrahams. Charlie Sheen, Cary Elwes, Valeria Golino, Lloyd Bridges, Kevin Dunn, Jon Cryer, William O'Leary, Kristy Swanson, Efrem Zimbalist, Jr., Bill Irwin, Judith Kahan, Pat Proft, Heidi Swedberg. Sheen plays a pilot trying to overcome his father's disastrous reputation in the cockpit in this zany, often hilarious takeoff on "flyboy" movies from ONLY ANGELS HAVE WINGS to TOP GUN. Surprisingly high quotient of successful gags, including sendups of movies ranging from DANCES WITH WOLVES to ROCKY, help this comedy soar at times. Bridges is a riot as an admiral with a loose propeller. Followed by a sequel. [PG-13] ▼▶

Hot Shots! Part Deux (1993) **C-89m.** **✱✱½** D: Jim Abrahams. Charlie Sheen, Lloyd Bridges, Valeria Golino, Richard Crenna, Brenda Bakke, Miguel Ferrer, Rowan Atkinson, Jerry Haleva, Mitchell Ryan, Gregory Sierra. Obligatory sequel with Rambo-like Sheen called into action to rescue U.S. soldiers who tried to rescue soldiers (and so on . . .) held captive after Desert Storm. Plenty of gags and countless movie parodies, but just as many misses as hits this time around, especially in the second half. The cast acquits itself nicely, particularly Sheen, Bridges, and Crenna (who kids his own RAMBO series role). [PG-13] ▼▶

Hot Spell (1958) **86m.** **✱✱** D: Daniel Mann. Shirley Booth, Anthony Quinn, Shirley MacLaine, Earl Holliman, Eileen Heckart, Warren Stevens. Quinn—not just a pig but a blue-ribbon hog—cheats on wife Booth, who spouts irritating platitudes like Hazel on speed. Well-acted but dated drama about the breakup's effect on their children; MacLaine shines as their daughter. Set in New Orleans. VistaVision ▼

Hot Spot SEE: **I Wake Up Screaming**

Hot Spot, The (1990) **C-130m.** **✱✱½** D: Dennis Hopper. Don Johnson, Virginia Madsen, Jennifer Connelly, Charles Martin Smith, William Sadler, Jerry Hardin, Barry Corbin, Leon Rippy, Jack Nance. Sounds as if it can't miss, but does: drifter Johnson, selling used cars in a nowhere Texas burg, gets involved with boss' wife Madsen, an R-rated descendant of Barbara Stanwyck from DOUBLE INDEMNITY. Overlong by 30 minutes and never once hits the bull's-eye, but there's so much ornery sex that you may be compelled to keep watching. Connelly plays the mysterious "nice girl" (with a sensuous body) who handles the car lot's financing. Based on Charles

Williams' 1952 novel *Hell Hath No Fury.* [R]▼▶

Hot Stuff (1979) **C-87m.** **✱✱½** D: Dom DeLuise. Dom DeLuise, Suzanne Pleshette, Jerry Reed, Luis Avalos, Ossie Davis, Marc Lawrence. Four Miami cops set up a "Sting"-like operation to fence stolen goods. Unexceptional but pleasant trifle that surprises by treating its characters as real human beings instead of cartoon stereotypes. Cowritten by Donald Westlake. [PG] ▼▶

Hot Sweat SEE: **Keetje Tippel**

Hottest State, The (2007) **C-116m.** **✱✱½** D: Ethan Hawke. Mark Webber, Catalina Sandino Moreno, Ethan Hawke, Michelle Williams, Sonia Braga, Laura Linney, Frank Whaley. Adapting his own semiautobiographical novel, writer-director Hawke infuses raw emotional intensity into a familiar story about the turbulent romance of two attractive twentysomethings—an aspiring actor (Webber) from Texas and a Latina pop singer (Sandino Moreno) from Connecticut—who fall madly in love much too quickly in N.Y.C. Best moments of uneven drama focus on male lead's increasingly frantic and self-humiliating attempts at reconciliation after he's dumped. Director Richard Linklater appears in a brief cameo. [R]▶

Hottie & The Nottie, The (2008) **C-90m.** BOMB D: Tom Putnam. Paris Hilton, Joel Moore, Christine Lakin, Adam Kulbersh, The Greg Wilson, Johann Urb. Vehicle for dubious acting talents of real-life celebrity heiress Hilton is complete nonsense as a young man tries to woo the "hottie," only to find true love could be with her incredibly ugly childhood friend, the "nottie." Get it? Actually, forget it. [PG-13]▶

Hot to Trot (1988) **C-83m.** BOMB D: Michael Dinner. Bob Goldthwait, Virginia Madsen, Dabney Coleman, Cindy Pickett, Jim Metzler, Tim Kazurinsky, Gilbert Gottfried, Jack Whitaker; voices of John Candy, Burgess Meredith. Here's a fresh concept for the 1980s: a comedy about a talking horse. Goldthwait plays a semi-imbecile who gets stock tips from a whinnying pal with the voice of John Candy. As comedies go, this is the equivalent of Black Monday. Coleman, courtesy of the makeup department, wears a pair of horse teeth here; they *are* funny. [PG]▼▶

Hot Tub Time Machine (2010) **C-99m.** **✱✱** D: Steve Pink. John Cusack, Clark Duke, Craig Robinson, Rob Corddry, Crispin Glover, Sebastian Stan, Lyndsy Fonseca, Chevy Chase, Charlie McDermott, Lizzy Caplan. Funny idea comes off as HANGOVER-lite when four guys suddenly find themselves transported by a mysterious hot tub back to a ski lodge vacation in the 1980s, where they get to meet their younger selves and assess the path their lives have taken in the past twenty years. Gross-out humor, frenetic pace, and generally sleazy production values short-circuit a clever premise that sadly doesn't meet its potential. Corddry is a standout but the others struggle for laughs that aren't there. Great title, though. Alternate version runs 111m. [R] ▶

Houdini (1953) **C-106m.** **½ D: George Marshall. Tony Curtis, Janet Leigh, Torin Thatcher, Ian Wolfe, Sig Ruman. Fanciful biography of famed escape artist; more fiction than fact, but entertaining. ▼●▶

Hound-Dog Man (1959) **C-87m.** *** D: Don Siegel. Fabian, Carol Lynley, Stuart Whitman, Arthur O'Connell, Dodie Stevens, Betty Field, Royal Dano, Margo Moore, Claude Akins, Edgar Buchanan, Jane Darwell, L.Q. Jones. Pleasant tale of Southern country boys Fabian (in film debut) and Whitman courting Stevens and Lynley. Fabian is surprisingly good; of course, he also sings. CinemaScope.

Hound of the Baskervilles, The (1939) **80m.** *** D: Sidney Lanfield. Basil Rathbone, Nigel Bruce, Richard Greene, Wendy Barrie, Lionel Atwill, John Carradine, Beryl Mercer, Mary Gordon, E. E. Clive. Rathbone made his first appearance as Sherlock Holmes in this grade-A production based on Conan Doyle's story about mysterious murders taking place at a creepy mansion on the moors (though he's off-screen for a good part of the story). Fairly faithful to the source material with the now classic closing line from cocaine-user Holmes: "Quick Watson, the needle!" (This was the fourth screen version of the oft-filmed novel.) ▼●▶

Hound of the Baskervilles, The (1959-British) **C-84m.** *** D: Terence Fisher. Peter Cushing, Christopher Lee, Andre Morell, Marla Landi, Miles Malleson, John LeMesurier. Cushing is well cast as Sherlock Holmes and Lee is fine as Sir Henry Baskerville in this atmospheric Hammer Films adaptation of the Conan Doyle classic. ▼●▶

Hound of the Baskervilles, The (1978-British) **C-84m.** BOMB D: Paul Morrissey. Dudley Moore, Peter Cook, Denholm Elliott, Joan Greenwood, Spike Milligan, Jessie Matthews, Roy Kinnear. Dreadful spoof of Conan Doyle story scripted by Cook (who plays Sherlock Holmes), Moore (as both Watson and Holmes' mother), and director Morrissey. After a few laughs it descends into dreariness and never recovers. What a waste of talent! U.S. version runs 78m., with sequences out of order. Technovision. ▼▶

Hour of the Assassin (1987) **C-93m.** ** D: Luis Llosa. Erik Estrada, Robert Vaughn, Alfredo Alvarez Calderon, Lourdes Berninzon. OK political thriller has Estrada called back from L.A. to South American nation of San Pedro to assassinate the newly elected democratic president. Vaughn is the CIA agent assigned to stop him. Filmed in Peru. [R] ▼

Hour of the Gun (1967) **C-100m.** ** D: John Sturges. James Garner, Jason Ro-

bards, Robert Ryan, Albert Salmi, Charles Aidman, Steve Ihnat, Michael Tolan, William Windom, William Schallert, Monte Markham, Frank Converse, Jon Voight. Western about Ike Clanton and the Earp Brothers after O.K. Corral shoot-up begins well, becomes increasingly tedious. Robards has a good time as Doc Holliday; flavorful score by Jerry Goldsmith. Panavision. ▼●▶

Hour of the Star, The (1986-Brazilian) **C-96m.** *** D: Suzana Amaral. Marcelia Cartaxo, Jose Dumont, Tamara Taxman, Fernanda Montenegro. Amaral's debut feature (made when she was 52 years old) is a subtle, touching neorealist drama about a plain, awkward, virginal country orphan (Cartaxo) and her experiences in São Paolo. Slow in spots, but still worthwhile. ▶

Hour of the Wolf (1968-Swedish) **88m.** *** D: Ingmar Bergman. Liv Ullmann, Max von Sydow, Erland Josephson, Gertrud Fridh, Gudrun Brost. Lesser Bergman about painter von Sydow, wife Ullmann, and apparitions he sees when they retreat to deserted island. The acting, as usual, is first-rate. ▼●▶

Hours, The (2002) **C-114m.** *** D: Stephen Daldry. Meryl Streep, Nicole Kidman, Julianne Moore, Ed Harris, Toni Collette, Claire Danes, Jeff Daniels, Stephen Dillane, Allison Janney, John C. Reilly, Miranda Richardson, Eileen Atkins, Margo Martindale. Demanding adaptation of Michael Cunningham's Pulitzer Prize–winning novel about three women whose emotional lives intersect: novelist Virginia Woolf (an unrecognizable Kidman in an Oscar-winning performance), 1950s American housewife Moore, and contemporary New Yorker Streep, who's throwing a party—much like Woolf's fictional Mrs. Dalloway—for a dying friend (Harris). Emotionally draining, to say the least, but redeemed by the luminescent performances of its three stars. Screenplay by David Hare, with a memorable score by Philip Glass. [PG-13] ▼▶

House (1986) **C-93m.** ** D: Steve Miner. William Katt, George Wendt, Richard Moll, Kay Lenz, Michael Ensign, Susan French, Mary Stavin. Horror novelist Katt, simultaneously suffering from the split-up of his marriage, son's disappearance, and Vietnam memories, is plagued by demonic fantasies when he moves to the Victorian home where his aunt hanged herself. Lots of horror effects that don't hang together, but a quirky attitude, and a sense of humor, buoy things enough to make this moderately entertaining. Followed by several sequels. [R] ▼●▶

House II: The Second Story (1987) **C-88m.** *½ D: Ethan Wiley. Arye Gross, Jonathan Stark, Royal Dano, Lar Park Lincoln, Bill Maher, John Ratzenberger. A follow-up rather than a sequel to HOUSE, this incoherent mess is, if anything, a step down. Another young hero moves into another weird house, and finds himself involved with living-dead gunslingers, crystal skulls, Aztec sacrifices, pterodactyls, and a sword-wielding electrician. Busy, but chaotic and boring. [PG-13]▼●◗

House III SEE: Horror Show, The

House IV (1992) **C-100m.** BOMB D: Lewis Abernathy. Terri Treas, Scott Burkholder, Denny Dillon, Melissa Clayton, William Katt, Ned Romero, Ned Bellamy, Dabbs Greer, John Santucci. When her husband is killed and her daughter confined to a wheelchair in a car wreck, a young wife holds onto the old house she inherited, despite spooky goings-on and efforts by her brother-in-law to get her out. Slow, overlong, thrill-less, this lurches from comedy to horror, and can't even match the shoddy effects of the first two. Although Katt has the same character name as in HOUSE, he doesn't seem to be playing the same person. [R]▼●

House Arrest (1996) **C-108m.** **½ D: Harry Winer. Jamie Lee Curtis, Kevin Pollak, Jennifer Tilly, Kyle Howard, Christopher McDonald, Sheila McCarthy, Wallace Shawn, Ray Walston, Caroline Aaron, Mooky Arizona, Colleen Camp, Russel Harper, Jennifer Love Hewitt, Amy Sakasitz, Ben Stein. Sensitive, put-upon teenage boy is so shocked that his parents are separating that he locks them in the basement, hoping to force them to talk out their problems; soon his scheme escalates as other kids bring their parents to join them. Not as bad as it sounds, a sometimes thoughtful comedy that should have been a one-hour TV show. [PG] ▼●◗

Houseboat (1958) **C-110m.** ***½ D: Melville Shavelson. Cary Grant, Sophia Loren, Martha Hyer, Harry Guardino, Eduardo Ciannelli, Murray Hamilton. Loren becomes Grant's housekeeper and takes his three motherless kids in hand. Predictable romance ensues, in this delightful comedy. Guardino hilarious as houseboat handyman. VistaVision.▼●◗

House Bunny, The (2008) **C-97m.** **½ D: Fred Wolf. Anna Faris, Colin Hanks, Emma Stone, Kat Dennings, Katharine McPhee, Rumer Willis, Monet Mazur, Kiely Williams, Tyson Ritter, Beverly D'Angelo, Christopher McDonald, Rick Swardson, Hugh Hefner. Ditzy but endearing Faris has had a perfect life as a Playmate at the Playboy mansion, so when she's kicked out she feels she has no identity. She becomes a den mother to the worst sorority at a nearby college, vowing to revamp its image and help its eccentric members fit in. Silly and predictable, but Faris and her castmates make this goofy yarn enjoyable. There are cameos by celebrities and Hefner's harem. HD Widescreen. [PG-13]◗

House by the Lake (1977-Canadian) **C-89m.** *½ D: William Fruet. Brenda Vaccaro, Don Stroud, Chuck Shamata, Richard Ayres, Kyle Edwards. Violent, ugly thriller. Four morons led by Stroud invade weekend retreat of lovers Vaccaro and Shamata. Stroud and Vaccaro good, though. Original title: DEATH WEEKEND. [R]▼

House by the River (1950) **84m.** *** D: Fritz Lang. Louis Hayward, Jane Wyatt, Lee Bowman, Ann Shoemaker, Kathleen Freeman. Strange, moody tale of larcenous husband (Hayward) who spins web of evil that involves his wife (Wyatt) and brother (Bowman). Overwrought at times—particularly near the end—but full of fascinating touches, striking atmosphere.◗

House Calls (1978) **C-98m.** ***½ D: Howard Zieff. Walter Matthau, Glenda Jackson, Art Carney, Richard Benjamin, Candice Azzara, Dick O'Neill, Thayer David. Matthau plays recently widowed doctor who tries to woo feisty Jackson without sacrificing his independence, in this laughing-outloud contemporary comedy. Cowritten by Max Shulman and Julius J. Epstein. Carney hilarious as addle-brained head of surgery at Matthau's hospital. Later a TV series. [PG]▼●◗

Houseguest (1995) **C-109m.** ** D: Randall Miller. Sinbad, Phil Hartman, Jeffrey Jones, Kim Greist, Stan Shaw, Tony Longo, Paul Ben-Victor, Mason Adams, Kim Murphy, Chauncey Leopardi, Talia Seider, Ron Glass. Deep-in-debt dreamer pursued by thuggish money collectors poses as a world-renowned oral surgeon and childhood friend of a suburban advertising exec. Sinbad is likable, but no funnier than the desperate rest. Woefully overextended comedy is mired in uninvolving subplots and burdened by two of the unfunniest break-ya-fingas comical thugs in screen history. The kind of movie that opens in January. [PG]▼●◗

Householder, The (1963-U.S.-Indian) **100m.** **½ D: James Ivory. Shashi Kapoor, Leela Naidu, Durga Khote, Hariendernath Chattopadaya. Fair comedy about perplexed schoolteacher Kapoor, coping with his arranged marriage and new obligations. Ivory's first fiction feature, and initial collaboration with longtime producer Ismail Merchant and scriptwriter Ruth Prawer Jhabvala; from her novel.▼●◗

Household Saints (1993) **C-124m.** *** D: Nancy Savoca. Tracey Ullman, Vincent D'Onofrio, Lili Taylor, Judith Malina, Michael Rispoli, Victor Argo, Michael Imperioli, Illeana Douglas, Joe Grifasi. Rich, almost folkloric portrait of three generations of Italian working-class N.Y.C. women: elderly immigrant Malina, whose life is ruled by old wives' tales; her daughter-in-law (Ullman), an old-maid-in-training won by Malina's son (D'Onofrio) in a pinochle game; and their religion-obsessed daughter (Taylor). As in her first feature, TRUE LOVE, director Savoca (who scripted with her husband, Richard Guay, from Francine Prose's novel) depicts Italian New Yorkers with uncanny accuracy. [R]▼

House in Nightmare Park, The SEE: **Crazy House**

Housekeeper, The (2002-French) **C-91m.** **½ D: Claude Berri. Jean-Pierre Bacri, Èmilie Dequenne, Brigitte Catillon, Jacques Frantz, Axelle Abbadie, Catherine Breillat. Shortly after separating from his wife a man hires a new housekeeper who does more for him than change the sheets. Typically French in attitude and style, this amusing if minor effort from director Berri manages to explore the ultimate male fantasy. Never fully meets the potential of its concept despite fine, understated performances from its two leads. French title: UNE FEMME DE MÉNAGE. Super 35. [R]▼❚

Housekeeping (1987) **C-116m.** **½ D: Bill Forsyth. Christine Lahti, Sara Walker, Andrea Burchill. Two orphaned girls meet their aunt for the first time when she comes to live with them; she turns out to be a free spirit who shuns responsibility and has a profound effect on the sisters' own relationship. Forsyth's first American film, set in the 1950s, is a quiet, offbeat, and melancholy story that unfolds like a novel but lacks a certain momentum. Still, there are many touching moments. Lahti is wonderful as always, and the girls (both movie newcomers) are excellent. Based on Marilynne Robinson's book. [PG]▼

House of Angels (1992-Swedish) **C-126m.** **½ D: Colin Nutley. Helena Bergstrom, Rikard Wolff, Per Oscarsson, Sven Wollter, Viveka Seldahl, Reine Brynolfsson, Jacob Eklund. Contemporary tale of sexy and liberal Bergstrom who, with her avant-garde pal, descends on a rural Swedish village to claim an inheritance and throws the straitlaced townfolk for a loop. Easygoing, offbeat (if longish) film is really not all that different from those classic Ealing comedies coming from 1950s Britain. U.S. theatrical version ran 119m. Aka COLIN NUTLEY'S HOUSE OF ANGELS. [R]▼

House of a Thousand Dolls (1967-British-Spanish) **C-83m.** *½ D: Jeremy Summers. Vincent Price, Martha Hyer, George Nader, Anne Smyrner, Wolfgang Kieling, Sancho Garcia. Vacationing couple in Tangiers befriended by young man convinced that his fiancée has been abducted into white slavery ring. Incredible dialogue, with Price walking through film in a daze. Techniscope.❚

House of Bamboo (1955) **C-102m.** **½ D: Samuel Fuller. Robert Ryan, Robert Stack, Shirley Yamaguchi, Cameron Mitchell, Sessue Hayakawa. Picturesque if not credible story of army officers and Japanese police tracking down a gang of former soldiers working for a well-organized syndicate. CinemaScope.❚

House of Cards (1969) **C-105m.** ** D: John Guillermin. George Peppard, Inger Stevens, Orson Welles, Keith Michell, Ralph Michael, Maxine Audley. Down-and-out boxer/ adventurer (Peppard) hired by rich widow (Stevens) to tutor her young son becomes pawn of Fascist millionaires and generals intent on retaking Europe. Sound familiar? One good chase, though. Techniscope. [G]

House of Cards (1993) **C-109m.** ** D: Michael Lessac. Kathleen Turner, Tommy Lee Jones, Park Overall, Shiloh Strong, Asha Menina, Esther Rolle, Michael Horse, Anne Pitoniak. Architect Turner and her two children return to the U.S. after several years of living among Mayan ruins (and the eerie spirituality of the Mayan Indians) of Central America. When her young daughter becomes increasingly withdrawn and shows signs of autism, Turner battles child psychologist Jones over therapy. Pokey story is less a treatise on the girl's trauma than it is on the benefits of having a well-to-do parent with lots of free time and a big backyard. [PG-13]▼❚

House of Crazies SEE: **Asylum** (1972)

House of D (2005) **C-97m.** **½ D: David Duchovny. Anton Yelchin, David Duchovny, Robin Williams, Téa Leoni, Erykah Badu, Frank Langella, Zelda Williams, Mark Margolis, Magali Amadei, Harold Cartier, Orlando Jones. Duchovny's debut as writer-director is a semiautobiographical story about a man looking back on his childhood growing up in 1970s Greenwich Village and the life-altering choice he makes when tragedy intervenes. Overly sentimental and shot with so many close-ups it can't be recommended for claustrophobics, this awkwardly structured memory play still has laughs and touching moments. Yelchin is a real find as the younger version of the man, played by Duchovny; Williams is good as the boy's mentally challenged friend and coworker. Williams' real-life daughter Zelda makes a charming first-love interest. [PG-13]❚

House of Dark Shadows (1970) **C-96m.** *** D: Dan Curtis. Jonathan Frid, Grayson Hall, Kathryn Leigh Scott, Roger Davis, Joan Bennett, John Karlen, Thayer David, Louis Edmonds, Nancy Barrett. Feature version of popular TV serial, recounting vampire Barnabas Collins' (Frid) quest for a cure so he can wed lovely Scott. Nothing new script-wise, but beautiful locations, flashy direction and camerawork, and some nice jolts make it an enjoyable chiller. Followed by NIGHT OF DARK SHADOWS. [PG]▼●

House of Dracula (1945) **67m.** **½ D: Erle C. Kenton. Onslow Stevens, Lon Chaney, Jr., John Carradine, Martha O'Driscoll, Jane Adams, Lionel Atwill, Glenn Strange, Skelton Knaggs. Sequel to HOUSE OF FRANKENSTEIN takes different tack: Stevens tries "real" science to cure various Universal monsters, but finds that some of their bad habits begin to rub off. Acting, direction, eerie set design compensate for overambitious script, hasty resolution. ▼●)

House of Evil (1971-Mexican-U.S.) **C-80m.** BOMB D: Juan Ibanez, Jack Hill. Boris Karloff, Julissa, Andres Garcia, Angel Espinosa, Beatriz Baz. The old heirs-being-killed-one-by-one story, involving crazy composer Karloff, his old house, killer toys, and an organ melody that heralds death. One of four films Karloff made back to back in 1968, constituting his last film work; this is the worst of the lot. Aka DANCE OF DEATH and SERANATA MACABRA. [PG] ▼●)

House of Exorcism, The SEE: **Lisa and the Devil**

House of Fear, The (1945) **69m.** ✱✱✱ D: Roy William Neill. Basil Rathbone, Nigel Bruce, Dennis Hoey, Aubrey Mather, Paul Cavanagh, Holmes Herbert, Gavin Muir. Sherlock Holmes is called in to investigate when members of an eccentric Scottish gentleman's club are knocked off one by one. Liberal, but ingenious, adaptation of Conan Doyle's "The Five Orange Pips." ▼●)

House of Flying Daggers (2004-Hong Kong-Chinese) **C-119m.** ✱✱½ D: Zhang Yimou. Takeshi Kaneshiro, Andy Lau, Zhang Ziyi, Song Dandan. China, A.D. 859: The notorious Flying Daggers have won renown for stealing from the rich and giving to the poor. Mei (Ziyi), a blind beauty and martial arts expert who is the daughter of the deceased leader of the Daggers, becomes the love object of two dashing Tang Dynasty government deputies; they compete for her amid many battles and fight scenes. Dazzling set pieces, special effects, and use of color, but long, boring at times, and downright silly toward the end; still, it's great to look at. Zhang's second foray into the martial arts genre, following HERO. Super 35. [PG-13] ▼)

House of Fools (2002-Russian) **C-104m.** ✱✱½ D: Andrei Konchalovsky. Yuliya Vysotskaya (Julia Vysotsky), Bryan Adams, Sultan Islamov, Stanislav Varkki, Vladas Bagdonas, Yevgeni Mironov. This thoroughly Russian film is set in a mental hospital where one of the patients is fixated on a fantasy life with pop singer Bryan Adams, only to see her dreams shattered by the real-life Chechen war in her midst. An odd cross between NO MAN'S LAND and ONE FLEW OVER THE CUCKOO'S NEST; the actors shine in spite of the film's dreary tone. Adams appears throughout, singing his hit "Have You Ever Really Loved a Woman" perhaps three times too many. [R] ▼)

House of Frankenstein (1944) **71m.** ✱✱½ D: Erle C. Kenton. Boris Karloff, J. Carrol Naish, Lon Chaney, Jr., John Carradine, Elena Verdugo, Anne Gwynne, Lionel Atwill, Peter Coe, George Zucco, Glenn Strange, Sig Rumann. Episodic all-star monster opus linked by evil scientist Karloff and hunchback Naish posing as traveling horror show operators. First third has them dealing with Dracula (wonderfully played by Carradine), the rest picks up where FRANKENSTEIN MEETS THE WOLF MAN left off. Contrived, to say the least, but tough to dislike. Strange's first appearance as the Frankenstein Monster. Sequel: HOUSE OF DRACULA. ▼●)

House of Fright SEE: **Two Faces of Dr. Jekyll, The**

House of Games (1987) **C-102m.** ✱✱✱½ D: David Mamet. Lindsay Crouse, Joe Mantegna, Mike Nussbaum, Lilia Skala, J.T. Walsh, Willo Hausman, Ricky Jay, Meshach Taylor, W. (William) H. Macy. Uptight female psychiatrist (and best-selling author) becomes involved with a slick confidence man and his "team," and quickly gets in over her head. Fascinating Hitchcockian tale by David Mamet, which also marks his film directing debut. Many of his stage cronies are on hand, notably Mantegna, in a dynamic performance, and Crouse, then Mamet's wife. [R] ▼●)

House of God, The (1979) **C-108m.** ✱½ D: Donald Wrye. Tim Matheson, Charles Haid, Bess Armstrong, Michael Sacks, Lisa Pelikan, George Coe, Ossie Davis, Howard Rollins, Jr., James Cromwell, Sandra Bernhard. Misfire black comedy about bunch of young interns coming to grips with reality of hospital pressures. A few scattered laughs, but mostly a waste of terrific (and then-unknown) talent. Adapted by Wrye from Samuel Shem's novel; never released theatrically. [R]

House of Mirth, The (2000-British-U.S.) **C-140m.** ✱✱½ D: Terence Davies. Gillian Anderson, Eric Stoltz, Dan Aykroyd, Eleanor Bron, Terry Kinney, Anthony LaPaglia, Laura Linney, Elizabeth McGovern, Jodhi May. Faithful but mirthless adaptation of Edith Wharton novel about a beautiful woman who is ostracized from N.Y. society at the turn of the 20th century because she doesn't "play the game." Deadly slow, the film gets more interesting as it goes along . . . but a more charismatic leading actress might have helped. Exquisitely mounted production. Arriscope. [PG] ▼)

House of 1000 Corpses (2003) **C-88m.** BOMB D: Rob Zombie. Sid Haig, Bill Moseley, Sheri Moon, Karen Black, Chris Hardwick, Erin Daniels, Jennifer Jostyn, Rainn Wilson, Tom Towles, Dennis Fimple, Michael J. Pollard, Jeanne Carmen. A night of blood-drenched terror begins when two morons and their girlfriends pay a visit to Captain Spaulding's Museum of Monsters and Madmen. This infantile ROCKY HORROR PICTURE SHOW/TEXAS CHAIN SAW MASSACRE wannabe sacrifices genuine scares for gratuitous gore and nonstop profanity. Rocker Zombie, who has a genuine fondness for horror films, pointlessly sprinkles in vintage movie/TV clips. Filmed in 2000. Followed by THE DEVIL'S REJECTS. [R]▼▶

House of Sand, The (2005-Brazilian) **C-115m.** *** D: Andrucha Waddington. Fernanda Montenegro, Fernanda Torres, Ruy Guerra, Seu Jorge, Luiz Melodia, Enrique Díaz, Stênio Garcia, Emiliano Queiroz. Sensuous story begins as a crazed man drags his wife (and her mother) to a remote spot in the Brazilian desert where he plans to build a home. The women remain and create a life for themselves away from civilization, spilling into the next generation—and in spite of the daughter's determination to get out. The female stars (who are real-life mother and daughter) exchange roles in a near-mystical passage of 59 years as this unique, cosmic drama unfolds. Super 35. [R]▶

House of Sand and Fog (2003) **C-126m.** ***½ D: Vadim Perelman. Jennifer Connelly, Ben Kingsley, Ron Eldard, Frances Fisher, Kim Dickens, Shohreh Aghdashloo, Jonathan Ahdout, Navi Rawat. A lost soul (Connelly) is evicted from her house overlooking the ocean. The county sells it, at a bargain price, to an Iranian ex-colonel now living in diminished circumstances who hopes to resell it for a profit. This sets Connelly and Kingsley on a collision course that wreaks havoc neither one can foresee. There's not a false move or a wasted moment in this exquisitely rendered, emotionally devastating film. Impressive feature debut for director Perelman, who adapted the screenplay with Shawn Otto from Andre Dubus III's best-selling novel. [R] ▼▶

House of Seven Corpses, The (1973) **C-90m.** ** D: Paul Harrison. John Ireland, Faith Domergue, John Carradine, Carole Wells, Charles Macaulay, Jerry Strickler. A movie crew uses a house with a notorious past for location work on a horror film, and learns to regret it; low budget, but not bad. [PG]▼▶

House of Strangers (1949) **101m.** *** D: Joseph L. Mankiewicz. Edward G. Robinson, Susan Hayward, Richard Conte, Luther Adler, Efrem Zimbalist, Jr., Debra Paget, Hope Emerson, Esther Minciotti. Dynamic drama of ruthless financier Robinson who uses his four sons to suit his own schemes. Unique plot line has been utilized in various disguises for many subsequent films—most memorably, five years later in the Western BROKEN LANCE and as THE BIG SHOW (1961). ▼▶

House of the Dead (2003-U.S.-German-Canadian) **C-92m.** BOMB D: Uwe Boll. Jonathan Cherry, Tyron Leitso, Clint Howard, Ona Grauer, Ellie Cornell, Will Sanderson, Enuka Okuma, Jürgen Prochnow. Low-grade horror movie, based on the video-game series, which charts the all-too-predictable fates of some addle-brained young people drawn to an island inhabited by zombies. Sloppily made and mind-numbingly

inept. Prochnow's character is named Captain Kirk. How clever! Followed by a TVM, HOUSE OF THE DEAD 2. [R] ▼▶

House of the Devil, The (2009) **C-95m.** **½ D: Ti West. Jocelin Donahue, Tom Noonan, Mary Woronov, Greta Gerwig, Dee Wallace, AJ Bowen. College sophomore Donahue, in dire need of cash, answers an ad for a babysitter—much to her regret. Refreshingly old-fashioned horror chiller is a throwback to late 1970s/early '80s shockers as it metes out scares without depending on graphic gore and computer-generated effects; if only it didn't have so many dull stretches along the way. West scripted and edited. [R] ▶

House of the Long Shadows (1983-British) **C-96m.** *½ D: Pete Walker. Vincent Price, Christopher Lee, Peter Cushing, Desi Arnaz, Jr., John Carradine, Sheila Keith, Julie Peasgood, Richard Todd. Arnaz, Jr. single-handedly sinks this sixth screen version of George M. Cohan's spoof, SEVEN KEYS TO BALDPATE, miscast as a mystery writer staying the night in a spooky mansion on a bet with Todd. Notable only for its historic teaming of four all-time horror masters, all wasted in small roles. [PG]▼▶

House of the Seven Gables, The (1940) **89m.** *** D: Joe May. George Sanders, Margaret Lindsay, Vincent Price, Nan Grey, Alan Napier, Cecil Kellaway, Dick Foran. Good adaptation of Hawthorne's classic novel. Set in 19th-century New England; conniving Sanders frames his brother, Price, for murder of their father in effort to cheat him out of inheritance. Fine performances from all. Price also appeared in TWICE-TOLD TALES, which includes abbreviated version of *Seven Gables* novel.▼▶

House of the Spirits, The (1993-German-Danish-Portuguese-U.S.) **C-138m.** ** D: Bille August. Jeremy Irons, Meryl Streep, Glenn Close, Winona Ryder, Vanessa Redgrave, Armin Mueller-Stahl, Antonio Banderas, Maria Conchita Alonso, Miriam Colon, Vincent Gallo, Jan Niklas, Teri Polo. Epic South American saga that follows a prominent family's turbulent life from the 1920s through the early '70s. Heavy with portent—and clearly written by someone for whom English is not a first language—this sprawling story tries to incorporate the mysticism of Isabel Allende's bestselling novel with sputtering results. Streep is badly miscast, and Irons struggles with his Hispanic role. Mamie Gummer, Streep's daughter, plays her character as a child. Opened in Europe at 145m. Panavision. [R]▼●▶

House of Usher (1960) **C-85m.** ***½ D: Roger Corman. Vincent Price, Mark Damon, Myrna Fahey, Harry Ellerbe. First-rate horror film based on classic tale by Edgar Allan Poe. When beautiful young girl's suitor arrives to ask her hand in marriage, the doors of the house of Usher fling open, and terror begins.

Filmed several times before and since, but never this effectively; a great tour de force for Price. First of Corman's eight Poe adaptations. Aka FALL OF THE HOUSE OF USHER. CinemaScope. ▼●▶

House of Usher, The (1988) C-90m. *½ D: Alan Birkinshaw. Oliver Reed, Donald Pleasence, Romy Windsor, Rufus Swart, Norman Coombes, Anne Stradi. Yet another telling of the Edgar Allan Poe saga is one big yawn, with Reed as Roderick Usher, and Windsor as his prey—the woman who can bear him a son and continue the family name. Filmed in South Africa. [R] ▼●

House of Wax (1953) C-88m. *** D: Andre de Toth. Vincent Price, Frank Lovejoy, Phyllis Kirk, Paul Picerni, Carolyn Jones, Paul Cavanagh, Charles Buchinsky (Bronson). Remake of MYSTERY OF THE WAX MUSEUM stars Price as vengeful sculptor who rebuilds his fire-destroyed showplace by using human victims as wax figures. Jones excellent as an early victim. Most popular of the era's 3-D films, a status it retains today. This is the film that launched Price on his horror film cycle after 15 years of "straight" roles. Love that paddleball man! Remade in 2005. 3-D. ▼●▶

House of Wax (2005-U.S.-Australian) C-105m. ** D: Jaume Collet-Serra. Elisha Cuthbert, Chad Michael Murray, Brian Van Holt, Paris Hilton, Jared Padalecki, Jon Abrahams, Damon Ri'chard, Damon Herriman. A group of friends heading to a college football game take a shortcut, find themselves stranded, get separated, stumble into a deserted town, and enter a house of wax with a "closed" sign on the door. Plays like a mediocre 1970s slasher flick, but with contemporary, "fleshed-out" characters. An in-name-only remake of the 1953 movie, though the wax sculptor *is* named Vincent. [R] ▼▶

House of Yes, The (1997) C-90m. **½ D: Mark Waters. Parker Posey, Josh Hamilton, Tori Spelling, Freddie Prinze, Jr., Genevieve Bujold, Rachael Leigh Cook. On a stormy night in 1983, a young man brings his fiancée home to meet his cracked Washington, D.C., family, including his demented twin sister, Jackie-O, whose fantasies about Jacqueline Kennedy have extended to reenacting the JFK assassination—with real bullets. Well-wrought black comedy, based on the stage play by Wendy MacLeod, here not quite escapes being a "play on film." Strong performances, led by Posey's, make this worth a look. [R] ▼●▶

House on Carroll Street, The (1988) C-100m. ** D: Peter Yates. Kelly McGillis, Jeff Daniels, Mandy Patinkin, Christopher Rhode, Jessica Tandy, Jonathan Hogan, Trey Wilson. McGillis, who's just lost her job after being branded a subversive during the McCarthy era, stumbles onto a strange espionage plot that's being covered up and gradually

persuades FBI agent Daniels that she's on to something big. Finely detailed period piece set in 1950s N.Y.C. starts off well, then chucks its relevance (and believability) for a melodramatic finale filmed à la Hitchcock at Grand Central Station . . . leaving a passel of plot holes and unanswered questions. A real disappointment from onetime blacklisted writer Walter Bernstein. Patinkin is excellent as Roy Cohn–type attorney. [PG] ▼●▶

House on Haunted Hill (1958) 75m. *** D: William Castle. Vincent Price, Carol Ohmart, Richard Long, Alan Marshal, Elisha Cook, Jr., Carolyn Craig, Leona Anderson. Zillionaire Price offers group of people $10,000 each if they'll spend a night in spooky old mansion with murder-laden history; he even provides loaded guns as party favors. Campy fun. Originally presented theatrically with flying skeleton gimmick "Emergo." Remade in 1999. ▼●▶

House on Haunted Hill (1999) C-93m. *½ D: William Malone. Geoffrey Rush, Famke Janssen, Taye Diggs, Bridgette Wilson, Peter Gallagher, Chris Kattan, Ali Larter, Max Perlich, Jeffrey Combs, Lisa Loeb. Dreary remake of the 1958 movie, with two obnoxious "hosts"—a venomous married couple (Rush, Janssen)—having a party whose guest list is comprised of five strangers. Each one can win a million dollars for surviving the night in a former sanitarium with a bloodstained past. Heavy-handed, and no fun at all. Followed by a direct-to-DVD sequel. [R] ▼●▶

House on 92nd Street, The (1945) 88m. ***½ D: Henry Hathaway. William Eythe, Lloyd Nolan, Signe Hasso, Gene Lockhart, Leo G. Carroll, Lydia St. Clair; narrated by Reed Hadley. Exciting, trend-setting documentary-style drama—based on fact and staged on actual locations—about FBI counterespionage activities during WW2: Nazi agents, operating in N.Y.C., attempt to pilfer part of the atom bomb formula. Charles G. Booth earned an Oscar for his original story. Screenplay by Booth, Barre Lyndon, and John Monks, Jr. Look for E. G. Marshall, in film debut. Followed by THE STREET WITH NO NAME (1948). ▼▶

House on Telegraph Hill, The (1951) 93m. **½ D: Robert Wise. Richard Basehart, Valentina Cortese, William Lundigan, Fay Baker. Good cast in intriguing tale of WW2 refugee assuming dead woman's identity so that she can come to San Francisco where wealthy relatives reside. ▶

House Party (1990) C-100m. *** D: Reginald Hudlin. Christopher Reid, Robin Harris, Christopher Martin, Martin Lawrence, Tisha Campbell, A. J. Johnson, Paul Anthony. Infectiously good-natured comedy about urban black teenagers and the events leading up to (and following) a house party one night. Upbeat and imaginative, cast with real-life music rappers (including

Reid, who plays the leading role of Kid). A solid feature debut for young writer-director Hudlin. Followed by animated TV series *Kid 'n Play* and three sequels. [R]▼●▶

House Party 2 (1991) **C-94m.** ** D: Doug McHenry, George Jackson. Christopher Reid, Christopher Martin, Eugene Allen, George Anthony Bell, Georg Stanford Brown, Tony Burton, Tisha Campbell, Iman, Kamron, Queen Latifah, Martin Lawrence, William Schallert. Uninspired sequel has Kid (Reid) heading off to college—if he can just hold on to the money his church congregation has raised to send him there. Reid is still appealing, but this fragmented film has little to offer, in spite of its social-consciousness rhetoric and get-an-education "message." [R]▼●▶

House Party 3 (1994) **C-94m.** *½ D: Eric Meza. Christopher Reid, Christopher Martin, David Edwards, Angela Means, Tisha Campbell, Bernie Mac, Gilbert Gottfried, Ketty Lester. Kid, amid jitters over his impending marriage, is trying to make it in music management by signing a feisty female rap group and dodging a vindictive tour promoter. Scattershot chuckles, but coarse, crude, and misogynistic, unlike the original. More hangover than beer blast. [R]▼●▶

HouseSitter (1992) **C-102m.** ** D: Frank Oz. Steve Martin, Goldie Hawn, Dana Delany, Julie Harris, Donald Moffat, Peter MacNicol, Richard B. Shull, Laurel Cronin, Christopher Durang, Cherry Jones. Unusual hybrid of comedy, farce, and screwball romance that doesn't know what it's trying to be. Martin plays a New England architect who meets kooky nonconformist Hawn; in no time she's moved into the vacant dream home he'd intended for Delany and begun spinning lies about being his Mrs. Laughs throughout, and the stars do their best, but the film is painfully Hollywood-cookie-cutter in form. [PG]▼●▶

House That Dripped Blood, The (1970-British) **C-101m.** **½ D: Peter Duffell. John Bennett, John Bryans, Denholm Elliott, Joanna Dunham, Tom Adams, Peter Cushing, Christopher Lee, Nyree Dawn Porter, Jon Pertwee, Ingrid Pitt. Entertaining four-part horror film written by Robert Bloch with a bit too much tongue in cheek, revolving around suitably creepy-looking mansion purchased by new, hesitant owner. Best segments: first and last. [PG]▼▶

House That Screamed, The (1970-Spanish) **C-94m.** *½ D: Narciso Ibanez Serrador. Lilli Palmer, Chistina Galbo, John Moulder-Brown, Mary Maude, Candida Losada. Grisly horror at a home for troubled girls, where disciplinarian Palmer and her sex-starved son (Brown) make life difficult—to say the least—for the young ladies. Franscope. [PG]▶

House Where Evil Dwells, The (1982) **C-88m.** ** D: Kevin Connor. Edward Albert, Susan George, Doug McClure, Amy Barrett, Mako Hattori, Toshiyuki Sasaki,

Toshiya Maruyama. American family moves into stylish old house in Kyoto, Japan, ignoring warnings that it's haunted by ghosts of doomed 19th-century love triangle. A few new twists can't relieve familiar formula and general air of silliness. Quite violent at times. [R]▼▶

How About You . . . (2007-Irish) **C-91m.** ** D: Anthony Byrne. Vanessa Redgrave, Imelda Staunton, Brenda Fricker, Hayley Atwell, Joss Ackland, Orla Brady, Joan O'Hara. Young Atwell comes to work in a residential home whose aging inhabitants are mostly eccentric or crotchety. What might have been an appealing tale of intergenerational bonding is ill conceived and often downright silly. Livens up in Atwell's all-too-brief scenes with elderly, dying O'Hara. Based on a short story by Maeve Binchy. Super 35.▶

Howards End (1992-British) **C-140m.** **** D: James Ivory. Anthony Hopkins, Vanessa Redgrave, Helena Bonham Carter, Emma Thompson, James Wilby, Sam West, Jemma Redgrave, Nicola Duffett, Prunella Scales. Sumptuous, stimulating adaptation of E. M. Forster's novel of class distinction—and what happens when members of different social strata collide in 1910 England. Thompson won an Oscar for her terrific performance as an audacious and independent young woman of no means who is ever-so-subtly seduced by Hopkins, a successful man whose social veneer masks an insidious (and even cruel) nature. Extraordinarily good on every level. Also won Oscars for Best Screenplay (by Ruth Prawer Jhabvala) and Art Direction–Set Decoration. Simon Callow appears unbilled as a lecturer. Super 35. [PG]▼●▶

Howards of Virginia, The (1940) **122m.** **½ D: Frank Lloyd. Cary Grant, Martha Scott, Cedric Hardwicke, Alan Marshal, Richard Carlson, Paul Kelly, Irving Bacon. Historical account of Revolutionary War is OK, but too long for such standard retelling. Look for young Peter Cushing.▼▶

Howard Stern's Private Parts SEE: **Private Parts**

Howard the Duck (1986) **C-111m.** BOMB D: Willard Huyck. Lea Thompson, Jeffrey Jones, Tim Robbins, Paul Guilfoyle, Holly Robinson, Miles Chapin, Virginia Capers, David Paymer, Thomas Dolby; voice of Richard Kiley. Steve Gerber's sarcastic comic-book creation is (unwisely) turned into a live-action character for this hopeless mess of a movie set in Cleveland. Gargantuan production produces gargantuan headache. Executive produced, but disowned, by George Lucas. [PG]▼●▶

How Do I Love Thee? (1970) **C-110m.** *½ D: Michael Gordon. Jackie Gleason, Maureen O'Hara, Shelley Winters, Rosemary Forsyth, Rick Lenz, Clinton Robinson. Pleasant cast can't do much for sloppily sentimental film about Gleason's inability to relate to his son, a philosophy professor. Plays like a TV show, a bad one at that. [PG]▼

How Do You Know (2010) **C-116m. *½** D: James L. Brooks. Reese Witherspoon, Owen Wilson, Paul Rudd, Jack Nicholson, Kathryn Hahn, Mark Linn-Baker, Lenny Venito, Molly Price, Ron McLarty, Tony Shalhoub. A highly motivated athlete who's just been dropped by her team (Witherspoon) and a somewhat dim-witted "nice guy" who's just been screwed by the company his father runs (Rudd) chance to meet and might be soul mates. Or maybe not. Or maybe they should talk about it some more. Muddled mess of a movie is not writer-director Brooks' finest two hours or a particularly good showcase for anyone except Witherspoon, who's never looked more glamorous. [PG-13] ◗

How Funny Can Sex Be? (1976-Italian) **C-97m. **½** D: Dino Risi. Giancarlo Giannini, Laura Antonelli, Alberto Lionello, Duilio Del Prete, Paola Borboni, Carla Mancini. Eight bawdy episodes on love, sex, and marriage. More misses than hits, but buoyed by Giannini's comic prowess and Antonelli's tantalizing beauty. Released here after Giannini's success in Wertmuller films. [R]▼

How Green Was My Valley (1941) **118m. ****** D: John Ford. Walter Pidgeon, Maureen O'Hara, Donald Crisp, Anna Lee, Master Roddy McDowall, John Loder, Sara Allgood, Barry Fitzgerald, Patric Knowles, Rhys Williams, Arthur Shields, Ann (E.) Todd, Mae Marsh; narrated by Irving Pichel; United Kingdom version narrated by Rhys Williams. Moving drama from Richard Llewellyn's story of Welsh coal miners, centering on Crisp's large, close-knit family. Beautifully filmed, lovingly directed, winner of five Academy Awards: Best Picture, Director, Supporting Actor (Crisp), Cinematography (Arthur Miller), Art Direction. Screenplay by Philip Dunne. ▼◗◗

How High (2001) **C-93m. **** D: Jesse Dylan. Method Man, Redman, Lark Voohries, Obba Babatundé, Mike Epps, Fred Willard, Anna Maria Horsford, Chuck Davis, Jeffrey Jones, Spalding Gray, Hector Elizondo, Tracey Walter, Tracy Morgan, Judah Friedlander. With Willard playing the chancellor of Harvard and Bob Dylan's son directing, this rare Ivy League stoner comedy has a curio advantage going in. Film's rapper leads play goof-offs who finesse their entrance exams by smoking the mind-expanding ashes of a dead friend. (Who says the spirit of Lubitsch is dead?) Movie has enough low-grade laughs to sustain its length, though there have probably been cockfights with more redeeming social value. [R]▼◗

How I Got Into College (1989) **C-89m. ** D: Savage Steve Holland. Anthony Edwards, Corey Parker, Lara Flynn Boyle, Finn Carter, Charles Rocket, Christopher Rydell, Brian Doyle-Murray, Richard Jenkins, Nora Dunn, Phil Hartman. Aimless senior applies to a small college because his high-achiever dream girl is doing the same, and gets caught up in the cutthroat recruitment machine. Mild execution of ripe satirical premise, buoyed by fantasy set pieces associated with director Holland's previous work. Has its moments, but not enough of them. [PG-13] ▼◗

How I Killed My Father (2001-French-Spanish) **C-95m. *** D: Anne Fontaine. Michel Bouquet, Charles Berling, Natacha Régnier, Amira Casar, Stéphane Guillon, Hubert Koundé, Karole Rocher, François Berléand. A doctor (Berling) whose specialty is slowing down the aging process among his wealthy clientele learns that his long-estranged father (Bouquet) has died unexpectedly. In a flash, he recalls their last extended meeting—or is this reunion all in his mind? Quietly devastating character study emphasizes the enduring impact parents have on children. Aka MY FATHER AND I.◗

How I Won the War (1967-British) **C-109m. *** D: Richard Lester. Michael Crawford, John Lennon, Roy Kinnear, Jack MacGowran, Michael Hordern, Lee Montague, Alexander Knox. Pungent, if occasionally overbaked, account of a middle-aged veteran whose pompous reminiscenses of his wartime heroics cannot obscure his ineptitude in battle. A deliciously cynical parody of the lunacy of war. Interesting to see Lennon in one of his very few acting roles, as the Cockney Gripweed. ▼◗◗

Howl (2010) **C/B&W-84m. *** D: Rob Epstein, Jeffrey Friedman. James Franco, David Strathairn, Jon Hamm, Bob Balaban, Alessandro Nivola, Treat Williams, Mary-Louise Parker, Jeff Daniels, Aaron Tveit, Todd Rotondi, Jon Prescott. Unusual, provocative, seminarrative film from documentarians Epstein and Friedman about the creation of Allen Ginsberg's landmark poem and its impact on the cultural landscape of the 1950s. Effectively blends a re-creation of Ginsberg (Franco) reading the poem at San Francisco's City Lights bookstore in 1955 and responding to an interviewer's questions about his life; the 1957 obscenity trial of *Howl*'s publisher, Lawrence Ferlinghetti; and some dazzling animation. Images of the real individuals portrayed are cleverly integrated with those of Franco and the other actors. [R] ◗

Howling, The (1981) **C-91m. *** D: Joe Dante. Dee Wallace, Patrick Macnee, Dennis Dugan, Christopher Stone, Belinda Balaski, Kevin McCarthy, John Carradine, Slim Pickens, Elisabeth Brooks, Robert Picardo, Noble Willingham, Kenneth Tobey, Dick Miller, Meshach Taylor. A female TV news reporter is sent to a strange California encounter-group community to recover from a sexual trauma, unaware that virtually everyone there is a werewolf. A hip, well-made horror film, brimming with film-buff jokes (almost every character is named after a werewolf-movie director) and Rob Bottin's amazing wolf transformations. Only complaint: Why set the horror against such a patently bizarre backdrop? Coscripter John Sayles has a funny cameo as a morgue attendant. Followed by several so-called sequels. [R]▼●▶

Howling II: Your Sister Is a Werewolf (1985) **C-90m.** BOMB D: Philippe Mora. Christopher Lee, Annie McEnroe, Reb Brown, Sybil Danning, Marsha A. Hunt, Ferdy Mayne. Ridiculous sequel is set in Transylvania where unlikely siblings Danning and Lee head up a family of werewolves. Attempt at sending up the genre falls flat. [R]▼●▶

Howling III (1987-Australian) **C-94m.** ** D: Philippe Mora. Barry Otto, Imogen Annesley, Dasha Blahova, Max Fairchild, Frank Thring, Michael Pate, Barry Humphries. OK horror spoof stars Annesley, a Kim Basinger-like beauty, as an Australian marsupial werewolf, who gives birth to a cute little creature that lives in a pouch on her belly. Unusual addition to werewolf genre features some funny cameos, including Thring as an Alfred Hitchcock–style director. [PG-13]▼●▶

Howling IV: The Original Nightmare (1988-British) **C-92m.** BOMB D: John Hough, Romy Windsor, Michael T. Weiss, Anthony Hamilton, Susanne Severeid. Being based somewhat more closely on Gary Bradner's original novel doesn't save this film from being a turkey in wolf's clothing. Isolated in a distant cabin, a young woman battles werewolves, including her boyfriend, a newly minted howler. Shot in South Africa, unsuccessfully passing itself off as California. Poor makeup effects. [R]▼●▶

Howling V: The Rebirth (1989) **C-99m.** ** D: Neal Sundstrom. Victoria Catlin, Elizabeth Silverstein, Mark Faulkner, Stephanie Shockley, William Stavin. Much better than II or IV, this still suffers from a very low budget—so low there are no werewolves to be seen! All the hairy monster stuff takes place off-screen in this variation on *Ten Little Indians,* as a group in a picturesque old castle is knocked off one by one by the secret werewolf among them. Some suspense, OK performances, and a genuine surprise at the end. [R]▼●▶

Howling VI—The Freaks (1991) **C-102m.** *½ D: Hope Perello. Brendan Hughes, Michelle Matheson, Bruce Martyn Payne, Jered Barclay, Sean Gregory Sullivan, Antonio Fargas, Carlos Cervantes. This time the werewolf is the hero, a drifter who turns up in a Southwestern desert town just ahead of a circus full of monsters. Intelligently written, especially for this series, but pretentious, with vague Ray Bradburyesque

overtones. Awkward and confusing, of appeal to buffs only. [R]▼●▶

Howl's Moving Castle (2004-Japanese) **C-119m.** ***½ D: Hayao Miyazaki. Voices of Christian Bale, Jean Simmons, Billy Crystal, Lauren Bacall, Emily Mortimer, Blythe Danner, Josh Hutcherson, Jena Malone, Moosie Drier. A girl falls under the spell of a witch and is transformed into a wrinkled old woman . . . but in her new form she acquires a sense of daring and wisdom she never had before, especially when she discovers a magical moving castle. This mystical fable offers a unique experience. It asks the viewer to take a leap of faith—and then offers constant surprise, turning from humor to sadness to a sense of wonder in the blink of an eye. Animation master Miyazaki adapted Diana Wynne Jones' novel. Simmons, Bacall, and Crystal contribute rich vocal performances to the U.S. version. [PG]▶

How She Move (2008-Canadian) **C-91m.** ** D: Ian Iqbal Rashid. Rutina Wesley, Tré Armstrong, Clé Bennett, Melanie Nicholls-King, Brennan Gademans, Dwain Murphy, Keyshia Cole, DeRay Davis. Utterly predictable story about a young girl who, after her sister's death, returns to her old neighborhood in the Caribbean projects of Toronto. To earn college tuition money she decides to compete in step-dancing competitions. Mediocre in every way; the dancing and music are uninspired, and they're supposed to drive the film. [PG-13]▶

How Stella Got Her Groove Back (1998) **C-124m.** ** D: Kevin Rodney Sullivan. Angela Bassett, Taye Diggs, Regina King, Whoopi Goldberg, Suzzanne Douglas, Michael J. Pagan, Sicily, Richard Lawson, Barry Shabaka Henley, Glynn Turman, Carl Lumbly. Tight-midriffed San Francisco stockbroker, age 40, romances the 20-year-old med-school hopeful she meets while vacationing in Jamaica, setting off a wave of *tsk-tsk*-ing among her friends and his parents. Overlong and dull, this occasionally lush version of Terry McMillan's novel might be more convincing if Bassett didn't look more like a 25-year-old knockout. Subplot about Goldberg's illness and subsequent hospitalization helps keep the film from getting *into* a groove. [R]▼●▶

How Sweet It Is! (1968) **C-99m.** *½ D: Jerry Paris. James Garner, Debbie Reynolds, Maurice Ronet, Paul Lynde, Marcel Dalio, Terry-Thomas. Married couple with teenage son goes to Europe to revitalize themselves, but Mom starts to dally with sexy Frenchman. Bland comedy looks like a TV show and is about as memorable. Watch for Penny Marshall as one of the Tour Girls. Panavision. ▼▶

How the Garcia Girls Spent Their Summer (2008) **C-128m.** *** D: Georgina Garcia Riedel. Elizabeth Peña, America

Ferrera, Lucy Gallardo, Steven Bauer, Jorge Cervera, Jr., Leo Minaya. Sharply observed and sympathetically detailed dramedy about the romantic entanglements of three generations of Mexican-American women—aging grandmother (Gallardo), divorced mother (Peña), 17-year-old daughter (Ferrera)—in a sleepy Arizona border town. Funny and insightful, but be forewarned: this SUMMER proceeds at the pace of someone amiably drifting through a hot August afternoon. Filmed before, but released after, Ferrera hit it big on TV's *Ugly Betty*. Panavision. [R]▶

How the Grinch Stole Christmas (2000) **C-105m.** *½ D: Ron Howard. Jim Carrey, Jeffrey Tambor, Christine Baranski, Bill Irwin, Molly Shannon, Clint Howard, Taylor Momsen; narrated by Anthony Hopkins. Cheerless bastardization of the beloved children's book by Dr. Seuss about a dastardly creature's attempt to rob Whoville of its yuletide holiday. Carrey is good, but the film is loud and cluttered, losing all the charm of the sweet, simple source material. Only good songs are two holdovers from the vastly superior 1966 animated TV special. Rick Baker and Gail Ryan won Oscars for Best Makeup. Full title is DR. SEUSS' HOW THE GRINCH STOLE CHRISTMAS. Later a Broadway musical. Bah, humbug! [PG]▼▶

How the West Was Won (1962) **C-155m.** ***½ D: John Ford ("The Civil War"), Henry Hathaway ("The Rivers, The Plains, The Outlaws"), George Marshall ("The Railroad"). Carroll Baker, Henry Fonda, Gregory Peck, George Peppard, Carolyn Jones, Eli Wallach, Robert Preston, Debbie Reynolds, James Stewart, John Wayne, Richard Widmark, All-Star Cast; narrated by Spencer Tracy. Blockbuster epic about three generations of Western pioneers isn't same experience seen at home as it is on a Cinerama screen, but great cast, first-rate photography and lovely Alfred Newman score still make it top entertainment. Peppard stands out with excellent portrayal. This won Oscars for Story and Screenplay (James R. Webb) and Editing (Harold F. Kress). Cinerama. ▼●▶

How to Beat the High Co$t of Living (1980) **C-110m.** *½ D: Robert Scheerer. Susan Saint James, Jane Curtin, Jessica Lange, Richard Benjamin, Cathryn Damon, Fred Willard, Dabney Coleman, Eddie Albert, Art Metrano, Garrett Morris. Thoroughly blah caper comedy by Bob Kaufman about three housewives who plot a heist at the local shopping center. Worth a glance to see Coleman in rare romantic lead . . . and Saint James and Curtin years before they clicked together as *Kate and Allie* on TV. [PG]▼▶

How to Be Very, Very Popular (1955) **C-89m.** **½ D: Nunnally Johnson. Betty Grable, Robert Cummings, Charles Coburn, Sheree North, Fred Clark, Alice Pearce, Orson Bean. Grable and North on the lam hide in a college fraternity in this semi-remake

of SHE LOVES ME NOT. Sheree does wild "Shake, Rattle and Roll" number, stealing Grable's spotlight. This was Betty's last movie. CinemaScope.

How to Commit Marriage (1969) **C-95m.** ** D: Norman Panama. Bob Hope, Jackie Gleason, Jane Wyman, Maureen Arthur, Tim Matheson, Leslie Nielsen, Tina Louise, Irwin Corey. Above average for later Hope movies, but still mediocre. Hope and Wyman are about to divorce when their daughter announces plans to marry Gleason's son. "Mod" elements of script were already dated when film came out. [M/PG]▼▶

How to Deal (2003) **C-101m.** ** D: Clare Kilner. Mandy Moore, Allison Janney, Trent Ford, Alexandra Holden, Dylan Baker, Nina Foch, Mackenzie Astin, Connie Ray, Mary Catherine Garrison. Dealing with a divorced mom and a pregnant best friend, a teenage girl vows never to fall in love. Dull attempt at dramedy isn't helped by Moore's uninteresting lead performance. Only the older generation here—Janney, Baker, and Foch as a grandmother who tokes marijuana for "medicinal" reasons—have any fun, though the dotty grandma bit has been overdone by now. Based on two of Sarah Dessen's popular teen novels. Peter Gallagher appears unbilled as Moore's hipster radio DJ dad. [PG-13]▼▶

How to Eat Fried Worms (2006) **C-83m.** **½ D: Bob Dolman. Luke Benward, Hallie Kate Eisenberg, Adam Hicks, Austin Rogers, Alexander Gould, Ryan Malgarini, Philip Daniel Bolden, Clint Howard, Ty Panitz, Kimberly Williams-Paisley, Tom Cavanagh, James Rebhorn. Cooked in Crisco. Mixed with marshmallow. Peanut butter and worm sandwich. These are some of the ways that the new kid in school must dine on phylum Annelida to win a bet and prove a point. Brightly adapted from Thomas Rockwell's 1973 classic novel of preadolescent crudity, this is one big gross-out joke that, while a family movie, is so not a popcorn movie. Young Benward is an appealing hero. Super 35. [PG]▶

How to Frame a Figg (1971) **C-103m.** ** D: Alan Rafkin. Don Knotts, Joe Flynn, Elaine Joyce, Edward Andrews, Yvonne Craig. Simplistic chap (Knotts) finds trouble behind every doorway as he is made patsy for crooked politicians. Usual unsubtle Knotts comedy. [G]▼▶

How to Get Ahead in Advertising (1989-British) **C-95m.** **½ D: Bruce Robinson. Richard E. Grant, Rachel Ward, Richard Wilson, Jacqueline Tong, John Shrapnel, Susan Wooldridge, Mick Ford. Advertising hotshot Grant is under so much pressure—and has become so negative about his manipulative profession—that his anxiety brings forth a talking boil on his shoulder with a mind of its own! Certifiably weird comedy by writer-director Robinson (reunited with the star of his first film, WITHNAIL AND I) has its share of funny and bizarre moments, but its attack on advertising is so heavy-handed that as satire it fizzles. [R]▼●)

How to Kill Your Neighbor's Dog (2001-U.S.-German) **C-107m.** *** D: Michael Kalesniko. Kenneth Branagh, Robin Wright Penn, Suzi Hofrichter, Lynn Redgrave, Jared Harris, Lucinda Jenney, Peter Riegert, Peri Gilpin, Tamala Jones, David Krumholtz, Johnathon Schaech. Sardonic playwright whose career is in a slump grapples with his wife's desire to have a baby. Meanwhile, a cute little girl moves in across the street and begins to affect the man's outlook—and even his work. Glib and funny, Kalesniko's screenplay deepens as it progresses with fine performances by Branagh, Penn, and young Hofrichter. Refreshingly unconventional comedy made its U.S. debut on cable TV. Daniel Stern appears unbilled. [R]▼)

How to Lose a Guy in 10 Days (2003) **C-115m.** ** D: Donald Petrie. Kate Hudson, Matthew McConaughey, Michael Michele, Shalom Harlow, Adam Goldberg, Bebe Neuwirth, Robert Klein, Kathryn Hahn, Thomas Lennon, Annie Parisse, Celia Weston, Liliane Montevecchi. Airy romantic comedy about a women's-magazine writer who takes on the challenge of attracting—and then driving away—a man, for the sake of an article, never dreaming that the man she chooses has taken a bet that he can woo and win her. The stars are attractive, though Hudson is obliged to act obnoxious—and is apparently shot through layers of gauze. Diverting for a while, but overlong, and there's barely an honest moment in the film. [PG-13]▼)

How to Lose Friends & Alienate People (2008-U.S.-British) **C-109m.** *** D: Robert Weide. Simon Pegg, Kirsten Dunst, Jeff Bridges, Danny Huston, Gillian Anderson, Megan Fox, Miriam Margolyes, Bill Paterson, Max Minghella, Diana Kent, Thandie Newton. Snarky British journalist Pegg desperately wants to be on the inside of the glamour scene and gets the opportunity when N.Y. magazine editor Bridges hires him. His obnoxious, bull-in-a-china-shop behavior is nearly his undoing until he learns to play the game—and gets to score with a sexy starlet (Fox). Drawn from Toby Young's book about working for *Vanity Fair*, with Bridges having fun as a Graydon Carter type. A sharp look at our celebrity culture. Alternately silly and clever; well cast from top to bottom. [R])

How to Make an American Quilt (1995) **C-116m.** ** D: Jocelyn Moorhouse. Winona Ryder, Ellen Burstyn, Anne Bancroft, Maya Angelou, Kate Nelligan, Jean Simmons, Samantha Mathis, Alfre Woodard, Lois Smith, Kate Capshaw, Johnathon Schaech, Holland Taylor, Maria Celedonio, Claire Danes, Loren Dean, Melinda Dillon, Dermot Mulroney, Derrick O'Connor, Esther Rolle, Rip Torn, Mykelti Williamson, Alicia (Lecy) Goranson, Adam Baldwin, Richard Jenkins, Jared Leto. Aimless young woman leaves her fiancé behind to spend the summer with her grandmother and great-aunt. Soon she's delving into their lives and the experiences of their female friends who work together in a non-stop quilting bee. Episodic "woman's film" (based on Whitney Otto's novel) offers at least one flashback too many in its quiltlike pattern. It's genteel, good looking, and well acted, but has no narrative momentum. [PG-13]▼●)

How to Make It SEE: **Target: Harry**

How to Marry a Millionaire (1953) **C-95m.** *** D: Jean Negulesco. Marilyn Monroe, Betty Grable, Lauren Bacall, William Powell, Rory Calhoun, David Wayne, Alex D'Arcy, Fred Clark, Cameron Mitchell. Terrific ensemble work in dandy comedy of three man-hunting females pooling resources to trap eligible bachelors. Nunnally Johnson scripted and produced this remake of THE GREEKS HAD A WORD FOR THEM, which is preceded by Alfred Newman conducting his famed "Street Scene" theme (a prologue designed to show off stereophonic sound). Look for George Chakiris in the chorus. CinemaScope.▼●)

How to Murder Your Wife (1965) **C-118m.** *** D: Richard Quine. Jack Lemmon, Virna Lisi, Terry-Thomas, Eddie Mayehoff, Claire Trevor, Sidney Blackmer, Max Showalter, Jack Albertson, Mary Wickes. Engaging comedy that almost holds up to finale. Cartoonist Lemmon marries Lisi while drunk and spends rest of film devising ways to get rid of her. Mayehoff is standout as Lemmon's lawyer friend.▼●)

How to Save a Marriage And Ruin Your Life (1968) **C-108m.** *½ D: Fielder Cook. Dean Martin, Stella Stevens, Eli Wallach, Anne Jackson, Betty Field, Jack Albertson. Typical 1960s sex farce has swinging bachelor Dino mistaking Stella for his best friend's mistress, with predictable complications. Stevens wasted again. Panavision.)

How to Steal a Million (1966) **C-127m.** *** D: William Wyler. Audrey Hepburn, Peter O'Toole, Charles Boyer, Eli Wallach, Hugh Griffith. Hepburn and O'Toole are a delightful match in this sophisticated comedy about a million-dollar theft in a Paris art museum. Boyer, O'Toole's boss, and Griffith, Hepburn's father, are equally good. Panavision. ▼●)

How to Stuff a Wild Bikini (1965) **C-93m.** ** D: William Asher. Annette Funicello, Dwayne Hickman, Brian Donlevy, Buster Keaton, Mickey Rooney, Harvey Lembeck, Beverly Adams, Jody McCrea, John Ashley, Bobbi Shaw. The fatigue is palpable in this sixth BEACH PARTY movie, which tries out another new leading man (with Frankie

Avalon again shunted to a cameo role). As usual, the veterans—especially Rooney—liven things a little, but overall, pretty mediocre. Followed by GHOST IN THE INVISIBLE BIKINI. Panavision. ▼❚

How to Succeed in Business Without Really Trying (1967) **C-121m.** ***½ D: David Swift. Robert Morse, Michele Lee, Rudy Vallee, Anthony Teague, Maureen Arthur, Sammy Smith, Robert Q. Lewis. Delightful musical from Broadway hit about ambitious window-washer (Morse) who uses wiles, and a handbook, to rise to prominence in Vallee's Worldwide Wicket Co. Superb farce, good Frank Loesser songs (including "Brotherhood of Man" and "I Believe in You"), imaginative staging of musical numbers by Bob Fosse. Panavision. ▼●❚

How to Train Your Dragon (2010) **C-98m.** *** D: Dean DeBlois, Chris Sanders. Voices of Jay Baruchel, Gerard Butler, Craig Ferguson, America Ferrera, Jonah Hill, Christopher Mintz-Plasse, T. J. Miller, Kristen Wiig. Viking warrior's wimpy son Hiccup (who speaks like a modern-day American boy, along with the other kids in the story), can't seem to do anything right—until he brings down a supposedly fearsome dragon who turns out to be a loving pet. His challenge: to keep this a secret from the villagers, and especially his father. Often-enthralling animated feature, adapted from a British series of books by Cressida Cowell; only resorts to formula storytelling at the climax. Inventively staged for the camera, especially in 3-D. Note the resemblance of the dragon, Toothless, to the filmmakers' earlier Disney creation, Stitch, in LILO & STITCH. 3-D Digital Widescreen. [PG]❚

How U Like Me Now (1992) **C-109m.** *** D: Darryl Roberts. Darnell Williams, Salli Richardson, Raymond Whitfield, Daniel Gardner, Byron Stewart, Darryl Roberts, Charnele Brown. Likable comedy of middle and working-class African-American twenty-somethings in Chicago, with the focus on live-in lovers Williams and Richardson, whose relationship is at a crossroads. Refreshingly, none of the characters are stereotypical ghetto cartoons. [R] ▼❚

Huckleberry Finn (1974) **C-118m.** ** D: J. Lee Thompson. Jeff East, Paul Winfield, Harvey Korman, David Wayne, Arthur O'Connell, Gary Merrill. Little of Mark Twain is left in this handsome but empty-headed musical version of his classic story. Score by Richard and Robert Sherman is as forgettable as their script. Panavision. [G] ▼●❚

Hucksters, The (1947) **115m.** *** D: Jack Conway. Clark Gable, Deborah Kerr, Sydney Greenstreet, Adolphe Menjou, Ava Gardner, Keenan Wynn, Edward Arnold. Glossy dig at advertising and radio industries, with Gable battling for integrity among yes-men. Greenstreet memorable as despotic head of soap company; Kerr's first

American movie. Also shown in computer-colored version. ▼●

Hud (1963) **112m.** **** D: Martin Ritt. Paul Newman, Patricia Neal, Melvyn Douglas, Brandon de Wilde, John Ashley. Excellent story of moral degradation set in modern West, with impeccable performances by all. Neal won Best Actress Oscar as family housekeeper who doesn't want to get involved with no-account Newman. Douglas received Best Supporting Oscar as Newman's ethical, uncompromising father, and James Wong Howe's cinematography also earned a statuette. Irving Ravetch and Harriet Frank, Jr. scripted from Larry McMurtry's novel *Horseman, Pass By.* Panavision. ▼●❚

Hudson Hawk (1991) **C-95m.** ** D: Michael Lehmann. Bruce Willis, Danny Aiello, Andie MacDowell, James Coburn, Richard E. Grant, Sandra Bernhard, Donald Burton, Don Harvey, David Caruso, Andrew Bryniarski, Lorraine Toussaint, Frank Stallone, Leonardo Cimino. Wildly overblown vanity film (Willis cowrote the story *and* the title song) about a cat burglar, just sprung from prison, who's blackmailed into performing several daring art heists, including one from the Vatican! Blissfully incoherent, with some good action scenes, but nothing to hang them on except a steady stream of Willis wisecracks, only some of which are funny. [R] ▼●❚

Hudsucker Proxy, The (1994) **C-111m.** *** D: Joel Coen. Tim Robbins, Jennifer Jason Leigh, Paul Newman, Charles Durning, John Mahoney, Jim True, William Cobbs, Bruce Campbell, Joe Grifasi, Peter Gallagher, Noble Willingham, Steve Buscemi, Anna Nicole Smith, Jon Polito. A country bumpkin arrives in the Big City and becomes the unwitting pawn in a scheme to ruin a thriving corporation. The Coen brothers' most extravagant creation to date, an eye-popping '50s fantasy of big business gone berserk, with Robbins absolutely perfect as the wide-eyed patsy who miraculously rises to the top. Newman is a crafty villain, and Leigh is fun (if a bit one-note) as a fast-talking, Kate Hepburn–ish reporter. Written by Ethan and Joel Coen with Sam Raimi; the Coens rival Fellini in the selection of unusual faces to populate their films. [PG] ▼●❚

Hue and Cry (1947-British) **82m.** *** D: Charles Crichton. Alastair Sim, Jack Warner, Valerie White, Harry Fowler, Jack Lambert, Frederick Piper, Joan Dowling. Snappy romp as young Fowler suspects that details in the stories published in his favorite weekly pulp magazine are being used as a code by a gang of crooks. Nicely filmed on location on the streets of post-WW2 London. The first of many good Ealing comedies; written by T.E.B. Clarke. Released in the U.S. in 1950.▼

Huggers SEE: **Crazy Moon**

Hugo Pool (1997) **C-94m.** ** D: Robert Downey. Alyssa Milano, Patrick Dempsey, Cathy Moriarty, Malcolm McDowell, Robert Downey, Jr., Richard Lewis, Sean Penn, Bert Remsen, Chuck Barris, Ann Magnuson. Strained whimsy about an L.A. pool cleaner (Milano) and her dealings with her dysfunctional parents and assorted oddball clients, one of whom—a man suffering from Lou Gehrig's disease—she falls in love with. Self-indulgent shaggy-dog farce comes off like an actors' improv exercise and varies wildly from deadpan absurdist comedy to mawkish sentimentality. Laura Downey (the director's wife) coscripted. [R]▼●◗

Hugo the Hippo (1976) **C-90m.** **½ D: William Feigenbaum. Voices of Burl Ives, Marie and Jimmy Osmond, Robert Morley, Paul Lynde. OK children's cartoon musical about a youngster's attempt to save a hippo from extinction in ancient Zanzibar. [G]▼

Hulk (2003) **C-138m.** **½ D: Ang Lee. Eric Bana, Jennifer Connelly, Sam Elliott, Josh Lucas, Nick Nolte, Kevin Rankin, Celia Weston. Research scientist Bruce Banner represses painful childhood memories that eventually explode and turn him into The Hulk. Only his ex-girlfriend seems to understand his agony, while her father, a general with an age-old chip on his shoulder, wants to bring the big green guy down. Takes its time building character and story, then spoils it with cardboard villains, a heavy-handed KING KONG homage, and a climax where the Hulk bounces around like a video-game character. Even director Lee's ingenious comic-book graphic style wears out its welcome in this overlong, overly serious saga. Lou Ferrigno (TV's The Incredible Hulk) and Marvel's Stan Lee have an amusing cameo together. Based on the comic book created by Lee and Jack Kirby. See also THE INCREDIBLE HULK (2008). [PG-13]▼◗

Hullabaloo Over Georgie and Bonnie's Pictures (1978-British) **C-89m.** *** D: James Ivory. Peggy Ashcroft, Victor Banerjee, Larry Pine, Saeed Jaffrey, Aparna Sen, Jane Booker. Wry comedy about the purpose and significance of art, set in an Indian palace where various people (including a British aristocrat, wonderfully played by Ashcroft) are attempting to acquire several miniature paintings. Deftly scripted by Ruth Prawer Jhabvala. Originally produced for British television.▼◗

Human Beast, The SEE: **La Bête Humaine**

Human Comedy, The (1943) **118m.** ***½ D: Clarence Brown. Mickey Rooney, Frank Morgan, Jackie "Butch" Jenkins, James Craig, Marsha Hunt, Fay Bainter, Ray Collins, Darryl Hickman, Donna Reed, Van Johnson. Memorable Americana, faithfully adapted from William Saroyan's sentimental Oscar-winning story of life in a small town during WW2. Unfolds like a novel, with many lovely vignettes, and one of Rooney's best performances as a teenager with growing responsibilities. Screenplay by Howard

Estabrook. P.S.: Keep an eye out for those three soldiers on leave: Barry Nelson, Don DeFore, and Robert Mitchum! Also shown in computer-colored version.▼●◗

Human Condition, The SEE: **No Greater Love**, **Road to Eternity**, and **Soldier's Prayer, A**

Human Contract, The (2009) **C-107m.** *½ D: Jada Pinkett Smith. Jason Clarke, Paz Vega, Idris Elba, T. J. Thyne, Joanna Cassidy, Steven Brand, Jada Pinkett Smith, Ted Danson, Anne Ramsay, Tava Smiley. Successful L.A. marketing exec (Clarke) on the verge of a big merger finds his life spinning out of control when he falls for a sexy mystery woman (Vega). Meanwhile, he is forced to face his family's troubled past and his own self-destructive impulses. Snail-paced, pretentious writing and directing debut for Pinkett Smith begins as a formulaic erotic thriller, then starts to feel like a therapy session as it veers off in a million different directions, none of them particularly interesting or insightful. Released direct to DVD. Super 35. [R]◗

Human Desire (1954) **90m.** **½ D: Fritz Lang. Glenn Ford, Gloria Grahame, Broderick Crawford, Edgar Buchanan, Kathleen Case, Diana DeLaire. Lang's follow-up to THE BIG HEAT is a well-directed but muddled account of railroad engineer Ford, just back from Korea, who becomes mixed up with married Grahame and murder. Based on Zola's La Bête Humaine, filmed in 1938 in France by Jean Renoir.▼◗

Human Experiments (1980) **C-82m.** *½ D: Gregory Goodell. Linda Haynes, Geoffrey Lewis, Ellen Travolta, Aldo Ray, Jackie Coogan, Darlene Craviotto. As the title says . . . [R]▼

Human Factor, The (1975-British-Italian) **C-96m.** *½ D: Edward Dmytryk. George Kennedy, John Mills, Raf Vallone, Rita Tushingham, Barry Sullivan, Arthur Franz. Violent, bloody chronicle of Kennedy tracking down the killers of his family. Decent cast wasted. [R]▼

Human Factor, The (1979) **C-115m.** ** D: Otto Preminger. Nicol Williamson, Iman, Derek Jacobi, Richard Attenborough, Robert Morley, Ann Todd, John Gielgud. Dry, unexciting filmization of Graham Greene's spy novel about a British double agent (Williamson) who's forced to defect to Russia. Top cast, script by Tom Stoppard, but results are mediocre. Preminger's final film. [R]▼

Human Gorilla, The SEE: **Behind Locked Doors**

Human Highway (1982) **C-88m.** *½ D: Bernard Shakey (Neil Young), Dean Stockwell. Neil Young, Russ Tamblyn, Dennis Hopper, Sally Kirkland, Dean Stockwell, Charlotte Stewart, Devo. Young and Tamblyn run a gas station in the middle of nowhere in this wacked-out, anti-nuke comedy. Notable for footage of Young in concert plus rock group Devo performing with a red, radioactive glow about them (caused by the nuclear power plant in the vicinity). **▼◐**

Humanité (2000-French) **C-148m.** *** D: Bruno Dumont. Emmanuel Schotté, Séverine Caneele, Philippe Tullier, Ghislain Ghesquère, Ginette Allègre. Morose police superintendent (Schotté) with a troubled past investigates the rape and murder of an 11-year-old girl in a rural French town. Slow but never boring, and more a character study than a mystery or crime drama; a potent portrait of loneliness and depravity in a quietly ugly world. Written by the director. HawkScope. **▼◖**

Human Nature (2001-French-U.S.) **C-96m.** **½ D: Michel Gondry. Tim Robbins, Patricia Arquette, Rhys Ifans, Miranda Otto, Rosie Perez, Robert Forster, Mary Kay Place, Miguel Sandoval, Paul Giamatti, Hilary Duff. Loopy film from Charlie Kaufman, who wrote BEING JOHN MALKOVICH, about a tunnel-visioned research scientist (Robbins) who hooks up with a woman just back from the wild (where she had moved because of embarrassment over her hairy body) to attempt to civilize a manbeast (Ifans). Too laid back, but engagingly silly and unpredictable. [R]**◖**

Humanoids from the Deep (1980) **C-80m.** *** D: Barbara Peeters. Doug McClure, Ann Turkel, Vic Morrow, Cindy Weintraub, Anthony Penya, Denise Galik. Mutated salmon monsters with penchant for bikinied beachgoers commit rape and other (graphic) mayhem in small oceanside town. Fast, occasionally hilarious gutter trash from the Roger Corman stable. The finale is not for squeamish viewers. Remade in 1996 for TV. [R] **▼◕◖**

Human Resources (2000-French) **C-100m.** *** D: Laurent Cantet. Jalil Lespert, Jean-Claude Vallod, Chantal Barré, Véronique de Pandelaère, Michel Begnez. Engrossing class-struggle drama about a business-school student who becomes a trainee at the factory where his father works, only to find that he has to fire him. Cantet achieves a seamless Ken Loach–style social realism. Cast of nonprofessionals—except for boyishly handsome lead Lespert—is impressive.**◖**

Human Stain, The (2003) **C-105m.** ***½ D: Robert Benton. Anthony Hopkins, Nicole Kidman, Ed Harris, Gary Sinise, Wentworth Miller, Jacinda Barrett, Harry Lennix, Clark Gregg, Anna Deavere Smith, Lizan Mitchell, Phyllis Newman, Margo Martindale, Mili Avital, Mimi Kuzyk. Moving, intelligent adaptation (by Nicholas Meyer) of Philip Roth's novel about a distinguished college professor whose life is shattered by a chance remark. As he reveals more about himself to a newfound friend (Sinise), we learn that he has been living a lie for most of his adult life. His chance for rebirth and redemption comes through an unlikely affair with a working-class woman much younger than he. Rich

in nuance, filled with pitch-perfect performances, and beautifully shot by the late Jean Yves Escoffier. Super 35. [R] **▼◖**

Human Traffic (1999-British) **C-86m.** ** D: Justin Kerrigan. John Simm, Lorraine Pilkington, Shaun Parkes, Nicola Reynolds, Danny Dyer, Dean Davies. Deeply unoriginal Gen X fare about five Welsh twentysomethings stuck in dead-end jobs; they work for the weekend, when life becomes one big Ecstasy-drenched, debauched rave. Meant to be adrenaline-pumped, nihilistic, TRAINSPOTTING meets Tarantino, but it's way too desperate to be rebel cool. [R] **▼◖**

Humboldt County (2008) **C-96m.** *** D: Darren Grodsky, Danny Jacobs. Jeremy Strong, Fairuza Balk, Peter Bogdanovich, Brad Dourif, Frances Conroy, Madison Davenport, Chris Messina. Abandoned by his flaky one-night stand, an uptight medical school student (Strong) finds himself among unreconstructed hippies and second-generation fringe dwellers who farm marijuana in the "Lost Coast" region of Northern California. There's a distinctively '70s flavor to this easygoing and ingratiating indie, a character-driven comedy-drama with standout performances by Dourif and Conroy as laid-back leaders of the counterculture community. Written by the directors, who also appear as Bob and Steve. [R]**◖**

Humongous (1981-Canadian) **C-93m.** *½ D: Paul Lynch. Janet Julian, David Wallace, Janit Baldwin, John Wildman, Joy Boushel, Layne Coleman. Slow-moving horror film opens with brutal rape and follows with every cliché in the book. A group of youths who wreck their boat on a small island are picked off one at a time by a raving manbeast. Most of the action occurs in complete darkness and you never even get a good look at the monster. [R]**▼**

Humoresque (1946) **125m.** ***½ D: Jean Negulesco. Joan Crawford, John Garfield, Oscar Levant, J. Carrol Naish, Craig Stevens, Tom D'Andrea, Peggy Knudsen, Paul Cavanagh. Ambitious violinist Garfield gets involved with wealthy, unstable patroness Crawford. No cardboard soap opera this; superb performances, handsome production, hilarious support from Levant, and a knockout finale. Perhaps Crawford's finest hour. Young Robert Blake plays Garfield as a child, and that's Isaac Stern's violin on the soundtrack. Filmed before in 1920. **▼◕◖**

Humpday (2009) **C-94m.** **½ D: Lynn Shelton. Mark Duplass, Joshua Leonard, Alycia Delmore, Lynn Shelton, Trina Willard. The lives of a conventional young married couple are upended with the unexpected arrival of the husband's reckless college pal. Well-intentioned exploration of male friendship and sexuality benefits from naturalistic performances, but is done in by the rambling scenario and direction. [R]**◖**

Hunchback of Notre Dame, The (1923) 117m. *** D: Wallace Worsley. Lon Chaney, Patsy Ruth Miller, Ernest Torrence, Tully Marshall, Norman Kerry. Lavish filming of Hugo classic, capturing flair of medieval Paris and strange attraction of outcast Chaney for dancing girl (Miller). Silent classic holds up well, with Chaney's makeup still incredible. Various prints survive with different running times. ▼◑◗

Hunchback of Notre Dame, The (1939) 115m. ***½ D: William Dieterle. Charles Laughton, Sir Cedric Hardwicke, Thomas Mitchell, Maureen O'Hara, Edmond O'Brien, Alan Marshal, Walter Hampden, Harry Davenport, George Zucco, Curt Bois, George Tobias, Rod La Rocque. Superb remake of Lon Chaney silent is even better than the original. Laughton, as Victor Hugo's misshapen bellringer Quasimodo, is haunting and unforgettable. Magnificently atmospheric studio re-creation of 15th-century Paris also a big plus. Film debut of O'Brien and U.S. debut of O'Hara. Also shown in computer-colored version. ▼◑◗

Hunchback of Notre Dame, The (1956-French) C-104m. **½ D: Jean Delannoy. Gina Lollobrigida, Anthony Quinn, Jean Danet, Alain Cuny. Quinn makes a valiant try in lead, but film misses scope and flavor of Hugo novel. CinemaScope. ▼◑◗

Hunchback of Notre Dame, The (1996) C-85m. *** D: Gary Trousdale, Kirk Wise. Voices of Tom Hulce, Demi Moore, Kevin Kline, Tony Jay, Jason Alexander, Heidi Mollenhauer, Paul Kandel, Charles Kimbrough, Mary Wickes, Jane Withers, David Ogden Stiers. Intensely dramatic, involving story about the pathetic, put-upon Quasimodo, his evil guardian Frollo, and the one person who shows him kindness, the gypsy Esmeralda. Disney's all-time strangest choice for an animated feature turns out surprisingly well: handsomely designed, dynamically staged, with songs that (if unmemorable) work within the fabric of the story; comic relief, however, involving Quasi's three gargoyle friends, seems contrived. Followed by a direct-to-video sequel. [G] ▼◑◗

Hunger, The (1983) C-97m. *½ D: Tony Scott. Catherine Deneuve, David Bowie, Susan Sarandon, Cliff DeYoung, Beth Ehlers, Dan Hedaya. Kinky trash masquerading as a horror film, with Deneuve as a vampire who needs fresh blood to survive. Bowie's quite good as Deneuve's companion—with an aging scene that's the film's highlight. As for the rest, beware, unless seeing Deneuve and Sarandon in bed together is your idea of a good time. Look for Ann Magnuson and Willem Dafoe in small roles. Panavision. [R] ▼◑◗

Hunger (2008-British-Irish) C-96m. ***½ D: Steve McQueen. Michael Fassbender, Liam Cunningham, Stuart Graham, Brian Milligan, Liam McMahon. Raw, riveting, minimalist account of jailed Irish Repub-

lican Army members who are horrifically abused by their British jailors. Based on the events surrounding the 1981 Maze Prison hunger strike, during which IRA detainees, including Bobby Sands (played here by Fassbender), starved themselves to death. Not for the faint of heart. Techniscope. ◗

Hunk (1987) C-102m. ** D: Lawrence Bassoff. John Allen Nelson, Steve Levitt, Deborah Shelton, Rebeccah Bush, James Coco, Robert Morse, Avery Schreiber. Youthful nerd sells his soul to become a California hunk—but still has to deal with the Devil (Coco) and his beautiful emissary (Shelton). Silly stuff benefits from an attractive and colorful cast. [PG] ▼◑◗

Hunted, The (1995) C-118m. *½ D: J. F. Lawton. Christopher Lambert, John Lone, Joan Chen, Yoshio Harada, Yoko Shimada. N.Y. businessman is chased by masked ninja assassins who actively conceal their identities, which at least puts them one-up on some of their fellow cast members. Slicing and dicing via DTS sound technology suggests an episode of *The Montel Williams Show* gone terribly wrong: titles of bona fide Japanese classics indicate what it's like sitting through this: GATE OF HELL, STREET OF SHAME and—in Lambert's case—AN ACTOR'S REVENGE. [R] ▼◑◗

Hunted, The (2003) C-94m. *** D: William Friedkin. Tommy Lee Jones, Benicio Del Toro, Connie Nielsen, Leslie Stefanson, John Finn, Jose Zuniga, Ron Canada, Lonny Chapman, Rex Linn. When a soldier (Del Toro) is suspected in a series of brutal murders, the FBI calls on the man (Jones) who helped train him as part of an elite corps of killers in Kosovo. Solid action/suspense yarn with breathtaking hand-to-hand combat scenes and kinetic camerawork (by Caleb Deschanel). Jones and Del Toro apparently did much of their own physical action—and it shows. [R] ▼◗

Hunter, The (1980) C-97m. BOMB D: Buzz Kulik. Steve McQueen, Eli Wallach, Kathryn Harrold, LeVar Burton, Ben Johnson. Incomprehensible bio of real-life contemporary bounty hunter Ralph (Pappy) Thorson has plot holes that Hannibal could have led elephants through. McQueen's last film and probably his worst. [PG] ▼◑◗

Hunters, The (1958) C-108m. **½ D: Dick Powell. Robert Mitchum, Robert Wagner, Richard Egan, Mai Britt, Lee Phillips. Veteran pilot falls for wife of younger flyer—who crashes behind enemy lines. Fair of its type. CinemaScope. ▼◗

Hunt for Red October, The (1990) C-135m. ***½ D: John McTiernan. Sean Connery, Alec Baldwin, Scott Glenn, Sam Neill, James Earl Jones, Joss Ackland, Richard Jordan, Peter Firth, Tim Curry, Courtney B. Vance, Jeffrey Jones, Fred Dalton Thompson, Timothy Carhart. Exciting, complex thriller from the best-seller by Tom Clancy. Connery stars as a Soviet submarine captain who may (or may not) be planning to defect to the U.S. during the maiden voyage of a supersecret nuclear sub; Baldwin is the American intelligence ace who tries to anticipate his every move. Long, potentially confusing at times, but always manages to make a course correction in the nick of time . . . and deliver another direct hit. Oscar winner for sound-effects editing. Followed by PATRIOT GAMES. Panavision. [PG]▼●❸

Hunting (1990-Australian) **C-97m.** **❊❊** D: Frank Howson. John Savage, Kerry Armstrong, Guy Pearce, Jeffrey Thomas, Rebecca Rigg, Rhys McConnochie. Ambitious but overwrought exercise in style, about beautiful but deeply troubled secretary Armstrong, who forsakes her self-pitying husband, and becomes involved with all-powerful (and predictably evil, hypocritical) empire-builder Savage. Panavision. [R]▼

Hunting Party, The (1971) **C-108m.** BOMB D: Don Medford. Oliver Reed, Candice Bergen, Gene Hackman, Simon Oakland, L. Q. Jones, Ronald Howard, G. D. Spradlin. When his wife is kidnapped and raped by Reed and his gang, Hackman sets out to kill them one by one. Fine cast wasted in repellently violent Western that adds nothing new to tired plot, unless you count the bordello-equipped train. [R]▼

Hunting Party, The (2007) **C-103m.** **❊❊½** D: Richard Shepard. Richard Gere, Terrence Howard, Jesse Eisenberg, James Brolin, Ljubomir Kerekeš, Kristina Krepela, Diane Kruger, Joy Bryant, Dylan Baker. TV producer Howard returns to Bosnia five years after the end of the war that he covered as a cameraman with daredevil reporter Gere. Reluctant at first, he allows himself (and tyro newsman Eisenberg) to be talked into joining a now-disgraced Gere on a wild scheme to flush out the world's most wanted war criminal, who's still at large in the Balkans. Gripping, forceful storytelling, dotted with absurdly funny moments; rings true (and is based on real-life journalist Scott Anderson's experiences) but deflates at the finale. Super 35. [R]❸

hurlyburly (1998) **C-122m.** **❊❊** D: Anthony Drazan. Sean Penn, Kevin Spacey, Robin Wright Penn, Chazz Palminteri, Garry Shandling, Anna Paquin, Meg Ryan. A seamy slice of life about a circle of L.A. friends—self-absorbed, smart-assy, driven, drug-infused people desperately looking for happiness in all the wrong places. David Rabe adapted his much-admired 1984 play, but it loses something in the transition to film, becoming more realistic and less funny despite a powerhouse cast. [R]▼●❸

Hurricane, The (1937) **102m.** **❊❊❊½** D: John Ford. Dorothy Lamour, Jon Hall, Mary Astor, C. Aubrey Smith, Raymond Massey, Thomas Mitchell, John Carradine,

Jerome Cowan. First-rate escapism on isle of Manikoora, where idyllic native life of Hall and Lamour is disrupted by vindictive governor Massey. Climactic hurricane effects have never been equaled. Lovely score by Alfred Newman. Screenplay by Dudley Nichols and Oliver H. P. Garrett, from the novel by Charles Nordhoff and James Norman Hall. Remade in 1979. ▼●❸

Hurricane (1979) **C-119m.** BOMB D: Jan Troell. Jason Robards, Mia Farrow, Max von Sydow, Trevor Howard, Dayton Ka'ne, Timothy Bottoms, James Keach. Look what just blew in: a $22 million remake of the 1937 classic that may well put you to sleep! Todd-AO 35. [PG]▼❸

Hurricane, The (1999) **C-125m.** **❊❊½** D: Norman Jewison. Denzel Washington, Vicellous Reon Shannon, Deborah Kara Unger, Liev Schreiber, John Hannah, Debbi Morgan, Dan Hedaya, Clancy Brown, Harris Yulin, David Paymer, Rod Steiger. Washington's powerful performance as wrongly imprisoned prizefighter Rubin "Hurricane" Carter makes this otherwise conventional drama worth seeing. Shannon plays a ghetto teenager who reads Carter's autobiography and determines to find a way to set him free. The boy's Canadian guardians are ill-defined characters and weaken the story, along with heavy-handed portrayals of Carter's victimizers. [R]▼●❸

Hurricane Streets (1998) **C-88m.** **❊❊❊** D: Morgan J. Freeman. Brendan Sexton III, Shawn Elliott, Isidra Vega, David Roland Frank, L. M. "Kit" Carson, Heather Matarazzo, Edie Falco. Moving drama of adolescents whose underlying decency is put to the test in a world of petty thievery in N.Y.C.'s East Village. Realistic, unsentimental acting highlights this excellent first feature from writer-director Freeman (not to be confused with the actor), who puts both angst and hope into his story. [R]▼●❸

Hurry Sundown (1967) **C-142m.** **❊❊** D: Otto Preminger. Michael Caine, Jane Fonda, John Phillip Law, Diahann Carroll, Robert Hooks, Faye Dunaway, Burgess Meredith, Robert Reed, George Kennedy, Frank Converse, Loring Smith, Beah Richards, Madeleine Sherwood, Rex Ingram, Jim Backus. Often ludicrous, overripe melodrama with ruthless Southerner Caine determined to buy up cousin's land, stopping at nothing to achieve goal. A curio for Fonda and Caine's offbeat casting, not to mention Horton Foote as one of the scripters. Jane's saxophone "solo," though, is worth checking out. Panavision.❸

Hurt Locker, The (2009) **C-131m.** **❊❊❊½** D: Kathryn Bigelow. Jeremy Renner, Anthony Mackie, Brian Geraghty, Guy Pearce, Ralph Fiennes, David Morse, Evangeline Lilly, Christian Camargo, Christopher Sayegh. Hotshot demolitions expert reports for duty in Baghdad and drives his two teammates crazy with his recklessness. They come to understand him, at least a bit, as they work together in tense, dangerous situations disarming unexploded bombs. Episodic but thoroughly absorbing character study has many suspenseful moments, and one breathtaking sequence in which the men fight fatigue while conducting a long-range rifle battle. Renner is perfect in the central role as a man for whom "war is a drug." Vivid, credible screenplay by Mark Boal, perfectly realized by Bigelow. Oscar winner for Best Picture, Director, Original Screenplay, Sound Mixing, Sound Editing, and Editing. [R] ❿

Husbands (1970) **C-138m.** **½ D: John Cassavetes. Ben Gazzara, Peter Falk, John Cassavetes, Jenny Runacre, Jenny Lee Wright, Noelle Kao. Cassavetes' follow-up to FACES is not nearly as good; story deals with trio of middle-aged buddies who take off for Europe when their best friend dies. Some good scenes, but plagued by Cassavetes' habitual self-indulgence. Originally released at 154m. [PG] ▼❿

Husbands and Wives (1992) **C-107m.** ***½ D: Woody Allen. Woody Allen, Blythe Danner, Judy Davis, Mia Farrow, Juliette Lewis, Liam Neeson, Sydney Pollack, Lysette Anthony, Cristi Conaway, Timothy Jerome, Ron Rifkin, Jerry Zaks, Bruce Jay Friedman, Benno Schmidt, Caroline Aaron, Nora Ephron. Long-married couple startles their best friends by announcing they're going to split up; meanwhile, the friends start to stray themselves. Perceptive, witty, knowing script by Allen is brilliantly performed (especially by Davis and Pollack), though Woody and Mia's headline-making scandal at the time of the film's release made it difficult not to grimace at some pointed dialogue. Only negative note: amateurish hand-held camera and jump-cuts are jarring and distracting. [R] ▼❂❿

Hush (1998) **C-97m.** *½ D: Jonathan Darby. Jessica Lange, Gwyneth Paltrow, Johnathon Schaech, Nina Foch, Debi Mazar, David Thornton, Hal Holbrook. Paltrow and wealthy boyfriend Schaech are manipulated by his neurotic horse-rancher mother (Lange). Viewers could read a novel while watching this "thriller" and still not miss anything. Lange appears to believe she's doing Blanche Dubois all over again. [PG-13] ▼❂❿

Hush . . . Hush, Sweet Charlotte (1964) **133m.** *** D: Robert Aldrich. Bette Davis, Olivia de Havilland, Joseph Cotten, Agnes Moorehead, Cecil Kellaway, Victor Buono, Mary Astor, Bruce Dern. Macabre story of a family with a skeleton in its closet, confusing at times but worth watching for its cast. Bette is Olivia's victimized cousin; Cotten is Olivia's boyfriend. ▼❂❿

Hussy (1980-British) **C-95m.** *½ D: Matthew Chapman. Helen Mirren, John Shea, Murray Salem, Paul Angelis, Jenny Runacre. Muddled, poorly directed melodrama centering on hooker Mirren, boyfriend Shea, and illicit drugs. [R] ▼❿

Hustle (1975) **C-120m.** BOMB D: Robert Aldrich. Burt Reynolds, Catherine Deneuve, Ben Johnson, Paul Winfield, Eileen Brennan, Eddie Albert, Ernest Borgnine, Jack Carter, Catherine Bach. Pretentious, foul-mouthed, foul-minded story about an L.A. cop and a high-class call-girl who dream of escaping from their gritty life but never make it. This one's the pits. [R] ▼❿

Hustle & Flow (2005) **C-115m.** *** D: Craig Brewer. Terrence Howard, Taryn Manning, Anthony Anderson, Taraji P. Henson, Paula Jai Parker, Elise Neal, DJ Qualls, Isaac Hayes, Ludacris (Chris Bridges). Potent drama about a small-time pimp in Memphis who, frustrated with his dead-end life, pursues his improbable dream to become a rap star. Despite the squalid setting and dialogue, this is a surprisingly old-fashioned (even corny) movie at times. First-time director Brewer lets his script and talented actors put it across without resorting to flashy editing techniques. Howard has a commanding presence from the film's opening monologue to the final shot. Oscar winner for Best Song, "It's Hard Out Here for a Pimp." [R] ❿

Hustler, The (1961) **135m.** **** D: Robert Rossen. Paul Newman, Jackie Gleason, Piper Laurie, George C. Scott, Myron McCormick, Murray Hamilton, Michael Constantine, Jake LaMotta, Vincent Gardenia. Newman is outstanding as disenchanted drifter and pool hustler who challenges legendary Minnesota Fats (Gleason). Dingy pool-hall atmosphere vividly realized in this incisive film. Cinematographer Eugen Shuftan won an Oscar. Walter Tevis novel adapted by Sidney Carroll and director Rossen. Followed years later by THE COLOR OF MONEY. CinemaScope. ▼❂❿

Hustler Squad SEE: **Doll Squad, The**

Hysteria (1965-British) **85m.** **½ D: Freddie Francis. Robert Webber, Anthony Newlands, Jennifer Jayne, Maurice Denham, Lelia Goldoni, Peter Woodthorpe, Sandra Boize. After a car accident, an amnesiac Yank in London finds himself entangled in a complex murder plot that may or may not be a figment of his imagination. Twisty, reasonably intriguing Hammer thriller starts out promisingly, but gets bogged down. ▼

Hysterical (1983) **C-87m.** BOMB D: Chris Bearde. William, Mark and Brett Hudson, Cindy Pickett, Richard Kiel, Julie Newmar, Bud Cort, Robert Donner, Murray Hamilton, Clint Walker, Franklin Ajaye, Charlie Callas, Keenan Wynn, Gary Owens. Lame parody of AMITYVILLE/EXORCIST type pictures; the start and finish of the Hudsons' screen career. [PG]▼●◗

I Accuse! (1958-British) **99m. **½** D: Jose Ferrer. Jose Ferrer, Anton Walbrook, Emlyn Williams, Viveca Lindfors, David Farrar, Leo Genn, Herbert Lom, Harry Andrews, Felix Aylmer, George Coulouris, Donald Wolfit. Sincere but pretentious treatment of the treason trial of Alfred Dreyfus (Ferrer), with Williams as his defender, Emile Zola. Screenplay by Gore Vidal. CinemaScope.
I Am a Camera (1955-British) **98m. ***½** D: Henry Cornelius. Julie Harris, Laurence Harvey, Shelley Winters, Ron Randell, Anton Diffring, Patrick McGoohan, Peter Prowse. Intelligent adaptation of John van Druten's play (based on Christopher Isherwood stories) about prewar Berlin, with Harris a delight as a fun-loving young woman who'll accept anything from anyone. Screenplay by John Collier. Basis of Broadway musical and film CABARET.▼
I Am a Fugitive from a Chain Gang (1932) **93m. ****** D: Mervyn LeRoy. Paul Muni, Glenda Farrell, Helen Vinson, Preston Foster, Edward Ellis, Allen Jenkins. Still packs a wallop after all these years, with Muni as innocent man brutally victimized by criminal justice system. Haunting finale is justly famous. Scripted by Sheridan Gibney and Brown Holmes, from Robert E. Burns' autobiographical story. Burns' plight is also dramatized in the made for cable TVM THE MAN WHO BROKE 1,000 CHAINS.▼●◗
I Am Cuba (1964-Russian-Cuban) **141m. ***½** D: Mikhail Kalatozov. Sergio Corrieri, Salvador Vud, Jose Gallardo, Raul Garcia. Luz Maria Collazo, Jean Bouise. Sweeping, eye-popping ode to Cuba and the Castro revolution. Vignettes idealize hardworking but exploited peasants and Castro's staunch, freedom-loving revolutionaries, depicting Americans as decadent, sexist swine. And the images are consistently dazzling; the film demands to be seen and savored by any lover of pure cinema. Scripted by Yevgeny Yevtushenko and Enrique Pineda Barnet; released in the U.S. in 1995. ▼●◗
I Am David (2004) **C-95m. ***** D: Paul Feig. Ben Tibber, Joan Plowright, Jim Caviezel, Marie Bonnevie, Viola Carinci, Silvia De Santis. In 1952, a young boy escapes from a Bulgarian labor camp and has to make his way through Italy and Switzerland to Denmark, and safety. The only life he's ever known is one of brutality, so he's easily rattled—and confused—during his journey. Genuinely moving story avoids cheap sentimentality and earns our emotional involvement, with a remarkable performance by young Tibber. Impressive feature directing debut for Feig, who adapted Anne Holm's novel. [PG] ▼◗
I Am Legend (2007) **C-101m. **½** D:

Francis Lawrence. Will Smith, Alice Braga, Charlie Tahan, Salli Richardson, Willow Smith, Darrell Foster, Dash Mihok. In the year 2012, scientist Smith is apparently the world's only human survivor, alone on the island of Manhattan, following a horrifying plague spread by the use of a chemical that was supposed to cure cancer. The only thing that keeps him going is his blind determination to find an antidote to the virus before he's destroyed by rampaging mutants. Third screen version of Richard Matheson's novel (following THE LAST MAN ON EARTH and THE OMEGA MAN) benefits from Smith's charisma and physicality but falls back on horror clichés when it comes to the zombies. Emma Thompson appears unbilled. Alternate version runs 107m. Panavision. [PG-13]◗
I Am Love (2010-Italian) **C-120m. ***** D: Luca Guadagnino. Tilda Swinton, Flavio Parenti, Edoardo Gabbriellini, Alba Rohrwacher, Pippo Delbono, Maria Paiato, Diane Fleri, Waris Ahluwalia, Mattia Zaccaro, Gabriele Ferzetti, Marisa Berenson. Patriarch of an upper-class Milanese clan announces his retirement from the family textile business, setting off a chain reaction among the younger generations. At the core of the story is his Russian-born daughter-in-law (Swinton) and her attraction to the young chef who is her son's friend and potential business partner. Studied tale of the importance of tossing tradition aside to follow your passions, no matter the consequences, is obvious at times (as it links food and sensuality), but undeniably provocative. Some viewers may find its operatic approach difficult to digest—pun intended. [R]◗
I Am Number Four (2011) **110m. *½** D: D. J. Caruso. Alex Pettyfer, Timothy Olyphant, Teresa Palmer, Dianna Agron, Callan McAuliffe, Jake Abel, Jeff Hochendoner. Alien teenager hides out on Earth trying to pass as a normal high schooler, hoping to avoid the enemy aliens who have already killed others like him. He's so dazzlingly handsome (not to mention his superpowers) that a teenage girl falls in love with him. Then the bad guys show up, as well as brusquely cynical Number Five, resulting in a flashy, CGI-intensive climax on the football field. Another attempt to create a TWILIGHT-like series, only this is pseudo–science fiction rather than pseudo-horror. Despite the trappings, it's inferior and exploits its target audience. A waste of time, except for the alien beagle. Based on a novel by Pittacus Lore (James Frey and Jobie Hughes). [PG-13]◗
i am sam (2001) **C-132m. ***½** D: Jessie Nelson. Sean Penn, Michelle Pfeiffer, Dianne Wiest, Dakota Fanning, Richard Schiff, Loretta Devine, Doug Hutchison, Laura Dern, Stanley DeSantis, Rosalind Chao, Mary Steenburgen, Brent Spiner. A

[656]

sweet, mentally retarded man becomes a father, but his devotion to his loving daughter runs aground when she reaches the age of 7 and a social services agency insists he isn't capable of raising her anymore. Then he finds an unlikely ally: a high-powered, self-absorbed attorney whose own life is a mess. Fine entertainment, with a great performance by Penn and equally good work by Pfeiffer and adorable young Fanning. Penn's fixation on the Beatles is reflected in a terrific soundtrack, with cover versions of their classic songs. [PG-13] ▼▶

I Am the Cheese (1983) **C-95m.** ****½** D: Robert Jiras. Robert MacNaughton, Hope Lange, Don Murray, Robert Wagner, Cynthia Nixon, Lee Richardson, John Fiedler, Sudie Bond. Paper-thin but occasionally appealing tale of alienated teenager who has witnessed his parents' death, and his fantasies while under psychiatric care. From Robert Cormier's novel. Remade as LAPSE OF MEMORY. [PG] ▼▶

I Became a Criminal SEE: **They Made Me a Fugitive**

I Can Do Bad All By Myself (2009) **C-113m.** ****½** D: Tyler Perry. Taraji P. Henson, Adam Rodriguez, Brian White, Hope Olaidé Wilson, Mary J. Blige, Gladys Knight, Marvin L. Winans, Freddy Siglar, Kwesi Boakye, Tyler Perry. Perry again plays Madea in another tonally dissonant dramedy based on one of his plays, but keeps the cantankerous old "lady" more or less in the background while focusing on a hard-drinking, self-destructive lounge singer (Henson) who gets a shot at redemption—and finally meets Mr. Right (Rodriguez)—while forced to care for her sister's three children. Atypically restrained (by Perry standards) in its mix of broad comedy, soapy melodrama, and spiritual uplift, and sporadically puts the plot on hold for some knockout musical sequences. Aka TYLER PERRY'S I CAN DO BAD ALL BY MYSELF. [PG-13] ▶

I Can Get It for You Wholesale (1951) **90m.** ******* D: Michael Gordon. Susan Hayward, Dan Dailey, Sam Jaffe, George Sanders, Randy Stuart, Marvin Kaplan, Harry Von Zell. Hayward is aces as a model-turned dress designer determined to make it in N.Y.C.'s garment industry. Jerome Weidman's flavorful novel was adapted by Vera Caspary and scripted by Abraham Polonsky. Aka: ONLY THE BEST.

I Capture the Castle (2003-British) **C-113m.** ******* D: Tim Fywell. Romola Garai, Rose Byrne, Henry Thomas, Marc Blucas, Bill Nighy, Tara Fitzgerald, Sinéad Cusack, Henry Cavill. In the mid-1930s, a wildly eccentric family living in a drafty old castle in the English countryside is changed by the arrival of two wealthy American brothers. Intelligent, involving comedy-drama from the novel by Dodie Smith (of *One Hundred*

and One Dalmatians fame). Beautifully photographed (by Richard Greatrex) and interesting throughout, but just a shade smug. Super 35. [R] ▼▶

Ice Age (2002) **C-81m.** ******* D: Chris Wedge. Voices of Ray Romano, John Leguizamo, Denis Leary, Goran Visnjic, Jack Black, Tara Strong, Cedric the Entertainer, Stephen Root, Jane Krakowski. Funny, imaginative computer-animated feature that's sort of a prehistoric THREE GODFATHERS, with a woolly mammoth and a loopy sloth named Sid trying to return a human baby to its tribe. They're joined by a saber-toothed tiger whose motives aren't so altruistic. Distinctively designed, with humor geared for young and old alike. Leguizamo's vocal performance as Sid is a riot. Wonderful score by David Newman. Followed by two sequels. [PG] ▼▶

Ice Age: Dawn of the Dinosaurs (2009) **C-93m.** ******* D: Carlos Saldanha. Voices of Ray Romano, John Leguizamo, Denis Leary, Simon Pegg, Queen Latifah, Seann William Scott, Josh Peck, Bill Hader, Chris Wedge, Jane Lynch, Kristen Wiig. There's a greater emphasis on thrills and spills in this third go-round, as our CG-animated heroes wander into an underground realm where supposedly extinct prehistoric creatures are alive and well—and, quite often, ravenously hungry. A swashbuckling weasel amusingly voiced by Pegg is the latest addition to the cast, but even he can't upstage old favorites Manny, Diego, and Sid. Neatly balances witty wordplay, rambunctious slapstick, and action sequences worthy of comparison to similar spectacle in live-action features. 3-D. [PG] ▶

Ice Age: The Meltdown (2006) **C-90m.** ****½** D: Carlos Saldanha. Voices of Ray Romano, John Leguizamo, Denis Leary, Queen Latifah, Seann William Scott, Josh Peck, Will Arnett, Jay Leno, Stephen Root, Renee Taylor, Joseph Bologna. In this sequel, our heroes learn that the ice around them is melting and they'd better move or be flooded out. Along the way, Manny, fearful that he's the last of his species, encounters a fetching female woolly mammoth who thinks she's a possum! CG-animated family fare lacks the freshness of the original (and makes Diego the sabertooth tiger rather toothless), but it's enjoyable enough. The misadventures of Scrat, the hapless rodent from the first film, punctuate this story. [PG] ▶

Ice Castles (1979) **C-109m.** ******* D: Donald Wrye. Lynn-Holly Johnson, Robby Benson, Colleen Dewhurst, Tom Skerritt, Jennifer Warren, David Huffman. Successful ice skating career of Iowa farm girl is interrupted after she is blinded in freak accident. Tops for the disease/affliction genre, with well-photographed skating sequences and good performances by all. Remade for DVD in 2010. [PG] ▼▶

Ice Cold in Alex SEE: **Desert Attack**

Ice Harvest, The (2005) C-88m. ** D: Harold Ramis. John Cusack, Billy Bob Thornton, Connie Nielsen, Oliver Platt, Randy Quaid, Mike Starr, T. J. Jagodowski. A recounting of how a "perfect" crime goes awry one Christmas Eve introduces us to a variety of lowlifes in Wichita, Kansas, including lawyer Cusack and porn purveyor Thornton, who've been skimming money from their boss. Mostly unfunny black comedy must have worked better on the pages of Scott Phillips' novel, adapted by the film's coexecutive producers, Richard Russo and Robert Benton. [R] ▼●

Iceman (1984) C-99m. ***½ D: Fred Schepisi. Timothy Hutton, Lindsay Crouse, John Lone, Josef Sommer, David Strathairn, Danny Glover, James Tolkan. A Neanderthal man is found frozen in ice. Scientists manage to bring him back to life, but only Hutton is interested in him as a human being and not a lab specimen. Fascinating, credible science fiction made all the more involving by Schepisi's fine direction. Haunting score by Bruce Smeaton; remarkable performance as the caveman by Lone. Story by John Drimmer; scripted by Chip Proser and Drimmer. Panavision. [PG] ▼●

Iceman Cometh, The (1973) C-178m. ***½ D: John Frankenheimer. Lee Marvin, Fredric March, Robert Ryan, Jeff Bridges, Martyn Green, Moses Gunn, Bradford Dillman, Evans Evans. Remarkably successful film of Eugene O'Neill's play about assorted barflies in a 1912 saloon; Marvin's Hickey is only adequate, but Ryan dominates an outstanding supporting cast. An American Film Theatre production. First shown at 239m. This was March's last film. [PG] ▼●

Ice Palace (1960) C-143m. **½ D: Vincent Sherman. Richard Burton, Robert Ryan, Carolyn Jones, Martha Hyer, Jim Backus, Ray Danton, Shirley Knight, Diane McBain, Karl Swenson, George Takei. Typically sprawling (and silly) Edna Ferber saga of two men whose friendship turns to bitter rivalry, and whose lives parallel the development of Alaska. Watchable, to be sure, but hokey from start to finish. ▼●

Ice Pirates, The (1984) C-91m. ** D: Stewart Raffill. Robert Urich, Mary Crosby, Michael D. Roberts, John Matuszak, Anjelica Huston, Ron Perlman, John Carradine, Robert Symonds. Spoofy blend of space opera and swashbuckler, set in an arid future where water has become the most precious of commodities. Script vacillates between clever and half-baked; claustrophobic direction keeps this from being more than passable rainy-afternoon fare. [PG] ▼●

Ice Princess (2005) C-92m. *** D: Tim Fywell. Joan Cusack, Kim Cattrall, Michelle Trachtenberg, Hayden Panettiere, Trevor Blumas, Connie Ray, Kirsten Olson, Juliana Cannarozzo, Jocelyn Lai. High school science whiz applies her intellectual curiosity to a study of ice skating and unexpectedly becomes a competitive skater, to the chagrin of her mom, a feminist teacher who has no respect for the sport. Entertaining film for young audiences realistically portrays teenage life, parental pressures, the harsh reality of competition, and the exhilaration of pursuing something you love. Real-life Olympic skating champs Michelle Kwan and Brian Boitano appear as themselves. [G] ▼●

Ice Rink, The (1999-French-Belgian-Italian) C-77m. *** D: Jean-Philippe Toussaint. Tom Novembre, Mireille Perrier, Bruce Campbell, Dolores Chaplin, Marie-France Pisier, Jean-Pierre Cassel, Gilbert Melki, Dominique Deruddere. Cineastes will savor this witty, allegorical film about the making of a movie, completely set in the title locale. Cast includes a sultry French leading lady (Chaplin, granddaughter of Charlie), a Hollywood action-hero leading man, and Lithuanian hockey players; the filmmaking process is amusingly portrayed as organized chaos. ●

Ice Station Zebra (1968) C-148m. **½ D: John Sturges. Rock Hudson, Ernest Borgnine, Patrick McGoohan, Jim Brown, Tony Bill, Lloyd Nolan. Standard Cold War nailbiter with all-male cast has Hudson a sub commander sailing for North Pole to await orders, not knowing that Cold War incident will ensue; McGoohan a British agent out to trap a Russian spy. Based on the Alistair MacLean novel; originally in Cinerama. Infamous as Howard Hughes' favorite movie! Super Panavision 70. [G] ▼●

Ice Storm, The (1997) C-113m. **½ D: Ang Lee. Kevin Kline, Joan Allen, Sigourney Weaver, Christina Ricci, Elijah Wood, Henry Czerny, Adam Hann-Byrd, Tobey Maguire, Jamey Sheridan, Kate Burton, Larry Pine, Katie Holmes, Allison Janney. Icy adaptation of Rick Moody's much-praised novel about a real-life ice storm in 1973 and how it parallels activities in upscale New Canaan, Connecticut. A sober and absorbing chronicle of sexuality—repressed and unleashed—in '70s suburbia (love those clothes!), but also somewhat clinical and off-putting, until the heartrending finale. A film one can admire without actually enjoying. [PG-13] ▼●

Icicle Thief, The (1989-Italian) C-85m. **½ D: Maurizio Nichetti. Maurizio Nichetti, Caterina Sylos Labini, Heidi Komárek, Renato Scarpa. Ingenious satire of contemporary commercialism—and disrespect for the art of film on television—has Nichetti's BICYCLE THIEF–type drama being presented on TV with so many commercials that soon no one can separate the program from the ads . . . including the actors in the film! Nichetti plays with his audience, often amusingly, but pulls the rug out from under a bit too often. ▼

I Come in Peace (1990) **C-92m.** ****** D: Craig R. Baxley. Dolph Lundgren, Brian Benben, Betsy Brantley, Matthias Hues, David Ackroyd, Jay Bilas, Michael J. Pollard, Jesse Vint. Black-clad alien, who looks like a giant surfer, arrives to harvest people for their endorphins; his race is addicted to them. Basically just another cop (Lundgren) and new partner (FBI agent Benben) movie, with lots of explosions. Routine and unimaginative. [R]▼●

I Confess (1953) **95m.** ****½** D: Alfred Hitchcock. Montgomery Clift, Anne Baxter, Karl Malden, Brian Aherne, Dolly Haas, O. E. Hasse. A priest hears a murderer's confession and is himself accused of the crime. Lesser Hitchcock film, made in Quebec, is nevertheless intriguing for its stark photography and symbolism. The shooting of the film plays a key role in LE CONFESSIONALE (1995). ▼●]

I Could Go on Singing (1963-British) **C-99m.** ****½** D: Ronald Neame. Judy Garland, Dirk Bogarde, Jack Klugman, Aline MacMahon, Gregory Phillips. Garland is famed singer returning to England to claim illegitimate son living with real father (Bogarde). Garland is exceptional in singing sequences revealing the true Judy; sadly, this was her last film. Panavision. ▼●]

I Could Never Be Your Woman (2007) **C-97m.** ***½** D: Amy Heckerling. Michelle Pfeiffer, Paul Rudd, Saoirse Ronan, Fred Willard, Jon Lovitz, Tracey Ullman, Stacey Dash, Sarah Alexander, Sally Kellerman, Wallace Shawn. Desperately unfunny mix of toothless showbiz satire, romantic-comedy clichés, and charm-free fantasy, about a 40-something TV producer (Pfeiffer) who falls for the 29-year-old star (Rudd) of her teen-centric TV series. Despite marquee names on both sides of the camera, this received no U.S. theatrical release. Henry Winkler appears unbilled. [PG-13]]

I Cover the War (1937) **68m.** ****** D: Arthur Lubin. John Wayne, Gwen Gaze, Major Sam Harris, James Bush, Don Barclay. Second-rate pulp fiction about correspondent Wayne tangling with Arab rebel leader.

I'd Climb the Highest Mountain (1951) **C-88m.** ******* D: Henry King. Susan Hayward, William Lundigan, Rory Calhoun, Gene Lockhart, Ruth Donnelly, Barbara Bates, Lynn Bari, Alexander Knox. Simple good-hearted slice of Americana filmed on location in Georgia, with Lundigan as a preacher whose bride must learn a new way of life in Southern hill country. ▼

Ideal Husband, An (1948-British) **C-96m.** ****½** D: Alexander Korda. Paulette Goddard, Michael Wilding, Diana Wynyard, C. Aubrey Smith, Glynis Johns, Michael Medwin. Oscar Wilde's drawing room comedy receives classy presentation but is slowmoving. Remade in 1999.▼

Ideal Husband, An (1999-British-U.S.) **C-**96m. ******* D: Oliver Parker. Cate Blanchett, Rupert Everett, Jeremy Northam, Julianne Moore, Minnie Driver, John Wood, Jeroen Krabbé, Peter Vaughan, Lindsay Duncan. Delightful revision of Oscar Wilde's classic 1895 comedy about a stalwart Member of Parliament who becomes a blackmail target—and can't stand the idea that his devoted wife will find him less than perfect. One couldn't ask for a more attractive or appealing cast, though Everett practically steals the film. [PG-13]▼]

I Deal in Danger (1966) **C-89m.** ****½** D: Walter Grauman. Robert Goulet, Christine Carere, Donald Harron, Werner Peters. Feature version of TV series *Blue Light* involves adventures of Goulet pretending to be Nazi convert in order to help Allies.]

Identification of a Woman (1982-Italian-French) **C-128m.** ****½** D: Michelangelo Antonioni. Tomas Milian, Daniela Silverio, Christine Boisson, Sandra Monteleoni, Giampaolo Saccarola. A familiar Antonioni theme—alienation and the difficulty of initiating relationships in contemporary society—is explored in this low-key tale of a movie director (Milian) and his involvement with two women. Atmospheric, allegorical film of interest mostly to Antonioni diehards. Released in the U.S. in 1996.▼

Identity (2003) **C-90m.** ***½** D: James Mangold. John Cusack, Ray Liotta, Amanda Peet, John Hawkes, Rebecca De Mornay, Alfred Molina, John C. McGinley, Clea DuVall, Jake Busey, William Lee Scott, Leila Kenzle, Pruitt Taylor Vince, Matt Letscher, Bret Loehr, Holmes Osborne. A group of seemingly unrelated people find themselves holed up in a fleabag motel on a stormy night with a psycho killer on the loose—or so it seems. Means to be clever but at its core is a harsh, unrelentingly ugly rip-off of Agatha Christie's *Ten Little Indians.* Also hampered by clichéd characters and some truly dumb dialogue. A good cast is wasted. Panavision. [R]▼]

Identity Crisis (1990) **C-98m.** BOMB D: Melvin Van Peebles. Mario Van Peebles, Ilan Mitchell-Smith, Nicholas Kepros, Shelley Burch, Rick Aviles, Stephen J. Cannell, Olivia Brown, Larry "Bud" Melman, Bobby Rivers. Crude, messy pseudo-farce, in which the spirit of a white, stereotypically effeminate fashion designer is mysteriously transferred into the body of black, stereotypically superhip rapper. Excruciating and, ultimately, boring. Scripted by Mario; produced by Melvin (who appears as a police inspector). [R]▼

I Died a Thousand Times (1955) **C-109m.** ****** D: Stuart Heisler. Jack Palance, Shelley Winters, Lori Nelson, Lee Marvin, Earl Holliman, Lon Chaney (Jr.), Dennis Hopper. Overblown remake of Bogart's HIGH SIERRA with Palance as mad killer with soft spot for crippled girl (Nelson). Winters is his moll in this gangster run-through. CinemaScope. ▼○●

Idiocracy (2006) **C-84m.** **½ D: Mike Judge. Luke Wilson, Maya Rudolph, Dax Shepard, Terry Alan Crews, David Herman, Andrew Wilson, Brad "Scarface" Jordan, Justin Long, Thomas Haden Church, Sara Rue; narrated by Earl Mann. It's as simple as this: stupid people procreate at a much greater rate than smart people, so in just a few years the U.S. will be overpopulated with idiots. When a military experiment sends Wilson and Rudolph 500 years into the future, even they are stupefied by the moronic state of affairs that has all but paralyzed society. Smart, funny ideas by Judge and cowriter Etan Cohen can't quite keep this scattershot movie afloat, but it's got some laugh-out-loud moments. Barely released to theaters. Stephen Root appears unbilled. [R]▌

Idiot, The (1951-Japanese) **166m.** *** D: Akira Kurosawa. Toshiro Mifune, Masayuki Mori, Setsuko Hara, Takashi Shimura. Kurosawa coscripted this updated version of the Dostoyevsky novel, about a prince and his friend who both love the same woman. Dramatically uneven (because the release version was edited down from Kurosawa's original cut), but there are enough flashes of brilliance to make it worthwhile. ▼▌

Idiots, The (1998-Danish-French) **C-114m.** *½ D: Lars von Trier. Bodil Jorgensen, Jens Albinus, Anne Louise Hassing, Troels Lyby, Nikolaj Lie Kaas, Henrik Prip. Pretending to be mentally handicapped, a group of 20-ish dropouts boorishly disrupt restaurants and swimming pools to gain gratis treatment. Too dull to be controversial, this was the first Danish film shot under the "pure cinema" manifesto called Dogma 95; the results look about as groundbreaking in a modern context as Vitaphone. One character talks about trying to find his "inner idiot," which, of course, Jerry Lewis has been doing for half a century. [R]▼

Idiot's Delight (1939) **105m.** *** D: Clarence Brown. Norma Shearer, Clark Gable, Edward Arnold, Charles Coburn, Joseph Schildkraut, Burgess Meredith, Virginia Grey. Disparate characters—including a tacky vaudevillian and his one-time flame, who's come up in the world—are forced to share each other's company in a hotel near the Italian border as WW2 is about to erupt. Robert E. Sherwood's Pulitzer Prize–winning play is badly dated, an interesting period piece, notable for its pacifist ideals . . . but frankly more interesting for Gable's famous song-and-dance routine to "Puttin' on the Ritz." Alternate ending for European release was added to U.S. laserdisc. ▼○●

Idle Hands (1999) **C-90m.** *½ D: Rodman Flender. Devon Sawa, Seth Green, Elden Henson, Jessica Alba, Fred Willard, Jack

Noseworthy, Vivica A. Fox. Lazy, dope-smoking teenager Sawa discovers that his right hand is possessed and a killer. He, or it, murders his parents and his two best friends, then he tries to remedy matters. Horror comedy (with ideas reminiscent of many other films, notably EVIL DEAD II) is doomed by too many crude and genuinely tasteless jokes. [R]▼○●

Idlewild (2006) **C-120m.** *½ D: Bryan Barber. André Benjamin, Antwan A. (Big Boi) Patton, Paula Patton, Terrence Howard, Malinda Williams, Macy Gray, Ben Vereen, Ving Rhames, Faizon Love, Patti LaBelle, Cicely Tyson, Bill Nunn, Paula Jai Parker. Train wreck of a musical featuring the hip-hop duo OutKast set in Prohibition-era Georgia. Big Boi Patton is a smooth talker who runs a nightclub and performs; Benjamin is a stifled mortician's son who moonlights as a pianist and songwriter. Writer-director Barber's self-consciously cool shots can't make up for long-winded, heavy-handed storytelling and clichéd dialogue. Fragmented song-and-dance numbers unsuccessfully try to merge 1930s swing and hip-hop. Benjamin's climactic song—performed during an embalming ceremony—has to be seen to be disbelieved. Super 35. [R]▌

Idol, The (1966) **107m.** ** D: Daniel Petrie. Jennifer Jones, Michael Parks, John Leyton, Jennifer Hilary, Guy Doleman. Trash about worthless type who makes it with both mother and girl of his best friend; interesting only as chance to see latter-day Jones and watch Parks try to ape James Dean. Filmed in England.▼

Idolmaker, The (1980) **C-119m.** **½ D: Taylor Hackford. Ray Sharkey, Tovah Feldshuh, Peter Gallagher, Paul Land, Joe Pantoliano, Maureen McCormick, Olympia Dukakis. Fictionalized bio of rock producer Bob Marcucci, who guided (pushed?) Frankie Avalon and Fabian to stardom in the late '50s. A great idea overcome by a script that builds momentum and then drops the ball. Good performances, sharp direction, though little period flavor (even in rock vet Jeff Barry's slick music score). [PG]▼○●

I Don't Buy Kisses Anymore (1992) **C-112m.** ** D: Robert Marcarelli. Jason Alexander, Nia Peeples, Lainie Kazan, Lou Jacobi, Eileen Brennan, Larry Storch. Chubby shoestore owner Alexander is befriended by psychology student Peeples; he wants romance, but she wants to study his compulsive eating disorder. Romantic comedy boasts a likable cast but slides too easily into caricature and stereotype. [PG]▼○●

I Don't Want to Be Born SEE: **Devil Within Her, The**

I Don't Want to Talk About It (1994-Argentine) **C-102m.** **½ D: Maria Luisa Bemberg. Marcello Mastroianni, Luisina

Brando, Alejandra Podesta. Memorable but not altogether compelling fable about a polished Casanova who finds himself attracted to a small town's most cultured woman—a dwarf whose physically attractive but repellently possessive mother has her own eyes set on this eligible bachelor. At 70, Mastroianni remains dashing. [PG-13]▼●

I Dood It (1943) **102m.** ** D: Vincente Minnelli. Red Skelton, Eleanor Powell, Richard Ainley, Patricia Dane, Lena Horne, Hazel Scott, Sam Levene, Butterfly McQueen, John Hodiak, Jimmy Dorsey and Orchestra. Strained, overlong musicomedy about a tailor's assistant obsessively in love with a stage star; good songs include "Star Eyes" and "Taking a Chance on Love," but patchwork film lifts its big finale from Powell's earlier BORN TO DANCE! A remake (more or less) of Buster Keaton's SPITE MARRIAGE (1929).▼▌

I Dreamed of Africa (2000) **C-112m.** ** D: Hugh Hudson. Kim Basinger, Vincent Perez, Eva Marie Saint, Liam Aiken, Garrett Strommen, Daniel Craig. Story of Kuki Gallmann, an Italian who moves with her young son and new husband to remote African ranch. She is determined to triumph over adverse conditions, and becomes passionate about animal rights. Basinger (an animal activist herself) is effective, but biopic is never quite as compelling as intended. Hawk-Scope. [PG-13]▼▌

I Drink Your Blood (1970) **C-72m.** ** D: David Durston. Bhaskar, Jadine Wong, Ronda Fultz, George Patterson. To get revenge on sadistic band of hippies, young boy gives them meat pies infected with rabies and they go homicidally crazy. Nuff said. [R]▼▌

I Eat Your Skin (1970) **82m.** BOMB D: Del Tenney. William Joyce, Heather Hewitt, Betty Hyatt Linton, Dan Stapleton, Walter Coy, Robert Stanton. Scientifically created zombies menace two-fisted hero on Caribbean island. Worthless. Filmed in 1964. Aka VOODOO BLOODBATH. [PG]▼▌

I Escaped from Devil's Island (1973) **C-89m.** BOMB D: William Witney. Jim Brown, Christopher George, Paul Richards, Rick Ely, Richard Rust, Jan Merlin. Produced by the Corman boys (Roger and Gene) in Mexico and the Caribbean, this actioner is an insult to vet director Witney's standing with buffs who know his earlier work. Violent, vulgar. [R]

if. . . . (1968-British) **C/B&W-111m.** **** D: Lindsay Anderson. Malcolm McDowell, David Wood, Richard Warwick, Robert Swann, Christine Noonan, Arthur Lowe, Mona Washbourne, Graham Crowden, Simon Ward. Magnificent, surrealistic study of students at boarding school who plot revolution—or do they? Originally X-rated, later trimmed for wider acceptance. Written by David Sherwin. [R]▼●▌

If a Man Answers (1962) **C-102m.** **½ D: Henry Levin. Sandra Dee, Bobby Darin, Micheline Presle, John Lund, Cesar Romero, Stefanie Powers, Christopher Knight, Charlene Holt. Trite pap of Dee and Darin (then married in real life) trying to outdo each other with jealousy-baiting antics.▌

If Ever I See You Again (1978) **C-105m.** *½ D: Joe Brooks. Joe Brooks, Shelley Hack, Jimmy Breslin, Jerry Keller, George Plimpton, Danielle Brisebois. Producer-director-writer-composer-arranger-conductor Brooks' follow-up to his mediocre YOU LIGHT UP MY LIFE is even worse; this time he stars, as a songwriter trying to rekindle old flame with Hack (in her starring movie debut). Breslin should stick to writing. [PG]▼

If He Hollers, Let Him Go (1968) **C-106m.** *½ D: Charles Martin. Raymond St. Jacques, Kevin McCarthy, Barbara McNair, Dana Wynter, Arthur O'Connell, John Russell, Ann Prentiss, Royal Dano. Prison escapee St. Jacques tries to clear himself of false rape-murder charge. Lots of clichés, plus McNair's celebrated nude scenes. Aka DEAD RIGHT. [R]▼

If I Had a Million (1932) **83m.** ***½ D: James Cruze, H. Bruce Humberstone, Stephen Roberts, William A. Seiter, Ernst Lubitsch, Norman Taurog, Norman Z. McLeod. Gary Cooper, George Raft, Mary Boland, Charles Laughton, W. C. Fields, Wynne Gibson, Gene Raymond, Charlie Ruggles, Alison Skipworth, Jack Oakie, Frances Dee, Richard Bennett. Wealthy Bennett gives that sum to various people; all the episodes are good, but the most famous are Laughton's worm-turning and Fields' revenge on road hogs.●

If It's Tuesday, This Must Be Belgium (1969) **C-99m.** *** D: Mel Stuart. Suzanne Pleshette, Ian McShane, Mildred Natwick, Murray Hamilton, Sandy Baron, Michael Constantine, Norman Fell, Peggy Cass, Joan Collins. Funny study of Americans abroad on quickie tour; filmed throughout Europe. Host of cameos sprinkled throughout. Rehashed as a TV movie in 1987. [G]▼●▌

If I Were King (1938) **101m.** *** D: Frank Lloyd. Ronald Colman, Frances Dee, Basil Rathbone, Ellen Drew, C. V. France, Henry Wilcoxon, Heather Thatcher, Sidney Toler. Colman (with that inimitable voice) is ideally cast as the French poet-rogue François Villon, who matches wits with the crafty King Louis XI (Rathbone) and falls hopelessly in love with a lady-in-waiting (Dee). Forget historical accuracy; this is just good entertainment. Scripted by Preston Sturges. Filmed before in 1920 and, as the operetta THE VAGABOND KING, in 1930 and again in 1956. Villon was also played by John Barrymore in THE BELOVED ROGUE (1927).▼

If Looks Could Kill (1991) **C-88m.** ** D:

William Dear. Richard Grieco, Linda Hunt, Roger Rees, Robin Bartlett, Gabrielle Anwar, Geraldine James, Carole Davis, Roger Daltrey. Class clown is mistaken for a top undercover agent while touring Paris with his high school class; standard flunk-out slapstick ensues. Negligible, though Hunt adds a touch of class as a whip-wielding villainess. [PG-13]▼●|

If Lucy Fell (1996) **C-94m.** *½ D: Eric Schaeffer. Sarah Jessica Parker, Eric Schaeffer, Ben Stiller, Elle Macpherson, James Rebhorn, Robert John Burke, David Thornton, Dominic Chianese, Mujibur Rahman, Sirajul Islam, Scarlett Johansson. Puerile "romantic comedy," with writer-director Schaeffer playing an artist of arrested emotional development who shares an apartment with Parker, a therapist (!) with whom he also shares a "death pact," if neither one has found the perfect mate by the age of 30. Any resemblance between these characters and actual human beings is strictly coincidental. Schaeffer isn't dumb, however; he wrote himself a makeout scene with supermodel Macpherson. [R]▼●|

If Winter Comes (1947) **97m.** ** D: Victor Saville. Walter Pidgeon, Deborah Kerr, Angela Lansbury, Binnie Barnes, Janet Leigh, Dame May Whitty, Reginald Owen. Good cast fails to enliven wooden drama about a crisis in the life of kindly, highly principled Pidgeon, living in a stuffy small town outside London and trapped in a marriage to coldhearted Lansbury.

If You Can't Say It, Just See It SEE: **Whore**

If You Could Only Cook (1935) **70m.** *** D: William A. Seiter. Herbert Marshall, Jean Arthur, Leo Carrillo, Lionel Stander, Alan Edwards. Arthur and Marshall are superb team in this delightful comedy of wealthy automobile tycoon/inventor and penniless woman who, for complex reasons, become mobster Carrillo's maid and butler. This film wrongly carried Frank Capra's name as director in many European prints as a fraudulent studio effort to exploit his massive popularity.|

If You Could See What I Hear (1982-Canadian) **C-103m.** ** D: Eric Till. Marc Singer, R. H. Thompson, Sarah Torgov, Shari Belafonte Harper, Douglas Campbell, Helen Burns. Well-intentioned but overly cute, ultimately unreal biography of Tom Sullivan (Singer), the writer, composer, athlete, TV personality and Renaissance man who happens to be blind. [PG]▼●

Igby Goes Down (2002) **C-97m.** **½ D: Burr Steers. Kieran Culkin, Ryan Phillippe, Claire Danes, Amanda Peet, Jeff Goldblum, Susan Sarandon, Bill Pullman, Celia Weston, Bill Irwin, Rory Culkin, Jared Harris. Somber comedy-drama about a screwed-up rich kid with a nutty mother and a schizophrenic father; he refuses to stay in school and won't listen to anyone, least of all his preppie older brother. As a result, he's kicked around by life in general and most of the people he meets. Some striking vignettes but not a successful film on the whole; Culkin's fine performance helps, along with a talented cast. Written by the director. Gore Vidal makes a cameo appearance. Super 35. [R] ▼|

I Girasoli SEE: **Sunflower** (1969)

Igor (2008) **C-87m.** ** D: Anthony Leondis. Voices of John Cusack, Jennifer Coolidge, John Cleese, Steve Buscemi, Molly Shannon, Sean Hayes, Eddie Izzard, Jay Leno, Christian Slater. Mad scientist's hunchbacked lab assistant takes over when his master unexpectedly dies. With the help of a sarcastic laboratory rabbit and a fussy robot, Igor creates a she-monster and later saves the kingdom from an evil ruler. Lots of lightning and electrical effects . . . but nothing comes to life. Mediocre computer-generated animated feature feels like a Tim Burton wannabe without any of Burton's style or appeal. [PG]|

I Got the Hook Up (1998) **C-93m.** BOMB D: Michael Martin. Master P, A.J. Johnson, Gretchen Palmer, Tommy "Tiny" Lister, Helen Martin, John Witherspoon, Ice Cube, Mia X, Snoop Doggy Dogg. Witless, interminable blaxploitation comedy about South Central L.A. con artists who hoodwink the whole hood when they get their hands on a truckload of "hot" beepers and cell phones. Dopey vehicle for rapper/producer Master P, and an unremarkable feature debut for R&B video director Martin. Makes FRIDAY look like RASHOMON. [R]▼●|

I Hate Actors (1986-French) **C/B&W-90m.** **½ D: Gerard Krawrzyk. Jean Poiret, Michel Blanc, Bernard Blier, Michel Galabru, Guy Marchand, Dominique Lavanant. Cute, slight little satire on Hollywood, with a series of murders comically disrupting the filming of a costume epic; agent Poiret is the prime suspect. Based on a novel by Ben Hecht and filmed mostly in beautiful black-and-white; set in Tinseltown, yet all of the dialogue is in French. Look very carefully for Gérard Depardieu. [PG]

I Hate Blondes (1981-Italian) **C-89m.** *** D: Giorgio Capitani. Enrico Montesano, Jean Rochefort, Corinne Clery, Marina Langner, Paola Tedesco, Ivan Desny. Funny comedy about ghostwriter Montesano, whose work inspires a series of real-life heists. Crammed with sight gags; highlighted by a sequence in which Montesano searches for stolen jewels at a party.▼

I Hate Your Guts! SEE: **Intruder, The**

i ♥ huckabees (2004) **C-105m.** **½ D: David O. Russell. Jason Schwartzman, Dustin Hoffman, Lily Tomlin, Jude Law, Mark Wahlberg, Naomi Watts, Isabelle Huppert, Jean Smart, Tippi Hedren, Bob Gunton, Shania Twain, Jonah Hill. Young man seeking the source of coincidences in his life hires a husband-and-wife team of existential detectives who try to show him that everything in life is interconnected. Amusing, impudent comedy about the search for life's imponderables resonates with the fun of watching so many good actors bring oddball characters to life. Doesn't necessarily lead anywhere, but the journey is enjoyable enough. Jon Brion offers an appropriately odd music score. Talia Shire, Schwartzman's real-life mom, plays his mother. Richard Jenkins appears unbilled. Panavision. [R] ▼❶

I Hope They Serve Beer in Hell (2009) **C-105m.** *½ D: Bob Gosse. Matt Czuchry, Jesse Bradford, Geoff Stults, Keri Lynn Pratt, Marika Dominczyk, Traci Lords. Against an anti-Proustian backdrop of video games, strip clubs, and public diarrhea, two socially stunted buds imperil the imminent wedding of a third by enticing him to take off on a boozy whim. A barrage of crudity in the early going evolves into all-too-predictable sentiment—and not the honest kind. A poor man's version of THE HANG-OVER, less directed than patched together. Based on Tucker Max's bestseller. [R] ❶

I Killed Rasputin (1967-French-Italian) **C-95m.** *½ D: Robert Hossein. Gert Frobe, Peter McEnery, Geraldine Chaplin, Robert Hossein, Ira Furstenberg, Ivan Desny. Well-mounted but ponderous story of the men who befriended and then murdered Rasputin. Frobe is simply awful. Franscope.▼

Ikiru (1952-Japanese) **143m.** **** D: Akira Kurosawa. Takashi Shimura, Nobuo Kaneko, Kyoko Seki, Miki Odagiri, Yunosuke Ito. Minor bureaucrat Shimura, dying of cancer, searches for meaning in his life. Thoughtful, poignant examination of loneliness, with a brilliant performance by Shimura. Serves as inspiration for LIFE AS A HOUSE. ▼❶

I Know What You Did Last Summer (1997) **C-100m.** ** D: Jim Gillespie. Jennifer Love Hewitt, Sarah Michelle Gellar, Ryan Phillippe, Freddie Prinze, Jr., Johnny Galecki, Bridgette Wilson, Anne Heche, Muse Watson. In coastal North Carolina, four friends accidentally run down a pedestrian on a lonely road. They dump the body into the sea and vow never to mention it again. But a year later, they each begin receiving the title message in the mail, and then the murders begin. . . . Scripter Kevin Williamson's attempt at a SCREAM follow-up is too routine to succeed overall. Followed by I STILL KNOW WHAT YOU DID LAST SUMMER. Panavision. [R] ▼❶

I Know Where I'm Going! (1945-British) **91m.** **** D: Michael Powell, Emeric Pressburger. Wendy Hiller, Roger Livesey, Finlay Currie, Pamela Brown, Valentine Dyall, Petula Clark. Simple film of headstrong girl (Hiller) who plans to marry for money, stranded in Scottish seacoast town for a week, where she meets and slowly falls in love with Livesey. Very little plot, but an abundance of charm and wit. A quiet gem. Beautifully scripted by the filmmakers. ▼❶

I Know Who Killed Me (2007) **C-105m.** BOMB D: Chris Sivertson. Lindsay Lohan, Julia Ormond, Neal McDonough, Brian Geraghty, Garcelle Beauvais-Nilon, Spencer Garrett, Gregory Itzin. Hopeless thriller in which a young woman is kidnapped and terrorized by a serial killer. When she wakes up in a hospital, she tries to convince everyone she is not who they think she is. Woefully inept, with an incoherent plot and incompetent cinematography. HD Widescreen. [R] ❶

Il Bell'Antonio SEE: **Bell'Antonio**

Il Bidone SEE: **Swindle, The** (1955)

Il Divo (2008-Italian-French) **C/B&W-118m.** *** D: Paolo Sorrentino. Toni Servillo, Anna Bonaiuto, Giulio Bosetti, Flavio Bucci, Carlo Buccirosso, Piera Degli Esposti, Massimo Popolizio, Aldo Ralli. Factual, contemporary saga of seven-time Italian Prime Minister Giulio Andreotti unfolds as if a Borgia were one of the President's Men. A seemingly mild-mannered hypochondriac, he secretly colludes with the Mafia while publicly decrying them, and thus is the concrete centerpiece in a flashy, violent gangster flick about deceptive, Machiavellian politicians. Helpful on-screen character IDs somewhat clarify an almost incomprehensibly complex epic that is otherwise delivered with bloody, juicy brio. Written by the director. Full title is IL DIVO: THE SPECTACULAR LIFE OF GIULIO ANDREOTTI. Super 35.❶

Il Grido (1957-Italian) **115m.** **½ D: Michelangelo Antonioni. Steve Cochran, Alida Valli, Dorian Gray, Betsy Blair, Lyn Shaw. Leisurely paced yet compelling study of Cochran's mental disintegration due to lack of communication with those he loves; Cochran is quite good. Aka THE OUTCRY. ▼❶

I Like It Like That (1994) **C-105m.** *** D: Darnell Martin. Lauren Velez, Jon Seda, Tomas Melly, Desiree Casado, Isaiah Garcia, Jesse Borrego, Lisa Vidal, Griffin Dunne, Rita Moreno. Fresh, vibrant little film about a Latino woman from the Bronx whose tumultuous, love/hate relationship with her husband and three kids is rocked when she stumbles into a job—an exciting one, no less—in the record business. Writer-director Darnell Martin examines real, everyday issues with zest, humor, and the ring of truth. [R] ▼❶

I Like Money (1960-British) **C-97m.** **½ D: Peter Sellers. Peter Sellers, Nadia Gray, Herbert Lom, Leo McKern, Martita Hunt, John Neville, Michael Gough, Billie Whitelaw. Subdued satirical remake of TOPAZE, with Sellers the timid schoolteacher who becomes an unscrupulous businessman. British title: MR. TOPAZE. CinemaScope.

I Live My Life (1935) 92m. ** D: W. S. Van Dyke, II. Joan Crawford, Brian Aherne, Frank Morgan, Aline MacMahon, Eric Blore, Fred Keating, Jessie Ralph, Arthur Treacher, Frank Conroy, Sterling Holloway, Vince Barnett, Hedda Hopper, Lionel Stander. Crawford and Aherne are in love, but she's flighty and he's an archaeologist. Glossy and empty. Scripted by Joseph L. Mankiewicz. ▼

Il Ladro di Bambini SEE: **Stolen Children**

I'll Be Home for Christmas (1998) C-86m. **½ D: Arlene Sanford. Jonathan Taylor Thomas, Jessica Biel, Adam LaVorgna, Sean O'Bryan, Gary Cole, Kathleen Freeman, Amzie Strickland. Conniving college kid tries to make his way cross-country to be home for Christmas dinner, only because his dad has promised him a Porsche if he does. Fairly predictable boy-gets-girl, boy-loses-girl, boy-gets-girl-again-and-learns-a-lesson comedy aimed at young fans of the teenage star. [PG] ▼ ●

I'll Be Seeing You (1945) 85m. **½ D: William Dieterle. Ginger Rogers, Joseph Cotten, Shirley Temple, Spring Byington, Tom Tully, Dare Harris (John Derek). Overblown David Selznick schmaltz. Rogers, convict home on parole, meets disturbed soldier Cotten and they fall in love. ▶

I'll Cry Tomorrow (1955) 117m. ***½ D: Daniel Mann. Susan Hayward, Richard Conte, Jo Van Fleet, Ray Danton, Eddie Albert, Margo. Superlative portrayal by Hayward of star Lillian Roth, her assorted marriages and alcoholic problems. Everything a movie biography should be. Helen Rose won an Oscar for her costumes. Also shown in computer-colored version. ▼ ●

I'll Do Anything (1994) C-115m. ** D: James L. Brooks. Nick Nolte, Albert Brooks, Julie Kavner, Joely Richardson, Tracey Ullman, Whittni Wright, Jeb Brown, Joely Fisher, Ian McKellen, Suzzanne Douglas, Robert Joy, Harry Shearer, Rosie O'Donnell, Ken Page, Woody Harrelson, Patrick Cassidy, Anne Heche. Self-absorbed actor whose career is on the ropes is suddenly forced to care for his 6-year-old daughter. Writer-director Brooks tries to weave a tale of fatherhood into a cutting look behind the scenes of Hollywood, with discouragingly spotty results. Some great "in" material shares screen time with an array of truly dislikeable characters. Kavner and Albert Brooks come off best, as a neurotic match made in heaven. Shot as a musical, before test screenings indicated all the musical numbers should come out! [PG-13] ▼ ●

Illegal (1955) 88m. **½ D: Lewis Allen. Edward G. Robinson, Nina Foch, Hugh Marlowe, Jayne Mansfield, Albert Dekker, Ellen Corby, DeForest Kelley, Howard St. John. Former D.A. Robinson becomes criminal attorney with gangster client, but lays reputation—and life—on the line to defend former assistant Foch for homicide. Valiant attempt to recapture spark of earlier Robinson vehicles; remake of THE MOUTHPIECE. ▼▶

Illegal in Blue (1994) C-94m. **½ D: Stu Segall. Stacey Dash, Dan Gauthier, Louis Giambalvo, Trevor Goddard, Michael Durrell, Sandra Reinhardt, David Groh, Raye Birk. Cop Gauthier, on leave without pay after turning in some crooked coworkers, becomes involved with a sultry nightclub singer (Dash) who may or may not have murdered her husband. Atmospheric 1990s film noir is occasionally illogical but fun nonetheless, and quite sexy. Unrated version also available. [R] ▼

Illegal Tender (2007) C-108m. ** D: Franc. Reyes. Rick Gonzalez, Wanda De Jesus, Dania Ramirez, Antonio Ortiz, Tego Calderon, Jessica Pimentel, Manny Perez. N.Y.C. drug dealer is gunned down the same night his wife gives birth. Twenty years later, the mother is living a nice life in a suburb with her college-student son. When thugs arrive to finish off a job started two decades earlier, she shows her true colors, turning into a pistol-packing mama. Pulpy, Latin-flavored melodrama has lots of fireworks and a good performance by De Jesus, but is brought down by mindless violence and an incredible plotline that wallows in stereotypes. Super 35. [R] ▶

Illegally Yours (1988) C-102m. BOMB D: Peter Bogdanovich. Rob Lowe, Colleen Camp, Harry Carey, Jr., Kenneth Mars, Kim Myers. Juror Lowe is shocked to see that defendant Camp was once the girl he lusted for in elementary school, and snoops around on his own to clear her of the charge. Barely released, painfully unfunny farce, with Bogdanovich still trying to emulate Howard Hawks; how bizarre to see pratfalling Lowe (in glasses) aping Ryan O'Neal in WHAT'S UP DOC?—who, in turn, was aping Cary Grant in BRINGING UP BABY. [PG] ▼▶

Illicit Interlude (1951-Swedish) 94m. **½ D: Ingmar Bergman. Maj-Britt Nilsson, Alf Kjellin, Birger Malmsten, Georg Funkquist. Moody film using flashback retells Nilsson's romance with now-dead lover, and its relationship to her present frame of mind. Original title: SUMMERPLAY; video title: SUMMER INTERLUDE. ▼

I'll Never Forget What's 'Isname (1967-British) C-99m. ***½ D: Michael Winner. Orson Welles, Oliver Reed, Carol White, Harry Andrews, Michael Hordern, Wendy Craig, Marianne Faithfull, Peter Graves, Frank Finlay, Edward Fox. Excellent comedy-drama in which one man rebels against his good life and tries vainly to go back to simpler days. Script by Peter Draper. ▼▶

I'll See You in My Dreams (1951) 110m.

**½ D: Michael Curtiz. Doris Day, Danny Thomas, Frank Lovejoy, Patrice Wymore, James Gleason. Warner Bros. formula musical biography at its hokiest: trite telling of Gus Kahn's life and times; songs include "Ain't We Got Fun," "It Had to Be You."▼○●

I'll sleep when I'm dead (2004-U.S.-British) **C-102m.** *½ D: Mike Hodges. Clive Owen, Charlotte Rampling, Jonathan Rhys Meyers, Malcolm McDowell. Sudden death of a young would-be hustler brings his brother—a former local crime boss—out of isolation, looking for explanations and revenge. Lugubrious drama doesn't lead anywhere especially interesting, and takes its time getting there, to boot. A disappointing reunion for the director and star of CROUPIER. [R] ●

illtown (1998) **C-97m.** *½ D: Nick Gomez. Michael Rapaport, Lili Taylor, Adam Trese, Kevin Corrigan, Paul Schulze, Angela Featherstone, Saul Stein, Tony Danza, Isaac Hayes. Good cast flounders in this downer of a drama about drug dealers Rapaport, Taylor, and Corrigan—they're the good guys—and a vengeance-seeking ex-partner (Trese) who's just been released from jail. Pretentious, boring, and crammed with fuzzy moralizing. Of note for Danza's offbeat casting as a gay crimelord. Filmed in 1995. [R] ▼●

Illuminata (1999) **C-111m.** ** D: John Turturro. John Turturro, Katherine Borowitz, Susan Sarandon, Christopher Walken, Rufus Sewell, Beverly D'Angelo, Donal McCann, Georgina Cates, Ben Gazzara, Aida Turturro. Life, love, lust, and ambition in a theatrical troupe in turn-of-the-20th-century N.Y.C. (although the flavor is distinctly European). Playwright Turturro is in love with the company's star/manager, and longs to have her perform his latest play. Lively, even campy, roles for a fine cast spark this good-looking but often lumbering production, which plays like a French farce in slow motion. Turturro coscripted with Brandon Cole, based on the latter's play. [R] ▼●

Illusionist, The (2006) **C-109m.** **½ D: Neil Burger. Edward Norton, Paul Giamatti, Jessica Biel, Rufus Sewell, Edward (Eddie) Marsan, Jake Wood, Tom Fisher. In turn-of-the-20th-century Vienna the imperious Crown Prince Leopold (Sewell) sees a master stage magician (Norton) as a threat—especially when it's clear that the Prince's fiancée (Biel) is smitten with the illusionist. Intriguing story lets down toward the end and becomes disappointingly ordinary. Giamatti is especially good as a tenacious police inspector. Based on a short story by Steven Millhauser. Music by Philip Glass. [PG-13]●

Illusionist, The (2010-British-French) **C-80m.** **½ D: Sylvain Chomet. A down-and-out vaudeville magician, who now

plays seedy theaters, finds acceptance on a Scottish island—and from a waiflike girl who attaches herself to him as a father figure. They move to Edinburgh and try to start a new life together, but fate pulls them in different directions. Chomet (THE TRIPLETS OF BELLEVILLE) brings Jacques Tati's Monsieur Hulot to vivid life again in animated form, adapting an unproduced Tati script (and providing the music score), but despite moments of charm and whimsy it's slow and emotionally distant. Combining animation techniques produces a strange visual effect as well . . . but the film has its fervent supporters. [PG] ●

Illusion Travels by Streetcar (1953-Mexican) **90m.** **½ D: Luis Buñuel. Lilia Prado, Carlos Navarro, Domingo Soler, Fernando Soto, Agustin Isunza. Two transit workers steal a streetcar destined for the scrap heap, take it on one last run, picking up odd assortment of passengers. Agreeable (if lesser) Buñuel fable. ▼●

Illustrated Man, The (1969) **C-103m.** ** D: Jack Smight. Rod Steiger, Claire Bloom, Robert Drivas, Don Dubbins, Jason Evers, Tim Weldon, Christie Matchett. Young wanderer Drivas meets tattooed man Steiger, searching for the strange woman (Bloom), who "illustrated" his entire body. The wanderer sees futuristic tales in three of the illustrations, all of which also star Steiger and/or Bloom and Drivas. Disappointing, slow-paced adaptation of stories from Ray Bradbury. Panavision. [M/PG] ▼●●

I Love Melvin (1953) **C-76m.** **½ D: Don Weis. Donald O'Connor, Debbie Reynolds, Una Merkel, Allyn Joslyn, Richard Anderson, Noreen Corcoran, Jim Backus, Robert Taylor. N.Y.C. location filming enhances cute musical about lowly photo assistant O'Connor's attempt to impress ambitious dancer Reynolds by pretending he can get her picture in *Look* magazine. ▼○●

I Love My . . . Wife (1970) **C-95m.** ** D: Mel Stuart. Elliott Gould, Brenda Vaccaro, Angel Tompkins, Dabney Coleman, Joan Tompkins. The kind of comedy for which the word "vehicle" was invented. Rarely funny chronicle of Gould's lifelong sexual hangups; witless script, bland direction. [R] ▼

I Love Trouble (1948) **94m.** *** D: S. Sylvan Simon. Franchot Tone, Janet Blair, Janis Carter, Adele Jergens, Glenda Farrell, Steven Geray, Tom Powers, Lynn Merrick, John Ireland, Eduardo Ciannelli, Raymond Burr. Businessman hires flippant private eye Tone to investigate his wife in this Raymond Chandleresque mystery written by Roy Huggins.

I Love Trouble (1994) **C-123m.** **½ D: Charles Shyer. Julia Roberts, Nick Nolte, Saul Rubinek, James Rebhorn, Robert Loggia, Kelly Rutherford, Olympia Dukakis, Marsha Mason, Eugene Levy, Charles Martin Smith, Dan Butler, Paul Gleason,

Jane Adams, Lucy Lu, Clark Gregg, Nora Dunn, Keith Gordon, Dorothy Lyman, Stuart Pankin, Megan Cavanagh, Jessica Lundy, Robin Duke. Rival Chicago newspaper reporters reluctantly join forces to investigate a mysterious train wreck—and, naturally, fall in love. Likable homage to vintage Hollywood bickering/bantering romantic comedies with a touch of adventure and suspense thrown in; there are even old-fashioned "wipes" between shots. Unfortunately, overlength hampers its cuteness, and reveals the degree of contrivance at work. [PG]▼●❙

I Love You (1981-Brazilian) **C-104m.** *½ D: Arnaldo Jabor. Sonia Braga, Paulo Cesar Pereio, Vera Fischer, Tarcisio Meira, Maria Lucia Dahl, Regina Case. Silly, pretentiously arty chronicle of relationship between Braga and Pereio, each of whom tries to manipulate the other. Sonia, however, is lovely to look at. [R]▼

I Love You Again (1940) **99m.** ***½ D: W. S. Van Dyke II. William Powell, Myrna Loy, Frank McHugh, Edmund Lowe, Donald Douglas, Nella Walker. Hilarious story of amnesiac Powell—solid citizen in a small town—reverting to former life as con man, but trying to forestall divorce proceedings by "his" wife (Loy). Ingenious script by Charles Lederer, George Oppenheimer, and Harry Kurnitz.▼●❙

I Love You, Alice B. Toklas (1968) **C-93m.** ***½ D: Hy Averback. Peter Sellers, Jo Van Fleet, Leigh Taylor-Young, Joyce Van Patten. Excellent comedy about the freaking out of mild-mannered L.A. lawyer. Sellers has never been better. Written by Larry Tucker and Paul Mazursky. [R]▼●❙

I Love You, Beth Cooper (2009-U.S.-Canadian) **C-102m.** **½ D: Chris Columbus. Hayden Panettiere, Paul Rust, Jack T. Carpenter, Lauren London, Lauren Storm, Shawn Roberts, Alan Ruck, Cynthia Stevenson. Mega-geek Rust spends a memorably episodic graduation night with former cheerleader Panettiere after outing his ardor for her in a humiliating senior speech. Frequently funny comedy recalls John Hughes' teen epics, and was adapted by *Simpsons* writer Larry Doyle from his 2007 autobiographical novel. More adult than it looks; parents should heed the rating. [PG-13]❙

I Love You, I Love You Not (1979) SEE: **Together?**

I Love You, I Love You Not (1996-French-German-British-U.S.) **C-92m.** ** D: Billy Hopkins. Jeanne Moreau, Claire Danes, Jude Law, James Van Der Beek, Kris Park, Lauren Fox, Emily Burkes-Nossiter, Robert Sean Leonard, Julia Stiles. Disappointingly overwrought drama about a shy teen (Danes) who attends a Manhattan prep school; she has a crush on the school hunk (Law), and encounters anti-Semitism when her classmates

learn that her beloved grandmother (the ever-resplendent Moreau) is a Holocaust survivor. Scripted by Wendy Kesselman, based on her play; Danes also plays the grandmother (as a young woman) in the Holocaust sequences.▼●❙

I Love You, Man (2009) **C-104m.** **½ D: John Hamburg. Paul Rudd, Jason Segel, Rashida Jones, Andy Samberg, J. K. Simmons, Jane Curtin, Jon Favreau, Jaime Pressly, Rob Huebel, Thomas Lennon, Sarah Burns, Lou Ferrigno. Straight-arrow nice guy Rudd plans to wed girlfriend Jones, but comes to realize he doesn't have any real buddies—and no one to serve as best man. In his quest to make friends he bonds with over-age adolescent Segel, who's fun to be with but turns out to be a very loose cannon. The two main characters are sharply drawn and well played in this comedy but the raunch factor is uncomfortably high. *Incredible Hulk* TV star Ferrigno plays . . . himself. [R]❙

I Love You Phillip Morris (2010-U.S.-French) **C-98m.** *** D: Glenn Ficarra, John Requa. Jim Carrey, Ewan McGregor, Leslie Mann, Rodrigo Santoro, Antoni Corone, Brennan Brown, Michael Mandell, Annie Golden, Mary Louise Burke, Aunjanue Ellis. A Southern churchgoer marries his high school sweetheart, then one day comes to the realization that he's gay. In order to support his new lavish lifestyle, he becomes a con artist—and a good one, although he winds up in jail. There he meets his soul mate (McGregor) and promises to find a way they can spend the rest of their lives together. Continuously surprising blend of comedy and drama features what is arguably Carrey's all-time best performance. And yes, it's based on a true story, as documented in Steve McVicker's book. Written by the directors. [R]❙

I Love Your Work (2005) **C-111m.** **½ D: Adam Goldberg. Giovanni Ribisi, Franka Potente, Joshua Jackson, Marisa Coughlan, Christina Ricci, Jared Harris, Elvis Costello, Jason Lee, Nicky Katt, Randall Batinkoff, Haylie Duff, Judy Greer, Shalom Harlow, Vince Vaughn, Lake Bell. Hot young film actor (Ribisi) has a tempestuous relationship with his movie-star wife while being constantly pawed at in public; as he yearns for an ordinary life, he becomes convinced he's being stalked by a fan. Obvious, occasionally rambling, but still an attention-grabbing exploration of the pitfalls of celebrity. Goldberg cowrote, coproduced, and collaborated on the music. Panavision. [R]▼❙

I Love You to Death (1990) **C-96m.** **½ D: Lawrence Kasdan. Kevin Kline, Tracey Ullman, Joan Plowright, River Phoenix, William Hurt, Keanu Reeves, James Gammon, Victoria Jackson, Miriam Margolyes, Heather Graham. Lumpy black comedy about a gregarious Italian-American pizzeria owner whose constant womanizing remains a secret to his wife—until one day when she learns the truth, and then attempts to murder him, with spectacular lack of success. Kline is fun, Plowright is hilarious as his mordant, Slavic mother-in-law, but unfortunately, the film goes flat. Director Kasdan plays a lawyer in the closing scenes; Kline's real-life wife, Phoebe Cates, has an unbilled part as one of his one-night stands. Amazingly, based on a real-life couple! [R]▼●◗

Il Postino SEE: **Postman, The** (1994)

Il Posto (1961-Italian) **93m. ***½** D: Ermanno Olmi. Sandro Panseri, Loredana Detto, Tullio Kezich, Mara Revel. This early Olmi feature has something of the feel of early Truffaut and Milos Forman in its portrayal of everyday life with its tiny triumphs and failures. Simple story concerns a teenaged boy getting his first job and meeting a girl, but the beauty of the film is in the loving and perceptive observation of human behavior. A small-scale gem. ◗

I, Madman (1989) **C-89m. **½** D: Tibor Takacs. Jenny Wright, Clayton Rohner, Randall William Cook, Steven Memel, Stephanie Hodge. A young woman's reading of a novel brings its murderous, supernatural author back to life. A nice, small surprise: the story is imaginative, scary and funny, the effects are clever, and the cast above average; there's also a wow of an ending. If it only made *sense* . . . [R]▼●◗

Imagemaker, The (1986) **C-93m. **** D: Hal Wiener. Michael Nouri, Jerry Orbach, Jessica Harper, Anne Twomey, Farley Granger, Maury Povich, Marcia Gay Harden. The President's ex-media adviser, still reeling from his wife's death, has an audio tape that could incriminate his former boss; genuine or bogus, people are literally dying to get their hands on it. A muddled mess, though a sometimes entertaining one; high point is a hilariously melodramatic scene on a Washington talk show. Twomey good as an ambitious TV reporter. [R]▼

Images (1972-U.S.-British) **C-101m. ***½** D: Robert Altman. Susannah York, Rene Auberjonois, Marcel Bozzuffi, Hugh Millais, Cathryn Harrison. Difficult but fascinating film about a troubled woman who tries to sort out her life; images of reality and fantasy clash in a kind of continuous hallucination. Off-putting at first, but worth the effort to hang on. Filmed in Ireland. Panavision. [R]◗

Imaginarium of Doctor Parnassus, The (2009-British-French-Canadian) **C-122m. **½** D: Terry Gilliam. Heath Ledger, Christopher Plummer, Verne Troyer, Andrew Garfield, Lily Cole, Tom Waits, Peter Stormare, Johnny Depp, Jude Law, Colin Farrell. An old man who harbors dark secrets presides over a quaint traveling show that offers spectators a chance to explore their imagination—be it dark or light—by stepping through a magic mirror. Visually impressive metaphoric muddle offers colorful set pieces, if not a fully satisfying story. Ledger died during production, so Depp, Law, and Farrell play his alter egos on the other side of the mirror—a conceit that actually works to the film's benefit. Gilliam coscripted with Charles McKeown. [PG-13]◗

Imaginary Crimes (1994) **C-105m. **½** D: Anthony Drazan. Harvey Keitel, Fairuza Balk, Kelly Lynch, Vincent D'Onofrio, Elisabeth Moss, Diane Baker, Chris Penn, Amber Benson, Seymour Cassel, Annette O'Toole. Thoughtful, moving (if ultimately overly familiar) coming-of-age story with Keitel doing well as a hustler-dreamer who tries to be the best father he can to his two motherless daughters: drab 17-year-old Balk and younger sister Moss. Lynch shines in her few flashback scenes as the family's deceased wife-mother. [PG]▼●◗

Imaginary Heroes (2004) **C-111m. **½** D: Dan Harris. Sigourney Weaver, Emile Hirsch, Jeff Daniels, Michelle Williams, Kip Pardue, Deirdre O'Connell, Ryan Donowho, Suzanne Santo, Jay Paulson. A shape-shifting drama laced with dark humor about a suburban family struck by tragedy. A strong-willed mother, a disconsolate father, and an emotionally fragile brother each struggles to cope with his own demons and each other. Writer-director Harris (in his feature debut) presents a dysfunctional family to match any in ancient Greek tragedy, with mixed results—but superior performances. Super 35. [R]▼◗

Imagine: John Lennon (1988) **C-103m. **½** D: Andrew Solt. Narrated by John Lennon. Unusual documentary, produced by Solt and David L. Wolper, assembled from 240 hours of footage from Yoko Ono's personal archives. Not exactly a puff job, but a bit discomforting given the obvious calculation that went into the project. Not to be missed are Lennon's confrontations with Al Capp and journalist Gloria Emerson. [R]▼◗

Imagine Me & You (2006-British-German) **C-93m. **½** D: Ol Parker. Piper Perabo, Lena Headey, Matthew Goode, Celia Imrie, Anthony (Stewart) Head, Darren Boyd, Sue Johnston, Eva Birthistle, Ruth Sheen. Amiable romance with a twist: Perabo weds her longtime boyfriend, only to question her feelings for him when she senses a mutual attraction with the woman hired to provide flowers for their nuptials. Generally winning exploration of the unpredictability of life and love is hampered only by the formulaic (and highly unlikely) finale. Super 35. [R]◗

Imagine That (2009-U.S.-British-German) **C-107m. **½** D: Karey Kirkpatrick. Eddie Murphy, Thomas Haden Church, Yara Shahidi, Ronny Cox, Nicole Ari Parker, Vanessa Williams, Martin Sheen, Stephen Root, Richard Schiff. Lightweight but likable fantasy about a stressed-for-success financial manager (Murphy) whose precocious preteen daughter (Shahidi) claims access to "invisible playmates" with exceptionally prescient investment advice. Mildly amusing, albeit a trifle bland; arguably the most innocuous movie of Murphy's career. Aptly chosen covers of Beatles songs pepper the soundtrack. Super 35. [PG]▶

Imagining Argentina (2004-British-Spanish-U.S.) **C-108m.** **½ D: Christopher Hampton. Antonio Banderas, Emma Thompson, Rubén Blades, María Canals, Kuno Becker, John Wood, Claire Bloom. A military dictatorship rules Argentina in 1976, and journalist-activist Thompson is among the thousands whom the authorities indiscriminately kidnap and imprison—or murder. Husband Banderas searches for her in vain, then begins having visions of the fates of other victims. Sobering, well-intentioned drama pointedly parallels the plight of Argentineans during this period to victims of the Holocaust . . . but despite some powerful sequences, the story lacks dramatic cohesion. Hampton scripted, based on a much-lauded novel by Lawrence Thornton. Barely released in the U.S. [R]▶

I'm All Right Jack (1959-British) **104m.** ***½ D: John Boulting. Ian Carmichael, Terry-Thomas, Peter Sellers, Richard Attenborough, Margaret Rutherford, Dennis Price, Irene Handl, Miles Malleson. Carmichael works for his uncle and unwittingly upsets an elaborate and crooked business scheme in this memorable comedy. Sellers wonderful as labor leader. Scripted by Frank Harvey, John Boulting, and Alan Hackney, from Hackney's novel *Private Life.* Sequel to PRIVATE'S PROGRESS (1956). Produced by Roy Boulting.▼▶

I Married a Communist (1950) **73m.** ** D: Robert Stevenson. Laraine Day, Robert Ryan, John Agar, Thomas Gomez, Janis Carter, Richard Rober, William Talman. Cornball acting and a "better-dead-than-Red" scenario sink this noirish melodrama, which has become a relic of its era. Ryan is a shipping executive and former political radical whose past comes back to haunt him. The "commies" (headed by Gomez) are depicted as two-bit gangsters, but Talman is especially good as a killer-for-hire. Retitled THE WOMAN ON PIER 13.▶

I Married a Dead Man SEE: **I Married a Shadow**

I Married a Monster from Outer Space (1958) **78m.** **½ D: Gene Fowler, Jr. Tom Tryon, Gloria Talbott, Ken Lynch, John Eldredge, Jean Carson, Maxie Rosenbloom. One of the silliest titles in film history obscures pretty good little rehash of INVASION OF THE BODY SNATCHERS: Talbott notices that husband Tryon (as well as some of his friends) has been behaving very peculiarly of late. Some nice, creepy moments in chiller which has slowly devel-

oped a cult following. Remade for TV in 1998.▼▶●

I Married an Angel (1942) **84m.** ** D: W. S. Van Dyke II. Jeanette MacDonald, Nelson Eddy, Edward Everett Horton, Binnie Barnes, Reginald Owen, Douglass Dumbrille. Playboy Eddy dreams he marries angel MacDonald in this bizarre adaptation of Rodgers and Hart musical. MacDonald and Eddy's last film together. Songs include "Spring Is Here," title tune.▼

I Married a Shadow (1982-French) **C-110m.** *** D: Robin Davis. Nathalie Baye, Francis Huster, Richard Bohringer, Madeleine Robinson, Guy Trejan. Engrossing if sometimes overwrought drama of abandoned, pregnant Baye taking on the identity of another after a train wreck. Baye is radiant, particularly in the scenes with her newborn baby. Based on a Cornell Woolrich story previously filmed as NO MAN OF HER OWN (1950). Remade in 1996 as MRS. WINTERBOURNE. Aka I MARRIED A DEAD MAN. [PG]▼

I Married a Strange Person! (1998) **C-74m.** **½ D: Bill Plympton. Voices of Charis Michelson, Tom Larson, Richard Spore, Toni Rossi, J. B. Adams, John Russo. Animator-director-cowriter Plympton invokes Picasso's famous quote disdaining "good taste," and follows through with this wild, freeform story of a man who acquires strange powers— and an overactive imagination—just as he embarks on married life. Brash, bizarre, full of deliberately "gross" sight gags involving body parts, and often howlingly funny . . . but not for prudish viewers. Plympton fans should revel in it.▼▶

I Married a Witch (1942) **76m.** *** D: René Clair. Fredric March, Veronica Lake, Robert Benchley, Susan Hayward, Cecil Kellaway, Elizabeth Patterson. Witch burned in Salem centuries ago (Lake) comes back to haunt descendants of Puritan (March) who sent her to her death. Saucy comedy-fantasy based on a story by Thorne (*Topper*) Smith. Good special effects, too.▼●

I'm Dancing as Fast as I Can (1982) **C-107m.** **½ D: Jack Hofsiss. Jill Clayburgh, Nicol Williamson, Dianne Wiest, Daniel Stern, Joe Pesci, Geraldine Page, James Sutorius, Cordis Heard, Richard Masur, Ellen Greene, John Lithgow. Successful Valium-addicted TV documentary filmmaker Clayburgh undergoes harrowing ordeal when she quits pills cold-turkey. Searing because of subject matter, but not particularly well made; still, Clayburgh and costars are first-rate. Screenplay by David Rabe (Clayburgh's husband), based on Barbara Gordon's memoir. [R]▼●

I'm Going Home (2001-French-Portuguese) **C-90m.** *** D: Manoel de Oliveira. Michel Piccoli, Catherine Deneuve, John Malkovich, Antoine Chappey, Jean Koeltgen. Poignant, carefully observed account of a celebrated actor (Piccoli) and his solitude upon learning that his family has been wiped out in a car crash, leaving only his grandson behind. A beautifully realized film, from a 93-year-old filmmaker, about the need to maintain one's personal and artistic integrity, the passage of time, and the fleeting nature of life. ▼▶

I'm Gonna Git You Sucka (1988) **C-87m.** *** D: Keenen Ivory Wayans. Keenen Ivory Wayans, Bernie Casey, Antonio Fargas, Steve James, Isaac Hayes, Jim Brown, Ja'net DuBois, Dawnn Lewis, John Vernon, Clu Gulager, Kadeem Hardison, Damon Wayans, Jester Hairston, Anne Marie Johnson, Gary Owens, Eve Plumb, Clarence Williams III, David Alan Grier, Kim Wayans, Robin Harris, Chris Rock. Hip spoof of '70s blaxploitation films with Wayans (who also wrote and directed) as Jack Spade, vowing to avenge the death of his brother, who died of an o.g. (overdose of gold chains). Loose and good-natured, with some laugh-out-loud gags. Jim Brown and Isaac Hayes, who made so many straight-faced films of this kind, contribute some of the funniest moments. Look for Robert Townsend in a cameo. [R] ▼▶

Imitation General (1958) **88m.** ** D: George Marshall. Glenn Ford, Red Buttons, Taina Elg, Dean Jones, Kent Smith, Tige Andrews. Tepid, occasionally tasteless WW2 comedy defeats its game cast. Ford is a sergeant who impersonates superior officer. CinemaScope.

Imitation of Life (1934) **109m.** **½ D: John M. Stahl. Claudette Colbert, Warren William, Rochelle Hudson, Louise Beavers, Fredi Washington, Ned Sparks, Alan Hale, Henry Armetta. Believable but dated first version of Fannie Hurst's soaper of working-girl Colbert who makes good with Beavers' pancake recipe; Washington is fine as latter's daughter who passes for white. Ultrasentimental. Adapted for the screen by Preston Sturges. ▼▶

Imitation of Life (1959) **C-124m.** ***½ D: Douglas Sirk. Lana Turner, John Gavin, Sandra Dee, Dan O'Herlihy, Susan Kohner, Robert Alda, Juanita Moore, Mahalia Jackson, Troy Donahue, Jack Weston. Plush remake of Fannie Hurst story, with Turner as career-driven actress; Moore is the good-hearted black woman who shares her life, and whose troubled daughter (Kohner) passes for white. Fine performances and direction overcome soap opera trappings to make this quite credible and moving. ▼▶

I'm Losing You (1999) **C-100m.** **½ D: Bruce Wagner. Frank Langella, Rosanna Arquette, Salome Jens, Andrew McCarthy, Elizabeth Perkins, Amanda Donohoe, Buck Henry, Laraine Newman, Daniel von Bargen. Interesting, adult film about a Hollywood producer who learns

he's dying just as his grown children (Arquette, McCarthy) are going through crises of their own. Full of incisive vignettes, though one is left wanting to know more about some of the characters. A creditable directing debut for Wagner, who adapted his own novel. Gina Gershon appears unbilled. [R] ▼▶

Immediate Family (1989) **C-95m.** **½ D: Jonathan Kaplan. Glenn Close, James Woods, Mary Stuart Masterson, Kevin Dillon, Linda Darlow, Jane Greer, Jessica James, Mimi Kennedy. Well-off professional marrieds yearn for a child and hook up with a pregnant, underprivileged teenager via an adoption agency. Watchable change of pace from a pair of often angst-ridden leads but more slick and rose-colored than need be. Masterson stands out in a solid acting quartet. [PG-13] ▼▶

Immortal Bachelor, The (1979-Italian) **C-95m.** **½ D: Marcello Fondato. Monica Vitti, Giancarlo Giannini, Vittorio Gassman, Claudia Cardinale, Renato Pozzetto. Cleaning woman Vitti is on trial for killing philandering husband Giannini; jury member Cardinale decides she'd prefer him to her boring husband (Gassman). Slight Neapolitan comedy. ▼

Immortal Battalion, The SEE: **Way Ahead, The**

Immortal Beloved (1994) **C-121m.** *** D: Bernard Rose. Gary Oldman, Jeroen Krabbé, Isabella Rossellini, Johanna Ter Steege, Marco Hofschneider, Miriam Margolyes, Barry Humphries, Valeria Golino. Handsome, absorbing biography is told in picture-puzzle style, as Beethoven's most ardent admirer and confidant (Krabbé) tries to learn the identity of the composer's "immortal beloved," addressed in a passionate letter found after his death. Filmed in and around Prague, it's a sumptuous-looking and sumptuous-*sounding* tale, but apparently takes as many liberties with the facts as those corny Hollywood composer biopics of yore. Oldman is ideal in the leading role. The director also scripted. Panavision. [R] ▼▶

Immortal Story, The (1968-French) **C-63m.** *** D: Orson Welles. Orson Welles, Jeanne Moreau, Roger Coggio, Norman Eshley, Fernando Rey. Intriguing tale (from an Isak Dinesen story) about a morally bankrupt merchant (Welles) who contrives to make a myth about a sailor seducing a wealthy man's wife come true. Generally well done and, at times, dazzling; originally made for French television. ▼

I'm No Angel (1933) **87m.** ***½ D: Wesley Ruggles. Mae West, Cary Grant, Edward Arnold, Gertrude Michael, Kent Taylor. West is in rare form as star of Arnold's sideshow who chases after playboy Grant. Builds to a hilarious courtroom climax.

Mae gets sole screenplay credit for this, one of her all-time best. ▼●◖

I'm Not Rappaport (1996) **C-136m.** **½ D: Herb Gardner. Walter Matthau, Ossie Davis, Amy Irving, Martha Plimpton, Craig T. Nelson, Guillermo Diaz, Boyd Gaines, Ron Rifkin, Irwin Corey. Too long—and too literal—adaptation of Gardner's 1986 Tony Award–winning Broadway play about a pair of old codgers who develop an adversarial friendship in Central Park. Strong performances by Matthau, as an aged radical and congenital tale-spinner, and Davis, as a nearly blind building superintendent just trying to hang on. The characters are so good and so likable that they almost overcome the silliness of the climactic sequence (standing up to drug pusher Nelson) . . . but not quite. [PG-13] ▼●◖

I'm Not Scared (2003-Italian-Spanish-British) **C-101m.** *** D: Gabriele Salvatores. Aitana Sánchez-Gijón, Dino Abbrescia, Giorgio Careccia, Giuseppe Cristiano, Mattia Di Pierro, Diego Abatantuono. A ten-year-old inadvertently discovers a boy hidden away in a covered hole in the ground near a spot where he and his friends play; neither one understands what's going on or why, though we in the audience put the pieces together one by one. Understated yet evocative film, set in rural Southern Italy in 1978, is told from an innocent child's point of view. Based on Niccòlo Ammaniti's best-selling book. Super 35. [R]◖

I'm Not There (2007-U.S.-German) **C/B&W-135m.** **½ D: Todd Haynes. Christian Bale, Cate Blanchett, Marcus Carl Franklin, Richard Gere, Heath Ledger, Ben Whishaw, Charlotte Gainsbourg, David Cross, Bruce Greenwood, Julianne Moore, Michelle Williams, Richie Havens; narrated by Kris Kristofferson. Fragmented portrait of Bob Dylan, with six actors (including Blanchett, who is extraordinary) playing different aspects of the musician's biographical and fictional personas. Provocative attempt to circumvent the clichés of a biopic; extremely well filmed and acted, but provides little insight into Dylan, his work, or his cultural impact. Dylan fans may find more to enjoy; film buffs will have fun spotting references to Fellini, Godard, and other directors. Super 35. [R]◖

I Mobster (1958) **80m.** **½ D: Roger Corman. Steve Cochran, Lita Milan, Robert Strauss, Celia Lovsky, Lili St. Cyr. Rugged account of gangster Cochran and events in his crime-filled life. Full title: I MOBSTER . . . THE LIFE OF A GANGSTER. CinemaScope. ▼◖

I, Monster (1971-British) **C-74m.** ** D: Stephen Weeks. Christopher Lee, Peter Cushing, Mike Raven, Richard Hurndall, George Merritt, Kenneth J. Warren. Good, atmospheric production and ensemble performances cannot completely redeem boring adaptation of Stevenson's *Dr. Jekyll and Mr. Hyde.* This time, early student of Freud develops serum to relieve human inhibitions. Intended to be shown in 3-D, which explains some of the camera movements. [PG]◖

Importance of Being Earnest, The (1952-British) **C-95m.** *** D: Anthony Asquith. Michael Redgrave, Michael Denison, Richard Wattis, Edith Evans, Margaret Rutherford, Joan Greenwood, Dorothy Tutin. Oscar Wilde's peerless comedy of manners set in Victorian England is given admirable treatment. Remade in 2002. ▼●◖

Importance of Being Earnest, The (2002-British-U.S.) **C-94m.** ** D: Oliver Parker. Rupert Everett, Colin Firth, Frances O'Connor, Reese Witherspoon, Judi Dench, Tom Wilkinson, Anna Massey, Edward Fox. Two lotharios pursue their women by adopting false identities in this remake of the Oscar Wilde comedy by the writer-director of AN IDEAL HUSBAND. This time, unfortunately, the tone is all wrong: the actors are terribly, terribly coy, the comedy much too self-aware. Fox fares best as a wry butler—but he's barely in the film. Witherspoon comes off quite well, British accent and all. Lively score by Charlie Mole. Dench's real-life daughter Finty Williams plays her mother's character in flashback scene. Panavision. [PG] ▼◖

Impossible Object SEE: **Story of a Love Story**

Impossible Years, The (1968) **C-92m.** BOMB D: Michael Gordon. David Niven, Lola Albright, Chad Everett, Ozzie Nelson, Cristina Ferrare. Stupid, leering sex farce from hit Broadway play about psychiatrist who has problems of his own with nubile young daughter; the most obscene G-rated film of all. Panavision. [G]▼◖

Impostor (2002) **C-95m.** BOMB D: Gary Fleder. Gary Sinise, Madeleine Stowe, Vincent D'Onofrio, Tony Shalhoub, Mekhi Phifer, Tim Guinee, Lindsay Crouse, Elizabeth Peña. *Is* Sinise an alien spy impersonating a scientist married to Stowe in 2079? The movie's distributor apparently didn't think anyone cared enough to find out, because this malnourished Philip K. Dick adaptation sat on the shelf for more than a year. Most interesting features are the neat home appliances in the early scenes, which include a voice-activated wall-screen TV that shuts off on command. You should be so lucky when watching this movie at home. Director's cut runs 102m. and is rated R. [PG-13] ▼◖

Impostors, The (1998) **C-100m.** *** D: Stanley Tucci. Stanley Tucci, Oliver Platt, Alfred Molina, Lili Taylor, Tony Shalhoub, Steve Buscemi, Allison Janney, Richard Jenkins, Isabella Rossellini, Campbell Scott, Billy Connolly, Dana Ivey, Hope Davis, Lewis J. Stadlen, Michael Emerson. A rare bird for our time: an old-fashioned farce, written and directed by and starring Tucci, who's teamed (providentially) with Platt, as unemployed actors whose audacious behavior toward popular ham actor Molina sends them scurrying—and hiding out on a luxury liner. Doors slam, people trip over each other, and fall in love at the drop of a hat. A treat to watch . . . especially with this cast of supremely gifted actors (including one surprise). [R] ▼●❍

Impromptu (1991-British) **C-109m.** ***½ D: James Lapine. Judy Davis, Hugh Grant, Mandy Patinkin, Bernadette Peters, Julian Sands, Ralph Brown, Georges Corraface, Anton Rodgers, Emma Thompson, Anna Massey. Intellectual romp, in the SMILES OF A SUMMER NIGHT mold, about 19th-century superstars—Chopin, Liszt, Delacroix, George Sand, and the like—on a country holiday. Spirited performances and some timeless satire of culture vultures on the make; compared to A SONG TO REMEMBER, they *do* make them better than they used to. Film debut of stage director Lapine; screenplay by Sarah Kernochan, his wife. [PG-13] ▼●❍

Improper Channels (1981-Canadian) **C-92m.** **½ D: Eric Till. Alan Arkin, Mariette Hartley, Sarah Stevens, Monica Parker, Harry Ditson. OK comedy with oddball architect Arkin erroneously accused of child abuse. Stevens, as his 5-year-old daughter, is cute; Hartley, as his estranged wife, is wasted. [PG] ▼●

Impulse (1974) **C-91m.** BOMB D: William Grefe. Ruth Roman, William Shatner, Harold Sakata, Kim Nicholas, Jenifer Bishop, James Dobson. Distasteful Florida-made cheapie with Shatner overacting as a lothario who cons, then kills, women. Truly awful. Originally titled WANT A RIDE, LITTLE GIRL? [PG] ▼●

Impulse (1984) **C-91m.** *½ D: Graham Baker. Tim Matheson, Meg Tilly, Hume Cronyn, John Karlen, Bill Paxton, Amy Stryker. Matheson visits girlfriend Tilly in a small farming community, finds the citizens are robbing banks, shooting children, urinating on cars. Plodding reverse variation on INVASION OF THE BODY SNATCHERS—here, everyone exhibits *too much* emotion. [R] ▼●❍

Impulse (1990) **C-108m.** *** D: Sondra Locke. Theresa Russell, Jeff Fahey, George Dzundza, Alan Rosenburg, Nicholas Mele, Eli Danker, Charles McCaughan, Lynne Thigpen, Shawn Elliott. Half-standard, half-fresh, and always tough: honest narc Russell, moonlighting as an L.A. streetwalker for the vice squad, briefly but fatefully yields to corruption after lousy hours and failed relationships combine to wear her down. Underrated sleeper doesn't exactly expand parameters of the cop genre, but has a memorable central character; arguably Russell's best performance. [R] ▼●

Impulsion SEE: **Stepmother, The**
Impure Thoughts (1985) **C-87m.** **½ D:

Michael A. Simpson. Brad Dourif, Lane Davies, Terry Beaver, John Putch, Joe Conley, Mary McDonough, Mary Nell Santacroce; narration by Dame Judith Anderson. A quartet of men has died; they meet in purgatory and recall their lives together as Catholic school students when JFK was president and no one had ever heard of Vietnam. Occasionally funny and insightful, with some truly wonderful moments, but it just doesn't hold together. [PG] ▼

I'm Still Here (2010) **C-107m.** *½ D: Casey Affleck. Words like "strange" and "self-indulgent" don't begin to describe this up-close-and-personal chronicle of Joaquin Phoenix, the Oscar-nominated actor who "retired" from his film career to enter the world of hip-hop. Is this a documentary or mockumentary? A comedy or tragedy? Is Phoenix a narcissist and boor, a deeply troubled soul—or both? The world is not breathlessly waiting for answers. Affleck, by the way, is Phoenix's brother-in-law. Many famous faces appear throughout. [R] ❍

I'm the One That I Want (2000) **C-96m.** ***½ D: Lionel Coleman. Margaret Cho. Terrific concert film of Cho's one-woman show at San Francisco's Warfield Theater details her rise, fall, and rebirth after barely living through *All-American Girl,* a TV sitcom based on her Korean-American family. Alternately poignant and hilarious material tackles the double standard that women—especially minority women—face in the entertainment industry. [R] ▼●

In a Better World (2010-Danish-Swedish) **C-113m.** ***½ D: Susanne Bier. Mikael Persbrandt, Trine Dyrholm, Ulrich Thomsen, Markus Rygaard, William Jøhnk Nielsen, Bodil Jørgensen. Altruistic Danish doctor who treats the sick in Africa returns home to find his son the victim of a bully at school. The boy is befriended by a new arrival from England who's got serious psychological problems of his own, angry over the death of his mother. Bier and screenwriter Anders Thomas Jensen create a story that's both gripping and harrowingly believable, an exploration of violence that simmers just below the surface of polite society. Oscar winner for Best Foreign Language Film. HD Widescreen. [R] ❍

Inadmissible Evidence (1968-British) **96m.** **½ D: Anthony Page. Nicol Williamson, Eleanor Fazan, Jill Bennett, Peter Sallis, David Valla, Eileen Atkins. John Osborne's play about barrister who has reached saturation point with everyone and everything preserves Williamson's fine stage performance, but still a photographed play, not a film. Music by Dudley Moore. [R]

In a Lonely Place (1950) **91m.** ***½ D: Nicholas Ray. Humphrey Bogart, Gloria Grahame, Frank Lovejoy, Robert Warwick, Jeff Donnell, Martha Stewart. Mature, powerful drama about a feisty, self-destructive screenwriter (Bogart) who has an affair with starlet Grahame while trying to clear himself of a murder rap. Excellent performances in this study of two turbulent characters set against realistic and cynical Hollywood backdrop. Written by Andrew Solt. ▼▶

In America (2003-Irish-British) **C-115m.** ***½ D: Jim Sheridan. Samantha Morton, Paddy Considine, Djimon Hounsou, Sarah Bolger, Emma Bolger, Juan Hernandez. Poignant, bittersweet fable of survival based on writer-director Sheridan's own experiences emigrating to the U.S. (through Canada) with his family. Seen largely through the eyes of two young sisters, who filter out the grunginess of their N.Y.C. existence (human and otherwise) and make a special connection with a seemingly hostile neighbor (Hounsou). Sheridan, always a gifted storyteller, wrote this very personal film with his daughters Naomi and Kirsten, and cast remarkable, real-life sisters as the children. [PG-13] ▼▶

In & Out (1997) **C-90m.** *** D: Frank Oz. Kevin Kline, Joan Cusack, Tom Selleck, Matt Dillon, Debbie Reynolds, Wilford Brimley, Bob Newhart, Gregory Jbara, Shalom Harlow, Lewis J. Stadlen, Ernie Sabella, Dan Hedaya, Joseph Maher, Shawn Hatosy, Selma Blair. When a young actor (Dillon) wins an Oscar, he thanks his small-town high school teacher—who, he says, is gay. The popular teacher, days away from his wedding, denies this emphatically but still has to deal with the tumult and media frenzy that erupt. Very funny script by Paul Rudnick, played to a fare-thee-well by an expert cast. Enjoyable cameos by Whoopi Goldberg and Glenn Close at the mock Oscar ceremony. [PG-13] ▼●▶

In a Shallow Grave (1988) **C-92m.** BOMB D: Kenneth Bowser. Michael Biehn, Maureen Mueller, Michael Beach, Patrick Dempsey, Thomas Boyd Mason. Gloomy, slow-moving tale of WW2 veteran Biehn, disfigured at Guadalcanal, who has retreated to his family's desolate Virginia homestead to brood about his condition (and wallow in self-pity). Biehn tries hard but is overpowered by film's snaillike pacing and bizarre, romantic storyline (involving drifter Dempsey, whose character is weird in the extreme). One of the oddest and most maudlin dramas ever made. An *American Playhouse* presentation. [R] ▼

In a Year with 13 Moons (1978-German) **C-129m.** ***½ D: Rainer Werner Fassbinder. Volker Spengler, Ingrid Caven, Gottfried John, Elisabeth Trissenaar, Eva Mattes. Extraordinary performance by Spengler in the difficult role of a pathetic transsexual conceived and abandoned by his mother while her husband was in a prison camp. Powerful, disturbing tale of loneliness, alienation, rejection, winningly written and directed by Fassbinder. ▼▶

In Bruges (2008-U.S.-British) **C-107m.** *** D: Martin McDonagh. Colin Farrell, Brendan Gleeson, Ralph Fiennes, Clémence Poésy, Jérémie Rénier, Thekla Reuten, Jordan Prentice, Željko Ivanek. Black comedy about two hit men who are exiled to the Belgian tourist city of Bruges until things cool off after a bungled job at home. Easygoing Gleeson is content to take in the sights but hotheaded Farrell is bored—and itchy. Eventually their mercurial boss (Fiennes) is forced to follow them there. Ingenious feature debut for playwright McDonagh, who creates truly original characters: hard-core criminals, each with his own moral code. All three leading actors are on top of their game. Exceptional score by Carter Burwell. Ciarán Hinds appears unbilled. Super 35. [R] ▶

In Celebration (1975-British) **C-110m.** *** D: Lindsay Anderson. Alan Bates, James Bolam, Brian Cox, Constance Chapman, Gabrielle Day, Bill Owen. Overly theatrical but still taut, vivid drama depicting the pain, anger, and intense relationship of three brothers who return to the coal-mining town of their youth for their parents' 40th anniversary. Based on a play by David Storey, which Anderson had directed on the stage; an American Film Theatre production. [PG] ▼▶

Incendiary (2008-British) **C-96m.** *½ D: Sharon Maguire. Ewan McGregor, Michelle Williams, Matthew Macfadyen, Nicholas Gleaves, Sidney Johnston, Usman Khokhar, Sasha Behar. Suicide bombers attack a North London stadium during a high-profile soccer match. One of the victims is Williams' young son; as she mourns, she fixates on a boy whose father she believes was one of the terrorists. Barely watchable drama accomplishes the near impossible: It portrays issues relating to terrorism and its impact on individual lives as hackneyed soap opera. Williams' gutsy performance is the sole interest here. Maguire scripted, from Chris Cleave's 2005 novel. Panavision. [R] ▶

Incendies (2010-Canadian-French) **C-130m.** ***½ D: Denis Villeneuve. Lubna Azabal, Mélissa Désormeaux-Poulin, Maxim Gaudette, Rémy Girard, Abdelghafour Elaaziz, Allen Altman. A brother and sister, who are twins, attend the reading of their mother's will and learn that they have a sibling they never knew about—and a father who, despite what they were told, is very much alive. The sister embarks on a journey of discovery to their homeland in the Middle East, retracing her mother's steps and learning how much the woman suffered at the hands of family, neighbors, and captors during her difficult life. A tough, spellbinding story that deals with forgiveness and resolution, adapted by the director from Wajdi Mouawad's play. Note that the Middle Eastern country is never named. [R] ▶

Incense for the Damned SEE: **Bloodsuckers** (1970)

Inception (2010) **C-148m.** **½ D: Christopher Nolan. Leonardo DiCaprio, Ken Watanabe, Joseph Gordon-Levitt, Marion

Cotillard, Ellen Page, Tom Hardy, Cillian Murphy, Tom Berenger, Michael Caine, Dileep Rao, Lukas Haas, Pete Postlethwaite. DiCaprio and his team are masters of a form of corporate spying: entering a selected target's dream state and extracting information, for which competitors pay huge sums. Underestimating the complexities of the tool, DiCaprio mishandled it to the point of severely rupturing his personal life, forcing him to flee the U.S. Now, at a psychological impasse, he's offered a challenging job he can't refuse by corporate giant Watanabe. But this means facing his demons by virtually retracing the same nightmarish territory that nearly destroyed him. Ambitious, exceedingly well-crafted film, written by Nolan, works too hard to show off its cleverness and intricacy and even betrays its own ground rules when it suits the filmmaker. Oscar winner for Cinematography (Wally Pfister), Sound Editing, Sound Mixing, and Visual Effects. Panavision/Panavision 70. [PG-13] ▶

Inchon! (1982-Korean-U.S.) **C-105m.** BOMB D: Terence Young. Laurence Olivier, Jacqueline Bisset, Ben Gazzara, Toshiro Mifune, Richard Roundtree. Empty-headed Korean war epic produced by Rev. Sung Myung Moon's Unification Church. Olivier looks like a wax museum figure in his makeup as Gen. Douglas MacArthur. Laughable script punctuated by epic-scale battle scenes. Cut from 140m. length. [PG]

Incident, The (1967) **107m.** *** D: Larry Peerce. Tony Musante, Martin Sheen, Beau Bridges, Jack Gilford, Thelma Ritter, Brock Peters, Ruby Dee, Ed McMahon, Diana Van Der Vlis, Mike Kellin, Jan Sterling, Gary Merrill, Donna Mills. Tough, brutal story of two drunken hoods who terrorize passengers in N.Y.C. subway. Well made but unpleasant—and still topical. Film debuts of Sheen and Mills.▼●

Incident at Oglala (1992) **C-89m.** *** D: Michael Apted. Narrated by Robert Redford. Incisive documentary detailing the alleged framing of Leonard Peltier, Native American who was jailed in the wake of a 1975 "incident" at South Dakota's Pine Ridge Reservation that resulted in the deaths of two FBI agents. Must viewing in tandem with the thematically related THUNDER-HEART, also directed by Apted. Redford also is executive producer. [PG]▼●

Incognito (1997-U.S.-British) **C-107m.** **½ D: John Badham. Jason Patric, Irène Jacob, Rod Steiger, Thomas Lockyer, Ian Richardson, Simon Chandler. An art forger (Patric) who's hired to create a fake Rembrandt goes to Europe and falls for an art expert (Jacob) who happens to be the world's foremost Rembrandt authority, and forces her to go on the run with him after he's framed for murder. Barely released, would-be Hitchcockian thriller. Ian Holm appears unbilled. Panavision. [R] ▼●

In Cold Blood (1967) **134m.** **** D: Richard Brooks. Robert Blake, Scott Wilson, John Forsythe, Paul Stewart, Gerald S. O'Loughlin, Jeff Corey, Will Geer. Excellent semidocumentary adaptation of Truman Capote's book, tracing stories of two young killers (Blake, Wilson), their motives and eventual arrest after slaughtering innocent family. Incisive, engrossing, unsensational; masterful script, direction by Brooks, fine black-and-white photography by Conrad Hall. Remade as a TV miniseries in 1996. The story of Capote researching this book is recounted in CAPOTE and INFAMOUS. Panavision.▼●

Inconvenient Truth, An (2006) **C-96m.** *** D: Davis Guggenheim. Intelligent filmed version of Al Gore's multimedia presentation on the phenomenon of global climate change, in which the former vice president clearly, succinctly explains global warming and its potentially disastrous consequences. While the film persuasively explores an issue that is relevant to the future of planet earth, it also serves as a celluloid press release for Gore by spotlighting the major events in his life, stressing his deep commitment to the issue at hand. Oscar winner for Best Documentary and Original Song "I Need to Wake Up" by Melissa Etheridge. [PG]▼

In Country (1989) **C-120m.** *½ D: Norman Jewison. Bruce Willis, Emily Lloyd, Joan Allen, Kevin Anderson, John Terry, Peggy Rea, Judith Ivey, Richard Hamilton, Patricia Richardson, Jim Beaver. Disappointing, poorly executed film of Vietnam vet Willis and niece Lloyd, two Kentuckians trying to come to terms with the war. Willis is good as a cynical, shell-shocked recluse, but script, from Bobbie Ann Mason's acclaimed novel, is flawed: character relationships are uneven, and too many questions are left unanswered (like Willis' medical condition). Beautifully handled concluding scenes, leading up to Washington, D.C., Veterans Memorial visit, can't redeem film. [R]▼●

Incredible Hulk, The (2008) **C-112m.** *** D: Louis Leterrier. Edward Norton, Liv Tyler, Tim Roth, William Hurt, Tim Blake Nelson, Ty Burrell, Christina Cabot. Bruce Banner lives in exile in Brazil, trying to figure out what causes him to become the Hulk when he gets angry. Then his old nemesis, General Ross (Hurt), tracks him down, with a ferocious fighting man (Roth) in tow, and sends him on the run—back to the college lab where he first experimented on himself (and fell in love). Straightforward comic-book movie has energy to spare and a first-rate performance by Norton. Monstrous street-fight finale is reminiscent of the climax of TRANSFORMERS. Offers pleasing nods to the vintage TV series and its stars. Robert Downey, Jr., appears unbilled.

The Hulk's cocreator Stan Lee cameos. See HULK (2003). Panavision. [PG-13]▶

Incredible Invasion SEE: **Sinister Invasion**

Incredible Journey, The (1963) **C-80m.** *** D: Fletcher Markle. Emile Genest, John Drainie, Tommy Tweed, Sandra Scott. Entertaining, well-made Disney story of three pets—two dogs and a cat—who make 250-mile journey across Canada on their own to be with their family of humans. Remade by Disney in 1993 as HOMEWARD BOUND: THE INCREDIBLE JOURNEY. ▼●▶

Incredible Melting Man, The (1978) **C-86m.** *½ D: William Sachs. Alex Rebar, Burr DeBenning, Myron Healey, Michael Aldredge, Ann Sweeney, Lisle Wilson. Rebar is only survivor of outer space mission which has turned his body into a melting muck. Cheap, old-fashioned B horror film whose only saving grace is Rick Baker's excellent makeup effects. [R]▼

Incredible Mr. Limpet, The (1964) **C-102m.** ** D: Arthur Lubin. Don Knotts, Jack Weston, Carole Cook, Andrew Duggan, Larry Keating. Knotts plays a milquetoast who dreams of becoming a fish—and miraculously gets his wish (turning into an animated cartoon figure). What's more, he helps the Navy spot Nazi submarines during WW2. Innocuous family fare goes on too long.▼●▶

Incredibles, The (2004) **C-115m.** *** D: Brad Bird. Voices of Craig T. Nelson, Holly Hunter, Samuel L. Jackson, Jason Lee, Wallace Shawn, Sarah Vowell, Spencer Fox, Elizabeth Peña, John Ratzenberger. Dynamic computer-animated film from Pixar about a family of superheroes who now live in a witness-protection program and have to suppress their superpowers . . . until a mysterious source calls on Mr. Incredible for help. Starts out as sharp comedy, then morphs into a comic-book–style action film; result is a shift in tone and a lengthening of the story, but it all comes together. Writer-director Bird provides the voice of costume designer Edna Mode, and includes a cameo by (and tribute to) legendary Disney animators Frank Thomas and Ollie Johnston. Snazzy music score by Michael Giacchino. Oscar winner for Best Animated Feature and Sound Editing. Digital widescreen. [PG] ▼▶

Incredible Sarah, The (1976) **C-106m.** ** D: Richard Fleischer. Glenda Jackson, Daniel Massey, Yvonne Mitchell, Douglas Wilmer, David Langton, Simon Williams. Broadly sketched portrait of legendary French actress Sarah Bernhardt; Jackson chews the scenery in a flamboyant performance, but someone should have chewed up the script instead. Filmed in England. [PG]▼●

Incredible Shrinking Man, The (1957) **81m.** ***½ D: Jack Arnold. Grant Williams, Randy Stuart, April Kent, Paul Langton,

William Schallert, Billy Curtis. Accidents result in Williams shrinking ever smaller; trapped in his own basement, he has memorable encounters with a cat and (even smaller) a spider. Intelligent, serious approach, exceptional effects for the period, and a vigorous leading performance result in a genuine sci-fi classic, unsurpassed by later attempts. No dialogue in the last third, just Williams' occasional narration. Director Arnold's best movie. Screenplay by Richard Matheson, from his own novel. ▼●▶

Incredible Shrinking Woman, The (1981) **C-88m.** ** D: Joel Schumacher. Lily Tomlin, Charles Grodin, Ned Beatty, Henry Gibson, Elizabeth Wilson, Mark Blankfield, Pamela Bellwood, John Glover, Mike Douglas. Semi-spoof of SHRINKING MAN with Tomlin in three roles, principally as a suburban housewife whose constant exposure to household products causes her to dwindle; she becomes a media darling, then the target of an evil corporation. Never as funny or pointed as it would like to be, but worth catching for really peculiar color schemes and an amazing performance by Rick Baker as a gorilla named Sidney. Schumacher's directorial debut. [PG] ▼●▶

Incredible 2-Headed Transplant, The (1971) **C-88m.** *½ D: Anthony M. Lanza. Bruce Dern, Pat Priest, Casey Kasem, Albert Cole, John Bloom, Berry Kroeger. The head of an insane murderer is attached to the head of a mental incompetent. But who can we blame for this movie? [PG] ▼▶

Incredibly Strange Creatures Who Stopped Living and Became Mixed-Up Zombies!!?, The (1963) **C-82m.** **½ D: Ray Dennis Steckler. Cash Flagg (Ray Dennis Steckler), Brett O'Hara, Atlas King, Sharon Walsh, Madison Clarke, Son Hooker. Legendary (thanks to that title) low-budget horror film about hideous goings-on at a carny sideshow, with lots of rock numbers thrown in. Truly bizarre film features gorgeously saturated color, awful acting, hideous dialogue, haunting atmosphere, and little plot. Cinematography by Joe Micelli (author of *American Cinematographers' Manual*) with very young Laszlo Kovacs and Vilmos Zsigmond helping. Aka THE TEENAGE PSYCHO MEETS BLOODY MARY.▼▶

Incredibly True Adventures of Two Girls in Love, The (1995) **C-94m.** ** D: Maria Maggenti. Laurel Holloman, Nicole Parker, Maggie Moore, Kate Stafford, Sabrina Artel. A grungily dressed, white tomboy from a lesbian household falls for a financially secure black beauty—a reciprocated romance that has the latter's snooty high school pals reeling. Given the physical characteristics of the two leads and the script's lack of mean streak, the tolerant may overlook this meagerly budgeted comedy's total lack of cinematic interest. Otherwise, it's more interminable than incredible. [R] ▼▶

"In" Crowd, The (1988) C-96m. **½ D: Mark Rosenthal. Donovan Leitch, Jennifer Runyon, Scott Plank, Joe Pantoliano, Bruce Kirby, Wendy Gazelle, Page Hannah. Surprisingly likable look at the lives and loves of those guys and gals who danced their hearts out on daily TV dance shows in the 1960s. Not as hip as John Waters' similarly themed HAIRSPRAY but fun anyway. Leitch is the son of '60s recording star Donovan. [PG]▼●

In Crowd, The (2000) C-104m. BOMB D: Mary Lambert. Lori Heuring, Susan Ward, Nathan Bexton, Matthew Settle, Daniel Hugh Kelly, Taylor Negron, Tess Harper, Jay R. Ferguson. Sub-par cross between a slasher pic and Aaron Spelling sludge about a troubled girl, fresh out of the loony bin, who takes a summer job at an exclusive country club. There she falls in with a homicidal, bisexual young woman and her 90210 hottie friends. The pinup cast pouts, glares, and shows off its tan lines with minimal conviction. [PG-13]▼▼

Incubus (1966) 74m. *** D: Leslie Stevens. William Shatner, Allyson Ames, Eloise Hardt, Robert Fortier, Ann Atmar, Milos Milos. First—and so far *only*—movie ever made in the language of Esperanto concerns a beautiful succubus who tries to corrupt a pure soul, only to fall in love instead. Long-lost, genuinely creepy curio written and directed by the creator of *The Outer Limits* plays like a feature-length episode of that series—as made by Ingmar Bergman. Conrad Hall's expressionistic b&w photography of the striking Big Sur locations is a major asset.▼▼

Incubus, The (1982-Canadian) C-90m. BOMB D: John Hough. John Cassavetes, Kerrie Keane, Helen Hughes, Erin Flannery, Duncan McIntosh, John Ireland. Repulsive, poorly made horror thriller about sex murders in small Wisconsin town. [R]▼●▼

In Custody (1993-British-Indian) C-123m. ** D: Ismail Merchant. Shashi Kapoor, Shabana Azmi, Om Puri, Sushma Seth, Neena Gupta, Tinnu Anand. Silly tale of a doltish college lecturer and intellectual (Puri) who writes poetry no one will publish; he sets out to interview India's "greatest living Urdu poet" (Kapoor), which quickly proves to be a disheartening experience. Means to be an allegory about the lack of respect for history, intellectualism, and scholarship in modern India, but the result is only nonsensical. Disappointing feature directorial debut from Merchant (better known as James Ivory's longtime producer). [PG]▼▼

Indecent Proposal (1993) C-118m. ** D: Adrian Lyne. Robert Redford, Demi Moore, Woody Harrelson, Oliver Platt, Seymour Cassel, Billy Bob Thornton, Rip Taylor, Joel Brooks, Billy Connolly, Sheena Easton, Herbie Hancock. A cocky high roller offers destitute couple Harrelson and Moore a million

dollars to sleep with her for one night. They accept, but are immediately plunged into a whirlpool of remorse, jealousy, and bitterness. Intriguing premise bogged down by sheer silliness (not to mention overlength), though it remains watchable. [R]▼●▼

Independence Day (1983) C-110m. ** D: Robert Mandel. Kathleen Quinlan, David Keith, Frances Sternhagen, Cliff DeYoung, Dianne Wiest, Josef Sommer, Bert Remsen, Richard Farnsworth, Brooke Alderson, Noble Willingham, Susan Ruttan. Interesting but unfocused little picture about a young woman who's aching to leave her claustrophobic hometown but held back (in part) by romance with car mechanic Keith. Subplot about battered wife (superbly played by Wiest) seems to be a separate film altogether. [R]▼

Independence Day (1996) C-145m. **½ D: Roland Emmerich. Will Smith, Bill Pullman, Jeff Goldblum, Mary McDonnell, Judd Hirsch, Margaret Colin, Randy Quaid, Robert Loggia, James Rebhorn, Harvey Fierstein, Adam Baldwin, Brent Spiner, James Duval, Vivica A. Fox, Lisa Jakub, Ross Bagley, Bill Smitrovich, Harry Connick, Jr. Spectacular—and spectacularly stupid—sci-fi saga of alien ships hovering over the earth and apparently planning to attack. U.S. President Pullman tries to determine how best to fight, as the stakes keep changing on an hour-to-hour basis. Big, Oscar-winning special effects are impressive, but the human stories are so dumb, the writing so lame, and some of the performances so broad they make some silly '50s sci-fi movies look brilliant by comparison. 15m. added for special edition. Super 35. [PG-13] ▼●▼

Independent, The (2001) C-85m. **½ D: Stephen Kessler. Jerry Stiller, Janeane Garofalo, Max Perlich, Andy Dick, John Lydon, Ginger Lynn Allen, Billy Burke, Fred Dryer, Richard Paul, Larry Hankin. Mockumentary about legendary schlock film producer Morty Fineman (Stiller), who enlists his estranged daughter to save his bankrupt production company. Uneven, but the cast is game and the clips from Morty's *extremely* prolific oeuvre are very funny. Many cameos from filmmakers like Ron Howard, Peter Bogdanovich, and Roger Corman, along with Stiller's wife, Anne Meara, and son, Ben. Stay through the credits for the entire Fineman filmography. [R] ▼▼

Indiana Jones and the Kingdom of the Crystal Skull (2008) C-122m. *** D: Steven Spielberg. Harrison Ford, Cate Blanchett, Karen Allen, Ray Winstone, John Hurt, Jim Broadbent, Shia LaBeouf, Igor Jijikine. After a 19-year hiatus, Indy returns with the same brand of high adventure that marked the original RAIDERS OF THE LOST ARK. In 1957 the intrepid archaeologist-professor runs afoul of Russian spies (including a wily Blanchett), then follows a young man (LaBeouf) who bears a letter from an old friend, now lost in the jungles of Peru, that may lead them to the Crystal Skull of Akator—and the lost city of El Dorado. Opens with slam-bang action, falls into a lull of exposition, then revs into high gear for an eye-filling finale. Ford reclaims the role he invented in fine fashion. Written by David Koepp from a story by George Lucas and Jeff Nathanson. Panavision. [PG-13]▐

Indiana Jones and the Last Crusade (1989) **C-127m.** **½ D: Steven Spielberg. Harrison Ford, Sean Connery, Denholm Elliott, Alison Doody, John Rhys-Davies, Julian Glover, River Phoenix, Michael Byrne, Alex Hyde-White. Follow-the-numbers adventure spectacle has Ford in fine form and Connery adding panache as Indy's archaeologist father, whose mysterious disappearance (while searching for the Holy Grail) sets the story in motion. This deliberately old-fashioned Saturday matinée yarn has everything money can buy, but never really generates a sense of wonder and excitement. A definite improvement over the second Indiana Jones outing, but it still bears the mark of one too many trips to the well. Oscar winner for sound effects editing. Followed by INDIANA JONES AND THE KINGDOM OF THE CRYSTAL SKULL. Panavision. [PG-13]▼●▌

Indiana Jones and the Temple of Doom (1984) **C-118m.** ** D: Steven Spielberg. Harrison Ford, Kate Capshaw, Ke Huy Quan (Jonathan Ke Quan), Amrish Puri, Roshan Seth, Philip Stone, Dan Aykroyd. Headache-inducing prequel to RAIDERS OF THE LOST ARK, but this time the 1930s archaeologist-adventurer has a weaker story and wimpier heroine. Re-creates (and outdoes) a bunch of great cliffhanger stunts, but never gives us a chance to breathe . . . and tries to top the snake scene in RAIDERS by coming up with a variety of new "gross-out" gags. Oscar winner for Visual Effects. Followed by INDIANA JONES AND THE LAST CRUSADE. Panavision. [PG] ▼●▌

Indian Fighter, The (1955) **C-88m.** *** D: Andre de Toth. Kirk Douglas, Walter Matthau, Elsa Martinelli, Walter Abel, Lon Chaney. Exciting account of Douglas leading wagon train through rampaging Indian country. CinemaScope.▼▌

Indian in the Cupboard, The (1995) **C-96m.** *** D: Frank Oz. Hal Scardino, Litefoot, Lindsay Crouse, Richard Jenkins, Rishi Bhat, Steve Coogan, David Keith, Sakina Jaffrey, Vincent Kartheiser, Nestor Serrano. A boy (Scardino) receives an old cupboard as a birthday present, and finds that when he puts a plastic Indian inside and turns the key, the Indian comes to life. *Then* he learns that the Indian is not a toy, but a real person, and complications ensue—especially when his best friend conjures up a real-life cowboy. First-rate adapta-

tion of Lynne Reid Banks' popular children's book, scripted by Melissa Mathison (of E.T. fame); full of wonder and simple wisdom . . . if a few too many giant closeups of the boy's face. [PG] ▼●▌

Indian Love Call SEE: **Rose Marie** (1936)

Indian Runner, The (1991) **C-125m.** *** D: Sean Penn. David Morse, Viggo Mortensen, Valeria Golino, Patricia Arquette, Charles Bronson, Sandy Dennis, Dennis Hopper, Benicio Del Toro, Kenny Stabler. Mood piece about a young man's desperate attempts to understand—and get closer to—his troubled kid brother, who's just returned from Vietnam. Lethargic at times, but filled with emotion and truth, and ultimately quite moving. Strong performances all around, with offbeat but effective casting of Bronson as the boys' melancholy father. Impressive achievement for first-time writer/director Penn. Penn's real-life mother, actress Eileen Ryan, plays Mrs. Baker. Inspired by Bruce Springsteen's song "Highway Patrolman." [R] ▼●▌

Indian Summer (1993) **C-97m.** *** D: Mike Binder. Alan Arkin, Matt Craven, Diane Lane, Bill Paxton, Elizabeth Perkins, Kevin Pollak, Vincent Spano, Julie Warner, Kimberly Williams. Good-natured yuppie nostalgia about thirtysomethings who return to the beloved summer camp of their youth for a reunion weekend. Arkin is wonderful as the camp director, and the cast couldn't be more appealing. Writer-director Binder based this on his own memories, and filmed at the actual Camp Tamakwa he attended in Canada. That's director Sam Raimi playing Arkin's flunky. Panavision. [PG-13] ▼●▌

Indian Summer (1995) SEE: **Alive and Kicking**

Indian Tomb, The (1959-German) **C-97m.** **½ D: Fritz Lang. Debra Paget, Paul Hubschmid, Walther Reyer, Claus Holm, Sabine Bethmann, René Deltgen. The pace picks up a bit in this second of Lang's Indian diptych, chronicling the events leading up to lovers Paget and Hubschmid's escape from the clutches of maharajah Reyer. Paget's exotic dance is a highlight. This and Part One (THE TIGER OF ESCHNAPUR) were originally dubbed, edited down to 95m., and released in the U.S. as JOURNEY TO THE LOST CITY.▐

Indigènes SEE: **Days of Glory** (2006)

Indiscreet (1958) **C-100m.** *** D: Stanley Donen. Cary Grant, Ingrid Bergman, Cecil Parker, Phyllis Calvert, David Kossoff, Megs Jenkins. Bergman is renowned actress whom American playboy Grant romances and can't forget. Delightful comedy from Norman Krasna play *Kind Sir.* Made in England. Remade as a 1988 TVM with Robert Wagner and Lesley-Anne Down. ▼▌

Indiscretion of an American Wife (1953-U.S.-Italian) **63m.** **½ D: Vittorio De Sica.

Jennifer Jones, Montgomery Clift, Gino Cervi, Richard Beymer. Turgid melodrama set in Rome's railway station, with Jones the adulterous wife meeting lover Clift for one more clinch. De Sica's original 87m. version, titled TERMINAL STATION, was restored in 1983. Remade in 1998 for TV. ▼)

Indochine (1992-French) **C-155m.** ** D: Régis Wargnier. Catherine Deneuve, Vincent Perez, Linh Dan Pham, Jean Yanne, Dominique Blanc, Henri Marteau, Carlo Brandt, Gerard Lartigau. Soap opera set against political upheaval in French Indochina during the 1930s. Deneuve plays a wealthy French landowner who's raised an orphaned Indochinese girl, and now must contend with the fact that she's grown— and has a mind of her own. Interesting historical elements, set against a fascinating landscape, but story is mostly tripe. Even so, nabbed the Foreign Film Oscar. [PG-13] ▼◑)

Indomitable Teddy Roosevelt, The (1983) **C-94m.** *** D: Harrison Engle. Narrated by George C. Scott. Excellent and innovative documentary about the remarkable, larger-than-life figure who became our 26th president. Artfully mixes newsreel footage with meticulous recreations featuring Bob Boyd in the role of T.R. Set to the stirring music of John Philip Sousa. ▼)

In Dreams (1999) **C-99m.** ** D: Neil Jordan. Annette Bening, Robert Downey, Jr., Aidan Quinn, Stephen Rea, Paul Guilfoyle, Dennis Boutsikaris, Katie Sagona, Krystal Benn. Massachusetts woman is haunted by disturbing dreams which turn out to be the thoughts of a sick man who's abducting and murdering children. Is she insane, or somehow psychically connected to the killer? Extremely unpleasant adult horror film is well made but hard to watch. It's also hard to top the opening sequence, based on the real-life incident of a town being flooded to create a reservoir. Jordan coscripted with Bruce Robinson. [R] ▼◑)

In Enemy Country (1968) **C-107m.** ** D: Harry Keller. Tony Franciosa, Anjanette Comer, Guy Stockwell, Paul Hubschmid, Tom Bell, Emile Genest. So-so programmer of WW2 intrigue, set in France and England, filmed on Universal's backlot. Not very convincing. Techniscope.

I Never Promised You a Rose Garden (1977) **C-96m.** *** D: Anthony Page. Bibi Andersson, Kathleen Quinlan, Ben Piazza, Lorraine Gary, Reni Santoni, Susan Tyrrell, Signe Hasso, Jeff Conaway, Diane Varsi, Barbara Steele, Sylvia Sidney, Dennis Quaid. Intelligent adaptation of Hannah Green's book about her treatment for schizophrenia as a teenager, focusing on relationship between her (Quinlan) and dedicated psychiatrist (Andersson). Graphic, clinical approach is often disturbing. [R] ▼)

I Never Sang for My Father (1970) **C-93m.** ***½ D: Gilbert Cates. Melvyn Douglas, Gene Hackman, Dorothy Stickney, Estelle Parsons, Elizabeth Hubbard, Lovelady Powell. Sensitive adaptation of Robert Anderson play about grown man (Hackman) faced with problem of caring for elderly father (Douglas). Fine job all around, but extremely depressing. Scripted by the playwright. [PG] ▼◑)

Inevitable Grace (1994) **C-103m.** BOMB D: Alex Canawati. Maxwell Caulfield, Stephanie Knights, Jennifer Nicholson, Tippi Hedren, Samantha Eggar, Sandra Knight, Rob Sheiffele, Taylor Negron. Lame psychological thriller about a psychiatrist at a mental institution who gets involved in a nasty (and ludicrous) triangle with her patient and the woman's husband. Seemingly endless movie offers a chance to check out Jack Nicholson and Sandra Knight's daughter Jennifer, but that's not much of a recommendation. ▼

Infamous (2006) **C-118m.** *** D: Douglas McGrath. Toby Jones, Sandra Bullock, Jeff Daniels, Sigourney Weaver, Daniel Craig, Hope Davis, Isabella Rossellini, Juliet Stevenson, Lee Pace, Gwyneth Paltrow, Peter Bogdanovich, John Benjamin Hickey. Writer Truman Capote (a superb Jones), darling of 1950s New York society, heads to Kansas with novelist pal Nelle Harper Lee (Bullock) when a random murder spree piques his interest. Based on a George Plimpton book, this film covers the same ground as 2005's CAPOTE, but on a broad canvas, with more humor and panache. Written by the director. [R] ◗

Infernal Affairs (2002-Hong Kong) **C-101m.** *** D: Andrew Lau, Alan Mak. Tony Leung Chiu-wai, Andy Lau, Anthony Wong, Eric Tsang, Chapman To, Lam Katung, Ng Ting-yip, Wan Chi-keung. Hong Kong cop goes deep undercover to infiltrate a Triad crime gang and spends 10 years rising to the top, then learns that the gang has planted a mole in the police department for the same amount of time. Tense game of cat and mouse ensues as each one tries to discover the other's identity. Stylish, character-driven thriller delivers plenty of action while dealing with philosophical notions of morality, identity, and loyalty. Followed by a prequel and a sequel. Remade by Martin Scorsese as THE DEPARTED. Arriscope. [R] ◗

Infernal Idol, The SEE: **Craze**

Inferno (1953) **C-83m.** **½ D: Roy (Ward) Baker. Robert Ryan, Rhonda Fleming, William Lundigan, Henry Hull, Carl Betz, Larry Keating. Fleming plots rich husband Ryan's demise, with surprising results. Good desert sequences. Remade as a TV movie, ORDEAL. 3-D. ◗

Inferno (1980-Italian) **C-107m.** **½ D: Dario Argento. Leigh McCloskey, Irene Miracle, Sacha Pitoeff, Daria Nicolodi, Eleonora Giorgi, Veronica Lazar, Alida

Valli. American returns to N.Y. from studies in Rome to investigate the gruesome murder of his sister, and discovers "evil mothers" wreaking supernatural havoc on both sides of Atlantic. Surreal, hypnotic shocker by Italian horror maestro Argento is short on sense, but long on style. Second in Argento's *Three Mothers* trilogy, following SUSPIRIA; followed by MOTHER OF TEARS. [R]▼◗

Infinity (1996) **C-117m.** **½ D: Matthew Broderick. Matthew Broderick, Patricia Arquette, Peter Riegert, Dori Brenner, Peter Michael Goetz, Željko Ivanek, Matt Mulhern, Joyce Van Patten, James LeGros. Sweet but uneven movie based on the life of Richard Feynman, whose relationship with Arline Greenbaum (Arquette) in pre-WW2 N.Y.C. takes a fateful turn when he is recruited to work on the Manhattan Project. (The theoretical physicist won the Nobel Prize in 1965.) Effective when dealing with the love story, but meanders when Feynman moves to Los Alamos. Broderick's directorial debut; scripted by his mother, Patricia Broderick. [PG]▼◗◗

Informant!, The (2009) **C-108m.** *** D: Steven Soderbergh. Matt Damon, Scott Bakula, Joel McHale, Melanie Lynskey, Rick Overton, Tom Papa, Tom Wilson, Clancy Brown, Tony Hale, Ann Cusack, Allan Havey, Rusty Schwimmer, Eddie Jemison, Candy Clark, Bob Zany, Scott Adsit, Patton Oswalt, Tom Smothers, Dick Smothers. Mark Whitacre (Damon), a rising executive at Midwestern biofuel corporation Archer Daniels Midland, decides to blow the whistle on some of its shady practices in the early 1990s, and works with the FBI to nail his greedy bosses. Whitacre has no idea of what lies in store for him, but it turns out the feds are in for some big surprises, too. A story so nutty it could only be true—although an opening title card cheekily admits that some elements have been fictionalized for dramatic effect. True-life saga gets better (and loopier) as it goes along, and Damon is terrific. Adapted from journalist Kurt Eichenwald's book. Delightfully puckish, "retro" score by Marvin Hamlisch. [R]◗

Informer, The (1935) **91m.** ***½ D: John Ford. Victor McLaglen, Heather Angel, Preston Foster, Margot Grahame, Wallace Ford, Una O'Connor, J. M. Kerrigan, Joseph Sauers (Sawyer), Donald Meek. Dated but still potent study of human nature tells of hard-drinking McLaglen, who informs on buddy to collect reward during Irish Rebellion of 1922. Powerful drama, based on Liam O'Flaherty's novel, with a memorable Max Steiner score. McLaglen's performance won the Oscar, as did Ford, Steiner, and Dudley Nichols (for Best Screenplay). Filmed before in England in 1929. Remade as UP TIGHT.▼◗◗

Informers, The (1965-British) SEE: **Underworld Informers**

Informers, The (2009) **C-98m.** BOMB D: Gregor Jordan. Billy Bob Thornton, Kim Basinger, Mickey Rourke, Winona Ryder, Brad Renfro, Jon Foster, Amber Heard, Rhys Ifans, Chris Isaak, Austin Nichols, Lou Taylor Pucci, Mel Raido, Theo Rossi. Returning to the bored, drug-addled, sex-obsessed L.A. deadheads he made famous in *Less Than Zero*, author and coscreenwriter Bret Easton Ellis' collection of familiar and wasted Hollywood types adds up to *way* less than zero this time. A good cast is lost in the fog of clichéd writing and indifferent direction. There's the sinister studio exec, the neglected wife having an affair with the pool boy, the aging newscaster, the low-level hood, and a host of beautiful, vapid young people who spend their days doing drugs and their nights in bed with each other. Yecccch. This was Renfro's last film. Super 35. [R]◗

In for Treatment (1979-Netherlands) **C-99m.** ***½ D: Eric van Zuylen, Marja Kok. Helmert Woudenberg, Frank Groothof, Hans Man In't Veld, Marja Kok, Joop Admiraal. Simple, pointed, powerful story of a middle-aged man who checks into a hospital for tests but is really dying of cancer; he must deal with a distant, maddeningly impersonal hospital system. Hard to watch because of the subject, but still poignant and never maudlin; a production of the Werkteater, a Dutch theater collective.▼

Infra-Man (1976-Hong Kong) **C-92m.** *** D: Hua-Shan. Li Hsiu-hsien, Wang Hsieh, Yuan Man-tzu, Terry Liu, Tsen Shuyi, Huang Chien-lung, Lu Sheng. Princess Dragon Mom (Liu) and her odd assortment of monster underlings attempt to take over the earth—and it's Infra-Man (Hsiu-hsien) to the rescue. Action-packed, with gloriously corny dialogue (dubbed), outlandish costumes and sets, adequate special effects. Great fun. Panavision. [PG]▼◗

Inglorious Bastards, The (1978-Italian) **C-100m.** ** D: Enzo G. Castellari. Bo Svenson, Fred Williamson, Peter Hooten, Ian Bannen, Michael Pergolani, Jackie Basehart, Michel Constantin, Debra Berger. Ragtag group of American soldiers, headed for court-martialing, escape during a German attack and make their way to the Swiss border. Dubious acting—and dubbing—make this Hollywood-wannabe action yarn something of a hoot, but some energetic action in the second half helps to redeem it. This inspired Quentin Tarantino's INGLOURIOUS BASTERDS, though the two films have almost nothing in common. [R]▼◗

Inglourious Basterds (2009-U.S.-German) **C-153m.** **½ D: Quentin Tarantino. Brad Pitt, Mélanie Laurent, Christoph Waltz, Eli Roth, Michael Fassbender, Diane Kruger, Daniel Brühl, Til Schweiger, Jacky Ido, B. J. Novak, Julie Dreyfus, Mike Myers, Rod Taylor. Cartoonish WW2 vignettes, each one teasingly tense but long, focus on a band of Jewish vigilante U.S.

soldiers who are out for Nazi blood . . . a French woman whose family was slaughtered and now runs a Paris movie theater . . . an operation involving a German movie star who's working undercover for the Allies . . . and a cheerfully sly S.S. officer who's one step ahead of his enemies. (Waltz's rich performance earned him a Best Supporting Actor Oscar.) In this boys' adventure-cum-fantasy, moviemaking plays a crucial role in the outcome of the war. A colorful, flamboyant concoction that's well-staged but awfully self-indulgent, a handful of scenes in search of a real movie. Inspired by THE INGLORIOUS BASTARDS (1978), directed by Enzo G. Castellari, who has a cameo here. Panavision. [R] ▌

In God's Hands (1998) **C-96m.** ** D: Zalman King. Matt George, Matty Liu, Patrick Shane Dorian, Shaun Tomson, Maylin Pultar, Bret Michaels. Three world-class surfers (played by three actual world-class surfers) embark on the ultimate global tour of duty. Fictional film suffers from amateurishness of its cast of nonperformers, but is marginally worth seeing for gorgeous cinematography and, of course, some breathtaking wave riding. A change of pace for soft-core auteur King. Super 35. [PG-13] ▼▌

In God We Tru$t (1980) **C-97m.** BOMB D: Marty Feldman. Marty Feldman, Peter Boyle, Louise Lasser, Richard Pryor, Andy Kaufman, Wilfrid Hyde-White, Severn Darden. Naïve monk Feldman treks to L.A. to raise money for his monastery. A comedy that is tragically unfunny—including Pryor, who plays God. Feldman also cowrote the script. [PG] ▼

In Good Company (2004) **C-109m.** *** D: Paul Weitz. Dennis Quaid, Topher Grace, Scarlett Johansson, Marg Helgenberger, Selma Blair, David Paymer, Clark Gregg, Philip Baker Hall, Frankie Faison, Ty Burrell, Kevin Chapman, Amy Aquino, Colleen Camp, Lauren Tom. Successful, happily married, 50-ish sales exec Quaid has his world turned inside out when a young 20-ish hotshot with no experience is installed as his boss—and even starts seeing Quaid's college-age daughter. Smart, relevant social comedy tackles a variety of modern-day ills in a consistently entertaining way. Breakout role for Grace, who's perfect as the corporate climber who finds that his life is empty. Weitz's solo debut as writer-director. Malcolm McDowell appears unbilled. [PG-13] ▼▌

In Harm's Way (1965) **165m.** **½ D: Otto Preminger. John Wayne, Kirk Douglas, Patricia Neal, Tom Tryon, Paula Prentiss, Henry Fonda, Brandon de Wilde, Jill Haworth, Dana Andrews, Stanley Holloway, Burgess Meredith, Franchot Tone, Patrick O'Neal, Carroll O'Connor, Slim Pickens, Barbara Bouchet, Hugh O'Brian, George Kennedy, Bruce Cabot, Larry Hagman. Overlong, melodramatic account of warfare in the South Pacific at the outset of WW2, focusing on the exploits of larger-than-life naval officer Wayne (whose character is nicknamed "Rock"). Most interesting for its cast of old-timers and up-and-coming stars. Panavision. ▼▌

Inheritance, The (1976-Italian) **C-105m.** **½ D: Mauro Bolognini. Anthony Quinn, Dominique Sanda, Fabio Testi, Adriana Asti, Luigi Proietti. Moody melodrama about dying patriarch (Quinn) who wants to disown everyone but his calculating daughter-in-law (Sanda), who offers him sexual comforts. Well-acted, handsome production with emphasis on eroticism. Originally 121m. Techniscope. [R] ▼▌

Inheritors, The (1998-Austrian) **C-95m.** *** D: Stefan Ruzowitzky. Simon Schwarz, Sophie Rois, Lars Rudolph, Julia Gschnitzer, Ulrich Wildgruber, Elizabeth Orth, Tilo Pruckner, Susanne Silverio. A landowner dies and bequeaths his assets to the seven lowly peasants who worked his farm. Spirited, pointed (if predictable) political allegory, set in an Austrian village in the 1930s. Vivid characterizations add punch to the proceedings. [R] ▼▌

Inherit the Wind (1960) **127m.** ***½ D: Stanley Kramer. Spencer Tracy, Fredric March, Gene Kelly, Florence Eldridge, Dick York, Harry Morgan, Donna Anderson, Elliott Reid, Claude Akins, Noah Beery, Jr., Norman Fell. Vocals by Leslie Uggams. Absorbing adaptation of Jerome Lawrence–Robert E. Lee play based on notorious Scopes Monkey Trial of 1925, when Clarence Darrow defended and William Jennings Bryan prosecuted a schoolteacher arrested for teaching Darwin's Theory of Evolution. Names are changed (Kelly's character is based on acid-tongued H. L. Mencken), but the issue is real and still relevant. An acting tour de force, with solid support from Morgan as the judge, Reid as a lawyer, Eldridge as March's devoted wife. Only offbeat casting of Kelly doesn't quite come off. Screenplay by Nathan E. Douglas (Nedrick Young) and Harold Jacob Smith. Remade as 1988 TVM with Kirk Douglas and Jason Robards. Also remade as a TVM in 1999 with Jack Lemmon and George C. Scott. ▼▌

In Her Shoes (2005) **C-129m.** *** D: Curtis Hanson. Cameron Diaz, Toni Collette, Shirley MacLaine, Mark Feuerstein, Ken Howard, Candice Azzara, Brooke Smith, Francine Beers, Norman Lloyd, Jerry Adler. A woman who struggles with her self-image is constantly undone by her sexy sister, whose life is an even bigger mess. Then her sibling travels to Florida and looks up their long-estranged grandmother, who's living at a senior community; here, of all places, she finds direction and purpose for the first time in her life. First-rate adaptation of Jennifer Weiner's best-seller by Susannah Grant, ideally cast with a great part for Diaz. MacLaine scores especially well by underplaying. Super 35. [PG-13]🅳

Initiation: Silent Night, Deadly Night 4
SEE: **Silent Night, Deadly Night 4**

Inkheart (2008-U.S.-German) **C-106m. ✱✱** D: Iain Softley. Brendan Fraser, Paul Bettany, Helen Mirren, Jim Broadbent, Andy Serkis, Eliza Hope Bennett, Rafi Gavron; narrated by Roger Allam. When Fraser reads aloud he brings characters from books to life—with often frightening results. He and his daughter go to Europe in search of the rare book that can free her mother from imprisonment within its pages. Elaborate fantasy based on Cornelia Funke's novel borrows from other, better, stories (including *The Wizard of Oz*) and never coalesces into a great yarn of its own. Nice in-joke has Jennifer Connelly, Bettany's real-life wife, doing a cameo as his spouse. Panavision. [PG]🅳

Inkwell, The (1994) **C-110m. ✱½** D: Matty Rich. Larenz Tate, Joe Morton, Suzzanne Douglas, Glynn Turman, Vanessa Bell Calloway, Adrienne-Joi Johnson, Morris Chestnut, Jada Pinkett, Duane Martin, Mary Alice, Phyllis Yvonne Stickney. A 16-year-old, whose toy doll confidante naturally worries his parents, learns about love, SUMMER OF '42-style, in this Summer of '76 nostalgia piece set in a black section of Martha's Vineyard. Clumsily written and directed and (doll aside) irritatingly derivative. Filmmakers groused that the result would have been better without studio interference. [R] ▼◑

Inland Empire (2006-U.S.-Polish-French) **C/B&W-179m. ✱✱½** D: David Lynch. Laura Dern, Jeremy Irons, Justin Theroux, Harry Dean Stanton, Peter J. Lucas, Karolina Gruszka, Jan Hench, Grace Zabriskie, Diane Ladd, Julia Ormond, Ian Abercrombie, William H. Macy, Mary Steenburgen, Laura Harring, Nastassja Kinski, Michael Paré; voice of Naomi Watts. Demanding, surreal Lynchian experiment is almost impossible to describe. Suffice it to say that Dern offers staggering performances in several roles (which may or may not be the same character), most prominently as an actress who is cast as the lead in a new movie. A digitally shot companion piece to MULHOLLAND DR. Not for every filmgoer; Lynch buffs will probably rate this higher. Dern also coproduced. [R]🅳

In-Laws, The (1979) **C-103m. ✱✱✱** D: Arthur Hiller. Peter Falk, Alan Arkin, Richard Libertini, Nancy Dussault, Penny Peyser, Arlene Golonka, Michael Lembeck, Ed Begley, Jr., Rosana (de) Soto, Art Evans, David Paymer. Wacky comedy about a dentist (Arkin) who becomes involved in the bizarre intrigues of his daughter's father-in-law-to-be (Falk), who claims to be a CIA agent. Andrew Bergman's script commendably unpredictable start to finish; Libertini hilarious as Latin dictator with a Señor Wences

fetish. Enjoyable score by John Morris. Remade in 2003. [PG]▼◑

In-Laws, The (2003) **C-98m. ✱✱½** D: Andrew Fleming. Michael Douglas, Albert Brooks, Robin Tunney, Ryan Reynolds, Candice Bergen, David Suchet, Lindsay Sloane, Maria Ricossa. Needless but amusing-enough remake of the fondly remembered 1979 comedy, bolstered by its well-cast stars. Douglas is a reckless CIA agent—and neglectful father of groom-to-be Reynolds—who takes Brooks, a timid, nebbishy father of the bride, on the adventure of his life in the days leading up to their kids' wedding. Suchet is a standout as the crazed French arms buyer and megalomaniac. [PG-13]▼◑

In Like Flint (1967) **C-114m. ✱✱½** D: Gordon Douglas. James Coburn, Lee J. Cobb, Jean Hale, Andrew Duggan, Anna Lee. Weak sequel to OUR MAN FLINT finds our hero going against secret society of women plotting to take over the world. CinemaScope.▼◑

In Love SEE: **Falling in Love Again**

In Love and War (1996-U.S.-British) **C-115m.** BOMB D: Richard Attenborough. Sandra Bullock, Chris O'Donnell, Mackenzie Astin, Emilio Bonucci, Ingrid Lacey, Margot Steinberg. Lumbering catastrophe chronicles Ernest Hemingway's WW1 love affair with Red Cross nurse Agnes von Kurowsky, eight years his senior and the inspiration for the character Catherine Barkley in *A Farewell to Arms*. Miscast O'Donnell might actually be more credible playing Ernest Borgnine, and the leads have no chemistry. The film leans on what used to be called "scenic values" like a bookie who's been stiffed. Panavision. [PG-13]▼◑

In My Country (2005-U.S.-British-Irish) **C-102m. ✱✱** D: John Boorman. Samuel L. Jackson, Juliette Binoche, Brendan Gleeson, Menzi Ngubane, Sam Ngakane, Lionel Newton. Reporter Jackson and poet Binoche are covering the Truth and Reconciliation Commission hearings in South Africa, an event where opposing sides from the Apartheid era confront each other. Despite a talented cast and director, important subject matter, and a provocative setting, it all goes awry and winds up being a 3-D movie: dull, dreary, and disappointing. Even Jackson is bland. Original British title: COUNTRY OF MY SKULL. [R]▼◑

In Name Only (1939) **94m. ✱✱✱** D: John Cromwell. Carole Lombard, Cary Grant, Kay Francis, Charles Coburn, Helen Vinson, Peggy Ann Garner. Solid soaper with wealthy, married Grant falling for widowed Lombard, trying desperately to obtain a divorce from bitchy, manipulative social climber Francis. Beautifully acted.▼◑

Inner Circle, The (1991) **C-134m. ✱✱½** D: Andrei Konchalovsky. Tom Hulce, Lolita Davidovich, Bob Hoskins, Alexandre Zbruev, Feodor Chaliapin, Jr., Bess Meyer,

Maria Baranova. Intriguing if ultimately obvious, disappointing saga of life in the Soviet Union under the iron rule of Stalin. Story follows naive, humble projectionist (Hulce) who gets to screen a film for the dictator. Much more subtlety is in order here, as Hulce's performance soon becomes grating and one-dimensional. Based on a true story; some sequences were shot inside the Kremlin, and even KGB headquarters. [PG-13]▼●

Inner Life of Martin Frost, The (2007-U.S.-French-Spanish-Portuguese) **C/B& W-93m.** *** D: Paul Auster. David Thewlis, Irène Jacob, Michael Imperioli, Sophie Auster. Work-weary novelist Thewlis, decompressing alone in a borrowed country home, is startled to wake up one morning next to lovely, cheerful Jacob. Romance blooms—how could it not?—but soon he learns she's not what she appears to be. Intriguing Orphic fable intimately addresses large themes of literature, philosophy, and the creative process, while delicately tiptoeing across the balance beam of fantasy. Adapted from his own novel and austerely narrated by director Auster.❚

Innerspace (1987) **C-120m.** **½ D: Joe Dante. Dennis Quaid, Martin Short, Meg Ryan, Kevin McCarthy, Fiona Lewis, Vernon Wells, Robert Picardo, Wendy Schaal, Harold Sylvester, William Schallert, Henry Gibson, Orson Bean, Kevin Hooks, Kathleen Freeman, Dick Miller, Ken Tobey. Diverting tale of rambunctious Navy test pilot (Quaid) who undergoes miniaturization experiment and is accidentally injected into the body of hypochondriac Short. Heady combination of science fiction and comedy, with an off-the-wall sensibility that keeps things unpredictable . . . though tightening would have helped. Short is a delight as the comic hero. Oscar winner for Best Visual Effects. [PG]▼●❶

Innocence (2000-Australian-Belgian) **C-94m.** ***½ D: Paul Cox. Julia Blake, Charles "Bud" Tingwell, Terry Norris, Robert Menzies, Marta Dusseldorp, Kristien Van Pellicom, Chris Haywood, Norman Kaye. Complex, poignant tale of a long-widowed man and a long-married woman (Tingwell, Blake) who rekindle a romance that first blossomed four decades earlier. This wise, nuanced tale explores the meaning of love, and dares to be both tender and sensuous while dealing with characters who are in the twilight of their lives. Cox also scripted.▼❚

Innocent, The (1976-Italian) **C-127m.** **** D: Luchino Visconti. Giancarlo Giannini, Laura Antonelli, Jennifer O'Neill. Director Visconti's final film is among his greatest, a lavishly mounted tragedy about a Sicilian aristocrat who has the tables turned on him by the luscious wife he has chosen to ignore. Digitally released in the U.S. at 115m. Technovision. [R]▼❚

Innocent, The (1985-British) **C-101m.** **½ D: John Mackenzie. Andrew Hawley, Kika Markham, Kate Foster, Liam Neeson, Patrick Daley, Tom Bell, Clive Wood, Miranda Richardson. Medium drama about a young boy (Hawley) on the edge of puberty, growing up in a Yorkshire town during the Depression. Occasionally striking but too often slow.

Innocent, The (1993-British-German) **C-107m.** ** D: John Schlesinger. Isabella Rossellini, Anthony Hopkins, Campbell Scott, Ronald Nitschke, Hart Bochner, James Grant, Jeremy Sinden. Blah Cold War/paranoia thriller, set in the 1950s, about an ingenuous British circuitry expert (Scott) sent to Berlin to help set up a complicated phone-tapping apparatus to be used against the East Germans; along the way, he becomes involved in a passionate romance. Hopkins is fine as usual (although he's miscast as a blustery American CIA official). The characters are strictly one-dimensional; a minor credit for all concerned. Unreleased in U.S. till 1996. [R]▼●❶

Innocent and the Damned SEE: **Girls Town**

Innocent Blood (1992) **C-112m.** *** D: John Landis. Anne Parillaud, Robert Loggia, Anthony LaPaglia, David Proval, Don Rickles, Chazz Palminteri, Rocco Sisto, Tony Sirico, Tony Lip, Kim Coates, Angela Bassett, Luis Guzmán, Leo Burmester, Linnea Quigley, Frank Oz. Guilty-pleasure time: a sexy French vampire (Parillaud) sinks her teeth into mob boss Loggia and unwittingly unleashes a brood of bloodsucking gangsters! Meanwhile, good cop LaPaglia tries to figure out just what's going on. Wild and woolly crossbreed of urban action thriller and vampire movie, with a wicked sense of humor; doesn't always make sense, but fun to watch (if you can take the blood). Rickles is terrific as Loggia's loyal lawyer. Landis casts other film directors, as usual, in cameo roles, including Dario Argento, Michael Ritchie, and Sam Raimi. [R]▼●❶

Innocent Bystanders (1973-British) **C-111m.** **½ D: Peter Collinson. Stanley Baker, Geraldine Chaplin, Donald Pleasence, Dana Andrews, Sue Lloyd, Derren Nesbitt. Baker plays James Bond–like character involved in international manhunt for Russian scientist who has escaped from Siberia. Well-made but standard fare, with heavy doses of sadism and violence. [PG]

Innocent Man, An (1989) **C-113m.** ** D: Peter Yates. Tom Selleck, F. Murray Abraham, Laila Robins, David Rasche, Richard Young, Badja Djola. Happily married airline mechanic is mistaken for a drug contact by a pair of on-the-take cops who've burst into his home; victim gets a hearty course of "Slammer 101" after both slugs frame him. Slick and soft at the center, despite some potentially compelling script elements; not too strong on credibility, either. [R]▼●❶

Innocents, The (1961-British) **100m.** ***½ D: Jack Clayton. Deborah Kerr, Michael Redgrave, Peter Wyngarde, Megs Jenkins, Pamela Franklin, Martin Stephens. First-rate thriller based on Henry James' "The Turn of the Screw," with Kerr as governess haunted by specters that may or may not be real. Script by William Archibald and Truman Capote, brilliantly realized on film. Photographed by Freddie Francis. Remade in 1992 as THE TURN OF THE SCREW. CinemaScope.▼●❶

Innocent Sleep, The (1996-British) **C-95m.** ** D: Scott Michell. Rupert Graves, Annabella Sciorra, Michael Gambon, Franco Nero, John Hannah, Graham Crowden. A drunken derelict in London finds himself being pursued by a corrupt cop after witnessing a murder and stumbling onto a high-level international conspiracy. Old-fashioned, would-be Hitchcockian "innocent-man-on-the-run" thriller is extremely slow moving and murkily plotted, with a cop-out finale that fails to wrap up the myriad loose ends. Super 35. [R]▼❶

Innocents with Dirty Hands SEE: **Dirty Hands**

Innocent Victim (1989-British) **C-89m.** **½ D: Giles Foster. Helen Shaver, Lauren Bacall, Malcolm Stoddard, Peter Firth, Paul McGann, Katie Hardie, Tony Haygarth, Phyllida Law. When the young son of unmarried writer Shaver unexpectedly dies, her disturbed mother (Bacall) kidnaps another boy, the abused son of a would-be singer (Hardie). Deliberately paced thriller with too many plot twists; well acted, but wears out its welcome. Based on a novel by Ruth Rendell. Original British title: TREE OF HANDS.▼

Innocent Voices (2005-Mexican-U.S.-Puerto Rican) **C-112m.** **½ D: Luis Mandoki. Carlos Padilla, Leonor Varela, Gustavo Muñoz, José María Yazpik, Ofelia Medina, Daniel Giménez Cacho, Jesús Ochoa. Heartfelt story of an 11-year-old boy who, with his brother, sister, and hardworking mother, struggles to survive in the midst of the civil war in 1980s El Salvador. It's not a matter of choosing sides when bullets fly through their makeshift house or when the government recruits schoolboys at the age of 12. Based on the experiences of writer Oscar Torres; simplistic at times, but still has the ring of truth and sincerity. [R]❶

Inn of the Damned (1974-Australian) **C-118m.** **½ D: Terry Bourke. Judith Anderson, Alex Cord, Michael Craig, Joseph Furst, Tony Bonner, John Meillon. Bounty hunter Cord investigates the disappearances of travelers at an inn operated by sickies Anderson and Furst. Fair of its type, uplifted immeasurably by Anderson's entertaining performance.▼❶

Inn of the Frightened People (1971-British) **89m.** ** D: Sidney Hayers. Joan Collins, James Booth, Ray Barrett, Sinead Cusack, Tom Marshall, Kenneth Griffith. Parents of young girl who was raped and murdered take revenge on man they believe guilty. Sordid, low-budget thriller with some interesting moments. British title: REVENGE. Aka TERROR FROM UNDER THE HOUSE. ▼

Inn of the Sixth Happiness, The (1958) **C-158m.** *** D: Mark Robson. Ingrid Bergman, Curt Jurgens, Robert Donat, Ronald Squire, Athene Seyler, Richard Wattis. True story of English servant (Bergman) who, despite her lack of credentials, realizes her dream of becoming a missionary in China. Bergman is wonderful and Donat memorable in final screen performance. Simple, effective score by Malcolm Arnold. CinemaScope.▼●❶

In Old California (1942) **88m.** ** D: William McGann. John Wayne, Binnie Barnes, Albert Dekker, Helen Parrish, Patsy Kelly, Edgar Kennedy, Dick Purcell, Harry Shannon. Wayne moves into Western town controlled by shifty Dekker, with inevitable confrontation. Also shown in computer-colored version.▼❶

In Old Chicago (1938) **95m.** ***½ D: Henry King. Tyrone Power, Alice Faye, Don Ameche, Alice Brady, Andy Devine, Brian Donlevy, Phyllis Brooks, Tom Brown, Berton Churchill, Sidney Blackmer, Gene Reynolds, Bobs Watson. Lavish period piece building up to Chicago fire of 1871; Oscar-winning Brady is Mrs. O'Leary, whose sons Power, Ameche, and Brown find their own adventures in the Windy City. Scripted by Lamar Trotti and Sonya Levien, based on a story by Niven Busch. Originally released at 115m.▼❶

In Old Oklahoma (1943) **102m.** **½ D: Albert S. Rogell. John Wayne, Martha Scott, Albert Dekker, Gabby Hayes, Marjorie Rambeau, Sidney Blackmer, Dale Evans. Slugger Wayne brooks no nonsense in this oil-drilling yarn; good action, obligatory romance. Rhonda Fleming's film debut. Aka WAR OF THE WILDCATS. ▼

In Our Time (1944) **110m.** **½ D: Vincent Sherman. Ida Lupino, Paul Henreid, Nazimova, Nancy Coleman, Mary Boland, Victor Francen, Michael Chekhov. Lupino and Henreid try to save Poland from Nazi takeover in plush soaper that seeks to be meaningful propaganda; Nazimova is touching as Henreid's aristocratic mother. Never quite hits the mark.

I Now Pronounce You Chuck and Larry (2007) **C-110m.** *½ D: Dennis Dugan. Adam Sandler, Kevin James, Jessica Biel, Dan Aykroyd, Ving Rhames, Steve Buscemi, Nicholas Turturro, Allen Covert, Rachel Dratch, Richard Chamberlain, Mary Pat Gleason, Rob Corddry, Lance Bass, Blake

Clark. In order to overcome bureaucratic red tape two single, heterosexual Brooklyn firefighters, one (Sandler) a ladies' man and the other (James) a widower, pretend to be a gay couple. Generally idiotic comedy hypocritically lambastes homophobia while featuring characters who are flagrant gay stereotypes. Rob Schneider and David Spade appear unbilled. [PG-13]▮

In Praise of Love (2001-French-Swiss) **C/B&W-97m.** **½ D: Jean-Luc Godard. Bruno Putzulu, Cécile Camp, Jean Davy, Françoise Verney, Audrey Klebaner, Jeremy Lippman, Jean Lacouture. Two-part film is a return to form for the ever-provocative director. Part one deals with discussions of a project in the works called *"Éloge de L'amour,"* from which the film took its original French title. In part two, set two years earlier, an elderly couple attempt to sell their story of fighting in the French Resistance to Hollywood. Doesn't always hit its mark, particularly when it takes potshots at Steven Spielberg and SCHINDLER'S LIST, but this challenging film is worth seeing, especially for Godard fans. [PG]▼▮

In Praise of Older Women (1978-Canadian) **C-108m.** BOMB D: George Kaczender. Tom Berenger, Karen Black, Susan Strasberg, Helen Shaver, Alexandra Stewart, Marilyn Lightstone. Hungarian stud recalls nearly two decades' worth of conquests, all of whom are paraded across the screen in various stages of undress. Strasberg and Stewart are particularly praiseworthy, but nothing else is in this tease of a movie. Remade in 1997. [R]▼▮

Inquiry, The (1987-Italian) **C-107m.** **½ D: Damiano Damiani. Keith Carradine, Harvey Keitel, Phyllis Logan, Lina Sastri. Intriguing story treats the resurrection of Christ as a mystery thriller. Carradine is a hardnosed investigator sent from Rome to find out what happened to the missing body of Jesus Christ; an official cover-up is presumed. Offbeat point of view holds interest. Excellent dubbing of the Italian supporting characters, but it's still distracting to hear Keitel's Bronx accent as Pontius Pilate.▼

In Search of Gregory (1970-British-Italian) **C-90m.** ** D: Peter Wood. Julie Christie, John Hurt, Michael Sarrazin, Adolfo Celi, Paola Pitagora. Muddled film set in Geneva, about two potential lovers who fantasize about, but never meet, each other. [M/PG]

In Search of the Castaways (1962) **C-100m.** **½ D: Robert Stevenson. Hayley Mills, Maurice Chevalier, George Sanders, Wilfrid Hyde-White, Michael Anderson, Jr., Keith Hamshire. Expedition tries to locate missing sea captain, in journey that encounters fire, flood, earthquake and other disasters. Disney adaptation of Jules Verne suffers from muddled continuity; good cast does its best.▼●▮

Insect SEE: **Blue Monkey**
Inseminoid SEE: **Horror Planet**
Inserts (1975-British) **C-99m.** BOMB D: John Byrum. Richard Dreyfuss, Jessica Harper, Veronica Cartwright, Bob Hoskins, Stephen Davies. Pretentious, unending nonsense played out by five characters on one set: decaying Hollywood mansion in early thirties where once-famous director now makes porno films. Dreadful. The British version runs 117m. [X]▼▮

Inside (1996) **C-94m.** ** D: Arthur Penn. Eric Stoltz, Nigel Hawthorne, Louis Gossett, Jr., Ian Roberts, Jerry Mofokeng. South African university professor Stoltz is accused of conspiring against the apartheid government and is subjected to ruthless interrogation by a sadistic colonel (Hawthorne). Years later, the colonel is subject to questioning by Gossett. The cast is first rate and the subject matter is interesting, but film lacks dramatic spark. First shown on cable TV. [R]▼●▮

Inside Daisy Clover (1965) **C-128m.** **½ D: Robert Mulligan. Natalie Wood, Robert Redford, Christopher Plummer, Roddy McDowall, Ruth Gordon, Katherine Bard. Potentially biting account of Wood's rise as Hollywood star in 1930s misfires; pat situations with caricatures instead of people. Gavin Lambert adapted his own novel. Panavision.▼●▮

Inside Deep Throat (2005) **C-92m.** **½ D: Fenton Bailey, Randy Barbato. Saga of DEEP THROAT, the 1972 porno film that became a landmark: the first such movie to enjoy huge mainstream success and a lightning rod for government attacks on obscenity. Neatly mixes archival footage, interviews with the participants (actors Linda Lovelace and Harry Reems, director Gerard Damiano), and popular-culture commentators (Hugh Hefner, Erica Jong, Norman Mailer, Helen Gurley Brown, John Waters, et al.). Interesting, to be sure, but not as profound as its filmmakers would have you believe. R-rated version also available. [NC-17]▮

Inside I'm Dancing SEE: **Rory O'Shea Was Here**

Inside Job (2010) **C-109m.** ***½ D: Charles Ferguson. Narrated by Matt Damon. Careful exploration of the economic meltdown of 2008 begins by showing what happened when unbridled greed overtook the long-stable economy of Iceland a decade earlier. That serves as prelude to a sea of bad decision-making and outright corruption in the U.S. and elsewhere, with seemingly no one minding the store, and no one being punished for the dire results except the public. A riveting, clearheaded, and infuriating film. Oscar winner for Best Documentary. HD Widescreen. [PG-13]▮

Inside Man (2006) **C-128m.** *** D: Spike Lee. Denzel Washington, Clive Owen,

Jodie Foster, Christopher Plummer, Willem Dafoe, Chiwetel Ejiofor, Carlos Andréas Gómez, Kim Director, James Ransone, Bernard Rachelle, Peter Gerety, Victor Colicchio, Peter Frechette, Daryl "Chill" Mitchell. Clever reinvention of a bank-heist story with a streetwise N.Y.C. detective (Washington) trying to figure out the real motive of the wily robber (Owen) who is staked out inside the bank building. Laced with uniquely New York–flavored moments of humor and character riffs, though it overplays its hand and goes on too long. Foster brings no color whatsoever to her role as a high-stakes power broker. Super 35. [R]▋

Inside Monkey Zetterland (1992) **C-93m.** **½ D: Jefery Levy. Steven Antin, Katherine Helmond, Patricia Arquette, Tate Donovan, Sandra Bernhard, Sofia Coppola, Rupert Everett, Bo Hopkins, Martha Plimpton, Debi Mazar, Ricki Lake, Lance Loud, Francis Bay. Hit-and-miss L.A. comedy about the title character (Antin), a young screenwriter, and his complex connections with family (most tellingly, soap opera star mom Helmond) and friends. Filled with moments of humor and insight, and tolerance for its various offbeat characters, but at other times affected and formulaic. Loosely autobiographical; star Antin scripted and coproduced. [R]▼●▋

Inside Moves (1980) **C-113m.** **½ D: Richard Donner. John Savage, David Morse, Diana Scarwid, Amy Wright, Tony Burton, Bill Henderson, Bert Remsen, Harold Russell. Offbeat drama about a young suicide survivor (Savage) who falls in with a group of upbeat misfits and learns about self-esteem. A well-meaning film with some excellent performances and emotional highpoints but a few too many story flaws—including the final scene. Russell's first film since THE BEST YEARS OF OUR LIVES. [PG]▼●▋

Inside Out (1975-British) **C-97m.** **½ D: Peter Duffell. Telly Savalas, James Mason, Robert Culp, Aldo Ray, Charles Korvin. Savalas engineers break-in at maximum security prison in East Germany to free notorious war criminal who knows whereabouts of a secret cache of gold. Notbad caper. Retitled HITLER'S GOLD and THE GOLDEN HEIST. [PG]▼▋

Insider, The (1999) **C-157m.** ***½ D: Michael Mann. Al Pacino, Russell Crowe, Christopher Plummer, Diane Venora, Philip Baker Hall, Lindsay Crouse, Debi Mazar, Stephen Tobolowsky, Colm Feore, Bruce McGill, Gina Gershon, Michael Gambon, Rip Torn, Lynne Thigpen, Hallie Kate Eisenberg, Wings Hauser, Pete Hamill. Dynamic fact-based story of a gutsy segment producer for TV's *60 Minutes* (Pacino) who sniffs out a story in disaffected scientist Crowe, who's just been fired by a major tobacco company.

Compelling, adult entertainment that finds great drama in the real-life machinations of TV journalism (and big business). Great performances all around. Screenplay by Mann and Eric Roth, based on a magazine story by Marie Brenner. Super 35. [R]▼▋

Insidious (2011) **C-103m.** **½ D: James Wan. Patrick Wilson, Rose Byrne, Barbara Hershey, Ty Simpkins, Andrew Astor, Lin Shaye, Leigh Whannell, Angus Sampson. A family moves into an aging house, then a fall from a ladder sends the son into a coma from which he can't seem to awaken. Meanwhile, the family is terrorized by a series of spooky apparitions. A medium (Shaye) is brought in, but things only get worse. Oldfashioned haunted-house thriller aimed at adults boasts effective scares and a dark, mysterious mood, but it plays as a belated knockoff of POLTERGEIST. Decent B melodrama from the creators of SAW, director Wan and writer Whannell, who also costars as Specs. Super 35. [PG-13]▋

Insignificance (1985-British) **C-110m.** ***½ D: Nicolas Roeg. Gary Busey, Tony Curtis, Theresa Russell, Michael Emil, Will Sampson. Striking, gloriously cinematic examination of the meaning of fame in America and the perils of atomic warfare. The stars are cast as unnamed celebrities—a ballplayer, senator, actress, and professor—who resemble Joe DiMaggio, Joseph McCarthy, Marilyn Monroe, and Albert Einstein, and meet in a N.Y.C. hotel room in 1954. Funny, ironic, thought provoking. Wonderfully acted by all. Screenplay by Terry Johnson. [R]▼●▋

In Society (1944) **75m.** ** D: Jean Yarbrough. Bud Abbott, Lou Costello, Marion Hutton, Arthur Treacher, Thomas Gomez, Thurston Hall, Kirby Grant. Minor A&C, with the boys as plumbers mistaken for members of society; hectic slapstick finale. Includes chase footage lifted from NEVER GIVE A SUCKER AN EVEN BREAK.▼▋

Insomnia (1997-Norwegian) **C-97m.** *** D: Erik Skjoldbjaerg. Stellan Skarsgård, Sverre Anker Ousdal, Gisken Armand, Bjorn Floberg, Maria Bonnevie, Kristian Figenschow. Moody police thriller with two criminal investigators traveling to remote, arctic Norway on a murder case; soon the relentless midnight sun and tactical missteps cause one of the men to unravel. Skarsgård is good, as always, in this psychological maelstrom. Remade in 2002.▼▋

Insomnia (2002) **C-118m.** ***½ D: Christopher Nolan. Al Pacino, Robin Williams, Hilary Swank, Maura Tierney, Martin Donovan, Nicky Katt, Paul Dooley, Jonathan Jackson. Famous LAPD detective Pacino and his partner (Donovan) are sent to small town in Alaska to help solve a grisly murder—and to get them away from the firing line of a department controversy. It turns out that whodunit is not the problem, but how to catch the culprit...especially when he starts playing a cat-and-mouse game with Pacino. Multilayered story is enhanced by Nolan's cunning use of visual and aural devices, plus top-notch performances. Remake of 1997 film of the same name, adapted by Hillary Seitz. Panavision. [R]▼●

Inspecteur Lavardin (1986-French) **C-99m. **½** D: Claude Chabrol. Jean Poiret, Jean-Claude Brialy, Bernadette Lafont, Jacques Dacqmine, Jean-Luc Bideau, Hermine Claire, Pierre-Francois Dumeniaud, Florent Gibassier, Guy Louret, Jean Depusse. Crime and comedy make for an unusual mix in this tale of quirky police detective Poiret's murder investigation in a French seaside village. Lafont—newly widowed, wealthy, and an old flame of the inspector's—and her wacky brother (Brialy) head the list of suspects. A sequel to Chabrol's COP AU VIN/POULET AU VINAIGRE (1984) which introduced Poiret's Lavardin character in a supporting role.◗

Inspector Calls, An (1954-British) **80m.** *** D: Guy Hamilton. Alastair Sim, Arthur Young, Olga Lindo, Eileen Moore. J. B. Priestley play detailing British police detective Sim's investigation of girl's suicide. Via flashbacks he learns a family's responsibility for her fate. Clever plot finale.

Inspector Clouseau (1968) **C-94m. ** D: Bud Yorkin. Alan Arkin, Delia Boccardo, Frank Finlay, Patrick Cargill, Beryl Reid, Barry Foster. Scotland Yard calls on inept French detective to crack potential robbery; in spite of Arkin's talents, Peter Sellers is too well identified with the role (from other Pink Panther movies) for one to fully accept this characterization. Besides, film isn't particularly funny. Made in England. Panavision. [G]◗

Inspector Gadget (1999) **C-80m. ** D: David Kellogg. Matthew Broderick, Rupert Everett, Joely Fisher, Michelle Trachtenberg, Andy Dick, Cheri Oteri, Michael G. Hagerty, Dabney Coleman, Rene Auberjonois, Frances Bay; voices of D. L. Hughley, Don Adams. Desperate gimmick comedy for kids based on the 1980s animated TV series. After a severe accident, Broderick's body is pieced back together with cutting-edge technology, just right for chasing bad guys like Everett (aka Claw). Gizmos and slapstick galore, but precious few laughs in this Disney concoction. Followed by a direct-to-video sequel. [PG]▼●◗

Inspector General, The (1949) **C-102m.** *** D: Henry Koster. Danny Kaye, Walter Slezak, Barbara Bates, Elsa Lanchester, Gene Lockhart, Alan Hale, Walter Catlett. Kaye plays a buffoon who pretends to be a visiting bureaucrat in an Eastern European village. Entertaining musical adaptation of the Gogol story.▼◗

Inspiration (1931) **74m. **½** D: Clarence

Brown. Greta Garbo, Robert Montgomery, Lewis Stone, Marjorie Rambeau, Beryl Mercer. Lesser Garbo vehicle about beautiful Parisian woman whose past makes her decide to leave Montgomery, even though she still loves him. A modern version of Alphonse Daudet's *Sappho.* ▼●

Instinct (1999) **C-124m. **½** D: Jon Turteltaub. Anthony Hopkins, Cuba Gooding, Jr., Donald Sutherland, Maura Tierney, George Dzundza, John Ashton, John Aylward. Ambitious psychiatric resident (Gooding) evaluates brilliant and/or insane primatologist (Hopkins), who's been living among the Rwandan gorillas he studied and who may have murdered some park rangers. Talky drama sets off a few sparks whenever the two leads square off, and has some CUCKOO'S NEST flourishes throughout. Panavision. [R]▼●

Insurance Man, The (1985-British) **C-77m.** *** D: Richard Eyre. Robert Hines, Daniel Day-Lewis, Jim Broadbent, Hugh Fraser, Tony Haygarth. Dramatically uneven yet still ambitious, impressive account of a young dyeworker named Franz (Hines), whose body develops a rash, and his dealings with both the bureaucracy and a man named Mr. Kafka (Day-Lewis), a claims assessor who also writes. A tribute to Kafka and his work, with a screenplay by Alan Bennett.

Intacto (2001-Spanish) **C-108m. ** D: Juan Carlos Fresnadillo. Max von Sydow, Leonardo Sbaraglia, Eusebio Poncela, Mónica López, Antonio Dechent, Guillermo Toledo. Ambitious but muddled thriller involving an aging high-stakes gambler/Holocaust survivor (von Sydow) who enjoys, and appears to be able to control, good fortune; he takes away the luck of an underling who's announced his wish to go off on his own. Means to be eerie and compelling, but is pretentious and confusing instead. Super 35. [R] ▼●

Intended, The (2003-Danish-British) **C-110m. ** D: Kristian Levring. Janet McTeer, Olympia Dukakis, Brenda Fricker, Tony Maudsley, JJ Feild, David Bradley, Philip Jackson. In 1920s Malaya, a miserable wretch who works as an ivory trading-post overseer (Fricker) makes life intolerable for one and all, including a youthful surveyor (Feild) and his older fiancée (McTeer). An altogether unpleasant—and unnecessary—experience, despite some good performances. Levring and McTeer coscripted. [R]◗

Interiors (1978) **C-93m. ***½** D: Woody Allen. Diane Keaton, Geraldine Page, E. G. Marshall, Maureen Stapleton, Kristin Griffith, Mary Beth Hurt, Richard Jordan, Sam Waterston. Allen's first screen drama as writer-director is an Ingmar Bergmanesque study of a family full of unhappy, frustrated men and women; drama of anguished lives is not for all tastes, but extremely well done. [PG] ▼●)

Interlude (1968-British) **C-113m.** ******* D: Kevin Billington. Oskar Werner, Barbara Ferris, Virginia Maskell, Donald Sutherland, Nora Swinburne, Alan Webb, John Cleese. Charming, sentimental tale of symphony conductor and reporter who have an affair; told in flashback. Previously filmed as WHEN TOMORROW COMES and INTERLUDE (1957). [M/PG]

Intermezzo (1939) **70m.** *****½** D: Gregory Ratoff. Leslie Howard, Ingrid Bergman, Edna Best, Cecil Kellaway, John Halliday. One of the best love stories ever filmed, as married Howard, renowned violinist, has an affair with musical protégée Bergman (in her first English-speaking film). Short and sweet, highlighted by Robert Henning– Heinz Provost love theme. Original title: INTERMEZZO, A LOVE STORY; Bergman played same role in Gustav Molander's 1936 Swedish version. Remade, after a fashion, as HONEYSUCKLE ROSE. ▼●)

Intermission (2003-Irish-British) **C-102m.** ******* D: John Crowley. Colin Farrell, Shirley Henderson, Kelly Macdonald, Colm Meaney, Cillian Murphy, Ger Ryan, Brían F. O'Byrne, Barbara Bergin, Michael McElhatton, Deirdre O'Kane, David Wilmot. A lively mosaic of stories in modern-day Dublin involving working-class people whose dysfunctional lives collide as they search for love, vent their anger, and commit crimes that can't possibly pay. Alternately furious and funny, shot with a great feeling of spontaneity on high-definition video by a first-time director. The girl with the ice cream cone in the film's first scene is Emma Bolger, who costars in IN AMERICA. [R]▼)

Internal Affairs (1990) **C-117m.** ****** D: Mike Figgis. Richard Gere, Andy Garcia, Nancy Travis, Laurie Metcalf, Richard Bradford, William Baldwin, Michael Beach, Annabella Sciorra, Elijah Wood. Smarmy, overripe, and overlong drama about a young cop who joins L.A.'s Internal Affairs Dept. and becomes obsessed with nailing a cocky, corrupt officer (Gere) who's a past master at manipulating people. Intriguing ideas get lost, and illogic takes over pretty quickly. [R]▼●)

International, The (2009-U.S.-German) **C-118m.** ****** D: Tom Tykwer. Clive Owen, Naomi Watts, Armin Mueller-Stahl, Ulrich Thomsen, Brian F. O'Byrne, Jack McGee, Felix Solis, James Rebhorn. Interpol agent Owen teams up with Manhattan D.A. Watts in an effort to get the goods on an international bank that's involved in all sorts of dirty deals. Slick suspense thriller circles the globe but is discouragingly sparse on suspense *or* thrills, except for a long, bravura shootout inside N.Y.C.'s Guggenheim Museum. Its seemingly topical subject mat-

ter has surprisingly little resonance. Super 35. [R]❙

International House (1933) **70m.** *****½** D: A. Edward Sutherland. W. C. Fields, Peggy Hopkins Joyce, Stuart Erwin, George Burns, Gracie Allen, Bela Lugosi, Franklin Pangborn, Rudy Vallee, Sterling Holloway, Cab Calloway, Baby Rose Marie. Offbeat, delightful film with early television experiment bringing people from all over the world to large Oriental hotel. Spotlight alternates between Fields and Burns & Allen, all in rare form, with guest spots by various radio entertainers. Short and sweet, a must-see film. Calloway sings the memorable "Reefer Man."▼●)

International Velvet (1978-British-U.S.) **C-127m.** ******* D: Bryan Forbes. Tatum O'Neal, Christopher Plummer, Anthony Hopkins, Nanette Newman, Dinsdale Landen. Long overdue sequel to NATIONAL VELVET has Velvet (Newman) a grown woman with a live-in lover (Plummer) and a niece (O'Neal) primed to follow in her footsteps as an Olympic horsewoman. Too lengthy and shunned by the critics, but deftly played by Hopkins and Plummer; exquisitely filmed, entertaining. [PG]▼)

Internecine Project, The (1974-British) **C-89m.** ****** D: Ken Hughes. James Coburn, Lee Grant, Harry Andrews, Ian Hendry, Michael Jayston, Keenan Wynn. Lackluster espionage drama with Coburn as opportunist who tries to eliminate skeletons in his closet by having a handful of industrial spies kill each other off. [PG]▼)

Interns, The (1962) **120m.** ******* D: David Swift. Michael Callan, Cliff Robertson, James MacArthur, Nick Adams, Suzy Parker, Haya Harareet, Stefanie Powers, Buddy Ebsen, Telly Savalas. Glossy, renovated DR. KILDARE soap opera, kept afloat by an interesting young cast. Followed by sequel THE NEW INTERNS. ▼●)

Interpreter, The (2005-U.S.-German) **C-128m.** ****½** D: Sydney Pollack. Nicole Kidman, Sean Penn, Catherine Keener, Jesper Christensen, Yvan Attal, Earl Cameron, Michael Wright, George Harris, Clyde Kusatsu, Hugo Speer. U.N. interpreter Kidman overhears what sounds like an assassination plot against the leader of her homeland, Matobo, who's about to visit N.Y.C. Federal agent Penn is assigned to investigate the credibility of her claim and becomes emotionally involved. Star wattage and filmmaking craftsmanship help compensate for many loose ends in this thriller (credited to three separate screenwriters, "with the help of" a novel), but it seems neither the CIA, FBI, Secret Service, U.N. security, nor the NYPD can keep an eye on a suspect for long! Pollack has a small role as Penn's boss. Technovision. [PG-13]▼)

Interrupted Melody (1955) **C-106m.** ******* D: Curtis Bernhardt. Eleanor Parker, Glenn Ford, Roger Moore, Cecil Kellaway, Ann

Codee, Stephan Bekassy. Fine biography of Marjorie Lawrence, Australian opera star, who made a comeback after being crippled by polio. Eileen Farrell sings for Parker. William Ludwig and Sonya Levien won Oscars for their story and screenplay. CinemaScope.▼○)

Intersection (1994) **C-98m.** *½ D: Mark Rydell. Richard Gere, Sharon Stone, Lolita Davidovich, Martin Landau, David Selby, Jenny Morrison, Ron White. Dreary romantic triangle of wealthy architect Gere, who has drifted apart from his aloof wife (Stone), and taken up with spunky Davidovich. Meanwhile, all involved feel terribly guilty about the teenage daughter they're hurting. Title comes from an accident site, which prompts all this moping around in a series of flashbacks. Derived from a 1970 French feature, LES CHOSES DE LA VIE (THE THINGS OF LIFE), directed by Claude Sautet. [R] ▼○)

Interval (1973-Mexican) **C-84m.** ** D: Daniel Mann. Merle Oberon, Robert Wolders, Claudio Brook, Russ Conway, Charles Bateman, Barbara Ransom. A globetrotting woman, running from her past, finds true love with a much younger man (Wolders, who became Oberon's husband in real life). Drippy May-December romance, filmed in Mexico and produced by Oberon, whose last film this was. [PG] ▼

Interview (2007) **C-86m.** *** D: Steve Buscemi. Sienna Miller, Steve Buscemi. Political reporter reluctantly carries out an assignment to interview a beautiful young actress who's put off by his obvious indifference to the task. Over the course of an evening, they take turns seducing and bamboozling each other. Remake of Theo van Gogh's Dutch movie of the same name, shot in a series of lengthy handheld takes, ebbs and flows but never completely loses its momentum because of the two stars' compelling performances. Buscemi and David Schechter adapted Theodor Holman's original screenplay. [R]

Interview With the Assassin (2002) **C-88m.** *** D: Neil Burger. Raymond J. Barry, Dylan Haggerty, Renee Faia, Kelsey Kemper, Dennis Lau, Jared McVay. An unemployed cameraman interviews and tapes his terminally ill next-door neighbor (Barry, in a riveting performance), who claims to be the so-called second gunman who assassinated John F. Kennedy. This documentary-style film is a bit gimmicky, but still interesting and disturbing, a worthy companion piece to Oliver Stone's JFK.▼)

Interview With the Vampire: The Vampire Chronicles (1994) **C-122m.** *½ D: Neil Jordan. Tom Cruise, Brad Pitt, Antonio Banderas, Stephen Rea, Christian Slater, Kirsten Dunst, Domiziana Giordano, Thandie Newton, Indra Ove. In contemporary San Francisco, a young man grants an interview about his 200-year existence as a vampire—a "life" with which he has never felt completely comfortable. Likely to satisfy fans of Anne Rice's popular novel, and female fans of its star "hunks," but this descent into the netherworld is unappealing, unrelenting, and (after a while) downright boring. The actors can't be faulted, nor can the handsome production design. Followed by QUEEN OF THE DAMNED. [R]▼)

Intervista (1987-Italian) **C-108m.** *** D: Federico Fellini. Sergio Rubini, Antonella Ponziani, Maurizio Mein, Paola Liguori, Lara Wendel, Antonio Cantafora, Nadia Ottaviani, Anita Ekberg, Marcello Mastroianni, Federico Fellini. Engaging, illuminating mock-documentary about the making of a film about Fellini; the master is depicted in production of an adaptation of Kafka's *Amerika*. Mastroianni and Ekberg (who costarred almost 30 years before in LA DOLCE VITA) appear as themselves. The film also serves as an homage to Cinecittà, the studio where Fellini shot all of his classics. ▼)

In the Army Now (1994) **C-91m.** *½ D: Daniel Petrie, Jr. Pauly Shore, Lori Petty, David Alan Grier, Andy Dick, Esai Morales, Lynn Whitfield, Art LeFleur, Tom Villard, Keith Coogan. Pauly is a pacifist who joins the army so he can "be all that he can be for free," only to learn that there's more to enlisting than receiving complimentary room and board. Latest in a long line of barracks comedies proves no competition for BUCK PRIVATES. Pauly's fans might disagree. Brendan Fraser appears unbilled. [PG] ▼○)

In the Bedroom (2001) **C-138m.** *** D: Todd Field. Sissy Spacek, Tom Wilkinson, Nick Stahl, Marisa Tomei, William Mapother, William Wise, Celia Weston, Karen Allen. An avuncular small-town Maine doctor and his wife, who teaches music in the local school, don't approve of the "older" woman their son has fallen in love with . . . but no one is prepared for the events that then unfold. Quiet, observant film explores how grief affects a longtime married couple and the people around them. Rock-solid performances by all the lead actors. Field's feature directing debut; he also coscripted with Rob Festinger, from a story by Andre Dubus. Super 35. [R] ▼)

In the Bleak Midwinter SEE: Midwinter's Tale, A

In the Company of Men (1997) **C-93m.** ** D: Neil LaBute. Aaron Eckhart, Stacy Edwards, Matt Malloy, Mark Rector. Provocative but stark and discomfiting low-budget film about two yuppie office workers who—frustrated by the world around them, and women in particular—make a pact that while they're on assignment in another city, they'll both date a woman and then dump her, just for the satisfaction of it. The slicker of the two (Eckhart) turns out to have a hidden agenda, however. Alternately absorbing, humdrum, and distasteful. Eckhart's creepy character does get under your skin. Highly praised in some circles. Written by the director. [R] **VO◖**

In the Cool of the Day (1963-British) **C-89m.** ** D: Robert Stevens. Peter Finch, Jane Fonda, Angela Lansbury, Arthur Hill, Constance Cummings, Alexander Knox, Nigel Davenport, Alec McCowen. Good cast flounders in turgid soaper, with Finch (who is married to bitchy Lansbury) mediating marital rift between Hill and his emotionally and physically fragile wife Fonda; soon Finch and Fonda fall in love. Location filming in Greece helps. Panavision.

In the Cut (2003-U.S.-Australian) **C-118m.** **½ D: Jane Campion. Meg Ryan, Mark Ruffalo, Jennifer Jason Leigh, Nick Damici, Sharrieff Pugh. An English teacher becomes involved with a homicide detective who's investigating a series of brutal murders of women in her Manhattan neighborhood. A daring look at a sexual relationship between two emotionally fragile people, set against the backdrop of a murder mystery. Provocative and doggedly antiromantic, the storytelling is faulty and drawn out, but the atmosphere and performances are first-rate. Adapted by Campion and Susanna Moore from the latter's novel. Kevin Bacon appears unbilled. Unrated version runs 119m. [R] **V◗**

In the Devil's Garden (1971-British) **C-89m.** *½ D: Sidney Hayers. Suzy Kendall, Frank Finlay, Freddie Jones, Lesley-Anne Down, James Laurenson, Tony Beckley. Undistinguished thriller of rapist-killer in girls' school; of interest mainly for the presence of Down, in an early role as one of the victims. Aka ASSAULT, THE CREEPERS, TOWER OF TERROR and SATAN'S PLAYTHINGS. Panavision. [R]**▼**

In the Electric Mist (2009-U.S.-French) **C-102m.** **½ D: Bertrand Tavernier. Tommy Lee Jones, John Goodman, Mary Steenburgen, Peter Sarsgaard, Kelly Macdonald, Pruitt Taylor Vince, Justina Machado, Ned Beatty, James Gammon, Levon Helm, Buddy Guy, Julio César Cedillo. Recovering alcoholic Louisiana detective Dave Robicheaux (Jones) is trying to solve a series of gruesome murders when the corpse of a black man killed 40 years ago surfaces in a nearby marsh. Atmospheric and well cast, this police procedural with mystical undertones is highly watchable, although some of the characters and relationships seem a bit sketchy (and may come to life more fully in James Lee Burke's novel or Tavernier's European cut, which runs 117m.). John Sayles has a hilarious cameo as a foulmouthed movie director. Alec Baldwin played Robicheaux in 1996's HEAVEN'S PRISONERS. Panavision. [R]**◗**

In the French Style (1963) **105m.** **½ D:

Robert Parrish. Jean Seberg, Stanley Baker, Philippe Forquet, Addison Powell, Jack Hedley, Maurice Teynac, James Leo Herlihy, Claudine Auger. Seberg is memorable as a young American who heads off to Paris to study painting and becomes romantically involved with Forquet and Baker. Based on two Irwin Shaw stories, "In the French Style" and "A Year to Learn the Language."

In the Good Old Summertime (1949) **C-102m.** *** D: Robert Z. Leonard. Judy Garland, Van Johnson, S. Z. "Cuddles" Sakall, Spring Byington, Clinton Sundberg, Buster Keaton. Musical remake of THE SHOP AROUND THE CORNER, with Garland and Johnson the pen pals who fall in love. Not up to most MGM Garland vehicles, but pleasant. That's young Liza Minnelli with Judy in the finale. **▼◗**

In the Heat of Passion (1992) **C-102m.** **½ D: Rodman Flender. Sally Kirkland, Nick Corri, Jack Carter, Michael Greene, Gloria LeRoy, Carl Franklin. Low-budget but diverting film noir, with Corri a young garage mechanic who puts the moves on wealthy, mysterious Kirkland. When her husband gets in the way, what's a lover to do? Twisty tale encompasses a serial rapist and the reality-TV show tracking him, with Corri's assistance. Genuinely suspenseful, sexually frank film hindered by mediocre production values. [R]**V◗**

In the Heat of the Night (1967) **C-109m.** **** D: Norman Jewison. Sidney Poitier, Rod Steiger, Warren Oates, Lee Grant, Scott Wilson, Larry Gates, Quentin Dean, James Patterson, Anthony James, William Schallert. Redneck Southern sheriff grudgingly accepts help from big-city black detective in solving bizarre murder. Marvelous social thriller hasn't dated one bit—tough, funny, and atmospheric, with unbeatable acting and splendid Quincy Jones score. Five Oscars include Best Picture, Actor (Steiger), Screenplay (Stirling Silliphant), Editing (Hal Ashby). Poitier reprised his character in THEY CALL ME *MISTER* TIBBS! and THE ORGANIZATION. Followed by a TV series 20 years later. **V◗**

In the Land of Women (2007) **C-98m.** ** D: Jonathan Kasdan. Adam Brody, Kristen Stewart, Meg Ryan, Olympia Dukakis, Makenzie Vega, Elena Anaya, Clark Gregg, JoBeth Williams, Dustin Milligan, Ginnifer Goodwin. A 26-year-old L.A. writer, feeling he's a failure, moves to Michigan to care for his elderly (i.e., frail but feisty) grandmother and soon gets to know/help/save an upscale (i.e., cold and empty) family across the street. Oh, yes—he also finds himself in the process. Brody (*The O.C.*) is good in his first film lead, but this is pretty predictable stuff. Feature writing and directing debut for Jonathan Kasdan (son of Lawrence, brother of Jake). Super 35. [PG-13]**◗**

In the Line of Fire (1993) **C-128m.** ***½

D: Wolfgang Petersen. Clint Eastwood, John Malkovich, Rene Russo, Dylan McDermott, Gary Cole, Fred Dalton Thompson, John Mahoney, Jim Curley, Clyde Kusatsu, Patrika Darbo, John Heard. Crackling, well-made thriller about a would-be presidential assassin who pulls Secret Service agent Eastwood—who failed to protect President Kennedy in 1963—into a cruel game of cat-and-mouse as he plans to murder the current president. Eastwood, as an older, vulnerable, piano-playing loner, has never been better, and Malkovich matches him as the superintelligent loony. Steve Railsback appears unbilled. Written by Jeff Maguire. Panavision. [R] ▼●)

In the Loop (2009-British) **C-106m.** *** D: Armando Iannucci. Tom Hollander, Peter Capaldi, James Gandolfini, Mimi Kennedy, Anna Chlumsky, Chris Addison, Gina McKee, Steve Coogan. British bureaucrat Hollander has a tendency to put his foot in his mouth every time he talks to the press, which is especially awkward as both the British and American governments are toying with the idea of going to war. Lively, often hilarious and very foul-mouthed look at backroom politics on both sides of the Pond. Inspired by the TV series *The Thick of It*, from the same director and writers, in which Capaldi played the same character, England's ultimate spin doctor.▶

In The Mix (2005) **C-95m.** BOMB D: Ron Underwood. Usher, Chazz Palminteri, Robert Costanzo, Robert Davi, Matt Gerald, Emmanuelle Chriqui, Anthony Fazio, Kevin Hart, Nick Mancuso, Deezer D, Geoff Stults. Lame vehicle for rap star Usher, who is adequate—and nothing more—in this gangsta nap about a club deejay recruited to guard a mob boss' daughter. When they get involved romantically, Dad gets ticked off. Predictable comedy-drama merges the worlds of hip-hop and the Mob in pedestrian manner. Super 35. [PG-13] ▼▶

In the Mood (1987) **C-99m.** **½ D: Phil Alden Robinson. Patrick Dempsey, Talia Balsam, Beverly D'Angelo, Michael Constantine, Betty Jinette, Kathleen Freeman, Peter Hobbs, Edith Fellows. Engaging if low-key comedy based on true story of 1944's "woo woo kid" Sonny Wisecarver, a 15-year-old California boy who made headlines because of his affairs with two "older" women, one of whom he actually married. Dempsey is ideal and Robinson's script is delightfully wry, but film lacks a certain punch. The real-life Wisecarver appears as a mailman in newsreel sequence (narrated by an uncredited Carl Reiner). Wonderful score by Ralph Burns, incorporating many vintage songs. [PG-13] ▼●)

In the Mood for Love (2000-Hong Kong-French) **C-97m.** **½ D: Wong Kar-wai. Maggie Cheung, Tony Leung, Lai Chin, Rebecca Pan, Siu Ping-lam, Chin Tsi-ang. In 1962 Hong Kong, two lonely, married people are drawn to each other, but dare not pursue their feelings. An intriguing study of repressed emotions, ingeniously filmed so we're often peeking around corners, only partially seeing what is going on. An exceptional mood piece that, like its characters, too often keeps us at an emotional distance. [PG] ▼▶

In the Mouth of Madness (1995) **C-95m.** **½ D: John Carpenter. Sam Neill, Jürgen Prochnow, Charlton Heston, David Warner, John Glover, Julie Carmen, Bernie Casey, Peter Jason, Frances Bay, Hayden Christensen. From his padded cell, desperate Neill relates his story to Warner: Hired to locate reclusive horror writer Prochnow, Neill finds him in a small New England town. But then people, places, and even reality begin undergoing horrific transformations. The first two-thirds is among Carpenter's best work as a director, and Neill is outstanding, but the last third becomes pointlessly obscure, and the ending is a pretentious letdown. Derived, without credit, from concepts created by H. P. Lovecraft. Panavision. [R] ▼●)

In the Name of the Father (1993-U.S.-Irish) **C-127m.** ***½ D: Jim Sheridan. Daniel Day-Lewis, Pete Postlethwaite, Emma Thompson, John Lynch, Corin Redgrave, Beatie Edney, Daniel Massey. Searing, fact-based account of youthful Belfast no-good who's picked up—along with a friend and most of his family—by British police and accused of a terrorist bombing he had nothing to do with. Director Sheridan grabs you by the collar and never lets go; Day-Lewis is extraordinarily intense and believable, Postlethwaite every bit as good as his simple, straightforward dad. Gerry Conlon's book *Proved Innocent* adapted by Sheridan and Terry George. [R] ▼●)

In the Name of the King: A Dungeon Siege Tale (2008-German-Canadian) **C-126m.** BOMB D: Uwe Boll. Jason Statham, John Rhys-Davies, Ray Liotta, Matthew Lillard, Leelee Sobieski, Burt Reynolds, Ron Perlman, Claire Forlani, Kristanna Loken. Reluctant warrior Statham joins forces with a brave king (Reynolds) to battle a treacherous usurper (Lillard) and a wicked wizard (Liotta). Another video-game–inspired fiasco from the unfortunately prolific Boll. Even with a bigger budget and better actors than usual, this is a plodding patchwork of derivative fantasy-adventure, with substandard CGI effects and haphazardly edited action sequences. Alternate version runs 162m. Super 35. [PG-13]▶

In the Navy (1941) **85m.** **½ D: Arthur Lubin. Bud Abbott, Lou Costello, Dick Powell, The Andrews Sisters, Claire Dodd, Dick Foran. Bud and Lou are somehow in the Navy; Lou has hallucinations and nearly wrecks the entire fleet. Powell and Andrews Sisters provide songs, and Costello shows Abbott how 7 fimp 13 fieq 28. ▼●)

In the Realm of Passion SEE: **Empire of Passion**

In the Realm of the Senses (1976-Japanese-French) **C-105m.** **½ D: Nagisa Oshima. Tatsuya Fuji, Eiko Matsuda, Aio Nakajima, Meika Seri. Sexually insatiable Matsuda will do anything to possess husband Fuji. Explicit, controversial, often erotic and well-acted, but overall a pretentious film. The story was previously told in A WOMAN CALLED SADA ABE: BEYOND THE REALM OF THE SENSES.▼▶

In the Shadow of the Moon (2007-U.S.-British) **C-100m.** **** D: David Sington. The story of the Apollo space program, as told by ten of the men who flew to (and in some cases walked on) the moon, illustrated by breathtaking NASA footage, some of which has never been seen before. The astronauts are candid, articulate, and reflective, nearly 40 years after their otherworldly exploits. (The most impressive: Mike Collins, who's kept a low profile since Apollo 11.) An unexpectedly moving reminder of a time when Americans were united in justifiable pride over a towering human achievement. [PG]▶

In the Shadow of the Stars (1991) **C-93m.** *** D: Irving Saraf, Allie Light. Absorbing documentary about members of the chorus of the San Francisco Opera Company—the drive that makes them want to sing, the yearning to take center stage, the sacrifices made, the dreams fulfilled. Even nonopera lovers will be caught up in this very human story, simply but eloquently told (with a healthy selection of operatic excerpts). Oscar winner for Best Documentary Feature.▼▶

In the Soup (1992) **C/B&W-90m.** **½ D: Alexandre Rockwell. Steve Buscemi, Seymour Cassel, Jennifer Beals, Pat Moya, Will Patton, Sully Boyar, Jim Jarmusch, Carol Kane, Stanley Tucci, Rockets Redglare, Elizabeth Bracco, Debi Mazar, Sam Rockwell. Absurdist comedy about a naive, ambitious writer (Buscemi) who's penned a 500-page screenplay and the eccentric small-time hood (Cassel, in a canny, award-caliber performance) who promises to produce his film. At times very funny, but also downright silly; coscripted by Rockwell. Filmed in color, released in b&w. Both versions available on video.▼▶

In the Spirit (1990) **C-94m.** ** D: Sandra Seacat. Marlo Thomas, Elaine May, Peter Falk, Jeannie Berlin, Olympia Dukakis, Melanie Griffith, Michael Emil, Christopher Durang. Oddball throwback to black comedies of the 1970s, as mystic Thomas and house guest May get targeted by the mysterious killer who's murdered the prostitute next door. Packed with characters and performances that tend to grate on the nerves, though it is fun to see Thomas and May doing Abbott and Costello (or is it a neurotic version of Lucy and Ethel?). Griffith has just one scene. [R]▼

In the Valley of Elah (2007) **C-120m.** ***½ D: Paul Haggis. Tommy Lee Jones, Charlize Theron, Susan Sarandon, Jason Patric, James Franco, Josh Brolin, Frances Fisher, Jonathan Tucker, Mehcad Brooks, Wes Chatham, Jake McLaughlin, Victor Wolf, Barry Corbin. Retired Army investigator Jones takes matters into his own hands when his son, just returned from duty in Iraq, is reported AWOL. In time he convinces police detective Theron that his suspicions are worth checking out, in spite of stonewalling from Army officials and the young man's fellow soldiers. Riveting whodunit takes us into dark, difficult terrain, all of it mirrored on Jones' haunted face; his exceptional performance anchors this outstanding film. Haggis scripted from a story he wrote with Mark Boal, inspired by real-life events. Super 35. [R]▶

In the White City (1983-Swiss-Portuguese) **C-108m.** ***½ D: Alain Tanner. Bruno Ganz, Teresa Madruga, Julia Vonderlinn, Jose Carvalho. Involving, thought-provoking, Kafkaesque tale of seaman Ganz's experiences while in Lisbon, highlighted by his relationship with chambermaid Madruga. The work of a filmmaker in complete command of his art.▼

In This Our Life (1942) **97m.** *** D: John Huston. Bette Davis, Olivia de Havilland, George Brent, Dennis Morgan, Charles Coburn, Frank Craven, Billie Burke, Hattie McDaniel, Lee Patrick, Ernest Anderson. Fine drama of neurotic family with husband-stealing Davis ruining sister de Havilland's life, and eventually her own; Davis at histrionic height. Based on Ellen Glasgow novel. Walter Huston has cameo role as bartender in one scene. Also shown in computer-colored version.▼▶

In This World (2003-British) **C-90m.** *** D: Michael Winterbottom. Jamal Udin Torabi, Enayatullah. Teenage Jamal and his slightly older uncle Enayat pool their resources for cross-country transportation from an Afghan refugee camp to London. They travel by truck, train, and boat with surprisingly few complications—but those few can be deadly. Intriguing, unscripted film was shot as the two protagonists, playing themselves, actually made the journey. This, coupled with handheld photography, creates a powerful sense of realism. Engrossing, almost hypnotic at times, though the ultimate point remains elusive. Digital Video Widescreen. [R] ▼▶

Intimate Affairs SEE: **Investigating Sex**

Intimate Lighting (1965-Czech) **72m.** *** D: Ivan Passer. Vera Kresadlova, Zdenek Brezusek, Karel Blazek, Jaroslava Stedra, Jan Vostrcil, Vlastmila Vlkova, Karel Uhlik. Unpretentious, day-in-the-life story of two old friends, professional musicians, reuniting after long absence at country home. Excellent performances.▼

Intimate Relations (1996-British-Canadian) **C-105m.** ******* D: Philip Goodhew. Julie Walters, Rupert Graves, Matthew Walker, Laura Sadler, Holly Aird, Les Dennis, Elizabeth McKechnie. Black comedy/melodrama of romantic obsession in 1954 England. Housewife Walters (wickedly effective) takes in sailor Graves as a lodger, and in no time passions are aroused throughout the household. Interesting British Empire tale (fact based, and for mature viewers) reminiscent in many ways of both A PRIVATE FUNCTION and HEAVENLY CREATURES. [R]▼●

Intimate Stranger, The SEE: **Finger of Guilt**

Intimate Strangers (2004-French) **C-105m.** ******* D: Patrice Leconte. Fabrice Luchini, Sandrine Bonnaire, Michel Duchaussoy, Anne Brochet, Gilbert Melki, Laurent Gamelon. A woman forces her way into a psychiatrist's office and pours her heart out about her marital woes; he doesn't have the heart to tell her that she's come to the wrong office, as he is a mere tax adviser. Their relationship blossoms just the same in this charming, often piquant film, with two masterly performances guided by the gifted Leconte. The girl who asks a question in the library is Aurore Auteuil, daughter of Daniel Auteuil and Emmanuelle Béart. Panavision. [R]▼●

Intolerable Cruelty (2003) **C-100m.** ****½** D: Joel Coen. George Clooney, Catherine Zeta-Jones, Geoffrey Rush, Cedric the Entertainer, Edward Herrmann, Paul Adelstein, Richard Jenkins, Billy Bob Thornton, Julia Duffy, Jonathan Hadary, Tom Aldredge. A swaggering divorce attorney meets his match in a gold digger who sets her cap for him as the ultimate conquest. Clooney is terrific, Zeta-Jones is luminous, and they're supported by canny costars and faces out of Fellini's old casting directory . . . but the fun turns sour after a while, as no one is "real" enough to root for. Still, there are many funny moments, especially with Herrmann, Rush, and Thornton. Bruce Campbell appears unbilled. [PG-13] ▼●

Intolerance (1916) **178m.** ******** D: D. W. Griffith. Lillian Gish, Robert Harron, Mae Marsh, Constance Talmadge, Bessie Love, Seena Owen, Alfred Paget, Eugene Pallette, many others. Landmark American epic interweaves four stories of prejudice and inhumanity, from the Babylonian era to the modern day. Melodramatic, to be sure, but gains in momentum and power as it moves toward its stunning climax. That's Lillian Gish as the mother rocking the cradle; Constance Talmadge gives a most appealing and contemporary performance as the sprightly Mountain Girl. Shown in a variety of prints with variant running times—as long as 208m. ▼●

In Too Deep (1999) **C-95m.** ****½** D: Michael Rymer. Omar Epps, LL Cool J, Nia Long, Stanley Tucci, Hill Harper, Pam Grier, Veronica Webb. Police academy grad (Epps) goes undercover to take on a ruthless crimelord known as "God" (LL Cool J) but finds he can't get out. Gritty, realistic gangsploitation actually avoids most of the clichés of the genre and has a commanding, understated performance from Epps at its core. Hip-hoppers Jermaine Dupri, Mya and Nas appear in cameos. Super 35. [R]▼●

Into the Arms of Strangers: Stories of the Kindertransport (2000) **C/B&W-117m.** *****½** D: Mark Jonathan Harris. Narrated by Judi Dench. Well-crafted documentary covers a heretofore unexplored subject: the extraordinary efforts to place Jewish children from Germany, Austria, and Czechoslovakia out of harm's way by sending them to live with families in England during WW2. Told in large part by the people who lived through this experience, with the help of some incredibly rare footage from the period. From the same writer-director responsible for THE LONG WAY HOME. Oscar winner for Best Documentary. [PG]▼●

Into the Blue (2005) **C-110m.** ***½** D: John Stockwell. Paul Walker, Jessica Alba, Scott Caan, Ashley Scott, Josh Brolin, James Frain, Tyson Beckford. While diving in the Bahamas, a quartet of Beautiful People encounters the remains of a crashed plane laden with a cache of cocaine. Picturesque scenery and plenty of eye candy don't compensate for a half-baked storyline, routine suspense, and mindless violence. Followed by a DVD sequel. Super 35. [PG-13] ▼●

Into the Fire (1987-Canadian) **C-93m.** ****** D: Graeme Campbell. Susan Anspach, Olivia d'Abo, Art Hindle. Old-fashioned murder/sex triangle thriller has the novelty of a wintry Canadian setting where lodge owner Anspach is an impressive seductress. Almost outdone by one too many plot twists. Precocious d'Abo is also a stunning, contrasting femme fatale. Aka LEGEND OF WOLF LODGE. [R]▼●

Into the Night (1985) **C-115m.** ******* D: John Landis. Jeff Goldblum, Michelle Pfeiffer, Richard Farnsworth, Irene Papas, Kathryn Harrold, Paul Mazursky, Roger Vadim, Dan Aykroyd, David Bowie, Bruce McGill, Vera Miles, Clu Gulager. Engaging, episodic film about a middle-class nerd who helps a beautiful woman who's being chased by killers. Convoluted story filled with offbeat vignettes and colorful characters, many of them played by Hollywood directors (Don Siegel, Jonathan Demme, Jack Arnold, Lawrence Kasdan, Paul Bartel, David Cronenberg, Richard Franklin, Colin Higgins, Andrew Marton, Jonathan Kaufer, Amy Heckerling). Landis himself is very funny as one of the Iranian bad guys.

Probably more appealing to film buffs than general audiences. [R]▼●🕮

Into the Sun (1992) C-100m. *½ D: Fritz Kiersch. Anthony Michael Hall, Michael Paré, Deborah Maria Moore, Terry Kiser, Brian Haley. Hall plays a conceited actor who tags along with U.S. pilot Paré in order to research an upcoming film role. Virtually identical in plot to the Michael J. Fox/James Woods comedy THE HARD WAY, with a change in milieu (and budget). Aerial stunts aren't bad considering the threadbare production values, but it's only for those who'll try anything. [R]▼●

Into the West (1993-Irish) C-97m. *** D: Mike Newell. Gabriel Byrne, Colm Meaney, Ellen Barkin, Ciaran Fitzgerald, Ruaidhri Conroy, David Kelly, Johnny Murphy, John Kavanagh, Pauline Delaney. Dark, melancholy fable about two young brothers who flee their drab Dublin life (with a morose, widowed father) on the back of a mystical white horse. A highly original film with equal parts charm, dour Irish moods, and the theme of family and its inexorable pull on us all. Written by Jim Sheridan. [PG]▼●🕮

Into the Wild (2007) C-148m. ***½ D: Sean Penn. Emile Hirsch, William Hurt, Marcia Gay Harden, Jena Malone, Catherine Keener, Vince Vaughn, Kristen Stewart, Hal Holbrook, Brian Dierker, Zach Galifianakis, Thure Lindhardt. Recent college graduate Chris McCandless spurns his parents—and America's capitalist society—in search of quieter, more personal fulfillment in the Alaskan wilderness. But along the road he meets a variety of people who become something like extended family. Idiosyncratic melding of hippie sensibility and nature documentary results in writer-director-coproducer Penn's most artistic and powerful release to date—and a heartbreaker. Working on a large canvas, Penn elicits some wonderful vignettes and expert performances and punctuates it all with music by Eddie Vedder, among others. Based on the nonfiction bestseller by Jon Krakauer. Super 35. [R]🕮

Introducing the Dwights (2007-Australian) C-105m. **½ D: Cherie Nowlan. Brenda Blethyn, Rebecca Gibney, Khan Chittenden, Richard Wilson, Frankie J. Holden, Russell Dykstra, Emma Booth, Katie Wall, Philip Quast. A soft-spoken teenage boy has put his own life on hold in order to shuttle his mother—a force of nature not to be trifled with—to engagements in comedy clubs around greater Sydney. But when he acquires a girlfriend for the first time, Mom goes ballistic. Mild comedy-drama about a messed-up family is easy to take and offers Blethyn a great showcase. Original Australian title: CLUBLAND. [R]🕮

Intruder, The (1962) 80m. *** D: Roger Corman. William Shatner, Frank Maxwell, Beverly Lunsford, Robert Emhardt, Leo Gordon, Jeanne Cooper, Charles Beaumont, George Clayton Johnson, William F. Nolan. Racist Shatner drifts from one small Southern town to another inciting townspeople to riot against court-ordered school integration. Corman's only "message" film—and one of his few box-office flops—still packs a punch; low budget and location filming aid authenticity. Script by Charles Beaumont. Reissued as I HATE YOUR GUTS! and SHAME.▼🕮

Intruder, The (2005-French) C-129m. *** D: Claire Denis. Michel Subor, Grégoire Colin, Katia Golubeva, Bambou, Florence Loiret-Caille, Beatrice Dalle. Unusual drama of one man's journey, both literal and metaphysical, as he leaves his hearty life behind on the French-Swiss border, arranges for a heart transplant, and moves to a remote South Seas island. Denis demands a great deal of the viewer as she interweaves past, present, and future and alternates between reality and a kind of dream-state. Difficult and fascinating at the same time; beautifully shot by Agnès Godard. Inspired by Jean-Luc Nancy's memoir. Super 35.🕮

Intruder in the Dust (1949) 87m. *** D: Clarence Brown. David Brian, Claude Jarman, Jr., Juano Hernandez, Porter Hall, Elizabeth Patterson. Black man (Hernandez, in a solid performance) is accused of murder in a Southern town, and a gathering mob wants to lynch him. First-rate adaptation of William Faulkner novel. Surprisingly strong for a mainstream Hollywood film of that period; good use of locations, superbly photographed by Robert Surtees. Biggest problem: Brian's character is always speechifying and moralizing. Screenplay by Ben Maddow.▼🕮

Invaders, The SEE: **49th Parallel**

Invaders From Mars (1953) C-78m. *** D: William Cameron Menzies. Helena Carter, Arthur Franz, Jimmy Hunt, Leif Erickson, Hillary Brooke, Bert Freed. Starkly stylish sci-fi told from little boy's point of view, as he alone witnesses arrival of aliens who capture and brainwash residents of average small town. Remade in 1986. Alternate British version runs 83m.—and changes the ending!▼🕮

Invaders From Mars (1986) C-100m. *½ D: Tobe Hooper. Karen Black, Hunter Carson, Timothy Bottoms, Laraine Newman, James Karen, Louise Fletcher, Bud Cort, Jimmy Hunt. Remake of '50s fantasy favorite about a boy's nightmarish experiences when aliens land in his back yard and overtake everyone around him—even his parents. Starts fine, rapidly goes downhill toward utter disaster. Hunt, the youngster in the original film, plays a police chief here; the boy this time is real-life son of costar Black. J-D-C Scope. [PG]▼●🕮

Invasion, The (2007) C-99m. *½ D: Oliver Hirschbiegel. Nicole Kidman, Daniel Craig, Jeremy Northam, Jackson Bond, Veronica Cartwright, Jeffrey Wright, Josef Sommer, Celia Weston, Roger Rees, Eric Benjamin, Adam LeFevre. Third remake of INVASION OF THE BODY SNATCHERS is not the charm, as this mess never comes together as both the sci-fi thriller and human drama it seeks to be. Kidman is a Washington, D.C., psychiatrist who slowly discovers that a mysterious disease taking over the planet may be alien-inspired. With the help of doctor Craig she must find the antidote before most of humankind is lost. Widely reported reshoots couldn't salvage this film. [PG-13]▐

Invasion Earth 2150 A.D. SEE: **Daleks—Invasion Earth 2150 A.D.**

Invasion Force SEE: **Hangar 18**

Invasion of the Bee Girls (1973) C-85m. *** D: Denis Sanders. Victoria Vetri, William Smith, Anitra Ford, Cliff Osmond, Wright King, Ben Hammer. Wonderfully campy (and sexy) sci-fi outing about a strange force that's transforming women into dangerous creatures who you-know-what men to death in a small California town. Written by Nicholas Meyer pre-SEVEN-PER-CENT SOLUTION. [R] ▼▐

Invasion of the Body Snatchers (1956) 80m. ***½ D: Don Siegel. Kevin McCarthy, Dana Wynter, Larry Gates, King Donovan, Carolyn Jones, Virginia Christine. Classic, influential, and still very scary science-fiction (with McCarthy-era subtext) about small-town residents who are being replaced by duplicates hatched from alien "pods." Tense script by Daniel Mainwaring from Jack Finney's *The Body Snatchers*; Sam Peckinpah can be glimpsed as a meter reader. Appropriately frightening musical score by Carmen Dragon. Reissued in 1979 at 76m., minus unnecessary, studio-imposed prologue and epilogue with Whit Bissell and Richard Deacon. Remade in 1978 and 1994 (as BODY SNATCHER), and in 2007 as THE INVASION. Also shown in computer-colored version. SuperScope. ▼●▐

Invasion of the Body Snatchers (1978) C-115m. *** D: Philip Kaufman. Donald Sutherland, Brooke Adams, Leonard Nimoy, Jeff Goldblum, Veronica Cartwright. Chilling remake of 1956 classic with many new twists and turns; unfortunately, it runs out of steam and offers one climax too many. Kevin McCarthy and Don Siegel, star and director of original film, have significant cameo roles; look fast for Robert Duvall. Weird score by Denny Zeitlin. [PG] ▼●▐

Invasion Siniestra SEE: **Sinister Invasion**

Invasion U.S.A. (1985) C-107m. BOMB D: Joseph Zito. Chuck Norris, Richard Lynch, Melissa Prophet, Alex Colon. Political-paranoia action film about retired CIA agent (Norris) back on the job when Rus-

sian terrorists invade Florida, try to overtake entire country by causing panic and turmoil. Repellent in the extreme. [R]▼●▐

Inventing the Abbotts (1997) C-120m. ** D: Pat O'Connor. Liv Tyler, Joaquin Phoenix, Jennifer Connelly, Billy Crudup, Joanna Going, Kathy Baker, Will Patton, Barbara Williams, Alessandro Nivola, Shawn Hatosy. Two working-class brothers try to woo the beautiful and wealthy Abbott sisters in 1950s Midwest America. Aspires to be a classic coming-of-ager like SPLENDOR IN THE GRASS, but despite a very attractive cast, the proceedings are pretty flaccid. Lush surroundings can't compensate for dull scripting; plays like an anemic Douglas Sirk melodrama or a return to Peyton Place. Michael Keaton narrates unbilled. [R]▼●▐

Invention of Lying, The (2009-U.S.-British) C-99m. ** D: Ricky Gervais, Matthew Robinson. Ricky Gervais, Jennifer Garner, Jonah Hill, Louis C.K., Jeffrey Tambor, Rob Lowe, Tina Fey, Fionnula Flanagan, Stephanie March, Nate Corddry, John Hodgman, Christopher Guest, Philip Seymour Hoffman, Edward Norton, Jason Bateman. Comedy is set in a hypothetical world where everyone tells the absolute truth, until one day when hard-luck Gervais utters a lie . . . and gets away with it. Yet somehow he can't seem to win over beautiful but superficial Garner. Clever premise is squandered, with funny moments adrift in an anemic story. Gervais cowrote and codirected, but deserves a better vehicle. [PG-13]▐

Investigating Sex (2006-U.S.-German) C-108m. ** D: Alan Rudolph. Dermot Mulroney, Julie Delpy, Robin Tunney, Neve Campbell, Jeremy Davies, Alan Cumming, Til Schweiger, John Light, Nick Nolte, Terrence Dashon Howard, Tuesday Weld, Emily Bruni. Talky film, set in the 1920s, in which a group of artists and intellectuals initiate a discourse on the subject of sexuality. Occasionally tart dialogue is overshadowed by long stretches of boredom and an outdated sense of daring. Hart Bochner appears unbilled. Completed in 2001. Aka INTIMATE AFFAIRS. [R]▐

Investigation of a Citizen Above Suspicion (1970-Italian) C-115m. *** D: Elio Petri. Gian Maria Volonté, Florinda Bolkan, Salvo Randone, Gianni Santuccio, Arturo Dominici. Oscar-winning foreign film about powerful police chief who slashes the throat of his mistress, then waits entire movie to see if he'll be caught. Interesting, but not overly gripping. Superbly creepy score by Ennio Morricone. [R]

Invictus (2009) C-137m. *** D: Clint Eastwood. Morgan Freeman, Matt Damon, Tony Kgoroge, Julian Lewis Jones, Adjoa Andoh, Patrick Mofokeng, Matt Stern, Leleti Khumalo. As Nelson Mandela is elected President of South Africa in 1994, he seizes an opportunity to unite the white and black people of his country by encouraging its (mostly white) rugby team to push itself and compete for the World Cup. Inspiring true story about the sound instincts of a remarkable man who understood the power of sports. Narrative offers no surprises but tells its story well; it's hard to imagine anyone playing Mandela better than Freeman, and Damon is completely believable as an Afrikaner rugby star. Based on John Carlin's book *Playing the Enemy*. Panavision. [PG-13]▐

Invincible (2002-British-German) **C-127m.** ** D: Werner Herzog. Tim Roth, Jouko Ahola, Anna Gourari, Jacob Wein, Max Raabe, Gustav Peter Wöehler, Udo Kier. A sweetly naïve young Polish Jew becomes a false symbol of hope for Jewry in pre-Hitler Berlin upon winning fame as a strongman in a cabaret show staged by Hanussen (Roth), the magician-clairvoyant. This fact-based account is overlong and by the numbers; it's a compelling tale that deserves a far more subtle, pointed treatment. Hanussen's story is told much more forcefully in Istvan Szabo's HANUSSEN. [PG-13] ▼▐

Invincible (2006) **C-104m.** *** D: Ericson Core. Mark Wahlberg, Greg Kinnear, Elizabeth Banks, Kevin Conway, Michael Rispoli, Michael Nouri, Kirk Acevedo, Dov Davidoff, Michael Kelly, Sal Darigo, Nicoye Banks. Working-class stiff who's been laid off from his job and dumped by his wife pursues a whim when the new coach of the Philadelphia Eagles football team holds an open tryout. Fact-based story of Vince Papale (well played by Wahlberg) captures the hold a team can have on its hometown fans, especially when they have little else to believe in. Solid entertainment. Super 35. [PG]▐

Invincible Six, The (1970) **C-96m.** **½ D: Jean Negulesco. Stuart Whitman, Elke Sommer, Curt Jurgens, James Mitchum, Ian Ogilvy. Energetic action film about a motley crew on the lam who come to the aid of isolated villagers under the thumb of a bandit gang. It's THE MAGNIFICENT SEVEN transplanted to present-day mid-East in this Iranian-made production. Widescreen. ▼

Invisible, The (2007) **C-97m.** *½ D: David S. Goyer. Justin Chatwin, Margarita Levieva, Marcia Gay Harden, Chris Marquette, Alex O'Loughlin, Callum Keith Rennie, Michelle Harrison, Ryan Kennedy, Andrew Francis. Dreary teen ghost story about a promising high school senior who is caught in limbo between life and death, "invisible" to all around him and headed for expiration unless he can solve the mystery of his own murder. Sort of a cross between GHOST and RIVER'S EDGE, this tries to be a spiritual whodunit but winds up a why-didtheymakeit instead. Based on a 2002

Swedish film of the same name. Super 35. [PG-13]▐

Invisible Boy, The (1957) **89m.** *** D: Herman Hoffman. Richard Eyer, Philip Abbott, Diane Brewster, Harold J. Stone, Robert H. Harris; voice of Marvin Miller. The movies' first supercomputer not only helps scientist Abbott's lonely son Eyer become invisible (briefly) but also makes him smarter, so he can reassemble FORBIDDEN PLANET's Robby the Robot. However, the computer wants to use Robby to control the world. Robot-loving kids will take this straight, but it's an amusing, intelligent, low-key spoof of itself. ▼●▐

Invisible Circus, The (2001) **C-92m.** ** D: Adam Brooks. Jordana Brewster, Christopher Eccleston, Cameron Diaz, Blythe Danner, Patrick Bergin, Camilla Belle, Moritz Bleibtreu. A teenage girl tries to retrace the footsteps of her older sister, a free spirit who died mysteriously in Europe seven years earlier. Diaz is excellent, but Brewster hits just one note in this unsatisfying film. Brooks adapted Jennifer Egan's novel. [R] ▼▌

Invisible Man, The (1933) **71m.** ***½ D: James Whale. Claude Rains, Gloria Stuart, Una O'Connor, William Harrigan, E. E. Clive, Dudley Digges, Dwight Frye. H. G. Wells' fantasy brilliantly materializes on screen in tale of mad scientist who makes himself invisible, wreaking havoc on British country village. Rains' starring debut is dated but still enjoyable. Look fast for John Carradine phoning in a "sighting"; that's Walter Brennan whose bicycle is stolen. ▼●▐

Invisible Man Returns, The (1940) **81m.** *** D: Joe May. Cedric Hardwicke, Vincent Price, John Sutton, Nan Grey, Cecil Kellaway, Alan Napier. Fine follow-up, with Price going invisible to clear himself of murder charge. Considered by many to be Price's first horror film.▼●▐

Invisible Man's Revenge, The (1944) **77m.** ** D: Ford Beebe. Jon Hall, Alan Curtis, Evelyn Ankers, Leon Errol, John Carradine, Gale Sondergaard, Ian Wolfe, Billy Bevan. Hall allows unsuspecting scientist Carradine to make him invisible so he can seek vengeance on former business partners. Mixed-up script, unfunny comic relief (Errol), and slightly below par special effects add up to weakest INVISIBLE MAN sequel.▼●▐

Invisible Ray, The (1936) **81m.** **½ D: Lambert Hillyer. Boris Karloff, Bela Lugosi, Frances Drake, Frank Lawton, Walter Kingsford, Beulah Bondi. Scientist Karloff contracts radiation poisoning that gives him touch of death (and makes him glow in the dark). Interesting yarn, but a notch below other Karloff-Lugosi vehicles. ▼●▐

Invisible Stripes (1939) **82m.** *** D: Lloyd Bacon. George Raft, Jane Bryan, William Holden, Flora Robson, Humphrey Bogart,

Paul Kelly, Moroni Olsen, Tully Marshall. Earnest account of parolee Raft trying to go straight, protecting brother Holden from gangster Bogart; subdued acting is effective. ▶

Invisible Woman, The (1941) 72m. *** D: A. Edward Sutherland. John Barrymore, Virginia Bruce, John Howard, Charlie Ruggles, Oscar Homolka, Margaret Hamilton, Donald MacBride, Edward Brophy, Shemp Howard, Charles Lane, Thurston Hall. Great cast in likable comedy about screwy professor Barrymore turning model Bruce invisible, arousing the curiosity of playboy sponsor Howard, as well as the more monetary interests of gangster Homolka. Slick and sprightly, with Ruggles terrific as Howard's long-suffering butler; Maria Montez has a bit as one of Bruce's fellow models. ▼●▶

Invitation to a Gunfighter (1964) C-92m. **½ D: Richard Wilson. Yul Brynner, George Segal, Janice Rule, Pat Hingle, Brad Dexter. Cast surpasses turgid, talky script about town that hires gunslinger to kill an outcast, with surprising results. ▼▶

Invitation to the Dance (1956) C-93m. **½ D: Gene Kelly. Gene Kelly, Igor Youskevitch, Claire Sombert, David Paltenghi, Daphne Dale, Claude Bessy, Tommy Rall, Carol Haney, Tamara Toumanova, Belita. Kelly's ambitious film tells three stories entirely in dance. Earnest but uninspired, until final "Sinbad" segment with Kelly in Hanna-Barbera cartoon world. Music by Jacques Ibert, Andre Previn, and Rimsky-Korsakov. Filmed in 1952. ▼▶

In Which We Serve (1942-British) 115m. **** D: Noel Coward, David Lean. Noel Coward, John Mills, Bernard Miles, Celia Johnson, Kay Walsh, Joyce Carey, Michael Wilding, James Donald, Richard Attenborough. Unlike many WW2 films, this masterpiece doesn't date one bit; superb film about men on a British fighting ship, told through flashback. Written, codirected, and scored by costar Coward (who was given a special Oscar "for his outstanding production achievement"). Lean's first directing credit. Film debuts of Johnson, Attenborough, young Daniel Massey, and infant Juliet Mills. ▼●▶

I Only Want You to Love Me (1976-West German) C-101m. **½ D: Rainer Werner Fassbinder. Vitus Zeplichal, Elke Aberle, Alexander Allerson, Ernie Mangold, Johanna Hofer. Intriguing morality tale of decent, hardworking young bricklayer, whose Bavarian upbringing was noticeably lacking in parental affection. When he marries and moves to Munich, the lure of the big-city consumer society (and the ability to buy on credit) proves disastrous. Deliberately paced but offbeat examination of a shattered psyche. Made for TV; unreleased in the U.S. until 1994. ▼▶

I Ought to Be in Pictures (1982) C-107m. ** D: Herbert Ross. Walter Matthau, Ann-Margret, Dinah Manoff, Lance Guest, Lewis Smith, Martin Ferrero, David Faustino, Michael Dudikoff. Poor formula Neil Simon sitcom, adapted from his play: 19-year-old Brooklynite Manoff hitches to L.A. to make it in movies—and establishes connection with her father (Matthau), screenwriter turned gambler-drinker. Matthau and Manoff do their best; Ann-Margret wasted as Walter's mistress. [PG] ▼

Ipcress File, The (1965-British) C-108m. ***½ D: Sidney J. Furie. Michael Caine, Nigel Green, Guy Doleman, Sue Lloyd, Gordon Jackson. First and best of Len Deighton's Harry Palmer series, with Caine as unemotional Cockney crook turned secret agent, involved in grueling mental torture caper. Eerie score by John Barry. Followed by two sequels—FUNERAL IN BERLIN and BILLION DOLLAR BRAIN —and a pair of cable TV follow-ups in 1997, BULLET TO BEIJING and MIDNIGHT IN ST. PETERSBURG. Techniscope. ▼▶

Iphigenia (1977-Greek) C-127m. **½ D: Michael Cacoyannis. Irene Papas, Tatiana Papamoskou, Costa Kazakos, Costa Carras, Christos Tsangas. Ambitious but over-directed adaptation of Euripides' *Iphigenia in Aulis*, in which Agamemnon becomes convinced that, to earn military victory, he will have to sacrifice his daughter Iphigenia (impressively played by young Papamoskou). The elements of high drama are present, but Cacoyannis opts for eye-popping visuals rather than focusing on the heart of the story. ▼▶

I.Q. (1994) C-95m. *** D: Fred Schepisi. Tim Robbins, Meg Ryan, Walter Matthau, Lou Jacobi, Gene Saks, Joseph Maher, Stephen Fry, Tony Shalhoub, Frank Whaley, Keene Curtis, Charles Durning, Alice Playten, Danny Zorn. Pleasant romantic comedy (perhaps too "cute" for some viewers) about a garage mechanic who falls in love with a customer at first sight, and gets some unusual matchmaking help from her uncle—Albert Einstein! Likable performances by well-matched Robbins and Ryan, with Matthau having fun as the cagey Professor. Set in 1950s Princeton, N.J. Super 35. [PG] ▼●▶

Ira & Abby (2007) C-100m. **½ D: Robert Cary. Chris Messina, Jennifer Westfeldt, Frances Conroy, Judith Light, Jason Alexander, Robert Klein, Fred Willard, Maddie Corman, Darrell Hammond, Chris Parnell, Jon Hamm, B. D. Wong. Westfeldt (KISSING JESSICA STEIN) wrote this "comedy of divorce" about neurotic New Yorker Ira (Messina), who can't ever make a decision. At the other end of the spectrum, Abby (Westfeldt) wants to get married minutes after meeting him. She's a warmhearted, outgoing person, and he gets caught up in her upbeat life—at least for a while. Light and Klein are funny as Messina's analyst parents, as are Conroy and Willard as Westfeldt's sunny mom and dad. Uneven but often very funny. Donna Murphy appears unbilled. [R]

Iraq in Fragments (2006) **C-94m.** ******* D: James Longley. Documentary takes its cameras from southern to northern Iraq to see the effect war—and opposing religious philosophies—has taken on the country, in three segments that spotlight Shiites, Sunnis, and Kurds. Using no intruding narration, filmmaker Longley tells the story through the eyes and words of the Iraqi people, painting a compelling portrait of a troubled country and presenting a largely nonpolitical view Americans have rarely seen. Longley photographed, coedited, co-produced, and scored the film.

I Remember Mama (1948) **134m.** *****½** D: George Stevens. Irene Dunne, Barbara Bel Geddes, Oscar Homolka, Philip Dorn, Cedric Hardwicke, Edgar Bergen, Rudy Vallee, Barbara O'Neil, Florence Bates, Ellen Corby. Beautifully realized, exquisitely detailed filming of John Van Druten's play, based on Kathryn Forbes' memoirs about growing up with her Norwegian immigrant family in San Francisco. A bit long, but richly rewarding, with top performances in each and every role. Screenplay by DeWitt Bodeen. Followed by the TV series *Mama.* Also shown in computer-colored version. ▼ⓞ

Irina Palm (2008-Belgian-French-German-British-Luxembourgian) **C-100m.** ******* D: Sam Garbarski. Marianne Faithfull, Miki Manojlovic, Kevin Bishop, Siobhân Hewlett, Dorka Gryllus, Jenny Agutter. A sixtyish widow (Faithfull), in a financial bind due to her grandson's illness, takes a job as a "hostess" (translation: sex worker) in a Soho, London, club. Simple, no-frills drama presents a hardnosed look at human relations in a cold, cynical world while offering an unusual, nonexploitive spin on the sex industry. Only falters during a couple of unnecessary scenes near the finale. [R]

Iris (2001-British-U.S.) **C-90m.** ****½** D: Richard Eyre. Judi Dench, Jim Broadbent, Kate Winslet, Hugh Bonneville, Penelope Wilton, Juliet Aubrey, Samuel West, Timothy West, Eleanor Bron. Dench plays noted British author and psychologist Dame Iris Murdoch, with Broadbent as her devoted husband; Winslet and Bonneville play the characters in flashbacks to the 1950s when they first met at Oxford. As Iris descends into the world of Alzheimer's, her husband loses his grip, and the results become difficult to watch, despite the fine performances. Broadbent won an Oscar for Best Supporting Actor. [R] ▼ⓞ

Irishman, The (1978-Australian) **C-108m.** ******* D: Donald Crombie. Michael Craig, Simon Burke, Robin Nevin, Lou Brown, Andrew Maguire. Effective, wonderfully acted drama of teamster Craig, his wife and sons, and his refusal to accept change and progress during the 1920s. A touching portrait of a family in turmoil. ▼ⓞ

Irma la Douce (1963) **C-142m.** ****½** D: Billy Wilder. Shirley MacLaine, Jack Lemmon, Lou Jacobi, Herschel Bernardi, Joan Shawlee, Hope Holiday, Bill Bixby. Wilder's straight comedy adaptation of Broadway musical is a Parisian fairy tale for adults. Gendarme Lemmon falls for prostitute MacLaine and will do anything to keep her for himself. Red Light District is vividly re-created, but reteaming of stars and director can't equal THE APARTMENT. André Previn won an Oscar for his scoring. Look fast for young James Caan in walk-on. Panavision. ▼ⓞ

Irma Vep (1996-French) **C-96m.** ******* D: Olivier Assayas. Maggie Cheung, Jean-Pierre Léaud, Nathalie Richard, Alex Descas, Nathalie Boutefeu, Dominique Faysse, Bulle Ogier, Arsinée Khanjian, Lou Castel. Keen, insightful satire of movies and the disorder surrounding the moviemaking process. Hong Kong action-film star Cheung (cast as herself) comes to Paris to star in a reworking of Louis Feuillade's 1915–16 serial LES VAMPIRES. However, the inspiration for her character is not so much Feuillade as Michelle Pfeiffer's Catwoman in BATMAN RETURNS. Crammed with cinematic references and biting criticisms of contemporary moviemaking. The title, incidentally, is an anagram. ▼ⓞ

I, Robot (2004) **C-115m.** ****½** D: Alex Proyas. Will Smith, Bridget Moynahan, Bruce Greenwood, James Cromwell, Chi McBride, Shia LaBeouf, Adrian L. Ricard, Alan Tudyk. In the year 2035, Chicago cop Smith harbors a deep resentment toward the robots that have become ubiquitous as servants and laborers in American society. When a prominent scientist dies, he (and he alone) suspects foul play, and won't rest until he connects the dots at the monopolistic corporation that manufactures and sells the robots. Interesting premise is squandered in this obvious and overlong film, with cartoonish special effects and too many Will Smith–isms. "Suggested" by Isaac Asimov's classic short story collection. Super 35. [PG-13] ▼ⓞ

Iron Cowboy SEE: **Fade-In**

Iron Curtain, The (1948) **87m.** ******* D: William Wellman. Dana Andrews, Gene Tierney, June Havoc, Berry Kroeger, Edna Best. Well-made, based-on-fact "anti-commie" saga of Igor Gouzenko (Andrews), who with wife Tierney attempts to defect to the West with top-secret documents. Filmed on location in Canada. Retitled: BEHIND THE IRON CURTAIN.

Iron Eagle (1986) **C-119m.** ***½** D: Sidney

J. Furie. Louis Gossett, Jr., Jason Gedrick, David Suchet, Tim Thomerson, Larry G. Scott, Caroline Lagerfelt, Jerry Levine. Dumdum comic-book movie about an 18-year-old who commandeers an F-16 fighter jet and flies to the Middle East (playing rock music on his Walkman all the way) in order to save his dad, who's been taken prisoner. Full of jingoistic ideals, dubious ethics, and people who die and miraculously come back to life. Not boring, just stupid. Followed by three sequels. [PG-13]▼●○

Iron Eagle II (1988-Canadian-Israeli) **C-105m.** *½ D: Sidney J. Furie. Louis Gossett, Jr., Mark Humphrey, Stuart Margolin, Alan Scarfe, Sharon H. Brandon, Maury Chaykin. Equally idiotic sequel, with General Gossett recruiting pilot Humphrey to team with his Soviet counterparts on a secret mission in the Mideast. Humphrey may be a Tom Cruise clone, but the film makes TOP GUN seem like FROM HERE TO ETERNITY. Sequels: ACES: IRON EAGLE III and IRON EAGLE IV. [PG]▼●○

Iron Giant, The (1999) **C-86m.** *** D: Brad Bird. Voices of Jennifer Aniston, Eli Marienthal, Harry Connick, Jr., Vin Diesel, Christopher McDonald, James Gammon, Cloris Leachman, John Mahoney, M. Emmet Walsh. Striking and original animated feature gently pokes fun at 1950s paranoia (and sci-fi movies), as a boy befriends a huge robotic creature from outer space. That writer-director Bird and his animators can bring such feeling to a metallic character is just one of this film's triumphs. Based on the book *The Iron Man* by Ted Hughes. Celco-Widescreen. [PG]▼●○

Iron Hand, The SEE: **Chinese Connection, The**

Iron Horse, The (1924) **119m.** *** D: John Ford. George O'Brien, Madge Bellamy, Cyril Chadwick, Fred Kohler, Gladys Hulette, J. Farrell MacDonald. Epic-scale silent film about building of transcontinental railroad, intertwined with predictable human-interest subplots involving surveyor O'Brien, sweetheart Bellamy, traitor Kohler, etc. May seem hackneyed today, but it's important to note that this movie *invented* what later became clichés. ▼●

Iron Man (2008) **C-126m.** **½ D: Jon Favreau. Robert Downey, Jr., Jeff Bridges, Gwyneth Paltrow, Terrence Howard, Leslie Bibb, Shaun Toub, Faran Tahir, Clark Gregg, Bill Smitrovich, Jon Favreau, Peter Billingsley, Tim Guinee; voice of Paul Bettany. When wealthy weapons manufacturer Tony Stark is taken prisoner on a trip to Afghanistan he cobbles together a super-suit . . . and vows to get out of the arms business, having seen the misery it produces firsthand. Notbad adaptation of the Marvel comic book, with Downey in good form as the brainy billionaire, but there are too many misfired ideas (like the Middle Eastern setting, un-

comfortably real for a piece of escapist entertainment) and a retro heroine in Paltrow's lovesick Girl Friday. As usual there's a cameo by the character's cocreator Stan Lee. Followed by a sequel. Super 35. [PG-13]●

Iron Man 2 (2010) **C-124m.** **½ D: Jon Favreau. Robert Downey, Jr., Gwyneth Paltrow, Don Cheadle, Scarlett Johansson, Sam Rockwell, Mickey Rourke, Samuel L. Jackson, Clark Gregg, John Slattery, Jon Favreau, Kate Mara, Leslie Bibb, Garry Shandling; voice of Paul Bettany. Now that everyone knows Tony Stark's alter ego, the U.S. government wants access to his suit, to use as a weapon, which he refuses to surrender. This puts Lt. Col. "Rhodey" Rhodes (Cheadle, replacing Terrence Howard) in an awkward position. Meanwhile, disaffected Russian Rourke confronts Iron Man using his high-tech knowledge and gadgetry to bring him down. There's no shortage of action or incident, and a slew of new characters, in this follow-up to the 2008 hit, but when all is said and done it's just a sequel, without the freshness and sense of discovery that made the original so popular. Super 35. [PG-13]●

Iron Mask, The (1929) **87m.** *** D: Allan Dwan. Douglas Fairbanks, Belle Bennett, Marguerite De La Motte, Dorothy Revier, Vera Lewis, William Bakewell, Nigel de Brulier, Ullrich Haupt. Entertaining Dumas tale (later filmed as THE MAN IN THE IRON MASK) told from point of view of D'Artagnan (Fairbanks), who becomes Louis XIV's protector from birth to later time when scheming Rochefort (Haupt) tries to pass off twin brother as heir to throne. Lavish silent swashbuckler originally had talkie sequences. Final scenes are especially poignant as this was Doug's farewell to the swashbuckling genre. Most current prints are of the 1940 reissue with narration by Douglas Fairbanks, Jr. ▼●

Iron Maze (1991-U.S.-Japanese) **C-102m.** *½ D: Hiroaki Yoshida. Jeff Fahey, Bridget Fonda, Hiroaki Murakami, J. T. Walsh, Gabriel Damon, John Randolph. Japanese industrialist Murakami, hoping to build an amusement park in a Pennsylvania steel town, is near-fatally assaulted; his American wife (Fonda) and a laid-off steelworker (Fahey) offer different perceptions of events leading to the incident. Muddled, pretentious RASHOMON remake, coexecutive-produced by Oliver Stone. [R]▼●

Iron Monkey (1993-Hong Kong) **C-87m.** *** D: Yuen Wo Ping. Yu Rong Guang, Donnie Yen, Jean Wang, Tsang Sze Man, Yuen Shun Yi, James Wong, Yen Yee Kwan. In medieval China, a kindly village doctor masquerades as Iron Monkey, a Robin Hood type who fights a corrupt governor and helps the downtrodden. Made years before CROUCHING TIGER, HIDDEN DRAGON (and directed by its action choreographer), this anticipates some of its high-flying action techniques but has no pretensions: just a fast, entertaining action yarn with the exaggerated acting style of Hong Kong escapist fare. Pure fun. Cowritten by Tsui Hark. New music score added for slightly edited U.S. release in 2001. [PG-13]▼❶

Iron Petticoat, The (1956-British-U.S.) C-87m. **½ D: Ralph Thomas. Bob Hope, Katharine Hepburn, James Robertson Justice, Robert Helpmann, David Kossoff. Curious comedy made in England tries to update NINOTCHKA theme with Hepburn as humorless Russian and Hope as American military man who tries to win her over. Stars' surprising rapport is film's chief value; mediocre script and direction kill the rest. VistaVision.

Iron Triangle, The (1989) C-91m. ** D: Eric Weston. Beau Bridges, Haing S. Ngor, Johnny Hallyday, Liem Whatley, James Ishida. A U.S. Army captain, serving in Vietnam in 1969, is captured by a 17-year-old Vietcong soldier, and the pair develop a bond. Intriguing at a look at the war from the side of the "enemy," but the result is confused and slight. [R]▼❶❶

Ironweed (1987) C-144m. **½ D: Hector Babenco. Jack Nicholson, Meryl Streep, Carroll Baker, Michael O'Keefe, Diane Venora, Fred Gwynne, Margaret Whitton, Tom Waits, Jake Dengel, Nathan Lane, James Gammon, Joe Grifasi, Bethel Leslie, Ted Levine, Frank Whaley. William Kennedy adapted his Pulitzer Prize–winning novel about street people, set in Albany, N.Y., 1938. Nicholson plays a man trying to come to terms with the life he turned his back on years ago. Streep is his longtime companion who, like him, can't stay off the bottle for long. Babenco's first American film is strong on atmosphere and filled with haunting images . . . but it's long and unremittingly bleak, with a few too many dramatic peaks. The salvation is Nicholson and Streep, whose rich performances are a privilege to watch. [R]▼❶❶

Iron Will (1994) C-109m. *½ D: Charles Haid. Mackenzie Astin, Kevin Spacey, August Schellenberg, David Ogden Stiers, Brian Cox, George Gerdes, John Terry. Youngster enters a Winnipeg-to-St. Paul dog-sled race in the WW1 era; result is so "by the numbers" that you almost expect the numerals to start flashing on the screen, à la John Waters' POLYESTER. Two additional writers polished the original script by veteran John Michael Hayes (REAR WINDOW), presumably to make it more like a bad Disney Channel entry. There's a faint pulse whenever Spacey (as a journalist) shows up on screen. [PG]▼❶❶

Irreconcilable Differences (1984) C-117m. *** D: Charles Shyer. Ryan O'Neal, Shelley Long, Drew Barrymore, Sam Wanamaker, Allen Garfield, Sharon Stone, David Paymer. Bittersweet comedy about a bright young couple who marry and prosper, until success in Hollywood causes them to lose sight of what's really important in their lives. Result: Their ten-year-old daughter sues them for divorce! Perceptive script by Nancy Meyers and first-time director Shyer, with especially funny jabs at Hollywood. Also the only film in memory to drop the name of Sig Rumann! [PG]▼❶❶

Irréversible (2002-French) C-95m. *½ D: Gaspar Noé. Monica Bellucci, Vincent Cassel, Albert Dupontel, Philippe Nahon, Jo Prestia. "Controversial" does not begin to describe this ugly, over-the-top rape-and-revenge tale, told in reverse a la MEMENTO, spotlighting events surrounding the defiling of beautiful Bellucci. Graphically violent, even by contemporary standards, this glorified exploitation film features an extended rape sequence and brutal murder that's hard to stomach. Though gimmicky and repugnant, some will admire the film for its audacity. Nahon's character, a butcher, appears in the director's earlier I STAND ALONE. Bellucci and Cassel are married in real life. Super 16.▼❶

Isadora (1968-British) C-131m. ***½ D: Karel Reisz. Vanessa Redgrave, James Fox, Jason Robards, Ivan Tchenko, John Fraser, Bessie Love, Cynthia Harris. Extremely long but gripping study of Isadora Duncan, first of modern dancers and most prominent free-thinker of her time. Interesting technique and carefully studied performances combine together in this offbeat biography. Originally released at 168m., later recut to 131m. and retitled THE LOVES OF ISADORA. A third version, supervised by the director, was released to television in 1987 under the original title. [M/PG]▼

I Sailed to Tahiti with an All Girl Crew (1968) C-95m. *½ D: Richard L. Bare. Gardner McKay, Fred Clark, Diane McBain, Pat Buttram, Edy Williams. One of the all-time camp classics, if only for its title. Unfortunately, film doesn't live down to its expectations.

Is Anybody There? (2009-U.S.-British) C-92m. **½ D: John Crowley. Michael Caine, Bill Milner, Anne-Marie Duff, David Morrissey, Rosemary Harris, Elizabeth Spriggs, Leslie Phillips, Sylvia Syms, Peter Vaughan, Linzey Cocker. Ten-year-old boy (Milner, from SON OF RAMBOW) has an insatiable curiosity about death, not surprising since he lives among elderly people in his parents' nursing home. His life changes with the arrival of the Amazing Clarence (Caine), a retired magician. Agreeable, if unremarkable, film buoyed by its two lead performances. British title: IS THERE ANYBODY THERE? Super 35. [PG-13]❶

I Saw What You Did (1965) 82m. *** D: William Castle. Sara Lane, Andi Garrett, John Ireland, Joan Crawford, Leif Erickson, Patricia Breslin. Tense, gimmick-free

Castle shocker about two teenage girls who dial phone numbers at random and whisper film's title; one of their "victims" is Ireland—who's just murdered his wife! Look out! Remade for TV in 1988.▼▶

I Sent a Letter to My Love (1981-French) **C-96m. ***½** D: Moshe Mizrahi. Simone Signoret, Jean Rochefort, Delphine Seyrig. A woman (Signoret) cares for her paralyzed brother (Rochefort); through a newspaper personals column, they unknowingly begin a romantic correspondence. Perceptive character study, highlighted by brilliant Signoret performance; fine work by Rochefort and Seyrig (as their spinsterish friend). Director Mizrahi and Gerard Brach adapted Bernice Rubens' novel. [PG]▼

I Served the King of England (2006-Czech) **C-119m. *** D: Jirí Menzel. Ivan Barnev, Oldrich Kaiser, Julia Jentsch, Martin Huba, Marián Labuda, Milan Lasica, Josef Abrhám, István Szabó. Wide-eyed young man works as a waiter in increasingly posh establishments during the 1930s, hoping to become a millionaire . . . but when the Germans invade Czechoslovakia his eye for pretty women gets him enmeshed in politics that will affect the rest of his life. Told in flashback as the leading character, now an old man just released from prison, looks back on his life. Alternately whimsical, sexy, and pointed parable about life in a country that has undergone more than its share of upheavals. Menzel adapted the novel by Bohumil Hrabal, who also wrote the director's signature film, CLOSELY WATCHED TRAINS.▶

I Shot Andy Warhol (1996-U.S.-British) **C-106m. *** D: Mary Harron. Lili Taylor, Jared Harris, Stephen Dorff, Martha Plimpton, Danny Morgenstern, Lothaire Bluteau, Michael Imperioli, Reg Rogers, Donovan Leitch, Tahnee Welch, Eric Mabius. In 1968, Valerie Solanas shot pop art icon Warhol, seriously wounding him. This film traces her bizarre life leading to that moment, including the writing of her "SCUM Manifesto" decreeing males biologically obsolete. Taylor is brilliant as the delusional Solanas, and the film depicts Warhol (Harris, son of actor Richard), his "Factory," and the period in convincing detail. Not for all tastes and slightly pretentious, but well made and fascinating. [R]▼●

I Shot Jesse James (1949) **81m. ** D: Samuel Fuller. Preston Foster, Barbara Britton, John Ireland, Reed Hadley, J. Edward Bromberg. Flamboyant directorial touches (in Fuller's first film) cannot redeem essential dullness of story about Bob Ford (Ireland), the man who plugged Jesse (Hadley) in the back.▼▶

Ishtar (1987) **C-107m. ** D: Elaine May. Warren Beatty, Dustin Hoffman, Isabelle Adjani, Charles Grodin, Jack Weston, Tess Harper, Carol Kane, Aharon Ipale. The

HEAVEN'S GATE of movie comedies made headlines because of its huge expense and costly delays, but the only thing wrong with it is that it isn't very funny. Beatty and Hoffman go the Hope and Crosby route as untalented singer-songwriters who get involved with international intrigue in North Africa (shades of ROAD TO MOROCCO!). A blind camel and a flock of vultures steal the show. Paul Williams' deliberately awful songs are funny, too, but not funny enough to overcome the flatness of director May's script. Produced by Beatty. [PG-13]▼●

Island, The (1980) **C-114m.** BOMB D: Michael Ritchie. Michael Caine, David Warner, Angela Punch McGregor, Frank Middlemass, Don Henderson, Zakes Mokae, Jeffrey Frank. Absolutely awful thriller about magazine reporter who investigates strange doings in the Caribbean and winds up a prisoner of primitive island tribe. You know you're in trouble when David Warner plays the most normal guy on the island! Peter Benchley scripted from his own novel. Panavision. [R]▼●

Island (1989-Australian) **C-93m. **½** D: Paul Cox. Irene Papas, Eva Sitta, Anoja Weerasinghe, Chris Haywood, Francois Bernard. Three women—each struggling with a personal emotional crisis—meet on a remote Greek island. Knowing they are only to cross paths briefly, they unburden their innermost feelings to each other. Atmospheric psychological drama lacks a strong central core.

Island, The (2005) **C-136m. ** D: Michael Bay. Ewan McGregor, Scarlett Johansson, Djimon Hounsou, Sean Bean, Steve Buscemi, Michael Clarke Duncan, Ethan Phillips, Brian Stepanek. In a futuristic underground city, society is rigidly controlled and a lottery decides who'll get to move to an idyllic island. When McGregor suspects something is amiss, he enlists Johansson's aid to escape into a world they didn't expect. Well-cast but overheated thriller burns itself up with increasingly unbelievable action scenes and an unconvincing plot similar to that of PARTS: THE CLONUS HORROR. Panavision. [PG-13]▼▶

Island at the Top of the World, The (1974) **C-93m. **½** D: Robert Stevenson. David Hartman, Donald Sinden, Jacques Marin, Mako, David Gwillim, Agneta Eckemyr. Disney's attempt to score again in Jules Verne territory misses bull's-eye; simplistic, derivative story of Arctic expedition which stumbles across "lost" Viking civilization. Mainly for kids. [G]▼▶

Island in the Sky (1953) **109m. ***½** D: William A. Wellman. John Wayne, Lloyd Nolan, Walter Abel, James Arness, Andy Devine, Allyn Joslyn, Jimmy Lydon, Harry Carey, Jr., Hal Baylor, Sean McClory, Wally Cassell, Regis Toomey, Louis Jean Heydt,

Bob Steele, Darryl Hickman, Touch (Mike) Connors, Gordon Jones, Frank Fenton, Paul Fix, Carl ("Alfalfa") Switzer, Ann Doran. Transport plane goes down in snowy Labrador, and the crew's flying buddies devote all their energies to locating them. Meanwhile, pilot Wayne has to keep his crew's spirits up as they try to survive in frigid weather with little food and no heat. Moving drama with a striking score by Hugo Friedhofer and Emil Newman. Ernest K. Gann based his screenplay (and novel) on a real-life incident from WW2. Gann, Wellman, and Wayne reteamed a year later for THE HIGH AND THE MIGHTY. Look fast for Fess Parker. ▶

Island in the Sun (1957) C-119m. ** D: Robert Rossen. James Mason, Joan Fontaine, Dorothy Dandridge, Joan Collins, Michael Rennie, Diana Wynyard, John Williams, Stephen Boyd, Harry Belafonte. Misfire adaptation of Alec Waugh's book about idyllic West Indies island torn by racial struggle. Good cast can't do much with unconvincing script. CinemaScope. ▼▶

Island of Dr. Moreau, The (1977) C-104m. *** D: Don Taylor. Burt Lancaster, Michael York, Nigel Davenport, Barbara Carrera, Richard Basehart. Handsomely produced remake of ISLAND OF LOST SOULS with Lancaster heading a solid cast as demented doctor who has spent years creating half-man, half-beast "humanimals." Good horror-fantasy chiller, based on H. G. Wells' novel. Remade in 1996. [PG]▼▶

Island of Dr. Moreau, The (1996) C-95m. *½ D: John Frankenheimer. Marlon Brando, Val Kilmer, David Thewlis, Fairuza Balk, Ron Perlman, Marco Hofschneider, Temuera Morrison. Heavy-handed retelling of H. G. Wells' novel, as Thewlis is rescued at sea and brought to Dr. Moreau's island, where he's horrified to discover experiments turning animals into humans. Grotesque in the extreme, obvious, and ultimately pointless, but Brando devotees will want to check out his flamboyantly silly performance, and makeup buffs should admire Stan Winston's remarkable creations. Director's cut version runs 99m. Super 35. [PG-13]▼●▶

Island of Lost Souls (1933) 70m. ***½ D: Erle C. Kenton. Charles Laughton, Bela Lugosi, Richard Arlen, Kathleen Burke, Stanley Fields, Leila Hyams. Strong adaptation of H. G. Wells' novel of a mad scientist isolated on a remote island, where he transforms jungle beasts into half-human abominations (". . . are we not men?"). Laughton hams it up a bit, but despite more explicit horror films of late, this retains its frightening aura, particularly in the grisly finale. Remade as THE ISLAND OF DR. MOREAU in 1977 and 1996. ▼●

Island of Terror (1966-British) C-90m. ** D: Terence Fisher. Peter Cushing, Edward Judd, Carole Gray, Niall MacGinnis. Sci-fi tale about cancer research gone wild and mutations that result is directed and acted by veterans of the field, but result is nothing special.▼

Island of the Blue Dolphins (1964) C-93m. *½ D: James B. Clark. Celia Kaye, George Kennedy, Ann Daniel, Carlos Romero, Larry Domasin. True story of Indian girl (Kaye) abandoned on small island, befriended only by wild dogs. Set in early 19th century. Well meaning but not very good. Based on the novel by Scott O'Dell. ▶

Island of the Burning Damned SEE: Island of the Burning Doomed

Island of the Burning Doomed (1967-British) C-94m. **½ D: Terence Fisher. Christopher Lee, Peter Cushing, Patrick Allen, Sarah Lawson, Jane Merrow, William Lucas. Aliens cause a massive heatwave during winter. Good sci-fi, with Lee and Cushing at their best. Also known as ISLAND OF THE BURNING DAMNED and NIGHT OF THE BIG HEAT.▼

Island of the Lost (1967) C-91m. *½ D: John Florea; Underwater sequences, Ricou Browning. Richard Greene, Luke Halpin, Mart Hulswit, Jose De Vega, Robin Mattson, Irene Tsu. Anthropologist Greene takes his family on an expedition to find an uncharted South Sea isle but becomes shipwrecked. Clean-cut, highly innocuous travelogue from the Ivan Tors studio, cowritten by Tors and actor Richard Carlson. Underwater expert Browning appeared with Carlson years before as the CREATURE FROM THE BLACK LAGOON. ▼▶

Islands in the Stream (1977) C-105m. **½ D: Franklin J. Schaffner. George C. Scott, David Hemmings, Claire Bloom, Susan Tyrrell, Gilbert Roland, Richard Evans, Hart Bochner, Julius Harris. Film version of Hemingway novel about an island-dwelling sculptor and his three sons begins well but falls apart completely in the final third. Still one of the better adaptations of this author, with one of Scott's best performances. Panavision. [PG]▼●▶

Isle of Fury (1936) 60m. ** D: Frank McDonald. Humphrey Bogart, Margaret Lindsay, Donald Woods, Paul Graetz, Gordon Hart, E. E. Clive. Mild remake of Somerset Maugham novel *The Narrow Corner*, involving love triangle on South Sea island.

Isle of Lost Women SEE: **99 Women**

Isle of the Dead (1945) 72m. *** D: Mark Robson. Boris Karloff, Ellen Drew, Marc Cramer, Katherine Emery, Helene Thimig, Jason Robards (Sr.). Eerie horror tale of assorted characters stranded on Greek island during quarantine—one of them possibly a vampire. Good Val Lewton production. ▼●▶

Isle of the Snake People SEE: **Snake People**

Isn't She Great (2000) C-95m. ** D: Andrew Bergman. Bette Midler, Nathan Lane,

Stockard Channing, David Hyde Pierce, John Cleese, John Larroquette, Amanda Peet. Ill-conceived film about highly driven actress turned authoress Jacqueline Susann (*Valley of the Dolls*) and the one man who believes in her, her press agent husband, Irving Mansfield. Not funny enough to succeed as a comedy, not serious or solid enough to work as a biography; Lane is awfully hard to resist, however, as the irrepressibly upbeat Mansfield. Screenplay by Paul Rudnick, from Michael Korda's magazine article. [R]▼❙

Is Paris Burning? (1966-French-U.S.) **173m. **** D: René Clement. Jean-Paul Belmondo, Charles Boyer, Leslie Caron, Jean-Pierre Cassel, Claude Dauphin, Alain Delon, Kirk Douglas, Glenn Ford, Gert Frobe, Daniel Gelin, Yves Montand, Anthony Perkins, Simone Signoret, Robert Stack, Orson Welles. Rambling pseudo-documentary–style re-creation of WW2 France, showing liberation of Paris and Nazis' attempt to burn the city. Cameos by international players confuse blotchy film made in Europe. Screenplay by Gore Vidal and Francis Ford Coppola, from the Larry Collins–Dominique Lapierre book. Panavision.▼●❙

I Spy (2002) **C-96m. *½** D: Betty Thomas. Eddie Murphy, Owen Wilson, Famke Janssen, Malcolm McDowell, Gary Cole, Phill Lewis. In-name-only reincarnation of the smart 1960s TV show (which starred Robert Culp and Bill Cosby). Here, Wilson is an inept NSA operative who uses cocky prizefighter Murphy as his cover to locate a secret weapon in Budapest. An object lesson in bad screenwriting, with an incoherent story and characters that make no sense; only the occasional comic riffs by Murphy and Wilson keep this from complete disaster. [PG-13] ▼❙

Istanbul (1957) **C-84m. **** D: Joseph Pevney. Errol Flynn. Cornell Borchers, John Bentley, Torin Thatcher, Leif Erickson, Martin Benson, Nat "King" Cole, Werner Klemperer. Dull drama of flyer Flynn returning to Istanbul, discovering his ladylove (whom he believed had perished in a fire) to be alive and an amnesiac. Sole bright spot: Cole singing "When I Fall in Love." Remake of SINGAPORE (1947). CinemaScope.▼

Istanbul (1990-Turkish-Swedish) **C-88m.** BOMB D: Mats Arehn. Timothy Bottoms, Twiggy, Emma Kilberg, Robert Morley, Lena Endre, Sverre Anker Ousdal. Journalist Bottoms arrives in Istanbul with his daughter to seek information on family of his wife's son, becomes enmeshed in confusing intrigue. Twiggy is a mystery woman. Murky, clumsy, international coproduction is about as interesting as watching camel spit dry. [PG-13] ▼●

Is There Sex After Death? (1971) **C-97m. ***** D: Jeanne Abel, Alan Abel. Buck Henry, Alan Abel, Marshall Efron, Holly Woodlawn, Earle Doud. Crude but funny satire of porn films. Famous hoaxer Abel (who, with his wife, also produced and scripted) plays a traveling sexologist; Efron hilarious as an X-rated-film director. [R—edited from original X rating]▼❙

I Still Know What You Did Last Summer (1998) **C-101m. *½** D: Danny Cannon. Jennifer Love Hewitt, Freddie Prinze, Jr., Brandy, Mekhi Phifer, Muse Watson, Matthew Settle, Bill Cobbs, Jeffrey Combs, Jennifer Esposito, John Hawkes. Hewitt and friends win a vacation to a Caribbean island, where they are pursued by the killer with a hook from the first movie, I KNOW WHAT YOU DID LAST SUMMER. Another film in which the cast runs around screaming while being killed, one by one. Plotless mess lacks any suspense, and makes the original look like a classic. Jack Black appears unbilled. Followed by DVD sequel, I'LL ALWAYS KNOW WHAT YOU DID LAST SUMMER. Panavision. [R] ▼●❙

It (1927) **72m. **½** D: Clarence Badger. Clara Bow, Antonio Moreno, William Austin, Jacqueline Gadsdon (Jane Daly), Priscilla Bonner. Bow is dazzling in this otherwise ordinary tale of a spirited, gold-digging department-store salesgirl with designs on her handsome boss (Moreno). Based on Elinor Glyn's trendy story of the same title; Madame Glyn appears briefly as herself. Look for Gary Cooper in a walk-on as a reporter.▼●❙

It! (1967) **C-96m. **** D: Herbert J. Leder. Roddy McDowall, Jill Haworth, Ernest Clark, Paul Maxwell, Aubrey Richards. McDowall brings hulking stone statue—the Golem, no less—to life and soon finds it makes a great murderer. Kill it! Filmed in England.❙

It Ain't Hay (1943) **80m. **½** D: Erle C. Kenton. Bud Abbott, Lou Costello, Patsy O'Connor, Grace McDonald, Leighton Noble, Cecil Kellaway, Eugene Pallette, Eddie Quillan. Pretty good A&C from Damon Runyon story, "Princess O'Hara," of racehorse Teabiscuit; good supporting cast helps.❙

I Take This Woman (1940) **97m. **** D: W. S. Van Dyke II. Spencer Tracy, Hedy Lamarr, Verree Teasdale, Kent Taylor, Laraine Day, Mona Barrie, Louis Calhern, Marjorie Main, Frances Drake, Jack Carson. Disappointing soaper with dedicated doctor Tracy sacrificing all for Lamarr, who at first isn't grateful. Long in production, with innumerable behind-the-scenes changes, this was a notorious dud in 1940. ❙

Italian, The (2005-Russian) **C-99m. **½** D: Andrei Kravchuk. Kolya Spiridonov, Maria Kuznetsova, Nikolai Reutov, Yriy Itskov, Denis Moiseenko. Six-year-old Vanya (Spiridonov) resides in an orphanage in contemporary Russia, whose administrators sell their charges for profit. Even though an Italian couple has adopted him, he remains determined to find his birth mother, who abandoned him. Dickensian slice-of-life about a youngster who is wise beyond his years and whose childhood has been stolen from him. Occasionally affecting, but not as involving as it should be. [PG-13] ▶

Italian Connection, The (1973-Italian) **C-92m.** ✻✻ D: Fernando Di Leo. Henry Silva, Woody Strode, Mario Adorf, Luciana Paluzzi, Sylva Koscina, Adolfo Celi. Violent gangster meller has Milanese hood Adorf set up by gang boss Celi for the blame in a six-million-dollar heroin heist. For action fans only. Aka MANHUNT (1973). [R] ▼▶

Italian for Beginners (2000-Danish) **C-99m.** ✻✻✻ D: Lone Scherfig. Anders W. Berthelsen, Anette Støvelbaek, Peter Gantzler, Ann Elonora Jørgensen, Lars Kaalund, Sara Indrio Jensen, Bent Mejding. Sweet, upbeat romantic comedy in which several lonely, vulnerable thirty-something singles mix and match while taking an Italian-language adult education class. Most enjoyable, and definitely not for cynics! Filmed using the "pure cinema" rules of Dogma 95. Originally shown at 112m. [R] ▼▶

Italian Job, The (1969-British) **C-101m.** ✻✻½ D: Peter Collinson. Michael Caine, Noel Coward, Maggie Blye, Benny Hill, Tony Beckley, Raf Vallone. $4,000,000 in gold bullion's the object in average caper film about prison-based mastermind Coward's plan to divert authorities in Turin, Italy, causing "history's biggest traffic jam." Wild chases galore, plus truly bizarre ending, but characterizations are pat, forgettable. Remade in 2003. Panavision. [G] ▼●▶

Italian Job, The (2003) **C-110m.** ✻✻✻ D: F. Gary Gray. Mark Wahlberg, Charlize Theron, Edward Norton, Seth Green, Jason Statham, Mos Def, Franky G, Donald Sutherland. Entertaining caper starts out with a daring robbery, then a traitor disrupts business as usual with the otherwise loyal band of thieves. Winds up in L.A. with a wild chase sequence through the city's streets and subway system. Slick script, superior action scenes, and an array of colorful, well-drawn characters make this fun from start to finish. Remake of the 1969 film includes a brief homage to its star, Michael Caine. Super 35. [PG-13] ▼▶

It All Came True (1940) **97m.** ✻✻½D: Lewis Seiler. Ann Sheridan, Humphrey Bogart, Jeffrey Lynn, ZaSu Pitts, Jessie Busley, Una O'Connor, Grant Mitchell, Felix Bressart. Offbeat story combines comedy, drama, music, and sentiment as gangster Bogart hides out in quaint boarding-house. Fine showcase for Sheridan, who sings "Angel in Disguise" and "The Gaucho Serenade."

It All Starts Today (1999-French) **C-117m.** ✻✻✻½D: Bertrand Tavernier. Philippe Torreton, Maria Pitarresi, Nadia Kaci, Véronique Ataly, Nathalie Bécue, Emmanuelle Bercot. Wrenchingly believable study of a dedicated schoolteacher in a working-class French community who tries to overcome one hurdle after another—from government bureaucracy to negligent parents—to provide his children with a decent education. No false dramatics here, just a potent slice of life. Written by the director, his daughter Tiffany, and her husband, Dominique Sampiero (based on his experience as a teacher). Super 35. ▼▶

It Always Rains on Sunday (1947-British) **92m.** ✻✻✻½ D: Robert Hamer. Googie Withers, Jack Warner, John McCallum, Edward Chapman, Jimmy Hanley, John Carol, John Slater, Susan Shaw, Sydney Tafler, Alfie Bass, Betty Ann Davies, Jane Hylton, Hermione Baddeley. Excellent mosaic of characters whose lives intertwine in a drab London neighborhood. McCallum is escaped convict seeking refuge with his ex-lover, Withers. (In real life, the two stars married the following year.) Arthur La Bern's novel was scripted by Henry Cornelius, Angus MacPhail, and Hamer.

It Came From Beneath the Sea (1955) **80m.** ✻✻✻ D: Robert Gordon. Kenneth Tobey, Faith Domergue, Donald Curtis, Ian Keith, Harry Lauter. Breathtaking special effects highlight this sci-fi thriller. Huge octopus emerges from Pacific Ocean and wreaks havoc on San Francisco. First film made by the team of Ray Harryhausen and producer Charles H. Schneer. Also available in computer-colored version. ▼●▶

It Came From Hollywood (1982) **C-80m.** ✻½ D: Malcolm Leo, Andrew Solt. Dan Aykroyd, John Candy, Cheech and Chong, Gilda Radner. Contemporary comedy stars are spectacularly *unfunny* introducing and narrating clips from some of Hollywood's worst movies—most of which are funny enough without additional wisecracks. What's more, this pointless, poorly constructed compilation includes scenes from *good* movies like WAR OF THE WORLDS and THE INCREDIBLE SHRINKING MAN! Even so, howlers like MARS NEEDS WOMEN and PLAN 9 FROM OUTER SPACE still offer some genuine laughs. [PG] ▼▶

It Came From Outer Space (1953) **81m.** ✻✻✻ D: Jack Arnold. Richard Carlson, Barbara Rush, Charles Drake, Russell Johnson, Joe Sawyer, Kathleen Hughes. Intriguing science-fiction based on a Ray Bradbury story. An alien ship crashes in the Arizona desert; its passengers assume the identities of nearby townspeople so they can effect repairs unnoticed—they think. Remarkably sober for its era, with crisp performances and real restraint, even in its use of 3-D. The 1996 TV movie IT CAME FROM OUTER SPACE II is a much inferior remake, rather than the sequel the title suggests. 3-D. ▼●▶

It Came Without Warning SEE: **Without Warning**

It Comes Up Murder SEE: **Honey Pot, The**

It Conquered the World (1956) **68m.** **½ D: Roger Corman. Peter Graves, Beverly Garland, Lee Van Cleef, Sally Fraser, Jonathan Haze, Dick Miller. Low-budget sci-fi which intelligently attempts to create atmospheric excitement in yarn of carrot-shaped monster from Venus, Paul Blaisdell's finest creation. One of Corman's best early quickies, well acted and interesting but awkwardly plotted. Remade as ZONTAR, THE THING FROM VENUS.▼

It Could Happen to You (1994) **C-101m.** *** D: Andrew Bergman. Nicolas Cage, Bridget Fonda, Rosie Perez, Wendell Pierce, Isaac Hayes, Victor Rojas, Seymour Cassel, Stanley Tucci, J. E. Freeman, Red Buttons, Richard Jenkins. Charming romantic comedy about a Good Samaritan cop who shares a lottery ticket with a hard-luck waitress—little dreaming it will make them both millionaires. Warm, winning performances by Cage and Fonda carry this N.Y.-based fairy tale, with a plot not intended for close scrutiny. Inspired by a true-life story. [PG]▼●)

It Happened at the World's Fair (1963) **C-105m.** *** D: Norman Taurog. Elvis Presley, Joan O'Brien, Gary Lockwood, Yvonne Craig. Entertaining Presley vehicle set at Seattle World's Fair, with Elvis and O'Brien brought together by little Ginny Tiu. Listenable tunes (including "One Broken Heart for Sale," "A World of Our Own" and "Happy Ending") help make this most enjoyable. Young Kurt Russell, who later played Elvis in a TV movie, makes his film debut in a small role. Panavision.▼)

It Happened Here (1966-British) **95m.** *** D: Kevin Brownlow, Andrew Mollo. Pauline Murray, Sebastian Shaw, Fiona Leland, Honor Fehrson. Imaginative fable of Britain taken over by the Nazis during WW2, made in semidocumentary style by two ingenious young filmmakers. To get along in a harsh time, most Brits collaborate with the invaders, including nurse Murray, who has personal reasons to hate the resistance movement.▼)

It Happened in Brooklyn (1947) **105m.** ** D: Richard Whorf. Frank Sinatra, Kathryn Grayson, Jimmy Durante, Peter Lawford, Gloria Grahame. Hokey musical with Brooklynite Sinatra returning to his beloved borough after WW2; complications follow as he falls for music teacher Grayson. Some good songs, including "Time After Time" and wonderful Sinatra-Durante duet, "The Song's Gotta Come From the Heart."▼●)

It Happened One Night (1934) **105m.** **** D: Frank Capra. Clark Gable, Claudette Colbert, Walter Connolly, Roscoe Karns, Alan Hale, Ward Bond. Legendary romantic comedy doesn't age a bit. Still as enchanting as ever, with reporter Gable and runaway heiress Colbert falling in love on rural bus trip. Hitch-hiking travails, the Walls of Jericho, other memorable scenes remain fresh and delightful. First film to win all five major Oscars: Picture, Actor, Actress, Director, and Screenplay (Robert Riskin). Based on Samuel Hopkins Adams' story "Night Bus," originally published in *Cosmopolitan.* Remade as musicals EVE KNEW HER APPLES and YOU CAN'T RUN AWAY FROM IT (1956). ▼●)

It Happened One Summer SEE: **State Fair** (1945)

It Happened to Jane (1959) **C-98m.** **½ D: Richard Quine. Doris Day, Jack Lemmon, Ernie Kovacs, Steve Forrest, Teddy Rooney, Russ Brown, Mary Wickes, Parker Fennelly. Breezy, likable comedy: Doris runs a Maine lobstery, and Jack is her lawyer; together they tangle with ultracheap villain Kovacs (who hams mercilessly). Aka TWINKLE AND SHINE.❱

It Happened Tomorrow (1944) **84m.** *** D: René Clair. Dick Powell, Linda Darnell, Jack Oakie, Edgar Kennedy, John Philliber, Edward Brophy, George Cleveland, Sig Ruman, Paul Guilfoyle. Diverting if somewhat static fantasy yarn about a turn-of-the-20th-century reporter who gets inside track on *tomorrow's* headlines, leading to unexpected complications. Low key, often charming.▼)

It Happens Every Spring (1949) **87m.** ***½ D: Lloyd Bacon. Ray Milland, Jean Peters, Paul Douglas, Ed Begley, Ted de Corsia, Ray Collins, Jessie Royce Landis, Alan Hale, Jr., Debra Paget. Clever little comedy of chemistry professor (Milland) accidentally discovering a chemical mixture which causes baseballs to avoid all wooden surfaces, namely baseball bats. He takes leave from academia and embarks on meteoric pitching career. A most enjoyable, unpretentious picture. Story by Shirley W. Smith and Valentine Davies; scripted by Davies.▼

I, the Jury (1953) **87m.** **½ D: Harry Essex. Biff Elliot, Preston Foster, Peggie Castle, Margaret Sheridan, Alan Reed, Mary Anderson, Tom Powers, Joe Besser, Paul Dubov, Elisha Cook, Jr., John Qualen. Screen debut of Mickey Spillane's Mike Hammer (and Elliot as well) finds the thuggish sleuth spending his Christmas holidays hunting down the killer of a close pal. Naturally, more corpses ensue. Dark-humored fun, with a moody Franz Waxman score and stunning 3-D photography by John Alton, including some eye-popping shots inside L.A.'s famed Bradbury Building. Screenplay by Essex. Remade in 1982. 3-D.

I, the Jury (1982) **C-111m.** ** D: Richard T. Heffron. Armand Assante, Barbara Carrera, Alan King, Laurene Landon, Geoffrey

Lewis, Paul Sorvino, Judson Scott. Mickey Spillane's hard-boiled Mike Hammer seems out of place in this updated remake, though contemporary levels of violence and nudity suit the material. Lots of action and some truly beautiful women help camouflage the holes in Larry Cohen's script; Assante is a sulky Hammer. [R]▼

I Think I Love My Wife (2007) **C-94m.** *½ D: Chris Rock. Chris Rock, Kerry Washington, Gina Torres, Steve Buscemi, Edward Herrmann, Welker White, Michael K. Williams, Stephen A. Smith, Wendell Pierce, Matthew Morrison. Director-cowriter-coproducer Rock plays a successful but bored suburban family man who is contacted at his N.Y.C. office by an old pal's smoking-hot former flame (Washington). Her flirty afternoon visits become more frequent, and he is sorely tempted to stray. Rock has loosely updated Eric Rohmer's CHLOE IN THE AFTERNOON with dismal results. His own performance is leaden, and even Washington's femme fatale is wasted here. [R]●

It Lives Again (1978) **C-91m.** *½ D: Larry Cohen. Frederic Forrest, Kathleen Lloyd, John Ryan, John Marley, Andrew Duggan, Eddie Constantine. Sequel to IT'S ALIVE offers not one but three murderous babies. More of a horror film than a thriller—and not a very good one. Constantine's first American film in many years. Aka IT'S ALIVE II; followed by IT'S ALIVE III: ISLAND OF THE ALIVE. [R]▼●●

It Only Happens to Others (1971-French-Italian) **C-88m.** ** D: Nadine Trintignant. Marcello Mastroianni, Catherine Deneuve, Serge Marquand, Dominique Labourier, Catherine Allegret. Loss of young child causes happily married couple to withdraw from society. Heavy on the syrup. Panoramica. [PG]

It Runs in My Family (1994) **C-85m.** ** D: Bob Clark. Charles Grodin, Kieran Culkin, Mary Steenburgen, Christian Culkin, Al Mancini, Troy Evans, Roy Brocksmith, Glenn Shadix, Dick O'Neill, Wayne Grace. Follow-up to A CHRISTMAS STORY—with a new cast—is a huge disappointment, chronicling the same family's adventures in the early '40s—from the boy's efforts to win at top-spinning to the Old Man's feud with his hillbilly neighbors. Culkin and Grodin are no match for Peter Billingsley and Darren McGavin in the earlier film, and many of writer/narrator Jean Shepherd's nostalgic musings don't come off nearly as well as they do in his writings and broadcasts. Barely released theatrically; retitled MY SUMMER STORY. [PG]▼●

It Runs in the Family (2003) **C-109m.** ** D: Fred Schepisi. Michael Douglas, Kirk Douglas, Cameron Douglas, Diana Douglas, Bernadette Peters, Rory Culkin, Michelle Monaghan, Sarita Choudhury. Superficial story about conflicts between fathers, sons, girlfriends, and spouses serves merely as an excuse to bring three generations of Douglases together on-screen (not to mention Kirk's ex, Diana). But this contrivance is just that, with a script that might not pass muster as a TV movie. Michael Douglas also produced. Super 35. [PG-13]▼●

I Trust You to Kill Me (2006) **C/B&W-90m.** **½ D: Manu Boyer. While on hiatus from shooting his hit TV series *24*, Kiefer Sutherland acts as road manager for a European tour for Rocco DeLuca & The Burden, the group he's signed to his independent record label. Frank, revealing documentary offers a candid look at a celebrity after hours, but is most effective when contrasting a famous face and a bunch of talented but unknown wannabes. Bogs down in parts, but holds your interest most of the way. Film's title is the name of one of DeLuca's songs. [R]●

It's a Big Country (1951) **89m.** **½ D: Charles Vidor, Richard Thorpe, John Sturges, Don Hartman, Don Weis, Clarence Brown, William Wellman. Ethel Barrymore, Keefe Brasselle, Gary Cooper, Nancy Davis (Reagan), Gene Kelly, Keenan Wynn, Fredric March, Van Johnson, James Whitmore; narrated by Louis Calhern. Dore Schary's plug for America uses several pointless episodes about the variety of people and places in U.S. Other segments make up for it in very uneven film. ●

It's a Bikini World (1967) **C-86m.** *½ D: Stephanie Rothman. Deborah Walley, Tommy Kirk, Bob Pickett, Suzie Kaye, The Animals, The Gentrys. Superlover Kirk loves bikinied Debbie, but she doesn't dig him until he masquerades as an intellectual. Not among the best of its kind, if there even *is* a best of its kind. The Animals, however, do perform "We Gotta Get Out of This Place." Techniscope.

It's a Gift (1934) **68m.** **** D: Norman Z. McLeod. W. C. Fields, Baby LeRoy, Kathleen Howard, Tommy Bupp, Morgan Wallace. Fields is a grocery store owner who goes West with his family. Beautiful comedy routines in one of the Great Man's unforgettable films. Charles Sellon as a blind man, T. Roy Barnes as a salesman looking for Carl LaFong, contribute some hilarious moments. A remake of Fields' silent film IT'S THE OLD ARMY GAME.▼●

It's a Great Feeling (1949) **C-85m.** **½ D: David Butler. Dennis Morgan, Doris Day, Jack Carson, Bill Goodwin. Gentle spoof of Hollywood with Carson's ego making filming difficult for himself and partner Morgan; guest appearances by many Warner Bros. players and directors, including Joan Crawford, Gary Cooper, Michael Curtiz, Jane Wyman, Sydney Greenstreet, Danny Kaye, Edward G. Robinson, King Vidor, Eleanor Parker, Patricia Neal, Raoul

Walsh, Ronald Reagan—and even Reagan and Wyman's daughter Maureen!▼●◗

It's Alive! (1974) **C-91m.** **★★½** D: Larry Cohen. John Ryan, Sharon Farrell, Andrew Duggan, Guy Stockwell, James Dixon, Michael Ansara. Schlocky thriller about a baby who goes on a murderous rampage. Has a devoted following, but not for all tastes. Effective score by Bernard Herrmann. Sequels: IT LIVES AGAIN and IT'S ALIVE III: ISLAND OF THE ALIVE. Remade direct to DVD in 2009. [PG]▼●◗

It's Alive II SEE: **It Lives Again**

It's Alive III: Island of the Alive (1987) **C-91m.** **★★½** D: Larry Cohen. Michael Moriarty, Karen Black, Laurene Landon, Gerrit Graham, James Dixon, Neal Israel, Macdonald Carey. Part 3 makes serious comments on issues ranging from the AIDS crisis to abortion as Moriarty, father of a monster baby, succeeds in preventing society from exterminating all the monster infants, who are quarantined on a desert island. Wild fun, loaded with dark humor.▼◗

It's All True (1993) **C/B&W-87m.** **★★★** D: Richard Wilson, Myron Meisel, Bill Krohn. Fascinating assemblage of the remaining "lost" footage from Orson Welles' abandoned three-part documentary he was shooting in Brazil in 1942 as RKO brass was taking a knife to THE MAGNIFICENT AMBERSONS back in Hollywood. Only tantalizing snippets remain of the *My Friend Bonito* episode (shot in Mexico by Norman Foster under Welles' supervision) and of the seductive Carnaval footage (some in color); virtually intact is what would have been the original's centerpiece: the *Four Men on a Raft* tribute to Brazilian fishermen. A major contribution to movie history, albeit one for specialized tastes; film concludes with an audio track of Welles with Carmen Miranda. For film buffs who think they've experienced it all.▼●◗

It's Always Fair Weather (1955) **C-102m.** **★★★** D: Gene Kelly, Stanley Donen. Gene Kelly, Dan Dailey, Michael Kidd, Cyd Charisse, Dolores Gray, David Burns. Three WW2 buddies meet ten years after their discharge and find they have nothing in common. Pungent Comden and Green script falls short of perfection but still has wonderful moments, and some first-rate musical numbers (like Cyd's "Baby, You Knock Me Out" and Dolores' "Thanks a Lot But No Thanks"). Best: the ash-can dance in widescreen. CinemaScope.▼●◗

It's a Mad Mad Mad Mad World (1963) **C-154m.** **★★½** D: Stanley Kramer. Spencer Tracy, Edie Adams, Milton Berle, Sid Caesar, Buddy Hackett, Ethel Merman, Mickey Rooney, Dick Shawn, Dorothy Provine, Phil Silvers, Jonathan Winters, Peter Falk, Jimmy Durante, Terry-Thomas, Eddie "Rochester" Anderson, William Demarest, many guest stars. Supercom-

edy cast in attempt at supercomedy, about group of people racing to find hidden bank loot under watchful eye of detective Tracy. Big, splashy, generally funny, but bigness doesn't equal greatness. Restored on video to 175m. Ultra Panavision 70. ▼●◗

It's a Wonderful Life (1946) **129m.** **★★★★** D: Frank Capra. James Stewart, Donna Reed, Lionel Barrymore, Thomas Mitchell, Henry Travers, Beulah Bondi, Frank Faylen, Ward Bond, Gloria Grahame, H. B. Warner, Frank Albertson, Todd Karns, Samuel S. Hinds, Mary Treen, Sheldon Leonard, Ellen Corby. Sentimental tale of Stewart, who works all his life to make good in small town, thinking he's failed and trying to end his life. Guardian angel Travers comes to show him his mistake. Only Capra and this cast could pull it off so well; this film seems to improve with age. Capra, Frances Goodrich, Albert Hackett, and Jo Swerling expanded Philip Van Doren Stern's short story "The Greatest Gift" (which had originally been written by Stern as a Christmas card!). Remade for TV as IT HAPPENED ONE CHRISTMAS. Also shown in computer-colored version.▼●◗

It's a Wonderful World (1939) **86m.** **★★★** D: W. S. Van Dyke II. Claudette Colbert, James Stewart, Guy Kibbee, Nat Pendleton, Frances Drake, Edgar Kennedy, Ernest Truex, Sidney Blackmer, Hans Conried. Screwball comedy with Colbert a runaway poetess, Stewart a fugitive chased by cops Pendleton and Kennedy. Very, very funny, with Stewart having a field day. Scripted by Ben Hecht, from his and Herman J. Mankiewicz' story. We swear by our eyes!◗

It's Complicated (2009) **C-120m.** **★★★** D: Nancy Meyers. Meryl Streep, Steve Martin, Alec Baldwin, John Krasinski, Lake Bell, Rita Wilson, Mary Kay Place, Alexandra Wentworth, Zoe Kazan, Hunter Parrish, Caitlin Fitzgerald, Nora Dunn, Bruce Altman. Light-as-air, easy-to-take romantic comedy about a successful woman and mother of three nearly grown-up kids who's survived her ten-year-old divorce—and then succumbs to her ex-husband's wooing, just as a new man has come into her life. Appealing performances by three fine actors in peak form, in the most attractive settings imaginable, make this highly pleasurable escapism from writer-director Meyers. [PG-13]◗

It Seemed Like a Good Idea at the Time (1975-Canadian) **C-106m.** **★★** D: John Trent. Anthony Newley, Stefanie Powers, Isaac Hayes, Lloyd Bochner, Yvonne De Carlo, Henry Ramer, Lawrence Dane, John Candy. Tired comedy with a mostly tired cast, centering on Newley's attempts to woo back his remarried ex-wife. Dane and Candy appear as a pair of bumbling cops, characters they replayed a year later in FIND THE LADY. Aka GOOD IDEA! [PG]▼◗

It Should Happen to You (1954) **87m.**

*** D: George Cukor. Judy Holliday, Peter Lawford, Jack Lemmon, Michael O'Shea, Vaughn Taylor. Holliday is Gladys Glover of Binghamton, N.Y., who has come to N.Y.C. to make a name for herself—and does so, by plastering her moniker across a Columbus Circle billboard. Judy is radiant in this charming romantic comedy/satire, scripted by Garson Kanin. Lemmon's first film.▼●)

It Shouldn't Happen to a Vet SEE: All Things Bright and Beautiful

It's Kind of a Funny Story (2010) C-101m. ** D: Anna Boden, Ryan Fleck. Keir Gilchrist, Emma Roberts, Zach Galifianakis, Viola Davis, Lauren Graham, Jim Gaffigan, Zoë Kravitz, Jeremy Davies, Aasif Mandvi, MacIntyre Dixon, Novella Nelson, Morgan Murphy. Stressed-out 16-year-old considers suicide but checks himself into a mental ward at the local hospital instead. There he's mentored by a savvy patient (Galifianakis) and develops a crush on a smart girl his own age (Roberts). What's more, he begins to see that he's not nearly as bad off as he thought. The directors adapted Ned Vizzini's semiautobiographical novel, but the results are superficial: not serious enough to have real weight or funny enough to work as a comedy. [PG-13] ❙

It's Love I'm After (1937) 90m. *** D: Archie Mayo. Bette Davis, Leslie Howard, Olivia de Havilland, Patric Knowles, Eric Blore, Bonita Granville, Spring Byington, Veda Ann Borg. Delightful, witty comedy of ego-struck actor Howard and his fiancée/costar Davis, who explodes when he becomes involved with infatuated admirer de Havilland. Reminiscent in spirit of TWENTIETH CENTURY; Blore is marvelous as Howard's ultra-dedicated valet.❙

It's My Party (1996) C-109m. **½ D: Randal Kleiser. Eric Roberts, Gregory Harrison, Margaret Cho, Bruce Davison, Lee Grant, Devon Gummersall, Marlee Matlin, Roddy McDowall, Olivia Newton-John, Bronson Pinchot, Paul Regina, George Segal, Dimitra Arlys (Arliss), Christopher Atkins, Ron Glass, Victor Love, Joel Polis, Nina Foch, Sally Kellerman, Greg Louganis. Roberts portrays a successful L.A. designer suffering from AIDS, who decides he'd prefer to die with dignity and throws himself a wild weekend party for a final fling. Quite moving and often very funny. Roberts is excellent in the lead. [R] ▼●)

It's My Turn (1980) C-91m. *** D: Claudia Weill. Jill Clayburgh, Michael Douglas, Charles Grodin, Beverly Garland, Steven Hill, Teresa Baxter, Joan Copeland, John Gabriel, Charles Kimbrough, Jennifer Salt, Daniel Stern, Dianne Wiest. Enjoyable, low-key romantic comedy-drama about a young woman trying to balance her life as a career·woman, mate, and daughter. A quirky and consistently surprising little film

with good performances, especially from Grodin as Clayburgh's aloof lover. Film debut of Dianne Wiest. [R]▼●

It's Not the Size That Counts (1974-British) C-90m. BOMB D: Ralph Thomas. Leigh Lawson, Elke Sommer, Denholm Elliott, Vincent Price, Judy Geeson, George Coulouris, Milo O'Shea. Abominable sequel to PERCY, even worse, if that's possible; Lawson replaces Hywel Bennett as penis-transplant recipient. Original title PERCY'S PROGRESS. [R]▼

It'$ Only Money (1962) 84m. *** D: Frank Tashlin. Jerry Lewis, Joan O'Brien, Zachary Scott, Jack Weston, Jesse White, Mae Questel. TV repairman Jerry wants to be a detective like his idol (White!), so he sets out to locate a missing heir—and guess who it turns out to be? Slick mystery-comedy is one of Lewis' best vehicles, thanks to solid script (by John Fenton Murray) and direction, fine cast, and memorable climax involving runaway army of robot lawn mowers.

It's Pat (1994) C-77m. BOMB D: Adam Bernstein. Julia Sweeney, David Foley, Charles Rocket, Kathy Griffin, Julie Hayden, Kathy Najimy, Larry Hankin, Tim Meadows, Camille Paglia. Sweeney's cheerfully obnoxious, androgynous character from *Saturday Night Live* skits was never a prime candidate for feature-film stardom. If you can get through the first five minutes, you may get through the whole movie, as Pat finds true love with the equally androgynous Chris (Foley). Barely released theatrically. Sweeney coscripted. [PG-13]▼●

It Started in Naples (1960) C-100m. **½ D: Melville Shavelson. Clark Gable, Sophia Loren, Vittorio De Sica, Marietto, Paolo Carlini, Claudio Ermelli. Gable is American lawyer, in Italy to bring nephew back to America, but sexy Aunt Sophia won't agree. Star duo never clicks as love match, but they do their best. Attractive fluff. VistaVision.▼❙

It Started With a Kiss (1959) C-104m. **½ D: George Marshall. Glenn Ford, Debbie Reynolds, Eva Gabor, Fred Clark, Edgar Buchanan, Harry Morgan. Airy comedy about wacky Reynolds and her Army officer husband Ford, trying to make a go of marriage; set in Spain. Incidentally, the Lincoln Futura that features so prominently in this film was later modified to become the Batmobile in the 1960s. CinemaScope.▼

It's the Rage (2000) C-97m. *½ D: James D. Stern. Joan Allen, Jeff Daniels, Andre Braugher, Gary Sinise, Josh Brolin, Robert Forster, Anna Paquin, Giovanni Ribisi, David Schwimmer. The lives of a group of seemingly disparate people are connected by personal crises . . . which lead to resolutions with guns. Loud, heavy-handed satire about individual and cultural violence gets worse as it goes along, despite the efforts of a good cast, of whom only Allen and Forster emerge unscathed. Keith Reddin adapted his own play. Made for theaters, but U.S. debut on cable TV. [R]▼●

It Takes All Kinds (1969-U.S.-Australian) **C-98m.** **✱✱** D: Eddie Davis. Robert Lansing, Vera Miles, Barry Sullivan, Sid Melton, Penny Sugg. Fair double-cross drama about Miles' shielding of Lansing when he accidentally kills sailor in a brawl in Australia.

It Takes Two (1995) **C-101m.** **✱✱½** D: Andy Tennant. Kirstie Alley, Steve Guttenberg, Mary-Kate Olsen, Ashley Olsen, Philip Bosco, Jane Sibbett, Michelle Grison, Desmond Robertson, Ernie Grunwald, Lawrence Dane. Surprisingly well-wrought comedy for kids about lookalikes who trade places in order to help each other. The fabulously wealthy girl has a father who's about to marry a patently awful woman, while the orphan is about to lose her best friend, the social worker who supervises the orphanage. The twins give very likable performances, as do their adult costars. A cross between THE PRINCE AND THE PAUPER and THE PARENT TRAP. [PG]▼●

It! The Terror From Beyond Space (1958) **69m.** **✱✱½** D: Edward L. Cahn. Marshall Thompson, Shawn Smith, Kim Spalding, Ann Doran, Dabbs Greer. The second spaceship to Mars heads for Earth with the sole survivor of the *first* expedition, accused of murdering his crewmates—but the real killer is a Martian monster (Ray "Crash" Corrigan), which has crept aboard the returning ship. ALIEN owes a lot to this tidy, suspenseful, but underproduced movie, scripted by sci-fi writer Jerome Bixby. ▼●

Ivanhoe (1952) **C-106m.** **✱✱✱** D: Richard Thorpe. Robert Taylor, Joan Fontaine, Elizabeth Taylor, Emlyn Williams, George Sanders, Robert Douglas, Finlay Currie, Felix Aylmer, Francis de Wolff, Guy Rolfe, Norman Wooland, Basil Sydney. Almost a classic spectacular, marred by draggy scripting of Walter Scott's epic of England in Middle Ages, in days of chivalrous knights; beautifully photographed on location in Great Britain. Remade as a TVM in 1982.▼●

Ivan's Childhood (1962-Russian) **94m.** **✱✱✱** D: Andrei Tarkovsky. Kolya Burlaiev, Valentin Zubkov, Ye Zharikov, Nikolai Grinko. Taut, poignant account of 12-year-old Burlaiev, whose family is slaughtered during WW2, and his plight as he's sent as a spy into Nazi territory. Tarkovsky's first feature. Retitled: THE YOUNGEST SPY. ▼●

ivansxtc. (2002) **C-94m.** **✱✱✱** D: Bernard Rose. Danny Huston, Peter Weller, James Merendino, Adam Krentzman, Lisa Enos, Joanne Duckman, Caroleen Feeney, Valeria Golino, Robert Graham, Tiffani-Amber Thiessen, Victoria Silvstedt. Raw, emotionally intense look at the last few weeks of a Hollywood talent agent. Inspired by real-life agent Jay Moloney and based on Tol-

stoy's *The Death of Ivan Ilyich*, the film is shot as if it were a cinema-verité documentary and never hits a false note. Huston is astonishingly good as the slick, hedonistic Hollywood agent who finally encounters something he can't finesse or "handle"—his mortality. [R]

Ivan the Terrible, Part One (1945-Russian) **99m.** **✱✱✱✱** D: Sergei Eisenstein. Nikolai Cherkassov, Ludmila Tselikovskaya, Serafima Birman. Film spectacle of the highest order. Eisenstein's incredibly lavish, detailed chronicle of Czar Ivan IV's life from coronation to defeat to reinstatement, forging fascinating image of the man and his country. Enhanced by Prokofiev's original score. Heavy going, but worthwhile; the story continues in IVAN THE TERRIBLE, PART TWO.▼●

Ivan the Terrible, Part Two (1946-Russian) **88m.** **✱✱✱½** D: Sergei Eisenstein. Nikolai Cherkassov, Serafima Birman, Mikhail Nazvanov, Pavel Kadochnikov, Andrei Abrikosov. Continuation of the saga of Czar Ivan IV, in which he takes on the boyars in a battle for power. Impressive film is just a shade below its predecessor. Banned by Stalin because of controversial depiction of Ivan's secret police, and not released until 1958. (The director had planned to shoot Part Three—which, needless to say, he never did.) Banquet-dance sequence was originally in color.▼●

I've Heard the Mermaids Singing (1987-Canadian) **C-81m.** **✱✱½** D: Patricia Rozema. Sheila McCarthy, Paule Baillargeon, Ann-Marie McDonald, John Evans. Wistful, original comedy-drama about a young woman who's never been successful at anything but lands a job as assistant to a chic, intelligent art gallery owner whom she comes to idolize. McCarthy's winning and empathetic performance, in her film debut, keeps us hooked even when the movie starts to wander, which it does, more than once, before redeeming itself with the final shot. A slight but impressive first feature for writer-director Rozema.▼●

I've Loved You So Long (2008-French-German) **C-117m.** **✱✱✱** D: Philippe Claudel. Kristin Scott Thomas, Elsa Zylberstein, Serge Hazanavicius, Laurent Grévill, Frédéric Pierrot, Lise Ségur, Jean-Claude Arnaud. Zylberstein brings her sister (Scott Thomas) home to live with her husband and family, to whom she is a stranger: she's been away for 15 years. As details of her absence are revealed we come to empathize with this fragile woman's tentative reentry into society. The story can't bear much scrutiny but it's worth seeing for Scott Thomas, who conveys so much through her facial expressions and body language; Zylberstein is also quite good as her well-meaning sister. Directing debut for novelist and screenwriter Claudel. [PG-13]●

I Vitelloni (1953-Italian) **107m. ****** D: Federico Fellini. Alberto Sordi, Franco Interlenghi, Franco Fabrizi, Leopoldo Trieste, Riccardo Fellini. Magnificent comedy-drama—arguably Fellini's masterpiece—about five shiftless male adolescents in a small Adriatic town who have to cope with emerging adulthood. Film's episodic structure brings to mind AMERICAN GRAFFITI; its love of humanity anticipates the director's own AMARCORD two decades later. In any event, a lovely film. ▼●◗

I Wake Up Screaming (1941) **82m. ***** D: H. Bruce Humberstone. Betty Grable, Victor Mature, Carole Landis, Laird Cregar, William Gargan, Alan Mowbray, Allyn Joslyn, Elisha Cook, Jr. Entertaining whodunit with Grable and Mature implicated in murder of Betty's sister (Landis), pursued by determined cop Cregar. Good twist finish. Remade as VICKI; originally titled HOT SPOT. ▼◗

I Walk Alone (1947) **98m. **** D: Byron Haskin. Burt Lancaster, Lizabeth Scott, Kirk Douglas, Wendell Corey, Kristine Miller, George Rigaud, Marc Lawrence. A prison term changes Lancaster's outlook on life, and return to outside world makes him bitter. Good cast, weak film.

I Walked with a Zombie (1943) **69m. ***½** D: Jacques Tourneur. Frances Dee, Tom Conway, James Ellison, Edith Barrett, Christine Gordon, Theresa Harris, James Bell. Nurse Dee comes to Caribbean island to treat zombielike wife of troubled Conway, finds skeletons in family closet, plus local voodoo rituals and legends that cannot be ignored. Exceptional Val Lewton chiller with rich atmosphere, mesmerizing story. Loosely adapted from *Jane Eyre*! Read small-print disclaimer in opening credits carefully. Remade as RITUAL. ▼●◗

I Walk the Line (1970) **C-95m. **½** D: John Frankenheimer. Gregory Peck, Tuesday Weld, Estelle Parsons, Ralph Meeker, Lonny Chapman, Charles Durning. Rural sheriff Peck falls for moonshiner's daughter Weld, thereby destroying both his professional and personal life. Offbeat but aimless drama, helped by excellent Weld performance. Johnny Cash sings five songs. Panavision. [PG] ▼◗

I Wanna Hold Your Hand (1978) **C-104m. ***** D: Robert Zemeckis. Nancy Allen, Bobby DiCicco, Marc McClure, Susan Kendall Newman, Theresa Saldana, Eddie Deezen, Wendie Jo Sperber, Will Jordan. Teenagers connive to get tickets for the Beatles' first appearance on *The Ed Sullivan Show*. If this original comedy seems occasionally silly and overbearing, that's the price it pays for being a generally accurate portrayal of a raucous event. Comedian Jordan is as hilariously Sullivan-like as ever. Steven Spielberg was executive producer. [PG] ▼●◗

I Want Her Dead SEE: W

I Want Someone to Eat Cheese With (2007) **C-80m. **½** D: Jeff Garlin. Jeff Garlin, Sarah Silverman, Bonnie Hunt, Amy Sedaris, David Pasquesi, Gina Gershon, Elle Fanning. Garlin makes an unassumingly engaging impression as an overweight, unlucky-in-love comic who thinks *he* would be perfect for the lead role in a proposed remake of MARTY (and not just because he still lives with his mother). Mildly amusing ensemble comedy (based on Garlin's stage show) includes fellow alumni of the famed Second City comedy troupe. Silverman is a standout as a crazy/sexy ice cream parlor waitress. ◗

I Want to Go Home (1989-French) **C-101m. BOMB** D: Alain Resnais. Adolph Green, Gérard Depardieu, Linda Lavin, Laura Benson, Micheline Presle, Geraldine Chaplin, John Ashton, Ludivine Sagnier. Musical writer-performer Green (SINGIN' IN THE RAIN) plays a neurotic American cartoonist who travels to Paris for an art gallery show—and to see his estranged daughter (Benson). Depardieu, an exuberant admirer, brings him to his mother's country home for the weekend. Written by Jules Feiffer, with a score by John Kander, this Franco-American curio is appallingly bad, marked by amateurish performances and stilted dialogue. ◗

I Want to Live! (1958) **120m. ***½** D: Robert Wise. Susan Hayward, Simon Oakland, Virginia Vincent, Theodore Bikel, John Marley, Dabbs Greer, Gavin MacLeod. Hayward won an Oscar for her gutsy performance as prostitute-crook Barbara Graham who (according to the film) is framed for murder and goes to gas chamber. Smart presentation, fine acting, memorable jazz score by Johnny Mandel. Nelson Gidding and Don Mankiewicz based script on articles about Graham. Look fast for Jack Weston, Brett Halsey. Remade as a 1983 TVM with Lindsay Wagner. ▼●◗

I Want What I Want (1972-British) **C-91m. **½** D: John Dexter. Anne Heywood, Harry Andrews, Jill Bennett, Nigel Flatley, Paul Rogers. Interesting little piece about sexual crisis in the life of man who wants a sex-change operation. ▼◗

I Want You (1951) **102m. ***** D: Mark Robson. Dana Andrews, Dorothy McGuire, Farley Granger, Peggy Dow, Robert Keith, Mildred Dunnock, Martin Milner, Ray Collins, Jim Backus. Dated yet still touching Americana detailing effects of the Korean War on a small-town family. An artifact of its era, with fine performances all around. Screenplay by Irwin Shaw. ▼

I Was a Communist for the FBI (1951) **83m. **½** D: Gordon Douglas. Frank Lovejoy, Dorothy Hart, Philip Carey, James Millican. Documentary-style counterspy caper, low key and effective. ◗

I Was a Male War Bride (1949) **105m.** ***
D: Howard Hawks. Cary Grant, Ann Sheridan, Marion Marshall, Randy Stuart, William Neff, Ken Tobey. Delightful comedy of errors has French Army officer Grant trying to accompany WAC wife Sheridan back to U.S. with hilarious results. Grant in drag makes this one worth watching. ▼❙

I Was a Teenage Boy SEE: **Something Special**

I Was a Teenage Frankenstein (1957) **72m.** *½ D: Herbert L. Strock. Whit Bissell, Gary Conway, Phyllis Coates, Robert Burton. Campy junk about mad scientist who pulls young Conway from an auto wreck and "repairs" him. Doesn't live up to that title; worth catching only for Bissell's immortal line, "Answer me! You have a civil tongue in your head! I know—I sewed it in there!" One sequence is in color. ▼

I Was a Teenage Werewolf (1957) **75m.** *** D: Gene Fowler, Jr. Michael Landon, Yvonne Lime, Whit Bissell, Vladimir Sokoloff, Guy Williams. Landon plays a hair-trigger-temper teen who's got a nut (Bissell) for a psychotherapist with dangerous ideas about hypnotic regression and man's prehistoric past. Result: a werewolf in a high school jacket. As good as a low-budget drive-in monster movie gets; it launched Landon's career. ▼

I Was a Teenage Zombie (1987) **C-92m.** BOMB D: John E. Michalakias. Michael Ruben, George Seminara, Steve McCoy, Cassie Madden. Low-grade horror spoof concerns teen zombie Ruben battling McCoy, the zombie version of a drug pusher who's been preying on adolescents. Amateur night at the movies. ▼❍❙

I Was Happy Here SEE: **Time Lost and Time Remembered**

I Was Monty's Double (1958-British) **100m.** ***½ D: John Guillermin. M. E. Clifton-James, John Mills, Cecil Parker, Marius Goring, Michael Hordern, Leslie Phillips, Bryan Forbes. Exciting, true WW2 story of actor persuaded to pose as Gen. Montgomery in order to divert German intelligence in North Africa. Cast is first-rate.

I Went Down (1997-Irish-British) **C-107m.** **½ D: Paddy Breathnach. Brendan Gleeson, Peter McDonald, Tony Doyle, Peter Caffrey, Antoine Byrne. A good but down-on-his-luck guy is forced to pull off a kidnapping in order to work off a large debt he owes some gangsters. Quirky Irish action comedy has genuine affection for its unlikely heroes but never really catches fire, despite a wily performance from Gleeson as an aging petty thug who can't even steal a car properly. A big hit in Ireland. [R]▼

I Will, I Will . . . For Now (1976) **C-96m.** ** D: Norman Panama. Elliott Gould, Diane Keaton, Paul Sorvino, Victoria Principal, Robert Alda, Warren Berlinger, Madge Sinclair, Candy Clark. Fair satire on frigidity, infidelity, marriage counselling and a sex clinic. Gould and ex-wife Keaton spend film rediscovering each other. Panavision. [R]▼

I Woke Up Early the Day I Died (1999) **C/B&W-90m.** BOMB D: Aris Iliopulos. Billy Zane, Abraham Benrubi, Sandra Bernhard, Karen Black, Conrad Brooks, Tippi Hedren, Eartha Kitt, Ann Magnuson, Andrew McCarthy, Ron Perlman, Will Patton, Max Perlich, Summer Phoenix, Tara Reid, Christina Ricci, John Ritter, Rick Schroeder, Nicolette Sheridan, Jonathan Taylor Thomas, Vampira, Steven Weber. An unproduced screenplay by Edward D. Wood, Jr., served as the "inspiration" for this tedious chronicle of a thief (Zane) who breaks out of a mental institution. The intention was to make a bad (read: unintentionally funny) movie in the style of Ed Wood, but the result is just boring. Made as a silent movie, with sound effects and music. Zane coproduced. ▼

I Wonder Who's Killing Her Now? (1976) **C-87m.** **½ D: Steven H. Stern. Bob Dishy, Joanna Barnes, Bill Dana, Vito Scotti. Luckless husband hires someone to bump off his wife for insurance money, then tries to call it off; uneven but often funny farce, written by Woody Allen's one-time collaborator Mickey Rose. [PG]▼❙

Jabberwocky (1977-British) **C-100m.** **½ D: Terry Gilliam. Michael Palin, Max Wall, Deborah Fallender, John Le Mesurier, Annette Badland. Gilliam and Palin of MONTY PYTHON AND THE HOLY GRAIL fame give us another satire of medieval times, but the humor is even more spotty than its predecessor's. For fans. [R]▼❍❙

J'Accuse (1938-French) **95m.** *** D: Abel Gance. Victor Francen, Jean Max, Delaitre, Renee Devillers. Very good—but not great—antiwar film, focusing on exploited war veteran Francen; in a vivid sequence, he calls on war casualties to rise from their graves. Previously filmed by Gance in 1919. ▼

Jack (1996) **C-113m.** ** D: Francis Ford Coppola. Robin Williams, Diane Lane, Jennifer Lopez, Brian Kerwin, Fran Drescher, Bill Cosby, Michael McKean, Don Novello, Allan Rich, Adam Zolotin, Todd Bosley. A boy born prematurely—but fully developed—turns out to be aging at four times normal rate. At 10, with the physical characteristics of a 40-year-old man, he leaves his cloistered home to go to school and deal with other kids his age for the first time in his life. Williams is the perfect choice to play this man-child, but the script goes nowhere. Overlong, too adult for kids, too redundant for grown-ups; destined to please no one. [PG-13]▼❍❙

Jackal, The (1997) **C-124m.** **½ D: Michael Caton-Jones. Bruce Willis, Richard Gere, Sidney Poitier, Diane Venora, Tess

Harper, J. K. Simmons, Mathilda May, Stephen Spinella, Richard Lineback, Jack Black, Sophie Okonedo. When the FBI and the KGB are stumped as to how to capture an international assassin called The Jackal, they turn to the one man who knows him—an Irish terrorist (Gere) who's serving time in a U.S. prison. Watchable globe-trotting thriller is weakened by lapses of credibility, but boosted by Gere's charismatic performance. Venora is also a standout as a no-nonsense Russian agent. Bears only the slightest resemblance to the superior THE DAY OF THE JACKAL, despite being "officially" based on that screenplay. Panavision. [R]▼●)

Jackals, The (1967) **C-105m.** ** D: Robert D. Webb. Vincent Price, Diana Ivarson, Robert Gunner, Bob Courtney, Patrick Mynhardt. William Wellman's striking YELLOW SKY reset in the South African Transvaal, with six bandits terrorizing a grizzled old miner (Price) and his granddaughter into surrendering their gold.▼)

Jack & Sarah (1995-British-French) **C-110m.** **½ D: Tim Sullivan. Richard E. Grant, Samantha Mathis, Judi Dench, Ian McKellen, Cherie Lunghi, Eileen Atkins, Imogen Stubbs. A London lawyer is crushed when his young wife dies in childbirth, but he finds a reason to live in his infant daughter. He hires a young American as a nanny, which leads to romance—and complications. Good performances, particularly by the two leads, keep this uneven film watchable and pleasant. Also available in PG version. [R]▼●)

Jack and the Beanstalk (1952) **C/B&W-78m.** **½ D: Jean Yarbrough. Bud Abbott, Lou Costello, Dorothy Ford, Barbara Brown, Buddy Baer. A&C version of fairy tale OK for kids, but not as funny as their earlier films. Begins in sepiatone, then changes to color, like THE WIZARD OF OZ.▼●)

jackass: the movie (2002) **C-85m.** ** D: Jeff Tremaine. Johnny Knoxville, Bam Margera, Chris Pontius, Steve-O, Dave England, Ryan Dunn, Jason "Wee Man" Acuña, Preston Lacy, Ehren McGhehey. R-rated expansion of the mysteriously popular MTV show in which guys gleefully injure themselves doing all manner of stupid, raunchy, goofball stunts. Artless frat-house–level humor that some people find hilarious . . . especially the participants. Followed by two sequels. [R]▼)

jackass number two (2006) **C-91m.** **½ D: Jeff Tremaine. Johnny Knoxville, Bam Margera, Steve-O, Chris Pontius, Preston Lacy, Ryan Dunn, Ehren McGhehey, Jay Chandrasekhar, Tony Hawk, Spike Jonze, Mike Judge, John Waters, Luke Wilson, Rip Taylor. The tagline, "When was the last time a movie made you beg for mercy?" pretty much sums up this sequel, a spinoff from the enormously successful MTV series. With stunts

that cross the line and a cast willing to do anything—and we mean *anything*—for a laugh, this tasteless but sometimes hilarious collection of body-bashing gags is not for everyone—and you all know who you are. Don't try this at home! Unrated version runs 93m. [R]❿

jackass 3D (2010) **C-94m.** ** D: Jeff Tremaine. Johnny Knoxville, Bam Margera, Ryan Dunn, Steve-O, Jason "Wee Man" Acuña, Preston Lacy, Chris Pontius, Ehren McGhehey, Dave England, Spike Jonze, Rip Taylor. The 3-D effects occasionally enhance the trademarked gross-out shenanigans on display, but, as usual, it's mostly a gimmick in search of a movie. Some of the bits include a guy in a flying outhouse and a sexual encounter with a barnyard animal. Having maxed out so many ideas in previous films, the emphasis here seems to be on how far to go without getting killed in the process. Still, this was a box-office hit and will likely please JACKASS devotees. Followed by an expanded DVD edition, JACKASS 3.5. 3-D. [R]❿

Jack Be Nimble (1993-New Zealand) **C-93m.** **½ D: Garth Maxwell. Alexis Arquette, Sarah Smuts-Kennedy, Bruno Lawrence, Tony Barry, Elizabeth Hawthorne. Weird, clever little chiller in which the title character is adopted into a family of cretins and abused beyond endurance; he sets out to find his long-lost sister and also to seek revenge. Doesn't quite work when it takes itself too seriously; otherwise, this is devilishly entertaining, and has cult possibilities. [R]▼●)

Jacket, The (2005-U.S.-German-Scottish) **C-103m.** ** D: John Maybury. Adrien Brody, Keira Knightley, Jennifer Jason Leigh, Kris Kristofferson, Daniel Craig, Kelly Lynch, Brad Renfro, Mackenzie Phillips, Jason Lewis. Following a violent 1991 incident while serving in the Gulf War, soldier Brody ends up in Vermont and later in a time-travel journey to 2007. There he deals with the ramifications of a good Samaritan deed he performed—before another act of violence—in his previous life. Ugly to look at and apparently conceived from body parts of previous movies, modest head-case story (with the obligatory shady shrink) is only worth the time if you're curious to see the normally well-scrubbed Knightley sporting the goth look. Super 35. [R]▼)

Jack Frost (1998) **C-95m.** **½ D: Troy Miller. Michael Keaton, Kelly Preston, Mark Addy, Joseph Cross, Henry Rollins, Dweezil Zappa. A neglectful dad dies in a car accident and comes to life one year later as a snowman in his son's front yard! Warm, likable performances and an absence of treacle make this an OK family film, but it never overcomes its fundamental problem: a *very* strange premise. Panavision. [PG]▼●)

Jack Goes Boating (2010) **C-89m.** ** D: Philip Seymour Hoffman. Philip Seymour Hoffman, Amy Ryan, Daphne Rubin-Vega,

John Ortiz, Richard Petrocelli, Thomas McCarthy. Hoffman's directorial debut is MARTY-lite, a cloying character study about an oafish lonelyheart (Hoffman) who is set up with an equally awkward plain Jane (Ryan). They go boating and try to forge a relationship; that's pretty much it. Based on a play Hoffman performed Off-Broadway, the film is slow and just as tentative as the people it portrays. [R] ▶

Jackie Brown (1997) **C-154m.** *** D: Quentin Tarantino. Pam Grier, Samuel L. Jackson, Robert Forster, Michael Keaton, Bridget Fonda, Robert De Niro, Michael Bowen, Chris Tucker, Sid Haig. Leisurely paced but enjoyable adaptation of Elmore Leonard's crime caper *Rum Punch,* reset in Southern California. Grier (in a stand-out performance) plays a flight attendant who's been trafficking in hot money for lowlife Jackson; when caught, she plays all the angles she can think of to keep herself out of jail, managing to keep the cops, her chief client, and everyone else on ice. Dynamite performances all around sustain film through its periodic lulls. [R] ▼●]

Jackie Chan's First Strike (1996-Hong Kong) **C-110m.** **½ D: Stanley Tong. Jackie Chan, Chen Chun Wu, Jackson Lou, Bill Tung, Jouri Petrov. Hong Kong's most physically agile cop finds himself in a James Bond–like intrigue involving the CIA, Russian mafia, a nuclear device, and of course, a good-looking female scuba diver. The dubbing here is typically wretched, yet in a lark like this it really doesn't matter; the last two thirds is almost wall-to-wall action, including a doozy of a donnybrook in which Chan makes memorable use of a ladder. Technovision and Panavision. [PG-13] ▼●]

Jackie Chan's Police Story SEE: **Police Story** (1985)

Jackie Chan's Who Am I? (1998-Hong Kong) **C-108m.** *** D: Jackie Chan, Benny Chan. Jackie Chan, Michelle Ferre, Mirai Yamamoto, Ron Smerczak, Ed Nelson, Tom Pompert. Chan is part of a secret military team sent on a fatal mission; although he survives, he loses his memory, and can't understand why so many people are pursuing him. Lame dialogue and cardboard performances are outshone by one fantastic action scene after another, including a unique episode involving wooden shoes in Rotterdam. Chan also wrote the screenplay. Filmed in English. Originally 117m. Aka WHO AM I? Panavision. [PG-13] ▼●]

Jackie Robinson Story, The (1950) **76m.** *** D: Alfred E. Green. Jackie Robinson, Ruby Dee, Minor Watson, Louise Beavers, Richard Lane, Harry Shannon, Ben Lessy, Joel Fluellen. Straightforward bio of Robinson, the first black man to play major-league baseball. Fascinating as a social history; pointed in its presentation of the racial issues involved. Interestingly, Robin-

son's Negro League ball club is called the Black Panthers! Dee plays Robinson's wife; 40 years later, she was cast as his mother in the TV movie THE COURT-MARTIAL OF JACKIE ROBINSON. ▼]

Jack London's Klondike Fever SEE: **Klondike Fever**

Jacknife (1989) **C-102m.** *** D: David Jones. Robert De Niro, Ed Harris, Kathy Baker, Charles Dutton, Loudon Wainwright III. Simple and involving story of a Vietnam vet (De Niro) who looks up an old Army buddy (Harris) and tries to get him to face up to his repressed memories of Nam, and their mutual best friend who died there. Meanwhile, a romance blossoms between De Niro and Harris' wallflower sister, with whom he lives. Three terrific performances make this a must. Stephen Metcalfe adapted his play *Strange Snow.* [R] ▼●]

Jack of Diamonds (1967-U.S.-German) **C-105m.** *½ D: Don Taylor. George Hamilton, Joseph Cotton, Marie Lafont, Maurice Evans, Carroll Baker, Zsa Zsa Gabor, Lilli Palmer. Hamilton plays a cat burglar who robs jewels from Baker, Gabor, and Palmer, who are "special guests" in this sorry film. Skip this and wait for TO CATCH A THIEF instead.

Jackpot, The (1950) **87m.** **½ D: Walter Lang. James Stewart, Barbara Hale, James Gleason, Fred Clark, Natalie Wood. Dated, minor comedy, uplifted by stars; Stewart is winner of radio contest but can't pay taxes on winnings. ▼

Jackpot (2001) **C-96m.** ** D: Michael Polish. Jon Gries, Daryl Hannah, Garrett Morris, Peggy Lipton, Crystal Bernard, Anthony Edwards, Mac Davis, Adam Baldwin. An over-the-hill desert rat (Gries) ditches his wife and baby daughter to become a traveling karaoke cowboy, playing the Nevada circuit with his clingy, overambitious manager (Morris). Shot on high-definition video, the film looks even more fantastic than Mark and Michael Polish's first feature, TWIN FALLS, IDAHO, but this irony-drenched movie about a failed American dream gets pretty dreary once we realize we're stuck in the company of an irredeemable loser. HD 24P Widescreen. [R] ▼]

Jack's Back (1988) **C-97m.** *½ D: Rowdy Herrington. James Spader, Cynthia Gibb, Rod Loomis, Rex Ryon, Robert Picardo, Chris Mulkey, Danitza Kingsley. Umpteenth retelling of the JACK THE RIPPER saga is updated to contemporary L.A. where young doctor Spader is the #1 suspect when prostitutes are killed in grisly fashion 100 years to the day after Bloody Jack's legendary crimes. Plot twist halfway through is preposterous; Spader is earnest but miscast. [R] ▼●

Jackson County Jail (1976) **C-89m.** **½ D: Michael Miller. Yvette Mimieux, Tommy Lee Jones, Robert Carradine, Frederic Cook, Severn Darden, Howard Hesseman, Mary Woronov. Prisoner Yvette, dumped on by everyone she meets, goes on the lam with fellow inmate in yet another chase pic. Livelier than most, this one has eveloped a cult reputation. Miller later remade it for TV as OUTSIDE CHANCE; it was remade again in 1996 as MACON COUNTY JAIL. [R]▼●)

Jack the Bear (1993) C-98m. **½ D: Marshall Herskovitz. Danny DeVito, Robert J. Steinmiller, Miko Hughes, Gary Sinise, Julia Louis-Dreyfus, Reese Witherspoon, Bert Remsen, Andrea Marcovicci. Sporadically affecting, but mostly muddled comedy-drama about the emotional unraveling of a widowed TV horror-movie host whose neighbor is a pro-Nazi psycho who poses a threat to children. Kept on track at least some of the time by Steinmiller's exceptional performance as DeVito's older son (age 12). Set in 1972; based on Dan McCall's novel. Super 35. [PG-13] ▼●)

Jack the Giant Killer (1962) C-94m. *** D: Nathan Juran. Kerwin Mathews, Judi Meredith, Torin Thatcher, Walter Burke. Marvelous Fantascope special effects make this costume adventure yarn (in the SINBAD tradition) great fun. Beware reissue, which was dubbed into an ersatz musical!▼●)

Jacob's Ladder (1990) C-114m. **½ D: Adrian Lyne. Tim Robbins, Elizabeth Peña, Matt Craven, Pruitt Taylor Vince, Jason Alexander, Patricia Kalember, Eriq La Salle, Danny Aiello, Ving Rhames, Brian Tarantina, S. Epatha Merkerson. Brooding, only occasionally effective psychological study of Robbins, who is maimed in combat in Vietnam and exists in a netherworld between life and death, refusing to die. Bruce Joel Rubin's script is reminiscent of Ambrose Bierce's classic "An Occurrence at Owl Creek Bridge," but not as good. Scenario also touches on issues relating to Vietnam combat soldiers being subjected to psychological experiments by their superiors. Macaulay Culkin appears unbilled in a key supporting role. Two deleted scenes were added for the film's cable TV debut. [R] ▼●)

Jacob the Liar (1974-East German) C-95m. *** D: Frank Beyer. Vlastimil Brodsky, Erwin Geschonneck, Manuela Simon, Henry Hubchen, Blanche Kommerell, Armin Mueller-Stahl. Touching, sometimes comic tale of Polish Jew Brodsky, whose false tales to fellow ghetto dwellers give some hope against their Nazi captors. Remade in 1999 as JAKOB THE LIAR. ▼)

Jacob Two Two Meets the Hooded Fang (1977-Canadian) C-80m. **½ D: Theodore J. Flicker. Stephen Rosenberg, Alex Karras, Guy L'Ecuyer, Joy Coghill, Earl Pennington, Claude Gail. Engaging fantasy for kids written by Mordecai Richler, about a boy who dreams he's sent to chil- dren's prison. Low-budget production values are unfortunate detriment. [G]▼

Jacqueline Susann's Once Is Not Enough (1975) C-121m. BOMB D: Guy Green. Kirk Douglas, Alexis Smith, David Janssen, Deborah Raffin, George Hamilton, Melina Mercouri, Brenda Vaccaro. Trashy film based on Susann's trashy novel of jet-set intrigue, and a blossoming young woman (Raffin) with a father-fixation. Incurably stupid, and surprisingly dull. Vaccaro offers brightest moments as unabashed man-chaser. Panavision. [R]▼)

Jacques Brel Is Alive and Well and Living in Paris (1975) C-98m. ** D: Denis Heroux. Elly Stone, Mort Shuman, Joe Masiell, Jacques Brel. Musical revue featuring 26 bittersweet songs on life, love, war and death by Belgian balladeer Jacques Brel. No plot, no dialogue. Based on 1968 stage show. An American Film Theater Production. [PG]▼)

Jacquot de Nantes (1991-French) C-118m. ***½ D: Agnès Varda. Philippe Maron, Edouard Joubeaud, Laurent Monnier, Brigitte de Villepoix. Deeply moving chronicle of the sum of a man's life, as Varda creates a portrait of her late husband, French filmmaker Jacques Demy. Varda cuts from interviews with Demy (lovingly photographed in extreme close-up), to clips from his films, to the re-created story of young "Jacquot" growing up in Nantes during the 1940s and developing a passion for cinema. A heartfelt valentine from one life partner to another. Released in U.S. in 1993 as JACQUOT. Varda has since directed several other celluloid tributes to Demy.▼

Jade (1995) C-101m. ** D: William Friedkin. David Caruso, Linda Fiorentino, Chazz Palminteri, Michael Biehn, Richard Crenna, Donna Murphy, Ken King, Holt McCallany, David Hunt, Angie Everhart, Kevin Tighe. While investigating the brutal murder of a wealthy San Franciscan, assistant D.A. Caruso realizes to his dismay that his old flame (Fiorentino, married to his good friend Palminteri) may be involved. Sordid mystery/thriller from the seedy pen of Joe Eszterhas; has its moments (including an exciting S.F. car chase) but never rises above the mire. Unrated video edition has 12m. additional footage. [R] ▼●)

Jagged Edge (1985) C-108m. **½ D: Richard Marquand. Jeff Bridges, Glenn Close, Peter Coyote, Robert Loggia, John Dehner, Leigh Taylor-Young, Karen Austin, Lance Henriksen, James Karen, Michael Dorn. Wealthy publishing magnate is accused of murdering his wife; hotshot lawyer Close will defend him only if she believes he's innocent. Not only is she convinced—she immediately falls in love with him! Credibility goes out the window in this otherwise well-made, often gripping combination of thriller and courtroom drama. How could such a "smart" movie allow so many silly loopholes? Loggia is terrific as usual as Close's street-smart leg man. [R]▼●❍

Jaguar Lives! (1979) **C-90m.** *½ D: Ernest Pintoff. Joe Lewis, Christopher Lee, Donald Pleasence, Barbara Bach, Capucine, Joseph Wiseman, Woody Strode, John Huston. Karate champ Lewis is featured in this predictable action cheapie as a special agent sent to dispatch narcotics biggies in various world capitals. Top cast, but don't be fooled. [PG]▼

Jail Bait (1954) **70m.** *½ D: Edward D. Wood, Jr. Timothy Farrell, Lyle Talbot, Steve Reeves, Herbert Rawlinson, Dolores Fuller, Clancey Malone, Theodora Thurman, Mona McKinnon. Farrell leads young Malone into life of crime; when the law closes in, he forces Malone's plastic surgeon father to change his face. Misleadingly titled thriller is less inept than Wood's "classics," and thus less funny, but inspired teaming of Talbot and Reeves (in his first speaking part) as cops is good for a few giggles.▼●❍

Jail Bait (1972-German) **C-99m.** *** D: Rainer Werner Fassbinder. Eva Mattes, Harry Baer, Jorg von Liebenfels, Ruth Drexel, Kurt Raab, Hanna Schygulla. Another provocative, controversial exploration of emptiness in post-WW2 Germany from the prolific Fassbinder. Here, a seductive 14-year-old (Mattes) becomes involved with Baer, eventually coaxing him into murdering her father. Originally made for German television; not released in the U.S. until 1977.

Jailhouse Rock (1957) **96m.** *** D: Richard Thorpe. Elvis Presley, Judy Tyler, Vaughn Taylor, Dean Jones, Mickey Shaughnessy. Elvis learns to pick a guitar in the Big House, later becomes a surly rock star. Presley's best film captures the legend in all his nostril-flaring, pre-Army glory. Great Leiber-Stoller score, including "Treat Me Nice," "Don't Leave Me Now," and terrific title song. Also shown in computer-colored version. CinemaScope.▼●❍

Jake Speed (1986) **C-104m.** BOMB D: Andrew Lane. Wayne Crawford, Dennis Christopher, Karen Kopins, John Hurt, Leon Ames, Roy London, Donna Pescow, Barry Primus, Monte Markham. Utter waste of time about a paperback hero who turns up in real life to help a damsel in distress. Crawford, who has all the star appeal of a can of tuna, presumably got the lead role because he also cowrote and coproduced the film. [PG]▼●❍

Jakob the Liar (1999) **C-114m.** **½ D: Peter Kassovitz. Robin Williams, Alan Arkin, Bob Balaban, Hannah Taylor Gordon, Armin Mueller-Stahl, Liev Schreiber, Michael Jeter, Nina Siemaszko, Mathieu Kassovitz. In a Polish ghetto in 1944, a wistful widower (Williams) raises hopes among his fellow townspeople after he accidentally hears an optimistic report about the war on a Nazi radio. Soon, he is besieged for more "radio reports," which he is forced to invent. Modest film from Jurek Becker's novel is only mildly successful, though Williams does his best. Mueller-Stahl also appeared in the 1974 version. [PG-13]▼▶

Jamaica Inn (1939-British) **98m.** ** D: Alfred Hitchcock. Charles Laughton, Maureen O'Hara, Leslie Banks, Robert Newton, Emlyn Williams, Mervyn Johns. Stodgy Victorian costumer of cutthroat band headed by nobleman Laughton; O'Hara is lovely, but plodding Hitchcock film is disappointing. Based on Daphne du Maurier novel; Hitch had far more success a year later with du Maurier's *Rebecca*. Remade for British TV in 1985 with Jane Seymour and Patrick McGoohan. ▼●❍

James and the Giant Peach (1996) **C-80m.** ***½ D: Henry Selick. Paul Terry, Miriam Margolyes, Joanna Lumley, Pete Postlethwaite, Mike Starr; voices of Simon Callow, Richard Dreyfuss, Jane Leeves, Susan Sarandon, Miriam Margolyes, David Thewlis. Wondrous adaptation of Roald Dahl's fantasy about a beleaguered boy, tended by two harridan aunts, who discovers a magic pathway inside a giant peach. Together with a grasshopper, a spider, a centipede, a worm, a glowworm, and a ladybug, he sets sail for the city of his dreams—N.Y. Starts in live action, then segues to stop-motion animation to bring Dahl's (typically) bizarre but delightful story to life. Gets better and better as it goes along, with impeccable voice characterizations and charming songs by Randy Newman. A rare movie that creates a world all its own and an even rarer children's film that has real wit and imagination. [PG]▼●❍

James Dean Story, The (1957) **82m.** ** D: George W. George, Robert Altman. Narrated by Martin Gabel. Uninspired use of available material makes this a slow-moving documentary on life of 1950s movie star. ▼●❍

Jamón Jamón (1992-Spanish) **C-93m.** *** D: José Juan Bigas Luna. Penélope Cruz, Stefania Sandrelli, Anna Galiena, Juan Diego, Jordi Molla, Javier Bardem. Clever, erotic black comedy-melodrama about sex and food, which also serves to mirror Spanish society in transition. The scenario focuses on the various members of two families from different classes, and what follows after beautiful Cruz falls for (and becomes pregnant by) her boss' spoiled son (Molla). A delight from start to finish, and a sleeper hit in Europe.▼

Jane Austen Book Club, The (2007) **C-106m.** *** D: Robin Swicord. Maria Bello, Emily Blunt, Kathy Baker, Amy Brenneman, Maggie Grace, Jimmy Smits, Hugh Dancy, Marc Blucas, Kevin Zegers, Lynn Redgrave, Nancy Travis. Agreeable fare about five women—and one unlikely man—who form a book club devoted to Jane Austen's novels, only to discover that the storylines parallel their own dealings with marriage, divorce, fidelity, etc. Likable cast propels this easy-to-take material, with Blunt a standout as a repressed (yet snooty) schoolteacher. Directing debut for screenwriter Swicord, who also adapted Karen Joy Fowler's novel. [PG-13]🄳

Jane Austen in Manhattan (1980) C-108m. *½ D: James Ivory. Robert Powell, Anne Baxter, Michael Wager, Tim Choate, John Guerrasio, Katrina Hodiak, Kurt Johnson, Sean Young. Dreary, confusing oddity about charismatic acting-teacher Powell and his rival Baxter, each trying to produce a newly discovered play written by Jane Austen. Overlong; a disappointment from director Ivory. Hodiak is the daughter of Baxter and John Hodiak.▼🄳

Jane Austen's Mafia! (1998) C-84m. **½ D: Jim Abrahams. Jay Mohr, Billy Burke, Christina Applegate, Lloyd Bridges, Pamela Gidley, Olympia Dukakis, Jason Fuchs, Joe Viterelli, Tony Lo Bianco. Parody from the AIRPLANE/NAKED GUN school takes aim at THE GODFATHER and CASINO but throws in gags referring to everything from FORREST GUMP to JURASSIC PARK. Disorganized, to say the least, but full of funny stuff—funny enough to overlook many of its shortcomings. Bridges' last film. Aka MAFIA! [PG-13]▼🄳

Jane Eyre (1934) 67m. ** D: Christy Cabanne. Virginia Bruce, Colin Clive, Beryl Mercer, Aileen Pringle, David Torrence, Lionel Belmore. Thin version of the oft-filmed Brontë novel, produced by Monogram, of all studios, with Bruce in the title role and Clive as Mr. Rochester. Still, it's not uninteresting as a curio.▼🄳

Jane Eyre (1944) 96m. *** D: Robert Stevenson. Orson Welles, Joan Fontaine, Margaret O'Brien, Henry Daniell, John Sutton, Agnes Moorehead, Elizabeth Taylor, Peggy Ann Garner, Sara Allgood, Aubrey Mather, Hillary Brooke. Artistically successful if slow-moving version of Charlotte Brontë novel about orphan girl who grows up to become a governess in a mysterious household. Young Taylor appears unbilled.▼🄳🄳

Jane Eyre (1996-French-Italian-U.S.-British) C-117m. ** D: Franco Zeffirelli. William Hurt, Charlotte Gainsbourg, Anna Paquin, Geraldine Chaplin, Fiona Shaw, Elle Macpherson, John Wood, Joan Plowright, Amanda Root, Charlotte Attenborough. Unremarkable remake of Brontë's classic romance features Gainsbourg as a very credible Jane. Unfortunately, there is a lack of chemistry between the leads, and a rushed ending that is completely out of sync with the rest of the film. The 1944 version remains the best attempt. [PG]▼🄳🄳

Jane Eyre (2011-British) C-115m. *** D:

Cary Joji Fukunaga. Mia Wasikowska, Michael Fassbender, Jamie Bell, Judi Dench, Sally Hawkins, Holliday Grainger, Tamzin Merchant, Imogen Poots, Amelia Clarkson, Simon McBurney. Wasikowska is well cast as the resilient heroine of Charlotte Brontë's classic, oft-filmed 19th-century novel. After a loveless childhood and harsh adolescence, she finds herself working as governess for an enigmatic, mercurial—but somehow magnetic—man named Mr. Rochester (well played by Fassbender). Exquisite but restrained interpretation rests largely on its talented leading lady's shoulders. Screenwriter Moira Buffini has juggled the chronology of the novel but retained its dramatic power. [PG-13]🄳

Janis (1975) C-96m. *** D: Howard Alk, Seaton Findlay. Documentary on Janis Joplin was filmed with cooperation of her family, so it ignores the singer's dark side. OK within its limits, with a dozen or so songs performed (including "Piece of My Heart," "Me and Bobby McGee," "Kozmic Blues," "Mercedes Benz"). [R]▼

Janky Promoters, The (2009) C-85m. ** D: Marcus Raboy. Ice Cube, Mike Epps, Young Jeezy, Lahmard Tate, Julio Oscar Mechoso, Tamala Jones, "Li'l" JJ James Lewis, Glenn Plummer, Juanita Jennings. Two chronically cash-strapped concert promoters resort to increasingly desperate measures while trying to organize a rap concert in beautiful downtown Modesto, California. Genially slapdash, brazenly unPC comedy was barely released in theaters, but is good for a few laughs. [R] 🄳

January Man, The (1989) C-97m. *½ D: Pat O'Connor. Kevin Kline, Mary Elizabeth Mastrantonio, Susan Sarandon, Harvey Keitel, Danny Aiello, Rod Steiger, Alan Rickman, Faye Grant, Tandy Cronyn. Appallingly wrongheaded mix of cop movie, romantic drama, and offbeat comedy written by John Patrick Shanley, with Kline as a self-styled eccentric whose brother, the police commissioner of N.Y.C., is forced to hire him to help catch a serial killer. Fine cast founders in this unfunny, illogical mess. [R]▼🄳🄳

Japanese Story (2003-Australian) C-99m. **½ D: Sue Brooks. Toni Collette, Gotaro Tsunashima, Matthew Dyktynski, Lynette Curran, Yumiko Tanaka, Kate Atkinson. Geologist Collette is chosen to escort a Japanese businessman to a remote area of Australia where her company operates. They share unexpected adventures and eventually break through their professional reserve; then fate steps in. Intriguing story about the role of chance in our lives; deliberately pulls the rug out from under the audience, but doesn't fully compensate us for that jarring experience. Collette is excellent as usual. Super 35. [R] ▼🄳

Jarhead (2005) C-123m. *** D: Sam Mendes. Jake Gyllenhaal, Peter Sarsgaard, Jamie Foxx, Lucas Black, Brian Geraghty, Jacob Vargas, Laz Alonso, Evan Jones, Chris Cooper, Dennis Haysbert, John Krasinski. Visual diary of a raw Marine recruit who's shipped to the Arabian desert in 1990, where he and fellow newbies are placed in a holding pattern called Operation Desert Shield, waiting to fight in what eventually became Operation Desert Storm. Absurdities mount up on a daily basis in this surreal, sun-baked atmosphere. William Broyles, Jr., adapted Anthony Swofford's best-selling memoir; Mendes consciously echoes FULL METAL JACKET, APOCALYPSE NOW, and others in this offbeat but compelling war film in which there is precious little combat. Super 35. [R]▼❷

Jason and the Argonauts (1963-British) **C-104m.** *** D: Don Chaffey. Todd Armstrong, Gary Raymond, Nancy Kovack, Honor Blackman, Nigel Green. Great special effects (by Ray Harryhausen) and colorful backgrounds in fable about Jason's search for golden fleece. Encounters with mythic monsters and gods highlight this sweeping adventure. Rich score by Bernard Herrmann. Remade for TV in 2000. ▼❶❶

Jason Goes to Hell: The Final Friday (1993) **C-88m.** *½ D: Adam Marcus. John D. LeMay, Kari Keegan, Kane Hodder, Steven Williams, Steven Culp, Erin Gray, Rusty Schwimmer, Billy Green Bush. Ninth entry in the FRIDAY THE 13TH series, ignores the plots of the last six or so, and opens with Jason being blown to pieces in an ambush. However, his evil spirit takes over a convenient bystander, and reborn, he heads for home to confront his (hitherto unmentioned) sister. Erratic, illogical, and pointlessly cruel; some fans liked it because of its delight in including elements from other contemporary horror movie series. Followed in 2002 by JASON X. [R]▼❶❶

Jason's Lyric (1994) **C-119m.** ** D: Doug McHenry. Allen Payne, Jada Pinkett, Forest Whitaker, Bokeem Woodbine, Treach, Lisa Carson, Suzzanne Douglas, Eddie Griffin, Lahmard Tate. Overly familiar (not to mention confusing) tale of good-and-evil brothers. Jason (Payne) is an honest and dependable workingman; Joshua (Woodbine) is a drug-abusing thief. Jason falls in love with an attractive waitress named Lyric (Pinkett)—more a romantic male fantasy than a real person—and you know what's coming. Several sex scenes were trimmed to avoid an NC-17 rating, but gruesome violence remains intact. [R]▼❶❶

Jason X (2002) **C-93m.** *½ D: Jim Isaac. Kane Hodder, Lexa Doig, Lisa Ryder, Chuck Campbell, Jonathan Potts, Peter Mensah, Melyssa Ade. In this, the tenth FRIDAY THE 13TH installment (and first since 1993's JASON GOES TO HELL: THE FINAL FRIDAY), cryogenically frozen Jason (Hodder) and a sexy scientist (Doig) are thawed while

on board a spacecraft in the year 2455. You can guess what happens next. For dedicated slasher fans only. David Cronenberg appears briefly as Dr. Wimmer. Not to be confused with MALCOLM X. Followed by FREDDY VS. JASON. [R]▼❷

Jawbreaker (1999) **C-90m.** *½ D: Darren Stein. Rose McGowan, Rebecca Gayheart, Julie Benz, Judy Evans Greer, Carol Kane, William Katt, Jeff Conaway, Tatyana Ali, Pam Grier, Brian Warner (Marilyn Manson), P.J. Soles, The Donnas. Monotonous—and unpleasant—black comedy about a tight-knit band of girls who rule their high school—until an accidental murder forces them to "adopt" a geeky student who could cause trouble for them. A short-subject idea padded to feature length. [R]▼❶❶

Jaws (1975) **C-124m.** **** D: Steven Spielberg. Roy Scheider, Robert Shaw, Richard Dreyfuss, Lorraine Gary, Murray Hamilton, Jeffrey Kramer, Susan Backlinie, Carl Gottlieb. A rare case of a bubble-gum story (by Peter Benchley) scoring as a terrific movie. The story: New England shore community is terrorized by shark attacks; local cop (Scheider), ichthyologist (Dreyfuss), and salty shark expert (Shaw) determine to kill the attacker. Hold on to your seats! Screenplay by Benchley and Gottlieb. Three Oscars include John Williams' now-classic score, Verna Fields' sensational editing. Benchley has cameo as reporter on beach. Followed by three sequels. Panavision. [PG]▼❶❶

Jaws 2 (1978) **C-117m.** **½ D: Jeannot Szwarc. Roy Scheider, Lorraine Gary, Murray Hamilton, Joseph Mascolo, Jeffrey Kramer, Collin Wilcox. Just when you thought it was safe to turn on your TV set again, here comes another gratuitous sequel. The shark scenes deliver the goods, but Robert Shaw and Richard Dreyfuss are sorely needed when film is on land. Panavision. [PG]▼❶❶

Jaws 3-D (1983) **C-97m.** ** D: Joe Alves. Dennis Quaid, Bess Armstrong, Simon MacCorkindale, Louis Gossett, Jr., John Putch, Lea Thompson. Road-company Irwin Allen–type disaster film, unrelated to first two JAWS except by contrivance; this time a shark's on the loose in Florida's Sea World. (Does this make it an unofficial remake of REVENGE OF THE CREATURE?) Might play on TV, but in theaters its only real assets were excellent 3-D effects. Retitled JAWS III for TV and homevideo. ArriVision. [PG]▼❶❶

Jaws the Revenge (1987) **C-89m.** *½ D: Joseph Sargent. Lorraine Gary, Lance Guest, Mario Van Peebles, Karen Young, Michael Caine, Lynn Whitfield. Watchable but mediocre retread of JAWS, the fourth time around, with Gary as the widow of sheriff Scheider (from the original film) who's convinced the great white shark is deliberately seeking out and killing off members of her family. Marginal movie really sunk by stupid, abrupt finale; Caine wasted in frivolous supporting role. Set mostly in the Bahamas. Super 35. [PG-13]▼●▶

Jaws of Death, The SEE: **Mako: The Jaws of Death**

Jay and Silent Bob Strike Back (2001) **C-104m. **** D: Kevin Smith. Kevin Smith, Jason Mewes, Ben Affleck, Shannon Elizabeth, Ali Larter, Eliza Dushku, Jennifer Schwalbach, Jason Lee, Will Ferrell, Judd Nelson, Seann William Scott, Carrie Fisher, Jon Stewart, Jason Biggs, James Van Der Beek, Chris Rock, Mark Hamill, Morris Day, Tracy Morgan. The two crude doper-slackers from CLERKS, MALLRATS, etc., journey to Hollywood to stop a movie being made about them—or at least collect some dough. Giant in-joke comedy where the people on screen are clearly having a better time than we are in the audience. Moviemaking scene with Affleck and Matt Damon is arguably the funniest; many cameos include stars of earlier Smith films. Super 35. [R]▼▶

Jazz on a Summer's Day (1959) **C-85m. ***½** D: Bert Stern. Louis Armstrong, Big Maybelle, Chuck Berry, Dinah Washington, Gerry Mulligan, Thelonious Monk, Anita O'Day, Mahalia Jackson, Sonny Stitt, Jack Teagarden. Candid, enjoyable filmed record of the 1958 Newport Jazz Festival. A must for jazz aficionados.▼▶

Jazz Singer, The (1927) **89m. **½** D: Alan Crosland. Al Jolson, May McAvoy, Warner Oland, Eugenie Besserer, Otto Lederer, William Demarest, Roscoe Karns. Legendary first talkie is actually silent with several sound musical and talking sequences. Story of Cantor Oland's son (Jolson) going into show business is creaky, but this movie milestone should be seen once. Songs: "My Mammy," "Toot Toot Tootsie Goodbye," "Blue Skies," etc. Look fast for Myrna Loy as a chorus girl. Remade twice (so far!).▼●▶

Jazz Singer, The (1953) **C-107m. **½** D: Michael Curtiz. Danny Thomas, Peggy Lee, Mildred Dunnock, Eduard Franz, Tom Tully, Allyn Joslyn. Slick remake benefits from Curtiz' no-nonsense direction and presence of Lee and Dunnock . . . but it's still just *so* schmaltzy.▼

Jazz Singer, The (1980) **C-115m.** BOMB D: Richard Fleischer. Neil Diamond, Laurence Olivier, Lucie Arnaz, Catlin Adams, Franklyn Ajaye, Paul Nicholas, Sully Boyar, Mike Kellin. Cantor Olivier shouts, "I hef no son!"—one of the highpoints of this moth-balled sudser in which Diamond becomes a rock star in about as much time as it takes to get a haircut. This remake may actually contain more clichés than the 1927 version! [PG]▼●▶

JCVD (2008-Belgian-Luxembourgian-French) **C-96m. ***** D: Mabrouk El Mechri. Jean-Claude Van Damme, François Damiens, Zinedine Soualem, Karim Belkhadra, Jean-François Wolff, Anne Paulicevich, François Beukelaers, Saskia Flanders. Down-on-his-luck action hero ditches Hollywood (and a costly child custody case) and returns to his European roots. By chance he walks straight into a bloody bank heist and becomes a celebrity, a hostage, and a suspect. Dour, desaturated art-house thriller—partly scripted, partly improvised—seems set in an alternate reality. Van Damme, playing "himself" but not himself, proves he's a real actor as well as a movie star. Who'da thunk it? Super 35. [R]▶

J. D.'s Revenge (1976) **C-95m. **** D: Arthur Marks. Glynn Turman, Joan Pringle, Lou Gossett, Carl Crudup, James Louis Watkins, Alice Jubert. Black horror melodrama: possession of innocent man by vengeful spirit. Fairly well executed. [R]▼▶

Jean de Florette (1986-French) **C-122m. ***½** D: Claude Berri. Yves Montand, Gérard Depardieu, Daniel Auteuil, Elisabeth Depardieu, Ernestine Mazurowna, Marcel Champel, Armand Meffre. Proud, cocky French farmer schemes with his simpleminded nephew to acquire some nearby farmland by making sure the new owners never discover an all-important natural spring on the property. Richly textured, emotionally powerful adaptation of Marcel Pagnol novel, exquisitely and meticulously filmed, with galvanizing performances—especially by Depardieu as the doggedly optimistic novice farmer. Story continues in MANON OF THE SPRING. Technovision. [PG] ▼●▶

Jeanne and the Perfect Guy (1999-French) **C-98m. **½** D: Olivier Ducastel. Virginie Ledoyen, Mathieu Demy, Valerie Bonneton, Jacques Bonnaffe. Musical comedy about a beautiful young woman who finally meets the love of her life, only to lose him when he disappears after learning he is HIV-positive. Unusual subject matter for a musical, to say the least, but Ducastel (seemingly inspired by Jacques Demy films) almost pulls it off. Downbeat subject is eclipsed by inventive use of songs and ultimately life-affirming message. Panavision. ▼▶

Jeanne Eagels (1957) **109m. **½** D: George Sidney. Kim Novak, Jeff Chandler, Agnes Moorehead, Gene Lockhart, Virginia Grey. Novak tries but can't rise to demands of portraying famed actress of 1920s. Chandler is her virile love interest. Veteran director Frank Borzage appears as himself. ▶

Jeepers Creepers (2001) **C-90m. **½** D: Victor Salva. Gina Philips, Justin Long, Jonathan Breck, Patricia Belcher, Eileen Brennan, Brandon Smith, Peggy Sheffield. A brother and sister driving across the American South stop to investigate what looks like a murder, but turns out to be something far worse. Well directed and exciting, with an imaginatively conceived monster. This is genuinely scary at times, but the ending is unsatisfying and unpleasantly cynical. Written by the director. Followed by a sequel. [R] ▼▶

Jeepers Creepers II (2003) **C-106m.**
** D: Victor Salva. Ray Wise, Jonathan Breck, Garikayi Mutambirwa, Eric Nenninger, Nicki Aycox, Travis Schiffner, Lena Cardwell, Billy Aaron Brown, Diane Delano, Luke Edwards, Justin Long. The Creeper returns to attack a school bus filled with teenagers returning from a football game. Well-crafted film creates a tangible sense of fear and dread, and has plenty of good scares . . . but after a while its bag of tricks empties out. Panavision. [R] ▼▶

Jefferson in Paris (1995) **C-144m.** ** D: James Ivory. Nick Nolte, Greta Scacchi, Thandie Newton, Gwyneth Paltrow, Seth Gilliam, James Earl Jones, Simon Callow, Michael Lonsdale, Nancy Marchand, Jean-Pierre Aumont, Daniel Mesguich. While serving as U.S. Ambassador to France in the 1780s, a widowed Thomas Jefferson (Nolte) begins to fall in love with an Italian-born Englishwoman (Scacchi), but also finds himself attracted to a black, teenaged slave (Newton) on his household staff; meanwhile, his strong-willed daughter (Paltrow) seems to want to be the only woman in his life. Story is framed, in flashback, by Jones as free black man who claims to be Jefferson's son. Ambitious, well-appointed drama is also long and sluggish. [PG-13] ▼▶

Jeffrey (1995) **C-92m.** **½ D: Christopher Ashley. Steven Weber, Michael T. Weiss, Patrick Stewart, Bryan Batt, Sigourney Weaver, Nathan Lane, Olympia Dukakis, Christine Baranski, Robert Klein, Kathy Najimy, Irma St. Paule, Camryn Manheim. Thirtyish New Yorker Jeffrey (Weber), who is gay, has sworn off sex in this era of AIDS—only to meet hunky gym rat Weiss. They launch into a relationship and encounter just about every sort of "type" (gay or straight) imaginable, including Stewart (very good as a homosexual interior designer with a biting wit). Paul Rudnick's off-Broadway success works best when going for laughs; the intended poignancy of this very '90s romantic comedy is more forced. Kevin Nealon appears unbilled. [R] ▼▶

Jekyll & Hyde . . . Together Again (1982) **C-87m.** *½ D: Jerry Belson. Mark Blankfield, Bess Armstrong, Krista Errickson, Tim Thomerson, Michael McGuire, George Chakiris. Nothing here that Jerry Lewis's Nutty Professor didn't do better, as Blankfield exaggerates on his druggist character from *Fridays* TV show in tasteless excursion into cheap sex and drug jokes. A few scattered laughs in disappointing directorial debut by veteran comedy writer Belson. [R] ▼▶

Jennifer (1978) **C-90m.** ** D: Brice Mack. Lisa Pelikan, Bert Convy, Nina Foch, Amy Johnston, John Gavin, Jeff Corey, Wesley Eure. Unusually good cast in blatant rip-off of CARRIE, with Pelikan as ostracized high-school girl whose powers include ability to unleash deadly snakes on her victims. Retitled JENNIFER (THE SNAKE GODDESS) for TV. [PG] ▼

Jennifer Eight (1992) **C-127m.** **½ D: Bruce Robinson. Andy Garcia, Uma Thurman, Lance Henriksen, Kathy Baker, Graham Beckel, Kevin Conway, John Malkovich, Perry Lang, Lenny von Dohlen. Taut, entertaining thriller in which burned-out L.A. cop Garcia relocates to a small Northern California town, where he promptly finds himself investigating a series of brutal murders. Will the next victim be beautiful, blind Thurman? Strong performances and eerie snowbound locations are plusses, but credibility dwindles as the story plays out. [R] ▼▶●

Jennifer on My Mind (1971) **C-90m.** BOMB D: Noel Black. Michael Brandon, Tippy Walker, Lou Gilbert, Steve Vinovich, Peter Bonerz, Renee Taylor, Chuck McCann, Barry Bostwick, Jeff Conaway. Probably the worst of many drug films released in the early '70s; rootless American drifter and rich American girl smoke grass in Venice, advance to hard drugs back home. Awful script by Erich Segal; of interest mainly for presence of Robert De Niro, in small, prophetic role of gypsy cab driver. [R]

Jennifer's Body (2009) **C-102m.** ** D: Karyn Kusama. Megan Fox, Amanda Seyfried, Johnny Simmons, Adam Brody, J. K. Simmons, Amy Sedaris, Cynthia Stevenson, Joshua Emerson. Nerdy high school girl's best friend is the student hottie, but after an encounter with a narcissistic rock band she begins acting very, very strange. Could she be involved with a series of murders in which teenage boys have been *eaten*? Attempt to layer horror-movie tropes onto a story of female friendship (and the roles young women inhabit) doesn't work. Written by Diablo Cody, but this teenage outsider isn't as easy to embrace as the heroine of JUNO. Lance Henriksen appears unbilled. Alternate version runs 107m. [R]●

Jennifer (The Snake Goddess) SEE: **Jennifer**

Jenny (1970) **C-88m.** BOMB D: George Bloomfield. Marlo Thomas, Alan Alda, Marian Hailey, Elizabeth Wilson, Vincent Gardenia, Stephen Strimpell. Sappy soaper about filmmaker who marries pregnant girl in order to avoid the draft. Opening scene includes a clip from A PLACE IN THE SUN, which is best thing in film. [M/PG] ▼

Jeopardy (1953) **69m.** **½ D: John Sturges. Barbara Stanwyck, Barry Sullivan, Ralph Meeker, Lee Aaker. Uneven thriller with Stanwyck, on vacation in Mexico, attempting to save husband Sullivan from drowning—and then being kidnapped herself by killer-on-the-lam Meeker. Starts off well, but then fizzles. Paging Alex Trebek!●

Jeremiah Johnson (1972) **C-116m.** *** D: Sydney Pollack. Robert Redford, Will

[717]

Geer, Stefan Gierasch, Allyn Ann McLerie, Charles Tyner, Josh Albee. Atmospheric chronicle of life of a mountain man, surviving wintry wilderness, Indians, rival trappers. Unfortunately, film doesn't know where to quit, rambling on to inconclusive ending. Geer is delightful as feisty mountain hermit. Script by John Milius and Edward Anhalt. Panavision. [PG]▼●)

Jeremy (1973) **C-90m.** ******* D: Arthur Barron. Robby Benson, Glynnis O'Connor, Len Bari, Leonard Cimino, Ned Wilson, Chris Bohn. Two shy teenagers in N.Y.C. meet, fall in love, then separate. Poignant and real; situations, characters, and atmosphere are memorable. [PG]▼)

Jericho SEE: **Dark Sands**

Jerk, The (1979) **C-94m.** ****½** D: Carl Reiner. Steve Martin, Bernadette Peters, Catlin Adams, Mabel King, Richard Ward, Dick Anthony Williams, Bill Macy, Jackie Mason. Martin's first starring feature is a hit-or-miss comedy about the misadventures of a terminally stupid man. Some very funny moments, but after a while they're spread pretty thin. Martin later produced a TV version, THE JERK, TOO. Rob Reiner has an unbilled cameo. [R]▼●)

Jerky Boys, The (1995) **C-82m.** ***½** D: James Melkonian. John G. Brennan, Kamal Ahmed, Alan Arkin, William Hickey, Alan North, Brad Sullivan, James Lorinz. Crank-call practitioners (who in real life had a hit record in N.Y.C.) who describe themselves as "two low-lifes from Queens" palm themselves off as Chicago hit men, thoroughly confusing N.Y. mobster Arkin. Result may appeal to the type of person who enjoys vandalizing suburban mailboxes. [R]▼●

Jerrico, The Wonder Clown SEE: **3 Ring Circus**

Jerry and Tom (1999) **C-92m.** ****** D: Saul Rubinek. Joe Mantegna, Sam Rockwell, Maury Chaykin, Ted Danson, Charles Durning, William H. Macy, Peter Riegert, Sarah Polley. Flashback film about a couple of hit men: a mentor and his protégé. A fine cast fires expectations, but despite some good moments, the film never really delivers. Rubinek's first directing effort debuted on U.S. cable. [R]▼)

Jerry Maguire (1996) **C-138m.** *****½** D: Cameron Crowe. Tom Cruise, Cuba Gooding, Jr., Renée Zellweger, Kelly Preston, Jerry O'Connell, Jay Mohr, Bonnie Hunt, Regina King, Jonathan Lipnicki, Glenn Frey, Eric Stoltz, Jann Wenner, Alexandra Wentworth, Lucy Alexis Liu. Cocky, super-successful sports agent has a crisis of conscience, which costs him his job and all but one of his clients—the most difficult one on the roster (Gooding, in a charismatic, Oscar-winning performance). His only ally is a young woman (with a little boy) who's devoted to him professionally and personally. Intelligent, original, layered screenplay

(by Crowe) with characters who are actually interesting and three-dimensional. Cruise's earnestness is perfect for the part, and Zellweger is a real find. Various sports figures play themselves; Beau Bridges appears unbilled. Only complaint: It goes on too long. Some prints have a *faux* athletic shoe commercial at the end. [R]▼●)

Jersey Girl (2004) **C-102m.** ***½** D: Kevin Smith. Ben Affleck, Liv Tyler, Jennifer Lopez, George Carlin, Jason Biggs, Raquel Castro, Mike Starr, Stephen Root, Jason Lee, Matt Damon, Will Smith. High-powered music-industry publicist is shattered by his wife's death in childbirth and moves back to his father's house in New Jersey to raise his daughter and lick his wounds . . . until he meets a free-spirited video-store clerk (Tyler) who shakes him out of his stupor. Ultra-sentimental modern-day fairy tale is false and hollow—and played that way by everyone but Tyler. Writer-director Smith's most atypical movie to date—and his worst. Panavision. [PG-13]▼)

Jerusalem (1996-Swedish-Danish) **C-166m.** ****½** D: Bille August. Maria Bonnevie, Ulf Friberg, Lena Endre, Pernilla August, Sven-Bertil Taube, Reine Brynolfsson, Olympia Dukakis, Max von Sydow. In late 19th-century Sweden, a poor, rural community is swept up in religious fervor; the town becomes bitterly divided, separating a pair of young sweethearts (Friberg, Bonnevie). When the converted emigrate to a Christian commune in Palestine, led by American Dukakis, they find new strife and strain. Long, fact-based epic (from Selma Lagerlof's novel) is earnest to a fault. Made for Swedish TV. [PG-13]▼

Jesse James (1939) **C-105m.** ******* D: Henry King. Tyrone Power, Henry Fonda, Nancy Kelly, Randolph Scott, Henry Hull, Brian Donlevy, John Carradine, Jane Darwell. Sprawling, glamorous Western with Power and Fonda as Jesse and Frank James; movie builds a case that the Old West's most notorious outlaw was misguided. Shot in Missouri. Sequel: THE RETURN OF FRANK JAMES. ▼●)

Jesse James Meets Frankenstein's Daughter (1966) **C-88m.** ***½** D: William Beaudine. John Lupton, Narda Onyx, Cal Bolder, Estelita, Jim Davis, Steven Geray, William Fawcett. Low-budget nonsense mixes horror and Western genres, with Dr. Frankenstein's daughter practicing brain experiments—including turning Jesse's pal into a new monster. ▼)

Jesus (1979) **C-117m.** ****½** D: Peter Sykes, John Krish. Brian Deacon, Rivka Noiman, Yossef Shiloah, Niko Nitai, Gadi Roi, David Goldberg; narrated by Alexander Scourby. Straightforward but unmemorable retelling of Jesus' life, produced by The Genesis Project; filmed in Israel. [G]▼)

Jesus Camp (2006) **C-87m.** ******* D: Heidi Ewing, Rachel Grady. Fascinating and frightening look at the evangelical movement as seen through the eyes of three kids from Missouri who spend the summer at a camp for future Jerry Falwells. Artfully shows the indoctrination of children with ideas about politics and religion at an early age, demonstrating how the movement plans to spread its word to future generations. Curriculum includes lectures on the evils of homosexuality and abortion and the importance of working toward a Supreme Court populated by "believers." [PG-13]▶

Jesus Christ Superstar (1973) **C-103m.** *** D: Norman Jewison. Ted Neeley, Carl Anderson, Yvonne Elliman, Barry Dennen, Joshua Mostel, Bob Bingham. From record album to Broadway show to motion picture—film retains the Tim Rice–Andrew Lloyd Webber score, adds some interesting settings and visual trappings. It's not everyone's cup of religious experience, but certainly innovative. Watch for ubiquitous porno star Paul Thomas in the chorus. Todd-AO 35. [G]▼●)

Jesus of Montreal (1989-Canadian-French) **C-119m.** ***½ D: Denys Arcand. Lothaire Bluteau, Catherine Wilkening, Johanne-Marie Tremblay, Remy Girard, Robert Lepage, Gilles Pelletier, Marie-Christine Barrault. A group of actors come together to stage an unconventional production of the Passion Play, and find themselves embroiled in controversy. Writer-director Arcand takes on religious hypocrisy, commercialism, and other social ills in this wise, profoundly moving and sometimes savagely funny film. A real gem. Arcand also appears in the role of the judge. [R]▼●)

Jesus' Son (1998-Canadian) **C-109m.** ** D: Alison Maclean. Billy Crudup, Samantha Morton, Denis Leary, Jack Black, Will Patton, Greg Germann, Holly Hunter, Dennis Hopper, Mike (Michael) Shannon, Miranda July. A stream-of-consciousness reminiscence by one young man who's swallowed up in the drug culture of the 1970s. Told in nonlinear flashback style, with vignettes involving a variety of characters who cross his path (played by Leary, Hopper, Hunter). Main problem: it's hard to care about the leading character. Based on Denis Johnson's acclaimed collection of short stories. Super 35. [R]▼▶

Jet Lag (2002-French-British) **C-82m.** **½ D: Danièle Thompson. Juliette Binoche, Jean Reno, Sergi López. A beautician and a chef meet randomly during an airport layover and over the course of 24 hours fall in love. Featherweight romance is just an excuse to see two star performers at the height of their charm . . . but what's wrong with that? Veteran screenwriter Thompson (COUSIN, COUSINE, QUEEN MARGOT) cowrote with her son Christopher. Super 35. [R]▼▶

Jet Li's Fearless (2006-Hong Kong-Chinese-

U.S.) **C-103m.** *** D: Ronny Yu. Jet Li, Shido Nakamura, Li Sun, Yong Dong, Hee Ching Paw, Nathan Jones, Brandon Rhea, Anthony De Longis. Li apparently caps his career in this genre playing martial arts legend Huo Yuanjia, China's most famous fighter at the turn of the 20th century, who nearly dies in a tragic incident in which he loses most of his family. In time he returns to the ring and is pitted against four imposing fighters who represent the major foreign powers dominating China at that time. Emotionally charged and visually striking; Li shows why he is a master of the art. Unrated version runs 104m. Aka FEARLESS. Super 35. [PG-13]▶

Jet Li's Hero SEE: **Hero** (2002)

Jet Pilot (1957) **C-112m.** ** D: Josef von Sternberg. John Wayne, Janet Leigh, Jay C. Flippen, Paul Fix, Richard Rober, Roland Winters, Hans Conried. One of Howard Hughes' movie curios, updating his HELL'S ANGELS interest in aviation with cold war theme, as American pilot Wayne falls in love with Russian jet ace Leigh. Ridiculous, to say the least, though some of its humor seems to have been intentional. Completed in 1950, unreleased for seven years! Incidentally, some of the stunt flying was done by Chuck Yeager.▼●)

Jetsons: The Movie (1990) **C-81m.** ** D: William Hanna, Joseph Barbera. Voices of George O'Hanlon, Penny Singleton, Mel Blanc, Tiffany, Don Messick, Patric Zimmerman. Disappointing expansion of the 1960s animated TV sitcom has nothing to offer now-grown-up fans of the series, but remains a palatable offering for very young children, with pro-social messages thrown in at the end. [G]▼●

Je Vous Aime (1981-French) **C-105m.** *½ D: Claude Berri. Catherine Deneuve, Jean-Louis Trintignant, Gérard Depardieu, Alain Souchon, Christian Marquand, Serge Gainsbourg. Shallow, solemn tale of liberated career woman Deneuve, who is unable to remain monogamous. Good cast can do little with material; disappointing.

Jeweller's Shop, The (1987-Italian-Canadian) **C-97m.** ** D: Michael Anderson. Burt Lancaster, Ben Cross, Olivia Hussey, Andrea Occhipinti. Lancaster is a mysterious old Polish jeweler at the start of WW2 who brings together two pairs of lovers. Of particular interest both as one of the star's last film appearances and for the fact that it's based on a play by Karol Wojtyla, who later became Pope John Paul II. Aka THE GOLDSMITH'S SHOP.

Jewel of the Nile, The (1985) **C-104m.** ** D: Lewis Teague. Michael Douglas, Kathleen Turner, Danny DeVito, Spiros Focas, Avner Eisenberg, The Flying Karamazov Brothers. Contrived "high adventure" involving an evil potentate and a precious "jewel." Sequel to ROMANCING THE

STONE can't capture charm of original, because the characters are set—and character change (particularly Turner's) is what made the first movie fun. Some good stunts and funny lines, but it all rings hollow. Widescreen. [PG]▼●◗

Jezebel (1938) 103m. ***½ D: William Wyler. Bette Davis, Henry Fonda, George Brent, Margaret Lindsay, Donald Crisp, Fay Bainter, Spring Byington, Richard Cromwell, Henry O'Neill. Davis won her second Oscar as tempestuous Southern belle who goes too far to make fiancé Fonda jealous; Bainter also received Oscar as Davis' sympathetic aunt. Fine production, entire cast excellent. John Huston was one of the writers. Also shown in computer-colored version. ▼●◗

Jezebels, The SEE: **Switchblade Sisters**

JFK (1991) **C/B&W-188m.** ***½ D: Oliver Stone. Kevin Costner, Sissy Spacek, Kevin Bacon, Tommy Lee Jones, Laurie Metcalf, Gary Oldman, Michael Rooker, Jay O. Sanders, Beata Pozniak, Joe Pesci, Donald Sutherland, John Candy, Jack Lemmon, Walter Matthau, Ed Asner, Vincent D'Onofrio, Sally Kirkland, Brian Doyle-Murray, Wayne Knight, Tony Plana, Tomas Milian, Sean Stone. Absolutely riveting film about New Orleans D.A. Jim Garrison and his gradual involvement (and eventual obsession) with finding the truth about President Kennedy's assassination. Full of startling scenes, and bravura acting; as dramatic moviemaking, it's superb. Not to be mistaken for a documentary, however, despite its sanctimonious attitude toward the truth. Oscar winner for Robert Richardson's cinematography and Joe Hutshing and Pietro Scalia's phenomenal editing. Screenplay by Oliver Stone and Zachary Sklar. The real Garrison can be glimpsed playing Earl Warren. Lolita Davidovich and Frank Whaley appear unbilled. Director's cut runs 205m. Panavision. [R]▼●◗

Jigsaw (1968) **C-97m.** **½ D: James Goldstone. Harry Guardino, Bradford Dillman, Hope Lange, Pat Hingle, Diana Hyland, Victor Jory, Paul Stewart, Susan Saint James, Michael J. Pollard, James Doohan, Kent McCord. Fast-paced, utterly confusing yarn about amnesiac Dillman trying to figure out his past and unravel murder caper he was involved in. Frantic editing and music don't help viewer; remake of MIRAGE. Made for TV but shown theatrically first.

Jigsaw Man, The (1984-British) **C-91m.** ** D: Terence Young. Michael Caine, Laurence Olivier, Susan George, Robert Powell, Charles Gray, Michael Medwin. Caine, an ex-British Secret Service honcho who defected to Russia, comes back to England (following rejuvenating plastic surgery) for one final mission. Will he serve one country, the other, or play both ends against the middle? Unfortunately this Caine-Olivier pairing is no SLEUTH, so you won't care. [PG]▼●

Jim Buck SEE: **Portrait of a Hitman**

Jimi Hendrix (1973) **C-102m.** **½ D: Joe Boyd, John Head, Gary Weis. Documentary on life of noted black rock guitarist; good segments from various concerts, interviews with those who knew him well. Songs include "Purple Haze," "Wild Thing," "Johnny B. Goode." [R]▼◗

Jiminy Glick in La La Wood (2005-Canadian) **C-90m.** ** D: Vadim Jean. Martin Short, Jan Hooks, John Michael Higgins, Elizabeth Perkins, Linda Cardellini, Janeane Garofalo, Corey Pearson, Peter Breck. Ill-conceived extension of *Primetime Glick*, Short's TV series, in which he plays a character introduced on *The Martin Short Show*: a thickheaded, roly-poly celebrity interviewer-critic from Butte, Montana. Here, Jiminy and his family attend the Toronto Film Festival and become involved in a complicated murder plot. Film buffs will enjoy Short's impersonation of David Lynch, and Jiminy is always hilarious, but he and guest star Steve Martin provide the only bright spots in this painfully unfunny comedy. Other stars appear on camera, caught at the Toronto festivities. [R]◗

Jimmy Carter: Man from Plains (2007) **C-126m.** *** D: Jonathan Demme. Intimate documentary portrait of the former U.S. president follows him on his 2006–07 book tour for *Palestine: Peace Not Apartheid*, in which he stresses that a Middle East peace only will come when the Israelis and Palestinians agree to live in harmony. Compelling account of Carter's life since leaving office in 1981. [PG]◗

Jimmy Hollywood (1994) **C-109m.** ** D: Barry Levinson. Joe Pesci, Christian Slater, Victoria Abril, Jason Beghe, John Cothran, Jr., Rob Weiss, Chad McQueen. Well-meaning but one-note tale of hard-luck middle-aged dreamer Pesci, a would-be actor who earns fame by playing out the role of a lifetime: Jericho, an urban vigilante. Obvious look at life in seedy, contemporary Hollywood, which once was a "mecca of dreams." Pesci is good, but his character quickly becomes wearying. Watch for director Levinson at the finale. Levinson also scripted. [R] ▼●◗

Jimmy Neutron: Boy Genius (2001) **C-83m.** **½ D: John A. Davis. Voices of Megan Cavanagh, Mark DeCarlo, Debi Derryberry, Patrick Stewart, Martin Short, Rob Paulsen, David L. Lander, Laraine Newman, Andrea Martin, Mary Hart, Bob Goen. Clever computer-generated cartoon produced by Nickelodeon. When a young inventor inadvertently causes alien invaders to kidnap all the parents in the neighborhood, it's up to him and his classmates to travel through space and mount a rescue. Cute kids' film with plenty of visual and verbal humor, but lavish settings (particularly in outer space) clash with weak character designs and low-budget animation. Followed by a TV series. [G]▼▶

Jimmy the Gent (1934) **67m.** **½ D: Michael Curtiz. James Cagney, Bette Davis, Alice White, Allen Jenkins, Philip Reed, Mayo Methot. Crooked businessman Cagney pretends to refine himself to impress Davis in this bouncy comedy.▶

Jimmy the Kid (1983) **C-85m.** *½ D: Gary Nelson. Gary Coleman, Paul LeMat, Walter Olkewicz, Dee Wallace, Ruth Gordon, Don Adams, Cleavon Little, Avery Schreiber. Bored, brilliant son of wealthy husband-and-wife singing team is kidnapped by gang of pathetically incompetent bunglers who teach him how to enjoy being a kid. Coleman returns favor by bringing good cast down to his level of nonacting, consisting of endless mugging and exaggerated eyeball rolling, in this lame comedy. Based on a Donald Westlake novel, with LeMat as the same character played by Robert Redford in THE HOT ROCK. [PG]▼

Jim Thorpe—All-American (1951) **107m.** **½ D: Michael Curtiz. Burt Lancaster, Charles Bickford, Steve Cochran, Phyllis Thaxter, Dick Wesson. The life of the famed American Indian athlete who was stripped of his Olympic medals for playing professional baseball. Lancaster lends dignified vigor to title role; Bickford is especially outstanding as Thorpe's mentor, legendary coach Pop Warner.▼●▮

Jindabyne (2006-Australian) **C-123m.** *** D: Ray Lawrence. Laura Linney, Gabriel Byrne, Deborra-lee Furness, John Howard, Leah Purcell, Stelios Yiakmis, Simon Stone, Betty Lucas. Gas station owner (Byrne) and three pals take off for an annual fishing weekend at a remote spot where there isn't cell phone reception. They come upon a woman's dead body floating in the river, and while they're shocked they figure there's nothing they can do to help her, so they continue fishing. That decision has unexpected repercussions not only with their families but with the community at large. Absorbing, multifaceted drama flavored by aboriginal mysticism. Based on Raymond Carver's story "So Much Water So Close To Home," which was also dramatized in Robert Altman's SHORT CUTS. Super 35. [R]▶

Jingle All the Way (1996) **C-88m.** ** D: Brian Levant. Arnold Schwarzenegger, Sinbad, Phil Hartman, Rita Wilson, Robert Conrad, Martin Mull, James Belushi, Harvey Korman, Laraine Newman, Jake Lloyd. Neglectful father promises his son a Turbo Man action figure, then frantically searches to find the sold-out toy the day before Christmas. His chief rival in the search (Sinbad) turns out to be not just a competitor but a major sicko. Even at 88 minutes this feels prolonged and protracted, a dubious '90s addition to the canon of holiday movies. Arnold gives it his best, but he simply isn't funny. [PG]▼●▮

Jinnah (1998-U.S.-Pakistani-British) **C-94m.** *** D: Jamil Dehlavi. Christopher Lee, James Fox, Maria Aitkin, Shashi Kapoor, Shireen Shah, Richard Lintern, Robert Ashby, Sam Dastor. Lee is outstanding as the dedicated, brittle and reserved Mohammed Ali Jinnah, founder of Pakistan, in this odd biography in which, on the verge of death, he's shown the events of his past in Ebenezer Scrooge style. Fox, Ashby, and Dastor are also fine as Mountbatten, Nehru, and Gandhi. A worthwhile, intelligent movie that deserves, like its subject, to be better known.▼

Jinxed! (1982) **C-103m.** ** D: Don Siegel. Bette Midler, Ken Wahl, Rip Torn, Val Avery, Jack Elam, Benson Fong. Messy black comedy about a Vegas lounge singer, the lout she lives with, and a young blackjack dealer the lout has managed to jinx at his own table. Though a characteristically ripped Rip provides some amusement, the much-reported lack of rapport between Midler/Wahl and Midler/Siegel comes through on the screen. Screenwriter "Bert Blessing" is really Frank D. Gilroy. [R]▼▶

J-Men Forever! (1979) **75m.** *** D: Richard Patterson. Philip Proctor, Peter Bergman; voice of M. G. Kelly. Clever stunt that really works—scenes from countless Republic serials are re-edited into new feature, with redubbed soundtrack and a few new scenes. Story (by Firesign Theatre's Proctor and Bergman) has The Lightning Bug ("From the Moon, Baby!") out to conquer Earth by flooding radio airwaves with rock; various heroes try to make the world safe for Lawrence Welk. Amazing job of editing by Gail Werbin; one great gag involves a young Leonard Nimoy. [PG]▼▶

Joanna (1968-British) **C-107m.** **½ D: Michael Sarne. Genevieve Waite, Christian Doermer, Calvin Lockhart, Donald Sutherland, Glenna Forster-Jones. Flashy story of wide-eyed girl falling in with loose-living London crowd, growing up through heartbreak, conflict. Sutherland steals film in flamboyant role as frail, wealthy young man trying to enjoy life to fullest. Panavision. [R]

Joan of Arc (1948) **C-100m.** **½ D: Victor Fleming. Ingrid Bergman, Jose Ferrer, Francis L. Sullivan, J. Carrol Naish, Ward Bond, Shepperd Strudwick, Hurd Hatfield, Gene Lockhart, John Emery, Cecil Kellaway, George Coulouris, John Ireland. Bergman is staunchly sincere in this overlong, faithful adaptation of Maxwell Anderson's play. Not enough spectacle to balance talky sequences. Originally released theatrically at 145m.▼●▮

Joan Rivers: A Piece of Work (2010) **C-84m.** *** D: Ricki Stern, Annie Sundberg. Veteran stand-up comic Rivers proves to be the hardest-working woman in show business, at the age of 75. By following her for the better part of a year, the filmmakers show us what drives her and explore what shaped her psyche and her incredible neediness. Rivers' remarkable candor makes this a fascinating portrait, but the foundation of her career (and this documentary) remains the fact that she is consistently, often brutally funny. One comes away with new, or renewed, respect for her. [R] ▶

Jocks (1987) **C-91m.** *½ D: Steve Carver. Scott Strader, Perry Lang, Mariska Hargitay, Richard Roundtree, R. G. Armstrong, Christopher Lee, Stoney Jackson, Adam Mills, Katherine Kelly Lang, Trinidad Silva, Don Gibb. Silly teen comedy of college tennis team's hijinx in Las Vegas. Despite oddball roles for vets Lee and Armstrong, picture only comes to life on the tennis court. Filmed in 1984. [R] ▼▶

Joe (1970) **C-107m.** **½ D: John G. Avildsen. Peter Boyle, Dennis Patrick, K. Callan, Audrey Caire, Susan Sarandon, Patrick McDermott. Sleeper film brought Boyle to prominence as hardhat bigot who practices genteel blackmail on executive Patrick, who's murdered his daughter's hippie boyfriend. Overrated film owes much to Boyle's characterization, not to contrived plot. Sarandon's film debut. [R] ▼●▶

Joe Cocker: Mad Dogs and Englishmen (1971-British) **C-119m.** *** D: Pierre Adidge. Joe Cocker, Leon Russell, Chris Stainton, Carl Radle, John Price, Bobby Keys, Rita Coolidge, Claudia Linnear. Excellent rockumentary of Cocker's '70 American tour, highlighted by Cocker, Russell, and Linnear in performance. Songs include "Feelin' Alright," "With a Little Help from My Friends," "Darlin' Be Home Soon," many others. Aka MAD DOGS AND ENGLISHMEN. Multiple Screen. [PG] ▼▶

Joe Dirt (2001) **C-91m.** *½ D: Dennie Gordon. David Spade, Dennis Miller, Brittany Daniel, Adam Beach, Kid Rock, Jaime Pressly, Christopher Walken, Caroline Aaron, Fred Ward. One would need more than a spade to dig up laughs in this mucky saga of a white-trash loser with a big heart and an even bigger mullet hairdo who's on a quest to find the parents who ditched him when he was eight. Charming comic bits involve frozen animal testicles, incest, excrement, vomit, and the amputation of limbs. Joe Don Baker, Rosanna Arquette, Kevin Nealon, and Carson Daly all appear sans credit, while Walken (as tap-dancing janitor Gert E. Frobe) may wish he had done the same. [PG-13] ▼▶

Joe Gould's Secret (2000) **C-104m.** *** D: Stanley Tucci. Ian Holm, Stanley Tucci, Patricia Clarkson, Hope Davis, Steve Martin, Susan Sarandon, Patrick Tovatt, Celia Weston, Allan Corduner. *New Yorker* profile writer Joseph Mitchell (Tucci) is introduced to "the king of the Bohemians," street savant Joe Gould (Holm), and becomes fascinated (and sucked in) by this bombastic Greenwich Village habitue. Notable for its loving re-creation of 1940s N.Y.C. and the world that Mitchell documented so vividly. Holm is simply superb. Screenplay by Howard A. Rodman. [R] ▼▶

Joe Hill (1971-Swedish) **C-114m.** *** D: Bo Widerberg. Thommy Berggren, Ania Schmidt, Kelvin Malave, Everl Anderson, Cathy Smith. Fabricated story of legendary labor leader has usual Widerberg matter-of-taste glossiness, but also some affecting scenes and pleasant performances. Joan Baez sings title song. [PG]

Joe Kidd (1972) **C-88m.** ** D: John Sturges. Clint Eastwood, Robert Duvall, John Saxon, Don Stroud, Stella Garcia, James Wainwright. Eastwood is hired to hunt down some Mexican-Americans by land baron Duvall in ordinary Western; nice photography and a rousing scene where Eastwood drives a train through a barroom. Written by Elmore Leonard. Panavision. [PG] ▼●▶

Joe Panther (1976) **C-110m.** *** D: Paul Krasny. Brian Keith, Ricardo Montalban, Alan Feinstein, Cliff Osmond, A Martinez, Ray Tracey. Good family film about modern-day Seminole youth (Tracey) striving to make his way in the white man's world. [G] ▼

Joe's Apartment (1996) **C-80m.** **½ D: John Payson. Jerry O'Connell, Megan Ward, Robert Vaughn, Don Ho, Shiek Mahmud-Bey, Jim Sterling, Sandra Denton, Toukie Smith, Scott "Bam Bam" Bigelow, Paul Bartel; voices of Billy West, Reginald Hudlin, Dave Chappelle, B. D. Wong. Joe (O'Connell) lives in a N.Y.C. slum apartment infested by thousands of singing, dancing, and talking cockroaches, who help him defeat the schemes of his evil landlord (Don Ho). To put it mildly, not for all tastes, but if you can handle break-dancing vermin, the effects are excellent, the musical numbers inventive, and the whole thing harmlessly silly. Written by the director. Based on a short that first aired on MTV in 1992. [PG-13] ▼●▶

Joe Somebody (2001) **C-98m.** **½ D: John Pasquin. Tim Allen, Julie Bowen, Kelly Lynch, Hayden Panettiere, Jim Belushi, Greg Germann, Robert Joy, Patrick Warburton. Beaten-down corporate worker finally stands up for his rights by fighting with a bully in the company parking lot—and discovers that he suddenly has the attention, and respect, of coworkers who never noticed him before. Allen is good in his comedic everyman role, but the concept is hazy and underdeveloped. [PG] ▼▶

Joe Strummer: The Future Is Unwritten (2007-Irish-British) **C-125m.** *** D: Julien Temple. Compelling documentary traces the life and death of Clash front man, showing his vast influence both musically and personally on those around him. Employing Super 8 home movies, photos, and current interviews (with everyone from Bono to Johnny Depp), Temple presents a telling portrait of a pioneering musician from his childhood influences to his heyday in the late '70s and '80s to his latter-day life as a star, husband, and father. Musical sequences are superbly chosen and edited in this worthwhile look at a true rock music legend.▐

Joe the King (1999) **C-83m.** **✻✻** D: Frank Whaley. Noah Fleiss, Val Kilmer, Karen Young, Ethan Hawke, John Leguizamo, Austin Pendleton, Max Ligosh, James Costa, Camryn Manheim, Amy Wright. A 14-year-old boy's life is one long, losing battle. With a drunken, irresponsible father (Kilmer) and an absentee mother (Young), he's descended into a life of theft and antisocial behavior. He's not really a bad kid, but there is no relief, and certainly no hope, in sight for him. Actor Whaley's writing-directing debut is a vivid portrait of working-class life, but is so dismal it might be retitled THE 800 BLOWS. [R]▼▐

Joe Versus the Volcano (1990) **C-102m.** **✻✻½** D: John Patrick Shanley. Tom Hanks, Meg Ryan, Lloyd Bridges, Robert Stack, Dan Hedaya, Abe Vigoda, Ossie Davis, Barry McGovern, Amanda Plummer, Carol Kane, Nathan Lane. Pleasant if pointless fable about a stressed-out nerd who learns he has six months to live, and accepts an eccentric millionaire's offer to enable him to live like a king—so long as he jumps into a volcano at the end of his "vacation." Unfortunately, the story also takes a dive. Writer Shanley's directorial debut turns out to be a shaggy-dog story that doesn't pay off. However, it *is* fun watching Ryan play three distinctively different women . . . and remember, luggage is everything. Panavision. [PG]▼●▐

Joey (1985) **C-97m.** **✻✻** D: Joseph Ellison. Neill Barry, James Quinn, Elisa Heinsohn, Linda Thorson, Ellen Hammill, Dan Grimaldi, Frankie Lanz. Hokey but harmless ode to Oldies and Doo Wop, chronicling the troubled personal life of teen rock musician Barry and his relationship with his dad (Quinn), who used to turn out hit records but now toils in a gas station and drinks away his paycheck. Otherwise minor item features cameo appearances by The Limelights (who perform "Daddy's Home"), Silhouettes ("Get a Job"), Ad-Libs ("Boy From New York City"), Elegants ("Little Star"), Screamin' Jay Hawkins ("I Put a Spell on You") and, fleetingly, Jimmy Merchant and Herman Santiago, the only surviving Teenagers ("Why Do Fools Fall in Love?"). [PG]▼

Joey Breaker (1993) **C-92m.** **✻✻½** D: Steven Starr. Richard Edson, Cedella Marley, Fred Fondren, Erik King, Gina Gershon, Philip Seymour Hoffman, Michael Imperioli, Parker Posey. Astute, candid, but too often dramatically static portrait of a suave, self-absorbed N.Y. talent agent (Edson),

and how his consciousness is raised. Marley (the daughter of Bob Marley) plays the romantic interest, a Jamaican nursing student. Starr, an ex-William Morris agent, also scripted and coproduced. [R]▼

John and Mary (1969) **C-92m.** **✻✻½** D: Peter Yates. Dustin Hoffman, Mia Farrow, Michael Tolan, Sunny Griffin, Stanley Beck, Tyne Daly, Alix Elias, Marian Mercer, Olympia Dukakis, Cleavon Little, Kristoffer Tabori. John and Mary meet, make love, but don't know if the relationship should end right there. Innocuous, uncompelling trifle. Hoffman seems to be sleepwalking; audience may join him. Panavision. [PG—originally rated R]▐

John Carpenter's Escape From L.A. SEE: **Escape From L.A.**

John Carpenter's Ghosts of Mars SEE: **Ghosts of Mars**

John Carpenter's Vampires SEE: **Vampires**

John Goldfarb, Please Come Home (1965) **C-96m.** **✻½** D: J. Lee Thompson. Shirley MacLaine, Peter Ustinov, Richard Crenna, Scott Brady, Jim Backus, Charles Lane, Jerome Cowan, Wilfrid Hyde-White, Fred Clark, Harry Morgan, Telly Savalas, Richard Deacon, Jackie Coogan, Jerome (Jerry) Orbach, Barbara Bouchet. Trapped in desert kingdom, two Americans (pilot, woman reporter) conspire to help Arabian chief Ustinov's football team beat Notre Dame. Notre Dame University found this spoof so offensive it sued in court; the viewer has an easier alternative. Screenplay by William Peter Blatty. Look for Teri Garr. CinemaScope.

John Grisham's The Rainmaker SEE: **Rainmaker, The** (1997)

John Loves Mary (1949) **96m.** **✻✻½** D: David Butler. Ronald Reagan, Jack Carson, Patricia Neal, Wayne Morris, Edward Arnold, Virginia Field. Genial adaptation of Norman Krasna's Broadway hit about a soldier (Reagan) who does his pal a favor by marrying the fellow's British girlfriend, so she can come to the U.S.—intending to get divorce upon arrival. Naive fluff was Neal's film debut.▼▐

Johnny Be Good (1988) **C-84m.** BOMB D: Bud Smith. Anthony Michael Hall, Robert Downey, Jr., Paul Gleason, Uma Thurman, Steve James, Seymour Cassel, Howard Cosell, Jim McMahon, Robert Downey, Sr., Jennifer Tilly. Offensive, bottom-of-the-barrel comedy about star high-school jock Hall and how various colleges attempt to illegally recruit him. The seriousness of the issue completely eludes the makers of this turkey. R-rated scenes were added for homevideo version. [PG-13—later reedited to R]▼●▐

Johnny Belinda (1948) **103m.** **✻✻✻½** D: Jean Negulesco. Jane Wyman, Lew Ayres, Charles Bickford, Jan Sterling, Agnes Moorehead, Stephen McNally, Rosalind Ivan, Alan Napier, Dan Seymour. Sensitively acted, atmospheric drama of young deaf-mute girl (Wyman) and doctor (Ayres) who works with her. Setting of provincial fishing-farming community vividly realized. Wyman won an Oscar for her fine performance. Elmer Harris's play was scripted by Irmgard von Cube and Allen Vincent. Remade for TV in 1982 with Rosanna Arquette. Also shown in computer-colored version. ▼▶

Johnny Concho (1956) 84m. **½ D: Don McGuire. Frank Sinatra, Keenan Wynn, William Conrad, Phyllis Kirk, Wallace Ford, Dorothy Adams, Jean Byron, Claude Akins, John Qualen. Plodding Western with novelty of Sinatra as cowardly soul who must build courage for inevitable shoot-out. Adapted from a *Studio One* TV play.

Johnny Cool (1963) 101m. *** D: William Asher. Henry Silva, Elizabeth Montgomery, Sammy Davis, Jr., Richard Anderson, Jim Backus, Wanda Hendrix, Brad Dexter, Joey Bishop, Marc Lawrence, John McGiver, Mort Sahl, Telly Savalas, Elisha Cook, Jr. Sadistic study of vicious gangster seeking revenge. Brutal account, realistically told.▶

Johnny Dangerously (1984) C-90m. *½ D: Amy Heckerling. Michael Keaton, Joe Piscopo, Marilu Henner, Maureen Stapleton, Peter Boyle, Griffin Dunne, Richard Dimitri, Glynnis O'Connor, Byron Thames, Danny DeVito, Dom DeLuise, Ray Walston, Sudie Bond. Lame comedy about Prohibition-era gangsters; looks like a TV show and plays that way, too, with scattershot jokes (only a few of them funny) instead of a script. [PG-13]▼▶

Johnny Eager (1941) 107m. *** D: Mervyn LeRoy. Robert Taylor, Lana Turner, Edward Arnold, Van Heflin, Robert Sterling, Patricia Dane, Glenda Farrell, Barry Nelson. Slick MGM melodrama with convoluted plot about sociology student (and daughter of D.A. Arnold) Turner falling in love with unscrupulous racketeer Taylor. Heflin won Best Supporting Actor Oscar as Taylor's alcoholic friend.▼▶

Johnny English (2003-British-U.S.) C-86m. *** D: Peter Howitt. Rowan Atkinson, John Malkovich, Natalie Imbruglia, Ben Miller, Douglas McFerran, Tim Pigott-Smith, Kevin McNally, Greg Wise. Very funny James Bond spoof with Atkinson as a hopelessly clumsy office functionary who gets to live out his fantasy and become a secret agent. His adversary: a wily French criminal named Pascal Sauvage, played with brio by Malkovich. Atkinson is in prime form in this engagingly silly sight-gag comedy. Based on a series of British TV commercials from the 1990s. [PG]▼▶

Johnny Got His Gun (1971) C-111m. ** D: Dalton Trumbo. Timothy Bottoms, Kathy Fields, Marsha Hunt, Jason Robards, Donald Sutherland, Diane Varsi, David Soul, Tony Geary. Morbid film version of Trumbo's novel about WW1 basket case has moving opening and climax, but everything in the middle is either talky, pretentious, or amateurish. [PG]▼▶

Johnny Guitar (1954) C-110m. ***½ D: Nicholas Ray. Joan Crawford, Sterling Hayden, Scott Brady, Mercedes McCambridge, Ward Bond, Ben Cooper, Ernest Borgnine, Royal Dano, John Carradine, Paul Fix, Frank Ferguson. The screen's great kinky Western, a memorable confrontation between saloonkeeper Crawford and righteous hellion McCambridge, who wants her run out of town and/or hanged. Simply fascinating with symbolism rampant throughout. Script by Philip Yordan. Later a stage musical. ▼▶

Johnny Handsome (1989) C-94m. ** D: Walter Hill. Mickey Rourke, Ellen Barkin, Elizabeth McGovern, Morgan Freeman, Forest Whitaker, Lance Henriksen, Scott Wilson, Blake Clark. Disfigured Rourke is imprisoned after his abandonment by fellow lowlifes during a heist; a doctor then proposes performing plastic surgery on his features, hoping to lower his recidivism potential. Eccentric, to say the least, and not totally without interest given the cast, but eventually wears out its welcome. Given Rourke's standard appearance, this must be the only skull surgery ever performed without benefit of a shampoo. [R]▼▶●

Johnny in the Clouds SEE: Way to the Stars, The

Johnny Mnemonic (1995-Canadian) C-98m. *½ D: Robert Longo. Keanu Reeves, Dolph Lundgren, Takeshi, Ice-T, Dina Meyer, Udo Kier, Denis Akiyama, Henry Rollins, Tracy Tweed, Don Francks. In the very ugly future of 2021, a world-weary courier (who carries info in his head) takes one final run from Beijing to Newark, his storage capacity dangerously overloaded with volatile data sought by a huge, ruthless corporation. Intriguing premise, written by William Gibson and directed by artist Longo, goes absolutely nowhere, as uninteresting characters mouth laughable dialogue against a landscape of urban hell. Despite the computer graphics, this is cyberclaptrap. Runs about 15m. longer in Japan. [R] ▼▶●

Johnny O'Clock (1947) 95m. **½ D: Robert Rossen. Dick Powell, Evelyn Keyes, Lee J. Cobb, Ellen Drew, Nina Foch, Jeff Chandler. Cast and director make script about high-class gambler in trouble with the law seem better than it is; Powell is fine in lead role.

Johnny Reno (1966) C-83m. BOMB D: R.G. Springsteen. Dana Andrews, Jane Russell, Lon Chaney (Jr.), John Agar, Lyle Bettger, Tom Drake, Richard Arlen, Robert Lowery. Laughably clichéd Western has Marshal Andrews trying to save accused killer from lynching. Only for buffs who want to play "spot the star." Techniscope.▼◗

Johnny Stecchino (1991-Italian) **C-100m.** *** D: Roberto Benigni. Roberto Benigni, Nicoletta Braschi, Paolo Bonacelli, Ignazio Pappalardo, Franco Volpi. A mild and meek school bus driver is the spitting image of a notorious gangster—Johnny Stecchino ("Toothpick"). When the latter's luscious girlfriend drags the naive look-alike down to her Sicilian villa all sorts of shenanigans ensue. Bright physical comedy was Italy's most successful film ever at the box office, and director-cowriter-star Benigni has thrown in a wide array of his trademark physical gags. Material wears a little thin after a while, but it's hard to dislike a film with a heroine whose favorite exclamation is "Holy Cleopatra!" [R]▼●

Johnny Suede (1991) **C-95m.** *** D: Tom DiCillo. Brad Pitt, Calvin Levels, Alison Moir, Catherine Keener, Tina Louise, Nick Cave, Samuel L. Jackson. Pitt is perfectly cast as Johnny Suede, who sports a glorious pompadour and dreams of stardom as a Ricky Nelson–type pop singer. Clever, winningly hip little film; at its best contrasting Johnny's dream world with the reality that surrounds him.▼●◗

Johnny Tiger (1966) **C-102m.** **½ D: Paul Wendkos. Robert Taylor, Geraldine Brooks, Chad Everett, Brenda Scott. Set in Florida, tame tale of teacher Taylor, doctor Brooks, and half-breed Seminole Everett trying to come to conclusions about Indians' role in modern world.▼

Johnny Tremain (1957) **C-80m.** *** D: Robert Stevenson. Hal Stalmaster, Luana Patten, Jeff York, Sebastian Cabot, Dick Beymer, Walter Sande. Excellent Disney film, from Esther Forbes' novel about a young boy who gets involved in the Revolutionary War; sprinkles fiction with fact to bring history to life.▼●◗

John Paul Jones (1959) **C-126m.** **½ D: John Farrow. Robert Stack, Marisa Pavan, Charles Coburn, Erin O'Brien, Macdonald Carey, Jean-Pierre Aumont, Peter Cushing, Bruce Cabot, Bette Davis. Empty spectacle of 18th-century American naval hero, with cameo by Davis as Russian empress, Catherine the Great. Look for Mia Farrow (daughter of film's director and Maureen O'Sullivan) in film debut. Technirama.▼

John Q (2002) **C-118m.** **½ D: Nick Cassavetes. Denzel Washington, James Woods, Robert Duvall, Anne Heche, Ray Liotta, Kimberly Elise, Eddie Griffin, Shawn Hatosy, Obba Babatunde, Troy Beyer, Paul Johansson, Daniel E. Smith. Factory worker who's struggling to make ends meet learns that his insurance will not cover his son's heart transplant surgery. Assaulted by red tape and uncaring bureaucrats, he commandeers the hospital's emergency room—willing to do anything to save his child's life. Story ingredients ring true, but the film shamelessly pushes emotional buttons, with speechifying and two-dimensional supporting characters. Redeemed, to a surprising extent, by Washington's powerful performance. [PG-13]▼◗

johns (1996) **C-94m.** ** D: Scott Silver. Lukas Haas, David Arquette, Arliss Howard, Keith David, Christopher Gartin, Elliott Gould, Terrence Dashon Howard, Richard Kind, John C. McGinley. Depressing tale of friendship between two hustlers on the L.A. scene, set on the day before Christmas. Gritty and bleak with solid performances by Haas and Arquette, but the subject and tone will remind viewers of the far superior MIDNIGHT COWBOY. [R]▼◗

Johnson Family Vacation (2004) **C-97m.** BOMB D: Christopher Erskin. Cedric the Entertainer, Vanessa Williams, Bow Wow, Shannon Elizabeth, Solange Knowles, Steve Harvey, Christopher B. Duncan, Jennifer Freeman, Gabby Soleil, Wade Williams, Aloma Wright, Shari Headley. Uptight insurance man takes his family—including his estranged wife—on a disaster-prone motor trip from L.A. to Missouri for a family reunion and competition. Amateurish comedy is played so broadly you expect Kingfish Stevens to turn up at any minute. Cedric stars and also plays a bombastic, mush-mouthed character named Uncle Earl. Followed by two DVD sequels. [PG-13]▼◗

John Tucker Must Die (2006) **C-90m.** *½ D: Betty Thomas. Jesse Metcalfe, Brittany Snow, Ashanti, Sophia Bush, Arielle Kebbel, Jenny McCarthy, Penn Badgley, Fatso-Fasano, Kevin McNulty, Patricia Drake. When three high school girls discover they have all been dating the same two-timing lothario, they convince an innocent classmate to seduce the smooth-talking jock and break his heart. Charmless and predictable teen comedy loses touch with reality about halfway through and winds up a ludicrous mess. Any similarity between these characters and actual human beings is purely coincidental. [PG-13]◗

Jo Jo Dancer, Your Life Is Calling (1986) **C-97m.** ** D: Richard Pryor. Richard Pryor, Debbie Allen, Art Evans, Fay Hauser, Barbara Williams, Carmen McRae, Paula Kelly, Diahnne Abbott, Scoey Mitchell, Billy Eckstine, Wings Hauser, E'lon Cox, Virginia Capers, Dennis Farina. Pryor examines his life, with the help of an alter-ego character; largely autobiographical film only sparks when chronicling the comedian's early life and first show-biz encounters. From there it's downhill: jumbled, at arm's-length, and boring. Pryor's directorial debut, if you don't count an earlier concert film (he also coscripted and produced). Super 35. [R]▼●◗

Joke of Destiny, A (1983-Italian) **C-105m.** *½ D: Lina Wertmuller. Ugo Tognazzi, Piera Degli Esposti, Gastone Moschin,

Renzo Montagnani, Valeria Golino. A high government official is accidentally locked in his computer-controlled limousine, and his dilemma is dealt with as if it's a national crisis. Loud, overwrought satire has a couple of laughs but will either put you to sleep or give you a headache. Full title: A JOKE OF DESTINY, LYING IN WAIT AROUND THE CORNER LIKE A BANDIT. [PG]▼

Joker Is Wild, The (1957) 126m. *** D: Charles Vidor. Frank Sinatra, Mitzi Gaynor, Jeanne Crain, Eddie Albert, Beverly Garland, Jackie Coogan, Sophie Tucker. Sinatra is fine in biography of nightclub performer Joe E. Lewis, with Crain and Gaynor diverting as his two loves. Cahn and Van Heusen song "All the Way" won an Oscar; in fact, the film was reissued as ALL THE WAY. VistaVision.

Jokers, The (1967-British) C-94m. *** D: Michael Winner. Michael Crawford, Oliver Reed, Gabriella Licudi, Harry Andrews, James Donald, Daniel Massey, Michael Hordern, Frank Finlay, Rachel Kempson, Edward Fox. Droll satire on the Establishment with Reed and Crawford two brothers from upper classes, putting everyone on and carrying out perfect caper; ironic results.

Jolene (2010) C-115m. **½ D: Dan Ireland. Jessica Chastain, Frances Fisher, Dermot Mulroney, Rupert Friend, Theresa Russell, Denise Richards, Michael Vartan, Chazz Palminteri, Zeb Newman. E. L. Doctorow's short story is given overlong—and overly melodramatic—screen treatment in this episodic road movie elevated by a fine cast. Chastain plays an orphaned teen who travels cross country, engaging in a lot of bad-end relationships and encounters with a variety of colorful if unsavory characters. Uneven film is rescued by a memorable performance by the young, promising Chastain. [R]▶

Jolson Sings Again (1949) C-96m. **½ D: Henry Levin. Larry Parks, Barbara Hale, William Demarest, Ludwig Donath, Tamara Shayne. Attempt to continue THE JOLSON STORY only partially succeeds, and is a curio at best . . . especially when Parks (playing Jolson) meets Parks (playing Parks). Jolson standards ("Baby Face," "Sonny Boy," "Back In Your Own Back Yard," and many others) are still great. ▼○▶

Jolson Story, The (1946) C-128m. ***½ D: Alfred E. Green. Larry Parks, Evelyn Keyes, William Demarest, Bill Goodwin, Ludwig Donath, Tamara Shayne. Hokey but very entertaining biography of all-time great Al Jolson, with Parks giving his all in story of brash vaudeville performer's rise in the show biz world. Songs: "April Showers," "Avalon," "You Made Me Love You," "My Mammy" plus many others, all dubbed by Jolson; that's the real Jolson in long shot on the runway during the "Swanee"

sequence. Morris Stoloff earned an Oscar for his scoring. Sequel: JOLSON SINGS AGAIN.▼○▶

Jonah: a VeggieTales Movie (2002) C-82m. **½ D: Phil Vischer, Mike Nawrocki. Voices of Phil Vischer, Mike Nawrocki, Tim Hodge, Lisa Vischer, Dan Anderson, Kristin Blegen. The VeggieTales gang learns a lesson in compassion and mercy in the story of Jonah, the messenger of God who is swallowed by a whale, then given a second chance to deliver his message to the wayward people of Nineveh. A feature-length spin-off from a popular series of direct-to-video programs, this low-budget computer-generated Bible-themed animated feature is OK for young kids. [G]▼▶

Jonah Hex (2010) C-81m. BOMB D: Jimmy Hayward. Josh Brolin, John Malkovich, Megan Fox, Michael Fassbender, Will Arnett, Aidan Quinn, John Gallagher, Jr., Tom Wopat, Michael Shannon, Wes Bentley. Dreadful comic-book/Western hybrid in which Brolin plays a disfigured bounty hunter enlisted to stop a Civil War–era rebel terrorist who has mass destruction on his mind. Buried beneath a mound of makeup, Brolin can't make the character (introduced in a 1972 DC comic book) come alive. Fox is embarrassingly bad and the script is incoherent. Brief running time suggests heavy cuts were made during production, but considering the mess on-screen that's probably a good thing. Panavision. [PG-13]▶

Jonah Who Will Be 25 in the Year 2000 (1976-Swiss) C-115m. ***½ D: Alain Tanner. Myriam Boyer, Jean-Luc Bideau, Miou-Miou, Roger Jendly, Jacques Denis. Sensitive, literate, engaging comedy about eight individuals affected by the political events of the late '60s. Miou-Miou is lovely as supermarket clerk with no qualms about liberating groceries. A companion to Tanner's later NO MAN'S LAND (1985).▼

Jonathan Livingston Seagull (1973) C-120m. **½ D: Hall Bartlett. Voices of James Franciscus, Juliet Mills, Hal Holbrook, Kelly Harmon, Dorothy McGuire, Richard Crenna. Unique film based on Richard Bach's best-seller about an existential seagull. Superb photography allows us to take bird's point of view as he forsakes his flock to explore wonders of flying. Dialogue doesn't work nearly as well, nor does Neil Diamond's overbearing score. Panavision. [G]▼▶

Joneses, The (2010-U.S.-British) C-96m. *** D: Derrick Borte. Demi Moore, David Duchovny, Amber Heard, Ben Hollingsworth, Gary Cole, Glenne Headly, Catherine Dyer, Chris Williams, Lauren Hutton. Pertinent, funny, and well-written comedy finds a fake "perfect" family-for-hire, actually employees of a stealth marketing firm, moving into an upscale neighborhood in order to impress the residents with their trendy clothes, fancy cars, neat gadgets, and cool lifestyle. Smart, original satire on our materialistic society doesn't completely work but still gets enough right to be well worth seeing. Super 35. [R]█

Joni (1980) **C-108m.** **½ D: James F. Collier. Joni Eareckson, Bert Remsen, Katherine De Hetre, Cooper Huckabee, John Milford, Michael Mancini, Richard Lineback. Earnest account of Eareckson's actual struggle to rebuild her life and find religion after breaking her spine in a diving mishap. Based on a book by Eareckson; financed by Billy Graham. [G]▼

Joseph and His Brethren (1960) **C-103m.** ** D: Irving Rapper. Marietto, Geoffrey Horne, Belinda Lee, Finlay Currie, Antonio Segurini, Charles Borromel, Carlo Giustini. Juvenile biblical tale, lavishly produced but empty-headed. Original U.S. title: THE STORY OF JOSEPH AND HIS BRETHREN. Totalscope.▼█

Joseph Andrews (1977-British) **C-103m.** ** D: Tony Richardson. Ann-Margret, Peter Firth, Michael Hordern, Beryl Reid, Jim Dale, Natalie Ogle, Peter Bull, Karen Dotrice. Director Richardson returns to Henry Fielding but TOM JONES lightning fails to strike again; well-photographed farce based on concealed identities is dull throughout. [R]▼█

Joseph Conrad's The Secret Agent SEE: Secret Agent, The (1996)

Josh and S.A.M. (1993) **C-98m.** ** D: Billy Weber. Jacob Tierney, Noah Fleiss, Martha Plimpton, Stephen Tobolowsky, Joan Allen, Chris Penn, Maury Chaykin, Udo Kier, Allan Arbus, Amy Wright, Jake Gyllenhaal, Christian Clemenson. Odd, unsatisfying road movie about a pair of emotionally put-upon brothers, the offspring of otherwise occupied (as well as divorced) parents, who end up stealing a car and picking up hitchhiker Plimpton. The scenario strains credibility, if only because the boys are aged 12 and 7. There's the germ of an engaging film here, but the result is just too silly. [PG-13]▼●

Joshua (1976) **C-75m.** *½ D: Larry Spangler. Fred Williamson, Isela Vega, Brenda Venus, Stacy Newton, Kathryn Jackson. Modest Western of Williamson patiently tracking down and killing one by one the bandits who murdered his mother, maid to a frontier family. Embarrassing, cynical script by Williamson insults the audience; Mexican superstar Vega is wasted. Originally titled: THE BLACK RIDER. [PG—reedited from original R rating]▼█

Joshua (2002) **C-91m.** ** D: John Purdy. Tony Goldwyn, F. Murray Abraham, Kurt Fuller, Stacy Edwards, Colleen Camp, Giancarlo Giannini. Bland religious parable of affable drifter Goldwyn, a woodworker whose presence in small American town makes nearly everyone happier except

grumpy, distrustful Catholic priest Abraham. Giannini plays the Pope! Music by Christian pop star Michael W. Smith. A good substitute if the babysitter cancels. [G]▼█

Joshua (2007) **C-106m.** ** D: George Ratliff. Sam Rockwell, Vera Farmiga, Jacob Kogan, Celia Weston, Dallas Roberts, Michael McKean, Haviland Morris. A precocious 9-year-old in an upper-middle-class N.Y.C. household appears to deeply resent the arrival of his newborn baby sister. Strong performances by indie faves Rockwell and Farmiga, as the understandably stressed-out parents, compensate for a storyline that, though chilling, is also a bit repetitious. Strong on atmosphere and production design but weak on logic. Young couples with dreams of enlarging their families might want to steer clear of young Josh. [R]█

Joshua Then and Now (1985-Canadian) **C-118m.** *** D: Ted Kotcheff. James Woods, Gabrielle Lazure, Alan Arkin, Michael Sarrazin, Linda Sorenson, Alan Scarfe, Alexander Knox, Robert Joy. Unorthodox life and times of a Jewish writer in Canada whose father was a small-time gangster and who marries into a politically and socially prominent WASP family. Uneven but entertaining comedy-drama, based on Mordecai Richler's semiautobiographical novel; Woods is fine in one of his first leading-man roles, Arkin terrific as his colorful dad. [R]▼

Josie and the Pussycats (2001) **C-95m.** ** D: Harry Elfont, Deborah Kaplan. Rachael Leigh Cook, Tara Reid, Rosario Dawson, Alan Cumming, Parker Posey, Gabriel Mann, Paulo Costanzo, Missi Pyle, Alex Martin, Carson Daly, Jann T. Carl, Russ Leatherman. Live-action treatment finds the Archie Comics girl group used by record execs and the government to front subliminal marketing campaigns to kids. Goofy send-up of trendy teen pop culture often misses the mark, but the occasional hit is straight on. Best part comes early on with the top boy band Dujour (Word!). Breckin Meyer, Seth Green, Donald Faison, and Eugene Levy appear unbilled. [PG-13]▼█

Jour de Fete (1949-French) **70m.** ***½ D: Jacques Tati. Jacques Tati, Guy Decomble, Paul Frankeur, Santa Relli, Maine Vallee, Roger Rafal. In this exquisite feature-film directorial debut French comedian/mime Tati plays a postman whose attempts to modernize delivery link up a series of delightful gags built around a small town's Bastille Day celebration. Tati's cleverness and timing make him one of the most accomplished cinematic comedians since Buster Keaton. Originally filmed in color, but released in b&w with color tinting. Restored to its original color version in 1997. Some prints run 87m. Aka THE BIG DAY.▼●

Journey, The (1959) **C-125m.** *** D: Anatole Litvak. Deborah Kerr, Yul Brynner, Jason Robards, Jr., Robert Morley, E. G.

Marshall, Anne Jackson, Ronny Howard, Kurt Kasznar, Gérard Oury, Anouk Aimée. Colorful and unexpected events (including romance) surround a group of Westerners as they attempt to leave Budapest after the anti-Soviet uprising in 1956. Glossy drama marked feature-film debuts of Robards and young Howard.

Journey (1972-Canadian) **C-87m.** BOMB D: Paul Almond. Genevieve Bujold, John Vernon, Gale Garnett, George Sperdakos, Elton Hayes. Young woman, saved from drowning by head of wilderness commune, believes that she brings bad luck to everyone with whom she comes in contact. Including the people who made this film. Heavy going. [PG]▼

Journey Back to Oz (1974) **C-90m.** **½ D: Hal Sutherland. Voices of Liza Minnelli, Milton Berle, Margaret Hamilton, Jack E. Leonard, Paul Lynde, Ethel Merman, Mickey Rooney, Rise Stevens, Danny Thomas, Mel Blanc. Long-delayed (made in 1964) animated sequel without the Wizard. Okay for the kids; main interest for grownups is familiar voices, including Minnelli in her late mother's role. [G]▼▌

Journey Into Autumn SEE: **Dreams** (1955)

Journey Into Fear (1943) **69m.** *** D: Norman Foster. Orson Welles, Joseph Cotten, Dolores Del Rio, Ruth Warrick, Agnes Moorehead, Everett Sloane, Jack Moss, Hans Conried. Often baffling WW2 spy drama started by Welles, taken out of his hands. Much of tale of smuggling munitions into Turkey still exciting. Cotten and Welles scripted this adaptation of the Eric Ambler novel. Remade in 1975. Also shown in computer-colored version.▼◖

Journey Into Fear (1975-Canadian) **C-103m.** ** D: Daniel Mann. Sam Waterston, Zero Mostel, Yvette Mimieux, Scott Marlowe, Ian McShane, Joseph Wiseman, Shelley Winters, Stanley Holloway, Donald Pleasence, Vincent Price. Muddled remake of 1943 film, shot throughout Europe, with Waterston as research geologist involved in international intrigue. [R]▼

Journey of August King, The (1995) **C-95m.** *** D: John Duigan. Jason Patric, Thandie Newton, Larry Drake, Sam Waterston, Sara-Jane Wylde, Eric Mabius. Troubled, widowed farmer August King (Patric) comes to the assistance of Annalees Williamsburg (Newton), a vulnerable young slave who has run away from her master in 1815 North Carolina. Contemplative and civilized tale, beautifully filmed and richly humanistic. Waterston (cast as a landowner) also coproduced. Scripted by John Ehle, based on his novel. [PG-13]▼◖

Journey of Hope (1990-Swiss) **C-110m.** ***½ D: Xavier Koller. Necmettin Cobanoglu, Nur Surer, Emin Sivas, Erdinc Akbas, Yaman Okay. Heartbreaking, based-on-fact account of what happens when a poor Turk-ish couple and their young son set off for Switzerland, in the hope of finding a better life. This could have wallowed in sentiment and clichés, but director-coscripter Koller consistently keeps it on the right emotional track. Deserving Best Foreign Film Academy Award winner packs a real wallop.▼●

Journey of Natty Gann, The (1985) **C-101m.** *** D: Jeremy Kagan. Meredith Salenger, John Cusack, Ray Wise, Lainie Kazan, Barry Miller, Scatman Crothers, Verna Bloom. Girl travels cross-country during the hardest days of the Depression, in order to be with her father; along the way she acquires an unlikely companion and protector—a wolf. Low-key but entertaining Disney film travels smoothly to expected conclusion. Rich 1930s atmosphere helps a lot, and the wolf (actually played by a dog!) is great. Widescreen. [PG]▼◖

Journey Through the Past (1972) **C-78m.** *½ D: Bernard Shakey (Neil Young). Crosby, Stills, Nash and Young, Buffalo Springfield, Carrie Snodgrass, Jack Nitzsche. Overblown, phony, pseudo-hip home movie centering on rock superstar Young. [R]

Journey to Shiloh (1968) **C-101m.** *½ D: William Hale. James Caan, Michael Sarrazin, Brenda Scott, Don Stroud, Paul Petersen, Harrison Ford. Limp Civil War programmer about young Texans anxious to engage in battle. Veterans Rex Ingram, John Doucette, and Noah Beery are lost in this jumble. Techniscope.

Journey to the Beginning of the World SEE: **Voyage to the Beginning of the World**

Journey to the Center of the Earth (1959) **C-132m.** *** D: Henry Levin. James Mason, Pat Boone, Arlene Dahl, Diane Baker, Thayer David, Alan Napier. Entertaining, old-fashioned fantasy-adventure, from Jules Verne's story of daring expedition headed by Mason; long in telling, with silly digressions, but generally fun. Remade in 1999 (for TV), 2008, and as WHERE TIME BEGAN. Best enjoyed in CinemaScope. ▼◖

Journey to the Center of the Earth (2008) **C-93m.** **½ D: Eric Brevig. Brendan Fraser, Josh Hutcherson, Anita Briem, Seth Meyers. Hoping to salvage the reputation of his vanished brother, scientist Fraser heads for Iceland with his bored nephew Hutcherson. They join forces with an attractive guide (Briem) and set out hiking, as the title says, on a journey to the earth's center, evading dinosaurs and other menaces along the way. Lively, ingratiating family-friendly comedy-adventure is so loosely based on Jules Verne's novel that a copy of the book is a plot element. Good effects and design help, especially when the movie is seen in the intended 3-D, imaginatively used throughout. 3-D. [PG]◖

Journey to the Center of Time (1967) **C-82m.** *½ D: D. L. Hewitt. Scott Brady, Gigi

Perreau, Anthony Eisley, Abraham Sofaer, Poupee Gamin, Lyle Waggoner. Very cheap sci-fi time travel adventure to future and past, using plot elements from earlier THE TIME TRAVELERS. Aka TIME WARP. ▼●

Journey to the Far Side of the Sun (1969-British) **C-99m.** ******* D: Robert Parrish. Roy Thinnes, Lynn Loring, Herbert Lom, Patrick Wymark. Entertaining exploration of planet hidden behind the sun. The ending makes the movie. Originally titled DOPPELGANGER. [G]▼●]

Journey to the Lost City SEE: **Indian Tomb, The** and **Tiger of Eschnapur, The**

Journey to the Seventh Planet (1961-Danish) **C-83m.** ***½** D: Sidney Pink. John Agar, Greta Thyssen, Ann Smyrner, Mimi Heinrich, Carl Ottosen. In year 2001, expedition to Uranus discovers hostile alien brain that can turn thoughts into reality. Cheap, clumsy, dull, with just a smidge of imagination. ▼●]

Joyeux Noël (2005-French-German) **C-116m.** *****½** D: Christian Carion. Diane Kruger, Benno Fürmann, Guillaume Canet, Gary Lewis, Dany Boon, Alex Ferns, Daniel Brühl, Bernard Le Coq, Michel Serrault, Suzanne Flon, Ian Richardson. Potent dramatization of a real-life incident in which French, German, and Scottish soldiers on the front lines in WW1 decide to risk court-martial—or worse—and call a one-night Christmas Eve truce. This simple act demonstrates a clear reason why sometimes the "rules of engagement" should be broken, despite what superiors far from the battlefields dictate. With a flawless international cast, this delivers a lesson worth remembering in any era. Written by the director. Super 35. [PG-13]●

Joy House (1964-French) **98m.** ****½** D: René Clement. Jane Fonda, Alain Delon, Lola Albright, Sorrell Booke. Living on his looks, a playboy on the run seeks refuge in gloomy French mansion run by two American women. Fate and quicker wits than his control this brooding tale of irony. Aka THE LOVE CAGE. Franscope.▼]

Joy in the Morning (1965) **C-103m.** ****** D: Alex Segal. Richard Chamberlain, Yvette Mimieux, Arthur Kennedy, Sidney Blackmer. Betty Smith's gentle novel of struggling law student and his marital problems becomes mild vehicle for Chamberlain, who crusades for human dignity amid stereotypes of a college town.

Joy Luck Club, The (1993) **C-135m.** ******* D: Wayne Wang. Kieu Chinh, Tsai Chin, France Nuyen, Lisa Lu, Ming-Na Wen, Tamlyn Tomita, Lauren Tom, Rosalind Chao, Andrew McCarthy, Diane Baker, Chao-Li Chi, Melanie Chang, Victor Wong, Irene Ng. Rich tapestry of eight stories; the incredible saga of four women who survived—and prevailed—against all odds in China, and their assimilated American daughters, whose troubles seem almost trivial by comparison. Starts losing its grip in the penultimate sequence, but soars again for a powerhouse finale that will have you reaching for a crying towel. Screenplay by Amy Tan and Ronald Bass, from Tan's best-selling novel. [R]▼●]

Joy of Sex (1984) **C-93m.** BOMB D: Martha Coolidge. Michelle Meyrink, Cameron Dye, Lisa Langlois, Charles Van Eman, Christopher Lloyd, Colleen Camp, Ernie Hudson. Virgin Meyrink, believing she has weeks to live, decides to "do it all" before she dies. Nothing of Alex Comfort's book—including his name—is left (and despite the title, no one seems to be having a good time) in embarrassingly bad high-school comedy. [R]▼

Joyride (1977) **C-92m.** ****** D: Joseph Ruben. Desi Arnaz, Jr., Robert Carradine, Melanie Griffith, Anne Lockhart, Tom Ligon, Cliff Lenz. Meandering tale of two young-and-footloose couples on the road to Alaska looking for adventure but drifting into crime. Four show-biz offspring play the leads: the sons of Desi Arnaz (and Lucy) and John Carradine, the daughters of Tippi Hedren and June Lockhart. [R]▼]

Joy Ride (2001) **C-97m.** ****½** D: John Dahl. Paul Walker, Leelee Sobieski, Steve Zahn, Jessica Bowman. Egged on by his no-account brother (Zahn), a young man (Walker) plays a prank on a trucker using his CB radio—but the victim of the joke doesn't find it funny and exacts terrifying revenge by stalking the two and the girlfriend who joins them on the road. Lots of action and suspense in this improbable yarn, but the fun drains a bit toward the end. Followed by a direct-to-DVD sequel. Super 35. [R]▼]

J. R. SEE: **Who's That Knocking at My Door**

Juarez (1939) **132m.** ******* D: William Dieterle. Paul Muni, Bette Davis, Brian Aherne, Claude Rains, John Garfield, Gale Sondergaard, Donald Crisp, Gilbert Roland, Louis Calhern, Grant Mitchell. Interesting biography of Mexican leader (Muni), with unforgettable performance by Rains as Napoleon III; also notable is Garfield's offbeat casting as Mexican General Diaz. Elaborately done, but never as inspiring as it's intended to be.▼

Jubal (1956) **C-101m.** ******* D: Delmer Daves. Glenn Ford, Ernest Borgnine, Rod Steiger, Valerie French, Felicia Farr, Noah Beery, Jr., Charles Bronson. It's Bard in the Saddle with this Western *Othello*: when jealous rancher Borgnine seeks some lovemaking advice from cowhand Ford, along comes Steiger hinting that Ford's giving Borgnine's wife (French) a few "lessons" as well. Brooding, intense drama is pretty good on its own terms, more intriguing if you know the original. CinemaScope. ▼●]

Judas Kiss (1999) **C-97m.** ******* D: Sebastian Gutierrez. Carla Gugino, Hal Holbrook, Emma Thompson, Alan Rickman, Roscoe Lee Browne, Lisa Eichhorn, Greg Wise, Philip Baker Hall, Gil Bellows, Simon Baker-Denny (Simon Baker). Young New Orleans pick-up gang kidnaps an important official of a computer company for a big ransom payoff—but there's more to this caper than first meets the eye. Sexy Gugino (who also coproduced the film) sparks a good cast, but the real treat is watching Thompson and Rickman drawling together as Southern investigators (one Federal, one local) on the case. Written by the director. Made for theaters; debuted on cable. Panavision. [R]▼)

Judas Was a Woman SEE: La Bête Humaine

Jude (1996-British) C-123m. ** D: Michael Winterbottom. Christopher Eccleston, Kate Winslet, Rachel Griffiths, Liam Cunningham, June Whitfield, Ross Colvin Turnbull. Dour, generally uninvolving adaptation of Thomas Hardy's final novel, *Jude the Obscure,* about an unschooled but intellectually ambitious 19th-century stonemason who endures a lifetime of smashed dreams. The early going wobbily telescopes many of the book's events into the opening half hour; the movie then gets a desperately needed shot in the arm when Winslet (terrific) shows up as the cousin, lover, and academic rebel trying to exist in a society that systematically crushes rebels. Panavision. [R]▼)

Judge and the Assassin, The (1975-French) C-121m. ***½ D: Bertrand Tavernier. Philippe Noiret, Michel Galabru, Isabelle Huppert, Jean-Claude Brialy, Renee Faure. In a way, the title tells all in this incisive, expertly directed and acted drama: Judge Noiret must determine whether murderer Galabru is insane or faking. Fascinating from start to finish. Panavision. ▼)

Judge Dredd (1995) C-96m. ** D: Danny Cannon. Sylvester Stallone, Armand Assante, Diane Lane, Rob Schneider, Joan Chen, Jürgen Prochnow, Max von Sydow, Balthazar Getty, Joanna Miles, Mitchell Ryan. Loud, ugly adaptation of the comic book set in a future world of urban chaos where new-age police are empowered to "judge"—and kill, if need be—on the spot. Judge Dredd (Stallone) is caught in a conspiracy much bigger and more insidious than he realizes. Some interesting plotting is lost in a sea of hard-edged violence, video game–like special effects, and overripe acting. James Earl Jones reads opening narration; James Remar and Scott Wilson appear unbilled. Panavision. [R]▼)

Judgement in Stone, A (1986-Canadian) C-102m. *½ D: Ousama Rawi. Rita Tushingham, Ross Petty, Tom Kneebone, Shelley Peterson, Jessica Stern, Jonathan Crombie, Jackie Burroughs. Tushingham is well cast in this otherwise tiresome, drawn-out chiller as a repressed, illiterate, and psychotic spinster who takes a job as a housemaid with tragic results. Aka THE HOUSEKEEPER. Remade in France as LA CÉRÉMONIE. [R]▼)

Judge Priest (1934) 80m. ***½ D: John Ford. Will Rogers, Tom Brown, Anita Louise, Henry B. Walthall, Stepin Fetchit, Hattie McDaniel. Exceptional slice of Americana with Rogers as commonsensical yet controversial judge in small town; full of warm and funny character vignettes, including Walthall's stirring courtroom scene. Ford remade it in 1953 as THE SUN SHINES BRIGHT.▼)

Judgment at Nuremberg (1961) 178m. **** D: Stanley Kramer. Spencer Tracy, Burt Lancaster, Richard Widmark, Marlene Dietrich, Judy Garland, Maximilian Schell, Montgomery Clift, William Shatner. Superior production revolving around U.S. judge Tracy presiding over German war-criminal trials. Schell, who originated the role in Abby Mann's 1959 TV play, won Oscar as defense attorney, as did Mann for his screenplay. Fine performances by Dietrich as widow of German officer, Garland as hausfrau, Clift as unbalanced victim of Nazi atrocities. Later a Broadway play. ▼)

Judgment in Berlin (1988) C-92m. ** D: Leo Penn. Martin Sheen, Sam Wanamaker, Sean Penn, Max Gail, Juerger Hemrich, Carl Lumbly, Max Volkert Martens. U.S. judge Sheen, thrown into one of those Spencer Tracy/Nuremberg situations, has to determine if the hijacking of an East German jet into Berlin is justified. Ragged but *just* watchable, with actor Penn (the director's son) turning in one unexpectedly heartfelt cameo during some climactic courtroom testimony. Shown on TV as ESCAPE TO FREEDOM. [PG]▼)

Judgment Night (1993) C-109m. **½ D: Stephen Hopkins. Emilio Estevez, Cuba Gooding, Jr., Denis Leary, Stephen Dorff, Jeremy Piven, Peter Greene. Sporadically tense, competently directed programmer about four suburban buddies who end up being chased through tenements and sewers after driving their fancy RV over a shooting victim in a very tough part of Chicago. Ultimately done in by standard genre clichés, but surprisingly absorbing in the early going. Leary is a standout as the chief heavy. Super 35. [R]▼)

Judith (1966) C-109m. BOMB D: Daniel Mann. Sophia Loren, Peter Finch, Jack Hawkins, Hans Verner, Zharira Charifai. Austrian Jewess Loren survives prison camp with makeup intact, comes to Israel in 1948 to locate Nazi husband who betrayed her. Film is both dull and unbelievable, a bad combination. Video title: CONFLICT. Panavision.▼

Ju Dou (1989-Chinese-Japanese) C-95m. ***½ D: Zhang Yimou. Gong Li, Li Wei, Li Bao-Tian, Zhang Yi, Zhen Ji-an. Striking, visually magnificent drama, set during the 1920s, telling the tragic story of a young peasant woman who's forced to wed an elderly, bitter factory owner, and commences an affair with his nephew. Banned in China, supposedly because of its focus on individual values and unflattering depiction of the old man (in a nation ruled by a small elite group of old men); authorities feared audiences would see it as a metaphor for the way China's leaders control society. First Chinese film ever to earn a Best Foreign Film Academy Award nomination—and those responsible for entering it in the competition were disciplined by their superiors. Controversy aside, a powerful, provocative film. ▼◑

Judy Berlin (2000) 96m. *** D: Eric Mendelsohn. Barbara Barrie, Bob Dishy, Edie Falco, Carlin Glynn, Aaron Harnick, Bette Henritze, Madeline Kahn, Julie Kavner, Anne Meara, Novella Nelson. Cross-section of residents of Long Island town dream of happiness while facing bleak reality—and a lingering solar eclipse. Original, often eloquent (if slow-paced) statement on contemporary life and love, depicted by top-notch cast of N.Y. actors, including Kahn in her final film. Writer-director Mendelsohn's feature directing debut. ▼◗

Judy Moody and the Not Bummer Summer (2011) C-91m. ** D: John Schultz. Jordana Beatty, Heather Graham, Parris Mosteller, Preston Bailey, Jaleel White, Janet Varney, Kristoffer Winters, Garrett Ryan. Frenetic comedy, based on the popular book series by Megan McDonald, about a spirited 8-year-old girl's attempts to alleviate boredom during summer vacation by challenging herself with adventures—tightrope walking, riding roller coasters, hunting for Bigfoot, etc.—scored on her very own "thrill chart." May be too aggressively wacky for most grown-ups, but newcomer Beatty is engaging as the young heroine, and Graham stops just short of going over the top as her eccentric Aunt Opal. [PG]

Juggernaut (1974-British) C-109m. *** D: Richard Lester. Richard Harris, Omar Sharif, David Hemmings, Anthony Hopkins, Shirley Knight, Ian Holm, Roy Kinnear, Freddie Jones. Surprisingly effective thriller about bomb threat on luxury ocean liner, and demolition experts' attempts to avoid disaster. Harris is first-rate and so is Lester's direction of a formula story. [PG] ▼◗

Juggler, The (1953) 86m. **½ D: Edward Dmytryk. Kirk Douglas, Milly Vitale, Paul Stewart, Alf Kjellin, Beverly Washburn. Sentimental account of Jewish refugee Douglas going to Israel to rebuild his life, overcoming bitterness from life in a concentration camp. Filmed in Israel.◗

Juice (1992) C-92m. ** D: Ernest R. Dickerson. Omar Epps, Jermaine Hopkins, Tupac Shakur, Khalil Kain, Cindy Herron, Vincent Laresca, Samuel L. Jackson. Impressively shot but overly contrived (and extremely violent) tale of four black teenage friends whose lives take a tragic turn when a store robbery goes out of control. Promising directorial debut for Spike Lee's talented cinematographer. Costar Herron (from the group En Vogue), Queen Latifah, and other rap stars appear, and perform on the soundtrack. [R] ▼◗

Jules and Jim (1961-French) 104m. **** D: François Truffaut. Jeanne Moreau, Oskar Werner, Henri Serre, Marie Dubois, Vanna Urbino. Truffaut's memorable tale of three people in love, and how the years affect their interrelationships. A film of rare beauty and charm. Screenplay by Truffaut and Jean Gruault, based on novel by Henri-Pierre Roché. Americanized by Paul Mazursky in WILLIE AND PHIL. Franscope. ▼◗

Julia (1977) C-118m. **** D: Fred Zinnemann. Jane Fonda, Vanessa Redgrave, Jason Robards, Maximilian Schell, Hal Holbrook, Rosemary Murphy, Meryl Streep, Lisa Pelikan, Cathleen Nesbitt, John Glover. Fonda plays Lillian Hellman in adaptation of author's story in *Pentimento* about her exuberant, unusual friend Julia, and how she drew Hellman into involvement with European resistance movement in 1930s. Fine storytelling in beautifully crafted film; Robards (as Dashiell Hammett), screenwriter Alvin Sargent, and radiant Redgrave won Oscars. Streep's feature debut. [PG] ▼◗

Julia (2008-French-U.S.-Mexican) C-138m. *** D: Erick Zonca. Tilda Swinton, Aidan Gould, Saul Rubinek, Kate del Castillo, Jude Ciccolella, Bruno Bichir. Swinton commands our attention playing a character unlike any she's tackled before: a self-destructive alcoholic and party girl. She's so desperate she hatches a harebrained scheme to kidnap a Mexican neighbor's young son and collect a ransom payoff from his wealthy grandfather. You never know where this audacious, fast-paced film is heading next, and it's a wild ride . . . but even at its most outlandish Swinton keeps it firmly anchored. French filmmaker Zonca made this as an homage to John Cassavetes' GLORIA. Super 35. [R]◗

Julia and Julia (1987-Italian) C-97m. **½ D: Peter Del Monte. Kathleen Turner, Gabriel Byrne, Sting, Gabriele Ferzetti, Angela Goodwin. Turner is compelling as a woman whose life splits in two, leaving her caught between a happily married existence with Byrne and a dangerous affair with photographer Sting. Intriguing, well-acted psychological thriller that unfortunately leads nowhere. Handsomely photographed by Giuseppe Rotunno, this theatrical release was made on high-definition video, then transferred to film. [R] ▼◗

Julia Has Two Lovers (1991) C-86m. **½ D: Bashar Shbib. Daphna Kastner, David Duchovny, David Charles, Tim Ray, Clare Bancroft, Martin Donovan. Children's author, who's "involved" with a man but convinced she can do better, develops a fantasy relationship with a telephone wrong number, who ends up engaging her in mutually stimulating chats. Cheaply made, unevenly acted, but solid-enough premise keeps you engrossed to the end. [R]▼

Julia Misbehaves (1948) **99m.** *** D: Jack Conway. Greer Garson, Walter Pidgeon, Peter Lawford, Elizabeth Taylor, Cesar Romero, Mary Boland, Nigel Bruce. Bouncy account of showgirl Garson returning to dignified husband Pidgeon when daughter Taylor is about to marry; Romero is fun as bragging acrobat. Stars seem right at home with slapstick situations.▼

Julie (1956) **99m.** ** D: Andrew L. Stone. Doris Day, Louis Jourdan, Barry Sullivan, Frank Lovejoy, Jack Kelly, Ann Robinson, Jack Kruschen, Mae Marsh. Overbaked soaper in which Day contends with jealous, psychopathic spouse Jourdan, who strangled her first husband and now threatens to kill her. Sometimes tense, but too often unintentionally funny. Also shown in computer-colored version.▼

Julie & Julia (2009) **C-123m.** *** D: Nora Ephron. Meryl Streep, Amy Adams, Stanley Tucci, Chris Messina, Linda Emond, Helen Carey, Mary Lynn Rajskub, Jane Lynch, Vanessa Ferlito, Jillian Bach, Frances Sternhagen, Deborah Rush; voice of Mary Kay Place. New Yorker Julie Powell (Adams), a failed novelist, finds inspiration by replicating every recipe in Julia Child's groundbreaking cookbook. As we follow her culinary adventure we learn how Child, the wife of a U.S. diplomat stationed in Paris, stumbled into the career that made her famous. Streep is a marvel to behold as the fabled chef (with Tucci a perfect partner as her loving husband), and Adams is well cast as her modern-day disciple. What might have been a great film goes on too long and doesn't provide a satisfying finale. Screenplay by Ephron, based on books by Child and Powell. [PG-13]❒

Julien Donkey-Boy (1999) **C-94m.** *½ D: Harmony Korine. Ewen Bremner, Chloë Sevigny, Werner Herzog, Evan Neumann, Joyce Korine, Chrissy Kobylak, Alvin Law. Korine (of KIDS fame and GUMMO infamy) scripted this disgustingly sordid freak show about a dysfunctional family including a schizophrenic (Bremner), his pregnant sis (Sevigny), and their sadistically cruel father (Herzog). The first American film to utilize the cinematic rules of Dogma 95. [R]▼❒

Juliet of the Spirits (1965-Italian) **C-148m.** *** D: Federico Fellini. Giulietta Masina, Sandra Milo, Mario Pisu, Valentina Cortese, Lou Gilbert, Sylva Koscina. Surrealistic fantasy triggered by wife's fears that her well-to-do husband is cheating on her. A film requiring viewer to delve into woman's psyche via a rash of symbolism; counterbalanced with rich visual delights.▼●❒

Julius Caesar (1953) **120m.** ***½ D: Joseph L. Mankiewicz. Marlon Brando, James Mason, John Gielgud, Louis Calhern, Edmond O'Brien, Greer Garson, Deborah Kerr, George Macready, Michael Pate, Alan Napier, Ian Wolfe, Douglass Dumbrille, Edmund Purdom. Superior adaptation of William Shakespeare's play of political power and honor in ancient Rome. Lavishly produced (by John Houseman), with an excellent cast and Oscar-winning art direction-set decoration. Screenplay by director Mankiewicz.▼●❒

Julius Caesar (1970) **C-117m.** **½ D: Stuart Burge. Charlton Heston, Jason Robards, John Gielgud, Richard Johnson, Robert Vaughn, Richard Chamberlain, Diana Rigg, Jill Bennett, Christopher Lee, Michael Gough, Andre Morell. Technically ragged, but acceptable version of Shakespeare play, negated somewhat by Robards' zombielike portrayal of Brutus. The 1953 version (also starring Gielgud) is much better. Panavision. [G]▼●❒

Jumanji (1995) **C-104m.** ** D: Joe Johnston. Robin Williams, Bonnie Hunt, Kirsten Dunst, Bradley Pierce, Bebe Neuwirth, Jonathan Hyde, David Alan Grier, Patricia Clarkson, Adam Hann-Byrd. In 1969 New England, a boy finds a board game buried underground and soon discovers that by playing it a world of terror is unleashed; 26 years later, in the same house, two kids start playing the very same game and bring that boy—now a full-grown man—back to life. A phantasmagoria of digital special effects (a virulent vine, a stampede of wild animals, giant attacking mosquitoes, etc.) seems to be this film's raison d'être. Unfortunately, we're all too aware that they *are* special effects. The story doesn't seem to have much of a point, except perhaps that one shouldn't play with ancient board games. Based on Chris Van Allsburg's book. Followed by an animated TV series. [PG] ▼●❒

Jumbo SEE: **Billy Rose's Jumbo**

Jumper (2008) **C-90m.** ** D: Doug Liman. Hayden Christensen, Samuel L. Jackson, Diane Lane, Jamie Bell, Rachel Bilson, Michael Rooker, AnnaSophia Robb, Max Thieriot, Tom Hulce, Kristen Stewart. Sci-fi and action-thriller genres awkwardly blend in this overblown (albeit fast-paced) account of Christensen, who can transport himself from locale to locale at will—but not without complications. Based on Steven Gould's novel. Super 35. [PG-13]❒

Jumpin at the Boneyard (1992) **C-107m.** *½ D: Jeff Stanzler. Tim Roth, Alexis Arquette, Danitra Vance, Samuel L. Jackson, Kathleen Chalfant, Luis Guzman, Elizabeth Bracco, Jeffrey Wright. Divorced, unemployed Bronx father's further burden: his younger brother, a crack addict he's reunited with after three years. Honorably intentioned but stillborn drama taking place over 24 hours. Thematically and aesthetically for masochists only. [R]▼●

Jumping Jacks (1952) **96m.** **★★½** D: Norman Taurog. Dean Martin, Jerry Lewis, Mona Freeman, Don DeFore, Robert Strauss. Daffy duo has good opportunity for plenty of sight gags when they join military paratroop squad. ▼●)

Jumping the Broom (2011) **C-112m.** **★★½** D: Salim Akil. Angela Bassett, Paula Patton, Laz Alonso, Loretta Devine, Meagan Good, Tasha Smith, Julie Bowen, DeRay Davis, Valarie Pettiford, Brian Stokes Mitchell, Mike Epps, Romeo Miller, Pooch Hall, Gary Dourdan. A young couple's wedding weekend will be the first time their families meet—and they couldn't be more different. The bride (Patton) and her people are wealthy and sophisticated, while the groom (Alonso) and his family, particularly his overbearing mother (Devine), are working-class and traditional. The situations the characters find themselves in ring true, with lessons about finding common ground between loved ones and learning to pick your battles. Unfortunately, the story becomes unnecessarily complicated and loses some of its authenticity. [PG-13]●

Jumpin' Jack Flash (1986) **C-100m.** **★½** D: Penny Marshall. Whoopi Goldberg, Stephen Collins, John Wood, Carol Kane, Annie Potts, Peter Michael Goetz, Roscoe Lee Browne, Sara Botsford, Jeroen Krabbé, Jonathan Pryce, Jon Lovitz, Phil Hartman, Tracy Reiner, Jim Belushi, Paxton Whitehead, Tracey Ullman, Jamey Sheridan. Computer programmer is pulled into international intrigue when spy who wants in from the cold contacts her on her terminal. Lively but stupid star vehicle for Goldberg, who's infinitely better than the script. Feature directing debut for Marshall, who cast her producer-director brother Garry as a police detective and former TV costar Michael McKean in an unbilled cameo as a British party guest. [R]▼●)

Jump Tomorrow (2001-U.S.-British) **C-95m.** **★★½** D: Joel Hopkins. Tunde Adebimpe, Natalia Verbeke, Hippolyte Girardot, James Wilby, Patricia Mauceri, Isiah Whitlock, Jr. Sweet, slight romantic comedy about an uptight office worker on his way to a family-planned marriage (to a girl from his homeland, Nigeria). When he chances to meet a charming Latina, he's smitten … and encouraged to pursue her by a lovesick Frenchman. Debut feature for writer-director Hopkins takes its time to win you over, but succeeds. Based on Hopkins' own award-winning short subject called JORGE. [PG] ▼●

June Bride (1948) **97m.** **★★★** D: Bretaigne Windust. Bette Davis, Robert Montgomery, Fay Bainter, Tom Tully, Barbara Bates, Jerome Cowan, Mary Wickes. Flippant comedy of magazine writers Davis and Montgomery inspired by story they are doing on June brides. Breezy script by Ranald MacDougall. Don't blink or you'll miss Debbie Reynolds in her film debut.▼

Junebug (2005) **C-106m.** **★★★½** D: Phil

Morrison. Amy Adams, Embeth Davidtz, Benjamin McKenzie, Alessandro Nivola, Frank Hoyt Taylor, Celia Weston, Scott Wilson. Exceptional character study of a sophisticated Chicago art dealer and her husband, who travel to his North Carolina home after a long absence and meet head-on with family pressures and chasms in culture. Direct, spare, and moving in a way that is most unusual for an American film, with director Morrison (making his feature debut) and screenwriter Angus MacLachlan quietly and powerfully examining the effects of environment on people and relationships. Adams stands out in a perfect cast. [R] ●

Jungle Book (1942) **C-105m.** **★★★** D: Zoltan Korda. Sabu, Joseph Calleia, John Qualen, Frank Puglia, Rosemary DeCamp, Noble Johnson. Colorful Kipling fantasy of boy (Sabu) raised by wolves. Exciting family fare, fine Miklos Rozsa score. Remade twice (by Disney). ▼●)

Jungle Book, The (1967) **C-78m.** **★★★** D: Wolfgang Reitherman. Voices of Phil Harris, Sebastian Cabot, Louis Prima, George Sanders, Sterling Holloway, J. Pat O'Malley, Verna Felton, Bruce Reitherman. Genial Disney animated feature freely adapted from Rudyard Kipling's stories. Mowgli, the boy raised by wolves, is befriended by a laid-back bear named Baloo (memorably voiced by Harris) who joins him in his jungle adventures. Handpicked cast of actors help create some vivid characterizations in this easygoing film. Songs include "The Bare Necessities," "I Wanna Be Like You," "Trust in Me." Followed by a sequel 36 years later. Remade in 1998 as a live-action direct-to-video movie: THE JUNGLE BOOK: MOWGLI'S STORY. ▼●)

Jungle Book 2, The (2003) **C-72m.** **★★** D: Steve Trenbirth. Voices of John Goodman, Haley Joel Osment, Mae Whitman, Connor Funk, Bob Joles, Tony Jay, John Rhys-Davies, Jim Cummings, Phil Collins, David Ogden Stiers. Retread of the 1967 Disney feature has Mowgli leaving the village where he now lives to rejoin his old friends in the jungle—in spite of the ever-present threat of the tiger Shere Khan. Sound-alikes for Phil Harris, George Sanders, and other voices from the original film, and reuse of its hit songs, only emphasize how pointless this sequel really is. [G] ▼●

Jungle Book, The (1994) SEE: **Rudyard Kipling's The Jungle Book**

Jungle Fever (1991) **C-132m.** **★★★** D: Spike Lee. Wesley Snipes, Annabella Sciorra, Spike Lee, Ossie Davis, Ruby Dee, Samuel L. Jackson, Lonette McKee, John Turturro, Frank Vincent, Anthony Quinn, Halle Berry, Tyra Ferrell, Veronica Webb, Tim Robbins, Brad Dourif, Debi Mazar, Nicholas Turturro, Queen Latifah. Engrossing look at a love affair that crosses over racial, ethnic, cultural, and geographic boundary lines, when upwardly mobile, happily married Snipes has a fling with his new temp secretary Sciorra. Less than perfect, with a drug subplot that throws the film off-kilter toward the end—but still utterly compelling. Lee doesn't have all the answers, but he certainly raises interesting questions. Terrific songs by Stevie Wonder and score by Terence Blanchard, although the music practically drowns out the dialogue in some scenes. What's the point of that? [R]▼●❍

Jungle Fighters SEE: **Long and the Short and the Tall, The**

Jungle Heat SEE: **Dance of the Dwarfs**

Jungle Jim series SEE: ***Leonard Maltin's Classic Movie Guide***

Jungle 2 Jungle (1997) C-105m. *** D: John Pasquin. Tim Allen, Martin Short, JoBeth Williams, Lolita Davidovich, David Ogden Stiers, Bob Dishy, Valerie Mahaffey, Leelee Sobieski. Very likable, if predictable, Disney comedy about a career-obsessed New Yorker who goes to the Amazon to get final divorce papers signed by his ex-wife and comes back with a son he never knew he had. The boy's jungle instincts are no match for life in Manhattan—though he does manage to score some points along the way. Good laughs throughout this family-oriented feature, a remake of the French hit LITTLE INDIAN, BIG CITY. [PG]▼●❍

Junior (1994) C-110m. **½ D: Ivan Reitman. Arnold Schwarzenegger, Danny DeVito, Emma Thompson, Frank Langella, Pamela Reed, Judy Collins, James Eckhouse, Aida Turturro, Welker White. Pleasant-enough comedy about a straitlaced scientist (Schwarzenegger) who's persuaded by an aggressive colleague (DeVito) to try injecting sperm into his body and becoming pregnant. Unexpected result: he doesn't want to give up his baby! This "politically correct farce" boasts enthusiastic performances from its three stars, and precious few laughs after the initial "joke" is presented. Instead, Arnold becomes a better man by experiencing childbearing like a woman. Sheesh. [PG-13]▼●❍

Junior Bonner (1972) C-100m. ***½ D: Sam Peckinpah. Steve McQueen, Robert Preston, Ida Lupino, Ben Johnson, Joe Don Baker, Barbara Leigh, Mary Murphy. Totally captivating rodeo comedy-drama as an aging McQueen returns to his home and family to take part in a local contest. Peckinpah's most gentle film is full of natural performances, particularly by Preston and Lupino as McQueen's estranged parents. Written by Jeb Rosebrook. Todd-AO 35. [PG]▼❍

Junkman (1982) C-96m. *½ D: H. B. Halicki. H. B. Halicki, Christopher Stone, Susan Shaw, Lang Jeffries, Hoyt Axton, Lynda Day George. Cars speed, crash, and practically bring each other to orgasm. Oh, yes, there *is* a story . . . [PG]▼❍

Juno (2007) C-96m. ***½ D: Jason Reitman. Ellen Page, Michael Cera, Jennifer Garner, Jason Bateman, Allison Janney, J.K.

Simmons, Olivia Thirlby, Rainn Wilson, Cameron Bright. Precocious 16-year-old girl discovers she is pregnant, and decides to deal with the situation herself, choosing the couple she wants to adopt her baby. With her too-cool demeanor and lingo, Juno may be off-putting at first, but we soon discover that she's all too human. Exceptional, Oscar-winning screenplay by Diablo Cody grows warmer at every turn, and leads us in surprising directions. Janney and Simmons are terrific as Juno's straight-shooting parents, and Page is peerless in the title role. Great title sequence and use of music throughout. [PG-13]❍

Juno and the Paycock (1930-British) 96m. ** D: Alfred Hitchcock. Sara Allgood, Edward Chapman, Sidney Morgan, Maire O'Neill, John Laurie, Dennis Wyndham, John Longden. Faithful but dull, stagebound adaptation (by Hitchcock and Alma Reville) of Sean O'Casey's play about a poor Dublin family's travails during the civil war. The straightforward material defeats the director; however, Allgood is a standout as Juno. That's Barry Fitzgerald as "The Orator," in his screen debut.▼❍

Ju-on: The Grudge (2003-Japanese) C-92m. *** D: Takashi Shimizu. Megumi Okina, Misaki Ito, Misa Uehara, Yui Ichikawa, Kanji Tsuda, Takako Fuji, Kayoko Shibata, Yukako Kukuri, Takashi Matsuyama, Yuya Ozeki. Ghosts of a brutally murdered mother and her son vengefully terrorize and kill a series of people who have a connection with the modest Tokyo home where the murders took place. Not a story as such, but a series of eerie images, some quietly creepy, others outright terrifying; made in the same unnerving style as RINGU. Part of a Japanese series with a dedicated following. The imaginative director remade the movie for Hollywood as THE GRUDGE. Followed by a sequel. [R]▼❍

Jupiter's Darling (1955) C-96m. **½ D: George Sidney. Esther Williams, Howard Keel, George Sanders, Marge and Gower Champion, Norma Varden. Lavish musical of Robert Sherwood's *Road to Rome*, which bogs down in tedium: Williams is temptress who dallies with Hannibal (Keel) to prevent attack on Rome. CinemaScope.▼●

Jupiter's Thigh (1979-French) C-90m. ** D: Philippe De Broca. Annie Girardot, Philippe Noiret, Frances Perrin, Catherine Alric. Blah sequel to DEAR DETECTIVE, with sleuth Girardot and professor Noiret becoming involved in intrigue while honeymooning in Greece. [PG]▼

Jupiter's Wife (1994) C-78m. ***½ D: Michel Negroponte. Compelling documentary about a middle-aged homeless woman whom filmmaker Negroponte chanced to encounter in N.Y.'s Central Park. She claims to have ESP and be the wife of the god Jupiter and daughter of the late actor

Robert Ryan! Negroponte delves into her past and discovers quite a few surprises in this extremely moving portrait of a shattered life. Shown on cable TV prior to its theatrical premiere. ▼①

Jurassic Park (1993) C-126m. ***½ D: Steven Spielberg. Sam Neill, Laura Dern, Jeff Goldblum, Richard Attenborough, Bob Peck, Martin Ferrero, B. D. Wong, Joseph Mazzello, Ariana Richards, Samuel L. Jackson, Wayne Knight. Billionaire Attenborough invites paleontologists Dern and Neill and mathematician Goldblum to inspect his island amusement park, populated with living dinosaurs; he even has his grandchildren tag along, blissfully unconvinced that anything could go wrong. Slam-bang thriller delivers the goods with action, suspense, hair-raising chills, and landmark special effects: the dinosaurs seem *alive*. The story can't bear such close scrutiny, but while this thrill ride is going, you won't mind. Michael Crichton cowrote the screenplay from his own novel. Won three Oscars, for Visual Effects, Sound, and Sound Effects Editing. Followed by THE LOST WORLD: JURASSIC PARK. [PG-13] ▼①●

Jurassic Park III (2001) C-93m. *** D: Joe Johnston. Sam Neill, William H. Macy, Téa Leoni, Alessandro Nivola, Trevor Morgan, Michael Jeter, John Diehl, Bruce A. Young, Laura Dern. Entertaining popcorn movie that takes a formula and plays it for all it's worth: professor-paleontologist Neill is persuaded to lead an air expedition to the forbidden island where dinosaurs roam, but of course he hasn't been told the truth, and the plane lands there . . . a very bad idea. Full of scares, and lots of fun: proof that a thrill-ride type of movie doesn't have to be dumb . . . or overlong. Script by Peter Buchman, Alexander Payne, and Jim Taylor. [PG-13] ▼①

Juror, The (1996) C-116m. ** D: Brian Gibson. Demi Moore, Alec Baldwin, Joseph Gordon-Levitt, Anne Heche, James Gandolfini, Lindsay Crouse, Tony Lo Bianco, Michael Constantine, Matt Craven, Todd Susman, Michael Rispoli, Jack Gilpin. Shady (and, it turns out, psychopathic) underworld figure Baldwin victimizes an unsuspecting Moore so that she will sway fellow jurors into acquitting a Mafia boss. Comparisons to TRIAL BY JURY are apt, but this one goes on (much) longer and gets more ridiculous by the minute. The stars can't be faulted, but the script certainly can. Panavision. [R] ▼①●

Jury Duty (1995) C-85m. BOMB D: John Fortenberry. Pauly Shore, Tia Carrere, Stanley Tucci, Brian Doyle-Murray, Abe Vigoda, Charles Napier, Richard Edson, Richard Riehle, Alex Datcher, Shelley Winters, Dick Vitale, Andrew (Dice) Clay. "BOMB" may be too high a rating for this inane, insulting "comedy" featuring Shore as a jerk who would much rather face duty

on a sequestered jury (and get a free hotel room) than find himself a job. Loaded with tasteless, gratuitous references to the O. J. Simpson trial. [PG-13] ▼①●

Jury of One (1974-French-Italian) C-97m. ** D: André Cayatte. Sophia Loren, Jean Gabin, Henri Garcin, Julien Bertheau, Michel Albertini. Plodding melodrama about a woman who goes to outrageous extremes to protect her son, on trial for murder and rape. Gabin plays the judge. Aka THE VERDICT. [R]

Just a Gigolo (1979-West German) C-105m. **½ D: David Hemmings. David Bowie, Sydne Rome, Kim Novak, David Hemmings, Maria Schell, Curt Jurgens, Marlene Dietrich. *Very* interesting cast is chief attraction of weird melodrama starring Bowie as Prussian war vet who drifts from job to job in Berlin before finally discovering his true calling. Dietrich, in her last film appearance, pops in long enough to croak the title song; Rome's spirited performance gives lift to uneven film that possibly made more sense in original 147m. version released in Europe. [R] ▼①

Just a Kiss (2002) C-90m. ** D: Fisher Stevens. Patrick Breen, Ron Eldard, Kyra Sedgwick, Marisa Tomei, Marley Shelton, Taye Diggs, Zoe Caldwell, Sarita Choudhury, Ron Rifkin. Love, sex, infidelity, and betrayal among a group of N.Y.C. hipsters, showing how a simple kiss between a philanderer (Eldard) and the girlfriend of his best pal (Breen) leads to a bizarre chain of disasters and deaths. Well-acted feature directing debut for actor Stevens is yet another self-indulgent indie riff on LA RONDE, pointlessly gimmicked up with animation, surreal flashbacks and flash-forwards, and a third-act rewind where the characters get a second chance. Unattractive digital video cinematography doesn't help. Written by Breen, based on his play. [R] ▼①

Just a Little Harmless Sex (1999) C-98m. **½ D: Rick Rosenthal. Alison Eastwood, Lauren Hutton, Kimberly Williams, Jonathan Silverman, Jessica Lundy, Rachel Hunter, William Ragsdale. After a wife kicks her husband out of the house (when he reluctantly picks up a hooker one night) their marriage is thrust into crisis mode. She calls her girlfriends together for advice, and he does the same with the guys; they all converge at a local club. Minor but entertaining, even insightful, low-budget romantic comedy with a very attractive cast. [R] ▼①

Just Another Girl on the I.R.T. (1993) C-92m. *½ D: Leslie Harris. Ariyan Johnson, Kevin Thigpen, Ebony Jerido, Chequita Jackson, William Badget, Jerard Washington. A bright, sassy 17-year-old African-American (Johnson) desires to escape from her stifling Brooklyn housing project by going to college and then medical school, but her dreams are shattered when she finds herself pregnant. Cinematically, this is strictly amateur night; plus, the film's two white characters are thoughtless, mean-spirited stereotypes (proving that an African-American filmmaker can be as insensitive and racist as a white one). Sole merit: Johnson, who offers a spirited performance. [R] ▼❿

Just Around the Corner (1938) **70m.** ★★ D: Irving Cummings. Shirley Temple, Joan Davis, Charles Farrell, Amanda Duff, Bill Robinson, Bert Lahr, Claude Gillingwater. Simpleminded corn with Shirley single-handedly ending the Depression, manipulating pessimistic tycoon Gillingwater into creating new jobs. But the musical numbers with Robinson are still a delight. Also shown in computer-colored version. ▼❿

Just Ask for Diamond (1988-British) **C-94m.** ★★★ D: Stephen Bayly. Susannah York, Patricia Hodge, Roy Kinnear, Michael Medwin, Peter Eyre, Nickolas Grace, Dursley McLinden, Colin Dale, Bill Paterson, Jimmy Nail, Saeed Jaffrey. Clever, if occasionally cartoonish, detective-film parody, about the kid brother of a dumbbell private eye and the mystery surrounding a box of candy. Best for older children (although they might not get all the references to 1940s Hollywood detective dramas). Screenplay by Anthony Horowitz, from his novel *The Falcon's Malteser.* Aka DIAMOND'S EDGE. [PG] ▼❿

Just Between Friends (1986) **C-110m.** ★★½ D: Allan Burns. Mary Tyler Moore, Ted Danson, Christine Lahti, Sam Waterston, Salome Jens, Jane Greer, James MacKrell. Genteel tearjerker about two women who strike up a friendship, unaware that they share the same man—one as wife, one as lover. Too pat, too neat and clean to really hit home, though the acting is first-rate, and Lahti is terrific as the single career woman. Nice role for Jane Greer, too, as Mary's mom. Directing debut for writer Burns. [PG-13] ▼❿

Just Cause (1995) **C-102m.** ★½ D: Arne Glimcher. Sean Connery, Laurence Fishburne, Kate Capshaw, Blair Underwood, Ed Harris, Christopher Murray, Ruby Dee, Scarlett Johansson, Daniel J. Travanti, Ned Beatty, Liz Torres, Lynne Thigpen, Kevin McCarthy, Hope Lange, Chris Sarandon, George Plimpton. Eminent Harvard Law School professor is persuaded to help a black man in Florida who's about to be executed for a heinous crime he swears he didn't commit. Starts out as an engrossing story, but goes so far afield—and becomes so preposterous (not to mention unpleasant) by the swampy climax that it winds up a huge waste of time. John Katzenbach's novel considerably changed. [R] ▼●❿

Just for You (1952) **C-104m.** ★★★ D: Elliott Nugent. Bing Crosby, Jane Wyman, Ethel Barrymore, Bob Arthur, Natalie Wood, Cora Witherspoon, Regis Toomey. Zesty musical of producer Crosby who can't be bothered with his growing children, till Wyman shows him the way. Pleasant Harry Warren–Leo Robin score, highlighted by "Zing a Little Zong." Based on Stephen Vincent Benet novel *Famous.* ▼❶❿

Just Friends (2005-U.S.-Canadian) **C-94m.** ★½ D: Roger Kumble. Ryan Reynolds, Amy Smart, Anna Faris, Chris Klein, Julie Hagerty, Stephen Root, Christopher Marquette. An unlikely airplane breakdown traps a handsome music industry bigwig (who was overweight and unpopular as a kid) and a deranged teen pop sensation in his New Jersey hometown. When he tries to get back together with his best friend from high school, who never returned his affections, the expected hijinks ensue. Caricatures, clichés, and painfully unfunny slapstick sequences ruin a potentially sweet love story. [PG-13] ▼❿

Just Go With It (2011) **C-117m.** ★★ D: Dennis Dugan. Adam Sandler, Jennifer Aniston, Brooklyn Decker, Nick Swardson, Nicole Kidman, Dave Matthews, Kevin Nealon, Rachel Dratch, Allen Covert, Minka Kelly, Bailee Madison, Griffin Gluck. After Sandler has a traumatic experience with a woman he decides to completely change his life, becoming a plastic surgeon and lying to all future prospects to keep them from hurting him again. When he falls for a beautiful schoolteacher (swimsuit model Decker), he enlists the help of his loyal assistant (Aniston) to try and fix the mess he's in. Predictable storyline is relatively entertaining for a while, but gets more ridiculous and unbelievable as it progresses. Sandler is still trying to find a happy medium between fart jokes and mushy love stories. Remake of CACTUS FLOWER. [PG-13] ❶

Just Imagine (1930) **109m.** ★½ D: David Butler. El Brendel, Maureen O'Sullivan, John Garrick, Marjorie White, Frank Albertson, Hobart Bosworth. Famous but utterly disappointing sci-fi musical set in 1980, with Brendel, officially dead since 1930, suddenly revived and unable to get used to phenomenal changes in living. Futuristic sets, gags, costumes made tremendous impression on everyone who saw film in 1930, but alas, it doesn't wear well at all. Songs by DeSylva-Brown-Henderson.

Justine (1969) **C-116m.** ★★½ D: George Cukor. Anouk Aimée, Dirk Bogarde, Robert Forster, Anna Karina, Philippe Noiret, Michael York, John Vernon, Jack Albertson, Cliff Gorman, Michael Constantine, Marcel Dalio, Michael Dunn, Abraham Sofaer. Jews and Moslems equal topicality, but this is merely exotic kitsch (though Cukor makes great use of widescreen). Tunisian settings and a lush brothel scene can't rescue this condensation of Lawrence Durrell's *Alexandria Quartet.* [R] ▼

Just Like a Woman (1992-British) **C-102m.**

**½ D: Christopher Monger. Julie Walters, Adrian Pasdar, Paul Freeman, Gordon Kennedy, Susan Wooldridge. Amiable (if a bit overlong) comedy featuring Pasdar as Gerald, a heterosexual American in London who derives pleasure from becoming "Geraldine" and wearing women's clothes. The film works because it's never condescending toward Gerald; he's not a caricature, but a guy with an unusual predilection. ▼

Just Like Heaven (2005) C-95m. **½ D: Mark Waters. Reese Witherspoon, Mark Ruffalo, Donal Logue, Ben Shenkman, Jon Heder, Dina Waters, Rosalind Chao, Ivana Milicevic. Widower Ruffalo moves into an apartment inhabited by Witherspoon's spirit and an unlikely connection begins. Amiable fluff is sustained by charming performances from the leads and a solid supporting cast. [PG-13] ▼▶

Just Looking (2000) C-97m. ** D: Jason Alexander. Ryan Merriman, Gretchen Mol, Patti LuPone, Peter Onorati, Amy Braverman. Bland coming-of-age sexcom about a 14-year-old Jewish kid (Merriman) who gets sent to his aunt and uncle in the country (read: Queens) for the summer. His mission is to watch two people in the act of love, so he starts spying on a pretty neighbor. Affectionate but disappointing memory trip plays out like an ethnic episode of TV's *The Wonder Years*. [R] ▼▶

Just Married (2003) C-94m. **½ D: Shawn Levy. Ashton Kutcher, Brittany Murphy, Christian Kane, David Moscow, Monet Mazur, David Rasche, Veronica Cartwright, Raymond J. Barry. Young couple sets off for a European honeymoon, where one disaster follows another—and the bride is pursued by her onetime boyfriend. Surprisingly likable formula comedy, with Murphy and Kutcher giving it 100 percent. Super 35. [PG-13] ▼▶

Just My Luck (2006) C-102m. **½ D: Donald Petrie. Lindsay Lohan, Chris Pine, Faizon Love, Missi Pyle, Bree Turner, Samaire Armstrong, Tovah Feldshuh, Carlos Ponce, Makenzie Vega, McFly. At a masked ball, the world's most naturally fortunate girl kisses a handsome stranger, who just happens to be the most ill-fated fellow alive. Their karmas magically cross, and the girl who used to beat the odds every time stumbles through the rest of the movie trying to figure out what to do about the guy who stole her luck. Romantic comedy's gimmicky switcheroo script has both good and bad gags, but it's Lohan who makes it a star vehicle. [PG-13] ▶

Just One of the Guys (1985) C-100m. *** D: Lisa Gottlieb. Joyce Hyser, Clayton Rohner, Billy Jacoby, Toni Hudson, William Zabka, Leigh McCloskey, Sherilyn Fenn, Arye Gross. Pretty high school senior, convinced that looks have kept patronizing male teachers from supporting her in citywide journalism competition, dons male

disguise and tries again at another school. Engagingly eccentric characterizations take this fast-paced sleeper out of the ordinary; performed with gusto by a cast that's aiming to please. [PG-13] ▼▶●

Just Tell Me What You Want (1980) C-112m. **½ D: Sidney Lumet. Ali MacGraw, Alan King, Myrna Loy, Keenan Wynn, Tony Roberts, Peter Weller, Judy Kaye, Dina Merrill, Joseph Maher, Michael Gross, Leslie Easterbrook, David Rasche, John Gabriel. Obnoxious tycoon King drives long-time mistress MacGraw into arms of younger man, then does everything he can to get her back. Bitchy upper-class comedy may be too strident for some tastes, but King's flamboyant performance is sensational, as is Loy's quiet one as his long-suffering secretary. Screenplay by Jay Presson Allen, from her novel. Loy's last theatrical feature. [R] ▼▶

Just the Ticket (1999) C-115m. **½ D: Richard Wenk. Andy Garcia, Andie MacDowell, Richard Bradford, Laura Harris, Andre Blake, Elizabeth Ashley, Patrick Breen, Fred Asparagus, Ron Leibman, Chris Lemmon, Don Novello, Abe Vigoda, Bill Irwin. Mostly likable but lumpy comedy-drama about ne'er-do-well ticket scalper Garcia and his on-again, off-again relationship with MacDowell—who loves him but can't tolerate his utter irresponsibility. Nice characterizations, vivid filming on the streets of N.Y.C.; hurt by uneven narrative and overlength. Garcia produced the film and composed much of its music. Written by the director. [R] ▼▶●

Just the Way You Are (1984) C-94m. *** D: Edouard Molinaro. Kristy McNichol, Michael Ontkean, Kaki Hunter, Andre Dussolier, Catherine Salviat, Robert Carradine, Lance Guest, Alexandra Paul, Timothy Daly, Patrick Cassidy. Episodic but likable film about crippled musician (McNichol) who goes to French ski resort with her leg in a cast—to see, for once, what it's like when people don't know she's handicapped. Elements of sharp comedy, escapist romance, and travelogue aren't seamlessly connected, but results are extremely pleasant, and McNichol has never been more appealing. Script by Allan Burns. [PG] ▼▶

Just Visiting (2001-French) C-89m. ** D: Jean-Marie Gaubert. Jean Reno, Christina Applegate, Christian Clavier, Malcolm McDowell, Matthew Ross, Tara Reid, Bridgette Wilson-Sampras, John Aylward, George Plimpton. A 12th-century French knight and his valet are transported to the 21st century, where their only ally is the descendant of the nobleman's bride-to-be. Americanization of France's 1993 box-office smash LES VISITEURS with the same director and stars, and screenplay revisions by John Hughes. Reno and Clavier (the film's cowriter) are terrific, but this remake is heavy-handed and only occasionally funny. Super 35. [PG-13] ▼▶

Just Wright (2010) **C-100m.** **½ D: Sanaa Hamri. Queen Latifah, Common, Paula Patton, James Pickens, Jr., Phylicia Rashad, Pam Grier, Laz Alonso, Mehcad Brooks. Big-hearted physical therapist (Latifah) never seems to land a guy, while her beautiful, ambitious stepsister (Patton) has men falling at her feet—like a hot N.J. Nets basketball star (Common). Then Latifah nurses the player back to health after a crippling injury and he begins to see things differently—or so it seems. Cinderella story is attractive, innocuous fluff with some serious plot holes and more than a few cheesy moments; Latifah's likability helps a lot. Super 35. [PG] ▶

Just You and Me, Kid (1979) **C-95m.** *½ D: Leonard Stern. George Burns, Brooke Shields, Lorraine Gary, Nicolas Coster, Burl Ives, Ray Bolger, Leon Ames, Carl Ballantine, Keye Luke. Burns struggles to keep awful comedy afloat, but it ain't easy. Shields plays a runaway who comes to stay with the ex-vaudevillian. Commercial interruptions might help this one. [PG]

Juwanna Mann (2002) **C-91m.** ** D: Jesse Vaughan. Miguel A. Nunez, Jr., Vivica A. Fox, Kevin Pollak, Tommy Davidson, Ginuwine, Kim Wayans, Jenifer Lewis, Lil' Kim (Kimberly Jones), Annie Corley. Egocentric basketball star torpedoes his own career and no one in the NBA will hire him—until he disguises himself as a woman and joins a female team. Naturally, he's attracted to one of his colleagues—and predictably, he suffers a crisis of conscience as the experience turns him into a better man. This is TOOTSIE light—or is it TOOTSIE dark? Similarities to that classic comedy are superficial at best. Several real-life sports figures appear as themselves. [PG-13] ▼▶

J. W. Coop (1972) **C-112m.** ***½ D: Cliff Robertson. Cliff Robertson, Geraldine Page, Cristina Ferrare, R. G. Armstrong, John Crawford. Vivid character study of none-too-bright drifter who sets his sights on becoming No. 1 rodeo star. Tour de force: director/cowriter/star Robertson scores in all departments. [PG]▼▶

Kabloonak (1994-Canadian-French) **C-105m.** **½ D: Claude Massot. Charles Dance, Adamie Quasiak Knukpuk, David Bursztein, Patty Hannock, Philippe Freturn, Peter Hudson, Geoffrey Bateman. Dance (who played D.W. Griffith in GOOD MORNING, BABYLON) here portrays pioneer documentarian Robert Flaherty, who spends one year in Alaska befriending Inuit eskimos in order to make NANOOK OF THE NORTH (1922). Interesting throughout, if not particularly inspired. Aka THE STRANGER.▼

Kabluey (2008) **C-86m.** ** D: Scott Prendergast. Lisa Kudrow, Scott Prendergast, Christine Taylor, Conchata Ferrell, Jeffrey Dean Morgan, Chris Parnell, Teri Garr, Cameron Wofford, Landon Henninger. Burnt-out Kudrow is attempting to raise her two bratty kids while her husband is fighting in Iraq. Her loser brother-in-law arrives on the scene to help out and gets a job that requires him to wear a large blue suit that makes him look like an overgrown extraterrestrial. Bizarre, ambitious, but mostly downright silly; doesn't know if it wants to be a quirky farce, a cynical portrait of corporate culture, or a social commentary on the inanity of contemporary America. [PG-13]▶

Kadosh (1999-Israeli) **C-117m.** ***½ D: Amos Gitai. Yael Abecassis, Yoram Hattub, Meital Barda, Sami Hori, Uri Ran Klausner, Yussef Abu Warda, Lea Koenig. Thoughtfully made, involving peek into the world of the Orthodox Jew, centering on two deeply troubled sisters who live in an ultrareligious community in Jerusalem and are oppressed by the dictates of their faith. A trenchant exploration of the nature of spirituality and the impact of blindly following the strictures of religion without considering the consequences.▼▶

Kafka (1991) **C/B&W-98m.** **½ D: Steven Soderbergh. Jeremy Irons, Theresa Russell, Joel Grey, Ian Holm, Jeroen Krabbé, Armin Mueller-Stahl, Alec Guinness, Brian Glover, Robert Flemyng. Strikingly photographed and designed film about mild-mannered insurance clerk Franz Kafka (Irons), who becomes both curious and assertive for the first time when he begins investigating a friend's disappearance. Teasing, darkly comic tale takes elements from various Kafka stories about oppression and paranoia, and weaves them into an expressionistic tapestry. Set in 1919 Prague. Not a total success, and not for all tastes, but offers many delights, including some choice character vignettes. Written by Lem Dobbs; photographed on location in Prague by Walt Lloyd. [PG-13]▼▶

Kagemusha (1980-Japanese) **C-159m.** **** D: Akira Kurosawa. Tatsuya Nakadai, Tsutomu Yamazaki, Kenichi Hagiwara, Jinpachi Nezu, Shuji Otaki. Sixteenth-century thief is spared execution if he will pose as secretly deceased warlord whose throne is coveted by others. Grand combination of humanism and spectacle from a great filmmaker in the twilight of his career. Released outside the U.S. at 179m. Aka KAGEMUSHA (THE SHADOW WARRIOR). [PG]▼●▶

Kairo SEE: **Pulse** (2001)

Kaleidoscope (1966) **C-103m.** ** D: Jack Smight. Warren Beatty, Susannah York, Clive Revill, Eric Porter, Murray Melvin. Idea of Beatty-York teaming can't miss, but does, in bland comedy about American playboy/card-shark forced to capture narcotics smuggler or go to jail. Flashy but forgettable. Filmed in England. ▼▶

Kalifornia (1993) **C-117m.** *** D: Dominic Sena. Brad Pitt, Juliette Lewis, David Duchovny, Michelle Forbes, Sierra Pecheur, Gregory Mars Martin. Offbeat road-movie thriller about a writer and a photographer, researching a coffee-table book on serial killers, who get a harsh dose of reality when they hook up with Pitt and Lewis. Effectively ironic, and well acted by its talented cast. Unrated version runs 118m. Super 35. [R] ▼●▶

Kama Sutra: A Tale of Love (1996-Indian) **C-114m.** *** D: Mira Nair. Indira Varma, Sarita Choudhury, Naveen Andrews, Ramon Tikaram, Rekha, Pearl Padamsee, Arundhati Rao. Frankly erotic, spirited feminist saga of sex and sexual politics in 16th-century feudal India, telling the story of Maya (Varma), an independent-minded servant who seduces a young king. He becomes obsessed with her, but weds a princess whom he does not love. A pointed portrait of a woman who is unwilling to accept a woman's "destiny" of being her father's property one day and her husband's property the next. R-rated version runs 113m. [NC-17] ▼●▶

Kamikaze '89 (1982-German) **C-106m.** *** D: Wolf Gremm. Rainer Werner Fassbinder, Gunther Kaufmann, Boy Gobert, Arnold Marquis, Richy Mueller, Brigitte Mira, Frank Ripploh, Franco Nero. Police lieutenant Fassbinder (in his final screen role) attempts to foil an alleged bomb plot, set in a futuristic Germany. Exciting if sometimes confusing thriller, from Per Wahloo novel. ▼

Kamilla (1981-Norwegian) **C-100m.** *** D: Vibeke Lokkeberg. Nina Knapskog, Vibeke Lokkeberg, Helge Jordal, Kenneth Johansen, Karin Zetlitz Haerem. Briskly paced yet quietly disturbing chronicle of 7-year-old Knapskog and the world around her: most distressingly, her constantly squabbling parents; most specially, the secret world she shares with a little boy. Knapskog is remarkable, and the film can be favorably compared to SMALL CHANGE and FORBIDDEN GAMES, the celluloid masterpieces about childhood.

Kanal (1956-Polish) **97m.** *** D: Andrzej Wajda. Teresa Izewska, Tadeusz Janczar, Wienczylaw Glinski, Wladyslaw (Vladek) Sheybal. Intense, almost unrelentingly graphic account of the final days of the September, 1944, Warsaw uprising in Nazi-occupied Poland. This is the second of Wajda's war trilogy, after A GENERATION and before ASHES AND DIAMONDS. Aka THEY LOVED LIFE. Not shown in U.S. until 1961. ▼▶

Kandahar (2001-Iranian-French) **C-85m.** **½ D: Mohsen Makhmalbaf. Nelofer Pazira, Sadou Teymouri, Hassan Tantaï, Hayatalah Hakimi. A journalist who fled Afghanistan during one of its many civil wars returns to her birthplace after receiving a suicidal letter from her despondent sister, who remained behind. Timely film of oppression and hypocrisy in a religiously charged country is hurt by amateur actors and an underdeveloped script. The stark photography, simultaneously showing the beauty and desolation of that part of the world, is a plus. Loosely based on Pazira's real life. Followed by a documentary sequel. ▼▶

Kangaroo (1986-Australian) **C-105m.** ** D: Tim Burstall. Colin Friels, Judy Davis, John Walton, Julie Nihill, Hugh Keays-Byrne. Muddled account of controversial British writer (Friels) who exiles himself and wife Davis to Australia in the early 1920s, and develops an intellectual attachment to a group of Fascists. Potentially fascinating, insightful portrait of a man of letters and his difficulties in dealing with the real world, but there's little feel for the characters and their motivations. Adapted from D. H. Lawrence's autobiographical novel. Friels and Davis are real-life husband and wife. Panavision. [R] ▼

Kangaroo Jack (2003) **C-89m.** ** D: David McNally. Jerry O'Connell, Anthony Anderson, Estella Warren, Michael Shannon, Christopher Walken, Bill Hunter, Marton Csokas. Lifelong odd-couple pals are ordered (by O'Connell's mob-boss stepfather) to deliver an envelope of money to Australia—but a kangaroo makes off with the cash. Juvenile comedy has a terrible script, but kids may still respond to the amiable leads and the Australian setting. Don't blink or you'll miss Dyan Cannon in the opening flashback as O'Connell's mother. Followed by an animated direct-to-video sequel. Panavision. [PG] ▼▶

Kansas (1988) **C-108m.** BOMB D: David Stevens. Matt Dillon, Andrew McCarthy, Leslie Hope, Brent Jennings, Brynn Thayer, Kyra Sedgwick. McCarthy gets stranded in the Midwest after his car and possessions blow up on the road, and takes it on the lam after boxcar acquaintance (and punk) Dillon implicates him in a bank robbery. Goes into fast free-fall around the time McCarthy rescues the governor's daughter from drowning (!)—and falls for the kind of farmer's daughter who wears makeup and pearls in the field. Second only to Toto as the Sunflower State's top movie dog. Super 35. [R] ▼●▶

Kansas City (1996-U.S.-French) **C-115m.** ** D: Robert Altman. Jennifer Jason Leigh, Miranda Richardson, Harry Belafonte, Michael Murphy, Dermot Mulroney, Steve Buscemi, Brooke Smith, Jane Adams, A. C. Smith. Vividly atmospheric but dramatically lackluster portrait of K.C. in the 1930s, a hotbed of racketeering, political machines, and jazz, focusing on local mob kingpin Belafonte, young upstart Mulroney, and his wife, Leigh. Lots of flavor but little substance and a redundant storyline. Best part: the jazz, which is played almost continuously (often on-camera) by an all-star lineup including Nicholas Payton, Joshua Redman, Mark Whitfield, Christian McBride, Cyrus Chestnut, and Ron Carter. [R]▼●◗

Kansas City Bomber (1972) **C-99m.** ** D: Jerrold Freedman. Raquel Welch, Kevin McCarthy, Helena Kallianiotes, Norman Alden, Jeanne Cooper, Dick Lane, Jodie Foster. Once you've seen five minutes, it doesn't pay to stay through the rest. Raquel stars as good-hearted roller derby star who has female colleagues jealous, male employers drooling. Dialogue, situations often unintentionally funny. [PG]◗

Kansas City Confidential (1952) **98m.** *** D: Phil Karlson. John Payne, Coleen Gray, Preston Foster, Neville Brand, Lee Van Cleef, Jack Elam, Dona Drake. Tough action drama with hard-luck ex-con Payne implicated in a bank heist, determined to quite literally unmask the real culprits. Quentin Tarantino must have seen this one prior to scripting RESERVOIR DOGS!▼◗

Karate Cop SEE: **Slaughter in San Francisco**

Karate Kid, The (1984) **C-126m.** ***½ D: John G. Avildsen. Ralph Macchio, Noriyuki (Pat) Morita, Elisabeth Shue, Randee Heller, Martin Kove, William Zabka, Chad McQueen, Tony O'Dell, Larry Drake. Teenager is beset by bullies until an unlikely mentor (the Japanese handyman in his apartment house) teaches him about self-confidence—and karate. Unabashedly old-fashioned, manipulative movie is a real audience-pleaser; from director of the original ROCKY. Winning performances by Macchio and Morita. If only they'd trimmed it a bit. Followed by three sequels (last is THE NEXT KARATE KID) and animated TV series. Remade in 2010. [PG]▼●◗

Karate Kid, The (2010-U.S.-Chinese) **C-140m.** *** D: Harald Zwart. Jaden Smith, Jackie Chan, Taraji P. Henson, Wenwen Han, Rongguang Yu, Zhenwei Wang. American boy and his mom move to China, where he is truly a fish out of water. After a girl he meets at school is friendly to him, he's tormented by a pack of bullies, until the reclusive janitor at his apartment building comes to his rescue and reluctantly agrees to teach him martial arts. Remake of the 1984 hit retains only the broad outline of the original and stretches out the story (and climactic tournament) much longer than necessary . . . but charismatic Smith (Will Smith's son) and the always appealing Chan generate rooting interest, and the movie works as feel-good entertainment. Super 35. [PG] ◗

Karate Kid, Part II, The (1986) **C-113m.** **½ D: John G. Avildsen. Ralph Macchio, Noriyuki (Pat) Morita, Nobu McCarthy, Danny Kamekona, Yuji Okumoto, Tamlyn Tomita, Martin Kove. Purposeless sequel takes main characters from original film to Japan, where they're confronted by Morita's long-ago arch-enemy and his nasty nephew. Corny in the extreme (all that's missing from climax is hounds and ice floes), but made palatable by performances of Macchio and Morita. Aimed strictly at kids. [PG]▼●◗

Karate Kid Part III, The (1989) **C-111m.** BOMB D: John G. Avildsen. Ralph Macchio, Noriyuki (Pat) Morita, Robyn Elaine Lively, Thomas Ian Griffith, Martin Kove, Sean Kanan, Jonathan Avildsen. Utterly stupid sequel has the "kid" (27-year-old Macchio) being set up for slaughter by nemesis Kove (in an obligatory appearance). When Morita refuses to train him, Macchio turns instead to Griffith—a sadistic millionaire Vietnam vet (who also turns out to be a buddy of Kove's!). Will Morita save him? Naturally . . . but this film is hopeless. [PG]▼●◗

Kate & Leopold (2001) **C-121m.** **½ D: James Mangold. Meg Ryan, Hugh Jackman, Liev Schreiber, Breckin Meyer, Natasha Lyonne, Bradley Whitford, Paxton Whitehead, Spalding Gray, Philip Bosco, Viola Davis. A genial crackpot (Schreiber) manages to find a portal in time and transport a 19th-century gentleman to 21st-century N.Y.C., where he meets a driven career woman who's as foreign to his acquaintance as he is to her. Cute, funny romantic comedy goes on longer than it should—given that the finale is a foregone conclusion. Jackman is charming, and Meyer is very funny as Ryan's actor brother. [PG-13]▼◗

Katie's Passion SEE: **Keetje Tippel**

Katyn (2007-Polish) **C-118m.** ***½ D: Andrzej Wajda. Andrzej Chyra, Maja Ostaszewska, Artur Zmijewski, Danuta Stenka, Jan Englert, Magdalena Cielecka, Agnieszka Glinska. Intense, epic drama set in Poland during and immediately following WW2. In 1940, thousands of Polish officers and civilians are massacred by the Russians in the Katyn forest, an event that the Germans use to propagandize the Poles while occupying the country. Once the war ends, the Soviets (who are building their postwar powerbase) attribute the atrocity to the Nazis . . . and heaven help anyone who disagrees. Scenario focuses on various individuals caught in the chaos; the final, extended sequence is heartbreaking. Octogenarian Wajda coscripted (based on Andrzej Mularczyk's novel); his father, a captain in the Polish infantry, died in the massacre. Super 35.◗

Katzelmacher (1969-German) **88m.** ** D: Rainer Werner Fassbinder. Hanna Schygulla, Lilith Ungerer, Elga Sorbas,

Doris Mattes, Rainer Werner Fassbinder, Harry Baer. Fassbinder's second film is an aimless seriocomic look at a group of suburban Munich slackers who spend their days sitting on the sidewalk while bitching, bickering, and putting down a Greek immigrant (Fassbinder). Interesting as an experiment in minimalism, but an artistic and dramatic dead end. Based on a play by the filmmaker. ▼◗

Kazaam (1996) **C-93m.** *½ D: Paul M. Glaser. Shaquille O'Neal, Francis Capra, Ally Walker, Marshall Manesh, James Acheson, Fawn Reed. Threadbare urban fantasy has a troubled kid accidentally summoning a friendly genie from his home—a boom box. Vehicle for basketball star O'Neal confirms his pleasing personality but gets mired in a story full of grimy and unpleasant characters; far from ideal family entertainment. Glaser also wrote the story. [PG] ▼●◗

Kazablan (1974-Israeli) **C-114m.** ***
D: Menahem Golan. Yehoram Gaon, Arie Elias, Efrat Lavie, Joseph Graber. Entertaining musical made in Old Jaffa and Jerusalem, based on a popular show that puts a love story against the backdrop of a cultural divide. Singing star Gaon repeats his stage role as a streetwise war hero out to save his neighborhood from being torn down. Filmed in both English and Hebrew-language versions. Panavision. ◗

Keane (2005) **C-93m.** *** D: Lodge Kerrigan. Damian Lewis, Amy Ryan, Abigail Breslin. Harrowing portrait of a desperately driven man who (we learn) fell apart after losing sight of his 6-year-old daughter at the Port Authority bus terminal in Manhattan many months ago. A chance meeting with a single mom and her young daughter offers him the first link to stability, and reality, he's had in a long time. A tour-de-force performance by Lewis propels this lean, intense, ultimately satisfying drama shot entirely with a handheld camera. Written by the director. [R]◗

Keep, The (1983) **C-96m.** *½ D: Michael Mann. Scott Glenn, Ian McKellen, Alberta Watson, Jürgen Prochnow, Robert Prosky, Gabriel Byrne. German soldiers try to defend a Rumanian mountain pass during WW2 by headquartering in an ancient fortress—ignoring villagers' warnings of a strange presence inside. Outlandish, incoherent, and mostly awful; recommended only for connoisseurs of Strange Cinema. Panavision. [R] ▼●◗

Keep 'Em Flying (1941) **86m.** **½ D: Arthur Lubin. Bud Abbott, Lou Costello, Carol Bruce, Martha Raye, William Gargan, Dick Foran. Good A&C mixed in with clichéd plot of stunt pilot Foran unable to accustom himself to Air Force discipline. Raye is fun playing twins. ▼●◗

Keeper of the Flame (1943) **100m.** ***
D: George Cukor. Spencer Tracy, Katha-

rine Hepburn, Richard Whorf, Margaret Wycherly, Forrest Tucker, Frank Craven, Audrey Christie, Horace (Stephen) McNally, Darryl Hickman, Howard da Silva, Donald Meek. Reporter Tracy sets out to write the true story of a beloved, just-deceased American patriot. Dated, somewhat heavy-handed treatment of a still-timely theme: the pitfalls of blind hero worship. Scripted by Donald Ogden Stewart, with some interesting echoes of CITIZEN KANE. ▼●◗

Keeper: The Legend of Omar Khayyam, The (2005) **C-95m.** *** D: Kayvan Mashayekh. Adam Echahly, Bruno Lastra, Moritz Bleibtreu, Rade Serbedzija, Vanessa Redgrave, Christopher Simpson, Marie Espinosa, Diane Baker, C. Thomas Howell, Daniel Black. Family-friendly double feature: first, a Houston 12-year-old of Iranian descent embarks on a vision quest to find his roots; then, the epic story of the 11th-century Persian poet-scientist of Rubaiyat fame. Eastern and Western halves—seamlessly and subtly braided—are equally engaging, tied together by the theme of passing cultural knowledge to successive generations. In a perfectly cast film, Bleibtreu stands out as the callow sultan. [PG]◗

Keeping Mum (2005-British) **C-103m.** *** D: Niall Johnson. Rowan Atkinson, Kristin Scott Thomas, Maggie Smith, Patrick Swayze, Tamsin Egerton, Toby Parkes, Liz Smith. British black comedy set in Little Wallop, where vicar Atkinson, his sexually frustrated wife, and their two children welcome an eccentric new housekeeper (Smith). Small but delightfully realized fun, sparked by a sterling cast. Scripted by American novelist Richard Russo but transposed to bucolic English countryside by director-cowriter Johnson. Panavision. [R]◗

Keeping the Faith (2000) **C-129m.** **½ D: Edward Norton. Ben Stiller, Edward Norton, Jenna Elfman, Anne Bancroft, Eli Wallach, Ron Rifkin, Milos Forman, Holland Taylor, Lisa Edelstein, Rena Sofer, Ken Leung, Brian George. N.Y.C. boyhood pals grow up to be a priest and a rabbi, both contemporary thinkers with great appeal to their congregations. Into their lives comes a savvy woman who was their best friend at age eight, before she moved away; now they become caught in a most unusual triangle. Smart (if predictable) comedy goes on much too long and wears out its welcome, though the trio of stars is likable throughout. Norton's directorial debut. [PG-13] ▼◗

Keeping Up with the Steins (2006) **C-90m.** **½ D: Scott Marshall. Jeremy Piven, Jami Gertz, Garry Marshall, Daryl Hannah, Daryl Sabara, Doris Roberts, Larry Miller, Cheryl Hines, Richard Benjamin. Utterly likable, if somewhat loose-jointed, comedy about a Hollywood overachiever (Piven) whose rivalry with an arch-nemesis

[741]

(Miller) reaches its apex as he plans a spectacular bar mitzvah for his son. But when the boy invites his long-estranged grandfather (Marshall) to stay with the family in the days leading up to the big bash, the older *mensch* sets the kid on a different path. A comedy of recognition for its target audience, though first-time director Marshall (like his father, Garry) is in fact a goy. Filmed in 2004. [PG-13]❱

Keep Your Powder Dry (1945) 93m. ** D: Edward Buzzell. Lana Turner, Laraine Day, Susan Peters, Agnes Moorehead, Bill Johnson, Natalie Schafer, Lee Patrick, Jess Barker, June Lockhart. Hackneyed tale of playgirl Turner, by-the-book Day, and soldier's wife Peters, and their exploits as they join the WACS during WW2.❱

Keetje Tippel (1975-Dutch) C-107m. **½ D: Paul Verhoeven. Rutger Hauer, Monique van de Ven, Eddie Brugman, Hannah De Leeuwe, Andrea Domburg. Slickly produced tale of a poor-but-determined young woman (van de Ven), and her struggles as she rises up the social ladder in 19th-century Amsterdam. Superficial social commentary on working class life. However, van de Ven is excellent as Keetje. Aka A GIRL NAMED KATJE TIPPEL, KATIE'S PASSION, CATHY TIPPEL, and HOT SWEAT. [R] ▼●❱

Kelly's Heroes (1970) C-145m. **½ D: Brian G. Hutton. Clint Eastwood, Telly Savalas, Don Rickles, Donald Sutherland, Carroll O'Connor, Gavin MacLeod, Stuart Margolin, (Harry) Dean Stanton. Large-scale WW2 film tries for Sergeant Bilko-ish atmosphere with middling results; hippie soldier Sutherland isn't credible in 1940s setting. Action-filled aspects of Savalas and Eastwood's far-fetched gold heist behind enemy lines make film worth watching. Panavision. [PG]▼●❱

Kentuckian, The (1955) C-104m. **½ D: Burt Lancaster. Burt Lancaster, Diana Lynn, Dianne Foster, Walter Matthau, John McIntire, Una Merkel, John Carradine. Minor but spirited frontier adventure set in 1820s with Lancaster (doing double duty as star and director) traveling to Texas with his son, hoping to start new life. Based on Felix Holt's novel *The Gabriel Horn.* Matthau's film debut. CinemaScope. ▼●❱

Kentucky Fried Movie, The (1977) C-84m. *** D: John Landis. Evan Kim, Master Bong Soo Han, Bill Bixby, George Lazenby, Henry Gibson, Donald Sutherland, Tony Dow, Boni Enten, Ursula Digard. Vulgar, often funny skits strung together. Best: a lengthy Bruce Lee takeoff, a b&w spoof of the old courtroom TV shows. Idea originated with Kentucky Fried Theatre, a Madison, Wisconsin, satirical group whose key members—Jim Abrahams, David Zucker, and Jerry Zucker—went on to do AIRPLANE! Followed a decade later by

AMAZON WOMEN ON THE MOON. [R] ▼●

Kes (1969-British) 113m. *** D: Kenneth Loach. David Bradley, Lynne Perrie, Freddie Fletcher, Colin Welland, Brian Glover, Bob Bowes. Refreshingly unsentimental account of a young working-class boy who finds release from the dreariness of his life by looking after and training a falcon. This is no typical boy-and-his-pet story; rather, it's a pointed commentary on the lack of opportunities for the lower classes in England—a theme that's been a constant in director Loach's work.❱

Key, The (1958-British) 125m. **½ D: Carol Reed. William Holden, Sophia Loren, Trevor Howard, Oscar Homolka, Kieron Moore, Bernard Lee. Jan de Hartog novel becomes pointless romance tale. Loren is disillusioned woman passing out key to her room to series of naval captains during WW2, hoping to make their dangerous lives a little happier. Michael Caine has a small role. CinemaScope.▼●

Key Exchange (1985) C-90m. *** D: Barnet Kellman. Ben Masters, Brooke Adams, Daniel Stern, Danny Aiello, Nancy Mette, Tony Roberts. Masters plays a neurotic New Yorker who exchanges apartment keys with Adams but can't commit himself to her alone. Amusing adaptation of Kevin Wade's off-Broadway play with fine performances and good use of N.Y.C. locations. [R]▼

Key Largo (1948) 101m. ***½ D: John Huston. Humphrey Bogart, Edward G. Robinson, Lauren Bacall, Lionel Barrymore, Claire Trevor, Thomas Gomez, Jay Silverheels, Marc Lawrence, Dan Seymour, Harry Lewis. Dandy cast in adaptation of Maxwell Anderson's play about tough gangster (Robinson) holding people captive in Florida hotel during tropical storm. Trevor won Best Supporting Actress Oscar as Robinson's boozy moll. Script by Huston and Richard Brooks. Score by Max Steiner. Also shown in computer-colored version. ▼●

Keys of the Kingdom, The (1944) 137m. *** D: John M. Stahl. Gregory Peck, Thomas Mitchell, Vincent Price, Edmund Gwenn, Roddy McDowall, Cedric Hardwicke, Peggy Ann Garner. Peck is fine in this long but generally good film about missionary's life (played as boy by McDowall); from A. J. Cronin novel.▼●

Keys to the House (2004-Italian-French) C-105m. **½ D: Gianni Amelio. Kim Rossi Stuart, Andrea Rossi, Charlotte Rampling, Alla Faerovich, Pierfrancesco Favino. Well-meaning, low-key story has a young father meeting his teenage handicapped son for the first time, slowly trying to establish the relationship they never had, and would never have had until fate intervened. Rampling is moving as a woman with a disabled daughter who teaches the man the joy of caring and responsibility. Film might have had more impact if the performance of leading actor Stuart were more affecting. Young Rossi, who is disabled in real life, does an exceptional job. ▼◗

Keys to Tulsa (1997) **C-113m.** *½ D: Leslie Greif. Eric Stoltz, James Spader, Deborah Kara Unger, Joanna Going, Michael Rooker, Randy Graff, Mary Tyler Moore, James Coburn, Peter Strauss, Cameron Diaz. Or, Time Spent with Low-lifes in Oklahoma. Tiresome crime melodrama about a perpetual screw-up (Stoltz) who gets involved with a blackmail scheme instigated by seedy Spader, who also happens to be married to Stoltz's longtime heartthrob Unger. Diaz is fun in the first scene, but then disappears—and with her, all hope for some form of entertainment. [R] ▼◗

Key to the City (1950) **101m.** **½ D: George Sidney. Clark Gable, Loretta Young, Frank Morgan, Marilyn Maxwell, Raymond Burr, James Gleason. Bland romance between Gable and Young, two mayors who meet at convention in San Francisco. ▼

Khartoum (1966-British) **C-134m.** *** D: Basil Dearden. Charlton Heston, Laurence Olivier, Richard Johnson, Ralph Richardson, Alexander Knox, Johnny Sekka, Michael Hordern, Nigel Green, Hugh Williams, Ralph Michael; narrated by Leo Genn. Intelligent, compelling widescreen historical spectacle unfortunately lost in the shadow of LAWRENCE OF ARABIA. Olivier is eerily effective as an 1885-era Osama bin Laden, Heston is first-rate as "Chinese" Gordon, with solid support from a charismatic Richard Johnson. Fabulous battle sequences were staged by the legendary Yakima Canutt. Ultra Panavision 70. ▼◗

Kick-Ass (2010-British-U.S.) **C-113m.** ** D: Matthew Vaughn. Aaron Johnson, Christopher Mintz-Plasse, Nicolas Cage, Mark Strong, Chloë Grace Moretz, Omari Hardwick, Xander Berkeley, Michael Rispoli, Clark Duke, Lyndsy Fonseca, Jason Flemyng, Randall Batinkoff. Nerdy high school teen fulfills his dream of becoming a superhero called Kick-Ass, though he has no superpowers, just nerve. He runs afoul of a crime kingpin, only to find two unexpected allies: a father-and-daughter vigilante duo. (She's an 11-year-old "hit man" with an alarming vocabulary.) Starts out as an engaging wish-fulfillment story, and Cage is fun as a Batman-like crime fighter . . . then goes to extremes, turning from guilty-pleasure entertainment to an orgy of excess that leaves a bad taste behind. Created in tandem with a comic book by Mark Millar and John S. Romita, Jr. Panavision. [R] ◗

Kickboxer (1989) **C-105m.** *½ D: Mark DiSalle, David Worth. Jean-Claude Van Damme, Denis Alexio, Dennis Chan, Tong Po, Haskell Anderson, Rochelle Ashana. Dull, dumb martial-arts time-killer. Van Damme seeks revenge against Thai fighter who crippled his brother. Strictly by the numbers. Followed by several unrelated sequels. [R] ▼◗

Kicked in the Head (1997) **C-88m.** BOMB D: Matthew Harrison. Kevin Corrigan, Linda Fiorentino, Michael Rapaport, James Woods, Lili Taylor, Burt Young. Woefully inept N.Y. comedy about a would-be author of a meaning-of-life book and the tiresome characters he meets in the passing parade—among them motormouthed uncle Woods and flight attendant Fiorentino. Scripted by the director and his star. [R] ▼◗

Kicking and Screaming (1995) **C-96m.** ** D: Noah Baumbach. Josh Hamilton, Eric Stoltz, Olivia d'Abo, Chris Eigeman, Parker Posey, Jason Wiles, Cara Buono, Carlos Jacott, Elliott Gould, Jessica Hecht. Guess what? It's another we-just-graduated-from-college-what-do-we-do-now film! This one centers on a group of young men and their life-and-death crises concerning relationships, jobs, parents, etc. Successful in spots, but should have been better. Funniest scene is the opening—a grad night lawn party. Eigeman virtually reprises the roles he had in Whit Stillman's METROPOLITAN and BARCELONA. [R] ▼◗

Kicking & Screaming (2005) **C-96m.** **½ D: Jesse Dylan. Will Ferrell, Robert Duvall, Mike Ditka, Kate Walsh, Musetta Vander, Dylan McLaughlin, Josh Hutcherson, Jeremy Bergman, Elliot Cho, Steven Anthony Lawrence, Laura Kightlinger. Frenetic family sports comedy is a perfect vehicle for Ferrell's everyman appeal and ballistic comic style. When his übercompetitive father (Duvall) dumps his own grandson from his kids' soccer team, Ferrell is drafted to coach their ragtag competitors. Less about movie-cute kids than out-of-control parents who adopt a "win at all cost" attitude, this upbeat trifle has some hilarious moments, as when an overcaffeinated Ferrell goes nuts in a coffee store. Former Chicago Bears legend Ditka has a sizeable and amusing role as himself, recruited to juice up Ferrell's timid coaching style. Super 35. [PG] ▼◗

Kickin' It Old Skool (2007) **C-108m.** BOMB D: Harv Glazer. Jamie Kennedy, Maria Menounos, Miguel A. Nunez, Jr., Michael Rosenbaum, Christopher McDonald, Debra Jo Rupp, Bobby Lee, Alan Ruck, Aris Alvarado, Vivica A. Fox. Think of it as BIG meets BREAKIN' 2: ELECTRIC BOOGALOO, but then *thinking* about this abysmal break-dancing comedy is not advised. Kennedy falls off a stage while bustin' some fancy moves at the age of 10 and doesn't wake from a coma until 20 years later. With his mind still in the '80s he puts together his old dance team to challenge a new generation of fancy footsteppers. This moronic exercise gets its only laughs from a David Hasselhoff cameo. TV's

Webster, Emmanuel Lewis, also appears. Super 35. [PG-13]🅓

Kid, The (1921) **50m. ***½ D:** Charles Chaplin. Charlie Chaplin, Jack (Jackie) Coogan, Edna Purviance, Chuck Reisner, Lita Grey. Chaplin's first real feature mixes slapstick and sentiment in a winning combination, as the Tramp raises a streetwise orphan. Wonderful film launched Coogan as major child star, and it's easy to see why. Alternate version (no different in content, but shown at a different speed) runs 69m. ▼🅞🅓

Kid, The (2000) SEE: **Disney's The Kid**

Kid and I, The (2005) **C-93m. ** D:** Penelope Spheeris. Tom Arnold, Eric Gores, Richard Edson, Linda Hamilton, Henry Winkler, Joe Mantegna, Brenda Strong, Shannon Elizabeth, Arielle Kebbel, Penelope Spheeris. Arnold plays a despondent, down-on-his-luck actor who reluctantly agrees to write and appear in a film with a nonpro: a 17-year-old boy with cerebral palsy (Gores) whose father is bankrolling the movie. Comedy mixes fact and fiction (in real life Gores proposed the idea to Arnold, who wrote and coproduced) and avoids becoming overly maudlin without excelling in any other way. A number of familiar faces appear in cameos. [PG-13]🅓

Kid Blue (1973) **C-100m. *½ D:** James Frawley. Dennis Hopper, Warren Oates, Ben Johnson, Peter Boyle, Janice Rule, Lee Purcell, Ralph Waite, Clifton James, Howard Hesseman, M. Emmet Walsh. Pseudo-hip Western comedy about misfit Hopper's faltering attempts to exist in small Texas town in early 20th century. Laughs, excitement, and interest are at a minimum here in spite of cast; Hopper is too old for his role. Panavision. [PG]

Kid Brother, The (1927) **82m. **** D:** Ted Wilde, J. A. Howe. Harold Lloyd, Jobyna Ralston, Walter James, Leo Willis, Olin Francis. Delightfully winning, beautifully filmed silent comedy with Harold as Cinderella-type kid brother in robust all-male family, who gets to prove his mettle in exciting finale where he subdues beefy villain. One of Lloyd's all-time best. ▼🅓

Kidco (1984) **C-105m. **½ D:** Ronald F. Maxwell. Scott Schwartz, Cinnamon Idles, Tristine Skyler, Elizabeth Gorcey. Okay comedy about the problems of preteen entrepreneur Schwartz and his cohorts, yuppies-in-training all. Ideal fare for the money-obsessed '80s yet barely released theatrically. Based on a true-life story; filmed in 1982. [PG]▼

Kid for Two Farthings, A (1955-British) **C-96m. *** D:** Carol Reed. Celia Johnson, Diana Dors, David Kossoff, Jonathan Ashmore, Brenda De Banzie, Primo Carnera, Sidney Tafler, Lou Jacobi. Imaginative fable of a poor little London boy (Ashmore) with a vivid imagination; he looks for a unicorn he believes will work miracles, and finds instead a sick, one-horned goat. Script by Wolf Mankowitz, based on his novel. ▼🅓

Kid From Brooklyn, The (1946) **C-113m. *** D:** Norman Z. McLeod. Danny Kaye, Virginia Mayo, Vera-Ellen, Steve Cochran, Eve Arden, Walter Abel, Lionel Stander, Fay Bainter. Comedy of milkman accidentally turned into prizefighter is often overdone but still a funny Kaye vehicle; remake of Harold Lloyd's THE MILKY WAY. ▼🅞

Kid Galahad (1937) **101m. *** D:** Michael Curtiz. Edward G. Robinson, Bette Davis, Humphrey Bogart, Wayne Morris, Jane Bryan, Harry Carey, Veda Ann Borg. Well-paced yarn with promoter Robinson making naive bellhop Morris a boxing star, tangling with mobster Bogart at every turn. Remade in 1941 (as THE WAGONS ROLL AT NIGHT) and in 1962. Shown on TV for years as BATTLING BELLHOP. ▼🅓

Kid Galahad (1962) **C-95m. *½ D:** Phil Karlson. Elvis Presley, Gig Young, Lola Albright, Joan Blackman, Charles Bronson, Ned Glass. This remake lacks wallop of the original. Elvis stars as a boxer who wins championship—and sings six forgettable songs—but prefers quiet life as garage mechanic. ▼🅞🅓

Kid Glove Killer (1942) **74m. *** D:** Fred Zinnemann. Van Heflin, Lee Bowman, Marsha Hunt, Samuel S. Hinds, Cliff Clark, Eddie Quillan. Solid B film about police chemist Heflin uncovering the killer of a mayor, with taut direction by Zinnemann. Look for Ava Gardner as a car hop.

Kid in King Arthur's Court, A (1995) **C-89m. **½ D:** Michael Gottlieb. Thomas Ian Nicholas, Joss Ackland, Art Malik, Paloma Baeza, Kate Winslet, Ron Moody, Daniel Craig. Innocuous kids' comedy about a teenaged boy who's magically transported to ancient Camelot, where he helps to redeem the doddering King Arthur and undo the archvillain Lord Belasco. Parents may yawn, but it's a pleasant-enough outing for kids. Young Nicholas is engaging and Ackland is solid as a rock, playing the good King. [PG]▼🅞🅓

Kidnapped (1938) **90m. **½ D:** Alfred L. Werker. Warner Baxter, Freddie Bartholomew, Arleen Whelan, C. Aubrey Smith, Reginald Owen, John Carradine, Nigel Bruce. Good adventure yarn of 1750s Scotland and England but not Robert Louis Stevenson; fine cast in generally entertaining script.

Kidnapped (1948) **80m. ** D:** William Beaudine. Roddy McDowall, Sue England, Dan O'Herlihy, Roland Winters, Jeff Corey. Disappointing low-budget adaptation of Robert Louis Stevenson novel. Look for Hugh O'Brian as a sailor.🅓

Kidnapped (1960) **C-97m. **½ D:** Robert Stevenson. Peter Finch, James MacArthur, Bernard Lee, Niall MacGinnis, John Laurie, Finlay Currie, Peter O'Toole. Disney feature filmed in England is faithful to Robert Louis Stevenson's classic novel, but surprisingly dull. Good cast and vivid atmosphere are its major assets. ▼●▶

Kidnapped (1971-British) **C-100m.** ** D: Delbert Mann. Michael Caine, Trevor Howard, Jack Hawkins, Donald Pleasence, Gordon Jackson, Vivien Heilbron. Disappointing version of Stevenson tale is made endurable by Caine's pleasing performance as Alan Breck. Panavision. [G]

Kidnapping of the President, The (1980-U.S.-Canadian) **C-113m.** **½ D: George Mendeluk. William Shatner, Hal Holbrook, Van Johnson, Ava Gardner, Miguel Fernandes, Cindy Girling. The title tells all: Third World terrorists kidnap president Holbrook, with Secret Service chief Shatner intervening. OK actioner is certainly topical; based on Charles Templeton's novel. [R] ▼▶

Kid Rodelo (1966) **91m.** *½ D: Richard Carlson. Don Murray, Janet Leigh, Broderick Crawford, Richard Carlson. After jail term, cowboys go off to search for hidden $50,000 in gold. You've seen it all before. Based on a Louis L'Amour novel. Filmed in Spain.

Kids (1995) **C-90m.** **½ D: Larry Clark. Leo Fitzpatrick, Justin Pierce, Chloe Sevigny, Rosario Dawson, Yakira Peguero, Harold Hunter, Sarah Henderson. Photographer/skateboardist Clark's filmmaking debut is a cinema verité–style look at aimless N.Y.C. teens, focusing on Telly (Fitzpatrick), who loves to deflower virgins, and Jennie (Sevigny), who's facing the consequences of one such encounter. A telling portrait of '90s-style hedonism and the results of kids growing up without parents to guide them. Utterly matter-of-fact and nonjudgmental about its sexual frankness and violence, (which is precisely what disturbed many viewers). Is it purely exploitive, or true to life? You be the judge. ▼●▶

Kids Are All Right, The (2010) **C-106m.** ***½ D: Lisa Cholodenko. Annette Bening, Julianne Moore, Mark Ruffalo, Mia Wasikowska, Josh Hutcherson, Yaya DaCosta, Kunal Sharma, Eddie Hassell, Rebecca Lawrence. Teenaged brother and sister have been raised by two loving moms but are curious to know about the man who made their birth possible, so they look up their sperm donor and—to their mothers' dismay—befriend him. Savvy, funny, and unexpectedly poignant look at an alternative family, with first-rate performances across the board. Cholodenko cowrote the screenplay with Stuart Blumberg. [R] ▶

Kids Are Alright, The (1979) **C-108m.** *** D: Jeff Stein. Overlong and disjointed, yet frequently exhilarating documentary on The Who that manages to capture the anarchic spirit of the group—and of rock 'n' roll. Brief appearances by Steve Martin, Tom Smothers, and Ringo Starr, along with wild interviews with Townshend, Daltrey, Moon, and Entwistle. Songs include

"Magic Bus," "Happy Jack," and several numbers from *Tommy*. [PG] ▼●▶

Kids in the Hall Brain Candy SEE: **Brain Candy**

Kid Stays in the Picture, The (2002) **C-93m.** ** D: Nanette Burstein, Brett Morgen. Narrated by Robert Evans. From garment-center hotshot to screen actor to movie mogul and ladies man, Robert Evans has lived a colorful (and often public) life. This documentary allows him to tell his story, but his self-absorption grows tiresome after a while, and only vintage video and film clips bring it to life. Not nearly as much fun as listening to Evans' audiobook version of his autobiography. Highlight: Dustin Hoffman's impression of Evans, shown during the closing credits. ▼▶

Kid Vengeance (1977) **C-94m.** *½ D: Joe Manduke. Lee Van Cleef, Jim Brown, John Marley, Leif Garrett, Glynnis O'Connor, Matt Clark. Bloody, gory, obnoxious Western about young Garrett seeking revenge against outlaws who killed his parents and kidnapped his sister. ▼▶

Kika (1993-Spanish) **C-111m.** *** D: Pedro Almodóvar. Peter Coyote, Veronica Forque, Victoria Abril, Alex Casanovas, Rossy de Palma, Santiago Lajusticia, Anabel Alonso, Bibi Andersson. Wacky, very adult story about free-spirited makeup artist Kika (Forque, whose performance is positively infectious) and the men in her life, including an American expatriate writer (Coyote) and a psychotic prison escapee. Almodóvar has given his favorite actress, Abril, the role of a lifetime: a tabloid TV hostess who cruises Madrid with a camera strapped to her head, seeking to capture criminal acts on videotape. Very funny, explicitly sexual film doesn't quite sustain its momentum to the end, but remains fresh and certainly different. ▼●▶

Kiki's Delivery Service (1989-Japanese) **C-103m.** ***½ D: Hayao Miyazaki. Voices of Kirsten Dunst, Phil Hartman, Matthew Lawrence, Debbie Reynolds, Janeane Garofalo, Tress MacNeille, Edie McClurg. Enchanting coming-of-age fable about a friendly, precocious witch who must leave home on her 13th birthday to find her place in life. With her talking cat in tow, she makes friends (and uses her powers and flying broom) as the delivery girl for a small-town bakery. Another beautifully animated, kindhearted gem from filmmaker Miyazaki. [G] ▼●▶

Kikujiro (1999-Japanese) **C-116m.** ** D: Takeshi Kitano. Beat Takeshi, Yasuke Sekiguchi, Kayoko Kishimoto, Yuko Daike, Beat Kiyoshi. Half road movie, half variation on the unhappy child/crusty adult genre, a listless story of a young boy's journey to seek out his long-gone mother—with a low-life chaperone. Title character (played by the director under his "Beat Takeshi" monicker) is an unsympathetic bully, while young Sekiguchi is a bit of a lump. By the time this very protracted story tries turning fanciful by introducing two of the most unlikely bikers in history, a cutting-edge action filmmaker has lost control of his picture. [PG-13]▼❶

Kill and Kill Again (1981) **C-100m.** ** D: Ivan Hall. James Ryan, Anneline Kriel, Ken Gampu, Norman Robinson, Michael Meyer. OK chop-socky actioner, with Ryan foiling scientist Meyer's plot to take over the world. Filmed in South Africa. [PG]▼❶

Kill, Baby, Kill (1966-Italian) **C-83m.** *** D: Mario Bava. Erika Blanc, Giacomo Rossi Stuart, Fabienne Dali, Giana Vivaldi, Piero Lulli, Max Lawrence. One of horror maestro Bava's best films, spoiled only by his overuse of a zoom lens. Suicide victims in a small Transylvanian village are found with gold coins embedded in their hearts. Stylish, witty and colorful, with many astonishing sequences. Also shown in cut version under title CURSE OF THE LIVING DEAD. [PG]▼❶

Kill Bill Vol. 1 (2003) **C-110m.** ***½ D: Quentin Tarantino. Uma Thurman, Lucy Liu, Vivica A. Fox, Michael Madsen, Daryl Hannah, David Carradine, Sonny Chiba, Chiaki Kuriyama, Gordon Liu (Chia-hui), Michael Parks, Julie Dreyfus, Bo Svenson. A blood-spattered bride vows revenge on her former boss and colleagues, a team of elite assassins who left her for dead. Tarantino channels a dizzying array of pop culture influences, including spaghetti Westerns, samurai films, vintage Hong Kong chop-socky vehicles, and anime, but the result is all his own: a wild, adrenaline-charged, operatically violent, comic-book action yarn. This would be indefensible if it pretended to be anything other than what it is. The women are all terrific, and the climactic swordfight is a knockout. Ends with a cliffhanger leading to VOL. 2, though originally planned to be one long film. Super 35. [R]▼❶

Kill Bill Vol. 2 (2004) **C-137m.** *** D: Quentin Tarantino. Uma Thurman, David Carradine, Daryl Hannah, Michael Madsen, Gordon Liu (Chia-hui), Michael Parks, Larry Bishop, Sid Haig, Samuel L. Jackson, Jeannie Epper, Bo Svenson. Perfect companion piece to VOL. 1 doesn't have the same energy or enormous set pieces but establishes its own pace and style. Thurman must eliminate two more assassins (Madsen and Hannah) before her ultimate showdown with the boss, Bill. Carradine gives the performance of his career as Thurman's wily, articulate, and deadly mentor. Parks and Liu play (albeit briefly) entirely different roles than in VOL. 1. Tarantino continues to pay homage to favorite films and genres; there's even a quick shot of Roy Rogers in a William Witney Western. Super 35. [R]▼❶

Killbots SEE: **Chopping Mall**
Kill Castro SEE: **Cuba Crossing**
Killer SEE: **Bulletproof Heart**
Killer, The (1989-Hong Kong) **C-110m.**

***½ D: John Woo. Chow Yun-Fat, Sally Yeh, Danny Lee, Kenneth Tsang, Chu Kong, Lam Chung, Shing Fui-On. Spectacular thriller about a hit man (Yun-Fat) who forms an unusual relationship with a singer (Yeh) he accidentally blinds and the cop (Lee) assigned to stop him. Pulp melodrama achieves near-operatic grandeur, thanks to multileveled characterizations and story, creative direction, and phenomenal action scenes that make most American films look anemic by comparison. Woo also wrote the screenplay.▼❶❷

Killer: A Journal of Murder (1996) **C-91m.** *½ D: Tim Metcalfe. James Woods, Robert Sean Leonard, Steve Forrest, Robert John Burke, Cara Buono, Ellen Greene, Jeffrey DeMunn, Christopher Petrosino, Richard Riehle, Harold Gould. In 1929, young Jewish prison guard Leonard befriends Leavenworth convict Carl Panzram (Woods), smuggling him forbidden writing supplies. Panzram, a habitual killer, writes his story, which we see in flashbacks. Woods is brilliant, but the point of view is hackneyed and outmoded. Badly written and directed. [R] ▼❶❷

Killer Bats SEE: **Devil Bat, The**
Killer Elite, The (1975) **C-122m.** ** D: Sam Peckinpah. James Caan, Robert Duvall, Arthur Hill, Bo Hopkins, Mako, Burt Young, Gig Young. Mercenary Duvall double-crosses partner Caan, leading to characteristic but lesser Peckinpah bloodbath involving the CIA. Trashy script slightly redeemed by director's flair for action sequences. Panavision. [PG]▼❶❷

Killer Fish (1979-Italian-Brazilian) **C-101m.** ** D: Anthony M. Dawson (Antonio Margheriti). Lee Majors, Karen Black, James Franciscus, Margaux Hemingway, Marisa Berenson, Gary Collins. Pursuit of stolen jewels dumped in lake full of deadly piranha fish forms basis for this predictable outing filmed in Brazil. Same fishy predators were used in much more enjoyable film, PIRANHA. Also known as DEADLY TREASURE OF THE PIRANHA. [PG]▼

Killer Force (1975) **C-101m.** ** D: Val Guest. Peter Fonda, Telly Savalas, Hugh O'Brian, Christopher Lee, Maud Adams, O. J. Simpson, Ian Yule. Dirty doings at diamond syndicate's desert mine in South Africa. Has cast and potential but overly diffuse and complex. [R]▼

Killer Grizzly SEE: **Grizzly**
Killer Inside Me, The (1976) **C-99m.** *** D: Burt Kennedy. Stacy Keach, Susan Tyrrell, Keenan Wynn, Tisha Sterling, Don Stroud, Charles McGraw. Bizarre opus about a psychotic deputy sheriff (flashbacks accounting for his present state) about to go off the deep end; saved and made believable by strong performance from Keach. Based on the Jim Thompson novel. Remade in 2010. Panavision. [R]▼❶❷

Killer Inside Me, The (2010-U.S.-British-Swedish) **C-109m.** ** D: Michael Winterbottom. Casey Affleck, Kate Hudson, Jessica Alba, Simon Baker, Bill Pullman, Ned Beatty, Elias Koteas, Tom Bower, Brent Briscoe, Jay R. Ferguson, Liam Aiken. In early 1950s Texas, a quiet deputy sheriff who's grown up in the community reveals a dark side no one in town has ever seen: He brutalizes women and does whatever it takes to cover up his misdeeds. Ostensibly faithful adaptation (by John Curran) of Jim Thompson's landmark 1952 novel succeeds in capturing only the externals and never allows us to get inside the protagonist's head. As a result the movie is remote and off-putting, smeared with truly repellent violence. Super 35. [R] ▌

Killer Is Loose, The (1956) **73m.** *** D: Budd Boetticher. Joseph Cotten, Rhonda Fleming, Wendell Corey, Alan Hale (Jr.), Michael Pate. Cop Cotten accidentally kills the wife of quiet bank-clerk-turned-robber Corey, who later escapes from prison with eye-for-an-eye revenge in mind. Fast-paced suspenseful sleeper, with excellent L.A. location photography and perhaps Corey's best performance: he's both scary and pathetic.▌

Killer Klowns From Outer Space (1988) **C-88m.** **½ D: Stephen Chiodo. Grant Cramer, Suzanne Snyder, John Vernon, John Allen Nelson, Peter Licassi, Michael Siegel, Royal Dano. One-of-a-kind alien invasion sci-fi featuring blood-drinking alien clowns harvesting a small city. Routinely plotted, but vividly designed, with cheeky humor, it plays its premise to the hilt, all circus bases touched. A cult favorite. [PG-13]▼●▌

Killer McCoy (1947) **104m.** *** D: Roy Rowland. Mickey Rooney, Brian Donlevy, Ann Blyth, James Dunn, Tom Tully, Sam Levene. Good drama of fighter Rooney accidentally involved in murder, with fine supporting cast of promoters and racketeers. Remake of THE CROWD ROARS (1938). ▌

Killer of Sheep (1977) **81m.** ***½ D: Charles Burnett. Henry Gayle Sanders, Kaycee Moore, Charles Bracy, Angela Burnett, Eugene Cherry, Jack Drummond. Starkly simple series of documentary-style vignettes set in the Watts district of L.A., focusing primarily on a working-class man (Sanders) who's become emotionally numb, especially with his wife. Could it be the result of his job at a slaughterhouse? These quiet slices of black ghetto life are connected by the thinnest possible thread, but offer a portrayal that's both profound and poetic. Barely released in 1977, when it was a thesis project at UCLA film school; theatrically released in 2007. Soundtrack features black artists ranging from Paul Robeson to Earth Wind & Fire. Burnett also photographed and edited.▌

Killers, The (1946) **105m.** **** D: Robert Siodmak. Burt Lancaster, Ava Gardner, Edmond O'Brien, Albert Dekker, Sam Levene, Virginia Christine, William Conrad, Charles McGraw. Compelling crime drama (based on Hemingway story) of ex-fighter found murdered, subsequent investigation. Film provides fireworks, early success of Lancaster (in film debut) and Gardner. Miklos Rozsa's dynamic score features the familiar dum-da-dum-dum theme later utilized by *Dragnet.* Screenplay by Anthony Veiller (and, uncredited, John Huston). Reworked in 1964.▼●▌

Killers, The (1964) **C-95m.** **½ D: Don Siegel. Lee Marvin, John Cassavetes, Angie Dickinson, Ronald Reagan, Clu Gulager, Claude Akins, Norman Fell. Two inquisitive hit men piece together the story of the man they've just murdered, in this free adaptation of Hemingway's short story. Originally shot for TV, it was rejected as "too violent" and released to theaters instead. Some latter-day notoriety derives from Reagan's casting as a brutal crime kingpin; it was his last movie role. Marvin has a great closing line.▼▌

Killers (2010) **C-100m.** BOMB D: Robert Luketic. Katherine Heigl, Ashton Kutcher, Tom Selleck, Catherine O'Hara, Katheryn Winnick, Kevin Sussman, Lisa Ann Walter, Casey Wilson, Rob Riggle, Martin Mull, Alex Borstein, Usher Raymond. Desperately unfunny, drearily frenetic action-comedy about an attractive but unobservant suburban wife who's shocked to discover her hunky husband (Kutcher) is a retired assassin—and her seemingly friendly neighbors want to collect the price on his head. Heigl is atypically unappealing here, acting at the top of her lungs to nerve-grating effect, while Kutcher simply mugs, shrugs, and skates through. HD Widescreen. [PG-13] ▌

Killer's Curse SEE: **Beyond the Living**
Killer's Kiss (1955) **67m.** ** D: Stanley Kubrick. Frank Silvera, Jamie Smith, Irene Kane, Jerry Jarret. Meandering account of revenge when boxer's courting of working-girl causes her boss to commit murder. Interesting early Kubrick; the inspiration for the film-within-a-film of STRANGERS KISS. Leading lady Kane became TV and newspaper journalist Chris Chase.▼●▌

Killers Three (1968) **C-88m.** BOMB D: Bruce Kessler. Robert Walker, Diane Varsi, Dick Clark, Norman Alden, Maureen Arthur, Merle Haggard. Knock-off of BONNIE AND CLYDE doesn't offer much by way of comparison, unless you find the idea of Dick Clark in wirerims a gas. [M/PG]

Killing, The (1956) **83m.** ***½ D: Stanley Kubrick. Sterling Hayden, Coleen Gray, Vince Edwards, Jay C. Flippen, Ted de Corsia, Marie Windsor, Joe Sawyer, Elisha Cook, Timothy Carey. The film that really put Kubrick on the map—a case study of a racetrack heist, with a colorful cast of characters, including the ultimate nebbish (Cook, married to vixenish Windsor) and a sinister sniper for hire (Carey). Major flaw: the *Dragnet*-style narration. Kubrick scripted from Lionel White's novel *Clean Break.* ▼●)

Killing Affair, A (1988) **C-100m.** *½ D: David Saperstein. Peter Weller, Kathy Baker, John Glover, Bill Smitrovich. Dreary goings on in the Southern backwoods, circa 1943, where Weller kills Baker's hateful husband, and then develops a turbulent relationship with her. Based on Robert Houston's novel *Monday, Tuesday, Wednesday,* this marks writer Saperstein's directing debut. Filmed in 1985. [R] ▼●)

Killing Box SEE: **Ghost Brigade**

Killing Fields, The (1984-British) **C-141m.** ***½ D: Roland Joffé. Sam Waterston, Haing S. Ngor, John Malkovich, Julian Sands, Craig T. Nelson, Bill Paterson, Athol Fugard, Spalding Gray. Highly charged drama based on the memoirs of *N.Y. Times* reporter Sidney Schanberg, who remained in Cambodia after American evacuation—putting his native translator and assistant Dith Pran in great jeopardy. Frighteningly realistic depiction of a country torn apart by war and terrorism; an emotional powerhouse. Long but worthwhile. Impressive feature debut for Malkovich and documentary director Joffé; Ngor (who lived through Cambodian turmoil in real life) won Best Supporting Actor Oscar for his acting debut. Oscars also went to cinematographer Chris Menges, editor Jim Clark. [R] ▼●)

Killing Game, The (1967-French) **C-94m.** **½ D: Alain Jessua. Jean-Pierre Cassel, Claudine Auger, Michael Duchaussoy, Eleanore Hirt. Mystery comic strip writer comes up with his ultimate puzzler. Not bad. ▼

Killing Heat SEE: **Grass Is Singing, The**

Killing Me Softly (2002-U.S.-British) **C-100m.** ** D: Chen Kaige. Heather Graham, Joseph Fiennes, Natascha McElhone, Ulrich Thomsen, Ian Hart, Jason Hughes, Kika Markham. American Graham, living in London and already in a relationship, is drawn to a handsome stranger. Will this attraction be fatal? Potentially intriguing tale of desire, obsession, and the fine line between ecstasy and terror starts off promisingly but falls apart, becoming just another predictable thriller. Kaige's English-language debut. Released direct to video in the U.S. Also available in an unrated version. [R] ▼

Killing of a Chinese Bookie, The (1976) **C-109m.** *½ D: John Cassavetes. Ben Gazzara, Timothy Agoglia Carey, Seymour Cassel, Azizi Johari, Meade Roberts, Alice Friedland. Strange, self-indulgent (even for Cassavetes) home movie centering around the owner of a strip joint, the mob and what used to be called "B-girls." Small cult may take to this; others beware. [R] ▼●)

Killing of Angel Street, The (1981-Australian) **C-101m.** **½ D: Donald Crombie. Liz Alexander, John Hargreaves, Alexander Archdale, Reg Lye, Gordon McDougall. Fair melodrama about corrupt real estate manipulators harassing homeowners to sell their property. Communist Hargreaves and geologist Alexander take on the villains when her activist father mysteriously dies. Supposedly based on actual events that also inspired HEATWAVE (1983).▼

Killing of Sister George, The (1968) **C-138m.** **½ D: Robert Aldrich. Beryl Reid, Susannah York, Coral Browne, Ronald Fraser, Patricia Medina. Overwrought but entertaining drama, with comedy touches, about soap opera actress Reid who fears her character (Sister George) is due to be "killed." Story follows her deteriorating lesbian relationship with dependent, child-like York, who's caught the eye of network executive Browne. Very good performances in this adaptation of Frank Marcus' play. [R—originally rated X] ▼)

Killing Time, The (1987) **C-94m.** ** D: Rick King. Beau Bridges, Kiefer Sutherland, Wayne Rogers, Joe Don Baker, Camelia Kath, Janet Carroll, Michael Madsen, Gracie Harrison. Stale noir-ish thriller about sex, sin, violence and duplicity in a small California town. Sutherland has murdered a deputy, assumed his identity, while new sheriff Bridges and mistress Kath plot to do in her evil husband (Rogers). DOUBLE INDEMNITY it ain't! [R] ▼●)

Killing Zoe (1994) **C-98m.** **½ D: Roger Avary. Eric Stoltz, Jean-Hugues Anglade, Julie Delpy, Tai Thai, Bruce Ramsey, Kario Salem, Salvator Xurev, Gary Kemp, Martin Raymond, Cecilia Peck. Writer-director Avary, coscripter of PULP FICTION, spreads mayhem and body tissue in his own Paris-set directorial debut—a Bastille Day bank caper in which some participants are preoccupied with drugs, and their imported Yank safecracker is preoccupied with a call girl who has surpassed all expectations. Plot twists and stylistic flourishes notwithstanding, zippy melodrama is too little, too late. *Extremely violent.* [R] ▼●)

Kill! Kill! Kill! (1972-French-Spanish-German-Italian) **C-90m.** *½ D: Romain Gary. Jean Seberg, James Mason, Stephen Boyd, Curt Jurgens, Daniel Emilfork. Interpol agent Mason, on the trail of Italian drug kingpins, gets competition from fellow agent Boyd, who believes in playing dirty. Hardened violence clashes with writer-director Gary's purple prose. Original title KILL, at 102m.

Kill Me Again (1989) **C-94m.** **½ D: John Dahl. Val Kilmer, Joanne Whalley-Kilmer, Michael Madsen, Jonathan Gries, Pat Mulligan, Nick Dimitri, Bibi Besch. Femme fatale Whalley-Kilmer makes like Jane Greer in this contemporary film noir, sexily scamming her way through the Nevada desert (and a couple of big cities) trying to steal gangland booty. Fans of detective genre will enjoy this mild send-up of crime flicks. Fun, but also inherently derivative. [R]▼▶

Kill Me Later (2001) C-105m. *** D: Dana Lustig. Selma Blair, Max Beesley, O'Neal Compton, Lochlyn Munro, D.W. Moffett, Brendan Fehr, Tom Heaton. Young woman who's sour on life is about to end it all when she's taken hostage by a bungling bank robber, who takes it on the lam. In time (of course), they drop their defenses and actually bring out the best qualities in each other, even as the cops close in. Modest but entertaining mix of black comedy and romance with good performances by the two leads. Director Lustig appears as Beesley's ex-wife. [R]▼▶

Kill-Off, The (1990) C-110m. ***½ D: Maggie Greenwald. Loretta Gross, Andrew Lee Barrett, Jackson Sims, Steve Monroe, Cathy Haase, William Russell. A miserable, manipulative, bedridden woman terrorizes her small seaside town by spreading malicious gossip over the phone. Clearly, this cannot last. First-rate realization of Jim Thompson's novel in this modest, moody film noir, scripted by Greenwald, perfectly photographed by Declan Quinn, with an ideal score by Evan Lurie. [R]▼

Kill or Be Killed (1980) C-90m. ** D: Ivan Hall. James Ryan, Norman Combes, Charlotte Michelle, Danie DuPlessis. Karate champions lock limbs as ex-Nazi coach seeks revenge against Japanese counterpart who bested him in a tournament during WW2. A cut above the usual martial arts fodder. [PG]▼

Killshot (2009) C-95m. ** D: John Madden. Diane Lane, Mickey Rourke, Thomas Jane, Joseph Gordon-Levitt, Rosario Dawson, Lois Smith, Don McManus, Hal Holbrook. Routine crime thriller based on Elmore Leonard's novel about a divorcing couple (Lane, Jane) forced to enter the Federal Witness Protection Program after running afoul of a weary, half-Indian hit man (Rourke) and his psychotic young partner (Gordon-Levitt). Quintessential B-movie material is drained of action and suspense via pretentious treatment from the director of SHAKESPEARE IN LOVE, although interesting cast keeps it watchable. Made in 2006 and barely released theatrically (at 84m.), film underwent extensive reshoots and recutting. Super 35. [R]▶

Kim (1950) C-113m. ***½ D: Victor Saville. Errol Flynn, Dean Stockwell, Paul Lukas, Thomas Gomez, Cecil Kellaway. Rousing actioner based on Kipling classic, set in 1880s India, with British soldiers combatting rebellious natives. Flavorful production. Remade for TV in 1984 with Peter O'Toole.▼▶

Kindergarten Cop (1990) C-111m. **½ D: Ivan Reitman. Arnold Schwarzenegger, Penelope Ann Miller, Pamela Reed, Linda Hunt, Richard Tyson, Carroll Baker, Cathy

Moriarty, Park Overall, Richard Portnow, Angela Bassett. Macho cop is forced to masquerade as a kindergarten teacher in order to find a youngster who's living with his mother incognito. Amusing but overly contrived Schwarzenegger vehicle blends elements of comedy, cop thriller, and romance. Despite the presence of cute kids, this is definitely not for children—especially the finale. [PG-13]▼▶

Kind Hearts and Coronets (1949-British) 104m. ***½ D: Robert Hamer. Dennis Price, Alec Guinness, Valerie Hobson, Joan Greenwood, Miles Malleson, Hugh Griffith, Jeremy Spenser, Arthur Lowe. Peerless black comedy of castoff member of titled family setting out to eliminate them all. Guinness plays all eight victims! Hamer and John Dighton adapted Roy Horniman's novel *Israel Rank.*▼▶

Kind of Loving, A (1962-British) 112m. *** D: John Schlesinger. Alan Bates, June Ritchie, Thora Hird, Bert Palmer, Gwen Nelson, Malcolm Patton, Leonard Rossiter, Peter Madden. Intelligent account of young couple forced to marry when girl becomes pregnant, detailing their home life; well acted.▼

Kindred, The (1987) C-97m. **½ D: Stephen Carpenter, Jeffrey Obrow. Rod Steiger, Kim Hunter, David Allen Brooks, Amanda Pays, Talia Balsam, Timothy Gibbs, Peter Frechette, Julia Montgomery. Enjoyable horror flick of teens in danger from a scientific experiment that resulted in a grotesque monster. OK special effects in a film marking Steiger's latter-day entry into Donald Pleasence–type horror roles. [R]▼●

King, The (2006) C-105m. ** D: James Marsh. Gael García Bernal, William Hurt, Pell James, Laura Harring, Paul Dano, Derek Alvarado, Milo Addica. A 21-year-old dreamer, just out of the Navy, returns to his hometown to seek out the father he has only heard about from his deceased Mexican mother. Now a happily married minister with two all-American kids, Dad wants nothing to do with him. Then the young man shatters taboos by taking up romantically with his unwitting half-sister. Dreary tale isn't helped by Bernal's less-than-appealing character and the sick nature of the film's evolving relationships. Predictably violent events unravel what little interest the film holds in its first half. Super 35.▶

King: A Filmed Record . . . Montgomery to Memphis (1970) 180m. ***½ D: No director credited. Superior documentary covering life of Dr. Martin Luther King from 1955 until his death in 1968 is marred only by the pretentious and unnecessary "bridges" featuring stars Paul Newman, Joanne Woodward, James Earl Jones, Harry Belafonte, Charlton Heston, Clarence Williams III, Ruby Dee, Ben Gazzara, Burt Lancaster, and Anthony Quinn. Otherwise, well-chosen compilation of news footage carries tremendous wallop. Sidney Lumet and Joseph L. Mankiewicz directed portions of the film. ●

King & Country (1964-British) **90m.** ***½ D: Joseph Losey. Dirk Bogarde, Tom Courtenay, Leo McKern, Barry Foster, James Villiers, Peter Copley. Vivid antiwar treatise beautifully acted by strong supporting cast. Bogarde is detached Army captain lawyer assigned to defend deserter private Courtenay during WW1. Score composed by harmonica virtuoso Larry Adler. ▼●

King and Four Queens, The (1956) **C-86m.** **½ D: Raoul Walsh. Clark Gable, Eleanor Parker, Jo Van Fleet, Jean Willes, Barbara Nichols, Sara Shane, Jay C. Flippen. Static misfire with Gable on the search for money hidden by husbands of four women he encounters. CinemaScope. ▼

King and I, The (1956) **C-133m.** ***½ D: Walter Lang. Deborah Kerr, Yul Brynner, Rita Moreno, Martin Benson, Terry Saunders, Rex Thompson, Alan Mowbray. Excellent film adaptation of Rodgers and Hammerstein Broadway musical, based on book filmed in 1946 as ANNA AND THE KING OF SIAM (and remade as ANNA AND THE KING). Kerr plays widowed English schoolteacher who travels to Siam to teach the King's many children, and finds dealing with His Highness her greatest challenge. Brynner gives the performance of a lifetime, and won an Oscar recreating his Broadway role. Kerr is charming; her singing voice was dubbed by Marni Nixon. Songs include "Hello, Young Lovers," "Getting to Know You," "Shall We Dance." Also won Oscars for art direction–set decoration, Irene Sharaff's costumes, Alfred Newman and Ken Darby's scoring. Screenplay by Ernest Lehman. CinemaScope 55. ▼●●

King and I, The (1999) **C-87m.** **½ D: Richard Rich. Voices of Miranda Richardson, Christiane Noll, Martin Vidnovic, Ian Richardson, Darrell Hammond, Adam Wylie, Allen D. Hong. Condensed animated kiddie version of classic Rodgers and Hammerstein musical now includes romps with animal chums, black magic by the king's evil minister, and unfunny slapstick with his racially stereotyped sidekick. Artwork and settings are colorful and lavish, but animation is erratic. Eight songs (out of twenty) survive somewhat unscathed; Barbra Streisand sings medley over end credits. [G] ▼●●

King Arthur (2004-U.S.-British-Irish) **C-126m.** **½ D: Antoine Fuqua. Clive Owen, Keira Knightley, Ioan Gruffudd, Stephen Dillane, Stellan Skarsgård, Ray Winstone, Hugh Dancy, Til Schweiger, Mads Mikkelsen, Ray Stevenson. Camelot is nowhere in sight in this revisionist look at the legend of King Arthur: the dark, gritty story concerns a warrior who fights long and hard,

only to be betrayed by his sovereign. Better than one might expect, with Owen an ideal lead and Winstone supplying welcome rough-and-tumble comedy relief, but Knightley is too young for the role of Guinevere (and her skimpy costume in the climactic battle scene is laughable). Unrated director's cut runs 138m. Super 35. [PG-13] ▼●

King Creole (1958) **116m.** **½ D: Michael Curtiz. Elvis Presley, Carolyn Jones, Dolores Hart, Dean Jagger, Liliane Montevecchi, Walter Matthau, Paul Stewart, Vic Morrow. Elvis is quite good as young New Orleans nightclub singer who is eventually dragged into the criminal underworld. Toned-down adaptation of Harold Robbins' *A Stone For Danny Fisher* (which was set in Chicago), co-scripted by Michael V. Gazzo. Songs include "Hard Headed Woman," "Trouble," title number. VistaVision. ▼●

King David (1985) **C-114m.** **½ D: Bruce Beresford. Richard Gere, Edward Woodward, Alice Krige, Denis Quilley, Niall Buggy, Cherie Lunghi, Hurd Hatfield, Jack Klaff. Solid biblical story traces young David's life from boyhood battle with Goliath to uneasy reign as king; only goes awry in second half, where abruptness undermines narrative. Visually striking, with Donald McAlpine's photography, Carl Davis' music strong assets—along with outstanding performance by Woodward as deposed King Saul. Panavision. [PG-13] ▼●●

Kingdom, The (1994-Danish) **C-271m.** ***½ D: Lars von Trier. Ernst-Hugo Jaregard, Kirsten Rolffes, Ghita Norby, Soren Pilmark, Holger Juul Hansen, Annevig Schelde Ebbe, Jens Okking, Otto Brandenburg, Baard Owe, Solbjorg Hojfeldt. Four-hour film is actually four Danish TV episodes strung together, set and shot at the real National State Hospital in Copenhagen (known as "The Kingdom"). As virtually every critic has pointed out, this is *ER* meets *Twin Peaks*, with crackpot doctors, paranormal goings-on, sex, black humor, etc. A must for those who think they've seen everything. Note: The unusual look of the film (a brownish, dirty-looking print texture) was achieved by shooting on 16mm, transferring to video, editing on video, transferring back to 16mm, and finally blowing up to 35mm! Alternate version runs 291m. Remade as a miniseries for TV in 2004. Followed by THE KINGDOM, PART 2. ▼●●

Kingdom, The (2007) **C-110m.** *** D: Peter Berg. Jamie Foxx, Jennifer Garner, Chris Cooper, Jason Bateman, Ashraf Barhom, Ali Suliman, Jeremy Piven, Danny Huston, Richard Jenkins, Frances Fisher, Anna Deavere Smith, Tim McGraw. The political thriller reinvented as an action movie: blood-pumping story of an elite FBI team that travels surreptitiously to Riyadh, Saudi Arabia, to investigate a massacre at a U.S. compound. Special Agent Foxx teams up with a sympathetic Saudi colonel (Barhom) who cuts through red tape to find the perpetrator of this atrocity. Plays like escapist action fare—except that the setting and political climate are all too real. Director Berg makes a cameo early on. Super 35. [R]◐

Kingdom Come (2001) **C-92m.** *** D: Doug McHenry. LL Cool J, Jada Pinkett Smith, Vivica A. Fox, Whoopi Goldberg, Loretta Devine, Anthony Anderson, Toni Braxton, Cedric the Entertainer, Darius McCrary, Richard Gant, Masasa, Clifton Davis. A funeral brings a raucous family together, but nothing can quell the tumult. Warmhearted, often broadly funny comedy-drama, adapted from the play *Dearly Departed* by its authors, David Dean Bottrell and Jessie Jones. Impressive performance by LL Cool J as a man coming to terms with his feelings about his father. Super 35. [PG] ▼◐

Kingdom of Heaven (2005-British-Spanish-U.S.-German) **C-145m.** *** D: Ridley Scott. Orlando Bloom, Liam Neeson, Eva Green, Jeremy Irons, David Thewlis, Brendan Gleeson, Marton Csokas, Ghassan Massoud, Edward Norton, Jon Finch, Iain Glen, Michael Sheen. A blacksmith, reeling from personal tragedy, is persuaded to join the Crusades by an illustrious knight, who reveals himself to be the young man's father. The new recruit shows his mettle by proving himself a man of the people who struggles to achieve peace between the Muslims and the Christians while defending Jerusalem. Impressive, epic-scale film manages to find nobility in the Crusades, but never loses sight of its main character's personal journey. Like the man he portrays, Bloom definitely carries his weight. Director's cut runs 194m. Super 35. [R]▼◐

Kingdom of the Spiders (1977) **C-94m.** *** D: John (Bud) Cardos. William Shatner, Tiffany Bolling, Woody Strode, Lieux Dressler, Altovise Davis. Unsurprising but well-made chiller about veterinarian Shatner and entomologist Bolling discovering that tarantulas are going on the warpath in Arizona. [PG] ▼◐

Kingfisher Caper, The (1975-South African) **C-90m.** **½ D: Dirk DeVilliers. Hayley Mills, David McCallum, Jon Cypher. Typical tale of intrigue, love and passion interwoven with a family feud over the running of a South African diamond empire. Aka DIAMOND LUST. [PG] ▼

King Gun SEE: **Gatling Gun, The**

King in New York, A (1957-British) **100m.** **½ D: Charles Chaplin. Charles Chaplin, Dawn Addams, Oliver Johnston, Maxine Audley, Harry Green, Michael Chaplin. Unseen in U.S. until 1973, supposedly anti-American film is rather mild satire of 1950s sensibilities, witch hunts, and technology. Chaplin overindulges himself, and film lacks focus, but there are good moments,

and interesting performance by son Michael as young malcontent.▼◐

King is Alive, The (2000-Danish-U.S.) **C-108m.** *½ D: Kristian Levring. Jennifer Jason Leigh, Janet McTeer, Bruce Davison, Miles Anderson, Romane Bohringer, David Bradley, David Calder, Brion James, Peter Kubheka, Vusi Kunene, Chris Walker, Lia Williams. Dreary, sun-baked drama about a group of exceptionally unpleasant people stranded in the African desert who, to pass the time, stage a production of *King Lear*. Supposedly inspired by *Lear*, it plays more like a cross between a Greek tragedy and an episode of *Survivor*. A Dogma 95 film, written and directed by one of the movement's founders. [R]▼◐

King Kong (1933) **103m.** **** D: Merian C. Cooper, Ernest B. Schoedsack. Fay Wray, Robert Armstrong, Bruce Cabot, Frank Reicher, Sam Hardy, Noble Johnson, James Flavin. Classic version of beauty-and-beast theme is a moviegoing must, with Willis O'Brien's special effects and animation of monster ape Kong still unsurpassed. Final sequence atop Empire State Building is now cinema folklore; Max Steiner music score also memorable. Followed immediately by THE SON OF KONG. Remade in 1976 and 2005. Also shown in computer-colored version.▼◐

King Kong (1976) **C-134m.** *½ D: John Guillermin. Jeff Bridges, Charles Grodin, Jessica Lange, John Randolph, Rene Auberjonois, Julius Harris, Jack O'Halloran, Ed Lauter, John Lone. Adle-brained remake of 1933 classic has great potential but dispels all the mythic, larger-than-life qualities of the original with idiotic characters and campy approach. Highly touted special effects (which earned a special Oscar) run hot-and-cold; real marvel is Rick Baker in a gorilla suit. Extra footage added for network showing. Lange's film debut; Joe Piscopo has a small role; look fast for Corbin Bernsen playing a reporter. Followed a decade later by KING KONG LIVES. Panavision. [PG]▼◐

King Kong (2005) **C-187m.** ***½ D: Peter Jackson. Naomi Watts, Jack Black, Adrien Brody, Thomas Kretschmann, Colin Hanks, Andy Serkis, Evan Parke, Jamie Bell, Kyle Chandler. In Depression-era N.Y.C. conniving movie producer Carl Denham (Black) shanghais a crew, a screenwriter (Brody), and a leading lady (Watts) for an ocean voyage to Skull Island on the biggest gamble of his career. They soon find themselves in a desperate struggle to survive in a jungle inhabited by predatory prehistoric creatures, while Kong is distracted by the feisty blonde girl. A rare remake that reinvents the original film while honoring it at the same time. Jackson pulls us into a world of wonder, both on Skull and Manhattan island, and takes us on a long but thrilling adventure that's hard to beat. He also cowrote with Fran Walsh and Philippa Boyens. Oscar winner for Sound Mixing, Sound Editing, and Visual Effects. Super 35. [PG-13]▶

King Kong Escapes (1967-Japanese) **C-96m.** BOMB D: Ishiro Honda. Rhodes Reason, Mie Hama, Linda Miller, Akira Takarada. Contrived new plot involving girl who wins ape's heart, battle against would-be world conqueror. Kong never had it so bad. Tohoscope. [G]▶

King Kong Lives (1986) **C-105m.** BOMB D: John Guillermin. Brian Kerwin, Linda Hamilton, John Ashton, Peter Michael Goetz, Frank Maraden, Alan Sader. Dino De Laurentiis sequel gives the ape a mate with everything he loves: She's tall, statuesque, with great mossy teeth. The Army tries to kill them (naturally), but not before a finale that actually rips off the final scene in SPARTACUS. Desperate. J-D-C Scope. [PG-13]▼●❙

King Kong Vs. Godzilla (1963-Japanese) **C-90m.** ** D: Ishirô Honda, Thomas Montgomery. Tadao Takashima, Kenji Sahara, Yu Fujiki, Ichirô Arishima, Mie Hama, Akihiko Hirata, Jun Tazaki. Essentially a KONG remake, with Tokyo subbing for N.Y.C. and Godzilla showing up to make that mess even bigger. (Oh yes, there's also a gigantic octopus.) Third Godzilla movie—the first in color and widescreen—was originally a clever satire of the worst excesses of TV journalism, but the U.S. version eliminates most of this (as well as Akira Ifukube's thrilling score), and adds awful new scenes with Michael Keith, Harry Holcombe, Byron Morrow, and Victor Milian. Still worth a look. (P.S.: Despite urban legend, only one ending was shot.) Japanese running time 98m. Tohoscope. ▼❙

King Lear (1971-British) **137m.** ***½ D: Peter Brook. Paul Scofield, Irene Worth, Jack MacGowran, Alan Webb, Cyril Cusack, Patrick Magee. This version of Shakespeare tragedy could be heavy going for the uninitiated, but often a strong and rewarding experience. Starkly photographed in Denmark. [PG]▼

King Lear (1987-U.S.-Swiss) **C-91m.** *½ D: Jean-Luc Godard. Peter Sellars, Burgess Meredith, Molly Ringwald, Jean-Luc Godard, Woody Allen, Norman Mailer, Kate Mailer. Bizarre, garish, contemporary punk-apocalyptic updating of Shakespeare classic. Little to be said about this pretentious mess except . . . avoid it. [PG]▼

King of California (2007) **C-93m.** ***½ D: Mike Cahill. Michael Douglas, Evan Rachel Wood, Willis Burks II, Laura Kachergus, Paul Lieber, Kathleen Wilhoite. Sixteen-year-old Wood's life turns chaotic when her father is released from a mental institution. A free spirit (to say the least), he is obsessed with locating an ancient Spanish treasure right under their noses in California and

pulls her into his crazy scheme—against her better judgment. Whimsically inventive story isn't easily pigeonholed, embracing comedy and drama, dreams and reality, and contrasting individuality vs. "progress." A genuine original, and an impressive debut film for writer-director Cahill. Douglas has never been better. [PG-13]▶

King of Comedy, The (1983) **C-109m.** ***½ D: Martin Scorsese. Robert De Niro, Jerry Lewis, Diahnne Abbott, Sandra Bernhard, Shelley Hack, Tony Randall, Ed Herlihy, Fred de Cordova. Pungent black comedy about a show-business hanger-on and world class loser who idolizes America's top TV comedian/talk-show host and figures out a bizarre scheme to get on the program. The denouement is a wow! Too mordant and "sick" for many viewers' taste, though it's all been done with a minimum of exaggeration . . . and a pair of knock-out performances by De Niro and Lewis. Written by Paul D. Zimmerman. Filmed in 1981. [PG]▼●❙

King of Hearts (1966-French-British) **C-102m.** *** D: Philippe De Broca. Alan Bates, Pierre Brasseur, Jean-Claude Brialy, Genevieve Bujold, Francoise Christophe, Adolfo Celi. Scotsman Bates walks into French town in WW1 that has been abandoned by everyone except those in the insane asylum. Stylish film isn't for all tastes, but has become a cult favorite. Offbeat. Techniscope.▼●❙

King of Kings, The (1927) **155m.** *** D: Cecil B. DeMille. H. B. Warner, Ernest Torrence, Jacqueline Logan, Joseph Schildkraut, Victor Varconi, Robert Edeson, William Boyd. Lavish silent film benefits from DeMille's superb storytelling skills and reverence for the subject. The Resurrection sequence is in two-color Technicolor. Some prints run 112m. Remade in 1961.▼●❙

King of Kings (1961) **C-168m.** ***½ D: Nicholas Ray. Jeffrey Hunter, Siobhan McKenna, Robert Ryan, Hurd Hatfield, Viveca Lindfors, Rita Gam, Rip Torn; narrated by Orson Welles. The life of Christ, intelligently told and beautifully filmed; full of deeply moving moments, such as the Sermon on the Mount, Christ's healing of the lame, and many others. Memorable Miklos Rozsa score. Not without flaws, but well worthwhile; grandly filmed in widescreen. SuperTechnirama 70.▼●❙

King of Kong: A Fistful of Quarters, The (2007) **C-82m.** ***½ D: Seth Gordon. Vastly entertaining documentary about Billy Mitchell, who has held the world's record for highest score on the first-generation video game Donkey Kong since 1982, and unassuming Seattle schoolteacher Steve Wiebe, who threatens to rob him of his title. Although the film takes us deep inside the video-game community it isn't really about the game at all, but a portrait of some amazing characters. Gordon wisely allows the viewer to make his own judgments. [PG-13]➤

King of Kong Island (1978-Italian) **C-92m.** BOMB D: Robert Morris. Brad Harris, Esmeralda Barros, Marc Lawrence, Adrianna Alben, Mark Farran. Mercenary Harris on the trail of loony scientist Lawrence, who's been monkeying around with the brains of apes, making them act like robots. Couldn't be any worse; not even good for laughs. Aka KONG ISLAND.▼➤

King of Marvin Gardens, The (1972) **C-104m.** ***½ D: Bob Rafelson. Jack Nicholson, Bruce Dern, Ellen Burstyn, Julia Anne Robinson, Scatman Crothers. Pretentious but genuinely haunting, original drama about Nicholson's failure to discourage brother Dern's outlandish financial schemes. Burstyn's performance as an aging beauty is chilling in its perfection, and Laszlo Kovacs' photography rates with the best of the decade. [R]▼●➤

King of Masks, The (1997-Chinese) **C-101m.** ***½ D: Wu Tianming. Chu Yuk, Chao Yim Yin, Zhang Riuyang, Zhao Zhigang. Beautifully realized story, set in 1930s Sichuan, about an aged street performer who realizes he has no heir to whom he can pass on his ancient tradition (and secrets) . . . so he purchases a child on the black market. Simple, eloquent, and moving. Written by Wei Minglun.▼➤

King of New York (1990) **C-103m.** ** D: Abel Ferrara. Christopher Walken, David Caruso, Larry Fishburne, Victor Argo, Wesley Snipes, Janet Julian, Joey Chin, Steve Buscemi, Paul Calderon, Giancarlo Esposito. Fidgety Walken plays the ex-con lord to a band of black drug dealers who regularly annihilate their Colombian-Italian-Chinese rivals. Cult director Ferrara offers style and little more in this ultraviolent outing; one extended monsoon shootout makes this presumably tongue-in-cheek effort worth a glance on a very draggy night. Walken's improbable headquarters, the Plaza Hotel, begs for a scene between his low-rent minions and Ivana Trump in the service elevator. [R]▼●➤

King of the Grizzlies (1970) **C-93m.** **½ D: Ron Kelly. John Yesno, Chris Wiggins, Hugh Webster, Jack Van Evera; narrated by Winston Hibler. Standard Disney animal-adventure about Indian who was "brother" to bear as a cub, and who now faces the full-grown grizzly in a different light. Filmed in the Canadian Rockies. [G]▼➤

King of the Gypsies (1978) **C-112m.** **½ D: Frank Pierson. Eric Roberts, Judd Hirsch, Susan Sarandon, Sterling Hayden, Annette O'Toole, Brooke Shields, Shelley Winters, Annie Potts, Michael V. Gazzo, Michael Higgins, Mary Louise Wilson, Matthew Laborteaux, Danielle Brisebois, Patti LuPone, Linda Manz; Tom Mason, Rachel Ticotin. Loose adaptation of Peter Maas' best-seller about three generations of gypsies in N.Y.C. Dying Hayden passes tribe leadership to grandson Roberts (in his film debut), skipping over sleazy son Hirsch, who promptly sets out to kill his offspring. Initially fascinating melodrama turns into conventional chase thriller, but still intriguing, with fine acting, moody Sven Nykvist photography, and infectious score by David Grisman and Stéphane Grappelli (who also appear in the film). [R]▼➤

King of the Hill (1993) **C-103m.** ***½ D: Steven Soderbergh. Jesse Bradford, Jeroen Krabbé, Lisa Eichhorn, Karen Allen, Spalding Gray, Elizabeth McGovern, Joseph Chrest, Adrien Brody, Cameron Boyd, Amber Benson, Kristin Griffith, Remak Ramsay, Katherine Heigl. A 12-year-old St. Louis boy, whose mother is ill and whose flaky father is often away, is forced to fend for himself in the depths of the Great Depression, using his wits to survive against extraordinary odds. One of the most vivid depictions of the Depression ever captured on film; full of rich, often harrowing detail that draws us in to vicariously experience everything young Aaron (Bradford) is going through. Director Soderbergh also scripted this adaptation of the memoir by A. E. Hotchner. Exceptional in every way. Super-35. [PG-13]▼●➤

King of the Khyber Rifles (1953) **C-100m.** **½ D: Henry King. Tyrone Power, Terry Moore, Michael Rennie, John Justin. Power is half-caste British officer involved in native skirmishes, Moore the general's daughter he loves. Film version of Talbot Mundy's novel lacks finesse or any sense of Kipling-style reality-fantasy. CinemaScope.

King of the Mountain (1981) **C-90m.** ** D: Noel Nosseck. Harry Hamlin, Joseph Bottoms, Deborah Van Valkenburgh, Richard Cox, Dennis Hopper, Dan Haggerty, Seymour Cassel. Garage mechanic Hamlin and friends guzzle beer and race their cars down L.A.'s treacherous Mulholland Drive. Pretentious, clichéd script and situations, with superficial and obvious finale. Hopper overacts outrageously as a burned-out former king of the Drive. Inspired by David Barry's feature in *New West* magazine. [PG]▼

King of the Roaring 20's—The Story of Arnold Rothstein (1961) **106m.** **½ D: Joseph M. Newman. David Janssen, Dianne Foster, Jack Carson, Diana Dors, Mickey Rooney. Slow-paced narrative of famous gambler's rise and fall miscasts lead role (real Rothstein was short and fat), slightly whitewashes him, and gets most of the facts wrong. Stray gangster-movie elements are inappropriately added. ▼➤

King of the Underworld (1939) **69m.** ** D: Lewis Seiler. Humphrey Bogart, Kay Francis, James Stephenson, John Eldredge, Jessie Busley. Far-fetched tale of doctor

Francis, falsely linked to gangster Bogart, the "last of the public enemies," setting out to prove her innocence. Remake of DR. SOCRATES.

Kingpin (1996) **C-113m.** *½ D: Peter Farrelly, Bobby Farrelly. Woody Harrelson, Randy Quaid, Vanessa Angel, Bill Murray, Chris Elliott, William Jordan, Richard Tyson, Rob Moran, Lin Shaye, Zen Gesner, Prudence Wright Holmes. Once-promising bowling champ whose career was ruined by a sleazy competitor sees his chance for reflected glory when he discovers a potential ace, who turns out to be Amish. Stupid and proud of it, this comedy goes the gross-out route and then, halfway through, asks us to care about these pinhead characters! Setups for laugh lines or visual punch lines are muffed time and time again. What a waste. 117m. R-rated version debuted on video in 1999. Super 35. [PG-13]▼●▶

King, Queen, Knave (1972-British) **C-92m.** BOMB D: Jerzy Skolimowski. David Niven, Gina Lollobrigida, John Moulder-Brown, Mario Adorf. Coarse, heavy-handed adaptation of Vladimir Nabokov novel about a klutzy youth who falls in love with his sexy aunt (Lollobrigida). Never released theatrically in the U.S. [R]▼

King Ralph (1991) **C-97m.** **½ D: David S. Ward. John Goodman, Peter O'Toole, John Hurt, Camille Coduri, Richard Griffiths, Leslie Phillips, James Villiers, Joely Richardson, Niall O'Brien, Julian Glover, Judy Parfitt. Mild, one-joke comedy about a Las Vegas lounge entertainer who is found to be the only living heir to the throne of England. Inoffensive but hardly inspired; Goodman's likability has to carry this a long, long way. Based on Emlyn Williams' novel *Headlong*. [PG]▼●▶

King Rat (1965) **133m.** *** D: Bryan Forbes. George Segal, Tom Courtenay, James Fox, Patrick O'Neal, Denholm Elliott, James Donald, John Mills, Alan Webb. James Clavell novel of WW2 Japanese POW camp, focusing on effect of captivity on Allied prisoners. Thoughtful presentation rises above clichés; many exciting scenes.▼▶

King Richard and the Crusaders (1954) **C-114m.** *½ D: David Butler. Rex Harrison, Virginia Mayo, George Sanders, Laurence Harvey, Robert Douglas. Cardboard costumer of Middle Ages, with laughable script. Indeed, Sanders as The Lion Heart and Harrison as a Saracen warrior do appear to be having a good time. CinemaScope.▼

Kings and Desperate Men (1983-Canadian) **C-118m.** *½ D: Alexis Kanner. Patrick McGoohan, Alexis Kanner, Andrea Marcovicci, Margaret Trudeau, Robin Spry, Frank Moore. Abrasive talkshow host McGoohan is held hostage in his studio by amateurish terrorists seeking public forum to debate plight of their comrade, convicted of manslaughter. Interesting premise sabotaged by poor direction, choppy editing. McGoohan overacts shamelessly. Trudeau has limited footage as his wife. [PG-13]▼

Kings Go Forth (1958) **109m.** *** D: Delmer Daves. Frank Sinatra, Tony Curtis, Natalie Wood, Leora Dana, Karl Swenson. Soapy but well-done three-cornered romance, set in WW2 France. Two GI buddies both fall for same girl, unaware that she is half-black. Script by Merle Miller; several jazz greats, including Red Norvo and Pete Candoli, put in appearances.▼●▶

King's Mistress, The SEE: **King's Whore, The**

Kings of the Road (1976-German) **176m.** ***½ D: Wim Wenders. Rudiger Vogler, Hanns Zischler, Lisa Kreuzer, Rudolf Schundler, Marquard Bohm. Deliberately slow, introspective, disarming tale (written by the director) of itinerant cinema mechanic Vogler, traveling with Zischler along the underpopulated, forgotten border regions between East and West Germany—a dying area that serves as a metaphor for the decline of the German film industry. It's also about cars, rock 'n' roll, and the American cultural imperialism of Wenders' homeland. The last (and best) in Wenders' "road movie" trilogy, after ALICE IN THE CITIES and WRONG MOVE.▼

Kings of the Sun (1963) **C-108m.** **½ D: J. Lee Thompson. Yul Brynner, George Chakiris, Shirley Anne Field, Richard Basehart, Brad Dexter. Skin-deep spectacle, badly cast, telling of Mayan leader who comes to America with surviving tribesmen and encounters savage Indians. Filmed in Mexico. Panavision.▶

King Solomon's Mines (1937-British) **80m.** *** D: Robert Stevenson. Paul Robeson, Cedric Hardwicke, Roland Young, John Loder, Anna Lee. Robust adventure given full-blooded treatment by fine cast, exploring Africa in search of treasure-filled mines. One of Robeson's best screen roles even allows him to sing. H. Rider Haggard story remade in 1950, 1985, and for TV in 2004.▶

King Solomon's Mines (1950) **C-102m.** ***½ D: Compton Bennett, Andrew Marton. Deborah Kerr, Stewart Granger, Richard Carlson, Hugo Haas. Remake of H. Rider Haggard story is given polished production, with Granger-Kerr-Carlson trio leading safari in search for legendary diamond mines. Scripted by Helen Deutsch. This won Oscars for Cinematography (Robert Surtees) and Editing; excess footage used in WATUSI and other later jungle films. Remade in 1985. ▼●▶

King Solomon's Mines (1985) **C-100m.** *½ D: J. Lee Thompson. Richard Chamberlain, Sharon Stone, Herbert Lom, John

Rhys-Davies, Ken Gampu. H. Rider Haggard's adventure yarn is updated for the Indiana Jones generation, but the results are unsuccessful. Cartoon characters and outlandish cliffhanger situations abound—but where's the charm? Followed by sequel (shot simultaneously), ALLAN QUATERMAIN AND THE LOST CITY OF GOLD. J-D-C Scope. [PG-13]▼●

King Solomon's Treasure (1977-Canadian-British) C-89m. *½ D: Alvin Rakoff. David McCallum, John Colicos, Patrick Macnee, Britt Ekland, Yvon Dufour, Ken Gampu, Wilfrid Hyde-White. Silly, low-budget adaptation of H. Rider Haggard's *Allan Quatermain* has miscast trio of Colicos, McCallum (with comedy-relief stutter) and Macnee hunting for African treasure, fighting off dinosaurs and meeting Phoenician queen Ekland. Despite obvious similarities, this is no RAIDERS OF THE LOST ARK.▼●

King's Pirate, The (1967) C-100m. **½ D: Don Weis. Doug McClure, Jill St. John, Guy Stockwell, Mary Ann Mobley. Cardboard, juvenile swashbuckler set in 18th century, with McClure the nominal hero. Remake of AGAINST ALL FLAGS.

King's Ransom (2005) C-97m. *½ D: Jeff Byrd. Anthony Anderson, Jay Mohr, Kellita Smith, Nicole Parker, Regina Hall, Loretta Devine, Donald Faison, Charlie Murphy, Jackie Burroughs. Stereotypes abound in this entirely unfunny comedy. A wealthy mogul (Anderson), hated by everyone around him, attempts to get out of paying off his ex-wife-to-be by having himself kidnapped, unaware that someone else is really planning to abduct him. Screwball antics and obvious mix-ups add up to naught, even with this talented cast. [PG-13]▼●

Kings Row (1942) 127m. ***½ D: Sam Wood. Ann Sheridan, Robert Cummings, Ronald Reagan, Betty Field, Charles Coburn, Claude Rains, Judith Anderson, Maria Ouspenskaya. Forerunner of PEYTON PLACE still retains its sweep of life in pre-WW1 Midwestern town, with the fates of many townsfolk intertwined. Beautiful Erich Wolfgang Korngold music score backs up plush production, fine characterizations. Notable, too, as Reagan's finest performance. Screenplay by Casey Robinson, from Henry Bellamann's best-selling book. Also shown in computer-colored version.▼●

King's Speech, The (2010-British-Australian-U.S.) C-118m. **** D: Tom Hooper. Colin Firth, Geoffrey Rush, Helena Bonham Carter, Guy Pearce, Timothy Spall, Derek Jacobi, Jennifer Ehle, Anthony Andrews, Claire Bloom, Eve Best, Michael Gambon. As it becomes increasingly evident that the Prince of Wales (Pearce) is not comfortable in his soon-to-be role as King of England in the mid-1930s, his more solid and responsible brother (Firth) is forced to deal with his greatest impediment to success: his stammer. He is eventually persuaded, by his wise and patient wife (Bonham Carter), to consult an unorthodox Australian speech therapist named Lionel Logue (Rush). Amazing—and inspiring—true story brought to life with verve and considerable wit in David Seidler's screenplay, enacted by a truly wonderful cast. Oscar winner for Best Picture, Director, Actor (Firth), and Original Screenplay. [R]●

King's Thief, The (1955) C-78m. *** D: Robert Z. Leonard. Ann Blyth, Edmund Purdom, David Niven, George Sanders, Roger Moore, John Dehner, Sean McClory. The king is England's Charles II (Sanders) and the thief is brash Purdom, whose pilfering of a valuable book sets off plenty of intrigue in this lavish costumer. Niven makes a fine villain. CinemaScope. ▼

King's Whore, The (1990-French-Austrian-British-Italian) C-115m. **½ D: Axel Corti. Timothy Dalton, Valeria Golino, Stephane Freiss, Feodor Chaliapin, Margaret Tyzack, Eleanor David, Robin Renucci. Lavishly filmed but dramatically uneven historical melodrama. In the royal court of Piedmont in Northern Italy, king Dalton becomes consumed by his burning desire for beautiful but unwilling Golino, the wife of his chamberlain. Scripted by Corti, Frederic Raphael, and Daniel Vigne. Aka THE KING'S MISTRESS. [R]▼●

Kinjite: Forbidden Subjects (1989) C-97m. ** D: J. Lee Thompson. Charles Bronson, Juan Fernandez, James Pax, Kumiko Hayakawa, Perry Lopez, Peggy Lipton, Amy Hathaway, Bill McKinney, Sy Richardson, Alex Hyde-White, Richard Egan, Jr. Glum urban thriller pitting supercop Bronson against scummy pimp Fernandez, who specializes in turning teenage girls to prostitution. Also involved is a Japanese businessman, newly come to L.A., whose daughter is kidnapped by the pimp. Some interesting ideas, but mostly formulaic. [R]▼●

Kinky Boots (2005-British) C-107m. **½ D: Julian Jarrold. Joel Edgerton, Chiwetel Ejiofor, Sarah-Jane Potts, Jemima Rooper, Linda Bassett, Nick Frost, Robert Pugh, Mona Hammond, Stephen Marcus. Comedy in the mold of such feel-good films as THE FULL MONTY and CALENDAR GIRLS, about a transvestite club entertainer who comes to the aid of a young man who's inherited his father's failing shoe factory. When they hatch an idea of creating outrageous boots for man-sized feet they set a course for reinventing the business and saving the soul (or is that sole?) of the company and its workforce. Worth seeing for the high-octane performance of Ejiofor, who looks great in heels and gets to perform such songs as "These

Boots Were Made for Walking." Super 35. [PG-13]▌

Kinsey (2004) **C-118m.** *** D: Bill Condon. Liam Neeson, Laura Linney, Chris O'Donnell, Peter Sarsgaard, Timothy Hutton, John Lithgow, Tim Curry, Oliver Platt, Dylan Baker, Julianne Nicholson, William Sadler, Heather Goldenhersh, John McMartin, Veronica Cartwright, Kathleen Chalfant, Dagmara Dominczyk, Lynn Redgrave, Katharine Houghton, John Krasinski. Provocative look at the life of Alfred Kinsey, who during a sexually repressed childhood developed a keen interest in biology that ultimately led to his great mission in life: freeing Americans from ignorance about sex, and publishing the results of a massive survey about sexual behavior. Startlingly frank, evocative biopic boasts superior performances and a keen sense of period detail, although it tries to cover too much ground, and much like its leading character, loses its way toward the end. Written by the director. J-D-C Scope. [R]▼●

Kipperbang (1982-British) **C-80m.** *½ D: Michael Apted. John Albasiny, Alison Steadman, Gary Cooper, Abigail Cruttenden, Maurice Lee. Annoyingly lightweight comedy detailing the romantic fantasies and predicaments of young teens and their elders—particularly, their English teacher—in 1948 Britain. Originally made for British television, released here theatrically in 1984. Original title: P'TANG YANG KIPPERBANG. [PG]▼

Kippur (2000-Israeli) **C-117m.** *** D: Amos Gitai. Liron Levo, Tomer Ruso, Uri Ran Klauzner, Yoram Hattab, Guy Amir, Ran Kauchinsky. A unique vision of the Yom Kippur War as seen through the eyes of two volunteer soldier brothers, both completely unprepared for battle. A painstaking, grueling picture of war.▼●

Kismet (1944) **C-100m.** **½ D: William Dieterle. Ronald Colman, Marlene Dietrich, Edward Arnold, Florence Bates, James Craig, Joy Ann Page, Harry Davenport. Colman tries a change of pace playing the "king of beggars," a wily magician whose daughter is wooed by the handsome young Caliph in this plot-heavy Arabian Nights–type tale. Passably entertaining but nothing special, despite opulent MGM production. Best of all is Dietrich, with tongue in cheek and body painted gold for one famous dance scene. Filmed before in 1920 and 1930; remade in 1955 after the Broadway musical version. Retitled ORIENTAL DREAM.▼●

Kismet (1955) **C-113m.** **½ D: Vincente Minnelli. Howard Keel, Ann Blyth, Dolores Gray, Monty Woolley, Sebastian Cabot, Vic Damone. Handsome but uninspired filming of the Broadway musical of this Arabian Nights–type tale. Robert Wright–George Forrest songs (based on

Borodin themes) include "Stranger in Paradise," "Baubles, Bangles, and Beads." CinemaScope.▼●

Kiss, The (1988) **C-101m.** ** D: Pen Densham. Joanna Pacula, Meredith Salenger, Mimi Kuzyk, Nicholas Kilbertus, Jan Rubes. Occasionally scary horror film builds up to but downplays the sexual implications of its CAT PEOPLE–style story of a family curse passed down to each generation by a woman-to-woman kiss. Salenger is the unlucky target of beautiful aunt Pacula's evil smooch. [R]▼●

Kiss and Kill SEE: **Blood of Fu Manchu, The**

Kiss and Tell (1945) **90m.** **½ D: Richard Wallace. Shirley Temple, Jerome Courtland, Walter Abel, Katherine Alexander, Robert Benchley, Porter Hall. Film of successful Broadway play about wacky teenager Corliss Archer is a bit forced but generally funny; one of Temple's better grown-up roles. Sequel: A KISS FOR CORLISS.

Kiss Before Dying, A (1956) **C-94m.** *** D: Gerd Oswald. Robert Wagner, Virginia Leith, Jeffrey Hunter, Joanne Woodward, Mary Astor, George Macready. Effective chiller with Wagner superb as psychopathic killer and Astor his devoted mother; well paced. Based on an Ira Levin novel. Remade in 1991. CinemaScope.▼

Kiss Before Dying, A (1991) **C-95m.** *½ D: James Dearden. Matt Dillon, Sean Young, Max von Sydow, Diane Ladd, James Russo, Martha Gehman, Ben Browder, Joie Lee, Adam Horovitz. Almost completely ineffectual thriller about an ambitious young sicko who charms—and murders—his way into a powerful family. Young plays twin sisters, enabling us to watch her give *two* bad performances. Writer-director Dearden even dares to have her looking at Hitchcock's VERTIGO on TV, a reminder (as if we needed one) of the right way to make this kind of film. Ira Levin's novel was filmed before in 1956. [R]▼●

Kiss Daddy Good Night (1987) **C-89m.** *½ D: Peter Ily Huemer. Uma Thurman, Paul Dillon, Paul Richards, Steve Buscemi, Annabelle Gurwitch, David Brisbin. Vague, forgettable melodrama-thriller about a young vamp (Thurman, in her screen debut), who seduces and robs men, and her strange relationship with older bohemian Richards. [R]▼●

Kissed (1996-Canadian) **C-73m.** *½ D: Lynne Stopkewich. Molly Parker, Peter Outerbridge, Jay Brazeau, Natasha Morley, Jessie Winter Mudie. A woman infatuated with corpses since childhood gets her dream job working in a mortuary, then meets a man who becomes obsessed with her flirtation with death. Dull, occasionally repulsive thought provoker seeks poetry in necrophilia. Only pluses are Parker and Morley's transfixing performances. Educational value: everything you ever wanted to know about embalming.▼▶

Kisses for My President (1964) **113m.** **½ D: Curtis Bernhardt. Fred MacMurray, Polly Bergen, Arlene Dahl, Edward Andrews, Eli Wallach. Thirties-style comedy of Bergen becoming President of the U.S., with MacMurray her husband caught in unprecedented protocol. Sometimes funny, often witless.▼▶●

Kiss for Corliss, A (1949) **88m.** ** D: Richard Wallace. Shirley Temple, David Niven, Tom Tully, Virginia Welles. Puffed-up comedy of teenager Temple convincing everyone that she and playboy Niven are going together; naïve fluff. Limp follow-up to KISS AND TELL with Shirley as Corliss Archer; this was her final film. Retitled ALMOST A BRIDE.▼▶

Kiss From Eddie, A SEE: **Arousers, The**
Kissin' Cousins (1964) **C-96m.** **½ D: Gene Nelson. Elvis Presley, Arthur O'Connell, Glenda Farrell, Jack Albertson, Pamela Austin, Yvonne Craig, Donald Woods. Elvis has a dual role as military officer trying to convince yokel relative to allow missile site to be built on homestead; good supporting cast, usual amount of singing—mostly forgettable—and dancing. Panavision.▼▶

Kissing a Fool (1998) **C-93m.** *½ D: Doug Ellin. David Schwimmer, Jason Lee, Mili Avital, Bonnie Hunt, Vanessa Angel, Kari Wuhrer, Bitty Schram. Thoroughly charmless romantic comedy, told via flashback in an irritating narrative form, about a betrothed Chicago sportscaster who badgers a novelist buddy into testing his fiancée's fidelity as he himself is playing around. Subliminally sleazy but wrapped in a cozily sentimental veneer, which means the film doesn't even have the courage of its convictions. Avital is appealing as the pretty book editor who deserves better. Schwimmer also coexecutive-produced. [R]▼▶●

Kissing Bandit, The (1948) **C-102m.** ** D: Laslo Benedek. Frank Sinatra, Kathryn Grayson, Ann Miller, J. Carrol Naish, Ricardo Montalban, Mildred Natwick, Cyd Charisse, Billy Gilbert. Frail Sinatra vehicle about son of Western kissing bandit who picks up where Dad left off; song "Siesta" sums it up.▼▶

Kissing Jessica Stein (2002) **C-97m.** *** D: Charles Herman-Wurmfeld. Jennifer Westfeldt, Heather Juergensen, Scott Cohen, Tovah Feldshuh, Jackie Hoffman, Michael Mastro, Carson Elrod, David Aaron Baker, Jon Hamm. A single Jewish woman in N.Y.C., tired of looking for Mr. Right, answers a personal ad and hooks up with a woman, which leads to unexpected emotional consequences. Smart, funny romantic comedy that balances sitcom-style moments with clever insights, good supporting characters, and terrific chemistry between Westfeldt

and Juergensen, who cowrote the screenplay based on their play *Lipschtick*. [R]▼▶

Kiss Kiss Bang Bang (1966-Spanish) **C-90m.** **½ D: Duccio Tessari. Giuliano Gemma, George Martin, Antonio Casas, Daniel Vargas. Routine spy yarn of British Secret Service efforts to prevent sale of secret formula to foreign powers. Techniscope.

Kiss Kiss, Bang Bang (2005) **C-102m.** ** D: Shane Black. Robert Downey, Jr., Val Kilmer, Michelle Monaghan, Corbin Bernsen, Dash Mihok, Larry Miller, Shannyn Sossamon. Thief-turned-actor and a gay detective team up with an aspiring actress (the actor's old flame) to solve several murders. Uneven neo-noir/screwball comedy starts out as mindless entertainment but quickly grows confusing and tiresome. LETHAL WEAPON scribe Black seems awfully impressed with himself for repeatedly having the protagonist break away from the story to mock the film's use of narrative and genre clichés. Enjoyably pulpy characters and charismatic stars make it somewhat bearable. Downey's real-life son plays his character as a boy. Loosely based on a Brett Halliday novel. Super 35. [R]

Kiss Me Deadly (1955) **105m.** ***½ D: Robert Aldrich. Ralph Meeker, Albert Dekker, Paul Stewart, Cloris Leachman, Wesley Addy, Nick Dennis, Maxine Cooper, Gaby Rodgers, Jack Elam, Strother Martin, Jack Lambert. Meeker is a perfect Mike Hammer in moody, fast, and violent adaptation of Mickey Spillane novel. Years ahead of its time, a major influence on French New Wave directors, and one of Aldrich's best films. Leachman's film debut. Some video versions have 82 seconds of additional footage that completely change the finale. ▼▶●

Kiss Me Goodbye (1982) **C-101m.** ** D: Robert Mulligan. Sally Field, James Caan, Jeff Bridges, Paul Dooley, Claire Trevor, Mildred Natwick, Dorothy Fielding, William Prince. Strained romantic comedy-fantasy about young woman who's visited by her dead husband just as she's about to remarry. Attractive cast is pretty much wasted in this reworking of the Brazilian film DONA FLOR AND HER TWO HUSBANDS. [PG]▼▶

Kiss Me, Guido (1997) **C-86m.** **½ D: Tony Vitale. Nick Scotti, Anthony Barrile, Anthony DeSando, Craig Chester, Dominick Lombardozzi, Molly Price, Christopher Lawford. Earnest comedy about a heterosexual Pacino/De Niro wannabe (Scotti) from the Bronx who moves to Manhattan and unknowingly takes a gay roommate. Occasionally funny, even though the set-up is artificial and the characters are stereotypes. Later a TV series: *Some of My Best Friends*. [R]▼▶●

Kiss Me Kate (1953) **C-109m.** ***½ D:

George Sidney. Kathryn Grayson, Howard Keel, Ann Miller, Bobby Van, Keenan Wynn, James Whitmore, Bob Fosse, Tommy Rall, Kurt Kasznar, Ron Randell. Bright filmization of Cole Porter's Broadway musical, adapted from Shakespeare's *The Taming of the Shrew*. Grayson and Keel are erstwhile married couple whose offstage and on-stage lives intertwine. Songs include "So in Love," "Always True to You in My Fashion," "Brush Up Your Shakespeare" (delightfully performed by Wynn and Whitmore); the "From This Moment On" number, highlighting Fosse and Carol Haney, is outstanding. 3-D.▼●)

Kiss Me, Stupid (1964) **122m.** ** D: Billy Wilder. Dean Martin, Ray Walston, Kim Novak, Felicia Farr, Cliff Osmond, Barbara Pepper, Doro Merande, Henry Gibson, John Fiedler, Mel Blanc. Martin plays womanizing crooner named "Dino" whose interest in unsuccessful songwriter Walston might increase if he gets a crack at his wife. Lewd farce (by Wilder and I. A. L. Diamond) was condemned as "smut" when first released, and hasn't improved very much—although it does have its defenders. DVD features the alternate European ending. Panavision. ▼●)

Kiss of Death (1947) **98m.** *** D: Henry Hathaway. Victor Mature, Brian Donlevy, Coleen Gray, Richard Widmark, Karl Malden, Taylor Holmes, Mildred Dunnock. Famous gangster saga is showing its age, with both the cops and robbers a little too polite—except, of course, for Widmark, in his notorious film debut as giggling, psychopathic killer who shoves a wheelchair-bound old woman (Dunnock) down a flight of stairs! Mature is solid as thief who turns state's evidence. Scripted by Ben Hecht and Charles Lederer; filmed on authentic N.Y.C. locations. Remade in 1995.▼)

Kiss of Death (1995) **C-101m.** **½ D: Barbet Schroeder. David Caruso, Nicolas Cage, Samuel L. Jackson, Helen Hunt, Kathryn Erbe, Stanley Tucci, Michael Rapaport, Ving Rhames, Philip Baker Hall, Anthony Heald, Anne Meara, Kevin Corrigan, Hope Davis. Mediocre '90s remake of '40s crime yarn (with Richard Price script) has Caruso as an ex-con trying to go straight who's swept back into the underworld—then forced to turn stoolie for the D.A. Caruso is OK—nothing more—in first starring film, but Cage is a parody of a mad-dog bad guy. Jackson shines, as usual, in a solid supporting role. Jay O. Sanders appears unbilled as a Federal agent. [R]▼●)

Kiss of the Dragon (2001-U.S.-French) **C-98m.** ** D: Chris Nahon. Jet Li, Bridget Fonda, Tchéky Karyo, Ric Young, Burt Kwouk, Laurence Ashley. In Paris on a secret mission, Chinese agent Li is framed for murder by a corrupt French official

and has to go on the run. His only ally is mistreated prostitute Fonda. Lots of fights, but not as well staged or photographed as Jet Li's Hong Kong movies. A convoluted plot slows the action, although Karyo is an entertaining villain. Overall, highly forgettable. Cowritten and coproduced by Luc Besson. Technovision. [R]▼)

Kiss of the Spider Woman (1985-U.S.-Brazilian) **C/B&W-119m.** *** D: Hector Babenco. William Hurt, Raul Julia, Sonia Braga, Jose Lewgoy, Nuno Leal Maia, Denise Dumont. Adaptation of Manuel Puig's highly regarded novel actually gets better as it goes along, revealing layers in story of gay man and political activist locked together in South American prison cell. Hurt is superb in Oscar-winning performance as man whose only food for survival is his memory of tacky Hollywood movies. Script by Leonard Schrader. Later a Broadway musical. [R]▼●)

Kiss of the Vampire, The (1963-British) **C-88m.** **½ D: Don Sharp. Clifford Evans, Edward De Souza, Noel Willman, Jennifer Daniel. Luckless honeymooners run out of petrol in eastern Europe and take refuge in the castle of Count Ravna, leader of a vampire cult. Ornate masked ball anticipates Polanski's FEARLESS VAMPIRE KILLERS. Intelligent Hammer production with many chilling sequences.▼●)

Kiss or Kill (1997-Australian) **C-93m.** *** D: Bill Bennett. Matt Day, Frances O'Connor, Chris Haywood, Barry Otto, Andrew S. Gilbert, Barry Langrishe, Max Cullen. Neat, noirish murder mystery with Day and O'Connor well cast as a pair of scam-artists who take it on the lam after their latest dupe unexpectedly dies. The style, impudence, and unusual characters overcome the formulaic story. [R]▼●

Kiss the Blood off My Hands (1948) **80m.** ** D: Norman Foster. Joan Fontaine, Burt Lancaster, Robert Newton. Disappointing romance-thriller follows the plight of two lost souls, lonely nurse–war widow Fontaine and deeply troubled ex-POW Lancaster, who's on the lam for murder in London. Some potent scenes and good Miklos Rozsa score cannot salvage tepid film.

Kiss the Girls (1997) **C-116m.** **½ D: Gary Fleder. Morgan Freeman, Ashley Judd, Cary Elwes, Tony Goldwyn, Bill Nunn, Brian Cox, Jeremy Piven, Roma Maffia, Jay O. Sanders, Alex McArthur, Mena Suvari. When a police forensic psychologist learns that his niece has been abducted, he uses his considerable skills to try and identify the culprit—a devious sicko who doesn't kill all his victims, but holds them captive instead. Surprisingly discreet for a '90s film—but in its final segments, increasingly conventional and formulaic. And too long. Freeman is—typically—solid as a rock; Judd is very good as a doctor who refuses to be treated as a victim. Followed by ALONG CAME A SPIDER. Panavision. [R]▼●◗

Kiss the Girls and Make Them Die (1966-Italian) **C-101m.** BOMB D: Henry Levin. Michael Connors, Dorothy Provine, Terry-Thomas, Raf Vallone, Beverly Adams, Oliver McGreevy. Dull spy spoof about power-crazy industrialist who has a satellite capable of sterilizing the world, which is something Bond, Flint, and Matt Helm wouldn't mind. Awful film.

Kiss Them for Me (1957) **C-105m.** **½ D: Stanley Donen. Cary Grant, Jayne Mansfield, Leif Erickson, Suzy Parker, Larry Blyden, Ray Walston. Forced comedy about romantic entanglements of navy officers on shore leave. CinemaScope.◗

Kiss Tomorrow Goodbye (1950) **102m.** **½ D: Gordon Douglas. James Cagney, Barbara Payton, Luther Adler, Ward Bond, Helena Carter, Steve Brodie, Barton Mac-Lane, Rhys Williams, Frank Reicher, John Litel, William Frawley, Neville Brand, Kenneth Tobey. Violent thriller in the wake of WHITE HEAT, with Cagney as criminal so ruthless he even blackmails crooked cops! Despite impressive cast, Jimmy's practically the whole show; only Adler as shyster lawyer gives him any competition. Cagney's brother William produced—and also plays his brother.▼●◗

Kitchen Stories (2003-Norwegian-Swedish) **C-95m.** *** D: Bent Hamer. Joachim Calmeyer, Tomas Nordström, Bjørn Floberg, Reine Brynolfsson, Sverre Anker Ousdal. Offbeat but warm human comedy set in a remote town in post-WW2 Norway has a research institute sending scientific "observers" to sit in tall chairs in the kitchen corner to study the cooking habits of single men. Although not allowed to speak to the subjects or interrupt any activities, one analyst bends the rules and learns more about himself in the process than he ever possibly imagined. Quirky, completely original movie grows on you as it goes along. Written by Hamer and Jörgen Bergmark.▼◗

Kitchen Toto, The (1987) **C-96m.** *** D: Harry Hook. Edwin Mahinda, Bob Peck, Phyllis Logan, Robert Urquhart, Kirsten Hughes, Edward Judd. Moving account of Kenya's final break from British rule in the mid-1950s. This complicated and violent struggle for freedom is told through the eyes of a young "kikuyu" boy slowly drawn into these events when he goes to work in the household of the British police chief after his father is murdered by terrorists. Demanding but ultimately rewarding; first-rate debut for director Hook, who grew up in Kenya during the period depicted here. [PG-13]▼◗

Kite Runner, The (2007) **C-128m.** *** D: Marc Forster. Khalid Abdalla, Homayoun Ershadi, Zekiria Ebrahimi, Ahmad Khan Mahmoodzada, Shaun Toub, Nabi Tanha, Saïd Taghmaoui, Atossa Leoni. Iranian man living in San Francisco receives a phone call summoning him home, where he tries to undo a wrong he committed years earlier. In flashback we learn about his boyhood friendship with the son of his father's household servant, their participation in Kabul's kite-flying competition, and the incident that changes both their lives. David Benioff adapted Khaled Hosseini's best-selling novel. Well done, although it never reaches the emotional heights the story calls for. The acting is exceptional, and the faces of the two boys are unforgettable. Super 35. [PG-13]

Kit Kittredge: An American Girl (2008) **C-100m.** *** D: Patricia Rozema. Abigail Breslin, Joan Cusack, Glenne Headly, Jane Krakowski, Chris O'Donnell, Julia Ormond, Wallace Shawn, Stanley Tucci, Max Thieriot, Willow Smith, Zach Mills. Unusually smart family film with Breslin as a plucky 10-year-old (and aspiring newspaper reporter) who experiences the effects of the Great Depression firsthand in 1934 Cincinnati. Her father leaves home in search of work and her mother is forced to take in boarders, including a magician (Tucci) who bears watching—and not just when he's performing tricks. Evocative look at everyday life in the 1930s has entertainment value for grown-ups as well as kids. Based on Valerie Tripp's stories, which were inspired by a popular line of dolls and books. [G]◗

Kitten With a Whip (1964) **83m.** ** D: Douglas Heyes. Ann-Margret, John Forsythe, Patricia Barry, Peter Brown, Ann Doran. Uninspired account of delinquent (Ann-Margret) and friends victimizing wannabe senator Forsythe and forcing him to drive to Mexico.▼◗

Kitty (1945) **104m.** *** D: Mitchell Leisen. Paulette Goddard, Ray Milland, Patric Knowles, Reginald Owen, Cecil Kellaway, Constance Collier. Overlong but entertaining costumer of girl's rise from guttersnipe to lady in 18th-century England with help of impoverished rake Milland; one of Goddard's best roles.

Kitty Foyle (1940) **107m.** ***½ D: Sam Wood. Ginger Rogers, Dennis Morgan, James Craig, Eduardo Ciannelli, Ernest Cossart, Gladys Cooper. Tender love story won Rogers an Oscar as Christopher Morley's working-girl heroine; Ciannelli memorable as speakeasy waiter.▼●◗

KKK SEE: **Klansman, The**

Klansman, The (1974) **C-112m.** BOMB D: Terence Young. Lee Marvin, Richard Burton, Cameron Mitchell, Lola Falana, Luciana Paluzzi, Linda Evans, O. J. Simpson. Thoroughly trashy racial melodrama casts Marvin as a Southern sheriff and Burton as a local landowner who get involved in a hotbed (and hot beds) of racial activity. Original director Sam Fuller (who is still credited as coscripter) wisely took an early hike. Aka THE BURNING CROSS and KKK. [R]▼▶

Klimt (2007-Austrian-German-British-French) **C-97m.** *½ D: Raúl Ruiz. John Malkovich, Veronica Ferres, Stephen Dillane, Saffron Burrows, Sandra Ceccarelli, Nikolai Kinski. Gorgeous but faux-artsy biopic of the Symbolist radical Gustav Klimt is fop cinema, set in *fin de siècle* Vienna. Pretentious, factually questionable, and annoyingly hallucinatory, elevated only by the luminous paintings and abundant nudity. A somnolent Malkovich makes not the slightest effort to sound anything but pure Illinoisan. Written by the director, whose version runs 131m.▶

Klondike Annie (1936) **80m.** *** D: Raoul Walsh. Mae West, Victor McLaglen, Philip Reed, Helen Jerome Eddy, Harry Beresford, Harold Huber, Soo Young, Lucille Webster Gleason. West and McLaglen are rugged team, with Mae on the lam from police, going to the Yukon and masquerading as Salvation Army worker. West chants "I'm An Occidental Woman in An Oriental Mood For Love."▼▶

Klondike Fever (1980) **C-106m.** *½ D: Peter Carter. Rod Steiger, Angie Dickinson, Jeff East, Lorne Greene, Barry Morse. Jack London (East) in Alaska during the Gold Rush. Poorly made adventure yarn. Aka JACK LONDON'S KLONDIKE FEVER. [PG]▼▶

Klute (1971) **C-114m.** ***½ D: Alan J. Pakula. Jane Fonda, Donald Sutherland, Charles Cioffi, Roy Scheider, Dorothy Tristan, Rita Gam, Jean Stapleton. Fine combination detective-thriller/character-study, with Sutherland a private-eye searching for suburban husband last seen in N.Y.C. Fonda won Oscar as call girl who once saw man in question. Panavision. [R]▼▶

Knack . . . and How to Get It, The (1965-British) **84m.** ***½ D: Richard Lester. Rita Tushingham, Ray Brooks, Michael Crawford, Donal Donnelly. One of the funniest comedies ever imported from Britain. One man's a whiz with the ladies, and his buddy simply wants to learn his secret. Fast-moving, constantly funny. Charles Wood adapted Ann Jellicoe's play. Look sharp for Charlotte Rampling (as a water skier) and Jacqueline Bisset.▼▶

Knife in the Head (1978-German) **C-113m.** ***½ D: Reinhard Hauff. Bruno Ganz, Angela Winkler, Hans Christian Blech, Hans Honig, Hans Brenner. Ganz is excellent as a biogeneticist who is paralyzed after being shot in the head in a police raid, then used as a pawn by both police and political radicals. Fascinating, disturbing drama.▼

Knife in the Water (1962-Polish) **94m.** **** D: Roman Polanski. Leon Niemczyk, Jolanta Umecka, Zygmunt Malanowicz.

Absorbing drama grows out of the tensions created when a couple off for a sailing weekend pick up a student hitchhiker. Polanski's first feature film is a brilliant piece of cinematic storytelling, and a must-see movie.▼▶

Knight and Day (2010) **C-109m.** *** D: James Mangold. Tom Cruise, Cameron Diaz, Peter Sarsgaard, Viola Davis, Jordi Mollà, Paul Dano, Maggie Grace, Marc Blucas, Celia Weston, Falk Hentschel, Lennie Loftin, Dale Dye. Woman finds herself on a flight with a man who claims to be a secret agent; mayhem erupts wherever he goes, but he swears he's one of the "good guys," and she's swept up in a worldwide whirlwind adventure. Entertaining vehicle for the two well-cast stars delivers exactly what it promises: pure escapism, not intended to be taken too seriously. Evokes such movies as NORTH BY NORTHWEST, and while it isn't in that league, it's still fun to watch. Super 35. [PG-13]▶

Knight Moves (1992) **C-96m.** **½ D: Carl Schenkel. Christopher Lambert, Diane Lane, Tom Skerritt, Daniel Baldwin. Chess master Lambert finds himself a murder suspect during a competition on an island in Washington state. Meanwhile, the killer teases Lambert by providing the chess champion with clues he must decipher for himself. OK thriller; has its moments, but also more than its share of lulls. Super 35. [R]▼▶

Knight of the Dragon, The SEE: **Star Knight**

Knightriders (1981) **C-145m.** *** D: George A. Romero. Ed Harris, Gary Lahti, Tom Savini, Amy Ingersoll, Patricia Tallman, Christine Forrest, Warner Shook, Brother Blue. Ambitious, unusual film about a traveling band that stages medieval fairs at which knights joust on motorcycles, and their self-styled King Arthur, who tries to get his followers to live under an old-fashioned code of honor. Finely crafted little change-of-pace for horror master Romero, who also wrote the screenplay; Stephen King has a funny cameo as a beer-guzzling spectator. [R]▼▶

Knights of the Round Table (1953) **C-115m.** **½ D: Richard Thorpe. Robert Taylor, Ava Gardner, Mel Ferrer, Stanley Baker, Felix Aylmer. MGM's first widescreen film (made in England) was excuse for this pretty but empty mini-spectacle of King Arthur's Court, revealing famous love triangle. CinemaScope.▼▶

Knight's Tale, A (2001) **C-132m.** ** D: Brian Helgeland. Heath Ledger, Mark Addy, Rufus Sewell, Paul Bettany, Shannyn Sossamon, Alan Tudyk, Christopher Cazenove. High-concept moviemaking at its screwiest: a gleefully anachronistic medieval tale of a would-be knight who becomes a jousting champion, set to rock 'n' roll music. If it had gone completely over the top it might be fun, but writer-director Helgeland wants us to care about his characters and story—while undermining them at every turn. Almost rescued by Ledger's star quality and strong supporting performances. (P.S. The jousting itself becomes surprisingly monotonous.) Super 35. [PG-13]▼◗

K-9 (1989) **C-102m.** BOMB D: Rod Daniel. James Belushi, Mel Harris, Kevin Tighe, Ed O'Neill, Jerry Lee, James Handy, Cotter Smith. Cop Belushi teams with a German shepherd (Jerry Lee) to crack a drug case. Dubbing this one a dog would be much too kind. Followed by two direct-to-video sequels. [PG-13]▼◗●

K-19 The Widowmaker (2002) **C-138m.** **½ D: Kathryn Bigelow. Harrison Ford, Liam Neeson, Peter Sarsgaard, Joss Ackland, John Shrapnel, Donald Sumpter, Tim Woodward. In 1961, a patriotic Russian naval officer (Ford) takes out a nuclear submarine on its maiden voyage, having just usurped command from a well-liked captain (Neeson) who stays on as executive officer. But the sub, and its crew, are ill prepared for the challenges they will face. Tense and exciting at times, but its main characters' motivations are not always understandable—even less so after a climactic showdown. Much Sturm und Drang in this very long movie, but not enough meaning. Based on a real-life incident. Super 35. [PG-13]▼◗

Knockaround Guys (2002) **C-93m.** **½ D: David Levien, Brian Koppelman. Barry Pepper, John Malkovich, Vin Diesel, Seth Green, Andrew Davoli, Dennis Hopper, Tom Noonan. Interesting variation on the usual gangster saga, examining the younger generation of today's remaining gangland dinosaurs. Pepper, the son of mob boss Hopper, doesn't have his father's respect, or a career to call his own. He begs for the chance to do something important, so his father finally gives him an assignment, which goes completely awry, sending him and his Brooklyn-based cousins to the wilds of Montana. Good cast and offbeat setting keep this lively, but the finale doesn't entirely add up. Filmed in 1999; released in Italy in 2001 as DANGEROUS COMPANY. Super 35. [R]▼◗

Knocked Up (2007) **C-129m.** *** D: Judd Apatow. Seth Rogen, Katherine Heigl, Paul Rudd, Leslie Mann, Jason Segel, Harold Ramis, Jay Baruchel, Joanna Kerns, Jonah Hill, Alan Tudyk, Kristen Wiig, Bill Hader, Ken Jeoung. Fast-rising entertainment reporter (Heigl) finds herself pregnant after a drunken one-night stand with an amiable, scruffy goof-off (Rogen). She decides to have the baby and, to the surprise of both, a wobbly relationship develops between them. Overlong but often hysterically funny comedy is also sweet, romantic, and, despite the exceedingly foul-mouthed dialogue, downright moral.

Written by the director. Numerous celebrities appear as themselves. Unrated version also available. [R]◗

Knock Off (1998-U.S.-Hong Kong) **C-91m.** *½ D: Tsui Hark. Jean-Claude Van Damme, Rob Schneider, Lela Rochon, Michael Fitzgerald Wong, Paul Sorvino, Carmen Lee. Van Damme teams up with American agents to combat terrorists. Having Van Damme play a Hong Kong clothing designer/importer in an action film pinned to a plot about designer jeans is peculiar but not interesting . . . which also describes the movie. Director Hark abandons his usual vivid fight choreography for standard swift intercutting instead. Samo Hung appears unbilled. Super 35. [R]▼◗●

Knock on Any Door (1949) **100m.** **½ D: Nicholas Ray. Humphrey Bogart, John Derek, George Macready, Allene Roberts, Susan Perry. More a showcase for young Derek—as a "victim of society" who turns to crime—than a vehicle for Bogart, as conscience-stricken attorney who defends him. Serious but dated drama. Sequel: LET NO MAN WRITE MY EPITAPH.▼●

Knock on Wood (1954) **C-103m.** *** D: Norman Panama, Melvin Frank. Danny Kaye, Mai Zetterling, Torin Thatcher, David Burns, Leon Askin, Abner Biberman. Superior Kaye vehicle, with ventriloquist Danny involved with beautiful Zetterling and international spies; good Kaye routines.◗

Knockout (2000) **C-100m.** *½ D: Lorenzo Doumani. Sophia-Adella Hernandez, Eduardo Yanez, Tony Plana, William McNamara, Maria Conchita Alonso, Paul Winfield. B movie about an East L.A. homegirl (Hernandez) who becomes a boxer, following in the footsteps of her dad (Plana), who gave up life in the ring to become a cop. Potentially intriguing subject matter KO'd by hammy performances (especially McNamara as a yuppie sleaze promoter), flat direction, and a clichéd script that would shame Syd Field. [R]▼◗

Knock Out Cop, The (1978-Italian-German) **C-113m.** ** D: Steno. Bud Spencer, Werner Pochat, Enzo Cannavale, Joe Stewardson, Bodo, Dagmar Lassander. Silly live-action comic strip with tough, beefy police inspector Spencer on the hunt for drug smugglers. For prepubescent boys only. Originally titled FLATFOOT. Video title: TRINITY: TRACKING FOR TROUBLE.▼

Knowing (2009) **C-121m.** ** D: Alex Proyas. Nicolas Cage, Rose Byrne, Chandler Canterbury, Ben Mendelsohn, Lara Robinson, Nadia Townsend, Alan Hopgood, Danielle Carter. In 1959, students in a Boston-area school draw pictures to put in a time capsule, but one spooky little girl scribbles down a bunch of numbers on a paper. Fifty years later, the paper winds up with a boy whose father, M.I.T. astrophysics professor Cage, discovers that the numbers accurately predicted the dates, locations, and death tolls of major catastrophes of the past—and quite possibly the future. Intriguing premise would have made a great *Twilight Zone* episode, but this New Age doomsday thriller becomes increasingly dour and tedious, with a particularly preposterous finale blending science fiction and biblical prophecy. Shot mostly in Australia. HD Widescreen. [PG-13]▶

Knute Rockne All American (1940) **96m.** *** D: Lloyd Bacon. Pat O'Brien, Gale Page, Donald Crisp, Ronald Reagan, Albert Bassermann, John Qualen. Corny but entertaining bio of famed Notre Dame football coach (O'Brien, in a standout performance), with Reagan as his star player, George Gipp. Several long-excised scenes, including O'Brien's famous locker-room pep talk and Reagan's "win just one for the Gipper" speech have now been restored to most prints. Also shown in computer-colored version.▼▶

Kolya (1996-Czech-British) **C-110m.** **½ D: Jan Sverak. Zdenek Sverak, Andrej Chalimon, Libuse Safrankova, Ondrez Vetchy, Stella Zazvorkova, Ladislav Smoljak, Irena Livanova. Sentimental tale of a mid-fiftyish cellist, an unattached lothario who unexpectedly is made guardian of a small Russian boy. Set in 1988 Prague, on the eve of independence from the Russians, this is a sweet-natured love story that unfortunately seems too pat and manufactured. You'll laugh and certainly cry, but same essential story has been told on film many times before. Lead actor/screenwriter is the director's father. Oscar winner as Best Foreign Film. [PG-13]▼▶

Konga (1961-British) **C-90m.** *½ D: John Lemont. Michael Gough, Margo Johns, Jess Conrad, Claire Gordon. *Very* mad scientist Gough, intent on creating a plant-animal hybrid, occasionally enlarges his chimpanzee friend to gorilla size, then sends the ape out to kill his enemies. A climactic overdose makes Konga king-sized for an exceptionally dull rampage. Brassy, silly Herman Cohen–produced knockoff of KING KONG has only Gough's juicy, hammy performance to recommend it.▼▶

Kong Island SEE: **King of Kong Island**
Kontroll (2003-Hungarian) **C-106m.** *** D: Nimród Antal. Sándor Csányi, Sándor Badár, Zoltán Mucsi, Zsolt Nagy, Csaba Pindroch, Eszter Balla. Highly original thriller set entirely in the Budapest underground system, where a ticket inspector has to deal with gangs of rival workers, a mystery woman who's caught his eye, and a fiendishly clever, elusive murderer. Cowriter-director Antal creates a dense, dynamic universe all his own. [R] ▼▶

Kopek and Broom SEE: **Find the Lady**
Korczak (1990-Polish) **118m.** *** D: Andrzej Wajda. Wojtek Pszoniak, Ewa Dalkowska, Teresa Budzisz-Krzyzanowska,

Piotr Kozlowski, Jan Peszek. Tremendously moving, real-life story of a truly remarkable man: Janusz Korczak (Pszoniak, in a powerful performance), a respected doctor, writer and children's rights advocate who operated a house for Jewish orphans in Warsaw during the 1930s and maintained his moral standards after the Nazis invaded his homeland. Simple, poignant script by Agnieszka Holland.▼

Kotch (1971) **C-113m.** *** D: Jack Lemmon. Walter Matthau, Deborah Winters, Felicia Farr, Charles Aidman, Ellen Geer, Darrell Larson, Lucy Saroyan, Larry Linville. Matthau is the entire show in this winning comedy-drama about a friendly, child-loving septuagenarian who is out of sync with the coolness of the contemporary world, and who helps a young unwed mother-to-be. Lemmon's lone film as director; look fast for him as a mustachioed sleeping passenger on a bus. Farr is Lemmon's wife; Saroyan is Matthau's stepdaughter. [PG] ▼▶

Koyaanisqatsi (1983) **C-87m.** **** D: Godfrey Reggio. Spellbinding, senses-staggering nonnarrative film soars across the United States in search of vistas both natural and man-made. Much of the photography is slow-motion or time-lapse (the title is Hopi Indian for "life out of balance"), all of it set to a mesmerizing score by Philip Glass. So rich in beauty and detail that with each viewing it becomes a new and different film. Should be seen in a theatre for maximum impact. Followed by POWAQQATSI and NAQOY-QATSI. ▼▶

K-PAX (2001) **C-120m.** ** D: Iain Softley. Kevin Spacey, Jeff Bridges, Mary McCormack, Alfre Woodard, David Patrick Kelly, Saul Williams, Peter Gerety, Celia Weston, Ajay Naidu, John Toles-Bey, Aaron Paul. A nutcase is brought to a N.Y.C. mental institution, claiming to be a visitor from the advanced planet K-Pax. Psychiatrist Bridges tries to figure him out, but begins to wonder if the guy isn't telling the truth. Is this movie a warm, fuzzy wish-fulfillment fantasy or a psychiatric case study? Ultimately it fails on both counts, despite the best efforts of its cast. Panavision. [PG-13] ▼▶

Krakatoa East of Java (1969) **C-101m.** **½ D: Bernard Kowalski. Maximilian Schell, Diane Baker, Brian Keith, Barbara Werle, John Leyton, Rossano Brazzi, Sal Mineo. Muddled epic-adventure of disparate group sailing for location of treasure-laden sunken ship. Attempt at Jules Verneish saga hampered by shallow characterizations, dialogue, but action footage is first-rate, climaxed by volcanic explosion and tidal wave. Heavily cut after premiere, leaving story more jumbled than before. P.S.: Krakatoa was *West* of Java. Retitled VOLCANO. Originally 136m. Super Panavision 70. [G]▼▶

Kramer vs. Kramer (1979) **C-104m.** **** D: Robert Benton. Dustin Hoffman, Meryl

Streep, Jane Alexander, Justin Henry, Howard Duff, George Coe, JoBeth Williams. Wife walks out on upwardly mobile husband, leaving him to fend for himself and young son; intelligent, beautifully crafted, intensely moving film. Adapted by Benton from Avery Corman's novel and acted to perfection by entire cast. Oscar winner for Best Picture, Actor, Screenplay, Director, Supporting Actress (Streep). [PG]▼●◗

Krays, The (1990-British) **C-119m.** *** D: Peter Medak. Billie Whitelaw, Gary Kemp, Martin Kemp, Susan Fleetwood, Charlotte Cornwell, Jimmy Jewel, Avis Bunnage, Kate Hardie, Alfred Lynch, Tom Bell, Steven Berkoff, Victor Spinetti, Barbara Ferris, Julia Migenes, John McEnery, Sadie Frost. Brutal but stylish bio of the real-life twins (one gay, one straight) who ruled London's underworld in the 1960s, aided immeasurably by the title-role casting of two sibling members (not twins) of the Brit pop group Spandau Ballet. Picks up, after an iffy beginning, when the Kemps take over from an assortment of child actors; would have been even stronger had it gone beyond character study and dealt more with the lowlife Mod milieu. Whitelaw is good, as usual, as the boys' smothering mother. [R]▼●

Kremlin Letter, The (1970) **C-120m.** *½ D: John Huston. Bibi Andersson, Richard Boone, Max von Sydow, Orson Welles, Patrick O'Neal, Barbara Parkins, Dean Jagger, George Sanders, Raf Vallone. Dull, complicated thriller based on best-seller concerns efforts to retrieve bogus treaty supposedly signed by U.S. and Soviet Union that will pit them against Red China. Good cast is thrown away; film does provide rare opportunity to see Sanders in drag. Panavision. [M/PG]◗

Kriemhild's Revenge SEE: **Die Nibelungen**

Krippendorf's Tribe (1998) **C-94m.** ** D: Todd Holland. Richard Dreyfuss, Jenna Elfman, Natasha Lyonne, Gregory Smith, Carl Michael Lindner, Stephen Root, Elaine Stritch, Tom Poston, David Ogden Stiers, Lily Tomlin, Zakes Mokae, Mila Kunis. Widowed anthropology professor, who's spent all his grant money, is forced to present his findings on an unknown tribe in New Guinea. Trouble is, he never found such a tribe, so he makes one up, then shoots bogus videos with his three kids to back up his claims. Farcical comedy fizzles with wildly inconsistent characters (particularly Elfman) and desperate plot devices. [PG-13]▼●◗

Kristin Lavransdatter (1995-Norwegian) **C-144m.** ** D: Liv Ullmann. Elisabeth Matheson, Bjorn Skagestad, Sverre Anker Ousdal, Henny Moan, Rut Tellefsen, Erland Josephson, Lena Endre. Intense, plodding drama, set in the 14th century, about the title character (Matheson) and how pressures from family and society thwart her from being with her true love and steer her to marry

another man instead. It's a conflict between religious obligation and "the sin of passion," and well acted, but never as profound or involving as intended. Ullmann also scripted, based on novel by Nobel Prize winner Sigrid Undset. Originally shown at 180m.▼◗

Kronos (1957) **78m.** **½ D: Kurt Neumann. Jeff Morrow, Barbara Lawrence, John Emery, George O'Hanlon, Morris Ankrum. Diverting science-fiction with unique monster: an enormous metallic walking machine capable of absorbing the Earth's energy. Occasionally shaky special effects are compensated for by nice touch of mysterioso and convincing performances, especially by Emery as the alien's catspaw. Regalscope.▼●◗

Kronos (1974) SEE: **Captain Kronos: Vampire Hunter**

Krull (1983) **C-117m.** ** D: Peter Yates. Ken Marshall, Lysette Anthony, Freddie Jones, Francesca Annis, David Battley, Liam Neeson, Robbie Coltrane. Overly familiar story elements and plodding treatment keep this traditional fantasy quest from going anywhere, despite its elaborate trappings. Marshall is the young hero who must recover a magic ornament to save damsel and kingdom. Panavision. [PG]▼●◗

Krush Groove (1985) **C-97m.** ** D: Michael Schultz. Blair Underwood, Joseph Simmons, Sheila E., Fat Boys, Daryll McDaniels, Kurtis Blow. Yet another rap musical, with a silly (almost nonexistent) story but lots of music, rapping, and street culture artifacts. Aficionados of this kind of music rate the soundtrack very highly. [R]▼●◗

K2 (1992-British) **C-111m.** **½ D: Franc Roddam. Michael Biehn, Matt Craven, Raymond J. Barry, Hiroshi Fujioka, Patricia Charbonneau, Luca Bercovici, Julia Nickson-Soul, Jamal Shah. A Seattle assistant D.A. (brash) and his physics-prof pal (gentle) attempt to climb the world's steepest and most remote mountain. Gritty outdoor expansion of Patrick Meyers' play, which won a Tony for its impressive mountain set; magnificent outdoor footage compensates for that, but not for the stock movie characterizations. Film never tops its first 15 minutes, which are spellbinding. [R]▼●◗

Kuffs (1992) **C-100m.** *½ D: Bruce Evans. Christian Slater, Tony Goldwyn, Milla Jovovich, Bruce Boxleitner, George De La Pena, Troy Evans, Lu Leonard, Leon Rippy, Mary Ellen Trainor, Ashley Judd. Smarmy Slater desperately needs a job after abandoning his pregnant girlfriend; as luck would have it, his brother gets shot in the line of duty as a private policeman in San Francisco. Unbearably flip, especially during frequent breaks for Slater's straight-to-camera narration. You keep waiting for Dirty Harry to show up and toss this kiddie cop one of his patented glares. [PG-13] ▼●◗

Kull the Conqueror (1997) **C-95m.** ****** D: John Nicolella. Kevin Sorbo, Tia Carrere, Karina Lombard, Thomas Ian Griffith, Litefoot, Roy Brocksmith, Harvey Fierstein, Edward Tudor-Pole, Douglas Henshall, Sven Ole Thorsen. In ancient times, Kull, a barbarian from Atlantis, unexpectedly becomes king of a troubled country, and soon finds himself involved in swordfights, magic, and palace intrigue. Passionless, incoherent, and routine, with a few good performances, very uneven effects and makeup, and not enough sorcery. Based on a character created by Conan creator Robert E. Howard; in fact, this began life as a script for a third Conan movie. Super 35. [PG-13]▼●〗

Kundun (1997) **C-134m.** ******* D: Martin Scorsese. Tenzin Thuthob Tsarong, Gyurme Tethong, Tulku Jamyang Kunga Tenzin, Tenzin Yeshi Paichang, Tencho Gyalpo, Tsewang Migyur Khangsar, Sonam Phuntsok, Robert Lin. The fascinating saga of the 14th Dalai Lama begins with the discovery that he has been reincarnated in the body of a two-year-old boy. We follow his journey through life, including education, exile, and a confrontation with the Chinese government, led by Mao Tse-tung. Search in vain for a Scorsese "edge"—this is just good, solid storytelling, from Melissa Mathison's script (written with the Dalai Lama's cooperation). A cast of nonprofessional actors is simply remarkable, and so is Philip Glass' score. Super 35. [PG-13]▼●〗

Kung Fu Hustle (2005-Hong Kong) **C-99m.** ****** D: Stephen Chow. Stephen Chow, Yuen Wah, Yuen Qiu, Leung Siu Lung, Dong Zhi Hua, Chiu Chi Ling, Xing Yu, Chan Kwok Kwan, Lam Tze Chung. In Pig Sty Alley, the brutal Axe Gang terrorizes the locals but doesn't know what to make of a young gangster-wannabe (Chow). Less a story than a series of action sequences, this heavy-handed mix of martial arts and slapstick (with a dollop of romance) pays homage to everything from THE SHINING and Road Runner cartoons to TOP HAT! The novelty of live-action cartoon violence wears thin pretty fast. Chow cowrote and coproduced; choreographed by Yuen Wo Ping (CROUCHING TIGER, HIDDEN DRAGON, THE MATRIX). Super 35. [R]▼〗

Kung Fu Panda (2008) **C-91m.** ******* D: John Stevenson, Mark Osborne. Voices of Jack Black, Dustin Hoffman, Angelina Jolie, Ian McShane, Jackie Chan, Seth Rogen, Lucy Liu, David Cross, Randall Duk Kim, James Hong, Dan Fogler, Michael Clarke Duncan, Laura Kightlinger. Entertaining animated feature about a panda who dreams of being a martial arts hero, instead of the son of a dumpling chef. Then, through a quirk of fate, he is chosen as the Dragon Warrior to help save a city that's about to be attacked by a ferocious leopard. Uncommonly handsome production design and exciting action scenes

enhance a simple storyline. Black's engaging performance as the schlump who wants to make good is matched by Hoffman's deadpan delivery as his kung fu master. Followed by a sequel. Digital Widescreen. [PG]〗

Kung Fu Panda 2 (2011) **C-90m.** ******* D: Jennifer Yuh Nelson. Voices of Jack Black, Angelina Jolie, Dustin Hoffman, Gary Oldman, Jackie Chan, Seth Rogen, Lucy Liu, David Cross, James Hong, Michelle Yeoh, Danny McBride, Victor Garber, Dennis Haysbert, Jean-Claude Van Damme. When he tries to ward off plunderers, alongside the Furious Five, Po finds himself blinded by images of his panda parents—and begins to wonder, for the first time, where he came from. This is his Achilles' heel as he tries to combat the evil peacock Lord Shen, who is bent on conquering China with his all-powerful cannons. Surprisingly good sequel to the 2008 feature minimizes Master Shifu's role and sacrifices laughs for more serious storytelling, in the vein of THE EMPIRE STRIKES BACK. Beautifully designed and realized. 3-D Digital Widescreen. [PG]

Kung Pow: Enter the Fist (2002) **C-81m.** ***½** D: Steve Oedekirk. Steve Oedekirk, Lung Fai, Leo Lee, Chen Hui Lou, Jennifer Tung. Writer-director Oedekirk redubs, and adds deliberately clunky new footage to, a 1976 Hong Kong martial arts movie, TIGER & CRANE FISTS (directed by Jimmy Wang Yu), turning the original into a parody of itself, with a nonstop barrage of gags—occasionally funny, but obvious and repetitive. Oedekirk also stars, as The Chosen One. Not nearly as good as WHAT'S UP, TIGER LILY?, but if you do watch, stay till the end of the credits. Panavision. [PG-13]▼〗

Kwaidan (1964-Japanese) **C-164m.** *****½** D: Masaki Kobayashi. Rentaro Mikuni, Michiyo Aratama, Keiko Kishi, Tatsuya Nakadai, Takashi Shimura. Four tales of the supernatural, based on works by Lafcadio Hearn, focusing on samurais, balladeers, monks, spirits. Subtle, moody, well staged; stunning use of color and widescreen. Released in U.S. in 1965 at 125m., with the second episode (featuring Kishi and Nakadai) deleted. Tohoscope.▼●〗

La Balance (1982-French) **C-102m.** ******* D: Bob Swaim. Nathalie Baye, Philippe Leotard, Richard Berry, Maurice Ronet, Christophe Malavoy, Jean-Paul Connart. Extremely tough, violent Parisian cop movie (directed and cowritten by an American) about effort to nail criminal kingpin by forcing one-time associate (Leotard) to turn informer. Baye is excellent as prostitute in love with victimized pimp. Winner of many Cesar Awards (France's Oscar) including Best Picture. [R]▼〗

La Bamba (1987) **C-108m.** ******* D: Luis Valdez. Lou Diamond Phillips, Esai Morales, Rosana De Soto, Elizabeth Pena, Danielle von Zerneck, Joe Pantoliano, Rick

Dees, Marshall Crenshaw, Brian Setzer. Solid musical biography of Ritchie Valens, a poor Mexican-American who became a rock 'n' roll sensation at age 17. Writer-director Valdez can't avoid some standard Hollywood bio trappings, but good-time music and Phillips' commanding, sympathetic performance more than compensate. Morales is excellent as Ritchie's troubled brother. Valens' music is performed by Los Lobos on soundtrack—they appear as the Tijuana band. Original music by Carlos Santana and Miles Goodman. [PG-13]▼●◗

La Belle Noiseuse (1991-French) **C-240m.** ***½ D: Jacques Rivette. Michel Piccoli, Jane Birkin, Emmanuelle Béart, Marianne Denicourt, David Bursztein, Gilles Arbona, Bernard Dufour. Riveting story of the relationship between a once-famed artist and the young woman who inspires him to paint after 10 years of inactivity, and becomes his model. A stunning examination of the artistic process and its accompanying obsessions, with outstanding performances by Piccoli as the artist and gorgeous Béart as his subject. Extremely long, deliberately paced but always involving; beautifully directed by Rivette and photographed by William Lubtchansky. Screenplay by Rivette, Pascal Bonitzer, and Christine Laurent. Dufour, by the way, supplies the artist's hand. A new version, reworked and with a new perspective, was released in 1993. Its title: DIVERTIMENTO, running 125m. ▼▷

La Bête Humaine (1938-French) **99m.** ***½ D: Jean Renoir. Jean Gabin, Julien Carette, Simone Simon, Fernand Ledoux, Blanchette Brunoy, Gerard Landry. Locomotive engineer Gabin displays fits of uncontrollable violence against women. When he forms a liaison with the flirtatious wife of a deputy stationmaster, he becomes entangled in a plot to kill the husband. Sublimely atmospheric adaptation of Emile Zola's novel suited the fatalistic mood of Europe in 1938, as the Nazis overran Czechoslovakia. That's Renoir himself in the role of Cabuche; he also scripted. Aka THE HUMAN BEAST and JUDAS WAS A WOMAN. Fritz Lang remade it in the U.S. as HUMAN DESIRE.▼▷

La Boum (1981-French) **C-100m.** **½ D: Claude Pinoteau. Claude Brasseur, Brigitte Fossey, Sophie Marceau, Denise Grey, Bernard Giraudeau. Clichéd but harmless chronicle of the life of pretty 13-year-old Marceau, whose parents (Brasseur, Fossey) are having marital difficulties. A French box-office smash. Sequel: LA BOUM 2.▼

La Boum 2 (1982-French) **C-109m.** **½ D: Claude Pinoteau. Sophie Marceau, Claude Brasseur, Brigitte Fossey, Pierre Cosso, Shiela O'Connor, Denise Grey. Here teenager Marceau is two years older and has a romance with another student. Her parents are still squabbling. A formula film, no better or worse than the original.

La Buche (1999-French) **C-107m.** *** D: Daniele Thompson. Charlotte Gainsbourg, Emmanuelle Béart, Sabine Azema, Claude Rich, Françoise Fabian, Christopher Thompson, Jean-Pierre Darroussin. Penetrating examination of three sisters who must deal with their problems and differences (not to mention their long-estranged parents) as the Christmas holiday approaches. A refreshing antidote to all those sugary seasonal films. Directorial debut for Thompson, a top French screenwriter, who coscripted with her son Christopher (who also plays Joseph). Super 35.▼▷

Labyrinth (1986) **C-101m.** *** D: Jim Henson. David Bowie, Jennifer Connelly, Toby Froud. Teenage girl's baby brother is kidnapped by the King of the Goblins (Bowie) in order to rescue him she must navigate a devilish labyrinth. Entertaining variation on *Alice in Wonderland* written by Monty Python's Terry Jones, executive produced by George Lucas, and filtered through the sensibilities of The Muppets' Jim Henson. A treat for kids and the young at heart (Muppet fans in particular); only weakness is that it does get slow at times. J-D-C Scope. [PG]▼●◗

Labyrinth of Passion (1982-Spanish) **C-100m.** *** D: Pedro Almodóvar. Celia Roth, Imanol Arias, Helga Line, Antonio Banderas. Zany, energetic sex farce, most of which is beyond the power of description. It does involve a gallery of comically outlandish characters scurrying about Madrid, including transvestites, punk rockers, nymphomaniacs—and Islamic fundamentalists. Occasionally crude, and always rude, but that's all part of the fun.▼◗

La Cage aux Folles (1978-French-Italian) **C-91m.** *** D: Edouard Molinaro. Ugo Tognazzi, Michel Serrault, Michel Galabru, Claire Maurier, Remy Laurent, Benny Luke. A gay couple tries to act straight for the sake of Tognazzi's son, who's bringing home his fiancée and her parents. Entertaining adaptation of French stage farce, with some hilarious moments and a wonderful performance by Serrault as the more feminine half of the middle-aged twosome—but why this became such a raging success is a mystery. Followed by two sequels, as well as a hit Broadway musical. Remade in 1996 as THE BIRDCAGE. [R]▼●◗

La Cage aux Folles II (1980-French) **C-101m.** **½ D: Edouard Molinaro. Michel Serrault, Ugo Tognazzi, Marcel Bozzuffi, Michel Galabru, Paola Borboni, Benny Luke. St. Tropez nightclub owner (Tognazzi) and his female-impersonator housemate (Serrault) become involved with a spy ring in this mild sequel. [R]▼●◗

La Cage aux Folles 3: The Wedding (1985-French-Italian) **C-87m.** *½ D: Georges Lautner. Michel Serrault, Ugo Tognazzi, Michel Galabru, Benny Luke, Stephane Audran, Antonella Interlenghi.

Pointless sequel has drag queen Albin (Serrault) in line for big inheritance—if he marries and produces a son. This farce has been milked dry by now. [PG-13]▼●

La Cérémonie (1995-French-German) C-111m. *** D: Claude Chabrol. Isabelle Huppert, Sandrine Bonnaire, Jacqueline Bisset, Jean-Pierre Cassel, Virginie Ledoyen, Valentin Merlet. Slow-moving but effective Chabrol thriller, with Huppert and Bonnaire as lower-class pals in rural Brittany, who resent the wealthy household in which Bonnaire is employed as maid. Nice turn by Bisset, as sympathetic matriarch. ▼)

La Chèvre (1982-French) C-91m. *** D: Francis Veber. Pierre Richard, Gérard Depardieu, Michel Robin, Pedro Armendariz, Jr., Corynne Charbit, Andre Valardy. Nononsense sleuth Depardieu sets out to locate an industrialist's daughter who's disappeared in Mexico, finds himself comically hampered by his employer's accountant (Richard), an amateur detective. Amiable, amusing comedy was a box-office smash in France. Veber also scripted. Aka THE GOAT. Americanized remake: PURE LUCK. ▼)

La Chienne (1931-French) 95m. **** D: Jean Renoir. Michel Simon, Janie Mareze, Georges Flamant, Madeleine Berubet. Renoir's first sound film, and first sound-film masterpiece: a terse, somber drama of mild-mannered bank cashier Simon, with an overbearing wife, who plays into the hands of prostitute Mareze and her scheming pimp. Renoir coscripted; Mareze died in a car accident a couple of weeks after filming was completed. Fritz Lang redid this as SCARLET STREET; what a double bill they would make! ▼●

La Chinoise (1967-French) C-95m. *** D: Jean-Luc Godard. Anne Wiazemsky, Jean-Pierre Léaud, Michel Semianko, Lex de Bruijn, Juliet Berto. Five young Maoists share an apartment and try to apply their politics to the reality of their lives. Godard aficionados will be fascinated; others may be bored.)

La Ciudad SEE: City, The

La Collectionneuse (1967-French) C-88m. *** D: Eric Rohmer. Patrick Bauchau, Haydee Politoff, Daniel Pommerulle, Alain Jouffroy, Mijanou Bardot. No. 3 of Rohmer's "Six Moral Tales" is less compelling than later films, still intriguing for fans of contemplative stories in this series, focusing on young man's attraction to aloof young girl sharing summer villa on the Mediterranean. ▼)

Lacombe Lucien (1974-French) C-137m. **** D: Louis Malle. Pierre Blaise, Aurore Clement, Holger Lowenadler, Therese Giehse. Brilliant, perceptive account of opportunist French peasant Blaise, who joins the Gestapo during the Nazi Occupation—after setting out to join the Resistance—and falls in love with a Jewish tailor's daughter.

Subtle, complex tale of guilt, innocence, and the amorality of power; masterfully directed. [R])

L.A. Confidential (1997) C-136m. ***½ D: Curtis Hanson. Kevin Spacey, Russell Crowe, Guy Pearce, James Cromwell, David Strathairn, Kim Basinger, Danny DeVito, Graham Beckel, Brenda Bakke, Paul Guilfoyle, Ron Rifkin, Simon Baker Denny (Simon Baker). Vividly atmospheric tale of L.A. in the early 1950s, run by corrupt cops—one of whom (Spacey) works hand in hand with the publisher of a sleazy tabloid (DeVito). Self-righteous Pearce, however, thinks he can rise above the murk in the department. Director Hanson and Brian Helgeland's Oscar-winning adaptation of the James Ellroy novel is overlong but compelling and richly detailed; a bleak worldview, to be sure. Basinger won a Best Supporting Actress Oscar as the Veronica Lake–ish call girl, but she's surrounded by Oscar-worthy costars. Super 35. [R] ▼●)

La Danse: Le Ballet de l'Opéra de Paris (2009-French-U.S.) C-158m. ***½ D: Frederick Wiseman. Deeply insightful documentary from veteran filmmaker Wiseman offers an up-close-and-personal look at the inner workings of the Paris Opera Ballet. Without commentary, Wiseman simply, straightforwardly records dancers in performance; just as significantly, he includes extensive footage of rehearsals, meetings, and other backstage business. A must for balletomanes and well worth seeing for anyone interested in the artistic process and the challenges inherent in operating a world-class cultural entity.

Ladder 49 (2004) C-114m. *** D: Jay Russell. Joaquin Phoenix, John Travolta, Jacinda Barrett, Robert Patrick, Morris Chestnut, Balthazar Getty, Tim Guinee. Straightforward story of a Baltimore fireman, from the day he reports for work as a rookie to his ultimate challenge inside a burning factory. Warm depiction of firemen's lives as brothers in an extended family. Full of white-knuckle sequences depicting daring (but realistic) rescue operations, which cumulatively pay tribute to some of the bravest men on earth. Solid, old-fashioned storytelling. [PG-13] ▼)

Ladies and Gentlemen, The Fabulous Stains (1982) C-87m. ** D: Lou Adler. Diane Lane, Ray Winstone, Peter Donat, David Clennon, John Lehne, Cynthia Sikes, Laura Dern, John (Fee) Waybill, Christine Lahti. Antisocial teenage girl decides to become a punk rock star and takes to the road. Unreleased major studio film is strident and unappealing, despite good cast. Lahti shines in her two scenes. Members of Clash and The Sex Pistols appear as a British punk band. [R])

Ladies in Lavender (2004-British) C-103m. *** D: Charles Dance. Judi Dench,

Maggie Smith, Natascha McElhone, Daniel Brühl, Miriam Margolyes, Freddie Jones, David Warner, Clive Russell. Dames Dench and Smith add luster to this lightly likable drama about a pair of aging sisters in pre-WW2 England whose lives are changed when a handsome young Polish man mysteriously washes ashore one morning near their seaside Cornwall cottage. Not a great film by any means, but it's as cozy and inviting as a warm blanket on a cold winter night. Actor Dance's screenwriting and big-screen directing debut. [PG-13]▐

Ladies' Man, The (1961) **C-96m.** *** D: Jerry Lewis. Jerry Lewis, Helen Traubel, Kathleen Freeman, Hope Holiday, Pat Stanley, Jack Kruschen, Doodles Weaver, Harry James and His Band. Pretty funny comedy with Jerry the handyman in a girls' boardinghouse run by Miss Wellenmelon (Traubel). Enormous set is the real star; Buddy Lester and George Raft have amusing cameo appearances.▼O▐

Ladies Man, The (2000) **C-84m.** ** D: Reginald Hudlin. Tim Meadows, Karyn Parsons, Billy Dee Williams, Kevin McDonald, Tiffani (Amber) Thiessen, Lee Evans, Will Ferrell, Jimmy Fallon, Julianne Moore, Eugene Levy. Kinky comedy about a sex-driven radio talk-show host who has a bad habit of sleeping with married women. Meadows is exceedingly funny, but the film once again proves that *Saturday Night Live* TV skits are meant to be just that: skits. Meadows coscripted. [R]▼▐

Ladies of Leisure (1930) **98m.** **½ D: Frank Capra. Barbara Stanwyck, Ralph Graves, Lowell Sherman, Marie Prevost, Nance O'Neill, George Fawcett. Stanwyck falls in love with playboy-artist Graves, but cannot shake her reputation as gold digger. Creaky story made worthwhile by Stanwyck's believable performance and Capra's fluent filmmaking technique. Remade as WOMEN OF GLAMOR.▼

La Discrète (1990-French) **C-94m.** *** D: Christian Vincent. Fabrice Luchini, Judith Henry, Maurice Garrel, Francois Toumarkine. Insightful allegory about a heartless writer/Don Juan (Luchini) who allows vengeful publisher Garrel to convince him to toy with the emotions of typist Henry, to extract raw material for a book. Solid performances (especially by Henry) help put this one over.▼

La Dolce Vita (1960-Italian) **175m.** ***½ D: Federico Fellini. Marcello Mastroianni, Anita Ekberg, Anouk Aimée, Yvonne Furneaux, Magali Noel, Alain Cuny, Annibale Ninchi, Walter Santesso, Lex Barker, Jacques Sernas, Nadia Gray. Lengthy trendsetting film, not as ambiguous as other Fellini works—much more entertaining, with strong cast. Mastroianni stars as tabloid reporter who sees his life in shallow Rome

society as worthless but can't change. Story and screenplay by Fellini, Ennio Flaiano, and Tullio Pinelli, with Brunello Rondi. Piero Gherardi's costumes won an Oscar. Totalscope.▼O▐

Ladrón que roba a ladrón . . . (2007) **C-99m.** **½ D: Joe Menendez. Fernando Colunga, Miguel Varoni, Gabriel Soto, Julie Gonzalo, Ivonne Montero, Sonya Smith, Saúl Lisazo. Innocuous U.S.-produced Spanish-language OCEAN'S ELEVEN–inspired caper comedy in which a pair of Robin Hood–like thieves plot to rip off a pompous L.A. infomercial king, who has built his fortune by duping poor Latino immigrants. Occasionally clever, but mostly covers familiar ground. Title's English translation is A THIEF WHO STEALS FROM A THIEF; the main actors are veterans of Spanish-language telenovelas. [PG-13]▐

Lady and the Duke, The (2001-French) **C-125m.** *** D: Eric Rohmer. Lucy Russell, Jean-Claude Dreyfus, Alain Libolt, Charlotte Véry, Léonard Cobiant, François Marthouret, Caroline Morin. Intelligent, provocative historical drama set during the French Revolution. The lady of the title is Grace Elliott (Russell), a Scottish blueblood expatriate; the duke is Philippe d'Orleans (Dreyfus), a cousin to Louis XVI. The two share a complex relationship as the politics and events of the period swirl around them. Conversation is the hallmark of a Rohmer film, and here it is never less than illuminating. Shot in digital video; the 81-year-old filmmaker also scripted (based on Elliott's memoirs). [PG-13]▼▐

Lady and the Outlaw, The SEE: **Billy Two Hats**

Lady and the Tramp (1955) **C-75m.** ***½ D: Hamilton Luske, Clyde Geronimi, Wilfred Jackson. Voices of Peggy Lee, Barbara Luddy, Bill Thompson, Bill Baucon, Stan Freberg, Verna Felton, Alan Reed. One of Walt Disney's most endearing animated features about a rakish dog named Tramp who helps pedigreed canine named Lady out of a jam—and into a romance. Elements of adventure and drama are masterfully blended with comedy and music in. this stylish film, the Disney studio's first feature cartoon in CinemaScope. Songs by Sonny Burke and Peggy Lee (who's the voice of Peg, Darling, Si and Am, the Siamese cats). Followed in 2001 by a direct-to-video sequel. CinemaScope.▼O▐

Lady Be Good (1941) **111m.** *** D: Norman Z. McLeod. Eleanor Powell, Ann Sothern, Robert Young, Lionel Barrymore, John Carroll, Red Skelton, Virginia O'Brien, Dan Dailey, Jimmy Dorsey and His Orchestra. Spunky musical of married songwriters Sothern and Young, with Powell and Skelton along for good measure. Fine score: title tune, "Fascinating Rhythm," "You'll Never

Know," Oscar-winning "Last Time I Saw Paris." ▼●◗

Lady Beware (1987) **C-108m.** **½ D: Karen Arthur. Diane Lane, Michael Woods, Cotter Smith, Viveca Lindfors, Peter Nevargic, Edward Penn, Tyra Ferrell. Lane's mildly kinky store-window displays arouse a married psychotic; he soon graduates from irritating phone calls and mail interception to breaking into her window-barred loft. Imperfect, but compelling, feminist exploitation film builds to a satisfying (and surprisingly nonviolent) conclusion; Lane's performance is uneven, but her rage convincing. Filmed and set in Pittsburgh. [R] ▼●

Ladybird, Ladybird (1994-British) **C-102m.** *** D: Kenneth Loach. Crissy Rock, Vladimir Vega, Ray Winstone, Sandie Lavelle, Mauricio Venegas, Clare Perkins. Shattering, based-on-fact account of a durable but deeply troubled single mother of four (extremely well played by Rock), who has a history of being abused by men; she becomes involved with kindly Vega, but this relationship will not be without its share of crises. Another impassioned look at British working class life from Loach. ▼

Ladybug Ladybug (1963) **84m.** *** D: Frank Perry. Jane Connell, William Daniels, James Frawley, Richard Hamilton, Kathryn Hays, Jane Hoffman, Elena Karam, Judith Lowry, Nancy Marchand, Estelle Parsons, Miles Chapin, Alice Playten. Ambitious and provocative (if a bit too obvious) account of some rural schoolchildren and their reactions when a civil defense system warns of an impending nuclear attack. Screenplay by Eleanor Perry; a follow-up of sorts to DAVID AND LISA. Based on an actual incident.

Ladybugs (1992) **C-89m.** *½ D: Sidney J. Furie. Rodney Dangerfield, Jackée, Jonathan Brandis, Ilene Graff, Vinessa Shaw, Tom Parks, Jeanetta Arnette, Nancy Parsons, Blake Clark, Tommy Lasorda. To placate his boss and secure a promotion, Rodney becomes the coach of a girls' soccer team—complete with an in-drag male player (the son of his fiancée). Slapdash execution of what sounds like a sure-fire Dangerfield premise; the best zingers concern rival female coach Parsons. [PG-13] ▼●◗

Lady Caroline Lamb (1972-British) **C-118m.** BOMB D: Robert Bolt. Sarah Miles, Jon Finch, Richard Chamberlain, John Mills, Margaret Leighton, Ralph Richardson, Laurence Olivier. Wretched filmization of famous story; wife of English politician scandalizes everyone by her open affair with Lord Byron. Bolt's banal script is often unintentionally funny. Panavision. [PG] ▼

Lady Chatterley (2006-French-Belgian) **C-168m.** *** D: Pascale Ferran. Marina Hands, Jean Louis Coullo'ch, Hippolyte Girardot, Hélène Alexandridis, Hélène Fillières, Bernard Verley, Sava Lolov. Beautifully filmed, leisurely adaptation of D. H. Lawrence's erotic novel about a wealthy woman's affair with the gamekeeper on her paralyzed husband's estate. Sensuous and startlingly fine performance by Hands as the Lady who explores her sexual feelings. Graphic, but tasteful, telling of the once-notorious book milks its romantic content for everything it's worth. Winner of five César awards including Best Film. European TV version runs 220m. Also available in R-rated version. ◗

Lady Chatterley's Lover (1981-French-British) **C-105m.** BOMB D: Just Jaeckin. Sylvia Kristel, Nicholas Clay, Shane Briant, Ann Mitchell, Elizabeth Spriggs, Peter Bennett. Dull, cheap version of the D. H. Lawrence classic, with Kristel as the lady and Clay as the lover. Kristel is beautiful, but still cannot act. From the director of EMMANUELLE. Previously filmed in France in 1955; remade in 2006. [R] ▼●◗

Lady Dances, The SEE: **Merry Widow, The** (1934)

Lady Dracula (1973) **C-80m.** BOMB D: Richard Blackburn. Cheryl Smith, Lesley Gilb, William Whitton, Richard Blackburn. Perfectly awful low-budgeter about a lady vampire with lesbian tendencies. Bring back Gloria Holden! Aka LEGENDARY CURSE OF LEMORA and LEMORA, THE LADY DRACULA. [PG]◗

Lady Eve, The (1941) **94m.** ***½ D: Preston Sturges. Barbara Stanwyck, Henry Fonda, Charles Coburn, Eugene Pallette, William Demarest, Eric Blore, Melville Cooper. Stanwyck is a con artist who sets her eyes on wealthy Fonda—the dolt to end all dolts, who proclaims "snakes are my life." Sometimes silly and strident, this film grows funnier with each viewing— thanks to Sturges's script, breathless pace, and two incomparable stars. Remade as THE BIRDS AND THE BEES (1946). ▼●◗

Lady for a Day (1933) **96m.** **** D: Frank Capra. Warren William, May Robson, Guy Kibbee, Glenda Farrell, Jean Parker, Walter Connolly, Ned Sparks, Nat Pendleton. Wonderful Damon Runyon fable of seedy apple vendor Robson transformed into perfect lady by softhearted racketeer William. Robert Riskin adapted Runyon's story "Madame La Gimp." Sequel: LADY BY CHOICE. Remade by Capra as POCKETFUL OF MIRACLES. ▼●◗

Lady for a Night (1942) **87m.** ** D: Leigh Jason. Joan Blondell, John Wayne, Ray Middleton, Philip Merivale, Blanche Yurka, Edith Barrett, Hattie Noel. Plodding costume drama of wealthy, status-seeking gambling queen Blondell and her plight upon marrying impoverished society drunk Middleton. Good cast seems out of place.▼

Lady Frankenstein (1971-Italian) **C-84m.** BOMB D: Mel Welles. Joseph Cotten,

Mickey Hargitay, Sarah Bey, Paul Muller, Peter Whiteman. Poor horror entry with Cotten a tired, ill-fated Baron; his daughter (Bey) takes up where he leaves off in the monster-making department. [R]▼❶

Lady From Louisiana (1941) 82m. **½ D: Bernard Vorhaus. John Wayne, Ona Munson, Ray Middleton, Henry Stephenson, Helen Westley, Jack Pennick, Dorothy Dandridge. Wayne and Munson fall in love, then discover they're on opposite sides of gambling controversy; so-so period piece.▼

Lady From Shanghai, The (1948) 87m. *** D: Orson Welles. Rita Hayworth, Orson Welles, Everett Sloane, Glenn Anders, Ted de Corsia, Erskine Sanford, Gus Schilling. The camera's the star of this offbeat thriller, with the cast incidental in bizarre murder mystery about an Irish adventurer (Welles) who joins seductive Hayworth and her husband (Sloane) on a Pacific cruise. The famous hall of mirrors climax is riveting. Cinematography by Charles Lawton, Jr. Based on novel by Sherwood King; scripted and produced by Welles. That's Errol Flynn's yacht, *Zaca,* in the seagoing scenes.▼❶

Lady Gambles, The (1949) 98m. *** D: Michael Gordon. Barbara Stanwyck, Robert Preston, Stephen McNally, Edith Barrett, John Hoyt, Leif Erickson. The LOST WEEKEND of gambling films, a well-acted drama chronicling Stanwyck's decline from respectable writer's wife to desperate, addicted gambler and all-around screwup. Look for Tony Curtis—then billed as "Anthony"—as a bellboy.❶

Lady Godiva (1955) C-89m. ** D: Arthur Lubin. Maureen O'Hara, George Nader, Victor McLaglen, Torin Thatcher, Robert Warwick. Cardboard costumer of famed lady and her horseback ride set in Middle Ages England—What a dull ride! Look for Clint Eastwood, billed as "First Saxon."❶

Lady Hamilton SEE: **That Hamilton Woman**

Ladyhawke (1985) C-124m. *** D: Richard Donner. Matthew Broderick, Rutger Hauer, Michelle Pfeiffer, Leo McKern, John Wood, Ken Hutchison, Alfred Molina. Overlong but generally entertaining medieval fantasy adventure about star-crossed lovers caught in an evil spell—and a young thief who becomes their unlikely ally. Hauer and Pfeiffer are perfectly cast as stalwart hero and heroine, but Broderick's manner and dialogue seem better suited to a Woody Allen movie! Thunderous music by Andrew Powell. Technovision. [PG-13]▼❶

Lady Ice (1973) C-93m. ** D: Tom Gries. Donald Sutherland, Jennifer O'Neill, Robert Duvall, Patrick Magee, Eric Braeden, Jon Cypher. Dull caper film pairs insurance investigator Sutherland and wealthy O'Neill, whose father is a major "fence"

for stolen jewels. Good cast wasted. Panavision. [PG]▼❶

Lady in a Cage (1964) 93m. *** D: Walter Grauman. Olivia de Havilland, Ann Sothern, Jeff Corey, James Caan, Jennifer Billingsley, Rafael Campos, Scatman Crothers. Bone-chilling psychological drama in which incapacitated widow de Havilland finds herself stuck in an elevator in her home, then is terrorized by thugs. Allegorical tale of alienation and mindless cruelty in an impersonal society; unpleasant to watch, but undeniably truthful and prophetic. Starkly directed and well acted.▼

Lady in Cement (1968) C-93m. ** D: Gordon Douglas. Frank Sinatra, Raquel Welch, Dan Blocker, Richard Conte, Martin Gabel, Lainie Kazan, Richard Deacon, Joe E. Lewis. Sequel to TONY ROME finds Sinatra discovering nude corpse with feet encased in cement. Typical private-eye hokum, with heavy doses of violence, leering sex. Panavision. [PG—originally rated R]▼❶

Lady in Red, The (1979) C-93m. **½ D: Lewis Teague. Pamela Sue Martin, Robert Conrad, Louise Fletcher, Robert Hogan, Laurie Heineman, Glenn Withrow, Christopher Lloyd, Dick Miller. Martin suffers a life on the lam, before and after her period of notoriety as girlfriend of John Dillinger (Conrad). Lurid, low-budget retread of familiar material is handled with surprising verve. A Roger Corman production; screenplay by John Sayles. Robert Forster appears uncredited in key supporting role. Retitled GUNS, SIN AND BATHTUB GIN. [R]▼❶

Lady in the Car With Glasses and a Gun, The (1970-French) C-105m. **½ D: Anatole Litvak. Samantha Eggar, Oliver Reed, John McEnery, Stephane Audran, Billie Dixon. Eggar is best thing about otherwise unexceptional film. Psychological thriller about attempt to drive young woman crazy is only occasionally interesting. Panavision. [R]

Lady in the Dark (1944) C-100m. **½ D: Mitchell Leisen. Ginger Rogers, Ray Milland, Jon Hall, Warner Baxter, Barry Sullivan, Gail Russell, Mischa Auer. Overproduced Technicolor adaptation of the groundbreaking Moss Hart Broadway show (minus most of the Kurt Weill–Ira Gershwin songs) about a career woman who undergoes psychoanalysis to find the root of her problems. Intriguing but ultimately ponderous.

Lady in the Lake (1946) 103m. **½ D: Robert Montgomery. Robert Montgomery, Audrey Totter, Lloyd Nolan, Tom Tully, Leon Ames, Jayne Meadows. Raymond Chandler whodunit has novelty of camera taking first-person point of view of detective Philip Marlowe (Montgomery); unfortunately, confusing plot is presented in more prosaic (and dated) manner.▼❶

Lady in the Water (2006) C-110m. *½ D: M. Night Shyamalan. Paul Giamatti, Bryce

Dallas Howard, Jeffrey Wright, Bob Balaban, Sarita Choudhury, Cindy Cheung, M. Night Shyamalan, Freddy Rodriguez, Bill Irwin, Mary Beth Hurt, Jared Harris, Tovah Feldshuh. Superintendent in an apartment complex discovers an ethereal young woman in the swimming pool and senses that she needs protection. As this fable (or bedtime story, as Shyamalan would have it) unfolds, we're given more and more "information" to swallow until it becomes laughably absurd. Giamatti's empathetic performance helps, but writer-director Shyamalan was unwise to put himself in a key role—as mankind's savior! [PG-13]▶

Lady in White (1988) C-112m. *** D: Frank LaLoggia. Lukas Haas, Len Cariou, Alex Rocco, Katherine Helmond, Jason Presson, Jared Rushton, Renata Vanni, Angelo Bertolini. Sleeper film combines 1960s nostalgia with supernatural horror in original fashion. An inquisitive youngster (Haas) becomes involved with ghosts in mystery story about an unsolved murder and the legendary Lady in White (Helmond) residing in a spooky house nearby. Villain's identity is a bit too easy to guess, but there are plenty of chills and great period atmosphere along the way. Director's cut version runs 6m. longer. [PG-13] ▼O●

Lady Is Willing, The (1942) 92m. *** D: Mitchell Leisen. Marlene Dietrich, Fred MacMurray, Aline MacMahon, Arline Judge, Stanley Ridges, Roger Clark. Agreeable comedy; glamorous Dietrich wants to adopt a baby, so she marries pediatrician MacMurray. Dramatic segment near the end spoils lively mood.▼

Lady Jane (1986-British) C-142m. *** D: Trevor Nunn. Helena Bonham Carter, Cary Elwes, John Wood, Michael Hordern, Jill Bennett, Jane Lapotaire, Sara Kestelman, Patrick Stewart, Warren Saire, Joss Ackland, Ian Hogg, Richard Johnson. Absorbing historical drama about the machinations that put a 16-year-old girl on the throne of England for just nine days. Exquisite looking, well acted, just a trifle slow at times. Same story told before in a 1936 film, TUDOR ROSE. [PG-13]▼O●

Lady Killer (1933) 74m. *** D: Roy Del Ruth. James Cagney, Mae Clarke, Leslie Fenton, Margaret Lindsay, Henry O'Neill, Raymond Hatton, George Chandler. Vintage Cagney, with tangy tale of mobster becoming Hollywood actor, torn between two professions; Cagney repeats his Clarke slapfest.▼O●

Ladykillers, The (1955-British) C-90m. ***½ D: Alexander Mackendrick. Alec Guinness, Katie Johnson, Cecil Parker, Herbert Lom, Peter Sellers, Danny Green, Frankie Howerd. Droll black comedy of not-so-bright crooks involved with seemingly harmless old lady. Guinness scores again (even his *teeth* are funny) with top-notch supporting cast in this little Ealing Studios gem, written by William Rose. Original British running time: 97m. Remade in 2004.▼O●

Ladykillers, The (2004) C-104m. *** D: Joel Coen, Ethan Coen. Tom Hanks, Irma P. Hall, Marlon Wayans, J.K. Simmons, Tzi Ma, Ryan Hurst, George Wallace, Diane Delano, Stephen Root. Obsequiously polite Southern gentleman rents a room from a churchgoing widow, then plots a daring heist in her basement with an ill-chosen group of accomplices. The Coens keep a sure hand on this farcical black comedy with impeccable casting, finely tuned performances, and a bedrock of Southern gospel music (produced by T-Bone Burnett). Remake of the well-remembered Ealing comedy of 1955. [R] ▼O●

Lady L (1965-British) C-107m. **½ D: Peter Ustinov. Sophia Loren, Paul Newman, David Niven, Claude Dauphin, Philippe Noiret, Michel Piccoli. Stars and sets are elegant, but this wacky comedy set in early 20th-century London and Paris fizzles, despite Ustinov's writing, directing, and cameo appearance. Panavision.▼

Lady Liberty (1971-Italian) C-95m. *½ D: Mario Monicelli. Sophia Loren, William Devane, Luigi Proietti, Beeson Carroll, Danny DeVito, David Doyle, Richard Libertini, Edward Herrmann, Alan Feinstein, Christopher Norris, Susan Sarandon. Dull comedy of immigrant bride-to-be who tries to get an enormous sausage through U.S. customs. Watch for Warhol's Candy Darling in transvestite cameo. Original Italian title: LA MORTADELLA. [PG]

Lady of Burlesque (1943) 91m. *** D: William Wellman. Barbara Stanwyck, Michael O'Shea, J. Edward Bromberg, Iris Adrian, Marion Martin, Pinky Lee, Frank Conroy, Gloria Dickson. Stanwyck attempts to uncover—no pun intended—killer of strippers in this amusing adaptation of Gypsy Rose Lee's *G-String Murders.*▼O●

Lady on the Bus (1978-Brazilian) C-102m. *½ D: Neville D'Almeida. Sonia Braga, Nuno Leal Maia, Paulo Cesar Pereio, Jorge Doria, Yara Amaral, Claudio Marzo. Braga, the least likely of all actresses to project frigidity, is unresponsive on her wedding night—but wait! Soon she begins sampling other men, and sampling, and sampling.... Follow-up to DONA FLOR AND HER TWO HUSBANDS has even more sex but far less wit and charm. A dull ride. [R]▼

Lady Sings the Blues (1972) C-144m. **½ D: Sidney J. Furie. Diana Ross, Billy Dee Williams, Richard Pryor, James Callahan, Paul Hampton, Sid Melton. Black version of Hollywood cliché-biography, sparked by superb performance by Ross (in her acting debut) as Billie Holiday, legendary jazz singer whose life was ruined by drug addiction. Valueless as biography, but OK as soap opera, with excellent support from Pryor as "Piano Man." Panavision. [R]▼●)

Lady Takes a Chance, A (1943) 86m. *** D: William A. Seiter. Jean Arthur, John Wayne, Charles Winninger, Phil Silvers, Mary Field, Don Costello. Wayne and Arthur make fine comedy team as burly rodeo star and wide-eyed city girl who falls for him; Silvers adds zip as bus-tour guide.▼❚

Lady Vanishes, The (1938-British) 97m. **** D: Alfred Hitchcock. Margaret Lockwood, Michael Redgrave, Paul Lukas, Dame May Whitty, Googie Withers, Cecil Parker, Linden Travers, Catherine Lacey. An old woman's disappearance during a train ride leads baffled young woman into a dizzying web of intrigue. Delicious mystery-comedy; Hitchcock at his best, with a witty script by Frank Launder and Sidney Gilliat, and wonderful performances by Naunton Wayne and Basil Radford, who scored such a hit as a pair of twits that they repeated those roles in several other films! Based on Ethel Lina White's novel *The Wheel Spins*. Remade in 1979.▼●)

Lady Vanishes, The (1979-British) C-99m. *½ D: Anthony Page. Elliott Gould, Cybill Shepherd, Angela Lansbury, Herbert Lom, Arthur Lowe, Ian Carmichael. Remake of Hitchcock classic retains basic story but is sabotaged by the obnoxious characterizations of its "screwball" stars, Gould and Shepherd. Screenplay by George Axelrod. Panavision. [PG]▼●

Lady Vengeance (2005-Korean) C-115m. **½ D: Park Chan-wook. Lee Yeong-ae, Choi Min-sik, Kim Si-hu, Nam Il-woo, Kim Byeong-ok, Oh Dal-Su. Conclusion of the director's "revenge trilogy" (preceded by SYMPATHY FOR MR. VENGEANCE and OLDBOY) focuses on a woman, wrongfully imprisoned for kidnapping and murdering a young boy when she was 19, who is released after serving 13 years. While trying to reunite with the daughter she was forced to give up for adoption, she executes an elaborate and grisly revenge against the killer for whom she took the fall. Dazzlingly directed film is an undeniable display of cinematic virtuosity, but also a deeply unpleasant experience that seems to revel in brutality and torture, much of it involving children. Super 35. [R]❚

Lafayette (1962-French-Italian) C-110m. ** D: Jean Dreville. Jack Hawkins, Orson Welles, Howard St. John, Edmund Purdom, Vittorio De Sica, Michel Le Royer. Overblown, badly scripted costumer of famed 18th- century Frenchman; an episodic minor spectacle. Super Technirama 70. ▼

Lafayette Escadrille (1958) 93m. ** D: William Wellman. Tab Hunter, Etchika Choureau, William Wellman, Jr., Jody McCrea, Dennis Devine, Marcel Dalio, David Janssen, Paul Fix, Will Hutchins, Clint Eastwood, Tom Laughlin, Brett Halsey.

Wellman's final film is a well-intentioned but flat account of the celebrated French flying legion of WW1, spotlighting the coming to maturity of wayward Hunter. Mostly of interest for its cast, with Wellman, Jr., playing his father (who actually was a pilot during the war). Wellman, Sr., wrote the story and narrates.

La Femme Infidèle (1969-French-Italian) C-98m. ***½ D: Claude Chabrol. Stephane Audran, Michel Bouquet, Maurice Ronet, Stephen Di Napolo, Michel Duchaussoy. Razor-sharp thriller about a husband who thinks his wife is cheating on him. Audran and Bouquet are well cast in one of writer-director Chabrol's finest films, which chips away at the façade of a seemingly ordinary marriage. Remade in 2002 as UNFAITHFUL. Aka THE UNFAITHFUL WIFE. [R]▼❚

La Femme Nikita (1990-French-Italian) C-117m. *** D: Luc Besson. Anne Parillaud, Jean-Hugues Anglade, Tchéky Karyo, Jeanne Moreau, Jean Reno, Jean Bouise. Slick, ultra-violent saga of a hedonistic young woman who runs with a punked-out gang—until she's recruited by a French intelligence officer, determined to make her an undercover agent and "hit man." Stylish and compelling, if not always believable, with a star-making role for Parillaud. Remade in the U.S. as POINT OF NO RETURN, and in Hong Kong as BLACK CAT; later a U.S. cable TV series. Technovision. [R]▼●)

Lagaan: Once Upon a Time in India (2001-Indian) C-224m. ***½ D: Ashutosh Gowariker. Aamir Khan, Gracy Singh, Rachel Shelley, Paul Blackthorne, Suhasini Mulay, Kulbhushan Kharbanda, Raghuveer Yadav. India, 1893: an arrogant British military commander offers to cancel the crippling land tax in a drought-ridden farming village for three years if the locals, led by defiant peasant Khan (who also produced the film) can beat his team in a cricket match. If the villagers lose, they'll have to pay triple tax! Long but entertaining historical drama is a quintessential Bollywood epic, expertly combining action, romance, humor, and songs in a resplendent widescreen package. Arriscope. [PG]▼❚

L'Age d'Or (1930-French) 63m. **** D: Luis Buñuel. Gaston Modot, Lya Lys, Max Ernst, Pierre Prévert. Bishops turn into skeletons and the cow wanders into the bedroom in Buñuel's first feature, a surrealistic masterpiece coscripted by Salvadore Dali. Right-wing agitators caused a riot at the film's first (and for a long time, only) public screening; its anticlericalism put it into the "banned film" category for decades. Still has the power to delight, if no longer shock.▼●)

La Grande Bouffe SEE: **Grande Bouffe, The**

La Grande Bourgeoise (1974-Italian) C-

**115m. **½ D: Mauro Bolognini. Catherine Deneuve, Giancarlo Giannini, Fernando Rey, Tina Aumont, Paolo Bonicelli. Strong cast adds some punch to true story about Giannini's murder of sister Deneuve's loutish husband and the political storm it generates. Stylish but not terribly compelling. [R]▼●

La Guerre Est Finie (1966-French-Swedish) **121m. ***½ D: Alain Resnais. Yves Montand, Ingrid Thulin, Genevieve Bujold, Jean Daste, Michel Piccoli. Aging, tired leftist Montand travels from Spain to Paris, reports to his political associates, and visits mistress Thulin. Complex, emotionally powerful drama, with striking direction, performances. Screenplay by Jorge Semprun.▼●

Lair of the White Worm, The (1988-British) **C-94m. **½ D: Ken Russell. Amanda Donohoe, Hugh Grant, Catherine Oxenberg, Peter Capaldi, Sammi Davis, Stratford Johns, Paul Brooke, Christopher Gable. Typically outrageous Ken Russell farce, adapted from a novel by Bram Stoker (of *Dracula* fame). Strange doings begin when an archaeologist unearths a huge wormlike skull on the grounds of an estate; they get *curiouser* and *curiouser* when it turns out worms are the stuff of legend in that area. Bizarre, campy, and altogether outlandish. [R]▼●●

Lakeboat (2001) **C-98m. **½ D: Joe Mantegna. Peter Falk, Tony Mamet, Robert Forster, Charles Durning, Denis Leary, J.J. Johnston, Jack Wallace, George Wendt, Saul Rubinek. A series of vignettes about the crew of a cargo freighter that travels Lake Michigan. David Mamet adapted his play, with younger brother Tony taking one of the leading roles as a student who signs on for the summer. Never quite becomes a movie, but does offer wonderful dialogue and superb performances. Forster is particularly good. Andy Garcia appears unbilled. Feature directing debut for veteran Mamet actor Mantegna. [R]▼●

Lake House, The (2006) **C-98m. **½ D: Alejandro Agresti. Keanu Reeves, Sandra Bullock, Dylan Walsh, Shohreh Aghdashloo, Christopher Plummer, Ebon Moss-Bachrach, Willeke van Ammelrooy, Lynn Collins. Chicago architect Reeves moves into a striking lakefront glass house and finds a letter from its former occupant—doctor Bullock—waiting for him. They begin to correspond, leaving their letters in the old-fashioned mailbox at the front of the property, and eventually discover that they are living two years apart. Romantic drama stretches credulity (to put it mildly) but still creates a moodiness that's intriguing . . . enough to allow a willing viewer to go along for the ride. Based on a Korean film, IL MARE (2000). Super 35. [PG]●

Lake of Fire (2007) **152m. ***½ D: Tony Kaye. It's shot in stark b&w, but this scrupulously balanced and profoundly troubling documentary depicts the ongoing debate over abortion in painfully ambiguous shades of gray. Filmed over a 17-year period, Kaye's emotionally and intellectually challenging film forces viewers on both sides of the issue to rethink assumptions while exposing them to archival footage, on-the-street interviews, and sometimes dispassionate, sometimes fanatical testimony from journalists, activists, philosophers, academics, ministers—and, of course, women who have chosen (and, in some cases, regretted their decisions) to have abortions.●

Lake Placid (1999) **C-82m. ** D: Steve Miner. Bill Pullman, Bridget Fonda, Oliver Platt, Brendan Gleeson, Betty White, David Lewis, Mariska Hargitay, Meredith Salenger. The creature terrorizing a Maine lake (which is *not* Lake Placid, N.Y.) turns out to be a very large crocodile. Between arguments, paleontologist Fonda, game warden Pullman, sheriff Gleeson, and irritating, wealthy academic Platt try to figure out what to do about it. David E. Kelley, writing down to the material, provides lots of wisecracks, but few scares. Brief but tiresome film tries—but fails—to be a monster movie and environmentally correct at the same time. Adam Arkin appears unbilled. Followed by 2007 TV sequel and DVD sequel, LAKE PLACID 3. Panavision. [R]▼●●

Lakeview Terrace (2008) **C-106m. **½ D: Neil LaBute. Samuel L. Jackson, Patrick Wilson, Kerry Washington, Ron Glass, Justin Chambers, Jay Hernandez, Robert Pine. Mixed-race couple moves into a suburban cul-de-sac next door to an angry veteran L.A. cop (and single father) who feels empowered to impose his moral code on everyone around him. Provocative and well acted, but film's constantly shifting sympathies make it difficult to know what the point is supposed to be. Super 35. [PG-13]●

La Lectrice (1988-French) **C-98m. *** D: Michel Deville. Miou-Miou, Christian Ruché, Sylvie Laporte, Michel Raskine, Brigitte Catillon, Régis Royer, Maria Casarés, Pierre Dux. Fascinating, multi-textured account of Miou-Miou reading a book aloud to her boyfriend and imagining herself the heroine in the story: a professional reader who becomes involved in the lives of her various clients. Scripted by Deville and his wife, Rosalinde. [R]▼●

La Marseillaise (1938-French) **130m. ***½ D: Jean Renoir. Pierre Renoir, Louis Jouvet, Julien Carette, Lisa Delamare. Renoir scripted this stirring account of the French Revolution, featuring dialogue extracted from documents of the 1790s. Begins with news of the fall of the Bastille reaching Louis XVI, ends with the Marseilles Battalion of the French Revolutionary Army storming the Tuilleries and marching to Valmy. Renoir opted for a humanist approach to history, avoiding what he considered the false solemnity of most historical epics. ▼●

Lamb (1985-British) **C-110m.** **½ D: Colin Gregg. Liam Neeson, Hugh O'Conor, Ian Bannen, Rouan Wilmot, Frances Tomelty, Dudley Sutton. Neeson is good in this otherwise obvious drama spotlighting the complex relationship between an idealistic Brother who teaches at a Roman Catholic school for problem boys and a deeply troubled pupil (O'Conor) who is maltreated by the authoritarian headmaster. Not released in the U.S. until 1995.▼❚

Lambada (1990) **C-98m.** BOMB D: Joel Silberg. J. Eddie Peck, Melora Hardin, Shabba-Dooʹ, Ricky Paull Goldin, Basil Hoffman, Dennis Burkley. By day, Peck teaches math to snots in a posh Beverly Hills high school; by night, he tries to "reach" barrio kids in an East L.A. lambada club. In other words, it's STAND AND DELIVER with better buns; avoid at all costs unless you never miss a Shabba-Doo movie. Super 35. [PG-13]▼❚

Lamerica (1994-Italian-French) **C-110m.** ***½ D: Gianni Amelio. Enrico Lo Verso, Michele Placido, Carmelo Di Mazzarelli, Piro Milkani, Elida Janushi. Deeply touching, laced-in-acid drama, set in the wake of Albania's emancipation from communism and detailing the manner in which fate links up a young, arrogant Italian capitalist (Lo Verso) and the just-liberated political prisoner (Di Mazzarelli) he is attempting to exploit. A politically savvy account of how the downtrodden go from one kind of exploitation to another as political systems change. Amelio effectively captures the feeling of what it's like to be a poor and powerless refugee. Technovision.▼❚

La Moustache (2005-French) **C-84m.** *** D: Emmanuel Carrère. Vincent Lindon, Emmanuelle Devos, Mathieu Amalric, Hippolyte Girardot, Cylia Malki, Macha Polikarpova, Fantine Camus. On a whim, a man shaves off his moustache and no one remembers that he ever had one— beginning with his wife. Disturbing, challenging allegorical drama that ponders the nature of intimate human relationships and asks how well two people ever really know each other. Carrère adapted his own novel with Jérôme Beaujour.❚

Lancelot and Guinevere SEE: **Sword of Lancelot**

Land and Freedom (1995-U.S.-Spanish-German) **C-109m.** *** D: Kenneth Loach. Ian Hart, Rosana Pastor, Iciar Bollain, Tom Gilroy, Marc Martines, Frederic Pierrot, Angela Clarke. Perceptive, passionate account of the Spanish Civil War, centered on a young, working-class British Communist (Hart) who comes to Spain to join the anti-fascists in their battle against Franco. Rich human drama of political idealism and reality, if a bit too moralistic at times. Highlight: that pseudo-documentary ad hoc town meeting.▼●

Land Before Time, The (1988) **C-69m.**

**½ D: Don Bluth. Voices of Pat Hingle, Gabriel Damon, Helen Shaver, Candace Hutson, Judith Barsi, Will Ryan, Burke Barnes. A young dinosaur is orphaned and must make his way to a valley green with vegetation where he and his tribe can survive. Along the way he meets other young friends of different dinosaur species, and they make the trek together. Enjoyable if leisurely paced (and plotted) cartoon feature for younger viewers. Followed by far too many video sequels. [G]▼❚

Land Before Time II: The Great Valley Adventure, The (1994) **C-74m.** *** D: Roy Allen Smith. Voices of Jeff Bennett, Heather Hogan, Kenneth Mars, John Ingle, Linda Gary, Candace Hutson, Scott McAfee. Charming direct-to-video sequel to earlier animated feature has young brontosaurus Littlefoot and his dino pals contending with omnivores and a baby T-Rex who wants to join their group! Kids will identify with the young reptiles in this delightful adventure. Songs by The Roches; original theme music by James Horner. Followed by several more video sequels. [G]▼❚

Land Girls, The (1998-British-French) **C-110m.** ** D: David Leland. Catherine McCormack, Rachel Weisz, Anna Friel, Steven Mackintosh, Tom Georgeson, Maureen O'Brien, Gerald Down. Disappointing soap opera based on the potentially fascinating story of the Women's Land Army, formed in 1941 to put women to work on English farms whose men had gone off to war. The three attractive young women who come to live with farmer Georgeson wind up dallying with his randy son (Mackintosh), and after a while it all seems rather silly. Leland coscripted from a novel by Angela Huth. Panavision. [R]▼●

Landlord, The (1970) **C-113m.** ***½ D: Hal Ashby. Beau Bridges, Pearl Bailey, Diana Sands, Louis Gossett, Lee Grant, Susan Anspach, Bob (Robert) Klein, Patricia (Trish) Van Devere. Vibrant comedy-drama with Bridges as aimless rich-kid who buys Brooklyn tenement planning to renovate it for himself, changing plans when he meets tenants. Delightful comic touches combined with perceptive sidelights on black experience. Ashby's first film as director. [PG—originally rated R]▼❚

Land of Plenty (2004-U.S.-German) **C-119m.** **½ D: Wim Wenders. John Diehl, Michelle Williams, Richard Edson, Wendell Pierce, Gloria Stuart, Burt Young, Shaun Toub, Bernard White. Psychologically disconnected Vietnam veteran (Diehl) cruises around L.A., looking for suspected terrorists. He and his niece (Williams), newly arrived in town and working in a homeless shelter, investigate the drive-by shooting of a destitute Middle Easterner. This mournful meditation on paranoia, homelessness, and violence in America is at best a plea for peace and understanding in our post-9/11 world, but it meanders and is way overlong. Digital Video Widescreen.▶

Land of the Dead (2005-U.S.-Canadian-French) **C-93m.** **½ D: George A. Romero. Simon Baker, John Leguizamo, Dennis Hopper, Asia Argento, Robert Joy, Eugene Clark, Joanne Boland, Tony Nappo. Survivors of a disaster that turned the dead into flesh-eating zombies hole up in a city on a river with barricades to keep the zombies out. Inside, tensions increase while outside the dead are getting smarter. Romero's fourth walking dead movie is well produced and suspenseful, with a dose of social satire and a standout performance by Leguizamo . . . but we've seen it all before, and it never really catches fire. Title on-screen is GEORGE A. ROMERO'S LAND OF THE DEAD. Also available in unrated version. Super 35. [R]▼▶

Land of the Lost (2009) **C-101m.** *½ D: Brad Silberling. Will Ferrell, Anna Friel, Danny McBride, Jorma Taccone, John Boylan, Bobb'e J. Thompson; voice of Leonard Nimoy. An obnoxious scientist, his assistant, and a redneck survivalist are sucked into a space-and-time vortex that takes them to an alternate universe populated by dinosaurs and a guy in a monkey suit named Chaka. Bloated, unfunny big-screen version of Sid and Marty Krofft's hokey but endearing Saturday morning kid show. Ferrell has a funny bit involving a prehistoric bee sting but mostly mugs his way through this ill-conceived mess. The dino effects are way overdone considering the juvenile shenanigans. You know it's bad when *Today Show* host Matt Lauer gets all the real laughs. [PG-13]▶

Land of the Minotaur (1976-U.S.-British) **C-88m.** *½ D: Costa Carayiannis. Donald Pleasence, Luan Peters, Peter Cushing, Nikos Verlekis, Costas Skouras. Tourists are kidnapped by Greek Minoan devil-worship cult, and a local priest tries to save them, in this draggy, uninteresting yarn. Aka MINOTAUR. Released in England at 94m. as THE DEVIL'S MEN. [PG]▼▶

Land of the Pharaohs (1955) **C-106m.** **½ D: Howard Hawks. Jack Hawkins, Joan Collins, James Robertson Justice, Dewey Martin, Alexis Minotis, Sydney Chaplin, James Hayter. Entertaining, if fruity spectacle about building of the Great Pyramid, filmed on an epic scale. Hawks claimed neither he nor his writers (including William Faulkner and Harry Kurnitz) "knew how a pharaoh talked" . . . and it shows. Still worth catching for great revenge ending and now-campy villainy by Collins. CinemaScope.▼●▶

Land Raiders (1970) **C-100m.** ** D: Nathan Juran. Telly Savalas, George Maharis, Arlene Dahl, Janet Landgard, Jocelyn Lane, George Coulouris, Guy Rolfe. Even if you can accept Savalas and Maharis as brothers, this Western about family feuds amidst Indian attacks has little to offer.▼▶

Landru SEE: **Bluebeard** (1962)

Land That Time Forgot, The (1975-British) **C-90m.** **½ D: Kevin Connor. Doug McClure, John McEnery, Susan Penhaligon, Keith Barron, Anthony Ainley. Edgar Rice Burroughs' 1918 sci-fi novel about Germans and Americans in WW1 submarine discovering unknown land in South America is not bad as adventure yarn, but special effects (dinosaurs, volcanic eruption) are not convincing. Sequel: THE PEOPLE THAT TIME FORGOT. Contemporized direct-to-DVD remake in 2009. [PG]▼▶

Langrishe, Go Down (1978-British) **C-112m.** *** D: David Jones. Judi Dench, Jeremy Irons, Annette Crosbie, Harold Pinter, Margaret Whiting, Susan Williamson. Dench is superb in this understated drama, set in the 1930s, as one of the daughters of a faded aristocratic Irish family; she experiences an array of emotions while immersing herself in an affair with a calculating Bavarian intellectual (Irons). Starts off slowly and becomes more involving as it goes along. Scripted by Pinter, from a novel by Aidan Higgins. Originally made for British television, this opened theatrically in the U.S. in 2002.▶

La Notte (1961-French-Italian) **120m.** **½ D: Michelangelo Antonioni. Jeanne Moreau, Marcello Mastroianni, Monica Vitti, Bernhard Wicki. Moreau is bored and troubled by one-dimensional husband Mastroianni in this study of noncommunication. Moody, introverted, abstract—and superficial—filled with "empty, hopeless images." The second of a trilogy, preceded by L'AVVENTURA and followed by L'ECLISSE. Aka THE NIGHT.▼▶

Lantana (2001-Australian-German) **C-121m.** ***½ D: Ray Lawrence. Anthony LaPaglia, Geoffrey Rush, Barbara Hershey, Kerry Armstrong, Rachael Blake, Vince Colosimo, Daniela Farinacci, Peter Phelps. Moving, adult story of relationships thwarted by boredom, habit, and lack of communication. LaPaglia plays a cop whose marriage has stagnated, leading him to sleep with another woman; meanwhile, he investigates the disappearance of a woman whose own marriage is in jeopardy. Beautifully nuanced at every turn. Screenplay by Andrew Bovell from his play *Speaking in Tongues*. Super 35. [R]▼▶

La Nuit de Varennes (1982-Italian-French) **C-133m.** *** D: Ettore Scola. Marcello Mastroianni, Jean-Louis Barrault, Hanna Schygulla, Harvey Keitel, Jean-Claude Brialy. Witty historical fable allows such famous figures as Casanova and Thomas Paine to cross paths at the time of the French Revolution. Original French running time 150m. Technovision. [R]▼

La Passante (1982-French-German) **C-106m.** *** D: Jacques Rouffio. Romy Schneider, Michel Piccoli, Wendelin Werner, Helmut Griem, Gerard Klein, Dominique Labourier, Mathieu Carriere, Maria Schell. Why does nonviolence advocate Piccoli kill a Paraguayan ambassador, an ex-Nazi living under an assumed name? Interesting drama is ambitious in scope, but could have been better. Schneider, in her final film, plays both Piccoli's wife and the woman who sheltered him as a boy. ▼●

La Pelle (1981-Italian-French) **C-131m.** *½ D: Liliana Cavani. Marcello Mastroianni, Burt Lancaster, Claudia Cardinale, Ken Marshall, Alexandra King, Carlo Giuffre. Distastefully bitter panorama of American troops in Naples after the Liberation, based on the memoirs of Curzio Malaparte (played here by Mastroianni). Overlong; poorly directed and scripted (by Cavani and Robert Katz). A disaster.

La Permission SEE: **Story of a Three Day Pass, The**

La Petite Lili (2003-French-Canadian) **C-104m.** *** D: Claude Miller. Nicole Garcia, Bernard Giraudeau, Jean-Pierre Marielle, Ludivine Sagnier, Robinson Stévenin, Julie Depardieu, Yves Jacques, Michel Piccoli. A family's country retreat becomes charged with emotion when the hotheaded son—an aspiring filmmaker/artiste—discovers that his girlfriend is intrigued with his mother's boyfriend, a successful director of mainstream movies. Ingenious film inspired by Chekhov's *The Seagull*, exploring the line between art and life, and how the two affect each other. Screenplay by Miller and Julien Boivent. ▶

La Prima Cosa Bella (2010-Italian) **C-118m.** *** D: Paolo Virzì. Valerio Mastandrea, Micaela Ramazzotti, Stefania Sandrelli, Claudia Pandolfi, Marco Messeri, Fabrizia Sacchi. Woman's radiant beauty and innocent charm are her blessing and her curse as they attract equal parts good and bad to her life. It especially affects her son, who takes all the mean-spirited, small-town gossip and domestic abuse of the father to heart, knowing that somehow his mother is the cause of it all. Now grown, he learns she is ill and is dragged to her bedside, where he is forced to reconcile his warring feelings about her and their relationship. Melancholy tale slips back and forth from past to present. Sandrelli as the elder and Ramazzotti as the younger Anna are luminous.

La Prisonniere (1968-French) **C-104m.** ** D: Henri-Georges Clouzot. Laurent Terzieff, Bernard Fresson, Elsabeth Wiener, Dany Carrel, Dario Moreno, Daniel Riviere. From the director of DIABOLIQUE comes this obscure, confused study of woman obsessed with a photographer of sadomasochism. Strikingly photographed.

La Promesse (1996-Belgian-French-Luxembourgian-Tunisian) **C-93m.** ***½ D: Jean-Pierre Dardenne, Luc Dardenne. Jérémie Renier, Olivier Gourmet, Assita Ouedraogo, Rasmané Ouedraogo. Harrowing tale of a boy being raised by a father who mercilessly ex-

ploits illegal immigrants—as their supposed savior, landlord, and employer. Trouble begins when the boy, who's always obeyed his father unquestioningly, develops a friendship with one of the illegals. Moving in its understated, matter-of-fact look at a young man at a moral crossroads in his life. Remarkably raw . . . and real. Written by the directors. ▼▶

La Provinciale SEE: **Girl From Lorraine, The**

Laputa: Castle in the Sky (1986-Japanese) **C-124m.** **** D: Hayao Miyazaki. Voices of James Van Der Beek, Anna Paquin, Cloris Leachman, Mark Hamill, Mandy Patinkin, Andy Dick. Magnificent animated adventure fantasy about an orphan girl who is pursued by sky pirates and an evil government agent who want to get their hands on the magical crystal that allows her to float—and also holds the secret to finding a mythical treasure-laden island above the clouds. Stunning visuals, thrilling set pieces and compelling characters make this a masterpiece of action filmmaking, animated or otherwise, inspiring a true sense of awe. Aka CASTLE IN THE SKY. ▼▶

Lara Croft Tomb Raider (2001) **C-100m.** *½ D: Simon West. Angelina Jolie, Jon Voight, Noah Taylor, Iain Glen, Daniel Craig, Christopher Barrie, Richard Johnson, Leslie Phillips. Jolie plays the sexy British archeologist-adventurer who follows her late father's instructions to find—and destroy—both pieces of an ancient relic that can control time. Perhaps the dullest action-adventure film ever made, with flat writing and performances (save for Jolie) and lifeless direction, sparked now and then by some flashy set pieces. Voight, Jolie's real-life father, plays Croft's dad. Based on a popular computer game. To quote a character in the film itself, "Enough of this twaddle!" Followed by a sequel. Super 35. [PG-13] ▼▶

Lara Croft Tomb Raider: The Cradle of Life (2003) **C-117m.** *½ D: Jan De Bont. Angelina Jolie, Gerard Butler, Noah Taylor, Ciarán Hinds, Djimon Hounsou, Til Schweiger, Christopher Barrie, Simon Yam. Pouting and plundering in a variety of revealing outfits, Jolie returns as the videogame adventuress who teams up with her shady ex in a race to find Pandora's Box before it falls into the hands of an evil scientist who wants to harness its power to create biological weapons. Astonishingly inept and interminable sequel gives new meaning to the word "boring." Game over. Panavision. [PG-13] ▼▶

Larceny, Inc. (1942) **95m.** ***½ D: Lloyd Bacon. Edward G. Robinson, Jane Wyman, Broderick Crawford, Jack Carson, Anthony Quinn, Edward Brophy. Hilarious little comedy of ex-cons Robinson, Crawford, and Brophy using luggage store as front for shady activities; villain Quinn tries to horn in. Look for Jackie Gleason in a small role as a soda jerk.▐

L'Argent (1983-French-Swiss) **C-81m.** ***½ D: Robert Bresson. Christian Patey, Sylvie van den Elsen, Michel Briguet, Caroline Lang, Jeanne Aptekman. How the petty maneuverings of some upper-class boys and shopkeepers result in the ruin of workingman Patey: the rich lie, and get their workers to lie for them, but are aghast when the workers lie to them. Subtle, powerful film, simply and effectively directed by a master filmmaker; based on a Tolstoy story. ▼▐

Larger Than Life (1996) **C-93m.** *½ D: Howard Franklin. Bill Murray, Janeane Garofalo, Matthew McConaughey, Linda Fiorentino, Keith David, Pat Hingle, Jeremy Piven, Maureen Mueller, Harve Presnell, Lois Smith, Tai. Disappointing comedic misfire of motivational speaker Murray trying to get an elephant cross-country in a hurry. One hysterical sequence of Murray's mishandling of a truck is the only real laugh. Promising possibilities fall flat, with McConaughey way over the top and Fiorentino completely wasted. [PG] ▼●▐

La Ronde (1950-French) **97m.** ***½ D: Max Ophuls. Anton Walbrook, Serge Reggiani, Simone Simon, Simone Signoret, Daniel Gelin, Danielle Darrieux, Fernand Gravet, Odette Joyeux, Jean-Louis Barrault, Isa Miranda, Gérard Philipe. Wise, witty account of various people having affairs, forming a chain that eventually comes full circle, all held together by sarcastic Walbrook. A film of style and charm, based on an Arthur Schnitzler play. Screenplay by Jacques Natanson and director Ophuls. Remade as CIRCLE OF LOVE and CHAIN OF DESIRE. ▼●▐

Larry Crowne (2011) **C-95m.** **½ D: Tom Hanks. Tom Hanks, Julia Roberts, Bryan Cranston, Cedric the Entertainer, Taraji P. Henson, Gugu Mbatha-Raw, Wilmer Valderrama, Pam Grier, Rita Wilson, George Takei, Rob Riggle, Bob Stephenson, Holmes Osborne, Rami Malek, Grace Gummer, Dale Dye. When a loyal store manager is fired because he never went to college, he's forced to take stock of his life and enrolls in a local community college. There he makes young friends who open him up to new experiences and falls under the spell of his teachers—especially Roberts, who offers a course in informal public speaking. Self-consciously whimsical and uneven; still lightly enjoyable as a vehicle for its stars and an agreeable ensemble. Hanks coscripted with Nia Vardalos (who's the voice of Roberts' GPS device and whose husband, Ian Gomez, plays restaurant owner Frank). Panavision. [PG-13]

Larry the Cable Guy: Health Inspector (2006) **C-89m.** *½ D: Trent Cooper. Larry the Cable Guy (Dan Whitney), Iris Bahr, Bruce Bruce, Joanna Cassidy, Brooke Dillman, Tony Hale, David Koechner, Lisa Lampanelli, Megyn Price, Tom Wilson, Joe

Pantoliano, Kid Rock, Jerry Mathers. Whitney brings his blue-collar "Larry" character—a beer-bellied, foulmouthed, endlessly flatulent dimwit—to the screen in this low-rent, low-laugh-quotient comedy about a bungling health inspector who investigates a series of restaurant food-poisonings. "Larry" fans and aficionados of redneck humor may rate this higher. [PG-13]▐

Lars and the Real Girl (2007) **C-106m.** *** D: Craig Gillespie. Ryan Gosling, Emily Mortimer, Patricia Clarkson, Kelli Garner, Paul Schneider. Sweet film about socially traumatized Gosling, who purchases a life-sized doll and treats her as if she's real—to the dismay of his older brother and sister-in-law (who feel protective of him) and the neighbors in their tight-knit community. Fortunately, a sympathetic doctor (Clarkson) steers them in the right direction. This could have been written as farce, but instead it's a story about caring and compassion in the face of genuinely odd behavior . . . and it's disarmingly effective. Written by Nancy Oliver. [PG-13]▐

Larsen, Wolf of the Seven Seas SEE: **Wolf Larsen**

La Salamandre (1971-Swiss) **125m.** *** D: Alain Tanner. Bulle Ogier, Jean-Luc Bideau, Jacques Denis. Simple, funny examination of truth: journalist Bideau and writer Denis research facts behind the case of mysterious Ogier, accused by her uncle of attempted murder. Fine performances by the three leads. ▼

La Separation (1994-French) **C-85m.** *** D: Christian Vincent. Isabelle Huppert, Daniel Auteuil, Jerome Deschamps, Karin Viard, Laurence Lerel. Knowingly detailed, beautifully acted chronicle of the simmering tensions between a married couple (Huppert and Auteuil) as their relationship disintegrates. In its best moments, this sobering film compares favorably with Bergman's SCENES FROM A MARRIAGE. Released in the U.S. in 1998. ▼▐

Laserblast (1978) **C-90m.** **½ D: Michael Raye. Kim Milford, Cheryl Smith, Roddy McDowall, Ron Masak, Keenan Wynn, Dennis Burkley. Low-budget sci-fi with teen Milford finding alien ray gun which enables him to become a creature who can destroy his enemies. David Allen's stop-motion effects are a highlight. [PG] ▼●▐

Laser Mission (1989-German-South African-U.S.) **C-83m.** ** D: Beau Davis. Brandon Lee, Debi Monahan, Ernest Borgnine, Werner Pochath, Graham Clarke, Maureen Lahoud, Pierre Knoessen. Freelance secret agent Lee and tough Monahan travel across a South African desert to rescue laser expert Borgnine, kidnapped by the Soviets. Lee is appealing, but this low-rent 007-type adventure has nothing new to offer. ▼●▐

Lassie (1994) **C-92m.** *** D: Daniel Petrie. Helen Slater, Thomas Guiry, Jon Tenney, Brittany Boyd, Frederic Forrest, Richard

Farnsworth, Michelle Williams, Charlie Hofheimer. A city family with some problems decides to start over again at the old family farm; along the way, a remarkably smart dog "adopts" them. Young Guiry is a standout as the troubled boy who (quite credibly) changes under the influences of Lassie and his new country environment. Painted in broad strokes, for its intended youthful audience. [PG]▼●)

Lassie (2005-British-Irish-French-U.S.) **C-100m.** *** D: Charles Sturridge. Peter O'Toole, Samantha Morton, John Lynch, Peter Dinklage, Steve Pemberton, Jemma Redgrave, Jonathan Mason, Edward Fox, John Standing, Gregor Fisher, Robert Hardy, Kelly Macdonald, Nicholas Lyndhurst. The setting is Yorkshire, 1938: young Joe (Mason) is heartbroken when his impoverished parents are forced to sell his beloved collie to the Duke of Rudling (O'Toole, in fine fettle). But Lassie has no intention of staying with the Duke, even after he brings the dog to his Glasgow estate, and makes the long journey home, meeting a variety of colorful characters along the way. Pleasing, straightforward retelling of Eric Knight's story, filmed before as LASSIE COME HOME (1943). Super 35. [PG]▌

Lassie Come Home (1943) **C-88m.** ***½ D: Fred M. Wilcox. Roddy McDowall, Donald Crisp, Dame May Whitty, Edmund Gwenn, Nigel Bruce, Elsa Lanchester, Elizabeth Taylor. Winning, wonderful film from Eric Knight's book about a poor family forced to sell their beloved dog, who undertakes several tortuous journeys to return to them. A tearjerker of the first order, and one of the all-time great family films. Lassie is played—quite remarkably—by a male collie named Pal. Sequel: SON OF LASSIE. Remade as GYPSY COLT (1954), THE MAGIC OF LASSIE, and LASSIE (2005).▼●)

Lassiter (1984) **C-100m.** **½ D: Roger Young. Tom Selleck, Jane Seymour, Lauren Hutton, Bob Hoskins, Joe Regalbuto, Ed Lauter, Warren Clarke. A second-story man is shanghaied into doing espionage work in London on the eve of WW2. Stylish and nicely acted, but too plodding to overcome its basic problem of ordinariness. Selleck's second star vehicle is at least an improvement over his first (HIGH ROAD TO CHINA). [R]▼●

Last Action Hero (1993) **C-130m.** ** D: John McTiernan. Arnold Schwarzenegger, F. Murray Abraham, Art Carney, Charles Dance, Frank McRae, Tom Noonan, Robert Prosky, Anthony Quinn, Mercedes Ruehl, Austin O'Brien, Ian McKellen, Toru Tanaka, Joan Plowright, Tina Turner, Rick Ducommun, Michael V. Gazzo. Noisy, smug, self-conscious blockbuster-wannabe about a boy whose "magic ticket" transports him into an action movie alongside his No. 1 hero, Jack Slater (Schwarzenegger). Genuinely bad

writing and an overall air of unpleasantness torpedo this film; good action scenes and occasional clever ideas can't save it. (And how exactly did an Ingmar Bergman picture work its way into the story?) A raft of cameo appearances add to the in-joke tone of the picture. Panavision. [PG-13] ▼●

Last Adventure, The (1967-French) **C-102m.** **½ D: Robert Enrico. Alain Delon, Lino Ventura, Joanna Shimkus, Hans Meyer. Two adventurers and a beautiful woman go on a very engaging treasure hunt. Techniscope.▼

Last Airbender, The (2010) **C-103m.** *½ D: M. Night Shyamalan. Noah Ringer, Dev Patel, Nicola Peltz, Jackson Rathbone, Shaun Toub, Aasif Mandvi, Cliff Curtis, Katharine Houghton. Live-action adaptation of popular Nickelodeon animated TV series *Avatar: The Last Airbender* is a near-total misfire, with sporadically impressive special effects offering inadequate compensation for flat performances, clunky pacing, and speechifying dialogue. Muddled fantasy-adventure plot pivots on efforts by 12-year-old would-be messiah (charisma-free Ringer) to master control of four elements—earth, fire, water, and, of course, air—to defend disparate tribes against a wicked warlord (Curtis). Last-minute conversion to 3-D is spectacularly ineffective. 3-D Super 35. [PG]▌

Last American Hero, The (1973) **C-100m.** *** D: Lamont Johnson. Jeff Bridges, Valerie Perrine, Geraldine Fitzgerald, Art Lund, Gary Busey, Ed Lauter, Ned Beatty. Unusual, engrossing saga of Junior Jackson, North Carolinian moonshiner and racing fanatic, pitting his ability against the System. Three-dimensional, believable characters enhance cynical point of view. Retitled HARD DRIVER. Panavision. [PG] ▼▌

Last Angry Man, The (1959) **100m.** *** D: Daniel Mann. Paul Muni, David Wayne, Betsy Palmer, Luther Adler, Joby Baker, Joanna Moore, Godfrey Cambridge, Billy Dee Williams. Sentimental story of an old, dedicated family doctor in Brooklyn whose life is going to be portrayed on TV. Muni (in his last film) makes it worth seeing. Adapted by Gerald Green from his novel. Look fast for a young Cicely Tyson. Remade as 1974 TVM with Pat Hingle.▼

Last Boy Scout, The (1991) **C-105m.** ** D: Tony Scott. Bruce Willis, Damon Wayans, Chelsea Field, Noble Willingham, Taylor Negron, Danielle Harris, Halle Berry, Bruce McGill. Hardcore action film with Willis as a fired Secret Service agent now supporting himself through sticky gumshoe hire-outs; Wayans is his buddy in bonding (and an ex-pro-football quarterback) who helps him investigate gridiron corruption. More of the same from LETHAL WEAPON screenwriter Shane Black. Violent, even by this genre's standards, but zippy enough to make it an OK view. Panavision. [R]▼●)

Last Butterfly, The (1991-Czech-British) C-110m. *** D: Karel Kachyna. Tom Courtenay, Brigitte Fossey, Ingrid Held, Freddie Jones, Milan Knazko, Josef Kemer, Linda Jablonska. Acidly ironic drama of famous French mime Courtenay, who is "hired" by the Nazis to give one performance for the children of Terezin, the infamous "city of the Jews," during WW2. It's meant for propaganda purposes, to show the world that Jews in concentration camps were living the Life of Riley. Occasionally heavy going because of subject matter, but always moving. [PG-13]▼●▌

Last Castle, The (2001) C-131m. ** D: Rod Lurie. Robert Redford, James Gandolfini, Mark Ruffalo, Steve Burton, Delroy Lindo, Paul Calderon, Clifton Collins, Jr., Samuel Ball, Frank Military. After a controversial court-martial, a highly respected general is sent to a military prison, where he squares off against the warden and ultimately leads a revolt. Redford plays the kind of quiet rebel he virtually invented in the 1970s, but the script is swimming in movie clichés, and Gandolfini is too obvious a target. Panavision. [R] ▼▌

Last Challenge, The (1967) C-96m. ** D: Richard Thorpe. Glenn Ford, Angie Dickinson, Chad Everett, Gary Merrill, Jack Elam, Delphi Lawrence, Royal Dano. Punk Everett is out to get Marshal Ford in well-cast but routine Western; Angie plays saloonkeeper, which makes one wonder why the two men don't just settle their problems over a drink. Panavision.

Last Chance Harvey (2008-U.S.-British) C-90m. *** D: Joel Hopkins. Dustin Hoffman, Emma Thompson, Kathy Baker, James Brolin, Eileen Atkins, Richard Schiff, Liane Balaban. A poor shlub (Hoffman) whose career is on the skids flies to London for his daughter's wedding but feels alienated from the festivities, presided over by his ex-wife and her new husband. Then he chances to meet a middle-aged working woman (Thompson) and strikes up a conversation. A poignant portrait of two mature people who form a kinship; this shows off the two stars at their very best. Super 35. [PG-13]▌

Last Chase, The (1981-Canadian) C-101m. *½ D: Martyn Burke. Lee Majors, Burgess Meredith, Chris Makepeace, Alexandra Stewart, Ben Gordon. Oil shortage causes the demise of auto travel during the 1980s; 20 years later, ex-race-car driver Majors reassembles his Porsche and becomes a "symbol of freedom" as he races across the country. Flimsy drama that reeks of Reaganomics. [PG]▼

Last Command, The (1928) 88m. **** D: Josef von Sternberg. Emil Jannings, Evelyn Brent, William Powell, Nicholas Soussanin, Michael Visaroff, Jack Raymond, Fritz Feld. Stunning silent drama of refugee Russian general Jannings, who is now reduced to working as a Hollywood extra—and destined to appear in a movie depicting the Russian revolution. A fascinating story laced with keen perceptions of life and work in Hollywood. Lajos Biros' story was based on an actual person; Jannings' gripping performance won him an Oscar (shared for his work in THE WAY OF ALL FLESH).▼▌

Last Command, The (1955) C-110m. **½ D: Frank Lloyd. Sterling Hayden, Anna Maria Alberghetti, Richard Carlson, Arthur Hunnicutt, Ernest Borgnine, J. Carrol Naish, Ben Cooper, John Russell, Virginia Grey, Jim Davis, Eduard Franz, Otto Kruger, Slim Pickens. Elaborate, sweeping account of the battle of the Alamo, hampered by tedious script. Story centers on wandering adventurer Jim Bowie (Hayden), who is galvanized by Mexican threats against Texas. All the historical Alamo set pieces are here, with Hunnicutt a refreshingly rustic Davy Crockett. Music by Max Steiner; "Jim Bowie" sung by Gordon MacRae.▼

Last Dance (1996) C-103m. **½ D: Bruce Beresford. Sharon Stone, Rob Morrow, Randy Quaid, Peter Gallagher, Jack Thompson, Jayne Brook, Pamala Tyson, Skeet Ulrich. Younger brother of governor's chief of staff arrives in state capitol and gets a makework job in the Clemency Office. He throws himself into his first case, launching a crusade to save a woman convicted of double murder from being executed. Stone gives a creditable performance in this severely deglamorized role, though it's hard to empathize with a murderer heroine. (By film's end, you can't help but feel *something*.) Morrow is good, too, but his character's motivations are muddy. Suffers from comparison to the previous year's superior DEAD MAN WALKING. Charles S. Dutton appears unbilled. [R]▼●▌

Last Days, The (1999) C-90m. ***½ D: James Moll. Exceptional documentary about five survivors of the Holocaust who suffered through Hitler's "final solution" in the last year of the war in Hungary. Brilliantly compiled from archive footage, vivid interviews and contemporary visits to Germany and Hungary, with five well-chosen subjects whose stories gradually meld into a mosaic. Produced by Steven Spielberg's Shoah Foundation. Oscar winner as Best Documentary. [PG-13]▼▌

Last Days (2005) C-97m. ** D: Gus Van Sant. Michael Pitt, Lukas Haas, Asia Argento, Scott Green, Nicole Vicius, Ricky Jay, Ryan Orion, Harmony Korine, Kim Gordon. Ambitious but ineffective minimalist drama chronicling the final hours in the life of a Kurt Cobain–like rock star (Pitt). Van Sant attempts to get inside the character's head and explore his mental and emotional state; despite some striking images, the result is meandering . . . and the religious references are preposterous. [R]▌

Last Days of Chez Nous, The (1993-

Australian) **C-96m.** **½ D: Gillian Armstrong. Lisa Harrow, Bruno Ganz, Kerry Fox, Miranda Otto, Kiri Paramore, Bill Hunter. Aspiring novelist with a teenage daughter endures marital discord when her aimless younger sister moves in. Director Armstrong returns to her roots for this interesting, if not entirely successful, film about relationships—between spouses, siblings, children and parents. (Biggest problem: an enigmatic and unappealing lead character.) A movie for real grown-ups, though it lacks the emotional power of MY BRILLIANT CAREER. Offers a view of Sydney (the bleaker part) that other movies usually don't show. [R]▼

Last Days of Disco, The (1998) **C-113m.** *** D: Whit Stillman. Chloë Sevigny, Kate Beckinsale, Chris Eigeman, Mackenzie Astin, Matt Keeslar, Robert Sean Leonard, Jennifer Beals, Burr Steers, David Thornton, Jaid Barrymore, Carolyn Farina. Two friends, naive but smart Sevigny and critical Beckinsale, hang out at a trendy disco in the early 1980s, trying—like everyone they know—to make the transition from group activity to pairing off. Sardonic but sympathetic to its characters, the movie is amusing and well acted but not particularly insightful. Said to be the last in Stillman's romantic-yuppies trilogy with METROPOLITAN and BARCELONA; some of the characters from those films turn up here. [R]▼●❍

Last Days of Frankie the Fly, The (1997) **C-95m.** BOMB D: Peter Markle. Dennis Hopper, Daryl Hannah, Kiefer Sutherland, Michael Madsen, Dayton Callie. Hopper is a lowly runner for a neighborhood thug (Madsen, surprise!) who's looking to get out from under the creep's thumb—as a screenwriter. Unsympathetic characters in a harsh and violent world, spouting quirky dialogue amidst the L.A. porn scene; yet another PULP FICTION wannabe. Debuted on U.S. cable TV. [R]▼

Last Days of Man on Earth, The (1973-British) **C-78m.** *½ D: Robert Fuest. Jon Finch, Jenny Runacre, Sterling Hayden, Patrick Magee, Hugh Griffith, Harry Andrews. Muddled sci-fi comedy set in Lapland, London, and Turkey as world nears its end. A few scattered laughs. Longer, original British version (called THE FINAL PROGRAMME, running 89m.) has more substance. Based on one of Michael Moorcock's "Jerry Cornelius" stories; film has gained cult reputation. [R]▼●❍

Last Days of Pompeii, The (1935) **96m.** *** D: Ernest B. Schoedsack. Preston Foster, Basil Rathbone, Dorothy Wilson, David Holt, Alan Hale, John Wood, Louis Calhern. Former blacksmith Foster aspires to wealth and power as gladiator; climactic spectacle scenes are thrilling and expertly done, by the same special effects team responsible for KING KONG. Also shown in computer-colored version.▼●❍

Last Days of Pompeii, The (1960-Italian) **C-105m.** **½ D: Mario Bonnard. Steve Reeves, Christine Kaufmann, Barbara Carroll, Anne Marie Baumann, Mimmo Palmara. New version of venerable tale focuses on muscleman Reeves and synthetic account of Christian martyrs. Very little spectacle. SuperTotalscope.▼❍

Last Detail, The (1973) **C-105m.** ***½ D: Hal Ashby. Jack Nicholson, Otis Young, Randy Quaid, Clifton James, Carol Kane, Michael Moriarty, Nancy Allen. Superior comedy-drama about two career sailors ordered to transport a kleptomaniac prisoner to the brig. Robert Towne's brilliant off-color dialogue contributes to a quintessential Nicholson performance. Based on a Darryl Ponicsan novel. Look quickly for Gilda Radner. [R]▼●❍

Last Dragon, The (1985) **C-109m.** ** D: Michael Schultz. Taimak, Vanity, Chris Murney, Julius J. Carry 3rd, Faith Prince, Ernie Reyes, Jr., Keshia Knight (Pulliam), William H. Macy. Juvenile film about would-be martial arts master who gets involved with glamorous video deejay (Vanity) and some overwrought gangsters. Campy and heavy-handed; strictly kid stuff, except for one gag: the name of the Chinatown warehouse. Released theatrically as BERRY GORDY'S THE LAST DRAGON. Look fast for Chazz Palminteri as a thug. [PG-13] ▼❍

Last Embrace (1979) **C-102m.** *** D: Jonathan Demme. Roy Scheider, Janet Margolin, John Glover, Sam Levene, Christopher Walken, Charles Napier. CIA agent Scheider sees wife ambushed, spends rest of the picture believing he's next. One of the better Hitchcock-influenced suspense thrillers offers good performances and a punchy climax at Niagara Falls. Fine Miklos Rozsa score; watch for Mandy Patinkin. [R]▼●

Last Emperor, The (1987-Italian-British-Chinese) **C-165m.** ***½ D: Bernardo Bertolucci. John Lone, Joan Chen, Peter O'Toole, Ying Ruocheng, Victor Wong, Dennis Dun, Ryuichi Sakamoto, Maggie Han, Ric Young. Remarkable film inspired by true story of Pu Yi, the last emperor of China, who is crowned at age three and lives a cloistered life in the Forbidden City until he is deposed (as a young man) during the revolution and forced to fend for himself in the outside world for the first time. A magnificent journey to another time and place, hampered by unanswered questions in the narrative and a main character who remains somewhat cold. Nothing can top the spectacle of life in the Forbidden City (where scenes were actually filmed)—or the twists of fate that fill Pu Yi's life. Photographed by Vittorio Storaro; music by Ryuichi Sakamoto, David Byrne, and Cong Su. Winner of nine Academy Awards including Best Picture, Director, Adapted Screenplay (Mark Peploe, Bertolucci), Cinematography, Art Direction, Editing, Costume Design, and Original Score.

Hong Kong–produced version, based on Pu Yi's autobiography, predates this. Alternate version runs 218m. Technovision. [PG-13] ▼◐)

Last Escape, The (1970) C-90m. *½ D: Walter Grauman. Stuart Whitman, John Collin, Pinkas Braun, Martin Jarvis, Gunther Neutze, Margit Saad. O.S.S. Captain Whitman is ordered to sneak rocket expert out of Germany near the end of WW2 with predictable results. [G]

Last Exit to Brooklyn (1989-W. German) C-102m. **½ D: Uli Edel. Stephen Lang, Jennifer Jason Leigh, Burt Young, Peter Dobson, Jerry Orbach, Stephen Baldwin, Sam Rockwell, Ricki Lake, John Costelloe, Alexis Arquette. Gritty, brutal but stylish adaptation of Hubert Selby, Jr.'s notorious slice-of-life novel set on the mean streets of 1952 Brooklyn, where violence—verbal, physical, sexual, and otherwise—rules. Crammed with local color, but all the characters are thoroughly repellent and the film is difficult to like and to take. Selby himself appears as a cab driver. [R] ▼●

Last Exorcism, The (2010-U.S.-French) 87m. **½ D: Daniel Stamm. Patrick Fabian, Ashley Bell, Iris Bahr, Louis Herthum, Caleb Landry Jones, Tony Bentley, John Wright, Jr. Phony evangelist/spiritualist (Fabian) is on the verge of revealing himself to documentary filmmakers when he decides to conduct one last exorcism, of an angelic teenaged farm girl (Bell). Things don't go as he planned. Faux documentary is very well acted, especially by Fabian and Bell, and remains interesting and occasionally absorbing, until it goes off the tracks near the end. Not particularly violent. [PG-13]▶

Last Flight of Noah's Ark, The (1980) C-97m. **½ D: Charles Jarrott. Elliott Gould, Genevieve Bujold, Ricky Schroder, Tammy Lauren, John Fujioka, Yuki Shimoda, Vincent Gardenia. Typical Disney sentimentality, somewhat effective. Pilot Gould, missionary Bujold, stowaway children, and a planeload of animals are forced down in the Pacific, where they unite with two Japanese soldiers, who didn't know WW2 was over, to convert the plane into an ark. Filmed largely on Waikiki Beach. Story by Ernest K. (THE HIGH AND THE MIGHTY) Gann. [G] ▼▶

Last Frontier, The (1956) C-98m. **½ D: Anthony Mann. Victor Mature, Guy Madison, Robert Preston, James Whitmore, Anne Bancroft. Three wilderness scouts see their lives change with the coming of cavalry outpost and military martinet (Preston). Offbeat characterizations in this cavalry drama. Aka SAVAGE WILDERNESS. CinemaScope. ▼▶

Last Good Time, The (1994) C-91m. *** D: Bob Balaban. Armin Mueller-Stahl, Maureen Stapleton, Lionel Stander, Olivia d'Abo, Adrian Pasdar, Zohra Lampert, Kevin Corrigan. Well-observed little chamber drama about an elderly widower who takes in a young woman hiding from her lowlife boyfriend. Well acted all around, and nicely detailed, with a fine score by Jonathan Tunick. [R]▼●

Last Hard Men, The (1976) C-103m. *½ D: Andrew V. McLaglen. Charlton Heston, James Coburn, Barbara Hershey, Michael Parks, Jorge Rivero, Larry Wilcox, Thalmus Rasulala, Morgan Paull, Robert Donner, Christopher Mitchum. Outlaw Coburn leads a gang of men on a jailbreak, then sets into motion plan of vengeance on sheriff Heston: kidnapping daughter Hershey and threatening to gang-rape her. Repellently violent and tasteless Western, loosely based on a Brian Garfield novel, saved only by Parks' interesting performance as reform-minded sheriff. Panavision. [R]▼▶

Last Holiday (1950-British) 89m. *** D: Henry Cass. Alec Guinness, Beatrice Campbell, Kay Walsh, Bernard Lee, Wilfrid Hyde-White, Sidney James, Ernest Thesiger. Ordinary man is told he is dying and decides to live it up at a swank resort. A droll, biting script by J. B. Priestley (who also co-produced) with sterling performances by all. Remade in 2006.▼

Last Holiday (2006) C-112m. **½ D: Wayne Wang. Queen Latifah, LL Cool J, Timothy Hutton, Giancarlo Esposito, Alicia Witt, Gérard Depardieu, Jane Adams, Mike Estime, Susan Kellermann, Ranjit Chowdhry, Michael Nouri, Emeril Lagasse, Smokey Robinson. Affable reworking of the 1950 Alec Guinness film (written by J. B. Priestley), with Latifah in good form as a shy department store salesclerk who decides to go for broke when she learns she is terminally ill. Squanders its good vibes by going on too long toward an obvious conclusion, but Latifah's warmhearted performance carries it most of the way. Super 35. [PG-13]▶

Last Hour, The (1991) C-85m. **½ D: William Sachs. Michael Paré, Shannon Tweed, Bobby Di Cicco, Robert Pucci, Robert Miano, George Kyle, Danny Trejo, Raye Hollitt. A gangster kidnaps the ex-wife of cop Paré and current wife of high-living Pucci, who previously double-crossed the gangster, and holds her hostage in an old L.A. building. Pretty good low-rent imitation DIE HARD with atmospheric photography and occasionally amusing dialogue. [R]▼●

Last House on the Left, The (1972) C-84m. *½ D: Wes Craven. David Hess, Lucy Grantham, Sandra Cassel, Marc Sheffler, Jeramie Rain, Fred Lincoln. Group of thugs rapes and kills two girls, then meets bloody vigilante justice from one girl's parents. Cheap, and looks it. Repellent but admittedly powerful and (for better or worse) influential horror shocker. Surprisingly, based on Bergman's THE VIRGIN SPRING. First film by director Wes Craven. Also available

in unrated version. Remade in 2009. [R]
▼●◗

Last House on the Left, The (2009) C-110m. *½ D: Dennis Iliadis. Garret Dillahunt, Michael Bowen, Joshua Cox, Riki Lindhome, Aaron Paul, Sara Paxton, Monica Potter, Tony Goldwyn, Spencer Treat Clark, Martha MacIsaac. Attractive teenage girl leaves her parents' vacation home with a friend, but they're captured by brutal prison escapees with rape and murder on their minds. Later, the killers take refuge from a storm—with the girl's parents. Remake of the 1972 horror film is better made but lacks its crude, direct power; this wastes such good actors as Dillahunt and Goldwyn. Not as violent as the original, but still more gruesome than some recent slasher movies. Unrated version runs 114m. [R]◗

Last House on the Left, Part II SEE: **Twitch of the Death Nerve**

Last Hunt, The (1956) C-108m. **½ D: Richard Brooks. Robert Taylor, Stewart Granger, Lloyd Nolan, Debra Paget, Russ Tamblyn, Constance Ford. In the Old West, Granger and Taylor form an uneasy partnership to hunt the last remaining herds of buffalo; Granger is sick of killing, Taylor likes it all too well. Complex characters and good dialogue help, but overlength and slow pace damage this serious Western. CinemaScope.▼

Last Hurrah, The (1958) 121m. ***½ D: John Ford. Spencer Tracy, Jeffrey Hunter, Dianne Foster, Basil Rathbone, Pat O'Brien, Donald Crisp, James Gleason, Ed Brophy, John Carradine, Ricardo Cortez, Frank McHugh, Jane Darwell, Anna Lee, Charles FitzSimmons, Ken Curtis, O. Z. Whitehead, Jack Pennick, Dan Borzage. Sentimental version of Edwin O'Connor novel of politics, loosely based on life of Boston's mayor James Curley who in this story is mounting his final election campaign. Top-notch veteran cast makes film sparkle. Remade for TV in 1977 by (and with) Carroll O'Connor.▼●◗

Last King of Scotland, The (2006-British-German) C-121m. *** D: Kevin Macdonald. Forest Whitaker, James McAvoy, Kerry Washington, Gillian Anderson, Simon McBurney, David Oyelowo, Stephen Rwangyezi. Aimless young Scottish doctor (McAvoy) travels to Uganda and, through odd circumstances, finds himself personal physician to General Idi Amin (Whitaker). He lives the high life until the dictator's brutal nature is revealed. Provocative story goes exactly where you expect it to but is powered by Whitaker's mesmerizing, Oscar-winning performance, which captures all of Amin's charm and danger. Peter Morgan and Jeremy Brock adapted Giles Foden's novel. Fiction feature debut for documentarian Macdonald. Super 35. [R]◗

Last Kiss, The (2001-Italian) C-114m.

*** D: Gabriele Muccino. Stefano Accorsi, Giovanna Mezzogiorno, Stefania Sandrelli, Claudio Santamaria, Marco Cocci, Giorgio Pasotti, Martina Stella, Pierfrancesco Favino. A man about to turn 30—and become a father with his lover—begins to regret that he no longer feels great passion. Meanwhile, his friends plan a way to escape their lives and flee, and his lover's mother (Sandrelli), wracked by fear of growing old, attempts to leave her husband. A very passionate, very Italian drama. Remade in 2006. Super 35. [R]▼▼

Last Kiss, The (2006) C-104m. *** D: Tony Goldwyn. Zach Braff, Jacinda Barrett, Casey Affleck, Rachel Bilson, Michael Weston, Blythe Danner, Tom Wilkinson, Eric Christian Olsen, Marley Shelton, Lauren Lee Smith, Harold Ramis. Braff has a good job and comfortable life, and is contemplating marriage to his pregnant girlfriend . . . but he and his pals are suffering a collective panic attack as they near the age of 30, still wary of accepting adult responsibility. Meanwhile, Braff's future in-laws (Danner and Wilkinson) are going through a crisis of their own. The characters are refreshingly human in this satisfying drama set in Madison, Wisconsin. Paul Haggis scripted this remake of the 2001 Italian film. Panavision. [R]◗

Last Laugh, The (1924-German) 87m. ***½ D: F. W. Murnau. Emil Jannings, Maly Delschaft, Max Hiller, Hans Unterkirchen. Silent-film classic told entirely by camera, without title cards. Jannings plays proud doorman at posh hotel who is suddenly demoted; film details his utter and grievous humiliation. Brilliantly filmed by pioneer cameraman Karl Freund, with towering performance by Jannings. Remade in Germany in 1955.▼●◗

Last Legion, The (2007-British-French-Italian) C-102m. **½ D: Doug Lefler. Colin Firth, Ben Kingsley, Aishwarya Rai, Peter Mullan, John Hannah, Thomas Sangster, Kevin McKidd, Iain Glen, Rupert Friend. After barbarian hordes invade the crumbling Roman Empire in A.D. 476, a loyal military officer (Firth) and his brave men escort the newly crowned 12-year-old emperor (Sangster) to relative safety in far-off Britannia. There are faint echoes of Robert Louis Stevenson in this fitfully rousing, amusingly retro action-adventure. Kingsley is well cast as a cryptic sage (and occasional wizard) who serves as mentor to Sangster's resilient young hero. Super 35. [PG-13]◗

Last Man on Earth, The (1964-U.S.-Italian) 86m. ** D: Sidney Salkow. Vincent Price, Franca Bettoia, Emma Danieli, Giacomo Rossi-Stuart, Tony Cerevi. Often crude chiller with Price the sole survivor of plague, besieged by victims who arise at night thirsting for his blood; erratic production. Based on Richard Matheson's *I Am*

Legend; remade as THE OMEGA MAN and I AM LEGEND. CinemaScope. ▼●◗

Last Man Standing (1996) **C-101m.** ** D: Walter Hill. Bruce Willis, Christopher Walken, Bruce Dern, Alexandra Powers, David Patrick Kelly, William Sanderson, Karina Lombard, Ned Eisenberg, Michael Imperioli, R. D. Call, Leslie Mann. Willis chances to pass through a dreary Texas town where two Chicago gangs are at each other's throats—and tries to work both sides of the street to his own advantage. Remake of YOJIMBO (which itself became FISTFUL OF DOLLARS), set in the 1930s, is rife with gunplay, but overcome by sheer boredom. Super 35. [R]▼●◗

Last Married Couple in America, The (1980) **C-103m.** *½ D: Gilbert Cates. George Segal, Natalie Wood, Richard Benjamin, Valerie Harper, Bob Dishy, Dom DeLuise. Likable cast in stupid sex comedy about happily married couple so upset by breakup of married friends that they begin to question their own relationship. Smutty and ridiculous. [R]▼

Last Metro, The (1980-French) **C-133m.** **½ D: François Truffaut. Catherine Deneuve, Gérard Depardieu, Jean Poiret, Heinz Bennent, Andrea Ferreol, Paulette Dubost. A beautiful actress struggles to keep her "exiled" husband's theater alive during the German occupation of Paris. A film with charm and style but no point—a problem underscored by its abrupt and quizzical finale. Watching the elegant Deneuve provides most of this film's appeal. [PG]▼●◗

Last Mimzy, The (2007) **C-90m.** *½ D: Bob Shaye. Chris O'Neil, Rhiannon Leigh Wryn, Joely Richardson, Timothy Hutton, Rainn Wilson, Kathryn Hahn, Michael Clarke Duncan. Two Seattle kids find a box sent back from the future; the devices inside increase their intelligence and give them abilities to help them change the future for the better. Treacly misfire tosses science fiction and fantasy elements into the same hopper; wants to be the new E.T. but falls far short. Loosely based on the short story "Mimsy Were the Borogoves" by Lewis Padgett. The director's day job is running New Line Cinema. Super 35. [PG]◗

Last Mogul: The Life and Times of Lew Wasserman, The (2005-U.S.-Canadian) **C-110m.** **½ D: Barry Avrich. Compelling documentary chronicles the life and career of MCA-Universal kingpin Wasserman from his early days to his huge success as an agent to his years as head of one of Hollywood's most important studios. Told in straightforward fashion, this unauthorized look does not shy away from controversial areas of his life, including his reputed association with mob figures. Still, while well made and researched, the film doesn't appear to cover the whole picture; key people, including family members and longtime as-

sociates, are conspicuous by their absence. [PG-13]◗

Last Movie, The (1971) **C-108m.** *½ D: Dennis Hopper. Dennis Hopper, Julie Adams, Peter Fonda, Kris Kristofferson, Sylvia Miles, John Phillip Law, Rod Cameron, Sam Fuller. Hopper's fatally pretentious follow-up to EASY RIDER is interesting only as curio; incomprehensible story of small Peruvian village after a movie company pulls out has lovely photography, good acting by Adams. Otherwise, you've been warned. Among the supporting cast: Dean Stockwell, Russ Tamblyn, Michelle Phillips. Kristofferson's film debut (he also wrote the music). Also known as CHINCHERO. [PG]▼

Last Night (1998-Canadian-French) **C-93m.** ** D: Don McKellar. Don McKellar, Sandra Oh, Sarah Polley, Callum Keith Rennie, David Cronenberg, Robin Gammel, Genevieve Bujold, Jackie Burroughs. Rumination on the last night of civilization, and how various people deal with their impending demise. Not exactly profound, though Oh's heartrending performance almost makes this worth watching. Written by leading actor McKellar, making his directorial debut. [R]▼◗

Last Night (2010-U.S.-French) **C-93m.** ** D: Massy Tadjedin. Keira Knightley, Sam Worthington, Eva Mendes, Griffin Dunne, Guillaume Canet, Scott Adsit, Daniel Eric Gold, Stephanie Romanov, Anson Mount. One fateful evening after a party, a young N.Y.C. couple suffers a divisive turning point during a fight about fidelity. The next night, on a Philly business trip, Worthington is tempted by a new colleague (Mendes), while at home Knightley unexpectedly meets up with an old amour (Canet). Realizing that once accused, guilty or not, you could just go for it, this morose quartet must puzzle out by morning who will or who won't. Talky characters, self-absorbed to a fault, inhabit an OK date movie. A glum sit for anyone who's been there. Panavision. [R]◗

Last Night at the Alamo (1983) **80m.** *** D: Eagle Pennell. Sonny Davis, Lou Perry, Steve Matilla, Tina Hubbard, Doris Hargrave. The last night at the Alamo, no famous battle site but a small, obscure Houston bar. A fascinating portrayal of the modern-era "cowboy" as henpecked, alcoholic, ultimately pathetic. Independently produced, with a hilariously profane script by Kim Henkel, author of THE TEXAS CHAINSAW MASSACRE. ▼

Last of Sheila, The (1973) **C-120m.** ***½ D: Herbert Ross. James Coburn, James Mason, Dyan Cannon, Ian McShane, Joan Hackett, Raquel Welch, Richard Benjamin. Super murder-puzzler about jet-set gamester who devises what turns into a deadly game of whodunit. Many red herrings make it all the more fun. Script by Anthony Perkins and Stephen Sondheim, real-life puzzle fans. [PG]▼❶

Last of the Cowboys, The SEE: **Great Smokey Roadblock, The**

Last of the Dogmen (1995) **C-120m. ★★** D: Tab Murphy. Tom Berenger, Barbara Hershey, Kurtwood Smith, Steve Reevis, Andrew Miller, Gregory Scott Cummins, Molly Parker; narrated by Wilford Brimley. Annoyingly clichéd, eminently forgettable adventure with crackerjack tracker Berenger setting out to bring back a trio of prison escapees who meet a horrible fate as he nears their campsite. Could it have been the work of the mysterious, legendary Cheyenne "dog soldiers"? You may not want to stick around to find out. Panavision. [PG]▼❶

Last of the Finest, The (1990) **C-106m. ★★** D: John Mackenzie. Brian Dennehy, Joe Pantoliano, Jeff Fahey, Bill Paxton, Deborah-Lee Furness, Guy Boyd, Henry Darrow, Lisa Jane Persky. Honest, independent-minded L.A. cop Dennehy and his comrades discover sinister forces at work while attempting to bust drug traffickers. Dennehy's usual solid performance can't overcome occasionally outlandish scenario, with obvious parallels to the Iran-Contra affair. [R]▼●

Last of the High Kings, The (1996-Irish-Danish) **C-104m. ★★★** D: David Keating. Gabriel Byrne, Catherine O'Hara, Jared Leto, Christina Ricci, Colm Meaney, Stephen Rea, Lorraine Pilkington, Emily Mortimer, Jason Barry, Ciaran Fitzgerald. Solid coming-of-age tale, set in Dublin, which tells the story of idealistic 17-year-old Frankie (Leto) and the individuals who affect his life—beginning with his eccentric, egocentric actor father (Byrne) and his comically pro-Protestant mom (O'Hara, who has never been better). Loaded with charm and thoughtfully scripted by Keating and Byrne. Aka SUMMER FLING. [R]▼❶

Last of the Mobile Hot-Shots (1970) **C-108m. ★★** D: Sidney Lumet. James Coburn, Lynn Redgrave, Robert Hooks, Perry Hayes, Reggie King. Ambitious flop from Tennessee Williams' *Seven Descents of Myrtle* about volatile interracial triangle set in Deep South. ("Mobile" refers to the Alabama town.) [R—edited from original X rating]▼❶

Last of the Mohicans, The (1936) **91m. ★★★** D: George B. Seitz. Randolph Scott, Binnie Barnes, Heather Angel, Hugh Buckler, Henry Wilcoxon, Bruce Cabot, Phillip Reed, Robert Barrat. Effective and exciting adaptation of James Fenimore Cooper novel about conflicts between British Army and Colonial settlers during the French and Indian War. Scott is a stout Hawkeye, Cabot an appropriately hissable Magua. Screenplay by Philip Dunne. Also shown in computer-colored version. ▼●

Last of the Mohicans, The (1992) **C-113m.**

★★★½ D: Michael Mann. Daniel Day-Lewis, Madeleine Stowe, Russell Means, Eric Schweig, Jodhi May, Steven Waddington, Wes Studi, Maurice Roëves, Patrice Chereau, Colm Meaney, Peter Postlethwaite. Rousing, kinetic update of the James Fenimore Cooper classic, replete with 1990s sensibilities, potent depiction of violence, and a charismatic central performance by Day-Lewis as Hawkeye. Wavers between sweep of historical fiction and smaller canvas of its love story, bput never fails to entertain. Oscar winner for Best Sound. Screenplay by Mann and Christopher Crowe from Philip Dunne's script for the 1936 film. Evocative score by Trevor Jones and Randy Edelman. Expanded version runs 117m. Panavision. [R]▼❶❶

Last of the Red Hot Lovers (1972) **C-98m.** BOMB D: Gene Saks. Alan Arkin, Sally Kellerman, Paula Prentiss, Renee Taylor. Appalling film version of typical Neil Simon play concerns Arkin's unsuccessful attempts to carry on sneaky love affair with three different women (not all at once). Actors scream at each other for more than an hour and a half in shoddy production for which the term "photographed stage play" must have been invented. [PG]▼❶

Last of the Secret Agents?, The (1966) **C-90m. ★½** D: Norman Abbott. Marty Allen, Steve Rossi, John Williams, Nancy Sinatra, Lou Jacobi. Tiring spoof on spy movies ends up unintentional self-mockery. Strictly for Allen and Rossi fans. Look for Harvey Korman as a German colonel.

Last Orders (2001-British) **C-109m. ★★½** D: Fred Schepisi. Michael Caine, Tom Courtenay, David Hemmings, Bob Hoskins, Helen Mirren, Ray Winstone, JJ Field, Cameron Fitch, Anatol Yusef, Kelly Reilly, Stephen McCole, George Innes, Laura Morelli, Sally Hurst, Denise Black, Sue James, Meg Wynn Owen. Four longtime friends agree to take a pal's remains to be scattered into the sea and recall their sometimes-rocky relationships. Inevitably entertaining, with such a strong cast, but not completely satisfying. Director Schepisi adapted prizewinning novel by Graham Swift. That's Hemmings' look-alike son Nolan playing him as a young man. Super 35. [R]▼❶

L.A. Story (1991) **C-95m. ★★½** D: Mick Jackson. Steve Martin, Victoria Tennant, Richard E. Grant, Marilu Henner, Sarah Jessica Parker, Kevin Pollak, Sam McMurray, Patrick Stewart, Iman. Martin wrote this amusing piece of fluff about a wacky TV weatherman trying to sort out his life. Slender story thread allows Martin to make comic observations about living in trend-conscious L.A., some of them mild, some of them worthy of laughing out loud. Several of Martin's comedy cronies make cameo appearances. A deleted scene with John Lithgow was added for the film's cable-TV debut. [PG-13]▼❶❶

[783]

Last Outpost, The (1951) **C-88m.** **½
D: Lewis R. Foster. Ronald Reagan, Rhonda
Fleming, Bruce Bennett, Bill Williams, Peter Hanson, Noah Beery, Jr. Burst of action
saves wornout yarn of two brothers on opposite sides of Civil War, teaming up to fight
off Indian attack. This was Reagan's first
starring Western. Video title: CAVALRY
CHARGE.▼⊃

Last Party, The (1993) **C-96m.** ★★★ D:
Mark Benjamin, Marc Levin. Robert
Downey, Jr., takes his video camera on an
odyssey of America, focusing on 1992 Democratic and Republican national conventions,
to get a sense of the country and its political attitudes. Along the way he interviews
such colleagues as Sean Penn and Mary
Stuart Masterson, and such varied notables
as Oliver Stone, Spike Lee, G. Gordon
Liddy, Jerry Falwell, and even his father,
filmmaker Robert Downey, Sr. Not quite a
documentary, but an entertaining journey
(in the ROGER & ME vein); ultimately, we
learn more about Downey, Jr., than we do
about the state of the union.▼⊃

Last Picture Show, The (1971) **118m.** ★★★★
D: Peter Bogdanovich. Timothy Bottoms,
Jeff Bridges, Ben Johnson, Cloris Leachman, Ellen Burstyn, Cybill Shepherd, Eileen
Brennan, Clu Gulager, Sam Bottoms, Randy
Quaid, John Hillerman, Noble Willingham.
Brilliant study of life in small Texas town
during 1950s, and how characters' lives intertwine, from Larry McMurtry's novel (he
and Bogdanovich wrote the script). Oscars
went to Johnson and Leachman for sensitive performances, but entire cast works at
same level. Beautifully photographed in
b&w by Robert Surtees. Shepherd's film
debut. Sequel: TEXASVILLE. "Special
Edition" reedited by Bogdanovich in 1990
includes 7m. of material originally cut from
the film. [R] ▼⊙)

La Strada (1954-Italian) **115m.** ★★★★ D:
Federico Fellini. Anthony Quinn, Giulietta Masina, Richard Basehart, Aldo
Silvani, Marcella Rovere, Livia Venturini.
Deceptively simple tale of brutish strongman Quinn taking simple-minded Masina
with him as he tours countryside, where he
encounters gentle acrobat Basehart. Best
Foreign Film Oscar winner; stunning performances, haunting Nino Rota score. Story
and screenplay by Fellini and Tullio Pinelli.
▼⊙)

Last Rebel, The (1971) **C-89m.** BOMB
D: Denys McCoy. Joe Namath, Jack Elam,
Woody Strode, Ty Hardin, Victoria George.
Namath plays Confederate soldier who raises
havoc in small Missouri town after the Civil
War. Film has obvious camp value, but it's
not enough; Joe makes Ty Hardin look like
John Gielgud. [PG]

Last Remake of Beau Geste, The (1977)
C-83m. ★★½ D: Marty Feldman. Marty
Feldman, Ann-Margret, Michael York, Peter

Ustinov, James Earl Jones, Trevor Howard,
Henry Gibson, Terry-Thomas, Spike Milligan, Roy Kinnear. After uproarious first
half, Feldman's Foreign Legion spoof falters and gropes its way to weak conclusion.
Enough belly-laughs to make it worthwhile,
and sidesplitting performance by butler
Milligan. Feldman also cowrote this, his
directorial debut. [PG]▼⊙)

Last Resort (1986) **C-80m.** ★★½ D: Zane
Buzby. Charles Grodin, Robin Pearson
Rose, John Ashton, Ellen Blake, Megan
Mullally, Christopher Ames, Jon Lovitz,
Gerrit Graham, Mario Van Peebles, Phil
Hartman. Newly unemployed Grodin de-
cides, on impulse, to take his family to a
Club Med–type vacation resort, with pre-
dictably comic results. Likable but iffy
comedy does have some genuine laughs.
First-time director Buzby also appears as
resort's baby sitter. [R] ▼⊙)

Last Resort (2000-British) **C-73m.** ★★★ D:
Pawel Pawlikowski. Dina Korzun, Artiom
Strelnikov, Paddy Considine, Lindsey Honey.
Abandoned by her British fiancé, a Russian
woman and her young son are detained in
England at a holding area for refugees and
befriended by an arcade manager. Spare, affecting story has few surprises, but is compellingly told in quasi-naturalistic style and
very well acted.

Last Rites (1988) **C-103m.** ★★ D: Donald P.
Bellisario. Tom Berenger, Daphne Zuniga,
Chick Vennera, Anne Twomey, Dane Clark,
Paul Dooley, Vassili Lambrinos. Routine
drama of a priest who uses the auspices of
the church to protect a girl on a Mafia hit
list. Of course, he falls in love with her. Of
course, he also happens to be the son of a
Mafia chieftain himself. And of course,
the studio sent this one straight to video.
[R]▼⊙)

Last Roman, The (1968-German-Ruma-
nian) **92m.** ★★ D: Robert Siodmak. Laurence Harvey, Orson Welles, Sylva Koscina,
Honor Blackman, Michael Dunn, Harriet
Andersson, Lang Jeffries, Robert Hoffman.
Big cast in spears and togas look baffled at
what has become of Felix Dann's German
bestseller *Kamf um Rom* about the decline
of the Roman Empire. Edited down from a
two-part spectacular. Techniscope.▼

Last Run, The (1971) **C-99m.** ★★½ D:
Richard Fleischer. George C. Scott, Tony
Musante, Trish Van Devere, Colleen Dew-
hurst. Mediocre tale of aging gangland
driver who has to make one more run for his
ego. Great photography by Sven Nykvist.
Started by John Huston, who left early on.
Panavision. [PG]

Last Safari, The (1967-British) **C-110m.**
★★ D: Henry Hathaway. Kaz Garas, Stew-
art Granger, Gabriella Licudi, Johnny
Sekka, Liam Redmond. Uninteresting ac-
tion tale with depressed professional hunter
(Granger) coming to terms with himself and

rich young couple who hire him. Good cast can't handle script.▼

Last Samurai, The (2003) **C-154m.** **★★★** D: Edward Zwick. Tom Cruise, Ken Watanabe, Tony Goldwyn, Timothy Spall, Billy Connolly, Hiroyuki Sanada, Masato Harada, Koyuki, Scott Wilson, William Atherton. Burnt-out U.S. cavalry officer is hired to go to Japan in 1876 and train the emperor's soldiers to fight the last samurai warriors, who oppose their emperor's decision to abandon their traditional way of life. When the American is taken prisoner, he and captor Watanabe develop a mutual respect as fellow warriors, and Cruise comes to appreciate traditional Japanese customs, especially their code of honor. Epic-scale film flirts with greatness but falls short because it succumbs to Hollywood clichés a few times too many. (There's even a scene uncomfortably reminiscent of a famous Cruise moment in RISKY BUSINESS!) Still, there is much to admire, including strong performances and a vivid sense of time and place. Zwick coscripted; Cruise coproduced. Panavision. [R]▼▶

Last Seduction, The (1994) **C-110m.** **★★★** D: John Dahl. Linda Fiorentino, Peter Berg, J. T. Walsh, Bill Nunn, Bill Pullman, Michael Raysses, Zach Phifer. Pathologically evil—and stunningly sexual—woman ditches her husband, grabs the cash he's made in a drug deal, and flees N.Y.C., encamping in a small upstate town where she attracts and mystifies a local man—her latest patsy. Fiorentino's fiery femme fatale makes Stanwyck in DOUBLE INDEMNITY look like Snow White! Sizzling, sexy thriller from modern film noir expert Dahl and writer Steve Barancik. Unrelenting meanness wears it down a bit toward the end. Made U.S. debut on cable. Followed by a direct-to-video sequel. [R]▼▶●

Last September, The (1999-British-Irish-French) **C-103m.** **★★** D: Deborah Warner. Maggie Smith, Michael Gambon, Jane Birkin, Fiona Shaw, Lambert Wilson, Keeley Hawes, David Tennant, Gary Lydon. A less-than-compelling look at the last days of the Anglo-Irish, the British ruling class who live in cloistered elegance in Ireland as a storm brews all around them. The year is 1920, and a wealthy couple's young ward (Hawes) enters into a forbidden relationship with a young Irishman who's wanted for murder. Based on Elizabeth Bowen's novel. [R]▼▶

Last Shot, The (2004) **C-93m.** **★★½** D: Jeff Nathanson. Matthew Broderick, Alec Baldwin, Toni Collette, Tony Shalhoub, Calista Flockhart, Tim Blake Nelson, Buck Henry, Ray Liotta, James Rebhorn, Jon Polito, Pat Morita. Entertaining farce, inspired by a true story, about an FBI agent (Baldwin) who pretends to produce a movie in order to snare a mobster with ties to the Teamsters

union. Baldwin begins to like his "role" as producer, as he brings hope into the life of sincere, would-be filmmaker Broderick. Uneven, but has some hilarious moments. Directing debut for screenwriter Nathanson. Joan Cusack appears unbilled; other actors turn up in gag cameos. [R]▶

Last Song, The (2010) **C-107m.** **★★½** D: Julie Anne Robinson. Miley Cyrus, Greg Kinnear, Bobby Coleman, Liam Hemsworth, Kelly Preston, Kate Vernon, Nick Searcy, Hallock Beals. Rebellious girl spends the summer in a small Southern beach town with her estranged father; there she finds first love, reignites her passion for music, and learns what's important in life. Cyrus vehicle cowritten for the young star by sapmeister Nicholas Sparks is surprisingly devoid of the usual clichés for this sort of sudsy drama. Cyrus acquits herself nicely in her first "grown-up" role, and Kinnear is touching as a dad reconnecting with his kids just in the nick of time. Super 35. [PG]

Last Starfighter, The (1984) **C-100m.** **★★½** D: Nick Castle. Lance Guest, Robert Preston, Dan O'Herlihy, Catherine Mary Stewart, Barbara Bosson, Norman Snow, Cameron Dye, Wil Wheaton. Sci-fi for kids, about a youngster whose video-game prowess makes him a prime recruit to help save real-life planet under attack. Likable but toothless adventure (with an arch-villain who simply disappears from the proceedings) benefits greatly from performances of old pros Preston and O'Herlihy, who's unrecognizable in lizardlike makeup. Preston's last film. Panavision. [PG]▼▶●

Last Station, The (2009-German-Russian-British) **C-113m.** **★★½** D: Michael Hoffman. James McAvoy, Christopher Plummer, Helen Mirren, Paul Giamatti, Anne-Marie Duff, Kerry Condon, Patrick Kennedy, John Sessions. Near the end of Leo Tolstoy's life, his loyal but mercurial wife tries to protect him from what she sees as exploitation by a sycophant (Giamatti) who believes that ownership of the great man's novels should be given to the Russian people. A soldier in the utopian Tolstoyan movement (McAvoy) is sent to monitor the situation. Hoffman adapted Jay Parini's intriguing historical novel, which is well served by two commanding performances (Plummer and Mirren), but the film loses its momentum and goes on far too long. McAvoy and Duff are real-life husband and wife. Super 35. [R]

Last Summer (1969) **C-97m.** **★★★½** D: Frank Perry. Richard Thomas, Barbara Hershey, Bruce Davison, Cathy Burns, Ralph Waite, Conrad Bain. Powerful story based on Evan Hunter novel of teenagers playing on the beach in a summer resort. Film follows their games, sexual awakenings, and how evil manifests itself with calculated determination. Cathy Burns a standout. [R—edited from original X rating]▼

Last Summer in the Hamptons (1995) **C-105m.** ✱✱ D: Henry Jaglom. Victoria Foyt, Viveca Lindfors, Jon Robin Baitz, Savannah Boucher, Roscoe Lee Browne, Andre Gregory, Nick Gregory, Melissa Leo, Roddy McDowall, Martha Plimpton, Holland Taylor, Ron Rifkin, Brooke Smith, Diane Salinger, Kristoffer Tabori. An insecure young movie star (Foyt) arrives in the summer community of East Hampton, Long Island, and becomes involved with the assorted theater folk who comprise a circle of friends-lovers-colleagues. Another of Jaglom's occasionally insightful talk-fest/confessionals in which the characters reveal their jealousies, neuroses, and feelings. For inveterate Jaglom fans only. Scripted by Jaglom and Foyt (who are husband and wife). [R]▼●)

Last Sunset, The (1961) **C-112m.** ✱✱✱ D: Robert Aldrich. Rock Hudson, Kirk Douglas, Dorothy Malone, Joseph Cotten, Carol Lynley, Neville Brand, Regis Toomey, Jack Elam. Strange on the Range, courtesy Aldrich and scripter Dalton Trumbo; philosophical outlaw Douglas and pursuing sheriff Hudson play cat-and-mouse with each other during lengthy cattle drive. Throws in everything from incest to Indians!●

Last Supper, The (1996) **C-94m.** ✱✱ D: Stacy Title. Cameron Diaz, Ron Eldard, Annabeth Gish, Jonathan Penner, Courtney B. Vance, Nora Dunn, Ron Perlman, Bill Paxton, Charles Durning, Mark Harmon, Jason Alexander, Bryn Erin, Elizabeth Moss. Five grad student friends decide to rid the world of antisocial extremists who don't happen to conform to their worldview. Intriguing premise plays itself out too soon and stretches credibility in the name of satire; ultimately unpleasant and unsatisfying, though the cast is excellent and some of the cameos (Paxton, Durning, Harmon, Perlman) are first-rate. Filmed in 1994. [R]▼●)

Last Tango in Paris (1972-French-Italian) **C-129m.** ✱✱✱½ D: Bernardo Bertolucci. Marlon Brando, Maria Schneider, Jean-Pierre Léaud, Darling Legitimus, Catherine Sola, Mauro Marchetti, Dan Diament. Expatriate American in Paris tries purging himself of bad memories after his wife's suicide, enters into a tragic "no questions asked" sexual liaison with a chance acquaintance. The most controversial film of its era is still explicit by today's standards, though it's mellowed somewhat with age. A sterling showcase for Bertolucci's camera mastery; Brando's performance is among the best of his career. [X—also shown in R-rated version]▼●)

Last Temptation of Christ, The (1988) **C-164m.** ✱✱✱ D: Martin Scorsese. Willem Dafoe, Harvey Keitel, Barbara Hershey, Harry Dean Stanton, David Bowie, Verna Bloom, Andre Gregory, Juliette Caton, Roberts Blossom, Irvin Kershner, Nehemiah Persoff, Barry Miller. Thought-provoking and deeply felt drama adapted from Nikos Kazantzakis' book which speculates about Jesus' self-doubts when he realizes he has been chosen by God to carry His message. Moments of great power and beauty are diminished somewhat by mundane dialogue and slow stretches; still worthwhile, with a genuine feeling for time and place that helps make the story vivid and real. Music by Peter Gabriel. [R]▼●)

Last Time, The (2007) **C-96m.** ✱✱ D: Michael Caleo. Michael Keaton, Brendan Fraser, Amber Valletta, Daniel Stern, Neal McDonough, Michael G. Hagerty, Michael Lerner, William Ragsdale. Country bumpkin Fraser is transferred to the N.Y. home office of a business where sales exec Keaton prides himself on his take-no-prisoners tactics. He mentors the naïve newcomer and winds up in bed with his beautiful wife. There's more going on than meets the eye . . . though the setup is awfully obvious. Minor-league stuff, but Keaton is good. Super 35. [R]●

Last Time I Committed Suicide, The (1997) **C-93m.** ✱½ D: Stephen Kay. Thomas Jane, Keanu Reeves, Adrien Brody, John Doe, Claire Forlani, Jim Haynie, Marg Helgenberger, Lucinda Jenney, Gretchen Mol. Mordantly stylized, cliché-laden story of beat icon Neal Cassady, ostensibly based on a letter he once wrote to Jack Kerouac. Totally unsympathetic, angst-filled characters are put to even greater disadvantage by a jittery camera and harsh lighting. [R]▼●)

Last Time I Saw Archie, The (1961) **98m.** ✱✱ D: Jack Webb. Robert Mitchum, Jack Webb, Martha Hyer, France Nuyen, Louis Nye, Richard Arlen, Don Knotts, Joe Flynn, Robert Strauss. Webb's sole attempt at comedy is less funny than some of his more serious films; a pity, because William Bowers' script—based on his own Army experiences—had real potential, and Mitchum nicely underplays as the titular con man. (By the way, the real Archie Hall sued for invasion of privacy!)

Last Time I Saw Paris, The (1954) **C-116m.** ✱✱✱ D: Richard Brooks. Elizabeth Taylor, Van Johnson, Donna Reed, Walter Pidgeon, Eva Gabor, George Dolenz, Roger Moore. Updated version of F. Scott Fitzgerald story, set in post-WW2 Paris, of ruined marriages and disillusioned people. MGM gloss helps. Moore's U.S. film debut. ▼●)

Last Train From Gun Hill (1959) **C-94m.** ✱✱✱ D: John Sturges. Kirk Douglas, Anthony Quinn, Carolyn Jones, Earl Holliman, Brad Dexter, Brian Hutton, Ziva Rodann. Superior Western of staunch sheriff determined to leave Gun Hill with murder suspect, despite necessity for shoot-out. VistaVision. ▼❚

Last Train Home (2010-Canadian-Chinese) **C-87m.** ***½ D: Lixin Fan. Once a year in China, 130 million people who have moved from farms to cities in order to earn money return home to be with their families for the New Year's holiday. With often startling intimacy, we witness the schism within one such family: the parents have sacrificed everything by leaving their children behind to become day laborers, but their older daughter is openly resentful and leaves school to earn her own living. Eye-opening and heart-rending; a thoroughly remarkable documentary, photographed and coedited by director Fan. ❚

Last Tycoon, The (1976) **C-125m.** ***½ D: Elia Kazan. Robert De Niro, Tony Curtis, Robert Mitchum, Jeanne Moreau, Jack Nicholson, Donald Pleasence, Peter Strauss, Ingrid Boulting, Ray Milland, Dana Andrews, Theresa Russell, John Carradine, Anjelica Huston. Low-keyed but effective Harold Pinter adaptation of F. Scott Fitzgerald's final novel benefits immeasurably from De Niro's great, uncharacteristic performance as 1930s movie producer (inspired by Irving Thalberg) who is slowly working himself to death. Along with Joan Micklin Silver's TV film BERNICE BOBS HER HAIR, the best Fitzgerald yet put on the screen. Lew Ayres appears unbilled; Kazan's final feature as director. [PG] ▼❍❚

Last Unicorn, The (1982-British) **C-92m.** **½ D: Arthur Rankin, Jr., Jules Bass. Voices of Alan Arkin, Jeff Bridges, Mia Farrow, Tammy Grimes, Robert Klein, Angela Lansbury, Christopher Lee, Keenan Wynn, Paul Frees, Rene Auberjonois. Set in the time of Robin Hood, this pleasing animated fable tells of the adventures of a beautiful white unicorn who enters a forest in search of others of its kind. The weakest element: those bland, forgettable Jimmy Webb songs. Scripted by Peter S. Beagle, and based on his novel. [G] ▼❚

Last Valley, The (1970-British) **C-128m.** ** D: James Clavell. Michael Caine, Omar Sharif, Florinda Bolkan, Nigel Davenport, Per Oscarsson, Arthur O'Connell. Thinking man's adventure epic is an unfortunate misfire; 17th-century story brings warrior Caine and his soldiers to peaceful valley which has remained untouched by the Thirty Years War. Todd-AO. [PG] ▼❚

Last Voyage, The (1960) **C-91m.** *** D: Andrew L. Stone. Robert Stack, Dorothy Malone, George Sanders, Edmond O'Brien, Woody Strode. Engrossing drama of luxury ship that goes down at sea, and the ways the crew and passengers are affected. (To heighten the realism of the film, they really sank a ship.) Sanders is ill-fated captain, Stack and Malone a married couple in jeopardy. ▼❍❚

Last Wagon, The (1956) **C-99m.** *** D: Delmer Daves. Richard Widmark, Felicia Farr, Susan Kohner, Tommy Rettig, Stephanie Griffin, Ray Stricklyn, Nick Adams, Timothy Carey. Widmark is condemned killer who saves remnants of wagon train after Indian attack, leading them to safety. Clichéd plot well handled. CinemaScope. ❚

Last Waltz, The (1978) **C-117m.** **** D: Martin Scorsese. The Band, Bob Dylan, Neil Young, Joni Mitchell, Van Morrison, Eric Clapton, Neil Diamond, The Staples, Muddy Waters, Emmylou Harris, Paul Butterfield, Dr. John, Ronnie Hawkins, Ringo Starr, Ron Wood. Truly wonderful documentary about The Band's Thanksgiving, 1976, farewell concert, filmed by state-of-the-art Hollywood talent. A pair of studio-shot numbers involving The Staples and Harris are as exciting to watch as listen to, but the whole film is beautifully done. [PG] ▼❍❚

Last Wave, The (1977-Australian) **C-106m.** *** D: Peter Weir. Richard Chamberlain, Olivia Hamnett, (David) Gulpilil, Frederick Parslow, Vivean Gray, Nanjiwarra Amagula. Fascinating chiller about Australian lawyer (Chamberlain) defending aborigine accused of murder. Modern symbolism and ancient tribal rituals make for unusual and absorbing film. [PG] ▼❚

Last Will of Dr. Mabuse, The SEE: Testament of Dr. Mabuse, The

Last Woman, The (1976-French) **C-112m.** ** D: Marco Ferreri. Gérard Depardieu, Ornella Muti, Michel Piccoli, Zouzou, Renato Salvatori, David Biffani, Nathalie Baye. Provocative subject matter is superficially handled in this pointlessly sensationalistic drama about macho, self-absorbed engineer Depardieu, insensitive to women and confused by a world of changing roles and relationships. His final act of self-mutilation is as ridiculous as it is shocking. [X]

Last Year at Marienbad (1961-French-Italian) **93m.** *** D: Alain Resnais. Delphine Seyrig, Giorgio Albertazzi, Sacha Pitoeff. Murky, difficult but oddly fascinating tale in which Albertazzi confronts bewildered Seyrig, claiming they'd had an affair "last year at Frederiksbad, or perhaps at Marienbad." An art-house hit in its day, beautifully photographed (by Sacha Vierny); scripted by Alain-Robbe Grillet. Dyaliscope. ▼❚

Las Vegas Hillbillys (1966) **C-90m.** *½ D: Arthur C. Pierce. Ferlin Husky, Jayne Mansfield, Mamie Van Doren, Richard Kiel, Sonny James, Del Reeves, Bill Anderson, Connie Smith. How does country hick Husky become a big-time Las Vegas entrepreneur? You don't want to know. A once-in-a-lifetime cast. Sequel: HILLBILLYS IN A HAUNTED HOUSE. ▼▶

Las Vegas Lady (1976) **C-87m.** BOMB D: Noel Nosseck. Stella Stevens, Stuart Whitman, George DiCenzo, Lynne Moody, Linda Scruggs, Joseph Della Sorte, Jesse White. Substandard heist pic about a security guard who flips for title femme. Even LAS VEGAS HILLBILLYS is better. [PG]▼▶

La Symphonie Pastorale (1946-French) **105m.** ***½ D: Jean Delannoy. Pierre Blanchar, Michele Morgan, Jean Desailly, Line Noro, Andree Clement. Quietly powerful classic about pastor Blanchar's all-consuming passion for blind girl Morgan, whom he takes under his wing and educates. This sensitive study of moral and spiritual corruption was coscripted by the director and based on an Andre Gide novel.▼

L'Atalante (1934-French) **89m.** **** D: Jean Vigo. Michel Simon, Dita Parlo, Jean Dasté, Gilles Margaritis, Louis Lefèvre, Diligent Raya. Naturalism and surrealist fantasy blend beautifully in all-time masterpiece about a young couple who begin their life together sailing down the Seine on a barge. Ultimate in romantic cinema also anticipated neorealist movement by more than a decade; Vigo died at 29, just as film premiered. Restored in 1990 to its full length; avoid 82m. version, which circulated for years.▼▶

Late August, Early September (1999-French) **C-112m.** *** D: Olivier Assayas. Mathieu Amalric, Virginie Ledoyen, François Cluzet, Jeanne Balibar, Arsinée Khanjian, Alex Descas, Nathalie Richard. Bittersweet, subtly rendered slice of life about various friends, lovers, and acquaintances who are unable to set down roots—professionally, personally, or romantically. The specter of mortality hangs over the proceedings as one of them, a novelist (Cluzet) who has just turned 40, suffers from an unnamed illness. A heartfelt and potent portrait of self-involvement and emotional stagnation.▼▶

Late Autumn (1960-Japanese) **C-127m.** *** D: Yasujiro Ozu. Setsuko Hara, Yoko Tsukasa, Mariko Okada, Keiji Sada, Shin Saburi. Widowed Hara seeks a husband for unmarried daughter Tsukasa. Solid Ozu drama reworking his LATE SPRING.▶

Late for Dinner (1991) **C-99m.** **½ D: W. D. Richter. Brian Wimmer, Peter Berg, Marcia Gay Harden, Peter Gallagher, Colleen Flynn, Kyle Secor, Michael Beach, Bo Brundin, Janeane Garofalo. Two friends, on the lam and in need of help, are frozen by a doctor who's experimenting with cryonics; when they're awakened 29 years later, physically unchanged, they stumble to put their lives back together. Offbeat, to say the least, and movingly acted, but the transition from loopy comedy to deeply felt sentiment

(in the film's denouement) doesn't quite come off. [PG]▼●▶

Late George Apley, The (1947) **98m.** *** D: Joseph L. Mankiewicz. Ronald Colman, Peggy Cummins, Vanessa Brown, Richard Haydn, Charles Russell, Richard Ney, Percy Waram, Mildred Natwick, Edna Best. John P. Marquand's gentle satire of Boston bluebloods is smoothly entertaining. Colman is perfectly cast as the stuffy patriarch who strives to uphold his family's social status.

Late Marriage (2001-Israeli-French) **C-102m.** **½ D: Dover Kosashvili. Lior Ashkenazi, Ronit Elkabetz, Moni Moshonov, Lili Kosashvili, Aya Steinovits Laor, Rozina Cambus. Handsome bachelor is caught in the cross fire of tradition and emotion. His Georgian Jewish heritage dictates that he must choose a young virgin to marry, but he is secretly in love with a divorcée who has a six-year-old daughter. Intriguing film contains graphic sexual scenes and nudity. ▼▶

La Terra Trema (1948-Italian) **154m.** **** D: Luchino Visconti. Narrated by Luchino Visconti, Antonio Pietrangeli. Powerful, lyrical neorealist classic about a poor family in a Sicilian fishing village, exploited by fish wholesalers and boat owners. Filmed on location, and in Sicilian dialect, with a nonprofessional cast. Francesco Rosi and Franco Zeffirelli were Visconti's assistant directors. Beware of severely edited versions.▼▶

Late Show, The (1977) **C-94m.** ***½ D: Robert Benton. Art Carney, Lily Tomlin, Bill Macy, Eugene Roche, Joanna Cassidy, John Considine, Howard Duff. Carney is an aging private eye who tries to solve murder of his ex-partner (Duff), "helped" by flaky, aimless young woman (Tomlin). Echoes of Chandler and Hammett resound in Benton's complex but likable script; chemistry between Carney and Tomlin is perfect. Later a short-lived TV series called *Eye to Eye*. [PG]▼●▶

Latin Lovers (1953) **C-104m.** **½ D: Mervyn LeRoy. Lana Turner, Ricardo Montalban, John Lund, Louis Calhern, Jean Hagen, Rita Moreno. Hokey romance yarn set in South America, with Turner seeking true love; pointless script.▼

Latino (1985) **C-105m.** *** D: Haskell Wexler. Robert Beltran, Annette Cardona, Tony Plana, Ricardo Lopez, Luis Torrentes, Juan Carlos Ortiz, Julio Medina, James Karen. Gut-wrenching drama of Vietnam replayed, with Chicano Green Beret Beltran "advising" the U.S.-backed Contras in their war against the Sandinistas in Nicaragua. Unabashedly left-wing; to some it will be propaganda, while to others it will be truth. Striking direction with a fine sense of irony; however, Beltran's relationship with Cardona just doesn't ring true. Filmed in Nicaragua; Wexler's first "fiction" film since MEDIUM COOL.▼●)

Latitude Zero (1969-Japanese) **C-99m.** ** D: Ishiro Honda. Joseph Cotten, Cesar Romero, Richard Jaeckel, Patricia Medina, Linda Haynes, Akira Takarada. Better than average imported cast helps usual wide-eyed sci-fi adventure of underwater civilization of benevolent geniuses fighting legions of Malic (Romero), out to control world. Some good sets, but action and suspense poorly handled. Based on the old (American) radio series. Tohoscope. [G]●

L'Atlantide SEE: **Journey Beneath the Desert**

La Traviata (1982-Italian) **C-112m.** **** D: Franco Zeffirelli. Teresa Stratas, Placido Domingo, Cornell MacNeil, Alan Monk, Axelle Gail. Verdi's opera, adapted from the Alexandre Dumas *Camille* saga, makes a magnificent film. If Domingo looks too old for Alfredo, he still sings beautifully, while Stratas' performance as the tragic Violetta matches her brilliant voice. The cinematography and production design are the equal of anything from the Golden Age of moviemaking in a film that even those who dislike opera will enjoy. [G]▼●)

La Truite SEE: **Trout, The**

Latter Days (2004) **C-97m.** **½ D: C. Jay Cox. Steve Sandvoss, Wes Ramsey, Joseph Gordon-Levitt, Rebekah Johnson (Jordan), Amber Benson, Khary Payton, Erik Palladino, Mary Kay Place, Dave Power, Jacqueline Bisset. A young Mormon missionary gets involved with a sexually aggressive gay party boy, causing lots of friction within his archconservative family. Very low budget independent effort doesn't score a dramatic bull's-eye, but interesting premise and solid acting from its attractive, mostly unknown cast make it worthwhile viewing for discerning adult audiences. [R]▼)

L'Auberge Espagnole (2002-French-Spanish) **C-116m.** ** D: Cédric Klapisch. Romain Duras, Judith Godrèche, Audrey Tautou, Cécile de France, Kelly Reilly, Cristina Brondo. A 25-year-old French grad student goes to Spain for his year abroad and winds up living in a cramped apartment with seven strangers of all different nationalities. Fictitious version of *The Real World* is bland and overlong despite an appealing cast. Disappointing follow-up from the writer-director of the infinitely more charming WHEN THE CAT'S AWAY. Title translates literally to SPANISH APARTMENT, or in French slang, EURO PUDDING. [R]▼)

Laughing Policeman, The (1973) **C-111m.** **½ D: Stuart Rosenberg. Walter Matthau, Bruce Dern, Lou Gossett, Albert Paulsen, Anthony Zerbe, Anthony Costello, Cathy Lee Crosby, Joanna Cassidy. Reasonably engrossing San Francisco cop drama about search for mass slayer of bus passengers. Matthau and Dern are good as cops with contrasting styles.

Based on the Martin Beck novel by Maj Sjowall and Per Wahloo. [R]▼)

Laughter in Paradise (1951-British) **95m.** **½ D: Mario Zampi. Alastair Sim, Joyce Grenfell, Hugh Griffith, Fay Compton, John Laurie. Notorious practical joker dies, and leaves hefty sum to four relatives if they will carry out his devilish instructions. Pleasant little comedy. Audrey Hepburn appears fleetingly as cigarette girl. Remade in 1969 as SOME WILL, SOME WON'T.

Laughter in the Dark (1969-British) **C-101m.** *½ D: Tony Richardson. Nicol Williamson, Anna Karina, Jean-Claude Drouot, Peter Bowles, Sian Phillips. Excruciating film from Nabokov novel about wealthy married man (Williamson) whose fascination with young girl (Karina) backfires at every turn, eventually ruining his life. Exceedingly unpleasant, and seemingly interminable. [X]

Laura (1944) **85m.** **** D: Otto Preminger. Gene Tierney, Dana Andrews, Clifton Webb, Vincent Price, Judith Anderson, Grant Mitchell, Lane Chandler, Dorothy Adams. Classic mystery with gorgeous Tierney subject of murder plot; detective Andrews trying to assemble crime puzzle. Fascinating, witty, classic, with Webb as standout as cynical columnist Waldo Lydecker and Price in his finest non-horror performance as suave Southern gigolo. Based on the Vera Caspary novel; also features David Raksin's theme. Rouben Mamoulian started directing film, Preminger took over. Screenplay by Jay Dratler, Samuel Hoffenstein, and Betty Reinhardt. Joseph LaShelle's cinematography earned an Oscar. ▼●

Laurel Canyon (2003) **C-101m.** **½ D: Lisa Cholodenko. Frances McDormand, Christian Bale, Kate Beckinsale, Natascha McElhone, Alessandro Nivola, Louis Knox Barlow, Russell Pollard. Med-school grad Bale and prim fiancée Beckinsale reluctantly move in with his flaky mother (McDormand), a rock-music producer. Soon the uptight young woman is seduced by the free-spirited lifestyle of her future mother-in-law . . . while the son is attracted to a beautiful doctor. Superficial but diverting hijinks with an attractive cast, and McDormand in a role unlike any she's done before. Follows the same pattern as Cholodenko's previous, more richly textured film, HIGH ART. [R]▼)

Lavender Hill Mob, The (1951-British) **82m.** ***½ D: Charles Crichton. Alec Guinness, Stanley Holloway, Sidney James, Alfie Bass, Marjorie Fielding, John Gregson, Edie Martin. Excellent comedy with droll Guinness a timid bank clerk who has perfect scheme for robbing a gold bullion truck, with a madcap chase climax. Won an Oscar for Best Story and Screenplay (T.E.B. Clarke); look for Audrey Hepburn in opening scene.▼●)

La Venexiana SEE: **Venetian Woman, The**
L'Aventure, C'est L'Aventure SEE:
Money Money Money
La Vie Continue (1981-French) **C-93m.**
*½ D: Moshe Mizrahi. Annie Girardot,
Jean-Pierre Cassel, Pierre Dux, Giulia Sal-
vatori, Emmanuel Gayet, Rivera Andres.
Dreary sudser wastes Girardot as middle-aged
woman whose husband suddenly drops dead
of a heart attack; she struggles with her new-
found widowhood. Loosely remade in U.S. as
MEN DON'T LEAVE. [PG]▼
La Vie de Bohème (1992-Finnish-French-
Swedish-German) **100m.** *** D: Aki Kaurismaki. Matti Pellonpaa, Andre Wilms, Kari
Vaananen, Christine Murillo, Evelyne Didi,
Samuel Fuller, Louis Malle, Jean-Pierre
Léaud. Pleasantly offbeat comic/absurdist
slice-of-life about three poor, struggling artists: a painter, composer and writer. While at
best mediocre talent-wise, each is dedicated to
the artistic life and values his books, piano, or
paint over all else. A loose updating of a novel
by Henri Murger, which was the inspiration
for Puccini's *La Bohème.* ▼
La Vie de Chateau SEE: **Matter of Resistance, A**
La Vie en Rose(2007-French-British-Czech)
C-140m. *** D: Olivier Dahan. Marion Cotillard, Clotilde Courau, Jean-Paul Rouve,
Sylvie Testud, Pascal Greggory, Jean-
Pierre Martins, Emmanuelle Seigner, Gérard Depardieu, Catherine Allégret. Not
a conventional biography, but a series of
snapshots (jumbled out of chronological
order) about the difficult life and transcen-
dent talent of French singer Edith Piaf.
Randomness of the narrative is a liability,
but a must-see for Cotillard's astonishing
Academy Award–winning performance.
She transforms herself into the Little Sparrow in her youth, at her peak, and during her
precipitous decline . . . and does a remarkable job lip-synching Piaf (and a sounda-
like who recorded songs from her early
years). Oscar winner for Best Makeup (Didier Lavergne, Jan Archibald). Piaf's relationship with boxer Marcel Cerdan, which
is detailed here, is also depicted in EDITH
AND MARCEL. Original French title: LA
MÔME. Super 35. [PG-13]❙
La Vie Privée SEE: **Very Private Affair, A**
La Vie Promise (2002-French) **C-93m.** **
D: Olivier Dahan. Isabelle Huppert, Pascal
Greggory, Maud Forget, André Marcon,
Fabienne Babe. A hooker must flee Nice
when her estranged daughter commits a violent crime. A new bond develops between
the two women as they travel the French
countryside, where the mother comes face-
to-face with gut-wrenching decisions she
made in the past as well as an uncertain
future. Exquisite cinematography, eclectic
music score, and a fine performance from
Huppert (as always) can't redeem this earnest but slow-moving and mostly uninvolv-

ing story of a woman at the crossroads of
a life that didn't go the way she planned.
Super 35.❙
L'Avventura (1960-French-Italian) **145m.**
***½ D: Michelangelo Antonioni. Monica
Vitti, Gabriele Ferzetti, Lea Massari, Dominique Blanchar, James Addams. Massari
mysteriously disappears on an uninhabited
island after arguing with boyfriend Ferzetti,
impelling him and her friend Vitti to look
for her. Subtle, incisive allegory of spiritual and moral decay makes for demanding
viewing. Antonioni's first international success was also the first of a trilogy (followed
by LA NOTTE and L'ECLISSE). ▼●❙
Law, The SEE: **Where the Hot Wind
Blows!**
Law Abiding Citizen (2009) **C-109m.** **
D: F. Gary Gray. Jamie Foxx, Gerard Butler, Bruce McGill, Colm Meaney, Leslie
Bibb, Regina Hall, Michael Irby, Gregory
Itzin, Christian Stolte, Annie Corley,
Richard Portnow, Viola Davis, Michael
Kelly. Loving husband and father (Butler)
sees his wife and daughter brutalized and
murdered in his own home; then an ambitious city prosecutor (Foxx) accepts a plea
bargain from one of the killers in order to
nail his partner. Ten years later, the crazed,
embittered man exacts his revenge, not
only on Foxx and the justice system but on
the entire city of Philadelphia! Outlandish
modern spin on DEATH WISH gets the
visceral response it seeks but makes less
and less sense as its story unfolds. Super
35. [R]❙
Law and Disorder (1974) **C-103m.** ***
D: Ivan Passer. Carroll O'Connor, Ernest
Borgnine, Ann Wedgeworth, Anita Dangler, Leslie Ackerman, Karen Black, Jack
Kehoe. Intelligent, original comedy-drama
of two middle-aged New Yorkers incensed
at rising crime who become auxiliary cops.
At first they treat it as a lark, but soon it be-
comes deadly serious. Full of fine percep-
tions, interesting vignettes. [R]▼❙
Law and Order (1953) **C-80m.** ** D:
Nathan Juran. Ronald Reagan, Dorothy
Malone, Alex Nicol, Preston Foster, Ruth
Hampton, Russell Johnson, Dennis Weaver,
Jack Kelly. Lawman Reagan wants to retire
to marry Malone, but first must tame bad
guy Foster. Standard Western was filmed far
more successfully in 1932. ▼❙
Lawless Breed, The (1952) **C-83m.** ***
D: Raoul Walsh. Rock Hudson, Julia (Julie)
Adams, John McIntire, Mary Castle, Hugh
O'Brian, Lee Van Cleef, Dennis Weaver,
Michael Ansara. Solid Western drama that
recounts the life and times of legendary
(and misunderstood) outlaw John Wesley
Hardin (well played by Hudson, in his star-
ring debut).▼❙
Lawless Heart (2001-British) **C-86m.** ***
D: Neil Hunter, Tom Hunsinger. Doug-
las Henshall, Tom Hollander, Bill Nighy,

Clémentine Célarié, Josephine Butler, Ellie Haddington, Stuart Laing, Sukie Smith. Clever three-part story about lives that intersect in a small seaside town when friends and family gather for a young man's funeral: first one person's story is told, then two others that overlap in interesting and unpredictable ways. Satisfying, well written, and original, with rich performances throughout. Written by the directors. [R] ▼▶

Lawless Street, A (1955) C-78m. **½ D: Joseph H. Lewis. Randolph Scott, Angela Lansbury, Warner Anderson, Jean Parker, Wallace Ford, Ruth Donnelly, Michael Pate. Hard-bitten marshal Scott tries to eliminate evil forces from western town, then confronts his bittersweet past when musical star Lansbury comes to town. Entertaining Western with disappointing resolution. ▼▶

Lawman (1971) C-98m. *** D: Michael Winner. Burt Lancaster, Robert Ryan, Lee J. Cobb, Robert Duvall, Sheree North, Albert Salmi, Joseph Wiseman, J.D. Cannon, Richard Jordan, John McGiver, Ralph Waite, John Beck, John Hillerman. Intriguing thought-Western about stoic marshal (Lancaster) who comes into unfamiliar town to bring back wanted men, refusing to sway from duty even though entire town turns against him. Unsatisfactory resolution mars otherwise compelling story; Ryan gives one of his finest performances as timid sheriff. [PG] ▼▶

Lawn Dogs (1998-U.S.-British) C-100m. **½ D: John Duigan. Kathleen Quinlan, Sam Rockwell, Christopher McDonald, Bruce McGill, Tom Aldredge, Mischa Barton. Odd but intriguing story of the unlikely relationship that develops between a misfit kid who lives in an antiseptic, gate-guarded community, and a drop-out gardener who grew up in the area but has long been an outcast in the community. Sometimes uneasy mix of black comedy and social satire, but marked by good performances and a piquant sense of humor. [R] ▼▶

Lawnmower Man, The (1992) C-105m. *½ D: Brett Leonard. Jeff Fahey, Pierce Brosnan, Jenny Wright, Mark Bringleson, Geoffrey Lewis, Jeremy Slate, Dean Norris, Austin O'Brien. Scientist Brosnan needs a guinea pig for hitherto failed experiments in drug therapy and computer instruction; who better than the grinning mental defective who mows his lawn? At least the pyrotechnics at the end (simulating "virtual reality") are full of visual buzz. Fahey in a blond wig is really tough to take. Has nothing to do with the Stephen King short story it's ostensibly based on. Alternate version runs 140m. Followed by a sequel. [R] ▼▶

Lawnmower Man 2: Beyond Cyberspace (1996-U.S.-British-Japanese) C-93m. ** D: Farhad Mann. Patrick Bergin, Matt Frewer, Austin O'Brien, Ely Pouget, Camille Cooper, Patrick La Brecque, Crystal Celeste Grant, Kevin Conway. Moron-turned-genius Jobe is back, still intent on ruling the world from cyberspace. This involves ruthless billionaire Conway, reclusive computer expert Bergin, doctor Pouget, and young O'Brien, returning from the original film. The plot is both complicated and simpleminded, and aimed primarily at teenage computer fans—but the standardized BLADE RUNNER future, routine action, and only intermittent computer graphics will likely leave them as disinterested as everyone else. Aka: LAWNMOWER MAN 2: JOBE'S WAR. Panavision. [PG-13] ▼▶

Law of Desire (1987-Spanish) C-100m. *** D: Pedro Almodóvar. Eusebio Poncela, Carmen Maura, Antonio Banderas, Miguel Molina, Bibi Andersson, Manuela Velasco, Nacho Martinez. Surreal, hedonistic, and hilarious comedy focusing on a gay love triangle, with equal doses of passion, sex, fantasy, and tragedy. Maura is a standout as a free-spirited transsexual; this film helped to cement Almodóvar's international reputation. ▼▶

Lawrence of Arabia (1962-British) C-216m. **** D: David Lean. Peter O'Toole, Alec Guinness, Anthony Quinn, Jack Hawkins, Claude Rains, Anthony Quayle, Arthur Kennedy, Omar Sharif, Jose Ferrer. Blockbuster biography of enigmatic adventurer T. E. Lawrence is that rarity, an epic film that is also literate. Loses some momentum in the second half, but still a knockout—especially in 1989 reissue version, which restored many cuts made over the years (and made a few judicious trims in the process). Still, the only way to really appreciate this film is on a big screen. Screenplay by Robert Bolt and Michael Wilson, based on Lawrence's book *The Seven Pillars of Wisdom.* Seven Oscars include Best Picture, Director, Cinematography (Freddie Young), Score (Maurice Jarre), Editing, and Art Direction. O'Toole's first leading role made him an instant star. Beware of shorter prints. Originally 222m. Super Panavision 70. ▼▶

Laws of Attraction (2004-British-Irish) C-90m. **½ D: Peter Howitt. Pierce Brosnan, Julianne Moore, Frances Fisher, Parker Posey, Michael Sheen, Nora Dunn, David Kelly. N.Y.C. divorce lawyer Moore has never lost a case but meets her match in wily opposing counsel Brosnan, who also manages to get her to let her guard down. Romantic comedy never nears the bull's-eye, but showcases Brosnan's easygoing charm and gives Moore a rare comedic opportunity. There are worse ways to spend some time than in their company. Panavision. [PG-13] ▼▶

Laws of Gravity (1991) C-100m. *** D: Nick Gomez. Peter Greene, Adam Trese, Edie Falco, Arabella Field, Paul Schulzie.

Intense, vivid chronicle of three momentous days in the lives of a pair of young blue-collar Brooklyn thieves and their girlfriends. Shot on a minuscule budget, and distinguished by gritty, Scorsese-like realism. The performances are collectively terrific, and Jean de Segonzac's hand-held camera is a major plus. [R]▼❶

Lawyer, The (1970) **C-117m.** **½ D: Sidney J. Furie. Barry Newman, Harold Gould, Diana Muldaur, Robert Colbert, Kathleen Crowley. Lively story loosely based on famous Dr. Sam Sheppard murder case; Newman is stubborn young lawyer defending doctor accused of murdering his wife, battling legal protocol and uncooperative client. Unexceptional but diverting; Newman later revived role in TV series *Petrocelli.* [R]

Layer Cake (2004-British) **C-105m.** **½ D: Matthew Vaughn. Daniel Craig, Colm Meaney, Kenneth Cranham, George Harris, Jamie Foreman, Sienna Miller, Michael Gambon, Marcel Iures, Tom Hardy, Jason Flemyng, Sally Hawkins. London drug dealer who tries to approach what he does on a strictly-business basis comes to learn that he has no control over his life or the actions of the people around him. Superficial crime yarn boasts a good cast but travels an all-too-familiar path. First-time director Vaughn (who produced LOCK, STOCK AND TWO SMOKING BARRELS and SNATCH) indulges in look-at-me camera shots that add nothing. Adapted by J. J. Connolly from his novel. J-D-C Scope. [R]▼❶

Leadbelly (1976) **C-126m.** ***½ D: Gordon Parks. Roger E. Mosley, Paul Benjamin, Madge Sinclair, Alan Manson, Albert P. Hall, Art Evans, Loretta Greene. Poignant biography of the legendary folksinger Huddie Ledbetter, master of the 12-string guitar and long-time convict on Texas and Louisiana chain gangs. Stunning musical performances (including "Rock Island Line," "Goodnight Irene" and many more classics), with Mosley effectively restrained in the title role. Superior entertainment. [PG]

Leading Man, The (1997-British) **C-100m.** *** D: John Duigan. Jon Bon Jovi, Anna Galiena, Lambert Wilson, Thandie Newton, Barry Humphries, David Warner. British backstage theater romance about an American movie star who seduces a playwright's lonely wife and his leading-lady mistress. While it can't quite make up its mind whether it's a comic drama or a light thriller, it's still very entertaining stuff. Bon Jovi is good as the brash, amoral Yankee, and Galiena and Newton are fetching as the women caught in his web. [R]▼❶

League of Extraordinary Gentlemen, The (2003) **C-110m.** ** D: Stephen Norrington. Sean Connery, Shane West, Stuart Townsend, Naseeruddin Shah, Richard Roxburgh, Peta Wilson, Tony Curran, Jason Flemyng, David Hemmings, Max Ryan. Intriguing premise—a gathering of notorious 19th-century fictional figures, from Dr. Jekyll and Dorian Gray to *Dracula*'s Mina Harker, whose various attributes combine to form a kind of Justice League—is undone by lumpy storytelling, poorly staged action, and outsized, cartoonish special effects sequences. Connery is charismatic as ever playing Allan Quatermain. Based on a graphic novel by Alan Moore and Kevin O'Neill. Panavision. [PG-13]▼❶

League of Gentlemen, The (1960-British) **114m.** ***½ D: Basil Dearden. Jack Hawkins, Nigel Patrick, Roger Livesey, Richard Attenborough, Bryan Forbes, Kieron Moore, Robert Coote, Nanette Newman. Ex-army colonel enlists the aid of former officers (through blackmail) to pull off big bank heist. High-class British humor makes this tale of crime a delight. Forbes also wrote the script. Look for Oliver Reed as a ballet dancer!▼❶

League of Their Own, A (1992) **C-128m.** *** D: Penny Marshall. Tom Hanks, Geena Davis, Madonna, Lori Petty, Jon Lovitz, David Strathairn, Garry Marshall, Megan Cavanagh, Rosie O'Donnell, Renee Coleman, Ann Cusack, Tracy Reiner, Janet Jones, Téa Leoni, Bill Pullman. Thoroughly entertaining comedy about the women's baseball league that sprang up when male ballplayers were off fighting in WW2. Davis and Madonna stand out in a first-rate cast, with Hanks giving a terrific comedy performance as the drunken ex-baseball star who manages their team. Good-natured fiction that sheds light on a neglected chapter of real-life sports history. Later, briefly a TV series. Panavision. [PG]▼❶❶

Lean on Me (1989) **C-109m.** **½ D: John G. Avildsen. Morgan Freeman, Beverly Todd, Robert Guillaume, Alan North, Lynne Thigpen, Robin Bartlett, Michael Beach, Ethan Phillips, Regina Taylor. The story of "Crazy Joe" Clark, the real-life baseball bat, bullhorn toting high school principal from New Jersey who whips his students into shape by alternately bolstering and bullying them. Freeman is riveting in the central role, making up for script's shortcomings and Avildsen's all-too-familiar approach. That's Michael Imperioli as one of the kids being kicked out of the school. [PG-13]▼❶❶

Leap Into the Void (1980-Italian) **C-120m.** *** D: Marco Bellocchio. Michel Piccoli, Anouk Aimée, Michele Placido, Gisella Burinato, Antonio Piovanelli. A compassionate comedy about a very unusual topic: suicide. Magistrate Piccoli uses Placido to try to induce his mentally ill sister (Aimée) to do herself in.

Leap of Faith (1992) **C-108m.** **½ D: Richard Pearce. Steve Martin, Debra

[792]

Winger, Lolita Davidovich, Liam Neeson, Lukas Haas, Meat Loaf, Philip Seymour Hoffman, M. C. Gainey, Delores Hall. Nicely textured look at an evangelist's traveling tent show—but Martin is never credible as a religious pitchman who connects with his gullible audiences. Director Pearce has a keen eye for detail and atmosphere, but the film's story flaws are hard to overlook. The real treat: watching Winger as Martin's savvy partner-in-crime. [PG-13]▼●)

Leap Year (2010-U.S.-Irish) **C-100m.** *½ D: Anand Tucker. Amy Adams, Matthew Goode, Adam Scott, John Lithgow, Noel O'Donovan, Tony Rohr, Pat Laffan. Charm-free romantic comedy brings out the worst in everyone involved. Even the usually appealing Adams is off-putting as a stressed-for-success Boston yuppie who, en route to a Dublin rendezvous with her longtime boyfriend, is repeatedly humiliated and unconvincingly "humanized" while forced to journey across most of Ireland with a hunky but cranky pub owner/cabdriver (Goode). Try to imagine what IT HAPPENED ONE NIGHT might have been like if Clark Gable and Claudette Colbert had little charisma and no chemistry. Panavision. [PG]❒

Learning Tree, The (1969) **C-107m.** **½ D: Gordon Parks. Kyle Johnson, Alex Clarke, Estelle Evans, Dana Elcar, Mita Waters. Parks called virtually every shot in brilliantly photographed but surprisingly mild film version of his autobiographical novel about young black growing up in Kansas. Film's appeal lies more in its intentions than in what it actually accomplishes. Panavision. [M/PG]▼❒

Leather Boys, The (1963-British) **105m.** *** D: Sidney J. Furie. Rita Tushingham, Colin Campbell, Dudley Sutton, Gladys Henson. Uncompromising study of impulsive Tushingham's incompatible marriage to motorcycle-loving mechanic, focusing on their opposing viewpoints and sleazy environment. CinemaScope.▼❒

Leatherface: Texas Chainsaw Massacre III (1990) **C-81m.** *½ D: Jeff Burr. Kate Hodge, Ken Foree, R. A. Mihailoff, Viggo Mortensen, William Butler, Joe Unger. Mostly a remake of the first film: cannibal clan battles three would-be dinners. Severely damaged by prerelease cuts designed to reduce gore but which only make the film incoherent. Followed by TEXAS CHAINSAW MASSACRE: THE NEXT GENERATION. [R]▼●)

Leatherheads (2008) **C-113m.** **½ D: George Clooney. George Clooney, Renée Zellweger, John Krasinski, Jonathan Pryce, Peter Gerety, Jack Thompson, Stephen Root, Wayne Duvall, Marian Seldes, Max Casella, Blake Clark. Hotshot gridiron player Clooney, desperate to keep his team afloat in the early ragtag days of pro football in 1925, recruits a WW1 hero (Krasinski) who's become a star college player. Meanwhile, hotshot reporter Zellweger is assigned to attach herself to the hero and expose him as a fraud. Attempt to replicate a smart, sassy 1930s Hollywood movie succeeds only sporadically; likable enough but overlong and slow. Film's composer, Randy Newman, appears briefly as a pianist. [PG-13]❒

Leather Jackets (1991) **C-90m.** BOMB D: Lee Drysdale. D. B. Sweeney, Bridget Fonda, Cary Elwes, Craig Ng, Marshall Bell, Christopher Penn, Jon Polito, James LeGros, Neil Giuntoli. Leather-jacketed Elwes and friends rip off and murder a Vietnamese mob bagman, whose associates vow vengeance—and plenty of it. Newly engaged Sweeney and Fonda try to help, and get caught in the crossfire, which they deserve for being in such a turkey. What a bloody mess! [R]▼●

Leave All Fair (1985-New Zealand) **C-88m.** *** D: John Reid. John Gielgud, Jane Birkin, Feodor Atkine, Simon Ward. Intelligent, rewarding account of the elderly John Middleton Murry (Gielgud), husband and editor of Katherine Mansfield, and his manipulative relationship with her. She's portrayed in flashback by Birkin, who also appears as a young woman who reminds Murry of her. Stick with this one.

Leave Her to Heaven (1945) **C-110m.** *** D: John M. Stahl. Gene Tierney, Cornel Wilde, Jeanne Crain, Vincent Price, Mary Philips, Ray Collins, Darryl Hickman, Gene Lockhart. Tierney's mother says, "There's nothing wrong with Ellen. It's just that she loves too much." In fact, she loves some people to death! Slick trash, expertly handled all around with Tierney breathtakingly photographed in Technicolor by Oscar winner Leon Shamroy. And how about those incredible homes in New Mexico and Maine! Remade for TV as TOO GOOD TO BE TRUE in 1988.▼●❒

Leave It to Beaver (1997) **C-89m.** *** D: Andy Cadiff. Christopher McDonald, Janine Turner, Cameron Finley, Erik von Detten, Adam Zolotin, Barbara Billingsley, Ken Osmond, Frank Bank, Erika Christensen, Alan Rachins. Cute family comedy based on the vintage TV series, with Finley an appealing Theodore Cleaver, for whom things never seem to go quite right . . . especially when he volunteers to play football in order to please his dad. Brother Wally (who experiences his first taste of puppy love) and unctuous Eddie Haskell are here, too. Billingsley, Osmond, and Bank (June, Eddie, and Lumpy from the original show) make token appearances. [PG] ▼●)

Leaves of Grass (2010) **C-105m.** ** D:

Tim Blake Nelson. Edward Norton, Keri Russell, Tim Blake Nelson, Josh Pais, Pruitt Taylor Vince, Melanie Lynskey, Maggie Siff, Ty Burrell, Lee Wilkof, Richard Dreyfuss, Susan Sarandon. Annoyingly uneven Coen Brothers knockoff is a showcase for Norton as identical twin brothers, one a rising star in academia and the other a scuzzy drug dealer who lures his sibling back to his Oklahoma roots. Potentially intriguing story wallows in silliness, and much of the quirky humor falls flat. Still, Norton does make two entirely different characters wholly believable. Nelson also scripted. [R] ▶

Leaving (2009-French) **C-86m.** **½ D: Catherine Corsini. Kristin Scott Thomas, Sergi López, Yvan Attal, Bernard Blancan, Aladin Reibel. Thomas' fine performance isn't quite enough to help this somewhat familiar adultery saga. At least there's a halfway credible reason (beyond a chilly walking ego of a husband) that her character risks a secure upscale existence for an ex-con handyman who's building her an office. Except for Scott, nothing really stands out here, but the compact running time keeps the drama from wearing down, and picks up its share of "melo-" as tragic events unfold. ▶

Leaving Las Vegas (1995) **C-111m.** ***½ D: Mike Figgis. Nicolas Cage, Elisabeth Shue, Julian Sands, Richard Lewis, Steven Weber, Valeria Golino, Graham Beckel, Carey Lowell, R. Lee Ermey, Mariska Hargitay, Laurie Metcalf, Julian Lennon, Lou Rawls, Ed Lauter, Xander Berkeley, Susan Barnes. Cage is a hopeless alcoholic who moves to Las Vegas, determined to drink himself to death, while Shue is a prostitute who demeans herself on a nightly basis. Their attachment to one another (and their willingness to accept each other as they are) makes this an unusually powerful and moving love story, in spite of the seamy trappings. Cage and Shue give brave, honest performances (Cage won the Best Actor Oscar). Figgis scripted from John O'Brien's novel and also composed the score, with vocals by Sting. Ironically, O'Brien committed suicide after selling the movie rights to his book. [R] ▼●▶

Leaving Normal (1992) **C-110m.** **½ D: Edward Zwick. Christine Lahti, Meg Tilly, Lenny Von Dohlen, Maury Chaykin, James Gammon, Patrika Darbo, Eve Gordon, James Eckhouse, Brett Cullen, Rutanya Alda. An aggressively cynical cocktail waitress and her quieter, twice-wed friend take off for Alaska after failing to find fulfillment in Normal, Wyoming. Smug collection of on-the-road episodes fails to build a solid foundation, though the film does improve marginally once the characters settle down at their destination. Tilly is well cast, but Lahti is atypically insuffer-

able. Cinematographer Ralf Bode's color vistas help. [R] ▼●

Le Bal (1982-Italian-French) **C-112m.** *** D: Ettore Scola. Christophe Allwright, Marc Berman, Regis Bouquet, Chantal Capron, Nani Noel, Jean-François Perrier. Original, stylish panorama of life, love, loneliness, war and peace, from the mid-'30s to '80s. Set in a ballroom, with no major characters; the actors play different roles, in different time periods. No dialogue, just music and sound effects. Quite different, but most definitely worthwhile. ▼

Lebanon (2009-Israeli-German-French-Lebanese) **C-93m.** *** D: Samuel Maoz. Yoav Donat, Itay Tiran, Oshri Cohen, Michael Moshonov, Zohar Strauss, Dudu Tassa, Ashraf Barhom. A portrait of four Israeli soldiers in a tank, in the earliest moments of their country's incursion into Lebanon in 1982. Hard-edged look at the brutality of war and the psychological impact on its combatants features endless scenes of gruesome violence while effectively capturing the fears and claustrophobia of the men. Maoz also scripted, based on his experiences during the Lebanon War. [R] ▶

Le Beau Mariage (1982-French) **C-97m.** ***½ D: Eric Rohmer. Beatrice Romand, Andre Dussollier, Feodor Atkine, Hugette Faget, Arielle Dombasle. Headstrong young woman rather arbitrarily decides she will be married (to no one in particular), initiates an embarrassing pursuit of male with other ideas. If you can accept this hard-to-swallow premise, film is a beautifully acted comedy of humiliation. Romand, incidentally, is the now-grown-up adolescent from Rohmer's CLAIRE'S KNEE, made 11 years earlier. Aka THE GOOD MARRIAGE. [PG] ▼▶

Le Beau Serge (1958-French) **97m.** *** D: Claude Chabrol. Jean-Claude Brialy, Gérard Blain, Michele Meritz, Bernadette Lafont, Edmond Beauchamp. Considered to be the first New Wave film, this rural tale also marked the feature directing debut of *Cahiers du Cinéma* film critic Claude Chabrol. When Brialy returns to his tiny home town, he is stunned to find how drastically his old school chum (Blain) has changed. Perceptive examination of the trials of life in a poor farming community and the moral questions raised by how one treats a friend. Brialy, Blain, and young Lafont (a teenaged nymphet) continued to collaborate with Chabrol (who also wrote and produced) for three decades. ▼▶

Le Bonheur (1965-French) **C-87m.** **½ D: Agnès Varda. Jean-Claude Drouot, Claire Drouot, Sandrine Drouot, Oliver Drouot, Marie-France Boyer. Happily married carpenter Drouot falls for postal clerk Boyer, feels he can love both her and wife and they will share him. Intriguing, but emotionally uninvolving and unbelievable.

Drouot's real wife and children portray his cinematic spouse and offspring. Aka HAPPINESS.▼❶

Le Bossu SEE: **On Guard**

Le Boucher (1969-French-Italian) **C-93m.** *** D: Claude Chabrol. Stephane Audran, Jean Yanne, Antonio Passallia, Mario Beccaria, Pasquale Ferone. Another good psychological thriller from Chabrol, focusing on sympathetic murderer and his relationship with beautiful schoolteacher in small French village. Aka THE BUTCHER. [PG] ▼❶

Le Cercle Rouge (1970-French-Italian) **C-140m.** ***½ D: Jean-Pierre Melville. Alain Delon, Gian-Maria Volonté, André Bourvil, Yves Montand, François Périer, Rene Berthier. Super-cool gangster Delon is released from prison on the same day another hood (Volonté) makes a daring escape from custody. The two hook up, along with Montand, for an ambitious heist, all the while humiliating a patient police inspector (marvelously played by Bourvil). Another winner from the star and writer-director of LE SAMOURAI. Originally released in U.S. as THE RED CIRCLE, at 100m. ▼❶

L'Eclisse SEE: **Eclipse**

Le Combat Dans L'île (1962-French) **104m.** ** D: Alain Cavalier. Jean-Louis Trintignant, Romy Schneider, Henri Serre, Diana Lepvrier, Robert Bousquet, Jacques Berlioz. Somewhat cold, aloof drama about a troubled couple: she's given up her acting career onstage because she feels she isn't good enough, while he's secretly become part of an extremist group that's training its members to use weapons against the government. Political parable is an interesting period piece but not terribly entertaining on any level. First released in the U.S. in 2010, when it received many rave reviews. ❶

Le Confessionnal (1995-Canadian-British-French) **C-100m.** **½ D: Robert Lepage. Lothaire Bluteau, Patrick Goyette, Jean-Louis Millette, Kristin Scott Thomas, Richard Frechette, Marie Gignac. Elaborate, challenging, but only intermittently successful tale which intercuts two scenarios set years apart, involving a pregnant adolescent in 1952 Quebec (as Alfred Hitchcock is in town shooting I CONFESS) who is determined not to reveal her lover's identity, and the adopted brother (Bluteau) of her natural father. Fluidly directed, with clever visual references to Hitch, but the result somehow seems disconnected and unnecessarily complex. Worth a look, especially for Hitchcock aficionados. Stage director Lepage's debut feature; he also scripted.▼

Le Crabe Tambour (1977-French) **C-120m.** ***½ D: Pierre Schoendoerffer. Jean Rochefort, Claude Rich, Jacques Dufilho, Jacques Perrin, Odile Versois, Aurore Clement. Expertly directed, detailed chronicle,

mostly told in flashback, of the complex relationship between dying naval captain Rochefort and legendary officer Perrin, a character out of *Soldier of Fortune* magazine. Both, along with Rich as the doctor and Dufilho as the chief engineer, offer top-notch performances, and Raoul Coutard's cinematography is breathtaking.▼●

Leda SEE: **Web of Passion**

Le Dernier Combat (1983-French) **90m.** ** D: Luc Besson. Pierre Jolivet, Jean Bouise, Fritz Wepper, Christiane Kruger, Jean Reno. Wildly overpraised science-fiction film is basically another post-apocalypse epic. Jolivet is curious survivor wandering around a devastated landscape having odd, pointless encounters with strange people. Novelty item is without dialogue, in b&w, with stereo sound. Widescreen Cinema-Scope. [R]▼❶

Le Deuxième Souffle (1966-French) **150m.** ***½ D: Jean-Pierre Melville. Lino Ventura, Paul Meurisse, Raymond Pellegrin, Christine Fabréga, Marcel Bozzufi, Paul Frankeur, Michel Constantin. Ventura means business as Gu, a tough crook who escapes from jail and becomes involved in a big heist, but is duped into helping the cops. Melville pulls out all the cinematic stops in his definitive caper film, a major reworking of his favorite themes of criminal loyalty, betrayal, and professionalism.❱

Le Divorce (2003-U.S.-French) **C-117m.** ** D: James Ivory. Kate Hudson, Naomi Watts, Leslie Caron, Stockard Channing, Glenn Close, Thierry Lhermitte, Sam Waterston, Melvil Poupaud, Stephen Fry, Matthew Modine, Bebe Neuwirth, Romain Duris, Jean-Marc Barr, Samuel Labarthe, Thomas Lennon, Nathalie Richard, Daniel Mesguich. Large, impressive cast flounders in this paper-thin comedy-of-manners about the sexual and romantic plight of an inexperienced American in Paris (Hudson) and her pregnant, abandoned sister (Watts). There are plenty of plot complications, but they don't add up to much; the potential for exploring the cultural differences between Americans and the French is wasted. Scripted by Ivory and Ruth Prawer Jhabvala, based on Diane Johnson's novel. Panavision. [PG-13]▼❶

Le Doulos (1962-French) **108m.** *** D: Jean-Pierre Melville. Jean-Paul Belmondo, Serge Reggiani, Jean Desailly, Fabienne Dali, Michel Piccoli, René Lefèvre, Monique Hennessy. Hard-boiled crime tale centering on the search for hidden loot stolen by Reggiani and whether or not fellow crook Belmondo ratted him out to the cops. Slick Melville imitation of an American film noir is a notch below his best, but still an entertaining study of duplicity and honor among thieves. Aka DOULOS—THE FINGER MAN.▼❶

Left Behind (2000) **C-100m.** *½ D: Vic

Sarin. Kirk Cameron, Brad Johnson, Janaya Stephens, Chelsea Noble, Clarence Gilyard. What do religion, international bankers, control of the world's food supply, and the sudden disappearance of millions of people have in common? They're all pieces of a puzzle intrepid reporter Cameron is trying to put together. Intriguing story (based on a best-selling book inspired by biblical prophecies) is defeated by one-dimensional treatment. Debuted on home video before theatrical release. Followed by two sequels. [PG-13] ▼▶

Left Handed Gun, The (1958) 102m. **½ D: Arthur Penn. Paul Newman, Lita Milan, John Dehner, Hurd Hatfield. Faltering psychological Western dealing with Billy the Kid's career, method-acted by Newman. Penn's first feature, based on a 1955 *Philco Playhouse* TV play by Gore Vidal in which Newman starred. See also GORE VIDAL'S BILLY THE KID. ▼▶

Left-Handed Woman, The (1978-German) C-119m. ** D: Peter Handke. Edith Clever, Bruno Ganz, Michel Lonsdale, Markus Muhleisen, Angela Winkler, Ines de Longchamps, Bernhard Wicki, Gérard Depardieu. Clever, as The Woman, demands that husband Ganz leave her. He complies. Time passes . . . and the audience falls asleep.

Left Hand of God, The (1955) C-87m. *** D: Edward Dmytryk. Humphrey Bogart, Gene Tierney, Lee J. Cobb, Agnes Moorehead, E. G. Marshall, Benson Fong. Bogart manages to be convincing as American caught in post-WW2 China, posing as clergyman with diverting results. CinemaScope. ▼

Left Luggage (1998-Dutch-Belgian-U.S.) C-97m. **½ D: Jeroen Krabbé. Isabella Rossellini, Maximilian Schell, Laura Fraser, Jeroen Krabbé, Marianne Sägebrecht, David Bradley, Adam Monty, Chaim Topol, Miriam Margolyes. In 1972 Antwerp, a free-spirited Jewish woman (Fraser), the daughter of Holocaust survivors, hires on as nanny for a Hasidic family and immediately bonds with a mute, cherubic 5-year-old who is terrified of his rigid father. Emotionally charged drama explores a host of issues, but despite some powerful moments, is far too obvious and even schmaltzy at times. Opened in the U.S. in 2000. ▼▶

Legacy, The (1979) C-100m. **½ D: Richard Marquand. Katharine Ross, Sam Elliott, John Standing, Ian Hogg, Margaret Tyzack, Charles Gray, Lee Montague, Roger Daltrey. Two Americans find themselves among group of people shanghaied to British mansion where strange deaths and an occult ceremony await. Acceptable fare for fans of this genre. Filmed in England; aka THE LEGACY OF MAGGIE WALSH. [R] ▼▶

Legacy (2010-Nigerian-British) C-93m. *½ D: Thomas Ikimi. Idris Elba, Eamonn

Walker, Monique Gabriela Curnen, Clarke Peters, Richard Brake, Julian Wadham, Lara Pulver. Betrayal and collateral damage lie at the heart of this psychological thriller involving a former military man turned private contractor for hire (Elba) and his fast-tracking, politically savvy brother (Walker), who had Elba sent overseas on a covert assignment that went horribly wrong. Returning stateside, Elba appears intent on exposing his brother's corrupt government dealings, even though it may put his own life at risk. Promising opening sequence leads to a claustrophobic and one-note, overly psychotic film; too tiresome to be effective. [R] ▶

Legacy of Blood SEE: **Blood Legacy**
Legacy of Maggie Walsh, The SEE: **Legacy, The**

Legacy of Rage (1986-Hong Kong) C-87m. **½ D: Ronny Yu. Brandon Lee, Michael Wong, Regina Kent, Onno Boelee (Bolo Yeung), Tanya George, Wai-Man Chan, Randy Mang. Lee's debut film has him framed for the murder of a cop by a mobster "friend" who then tries to steal his fiancée; eight years later he's released from prison and is out for blood. Martial arts mayhem is surprisingly kept to a bare minimum in this imitation John Woo crime drama filled with gory shootouts, bone-crushing violence and hyperkinetic car chases and explosions. ▼▶

Legal Eagles (1986) C-114m. **½ D: Ivan Reitman. Robert Redford, Debra Winger, Daryl Hannah, Brian Dennehy, Terence Stamp, Steven Hill, David Clennon, John McMartin, Jennie Dundas, Roscoe Lee Browne, Christine Baranski, Christian Clemenson, Jay Thomas. Underwritten, overproduced romantic comedy about assistant D.A. who becomes involved with flaky lawyer (Winger) and her even flakier client (Hannah). Redford's charisma is at its brightest, which helps make up for lack of spark between him and Winger and film's other weaknesses. Panavision. [PG] ▼▶

Legally Blonde (2001) C-96m. **½ D: Robert Luketic. Reese Witherspoon, Luke Wilson, Selma Blair, Matthew Davis, Victor Garber, Jennifer Coolidge, Holland Taylor, Ali Larter, Jessica Cauffiel, Alanna Ubach, Oz Perkins, Raquel Welch. A way-perky sorority girl gets accepted at Harvard Law School in order to win her ex-boyfriend back, then discovers she has the right stuff to become a lawyer. Witherspoon is practically the whole show in this very predictable but engagingly silly comedy that, like its heroine, has more smarts than you'd expect. Later a Broadway musical. Followed by a sequel. Super 35. [PG-13] ▼▶

Legally Blonde 2: Red White & Blonde (2003) C-94m. *½ D: Charles Herman-Wurmfeld. Reese Witherspoon, Sally Field, Regina King, Jennifer Coolidge, Bruce Mc-

Gill, Dana Ivey, Mary Lynn Rajskub, Jessica Cauffiel, Alanna Ubach, Bob Newhart, Luke Wilson. Appallingly imbecilic sequel sends Witherspoon's effervescent Elle Woods to Washington (like Mr. Smith, who is briefly invoked) to push through a bill that will prevent chemical testing on animals. She gets some quick lessons on "playing the game," capitol-style. Any film that begins with its heroine hiring a detective to locate her dog's birth mother isn't going for credibility . . . but this one can't even give us an emotionally satisfying climax when Elle addresses Congress! Followed by a DVD sequel. [PG-13] ▼❚

Legend (1985-British) **C-89m.** ** D: Ridley Scott. Tom Cruise, Mia Sara, Tim Curry, David Bennent, Alice Playten, Billy Barty. Lavishly mounted fantasy, in the Grimm's Fairy Tale mold, about the demon Darkness trying to gain control over young girl who represents absolute innocence. Incredibly handsome but story lacks momentum and characters are not well defined. Kids might enjoy it. Released in U.S. in 1986 with Tangerine Dream score; European version had a Jerry Goldsmith score. Director's cut runs 113m. J-D-C Scope. [PG] ▼●❚

Legendary (2010) **C-107m.** ** D: Mel Damski. Patricia Clarkson, John Cena, Devon Graye, Madeleine Martin, Danny Glover, John Posey, Tyler Posey, Teo Olivares, Kareem Grimes. Nerdy teen, fatherless and harassed by a school bully, finds salvation in wrestling and establishes a connection with his older brother (World Wrestling Entertainment champion Cena), a once celebrated high school jock who's now on the skids. Innocuous "inspirational" tale is formulaic to an extreme; worth watching only for Clarkson, who is aces as the boys' mom. No surprise that this was produced by the WWE. [PG-13] ❚

Legendary Curse of Lemora SEE: **Lady Dracula**

Legend in Leotards SEE: **Return of Captain Invincible, The**

Legend of Bagger Vance, The (2000) **C-127m.** *** D: Robert Redford. Will Smith, Matt Damon, Charlize Theron, Bruce McGill, Joel Gretsch, Lane Smith, Harve Presnell, J. Michael Moncrief. A once-promising golfer from Savannah, Georgia, shattered by his experiences in WW1, is goaded into competing against champions Bobby Jones and Walter Hagen in an exhibition match . . . with the help of a mysterious caddy named Bagger Vance. Leisurely paced, beautifully rendered fable; fortunately, some undercooked mysticism doesn't get in the way. Jack Lemmon appears unbilled. [PG-13] ▼❚

Legend of Billie Jean, The (1985) **C-96m.** ** D: Matthew Robbins. Helen Slater, Keith Gordon, Christian Slater, Richard Brad-

ford, Peter Coyote, Martha Gehman, Dean Stockwell. Texas girl and her brother are implicated in a shooting; unjustly accused of other crimes, they run from police and soon become rebel heroes. Slater is very good, and film is watchable, but its adult characters come out as caricatures and the "message" gets muddy. Christian Slater's first feature film. [PG-13] ▼

Legend of Boggy Creek, The (1972) **C-90m.** ** D: Charles B. Pierce. Willie E. Smith, John P. Nixon, John W. Gates, Jeff Crabtree, Buddy Crabtree. Docudrama about sightings of a horrifying swamp monster in an Arkansas community. This modest but well-touted endeavor became a huge success, inspiring many similar films—including RETURN TO BOGGY CREEK and THE BARBARIC BEAST OF BOGGY CREEK PART II (which is actually the third in the series). Technicope. [G] ▼❚

Legend of Drunken Master, The SEE: **Drunken Master II**

Legend of Frenchie King, The (1971-French-Spanish-Italian-British) **C-97m.** *½ D: Christian-Jaque, Guy Casaril. Brigitte Bardot, Claudia Cardinale, Michael J. Pollard, Patty Shepard, Micheline Presle. Clumsy attempt at bawdy Western in the style of VIVA MARIA, with Bardot and her sisters as female outlaws at a French settlement in New Mexico, circa 1880. Badly dubbed. Aka PETROLEUM GIRLS. [R] ▼

Legend of Hell House, The (1973-British) **C-95m.** *** D: John Hough. Roddy McDowall, Pamela Franklin, Clive Revill, Gayle Hunnicutt, Roland Culver, Peter Bowles. Harrowing story of occult phenomena as four researchers agree to spend one week in house known to be inhabited by malignant spirits. Not the usual ghost story, and certain to curl a few hairs. Michael Gough turns up as a corpse at conclusion. Written by Richard Matheson from his novel *Hell House*. [PG] ▼●❚

Legend of Lylah Clare, The (1968) **C-130m.** ** D: Robert Aldrich. Kim Novak, Peter Finch, Ernest Borgnine, Milton Selzer, Valentina Cortese, Michael Murphy, Lee Meriwether, Coral Browne, Ellen Corby. Has-been Hollywood director fashions young woman into the image of his late wife for screen biography; flamboyantly awful, but some think it's so bad it's good. Judge for yourself. Based on a 1963 *Dupont Show of the Week* TV play by Robert Thom. [R]

Legend of Nigger Charley, The (1972) **C-98m.** **½ D: Martin Goldman. Fred Williamson, D'Urville Martin, Don Pedro Colley, Gertrude Jeanette, Marcia McBroom, Alan Gifford. Violent, routine black Western about Virginia slave who becomes a fugitive after killing treacherous overseer; Lloyd Price sings title tune. Sequel: THE SOUL OF NIGGER CHARLEY. [PG]

Legend of 1900, The (1998-Italian) C-116m. ** D: Giuseppe Tornatore. Tim Roth, Pruitt Taylor Vince, Bill Nunn, Clarence Williams III, Melanie Thierry, Harry Ditson. Expansive fable about an infant named 1900, born (and abandoned) on a huge ocean liner at the turn of the 20th century; he spends his entire life on that ship, and turns out to be a uniquely gifted pianist. Ambitious tale has some wonderful moments—including a piano duel with Jelly Roll Morton (Williams)—but rambles inconclusively. Italian title: THE LEGEND OF THE PIANIST ON THE OCEAN, which runs 170m. Technovision. [R]▼❚

Legend of Rita, The (2000-German) C-103m. *** D: Volker Schlöndorff. Bibiana Beglau, Martin Wuttke, Nadja Uhl, Harald Schrott, Alexander Beyer, Jenny Schilly, Mario Irrek. Trenchant look at the youthful idealism of headline-grabbing political firebrands who were active in West Germany during the 1970s. The fictional title character (Beglau) is a radical/zealot who finds herself in East Germany living under a false identity and toiling alongside drab, discontented fellow workers. With much irony, Schlöndorff examines the era's politics, passions, and harsh realities.▼❚

Legend of Sea Wolf SEE: **Wolf Larsen**

Legend of the Bayou SEE: **Eaten Alive**

Legend of the Guardians: The Owls of Ga'Hoole (2010-U.S.-Australian) C-97m. ** D: Zack Snyder. Voices of Helen Mirren, Geoffrey Rush, Jim Sturgess, Hugo Weaving, Emily Barclay, Abbie Cornish, Sam Neill, Ryan Kwanten, Anthony La Paglia, David Wenham, Richard Roxburgh, Miriam Margolyes, Joel Edgerton, Deborra-Lee Furness, Bill Hunter, Barry Otto. An owlet named Soren has always been inspired by his father's stories of their species' magnificent guardians. After he and his competitive brother are kidnapped by "the pure ones," who seek absolute power, Soren escapes and finds that the legend is true. Now he must find strength in himself to protect his family and fellow owls. Impressive-looking CGI animated feature stuffs a lot of story—and warfare—into its narrative, but everything feels secondhand and contrived, including the sparse comedy relief. It's also pretty bleak for a so-called family film. Based on Kathryn Lasky's series of novels for kids. 3-D Digital Widescreen. [PG]❚

Legend of the Holy Drinker, The (1988-Italian) C-125m. ***½ D: Ermanno Olmi. Rutger Hauer, Anthony Quayle, Sandrine Dumas, Dominique Pinon, Sophie Segalen. Subtle, poetic tale of a down-and-out man (Hauer, in a very uncharacteristic performance), who drinks too much, sleeps under a bridge, and is haunted by his past. The scenario chronicles what happens when he's presented 200 francs by a stranger. As in Olmi's best films, there are often long silences—but those silences are golden.

Legend of the Lone Ranger, The (1981) C-98m. ** D: William A. Fraker. Klinton Spilsbury, Michael Horse, Christopher Lloyd, Jason Robards, Matt Clark, Juanin Clay, Richard Farnsworth, John Bennett Perry, John Hart. A middling effort to tell the origin of the Masked Man, which wavers between seriousness and tongue-in-cheek. Some fine action, great scenery, and a promising storyline, but sabotaged by awkward handling, uncharismatic leads (Spilsbury was dubbed to no great effect), and an awful "ballad" narration by Merle Haggard. Bring back Clayton Moore and Jay Silverheels! Panavision. [PG]▼❚

Legend of the Lost (1957) C-109m. ** D: Henry Hathaway. John Wayne, Sophia Loren, Rossano Brazzi, Kurt Kasznar, Sonia Moser. Incredibly insipid hodgepodge interesting as curio: Wayne and Brazzi on treasure hunt in Sahara battle over rights to Loren. Technirama.▼❚

Legend of the 7 Golden Vampires, The SEE: **Seven Brothers Meet Dracula, The**

Legend of the Werewolf (1975-British) C-87m. ** D: Freddie Francis. Peter Cushing, Ron Moody, Hugh Griffith, Roy Castle, David Rintoul, Lynn Dalby. Trite version has handsome Rintoul as the hairy guy, working in French zoo, tracked down by coroner-investigator Cushing. Man-to-Wolf transformation scenes are subpar.▼

Legend of Wolf Lodge SEE: **Into the Fire**

Legend of Zorro, The (2005) C-129m. **½ D: Martin Campbell. Antonio Banderas, Catherine Zeta-Jones, Rufus Sewell, Nick Chinlund, Julio Oscar Mechoso, Shuler Hensley, Michael Emerson, Adrian Alonso, Mary Crosby. In this sequel to THE MASK OF ZORRO, our hero, now married and the father of a son, is persuaded to retire by his wife as Californians vote to become part of the U.S., but the arrival of a mysterious stranger from Europe signals a need for him to return to action. Escapism with a capital E, made with a family audience in mind, full to overflowing with grandiose action and stunts . . . but like the first film, there's too much of everything. The charismatic stars do their best to combat a plot-heavy script. Super 35. [PG]▼❚

Legend of Zu, The SEE: **Zu Warriors**

Legends of the Fall (1994) C-134m. ** D: Edward Zwick. Brad Pitt, Anthony Hopkins, Aidan Quinn, Julia Ormond, Henry Thomas, Karina Lombard, Gordon Tootosis, Tantoo Cardinal, Paul Desmond. Sprawling family saga about three brothers raised in Montana by their iconoclastic father—a former cavalry officer who turned his back on bloodshed and the exploitation of Indians. Lumbering, Edna Ferber-esque plot is rife with sibling rivalry, pregnant looks, and heated exchanges. Many moviegoers—especially fans of red-hot Pitt—embraced this film, but its earnest, straight-faced story gets sillier as it goes along. Performances are fairly one-note, as well, except for Thomas as the youngest brother. Based on a novella by Jim Harrison. Oscar winner for John Toll's cinematography. [R]▼●)

Legion (2010) **C-104m.** ** D: Scott Stewart. Paul Bettany, Dennis Quaid, Lucas Black, Tyrese Gibson, Adrianne Palicki, Charles S. Dutton, Jon Tenney, Kevin Durand, Willa Holland, Kate Walsh. When God decides—in an apparent fit of pique—to destroy humankind, rebellious archangel Michael (Bettany) descends to Earth, clips his own wings, and speeds to a remote desert café to protect a besieged cross-section of lost souls. (Think of it as THE PROPHECY meets THE PETRIFIED FOREST.) As Michael smites the wicked with automatic weaponry while rival angel Gabriel (Durand) launches attacks by zombiefied bit players, it's hard not to laugh out loud. Admirably straight-faced performances and first-rate action scenes laced with nifty special effects keep this biblical-themed fantasy-thriller from toppling irrevocably into absurdity. Super 35. [R]❙

Legionnaire (1998) **C-99m.** *½ D: Peter MacDonald. Jean-Claude Van Damme, Adewale Akinnuoye-Agbaje, Steven Berkoff, Nicholas Farrell, Jim Carter, Ana Sofrenovic. Boxer Van Damme joins the French Foreign Legion in 1925 and flees to Morocco after defying a mobster who orders him to take a dive. The script is so dated and unintentionally hilarious that you keep expecting to see Ramon Novarro show up in a turban, or at least Marty Feldman; but alas, it's all played with numbing seriousness and a lack of style and imagination. Released straight to video in the U.S. Super 35. [R]▼●)

Le Grand Chemin SEE: **Grand Highway, The**

Le Haine SEE: **Hate**

Le Jouet (1976-French) **C-92m.** **½ D: Francis Veber. Pierre Richard, Michel Bouquet, Fabrice Greco, Suzy Dyson, Jacques Francois. To show up his cutthroat father, a rich boy buys a human toy. Sometimes funny, sometimes not . . . but it's miles ahead of the American remake, THE TOY. Veber also scripted. [PG]

Le Jour Se Lève (1939-French) **93m.** ***½ D: Marcel Carné. Jean Gabin, Jacqueline Laurent, Jules Berry, Arletty, Mady Berry. A staple of French cinema, from the writer-director team that later created CHILDREN OF PARADISE; factory worker Gabin, trapped in a building, flashes back on events that drove him to murder. Generally holds up, while going a long way toward defining Gabin's screen persona. Written by Jacques Prévert, from Jacques Viot's story.

U.S. title: DAYBREAK. Later remade here as THE LONG NIGHT.▼❙

Le Mans (1971) **C-106m.** *** D: Lee H. Katzin. Steve McQueen, Siegfried Rauch, Elga Andersen, Ronald Leigh-Hunt. Exciting study of Grand Prix auto racing with exceptionally fine camera work on the track. Panavision. [G]▼)

Le Mentale SEE: **Code, The** (2002)

Le Million (1931-French) **85m.** ***½ D: René Clair. Annabella, René Lefevre, Vanda Greville, Paul Olivier, Louis Allibert. A chase after a lost lottery ticket propels this charming, whimsical, innovative gem from Clair. The actors sing some of their dialogue; as much fun today as when first released.▼●)

Lemonade Joe (1964-Czech) **C-84m.** *** D: Oldrich Lipsky. Carl Fiala, Olga Schoberova, Veta Fialova, Miles Kopeck, Rudy Dale, Joseph Nomaz. Sometimes repetitious but often quite funny spoof of the American Western; title refers to hero, who drinks Kola Loca lemonade instead of booze. Original running time is 99m. Filmed in b&w but makes use of color tinting. CinemaScope. ▼❙

Lemon Drop Kid, The (1951) **91m.** *** D: Sidney Lanfield. Bob Hope, Marilyn Maxwell, Lloyd Nolan, Jane Darwell, William Frawley. Hope is hilarious as racetrack tout who owes big money to gangster Nolan and must pay or else. Adapted from Damon Runyon story, filmed before in 1934. Film introduced Livingston-Evans Christmas hit "Silver Bells."▼●)

Lemon Sisters, The (1990) **C-93m.** *½ D: Joyce Chopra. Diane Keaton, Carol Kane, Kathryn Grody, Elliott Gould, Ruben Blades, Aidan Quinn, Estelle Parsons, Richard Libertini, Nathan Lane. Dopey female buddy comedy involving three women; doesn't take off despite an impressive cast. Although the laughs are few, the scene in which Kane sings "Rawhide" is almost worth a look. This film sat on the shelf awhile before its desultory release to theaters. [PG-13]▼●)

Lemony Snicket's A Series of Unfortunate Events (2004) **C-107m.** *** D: Brad Silberling. Jim Carrey, Liam Aiken, Emily Browning, Kara Hoffman, Shelby Hoffman, Meryl Streep, Jude Law, Timothy Spall, Catherine O'Hara, Billy Connolly, Luis Guzman, Jamie Harris, Craig Ferguson, Jennifer Coolidge, Jane Adams, Cedric the Entertainer, Jane Lynch. Three newly orphaned siblings are sent to live with their very strange uncle, would-be actor Count Olaf, who intends to do them in and steal their inheritance. When they manage to escape from his clutches, they are taken in by a series of odd and unusual guardians. Grand Guignol family fodder based on three Lemony Snicket novels (written by Daniel Handler), impeccably designed by longtime Tim Burton colleague

Rick Heinrichs. Unbeatable cast strikes just the right darkly comic tone, led by Carrey in one of his richest performances. Oscar winner for Valli O'Reilly and Bill Corso's makeup. Stick around for the ingenious, entertaining closing credits. Dustin Hoffman appears unbilled. [PG]▼▶

Lemora, The Lady Dracula SEE: **Lady Dracula**

L'Enfant (2005-Belgian-French) **C-95m.** ******* D: Jean-Pierre Dardenne, Luc Dardenne. Jérémie Renier, Déborah François, Jérémie Segard, Fabrizio Rongione, Olivier Gourmet. A young, amoral thief and his girlfriend have a baby, but responsibility is such a foreign concept to him that he sells the child to a black-market ring, with unexpected consequences. As forceful and naturalistic as the Dardennes' other films, but the story is uncharacteristically schematic, which dilutes its impact somewhat. Said to be inspired by *Crime and Punishment* and Robert Bresson's PICKPOCKET. The leading actor starred in the filmmakers' LA PROMESSE when he was a boy. [R]▶

L'Enfer (1994-French) **C-105m.** ** D: Claude Chabrol. Emmanuelle Béart, François Cluzet, Marc Lavoine, Nathalie Cardone, Andre Wilms, Christiane Minazzoli, Dora Doll, Jean-Pierre Cassel. Cluzet and sexy Béart marry, become settled in domesticity and seem very happy—until the husband becomes convinced that the wife is cheating on him. Chabrol ponders some interesting questions—how well can two people know each other? how far can they trust each other?—but result is one-note, with Cluzet becoming a laughable caricature of an insanely jealous man. Scripted by Chabrol, from original screenplay by Henri-Georges Clouzot (which the latter had started filming in 1964 but never completed). [R]▼▶

Leningrad Cowboys Go America (1989-Finnish) **C-80m.** *** D: Aki Kaurismaki. Matti Pellonpaa, Kari Vaananen, Jim Jarmusch, Nicky Tesco. Straight-faced comedy from Kaurismaki about a group of dreadful musicians from Finland; they're so bad that they decide to head for the U.S.—where people will listen to "anything"—and they set out on tour through the modern wasteland of small-town America. Shot in the U.S. and Finland, and scripted by the prolific Kaurismaki; while his films have become known and admired at festivals, this was the first to have a major theatrical release in the U.S. [PG-13]▼●

Lenny (1974) **112m.** **** D: Bob Fosse. Dustin Hoffman, Valerie Perrine, Jan Miner, Stanley Beck, Gary Morton. Powerful biography of troubled nightclub comic Lenny Bruce, whose hip humor and scatological dialogue made him a controversial figure in the 1950s. Fine direction, evocative b&w camerawork (by Bruce Surtees) showcase excellent performances by Hoffman and Perrine (as Lenny's wife, stripper Honey Harlowe). Script by Julian Barry, expanded from his Broadway play. [R]▼●▶

Le Notti Bianche SEE: **White Nights** (1957)

Lensman (1984-Japanese) **C-107m.** **½ D: Yoshiaki Kawajiri, Kazuyuki Hirokawa. Voices of Kerrigan Mahan, Tom Wyner, Greg Snegoff, Michael McConnohie. Animated feature loosely based on classic sci-fi novels of American E. E. "Doc" Smith, which also inspired STAR WARS. Unfortunately, this film plays like a mediocre rip-off of the George Lucas film; computer-generated animation sequences are interesting to watch but don't move the story along. For comic book buffs only.▼

Léolo (1992-Canadian-French) **C-107m.** *** D: Jean-Claude Lauzon. Maxime Collin, Ginette Reno, Roland Blouin, Julien Guiomar, Pierre Bourgault, Giuditta Del Vecchio, Denys Arcand; narrated by Gilbert Sicotte. Bizarrely funny black comedy about a boy, on the verge of adolescence, surviving in the slums of Montreal. He's stifled by a family he aptly describes as a "black hole," and is convinced he's the offspring of a contaminated, sperm-laden tomato! Lauzon penned the semiautobiographical script.▼●▶

Leonard Cohen: I'm Your Man (2005) **C/B&W-105m.** **½ D: Lian Lunson. Agreeable if unspectacular documentary-concert film that charts the life and times of the famed Canadian songwriter-novelist-poet. Most interesting are Cohen's recollections of his early success and his decision to interrupt his career to pass time in a Zen monastery. Cohen and others (including Nick Cave, Rufus Wainwright, Kate and Anna McGarrigle, Beth Orton, and Jarvis Cocker) perform in a tribute concert at the Sydney Opera House. [PG-13]▶

Leonard Part 6 (1987) **C-85m.** BOMB D: Paul Weiland. Bill Cosby, Tom Courtenay, Joe Don Baker, Moses Gunn, Pat Colbert, Gloria Foster, Victoria Rowell. With a band of mad animals knocking off the government's top-secret agents, restaurateur Cos comes out of retirement to avenge his onetime colleagues by foiling the villainess responsible. Even Cosby warned audiences to stay away from this megabomb (for which he receives story and producer credit). [PG]▼●▶

Leon Morin, Priest (1961-French) **116m.** **½ D: Jean-Pierre Melville. Jean-Paul Belmondo, Emmanuele Riva, Patricia Gozzi, Irene Tunc. Belmondo gives subdued, offbeat performance as clergyman trying to set shady woman onto the path of righteousness. ▼▶

Leonor (1975-French-Spanish-Italian) **C-90m.** BOMB D: Juan Buñuel. Michel Piccoli, Liv Ullmann, Ornella Muti, Antonio Ferrandis, Jorge Rigaud. Medieval mishmash with Lady Liv rising from the dead a decade after husband Piccoli seals her in a tomb. Deadening and idiotic. Directed by the son of Luis Buñuel. [PG]▼

Leopard, The (1963-French-Italian) **C-187m. ****** D: Luchino Visconti. Burt Lancaster, Alain Delon, Claudia Cardinale, Rina Morelli, Paolo Stoppa. Magnificent spectacle, set in 1860 Sicily, about an aristocrat who tries coming to terms with the unification of Italy. Originally screened at 195m., then released in the U.S. in a badly dubbed 165m. version. Visconti tinkered with the film repeatedly over the years, finally pronouncing the 187m. print "definitive" (although Lancaster's voice is still dubbed by another actor in the original *foreign* version). Delon and Cardinale are close to the final word in romantic pairings; concluding hour-long banquet scene is among the great set pieces in movie history. Technirama.▶

Leopard in the Snow (1978-Canadian-British) **C-90m. **½** D: Gerry O'Hara. Keir Dullea, Susan Penhaligon, Kenneth More, Billie Whitelaw, Jeremy Kemp, Yvonne Manners. First movie produced by publishers of Harlequin Romance paperbacks is predictably tearful love story about English girl who falls for a testy, reclusive American who's afraid to admit his feelings. [PG]▼▶

Leopard Man, The (1943) **66m. **½** D: Jacques Tourneur. Dennis O'Keefe, Margo, Jean Brooks, Isabel Jewell, James Bell, Margaret Landry, Abner Biberman. Intriguing but flawed Val Lewton thriller about series of murders in small New Mexico town blamed on escaped leopard. Based on novel *Black Alibi* by Cornell Woolrich. ▼▶●

Leopard Son, The (1996) **C-84m. ***½** D: Hugo Van Lawick. Narrated by John Gielgud. Sweeping, beautifully filmed documentary following the birth, growing pains, and coming-of-age of a leopard cub. Shot over a two-year period in Africa's Serengeti Plain, this eye-opening film shows just how much luck plays a part in any animal's survival. Parents should know that there are disturbing scenes of animal death, though handled with discretion. Music by Stewart Copeland. Discovery Channel's first theatrical release. [G]▼●

Leo the Last (1970-British) **C-103m. **** D: John Boorman. Marcello Mastroianni, Billie Whitelaw, Calvin Lockhart, Glenna Forster-Jones, Graham Crowden. Oddball film about reticent Mastroianni, last in a line of princes, who gradually emerges from decaying London mansion to become involved with people living on his black ghetto block. Enigmatic, unsatisfying film, with occasional bright touches. Boorman explored some of the same ideas 20 years later in WHERE THE HEART IS. [R]▶

Leo Tolstoy's Anna Karenina (1997) **C-108m. **** D: Bernard Rose. Sophie Marceau, Sean Bean, Alfred Molina, Mia Kirshner, James Fox, Fiona Shaw, Danny Huston, Phyllida Law, David Schofield, Saskia Wickham, Jennifer Hall. Practically passionless recounting of the oft-filmed tale of the title character (Marceau), a wife and mother who commences an illicit affair with dashing Count Vronsky (Bean) in 19th-century Russia. Handsomely mounted, but dramatically flat. Notable only as the first Western-produced ANNA to be filmed in Russia—in St. Petersburg, to be exact. Panavision. [R]▼●

Le Petit Lieutenant (2005-French) **C-111m. ***** D: Xavier Beauvois. Nathalie Baye, Jalil Lespert, Roschdy Zem, Antoine Chappey, Jacques Perrin, Patrick Chauvel, Xavier Beauvois. Engrossing, low-key account of life in a Parisian criminal investigation police unit. The main characters are the title one (Lespert), newly graduated from the police academy, who's been assigned to the unit, and his superior officer (Baye), a world-weary recovering alcoholic who's haunted by the death of her son. There's a plot, involving the tracking of a pair of Russian thugs, but the emphasis is on the drudgery—and heartbreak—of everyday police work. Beauvois, who coscripted, also plays one of the cops.▶

Le Petit Soldat (1960-French) **88m. ***** D: Jean-Luc Godard. Michel Subor, Anna Karina, Henri-Jacques Huet, Paul Beauvais, László Szabó, Georges de Beauregard. Godard's second feature concerns the terrorist activities of Algerian rebels who capture French army deserter Subor and blackmail him into committing an assassination. Godard's future wife Karina makes her feature debut as a leftist activist with whom Subor falls in love. Featuring an unforgettable torture scene, this powerful film was banned in France until 1963; less about politics than personal freedom and the banality of evil. ▼▶

Le Petit Théâtre de Jean Renoir SEE: **Little Theatre of Jean Renoir, The**

Lepke (1975) **C-110m. **½** D: Menahem Golan. Tony Curtis, Anjanette Comer, Michael Callan, Warren Berlinger, Milton Berle, Vic Tayback. Cut above usual gangster film, with Curtis surprisingly convincing as title character, head of '30s Murder, Inc. Berle has serious cameo as Comer's father. Recut to 98m. by Golan for cable TV release. Panavision. [R]▼▶

Le Plaisir (1951-French) **97m. ***½** D: Max Ophuls. Jean Gabin, Danielle Darrieux, Simone Simon, Claude Dauphin, Gaby Morlay, Pierre Brasseur, Pauline Dubost, Madeleine Renaud, Daniel Gelin. The joy and heartache of *l'amour* and the pursuit of pleasure is explored with subtlety and sophistication in a trilogy of stories by Guy de Maupassant: in "Le Masque," a vain old man tries to regain his youth by donning a mask to a ball; in "Le Maison Tellier," a group of prostitutes travels to the country to attend the first communion of the madam's niece; in "Le Modele," a free-living artist's affair with a model takes a tragic turn. Brilliantly acted by a superb cast and directed with customary virtuosity and a dazzlingly fluid style. Jean Marais narrates the French version of the film as de Maupassant (Peter Ustinov narrates the English version; Anton Walbrook narrates the German version). ▼◗

Leprechaun (1993) **C-92m.** BOMB D: Mark Jones. Warwick Davis, Jennifer Aniston, Ken Olandt, Mark Holton, Robert Gorman, John Sanderford, Shay Duffin. Inept horror drama in which a pint-sized Irish fairy (Davis) goes on a rampage after being ripped off of a hundred gold-pieces. Gratuitous gore and cheap shocks take the place of moviemaking skill. [R] ▼◗

Leprechaun 2 (1994) **C-85m.** *½ D: Rodman Flender. Warwick Davis, Charlie Heath, Shevonne Durkin, Sandy Baron, Adam Biesk, James Lancaster, Clint Howard, Kimmy Robertson. A spurned, vengeful leprechaun arrives in L.A. from ancient Ireland to claim his bride—the descendant of a lass he was tricked out of 1,000 years ago. Just another excuse for high-body-count gratuitous gore, begorrah! [R] ▼◗

Le Samourai (1967-French) **C-101m.** ***½ D: Jean-Pierre Melville. Alain Delon, Nathalie Delon, François Perier, Cathy Rosier, Jacques Leroy, Jean-Pierre Posier, Catherine Jourdan. Delon is the ultimate existential hit man in this tale of an assassin who's hired to kill a nightclub owner, but is double-crossed by his mysterious employers. Alain Delon was never better than in this quintessential Melville *policier,* a marvelously stylish meditation on crime and solitude that was a direct influence on John Woo's THE KILLER. First released in U.S. as THE GODSON. ▼◗

Le Sauvage SEE: **Lovers Like Us**

Les Biches (1968-French-Italian) **C-94m.** ***½ D: Claude Chabrol. Jean-Louis Trintignant, Jacqueline Sassard, Stephane Audran, Nane Germon. Excellent film of rich, aging lesbian who picks up unformed waif who earns her living drawing on the sidewalks of Paris. [R] ▼◗

Les Bonnes Femmes (1960-French) **93m.** *** D: Claude Chabrol. Bernadette Lafont, Clotilde Joano, Stephane Audran, Lucile Saint-Simon, Pierre Bertin, Jean-Louis Maury, Claude Berri, Mario David. Offbeat, intriguing Chabrol concoction, an important film of the early French New Wave, about a quartet of French shopgirls and their varied hopes and dreams. The most interesting storyline spotlights dreamy Joano and her fascination with a mysterious motorcyclist. The finale is a real knockout. ▼◗

Les Carabiniers (1963-French-Italian) **80m.** *** D: Jean-Luc Godard. Albert Juross, Marino Masé, Genevieve Galea, Catherine

Ribeiro, Gérard Poirot, Jean Brassat, Alvaro Gheri, Barbet Schroeder. In an unspecified time and place, two peasants are offered money and the promise of great adventures if they fight for the king; they accept, but are executed when a peace treaty is signed. Critically lambasted upon its release, this (intentionally) crudely made and anachronistic fable remains one of the few honest films about the insanity and immorality of war: it refuses to romanticize its subject. Written by Godard, Jean Gruault, and Roberto Rossellini. ▼◗

Les Choristes (2004-French-Swiss) **C-97m.** **½ D: Christophe Barratier. Gérard Jugnot, François Berléand, Kad Merad, Jacques Perrin, Jean-Baptiste Maunier, Marie Bunel, Jean-Paul Bonnaire, Maxence Perrin. New supervisor reports for work at a reform school for "difficult" boys run by a severe and unenlightened man. By starting a choir, the new man gives his young charges unity and hope. Well made, but obvious from the word go, which undercuts its emotional impact. Coproducer Jacques Perrin plays the conductor in the opening scene; that's his son Maxence as Pépinot. Remake of LA CAGE AUX ROSSIGNOLS (1947). Aka THE CHORUS. Super 35. [PG-13]◗

Les Compères (1984-French) **C-92m.** *** D: Francis Veber. Pierre Richard, Gérard Depardieu, Anny Duperey, Michel Aumont, Stephane Bierry. Endearing comedy in which beautiful, desperate Duperey manipulates former boyfriends Richard and Depardieu into searching for runaway son Bierry by making each think that the boy is his. This one works primarily because of the stars' knowing performances. Veber also scripted. Remade in the U.S. as FATHERS' DAY. [PG]▼◗

Les Destinées (2000-French-Swiss) **C-174m.** **½ D: Olivier Assayas. Emmanuelle Béart, Charles Berling, Isabelle Huppert, Olivier Perrier, Dominique Reymond, André Marcon, Alexandra London, Julie Depardieu, Catherine Mouchet. Heartfelt, sumptuously filmed but disappointing epic set during the first decades of the 20th century, centering on small-town minister Berling, who agrees to take over his family's porcelain-manufacturing business, and his evolving relationship with beautiful Béart. Sporadically on target when spotlighting the importance of love in a cold, fast-changing world, but never as involving as it should be . . . and terribly overlong. Originally titled LES DESTINÉES SENTIMENTALES. Widescreen. ▼◗

Les Diaboliques SEE: **Diabolique** (1955)

Le Sex Shop (1972-French) **C-92m.** *** D: Claude Berri. Claude Berri, Juliet Berto, Nathalie Delon, Jean-Pierre Marielle, Beatrice Romand, Catherine Allegret. Amiable spoof of our preoccupation with sex; failing bookstore owner starts selling porno material, becomes increasingly fascinated by it. Clever idea well done; originally rated X because of its candid (yet unsensational) scenes. [R—edited from original X rating]▼

Les Girls (1957) **C-114m.** ***½ D: George Cukor. Gene Kelly, Mitzi Gaynor, Kay Kendall, Taina Elg, Jacques Bergerac, Leslie Phillips, Henry Daniell, Patrick Macnee. Charming, sprightly musical involving three show girls who (via flashback) reveal their relationship to hoofer Kelly; chicly handled in all departments, with Cole Porter tunes and Oscar-winning Orry-Kelly costumes. John Patrick adapted Vera Caspary's novel. CinemaScope.▼●▶

Les Miserables (1935) **108m.** ***½ D: Richard Boleslawski. Fredric March, Charles Laughton, Cedric Hardwicke, Rochelle Hudson, Frances Drake, John Beal, Florence Eldridge, Jessie Ralph, Leonid Kinskey. Meticulous production of Victor Hugo's oft-filmed classic tale. Minor thief March tries to bury past and become respectable town mayor, but police inspector Javert (Laughton) won't let him. John Carradine has bit part as student radical. Screenplay by W. P. Lipscomb.▼●▶

Les Miserables (1947-Italian) **118m.** *** D: Riccardo Freda. Gino Cervi, Valentina Cortesa, John Hinrich, Aldo Nicodemi, Duccia Giraldi, Marcello Mastroianni. Intelligent, handsomely mounted version of the oft-filmed Victor Hugo story, with Cervi making a fine Jean Valjean. Mario Monicelli was one of the scripters. Originally 140m. ▼

Les Miserables (1952) **104m.** *** D: Lewis Milestone. Michael Rennie, Debra Paget, Robert Newton, Sylvia Sidney, Edmund Gwenn, Cameron Mitchell, Elsa Lanchester, Florence Bates. Glossy but thoughtful remake of the venerable Victor Hugo classic.▶

Les Misérables (1957-French-German) **C-210m.** **½ D: Jean-Paul Le Chanois. Jean Gabin, Daniele Delorme, Bernard Blier, Bourvil, Gianni Esposito, Serge Reggiani. Victor Hugo tale, with Gabin as Jean Valjean, Blier as Javert. Respectful but uninspiring. Often shown in two parts. Technirama.▼▶

Les Misérables (1995-French) **C-178m.** ***½ D: Claude Lelouch. Jean-Paul Belmondo, Michel Boujenah, Alessandra Martines, Annie Girardot, Clementine Celarie, Philippe Leotard, Rufus, Jean Marais, Micheline Presle, Darry Cowl, Salome, Ticky Holgado, Philippe Kohrsand, Nicole Croisille, Paul Belmondo. Extraordinary recycling of Victor Hugo's sprawling novel into a 20th-century landscape, culminating in a story of WW2 France. Belmondo plays a simple man who takes on the qualities of Jean Valjean as he helps a Jewish family fleeing from the Nazis. Lelouch's modern parable/adaptation emphasizes the impact that one good man can have on the lives of people around him; the result is absolutely riveting. Great, humanistic storytelling. Marais (from the Cocteau classics of the 1940s) plays the Monseigneur; Presle plays the Mère Supérieure. The ballerina and her daughter are played by Lelouch's real-life wife and daughter. Super 35. [R] ▼●

Les Misérables (1998) **C-131m.** **½ D: Bille August. Liam Neeson, Geoffrey Rush, Uma Thurman, Claire Danes, Hans Matheson, Reine Brynolfsson, Mimi Newman. Respectful, well-made adaptation of the Hugo classic, with strong performances from Neeson (as Jean Valjean), Thurman (as Fantine), Danes (as Cosette), and of course Rush (as the villainous Javert). Location filming in Paris (and Prague) is another asset. Yet there is a certain fire missing, especially at the finale, which keeps this from soaring. Panavision. [PG-13]▼●▶

Les Parents Terribles (1948-French) **98m.** *** D: Jean Cocteau. Jean Marais, Josette Day, Yvonne de Bray, Marcel Andre, Gabrielle Dorziat. Absorbing drama of a dysfunctional middle-class family, with in-experienced young Marais falling in love with Day, unaware that she's been his father's mistress. De Bray is outstanding as Marais's neurotic mother, who subtly expresses incestuous feelings toward her son. Cocteau scripted based on his play (which featured these same actors). Remade in England as INTIMATE RELATIONS.▼●

Lesson in Love, A (1954-Swedish) **95m.** *** D: Ingmar Bergman. Gunnar Bjornstrand, Eva Dahlbeck, Yvonne Lombard, Harriet Andersson, Ake Gronberg. Obstetrician Bjornstrand, happily married for 15 years to Dahlbeck, has an affair with a patient; Dahlbeck then returns to *her* former lover—the husband's best friend. Medium Bergman.▼

Less Than Zero (1987) **C-96m.** ** D: Marek Kanievska. Andrew McCarthy, Jami Gertz, Robert Downey, Jr., James Spader, Tony Bill, Nicholas Pryor, Brad Pitt. Bret Easton Ellis' nihilistic novel about young, disengaged L.A. have-it-alls is sanitized into pointlessness, though a faithful adaptation would have turned off everyone; try to imagine it with Eddie Bracken, Veronica Lake, and Sonny Tufts. The two leads are awful, but Spader is creepy as a drug-dealing slug, Downey exceptional as a wealthy addict. *Almost* good-bad. [R]▼●▶

Les Visiteurs SEE: **Visitors, The** (1993-French)

Les Voleurs (1996-French) **C-117m.** ** D: André Téchiné. Catherine Deneuve, Daniel Auteuil, Laurence Côte, Fabienne Babe, Julien Rivière, Benoît Magimel, Didier Bezace, Ivan Desny. Something different from Téchiné (who last teamed with these two stars on MA SAISON PRÉFÉRÉE): a crime picture, laced with his usual emotional/sexual twists. Here, as a boy pieces together his father's death, the viewer meets his outcast uncle, a cop (Auteuil), a cipher-like professor (Deneuve), and the young woman who comes between them (Côte). More an acting exercise than a cogent drama. Aka THIEVES.▼●]

Lethal Terminator SEE: **Glove, The**
Lethal Weapon (1987) **C-110m.** ******* D: Richard Donner. Mel Gibson, Danny Glover, Gary Busey, Mitchell Ryan, Tom Atkins, Darlene Love, Traci Wolfe. Under-cover cop Gibson, a borderline psychopath who's always on the edge, is partnered with stable family man Glover, and they prove a good team as they go after a particularly scummy drug ring. Loud, violent, trashy cop movie done to a turn; fast paced and enter-taining so long as you don't think about it too much. Director's cut runs 117m. Fol-lowed by three sequels. [R]▼●]
Lethal Weapon 2 (1989) **C-113m.** ******* D: Richard Donner. Mel Gibson, Danny Glover, Joe Pesci, Joss Ackland, Derrick O'Connor, Patsy Kensit, Darlene Love, Traci Wolfe, Steve Kahan. Ultraviolent, superslick sequel is just as cartoonish as the first—and possibly even more entertaining. This time around, our heroes tangle with a nefarious smuggling kingpin hiding behind diplomatic immunity, but doesn't reckon with Gibson's reckless ways. A must for action fans. Director's cut runs 118m. Panavision. [R]▼●]
Lethal Weapon 3 (1992) **C-115m.** ****½** D: Richard Donner. Mel Gibson, Danny Glover, Joe Pesci, Rene Russo, Stuart Wilson, Steve Kahan, Darlene Love, Traci Wolfe, Gregory Millar, Jason Meshover-Iorg, Delores Hall. Glover is about to retire when he and partner Gibson find themselves in the midst of an escalating war with a former cop turned criminal mastermind. Despite lazy writing and pointless plot turns, manages to crank out enough thrills, laughs, and vio-lent action to rate as acceptable escapism. Director's cut runs 117m. Panavision. [R]▼●]
Lethal Weapon 4 (1998) **C-127m.** ******* D: Richard Donner. Mel Gibson, Danny Glover, Joe Pesci, Rene Russo, Chris Rock, Jet Li, Steve Kahan, Kim Chan, Darlene Love, Traci Wolfe. Those wacky cops are at it again, this time battling a Chinese ganglord—and facing domestic crises in-volving pregnancy and marriage. Added this time: Rock, as an overzealous cop, and Li, as a formidable bad guy. The cast is so likable and their energy so infectious that the filmmakers get away with murder, presenting an overlong, incoherent story and peppering it with supercharged action sequences. Fans of the series won't be dis-appointed; others needn't bother. Richard Libertini appears unbilled. Panavision. [R]▼●]
Let Him Have It (1991-British) **C-115m.** ******* D: Peter Medak. Chris Eccleston, Paul Reynolds, Tom Courtenay, Tom Bell, Eileen Atkins, Clare Holman, Mark McGann, Mi-chael Gough, Ronald Fraser, James Villiers, Murray Melvin, Norman Rossington, Clive Revill. Absorbing drama based on the true story of Derek Bentley, a slow-witted youth who was pulled into a life of crime in postwar England and sentenced to death for a murder actually committed by his youthful cohort. Medak's sympathetic point of view is abetted by vivid performances, including Eccleston in the lead, and a gallery of top British actors in supporting roles. [R]▼●]
Let It Be (1970-British) **C-80m.** ******* D: Michael Lindsay-Hogg. John Lennon, Paul McCartney, Ringo Starr, George Harrison. Uneven, draggy documentary is rescued and abetted by brilliant, Oscar-winning score by The Beatles. When they perform it becomes magical; when others are thrown in it be-comes a bore. [G]▼●
Let It Ride (1989) **C-86m.** ****** D: Joe Pytka. Richard Dreyfuss, Teri Garr, Da-vid Johansen (Buster Poindexter), Jennifer Tilly, Allen Garfield, Ed Walsh, Michelle Phillips, Mary Woronov, Robbie Coltrane, Richard Edson, Cynthia Nixon. Disjointed, only sporadically funny tale of a compulsive gambler who finally hits a winning streak at a Florida racetrack. First-time director Pytka tries for a Damon Runyon flavor and a fast pace, but it doesn't come off; screenwriter Nancy Dowd had her name removed from credits. [PG-13]▼●]
Let Me In (2010-U.S.-Swedish-British) **C-116m.** ******* D: Matt Reeves. Kodi Smit-McPhee, Chloë Grace Moretz, Richard Jenkins, Elias Koteas, Cara Buono, Sasha Barrese, Ritchie Coster. Lonely, bullied boy finds an unusual friend in his new next-door neighbor, who turns out to be a vampire. Writer-director Reeves has crafted one of Hollywood's best adaptations of a foreign film, remaining faithful to the Swedish original but placing greater emphasis on the attraction between his two main characters. Still, if you've seen the 2008 original, LET THE RIGHT ONE IN, there aren't any real surprises. Terrifically effective score by Mi-chael Giacchino. Panavision. [R]❿
Let No Man Write My Epitaph (1960) **106m.** ******* D: Philip Leacock. Burl Ives, Shelley Winters, James Darren, Jean Seberg, Ricardo Montalban, Ella Fitzgerald. Bi-zarre account of slum life, focusing on Dar-ren and his dope-addicted mother involved with a variety of corrupt individuals. Sequel to KNOCK ON ANY DOOR.▼
L'Etoile du Nord (1982-French) **C-101m.** ***½** D: Pierre Granier-Deferre. Simone Si-gnoret, Philippe Noiret, Fanny Cottencon, Julie Jezequel, Gamil Ratib. Boring tale of down-and-out Noiret murdering wealthy businessman Ratib, and his relationships with gold digger Cottencon and her mother (Signoret). Just talk, flashbacks, and more

talk, with insufficient action or character development. Signoret can't save this one. Based on a Georges Simenon novel. [PG]▼

Let's Dance (1950) **C-112m.** **½ D: Norman Z. McLeod. Betty Hutton, Fred Astaire, Roland Young, Ruth Warrick, Shepperd Strudwick, Lucile Watson, Barton MacLane, Melville Cooper. Lesser-known Astaire vehicle is still fun, with war widow Hutton attempting to shield her young son from the clutches of his wealthy, stuffy great-grandmother. Astaire is the man who loves her, and his dancing (particularly in the "Piano Dance" number) is wonderful. Songs by Frank Loesser.▼●

Let's Do It Again (1975) **C-112m.** *** D: Sidney Poitier. Sidney Poitier, Bill Cosby, Jimmie Walker, Calvin Lockhart, John Amos, Denise Nicholas, Lee Chamberlain. Hilarious follow-up to UPTOWN SATURDAY NIGHT; lodge brothers Poitier and Cosby hypnotize Walker into becoming great boxer, figuring they can clean up on bets. Yes, it's an old *Bowery Boys* plot, but still well done. Followed by A PIECE OF THE ACTION. [PG]▼❙

Let's Get Harry (1986) **C-107m.** *½ D: Alan Smithee. Michael Schoeffling, Tom Wilson, Glen Frey, Gary Busey, Robert Duvall, Rick Rossovich, Ben Johnson, Mátt Clark, Gregory Sierra, Elpidia Carrillo, Mark Harmon, Jere Burns. Inherently stupid, unbelievable action yarn about a soldier of fortune's attempt to rescue pipeline worker Harmon, who's been kidnapped (along with an ambassador) by an underground group of drug dealers in South America. Busey and Duvall give lively performances, but that's all one can recommend about this turkey. Director Stuart Rosenberg had his name removed from the credits. Barely received theatrical release. Video title: THE RESCUE. [R]▼●

Let's Get Lost (1989) **119m.** *** D: Bruce Weber. Chet Baker, jazz trumpeter and singer from the "cool" school of the 1950s, is the subject of photographer Weber's high-style, b&w documentary. It's a fascinating (and sometimes disquietingly personal) look at the charismatic musician once referred to as the James Dean of jazz, whose long involvement with drugs never seemed to deter him from making beautiful music. Overlong, but worthwhile.▼

Let's Go to Prison (2006) **C-90m.** BOMB D: Bob Odenkirk. Dax Shepard, Will Arnett, Chi McBride, David Koechner, Dylan Baker, Michael Shannon. Prisoner vows to get revenge on the judge who put him behind bars by framing his wealthy, spoiled son and introducing him to the horrors of penitentiary life. Quirky, charismatic performers are trapped in a humorless, poorly directed, generally deadening film. Even people who find "don't drop the soap in the shower" jokes amusing will probably be bored. Very loosely based on Jim Hogshire's book *You Are Going to Prison*. Also available in unrated version. [R]❙

Let's Hope It's a Girl (1985-Italian) **C-114m.** *** D: Mario Monicelli. Liv Ullmann, Philippe Noiret, Catherine Deneuve, Bernard Blier, Giuliana De Sio, Athina Cenci, Stefania Sandrelli. Complex, funny, seriocomic account of what happens when Count Noiret returns to his former wife (Ullmann) and family and attempts to sell part of their estate. The men all have a variety of faults, and the women can very well live without them. Blier is great as the elderly, hilariously senile uncle.

Let's Kill Uncle (1966-British) **C-92m.** **½ D: William Castle. Nigel Green, Mary Badham, Pat Cardi, Robert Pickering, Linda Lawson, Reff Sanchez, Nestor Paiva. Green's ham is just right for this outrageous tale of 12-year-old who tries to kill his uncle because his uncle is trying to kill him over a $5 million inheritance. Lots of hokey thrills involving sharks, tarantulas, and the like. Loosely based on Rohan O'Grady novel.

Let's Make It Legal (1951) **77m.** ** D: Richard Sale. Claudette Colbert, Macdonald Carey, Zachary Scott, Robert Wagner, Barbara Bates, Marilyn Monroe. Trifling comedy in which Colbert divorces Carey and is tempted to wed ex-beau Scott. Monroe is wasted as a bathing beauty.▼❙

Let's Make Love (1960) **C-118m.** *** D: George Cukor. Marilyn Monroe, Yves Montand, Tony Randall, Frankie Vaughan, Wilfrid Hyde-White, David Burns. Billionaire Montand hears of show spoofing him, wants to stop it, then meets the show's star, Monroe. To charm her, he hires Bing Crosby to teach him to sing, Milton Berle to coach on comedy, Gene Kelly to make him dance. Bubbly cast, snappy musical numbers. CinemaScope.▼●❙

Let's Scare Jessica to Death (1971) **C-89m.** **½ D: John Hancock. Zohra Lampert, Barton Heyman, Kevin O'Connor, Mari-Claire Costello, Gretchen Corbett. Creepy little tale of murder and deception as unstable girl gets full fright-treatment at country home. [PG]▼❙

Let's Spend the Night Together (1982) **C-94m.** ** D: Hal Ashby. Tired concert film, edited from three separate performances from the Rolling Stones' 1981 tour. Flirts with excitement only when lookers in appropriate garb help Mick Jagger perform "Honky Tonk Woman." This is at least the *third* Stones concert film, followed in 2008 by SHINE A LIGHT. [PG]▼●❙

Let's Talk About Men (1965-Italian) **93m.** *** D: Lina Wertmuller. Nino Manfredi, Luciana Paluzzi, Margaret Lee, Milena Vukotic, Patrizia DeClara, Alfredo Baranchini. Amusing episodic film (four stories tied to a fifth): Manfredi competently and comically plays five different men involved with different women and situations. Made right after Ettore Scola's LET'S TALK ABOUT

WOMEN, this took 11 years to cross the ocean but was worth the wait.

Let's Talk About Sex (1998) **C-82m.** *½ D: Troy Beyer. Troy Beyer, Paget Brewster, Randi Ingerman, Joseph C. Phillips, Michaline Babich, Tina Nguyen. Let's not and say we did. Miami advice columnist enlists her two roomies to help make a documentary about what women really think about men and sex. Intriguing concept is poorly handled with lame attempts at shock humor and mawkish dramatic material. This film would lead you to believe that the peak of sexual freedom derives from all-night, frozen-yogurt–bingeing, teary-eyed confessionals. Directorial debut for actress Beyer, who also wrote the infantile B*A*P*S. [R]▼●

Let's Talk About Women (1964-Italian-French) **108m.** **½ D: Ettore Scola. Vittorio Gassman, Maria Fiore, Donatella Mauro, Giovanna Ralli, Antonella Lualdi, Sylva Koscina, Heidi Stroh, Rosanna Ghevardi, Walter Chiari, Eleonora Rossi-Drago, Jean Valerie. Nine-episode comedy with Gassman starring in each, and encountering a variety of women. Some segments better than others; one of the best has Gassman discovering that the prostitute he's hired is married to an old friend of his! Lina Wertmuller's LET'S TALK ABOUT MEN came a year later.

Letter, The (1940) **95m.** ***½ D: William Wyler. Bette Davis, Herbert Marshall, James Stephenson, Frieda Inescort, Gale Sondergaard. Lushly photographed Somerset Maugham drama set in Malaya, tells of murderess (Davis) who tries to cover up her deed by pleading self-defense. Davis quite appealing in her unsympathetic role. DVD offers an alternate ending. Previously filmed in 1929 (with Herbert Marshall in cast); remade as THE UNFAITHFUL and for TV in 1982 with Lee Remick. ▼●

Letter From an Unknown Woman (1948) **90m.** *** D: Max Opuls (Ophuls). Joan Fontaine, Louis Jourdan, Mady Christians, Marcel Journet, Art Smith. Lush romantic flavor of direction and performances obscures clichés and improbabilities in story of Fontaine's lifelong infatuation with musician Jourdan. Based on a Stefan Zweig story filmed in Germany as NARKOSE (1929). ▼●

Letters From Iwo Jima (2006) **C-141m.** ***½ D: Clint Eastwood. Ken Watanabe, Kazunari Ninomiya, Tsuyoshi Ihara, Ryo Kase, Shido Nakamura, Hiroshi Watanabe, Takumi Bando, Nae (Yuuki), Mark Moses, Roxanne Hart, Ryan Carnes. Exceptional companion piece to FLAGS OF OUR FATHERS depicts the battle of Iwo Jima from the Japanese point of view: General Kuribayashi (Watanabe) is sent to the desolate island to shore up defenses against incoming American forces, knowing full well that few, if any, of his soldiers are expected to survive. Spare, almost pointilistic examination of human behavior in the shadows of war and death, with Watanabe a tower of quiet strength. Cinematographer Tom Stern's desaturated colors lend grave elegance to the historic events. Screenplay by Iris Yamashita; story by Yamashita and Paul Haggis, inspired by Kuribayashi's published letters. Eastwood's son Kyle cowrote the score. Coproduced by Eastwood and Steven Spielberg. Oscar winner for Sound Editing. Panavision. [R]●

Letters to Juliet (2010) **C-105m.** **½ D: Gary Winick. Amanda Seyfried, Vanessa Redgrave, Christopher Egan, Gael García Bernal, Franco Nero, Luisa Ranieri. Aspiring author (Seyfried) and her up-and-coming restaurateur fiancé (Bernal) decide to take a pre-honeymoon trip to Verona. She's hoping for romance but he'd rather meet with his food and wine vendors. While roaming the city alone she discovers a group of women who voluntarily answer all of the ladies who write to Shakespeare's Juliet seeking her advice on love. Little does she expect that her own response to one of the letters will be the catalyst for a life-changing adventure. Sappy and completely predictable, but it's pleasant enough and filmed on gorgeous locations. Redgrave and Nero are a longtime couple in real life. Oliver Platt appears unbilled. Super 35. [PG]●

Letter to Brezhnev (1985-British) **C-94m.** *** D: Chris Bernard. Peter Firth, Alfred Molina, Alexandra Pigg, Margi Clarke, Neil Cunningham, Ken Campbell, Angela Clarke, Tracy Lea. Bored, unemployed Pigg and zany girlfriend Margi Clarke meet Russian sailors Firth and Molina, who are on leave in dreary Liverpool. There's the potential for love, yet in a few hours they'll be far apart, perhaps forever. Charming, disarming fable about taking risks and dreaming dreams, whose many assets far outweigh its few defects. Very much a product of Liverpool. [R]▼●

Letter to Three Wives, A (1949) **103m.** **** D: Joseph L. Mankiewicz. Jeanne Crain, Linda Darnell, Ann Sothern, Kirk Douglas, Paul Douglas, Jeffrey Lynn, Barbara Lawrence, Connie Gilchrist, Florence Bates, Thelma Ritter. Delicious Americana showing reactions of three women who receive a letter from town flirt who has run off with one of their husbands. Celeste Holm provides the voice of the letter's authoress. Mankiewicz won Oscars for his terrific script and direction. Based on a novel by John Klempner, adapted by Vera Caspary. Remade as a TVM in 1985.▼●●

Let the Devil Wear Black (2000) **C-89m.** **½ D: Stacy Title. Jonathan Penner, Jacqueline Bisset, Mary-Louise Parker, Jamey Sheridan, Philip Baker Hall, Jonathan Banks, Maury Chaykin, Chris Sarandon. Son of a deceased millionaire returns to L.A. and comes to believe his shady uncle, now linked to his mother, murdered his father. Urban thriller based on *Hamlet* is alternately insightful and silly (the Hamlet character meets his father's ghost in a toilet). Penner coscripted with his wife, Title. Worth a look. **▼❿**

Let the Good Times Roll (1973) **C/B&W-98m.** *** D: Sid Levin, Bob Abel. Chuck Berry, Chubby Checker, Bo Diddley, Little Richard, Five Satins, Shirelles, Coasters, Bill Haley and The Comets. Rockumentary with flavor and wit. Study of 1950s told through incredible compilation of film footage, and some fine performances by leading rock 'n' rollers of the period in revival concerts, highlighted by terrific finale with Berry and Diddley dueting on "Johnny B. Goode." Imaginative multi-image widescreen effects are letterboxed on most TV prints. Multi-Screen. [PG]

Let the Right One In (2008-Swedish) **C-115m.** ***½ D: Tomas Alfredson. Kåre Hedebrant, Lina Leandersson, Per Ragnar, Henrik Dahl, Karin Bergquist, Peter Carlberg, Ika Nord, Mikael Rahm, Karl-Robert Lindgren, Patrik Rydmark. Unique gothic horror tale set against the snowy backdrop of a suburban town outside of Stockholm. There, a lonely 12-year-old boy who's bullied at school finds an unlikely soul mate in a strange girl who lives in the apartment next door—and turns out to be a vampire. Unusual melding of horror and adolescent angst in an utterly ordinary setting; adapted by John Ajvide Lindqvist from his novel. Artfully staged and photographed in widescreen, this doles out its moments of shock in leisurely fashion—which magnifies their impact when they occur. U.S. remake: LET ME IN. Super 35. [R]❿

Leviathan (1989) **C-98m.** *½ D: George Pan Cosmatos. Peter Weller, Richard Crenna, Amanda Pays, Daniel Stern, Ernie Hudson, Michael Carmine, Lisa Eilbacher, Hector Elizondo, Meg Foster. Yet one more dreadful ALIEN clone, this one set underwater (like several other 1989 releases), with a team of men and women imperiled as they toil in the depths of the Atlantic. Skip it. J-D-C Scope. [R]**▼❶**

Levity (2003) **C-100m.** *** D: Ed Solomon. Billy Bob Thornton, Morgan Freeman, Holly Hunter, Kirsten Dunst, Dorian Harewood, Geoffrey Wigdor, Luke Robertson. Released from prison after 23 years, a shell-shocked Thornton seeks out the sister of the young man he murdered and is taken in by a storefront preacher/neighborhood activist (Freeman). Thoughtful, slow-paced rumination on guilt, shame, responsibility, and redemption doesn't give its characters easy solutions to their dilemmas. Directing debut for screenwriter Solomon, better known for cowriting the BILL & TED movies and MEN IN BLACK. Freeman also executive-produced. [R]**▼❿**

Le Voyage en Douce (1980-French) **C-98m.** **½ D: Michel Deville. Dominique Sanda, Geraldine Chaplin. What do women talk about when men aren't around? Friends Sanda and Chaplin travel to the South of France; they gab, flirt, tell each other lies. Sometimes witty, but ultimately disappointing; director Deville asked 15 French writers of both sexes to provide him with sexual anecdotes, which he worked into screenplay. Aka VOYAGE EN DOUCE. **▼❿**

Liam (2001-British-German) **C-90m.** **½ D: Stephen Frears. Ian Hart, Claire Hackett, Anthony Borrows, Anne Reid, David Hart, Megan Burns, Russell Dixon, Julia Deakin, Bernadette Shortt. Vivid evocation of 1930s working-class England, seen through the eyes of a young boy (Borrows) who watches his father lose his job, his mother try to maintain her pride, his sister take a job, and his priest and schoolteacher warn him about the sins that will have him burning in hell forever. Well done in every respect, with a sharp-eyed script by Jimmy McGovern . . . but damaged by an unsatisfying conclusion. [R]**▼❿**

Lianna (1983) **C-110m.** *** D: John Sayles. Linda Griffiths, Jane Hallaren, Jon DeVries, Jo Henderson, Jessica Wight MacDonald, Jesse Solomon, Maggie Renzi. Young woman, trapped in an unhappy marriage, finds herself attracted to another woman, and tries to come to grips with being lesbian. Writer-director Sayles hasn't a false note or an unsure line of dialogue, though the film goes on a bit too long. As usual, he's written himself a good role, as a film professor; look for Chris Elliott as a lighting technician. [R]**▼❿**

Liar Liar (1997) **C-87m.** **½ D: Tom Shadyac. Jim Carrey, Maura Tierney, Jennifer Tilly, Swoosie Kurtz, Amanda Donohoe, Jason Bernard, Mitchell Ryan, Anne Haney, Justin Cooper, Cary Elwes, Randall "Tex" Cobb, Cheri Oteri. Unscrupulous lawyer with a penchant for lying gets his just deserts when his neglected son makes a birthday wish that his dad has to tell the truth for 24 hours—and it comes true. Carrey vehicle delivers the laughs for his fans, but once the premise unfolds it's pretty formulaic. Bob Hope lived through a similar 24 hours in NOTHING BUT THE TRUTH (1941). [PG-13]**▼❶**

Liar's Moon (1981) **C-105m.** **½ D: David Fisher. Matt Dillon, Cindy Fisher, Christopher Connelly, Hoyt Axton, Maggie Blye, Susan Tyrrell, Yvonne DeCarlo, Broderick Crawford, Mark Atkins, Molly McCarthy. Hokey and obvious but still engaging soaper of poor Dillon and wealthy Fisher falling in love, with a "terrible secret" between them. Director Fisher also wrote the screenplay. Filmed with two different endings; both were released. [PG]**▼**

Libel (1959-British) **100m.** **½ D: Anthony Asquith. Dirk Bogarde, Olivia de Havilland, Robert Morley, Paul Massie, Wilfrid Hyde-White, Anthony Dawson,

Richard Wattis, Millicent Martin. Engrossing if uninspired filming of Edward Wooll's vintage play about a baronet (and former prisoner of war) who is challenged in court to prove his identity—which turns out to be unusually difficult. Metroscope.◗

Libeled Lady (1936) 98m. **** D: Jack Conway. Jean Harlow, William Powell, Myrna Loy, Spencer Tracy, Walter Connolly, Charley Grapewin, Cora Witherspoon. Wonderful comedy with the four stars working at full steam: conniving newspaper editor Tracy uses his fiancee (Harlow) and ex-employee (Powell) to get the goods on hot-headed heiress Loy—but everything goes wrong. Sit back and enjoy. Screenplay by Maurine Watkins, Howard Emmett Rogers, and George Oppenheimer. Remade as EASY TO WED.▼◗●

Liberation of L. B. Jones, The (1970) C-102m. **½ D: William Wyler. Lee J. Cobb, Anthony Zerbe, Roscoe Lee Browne, Lola Falana, Lee Majors, Barbara Hershey, Yaphet Kotto, Chill Wills. Wyler's final film is militant tale of racism in the South. Some good performances, especially Falana's, but slow pace and many subplots hurt. [R]▼◗

Libertine, The (2005-U.S.-British) C-114m. **½ D: Laurence Dunmore. Johnny Depp, Samantha Morton, John Malkovich, Rosamund Pike, Tom Hollander, Johnny Vegas, Kelly Reilly, Jack Davenport, Richard Coyle, Francesca Annis, Rupert Friend, Claire Higgins. The Earl of Rochester (Depp) promises, "You will not like me." Moreover, this witty social gadfly doesn't like himself, as he proves through his creatively and sexually self-destructive behavior. He squanders the goodwill bestowed upon him by King Charles II (Malkovich) and tests our patience in this often leaden, drawn-out drama . . . but there's still something magnetic about the character as written by Stephen Jeffreys (from his play) and portrayed by Depp. Super 35. [R]◗

Liberty Heights (1999) C-127m. **½ D: Barry Levinson. Adrien Brody, Ben Foster, Orlando Jones, Bebe Neuwirth, Joe Mantegna, Rebekah Johnson, David Krumholtz, Richard Kline, Vincent Guastaferro, Justin Chambers, Carolyn Murphy, James Pickens, Jr., Shane West. A family living in a Jewish suburb in 1954 Baltimore must deal with changing times and values represented by "the other kind," i.e., gentiles and African Americans. Director-writer Levinson's fourth Baltimore tale (following DINER, TIN MEN and AVALON) is well mounted and has many insightful and humorous moments, but is also surprisingly bland, with rather pedestrian plot turns and revelations of character and theme. [R]▼◗●

Liberty Kid (2008) C-92m. *** D: Ilya Chaiken. Al Thompson, Kareem Saviñon, Johnny Rivera, Fly Williams, Rayniel Rufino, Anny Mariano, Raquel Jordan, Rosa Ramos. Frank, flavorful slice-of-life about two young New Yorkers, blue-collar workers on Liberty Island (home of the Statue of Liberty), and their plight upon losing their jobs after 9/11. Rambles a bit but offers a sobering look at the struggles of the N.Y.C. underclasses.◗

Licence to Kill (1989-British) C-133m. *** D: John Glen. Timothy Dalton, Carey Lowell, Robert Davi, Talisa Soto, Anthony Zerbe, Frank McRae, Everett McGill, Wayne Newton, Benicio Del Toro, Desmond Llewelyn, David Hedison, Priscilla Barnes. Tough, mean James Bond adventure, with Dalton pursuing a drug kingpin to avenge an attack on his best friend. Dazzling stunts, high adventure, and a sexy companion for Bond (Lowell) make this one of the best of the series since Sean Connery's departure (yet it still lacks that old-time panache). Panavision. [PG-13]▼◗

License to Drive (1988) C-88m. ** D: Greg Beeman. Corey Haim, Corey Feldman, Carol Kane, Richard Masur, Heather Graham, Michael Manasseri, Harvey Miller, Nina Siemaszko, Grant Goodeve, Parley Baer. Noisy teen comedy about a 16-year-old who's just flunked his driver's test, and sneaks his grandfather's prized car out for a "dream" date that turns into a nightmare. Appealing performance by Haim, and a terrific one by the underrated Masur. Uneven comedy; low point: a long, tasteless sequence involving a drunk driver. [PG-13]▼◗

License to Wed (2007) C-91m. BOMB D: Ken Kwapis. Robin Williams, John Krasinski, Mandy Moore, Christine Taylor, Eric Christian Olsen, Peter Strauss, Josh Flitter, DeRay Davis, Grace Zabriskie, Roxanne Hart, Rachael Harris. Embarrassing comedy wastes a talented cast in a laughless story about a reverend who puts an unsuspecting engaged couple through a series of "tests" to determine if they are ready to be married. Gag after gag falls hopelessly flat, with one involving mechanical babies hitting a new low, even for this kind of lame-brained affair. A comic misfire for Williams, who is basically straitjacketed here. Wanda Sykes appears unbilled. Panavision. [PG-13]◗

L.I.E. (2001) C-100m. ***½ D: Michael Cuesta. Brian Cox, Paul Franklin Dano, Billy Kay, Bruce Altman, James Costa, Tony Donnelly. Challenging, perceptive mood piece about an upper-middle-class 15-year-old boy who lives near the Long Island Expressway: his mother recently died, his sleazy father is mostly absent, and he has become a lost soul. This would seem to make him easy prey for a local Fagin-like pederast named Big John . . . but things aren't that simple. Intelligent, believable drama whose characters reveal themselves layer by layer. Great performances by Cox and young Dano. Written by the director, Gerald Cuesta, and Stephen M. Ryder. [NC-17] ▼▶

Liebestraum (1991) **C-109m.** **½ D: Mike Figgis. Kevin Anderson, Pamela Gidley, Bill Pullman, Kim Novak, Graham Beckel, Zach Grenier, Thomas Kopache, Max Perlich, Catherine Hicks, Taina Elg. An architectural writer visits his dying mother in a small town, only to get involved in a 40-year-old sex scandal, his own adultery, and the demolition of the town's most distinctive building by his lover's husband. So-so material with a truly insane title; directed (overdirected?) with some style by the maker of STORMY MONDAY. Novak, who's wasted, spends most of the film bedridden in a gloomy hospital. Also available in unrated version. [R] ▼▶●

Lies & Alibis (2006) **C-90m.** **½ D: Kurt Mattila, Matt Checkowski. Steve Coogan, Rebecca Romijn, Selma Blair, James Brolin, Sam Elliott, Jaime King, John Leguizamo, James Marsden, Debi Mazar, Henry Rollins, Deborah Kara Unger, Sharon Lawrence, Jerry O'Connell, Allan Rich, Jon Polito. Coogan plays an entrepreneur who runs a service that provides alibis for cheating spouses, but gets in over his head when a longtime client's randy son accidentally kills a woman. Not great by any means but very watchable, with a clever denouement in which all its story threads and characters intersect. It's also unusual to find a modest film in which virtually every part, no matter how small, is filled by a familiar actor! Completed in 2004. Super 35. [R] ▶

Lies My Father Told Me (1975-Canadian) **C-102m.** ***½ D: Jan Kadar. Yossi Yadin, Len Birman, Marilyn Lightstone, Jeffrey Lynas. Tender film about young boy in Canadian-Jewish ghetto of the 1920s who idolizes his grandfather, a simple, old-fashioned junk collector. Author Ted Allan plays Mr. Baumgarten. Simple and moving drama. [PG] ▼

Lieutenant Wore Skirts, The (1956) **C-99m.** **½ D: Frank Tashlin. Tom Ewell, Sheree North, Rita Moreno, Rick Jason, Les Tremayne, Jean Willes. Ewell makes nonsense acceptable as he chases after wife who reenlisted in service thinking he'd been drafted again. CinemaScope.

Life (1999) **C-108m.** **½ D: Ted Demme. Eddie Murphy, Martin Lawrence, Obba Babatundé, Ned Beatty, Bernie Mac, Miguel A. Nuñez, Jr., Clarence Williams III, Bokeem Woodbine, Nick Cassavetes, Anthony Anderson, Barry Shabaka Henley, Poppy Montgomery, Noah Emmerich, Rick James, R. Lee Ermey, Lisa Nicole Carson. A slick Harlem pickpocket and a none-too-bright patsy meet up in the early 1930s and are railroaded into a Mississippi prison, where they spend the next 55 years. Broad comedy is juxtaposed against unexpectedly poignant and serious moments in this episodic film; not always on target, but entertaining just the same. Murphy and Lawrence are very funny, and age believably in Rick Baker's makeup. [R] ▼▶●

Life and Adventures of Nicholas Nickleby, The SEE: **Nicholas Nickleby** (1947)

Life and Death of Colonel Blimp, The (1943-British) **C-163m.** **** D: Michael Powell, Emeric Pressburger. Roger Livesey, Deborah Kerr, Anton Walbrook, John Laurie, James McKechnie, Neville Mapp. Superb, sentimental story of a staunch British soldier, and incidents that dovetail in his long, eventful life. Opens in WW2 and flashes back as far as the Boer War. Kerr charming as three different women in the Colonel's life. (Title character bears no relation to famous David Low caricature buffoon on whom he's supposedly based.) Heavily cut for various reissues; often shown in b&w. ▼▶●

Life and Nothing But (1990-French) **C-135m.** *** D: Bertrand Tavernier. Philippe Noiret, Sabine Azema, Pascale Vignal, Maurice Barrier, François Perrot. Two years after the WW1 armistice, French Army officer Noiret is still tabulating French casualties and identifying bodies, a job which brings him into contact with a wealthy and repressed young woman who's been searching obsessively for her husband. Subject matter is more compelling than the script, which loses its edge; still worthwhile. Panavision. [PG] ▼▶●

Life and Times of Grizzly Adams, The (1976) **C-93m.** *½ D: Richard Friedenberg. Dan Haggerty, Don Shanks, Lisa Jones, Marjorie Harper, Bozo. Poorly made, clumsily scripted family/wilderness saga, about fur trapper innocently pursued for crime, who finds peace in the mountains where he befriends a massive bear. Followed by THE MARK OF THE BEAR in 1991, GRIZZLY MOUNTAIN in 1998, the 1982 made-for-TV movie THE CAPTURE OF GRIZZLY ADAMS and a TV series. [G] ▼

Life and Times of Hank Greenberg, The (2000) **C/B&W-95m.** **½ D: Aviva Kempner. Heartfelt but flawed documentary about Hall of Fame baseball player Greenberg. Spotlights his humanity and his travails as a Jew playing in the major leagues during the 1930s and '40s—but leaves the erroneous impression that he was the only Jewish ballplayer of this period. Among the interviewees: Alan Dershowitz, Walter Matthau, and several of Greenberg's ballplayer contemporaries. ▼▶

Life and Times of Judge Roy Bean, The (1972) **C-120m.** *** D: John Huston. Paul Newman, Ava Gardner, Victoria Principal, Jacqueline Bisset, Anthony Perkins, Tab Hunter, John Huston, Stacy Keach, Roddy McDowall, Ned Beatty, Dick (Richard) Farnsworth. Tongue-in-cheek Western saga with surrealistic touches. Newman plays self-appointed "Judge" who rules over barren territory, encountering various colorful characters as town grows and matures. Engaging cameos by Keach, Huston, McDowall, and Gardner as Lillie Langtry. Written by John Milius. [PG]▼●◑

Life Aquatic with Steve Zissou, The (2004) **C-118m.** **½ D: Wes Anderson. Bill Murray, Owen Wilson, Cate Blanchett, Anjelica Huston, Willem Dafoe, Jeff Goldblum, Michael Gambon, Bud Cort, Seu Jorge, Seymour Cassel. A Jacques Cousteau–like figure who's seen better days tries to regain his professional footing when into his life comes a young man who may or may not be his son from a 30-year-old relationship. Droll, quirky comedy expands on ideas and themes from Anderson's other films, but it's his oddest, most elusive, and self-indulgent work to date. Devotees will enjoy Murray's deadpan performance, the vocal-and-guitar renditions of David Bowie songs by Jorge (from CITY OF GOD), and Henry Selick's animated sea creatures; others may flounder. Panavision. [R]▼◑

Life as a House (2001) **C-124m.** **½ D: Irwin Winkler. Kevin Kline, Kristin Scott Thomas, Hayden Christensen, Jena Malone, Mary Steenburgen, Mike Weinberg, Jamey Sheridan, Scott Bakula, Sam Robards. Talk about a midlife crisis: Kline is divorced, his teenage son won't speak to him (or anyone else in the family), he's just been fired, and he learns he's dying of cancer. So he decides to build his dream house and enlist his son's help, in order to bond with the boy. Uneven film benefits from Kline's commanding performance; manages to push some emotional buttons, but goes for the obvious and wraps things up too neatly. Inspired by Akira Kurosawa's IKIRU. Panavision. [R] ▼◑

Life As We Know It (2010) **C-114m.** **½ D: Greg Berlanti. Katharine Heigl, Josh Duhamel, Christina Hendricks, Josh Lucas, Hayes MacArthur, Sarah Burns, Jessica St. Clair, Melissa McCarthy, Faizon Love. Two single adults with nothing in common but a one-time disastrous dating experience have their lives turned upside down when their married mutual best friends are tragically killed and leave the mismatched pair as guardians of their baby girl. Predictable storyline is usually the stuff of cable TV movies, but this warm comedy-drama works fairly well thanks to the chemistry of the two attractive stars. Jean Smart appears unbilled. Super 35. [PG-13]◑

Life at the Top (1965-British) **117m.** **½ D: Ted Kotcheff. Laurence Harvey, Jean Simmons, Honor Blackman, Michael Craig, Donald Wolfit, Robert Morley, Margaret Johnston, Nigel Davenport. Follow-up to ROOM AT THE TOP picks up the account a decade later; film lacks flavor or life—best moments are flashbacks to Signoret-Harvey romance.▼

Life Before Her Eyes, The (2008) **C-90m.** **½ D: Vadim Perelman. Uma Thurman, Evan Rachel Wood, Eva Amurri, Gabrielle Brennan, Brett Cullen, Oscar Isaac, Jack Gilpin, Maggie Lacey. Two girlfriends (Wood and Amurri) share their hopes and dreams—until an outbreak of violence at their high school changes the course of their lives in an instant. This is paralleled by scenes from Wood's later life as a wife and mother (Thurman) who is tormented by the upcoming anniversary of that school incident. Compelling but elliptical drama, based on Laura Kasischke's novel, leads to an unsatisfying conclusion that poses more questions than it answers . . . yet it can't completely negate the interesting drama that has unfolded. Panavision. [R]◑

Lifeboat (1944) **96m.** ***½ D: Alfred Hitchcock. Tallulah Bankhead, William Bendix, Walter Slezak, Mary Anderson, John Hodiak, Henry Hull, Heather Angel, Hume Cronyn, Canada Lee. Penetrating revelations about shipwreck survivors adrift in lonely lifeboat during WW2. Bankhead remarkable as spoiled journalist, Slezak fine as Nazi taken aboard. Only Hitchcock would take on the challenge of such a film—and succeed. Jo Swerling adapted John Steinbeck's original story. Remade as a 1993 TVM, LIFEPOD. ▼◑

Life During Wartime (2010) **C-98m.** ***½ D: Todd Solondz. Shirley Henderson, Ciarán Hinds, Allison Janney, Michael Lerner, Chris Marquette, Rich Pecci, Charlotte Rampling, Paul Reubens, Ally Sheedy, Dylan Riley Snyder, Renée Taylor, Michael Kenneth Williams, Gaby Hoffmann. Writer-director Solondz revisits the characters from his 1998 film HAPPINESS (all recast here) and finds them still mired in guilt, self-doubt, and yearning. Most tellingly, a boy (Snyder) about to be bar mitzvahed has vexing questions about manhood, sexuality, and his father, a pederast. A series of nearly self-contained vignettes, the film opens on a comic note, then comes full circle emotionally as it pulls its many threads together for a poignant finale. Notable production design by Roshelle Berliner; photographed by Ed Lachman. [R]◑

Lifeforce (1985) **C-101m.** ** D: Tobe Hooper. Steve Railsback, Peter Firth, Frank Finlay, Mathilda May, Patrick Stewart, Michael Gothard. Completely crazy science-fiction yarn starts as outer space saga, then becomes a vampire movie, then turns into an end-of-the-world story! Ridiculous, to say the least, but so bizarre, it's fascinating: people disintegrate, London is overrun by zombies, and controlling it all is a beautiful nude space vampiress! Don't say we didn't warn you. Based on Colin Wilson's novel *Space Vampires*. Foreign release version running 116m. available on video. J-D-C Scope. [R]▼●◑

Lifeguard (1976) **C-96m.** **½ D: Daniel Petrie. Sam Elliott, Anne Archer, Kathleen Quinlan, Stephen Young, Parker Stevenson, Steve Burns, Sharon Weber. After his 15-year high school reunion, Elliott can't decide whether to chuck the title job to become a salesman. Slight drama resembles made-for-TV movie, but attractive cast and locations make it pleasant enough. [PG]▼▶

Life Is a Bed of Roses (1983-French) **C-111m.** ***½ D: Alain Resnais. Vittorio Gassman, Ruggero Raimondi, Geraldine Chaplin, Fanny Ardant, Pierre Arditi, Sabine Azema. Enchanting, magical, original fable paralleling the stories of wealthy Raimondi building a "temple of happiness" circa WW1, and a conference on alternative education at that site in the present day. Resnais and screenwriter Jean Gruault beautifully illustrate that there are no simple solutions to problems, that those who impose their ideas of perfection on the world are just as dangerous as those who cause disorder. [PG]▶

Life Is a Long Quiet River (1987-French) **C-95m.** *** D: Etienne Chatiliez. Benoit Magimel, Valerie Lalande, Tara Romer, Jerome Floch, Sylvie Cubertafon, Emmanuel Cendrier. A mixup of babies is revealed 12 years after the fact, and two very different families must learn to deal with the life-changing events it causes. Delightful French comedy that examines the differences between the lower class and the bourgeoisie. Wry, winning directorial debut for Chatiliez.▼

Life Is Beautiful (1997-Italian) **C-116m.** ***½ D: Roberto Benigni. Roberto Benigni, Nicoletta Braschi, Giorgio Cantarini, Giustino Durano, Sergio Bustric, Marisa Paredes, Horst Buchholz. Extraordinary film by comedy star Benigni about an irrepressible spirit who refuses to ever give in to adversity, even when he is taken to a concentration camp with his wife (Benigni's real-life wife, Braschi) and young son. He determines that the boy will be shielded from the horrors around them—and somehow finds a way to do it. A unique and beguiling fable that celebrates the human spirit. Benigni cowrote with Vincenzo Cerami. Oscar winner for Best Foreign Language Film, Best Actor, Best Score (Nicola Piovani). Original title: LA VITA E BELLA. [PG-13]▼▶●

Life Is Cheap . . . but Toilet Paper Is Expensive (1990) **C-89m.** ** D: Wayne Wang. Spenser Nakasako, Lo Wai, Cora Miao, Victor Wong, Cheng Kwan Min. Courier is sent to Hong Kong with metal briefcase handcuffed to his wrist; upon arrival, he's unable to deliver his mysterious attaché, so he decides to take in the colorful sights of the city instead. Extremely bizarre, graphic, and dense little film, of interest mainly to fans of filmmaker Wang. Some bloody scenes threatened to earn this an

X rating, so the film was released unrated and visually intact.

Life Is Sweet (1991-British) **C-102m.** *** D: Mike Leigh. Alison Steadman, Jim Broadbent, Claire Skinner, Jane Horrocks, Stephen Rea, Timothy Spall, David Thewlis. Another slice of working-class life from Leigh, focusing on an endearing couple and their iconoclastic twin daughters—one of whom (Horrocks) is waist-deep in self-loathing. More a series of vignettes than a conventional story and filled with deliciously offbeat humor; not for every taste, but a bittersweet treat for fans of Leigh's work. Leading lady Steadman was then the director's wife.▼●

Life Less Ordinary, A (1997-British) **C-103m.** **½ D: Danny Boyle. Ewan McGregor, Cameron Diaz, Holly Hunter, Delroy Lindo, Ian Holm, Ian McNeice, Stanley Tucci, Dan Hedaya, Tony Shalhoub, Maury Chaykin, Judith Ivey. Black comedy about a janitor who kidnaps his ex-boss' daughter, a spoiled heiress who finds life a bore. Meanwhile, two emissaries from Heaven (Hunter and Lindo) have to find a way to make these two fated souls fall in love. Fans of the two likable stars will perhaps be more forgiving than others of this oddball, sporadically funny outing from the SHALLOW GRAVE/TRAINSPOTTING team. Super 35. [R]▼●

Life of Brian (1979-British) **C-93m.** *** D: Terry Jones. Graham Chapman, John Cleese, Terry Gilliam, Eric Idle, Terry Jones, Michael Palin. This Monty Python religious parable will probably offend every denomination equally, but it shouldn't. Story of a man whose life parallels Christ is the funniest and most sustained feature from Britain's bad boys. [R]▼●

Life of David Gale, The (2003) **C-130m.** *** D: Alan Parker. Kevin Spacey, Kate Winslet, Laura Linney, Gabriel Mann, Matt Craven, Rhona Mitra, Leon Rippy, Elizabeth Gast, Cleo King, Jim Beaver. Absorbing tale of a man on death row (Spacey) who requests a specific newsmagazine reporter (Winslet) to interview him during the last days of his life. In flashback, we learn the story of this passionate activist for the abolition of capital punishment and how his life fell apart, but that still doesn't explain his conviction for murder—at first. A good yarn that may not stand up to close scrutiny. J-D-C Scope. [R]▼▶

Life of Emile Zola, The (1937) **116m.** **** D: William Dieterle. Paul Muni, Gale Sondergaard, Joseph Schildkraut, Gloria Holden, Donald Crisp, Erin O'Brien-Moore, Morris Carnovsky, Louis Calhern, Harry Davenport, Marcia Mae Jones, Dickie Moore, Ralph Morgan. Sincere biography of famed 19th-century French writer who rose to cause of wrongly exiled Captain Dreyfus (Schildkraut); detailed production filled with fine vignettes. Won Oscars for Best Picture, Screenplay (Norman Reilly Raine, Geza Herczeg, and Heinz Herald), Supporting Actor (Schildkraut).▼●❍

Life of Her Own, A (1950) **108m. **½** D: George Cukor. Lana Turner, Ray Milland, Tom Ewell, Louis Calhern, Ann Dvorak, Margaret Phillips, Jean Hagen, Barry Sullivan, Phyllis Kirk. Turner is at the center of three-cornered romance leading to heartbreak for all. MGM fluff; Dvorak wraps it up with her expert portrayal of an aging model. Bronislau Kaper's musical theme was later reused for his classic INVITATION.▼

Life of Oharu, The (1952-Japanese) **146m. **½** D: Kenji Mizoguchi. Kinuyo Tanaka, Toshiro Mifune, Hisako Yamane, Yuriko Hamada, Ichiro Sugai. Clichéd account of beautiful Tanaka, banished for loving a samurai (Mifune, in a small role) below her station, ending up an aged prostitute. Also shown at 118m. and known as DIARY OF OHARU.▼●

Life on a String (1991-Chinese-British-German) **C-110m. *** D: Chen Kaige. Liu Zhong Yuan, Huang Lei, Xu Qing, Ma Ling, Zhang Zhengguan. Lyrical, beautifully filmed tale of a blind boy who's told by his master that his sight will be restored if he devotes his life to music; he becomes a saintly old man (still without sight) who travels from village to village with his young disciple singing songs, which he finds spiritually nurturing. Thoughtful film crammed with poetic imagery, soundtrack of wonderful folk songs.▼❍

Life or Something Like It (2002) **C-103m. ** D: Stephen Herek. Angelina Jolie, Edward Burns, Tony Shalhoub, Christian Kane, James Gammon, Melissa Errico, Stockard Channing, Lisa Thornhill, Gregory Itzin. Career-driven Seattle TV reporter is told by a street prophet that she has one week to live. A down-to-earth cameraman tries to show her what life is really about, even as a tempting job offer looms in N.Y.C. Romantic comedy gives Jolie a good opportunity to show her lighter side, with Burns a likable leading man, but logic goes out the window as the story builds to a pat and improbable resolution. Panavision. [PG-13]▼❍

Life Stinks (1991) **C-95m. ** D: Mel Brooks. Mel Brooks, Lesley Ann Warren, Jeffrey Tambor, Stuart Pankin, Howard Morris, Rudy De Luca, Teddy Wilson, Michael Ensign, Matthew Faison, Billy Barty, Carmine Caridi. Money-hungry developer Brooks takes a bet that he won't survive on the streets of L.A. for one month without a cent. Usual Brooks smorgasbord of gags, but the success rate is pretty low. Attempts to make meaningful statement about homelessness are thin at best, tasteless at worst. Brooks also cowrote the screenplay. [PG-13]▼●❍

Life With Father (1947) **C-118m. **** D: Michael Curtiz. William Powell, Irene Dunne, Elizabeth Taylor, Edmund Gwenn, ZaSu Pitts, Jimmy Lydon, Martin Milner. Rich adaptation of long-running Broadway play (by Howard Lindsay and Russel Crouse) based on Clarence Day's story of growing up in turn-of-the-20th-century N.Y.C. with his loving but eccentric father. Utterly delightful, and a handsome production as well. Screenplay by Donald Ogden Stewart.▼❍

Life With Mikey (1993) **C-91m. *** D: James Lapine. Michael J. Fox, Christina Vidal, Nathan Lane, Cyndi Lauper, David Krumholtz, David Huddleston, Victor Garber, Tony Hendra. Former child TV star Fox lackadaisically runs a Manhattan talent agency for kids with his more dedicated brother. Then he tries to turn 10-year-old pickpocket Vidal into a star of cookie commercials and finds himself fired up in the process. Funny film, with serious overtones, is a perfect vehicle for Fox and appealing newcomer Vidal. Audition scenes are particularly good. Ruben Blades appears unbilled as Vidal's father. [PG]▼❍

Lift, The (1983-Dutch) **C-98m. **½** D: Dick Maas. Huub Stapel, Willeke Van Ammelrooy, Josine Van Dalsum, Pret Romer, Gerard Thoolen, Hans Veerman. Sleek horror thriller set in a new highrise, where the elevators are involved in a suspicious number of accidents. Maas is a better director than writer; smoothly made, suspenseful, and witty, but talky, with no satisfactory explanation for the bizarre events. Remade by the director in 2001 as THE SHAFT. [R] ▼❍

Light at the Edge of the World, The (1971-Spanish-Liechtensteinian) **C-119m. *½** D: Kevin Billington. Kirk Douglas, Yul Brynner, Samantha Eggar, Jean-Claude Druout, Fernando Rey. Amidst their fight for possession of an island, lighthouse keeper Douglas and sea pirate Brynner battle it out for affections of shipwreck victim Eggar. Jules Verne tale has some excitement, but is more often unintentionally funny. Panavision. [PG]▼❍

Lighthorsemen, The (1987-Australian) **C-111m. **½** D: Simon Wincer. Jon Blake, Peter Phelps, Nick Wateres, Tony Bonner, Bill Kerr, John Walton, Tim McKenzie, Sigrid Thornton, Anthony Andrews. Saga of the Australian Light Horse Brigade, and their involvement in a daunting desert campaign during WW1. Sweeping widescreen adventure, stunningly filmed, but marred by simplistic characterizations, and overlength (though trimmed for U.S. release). Climactic charge on Beersheba is genuinely exciting. Original Australian running time: 128m. Panavision. [PG]▼❍

Light in the Jungle (1990) **C-89m. ** D: Gray Hofmeyer. Malcolm McDowell, Susan Strasberg, Andrew Davis, John Carson, Helen Jessop, Henry Cele, Patrick Shai. Languid story of Nobel prize winner Albert Schweitzer's years as a doctor in

Africa, where he battles both the superstitions of the natives and the interference of his European benefactors. Inspired visuals, but choppy storytelling hampers this potentially interesting bio. [PG]▼

Light in the Piazza (1962) **C-101m.** ***½ D: Guy Green. Olivia de Havilland, Rossano Brazzi, Yvette Mimieux, George Hamilton, Barry Sullivan. Splendid soaper about mother who's anxious to marry off retarded daughter but isn't sure she's being fair to suitor. Beautifully filmed on location in Italy. Screenplay by Julius Epstein, from Elizabeth Spencer's novel. Later a Broadway musical. CinemaScope.

Light It Up (1999) **C-99m.** **½ D: Craig Bolotin. Usher Raymond, Forest Whitaker, Marcello Robinson, Rosario Dawson, Robert Ri'chard, Judd Nelson, Fredro Starr, Sara Gilbert, Glynn Turman, Vanessa L. Williams. Well-intentioned but preachy drama about a group of N.Y.C. students who occupy their high school after their favorite teacher is unfairly suspended and a police officer is accidentally shot. Attempts to deal with a number of serious issues, but results are forced and melodramatic. Written by the director. [R]▼◗

Lightning in a Bottle (2004) **C-106m.** ***½ D: Antoine Fuqua. Spirited Blues-tribute concert film, staged in 2003 at Radio City Music Hall, opens with an onstage intro by Martin Scorsese (who also coexecutive produced). Then it rips up the joint. What little backstage material there is proves compelling, but director Fuqua wisely lets the performers dominate a roughly chronological history featuring both veteran and contemporary performers. For a blues movie, smiley-face moments abound: Natalie Cole surprises with a super-charged "St. Louis Blues," while veterans B. B. King and Solomon Burke prove they can still belt, even though they're sitting down. [PG-13]◗

Lightning Jack (1994-Australian) **C-93m.** ** D: Simon Wincer. Paul Hogan, Cuba Gooding, Jr., Beverly D'Angelo, Kamala Dawson, Pat Hingle, Richard Riehle, Frank McRae, Roger Daltrey, L. Q. Jones, Max Cullen. Hogan attempts to repeat his "CROCODILE" DUNDEE success with this amiable but obvious, undistinguished Western/comedy. He's the whole show in his role as two-bit desperado Lightning Jack Kane, but all his charm can't save it. Gooding is his mute sidekick. Hogan also scripted and coproduced. Panavision. [PG-13]▼◗

Lightning Swords of Death (1974-Japanese) **C-83m.** *** D: Kenji Misumi. Tomisaburo Wakayama, Masahiro Tomikawa, Goh Kato. Discredited samurai roams medieval Japan pushing his young son ahead of him in baby cart in this edited entry from *Sword of Vengeance* series. Unending action and beautifully staged fights, with climactic battle rivaling finale of THE WILD BUNCH. Very bloody, though; followed by SHOGUN ASSASSIN. Inexplicably available on DVD as SHOGUN ASSASSIN II. Shawscope. [R]◗

Lightning the White Stallion (1986) **C-95m.** *½ D: William A. Levey. Mickey Rooney, Isabel Lorca, Susan George, Billy Wesley. Extremely weak family fare with Rooney a wealthy man whose racehorse is stolen. The Mick can't save it. [PG]▼◗

Light of Day (1987) **C-107m.** ** D: Paul Schrader. Michael J. Fox, Gena Rowlands, Joan Jett, Michael McKean, Thomas G. Waites, Cherry Jones, Michael Dolan, Jason Miller, Michael Rooker. Family angst movie masquerading as a rock 'n' roll tale. Jett and Fox are sister and brother who perform together in a local Cleveland band that starts to gain some recognition, just as personal problems threaten to tear the family apart. Rowlands, in a gratuitous subplot, plays their dying mother. Real-life rock star Jett steals the movie with her compelling performance, but the film degenerates as it goes along. Occasional sparks can't save Schrader's muddled script. [PG-13]▼◗

Lightship, The (1985) **C-89m.** ** D: Jerzy Skolimowski. Robert Duvall, Klaus Maria Brandauer, Tom Bower, Robert Costanzo, Badja Djola, William Forsythe, Arliss Howard, Michael Lyndon. Duvall, practically unrecognizable, gives an outrageously inventive performance as a slimy homosexual thug in this otherwise muddled, pretentiously symbolic saga of a trio of criminals who besiege Brandauer's lightship. Narration, spoken by Brandauer's son (Lyndon—real-life son of Skolimowski), is laughably hokey. [PG-13]▼◗

Light Sleeper (1992) **C-103m.** *** D: Paul Schrader. Willem Dafoe, Susan Sarandon, Dana Delany, David Clennon, Mary Beth Hurt, Victor Garber, Jane Adams, Paul Jabara, Sam Rockwell, David Spade. Quintessential Schrader Lonely Guy film, with Dafoe an aging sadsack who wants more out of life than his dead-end job taxi-ing cocaine to upscale users in N.Y. Well performed by all, and with surprising dashes of loopy humor—though leading to an inevitable bloodbath given the standard blueprint for most Schrader movies. Quite the image-altering showcase for Delany. [R] ▼◗

Light Years (1988-French) **C-71m.** ** D: Rene Laloux. Voices of Glenn Close, Christopher Plummer, Jennifer Grey, John Shea, David Johansen, Terrence Mann, Penn and Teller. Pretentious animated sci-fi fantasy, about a prince who time-travels into the future; he's surrounded by characters named Ambisextra, Metamorphosis, Chief of the Deformed, and The Collective Voice (so you know this wasn't made with young children in mind). The animation is nothing special, and the talky script is by none other than Isaac Asimov. [PG]▼◗

Light Years Away (1981-French-Swiss) **C-105m. *** D:** Alain Tanner. Trevor Howard, Mick Ford, Bernice Stegers, Henri Vorlogeux. Irritable old Howard, who resides in a deserted, dilapidated gas station, becomes the mentor of drifter Ford. Thoughtful yarn is well acted by its two leads. Filmed in Ireland.

Like a Turtle on Its Back (1978-French) **C-110m. **½ D:** Luc Beraud. Jean-Francois Stevenin, Bernadette Lafont, Virginie Thevenet, Veronique Silver, Claude Miller. Uneven yet absorbing tale of blocked writer Stevenin's efforts to create, offering a hint of the real struggle a writer must make to pound out meaningful sentences on his typewriter.

Like Father, Like Son (1987) **C-98m. BOMB D:** Rod Daniel. Dudley Moore, Kirk Cameron, Margaret Colin, Catherine Hicks, Patrick O'Neal, Sean Astin. Heart surgeon accidentally sprinkles an ancient Indian potion into his Bloody Mary and presto!—he and his teenage son have somehow switched identities. Moore's mugging talents get a major workout in this Hall of Fame embarrassment, first of four 1987/1988 comedies to utilize an adult-teen switcheroo theme. [PG-13]▼●]

Like Mike (2002) **C-99m. *** D:** John Schultz. Lil' Bow Wow, Morris Chestnut, Jonathan Lipnicki, Robert Forster, Crispin Glover, Eugene Levy, Brenda Song, Jesse Plemons, Anne Meara. Cute film for kids about an orphaned boy who acquires sneakers that may have belonged to Michael Jordan and turns into a basketball-playing phenomenon . . . but what he really wants is a father. Engaging, well cast, and family friendly, with a notable absence of crude humor, bad language, and violence. Film debut for hip-hop recording sensation Lil' Bow Wow. Many basketball stars appear as themselves. Followed by a direct-to-video sequel. [PG] ▼]

Like Water for Chocolate (1992-Mexican) **C-113m. *** D:** Alfonso Arau. Lumi Cavazos, Marco Leonardi, Regina Torne, Mario Ivan Martinez, Ada Carrasco. Striking and sensuous film (from a novel by Laura Esquivel, the director's then-wife), set in the early part of the 20th century: a young woman's life is shaped first by her stern and unyielding mother, and more important, by the overwhelming power of cooking. Sumptuous fable—not without humor—with a good cast and a top-notch performance from lead actress Cavazos. Piquant, sometimes mystical, and enjoyably unpredictable. Original running time was 144m. ●]

Li'l Abner (1959) **C-113m. *** D:** Melvin Frank. Peter Palmer, Leslie Parrish, Stubby Kaye, Howard St. John, Julie Newmar, Stella Stevens, Billie Hayes, Robert Strauss. Lively Gene DePaul–Johnny Mercer musical based on Broadway version of Al Capp's comic strip; loud and brassy, with corny comedy, some good songs. Stubby

Kaye is fine as Marryin' Sam; other Dogpatch characters vividly enacted. Look sharp for young Valerie Harper and Beth Howland among the chorus girls. VistaVision.

Lila Says (2005-French-Italian-British) **C-90m. **½ D:** Ziad Doueiri. Vahina Giocante, Mohammed Khouas, Karim Ben Haddou, Lotfi Chakri, Hamid Dkhissi, Carmen Lebbos, Edmonde Franchi. A Marseille teenager on the brink of manhood thinks about becoming a writer, but he's broke, ghettoized, and pressured by his peers to remain a loser . . . until he meets a blonde bombshell who sparks his literary fuse, and then some. Faintly surreal saga of contemporary French-Arabian relations stays lightweight and nymphet-fixated until its inevitable bittersweet ending. [R]

Lili (1953) **C-81m. **** D:** Charles Walters. Leslie Caron, Mel Ferrer, Zsa Zsa Gabor, Jean-Pierre Aumont, Amanda Blake, Kurt Kasznar. Enchanting musical with Leslie as French orphan who attaches herself to carnival and self-pitying puppeteer Ferrer. Bronislau Kaper's Oscar-winning score includes "Hi Lili, Hi Lo." Helen Deutsch scripted, from Paul Gallico's story, and provided lyrics for the title song. ▼●]

Lilies of the Field (1963) **93m. *** D:** Ralph Nelson. Sidney Poitier, Lilia Skala, Lisa Mann, Isa Crino, Stanley Adams. A "little" film that made good, winning Poitier an Oscar as handyman who helps build chapel for Skala and her German-speaking nuns. Quiet, well acted, enjoyable. Director Nelson followed this with a TV movie, CHRISTMAS LILIES OF THE FIELD. ▼●]

Lili Marleen (1981-German) **C-120m. **½ D:** Rainer Werner Fassbinder. Hanna Schygulla, Giancarlo Giannini, Mel Ferrer, Karl Heinz von Hassel, Christine Kaufmann, Hark Bohm, Karin Baal, Udo Kier. Second-rate Fassbinder about third-rate cabaret singer Schygulla, whose recording of the title song becomes a hit in Nazi Germany. Intriguing subject matter is pretentiously handled. [R]

Lilith (1964) **114m. **½ D:** Robert Rossen. Warren Beatty, Jean Seberg, Peter Fonda, Kim Hunter, Jessica Walter, Anne Meacham, Gene Hackman, Rene Auberjonois. Fairly faithful version of controversial J. R. Salamanca novel about a novice therapist who falls in love with a troubled patient. A probing if not altogether satisfying look at the many facets of madness—and love. Director-writer Rossen's last film. ▼]

Lillian Russell (1940) **127m. ** D:** Irving Cummings. Alice Faye, Don Ameche, Henry Fonda, Edward Arnold, Warren William, Leo Carrillo, Nigel Bruce. Strained bio of early 20th-century star; lavish backgrounds and weak plotline diminish Faye's vehicle; Arnold repeats his Diamond Jim Brady role with gusto. ▶]

Lilo & Stitch (2002) **C-85m. *** D:** Chris Sanders, Dean DeBlois. Voices of Daveigh

Chase, Christopher Michael Sanders, Tia Carrere, Kevin McDonald, Ving Rhames, David Ogden Stiers, Zoe Caldwell, Jason Scott Lee, Kevin Michael Richardson. Forlorn Hawaiian girl being raised by her older sister finds an unlikely friend at the dog pound: a monstrous alien whom she names Stitch. Meanwhile, emissaries from Stitch's planet have landed on earth to retrieve the destructive little fellow. Lively Disney cartoon feature takes time to warm up to—since Stitch is so mean-spirited—but eventually wins you over. Unique character design and beautiful watercolor backgrounds are major assets. Followed by two direct-to-video sequels and a TV series. [PG] ▼▶

Lilya 4-Ever (2002-Swedish) **C-109m.** ★★★ D: Lukas Moodysson. Oksana Akinshina, Artiom Bogucharskij, Elina Benenson, Lilia Sinkarjova, Pavel Ponomarjov. Obvious but stinging account of an adolescent girl (Akinshina) who lives in what once was the Soviet Union and yearns to go to America, but is abandoned and abused by everyone around her, starting with her mother. Of the countless films that have focused on child abuse, few are as edgy or as memorable. [R]

Lily in Love (1985-U.S.-Hungarian) **C-103m.** ★½ D: Karoly Makk. Christopher Plummer, Maggie Smith, Elke Sommer, Adolph Green, Szabo Sandor. Flat, unfunny (and uncredited) reworking of Molnar's THE GUARDSMAN and THE CHOCO-LATE SOLDIER. Egotistical actor Plummer disguises himself as an Italian and courts wife Smith. Tries to be charming and sophisticated, but fails dismally despite Plummer and Smith's efforts. [PG-13] ▼●

Limbo (1972) **C-112m.** ★★ D: Mark Robson. Kathleen Nolan, Kate Jackson, Katherine Justice, Stuart Margolin, Hazel Medina, Russell Wiggins. Emotional melodrama about three women, whose husbands are either missing or captured in Vietnam, who become friends. One of the first major Hollywood productions to examine homefront repercussions of the war, but its intentions are better than its results. Screenplay by Joan (Micklin) Silver and James Bridges. Aka WOMEN IN LIMBO. [PG]

Limbo (1999) **C-126m.** ★★★½ D: John Sayles. Mary Elizabeth Mastrantonio, David Strathairn, Vanessa Martinez, Kris Kristofferson, Casey Siemaszko, Leo Burmester, Kathryn Grody, Rita Taggart. Novelistic film by writer-director Sayles set in modern-day Alaska about characters who find themselves at emotional crossroads: a quiet man with a skeleton in his closet (Strathairn), an itinerant nightclub singer (Mastrantonio) with a habit of picking rotten male companions, and her teenage daughter (Martinez), who's filled with self-loathing and tired of her mother's mercurial relationships. Surprising, intelligent, and richly textured. [R] ▼▶

Limelight (1952) **145m.** ★★★ D: Charles Chaplin. Charles Chaplin, Claire Bloom, Nigel Bruce, Buster Keaton, Sydney Chaplin, Norman Lloyd. Sentimental story of aging, washed-up music hall clown (Chaplin) who saves ballerina Bloom from suicide and regains his own confidence while building her up. Overlong, indulgent Chaplin effort still has many moving scenes, historic teaming of Chaplin and Keaton in comedy skit. Young Geraldine Chaplin (the director's daughter) makes her film debut as a street urchin. This won an Oscar for its score in 1972, the year in which it was first eligible for the competition—because it had not been shown in an L.A. theater until then! ▼●

Limey, The (1999) **C-90m.** ★★½ D: Steven Soderbergh. Terence Stamp, Peter Fonda, Lesley Ann Warren, Luis Guzman, Barry Newman, Joe Dallesandro, Nicky Katt, Amelia Heinle. A taciturn Britisher, just out of prison, comes to L.A. to avenge the suspicious death of his daughter, who fell under the spell of a sleazy music magnate (Fonda). Stylish and understated, with great use of L.A. locations, but the story at the core isn't all that interesting. Stamp appears in flashbacks lifted from his 1967 film POOR COW. [R] ▼●

Limitless (2011) **C-105m.** ★★★ D: Neil Burger. Bradley Cooper, Abbie Cornish, Robert De Niro, Andrew Howard, Anna Friel, Johnny Whitworth, Robert John Burke, Ned Eisenberg, T.V. Carpio. Imaginative, propulsively paced thriller about an underachieving author (Cooper) who becomes an overachieving genius after obtaining experimental pills that turbo-charge his cognitive abilities. As his fortunes rise, however, he's drawn dangerously close to an autocratic Wall Street tycoon (De Niro) and a borderline-psychotic Russian loan shark (Howard). Cooper evidences unmistakable star power with a performance that neatly balances witty swagger and skittish paranoia. Adapted from Alan Glynn's novel *The Dark Fields.* Super 35. [PG-13]▶

Limits of Control, The (2009) **C-116m.** ★½ D: Jim Jarmusch. Isaach De Bankolé, Alex Descas, Jean-François Stévenin, Óscar Jaenada, Luis Tosar, Paz de la Huerta, Tilda Swinton, Youki Kudoh, John Hurt, Gael García Bernal, Hiam Abbass, Bill Murray. Incomprehensible and downright boring drama about a mysterious man with a criminal past who arrives in Spain, ostensibly to finish a job. His journey is never quite clear, taking him to places that may be real or imagined. Mainly he walks around a lot, encountering people who utter clues like, "Wait three days until you see the bread and the guitar will find you." Indulgent exercise by Jarmusch wastes a talented cast, although Swinton, in too brief a cameo, is vibrant and original. Her character sums the whole thing up by saying, "Sometimes there are films where people just sit there." [R]▶

Lincoln Lawyer, The (2011) **C-118m. **½** D: Brad Furman. Matthew McConaughey, Marisa Tomei, Ryan Phillippe, Josh Lucas, William H. Macy, John Leguizamo, Michael Peña, Bob Gunton, Frances Fisher, Bryan Cranston, Trace Adkins, Shea Whigham, Michael Paré. L.A. criminal lawyer Mick Haller, who works out of his chauffeured Lincoln Continental, takes on an unusually high-profile case defending Phillippe, the scion of a wealthy family who's accused of raping a prostitute. There's clearly more to it than meets the eye, and it may tie into a case he tried some years ago. Adaptation of Michael Connelly's best-selling novel is well cast and neatly plotted but loses its spark long before the unexpected finale. Not bad, but not as solid as it promises to be at the outset. Makes creative use of offbeat L.A. locations. HD Widescreen. [R]▶

Line King: The Al Hirschfeld Story, The (1996) **C-87m. ***½** D: Susan Warms Dryfoos. Outstanding documentary about Al Hirschfeld, the most famous—and durable—caricaturist of the 20th century. The articulate artist is seen throughout and some of his admiring, amused subjects appear, including Lauren Bacall, Carol Channing, Joan Collins and Robert Goulet. Jules Feiffer offers commentary as well. The highest praise possible: the film is truly worthy of its subject. Beware the hour-long broadcast TV version. ▼▶

Line of Fire SEE: **Sam's Song**

Lineup, The (1958) **86m. **½** D: Don Siegel. Warner Anderson, Emile Meyer, Eli Wallach, Richard Jaeckel, Robert Keith. Expanded version of TV series set in San Francisco, focusing on gun-happy hoodlum after a cache of dope. Cult favorite with fans of director Siegel. Pretty ordinary except for final car-chase stunt.▶

Linguini Incident, The (1992) **C-98m. *½** D: Richard Shepard. Rosanna Arquette, David Bowie, Eszter Balint, Andre Gregory, Buck Henry, Viveca Lindfors, Marlee Matlin, Lewis Arquette. Even pasta lovers should probably steer clear of this dismal trendy-cutesy-quirky caper comedy. Arquette (quite appealing) is a Houdini-obsessed waitress at a N.Y.C. restaurant who wants to rob the place, Bowie is an illegal alien bartender, and Matlin is a cashier. Story concerns magic acts, wagers, and an antique wedding ring. Julian Lennon and Iman have cameos. [R]▼▶

Link (1986-British) **C-103m.** BOMB D: Richard Franklin. Terence Stamp, Elisabeth Shue, Steven Pinner, Richard Garnett. Primatologist Stamp is experimenting on chimps . . . and his activities get predictably out of hand. A horror film that's not horrifying, or suspenseful, or even mildly entertaining. [R]▼▶

L'Innocente (1976-Italian) SEE: **The Innocent**

Lion, The (1962) **C-96m. ** D: Jack Cardiff. William Holden, Trevor Howard, Capucine, Pamela Franklin, Samuel Romboh, Christopher Agunda. Beautiful scenery of Kenya is far better than melodrama about young girl attached to pet lion, with family concerned it is turning her into a savage. CinemaScope.

Lionheart (1987) **C-104m. *** D: Franklin J. Schaffner. Eric Stoltz, Gabriel Byrne, Nicola Cowper, Dexter Fletcher, Deborah Barrymore, Nicholas Clay. Seeking Richard the Lionhearted, who's passing through France headed for the Crusades, runaway young knight Stoltz gradually forms his own children's crusade as more and more homeless children follow him. Richly produced, well acted, with a superb Jerry Goldsmith score, it's a shame this sincere, if slight, film received almost no theatrical release. [PG]▼▶

Lionheart (1991) **C-105m. ** D: Sheldon Lettich. Jean-Claude Van Damme, Deborah Rennard, Harrison Page, Lisa Pelikan, Ashley Johnson. By-the-numbers programmer with Van Damme deserting the foreign legion, becoming a professional streetfighter, and battling a variety of villains. Only for those who like films in which fights are staged ad nauseam. Aka A.W.O.L. and WRONG BET. [R]▼▶

Lion in Winter, The (1968-British) **C-135m. **** D: Anthony Harvey. Peter O'Toole, Katharine Hepburn, Jane Merrow, Anthony Hopkins, Nigel Terry, Timothy Dalton, Nigel Stock, John Castle. Brilliant, fierce, and personal drama (adapted by James Goldman from his play) of Henry II deliberating over a successor on fateful Christmas Eve. Hepburn co-won Best Actress Oscar for her strong performance as Eleanor of Aquitaine. Oscars also went to Goldman and composer John Barry. Film debuts of Hopkins and Dalton. O'Toole also played Henry II in BECKET. Remade for cable TV in 2004. Panavision. ▼▶

Lion Is in the Streets, A (1953) **C-88m.**½** D: Raoul Walsh. James Cagney, Barbara Hale, Anne Francis, Warner Anderson, John McIntire, Jeanne Cagney, Lon Chaney, Jr., Frank McHugh. Cagney, in a Huey Long take-off, is lively as a swamp peddler turned politician, but rambling screenplay prevents film from having much impact. Well photographed by Harry Stradling. ▼▶

Lion King, The (1994) **C-88m. *** D: Roger Allers, Rob Minkoff. Voices of Jonathan Taylor Thomas, Matthew Broderick, James Earl Jones, Jeremy Irons, Moira Kelly, Niketa Calame, Ernie Sabella, Nathan Lane, Robert Guillaume, Rowan Atkinson, Madge Sinclair, Whoopi Goldberg, Cheech Marin, Jim Cummings. A lion cub raised to take his father's place someday as king of the jungle is sabotaged by his evil uncle—

and lives in exile until he realizes his rightful place in the circle of life. With distant echoes of BAMBI, this entertaining Disney cartoon feature (highlighted by Oscar-winning Elton John–Tim Rice songs and Oscar-winning music score by Hans Zimmer) has dazzling scenics, some show-stopping animation, and outstanding voice work—but drama so intense (and comedy so hip), it's not really for very young viewers. Followed by animated TV series, two direct-to-video sequels, and a Broadway musical. Rereleased in Imax in 2002 at 89m. [G] ▼●◗

Lion of the Desert (1981-Libyan-British) **C-162m.** ******* D: Moustapha Akkad. Anthony Quinn, Oliver Reed, Rod Steiger, John Gielgud, Irene Papas, Raf Vallone, Gastone Moschin. Sweeping "David vs. Goliath" spectacle, with Quinn as Omar Mukhtar, guerrilla leader who stymied Italian forays into Libya between 1911 and 1931. Steiger is Benito Mussolini. Panavision. [PG] ▼◗

Lions for Lambs (2007) **C-88m.** ******* D: Robert Redford. Tom Cruise, Meryl Streep, Robert Redford, Andrew Garfield, Michael Peña, Derek Luke, Peter Berg, Kevin Dunn. Hotshot senator (Cruise) summons a star reporter (Streep) to unveil his plan to attack terrorists in Afghanistan. Meanwhile, a college professor (Redford) tries to inspire a student with great potential who seems to have drifted, even though his last two protégés took his call for involvement to extremes. Unusual chamber piece allows three commanding actors to make long, pointed speeches about everything from Washington games-playing to empty-headed TV journalism. Short on subtlety but obviously impassioned. Screenplay by Matthew Michael Carnahan. Panavision. [R]◗

Lipstick (1976) **C-89m.** BOMB D: Lamont Johnson. Margaux Hemingway, Chris Sarandon, Perry King, Anne Bancroft, Robin Gammell, Mariel Hemingway. Gorgeous model is brutally raped, must ultimately take justice into her own hands. Totally wretched film gives new dimension to term "exploitation picture." Mariel's film debut. [R] ▼●◗

Liquidator, The (1966-British) **C-105m.** ****½** D: Jack Cardiff. Rod Taylor, Trevor Howard, Jill St. John, Wilfrid Hyde-White. Nice location photography and adequate acting add up to a rather limp Bondian imitation. Even Taylor can't save this one. Panavision.

Liquid Dreams (1991) **C-92m.** ****½** D: Mark Manos. Richard Steinmetz, Candice Daly, Barry Dennen, Juan Fernandez, Tracey Walter, Frankie Thorn, Paul Bartel, Mink Stole, John Doe. Beautiful Daly, determined to uncover her sister's killer, becomes immersed in a world of decadent, nightmarish dance halls and clubs, and various hidden evils. Provocative if overly slick thriller with sci-fi elements. Also available in unrated version. [R]▼

Liquid Sky (1983) **C-112m.** ******* D: Slava Tsukerman. Anne Carlisle, Paula E. Sheppard, Susan Doukas, Otto Von Wernherr, Bob Brady. Gleefully nasty original about a lesbian punker whose Manhattan penthouse patio is trespassed by a UFO. A one-joke movie, but a pretty good joke; Carlisle, who also plays a gay male model, is remarkable, and there's some potent imagery despite the minuscule budget. Not for every taste, but you knew that when you read the plot synopsis. [R]▼●◗

Lisa and the Devil (1972-Italian-Spanish-West German) **C-95m.** ****½** D: Mario Bava. Elke Sommer, Telly Savalas, Sylva Koscina, Alida Valli, Alessio Orano, Gabriele Tinti, Kathy Leone, Eduardo Fajardo. A tourist (Sommer) gets lost in an unidentified European town and winds up at an eerie mansion replete with rotting corpses, wax dummies, a blind woman, and a man who thinks she's the reincarnation of his dead wife. Oh yes, there's also an evil lollipop-sucking butler (Savalas), who just happens to be Satan. Truly strange, surreal psychological horror tale filled with hallucinatory imagery. Re-edited in 1975 as THE HOUSE OF EXORCISM, with gory new footage and unrelated scenes with Robert Alda as a priest. ▼●◗

Lisa Picard is Famous (2001) **C-87m.** ****½** D: Griffin Dunne. Laura Kirk, Nat DeWolf, Griffin Dunne, Daniel London. Kirk is a struggling N.Y.C. actress whose (painfully) ordinary life is being documented by filmmaker Dunne. DeWolf is her gay pal, whose success is equally meager. Satire of fame, actors, and the show-business milieu has many sharp moments but wears thin after a while. Written by costars Kirk and DeWolf. Mira Sorvino and Fisher Stevens are two of the producers; they are among many celebrities who pop up in choice cameos. [PG-13]▼◗

Listen to Me (1989) **C-107m.** ***½** D: Douglas Day Stewart. Kirk Cameron, Jami Gertz, Roy Scheider, Amanda Peterson, Tim Quill, George Wyner, Anthony Zerbe, Christopher Atkins. Slick travesty about a renowned small-college debating squad, set on the kind of party-school campus where Dick Dale and The Del-Tones wouldn't be out of place. Climactic abortion debate—before the Supreme Court, no less—is cheap and hokey in roughly equal measure. Beware of Cameron's shifting Oklahoma accent. [PG-13] ▼●

Listen Up: The Lives of Quincy Jones (1990) **C-114m.** ****½** D: Ellen Weissbrod. Ultraslick look at the life and times of Quincy Jones, the famed musician-composer-arranger-producer. Not so much a documentary as a visual and musical collage; sometimes effective, but too often plays like a music video—and is much too self-congratulatory. Dozens of Jones' friends, associates, and admirers appear, including Dizzy

Gillespie, Lionel Hampton, Jesse Jackson, Frank Sinatra, Barbra Streisand, Miles Davis, Steven Spielberg, Sidney Lumet, Ella Fitzgerald, Oprah Winfrey, Ray Charles, Ice T, Melle Mel, Big Daddy Kane. [PG-13]▼●◗

List of Adrian Messenger, The (1963) **98m.** ***** D: John Huston. George C. Scott, Clive Brook, Dana Wynter, Herbert Marshall, Tony Curtis, Kirk Douglas, Burt Lancaster, Robert Mitchum, Frank Sinatra, John Huston, Bernard Fox. Good murder mystery has a gimmick: Curtis, Douglas, Lancaster, Mitchum, and Sinatra are all heavily disguised in character roles. All that trouble wasn't necessary; the mystery is good on its own. The director's son Tony (billed as Anthony Walter Huston) plays Wynter's son. ▼●◗

Lisztomania (1975-British) **C-105m.** *½ D: Ken Russell. Roger Daltrey, Sara Kestelman, Paul Nicholas, Fiona Lewis, Ringo Starr. So-called biography of Franz Liszt is, in truth, one of Ken Russell's most outlandish extravaganzas; director's devotees may enjoy this visual, aural (and sexual) assault. Others beware! Panavision. [R]▼●

Little Ark, The (1972) **C-100m.** ***** D: James B. Clark. Theodore Bikel, Philip Frame, Genevieve Ambas, Max Croiset, Johan De Slaa. Another good children's film from producer Robert Radnitz; this one concerns two Dutch youngsters who try to find their father after being separated from him during a flood. Panavision. [G]

Little Ashes (2009-Spanish-British) **C-112m.** ** D: Paul Morrison. Robert Pattinson, Javier Beltrán, Matthew McNulty, Marina Gatell, Arly Jover. It's Madrid in the jazz age of the anything-goes '20s when 18-year-old artist Salvador Dali arrives at the university and strikes up a friendship with two other aspiring young talents, director Luis Buñuel and poet Federico García Lorca. As time and events drag on Dali is increasingly attracted (intellectually and otherwise) to García Lorca. Loosely structured quasi-biopic takes mucho liberties with its key subjects and never gets below the surface. Soft-core gay love scene may surprise Pattinson's rabid fans from TWILIGHT, but he does show acting chops as well. [R]◗

Little Big League (1994) **C-119m.** ** D: Andrew Scheinman. Luke Edwards, Timothy Busfield, John Ashton, Ashley Crow, Kevin Dunn, Jonathan Silverman, Dennis Farina, Jason Robards, Wolfgang Bodison, Scott Patterson. A 12-year-old boy inherits the Minnesota Twins from his grandfather, and decides to manage the baseball team himself. Could have and should have been a cute family movie, but it has no energy—and goes on forever. Special appearances by real-life major leaguers Ken Griffey, Jr., Lou Piniella, Sandy Alomar, Jr., Tim Raines, Wally Joyner, and others. Directing debut for producer Scheinman. [PG]▼●◗

Little Big Man (1970) **C-139m.** **** D: Arthur Penn. Dustin Hoffman, Faye Dunaway, Martin Balsam, Richard Mulligan, Chief Dan George, Jeff Corey, Alan Oppenheimer, Aimee Eccles, William Hickey. Sprawling, superb filmization of Thomas Berger's novel about Jack Crabb, 121-year-old man who reminisces about his life as young pioneer, adopted Indian, drinking pal of Wild Bill Hickok, medicine-show hustler, and survivor of Custer's Last Stand. Rich humor, colorful characterizations, moving tragedy are among ingredients, and they all click. Screenplay by Calder Willingham. Originally released at 150m. Panavision. [PG]▼●◗

Little Bit of Soul, A (1998-Australian) **C-85m.** ** D: Peter Duncan. Geoffrey Rush, David Wenham, Frances O'Connor, Heather Mitchell, John Gaden. Wacko Aussie black comedy about two scientists (and ex-lovers) working on an immortality serum who make a pact with their married benefactors—who just happen to be your average, everyday Satanists! Attempted satire of science and religion is ultimately too shrill and strained to generate many laughs despite a capable cast. Soundtrack of Louis Jordan oldies helps liven things up. [R]▼

Little Black Book (2004) **C-106m.** *½ D: Nick Hurran. Brittany Murphy, Holly Hunter, Ron Livingston, Kathy Bates, Stephen Tobolowsky, Julianne Nicholson, Josie Maran, Sharon Lawrence. Murphy lands a job at a trash-TV talk show and becomes a protégée of ambitious staffer Hunter, who encourages her to spy on her boyfriend using his handheld PDA. Vehicle for Murphy has too many plot threads, many of them dark and unpleasant, and doesn't seem to have a point . . . except to pay homage to better movies like WORKING GIRL and BROADCAST NEWS. The actors (other than Murphy) are photographed in the most unflattering manner imaginable. Super 35. [PG-13]▼◗

Little Boy Lost (1953) **95m.** ***** D: George Seaton. Bing Crosby, Claude Dauphin, Nicole Maurey, Gabrielle Dorziat. Synthetic tear-jerker set in post-WW2 France, where newspaperman Crosby is trying to locate his son, not knowing which boy at orphanage is his.

Little Buddha (1993) **C-123m.** ** D: Bernardo Bertolucci. Keanu Reeves, Chris Isaak, Bridget Fonda, Alex Wiesendanger, Ying Ruocheng, Raju Lal, Rudraprsad, Jo Champa. Disappointing, dramatically muddled Bertolucci epic with obvious similarities to THE LAST EMPEROR, telling the parallel stories of aged Tibetan monk (Ruocheng) who believes that a young Seattle boy (Wiesendanger) is the reincarnation of his respected mentor, and the young Prince Siddhartha (Reeves), who lived 2,500 years ago. Pretty to look at, but otherwise pretty much of a bore. Technovision (35mm), Arriflex (70mm). [PG]▼●◗

Little Caesar (1930) **80m.** ***½ D: Mervyn LeRoy. Edward G. Robinson, Douglas Fairbanks, Jr., Glenda Farrell, Stanley Fields, Sidney Blackmer, Ralph Ince, George E. Stone. Small-time hood becomes underworld big shot; Robinson as Caesar Enrico Bandello gives star-making performance in classic gangster film, still exciting. Francis Faragoh and Robert E. Lee adapted W. R. Burnett's novel. ▼●❙

Little Children (2006) **C-137m.** **** D: Todd Field. Kate Winslet, Patrick Wilson, Jennifer Connelly, Gregg Edelman, Noah Emmerich, Jackie Earle Haley, Phyllis Somerville, Trini Alvarado, Helen Carey, Mary B. McCann, Jane Adams, Raymond J. Barry; narrated by Will Lyman. Intensely emotional story, which unfolds in novelistic fashion (complete with narration) about lives that crisscross in an upscale Massachusetts town: a woman who's unhappy as a wife and mother (Winslet), a househusband who can't get his act together (Wilson), a sex offender (Haley) just released from prison who still lives with his mother, and an ex-cop (Emmerich) who's obsessed with the predator in their midst. Spellbinding look at how frustrated people act out without thinking about the consequences, told with an ironic point of view. Tom Perrotta adapted his own novel with director Field. Super 35. [R]❙

Little Cigars (1973) **C-92m.** *** D: Chris Christenberry. Angel Tompkins, Billy Curtis, Jerry Maren, Frank Delfino, Emory Souza, Felix Silla, Joe De Santis. Crime-caper comedy with a midget gang committing the mayhem. Fast and funny, with Tompkins especially good as a former mistress to gangster De Santis, and Curtis, the leader of the tiny troupe. Look for a funny bit by dwarf Angelo Rossitto during a police lineup. [PG]

Little City (1999) **C-89m.** ** D: Roberto Benabib. Jon Bon Jovi, Penelope Ann Miller, Josh Charles, Annabella Sciorra, JoBeth Williams, Joanna Going. Life and loves—gay and straight, platonic and passionate—among a group of young people in San Francisco. Pleasant-enough time-filler, with an attractive cast and postcard views of the city, but nothing special. Released direct to video. [R]▼❙

Little Colonel, The (1935) **80m.** *** D: David Butler. Shirley Temple, Lionel Barrymore, Evelyn Venable, John Lodge, Sidney Blackmer, Bill Robinson. Even non-fans should like this, one of Shirley's best films, as she mends broken ties between Grandpa Barrymore and Mama Venable in the Reconstruction South . . . and does that famous step dance with Robinson. Final scene was filmed in Technicolor. Also shown in computer-colored version. ▼●❙

Little Darlings (1980) **C-95m.** ** D: Ronald F. Maxwell. Tatum O'Neal, Kristy McNichol, Armand Assante, Matt Dillon, Maggie Blye, Nicolas Coster, Krista Erickson, Alexa Kenin, Cynthia Nixon. Tatum and Kristy wager which one will be the first to lose her virginity at summer camp. Not quite as sleazy as it sounds, but not very inspiring, either. McNichol easily out-acts her costar with a solid performance. Panavision. [R]▼●

Little Dorrit (1988-British) ** D: Christine Edzard. Derek Jacobi, Alec Guinness, Roshan Seth, Sarah Pickering, Miriam Margolyes, Cyril Cusack, Max Wall, Eleanor Bron, Michael Elphick, Joan Greenwood, Patricia Hayes, Robert Morley, Sophie Ward, Bill Fraser. PART ONE: NOBODY'S FAULT (**C-177m.**) Ambitious adaptation of Charles Dickens' satiric novel concerns upstanding but ineffectual Jacobi, and the young seamstress Little Dorrit (Pickering) who lives with her father (Guinness) in debtors' prison. Low-budget production is painstakingly slow moving: viewers will either adore this or despise it. PART TWO: LITTLE DORRIT'S STORY (**C-183m.**) Second half of saga unfortunately insists on recreating almost the entire first half *scene for scene* before moving forward. As in first part, there are several good performances (notably Guinness') but screenplay is inadequate. [G]▼●

Little Dorrit's Story SEE: **Little Dorrit**

Little Dragons, The (1980) **C-90m.** *½ D: Curtis Hanson. Charles Lane, Ann Sothern, Chris Petersen, Pat Petersen, Sally Boyden, Rick Lenz, Sharon Weber, Joe Spinell, Tony Bill. Junior Kung Fu aficionados solve a kidnapping mystery. May appeal to the less discriminating 9-year-old. Lane and particularly Sothern are wasted. [PG]▼

Little Drummer Girl, The (1984) **C-130m.** *** D: George Roy Hill. Diane Keaton, Yorgo Voyagis, Klaus Kinski, Sami Frey, Michael Cristofer, Thorley Walters, Anna Massey, Bill Nighy. Adaptation of John le Carré's best-selling spy thriller is long, slow, confusing, not always believable—but still worthwhile, if only for Keaton's strong performance as a mercurial pro-Palestinian actress recruited to perform as Israeli agent. Globe-trotting story about a novice caught in the world of terrorists holds interest throughout, even with its flaws. Kinski is first-rate as Israeli counter-intelligence officer. [R]▼●

Little Fauss and Big Halsy (1970) **C-97m.** **½ D: Sidney J. Furie. Robert Redford, Michael J. Pollard, Lauren Hutton, Noah Beery, Lucille Benson. So-so character study of two motorcycle racers, one timid and gullible (Pollard), the other a self-centered braggart (Redford) who takes advantage of cohort. Beery and Benson outstanding as Pollard's folks; flavorful song score by Johnny Cash. Panavision. [R]

Little Fish (2005-Australian) **C-114m.** ★★★ D: Rowan Woods. Cate Blanchett, Sam Neill, Hugo Weaving, Martin Henderson, Dustin Nguyen, Noni Hazlehurst, Joel Tobeck, Lisa McCune, Susie Porter. Gritty kitchen-sink drama with the always-watchable Blanchett playing an ex–heroin addict who faces all sorts of pressures and temptations while struggling to stay straight. She's surrounded by an array of vividly etched characters, with Weaving and Neill especially good as an addict and a gang lord. [R]●

Little Fockers (2010) **C-98m.** BOMB D: Paul Weitz. Robert De Niro, Ben Stiller, Owen Wilson, Blythe Danner, Jessica Alba, Teri Polo, Dustin Hoffman, Barbra Streisand, Laura Dern, Colin Baiocchi, Daisy Tahan, Kevin Hart, Yul Vazquez, Harvey Keitel. Greg (Stiller), now the father of twins, continues to run afoul of dad-in-law Jack (De Niro), climaxing in the fisticuffs teased at in MEET THE PARENTS and promised in MEET THE FOCKERS. With enema, vomit, wee-wee, and e.d. gags, and tedious sitcomplications over building a house, planning a birthday party, and maybe or maybe not having an affair, the whole dispiriting endeavor leads to an alarming ensemble finale that sets up yet another sequel. [PG-13] ●

Little Foxes, The (1941) **116m.** ★★★½ D: William Wyler. Bette Davis, Herbert Marshall, Teresa Wright, Richard Carlson, Patricia Collinge, Dan Duryea, Charles Dingle. Outstanding filmization of Lillian Hellman's play of greed and corruption within a crumbling Southern family on the financial outs, headed by majestic Davis as ruthless Regina. Collinge, Duryea, Dingle, Carl Benton Reid, and John Marriott all re-create their Broadway roles, with Collinge, Duryea, Reid, and Teresa Wright making their film debuts. Scripted by Hellman. Prequel: ANOTHER PART OF THE FOREST.▼●

Little Fugitive (1953) **80m.** ★★★ D: Ray Ashley, Morris Engel, Ruth Orkin. Richie Andrusco, Rickie Brewster, Winifred Cushing, Will Lee. A young boy who thinks he has killed his brother wanders lost through Coney Island. A lyrical little comedy-drama, produced independently and on a threadbare budget. A minor classic. Remade in 2006. ▼●

Little Giant (1946) **91m.** ★★ D: William A. Seiter. Bud Abbott, Lou Costello, Brenda Joyce, Jacqueline de Wit, George Cleveland, Elena Verdugo, Mary Gordon, Margaret Dumont. Bud and Lou don't work as a team in this atypical comedy with Lou becoming a vacuum cleaner salesman; filled with amusing, tried-and-true routines.▼●

Little Giants (1994) **C-105m.** ★★½ D: Duwayne Dunham. Rick Moranis, Ed O'Neill, Shawna Waldron, Mary Ellen Trainor, Matthew McCurley, Susanna Thompson, Brian Haley, Devon Sawa, Michael Zwiener, John Madden, Harry Shearer, Dabbs Greer. Moranis has always lived in the shadow of big brother O'Neill, a swaggering football star; when Moranis' daughter—a first-rate player—doesn't get picked for O'Neill's Pop Warner football team, she persuades her dad to launch a rival team, as a haven for all the town's misfit kids. Amiable juvenile comedy is formula to the max, but knows how to please its youthful audience. Several real-life football players appear as themselves. [PG]▼●

Little Girl Who Lives Down the Lane, The (1976-Canadian) **C-94m.** ★★★ D: Nicolas Gessner. Jodie Foster, Martin Sheen, Scott Jacoby, Mort Shuman, Alexis Smith. Complex, unique mystery with Foster as young girl whose father never seems to be home—and she gets very nervous when anyone goes near the basement. Think you've figured it out? Forget it, Charlie; you haven't even scratched the surface. Engrossing, one-of-a-kind film written by Laird Koenig. [PG]▼●

Little Hut, The (1957-British) **C-90m.** ★★ D: Mark Robson. Ava Gardner, Stewart Granger, David Niven, Finlay Currie, Walter Chiari. Busy husband Granger takes sexy wife Gardner for granted. Will her friendship with Niven stay platonic when all three are stranded on an island? Static, flat, talky sex farce, from the Andre Roussin play.

Little Indian, Big City (1994-French) **C-90m.** *½ D: Hervé Palud. Thierry Lhermitte, Ludwig Briand, Patrick Timsit, Arielle Dombasle. Dopey French kiddie comedy about a stockbroker who goes to the Amazon to divorce his estranged wife and discovers he has a 13-year-old son, whom he brings back to Paris. A big hit in France, Disney released it in the U.S., with terrible American dubbing. Jokes are mainly of the scatological variety: the little kid's name Mimi-Siku means "cat pee" in his native tongue. Americanized in 1997 as JUNGLE 2 JUNGLE. [PG]▼

Little Kidnappers, The (1953-British) **95m.** ★★★½ D: Philip Leacock. Jon Whiteley, Vincent Winter, Adrienne Corri, Duncan Macrae, Jean Anderson, Theodore Bikel. Splendid children's story set in Nova Scotia, 1900. Two orphan youngsters "adopt" abandoned baby when strict grandfather forbids them having a dog. Whiteley and Winter won special Oscars for outstanding juvenile performances. British title: THE KIDNAPPERS. Remade for cable TV in 1990 with Charlton Heston.

Little Laura & Big John (1973) **C-82m.** ★★½ D: Luke Moberly, Bob Woodburn. Fabian Forte, Karen Black, Ivy Thayer, Ken Miller, Paul Gleason, Cliff Frates. Surprisingly engaging road company BONNIE AND CLYDE set in Everglades country. One-time teen rock 'n' roll idol Fabian made his acting comeback in this one, although Warren Beatty needn't be too concerned about the competition. [R]▼●

Little Lord Fauntleroy (1936) **98m.** ******* D: John Cromwell. Freddie Bartholomew, C. Aubrey Smith, Guy Kibbee, Dolores Costello, Mickey Rooney, Jessie Ralph. Young New Yorker Bartholomew suddenly finds himself a British lord in this charming film from classic story. Handsome, well-cast production. Previously filmed in England in 1914 and in 1921; remade for TV in 1980 with Ricky Schroder and Alec Guinness, and in Russia in 2003. Also shown in computer-colored version.▼◗

Little Malcolm (1974-British) **C-112m.** ****** D: Stuart Cooper. John Hurt, John McEnery, David Warner, Rosalind Ayres, Raymond Platt. Hurt is prototypical angry young man (booted out of art school) who forms neofascist cult and rails out against society in this well-acted adaptation of David Halliwell's play criticizing 1960s protest movements. Warner takes acting honors as Hurt's obsessive verbal adversary. Ex-Beatle George Harrison's first venture into film production. Original British title: LITTLE MALCOLM AND HIS STRUGGLE AGAINST THE EUNUCHS.

Little Man (2006) **C-98m.** BOMB D: Keenen Ivory Wayans. Marlon Wayans, Shawn Wayans, Tracy Morgan, Kerry Washington, John Witherspoon, Chazz Palminteri, Molly Shannon, David Alan Grier. Diminutive criminal drops a stolen diamond in a woman's purse and is forced to disguise himself as a baby left on her doorstep to get it back. Idiotic gags involving breast feeding, anal thermometers, and dirty diapers ensue. A running joke in which "the baby" molests unsuspecting women is particularly offensive. The three Wayans who wrote this admit they were inspired by the Bugs Bunny cartoon "Baby Buggy Bunny"—which is funnier (and shorter). See also the *Our Gang* comedy "Free Eats." Rob Schneider appears unbilled. [PG-13]◗

Little Manhattan (2005) **C-90m.** ******* D: Mark Levin. Josh Hutcherson, Charlie Ray, Bradley Whitford, Cynthia Nixon, Talia Balsam, Josh Pais, Willie Garson, Tonye Patano, J. Kyle Manzay, Josh Pais. In an ideal N.Y.C. where nothing bad ever happens, 10-year-old Gabe and Rosemary discover a mutual attraction during karate class, though they've known each other since kindergarten. *Wonder Years*–style narration and bright, imaginative visual design combine with sweet performances in an Upper West Side story filled with bubbles and balloons. The dialogue is a bit precocious, but this miniaturized romantic comedy is genuinely cute. Super 35. [PG]◗

Little Man Tate (1991) **C-99m.** ******* D: Jodie Foster. Jodie Foster, Dianne Wiest, Adam Hann-Byrd, Harry Connick, Jr., David Pierce, P.J. Ochlan, Debi Mazar, Celia Weston, Danitra Vance, Josh Mostel, George Plimpton. Moving, extraordinarily empathic look at a child genius; his single, working-class mom (Foster) can't give him the support and stimulation he needs—but neither can the director (Wiest) of a school for exceptional children who takes him under her wing. Beautifully realized by Foster in her directing debut; her performance is equally strong. Bittersweet screenplay by Scott Frank; solid jazz score by Mark Isham. Bob Balaban appears unbilled as a quizmaster. [PG]▼◗

Little Men (1940) **84m.** ****** D: Norman Z. McLeod. Kay Francis, Jack Oakie, George Bancroft, Jimmy Lydon, Ann Gillis, Charles (Carl) Esmond, William Demarest. Slight, predictable adaptation of the Louisa May Alcott novel, focusing on rough adolescent Lydon "learning the ways" at Francis' school. Oakie easily steals the film as an irrepressible con man. Remade in 1998. ▼◗

Little Men (1998-Canadian) **C-98m.** ****½** D: Rodney Gibbons. Mariel Hemingway, Chris Sarandon, Michael Caloz, Ben Cook, Ricky Mabe, Gabrielle Boni; narrated by Kathleen Fee. Pleasant TV-style period piece based on Louisa May Alcott's followup to *Little Women*. Jo and Mr. Bhaer are now married and running a home for wayward boys; they turn their kind attention to a newly orphaned street urchin and his rowdy friend. Official title is: LOUISA MAY ALCOTT'S LITTLE MEN. [PG]▼

Little Mermaid, The (1989) **C-82m.** ******* D: John Musker, Ron Clements. Voices of Jodi Benson, Pat Carroll, Samuel E. Wright, Kenneth Mars, Buddy Hackett, Christopher Daniel Barnes, Rene Auberjonois, Ben Wright. Delightful Disney animated feature loosely based on Hans Christian Andersen story about a young mermaid named Ariel who longs to be human. One could squabble about certain story points, but the film is so enjoyable it's foolish to try. Buoyant musical numbers include "Kiss The Girl," "Part of Your World," and "Under the Sea," sung by a Jamaican crab named Sebastian (Wright). Won Oscars for Best Original Score (Alan Menken) and Song ("Under the Sea," by Menken and Howard Ashman). Followed by an animated TV series and a DVD sequel. Later a Broadway musical. [G] ▼◗

Little Minister, The (1934) **110m.** *****½** D: Richard Wallace. Katharine Hepburn, John Beal, Donald Crisp, Andy Clyde, Beryl Mercer. Charming film of James M. Barrie story about Scottish pastor falling in love, with Hepburn radiant in period romance. ▼◗

Little Miss Broadway (1938) **70m.** ****** D: Irving Cummings. Shirley Temple, George Murphy, Jimmy Durante, Phyllis Brooks, Edna May Oliver, George Barbier. Not bad Temple, with Shirley bringing Oliver's theatrical boardinghouse to life; Shirley and Durante are good together. Also shown in computer-colored version.▼◗

Little Miss Marker (1934) **80m.** ******* D:

Alexander Hall. Adolphe Menjou, Shirley Temple, Dorothy Dell, Charles Bickford, Lynne Overman, Warren Hymer. Winning Damon Runyon tale of bookie Menjou and N.Y.C. gambling colony reformed by adorable little Shirley, left as IOU for a debt. Remade as SORROWFUL JONES (1949) and 40 POUNDS OF TROUBLE, and again in 1980. Also shown in computer-colored version. ▼●

Little Miss Marker (1980) **C-103m.** ** D: Walter Bernstein. Walter Matthau, Julie Andrews, Tony Curtis, Bob Newhart, Sara Stimson, Lee Grant, Brian Dennehy, Kenneth McMillan. Boring remake of the Damon Runyon story, with Matthau as the bookie, Stimson the little girl, Andrews the love interest, Curtis the heavy. Veteran screenwriter Bernstein's first directing credit. [PG] ▼▶

Little Miss Sunshine (2006) **C-101m.** ***½ D: Jonathan Dayton, Valerie Faris. Greg Kinnear, Toni Collette, Steve Carell, Alan Arkin, Abigail Breslin, Paul Dano, Bryan Cranston, Beth Grant, Wallace Langham, Julio Oscar Mechoso, Mary Lynn Rajskub, Gordon Thomson. Winning comedy-drama about a seriously off-kilter family, including a 7-year-old girl who wants to enter beauty contests. Each family member undergoes a change during an eventful road trip to California in an old Volkswagen bus to get the little girl to an all-important pageant. Impressive feature debut for top TV commercial directors Dayton and Faris, who capture all the telling details in the script by first-time screenwriter Michael Arndt. The cast simply couldn't be better. Oscar winner for Best Original Screenplay and Supporting Actor (Arkin). Super 35. [R]▶

Little Monsters (1989) **C-100m.** *½ D: Richard Alan Greenberg. Fred Savage, Howie Mandel, Ben Savage, Daniel Stern, Margaret Whitton, Rick Ducommun, Frank Whaley. BEETLE JUICE–inspired fantasy comedy suffers from clumsy script and obvious post-production cuts. Boy finds prankish monster (Mandel) under his bed; their friendship leads to various crises, in our world and in the dimly lit land of the monsters. Premise was promising but results are dismal. [PG] ▼●

Little Murders (1971) **C-110m.** *** D: Alan Arkin. Elliott Gould, Marcia Rodd, Vincent Gardenia, Elizabeth Wilson, Jon Korkes, Donald Sutherland, Lou Jacobi, Alan Arkin. Jules Feiffer's ultrablack comedy about life in nightmarish N.Y.C. focuses on aggressive urbanite (Rodd) who lassoes passive photographer Gould into marriage. Superb performance by Gardenia as Rodd's father, hilarious cameo by Arkin as mind-blown detective, but even funniest moments are overshadowed by frighteningly depressing atmosphere. [PG— edited from original R rating] ▼▶

Little Nellie Kelly (1940) **100m.** **½ D: Norman Taurog. Judy Garland, George Murphy, Charles Winninger, Douglas McPhail. Lightweight musical based on George M. Cohan play about Judy patching up differences between father Murphy and grandfather Winninger. Garland sings "It's A Great Day For The Irish."▼●

Little Nemo: Adventures in Slumberland (1990-Japanese) **C-85m.** **½ D: Masami Hata, William T. Hurtz. Voices of Gabriel Damon, Mickey Rooney, Rene Auberjonois, Danny Mann, Laura Mooney, Bernard Erhard. Beautifully rendered animation about a young boy's odyssey into the world of dreams—and the perils of Nightmare Land. Starts with a knockout opening sequence, and has much to entertain youngsters (and animation buffs), but its story loses momentum. Inspired by Winsor McCay's comic strip classic. Songs by Richard M. and Robert B. Sherman. Concept for the screen by Ray Bradbury. Not released in the U.S. until 1992. [G] ▼●

Little Nicky (2000) **C-90m.** ** D: Steven Brill. Adam Sandler, Patricia Arquette, Harvey Keitel, Rhys Ifans, Tommy "Tiny" Lister, Jr., Rodney Dangerfield, Robert Smigel, Allen Covert, Blake Clark, Kevin Nealon, Reese Witherspoon, Quentin Tarantino. The sweetest of the Devil's three sons must go to Earth and bring back his two errant brothers or his father will die. Meanwhile, his siblings are turning N.Y.C. into a living hell. Outrageous, sometimes appalling, occasionally funny comedy revels in extraordinary crudeness. Full of gag cameos (many by Sandler's onetime *Saturday Night Live* costars). Sandler cowrote. [PG-13] ▼▶

Little Night Music, A (1978) **C-124m.** *½ D: Harold Prince. Elizabeth Taylor, Diana Rigg, Len Cariou, Lesley-Anne Down, Hermione Gingold, Lawrence Guittard, Christopher Guard, Chloe Franks. Laughably stilted film version of the Stephen Sondheim–Hugh Wheeler stage musical which in turn was based on Ingmar Bergman's sex-at-a-country-estate comedy, SMILES OF A SUMMER NIGHT. Liz's rendition of "Send in the Clowns" is no chart buster. Filmed in Austria. [PG] ▼●

Little Nikita (1988) **C-98m.** ** D: Richard Benjamin. Sidney Poitier, River Phoenix, Richard Jenkins, Caroline Kava, Richard Bradford, Richard Lynch, Loretta Devine, Lucy Deakins. Intriguing premise—young, all-American Phoenix learning that his parents are Soviet agents—fails to catch fire in this sometimes entertaining but ultimately incoherent thriller. Poitier adds a bit of spark as an FBI agent. [PG] ▼●

Little Noises (1991) **C-110m.** **½ D: Jane Spencer. Crispin Glover, Tatum O'Neal, Rik Mayall, Tate Donovan, John C. McGinley, Nina Siemaszko, Carole Shelley, Steven Schub. Ambitious but muddled account of Glover, a failure who calls himself a writer (even though he's never penned anything); he finds status and monetary reward after passing off the poetry of a deaf mute orphan as his own.▼●)

Little Odessa (1994) C-98m. *** D: James Gray. Tim Roth, Edward Furlong, Moira Kelly, Vanessa Redgrave, Maximilian Schell, Paul Guilfoyle, Natasha Andreichenko, David Vadim, Mina Bern. Melancholy drama set during a bleak Brooklyn winter, about Joshua (Roth), a hitman whose Russian-Jewish family resides in Brighton Beach. He has been disowned by his adulterous father (Schell), and his mother (Redgrave) is dying; his kid brother (Furlong) is caught between Russian and American cultures, and between his love for Joshua and the knowledge that his brother is evil. Grim, disturbing, brilliantly directed with a distinctive visual style by 24-year-old Gray (who also scripted). Super 35. [R]▼●)

Little Old New York (1940) 100m. **½ D: Henry King. Alice Faye, Brenda Joyce, Fred MacMurray, Richard Greene, Henry Stephenson. Claims to be story of Robert Fulton and his steamboat; merely serves as framework for standard romance.

Little Prince, The (1974-British) C-88m. **½ D: Stanley Donen. Richard Kiley, Steven Warner, Bob Fosse, Gene Wilder, Joss Ackland, Clive Revill, Donna McKechnie, Victor Spinetti. Antoine de St. Exupery's children's book is considered a classic, but this musical fantasy doesn't do it justice. Kiley plays aviator who counsels and guides a young boy who wants to learn about life. Unmemorable score by Lerner and Loewe is just one of this fable's major letdowns. [G]▼●)

Little Princess, The (1939) C-91m. *** D: Walter Lang. Shirley Temple, Richard Greene, Anita Louise, Ian Hunter, Cesar Romero, Arthur Treacher, Marcia Mae Jones, Sybil Jason. Shirley stars as a Victorian waif who makes good in this lavishly mounted, colorful production. Remade (twice) in 1995, again in 1997, and for TV. ▼●)

Little Princess, A (1995) C-97m. *** D: Alfonso Cuaron. Eleanor Bron, Liam Cunningham, Liesel Matthews, Rusty Schwimmer, Arthur Malet, Vanessa Lee Chester, Errol Sitahal, Vincent Schiavelli. A little jewel of a movie about a fanciful young girl (Matthews) whose father deposits her at a boarding school while he goes off to fight in WW1—unaware that the headmistress is a spiteful woman. Devotees of Frances Hodgson Burnett's classic novel (filmed before with Shirley Temple) may be dismayed at liberties taken with the original—moving it to N.Y.C. in the teens, for instance—but its spirit is intact. Hard to believe this handsome production was filmed almost entirely on a Burbank studio backlot! [G] ▼●)

Little Rascals, The (1994) C-72m. ** D: Penelope Spheeris. Travis Tedford, Bug Hall, Brittany Ashton Holmes, Kevin Jamal Woods, Zachary Mabry, Ross Elliot Bagley, Sam Saletta, Blake Jeremy Collins. Spanky and the members of the He-Man Woman Haters Club try to sabotage Alfalfa's budding romance with Darla. Aimed squarely at young children, who will probably enjoy it, though it's no match for the original 1930s Hal Roach comedy shorts. The kids are cute, but Alfalfa (played by Hall) is the only standout—along with Pete the Pup. Gag cameos by a few stars and celebrities seem extraneous. [PG]▼●)

Little Romance, A (1979) C-108m. *** D: George Roy Hill. Laurence Olivier, Diane Lane, Thelonious Bernard, Arthur Hill, Sally Kellerman, David Dukes, Broderick Crawford. Engaging film about relationship of young American girl (Lane, in her film debut) living in Paris and running off with a charming French boy (Bernard), chaperoned by wily old con man (Olivier, wonderfully hammy). A throwback to director Hill's WORLD OF HENRY ORIENT in its winning treatment of adolescence, but not quite as good. Crawford has funny cameo as himself. Georges Delerue's music score won a well-deserved Oscar. Panavision. [PG]▼●)

Little Sex, A (1982) C-95m. ** D: Bruce Paltrow. Tim Matheson, Kate Capshaw, Edward Herrmann, John Glover, Joan Copeland, Susanna Dalton, Wendie Malick, Wallace Shawn, Melinda Culea, Bill Smitrovich. MTM Enterprises' first theatrical feature is basically an R-rated TV-movie, with Matheson marrying long-time girlfriend Capshaw hoping it will cure him of his womanizing. It doesn't. Tired but watchable comedy-drama has pretty N.Y.C. locations and pleasing performances, particularly by Herrmann as Matheson's wiser older brother. Capshaw's film debut. [R]▼●

Little Shop of Horrors, The (1960) 70m. ***½ D: Roger Corman. Jonathan Haze, Jackie Joseph, Mel Welles, Dick Miller, Myrtle Vail, Jack Nicholson. Classic black comedy about young schnook who develops bloodthirsty plant and is forced to kill in order to feed it. Initially infamous as The Film Shot In Two Days, but now considered one of Corman's best pictures. Nicholson has hilarious bit as masochist who thrives on dental pain; delightful screenplay by Charles Griffith (who also plays the hold-up man and is the voice of "Audrey, Jr."). Later a stage musical, which was filmed in 1986. Also shown in computer-colored version. ▼●)

Little Shop of Horrors (1986) C-88m. **½ D: Frank Oz. Rick Moranis, Ellen Greene, Vincent Gardenia, Steve Martin, James Belushi, John Candy, Christopher Guest, Bill Murray, voice of Levi Stubbs. Very entertaining black comedy/musical about a nebbish (played to perfection by Moranis) whose "unusual" new plant brings him good fortune—but turns into a Frankenstein. Greene (repeating her stage role) is a delight as his squeaky-voiced heartthrob, Martin hilarious as her macho boyfriend. But when Audrey II, the plant, turns *really* mean and monstrous, with super-duper special effects, the fun drains away. Based on the off-Broadway musical by Howard Ashman and Alan Menken, which in turn was based on Roger Corman's 1960 low-budget black comedy (written by Charles B. Griffith). [PG-13]▼●♪

Littlest Horse Thieves, The (1977) C-104m. *** D: Charles Jarrott. Alastair Sim, Peter Barkworth, Maurice Colbourne, Susan Tebbs, Andrew Harrison, Chloe Franks. Well-made Disney period piece, filmed in England, about three children's efforts to save pit-ponies who work the mines from abuse and death. Set at the turn of the century. Good location photography. Originally titled ESCAPE FROM THE DARK. [G]▼▶

Littlest Rebel, The (1935) 73m. *** D: David Butler. Shirley Temple, John Boles, Jack Holt, Karen Morley, Bill Robinson, Stepin Fetchit, Guinn "Big Boy" Williams. One of Shirley's best films, a Civil War saga set in the Old South, with our heroine managing to wrap Union officer Holt around her little finger and protect her Confederate officer father (Boles). Temple and Robinson do some delightful dancing as well. Also shown in computer-colored version. ▼▶

Little Theatre of Jean Renoir, The (1971-French) C-100m. *** D: Jean Renoir. Jeanne Moreau, Fernand Sardou, Francoise Arnoul, Jean Carmet, Marguerite Cassan, Dominique Labourier. Quartet of short sketches about human dignity and goodness of country life (as opposed to surviving in a dehumanized urban wilderness). Renoir's celluloid swan song may not be among his best, but still has much to offer. Made for television in 1969.▼●

Little Thief, The (1989-French) C-104m. **½ D: Claude Miller. Charlotte Gainsbourg, Didier Bezace, Simon de la Brosse, Nathalie Cardone, Raoul Billerey. So-so character portrait of the title lass, an alienated, amoral teen drifting through life in postwar France. If she comes off as a female Antoine Doinel, it's because the original story was cowritten by François Truffaut, who was supposedly planning to film this at the time of his death; resulting film lacks the director's inimitable touch. Miller was for ten years Truffaut's assistant; Gainsbourg is the daughter of Jane Birkin. [R]▼●

Little Treasure (1985) C-95m. *½ D: Alan Sharp. Margot Kidder, Ted Danson, Burt Lancaster, Joseph Hacker, Malena Doria, John Pearce. A stripper ventures to Mexico to meet her long-lost father but spends most of her time searching for treasure

with a dropout American. Unsatisfying story marked directing debut for writer Sharp. Danson comes off best. [R]▼●

Little Vampire, The (2000-German-Dutch-U.S.) C-96m. **½ D: Uli Edel. Jonathan Lipnicki, Richard E. Grant, Alice Krige, Anna Popplewell, Jim Carter, John Wood, Pamela Gidley, Rollo Weeks. A nine-year-old California schoolboy moves to Scotland and makes friends with a nine-year-old vampire who sucks him into his world and shows him the time of his life. Good-natured if uninspired adaptation of Angela Sommer-Bodenburg's popular German children's books. Lipnicki is cute as always, but Weeks steals the show as his vampire pal. [PG]▼▶

Little Vegas (1990) C-91m. ** D: Perry Lang. Anthony John Denison, Catherine O'Hara, Jerry Stiller, Michael Nouri, Perry Lang, Bruce McGill, John Sayles, Jay Thomas, Bob Goldthwait. Subtle comedy revolving around offbeat characters in trailer park located in desolate area that Mafia developers want to turn into a "little" Las Vegas. Intriguing possibilities, but it doesn't quite gel. [R]▼●

Little Vera (1988-Russian) C-133m. *** D: Vassili Pitchul. Natalia Negoda, Andrei Sokolov, Yuri Nazarov, Ludmila Zaisova, Alexander Niegreva. Groundbreaking, post-*glasnost* look at life in modern Russia. Negoda offers a fresh performance as an alienated, working-class, rock music-loving young woman; the depiction of her sexual relationship with Sokolov, plus the manner in which Western culture has affected her life, make this unlike any other Soviet film you've ever seen. Not surprisingly, it was a smash hit in its homeland. ▼●♪

Little Voice (1998-British-U.S.) C-96m. *** D: Mark Herman. Jane Horrocks, Michael Caine, Brenda Blethyn, Jim Broadbent, Ewan McGregor, Annette Badland, Philip Jackson. When a sleazy talent agent (Caine) and an equally greasy nightclub owner (Broadbent) discover that the reclusive daughter of a middle-aged shrew has the uncanny ability to sing like Judy Garland and other show-business greats, they smell money. But the mousy girl, known as Little Voice, sings for other reasons entirely. Vivid adaptation of Jim Cartwright's London play *The Rise and Fall of Little Voice*, with Horrocks re-creating her sensational performance, joined by a superb cast that (to put it mildly) doesn't hold back. [R]▼●♪

Little Women (1933) 115m. **** D: George Cukor. Katharine Hepburn, Joan Bennett, Paul Lukas, Frances Dee, Jean Parker, Edna May Oliver, Douglass Montgomery, Spring Byington. Film offers endless pleasure no matter how many times you've seen it; a faithful, beautiful adaptation of Alcott's book by Victor Heerman and Sarah Y. Mason, who deservedly received Oscars. The cast is uniformly superb. Remade in 1949, 1978 (for TV), and 1994.▼●◗

Little Women (1949) **C-121m.** **½ D: Mervyn LeRoy. June Allyson, Peter Lawford, Margaret O'Brien, Elizabeth Taylor, Janet Leigh, Mary Astor. Glossy remake of Louisa May Alcott's gentle account of teenage girls finding maturity and romance—patly cast.▼●◗

Little Women (1994) **C-118m.** **** D: Gillian Armstrong. Winona Ryder, Susan Sarandon, Gabriel Byrne, Trini Alvarado, Samantha Mathis, Kirsten Dunst, Claire Danes, Christian Bale, Eric Stoltz, John Neville, Mary Wickes. Exquisite rendering of Louisa May Alcott's Civil War–era classic about four devoted sisters who eventually have to leave their New England nest. A perfect cast is led by Ryder as the headstrong Jo, with Sarandon as that tower of strength, Marmee. Not a false moment or false move in the entire film, though purists may object to Marmee mouthing 1990s-style feminist doctrine. Veteran character actress Wickes threatens to steal every scene she's in, as crotchety Aunt March. Screenplay by Robin Swicord. [PG]▼●◗

Live a Little, Love a Little (1968) **C-90m.** ** D: Norman Taurog. Elvis Presley, Michele Carey, Don Porter, Rudy Vallee, Dick Sargent, Sterling Holloway, Eddie Hodges. Elvis manages to land two well-paying photographer's jobs and work them both by hopping back and forth from office to office. Pleasant, if standard, Presley fare. Panavision.▼●◗

Live a Little, Steal a Lot (1975) **C-101m.** **½ D: Marvin Chomsky. Robert Conrad, Don Stroud, Donna Mills, Robyn Millan, Luther Adler, Burt Young, Paul Stewart. Unremarkable but engrossing tale based on real-life story of two Florida beach bums who engineered "impossible" heist of 564-carat Star of India. Fine TOPKAPI-like caper scenes, plus good speedboat chase. Originally titled MURPH THE SURF and retitled YOU CAN'T STEAL LOVE. [PG]▼◗

Live and Let Die (1973-British) **C-121m.** **½ D: Guy Hamilton. Roger Moore, Yaphet Kotto, Jane Seymour, Clifton James, Geoffrey Holder, Bernard Lee, Lois Maxwell. Barely memorable, overlong James Bond movie seems merely an excuse to film wild chase sequences; superagent goes after master criminal subverting U.S. economy via drugs. Works on level of old-time serial. This was Moore's first appearance as 007; title song by Paul McCartney. [PG]▼●◗

Live Flesh (1997-Spanish-French) **C-100m.** ***½ D: Pedro Almodóvar. Liberto Rabal, Francesca Neri, Javier Bardem, Angela Molina, Jose Sancho, Penélope Cruz. Smitten son of a prostitute is jailed for accidentally shooting and paralyzing a cop during an altercation with a dishy drug user. Upon his release, he discovers that the woman is married to his victim! What might have

been a melodramatic howler is instead Almodóvar's best feature since WOMEN ON THE VERGE OF A NERVOUS BREAKDOWN. After a bumpy start, film becomes a model of how to change moods. The director scripted from the novel by Ruth Rendell. Panavision. [R]▼●◗

Live for Life (1967-French-Italian) **C-130m.** **½ D: Claude Lelouch. Yves Montand, Annie Girardot, Candice Bergen, Irene Tunc, Anouck Ferjac. TV documentary producer Montand leaves wife Girardot for fashion model Bergen in glossy film helped by some good acting; picture was follow-up to Lelouch's A MAN AND A WOMAN.

Live Free or Die (2007) **C-90m.** ** D: Gregg Kavet, Andy Robin. Aaron Stanford, Paul Schneider, Michael Rapaport, Ebon Moss-Bachrach, Judah Friedlander, Kevin Dunn, Zooey Deschanel. Quirky comedy spotlighting John "Rugged" Rudgate (Stanford), a "legendary" criminal who thinks he's a modern-day Al Capone/Billy the Kid but is actually a tenth-rate, self-deluded loser. Schneider does a Will Ferrell imitation as Rudgate's trusting, mentally challenged protégé, and the bizarre scenario consists of an escalating series of misadventures and coincidences. The only problem is that none of it is particularly funny. The directors, who also coscripted, were occasional writers of *Seinfeld*. [R]◗

Live Free or Die Hard (2007) **C-129m.** *** D: Len Wiseman. Bruce Willis, Justin Long, Timothy Olyphant, Cliff Curtis, Mary Elizabeth Winstead, Maggie Q, Kevin Smith, Željko Ivanek, Yancey Arias, Christina Chang. While snooping on his daughter, NYPD cop (and overprotective father) John McClane picks up a N.J. suspect for a federal sweep of computer geeks and brings him to Washington, just as cyber-lord Olyphant initiates a plan to shut down the entire country. DIE HARD is effectively reinvented for a post-9/11 world, with the techies proving no match for an indestructible old-school cop. Credibility gives way to preposterous action scenes toward the end, but it's still fun to watch. Released overseas as DIE HARD 4.0. Also available in unrated version. Super 35. [PG-13]◗

Live Nude Girls (1995) **C-92m.** ** D: Julianna Lavin. Dana Delany, Kim Cattrall, Cynthia Stevenson, Laila Robins, Lora Zane, Olivia d'Abo, Glenn Quinn, Tim Choate, Amber (Rose) Tamblyn. A bunch of galpals come together for a bachelorette party and pass the time talking, at which point assorted jealousies, fantasies, and feelings come to the surface. Well intentioned, to be sure, but oh so predictable. [R]▼●◗

Lives of a Bengal Lancer, The (1935) **109m.** **** D: Henry Hathaway. Gary Cooper, Franchot Tone, Richard Cromwell, Sir Guy Standing, C. Aubrey Smith, Monte Blue,

Kathleen Burke, Noble Johnson, Lumsden Hare, Akim Tamiroff, J. Carrol Naish, Douglass Dumbrille. Delightful Hollywood foray into empire building in Northwest India. Cooper and Tone are pals. in famed British regiment, Cromwell the callow son of commander Standing whom they take under their wing. Top story, action, repartee—and wonderful snake-charming scene. Grover Jones, William Slavens McNutt, Achmed Abdullah, Waldemar Young, and John Balderston coscripted; from the novel by Major Francis Yeats-Brown. Remade, with obvious changes, as GERONIMO (1939). ▼●▶

Lives of Others, The (2006-German) **C-137m.** ***½ D: Florian Henckel von Donnersmarck. Martina Gedeck, Ulrich Mühe, Sebastian Koch, Ulrich Tukur, Thomas Thieme, Hans-Uwe Bauer, Volkmar Kleinert. In 1984 East Berlin a single-minded officer (Mühe) in the Stasi, the country's well-staffed secret police, is assigned to eavesdrop on playwright Koch, refusing to believe that the popular writer is completely loyal to his government. But this obsessive quest has an unexpected effect on the professional spy. Fascinating drama deals with the poisonous nature of a society built on suspicion and doubt. Outstanding performances in this impressive writing and directing debut for von Donnersmarck. Oscar winner as Best Foreign Language Film. Hawk-Scope. [R]▶

Live Wire (1992) **C-85m.** **½ D: Christian Duguay. Pierce Brosnan, Ron Silver, Ben Cross, Lisa Eilbacher, Brent Jennings, Tony Plana, Al Waxman, Philip Baker Hall, Michael St. Gerard. FBI bomb expert Brosnan is puzzled when several people in Washington literally explode; his nemesis is terrorist Cross. Silver is a crooked senator, one of Cross' targets. OK thriller with good performances and an unusual, if absurd, premise. Debuted on cable TV. Also available in 87m. unrated version. [R] ▼●▶

Living Daylights, The (1987-British) **C-130m.** **½ D: John Glen. Timothy Dalton, Maryam d'Abo, Jeroen Krabbé, Joe Don Baker, John Rhys-Davies, Art Malik, Andreas Wisniewski, Desmond Llewelyn, Robert Brown. Dalton makes an impressive debut as James Bond in this entertaining, globe-trotting spy story about a double-dealing Russian general; it's brimming with great stunts and gimmicks, and eschews the smirking comic attitude of other recent Bond outings. But like some other Bonds, this one goes on far too long. Caroline Bliss debuts as Miss Moneypenny. Panavision. [PG]▼●▶

Living Desert, The (1953) **C-69m.** *** D: James Algar. Narrated by Winston Hibler. Disney's first True-Life Adventure feature has dazzling footage of the American desert and its inhabitants, but attracted justifiable criticism for its gimmicky treatment of some material like the famous "scorpion

dance." Still worthwhile. Academy Award winner. ▼▶

Living End, The (1992) **C-92m.** *** D: Gregg Araki. Mike Dytri, Craig Gilmore, Mark Finch, Mary Woronov, Johanna Went, Darcy Marta, Nicole Dillenberg, Paul Bartel. Frank, impertinent black comedy–road movie about Dytri and Gilmore. Each is twentyish, gay, and HIV-positive, and they set out on a nihilistic journey. Despite the characters' situation, the film is spirited and devilishly funny, but there's still no shortage of rage over their circumstances. Araki also scripted, photographed, and edited this ultra-low-budget gem. ▼▶

Living Free (1972-British) **C-91m.** **½ D: Jack Couffer. Susan Hampshire, Nigel Davenport, Geoffrey Keen. Sequel to BORN FREE details further adventures of lioness Elsa and her three cubs. Nice photography but far too leisurely. [G]▼▶

Living in a Big Way (1947) **103m.** ** D: Gregory La Cava. Gene Kelly, Marie McDonald, Charles Winninger, Phyllis Thaxter, Spring Byington. Kelly returns from WW2 to get to know his war bride for the first time and clashes with her *nouveau riche* family. A notorious flop in its day, but not all that bad; Kelly does a couple of first-rate dance numbers. ▼

Living in Oblivion (1995) **C/B&W-91m.** *** D: Tom DiCillo. Steve Buscemi, Catherine Keener, Dermot Mulroney, Danielle Von Zerneck, James Le Gros, Rica Martens, Peter Dinklage, Hilary Gilford, Michael Griffiths, Matthew Grace, Robert Wightman. Clever, amusing look at a low-budget movie in progress, from several points of view. Writer-director DiCillo has several tricks up his sleeve to go along with his pointed perceptions about how egos collide—and how things go wrong on every movie set. Most of the cast also worked behind the scenes. [R]▼●▶

Living It Up (1954) **C-95m.** *** D: Norman Taurog. Dean Martin, Jerry Lewis, Janet Leigh, Edward Arnold, Fred Clark, Sheree North, Sig Ruman. Bright remake of NOTHING SACRED. Jerry has Carole Lombard's role as supposed radiation victim brought to N.Y.C. as publicity stunt by reporter Leigh; Martin is Jerry's doctor. Scene at Yankee Stadium is a classic. That's sexy Sheree North, in her film debut, doing what was billed as "the first rock 'n' roll dance on the screen."▶

Living Out Loud (1998) **C-100m.** **½ D: Richard LaGravenese. Holly Hunter, Danny DeVito, Queen Latifah, Martin Donovan, Richard Schiff, Elias Koteas, Suzanne Shepherd, Rachael Leigh Cook. Deeply felt comedy-drama about loneliness, focusing on a woman who can't get over the breakup of her marriage and an elevator operator in her Manhattan building who falls in love with her. Because there's no strong storyline it bobs and weaves a bit, but there are many fine vignettes and moments of truth . . . and a dynamite opening, with Latifah singing a beautiful rendition of "Lush Life." Inspired in part by two Chekhov short stories. Directing debut for top screenwriter LaGravenese. Panavision. [R]▼●)

Livin' Large (1991) **C-96m.** ** D: Michael Schultz. Terrence "T.C." Carson, Lisa Arrindell, Blanche Baker, Nathaniel "Afrika" Hall, Julia Campbell, Bernie McInerney, Loretta Devine. Young streetwise black desperately wants to be a TV newsman—and gets his chance by sheer fluke; then he learns that staying on top in the TV game means selling his soul. Farcical comedy has moments, but grows increasingly shallow, predictable; only energetic, likable cast keeps it alive. [R]▼●)

Lizzie (1957) **81m.** **½ D: Hugo Haas. Eleanor Parker, Richard Boone, Joan Blondell, Hugo Haas, Ric Roman, Marion Ross, Johnny Mathis. Interesting, if ultimately pedantic, adaptation of Shirley Jackson's *The Bird's Nest*, with Parker as a mousy woman who turns out to have three distinct personalities. Boone is a psychiatrist trying to help her. A project of rare distinction for cultish director Haas, though he injects his familiar personality by playing a kibitzing neighbor. Parker is excellent. Eclipsed by release of similar (and superior) THE THREE FACES OF EVE soon after.

Lizzie McGuire Movie, The (2003) **C-90m.** **½ D: Jim Fall. Hilary Duff, Adam Lamberg, Hallie Todd, Robert Carradine, Jake Thomas, Ashlie Brillault, Clayton Snyder, Alex Borstein, Yani Gellman. A teenage girl travels to Rome with her classmates and meets a handsome Italian pop star who offers her romance and adventure—not to mention the chance of posing as his singing partner. Innocuous feature film based on the popular Disney Channel TV series for preadolescent girls. Punctuated by amusing animated vignettes designed by Debra Solomon—including a final nod to Tinker Bell. Super 35. [PG]▼▌

Lloyd's of London (1936) **115m.** ***½ D: Henry King. Freddie Bartholomew, Madeleine Carroll, Sir Guy Standing, Tyrone Power, C. Aubrey Smith, Virginia Field, George Sanders. Handsomely mounted fiction of rise of British insurance company; young messenger boy Bartholomew grows up to be Power, who competes with Sanders for affection of Carroll.▼

Loaded (1994-British-New Zealand) **C-105m.** **½ D: Anna Campion. Oliver Milburn, Nick Patrick, Catherine McCormack, Thandie Newton, Mathew Eggleton, Danny Cunningham, Biddy Hodson, Dearbhla Molloy. Seven young-adult friends spend a weekend in the British countryside to make an amateur horror movie. They are by turns aimless, repressed, rebellious, scared (etc.); before the weekend ends, recklessness and tragedy permanently alter their relationships. Slow-moving but worthwhile film. Feature directing debut for Anna Campion, sister of director Jane. [R]▼●)

Local Color (2006) **C-107m.** *** D: George Gallo. Armin Mueller-Stahl, Trevor Morgan, Ray Liotta, Diana Scarwid, Samantha Mathis, Ron Perlman, Julie Lott, Charles Durning. Teenaged boy with a passion to paint attaches himself to a Russian émigré who's a great artist—and a foul-mouthed iconoclast. Over the course of a season at the painter's rural summer home the boy soaks up life lessons that will inform his art. Mueller-Stahl is wonderful, and the youthful Morgan keeps up with him at every turn. Deeply felt autobiographical drama by Gallo. Digital Widescreen.▌

Local Hero (1983-British) **C-111m.** ***½ D: Bill Forsyth. Peter Riegert, Burt Lancaster, Fulton MacKay, Denis Lawson, Norman Chancer, Peter Capaldi, Jenny Seagrove. Enchantingly off-kilter comedy about an oil company rep (Riegert) who's assigned to buy up a Scottish coastal village which is badly needed for a refinery site. Nothing normal or predictable happens from that point on; writer-director Forsyth is more interested in quirkiness than belly-laugh gags, and his film is overflowing with ingenious characters and incidents. A little gem. [PG]▼●)

Local Stigmatic, The (1990) **C-54m.** **½ D: David Wheeler. Al Pacino, Paul Guilfoyle, Joe (Joseph) Maher, Michael Higgins, Brian Mallon. Lots of chatter in this mostly two-character exploration of envy and evil, centering on a pair of disaffected British hooligans (Pacino, Guilfoyle) who converse, go to a movie, drink in a pub—and commit a senseless act of violence. Not terribly cinematic—which was Pacino's intention—but a must for Pacino completists, as he offers a bravura performance. Based on a one-act play by Heathcote Williams (in which Pacino starred onstage in 1969). Never released theatrically.▌

Loch Ness (1996-British) **C-101m.** **½ D: John Henderson. Ted Danson, Joely Richardson, Ian Holm, Harris Yulin, James Frain, Kirsty Graham, Keith Allen, Nick Brimble. Lighthearted adventure-fantasy with jaded scientist Danson going to Scotland to prove Loch Ness monster is a hoax, only to discover some real magic and fall in love with single mom Richardson. Innocuous, but amiable, family fare. U.S. debut on network TV. Filmed in 1994. Panavision. [PG]▼●)

Lock, Stock and Two Smoking Barrels (1998-U.S.-British) **C-106m.** **½ D: Guy Ritchie. Jason Flemyng, Dexter Fletcher, Nick Moran, Jason Statham, Steven Mackintosh, Vinnie Jones, Sting, Lenny McLean, P. H. Moriarty. PULP FICTION, British style: a young smart aleck tries to beat a professional gambling ring and sinks in over his head, while others peripheral to this action are drawn into a vortex of coincidence, misunderstanding, and violence. Outlandish, audacious, and funny, though it wears thin after a while, and its ultimate resolution is apparent a bit too soon. Followed by SNATCH. [R]▼●)

Lock Up (1989) **C-106m.** *½ D: John Flynn. Sylvester Stallone, Donald Sutherland, Darlanne Fluegel, John Amos, Sonny Landham, Tom Sizemore, Frank McRae. With six months to go on his sentence, convict Stallone gets abducted from his country-club cell and transported to a hellhole run by old Hun-like adversary Sutherland. Missing are Linda Blair, John Vernon, a lesbian guard, and 15 gratuitous showers; you *do* get a body-shop montage backed by Ides of March's "Vehicle." Bottom of the world, ma. [R]▼●)

Lock Up Your Daughters! (1969-British) **C-102m.** BOMB D: Peter Coe. Christopher Plummer, Susannah York, Glynis Johns, Ian Bannen, Tom Bell, Elaine Taylor. Film version of Henry Fielding play tries to be another TOM JONES, but tale of mistaken identities in 18th-century England couldn't be more forced. [R]

Locusts, The (1997) **C-124m.** *½ D: John Patrick Kelley. Ashley Judd, Kate Capshaw, Paul Rudd, Jeremy Davies, Vince Vaughn, Jessica Capshaw. A hunk of a drifter comes to town and is hired by oversexed ranch queen Kate Capshaw to work for her, both day *and* night; along the way, he develops a friendship with her highly disturbed son. Brooding drama of cruel family secrets gives viewers a reprieve whenever local-girl-with-a-heart-of-gold Judd is on-screen. Set in 1950s Kansas. Super 35. [R]▼●)

Lodger, The (1926-British) **75m.** *** D: Alfred Hitchcock. Ivor Novello, Malcolm Keen, June, Marie Ault, Arthur Chesney. The director's first suspense thriller, with a classic Hitchcockian theme: lodger Novello is accused by jealous detective Keen of being a killer. Memorable finale: Novello chased by bloodthirsty mob. Remade in 1932 (again with Novello), 1944, and in 1953 as MAN IN THE ATTIC. Look for Hitchcock's first cameo. Full title on-screen is THE LODGER A STORY OF THE LONDON FOG. ▼)

Lodger, The (1944) **84m.** *** D: John Brahm. Merle Oberon, George Sanders, Laird Cregar, Sir Cedric Hardwicke, Sara Allgood, Aubrey Mather, Queenie Leonard, Doris Lloyd, Billy Bevan. That new lodger at a turn-of-the-20th-century London boarding house may be Jack the Ripper. Good, atmospheric chiller with fine performances. Remade as MAN IN THE ATTIC (1953). Again remade as THE LODGER (2008), reset in Los Angeles.❯

Logan's Run (1976) **C-120m.** ** D: Michael Anderson. Michael York, Jenny Agutter, Richard Jordan, Peter Ustinov, Farrah Fawcett-Majors, Roscoe Lee Browne. Dazzling first half, showing life of unending pleasure and extinction at age 30 in the year 2274, canceled out by dreary second half. Earned a special Oscar for visual effects. From novel by William F. Nolan and George Clayton Johnson. Later a brief TV series. Todd-AO 35. [PG]▼●)

Loggerheads (2005) **C-96m.** *** D: Tim Kirkman. Bonnie Hunt, Kip Pardue, Tess Harper, Chris Sarandon, Michael Learned, Michael Kelly, Robin Weigert. Sincere, low-key drama of several lives that intersect in North Carolina during the 1990s: a drifter who knows he hasn't long to live strives to help endangered turtles on the Carolina shore . . . a woman who's haunted by thoughts of the child she gave up for adoption nearly 20 years earlier . . . and a preacher's wife who has regrets about having driven away her gay son. Everyone hits the right notes in this simply told drama, inspired by a real woman's encounter with adoption bureaucracy in her state. Kirkman also scripted. [PG-13]❯

Lola (1961-French) **90m.** *** D: Jacques Demy. Anouk Aimée, Marc Michel, Jacques Harden, Alan Scott, Elina Labourdette. Contemporary fable of love, with several disparate people's lives intertwining in port city of Nantes. Aimée is enchanting as cabaret dancer and carefree single mother; Michel is young man looking for life's meaning—and romance. Demy's first feature successfully links coincidence and Hollywood-movie fantasy with '60s realism and sexual frankness. References to Lola pop up in Demy's later films. Music score by Michel Legrand; film is dedicated to Max Ophuls. Franscope.▼)

Lola (1969-British-Italian) **C-88m.** ** D: Richard Donner. Charles Bronson, Susan George, Trevor Howard, Michael Craig, Honor Blackman, Lionel Jeffries, Robert Morley, Jack Hawkins, Orson Bean, Kay Medford, Paul Ford. Sixteen-year-old nymphet initiates relationship with 38-year-old porno book writer; hyperkinetic film misses target, despite good cast and likable performance by Bronson. Released in England as TWINKY, at 98m. Aka STATUTORY AFFAIR. [PG]▼)

Lola (1981-German) **C-114m.** ***½ D: Rainer Werner Fassbinder. Barbara Sukowa, Armin Mueller-Stahl, Mario Adorf, Mathias Fuchs, Helga Feddersen, Karin Baal, Ivan Desny. Brilliantly directed and edited chronicle of repercussions when cynical, calculating singer-whore Sukowa sets sights on respectable Mueller-Stahl, the new Building Commissioner and only honest politician in town. Striking, unusual use of lighting and color. One-third of Fassbinder's trilogy of life in postwar Germany (with THE MAR-

RIAGE OF MARIA BRAUN and VERON-
IKA VOSS). [R]▌

Lola Montes (1955-French) **C-115m.**
★★★ D: Max Ophuls. Martine Carol, Peter
Ustinov, Anton Walbrook, Oskar Werner,
Ivan Desny. Legendary film about beautiful
circus performer and her effect on various
men nonetheless suffers from Carol's lack
of magnetism in title role. Ophuls makes
superb use of widescreen and color; the
celebrated director's last film. Aka THE
SINS OF LOLA MONTES. CinemaScope.
▼●◗

Lolita (1962-British) **152m.** **★★★** D: Stanley
Kubrick. James Mason, Shelley Winters, Peter Sellers, Sue Lyon, Marianne Stone, Diana
Decker. Sexually precocious Lyon becomes
involved with stolid professor Mason, and bizarre Sellers provides peculiar romance leading to murder and lust. Screenplay for this
genuinely strange film is credited to Vladimir
Nabokov, who wrote the novel of the same
name, but bears little relation to his actual
script, later published. Winters is outstanding as Lyon's sex-starved mother. Reissued
in U.S. with 1m. of additional dialogue from
British version. Remade in 1997. ▼●◗

Lolita (1997-British-French) **C-137m.** **★★★½**
D: Adrian Lyne. Jeremy Irons, Melanie
Griffith, Dominique Swain, Frank Langella,
Suzanne Shepherd. Exceptional remake of
Vladimir Nabokov's notorious novel about
a man's overwhelming (and ultimately, self-
destructive) infatuation with a nymphet. In
this version we're told the source of his obsession, which is just one reason it stands up
against Kubrick's 1962 version and in some
ways surpasses it . .'. though Peter Sellers is
sorely missed. Irons is a perfect Humbert,
Swain ideal as his object of desire. Screenplay by Stephen Schiff. [R] ▼◗

Lolly Madonna XXX (1973) **C-103m.** **★★**
D: Richard C. Sarafian. Rod Steiger, Robert Ryan, Jeff Bridges, Scott Wilson, Season Hubley, Katherine Squire, Ed Lauter,
Gary Busey, Randy Quaid. Modern-day
Hatfield-McCoy feud erupts between two
backwoods families, prompted by mistaken
identity situation involving innocent girl
(Hubley). Histrionics galore, but no point
to it at all. Aka THE LOLLY-MADONNA
WAR. Panavision. [PG]

Lolly-Madonna War, The SEE: **Lolly
Madonna XXX**

London (2006) **C-92m.** BOMB D: Hunter
Richards. Chris Evans, Jessica Biel, Jason
Statham, Joy Bryant, Kelli Garner, Isla Fisher,
John Newton, Dane Cook, Leelee Sobieski.
Poorly written movie about coke-heads. Biel
plays a woman named London, the object of
Evans' affection who broke up with him; as
the film goes on it's easy to see why. Most of
the action occurs in the bathroom as Evans
and Statham do drugs, drink, and discuss God,
love, and all of life's Big Questions. Depressing and drawn out, with graphic sex and nu-

dity, but there are no revelations, resolutions,
or warm feelings here. Super 35. [R]▌

London Kills Me (1991-British) **C-107m.**
BOMB D: Hanif Kureishi. Justin Chadwick,
Steven Mackintosh, Fiona Shaw, Emer Mc-
Court, Brad Dourif, Roshan Seth, Tony
Haygarth, Stevan Rimkus, Eleanor David,
Alun Armstrong. Glossy, phony tale of a
homeless, rootless young man who steals
and deals drugs, and decides he wants to go
straight. This shallow cop-out of a movie does
little more than serve as a recruiting poster for
thieving and shooting heroin. Directorial de-
but of playwright-screenwriter Kureishi (MY
BEAUTIFUL LAUNDRETTE, SAMMY
AND ROSIE GET LAID). [R]▼

**Loneliness of the Long Distance Runner,
The** (1962-British) **103m.** **★★★★** D: Tony
Richardson. Michael Redgrave, Tom Courtenay, Avis Bunnage, Peter Madden, Alec
McCowen, James Fox, Julia Foster, John
Thaw. Engrossing story of rebellious young
man chosen to represent reform school in
track race. Superbly acted film confronts
society, its mores and institutions. Screenplay by Alan Sillitoe, from his own story.
Key British film of 1960s. ▼●◗

Lonely Are the Brave (1962) **107m.** **★★★**
D: David Miller. Kirk Douglas, Gena Rowlands, Walter Matthau, Michael Kane, Carroll O'Connor, William Schallert, George
Kennedy, Bill Bixby. Penetrating study of rebellious cowboy Douglas escaping from jail,
pursued by posse utilizing modern means of
communications and transportation. Script by
Dalton Trumbo, from Edward Abbey's novel,
Brave Cowboy. Panavision. ▼◗

Lonely Guy, The (1984) **C-90m.** **★★½** D:
Arthur Hiller. Steve Martin, Charles Grodin, Judith Ivey, Robyn Douglass, Steve
Lawrence, Merv Griffin, Dr. Joyce Brothers. Unusually subdued and offbeat vehicle
for Martin, who's quite likable as a nerd-ish
type who's just been thrown out by his girlfriend . . . only to find he's not alone. Grodin
is a delight as a melancholy soulmate who
inducts him into the society of Lonely Guys
in N.Y.C. Too prolonged and uneven. Based
on Bruce Jay Friedman's book *The Lonely
Guy's Book of Life*. Adapted by Neil Simon,
scripted by Ed. Weinberger and Stan Daniels. [R] ▼●◗

Lonelyhearts (1958) **101m.** **★★½** D: Vincent
J. Donehue. Montgomery Clift, Robert
Ryan, Myrna Loy, Dolores Hart, Maureen
Stapleton, Frank Maxwell, Jackie Coogan,
Mike Kellin. Superior cast in interesting
adaptation of Nathanael West's book and
Howard Teichmann's play, both titled *Miss
Lonelyhearts*. Clift is would-be reporter
assigned to title column and becomes too
deeply involved in the problems of his
readers. A bit dated by today's standards,
but watchable; scripted and produced by
Dore Schary. West's book had previously
been filmed as ADVICE TO THE LOVE-

LORN. Film debuts of Stapleton and director Donehue.▼

Lonely Hearts (1981-Australian) **C-95m.** *** D: Paul Cox. Wendy Hughes, Norman Kaye, Jon Finlayson, Julia Blake, Jonathan Hardy. Delightfully quirky romantic comedy about an unlikely match—a middle-aged piano tuner with a flair for theatrics and a painfully shy office worker. Lovely performances match director Cox's offbeat screenplay. [R]▼●]

Lonely Hearts (2007-U.S.-German) **C-107m.** ** D: Todd Robinson. John Travolta, Salma Hayek, James Gandolfini, Jared Leto, Scott Caan, Laura Dern, Alice Krige, Dagmara Dominczyk, Michael Rispoli, Ellen Travolta. Real-life story of Ray Fernandez (Leto), who conned women who advertised in "lonely hearts" newspaper ads, and how his twisted relationship with Martha Beck (Hayek) led to a series of grisly murders in the 1940s. Travolta plays Nassau County detective Elmer Robinson (grandfather of this film's writer-director), who became obsessed with capturing these heartless killers. Uninspired treatment of acutely unpleasant material, dramatized before in THE HONEYMOON KILLERS and DEEP CRIMSON. Super 35. [R]▌

Lonely Lady, The (1983) **C-92m.** BOMB D: Peter Sasdy. Pia Zadora, Lloyd Bochner, Bibi Besch, Joseph Cali, Anthony Holland, Jared Martin, Ray Liotta, Kenneth Nelson. Terrible movie about an aspiring screenwriter who's used and abused while on her way to the Top in Hollywood; adapted from the Harold Robbins novel. Pia does her best, but this is rock-bottom stuff, not even fun on a trash level (although there's campy dialogue to spare). Filmed mostly in Italy. [R]▼●

Lonely Passion of Judith Hearne, The (1987-British) **C-116m.** **½ D: Jack Clayton. Maggie Smith, Bob Hoskins, Wendy Hiller, Marie Kean, Ian McNeice, Alan Devlin, Rudi Davies, Prunella Scales. Smith gives a knockout performance as a lonely, driven Irish woman whose life takes another turn for the worse after moving into a boardinghouse run by snippy Kean. Hoskins is equally fine as a garrulous gentleman with whom she sparks a relationship based on mutual misunderstanding. All the performances are superb in this adaptation of Brian Moore's 1955 novel about a woman's blind faith in the church—and total lack of faith in herself . . . but the story has a few too many peaks and valleys. [R]▼▌

Lone Ranger, The (1956) **C-86m.** **½ D: Stuart Heisler. Clayton Moore, Jay Silverheels, Lyle Bettger, Bonita Granville, Perry Lopez, Robert J. Wilke. Action-packed feature version of the popular TV series, focusing on the Masked Man and Tonto as they tangle with scheming rancher Bettger, who has been stirring up trouble with the Indians.▼▌

Lone Ranger and the Lost City of Gold, The (1958) **C-80m.** ** D: Lesley Selander. Clayton Moore, Jay Silverheels, Douglas Kennedy, Charles Watts. Typical Lone Ranger Western is fine for younger audiences, involving hooded killers and mysterious clues to a hidden treasure city.▼▌

Loners, The (1972) **C-79m.** ** D: Sutton Roley. Dean Stockwell, Todd Susman, Scott Brady, Gloria Grahame, Pat Stich, Alex Dreier, Tim Rooney. Standard bike movie with several screen veterans and a plot involving three drop-out cyclists who turn their backs on society and take it on the lam across the Southwest. [R]▼

Lonesome Jim (2006) **C-91m.** *** D: Steve Buscemi. Casey Affleck, Liv Tyler, Mary Kay Place, Seymour Cassel, Kevin Corrigan, Jack Rovello, Mark Boone Junior. A young man of vague ambition who's failed in N.Y.C. has nowhere to go but home to Indiana, where he is less than thrilled to be with his parents again. Suffering from "chronic despair," he doesn't know how to deal with a nice, non-neurotic woman he meets. So low-key it makes a Jim Jarmusch film seem like PEARL HARBOR, but grows on you, especially if you share its sly, specific (and dark) sense of humor. Affleck is terrific. Written by novelist James C. Strouse. [R]▌

Lone Star (1952) **94m.** **½ D: Vincent Sherman. Clark Gable, Ava Gardner, Broderick Crawford, Lionel Barrymore, Beulah Bondi, Ed Begley, James Burke, William Farnum, Moroni Olsen, William Conrad. Glossy MGM western about conflict over Texas joining the Union. Sam Houston (Olsen) wins wealthy, powerful Gable to his cause, which pits him against state senator Crawford (and his crusading newspaper-editor girlfriend Gardner). Also shown in computer-colored version. ▼

Lone Star (1996) **C-134m.** *** D: John Sayles. Kris Kristofferson, Chris Cooper, Elizabeth Peña, Joe Morton, Ron Canada, Miriam Colon, Clifton James, Matthew McConaughey, Stephen J. Lang, Tony Plana, Frances McDormand, LaTanya Richardson, Chandra Wilson. Absorbing multi-character story set in small Texas border town, where the memory of a former sheriff looms large—especially to his son, who's the current lawman. Keenly observed character studies are woven together by writer-director Sayles with his usual eye for detail and ear for good dialogue. Super 35. [R]▼●▌

The Lone Wolf series SEE: *Leonard Maltin's Classic Movie Guide*

Lone Wolf & Cub: Sword of Vengeance (1972-Japanese) **C-83m.** *** D: Kenji Misumi. Tomisaburo Wakayama, Yunosuke Itoo, Fumio Watanabe, Shigeru Tsuyuguchi, Tomoko Mayama, Tomoo Uchida. In 17th-century Japan, Itto Ogami (Wakayama), the Shogun's executioner, is framed by the Yagyu clan, who also murder his wife. Embittered, he becomes a traveling assassin for hire, wheeling his young son Daigoro around Japan in a baby cart loaded with more gadgets than James Bond's Aston-Martin. First in the outstanding series is largely a setup for the sequels; beautifully stylized, gorily violent, and intelligent. Based on a long-running *manga* series written by Kazuo Koike, illustrated by Goseki Kojima. LIGHTNING SWORDS OF DEATH and SHOGUN ASSASSIN were composed of segments from this and/or the sequels. Tohoscope.▼●)

Lone Wolf and Cub 2: Baby Cart at the River Styx (1972-Japanese) **C-81m.** ***½ D: Kenji Misumi. Tomisaburo Wakayama, Kayo Matsuo, Minoru Ooki, Shooji Kobayashi, Shin Kishida, Akihiro Tomikawa. Ogami is hired to kill a defecting worker who knows the secret of a dye process, the basis of the prosperity of a province. Best in the series, with amazing fights (Ogami is attacked with a *radish* at one point), photography, period atmosphere, and a sense of humor about itself. As with all in the series, very violent and bloody. Tohoscope.▼●)

Lone Wolf & Cub 3: Baby Cart to Hades (1972-Japanese) **C-89m.** *** D: Kenji Misumi. Tomisaburo Wakayama, Goo Katoo, Yuuko Hama, Isao Yamagata, Michitaro Mizushima, Ichiroo Takatani. A man whose insane lord was betrayed hires Ogami to kill the betrayer, now an important official. First in the series to climax with Wakayama defeating a virtual army singlehanded. More conventional than usual, it's still an accomplished, stylish film. Tohoscope.▼●)

Lone Wolf & Cub 4: Baby Cart in Peril (1972-Japanese) **C-81m.** **½ D: Buiichi Saito. Tomisaburo Wakayama, Yooichi Hayashi, Michie Azuma, Akihiro Tomikawa, So Yamamura. Ogami is hired to kill a tattooed woman, an expert with a short sword, who's carving up those connected to the man who raped her. Meanwhile, more Yagyu assassins try to kill our stone-faced hero. Stylistically overblown, with flashbacks, narration, and voice-overs galore; slowly paced, but has a great climactic fight. Tohoscope.▼●)

Lone Wolf & Cub 5: Baby Cart in the Land of Demons (1973-Japanese) **C-89m.** *** D: Kenji Misumi. Tomisaburo Wakayama, Michiyo Yasuda, Akihiro Tomikawa, Shingo Yamashiro, Tomomi Satoo, Akira Yamauchi. One by one, five samurai face Ogami to test his skills before hiring him. As each one dies, he gives Ogami another part of his instructions: to kill their lord, his concubine, and their five-year-old daughter. Grimmest of the lot, but also graced with the finest photography in the series and a powerful incident centering on Ogami's young son. Tohoscope.▼●)

Lone Wolf & Cub 6: White Heaven in Hell (1974-Japanese) **C-83m** *** D: Yoshiyuki Kuroda. Tomisaburo Wakayama, Akihiro Tomikawa, Junko Hitomi, Goroo

Mutsumi, Minoru Ooki, Isao Kimura. Ogami is confronted by the last remaining son of his archenemy; this time, the supernatural plays a part, and for the first time the Lone Wolf is afraid—but not for long. Particularly resembles the comic books. Robust battle on a snowy mountain climaxes the series, one of the best, not just in Japanese cinema history, but *world* cinema. Tohoscope.▼●)

Lone Wolf McQuade (1983) **C-107m.** **½ D: Steve Carver. Chuck Norris, David Carradine, Barbara Carrera, Leon Isaac Kennedy, Robert Beltran, L.Q. Jones, R.G. Armstrong, Sharon Farrell. Maverick Texas Ranger Norris takes on gun-running operation headed by Carradine. Played as a spaghetti Western, providing perfect milieu for Norris' fighting skills. A little long, with a sappy emotional sub-plot. [PG]▼●)

Long Ago Tomorrow (1970-British) **C-100m.** ** D: Bryan Forbes. Malcolm McDowell, Nanette Newman, Georgia Brown, Bernard Lee, Gerald Sim, Michael Flanders. Rather wrong-headed drama of love between paraplegics. Could have been sensitive if script and direction weren't so porous and obvious. Original British title: THE RAGING MOON. [PG]▼

Long and the Short and the Tall, The (1961-British) **105m.** *** D: Leslie Norman. Richard Todd, Laurence Harvey, Richard Harris, David McCallum, Ronald Fraser. Well-delineated account of British patrol unit during WW2, focusing on their conflicting personalities and raids on Japanese. Retitled: JUNGLE FIGHTERS.

Long Arm, The SEE: **Third Key, The**

Long, Dark Night, The SEE: **Pack, The**

Long Day Closes, The (1992-British) **C-83m.** *** D: Terence Davies. Leigh McCormack, Marjorie Yates, Anthony Watson, Aysee Owens, Nicholas Lamont, Tina Malone. Poignant, painterly slice-of-life remembrance by writer-director Davies of working-class England in the 1950s. The depiction of family life is far rosier than in Davies' DISTANT VOICES, STILL LIVES, as a dreary postwar England yearns for an idealized beauty found in Hollywood movies and romantic pop songs. [PG]▼

Long Day's Dying, The (1968-British) **C-93m.** *½ D: Peter Collinson. David Hemmings, Tom Bell, Tony Beckley, Alan Dobie. Dull story of three British soldiers and their German captive during weary trek through European countryside. Techniscope. [R]

Long Day's Journey Into Night (1962) **174m.** ***½ D: Sidney Lumet. Katharine Hepburn, Ralph Richardson, Jason Robards, Jr., Dean Stockwell, Jeanne Barr. Faithful, stagy adaptation of Eugene O'Neill's detailed study of family in the 1910s. Hepburn is dope-addicted wife, Richardson her pompous actor husband, Stockwell the son dying of TB, and Robards the alcoholic son.

Later cut to 136m. Remade for TV in 1987 with Jack Lemmon. ▼●)

Long Duel, The (1967-British) **C-115m.** **½ D: Ken Annakin. Yul Brynner, Trevor Howard, Harry Andrews, Andrew Keir, Charlotte Rampling. Brynner leads peasant revolt against British raj in 1920s India; routine adventure saga. Look for Edward Fox. Panavision.

Longest Day, The (1962) **180m.** **** D: Ken Annakin, Andrew Marton, Bernhard Wicki. John Wayne, Rod Steiger, Robert Ryan, Peter Lawford, Henry Fonda, Robert Mitchum, Richard Burton, Richard Beymer, Jeffrey Hunter, Sal Mineo, Roddy McDowall, Eddie Albert, Curt Jurgens, Gert Frobe, Sean Connery, Robert Wagner, Red Buttons, Mel Ferrer, many others. One of the all-time great epic WW2 films. Brilliant retelling of the Allied invasion of Normandy, complete with all-star international cast, re-creation of historical events on a grand scale; Oscar-winning special effects and cinematography. Also shown in computer-colored version. CinemaScope. ▼●)

Longest Yard, The (1974) **C-123m.** ***½ D: Robert Aldrich. Burt Reynolds, Eddie Albert, Ed Lauter, Michael Conrad, Jim Hampton, Bernadette Peters, Charles Tyner, Mike Henry, Harry Caesar, Richard Kiel, Robert Tessier, Malcolm Atterbury. Convict Reynolds, a former football pro, quarterbacks a squad of dirty players against warden Albert's hand-picked team. An audience picture if there ever was one; hilarious bone-crunching comedy written by Tracy Keenan Wynn. Remade in 2001 as MEAN MACHINE (the original film's British title) and in 2005. [R] ▼●)

Longest Yard, The (2005) **C-107m.** **½ D: Peter Segal. Adam Sandler, Chris Rock, Burt Reynolds, William Fichtner, Nelly, Michael Irvin, James Cromwell, Nick Turturro, Terry Crews, Cloris Leachman, Courteney Cox, Tracy Morgan. By-the-numbers remake (the second, after MEAN MACHINE) with Sandler as the disgraced former pro quarterback who is sent up the river. There, he is coerced by the hard-nosed warden (Cromwell) into creating a football team out of fellow inmates. Blends comedy and violence as well as the 1974 film, but lacks its freshness and spark. Reynolds takes over the Michael Conrad role with a knowing wink. (Ed Lauter shows up, too.) Populated with many recognizable sports figures . . . and, yes, Rob Schneider. Panavision. [PG-13] ▼)

Long Goodbye, The (1973) **C-112m.** **½ D: Robert Altman. Elliott Gould, Nina Van Pallandt, Sterling Hayden, Henry Gibson, Mark Rydell, Jim Bouton, David Arkin, Warren Berlinger. Strange, almost spoofy updating of Raymond Chandler's novel, with Gould as a shabby Philip Marlowe involved with mysterious Van Pallandt, alcoholic Hayden, evil Gibson, missing pal

Bouton, and Jewish gangster Rydell. Some nice touches, especially John Williams' jokey score, but Altman's attitude toward the genre borders on contempt. Screenplay by Leigh Brackett, who had earlier coscripted THE BIG SLEEP. Look for Arnold Schwarzenegger as a muscleman, David Carradine as a prisoner. Panavision. [R] ▼●)

Long Good Friday, The (1980-British) **C-114m.** ***½ D: John Mackenzie. Bob Hoskins, Helen Mirren, Eddie Constantine, Dave King, Bryan Marshall, Derek Thompson, George Coulouris, Stephen Davies, Pierce Brosnan. Occasionally confusing but otherwise terrific portrait of hoodlum rivalry in contemporary London; takes its rightful place with the best gangster movies of all time. Hoskins, brilliant as underworld entrepreneur, is matched by Mirren as subtly sexy mistress. Original screenplay by Barrie Keeffe. [R] ▼●)

Long Gray Line, The (1955) **C-138m.** *** D: John Ford. Tyrone Power, Maureen O'Hara, Robert Francis, Ward Bond, Donald Crisp, Betsy Palmer, Phil Carey, Harry Carey, Jr. Lengthy sentimental melodrama of West Point athletic trainer Power and his many years at the Academy. O'Hara is radiant as his wife. CinemaScope. ▼)

Long, Hot Summer, The (1958) **C-117m.** *** D: Martin Ritt. Paul Newman, Joanne Woodward, Anthony Franciosa, Orson Welles, Lee Remick, Angela Lansbury. Well-blended William Faulkner short stories make a flavorful, brooding drama of domineering Southerner (Welles) and a wandering handyman (Newman), who decides to stick around and marry daughter Woodward. Excellent Alex North score, weak finish to strong film; the Newmans' first film together. Remade for TV with Don Johnson. CinemaScope. ▼●)

Long John Silver (1954-Australian) **C-109m.** **½ D: Byron Haskin. Robert Newton, Connie Gilchrist, Kit Taylor, Grant Taylor. Newton reprises title role from TREASURE ISLAND (with same director as the Disney film) and chews the scenery in this loose adaptation of Robert Louis Stevenson. Look for Rod Taylor in a small role. Aka RETURN TO TREASURE ISLAND. CinemaScope. ▼)

Long Kiss Goodnight, The (1996) **C-120m.** **½ D: Renny Harlin. Geena Davis, Samuel L. Jackson, Craig Bierko, Yvonne Zima, Tom Amandes, Brian Cox, Patrick Malahide, David Morse, Joseph McKenna, G. D. Spradlin, Alan North. If you find a kitchen sink, it's the one screenwriter Shane Black forgot to throw into this over-the-top action yarn, which starts out seriously, then changes tone. Davis plays an amnesiac with a young daughter, whose happy life is disrupted when she's forced to confront her past—as a professional undercover assassin! Jackson is a low-rent private eye who goes along for this roller-coaster ride, full of large-scale stunts and humor with Davis as a combination Pauline (as in PERILS OF . . .) and Rambo. No one seems to mind or care that a child is also part of the mayhem. Super 35. [R] ▼●◗

Long Live Your Death SEE: **Don't Turn the Other Cheek**

Long, Long Trailer, The (1954) **C-96m.** **½ D: Vincente Minnelli. Lucille Ball, Desi Arnaz, Marjorie Main, Keenan Wynn, Gladys Hurlbut. Lucy and Desi decide to spend their honeymoon visiting scenic spots in the West, traveling and living in the 50-foot house trailer of the title (a perfect "vehicle" for a CinemaScope movie). Though based on the popular novel by Clinton Twiss, this enduringly popular slapstick comedy is almost an *I Love Lucy* episode on wheels. CinemaScope. ▼●◗

Long Night, The (1947) **101m.** ** D: Anatole Litvak. Henry Fonda, Barbara Bel Geddes, Vincent Price, Ann Dvorak, Howard Freeman, Elisha Cook, Jr., Queenie Smith, Charles McGraw. Factory worker Fonda kills Price, then holes up in his boarding house (besieged by police) and relives in flashbacks, and flashbacks within flashbacks, the events leading up to his predicament. Plodding and sullen; a long night indeed. Remake of Jean Gabin film LE JOUR SE LEVE. ▼▶

Long Ride from Hell, A (1970-Italian) **C-94m.** *½ D: Alex Burks (Camillo Bazzoni). Steve Reeves, Wayde Preston, Dick Palmer, Silvana Venturelli, Lee Burton, Ted Carter. Title is another instance of truth-in-advertising; dreary Western co-authored by Reeves has to do with rancher who tries to clear himself of phony train-robbery charge. [R]◗

Long Ride Home, The SEE: **Time for Killing, A**

Long Riders, The (1980) **C-100m.** *** D: Walter Hill. David, Keith and Robert Carradine, Stacy and James Keach, Randy and Dennis Quaid, Nicholas and Christopher Guest, Pamela Reed, Savannah Smith, James Whitmore, Jr., Harry Carey, Jr. *All in the Family* The Carradines, Keaches, Quaids, and Guests portray, respectively, the Younger, James, Miller, and Ford brothers in this stylish but extremely bloody film. Typically meticulous direction by Hill, with David Carradine and Reed igniting sparks as Cole Younger and Belle Starr. Excellent score by Ry Cooder. [R] ▼●◗

Long Ships, The (1964-British-Yugoslavian) **C-125m.** ** D: Jack Cardiff. Richard Widmark, Sidney Poitier, Rosanna Schiaffino, Russ Tamblyn, Oscar Homolka, Colin Blakely. Fairly elaborate but comic-book–level costume adventure of Vikings battling Moors for fabled treasure. Good cast deserves better. Super Technirama 70. ▼▶

Long Shot, The (1976) SEE: **Target of an Assassin**

Longshot, The (1986) **C-89m.** BOMB D: Paul Bartel. Tim Conway, Jack Weston, Harvey Korman, Ted Wass, Jonathan Winters, Stella Stevens, Anne Meara, George DiCenzo. Four lower-middle-class losers borrow $5,000 from the local break-ya-fingas financier to finance a sure thing at the track. Pathetic comedy is full of toilet gags and can't even coast on the good will established by the cast in better days. Mike Nichols *(Mike Nichols!!!)* executive-produced. [PG-13] ▼▶

Longshots, The (2008) **C-94m.** ** D: Fred Durst. Ice Cube, Keke Palmer, Tasha Smith, Dash Mihok, Matt Craven, Glenn Plummer, Garrett Morris, Jill Marie Jones, Michael Colyar, Malcolm Goodwin. Routine "inspirational" drama based on true story of a young girl who becomes the only female on a Pop Warner football team. Urged on and later coached by her ne'er-do-well uncle, a former pro player now fallen on hard times, she quarterbacks a footloose, ragtag group right to the cusp of junior pigskin glory. As she proved in AKEELAH AND THE BEE, Palmer is endearing and irresistible, while Cube gets his best screen outing in a while . . . but neither of them can rescue this by-the-numbers family film swimming in sports-movie clichés. Super 35. [PG]◗

Longtime Companion (1990) **C-96m.** *** D: Norman René. Stephen Caffrey, Patrick Cassidy, Brian Cousins, Bruce Davison, John Dossett, Mark Lamos, Dermot Mulroney, Mary-Louise Parker, Michael Schoeffling, Campbell Scott, Robert Joy, Tony Shalhoub. Emotional pre-PHILADELPHIA examination of AIDS in the '80s, focusing on a closely knit group of gay men in N.Y.C. Film spans the entire decade, from first reports of a mystery illness to a time when the disease became a tragic part of everyday life. Craig Lucas' script is insightful, heartwrenching, and funny. Entire cast is excellent, especially Davison. A PBS *American Playhouse* presentation. [R] ▼●◗

Long Tomorrow, The SEE: **Cry For Me, Billy**

Long Voyage Home, The (1940) **105m.** ***½ D: John Ford. John Wayne, Thomas Mitchell, Ian Hunter, Ward Bond, Barry Fitzgerald, Wilfrid Lawson, Mildred Natwick, John Qualen, Arthur Shields, Joe Sawyer, J. M. Kerrigan. Evocative look at men who spend their lives at sea, adapted (by Dudley Nichols) from four short O'Neill plays. Richly textured drama with many beautiful vignettes; exquisitely photographed by Gregg Toland. ▼●◗

Long Walk Home, The (1990) **C-97m.** *** D: Richard Pearce. Sissy Spacek, Whoopi Goldberg, Dwight Schultz, Ving Rhames, Dylan Baker; narrated by Mary Steenburgen. Perceptive, extremely well-acted account of the life and changing times in the segregated American South of the mid-1950s. The focus is on the consciousness-raising of Spacek, a privileged pillar of

Southern womanhood; Goldberg is her hard-working housekeeper, who's struggling to help support her own family. Fine sense of period detail; most intriguing of all, John Cork's script mirrors the connection between feminism and the civil rights movement. [PG]▼●◗

Long Way Home, The (1997) **C-119m.** ***½ D: Mark Jonathan Harris. Narrated by Morgan Freeman. Exceptional, Oscar-winning documentary about the incredible story of Jews who—once freed from Nazi concentration camps—were forced to endure yet another ordeal. Unwelcome in their homelands, bereft of families, they were held in squalid detention camps or arrested for illegal immigration until the formation of the state of Israel in 1948. Well told through the use of archival footage, on-camera interviews, and the words of survivors and participants. ▼●◗

Look At Me (2004-French) **C-110m.** *** D: Agnès Jaoui. Marilou Berry, Jean-Pierre Bacri, Agnès Jaoui, Laurent Grévill, Virginie Desarnauts, Keine Bouhiza. Another smart, sophisticated comedy from Jaoui (THE TASTE OF OTHERS) about a group of people who have all the answers for improving each other's lives but not a clue of what to do about their own. Flawless ensemble includes real-life husband and wife Jaoui and Bacri, who also cowrote the screenplay, set in the world of literature and music, but shining an all-knowing light on the mystery (and fragility) of human nature. Super 35. [PG-13]◗

Look Back in Anger (1959-British) **99m.** ***½ D: Tony Richardson. Richard Burton, Claire Bloom, Edith Evans, Mary Ure, Gary Raymond, Glen Byam Shaw, Donald Pleasence. John Osborne's trend-setting angry-young-man play, with Burton rebelling against life and wife, realistically filmed and acted; dialogue bristles. Remade for British TV in 1989. ▼●◗

Look Both Ways (2005-Australian) **C-100m.** *** D: Sarah Watt. Justine Clarke, William McInnes, Anthony Hayes, Lisa Flanagan, Andrew S. Gilbert, Daniela Farinacci, Sacha Horler, Maggie Dence. A woman who sees disaster lurking around every corner and a photojournalist who's facing a genuine health crisis meet under unusual circumstances and feel a connection between them. Meanwhile, everyone around them is dealing with their mortality in one way or another. Fresh, likeable comedy-drama tackles the biggest subjects of all—life and death—using animation to illustrate the characters' deepest fears. Feature debut for animator Watt, who also scripted. Winner of multiple Australian Film Institute awards, including Best Film. [PG-13]◗

Look Down and Die SEE: **Steel** (1980)
Looker (1981) **C-94m.** BOMB D: Michael Crichton. Albert Finney, James Coburn,

Susan Dey, Leigh Taylor-Young, Dorian Harewood, Tim Rossovich, Darryl Hickman. Conglomerate head Coburn produces the computerized images of gorgeous models to hawk products and political candidates on TV—and also murders his subjects. As he is losing all his clients, Beverly Hills plastic surgeon Finney investigates. Intriguing premise is illogically and boringly handled; even Finney cannot save this turkey. Watch for Vanna White. Panavision. [PG]▼●◗

Look for the Silver Lining (1949) **C-100m.** **½ D: David Butler. June Haver, Ray Bolger, Gordon MacRae, Charles Ruggles, Rosemary DeCamp. Superficial biography of Marilyn Miller's career in show business, with vintage vaudeville numbers bolstering trivial plot line.▼◗

Looking for Comedy in the Muslim World (2006) **C-96m.** **½ D: Albert Brooks. Albert Brooks, Sheetal Sheth, John Carroll Lynch, Jon Tenney, Amy Ryan, Homie Doroodian, Fred Dalton Thompson, Penny Marshall. Brooks (playing his usual on-screen self) is asked by the U.S. government to bridge a vital cultural gap in the post-9/11 world by traveling to India and Pakistan to learn what makes Muslim people laugh. What might have been brilliant as a short is a bit mild at feature length but still has many funny and inspired moments as Brooks targets show-business egotists, government drones . . . and himself. Super 35. [PG-13]◗

Looking for Eric (2009-British-French-Italian-Belgian-Spanish) **C-117m.** *** D: Ken Loach. Steve Evets, Eric Cantona, Stephanie Bishop, Gerard Kearns, Stefan Gumbs, Lucy-Jo Hudson, John Henshaw, Justin Moorhouse. Depressed postal worker, traumatized by a car crash, seeks spiritual healing from an unlikely source: U.K. football league Manchester United's #7, the French center forward Cantona, known for his pithy philosophizing as well as his fine kicking. Through a series of spliff-fueled fantasy therapy sessions, the bloke learns to reconnect with his ex-wife, his stepsons, his best mates, and himself. Likable, and lighter than most Loach movie fodder, but not without his usual bleak stamp.◗

Looking for Mr. Goodbar (1977) **C-135m.** *½ D: Richard Brooks. Diane Keaton, Richard Gere, William Atherton, Tuesday Weld, Richard Kiley, LeVar Burton, Tom Berenger, Brian Dennehy. Sordid rewrite (by director Brooks) of Judith Rossner's novel begins as intelligent study of repressed young girl, then wallows endlessly in her new "liberated" lifestyle. Keaton's performance outclasses this pointless movie. Story recycled in the TVM TRACKDOWN: FINDING THE GOODBAR KILLER. [R]▼●

Looking for Richard (1996) **C-109m.** ***½ D: Al Pacino. Al Pacino, Frederic Kimball, Harris Yulin, Penelope Allen, Alec

Baldwin, Kevin Spacey, Estelle Parsons, Winona Ryder, Aidan Quinn. Fascinating documentary-style film about Pacino's staging of *Richard III* and his simultaneous exploration of the relevance of Shakespeare to people in every walk of life. Every scene is dissected—by actors and scholars—before we see it performed, bringing this play to vivid life, especially for those of us who aren't already Shakespeare buffs. A treat from start to finish. Among the interviewees: Kenneth Branagh, Kévin Kline, James Earl Jones, Rosemary Harris, Peter Brook, Derek Jacobi, Vanessa Redgrave, and John Gielgud. [PG-13] ▼●▮

Looking Glass War, The (1969-British) C-108m. *½ D: Frank R. Pierson. Christopher Jones, Pia Degermark, Ralph Richardson, Anthony Hopkins, Paul Rogers, Susan George, Anna Massey, Ray McAnally, Vivien Pickles. Dull film version of John le Carré's best-seller has Jones risking his life to photograph a rocket in East Berlin. Good opportunity to study the leads' bone structure, since they never change facial expressions. Panavision. [M/PG] ▼▮

Lookin' to Get Out (1982) C-104m. BOMB D: Hal Ashby. Jon Voight, Burt Young, Ann-Margret, Bert Remsen, Jude Farese, Allen Keller, Richard Bradford, Angelina Jolie. Implausible, often embarrassing comedy about two losers who talk their way into a suite at the MGM Grand in Las Vegas with a plan to win big at blackjack. Remsen's performance as a wily old card shark is the only bright spot in this utter catastrophe. Voight coscripted, coproduced, and seems to be trying out his Al Pacino impression. In 2009 an alternate version of the film surfaced, edited by Ashby before his untimely death; it runs 120m. and is a definite improvement. Incidentally, the little girl at the end is Voight's four-year-old daughter, Angelina Jolie. [R] ▼▮

Lookout, The (2007) C-102m. ***½ D: Scott Frank. Joseph Gordon-Levitt, Jeff Daniels, Matthew Goode, Isla Fisher, Carla Gugino, Bruce McGill, Alberta Watson, Alex Borstein, Sergio Di Zio, David Huband. Onetime Midwest high school prince (Gordon-Levitt) now struggles through every day since surviving a devastating car accident. He shares an apartment with a sardonic blind man (Daniels) and holds down a simple job as night janitor at the local bank. This makes him a prime target for crafty Goode, who's planning a bank heist and needs an inside man to help. Crackerjack thriller is also a superb (if dark) character study. Every person on-screen is well drawn, no matter how small the part; Gordon-Levitt is terrific as usual. Directing debut for screenwriter Frank. HD Widescreen. [R]▮

Looks and Smiles (1981-British) **104m.** *** D: Kenneth Loach. Graham Green, Carolyn Nicholson, Tony Pitts, Phil Askham,

Cilla Mason. Working-class teenager Green cannot find a job or place for himself in society. Solid, realistic story of alienation, frustration, anger.▮

Look Who's Talking (1989) **C-90m.** *** D: Amy Heckerling. John Travolta, Kirstie Alley, Olympia Dukakis, George Segal, Abe Vigoda; voice of Bruce Willis. Amiable comedy about an unmarried woman who has a baby (by her no-good married boyfriend) and then sets out to find a suitable "daddy" for him. Good showcase for costars Alley and Travolta. Written by director Heckerling. One quibble: though set in N.Y.C., it's all too obvious that it was shot somewhere else (Vancouver, to be precise). Followed by two sequels and the TV series *Baby Talk.* [PG-13]▼●▮

Look Who's Talking Now (1993) **C-92m.** ** D: Tom Ropelewski. John Travolta, Kirstie Alley, George Segal, Olympia Dukakis, David Gallagher, Tabitha Lupien, Lysette Anthony; voices of Danny DeVito, Diane Keaton. Third entry in the series isn't bad, thanks to some cute dogplay and the delightful voice-over work by DeVito and Keaton, as a kind of live-action LADY AND THE TRAMP, who wreak havoc on the lives of the Umbriacco family. Passable family entertainment. [PG-13]▼●▮

Look Who's Talking Too (1990) **C-81m.** BOMB D: Amy Heckerling. John Travolta, Kirstie Alley, Olympia Dukakis, Elias Koteas, Twink Caplan, Gilbert Gottfried, Lorne Sussman; voices of Bruce Willis, Roseanne Barr, Damon Wayans, Mel Brooks. Militantly offensive sequel adds a baby girl to the formula—with the voice of Barr. It took a million bad poo-poo jokes and a gratuitous Travolta dance number to pad the running time. Climactic apartment fire may traumatize young children. [PG-13]▼●▮

Looney, Looney, Looney Bugs Bunny Movie, The (1981) **C-80m.** **½ D: Friz Freleng. Voice of Mel Blanc. Feature-length compilation of classic Warner Bros. cartoons is divided into three parts. In the first, Yosemite Sam must return Bugs Bunny to the Devil in order to save his own soul. Second part has Bugs rescuing Tweety from gangsters Rocky and Muggsy. Third and best segment is a parody of Hollywood award shows featuring Freleng's wonderful 1957 cartoon THE THREE LITTLE BOPS. Also includes Bugs Bunny's Oscar-winning KNIGHTY KNIGHT BUGS (1958). Official billing is FRIZ FRELENG'S LOONEY, LOONEY, LOONEY BUGS BUNNY MOVIE. [G] ▼▮

Looney Tunes: Back in Action (2003) **C-91m.** **½ D: Joe Dante. Brendan Fraser, Jenna Elfman, Steve Martin, Timothy Dalton, Joan Cusack, Heather Locklear, Mary Woronov, Robert Picardo, Marc Lawrence; voices of Joe Alaskey, Billy West, Jeff Glenn Bennett, Bob Bergen. Humorless Warner Bros. V.P. of Comedy Elfman is forced to join forces with ex-studio guard Fraser to bring the recently fired Daffy Duck back to the studio, unaware that he's fallen prey to the machinations of the Acme Company's evil chairman (Martin). Bugs Bunny, Daffy, and friends are just as funny as ever, but the live-action story line is strained at best. Even obscure WB cartoon characters make brief but welcome appearances. As always, Dante fills his movie with in-jokes for buffs (watch carefully!) and cameos. Super 35. [PG] ▼▶

Loophole (1980-British) **C-105m.** **½ D: John Quested. Albert Finney, Martin Sheen, Susannah York, Colin Blakely, Jonathan Pryce, Robert Morley, Alfred Lynch, Christopher Guard. Slick but very ordinary caper film about an unemployed architect who's persuaded to participate in an ambitious break-in of "impenetrable" London bank. Aka BREAK IN. ▼▶

Loose Cannons (1990) **C-94m.** *½ D: Bob Clark. Gene Hackman, Dan Aykroyd, Dom DeLuise, Ronny Cox, Nancy Travis, Robert Prosky, Paul Koslo, Dick O'Neill, Jan Triska, David Alan Grier. Below-rock-bottom car-chase excuse about two D.C. cops caught between ex-Nazis and Israeli adversaries scuffling over a mysterious Hitler home movie. Unfunny and offensive, film stagnated on the shelf while the studio figured out what to do with it. Career nadir for most of its participants. Panavision. [R] ▼●▶

Loose Shoes (1980) **C-74m.** **½ D: Ira Miller. Bill Murray, Howard Hesseman, David Landsburg, Ed Lauter, Susan Tyrrell, Avery Schreiber, Misty Rowe, Jaye P. Morgan, Buddy Hackett, Murphy Dunne. Very mixed bag of spoofs of coming-attractions previews, some hilarious, some duds. Highlights: "Skateboarders From Hell," "The Yid and the Kid" (Chaplin), "The Sneaker" (Woody Allen), "Welcome to Bacon County," "Jewish Star Wars," and unbearably funny "Darktown After Dark." Dunne also composed score and songs. Filmed mostly in 1977. Originally titled COMING ATTRACTIONS. Aka QUACKERS. [R] ▼▶

Loot (1970-British) **C-101m.** **½ D: Silvio Narizzano. Lee Remick, Richard Attenborough, Roy Holder, Hywel Bennett, Milo O'Shea, Dick Emery, Joe Lynch. Frantic black comedy from Joe Orton's stage hit. Holder and Bennett knock over a bank, hide the swag in the coffin of the former's mother, and then have a spot of trouble retrieving it. Despite Mod trappings, basically an old-fashioned, door-slamming farce; funny for those in the mood. [PG—originally rated R] ▼

Lord Jim (1965) **C-154m.** **½ D: Richard Brooks. Peter O'Toole, James Mason, Curt Jurgens, Eli Wallach, Jack Hawkins, Paul Lukas, Daliah Lavi, Akim Tamiroff. Overlong, uneven adaptation of Joseph Conrad's story about idealistic young man in British Merchant Marine in the 19th century dis-

credited as a coward who lives with scar for the rest of his life. Film's great moments provided by outstanding supporting cast. Super Panavision 70. ▼▶

Lord Love a Duck (1966) **105m.** *** D: George Axelrod. Tuesday Weld, Roddy McDowall, Lola Albright, Martin West, Ruth Gordon, Harvey Korman, Martin Gabel, Sarah Marshall, Lynn Carey. Madcap black comedy about progressive Southern California high school where botany is called "plant skills." Film wavers uncomfortably between comedy and drama at times, but really delivers some belly laughs. Terrific performances in movie that was ahead of its time. Directorial debut of co-writer Axelrod. ▼▶

Lord of Illusions (1995) **C-108m.** **½ D: Clive Barker. Scott Bakula, Kevin J. O'Connor, Famke Janssen, Vincent Schiavelli, Barry Del Sherman, Sheila Tousey, Joel Swetow, Joseph Latimore, Susan Traylor, Daniel Von Bargen, Barry Shabaka Henley. Private eye Bakula, a specialist in the supernatural, is in L.A. on a "normal" case when a stage magician is apparently killed during a performance. This is linked to the pending resurrection of an evil sorcerer, and soon Bakula is battling the forces of darkness again. Intelligent thriller, written by the director, is better than the usual genre fodder, but it's thinly plotted, and condescends slightly to its audience. Unrated version runs 122m. [R] ▼●▶

Lord of the Flies (1963-British) **90m.** *** D: Peter Brook. James Aubrey, Tom Chapin, Hugh Edwards, Roger Elwin, Tom Gaman. Unique story of a group of British schoolboys stranded on remote island. Their gradual degeneration into a savage horde is compelling. Adapted from William Golding's novel. Remade in 1990. ▼●▶

Lord of the Flies (1990) **C-90m.** **½ D: Harry Hook. Balthazar Getty, Chris Furrh, Danuel Pipoly, Badgett Dale, Edward and Andrew Taft. Color update of the novel-to-film turns William Golding's savage schoolboys into TV-savvy American kids; it may make the story more immediate (though even that's arguable), but it also purges the original of its poetry. Visceral, and improves as it progresses, but inferior to Peter Brook's 1963 version whose amateur actors, by and large, were superior to this brood. [R] ▼●▶

Lord of the Rings, The (1978) **C-133m.** **½ D: Ralph Bakshi. Voices of Christopher Guard, William Squire, John Hurt, Michael Sholes, Dominic Guard. Ambitious animated version of J.R.R. Tolkien's fantasy saga covers 1½ books of his trilogy (ending rather abruptly). Story of different races in Middle-earth competing for ownership of all-powerful Rings is inspired and exciting, but begins to drag—and confuse—during last hour. Bakshi's technique awkwardly combines animation and live-action tracings. Remade in 2001. [PG]▼▶

Lord of the Rings: The Fellowship of the Ring, The (2001) **C-178m. *** D:** Peter Jackson. Elijah Wood, Ian McKellen, Liv Tyler, Viggo Mortensen, Sean Astin, Cate Blanchett, John Rhys-Davies, Billy Boyd, Dominic Monaghan, Orlando Bloom, Christopher Lee, Hugo Weaving, Sean Bean, Ian Holm. Sprawling, epic adaptation of the first part of J.R.R. Tolkien's trilogy about Frodo Baggins, the Hobbit chosen to destroy a powerful ring that threatens Middle-earth. Moves in fits and starts, but intelligent and beautifully executed by director/cowriter Jackson, with phenomenal production values and a fine cast, led by McKellen, perfect as the wizard Gandalf. Won Oscars for Makeup, Visual Effects, Cinematography (Andrew Lesnie), and Original Score (Howard Shore). Extended video version runs 208m. Followed by THE LORD OF THE RINGS: THE TWO TOWERS. Super 35. [PG-13] ▼▶

Lord of the Rings: The Return of the King, The (2003) **C-200m. ***½ D:** Peter Jackson. Elijah Wood, Ian McKellen, Liv Tyler, Viggo Mortensen, Sean Astin, Cate Blanchett, John Rhys-Davies, Bernard Hill, Billy Boyd, Dominic Monaghan, Orlando Bloom, Hugo Weaving, Miranda Otto, David Wenham, Karl Urban, John Noble, Andy Serkis, Ian Holm, Sean Bean. Final film in the J.R.R. Tolkien trilogy ends on a high note as Frodo approaches his destiny at Mount Doom and the forces of good prepare for final battle against the evil minions of Sauron. Long, to be sure, with a few too many endings, but still a staggering achievement—alone and in concert with the previous two films. Cast, production, and direction are splendid and the astounding visual effects are always at the service of a story that scales heroic and very human heights. Winner of 11 Oscars: Best Picture, Director, Adapted Screenplay (by Jackson, Fran Walsh, and Philippa Boyens), Costumes (Ngila Dickson, Richard Taylor), Art Direction (Grant Major, Dan Hennah, Alan Lee), Score (Howard Shore), Song ("Into the West"), Sound Mixing, Editing, Makeup, and Visual Effects. Extended version runs 250m. Super 35. [PG-13] ▼▶

Lord of the Rings: The Two Towers, The (2002) **C-179m. ***½ D:** Peter Jackson. Elijah Wood, Ian McKellen, Liv Tyler, Viggo Mortensen, Sean Astin, Cate Blanchett, John Rhys-Davies, Bernard Hill, Christopher Lee, Billy Boyd, Dominic Monaghan, Orlando Bloom, Hugo Weaving, Miranda Otto, Brad Dourif, Karl Urban, Andy Serkis. Spectacular continuation of J.R.R. Tolkien's trilogy, with Frodo and a far-ranging group of warriors plunging ahead in the quest to prevent evil Lord Sauron from destroying Middle-earth. Darker, more focused, more deeply emotional, and more exciting than the first

installment, with a stunning array of technical wizardry and an ideal cast. Highlighted by the presence of Gollum, an amazing blend of CGI and Serkis' performance. Rhys-Davies also provides the voice of Treebeard. Oscar winner for Visual Effects and Sound Editing. Extended video version runs 223m. Followed by THE LORD OF THE RINGS: THE RETURN OF THE KING. Super 35. [PG-13] ▼▶

Lord of War (2005) **C-122m. *** D:** Andrew Niccol. Nicolas Cage, Jared Leto, Bridget Moynahan, Ian Holm, Ethan Hawke, Eamonn Walker, Sammi Rotibi. Biting satire of the arms industry with Cage as a Russian immigrant who's desperate to escape his dead-end life in 1980s Brooklyn, and sees a way out: selling guns, without regard to the consequences of who buys them or why. Ultimately he learns that there is a price to pay for his success. Raw and relevant, this cuts awfully close to the bone, which is why it's no candidate for Feel Good Movie of the Year. Written by the director. Super 35. [R] ▼▶

Lords of Discipline, The (1983) **C-102m. **½ D:** Franc Roddam. David Keith, Robert Prosky, G. D. Spradlin, Rick Rossovich, John Lavachielli, Mitchell Lichtenstein, Mark Breland, Michael Biehn, Barbara Babcock, Judge Reinhold, Bill Paxton, Jason Connery, Matt Frewer, Sophie Ward. Familiar but satisfactory military school drama, set in 1964 South Carolina. Keith plays senior asked to keep an eye on first black cadet (Breland) who's being systematically tortured by secret society called "The Ten." Good performances, especially by Prosky as school's number-two officer; based on the Pat Conroy novel. Unbelievable as it may appear, most of the film was shot in England! [R] ▼▶

Lords of Dogtown (2005-U.S.-German) **C-107m. ** D:** Catherine Hardwicke. Emile Hirsch, Victor Rasuk, John Robinson, Michael Angarano, Nikki Reed, Rebecca De Mornay, Heath Ledger, Johnny Knoxville, Vincent Laresca, Julio Oscar Mechoso, Sofia Vergara, Pablo Schreiber, Elden Henson, America Ferrera, Jeremy Renner, William Mapother, Bai Ling, Charles Napier. Venice, California, 1975: a group of raucous teens find themselves on the cutting edge of the skateboarding craze. High-energy account is inspired by a true story, and scripted by one of the "lords," Stacy Peralta (played here by Robinson), who made the documentary DOGTOWN AND Z-BOYS, but there's not enough material to sustain a feature film. Attempts to capture the purity and joy of skateboarding, but instead merely glorifies insufferable behavior. Unrated version also available. [PG-13] ▼▶

Lord's of Flatbush, The (1974) **C-88m. *** D:** Stephen F. Verona, Martin Davidson. Perry King, Sylvester Stallone, Henry Winkler, Paul Mace, Susan Blakely, Paul Jabara, Dolph Sweet. Fun story of a Flatbush gang, circa 1957, with original music score. Training ground for two future stars, with Stallone writing some of the dialogue and Winkler trying out his Fonzie character. Look for Ray Sharkey as a student, Armand Assante as a wedding guest. [PG]▼●

Lords of the Deep (1989) **C-79m.** BOMB D: Mary Ann Fisher. Bradford Dillman, Priscilla Barnes, Daryl Haney, Melody Ryane, Eb Lottimer, Stephen Davies. In undersea base of future, menace seems to be manta-shaped aliens, but it's really loony leader Dillman. Clumsy, cheap, and amateurish, this was the fourth and last of 1989's undersea sci-fi thrillers, and the worst by far. Roger Corman appears unbilled (which is just as well). [PG-13]▼

Lords of Treason SEE: **Secret Honor**

Lorenzo's Oil (1992) **C-135m.** *** D: George Miller. Nick Nolte, Susan Sarandon, Peter Ustinov, Kathleen Wilhoite, Gerry Bamman, Margo Martindale, James Rebhorn, Ann Hearn, Zack O'Malley Greenburg, Laura Linney. True-life story of Michaela and Augusto Odone, who learned their son had adrenoleukodystrophy, an incurable degenerative disease, and proceeded to turn the medical community upside down to keep him alive. Powerful film transcends its "disease of the week" roots, thanks to a highly cinematic visual style and an intelligent script (cowritten by director Miller, a physician by training, and Nick Enright). Nolte and Sarandon are excellent, and Ustinov offers fine support as a sympathetic doctor. The physical torture that Lorenzo goes through is often painful to watch. [PG-13] ▼●

Lorna's Silence (2008-Belgian-French-Italian-German) **C-105m.** **½ D: Jean-Pierre Dardenne, Luc Dardenne. Arta Dobroshi, Jérémie Renier, Fabrizio Rongione, Alban Ukaj, Morgan Marinne, Olívier Gourmet. Sobering drama, told in the Dardennes' usual documentary-like style, follows an Albanian woman who has married a junkie in order to acquire citizenship papers in Belgium. This will enable her to earn a tidy sum by marrying a Russian—after the junkie is disposed of. Trouble brews when she develops a conscience about her actions. Engrossing and believable, but lacks the dramatic impact of other Dardenne films. [R]●

Los Amigos SEE: **Deaf Smith & Johnny Ears**

Loser (2000) **C-95m.** ** D: Amy Heckerling. Jason Biggs, Mena Suvari, Greg Kinnear, Zak Orth, Thomas Sadoski, Dan Aykroyd, Twink Caplan, Andy Dick, Steven Wright, David Spade, Colleen Camp. Disappointing teen romantic comedy from the director of FAST TIMES AT RIDGEMONT HIGH and CLUELESS about a nice small-town kid who goes to college in N.Y.C. He's branded a loser by his roommates, and falls in love with a classmate who's caught in a bad relationship with an English professor. Gen Y variation of THE APARTMENT has adorable leads but they seem way too smart to endure the contrivances in Heckerling's script. Not helped by abrupt ending. [PG-13]▼●

Losers, The (2010) **C-98m.** ** D: Sylvain White. Jeffrey Dean Morgan, Zoë Saldana, Chris Evans, Idris Elba, Columbus Short, Jason Patric, Oscar Jaenada. After being set up and left for dead in the remote jungles of Bolivia, a group of elite U.S. Special Forces seek revenge on the powerful man who tried to have them killed. Things get complicated when Saldana, a take-no-prisoners operative, gets involved romantically and professionally. Lots of explosions, chases, and gunplay can't disguise this A-TEAM/DIRTY DOZEN hybrid as anything more than a mediocre adaptation of a comic book franchise. Maybe they should have just called it THE B TEAM instead. Super 35. [PG-13]●

Losing Chase (1996) **C-92m.** *** D: Kevin Bacon. Helen Mirren, Kyra Sedgwick, Beau Bridges, Michael Yarmush, Lucas Denton, Nancy Beatty. Well-acted character-driven drama, set on Martha's Vineyard, about a psychologically troubled woman (Mirren) and her complex relationship with the new mother's helper (Sedgwick) hired to look after her children. This premiered on cable TV prior to theatrical release; Bacon's feature directing debut. Sedgwick (Bacon's wife) executive-produced. [R]▼●

Losing Isaiah (1995) **C-108m.** *** D: Stephen Gyllenhaal. Jessica Lange, Halle Berry, David Strathairn, Cuba Gooding, Jr., Daisy Eagan, Marc John Jeffries, Samuel L. Jackson, Joie Susannah Lee, Regina Taylor, La Tanya Richardson, Jacqueline Brookes. Dedicated white Chicago social worker adopts a black infant who's been thrown in the trash (literally) by his crack-addicted mother; several years later, when the young woman straightens out her life, she goes to court to reclaim her son. Wrenching (and believable) drama scores points by making all of its characters human and flawed; first-rate performances make the most of Naomi Foner's intelligent script. Only disappointment is the final scene. Jackson and Richardson, who play opposing attorneys, are real-life husband and wife. [R]▼●

Losin' It (1983) **C-104m.** **½ D: Curtis Hanson. Tom Cruise, Jackie Earle Haley, John Stockwell, Shelley Long, John P. Navin, Jr., Henry Darrow, Hector Elias, Rick Rossovich. Pleasant enough but predictable film about three teenagers out for a wild time in Tijuana—with more bluster than experience. Appealing cast gives it extra value. [R]▼●

Los Olvidados (1950-Mexican) **88m.** ***½ D: Luis Buñuel. Alfonso Mejia, Roberto

Cobo, Stella Inda, Miguel Inclan. Gripping story of juvenile delinquency among slums of Mexico, with surreal dream sequences interspersed. An offbeat winner from Buñuel. Buñuel shot an alternate "happy" ending that was rediscovered in 2005 for reissue and video release. Aka THE YOUNG AND THE DAMNED. ▼●

Loss of a Teardrop Diamond, The (2009) **C-103m.** *½ D: Jodie Markell. Bryce Dallas Howard, Chris Evans, Ellen Burstyn, Ann-Margret, Will Patton, Peter Gerety, Jennifer Sipes, Mamie Gummer. It's 1923 and Southern heiress Howard is obsessed with poor but educated Evans, the son of her wicked father's drunken commissary caretaker. Vocally scornful of snobbish Memphis high society, Howard seeks their favor all the same. Southern soapy stew is seasoned with, mostly, two types of people: vapid and noxious. Based on a recently rediscovered, unproduced Tennessee Williams play. Too bad someone produced it. Panavision. [PG-13]▐

Loss of Sexual Innocence, The (1999-British) **C-106m.** BOMB D: Mike Figgis. Julian Sands, Saffron Burrows, Stefano Dionisi, Kelly MacDonald, Gina McKee, Jonathan Rhys-Meyers, Bernard Hill. An outlandish, pretentious, and pointless film with parallel story threads from different phases of a man's life contrasting contemporary sexual relations and the first loss of innocence in the Garden of Eden. Almost plays like a parody of an "art" film. ▼▐

Lost and Delirious (2001-Canadian) **C-103m.** **½ D: Léa Pool. Piper Perabo, Jessica Paré, Mischa Barton, Graham Greene, Jackie Burroughs, Mimi Kuzyk. Sensitive coming-of-age tale about two budding lesbians at a Canadian girls boarding school and the reverberations of their secret relationship. Though it makes an awkward shift into Gothic melodrama in its second half, the film features handsome production values and a magnetic lead performance from Perabo as a jilted lover. [R]▼▐

Lost and Found (1979) **C-112m.** ** D: Melvin Frank. George Segal, Glenda Jackson, Maureen Stapleton, Hollis McLaren, John Cunningham, Paul Sorvino, John Candy, Martin Short. Widowed college prof and British divorcee meet in a French ski resort and quickly cool their romance by marrying. Attempt to recapture the success of the overrated A TOUCH OF CLASS is just more old-fashioned nonsense posing as hip comedy. [PG]▼

Lost & Found (1999) **C-95m.** *½ D: Jeff Pollack. David Spade, Sophie Marceau, Patrick Bruel, Artie Lange, Mitchell Whitfield, Martin Sheen, Jon Lovitz, Estelle Harris, Rose Marie, Marla Gibbs, Christian Clemenson, Carole Cook. Spade plots to win his beautiful new neighbor's affections while they search for her missing dog—which he

has kidnapped. Crude, offensive, unoriginal, often painful to watch; only redeeming feature is an engaging Marceau. Fundamental error: her "slimy" ex-boyfriend is more likable than the leading man. Spade also takes credit as cowriter. [PG-13] ▼●▐

Lost Angels (1989) **C-116m.** ** D: Hugh Hudson. Donald Sutherland, Adam Horovitz, Amy Locane, Don Bloomfield, Celia Weston, Graham Beckel, Kevin Tighe, John C. McGinley, Park Overall. Sincere but obvious and compromised drama of teenager Horovitz, unjustly sent to a mental clinic treating teenagers far more troubled than he. Sutherland is sole sympathetic psychiatrist. Shallow story grows increasingly incoherent and uninvolving. Horovitz, of singing group Beastie Boys, is good in acting debut. Super 35. [R]▼●

Lost Boundaries (1949) **99m.** *** D: Alfred L. Werker. Beatrice Pearson, Mel Ferrer, Richard Hylton, Susan Douglas, Canada Lee, Rev. Robert Dunn, Carleton Carpenter. Penetrating, well-meaning if slow-moving account of a dedicated, light-skinned Negro doctor (Ferrer, in his screen debut) who (with his family) passes for white in a small New Hampshire town. A clear-eyed look at segregated America. ▼▐

Lost Boys, The (1987) **C-97m.** ** D: Joel Schumacher. Jason Patric, Corey Haim, Dianne Wiest, Barnard Hughes, Edward Herrmann, Kiefer Sutherland, Jami Gertz, Corey Feldman, Jamison Newlander. Family moves to California town where the local teenage gang turns out to be a pack of vampires! Slick movie aimed at juvenile audiences; both the humor and the plotting are pretty obvious. Only real fireworks come at the end during final showdown. Followed by two DVD sequels. Panavision. [R]▼●▐

Lost City, The (2006) **C-138m.** **½ D: Andy Garcia. Andy Garcia, Bill Murray, Inés Sastre, Tomás Milian, Dustin Hoffman, Steven Bauer, Enrique Murciano, Danny Pino, Julio Oscar Mechoso, Nestor Carbonell, Millie Perkins, Richard Bradford, Lorena Feijóo, Tony Plana, Elizabeth Peña, Victor Rivers. Heartfelt attempt to bring Guillermo Cabrera Infante's sweeping saga of 1950s Cuban revolution to life through the story of one family (a university professor and his three sons, one an apolitical cabaret owner, the others fighting for social change). Captures the spirit of that time and place, and its music and color, but bites off more than it can chew, and goes on far too long. Romantic story seems trivial and Murray's wisecracks (as a character inspired by Infante) seem out of place. Hoffman is amusing as Meyer Lansky. Labor of love for writer-director-producer-composer-actor Garcia. [R]

Lost Command (1966) **C-130m.** *** D: Mark Robson. Anthony Quinn, Alain Delon, George Segal, Michele Morgan, Maurice

[839]

Ronet, Claudia Cardinale, Gregoire Aslan, Jean Servais. Taut, well-made story of French-Algerian guerrilla warfare in North Africa, with Quinn as the peasant who has risen to a position of command. Fine international cast, good direction, and some top-notch action sequences blend very well. Panavision.▼❶

Lost Continent, The (1968-British) **C-89m.** **½ D: Michael Carreras. Eric Porter, Hildegard Knef, Suzanna Leigh, Tony Beckley, Nigel Stock, Neil McCallum. Tramp steamer wanders into the seaweed-choked Sargasso Sea and finds isolated freak civilization derived from Spanish monarchy. Good cast handles lopsided script straightfaced; occasional good action. Based on Dennis Wheatley's novel *Uncharted Seas*. [G]▼❶

Lost Highway (1997-U.S.-French) **C-135m.** **½ D: David Lynch. Bill Pullman, Patricia Arquette, Balthazar Getty, Robert Blake, Natasha Gregson Wagner, Richard Pryor, Lisa Boyle, Michael Massee, Jack Nance, Henry Rollins, Gary Busey, Robert Loggia, Marilyn Manson, Giovanni Ribisi. Bizarre Lynchian story that makes *Twin Peaks* seem as easy to follow as a *Sesame Street* episode. Basic plot involves Pullman as a jazz musician who, believing his wife is having an affair, suddenly finds himself the main suspect in her murder. Or is he? Or was she? Lynch fans will have fun trying to figure it out; others will find it incomprehensible. Blake is particularly enigmatic as a mystery man with a bad makeup job. Panavision. [R]▼❶

Lost Honor of Katharina Blum, The (1975-German) **C-106m.** ***½ D: Volker Schlöndorff, Margarethe von Trotta. Angela Winkler, Mario Adorf, Dieter Laser, Heinz Bennent, Jürgen Prochnow. Solid drama about a woman persecuted because she is suspected of aiding terrorists that is also a stinging commentary on individual freedom, political repression, and the dangers of media manipulation. Based on the Henrich Boll novel; remade as a TVM, THE LOST HONOR OF KATHRYN BECK with Marlo Thomas. [R]▼❶

Lost Horizon (1937) **132m.** **** D: Frank Capra. Ronald Colman, Jane Wyatt, John Howard, Edward Everett Horton, Margo, Sam Jaffe, H. B. Warner, Isabel Jewell, Thomas Mitchell. James Hilton's classic story about five people stumbling into strange Tibetan land where health, peace, and longevity reign. A rare movie experience, with haunting finale. Screenplay by Robert Riskin. After being shown in edited reissue prints for years, this classic has been restored to its original length—though several scenes are still missing, and are represented by dialogue only, illustrated with stills. Won Oscars for Art Direction (Stephen Goosson) and Film Editing (Gene Havlick, Gene Milford). Remade with music in 1973.▼❶

Lost Horizon (1973) **C-143m.** *½ D: Charles Jarrott. Peter Finch, Liv Ullmann, Sally Kellerman, George Kennedy, Michael York, Olivia Hussey, Bobby Van, James Shigeta, Charles Boyer, John Gielgud. First half hour copies 1937 film scene-for-scene, and everything's fine; then we get to Shangri-La and awful Burt Bacharach–Hal David songs, and it falls apart. "Lost" is right. Originally released at 150m. Panavision. [G]

Lost in a Harem (1944) **89m.** **½ D: Charles Riesner. Bud Abbott, Lou Costello, Marilyn Maxwell, John Conte, Douglass Dumbrille, Lottie Harrison, Jimmy Dorsey Orchestra. Slicker-than-usual A&C (made on infrequent trip to MGM), but strictly routine. Some good scenes here and there with sultan Dumbrille; Maxwell is perfect harem girl.▼❶

Lost in Alaska (1952) **76m.** *½ D: Jean Yarbrough. Bud Abbott, Lou Costello, Mitzi Green, Tom Ewell, Bruce Cabot. Unremarkable slapstick set in 1890s, with A&C off to the wilds to help a friend but doing more hindering.▼❶

Lost in America (1985) **C-91m.** *** D: Albert Brooks. Albert Brooks, Julie Hagerty, Garry Marshall, Art Frankel, Michael Greene. Two yuppies drop out of the rat race and take to the road ("just like EASY RIDER") in this low-key, often hilarious satire of upwardly mobile types. Written by Brooks and Monica Johnson. And isn't that Albert's voice on the phone as the Mercedes salesman? [R]▼❶

Lost in La Mancha (2002-U.S.-British) **C-92m.** *** D: Keith Fulton, Louis Pepe. Narrated by Jeff Bridges. Fascinating documentary case study of a movie production where everything goes wrong, as filmmaker and dreamer Terry Gilliam prepares to shoot his longtime pet project, THE MAN WHO KILLED DON QUIXOTE, with Jean Rochefort and Johnny Depp. The director's own drawings, brought to life through animation, give us an idea of what might have been. A unique, close-up study of the many factors—including human folly—that go into making a film. [R]▼❶

Lost in Space (1998) **C-122m.** ** D: Stephen Hopkins. Gary Oldman, William Hurt, Matt LeBlanc, Mimi Rogers, Heather Graham, Lacey Chabert, Jack Johnson, Jared Harris, Edward Fox; voice of Dick Tufeld. In 2058, with the hope of opening a gateway to a new planet for denizens of the overcrowded Earth, a family is launched into space, accompanied by a he-man pilot and the weasely doctor who tried to sabotage the journey. The 1960s TV series is re-created on a lavish scale, but hurt by crudely episodic story, grim tone, and paper-thin characters. Oldman, curiously, *underplays* the role of Dr. Smith. Angela Cartwright, Mark Goddard, Marta Kristen, and June Lockhart, stars of the original TV series,

have cameo roles. Also available in PG version. Panavision. [PG-13]▼○●
Lost in the Stars (1974) C-114m. *** D: Daniel Mann. Brock Peters, Melba Moore, Raymond St. Jacques, Clifton Davis, Paula Kelly. Good American Film Theatre version of the Kurt Weill–Maxwell Anderson musical, based on Alan Paton's CRY, THE BELOVED COUNTRY (filmed on its own in 1951). Owes much of its power to Peters' portrayal of the South African minister. Filmed in Jamaica, B.W.I., and Hollywood. [G]▼●
Lost in Translation (2003) C-105m. ***½ D: Sofia Coppola. Bill Murray, Scarlett Johansson, Giovanni Ribisi, Anna Faris, Fumihiro Hayashi, Catherine Lambert. Beguiling mood piece about a wry movie star who travels to Tokyo on business, without his family, and forms a friendship with the young wife of a busy American photographer. A wistful, telling, often very funny film about two lonely people, far from home, who find solace in each other's company. Writer-director Coppola captures the poignancy of that unique life experience, the chance meeting, while observing the natural humor of Americans bumbling their way through the Japanese culture. A perfect showcase for Murray, who seems to ad-lib many of his best lines; Johansson comes across equally well. Oscar winner for Best Original Screenplay. Francis Ford Coppola coexecutive produced. [R]▼●
Lost in Yonkers (1993) C-112m. **½ D: Martha Coolidge. Richard Dreyfuss, Mercedes Ruehl, Irene Worth, David Strathairn, Brad Stoll, Mike Damus, Robert Guy Miranda, Jack Laufer, Susan Merson. Struggling widower leaves his two sons with his steely German mother, and his sweet but simple-minded grown-up sister, while he goes off to make a living during WW2. Faithful adaptation of Neil Simon's Pulitzer Prize–winning comedy-drama. Simon's script and Coolidge's direction try to make you forget it's a photographed play, and they almost succeed. Worth seeing if only to watch Ruehl and Worth repeat their moving, Tony Award–winning stage performances. [PG]▼●●
Lost Man, The (1969) C-122m. **½ D: Robert Alan Aurthur. Sidney Poitier, Joanna Shimkus, Al Freeman, Jr., Michael Tolan, Leon Bibb, Richard Dysart, David Steinberg, Paul Winfield. Uncomfortable updating of ODD MAN OUT to present-day black underground has some tension, but doesn't really work. Three stars are good. Panavision. [M/PG]▼
Lost Patrol, The (1934) 73m. **** D: John Ford. Victor McLaglen, Boris Karloff, Wallace Ford, Reginald Denny, Alan Hale, J. M. Kerrigan, Billy Bevan. McLaglen's small British military group lost in Mesopotamian desert, as Arabs repeatedly

attack the dwindling unit. Classic actioner filled with slice-of-life stereotypes, headed by religious fanatic Karloff. Fast-moving fun, great Max Steiner score. Scripted by Dudley Nichols, from Philip MacDonald's novel *Patrol*. Previously filmed in 1929, as a British silent starring Victor McLaglen's brother, Cyril, in the lead role; reworked many times (BAD LANDS, SAHARA, BATAAN, etc.).▼●
Lost Skeleton of Cadavra, The (2004) 89m. **½ D: Larry Blamire. Larry Blamire, Fay Masterson, Andrew Parks, Susan McConnell, Brian Howe, Jennifer Blaire, Dan Conroy. Genial spoof of tacky, low-budget 1950s sci-fi films, with writer-director Blamire as an earnest scientist scouring the countryside (with his wife in tow) in search of a meteor. Along the way they encounter an alien couple who try their best to blend in. The actors never wink at the audience in this affectionate homage, made on a shoestring. Most inspired decision: using authentic 1950s "stock library" music. Followed by a direct-to-DVD sequel. [PG]▼●
Lost Souls (2000) C-97m. *½ D: Janusz Kaminski. Winona Ryder, Ben Chaplin, Sarah Wynter, Philip Baker Hall, Elias Koteas, John Hurt, John Beasley, Victor Slezak, John Diehl. Ryder, survivor of a childhood exorcism, becomes convinced that atheist true-crime writer Chaplin will become Satan incarnate on his 33rd birthday. As the directional debut of famed cinematographer Kaminski, it's not surprising that this *looks* great, and it's well acted, but it's just another religious-themed horror film, more pretentious—and boring—than most. Super 35. [R]▼●
Lost Weekend, The (1945) 101m. **** D: Billy Wilder. Ray Milland, Jane Wyman, Phillip Terry, Howard da Silva, Doris Dowling, Frank Faylen, Mary Young. An unsuccessful novelist battles the bottle. Unrelenting drama of alcoholism—and a landmark of adult filmmaking in Hollywood. Milland's powerful performance won him an Oscar; there's fine support from bartender da Silva, sanitarium aide Faylen. Won Academy Awards for Best Picture, Director, Actor, Screenplay (Wilder and Charles Brackett).▼●
Lost World, The (1925) 93m. **½ D: Harry Hoyt. Bessie Love, Wallace Beery, Lewis Stone, Lloyd Hughes. Silent film version of A. Conan Doyle adventure yarn is remarkable for special effects recreating prehistoric beasts encountered on scientific expedition to remote plateau. Interesting as precursor to KING KONG—in story structure and in Willis O'Brien's special effects. Shown in severely truncated prints for years; two restored versions now exist. Remade twice.▼●
Lost World, The (1960) C-98m. ** D: Irwin Allen. Michael Rennie, Jill St. John, David Hedison, Claude Rains, Fernando Lamas, Richard Haydn. Despite cinematic advances, this remake of the 1925 film

doesn't match original's special effects. OK juvenile entry of an expedition into remote territory hopefully inhabited by prehistoric monsters ("played" by photographically enlarged lizards). CinemaScope. ▼▶

Lost World, The (1993-Canadian) **C-99m.** *½ D: Timothy Bond. John Rhys-Davies, David Warner, Eric McCormack, Nathania Stanford, Darren Peter Mercer, Tamara Gorski, Innocent Chosa, Kate Egan. In 1912, an expedition journeys to an African plateau where dinosaurs still live. Rhys-Davies as Professor Challenger and Warner as his rival are good, but others in the too-large cast are amateurish, and the dinosaurs are not only badly done, but extremely scarce. A cheap, insignificant version of Conan Doyle's wonderful novel, which still deserves a lavish remake. Sequel, RETURN TO THE LOST WORLD (1994), was shot simultaneously. ▼

Lost World: Jurassic Park, The (1997) **C-134m.** **½ D: Steven Spielberg. Jeff Goldblum, Julianne Moore, Pete Postlethwaite, Arliss Howard, Richard Attenborough, Vince Vaughn, Vanessa Lee Chester, Peter Stormare, Harvey Jason, Richard Schiff, Thomas F. Duffy, Joseph Mazzello, Ariana Richards. It turns out that madman Attenborough left a menagerie of dinosaurs behind on a *second* island—and wants to sponsor an expedition there. Goldblum knows the dangers, but his girlfriend is already there and he's forced to follow, along with assorted others. Havoc ensues. Completely contrived sequel to JURASSIC PARK benefits from Goldblum's deprecating dialogue and superior special effects. Enough cliffhanger-style action scenes to make up for the lulls. Followed in 2001 by JURASSIC PARK III. [PG-13] ▼▶●

Lot Like Love, A (2005) **C-107m.** **½ D: Nigel Cole. Ashton Kutcher, Amanda Peet, Kathryn Hahn, Kal Penn, Ali Larter, Taryn Manning, Gabriel Mann, Jeremy Sisto, Molly Cheek, Amy Aquino, Holmes Osborne. Romantic comedy about how, after a chance airport meeting, two people who are attracted to each other *don't* get together, for a variety of reasons, over a period of years. The stars are affable enough to keep this afloat, but the story seems one episode too long. [PG-13] ▼▶

Lottery Ticket (2010) **C-99m.** BOMB D: Erik White. Bow Wow, Brandon T. Jackson, Naturi Naughton, Loretta Devine, Ice Cube, Teairra Mari, Keith David, Terry Crews, Gbenga Akinnagbe, Mike Epps, Charlie Murphy, Bill Bellamy, T-Pain. Young man (Bow Wow), growing up in the projects with his grandmother (Devine), has to survive a three-day weekend when his opportunistic neighbors find out he's holding on to a lottery ticket worth $370 million. Tired plot with stereotypical characters is punctuated with scenes of sex and violence; the results waver between being boring and offensive.

Tries to be too many things all at once. Super 35. [PG-13] ▶

Lotus Eaters, The (1993-Canadian) **C-101m.** *** D: Paul Shapiro. Sheila McCarthy, R. H. Thomson, Michele-Barbara Pelletier, Aloka McLean, Tara Frederick, Frances Hyland, Andrea Libman, Gabe Khouth, Paul Soles. Amiably amusing 1960s nostalgia set on an island in Western Canada, where a change of wind (signified by the arrival of a new schoolteacher) blows a gust of drama into the lives of a mildly eccentric school principal, his wife, and their two impressionable daughters. Winner of three Genie Awards including Best Actress for McCarthy and Best Screenplay (Peggy Thomson). [PG-13] ▼

Louisa (1950) **90m.** *** D: Alexander Hall. Ronald Reagan, Charles Coburn, Ruth Hussey, Edmund Gwenn, Spring Byington, Piper Laurie, Scotty Beckett, Martin Milner. Delightful romantic yarn of Byington seeking to become a December bride, undecided between Coburn and Gwenn; most disarming. Film debut of Piper Laurie.

Louisa May Alcott's Little Men SEE: **Little Men** (1998)

Louisiana Story (1948) **77m.** **** D: Robert Flaherty. Classic, influential documentary set in the Louisiana bayous, with a young boy observing oil drillers at work. Beautifully made; produced by the Standard Oil Company. Music by Virgil Thomson. ▼▶

Loulou (1980-French) **C-110m.** ***½ D: Maurice Pialat. Isabelle Huppert, Gérard Depardieu, Guy Marchand, Humbert Balsan, Bernard Tronczyk. Huppert leaves stable hubby for topsy-turvy life with loutish Depardieu. Two leads have terrific sexual rapport in dynamic star vehicle. ▼▶

Love Actually (2003-U.S.-British-French) **C-135m.** **½ D: Richard Curtis. Hugh Grant, Emma Thompson, Liam Neeson, Laura Linney, Alan Rickman, Colin Firth, Bill Nighy, Martine McCutcheon, Keira Knightley, Rowan Atkinson, Andrew Lincoln, Billy Bob Thornton, Shannon Elizabeth, Denise Richards, Chiwetel Ejiofor, Heike Makatsch, Rodrigo Santoro, Lúcia Moniz, Martin Freeman, Joanna Page, Thomas Sangster, January Jones, Elisha Cuthbert, Claudia Schiffer. It seems as if every Brit from the prime minister to a fading rock star to a widower is falling in love, which helps to explain a mild comedy's grandiose running time. Full of charm and wit but also highly uneven, and the hopscotching stories turn into overkill actually. Highlights include Nighy's original performance as the aging rocker, Thompson's portrayal of a wife betrayed, and funny bits by P.M. Grant. Directing debut for screenwriter Curtis (FOUR WEDDINGS AND A FUNERAL, NOTTING HILL, et al.). Super 35. [R] ▼▶

Love Affair (1939) **87m.** ***½ D: Leo

McCarey. Irene Dunne, Charles Boyer, Maria Ouspenskaya, Lee Bowman, Astrid Allwyn, Maurice Moscovich, Joan Brodel (Leslie). Superior comedy-drama about shipboard romance whose continuation on-shore is interrupted by unforseen circumstances. Dunne and Boyer are a marvelous match. Screenplay by Delmer Daves and Donald Ogden Stewart, from story by Mildred Cram and Leo McCarey. Remade by McCarey as AN AFFAIR TO REMEMBER, and a second time (by Warren Beatty). Beware public-domain copy with entirely new music score. ▼●

Love Affair (1994) **C-108m.** **½ D: Glenn Gordon Caron. Warren Beatty, Annette Bening, Katharine Hepburn, Garry Shandling, Chloe Webb, Pierce Brosnan, Kate Capshaw, Paul Mazursky, Brenda Vaccaro, Glenn Shadix, Barry Miller, Harold Ramis, Elya Baskin, Taylor Dayne, Carey Lowell, Dan Castellaneta, Rosalind Chao, Wendie Jo Sperber, Frank Campanella, Ray Charles, Mary Hart, John Tesh. Soulless remake of the 1939 weepie (itself remade as AN AFFAIR TO REMEMBER), with Beatty as an ex-jock-turned-sportscaster and ladies man who chances to meet Bening on an eventful plane ride. Frustrating film runs hot and cold; high point is the sequence with Hepburn (in her final feature film) as Beatty's feisty aunt. Intrusive songs on the soundtrack are a debit, Conrad Hall's silky cinematography is a plus, but the biggest letdown is the ending, which stops short of a big, old-fashioned sentimental Hollywood finish—just what the movie really needs. Beatty produced and cowrote with Robert Towne. [PG-13] ▼●

Love and a .45 (1994) **C-101m.** **½ D: C. M. Talkington. Gil Bellows, Renée Zellweger, Rory Cochrane, Jeffrey Combs, Jace Alexander, Michael Bowen, Ann Wedgeworth, Peter Fonda. Derivative (although not uninteresting) young-lovers-on-the-lam melodrama, about a white-trash couple who become criminals and outlaws. Features the same over-the-top comic-book violence that made RESERVOIR DOGS an instant cult favorite. [R] ▼●

Love and Anarchy (1973-Italian) **C-108m.** *** D: Lina Wertmuller. Giancarlo Giannini, Mariangela Melato, Lina Polito, Eros Pagni, Pina Cel, Elena Fiore. Italian bumpkin Giannini tries to assassinate Mussolini in 1932, falls for a prostitute in the brothel serving as his base of operation. Uneven but stylish drama helped establish Wertmuller's reputation in the U.S. [R] ▼●

Love and Basketball (2000) **C-124m.** *** D: Gina Prince-Bythewood. Sanaa Lathan, Omar Epps, Alfre Woodard, Dennis Haysbert, Debbi Morgan, Harry J. Lennix, Kyla Pratt, Glenndon Chatman. A most agreeable hybrid of love story and coming-of-age saga. Lathan plays a precocious, tal-

ented basketball player, Epps the cocky son of an NBA professional; their relationship goes through many phases from the time they're 11 years old to young adulthood, as the story breaks down into four "quarters." A crowd-pleaser from start to finish, if a little long; only the final resolution seems contrived. Feature debut for writer-director Prince-Bythewood. [R] ▼●

Love and Bullets (1979-British) **C-103m.** ** D: Stuart Rosenberg. Charles Bronson, Rod Steiger, Jill Ireland, Strother Martin, Bradford Dillman, Henry Silva, Michael V. Gazzo. Bronson is supposed to nab gangster's moll Ireland for the FBI, but falls in love with her during his pursuit in Switzerland. Routine action yarn . . . for Bronson fans only. Panavision. [PG] ▼

Love and Death (1975) **C-82m.** *** D: Woody Allen. Woody Allen, Diane Keaton, Harold Gould, Alfred Lutter, Olga Georges-Picot, Zvee Scooler. One of Woody's most pretentious films won applause for its spoofs of Russian literature and foreign films, but this tale of a devout coward in the Napoleonic wars is more like a remake of Bob Hope's MONSIEUR BEAUCAIRE. Funny but uneven, with music by Prokofiev. [PG] ▼●

Love and Death on Long Island (1997-Canadian-British) **C-93m.** ***½ D: Richard Kwietniowski. John Hurt, Jason Priestley, Fiona Loewi, Sheila Hancock, Maury Chaykin, Gawn Granger, Elizabeth Quinn. Quiet gem about an eccentric, reclusive British writer who stumbles into the wrong movie theater and, while watching HOT PANTS COLLEGE II, becomes intrigued, and then obsessed, with one of its cast members (Priestley). Before long, he flies to Long Island, N.Y., in the hope of somehow consummating his fantasy relationship with the actor. A marvel of nuance and quiet observation, with Hurt simply perfect in the lead; impressive feature directing debut for Kwietniowski, who also scripted (from Gilbert Adair's novel). [PG-13] ▼●

Love and Fear (1988-Italian-German-French) **C-114m.** *** D: Margarethe von Trotta. Fanny Ardant, Greta Scacchi, Valeria Golino, Peter Simonischek, Sergio Castellito, Agnes Sorel, Paolo Hendel. Involving if occasionally melodramatic account of the lives and loves of a trio of sisters: the oldest (Ardant) is an intellectual and all too aware of passing time and advancing age; the middle one (Scacchi) has no professional identity and lives by her emotions; the youngest (Golino) is a passionate, idealistic premed student. Crammed with ideas and observations about how life is in constant flux; loosely based on Chekhov's *Three Sisters.*

Love & Human Remains (1993-Canadian) **C-100m.** *** D: Denys Arcand. Thomas Gibson, Ruth Marshall, Cameron Bancroft, Mia Kirshner, Joanne Vannicola, Matthew Ferguson, Rick Roberts. Arcand's first English-language film is a provocative portrait of confused, restless urban singles, focusing on a pair of ex-lovers who are still roommates: Gibson, a gay, 30-ish former teen TV star who now works as a waiter, and Marshall, who's straight and desperate for tenderness. Meanwhile, there's a maniac on the loose murdering unsuspecting women! An astute look at what it means to fall in love in the era of AIDS, ambiguous sexuality, and pervasive violence. Scripted by Brad Fraser, based on his play. ▼●◗

Love and Money (1982) **C-90m.** ** D: James Toback. Ray Sharkey, Ornella Muti, Klaus Kinski, Armand Assante, King Vidor, Susan Heldfond, William Prince. Convoluted drama about Sharkey's entanglement in international scheme plotted by billionaire businessman Kinski; has its bright spots, but disappoints nonetheless because director Toback distances himself from his material. Sex scenes with Sharkey and Muti were toned down before film's release. Of interest mainly for presence of legendary director Vidor as Sharkey's senile grandfather. Completed in 1980. [R]◗

Love and Other Catastrophes (1996-Australian) **C-76m.** **½ D: Emma-Kate Croghan. Frances O'Connor, Alice Garner, Radha Mitchell, Matt Day, Matthew Dyktynski. Agreeable comedy about the various crises, crushes and romances among a group of twentysomething Melbourne University students who are male and female, straight and gay. An amusing look at a point in young adulthood in which switching one's major is a pivotal life decision; also refreshing in its depiction of the easy mixing and socializing between characters with different sexual preferences. A promising debut for 23-year-old director/coscripter Croghan. [R] ▼

Love and Other Drugs (2010) **C-112m.** *** D: Edward Zwick. Jake Gyllenhaal, Anne Hathaway, Oliver Platt, Hank Azaria, Josh Gad, Gabriel Macht, Judy Greer, George Segal, Jill Clayburgh, Kate Jennings Grant, Katheryn Winnick, Kimberly Scott. Gyllenhaal comes from a family of achievers but is something of a screwup, until he takes a job as a pharmaceutical salesman and finds he has what it takes, especially when he starts breaking rules. He pursues a beautiful woman he meets on his rounds but finds her to be his biggest challenge yet: she loves having sex but doesn't want a relationship, for reasons she won't reveal (at first). Sexy, adult romantic drama is unusually (and refreshingly) frank for a Hollywood movie, and its two stars hold nothing back. Loosely based on Jamie Reidy's book, *Hard Sell: The Evolution of a Viagra Salesman.* [R] ◗

Love and Pain (and the Whole Damn Thing) (1972) **C-110m.** *** D: Alan J. Pakula. Maggie Smith, Timothy Bottoms. Charming story of two introverts who mi-

raculously and humorously find each other, fall in love while touring Spain; written by Alvin Sargent. [PG]◗

Love & Sex (2000) **C-82m.** **½ D: Valerie Breiman. Famke Janssen, Jon Favreau, Noah Emmerich, Cheri Oteri, Ann Magnuson, Josh Hopkins, Robert Knepper, David Steinberg. Romantic comedy in which a magazine writer (Janssen), doing a piece on how to maintain a relationship, recalls her own involvement with a wisecracking, neurotic painter (Favreau). Director-writer Breiman provides some snappy, sitcom-style one-liners, although the results are predictable. David Schwimmer appears uncredited. ▼◗

Love at First Bite (1979) **C-96m.** *** D: Stan Dragoti. George Hamilton, Susan St. James, Richard Benjamin, Dick Shawn, Arte Johnson, Sherman Hemsley, Isabel Sanford, Barry Gordon, Ronnie Schell, Eric Laneuville. Silly but likable comedy about Count Dracula's adventures in N.Y.C., and love affair with fashion model St. James. Hamilton's comic performance is bloody good. Written by Robert Kaufman. [PG] ▼◗

Love at Large (1990) **C-97m.** ** D: Alan Rudolph. Tom Berenger, Anne Archer, Elizabeth Perkins, Kate Capshaw, Annette O'Toole, Ted Levine, Ann Magnuson, Kevin J. O'Connor, Ruby Dee, Barry Miller, Neil Young. A challenge to Rudolph cultists everywhere, this coy mess involves rival private detectives (male and female) who keep tripping over each other while following a case plagued by problems of mistaken identity. Made watchable by the director's typically beguiling use of color and decor, plus his penchant for offbeat casting. Rocker Neil Young has a straight part (uh . . . so to speak). [R]▼●◗

Love at Stake (1987) **C-83m.** **½ D: John Moffitt. Patrick Cassidy, Kelly Preston, Bud Cort, Barbara Carrera, Stuart Pankin, Dave Thomas, Georgia Brown, Annie Golden. Wacky, overlooked comedy spoofs the Salem witch trials in the irreverent Mel Brooks tradition (producer Michael Gruskoff coproduced several Brooks pictures). Ingenues Cassidy and Preston (who plays baker Sarah Lee) are appealing, but the show is stolen by Carrera as a very sexy witch and Pankin and Thomas as corrupt officials. [R]▼●◗

Love at the Top (1974-French) **C-105m.** ** D: Michel Deville. Jean-Louis Trintignant, Jean-Pierre Cassel, Romy Schneider, Jane Birkin, Florinda Bolkan. Slick but superficial, muddled account of club-footed writer Cassel advising Trintignant on how to become rich and sleep with lots of women. Birkin, Bolkan, and Schneider are attractive, but it's all window dressing. Aka THE FRENCH WAY IS. [R]◗

Love at Twenty (1962-International) **113m.** **½ D: François Truffaut, Renzo Rossellini, Shintaro Ishihara, Marcel Ophuls, Andrzej Wajda. Jean-Pierre Léaud, Eleonora Rossi-Drago, Zbigniew Cybulski, Nami Tamura, Marie-France Pisier, Barbara Lass. Quintet of middling stories produced in France, Germany, Italy, Japan, Poland; variations on theme of love among younger generation. Truffaut's ANTOINE ET CO-LETTE is a sequel to THE FOUR HUN-DRED BLOWS (the first of his Antoine Doinel films). Original French running time: 123m. Totalscope.

Love Bug, The (1969) **C-107m.** ***½ D: Robert Stevenson. Dean Jones, Michele Lee, Buddy Hackett, David Tomlinson, Joe Flynn, Benson Fong, Iris Adrian. Delightful Disney comedy about a Volkswagen with a mind of its own; subtle it ain't, but the slapstick and stunts are great fun to watch. Followed by four HERBIE sequels and a 1997 made-for-TV movie. ▼●)

Love Cage, The SEE: **Joy House**

Love Child (1982) **C-96m.** ** D: Larry Peerce. Amy Madigan, Beau Bridges, Mackenzie Phillips, Albert Salmi, Joanna Merlin, Rhea Perlman. Trifling melodrama of prisoner Madigan who has baby by Bridges and fights for the right to mother-hood. Plays like an R-rated made-for-TV movie; based on a true story. [R]▼●)

Love Crimes (1992) **C-85m.** BOMB D: Lizzie Borden. Sean Young, Patrick Bergin, Arnetia Walker, James Read, Ron Orbach, Wayne Shorter. Astonishingly inept, confusing thriller with Young (in a lifeless performance) playing an assistant district attorney who becomes involved with Bergin who, posing as a fashion photographer, exploits and rips off unsuspecting women. The director's cut (which is unrated and runs 97m.) is far more coherent. However, the scenario remains obvious and superficial. That version is rated **. [R]▼

Loved One, The (1965) **121m.** ***½ D: Tony Richardson. Robert Morse, Jonathan Winters, Anjanette Comer, Rod Steiger, Dana Andrews, Milton Berle, James Coburn, John Gielgud, Tab Hunter, Margaret Leighton, Liberace, Roddy McDowall, Robert Morley, Lionel Stander, Ayllene Gibbons, Bernie Kopell, Alan Napier, Jamie Farr. Correctly advertised as the picture with something to offend everyone. Britisher Morse attends to uncle's burial in California, encountering bizarre aspects of funeral business. Often howlingly funny, and equally gross. Once seen, Mrs. Joyboy can never be forgotten. Based on the Evelyn Waugh novel, adapted by Terry Southern and Christopher Isherwood. ▼●)

Love Don't Cost a Thing (2003) **C-101m.** ** D: Troy Beyer. Nick Cannon, Christina Milian, Kenan Thompson, Kal Penn, Steve Harvey, Vanessa Bell Calloway, Dante Basco. Remake of the similarly forgettable 1987 comedy CAN'T BUY ME LOVE with a change of color. High school nerd (Cannon)

hires the most popular girl in class to pretend to be his girlfriend, and undergoes an extreme personality change once he's perceived as being cool by his classmates. Cannon's character quickly becomes a caricature in this low-grade, superficial teen comedy. [PG-13] ▼)

Love Field (1992) **C-104m.** **½ D: Jonathan Kaplan. Michelle Pfeiffer, Dennis Haysbert, Stephanie McFadden, Brian Kerwin, Louise Latham, Peggy Rea, Mark Miller. Small, sensitive film of Dallas beautician (a platinum-blond Pfeiffer) who is enthralled by President and Mrs. Kennedy—and is like an excited schoolgirl at the thought of their fateful 1963 visit to her hometown. (Love Field is the name of Dallas' airport.) Really a road movie, with Pfeiffer deserting her husband and traveling halfway across the country with the unlikely duo of black father and daughter (Haysbert and McFadden). Rich performances (especially Pfeiffer's), rural flavor, and an unflinching look at race relations almost compensate for the sometimes overly contrived plot. [PG-13] ▼●)

Love God?, The (1969) **C-101m.** ** D: Nat Hiken. Don Knotts, Anne Francis, Edmond O'Brien, James Gregory, Maureen Arthur, Maggie Peterson, Jesslyn Fax. Comedy for those who are amused by Knotts playing Hugh Hefner type; film is final work of Nat Hiken, who created Sergeant Bilko in better days. [M]▼)

Love Guru, The (2008) **C-86m.** ** D: Marco Schnabel. Mike Myers, Jessica Alba, Justin Timberlake, Romany Malco, Meagan Good, Verne Troyer, Ben Kingsley, Manu Narayan, John Oliver, Stephen Colbert, Jim Gaffigan. Myers hams it up as an American-born self-help guru raised in India, who is hired by the fetching owner (Alba) of the Toronto Maple Leafs hockey team to help a struggling star player regain his confidence. Myers also cowrote this silly little farce that has a few laughs but is mostly filled with juvenile double entendres and recycled Austin Powers shtick. A number of celebrities appear as themselves. Super 35. [PG-13]❙

Love Happens (2009) **C-109m.** ** D: Brandon Camp. Aaron Eckhart, Jennifer Aniston, Dan Fogler, Judy Greer, John Carroll Lynch, Frances Conroy, Martin Sheen, Joe Anderson, Sasha Alexander. Eckhart plays a long-grieving widower who can't seem to marshal his own skills as a self-help guru to solve his personal problems. Into his life comes unlucky-in-love florist Aniston, who slowly warms to the idea of a new relationship with guess who. Thoroughly flat, sometimes melodramatic romantic drama unfortunately lacks much drama or romance. Eckhart is fine, while Aniston is shuffled off to the sidelines. [PG-13]❙

Love Happy (1949) **91m.** **½ D: David Miller. Harpo, Chico, and Groucho Marx,

Ilona Massey, Vera-Ellen, Marion Hutton, Raymond Burr, Eric Blore. No NIGHT AT THE OPERA, but even diluted Marx Brothers are better than none. Putting on a musical forms background for Harpo's antics, with Chico in support, Groucho in a few unrelated scenes. Marilyn Monroe has a brief bit. Among the writers were Ben Hecht and Frank Tashlin. ▼0▶

Love Has Many Faces (1965) C-105m. **½ D: Alexander Singer. Lana Turner, Cliff Robertson, Hugh O'Brian, Ruth Roman, Stefanie Powers, Virginia Grey. Timid attempt at lurid soaper; playgirl Turner's costume changes are the highlights. O'Brian and Robertson are gigolos. Filmed in Acapulco. ▼▶

Love Hurts (1990) C-106m. ** D: Bud Yorkin. Jeff Daniels, Judith Ivey, Cynthia Sikes, John Mahoney, Cloris Leachman, Amy Wright, Mary Griffin, Brady Quaid. Unhappily divorced Daniels goes home for his sister's wedding, only to find his ex-wife and their kids staying with his folks. Bittersweet comedy-drama has some good moments, but not enough. Mahoney and Leachman's performances as Daniels' parents border uncomfortably on caricature. [R] ▼▶

Love Hurts (2009) C-95m. *½ D: Barra Grant. Richard E. Grant, Carrie-Anne Moss, Johnny Pacar, Jenna Elfman, Janeane Garofalo, Camryn Manheim, Caroline Aaron, Jeffrey Nordling, Rita Rudner, Olga Fonda. Grant and Moss once were young and in love. Now they are married, middle-aged, and miserable. She's frustrated by his patronizing demeanor; he acts like a blithering idiot when she leaves him. Astonishingly bad romantic comedy. A subplot involving their teenage son's infatuation with a ballet dancer seems to be taken from another film, and the touchy-feely finale is highly improbable. [PG-13]

Love in Germany, A (1983-German) C-110m. **½ D: Andrzej Wajda. Hanna Schygulla, Marie-Christine Barrault, Armin Mueller-Stahl, Elisabeth Trissenaar, Daniel Olbrychski, Piotr Lysak, Bernhard Wicki. German shopkeeper, her husband off fighting at the front, risks life and reputation by romancing a much younger Polish POW. Wimpy Lysak doesn't look as if he could drive a girl's hopscotch team into sexual delirium, creating severe credibility problems in this subpar Wajda effort. Barrault is effectively cast against type as conniving Nazi sympathizer. [R] ▼

Love-Ins, The (1967) C-92m. BOMB D: Arthur Dreifuss. James MacArthur, Susan Oliver, Richard Todd, Mark Goddard, Carol Booth. Professor Timothy Leary—er, Richard Todd—advocates LSD, becomes a hippie messiah. A bad trip. ▶

Love in the Afternoon (1957) 130m. ***½ D: Billy Wilder. Gary Cooper, Audrey Hepburn, Maurice Chevalier, John McGiver. Forget age difference between Cooper and Hepburn and enjoy sparkling romantic comedy, with Chevalier as Audrey's private-eye dad. McGiver lends good support in witty comedy set in Paris. Wilder's first film cowritten with I.A.L. Diamond, and a tribute to his idol, Ernst Lubitsch. ▼0▶

Love in the City (1953-Italian) 90m. ** D: Michelangelo Antonioni, Federico Fellini, Dino Risi, Carlo Lizzani, Alberto Lattuada, Francesco Maselli, Cesare Zavattini. Ugo Tognazzi, Maresa Gallo, Caterina Rigoglioso, Silvio Lillo, Angela Pierro. The title tells all in this episodic, six-part neorealist chronicle—filmed cinéma verité style—of various aspects of romance in Rome. This was supposed to be the first edition of a film journal, known as "The Spectator." Originally 110m.; the Lizzani-directed sequence, about prostitution, was deleted from foreign-release prints. ▼

Love in the Time of Cholera (2007) C-138m. ***½ D: Mike Newell. Javier Bardem, Giovanna Mezzogiorno, Benjamin Bratt, Catalina Sandino Moreno, Hector Elizondo, Liev Schreiber, Ana Claudia Talancón, Fernanda Montenegro, Unax Ugalde, John Leguizamo, Laura Harring. Mild-mannered young man falls in love with a woman on sight, and though she marries a wealthy doctor, he never abandons his obsessive dream of being with her. Robust interpretation of Gabriel García Márquez novel captures its "magical realism"—and disarming sense of humor—as it spans 50 years. Filled with colorful characters, beautiful women, and a quixotic central character beautifully played by Bardem. Inspired adaptation by Ronald Harwood; exquisite production design (by Wolf Kroeger) and costumes (by Marit Allen). Super 35. [R]▶

Love in the Time of Hysteria SEE: **Sólo Con Tu Pareja**

Love Is All There Is (1996) C-90m. *½ D: Renee Taylor, Joseph Bologna. Renee Taylor, Joseph Bologna, Lainie Kazan, Paul Sorvino, Barbara Carrera, Angelina Jolie, Nathaniel Marston, William Hickey, Abe Vigoda, Connie Stevens, Dick Van Patten. Taylor and Bologna scripted this loud, sentimental, silly romantic comedy of two rival Italian catering families whose children fall in love. This modern-day *Romeo and Juliet* makeover is set in City Island, The Bronx, where the scenery upstages the largely wasted cast. Filmed in 1994. [R] ▼0▶

Love Is a Many Splendored Thing (1955) C-102m. *** D: Henry King. William Holden, Jennifer Jones, Murray Matheson, Torin Thatcher, Jorja Curtright, Virginia Gregg, Isobel Elsom, Richard Loo, Soo Yong, Philip Ahn, James Hong, Keye Luke. Well-mounted soaper set in Hong Kong at time of Korean War. Eurasian doctor Jones falls in love with war correspondent Holden. Effective telling of true story, beautifully executed, with Oscar-winning costumes (Charles Le-Maire), scoring (Alfred Newman), and title song (Sammy Fain and Paul Francis Webster). CinemaScope.▼O◗

Love Is Better Than Ever (1952) 81m. **½ D: Stanley Donen. Elizabeth Taylor, Larry Parks, Josephine Hutchinson, Tom Tully, Ann Doran, Elinor Donahue, Kathleen Freeman. Forgettable froth involving talent agent Parks and dance teacher Taylor. Mild MGM musical, but Liz looks terrific. Gene Kelly has an unbilled cameo. ▼◗

love jones (1997) C-110m. **½ D: Theodore Witcher. Larenz Tate, Nia Long, Isaiah Washington, Bill Bellamy, Bernadette Clark, Lisa Nicole Carson, Khalil Kain. Age-old boy-meets-girl love story given '90s treatment, set in the upwardly mobile black culture of Chicago. Slightly overlong but refreshing date movie is energized by the chemistry of leads Tate and Long, and fine supporting performances. [R]▼O◗

Loveless, The (1983) C-84m. **½ D: Kathryn Bigelow, Monty Montgomery. J. Don Ferguson, Willem Dafoe, Marin Kanter, Robert Gordon, Tina L'Hotsky, Liz Gans. A group of bikers stop in a small Southern town while on their way to the races at Daytona. Uneven homage to THE WILD ONE: pretentious and practically plotless, with about five times as much rockabilly music as dialogue; still, visually stunning, like an Edward Hopper painting of the 1950s. [R]▼◗

Love Letter, The (1999) C-88m. ** D: Peter Ho-sun Chan. Kate Capshaw, Blythe Danner, Ellen DeGeneres, Geraldine McEwan, Julianne Nicholson, Tom Everett Scott, Tom Selleck, Gloria Stuart. Low-key romantic comedy of New England seaside hamlet; bookstore owner/single mom Capshaw finds a love letter that inadvertently gets passed around town. Fun at first, but slows to a crawl at the midway point. Capshaw coproduced; her daughters Jessica Capshaw and Sasha Spielberg briefly appear. Based on the novel by Cathleen Schine. Jack Black appears unbilled. [PG-13]▼O◗

Love Letters (1945) 101m. ** D: William Dieterle. Jennifer Jones, Joseph Cotten, Ann Richards, Anita Louise, Cecil Kellaway, Gladys Cooper, Reginald Denny. Artificial soaper of amnesiac Jones cured by Cotten's love; only real asset is Victor Young's lovely title song. Ayn Rand adapted Chris Massie's book, *Pity My Simplicity*. ▼

Love Letters (1983) C-98m. *** D: Amy Jones. Jamie Lee Curtis, James Keach, Amy Madigan, Bud Cort, Matt Clark, Bonnie Bartlett, Sally Kirkland. Moving drama about a young single woman (nicely played by Curtis) who discovers deceased mother's

correspondence with lover, then takes up with a married man of her own (Keach). Originally titled MY LOVE LETTERS. Aka PASSION PLAY. [R]▼O◗

Love Liza (2002-U.S.-French) C-90m. **½ D: Todd Louiso. Philip Seymour Hoffman, Kathy Bates, Jack Kehler, Sarah Koskoff, Stephen Tobolowsky, Erika Alexander. Offbeat story of a man desperately trying to cope with an unthinkable tragedy—the suicide of his wife, who's left behind a letter he can't bear to read. Unlike mainstream movies, this one doesn't try to solve its character's problems in a neat and tidy way, which is admirable but also off-putting at times. Interesting and surprising from start to finish. Written by the star's brother, playwright Gordy Hoffman. [R]▼◗

Lovely & Amazing (2002) C-89m. **½ D: Nicole Holofcener. Catherine Keener, Brenda Blethyn, Emily Mortimer, Raven Goodwin, Aunjaue Ellis, Clark Gregg, Jake Gyllenhaal, James LeGros, Michael Nouri, Dermot Mulroney. A laid-back character study of two dysfunctional sisters and their well-meaning but screw-loose mother. Keener approaches the world with unbridled anger, while Mortimer has no self-esteem; young children affect the lives of all the women in the story. Uneven seriocomedy from the creator of WALKING AND TALKING is strident at times, but resolves itself quite movingly.▼◗

Lovely Bones, The (2009-U.S.-New Zealand-British) C-135m. **½ D: Peter Jackson. Mark Wahlberg, Rachel Weisz, Susan Sarandon, Stanley Tucci, Michael Imperioli, Saoirse Ronan, Rose McIver, Christian Ashdale, Reece Ritchie, Andrew James Allen. A 14-year-old girl (a luminous Ronan) has a typical 1970s existence with her family in a small Pennsylvania town—until she is murdered. It's her voice narrating the story as she moves on to her next life, unable to surrender her earthly ties or forget about the man who killed her. Well-made, well-acted adaptation of Alice Sebold's bestseller suffers from overabundant, heavy-handed images of an Edenic afterlife that don't connect with the rest of the film. HD Widescreen. [PG-13]◗

Lovely, Still (2009) C-92m. *** D: Nik Fackler. Martin Landau, Ellen Burstyn, Elizabeth Banks, Adam Scott. Elderly man, about to spend yet another Christmas alone, meets and falls in love with a sweet, kind woman, but there are surprises in store—and they're not what you think. Heartfelt, moving drama of old age and enduring love features superlative performances by Burstyn and especially Landau. Debut feature for Fackler, who scripted with additional material by Tim Kasher. [PG]◗

Lovely To Look At (1952) C-105m. **½ D: Mervyn LeRoy. Kathryn Grayson, Red Skelton, Howard Keel, Ann Miller, Marge & Gower Champion, Zsa Zsa Gabor. Second screen version of ROBERTA is a lesser MGM musical, but definitely has its moments as American comic Skelton inherits half-interest in a Paris dress salon run by Grayson and Marge Champion. Miller and the Champions add punch to the musical sequences; Vincente Minnelli directed the fashion show sequence. Songs include "Smoke Gets in Your Eyes," "I Won't Dance," and title tune.▼●▶

Lovely Way to Die, A (1968) **C-103m.** **½ D: David Lowell Rich. Kirk Douglas, Sylva Koscina, Eli Wallach, Kenneth Haigh, Sharon Farrell, Gordon Peter, Martyn Green. Odd detective suspenser. Douglas is likable cop turned private eye assigned by D.A. (Wallach) to protect Koscina, awaiting murder trial. Pacing and script offbeat at right moments, otherwise standard. Look for Ali MacGraw in screen debut. Techniscope. ▶

Love Machine, The (1971) **C-108m.** *½ D: Jack Haley, Jr. John Phillip Law, Dyan Cannon, Robert Ryan, Jackie Cooper, David Hemmings, Shecky Greene, Maureen Arthur. Ridiculous screen version of Jacqueline Susann's best-seller about Robin Stone (Law), ruthless TV executive who uses others for self-gain. [R]▼▶

Love Maniac, The SEE: **Blood of Ghastly Horror**

Love Me if You Dare (2003-French-Belgian) **C-94m.** ** D: Yann Samuell. Guillaume Canet, Marion Cotillard, Thibault Verhaeghe, Joséphine Lebas-Joly, Gérard Watkins, Gilles Lellouche. Alternately whimsical and cruel romantic comedy chronicling the twisted, hypnotic relationship of a boy and girl through adulthood. As children they begin daring each other to commit silly pranks in defiance of authority; years later the challenges become increasingly dangerous, both physically and psychologically. Feature directing debut from animator Samuell employs many gimmicks in this complex tale of love, but it eventually becomes tiresome. [R]▼▶

Love Me or Leave Me (1955) **C-122m.** ***½ D: Charles Vidor. Doris Day, James Cagney, Cameron Mitchell, Robert Keith, Tom Tully. Engrossing musical bio (from an Oscar-winning story by Daniel Fuchs) of singer Ruth Etting, whose life and career were dominated by a gangster called the Gimp. Day and Cagney give strong performances. Score includes Doris' hit "I'll Never Stop Loving You," plus oldies like "Ten Cents a Dance," "Shaking the Blues Away." CinemaScope.▼●▶

Love Me Tender (1956) **89m.** **½ D: Robert D. Webb. Richard Egan. Debra Paget, Elvis Presley, Robert Middleton, William Campbell, Neville Brand, Mildred Dunnock. Presley's film debut is Civil War yarn of conflicting politics among sons in a Southern family, and their mutual love for Paget. Elvis' singing ("Let Me," "We're

Gonna Move (to a Better Home)," "Poor Boy," and the title tune) highlights so-so Western. Elvis' swivel hips *might* not be authentic period detail! CinemaScope.▼▶

Love Me Tonight (1932) **96m.** **** D: Rouben Mamoulian. Maurice Chevalier, Jeanette MacDonald, Charlie Ruggles, Myrna Loy, C. Aubrey Smith, Charles Butterworth, Robert Greig. One of the best musicals ever made; Chevalier plays a tailor who falls in love with a princess (MacDonald). Along the way they get to sing Rodgers and Hart's "Lover," "Mimi," "Isn't It Romantic?," among others. Mamoulian's ingenious ideas, and mobile camera, keep this fresh and alive. Screenplay by Samuel Hoffenstein, Waldemar Young, and George Marion, Jr., from a play by Leopold Marchand and Paul Armont. Originally released at 104m.▼▶

Love N' Dancing (2009) **C-95m.** *½ D: Robert Iscove. Amy Smart, Tom Malloy, Billy Zane, Nicola Royston, Caroline Rhea, Rachel Dratch, Betty White, Leila Arcieri, Gregory Harrison, Catherine Mary Stewart. Grade-school teacher Smart hires two-time U.S. Open Swing Dance champion Malloy to give her and her fiancé dance lessons for their impending wedding. Big on dance, short on plot. Advanced dance skills of the champion West Coast swingers used throughout the film merely underscore the weak skills of the leads, especially Malloy, who's supposed to be one of the best. (He also wrote the film.) [PG-13]▶

Love Nest (1951) **84m.** ** D: Joseph M. Newman. June Haver, William Lundigan, Frank Fay, Marilyn Monroe, Jack Paar, Leatrice Joy. Cheerful but bland comedy about an Army returnee whose wife has bought a broken-down brownstone apartment, and whose tenants become part of their lives. Interesting only for early looks at Monroe and future TV host Paar.▼▶

Love on a Pillow (1962-French) **C-102m.** ** D: Roger Vadim. Brigitte Bardot, Robert Hossein, James Robertson Justice, Jean-Marc Bory. Charitable Bardot bestows her pleasures on young man, hoping to divert his intended suicide; saucy little comedy. Franscope.▼▶

Love on the Ground (1984-French) **C-126m.** *½ D: Jacques Rivette. Geraldine Chaplin, Jane Birkin, Andre Dussollier, Jean-Pierre Kalfon, Facundo Bo, Laszlo Szabo. Boring, confusing, pretentious story of actresses Chaplin and Birkin, hired by Kalfon to rehearse and perform his play—whose ending has not yet been written. For Rivette admirers only.

Love on the Run (1979-French) **C-90m.** *** D: François Truffaut. Jean-Pierre Léaud, Marie-France Pisier, Claude Jade, Dani, Dorothee, Rosy Varte, Julien Bertheau, Daniel Mesguich. Further romantic adventures of Truffaut's alter ego, Antoine Doinel (Léaud): Here, he divorces wife Jade and sets out again on his hopeless chase after love. Fine, but not top-notch Truffaut. Fifth entry in series, following BED AND BOARD; included are clips of others, which don't work here. Léaud's final appearance as Doinel. [PG]▼●)

Love Parade, The (1929) 110m. *** D: Ernst Lubitsch. Maurice Chevalier, Jeanette MacDonald, Lillian Roth, Lionel Belmore, Lupino Lane, Ben Turpin. Initial teaming of Chevalier and MacDonald is enjoyable operetta with chic Lubitsch touch, about love among the royalty of Sylvania. Acrobatic comedian Lane and personality performer Roth make wonderful second leads. Virginia Bruce is one of Jeanette's ladies-in-waiting. "Dream Lover" is film's best song. Score by Victor Schertzinger (later a film director himself) and Clifford Grey. MacDonald's film debut. Jean Harlow is an extra. ●)

Love Potion No. 9 (1992) C-96m. ** D: Dale Launer. Tate Donovan, Sandra Bullock, Mary Mara, Dale Midkiff, Hillary Bailey Smith, Dylan Baker, Anne Bancroft. Sluggish, often silly comedy in which two timid people, biochemist Donovan and animal psychologist Bullock, become human guinea pigs for a love potion. Launer also produced and scripted. [PG-13]▼●)

Lover, The (1992-French) C-110m. **½ D: Jean-Jacques Annaud. Jane March, Tony Leung, Frédérique Meininger, Arnaud Giovaninetti, Melvil Poupaud, Lisa Faulkner, Xiem Mang; narrated by Jeanne Moreau. Exotic, soft-core adaptation of Marguerite Duras' autobiographical novel about a teenage girl who's initiated into sex by an older Chinese dandy in 1929 Indochina. Borderline tedious, yet offbeat and well mounted enough to amuse anyone inclined to see it in the first place. Peripheral characters are more interesting than the two leads (at least when clothed). Sexier European version is available unrated. [R]▼●)

Love Ranch (2010-U.S.-British) C-118m. ** D: Taylor Hackford. Helen Mirren, Joe Pesci, Sergio Peris-Mencheta, Gina Gershon, Bai Ling, Taryn Manning, Scout Taylor-Compton, Elise Neal, Emily Rios, Gil Birmingham, Raoul Trujillo, Bryan Cranston, Rick Gomez, M. C. Gainey, Melora Walters, Harve Presnell. In the 1970s, husband and wife Pesci and Mirren run the first legal brothel in Nevada, although keeping the law and protestors at bay is a full-time job. Pesci is also a serial womanizer, but when he decides to back a Spanish prizefighter, the last thing he expects is that his wife will fall in love with him. Pesci's character is so thoroughly unlikable that he throws this already ragtag film way off-kilter, in spite of a typically solid performance by Mirren and a credible one by Peris-Mencheta. Inspired by real people, but not inspired enough. [R])

Lover Boy (1989) C-98m. *½ D: Joan Micklin Silver. Patrick Dempsey, Kate Jackson, Robert Ginty, Nancy Valen, Charles Hunter Walsh, Barbara Carrera, Bernie Coulson, Ray Girardin, Robert Camilletti, Vic Tayback, Kim Miyori, Kirstie Alley, Carrie Fisher. Paper-thin comedy of pizza delivery boy Dempsey turning on a bevy of frustrated older women, with resulting predictable complications. Curiously anachronistic, and not even up to sitcom level; a major disappointment from the otherwise dependable Silver. [PG-13]▼●)

Loverboy (2005) C-84m. *½ D: Kevin Bacon. Kyra Sedgwick, Kevin Bacon, Blair Brown, Matt Dillon, Oliver Platt, Campbell Scott, Marisa Tomei, Melissa Errico, Dominic Scott Kay, Sandra Bullock. Story of a woman whose sole goal in life is to have a child. She feeds her obsession by smothering her son with attention and affection in all the wrong ways while everyone around her is oblivious—or just moronic. Director Bacon turns Victoria Redel's novel of an unbalanced woman into an unbalanced film, with his wife in the leading role. He tries hard but can't make this offbeat tale engrossing or believable. Bacon and Sedgwick coproduced; their children Sosie and Travis Bacon have small roles. [R])

Lover Come Back (1961) C-107m. ***½ D: Delbert Mann. Rock Hudson, Doris Day, Tony Randall, Edie Adams, Jack Oakie, Jack Kruschen, Ann B. Davis, Joe Flynn, Jack Albertson, Howard St. John, Donna Douglas. Early Day-Hudson vehicle is one of the best. Funny, fast-moving comedy has ad exec Doris trying to get account away from rival Rock—unaware that the product doesn't exist! Edie Adams stands out in fine supporting cast.▼●)

Lovers, The (1958-French) 88m. *** D: Louis Malle. Jeanne Moreau, Alain Cuny, Jose Luis de Villalonga, Jean-Marc Bory, Gaston Modot. Chic, once-controversial tale of wealthy, married, spiritually empty Moreau and her two very different extramarital involvements. Malle's first major international success, and one of Moreau's most important early credits. Dyaliscope. ▼)

Lovers (1991-Spanish) C-103m. ***½ D: Vicente Aranda. Victoria Abril, Jorge Sanz, Maribel Verdu. Handsome youth snuggles up with his sexy older landlady, while leaving his deceptively innocent fiancée in the lurch. Erotic true-crime saga, based on a murder case from 1955 Franco Madrid. Impressively acted and photographed. Screenplay by director Aranda, Alvaro Del Amo, and Carlos Perez Merinero.▼

Lovers and Liars (1979-Italian) C-96m. ** D: Mario Monicelli. Goldie Hawn, Giancarlo Giannini, Claudine Auger, Aurore Clement, Laura Betti, Andrea Ferreol. Forgettable black comedy centering on complications surrounding romance between American tourist Hawn and Italian bank exec Giannini. Aka TRAVELS WITH ANITA; originally ran 125m. [R]▼◗

Lovers and Other Strangers (1970) C-106m. ***½ D: Cy Howard. Gig Young, Bea Arthur, Bonnie Bedelia, Anne Jackson, Harry Guardino, Michael Brandon, Richard Castellano, Bob Dishy, Marian Hailey, Cloris Leachman, Anne Meara. Vividly real, genuinely funny movie about side effects, reverberations when young couple gets married. Film won fame for Castellano, with catch-line "So what's the story?" just one of many memorable vignettes. Gig Young delightful as perennially cheerful father of the bride. From the play by Renee Taylor and Joseph Bologna (they scripted with David Z. Goodman); with Oscar-winning song, "For All We Know." Diane Keaton's film debut. [PG—originally rated R]▼◗

Lover's Knot (1996) C-88m. *½ D: Pete Shaner. Bill Campbell, Jennifer Grey, Tim Curry, Adam Baldwin, Dr. Joyce Brothers, Anne Francis, Zelda Rubinstein, Dawn Wells. Cutesy romantic trifle in which cupid Curry must bring together a poetry scholar and a beautiful doctor, then keep them an item for the rest of this movie's seemingly endless running time. Cupid's arrow definitely misses the funny bone here. [R]▼

Lovers Like Us (1975-French) C-103m. **½ D: Jean-Paul Rappeneau. Catherine Deneuve, Yves Montand, Luigi Vanucchi, Tony Roberts, Dana Wynter. Globetrotting screwball comedy has Deneuve and Montand running away from their respective spouses, meeting and falling in love with each other. Nothing special, but easy to take. Original title: LE SAUVAGE. [PG]▼◗

Lovers of the Arctic Circle (1998-Spanish) C-112m. *** D: Julio Medem. Najwa Nimri, Fele Martinez, Nancho Novo, Maru Valdivielso, Kristel Díaz, Victor Hugo Oliveira. Beguiling romantic drama about two young people who first meet as eight-year-old schoolmates and gradually realize they are destined to be together; in fact, their entire lives are linked by a series of odd parallels. It's no coincidence that the main characters' names, Anna and Otto, are palindromes; director Medem's conceit is that love is circular and eternal. Only sour note is film's conclusion. Super 35. [R]▼◗

Lovers on the Bridge, The (1991-French) C-129m. **½ D: Léos Carax. Juliette Binoche, Denis Lavant, Klaus-Michael Grüber, Daniel Buain, Marion Stalens, Edith Scob. Binoche is a lustrous presence in this otherwise hot-and-cold tale as a homeless, half-blind painter who, with manipulative street-performer Lavant, camps out on Paris' crumbling Pont Neuf Bridge while it's closed down for restoration. Some dazzling imagery combined with an air of pretension make this a decidedly mixed bag.

Lavant plays the same character in BOY MEETS GIRL and BAD BLOOD (1987). Released in the U.S. in 1999. [R]▼◗

Loves and Times of Scaramouche, The (1975-Italian) C-95m. *½ D: Enzo G. Castellari. Michael Sarrazin, Ursula Andress, Aldo Maccione, Giancarlo Prete, Michael Forest. Scaramouche has his way with women, and runs afoul of an oafish Napoleon in this energetic but empty-headed farce. Maccione adds some laughs as Bonaparte. Poorly dubbed. Filmed in Rome and Zagreb.▼◗

Love Serenade (1996-Australian) C-101m. **½ D: Shirley Barrett. Miranda Otto, Rebecca Frith, George Shevtsov, John Alansu, Jessica Napier. Oddball black comedy about a desperate, clingy beautician (Frith) and her reclusive younger sister (Otto) vying for the affections of a self-centered hipster deejay (Shevtsov)—who seems to be the only eligible man in town. Often poignant and deadpan funny, but the ending is unsatisfying. Worth seeing for the performances, especially Otto, a compendium of hilariously paranoid body tics. Film takes its title from a Barry White song, one of many featured on the groovy '70s soundtrack. Written by the director. Super 35. [R]▼◗

Lovesick (1983) C-95m. ** D: Marshall Brickman. Dudley Moore, Elizabeth McGovern, Alec Guinness, John Huston, Wallace Shawn, Alan King, Renee Taylor, Ron Silver, Gene Saks, David Strathairn. "Sick" is right; this romantic comedy (about a psychiatrist who falls in love with his newest patient) needs a shot of adrenalin. Fine cast founders; Guinness' turn as the shade of Sigmund Freud is a waste. Only Silver gets real laughs as a Pacino-like actor. [PG]▼◗●

Love's Labour's Lost (2000-U.S.-British-French) C-95m. *½ D: Kenneth Branagh. Kenneth Branagh, Natascha McElhone, Alicia Silverstone, Nathan Lane, Adrian Lester, Alessandro Nivola, Matthew Lillard, Timothy Spall, Carmen Ejogo, Emily Mortimer, Geraldine McEwan, Richard Briers. Shakespeare's comic romp becomes a 1930s musical. The King of Navarre (Nivola) and three comrades swear off women—just as the King of France's daughter (Silverstone) arrives with three attractive friends. Hollywood-inspired production numbers are downright embarrassing at times; everyone tries hard, but only Lane emerges unscathed. Uses old Fred & Ginger songs, but reminds one more of Burt & Cybill (from AT LONG LAST LOVE). Full title on-screen is LOVE'S LABOUR'S LOST A ROMANTIC MUSICAL COMEDY. Panavision. [PG]▼◗

Loves of a Blonde (1965-Czech) 88m. ***½ D: Milos Forman. Hana Brejchova, Josef Sebanek, Vladimir Pucholt, Jan Vostrell, Vladimir Mensik. Sweet, poignant tale of idealistic shoe-factory worker Brejchova, and what happens after she spends the night with—and falls in love with—womanizing pianist Pucholt. Gentle comedy-drama is both entertaining and revealing. **▼O◗**

Loves of Carmen, The (1948) **C-99m.** **½** D: Charles Vidor. Rita Hayworth, Glenn Ford, Ron Randell, Victor Jory, Luther Adler. Hayworth's beauty is all there is in this colorful but routine retelling of the story of a gypsy man-killer, minus Bizet's music. **▼O◗**

Loves of Count Iorga, Vampire, The SEE: **Count Yorga, Vampire**

Loves of Isadora, The SEE: **Isadora**

Love Song for Bobby Long, A (2004) **C-119m.** ** D: Shainee Gabel. John Travolta, Scarlett Johansson, Gabriel Macht, Deborah Kara Unger, Dane Rhodes, David Jensen. Upon the death of her mother, from whom she was estranged, a young woman returns to her New Orleans home, which is now occupied by two of her mother's friends: a boozy Southern character, once an admired professor of English literature, and his emotionally paralyzed protégé. Picaresque, richly imbued with Louisiana flavor, but overlong and unconvincing. Feature debut for writer-director Gabel, inspired by Ronald Everett Capps' novel *Off Magazine Street.* [R] **▼◗**

Love Songs (1986-Canadian-French) **C-107m.** ** D: Elie Chouraqui. Catherine Deneuve, Richard Anconina, Christopher Lambert, Jacques Perrin, Nick Mancuso, Dayle Haddon, Charlotte Gainsbourg. Lightweight, predictable soap opera about the loves and ambitions of rock singers (Anconina, Lambert), focusing mostly on the latter's relationship with an older woman (Deneuve). Attempts to be touching and bittersweet but doesn't ring true. **▼◗**

Love Songs (2007-French) **C-100m.** *** D: Christophe Honoré. Louis Garrel, Ludivine Sagnier, Chiara Mastroianni, Clotilde Hesme, Grégoire Leprince-Ringuet, Brigitte Roüan, Jean-Marie Winling, Yannick Renier. Ambitious, generally winning (and *very* French) romantic musical in which Garrel and Sagnier commence—he wholeheartedly, she reluctantly—a ménage à trois with Hesme. Then tragedy strikes. Bold attempt to explore the way people are drawn to each other, how they deal with their feelings, and the curveballs that life tosses at them. Stylistically, Honoré pays homage to the French New Wave; musical interludes are reminiscent of Demy's THE UMBRELLAS OF CHERBOURG. **◗**

Lovespell (1979) **C-91m.** BOMB D: Tom Donovan. Richard Burton, Kate Mulgrew, Nicholas Clay, Cyril Cusack, Geraldine Fitzgerald, Niall Toibin, Diana Van Der Vlis, Niall O'Brien. Thoroughly inept retelling of the romantic Tristan and Isolde legend. One-take-only filming on Irish locations has static direction and writing from a *Classics Illustrated* comic book. Mulgrew is too old for the Isolde role, and her American accent clashes with the rest of the cast. Aka TRISTAN AND ISOLDE. **▼◗**

Love Stinks (1999) **C-93m.** *½ D: Jeff Franklin. French Stewart, Bridgette Wilson, Bill Bellamy, Tyra Banks, Steve Hytner, Jason Bateman, Tiffani-Amber Thiessen, Colleen Camp. Love is not the only thing that stinks in this barely funny (and mean-spirited) tale of a television comedy writer (Stewart) who becomes romantically involved with a sociopathic beauty-from-hell (Wilson). Plays like a one-note, R-rated TV sitcom episode. [R] **▼◗**

Love Story (1970) **C-99m.** *** D: Arthur Hiller. Ali MacGraw, Ryan O'Neal, Ray Milland, John Marley, Katherine Balfour, Russell Nype, Tom (Tommy) Lee Jones. Just what it says: simple, modern boy-meets-girl story set against New England college backdrop, tinged with tragedy of girl's sudden illness. Can't hold a candle to older Hollywood schmaltz, but on its own terms, pretty good (and a box-office smash). Screenplay by Erich Segal, who also wrote the bestselling novel. Francis Lai won an Oscar for his score. Followed by OLIVER'S STORY. [PG] **▼◗**

Love Streams (1984) **C-141m.** ** D: John Cassavetes. Gena Rowlands, John Cassavetes, Diahnne Abbott, Risa Martha Blewitt, Seymour Cassel, Margaret Abbott. Typical Cassavetes fodder about a brother and sister with a strong emotional bond: for her, love never ends; and for him, love is an abstract undone by the harsh realities of life. Cassavetes aficionados will probably like it; for others, only marginally bearable. Based on a play by Ted Allan, who cowrote screenplay with Cassavetes. [PG-13] **▼**

Love the Hard Way (2003-U.S.-German) **C-104m.** ** D: Peter Sehr. Adrien Brody, Charlotte Ayanna, Jon Seda, August Diehl, Pam Grier, Katherine Moennig. Dull noir about a two-bit grifter who seduces a prim college coed into a life of crime, with tragic results. Brody and Ayanna have chemistry (and some steamy sex scenes) but the script fails to make their relationship plausible. Gritty Manhattan atmosphere helps somewhat, as does some off-the-wall comic dialogue (but not enough). Oddly, based on a Chinese pulp novel. [R] **▼◗**

Love! Valour! Compassion! (1997) **C-110m.** **½ D: Joe Mantello. Jason Alexander, Randy Becker, Stephen Bogardus, John Glover, John Benjamin Hickey, Justin Kirk, Stephen Spinella. Entertaining but overlong adaptation of Terrence McNally's Tony Award–winning play about eight gay male acquaintances who spend countryside weekends at their host's dream Victorian home over three summer holidays. Too much of the text tiresomely depends on Backbiting! Pettiness! and Sniping!, though

Glover (reprising his Tony Award–winning performance) is impressive in a dual role as twins of wildly differing dispositions (last name, uh, Jeckyll). [R]▼◉●

Love Walked In (1998-U.S.-Argentinian) **C-90m.** ** D: Juan J. Campanella. Denis Leary, Terence Stamp, Aitana Sanchez-Gijon, Danny Nucci, Moira Kelly, Michael Badalucco, Marj Dusay. Routine, low-rent film noir about a sour nightclub pianist who agrees to use his beautiful girlfriend as bait to entrap a wealthy admirer. Object: a big cash payoff. Adequate but uninspired time filler. [R]▼

Love With the Proper Stranger (1963) **100m.** *** D: Robert Mulligan. Natalie Wood, Steve McQueen, Edie Adams, Herschel Bernardi, Tom Bosley. Nifty, cynical romance tale of working girl Wood and trumpet player McQueen. Much N.Y.C. on-location filming, nice support from Adams. Written by Arnold Schulman. Good bit: the title tune.▼◉

Love Your Mama (1993) **C-92m.** ** D: Ruby Oliver. Carol E. Hall, Audrey Morgan, Andre Robinson, Earnest Rayford III, Kearo Johnson, Jacqueline Williams. Low-budget, semi-autobiographical melodrama about a mother in a Southside Chicago ghetto whose tribulations include an unfaithful, alcoholic husband, a pregnant teenage daughter, and two sons whose lives seem to be headed nowhere. Debuting writer-director Oliver must be commended for surmounting all obstacles to get her vision on the screen; in point of fact, her saga of getting the movie made is more inspiring than the film itself. [PG-13]▼

Loving (1970) **C-90m.** ***½ D: Irvin Kershner. George Segal, Eva Marie Saint, Sterling Hayden, Keenan Wynn, Nancie Phillips, Janis Young, Roy Scheider, Sherry Lansing. Extremely good drama chronicles Segal's marital and occupational problems. Director Kershner has great feeling for day-to-day detail; film's superb climax involves public lovemaking. [R]▼▼

Loving Couples (1980) **C-97m.** ** D: Jack Smight. Shirley MacLaine, James Coburn, Susan Sarandon, Stephen Collins, Sally Kellerman, Nan Martin. Couples MacLaine/Coburn and Sarandon/Collins switch partners. A titillating title for a predictable comedy. [PG]▼▼

Loving Jezebel (2000) **C-90m.** *½ D: Kwyn Bader. Hill Harper, Nicole Ari Parker, Laurel Holloman, Sandrine Holt, Phylicia Rashad, David Moscow. Shrill romantic comedy about a frustrated waiter/writer and his penchant for sleeping with neurotic, unavailable women. Deserves some points for its casual depiction of interracial relationships, but is full of irritating characters and substitutes histrionics for hilarity. The women are gorgeous but are reduced to man-crazed, screaming harpies. [R]▼▼●

Loving You (1957) **C-101m.** **½ D: Hal Kanter. Elvis Presley, Lizabeth Scott, Wendell Corey, Dolores Hart, James Gleason. Publicist Liz and country-western musician Corey discover gas station attendant Presley and promote him to stardom. Elvis' second movie is highlighted by his performance of "Teddy Bear" and the title tune. VistaVision.▼◉

Lovin' Molly (1974) **C-98m.** ** D: Sidney Lumet. Anthony Perkins, Beau Bridges, Blythe Danner, Edward Binns, Susan Sarandon, Conard Fowkes. Danner is just right in otherwise indifferent filmization of Larry McMurtry's novel *Leaving Cheyenne*, about two friends in Texas and their lifelong love for the same woman. [R]

Low Down, The (2001-British) **C-96m.** ** D: Jamie Thraves. Aidan Gillen, Kate Ashfield, Dean Lennox Kelly, Tobias Menzies, Rupert Proctor, Samantha Power. Low-low-low-key slice of slacker London life about a successful artist in his late 20s who lives in a slum neighborhood and grapples with moving up and moving on. Gillen makes for an appealing commitment-phobe but it's hard to care when all he and his mates do is sit around, drink beer and smoke cigarettes. Feature-film debut for music video director Thraves.

Low Down Dirty Shame, A (1994) **C-108m.** **½ D: Keenen Ivory Wayans. Keenen Ivory Wayans, Charles S. Dutton, Jada Pinkett, Salli Richardson, Andrew Divoff, Corwin Hawkins, Gary Cervantes, Gregory Sierra, Kim Wayans. Occasionally amusing comedy-actioner with Wayans as a private detective hired by the DEA to uncover some missing drug money. However, you might say that it's a low-down dirty shame that this film isn't funnier—or that Wayans (who also scripted) so often resorts to unsubtle stereotyping for cheap laughs. Pinkett really scores as Wayans' loyal assistant. [R]▼◉

Lower City (2005-Brazilian) **C-98m.** **½ D: Sérgio Machado. Alice Braga, Lázaro Ramos, Wagner Moura. Two lifelong pals operate a cargo boat, leading a rough-and-tumble existence. Their relationship changes after they give a lift to a beautiful young prostitute in return for sexual favors: both men are deeply attracted to her, and she refuses to choose between them. Resolution isn't terribly satisfying, but story takes a backseat to the atmosphere in this striking, sexy slice-of-life drama. Debut feature for documentary filmmaker Machado, who also coscripted. Walter Salles coproduced. Braga is the niece of actress Sônia. [R]◉

Lower Depths, The (1936-French) **92m.** **½ D: Jean Renoir. Jean Gabin, Louis Jouvet, Suzy Prim, Vladimir Sokoloff, Junie Astor, Robert Le Vignan. Sordid drama about assorted characters in a squalid home for derelicts. Pepel (Gabin), a professional thief, loves the younger sister of his mistress, and commits murder to save her from the clutches of a police officer to whom she has been "given" as a bribe. Loose adaptation of the 1902 Maxim Gorki play changes the setting from Czarist Russia to an imaginary land. Renoir scripted with Charles Spaak. Remade 21 years later by Akira Kurosawa, who was more faithful to the play. Original title: LES BAS-FONDS. ▼▶

Lower Depths, The (1957-Japanese) 125m. *** D: Akira Kurosawa. Toshiro Mifune, Isuzu Yamada, Ganjiro Nakamura, Kyoko Kagawa. Well-directed and acted but endlessly talky drama of tortured, poverty-stricken souls, with Mifune a thief who becomes involved with Kagawa. Based on a Maxim Gorki play. ▼▶

Low Life, The (1996) C-98m. ** D: George Hickenlooper. Rory Cochrane, Kyra Sedgwick, Sean Astin, Ron Livingston, Christian Meoli, Sara Melson, James Le Gros, Shawnee Smith, J.T. Walsh, Renée Zellweger. Wannabe writer Cochrane comes to L.A. and finds himself surrounded by aimless companions and a woman (Sedgwick) who cannot commit. Well acted, but depressing and unfulfilling. [R] ▼●▶

Loyal 47 Ronin, The SEE: **47 Ronin, Part I and Part II, The**

L. 627 (1992-French) C-145m. *** D: Bertrand Tavernier. Didier Bezace, Charlotte Kady, Philippe Torreton, Nils Tavernier, Jean-Paul Comart, Jean-Roger Milo, Lara Guirao. "Lulu" Marguet is a career cop who fights drug dealers with a keen sense of commitment—which is more than can be said for many of his colleagues. Pungent satire of contemporary French police force, and the way an "elite" drug-busting unit tries to function amid the absurdities of red tape and administrative bungling. Funny, yet frightening. Director Tavernier's son plays Vincent. ▼

L-Shaped Room, The (1962-British) 125m. *** D: Bryan Forbes. Leslie Caron, Tom Bell, Brock Peters, Avis Bunnage, Emlyn Williams, Cicely Courtneidge, Bernard Lee, Patricia Phoenix, Nanette Newman. French woman crosses the Channel to face pregnancy alone, comes to meet interesting assortment of characters in shabby London boarding house. Caron is superb in the lead. ▼

Lt. Robin Crusoe, USN (1966) C-110m. BOMB D: Byron Paul. Dick Van Dyke, Nancy Kwan, Akim Tamiroff, Arthur Malet, Tyler McVey. Labored Disney comedy is unworthy of Van Dyke, who plays modern-day Robinson Crusoe, a Navy pilot who drifts onto deserted island, becomes involved with pretty native girl. Film has virtually nothing of merit to recommend. Story by Retlaw Yensid (spell it backwards). ▼▶

Lucas (1986) C-100m. *** D: David Seltzer. Corey Haim, Kerri Green, Charlie Sheen, Courtney Thorne-Smith, Winona Ryder, Thomas E. Hodges, Jeremy Piven. Thoroughly winning story of a precocious 14-year-old boy who develops a serious crush on the new girl in town—and the various ramifications that follow. One of the few Hollywood films about young people in the '80s that doesn't paint its characters in black and white only. A real sleeper, marking writer Seltzer's directing debut as well as screen debut for Ryder. [PG-13] ▼▶

Lucia, Lucia (2002-Mexican-Spanish) C-110m. **½ D: Antonio Serrano. Cecilia Roth, Carlos Álvarez-Novoa, Kuno Becker. An unhappily married middle-aged author gets a new lease on life when her husband disappears. Two men—one older, one younger—fall in love with her while helping her track him down. Curious romantic comedy-thriller set in Mexico City can't figure out what it wants to be; still a dynamic vehicle for Roth (ALL ABOUT MY MOTHER), who's never been more appealing. Super 35. [R] ▼▶

Lucie Aubrac (1997-French) C-116m. **½ D: Claude Berri. Carole Bouquet, Daniel Auteuil, Patrice Chereau, Jean-Roger Milo, Heino Ferch, Pascal Greggory. Married couple Auteuil and Bouquet are members of the Resistance in Lyon, France. When he is captured by the Gestapo, she determines to free him. WW2 drama emphasizes real-life love story but suffers from deliberate pacing. Based on the book *Outwitting the Gestapo* by Lucie Aubrac herself. Leading French director Chereau portrays Max. Technovision. [R] ▼

Luckiest Man in the World, The (1989) C-82m. *** D: Frank D. Gilroy. Philip Bosco, Doris Belack, Joanne Camp, Matthew Gottlieb, Arthur French, Stan Lachow. Scrooge-like businessman Bosco is almost killed in a plane crash, and abruptly decides to change his ways. Gilroy also scripted this unpretentious, well-acted little tale; the "voice" in the bathroom is that of Moses Gunn.

Luck of Ginger Coffey, The (1964-Canadian-U.S.) 100m. *** D: Irvin Kershner. Robert Shaw, Mary Ure, Liam Redmond, Tom Harvey, Libby McClintock. Effective kitchen-sink drama with Shaw in one of his best performances as an out-of-work Irish-born dreamer, approaching middle age, who moves to Montreal with wife Ure and their teenage daughter, hoping to find success. Scripted by Brian Moore, based on his novel. ▼

Lucky Break (2001-British-German) C-107m. **½ D: Peter Cattaneo. James Nesbitt, Olivia Williams, Timothy Spall, Bill Nighy, Lennie James, Ron Cook, Frank Harper, Christopher Plummer. Cattaneo's follow-up picture to THE FULL MONTY is at best an amusing story of inmates who literally *stage* an escape by producing and appearing in a musical written by the prison governor.

Slight but diverting, well-acted tale should please fans of British comedy, especially when it finally gets around to the night of the big show. Lyrics for that show were written by Stephen Fry. Super 35. [PG-13]▼◗

Lucky Lady (1975) **C-118m.** ** D: Stanley Donen. Gene Hackman, Liza Minnelli, Burt Reynolds, Geoffrey Lewis, John Hillerman, Robby Benson, Michael Hordern. Star trio make an engaging team, as amateur rum-runners in the 1930s who practice a ménage-à-trois after business hours . . . script goes astray and drags along to a limp, hastily refilmed conclusion. Unfortunate waste of talent; written by Willard Huyck and Gloria Katz. [PG]◗

Lucky Luciano (1973-Italian-French-U.S.) **C-110m.** ** D: Francesco Rosi. Gian-Maria Volonté, Rod Steiger, Edmond O'Brien, Vincent Gardenia, Charles Cioffi. Fair international coproduction about the deported crime kingpin, given a good interpretation by Volonte. Former federal narcotics agent Charles Siragusa, Luciano's real-life nemesis, plays himself. [R]▼

Lucky Me (1954) **C-100m.** ** D: Jack Donohue. Doris Day, Robert Cummings, Phil Silvers, Eddie Foy, Nancy Walker, Martha Hyer, Bill Goodwin. Bright-faced but doggedly mediocre musical set in Miami, with Doris as star of Silvers' third-rate theatrical troupe who attracts the attention of Broadway songwriter Cummings. Look for young Angie Dickinson in first film appearance. CinemaScope. ▼◗◗

Lucky Numbers (2000) **C-105m.** *½ D: Nora Ephron. John Travolta, Lisa Kudrow, Tim Roth, Ed O'Neill, Michael Rapaport, Daryl Mitchell, Bill Pullman, Richard Schiff, Michael Moore, Michael Weston, Sam McMurray. Hapless local TV weatherman Travolta, who's in debt, is persuaded to try rigging the station's weekly state lottery drawing, with the help of "lottery girl" Kudrow. Witless comedy full of unpleasant characters; a total turn-off. [R]▼◗

Lucky Number Slevin (2006) **C-110m.** **½ D: Paul McGuigan. Josh Hartnett, Bruce Willis, Morgan Freeman, Ben Kingsley, Lucy Liu, Stanley Tucci, Danny Aiello, Kevin Chamberlin, Mykelti Williamson, Robert Forster. A mysterious figure (Willis) tells a stranger about a crime committed long ago; the rest of the film reveals the other side of that coin. Hartnett is mistaken for a friend he's visiting in N.Y.C. and is summoned by two rival crime bosses (Freeman, cast against type, and Kingsley, as a rabbi-crimelord with a New York accent) who expect him to do their bidding in order to save his life. Challenging, puzzlelike script is never dull but is too self-consciously clever. Liu is a standout as Hartnett's love interest who's also the city coroner. Super 35. [R]◗

Lucky Ones, The (2008) **C-113m.** **½ D: Neil Burger. Rachel McAdams, Tim Rob-

bins, Michael Peña, Annie Corley, John Diehl, John Heard, Molly Hagan, Spencer Garrett, Arden Myrin. Three lost souls who have just returned to the U.S. after serving in Iraq take off on a cross-country road trip and discover an America that is at best appreciative of—but mostly indifferent to—their sacrifices. Episodic tale features touching moments and solid performances (particularly by McAdams), but some unnecessary attempts at comic relief fall flat. [R]◗

Lucky Partners (1940) **99m.** ** D: Lewis Milestone. Ronald Colman, Ginger Rogers, Jack Carson, Spring Byington, Cecilia Loftus, Harry Davenport. Far-fetched comedy about Colman and Rogers winning sweepstakes together, then taking "imaginary" honeymoon. Stars try to buoy mediocre script. ▼◗

Lucky Star, The (1980-Canadian) **C-110m.** *** D: Max Fischer. Louise Fletcher, Rod Steiger, Lou Jacobi, Brett Marx, Helen Hughes. Entertaining tale of a young Jewish boy (Marx) whose parents are taken away by the Nazis. He is sheltered on a Rotterdam farm and singlehandedly goes up against German Colonel Steiger. A sleeper. [PG]

Lucky Stiff (1988) **C-82m.** ** D: Anthony Perkins. Joe Alaskey, Donna Dixon, Jeff Kober, Morgan Sheppard, Barbara Howard, Charles Frank, Fran Ryan, Leigh McCloskey, Bill Quinn. Uneven black comedy about cannibalism improves as it goes along. Fat Alaskey, full of jokes and yearning to be married, is romanced by gorgeous Dixon, but doesn't know that she's selected him as Mr. Christmas Dinner for her inbred family. Awkwardly structured script and odd rhythms of film are helped by Alaskey's ingratiating performance. [PG]▼◗

Lucky You (2007) **C-124m.** ** D: Curtis Hanson. Eric Bana, Drew Barrymore, Robert Duvall, Debra Messing, Horatio Sanz, Charles Martin Smith, Joey Kern, Jean Smart, Phyllis Somerville, Robert Downey, Jr., Saverio Guerra, Madeleine Peyroux, Michael Shannon. Poker-faced study of professional gambler Bana, who lives in Las Vegas and plays cards for a living—but can't step out of the shadow of his estranged father (Duvall), a revered poker champion. Movie gets everything right when it comes to the game (even re-creating the 2003 World Series of Poker, with many key players as themselves) but fails to ignite an interesting story for its characters. Amazingly dull. Written by Hanson and Eric Roth. Super 35. [PG-13]◗

Lucy Gallant (1955) **C-104m.** **½ D: Robert Parrish. Charlton Heston, Jane Wyman, Thelma Ritter, Claire Trevor, William Demarest, Wallace Ford. Spiritless soaper of success-bent Wyman rejecting suitors Heston et al., wanting to get ahead instead; set in Western oil town. Wyman plays dressmaker, and veteran Hollywood costume designer Edith Head makes a rare on-screen appearance near the end. VistaVision.

Ludwig (1972-Italian-French-German) C-173m. ** D: Luchino Visconti. Helmut Berger, Romy Schneider, Trevor Howard, Silvana Mangano, Helmut Griem, Gert Frobe. Lavish film about Mad King of Bavaria keeps main character so cold, aloof that one feels no sympathy; after nearly three hours, effect is deadening. Authentic locations are breathtaking. Schneider and Howard excellent, but slow-moving film doesn't work. Incredibly, the original version of this runs 246m.! Video runs 237m. Panavision. [PG]▼▶

Lullaby of Broadway (1951) C-92m. **½ D: David Butler. Doris Day, Gene Nelson, Gladys George, S. Z. Sakall, Billy de Wolfe, Florence Bates, Anne Triola. Musical comedy star Day returns to N.Y.C., unaware that her singer mother has hit the skids. Warner Bros. musical is decent but no big deal; good cast and lots of great old songs keep it moving.▼◐

Lulu on the Bridge (1999) C-103m. *** D: Paul Auster. Harvey Keitel, Mira Sorvino, Willem Dafoe, Gina Gershon, Mandy Patinkin, Vanessa Redgrave, Don Byron, Richard Edson, Victor Argo, Kevin Corrigan, Harold Perrineau, Lou Reed, David Byrne; voice of Stockard Channing. Jazz saxophonist Keitel's career abruptly ends after he is a victim of random violence. After coming upon a magic stone on a Manhattan street, he enters into an unusual, intensely romantic relationship with a struggling actress (Sorvino). Jarring, provocative film is crammed with twists and surprises and explores the roles that coincidence and fate play in everyday life. Sorvino has never been lovelier. Solo directing debut for novelist Auster, who also scripted. [PG-13]▼▶

Lulu the Tool SEE: **Working Class Goes to Heaven, The**

Lumiere (1976-French) C-95m. **½ D: Jeanne Moreau. Jeanne Moreau, Francine Racette, Lucia Bose, Caroline Cartier, Marie Henriau, Keith Carradine, Bruno Ganz, François Simon. Elaborate but not very involving drama about four actresses of different ages and status and their relationships with careers, men, each other. Curio is worth seeing for Moreau's directorial debut. [R]▼

Luminarias (2000) C-100m. *** D: Jose Luis Valenzuela. Evelina Fernandez, Marta DuBois, Angela Moya, Diana Ortelli, Sal Lopez, Scott Bakula, Cheech Marin, Robert Beltran, Andrew Kim, Pepe Serna, Liz Torres. Four L.A. Latina women of a certain age cling to one another as they try to find the right men—while battling their own social prejudices. A sharply observed portrait of women with ethnic identity crises, told with vigor and humor. Written

by its impressive leading lady, Fernandez. [R]▼▶

Lumumba (2000-French-Belgian-German-Haitian) C-115m. ***½ D: Raoul Peck. Eriq Ebouaney, Alex Descas, Théophile Sowié, Maka Kotto, Dieudonné Kabongo, Pascal N'Zonzi. Powerful account of the life and times of Patrice Lumumba (Ebouaney, who is magnetic), the dedicated but ill-fated first prime minister of the Congo (now Zaire) after it was granted independence from Belgium in 1960. Both a top-notch thriller and a fair-minded biography of a courageous, charismatic individual and the complex time in which he lived. Written by Peck and Pascal Bonitzer.▼▶

Luna (1979) C-144m. *** D: Bernardo Bertolucci. Jill Clayburgh, Matthew Barry, Veronica Lazar, Renato Salvatori, Fred Gwynne, Alida Valli, Roberto Benigni. Initially dazzling tale of male adolescent's identity crisis becomes ponderous when it turns into a mother-son soap opera with incestuous implications. Cinematically exciting, though, with a bravura finale. [R]

Lunatics: A Love Story (1992) C-87m. **½ D: Josh Becker. Theodore Raimi, Deborah Foreman, Bruce Campbell, Brian McCree, Eddie Rosmaya, Michele Stacey. Raimi is a gentle paranoid, confined by his fears to his lonely, foil-lined L.A. apartment; Foreman is convinced she causes the death of everyone she loves. Odd low-budget comedy has real, if eccentric, charm. "Presented" by Sam Raimi. [PG-13]▼

Lunatics and Lovers (1976-Italian) C-93m. *½ D: Flavio Mogherini. Marcello Mastroianni, Claudia Mori, Lino Morelli, Flora Carabella, Adriano Celentano. Aristocrat Mastroianni has an imaginary wife; an organ grinder convinces prostitute Mori to "impersonate" her. When it's not silly, it's dull.▼

Lunch Wagon (1980) C-88m. **½ D: Ernest Pintoff. Pamela Jean Bryant, Rosanne Katon, Candy Moore, Rick Podell, Rose Marie, Chuck McCann, Vic Dunlop, Jimmy Van Patten, Dick Van Patten. Above average drive-in comedy about trio of young lovelies who set up their lunch truck at a prime construction site, unaware that their competition is really a cover for a planned bank robbery. Good cast, spirited direction; Dale Bozzio sings "Mental Hopscotch." Reissued as LUNCH WAGON GIRLS and COME 'N' GET IT. [R]▼

Lunch Wagon Girls SEE: **Lunch Wagon**

Lured (1947) 102m. **½ D: Douglas Sirk. George Sanders, Lucille Ball, Charles Coburn, Alan Mowbray, Cedric Hardwicke, Boris Karloff, George Zucco. Ball turns detective in this melodrama, encounters strange characters and harrowing experiences while tracking murderer; pretty good, with top cast. Remake of Robert Siodmak's 1939 French film PIÈGES.▼▶

Lurking Fear (1994) **C-76m.** *½ D: C. Courtney Joyner. Jon Finch, Blake Bailey, Ashley Lauren, Jeffrey Combs, Allison Mackie, Paul Mantee, Vincent Schiavelli. On a hot, sunny Christmas in Massachusetts, crooks and monster fighters confront one another in an old church, waiting for the creatures who live in tunnels below to make their annual attack. Seedy and tiresome, this seems more derived from KEY LARGO than from H. P. Lovecraft's story. Shot in Romania, and looks it. From Full Moon.▼●◗

Lust, Caution (2007-Hong Kong-U.S.-Chinese) **C-157m.** *** D: Ang Lee. Tony Leung Chiu-Wai, Wei Teng, Joan Chen, Lee-Hom Wang, Chung Hua Tou, Chih-ying Chu, Ying-hsien Kao, Anupam Kher. Idealistic student in late 1930s Shanghai is recruited to join a resistance movement against Chinese people who are collaborating with the Japanese invaders. Her job is to win over a hardened official in order to set him up for assassination, but their relationship becomes so intense—sexually *and* psychically—that her emotions are blurred. Unusual story unfolds at great length yet maintains an almost hypnotic mood; sex scenes are graphic, but it's the looks in the leading actors' eyes that really tell the tale. Exquisite score by Alexandre Desplat. R-rated version runs 148m. [NC-17]◗

Lust for a Vampire (1971-British) **C-95m.** *½ D: Jimmy Sangster. Ralph Bates, Yutte Stensgaard, Barbara Jefford, Michael Johnson, Suzanna Leigh, Mike Raven, Christopher Neame. Carmilla, the seductress from THE VAMPIRE LOVERS, preys on students at a girls' school. Third-rate Hammer horror, anemically produced. Followed by TWINS OF EVIL. Original title: TO LOVE A VAMPIRE. [R]▼◗

Lust for Life (1956) **C-122m.** **** D: Vincente Minnelli. Kirk Douglas, Anthony Quinn, James Donald, Pamela Brown, Everett Sloane, Niall MacGinnis, Noel Purcell, Henry Daniell, Jill Bennett, Lionel Jeffries, Eric Pohlmann. Brilliant adaptation of Irving Stone's biography of painter Van Gogh, vividly portraying his anguished life. Quinn won well-deserved Oscar for performance as painter-friend Gauguin, in this exquisite color production. Script by Norman Corwin. Produced by John Houseman. Fine music score by Miklos Rozsa. CinemaScope.▼●◗

Lust in the Dust (1985) **C-85m. BOMB** D: Paul Bartel. Tab Hunter, Divine, Lainie Kazan, Geoffrey Lewis, Henry Silva, Cesar Romero, Gina Gallego, Woody Strode, Pedro Gonzales-Gonzales. Hunter and Divine descend on a New Mexico hellhole—he (like most of the cast) to locate some buried treasure, she (he?) to fulfill a dream of becoming a saloon singer. Dreadful attempt at camp despite an apparently whimsical casting

director; what's to say about a movie where Divine's warbling is the comical highlight? Techniscope. [R]▼●◗

Lusty Men, The (1952) **113m.** *** D: Nicholas Ray. Susan Hayward, Robert Mitchum, Arthur Kennedy, Arthur Hunnicutt, Frank Faylen. Intelligent, atmospheric rodeo drama, with ex-champ Mitchum becoming mentor of novice Kennedy—and finding himself attracted to Kennedy's no-nonsense wife (Hayward). Solid going most of the way—until that hokey finale. Well directed by Ray.▼●

Luther (1973-British) **C-112m.** **½ D: Guy Green. Stacy Keach, Patrick Magee, Hugh Griffith, Robert Stephens, Alan Badel, Judi Dench. Sincere but placid American Film Theatre re-creation of John Osborne's play about Martin Luther (Keach), leader of the Protestant Reformation.▼◗

Luther (2003-U.S.-German) **C-113m.** ** D: Eric Till. Joseph Fiennes, Alfred Molina, Bruno Ganz, Jonathan Firth, Peter Ustinov, Claire Cox, Benjamin Sadler. Handsomely mounted but one-dimensional historical soap opera about the life and times of Martin Luther (Fiennes), the father of the Protestant Reformation. Dramatically over-the-top and filled with corny dialogue, but its major failing is that it reduces complex historical issues to good-versus-evil simplicity. [PG-13]▼◗

Luv (1967) **C-95m.** *½ D: Clive Donner. Jack Lemmon, Peter Falk, Elaine May, Eddie Mayehoff, Paul Hartman, Severn Darden. Murray Schisgal's three-character hit play about pseudo-intellectuals was not a natural for the screen anyway, but this version is truly an abomination. The cast tries. Look for a young Harrison Ford. Panavision.▼●

Luzhin Defence, The (2000-British-French) **C-106m.** *** D: Marleen Gorris. John Turturro, Emily Watson, Geraldine James, Stuart Wilson, Christopher Thompson, Fabio Sartor. Intriguing adaptation of Vladimir Nabokov novel about a Russian chess master who falls in love while attending a world tournament in Italy during the 1920s. But his longtime teacher knows his dark secret: chess is not a game for him, but a compulsion. A treat to watch Turturro and Watson in this modest but well-made period piece. [PG-13]▼◗

Lymelife (2009) **C-94m.** *** D: Derick Martini. Alec Baldwin, Rory Culkin, Jill Hennessy, Timothy Hutton, Cynthia Nixon, Kieran Culkin, Emma Roberts. Meek, adolescent boy (Rory Culkin) sees his parents' strained marriage dissolve before his eyes, even as he falteringly initiates his first relationship—with the pretty girl next door (Roberts). Coming-of-age tale set in Long Island in 1979, as the boy's father (Baldwin) brashly pursues the American dream, covers familiar turf with some original touches and winning performances. Lean, independent film written by the director and his brother Steve Martini; the real-life Culkin brothers play siblings on-screen. Panavision. [R]▶

M (1931-German) **111m.** ******** D: Fritz Lang. Peter Lorre, Otto Wernicke, Ellen Widmann, Inge Landgut, Theodor Loos, Gustaf Gründgens. Harrowing melodrama about psychotic child murderer brought to justice by Berlin underworld. Riveting and frighteningly contemporary; cinematically dazzling, especially for an early talkie. Lorre's performance is unforgettable. Older 99m. prints still circulate—with a truncated ending. Remade in 1951. ▼●▮

M (1951) **88m.** ******* D: Joseph Losey. David Wayne, Howard da Silva, Luther Adler, Karen Morley, Jorja Curtright, Martin Gabel, Norman Lloyd. Interesting, intelligent re-thinking of Fritz Lang classic set in L.A., with Wayne as child killer hunted down by community of criminals.

Ma and Pa Kettle series SEE *Leonard Maltin's Classic Movie Guide*

Mac (1992) **C-118m.** ******* D: John Turturro. John Turturro, Michael Badalucco, Carl Capotorto, Katherine Borowitz, John Amos, Olek Krupa, Ellen Barkin, Joe Paparone, Nicholas Turturro. Rock-solid tale of a trio of Italian-American brothers in Queens, New York, during the mid-1950s. The eldest, a carpenter, is fiercely determined to realize his American Dream, so he starts up his own construction company. Crammed with offbeat humor, but most refreshing as a sincere depiction of the lives and struggles of blue-collar Americans. Turturro's directorial debut; he coscripted with Brandon Cole. The film is dedicated to Turturro's father, a carpenter, and inspired by the senior Turturro's life. [R] ▼●

Macabra SEE: **Demonoid, Messenger of Death**

Macabre (1958) **73m.** ****** D: William Castle. William Prince, Jim Backus, Christine White, Jacqueline Scott. Weird goings-on in small town where doctor's young daughter mysteriously vanishes—and an anonymous phone caller announces that the child has been buried alive. Film promises much, delivers little. Famous for Castle's gimmick of handing out policies insuring moviegoers for $1,000 against death by fright.▮

Mac and Me (1988) **C-93m.** ***½** D: Stewart Raffill. Christine Ebersole, Jonathan Ward, Katrina Caspary, Lauren Stanley, Jade Calegory. Slight E.T. clone about Mac, an outer space creature, and his plight in suburban L.A. More a TV commercial than a movie: There's a production number set in a McDonald's, and the alien survives by sipping Coca-Cola. [PG]▼●▮

Macao (1952) **80m.** ****** D: Josef von Sternberg. Robert Mitchum, Jane Russell, William Bendix, Gloria Grahame, Thomas Gomez, Philip Ahn. Flat yarn supposedly set in murky title port, with Russell a singer and Mitchum the action-seeking man she loves. ▼●▮

Macaroni (1985-Italian) **C-104m.** ****½** D: Ettore Scola. Jack Lemmon, Marcello Mastroianni, Daria Nicolodi, Isa Danieli, Maria Luisa Saniella. Uptight American businessman goes to Naples and finds some unfinished personal business left over from his last visit—when he was an amorous soldier during WW2. Two of the world's most endearing actors try to keep this soufflé from falling and almost succeed. [PG]▼●

MacArthur (1977) **C-130m.** ******* D: Joseph Sargent. Gregory Peck, Dan O'Herlihy, Ed Flanders, Sandy Kenyon, Dick O'Neill, Marj Dusay, Art Fleming. Solid, absorbing saga of flamboyant military chief during WW2 and Korean War. Peck is excellent but film doesn't pack the punch of PATTON. Originally trade-screened at 144m. then cut for release. [PG]▼●

MacArthur's Children (1985-Japanese) **C-115m.** *****½** D: Masahiro Shinoda. Masako Natsume, Shima Iwashita, Hiromi Go, Takaya Yamauchi, Yoshiyuka Omori, Shiori Sakura, Juzo Itami, Ken Watanabe. Extremely poignant, proud, loving remembrance of life in a small Japanese fishing village immediately following that nation's defeat in WW2. Most effectively delineated are the Japanese reaction to losing the war, as well as the cultural effects of the American occupation—from styles of dress to baseball. [PG]▼●

Macbeth (1948) **89m.** ******* D: Orson Welles. Orson Welles, Jeanette Nolan, Dan O'Herlihy, Edgar Barrier, Roddy McDowall, Robert Coote, Erskine Sanford, Alan Napier, Peggy Webber, John Dierkes. Welles brought the Bard to Republic Pictures with this moody, well-done adaptation, filmed entirely on bizarre interiors (which deliberately emphasize its theatricality). Most revival houses now show Welles' original version, which runs 105m. and has the actors speaking with authentic Scot accents. ▼●

Macbeth (1971-British) **C-140m.** *****½** D: Roman Polanski. Jon Finch, Francesca Annis, Martin Shaw, Nicholas Selby, John Stride, Stephan Chase. Gripping, atmospheric, and extremely violent re-creation of Shakespeare tragedy of young Scots nobleman lusting for power, driven onward by crazed wife and prophecies. Great example of film storytelling, thanks to excellent direction. Todd-AO 35. [R]▼●

Macbeth (2006-Australian) **C-109m.** ****** D: Geoffrey Wright. Sam Worthington, Victoria Hill, Lachy Hulme, Gary Sweet, Steve Bastoni, Mick Molloy, Matt Doran. Ill-conceived retelling of the Shakespeare classic set among warring gangsters in contemporary Melbourne (but with Shakespearean dialogue intact). Macbeth is depicted as a shaggy-haired hood who resembles a grunge rock star; Lady Macbeth is a cocaine-snorting, mentally unhinged schemer. There's precious little conversation during the film's first nine minutes, but plenty of bloody corpses. Adapted by Wright and Hill (who plays Lady M.). ▶

MacGruber (2010) **C-90m.** **✲✲½** D: Jorma Taccone. Will Forte, Kristen Wiig, Ryan Phillippe, Powers Boothe, Maya Rudolph, Val Kilmer. How much mileage can a comedy get from a single joke? Quite a bit, judging from the guffaws-to-groaners ratio in this broadly played, raunchily written farce inspired by *Saturday Night Live* sketches spoofing the 1985–92 *MacGyver* TV series. Forte is undeniably funny as a lost-in-the-'80s action hero who somehow tries (with a little help from allies Phillippe and Wiig) to prevent an over-the-top bad guy (Kilmer) from nuking Washington, D.C. Unrated version runs 95m. HD Widescreen. [R] ▶

Machete (2010) **C-105m.** **✲✲** D: Robert Rodriguez, Ethan Maniquis. Danny Trejo, Robert De Niro, Jessica Alba, Steven Seagal, Michelle Rodriguez, Jeff Fahey, Cheech Marin, Don Johnson, Lindsay Lohan, Shea Whigham, Daryl Sabara, Tom Savini, Gilbert Trejo, Billy Blair, Nimród Antal, Stacy Keach. Feature-length extension of one of the fake coming-attractions trailers from 2007's GRINDHOUSE, with Danny Trejo as the titular character, a former Mexican federale who seeks revenge on those who set him up to "assassinate" a Texas legislator (De Niro). It's fun to see the imposing Trejo in a leading role, but cowriter-codirector-coeditor Rodriguez's usual over-the-top mock-exploitation genre excesses—and undernourished plot—quickly become wearying. Amusing casting choices, although De Niro is wasted in a no-account part. [R] ▶

Machine, The (1994-French-German) **C-96m.** **✲✲✲** D: François Dupeyron. Gérard Depardieu, Nathalie Baye, Didier Bourdon, Natalia Woerner, Erwan Baynaud, Marc Andreoni, Julie Depardieu. Scientist Depardieu's experiment works better than he expected, and he switches minds with a psychotic killer of women. Suspenseful, well-plotted Gallic variation on old themes; good direction, better acting. From the novel *La Machine* by Rene Belletto. ▼●

Machine-Gun Kelly (1958) **80m.** **✲✲½** D: Roger Corman. Charles Bronson, Susan Cabot, Barboura Morris, Morey Amsterdam, Wally Campo, Jack Lambert, Connie Gilchrist. With typical efficiency, Corman gives this gangster chronicle pacing and more than passing interest. Bronson is fine in title role. Superama. ▼

Machine Gun McCain (1968-Italian) **C-94m.** **✲✲** D: Giuliano Montaldo. John Cassavetes, Britt Ekland, Peter Falk, Gabriele Ferzetti, Salvo Randone, Gena Rowlands.

Junk about just-released gangster who tries to rob Mafia-controlled casino in Las Vegas. Techniscope.[PG] ▶

Machinist, The (2004-Spanish) **C-102m.** **✲✲✲** D: Brad Anderson. Christian Bale, Jennifer Jason Leigh, Aitana Sánchez-Gijón, John Sharian, Michael Ironside, Larry Gilliard, Reg E. Cathey, Anna Massey. Machine shop worker Bale is deeply troubled: he hasn't slept in a year . . . mysterious notes appear on his refrigerator . . . he converses with a coworker who doesn't appear to exist . . . and he's losing weight at an alarming rate. Eerie, weirdly compelling psychological thriller is beautifully designed and shot. If Franz Kafka ever scripted a movie, this might have been it. Bale's mere presence is disturbing: he shed 63 pounds for this role and moves through the film like a walking skeleton. Super 35. [R] ▶

Macho Callahan (1970) **C-99m.** **✲✲½** D: Bernard Kowalski. David Janssen, Lee J. Cobb, Jean Seberg, David Carradine, Pedro Armendariz, Jr., James Booth, Richard Anderson. Janssen miscast as Civil War POW-escapee, out to kill man who got him arrested in first place; will recognize latter by his yellow shoes. Interesting view of West, but dialogue often unbelievable. Panavision. [R] ▼

Mack, The (1973) **C-110m.** **✲✲** D: Michael Campus. Max Julien, Don Gordon, Richard Pryor, Carol Speed, Roger E. Mosley, William C. Watson. Extremely violent melodrama about a black pimp in Oakland was one of the most popular blaxploitation films; strange, because it's utterly ordinary. [R] ▼●

Mackenna's Gold (1969) **C-128m.** **✲✲½** D: J. Lee Thompson. Gregory Peck, Omar Sharif, Telly Savalas, Camilla Sparv, Keenan Wynn, Julie Newmar, Lee J. Cobb, Raymond Massey, Burgess Meredith, Anthony Quayle, Edward G. Robinson, Eli Wallach, Ted Cassidy, Eduardo Ciannelli; narrated by Victor Jory. Overblown adventure saga about search for lost canyon of gold, with double-crosses, conflicts, mysterious clues, etc. Super cast saddled with ludicrous script, made worse by pre-release tampering that cut extremely long film, leaving abrupt denouement, several loose ends. Fine Quincy Jones score; produced by Carl Foreman (who also scripted) and Dimitri Tiomkin. Super Panavision 70. [M] ▼●

Mackintosh and T.J. (1975) **C-96m.** **✲✲** D: Marvin J. Chomsky. Roy Rogers, Clay O'Brien, Billy Green Bush, Andrew Robinson, Joan Hackett. Old-fashioned modern-day Western about an aging ranch hand and a young boy. Those charmed by idea of Roy Rogers' comeback will want to see it; others beware. Music by Waylon Jennings. [PG]

Mackintosh Man, The (1973) **C-105m.** **✲✲½** D: John Huston. Paul Newman, Dominique Sanda, James Mason, Harry Andrews, Ian Bannen, Nigel Patrick, Michael Hordern.

Well-made espionage thriller has only one problem: it's all been done before. Filmed in Ireland, England, and Malta; screenplay credited to Walter Hill. [PG] ▼●]

Mack the Knife (1989) C-120m. BOMB D: Menahem Golan. Raul Julia, Richard Harris, Julia Migenes, Roger Daltrey, Julie Walters, Rachel Robertson, Clive Revill, Bill Nighy. Name cast overemotes in this ill-conceived, overly stylized version of *The Threepenny Opera.* More a filmed stage revue than anything else, and not a very good one; Golan adapted the script, and completely misses the spirit of the original. This one blots the memory of Brecht and Weill (not to mention Bobby Darin). [PG-13] ▼●

Macomber Affair, The (1947) 89m. ***½ D: Zoltan Korda. Gregory Peck, Joan Bennett, Robert Preston, Reginald Denny, Carl Harbord. Penetrating, intelligent filmization of Hemingway story about conflicts that develop when hunter Peck takes married couple (Preston, Bennett) on safari. Bristling performances help make this one of the most vivid screen adaptations of a Hemingway work. Based on "The Short Happy Life of Francis Macomber"; scripted by Casey Robinson and Seymour Bennett.

Macon County Line (1974) C-89m. *** D: Richard Compton. Alan Vint, Cheryl Waters, Max Baer, Jr., Jesse Vint, Joan Blackman, Geoffrey Lewis, James Gammon, Leif Garrett. In 1954, two fun-loving brothers from Chicago roam the South before military service, but get into trouble with a Georgia sheriff. Drive-in classic was a huge hit and created a sub-genre. Intelligent, well acted and suspenseful; shot around Sacramento, California. And despite the introductory claim, it's *not* based on a true story. Baer produced and scripted. Followed by RETURN TO MACON COUNTY. [R]▼●

Mad About Mambo (1999-British) C-92m. **½ D: John Forte. William Ash, Keri Russell, Brian Cox, Theo Fraser Steele, Rosaleen Linehan, Maclean Stewart. Belfast lad desperately wants to play football (Americans: read "soccer"), but isn't any good—until he hears a Brazilian pro say it's all in the rhythm, which inspires him to take Latin dance lessons. There he meets a rich girl who's determined to win an upcoming competition. Utterly predictable fluff, but nicely done, with a dollop of social commentary and a radiant Russell. P.S. The film is about the samba, not the mambo. [PG-13]▼

Madadayo (1993-Japanese) C-134m. *** D: Akira Kurosawa. Tatsuo Matsumura, Kyoko Kagawa, Hisashi Igawa, George Tokoro. Kurosawa's final film, made when he was 83, is a gentle and contemplative series of vignettes depicting two decades in the life of a revered professor—his retirement in 1943, the bombing of his house during an air raid, building a new home, finding and losing a stray cat, etc.—all

centered around a string of birthday parties thrown for him by his ex-students at which he shouts "madadayo!" ("not yet!") to indicate he's not ready to be taken by death. A warmhearted and life-affirming finale to the career of a cinematic master. Released in the U.S. in 1998. ▼]

Mad Adventures of "Rabbi" Jacob, The (1973-French) C-96m. *** D: Gerard Oury. Louis De Funes, Suzy Delair, Marcel Dalio, Claude Giraud, Claude Pieplu. Broad slapstick comedy about hotheaded, bigoted businessman who—for complicated reasons—is forced to disguise himself as a rabbi. Uneven but often quite funny, with echoes of silent-screen humor. [G]▼]

Madagascar (2005) C-86m. ** D: Eric Darnell, Tom McGrath. Voices of Ben Stiller, Chris Rock, David Schwimmer, Jada Pinkett Smith, Sacha Baron Cohen (Ali G), Cedric the Entertainer, Andy Richter. A zebra wants to leave his comfy home at N.Y.C.'s Central Park Zoo. His best friends (a lion, a hippo, and a giraffe) try to stop him, which leads to a series of misadventures—and finds them all deposited in the wilds of Madagascar. Computer-animated feature has all the moves and rhythms of a sitcom, with "clever" references for grown-ups in the audience, but it isn't very funny. Instantly forgettable. Co-director McGrath provides the voice of the head penguin. Followed by a sequel. [PG] ▼]

Madagascar: Escape 2 Africa (2008) C-89m. **½ D: Eric Darnell, Tom McGrath. Voices of Ben Stiller, Chris Rock, David Schwimmer, Jada Pinkett Smith, Sacha Baron Cohen, Cedric the Entertainer, Andy Richter, Bernie Mac, Alec Baldwin, Sherri Shepherd, Will I. Am, Tom McGrath. The animal characters of the original attempt to return to N.Y.C. but instead find themselves in Africa, where they mix with their wild (rather than zoo-raised) brethren. Computer-animated comedy is a rarity for kids' movies: a sequel that improves on the original. [PG]❘

Madame Bovary (1934-French) 102m. ** D: Jean Renoir. Valentine Tessier, Pierre Renoir, Max Dearly, Daniel Lecourtois, Fernand Fabre, Alice Tissot, Helena Manson. Uneven, unsatisfying version of the oft-filmed Flaubert story, about the romantic, ill-fated title character. Originally three hours long, Renoir (who also scripted) was forced to drastically edit it. While the first version may have been more compelling than the existing film, the fact remains that Tessier is miscast as Emma Bovary.▼

Madame Bovary (1949) 115m. ***½ D: Vincente Minnelli. Jennifer Jones, James Mason, Van Heflin, Louis Jourdan, Christopher Kent (Alf Kjellin), Gene Lockhart, Gladys Cooper, George Zucco, Henry (Harry) Morgan. Gustave Flaubert's 19th-century heroine sacrifices her husband and their security for love, meets a horrible end. Once-controversial adaptation looks better every year, despite an odd "framing" device involving Flaubert's morals trial. Justifiably celebrated ball sequence is among the greatest set pieces of Minnelli's—or anyone else's—career. Screenplay by Robert Ardrey. Previously filmed in 1932 (as UNHOLY LOVE) and 1934 (in France, by Jean Renoir); remade in France in 1991.▼●◗

Madame Bovary (1991-French) **C-130m.** ** D: Claude Chabrol. Isabelle Huppert, Jean-Francois Balmer, Christopher Malavoy, Jean Yanne, Lucas Belvaux, Jean-Claude Bouilland. Huppert's persona is far too chilly to convey the passion of Emma Bovary in this faithful but exhaustingly dull rendering of Flaubert's classic. Vincente Minnelli's version may turn the novel upside down, but it's a far more significant movie. Even viewers with unusually refined auteurist radar would have a tough time pegging this as a Chabrol. [PG-13] ▼●◗

Madame Curie (1943) **124m.** *** D: Mervyn LeRoy. Greer Garson, Walter Pidgeon, Henry Travers, Albert Basserman, Robert Walker, C. Aubrey Smith. Despite stretches of plodding footage, bio of famed female scientist is generally excellent. Garson and Pidgeon team well, as usual.▼●◗

Madame Rosa (1977-French) **C-105m.** **½ D: Moshe Mizrahi. Simone Signoret, Samy Ben Youb, Claude Dauphin, Gabriel Jabbour, Michal Bat-Adam, Costa-Gavras. Signoret's magnetic performance gives substance to interesting but aimless film about an aging madam who earns her keep sheltering prostitutes' children. Won Best Foreign Film Oscar. [PG]▼

Madame Sousatzka (1988) **C-122m.** *** D: John Schlesinger. Shirley MacLaine, Navin Chowdhry, Peggy Ashcroft, Twiggy, Shabana Azmi, Leigh Lawson, Geoffrey Bayldon, Lee Montague. Eccentric, reclusive London piano teacher (MacLaine, wearing clanky jewelry and piles of makeup) implores her students to cultivate their artistic spirit and bring passion to their music. She meets her match in her star pupil, a 15-year-old boy of Indian heritage. Beautifully made film succeeds largely due to the strong emotions being played out, and to the superb supporting cast (especially young Chowdhry and mother Azmi—the latter a major star in her native India). [PG-13]▼●

Madame X (1929) **90m.** ** D: Lionel Barrymore. Ruth Chatterton, Lewis Stone, Raymond Hackett, Holmes Herbert, Eugenie Besserer, Sidney Toler. Leaden weeper, filmed previously in 1906, 1916, and 1920, about cold, cruel husband Stone forcing wife Chatterton onto the streets. Their son comes of age believing she's dead . . . and then gets to defend her on a murder charge. A curio at best; the remakes are better.●◗

Madame X (1937) **71m.** **½ D: Sam Wood. Gladys George, John Beal, Warren William, Reginald Owen, William Henry, Henry Daniell, Phillip Reed, Ruth Hussey. Alexandre Bisson's stalwart soap opera gets polished MGM treatment and a fine performance by Gladys George as the woman whose ultimate sacrifice is never detected by her son. Goes astray toward the end (with Beal a bit much), but worth a look.▼◗

Madame X (1966) **C-100m.** **½ D: David Lowell Rich. Lana Turner, John Forsythe, Constance Bennett, Ricardo Montalban, Burgess Meredith, Keir Dullea, Virginia Grey. Plush remake of perennial soaper of attorney defending a woman accused of murder, not knowing it's his mother. Fine cast and varied backgrounds bolster Turner's pivotal performance. Constance Bennett's last film. Remade for TV in 1981 with Tuesday Weld.▼◗

Mad Checkmate SEE: **It's Your Move**

Mad City (1997) **C-114m.** ** D: Costa-Gavras. John Travolta, Dustin Hoffman, Alan Alda, Mia Kirshner, William Atherton, Raymond J. Barry, Ted Levine, Robert Prosky, Blythe Danner. Recently fired museum guard Travolta tries to get his job back at gunpoint, accidentally taking some children hostage and giving disgraced TV newsman Hoffman a chance to get back into the big time. Well-crafted movie with a knockout performance by Hoffman is unfortunately routine and obvious. Does anyone still find it outrageous that a TV newsman might exploit his subjects for self-gain? Bill Nunn appears unbilled. Super 35. [PG-13]▼●◗

Maddening, The (1996) **C-97m.** *½ D: Danny Huston. Burt Reynolds, Angie Dickinson, Mia Sara, Brian Wimmer, Josh Mostel, William Hickey. Addled Angie and brutal Burt hold Mia and her young daughter captive in backwoods Florida, while her estranged husband searches for her. Over-the-top Southern gothic saddled with a familiar, predictable plot and uneven acting. Filmed in 1994. [R]▼●

Mad Dog SEE: **Mad Dog Morgan**

Mad Dog and Glory (1993) **C-96m.** *** D: John McNaughton. Robert De Niro, Uma Thurman, Bill Murray, Kathy Baker, David Caruso, Mike Starr, Tom Towles, J. J. Johnston, Richard Belzer. Offbeat concoction from street-smart writer Richard Price, about a nerdy cop (De Niro) who does a favor for a Chicago hood (Murray), and is repaid by having Thurman delivered to him as a "present" for one week. Though it's low-key, and doesn't quite hit the bull's-eye, it's still oddly endearing. Coproduced by Price, Martin Scorsese, and Barbara De Fina. [R]▼●◗

Mad Dog Morgan (1976-Australian) **C-102m.** *** D: Philippe Mora. Dennis Hopper, Jack Thompson, David Gulpilil, Frank Thring, Michael Pate. Hopper gives lively performance as legendary Australian outlaw of the 1800s in this moody, well-made, but extremely violent film. Retitled: MAD DOG. Panavision. [R]▼▋

Mad Dogs and Englishmen SEE: **Joe Cocker: Mad Dogs and Englishmen**

Mad Dog Time (1996) **C-93m.** ** D: Larry Bishop. Ellen Barkin, Gabriel Byrne, Richard Dreyfuss, Jeff Goldblum, Diane Lane, Gregory Hines, Kyle MacLachlan, Burt Reynolds, Christopher Jones, Henry Silva, Michael J. Pollard, Billy Idol, Billy Drago, Paul Anka, Rob Reiner, Richard Pryor, Angie Everhart. On another, but almost identical, Earth, gangsters rule supreme. Sleek Goldblum is continually challenged by upstarts, primarily MacLachlan, but his real rival is big boss Dreyfuss, fresh out of prison. Dry and intelligent, but slow and ostentatiously stylish. Goldblum is sensational, however. Written by the director, the son of Joey Bishop, who appears unbilled. Retitled TRIGGER HAPPY. [R]▼●

Made (2001) **C-95m.** *** D: Jon Favreau. Jon Favreau, Vince Vaughn, Famke Janssen, Peter Falk, Sean Combs, Faizon Love, Vincent Pastore, Jonathan Silverman. Favreau and Vaughn (who worked so well together in SWINGERS) play L.A. slackers hired by Falk to handle some shady business in N.Y.C. involving big-shot Combs (in his screen-acting debut). The stars' rapport, especially Vaughn's inept character, make MADE a whole lot funnier than many bigger movie comedies. The two stars also produced; Favreau wrote the script. Bud Cort and Sam Rockwell appear unbilled. [R]▼▋

Madea Goes to Jail (2009) **C-103m.** *½ D: Tyler Perry. Tyler Perry, Derek Luke, Keshia Knight Pulliam, David Mann, Tamela Mann, Ion Overman, Viola Davis, Sofia Vergara. Adapting yet another of his popular stage plays, writer-director Perry again stars as Madea, the trash-talking, quick-tempered matriarch of an extended Atlanta family, for his customary mix of broad comedy, sudsy sentimentality, violent slapstick, and spiritual uplift. Movie lurches clumsily between parallel plotlines: While Madea's sassy, self-absorbed antics dismay loved ones and anger law-enforcement officials, a sincere assistant DA (Luke) tries to help a fallen-from-grace former classmate (Pulliam, all grown up since *The Cosby Show*), greatly annoying his snooty fiancée (Overman). Madea is more obnoxious than usual, but undeniably funny in a verbal showdown with TV's Dr. Phil. Other TV personalities appear as themselves. Aka TYLER PERRY'S MADEA GOES TO JAIL. [PG-13]▋

Madea's Big Happy Family (2011) **C-106m.** ** D: Tyler Perry. Tyler Perry, Loretta Devine, Shad "Bow Wow" Moss, David Mann, Cassi Davis, Shannon Kane, Isaiah Mustafa, Teyana Taylor, Lauren London, Natalie Desselle Reid. Perry's cross-dressing antics as the irrepressible,

language-mangling matriarch Madea are back in full force as she tries to bring her extended dysfunctional family back together when her niece gets distressing health news and needs help in dealing with it, Perry's awkward, sometimes mawkish blend of broad comedy and overwrought melodrama is tempered by a game cast who make the most of the director's formulaic script. If you're a fan, however, the prolific Perry serves up just what you're expecting. Aka TYLER PERRY'S MADEA'S BIG HAPPY FAMILY. [PG-13]▋

Madea's Family Reunion (2006) **C-107m.** *½ D: Tyler Perry. Lynn Whitfield, Tyler Perry, Blair Underwood, Rochelle Aytes, Lisa Arrindell Anderson, Boris Kodjoe, Henry Simmons, Cicely Tyson, Maya Angelou, Keke Palmer, Jenifer Lewis. Cliché-ridden comedy-soaper about a class-conscious louse (Whitfield) who relishes manipulating her daughters. One is engaged to an abusive scoundrel, the other is a single mom who's been burned in previous relationships. Like writer-director-star Perry's DIARY OF A MAD BLACK WOMAN, this is based on his play, and he appears in three roles, most prominently the title character, a feisty matriarch. Uneasy mixture of shameless moralizing and crude humor is as subtle as a sledgehammer. Aka TYLER PERRY'S MADEA'S FAMILY REUNION. [PG-13]▋

Made For Each Other (1939) **93m.** *** D: John Cromwell. Carole Lombard, James Stewart, Charles Coburn, Lucile Watson, Alma Kruger, Esther Dale, Ward Bond, Louise Beavers. First-rate soaper of struggling young marrieds Stewart and Lombard battling illness, lack of money, Stewart's meddling mother Watson. Fine acting makes this all work. Also shown in computer-colored version.▼▋

Made for Each Other (1971) **C-101m.** *** D: Robert B. Bean. Renee Taylor, Joseph Bologna, Paul Sorvino, Olympia Dukakis, Adam Arkin. Exceptionally funny tale of two oddball types who meet at encounter session and fall in love. Screenplay by Taylor and Bologna. [PG]

Made in America (1993) **C-110m.** ** D: Richard Benjamin. Whoopi Goldberg, Ted Danson, Will Smith, Nia Long, Paul Rodriguez, Jennifer Tilly, Peggy Rea, Clyde Kusatsu, Lu Leonard. Fiercely proud, independent Goldberg is forced to reveal to her teenage daughter that she was conceived from a sperm bank. The daughter then learns that her "father" is a blowhard car salesman—who's white. Dishearteningly stupid movie based on a clever premise. The two ladies trapped in Whoopi's store, by the way, are Frances Bergen (Candice's mother) and '50s TV leading lady Phyllis Avery. [PG-13]▼●

Made in Dagenham (2010-British) **C-113m.** ** D: Nigel Cole. Sally Hawkins, Bob Hoskins, Miranda Richardson, Geraldine James,

Rosamund Pike, Andrea Riseborough, Jaime Winstone, Daniel Mays, Richard Schiff, Kenneth Cranham, Rupert Graves, John Sessions, Roger Lloyd-Pack; voice of Danny Huston. Routine dramatization of a meaty, true-life story about women who went on strike at a Ford Motor Co. plant outside of London in 1968, causing unexpected repercussions. The film gives its audience no credit for understanding anything that isn't spelled out and underlined. Good performances, especially by Hawkins as the unlikely labor leader, make it watchable. Super 35. [R] ◗

Made in Heaven (1987) C-103m. ** D: Alan Rudolph. Timothy Hutton, Kelly McGillis, Maureen Stapleton, Don Murray, Marj Dusay, Ray Gideon, Amanda Plummer, Mare Winningham, Timothy Daly. Young man dies and goes to heaven, where he meets a yet-unborn beauty and falls in love. The Big Question: how long will it take for them to meet, in their new identities on earth, and realize that they were "made for each other"? Potentially sweet fantasy-romance is undermined by too many kinky touches and inside-joke cameos (Debra Winger, in drag, plays Hutton's guardian angel). This is apparently director Rudolph's idea of a mainstream Hollywood movie. Among the other cameos: Neil Young, Tom Petty, Ellen Barkin, Ric Ocasek, David Rasche, Tom Robbins, Gary Larson. [PG] ▼◗

Made in Paris (1966) C-101m. **½ D: Boris Sagal. Ann-Margret, Louis Jourdan, Richard Crenna, Edie Adams, Chad Everett. Witless, unpolished shenanigans of Ann-Margret, fashion designer in France, falling for Jourdan. Panavision. ◗

Made in U.S.A (1966-French-Italian) C-85m. *** D: Jean-Luc Godard. Anna Karina, Jean-Pierre Léaud, Lászlo Szabó, Yves Afonso, Ernest Menzer, Marianne Faithfull. Journalist Karina turns into a trench-coated shamus to discover who killed her lover and gets mixed up in a labyrinthine mystery in a place called Atlantic City (even though the action is clearly set in France). Thoroughly whacked-out and completely unauthorized adaptation of a Richard Stark (Donald E. Westlake) novel is a bracing (if sometimes incomprehensible) homage to American noir, filled with typical Godardian movie references, allusions to political conspiracies and assassinations, and characters named Richard Widmark, Donald Siegel, Inspector Aldrich, David Goodis, Robert McNamara, and Richard Nixon. Techniscope. ◗

Madeleine (1950-British) 114m. **½ D: David Lean. Ann Todd, Leslie Banks, Elizabeth Sellars, Ivor Barnard. Superior cast improves oft-told drama of woman accused of murdering her lover. A vehicle for Lean's then wife, Ann Todd, and one of the filmmaker's few disappointments. Retitled: STRANGE CASE OF MADELEINE. ▼◗

Madeline (1998) C-90m. *** D: Daisy von Scherler Mayer. Frances McDormand, Hatty Jones, Nigel Hawthorne, Ben Daniels, Stéphane Audran. Genteel adaptation of Ludwig Bemelmans' beloved children's books about a mischievous orphan girl and the wise nun, Miss Clavel (McDormand), who looks after her and her classmates. Combining elements from several stories with new plot devices, the film captures the spirit of the books and benefits from location filming in Paris. Too bland for older children—and, most likely, their parents—but just right for young ones. [PG] ▼◗

Mademoiselle (1966-British-French) 103m. ** D: Tony Richardson. Jeanne Moreau, Ettore Manni, Keith Skinner, Umberto Orsini, Jane Berretta, Mony Rey. Ponderous, sometimes hilariously pretentious film written by Jean Genet, about a sexually repressed schoolteacher in a small French village who secretly poisons animals, sets fires, and tries to destroy an Italian woodcutter whom she can't seduce. Woeful foray into arty s&m was shot in both French and English-language versions. Panavision. ▼◗

Made of Honor (2008) C-101m. **½ D: Paul Weiland. Patrick Dempsey, Michelle Monaghan, Kevin McKidd, Kathleen Quinlan, Sydney Pollack, Kadeem Hardison, Chris Messina, Richmond Arquette, Busy Philipps, Whitney Cummings, Emily Nelson, James B. Sikking, Kevin Sussman. Dempsey is a serial womanizer but loves spending time with best friend Monaghan. Only when she announces that she's getting married (to a Scotsman she's just met) does he realize he's going to lose her. As her "maid of honor" he determines to undo her wedding plans. Slick romantic comedy covers familiar ground, but does it with brio—and great Scottish scenery. Dempsey's first star vehicle since his reemergence on TV's *Grey's Anatomy*. Super 35. [PG-13] ◗

Made-Up (2004) C-96m. **½ D: Tony Shalhoub. Brooke Adams, Lynne Adams, Eva Amurri, Kalen Conover, Light Eternity, Tony Shalhoub, Gary Sinise, Jim Issa, Lance Krall. Actor Shalhoub's directing debut purports to show us the making of a mockumentary about the extremes people go to to counterattack the aging process with all sorts of cosmetic help. A genuine family affair benefits from occasionally amusing script from Shalhoub's real-life sister-in-law Lynne Adams and fine lead performance from his wife, Brooke Adams, as a former actress who's put family ahead of show business. Overdone faux-documentary form is weakly employed here, but rescued by smart, funny dialogue, especially from Amurri's character. ◗

Mad Hot Ballroom (2005) C-105m. *** D: Marilyn Agrelo. Irresistible documentary about public elementary school students who learn ballroom dancing, with the hope of participating in a citywide competition. Upbeat without being saccharine, this film says a lot about the possibilities that unfold for children when given an opportunity to learn poise, politeness, and self-confidence through dance. The very embodiment of a feel-good movie. [PG]▷

Madhouse (1974-British) **C-89m.** ✱✱✱ D: Jim Clark. Vincent Price, Peter Cushing, Robert Quarry, Adrienne Corri, Natasha Payne, Linda Hayden. Price plays horror-film actor making a TV comeback after a long mental breakdown—until he's implicated in a series of grisly homicides. Good, if somewhat unimaginative, adaptation of Angus Hall novel *Devilday*. [PG]▼▷

Madhouse (1990) **C-90m.** ✱½ D: Tom Ropelewski. John Larroquette, Kirstie Alley, Alison LaPlaca, John Diehl, Jessica Lundy, Bradley Gregg, Dennis Miller, Robert Ginty. Larroquette and Alley find themselves unable to enjoy their new home when unwanted house guests drop in and *never* leave. Gags are drawn out endlessly; though Larroquette is a talented farceur, he can't sustain the whole film. Humor here would never pass muster on the stars' later TV series. [PG-13]▼▷

Madigan (1968) **C-101m.** ✱✱✱½ D: Donald Siegel. Richard Widmark, Henry Fonda, Harry Guardino, Inger Stevens, James Whitmore, Susan Clark, Michael Dunn, Sheree North. Excellent, unpretentious film blends day-to-day problems of detective Madigan (Widmark) with endless dilemmas facing police commissioner Fonda. Fine work by Guardino, Whitmore, and supporting cast. Adapted as TV series. Techniscope.▼▷

Madigan's Million (1968) **C-86m.** BOMB D: Stanley Prager. Dustin Hoffman, Elsa Martinelli, Cesar Romero. Pre-GRADUATE Hoffman is caught in amateurish movie released to capitalize on later success; he plays bumbling Treasury agent sent to Italy to recover money stolen by recently murdered gangster Romero. Inept. [G]▼▷

Madison (2005) **C-94m.** ✱✱½ D: William Bindley. Jake Lloyd, Mary McCormack, James (Jim) Caviezel, Bruce Dern, Reed Diamond, Richard Lee Jackson, Brent Briscoe, Paul Dooley, Chelcie Ross. Old-fashioned underdog story about a man's attempt to overcome a troubling memory and win an annual hydroplane race. Loosely based on a true story; set in Madison, Indiana, in 1971. Sincere and straightforward; definitely not for cynics. Made in 1999. Panavision. [PG]▷

Mad Little Island (1957-British) **C-94m.** ✱✱½ D: Michael Relph. Jeannie Carson, Donald Sinden, Roland Culver, Noel Purcell, Ian Hunter, Duncan MacRae, Catherine Lacey, Jean Cadell, Gordon Jackson. Sequel to TIGHT LITTLE ISLAND finds that little Scottish isle's tranquility disturbed again, this time by imminent installation of missile base. Not up to its predecessor, but on its own terms, decent enough. Original title: ROCKETS GALORE.

Mad Love (1935) **70m.** ✱✱✱ D: Karl Freund. Peter Lorre, Frances Drake, Colin Clive, Ted Healy, Sara Haden, Edward Brophy, Keye Luke. Famous *Hands of Orlac* story refitted for Lorre as mad Paris surgeon in love with married Drake. He agrees to operate on her pianist husband's injured hands, with disastrous results. Stylishly directed by legendary cameraman Freund; only debit is unwelcome comedy relief by Healy.▼▷

Mad Love (1995) **C-95m.** ✱½ D: Antonia Bird. Chris O'Donnell, Drew Barrymore, Joan Allen, Jude Ciccolella, Kevin Dunn, Liev Schreiber, Richard Chaim, Robert Nadir, Matthew Lillard. Teen-lovers-on-the-lam movie with a difference: she's mentally unstable. Attractive young stars do the best they can, but the script peters out and leaves them nothing to work with. A waste of time. By the way, this is not a remake of the 1935 movie; too bad—they could have used a dose of Peter Lorre. [PG-13] ▼▷

Mad Magazine Presents Up the Academy SEE: **Up the Academy**

Mad Magician, The (1954) **72m.** ✱✱½ D: John Brahm. Vincent Price, Mary Murphy, Patrick O'Neal, Eva Gabor, John Emery, Lenita Lane, Donald Randolph, Jay Novello. Amusing knockoff of HOUSE OF WAX, made by many of the same hands (and also shot in 3-D). This time Price is an illusionist, but otherwise the plots are pretty much alike. Much better than it has any right to be; Brahm, no stranger to Victorian-era melodrama, keeps it moving swiftly, with Lane upstaging the stars as a nosy crime novelist. Lyle Talbot appears unbilled as a program hawker. 3-D.

Madman (1978-Israeli) **C-92m.** ✱½ D: Dan Cohen. Michael Beck, F. Murray Abraham, Alan Feinstein, Sigourney Weaver, Esther Zevko. Bitterly vengeful Soviet-Jewish mental patient joins the Israeli army, intent on killing Russians. Slow, poorly directed film lacks conviction. Casting of Weaver, in her first leading role, and future Oscar-winner Abraham, gives this film its only distinction. [R]▼

Mad Max (1979-Australian) **C-93m.** ✱✱✱½ D: George Miller. Mel Gibson, Joanne Samuel, Hugh Keays-Byrne, Steve Bisley, Tim Burns, Roger Ward. In the desolate near-future, the police have their hands full keeping roads safe from suicidally daring drivers and roving gangs. Top cop Gibson tires and quits, but when his wife and child are murdered by vicious cyclists, he embarks on high-speed revenge. Weird atmosphere and characters combine with amazing stunt work in this remarkable action film. Thrown away by its U.S. distributor (which also redubbed it with American voices), later found its audience in the wake of successful sequel. Todd-AO 35. [R]▼▷

Mad Max 2 SEE: **Road Warrior, The**
Mad Max Beyond Thunderdome (1985-

[863]

Australian) **C-106m.** **★★½** D: George Miller, George Ogilvie. Mel Gibson, Tina Turner, Angelo Rossitto, Helen Buday, Rod Zuanic, Frank Thring, Angry Anderson. In the desolate future Mad Max comes upon Turner's cutthroat city of Bartertown, survives a battle-to-the-death in Roman-style Thunderdome arena, and is exiled to the desert, where he's rescued by tribe of wild children. Thunderous film has lots of action and stunts, and even some philosophical moments, but lacks the kinetic energy of THE ROAD WARRIOR (MAD MAX 2). Panavision. [PG-13]▼●❘

Madmen of Mandoras SEE: **They Saved Hitler's Brain**

Mad Money (2008) **C-104m.** **★★★** D: Callie Khouri. Diane Keaton, Queen Latifah, Katie Holmes, Ted Danson, Adam Rothenberg, Roger Cross, Stephen Root, Christopher McDonald, Finesse Mitchell, Meagen Fay. Entertaining comedy about a nouveau poor suburbanite (Keaton) who goes to work as a janitor at the Federal Reserve Bank in Kansas City and realizes there is a way to steal money so it will never be traced or even missed. She recruits two other workers to be her partners in crime, and off they go! Engaging farce is played with verve by the three female costars. Remake of a 2001 British TV movie called HOT MONEY. Super 35. [PG-13]❘

Mad Monkey, The SEE: **Twisted Obsession**

Mad Monster Party? (1967) **C-94m.** **★★** D: Jules Bass. Voices of Boris Karloff, Phyllis Diller, Gale Garnett, Ethel Ennis. Famous monsters are brought together by Baron von Frankenstein (voice of Karloff), who wants to announce his retirement, in this silly animated kiddie feature from Rankin/Bass. ▼❘

Madness of King George, The (1994-British-U.S.) **C-107m.** **★★★** D: Nicholas Hytner. Nigel Hawthorne, Helen Mirren, Ian Holm, Rupert Everett, Rupert Graves, John Wood, Amanda Donohoe, Julian Rhind-Tutt. In the late 18th century, England's benevolent King George (Hawthorne) suddenly takes ill, and shows signs of mental instability—opening the door for court intrigue and the usurping of the throne by his ne'er-do-well son, the Prince of Wales (Everett). Hawthorne vividly recreates his stage performance (surrounded by a first-rate cast) in Alan Bennett's adaptation of his witty and intriguing play; Bennett also appears in a cameo near the end as a member of Parliament. First film for theater director Hytner. Oscar winner for Art Direction. ▼●❘

Madonna Truth or Dare SEE: **Truth or Dare**

Madron (1970) **C-93m.** **★★** D: Jerry Hopper. Richard Boone, Leslie Caron, Paul Smith, Gabi Amrani, Chaim Banai, Avraham Telya. A nun who survived wagon-train massacre and a scowling gunslinger try to elude Apaches on the warpath in this ho-hum Western shot in Israel's Negev Desert. [PG]▼❘

Mad Room, The (1969) **C-92m.** **★★** D: Bernard Girard. Stella Stevens, Shelley Winters, James Ward, Carol Cole, Severn Darden, Beverly Garland, Michael Burns. Mild but unexceptional remake of LADIES IN RETIREMENT concerns the skeletons in Stella's closet. Grisly tale has a few shocking scenes. [M]▼❘

Mad Wednesday SEE: **Sin of Harold Diddlebock, The**

Madwoman of Chaillot, The (1969) **C-132m.** **★★** D: Bryan Forbes. Katharine Hepburn, Charles Boyer, Claude Dauphin, Edith Evans, John Gavin, Paul Henreid, Oscar Homolka, Margaret Leighton, Giulietta Masina, Nanette Newman, Richard Chamberlain, Yul Brynner, Donald Pleasence, Danny Kaye. Unfortunate misfire, with Hepburn as eccentric woman who refuses to believe the world no longer beautiful. Stellar cast wasted in heavy-handed allegory that just doesn't work; adapted from Jean Giraudoux's play. [G] ▼●

Mädchen in Uniform (1958-German) **C-91m.** **★★½** D: Geza von Radvanyi. Lilli Palmer, Romy Schneider, Christine Kaufmann, Therese Giehse. Rather talky story of girls' school and one particularly sensitive youngster (Schneider) who is attracted to her teacher (Palmer). Remake of famous 1931 movie is a shade above average.

Maestro, The SEE: **Home Movies**

Mafia! SEE: **Jane Austen's Mafia!**

Mafioso (1962-Italian) **99m.** **★★★** D: Alberto Lattuada. Alberto Sordi, Norma Bengell, Gabriella Conti, Ugo Attanasio, Cinzia Bruno, Katiusca Piretti, Armando Tine. Sicilian Sordi has a good job in Milan and is about to embark on his first vacation in years: a visit home to show off his Northern Italian wife and children to his skeptical family and friends. He soon learns that the village Mafia don, now a grandfatherly figure, has lost none of his power. You'll never guess where this story is headed! Fascinating blend of comedy and drama and a tailor-made vehicle for Sordi, who personifies the Italian working-class hero. Released in the U.S. in 1964; a restored version was released theatrically in 2007.❘

Mafu Cage, The (1978) **C-102m.** **★½** D: Karen Arthur. Lee Grant, Carol Kane, Will Geer, James Olson. Grant and Kane are sisters in this offbeat, unfocused melodrama of incest, jealousy, and murder. Mafu is Kane's pet orangutan; each protagonist in turn assumes animal's caged, victimized role. Retitled MY SISTER, MY LOVE and THE CAGE. [R]▼❘

Magdalene Sisters, The (2002-British-Irish) **C-119m.** **★★★½** D: Peter Mullan. Geraldine McEwan, Anne-Marie Duff, Nora-

Jane Noone, Dorothy Duffy, Eileen Walsh, Mary Murray, Britta Smith, Frances Healy, Eamonn Owens. Harrowing, fact-based drama set in 1960s Ireland in a convent where young women are incarcerated for committing such "misdeeds" as flirting with boys, becoming pregnant out of wedlock, and being raped. They are physically and psychologically abused by the head nun and her sadistic staff, who are convinced they are doing the Lord's work. Sometimes painful to watch, but it's a story that needs to be told. Director Mullan plays one girl's furious father; he based his screenplay on the experiences of actual Magdalene inmates. [R]▼❶

Magic (1978) **C-106m.** ** D: Richard Attenborough. Anthony Hopkins, Ann-Margret, Burgess Meredith, Ed Lauter, Jerry Houser, David Ogden Stiers. Ludicrous thriller about demented ventriloquist Hopkins who's tormented by his dummy—even as he tries to rekindle romance with high-school sweetie Ann-Margret. Wait for a rerun of DEAD OF NIGHT (1945) instead. Screenplay by William Goldman, from his novel. [R]▼❶❷

Magic Bubble, The SEE: **Unbecoming Age**

Magic Christian, The (1969-British) **C-93m.** *** D: Joseph McGrath. Peter Sellers, Ringo Starr; guest stars Richard Attenborough, Christopher Lee, Raquel Welch, Laurence Harvey, Yul Brynner, Wilfrid Hyde-White, Spike Milligan, Dennis Price, John Cleese, Graham Chapman, Roman Polanski. In series of wacky schemes, world's wealthiest man and his protégé wreak havoc on society by demonstrating how people will do *anything* for money. Fiendishly funny adaptation of Terry Southern's insane novel, scripted by Southern and McGrath, with contributions from Sellers, Cleese, and Chapman. Some prints run 88m. [M/PG]▼❶❷

Magic Flute, The (1974-Swedish) **C-134m.** ***½ D: Ingmar Bergman. Ulric Cold, Josef Kostlinger, Erik Saeden, Birgit Nordin, Irma Urrila, Hakan Hagegard. Lively, intelligent filmization of Mozart's opera of activities surrounding the kidnapping of Urrila, the Queen's daughter, by sorcerer Cold. Shot for Swedish TV, released as a feature in the U.S. Kenneth Branagh directed his own version of this in 2006. [G]▼❶❷

Magic Garden of Stanley Sweetheart, The (1970) **C-117m.** *½ D: Leonard Horn. Don Johnson, Linda Gillin, Michael Greer, Dianne Hull, Holly Near, Victoria Racimo. Vapid film from Robert Westbrook's novel about sexual and drug-oriented experiences of aimless college student trying to put his head together. A yawn, except for Greer, and Stanley's underground film "Headless." [R]

Magician, The (1958-Swedish) **102m.** *** D: Ingmar Bergman. Max von Sydow, Ingrid Thulin, Gunnar Bjornstrand, Naima

Wifstrand, Bibi Andersson, Erland Josephson. Complex, provocative account of Albert Emanuel Vogler (von Sydow), a 19th-century hypnotist-magician who has studied with Mesmer but finds himself debt-ridden and charged with blasphemy. A thoughtful (and too-long underrated) portrait of a man who is part-faker, part-genius.▼❶

Magician of Lublin, The (1979) **C-105m.** *½ D: Menahem Golan. Alan Arkin, Louise Fletcher, Valerie Perrine, Shelley Winters, Lou Jacobi, Maia Danziger, Lisa Whelchel. Turn-of-the-century Jewish magician tries for the big time in stilted, poorly acted version of Isaac Bashevis Singer's Polish-based novel. However, you do get to see Winters destroy a jailhouse even more impressively than Sam Jaffe's elephant did in GUNGA DIN. [R]▼

Magic in the Water (1995-Canadian) **C-101m.** *½ D: Rick Stevenson. Mark Harmon, Harley Jane Kozak, Joshua Jackson, Sarah Wayne, Willie Nark-Orn, Thomas (Tom) Cavanagh, David Rasche. In the laid-back community of Glenorky a number of residents believe there's a monster that lives in the lake; a vacationing family comes to learn there is some "truth" to the myth. All the magic *must* be in the water; there's certainly none on the screen. Routine family film feels like recycled Spielberg. [PG]▼❶

Magic of Lassie, The (1978) **C-100m.** **½ D: Don Chaffey. James Stewart, Lassie, Mickey Rooney, Alice Faye, Stephanie Zimbalist, Pernell Roberts, Michael Sharrett, Mike Mazurki. Stewart is worth watching in this bland remake of LASSIE COME HOME, as grandfather of Zimbalist and Sharrett, who are forced to turn over their beloved Lassie to mean owner Roberts. Songs performed by Pat and Debby Boone, plus Faye and even Stewart. [G]▼

Magic Sword, The (1962) **C-80m.** **½ D: Bert I. Gordon. Basil Rathbone, Estelle Winwood, Gary Lockwood, Anne Helm, Liam Sullivan, Jacques Gallo. Entertaining, often (unintentionally) hilarious adventure. Young knight Lockwood sets out to rescue beautiful princess Helm, who's been kidnapped by evil sorcerer Rathbone. In their better moments, Lockwood and Helm seem like refugees from a Beach Party movie; Rathbone and Winwood offer knowingly hammy performances.▼❶

Magic Town (1947) **103m.** *** D: William Wellman. James Stewart, Jane Wyman, Kent Smith, Regis Toomey, Donald Meek. Intriguing satire of pollster Stewart finding perfect average American town, which ruins itself when people are told his discovery. Doesn't always hit bull's-eye but remains engrossing throughout; written by Frank Capra's frequent scripter, Robert Riskin. Also shown in computer-colored version.▼❶

Magnificent Ambersons, The (1942) **88m.** **** D: Orson Welles. Tim Holt, Joseph

Cotten, Dolores Costello, Anne Baxter, Agnes Moorehead, Ray Collins, Richard Bennett, Erskine Sanford. Brilliant drama from Booth Tarkington novel of family unwilling to change its way of life with the times; mother and son conflict over her lover. Welles' follow-up to CITIZEN KANE is equally exciting in its own way, though film was taken out of his hands, recut and reshot by others. Previously filmed in 1925 as PAMPERED YOUTH. Also shown in computer-colored version. Remade for cable TV in 2001. ▼●▶

Magnificent Cuckold, The (1964-Italian) **111m.** **½ D: Antonio Pietrangeli. Claudia Cardinale, Ugo Tognazzi, Michele Girardon, Bernard Blier. Saucy sex comedy of marital infidelity, with Tognazzi, the businessman husband of Cardinale, outwitted by his curvaceous wife.

Magnificent Matador, The (1955) **C-94m.** **½ D: Budd Boetticher. Anthony Quinn, Maureen O'Hara, Manuel Rojas, Thomas Gomez, Richard Denning, Lola Albright. Another of director Boetticher's bullfighting films has Quinn an aging matador who re-examines his commitment to bullfighting, while protecting his young "protégé" (Rojas) and being romanced by American O'Hara. CinemaScope. ▼

Magnificent Obsession (1935) **101m.** *** D: John M. Stahl. Irene Dunne, Robert Taylor, Betty Furness, Charles Butterworth, Sara Haden, Ralph Morgan, Arthur Treacher. Dated but sincere adaptation of Lloyd Douglas' story about drunken playboy who mends his ways, becomes respected surgeon in order to restore the eyesight of a woman (Dunne) he blinded in an auto accident. Soap opera gave Taylor his first important lead—and made him a star. Original running time was 112m. Remade in 1954. ▶

Magnificent Obsession (1954) **C-108m.** *** D: Douglas Sirk. Jane Wyman, Rock Hudson, Barbara Rush, Otto Kruger, Agnes Moorehead, Gregg Palmer. Director Sirk pulls out all the stops in this baroque, melodramatic remake of 1935 film which remains faithful to original story. Like its predecessor, a smash hit which (once again) boosted its male lead to stardom. ▼▶

Magnificent Seven, The (1960) **C-126m.** ***½ D: John Sturges. Yul Brynner, Steve McQueen, Eli Wallach, Horst Buchholz, James Coburn, Charles Bronson, Robert Vaughn, Brad Dexter. Enduringly popular Western remake of SEVEN SAMURAI, about paid gunslingers who try to rout the bandits who are devastating a small Mexican town. Great cast of stars-to-be; memorable Elmer Bernstein score. Followed by three sequels, starting with RETURN OF THE SEVEN, and a TV series. Remade as a TVM in 1998. Panavision. ▼●▶

Magnificent Seven Ride!, The (1972) **C-100m.** **½ D: George McCowan. Lee Van Cleef, Stefanie Powers, Mariette Hartley, Michael Callan, Luke Askew, Pedro Armendariz, Jr. Newly married gunfighter decides to help his buddy fight bandits after they kidnap his wife. Fourth "ride" for the Seven isn't bad. [PG]▶

Magnificent Yankee, The (1950) **80m.** *** D: John Sturges. Louis Calhern, Ann Harding, Eduard Franz, James Lydon, Philip Ober, Richard Anderson, Hayden Rorke, John Hamilton. Genteel, entertaining saga of Oliver Wendell Holmes and his devoted wife, spanning many decades from the day they arrive in Washington, D.C., in 1902 so he may join the Supreme Court. A pleasure from start to finish, with Calhern re-creating his triumphant Broadway role. ▼▶

Magnolia (1999) **C-188m.** *** D: Paul Thomas Anderson. Tom Cruise, Julianne Moore, John C. Reilly, Jason Robards, Philip Seymour Hoffman, Melora Walters, William H. Macy, Philip Baker Hall, Jeremy Blackman, Michael Bowen, Melinda Dillon, April Grace, Luis Guzmán, Ricky Jay, Alfred Molina, Michael Murphy, Henry Gibson, Felicity Huffman, Eileen Ryan, Thomas Jane, Clark Gregg. A mosaic of misery, with an array of characters—ranging from a dying man and his angelic male nurse to a precocious kid pressured to perform on a TV game show—who must deal with anger, guilt, isolation, the sins of the fathers, and ultimately, forgiveness, on an almost biblical level. Fine performances in this emotionally exhausting film, including a dynamic Cruise as a self-invented Pied Piper of satyrdom. Overall impact is muted by the film's sheer length. Haunting songs by Aimee Mann. Written by the director. Robards' final film. Panavision. [R]▼▶

Magnum Force (1973) **C-124m.** **½ D: Ted Post. Clint Eastwood, Hal Holbrook, Mitchell Ryan, David Soul, Felton Perry, Robert Urich, Kip Niven, Tim Matheson. Eastwood's second go-round as individualistic San Francisco cop Dirty Harry Callahan. This time he traces a series of mysterious slayings to the police department itself, and finds himself in extra-hot water. Some brutal scenes; not nearly as stylish as the original. Written by John Milius and Michael Cimino. Look for Suzanne Somers at gangster's pool party. Followed by THE ENFORCER. Panavision. [R]▼●▶

Magus, The (1968-British) **C-117m.** BOMB D: Guy Green. Anthony Quinn, Michael Caine, Candice Bergen, Anna Karina, Paul Stassino, Julian Glover. Pretentious, hopelessly confusing story from John Fowles' novel about a magus, or magician (Quinn), who tries to control destiny of Caine, new arrival on his Greek island. At first mazelike story is fun, but with no relief it grows tiresome. Panavision.▶

Mahler (1974-British) **C-115m.** ∗∗∗ D: Ken Russell. Robert Powell, Georgina Hale, Richard Morant, Lee Montague, Rosalie Crutchley. Not for every taste (could it be a Russell film if it were?) but one of the director's best films; a gorgeously shot, set, and costumed bio about the turn-of-the-20th-century composer and his tormented life. If you think this means it's refined, check out the purposely anachronistic Nazi humor. Energetic to a fault. [PG]▼▶

Mahogany (1975) **C-109m.** ∗½ D: Berry Gordy. Diana Ross, Billy Dee Williams, Anthony Perkins, Jean-Pierre Aumont, Beah Richards, Nina Foch. Silly, contrived affair about fashion designer who becomes world famous, then finds happiness only in arms of unsuccessful boy friend. Wooden performances except for Perkins' extension of PSYCHO role. Panavision. [PG]▼●▶

Maid, The (1991-U.S.-French) **C-91m.** ∗∗ D: Ian Toynton. Martin Sheen, Jacqueline Bisset, Jean-Pierre Cassel, Victoria Shalet, James Faulkner. Wall Street ladies' man Sheen poses as a "maid" to ingratiate himself with French businessmom Bisset and her spoiled young daughter. Warm but predictable romantic comedy which gets off to a faulty start. [PG]▼

Maid, The (2009-Chilean) **C-96m.** ∗∗∗½ D: Sebastián Silva. Catalina Saavedra, Claudia Celedón, Mariana Loyola, Andrea García-Huidobro, Alejandro Goic, Agustín Silva, Anita Reeves, Delfina Guzmán. Raquel (Saavedra) has been housemaid, cook, and nanny for a busy, affluent Chilean family for more than 20 years. She's "part of the family" but also moody, paranoid, and highly territorial, an almost inscrutable loner—until one person penetrates her outer shell. Startlingly intimate (to a point of discomfort at times) and bracingly real, with an unexpected and cathartic resolution. Written by the director and Pedro Peirano. ▶

Maiden Heist, The (2009) **C-90m.** ∗∗∗ D: Pete Hewitt. Morgan Freeman, Christopher Walken, William H. Macy, Marcia Gay Harden, Breckin Meyer, Wynn Everett, Joseph McKenna. Lifer security guards (Walken, Freeman, Macy) devise a risky, high-tech museum heist when the art exhibit they've protected for years is callously sold out from under them to an overseas gallery. Not a gut-buster, but stellar performances turn this comedic caper into a very enjoyable romp. Released direct to DVD. [PG-13]▶

Maid in Manhattan (2002) **C-105m.** ∗∗∗ D: Wayne Wang. Jennifer Lopez, Ralph Fiennes, Natasha Richardson, Stanley Tucci, Bob Hoskins, Tyler Garcia Posey, Frances Conroy, Chris Eigeman, Marissa Matrone, Amy Sedaris. Fiennes and Lopez meet cute in a frothy, old-fashioned Cinderella story about a wealthy senatorial candidate who has a whirlwind affair with a hotel chambermaid (and single mother) who he believes to be a socialite. Formulaic to be sure, but Fiennes' charm and Lopez's believability as a hardworking mom make it an enjoyable romantic fantasy. Panavision. [PG-13] ▼▶

Maids, The (1975-British) **C-95m.** ∗∗ D: Christopher Miles. Glenda Jackson, Susannah York, Vivien Merchant, Mark Burns. Jean Genet's windy, pointless, exasperating play about two maids who hate their mistress. Excellent acting wasted on tripe. An American Film Theater Production. [PG]▼▶

Maid to Order (1987) **C-96m.** ∗∗½ D: Amy Jones. Ally Sheedy, Beverly D'Angelo, Michael Ontkean, Valerie Perrine, Dick Shawn, Tom Skerritt, Merry Clayton. Cute fairytale comedy about spoiled rich girl who's robbed of her identity, and forced to work as a maid for a gaudy and self-centered Malibu couple (played to perfection by Perrine and Shawn). D'Angelo is fun as her fairy godmother, and Ontkean is a sweet Prince Charming. Clayton scores as the household cook who belts out two numbers. Film's good-heartedness makes up for its shortcomings. [PG]▼●▶

Main Event, The (1979) **C-112m.** ∗½ D: Howard Zieff. Barbra Streisand, Ryan O'Neal, Paul Sand, Whitman Mayo, Patti D'Arbanville, Richard Lawson, James Gregory, Rory Calhoun, Ernie Hudson. Tortuous farce about a bankrupt executive who inherits a hapless boxer and goads him into resuming his career. O'Neal comes off slightly better than Streisand, but only because his yelling and screaming isn't as abrasive as hers; D'Arbanville tops them both as a girl with a *really* bad cough. [PG] ▼●▶

Maisie series SEE: *Leonard Maltin's Classic Movie Guide*

Maîtresse (1975-French) **C-112m.** ∗∗∗ D: Barbet Schroeder. Gérard Depardieu, Bulle Ogier, Andre Rouyer, Nathalie Keryan, Roland Bertin, Tony Taffin. Wickedly amusing comedy about a woman (Ogier) who earns her keep as a dominatrix, and puts her profession aside in her romantic relationship with Depardieu. Decidedly not for all tastes, but delicious fun for those who are game.▼●▶

Majestic, The (2001) **C-152m.** ∗∗ D: Frank Darabont. Jim Carrey, Martin Landau, Laurie Holden, David Ogden Stiers, James Whitmore, Jeffrey DeMunn, Ron Rifkin, Hal Holbrook, Bob Balaban, Brent Briscoe, Gerry Black, Susan Willis, Chelcie Ross, Allen Garfield, Daniel von Bargen, Bruce Campbell. A Capraesque approach to the Hollywood witch hunt of the 1950s. Apolitical screenwriter Carrey loses his memory in an accident and winds up in an idyllic coastal town where he is mistaken for Landau's long-missing son, a WW2 hero. Carrey is good in a Jimmy Stewart–ish role, but the film is long, slow, and maddeningly uneven, relying too often on secondhand emotions. Landau stands out as the owner of the town's dilapidated movie theater. Features the voices of Matt Damon, Rob Reiner, Garry Marshall, Paul Mazursky, and Sydney Pollack. [PG] ▼▶

Major and the Minor, The (1942) **100m.** ***½ D: Billy Wilder. Ginger Rogers, Ray Milland, Rita Johnson, Robert Benchley, Diana Lynn, Frankie Thomas, Jr., Charles Smith, Larry Nunn, Norma Varden. Memorable comedy of working girl Rogers disguised as 12-year-old to save train fare, becoming involved with Milland's military school. Wilder's first directorial effort (written with Charles Brackett) is still amusing. Story suggested by Edward Childs Carpenter's play *Connie Goes Home* and *Saturday Evening Post* story "Sunny Goes Home" by Fannie Kilbourne. That's Ginger's real-life mom playing her mother near the end of the film. Remade as YOU'RE NEVER TOO YOUNG. ▼▶

Major Barbara (1941-British) **131m.** **** D: Gabriel Pascal. Wendy Hiller, Rex Harrison, Robert Morley, Robert Newton, Emlyn Williams, Sybil Thorndike, Deborah Kerr, David Tree, Stanley Holloway. Topnotch adaptation of Shaw play about wealthy girl who joins Salvation Army; Harrison is a professor who woos her. Excellent cast in intelligent comedy (scripted by Anatole de Grunwald and Shaw). Kerr's film debut. Also shown at 115m. ▼▶

Major Dundee (1965) **C-124m.** **½ D: Sam Peckinpah. Charlton Heston, Richard Harris, Jim Hutton, James Coburn, Michael Anderson, Jr., Senta Berger, Mario Adorf, Brock Peters, Warren Oates, Slim Pickens, Ben Johnson, R.G. Armstrong, L.Q. Jones, Michael Pate, Dub Taylor. Obsessive Union officer Heston leads a ragtag brigade (including recently sprung Confederate prisoner Harris) to Mexico to rescue three children who've been kidnapped by Apaches. Sweeping, violent, epic-scale Western with an Ahab-like protagonist was severely cut prior to release; Peckinpah disowned the film and its score. In 2005 it was reconstituted to 136m., 6m. shy of its intended length, with a supportive new score by Christopher Caliendo. This version is more meaningful if no less flawed. Panavision. ▼▶

Majority of One, A (1962) **C-153m.** **½ D: Mervyn LeRoy. Rosalind Russell, Alec Guinness, Ray Danton, Madlyn Rhue, Mae Questel. Compared to Broadway play, this is overblown, overacted account of Jewish matron Russell falling in love with Japanese widower Guinness. Written by Leonard Spiegelgass. ▼▶

Major League (1989) **C-107m.** **½ D: David S. Ward. Tom Berenger, Charlie Sheen, Corbin Bernsen, Margaret Whitton, James Gammon, Rene Russo, Wesley Snipes, Dennis Haysbert, Charles Cyphers, Bob Uecker. Bitchy baseball team owner Whitton seeks to get out of her Cleveland franchise by organizing a team that's guaranteed to lose games—and fans. Pleasant but completely unremarkable baseball comedy, with no surprises whatsoever. Followed by two sequels. [R] ▼▶●

Major League II (1994) **C-104m.** *½ D: David S. Ward. Charlie Sheen, Tom Berenger, Corbin Bernsen, Dennis Haysbert, James Gammon, Omar Epps, Eric Bruskotter, Bob Uecker, David Keith, Alison Doody, Margaret Whitton, Takaaki Ishibashi, Michelle Burke, Randy Quaid. Excruciatingly unfunny, decidedly minor-league sequel, with most of the principals returning for a second season; the key exclusion is Wesley Snipes, replaced by Epps as Willie Mays Hayes. Crammed with cheap jokes; except for Uecker's quips, there's barely a laugh in sight. What's more, it's shamelessly loaded with plugs for commercial products. [PG] ▼▶●

Major League: Back to the Minors (1998) **C-100m.** ** D: John Warren. Scott Bakula, Corbin Bernsen, Dennis Haysbert, Takaaki Ishibashi, Jensen Daggett, Eric Bruskotter, Ted McGinley, Bob Uecker, Walt Goggins, Kenneth Johnson, Peter MacKenzie. Ex-ballplayer Bakula hires on as manager of a minor league team, transforming it from loser to contender. Sound familiar? Hohum comedy isn't as irritating as MAJOR LEAGUE II and does have Uecker around for laughs. [PG-13] ▼▶●

Major Payne (1995) **C-97m.** *½ D: Nick Castle. Damon Wayans, Karyn Parsons, William Hickey, Michael Ironside, Albert Hall, Steven Martini, Orlando Brown, Andrew Harrison Leeds, Damien Wayans. Major Benson Payne is a warrior without a war, a disciplinarian with a rigid military mentality who is oblivious to humanity and feeling. This is about to change upon his taking command of a group of underage cadets. Inane, by-the-numbers comedy, with a miscast Wayans too often hard to take in the title role. Remake of THE PRIVATE WAR OF MAJOR BENSON. Wayans coscripted. [PG-13] ▼▶●

Make Mine Mink (1960-British) **100m.** *** D: Robert Asher. Terry-Thomas, Athene Seyler, Hattie Jacques, Billie Whitelaw, Elspeth Duxbury, Raymond Huntley, Ron Moody, Jack Hedley, Kenneth Williams, Sidney Tafler. Former military man Terry-Thomas organizes unlikely band of fur thieves in this delightful British farce. Beware of shorter version on tape. ▼▶

Make Mine Music (1946) **C-74m.** **½ D: Joe Grant (production supervisor). Voices of Nelson Eddy, Dinah Shore, Jerry Colonna, The Andrews Sisters, Andy Russell, Sterling Holloway, and music by The Benny Goodman Quartet. Ten-part Walt Disney animated feature with such segments as "Peter and the Wolf," "Johnny Fedora and Alice Blue Bonnet," and "Casey at the Bat." At its worst when it tries to be "arty," and at its best when it offers bright, original pieces like "The Whale Who Wanted to Sing at the Met," and the dazzling Benny Goodman number "After You've Gone." A mixed bag, to be sure. Video release is missing "The Martins and the Coys" segment.▼❙

Maker, The (1997) **C-98m.** ** D: Tim Hunter. Matthew Modine, Mary-Louise Parker, Jonathan Rhys-Meyers, Fairuza Balk, Jesse Borrego, Michael Madsen, Lawrence Pressman. Troubled teenager, just coming of age, falls prey to his long-lost older brother who leads him into a life of crime. Off-putting at first, interesting for a while, but overall an unsatisfying brew. Never released theatrically. Panavision. [R]▼❙

Make Way For Tomorrow (1937) **92m.** ***½ D: Leo McCarey. Victor Moore, Beulah Bondi, Fay Bainter, Thomas Mitchell, Porter Hall, Barbara Read, Louise Beavers. Sensitive film of elderly couple in financial difficulty, shunted aside by their children, unwanted and unloved; shatteringly true, beautifully done. Screenplay by Vina Delmar, based on Josephine Lawrence's novel *The Years Are So Long* and a play adaptation by Helen and Nolan Leary.❙

Making It (1971) **C-97m.** ** D: John Erman. Kristoffer Tabori, Joyce Van Patten, Marlyn Mason, Bob Balaban, Lawrence Pressman, Louise Latham, Dick Van Patten. Uneven, seriocomic "youth picture" with Tabori (son of Viveca Lindfors, impressive in his first starring role) as a 17-year-old with little but sex on his mind—until he shares a traumatic experience with his mother. Filmed in Albuquerque. [R]

Making Love (1982) **C-113m.** **½ D: Arthur Hiller. Michael Ontkean, Kate Jackson, Harry Hamlin, Wendy Hiller, Arthur Hill, Nancy Olson, Terry Kiser. Repressed homosexual doctor jeopardizes 8-year marriage by coming out of the closet with sexually carefree novelist. Soaper is easy to take, but that's its problem; script, direction, nonstereotyped performances, lack edge in bland attempt to avoid offending anyone. From the director of LOVE STORY. [R]▼❙

Making Mr. Right (1987) **C-95m.** **½ D: Susan Seidelman. John Malkovich, Ann Magnuson, Glenne Headly, Ben Masters, Laurie Metcalf, Polly Bergen, Harsh Nayyar, Hart Bochner, Polly Draper, Christian Clemenson, Susan Anton. Nerdy scientist Malkovich has created a nearly human android in his own image; public relations whiz Magnuson is hired to sell the concept of Ulysses to the public. Hit-or-miss comedy has good performances and many effective moments, but misses the bull's-eye. Filmed and set in Miami Beach. [PG-13]▼❍

Making the Grade (1984) **C-105m.** *½ D: Dorian Walker. Judd Nelson, Jonna Lee, Carey Scott, Dana Olsen, Gordon Jump, Walter Olkewicz, Ronald Lacey, Scott McGinnis. Spoiled rich kid hires young hustler to take his place at prep school. Better than the average raunchy youth comedies of the '80s, but that's faint praise. Andrew Clay plays a character here named Dice. [R]▼❙

Makioka Sisters, The (1985-Japanese) **C/B&W-140m.** ** D: Kon Ichikawa. Keiko Kishi, Yoshiko Sakuma, Sayuri Yoshinaga, Yuko Kotegawa, Juzo Itami. Emotionally distant, occasionally confusing tale of four upper-class sisters, two married and two single, and the manner in which they contend with tradition and social change in pre-WW2 Osaka. Ichikawa coscripted, from a highly regarded novel by Junichiro Tanizaki.▼❍

Mako: The Jaws of Death (1976) **C-93m.** **½ D: William Grefe. Richard Jaeckel, Jenifer Bishop, Harold Sakata, John Chandler, Buffy Dee. Good horror premise has Jaeckel a friend and protector of sharks who goes berserk when both he and his "friends" are exploited. Shown theatrically as THE JAWS OF DEATH. [PG]▼

Malaya (1949) **98m.** **½ D: Richard Thorpe. Spencer Tracy, James Stewart, Valentina Cortese, Sydney Greenstreet. Routine WW2 melodrama set in the Pacific, about Allies' efforts to smuggle out rubber. Good cast let down by so-so script.▼❙

Malcolm (1986-Australian) **C-86m.** *** D: Nadia Tass. Colin Friels, John Hargreaves, Lindy Davies, Chris Haywood, Charles "Bud" Tingwell, Beverly Phillips, Judith Stratford. Charming, disarmingly offbeat comedy about a slow-witted young man with a genius for Rube Goldberg–like mechanical devices and his unusual entry into a life of crime. Surefooted directorial debut for actress Tass, whose husband David Parker wrote the screenplay (and designed the Tinkertoys) and whose real-life brother was the inspiration for the character of Malcolm. Infectious music score performed by The Penguin Cafe Orchestra. Australian Film Institute winner for Best Picture and other awards. [PG-13]▼❍

Malcolm X (1972) **92m.** *** No director credited. Excellent documentary about the life and times of the black revolutionary leader, which allows him to speak for himself. (Passages from his autobiography are spoken by James Earl Jones; his eulogy is read, as it was in real life, by Ossie Davis.) A fascinating time capsule and history lesson. Particularly interesting to see alongside Spike Lee's later film, which was produced and cowritten by Marvin Worth and Arnold Perl, the same partnership responsible for this Oscar-nominated documentary. [PG]▼❍

Malcolm X (1992) **C-201m.** ***½ D: Spike Lee. Denzel Washington, Angela Bassett, Albert Hall, Al Freeman, Jr., Delroy Lindo, Spike Lee, Theresa Randle, Kate Vernon,

Lonette McKee, Tommy Hollis, Giancarlo Esposito, Craig Wasson, John Ottavino, David Patrick Kelly, Shirley Stoler, Christopher Plummer, Peter Boyle, Karen Allen, Nick (Nicholas) Turturro. Sweeping biography of the black leader, tracing his transformation from street hustler to prison inmate to religious convert—and his ascension to national leadership while preaching the words of Elijah Muhammad. Compelling every step of the way, with a superb performance by Washington and sure-footed guidance from director/co-writer Lee. A surprisingly measured and intelligent portrait of a still-controversial figure, with Lee's expected indulgences limited to the main title sequence and epilogue. Screenplay by Lee and Arnold Perl, based on the book *The Autobiography of Malcolm X,* as told to Alex Haley. Many famous people appear as themselves. [PG-13]▼●)

Male Animal, The (1942) 101m. ***½ D: Elliott Nugent. Henry Fonda, Olivia de Havilland, Joan Leslie, Jack Carson, Herbert Anderson, Don DeFore, Hattie McDaniel, Eugene Pallette. Intelligent, entertaining Elliott Nugent–James Thurber comedy of college professor Fonda defending his rights, while losing wife de Havilland to old flame Carson. Excellent performances in this fine, contemporary film, with spoof on typical football rallies a highlight. Remade as SHE'S WORKING HER WAY THROUGH COLLEGE.▼●

Malena (2000-Italian-U.S.) C-94m. **½ D: Giuseppe Tornatore. Monica Bellucci, Giuseppe Sulfaro, Luciano Federico, Matilde Piana, Pietro Notarianni, Gaetano Aronica. Maddeningly uneven farce, set in 1941 Sicily, about an earthy, stunningly beautiful woman (Bellucci) whose husband has gone off to war and who must suffer the brunt of small-town sexism, jealousy, and gossip; one of her ardent admirers is an imaginative, obsessive 13-year-old boy (Sulfaro). A decidedly mixed bag, at once bittersweet and simplistic. Panavision. [R]▼●)

Male of the Century, The (1975-French) C-90m. **½ D: Claude Berri. Juliet Berto, Claude Berri, Hubert Deschamps, Laszlo Szabo, Yves Afonso. Writer-director Berri stars in this slight, occasionally perceptive comedy as a jealous chauvinistic husband; his wife is taken hostage during a bank robbery . . . and he's positive that she's becoming sexually involved with her captor.

Malibu Express (1985) C-101m. ** D: Andy Sidaris. Darby Hinton, Sybil Danning, Art Metrano, Shelley Taylor Morgan, Lori Sutton, Barbara Edwards. Hinton is a private detective working on a complex espionage and blackmail case, but this film is just an excuse to showcase the charms of numerous *Playboy* centerfold models (accounting for its frequent programming on

pay-cable services). A loose remake of Sidaris' 1973 STACEY. [R]▼●

Malibu's Most Wanted (2003) C-86m. ** D: John Whitesell. Jamie Kennedy, Taye Diggs, Anthony Anderson, Blair Underwood, Regina Hall, Damien Dante Wayans, Ryan O'Neal, Bo Derek, Jeffrey Tambor, Kellie Martin; voice of Snoop Dogg. B-Rad (a character Kennedy introduced on his self-named TV series) is a pampered white boy from Malibu, California, who has adopted the personality and patois of an urban black rapper. His father (O'Neal) is running for governor, so campaign manager Underwood hires two black actors to kidnap B-Rad and scare him out of his pose. Diggs and Anderson, as the "homies for hire," bring the most laughs to this one-joke comedy. Super 35. [PG-13]▼●

Malice (1993) C-107m. **½ D: Harold Becker. Alec Baldwin, Nicole Kidman, Bill Pullman, Bebe Neuwirth, George C. Scott, Anne Bancroft, Peter Gallagher, Josef Sommer, Tobin Bell, Debrah Farentino, Gwyneth Paltrow. A professor at a New England college finds himself undermined—and overshadowed—by the arrival in town of a hotshot surgeon who rents a room from him and his wife. The plot thickens, and gets progressively sillier, in this slick, engrossing, sexy thriller. Good performances help disguise story holes until the denouement, when it all goes to pieces. Overheated and fairly absurd. [R]▼●)

Malicious (1973-Italian) C-97m. **½ D: Salvatore Samperi. Laura Antonelli, Turi Ferro, Alessandro Momo, Angela Luce, Pino Caruso, Tina Aumont. Seriocomic slice of life about a sexy, though innocent young woman who comes to work as housekeeper for a widower and his three sons—and tantalizes both the father and one of his teenage boys. Intriguing but often unpleasant look at mores, morals, and hypocrisy, with typically titillating role for Antonelli. Originally titled MALIZIA. Techniscope. [R]▼

Malizia SEE: **Malicious**

Mallrats (1995) C-95m. *½ D: Kevin Smith. Shannen Doherty, Jeremy London, Jason Lee, Claire Forlani, Jason Mewes, Kevin Smith, Michael Rooker, Renee Humphrey, Ethan Suplee, Ben Affleck, Joey Lauren Adams, Priscilla Barnes. Inert, unfunny film, from the creator of CLERKS, about a band of friends, enemies, former girl- and boyfriends, and geeks who hang out at a suburban mall. Don't look for more story than that . . . or much else. Comic book legend Stan Lee plays himself in a rather contrived subplot. Extended edition runs 123m. [R]▼●

Malone (1987) C-92m. *½ D: Harley Cokliss. Burt Reynolds, Cliff Robertson, Kenneth McMillan, Cynthia Gibb, Scott Wilson, Lauren Hutton. Robertson is a megalomaniac plotting to take over America;

lucky for us the mountain-town gas station essential to his plans is the same one ex-CIA agent Reynolds stops at for a fill-up. Hybrid of SHANE and a modern-day shoot-em-up turns pretty ludicrous after a passable beginning; note how quickly Burt recovers from a golf ball–size bullet wound. [R] ▼●

Maltese Bippy, The (1969) C-88m. ** D: Norman Panama. Dan Rowan, Dick Martin, Carol Lynley, Julie Newmar, Mildred Natwick, Fritz Weaver, Robert Reed. Werewolves, haunted houses, good cast, but few true laughs in tired horror-movie spoof. Film tried to cash in on the great success of Rowan and Martin's *Laugh-In* TV show—and their "bippy" catchword. Panavision. [G]

Maltese Falcon, The (1931) 80m. *** D: Roy Del Ruth. Bebe Daniels, Ricardo Cortez, Dudley Digges, Robert Elliott, Thelma Todd, Una Merkel, Dwight Frye. First film version of Dashiell Hammett story is quite good, with Cortez more of a ladies' man than Bogart; otherwise very similar to later classic. Remade in 1936 (as SATAN MET A LADY) and 1941. ▼❚

Maltese Falcon, The (1941) 100m. **** D: John Huston. Humphrey Bogart, Mary Astor, Peter Lorre, Sydney Greenstreet, Ward Bond, Gladys George, Barton MacLane, Elisha Cook, Jr., Lee Patrick, Jerome Cowan. Outstanding detective drama improves with each viewing; Bogey is Dashiell Hammett's "hero" Sam Spade, Astor his client, Lorre the evasive Joel Cairo, Greenstreet (in his talkie film debut) the Fat Man, and Cook the neurotic gunsel Wilmer. Huston's first directorial effort (which he also scripted) moves at lightning pace, with cameo by his father Walter Huston as Captain Jacobi. Previously filmed in 1931 and in 1936 (as SATAN MET A LADY). Also shown in computer-colored version. ▼●❚

Mama's Boy (2007) C-92m. *½ D: Tim Hamilton. Jon Heder, Diane Keaton, Jeff Daniels, Anna Faris, Eli Wallach, Mary Kay Place, Sarah Chalke, Laura Kightlinger. Irredeemably clunky "comedy" with Heder as a self-absorbed 29-year-old slacker whose emotional bullying of his widowed mother (Keaton) is far too creepy to be funny. When mom falls for a motivational speaker (Daniels), the son rightly senses a rival for her attention and sets out to sabotage the budding romance. Keaton and Daniels are better than the movie deserves. Barely released, and with good reason. [PG-13]❚

Mama, There's a Man in Your Bed (1989-French) C-111m. *** D: Coline Serreau. Daniel Auteuil, Firmine Richard, Pierre Vernier, Maxime Leroux, Gilles Privat, Muriel Combeau, Catherine Salviat. Unlikely romance between the harried CEO of a yogurt company and the financially strapped cleaning woman who will do any-

thing to keep her five children (from five different marriages) from going hungry. Clever, heartwarming story from the director of THREE MEN AND A CRADLE has a lot to say about class and color differences in a world none too tolerant of either. Original French title: ROMUALD ET JULIET. ▼●

Mambo (1954-U.S.-Italian) 94m. **½ D: Robert Rossen. Silvana Mangano, Michael Rennie, Shelley Winters, Vittorio Gassman, Eduardo Ciannelli, Mary Clare, Katherine Dunham. Offbeat romance set in Venice; young saleswoman, her love life complicated by a penniless gambler and a sickly count, becomes a famous dancer. Strong cast keeps it watchable. Original Italian running time 107m. ▼

Mambo Italiano (2003-Canadian) C-89m. *½ D: Émile Gaudreault. Luke Kirby, Paul Sorvino, Ginette Reno, Claudia Ferri, Peter Miller, Mary Walsh, Sophie Lorain. Or, *My Big Fat Gay Wedding*. Bombastic, by-the-numbers comedy about a nice Italian-Canadian boy (Kirby) who's struggling to find a way to tell his stereotypically ethnic parents that he's gay. Plays like a tired, dated TV sitcom, though it's based on a play by Steve Galluccio. [R] ▼❚

Mambo Kings, The (1992) C-104m. **½ D: Arne Glimcher. Armand Assante, Antonio Banderas, Cathy Moriarty, Maruschka Detmers, Desi Arnaz, Jr., Celia Cruz, Roscoe Lee Browne, Vondie Curtis-Hall, Tito Puente, Talisa Soto. Two brothers leave Cuba for the U.S. in the early 1950s and try to establish their own band. Colorful adaptation of Oscar Hijuelos' Pulitzer Prize–winning novel *Mambo Kings Play Songs of Love* is disappointingly underwritten and one-dimensional. Most intriguing sequence involves Desi Jr. playing his father and inviting the brothers to appear on an episode of *I Love Lucy*. Adapted for the stage in 2005. [R] ▼●

Mame (1974) C-131m. BOMB D: Gene Saks. Lucille Ball, Robert Preston, Beatrice Arthur, Bruce Davison, Joyce Van Patten, Don Porter, Audrey Christie, Jane Connell, Kirby Furlong, John McGiver. Hopelessly out-of-date musical taken from Jerry Herman's Broadway hit and based on AUNTIE MAME will embarrass even those who love Lucy. Calling Fred and Ethel Mertz! Bea Arthur re-creates her Tony-winning stage role; Lucy's final feature film. Panavision. [PG]▼●

Mamma Mia! (2008) C-108m. *** D: Phyllida Lloyd. Meryl Streep, Pierce Brosnan, Colin Firth, Stellan Skarsgård, Julie Walters, Dominic Cooper, Amanda Seyfried, Christine Baranski. Cheerful adaptation of the internationally successful stage show based on the enduring songs of Swedish pop group ABBA. Seyfried has been raised by her mom (Streep) on a Greek island; now that she's going to be married, she sends wedding invitations to the three men who might be her father. Thin story strings together a parade of songs by an attractive cast (though Streep's pipes outshine her costars'), with beautiful Greek scenery as the backdrop. The creators of the show also put together this feel-good film, which seemingly has four or five finales . . . but they're all fun. Panavision. [PG-13]▶

Mamma Roma (1962-Italian) **110m. ***½** D: Pier Paolo Pasolini. Anna Magnani, Ettore Garofolo, Franco Citti, Silvana Corsini, Luisa Orioli, Paolo Volponi. Magnani dominates the screen as the title character, an earthy, larger-than-life woman attempting to abandon her career as a prostitute and enter the middle class. The scenario charts her complex relationship with (and high hopes for) her adolescent son, with whom she is reunited after many years. Pasolini scripted this fascinating, intensely involving drama which is loaded with cinematic references; Mamma Roma would be the same character Magnani played in Rossellini's OPEN CITY had that character not been killed at the finale! Watch for Lamberto Maggiorani, the star of De Sica's BICYCLE THIEVES, in a small but pivotal role. Released theatrically in the U.S. in 1994.▼▶

Mammoth (2009-Swedish-Danish-German) **C-125m. **½** D: Lukas Moodysson. Gael García Bernal, Michelle Williams, Marife Necesito, Sophie Nyweide, Run Srinikornchot, Tom McCarthy, Jan Nicdao. Complex, ambitious, but flawed account of an affluent N.Y.C. couple: businessman Bernal and doctor Williams. They have a young daughter and a caring Filipino nanny, whose own children remain in her homeland, thousands of miles away and wallowing in poverty. Plot threads involve Bernal's trip to Bangkok, where he helps out an exploited young hooker, and Williams' reaction as she doctors a child who has been stabbed by his mother. Overlong, meandering film still offers astute commentary on how all children are not created equal. Moodysson also scripted. ▶

Man, The (1972) **C-93m. **** D: Joseph Sargent. James Earl Jones, Martin Balsam, Burgess Meredith, Lew Ayres, William Windom, Barbara Rush, Janet MacLachlan. Black Senator Jones becomes President of U.S. after freak disaster kills chief executive in Europe. Originally made for TV but released theatrically; marginally interesting Rod Serling adaptation of Irving Wallace best-seller plus acceptable performances add up to forgettable experience. Cameo appearance by Jack Benny. [G]

Man, The (2005) **C-83m. BOMB** D: Les Mayfield. Samuel L. Jackson, Eugene Levy, Luke Goss, Miguel Ferrer, Susie Essman, Anthony Mackie, Horatio Sanz, Rachael Crawford. A case of mistaken identity forces a tough ATF agent (Jackson) to team up with a nerdy dental-supply salesman (Levy) to pull off a sting operation. Contrived, derivative, mismatched-buddies romp mixes lame action and juvenile humor. Yet another waste of Levy's comic talent. [PG-13]▶

Man About Town (2005-U.S.-Canadian) **C-98m. *** D: Mike Binder. Ben Affleck, Rebecca Romijn, John Cleese, Gina Gershon, Adam Goldberg, Howard Hesseman, Bai Ling, Jerry O'Connell, Kal Penn, Samuel Ball, Damien Dante Wayans. As both clients and wife slip away, a disaffected talent agent starts keeping a secret daily journal to examine his smileless existence . . . only to have it stolen by a ruthless, amoral reporter. Affleck gives a fine performance as a loser who has everything, but this act of Hollywood self-flagellation, though optically clever, is an unlikable pageant of past and present pain. Written by the director, who also plays a fellow rep. Super 35. [R]▶

Management (2009) **C-93m. *** D: Stephen Belber. Jennifer Aniston, Steve Zahn, Woody Harrelson, Margo Martindale, Fred Ward, James Liao, Mark Boone Junior, Tzi Ma. Whimsical comedy-drama of an almost childlike 30-something misfit (Zahn) who lives and works at his parents' Arizona motel. When businesswoman Aniston checks in he is instantly smitten, and though she's unresponsive at first, he is undeterred. How—and why—their relationship develops is the heart and soul of this small-scale, entertaining film. At turns disarming, poignant, and funny. Playwright Belber's debut feature as writer-director. [R]▶

Man and a Woman, A (1966-French) **C-102m. ***½** D: Claude Lelouch. Anouk Aimée, Jean-Louis Trintignant, Pierre Barouh, Valerie Lagrange. Moving romantic drama about young widow and widower who fall in love; one of the 1960s' most popular love stories, thanks to intelligent script, winning performances, innovative direction and camerawork, Francis Lai's music score. Oscar winner for Best Foreign Film, Best Original Screenplay. Remade by cowriter/director Lelouch in 1977 as ANOTHER MAN, ANOTHER CHANCE, and followed by A MAN AND A WOMAN: 20 YEARS LATER.▼▶

Man and a Woman: 20 Years Later, A (1986) **C-108m. *½** D: Claude Lelouch. Anouk Aimée, Jean-Louis Trintignant, Richard Berry, Evelyne Bouix, Robert Hossein, Marie-Sophie Pochat. Badly misconceived sequel to one of the '60s' essential "date" movies finds former script girl Aimee now a film producer, race driver Trintignant involved in a Paris-to-Dakar rally. Silly film-within-a-film pays homage to DIAL M FOR MURDER and—in one desert scene—the opening to HATARI! Someone should have reminded Lelouch

that "hatari!" means "danger" in Swahili.
[PG]▼▶

Man and Boy (1972) C-98m. **½ D: E.
W. Swackhamer. Bill Cosby, Gloria Fos-
ter, Leif Erickson, George Spell, Douglas
Turner Ward, John Anderson, Yaphet Kotto,
Henry Silva, Dub Taylor. Civil War vet and
young son take after the thief who has sto-
len their horse in a kind of black BICYCLE
THIEF. Decent enough family film with
Cosby in rare dramatic role. [G]▼▶

Man Apart, A (2003) C-109m. ** D:
F. Gary Gray. Vin Diesel, Larenz Tate,
Timothy Olyphant, Geno Silva, Jacqueline
Obradors, Steve Eastin, Juan Fernandez,
Jeff Kober. Undercover DEA operatives
Diesel and Tate bust a Mexican drug lord
whose replacement—a fiendish, mysterious figure called El Diablo—is even
more ruthless than his predecessor. Slick,
bullet-riddled action yarn gives Diesel
a star vehicle in the mold of earlier Stallone movies, but yields to predictability at
every turn. Diesel coexecutive-produced.
Super 35. [R]▼

Man at the Top (1973-British) C-92m. ***
D: Mike Vardy. Kenneth Haigh, Nanette
Newman, Harry Andrews, John Quentin,
Mary Maude. Feature spin-off of British TV
show which in turn is a spin-off of ROOM
AT THE TOP, with Haigh as Joe Lampton,
now caught in EXECUTIVE SUITE–type
business conflicts.

Man, a Woman and a Bank, A (1979-
Canadian) C-100m. **½ D: Noel Black.
Donald Sutherland, Brooke Adams, Paul
Mazursky, Allen Magicovsky, Leigh
Hamilton. Needless but inoffensive caper
movie about a $4 million bank heist, with
pleasing performances by the three leads.
Magicovsky isn't too appealing as a suicidal whipped cream freak, but how many
suicidal whipped cream freaks do you know
that *are*? [PG]▼▶

Man Betrayed, A (1941) 83m. ** D:
John H. Auer. John Wayne, Frances Dee,
Edward Ellis, Wallace Ford, Ward Bond,
Harold Huber, Alexander Granach. Coun-
try lawyer crusades against father of girl-
friend to prove that he's crooked politician.
Minor melodrama with the Duke in one
of his oddest roles. Retitled: WHEEL OF
FORTUNE.▼

Man Bites Dog (1992-Belgian) 88m. ***
D: Rémy Belvaux, André Bonzel, Benôt
Poelvoorde. Benôt Poelvoorde, Jacqueline
Poelvoorde Pappaert, Nelly Pappaert, Hector Pappaert. Controversial, no-holds-barred
portrait of an unashamedly brutal serial
killer (played by codirector Poelvoorde).
The nonstop, graphic brutality can be
viewed either as sensationalism, a sick joke,
or as a comment on violence on-screen and
in society. Shot in cinéma-vérité documentary style; codirectors Belvaux and Bonzel
play a reporter and cameraman making a

film about the killer (whose actions clearly
are spurred on by their presence). Definitely
not for all tastes. Also available in unrated
version. [NC-17]▼▶

Man Called Adam, A (1966) 102m. ** D:
Leo Penn. Sammy Davis, Jr., Ossie Davis,
Cicely Tyson, Louis Armstrong, Frank Sinatra, Jr., Peter Lawford, Mel Torme, Lola
Falana, Gerald O'Loughlin. Pretentious
melodrama of trumpet-player Davis trying
to find some purpose in life; amateurishly
produced.▼▶

Man Called Dagger, A (1968) C-86m.
BOMB D: Richard Rush. Terry Moore, Jan
Murray, Sue Ane Langdon, Paul Mantee,
Eileen O'Neill, Maureen Arthur. Ex-Nazi
scientist journeys to L.A. followed by se-
cret agent Richard Dagger to assist former
S.S. colonel (Murray!) in world-conquering
plan. Embarrassing script, acting.

Man Called Flintstone, The (1966) C-
87m. **½ D: Joseph Barbera, William
Hanna. Voices of Alan Reed, Mel Blanc,
Jean Vander Pyl, June Foray. Feature-length
cartoon based on TV series of Stone Age
characters satirizes superspy films. Mainly
for kids.▼▶

Man Called Horse, A (1970) C-114m.
**½ D: Elliot Silverstein. Richard Harris,
Judith Anderson, Jean Gascon, Manu Tupou, Corinna Tsopei, Dub Taylor. English
aristocrat gets captured by Sioux Indians,
undergoes torture to prove his worth. Sometimes gripping, sometimes gory; fine score
by Leonard Rosenman. Followed by THE
RETURN OF A MAN CALLED HORSE
and TRIUMPHS OF A MAN CALLED
HORSE. Panavision. [M/PG]▼▶

Man Called Peter, A (1955) C-119m. ***
D: Henry Koster. Richard Todd, Jean Pe-
ters, Marjorie Rambeau, Doris Lloyd, Em-
mett Lynn. Moving account of Scotsman
Peter Marshall who became clergyman and
U.S. Senate chaplain; sensitively played by
Todd, with fine supporting cast. Cinema-
Scope.▼▶

Man Called Sledge, A (1970-Italian) C-
93m. ** D: Vic Morrow. James Garner,
Dennis Weaver, Claude Akins, John Marley, Laura Antonelli, Wade Preston. Violent
Western about a gunman whose gang goes
after a cache of gold stored in a prison, and
then fights over the loot. Notable mainly
for Garner's atypical role as brutal outlaw.
Techniscope. [R]▼▶

**Manchu Eagle Murder Caper Mystery,
The** (1973) C-80m. **½ D: Dean Har-
grove. Gabriel Dell, Will Geer, Joyce Van
Patten, Anjanette Comer, Jackie Coogan,
Huntz Hall, Barbara Harris. Fairly successful satire of tough private eye melodramas
of 1940s. Cast and director on top of their
material help make up for cheapness of production. [PG]

Manchurian Candidate, The (1962)
126m. ***½ D: John Frankenheimer. Frank

Sinatra, Laurence Harvey, Janet Leigh, Angela Lansbury, Henry Silva, James Gregory, John McGiver, Leslie Parrish, Khigh Dhiegh. Tingling political paranoia thriller about strange aftermath of a Korean war hero's decoration and his mother's machinations to promote her Joseph McCarthy-like husband's career. Harrowing presentation of Richard Condon story (adapted by George Axelrod). Score by David Amram. Rereleased theatrically in 1987; remade in 2004. ▼●◗

Manchurian Candidate, The (2004) C-130m. **½ D: Jonathan Demme. Denzel Washington, Meryl Streep, Liev Schreiber, Jon Voight, Kimberly Elise, Jeffrey Wright, Ted Levine, Bruno Ganz, Miguel Ferrer, Dean Stockwell, Jude Ciccolella, Simon McBurney, Vera Farmiga, Obba Babatundé, Željko Ivanek, John Bedford Lloyd, Anthony Mackie, Robyn Hitchcock, Bill Irwin, Charles Napier, Roger Corman, Tracey Walter. Washington, a veteran of Operation Desert Storm, is obsessed by the feeling that something isn't right about his memories of combat or the decorations given his comrade in arms (Schreiber), who's now running for Vice-President, with his powerful mother, a Senator (Streep), pushing him along. Remake of a genuinely great film puts an intriguing, modern spin on the depiction of backroom power brokers but lacks the chilling edge—and starkness—that marked the original. Tina Sinatra coproduced. [R] ▼◗

Man Could Get Killed, A (1966) C-99m. **½ D: Ronald Neame, Cliff Owen. James Garner, Melina Mercouri, Sandra Dee, Tony Franciosa, Robert Coote, Roland Culver. Businessman Garner is mistaken for international spy in this so-so secret agent spoof with beautiful Rome and Lisbon locations. Bert Kaempfert's score introduces the hit tune "Strangers in the Night." Panavision.

Mandela (1996) C-120m. *** D: Jo Menell, Angus Gibson. Documentary chronicling the life of one of South Africa's greatest leaders, famed political prisoner and Nobel prizewinner Nelson Mandela. From his tribal upbringing to his work with the African National Congress, viewers are given a sense of what shaped his future role under apartheid rule to then become South Africa's first black president. Insightful and inspiring. Coproduced by Jonathan Demme. ▼●◗

Manderlay (2005-Danish-Swedish-Dutch-French-German-British) C-139m. *½ D: Lars von Trier. Bryce Dallas Howard, Isaach de Bankolé, Danny Glover, Willem Dafoe, Jeremy Davies, Lauren Bacall, Chloë Sevigny, Jean-Marc Barr, Udo Kier, Zeljko Ivanek; narrated by John Hurt. Venal followup to DOGVILLE, with the same bare-bones staging, finds righteous idealist Grace (now played by Howard) in the Deep South in 1933; she and her gangster father discover a plantation where blacks still live as slaves.

Grace opts to remain at Manderlay as liberator, but obstacles and dysfunction make that exceedingly difficult. Writer-director von Trier's contempt for the U.S. practically oozes from the screen. Title may refer to the Manderley estate in REBECCA, with its own themes of domination, and possibly also MANDINGO. HD 24P Widescreen. ◗

Mandingo (1975) C-127m. BOMB D: Richard Fleischer. James Mason, Susan George, Perry King, Richard Ward, Brenda Sykes, Ken Norton, Lillian Hayman, Roy Poole, Ji-Tu Cumbuka, Paul Benedict, Ben Masters. Trashy potboiler will appeal only to the s&m crowd. Mason is a bigoted plantation patriarch, George his oversexed daughter, Norton—what else?—a fighter. Stinko! Based on the Kyle Onstott novel, the first of a long series, although only one more—DRUM—was filmed. [R] ▼●◗

Man-Eater SEE: **Shark!**

Man for All Seasons, A (1966-British) C-120m. **** D: Fred Zinnemann. Paul Scofield, Wendy Hiller, Leo McKern, Robert Shaw, Orson Welles, Susannah York, John Hurt, Nigel Davenport, Vanessa Redgrave. Splendid film based on Robert Bolt's play about Sir Thomas More's personal conflict when King Henry VIII asks his support in break with Pope and formation of Church of England. Scofield's rich characterization matched by superb cast, vivid atmosphere. Six Oscars: Best Actor, Director, Picture, Screenplay (Robert Bolt), Cinematography (Ted Moore), Costumes. Remade for TV in 1988 with Charlton Heston. ▼●◗

Man Friday (1976-British) C-115m. *½ D: Jack Gold. Peter O'Toole, Richard Roundtree, Peter Cellier, Christopher Cabot, Joel Fluellen. Defoe classic rewritten to conform to today's racial standards. Amid gore and confusing flashbacks, Friday revolts against bondage, outwits master Crusoe, and also drives him mad (as shown in Cannes, Crusoe, having failed to "educate" Friday to British standards, and himself refused admission to Friday's tribe, blows his brains out!). [PG] ▼◗

Man from Elysian Fields, The (2002) C-105m. *** D: George Hickenlooper. Andy Garcia, Mick Jagger, Julianna Margulies, Olivia Williams, James Coburn, Anjelica Huston, Michael Des Barres, Richard Bradford, Xander Berkeley, Rosalind Chao, Joe Santos. A failed novelist with a loving wife and son is so desperate that he accepts a stranger's offer to work for his escort service. He becomes involved with a beautiful woman and, unexpectedly, her husband, a gruff, Pulitzer Prize–winning novelist who is nearing the end of his life. Consistently intriguing fable creates a world of its own, and has enough going for it (including strong, sincere performances) to forgive it its imperfections. Garcia also coproduced. [R] ▼◗

Man From Laramie, The (1955) C-104m.

*** D: Anthony Mann. James Stewart, Arthur Kennedy, Donald Crisp, Cathy O'Donnell, Alex Nicol, Aline MacMahon, Wallace Ford. Taut action tale of revenge, with Stewart seeking those who killed his brother. CinemaScope.▼▶

Man From O.R.G.Y. (1970) C-92m. *½ D: James A. Hill. Robert Walker, Steve Rossi, Slappy White, Louisa Moritz. Banal counterespionage comedy-drama. Who's got the secrets? [R]

Man From Planet X, The (1951) 70m. **½ D: Edgar G. Ulmer. Robert Clarke, Margaret Field, Raymond Bond, William Schallert. Scottish Highlands are visited by alien from wandering planet; at first he is benign, but evil designs of Schallert turn him against human race. Extremely cheap, but atmospheric; script is stilted but story is strong and somewhat unusual.▼●▶

Man From Snowy River, The (1982-Australian) C-115m. ***½ D: George Miller. Kirk Douglas, Tom Burlinson, Sigrid Thornton, Jack Thompson, Lorraine Bayly, Tommy Dysart, Bruce Kerr. Grand, old-fashioned Western saga, based on epic Australian poem, about strong-willed young man who goes to work for an empire-building cattleman, and falls in love with his daughter. Hokey, simplistic, but great fun, with eye-filling scenery and incredible action scenes with some wild horses. Douglas has fun in a dual role; Thompson's part is virtually a cameo. Followed by RETURN TO SNOWY RIVER. Panavision. [PG]▼●▶

Man From the Alamo, The (1953) C-79m. *** D: Budd Boetticher. Glenn Ford, Julia (Julie) Adams, Chill Wills, Hugh O'Brian, Victor Jory, Neville Brand, Jeanne Cooper, Dennis Weaver. Ford leaves the Alamo to protect his family and others but is branded a coward and is forced to prove his heroism while battling lawless Jory. Typically offbeat Boetticher Western. ▼▶

Man from the Diner's Club, The (1963) 90m. ** D: Frank Tashlin. Danny Kaye, Martha Hyer, Cara Williams, Telly Savalas, George Kennedy, Ann Morgan Guilbert. Labored slapstick comedy about a bungling credit-card company clerk who inadvertently OKs an account for gangster Savalas. Look for Harry Dean Stanton as a beatnik. Cowritten by Bill (William Peter) Blatty. Title song sung (and cowritten) by Steve Lawrence.

Mangler, The (1995) C-106m. *½ D: Tobe Hooper. Robert Englund, Ted Levine, Daniel Matmor, Jeremy Crutchley, Vanessa Pike. An evil, gargantuan steam iron and speed-folder at a rural industrial laundry has been eating the employees lately; a local cop tries to exorcise the demons responsible. Englund is good as the laundry's crazed owner, but ridiculous "scares" and lack of logic defeat this forgettable genre entry based on a Stephen King short story. Horror fans will be disappointed with the results of this Englund-Hooper-King convergence. Unrated version available on video. Followed by two in-name-only sequels. [R]▼●▶

Mango Tree, The (1977-Australian) C-93m. **½ D: Kevin Dobson. Christopher Pate, Geraldine Fitzgerald, Robert Helpmann, Diane Craig, Gerald Kennedy, Gloria Dawn. A young man's coming of age in Australia, around the time of WW1; pictorially pleasing, with a warm performance by Fitzgerald as the young man's wise, gentle grandmother, but nothing out of the ordinary. Written and produced by former actor Michael Pate, whose son plays the lead. Panavision.▼

Manhattan (1979) 96m. ***½ D: Woody Allen. Woody Allen, Diane Keaton, Michael Murphy, Mariel Hemingway, Meryl Streep, Anne Byrne, Tisa Farrow. Bittersweet slice-of-life about a N.Y.C. comedy writer and his cerebral friends; blisteringly accurate and ultimately poignant, a worthy follow-up to Woody's ANNIE HALL. Magnificently photographed (in b&w) by Gordon Willis, with splendid use of Gershwin music on the soundtrack. Wallace Shawn's role is especially funny; that's Mark Linn-Baker as one of the Shakespearean actors and Karen Allen (in blonde wig) and David Rasche on TV show. Panavision. [R]▼●▶

Manhattan Melodrama (1934) 93m. *** D: W. S. Van Dyke II. Clark Gable, William Powell, Myrna Loy, Leo Carrillo, Isabel Jewell, Mickey Rooney, Nat Pendleton. Boyhood pals remain adult friends though one is a gangster and the other a D.A. (a plot device reused many times). What might be unbearably corny is top entertainment, thanks to this star trio and a director with gusto. Arthur Caesar's original story won an Oscar. Footnoted in American history as the film John Dillinger saw just before being gunned down at the Biograph Theatre in Chicago, as illustrated in 2009's PUBLIC ENEMIES. Reworked as a 1942 B movie, NORTHWEST RANGERS. Also shown in computer-colored version.▼●▶

Manhattan Murder Mystery (1993) C-108m. *** D: Woody Allen. Woody Allen, Diane Keaton, Alan Alda, Anjelica Huston, Jerry Adler, Lynn Cohen, Ron Rifkin, Joy Behar, Marge Redmond, Aida Turturro. Slight but enjoyable caper, with Allen and Keaton as a married couple who suspect their seemingly harmless neighbor has murdered his wife. A return (of sorts) to "earlier, funnier" filmmaking for Allen, this is no classic but it is consistently entertaining, with the usual quota of one-liners and some very funny set pieces. Best of all is the marvelous chemistry between Allen and Keaton (taking over the role originally intended for Mia Farrow), who play off each other's neuroses with intuitive ease. Allen cowrote the screenplay with his ANNIE HALL and MANHATTAN collaborator Marshall Brickman. [PG]▼●)

Manhattan Project, The (1986) **C-117m.** ** D: Marshall Brickman. John Lithgow, Christopher Collet, Cynthia Nixon, Jill Eikenberry, John Mahoney, Sully Boyar, Gregg Edelman, Robert (Sean) Leonard, Richard Jenkins. Precocious teenager breaks into top-secret plant, steals some plutonium, and builds his own nuclear reactor, ostensibly to make a point but also to show off. Slick, extremely well-acted film is blatantly irresponsible and has us cheering for the kid as he outwits the dopey grownups and nearly blows up the world! [PG-13]▼●)

Man Hunt (1941) **105m.** ***½ D: Fritz Lang. Walter Pidgeon, Joan Bennett, George Sanders, John Carradine, Roddy McDowall. Farfetched yet absorbing drama of man attempting to kill Hitler, getting into more trouble than he bargained for. Tense, well done. Screenplay by Dudley Nichols, from Geoffrey Household's novel. Remade as ROGUE MALE.▶

Manhunt (1973) SEE: **The Italian Connection**

Manhunter (1986) **C-121m.** *** D: Michael Mann. William L. Petersen, Kim Greist, Joan Allen, Brian Cox, Dennis Farina, Stephen Lang, Tom Noonan. Forceful contemporary cops-and-robbers melodrama told with *Miami Vice* stylistics (and hard-pounding music) by that show's creator, writer-director Mann. Petersen plays a troubled former FBI agent who's called back to service to capture a serial killer, which he does by getting himself to think just like the murderer! Gripping all the way and surprisingly nonexploitive. Don't examine story too carefully or the holes start to show through. Jailed killer Hannibal Lecter figures in the story; later he'd become the subject of his own story, THE SILENCE OF THE LAMBS. Based on Thomas Harris' novel *Red Dragon*. Director's cut runs 124m. Aka RED DRAGON, also the name of the 2002 remake. Super 35. [R]▼●)

Mania (1960-British) **87m.** *** D: John Gilling. Peter Cushing, Donald Pleasence, George Rose, June Laverick, Dermot Walsh, Billie Whitelaw. Deliciously lurid shocker with Cushing going all out as an Edinburgh scientist who employs graverobbers Pleasence and Rose to supply him with corpses for his experiments. Originally titled THE FLESH AND THE FIENDS (and released at 93m.; European version has nudity and violence). Aka PSYCHO KILLERS and THE FIENDISH GHOULS (running 74m.). Dyaliscope. ▼▶

Maniac (1977) SEE: **Ransom** (1977)

Maniac (1980) **C-87m.** BOMB D: William Lustig. Joe Spinell, Caroline Munro, Gail

Lawrence (Abigail Clayton), Kelly Piper, Rita Montone, Tom Savini. Unrelenting exercise in nihilistic gore about a cretin who murders women and then scalps them so that he can dress up his mannequins. Although an excellent character actor, coscriptwriter-producer-star Spinell bears most of the blame for this claustrophobic, sickening film. [R]▼●)

Maniac Cop (1988) **C-85m.** *½ D: William Lustig. Tom Atkins, Bruce Campbell, Laurene Landon, Richard Roundtree, William Smith, Robert Z'dar, Sheree North. Potentially intriguing premise, of a killer on the police force striking terror in the hearts of N.Y.C. residents, is bungled by failed black humor and ham-fisted direction into standard stalk-and-slash fare. Best work is done by North as a crippled, embittered policewoman. Followed by several sequels. [R]▼●)

Manic (2003) **C-100m.** ** D: Jordan Melamed. Joseph Gordon-Levitt, Zooey Deschanel, Michael Bacall, Don Cheadle, Elden Henson, Sara Rivas, Blayne Weaver, Cody Lightning. Interesting but uneven drama about emotionally troubled teens in a mental hospital. Shot with handheld digital cameras, the film has a feeling of spontaneity, which works best in group therapy scenes (led by the rock-solid Cheadle), but the constant use of ultra-tight close-ups becomes tiresome after a while. Written by two of the film's actors, Bacall and Weaver. [R]▼

Manifesto (1988-U.S.-Yugoslavian) **C-96m.** **½ D: Dusan Makavejev. Camilla Søeberg, Alfred Molina, Simon Callow, Eric Stoltz, Lindsay Duncan, Rade Šerbedžija, Svetozar Svetković, Chris Haywood, Patrick Godfrey, Linda Marlowe, Gabrielle Anwar, Ronald Lacey. Set in the 1920s, this anarchic dark comedy depicts a small Balkan community that's a hotbed of assassination plots, sexual freedom, and repressive ideas. Loosely derived from a story by Emile Zola, the film is brightly colored and impishly written (by the director), but eventually becomes *too* anarchic for its own good. More notable for what it attempts than what it achieves. Makavejev's first film in Yugoslavia after a 17-year exile. Video title: A NIGHT OF LOVE. [R]▼

Man I Love, The (1946) **96m.** *** D: Raoul Walsh. Ida Lupino, Robert Alda, Bruce Bennett, Andrea King, Dolores Moran, Martha Vickers, Alan Hale. Slick, well-acted melodrama casts Ida as nightclub singer pursued by no-good mobster Alda. Forget logic and just enjoy. This film inspired Scorsese's NEW YORK NEW YORK.▼●)

Man in a Cocked Hat (1959-British) **88m.** *** D: Jeffrey Dell, Roy Boulting. Terry-Thomas, Peter Sellers, Luciana Paluzzi, Thorley Walters, Ian Bannen, John Le Mesurier, Miles Malleson. Screwball farce about Island of Gallardia, a British protectorate forgotten for 50 years; when rediscovered, bumbling Terry-Thomas of the Foreign Office is left in charge. British title: CARLTON-BROWNE OF THE F.O.▼◗▶

Man in a Uniform (1993-Canadian) C-99m. *** D: David Wellington. Tom McCamus, Brigitte Bako, Kevin Tighe, David Hemblen, Graham McPherson. Startlingly effective TAXI DRIVER variation about an actor (McCamus, who is excellent) who wins a role as a cop on a TV series and begins wearing his costume uniform in public, with jarring results. Film effectively examines the difference between real and reel life in an impersonal, randomly violent society. Well worth watching. Original title: I LOVE A MAN IN UNIFORM. ▼◗▶

Man in Love, A (1987-French-Italian) C-117m. *** D: Diane Kurys. Peter Coyote, Greta Scacchi, Peter Riegert, Claudia Cardinale, Jamie Lee Curtis, John Berry, Vincent Lindon, Jean Pigozzi. Full-blooded romance about a married American actor who falls in love with his leading lady while making a movie in Rome. Coyote and Scacchi are believable (and extremely sexy) in this sensual and intelligent film, written by Israel Horovitz and director Kurys, whose first English language film this is. Technovision. [R]▼◗

Man Inside, The (1990-U.S.-French) C-93m. ** D: Bobby Roth. Jürgen Prochnow, Peter Coyote, Nathalie Baye, Dieter Laser, Monique van de Ven, Phillip Anglim, Henry G. Sanders. Crusading West German investigative reporter infiltrates a scandal-sheet newspaper in order to write an indictment of their sleazy practices. A misfire, despite its intriguing premise and cast; it may just be that the film bites off more than it can chew. Story seems dated already. [PG]▼◗

Man in the Chair (2007) C-107m. **½ D: Michael Schroeder. Christopher Plummer, Michael Angarano, M. Emmet Walsh, Robert Wagner, George Murdock, Mimi Kennedy, Joshua Boyd, Allan Rich, Mitch Pileggi, Tracey Walter, Ellen Geer. Alcoholic down-on-his-luck former studio gaffer meets a rebellious young filmmaker at a fading revival movie theater. They forge a friendship that leads to a collaboration, which also reinvigorates the lives of several residents of a motion-picture retirement home. Well-meaning drama is awkward at times but Plummer's tour-de-force performance (and a fine supporting cast) make it worth a look. Super 35. [PG-13]

Man in the Dark (1953) 70m. **½ D: Lew Landers. Edmond O'Brien, Audrey Totter, Ruth Warren, Ted de Corsia, Horace McMahon, Nick Dennis. Convict O'Brien undergoes brain surgery to eliminate criminal bent and loses memory in the process; his old cohorts only care that he remember where he stashed their stolen loot. OK remake of THE MAN WHO LIVED TWICE (and CRIME DOCTOR). 3-D.

Man in the Glass Booth, The (1975) C-117m. **½ D: Arthur Hiller. Maximilian Schell, Lois Nettleton, Luther Adler, Lawrence Pressman, Henry Brown, Richard Rasof. American Film Theatre version of Robert Shaw's play about a glib Jewish industrialist brought to trial for Nazi war crimes. Schell is good, but overall effect is contrived. Shaw had his name removed from credits of film. [PG]▼◗

Man in the Gray Flannel Suit, The (1956) C-153m. ***½ D: Nunnally Johnson. Gregory Peck, Jennifer Jones, Fredric March, Marisa Pavan, Lee J. Cobb, Keenan Wynn, Gene Lockhart, Gigi Perreau, Arthur O'Connell, Henry Daniell. Sloan Wilson's slick novel of Madison Avenue executive struggling to get ahead and to find meaning in his home life. Nice cameo by Ann Harding as March's wife. Scripted by the director; music by Bernard Herrmann. CinemaScope.▼◗

Man in the Iron Mask, The (1939) 110m. *** D: James Whale. Louis Hayward, Joan Bennett, Warren William, Joseph Schildkraut, Alan Hale, Walter Kingsford, Marion Martin. Rousing adventure of twin brothers: one becomes King of France, the other a carefree gay blade raised by D'Artagnan (William) and the Three Musketeers. Fine swashbuckler. Filmed in 1929 with Douglas Fairbanks as THE IRON MASK.▼

Man in the Iron Mask, The (1998) C-132m. *** D: Randall Wallace. Leonardo DiCaprio, Jeremy Irons, John Malkovich, Gérard Depardieu, Gabriel Byrne, Anne Parillaud, Judith Godreche, Edward Atterton, Peter Sarsgaard, Hugh Laurie. Handsome retelling of the durable Alexandre Dumas tale of a man unjustly imprisoned and encased in an iron mask—because his very existence threatens the reigning king of France, the young, selfish Louis XIV. The fate of both are soon in the hands of the aging but still passionate Musketeers. It would be hard to miss with that cast; the film is quite enjoyable, but it does go on too long. [PG-13]▼◗▶

Man in the Moon, The (1991) C-99m. *** D: Robert Mulligan. Sam Waterston, Tess Harper, Gail Strickland, Reese Witherspoon, Jason London, Emily Warfield, Bentley Mitchum, Ernie Lively. Ingratiatingly old-fashioned weeper set in rural Louisiana in 1957, about a 14-year-old girl in love with an older boy, who in turn prefers her college-bound sis. Newcomer Witherspoon is unforgettable as the younger sister—more early adolescent lightning for director Mulligan, who guided TO KILL A MOCKINGBIRD and SUMMER OF '42. Nicely shot by Freddie Francis. Waterston has some effective scenes as the girls' father. Mulligan's last film. [PG-13]▼●◗

Man in the White Suit, The (1951-British) **84m.** ***½ D: Alexander Mackendrick. Alec Guinness, Joan Greenwood, Cecil Parker, Michael Gough, Ernest Thesiger, Vida Hope, George Benson, Edie Martin. Guinness is inventor who discovers a fabric that can't wear out or soil; dismayed garment manufacturers set out to bury his formula. Most engaging comedy. Screenplay by Roger Macdougall, John Dighton, and Mackendrick, from Macdougall's play. ▼●◗

Man in the Wilderness (1971) **C-105m.** *** D: Richard C. Sarafian. Richard Harris, John Huston, John Bindon, Ben Carruthers, Prunella Ransome, Henry Wilcoxon. Trapper Harris abandoned in wasteland, must fight for survival, and revenge as well. Well-made, engrossing, but bloody film. Panavision. [PG]▼▶

Manitou, The (1978) **C-104m.** BOMB D: William Girdler. Tony Curtis, Susan Strasberg, Michael Ansara, Ann Sothern, Burgess Meredith, Stella Stevens. Long-dead Indian medicine man gets himself resurrected through a fetus on Strasberg's neck. Veterans Curtis, Sothern, and Meredith look properly embarrassed. Based on a novel by Graham Masterson. Panavision. [PG]▼●◗

Mannequin (1937) **95m.** **½ D: Frank Borzage. Joan Crawford, Spencer Tracy, Alan Curtis, Ralph Morgan, Leo Gorcey, Elisabeth Risdon. Prototype rags-to-riches soaper, with working-girl Crawford getting ahead via wealthy Tracy. Predictable script, but nice job by stars, usual MGM gloss (even in the tenements!). ▼●◗

Mannequin (1987) **C-89m.** BOMB D: Michael Gottlieb. Andrew McCarthy, Kim Cattrall, Estelle Getty, G. W. Bailey, James Spader, Meshach Taylor, Carole Davis. Cattrall is an ancient Egyptian spirit who embodies a department store mannequin; McCarthy is the only one who sees her come to life, and falls in love with her. Attempt to re-create the feeling of old screwball comedies is absolute rock-bottom fare. Dispiriting to anyone who remembers what movie comedy ought to be. Followed by a sequel. [PG]▼●◗

Mannequin Two: On the Move (1991) **C-95m.** BOMB D: Stewart Raffill. Kristy Swanson, William Ragsdale, Meshach Taylor, Terry Kiser, Stuart Pankin, Cynthia Harris. This inept sequel to MANNEQUIN makes you think the original was not so bad by comparison. Again, a window dresser (Ragsdale) in a department store frees the spirit of a medieval peasant (Swanson) who has been imprisoned inside a mannequin's form for—quite logically—1,000 years. Torpor ensues. [PG]▼●◗

Manny & Lo (1996) **C-97m.** *** D: Lisa Krueger. Scarlett Johansson, Aleksa Palladino, Mary Kay Place, Paul Guilfoyle, Glenn Fitzgerald, Novella Nelson. Orphaned 11-year-old Manny (Johansson) and her more naive 16-year-old sister Lo (Palladino) sleep in model homes and drive about in an old station wagon, until it's obvious Lo is pregnant, so they kidnap prissy Place to help with the delivery while hiding out in a woodsy cabin. Wise, warm comedy-drama is fresh and unexpected; a notable debut for writer-director Krueger. Place is particularly good. [R]▼●◗

Man of Aran (1934-British) **73m.** **** D: Robert Flaherty. Colman (Tiger) King, Maggie Dillane. Superb, classic documentary about day-to-day existence, and constant fight for survival, of fisherman in remote Irish coastal community. Scenes at sea are breathtaking.▼▶

Man of a Thousand Faces (1957) **122m.** ***½ D: Joseph Pevney. James Cagney, Dorothy Malone, Jane Greer, Marjorie Rambeau, Jim Backus, Jeanne Cagney, Robert J. Evans, Roger Smith, Jack Albertson, Snub Pollard. Surprisingly good, well-acted biography of silent star Lon Chaney. Cagney as Chaney, Malone as disturbed first wife, Greer as wife who brings him happiness, are all fine. Chaney's life and career are re-created with taste (if not accuracy). Touching portrayal of movie extra by Rambeau. Ralph Wheelwright's story was adapted by R. Wright Campbell, Ivan Goff, and Ben Roberts. CinemaScope. ▼●◗

Man of Flowers, A (1984-Australian) **C-91m.** **½ D: Paul Cox. Norman Kaye, Alyson Best, Chris Haywood, Sarah Walker, Julia Blake, Bob Ellis, Barry Dickins. Kaye, a wealthy flower-loving bachelor with a mother fixation, pays artist's model Best $100 a week to disrobe for him on call. Original but monotonal mix of somberness and silliness; may catch your interest if you're in the right mood. Werner Herzog plays Kaye's father in flashback. ▼●◗

Man of Iron (1981-Polish) **C-152m.** ***½ D: Andrzej Wajda. Jerzy Radziwilowicz, Krystyna Janda, Marian Opiana. Sequel to MAN OF MARBLE finds documentary filmmaker Janda married to son of the fallen hero whose life she had been researching. Rousing march for Solidarity is not quite up to its predecessor, but two films taken together are as epic in scope as our own GODFATHER sagas. Lech Walesa appears briefly as himself. [PG]▼●◗

Man of La Mancha (1972) **C-130m.** BOMB D: Arthur Hiller. Peter O'Toole, Sophia Loren, James Coco, Harry Andrews, John Castle. Plodding, abysmal adaptation of Dale Wasserman's popular musical based on Cervantes' *Don Quixote*, with Joe Darion–Mitch Leigh score. Beautiful source material has been raped, murdered, and buried. [PG]▼●◗

Man of Marble (1977-Polish) **C-160m.** **** D: Andrzej Wajda. Krystyna Janda, Jerzy Radziwilowicz, Tadeusz Lomnicki, Jacek Lomnicki, Krystyna Zachwatowicz. Compelling, controversial, brilliantly directed tale of determined filmmaker Janda retracing the life of Radziwilowicz, naive bricklayer lionized in the 1950s as a worker-hero of the State. Wajda celebrates the role of filmmaker as a speaker of truth; ironically, the film's finale, an explanation of the bricklayer's fate, was excised by the Polish censors. Followed by MAN OF IRON. ▼▶

Man of No Importance, A (1994-British) **C-98m.** **½ D: Suri Krishnamma. Albert Finney, Brenda Fricker, Michael Gambon, Tara Fitzgerald, Rufus Sewell, Patrick Malahide, David Kelly, Mick Lally, Jonathan Rhys-Myer (Meyers). While staging Oscar Wilde's controversial *Salome* at his local Dublin church, a theater-loving bus conductor examines his repressed sexual feelings—toward both his leading actress and the bus' handsome driver. Initially lightweight comedy-drama gradually becomes more complex, possibly taking on more than it can handle; Finney, however, devours the role with his usual feeling and conviction. Later a stage musical. [R] ▼●

Man of the Century (1999) **80m.** ** D: Adam Abraham. Gibson Frazier, Susan Egan, David Margulies, Frank Gorshin, Bobby Short, Anne Jackson, Gary Beach, Marisa Ryan, Lester Lanin. A snappy-talking newspaper reporter named Johnny Twennies (Frazier) lives in a 1920s world, immersed in its slang, customs, and music, unaware of the realities around him, or the very contemporary sexual longing of his girlfriend (Egan). An obvious labor of love, this somewhat amateurish film has enthusiasm to spare, and some amusing cameos, but one overriding problem: it makes no sense. Written by the director and his star. [R] ▼▶

Man of the House (1995) **C-96m.** ** D: James Orr. Chevy Chase, Farrah Fawcett, Jonathan Taylor Thomas, George Wendt, David Shiner, Art LaFleur, Richard Portnow. Thomas is the center of attention in this tepid comedy, as the sometimes overbearing son of Fawcett, whom district attorney Chase intends to marry. Stepdad-to-be attempts to ingratiate himself with the boy, who plots to eliminate the man from his mom's life. The humor—what there is of it—is plenty predictable, but kids will probably lap it up. [PG] ▼●▶

Man of the House (2005) **C-97m.** *½ D: Stephen Herek. Tommy Lee Jones, Anne Archer, Cedric the Entertainer, Christina Milian, Paula Garcés, Monica Keena, Vanessa Ferlito, Kelli Garner, R. Lee Ermey, Curtis Armstrong, Paget Brewster. Destined to go down in history as the movie in which Jones buys tampons, this lamer-than-lame comedy casts him as a Texas Ranger house-sitting a band of cheerleaders who've witnessed a murder. Though there's potential in the idea of the girls giving Jones a makeover, the actor's dyspeptic facial expression seems to have been exacerbated by reading the script. Panavision. [PG-13] ▼▶

Man of the West (1958) **C-100m.** *** D: Anthony Mann. Gary Cooper, Julie London, Lee J. Cobb, Arthur O'Connell, Jack Lord, John Dehner, Royal Dano. Dismissed in 1958, this powerful story deserves another look. Cooper plays a reformed outlaw who is forced to rejoin his ex-boss (Cobb) to save himself and other innocent people from the gang's mistreatment. Strong, epic-scale Western, with script by Reginald Rose. CinemaScope. ▼▶

Man of the Year (2006) **C-108m.** ** D: Barry Levinson. Robin Williams, Laura Linney, Christopher Walken, Lewis Black, Jeff Goldblum, Rick Roberts, David Alpay. Glib talk-show host Williams runs for President as a lark, then finds himself elected. The reason: there's a flaw in a new computer voting program, and the firm that created it can't afford to admit the mistake. Linney tries to go public with the information, but only Williams seems to believe her. Muddled mess of a movie tries to be topical, funny, suspenseful, and romantic. Scattered sharp, funny moments can't salvage Levinson's unwieldy screenplay. Various TV personalities and politicos appear as themselves. Super 35. [PG-13] ▶

Man on a Swing (1974) **C-110m.** **½ D: Frank Perry. Cliff Robertson, Joel Grey, Dorothy Tristan, Elizabeth Wilson, George Voskovec. Mysterious clairvoyant (Grey) offers to help a cop (Robertson) solve sex-slaying that's been troubling him, but generates more questions than answers. Intriguing idea sadly misses the mark by building up to an unsatisfying conclusion. Based on a true story. [PG]

Man on a Tightrope (1953) **105m.** **½ D: Elia Kazan. Fredric March, Gloria Grahame, Terry Moore, Cameron Mitchell, Adolphe Menjou, Richard Boone, Robert Beatty. Passable based-on-fact account of an obscure, downtrodden little circus troupe and its escape from Communist-ruled Czechoslovakia to freedom in Bavaria. Has its moments, but the characters are far too broadly drawn. Scripted by Robert E. Sherwood. ▶

Man on Fire (1957) **95m.** **½ D: Ranald MacDougall. Bing Crosby, Mary Fickett, Inger Stevens, E.G. Marshall, Malcolm Broderick, Anne Seymour, Richard Eastham. Divorced father (Crosby) refuses to grant his remarried ex-wife partial custody of their son in this modest domestic drama.

Man on Fire (2004) **C-146m.** ** D: Tony Scott. Denzel Washington, Dakota Fanning, Marc Anthony, Radha Mitchell, Christopher Walken, Giancarlo Giannini, Rachel Ticotin,

Jesus Ochoa, Mickey Rourke. Guilt-ridden military ops veteran Washington is hired as a bodyguard for young Fanning to protect her from the constant threat of kidnapping in Mexico City. After a good first hour the film becomes a vigilante saga, urging us to cheer on the violent deaths of scummy characters who "deserve" it. Told in director Scott's self-indulgent style, with uncomfortable ultra-close-ups, smash cuts with loud sound effects, and handheld grainy shots in the middle of scenes for no reason at all. Too bad. Super 35. [R]▼▶

Manon of the Spring (1986-French) C-113m. *** D: Claude Berri. Yves Montand, Emmanuelle Béart, Daniel Auteuil, Hippolyte Girardot, Elisabeth Depardieu, Gabriel Bacquier. Conclusion of the story begun in JEAN DE FLORETTE resumes with Manon, now a beautiful, free-spirited young shepherdess, learning the truth behind her father's death, and plotting her revenge on the pathetic Auteuil and the scheming Montand. Berri spins his story slowly, deliberately, savoring every moment leading to the unexpected conclusion. Only thing missing in this second half is the strong presence of Gérard Depardieu. Filmed before in 1952 by Marcel Pagnol. Technovision. [PG]▼▶●

Man on the Flying Trapeze (1935) 65m. ***½ D: Clyde Bruckman. W. C. Fields, Mary Brian, Kathleen Howard, Grady Sutton, Vera Lewis, Walter Brennan. Hilarious Fieldsian study in frustration, with able assistance from hardboiled wife Howard, good-for-nothing Sutton. Best sequence has W. C. receiving four traffic tickets in a row!▶

Man on the Moon (1999) C-118m. ** D: Milos Forman. Jim Carrey, Danny DeVito, Courtney Love, Paul Giamatti, Vincent Schiavelli, Peter Bonerz, Gerry Becker, Leslie Lyles. The writers of ED WOOD and THE PEOPLE VS. LARRY FLYNT, reteamed with FLYNT director Forman, strike out with this bio of the late comedy performer Andy Kaufman. Carrey perfectly embodies his subject, but it's impossible to get inside Kaufman's head and understand what made him so very, very strange, on-stage and off . . . if indeed it's even worth the effort. Some of Kaufman's real-life acting colleagues appear as themselves. Panavision. [R]▼▶●

Man on the Roof (1977-Swedish) C-110m. ***½ D: Bo Widerberg. Carl-Gustaf Lindstedt, Hakan Serner, Sven Wollter, Thomas Hellberg. A cop killer is the subject of a Stockholm manhunt in this police film with substance and style. Absorbing for its look at police methodology as well as its suspense and action. Based on the Martin Beck novel by Maj Sjowall and Per Wahloo (Walter Matthau played Beck in THE LAUGHING POLICEMAN). [R]▼

Man on the Train (2002-French) C-90m.

*** D: Patrice Leconte. Jean Rochefort, Johnny Hallyday, Jean-François Stevenin, Charlie Nelson, Pascal Parmentier, Isabelle Petit-Jacques. A gun-toting stranger comes to a small town and rooms with a retired schoolteacher; the two men couldn't be more different, but as they get to know each other each one sees in the other qualities he's always longed for in his own life. A minor but entertaining fable that makes the most of its two stars' exceptional screen presence. Super 35. [R]▼●

Man on Wire (2008-U.S.-British) C-94m. ***½ D: James Marsh. On August 7, 1974, daredevil Philippe Petit made big news as he took a leisurely 45-minute stroll back and forth on a steel cable between New York's World Trade Center towers. Vertiginous documentary, based on Petit's 2002 memoir, *To Reach the Clouds*, unveils his support crew's rehearsals, subterfuge, and reservations, while questioning the sanity of a gutsy artist whose arrest report provides the title. Literally breathtaking account is all a thriller should be, yet it's real, aside from a few dramatic reenactments and one nutty sex scene. Not for the acrophobic. Oscar winner as Best Documentary. [PG-13]●

Man Outside (1986) C-109m. *½ D: Mark Stouffer. Robert Logan, Kathleen Quinlan, Bradford Dillman, Levon Helm, Andrew Barach. Why has Logan dropped out and chosen to isolate himself and live off the land in rural Arkansas? Anthropology professor Quinlan decides to find out and promptly falls for him . . . even as he's accused of kidnapping a young boy. Slickly made but obvious, overbaked, and a bore. In addition to Helm, other former members of The Band (Rick Danko, Garth Hudson, Richard Manuel) appear. [PG-13]▼●

Man Push Cart (2006) C-87m. *** D: Ramin Bahrani. Ahmad Razvi, Leticia Dolera, Charles Daniel Sandoval, Ali Reza, Farooq "Duke" Muhammad. Pakistani immigrant hauls his food cart into place every morning to sell coffee and snacks to a myriad of New Yorkers. His private life isn't nearly as orderly: he's battling his in-laws for custody of his young son, he's abandoned a once-thriving musical career, and his inner turmoil prevents him from making the most of new contacts and acquaintances. Penetrating character study in which location, looks, and silences tell more than dialogue. Writer-director Bahrani's feature debut. Also Razvi's acting debut; he used to work as a pushcart vendor.▶

Man's Best Friend (1993) C-97m. **½ D: John Lafia. Ally Sheedy, Lance Henriksen, Robert Costanzo, Fredric Lehne, John Cassini, J. D. Daniels, William Sanderson, Trula Marcus, Rick Barker. Investigative reporter Sheedy rescues big doggy, Max, from scientist Henricksen's vivesection lab . . . but Max is genetically engineered with many odd abilities—and a bad attitude. Modestly clever thriller pushes clichés associated with dogs (mailmen, junkyards, cats) to amusingly violent extremes. Derivative but fun. Written by the director. [R]▼●◗

Man's Favorite Sport? (1964) C-120m. **½ D: Howard Hawks. Rock Hudson, Paula Prentiss, John McGiver, Maria Perschy, Roscoe Karns, Charlene Holt. Amusing, often labored variation on Hawks' own BRINGING UP BABY. Fishing "expert" Hudson, who in reality has never fished, is forced to enter big tournament by pushy Prentiss (in her best performance). Loaded with slapstick and sexual innuendo; Norman Alden is hilarious as wisecracking Indian guide.▼◗

Mansfield Park (1999-British) C-99m. **½ D: Patricia Rozema. Frances O'Connor, Embeth Davidtz, Jonny Lee Miller, Alessandro Nivola, Harold Pinter, Lindsay Duncan, Sheila Gish. In early 19th-century England, an impoverished girl is sent to live with wealthy relatives. Working as their servant she grows to be an astute, imaginative and surprisingly independent-minded woman. Very loosely based on Jane Austen's novel and personal journals. O'Connor shines as the heroine among a top-notch cast, but story lacks the wit and satirical edge of other Austen adaptations. [PG-13]▼◗

Man They Could Not Hang, The (1939) 65m. **½ D: Nick Grinde. Boris Karloff, Lorna Gray (Adrian Booth), Robert Wilcox, Roger Pryor, Ann Doran. One of five Karloff films with the same basic premise: hanged man brought back to life seeks revenge on judge, jury, et al. Good of its type.▼◗

Man Trouble (1992-U.S.-Italian) C-100m. *½ D: Bob Rafelson. Jack Nicholson, Ellen Barkin, Beverly D'Angelo, Harry Dean Stanton, Michael McKean, Veronica Cartwright, David Clennon, Paul Mazursky, Saul Rubinek, Lauren Tom. Opera singer Barkin is troubled by a frightening break-in and other harassment so she hires guard-dog specialist Nicholson to beef up security. This mongrel of a screwball comedy consistently misses the target. Particularly disappointing in light of reteaming Nicholson with FIVE EASY PIECES director Rafelson and writer Carole Eastman. Way below par for all concerned. [PG-13]▼●◗

Manufactured Landscapes (2007-Canadian) C/B&W-87m. *** D: Jennifer Baichwal. Provocative documentary portrait of photographer Edward Burtynsky, who takes stark, stunning images that reflect on how natural landscapes are altered by industrialization while showing the impact that industrial waste is having on the environment and the future of humankind. Well worth watching—and pondering.◗

Man Under Suspicion (1984-German) C-126m. **½ D: Norbert Kuckelmann. Maximilian Schell, Lena Stolze, Robert Aldini, Wolfgang Kieling, Kathrin Ackermann, Reinhard Hauff. Lawyer Schell investigates the motives behind a young man's act of violence at a political rally. Provocative subject matter—how the roots of fascism must be destroyed before they are given the opportunity to blossom—but low-keyed to the point of tedium, and much too long, though final twenty minutes are fairly effective.

Man Who Came to Dinner, The (1941) 112m. ***½ D: William Keighley. Bette Davis, Ann Sheridan, Monty Woolley, Billie Burke, Jimmy Durante, Richard Travis, Grant Mitchell, Mary Wickes, Elizabeth Fraser, Reginald Gardiner. Acerbic radio commentator Woolley (re-creating his Broadway role) is forced to stay with Burke's Midwestern family for the winter, driving them crazy with assorted wacky friends passing through. Delightful adaptation of George S. Kaufman–Moss Hart play, inspired by the celebrated critic and columnist Alexander Woollcott. Scripted by the Epstein brothers. Also shown in computer-colored version. ▼●◗

Man Who Could Work Miracles, The (1936-British) 82m. ***½ D: Lothar Mendes. Roland Young, Ralph Richardson, Edward Chapman, Ernest Thesiger, Joan Gardner, George Zucco, Wallace Lupino, Joan Hickson, George Sanders, Torin Thatcher. H. G. Wells' fantasy of timid British department store clerk (Young) endowed with power to do anything he wants. Special effects are marvelous, supported by good cast, in charming film.▼●◗

Man Who Cried, The (2000-British-French) C-100m. ** D: Sally Potter. Christina Ricci, Johnny Depp, Cate Blanchett, John Turturro, Harry Dean Stanton, Oleg Yankovskiy, Claudia Lander-Duke. Strange, unsatisfying saga—with a capital *S*—about a girl separated from her father in 1920s Russia. She grows up in England and winds up in Paris during the 1930s, where she's taken under the wing of a flamboyant nightclub dancer (Blanchett, almost unrecognizable), pursued by a self-important Italian tenor (Turturro), and charmed by a quiet, self-assured gypsy (Depp) as storm clouds gather over Europe. What's the point? We still don't know. Her costars act rings around a blank-faced Ricci. Written by the director. [R]▼◗

Man Who Fell to Earth, The (1976-British) C-140m. ***½ D: Nicolas Roeg. David Bowie, Rip Torn, Candy Clark, Buck Henry, Bernie Casey, Jackson D. Kane. Title character ostensibly heads world conglomerate, but is actually here to find water for his planet. Highly original, fabulously photographed adaptation of Walter Tevis' classic fantasy novel is riveting for the first two-thirds, goes downhill toward the end. Still tops of its kind. Originally released in the U.S. at 118m. Remade as 1987 TVM. Panavision. [R]▼●)

Man Who Had Power Over Women, The (1970-British) C-89m. **½ D: John Krish. Rod Taylor, James Booth, Carol White, Penelope Horner, Charles Korvin, Clive Francis, Magali Noel. Seriocomic satire about an executive with ethics in a London talent agency. Andrew Meredith's script (from the Gordon Williams novel) tends toward overstatement, which a good cast tries to moderate. [R]▼

Man Who Haunted Himself, The (1970-British) C-94m. ** D: Basil Dearden. Roger Moore, Hildegarde Neil, Alastair Mackenzie, Hugh Mackenzie, Kevork Malikyan. Strange psychological drama about Moore encountering a duplicate of himself in the aftermath of a car crash. Mildly interesting; good location footage of London. [PG]▼)

Man Who Knew Too Little, The (1997) C-94m. ** D: Jon Amiel. Bill Murray, Peter Gallagher, Joanne Whalley, Alfred Molina, Richard Wilson, Geraldine James, John Standing, Anna Chancellor, Nicholas Woodeson, Eddie Marsan. Curiously flat Murray vehicle about a dolt who visits his brother in England, is signed up for an "interactive theater" experience, but walks instead into the midst of a complex espionage scheme. Murray is game as always, in the kind of situation that used to serve Bob Hope and Danny Kaye so well, but the script lets him down. The title is the funniest part of the picture. [PG]▼●)

Man Who Knew Too Much, The (1934-British) 75m. *** D: Alfred Hitchcock. Leslie Banks, Edna Best, Peter Lorre, Nova Pilbeam, Frank Vosper, Pierre Fresnay. Film buffs argue which version of exciting story is better. We vote this one, with Hitchcock in fine form weaving dry British humor into a story of heart-pounding suspense; young girl is kidnapped to prevent her parents from revealing what they've learned about assassination plot.▼●)

Man Who Knew Too Much, The (1956) C-120m. **½ D: Alfred Hitchcock. James Stewart, Doris Day, Brenda De Banzie, Bernard Miles, Ralph Truman, Daniel Gelin, Alan Mowbray, Carolyn Jones, Hillary Brooke. Hitchcock's remake of his 1934 film is disappointing. Even famous Albert Hall assassination sequence rings flat in tale of American couple accidentally involved in international intrigue. Doris's "Que Sera, Sera" won Jay Livingston and Ray Evans Best Song Oscar. Composer Bernard Herrmann is conducting orchestra at the climax. VistaVision.▼●)

Man Who Loved Cat Dancing, The (1973) C-122m. *** D: Richard C. Sarafian. Burt Reynolds, Sarah Miles, George Hamilton,

Lee J. Cobb, Jack Warden, Bo Hopkins, Robert Donner, Jay Silverheels. Western tale of defiant woman who leaves her husband and takes up riding along with a band of outlaws. Sluggish in spots, but enjoyable; script by Eleanor Perry. Panavision. [PG]▼)

Man Who Loved Women, The (1977-French) C-119m. *** D: François Truffaut. Charles Denner, Brigitte Fossey, Nelly Borgeaud, Leslie Caron, Genevieve Fontanel. Charming, sophisticated comedy about a bachelor who is obsessed with women and, it turns out, they with him. To make sense of the fact that he falls in love with almost every woman he meets, he writes his autobiography. Remade in 1983.▼●)

Man Who Loved Women, The (1983) C-110m. ** D: Blake Edwards. Burt Reynolds, Julie Andrews, Kim Basinger, Marilu Henner, Barry Corbin, Cynthia Sikes, Jennifer Edwards, Tracy Vaccaro. Lackluster, snail's pace remake of the François Truffaut film—minus the climactic revelation that gave the earlier movie its point. Reynolds gives one of his most appealing performances, but spends an eternity discussing his adoration of women with stone-faced psychoanalyst Andrews. Director-writer Edwards gave coscreenplay credit to his own psychiatrist! [R]▼●)

Man Who Shot Liberty Valance, The (1962) 123m. **** D: John Ford. James Stewart, John Wayne, Vera Miles, Lee Marvin, Edmond O'Brien, Andy Devine, Woody Strode, Jeanette Nolan, Ken Murray, John Qualen, Strother Martin, Lee Van Cleef, John Carradine, Carleton Young. Tenderfoot lawyer Stewart helps civilize the West, but needs help from he-man Wayne to do so. Panned and patronized upon original release, but now regarded as an American classic; one of the great Westerns. Producer Willis Goldbeck and James Warner Bellah adapted Dorothy Johnson's story.▼●)

Man Who Wasn't There, The (1983) C-111m. BOMB D: Bruce Malmuth. Steve Guttenberg, Jeffrey Tambor, Lisa Langlois, Art Hindle, Morgan Hart, Bill Forsythe, Vincent Baggetta. Inept—not to mention inane—invisibility comedy that touted its 3-D effects but offered little in *any* dimension. Better writing, directing, and acting can be found at a nursery school pageant. 3-D Panavision. [R]▼

Man Who Wasn't There, The (2001) 116m. **½ D: Joel Coen. Billy Bob Thornton, Frances McDormand, James Gandolfini, Michael Badalucco, Katherine Borowitz, Jon Polito, Scarlett Johansson, Richard Jenkins, Tony Shalhoub, Adam Alexi-Malle, Christopher McDonald. Exquisitely detailed b&w homage to film noir, and James M. Cain in particular, set in the 1940s. Thornton gives a striking performance as a taciturn small-town barber who gets involved in a crime that snowballs out of control. Unfortunately, the script takes one of those Coen Brothers left turns, changes gears, and goes on much longer than it should. Still, there's incredible production design, Roger Deakins' cinematography, and a gallery of rich, colorful performances to compensate. [R] ▼●

Man Who Watched Trains Go By SEE: **Paris Express, The**

Man Who Would Be King, The (1975) C-129m. ***½ D: John Huston. Sean Connery, Michael Caine, Christopher Plummer, Saeed Jaffrey, Shakira Caine. Old-fashioned adventure and derring-do from Kipling via Huston: two British soldier-pals try to bamboozle high priests of remote Kafiristan into turning over their riches by convincing them that Connery is a god. Caine and Connery are ideal, script is superb, and film is entertaining, if not quite in the realm of GUNGA DIN. Panavision. [PG] ▼●

Man With Bogart's Face, The (1980) C-106m. **½ D: Robert Day. Robert Sacchi, Michelle Phillips, Olivia Hussey, Franco Nero, Misty Rowe, Victor Buono, Herbert Lom, Sybil Danning, Dick Bakalyan, George Raft, Mike Mazurki, Yvonne DeCarlo, Henry Wilcoxon, Victor Sen Yung, Jay Robinson. Offbeat mystery about present-day detective who has plastic surgery to resemble his idol and immediately becomes involved in MALTESE FALCON-esque case. Not really a comedy, although it has its lighter moments; good fun, especially for buffs. Adapted from his own novel and produced by Andrew J. Fenady; Raft's final film. Aka SAM MARLOW, PRIVATE EYE. [PG] ▼●

Man With Connections, The (1970-French) C-93m. **½ D: Claude Berri. Guy Bedos, Yves Robert, Rosy Varte, Georges Geret, Zorica Lozic. Good-natured comedy about young Frenchman who tries to use "pull" to make Army hitch as pleasant as possible. Autobiographical film is, like Berri's others, amiable, quietly entertaining. [R]

Man With Nine Lives, The (1940) 74m. **½ D: Nick Grinde. Boris Karloff, Roger Pryor, Jo Ann Sayers, Stanley Brown, John Dilson, Hal Taliaferro. Scientist Karloff seeks cure for cancer by freezing bodies in suspended animation. Hokey, but fun when Karloff himself thaws out. ▼●

Man With One Red Shoe, The (1985) C-93m. ** D: Stan Dragoti. Tom Hanks, Dabney Coleman, Lori Singer, Charles Durning, Carrie Fisher, Edward Herrmann, Jim Belushi, Irving Metzman, Gerrit Graham, David L. Lander, David Ogden Stiers. Flat remake of THE TALL BLOND MAN WITH ONE BLACK SHOE, about an innocent guy wrongly targeted by CIA types for elimination. Wastes the considerable comic talents of its cast—and doesn't allow leading man Hanks to be funny at all! [PG] ▼●

Man Without a Face, The (1993) C-114m. *** D: Mel Gibson. Mel Gibson, Nick Stahl, Margaret Whitton, Fay Masterson, Gaby Hoffmann, Geoffrey Lewis, Richard Masur, Michael DeLuise, Ethan Phillips, Jean De Baer, Viva. Literate, absorbing drama exploring the evolving relationship between lonely 12-year-old Stahl, who's intent on gaining entrance to a military academy, and reclusive, facially scarred ex-teacher Gibson, who becomes his mentor. Despite some dramatic lapses, Gibson's directorial debut is more than respectable; he and Stahl offer excellent performances. From Isabelle Holland's novel. [PG-13] ▼●

Man Without a Past, The (2002-Finnish-German-French) C-97m. ***½ D: Aki Kaurismäki. Markku Peltola, Kati Outinen, Juhani Niemelä, Kaija Pakarinen, Sakari Kuosmanen, Esko Nikkari. After being brutally beaten by muggers upon his arrival in Helsinki and miraculously cheating death, a middle-aged man becomes a penniless amnesiac. Without knowing a single person, "The Man" must try to survive. Existential black comedy contrasts society's emphasis on the importance of identity with the individual and idiosyncratic imprint that makes each of us spiritually unique. Fascinating and funny; written and produced by the prolific Kaurismäki. [PG-13] ▼●

Man Without a Star (1955) C-89m. *** D: King Vidor. Kirk Douglas, Jeanne Crain, Claire Trevor, Richard Boone, Jay C. Flippen, William Campbell. Boisterous Western with drifter Douglas befriending young Campbell, tangling with manipulative rancher Crain. Kirk gets to sing and play the banjo in this one. Remade as A MAN CALLED GANNON. ▼

Man with the Golden Arm, The (1955) 119m. *** D: Otto Preminger. Frank Sinatra, Kim Novak, Eleanor Parker, Darren McGavin, Arnold Stang, Doro Merande. Nelson Algren's novel, the first to win the National Book Award, was presumed to be unfilmable until Preminger ignored and thus busted Hollywood's Production Code. The taboo subject was heroin addiction, and Sinatra's performance is still provocative, especially in the actor's famed gets-the-shakes withdrawal scene. Otherwise, the film (which appears to have been shot on the cheap) has lost some, though hardly all, of its power. Two other landmarks: Saul Bass's trendsetting opening credits and Elmer Bernstein's jazz score, which put the composer on the map. ▼●

Man With the Golden Gun, The (1974-British) C-125m. *** D: Guy Hamilton. Roger Moore, Christopher Lee, Britt Ekland, Maud Adams, Herve Villechaize, Clifton James, Richard Loo, Marc Lawrence, Bernard Lee, Lois Maxwell, Desmond Llewelyn. Moore's second shot as super agent James Bond is good, gimmicky fun but the actor had one more film to go (THE SPY WHO LOVED ME) before actually growing into the character; Lee is excellent as assassin Scaramanga. Great car stunts, worldwide locales. [PG]▼●)

Man With the Synthetic Brain, The SEE: **Blood of Ghastly Horror**

Man With Two Brains, The (1983) **C-93m.** ******* D: Carl Reiner. Steve Martin, Kathleen Turner, David Warner, Paul Benedict, Richard Brestoff, James Cromwell, George Furth, Randi Brooks. While trapped in a loveless marriage with venal Turner, brilliant surgeon Michael Hfuhruhurr (Martin) falls in love with a brain in a jar (voiced by Sissy Spacek) and immediately starts searching for a new "home" for it. As silly as it sounds, but put your brain in neutral and the laughs are there, particularly the decor of Warner's condo and the identity of "The Elevator Killer." [R]▼●)

Man, Woman and Child (1983) **C-99m.** ******* D: Dick Richards. Martin Sheen, Blythe Danner, Sebastian Dungan, Arlene McIntyre, Missy Francis, Craig T. Nelson, David Hemmings, Nathalie Nell. Unabashed tearjerker (from Erich Segal's book) about a happily married man, with two children, who learns that a brief affair he had with a Frenchwoman 10 years ago produced a son—and that the boy has just been orphaned. Simple, honestly sentimental movie. [PG]▼●

Manxman, The (1929-British) **90m.** ****½** D: Alfred Hitchcock. Carl Brisson, Malcolm Keen, Anny Ondra, Randle Ayrton. Fisherman Brisson and lawyer Keen, best friends since childhood, both love Ondra. OK melodrama was Hitchcock's last silent film.▼●

Mao's Last Dancer (2009-Australian) **C-117m.** ****½** D: Bruce Beresford. Bruce Greenwood, Kyle MacLachlan, Joan Chen, Chi Cao, Amanda Schull, Wang Shuang Bao, Cheng Wu Guo, Camilla Vergotis, Jack Thompson, Huang Wen Bin. At age 11, a scrawny boy is taken from his family in a rural Chinese village and brought to Beijing to learn ballet. Years later he is sent to Houston, Texas, as part of a cultural exchange program, and though he's been indoctrinated by his Communist government, he finds he likes America—and especially likes the freedom he feels when he dances. Absorbing true-life story, adapted from Li Cunxin's autobiography, is flattened by uninspired treatment and plays like a corny Hollywood movie of years gone by. Chi Cao's impressive dancing helps redeem the film. [PG]●

Map of the Human Heart (1993-British-Australian-French-Canadian) **C-126m.** ******* D: Vincent Ward. Jason Scott Lee, Anne Parillaud, Patrick Bergin, John Cusack, Robert Joamie, Annie Galipeau, Jeanne

Moreau, Ben Mendelson, Clotilde Courau. Fascinating, if not altogether successful, fable about an Inuit Eskimo boy plucked from his Canadian homeland and taken to "civilization" by a mapmaker in the 1930s. The rest of the young man's life unfolds like a strange dream. Director Ward's sometimes hallucinatory images and a mystical atmosphere make this a compelling film to watch even when it falters storywise. Filled with extraordinary performances, including a cameo by the always wonderful Moreau. Super 35. [R]▼●

Map of the World, A (1999) **C-126m.** ******* D: Scott Elliott. Sigourney Weaver, Julianne Moore, David Strathairn, Ron Lea, Arliss Howard, Chloë Sevigny, Louise Fletcher. School nurse Weaver, whose family life is fragmented, observes the world with ironic detachment until she's imprisoned for abusing a student. She regards jail as almost a vacation from her responsibilities, but cannot evade her own memories. Excellent performances, especially by Weaver, enliven this intelligent adaptation of the novel by Jane Hamilton. The middle seems to mark time, but the first third is outstanding. [R]▼●

Marathon Man (1976) **C-125m.** ****½** D: John Schlesinger. Dustin Hoffman, Laurence Olivier, Roy Scheider, William Devane, Marthe Keller, Fritz Weaver, Marc Lawrence, Richard Bright. Glossy thriller adapted by William Goldman from his book. Basic premise of graduate student Hoffman propelled into dizzying world of international intrigue spoiled by repellent violence and some gaping story holes. Hoffman and arch-villain Olivier are superb but film doesn't do them justice. [R]▼●

Marat/Sade (Persecution and Assassination of Jean-Paul Marat as Performed by the Inmates of the Asylum at Charenton Under the Direction of the Marquis de Sade, The) (1966-British) **C-115m.** ******** D: Peter Brook. Patrick Magee, Clifford Rose, Glenda Jackson, Ian Richardson, Brenda Kempner, Ruth Baker, Michael Williams, Freddie Jones. Chilling adaptation of Peter Weiss play about "performance" staged by inmates of French insane asylum, under direction of Marquis de Sade. Lurid atmosphere is so vivid that it seems actors are breathing down your neck; brilliantly directed by Brook. Not for weak stomachs. Screenplay by Adrian Mitchell.▼●)

Marcello Mastroianni: I Remember, Yes I Remember (1997-Italian) **C/B&W-98m.** ******* D: Anna Maria Tató. Film lovers in general and fans of the late actor in particular should savor this full-bodied documentary portrait, made by Mastroianni's longtime companion, who filmed him not long before his death in 1996. Mastroianni reminisces, jokes, reflects on his career and the directors with whom he worked—and, most tellingly, exudes a love of and passion for life. Originally 199m.; made for Italian television. ▼▶

March of the Penguins (2005-French) **C-80m.** ******* D: Luc Jacquet. Narrated by Morgan Freeman. Entertaining, beautifully filmed documentary about the journey of the Emperor penguins and their cycle of mating, breeding, and surviving in the unbelievably harsh climate of the Antarctic. A simple story compellingly told, with the title characters an endearing, scrappy, and endlessly photogenic lot. Original 85m. French version had actors providing "voices" for the penguins; the American release (wisely) dropped this, added a new music score by Alex Wurman and Freeman's narration. Stay through the credits to get an idea of the conditions the filmmakers faced. Oscar winner for Best Documentary. [G]▶

March of the Wooden Soldiers SEE: **Babes in Toyland** (1934)

March or Die (1977) **C-104m.** ****** D: Dick Richards. Gene Hackman, Terence Hill, Max von Sydow, Catherine Deneuve, Ian Holm. Homage to French Foreign Legion adventures of filmdom's past. Good cast wages losing battle with static script and walks downheartedly through action scenes. Disappointing epic-that-might-have-been. Additional footage tacked on for network showing. [PG]▼▶

Marci X (2003) **C-84m.** BOMB D: Richard Benjamin. Lisa Kudrow, Damon Wayans, Richard Benjamin, Christine Baranski, Paula Garcés, Jane Krakowski, Veanne Cox, Sherie Rene Scott, Billy Griffith, Charles Kimbrough, Matthew J. Morrison. Abysmal satire involving a vapid, aging Jewish-American Princess (Kudrow), who is forced by circumstance to enter the uptown world of a controversial bad-boy rap star (Wayans). Offers nary a laugh, not to mention some mind-bogglingly tasteless stereotypes. Written by Paul Rudnick. Completed in 2001. [R] ▼▶

Marco (1973) **C-109m.** ****** D: Seymour Robbie. Desi Arnaz, Jr., Jack Weston, Zero Mostel. Lavish but lumbering musical, filmed on Oriental locations, with Arnaz as young Marco Polo and Mostel as Kublai Khan. Disappointing. [G]▼▶

Marc Pease Experience, The (2009) **C-83m.** ****** D: Todd Louiso. Jason Schwartzman, Ben Stiller, Anna Kendrick, Ebon Moss-Bachrach, Gabrielle Dennis, Jay Paulson, Amber Wallace. Mirthfully delusional doofus (a goony Schwartzman) pesters long-ago high school music teacher (a slick, smarmy Stiller) to produce a demo CD of his a cappella group, unaware that they share a senior-year girlfriend (Kendrick, in an underdeveloped role). Painful satire of teen FAME-mania, cowritten by the director, finds its sparse laughs in goofy theater games and vocal exercises, but easily could have been a horror movie in other hands. Viewers may catch more of *The Wiz* than they wish. [PG-13] ▶

Marebito (2004-Japanese) **C-92m.** ****½** D: Takashi Shimizu. Shinya Tsukamoto, Tomomi Miyashita, Kazuhiro Nakahara, Miho Ninagawa, Shun Sugata. Freelance video journalist totes his camcorder deep into the Tokyo subway system to solve a grisly suicide. There, the electronic-age Orpheus finds his unlikely Eurydice: a chained-up naked girl. With fangs. He takes her home. Subtitled A STRANGER FROM AFAR, this morbid study of a man who shouldn't have thrown away his Prozac is both a descent into the netherworld and an ascent into the metaphysical. Morose and unsettling, but a mundane resolution drags the disturbing back into the ordinary. Script by Chiaki Konaka, from his novel. [R]▶

Margaret Cho: Assassin (2005) **C-85m.** ****** D: Kerry Asmussen. Cho's fourth concert film, taped in Washington, D.C., is strictly by-the-numbers, with the comedian offering commentary on gay marriage and animal activists, Martha Stewart and Arnold Schwarzenegger, Ronald Reagan, Zhang Ziyi . . . and Laura and George W. Bush. What once was fresh now seems tired, preachy, and only intermittently funny. Strictly for diehard Cho fans.▶

Margaret's Museum (1995-Canadian) **C-118m.** ****½** D: Mort Ransen. Helena Bonham Carter, Kate Nelligan, Clive Russell, Craig Olejnik, Andrea Morris, Peter Boretski, Kenneth Welsh. Bonham Carter is terrific as a maverick who lives in a Nova Scotia mining town that seems to be on the edge of civilization; she despises the mines, which have killed her father and brother and embittered her mother (Nelligan). Then she falls in love with a burly former miner (Russell). Well meaning—with some strong moments—but gloomy and predictable. [R] ▼▶

Margot at the Wedding (2007) **C-91m.** ****** D: Noah Baumbach. Nicole Kidman, Jennifer Jason Leigh, Jack Black, John Turturro, Ciarán Hinds, Zane Pais, Flora Cross, Halley Feiffer. Margot (Kidman) hasn't talked to her sister (Leigh) in a long time, but agrees to attend her wedding—to a layabout "artist" (Black)—at the home where they grew up in the Hamptons. Yet from the minute she arrives Margot's poisonous mind, and mouth, take over, with little regard for the turmoil she creates—or the effect it has on her vulnerable, adolescent son. Spending time with this spectacularly neurotic family is no fun at all. Occasional insights and observations can't make up for the lack of story, or the loathsome cast of characters, in Baumbach's Chekhovian comedy-drama. [R] ▶

Maria Full of Grace (2004-U.S.-Colombian) **C-101m.** *****½** D: Joshua Marston. Catalina Sandino Moreno, Wilson Guerrero, Yenny Paola Vega, Jhon Álex Toro, Jaime Osorio Gómez, Guilied López, Patricia Rae. Exceptional film about a 17-year-old Colombian girl, dissatisfied with her dead-end life, who accepts a job as a "mule," digesting packets of drugs and smuggling them into the U.S. She has no idea what lies in store for her . . . and neither do we. There is no artifice in debuting writer-director Marston's presentation of the story, nor is there a feeling of "acting" in any of the utterly believable performances. A knockout. [R]▼❶

Marianne and Juliane (1981-German) **C-106m. ***½** D: Margarethe von Trotta. Jutta Lampe, Barbara Sukowa, Rudiger Vogler, Doris Schade, Franz Rudnick. Profound, multileveled, and memorable chronicle of the relationship between two sisters, alike in some ways yet so very different in others. Juliane (Lampe) is a feminist editor working within the system; Marianne (Sukowa) is a radical political terrorist. Superbly acted, a must-see.▼

Maria's Lovers (1984) **C-100m. ** ** D: Andrei Konchalovsky. Nastassia Kinski, John Savage, Robert Mitchum, Keith Carradine, Anita Morris, Bud Cort, Karen Young, Tracy Nelson, John Goodman, Vincent Spano, Bill Smitrovich. Young soldier returns home from WW2, after suffering nervous breakdown, and finds himself unable to consummate his love with new bride. Richly atmospheric film, set in Pennsylvania mining town, has fine performances and other attributes, but is unrelievedly ponderous. Opening sequence cleverly integrates footage from John Huston's famous documentary LET THERE BE LIGHT with newly shot material of Savage. [R]▼❶

Marie (1985) **C-112m. *** D: Roger Donaldson. Sissy Spacek, Jeff Daniels, Keith Szarabajka, Morgan Freeman, Fred (Dalton) Thompson, Don Hood, John Cullum. Solid drama about divorcée and mother of three who takes a job in Tennessee state government, then blows the whistle on corruption and finds herself in very hot water. Might be hard to believe if it wasn't true (though knowing the outcome of the case will certainly remove a lot of the suspense). Based on Peter Maas' book; defense attorney Thompson plays himself. J-D-C Scope. [PG-13]▼❶

Marie Antoinette (1938) **149m. **½** D: W. S. Van Dyke II. Norma Shearer, Tyrone Power, John Barrymore, Robert Morley, Gladys George, Anita Louise, Joseph Schildkraut. Opulent MGM production of life of 18th-century French queen lacks pace but has good acting, with great performance by Morley as Louis XVI. Shearer captures essence of title role as costumer retells her life from Austrian princess to doomed queen of crumbling empire. ▼❶❶

Marie Antoinette (1955-French) **C-108m. **½** D: Jean Delannoy. Michele Morgan, Richard Todd, Jean Morel. Epic on life of famed 18th-century French queen has marvelous Morgan in title role but lacks perspective and scope.

Marie Antoinette (2006) **C-123m. ***½** D: Sofia Coppola. Kirsten Dunst, Jason Schwartzman, Judy Davis, Rip Torn, Steve Coogan, Rose Byrne, Asia Argento, Molly Shannon, Shirley Henderson, Danny Huston, Marianne Faithfull, Mary Nighy, Sarah Adler. Visually sumptuous account of a teenager's journey from Vienna to the Palace at Versailles and the throne of France. Writer-director Coppola's Marie (as played by Dunst) is a contemporary girl, with modern music set against the pomp and detail of the 18th-century life in the fast lane. Starts to tire after a while and ends with a whimper, not a bang . . . but there's much to enjoy here. Based on Antonia Fraser's book *Marie Antoinette: The Journey*. Oscar winner for Costume Design (Milena Canonero). Francis Ford Coppola coexecutive-produced. [PG-13]❶

Marigold (2007-U.S.-Indian) **C-112m. ** ** D: Willard Carroll. Ali Larter, Salman Khan, Nandana Sen, Ian Bohen, Helen Khan, Suchitra Pillai, Shari "Truth Hurts" Watson. Obnoxious grade-Z Hollywood actress ("I don't do 'grateful' very well," she admits) flies to India to make a movie, only to find that the production has fallen apart. Before long she's hired to participate in a Bollywood musical, and a mutual attraction grows between her and the handsome choreographer . . . but he isn't forthcoming about his family background. Opening scenes with Larter are incredibly off-putting; the rest is innocuous but trite. Super 35. [PG-13]❶

"Marihuana" (1936) **58m. BOMB** D: Dwain Esper. Harley Wood, Hugh McArthur, Pat Carlyle, Paul Ellis, Dorothy Dehn, Richard Erskine. Some naive, fun-loving kids puff on the title weed, offered them by a man you know is evil incarnate because he has a mustache, and the result is nude swimming, a drowning . . . and worse! This exploitation fare is almost mind-boggling in its dopiness. And don't forget that it was researched "with the help of federal, state and police narcotic officers." A companion piece to REEFER MADNESS. Originally titled "MARIJUANA"—THE DEVIL'S WEED.▼❶

Marilyn Hotchkiss' Ballroom Dancing & Charm School (2006) **C-103m. *½** D: Randall Miller. Robert Carlyle, Marisa Tomei, Sean Astin, John Goodman, Mary Steenburgen, Donnie Wahlberg, David Paymer, Camryn Manheim, Adam Arkin, Sonia Braga, Elden Henson, Ernie Hudson, Miguel Sandoval, Danny DeVito, Ian Abercrombie. When a recent widower aids a dying accident victim it sets in motion a quest to find that man's long-lost love at a school reunion. This leads to a ballroom dance school and a dreary, hokey, overly sentimentalized story. Based on Miller's 1990 short film, there's more padding here than in a Wonderbra. Meant to be romantic and moving, but succeeds only in wasting its considerable on-screen talent. Panavision. [PG-13]◗

Marine, The (2006) **C-93m.** ****** D: John Bonito. John Cena, Robert Patrick, Kelly Carlson, Anthony Ray Parker, Abigail Bianca, Jerome Ehlers, Manu Bennett, Damon Gibson. In South Carolina, fleeing diamond robbers make the mistake of kidnapping the wife (Carlson) of a recently discharged Marine (Cena), who doggedly pursues them down highways and through swamps, despite everything in sight exploding in impressive fireballs. Backed by World Wrestling Entertainment, this didn't turn poker-faced wrestler Cena into a movie star; occasionally lively, jokey throwback to 1980s-style action adventures. Patrick is fun as the sarcastic villain. Also available in unrated version. Followed by a direct-to-DVD sequel. [PG-13]◗

Marius (1931-French) **125m.** ******* D: Alexandre (Alexander) Korda. Raimu, Pierre Fresnay, Charpin, Alida Rouffe, Orane Demazis. Amusing, flavorful if a bit too theatrical satire of provincial life, centering on the love of Marius (Fresnay) for Fanny (Demazis). Raimu is wonderful as Cesar, cafe owner and father of Marius. Screenplay by Marcel Pagnol; first of a trilogy, followed by FANNY and CESAR. All three were the basis of the play and movie FANNY (1961).▼●

Marjoe (1972) **C-88m.** ***½** D: Howard Smith, Sarah Kernochan. Oscar-winning documentary about life of fake evangelist Marjoe Gortner is certainly interesting, but is a little too pleased with itself, a little too pat to be totally convincing. Marjoe himself is likable enough. [PG]▼◗

Marjorie Morningstar (1958) **C-123m.** ****½** D: Irving Rapper. Gene Kelly, Natalie Wood, Claire Trevor, Ed Wynn, Everett Sloane, Carolyn Jones, Martin Milner, George Tobias, Martin Balsam, Ruta Lee, Edward (Edd) Byrnes, Shelley Fabares. Diluted adaptation of Herman Wouk's bestseller about a well-to-do Jewish girl, conflicted about her religion and background, who's swept off her feet by a musical theater director-performer at a Catskills resort one summer. Kelly is perfectly cast. ▼●

Mark, The (1961-British) **127m.** *****½** D: Guy Green. Stuart Whitman, Maria Schell, Rod Steiger, Brenda De Banzie, Maurice Denham, Donald Wolfit, Paul Rogers, Donald Houston. Whitman is excellent in his portrayal of emotionally broken sex criminal who has served time, now wants to make new start. Thoughtful, well-acted adult drama written by Sidney Buchman and Stanley Mann. CinemaScope.▼●

Marked for Death (1990) **C-94m.** ****** D: Dwight H. Little. Steven Seagal, Basil Wallace, Keith David, Tom Wright, Joanna Pacula, Elizabeth Gracen, Bette Ford, Danielle Harris, Al Israel, Arlen Dean·Snyder, Jimmy Cliff. Familiar, brainless actioner with ex-drug agent Seagal taking on Jamaican dope pushers who've, as the title says, marked him and his family for extinction. Cliff and band appear briefly and perform on soundtrack. Super 35. [R]▼●

Marked Woman (1937) **99m.** ******* D: Lloyd Bacon. Bette Davis, Humphrey Bogart, Lola Lane, Isabel Jewell, Jane Bryan, Eduardo Ciannelli, Allen Jenkins, Mayo Methot. Bristling gangster drama of D.A. Bogart convincing Davis and four girlfriends to testify against their boss, underworld king Ciannelli.▼●

Mark of the Hawk, The (1957-British) **C-83m.** ******* D: Michael Audley. Eartha Kitt, Sidney Poitier, Juano Hernandez, John McIntire. Unusual tale intelligently acted, set in contemporary Africa, with peaceful vs. violent means for racial equality the main theme. Originally titled ACCUSED. Aka SHAKA ZULU. SuperScope 235.▼●

Mark of the Vampire (1935) **61m.** ******* D: Tod Browning. Lionel Barrymore, Elizabeth Allan, Bela Lugosi, Lionel Atwill, Carol (Carroll) Borland, Jean Hersholt, Donald Meek. Delightful, intriguing tale of vampires terrorizing European village; inspector Atwill, vampire expert Barrymore investigate. Beautifully done, with an incredible ending. Remake of Browning's silent LONDON AFTER MIDNIGHT.▼●

Mark of Zorro, The (1920) **90m.** *****½** D: Fred Niblo. Douglas Fairbanks, Sr., Marguerite De La Motte, Noah Beery, Robert McKim, Charles Mailes. Silent classic with Fairbanks as the masked hero of old California; perhaps Doug's best film—his first swashbuckler. Nonstop fun.▼●

Mark of Zorro, The (1940) **93m.** *****½** D: Rouben Mamoulian. Tyrone Power, Linda Darnell, Basil Rathbone, Gale Sondergaard, Eugene Pallette, J. Edward Bromberg, Montagu Love. Lavish swashbuckler with Power as son of California aristocrat in 1800s, alternately a foppish dandy and a dashing masked avenger of evil: climactic swordplay with Rathbone a swashbuckling gem. Great score by Alfred Newman. Remade for TV in 1974.▼●

Marlene (1984-German) **C/B&W-96m.** ******* D: Maximilian Schell. Utterly, unexpectedly fascinating look at Marlene Dietrich, built on unusual foundation of a tape-recorded interview with Schell that she refused to allow to be filmed! How Schell turns this liability into an asset for the film—just one of its layers—and how Dietrich reveals so much about herself even in her stubborn rejection of basic interview questions, is all part of the film's mystique (and Marlene's). Includes most of her finest moments on screen.▼●◗

Marley & Me (2008) **C-116m.** ******* D:

David Frankel. Owen Wilson, Jennifer Aniston, Eric Dane, Kathleen Turner, Alan Arkin, Nathan Gamble, Haley Bennett, Joyce Van Patten. Sweet film about the life of a rambunctious dog and how he affects a young couple and their growing family. Wilson plays a happily married newspaper reporter whose career takes an unexpected turn when he starts writing a column drawn from his own life. Parents and dog lovers should approach with caution: the movie follows the dog's life to its very end. Based on the autobiographical book by newspaperman John Grogan; screenplay by Scott Frank and Don Roos. Followed by a direct-to-DVD sequel. Super 35. [PG] ▶

Marlowe (1969) C-95m. *** D: Paul Bogart. James Garner, Gayle Hunnicutt, Carroll O'Connor, Rita Moreno, Sharon Farrell, William Daniels, Jackie Coogan, Bruce Lee. Slick updating of Raymond Chandler's *The Little Sister* with Garner as Philip Marlowe, hired by girl to find missing brother. Really belongs in 1940s, but works fairly well; Moreno memorable as stripper who helps solve case in exciting finale, plus hilarious scene where Lee reduces Marlowe's office to rubble. [M/PG] ▼●

Marmaduke (2010) C-88m. *½ D: Tom Dey. Lee Pace, Judy Greer, William H. Macy, David Walliams; voices of Owen Wilson, Emma Stone, George Lopez, Kiefer Sutherland, Christopher Mintz-Plasse, Steve Coogan, Fergie, Marlon Wayans, Damon Wayans, Jr., Sam Elliott. Fans of the long-running comic strip by Brad Anderson and Phil Leeming may be surprised to learn that Marmaduke, the humongous Great Dane who often tests the patience of his "two-legger" owners, speaks in a lazy-hipster voice (supplied by Wilson) that suggests a California stoner. Unfortunately, that's one of the very few novelties in this otherwise derivative, unimaginative comedy that relies heavily on the intermingling of human actors in thankless parts and CGI-tweaked live animals voiced by familiar actors. Strictly kid stuff. Super 35. [PG] ▶

Marnie (1964) C-129m. *** D: Alfred Hitchcock. Sean Connery, Tippi Hedren, Diane Baker, Martin Gabel, Louise Latham, Alan Napier. This story of a habitual thief (Hedren) whose employer (Connery) is determined to understand her illness was considered a misfire in 1964 . . . but there's more than meets the eye, especially for Hitchcock buffs. Script by Jay Presson Allen. Look for Bruce Dern, Mariette Hartley, and Melody Thomas Scott in small roles. ▼●

Maroc 7 (1967-British) C-91m. ** D: Gerry O'Hara. Gene Barry, Elsa Martinelli, Cyd Charisse, Leslie Phillips. Slow robbery-murder tale of secret agent out to catch split-personality thief. Panavision. ▼

Marooned (1969) C-134m. ** D: John Sturges. Gregory Peck, Richard Crenna, James Franciscus, David Janssen, Gene Hackman, Lee Grant, Nancy Kovack, Mariette Hartley. Glossy but disappointing story of astronauts unable to return to earth, while space agency head Peck tries to keep lid from blowing off. Alternately boring and excruciating; climactic scenes in space produce agony, not excitement. Oscar-winning special effects are chief asset. Retitled SPACE TRAVELLERS. Panavision. [M/PG] ▼●

Marquise of O, The (1976-French-German) C-102m. *** D: Eric Rohmer. Edith Clever, Bruno Ganz, Peter Luhr, Edda Seippel, Otto Sander. Delicate, disarmingly simple story set in 18th-century Italy; a young widow saved from rape by a Russian soldier during Franco-Prussian war finds herself pregnant some months later, and doesn't understand how. Beautiful period flavor, but film's charm is very low-key. Based on a novella by Heinrich von Kleist. [PG] ▼●

Marriage-Italian Style (1964-Italian) C-102m. *** D: Vittorio De Sica. Sophia Loren, Marcello Mastroianni, Aldo Puglisi, Pia Lindstrom, Vito Moriconi, Marilu Tolo. Spicy account of Loren's efforts to get long-time lover Mastroianni to marry her and stay her husband. Based on Eduardo De Filippo's 1946 play *Filumena*. ▼●

Marriage of a Young Stockbroker, The (1971) C-95m. **½ D: Lawrence Turman. Richard Benjamin, Joanna Shimkus, Elizabeth Ashley, Adam West, Patricia Barry, Tiffany Bolling. Humorous and sad depiction of marital breakdown; husband indulges in voyeurism, wife has own problems. Good cast working with script that seems uncertain as to what point it wants to drive across. Director Turman, who'd produced THE GRADUATE, hoped lightning would strike twice with this adaptation of novel by same author, Charles Webb. [PG— edited from original R rating] ▼

Marriage of Maria Braun, The (1979-German) C-120m. ***½ D: Rainer Werner Fassbinder. Hanna Schygulla, Ivan Desny, Gottfried John, Klaus Lowitsch, Gisela Uhlen. Schygulla shines in the Joan Crawfordesque role of a penniless soldier's wife who builds an industrial empire after the end of WW2. Riveting; the first of Fassbinder's three parables of postwar Germany, followed by LOLA and VERONIKA VOSS. [R] ▼●

Marriage on the Rocks (1965) C-109m. **½ D: Jack Donohue. Frank Sinatra, Deborah Kerr, Dean Martin, Cesar Romero, Hermione Baddeley, Tony Bill, Nancy Sinatra, John McGiver, Trini Lopez. Frank and Deborah have marital spat, get quickie Mexican divorce, she ends up married to his best pal, Dino. A waste of real talent. Panavision. ▼●

Married Life (2008) **C-90m.** **½ D: Ira Sachs. Chris Cooper, Patricia Clarkson, Pierce Brosnan, Rachel McAdams, David Wenham, David Richmond-Peck. Successful businessman Cooper tells his best friend (Brosnan) that he plans to leave his wife (Clarkson) and disrupt their apparently happy marriage, because he's found a (younger) woman (McAdams) who truly loves him. He just can't figure out how to break the news to his spouse. Intriguing blend of social commentary, soap opera, and noirish melodrama set in 1949 plays like one long pregnant pause; elevated by a quartet of good actors in top form. Adapted from John Bingham's novel *Five Roundabouts to Heaven* by Sachs and Oren Moverman. [PG-13]▶

Married to It (1993) **C-112m.** ** D: Arthur Hiller. Beau Bridges, Stockard Channing, Robert Sean Leonard, Mary Stuart Masterson, Cybill Shepherd, Ron Silver, Don Francks, Donna Vivino. Several married couples meet in Manhattan and become the unlikeliest of friends. Each spouse manages to embrace several annoyingly bland clichés: yuppie, young newlywed, ex-hippie, bitchy stepmother—you get the picture. Cast of decent actors can't begin to save the pedestrian script. This one sat on the shelf for a couple of years. [R]▼●

Married to the Mob (1988) **C-103m.** *** D: Jonathan Demme. Michelle Pfeiffer, Matthew Modine, Dean Stockwell, Mercedes Ruehl, Alec Baldwin, Joan Cusack, Trey Wilson, Charles Napier, Tracey Walter, Al Lewis, Nancy Travis, David Johansen (Buster Poindexter), Chris Isaak, Oliver Platt, Todd Solondz. A woman tries to escape from the Mafia after the death of her hit man husband, only to find that the local boss has the hots for her. Amiable, entertaining farce with right-on performances by Pfeiffer and Stockwell (in a neat comic turn as the mafioso). Only director Demme could make a mob movie with likable characters in it! Score by David Byrne. [R]▼●

Married Woman, A (1964-French) **94m.** ** D: Jean-Luc Godard. Macha Meril, Philippe Leroy, Bernard Noel. Turgid three-cornered romance, with Meril unable to decide between husband Leroy and lover Noel; then, she finds herself pregnant. Godard narrates this pretentious allegory of middle-class alienation.▼●

Marrying Kind, The (1952) **93m.** *** D: George Cukor. Judy Holliday, Aldo Ray, Madge Kennedy, Sheila Bond, John Alexander, Rex Williams, Phyllis Povah, Peggy Cass, Mickey Shaughnessy, Griff Barnett. Bittersweet drama of young couple on verge of divorce recalling their life together via flashbacks; sensitive performers outshine talky script—but story and situations haven't dated one bit. Look for Charles Bronson as postal worker.▼●

Marrying Man, The (1991) **C-115m.** **½ D: Jerry Rees. Kim Basinger, Alec Baldwin, Robert Loggia, Elisabeth Shue, Armand Assante, Paul Reiser, Fisher Stevens, Peter Dobson, Gretchen Wyler. Engaged L.A. playboy joyrides with buddies to post-WW2 Las Vegas—and falls for a gorgeous chanteuse who happens to be Bugsy Siegel's mistress. Neil Simon original was notorious for its on-set hijinks, in-fighting, and star egos, causing just about everyone down to the Key Grip to disown the thing. In truth, the picture's fairly entertaining, with sexy Baldwin and super-sultry Basinger hard to resist. [R]▼●

Marry Me, Marry Me (1969-French) **C-87m.** *** D: Claude Berri. Elisabeth Wiener, Regine, Claude Berri, Luisa Colpeyn. Delightful story of love and (what else?) marriage, Berri-style. [M/PG]▼

Mars Attacks! (1996) **C-103m.** **½ D: Tim Burton. Jack Nicholson, Glenn Close, Annette Bening, Pierce Brosnan, Danny DeVito, Martin Short, Sarah Jessica Parker, Michael J. Fox, Rod Steiger, Tom Jones, Lukas Haas, Natalie Portman, Jim Brown, Pam Grier, Paul Winfield, Sylvia Sidney, Jack Black, Lisa Marie, Joe Don Baker, Christina Applegate, Barbet Schroeder. Overly self-satisfied spoof of '50s alien-invasion movies (and '50s attitudes) has Martians landing in flying saucers. President Nicholson urges calm and reason, but the little guys turn out to be predators . . . nasty ones at that! Great effects and animation (of the Martian characters) but awfully broad and one-note in tone, spoofing something that's already funny in the straight-faced originals of the period. One can't completely dislike a film in which Slim Whitman figures so prominently, however. Inspired by a gum card series of the same name. Panavision. [PG-13]▼●

Marseille Contract, The SEE: **Destructors, The** (1974)

Mars Invades Puerto Rico SEE: **Frankenstein Meets the Space Monster**

Mars Needs Moms (2011) **C-88m.** *** D: Simon Wells. Seth Green, Dan Fogler, Joan Cusack, Elisabeth Harnois, Mindy Sterling, Kevin Cahoon, Tom Everett Scott. Engaging adaptation of Berkeley Breathed's children's book about a boy named Milo who resents his mother's nagging and insistence that he do chores around the house—until she's swept away by a Martian spaceship. He manages to tag along and discovers that Mars needs his mother's brain matter in order to sustain its baby life forms. Funny, imaginative, and well-paced animated yarn was filmed in motion-capture medium; it isn't hard to recognize the leading actors in "cartoon" form—except for Green, whose facial features have been morphed onto a little boy. 3-D Digital Widescreen. [PG]▶

Mars Needs Women (1968) **C-80m.** *½

D: Larry Buchanan. Tommy Kirk, Yvonne Craig, Byron Lord, Roger Ready, Warren Hammack, Anthony Houston. Just as the title suggests, Martians Kirk and four pals, hoping to increase birthrate on their planet, arrive here to capture live women. Strangely sincere but extremely silly and distended. Texas-made film written by the director. Most important revelation: Mars abandoned neckties 50 years ago. ▼●)

Marsupials, The: The Howling III SEE: **Howling III**

Martha (1973-West German) **C-112m.** **½ D: Rainer Werner Fassbinder. Margit Carstensen, Karlheinz Bohm, Gisela Fackeldey, Adrian Hoven, Peter Chatel. Unsubtle account of spinsterish Carstensen, who has spent her life under the control of her father. He dies and she immediately marries, with disastrous results. Very much of its time, when women were discovering feminism. Cineastes take note: Martha's last name is Heyer (as in Martha Hyer), and she lives on Douglas Sirk Street! First made available in the U.S. in 1994.●

Martha, Meet Frank, Daniel and Laurence SEE: **Very Thought of You, The**

Martian Child (2007) **C-106m.** ** D: Menno Meyjes. John Cusack, Bobby Coleman, Amanda Peet, Joan Cusack, Oliver Platt, Anjelica Huston, Sophie Okonedo, Richard Schiff, Howard Hesseman. By turns annoyingly sappy and affectingly sentimental, uneven comedy-drama focuses on the father-son bond that develops between a recently widowed sci-fi author (John Cusack) and an orphaned youngster (Coleman) who claims to be an extraterrestrial. Joan Cusack, John's real-life sibling, offsets the schmaltz with her sassy supporting performance as the writer's sister. Based on David Gerrold's novella. [PG]●

Martians Go Home (1990) **C-89m.** *½ D: David Odell. Randy Quaid, Margaret Colin, Anita Morris, Barry Sobel, Vic Dunlop, John Philbin, Gerrit Graham, Ronny Cox, Harry Basil. TV songwriter Quaid accidentally summons a billion green wisecracking Martians to Earth; chaos (limited by the film's low budget) ensues. Fredric Brown's classic sci-fi humor novel misfires on the screen, partly because the pesky Martians are all played by mediocre standup comics. [PG-13] ▼●

Martin (1978) **C-95m.** *** D: George A. Romero. John Amplas, Lincoln Maazel, Christine Forrest, Elayne Nadeau, Tom Savini, Sarah Venable, George A. Romero. Typical Romero mix of social satire and stomach-churning gore: 17-year-old Amplas thinks he's a vampire (lacking fangs, he must resort to razor blades); thanks to his frequent calls to a late-night radio show, he's also something of a local celebrity! Intriguing little shocker is worth seeing, but not right after dinner. [R] ▼●)

Martin Lawrence Live: Runteldat SEE: **Runteldat**

Martin Lawrence: You So Crazy SEE: **You So Crazy**

Martin's Day (1984-Canadian) **C-98m.** ** D: Alan Gibson. Richard Harris, Lindsay Wagner, James Coburn, Justin Henry, Karen Black, John Ireland. Utterly ordinary "family film" about escaped prisoner who kidnaps (and ultimately befriends) young boy. Bland and unconvincing. [PG]▼

Marty (1955) **91m.** ***½ D: Delbert Mann. Ernest Borgnine, Betsy Blair, Joe Mantell, Joe De Santis, Esther Minciotti, Augusta Ciolli, Karen Steele, Jerry Paris, Frank Sutton. Borgnine shines as a Bronx butcher who unexpectedly finds love. Paddy Chayefsky adapted his TV play for the screen. Oscar winner for Borgnine, Chayefsky, Mann, and Best Picture. Some prints include a scene with Blair and her parents that's inexplicably missing from other versions. ▼●)

Marvin and Tige (1983) **C-104m.** **½ D: Eric Weston. John Cassavetes, Gibran Brown, Billy Dee Williams, Denise Nicholas Hill, Fay Hauser. Tearjerker about a loser (Cassavetes) who takes in an aimless 11-year-old (Brown) who tried to kill himself. Well acted, and well intentioned, but pretty standard stuff. Aka LIKE FATHER AND SON, running 109m. [PG]▼

Marvin's Room (1996) **C-98m.** ***½ D: Jerry Zaks. Meryl Streep, Leonardo DiCaprio, Diane Keaton, Robert De Niro, Hume Cronyn, Gwen Verdon, Dan Hedaya, Hal Scardino, Cynthia Nixon, Kelly Ripa. Affecting adaptation of Scott McPherson's Off-Broadway play about a woman who's devoted her adult life to caring for her stroke-ridden father and a dithery aunt; now she must call on her long-estranged sister and nephews to help out in her own health emergency. A poignant and pointed look at family ties, old wounds, love, and responsibility, with uniformly fine performances. Cronyn adds immeasurable strength, though he says not a word. Rachel Portman's beautiful score is another asset. Broadway director Zaks' film debut. Victor Garber appears unbilled. [PG-13] ▼●

Marx Brothers at the Circus SEE: **At the Circus**

Marx Brothers Go West SEE: **Go West**

Maryjane (1968) **C-96m.** *½ D: Maury Dexter. Fabian, Diane McBain, Michael Margotta, Kevin Coughlin, Patty McCormack, Terri (Teri) Garr. 1960s version of REEFER MADNESS casts Fabian as high school art teacher who tries to keep his students from smoking grass; terrible, but may play better if you're stoned. Look quickly for Garry Marshall and the film's cowriters, Dick Gautier and Peter Marshall.

Mary of Scotland (1936) **123m.** ***½ D: John Ford. Katharine Hepburn, Fredric

March, Florence Eldridge, Douglas Walton, Moroni Olsen, John Carradine, Robert Barrat, Ian Keith, Ralph Forbes, Alan Mowbray, Donald Crisp. Lavish historical drama in which Mary, Queen of Scots (Hepburn), returns to her homeland from France, to rule "fairly and justly." She falls in love with lord March and contends with various treacheries. Based on a play by Maxwell Anderson. ▼●)

Mary Poppins (1964) **C-140m.** ******** D: Robert Stevenson. Julie Andrews, Dick Van Dyke, David Tomlinson, Glynis Johns, Ed Wynn, Hermione Baddeley, Karen Dotrice, Matthew Garber, Arthur Treacher, Reginald Owen. There's charm, wit, and movie magic to spare in Walt Disney's adaptation of P. L. Trayers' book about a "practically perfect" nanny who brings profound change to the Banks family of London, circa 1910. Oscars went to Richard and Robert Sherman for their tuneful score, the song "Chim-Chim-Cheree," the formidable Visual Effects team, Cotton Warburton for his editing, and Andrews, in her film debut (though Van Dyke is equally good as Bert, the whimsical jack of all trades). That's Jane Darwell, in her last screen appearance, as the bird lady. A wonderful movie. Scripted by coproducer Bill Walsh and Donald Da Gradi. Adapted for the stage in 2004. ▼●)

Mary, Queen of Scots (1971) **C-128m.** ******* D: Charles Jarrott. Vanessa Redgrave, Glenda Jackson, Patrick McGoohan, Timothy Dalton, Nigel Davenport, Trevor Howard, Daniel Massey, Ian Holm. Inaccurate history lesson but good costume drama, with strong performances from Redgrave as Mary, Jackson as Queen Elizabeth, rivals for power in Tudor England. Panavision. [PG]▼●)

Mary Reilly (1996) **C-108m.** ****½** D: Stephen Frears. Julia Roberts, John Malkovich, Glenn Close, George Cole, Michael Gambon, Kathy Staff, Michael Sheen, Bronagh Gallagher, Linda Bassett, Ciarán Hinds. Intriguing premise: the story of Dr. Jekyll and Mr. Hyde from the point of view of a housemaid in his employ. Unfortunately, this chamber drama is played out in ponderous fashion and almost sinks under its own weight, despite the interesting performances by its stars. (Admittedly, Roberts' Irish accent comes and goes at whim.) Close is fun in a flamboyant part as a madam. Screenplay by Christopher Hampton from the novel by Valerie Martin. [R]▼●)

Mary Shelley's Frankenstein (1994) **C-128m.** ****** D: Kenneth Branagh. Robert De Niro, Kenneth Branagh, Tom Hulce, Helena Bonham Carter, Aidan Quinn, Ian Holm, Richard Briers, John Cleese, Robert Hardy, Cherie Lunghi. Hugely disappointing, "faithful" rendition of the Frankenstein saga. Energetic to a fault, with a camera that refuses to stand still. Branagh allows us to understand what makes Dr. F. tick, but the story goes askew once his creation is unleashed. De Niro's monster remains doggedly De Niroish, and makes one yearn for Karloff. (Even Peter Boyle would do.) [R]▼●)

Ma Saison Préférée (1993-French) **C-124m.** ******* D: André Téchiné. Catherine Deneuve, Daniel Auteuil, Marthe Villalonga, Jean-Pierre Bouvier, Chiara Mastroianni, Carmen Chaplin, Anthony Prada. Story of intertwining relationships, and more interestingly, familial bonds and duties. Deneuve (married, with successful small business but stress at home) and eccentric brother Auteuil (a bachelor and neurosurgeon) make realistic, offbeat leads as adults trying to understand and enjoy life. Deneuve and Marcello Mastroianni's real-life daughter, Chiara, makes her film debut, playing Deneuve's daughter. Talky, but worthwhile. Panavision. ▼●)

Masculine-Feminine (1966-French-Swedish) **103m.** ******* D: Jean-Luc Godard. Jean-Pierre Léaud, Chantal Goya, Marlene Jobert, Michel Debord, Catherine-Isabelle Duport, Eva-Britt Strandberg, Brigitte Bardot. Engaging, original concoction mixes politics, sex, comedy, nostalgia with standard boy-meets-girl theme. Interviewer/journalist Léaud has affair with would-be rock star singer Goya; they're Godard's "children of Marx and Coca-Cola." Adapted, oddly enough, from a Guy de Maupassant story! ▼|

MASH (1970) **C-116m.** ******** D: Robert Altman. Donald Sutherland, Elliott Gould, Tom Skerritt, Sally Kellerman, Robert Duvall, Jo Ann Pflug, Rene Auberjonois, Roger Bowen, Gary Burghoff, Fred Williamson, John Schuck, Bud Cort, G. Wood. Altman's first major success gave new meaning to the word "irreverence," set new style for contemporary filmmaking; follows black-comedy exploits of wild and woolly medical unit during Korean War in hilarious, episodic fashion. Oscar-winning screenplay by Ring Lardner, Jr.; reissued in 1973 at 112m., with new title music by Ahmad Jamal. Later a hit TV series (*M*A*S*H*). Panavision. [PG—edited from original R rating]▼●)

Mask, The (1961-Canadian) **83m.** ***½** D: Julian Roffman. Paul Stevens, Claudette Nevins, Bill Walker, Anne Collings, Martin Lavut, Jim Moran. Low-budget shocker about an ancient Aztec mask that causes wearer to hallucinate and murder. 3-D scenes were put together by famed montage expert Slavko Vorkapich. Retitled EYES OF HELL. 3-D. ▼●

Mask (1985) **C-120m.** *****½** D: Peter Bogdanovich. Cher, Sam Elliott, Eric Stoltz, Estelle Getty, Richard Dysart, Laura Dern, Harry Carey, Jr., Lawrence Monoson, Marsha Warfield, Barry Tubb, Andrew Robinson. Irresistible film based on true story of Rocky Dennis, teenage boy whose face has been terribly disfigured by a rare disease, and his mother Rusty, who's instilled a sense of confidence and love in her son, though her own defenses are easily broken down. Anna Hamilton Phelan's script dodges cliché, while Cher and Stoltz make their characters warm and real. A winner. Director's cut runs 127m. [PG-13] ▼●▶

Mask, The (1988-Italian) **C-90m.** *½ D: Fiorella Infascelli. Helena Bonham Carter, Michael Maloney, Feodor Chaliapin, Roberto Herlitzka. Trivial, dull account of self-centered count's son who becomes obsessed with pretty young actress Carter. She's put off by him, so he woos her by donning various masks and changing his identity. Extremely slow-moving.

Mask, The (1994) **C-101m.** **½ D: Charles Russell. Jim Carrey, Cameron Diaz, Peter Riegert, Peter Greene, Amy Yasbeck, Richard Jeni, Orestes Matacena, Timothy Bagley, Nancy Fish, Ben Stein. A wimpy bank clerk discovers a mask that turns him into a sizzling Superdude who acts out his alter ego's fantasies. Pretty entertaining, though it's seamier (and more violent) than it needs to be, and has some real lulls during its plottier moments. The already rubber-faced Carrey is aided and abetted by stunning digital computer effects, inspired by the manic 1940s cartoons of Tex Avery. Based on the comic book. Followed by SON OF THE MASK and an animated TV series. Also available in PG version. [PG-13] ▼●▶

Masked and Anonymous (2003-U.S.-British) **C-112m.** *½ D: Larry Charles. Bob Dylan, Jeff Bridges, Penélope Cruz, John Goodman, Jessica Lange, Luke Wilson. A faded music legend is freed from jail to headline a televised benefit concert. Dylan and Charles (using pseudonyms) penned this misfire, set in a fictional America that's become a police state. Shaggy storytelling, Dylan's nonperformance, and an air of pomposity do this in. Angela Bassett, Bruce Dern, Ed Harris, Val Kilmer, Cheech Marin, Chris Penn, Giovanni Ribisi, Mickey Rourke, Christian Slater, and Fred Ward are among those who appear in cameos. [PG-13] ▼▶

Mask of Dimitrios, The (1944) **95m.** *** D: Jean Negulesco. Peter Lorre, Sydney Greenstreet, Zachary Scott, Faye Emerson, Victor Francen, George Tobias, Steve Geray, Eduardo Ciannelli, Florence Bates. Fine, offbeat melodrama with mild-mannered mystery writer Lorre reviewing life of notorious scoundrel Scott (in film debut). Frank Gruber adapted Eric Ambler's novel *A Coffin for Dimitrios*. As always, Lorre and Greenstreet make a marvelous team. ▼

Mask of Fu Manchu, The (1932) **68m.** **½ D: Charles Brabin. Boris Karloff,

Lewis Stone, Karen Morley, Myrna Loy, Charles Starrett, Jean Hersholt. Elaborate chiller of Chinese madman Karloff menacing expedition that plundered the tomb of Genghis Khan. Adaptation of Sax Rohmer novel is ornate and hokey, but fun; Loy is terrific as Fu's deliciously evil daughter. ▼●▶

Mask of Zorro, The (1998) **C-136m.** *** D: Martin Campbell. Antonio Banderas, Anthony Hopkins, Catherine Zeta-Jones, Stuart Wilson, Matt Letscher, Maury Chaykin, Tony Amendola, Pedro Armendariz, L.Q. Jones, Victor Rivers. An aging Zorro passes the mantle of public protector to a younger man, who's reluctant at first but soon relishes his secret identity with cape and sword. Exquisite, exciting, with great swordplay and horse action—but has too much of everything, as if the filmmakers want to wear you out. Banderas is an ideal Zorro, Hopkins a surprisingly engaging one, Zeta-Jones a saucy and beautiful heroine. Followed by THE LEGEND OF ZORRO. Panavision. [PG-13] ▼●▶

Masque of the Red Death, The (1964) **C-86m.** ***½ D: Roger Corman. Vincent Price, Hazel Court, Jane Asher, David Weston, Patrick Magee, Skip Martin, Nigel Green, John Westbrook. The most Bergman-like of Corman's films, an ultrastylish adaptation of the Poe tale (with another, *Hop Frog,* worked in as a subplot), starring Price as evil Prince Prospero, living it up in eerie, timeless castle while Plague ravages the countryside. Beautifully photographed in England by Nicolas Roeg. Remade in 1989. Panavision. ▼●▶

Masque of the Red Death (1989) **C-83m.** ** D: Larry Brand. Adrian Paul, Clare Hoak, Jeff Osterhage, Patrick Macnee, Tracy Reiner. Roger Corman produced this remake of one of his best films. Poe's Prince Prospero (Paul) is still dissipated, but this time more thoughtful and troubled. Despite an interesting approach to figure of the Red Death and literate (if talky) script, overall cheapness and very slow pace cripple this medieval melodrama. [R] ▼

Masquerade (1988) **C-91m.** **½ D: Bob Swaim. Rob Lowe, Meg Tilly, Kim Cattrall, Doug Savant, John Glover, Dana Delany, Erik Holland. Lowe essentially has the ambiguous Cary Grant SUSPICION role: Does he really love delicate (and in this case, filthy rich) spouse Tilly—or is he planning to murder her at the first opportunity? Romantic suspense thriller has its moments, and might have had more with a better leading man. Merely OK, with Tilly, Glover, Delany and lovely Hamptons scenery offering compensation. [R] ▼●▶

Massacre at Central High (1976) **C-85m.** *** D: Renee Daalder. Derrel Maury, Andrew Stevens, Kimberly Beck, Robert

Carradine, Roy Underwood, Steve Bond. Newcomer to California high school doesn't like the way students are being terrorized by a gang, so he decides to eliminate them, in ultra-violent fashion . . . but that's not the end of the story. Seemingly typical blend of teen and revenge formulas given offbeat twists by writer-director Daalder. [R]▼

Massacre at Fort Holman SEE: **Reason to Live, a Reason to Die, A**

Massacre in Rome (1973-French-Italian) **C-103m.** ******* D: George Pan Cosmatos. Richard Burton, Marcello Mastroianni, Leo McKern, John Steiner, Anthony Steel. Good drama: priest Mastroianni opposed to idealistic German Colonel Burton, who must execute 330 Roman hostages in retaliation for deaths of 33 Nazi soldiers. [PG]▼❍

Massacre Mansion SEE: **Nesting, The**

Mass Appeal (1984) **C-100m.** ******* D: Glenn Jordan. Jack Lemmon. Zeljko Ivanek, Charles Durning, Louise Latham, Lois de Banzie, James Ray, Talia Balsam, Gloria Stuart. Feisty young seminarian rattles the complacency of a popular parish priest in this entertaining filmization of Bill C. Davis' glib Broadway play. Lemmon is first-rate as usual, and though film belies its stage origins it still works fine. [PG]▼❍

Master and Commander: The Far Side of the World (2003) **C-139m.** ******* D: Peter Weir. Russell Crowe, Paul Bettany, Billy Boyd, James D'Arcy, Lee Ingleby, George Innes, Mark Lewis Jones, Chris Larkin, Richard McCabe, Robert Pugh, David Threlfall. Lavish adaptation of Patrick O'Brian's series of naval novels, with Crowe as British Captain Jack Aubrey of the HMS *Surprise* against a dangerous enemy during the Napoleonic era. Heavier on atmosphere than on story, but Crowe is an ideal commander, the human element is nicely played, and the physical production is impressive. Screenplay by Weir and John Collee. Oscar winner for Best Cinematography (Russell Boyd) and Sound Editing. Super 35. [PG-13]▼❍

Master Gunfighter, The (1975) **C-121m.** BOMB D: Frank Laughlin. Tom Laughlin, Ron O'Neal, Lincoln Kilpatrick, Geo Anne Sosa, Barbara Carrera, Victor Campos. BILLY JACK'S creator-star is an intense gunfighter who hates to kill but does it just the same. Lots of rhetoric. Remake of a 1969 Japanese samurai film, GOYOKIN. Panavision. [PG]▼❍

Mastermind (1976) **C-131m.** ******* D: Alex March. Zero Mostel, Bradford Dillman, Keiko Kishi, Gawn Grainger, Herbert Berghof, Jules Munshin, Sorrell Booke. Enjoyable spoof of Charlie Chan films with Mostel as Inspector Hoku, who tries to protect robotlike invention sought by international interests. Some good slapstick,

rousing car chase. Received limited release after sitting on shelf since 1969. [G]▼

Masterminds (1997) **C-105m.** ***½** D: Roger Christian. Patrick Stewart, Vincent Kartheiser, Brenda Fricker, Brad Whitford, Matt Craven, Annabelle Gurwitch. High-tech action/adventure yarn finds evil genius Stewart taking over an exclusive private school for ransom, but former student and computer whiz kid Kartheiser stands in his way. Kids might find the attitude-driven script harmless fantasy, but adults may cringe watching this DIE HARD for preteens. Super 35. [PG-13]▼❍

Master of Ballantrae, The (1953) **C-89m.** ****½** D: William Keighley. Errol Flynn, Roger Livesey, Anthony Steel, Yvonne Furneaux. Robert Louis Stevenson's historical yarn has Flynn involved in plot to make Bonnie Prince Charles king of England; on-location filming in Scotland, Sicily, and England adds scope to costumer. Remade for TV in 1984.▼❍

Master of Disguise, The (2002) **C-80m.** ***½** D: Perry Andelin Blake. Dana Carvey, Brent Spiner, Jennifer Esposito, Harold Gould, James Brolin, Maria Canals, Mark Devine, Edie McClurg, Austin Wolff. Simpleminded Italian waiter named Pistachio Disguisey must rescue his kidnapped parents from a super-criminal after learning that he's descended from a long line of secret agent–type disguise masters. Purportedly aimed at little kids, yet packed with spoofs of SCARFACE, THE EXORCIST, and other grown-up movies. Silly, fart-filled, often embarrassingly unfunny pretext for Carvey (who also cowrote) to do goofy impersonations and act like an imbecile. Cameos include Bo Derek, Jesse Ventura, and Kevin Nealon. [PG]▼❍

Master of the World (1961) **C-104m.** ******* D: William Witney. Vincent Price, Charles Bronson, Mary Webster, Henry Hull, Richard Harrison. Sci-fi adventure adapted from two Jules Verne novels about a 19th-century genius (Price) seeking to stop war from his ingenious flying machine, a cross between a zeppelin and a helicopter. Bronson (oddly cast) admires his ends, deplores his methods, and sets out to stop him. Very well done. Screenplay by Richard Matheson.▼❍

Masters of the Universe (1987) **C-106m.** ****** D: Gary Goddard. Dolph Lundgren, Frank Langella, Courteney Cox, James Tolkan, Meg Foster, Christina Pickles, Billy Barty, Jon Cypher. He-Man (Lundgren) comes to Earth seeking a key that controls the power of the universe, stolen by cosmic crud Skeletor (unrecognizable Langella); somehow two teen puppy-lovers get involved. Elaborate comic book nonsense (which has had another life in kiddie animation) is dumb but inoffensive. [PG]▼❍

Master Touch, The (1972-Italian-German) **C-96m.** ****** D: Michele Lupo. Kirk Douglas,

Florinda Bolkan, Giuliano Gemma, Rene Koldehoff. Safecracker Douglas, just out of jail, attempts to trip up a foolproof alarm and rip off a safe for $1 million. Deadening. Aka A MAN TO RESPECT. Techniscope. [PG]▼▶

Matador (1986-Spanish) **C-106m.** ✳✳✳ D: Pedro Almodóvar. Assumpta Serna, Antonio Banderas, Nacho Martinez, Carmen Maura, Eva Cobo, Julieta Serrano, Chus Lampreave. Dazzling black comedy chronicles plight of retired matador Martinez, passing time by compulsively watching snuff films—and his young, troubled protégé (Banderas). Opening sequence is a real stunner.▼●▶

Matador, The (2005) **C-97m.** ✳✳✳ D: Richard Shepard. Pierce Brosnan, Greg Kinnear, Hope Davis, Philip Baker Hall, Dylan Baker, Adam Scott. Amusing black comedy/character study about a paid assassin who strikes up an acquaintance with a straitlaced American businessman while on assignment in Mexico. The two men couldn't be more different, but at a moment of crisis, the hit man realizes that the square is in fact his only friend. Low-key from start to finish, but sharply defined performances by Brosnan, Kinnear, and Davis and Shepard's offbeat script make this worth watching. Super 35. [R]▶

Mata Hari (1931) **90m.** ✳✳✳ D: George Fitzmaurice. Greta Garbo, Ramon Novarro, Lionel Barrymore, Lewis Stone, C. Henry Gordon, Karen Morley. Garbo is the alluring spy of WW1, beguiling everyone from Novarro to Barrymore. Highlights: Garbo's exotic dance sequence, Morley stalked by gang executioner. That's an unbilled Mischa Auer in opening scene as condemned man who won't betray Garbo's love.▼●▶

Match Factory Girl, The (1990-Finnish) **C-70m.** ✳✳✳ D: Aki Kaurismaki. Kati Outinen, Elina Salo, Esko Nikkari, Vesa Vierikko. A drab, oppressed young woman allows herself to fall for the wrong man; he unceremoniously dumps her, but her reaction is anything but passive. Clever, ironic pitch-black comedy from prolific Kaurismaki. ▼▶

Matchmaker, The (1958) **101m.** ✳✳✳ D: Joseph Anthony. Shirley Booth, Anthony Perkins, Shirley MacLaine, Paul Ford, Robert Morse, Wallace Ford. Endearing Thornton Wilder comedy about middle-aged widower deciding to re-wed . . . but the matchmaker he consults has plans of her own. Solid performances, fine period detail; later musicalized as HELLO, DOLLY! VistaVision.▼●▶

Matchmaker, The (1997-U.S.-Irish) **C-96m.** ✳✳✳ D: Mark Joffe. Janeane Garofalo, David O'Hara, Milo O'Shea, Denis Leary, Jay O. Sanders, Rosaleen Linehan, Paul Hickey, Maria Doyle Kennedy, Robert Mandan. Cute comedy about a campaign worker for a less than exemplary U.S. Sena-

tor from Massachusetts, who's given the job of tracing his relatives to a small village in Ireland and setting up a photo opportunity to entice the state's Irish-American vote. Garofalo arrives in the remote village during its annual matchmaking festival and, despite everything, gets caught up in a relationship. Fanciful, rather than realistic, but entertaining. Super 35. [R] ▼●▶

Match Point (2005-U.S.-British) **C-124m.** ✳✳✳ D: Woody Allen. Jonathan Rhys Meyers, Scarlett Johansson, Emily Mortimer, Matthew Goode, Brian Cox, Penelope Wilton, Ewen Bremner, James Nesbitt, Rupert Penry-Jones, Margaret Tyzack. Dramatic effort from Allen about an ambitious young tennis coach in London who gets involved with the daughter of a prominent family as well as a sexy American actress, with consequences that no one—he least of all—can foresee. Dark examination of chance and fate covers familiar ground, but Allen responds to the fresh British milieu with some of his most urgent and (surprisingly) passionate filmmaking. Echoes of *Crime and Punishment* and *An American Tragedy* abound. [R]▶

Matchstick Men (2003) **C-116m.** ✳✳✳ D: Ridley Scott. Nicolas Cage, Sam Rockwell, Alison Lohman, Bruce Altman, Bruce McGill, Sheila Kelley, Beth Grant. Phobic con artist discovers he has a teenage daughter, which casts a new light on his work, his relationship with his protégé-partner, and his life in general. Lively, engaging yarn with pinpoint performances and a nice eye for detail, though it goes on a bit longer than it should . . . and then pulls the rug out. Inventive score by Hans Zimmer and great use of source music, too. Based on the novel by Eric Garcia. Panavision. [PG-13] ▼▶

Material Girls (2006) **C-97m.** ✳✳ D: Martha Coolidge. Hilary Duff, Haylie Duff, Maria Conchita Alonso, Anjelica Huston, Brent Spiner, Lukas Haas, Marcus Coloma, Obba Babatunde, Colleen Camp, Judy Tenuta. Two spoiled cosmetics industry heiresses lose their money after a controversy involving face cream and a disfiguring skin disease. Forced to suffer indignities like riding the bus and wearing last year's fashions, they eventually learn the value of hard work and fight to reclaim their company's reputation. This movie glorifies "the high life" while praising its heroines for transcending it. Filled with absurdities, but fast paced, colorful, and painless. Super 35. [PG]▶

Matewan (1987) **C-130m.** ✳✳✳½ D: John Sayles. Chris Cooper, Will Oldham, Mary McDonnell, Bob Gunton, James Earl Jones, Kevin Tighe, Gordon Clapp, Josh Mostel, Joe Grifasi, Maggie Renzi, David Strathairn. Compelling and compassionate drama about labor troubles in the heart of coal-mining country, Matewan, West Virginia, in the 1920s. As usual, writer-director

Sayles (who appears briefly as a preacher) makes every note ring true in this meticulous period piece; he even cowrote some phony labor songs! Beautifully photographed by Haskell Wexler. [PG-13]▼●)

Matilda (1978) C-103m. BOMB D: Daniel Mann. Elliott Gould, Robert Mitchum, Harry Guardino, Clive Revill, Karen Carlson, Lionel Stander, Larry Pennell, Art Metrano. Good cast wasted in awful kiddie pic about a boxing kangaroo, played by a man in a suit (Gary Morgan). Paul Gallico's novel loses everything in translation. [G]▼

Matilda (1996) C-93m. **½ D: Danny DeVito. Danny DeVito, Rhea Perlman, Embeth Davidtz, Pam Ferris, Mara Wilson, Paul Reubens, Tracey Walter, Kiami Davael. Cursed with a cretinous family and a witch of a school principal, a bright young girl learns self-reliance—and develops unusual powers. Wilson's irresistible charm anchors this very black comedy from the book by Roald Dahl. The bizarre goings-on, and the strange sensibilities, may play better on the printed page (and in a reader's imagination) than they do when acted out literally on-screen. Anne Ramsey bing dead, DeVito had to find another harpy—in this case the furious Ferris. Jon Lovitz appears unbilled; DeVito narrates. Super 35. [PG]▼●)

Matinee (1993) C-98m. *** D: Joe Dante. John Goodman, Cathy Moriarty, Simon Fenton, Omri Katz, Lisa Jakub, Kellie Martin, Jesse Lee, Lucinda Jenney, James Villemaire, Robert Picardo, Jesse White, Dick Miller, John Sayles, David Clennon, Luke Halpin, Naomi Watts. Goodman is delightful as a movie schlockmeister (inspired by real-life producer William Castle) previewing his latest scare-the-pants-off-'em horror movie at a Key West theater—the very weekend of the Cuban missile crisis, when everyone's nerves are on edge. Sweet-natured film, full of nostalgia and in-jokes for film buffs, but a little slow (and soft) until it gets rolling. Film-within-a-film, MANT, is a real hoot, with appearances by sci-fi stalwarts William Schallert, Kevin McCarthy, Robert Cornthwaite. [PG]▼●)

Mating Game, The (1959) C-96m. *** D: George Marshall. Debbie Reynolds, Tony Randall, Paul Douglas, Fred Clark, Una Merkel, Philip Ober, Charles Lane. Zippy comedy romp of tax agent Randall falling in love with farm girl Reynolds, with Douglas rambunctious as Debbie's father. CinemaScope.▼)

Mating Season, The (1951) 101m. ***½ D: Mitchell Leisen. Gene Tierney, John Lund, Miriam Hopkins, Thelma Ritter, Jan Sterling, Larry Keating, James Lorimer. Excellent, underrated comedy with cynical undertones about the American dream. Hardworking Lund marries socialite Tierney, suffers embarrassment when his plain-talking mother (Ritter) comes to town and is mistaken

for servant. Ritter is simply superb. Written by Walter Reisch, Richard Breen, and producer Charles Brackett.

Matrix, The (1999) C-136m. **½ D: The Wachowski Brothers. Keanu Reeves, Laurence Fishburne, Carrie-Anne Moss, Hugo Weaving, Gloria Foster, Joe Pantoliano, Marcus Chong. A computer hacker (Reeves) discovers the world he is living in is an illusion maintained by computers that have taken over the world . . . and he is thought to be "the chosen one" to save humanity. Cutting-edge visuals and production design compete with an overlong script, written by the directors, that's got a high MJQ (Mumbo-Jumbo Quotient), and a tendency to keep changing its own complicated "rules." Martial arts scenes staged by Yuen Wo Ping are highlights. Oscar winner for Film Editing, Sound, Sound Effects Editing, and Visual Effects. Followed by THE MATRIX: RELOADED and the DVD collection of animated shorts, THE ANIMATRIX. Super 35. [R]▼●)

Matrix: Reloaded, The (2003) C-138m. **½ D: The Wachowski Brothers. Keanu Reeves, Laurence Fishburne, Carrie-Anne Moss, Hugo Weaving, Jada Pinkett Smith, Gloria Foster, Harold Perrineau, Jr., Monica Bellucci, Harry Lennix, Lambert Wilson, Randall Duk Kim, Anthony Zerbe. Big, booming sequel is more straightforward in its storytelling than the original, as our heroes race against time to stop a marauding army from overtaking the last outpost of humankind, Zion. Doesn't have the feeling of stylistic innovation that the first film did, but there's plenty of action and special effects to compensate. Ironically, the highlight of this dense, futuristic saga is a car chase on a California freeway! Followed by THE MATRIX: REVOLUTIONS. Super 35. [R]▼●)

Matrix Revolutions, The (2003) C-130m. *½ D: The Wachowski Brothers. Keanu Reeves, Laurence Fishburne, Carrie-Anne Moss, Hugo Weaving, Jada Pinkett Smith, Mary Alice, Harold Perrineau, Jr., Monica Bellucci, Harry Lennix, Lambert Wilson, Nona Gaye, Anthony Zerbe. No one expected the third JAWS movie to be any good, but the Wachowski Brothers' failure to cap their franchise with any real meaning was one of 2003's bigger disappointments. Like Santa Anna's troops at the Alamo or the Blob in any neighborhood, the so-called Machines are on the march to outpost Zion, with only Neo and the remaining humans left to stop them. Pinkett Smith's piloting of a tricky aircraft is actually more compelling than the love story between Reeves and Moss. BILL & TED'S BOGUS JOURNEY should not be the better sequel on Reeves' resumé. Super 35. [R]▼)

Matter of Innocence, A (1967-British) C-102m. **½ D: Guy Green. Hayley Mills, Trevor Howard, Shashi Kapoor, Brenda De Banzie. Plain Jane (Mills) travels to

Singapore with aunt, has an affair with Eurasian Kapoor and becomes a woman. Trite soaper with unusual role for suave Howard; from Noel Coward story "Pretty Polly." Techniscope.

Matter of Life and Death, A (1946-British) **C-104m.** ******** D: Michael Powell, Emeric Pressburger. David Niven, Kim Hunter, Raymond Massey, Roger Livesey, Robert Coote, Marius Goring, Richard Attenborough. Powell and Pressburger manage to straddle reality and fantasy in a most disarming manner in this unusual story of a pilot during WW2 who claims he was accidentally chosen to die, and must now plead for his life in a Heavenly court. Like most films by this writer-director team, an absolute original—and a gem, too. Original U.S. title: STAIRWAY TO HEAVEN. ▼▶

Matter of Resistance, A (1966-French) **92m.** ****½** D: Jean-Paul Rappeneau. Catherine Deneuve, Philippe Noiret, Pierre Brasseur, Mary Marquet, Henri Garcin, Carlos Thompson. Pleasant French comedy of bored housewife (Deneuve) who welcomes arrival of soldiers to her village prior to Normandy invasion. Originally titled LA VIE DE CHATEAU. ▼▶

Matter of Time, A (1976) **C-99m.** BOMB D: Vincente Minnelli. Liza Minnelli, Ingrid Bergman, Charles Boyer, Spiros Andros, Tina Aumont, Anna Proclemer. Depressing schmaltz about a chambermaid in pre-WW1 Europe taught to love life by a batty contessa. Director Minnelli's worst film, though, for his part, he denounced this version as edited. Final film for both Boyer and the director. Bergman's daughter, Isabella Rossellini, makes her screen debut as a nun. [PG]▼

Maurice (1987-British) **C-135m.** ******* D: James Ivory. James Wilby, Hugh Grant, Rupert Graves, Denholm Elliott, Simon Callow, Billie Whitelaw, Ben Kingsley, Judy Parfitt, Phoebe Nicholls, Barry Foster. Typically meticulous Merchant-Ivory production of a literary work (by E. M. Forster) about a young Britisher's coming of age in the 1910s, and coming to terms with his homosexuality. Beautifully realized and extremely well acted all around . . . but overlong. Helena Bonham Carter makes a cameo appearance. [R]▼▶

Maurie (1973) **C-113m.** ****** D: Daniel Mann. Bernie Casey, Bo Svenson, Janet MacLachlan, Stephanie Edwards, Paulene Myers, Bill Walker. Well-meaning but downbeat tearjerker based on true story of basketball star Maurice Stokes (Casey). His sudden paralysis spurs teammate Jack Twyman (Svenson) to devote himself to Maurie's rehabilitation. Too similar to other sports-tragedy films to stand out. Shown on TV as BIG MO. [G]▼

Maverick (1994) **C-129m.** ****½** D: Richard Donner. Mel Gibson, Jodie Foster, James Garner, Graham Greene, James Coburn, Alfred Molina, Paul Smith, Geoffrey Lewis, Max Perlich, Dub Taylor. Lackadaisical update of the fondly remembered '60s TV show relies heavily on personal charm to carry a thin storyline that moseys along much too slowly—and much too long. Gibson is fun as a wily cardsharp on his way to a big-stakes poker game, and the cast is peppered with familiar faces from the world of vintage TV Westerns and contemporary country music; look for a couple of cameos by stars of earlier movies from director Donner. Garner, who starred in the old TV series, is cast here as a marshal. Script by William Goldman. Panavision. [PG]▼▶

Maverick Queen, The (1956) **C-92m.** ****½** D: Joseph Kane. Barbara Stanwyck, Barry Sullivan, Scott Brady, Mary Murphy, Wallace Ford. Stanwyck is peppy as outlaw who's willing to go straight for lawman Sullivan. Filmed in Naturama.▼

Ma Vie en Rose (1997-Belgian-French-British) **C-88m.** ******* D: Alain Berliner. Michele Laroque, Jean-Philippe Ecoffey, Helene Vincent, Georges Du Fresne, Julien Riviere. Ludovic (Du Fresne), a sweet little boy who resides with his parents in a Belgian suburb, has decided that, when he grows up, he wants to be a girl. To him this is perfectly logical; he already favors wearing dresses and makeup, and is determined to eventually wed the boy-next-door. Needless to say, mom and dad are perplexed and none too pleased. All points of view are well served in this charming and compassionate comedy-drama. [R]▼▶

Max (2002-Hungarian-British-Canadian) **C-109m.** ***½** D: Menno Meyjes. John Cusack, Noah Taylor, Leelee Sobieski, Molly Parker, Ulrich Thomsen, David Horovitch, Janet Suzman, Caroleen Feeney. What might have happened if Adolf Hitler had been encouraged to pursue a career in art in the days following WW1? Fascinating idea is bungled by writer-director Meyjes, with a miscast Cusack (spouting incongruously modern vernacular) as a German-Jewish art dealer who is drawn to the angry young artist (well played by Taylor). Best/worst line: "Hitler, come on, I'll buy you a glass of lemonade." [R] ▼▶

Max Dugan Returns (1983) **C-98m.** ******* D: Herbert Ross. Marsha Mason, Jason Robards, Donald Sutherland, Matthew Broderick, Dody Goodman, Sal Viscuso, David Morse, Kiefer Sutherland, Charlie Lau. Sweet, simple Neil Simon comedy about a long-lost father who tries to make amends to his daughter (a struggling schoolteacher and single parent) by showering her with presents—using money he's obtained by slightly shady means. Acted with verve and sincerity by a perfect cast. Film debuts of Matthew Broderick and Kiefer Sutherland. [PG]▼▶

Maxed Out (2007) **C/B&W-87m.** ****½** D: James D. Scurlock. Outraged, muckraking documentary about our country's consumer-lending industry and the vicious cycle of profit and debt it has created and gladly fuels. Frequently compelling, even eye-opening, but resorts to obvious tactics a bit too much and often confuses self-righteousness with effective reportage. Stay through the end credits.▶

Max et les Ferrailleurs (1971-French) **C-110m.** *****½** D: Claude Sautet. Michel Piccoli, Romy Schneider, Bernard Fresson, Georges Wilson, François Périer, Maurice Auzel, Philippe Léotard. Top-notch film about a moralistic police inspector who, tired of seeing a gang of bank robbers escape, decides to set up a situation where he can be assured of capturing some thieves. This involves forming a relationship with the girlfriend of his target thief, but he doesn't foresee how living a lie will affect his own integrity. A crackling, diamond-hard story, perfectly enacted by Piccoli, Schneider, and Fresson. Written by Sautet and Claude Néron. Aka MAX AND THE JUNKMEN.

Maxie (1985) **C-90m.** ****** D: Paul Aaron. Glenn Close, Mandy Patinkin, Ruth Gordon, Barnard Hughes, Valerie Curtin, Googy Gress, Harry Hamlin. Roaring twenties flapper inhabits the body of hardworking eighties woman, and titillates her husband to boot! *Very* old-fashioned screwball comedy-fantasy just doesn't come off, despite good intentions. Incidentally, the actress playing Maxie in authentic silent movie footage is Carole Lombard. [PG]▼●▮

Maximum Overdrive (1986) **C-97m.** BOMB D: Stephen King. Emilio Estevez, Pat Hingle, Laura Harrington, Yeardley Smith, John Short, J. C. Quinn. Customers and employees of interstate truck stop are terrorized by the trucks themselves, which have come to demonic life as part of a global rebellion of machines. Novelist King, making his directing debut, said he set out to create a junk movie, nothing more . . . but he made it stupid and boring. Remade as a 1997 cable movie, TRUCKS. J-D-C Scope. [R]▼●▮

Maximum Risk (1996) **C-100m.** ****½** D: Ringo Lam. Jean-Claude Van Damme, Natasha Henstridge, Jean-Hugues Anglade, Zach Grenier, Paul Ben-Victor, Frank Senger. The FBI and the Russian mafia are both after former French soldier Van Damme, who's out to avenge the death of an identical twin brother that everyone seems to think he is. He even inherits the brother's dishy girlfriend in the deal. Marginally closer to a real movie than most Van Damme efforts, thanks to some stylish touches by Hong Kong action specialist Lam. Super 35. [R]▼●▮

Max Keeble's Big Move (2001) **C-86m.** ****** D: Tim Hill. Alex D. Linz, Larry Miller, Jamie Kennedy, Nora Dunn, Zena Grey, Josh Peck, Robert Carradine, Clifton Davis,

Noel Fisher, Orlando Brown. Loud, often obnoxious cookie-cutter comedy about seventh-grader Max (Linz), who is harassed at school by fellow students and even the principal. Upon learning that his family is moving out of town, he plots a hit-and-run–style revenge, but there are predictable complications. [PG]▼▮

Max Payne (2008) **C-100m.** ****** D: John Moore. Mark Wahlberg, Mila Kunis, Beau Bridges, Chris "Ludacris" Bridges, Chris O'Donnell, Donal Logue, Amaury Nolasco, Kate Burton, Olga Kurylenko, Joel Gordon, Jamie Hector, Nelly Furtado. A Dirty Harry–like homicide cop (Wahlberg) seeks revenge against the killers of his loved ones. Good-looking film falls flat dramatically. There's plenty of gore, though it's not graphic enough to earn this an R rating. Based on a popular video game. Unrated version runs 103m. Super 35. [PG-13]▮

May (2002) **C-93m.** ****** D: Lucky McKee. Angela Bettis, Jeremy Sisto, Anna Faris, James Duval, Nichole Hiltz, Kevin Gage, Merle Kennedy. Wacko who grew up with only a doll for a best friend wigs out in adulthood and goes to gruesome lengths to make a friend . . . literally. Yucky chiller is well acted, but is way too pleased with its own cruelty to be able to watch on a full stomach. The writer-director cameos in a couple of self-serving scenes in an elevator. [R]▼▮

Maya (1966) **C-91m.** ****** D: John Berry. Clint Walker, Jay North, I. S. Johar, Sajid Kahn, Jairaj, Sonia Sahni. Silly juvenile jungle tale has young North temporarily losing respect for his big-game hunter father Walker, who has lost his nerve. Panavision.▼

Maya Lin: A Strong Clear Vision (1994) **C-96m.** ****½** D: Freida Lee Mock. Respectful, Oscar-winning documentary about artist Maya Lin, best known as the designer of the Washington, D.C., Vietnam Veterans Memorial. While effective as a record of the artist's creative process, her conception for the Memorial and the controversy it created, this is not a particularly insightful or memorable film.▼▮

Maybe Baby (2000-British-French) **C-93m.** ****½** D: Ben Elton. Hugh Laurie, Joely Richardson, Adrian Lester, James Purefoy, Tom Hollander, Joanna Lumley, Rowan Atkinson, Matthew Macfadyen, Dawn French, Emma Thompson. BBC-TV executive and his talent-agent wife are desperately trying to have a baby while dealing with the vicissitudes of their show-business careers. Anyone who's faced difficulty getting pregnant will recognize the truth in Elton's amusing screenplay; his leading actors' charm helps make up for the unevenness of surrounding story elements. Cameos by the likes of Thompson and Atkinson don't hurt, either. [R]▼▮

Maybe . . . Maybe Not (1995-German) **C-93m.** ****** D: Sönke Wortmann. Til Schweiger, Katja Riemann, Joachim Król, Rufus

Beck, Antonia Lang, Armin Rohde. Thrown out for cheating on his girlfriend, a heterosexual male finds respite at the home of a gay acquaintance. While the ensuing advances of gay suitors are somewhat humorous, the film is filled with characters about whom we care very little. Based on a series of German comic books, entitled "Der Bewegte Mann" and "Pretty Baby," by comic artist Ralf König. [R]▼●

Mayerling (1936-French) **92m.** ******* D: Anatole Litvak. Charles Boyer, Danielle Darrieux, Suzy Prim, Jean Dax, Vladimir Sokoloff. Touching, well-made romantic tragedy based on true story of Austrian Crown Prince Rudolph, who dared to fall in love with a commoner. Good performances spark international hit; miles ahead of 1969 remake.▼●

Mayerling (1968-British) **C-140m.** ****½** D: Terence Young. Omar Sharif, Catherine Deneuve, James Mason, Ava Gardner, James Robertson Justice, Genevieve Page. Remake of 1936 version casts Sharif as Austrian prince who defies convention, and his father (Mason), by falling in love with commoner Deneuve. Old-fashioned tragic romance is pleasant but uncompelling. Justice steals film as spirited Prince of Wales. Panavision. [M/PG] ▼

May Fools (1990-French-Italian) **C-108m.** ****½** D: Louis Malle. Michel Piccoli, Miou-Miou, Michel Duchaussoy, Dominique Blanc, Bruno Carette, Harriet Walter, Francois Berleand, Martine Gautier, Paulette Dubost. Ensemble piece, set in the French countryside in 1968. A grandmother's death brings assorted relatives to their ancestral home; most of them, like MiouMiou, are more money grubbing than grieving. Piccoli is splendid as the head of the clan, a contented vintner who truly mourns his late mother. There are romantic entanglements, an interesting subtext of Paris student rebellion, jazzy Stephane Grappelli score—but it's all rather slight. Not top-notch Malle, but still diverting. [R]▼●

Maytime (1937) **132m.** ******* D: Robert Z. Leonard. Jeanette MacDonald, Nelson Eddy, John Barrymore, Herman Bing, Tom Brown, Lynne Carver, Rafaela Ottiano, Paul Porcasi, Sig Ruman, Walter Kingsford, Harry Davenport. One of singing duo's best films, despite occasional heavy-handedness and piercing operatic sequence near the end (composed especially for film, based on Tchaikovsky's Fifth Symphony). Exquisite filming of simple story: opera star and penniless singer fall in love in Paris, but her husband/mentor (Barrymore) interferes. Only song retained from Sigmund Romberg's hit Broadway score is "Will You Remember (Sweetheart)."▼●

Maze, The (1953) **81m.** ****** D: William Cameron Menzies. Richard Carlson, Veronica Hurst, Michael Pate, Katherine Emery, Hillary Brooke. Mysterious doings at a Scottish castle; a low-budgeter with a ludicrous (and unsatisfying) payoff. Stylishly composed as a 3-D movie by designer-director Menzies. 3-D.

Maze (2000) **C-97m.** ****½** D: Rob Morrow. Rob Morrow, Laura Linney, Craig Sheffer, Rose Gregorio, Gia Carides, Robert Hogan. While his best friend's away, an artist with Tourette Syndrome falls in love with his pregnant girlfriend. Lightweight romantic drama and personal project for Morrow isn't as bad as it sounds. Linney, in a lovely low-key performance, steals the show. Playwright Jon Robin Baitz cameos as an art gallery patron. [R]▼●

M. Butterfly (1993) **C-101m.** ****** D: David Cronenberg. Jeremy Irons, John Lone, Barbara Sukowa, Ian Richardson, Annabel Leventon, Shizuko Hoshi, The Beijing Opera Troupe. Surprisingly tame and conventional Cronenberg rendering of David Henry Hwang's Tony-winning Broadway play—about the bizarrely extended relationship between a French diplomatic functionary and a Chinese diva/spy who managed to conceal the fact from him that she was a man. Cinematic closeups blatantly telegraph Lone's maleness; it's symptomatic of the movie's failure that office politics and even Irons' weary marriage are more compelling than the central ruse. [R]▼●●

McBain (1991) **C-102m.** ****** D: James Glickenhaus. Christopher Walken, Maria Conchita Alonso, Michael Ironside, Steve James, Jay Patterson, T.G. Waites, Victor Argo, Chick Vennera. To pay back a debt, ex-Vietnam P.O.W. Walken joins rebels in a battle against a corrupt Colombian dictatorship. Predictable, by-the-numbers actioner. [R]▼●

McCabe & Mrs. Miller (1971) **C-121m.** *****½** D: Robert Altman. Warren Beatty, Julie Christie, Rene Auberjonois, John Schuck, Bert Remsen, Keith Carradine, William Devane, Shelley Duvall, Michael Murphy, Hugh Millais, Jack Riley. Richly textured mood piece about an ambitious small-timer who opens bordello in turn-of-the-20th-century boom town. Altman deglamorizes Hollywood image of period with his realistic visions. Beatty is first-rate as the two-bit braggart McCabe. Edmund Naughton's novel *McCabe* adapted by Brian McKay and Altman. Panavision. [R]▼●●

McCullochs, The SEE: **Wild McCullochs, The**

McGuffin, The (1985-British) **C-95m.** ****** D: Colin Bucksey. Charles Dance, Ritza Brown, Francis Matthews, Brian Glover, Phyllis Logan, Jerry Stiller, Anna Massey, Ann Todd, Bill Shine. Meandering, confusing thriller about film critic Dance, whose curiosity about a couple of his neighbors leads to his involvement in murder and mayhem. Starts off nicely but goes downhill all too quickly. An homage to Hitchcock in general, REAR WINDOW in particular.▼

McHale's Navy (1964) **C-93m.** **½ D: Edward J. Montagne. Ernest Borgnine, Joe Flynn, Tim Conway, George Kennedy, Claudine Longet, Bob Hastings, Carl Ballantine, Billy Sands, Gavin MacLeod, Jean Willes. Theatrical feature inspired by popular TV series finds the PT-73 crew doing everything possible to try and raise money to pay off gambling debts. Usual blend of slapstick and snappy dialogue; entertaining for fans.▼❍

McHale's Navy (1997) **C-109m.** ** D: Bryan Spicer. Tom Arnold, Dean Stockwell, Ernest Borgnine, Debra Messing, David Alan Grier, Tim Curry, Brian Haley, French Stewart, Bruce Campbell, Tommy Chong. Former Navy man who now wheels and deals from a remote Pacific island is called back to service to do battle with "the second-best terrorist in the world." Broad approach, simplistic script make this strictly a juvenile outing. Very loosely based on the 1960s TV series; Borgnine, who played McHale back then, appears here as a Pentagon security chief. [PG] ▼❍❍

McHale's Navy Joins the Air Force (1965) **C-90m.** **½ D: Edward J. Montagne. Tim Conway, Joe Flynn, Bob Hastings, Ted Bessell, Susan Silo, Henry Beckman, Billy Sands, Gavin MacLeod, Tom Tully, Jacques Aubuchon. Rather unusual comedy with little relation to either the first feature or the TV series (including no Borgnine). Ensign Parker (Conway) is mistaken for an Air Force hot shot, and the more he screws up, the higher he's promoted! John Fenton Murray's intricate script adds some mild satire to normal quota of slapstick; a genuine curio.▼

McKenzie Break, The (1970) **C-106m.** *** D: Lamont Johnson. Brian Keith, Helmut Griem, Ian Hendry, Jack Watson, Patrick O'Connell. Daring escape from a P.O.W. camp for Germans in Scotland makes for engrossing movie fare. Aka ESCAPE. [PG] ▼❍

McLintock! (1963) **C-127m.** *** D: Andrew V. McLaglen. John Wayne, Maureen O'Hara, Patrick Wayne, Stefanie Powers, Yvonne De Carlo, Chill Wills, Bruce Cabot, Jack Kruschen, Jerry Van Dyke, Perry Lopez, Strother Martin. Brawling cattle baron G. W. McLintock (Wayne) locks horns with his feisty, estranged wife (O'Hara) who has returned home to get a divorce; their daughter visiting from college only complicates matters. Rowdy slapstick seldom stops—a giant mud pit free-for-all and a public spanking for O'Hara are just a few of the stops along the way in this Western version of *The Taming of the Shrew.* Not recommended for feminists. Produced by Michael Wayne. Panavision.▼❍❍

McMasters, The (1970) **C-89/97m.** **½ D: Alf Kjellin. Burl Ives, Brock Peters, Da-

vid Carradine, Nancy Kwan, Jack Palance, John Carradine. Pretty grim drama of bigotry and violence gone crazy as black Union soldier (Peters) returns to ranch of former master (Ives), eventually made co-owner of land. Dual running times indicate two different endings: bad guys (led by Palance) win out or good guys emerge victorious. Both versions were released to theaters. [PG] ▼

McQ (1974) **C-116m.** ** D: John Sturges. John Wayne, Eddie Albert, Diana Muldaur, Colleen Dewhurst, Clu Gulager, David Huddleston, Al Lettieri, Julie Adams. An aging Duke tries to be Clint Eastwood as a Firebird-driving cop out to get the gangster who murdered his partner. Good action, but that's about all. Panavision. [PG] ▼❍❍

McVicar (1980-British) **C-111m.** *** D: Tom Clegg. Roger Daltrey, Adam Faith, Cheryl Campbell, Brian Hall, Steven Berkoff, Jeremy Blake, Ian Hendry. Impressive drama about John McVicar (Daltrey), England's Public Enemy Number 1, and his escape from prison. Screenplay by McVicar, who adapted his book; Daltrey is surprisingly good; Faith and Campbell fine as his prison buddy/fellow escapee and his common-law wife. [R] ▼❍

Mean Creek (2004) **C-90m.** **½ D: Jacob Aaron Estes. Rory Culkin, Ryan Kelly, Scott Mechlowicz, Carly Schroeder, Trevor Morgan, Josh Peck. Surprisingly adept tale of a bullied boy (Culkin) who plots revenge, with his older brother and friends, on his tormentor. The performances are realistic, with unforced emotional revelations and insight, but the film can't escape echoes of similar stories. Still, a promising feature debut for writer-director Estes. [R] ▼❍

Me and Him (1989-U.S.-West German) **C-94m.** BOMB D: Doris Dörrie. Griffin Dunne, Ellen Greene, Kelly Bishop, Carey Lowell, Craig T. Nelson, Mark Linn-Baker. Embarrassingly unfunny story of a man and his talking sex organ. Based on an Italian novel, clever idea goes absolutely limp. Linn-Baker supplies the voice of Dunne's "special friend." [R] ▼❍

Mean Dog Blues (1978) **C-108m.** **½ D: Mel Stuart. George Kennedy, Gregg Henry, Kay Lenz, Scatman Crothers, Tina Louise, Felton Perry, Gregory Sierra, James Wainwright, William Windom. Henry is railroaded onto prison farm run by Kennedy and a team of bloodthirsty Dobermans; unsurprising but well-made action film. [R] ▼

Me and Orson Welles (2009-British-U.S.) **C-114m.** *** D: Richard Linklater. Zac Efron, Claire Danes, Christian McKay, Ben Chaplin, Eddie Marsan, Zoe Kazan, James Tupper, Leo Bill, Kelly Reilly, Saskia Reeves. Teenager with an artistic bent stumbles into a job with Orson Welles' Mercury Theatre troupe as they're preparing their groundbreaking stage production of *Julius Caesar* in 1937. Quite suddenly he finds himself in fast company, attracted to the ensemble's girl Friday (Danes) and in the orbit of the mercurial but brilliant Welles. Wonderfully vivid evocation of a storied time in Welles' career. McKay is a standout in the fine ensemble as the larger-than-life boy genius. Based on a novel by Robert Kaplow. Super 35. [PG-13] ▶

Me and the Colonel (1958) 109m. **½ D: Peter Glenville. Danny Kaye, Curt Jurgens, Nicole Maurey, Françoise Rosay. Franz Werfel's *Jacobowsky and the Colonel* is source for spotty satire; Jacobowsky is played by Kaye, and Jurgens is the anti-Semitic military officer, both brought together during crisis in WW2. Filmed in France.▼

Me and the Kid (1993) C-94m. *½ D: Dan Curtis. Danny Aiello, Alex Zuckerman, Joe Pantoliano, Cathy Moriarty, David Dukes, Anita Morris, Abe Vigoda, Demond Wilson, Rick Aiello, Ben Stein. Rich kid is kidnapped in a bungled robbery attempt and sets out on the road with a couple of cons—who get more than they bargained for. Low-budget attempt to cash in on the HOME ALONE bonanza, with a decent cast wasted; recommended only for the most undemanding young viewers. [PG]▼●)

Me and You and Everyone We Know (2005) C-90m. *** D: Miranda July. John Hawkes, Miranda July, Miles Thompson, Brandon Ratcliff, Carlie Westerman, Natasha Slayton, Najarra Townsend, Hector Elias, Tracy Wright, JoNell Kennedy, Brad Henke, Ellen Geer, James Mathers. Highly original, observational comedy-drama about lonely people of all ages—from children to senior citizens—who are desperately trying to connect. Hawkes is a newly divorced shoe salesman trying to raise two boys (the younger of whom is making "friends" on the Internet); July plays a struggling artist who's more comfortable creating videos than dealing with people in person. Earns its R rating with some sexually explicit material. Debut feature as writer-director for performance artist July. [R]▶

Mean Girls (2004) C-97m. **½ D: Mark Waters. Lindsay Lohan, Tina Fey, Rachel McAdams, Tim Meadows, Ana Gasteyer, Amy Poehler, Lacey Chabert, Amanda Seyfried, Jonathan Bennett, Lizzy Caplan, Daniel Franzese, Neil Flynn. Sixteen-year-old who's been home-schooled (in Africa!) goes to Illinois public school for the first time. She's immediately torn between two outcasts who adopt her as a friend and a clique of popular girls who set their own agenda and make fun of almost everyone else. Sounds awfully familiar, but the script by Fey (based on Rosalind Wiseman's book *Queen Bees and Wannabes*) has sharp, funny moments one doesn't usually find in teen movies; she also plays a sympathetic

teacher. Reverts to formula, but still a cut above the norm. Followed by a direct-to-DVD sequel. [PG-13]▼▶

Mean Johnny Barrows (1976) C-85m. ** D: Fred Williamson. Fred Williamson, Jenny Sherman, Aaron Banks, Anthony Caruso, Luther Adler, Stuart Whitman, Roddy McDowall, Elliott Gould. Mean but dull; Vietnam vet gets involved with the Mafia. Slow-paced, notable for unlikely cast and Gould's incongruous comedy relief. [R] ▼▶

Mean Machine (2001-British-U.S.) C-98m. *½ D: Barry Skolnick. Vinnie Jones, David Kelly, David Hemmings, Ralph Brown, Vas Blackwood, Robbie Gee, Geoff Bell, Jason Flemyng, Jason Statham. Disgraced ex– soccer star Jones winds up in a high-security prison, where he is caught between brutal guards and embittered fellow prisoners and ends up involved in a cons-versus-guards soccer match. By-the-numbers remake of THE LONGEST YARD (which was titled THE MEAN MACHINE in the U.K.) is as subtle as a jackhammer and sorely missing the spunk of the original. Strictly for those who delight in bone-crunching brutality. [R]▼▶

Mean Season, The (1985) C-103m. **½ D: Phillip Borsos. Kurt Russell, Mariel Hemingway, Richard Jordan, Richard Masur, Joe Pantoliano, Andy Garcia. Miami newspaper reporter (Russell, in a very credible performance) becomes sole contact for crazed killer, but as the headlines (and murders) continue, it becomes a question of who is "using" whom. Intriguing and initially believable idea goes awry in latter half of this mean movie. [R]▼●

Mean Streets (1973) C-110m. **** D: Martin Scorsese. Robert De Niro, Harvey Keitel, David Proval, Amy Robinson, Richard Romanus, Cesare Danova, George Memmoli, Robert Carradine, David Carradine. Masterpiece about small-time hood Keitel, irresponsible friend De Niro, and their knockabout cronies in N.Y.C.'s Little Italy. Technically dazzling film put director Scorsese on the map and deservedly so. [R]▼●

Meantime (1983-British) C-104m. **½ D: Mike Leigh. Marion Bailey, Phil Daniels, Tim Roth, Pam Ferris, Jeff Robert, Alfred Molina, Gary Oldman. Downbeat kitchen-sink drama about the problems of a working-class London family; no one captures this milieu quite like director Leigh, though it can be pretty bleak. Made for TV. Molina and Oldman later costarred in PRICK UP YOUR EARS.▼▶

Meatballs (1979-Canadian) C-92m. *½ D: Ivan Reitman. Bill Murray, Harvey Atkin, Kate Lynch, Russ Banham, Kristine DeBell, Sarah Torgov. Alternately cruel and sloppily sentimental comedy about summer camp will no doubt wow fifth graders of all ages, though myopic screen characters named "Spaz" aren't really all that funny.

Pretty desperate. Followed by several so-called sequels. [PG] ▼●)

Meatballs Part II (1984) **C-87m.** ** D: Ken Wiederhorn. Richard Mulligan, John Mengatti, Hamilton Camp, Kim Richards, Tammy Taylor, John Larroquette, Archie Hahn, Misty Rowe, Paul Reubens (Pee-wee Herman), Elayne Boosler. In-name-only sequel throws in everything from Jewish aliens to FROM HERE TO ETERNITY take-off, as the fate of Camp Sasquatch rides on a boxing match against nearby Camp Patton ("Where Outdoor Living Molds Killers"). Slightly better than its predecessor (which isn't saying much). [PG] ▼●)

Meatballs III (1987) **C-94m.** *½ D: George Mendeluk. Sally Kellerman, Patrick Dempsey, Al Waxman, Isabelle Mejias, Shannon Tweed, Ian Taylor, George Buza. What do you say about a movie dealing with a dead porno star who coaches a teenage nerd on how to lose his virginity at summer camp? As little as possible. [R] ▼●

Mechanic, The (1972) **C-100m.** **½ D: Michael Winner. Charles Bronson, Keenan Wynn, Jan-Michael Vincent, Jill Ireland. Detailed study of James Bond-type assassin and youth he trains to take his place. Worth it for the double-twist ending; terse script by Lewis John Carlino. Remade in 2011. [PG] ▼●)

Mechanic, The (2011) **C-93m.** ** D: Simon West. Jason Statham, Ben Foster, Donald Sutherland, Tony Goldwyn, Jeff Chase, Mini Anden, James Logan, Christa Campbell. Remake of Charles Bronson's 1972 crime thriller about an elite assassin who takes his mentor's aimless son and teaches him the trade. Souped-up and contemporized, this basically retains the same elements as the original. First half is heavy on exposition and character development; then, as the new partners prepare for a hit, inevitable complications arise. Plenty of action, but the brutal violence becomes deadening after a while. Foster is good in an underwritten role, and Statham has undeniable presence, but it's hard to care about any of these people. Super 35. [R] ▶

Medallion, The (2003-Hong Kong-U.S.) **C-90m.** *½ D: Gordon Chan. Jackie Chan, Lee Evans, Claire Forlani, Julian Sands, Jonathan Rhys-Davies, Anthony Wong, Christy Chung. Hong Kong cop joins forces with Interpol to capture a nefarious villain who has kidnapped a mystic child; his medallion holds the key to immortality. OK story framework is pounded into senselessness by bad writing, overacting, hammy comedy touches, and incongruous special effects. Chan is still fun to watch, and a handful of action scenes (sans fx) show what he's capable of. Action directed by Sammo Hung. Super 35. [PG-13] ▼ ▶

Medicine Ball Caravan (1971) **C-90m.** **½ D: Francois Reichenbach. B. B. King, Alice Cooper, Delaney and Bonnie, Doug Kershaw,

David Peel. The Caravan is a 150-member troupe that traveled the U.S. during the summer of '70 to spread peace, love, music—and make a movie. Superficially arty direction; Martin Scorsese was associate producer and supervising editor. Techniscope. [R]

Medicine Man (1992) **C-106m.** **½ D: John McTiernan. Sean Connery, Lorraine Bracco, José Wilker. Connery plays a research scientist, sequestered in the Brazilian rain forest, who's found the cure for cancer—but can't duplicate it. Bracco is his brainy superior from the U.S. who's come to check up on him. Connery carries this movie singlehandedly, and as usual he's commanding to watch, but the film is weak, and Bracco's abrasive performance (and poorly written character) practically sink it. Panavision. [PG-13] ▼●)

Mediterraneo (1991-Italian) **C-92m.** *** D: Gabriele Salvatores. Diego Abatantuono, Claudio Bigagli, Giuseppe Cederna, Claudio Bisio, Gigio Alberti, Vanna Barba. It's 1941 and Greek-island males are off fighting in WW2, so some stranded Italian soldiers partake in la dolce vita—for years. Sweet memory movie with double-digit guffaws, though a slight choice to have won the Best Foreign Film Oscar. ▼●

Medium Cool (1969) **C-110m.** **** D: Haskell Wexler. Robert Forster, Verna Bloom, Peter Bonerz, Marianna Hill, Harold Blankenship, Peter Boyle. Arresting, unique film of TV cameraman who remains detached though surrounded by events demanding his involvement. Director/writer/cameraman Wexler used real footage of his actors at 1968 Democratic convention in Chicago, and subsequent riots, as basis for ultrarealistic film. Score by Mike Bloomfield; Paul Butterfield and The Mothers of Invention are among the artists on the soundtrack. [R] ▼●)

Medusa Touch, The (1978-British-French) **C-110m.** ** D: Jack Gold. Richard Burton, Lino Ventura, Lee Remick, Harry Andrews, Alan Badel, Marie-Christine Barrault, Jeremy Brett, Michael Hordern, Gordon Jackson, Derek Jacobi. Burton has spent his whole life willing people's deaths, and now he's completely out of control; Remick is his psychiatrist in this derivative, unappealing film. [PG] ▼

Meek's Cutoff (2011) **C-104m.** *** D: Kelly Reichardt. Michelle Williams, Bruce Greenwood, Will Patton, Zoe Kazan, Paul Dano, Shirley Henderson, Neal Huff, Tommy Nelson, Rod Rondeaux. In 1845, three families of settlers follow their garrulous tracker (an unrecognizable Greenwood) across Oregon Territory, but begin to suspect that in spite of their leader's outward confidence, they're lost. Arid and slowly paced, like Reichardt's other features, which will turn some people off. Still, without ever raising a fuss or showing off the incredible degree of detail that went into every shot, the filmmaker and her cast make us feel as if we're right there alongside them. No movie has ever captured the harshness of life on the trail quite like this before. Screenplay by Reichardt's frequent collaborator Jon Raymond. [PG]

Meet Bill (2008) **C-92m.** **½ D: Bernie Goldmann, Melisa Wallack. Aaron Eckhart, Elizabeth Banks, Logan Lerman, Timothy Olyphant, Holmes Osborne, Jessica Alba, Reed Diamond, Craig Bierko, Kristen Wiig, Marisa Coughlan, Jason Sudeikis. Bill's life is a mess; he hates his job, his wife is cheating on him, and he's unhappy. It isn't until he (reluctantly) begins mentoring a remarkably intelligent but rebellious teenager (Lerman) that he finally gains confidence in himself. Though uneven in tone, this is an honest and relatable comedy with strong performances by Eckhart and Lerman. [R]◗

Meet Dave (2008) **C-90m.** ** D: Brian Robbins. Eddie Murphy, Elizabeth Banks, Gabrielle Union, Scott Caan, Ed Helms, Kevin Hart, Mike O'Malley, Pat Kilbane, Judah Friedlander, Marc Blucas, Jim Turner, Austyn Lind Myers. High-concept fish-out-of-water family fantasy about tiny aliens who construct a spacecraft in the image of a man (who looks amazingly like Murphy) and come to Earth on a mission to drain its oceans in order to save their own planet. Predictable complications arise in the form of a pretty single mom (Banks), her bullied son, and the discovery of such human emotions as love. Innocuous and overstretched, but easily amused kids may go for it. [PG]◗

Meetings With Remarkable Men (1979-British) **C-110m.** **½ D: Peter Brook. Terence Stamp, Dragan Maksimovic, Mikica Dimitrijevic, Athol Fugard, Warren Mitchell, Gerry Sundquist, Bruce Myers, Natasha Parry, Martin Benson. Uneven account of G. I. Gurdjieff (Maksimovic), the famed, inspirational cult leader, focusing on his quest through Asia to uncover the meaning of human existence. Has its moments of insight, but will ultimately be of interest only to those fascinated by the subject. Based on Gurdjieff's memoirs. [G]▼

Meeting Venus (1991-British) **C-117m.** *** D: Istvan Szabo. Glenn Close, Niels Arestrup, Erland Josephson, Johanna Ter Steege, Jay O. Sanders, Maria de Medeiros, Ildiko Bansagi. During the tumultuous preparations for a multinational production of Wagner's *Tannhauser*, a Hungarian conductor (Arestrup) and a Swedish diva (Close, who's outstanding) find themselves involved in an affair. Witty, knowing romantic farce about the politics of art, which also works as a metaphor for the aftereffects of European reunification. Veteran Hungarian director Szabo's first film in English.

Close's singing voice is dubbed by Kiri Te Kanewa. [PG-13]▼◗

Meet Joe Black (1998) **C-178m.** ** D: Martin Brest. Anthony Hopkins, Brad Pitt, Claire Forlani, Jake Weber, Marcia Gay Harden, Jeffrey Tambor, David S. Howard. Death comes to claim a billionaire industrialist (Hopkins), and decides to take human form (Pitt), emerging as a mysterious stranger with a childlike manner and a fondness for peanut butter. Odd rethinking of DEATH TAKES A HOLIDAY adds subplots that make it go on for days, toward a preposterous and unsatisfying conclusion. Hopkins is terrific, but Death's character simply makes no sense. Sumptuous production design. [PG-13] ▼◗

Meet John Doe (1941) **132m.** *** D: Frank Capra. Gary Cooper, Barbara Stanwyck, Edward Arnold, Walter Brennan, Spring Byington, James Gleason, Gene Lockhart. Overlong but interesting social commentary, with naive Cooper hired to spearhead national goodwill drive benefiting corrupt politician Arnold. Wordy idealism can't bury good characterizations; usual Capra touches exulting populism. Virtually all existing prints (from reissue) run 123m. Also shown in computer-colored version.▼◗

Meet Me in St. Louis (1944) **C-113m.** **** D: Vincente Minnelli. Judy Garland, Margaret O'Brien, Lucille Bremer, Tom Drake, Mary Astor, Leon Ames, Marjorie Main, June Lockhart, Harry Davenport, Joan Carroll, Hugh Marlowe. Captivating musical based on Sally Benson's slice of Americana about a family's experiences during the year of the St. Louis World's Fair, 1903. Judy sings wonderful Ralph Blane–Hugh Martin songs "The Boy Next Door," "Have Yourself a Merry Little Christmas," "The Trolley Song," while Margaret O'Brien steals every scene she's in as little sister Tootie. (In fact, she won a special Oscar, as the year's best child actress.) Screenplay by Irving Brecher and Fred F. Finklehoffe. Years later adapted for Broadway.▼◗

Meet Me Tonight SEE: **Tonight at 8:30**

Meet the Applegates (1991) **C-90m.** **½ D: Michael Lehmann. Ed Begley, Jr., Stockard Channing, Dabney Coleman, Bobby Jacoby, Cami Cooper, Glenn Shadix, Susan Barnes. Brazilian beetles in human form assimilate (sort of) in U.S. suburbia, but still manage to stock their quota of human prey in the basement. Spotty, but sometimes funny comedy, wittily designed but marred by a weak conclusion. Released on video, for no apparent reason, as THE APPLEGATES. [R] ▼◗

Meet the Browns (2008) **C-100m.** ** D: Tyler Perry. Angela Bassett, David Mann, Rick Fox, Irma P. Hall, Jenifer Lewis, Tamela J. Mann, Frankie Faison, Margaret Avery, Lance Gross, Chloe Bailey, Mariana Tolbert, Sofia Vergara, Tyler Perry. Single mother barely making ends meet gets talked into taking her family to the funeral of the father she never met. She gets more than she bargained for: a boisterous extended family, a new romance, and a surprise piece of ol' dad's "estate." Bassett tries to elevate this but it's typical Perry fodder, veering wildly between broad comedy and overwrought melodrama. Perry appears briefly toward the end in cross-dressing mode as Madea in a shameless preview for his next feature. Aka TYLER PERRY'S MEET THE BROWNS. [PG-13]▌

Meet the Deedles (1998) **C-92m.** *½ D: Steve Boyum. Steve Van Wormer, Paul Walker, A. J. Langer, John Ashton, Dennis Hopper, Megan Cavanaugh, Eric Braeden, Richard Lineback, M. C. Gainey, Robert Englund. Idiotic BILL & TED clone about twin surfer dude brothers from Hawaii whose filthy rich father schemes to teach them responsibility by dispatching them to a summer camp. Bottom-of-the-barrel Disney wipeout; less discriminating teens might go for it for about three minutes. Hopper plays a villainous ex-park ranger, and Bart the Bear has a cameo. [PG]▼●

Meet the Fockers (2004) **C-115m.** *½ D: Jay Roach. Robert De Niro, Ben Stiller, Dustin Hoffman, Barbra Streisand, Blythe Danner, Teri Polo, Alanna Ubach, Tim Blake Nelson, Shelley Berman, Owen Wilson. Unnecessary follow-up to MEET THE PARENTS has Stiller taking his future in-laws and fiancée Polo to meet *his* parents. Hoffman and Streisand are the wacky, liberal, free-spirited Fockers; De Niro and Danner are the stuffed-shirt, conservative Byrneses. Together they make humiliation, embarrassment, and misunderstandings the foundation of a lame comedy . . . but the public loved it! Followed by LITTLE FOCKERS. [PG-13]▌

Meet the Parents (2000) **C-108m.** **½ D: Jay Roach. Robert De Niro, Ben Stiller, Blythe Danner, Teri Polo, James Rebhorn, Jon Abrahams, Owen Wilson, Phyllis George. A male nurse spends a weekend with his girlfriend's parents, hoping to ask her uptight father for her hand in marriage . . . but the dad is so intimidating that he starts bungling things and can't seem to stop. Funny setup, ideal cast, but the results are frustratingly uneven. Based on a low-budget film of the same name from 1992. Followed by MEET THE FOCKERS. [PG-13]▼▌

Meet the Robinsons (2007) **C-96m.** **½ D: Stephen Anderson. Voices of Daniel Hansen, Jordan Fry, Wesley Singerman, Angela Bassett, Tom Selleck, Harland Williams, Laurie Metcalf, Adam West, Ethan Sandler, Tom Kenney. Orphaned boy becomes a science whiz; then one day he's whisked off to the future by a kid in a time-traveling space vehicle. There he meets a family just like the one he's always longed for. Disney CGI cartoon feature follows a wildly uneven story path,

and suffers from some lackluster voice performances (including director Anderson as the villain), but finally hits its emotional stride for the home stretch. Based on the book *A Day With Wilbur Robinson* by William Joyce. 3-D. [G]▌

Meet the Spartans (2008) **C-84m.** BOMB D: Jason Friedberg, Aaron Seltzer. Sean Maguire, Carmen Electra, Ken Davitian, Kevin Sorbo, Diedrich Bader, Method Man, Jareb Dauplaise, Travis Van Winkle, Nicole Parker. The creators of DATE MOVIE and EPIC MOVIE concocted this moronic, product-placement-laden spoof of the homoeroticism of 300, aimed at adolescent boys. Plot involves King Leonidas of Sparta (Maguire) and his self-adoring, scantily clad warriors as they battle the Persians. Oodles of pop-cultural references are complete duds. Unrated version runs 87m. [PG-13]▌

Meet Wally Sparks (1997) **C-104m.** *½ D: Peter Baldwin. Rodney Dangerfield, Debi Mazar, Cindy Williams, Burt Reynolds, David Ogden Stiers, Alan Rachins. Embarrassingly unfunny vehicle for Dangerfield, as a trashy TV talk show host attempting to save his program. Instead of successfully satirizing elements of the morally bankrupt TV talk genre, the screenplay (cowritten by Dangerfield) sinks to its level. Look for mercifully short cameos from Tony Danza, Tim Allen, Roseanne, Jay Leno, and Gilbert Gottfried. [R]▼●

Megaforce (1982) **C-99m.** BOMB D: Hal Needham. Barry Bostwick, Persis Khambatta, Michael Beck, Edward Mulhare, George Furth, Henry Silva. Atrocious bubble-gum movie about an ultra-modern fighting force headed by one Ace Hunter (Bostwick, badly miscast). Embarrassing performances, clunky hardware, uninspired action scenes. [PG]▼

Megamind (2010) **C-96m.** **½ D: Tom McGrath. Voices of Will Ferrell, Tina Fey, Brad Pitt, Jonah Hill, David Cross, Ben Stiller, J. K. Simmons. Two infants are rocketed to Earth—just like you-know-who—before their planets are destroyed. One becomes a handsome hero called Metro Man, while the other leads a star-crossed life as Megamind, inept master villain. When Megamind finally manages to subdue his adversary, life loses all meaning—until he gets to know a crusading female TV reporter. CGI-animated feature is long on wisecracks and attitude (over the heads of little kids), but when the story finally kicks into gear it's fun to watch. 3-D Digital Widescreen. [PG]▼

Megiddo (2001) **C-106m.** *½ D: Brian Trenchard-Smith. Michael York, Michael Biehn, Diane Venora, R. Lee Ermey, Udo Kier, Franco Nero, Jim Metzler. From the people who brought you THE OMEGA CODE (this was subtitled in ads as OMEGA CODE 2) comes another tale of York's desire for world domination. This one includes a flashback of the bad seed's childhood, and his relationship with his brother (Biehn). Silly, pathetic; just another attempt to capitalize on the intriguing premise of Armageddon. [PG-13]▼▶

Melinda and Melinda (2005) **C-100m.** ** D: Woody Allen. Radha Mitchell, Will Ferrell, Chloë Sevigny, Jonny Lee Miller, Amanda Peet, Chiwitel Ejiofor, Brooke Smith, Josh Brolin, Gene Saks, Vinessa Shaw, Wallace Shawn, Larry Pine, Steve Carell. Two playwrights discuss how they would approach a story they've heard about a young woman who shows up unannounced on an old friend's Manhattan doorstep—one in comedic terms, the other dramatic. Both stories unfold but don't lead anywhere; meandering film offers echoes and reminders of earlier, better Allen movies, though it serves as a good showcase for Mitchell. Ferrell's dialogue is stuffed with Woodyesque one-liners. [PG-13]▼▶

Mélo (1986-French) **C-110m.** *** D: Alain Resnais. Sabine Azéma, Pierre Arditi, Andre Dussollier, Fanny Ardant, Jacques Dacqmine, Catherine Arditi. Different sort of film experiment from innovator Resnais, rigorously adapting Henry Bernstein's 1929 play about a tragic love triangle. Top-notch acting and direction make this one a winner, but the (intentionally) stagy production makes it not for all tastes. Previously filmed as MÉLO (1932); DER TRÄUMENDE MUND (1932) and DREAMING LIPS (1937), both with Elisabeth Bergner; and DER TRÄUMENDE MUND (1953).▶

Melody (1971-British) **C-103m.** *** D: Waris Hussein. Jack Wild, Mark Lester, Tracy Hyde, Sheila Steafel, Kate Williams, Roy Kinnear. Adolescent view of life, disarmingly played by Lester and Wild (from OLIVER!) as friends who rebel against adult establishment, particularly when Lester and girlfriend Hyde decide they want to get married. Music by The Bee Gees. [G]▼

Melvin and Howard (1980) **C-95m.** ***½ D: Jonathan Demme. Paul LeMat, Jason Robards, Mary Steenburgen, Jack Kehoe, Pamela Reed, Dabney Coleman, Michael J. Pollard, Gloria Grahame, Elizabeth Cheshire, Martine Beswicke, Charles Napier, John Glover. Wonderful slice-of-life comedy based on the story of Melvin Dummar, who once gave a lift to a grizzled Howard Hughes and later produced a will naming himself as heir to the Hughes fortune. An endearing, bittersweet American fable, with Oscar winner Steenburgen providing most of the comic highlights, including a memorable TV talent contest. Bo Goldman's script also won an Academy Award. (That's the real Melvin Dummar behind a bus station lunch counter.) [R]▼▶

Member of the Wedding, The (1952) **91m.** *** D: Fred Zinnemann. Ethel Waters, Julie Harris, Brandon de Wilde, Arthur Franz, Nancy Gates, James Edwards. Carson McCullers' sensitive account of child Harris prodded into growing up by her brother's forthcoming marriage. Waters, Harris, and de Wilde movingly re-create their Broadway roles, the latter two making their film debuts. Slow but worthwhile. Remade for cable TV in 1997.▼▶

Memento (2001) **C/B&W-113m.** *½ D: Christopher Nolan. Guy Pearce, Carrie-Anne Moss, Joe Pantoliano, Mark Boone, Jr., Stephen Tobolowsky, Jorja Fox, Callum Keith Rennie. A man with short-term memory loss tries to keep his life in order while avenging his wife's murder. Is he being helped, or manipulated, by the people around him? Pretentious pap plays with storytelling conventions and juggles "real time," but adds up to zero (though the film has many ardent fans). Panavision. [R]▼▶

Memoirs of a Geisha (2005) **C-144m.** **½ D: Rob Marshall. Ziyi Zhang, Ken Watanabe, Michelle Yeoh, Gong Li, Kôji Yakusho, Youki Kudoh, Kaori Momoi, Tsai Chin, Cary-Hiroyuki Tagawa, Randall Duk Kim, Mako, Ted Levine. Sumptuous adaptation of Arthur Golden's bestseller about a young peasant woman's training in the art of the geisha, even as its traditions collide with the demands of increasingly modern times and WW2. Intriguing story is Hollywoodized at every turn but still reasonably entertaining thanks to the presence of Zhang, Yeoh, and Li. Spectacular production earned Oscars for Art Direction and Set Decoration (John Myhre, Gretchen Rau), Costumes (Colleen Atwood), and Cinematography (Dion Beebe). Panavision. [PG-13]▶

Memoirs of an Invisible Man (1992) **C-99m.** ** D: John Carpenter. Chevy Chase, Daryl Hannah, Sam Neill, Michael McKean, Stephen Tobolowsky, Rosalind Chao. Clever (but endless) special effects are the star of this stale, paper-thin dud. Chase plays a securities analyst who's rendered invisible after an accident, and finds himself involved in a by-the-numbers spy scenario. Panavision. [PG-13]▼◉

Memoirs of a Survivor (1981-British) **C-117m.** *½ D: David Gladwell. Julie Christie, Christopher Guard, Leonie Mellinger, Debbie Hutchings, Nigel Hawthorne, Pat Keen. Christie's presence cannot save this dismal, badly directed fantasy about a woman and a teenager (Mellinger) surviving in a decayed urban civilization. Good idea—film is based on a Doris Lessing novel—but poorly realized.▼

Memories of Me (1988) **C-105m.** ** D: Henry Winkler. Billy Crystal, Alan King, JoBeth Williams, Janet Carroll, David Ackroyd, Phil Fondacaro, Robert Pastorelli, Sidney Miller. A heart surgeon, who recently suffered a heart attack himself, seeks out his father, from whom he's been estranged, hoping to put his life in order. Contrived comedy-drama combines comic shtick with mawkish emotional scenes and never quite manages to be convincing. Crystal cowrote the screenplay and coproduced with King. [PG-13] ▼●◗

Memory of a Killer, The (2003-Belgian-Dutch) **C-123m.** *** D: Erik Van Looy. Jan Decleir, Koen De Bouw, Werner De Smedt, Hilde De Baerdemaeker, Geert Van Rampelberg, Jo De Meyere. An aging professional assassin (Decleir) in the early stages of Alzheimer's disease refuses to carry out a hit on a 12-year-old prostitute and tries to help the cops nail the powerful baron who hired him—before he loses his memory. Gripping police procedural/character study is as slick and stylish as any American crime thriller, while offering stinging social commentary with a worldly European sensibility. Super 35. [R]◗

Memory of Justice, The (1976-German-U.S.) **C-278m.** **** D: Marcel Ophuls. Outstanding documentary from the director of THE SORROW AND THE PITY questions how one country can pass judgment on the atrocities of others by examining the Nuremberg trials and their aftermath, the French performance in Algeria and the American intervention in Vietnam. Always riveting in spite of its mammoth length. [PG]

Memory of Us (1974) **C-93m.** **½ D: H. Kaye Dyal. Ellen Geer, Jon Cypher, Barbara Colby, Peter Brown, Robert Hogan, Rose Marie, Will Geer. Modest, interesting contemporary drama about a happily married woman who begins to question her role as wife and mother; script by star Ellen Geer, whose father Will makes brief appearance. [PG]▼

Memphis Belle (1990-British) **C-101m.** ** D: Michael Caton-Jones. Matthew Modine, Eric Stoltz, Tate Donovan, D.B. Sweeney, Billy Zane, Sean Astin, Harry Connick, Jr., Reed Edward Diamond, Courtney Gains, Neil Giuntoli, David Strathairn, John Lithgow, Jane Horrocks. If you can make it through the first hour (a virtual catalogue of war-movie clichés) this film ultimately provides an exciting fictional reenactment of the famous B-17's final bombing raid over Germany during WW2. Still, it's hard to believe that such a cornball script could be concocted in 1990. Coproduced by Catherine Wyler, whose father, William Wyler, made the 1944 documentary THE MEMPHIS BELLE. [PG-13]▼●◗

Me Myself and I (1992) **C-97m.** **½ D: Pablo Ferro. JoBeth Williams, George Segal, Don Calfa, Shelley Hack, Betsy Lynn George, Bill Macy, Sharon McNight, Ruth Gilbert. Novelist-TV writer Segal becomes involved with his next-door neighbor, a schizophrenic (well played by Williams) who is intelligent and nurturing when "sane," but otherwise totally off-the-wall.

Bizarre comedy is uneven, sometimes enjoyable and other times annoying.▼

Me, Myself & Irene (2000) **C-100m.** ** D: Bobby Farrelly, Peter Farrelly. Jim Carrey, Renée Zellweger, Robert Forster, Tony Cox, Anthony Anderson, Mongo Brownlee, Jerod Mixon, Chris Cooper, Michael Bowman, Richard Jenkins, Rob Moran. A mild-mannered Rhode Island state trooper suddenly develops an alter ego, unleashing years of pent-up fury. Revealing more of the "plot" would be pointless. A typical Farrelly mishmash of oddball characters and non sequitur bad-taste gags, this one has an air of desperation about it. [R]▼◗

Me Myself I (1999-Australian-French) **C-104m.** **½ D: Pip Karmel. Rachel Griffiths, David Roberts, Sandy Winton, Yael Stone, Shaun Loseby, Trent Sullivan. Fiercely independent career woman realizes that she may have made a mistake putting off marriage and family. She gets to see how the other half lives when she comes face-to-face with the husband and kids she would have experienced had she gone the "soccer mom" route. Comedy-drama takes its time unfolding, but Griffiths is good as always in a "dream" role. Directing debut for Karmel, the editor of SHINE. [R]▼◗

Men, The (1950) **85m.** ***½ D: Fred Zinnemann. Marlon Brando, Teresa Wright, Everett Sloane, Jack Webb, Richard Erdman, Dorothy Tree, Howard St. John, DeForest Kelley. Brando excels in film debut as ex-GI adjusting to life in wheelchair after wartime injury; low-key acting is most effective. Story and screenplay by Carl Foreman. Retitled: BATTLE STRIPE. ▼●◗

Men... (1985-German) **C-95m.** ***½ D: Doris Dörrie. Heiner Lauterbach, Uwe Ochsenknecht, Ulrike Kriener, Janna Marangosoff. Ingenious comedy-satire about an uptight adman who becomes haplessly jealous when he learns that his wife's having an affair. He promptly befriends her lover and becomes his roommate, with hilarious results.▼

Men (1998) **C-93m.** ** D: Zoe Clarke-Williams. Sean Young, John Heard, Dylan Walsh, Richard Hillman, Jr., Karen Black, Beau Starr, Shawnee Smith, Glenn Shadix, Annie McEnroe. Trite, pretentious tearjerker about a young woman whose journey of self-discovery and sexual fulfillment takes her from N.Y. to California, where she gets involved with a married middle-aged man and a radical young photographer. Young is good, even if she's too old for the part, but much of her dialogue is unintentionally funny. Karen Black, who cowrote the script, livens things up with a cameo as a blind lesbian with an indecipherable accent. [R]▼●◗

Menace II Society (1993) **C-97m.** *** D: Allen and Albert Hughes. Tyrin Turner, Larenz Tate, Jada Pinkett, Vonte Sweet, MC Eiht, Ryan Williams, Too $hort, Samuel L. Jackson, Charles Dutton, Glenn Plummer,

Bill Duke. Powerful, unflinching story of life in the Watts district of Los Angeles and one teenager (Turner) who is too immersed in that violent world to get out. Social points are often hammered home, but the atmosphere of tension and random brutality is captured with searing authenticity. Extremely bloody (and profane) but gripping and well acted in naturalistic fashion. Strong debut by Hughes Brothers, who also cowrote story with screenwriter Tyger Williams. [R]▼●)

Ménage (1986-French) **C-84m.** *** D: Bertrand Blier. Gérard Depardieu, Michel Blanc, Miou-Miou, Bruno Cremer, Jean-Pierre Marielle. Outrageous, fast-paced farce about a roguish, gay crook (Depardieu), who thoroughly disrupts the lives of an impoverished couple (Blanc and Miou-Miou)—sexually and otherwise. Peters out at the end but still worth a look. Original French title: TENUE DE SOIRÉE. Panavision.▼)

Me, Natalie (1969) **C-111m.** **½ D: Fred Coe. Patty Duke, James Farentino, Martin Balsam, Elsa Lanchester, Salome Jens, Nancy Marchand, Deborah Winters, Al Pacino. Soap opera-ish tale about unattractive N.Y.C. girl struggling to find herself gets tremendous boost by Duke's great performance; otherwise, film wavers uncomfortably between comedy and drama. Pacino's feature debut. [M/PG]

Men at Work (1990) **C-99m.** ** D: Emilio Estevez. Charlie Sheen, Emilio Estevez, Leslie Hope, Keith David, Dean Cameron, John Getz, Cameron Dye, John Putch. Estevez and real-life brother Sheen play garbage men whose freewheeling lifestyle is interrupted when they discover a dead body along their route. Estevez also wrote the screenplay. Laurel and Hardy they're not, but this sibling duo does provide some undemanding fun—if you check your brain at the door. [PG-13]▼●)

Men Don't Leave (1990) **C-115m.** *** D: Paul Brickman. Jessica Lange, Arliss Howard, Joan Cusack, Chris O'Donnell, Charlie Korsmo, Kathy Bates. Widowed Lange, left broke with two sons, relocates from small-town Maryland to downtown Baltimore high rise. Erratic but well-performed comedy-drama is compromised by introduction of movie-predictable Mr. Right. Good moments abound, though, particularly between Lange and Cusack. And ultimately, film offers a good cry. Brickman's second directorial credit, following a seven-year layoff after RISKY BUSINESS. Remake of French film LA VIE CONTINUE. [PG-13]▼●)

Men in Black (1997) **C-98m.** *** D: Barry Sonnenfeld. Tommy Lee Jones, Will Smith, Linda Fiorentino, Rip Torn, Vincent D'Onofrio, Tony Shalhoub, Siobhan Fallon. Hip, funny spin on the usual sci-fi invasion saga. Street-smart NYPD cop Smith is recruited to join Jones on the super-secret team that

keeps an eye on thousands of aliens who already populate our planet, without most of us knowing it. When one especially violent visitor starts acting up, it's a race to find the prize he's looking for before Earth is destroyed. Outrageous and original at every turn, with great aliens by Rick Baker (Academy Award winner for Best Makeup, with David LeRoy Anderson), sharp pacing that never lets up, and a snappy script by Ed Solomon, based on the Malibu comic by Lowell Cunningham. Followed by a sequel and an animated TV series. [PG-13]▼●)

Men in Black II (2002) **C-88m.** ** D: Barry Sonnenfeld. Tommy Lee Jones, Will Smith, Rip Torn, Lara Flynn Boyle, Rosario Dawson, Tony Shalhoub, Patrick Warburton, Johnny Knoxville. Agent Smith tries to coax Agent Jones out of retirement to help fight humankind's latest enemy, an alien in the form of a seductress who can morph into other less-appealing creatures at will. All the fun and freshness of the first film have evaporated in this sequel, which feels as if it was manufactured, like so much product. Cheesy, unconvincing special effects don't help, and celebrity cameos offer only fleeting chuckles. A talking dog gets most of the good lines. [PG-13] ▼)

Men in War (1957) **102m.** *** D: Anthony Mann. Robert Ryan, Aldo Ray, Robert Keith, Phillip Pine, Nehemiah Persoff, Vic Morrow, James Edwards, L. Q. Jones. In Korea, an American platoon, separated from the main force, joins with a sergeant and nearly-comatose general in an effort to rejoin the main group. Grim, low-key, and psychologically valid, this well-acted film is devoid of stereotypes and clichés; deserves to be better known.▼●)

Men of Honor (2000) **C-129m.** *** D: George Tillman, Jr. Robert De Niro, Cuba Gooding, Jr., Charlize Theron, Aunjanue Ellis, Hal Holbrook, David Keith, Michael Rapaport, Powers Boothe, Joshua Leonard, Glynn Turman, Carl Lumbly, Lonette McKee. Old-fashioned but rock-solid biopic of Carl Brashear, the first African-American to become a Navy diver, in the 1950s. Gooding is sincere and believable as a young man of extraordinary determination, in the face of abuse from his superiors—including diver-turned-instructor De Niro. A real crowd-pleaser, if not exactly true to life. Super 35. [PG-13]▼)

Men of Respect (1991) **C-113m.** *½ D: William Reilly. John Turturro, Katherine Borowitz, Dennis Farina, Peter Boyle, Rod Steiger, Lilia Skala, Steven Wright, Stanley Tucci. Pretentious modern-day *Macbeth*: Hood Turturro, pushed by an ambitious wife, rises to the top by helping blow away mob rivals. The classic sleepwalking scene (you keep wondering how it will be staged) takes place in a courtyard with Borowitz carrying a flashlight! Overacted and underlit. Columbia Pictures' first gangster/Shakespeare hybrid since JOE MACBETH; we're in no hurry for them to try it again. [R]▼●)

Men of Steel SEE: **Steel** (1980)

Men's Club, The (1986) **C-100m.** BOMB D: Peter Medak. David Dukes, Richard Jordan, Harvey Keitel, Frank Langella, Roy Scheider, Craig Wasson, Treat Williams, Stockard Channing, Cindy Pickett, Gwen Welles, Ann Dusenberry, Jennifer Jason Leigh, Ann Wedgeworth. Jumbled, barely released expansion of Leonard Michaels' novel (scripted by the author) about seven males who try starting an encounter group in Jordan's home. Undistinguished performances despite that interesting cast; only noteworthy aspect is the elegant brothel for high-rollers, "The House of Affection." Ridiculous finale. [R]▼●

Men Who Stare at Goats, The (2009-U.S.-British) **C-94m.** ** D: Grant Heslov. George Clooney, Ewan McGregor, Jeff Bridges, Kevin Spacey, Stephen Root, Robert Patrick, Stephen Lang, Rebecca Mader, Glenn Morshower. Reporter McGregor stumbles onto the story of a bold, New Agey experimental unit formed by the U.S. Army in the 1980s to train so-called Jedi warriors to use paranormal powers in the cause of peace. Then he meets one of the unit's "stars" (Clooney), now supposedly retired, and tags along for a series of misadventures in Iraq. Sporadically amusing but never quite delivers on its promise and squanders an A-list quartet of stars. Based on Jon Ronson's nonfiction book. Panavision. [R]▼

Men With Guns (1998) **C-126m.** *** D: John Sayles. Federico Luppi, Damián Delgado, Dan Rivera González, Damián Alcázar, Mandy Patinkin, Katherine Grody, Tania Cruz. Dedicated, idealistic Central American doctor decides to track down former students from a government-sponsored program to bring good medicine to remote villages and tribes. This trek becomes an odyssey of discovery for the affluent but naive doctor, who acquires some unlikely companions along the way. Writer-director Sayles takes us on a road we've never traveled before—in Spanish, no less—and though it's long, it's a fascinating journey. [R]▼●)

Mephisto (1981-Hungarian) **C-135m.** *** D: Istvan Szabo. Klaus Maria Brandauer, Krystyna Janda, Ildiko Bansagi, Karin Boyd, Rolf Hoppe. Brandauer is magnetic as a vain, brilliant German actor who sells himself to gain prestige when the Nazis come to power. Engrossing drama is handsomely produced if a bit uneven. Based on a novel by Klaus Mann, son of Thomas, who committed suicide allegedly because he could not get the book published. Oscar winner for Best Foreign Film. First of a trilogy, followed by COLONEL REDL and HANUSSEN.▼)

Mephisto Waltz, The (1971) **C-108m.** *** D: Paul Wendkos. Alan Alda, Jacque-

line Bisset, Barbara Parkins, Curt Jurgens, Brad Dillman, William Windom, Kathleen Widdoes. Chiller about young journalist who falls prey to Satanic cult after meeting dying concert pianist Jurgens; good occult story with some truly frightening moments. Adapted by Ben Maddow from the Fred Mustard Stewart novel. [R]▼)

Mercenaries, The SEE: **Cuba Crossing**

Mercenary, The (1968-Italian) **C-105m.** **½ D: Sergio Corbucci. Franco Nero, Tony Musante, Jack Palance, Giovanna Ralli. Better-than-average Italian pasta Western with loads of action and violence and a welcome serving of humor. At odds with one another: a stalwart mercenary (Nero), his sadistic rival (Palance), a patriotic revolutionary (Musante), a lusty peasant girl, a greedy mineowner. Video title: A PROFESSIONAL GUN. Techniscope. [PG]▼)

Merchant of Four Seasons, The (1971-German) **C-88m.** *** D: Rainer Werner Fassbinder. Hans Hirschmuller, Irm Hermann, Hanna Schygulla, Andrea Schober. Fruit peddler trapped in unhappy marriage and frustrated with life disintegrates mentally and emotionally in this surprisingly rich and poignant meditation on mundane existence and failed dreams.▼)

Merchant of Venice, The (2004-U.S.-Italian-British-Luxembourg) **C-131m.** ***½ D: Michael Radford. Al Pacino, Jeremy Irons, Joseph Fiennes, Lynn Collins, Zuleikha Robinson, Kris Marshall, Charlie Cox, Heather Goldenhersh, Mackenzie Crook, John Sessions, Gregor Fisher, Ron Cook, Allan Corduner. Intelligent, frequently riveting adaptation of Shakespeare's controversial tale of Shylock (Pacino), a Jewish moneylender in 1596 Venice, and his plight after advancing 3,000 ducats to merchant Irons. Shylock may have been fashioned as a caricature, but Radford (who also adapted the play) presents the character sympathetically and emphasizes that, in 16th-century Venice, Jews were the victims of prejudice. Exceedingly well acted, particularly by Pacino (despite his New York accent). Aka WILLIAM SHAKESPEARE'S THE MERCHANT OF VENICE. Super 35. [R]▼)

Merchants of Death SEE: **B.O.R.N.**

Merci Docteur Rey (2003-U.S.-French) **C-91m.** ** D: Andrew Litvack. Dianne Wiest, Jane Birkin, Stanislas Merhar, Bulle Ogier, Karim Salah, Simon Callow, Jerry Hall, Vanessa Redgrave. Campy mystery-comedy involving a young phone-sex fanatic, his diva mother, and several other oddball characters, including a Vanessa Redgrave wannabe (and the star herself, in a brief cameo). Murder, mayhem, and, sadly, a shortage of real wit fill this mixed bag. Without the talents of the glorious Wiest and the sublime Paris locations there would be little to recommend here. A Merchant-Ivory production.)

Merci Pour le Chocolat (2000-French-Swiss). **C-99m.** **½ D: Claude Chabrol. Isabelle Huppert, Jacques Dutronc, Anna Mouglalis, Rodolphe Pauly, Brigitte Catillon. Swiss heiress remarries her first husband, a piano virtuoso. Then an attractive young female pianist shows up and reveals she may be part of the family. Subdued psychological thriller is mostly nuanced talk, with Chabrol favorite Huppert well suited to the role of perverse matriarch. Aka NIGHTCAP.▼▶

Mercury Rising (1998) **C-112m.** **½ D: Harold Becker. Bruce Willis, Alec Baldwin, Miko Hughes, Chi McBride, Kim Dickens, Robert Stanton, Bodhi Pine Elfman, Carrie Preston, L. L. Ginter, Camryn Manheim. An autistic nine-year-old boy innocently cracks a top-secret government code; cold-eyed bureaucrat Baldwin orders him killed, while over-the-hill FBI agent Willis tries to protect him. Except for the boy's autism, a routine suspense thriller, but well made and interesting throughout. Willis's standard action hero character shows a softer side here, while Baldwin plays an out-and-out heavy. Panavision. [R]▼●▶

Meridian (1990) **C-85m.** ** D: Charles Band. Sherilyn Fenn, Malcolm Jamieson, Charlie, Hilary Mason, Alex Daniels. Gothic tale about art student (Fenn) who becomes heiress to Italian castle—and its curse. OK variation on *Beauty and the Beast* doesn't hold up past the first hour, in spite of extensive nudity. Aka KISS OF THE BEAST. From Full Moon. [R]▼●▶

Mermaids (1990) **C-111m.** *** D: Richard Benjamin. Cher, Bob Hoskins, Winona Ryder, Michael Schoeffling, Christina Ricci, Caroline McWilliams, Jan Miner. Saucy, sexy single mother of two is a source of constant embarrassment to her teenage daughter, who's trying to deal with her own sexual awakening—and not having an easy time of it. Lively mix of comedy and drama set in New England in the early 1960s. Funny and affecting, with a standout performance by Ryder; based on a novel by Patty Dann. [PG-13]▼●▶

Merrill's Marauders (1962) **C-98m.** **½ D: Samuel Fuller. Jeff Chandler, Ty Hardin, Peter Brown, Andrew Duggan, Will Hutchins, Claude Akins, John Hoyt. Gritty war film; a WW2 actioner with Chandler (his last screen role) cast as Brig. Gen. Frank Merrill, leader of a band of GIs battling the Japanese in the Burmese jungle. Fuller coscripted. CinemaScope.▼●▶

Merry Christmas Mr. Lawrence (1983-British-Japanese) **C-122m.** *** D: Nagisa Oshima. Tom Conti, David Bowie, Ryuichi Sakamoto, Takeshi, Jack Thompson. Oshima's first film in English (for the most part) is strange, haunting drama set in Japanese POW camp, centering on test of wills between martinet commander Sakamoto and

British major Bowie. Quite rewarding for those willing to stick with it, but it does take some effort; splendid performances all around, especially Takeshi as tough sergeant and Conti as title character, camp's only bilingual prisoner. Japanese music superstar Sakamoto also composed the score. [R]▼

Merry Gentleman, The (2009) **C-96m.** *** D: Michael Keaton. Michael Keaton, Kelly Macdonald, Tom Bastounes, Bobby Cannavale, Darlene Hunt, Guy Van Swearingen, William Dick. Austere but stylish chamber thriller about a woman (Macdonald) fleeing an abusive husband (Cannavale) who tries to start a new life in Chicago. Extremely vulnerable, she keeps to herself but strikes up a relationship with another loner (Keaton) who, unbeknownst to her, works as a hit man. Impressive directorial debut for Keaton, working from Ron Lazzeretti's screenplay, but it's Macdonald who really makes the film worth seeing. Super 35. [R]▶

Merry War, A (1997-British) **C-102m.** *** D: Robert Bierman. Richard E. Grant, Helena Bonham Carter, Julian Wadham, Jim Carter, Harriet Walter, Lesley Vickerage, Liz Smith, Barbara Leigh-Hunt. Sweet, enjoyable comedy-satire about an advertising man (Grant) who is captivated by the concept of offering his life to "art." He quits his day job and embraces a Bohemian lifestyle as he sets out to become a full-time poet, all the while maintaining a relationship with his ex–coworker/girlfriend (Bonham Carter). Based on *Keep the Aspidistra Flying*, a semi-autobiographical novel by George Orwell; it played the film festival circuit under that title.▼▶

Merry Widow, The (1934) **99m.** *** D: Ernst Lubitsch. Maurice Chevalier, Jeanette MacDonald, Una Merkel, Edward Everett Horton, George Barbier, Herman Bing. Chevalier (as Count Danilo) is sent to Paris to lure a wealthy widow (MacDonald) back to her homeland of Marshovia, where her taxes keep the tiny country afloat. Charming reinvention of the famous operetta gets the fabled Lubitsch touch. Many of the original Franz Lehar songs remain, with new lyrics by Lorenz Hart and Gus Kahn. Filmed before in 1925, again in 1952.▼●

Merry Widow, The (1952) **C-105m.** **½ D: Curtis Bernhardt. Lana Turner, Fernando Lamas, Una Merkel, Richard Haydn. Franz Lehar's operetta has been rewritten (the widow is now a glamorous American who poses as a Parisian chorus girl) and the production is sumptuous, but there's no zing in this glossy remake.▼

Mesmerized (1986-British-Australian-New Zealand) **C-97m.** *½ D: Michael Laughlin. Jodie Foster, John Lithgow, Michael Murphy, Harry Andrews, Dan Shor, Reg Evans. Weird, ultimately silly drama about innocent orphan Foster who weds older man Lithgow in late-19th-century New Zealand. Laughlin adapted from Jerzy Skolimowski story. Aka SHOCKED. Panavision. [PG]▼●❍

Mesrine: Part 1—Killer Instinct (2008-French-Canadian-Italian) **C-113m. *** ** D: Jean-François Richet. Vincent Cassel, Cécile de France, Gérard Depardieu, Roy Dupuis, Gilles Lellouche, Elena Anaya, Michel Duchaussoy, Myriam Boyer, Ludivine Sagnier. Opening with the ambush that brought down notorious criminal Jacques Mesrine in 1979, film flashes back to the character's experiences while fighting in Algeria, which steep him in violence and make it impossible for him to readjust to "normal" life at home. He begins a life of crime, brashly climbing his way to the top—mentored by Depardieu, then teaming up with de France—until he is both celebrated and feared, first in France, then in Canada. Cassel is exceptionally charismatic as the antihero in this breathless biopic, based on Mesrine's best-selling memoir. Super 35. [R]❍

Mesrine: Part 2—Public Enemy Number 1 (2008-French-Canadian) **C-133m. *** ** D: Jean-François Richet. Vincent Cassel, Ludivine Sagnier, Mathieu Amalric, Samuel Le Bihan, Gérard Lanvin, Olivier Gourmet, Georges Wilson, Michel Duchaussoy, Anne Consigny, Myriam Boyer. The "man of a hundred faces" continues to fascinate his countrymen with audacious crimes committed in broad daylight, impudent encounters with courtroom judges, and repeated jailbreaks. Sagnier is his latest partner in crime, and, although there is no question where all this will lead, Mesrine refuses to live his life any other way. Richet maintains the same terrific pace he set in Part 1, and again Cassel dominates the action with his bold performance. He gets great support from Amalric and Sagnier. Super 35. [R]❍

Message, The SEE: **Mohammad, Messenger of God**

Message from Space (1978-Japanese) **C-105m. **½** D: Kinji Fukasaku. Vic Morrow, Sonny Chiba, Philip Casnoff, Peggy Lee Brennan, Sue Shiomi, Tetsuro Tamba. Embattled planet sends SOS, and intergalactic team comes to its rescue. Cardboard performances take back seat to special effects and "cute" robot, both obviously patterned after STAR WARS. Toeiscope. [PG]

Message in a Bottle (1999) **C-132m. **½** D: Luis Mandoki. Kevin Costner, Robin Wright Penn, Paul Newman, John Savage, Illeana Douglas, Robbie Coltrane, Jesse James, Bethel Leslie, Tom Aldredge, Viveka Davis, Raphael Sbarge, Rosemary Murphy. Sappy, old-fashioned romance based on Nicholas Sparks' novel about a Chicago newspaper researcher who finds a bottle washed ashore and in it a passionate letter from a man to his lover. She becomes obsessed with tracking down the writer, and when she finds him (widower Costner) she

doesn't reveal that their meeting was not by chance. Too long, too slow, but enjoyable escapism if you buy into it, with Wright Penn nicely cast against type, and Newman in fine form as Costner's starchy father. Panavision. [PG-13]▼●❍

Message to Love: The Isle of Wight Music Festival (1996) **C-128m. *** ** D: Murray Lerner. The Who, The Doors, Joan Baez, Joni Mitchell, Jimi Hendrix, Jethro Tull, Emerson, Lake and Palmer, Tiny Tim, The Moody Blues, Kris Kristofferson, Miles Davis, Donovan. Top-notch documentary chronicling the on- and offstage activities at Great Britain's version of Woodstock/Altamont: the 1970 Isle of Wight Festival, a musical smorgasbord that was as ineptly organized as it was musically significant. Priceless footage of rock acts, including Hendrix and The Doors' Jim Morrison just before their deaths. Because of financing problems, it took Lerner a quarter-century to complete this.▼●❍

Messenger, The (2009) **C-103m. ***½** D: Oren Moverman. Ben Foster, Woody Harrelson, Samantha Morton, Jena Malone, Steve Buscemi, Eamonn Walker. Decorated Iraq war veteran Foster, back home and dealing with various ailments, is assigned to the Casualty Notification Office, where he and his superior (Harrelson) have the unwelcome task of informing next of kin whenever a soldier dies. Episodic but moving look at the different ways people deal with anger, pain, repressed emotions, and grief—which includes these two messengers as well as the people who receive the dreaded news. Foster and Harrelson are first-rate, along with a fine ensemble who often have just moments to create their performances. Written by the (first-time) director and Alessandro Camon. Super 35. [R]❍

Messenger of Death (1988) **C-91m. *½** D: J. Lee Thompson. Charles Bronson, Trish Van Devere, Laurence Luckinbill, Jeff Corey, Marilyn Hassett, John Ireland, Daniel Benzali. Boring Bronson vehicle casts him as a reporter determined to get to the bottom of an odd murder case involving two warring Mormon sects led by Corey and Ireland. By-the-numbers filmmaking wastes a potentially interesting look at a different culture. [R]▼●❍

Messengers, The (2007) **C-90m. ** ** D: Danny Pang, Oxide Pang. Kristen Stewart, Dylan McDermott, Penelope Ann Miller, John Corbett, Dustin Milligan. A family trying to make a fresh start moves from the city to an abandoned farm (where, it turns out, the prior owners were mysteriously murdered). Troubled teenage daughter Stewart immediately sees and senses things that her parents are unaware of; before long, these nasty spirits close in on her and her baby brother. Anemic horror film is all setup with little payoff, eerie but not scary. American debut for Hong Kong directors the Pang Brothers. Followed by a DVD sequel. [PG-13]▼▶

Messenger: The Story of Joan of Arc, The (1999-French-U.S.) C-148m. **½ D: Luc Besson. Milla Jovovich, John Malkovich, Faye Dunaway, Dustin Hoffman, Pascal Greggory, Vincent Cassel, Tchéky Karyo, Richard Ridings, Desmond Harrington, Timothy West. Arresting approach to the story of Joan of Arc, with a vibrant Jovovich as the peasant girl who leads her countrymen into battle. But in this version (scripted by Besson and Andrew Birkin) she also questions herself, which causes the film to lose momentum after a rousing first half that's filled with vivid, in-your-face battle scenes. Alternate version runs 158m. Super 35. [R]▼▶

Meteor (1979) C-103m. *½ D: Ronald Neame. Sean Connery, Natalie Wood, Karl Malden, Brian Keith, Henry Fonda, Martin Landau, Trevor Howard, Richard Dysart. Switzerland, Hong Kong, and Manhattan all get a big piece of the rock when a giant meteor comes crashing to Earth. Late entry in Hollywood's disaster cycle wastes fine cast with dull script, shoddy effects. Panavision. [PG]▼▶

Meteor Man, The (1993) C-100m. *½ D: Robert Townsend. Robert Townsend, Marla Gibbs, Eddie Griffin, Robert Guillaume, James Earl Jones, Roy Fegan, Cynthia Belgrave, Marilyn Coleman, Don Cheadle, Bill Cosby, Frank Gorshin, Sinbad, Luther Vandross, Samuel L. Jackson. Townsend plays a timid inner-city schoolteacher (with a fear of heights) who's hit by an odd emerald meteor that turns him into a superhero. Townsend also wrote this "Superman N the Hood" tale, full of pro-social values— but not many laughs. As a comedy it just doesn't fly. [PG]▼▶

Metro (1997) C-117m. **½ D: Thomas Carter. Eddie Murphy, Michael Rapaport, Michael Wincott, Carmen Ejogo, Denis Arndt, Art Evans, Donal Logue, Kim Miyori. Murphy is a self-assured hostage negotiator for the San Francisco police, but this action film needs his thousand-watt personality to keep it afloat. Plotting is cluttered and predictable, with a heinous villain (Wincott) who proves so indestructible that when he finally dies, there's no satisfaction because we're not sure he's really finished! Action highlight: a runaway cable car. Panavision. [R]▼▶

Metroland (1998-British) C-97m. **½ D: Philip Saville. Christian Bale, Emily Watson, Lee Ross, Elsa Zylberstein, Rufus, Jonathan Aris, Ifan Meredith, Amanda Ryan, John Wood. 1977: Chris (Bale), a comfortably married man, is visited by his oldest friend, a vagabond poet, who forces him to reflect on his Bohemian days in late '60s Paris and question the value of middle-class existence in London suburbia. A thoughtful though basically unsurprising examination of compromised dreams, bolstered by the performances of Bale and Watson. Adrian Hodges adapted Julian Barnes' novel. ▼▶

Metropolis (1927-German) 124m. **** D: Fritz Lang. Brigitte Helm, Alfred Abel, Gustav Froelich, Rudolf Klein-Rogge, Fritz Rasp. Classic silent-film fantasy of futuristic city and its mechanized society, with upper-class young man abandoning his life of luxury to join oppressed workers in a revolt. Heavy going at times, but startling set design and special effects command attention throughout. Innumerable shorter versions of this film exist, including a 1984 reissue with color tints and a Giorgio Moroder score. Major 2010 restoration, with much long-missing footage, runs 153m. ▼▶

Metropolis (2001-Japanese) C-106m. *** D: Rintaro. Voices of Yuka Imoto, Kei Kobayashi, Kohki Okada, Taro Ishida, Kousei Tomita. A private detective and his nephew track a suspect to futuristic Metropolis, meet a mysterious girl who is actually a very powerful robot, and unravel a plot by a military leader who plans to take over the city. Spectacular Japanese anime with original story inspired by Fritz Lang's classic film. Written by Katsuhiro Otomo (AKIRA), based on a graphic novel by Osamu Tezuka (*Astro Boy*). Opulent backdrops contrast with cartoony-looking lead characters, but dramatic storytelling and powerful visuals overcome film's shortcomings. [PG-13]▼▶

Metropolitan (1990) C-98m. *** D: Whit Stillman. Carolyn Farina, Edward Clements, Christopher Eigeman, Taylor Nichols, Allison Rutledge-Parisi, Dylan Hundley, Isabel Gillies, Bryan Leder, Will Kempe, Elizabeth Thompson. Title might suggest teeming masses, but this thoroughly original little film looks instead at N.Y.C.'s upper crust—specifically, the inner circle of debutantes (who haven't yet "come out"), preppies, and their way of life. Social comedy, brimming with irony, is set during Christmas season, with loner Clements drawn into small clique of friends. Sharply written by first-time director Stillman, and well acted by cast of newcomers; Eigeman, as Nick, is a standout. [PG-13]▼▶

Me Without You (2001-British-German) C-107m. **½ D: Sandra Goldbacher. Anna Friel, Michelle Williams, Oliver Milburn, Trudie Styler, Marianne Denicourt, Steve John Shepherd, Nicky Henson, Allan Corduner, Kyle MacLachlan, Anna Popplewell. Shy, sensitive Williams and loose, outgoing Friel have been best pals since childhood, but as they come of age their friendship is compromised. Potentially intriguing female buddy film has some forceful moments, but it doesn't gel. [R]▼▶

Mexican, The (2001) C-123m. ** D: Gore Verbinski. Brad Pitt, Julia Roberts, James

Gandolfini, J.K. Simmons, Michael Cerveris, Bob Balaban, David Krumholtz, Steve Rossi. Barely adequate, overlong caper comedy starring America's sweethearts as a bickering couple who (separately) get involved with thugs all over the Southwest and Mexico. While Pitt hunts down the titular weapon, an antique pistol, amid every conceivable calamity, Roberts and mobster Gandolfini become irrepressible buddies. Gandolfini, predictably, steals the show. Gene Hackman appears unbilled. Super 35. [R] ▼●

Mexican Hayride (1948) 77m. ** D: Charles Barton. Bud Abbott, Lou Costello, Virginia Grey, Luba Malina, John Hubbard, Pedro de Cordoba, Fritz Feld. Lackluster A&C vehicle, with the boys on a wild goose chase with a mine deed in Mexico. Based on a Cole Porter Broadway musical, but without the songs! ▼●

Mexican Spitfire series SEE: *Leonard Maltin's Classic Movie Guide*

Miami Blues (1990) C-99m. ** D: George Armitage. Fred Ward, Alec Baldwin, Jennifer Jason Leigh, Nora Dunn, Charles Napier, Jose Perez, Paul Gleason, Obba Babatunde, Martine Beswicke. Psychopathic thief and murderer (Baldwin) arrives in Miami, hooks up with a naive young woman who's blind to his problems, and sets a world-weary cop on his trail by stealing the detective's badge and I.D. Three dynamic performances and some hip, high-style filmmaking command your attention—but the rampant amorality and violence leave a bad taste. Jonathan Demme and costar Ward were among the producers. From the Charles Willeford novel. [R] ▼●❸

Miami Rhapsody (1995) C-95m. ** D: David Frankel. Sarah Jessica Parker, Mia Farrow, Antonio Banderas, Gil Bellows, Paul Mazursky, Carla Gugino, Naomi Campbell, Jeremy Piven, Kevin Pollak, Mark Blum, Ben Stein. Young woman is afraid of committing to marriage, given the tumult of her parents' and siblings' marital lives. Only problem is that she can't seem to stop *talking* about it. Light comedy, with serious undertones, almost sinks under the weight of talk: an incessant stream of one-line, sitcom-style jokes. Written by the director. Overbearing big band–style score by Mark Isham. [PG-13] ▼●

Miami Vice (2006) C-134m. **½ D: Michael Mann. Jamie Foxx, Colin Farrell, Gong Li, Naomie Harris, Ciarán Hinds, Justin Theroux, Barry Shabaka Henley, Luis Tosar, John Ortiz, Elizabeth Rodriguez, Eddie Marsan, John Hawkes, Isaach De Bankolé. Miami detectives Crockett and Tubbs are back from the stylish 1980s TV series, but this time their pursuit of a ruthless drug lord takes them to Central and South America . . . and Crockett pursues an improbable relationship with the drug czar's sexy business partner. Super-cool

cars, boats, planes keep this fantasy version of cops-and-robbers watchable on a make-believe level, but the final showdown is awfully conventional. Mann, who coexecutive produced the original series, also wrote this screenplay. Director's cut runs 140m. HD Widescreen/Super 35. [R]❸

Michael (1996) C-105m. *** D: Nora Ephron. John Travolta, Andie MacDowell, William Hurt, Robert Pastorelli, Bob Hoskins, Jean Stapleton, Teri Garr, Wally Ward, Joey Lauren Adams, Carla Gugino, Tom Hodges, Wallace Langham. A pair of cynical reporters and a phony "angel expert" discover that a dotty old lady's claim that the archangel Michael is living with her is true. Michael, however, turns out not to be your average angel. Genial, wry movie never goes quite where you expect and takes its sweet time getting there, but the trip is charming, and Travolta, as the seedy, randy Michael, is perfectly cast. Ideal music score by Randy Newman. [PG] ▼●❸

Michael Clayton (2007) C-120m. *** D: Tony Gilroy. George Clooney, Tom Wilkinson, Tilda Swinton, Sydney Pollack, Michael O'Keefe, Ken Howard, David Lansbury, Denis O'Hare, Austin Williams. The morals of a corporate law firm's "fixer" (Clooney) are put to the test when one of its lead attorneys (Wilkinson) reveals damaging evidence in a huge class-action lawsuit. Rock-solid thriller and character study may fall back on some stock elements, but writer/first-time director Gilroy tells his story with supreme assurance, avoiding a lot of obvious melodramatic pitfalls. Wilkinson is tops in an excellent cast and Clooney offers a textbook lesson in understated acting by a Movie Star. Swinton's performance earned her a Best Supporting Actress Oscar. Be sure to sit through the credits. Panavision. [R]❸

Michael Collins (1996-U.S.-Irish) C-132m. *** D: Neil Jordan. Liam Neeson, Aidan Quinn, Julia Roberts, Stephen Rea, Alan Rickman, Ian Hart, Brendan Gleeson, Charles Dance, Gerard McSorley, Jonathan Rhys Myers (Meyers). Politically charged story of Irish rebel leader Collins (Neeson), who with charm, guts, and idealistic fervor leads the fight against British rule in the teens and '20s. Dynamic and powerful first half gives way to more sober and inevitable conclusion, in which Collins is forced to become a diplomat and compromiser—sowing the seeds of his own demise. Neeson is excellent and surrounded by a first-rate cast in this persuasive, believable, and violent period piece, beautifully filmed by Chris Menges. Jordan also scripted. [R] ▼●

Michael Shayne series SEE: *Leonard Maltin's Classic Movie Guide*

Mickey Blue Eyes (1999-U.S.-British) C-103m. **½ D: Kelly Makin. Hugh Grant, James Caan, Jeanne Tripplehorn, Burt

Young, James Fox, Joe Viterelli, Gerry Becker, Maddie Corman. Fitfully amusing farce about a N.Y.C. art auctioneer who asks his girlfriend to marry him—never dreaming that she's part of an Italian mob family. Soon, he's pressed into doing favors for some of "the boys." Starts out funny but soon sputters. [PG-13] ▼O◖

Mickey One (1965) **93m.** **½ D: Arthur Penn. Warren Beatty, Hurd Hatfield, Alexandra Stewart, Franchot Tone, Teddy Hart, Jeff Corey, Kamatari Fujiwara, Donna Michelle. Nightclub comic in trouble with mob takes it on the lam and assumes a new identity. Offbeat, to say the least; Penn's version of a French New Wave film; heavy with visual symbols but we're not quite sure what it's all about. Fine jazz score by Eddie Sauter with solos by Stan Getz. ▼O◖

Micki + Maude (1984) **C-118m.** **½ D: Blake Edwards. Dudley Moore, Amy Irving, Ann Reinking, Richard Mulligan, George Gaynes, Wallace Shawn, John Pleshette, Lu Leonard, Priscilla Pointer, George Coe. Dudley has a wife and a girlfriend—and they're both pregnant! Surprisingly warmhearted comedy that turns into old-fashioned farce. Runs out of steam somewhere along the line but benefits from winning performances by all three leads. Panavision. [PG-13] ▼O◖

Micmacs (2009-French) **C-105m.** ** D: Jean-Pierre Jeunet. Dany Boon, André Dussolier, Nicolas Marié, Jean-Pierre Marielle, Yolande Moreau, Julie Ferrier, Omar Sy, Dominique Pinon, Michel Crémadès, Marie-Julie Baup. A soldier dies while uncovering a land mine; years later a stray bullet punctures the skull of his son, who decides to seek revenge on the arms manufacturers he holds accountable for both incidents. He teams up with a motley gang of misfits, each with a specialty, to pull off a series of ingenious dirty tricks on the two tycoons of weaponry. Jeunet's visual flair and fondness for mechanical gimmickry make this fun at first, but the whimsy is smothered as the film goes on and the "warfare" grows larger in scope. A frustrating misfire with some good ingredients. Super 35. [R]◖

Microcosmos (1996-French-Swiss-Italian) **C-77m.** ***½ D: Claude Nuridsany, Marie Perennou. Strikingly visual nature documentary using high-powered lenses to record a magical universe that hardly can be seen by the human eye: the world of insects, in which beetles, snails, caterpillars, ladybugs, and dragonflies exist amid grass and vines, dewdrops and poppies. An immensely entertaining, endlessly fascinating visual treat; stunningly photographed and edited. U.S. prints feature narration by Kristen Scott Thomas. [G] ▼O◖

Midaq Alley (1995-Mexican) **C-144m.** ** D: Jorge Fons. Ernesto Gómez Cruz, María Rojo, Salma Hayek, Bruno Bichir, Delia Casanova, Margarita Sanz, Claudio Obregón.

Overwrought soap opera featuring several storylines involving characters who frequent a bar at the title locale in Mexico City. Although based on a novel by Nobel Prize winner Naguib Mahfouz, the characters are disappointingly one-dimensional. Hayek is a striking presence as Alma, a poor beauty driven to desperate acts. ▼◖

Midas Run (1969) **C-106m.** **½ D: Alf Kjellin. Fred Astaire, Richard Crenna, Anne Heywood, Ralph Richardson, Roddy McDowall, Cesar Romero. British secret serviceman plots a daring gold heist in this routine caper film, enlivened by Astaire's peerless presence in lead. Fred Astaire, Jr., appears briefly as plane's copilot. [M/PG]

Mid-August Lunch (2008-Italian) **C-76m.** *** D: Gianni Di Gregorio. Gianni Di Gregorio, Valeria De Franciscis, Marina Cacciotti, Maria Calì, Grazia Cesarini Sforza, Alfonso Santagata. Disarming observational comedy about a man who lives with his aged mother in a Rome apartment they can no longer afford. As people prepare to leave town for the Ferragosto holiday on August 15, Gianni finds himself tending to other people's elderly mothers and aunts, in return for rent money and medical services. Leisurely and utterly charming. Leading actor Di Gregorio's directorial debut; he also wrote the semi-autobiographical screenplay (from a story he developed with Simone Riccardini). ◖

Middle Age Crazy (1980-Canadian) **C-95m.** *½ D: John Trent. Bruce Dern, Ann-Margret, Graham Jarvis, Eric Christmas, Deborah Wakeham. Title tells all: 40-year-old Dern buys a Porsche, some new threads, and leaves wife Ann-Margret for pro-football cheerleader Wakeham. Nothing new; inspired by the hit song. [R]▼

Middle Men (2010) **C-109m.** **½ D: George Gallo. Luke Wilson, Giovanni Ribisi, Gabriel Macht, James Caan, Jacinda Barrett, Kevin Pollak, Laura Ramsey, Rade Serbedzija, Terry Crews, Kelsey Grammer, Graham McTavish, Jason Antoon, Robert Forster, John Ashton, Martin Kove. What would seem to be a tall tale is in fact based on the true story of a straight-arrow businessman (Wilson) who pioneered Internet transactions—but happened to do so for a pair of airheads who had the idea of selling pornography online. Happily married family man Wilson tells himself he can remain above the sleaze, but it doesn't turn out that way. Lively, often boisterously funny film is wildly uneven, providing more plot detail than we really need and turning unpleasant in the process. Super 35. [R] ◖

Middle of the World, The (1974-French-Swiss) **C-115m.** *** D: Alain Tanner. Olimpia Carlisi, Philippe Léotard, Juliet Berto, Jacques Denis, Roger Jendly. Intelligent, quietly effective tale of married engineer Léotard, running for political office, who has scandalous affair with waitress Carlisi.

Midnight (1939) **94m.** ***½ D: Mitchell Leisen. Claudette Colbert, Don Ameche, John Barrymore, Francis Lederer, Mary Astor, Hedda Hopper, Monty Woolley. Penniless Colbert masquerades as Hungarian countess in chic Parisian marital mixup; near-classic comedy written by Billy Wilder and Charles Brackett. Barrymore's antics are especially memorable. Remade as MASQUERADE IN MEXICO.▼●

Midnight (1981) **C-94m.** **½ D: John Russo. Lawrence Tierney, Melanie Verliin, John Amplas, John Hall, Charles Jackson, Doris Hackney. Low-budget horror, shot in Pennsylvania, isn't bad. Unfortunate teenager Verliin, driven out of her home by a lecherous policeman stepfather (Tierney), meets two young thieves and then a family of cultists who sacrifice young women. Russo adapted his own novel. Aka BACK-WOODS MASSACRE. Followed by a sequel. [R]▼●

Midnight (1989) **C-86m.** *½ D: Norman Thaddeus Vane. Lynn Redgrave, Tony Curtis, Steven Parrish, Frank Gorshin, Wolfman Jack, Rita Gam. Tiresome story of TV horror-movie hostess who finds people around her mysteriously dying. Always-watchable Redgrave does her best, but meager, slow-moving script does her in. A longer "director's cut" had theatrical showings following its video release. [R]

Midnight Auto Supply SEE: **Love and the Midnight Auto Supply**

Midnight Clear, A (1992) **C-107m.** ***½ D: Keith Gordon. Peter Berg, Kevin Dillon, Arye Gross, Ethan Hawke, Gary Sinise, Frank Whaley, John C. McGinley, Larry Joshua, Curt Lowens. Top-notch anti-war drama, about a squad of young American GI's (led by Hawke) on a mission in the Ardennes Forest near the end of WW2. Refreshingly unhurried film is filled with insight, irony, and eloquence. Extremely well acted and directed; Gordon also scripted, from William Wharton's novel. [R]▼●

Midnight Cop (1989-West German) **C-96m.** **½ D: Peter Patzak. Armin Mueller-Stahl, Michael York, Morgan Fairchild, Frank Stallone, Julia Kent, Monica Bleibtreu, Allegra Curtis. Slow but interesting murder mystery pitting quirky Berlin cop against both a serial killer and a blackmailer. Overdone tenor sax jazz score and murky plot developments hamper things, but Mueller-Stahl is very good. [R]▼●

Midnight Cowboy (1969) **C-113m.** **** D: John Schlesinger. Dustin Hoffman, Jon Voight, Sylvia Miles, John McGiver, Brenda Vaccaro, Barnard Hughes, Ruth White, Jennifer Salt, Bob Balaban. Emotionally shattering dramatization of James Leo Herlihy's novel was rated X in 1969, but it's essentially an old-fashioned story with some unusual modern twists: hayseed Voight comes to N.Y.C. in hopes of becoming a freelance stud, and develops unusual and deep friendship with seedy Ratso Rizzo (Hoffman). Seamiest side of N.Y.C. is backdrop for compelling, keen-eyed character study that if anything looks better today than it did when it came out. Won Best Picture, Director, Screenplay (Waldo Salt) Oscars. Graphic effects by Pablo Ferro. [R—edited from original X rating]▼●●

Midnight Crossing (1988) **C-104m.** *½ D: Roger Holzberg. Faye Dunaway, Daniel J. Travanti, Kim Cattrall, Ned Beatty, John Laughlin. Hokey, boring, needlessly violent soaper-adventure, with insurance agent Travanti intent on recovering some booty he and his late pal buried years before. Dunaway is thanklessly cast as his wife, who is blind. [R]▼●●

Midnight Express (1978) **C-121m.** ***½ D: Alan Parker. Brad Davis, Irene Miracle, Bo Hopkins, Randy Quaid, John Hurt, Mike Kellin, Paul Smith. Riveting, harshly violent story of young American Billy Hayes (Davis), who faces physical and emotional brutalization in Turkish prison after being caught drug-smuggling. Great moviemaking, though not as faithful to Hayes' true story as filmmakers would have us believe. Oscar winner for Oliver Stone's script and Giorgio Moroder's score. [R]▼●

Midnight in Paris (2011-U.S.-Spanish) **C-100m.** *** D: Woody Allen. Owen Wilson, Rachel McAdams, Marion Cotillard, Michael Sheen, Kathy Bates, Adrien Brody, Mimi Kennedy, Kurt Fuller, Alison Pill, Tom Hiddleston, Léa Seydoux, Corey Stoll, Carla Bruni, Gad Elmaleh. Hack Hollywood writer Wilson travels to Paris with his fiancée, hoping to find inspiration for a novel from the city that was home to so many legendary artists and writers in the 1920s. Then, magically, he is transported back to that time and meets them face-to-face. A *divertissement* from Allen filled with wistful charm, although it won't stand up to scrutiny; either you go along with its fantasy premise or you don't. Wilson is the best in a long line of Woody surrogates because he truly makes the part his own. [PG-13]

Midnight in the Garden of Good and Evil (1997) **C-155m.** ** D: Clint Eastwood. Kevin Spacey, John Cusack, Jack Thompson, The Lady Chablis, Alison Eastwood, Irma P. Hall, Paul Hipp, Jude Law, Dorothy Loudon, Anne Haney, Kim Hunter, Geoffrey Lewis, Richard Herd, James Moody. Meandering adaptation of John Berendt's best-seller about some of the more eccentric denizens of Savannah, Georgia. Cusack plays a N.Y. reporter assigned to cover Spacey's A-list Christmas party; when that gracious, noveau riche bon vivant is accused of murder later the same night, Cusack decides to stick around and see what happens. Never terribly compelling, despite several likable performances, and fatally overlong. [R]▼●●

Midnight Lace (1960) **C-108m.** *** D:

David Miller. Doris Day, Rex Harrison, John Gavin, Myrna Loy, Roddy McDowall, Herbert Marshall, Natasha Parry, Anthony Dawson. Shrill murder mystery; unbelievable plot line, but star cast and decor smooth over rough spots. Set in London; redone as a TVM in 1980.▼

Midnight Madness (1980) **C-110m.** BOMB D: David Wechter, Michael Nankin. David Naughton, Debra Clinger, Eddie Deezen, Brad Wilkin, Maggie Roswell, Stephen Furst. Idiotic comedy about college students participating in an all-night scavenger hunt. Nothing to stay up for (unless you want to see Michael J. Fox in his feature film debut). [PG]▼●

Midnight Man, The (1974) **C-117m. **½** D: Roland Kibbee, Burt Lancaster. Burt Lancaster, Susan Clark, Cameron Mitchell, Morgan Woodward, Joan Lorring, Ed Lauter, Catherine Bach, Linda Kelsey, Harris Yulin. Involved, overlong mystery with Lancaster as college security officer looking into a coed's murder. Lancaster and Kibbee also cowrote and coproduced. [R]

Midnight Run (1988) **C-122m. ***½** D: Martin Brest. Robert De Niro, Charles Grodin, Yaphet Kotto, John Ashton, Dennis Farina, Joe Pantoliano, Wendy Phillips, Richard Foronjy. Socko action-comedy with bounty hunter (and ex-cop) De Niro determined to bring bail-jumper Grodin, an embezzling accountant, from N.Y. to L.A. What De Niro *doesn't* know is that the Mob is also on Grodin's trail—with orders to kill. Sensational byplay between the stars is matched by first-rate action and a sharply written script by George Gallo. Director Brest handles the blend of violence and comedy as well as he did in BEVERLY HILLS COP. Dynamic music score by Danny Elfman. Followed by a TV series. [R]▼●

Midsummer Night's Dream, A (1935) **117m. ***** D: Max Reinhardt, William Dieterle. James Cagney, Dick Powell, Joe E. Brown, Jean Muir, Hugh Herbert, Olivia de Havilland, Ian Hunter, Frank McHugh, Victor Jory, Ross Alexander, Verree Teasdale, Anita Louise, Mickey Rooney, Arthur Treacher, Billy Barty. Hollywood-Shakespeare has good and bad points; Cagney as Bottom and the Mendelssohn music are among good parts; Hugh Herbert and other incongruous cast members make up the latter. After a while Rooney (as Puck) gets to be a bit too much. Hal Mohr's glistening cinematography won an Oscar—the only one ever awarded on a write-in. This was the only sound film of esteemed European stage director Reinhardt. Film debut of Olivia de Havilland (who had appeared in Reinhardt's Hollywood Bowl production of the play a year earlier). Originally 132m.▼●

Midsummer Night's Dream, A (1966) **C-93m. **½** D: Dan Eriksen. Suzanne Farrell, Edward Villella, Arthur Mitchell, Mimi

Paul, Nicholas Magallanes. Filmed record of New York City Ballet's presentation of Shakespeare's comedy is mostly for dance buffs; makes some attempt to be cinematic, but not enough. Panavision.

Midsummer Night's Dream, A (1968-British) **C-124m. **½** D: Peter Hall. Diana Rigg, David Warner, Michael Jayston, Ian Richardson, Judi Dench, Ian Holm, Bill Travers, Helen Mirren. Fine cast of England's Royal Shakespeare Co. in middling performance of the Shakespeare classic.▼●

Midsummer Night's Dream, A (1999) **C-115m. **½** D: Michael Hoffman. Kevin Kline, Michelle Pfeiffer, Rupert Everett, Stanley Tucci, Calista Flockhart, Anna Friel, Christian Bale, Dominic West, David Strathair, Sophie Marceau, Roger Rees, Max Wright, Gregory Jbara, Bill Irwin, Sam Rockwell, Bernard Hill, John Sessions. Shakespeare's classic comedy transported from ancient Greece to late-19th-century Italy (complete with newly invented bicycles). Young love runs wild, with Everett and Pfeiffer as King and Queen of the Fairies, Tucci a spirited Puck and Kline (in his element) a buffoonish Bottom. Works better in parts than as a whole, but still enjoyable for lovers of the play. Full on-screen title is WILLIAM SHAKESPEARE'S A MIDSUMMER NIGHT'S DREAM. 2.35 Research PLC. [PG-13]▼●

Midsummer Night's Sex Comedy, A (1982) **C-88m. **** D: Woody Allen. Woody Allen, Mia Farrow, Jose Ferrer, Mary Steenburgen, Tony Roberts, Julie Hagerty. SMILES OF A SUMMER NIGHT, Woody Allen–style; a quirky, entertaining diversion about sexual byplay among three couples on a summer weekend in the country, circa 1900. Appealing cast (including Farrow, in first film with Woody), exquisite Gordon Willis photography. [PG]▼●

Midway (1976) **C-132m. **** D: Jack Smight. Charlton Heston, Henry Fonda, James Coburn, Glenn Ford, Hal Holbrook, Robert Mitchum, Cliff Robertson, Toshiro Mifune, Robert Wagner, Edward Albert, Robert Webber, Ed Nelson, James Shigeta, Monte Markham, Christopher George, Glenn Corbett. Prominent cast acts to reels of stock shots from THIRTY SECONDS OVER TOKYO, antique Japanese war films, and actual wartime footage. Silly soap opera (Heston's ensign son in love with Japanese girl) doesn't help. Still, some of the drama and impact of the great naval battle comes through. *Many* familiar faces in cast: Tom Selleck, Kevin Dobson, Pat Morita, Dabney Coleman, Erik Estrada, Steve Kanaly, etc. Paul Frees dubbed Mifune's English dialogue. Panavision. [PG] ▼●

Midwinter's Tale, A (1995-British) **98m. **½** D: Kenneth Branagh. Michael Maloney, Richard Briers, Mark Hadfield, Nicholas Farrell, Gerard Horan, John Sessions, Celia

Imrie, Hetta Charnley, Julia Sawalha, Joan Collins, Jennifer Saunders. Unemployed actor decides to mount a free-form production of *Hamlet* in a remote English town with an all-volunteer cast and crew. Uneven comedy hits its stride in the final portion of the film as the cast and production for the play come together and the parallels between their real lives and their stage lives are revealed. A little too pat, but likable. Original screenplay by Branagh, who tailored many of the parts for these specific actors. Original British title: IN THE BLEAK MIDWINTER. [R] ▼●◗

Mifune (1999-Danish) **C-99m.** **½ D: Soren Kragh-Jacobsen. Anders W. Berthelsen, Iben Hjejle, Jesper Asholt, Emil Tarding, Anders Hove, Sofie Gråbol, Paprika Steen, Mette Bratlann. A newly married businessman returns home to take care of his mentally handicapped brother after their father dies. Complications follow when the housekeeper he hires turns out to be an ex-hooker with problems of her own. Filmed according to the spartan cinematic rules of Dogma 95, this has good acting and lovely isolated moments, but not enough to overcome a thin story with few surprises. Mifune, by the way, refers to actor Toshiro. [R] ▼▮

Mighty, The (1998) **C-100m.** ***½ D: Peter Chelsom. Kieran Culkin, Elden Henson, Sharon Stone, Gena Rowlands, Harry Dean Stanton, Gillian Anderson, James Gandolfini, Meat Loaf, Jenifer Lewis. Beautifully realized story of two young misfits who bond together and become, in their hearts and imaginations, invincible as the knights of old. Poetic and heart-rending, with remarkable performances by the youthful leading actors. Screenplay by Charles Leavitt from the novel *Freak the Mighty* by Rodman Philbrick. [PG-13] ▼●◗

Mighty Aphrodite (1995) **C-95m.** *** D: Woody Allen. F. Murray Abraham, Woody Allen, Claire Bloom, Helena Bonham Carter, Olympia Dukakis, Michael Rapaport, Mira Sorvino, David Ogden Stiers, Jack Warden, Peter Weller, Steven Randazzo, Donald Symington, Rosemary Murphy, Tony Sirico, Paul Giamatti. Highly entertaining fluff with Woody as a happily married man whose wife convinces him to adopt a baby; then, years later, he becomes obsessed with learning about (and getting to know) the boy's real mother. Sorvino is sensational in an Oscar-winning performance as the woman in question. [R] ▼●◗

Mighty Ducks, The (1992) **C-100m.** ** D: Stephen Herek. Emilio Estevez, Joss Ackland, Lane Smith, Heidi Kling, Josef Sommer, Joshua Jackson, Elden Ratliff (Hansen), Shaun Weiss, Matt Doherty. Harmless, clichéd Disney yarn of self-centered yuppie lawyer Estevez who's busted for drunk-driving, ordered to do community service, and assigned to coach a ragtag inner-

city peewee hockey team. Guess what happens next. (Anaheim-based pro hockey team was formed by Disney in 1993 called . . . you guessed it.) Followed by D2: THE MIGHTY DUCKS, D3: THE MIGHTY DUCKS, an animated series, and a TVM based on that series. [PG] ▼●◗

Mighty Heart, A (2007) **C-108m.** *** D: Michael Winterbottom. Angelina Jolie, Dan Futterman, Archie Panjabi, Irrfan Khan, Will Patton, Denis O'Hare, Adnan Siddiqui, Gary Wilmes, Alyy Khan. Gripping account of *Wall Street Journal* reporter Daniel Pearl's 2002 kidnapping in Pakistan and the desperate efforts of his journalist wife Mariane (Jolie) and others to find him. Jolie is excellent in this superbly crafted film, which unfolds in documentary style that does not cheapen the tragic subject matter but tends to keep the viewer at an emotional distance. Based on Mariane's memoir. Brad Pitt coproduced. Super 35. [R] ▮

Mighty Joe Young (1949) **94m.** *** D: Ernest B. Schoedsack. Terry Moore, Ben Johnson, Robert Armstrong, Mr. Joseph Young, Frank McHugh. Updating of KING KONG theme has comparable (and Oscar-winning) stop-motion special effects by Willis O'Brien and Ray Harryhausen, but no matching storyline, and Moore is no Fay Wray. Mr. Young is good, though. Last sequence was originally shown with color tints, which have been restored for most prints. Also shown in computer-colored version. Remade in 1998. ▼●◗

Mighty Joe Young (1998) **C-114m.** *** D: Ron Underwood. Bill Paxton, Charlize Theron, David Paymer, Regina King, Rade Sherbedgia (Serbedzija), Peter Firth, Linda Purl, Robert Wisdom, Lawrence Pressman, John Alexander, Naveen Andrews, Christian Clemenson. Entertaining update of the 1949 movie: Theron is raised in the jungle alongside a giant gorilla. In order to protect Joe from poachers, she agrees to bring him to an L.A. animal habitat—but no one understands the big guy as she does. What is more, a bad guy is out to get him, leading to an inevitable rampage. Good fun, earnestly done. Terry Moore (star of the 1949 film) and Ray Harryhausen (who helped animate the original Joe) have a cameo together; so does Dina Merrill, whose husband produced the film. Joe was designed by Rick Baker. [PG] ▼●◗

Mighty Morphin Power Rangers: The Movie (1995-U.S.-Japanese) **C-95m.** **½ D: Bryan Spicer. Karan Ashley, Johnny Yong Bosch, Steve Cardenas, Jason David Frank, Amy Jo Johnson, David Yost, Paul Schrier, Jason Narvy, Paul Freeman, Gabrielle Fitzpatrick, Nicholas Bell. The teenage Rangers temporarily lose their powers when primordial bad guy Ivan Ooze reappears after centuries of captivity and attacks their mentor, sending them on a quest for renewed power. Juvenile fantasy/adventure aimed squarely at the huge audience of the same-named TV series . . . and not bad, for what it is. Followed by TURBO: A POWER RANGERS MOVIE, then in 1999 a direct-to-video sequel. [PG] ▼●)

Mighty Quinn, The (1989) C-98m. **½ D: Carl Schenkel. Denzel Washington, Robert Townsend, James Fox, Mimi Rogers, M. Emmet Walsh, Sheryl Lee Ralph, Art Evans, Esther Rolle, Norman Beaton, Keye Luke. Washington plays the independent-minded police chief of a Caribbean island who's determined to get to the bottom of a murder, even though it apparently involves political sensitivities—and his boyhood pal, a now-notorious character played by Townsend. Colorful locale spices this ordinary tale and makes it a pleasant time-filler. [R] ▼●)

Mighty Wind, A (2003) C-92m. *** D: Christopher Guest. Christopher Guest, Michael McKean, Harry Shearer, Eugene Levy, Catherine O'Hara, Bob Balaban, Fred Willard, Parker Posey, Jane Lynch, John Michael Higgins, Jennifer Coolidge, Ed Begley, Jr., Larry Miller, Michael Hitchcock, Paul Dooley. When a veteran folk-music promoter dies, one of his sons launches a reunion concert of disparate folkies at N.Y.C.'s Town Hall. So droll that you have to pinch yourself to realize just how dead-on its satirical skewering is, including a host of bogus '60s folk songs (and even album covers). Treats its targets a bit more gently than WAITING FOR GUFFMAN and BEST IN SHOW; it's even touching at times. Willard is a scream as a showbiz promoter and "idea man" whose ideas could sink a continent. Screenplay by Guest and Levy. [PG-13] ▼)

Mike's Murder (1984) C-109m. *½ D: James Bridges. Debra Winger, Mark Keyloun, Darrell Larson, Paul Winfield, Brooke Alderson, William Ostrander, Dan Shor. One of the worst movies ever made by a filmmaker of Bridges' stature; after an acquaintance is butchered in a drug deal, Winger decides to investigate for herself. Filmed in 1982, followed by years at the editing table to no avail; Winfield provides only life as jaded record exec. Escapes BOMB rating only because several critics thought highly of it. [R] ▼

Mikey and Nicky (1976) C-116m. **½ D: Elaine May. Peter Falk, John Cassavetes, Ned Beatty, Rose Arrick, Carol Grace, Joyce Van Patten. Ragged film (in the editing room for several years) improves as it goes along, examining relationship between small-time hoods who were childhood pals, one of whom may be fingering the other for hit man Beatty. Superb performances by Falk and Cassavetes. [R] ▼)

Milagro Beanfield War, The (1988) C-117m. ***½ D: Robert Redford. Ruben Blades, Richard Bradford, Sonia Braga, Julie Carmen, James Gammon, Melanie Griffith, John Heard, Carlos Riquelme, Daniel Stern, Chick Vennera, Christopher Walken, Freddy Fender, Robert Carricart, M. Emmet Walsh, Trinidad Silva. Spirited, fanciful tale of a rugged individualist (dirt-poor, hard-luck Vennera) who decides to stand up to the big, brash developers who plan to milk his (and his neighbors') New Mexico land for all it's worth. Distilled from John Nichols' sprawling novel by Nichols and David Ward, this film takes a whimsical tone that's positively infectious . . . aided by a top ensemble cast, beautiful scenery, and Dave Grusin's lyrical, Oscar-winning score. [R] ▼●)

Mildred Pierce (1945) 109m. ***½ D: Michael Curtiz. Joan Crawford, Jack Carson, Zachary Scott, Eve Arden, Ann Blyth, Bruce Bennett, Lee Patrick, Butterfly McQueen. Crawford won an Oscar as housewife-turned-waitress who finds success in business but loses control of ungrateful daughter Blyth—especially when she finds they're competing for the love of the same man. Solid adaptation (scripted by Ranald MacDougall) of James M. Cain's novel with top supporting cast. Also shown in computer-colored version. Remade as a cable miniseries in 2011. ▼●)

Miles From Home (1988) C-114m. *½ D: Gary Sinise. Richard Gere, Kevin Anderson, Penelope Ann Miller, Laurie Metcalf, John Malkovich, Brian Dennehy, Judith Ivey, Helen Hunt, Terry Kinney. The "Farm of the Year" from 1959 goes bankrupt in 1988; heir Gere burns it down rather than see it taken over by the bank, then takes off on a Midwest spree accompanied by acquiescent brother Anderson. Gere's actions (and performance) are so off-putting that you begin to wonder if he doesn't deserve his fate, which can hardly be the point. Miller and Metcalf put spins on marginal roles. [R] ▼●

Milk (2008) C-127m. ***½ D: Gus Van Sant. Sean Penn, James Franco, Emile Hirsch, Josh Brolin, Diego Luna, Alison Pill, Victor Garber, Denis O'Hare, Joseph Cross, Stephen Spinella. Exceptional biopic about Harvey Milk, America's pioneering openly gay elected official, who changed both laws and perceptions as a San Francisco city supervisor in the 1970s. Penn disappears into the character of the sweet but forceful man who never gave up, despite repeated setbacks—and the knowledge that he might be cut down in his prime. Dustin Lance Black's expansive screenplay covers a lot of territory, both personal and public, while Van Sant's seamless interweaving of vintage news footage and re-creations transports us back in time. Milk's crusade, and the vitriolic response to it, has uncanny modern-day resonance. Oscar winner for Best Actor (Penn) and Best Original Screenplay. See also: THE TIMES OF HARVEY MILK. [R]❱

[916]

Milk Money (1994) **C-102m.** *½ D: Richard Benjamin. Melanie Griffith, Ed Harris, Michael Patrick Carter, Malcolm McDowell, Anne Heche, Casey Siemaszko, Philip Bosco. "Family-values" comedy about a 12-year-old who raises funds to ogle a sexy hooker—who later turns up in his hometown! Not as grubby as it sounds, but still an unlikely candidate to contribute to anyone's Irving G. Thalberg Award chances. McDowell overplays it, if that's possible in this kind of DOA dud, as a mobster. [PG-13] ▼●〗

Milky Way, The (1969-French) **C-102m.** ***½ D: Luis Buñuel. Paul Frankeur, Laurent Terzieff, Alain Cuny, Bernard Verley, Michel Piccoli, Pierre Clementi, Georges Marchal, Delphine Seyrig. Two men making religious pilgrimage through France form basis for string of Buñuel "jokes," parables, surrealistic visions. Heretical, funny, haunting, thoroughly enjoyable. [M/PG] ▼●〗

Millennium (1989) **C-108m.** ** D: Michael Anderson. Kris Kristofferson, Cheryl Ladd, Robert Joy, Daniel J. Travanti, Brent Carver, Maury Chaykin, David McIlwraith, Al Waxman, Lloyd Bochner. Intriguing premise features time travelers from the future kidnapping doomed passengers from crashing airliners; suspicious crash investigator Kristofferson becomes involved with Ladd, one of the time travelers. Story slowly falls apart, decaying into sheer corn. Highly regarded sci-fi writer John Varley adapted his own short story "Air Raid," but someone didn't trust the audience's intelligence. [PG-13] ▼●〗

Millennium Actress (2002-Japanese) **C/B&W-87m.** **½ D: Satoshi Kon. Voices of Miyoko Shôji, Mami Koyama, Fumiko Orikasa, Shozo Iizuka, Masaya Onosaka. A legendary actress agrees to give a rare interview to a documentary filmmaker and reveals personal secrets that allow the director and his cameraman to vicariously experience her life and times. Mature, literate Japanese animated feature makes innovative use of flashbacks but never quite lives up to the potential inherent in the story. Especially interesting to anyone who knows Japanese film history, as the actress spans the eras of propaganda films, Samurai sagas, and monster movies. [PG] ▼〗

Millennium Mambo (2001-French-Taiwanese) **C-119m.** *½ D: Hou Hsiao Hsien. Shu Qi, Jack Kao, Tuan Chun-Hao, Chen Yi-Hsuan, Maggie Cheung. Disappointing downer from acclaimed director concerns a young, beautiful girl caught in a dead-end life in Taipei. Scenes with her drugged-out boyfriend and a small-time mobster at the club where she occasionally works don't add up to much. Film's apparent point is that it's tough being young nowadays. Hip score and flashy camerawork

can't really compensate for the empty tale being told. [R] ▼〗

Miller's Crossing (1990) **C-115m.** **½ D: Joel Coen. Gabriel Byrne, Albert Finney, Marcia Gay Harden, John Turturro, Jon Polito, J.E. Freeman, Mike Starr, Al Mancini, Michael Jeter, Steve Buscemi. Moody, stylish, and pretentious take on gangster films by the Coen brothers (Joel directed and cowrote with producer-brother Ethan). Byrne plays a black-hearted Irish mobster with a code of ethics known only to himself, and a vow of loyalty to crime kingpin Finney. Dense and dour, it's almost doggedly off-putting at first, but gets more involving as its serpentine story unfolds. Some bravura moments, along with Barry Sonnenfeld's compelling cinematography. Frances McDormand has unbilled bit as a secretary. [R] ▼●〗

Millionairess, The (1960-British) **C-90m.** **½ D: Anthony Asquith. Sophia Loren, Peter Sellers, Alastair Sim, Vittorio De Sica, Dennis Price. Loren is an heiress who thinks money can buy anything, until she meets Indian doctor Sellers, who won't sell his principles, or his love. Sophia is stunning, but this adaptation of G. B. Shaw's play is heavy-handed comedy. CinemaScope. ▼〗

Million Dollar Baby (2004) **C-133m.** *** D: Clint Eastwood. Clint Eastwood, Hilary Swank, Morgan Freeman, Anthony Mackie, Jay Baruchel, Mike Colter, Lucia Rijker, Brian O'Byrne, Margo Martindale. Aging fight manager/trainer reluctantly takes on a 31-year-old woman as his newest client and is soon won over by her heart, determination, and talent. Entertaining, picaresque look at emotionally wounded people who find comfort in each other's protection; propelled by strong performances and flavorful narration by Freeman. Screenplay by Paul Haggis, from stories in *Rope Burns* by F. X. Toole. Oscar winner for Best Picture, Director, Actress, and Supporting Actor (Freeman). Panavision. [PG-13] ▼〗

Million Dollar Duck, The (1971) **C-92m.** **½ D: Vincent McEveety. Dean Jones, Sandy Duncan, Joe Flynn, Tony Roberts, James Gregory, Lee H. Montgomery. A duck who lays golden eggs spurs predictable twists and turns in this standard Disney comedy. [G] ▼〗

Million Dollar Hotel, The (2000-German-U.S.) **C-122m.** **½ D: Wim Wenders. Jeremy Davies, Milla Jovovich, Mel Gibson, Jimmy Smits, Donal Logue, Gloria Stuart, Bud Cort, Amanda Plummer, Julian Sands, Peter Stormare, Charlayne Woodard, Ellen Cleghorne, Harris Yulin, Tim Roth. Wacko, DAVID AND LISA–type story of two mentally ill young lovers in an L.A. welfare hotel. Bono (of U2) cowrote the confounding, convoluted script, which will try your patience, but Wenders' lensing has its share of visual poetry, and Davies and Jovovich are effective leads. Colorful supporting cast helps, too. (Gibson, as an FBI agent with a Frankenstein-like back brace, seems to be in a different movie altogether.) Panavision. [R]▼▶

Million Dollar Legs (1932) 61m. ***½ D: Edward Cline. W. C. Fields, Jack Oakie, Susan Fleming, Lyda Roberti, Andy Clyde, Ben Turpin, Dickie Moore, Billy Gilbert, Hugh Herbert. Wacky nonsense with Fields as President of Klopstokia, a nutty country entering the Olympics. Oakie is a young American pursuing W. C.'s daughter (Fleming). Joseph Mankiewicz was one of the writers of this little gem. Title on-screen is MILLION $ LEGS.▼

Million Dollar Mermaid (1952) C-115m. **½ D: Mervyn LeRoy. Esther Williams, Victor Mature, Walter Pidgeon, David Brian, Donna Corcoran, Jesse White, Maria Tallchief. Williams does OK as real-life aquatic star Annette Kellerman, alternating her swimming with romancing Mature. Some typically elaborate production numbers by Busby Berkeley.▼◆❚

Million Dollar Mystery (1987) C-95m. ** D: Richard Fleischer. Eddie Deezen, Penny Baker, Tom Bosley, Rich Hall, Wendy Sherman, Rick Overton, Mona Lyden, Kevin Pollak. Bosley, in his dying breath, informs customers at a roadside diner that $4 million is hidden nearby—giving them just enough clues to send the rabid group scrambling. Shameless rip-off of IT'S A MAD MAD MAD MAD WORLD is directed with more gusto than you'd expect from Fleischer. See how many plugs for Glad Bags (cosponsor, along with De Laurentiis Entertainment Group, of a real-life promotional million-dollar treasure hunt) you can spot. J-D-C Scope. [PG]▼◆❚

Million Eyes of Su-Muru, The (1967) C-95m. ** D: Lindsay Shonteff. Frankie Avalon, George Nader, Shirley Eaton, Wilfrid Hyde-White, Klaus Kinski. Tongue-in-cheek tale of murder and women's organization bent on enslaving all of mankind. From a Sax Rohmer story. Techniscope.

Millions (2005-British) C-98m. *** D: Danny Boyle. Alexander Nathan Etel, Lewis Owen McGibbon, James Nesbitt, Daisy Donovan, Christopher Fulford, Jane Hogarth. A smart, surprising and spiritual change of pace for TRAINSPOTTING director Boyle. Two young brothers have one week to spend a bagful of money they've come across, before the British pound switches over to the Euro. The choices the boys make not only say a lot about each of them but serve as a reflection of how society views the conflict between instant wealth and moral values. Newcomer Etel provides genuinely touching moments that are never maudlin. Boyle's zippy visuals are another plus; he forgoes the usually dreary movie look of British neighborhoods to make these sunny English 'burbs look like a Technicolor haven. Super 35. [PG]▼▶

Million to Juan, A (1993) C-97m. **½ D: Paul Rodriguez. Paul Rodriguez, Tony Plana, Bert Rosario, Polly Draper, Jonathan Hernandez, Larry Linville, Victor Rivers, David Rasche, Edward James Olmos, Pepe Serna, Paul Williams, Cheech Marin, Ruben Blades. Poor but honest, much put-upon Rodriguez, widowed with a ten-year-old son, is inexplicably given a check for $1 million. Predictable comedy-fantasy is uplifted by some sweet, touching moments. Based on a Mark Twain story, "The Million Pound Bank Note"; previously filmed as MAN WITH A MILLION. [PG]▼▶

Milwaukee, Minnesota (2005) C-95m. ** D: Allan Mindel. Troy Garity, Alison Folland, Randy Quaid, Bruce Dern, Hank Harris, Debra Monk, Josh Brolin, Holly Woodlawn. Paper-thin account of a mentally challenged young man who is an expert ice fisherman and the con artists who attempt to exploit him. Aims for a quirky tone, but turns out to be conventional—and forgettable. [R]❚

Mimic (1997) C-105m. *** D: Guillermo del Toro. Mira Sorvino, Jeremy Northam, Charles S. Dutton, Alexander Goodwin, Giancarlo Giannini, Josh Brolin, F. Murray Abraham. Entomologist Sorvino creates a non-breeding insect to wipe out a plague of disease-carrying cockroaches. This works, but three years later, the *cure* is getting out of hand. The hybrids bred after all, and have become giants, capable of disguising themselves as their favorite prey: people. Lively, scary sci-fi thriller becomes conventional in the last third; until then it's great fun. From Donald A. Wollheim's short story. Followed by two direct-to-video sequels. [R] ▼◆❚

Mina Tannenbaum (1994-French) C-123m. *** D: Martine Dugowson. Romane Bohringer, Elsa Zylberstein, Florence Thomassin, Jean-Philippe Ecoffey, Nils Tavernier, Stephane Slima, Hugues Quester. Entertaining melodrama about the friendship between two Jewish Parisian girls, an introspective artist and a brash reporter, and its disintegration when they fall in love with the same man. First half plays like a Nora Ephron coming-of-age comedy, while the rest is pure Max Ophuls. Despite the unevenness, the film is buoyed by two great performances from Zylberstein and Bohringer (in the title role). [R]▼

Minbo: Anti-Extortion Woman (1992-Japanese) C-123m. *** D: Juzo Itami. Nobuku Miyamoto, Akira Takarada, Masahiro Murata, Yasuo Daichi, Hideji Otaki, Hoboru Mitani, Shiro Ito, Akira Nakao. Wonderful wish-fulfillment comedy with the canny, super-competent (but diminutive) Miyamoto helping hapless hotel managers to confront the most intimidating Yakuza members in Hong Kong. A big hit in Japan, this film also inspired real-life Yakuza to attack writer-director Itami. Aka MINBO: THE GENTLE ART OF JAPANESE EXTORTION.▼

Mind Benders, The (1963-British) **101m.** *** D: Basil Dearden. Dirk Bogarde, Mary Ure, John Clements, Michael Bryant, Wendy Craig, Edward Fox. Top cast in slow-moving but compelling account of experiments in sensory deprivation, with espionage theme worked into plot.▶

Mind Field (1990-Canadian) **C-92m.** ** D: Jean-Claude Lord. Michael Ironside, Lisa Langlois, Sean McCann, Christopher Plummer, Stefan Wodoslawsky, Harvey Atkin, Eugene Clark. Montreal cop Ironside is plagued by problems on the job, mysterious killings, and strange LSD-like flashbacks connected to CIA researcher Plummer. Complicated, slow movie tries to cover too much ground (including police unions and JFK's assassination). [R]▼●

Mind Games SEE: **Agency**

Mindhunters (2004-British-Dutch-Finnish-U.S.) **C-106m.** ** D: Renny Harlin. Eion Bailey, Patricia Velasquez, Clifton Collins, Jr., Will Kemp, Val Kilmer, Jonny Lee Miller, Kathryn Morris, Christian Slater, James Todd Smith (LL Cool J), Cassandra Bell. A group of FBI agents-in-training are left on an isolated island designed to test their skills as profilers—but one of them is a serial killer intent on murdering the others, one by one. Moderately suspenseful and well-acted thriller sticks too closely to the TEN LITTLE INDIANS formula. Filmed in 2002. Super 35. [R]▶

Mind of Mr. Soames, The (1970-British) **C-95m.** ***½ D: Alan Cooke. Terence Stamp, Robert Vaughn, Nigel Davenport, Christian Roberts. Exceptionally fine sci-fi tale of man who has been in a coma since birth; finally revived, he must be taught 30 years' worth of knowledge in brief span of time. [M/PG]▶

Mind Snatchers, The SEE: **Happiness Cage, The**

Mindwalk (1991) **C-110m.** ** D: Bernt Capra. Liv Ullmann, Sam Waterston, John Heard, Ione Skye. Unusual ecological talkfest may be the MY DINNER WITH ANDRE of the environmental movement. Mainly a conversation on the sad state of the world among three people (a poet, a physicist, and a politician) roaming a picturesque French isle. Sometimes fascinating; mostly static, pretentious. If you met up with any of these people at a party, you'd be fumbling for the car keys. [PG]▼

Mindwarp: An Infinity of Terror SEE: **Galaxy of Terror**

Mini's First Time (2006) **C-91m.** *½ D: Nick Guthe. Alec Baldwin, Nikki Reed, Carrie-Anne Moss, Jeff Goldblum, Luke Wilson, Svetlana Metkina, Sprague Grayden, Rick Fox. Slutty teen (THIR-TEEN's Reed), living in a hilltop L.A. mansion, opts to turn tricks to spite her mother. Soon stepfather Baldwin gets involved—in more ways than one. Tantalizingly overripe performances from the strong cast cannot overcome this unconvincingly scripted satire. [R]▶

Miniskirt Mob, The (1968) **C-82m.** *½ D: Maury Dexter. Jeremy Slate, Diane McBain, Sherry Jackson, Patty McCormack, Ross Hagen, Harry Dean Stanton, Ronnie Rondell. McBain plays leader of female motorcycle gang, even though she looks as if she'd be more comfortable on a Tournament of Roses float. Those who like the title will probably like the film.▶

Ministry of Fear (1944) **85m.** *** D: Fritz Lang. Ray Milland, Marjorie Reynolds, Carl Esmond, Dan Duryea, Hillary Brooke, Alan Napier, Percy Waram. Atmospheric thriller of wartime London, with Milland framed in complicated espionage plot; good cast, fine touches by director Lang. From the Graham Greene novel.▼

Miniver Story, The (1950) **104m.** **½ D: H. C. Potter. Greer Garson, Walter Pidgeon, John Hodiak, Leo Genn, Cathy O'Donnell, Henry Wilcoxon, Reginald Owen, Peter Finch. Sequel to MRS. MINIVER (filmed this time in England) doesn't work as well, but Garson and Pidgeon have some poignant scenes as family reunited in post-WW2 England. Young James Fox, billed as William, makes his film debut.▼

Minnie and Moskowitz (1971) **C-114m.** *** D: John Cassavetes. Gena Rowlands, Seymour Cassel, Val Avery, Timothy Carey, Katherine Cassavetes, Elsie Ames. One of Cassavetes' most likable films chronicles manic romance between lonely museum curator (Rowlands) and crazy parking-lot attendant (Cassel). Touching, amusing, and most enjoyable. [PG]▼▶

Minority Report (2002) **C-144m.** **½ D: Steven Spielberg. Tom Cruise, Colin Farrell, Samantha Morton, Max von Sydow, Lois Smith, Peter Stormare, Tim Blake Nelson, Kathryn Morris, Jessica Capshaw, Jessica Harper, Arye Gross. In the year 2054, Cruise is the top cop in an elite D.C. unit that uses seers to predict and stop crimes before they occur, but the controversial program is under fire by the Feds. High-tech, highly charged sci-fi saga has many fine ingredients, but goes on far too long (especially considering it was adapted from a short story, by Philip K. Dick). Multiple endings, and growing confusion, diminish the effectiveness of the film, one of Spielberg's harshest. Excellent score by John Williams. Super 35. [PG-13] ▼▶

Minotaur (1976) SEE: **Land of the Minotaur**

Minus Man, The (1999) **C-112m.** **½ D: Hampton Fancher. Owen Wilson, Janeane Garofalo, Brian Cox, Sheryl Crow,

Mercedes Ruehl, Dennis Haysbert, Dwight Yoakam. Serial killer takes up residence in a middle-age suburban couple's spare room and hires on as a fellow postal worker with his landlord. Film's low-budget creepiness, though fairly effective, would have played better years ago before the screen's oversaturation with quiet, sensitive psychotics. Interesting for its sometimes-successful casting against type: comedic Wilson as the killer, the usually acerbic Garofalo as a lonely alcoholic, and rocker Crow as a bar-hopper with asthma. [R]▼❚

Minute to Pray, a Second to Die, A (1967-Italian) **C-97m.** *** D: Franco Giraldi. Alex Cord, Arthur Kennedy, Robert Ryan, Mario Brega. Outlaw seeks refuge in Escondido from outlaws, bounty hunters, territorial lawmen, and anyone out to take advantage of his occasional paralytic seizures. Outstanding color photography adds to great atmosphere. Aka OUTLAW GUN. [R]▼❚

Miracle, The (1959) **C-121m.** **½ D: Irving Rapper. Carroll Baker, Roger Moore, Walter Slezak, Vittorio Gassman, Katina Paxinou, Dennis King, Isobel Elsom. Claptrap vehicle resurrected as glossy, empty spectacle of 1810s Spain, with Baker the would-be nun unsure of her decision, Moore the soldier she romances. Technirama.▼

Miracle, The (1991-British) **C-100m.** *** D: Neil Jordan. Beverly D'Angelo, Donal McCann, Niall Byrne, Lorraine Pilkington, J. G. Devlin. Evocative coming-of-age drama about Byrne and Pilkington, a pair of bright, bored Irish teens who view the world with youthful cynicism, and become intrigued by a beautiful mystery woman (D'Angelo) arriving in town. Soon Byrne is pursuing her romantically, but he has no idea how her presence will affect his life. Collectively well acted, with intelligent, precise script by Jordan. [R]▼●

Miracle (2004) **C-135m.** *** D: Gavin O'Connor. Kurt Russell, Patricia Clarkson, Noah Emmerich, Sean McCann, Kenneth Welsh, Eddie Cahill, Patrick O'Brien Demsey, Michael Mantenuto, Nathan West. The story of coach Herb Brooks, who's hired to prepare a U.S. hockey team to compete with the unassailable Soviets in the 1980 Winter Olympics. He knows that the only way to do this is to beat them at their own game—and build a team that breathes as one, no matter what sacrifices that requires along the way. Exciting, even though the conclusion is a given. Russell has never been better; most of the younger cast members are athletes making their acting debuts. Karl Malden played Brooks in the 1981 TV movie MIRACLE ON ICE. Super 35. [PG]▼❚

Miracle at St. Anna (2008-U.S.-Italian) **C-160m.** ***½ D: Spike Lee. Derek Luke, Michael Ealy, Laz Alonso, Omar Benson Miller, Pierfrancesco Favino, Valentina Cervi, Matteo Sciabordi, John Turturro, Joseph Gordon-Levitt, John Leguizamo, Kerry Washington, D. B. Sweeney, Walton Goggins, Robert John Burke, Omero Antonutti, Sergio Albelli. A modern crime story cues a flashback to 1944: four black members of the Buffalo Soldiers division of the U.S. Army are separated from their unit in Italy. As they fend for themselves in a Tuscan village, they contend with internal friction—and questions about their role in the war—as well as partisans, Fascists, racist superiors, a Nazi prisoner, and a frightened boy whom one of them adopts. Long but picaresque, rich with detail about this unique chapter of WW2 history. James McBride adapted his own novel. Super 35. [R]❚

Miracle in Milan (1951-Italian) **95m.** ***½ D: Vittorio De Sica. Francesco Golisano, Paolo Stoppa, Emma Gramatica, Guglielmo Barnabo. Toto the Good (Golisano) brings cheer to a dreary village of poor people, aided by the old lady who raised him, who is now in heaven. Bitingly comic condemnation of the manner in which displaced Europeans were treated after WW2.▼●

Miracle in the Rain (1956) **107m.** **½ D: Rudolph Maté. Jane Wyman, Van Johnson, Peggie Castle, Fred Clark, Eileen Heckart, Josephine Hutchinson, Barbara Nichols, William Gargan, Alan King, Arte Johnson. Above-par soaper of two lost souls, Wyman and Johnson, falling in love in N.Y.C. during WW2.❚

Miracle Mile (1989) **C-87m.** *½ D: Steve DeJarnatt. Anthony Edwards, Mare Winningham, John Agar, Lou Hancock, Mykel T. Williamson, Kelly Minter, Kurt Fuller, Denise Crosby, Robert Doqui, Danny De La Paz. Good-natured musician who's just gotten to first base with a coffee shop waitress picks up a ringing pay phone and learns that the U.S. has fired a nuclear warhead—which means that the end of the world is about an hour away. Artificial and overwrought from the word go. Credible costars Edwards and Winningham can't do anything with this material. [R]▼●❚

Miracle of Fatima SEE: **Miracle of Our Lady of Fatima, The**

Miracle of Morgan's Creek, The (1944) **99m.** **** D: Preston Sturges. Eddie Bracken, Betty Hutton, William Demarest, Diana Lynn, Brian Donlevy, Akim Tamiroff, Porter Hall, Almira Sessions, Jimmy Conlin. Frantic, hilarious comedy of Betty attending all-night party, getting pregnant and forgetting who's the father. Bracken and Demarest have never been better than in this daring wartime farce. Filmed in 1942; sort of remade as ROCK-A-BYE BABY.▼●❚

Miracle of Our Lady of Fatima, The (1952) **C-102m.** *** D: John Brahm. Gilbert Roland, Angela Clarke, Frank Silvera, Jay Novello, Sherry Jackson. Thoughtful account of religious miracle witnessed by farm children in 1910s; intelligent script. Retitled: MIRACLE OF FATIMA. ▼●▮

Miracle of the Bells, The (1948) 120m. *½ D: Irving Pichel. Fred MacMurray, Valli, Frank Sinatra, Lee J. Cobb, Charles Meredith. Contrived story of miracle occurring when movie star is laid to rest in coal-mining home town; often ludicrous, despite sincere cast. Screenplay by Ben Hecht and Quentin Reynolds. Also shown in computer-colored version.▼

Miracle on 34th Street (1947) 96m. ***½ D: George Seaton. Maureen O'Hara, John Payne, Edmund Gwenn, Gene Lockhart, Natalie Wood, Porter Hall, William Frawley, Jerome Cowan. Classic Valentine Davies fable of Kris Kringle (Gwenn) working in Macy's, encountering an unbelieving child (Wood), and going on trial to prove he's Santa. Delightful comedy-fantasy won Oscars for Gwenn, Davies, and screenwriter Seaton. Thelma Ritter's auspicious screen debut; an amusing bit for young Jack Albertson, as a postal employee. Remade in 1973 (for TV) and 1994. Also shown in computer-colored version. ▼●▮

Miracle on 34th Street (1994) C-114m. **½ D: Les Mayfield. Richard Attenborough, Elizabeth Perkins, Dylan McDermott, Mara Wilson, Robert Prosky, J. T. Walsh, James Remar, Jane Leeves, Simon Jones, William Windom, Allison Janney, Horatio Sanz. Pretty good remake of the 1947 charmer. Attenborough is wonderful as the man who calls himself Kris Kringle, and Wilson is irresistible as the little girl who doesn't believe in Santa. Loses its way whenever it veers from the original script—as in the relationship between Mara's mom (Perkins) and her neighbor/friend (McDermott) . . . and when it manages to keep the adorable youngster off-screen. Tellingly, this version is almost 20 minutes longer than the earlier film. Produced and written by John Hughes. Joss Ackland appears unbilled. [PG] ▼●▮

Miracles (1986) C-86m. *½ D: Jim Kouf. Tom Conti, Teri Garr, Paul Rodriguez, Christopher Lloyd, Adalberto Martinez, Jorge Russek. Conti and Garr, newly divorced, are whisked away to South American hellhole by jewel thief Rodriguez in this clone of ROMANCING THE STONE. The stars do their best, but we've seen it all before, and better. Written by first-time director Kouf. Super Techniscope. [PG]▼

Miracles (1989-Hong Kong) C-127m. **½ D: Jackie Chan. Jackie Chan, Anita Mui, Wu Ma, Richard Ng, Bill Tung, Gui Ya-Lei, Gloria Yip, Billy Lau, Lo Lieh, Ko Chuen-Hsiang, Yuen Biao, Jacky Cheung, Ricky Hui, Amy Yip. A naïve newcomer to 1930s Hong Kong accidentally becomes head of a powerful mob and battles a rival racketeer. Meanwhile, he befriends a flower seller and agrees to help her impress her visiting daughter, who thinks she's wealthy. Uncredited remake of Frank Capra's LADY FOR A DAY and POCKETFUL OF MIRACLES follows that part of the story faithfully—punctuated by mindboggling fight scenes! An amusing oddity. Aka MR. CANTON AND LADY ROSE, later retitled BLACK DRAGON. Technovision. [PG-13] ▼▮

Miracle Woman, The (1931) 90m. *** D: Frank Capra. Barbara Stanwyck, David Manners, Sam Hardy, Beryl Mercer, Russell Hopton. Stanwyck plays an evangelist (patterned after Aimee Semple McPherson) whose splashy sermons become big business. Manners is a blind man who falls in love with her. Story contrivances overcome by fine performances, direction, and camerawork (by Joseph Walker).▼

Miracle Worker, The (1962) 107m. ***½ D: Arthur Penn. Anne Bancroft, Patty Duke, Victor Jory, Inga Swenson, Andrew Prine, Beah Richards, Kathleen Comegys. Austerely beautiful treatment of William Gibson's play about Annie Sullivan (Bancroft), the remarkable woman who accepts the challenge of getting through to blind, deaf Helen Keller (Duke). There is absolutely no sentiment, which only increases the emotional power of the piece. Bancroft and Duke had been playing these parts on Broadway for over a year, but you'd never know it from their spontaneous and totally compelling performances, which earned them both Oscars. Originally staged as a 1957 *Playhouse 90* on TV, also directed by Penn. Remade for TV in 1979, with Duke in the role of Sullivan, and again in 2000.▼●▮

Mirage (1965) 109m. *** D: Edward Dmytryk. Gregory Peck, Diane Baker, Walter Matthau, Kevin McCarthy, Jack Weston, Leif Erickson, Walter Abel, George Kennedy. Fine Hitchcock-like thriller, with Peck the victim of amnesia, and everyone else out to get him. Matthau steals film as easygoing private-eye; interesting on-location footage in N.Y.C. Remade as JIGSAW (1968).▼●▮

Miral (2010-French-Israeli-Italian-Indian) C-112m. ** D: Julian Schnabel. Freida Pinto, Hiam Abbass, Jamil Khoury, Willem Dafoe, Vanessa Redgrave, Alexander Siddig, Yasmine Al Massri, Omar Metwally, Ruba Blal. Uneven saga dives into Israeli-Palestinian conflict by focusing on four women from different generations whose lives parallel the tumultuous relationship between the warring neighbors. Instantly controversial, the simplistic storyline about women of different eras living under Israeli occupation is actually benign, bolstered by the performances of a sterling international cast. Segmented, confused plotting doesn't help matters as film ambles along, never allowing the audience to get inside its complex subjects. Schnabel does at least try to offer some modicum of hope through the eyes of the title character, well played by Pinto. Screenplay by Rula Jebreal, from her novel. Techniscope. [PG-13] ▶

Miranda (1948-British) **80m.** **½ D: Ken Annakin. Googie Withers, Glynis Johns, Griffith Jones, John McCallum, David Tomlinson, Margaret Rutherford, Maurice Denham. Cute movie (adapted by Peter Blackmore from his play) about a happily married doctor who's abducted by a mermaid; she agrees to send him back to dry land only if she can accompany him to see what the human world is like. Charming fluff. Amusing to see Johns and Tomlinson together years before they were husband and wife in MARY POPPINS. Title song by Jean Sablon. Followed by a sequel, MAD ABOUT MEN. ▶

Mirror, The (1975-Russian) **C-106m.** ***½ D: Andrei Tarkovsky. Margarita Terekhova, Philip Yankovsky, Ignat Daniltsev, Oleg Yankovsky. Extremely personal, moving tale of life in Russia during WW2. Superbly directed; overall, it works most effectively as an homage to childhood innocence. ▼▶

Mirror Crack'd, The (1980-British) **C-105m.** **½ D: Guy Hamilton. Angela Lansbury, Elizabeth Taylor, Rock Hudson, Kim Novak, Tony Curtis, Edward Fox, Geraldine Chaplin, Wendy Morgan, Charles Gray, Pierce Brosnan. A mild Agatha Christie whodunit made enjoyable by its quartet of 1950s stars, particularly Taylor and Novak, fun as catty rival movie stars. Lansbury is a crisp Miss Marple. A highlight: the b&w movie-within-a-movie, *Murder at Midnight.* [PG] ▼●▶

Mirror Has Two Faces, The (1996) **C-126m.** **½ D: Barbra Streisand. Barbra Streisand, Jeff Bridges, Lauren Bacall, Mimi Rogers, George Segal, Pierce Brosnan, Brenda Vaccaro, Austin Pendleton, Elle Macpherson. A nerdy college prof, smarting from love affairs gone bad, enters into a cerebral relationship with fellow professor Streisand in which sex plays no part. Then she begins to long for something more. A Very Barbra Movie—she even cowrote the love theme—that deals with self-image and the impact of physical beauty, then undermines its own convictions in a nonsensical climax. Still, entertaining and attractively cast, with Bacall terrific as Streisand's self-absorbed mother. Based on the 1958 French movie. [PG-13] ▼●

Mirrormask (2005-U.S.-British) **C-101m.** *** D: David McKean. Stephanie Leonidas, Jason Barry, Rob Brydon, Gina McKee, Stephen Fry. Teenage girl who feels alienated from her parents—and their threadbare traveling circus—expresses her frustrations through drawing. When her mother takes ill, the guilt-ridden girl goes into a dream state inspired by those drawings and embarks on an odyssey to keep the world from being overtaken by dark forces.

Wildly imaginative fantasy uses THE WIZARD OF OZ as a template, but the visuals are utterly original, the work of famed artist/designer McKean, making his directing debut. Screenplay by McKean's frequent collaborator Neil Gaiman, from a story they cowrote. Presented by the Jim Henson Company. [PG] ▶

Mirrors (2008) **C-110m.** ** D: Alexandre Aja. Kiefer Sutherland, Amy Smart, Paula Patton, Cameron Boyce, Erica Gluck, Mary Beth Peil, John Shrapnel, Jason Flemyng. Aja, director of the 2006 THE HILLS HAVE EYES remake, has apparently decided that mirrors have eyes, too. Troubled ex-cop Sutherland takes a job as a night security guard in an abandoned department store, where evil mirrors seem to take on a life of their own. Haunted by the deaths of the previous guard and a family member, and contending with problems at home, Sutherland must convince everyone he's not crazy before it's too late. Pretty lame attempt at horror bungles what could have been a decent psychological tale of a man in crisis. Based on a 2001 Korean film, INTO THE MIRROR. Followed by a DVD sequel. Super 35. [R]▶

Misadventures of Merlin Jones, The (1964) **C-88m.** *½ D: Robert Stevenson. Tommy Kirk, Annette Funicello, Leon Ames, Stuart Erwin, Alan Hewitt, Connie Gilchrist. Skimpy Disney comedy about college brain (Kirk) and his misadventures with mind-reading and hypnotism. Sequel: THE MONKEY'S UNCLE. ▼▶

Misadventures of Mr. Wilt, The (1989-British) **C-92m.** **½ D: Michael Tuchner. Griff Rhys-Jones, Mel Smith, Alison Steadman, Diana Quick, Jeremy Clyde, Roger Allam. Two stars of the hit British TV series *Alas Smith and Jones* are featured in this silly farce about college lecturer Henry Wilt (Rhys-Jones), who hates his bitchy wife— and becomes the prime suspect when the police think she's been murdered. Smith is the twit of an inspector assigned to the case. Funny—if it hits you in the right mood. Based on Tom Sharpe's best-seller. Original British title: WILT. ▼

Mischief (1985) **C-93m.** ** D: Mel Damski. Doug McKeon, Catherine Mary Stewart, Kelly Preston, Chris Nash, D. W. Brown, Jami Gertz, Terry O'Quinn. Amiable but leaden-paced teen movie set in 1950s. Likable cast and vivid period atmosphere are chief assets—but any film that shows a clip from REBEL WITHOUT A CAUSE and then tries to duplicate the scene is asking for trouble. [R]▼●

Misery (1990) **C-107m.** **½ D: Rob Reiner. James Caan, Kathy Bates, Richard Farnsworth, Frances Sternhagen, Lauren Bacall, Graham Jarvis. Stephen King white-knuckler about a successful romance novelist who's nursed back to health after a snowy car crash by his Number One

Fan—who turns out to be a serious sicko. Extremely well acted, but the suspense ebbs and flows; there was much more nuance, and more interesting development of the relationship between fan and prisoner, in the novel. Bates won an Oscar for her unforgettable performance. Screenplay by William Goldman; striking cinematography by Barry Sonnenfeld. J. T. Walsh has unbilled cameo as a park ranger. Later adapted as a stage play in London. [R]▼●◗

Misfit Brigade, The (1987-U.S.-British) **C-99m.** ** D: Gordon Hessler. Bruce Davison, David Patrick Kelly, David Carradine, D. W. Moffett, Jay O. Sanders, Keith Szarabajka, Oliver Reed. At once clichéd and lighthearted (!) DIRTY DOZEN variation, about a group of German prisoners who find themselves recruited into the military by the Nazis (who are desperate for fighting men). Aka WHEELS OF TERROR. [R]▼

Misfits, The (1961) **124m.** *** D: John Huston. Clark Gable, Marilyn Monroe, Montgomery Clift, Thelma Ritter, Eli Wallach, James Barton, Estelle Winwood, Kevin McCarthy. Unsatisfying but engrossing parable authored by Arthur Miller, involving disillusioned divorcee Monroe and her brooding cowboy friends. Both Monroe's and Gable's last film.▼●◗

Mishima (1985) **C/B&W-120m.** *** D: Paul Schrader. Ken Ogata. Narration read by Roy Scheider. Ambitious, highly stylized drama about Japan's most controversial post-WW2 author, playwright, actor, director, and militarist, Yukio Mishima, whose passion to merge life and art led to his ritualistic suicide in 1970. Scenes of Mishima's life (shot in black & white) are contrasted with vivid dramatizations (in opulent color) of key fictional works that grappled with his emotional crises. Long, difficult, not always successful, but fascinating. Beautifully photographed by John Bailey, swept along by stunning Philip Glass score. [R]▼●◗

Miss Congeniality (2000) **C-111m.** **½ D: Donald Petrie. Sandra Bullock, Michael Caine, Benjamin Bratt, William Shatner, Ernie Hudson, John DiResta, Candice Bergen, Heather Burns. All-too-predictable comedy about a tomboyish FBI agent who goes undercover as a contestant in the Miss United States beauty pageant to find a dangerous criminal. Likable cast (with Caine a standout) does its best with a disappointing script. Followed by a sequel. [PG-13]▼◗

Miss Congeniality 2 Armed & Fabulous (2005) **C-115m.** *½ D: John Pasquin. Sandra Bullock, Regina King, William Shatner, Ernie Hudson, Enrique Murciano, Heather Burns, Treat Williams, Diedrich Bader, Eileen Brennan, Abraham Benrubi, Stephen Tobolowsky. Bullock returns as FBI agent Gracie Hart who, for public relations purposes, becomes the "face of the FBI." When Burns and Shatner are kidnapped, the bureau's beauty and her bodyguard (King) abandon their PR duties and try to find the hostages. Forced (and redundant) sequel has only a couple of bright moments, and never hits a comedic stride. Several celebrities have bit parts. Super 35. [PG-13]▼◗

Miss Europe SEE: **Prix de Beauté**

Miss Firecracker (1989) **C-102m.** *** D: Thomas Schlamme. Holly Hunter, Mary Steenburgen, Tim Robbins, Alfre Woodard, Scott Glenn, Ann Wedgeworth, Trey Wilson, Amy Wright, Bert Remsen. Beth Henley's Off-Broadway play, *The Miss Firecracker Contest*, becomes a most enjoyable movie, with a peerless Hunter re-creating her stage role. In a Mississippi hamlet, lonely, pitiful (and hilarious) Hunter yearns for love and self-esteem. Cast is first-rate in this sweet-natured comedy-drama, scripted by Henley; reminiscent of 1930s screwball films. Director Schlamme's feature debut; that's his real-life wife, Christine Lahti, as a neighbor (holding their own newborn baby!). [PG]▼●◗

Missing (1982) **C-122m.** ***½ D: Constantin Costa-Gavras. Jack Lemmon, Sissy Spacek, Melanie Mayron, John Shea, Charles Cioffi, David Clennon, Joe Regalbuto, Richard Venture, Janice Rule. A carefully manipulated drama that works, because of Costa-Gavras' convincing direction and Lemmon's emphatic performance as a stiff-backed father who comes to a politically volatile Latin American country in search of his missing son—unable and unwilling to believe that American representatives there might not be telling him the truth. Based on the true experiences of Ed Horman; Costa-Gavras and Donald Stewart earned Oscars for their screenplay adaptation. [PG]▼●◗

Missing, The (2003) **C-135m.** *** D: Ron Howard. Tommy Lee Jones, Cate Blanchett, Eric Schweig, Evan Rachel Wood, Jenna Boyd, Steve Reevis, Ray McKinnon, Val Kilmer, Aaron Eckhart, Max Perlich, Simon Baker, Jay Tavare, Sergio Calderón, Elizabeth Moss, Clint Howard, Rance Howard. Grim, gritty Western story of a healer (Blanchett), long estranged from her father (Jones), who reluctantly joins him in order to rescue her daughter from the clutches of a mystical Apache and his gang of savages. Engrossing and unpredictable, but also unexpectedly brutal. Strong performances and unfamiliar-looking New Mexico scenery are major assets; overlength is a liability. Based on Thomas Eidson's novel *The Last Ride*. Unrated version runs 154m. Super 35. [R]▼◗

Missing in Action (1984) **C-101m.** ** D: Joseph Zito. Chuck Norris, M. Emmet Walsh, David Tress, Lenore Kasdorf, James Hong. Colonel Norris, an ex-POW in Vietnam, returns to Asia to liberate American prisoners.

A simplistic, revisionist fantasy-actioner, in the mold of UNCOMMON VALOR and RAMBO: FIRST BLOOD PART 2. Followed by a prequel. [R] ▼●●

Missing in Action 2—The Beginning (1985) C-96m. *½ D: Lance Hool. Chuck Norris, Soon-Teck Oh, Steven Williams, Bennett Ohta, Cosie Costa. In this limp prequel to you-know-what, Norris escapes from a POW camp in Vietnam. For Norris lovers only. Followed by BRADDOCK: MISSING IN ACTION III. [R] ▼●●

Missing Pieces (1996) C-93m. ** D: Leonard Stern. Eric Idle, Robert Wuhl, Lauren Hutton, Richard Belzer, Bernie Kopell, James Hong. Silly slapstick farce about two pals who try to solve the riddle of a mysterious inheritance that's made them a target for some deadly criminals. Amiable enough, but the gags are hit-or-miss. Filmed in 1990, never released theatrically in the U.S. [PG] ▼●

Mission, The (1986-British) C-125m. **½ D: Roland Joffé. Robert De Niro, Jeremy Irons, Ray McAnally, Aidan Quinn, Cherie Lunghi, Ronald Pickup, Chuck Low, Liam Neeson, Daniel Berrigan. Productive (and profitable) Jesuit mission in the jungles of Brazil is threatened by greedy merchants and political factions within the church, in the late 18th century. Magnificent-looking film (Chris Menges' cinematography won an Oscar), rich in imagery, goes on so long—to such an inevitable conclusion—that its dramatic power is drained. Literate, high-minded screenplay by Robert Bolt; fine performances by Irons and De Niro. J-D-C Scope. [PG] ▼●●

Missionary, The (1982-British) C-90m. ** D: Richard Loncraine. Michael Palin, Maggie Smith, Phoebe Nicholls, Trevor Howard, Denholm Elliott, Michael Hordern, Graham Crowden. Fans of Monty Python's Palin may be surprised by this mild comedy, which he also wrote and coproduced. Returning from Africa, young man of the cloth is recruited to run a home for fallen women ("Women who've tripped?") and quickly finds himself the recipient of, uh, fringe benefits. Great supporting cast, gorgeous locations, beautiful cinematography (by Peter Hannan) overwhelm modest picture. Panavision. [R] ▼●●

Mission: Impossible (1996) C-110m. **½ D: Brian De Palma. Tom Cruise, Jon Voight, Emmanuelle Béart, Henry Czerny, Jean Reno, Ving Rhames, Kristin Scott Thomas, Vanessa Redgrave. Slick update of the vintage TV spy series about a crack undercover unit is full of high-tech hijinks, as "team leader" Cruise tries to learn what went wrong on a crucial mission in Prague—and discover who set them up. Energy wanes at several junctions, only to be revved up again for a train-and-helicopter chase finale. Lalo Schifrin's

memorable TV theme is reused here, at a much higher decibel level. Emilio Estevez appears unbilled. Followed by two sequels. Panavision. [PG-13] ▼●●

Mission: Impossible II (2000) C-126m. ** D: John Woo. Tom Cruise, Thandie Newton, Dougray Scott, Ving Rhames, Richard Roxburgh, John Polson, Brendan Gleeson, Radé Sherbedgia. Cruise is called into action in Sydney when a ruthless renegade spy (Scott) captures a virus and its antidote and murders its creator. Cruise looks great, performs nifty martial-arts stunts and engages in hair-raising car and motorcycle chases, but there isn't a character to care about, or a story worth two hours' time; after a while it's simply boring, in spite of Woo's flamboyant treatment (and a script by Robert Towne). Anthony Hopkins appears unbilled. Panavision. [PG-13] ▼●

Mission: Impossible III (2006) C-125m. *** D: J. J. Abrams. Tom Cruise, Philip Seymour Hoffman, Ving Rhames, Billy Crudup, Michelle Monaghan, Jonathan Rhys Meyers, Keri Russell, Maggie Q, Laurence Fishburne, Simon Pegg, Eddie Marsan, Aaron Paul. Slam-bang action yarn and Cruise-controlled star vehicle has the deep-cover agent trying to hide his activities from fiancée Monaghan while jetting around the globe to rescue his protégée (Russell) and deal with a nefarious arms dealer (Hoffman). Debuting feature writer-director Abrams, creator of TV's *Felicity, Alias,* and *Lost,* favors ultra-close-ups and handheld camerawork but knows how to stage big action scenes—just as Cruise knows how to work his Movie Star persona. Highlight: a Cruise-Hoffman doppelgänger sequence. Panavision. [PG-13] ●

Mission Mars (1968) C-95m. *½ D: Nick Webster. Darren McGavin, Nick Adams, George DeVries, Heather Hewitt, Michael DeBeausset, Shirley Parker. Typical astronaut drama has three U.S. space men battling unseen forces while on a mission. ▼

Mission to Mars (2000) C-112m. ** D: Brian De Palma. Gary Sinise, Tim Robbins, Don Cheadle, Connie Nielsen, Jerry O'Connell, Kim Delaney, Elise Neal. Stupefyingly dull drama about a pioneering voyage to Mars in the year 2020, marked by mishap, tragedy, and some mind-blowing cosmic discoveries. Film takes a matter-of-fact approach to space travel that soon becomes deadening, with a spell-it-all-out climax for those who still don't get 2001: A SPACE ODYSSEY. There is, however, an ingenious bit of product placement for Dr Pepper. Armin Mueller-Stahl appears unbilled. Panavision. [PG] ▼●●

Mississippi Blues (1983) C-96m. *** D: Bertrand Tavernier, Robert Parrish. Easygoing documentary from American Parrish and Frenchman Tavernier about the American South—its country folk, its landscape, its customs and, most wonderfully, its music.

Mississippi Burning (1988) C-125m. *** D: Alan Parker. Gene Hackman, Willem Dafoe, Frances McDormand, Brad Dourif, R. Lee Ermey, Gailard Sartain, Stephen Tobolowsky, Michael Rooker, Pruitt Taylor Vince, Park Overall. Two FBI agents—one a tight-jawed, by-the-book type, the other an experienced Southern lawman who knows how to handle people—head the government investigation into the disappearance of three civil rights workers in Mississippi during the summer of 1964. Vivid re-creation of the period and setting helps carry a less-than-perfect script (inspired by real-life events); Hackman gives a dynamic performance as the former small-town sheriff who figures out how to crack the case. Peter Biziou's cinematography won an Oscar. [R]▼●)

Mississippi Masala (1992) C-118m. **½ D: Mira Nair. Denzel Washington, Sarita Choudhury, Roshan Seth, Sharmila Tagore, Charles S. Dutton, Joe Seneca, Ranjit Chowdhry. Affecting, leisurely paced story of interracial romance between Washington and Choudhury and the problems it causes their respective communities in Greenwood, Mississippi. Starts out fine, with lively characters and interesting observations of a transplanted Indian lifestyle in the Deep South, then bogs down in standard—and extenuated—melodrama. Good performances by Washington (as always) and especially by Seth as Choudhury's proud lawyer father who wants to return home to Uganda. "Masala," by the way, is a collection of hot and colorful spices. Director Nair also appears as a gossipmonger. [R]▼●)

Mississippi Mermaid (1969-French-Italian) C-123m. *** D: François Truffaut. Jean-Paul Belmondo, Catherine Deneuve, Michel Bouquet, Nelly Borgeaud. One of the director's few flops, but any film with Belmondo-Deneuve-Truffaut combo is of interest; story concerns tobacco planter whose mail-order bride turns out to be Deneuve. Always buy brand names. Based on the Cornell Woolrich novel *Waltz Into Darkness*. Originally shown in the U.S. at 110m. Remade as ORIGINAL SIN. Dyaliscope. [PG]▼●)

Miss Julie (1951-Swedish) 87m. *** D: Alf Sjoberg. Anita Bjork, Ulf Palme, Marta Dorff, Anders Henrikson. Masterful adaptation of August Strindberg's tragic play about the love affair between an aristocratic young woman and a commoner. Superbly acted and photographed, with imaginative use of flashbacks. A milestone in Swedish cinema. Remade in 1999. ▼)

Miss Julie (1999-British-U.S.) C-103m. **½ D: Mike Figgis. Saffron Burrows, Peter Mullan, Maria Doyle Kennedy. Pungent

adaptation of August Strindberg's fiery 19th-century play about the mistress of a household who toys with the affections of her footman—who in turn plays sexual games with her. Well acted, vigorously filmed, but awfully dismal. [R]▼)

Miss March (2009) C-89m. *½ D: Zach Cregger, Trevor Moore. Zach Cregger, Trevor Moore, Raquel Alessi, Craig Robinson, Molly Stanton, Hugh M. Hefner, Geoff Meed, Cedric Yarbrough, Eve Mauro, Alexis Raben. Young man has a terrible accident moments before he is about to lose his virginity to his high school sweetheart. He awakens four years later to discover that she is now a *Playboy* Playmate. If you're a fan of the stars' work on the TV show *The Whitest Kids U' Know* you might find this movie funny, but when you don't care about the characters or their objectives, it's hard to enjoy. Alternate version runs 90m. [R]▼)

Miss Mary (1986-Argentine) C-100m. **½ D: Maria Luisa Bemberg. Julie Christie, Nacha Guevara, Luisina Brando, Iris Marga, Eduardo Pavlovsky, Gerardo Romano. Proper, prim British governness Christie arrives in Argentina in 1938, to look after the children in a proper, prim, upper-class family. A few nice touches but mostly forgettable tale of unreleased passion and emerging sexuality. An offbeat role for Christie.▼

Missouri Breaks, The (1976) C-126m. BOMB D: Arthur Penn. Marlon Brando, Jack Nicholson, Kathleen Lloyd, Randy Quaid, Frederic Forrest, Harry Dean Stanton. Dynamite star combo in hired gun vs. horse thief confrontation—all for naught. Jumbled, excessively violent pseudo-event; a great director's worst film and one of the worst "big" movies ever made. [PG]▼●)

Miss Pettigrew Lives for a Day (2008-U.S.-British) C-92m. ** D: Bharat Nalluri. Frances McDormand, Amy Adams, Lee Pace, Ciarán Hinds, Shirley Henderson, Mark Strong, Tom Payne. Headstrong Guinevere Pettigrew (McDormand) has lost one job after another and winds up penniless on the streets of London in 1939, until she bluffs her way into a job as social secretary for flighty would-be actress Delysia Lafosse (Adams), who's juggling three men in her life. Arch, self-consciously cute rendering of Winifred Watson's 1930s novel, though the two female stars give it their all. Super 35. [PG-13]●)

Miss Potter (2006-U.S.-British) C-91m. *** D: Chris Noonan. Renée Zellweger, Ewan McGregor, Emily Watson, Barbara Flynn, Bill Paterson, Matyelok Gibbs, Anton Lesser, David Bamber, Phyllida Law, Lloyd Owen, Lucy Boynton. Lifelong dreamer Beatrix Potter marches to her own drummer, to the dismay of her Victorian parents, but the feisty young woman surprises everyone by landing a publisher for her whimsical stories and watercolors about Peter Rabbit. Warm, genteel, and whimsical film about the famous author, with an utterly charming performance by McGregor as the gentleman-publisher who falls in love with his author. Written by Broadway veteran Richard Maltby, Jr. Noonan's first directorial effort since BABE in 1995. Panavision. [PG]◐

Miss Sadie Thompson (1953) **C-91m.** *** D: Curtis Bernhardt. Rita Hayworth, Jose Ferrer, Aldo Ray, Russell Collins, Charles Bronson. Rita gives a provocative performance in musical of Somerset Maugham's RAIN, previously made as SADIE THOMPSON and DIRTY GERTIE FROM HARLEM U.S.A. 3-D. ▼●◐

Mist, The (2007) **C-127m.** *** D: Frank Darabont. Thomas Jane, Marcia Gay Harden, Laurie Holden, Andre Braugher, Toby Jones, William Sadler, Jeffrey DeMunn, Frances Sternhagen, Nathan Gamble. After a fierce storm and the arrival of a mysterious mist, an artist (Jane) and his young son (Gamble) are among those forced to take refuge in a Maine supermarket. Then they learn that there are strange things out in that mist—things that kill. The people in the market gradually form into antagonistic factions. Suspenseful and graced with very good effects, this is a monster movie in the classic mode. It also has some social commentary, ported over from Stephen King's novella by director-writer Darabont. Controversial ending is changed from the story. Also available on DVD in the director's preferred b&w version. Aka STEPHEN KING'S THE MIST. [R]◐

Mister Buddwing (1966) **100m.** ** D: Delbert Mann. James Garner, Jean Simmons, Suzanne Pleshette, Angela Lansbury, Katharine Ross, Raymond St. Jacques, Nichelle Nichols. Misfire; overfamiliar amnesia plot with Garner trying to fill in his past, meeting assorted women who might have been part of his prior life. ◐

Mister Cory (1957) **C-92m.** **½ D: Blake Edwards. Tony Curtis, Charles Bickford, Martha Hyer, Kathryn Grant (Crosby). Curtis does OK as poor-boy-turned-rich-gambler who returns to home town to show off his wealth. CinemaScope.

Mister 880 (1950) **90m.** *** D: Edmund Goulding. Dorothy McGuire, Burt Lancaster, Edmund Gwenn, Millard Mitchell, Minor Watson. Easygoing comedy, with Gwenn an elderly N.Y.C. counterfeiter tracked down by federal agent Lancaster. Script by Robert Riskin, based on a true story.

Mister Frost (1990-French-British) **C-92m.** ** D: Philip Setbon. Jeff Goldblum, Alan Bates, Kathy Baker, Jean-Pierre Cassel, Daniel Gelin, Francois Negret, Maxime Leroux, Vincent Schiavelli, Catherine Allegret, Charley Boorman. Goldblum is blithe, cheerful serial killer who tells psychiatrist Baker that he's really the Devil, something

ex-cop Bates already believes. It all has to do with Lucifer's annoyance over lack of belief in him. Goldblum is clearly having a great time, but you're not likely to. [R]▼●◐

Mister Johnson (1991) **C-101m.** **½ D: Bruce Beresford. Pierce Brosnan, Edward Woodward, Maynard Eziashi, Beatie Edney, Denis Quilley, Nick Reding. Africa, 1923: an ambitious, educated (and larcenous) black man who works for the local British magistrate continually gets into trouble by being too smart for his own good. Handsome, well-made, well-acted film still leaves one wanting to know more about Mister Johnson and what makes him tick. Based on a novel by Joyce Cary. [PG-13]▼●◐

Mister Lonely (2008-U.S.-British-French-Irish) **C-112m.** BOMB D: Harmony Korine. Diego Luna, Samantha Morton, Denis Lavant, James Fox, Melita Morgan, Anita Pallenberg, Rachel Korine, Jason Pennycooke, Richard Strange, Werner Herzog, Leos Carax, David Blaine. When a Michael Jackson impersonator meets a Marilyn Monroe look-alike in Paris, she invites him to join her at a mountainside commune filled with doppelgangers (for everyone from Buckwheat to the Pope). Meanwhile, in a jungle somewhere in Latin America, nuns are taking to the skies. Achingly awful movie, though as one character says of her comrades, "It isn't the Stooges' fault!" Super 35. ◐

Mister Moses (1965-British) **C-113m.** **½ D: Ronald Neame. Robert Mitchum, Carroll Baker, Ian Bannen, Alexander Knox, Raymond St. Jacques, Reginald Beckwith. Malarkey of rugged Mitchum and virtuous Baker leading African native tribe to their new homeland. Panavision.

Mister Roberts (1955) **C-123m.** **** D: John Ford, Mervyn LeRoy. Henry Fonda, James Cagney, William Powell, Jack Lemmon, Betsy Palmer, Ward Bond, Nick Adams, Philip Carey, Harry Carey, Jr., Ken Curtis, Martin Milner, Jack Pennick, Perry Lopez, Pat Wayne. Superb comedy-drama with Fonda recreating his favorite stage role as restless officer on WW2 cargo ship who yearns for combat action but has to contend with an irascible and eccentric captain (Cagney) instead. Fonda, Cagney, Powell (in his last screen appearance) as a philosophical doctor, and Lemmon (in an Oscar-winning performance) as the irrepressible Ensign Pulver, are all terrific. Thomas Heggen and Joshua Logan's Broadway hit was adapted for film by Logan and Frank Nugent. LeRoy replaced Ford as director sometime during production . . . but it certainly doesn't show. Sequel: ENSIGN PULVER. Remade for TV in 1984 with Kevin Bacon. CinemaScope.▼●◐

Mister Superinvisible (1973-Italian-German-Spanish) **C-91m.** **½ D: Anthony M. Dawson (Antonio Margheriti). Dean Jones, Ingeborg Schoener, Gastone Moschin, Peter Carsten. Engaging comedy made in Geneva has American researcher Jones becoming invisible as he seeks a cure for the common cold. Good for kids, okay for grownups. Techniscope. [G]▼●

Mister V SEE: **"Pimpernel" Smith**

Mistress (1991) **C-109m.** ** D: Barry Primus. Robert Wuhl, Martin Landau, Jace Alexander, Robert De Niro, Danny Aiello, Eli Wallach, Laurie Metcalf, Sheryl Lee Ralph, Jean Smart, Tuesday Knight, Christopher Walken, Ernest Borgnine, Stefan Gierasch, Roberta Wallach. Hollywood comedy-drama about a washed-up writer (Wuhl) who gets a chance to try to realize his dream—thanks to a has-been producer (Landau, who's marvelous). Plot concerns rounding up the money—and placating the money-men's mistresses. Paper-thin story has several choice moments, but never builds to a satisfying result. Veteran actor Primus' feature directing debut. [R] ▼●

Misunderstood (1984) **C-91m.** **½ D: Jerry Schatzberg. Gene Hackman, Henry Thomas, Rip Torn, Huckleberry Fox, Maureen Kerwin, Susan Anspach. Boy cries out for the love of his father, who's too busy (and too consumed by the loss of his wife) to understand how much the boy needs his attention—and affection. Extremely well acted but emotionally uneven drama. Filmed in Tunisia in 1982. [PG]▼

Mitchell (1975) **C-96m.** **½ D: Andrew V. McLaglen. Joe Don Baker, Martin Balsam, Linda Evans, John Saxon, Merlin Olsen, Morgan Paull. Baker plays tough cop whose singleminded pursuit of drug ring leads to expected action and violence; slick handling of typical action fodder. [R]▼●

Mi Vida Loca (My Crazy Life) (1994) **C-92m.** *** D: Allison Anders. Angel Aviles, Seidy Lopez, Jacob Vargas, Marlo Marron, Jessie Borrego, Magali Alvarado, Julian Reyes, Salma Hayek. Powerful look at hopes and realities of Latina gang girls in L.A.'s Echo Park area. Episodic structure takes some getting used to (as do some of the performances), but writer-director Anders ultimately succeeds in capturing the frustrations of the characters' world and the cycle of social rituals and violence affecting them daily. ▼●

Mixed Company (1974) **C-109m.** **½ D: Melville Shavelson. Barbara Harris, Joseph Bologna, Tom Bosley, Lisa Gerritsen, Dorothy Shay. Less than heartwarming but still entertaining comedy of losing basketball coach Bologna coping with wife Harris' adopting orphans of mixed ethnic backgrounds. [PG]

Mixed Nuts (1994) **C-97m.** *½ D: Nora Ephron. Steve Martin, Madeline Kahn, Rita Wilson, Robert Klein, Anthony LaPaglia, Juliette Lewis, Rob Reiner, Adam Sandler, Liev Schreiber, Joely Fisher, Parker Posey, Jon Stewart, Haley Joel Osment, Garry Shandling, Steven Wright. Genuinely strange black comedy (or is it black farce?) about the genially bumbling staff of a suicide helpline in Venice, California, and their misadventures on Christmas Eve. Occasional laughs sputter through the haze, but this oddity never really finds its comic center. Written by Ephron and her sister Delia, based on a 1982 French film, LE PERE NOEL EST UNE ORDURE. [PG-13]▼●

Miyazaki's Laputa SEE: **Laputa**

Miyazaki's Spirited Away SEE: **Spirited Away**

Mob, The (1951) **87m.** *** D: Robert Parrish. Broderick Crawford, Betty Buehler, Richard Kiley, Otto Hulett, Neville Brand, Ernest Borgnine, John Marley, Charles Bronson. Crawford is tough as nails as undercover cop on the trail of waterfront racketeers and their mystery boss. Sharp dialogue (by William Bowers), good suspense in this combination crime drama-whodunit.

Mo' Better Blues (1990) **C-127m.** ** D: Spike Lee. Denzel Washington, Spike Lee, Wesley Snipes, Giancarlo Esposito, Robin Harris, Joie Lee, Bill Nunn, John Turturro, Dick Anthony Williams, Cynda Williams, Nicholas Turturro, Samuel L. Jackson, Ruben Blades, Abbey Lincoln, Joe Seneca. Backstage look at a self-centered jazz trumpeter who manages to keep everyone at arm's length—including the two ladies in his life. Colorful, musically alive, with some good vignettes from members of Lee's stock company, but it goes on forever— with barely enough story to keep it afloat. Branford Marsalis' Quartet with Terence Blanchard is featured on the soundtrack; music score by Bill Lee (Spike's father). [R]▼●

Mobsters (1991) **C-104m.** ** D: Michael Karbelnikoff. Christian Slater, Patrick Dempsey, Costas Mandylor, Richard Grieco, F. Murray Abraham, Michael Gambon, Lara Flynn Boyle, Anthony Quinn, Christopher Penn, Nicholas Sadler. What promised to be YOUNG TOMMY GUNS turns out to be simply boring: a fanciful rehash of the Prohibition Era, with youthful actors as Lucky Luciano, Frank Costello, Bugsy Siegel, and Meyer Lansky. Long, convoluted, and unrewarding. Only distinction: Richard Sylbert's handsome production design. [R]▼●

Moby Dick (1956) **C-116m.** *** D: John Huston. Gregory Peck, Richard Basehart, Friedrich Ledebur, Leo Genn, Orson Welles, James Robertson Justice, Harry Andrews, Bernard Miles, Royal Dano. Moody version of Herman Melville sea classic, with Peck lending a deranged dignity to the role of Captain Ahab. Fine scenes throughout, including second-unit camera work by the great Freddie Francis. Screenplay by Huston and Ray Bradbury. Francis Ford Coppola executive produced 1998 remake as a TV miniseries with Patrick Stewart. ▼●◗

Model and the Marriage Broker, The (1951) 103m. *** D: George Cukor. Jeanne Crain, Scott Brady, Thelma Ritter, Zero Mostel, Michael O'Shea, Frank Fontaine, Nancy Kulp. Poignant, perceptive little comedy-drama chronicling the affairs of marriage broker Ritter, who plays Cupid for model Crain and X-ray technician Brady. However, most of her clients don't have pretty faces: they're shy, lonely, desperate for companionship. A winner.

Model Shop (1969-French) C-95m. *** D: Jacques Demy. Anouk Aimée, Gary Lockwood, Alexandra Hay, Carole Cole, Severn Darden, Tom Fielding. Twenty-four hours in life of disenchanted young architect (Lockwood), his affair with recently abandoned fashion model (Aimée). Director Demy's eye for L.A. is striking, but overall feel to story is ambiguous. [M/PG] ◗

Modern Affair, A (1996) C-90m. ** D: Vern Oakley. Lisa Eichhorn, Stanley Tucci, Caroline Aaron, Wesley Addy, Robert LuPone, Tammy Grimes, Robert Joy. Small, moderately amusing comedy about a successful corporate executive who undergoes artificial insemination, gets pregnant, and then impulsively tracks down the anonymous sperm donor. Results are predictable, but Tucci and Eichhorn lift the material up a couple of notches. This forgettable concoction may play better on the small screen. [R]▼

Modern Love (1990) C-109m. ** D: Robby Benson. Robby Benson, Karla DeVito, Rue McClanahan, Burt Reynolds, Frankie Valli, Louise Lasser, Kaye Ballard, Lou Kaplan. Paper-thin comedy which director-star Benson also produced and scripted. The film should be titled FAMILY AFFAIR: DeVito, Benson's wife, plays his on-screen mate, and their daughter Lyric is cast as the couple's offspring. The scenario—the duo meet, fall in love, wed, and deal with various "modern problems"—is run-of-the-mill. Filmed in South Carolina, while Benson was teaching a university moviemaking class. [R]▼

Modern Problems (1981) C-91m. *½ D: Ken Shapiro. Chevy Chase, Patti D'Arbanville, Mary Kay Place, Nell Carter, Brian Doyle-Murray, Dabney Coleman, Mitch Kreindel. Air-traffic controller Chase acquires telekinetic powers. A couple of funny bits; mostly flat, boring. [PG]▼◗

Modern Romance (1981) C-93m. **½ D:

Albert Brooks. Albert Brooks, Kathryn Harrold, Bruno Kirby, Jane Hallaren, James L. Brooks, George Kennedy. Writer-director Brooks plays a world-class neurotic who's obsessively devoted to Harrold but unable to maintain a normal - relationship with her. Alternately obnoxious and hilarious, with wonderful in-jokes about moviemaking (Brooks plays a film editor); Brooks' brother Bob Einstein plays a sporting-goods salesman in a nice cameo. Real-life writer-director James L. Brooks plays a director; he returned the favor by writing Albert a plum role in BROADCAST NEWS several years later. [R]▼●◗

Moderns, The (1988) C-128m. **½ D: Alan Rudolph. Keith Carradine, Linda Fiorentino, John Lone, Genevieve Bujold, Geraldine Chaplin, Wallace Shawn, Kevin J. O'Connor. Beautifully mounted but dramatically flawed period piece about a community of "artistes" in 1926 Paris. Bland Carradine is a major liability as an art forger; portraits of Hemingway and Gertrude Stein are less than half baked. Lone and Fiorentino are standouts as a menacing U.S rubber baron and wife, she a lost love of Carradine's. Worthy but iffy. [R]▼●◗

Modern Times (1936) 89m. **** D: Charlie Chaplin. Charlie Chaplin, Paulette Goddard, Henry Bergman, Chester Conklin, Stanley "Tiny" Sandford. Charlie attacks the machine age in inimitable fashion, with sharp pokes at other social ills and the struggle of modern-day survival. Goddard is the gamine who becomes his partner in life. Chaplin's last silent film (with his own music—including "Smile"—sound effects and gibberish song) is consistently hilarious, and unforgettable. Final shot is among Chaplin's most famous and most poignant. One of Goddard's sisters early on is young Gloria DeHaven (daughter of Chaplin's assistant director). ▼●◗

Modesty Blaise (1966-British) C-119m. ** D: Joseph Losey. Monica Vitti, Dirk Bogarde, Terence Stamp, Harry Andrews, Michael Craig, Scilla Gabel, Tina Marquand, Clive Revill, Alexander Knox. Director Losey ate watermelon, pickles, and ice cream, went to sleep, woke up, and made this adaptation of the comic strip about a sexy female spy. Filmed at the height of the pop-art craze, it tries to be a spoof at times, doesn't know what it's supposed to be at other moments.▼◗

Mod Squad, The (1999) C-94m. *½ D: Scott Silver. Claire Danes, Giovanni Ribisi, Omar Epps, Dennis Farina, Josh Brolin, Michael Lerner, Steve Harris, Richard Jenkins, Bodhi Elfman. Brain-dead rehash of the late '60s–early '70s TV series. Here, the title trio—all young delinquents recruited to work undercover in the LAPD—go into action in a scenario involving the theft of confiscated drugs and other mayhem. Plays like an extended, R-rated episode that was spit out of a computer. [R] ▼●◗

Mogambo (1953) **C-115m.** ***½ D: John Ford. Clark Gable, Ava Gardner, Grace Kelly, Donald Sinden, Philip Stainton, Eric Pohlmann, Laurence Naismith, Denis O'Dea. Lusty remake of RED DUST. Gable repeats his role, Ava replaces Harlow, Kelly has Mary Astor's part. John Lee Mahin reworked his 1932 screenplay. Romantic triangle in Africa combines love and action; beautifully filmed by Robert Surtees and Freddie Young. Title is Swahili for "Passion." ▼●◗

Mohammad, Messenger of God (1977-Arabic) **C-180m.** *** D: Moustapha Akkad. Anthony Quinn, Irene Papas, Michael Ansara, Johnny Sekka, Michael Forest, Neville Jason. Spectacle of the beginnings of Moslem religion is sincere effort, more impressive with action than religious angles. In accordance with the religion, Mohammad is never shown. Aka THE MESSAGE. Panavision. [PG] ▼◗

Mole People, The (1956) **78m.** ** D: Virgil Vogel. John Agar, Cynthia Patrick, Hugh Beaumont, Alan Napier. Agar and others find lost underground civilization of albino Sumerians, who have half-human creatures as their slaves. Probably the worst of Universal-International's '50s sci-fi movies. ▼●◗

Molière (2007-French) **C-120m.** ***½ D: Laurent Tirard. Romain Duris, Fabrice Luchini, Laura Morante, Edouard Baer, Ludivine Sagnier, Fanny Valette. The great 17th-century French playwright (Duris) learns a valuable life lesson at a crucial moment in his career. He's rescued from debtor's prison by a wealthy man (Luchini) who needs coaching for his first, stumbling effort as an actor-playwright, which is designed to impress the beautiful Sagnier. Meanwhile, Molière becomes involved with the smitten man's neglected wife (Morante). Hints of Molière plays to come are cleverly sprinkled throughout the elegant, bittersweet screenplay by director Tirard and Grégoire Vigneron. A delight. Panavision. [PG-13] ◗

Moll Flanders (1996) **C-123m.** **½ D: Pen Densham. Robin Wright, Morgan Freeman, Stockard Channing, John Lynch, Brenda Fricker, Geraldine James, Aisling Corcoran, Jeremy Brett. Daniel Defoe's 18th-century heroine was the inspiration for this newly spun tale of a girl, born to poverty and abuse, who spends her whole life standing up to men (and women) who would "use" her. Wright is rock-solid as Moll, but the interesting story has its share of lulls. Filmmaker Jim Sheridan plays a priest. Panavision. [PG-13] ▼●◗

Molly (1999) **C-91m.** *½ D: John Duigan. Elisabeth Shue, Aaron Eckhart, Thomas Jane, Jill Hennessy, D.W. Moffett, Elizabeth Mitchell, Lucy Liu. Female spin on

CHARLY is a saccharine vehicle for Shue as a childlike autistic person who gets a major brain upgrade. Solid support from Eckhart as her reluctant older brother and Jane as her shy boyfriend can't make up for a major case of the cutes. Film preaches endlessly (and irresponsibly) about how kooky and free-spirited autistic people can be and how wretched we are for not enjoying the simple things in life as they do. Made its U.S. debut as an inflight movie! [PG-13] ▼◗

Molly and Lawless John (1971) **C-97m.** ** D: Gary Nelson. Vera Miles, Sam Elliott, Clu Gulager, John Anderson. Slow-moving but not-uninteresting feminist Western, with Miles doing well as a repressed sheriff's wife who chooses to assist a brash young killer (Elliott) in a prison escape. Their developing relationship forms the basis of the story. [PG] ▼◗

Molly Maguires, The (1970) **C-123m.** **½ D: Martin Ritt. Sean Connery, Richard Harris, Samantha Eggar, Frank Finlay, Art Lund, Anthony Costello. Well-crafted film about secret society of Irish mineworkers in Pennsylvania, circa 1876, led by Connery; newcomer Harris is working as informer. Vivid atmosphere, good performances, but downbeat film lacks appeal, and is hurt by inconclusive ending. Panavision. [M/PG] ▼●◗

Molokai: The Story of Father Damien (1999-Australian-Dutch) **C-113m.** **½ D: Paul Cox. David Wenham, Derek Jacobi, Alice Krige, Kris Kristofferson, Sam Neill, Peter O'Toole, Leo McKern. True story of Father Damien and his battle to get proper medical and religious care for the outcast inhabitants of a leper colony in the Hawaiian islands. Hansen's disease is graphically shown; not for the fainthearted. Beautifully filmed on the site of the original colony, but given the subject matter, film is never as compelling as it ought to be. Super 35. ▼◗

Mom and Dad Save the World (1992) **C-88m.** *½ D: Greg Beeman. Teri Garr, Jeffrey Jones, Jon Lovitz, Thalmus Rasulala, Wallace Shawn, Eric Idle, Dwier Brown, Kathy Ireland. Perfectly dreadful comedy/fantasy about the megalomaniacal ruler of a tiny planet (Lovitz) who's about to blow up Earth. He becomes attracted to a suburban Mom (Garr) and spirits her and her husband (Jones) to his planet so she can be his bride. Some imaginative visuals can't buoy this strained and unfunny concoction. [PG] ▼●◗

Moment by Moment (1978) **C-102m.** BOMB D: Jane Wagner. Lily Tomlin, John Travolta, Andra Akers, Bert Kramer, Shelley R. Bonus. Role-reversal romance with Travolta as sex object, Tomlin as bored Malibu resident gives new dimension to the word "dreary." Panavision. [R]

Moment to Moment (1966) **C-108m.** **½ D: Mervyn LeRoy. Jean Seberg, Honor

Blackman, Sean Garrison, Arthur Hill. Unconvincing, confused murder mystery set on the Riviera, but filmed largely on Universal's sound stage.▼

Mommie Dearest (1981) **C-129m.** **½ D: Frank Perry. Faye Dunaway, Diana Scarwid, Steve Forrest, Howard da Silva, Mara Hobel, Rutanya Alda, Harry Goz. Vivid, well-crafted filmization of Christina Crawford's book about growing up the adopted and abused daughter of movie queen Joan Crawford (brilliantly played by Dunaway). Knowing that the story is (allegedly) real makes watching this film a creepy experience, something akin to voyeurism . . . though now it's seen as a camp classic! [PG]▼●)

Mommy (1995) **C-89m.** **½ D: Max Allan Collins. Patty McCormack, Jason Miller, Brinke Stevens, Majel Barrett, Mickey Spillane, Rachel Lemieux, Sarah Jane Miller. Pretty good little thriller set (and shot) in Muscatine, Iowa, with McCormack as The Bad Seed grown up: a smothering mommy who murders freely to get her way (and to protect her beloved daughter). Now the daughter starts to wonder how to deal with Mommy. McCormack is chillingly good, and the film seldom betrays its low-budget status. Scripted by the director, who also wrote (and sings) several songs on the soundtrack! Followed by MOMMY 2: MOMMY'S DAY. ▼●)

Mo'Money (1992) **C-91m.** ** D: Peter Macdonald. Damon Wayans, Marlon Wayans, Stacey Dash, Joe Santos, John Diehl, Harry J. Lennix, Almayvonne. Slapdash, needlessly violent comedy-actioner which barely runs on the energy of its talented stars. Damon Wayans plays a streetwise jerk who, in order to woo Dash, takes a job on the bottom rung of the credit card company where she works, and (with kid brother Marlon) becomes involved with fraud, blackmail, and mayhem. Look for Bernie Mac as a doorman. Damon Wayans also scripted and executive produced. [R]▼●)

Mona Lisa (1986-British) **C-104m.** *** D: Neil Jordan. Bob Hoskins, Cathy Tyson, Michael Caine, Robbie Coltrane, Clarke Peters, Kate Hardie, Zoe Nathenson, Sammi Davis. Absorbing adult drama about a small-time hood who's given a job driving around a high-priced callgirl but remains naive about the life she leads, and about the degree of depravity his underworld chums have sunk to. Director Jordan (who cowrote screenplay with David Leland) leads us into this nether world along with Hoskins, allowing us to discover things at the same time. Hoskins and newcomer Tyson are terrific; Caine is wonderfully slimy in support. [R]▼●)

Mona Lisa Smile (2003) **C-119m.** ** D: Mike Newell. Julia Roberts, Kirsten Dunst, Julia Stiles, Maggie Gyllenhaal, Juliet Stevenson, Dominic West, Ginnifer Goodwin, Topher Grace, Marcia Gay Harden, John Slattery, Jordan Bridges, Marian Seldes. Dedicated, freethinking art history prof Roberts molds young Wellesley women—even spoiled, mouthy Dunst—in the culturally stifling 1950s, but quickly learns that she's bucking the system in and out of the classroom. There's some fun seeing contemporary young actresses in a period setting, but the movie is so smug and condescending that even anti-nostalgists may be put off. Pop culture reminders of the 1950s are laid on with a trowel . . . and even the villains in DELIVERANCE would know Columbia Records' superstar Doris Day did not record for RCA Victor, though one close-up implies that she did. [PG-13]▼)

Monarch of the Moon (2005) **C-98m.** *** D: Richard Lowry. Blane Wheatley, Monica Himmelheber, Brent Moss, Kimberly Page, Will McMillan, Penny Drake, Kyle Vogt. Entertaining parody of 1940s Saturday matinee serials (divided into six chapters), with the heroic Yellowjacket using his winged backpack to soar into action at a moment's notice to protect the interests of the U.S.A.—and locking horns with the evil villainess Dragonfly. Executed on a microbudget with great verve and humor; even the sometimes-primitive special effects are fun to watch. This is the film SKY CAPTAIN AND THE WORLD OF TOMORROW aspired to be. Made by the same team that created DESTINATION MARS!▶

Mondays in the Sun (2002-Spanish) **C-113m.** *** D: Fernando León de Aranoa. Javier Bardem, Luis Tosar, José Ángel Egido, Nieve de Medina, Enrique Villén, Celso Bugallo, Aida Folch, Joaquín Climent. Fine if somber study of men who have lost their jobs as dockworkers and manage to survive on little more than hope. Bardem is very effective, and the film has something universally important to say. Based on a true story. Winner of the Goya, Spain's Oscar, for Best Picture.▼)

Mondo Cane (1962-Italian) **C-105m.** **½ Producer: Gualtiero Jacopetti. First and best of Italian shockumentaries, with dubbed American narration; focuses on bizarre peculiarities of man in various parts of the world. Features hit song "More."▼●)

Money for Nothing (1993) **C-100m.** ** D: Ramon Menendez. John Cusack, Debi Mazar, Michael Madsen, Benicio Del Toro, Michael Rapaport, Maury Chaykin, James Gandolfini, Fionnula Flanagan, Philip Seymour Hoffman. True story of unemployed longshoreman who finds over a million bucks which has fallen out of an armored car; he sees it as his ticket to the good life, but it doesn't work out that way. Earnest but drab treatment of an interesting story; promoted as a comedy, which it is not. The real-life Joey Coyle, on whom the film is based, committed suicide shortly before its release. Panavision. [R]▼●)

Money From Home (1953) C-100m. ** D: George Marshall. Dean Martin, Jerry Lewis, Marjie Millar, Pat Crowley, Richard Haydn, Robert Strauss, Gerald Mohr, Sheldon Leonard, Jack Kruschen. One of Dean and Jerry's weakest outings is slickly made but wanders all over the place, with Jerry as an aspiring veterinarian who gets involved with gangsters, steeplechase racing, an Arab ruler and his harem. Based on a Damon Runyon story. 3-D.◗

Money Money Money (1973-French) C-113m. *** D: Claude Lelouch. Lino Ventura, Jacques Brel, Charles Denner, Aldo Maccione, Charles Gerard. Gang of successful thieves decide that changing times demand their switch to political crimes, which pay more handsomely. Clever, funny spoof of our heated political era as seen through eyes of men whose only belief is in money. Aka L'AVENTURE, C'EST L'AVENTURE. [PG]◗

Money Pit, The (1986) C-91m. ** D: Richard Benjamin. Tom Hanks, Shelley Long, Alexander Godunov, Maureen Stapleton, Joe Mantegna, Philip Bosco, Josh Mostel. A young couple's slapstick misadventures trying to repair and remodel a lemon of a house. Hanks and Long are very likable, but this yuppie update of MR. BLANDINGS BUILDS HIS DREAM HOUSE loses all contact with reality (and humor). Starts out funny but just gets worse and worse. Produced by Steven Spielberg and Co. [PG]▼●◗

Money Talks (1997) C-95m. ** D: Brett Ratner. Chris Tucker, Charlie Sheen, Heather Locklear, Paul Sorvino, Veronica Cartwright, Gerard Ismael, Paul Gleason, David Warner. TV newsman Sheen stumbles into a big story involving fugitive Tucker, and is forced to palm off the hustler as a longtime friend to fiancée Locklear and her rich parents. Surprise box-office success is familiar and lightweight, but has one genuine spark of whimsy: Tucker's phony masquerade as "Vic Damone, Jr.," brought on by the movie's amusingly concocted TV ad for an album of Vic Sr.'s hit recordings. Super 35. [R]▼●◗

Money Train (1995) C-103m. ** D: Joseph Ruben. Wesley Snipes, Woody Harrelson, Jennifer Lopez, Robert Blake, Chris Cooper, Joe Grifasi. The costars of WHITE MEN CAN'T JUMP try to reignite their chemistry as randy N.Y.C. transit cops—and brothers (!)—who fight over the same woman, argue over Woody's gambling fever, and get involved in the theft of a money-laden subway car. Violent, overly contrived buddy flick with some big subterranean action scenes. The stars are funny together, but Blake is way over the top as the boys' megalomaniac supervisor. All in all, "token" entertainment. Super 35. [R]▼●◗

Money Trap, The (1966) 92m. **½ D: Burt Kennedy. Glenn Ford, Rita Hayworth,

Elke Sommer, Joseph Cotten, Ricardo Montalban. Ford is detective turned crook in pedestrian murder yarn. Hayworth most convincing as middle-aged woman no longer self-sufficient. Rare non-Western from Kennedy; adapted by Walter Bernstein from Lionel White's novel. Panavision.◗

Mongol (2007-Kazakhstanian-German-Russian-Mongolian) C-126m. *** D: Sergei Bodrov. Tadanobu Asano, Khulan Chuluun, Honglei Sun. Surprisingly personal portrait of the man who would be known as Genghis Khan—warrior and conqueror—and his extraordinary bond with the woman he chose to be his wife when he was nine years old. Vivid character portrait is played out on an enormous canvas, with eye-filling images and massive battle scenes, though the film's storytelling momentum flags from time to time. Super 35. [R]◗

Mon Homme (1996-French) C-95m. *** D: Bertrand Blier. Anouk Grinberg, Gérard Lanvin, Valeria Bruni Tedeschi, Olivier Martinez, Sabine Azema, Bernard Le Coq. Gleefully amoral sex fable about a sweet-natured, nymphomaniac prostitute (Grinberg) and what happens when she falls in love with a homeless man and turns him into her pimp. Full of typically perverse and surreal Blier touches, but also surprisingly affecting. Aka MY MAN. Panavision. ▼

Monika SEE: **Summer With Monika**

Monitors, The (1969) C-92m. ** D: Jack Shea. Guy Stockwell, Susan Oliver, Avery Schreiber, Larry Storch, Ed Begley, Keenan Wynn, Alan Arkin, Xavier Cugat, Stubby Kaye, Jackie Vernon, Everett Dirksen. Great cast wasted in this failed attempt at science fiction satire filmed in Chicago by Second City company. Alien Monitors control Earth and keep everything peaceful, but rebels plot against them. From novel by sci-fi writer Keith Laumer. [M/PG]▼

MonkeyBone (2001) C-92m. *½ D: Henry Selick. Brendan Fraser, Bridget Fonda, Dave Foley, Whoopi Goldberg, Giancarlo Esposito, Rose McGowan, Megan Mullally, Lisa Zane, Chris Kattan; voice of John Turturro. Simply awful fantasy-comedy about a cartoonist who's created a mischievous-monkey cartoon alter ego. When he slips into a coma, he enters a bizarre, nightmarish netherworld in which the monkey runs rampant; then the creature wreaks havoc in his "real life" too. Overblown, ugly, unfocused mess; Kattan steals the show in a small but hilarious part. Thomas Haden Church appears uncredited. Based on the graphic novel *Dark Town*. [PG-13]▼◗

Monkey Business (1931) 77m. ***½ D: Norman Z. McLeod. Groucho, Harpo, Chico, Zeppo Marx, Thelma Todd, Ruth Hall, Harry Woods. Four brothers stow away on luxury liner; Groucho goes after gangster's wife Thelma Todd, all four pretend to be Maurice Chevalier to get off ship. Full quota of sight gags and puns in typically wacky comedy, coscripted by S. J. Perelman; their first film written directly for the screen.▼●▶

Monkey Business (1952) **97m.** ******* D: Howard Hawks. Ginger Rogers, Cary Grant, Charles Coburn, Marilyn Monroe, Hugh Marlowe. Grant discovers rejuvenation serum, which affects him, wife Rogers, boss Coburn, and secretary Monroe in this zany comedy. Coburn's classic line to MM: "Find someone to type this." Written by Ben Hecht, Charles Lederer, and I.A.L. Diamond; that's Hawks' voice during the opening credits.▼●▶

Monkey Grip (1982-Australian) **C-101m.** ****½** D: Ken Cameron. Noni Hazlehurst, Colin Friels, Alice Garner, Harold Hopkins, Candy Raymond. Unmemorable drama detailing the trials of singleminded single mother Hazlehurst, particularly her relationship with obnoxious drug addict boyfriend Friels. Nice performance by Hazlehurst, but ultimately just a superficial soap opera.▼

Monkey Hustle (1977) **C-90m.** ***½** D: Arthur Marks. Yaphet Kotto, Rosalind Cash, Rudy Ray Moore, Kirk Calloway, Randy Brooks. Appealing cast is only saving grace of dumb comedy actioner designed for black audiences, shot in Chicago. Kotto is a black Fagin; ghetto neighborhood's impending demise for an expressway forms a bit of plot. [PG]▼▶

Monkeys, Go Home! (1967) **C-101m.** ****** D: Andrew V. McLaglen. Maurice Chevalier, Dean Jones, Yvette Mimieux, Bernard Woringer, Clement Harari, Yvonne Constant. Disney trivia about a man who inherits French olive farm and trains monkeys to pick his crop. Gossamer-thin, for kids only. Chevalier's final film appearance.▼▶

Monkey Shines: An Experiment in Fear (1988) **C-115m.** ****** D: George Romero. Jason Beghe, John Pankow, Kate McNeil, Joyce Van Patten, Christine Forrest, Stephen Root, Stanley Tucci, Janine Turner. A cute monkey (injected with human brain cells) is enlisted to help a quadraplegic get on with his life. From that premise writer-director Romero tries to build horror and suspense, but it only works in spurts, and taxes our credibility (and our patience) far too often. [R]▼●▶

Monkey's Uncle, The (1965) **C-87m.** ****** D: Robert Stevenson. Tommy Kirk, Annette Funicello, Leon Ames, Frank Faylen, Arthur O'Connell, Norman Grabowski. Juvenile Disney comedy has Kirk again as Merlin Jones, college whiz-kid who first tries sleeplearning method on monkey, then sets himself up in makeshift flying machine. Flight sequences provide brightest moments. Unforgettable title song warbled by Annette and The Beach Boys. Sequel to THE MISADVENTURES OF MERLIN JONES.▼▶

Monkey Trouble (1994) **C-95m.** ******* D: Franco Amurri. Thora Birch, Harvey Keitel, Mimi Rogers, Christopher McDonald, Kevin Scannell. Nicely done family film about Eva (Birch), a clever nine-year-old who yearns for a pet; she adopts a Capuchin monkey, whom she hides from her parents. Splendid change-of-pace for Keitel, as a gypsy who'd been using the monkey to pick pockets; the monkey, whom Eva names "Dodger" (played by "Finster"), is a real scene-stealer. Kids Eva's age should love it. Amurri scripted, with Stu Krieger. Ridley Scott executive-produced. [PG]▼▶

Monogamy (2011) **C-96m.** ****** D: Dana Adam Shapiro. Chris Messina, Rashida Jones, Meitel Dohan, Zak Orth, Ivan Martin. Feeling in a rut shooting wedding photos amid the mundane details of planning his own coming marriage, Brooklyn photographer Messina starts a sideline service where clients hire him to take covert pics of them (shot from afar) in their everyday lives. Derivative premise (think BLOWUP and its progeny) gets somewhat of a fresh slant (wounded fiancée Jones senses that her intended is, well . . . becoming distracted). A virtuoso filmmaker could have gone to town with this obsession-spurred hook; the payoff here is middling and on the labored side.▶

Monolith (1994) **C-95m.** BOMB D: John Eyres. Bill Paxton, Lindsay Frost, John Hurt, Louis Gossett, Jr., Paul Ganus, Musetta Vander, Andrew Lamond. Nonsensical sci-fi/action adventure of cops Paxton and Frost chasing an invincible killer alien. Attempts at repartee are embarrassing. [R]▼●

Mon Oncle (1958-French) **C-126m.** ******** D: Jacques Tati. Jacques Tati, Jean-Pierre Zola, Adrienne Servantie, Alain Bercourt. Tati's first color film is a masterpiece. M. Hulot's simple, uncluttered life is sharply contrasted to that of his sister and brother-in-law, who live in an ultramodern, gadget-laden home reminiscent of those in Buster Keaton's silent classics. Continuous flow of sight gags (including the funniest fountain you'll ever see) makes this easygoing, nearly dialogue-less comedy a total delight. Oscar winner as Best Foreign Film. Also available in 115m. English-language version called MY UNCLE. ▼●▶

Mon Oncle Antoine SEE: **My Uncle Antoine**

Mon Oncle d'Amerique (1980-French) **C-123m.** *****½** D: Alain Resnais. Gérard Depardieu, Nicole Garcia, Roger Pierre, Marie Dubois, Nelly Bourgeaud, Henri Laborit. Intensely directed, acted, and written (by Jean Gruault) film illustrating research scientist Laborit's theories on human conduct. The focus is on the intertwined lives of a plant manager (Depardieu), actress (Garcia), and media executive (Pierre). Intelligent, thought-provoking. [PG]▼▶

Monsieur Beaucaire (1946) **93m.** *** D: George Marshall. Bob Hope, Joan Caulfield, Patric Knowles, Marjorie Reynolds, Cecil Kellaway, Joseph Schildkraut, Reginald Owen, Constance Collier. Pleasing Hope vehicle with Bob in costume as barber sent on mission as dead duck sure to be murdered. Plush settings, funny gags. Remake of Rudolph Valentino's 1924 drama. ▼◑

Monsieur Hire (1989-French) **C-88m.** ***½ D: Patrice Leconte. Michel Blanc, Sandrine Bonnaire, Luc Thuillier, Eric Berenger. Bald, middle-aged Peeping Tom falls in love with the object of his obsession—a young woman, peripherally involved in a murder, who lives across the courtyard. Cold, but involving and terrifically acted version of a Georges Simenon novel; the short running time helps. Previously filmed in 1946 as PANIQUE. Panavision. [PG-13]▼◑

Monsieur Ibrahim (2003-French) **C-94m.** **½ D: François Dupeyron. Omar Sharif, Pierre Boulanger, Gilbert Melki, Isabelle Renauld, Lola Naymark, Anne Suarez, Mata Gabin, Isabelle Adjani. A resourceful Jewish teen (Boulanger) in 1960s Paris gets to know the philosophical Muslim shopkeeper across the street . . . and the neighborhood prostitutes as well. The growing friendship between the elder and the adolescent, along with the life lessons, are nicely played, but story is rather slight and leisurely paced. Adjani has a bit as a movie star. [R]▼◐

Monsieur N. (2003-French-British) **C-128m.** ** D: Antoine de Caunes. Philippe Torreton, Richard E. Grant, Jay Rodan, Elsa Zylberstein, Roschdy Zem, Bruno Putzulu, Stéphane Freiss, Frédéric Pierrot, Siobhan Hewlett. Fanciful yarn set on the island of St. Helena, where a British military martinet (Grant) is sent to guard Napoleon Bonaparte (Torreton) in 1815, certain that the ingenious emperor is planning to escape. Told through the eyes of a British lieutenant (Rodan) who suspects, 20 years later, that history has been hoodwinked. Promising story actually grows less interesting as it develops, despite impressive production values. Super 35.◐

Monsieur Verdoux (1947) **123m.** ***½ D: Charles Chaplin. Charles Chaplin, Martha Raye, Isobel Elsom, Marilyn Nash, Irving Bacon, William Frawley. Chaplin's controversial black comedy about a Parisian Bluebeard who murders wives for their money was years ahead of its time; its wry humor and pacifist sentiments make it quite contemporary when seen today. Broad comic sequence with Raye is particular highlight.▼◑

Monsieur Vincent (1947-French) **114m.** *** D: Maurice Cloche. Pierre Fresnay, Aimé Clariond, Jean Debucourt, Lise Delamare, Germaine Dermoz, Gabrielle Dorziat, Pierre Dux, Yvonne Gaudeau. Absorbing biography of Vincent de Paul (Fresnay), the selfless 17th-century French priest who earned fame (and sainthood) for his devotion to and advocacy of the poor. Occasionally slow-moving but not without powerful dramatic moments; film mirrors the time in which it was made as it offers the point of view that the wealthy should take responsibility for those less fortunate in a war-torn world. Coscripted by Jean Anouilh and Jean Bernard-Luc. Winner of a special Academy Award, given before there was a Best Foreign Language Film category. ▼◐

Monsignor (1982) **C-122m.** ** D: Frank Perry. Christopher Reeve, Genevieve Bujold, Fernando Rey, Jason Miller, Joe Cortese, Adolfo Celi, Leonardo Cimino, Tomas Milian, Robert J. Prosky. Saga of ambitious priest who commits every heresy imaginable (including having an affair with a nun!) while operating as the Vatican's business manager. Grows more ridiculous as it goes along—with unintentional comedy on a grand scale—culminating in an astonishing final shot involving the Pope. Another camp classic from the producer and director of MOMMIE DEAREST. [R]▼

Monsignor Quixote (1988-British) **C-118m.** **½ D: Rodney Bennett. Alec Guinness, Leo McKern, Ian Richardson, Graham Crowden, Maurice Denham, Philip Stone, Rosalie Crutchley, Valentine Pelka, Don Fellows. To his surprise, a quiet, provincial Spanish priest (Guinness), a descendant of Don Quixote, is appointed monsignor. To celebrate, he and a local Communist politician (McKern) take a journey that mirrors the adventures of Cervantes' knight errant. Gentle film features fine acting and an interesting story but never engages the emotions. Based on a Graham Greene novel. Made for British television.▼

Monsoon Wedding (2002-Indian-U.S.) **C-113m.** *** D: Mira Nair. Naseeruddin Shah, Lillete Dubey, Shefali Shetty, Vasundhara Das, Parvin Dabas, Vijay Raaz, Tilotama Shome, Rajat Kapoor. A middle-class Punjabi man plans an elaborate wedding that is well beyond his means for his daughter, who has only met the groom weeks ago. In the days leading up to the event, the tangled relationships of his extended family—and his daughter's own doubts—lead to tumult. Long but richly textured comedy-drama emphasizing how love, betrayal, and ambition impose themselves on even the most tradition-bound societies.▼◐

Monster, The (1994-Italian) **C-112m.** **½ D: Roberto Benigni. Roberto Benigni, Michel Blanc, Nicoletta Braschi, Jean-Claude Brialy, Massimo Girotti, Dominique Lavanant, Ivano Marescotti. Bumbling Benigni is mistaken by the police for a wanted serial killer, and he's followed by an attractive female cop hoping to get the goods on him. Moderately amusing comedy will mostly please those who already adore Benigni; others will find fewer laughs. Original title: IL MOSTRO.▼❙

Monster (2003) **C-109m.** *** D: Patty Jenkins. Charlize Theron, Christina Ricci, Bruce Dern, Scott Wilson, Pruitt Taylor Vince, Lee Tergesen, Annie Corley. Theron won an Oscar for her raw, no-holds-barred performance as Aileen Wuornos, the infamous prostitute and serial killer who murdered seven men and was executed in 2002. The film works better as a love story between the emotionally scarred Wuornos and a young woman she grows to trust (Ricci) than as an incisive social commentary. Impressive feature debut for writer-director Jenkins. Theron's extraordinary makeup was crafted by Toni G. [R] ▼❙

Monster Club, The (1980-British) **C-97m.** *½ D: Roy Ward Baker. Vincent Price, John Carradine, Donald Pleasence, Stuart Whitman, Warren Saire, Richard Johnson, Britt Ekland, Simon Ward, Anthony Steel, Patrick Magee. A trio of horror stories, all told by vampire Price. Disappointing and unimaginative, with only the barest of shudders; never released theatrically in the U.S. The club, by the way, is a disco patronized by Transylvanians.▼●❙

Monster House (2006) **C-91m.** **½ D: Gil Kenan. Steve Buscemi, Maggie Gyllenhaal, Kevin James, Nick Cannon, Jason Lee, Jon Heder, Catherine O'Hara, Fred Willard, Kathleen Turner, Mitchel Musso, Sam Lerner, Spencer Locke. Two adolescent boys and a girl they've just met realize that the spooky house across the street is actually alive and swallowing up people! Story gets stranger as it goes along (try explaining it to *your* kids) but offers some good, spooky moments for juvenile audiences. Why it's done with "motion capture," to make animated characters act like real people, is a question adults will have to grapple with. 3-D Digital Widescreen. [PG]❙

Monster in a Box (1992) **C-96m.** *** D: Nick Broomfield. The second film adaptation of a Spalding Gray monologue, this one chronicling various adventures from L.A. to the Soviet Union which interrupt Gray's efforts to write a huge autobiographical novel (the monster of the title). The direction and the music are more obtrusive than in the previous SWIMMING TO CAMBODIA, but Gray's stories and observations are still funny, profound, and extremely compelling. Our favorite anecdote: Gray's semi-disastrous stint as the Stage Manager in a N.Y. revival of *Our Town.*▼❙

Monster-in-Law (2005) **C-95m.** ** D: Robert Luketic. Jennifer Lopez, Jane Fonda, Michael Vartan, Wanda Sykes, Adam Scott, Monet Mazur, Annie Parisse, Will Arnett, Elaine Stritch. Nice girl meets nice guy, and he asks her to marry him. Now she has to contend with the mother-in-law from hell, a vain, controlling woman who'll stop at nothing to prevent the nuptials from taking place. Professionalism (and Sykes' well-calculated one-liners) just barely sustain this obvious, heavy-handed comedy. Fonda is still a formidable presence after 15 years off-screen; too bad she couldn't have found a better script for her return. Super 35. [PG-13]▼❙

Monster in the Closet (1986) **C-87m.** *** D: Bob Dahlin. Donald Grant, Denise DuBarry, Claude Akins, Howard Duff, Henry Gibson, Donald Moffat, Paul Dooley, John Carradine, Jesse White, Stella Stevens. Perceptive and funny homage to 1950s sci-fi flicks. Clark Kent–type reporter Grant and scientist DuBarry team up to track down and destroy California monsters who pop out of closets and kill people. A must for buffs. Filmed in 1983. [PG]▼❙

Monster Island (1981-U.S.-Spanish) **C-100m.** *½ D: Juan Piquer Simon. Terence Stamp, Peter Cushing, Ian Serra, David Hatton, Blanca Estrada. Humdrum actioner, with Serra and Hatton shipwrecked on an island loaded with gold and strange creatures. Based on a story by Jules Verne.

Monsters (2010-British) **C-94m.** **½ D: Gareth Edwards. Scoot McNairy, Whitney Able, Annalee Jefferies, Justin Hall, Victor Vejan. Alien life accidentally brought to Earth has multiplied, overrunning northern Mexico, but it's kept isolated by the regional governments. Years later, two young Americans have to travel overland from central Mexico back to the U.S. across an alien-infested wilderness populated by a few scattered locals. The two become close as they make their dangerous trek. Unusually conceived, ultra-low-budget film is surprisingly intelligent and occasionally suspenseful, though it's overlong, inconclusive, and the acting level varies sharply. Still, an impressive debut for writer-director-cinematographer-production designer Edwards. HD Widescreen. [R]❙

Monster's Ball (2001) **C-112m.** ***½ D: Marc Forster. Billy Bob Thornton, Halle Berry, Peter Boyle, Heath Ledger, Sean Combs, Mos Def, Coronji Calhoun. A soft-spoken Georgia prison functionary who's repressed his feelings for years—through family tragedies and the emotional upheavals of his job—begins to change after his son, a fellow prison guard, reacts badly to their latest execution. Challenging film tackles issues of darkness and light with great feeling and nuance, as Thornton becomes involved with the unstable widow of the man he just put to death. Unlike some dramas that wallow in misery, this one provides a meaningful—and plausible—catharsis, with superb acting right down the line. Berry's shattering performance earned her a Best Actress Oscar. Written by Milo Addica and Will Rokos. Super 35. [R]▼❙

Monsters, Inc. (2001) **C-92m.** ******* D: Peter Docter. Voices of John Goodman, Billy Crystal, Mary Gibbs, Steve Buscemi, James Coburn, Jennifer Tilly, John Ratzenberger, Frank Oz, Bonnie Hunt. Clever, funny computer-animated tale of life in Monstropolis, a city powered by the screams of children frightened by monsters who come out of their closets at night. Trouble begins when a little girl named Boo invades this world—to the dismay of furry monster Sulley and his talkative squire, Mike Wazowski. Goodman and Crystal give wonderful vocal performances; full of laughs for kids and grownups alike. Randy Newman's song "If I Didn't Have You" won an Oscar. Another winner from Pixar and Disney. [G] ▼◗

Monster Squad, The (1987) **C-81m.** ****½** D: Fred Dekker. Andre Gower, Robby Kiger, Stephen Macht, Duncan Regehr, Tom Noonan, Brent Chalem, Ryan Lambert, Ashley Bank. Young friends belong to a club that's devoted to monsters, but they unexpectedly encounter the horror heavies in real life when Dracula (accompanied by the Frankenstein monster, the Mummy, the Wolf Man, and the Gill Man) comes to their town in search of an amulet vital to his continued existence. Affectionate homage to classic horror films and their monster stars is ultimately too bland and unbelievable (even for a kiddie horror film). Climactic showdown boasts Richard Edlund's superduper special effects. Panavision. [PG-13] ▼◗

Monsters vs Aliens (2009) **C-95m.** ****½** D: Rob Letterman, Conrad Vernon. Voices of Reese Witherspoon, Seth Rogen, Hugh Laurie, Will Arnett, Kiefer Sutherland, Rainn Wilson, Stephen Colbert, Paul Rudd, Julie White, Jeffrey Tambor, Amy Poehler, Ed Helms, Renée Zellweger, John Krasinski. Young woman who's about to be married has a close encounter with a meteorite and becomes a giant. The government seizes her and closets her away with other assorted monsters—then realizes that these creatures might be just the ones to fend off an alien invasion. Jokey monster movie is also (no kidding) a female empowerment story. Innocuous animated family entertainment (especially good in 3-D) but the final gags fall curiously flat. 3-D Digital Widescreen. [PG]◗

Monster Zero (1966-Japanese) **92m.** ***½** D: Ishiro Honda. Nick Adams, Akira Takarada. Godzilla and Rodan are swiped from Earth to battle Ghidrah on an alien planet. Lesser monster movie from the Toho Studio. Aka GODZILLA VS. MONSTER ZERO. Tohoscope. ▼◗

Monte Carlo (1930) **90m.** ******* D: Ernst Lubitsch. Jeanette MacDonald, Jack Buchanan, ZaSu Pitts, Claude Allister. Dated but enjoyable musical froth with Jeanette an impoverished countess wooed by royal Buchanan, who's incognito, of course. Lubitsch's methods of integrating songs into the film were innovations in 1930; most memorable is "Beyond the Blue Horizon." ◗|

Monte Carlo or Bust SEE: **Those Daring Young Men in Their Jaunty Jalopies**

Montenegro (1981-Swedish-British) **C-98m.** ******* D: Dusan Makavejev. Susan Anspach, Erland Josephson, Per Oscarsson, John Zacharias, Svetozar Cvetkovic, Patricia Gelin. Bored middle-class housewife Anspach becomes sexually liberated when she accidentally falls in with Yugoslav workers who frequent a boisterous bar. Funny and entertaining. Aka MONTENEGRO OR PIGS AND PEARLS. [R] ▼◗|

Monterey Pop (1969) **C-88m.** *****½** D: James Desmond, Barry Feinstein, D.A. Pennebaker, Albert Maysles, Roger Murphy, Richard Leacock, Nick Proferes. Otis Redding, Mamas and Papas, Jimi Hendrix, The Who, Janis Joplin, Animals, Jefferson Airplane. First major rock concert film, shot at 1967 Monterey Pop Festival, is still one of the best ever, with Joplin's "Ball and Chain" and Hendrix's pyrotechnical "Wild Thing" among the highlights. Video version includes 9m. extra footage. ▼◗

Monte Walsh (1970) **C-106m.** ******* D: William Fraker. Lee Marvin, Jeanne Moreau, Jack Palance, Mitch Ryan, Jim Davis, Allyn Ann McLerie, Richard Farnsworth. Melancholy Western with Marvin a veteran cowboy who finds himself part of a dying West. Sensitive filming of novel by Jack Schaefer (who wrote SHANE). Fine performance by Palance in atypical good-guy role. Directorial debut for noted cinematographer Fraker. Remade for TV in 2003. Panavision. [PG]▼

Month by the Lake, A (1995) **C-94m.** ****½** D: John Irvin. Vanessa Redgrave, Edward Fox, Uma Thurman, Alida Valli, Alessandro Gassman. Garrulous, unmarried Brit (Redgrave) vacations at Italy's Lake Como on the eve of WW2. She's interested in a fellow hotel guest, stiff-upper-lip Fox, but her hesitancy opens the door for flirtatious American Thurman. Sweetly entertaining (and picturesque), if painted in very broad strokes. That's Vittorio Gassman's son as the young lothario. Based on the novella by H. E. Bates. [PG]▼◗

Month in the Country, A (1987-British) **C-96m.** ******* D: Pat O'Connor. Colin Firth, Kenneth Branagh, Natasha Richardson, Patrick Malahide, Tony Haygarth, Jim Carter. Occasionally slow but still thoughtful, rewarding drama about shellshocked WW1 vet Firth, and his experiences while uncovering a medieval painting on a church wall in a remote Yorkshire town. Screenplay by Simon Gray, from a novel by J. R. Carr. Stick with this one. [PG]▼●

Monty Python and the Holy Grail (1975-

British) **C-90m.** **½ D: Terry Gilliam, Terry Jones. Graham Chapman, John Cleese, Terry Gilliam, Eric Idle, Terry Jones, Michael Palin. The Python troupe's second feature is wildly uneven, starting out well and then getting lost—in the "story" of a medieval quest. Some inspired lunacy, and a lot of dry stretches; awfully bloody, too. Recommended for fans only. Adapted into a stage musical, *Spamalot*, in 2004. [PG]▼●〗

Monty Python Live at the Hollywood Bowl (1982-British) **C-77m.** *** D: Terry Hughes, "Monty Python." Graham Chapman, John Cleese, Terry Gilliam, Eric Idle, Terry Jones, Michael Palin, Neil Innes, Carol Cleveland. Britain's bad boys invade Los Angeles with this madcap series of sketches and routines, including many old favorites. A must for Python aficionados. Videotaped, then transferred to film. Aka MONTY PYTHON LIVE. [R]▼●〗

Monty Python's Life of Brian SEE: **Life of Brian**

Monty Python's The Meaning of Life (1983-British) **C-103m.** *** D: Terry Jones. Graham Chapman, John Cleese, Terry Gilliam, Eric Idle, Terry Jones, Michael Palin, Carol Cleveland, Simon Jones. Original, outrageous comedy exploring various facets of life and death—from procreation to the Grim Reaper himself—with typical Python irreverence. Highlights include the world's most obese man (an unforgettable scene, like it or not) and a cheerful, elaborate production number about sperm! A barrel of bellylaughs for Python fans; others beware. [R]▼●〗

Monument Ave. (1998) **C-90m.** ** D: Ted Demme. Denis Leary, Billy Crudup, Ian Hart, Jason Barry, Colm Meaney, Martin Sheen, Jeanne Tripplehorn, Famke Janssen, Noah Emmerich, John Diehl. Substitute Boston-Irish hoods for Martin Scorsese's Italian counterparts, and you get a sense of what this aspires to be. Serviceable drama deals with the tension between an older mentor and his band of younger car thieves, as well as the women who mourn at the funerals their actions have engendered. Might have been more impressive had it come out ten years earlier. [R]▼●〗

Moolaadé (2005-Senegalese-French-Moroccan-Tunisian-Burkina Faso-Cameroon) **C-124m.** ***½ D: Ousmane Sembene. Fatoumata Coulibaly, Maïmouna Hélène Diarra, Salimata Traoré, Dominique T. Zeïda, Mah Compaoré. Deceptively simple but riveting account of a single-minded wife/mother in a small West African village, who defiantly gives refuge to some terrified young girls who want to avoid the ritualistic mutilation of their genitals—a custom throughout many parts of Africa. Difficult subject matter is potently handled by octogenarian Senegalese writer-director Sembene, who has fashioned a multilayered, politically savvy

drama that also brims with charm and wit. This is his final film.〗

Moon (2009) **C-97m.** *** D: Duncan Jones. Sam Rockwell, Dominique McElligott, Kaya Scodelario; voice of Kevin Spacey. On the eve of his expiring contract and a return home to his loved ones, a moon-based maintenance man for a mining company (Rockwell) begins to sense that matters are not as they seem. Adding to his disorientation is a computer/robot (Spacey) whose resemblance to 2001: A SPACE ODYSSEY's duplicitous HAL is obviously very much on the minds of the filmmakers. A good example of how to make a resourceful movie and maintain viewer interest with minimal production components. Director Jones is the son of rock royalty and occasional actor David Bowie. Super 35. [R]〗

Moon and Sixpence, The (1942) **89m.** *** D: Albert Lewin. George Sanders, Herbert Marshall, Doris Dudley, Eric Blore, Albert Bassermann, Molly Lamont, Elena Verdugo, Florence Bates, Heather Thatcher. Surprisingly adult adaptation of W. Somerset Maugham's novel based on the life of Paul Gauguin, with Sanders as the restless (and selfish) spirit who turns his back on his family, and society, to become a painter. A postscript, tacked on to satisfy Hollywood's moral code, weakly tries to undermine the character that Sanders and writer-director Lewin have just portrayed so well! Climactic scene of paintings originally shown in color.▼〗

Moonfleet (1955) **C-87m.** **½ D: Fritz Lang. Stewart Granger, George Sanders, Joan Greenwood, Viveca Lindfors, Jon Whiteley, Melville Cooper, Liliane Montevecchi. Moderately entertaining costumer, set in Southern England, with suave gentleman bootlegger Granger forging a father-son relationship with orphaned Whiteley amid much intrigue. CinemaScope. ●

Moon 44 (1990-West German) **C-102m.** *½ D: Roland Emmerich. Michael Paré, Lisa Eichhorn, Malcolm McDowell, Dean Devlin, Brian Thompson, Stephen Geoffreys, Mechmed Yilmaz, Leon Rippy, Roscoe Lee Browne. In the 21st century, a multinational company forces its prisoners to protect their claim on a "moon" from takeover attempt by rival company. Paré plays a tough undercover agent. Annoyingly derivative, drearily obvious sci-fi epic. Panavision. [R]▼●〗

Moon in the Gutter, The (1983-French) **C-126m.** *½ D: Jean-Jacques Beineix. Nastassia Kinski, Gerard Depardieu, Victoria Abril, Vittorio Mezzogiorno, Dominique Pinon. Overbaked, pompously surreal tale of dockworker Depardieu, seeking his sister's rapist, and his involvement with wealthy, beautiful Kinski. Both stars couldn't be worse. Panavision. [R]▼〗

Moon Is Blue, The (1953) **99m.** **½ D: Otto Preminger. William Holden, David

Niven, Maggie McNamara, Tom Tully, Dawn Addams, Gregory Ratoff. Once-saucy sex comedy about a young woman who flaunts her virginity now seems tame, too much a filmed stage play, with most innuendoes lacking punch. Adapted by F. Hugh Herbert from his stage hit. Hardy Kruger (who has a small part here) played the lead in a German-language version that Preminger filmed simultaneously.▼○)

Moonlight and Valentino (1995) **C-104m.** *** D: David Anspaugh. Elizabeth Perkins, Whoopi Goldberg, Kathleen Turner, Gwyneth Paltrow, Jon Bon Jovi, Jeremy Sisto, Josef Sommer. A young woman cannot deal with the reality of suddenly being widowed—despite the support of her best friend, her younger sister, and her ex-stepmother, who rally around her. Unusual subject matter portrayed with skill and unpredictability, though some will find it too talky and/or too studied in its quirkiness. Perkins gives an outstanding performance. Ellen Simon (daughter of Neil) adapted her stage play, based on her own experience. Peter Coyote appears unbilled as Goldberg's husband. Panavision. [R] ▼○)

Moonlighter, The (1953) **75m.** ** D: Roy Rowland. Barbara Stanwyck, Fred MacMurray, Ward Bond, William Ching, John Dierkes, Jack Elam. Drifter MacMurray returns home to find that sweetheart Stanwyck is about to marry his brother. Complications ensue but there are no sparks, though Stanwyck is convincing as a rugged woman of the West. Mediocre Western written by Niven Busch. 3-D.❙

Moonlighting (1982-British) **C-97m.** **** D: Jerzy Skolimowski. Jeremy Irons, Eugene Lipinski, Jiří Stanislav, Eugeniusz Haczkiewicz. Slow-paced but mesmerizing allegory about a Polish man sent to London with a trio of workmen to renovate a wealthy man's apartment. The supervisor (Irons) must keep their job a secret, since they have no work permits; the pressure increases when he learns that Poland has imposed martial law. Fascinating study of loneliness and desperation, full of irony and bittersweet humor; Irons is superb. Written and directed by Polish emigré Skolimowski. [PG] ▼○)

Moonlight Mile (2002) **C-117m.** **½ D: Brad Silberling. Jake Gyllenhaal, Dustin Hoffman, Susan Sarandon, Holly Hunter, Ellen Pompeo, Richard T. Jones, Allan Corduner, Dabney Coleman. Young man whose fiancée was murdered just before their wedding continues to live with the girl's parents as they all try to deal with their grief—and he grapples with feelings of guilt and indecision. Delicate material is handled with skill and good humor, until the young hero meets a woman who's too good to be true, and the story's credibility is derailed. Salvaged, to a great degree, by superior acting from Hoffman and Sarandon. Silberling wrote this

in response to the murder of his girlfriend, actress Rebecca Schaffer, in 1989. Panavision. [PG-13] ▼❙

Moon Over Broadway (1997) **C-92m.** *** D: D. A. Pennebaker, Chris Hegedus. Revealing—and entertaining—documentary about the Broadway production of Ken Ludwig's comedy *Moon Over Buffalo,* starring Carol Burnett, in her first Broadway play in many years, and Philip Bosco. The assorted behind-the-scenes power trips, emotions, and distresses are captured in vivid detail; a fascinating look at what goes into creating a high-profile Broadway production. A must for theater buffs. ▼❙

Moon Over Miami (1941) **C-91m.** *** D: Walter Lang. Don Ameche, Betty Grable, Robert Cummings, Carole Landis, Charlotte Greenwood, Jack Haley. Grable, sister Landis, and Greenwood go fortune-hunting in Miami, come up with more than they bargained for in smoothly entertaining musical romance, especially nice in Technicolor. Tuneful songs include title number, "You Started Something." Remake of THREE BLIND MICE, also remade as THREE LITTLE GIRLS IN BLUE.▼❙

Moon Over Parador (1988) **C-105m.** **½ D: Paul Mazursky. Richard Dreyfuss, Raul Julia, Sonia Braga, Jonathan Winters, Michael Greene, Polly Holliday, Charo, Marianne Sägebrecht, Sammy Davis, Jr., Dick Cavett, Ed Asner. Amiable comedy about an American actor who's shanghaied into portraying a recently deceased Latin American dictator; reluctant at first, he soon finds he enjoys the charade (and the despot's sexy companion). Entertaining enough, but never hits the bull's-eye. Cowriter/director Mazursky has a hilarious cameo in drag. Inspired by THE MAGNIFICENT FRAUD (1939). [PG-13] ▼○)

Moon Pilot (1962) **C-98m.** *** D: James Neilson. Tom Tryon, Brian Keith, Edmond O'Brien, Dany Saval, Tommy Kirk, Bob Sweeney, Kent Smith. Dated but enjoyable Disney comedy about astronaut Tryon who meets mysterious girl from another planet (Saval) just before his mission.▼❙

Moonraker (1979) **C-126m.** ** D: Lewis Gilbert. Roger Moore, Lois Chiles, Michael Lonsdale, Richard Kiel, Corinne Clery, Bernard Lee, Desmond Llewelyn, Lois Maxwell. James Bond no longer resembles Ian Fleming's creation; now he's a tired punster pursuing an intergalactic madman. Overblown comic-strip adventure is strictly for the bubble-gum set . . . but tune in for eye-popping free-fall opening, the best part of this movie. Lee's last appearance as "M." Panavision. [PG]▼○)

Moonrise (1948) **90m.** **½ D: Frank Borzage. Dane Clark, Gail Russell, Ethel Barrymore, Allyn Joslyn, Henry (Harry) Morgan, Lloyd Bridges, Selena Royle, Rex Ingram, Harry Carey, Jr. Uneven script does in this psychological melodrama of angry, alienated Clark and his plight after accidentally killing the banker's son who's been taunting him for years. But it's beautifully directed; check out stunning opening shot, and opening sequence. ▼●

Moonrunners (1974) **C-102m.** ** D: Gy Waldron. James Mitchum, Kiel Martin, Arthur Hunnicutt, Joan Blackman, Waylon Jennings, Chris Forbes. Action-comedy about modern day bootleggers sputters because of Mitchum's lethargic acting and the script's lack of credibility. Later developed into the *Dukes of Hazzard* TV series. [PG]

Moonshine County Express (1977) **C-95m.** **½ D: Gus Trikonis. John Saxon, Susan Howard, William Conrad, Morgan Woodward, Claudia Jennings, Jeff Corey, Dub Taylor, Maureen McCormick. Murdered moonshiner's three sexy daughters decide to compete with local biggie (Conrad) whom they believe caused their father's death. Strong cast buoys good action programmer. [PG]▼

Moonshine War, The (1970) **C-100m.** ** D: Richard Quine. Richard Widmark, Alan Alda, Patrick McGoohan, Melodie Johnson, Will Geer, Joe Williams, Lee Hazlewood. Tediously plotted mixture of comedy and drama during late Prohibition era enlivened by unusual cast and honest attempt to evoke country atmosphere. Script by Elmore Leonard, from his novel. Look for Teri Garr as the tourist's wife. Panavision. [PG]

Moon-Spinners, The (1964) **C-118m.** **½ D: James Neilson. Hayley Mills, Eli Wallach, Pola Negri, Peter McEnery, Joan Greenwood, Irene Papas. Disney's attempt at Hitchcock-like intrigue with a light touch has Hayley a vacationer in Crete who becomes involved with jewelry-smuggling ring. Too long and muddled, but still entertaining, with Negri (off-screen since 1943) an enjoyable villainess. ▼●▶

Moonstruck (1987) **C-102m.** **** D: Norman Jewison. Cher, Nicolas Cage, Vincent Gardenia, Olympia Dukakis, Danny Aiello, Julie Bovasso, John Mahoney, Louis Guss, Feodor Chaliapin, Anita Gillette. A gem of a movie that unfolds like a good play, without ever seeming static or stagy. Cher plays an independent young widow who agrees to marry an older man (Aiello) —and then finds herself inexorably drawn to his misfit younger brother (Cage). John Patrick Shanley's script is brimming with wonderful vignettes and acute observations about Italian-American families. Cher, Dukakis (terrific as the mother), and Shanley won Oscars for their work. [PG]▼●▶

Moontrap (1989) **C-92m.** **½ D: Robert Dyke. Walter Koenig, Bruce Campbell, Leigh Lombardi, Robert Kurcz. OK entertainment, as aging space shuttle pilot and younger partner are sent to the Moon to investigate alien artifacts, but inadvertently

restart alien machinery designed to invade the Earth. Very low-budget production shows ingenuity in its special effects and imagination in the story, but dramatic values are highly variable. [R]▼●

Moon Zero Two (1969-British) **C-100m.** *½ D: Roy Ward Baker. James Olson, Catherina Von Schell (Catherine Schell), Warren Mitchell, Adrienne Corri, Ori Levy, Dudley Foster. Sci-fi adventure is almost like a Western, with people making mining claims on the moon and having to fight for their rights. You've seen it before without the craters. ▼▶

More American Graffiti (1979) **C-111m.** *½ D: B. W. L. Norton. Candy Clark, Bo Hopkins, Ron Howard, Paul Le Mat, Mackenzie Phillips, Charles Martin Smith, Cindy Williams, Anna Bjorn, Scott Glenn, Mary Kay Place, Rosanna Arquette, Delroy Lindo. More is less, in this sequel to 1973 hit, placing that film's likable characters in a quartet of pointless vignettes. Look sharp for Harrison Ford as a motorcycle cop. Panavision (part). [PG]▼●▶

More Than a Game (2009) **C-105m.** *** D: Kristopher Belman. Inspiring sports documentary follows NBA legend-in-the-making LeBron James and four of his teammates (Dru Joyce, Romeo Travis, Sian Cotton, and Willie McGee) as they conquer high school basketball in Akron, Ohio, anticipating James' remarkable pro career. Although hoop fans are the likely audience, the film's title indicates filmmakers have more on their mind in chronicling this likable group. Using a mix of real footage and CGI enhancements, director Belman depicts a story of true camaraderie and a love for the game. [PG]▶

More Than a Miracle (1967-Italian-French) **C-105m.** ** D: Francesco Rosi. Sophia Loren, Omar Sharif, Dolores Del Rio, Georges Wilson, Leslie French, Marina Malfatti. Sophia has never looked better but this absurd fairy tale about a prince and a peasant girl is just a waste of time. Franscope.

More the Merrier, The (1943) **104m.** *** D: George Stevens. Jean Arthur, Joel McCrea, Charles Coburn, Richard Gaines, Bruce Bennett, Ann Savage, Ann Doran, Frank Sully, Grady Sutton. The wartime housing shortage forces Arthur to share a Washington, D.C., apartment with McCrea and crafty old codger Coburn (who won an Oscar for this comic performance). Highly entertaining, with Arthur at her peerless best. Remade as WALK, DON'T RUN. ▼●▶

Morgan! (1966-British) **97m.** ***½ D: Karel Reisz. Vanessa Redgrave, David Warner, Robert Stephens, Irene Handl. Decidedly offbeat gem. Artist Warner verges on insanity, keyed off by wife Redgrave's divorcing him, and goes on eccentric escapades. Script by David Mercer, from his play. Vanessa's film debut. Complete title is MORGAN—A SUITABLE CASE FOR TREATMENT.▼○❶

Morgan Stewart's Coming Home (1987) **C-96m.** *½ D: Alan Smithee. Jon Cryer, Lynn Redgrave, Nicholas Pryor, Viveka Davis, Paul Gleason. Inane comedy from the notorious, and pseudonymous, director Smithee (in this case Paul Aaron) about a teenager who returns home from boarding school and tries to change the ways of his obnoxious, politically ambitious parents. Plays like an unsold sitcom pilot. Redgrave is wasted, and even Cryer's considerable charm can't make this worth coming home to see. [PG-13]▼○❶

Morituri (1965) **123m.** **½ D: Bernhard Wicki. Marlon Brando, Yul Brynner, Janet Margolin, Trevor Howard, Wally Cox, William Redfield, Carl Esmond. Brando highlights great cast in study of anti-Nazi German who helps British capture cargo ship. Cast and Conrad Hall's photography are only assets; script degenerates. Aka THE SABOTEUR, CODE NAME MORITURI. ▼❶

Morning After, The (1986) **C-103m.** ** D: Sidney Lumet. Jane Fonda, Jeff Bridges, Raul Julia, Diane Salinger, Richard Foronjy, Geoffrey Scott, James (Gypsy) Haake, Kathleen Wilhoite, Frances Bergen, Rick Rossovich. So-called thriller about alcoholic actress waking in bed with a dead man and not knowing how it happened. Tiresome story and ill-defined characters send this one down the tubes, despite promising star combo. Look fast for Kathy Bates as neighbor of victim. [R]▼○❶

Morning Glory (1933) **74m.** *** D: Lowell Sherman. Katharine Hepburn, Adolphe Menjou, Douglas Fairbanks, Jr., C. Aubrey Smith, Mary Duncan. Dated but lovely film from Zoe Akins' play about stagestruck young girl called Eva Lovelace who tries to succeed in N.Y.C. Good cast, sharp script, but it's magically compelling Hepburn who makes this memorable; she won her first Oscar for her work. Remade in 1958 as STAGE STRUCK.▼○❶

Morning Glory (2010) **C-107m.** *** D: Roger Michell. Rachel McAdams, Harrison Ford, Diane Keaton, Patrick Wilson, Jeff Goldblum, John Pankow, Matt Malloy, Patti D'Arbanville, Ty Burrell. Hardworking local TV producer (McAdams) gets a shot at the big time at a struggling network morning show in N.Y.C. The catch: she has to deal with the unbridled ego of the female host (Keaton) and the overwhelming surliness of her new partner, a past-his-prime anchorman (Ford) who finds his new assignment beneath his dignity. Bright, funny comedy written by Aline Brosh McKenna (who scripted another "inside" comedy, THE DEVIL WEARS PRADA). All three stars hit the bull's-eye, but it's a special treat to see Ford in such an atypical role. Many famous TV figures appear as themselves. Super 35. [PG-13]▼❶

Morning Light (2008) **C-97m.** ** D: Mark Monroe, Paul Crowder. Narrated by Patrick Warburton. Longtime sailing enthusiast (and racing cup holder) Roy E. Disney sponsors a competition to select 15 young people from various backgrounds to participate in the Transpac, a grueling 2,200-mile race across the Pacific Ocean to Hawaii. Curiously uninvolving reality-TV–type fare in which even the finale fails to pack a punch. [PG]❶

Morocco (1930) **92m.** *** D: Josef von Sternberg. Gary Cooper, Marlene Dietrich, Adolphe Menjou, Francis McDonald, Eve Southern, Paul Porcasi. Dietrich is alluring and exotic in her first Hollywood film, as a cabaret singer (improbably stuck in Morocco) who must choose between wealthy Menjou and Foreign Legionnaire Cooper. A treat. Marlene sings three numbers, including "What Am I Bid."▼○❶

Morons From Outer Space (1985-British) **C-87m.** **½ D: Mike Hodges. Griff Rhys Jones, Mel Smith, James B. Sikking, Dinsdale Landen, Jimmy Nail, Joanne Pearce, Paul Brown. Chaos reigns supreme in this inventive, uneven, but sometimes hilarious comedy about some very human aliens with British accents—who also happen to be brainless twits—and what happens when their spaceship crash-lands on Earth. Sight gags galore. [PG-13]▼❶

Mortadella SEE: **Lady Liberty**

Mortal Kombat (1995) **C-102m.** *½ D: Paul Anderson. Christopher Lambert, Robin Shou, Linden Ashby, Cary-Hiroyuki Tagawa, Bridgette Wilson, Talisa Soto. Shou, Ashby, and Wilson are among those kompeting in a martial arts tournament with nothing less than the fate of Earth in the balance. Elaborate special effects and impressive set design are helpless against a weak story, uneven akting, and komikally thin karakters. Mostly one fight after another, as you might expect from a movie based on a video game. Followed by a sequel. [PG-13]▼○❶

Mortal Kombat: Annihilation (1997) **C-95m.** BOMB D: John Leonetti. Robin Shou, Talisa Soto, James Remar, Brian Thompson, Lynn "Red" Williams, Irina Pantaeva. Mind-numbing sequel rehashes battle between good and evil for the fate of mankind (*yawn*). OK visual effects but endless fight scenes and dreadful acting stop film dead in its tracks. Of interest only to *American Gladiator* fanatics and vidkids with really low attention spans. Remar's morph from David Carradine–style kung fu sensei to turbo warrior is unintentionally hilarious. [PG-13] ▼○❶

Mortal Storm, The (1940) **100m.** ***½ D: Frank Borzage. Margaret Sullavan, James Stewart, Robert Young, Frank Morgan, Robert Stack, Bonita Granville, Irene Rich, Maria Ouspenskaya, Gene Reynolds, Ward

Bond. Nazi takeover in Germany splits family, ruins life of father, professor Morgan; Stewart tries to leave country with professor's daughter (Sullavan). Sincere filming of Phyllis Bottome's novel is beautifully acted, with one of Morgan's finest performances. Screenplay by Claudine West, Andersen Ellis, and George Froeschel. Film debut of Dan Dailey (billed as Dan Dailey, Jr.); look sharp in second classroom scene for Tom Drake.▼▶

Mortal Thoughts (1991) **C-104m.** **½ D: Alan Rudolph. Demi Moore, Glenne Headly, Bruce Willis, John Pankow, Harvey Keitel, Billie Neal. Two police detectives question a woman about the incidents surrounding the murder of her best friend's husband, an abusive lout. Interesting, flashback-framed film boasts some good performances, but a cast of characters it's hard to care much about, and a conclusion that pulls the rug out from everything else we've just seen. Meaningless "touches" (like use of slow-motion) don't add anything. Moore coproduced. [R]▼●

Morvern Callar (2002-British) **C-97m.** *** D: Lynne Ramsay. Samantha Morton, Kathleen McDermott, Raife Patrick Burchell, Dan Cadan, Carolyn Calder, Jim Wilson, Dolly Wells, Ruby Milton. Effectively moody, stunningly visual portrait of reckless youth and aimlessness. Morton is a Scottish supermarket clerk floating through a club-hopping, booze-swilling, pill-popping youth scene; her writer-boyfriend has killed himself, and she shamelessly claims to be the author of his unpublished novel. This cautionary tale about not having goals and accepting responsibilities exudes a quiet, poignant sadness. Based on the novel by Alan Warner. ▼▶

Moscow Does Not Believe in Tears (1980-Russian) **C-152m.** *** D: Vladimir Menshov. Vera Alentova, Irina Muravyova, Raisa Ryazonova, Natalia Vavilova, Alexei Batalov. A trio of young women come to Moscow during the late '50s to seek love and work. Enjoyable if slow moving; closer in spirit to THE BEST OF EVERYTHING than WAR AND PEACE. Oscar winner as Best Foreign Film.▼▶

Moscow on the Hudson (1984) **C-115m.** ***½ D: Paul Mazursky. Robin Williams, Maria Conchita Alonso, Cleavant Derricks, Alejandro Rey, Savely Kramarov, Elya Baskin. Fine original comedy-drama by Mazursky and Leon Capetanos about a Russian musician who defects during a trip to N.Y.C.—in Bloomingdale's, no less—and tries to come to grips with his new life in a new land. Full of endearing performances, perceptive and bittersweet moments—but a few too many false endings. Williams is superb in the lead. [R]▼●

Mosquito Coast, The (1986) **C-117m.** ***½ D: Peter Weir. Harrison Ford, Helen Mirren, River Phoenix, Jadrien Steele, Hilary Gordon, Rebecca Gordon, Conrad Roberts, Andre Gregory, Dick O'Neill, Martha Plimpton, Butterfly McQueen, Jason Alexander. Utterly compelling, novelistic saga of iconoclastic inventor and idealist (Ford, in a knockout performance) who moves his family to remote village in Central America where he creates an incredible utopia . . . and proceeds to play God. Not for all tastes, since Ford's character is unsympathetic (though he was even worse in Paul Theroux's novel!). Beautifully crafted, with fine screenplay by Paul Schrader. A serious and emotionally gripping film. [PG]▼●▶

Mosquito Squadron (1969-British) **C-90m.** **½ D: Boris Sagal. David McCallum, Suzanne Neve, David Buck, David Dundas, Dinsdale Landen, Charles Gray. Good ensemble performances in tired story of Canadian-born RAF pilot (McCallum)'s crucial behind-the-lines mission to destroy Germany's ultimate weapon project. [G]▶

Most Dangerous Game, The (1932) **63m.** *** D: Ernest B. Schoedsack, Irving Pichel. Joel McCrea, Fay Wray, Leslie Banks, Robert Armstrong, Noble Johnson. Vivid telling of Richard Connell's famous, oft-filmed story about a megalomaniac named Count Zaroff who hunts human beings on his remote island. Banks is a florid, sometimes campy villain. Made at the same time as KING KONG by many of the same people. Remade as A GAME OF DEATH and RUN FOR THE SUN, and ripped off many other times.▼●

Most Dangerous Sin, The SEE: **Crime and Punishment** (1958)

Mostly Martha (2002-German) **C-105m.** *** D: Sandra Nettelbeck. Martina Gedeck, Maxime Foerste, Sergio Castellitto, August Zirner, Sibylle Canonica, Katja Studt. Food, love and human relationships blend seamlessly in this tasty concoction about a neurotically obsessive chef (Gedeck), whose life of order and isolation is jolted upon the arrival of her 8-year-old niece (Foerste) and a charming new coworker (Castellitto). Nothing spectacular or innovative here, just a diverting entertainment that's as fun to watch as the mouthwatering dishes Martha concocts. Remade as NO RESERVATIONS. [PG]▼▶

Most Wanted (1997) **C-99m.** ** D: David Glenn Hogan. Keenen Ivory Wayans, Jon Voight, Jill Hennessy, Paul Sorvino, Robert Culp, Wolfgang Bodison, Simon Baker Denny, David Groh, John Diehl, Eric Roberts. Wayans coexecutive-produced and scripted this slick but boring, predictable, and instantly forgettable actioner about a G.I., trained as a government assassin, who takes it on the lam after being framed for murdering the First Lady. Voight makes the most of his role as a creepy, power-obsessed general. Super 35. [R]▼●

Motel Hell (1980) **C-92m.** *½ D: Kevin

Connor. Rory Calhoun, Paul Linke, Nancy Parsons, Nina Axelrod, Wolfman Jack, Elaine Joyce, Dick Curtis, John Ratzenberger. Just *what* are Calhoun and his rotund sister putting in their smoked sausage out there in the boondocks? Good to see Rory and Wolfman sharing screen credit, but scattered laughs and a lively finish fail to distinguish this gory horror comedy. [R]▼●◗

Mother (1996) **C-104m.** *** D: Albert Brooks. Albert Brooks, Debbie Reynolds, Rob Morrow, Lisa Kudrow, John C. McGinley, Isabel Glasser, Peter White. Typically low-key but likable Brooks movie about a twice-divorced man who decides to move back in with his mother in an attempt to understand the root of his problems with women. A benign comedy of recognition, with Brooks as endearing as ever and Reynolds in a well-modulated, nonjokey performance as Mother. Brooks scripted with frequent collaborator Monica Johnson. [PG-13]▼●◗

Mother, The (2003-British) **C-112m.** *** D: Roger Michell. Anne Reid, Daniel Craig, Peter Vaughan, Cathryn Bradshaw, Anna Wilson-Jones, Danira Govich. During a family visit to London a recently widowed grandmother explores rediscovered sexual desire when she secretly carries on a red-hot affair with her whiny daughter's boyfriend, a carpenter half her age. Absorbing and explicit drama benefits from Reid's luminous performance as an older woman not fulfilled just playing with the grandkids. Dramatic sparks between her and Craig (as her hunky lover) lift what could have been perverse melodrama into a different league. Challenging, well-written script by Hanif Kureishi. [R]▼◗

Mother (2009-South Korean) **C-128m.** ***½ D: Joon-ho Bong. Hye-ja Kim, Bin Won, Goo Jin, Yoon Jae-Moon, Mi-sun Jun, Young-Suck Lee, Sea-Beauk Song, Munhee Na. Gripping tale of a poor working woman who's always looking out for her slow-witted son. When he is arrested and accused of brutally murdering a girl in their village, she does everything she can to defend him—and get him to concentrate, so he can remember what actually happened that fateful night. More than a mere whodunit, this multilayered story also evokes life in a tight-knit community with all its alliances, prejudices, and corruption. Kim gives a riveting performance as the desperate mother. The director also coscripted. Hawk Scope. [R]◗

Mother and Child (2010) **C-126m.** *** D: Rodrigo García. Naomi Watts, Annette Bening, Kerry Washington, Jimmy Smits, Samuel L. Jackson, S. Epatha Merkerson, Cherry Jones, Eileen Ryan, Elpidia Carrillo, Marc Blucas, David Ramsey, Shareeka Epps, Lisa Gay Hamilton, David Morse, Michael Warren, LaTanya Richardson, Amy Brenneman, Carla Gallo, Tatyana Ali, Elizabeth Peña, Lawrence Pressman. Long but absorbing drama about three women involved with adoption from completely different perspectives: prickly caregiver Bening (who gave up her baby as a teenage mother), ambitious attorney Watts (who never knew her parents), and Washington, who desperately wants to have a child. Some of the plot turns are contrived, but the emotions all ring true in director García's screenplay—and the performances are exceptional. HD Widescreen. [R]◗

Mother Ghost (2007) **C-76m.** *** D: Rich Thorne. Mark Thompson, Kevin Pollak, Dana Delany, Jere Burns, Charles Durning, Joe Mantegna, Garry Marshall, James Franco, David Keith. Self-assured businessman has been acting strange since the death of his mother a year ago; his wife and best friend tell him he needs help, but he's in denial. Then he chances to hear a radio psychiatrist and impulsively calls in; before long he's spilling his guts. Modestly made film does what few major movies accomplish, focusing on a character who lays bare his emotions. Pollak is especially good as the shrink. Thompson (half of the morning-radio team Mark & Brian) also wrote the script. Made in 2002.◗

Motherhood (2009) **C-89m.** ** D: Katherine Dieckmann. Uma Thurman, Anthony Edwards, Minnie Driver, Daisy Tahan, Alice Drummond, Samantha Bee, Stephanie Szostak, Dale Soules, Clea Lewis, Arjun Gupta. One long hot day in the life of a struggling Greenwich Village mom, as she juggles an eccentric hubby, two toddlers, an incontinent dog, an impending birthday party, a towed Volvo, a bitter best friend, and a midnight deadline for a competition at a parenting blog. Agitated, mildly satiric seriocomedy, written by the director, may work best for grown-ups who have been there. Jodie Foster has an odd wordless cameo as herself. [PG-13]◗

Mother, Jugs & Speed (1976) **C-95m.** *** D: Peter Yates. Bill Cosby, Raquel Welch, Harvey Keitel, Allen Garfield, Larry Hagman, Bruce Davison, Dick Butkus, L.Q. Jones, Toni Basil. Hilarious black comedy about a rundown ambulance service more interested in number of patients serviced than their welfare. Hagman especially good as oversexed driver. Panavision. [PG]▼◗

Mother Kusters Goes to Heaven (1975-German) **C-108m.** *** D: Rainer Werner Fassbinder. Brigitte Mira, Ingrid Caven, Margit Carstensen, Karl-Heinz Böhm (Carl Boehm), Irm Hermann, Gottfried John. When a factory worker goes berserk and commits suicide after killing his boss' son, his shocked widow tries to learn how such a thing could occur, only to find herself being exploited by both right- and left-wing groups as well as her own family. Darkly satirical, politically charged fable is one of Fassbinder's most straightforward, accessible films. ▼◗

Mother Lode (1982) **C-101m.** ****** D: Charlton Heston. Charlton Heston, Nick Mancuso, Kim Basinger, John Marley. Heston's a meanie here—in twin brother roles—playing a Scottish miner who'll stop at nothing to get his sullied hands on a mother lode of gold in the mountains of British Columbia. Lackluster script was written by his son, Fraser Clarke Heston, who also produced the film. Reissued as SEARCH FOR THE MOTHER LODE: THE LAST GREAT TREASURE. [PG]**▼)**

Mother Night (1996) **C/B&W-110m.** ******* D: Keith Gordon. Nick Nolte, Sheryl Lee, Alan Arkin, John Goodman, Kirsten Dunst, Arye Gross, Frankie Faison, David Strathairn, Bernard Behrens, Brawley Nolte. American prisoner in an Israeli jail writes his memoirs, flashing back to his upbringing in Germany, where his career as a successful playwright was interrupted by his recruitment as a U.S. spy. His mission: to pose as a Nazi propagandist on the radio. Nolte takes on the challenging role in this adaptation of Kurt Vonnegut's provocative novel by writer-producer Robert B. Weide. Somber, fascinating, and unsettling. Vivid contributions by Arkin, Goodman, and others in supporting roles. Vonnegut does a cameo near the end of the film. [R]**▼●)**

Mother of Tears (2007-U.S-Italian) **C-102m.** ***½** D: Dario Argento. Asia Argento, Cristian Solimeno, Adam James, Moran Atias, Valeria Cavalli, Udo Kier. American archaeologist in Rome opens an ancient urn, releasing the last witch on Earth, and must elicit her own unsuspected psychic power to rout the evil flooding the city with waves of murder and mayhem. Gory, nonsensical eye-roller was made (unconvincingly) in English, delivering cliché after cliché with little of Argento's usual rococo élan. Third entry in director's "Three Mothers" trilogy, preceded by SUSPIRIA (1977) and INFERNO (1980), and drawn from Thomas De Quincey's 1845 *Suspiria De Profundis*. Daria Nicolodi, Asia's mother, plays her ghost mom. Super 35. [R]**❱**

Mother's Boys (1994) **C-95m.** ****** D: Yves Simoneau. Jamie Lee Curtis, Peter Gallagher, Joanne Whalley-Kilmer, Vanessa Redgrave, Luke Edwards, Colin Ward, Joey Zimmerman, Joss Ackland. Curtis makes an unwise return to the horror genre in this silly mom-who-deserted-family-wants-them-back revenge film. Gallagher, in a rare sympathetic turn, plays the husband, and Edwards is the eldest of three sons (and the one whose buttons Mother tries her best to push). Suspense is minimal, and story is too undernourished to have much bite. Despite one (odd) nude scene, Jamie Lee fans would fare better re-renting HALLOWEEN. [R]**▼●)**

Mother's Day (1980) **C-98m.** ***½** D: Charles Kaufman. Tiana Pierce, Nancy Hendrickson, Deborah Luce, Rose Ross,

Holden McGuire, Billy Ray McQuade. Just about the final word in the horror-misogyny genre. Three college chums are victimized by, then turn the tables on, a hillbilly mother and her two sons. No MURDER, HE SAYS, but Drano/electric carving-knife finale does boast showmanship.**▼●)**

Mother Wore Tights (1947) **C-107m.** ******* D: Walter Lang. Betty Grable, Dan Dailey, Mona Freeman, Connie Marshall, Vanessa Brown, Veda Ann Borg; narrated by Anne Baxter. One of Grable's most popular films, about a vaudeville family. Colorful production, costumes, nostalgic songs, Oscar-winning Alfred Newman score, plus specialty act by the great Señor Wences.**▼**

Mothman Prophecies, The (2002) **C-119m.** ****** D: Mark Pellington. Richard Gere, Laura Linney, Debra Messing, Will Patton, Lucinda Jenney, Alan Bates, David Eigenberg, Ann McDonough. Newspaper reporter Gere's wife has a paranormal experience. Then, several years later, he finds himself in a West Virginia town where scary, unexplainable incidents are happening right and left. Science-fiction meets conspiracy thriller in this muddled film; creepy at first, then simply tiresome. Based on real-life events, but so what? Super 35. [PG-13] **▼)**

Mothra (1961-Japanese) **C-100m.** ****½** D: Ishirô Honda, Lee Kresel. Franky Sakai, Hiroshi Koizumi, Kyoko Kagawa, Emi Itoh, Yumi Itoh, Jelly Itoh. Colorful Japanese monster movie about a giant caterpillar who invades Tokyo to rescue tiny twin girls, who are guiding it with their supernatural powers. Caterpillar then turns into a giant moth (natch), which carries on the destruction. Mothra (or its descendants) turned up in later films too. Tohoscope.**▼)**

Motorcycle Diaries, The (2004-U.S.-British-Argentinian) **C-126m.** ******** D: Walter Salles. Gael García Bernal, Rodrigo de la Serna, Mia Maestro, Gustavo Bueno, Jorge Chiarella. Two friends set off from Buenos Aires in 1952 on a beat-up motorcycle to see South America before they settle down. We share a journey of self-discovery (and political awakening) with these passionate young men as they travel through Chile, Peru, and Venezuela, winding up at a leper colony where they have volunteered their services. One of them will become famous as Che Guevara, but that lies far ahead. Jose Rivera's screenplay is based on the two friends' published memoirs, beautifully realized by director Salles. A profoundly moving film. Oscar winner for Jorge Drexler's song "Al Otro Lado Del Rio." [R] **▼)**

Mouchette (1967-French) **90m.** ******* D: Robert Bresson. Nadine Nortier, Marie Cardinal, Paul Hébert, Jean Vimenet, Jean-Claude Guilbert. Affecting tale of a 14-year-old girl who tries to escape her unhappy life with an abusive, alcoholic father and invalid mother, but only finds more cruelty and misery in the outside world. Sensitive Bresson study about the inherent pain of existence is relentlessly bleak, but essential viewing for serious students of cinema; beautifully shot by Ghislain Cloquet. From the novel by Georges Bernanos. ▼❚➤

Moulin Rouge (1952) **C-119m.** ***½ D: John Huston. Jose Ferrer, Zsa Zsa Gabor, Suzanne Flon, Eric Pohlmann, Colette Marchand, Christopher Lee, Michael Balfour, Peter Cushing. Rich, colorful film based on life of Henri de Toulouse-Lautrec, the 19th century Parisian artist whose growth was stunted by childhood accident. Huston brilliantly captures the flavor of Montmartre, its characters, and Lautrec's sadly distorted view of life. Excellent cast; memorable theme song by Georges Auric. Oscar winner for its stunning art direction–set decoration and costumes. ▼❚➤

Moulin Rouge! (2001-U.S.-Australian) **C-128m.** ** D: Baz Luhrmann. Nicole Kidman, Ewan McGregor, John Leguizamo, Jim Broadbent, Richard Roxburgh, Garry McDonald, Kylie Minogue, Lara Mulcahy. Visually dazzling but maddening, hyperkinetic musical about a star-crossed love affair at Paris' Moulin Rouge circa 1900. A hybrid of Luhrmann's earlier films (STRICTLY BALLROOM and WILLIAM SHAKESPEARE'S ROMEO & JULIET), this one is full of extraordinary images—but the "story" is anemic and aloof, leaving the two leads to attempt sincerity in the midst of a grotesque circus. Kidman and McGregor sing quite well; the songs are mostly a pastiche of past pop hits. Oscar winner for Art Direction and Costume Design. Panavision. [PG-13] ▼❚➤

Mountain, The (1956) **C-105m.** **½ D: Edward Dmytryk. Spencer Tracy, Robert Wagner, Claire Trevor, William Demarest, Richard Arlen, E. G. Marshall. Turgid tale of brothers Tracy and Wagner climbing Alpine peak to reach plane wreckage, for different reasons. VistaVision. ▼❚➤

Mountain Men, The (1980) **C-102m.** BOMB D: Richard Lang. Charlton Heston, Brian Keith, Victoria Racimo, Stephen Macht, John Glover, Seymour Cassel, David Ackroyd, Victor Jory. Heston and Keith star as fur trappers in this unnecessarily bloody, crude, tiresome good-guys-vs.-Indians epic. Screenplay by Fraser Clarke Heston, the star's son. Panavision. [R] ▼❚➤

Mountain of the Cannibal God SEE: **Slave of the Cannibal God**

Mountain Road, The (1960) **102m.** **½ D: Daniel Mann. James Stewart, Lisa Lu, Glenn Corbett, Henry (Harry) Morgan, Frank Silvera, James Best. Stewart is always worth watching, but this saga of American squadron working in China during waning days of WW2 is pretty flat. ▼

Mountains of the Moon (1990) **C-135m.** ***½ D: Bob Rafelson. Patrick Bergin, Iain Glen, Richard E. Grant, Fiona Shaw, John Savident, James Villiers, Adrian Rawlins, Delroy Lindo, Paul Onsongo, Bernard Hill, Roshan Seth, Anna Massey, Leslie Phillips, Roger Rees. Captivating saga of explorer Sir Richard Burton and his search for the source of the Nile River in the late 1800s. Bergin is a charismatic lead, with Glen as John Hanning Speke, the dilettante who accompanies him. Vivid, stimulating, and satisfying; manages to embrace the sweep of an epic film along with a compellingly personal story. Screenplay by Rafelson and William Harrison, based on the latter's biographical novel *Burton and Speke* and on actual journals of the two explorers. [R] ▼❚➤

Mourning Becomes Electra (1947) **173m.** **½ D: Dudley Nichols. Rosalind Russell, Michael Redgrave, Raymond Massey, Katina Paxinou, Nancy Coleman, Leo Genn, Kirk Douglas. Eugene O'Neill's play set in New England and adapted from the Greek tragedy *Oresteia*. Civil War general is killed by wife and their children seek revenge. Heavy, talky drama, even in 105m. version. British version runs 159m. ▼❚➤

Mouse and His Child, The (1977) **C-83m.** BOMB D: Fred Wolf, Chuck Swenson. Voices of Peter Ustinov, Alan Barzman, Marcy Swenson, Cloris Leachman, Andy Devine, Sally Kellerman. Boring animated film about a toy mouse and his child, and their adventures in the real world. Talk, talk, talk and no action. [G] ▼

Mouse Hunt (1997) **C-97m.** **½ D: Gore Verbinski. Nathan Lane, Lee Evans, Vicki Lewis, Maury Chaykin, Eric Christmas, Michael Jeter, Debra Christofferson, Camilla Soeberg, William Hickey, Christopher Walken. Two hapless brothers inherit a musty old house and a string factory from their father; the house has promise but is inhabited by one small, very crafty rodent who defies extermination. Black comedy and slapstick combine for surprisingly clever results, but after a while it's simply exhausting. Lane and Evans are an ideal (and very funny) team, but Laurel & Hardy and The Three Stooges did this sort of thing in 20 minutes flat. [PG] ▼❚➤

Mouse on the Moon, The (1963-British) **C-82m.** ***½ D: Richard Lester. Margaret Rutherford, Bernard Cribbins, Ron Moody, Terry-Thomas, Michael Crawford. Hilarious sequel to THE MOUSE THAT ROARED, about Duchy of Grand Fenwick. Tiny country enters space race, with little help from its befuddled Grand Duchess, Margaret Rutherford. ▼❚➤

Mouse That Roared, The (1959-British) **C-83m.** ***½ D: Jack Arnold. Peter Sellers, Jean Seberg, David Kossoff, William Hartnell, Monty Landis, Leo McKern. Hilarious satire about the Duchy of Grand Fenwick declaring war on the U. S. Sellers stars in three roles, equally amusing. Gag before opening titles is a masterpiece. Roger Macdougall and Stanley Mann adapted Leonard Wibberley's novel. Sequel: THE MOUSE ON THE MOON. ▼●)

Mouth to Mouth (1978-Australian) **C-95m.** ***½ D: John Duigan. Kim Krejus, Sonia Peat, Ian Gilmour, Sergio Frazetto, Walter Pym. A pair of unemployed, aimless teenage couples steal and hustle to survive. Fascinating, funny, sad, with lively direction by Duigan.

Mouth to Mouth (1995-Spanish) **C-105m.** **½ D: Manuel Gomez Pereira. Javier Bardem, Maria Barranco, Aitana Sanchez-Gijon, Josep Maria Flotats, Myriam Mezieres. Moderately amusing comedy about an out-of-work actor who soon finds his thespian talents in hot demand on a phone-sex line. Complications arise when he becomes romantically involved with one of his customers. Attractive cast makes this erotic romp actually funnier than it has a right to be. Original title: BOCA A BOCA. Panavision. [R] ▼●

Move (1970) **C-90m.** BOMB D: Stuart Rosenberg. Elliott Gould, Paula Prentiss, Genevieve Waite, John Larch, Joe Silver, Ron O'Neal. One of those comedies that helped to kill Gould's career within a year; porn-writer/dog-walker has problems when he moves from one apartment to another, but not as many as viewers will have trying to make sense out of the film. Panavision. [R]

Move Over, Darling (1963) **C-103m.** **½ D: Michael Gordon. Doris Day, James Garner, Polly Bergen, Chuck Connors, Thelma Ritter, Fred Clark, Don Knotts, Elliott Reid, John Astin, Pat Harrington, Jr. Woman long thought dead returns from desert island sojourn, to find her husband has remarried. Slick, amusing remake of MY FAVORITE WIFE, with strong cast of character actors milking every laugh. Film was intended to star Marilyn Monroe and Dean Martin, under the title SOMETHING'S GOT TO GIVE, but production was halted early on, and Marilyn died shortly thereafter. CinemaScope. ▼●

Movers & Shakers (1985) **C-79m.** *½ D: William Asher. Walter Matthau, Charles Grodin, Vincent Gardenia, Tyne Daly, Bill Macy, Gilda Radner. Satiric look at moviemaking in the '80s, written and coproduced by Grodin, who spent years trying to get it made. Talented cast (including cameos by Steve Martin and Penny Marshall) largely wasted in this unfunny comedy sprinkled with just an occasional insight or laugh. Too bad . . . *Love in Sex* had great possibilities. [PG]▼

Movie Crazy (1932) **84m.** *** D: Clyde Bruckman. Harold Lloyd, Constance Cummings, Kenneth Thomson, Sydney Jarvis, Eddie Fetherston. Lloyd's best talkie recaptures the spirit of his silent-comedy hits, telling story of small-town boy who goes to Hollywood with stars in his eyes, gets rude awakening but finally makes good. Includes his famous magician's coat scene. Cummings is a charming leading lady.▶

Movie Movie (1978) **C/B&W-107m.** *** D: Stanley Donen. George C. Scott, Trish Van Devere, Eli Wallach, Red Buttons, Barbara Harris, Barry Bostwick, Harry Hamlin, Art Carney, Rebecca York, Ann Reinking, Kathleen Beller. Affectionate parody of 1930s double feature: "Dynamite Hands" is b&w boxing saga with Hamlin in the John Garfield–ish role; "Baxter's Beauties of 1933" is Busby Berkeley–type musical, with numbers staged by Michael Kidd (who plays Hamlin's father in first story). There's even a Coming Attractions prevue! Introduced by George Burns. [PG]▼

Moving (1988) **C-89m.** *½ D: Alan Metter. Richard Pryor, Beverly Todd, Randy Quaid, Dave Thomas, Dana Carvey, Stacey Dash, Gordon Jump, Morris Day, Rodney Dangerfield, King Kong Bundy. Mass transit engineer Pryor falls into a dream job following his unexpected and unceremonious firing—only hitch: he and the family must relocate from New Jersey to Boise, Idaho. Wallows in the predictable (kids rebel, the movers are psychos), with a modest chuckle every half-hour or so. Pryor seems uncomfortable as Ozzie Nelson. [R]▼●)

Moving the Mountain (1994-British) **C/B&W-83m.** ***½ D: Michael Apted. Life-affirming documentary about young Chinese student Li Lu and others of his generation who became demonstrators at Tiananmen Square in 1989. The film also chronicles Li Lu's life during the Cultural Revolution and his reasons for deciding to defy his government. Revealing, never less than riveting; the "mountain" of the title is communist Chinese authorities. ▼●)

Moving Violation (1976) **C-91m.** ** D: Charles S. Dubin. Stephen McHattie, Kay Lenz, Eddie Albert, Lonny Chapman, Will Geer, Jack Murdock, John S. Ragin. Redneck sheriff goes after young couple, leading to usual car chases. So what else is new? [PG]▼

Moving Violations (1985) **C-90m.** *½ D: Neal Israel. John Murray, Jennifer Tilly, James Keach, Brian Backer, Sally Kellerman, Fred Willard, Lisa Hart Carroll, Wendie Jo Sperber, Clara Peller, Nedra Volz, Ned Eisenberg, Don Cheadle. Threadbare comedy of adventures in traffic violations school; more potholes than laughs. Wiseacre star Murray is Bill M.'s brother. [PG-13] ▼●)

Mozart and the Whale (2006) **C-93m.** **½ D: Petter Næss. Josh Hartnett, Radha Mitchell, Gary Cole, Sheila Kelley, Erica Leerhsen, John Carroll Lynch, Nate Mooney, Rusty Schwimmer, Robert Wisdom. Hartnett and Mitchell meet and begin dating. They have much in common: both like animals, both are fragile and vulnerable, and both suffer from Asperger syndrome, a form of autism. Well-intentioned "fictional story inspired by true events" (scripted by Ronald Bass) strives to be meaningful but seems unreal, particularly when people stand by passively as the lead characters are conspicuously loud and emotional in public. While touching at times and well acted, it's just too formulaic. [PG-13]▶

Mr. & Mrs. Bridge (1990) C-124m. ** D: James Ivory. Paul Newman, Joanne Woodward, Blythe Danner, Simon Callow, Kyra Sedgwick, Robert Sean Leonard, Margaret Welsh, Saundra McClain, Diane Kagan, Austin Pendleton, Remak Ramsay. Portrait of straitlaced, well-to-do Kansas City couple, and how they are affected by the demands of their growing children and the changes that overtake them in the 1930s and '40s. A plethora of intriguing but undeveloped, half-baked story threads make it frustrating and unsatisfying. Newman and Woodward are excellent, as usual. Based on two novels by Evan S. Connell, *Mrs. Bridge* (1959) and *Mr. Bridge* (1969). [PG-13]▼●)

Mr. & Mrs. Smith (1941) 95m. *** D: Alfred Hitchcock. Carole Lombard, Robert Montgomery, Gene Raymond, Jack Carson, Philip Merivale, Betty Compson, Lucile Watson. Madcap comedy of Lombard and Montgomery discovering their marriage wasn't legal. One of Hitchcock's least typical films, but bouncy nonetheless; written by Norman Krasna.▼●)

Mr. & Mrs. Smith (2005) C-120m. *** D: Doug Liman. Brad Pitt, Angelina Jolie, Vince Vaughn, Adam Brody, Kerry Washington, Keith David, Chris Weitz, Rachael Huntley, Michelle Monaghan; voices of Angela Bassett, William Fichtner. Not your parents' romantic star vehicle: a slick, sexy, supercharged showcase for the well-paired Pitt and Jolie, as a bored married couple who discover that they both work as undercover assassins. Never before have a man and woman engaged in a slugfest like the one in this film, but it's not to be taken seriously (or literally). Director Liman attempts to outdo his car chase from THE BOURNE IDENTITY—and succeeds. Dynamic score by John Powell. Super 35. [PG-13]▼▶

Mr. Arkadin (1955-Spanish-French) 99m. **½ D: Orson Welles. Orson Welles, Michael Redgrave, Patricia Medina, Akim Tamiroff, Mischa Auer, Katina Paxinou, Robert Arden. Overblown Welles curiosity (thematically similar to CITIZEN KANE) in which he stars as a famed tycoon with a shady past; the scenario follows his actions after being threatened with blackmail by his daughter's suitor. Filmed in English and Spanish-language versions. Variant prints run 98m. and 105m. Aka CONFIDENTIAL REPORT.▼●)

Mr. Baseball (1992) C-113m. **½ D: Fred Schepisi. Tom Selleck, Ken Takakura, Aya Takanashi, Toshi Shioya, Dennis Haysbert. Pleasant if uninspired comedy about a washed-up big leaguer who's traded to Japan, where his smart-ass attitude almost

does him in with his team, his manager, and the young Japanese woman who takes a liking to him. Selleck is ingratiating as usual. Panavision. [PG-13]▼●)

Mr. Bean's Holiday (2007-U.S.-British) C-88m. *** D: Steve Bendelack. Rowan Atkinson, Emma de Caunes, Max Baldry, Willem Dafoe, Jean Rochefort, Karel Roden, Steve Pemberton. Bumbling Mr. Bean wins a dream vacation to the south of France, but from the moment he arrives in Paris he finds himself in one jam after another. He also acquires a traveling companion, a boy who's been separated from his father, and becomes the *bête noire* of a pompous filmmaker (Dafoe) whose latest opus is playing at the Cannes Film Festival. Thoroughly enjoyable sight-gag comedy and follow-up to 1997's BEAN; the last word comes at the end of the credits. [G]▶

Mr. Billion (1977) C-93m. ** D: Jonathan Kaplan. Terence Hill, Valerie Perrine, Jackie Gleason, Slim Pickens, Chill Wills, William Redfield. Uninspired comedy about a lowly Italian mechanic (Hill, in his American debut) on a mad, cross-country scramble to claim a billion-dollar legacy, and the attempts of scoundrels to swindle him out of it. [PG] ▼▶

Mr. Blandings Builds His Dream House (1948) 94m. *** D: H. C. Potter. Cary Grant, Myrna Loy, Melvyn Douglas, Reginald Denny, Sharyn Moffett, Connie Marshall, Louise Beavers, Ian Wolfe, Lurene Tuttle, Lex Barker. Slick comedy of city couple attempting to build a house in the country; expertly handled, with Grant at his peak. And no one ever described room colors better than Loy! Norman Panama and Melvin Frank scripted, from Eric Hodgins' novel. Also shown in computer-colored version. Remade in 2007 as ARE WE DONE YET? ▼●)

Mr. Brooks (2007) C-120m. **½ D: Bruce A. Evans. Kevin Costner, Demi Moore, Dane Cook, William Hurt, Marg Helgenberger, Ruben Santiago-Hudson, Danielle Panabaker, Aisha Hinds, Lindsay Crouse, Jason Lewis, Michael Cole. Respected businessman, husband, and father (Costner) has a deadly secret: he's a serial killer. He battles his addiction just as an alcoholic would, but he's egged on by his evil alter ego (Hurt). Detective Moore, whose private life is a wreck, is determined to catch the multiple murderer, while eyewitness Cook has a different reaction: he wants in on the adrenaline rush of killing. Interesting ingredients, but a lumpy stew; sometimes laughably absurd. Costner coproduced. [R]▶

Mr. Bug Goes to Town SEE: **Hoppity Goes to Town**

Mr. Canton and Lady Rose SEE: **Miracles** (1989)

Mr. Death: The Rise and Fall of Fred A. Leuchter, Jr. (1999) C-92m. *** D: Errol Morris. Documentarian Morris has found another oddball to profile: a milquetoast type who's had a lifelong fascination with instruments of death. After becoming an expert at building and repairing electric chairs and the like, he's hired by Holocaust deniers to gather "evidence" as to whether Hitler's gas chambers in Poland were really used for their stated purpose. Leuchter strikes the viewer as amusing at first, then misguided, possibly insidious, and ultimately pathetic. Music by Caleb Sampson. [PG-13]▼❶

Mr. Deeds (2002) C-96m. BOMB D: Steven Brill. Adam Sandler, Winona Ryder, Peter Gallagher, Jared Harris, Allen Covert, John Turturro, Steve Buscemi, Conchata Ferrell, Harve Presnell, Erick Avari, Blake Clark. Sloppy remake of MR. DEEDS GOES TO TOWN follows the original's basic outline, with small-town good guy Sandler brought to N.Y.C., where he's taken advantage of by tycoon Gallagher and reporter Ryder, who falls in love with him. The new ingredients: Sandler's imbecilic persona and fondness for crude humor. You don't have to know Frank Capra's 1936 classic to know this one stinks; it doesn't even believe in its own story. Rob Schneider appears unbilled. [PG-13]▼❶

Mr. Deeds Goes to Town (1936) 115m. ✶✶✶✶ D: Frank Capra. Gary Cooper, Jean Arthur, George Bancroft, Lionel Stander, Douglass Dumbrille, Mayo Methot, Raymond Walburn, Walter Catlett, H. B. Warner. Cooper is Longfellow Deeds, who inherits 20 million dollars and wants to give it all away to needy people. Arthur is appealing as the hard-boiled big-city reporter who tries to figure out what makes him tick. Capra won his second Oscar for this irresistible film, written by Robert Riskin (from Clarence Budington Kelland's story "Opera Hat"). Later a short-lived TV series. Remade in 2002.▼●❶

Mr. Destiny (1990) C-110m. ✶✶ D: James Orr. James Belushi, Linda Hamilton, Michael Caine, Jon Lovitz, Hart Bochner, Rene Russo, Bill McCutcheon, Pat Corley, Courteney Cox, Kathy Ireland. Blah, by-the-numbers fantasy with Belushi an average, bored working stiff who gets to go back in time and replay an at-bat in a high school baseball game—which significantly alters his fate. Well intentioned but heavy-handed; comparisons to IT'S A WONDERFUL LIFE are more hopeful than actual. [PG-13]▼●❶

Mr. Forbush and the Penguins SEE: Cry of the Penguins

Mr. Hobbs Takes a Vacation (1962) C-116m. ✶✶½ D: Henry Koster. James Stewart, Maureen O'Hara, Fabian, John Saxon, Marie Wilson, Reginald Gardiner, Lauri Peters, John McGiver. Glossy Hollywood family fare, '60s-style, about various misadventures as Stewart and O'Hara's clan rent a house by the ocean for the summer. Based on a novel by Edward Streeter, the same man who wrote *Father of the Bride*. CinemaScope.▼❶

Mr. Holland's Opus (1995) C-142m.

✶✶✶ D: Stephen Herek. Richard Dreyfuss, Glenne Headly, Jay Thomas, Olympia Dukakis, W. (William) H. Macy, Alicia Witt, Terrence Howard, Jean Louisa Kelly, Nicholas John Renner, Joseph Anderson, Anthony Natale, Joanna Gleason. Disney dips into GOODBYE, MR. CHIPS for this sentimental, old-fashioned story of a musician who reluctantly takes a job as a high school music teacher, then spends the next thirty years of his life dedicated to imbuing students with a love of music. It's his own family that suffers. Too much time is spent on the climactic school play, but it's still a heartwarming tearjerker and Dreyfuss is perfect in the lead. Panavision. [PG] ▼●❶

Mr. Hulot's Holiday (1953-French) 87m. ✶✶✶½ D: Jacques Tati. Jacques Tati, Nathalie Pascaud, Michelle Rolla, Valentine Camax, Louis Perrault. Tati introduced his delightful Hulot character in this amusing excursion to a French resort town; a fond throwback to the days of silent-screen comedy. ▼●❶

Mr. Jealousy (1998) C-105m. ✶✶½ D: Noah Baumbach. Eric Stoltz, Annabella Sciorra, Chris Eigeman, Carlos Jacott, Marianne Jean-Baptiste, Brian Kerwin, Peter Bogdanovich, Bridget Fonda. Stoltz meets Sciorra and they hit it off, but his suspicions and jealousy over her former boyfriend start driving them both crazy. Talky but humorous romance with real N.Y.C. flavor and some priceless group therapy sequences. Stoltz also executive-produced. [R] ▼❶

Mr. Jones (1993) C-114m. ✶½ D: Mike Figgis. Richard Gere, Lena Olin, Anne Bancroft, Tom Irwin, Delroy Lindo, Bruce Altman, Lauren Tom, Anna Maria Horsford, Lucinda Jenney, Taylor Negron. A manic depressive and a shrink on the rebound have a professionally taboo romance. Gere's behavior—bounding on stage during a concert, tightrope-walking a high construction beam—turns this into THE JESTER OF TIDES. Gere is OK; Olin gives an awkward performance and is horribly lit. Sat on the shelf for a year. [R]▼●❶

Mr. Kingstreet's War (1973) C-92m. ✶✶½ D: Percival Rubens. John Saxon, Tippi Hedren, Rossano Brazzi, Brian O'Shaughnessy. Loner and his wife find idyllic life at African game preserve disrupted by WW2 and set out to do something about it. Interesting and unusual. Aka HEROES DIE HARD.▼

Mr. Klein (1976-French) C-122m. ✶✶✶ D: Joseph Losey. Alain Delon, Jeanne Moreau, Francine Bergé, Michel Lonsdale, Juliet Berto, Suzanne Flon, Massimo Giroti, Michel Aumont. A French art dealer exploits Jews who are desperately in need of money during WW2, then finds he is mistaken for a Jew with the same name. Enigmatic, interesting parable about the nature of identity. [PG] ▼❶

Mr. Love (1985-British) C-98m. ✶✶✶ D:

Roy Battersby. Barry Jackson, Maurice Denham, Christina Collier, Helen Cotterill, Julia Deakin, Linda Marlowe, Margaret Tyzack. Gentle, winning tale of quiet, reserved gardener, in a loveless marriage for almost 30 years and whom most everybody thinks is a joke—so why do all those women appear at his funeral? The CASABLANCA scene is a gem. [PG-13]▼

Mr. Lucky (1943) **100m. ***** D: H. C. Potter. Cary Grant, Laraine Day, Charles Bickford, Gladys Cooper, Alan Carney, Henry Stephenson, Paul Stewart, Kay Johnson, Florence Bates. Gambling-ship-owner Grant intends to fleece virtuous Day, instead falls in love and goes straight. Basis for later TV series has spirited cast, engaging script. Love that rhyming slang!▼●⊙

Mr. Magoo (1997) **C-87m. *½** D: Stanley Tong. Leslie Nielsen, Kelly Lynch, Matt Keeslar, Nick Chinlund, Stephen Tobolowsky, Ernie Hudson, Jennifer Garner, Malcolm McDowell, Miguel Ferrer. Alarmingly unfunny feature based on the famous nearsighted cartoon character (revived in the animated credits, with Greg Burson filling in for Jim Backus as the voice of Magoo). Nielsen does his best, as always, but the pointlessly complicated plot—about the theft of a precious ruby—just goes on and on. And there are an awful lot of mean-spirited characters for a kids' movie. Inauspicious Hollywood debut for Jackie Chan's frequent director and collaborator; even the closing outtakes aren't funny! [PG]▼●⊙

Mr. Magorium's Wonder Emporium (2007) **C-93m. **½** D: Zach Helm. Dustin Hoffman, Natalie Portman, Zach Mills, Jason Bateman, Ted Ludzik. A 243-year-old proprietor of a magical toy store prepares to leave his lifelong business and bequeaths it to his number-one clerk. When financial problems are revealed, a crisis ensues as dark and strange things begin to happen to the toys . . . until a young customer takes matters into his own hands. Harmless family fare with amusing, old-fashioned toy creations will appeal primarily to the under-8 set, but the sugar-coated plot may find adults wanting to fast-forward. Hoffman seems to be channeling Ed Wynn. Super 35. [G]▶

Mr. Majestyk (1974) **C-103m. **½** D: Richard Fleischer. Charles Bronson, Al Lettieri, Linda Cristal, Lee Purcell, Paul Koslo, Alejandro Rey. Above average Bronson thriller, casting him as Colorado watermelon farmer (!) marked for destruction by syndicate hit man Lettieri; surprisingly tongue-in-cheek script by Elmore Leonard. [PG]▼●

Mr. Mom (1983) **C-91m. **½** D: Stan Dragoti. Michael Keaton, Teri Garr, Martin Mull, Ann Jillian, Christopher Lloyd, Frederick Koehler, Taliesin Jaffe, Graham Jarvis, Jeffrey Tambor. Pleasant enough rehash of age-old sitcom premise: Mom gets a job when dad gets fired, leaving him to learn the perils of running a household. Likable stars make it palatable, but you've seen it all before. [PG]▼●⊙

Mr. Moto series SEE: *Leonard Maltin's Classic Movie Guide*

Mr. Music (1950) **113m. **½** D: Richard Haydn. Bing Crosby, Nancy Olson, Charles Coburn, Ruth Hussey, Marge and Gower Champion, Peggy Lee, Groucho Marx. Easygoing vehicle for crooner Crosby as Broadway songwriter who wants to live the easy life. Remake of ACCENT ON YOUTH.▼●

Mr. Nanny (1993) **C-84m. *½** D: Michael Gottlieb. Terry "Hulk" Hogan (Bollea), Sherman Hemsley, Austin Pendleton, Robert Gorman, Madeline Zima, David Johansen, Mother Love. Lamebrained comedy featuring Hogan as a struggling wrestler hired to look after a pair of spoiled, ignored rich kids (whom weirdo Johansen is plotting to kidnap). Strictly for die-hard fans of the Hulkster. Hemsley and Hogan are no threat to Clark and McCullough. [PG]▼●⊙

Mr. Nice Guy (1997-Hong Kong) **C-113m. ***** D: Samo Hung. Jackie Chan, Richard Norton, Miki Lee, Karen McLymont, Gabrielle Fitzpatrick, Vince Poletto. Jackie, a TV chef(!), is pursued by two sets of bad guys who are after an incriminating videotape that's fallen into his hands. One of Jackie's better later films, set in Melbourne and, like almost all his best movies, an action comedy. Dazzling and exciting fights abound, the best (and funniest) staged at a construction site. Only the climax, involving a colossal truck flattening a luxury home, is below par for the astounding Mr. Chan. Director Samo, Jackie's lifelong friend, has a cameo as an irritated bicyclist. Technovision. [PG-13]▼●⊙

Mr. North (1988) **C-92m. **½** D: Danny Huston. Anthony Edwards, Robert Mitchum, Lauren Bacall, Harry Dean Stanton, Anjelica Huston, Mary Stuart Masterson, Virginia Madsen, Tammy Grimes, David Warner, Hunter Carson, Christopher Durang, Mark Metcalf, Katharine Houghton. Bright but penniless young man makes a major impact on Newport high society in the 1920s by being forthright, ingenious, and possessing an unusual amount of electricity in his body! Agreeable fable based on Thornton Wilder's *Theophilus North* has many assets (fine cast, beautiful locations) as well as some liabilities (uneven performances, shifts of tone). Coscripted by John Huston, just before his death; this marks his son's theatrical feature debut as director. [PG] ▼●⊙

Mr. Patman (1980-Canadian) **C-105m. *½** D: John Guillermin. James Coburn, Kate Nelligan, Fionnula Flanagan, Les Carlson, Candy Kane, Michael Kirby. Coburn is well cast in this convoluted, poorly made tale of a charming but slightly mad psycho-ward orderly and his shenanigans. Aka CROSS-OVER.▼

Mr. Peabody and the Mermaid (1948) 89m. **½ D: Irving Pichel. William Powell, Ann Blyth, Irene Hervey, Andrea King, Clinton Sundberg. Mild comedy-fantasy by Nunnally Johnson has its moments, with unsuspecting Powell coming across a lovely mermaid while fishing. Powell makes anything look good.▼

Mr. Popper's Penguins (2011) C-95m. **½ D: Mark Waters. Jim Carrey, Carla Gugino, Angela Lansbury, Ophelia Lovibond, Madeline Carroll, Clark Gregg, Jeffrey Tambor, David Krumholtz, Philip Baker Hall, Maxwell Perry Cotton, James Tupper, Dominic Chianese, William C. Mitchell. Divorced N.Y.C. real estate manipulator Carrey—who's never gotten over the fact that his father was always away from home on travel adventures—inherits a penguin and then gets sent five more. This not only changes his relationship with his two kids and ex-wife but his outlook on life itself. Complete reinvention of Richard and Florence Atwater's beloved 1938 book is an OK comedy vehicle for Carrey, and the penguins (both real and CG-animated) are irresistible . . . but the story makes strange, sudden turns that undermine its emotional impact as it stumbles toward the finale. [PG]

Mr. Quilp (1975-British) C-118m. *** D: Michael Tuchner. Anthony Newley, David Hemmings, David Warner, Michael Hordern, Jill Bennett, Sarah Jane Varley. Entertaining musical version of Dickens' *The Old Curiosity Shop* with songs by Newley and musical score by Elmer Bernstein. Lighthearted until last reel when it goes serious in the Dickens vein. Retitled THE OLD CURIOSITY SHOP. Remade for cable in 1995. Panavision. [G]

Mr. Ricco (1975) C-98m. ** D: Paul Bogart. Dean Martin, Eugene Roche, Thalmus Rasulala, Geraldine Brooks, Denise Nicholas, Cindy Williams, Philip Michael Thomas. Martin in offbeat casting as criminal lawyer involved with racist killings, sex and assorted violence, but looks too tired to care. Good mystery angle. Panavision. [PG]

Mr. Rock and Roll (1957) 86m. ** D: Charles Dubin. Alan Freed, Little Richard, Clyde McPhatter, Frankie Lymon and the Teenagers, Teddy Randazzo, Chuck Berry, Rocky Graziano, Lois O'Brien, Lionel Hampton, Ferlin Husky, The Moonglows, Brook Benton, LaVern Baker. The saga of how Alan Freed "discovered" rock 'n' roll. In AMERICAN HOT WAX, Berry played opposite Tim McIntire portraying Freed; here, he acts with the real McCoy. Vintage footage of McPhatter, Lymon, Little Richard; Rocky Graziano is along for comic relief. Also of note: The 1999 TVM MR. ROCK 'N' ROLL: THE ALAN FREED STORY.

Mr. Sardonicus (1961) 89m. ** D: William Castle. Ronald Lewis, Audrey Dalton, Guy Rolfe, Oscar Homolka. Recluse count with face frozen in hideous grin lures wife's boyfriend/doctor to castle to cure him. Minor fare despite good ending; Castle gave the theatrical audiences the option of voting "thumbs up" or "thumbs down" via a "Punishment Poll" (but only one conclusion was filmed). Screenplay by Ray Russell from his novella *Sardonicus*.▼◗

Mr. Saturday Night (1992) C-119m. **½ D: Billy Crystal. Billy Crystal, David Paymer, Julie Warner, Helen Hunt, Mary Mara, Jerry Orbach, Ron Silver, Sage Allen, Jackie Gayle, Carl Ballantine, Slappy White, Conrad Janis, Jerry Lewis. Saga of a comedian who turns out to be his own worst enemy. Many moments of truth and insight, but too long, with too many climaxes, and Crystal's old-age makeup is garish and unbelievable. It's also tough to make an appealing movie about an unappealing character. The real treat is watching Paymer in a terrific performance as Crystal's long-suffering brother. Crystal's directing debut; he also cowrote with Lowell Ganz and Babaloo Mandel (both of whom appear fleetingly as inept TV writers). [R]▼◗

Mrs. Brown (1997-British-U.S.-Irish) C-103m. *** D: John Madden. Judi Dench, Billy Connolly, Geoffrey Palmer, Antony Sher, Gerard Butler, Richard Pasco, David Westhead. Rewarding drama, set in the 1860s. Queen Victoria (Dench) has been in mourning for years, following the death of her beloved husband Albert; living in Windsor Castle, away from London and public life, she only comes out of her shell when her husband's trusted Highland horseman, John Brown (Connolly), refuses to coddle her. An unusual relationship develops between the two—much to the consternation of everyone else on the Queen's staff. Richly detailed, with two superb performances at the forefront; Sher is also impressive as the bemused Benjamin Disraeli. Screenplay by Jeremy Brock. [PG]▼◗

Mrs. Brown You've Got a Lovely Daughter (1968-British) C-95m. ** D: Saul Swimmer. Herman's Hermits, Stanley Holloway, Mona Washbourne, Sara Caldwell, Lance Percival. A silly excuse for a movie, with Herman and his Hermits heading for London to enter their greyhound in a race. In between the suspense they sing "There's a Kind of Hush All Over the World" and the title tune. Panavision. [G]▼◗

Mrs. Dalloway (1998-British-Dutch) C-97m. *** D: Marleen Gorris. Vanessa Redgrave, Natascha McElhone, Rupert Graves, Michael Kitchen, Alan Cox, Lena Headey, Amelia Bullmore, Sarah Badel, Oliver Ford Davies, Katie Carr, John Standing, Robert Hardy, Margaret Tyzack, Phyllis Calvert. Redgrave is radiant as the wife of a British M.P. who, on the day of a major soiree, thinks back to her youth when she chose between a safe, secure life and a more daring existence with a man who truly loved her. McElhone is an excellent match for Redgrave in the flashback scenes. Thoughtful, intelligent drama adapted by actress Eileen Atkins from the Virginia Woolf novel. [PG-13] ▼●▐

Mrs. Doubtfire (1993) **C-125m.** ******* D: Chris Columbus. Robin Williams, Sally Field, Pierce Brosnan, Harvey Fierstein, Polly Holliday, Lisa Jakub, Matthew Lawrence, Mara Wilson, Robert Prosky, Anne Haney, Scott Capurro. Crowd-pleasing comedy (with serious overtones) about a free spirit whose wife divorces him after fourteen years; he can't bear being separated from his three kids, so he disguises himself as a dowdy British housekeeper (under an Oscar-winning makeup job) and gets himself hired to look after them. Williams is in peak form, and director Columbus keeps story and characters reasonably realistic in order to drive home a humanistic message. Based on the book *Alias Madame Doubtfire* by Anne Fine. Panavision. [PG-13] ▼●▐

Mr. Sebastian SEE: Sebastian

Mrs. Henderson Presents (2005-British) **C-103m.** ****½** D: Stephen Frears. Judi Dench, Bob Hoskins, Will Young, Christopher Guest, Kelly Reilly, Thelma Barlow, Anna Brewster, Rosalind Halstead. Recently widowed Dench decides to assert her newfound independence by buying a London theater, The Windmill, and hitting on the idea of staging nude tableaux. With the coming of WW2, the theater becomes a haven for soldiers and war-weary Londoners. Entertaining fluff based on a true story (which inspired the 1945 movie TONIGHT AND EVERY NIGHT). Bright musical numbers, good period flavor, but a bit calculated in its cuteness. Super 35. [R]▐

Mr. Skeffington (1944) **146m.** ******* D: Vincent Sherman. Bette Davis, Claude Rains, Walter Abel, Richard Waring, Jerome Cowan, Charles Drake, Gigi Perreau. Grand soap opera spanning several decades of N.Y.C. life from 1914 onward. Davis is vain society woman who marries stockbroker Rains for convenience, discovering his true love for her only after many years. Lavish settings, bravura Davis performance. ▼●▐

Mrs. Miniver (1942) **134m.** *****½** D: William Wyler. Greer Garson, Walter Pidgeon, Dame May Whitty, Teresa Wright, Reginald Owen, Henry Travers, Richard Ney, Henry Wilcoxon, Helmut Dantine, Peter Lawford. Moving drama about middle-class English family learning to cope with war. Winner of six Academy Awards—for Garson, Wright, director Wyler, and Best Picture, among others—this film did much to rally American support for our British allies during WW2, though its depiction of English life was decidedly Hollywoodized. Screenplay by Arthur Wimperis, George Froeschel, James Hilton, and Claudine West; based on Jan Struther's short stories. Se-

quel: THE MINIVER STORY. Also shown in computer-colored version. ▼●▐

Mr. Smith Goes to Washington (1939) **129m.** ******** D: Frank Capra. James Stewart, Jean Arthur, Claude Rains, Edward Arnold, Guy Kibbee, Thomas Mitchell, Eugene Pallette, Beulah Bondi, Harry Carey, H. B. Warner, Charles Lane, Porter Hall, Jack Carson. Stewart is young idealist who finds nothing but corruption in U.S. Senate. Fine Capra Americana, with Stewart's top performance bolstered by Arthur as hard-boiled dame won over by earnest Mr. Smith, and a stellar supporting cast; Carey is magnificent as the Vice President. Brilliant script by Sidney Buchman; however, Lewis R. Foster's Original Story received the Oscar. Later a brief TV series. Remade as BILLY JACK GOES TO WASHINGTON. ▼●▐

Mrs Palfrey at The Claremont (2005-British) **C-108m.** ******* D: Dan Ireland. Joan Plowright, Rupert Friend, Zoe Tapper, Anna Massey, Robert Lang, Marcia Warren, Millicent Martin, Lorcan O'Toole. An elderly widow moves into a residential hotel in London to live out her days. A chance meeting with a charming if rootless young writer develops into genuine friendship, and makes Mrs. Palfrey the most envied member of the sedate but gossipy Claremont "family." Played in broad strokes at first, this comedy-drama deepens and becomes more satisfying as it goes along. A sweet film with a typically commanding—and honest—performance by Plowright. That's Peter O'Toole's son playing Plowright's grandson. Adapted from Elizabeth Taylor's novel by Ruth Sacks.▐

Mrs. Parker and the Vicious Circle (1994) **C/B&W-125m.** ****½** D: Alan Rudolph. Jennifer Jason Leigh, Campbell Scott, Matthew Broderick, Andrew McCarthy, Peter Gallagher, Jennifer Beals, Gwyneth Paltrow, Sam Robards, Martha Plimpton, Tom McGowan, Stephen Baldwin, Wallace Shawn, Lili Taylor, James Le Gros, Keith Carradine, Nick Cassavetes, Jane Adams, Gary Basaraba, Rebecca Miller, Heather Graham, Jake Johannsen, Chip Zien. Closeup look at Dorothy Parker, fabled writer and charter member of the Algonquin Round Table in the 1920s; a vivid re-creation of that period and those celebrated wits, but Parker's chronic unhappiness (and Leigh's often mannered performance) makes for tough going in this longish film. Scott is a standout as Robert Benchley in the well-chosen supporting cast; the famous humorist's grandson, author Peter Benchley, appears early on as editor Frank Crowninshield. Stanley Tucci appears unbilled. Super 35. [R] ▼●▐

Mrs. Parkington (1944) **124m.** ****½** D: Tay Garnett. Greer Garson, Walter Pidgeon, Edward Arnold, Gladys Cooper, Agnes Moorehead, Frances Rafferty, Selena Royle, Dan Duryea, Lee Patrick, Rod Cameron, Tom Drake, Cecil Kellaway, Peter Lawford. Overlong but well-mounted soaper involving poor, naive Garson and how she changes after marrying wealthy, charismatic Pidgeon.▼▷

Mrs. Pollifax—Spy (1971) C-110m. *½ D: Leslie Martinson. Rosalind Russell, Darren McGavin, Nehemiah Persoff, Harold Gould, John Beck, Dana Elcar. A bored widow volunteers as a CIA agent—and gets accepted—in this lame comedy spy caper. Russell's last theatrical film (for which she did the screenplay, under pseudonym) is also one of her worst. [G]

Mrs. Soffel (1984) C-110m. ** D: Gillian Armstrong. Diane Keaton, Mel Gibson, Matthew Modine, Edward Herrmann, Trini Alvarado, Jennie Dundas, Danny Corkill, Terry O'Quinn. Interesting but gloomy, emotionally aloof rendering of true story, set in 1901, when wife of Pittsburgh prison warden falls in love with convicted murderer Gibson. Well made, but a pall hangs over entire film. [PG-13]▼▷

Mrs. Wiggs of the Cabbage Patch (1934) 80m. *** D: Norman Taurog. W. C. Fields, Pauline Lord, ZaSu Pitts, Evelyn Venable, Kent Taylor, Donald Meek, Virginia Weidler. Venerable melodrama about a good-hearted woman and her ever-growing brood gets a shot of comic adrenalin from Fields, who's perfectly matched with Pitts. Not a typical Fields vehicle by any means. Based on the 1901 novel by Alice Hegan Rice; filmed before in 1914 and 1919; remade in 1942.▼

Mrs. Winterbourne (1996) C-104m. **½ D: Richard Benjamin. Shirley MacLaine, Ricki Lake, Brendan Fraser, Miguel Sandoval, Loren Dean, Peter Gerety, Jane Krakowski, Susan Haskell. Wide-eyed Lake is impregnated by her sleazy boyfriend, who then kicks her out; a coincidental meeting with another pregnant woman on a train leads to mistaken identity, and she's taken in by a wealthy Boston family who think she's one of their own. Likable comedy goes flat, but benefits from earnest performances. Based on Cornell Woolrich's *I Married a Dead Man*, which was filmed before, more seriously, as NO MAN OF HER OWN (1950) and I MARRIED A SHADOW (1982). Paula Prentiss appears unbilled as an obnoxious nurse. [PG-13]▼▷

Mr. Sycamore (1974) C-88m. *½ D: Pancho Kohner. Jason Robards, Sandy Dennis, Jean Simmons, Robert Easton, Mark Miller. A milquetoasty mailman with a nagging wife (and a crush on local librarian) decides to escape rat race by turning into a tree! A definite curio, sadly defeated by heavy-handed treatment of material.▼

Mr 3000 (2004) C-102m. *** D: Charles Stone III. Bernie Mac, Angela Bassett, Paul Sorvino, Chris Noth, Michael Rispoli, Brian J. White. A Milwaukee Brewers baseball star with a giant ego retires after making his 3000th hit . . . but is forced to return years later when the statistic is found to be erroneous. Mac somehow makes this insufferable braggart appealing, and the script treats his relationship with sports reporter Bassett in a surprisingly refreshing, adult manner. Entertaining comedy manages to touch all the bases. Various celebrities and sports figures appear as themselves. [PG-13]▼▷

Mr. Toad's Wild Ride SEE: **Wind in the Willows, The**

Mr. Untouchable (2007) C-92m. ** D: Marc Levin. Uneven, occasionally unsettling chronicle of the rise, fall, and ongoing survival of 1970s Harlem drug kingpin Leroy "Nicky" Barnes, who continues to hide from former accomplices he "ratted out" to authorities. Even though Barnes is filmed only in silhouette—director Levin duly notes that his reclusive subject has a $1 million bounty on his head—the unrepentant gangster, living large in exile, has an undeniable star power, which this documentary does little to diminish. [R]

Mr. Wonderful (1993) C-98m. **½ D: Anthony Minghella. Matt Dillon, Annabella Sciorra, Mary-Louise Parker, William Hurt, Vincent D'Onofrio, David Barry Gray, Bruce Kirby, Dan Hedaya, Bruce Altman, Luis Guzman, Jessica Harper, James Gandolfini. Onetime childhood sweethearts Dillon and Sciorra get divorced, after she broadens her blue-collar horizons; to get out of paying her alimony, he tries to marry her off. Takes its time, but succeeds when exploring its characters' feelings. The attractive (and competent) cast helps. [PG-13]▼▷

Mr. Wong series SEE: *Leonard Maltin's Classic Movie Guide*

Mr. Woodcock (2007) C-88m. *½ D: Craig Gillespie. Billy Bob Thornton, Seann William Scott, Susan Sarandon, Amy Poehler, Melissa Sagemiller, Ethan Suplee, M. C. Gainey, Brent Briscoe, Bill Macy, Melissa Leo. Successful self-help book author is confronted with painful high school memories when he comes home to discover his mother is engaged to his terrifying phys. ed. coach. One-joke premise thrusts him into a series of competitions with the gym teacher, who seems to take joy in humiliating his future son-in-law. Gillespie's original version was heavily reshot and retooled by the studio, but it's still a mess, despite Thornton's game efforts. Super 35. [PG-13]▷

Mr. Write (1994) C-89m. BOMB D: Charlie Loventhal. Paul Reiser, Jessica Tuck, Martin Mull, Doug Davidson, Jane Leeves, Calvert De Forest, Gigi Rice, Tom Wilson, Wendie Jo Sperber, Darryl M. Bell; voice of Ben Stein. Astonishingly awful comedy about a would-be writer with no talent who falls head over heels for an advertising executive (Tuck) when he chances to work on a TV commercial. Clichéd at best, annoyingly amateurish at worst. This was completed in 1992 before Reiser launched his TV series *Mad About You*. [PG-13]▼●

Mr. Wrong (1985) SEE: **Dark of the Night**

Mr. Wrong (1996) **C-92m.** ** D: Nick Castle. Ellen DeGeneres, Bill Pullman, Joan Cusack, Dean Stockwell, Joan Plowright, Ellen Cleghorne, John Livingston, Robert Goulet, Polly Holliday, Louie Anderson, Hope Davis. Single DeGeneres finds the perfect man in Pullman . . . or so she thinks. Not the light, funny romantic comedy you might expect, but a dark-humored attempt at satire on stalking. DeGeneres, in her starring debut, turns in a fine performance opposite the always reliable Pullman, but an uneven script works against the cast. [PG-13]**▼●|**

Ms. Don Juan (1973-French) **C-87m.** *½ D: Roger Vadim. Brigitte Bardot, Maurice Ronet, Robert Hossein, Mathieu Carriere, Jane Birkin, Michele Sand. Bardot, in title role, seduces and/or humiliates everyone in her sight: a priest (who's also her cousin), a politician, a businessman. Glossy but limp; may be good for some unintended laughs.**▼|**

Ms. 45 (1981) **C-84m.** **½ D: Abel Ferrara. Zoe Tamerlis, Steve Singer, Jack Thibeau, Peter Yellen, Darlene Stuto. Tamerlis is raped twice, gets her "revenge" by murdering every male in sight. Well-made, violent role-reversal formula film with echoes of PSYCHO, REPULSION, CARRIE, etc., which won some strong reviews and a cult reputation. Aka ANGEL OF VENGEANCE. [R]**▼●|**

Much Ado About Nothing (1993-British-U.S.) **C-111m.** *** D: Kenneth Branagh. Kenneth Branagh, Michael Keaton, Robert Sean Leonard, Keanu Reeves, Emma Thompson, Denzel Washington, Richard Briers, Kate Beckinsale, Brian Blessed, Richard Clifford, Ben Elton, Gerard Horan, Phyllida Law, Imelda Staunton, Jimmy Yuill. Shakespeare's comedy of the wooing of Benedick (played by actor-director-screenwriter Branagh) and Beatrice (his then wife, Thompson) is set and shot entirely in and around an Italian villa in Tuscany and features a top-notch supporting cast. Rowdy, high spirited, and remarkably fast paced; this brings vigor to the Bard's text, though the poetry sometimes gets lost in the shenanigans. Branagh does impressive job, but cannot match earlier Shakespearean effort, HENRY V (1989). [PG-13]**▼●|**

Mudlark, The (1950) **99m.** *** D: Jean Negulesco. Irene Dunne, Alec Guinness, Finlay Currie, Anthony Steel, Andrew Ray, Beatrice Campbell, Wilfrid Hyde-White. Offbeat drama of Queen Victoria (Dunne), a recluse since her husband's death, coming back to reality after meeting waif who stole into her castle. Dunne does quite well as Queen, with Guinness a joy as Disraeli. Filmed in England.

Mulan (1998) **C-88m.** *** D: Barry Cook, Tony Bancroft. Voices of Ming-Na Wen, Lea Salonga, Eddie Murphy, B. D. Wong, Donny Osmond, Harvey Fierstein, Miguel Ferrer, Pat Morita, June Foray, Miriam Margolyes, George Takei, James Shigeta, Gedde Watanabe, James Hong. Disney's animated musical rendering of an ancient Chinese legend, about a headstrong daughter who disguises as a boy in order to take her father's place in the Imperial Army—and bring honor to her family. Strikingly staged and designed, with a strong and appealing leading character; the constant comedy "relief," while funny, seems jarring and unnecessary in such a strong dramatic tale. Followed by a direct-to-video sequel. [G] **▼●|**

Mulholland Dr. (2001-U.S.-French) **C-145m.** ***½ D: David Lynch. Justin Theroux, Naomi Watts, Laura Elena Harring, Ann Miller, Scott Wulf, Robert Forster, Brent Briscoe, Dan Hedaya, Michael Des Barres, Billy Ray Cyrus, Katharine Towne, Lee Grant, James Karen, Chad Everett. A plucky young actress arrives in Hollywood and tries to solve the mystery of an amnesiac woman's identity. Hypnotic, full-bore Lynchian strangeness, loaded with the writer-director's trademark visual fetishes and unexplainable dream logic, anchored by a knockout performance from Watts. Certainly not for all tastes. Originally a rejected TV pilot (!), later reshot and expanded to present length. Miller's final film. [R] **▼|**

Mulholland Falls (1996) **C-107m.** ** D: Lee Tamahori. Nick Nolte, Melanie Griffith, Chazz Palminteri, Michael Madsen, Chris Penn, Treat Williams, Jennifer Connelly, Andrew McCarthy, John Malkovich, Daniel Baldwin, Kyle Chandler, Ed Lauter, Aaron Neville. L.A. period piece (and CHINATOWN wannabe) about an elite squad of cops who make their own rules . . . until their leader (Nolte) becomes personally involved in a murder case with far-reaching consequences. Story unfolds in an obvious, heavy-handed way, and much of the cast is wasted. Tiresome, redundant score by Dave Grusin. That's production designer Richard Sylbert (who also worked on CHINATOWN) as the coroner. William L. Petersen, Rob Lowe, Louise Fletcher, and Bruce Dern appear unbilled. [R]**▼●|**

Multiplicity (1996) **C-117m.** **½ D: Harold Ramis. Michael Keaton, Andie MacDowell, Harris Yulin, Richard Masur, Eugene Levy, Ann Cusack, Brian Doyle-Murray. Working stiff who feels pulled in all directions by his job and his family finds a solution: he clones himself—again and again and again. Amusing gimmick comedy, in the same vein as Ramis' GROUNDHOG DAY, but not quite as good. Keaton has a field day with his multiple characters, but the premise is stretched way beyond credibility and wears thin. Panavision. [PG-13]**▼●|**

Mumford (1999) **C-112m.** **½ D: Lawrence Kasdan. Loren Dean, Hope Davis, Jason Lee, Alfre Woodard, Mary McDonnell, Pruitt Taylor Vince, Zooey Deschanel, Martin Short, David Paymer, Jane Adams, Ted Danson, Kevin Tighe, Dana Ivey, Elizabeth Moss. Quirky, novelistic film about a quiet, clean-cut psychologist who wins over a small town with his common-sense approach to their problems—while remaining an enigma himself. Original and amusing in a nice, old-fashioned way, but awfully tidy. Written by Kasdan. Super 35. [R]▼●▶

Mummy, The (1932) 72m. ***½ D: Karl Freund. Boris Karloff, Zita Johann, David Manners, Arthur Byron, Edward Van Sloan, Bramwell Fletcher, Noble Johnson. Horror classic stars Karloff as Egyptian mummy, revived after thousands of years, believing Johann is reincarnation of ancient mate. Remarkable makeup and atmosphere make it chills ahead of many follow-ups.▼●▶

Mummy, The (1959-British) C-88m. **½ D: Terence Fisher. Peter Cushing, Christopher Lee, Yvonne Furneaux, Eddie Byrne, Felix Aylmer, Raymond Huntley. Against warnings of severe consequences, archaeologists desecrate ancient tomb of Egyptian Princess Ananka. They return to England and those consequences. Stylish Hammer resurrection of Universal's Kharis series.▼●▶

Mummy, The (1999) C-124m. *½ D: Stephen Sommers. Brendan Fraser, Rachel Weisz, John Hannah, Arnold Vosloo, Kevin J. O'Connor, Jonathan Hyde, Oded Fehr. Hokey, jokey, Indiana Jones–ish adventure yarn has little to do with earlier Mummy movies. Librarian and Egyptologist Weisz (a clumsy character in the first scene—then, oddly, never again) hires Fraser to lead her to the "lost" city of Hamunaptra, where the tomb of Imhotep (Vosloo) is desecrated, to everyone's regret. Special effects galore, but no sense of awe or wonder; what's more, it goes on forever. Is that Dick Foran in the mummy attack scene? Followed by THE MUMMY RETURNS. Panavision. [PG-13] ▼●▶

Mummy Returns, The (2001) C-129m. *½ D: Stephen Sommers. Brendan Fraser, Rachel Weisz, John Hannah, Arnold Vosloo, Oded Fehr, Patricia Velasquez, Freddie Boath, Alun Armstrong, The Rock. Fraser and wife Weisz (with a precocious son in tow) desecrate an ancient crypt and inadvertently discover the means to raise an ancient army from the dead. Big Dumb Sequel to the original Big Dumb Hit has all the same ingredients (plus skeletal pygmy warriors!). A long, noisy action-adventure film made up entirely of climaxes. Followed by THE SCORPION KING and an animated TV series. Panavision. [PG-13]▼●▶

Mummy: Tomb of the Dragon Emperor, The (2008 - U.S. - German - Canadian) C-112m. *½ D: Rob Cohen. Brendan Fraser, Jet Li, Maria Bello, John Hannah, Michelle Yeoh, Luke Ford, David Calder, Isabella

Leong, Chau Sang Anthony Wong, Russell Wong, Liam Cunningham. Third in the series that began with the 1999 MUMMY finds adventurer Fraser, his wife (Bello), and son (Ford), plus hangers-on, in China battling the resurrected Emperor Han (Li), who's after an immortality formula. Fast-paced, with lots of effects, but a dopey story and ruinously overedited action sequences sink what might have been a fun film. Li and Yeoh are badly used. Bring back Kharis! Super 35. [PG-13]▶

Mummy's Curse, The (1944) 62m. **½ D: Leslie Goodwins. Lon Chaney, Jr., Peter Coe, Virginia Christine, Kay Harding, Dennis Moore, Martin Kosleck, Kurt Katch. Kharis and the reincarnated Ananka, last seen slipping into a New England swamp in THE MUMMY'S GHOST, are unaccountably dug up in a Louisiana bayou, where he's soon strangling people again. Surprisingly eerie and effective, with a good performance by Christine. Silent star William Farnum has a bit role as a caretaker. Last of the series.▼●▶

Mummy's Ghost, The (1944) 60m. *½ D: Reginald LeBorg. Lon Chaney, Jr., John Carradine, Ramsay Ames, Robert Lowery, Barton MacLane, George Zucco. Sequel to THE MUMMY'S TOMB finds seemingly unkillable Kharis and his mentor (Carradine) on the trail of a woman who is the reincarnation of Princess Ananka. Least interesting of the series, with nothing new or different to offer. Followed by THE MUMMY'S CURSE.▼●▶

Mummy's Hand, The (1940) 67m. *** D: Christy Cabanne. Dick Foran, Wallace Ford, Peggy Moran, Cecil Kellaway, George Zucco, Tom Tyler, Eduardo Ciannelli, Charles Trowbridge. Archeologists seeking lost tomb of Egyptian princess get more than they bargained for when they find it guarded by a living—and very deadly—mummy (Tyler). First of the "Kharis" series is entertaining blend of chills and comedy, with good cast, flavorful music and atmosphere. Not a sequel to THE MUMMY (1932), although it does utilize flashback footage; itself followed by three sequels, starting with THE MUMMY'S TOMB.▼●▶

Mummy's Shroud, The (1967-British) C-90m. BOMB D: John Gilling. Andre Morell, John Phillips, David Buck, Elizabeth Sellars, Maggie Kimberley, Michael Ripper. British expedition takes mummy of child pharaoh back to Cairo; boy's guardian, also a mummy, murders those responsible. One of the least of the Hammer horrors.▼●▶

Mummy's Tomb, The (1942) 61m. ** D: Harold Young. Lon Chaney, Jr., Elyse Knox, John Hubbard, Turhan Bey, Dick Foran, Wallace Ford, George Zucco, Mary Gordon. Sequel to THE MUMMY'S HAND finds Kharis (now played by Chaney) transported to

America to kill off surviving members of the expedition. Weak script and too much stock footage are the real villains. ▼●)

Mumsy, Nanny, Sonny and Girly (1970-British) **C-101m.** BOMB D: Freddie Francis. Vanessa Howard, Michael Bryant, Ursula Howells, Pat Heywood, Howard Trevor. Rock-bottom murder tale of eccentric family where children's "game-playing" has lethal overtones. Stupid. Aka GIRLY. [R]▼

Munich (2005) **C-164m.** **½ D: Steven Spielberg. Eric Bana, Daniel Craig, Ciarán Hinds, Mathieu Kassovitz, Hanns Zischler, Ayelet Zurer, Geoffrey Rush, Michael Lonsdale, Gila Almagor, Mathieu Almaric, Lynn Cohen, Valeria Bruni-Tedeschi, Yvan Attal. In the wake of the 1972 massacre of the Israeli Olympic team, the government of Israel hires a low-level operative (Bana) to head a secret squad. Its mission: to murder the terrorists responsible for the attack. Bana and his cohorts immerse themselves in the cloak-and-dagger world, but before long begin to question their own motives—and the toll the job may be taking on their humanity. Despite a script by Tony Kushner and Eric Roth (based on George Jonas' book *Vengeance,* which inspired the 1986 TV movie SWORD OF GIDEON), there is less here than meets the eye. A seeming lack of focus, and a feeling of treading familiar ground, dissipates the impact of key suspense scenes. Super 35. [R]▮

Munster, Go Home! (1966) **C-96m.** **½ D: Earl Bellamy. Fred Gwynne, Yvonne De Carlo, Terry-Thomas, Hermione Gingold, John Carradine, Debby Watson, Butch Patrick, Al Lewis. Monster family goes to England to claim a castle they've inherited; juvenile production based on the popular TV sitcom. Followed by TV movies in 1981 and 1995. ▼▮

Muppet Christmas Carol, The (1992) **C-85m.** *** D: Brian Henson. Michael Caine, Kermit the Frog, Miss Piggy, Fozzie Bear, The Great Gonzo, Animal, Rizzo the Rat (Frank Oz, Dave Goelz, Steve Whitmire, Jerry Nelson). Delightful adaptation of the Dickens perennial, with a human Scrooge (Caine, in a nicely modulated performance) surrounded by mostly Muppet characters. Jerry Juhl's script neatly balances humor with the story's robust melodrama, and Paul Williams' songs add perfect punctuation. [G]▼●▮

Muppet Movie, The (1979) **C-94m.** *** D: James Frawley. Kermit the Frog, Miss Piggy, Fozzie Bear, and the Muppets (Jim Henson, Frank Oz, Jerry Nelson, Richard Hunt, Dave Goelz), Charles Durning, Austin Pendleton; 15 guest stars. Enjoyable showcase for Jim Henson's irresistible characters, charting Kermit's odyssey from a Georgia swamp to Hollywood. Unnecessary movie-star cameos can't dim Muppets'

appeal in their first feature film. Trimmed from 97m. after initial release. [G]▼●▮

Muppets from Space (1999) **C-82m.** **½ D: Tim Hill. Gonzo, Kermit the Frog, Miss Piggy (Dave Goelz, Steve Whitmire, Frank Oz), Jeffrey Tambor, F. Murray Abraham, Ray Liotta, David Arquette, Andie MacDowell, Pat Hingle, Hollywood (Hulk) Hogan. Gonzo learns that he's really a stranded alien, and that others of his race are on the way. Conspiracy-minded Tambor is sure this means an invasion. Weak Muppet outing turns the story over to supporting characters, and loses the edge that sparked their earlier adventures. OK overall. [G]▼▮

Muppets Take Manhattan, The (1984) **C-94m.** *** D: Frank Oz. Kermit the Frog, Miss Piggy, Fozzie Bear, Gonzo, et al. (Jim Henson, Frank Oz, Jerry Nelson, Richard Hunt, Dave Goelz, Steve Whitmire), Dabney Coleman, Art Carney, James Coco, Joan Rivers, Gregory Hines, Linda Lavin, surprise guest stars. The Muppets try to crash Broadway with their college show, but Kermit soon discovers there's a broken heart for every light . . . Enjoyable outing with bouncy songs, nice use of N.Y.C. locations. [G]▼▮

Muppet Treasure Island (1996) **C-99m.** **½ D: Brian Henson. Kermit the Frog, Miss Piggy, Gonzo, Fozzie Bear (Steve Whitmire, Frank Oz, Dave Goelz), Tim Curry, Kevin Bishop, Billy Connolly, Jennifer Saunders. The Muppets take on Robert Louis Stevenson's classic pirate story, with Kermit the Frog as Captain Smollett and Miss Piggy as "Benjamina" Gunn. Good fun, but seems longer than it is, and Curry is—of all things—a bit more subdued as Long John Silver than you'd expect. Of course, after Robert Newton, anyone would seem subdued! [G]▼▮

Murder! (1930-British) **104m.** *** D: Alfred Hitchcock. Herbert Marshall, Norah Baring, Phyllis Konstam, Edward Chapman. Good early Hitchcock casts Marshall as actor who serves on jury at murder trial and believes accused woman innocent. Some prints run as short as 92m. Hitchcock also made a German-language version called MARY starring Alfred Abel. ▼▮

Murder Ahoy (1964-British) **93m.** ***½ D: George Pollock. Margaret Rutherford, Lionel Jeffries, Charles Tingwell, William Mervyn, Joan Benham, Stringer Davis, Miles Malleson. This time out, Miss Marple investigates murder on a naval cadet training-ship. Original screenplay (by David Persall and Jack Seddon) based on wonderful Agatha Christie character. ▼●▮

Murder at 1600 (1997) **C-107m.** ** D: Dwight Little. Wesley Snipes, Diane Lane, Alan Alda, Daniel Benzali, Ronny Cox, Dennis Miller, Tate Donovan, Diane Baker, Charles Rocket, Harris Yulin, Nicholas Pryor. Muddled, predictable mystery thriller in which Washington, D.C., homicide cop Snipes wades his way through assorted cover-ups and intrigue upon discovery of the bloody corpse of a beautiful White House staffer in an Oval Office bathroom. One Good Cop vs. Big Bad Bureaucracy scenario is done in by its endless plot holes, not to mention ludicrous finale. [R] ▼●▶

Murder at the Gallop (1963-British) **81m.** ***½ D: George Pollock. Margaret Rutherford, Robert Morley, Flora Robson, Charles Tingwell, Duncan Lamont, Stringer Davis, James Villiers, Robert Urquhart. Amateur sleuth Miss Marple suspects foul play when wealthy old recluse dies. Based on Agatha Christie's *After the Funeral.* ▼●▶

Murderball (2005) **C-88m.** ***½ D: Henry Alex Rubin, Dana Adam Shapiro. Electrifying documentary look at a group of gung-ho athletes who play their sport with the same competitive fire as the best pro and amateur jocks—only they are quadriplegics, and their game is rugby in wheelchairs. While the game sequences are riveting, the film is at its best when it focuses on the players' personalities and challenges off the field. [R] ▼▶

Murder by Contract (1958) **81m.** ** D: Irving Lerner. Vince Edwards, Philip Pine, Herschel Bernardi, Caprice Toriel. Intriguing little film about a hired killer and what makes him tick; ultimately sabotaged by pretentious dialogue and posturing.▶

Murder by Death (1976) **C-94m.** *** D: Robert Moore. Peter Sellers, Peter Falk, David Niven, Maggie Smith, James Coco, Alec Guinness, Elsa Lanchester, Eileen Brennan, Nancy Walker, Estelle Winwood, Truman Capote. Capote invites world's greatest detectives to his home and involves them in a baffling whodunit. Neil Simon spoofs such characters as Charlie Chan, Miss Marple, and Sam Spade in this enjoyable all-star comedy, with marvelous sets by Stephen Grimes. Simon followed this with THE CHEAP DETECTIVE. [PG] ▼●▶

Murder by Decree (1979-Canadian-British) **C-121m.** *** D: Bob Clark. Christopher Plummer, James Mason, Donald Sutherland, Genevieve Bujold, Susan Clark, David Hemmings, Frank Finlay, John Gielgud, Anthony Quayle. Sherlock Holmes investigates slayings of prostitutes by Jack the Ripper, with surprising results. Involved, often lurid story doesn't sustain through conclusion, but flaws overshadowed by warm interpretations of Holmes and Watson by Plummer and Mason. For another version of Holmes vs. the Ripper, see A STUDY IN TERROR. [PG] ▼●▶

Murder by Numbers (2002) **C-120m.** **½ D: Barbet Schroeder. Sandra Bullock, Ben Chaplin, Ryan Gosling, Michael Pitt, Agnes Bruckner, Chris Penn, R.D. Call. Homicide detective Bullock—a brilliant loner with heavy emotional baggage—works with her new partner (Chaplin) on a brutal

murder committed by two high schoolers out to stage the perfect crime, a la Leopold and Loeb. Yet another contemporary thriller that squanders all its good qualities by tacking on a silly, old-fashioned Hollywood finale. By that time, the two sick teenage criminals have worn out their welcome anyway. [R]▼▶

Murder by Phone (1980-Canadian) **C-79m.** ** D: Michael Anderson. Richard Chamberlain, John Houseman, Sara Botsford, Robin Gammell, Gary Reineke, Barry Morse. Talented cast and director go slumming in this hoary horror exercise involving a crazed killer who literally phones in his murders, doing in his victims by ingenious long distance device. Filmed as BELLS. [R]▼

Murder, Czech Style (1968-Czech) **90m.** **½ D: Jiri Weiss. Rudolf Hrusinsky, Kyeta Fialova, Vaclav Voska, Vladimir Mensik. Clever, gentle spoof of romantic triangle melodramas, with pudgy middle-aged clerk (Hrusinsky) marrying beautiful woman, realizing she's been cheating on him, planning revenge, via dream sequences.▼

Murderers' Row (1966) **C-108m.** BOMB D: Henry Levin. Dean Martin, Ann-Margret, Karl Malden, Camilla Sparv, James Gregory, Beverly Adams. Malden kidnaps A-M's father, threatens to melt Washington, D.C., with a "helio beam"; only Matt Helm can save both. (What if he'd had to make a choice?) Second Helm caper—after THE SILENCERS—offers one funny jibe at Frank Sinatra, absolutely nothing else. Sequel: THE AMBUSHERS.▼▶

Murder, He Says (1945) **93m.** *** D: George Marshall. Fred MacMurray, Helen Walker, Marjorie Main, Jean Heather, Porter Hall, Peter Whitney, Barbara Pepper, Mabel Paige. Zany slapstick of pollster MacMurray encountering Main's family of hayseed murderers. Too strident at times, but generally funny; clever script by Lou Breslow.▼▶

Murder, Inc. (1960) **103m.** *** D: Burt Balaban, Stuart Rosenberg. Stuart Whitman, May Britt, Henry Morgan, Peter Falk, David J. Stewart, Simon Oakland, Morey Amsterdam, Sarah Vaughan, Joseph Campanella. Solid little fact-based chronicle of the title crime organization, with Falk in particular scoring as Abe Reles, the syndicate's ill-fated number-one killer. Lots of familiar faces (Vincent Gardenia, Sylvia Miles, Seymour Cassel) in supporting roles. CinemaScope.▶

Murder in the First (1995) **C-122m.** **½ D: Marc Rocco. Christian Slater, Kevin Bacon, Gary Oldman, Embeth Davidtz, William H. Macy, Stephen Tobolowsky, Brad Dourif, R. Lee Ermey, Mia Kirshner, Stefan Gierasch. Young lawyer in the public defender's office is given his first assignment: defending an Alcatraz prisoner who murdered a fellow inmate. Only extenuating circumstance: the young prisoner was driven to madness by unspeakably brutal treatment for three straight years. Bacon's bravura performance is the centerpiece of this imperfect but commanding drama, which is a bit too self-satisfied and manipulative. Based on a true story, and set in the 1930s and '40s. Bacon's wife Kyra Sedgwick is amusingly cast in a cameo. With this film, director Rocco has used up his moving-camera allotment for at least 10 years. [R]▼⦿◗

Murder in the Ring SEE: **Ripped Off**

Murder Most Foul (1964-British) **90m.** *** D: George Pollock. Margaret Rutherford, Ron Moody, Charles Tingwell, Andrew Cruickshank, Stringer Davis, Francesca Annis, Dennis Price, James Bolam. When Miss Marple is lone jury member who believes defendant is innocent, she sets out to prove it. Based on Agatha Christie's *Mrs. McGinty's Dead.*▼⦿◗

Murder, My Sweet (1944) **95m.** ***½ D: Edward Dmytryk. Dick Powell, Claire Trevor, Anne Shirley, Otto Kruger, Mike Mazurki, Miles Mander. Adaptation of Raymond Chandler's book *Farewell My Lovely* gave Powell new image as hard-boiled detective Philip Marlowe, involved in homicide and blackmail. Still packs a wallop. Scripted by John Paxton. Story previously used for THE FALCON TAKES OVER; remade as FAREWELL, MY LOVELY in 1975. Also shown in computer-colored version.▼⦿◗

Murder on Monday SEE: **Home at Seven**

Murder on the Orient Express (1974-British) **C-128m.** *** D: Sidney Lumet. Albert Finney, Lauren Bacall, Martin Balsam, Ingrid Bergman, Jacqueline Bisset, Jean-Pierre Cassel, Sean Connery, John Gielgud, Wendy Hiller, Anthony Perkins, Vanessa Redgrave, Rachel Roberts, Richard Widmark, Michael York, Colin Blakely, George Coulouris. Elegant all-star production of Agatha Christie's whodunit set in the 1930s, with unrecognizable Finney as super-sleuth Hercule Poirot, and all his suspects on the same railroad train. Colorful entertainment, but awfully sluggish; sharp viewers will be able to guess the denouement, as well. Bergman won Best Supporting Actress Oscar. First of several lavish Christie adaptations; followed by DEATH ON THE NILE. Remade for TV in 2001. [PG]▼⦿◗

Murderous Maids (2000-French) **C-94m.** *** D: Jean-Pierre Denis. Sylvie Testud, Julie-Marie Parmentier, Isabelle Renauld, François Levantal, Dominique Labourier, Jean-Gabriel Nordmann, Marie Donnio. A new take on the notorious 1933 murder case that rocked all of France. Christine Papin (Testud) and her younger sister Léa, like their mother before them, work as house-

maids, but Christine's simmering resentment of her mother, her situation, and her employers boils over in various destructive ways. Denis' unsparing approach to the material doesn't even allow for a music score; Testud's performance is riveting and real. Super 35.◗

Murder She Said (1961-British) **87m.** *** D: George Pollock. Margaret Rutherford, Arthur Kennedy, Muriel Pavlow, James Robertson Justice, Charles Tingwell, Thorley Walters, Joan Hickson. Miss Marple takes a job as a domestic in order to solve a murder she witnessed. Based on Agatha Christie's *4:50 From Paddington*; first of four films starring Rutherford as Marple. Trivia note: Rutherford has several scenes with Hickson, later to play Miss Marple herself in a fine British TV series.▼⦿◗

Murders in the Rue Morgue (1932) **62m.** **½ D: Robert Florey. Bela Lugosi, Sidney Fox, Leon Waycoff (Ames), Bert Roach, Noble Johnson, Brandon Hurst, Arlene Francis. Expressionistic horror film based on Poe story, with Lugosi as fiendish Dr. Mirakle, with eyes on lovely Fox as the bride of his pet ape in 1845 Paris. Considered strong stuff back then. John Huston was one of the writers. Remade as PHANTOM OF THE RUE MORGUE, and twice more (once for TV in 1986) under original title.▼⦿◗

Murders in the Rue Morgue (1971) **C-87m.** *½ D: Gordon Hessler. Jason Robards, Herbert Lom, Christine Kaufmann, Lilli Palmer, Adolfo Celi, Maria Perschy, Michael Dunn. Sensationalistic reworking of Poe story; players at Grand Guignol–type theater suddenly become victims of real-life murders, gory goings-on. Set in Paris, but filmed in Spain. [PG]▼◗

Muriel (1963-French-Italian) **C-115m.** *** D: Alain Resnais. Delphine Seyrig, Jean-Pierre Kérien, Nita Klein, Claude Sainval, Jean-Baptiste Thierée. Poignant drama of alienation, about a widow (Seyrig) and her stepson (Thierée); she's haunted by the memory of her first love, he by his involvement in the torture and death of a woman named Muriel during the Algerian War.▼◗

Muriel's Wedding (1994-Australian) **C-105m.** ***½ D: P. J. Hogan. Toni Collette, Bill Hunter, Rachel Griffiths, Jeanie Drynan, Gennie Nevinson, Matt Day, Chris Haywood, Daniel Lapaine. Ugly duckling with a strikingly dysfunctional family (and a blustery, small-time politico father) yearns for a happier life, and starts on that road by leaving her home town of Porpoise Spit for Sydney, in the company of her fast-track girlfriend. Not the simple, straight-ahead "feel good" movie you might expect, but a darker, more idiosyncratic comedy-drama about friendship, dreams, reality, and the joys of ABBA music. A very satisfying film, full of wonderful performances; written by the director. [R] ▼●)

Murmur of the Heart (1971-French-German-Italian) **C-118m.** ***½ D: Louis Malle. Lea Massari, Benoit Ferreux, Daniel Gelin, Marc Winocourt, Michel Lonsdale. Fresh, intelligent, affectionately comic tale of bourgeois, sensuous Massari and her precocious 14-year-old son (Ferreux), builds to a thoroughly delightful resolution. Wonderful performances. [R] ▼●)

Murph the Surf SEE: **Live a Little, Steal a Lot**

Murphy's Law (1986) **C-100m.** *½ D: J. Lee Thompson. Charles Bronson, Kathleen Wilhoite, Carrie Snodgress, Robert F. Lyons, Richard Romanus, Angel Tompkins, Bill Henderson, James Luisi, Janet MacLachlan, Lawrence Tierney. All-too-typical Bronson vehicle about a cop framed for murders by psychopathic ex-con he originally sent to prison; only novelty is that the psycho is a woman (Snodgress). Strictly formula; violent and unpleasant. [R] ▼●)

Murphy's Romance (1985) **C-107m.** *** D: Martin Ritt. Sally Field, James Garner, Brian Kerwin, Corey Haim, Dennis Burkley, Georgann Johnson, Charles Lane. Young divorcée (with 12-year-old son) makes fresh start in small Arizona community, where she's attracted to older, laid-back, widowed pharmacist—and vice versa. Charming, easygoing comedy written by Irving Ravetch and Harriet Frank, Jr. (from Max Schott's novella), with Garner in a standout performance as Murphy, the last of the rugged individualists. In fact, this earned him his first Oscar nomination. [PG-13] ▼●)

Murphy's War (1971-British) **C-108m.** *** D: Peter Yates. Peter O'Toole, Sian Phillips, Philippe Noiret, Horst Janson, John Hallam, Ingo Morgendorf. Well-staged, gripping action sequences combine with psychological study of Irish seaman (O'Toole) only survivor of German massacre, out to get revenge. Good idea, but nonaction sequences tend to bog film down; script by Stirling Silliphant. Panavision. [PG] ▼●)

Muscle Beach Party (1964) **C-94m.** **½ D: William Asher. Frankie Avalon, Annette Funicello, Buddy Hackett, Luciana Paluzzi, Don Rickles, John Ashley, Jody McCrea, Morey Amsterdam, Peter Lupus, Candy Johnson, Dan Haggerty. Follow-up to BEACH PARTY picks up the pace as the gang finds the beach has been invaded by Rickles and his stable of body-builders. Usual blend of surf, sand, and corn; Rickles' first series appearance and the screen debut of "Little" Stevie Wonder. Sequel: BIKINI BEACH. Panavision. ▼●)

Muse, The (1999) **C-96m.** *** D: Albert Brooks. Albert Brooks, Sharon Stone, Andie MacDowell, Jeff Bridges, Mark Feuerstein, Steven Wright, Bradley Whitford. Brooks plays a Hollywood screenwriter who's told that he's out of touch—until he hooks up with a bona fide muse (Stone), a capricious woman whose working methods are unconventional at best. As with so many of Brooks's movies, the parts are greater than the whole, but his gibes at Hollywood are priceless, and some of the cameo appearances (which we won't give away) are very funny indeed. [PG-13] ▼●)

Muse Concert: No Nukes, The SEE: **No Nukes**

Music and Lyrics (2007) **C-96m.** **½ D: Marc Lawrence. Hugh Grant, Drew Barrymore, Brad Garrett, Kristen Johnston, Campbell Scott, Haley Bennett, Aasif Mandvi, Adam Grupper, Matthew Morrison. Paper-thin but cute romantic comedy about a washed-up '80s pop star (Grant) who's presented with a big break—getting to perform an original song with a contemporary music star (Bennett)—if he can only find a lyricist with whom he can collaborate. She appears in the unlikely person of a ditzy woman who's supposed to take care of the plants in his N.Y.C. apartment. Grant is at his best, tossing off a steady stream of funny lines. Written by the director. [PG-13])

Music Box (1989) **C-123m.** **½ D: Costa-Gavras. Jessica Lange, Armin Mueller-Stahl, Frederic Forrest, Donald Moffat, Lukas Haas, Cheryl Lynn Bruce, Michael Rooker. Chicago criminal attorney Lange is thrown for a loop when her Hungarian-immigrant dad is accused of heinous war crimes and threatened with deportation. She defends him in a sensational trial but has trouble—legally and emotionally—proving his innocence. What could have been a crackling political thriller becomes a high-gloss melodrama instead, plodding and far-fetched, though Lange is good in (rare) ethnic role, and Mueller-Stahl is strong as the enigmatic elder. A disappointment from the director of Z and MISSING. Panavision. [PG-13] ▼●)

Music for Millions (1944) **120m.** **½ D: Henry Koster. Margaret O'Brien, Jimmy Durante, June Allyson, Marsha Hunt, Hugh Herbert, Jose Iturbi, Connie Gilchrist, Harry Davenport, Marie Wilson, Larry Adler, Ethel Griffies. Teary tale of war-bride Allyson, a cellist in Iturbi's orchestra, gallantly waiting to have a baby—and for husband's return. O'Brien is her precocious kid sister. While there's plenty of Chopin and Debussy, Durante steals film with "Umbriago." Watch for Ava Gardner in a bit.

Music in Darkness SEE: **Night Is My Future**

Music in My Heart (1940) **70m.** ** D: Joseph Santley. Tony Martin, Rita Hayworth, Edith Fellows, Alan Mowbray, Eric Blore, George Tobias. Routine musical of Continental Martin cast in show where he meets lovely Hayworth. One good song, "It's a Blue World." ▼◗

Music Lovers, The (1970-British) **C-122m.** ****½** D: Ken Russell. Glenda Jackson, Richard Chamberlain, Max Adrian, Christopher Gable, Kenneth Colley. Occasionally striking but self-indulgent and factually dubious account of Tchaikovsky (Chamberlain), who marries and abandons the whorish Nina (Jackson). Overacted, overdirected. Panavision. [R]▼◗

Music Man, The (1962) **C-151m.** *****½** D: Morton Da Costa. Robert Preston, Shirley Jones, Buddy Hackett, Hermione Gingold, Paul Ford, Pert Kelton, Ronny Howard. Peerless Preston reprises his Broadway performance as super salesman/ con man Prof. Harold Hill, who mesmerizes Iowa town with visions of uniformed marching band. Faithful filmization of Meredith Willson's affectionate slice of Americana. Score includes "76 Trombones," "Till There Was You," and showstopping "Trouble." Remade for TV in 2003. Technirama. ▼◗

Music of Chance, The (1993) **C-98m.** ****½** D: Philip Haas. James Spader, Mandy Patinkin, M. Emmet Walsh, Charles Durning, Joel Grey, Samantha Mathis, Christopher Penn. A man gives a lift to a fellow stumbling alongside a country road, learns he's a high-stakes poker player, and decides to back him in an upcoming game against two eccentric millionaires. Low-key adaptation of Paul Auster's existential novel offers as many questions as answers while it spins its interesting—but oddball—tale. Coscripted by director Haas, a documentarian making his feature debut. Superior performances by a hand-picked cast; Spader is a particular standout as a slimeball with his own peculiar code of ethics. ▼●

Music of the Heart (1999) **C-124m.** ******* D: Wes Craven. Meryl Streep, Aidan Quinn, Angela Bassett, Gloria Estefan, Jane Leeves, Cloris Leachman, Kieran Culkin, Charlie Hofheimer, Jay O. Sanders. Newly single woman moves to East Harlem and starts a violin class, against all odds, giving her kids a sense of discipline, purpose, and pride. Pamela Gray's script sidesteps the obvious as often as possible, and makes many of the student characters worth caring about. Reaches its emotional peak before the climactic concert—but still a sweet, upbeat film. Inspired by the documentary SMALL WONDERS about the real-life Roberta Guaspari. Isaac Stern, Itzhak Perlman, and many other noted musicians appear as themselves. [PG]▼◗

Music Teacher, The (1988-Belgian) **C-95m.** ****½** D: Gerard Corbiau. Jose Van Dam, Anne Roussel, Philippe Volter, Sylvie Fennec, Patrick Bauchau, Johan Leyson. A familiar plot and stale script sink this musical drama detailing what happens when opera star Van Dam retires at the pinnacle of his fame to train fetching young Roussel and petty thief Volter. The charisma and magnificent singing voice of Van Dam, the Belgian bass-baritone, almost (but not quite) redeem this. [PG]▼●

Music Within (2007) **C-93m.** ****½** D: Steven Sawalich. Ron Livingston, Melissa George, Michael Sheen, Yul Vázquez, Rebecca De Mornay, Hector Elizondo, Leslie Nielsen, Marion Ross, Clint Howard, Dale Dye. Young man from Portland, Oregon, is stymied in pursuing his dream of public speaking, goes to Vietnam instead, and loses his hearing in an explosion. Back home he overcomes his impairment and becomes a celebrated advocate for the disabled, but doesn't fare as well in his private life. True story of Richard Pimentel seems to have the right stuff—including a showy performance by Sheen as a man with cerebral palsy—but winds up resembling a pat TV movie. Further hampered by a heavy-handed '70s jukebox score. [R]◗

Musketeer, The (2001-German-U.S.-Luxembourg) **C-105m.** BOMB D: Peter Hyams. Catherine Deneuve, Mena Suvari, Stephen Rea, Tim Roth, Justin Chambers, Bill Treacher, Daniel Mesguich, Nick Moran, Steven Speirs, Jan Gregor Kremp. Clumsily revamped version of THE THREE MUSKETEERS crams in Hong Kong–style martial arts action, but loses many of the characters—not to mention the charm and wit—from the novel. The Three Musketeers barely get a word in! Drab looking, badly photographed (by the director), and seemingly endless, this unattractive film may be the worst version ever of Dumas' evergreen. Super 35. [PG-13] ▼◗

Mustang Country (1976) **C-79m.** ******* D: John Champion. Joel McCrea, Robert Fuller, Patrick Wayne, Nika Mina. Excellent Western set along Montana-Canadian border in 1925. 70-year-old McCrea most convincing as ex-rancher and rodeo star who shares adventures with runaway Indian boy while hunting a wild stallion. [G]

Must Love Dogs (2005) **C-98m.** ****½** D: Gary David Goldberg. Diane Lane, John Cusack, Elizabeth Perkins, Dermot Mulroney, Christopher Plummer, Stockard Channing, Tony Bill, Ben Shenkman, Brad Hall, Steven R. Schirripa. Amiable if unremarkable romantic comedy about two divorced people who meet through an Internet personals ad: a woman whose family insists she start dating again, and a guy whose best friend does likewise. Sheer likability of the two stars carries this a long way over familiar territory. Panavision. [PG-13] ▼◗

Must Read After My Death (2009) **C/B&W-73m.** ****½** D: Morgan Dews. A woman dies, leaving behind hours of audio recordings and home movies. Dews is her grandson; from this material, he has fashioned an unsettling portrait of an outwardly happy but tragically dysfunctional American family. While the film offers the point of view that families suffered greatly because of predetermined gender roles in prefeminist 1960s America, there also is the sense that Dews is disrespecting his relatives' privacy. Watching this film is akin to peeking through a window and staring at an open wound. Dews wrote, directed, produced, and edited.

Mutant (1982) SEE: **Forbidden World**

Mutant (1984) SEE: **Night Shadows**

Mutant Chronicles (2008-U.S.-British) **C-101m.** *½ D: Simon Hunter. Ron Perlman, Thomas Jane, Devon Aoki, Sean Pertwee, Benno Fürmann, John Malkovich, Anna Walton, Tom Wu, Steve Toussaint, Luis Echegaray. Necromutants unleashed on the planet Earth strive (for no apparent reason other than it's what they do) to turn all humans into violent, blood-lusting creatures like themselves. Perlman plays a monk who believes he's the one to bring the mutants down, and rounds up a group of miscreant soldiers to help. By the time they do, who cares? Futuristic blood-and-guts thriller takes itself much too seriously; not even worth watching for a laugh. Drawn from the popular role-playing board game. [R]■

Mutations, The (1974-British) **C-92m.** ** D: Jack Cardiff. Donald Pleasence, Tom Baker, Brad Harris, Julie Ege, Michael Dunn, Jill Haworth. Scientist Pleasence crossbreeds humans with plants—and his unsuspecting university students are abducted as guinea pigs. Predictable story with truly grotesque elements and characters. Not recommended for dinnertime viewing. Video title: THE FREAKMAKER. [R]▼■

Mute Witness (1995-British-German-Russian) **C-98m.** **½ D: Anthony Waller. Marina Sudina, Fay Ripley, Evan Richards, Oleg Jankowskij, Igor Volkow, Sergei Karlenkov, Alex Bureew. The mute makeup artist on an American horror movie being shot in Moscow sees a snuff film being shot after-hours, and soon finds hit men from the Russian Mafia out to kill her. Impressive directing debut for Waller, who makes superb use of locations, but his script is second-rate; the story goes on too long, and is riddled with coincidences. Alec Guinness, in his final film, appears unbilled as a master criminal. Super 35. [R]▼■

Mutilator, The SEE: **Dark, The**

Mutiny on the Bounty (1935) **132m.** **** D: Frank Lloyd. Charles Laughton, Clark Gable, Franchot Tone, Herbert Mundin, Eddie Quillan, Dudley Digges, Donald Crisp, Movita, Henry Stephenson, Spring Byington, Ian Wolfe, Mamo. Storytelling at its best, in this engrossing adaptation of the Nordhoff-Hall book about mutiny against tyrannical Captain Bligh (Laughton) on voyage to the South Seas. Whole cast is good, but Laugh-

ton is unforgettable. Scripted by three top writers: Talbot Jennings, Jules Furthman, and Carey Wilson. Oscar winner for Best Picture; leagues ahead of its 1962 remake and the 1984 film THE BOUNTY. Also shown in computer-colored version.▼■

Mutiny on the Bounty (1962) **C-179m.** **½ D: Lewis Milestone. Marlon Brando, Trevor Howard, Richard Harris, Hugh Griffith, Richard Haydn, Tim Seely, Percy Herbert, Tarita, Gordon Jackson. Lavish remake of 1935 classic can't come near it, although visually beautiful; Howard good as Captain Bligh, but Brando is all wrong as Fletcher Christian. Best thing about this version is spectacular score by Bronislau Kaper. Ultra Panavision 70.▼■

Mutual Appreciation (2006) **110m.** *** D: Andrew Bujalski. Justin Rice, Rachel Cliff, Andrew Bujalski, Seung-Min Lee, Kevin Micka, Bill Morrison. Deadpan indie about an alternative rock musician who moves to N.Y.C. in search of a gig, stays with an old buddy and his girlfriend, and frets about romance and life. Ultra-*ultra* low-budget film has some stretches of tedium, but writer/director/editor Bujalski creates an improvisational mood of quiet, gently comic 20-something angst that few films achieve. The characters look, sound, and feel like real human beings. [R]■

MVP: Most Valuable Primate (2000-U.S.-Canadian) **C-93m.** *½ D: Robert Vince. Kevin Zegers, Jaime Renée Smith, Oliver Muirhead, Russell Ferrier, Dave Thomas, Ric Ducommun, Jay Brazeau, Patrick Cranshaw, Bernie, Mac, Louie. Contrived time-filler about a trained chimp who becomes the star player on a minor-league hockey team. This boring AIR BUD on ice may serve as perfect bedtime viewing for young tykes of worn-out parents. Followed by two direct-to-video sequels. [PG] ▼■

My American Cousin (1985-Canadian) **C-95m.** *** D: Sandy Wilson. Margaret Langrick, John Wildman, Richard Donat, Jane Mortifee. Well-acted, nostalgic coming-of-age story set in British Columbia in the summer of 1959, about a young girl's infatuation with her James Dean-like California cousin. Winner of six Genie awards (Canada's Oscar) including Best Picture. Donat is Robert Donat's nephew. Followed by a sequel, AMERICAN BOYFRIENDS. [PG]▼■

My Architect (2003) **C-116m.** **** D: Nathaniel Kahn. The illegitimate son of noted American architect Louis Kahn sets out to learn about his father, who died when the boy was 11. He visits his father's buildings around the world, talks to friends, colleagues (including such admiring architects as Philip Johnson, I. M. Pei, and Frank Gehry), and members of Kahn's "alternate" families. In making such a personal odyssey, the younger Kahn comes up with something much more resonant and universal; a quietly profound and beautiful film about dreams, goals, disappointments, and realities. ▼◻

My Baby's Daddy (2004) **C-86m.** BOMB D: Cheryl Dunye. Eddie Griffin, Anthony Anderson, Michael Imperioli, Paula Jai Parker, Joanna Bacalso, Bai Ling, Marsha Thomason, Bobb'e J. Thompson, Method Man, Amy Sedaris, John Amos, Tom "Tiny" Lister, Jr. "Comedy" with alleged heart is story of three buddies (and roommates) whose three girlfriends all become pregnant around the same time. All-too-predictable antics ensue as they grapple with raising infants while still trying to grow up themselves. Griffin also cowrote this time waster. [PG-13] ▼◻

My Beautiful Laundrette (1985-British) **C-98m.** ***½ D: Stephen Frears. Saeed Jaffrey, Roshan Seth, Daniel Day-Lewis, Gordon Warnecke, Derrick Branche, Shirley Anne Field. Extremely entertaining, perceptive examination of both race relations and the economic state in Britain, centering on a pair of young friends, Omar (Warnecke) and Johnny (Day-Lewis), and what happens when they take over a beat-up laundrette. On-target script by Hanif Kureishi, a Pakistani playwright who resides in England. Originally made for British TV. [R] ▼◻◐

My Best Fiend (1999-German-British) **C-95m.** ***½ D: Werner Herzog. Klaus Kinski starred in many of Werner Herzog's most notable films, but his intensity, ego and near-demented behavior made the productions tough going for everyone; at times the director and star actually plotted to murder each other. Hosting this unique documentary, Herzog revisits the locations of his Kinski films, musing over the actor's bizarre behavior. Funny, insightful, touching and deeply engrossing, it can't really explain Kinski, but it's a grand journey. Claudia Cardinale and Eva Mattes are among those interviewed. ▼◻

My Best Friend (2006-French) **C-94m.** *** D: Patrice Leconte. Daniel Auteuil, Dany Boon, Julie Gayet, Julie Durand, Henri Garcin, Jacques Mathou, Marie Pillet, Jacques Spiesser. Charming comedy about an antique dealer (Auteuil) who pays more attention to objects than human beings. Challenged by business associates who claim he has no personal life, he claims that he can produce a "best friend" and then desperately tries to find one, settling on talkative, outgoing cabdriver Boon. Super 35. [PG-13]◐

My Best Friend Is a Vampire (1988) **C-90m.** *½ D: Jimmy Huston. Robert Sean Leonard, Evan Mirand, Cheryl Pollak, René Auberjonois, Cecilia Peck, Fannie Flagg, Kenneth Kimmins, David Warner, Paul Wilson. One-joke comedy, in the wake of TEEN WOLF, has a high-school kid transformed into a vampire and trying to cope with it as a fact of life. Solid supporting cast does what it can. [PG] ▼◻

My Best Friend's Girl (1983-French) **C-99m.** **½ D: Bertrand Blier. Coluche, Isabelle Huppert, Thierry Lhermitte, Daniel Colas, Francois Perrot. Medium sex comedy with Lhermitte bringing home pick-up Huppert; she moves in, and his best friend (Coluche) falls for her. A familiar Blier theme (the sexual relationship between one woman and two men) is indifferently handled. Panavision. ▼

My Best Friend's Girl (2008) **C-102m.** ** D: Howard Deutch. Dane Cook, Kate Hudson, Jason Biggs, Alec Baldwin, Diora Baird, Lizzy Caplan. In the world according to this aggressively foulmouthed but only fitfully funny comedy, any guy who's dumped by his girlfriend can win her back simply by paying Tank (Cook), a smooth-talking rogue, to treat her to the worst date of her life. Complications arise when Tank genuinely falls for the lovely former flame (Hudson) of his best buddy (Biggs). Baldwin steals scenes right and left as Cook's equally swinish college-professor father. Cop-out ending plays like a last-minute improvised compromise. Unrated version runs 112m. [R]◐

My Best Friend's Wedding (1997) **C-105m.** *** D: P. J. Hogan. Julia Roberts, Dermot Mulroney, Cameron Diaz, Rupert Everett, Philip Bosco, M. Emmet Walsh, Rachel Griffiths, Carrie Preston, Susan Sullivan, Chris Masterson, Paul Giamatti, Harry Shearer. Roberts and Mulroney are old friends, and former lovers, who have pacted to wed at age 28 if they're both still single. When Mulroney springs fiancée Diaz on Julia, she starts to freak out and tries to sabotage the nuptials. Smart and funny romantic comedy (written by Ronald Bass) with Roberts scoring in a tailor-made role, and Everett stealing every scene he's in as her gay pal. Panavision. [PG-13] ▼◐

My Big Fat Greek Wedding (2002) **C-95m.** **½ D: Joel Zwick. Nia Vardalos, John Corbett, Michael Constantine, Lainie Kazan, Andrea Martin, Joey Fatone, Gia Carides, Louis Mandylor. Amiable comedy about a Greek-American woman trying to break free of her family's stifling adherence to old-world customs and falling in love with a WASP. You don't have to be Greek to relate to her story, especially with old pros like Constantine and Kazan as her parents. Expansion of Vardalos' one-woman show is slight, predictable, and sometimes broad, but entertaining, and became an unexpected box-office smash. Written by its star. Later a TV series. [PG] ▼◻

My Big Fat Independent Movie (2005) **C-80m.** BOMB D: Philip Zlotorynski. Paget Brewster, Neil Barton, Ashley Head, Eric Hoffman, Brian Krow, Clint Howard; voice of Jason Mewes. Two hit men hook up with a man mistaken for a fellow professional to pull off a "botched robbery" in Las Vegas. SCARY MOVIE–style treatment of independent cinema (PULP FICTION, SWINGERS, etc.) is unfunny, self-indulgent, and a struggle to watch. Brought to you, in part, by the folks at *Film Threat*. [R]▼❙

My Bloody Valentine (1981-Canadian) **C-91m. *½** D: George Mihalka. Paul Kelman, Lori Hallier, Neil Affleck, Keith Knight, Alf Humphreys, Cynthia Dale. Another gory HALLOWEEN/FRIDAY THE 13TH clone. Coal miner axes various victims (male as well as female) in the friendly little town of Valentine Bluffs. Ecch. Remade in 2009. [R]▼❙

My Bloody Valentine (2009) **C-101m. *½** D: Patrick Lussier. Jensen Ackles, Jaime King, Kerr Smith, Betsy Rue, Tom Atkins, Kevin Tighe. Remake of notorious 1981 slasher flick relied on 3-D gimmickry to increase the shock value of its full-bore gore in theatrical release. In 2-D it's just a routine reprise of a low-budget horror opus that wasn't very good to begin with. While a masked killer fatally applies a pickaxe to various unfortunates in a small mining town, local sheriff Smith suspects a recently returned mining-company heir (Ackles), the ex-boyfriend of the sheriff's wife (King), is behind the killing spree. Rue deserves some sort of good sport prize for remaining feisty and formidable during one of the longest displays of gratuitous nudity in the history of horror movies. Released to theaters as MY BLOODY VALENTINE 3D. 3-D. [R]❙

My Blueberry Nights (2008-Hong Kong-French) **C-90m. *½** D: Wong Kar Wai. Norah Jones, Jude Law, Rachel Weisz, David Strathairn, Natalie Portman, Frankie Faison, Chan Marshall. Jones is a sweet, sensitive young woman in N.Y.C. with romantic problems who makes a friend in cafe owner Law—the dreamiest, most unlikely counter man in all of Manhattan. Balance of film takes place in Memphis and out West, with Jones on a personal, solo odyssey to . . . nowhere. Good cast is wasted; jazz-pop sensation Jones is all too obviously an acting tyro. Inauspicious English-language debut for the noted Hong Kong filmmaker, for whom style often trumps story. Super 35. [PG-13]▼

My Blue Heaven (1990) **C-95m. ***** D: Herbert Ross. Steve Martin, Rick Moranis, Joan Cusack, Melanie Mayron, Bill Irwin, Carol Kane, William Hickey, Deborah Rush, Daniel Stern, Ed Lauter, Julie Bovasso, Colleen Camp. Lightweight but entertaining comedy about an Italian hood from N.Y.C. who's moved to suburban California as part of the FBI's witness protection program, where he's watched over by straight-arrow G-man Moranis. No

fireworks, but does have some good laughs, and enjoyable performances. Written by Nora Ephron. [PG-13]▼❙❙

My Bodyguard (1980) **C-96m. **½** D: Tony Bill. Chris Makepeace, Adam Baldwin, Martin Mull, Ruth Gordon, Matt Dillon, John Houseman, Joan Cusack, Craig Richard Nelson. Pleasant little film about high-school boy who hires a behemoth classmate to protect him from toughs at school. Totally likable but ultimately simplistic comedy-drama. Filmed in and around Chicago; look for Tim Kazurinsky, George Wendt, and Jennifer Beals as a classmate. Bill's directorial debut. [PG]▼

My Boss's Daughter (2003) **C-86m.** BOMB D: David Zucker. Ashton Kutcher, Tara Reid, Jeffrey Tambor, Andy Richter, Michael Madsen, Terence Stamp, Jon Abrahams, David Koechner, Carmen Electra, Molly Shannon, Kenan Thompson. Smitten with the title girl of his dreams (Reid), Kutcher is trapped into house-sitting for her wealthy father, a clean-freak who warns him against letting the inevitable happen: the thorough trashing of the family mansion. The leads have no chemistry in this trendily crude comedy that makes a short running time seem longer than the uncut GREED. This sat on the shelf for a couple of years before being dumped on the market. R-rated version also available. [PG-13]▼❙

My Boyfriend's Back (1993) **C-84m. *½** D: Bob Balaban. Andrew Lowery, Traci Lind, Danny Zorn, Edward Herrmann, Mary Beth Hurt, Matthew Fox, Philip Seymour Hoffman, Austin Pendleton, Cloris Leachman, Jay O. Sanders, Paul Dooley, Bob Dishy, Paxton Whitehead, Renée Zellweger. Terminally moronic comedy about a teen (Lowery) who is killed and comes back to life to take pretty Lind to the prom. Easy-to-please 13-year-olds might like it; others, beware. Talented cast is wasted. [PG-13]▼❙

My Boys Are Good Boys (1978) **C-90m. *½** D: Bethel Buckalew. Ralph Meeker, Ida Lupino, Lloyd Nolan, David F. Doyle, Sean T. Roche. Odd little film mixes 1940s approach to juvenile delinquency with far-fetched story of teenagers robbing armored car. [PG]▼❙

My Brilliant Career (1979-Australian) **C-101m. ***½** D: Gillian Armstrong. Judy Davis, Sam Neill, Wendy Hughes, Robert Grubb, Max Cullen, Pat Kennedy. Excellent portrait of a headstrong young woman determined to live a life of independent and intelligent pursuits in turn-of-the-century Australia. Armstrong's eye for detail and Davis' performance dominate this fine import, based on a true story. [G]▼❙

My Brother is an Only Child (2007-Italian-French) **C-108m. ***** D: Daniele Luchetti. Elio Germano, Riccardo Scamarcio, Diane Fleri, Angela Finocchiaro, Alba

Rohrwacher, Vittorio Emanuele Propizio. Absorbing tale of two brothers' relationship through the tumultuous 1960s and '70s. The older sibling (Scamarcio) is a Communist agitator, while the younger one (Germano) aligns himself—at first—with old-line Fascists. They also come to care for the same woman. From raucously funny family scenes to highly dramatic events, the film remains more personal than political, which is why it's so affecting. Screenplay by Luchetti and the team that wrote THE BEST OF YOUTH, Sandro Petraglia and Stefano Rulli.▶

My Brother's Wedding (1983) **C-118m.** ******* D: Charles Burnett. Everett Silas, Jessie Holmes, Gaye Shannon-Burnett, Ronnie Bell, Dennis Kemper, Sally Easter. Impressive, knowing tragicomedy from the talented director of KILLER OF SHEEP, about a 30-year-old product of the Watts ghetto who is pleased with his lot in life and despises his lawyer brother's upward mobility. Now he reluctantly agrees to be best man at his brother's nuptials. Impressively captures the urban black experience. 2007 director's cut runs 81m.▶

My Chauffeur (1986) **C-97m.** ****** D: David Beaird. Deborah Foreman, Sam Jones, E.G. Marshall, Sean McClory, Howard Hesseman. Heavily male chauvinist chauffeur service has to contend not only with Foreman's hiring, but her emergence as the most popular employee on the staff. Strange mix of '30s screwball with today's cruder comedies doesn't really come off, yet is enough of a curiosity to keep you watching. [R]▼○●

My Country, My Country (2006) **C-90m.** *****½** D: Laura Poitras. Heartrending (and eye-opening) documentary follows a civic-minded humanitarian Sunni doctor during the months leading up to the January 2005 elections in Iraq. Dr. Riyadh feels it is his obligation to run for office, to serve his community and his country, but the inherent danger frightens his family, and the actions of the U.S. forces cause nothing but anger and frustration. An intimate look at the ripple effect of the American occupation on the Iraqi people. Originally aired on PBS' series *P.O.V.*▶

My Cousin Rachel (1952) **98m.** ******* D: Henry Koster. Olivia de Havilland, Richard Burton, Audrey Dalton, John Sutton, Ronald Squire. Successful filmization of Daphne du Maurier mystery, with Burton (in his American debut) trying to discover if de Havilland is guilty or innocent of murder and intrigue.

My Cousin Vinny (1992) **C-119m.** ****½** D: Jonathan Lynn. Joe Pesci, Ralph Macchio, Marisa Tomei, Mitchell Whitfield, Fred Gwynne, Lane Smith, Austin Pendleton, Bruce McGill. Very likable (if much too lackadaisical) comedy about Brooklyn "lawyer" Pesci's attempt to defend his in-

nocent cousin (Macchio) and a friend on a murder charge in the Deep South. Pesci is perfect in a tailor-made part, and Tomei (in an Oscar-winning performance) is a delight to watch as his girlfriend. But there's no reason for this simple comedy to take so long to get where it's going. [R]▼○●

My Crazy Life SEE: **Mi Vida Loca**

My Darling Clementine (1946) **97m.** ******** D: John Ford. Henry Fonda, Linda Darnell, Victor Mature, Walter Brennan, Cathy Downs, Tim Holt, Ward Bond, Alan Mowbray, John Ireland, Jane Darwell, Grant Withers, J. Farrell MacDonald. Beautifully directed, low-key Western about Wyatt Earp (Fonda) and Doc Holliday (Mature), leading to inevitable gunfight at O.K. Corral. Full of wonderful details and vignettes; exquisitely photographed by Joseph P. MacDonald. One of director Ford's finest films, and an American classic. Screenplay by Samuel G. Engel and Winston Miller, from a story by Sam Hellman. Based on a book by Stuart N. Lake. Remake of FRONTIER MARSHAL (1939). In 1994 an archival print was found of the 104m. preview version, containing a number of minor differences and a slightly different finale.▼○●

My Darling Shiksa SEE: **Over the Brooklyn Bridge**

My Demon Lover (1987) **C-86m.** ****** D: Charles Loventhal. Scott Valentine, Michelle Little, Arnold Johnson, Gina Gallego, Robert Trebor. Trendy horror comedy has Valentine turning into a variety of monsters whenever he becomes sexually aroused, with Little the modern girl who tries to save him. Cast, including knockout beauty Gallego, is far better than the special effects-oriented material would indicate. [PG-13] ▼○●

My Dinner With Andre (1981) **C-110m.** ****½** D: Louis Malle. Andre Gregory, Wallace Shawn. Playwright-actor Shawn has dinner with his old friend, theater director Gregory, who's been having a series of strange life experiences; they talk about them and their philosophies for nearly two hours. A daring and unique film, written by its two principals, with moments of insight, drama, and hilarity—but not enough to sustain a feature-length film. [PG]▼○●

My Dog Skip (2000) **C-95m.** ******* D: Jay Russell. Frankie Muniz, Diane Lane, Kevin Bacon, Luke Wilson, Caitlin Wachs, Bradley Coryell, Clint Howard; narrated by Harry Connick, Jr. Sweet (but not cloying) family film based on Mississippi-born author Willie Morris' memoir of growing up in the 1940s with his beloved English fox terrier, who helps see him through childhood, boyhood, adolescence and young manhood. Warm and winning for grownups as well as children . . . but have a handkerchief handy! [PG]▼○●

My Dog Tulip (2010) **C-82m.** ****½** D: Paul Fierlinger, Sandra Fierlinger. Voices of Christopher Plummer, Lynn Redgrave, Isabella Rossellini, Peter Gerety, Brian Murray, Paul Hecht. Hand-crafted animated feature based on J. R. Ackerley's famous book about his enduring love for a German shepherd. Plummer narrates as the witty and iconoclastic author, for whom Tulip could do no wrong. Visually striking but awfully low-key; alternately amusing and arch. ▶

My Dream Is Yours (1949) **C-101m.** ****½** D: Michael Curtiz. Jack Carson, Doris Day, Lee Bowman, Adolphe Menjou, Eve Arden. Carson makes Day a radio star in standard musicomedy; highlights are Bugs Bunny dream sequence, Edgar Kennedy's performance as Day's uncle. Remake of TWENTY MILLION SWEETHEARTS, with Doris stepping into Dick Powell's role (and reprising the 1934 hit "I'll String Along With You"). ▼●◗

My Fair Lady (1964) **C-170m.** *****½** D: George Cukor. Rex Harrison, Audrey Hepburn, Stanley Holloway, Wilfrid Hyde-White, Gladys Cooper, Jeremy Brett, Theodore Bikel, Henry Daniell, Mona Washbourne, Isobel Elsom. Ultrasmooth filmization of Lerner and Loewe's enchanting musical from Shaw's PYGMALION, with Prof. Henry Higgins (Harrison) transforming guttersnipe Hepburn into regal lady, to win a bet. Sumptuously filmed, with "The Rain in Spain," Harrison's soliloquys among highlights. Eight Oscars include Picture, Actor, Director, Cinematography (Harry Stradling), Costumes (Cecil Beaton), Score Adaptation (Andre Previn), Art Direction (Beaton and Gene Allen). Super Panavision 70. ▼●◗

My Family/Mi Familia (1995) **C-128m.** ******* D: Gregory Nava. Jimmy Smits, Esai Morales, Edward James Olmos, Eduardo Lopez Rojas, Jenny Gago, Elpidia Carrillo, Lupe Ontiveros, Jacob Vargas, Jennifer López, Maria Canals, Leon Singer, Michael De Lorenzo, Jonathan Hernandez, Constance Marie, Mary Steenburgen, Scott Bakula, DeDee Pfeiffer. A Mexican-American writer (Olmos) looks back at his family's colorful history since immigrating to L.A. in the 1920s. Evocative, well-cast, multigenerational saga indulges in melodrama at times, but never seems false, and redeems itself with a healthy sense of humor. Written by Nava and producer Anna Thomas, who also made EL NORTE. [R] ▼●◗

My Father and I SEE: **How I Killed My Father**

My Father Is Coming (1991-German) **C-82m.** ******* D: Monika Treut. Alfred Edel, Shelley Kastner, Mary Lou Graulau, David Bronstein, Michael Massee, Annie Sprinkle, Fakir Musafar. Engrossing low-budget drama of German-born Kastner, who's struggling to find someone to love (whether it be male or female), and make it as an actress in N.Y.C.; her father's visit proves to be an awakening for both parent and child. In its best moments, an astute commentary on the importance of accepting who you are, as well as the differences in others. Notable for the appearances of porn star/performance artist Annie Sprinkle and "modern primitive" Fakir Musafar (who must be seen to be believed). ▼

My Father's Glory (1990-French) **C-110m.** *****½** D: Yves Robert. Philippe Caubere, Nathalie Roussel, Didier Pain, Therese Liotard, Julien Caimaca. Richly rewarding reminiscence, set in rural France at the turn of the century, chronicling the life of a precocious little boy and his family and a summer trip to Provence, where the child becomes immersed in the country and village life. Based on Marcel Pagnol's childhood memoirs. This is storytelling, and moviemaking, of the first order. The story continues in MY MOTHER'S CASTLE. [G] ▼▶

My Father The Hero (1994) **C-90m.** ******* D: Steve Miner. Gérard Depardieu, Katherine Heigl, Dalton James, Lauren Hutton, Faith Prince, Stephen Tobolowsky, Ann Hearn, Robyn Peterson, Frank Renzulli. Longtime absentee father takes his resentful 14-year-old daughter on a Caribbean vacation, where (to impress potential suitors) she spins a web of lies—starting with the "fact" that he's not her father, but her lover. Depardieu re-creates his role from the 1991 French film MON PÈRE, CE HÉROS, and brings his considerable charisma and credibility to a potentially silly comedy, making it a lot of fun. [PG] ▼●◗

My Favorite Blonde (1942) **78m.** ******* D: Sidney Lanfield. Bob Hope, Madeleine Carroll, Gale Sondergaard, George Zucco, Victor Varconi. Bob and his trained penguin become sitting ducks when spy Madeleine uses them to help deliver secret orders; very funny WW2 Hope vehicle. ▼◗

My Favorite Brunette (1947) **87m.** ******* D: Elliott Nugent. Bob Hope, Dorothy Lamour, Peter Lorre, Lon Chaney, John Hoyt, Reginald Denny. Better-than-usual Hope nonsense with Bob as a photographer mixed up with mobsters; Lorre and Chaney add authenticity. Two very funny surprise cameos at beginning and end of film. Also shown in computer-colored version. ▼●◗

My Favorite Martian (1999) **C-93m.** ****** D: Donald Petrie. Christopher Lloyd, Jeff Daniels, Elizabeth Hurley, Daryl Hannah, Wallace Shawn, Christine Ebersole, Michael Lerner, Ray Walston. Strictly juvenile update of the 1960s TV sitcom, with Lloyd as the Martian who lands on Earth and moves in with good-natured lunkhead Daniels, a TV news producer. Broad, sometimes crass special-effects comedy for undemanding kids. The presence of Walston

[962]

(from the original show) may bring a smile to those who remember the series. An unbilled Wayne Knight provides the voice of the Suit. [PG]▼●◗

My Favorite Season SEE **Ma Saison Préférée**

My Favorite Spy (1951) **93m.** ✱✱✱ D: Norman Z. McLeod. Bob Hope, Hedy Lamarr, Francis L. Sullivan, Mike Mazurki, John Archer, Iris Adrian, Arnold Moss. Bob resembles murdered spy, finds himself thrust into international intrigue. Fast-moving fun, with glamorous Hedy aiding Bob on all counts.◗

My Favorite Wife (1940) **88m.** ✱✱✱ D: Garson Kanin. Cary Grant, Irene Dunne, Gail Patrick, Randolph Scott, Ann Shoemaker, Scotty Beckett, Donald MacBride. Dunne, supposedly dead, returns to U.S. to find hubby Grant remarried to Patrick, in familiar but witty marital mixup, remade as MOVE OVER, DARLING. Inspired by *Enoch Arden*; Grant's character even has the same last name. Produced and cowritten (with Sam and Bella Spewack) by Leo McCarey. Also shown in computer-colored version.▼●◗

My Favorite Year (1982) **C-92m.** ✱✱✱ D: Richard Benjamin. Peter O'Toole, Mark Linn-Baker, Jessica Harper, Joseph Bologna, Bill Macy, Lainie Kazan, Anne DeSalvo, Lou Jacobi, Adolph Green, George Wyner, Selma Diamond, Cameron Mitchell. Enjoyable comedy about a young writer on TV's top comedy show in 1954 who's given the job of chaperoning that week's guest star, screen swashbuckler and off-screen carouser Alan Swann (O'Toole, in a tailor-made role). Shifts gears, and focus, a bit too often, but has many good moments, and likable performances (including Bologna as Sid Caesar–ish TV star). The woman O'Toole dances with in night club is 1930s leading lady Gloria Stuart. Benjamin's directorial debut. Musicalized on Broadway a decade later (also with Kazan). [PG]▼●◗

My Fellow Americans (1996) **C-101m.** ✱✱✱ D: Peter Segal. Jack Lemmon, James Garner, Dan Aykroyd, Lauren Bacall, John Heard, Bradley Whitford, Sela Ward, Wilford Brimley, Esther Rolle. Two ex-presidents of the U.S.—longtime enemies—are forced to work together to uncover a plot to blame one of them for a dirty deal conducted by the current head of state. On the lam and left to their own devices, they have to deal with ordinary citizens for the first time in years. Breezy comedy, short on subtlety and long on punchlines and occasional bathroom humor . . . but it works, thanks to the charisma and professionalism of Lemmon and Garner. Bacall (as Lemmon's wife) has almost nothing to do. [PG-13]▼●◗

My First Mister (2001) **C-109m.** ✱✱✱½

D: Christine Lahti. Leelee Sobieski, Albert Brooks, Desmond Harrington, Carol Kane, Mary Kay Place, John Goodman, Michael McKean, Rutanya Alda. A suicidal teenaged girl who hates her life, and especially hates her parents, is unexpectedly attracted to a schlumpy middle-aged clothing salesman. Soon, she is affecting his outlook on life as much as he is hers. A wonderfully fresh comedy-drama written by Jill Franklyn, with great performances by the two stars. An impressive feature directing debut for Lahti. Panavision. [R]▼◗

My First Wife (1984-Australian) **C-95m.** ✱✱½ D: Paul Cox. John Hargreaves, Wendy Hughes, Lucy Angwin, Anna Jemison, David Cameron. Painful, provocative drama about self-centered man who literally goes crazy when his wife leaves him after 10 years. Achingly real, superbly acted, but slow and talky at times. Cox coscripted with Bob Ellis, based on his own experiences.▼

My Friend Flicka (1943) **C-89m.** ✱✱✱ D: Harold Schuster. Roddy McDowall, Preston Foster, Rita Johnson, Jeff Corey, James Bell. Sentimental story of boy who loves rebellious horse; nicely done, beautifully filmed in color. Followed by sequel THUNDERHEAD, SON OF FLICKA and a TV series. Remade in 2006 as FLICKA.▼◗

My Friend Irma (1949) **103m.** ✱✱ D: George Marshall. Marie Wilson, John Lund, Diana Lynn, Don DeFore, Dean Martin, Jerry Lewis, Hans Conried. Based on radio series, movie concerns Wilson in title role as dumb blonde, Lynn as her level-headed pal, encountering wacky Martin and Lewis in their film debut. Followed by a sequel. Later a TV series.▼●◗

My Friend Irma Goes West (1950) **90m.** ✱✱½ D: Hal Walker. John Lund, Marie Wilson, Dean Martin, Jerry Lewis, Corinne Calvet, Diana Lynn, Lloyd Corrigan, Don Porter, Kenneth Tobey. Daffy Irma (Wilson) and pals join Martin and Lewis on their trek to Hollywood.◗

My Geisha (1962) **C-120m.** ✱✱½ D: Jack Cardiff. Shirley MacLaine, Yves Montand, Edward G. Robinson, Bob Cummings, Yoko Tani. Occasionally amusing comedy. MacLaine is movie star who tries the hard way to convince husband-director Montand that she's right for his movie. Loosely based on MacLaine's relationship with husband Steve Parker (who produced the film). Filmed in Japan. Technirama.▼●◗

My Giant (1998) **C-97m.** ✱✱½ D: Michael Lehmann. Billy Crystal, Gheorghe Muresan, Kathleen Quinlan, Joanna Pacula, Zane Carney, Jere Burns, Dan Castellaneta, Harold Gould, Doris Roberts, Lorna Luft, Estelle Harris, Steven Seagal. Ne'er-do-well showbiz agent chances to meet a 7'7" giant in Romania—and sees in him a way to resurrect his career and win back his estranged wife and kid. Sweet and amusing as long as Muresan's stomping around but the film turns borderline mawkish toward the end. Crystal is likeable as always, and then real-life Washington Wizards center Muresan is winning in the title role. That's Crystal's daughter Lindsay as a put-upon production assistant. [PG-13] ▼●◗

My Girl (1991) **C-102m.** **½ D: Howard Zieff. Dan Aykroyd, Jamie Lee Curtis, Macaulay Culkin, Anna Chlumsky, Richard Masur, Griffin Dunne, Ann Nelson, Peter Michael Goetz, Tom Villard, Ray Buktenica. Likable if soft-centered tale of an 11-year-old girl crying for attention from her widowed father, a mortician who doesn't know how to reach out to his precocious daughter. Bittersweet comedy touches on love, friendship, puberty, and most of all, death, but its telling moments are muted by an overall air of predictability. Appealing cast sparked by Chlumsky's mature performance. Followed by a Culkin-less sequel. [PG] ▼●◗

My Girl 2 (1994) **C-99m.** **½ D: Howard Zieff. Dan Aykroyd, Jamie Lee Curtis, Anna Chlumsky, Austin O'Brien, Richard Masur, Christine Ebersole, John David Souther, Angeline Ball, Aubrey Morris, Gerrit Graham, Ben Stein, Richard Beymer, George D. Wallace. Budding teenager Chlumsky travels to L.A. (where her uncle lives) to try and learn something about her mother, who died giving birth to her; her companion on this odyssey is the son of her uncle's girlfriend. Bland but likeable fodder aimed squarely at young viewers. [PG] ▼●◗

My Girlfriend's Boyfriend SEE: **Boyfriends and Girlfriends**

My Heroes Have Always Been Cowboys (1991) **C-106m.** **½ D: Stuart Rosenberg. Scott Glenn, Kate Capshaw, Ben Johnson, Balthazar Getty, Tess Harper, Gary Busey, Mickey Rooney, Clarence Williams III, Dub Taylor, Clu Gulager, Dennis Fimple. Aging collection of contusions (Glenn) comes home from the rodeo circuit to care for his father, only to battle sis and her husband, who'd just as soon the old man be put away. If you've seen Sam Peckinpah's sublime JUNIOR BONNER (which also featured Johnson) this has got to ring a bit hollow. Capable cast looks good in blue jeans, but cowpie cinema has been better served. [PG] ▼●

My Kid Could Paint That (2007) **C-84m.** *** D: Amir Bar-Lev. Fascinating documentary about Marla Olmstead, a 4-year-old girl whose abstract paintings became the hit of the New York art world until questions surfaced about their authenticity. What begins as an amusing look at modern art becomes an unsettling examination of the nature of documentary filmmaking itself, unintended by director Bar-Lev, who found himself caught between his relationship with the Olmstead family and the facts he felt obliged to pursue. The film allows the viewer to draw his own conclusions, and raises questions that are troubling and well worth considering. [PG-13] ◗

My Left Foot (1989-Irish) **C-103m.** ***½ D: Jim Sheridan. Daniel Day-Lewis, Brenda Fricker, Ray McAnally, Hugh O'Conor, Fiona Shaw, Cyril Cusack, Adrian Dunbar, Ruth McCabe, Alison Whelan. Exhilarating film with Day-Lewis in a tour de force as Christy Brown, feisty Irish artist-writer who was born with cerebral palsy. This is no disease-of-the-week weeper; it's an intensely moving story with just the right touches of humor, warmth, and poignancy. Fricker and McAnally are ideal as Christy's parents, and O'Conor is absolutely remarkable as the young Christy. Sheridan coscripted (with Shane Connaughton) from Brown's autobiography. Lovely score by Elmer Bernstein. Both Day-Lewis and Fricker won Oscars for their performances. [R] ▼●◗

My Life (1993) **C-112m.** **½ D: Bruce Joel Rubin. Michael Keaton, Nicole Kidman, Haing S. Ngor, Bradley Whitford, Queen Latifah, Michael Constantine, Rebecca Schull, Mark Lowenthal, Lee Garlington, Toni Sawyer. Successful ad executive, whose wife is pregnant, learns he's dying and doesn't know how to deal with the unfinished business in his life (particularly his feelings of anger toward his family) or the fact that he may never see his child. Many truthful and poignant moments in this unabashed tearjerker, but contrivances ultimately take over—especially toward the finale. Directing debut for screenwriter Rubin (the screenwriter of another misty-eyed Hollywood concoction, GHOST). [PG-13] ▼●◗

My Life and Times with Antonin Artaud (1994-French) **93m.** ** D: Gérard Mordillat. Sami Frey, Marc Barbé, Julie Jézéquel, Valerie Jeannet, Clotilde de Bayser, Charlotte Valandrey. Slow-moving fiction set in 1946, depicting the curious friendship between Jacques Prevel (Barbé), an eager, starving young poet, and Artaud (Frey), the brilliant but tortured, self-involved, and drug-addicted writer/actor/intellectual who has just been released from an asylum. A real downer, of interest mainly to aficionados of Artaud. Crisply filmed in b&w; also in 1993, Mordillat codirected a companion documentary, THE TRUE STORY OF ARTAUD THE MOMO. ▼◗

My Life as a Dog (1985-Swedish) **C-101m.** *** D: Lasse Hallström. Anton Glanzelius, Tomas von Brömssen, Anki Liden, Melinda Kinnaman, Kicki Rundgren, Ing-mari Carlsson. Warm-hearted look at the tumultuous life of an irrepressibly mischievous 12-year-old boy who's shipped off to live with relatives in a rural village in 1950s Sweden. Both comedic and poignant, this is ultimately an honest depiction of the often confusing nature of childhood. Glanzelius is excellent in the lead; based on an autobiographical novel by Reidar Jönsson. Later a cable-TV series. ▼◐▶

My Life in Ruins (2009-U.S.-Spanish) **C-95m.** *½ D: Donald Petrie. Nia Vardalos, Richard Dreyfuss, Alexis Georgoulis, Alistair McGowan, Harland Williams, Rachel Dratch, Caroline Goodall, Ian Ogilvy, Sophie Stuckey, María Botto, María Adánez, Brian Palermo, Rita Wilson. Lame comedy doubling as a travelogue has gorgeous Greek locations . . . and nothing else to recommend it. Vardalos is a sweet rookie guide who must deal with a group of stereotypical tourist "types," underhanded competitors, and a budding romance with her macho driver during a summer in Greece. At best it comes off as *Love Boat*–lite, although Vardalos is appealing as ever. [PG-13] ▶

My Life's in Turnaround (1994) **C-84m.** *½ D: Eric Schaeffer, Donal Lardner Ward. Eric Schaeffer, Donal Lardner Ward, Lisa Gerstein, Dana Wheeler Nicholson, Debra Clein, Sheila Jaffe, John Dore, John Sayles, Martha Plimpton, Phoebe Cates, Casey Siemaszko. Tired inside-Hollywood (or fringes-of-Hollywood) comedy might elicit a few approving snorts from the rarefied audience for which it's intended. Aspiring filmmakers exploit any presumed break that comes their way, be it a taxicab encounter with Phoebe Cates or a restaurant encounter with Martha Plimpton. Someone should have put *this* in turnaround. ▼▶

My Life So Far (1999-English-Scottish) **C-93m.** *** D: Hugh Hudson. Colin Firth, Mary Elizabeth Mastrantonio, Malcolm McDowell, Rosemary Harris, Irène Jacob, Robert Norman, Tchéky Karyo, Brendan Gleeson. Delightful memoir of growing up in an eccentric family, set in the Scottish highlands during the 1920s and '30s. Firth is a dreamer/inventor, Mastrantonio his patient wife, McDowell his scheming man-about-town brother who has no patience for Firth's peccadilloes; and Jacob the alluring Frenchwoman who captures the imagination of every male in the household. Spirited, funny, and handsomely made. Based on the book *Son of Adam* by Sir Denis Forman. [PG-13] ▼▶

My Life to Live (1962-French) **85m.** *** D: Jean-Luc Godard. Anna Karina, Saddy Rebbot, Andre S. Labarthe, Guylaine Schlumberger. Complex, fascinating 12-chapter portrait of a prostitute (Karina, who was then wed to Godard), told in documentary style. Probing look at the manner in which women and men view one another—and a celluloid valentine to Karina, upon whose mere presence Godard seems to be transfixed. Aka VIVRE SA VIE. ▼◐▶

My Life Without Me (2003-Spanish-Canadian) **C-106m.** *** D: Isabel Coixet. Sarah Polley, Scott Speedman, Deborah Harry, Mark Ruffalo, Leonor Watling, Amanda Plummer, Julian Richings, Maria de Medeiros. A trailer-dwelling mom in her early '20s (Polley) learns that she has incurable cancer. She makes a list of things she wants to accomplish in her remaining time on earth, including preparing her children for her absence and having an affair—in this case, with a Laundromat acquaintance (Ruffalo). Polley nips the potential for any mawkish excess, but modestly moving drama isn't a one-woman show. Richings is a standout as a shy, gentle doctor mortified by his bad-news plight. Adapted by the director from a short story by Nanci Kincaid. Alfred Molina appears unbilled. [R] ▼▶

My Little Chickadee (1940) **83m.** **½ D: Edward Cline. Mae West, W. C. Fields, Joseph Calleia, Dick Foran, Ruth Donnelly, Margaret Hamilton, Donald Meek. Team of West and Fields out West is good, but should have been funnier; W. C.'s saloon scenes are notable. The two stars also wrote screenplay. ▼◐▶

My Little Girl (1986) **C-113m.** *** D: Connie Kaiserman. Mary Stuart Masterson, James Earl Jones, Geraldine Page, Pamela Payton Wright, Anne Meara, Peter Gallagher, Page Hannah, Erika Alexander, Traci Lin, Jordan Charney, Jennifer Lopez. Subtle, perceptive account of affluent, romantic, naive young Masterson, who volunteers to work one summer in a children's detention center. Extremely well played by all, with a special nod to Alexander and Lin (as a pair of troubled, abused girls). [R] ▼◐

My Little Pony (1986) **C-89m.** ** D: Michael Joens. Voices of Danny DeVito, Madeline Kahn, Tony Randall, Cloris Leachman, Rhea Pearlman. Animated fantasy pits the good Little Ponies against an evil witch. Highlight is an encounter with the Smooze, an evergrowing mass of living lava—a good idea hampered by bad animation. Too "cute" for anyone over the age of 7. Followed by a TV series. [G] ▼▶

My Love Letters SEE: **Love Letters** (1983)

My Main Man From Stony Island SEE: **Stony Island**

My Man SEE: **Mon Homme**

My Man Adam (1985) **C-84m.** ** D: Roger L. Simon. Raphael Sbarge, Page Hannah, Veronica Cartwright, Larry B. Scott, Dave Thomas, Charlie Barnett, Austin Pendleton. Yet another youth wish-fulfillment comedy, done as a teen version of UP THE SANDBOX. Sbarge is a pizza delivery boy who fantasizes about dreamgirl Hannah (Daryl's redheaded sister, in her first starring role) and becomes involved in a real-life murder adventure. Barely released film is pleasant but uneventful. [R] ▼

My Man and I (1952) **99m.** **½ D: William A. Wellman. Shelley Winters, Ricardo Montalban, Wendell Corey, Claire Trevor,

Robert Burton, Jack Elam. Interesting curio about cheerful, kindly Mexican-born Montalban, who despite his trials and struggles is fiercely proud of his American citizenship.

My Man Godfrey (1936) 95m. ***½ D: Gregory La Cava. William Powell, Carole Lombard, Gail Patrick, Alice Brady, Eugene Pallette, Alan Mowbray, Mischa Auer, Franklin Pangborn. Delightful romp with Lombard and crazy household hiring Powell as butler thinking he's a tramp who needs a job; he teaches them that money isn't everything. Auer is impressive as starving artist, sheltered by patroness Brady. But Pallette—as harried head of household—has some of the best lines. Screenplay by Morrie Ryskind and Eric Hatch, from Hatch's novel. Jane Wyman is an extra in the party scene. Classic screwball comedy; remade in 1957. ▼▶

My Man Godfrey (1957) C-92m. **½ D: Henry Koster. June Allyson, David Niven, Martha Hyer, Eva Gabor, Jeff Donnell. Shallow compared to original, but on its own a harmless comedy of rich girl Allyson finding life's truths from butler Niven. CinemaScope. ▼

My Mom's New Boyfriend (2008) C-97m. ** D: George Gallo. Antonio Banderas, Meg Ryan, Colin Hanks, Selma Blair, Trevor Morgan, John Valdeterro, Eli Danker, Keith David, Enrico Colantoni, Marco St. John. Flatfooted comedy casts a willing Ryan as Hanks' fat, depressed mother who—while he's gone, training as an FBI agent—slims down and rejuvenates her life. But when he brings his fiancée home he discovers that his now-hot mom is being wooed by a slick art thief (Banderas), who's a wanted man. This might have played better as a broad farce; as it is it just lies there. Released direct to DVD. Super 35. [PG-13]▶

My Mother's Castle (1990-French) C-98m. *** D: Yves Robert. Julien Caimaca, Philippe Caubere, Nathalie Roussel, Didier Pain, Therese Liotard. Sweet, warm continuation of the story which begins in MY FATHER'S GLORY. Here, young Marcel further enjoys weekend family outings to his beloved Provence. Based on Marcel Pagnol's childhood memoirs; a notch below the first film, but still most worthwhile (and must-viewing in tandem with its predecessor, as well as with Claude Berri's JEAN DE FLORETTE and MANON OF THE SPRING).▼▶

My Name is Joe (1998-British-German) C-105m. **½ D: Ken Loach. Peter Mullan, Louise Goodall, Gary Lewis, Lorraine McIntosh, David McKay, Anne-Marie Kennedy, David Hayman, Scott Hannah. Likable loser Mullan is a recovering alcoholic eking out a life in Glasgow, Scotland. Mullan's tentative romance with health-care worker Goodall is worth a look . . .

and more engaging than the melodramatic turn the story takes involving local thugs. [R]▼

My Name Is John SEE: **Legend of Hillbilly John, The**

My Name Is Julia Ross (1945) 65m. *** D: Joseph H. Lewis. Nina Foch, Dame May Whitty, George Macready, Roland Varno, Anita Bolster, Doris Lloyd. An unsuspecting young woman answers a London newspaper ad for a job and winds up the prisoner of a crazy family. Often cited as a model B movie, it does go a long way on a low budget, though it's a bit more obvious now than it must have been in 1945. Foch's performance is still a standout. Later the inspiration for DEAD OF WINTER.

My Name Is Nobody (1973-Italian-French-German) C-115m. *** D: Tonino Valerii. Henry Fonda, Terence Hill, Jean Martin, Leo Gordon, R. G. Armstrong, Steve Kanaly, Geoffrey Lewis. Underrated, enjoyable if overlong Western spoof with Hill as an easygoing gunman who worships aging Fonda, a gunfighter who wants to retire. Filmed in the U.S. and Spain; produced by Sergio Leone. Released in Italy at 130m. Panavision. [PG]▼▶

My Neighbor Totoro (1988-Japanese) C-88m. ***½ D: Hayao Miyazaki. Voices of Dakota Fanning, Elle Fanning, Tim Daly, Pat Carroll, Paul Butcher, Lea Salonga, Frank Welker. Gentle, infectious animated tale of two young sisters in rural Japan and their magical adventures with Totoro, a giant furry forest spirit. Beautiful art direction and excellent English-language treatment make this a treat for small children and parents; older kids may chafe at the story's leisurely pace. Wait till you see the 12-legged cat-bus! Written by Miyazaki. First released in the U.S. in 1993; this revised English-language version (with an all-new voice cast) came out in 2006. [G] ▼▶

My New Gun (1992) C-99m. **½ D: Stacy Cochran. Diane Lane, James LeGros, Stephen Collins, Tess Harper, Bill Raymond, Bruce Altman, Maddie Corman, Natasha Lyonne, Philip Seymour Hoffman. Deadpan comedy about a quietly put-upon suburban housewife whose life takes unexpected turns when her loutish husband insists on buying her a .38 pistol. Some amusing moments and wry performances, but the film seems a bit undernourished. Feature debut for writer-director Cochran. [R] ▼▶

My New Partner (1984-French) C-106m. **½ D: Claude Zidi. Philippe Noiret, Thierry Lhermitte, Regine, Grace de Capitani, Claude Brosset. So-so comedy-drama about corrupt veteran cop Noiret, and how he responds when teamed with by-the-book rookie Lhermitte. Noiret is fine as always, but the film is strictly standard (despite its great popularity in France and its Best Picture/Director César awards). Followed by a sequel. [R]▼●

My New Partner 2 (1990-French) **C-107m.** **½ D: Claude Zidi. Philippe Noiret, Thierry Lhermitte, Guy Marchand, Line Renaud, Grace de Capitani, Michel Aumont, Jean-Pierre Castaldi, Jean-Claude Brialy. Intricately plotted sequel finds the amiably corrupt French cops suspended from the force and plotting to oust their replacements, who turn out to be even more corrupt than they were! Breezy farce deals frivolously with such serious issues as police brutality, but has several amusing sequences and the comic chemistry of its stars. Not released in the U.S. until 1997. Aka MY NEW PARTNER AT THE RACES.

My Night at Maud's (1969-French) **105m.** *** D: Eric Rohmer. Jean-Louis Trintignant, Françoise Fabian, Marie-Christine Barrault, Antoine Vitez. No. 3 of Rohmer's "Six Moral Tales" is most intellectual, with Trintignant as moral Catholic man infatuated with woman completely unlike himself. Talky, fascinating, more specialized in appeal than later entries in series. Barrault's first film. [PG]▼●

My Old Man's Place (1972) **C-93m.** **½ D: Edwin Sherin. Mitchell Ryan, Arthur Kennedy, William Devane, Michael Moriarty, Topo Swope. Moriarty (in his first film) returns home from war with two soldier pals; inevitable tensions lead to rape and murder. Not profound, but moody and interesting. Original title: GLORY BOY. [R]▼

My One and Only (2009) **C-85m.** ** D: Richard Loncraine. Renée Zellweger, Kevin Bacon, Logan Lerman, Mark Rendall, Chris Noth, Nick Stahl, Eric McCormack, Steven Weber, David Koechner, Troy Garity. In 1953, a flighty woman walks out on her philandering husband, takes her two adolescent sons, buys a Cadillac, and leaves N.Y.C. for points unknown in search of a new meal ticket. Seriocomic road trip hits familiar notes from start to finish and rings hollow, even though the story was inspired by real-life incidents in the young life of actor George Hamilton. [PG-13]▶

My Own Private Idaho (1991) **C-102m.** **½ D: Gus Van Sant. River Phoenix, Keanu Reeves, James Russo, William Richert, Rodney Harvey, Flea, Grace Zabriskie, Tom Troupe, Udo Kier. Uniquely distinctive portrayal of male street-hustling in the American Northwest, with Phoenix as a narcoleptic sex-for-hiree and Reeves as the son of Portland's mayor—slumming in the trade. Film opens terrifically, promising to surpass even Van Sant's DRUGSTORE COWBOY—then gets bogged down in a long, dreadfully conceived gay variation on Shakespeare's *Henry IV, Part I*, from which it never fully recovers. Many potent scenes,

though, and Phoenix is excellent; cult status is assured. [R]▼●▶

My Pleasure Is My Business (1974-Canadian) **C-85m.** BOMB D: Al Waxman. Xaviera Hollander, Henry Ramer, Colin Fox, Kenneth Lynch, Jayne Eastwood. "The Happy Hooker" makes her own attempt at acting in this witless comedy which purports to tell her true story (albeit just as cleaned-up as THE HAPPY HOOKER itself). Hollander is so expressionless she can't even play herself well. [R]▼

Myra Breckinridge (1970) **C-94m.** BOMB D: Michael Sarne. Mae West, John Huston, Raquel Welch, Rex Reed, Roger Herren, Farrah Fawcett, Jim Backus, John Carradine, Andy Devine, Grady Sutton. Gore Vidal's loosely structured comic novel about sex-change operation was probably unfilmable, but this version doesn't even give book a chance; as bad as any movie ever made, it tastelessly exploits many old Hollywood favorites through film clips. That's Tom Selleck—minus mustache—as one of Mae's "studs." Panavision. [R—edited from original X rating]▼▶

My Science Project (1985) **C-94m.** BOMB D: Jonathan Beteul. John Stockwell, Danielle Von Zerneck, Fisher Stevens, Raphael Sbarge, Dennis Hopper, Barry Corbin, Ann Wedgeworth, Richard Masur. Laughless, often tasteless comedy about high school kids who unearth an other-worldly device that can create time and space warps. Lost in the quagmire is Hopper in funny role as a latter-day hippie science teacher. Panavision. [PG]▼●▶

My Side of the Mountain (1969) **C-100m.** **½ D: James B. Clark. Ted Eccles, Theodore Bikel, Tudi Wiggins, Frank Perry, Peggi Loder. Children should enjoy this tale about 13-year-old Canadian boy who runs away from home to get closer to nature. Panavision. [G]▼▶

My Sister Eileen (1942) **96m.** **½ D: Alexander Hall. Rosalind Russell, Brian Aherne, Janet Blair, George Tobias, Allyn Joslyn, Elizabeth Patterson, June Havoc. Amusing tale of two Ohio girls trying to survive in Greenwich Village apartment; strained at times. Belongs mainly to Russell as older sister of knockout Blair. Ruth McKinney, Joseph Fields, and Jerome Chodorov adapted their Broadway hit (based on McKinney's autobiographical book). Remade as a musical in 1955 (and musicalized on Broadway as *Wonderful Town*). Finale features a gag cameo. ▼●▶

My Sister Eileen (1955) **C-108m.** ***½ D: Richard Quine. Betty Garrett, Janet Leigh, Jack Lemmon, Kurt Kasznar, Dick York, Horace McMahon, Robert (Bob) Fosse, Tommy Rall. Delightful, unpretentious musical version of 1942 movie about Ohio girls seeking success in the big city, moving into nutty Greenwich Village apartment. Especially interesting to see young Lemmon singing and equally young Fosse dancing; this was the first film he choreographed on his own. Not to be confused with the Broadway musical *Wonderful Town*, based on the same source. CinemaScope. ▼◉●

My Sister, My Love SEE: **Mafu Cage, The**

My Sister's Keeper (2009) C-106m. **½ D: Nick Cassavetes. Cameron Diaz, Abigail Breslin, Alec Baldwin, Jason Patric, Joan Cusack, Sofia Vassilieva, Evan Ellingson, Thomas Dekker, Heather Wahlquist, Emily Deschanel. When a couple discovers their 2-year-old daughter has leukemia, they have another child who can help to keep their firstborn alive. Now 11, the "donor child" sues them for medical emancipation so she won't have to supply a kidney. Heartrending material, from Jodi Picoult's best-selling novel, never quite reaches the emotional heights for which it aims, despite good performances. Vassilieva is incredible as the ailing adolescent. Panavision. [PG-13] ●

My Son John (1952) 122m. **½ D: Leo McCarey. Helen Hayes, Robert Walker, Dean Jagger, Van Heflin, Frank McHugh, Richard Jaeckel. Archetypal apple-pie parents (Hayes, Jagger) suspect their son (Walker) of being a Communist in this reactionary period piece. Dramatically overwrought, but fascinating as social history. Walker (who's superb) died before film was finished; most shots of him in final reel are cribbed from STRANGERS ON A TRAIN.

My Son, My Son, What Have Ye Done (2009-U.S.-German) C-91m. ** D: Werner Herzog. Michael Shannon, Willem Dafoe, Chloë Sevigny, Udo Kier, Michael Peña, Grace Zabriskie, Irma (P.) Hall, Loretta Devine, Brad Dourif. In San Diego, a strange young man (Shannon) stabs his mother to death with a sword and takes a couple of his "neighbors" hostage. What's his story? Is he seeking something spiritual in a world that is cold and corrupt, or has he simply gone mad? Genuinely odd film is ambitious but only intermittently successful, as it leaves too many unanswered questions about its characters. Inspired by a true story; Herzog coscripted. Given the film's general weirdness, it's no surprise that David Lynch is an executive producer. [R] ●

My Son the Fanatic (1997-British) C-89m. *** D: Udayan Prasad. Om Puri, Rachel Griffiths, Stellan Skarsgård, Akbar Kurtha, Gopi Desai, Harish Patel, Bhasker Patel. Writer Hanif Kureishi again examines a Pakistani coming to terms with his life in England. In this case it's a taxi driver (Puri) who's alienated from his wife, and whose son is rebelling against him for reasons he can't understand—even while he fosters a relationship with prostitute Grif-

fiths. A multi-layered story, pointed and insightful. ▼●

My Soul to Take (2010) C-107m. BOMB D: Wes Craven. Max Thieriot, John Magaro, Denzel Whitaker, Zena Grey, Nick Lashaway, Paulina Olszynski, Jeremy Chu, Emily Meade, Raúl Esparza, Shareeka Epps, Harris Yulin, Jessica Hecht. In a small Connecticut town, a wounded serial killer disappears after being captured. Sixteen years later, the seven youngsters born on the day the serial killer vanished (or died) begin to be murdered one by one. Is one of them the culprit? Boring, routine slasher film with unappealing characters; a real comedown for horror vet Craven, who also scripted. 3-D adds little, if anything, to the picture. Super 35. [3-D] [R] ●

My Stepmother Is an Alien (1988) C-108m. *½ D: Richard Benjamin. Dan Aykroyd, Kim Basinger, Jon Lovitz, Alyson Hannigan, Joseph Maher, Ann Prentiss (voice of purse), Seth Green, Wesley Mann, Harry Shearer (voice of Carl Sagan). Luscious Basinger, who knows nothing of romance or sex, marries widowed scientist (Aykroyd); he wants to settle into domesticity, while her mind is only on saving her planet from destruction. Somehow, Jimmy Durante imitations get worked into this lowbrow, high-concept comedy. [PG-13] ▼●

Mysterians, The (1957-Japanese) C-85m. **½ D: Ishirô Honda. Kenji Sahara, Yumi Shirakawa, Momoko Kochi, Akihiko Hirata. Centuries after the destruction of their planet, the title aliens land on Earth, install an impregnable dome by a lake, and demand women. The world does not take this well. Colorful special effects and fast pace make this one of the better Japanese sci-fis. Tohoscope. ▼●

Mysterious Island (1961-British) C-101m. *** D: Cy Endfield. Michael Craig, Joan Greenwood, Michael Callan, Gary Merrill, Herbert Lom. Deliberately paced fantasy adventure based on two-part Jules Verne novel, a sequel to his *20,000 Leagues Under the Sea*. Confederate prison escapees hijack observation balloon and are blown off course; find uncharted island with gigantic animals. Great special effects by Ray Harryhausen; rousing Bernard Herrmann score. Filmed before in 1929. Remade for cable TV in 2005. ▼●

Mysterious Skin (2004) C-99m. *** D: Gregg Araki. Brady Corbet, Joseph Gordon-Levitt, Elisabeth Shue, Mary Lynn Rajskub, Michelle Trachtenberg, Jeffrey Licon, Lisa Long, Bill Sage, George Webster, Chase Ellison, Richard Riehle, Billy Drago, Chris Mulkey. Absorbing, disturbing drama about two adolescents who are linked by a painful incident in their past. One (Gordon-Levitt) is a reckless, jaded gay hustler; the other (Corbet) is a deeply troubled introvert who has erased the occurrence from his memory. Often difficult to watch, but well worth seeing and pondering. The director scripted, based on a novel by Scott Heim. [NC-17]▎

Mystery, Alaska (1999) **C-118m.** ** D: Jay Roach. Russell Crowe, Burt Reynolds, Hank Azaria, Mary McCormack, Lolita Davidovich, Colm Meaney, Maury Chaykin, Ron Eldard, Michael McKean, Mike Myers, Little Richard. Remote Alaskan town's hockey team is given the chance to play against the professional N.Y. Rangers as a publicity stunt. A hodgepodge of characters and an inevitable big-game finale, coupled with derivative storylines, prove that David E. Kelley (who coscripted and coproduced) should stick to TV. Crowe is the only one to rise above the material. Super 35. [R]▼●▎

Mystery Date (1991) **C-99m.** **½ D: Jonathan Wacks. Ethan Hawke, Teri Polo, Brian McNamara, Fisher Stevens, B. D. Wong, Tony Rosato, Don Davis, James Hong, Victor Wong. Shy Hawke dreams of dating a dishy neighbor, so older brother McNamara rings her up and arranges a date . . . but it turns out he has an agenda of his own, which includes a corpse in the trunk of the car Hawke is driving. Surprisingly black youth comedy with more than a few unexpected twists. Wong is a scream as a criminal rival in McNamara's highstakes schemes. [PG-13]▼●▎

Mystery Men (1999) **C-111m.** **½ D: Kinka Usher. Hank Azaria, Claire Forlani, Janeane Garofalo, Greg Kinnear, William H. Macy, Kel Mitchell, Lena Olin, Paul Reubens, Geoffrey Rush, Ben Stiller, Wes Studi, Tom Waits, Jenifer Lewis, Ricky Jay, Louise Lasser, Eddie Izzard. Silly, flimsy story of wannabe superheroes with specious powers uniting to rescue a genuine hero from an evil villain. Good dialogue and a fun cast make up for the overblown special effects and cluttered array of characters. [PG-13]▼●▎

Mystery of Edwin Drood (1935) **87m.** **½ D: Stuart Walker. Claude Rains, Douglass Montgomery, Heather Angel, David Manners, E. E. Clive, Francis (L.) Sullivan, Valerie Hobson. Seemingly respectable English choirmaster Rains is actually responsible for horrible murder. Pretty good Hollywood adaptation of Charles Dickens' unfinished novel, which inspired a Broadway musical in the 1980s. Remade in 1993.▼

Mystery of Edwin Drood, The (1993-British) **C-102m.** ** D: Timothy Forder. Robert Powell, Michelle Evans, Jonathan Phillips, Rupert Rainsford, Finty Williams, Peter Pacey, Nanette Newman, Freddie Jones, Gemma Craven, Rosemary Leach, Ronald Fraser. Dickens' unfinished novel of a suspicious choirmaster,

whose deadly jealousy over his fiancée gets him into hot water, gets another goround here, but the results are mediocre at best. Powell is an uncharismatic lead, but the cast is peppered with familiar British actors.▼

Mystery of Kaspar Hauser, The SEE: **Every Man for Himself and God Against All**

Mystery of Oberwald, The (1980-Italian) **C-129m.** ** D: Michelangelo Antonioni. Monica Vitti, Ahmad Saha Alan, Paolo Bonacelli, Franco Branciaroli, Luigi Diberti, Elisabetta Pozzi. Static adaptation of Cocteau's play *The Eagle Has Two Heads*, about a queen who protects and gradually falls in love with an assassin sent to kill her. Notable for being shot on video and then transferred to 35mm., as well as for the director's experiments with some odd and rather labored color effects, which do little to relieve the tedium of the melodramatic plot. ▼

Mystery of Picasso, The (1956-French) **C-85m.** ***½ D: Henri-Georges Clouzot. Fascinating documentary about Pablo Picasso, who discusses his work and creates a number of paintings before the camera (all of which were destroyed after shooting ended, meaning that they exist only on film). Photographed by Claude (nephew of Jean and grandson of Auguste) Renoir. CinemaScope (part).▼●

Mystery of Rampo, The SEE: **Rampo**

Mystery of the Wax Museum (1933) **C-77m.** **½ D: Michael Curtiz. Lionel Atwill, Fay Wray, Glenda Farrell, Allen Vincent, Frank McHugh, Arthur Edmund Carewe. Vintage horror film strays somewhat into excess "comic relief" and contrivances, but plot of madman Atwill encasing victims in wax, with Wray next on his list, is still exciting. Filmed in early two-color Technicolor. Remade as HOUSE OF WAX. ▼●

Mystery Science Theater 3000: The Movie (1996) **C-73m.** *** D: Jim Mallon. Michael J. Nelson, Trace Beaulieu, Kevin Murphy, Jim Mallon, John Brady. Theatrical presentation of cable TV cult favorite has shorter running time than an average episode but just as many laughs. Nelson plays a hapless human trapped on orbiting spaceship with crew of wisecracking puppet robots, forced to watch an edited version of 1955's sci-fi outing THIS ISLAND EARTH. Silhouettes of Nelson and robots appear at lower right of screen, and their running commentary during the film is often hilarious. Brief framing setup and occasional break segments throughout are not so clever, especially compared to original series created by comedian Joel Hodgson. [PG-13]▼●

Mystery Train (1989) **C-113m.** *** D: Jim Jarmusch. Masatoshi Nagase, Youki Kudoh, Screamin' Jay Hawkins, Cinque Lee, Nicoletta Braschi, Elizabeth Bracco,

Joe Strummer, Rick Aviles, Steve Buscemi, Tom Noonan, Rockets Redglare, Rufus Thomas; voice of Tom Waits. Typically quirky slice-of-life film from Jarmusch, one of stories depicts foreigners' stays in sleazy Memphis hotel. Jarmusch's minimalist style results in some slow stretches, but there are enough genuinely funny moments to make this worth seeing. [R] ▼●▶

Mystic Masseur, The (2002-U.S.-French) **C-117m.** ** D: Ismail Merchant. Aasif Mandvi, Om Puri, Ayesha Dharker, James Fox, Jimi Mistry, Sakina Jaffrey, Zohra Segal. Rare directorial effort from the producing half of the Merchant-Ivory team is an adaptation of Nobel laureate V.S. Naipaul's novel about a fledgling author who suddenly becomes known for his "mystical" abilities to heal people. First part of the film is more successful than the second, when it gets bogged down in politics. Acting is first-rate, however, and colorful locations in the Indian community of mid-20th-century Trinidad add flavor. [PG] ▼▶

Mystic Pizza (1988) **C-104m.** ** D: Donald Petrie. Annabeth Gish, Julia Roberts, Lili Taylor, Vincent D'Onofrio, William R. Moses, Adam Storke, Conchata Ferrell, Joanna Merlin, Matt Damon. The amorous adventures of three young women who work at a pizzeria in Mystic, Connecticut. Superficial in the extreme but geared for a young female audience. A "nice little film" that isn't all that good. [R] ▼●▶

Mystic River (2003) **C-138m.** ***½ D: Clint Eastwood. Sean Penn, Tim Robbins, Kevin Bacon, Laurence Fishburne, Marcia Gay Harden, Laura Linney, Kevin Chapman, Thomas Guiry, Emmy Rossum. The lives of three boyhood pals from a tight-knit, working-class Boston neighborhood intersect years later: one is now a cop, another a potent figure in the community, and the other still bears deep emotional scars from a tragic childhood incident. Brian Helgeland expertly adapted Dennis Lehane's powerful novel about friendship, murder, neighborhood ties, and a criminal code of honor. Penn and his costars are exceptional, and Eastwood's handling of the material is masterful, if perhaps too leisurely at times. Penn and Robbins won Oscars for their performances. Eli Wallach and Kevin Conway appear unbilled. Panavision. [R] ▼▶

Mystique SEE: **Circle of Power**
My Summer Story SEE: **It Runs in My Family**

My Summer of Love (2004-British) **C-86m.** *** D: Pawel Pawlikowski. Nathalie Press, Emily Blunt, Paddy Considine, Dean Andrews, Michelle Byrne, Paul Antony-Barber, Lynette Edwards, Kathryn Sumner. Emotion-packed coming-of-age drama that happily veers from formula. Two adolescent girls meet one summer at a Yorkshire village and become fast friends: working-class Mona (Press), who is shy and lives with her ex-con, born-again Christian brother, and Tamsin (Blunt), who is aggressive and presents herself as experienced and sophisticated. As their relationship deepens, their story becomes intricate in ways that are better seen than described. Based on a novel by Helen Cross. [R] ▶

My Super Ex-Girlfriend (2006) **C-96m.** ** D: Ivan Reitman. Uma Thurman, Luke Wilson, Rainn Wilson, Anna Faris, Eddie Izzard, Wanda Sykes, Stelio Savante, Mike Iorio, Mark Consuelos. After breaking up with a needy art gallery owner with emotional problems, an architect learns the hard way that hell hath no fury like a woman scorned—especially when that woman is actually a superhero bent on revenge. The cast is likable and the concept of a neurotic female superhero is amusing, but the film fizzles out in a welter of mechanical plotting, perfunctory action scenes, and shoddy special effects. Super 35. [PG-13] ▶

Myth of Fingerprints, The (1997) **C-90m.** ** D: Bart Freundlich. Blythe Danner, Roy Scheider, Julianne Moore, Noah Wyle, Arija Bareikis, Brian Kerwin, Michael Vartan, Laurel Holloman, Hope Davis, James Le Gros. A dysfunctional New England family reunion at Thanksgiving reveals WASP angst simmering below the surface of gentility. Too many characters leave little time for any depth of understanding. Notable casting includes Wyle as Scheider's son; he was also associate producer. [R] ▼▶

My Tutor (1983) **C-97m.** ** D: George Bowers. Matt Lattanzi, Caren Kaye, Kevin McCarthy, Arlene Golonka, Clark Brandon, Bruce Bauer, Crispin Glover. Rich, hunky (but still virginal) Lattanzi won't graduate high school unless he passes French, so his folks hire beautiful Kaye to spend the summer tutoring him. Earns points for sincerity, but credulity is low. [R] ▼●▶

My 20th Century (1989-Hungarian) **92m.** *** D: Ildiko Enyedi. Dorotha Segda, Oleg Jankovskij, Paulus Manker, Peter Andorai, Gabor Maté. Compelling tale of twin sisters, born in 1880 Budapest, who are separated during childhood; one becomes a seductress, the other an anarchist. Enyedi incisively depicts an era that begins with promise, as Thomas Edison (Andorai) demonstrates the wonders of electricity, but develops into an age in which human relations do not keep pace with technological innovation. Segda is excellent as both sisters, and also appears as their mother. Enyedi also scripted. ▼●

My Uncle SEE: **Mon Oncle**
My Uncle Antoine (1971-Canadian) **C-104m.** **½ D: Claude Jutra. Jean Duceppe, Olivette Thibault, Claude Jutra, Jacques Gagnon, Helene Loiselle. Fifteen-year-old Gagnon observes those around him while

growing up in a small mining town during the 1940s. Not bad, but nothing special. Video title: MON ONCLE ANTOINE. ▼▷

My Uncle, Mr. Hulot SEE: **Mon Oncle**
My Wife is an Actress (2001-French) **C-95m.** **½ D: Yvan Attal. Charlotte Gainsbourg, Yvan Attal, Terence Stamp, Noémie Lvovsky, Laurent Bateau, Ludivine Sagnier. Sportswriter married to a Julia Roberts–type star must deal with her fame, his jealousies, and trying to live a normal life away from the spotlight. Entertaining froth with star-writer-director Attal (who resembles Al Pacino) delightful as the befuddled hubby. Stamp also scores as the star's latest leading man. Incidentally, Gainsbourg and Attal are married in real life. [R]▼▷

My Winnipeg (2008-Canadian) **C/B&W-80m.** ***½ D: Guy Maddin. Darcy Fehr, Ann Savage, Amy Stewart, Louis Negin, Brendan Cade, Wesley Cade. Another ingenious, deeply personal cinematic exercise from Maddin, a self-described "docufantasia" in which he plays tour guide on a journey through his Winnipeg, Manitoba, hometown. Maddin narrates and offers up a subjective portrait of his childhood and the city in which he came of age (and which defines him). What is fact and what is exaggeration? Who cares? Just sit back and enjoy. Great to see Savage (of DETOUR fame) as Maddin's mother.▷

Nacho Libre (2006) **C-91m.** **½ D: Jared Hess. Jack Black, Ana de la Reguera, Héctor Jiménez, Troy Gentile, Moises Arias, Lauro Chartrand, Peter Stormare, Richard Montoya. Extremely offbeat concept for a comedy feature casts Black as a Mexican friar who moonlights as a masked wrestler to raise money for the orphanage where he works. Black's engaging silliness is showcased against the kind of deadpan-humor landscape you'd expect from the director and writers of NAPOLEON DYNAMITE, but it doesn't jell as one might like. Black also coproduced. [PG]▷

Nada (1974-French-Italian) **C-107m.** ***½ D: Claude Chabrol. Fabio Testi, Michel Duchaussoy, Maurice Garrel, Michel Aumont, Lou Castel, Didier Kaminka, Viviane Romance, Mariangela Melato. Riveting political thriller about a group of hapless left-wing terrorists who kidnap the American Ambassador to France, but then have to deal with a fascistic police chief who's even more violent than they are and doesn't care about getting the hostage back alive. Chabrol is at the top of his cool, calculated, and ultra-cynical form in this superbly filmed blend of razor-sharp action and absurdist humor. Written by Chabrol and Jean Patrick Manchette, from the latter's novel. Original running time: 134m. Aka THE NADA GANG.▼▷

Nadine (1987) **C-82m.** *** Robert Benton. Jeff Bridges, Kim Basinger, Rip Torn, Gwen Verdon, Glenne Headly, Jerry Stiller, Jay Patterson. Lightweight but pleasing comedy set in 1954 Austin, about a pregnant but nearly divorced hairdresser who accidentally witnesses a murder while trying to retrieve some nude "art studies" she posed for in a weak moment. Very well cast, with Basinger a surprising standout; catchy credit tune is performed by Sweethearts of the Rodeo. [PG]▼●▷

Nadja (1994) **92m.** *** D: Michael Almereyda. Elina Lowensohn, Peter Fonda, Suzy Amis, Galaxy Craze, Martin Donovan, Jared Harris, Karl Geary. Cleverly amusing vampire movie with the vampirish title character (perfectly played by Lowensohn) stalking the streets and late-night clubs of Manhattan's East Village. Fonda is a hoot as "Dr. Van Helsing," who has murdered Nadja's father and now is after her and her twin brother. Most enjoyable, but the stylish visuals sometimes swallow up the story. Filmed in b&w, in part using a plastic toy Pixelvision video camera! Executive produced by David Lynch, who appears as a morgue attendant. [R]▼●▷

Nails (1992) **C-100m.** **½ D: John Flynn. Dennis Hopper, Anne Archer, Tomas Milian, Keith David, Carlos Carrasco, Charles Hallahan, Cliff De Young. Wired Hopper slips into his profane, law-bending cop bit, battling druggies and crooked politicians. Misplaced theatrical release debuted on cable.▼●

Naked (1993-British) **C-131m.** *** D: Mike Leigh. David Thewlis, Lesley Sharp, Katrin Cartlidge, Greg Cruttwell, Claire Skinner, Peter Wight, Ewen Bremner. Unique, contemporary, energized examination of a drifter from Manchester (Thewlis) who arrives unannounced at an ex-girlfriend's London flat and proceeds to verbally abuse and amuse everyone in sight. Bleak, often brutal, and frequently hilarious look at people drifting in an alienated modern society, with a very impressive performance by Thewlis; its only real shortcoming is its overlength. Another challenging film from writer-director Leigh.▼●▷

Naked and the Dead, The (1958) **C-131m.** *** D: Raoul Walsh. Aldo Ray, Cliff Robertson, Raymond Massey, William Campbell, Richard Jaeckel, James Best, Joey Bishop, L. Q. Jones, Robert Gist, Lili St. Cyr, Barbara Nichols. Norman Mailer's intensive novel about WW2 soldiers in the Pacific gets superficial but rugged filmization. Ray is the tough sergeant, Robertson the rich-kid lieutenant, Bishop the comic Jew, Jones the thick, Gist the loner, etc. RKO-Scope/WarnerScope.▼

Naked Ape, The (1973) **C-85m.** *½ D: Donald Driver. Johnny Crawford, Victoria Principal, Dennis Oliveri, Diana Darrin.

Tongue-in-cheek *Playboy* production loosely based on the pop anthropology of Desmond Morris's nonfiction best-seller. Snickering sex jokes and mediocre animation (by Charles Swenson) add nothing to this episodic summary of 10 million years of Man's evolution. Musical score by Jimmy Webb. [PG]

Naked Cage, The (1986) **C-97m.** ** D: Paul Nicholas. Shari Shattuck, Angel Tompkins, Lucinda Crosby, Faith Minton, Christina Whitaker, John Terlesky. Standard women's prison drama as innocent Stattuck is framed for a bank robbery and ends up in the slammer. [R]▼

Naked City, The (1948) **96m.** *** D: Jules Dassin. Barry Fitzgerald, Howard Duff, Don Taylor, Dorothy Hart, Ted de Corsia, House Jameson, Frank Conroy, David Opatoshu, Molly Picon, Celia Adler. Time (and decades of TV cop shows) have dulled the edge of this once-trendsetting crime drama, produced by columnist Mark Hellinger on the streets of N.Y.C., following the investigation of a murder case step by step. Fitzgerald is still first-rate, cast against type as the detective in charge, and the cast is peppered with soon-to-be-familiar character actors (Arthur O'Connell, Paul Ford, James Gregory, et al.). Cinematographer William Daniels and editor Paul Weatherwax won Oscars for their work. Screenplay by Albert Maltz and Malvin Wald. Later a TV series.▼●

Naked Dawn, The (1955) **C-82m.** **½ D: Edgar G. Ulmer. Arthur Kennedy, Betta St. John, Roy Engel, Eugene Iglesias, Charita. Modern Western about a snowballing series of crimes. Based on a story by Gorky, and much admired by Ulmer buffs.

Naked Edge, The (1961) **99m.** **½ D: Michael Anderson. Gary Cooper, Deborah Kerr, Eric Portman, Diane Cilento, Hermione Gingold, Michael Wilding, Peter Cushing. Uneven suspenser of Kerr thinking husband Cooper is guilty of murder. Cooper's last film, made in London.▼

Naked Face, The (1984) **C-103m.** **½ D: Bryan Forbes. Roger Moore, Rod Steiger, Elliott Gould, Anne Archer, David Hedison, Art Carney. Change of pace for Moore, playing a psychiatrist suspected of murdering one of his patients. Low-budget adaptation of Sidney Sheldon novel crudely injects clues and red herrings. [R]▼

Naked Gun: From the Files of Police Squad!, The (1988) **C-85m.** *** D: David Zucker. Leslie Nielsen, George Kennedy, Priscilla Presley, Ricardo Montalban, O.J. Simpson, Nancy Marchand. A failed (but loyally supported) TV sitcom, *Police Squad*, is reincarnated as a hilarious feature film, with a deadpan, dead-perfect Nielsen as Lt. Frank Drebin, the stupidest law officer since Inspector Clouseau. Writers David and Jerry Zucker, Jim Abrahams, and Pat Proft can't keep their momentum from slowing a bit during the baseball game finale, but they provide solid, silly laughs from start to finish. Followed by two sequels. [PG-13]▼●

Naked Gun 2½: The Smell of Fear, The (1991) **C-85m.** **½ (what else?) D: David Zucker. Leslie Nielsen, Priscilla Presley, George Kennedy, O. J. Simpson, Robert Goulet, George Kennedy, Jacqueline Brookes, Lloyd Bochner, Tim O'Connor, Peter Mark Richman. Frank Drebin is back, this time to save America from a plot hatched by oil, coal, and nuclear power brokers to keep the country from adopting a new energy policy. Lots of gags, some of them funny, but film lacks the freshness of its predecessor and empties out its bag of tricks sooner than it should. [PG-13]▼●

Naked Gun 33⅓: The Final Insult (1994) **C-82m.** **1/3 (what else?) D: Peter Segal. Leslie Nielsen, Priscilla Presley, George Kennedy, O.J. Simpson, Fred Ward, Kathleen Freeman, Anna Nicole Smith, Ellen Greene, Ed Williams, Randall "Tex" Cobb. Sloppy sequel in which a now retired Frank Drebin returns to Police Squad for one more case . . . losing the love of his wife in the process. The most slapdash slapstick yet, with some real laughs here and there, and a passel of cameo appearances at the climactic Oscar ceremony. [PG-13]▼●

Naked in New York (1994) **C-91m.** **½ D: Dan Algrant. Eric Stoltz, Mary-Louise Parker, Ralph Macchio, Kathleen Turner, Tony Curtis, Timothy Dalton, Jill Clayburgh, Roscoe Lee Browne. Unsuccessful, but generally watchable backstage comedy about an aspiring playwright who can't decide whether to pursue his career in N.Y.C. or remain with the woman he loves in their Ivy League environment. Stoltz and Macchio aren't aggressive enough for their roles, but Turner (as a soap actress) and Curtis (a Broadway producer) give mild film a boost. Amusing literati cameos. [R]▼●

Naked Jungle, The (1954) **C-95m.** *** D: Byron Haskin. Eleanor Parker, Charlton Heston, Abraham Sofaer, William Conrad. High-class South American jungle adventure, with Heston and wife Parker surrounded on their plantation by advancing army of ants. Produced by George Pal.▼●

Naked Kiss, The (1964) **93m.** *** D: Samuel Fuller. Constance Towers, Anthony Eisley, Michael Dante, Virginia Grey, Patsy Kelly, Betty Bronson. In-your-face melodrama opens with a bang and never lets up, as prostitute Towers arrives in a small town hoping to start a new life. By turns lurid, sentimental, romantic, surprising; a mélange that could only have been concocted by writer-director Fuller.▼●

Naked Lunch (1991-Canadian-British) **C-115m.** *** D: David Cronenberg. Peter Weller, Judy Davis, Ian Holm, Julian Sands, Roy Scheider, Monique Mercure, Nicholas Campbell, Michael Zelniker, Robert A. Silverman, Joseph Scorsiani. A no-holds-barred, graphic filming of William S. Burroughs' thoroughly unfilmable 1959 novel, weaving elements of the author's life in with the fictional material. Weller is an aspiring writer and N.Y.C. exterminator in 1953; when his loony drug-addict wife (Davis, who's great) dies, the real story takes off. He is immersed in an extended, drug-laced odyssey to a Casablanca-like community that's seething with oddballs and weirdos. Cronenberg was undeniably the right person to direct this, but be warned: mutating, oozing typewriter-size talking bugs fill the screen throughout. [R]▼●▶

Naked Maja, The (1959) **C-111m.** ** D: Henry Koster. Ava Gardner, Anthony Franciosa, Amedeo Nazzari, Gino Cervi, Massimo Serato, Lea Padovani, Carlo Rizzo. Mishmash involving 18th-century Spanish painter Goya and famed model for title painting. Filmed in Italy. Technirama.▼

Naked Night, The SEE: **Sawdust and Tinsel**

Naked Prey, The (1966) **C-94m.** *** D: Cornel Wilde. Cornel Wilde, Gert Van Den Bergh, Ken Gampu. Harrowing, well-done safari movie. African natives give prisoner Wilde headstart before they close in on him for kill, forcing Wilde to combat them with savage tactics; memorable brutal sequences. Panavision.▼●▶

Naked Runner, The (1967-British) **C-104m.** *½ D: Sidney J. Furie. Frank Sinatra, Peter Vaughan, Toby Robins, Edward Fox. Dull spy melodrama focusing on American who is pawn in bizarre plot to get him to assassinate enemy agent. Farfetched, too heavily plotted. Techniscope.▼

Naked Space SEE: **Creature Wasn't Nice, The**

Naked Spur, The (1953) **C-91m.** ***½ D: Anthony Mann. James Stewart, Janet Leigh, Ralph Meeker, Robert Ryan, Millard Mitchell. One of the best Westerns ever made: a tough, hard little film about self-styled bounty hunter Stewart trying to capture Ryan, who stirs tension among Stewart's newly acquired "partners." Strikingly directed and photographed (by William Mellor) on location in the Rockies. Written by Sam Rolfe and Harold Jack Bloom.▼▶

Naked Tango (1991) **C-90m.** ** D: Leonard Schrader. Vincent D'Onofrio, Mathilda May, Esai Morales, Fernando Rey, Cipe Lincovski, Josh Mostel, Constance McCashin. Very dark look at the Tango underground of 1920s Buenos Aires, in which the famous dance symbolizes the obsessive and strange passions of three people caught up in this forbidden world. Uneasy mixture of sex and violence, with an unconvincing central performance by D'Onofrio, though stunning production design and cinematography compensate a little for the murky storytelling. A real letdown from the producer (David Weisman) and screenwriter (Schrader) of KISS OF THE SPIDER WOMAN. [R]

Naked Truth, The SEE: **Your Past Is Showing**

Naked Under Leather SEE: **Girl on a Motorcycle**

Naked Warriors SEE: **Arena, The**

Naked Weekend, The SEE: **Circle of Power**

Name of the Rose, The (1986-Italian-German-French) **C-130m.** ** D: Jean-Jacques Annaud. Sean Connery, F. Murray Abraham, Christian Slater, Elya Baskin, Feodor Chaliapin, Jr., William Hickey, Michael Lonsdale, Ron Perlman; narrated by Dwight Weist. Unusual film (to say the least) based on Umberto Eco's best-seller, which places a Sherlock Holmesian monk (Connery) in the midst of a mysterious Italian abbey during the inquisition of the 13th century. Too provocative to dismiss, too lumbering to thoroughly enjoy, buoyed considerably by Connery's charismatic performance. [R]▼●▶

Namesake, The (2007) **C-122m.** *** D: Mira Nair. Kal Penn, Tabu, Irrfan Khan, Jacinda Barrett, Zuleikha Robinson, Ruma Guha Thakurta, Tamal Roy Choudhury, Glenne Headly, Daniel Gerroll, Linus Roache, Brooke Smith, Amy Wright, Heather MacRae. Richly layered saga of a Bengali family's cultural journey, spanning two generations. After an arranged marriage in Calcutta, a young man and his wife move to N.Y.C., where he pursues a career and she must adjust to life in a strange new land. Their son (Penn) grows up an assimilated American and has mixed feelings about his heritage, his identity, and even his name. Episodic drama covers some familiar territory about the clash of cultures but delves beneath the surface and is ultimately quite moving. Based on a novel by Jhumpa Lahiri. [PG-13]▶

Namu, the Killer Whale (1966) **C-88m.** **½ D: Laslo Benedek. Robert Lansing, John Anderson, Lee Meriwether, Richard Erdman, Robin Mattson. Intriguing tale, based on true story of naturalist Lansing capturing and training a killer whale. Nicely done, good family fare. Aka NAMU, MY BEST FRIEND. ▼▶

Nancy Drew series SEE: *Leonard Maltin's Classic Movie Guide*

Nancy Drew (2007) **C-99m.** **½ D: Andrew Fleming. Emma Roberts, Josh Flitter, Max Thieriot, Rachael Leigh Cook, Tate Donovan, Amy Bruckner, Barry Bostwick, Laura Elena Harring, Caroline Aaron, Pat Carroll, Adam Goldberg. Pleasant, somewhat bland movie about the teenage sleuth (created in the 1930s by "Carolyn Keene") who accompanies her father to L.A. and moves into a creepy old house; it once belonged to a glamorous movie star whose murder was never explained. Nancy has promised her dad she won't "sleuth" anymore but she just can't help it. Roberts is good as Nancy, who's portrayed as the ultimate square. Bruce Willis, Eddie Jemison, and Chris Kattan appear unbilled. Super 35. [PG]◗

Nanny, The (1965-British) **93m.** *** D: Seth Holt. Bette Davis, Wendy Craig, Jill Bennett, James Villiers, Pamela Franklin, William Dix, Maurice Denham. Twisting, scary plot plus fine direction reap results. Suspects of child murder narrowed to governess Davis and disturbed youngster Dix. Unusual Hammer production, written by Jimmy Sangster. From the novel by Evelyn Piper.▼◗

Nanny Diaries, The (2007) **C-105m.** ** D: Shari Springer Berman, Robert Pulcini. Scarlett Johansson, Laura Linney, Alicia Keys, Chris Evans, Donna Murphy, Paul Giamatti, Nicholas Reese Art, Nathan Corddry, Cady Huffman, Julie White. Aimless working-class college grad stumbles into a job as a nanny for pampered "perfect wife" Linney, who has virtually nothing to do with her little boy. Bland, defanged adaptation of Emma McLaughlin and Nicola Kraus' delicious book, which was based on their real-life experiences tending to spoiled children, impossibly demanding women, and emotionally detached fathers. [PG-13]◗

Nanny McPhee (2005-British) **C-96m.** **½ D: Kirk Jones. Emma Thompson, Colin Firth, Kelly Macdonald, Derek Jacobi, Patrick Barlow, Imelda Staunton, Celia Imrie, Angela Lansbury, Thomas Sangster. Widower with seven unruly children finds the perfect nanny on his doorstep: a serene, strange-looking woman who has almost magical powers to calm the kids and bring out the best in them. Raucous period variation on MARY POPPINS has an abundance of slapstick and grotesquerie, enacted by a first-class ensemble, but the end result is unmemorable. Thompson scripted from the *Nurse Matilda* books by Christianna Brand. Followed by NANNY McPHEE RETURNS. Super 35. [PG]◗

Nanny McPhee Returns (2010-U.S.-French-British) **C-109m.** **½ D: Susanna White. Emma Thompson, Maggie Gyllenhaal, Rhys Ifans, Maggie Smith, Rosie Taylor-Ritson, Bill Bailey, Sam Kelly, Daniel Mays, Ewan McGregor, Ralph Fiennes. Writer-star Thompson goes back to the well with this MARY POPPINS wannabe (based on Christianna Brand's books) in this sequel to her 2005 hit, set during WW2. This time the magical nanny shows up to help a young farm wife tend to her children and their rambunctious cousins while her husband is away at war. Full of slapstick and mayhem, which kids ought to eat up, and an inspired takeoff on synchronized swimming with pigs. As usual there's a moral to the tale, but Thompson's blend of warmth and wit makes it bearable. Original British title: NANNY McPHEE AND THE BIG BANG. Super 35. [PG]◗

Nanook of the North (1922) **79m.** ***½ D: Robert Flaherty. Pioneer documentary of Eskimos' daily life withstands the test of time quite well, remains as absorbing saga, well filmed. Set the standard for many documentaries to follow. Soundtrack added in 1939. The film's production is re-created in KABLOONAK.▼◗

Napoleon (1927-French) **235m.** **** D: Abel Gance. Albert Dieudonné, Antonin Artaud, Pierre Batcheff, Armand Bernard, Harry Krimer, Albert Bras, Abel Gance. Hard to put into words the impact of this monumental silent epic. Dieudonné mesmerizingly plays the famed emperor; notable sequences include snowball fight, the Reign of Terror, and eye-popping three-screen Polyvision finale. Recut and shortened many times over the years (often by Gance himself), finally painstakingly pieced together by historian Kevin Brownlow and reissued in 1981 with a serviceable music score by Carmine Coppola. Not the kind of film one can best appreciate on TV. Filmed in part-widescreen triptych.▼●

Napoleon and Samantha (1972) **C-92m.** **½ D: Bernard McEveety. Michael Douglas, Jodie Foster, Johnny Whitaker, Will Geer, Arch Johnson, Henry Jones. Disney tale of two kids who run away with pet lion is OK family fare. Foster's film debut. [G]◗

Napoleon Dynamite (2004) **C-90m.** *** D: Jared Hess. Jon Heder, Jon Gries, Aaron Ruell, Efren Ramirez, Tina Majorino, Diedrich Bader, Haylie Duff, Trevor Snarr, Shondrella Avery. Deadpan comedy about a geeky high school kid (Heder), his family, and friends, who inhabit an alternate universe but struggle to get by in the real world of rural Idaho. Trying to connect with a female classmate, contending with a macho uncle who moves in when his guardian grandma gets injured, or resentfully feeding the family's pet llama, Napoleon is one of a kind. Not for every taste, but it's the sort of film that gets funnier with repeated viewing. Five-minute epilogue was added after closing titles midway during the film's theatrical run. Vote for Pedro! Written by Hess and his wife Jerusha. [PG]▼◗

Narc (2002) **C-105m.** **½ D: Joe Carnahan. Ray Liotta, Jason Patric, Chi McBride, Busta Rhymes, Anne Openshaw, Richard Chevolleau, John Ortiz, Krista Bridges. Disgraced Detroit narcotics detective (Patric) gets a chance to redeem himself when he is asked to probe the murder of a cop with the man's former partner (Liotta), a violent maverick who may know more than he is telling. Visceral look at the brutal realities of undercover work is relentlessly grim, although the two stars give forceful performances, and the opening sequence is certainly a grabber. Scripted by the director. [R]▼◗

Narrow Margin, The (1952) **70m.** ***½ D: Richard Fleischer. Charles McGraw,

Marie Windsor, Jacqueline White, Queenie Leonard. Hard-boiled cop, transporting a gangster's widow to the trial in which she'll testify, must dodge hit men aboard their train who are trying to silence her. One of the best B's ever made—fast paced, well acted, impressively shot in claustrophobic setting. Photographed by George E. Diskant; scripted by Earl Felton, from a story by Martin Goldsmith and Jack Leonard. Remade in 1990. Also shown in computer-colored version.▼●◗

Narrow Margin (1990) **C-97m.** **½ D: Peter Hyams. Gene Hackman, Anne Archer, James B. Sikking, J.T. Walsh, M. Emmet Walsh, Susan Hogan, Nigel Bennett, J.A. Preston, Harris Yulin. Hackman is superb as an assistant D.A. who accompanies murder witness Archer on an eventful train ride through the Canadian Rockies—pursued by henchmen of the gangster who set up the killing she saw. Some sharp dialogue for Hackman and a great action climax atop the train, but dramatically it misses the bull's-eye—and cannot top the original 1952 film. Panavision. [R]▼●◗

Nashville (1975) **C-159m.** **** D: Robert Altman. Henry Gibson, Karen Black, Ronee Blakley, Keith Carradine, Geraldine Chaplin, Lily Tomlin, Michael Murphy, Barbara Harris, Allen Garfield, Ned Beatty, Barbara Baxley, Shelley Duvall, Keenan Wynn, Scott Glenn, Jeff Goldblum, Gwen Welles, Bert Remsen, Robert Doqui. Altman's brilliant mosaic of American life as seen through 24 characters involved in Nashville political rally. Full of cogent character studies, comic and poignant vignettes, done in seemingly free-form style. Carradine's song "I'm Easy" won an Oscar; Elliott Gould and Julie Christie appear as themselves. Screenplay by Joan Tewkesbury. Panavision. [R]▼●◗

Nashville Girl (1976) **C-93m.** ** D: Gus Trikonis. Monica Gayle, Glenn Corbett, Roger Davis, Johnny Rodriguez, Jesse White. OK low-budgeter about small-town girl who wants to make it big as a singer and falls in with typical no-good types in the music biz. Country superstar Rodriguez makes his movie debut. Reissued as COUNTRY MUSIC DAUGHTER. [R]▼

Nasty Girl, The (1990-German) **C/B&W-92m.** ***½ D: Michael Verhoeven. Lena Stolze, Monika Baumgartner, Michael Gahr, Fred Stillkrauth, Elisabeth Bertram, Robert Giggenbach. Biting serio-comic story of a young woman (Stolze) from a small Bavarian town whose attempts to enter a national essay contest on the subject of "My Hometown During the Third Reich" results in her obsessive quest for the truth. Stolze convincingly ages from adolescence to womanhood in this remarkable film, which is based on a true story (and scripted by the director). Verhoeven's visual style is equally striking, mixing real locations and theatrical backdrops for his actors. [PG-13]▼●

Nasty Habits (1977) **C-96m.** *½ D: Michael Lindsay-Hogg. Glenda Jackson, Melina Mercouri, Geraldine Page, Sandy Dennis, Anne Jackson, Anne Meara, Susan Penhaligon, Edith Evans, Rip Torn, Eli Wallach, Jerry Stiller. Labored comedy sets allegory of Nixon and Watergate scandal in Philadelphia convent, with Jackson as conniving Mother Superior, Dennis a dead ringer for John Dean. A one-joke film. [PG]▼◗

Nate and Hayes (1983-U.S.-New Zealand) **C-100m.** ** D: Ferdinand Fairfax. Tommy Lee Jones, Michael O'Keefe, Max Phipps, Jenny Seagrove, Grant Tilly, Peter Rowley. An adventure movie for people who've never seen a *real* adventure movie: watchable enough but pretty pale. Seagoing rogue "Bully" Hayes (Jones) helps a young missionary rescue his fiancée, who's been kidnapped by a scurrilous pirate. Lots of serial-type action, but the leading characters lack charisma. Cowritten by John Hughes. [PG]▼●◗

Nathalie . . . (2004-French-Spanish) **C-101m.** ** D: Anne Fontaine. Fanny Ardant, Emmanuelle Béart, Gérard Depardieu, Wladimir Yordanoff, Judith Magre, Aurore Auteuil. Muddled account of the evolving relationship between two women: a married gynecologist and the prostitute she hires to seduce her philandering husband. Even the hooker's vivid descriptions of their sexual encounters fail to light a spark under this pretentious character study. Remade as CHLOE. Super 35.◗

National Lampoon Goes to the Movies (1981) **C-89m.** BOMB D: Henry Jaglom, Bob Giraldi. Peter Riegert, Diane Lane, Candy Clark, Teresa Ganzel, Ann Dusenberry, Robert Culp, Bobby DiCicco, Fred Willard, Joe Spinell, Mary Woronov, Dick Miller, Robby Benson, Richard Widmark, Christopher Lloyd, Elisha Cook, Julie Kavner, Henny Youngman. Incredibly idiotic parody of the movies, presented in three excruciating parts, each one worse than the next. "Personal growth" films, Harold Robbins/Sidney Sheldon soap operas and police movies are spoofed; a fourth segment, parodying disaster films and featuring Allen Goorwitz (Garfield), Marcia Strassman, and Kenneth Mars, was excised. It's easy to see why this never received theatrical release. Aka NATIONAL LAMPOON'S MOVIE MADNESS. [R]▼◗

National Lampoon's Animal House (1978) **C-109m.** ** D: John Landis. John Belushi, Tim Matheson, John Vernon, Verna Bloom, Thomas Hulce, Cesare Danova, Peter Riegert, Stephen Furst, Donald Sutherland, Karen Allen, Sarah Holcomb, Bruce McGill, Martha Smith, Mary Louise Weller, James Daughton, Kevin Bacon, Mark Metcalf, James Widdoes. Spoof of early 1960s college life is only sporadically funny, depends largely on Belushi's mugging as frat-house animal. Not nearly as roisterous or amusing as any issue of the *Lampoon*, but it became a tremendous hit—and spawned a number of truly terrible imitations—as well as a short-lived TV series, *Delta House*. [R] ▼●)

National Lampoon's Christmas Vacation (1989) **C-97m.** *** D: Jeremiah S. Chechik. Chevy Chase, Beverly D'Angelo, Randy Quaid, Diane Ladd, John Randolph, E. G. Marshall, Doris Roberts, Julia Louis-Dreyfus, Mae Questel, William Hickey, Brian Doyle-Murray, Juliette Lewis, Johnny Galecki, Nicholas Guest, Miriam Flynn. Funny (if typically spotty, sometimes tasteless) saga of the Griswold family's disaster-filled holiday season, with Chase as the terminally stupid head of the household. Sprinkles some believably poignant moments into its slapstick brew with surprising deftness. Third in the VACATION series. Written by John Hughes. Followed by VEGAS VACATION and a direct-to-video spinoff. [PG-13] ▼●)

National Lampoon's Class Reunion (1982) **C-84m.** BOMB D: Michael Miller. Gerrit Graham, Michael Lerner, Fred McCarren, Miriam Flynn, Stephen Furst, Marya Small, Shelley Smith, Zane Buzby, Anne Ramsey. Spectacularly unfunny comedy about a high school reunion shaken by mad killer on the prowl. If you went to school with people like this, no jury in the world would convict you for turning homicidal, either. [R] ▼●

National Lampoon's European Vacation (1985) **C-94m.** *½ D: Amy Heckerling. Chevy Chase, Beverly D'Angelo, Jason Lively, Dana Hill, Eric Idle, Victor Lanoux, John Astin, Paul Bartel, Mel Smith, Robbie Coltrane. Pretty sorry sequel to VACATION, with idiotic Chase and his family stumbling through Europe. Misfire gags right and left, and surprising sexism in a film directed by a woman. Followed by NATIONAL LAMPOON'S CHRISTMAS VACATION. [PG-13] ▼●)

National Lampoon's Gold Diggers (2004) **C-87m.** BOMB D: Gary Preisler. Will Friedle, Chris Owen, Louise Lasser, Renee Taylor, Rudy De Luca, Nikki Ziering. Two inept overgrown teenagers arrive in L.A. hoping to con their way into the good life. They select a pair of creepily libidinous elderly sisters as their prey. If it's possible to insult the *National Lampoon* brand, this is the proof. Taylor's husband, Joe Bologna, is credited as "creative consultant"; their son Gabriel plays a jail guard. Unrated version also available. [PG-13] ▼)

National Lampoon's Loaded Weapon 1 (1993) **C-83m.** ** D: Gene Quintano. Emilio Estevez, Samuel L. Jackson, Jon Lovitz, Tim Curry, Kathy Ireland, Frank McRae, William Shatner, James Doohan, Charlie Sheen, Bill Nunn, F. Murray Abraham, Richard Moll, Denis Leary, Corey Feldman, Phil Hartman, J.T. Walsh, Erik Estrada, Larry Wilcox, Paul Gleason, Allyce Beasley, Rick Ducommun, Charles Napier, Beverly Johnson, Denise (Lee) Richards. Lethal Weapon, Loaded Weapon, get it? Quality-caboose of the movie-spoof genre has at least a few laugh-out-loud gags: a takeoff on the BASIC INSTINCT interrogation scene and a skewering of the standard cop film convenience-store shootup. Estevez is no Leslie Nielsen, but you knew that. [PG-13] ▼●)

National Lampoon's Movie Madness SEE: **National Lampoon Goes to the Movies**

National Lampoon's Senior Trip (1995) **C-91m.** ** D: Kelly Makin. Matt Frewer, Valerie Mahaffey, Lawrence Dane, Tommy Chong, Jeremy Renner, Rob Moore. Conniving senator is exposed by expected array of *Lampoon* honor-rollers: dopers, drop-outs, the class tramp, a Cheetos freak, a self-described "frigid head case," etc. Lower-than-low humor, but fairly fast paced. [R] ▼●)

National Lampoon's Vacation (1983) **C-98m.** *** D: Harold Ramis. Chevy Chase, Beverly D'Angelo, Anthony Michael Hall, Imogene Coca, Randy Quaid, Dana Barron, Christie Brinkley, John Candy, Eddie Bracken, Brian Doyle-Murray, Eugene Levy, Jane Krakowski. Enjoyable comedy about a sappy middle-class family's cross-country trip by car. Given the obvious premise, there are a surprising number of genuine laughs—including the ultimate fate of Aunt Edna. Written by John Hughes. Followed by three sequels, starting with NATIONAL LAMPOON'S EUROPEAN VACATION. [R] ▼●)

National Lampoon's Van Wilder (2002) **C-95m.** *½ D: Walt Becker. Ryan Reynolds, Tara Reid, Tim Matheson, Kal Penn, Teck Holmes, Daniel Cosgrove, Paul Gleason, Erik Estrada, Curtis Armstrong, Aaron Paul, Edie McClurg. Reynolds is the title character, a slick campus wheeler-dealer who never wants to graduate. Homage to ANIMAL HOUSE and other, better teen comedies even casts actors associated with those films in supporting roles . . . but just a rehash of the same old stuff with new gross-out gags. Tom Everett Scott appears unbilled. Followed by two sequels. [R] ▼)

National Lampoon's Van Wilder 2: The Rise of Taj (2006) **C-97m.** BOMB D: Mort Nathan. Kal Penn, Lauren Cohan, Daniel Percival, Holly Davidson, Anthony Cozens, Steven Rathman, Glen Barry. Taj (Penn), a protégé of Van Wilder, heads off to England to attend grad school, where he butts heads with an elitist aristocrat while somehow attracting the attention of a sexy scholar. Charmless male-fantasy comedy is sloppily made, with lame humor that will appeal only to the most undiscriminating beer guzzlers. Unrated version also available. Followed by a DVD sequel. [R]●)

National Security (2003) **C-88m.** **½ D: Dennis Dugan. Martin Lawrence, Steve Zahn, Colm Feore, Bill Duke, Eric Roberts, Timothy Busfield, Robinne Lee, Matt McCoy, Brett Cullen, Stephen Tobolowsky, Joe Flaherty. Two adversarial ex-cops discover malfeasance in high legal places while working as security guards. Buddy comedy doesn't make much sense even on its predictably moronic level, yet Lawrence and Zahn are surprisingly in sync, and as funny as they've ever been. The scene that leads to Zahn getting ousted from the force is first-rate; everything else is pretty much recycled. [PG-13] ▼●

National Treasure (2004) **C-130m.** *** D: Jon Turteltaub. Nicolas Cage, Diane Kruger, Jon Voight, Sean Bean, Christopher Plummer, Harvey Keitel, Hunter Gomez, Justin Bartha. Surprisingly entertaining yarn about a man who's devoted (some say "wasted") his life to the pursuit of a hidden treasure, its clues on the back of the Declaration of Independence. *The Da Vinci Code* lite, this thoroughly engaging action-adventure offers a clever script, good characters, and imaginative use of its Washington, D.C., Boston, Philadelphia, and N.Y.C. locations. Longer than it needs to be, but still fun. Followed by a sequel. Super 35. [PG] ▼●

National Treasure: Book of Secrets (2007) **C-124m.** **½ D: Jon Turteltaub. Nicolas Cage, Jon Voight, Harvey Keitel, Ed Harris, Helen Mirren, Diane Kruger, Justin Bartha, Bruce Greenwood, Ty Burrell, Brent Briscoe, Randy Travis. Treasure hunter Cage has a personal stake in his latest quest: proving the innocence of an ancestor who may have been involved in planning Abraham Lincoln's assassination. Pretty good premise is given slick treatment, with lots of action set pieces and a first-rate cast, although it's all too obvious that it's a sequel, with contrived plotting at every turn. Super 35. [PG]●

National Velvet (1944) **C-125m.** **** D: Clarence Brown. Mickey Rooney, Elizabeth Taylor, Donald Crisp, Anne Revere, Angela Lansbury, Reginald Owen, Norma Varden, Jackie "Butch" Jenkins, Terry Kilburn. Outstanding family film about a girl who determines to enter her horse in the famed Grand National Steeplechase. Taylor is irresistible, Rooney was never better, and they're surrounded by a perfect supporting cast. Revere won a Best Supporting Actress Oscar as Taylor's mother. Screenplay by Theodore Reeves and Helen Deutsch, from Enid Bagnold's novel. Followed years later by INTERNATIONAL VELVET and a TV series. ▼●

Native Son (1986) **C-112m.** **½ D: Jerrold Freedman. Victor Love, Matt Dillon, Elizabeth McGovern, Geraldine Page, Oprah Winfrey, Akosua Busia, Carroll Baker, John McMartin, Art Evans, John Karlen, Willard

E. Pugh, David Rasche, Ving Rhames. Second, star-studded filming of Richard Wright's landmark 1940 novel. Nineteen-year-old Bigger Thomas (played by newcomer Love) is a poor black in 1930s Chicago whose life takes a tragic turn. Capable cast and serviceable script cannot overcome film's deliberate alterations and softening of some of the novel's key plot points and themes. Still, for those unfamiliar with the book, an OK melodrama. A coproduction of PBS' *American Playhouse.* Previously filmed in 1950, with author Wright himself as Bigger Thomas. [PG] ▼●

Nativity Story, The (2006) **C-101m.** **½ D: Catherine Hardwicke. Keisha Castle-Hughes, Oscar Isaac, Hiam Abbass, Shaun Toub, Alexander Siddig, Ciarán Hinds, Shohreh Aghdashloo. Familiar saga of Mary, Joseph, and Jesus gets a reverent (if uninspired) mounting that endows well-known figures with emotional cores. Set in a time—circa 9 months B.C.—when conceiving a child of mysterious parentage is punishable by death, 16-year-old Mary has to deal not only with the imminent birth of the Israelites' deliverer but also how to explain things to her skeptical husband. Detailed script even provides a reasonable explanation for the Star of Bethlehem, but screenwriter Mike Rich fails to credit the original author. Super 35. [PG]●

Natural, The (1984) **C-134m.** **½ D: Barry Levinson. Robert Redford, Robert Duvall, Glenn Close, Kim Basinger, Wilford Brimley, Richard Farnsworth, Barbara Hershey, Robert Prosky, Joe Don Baker. Serpentine saga of a young man with a gift for baseball, whose life takes more than a few surprising turns. Freely adapted from Bernard Malamud's offbeat novel, with heavy doses of sentiment and larger-than-life imagery (courtesy of cinematographer Caleb Deschanel). Some effective moments, with a fine cast, but too long and inconsistent. Best of all: Randy Newman's score. Darren McGavin appears unbilled. Director's cut runs 144m. [PG] ▼●

Natural Born Killers (1994) **C-119m.** *½ D: Oliver Stone. Woody Harrelson, Juliette Lewis, Robert Downey, Jr., Tommy Lee Jones, Tom Sizemore, Russell Means, Rodney Dangerfield, Edie McClurg, Steven Wright, Joe Grifasi, Pruitt Taylor Vince, Balthazar Getty, Dale Dye, James Gammon, Arliss Howard. Supposed satire of America's infatuation with outlaws and social miscreants, focusing on a hedonistic couple who murder more than 50 people on their "honeymoon." Whatever points Stone wants to make are delivered early on, with a bludgeon; the rest is all sound and fury. Sixties-inspired hyperkinetic filmmaking style soon becomes boring and repetitious. Story by Quentin Tarantino; three others (including Stone) are credited with the screenplay. Director's cut (with 3m. of new footage) available on video. [R]▼●▶

Natural Enemies (1979) C-100m. *½ D: Jeff Kanew. Hal Holbrook, Louise Fletcher, Peter Armstrong, Beth Berridge, Steve Austin, Jose Ferrer, Viveca Lindfors. Successful publisher Holbrook wakes up one day with the urge to kill his family. Cold, uninvolving, and (needless to say) strange little film, written, directed and edited by Kanew. [R]▼

Nature's Mistakes SEE: **Freaks**

Naughty Marietta (1935) 106m. **½ D: W. S. Van Dyke II. Jeanette MacDonald, Nelson Eddy, Frank Morgan, Elsa Lanchester, Douglass Dumbrille, Cecilia Parker. First teaming of Eddy and MacDonald has her a French princess running off to America, falling in love with Indian scout Eddy. Agreeable operetta with Victor Herbert score, including "The Italian Street Song," "Tramp, Tramp, Tramp," and the immortal "Ah, Sweet Mystery of Life."▼●▶

Naughty Nineties, The (1945) 76m. ** D: Jean Yarbrough. Bud Abbott, Lou Costello, Alan Curtis, Rita Johnson, Henry Travers, Lois Collier, Joe Sawyer, Joe Kirk. Ordinary A&C comedy of riverboat gamblers, sparked by duo's verbal exchanges (including "Who's on First?") and slapstick finale.▼●▶

Nausicaä of the Valley of the Wind (1984-Japanese) C-116m. ***½ D: Hayao Miyazaki. Voices of Alison Lohman, Uma Thurman, Patrick Stewart, Shia LaBeouf, Chris Sarandon, Edward James Olmos, Mark Hamill, Jodi Benson. Imaginative anime feature set in a postapocalyptic world. When a peaceful kingdom is invaded by an evil race determined to retrieve a deadly weapon that has crashed into its valley, a princess leads the defense against all manner of invading hordes, giant insects, and poisonous plants. Based on his own graphic novel, Miyazaki's sci-fi epic blends terrific action set pieces with poignant emotional confrontations, and even an important ecological message. Originally released in the U.S. in 1985, heavily edited, as WARRIORS OF THE WIND. This superior English-language version, supervised by Pixar, was released in 2005. ▼▶

Navajo Joe (1966-Italian-Spanish) C-92m. *½ D: Sergio Corbucci. Burt Reynolds, Aldo Sanbrell, Tanya Lopert, Fernando Rey. Sole survivor of massacre swears revenge on his enemies in this tepid Western, of interest only for Reynolds' presence. Techniscope.▼▶

Navigator, The (1924) 69m. **½ D: Buster Keaton, Donald Crisp. Buster Keaton, Kathryn McGuire, Frederick Vroom. Buster plays (yet again) a pampered millionaire who—by sheer circumstance, with a dash of stupidity—winds up on a huge, deserted ship with the woman he wants to marry. Many great gags and amusing sequences,

but this silent doesn't have the momentum of Buster's best comedies. ▼●▶

Navigator: A Medieval Odyssey, The (1988-New Zealand) C/B&W-92m. *** D: Vincent Ward. Hamish McFarlane, Bruce Lyons, Chris Haywood, Marshall Napier, Noel Appleby, Paul Livingston, Sarah Pierse. Engrossing, very imaginative tale of psychic boy in tiny medieval English village who, to protect villagers from the plague, leads a tunneling expedition—which emerges in a modern city in 1988. Directed and written with great clarity, the film has much of the feel of a genuine medieval fable. Beautifully produced on a low budget. [PG]▼▶

Navy SEALS (1990) C-113m. ** D: Lewis Teague. Charlie Sheen, Michael Biehn, Joanne Whalley-Kilmer, Rick Rossovich, Cyril O'Reilly, Bill Paxton, Dennis Haysbert, Paul Sanchez. Middle Eastern terrorists are mere putty in the hands of U.S. Navy's elite commando unit (SEa, Air, Land); "inspired" by the actual team formed under J.F.K.'s administration. G.I. Joe-level action is name of the game here. Sheen's character operates at the maturity level of Dennis the Menace. [R]▼●▶

Navy vs. the Night Monsters, The (1966) C-90m. BOMB D: Michael Hoey. Mamie Van Doren, Anthony Eisley, Pamela Mason, Bill Gray, Bobby Van, Walter Sande, Edward Faulkner, Phillip Terry. 1) Look at the title. 2) Examine the cast. 3) Be aware that the plot involves omniverous trees. 4) Don't say you weren't warned.▼

Nazarin (1958-Mexican) 92m. *** D: Luis Buñuel. Francisco Rabal, Rita Macedo, Marga Lopez, Ignacio Lopez Tarso, Ofelia Guilmain. Powerful and pointed (if relentlessly grim) drama about saintly priest Rabal, and how hypocritical peasants deal with him as he tries to interpret the lessons of Christ. ▼●▶

Near Dark (1987) C-95m. **½ D: Kathryn Bigelow. Adrian Pasdar, Jenny Wright, Lance Henriksen, Bill Paxton, Jenette Goldstein, Tim Thomerson. Better-than-average vampire yarn actually plays more like a werewolf film. Cowboy Pasdar is literally bitten by Wright and joins a band of hillbilly bloodsuckers who roam the West in a van. Stylishly directed horror film reunites three cast members from ALIENS: Henriksen, Paxton, and Goldstein. [R]▼●▶

Necessary Roughness (1991) C-108m. *½ D: Stan Dragoti. Scott Bakula, Robert Loggia, Hector Elizondo, Harley Jane Kozak, Larry Miller, Sinbad, Fred Dalton Thompson, Rob Schneider, Jason Bateman. A 34-year-old quarterback at a Texas college reeling from NCAA penalties discovers that his cute no-nonsense prof is closet football junkie. Formulaic enough to insult anyone's intelligence, with a cast of quirky teammates transparently contrived (swimsuit model Kathy Ireland is the squadron's placekicker). Beware of Bill Conti's feel-good score. [PG-13]▼○▶

Necromancy (1972) **C-83m.** *½ D: Bert I. Gordon. Orson Welles, Pamela Franklin, Michael Ontkean, Lee Purcell, Harvey Jason. High priest Welles tries to manipulate Franklin into becoming a witch. Mindless, poorly crafted thriller was originally released without its nude coven scenes, if anybody cares. Some prints run 75m. Video titles: THE WITCHING and ROSEMARY'S DISCIPLES. [PG]▼

Ned Kelly (1970-British) **C-100m.** **½ D: Tony Richardson. Mick Jagger, Clarissa Kaye, Mark McManus, Frank Thring. Ambitious telling of the life and adventures of Australia's most famous outlaw, emphasizing the Irish-British conflict at the heart of his story. Many good songs on the soundtrack, written by Shel Silverstein. Retitled NED KELLY, OUTLAW. [PG]▼▶

Ned Kelly (2003-Australian-British) **C-109m.** **½ D: Gregor Jordan. Heath Ledger, Orlando Bloom, Naomi Watts, Geoffrey Rush, Rachel Griffiths, Laurence Kinlan, Philip Barantini, Joel Edgerton, Kiri Paramore. When he responds to brutal mistreatment from Protestant "policemen," Irish Catholic farmer Ned Kelly is thrown into prison; after serving his time, it doesn't take much to transform him into an outlaw who becomes a folk hero to all the oppressed immigrants of Australia during the late 1800s. Ledger's sturdy performance anchors this well-crafted but dour film. Same story was done in 1970 with Mick Jagger. Super 35. [R]▼▶

Needful Things (1993) **C-120m.** *½ D: Fraser C. Heston. Max von Sydow, Ed Harris, Bonnie Bedelia, Amanda Plummer, J. T. Walsh, Ray McKinnon, Duncan Fraser, Valri Bromfield. Bottom-of-the-barrel bore about a devilish old man (von Sydow) who opens a curiosity shop in a small Maine town, with predictably horrific results. Scripted by W. D. Richter, based on the best-seller by (who else?) Stephen King. [R]▼○▶

Negatives (1968-British) **C-90m.** ** D: Peter Medak. Peter McEnery, Diane Cilento, Glenda Jackson, Maurice Denham, Steven Lewis, Norman Rossington. Strange movie about unmarried couple who dress up like notorious Dr. Crippen and his wife for kicks; he later switches his characterization to Baron von Richtofen. Jackson is good, but direction is too mannered. [R]▼

Negotiator, The (1998) **C-138m.** *** D: F. Gary Gray. Samuel L. Jackson, Kevin Spacey, David Morse, Ron Rifkin, John Spencer, J.T. Walsh, Regina Taylor, Siobhan Fallon, Paul Giamatti, Brad Blaisdell. One of Chicago's top police hostage negotiators (Jackson) is framed for embezzling money from his union's pension fund—and has a murder pinned on him, to boot. His only chance is to take hostages and clear himself with the help of another crack negotiator (Spacey). Highly watchable, if not 100% credible, but the two stars (and a strong supporting cast) make the most of it. Super 35. [R]▼○▶

Neighbors (1981) **C-94m.** BOMB D: John G. Avildsen. John Belushi, Dan Aykroyd, Cathy Moriarty, Kathryn Walker, Lauren-Marie Taylor, Tim Kazurinsky. Appallingly unfunny and tiresome "comedy" based on Thomas Berger's novel about a middle-class milquetoast whose suburban existence is shaken by the arrival of bizarre and destructive neighbors. Screenplay credited to Larry Gelbart. Pointless; sadly, Belushi's last film. [R]▼○

Neil Simon's Odd Couple II SEE: **Odd Couple II, The**

Neil Young: Heart of Gold (2006) **C-103m.** ***½ D: Jonathan Demme. Baby boomers in general and Young fans in particular will savor this sublime concert film, shot during two 2005 performances at Nashville's Ryman Auditorium. Young and his band members perform songs both old and new. What makes the film especially poignant is the knowledge that the folk rocker penned his newer compositions after learning he had a brain aneurysm, for which he successfully underwent surgery. [PG]▶

Nell (1994) **C-113m.** ** D: Michael Apted. Jodie Foster, Liam Neeson, Natasha Richardson, Richard Libertini, Nick Searcy, Robin Mullins, Jeremy Davies. The death of a hermit woman brings a small-town Southern doctor into the backwoods, where he discovers she had a daughter who's been raised completely apart from civilization. He becomes fascinated—and so does a research scientist at a nearby university, who wants to "capture" the woman. Intriguing premise goes flat as the story loses focus, and the characters' motivations and relationships grow fuzzy. Foster gives a bravura performance but it's hard to forget it *is* a performance. Panavision. [PG-13]▼○▶

Nelly & Monsieur Arnaud (1995-French-Italian-German) **C-106m.** *** D: Claude Sautet. Emmanuelle Béart, Michel Serrault, Jean-Hugues Anglade, Claire Nadeau, Françoise Brion, Michel Lonsdale. Subtle, beautifully acted story of a 25-year-old woman in debt and stuck in a nowhere marriage, who meets an elegant and instantly infatuated man some 40 years her senior who offers to pay her bills and give her a job typing his memoirs. Sautet proves that in his 70s he's still as effective as ever in painting the difficulties and heartbreak of human relationships. ▼▶

Nelson Affair, The (1973-British) **C-118m.** **½ D: James Cellan Jones. Glenda Jackson, Peter Finch, Michael Jayston, Anthony Quayle, Margaret Leighton, Dominic Guard, Nigel Stock, Barbara Leigh-Hunt.

Handsome retelling of Lord Nelson-Lady Hamilton affair, making the "Lady" a slut; interesting but claustrophobic—even climactic sea battle was shot indoors! British title: A BEQUEST TO THE NATION. Panavision. [PG]

Nemesis (1993) **C-94m.** *½ D: Albert Pyun. Olivier Gruner, Tim Thomerson, Marjorie Monaghan, Merle Kennedy, Brion James, Deborah Shelton, Cary-Hiroyuki Tagawa, Nicholas Guest, Jackie Earle Haley, Tom Janes (Thomas Jane). In 2027, tough cop Gruner, who's had many body parts replaced with mechanical duplicates, fights a group of androids (here called "cyborgs") intent on conquering world. Just another amalgam of ideas borrowed from better movies. Gruner has some appeal, though. Followed by two direct-to-video sequels. Super 35. [R]▼●)

Nenette et Boni (1996-French) **C-103m.** *** D: Claire Denis. Alice Houri, Gregoire Colin, Valeria Bruni-Tedeschi, Vincent Gallo, Jacques Nolot. Arresting, emotionally involving chronicle of two children of divorced parents: Nenette (Houri), who is 15 and very pregnant, and lonely 18-year-old Boni (Colin), who is erotically obsessed with a baker's wife. A potent exploration of a brother-sister bond and how a dysfunctional family damages its youngest and most vulnerable members.▼▶

Neon Bible, The (1995-U.S.-British) **C-92m.** ** D: Terence Davies. Gena Rowlands, Denis Leary, Diana Scarwid, Jacob Tierney, Leo Burmester, Frances Conroy, Peter McRobbie. Slow-as-molasses Truman Capote–like reminiscence about a young boy coming of age in the American South and his eccentric, melancholy Aunt Mae (Rowlands, who is good as always). Despite its abundant atmosphere and good intentions, this cannot compare with Davies' earlier works. He scripted, based on a novel by John Kennedy Toole. J-D-C Scope.▼●)

Neptune Disaster, The SEE: **Neptune Factor, The**

Neptune Factor, The (1973-Canadian) **C-98m.** ** D: Daniel Petrie. Ben Gazzara, Yvette Mimieux, Walter Pidgeon, Ernest Borgnine. Deep-sea-diving sub races to save three men trapped by an earthquake in ocean floor laboratory. Soggy underwater yarn lifts its plot almost in toto from MAROONED. Aka AN UNDERWATER ODYSSEY and THE NEPTUNE DISASTER. Panavision. [G]▼▶

Neptune's Daughter (1949) **C-93m.** *** D: Edward Buzzell. Esther Williams, Red Skelton, Keenan Wynn, Betty Garrett, Ricardo Montalban, Mel Blanc. Musical romance with Esther a bathing-suit designer, Skelton a no-account mistaken for polo star by Garrett. Bubbly fun, with Academy Award–winning song: "Baby It's Cold Outside."▼●)

Nest, The (1980-Spanish) **C-109m.** *** D: Jaime De Arminan. Hector Alterio, Ana Torrent, Luis Politti, Agustin Gonzalez, Patricia Adriani. Diverting but predictable drama detailing the relationship between wealthy, aging widower Alterio and alienated 13-year-old Torrent. Helped immeasurably by Arminan's precise script and direction. [PG]▼

Nest, The (1988) **C-88m.** ** D: Terence H. Winkless. Robert Lansing, Lisa Lang-lois, Franc Luz, Terri Treas, Stephen Davies, Diana Bellamy, Nancy Morgan. Trifling, ever so familiar chronicle of a failed scientific experiment resulting in the creation of large, hungry cockroaches. [R]▼▶

Nesting, The (1981) **C-104m.** ** D: Armand Weston. Robin Groves, Christopher Loomis, Michael David Lally, John Carradine, Gloria Grahame, Bill Rowley. Gothic novelist moves into eerie Victorian mansion to which she's mysteriously drawn. Starts off interestingly but wanders and drags on to unsatisfying finish. Aka MASSACRE MANSION. [R]▼▶

Net, The (1995) **C-118m.** **½ D: Irwin Winkler. Sandra Bullock, Jeremy Northam, Dennis Miller, Diane Baker, Wendy Gazelle, Ken Howard, Ray McKinnon. The techno-thriller as plodding Sandra Bullock vehicle: She plays a mousy, vulnerable computer whiz. When bad guys need a disc she possesses, they stop at nothing—including deleting, then manipulating her identity on official computer records. Anyone who's ever seen a *real* thriller will be ahead of this story at every turn. Later a cable TV series. Followed by a direct-to-video sequel in 2005. [PG-13]▼●)

Network (1976) **C-121m.** **** D: Sidney Lumet. William Holden, Faye Dunaway, Peter Finch, Robert Duvall, Ned Beatty, Beatrice Straight, Wesley Addy, Darryl Hickman, Ken Kercheval, William Prince, Marlene Warfield. Paddy Chayefsky's outrageous satire on television looks less and less like fantasy as the years pass; uninhibited tale chronicles fourth-place network that will air anything for a big rating, including a patently insane, profanity-shouting "mad prophet of the airwaves" (Finch). Entire cast explodes, particularly Dunaway as ruthless programmer, Holden as conscientious newsman, Duvall as shark-like v.p., and Beatty as evangelistical board chairman. Well-deserved Oscars went to Finch (posthumously), Dunaway, Straight, and Chayefsky. [R]▼●)

Nevada Smith (1966) **C-135m.** *** D: Henry Hathaway. Steve McQueen, Karl Malden, Brian Keith, Arthur Kennedy, Suzanne Pleshette, Raf Vallone, Pat Hingle, Howard da Silva, Martin Landau. Good Western story. Smith swears revenge for senseless murder of his parents at the hands of outlaw gang. Based on character from

THE CARPETBAGGERS. Remade as a TVM in 1975. Panavision.▼◐)

Never a Dull Moment (1968) **C-100m.** ** D: Jerry Paris. Dick Van Dyke, Edward G. Robinson, Dorothy Provine, Henry Silva, Joanna Moore, Tony Bill. Tired Disney comedy belies title, as TV performer Van Dyke gets involved with gangsters; even Robinson's performance is lifeless.▼▶

Never Back Down (2008) **C-113m.** ** D: Jeff Wadlow. Sean Faris, Djimon Hounsou, Amber Heard, Cam Gigandet, Evan Peters, Leslie Hope. Faris plays a hardheaded high school jock whose single-parent family moves from Iowa to Orlando, where it seems every teen lives in nouveau riche decadence. Happily, he stumbles into an underground mixed–martial arts world and starts training at a gym run by spiritual loner Hounsou. Wildly improbable plot piles cliché on cliché but should entertain its target action audience. Nemesis Gigandet can glare with the best of them. Super 35. [PG-13]▶

Never Been Kissed (1999) **C-107m.** **½ D: Raja Gosnell. Drew Barrymore, David Arquette, Michael Vartan, Molly Shannon, John C. Reilly, Garry Marshall, Leelee Sobieski, Sean Whalen, Jordan Ladd, Jessica Alba, James Franco. Twenty-five-year-old newspaper copy editor gets her first chance as a reporter by going undercover and pretending to be a 17-year-old high school student. All this does is bring back vivid memories of her nerdy school days, while the assignment remains vague and unfulfilled. Star vehicle, if ever there was one, is buoyed by Barrymore's charm, but burdened with a muddled and barely believable story. Super 35. [PG-13] ▼◐)

Never Cry Wolf (1983) **C-105m.** *** D: Carroll Ballard. Charles Martin Smith, Brian Dennehy, Zachary Ittimangnaq, Samson Jorah. Smith plays real-life Canadian author Farley Mowat who braved the Arctic, alone, to study behavior of wolves . . . and wound up learning as much about himself. Uneven, but filled with striking moments and passages, plus a wonderful performance by Smith. There's also the irony of a Walt Disney production in which the leading character takes to eating mice! Two decades later, Smith directed THE SNOW WALKER, based on a Mowat short story. [PG] ▼◐)

Never Die Alone (2004) **C-88m.** ** D: Ernest Dickerson. DMX, David Arquette, Michael Ealy, Reagan Gomez-Preston, Clifton Powell, Jennifer Sky, Drew Sidora, Antwon Tanner, Tommy "Tiny" Lister, Aisha Tyler. Narrated by a shot-to-death corpse (all similarities to SUNSET BLVD. end here), off-the-cuff drug melodrama from a Donald Goines novel traces the semi-rise but unambiguous fall of a dealer named King David (DMX), who tricks his girlfriends into

snorting truly horrific substances. Arquette is the wannabe journalist who, by stumbling onto David's story, hopes to parlay it into the Bob Woodward big time. Moderately watchable in its tawdriness, but lacks the momentous central figure it thinks it has and the commanding lead actor it needs. Super 35. [R] ▼▶

NeverEnding Story, The (1984-West German-British) **C-92m.** *** D: Wolfgang Petersen. Noah Hathaway, Barret Oliver, Tami Stronach, Moses Gunn, Patricia Hayes, Sydney Bromley, Gerald McRaney; voice of Alan Oppenheimer. Magical, timeless fantasy built around young Oliver visualizing what he's reading from a mystical book: boy warrior Hathaway is the only hope of saving the empire of Fantasia from being swallowed up by The Nothing. Amazing, unique effects, characters, and visual design (and a not-so-subtle message that Reading Is Good). Followed by two live-action sequels and an animated TV movie and series. U.S. version was cut by 7m. Technovision. [PG] ▼◐)

NeverEnding Story II: The Next Chapter, The (1990-U.S.-German) **C-89m.** *½ D: George Miller. Jonathan Brandis, Kenny Morrison, Clarissa Burt, John Wesley Shipp, Martin Umbach. Mom's dead, dad's busy, and the swim coach says he suffers from a "high wimp factor." So, it's back to Fantasia (a magic land) for the young boy who loses himself in a storybook, where a child empress (as childlike as Drew Barrymore) is in danger. Poky and cheesy, though kids might take to some of the animal sidekicks. Followed by a direct-to-video sequel. Panavision. [PG]▼◐)

Never Fear (1950) **82m.** **½ D: Ida Lupino. Sally Forrest, Keefe Brasselle, Hugh O'Brian, Eve Miller, Lawrence Dobkin. Young dancer Forrest's life comes apart when she develops polio. Sincere drama scripted by Lupino and her then-husband, Collier Young. Aka THE YOUNG LOVERS. ▼▶

Never Forever (2007-U.S.-South Korean) **C-101m.** **½ D: Gina Kim. Vera Farmiga, Jung-Woo Ha, David Lee McInnis. A couple's inability to conceive a child is the only contentious issue in their otherwise happy marriage. Farmiga's oddly curious solution is risky at best. Film rests on the relationship between Farmiga and Jung-Woo, whose likability as a mismatched pair makes it worth watching. [R]▶

Never Give a Inch SEE: **Sometimes a Great Notion**

Never Give a Sucker an Even Break (1941) **71m.** ***½ D: Edward Cline. W. C. Fields, Gloria Jean, Leon Errol, Susan Miller, Franklin Pangborn, Margaret Dumont. Completely insane comedy with Fields (in his last starring film) playing himself; no coherent plot, but a lot of funny scenes. Dumont plays "Mrs. Hemoglobin." Climactic chase is a classic, reused by Abbott and

Costello in IN SOCIETY. Story by "Otis Criblecoblis." ▼●

Never Let Go (1960-British) **90m.** ****** D: John Guillermin. Richard Todd, Peter Sellers, Elizabeth Sellars, Carol White, Mervyn Johns. Sellers gives heavy-handed performance as ruthless and sadistic racketeer in weak story about car thievery. Billed as his first dramatic role, it was a poor choice. ▼●

Never Let Me Go (1953) **94m.** ****½** D: Delmer Daves. Clark Gable, Gene Tierney, Bernard Miles, Richard Haydn, Kenneth More, Belita, Theodore Bikel. Unconvincing yet smooth account of Gable trying to smuggle ballerina-wife Tierney out of Russia. ▼

Never Let Me Go (2010-British-U.S.) **C-103m.** ******* D: Mark Romanek. Carey Mulligan, Andrew Garfield, Keira Knightley, Charlotte Rampling, Sally Hawkins, Isobel Meikle-Small, Ella Purnell, Charlie Rowe. Students lead a fairly typical life at a traditional English boarding school, but these children are anything but ordinary, as we soon discover: they have no control over their lives, which are destined to be cut short (for reasons we won't reveal here). Somber but moving adaptation by Alex Garland of Kazuo Ishiguro's highly acclaimed novel turns on its leading actors' deeply felt performances and a haunting music score by Rachel Portman. Super 35. [R] ❒

Never Never Land (1980-British) **C-86m.** ******* D: Paul Annett. Petula Clark, Cathleen Nesbitt, John Castle, Anne Seymour, Evelyn Laye, Roland Culver, Heather Miller. Nice little film about lonely child (Miller), her fascination with Peter Pan and connection with elderly Nesbitt. Best for the kids. [G]

Never on Sunday (1960-Greek) **91m.** *****½** D: Jules Dassin. Melina Mercouri, Jules Dassin, Georges Foundas, Titos Vandis, Mitsos Liguisos, Despo Diamantidou. Charming idyll of intellectual boob coming to Greece, trying to make earthy prostitute Mercouri cultured. Grand entertainment, with Oscar-winning title song by Manos Hadjidakis. Later a Broadway musical, *Illya Darling.* ▼●

Never Say Goodbye (1956) **C-96m.** ****½** D: Jerry Hopper. Rock Hudson, Cornell Borchers, George Sanders, Ray Collins, David Janssen, Shelley Fabares. Spotty tearjerker of Hudson and Borchers, long separated, discovering one another again and creating fit home for their child. Remake of THIS LOVE OF OURS. Clint Eastwood is cast as Rock's lab assistant. ❒

Never Say Never Again (1983) **C-137m.** ****½** D: Irvin Kershner. Sean Connery, Klaus Maria Brandauer, Max von Sydow, Barbara Carrera, Kim Basinger, Bernie Casey, Alec McCowen, Edward Fox, Rowan Atkinson. Connery's stylish performance and self-deprecating humor make his return performance as James Bond (after 12

years) a real treat—but the film, a remake of THUNDERBALL, is uneven and overlong. Brandauer is a smooth villain, and Carrera a memorably sexy villainess, Fatima Blush. Panavision. [PG] ▼●

Never So Few (1959) **C-124m.** ****½** D: John Sturges. Frank Sinatra, Gina Lollobrigida, Peter Lawford, Steve McQueen, Richard Johnson, Paul Henreid, Brian Donlevy, Dean Jones, Charles Bronson. WW2 action/romance tale; salty performances which make one forget the clichés and improbabilities. CinemaScope. ▼●

Never Steal Anything Small (1959) **C-94m.** ****½** D: Charles Lederer. James Cagney, Shirley Jones, Roger Smith, Cara Williams, Nehemiah Persoff, Royal Dano, Horace McMahon. Odd musical comedy-drama, with Cagney a waterfront union racketeer who'll do anything to win union election. From Maxwell Anderson–Rouben Mamoulian play *The Devil's Hornpipe.* CinemaScope. ▼

Never Talk to Strangers (1995-U.S.-Canadian) **C-102m.** ***½** D: Peter Hall. Rebecca De Mornay, Antonio Banderas, Dennis Miller, Len Cariou, Beau Starr, Tim Kelleher, Harry Dean Stanton. Criminal psychologist falls for a charming, mysterious stranger, while at the same time unexplained, terrifying incidents begin occurring. Standard-issue thriller would be more at home on television. De Mornay also coexecutive-produced. [R] ▼●

Never to Love SEE: **Bill of Divorcement, A** (1940)

Never Too Young To Die (1986) **C-92m.** ***½** D: Gil Bettman. John Stamos, Vanity, Gene Simmons, George Lazenby, Peter Kwong, Ed Brock, John Anderson, Robert Englund. Stamos, son of a spy, takes up with Vanity, one of his father's associates, to find out who murdered his dad. Pretty awful, though Simmons scores a few points for outrageousness in his portrayal of a power-crazed hermaphrodite. [R] ▼●

Neverwas (2007) **C-108m.** ****** D: Joshua Michael Stern. Aaron Eckhart, Ian McKellen, Brittany Murphy, William Hurt, Nick Nolte, Alan Cumming, Jessica Lange, Bill Bellamy, Vera Farmiga, Michael Moriarty, Cynthia Stevenson, Ryan Drescher. Fantasy and reality fail to blend in this account of psychiatrist Eckhart, who comes to work at the facility where his father, a mentally ill children's book author, once was treated. It's no wonder that, despite its A-list cast, this paper-thin fairy tale failed to earn U.S. theatrical distribution. Eckhart coproduced. Super 35. [PG-13] ❒

New Adventures of Pippi Longstocking, The (1988) **C-100m.** ****** D: Ken Annakin. Tami Erin, Eileen Brennan, Dennis Dugan, Dianne Hull, George DiCenzo, John Schuck, Dick Van Patten. Dreary Americanization of Astrid Lindgren's popular books about a plucky young girl—here, transformed into a tiresome troublemaker. May entertain undiscriminating children; adults should avoid at all costs. [G]▼●▐

New Age, The (1994) **C-110m.** *½ D: Michael Tolkin. Peter Weller, Judy Davis, Patrick Bauchau, Corbin Bernsen, Jonathan Hadary, Patricia Heaton, Samuel L. Jackson, Audra Lindley, Paula Marshall, Adam West. Deadening deadpan satire, which its studio barely released, about a married couple who launch a born-to-go-bust boutique after they both lose their glitzy jobs on the same Recession-era day. Tolkin wrote THE PLAYER; perhaps this film would have benefitted from Robert Altman's wag-in-the-moon viewpoint. Jackson's sequence, in which he "motivates" some scam-artist telemarketers, is the only one with any real juice. [R]▼●

New Best Friend (2002) **C-91m.** BOMB D: Zoe Clarke-Williams. Meredith Monroe, Rachel True, Dominique Swain, Mia Kirshner, Taye Diggs, Scott Bairstow, Glynnis O'Connor, Oliver Hudson, Eric Michael Cole. Interminable would-be thriller about a sociopath working-class coed (Kirshner) determined to score with the rich and popular at an exclusive North Carolina college. Dreary teen exploitation is full of RASHOMON-like flashbacks and lesbian sex scenes but is so anemic you're unlikely to care. Terrible performances, with Diggs as a sheriff with an intermittent Southern accent. [R]▼▐

New Centurions, The (1972) **C-103m.** *** D: Richard Fleischer. George C. Scott, Stacy Keach, Jane Alexander, Rosalind Cash, Scott Wilson, Erik Estrada, Clifton James, Isabel Sanford, James B. Sikking, Ed Lauter, William Atherton, Roger E. Mosley. Fine, episodic adaptation by Stirling Silliphant of Joseph Wambaugh novel of rookie cops on modern-day L.A. police force, ultimately pessimistic in outlook. Great casting, performances; good storytelling. Panavision. [R]▼●▐

New Guy, The (2002) **C-89m.** *½ D: Ed Decter. DJ Qualls, Eliza Dushku, Zooey Deschanel, Lyle Lovett, Eddie Griffin, Jerod Mixon, Parry Shen, Gene Simmons, M.C. Gainey, Geoffrey Lewis, Illeana Douglas, Jerry O'Connell, Charlie O'Connell, Tommy Lee, Vanilla Ice, Henry Rollins, David Hasselhoff, Kool Mo Dee, Tony Hawk, Horatio Sanz. A harassed teenage nerd (Qualls) is transformed into an intimidating new person by a prison inmate (Griffin) and proceeds to live the cool life at a different high school. Revenge/teensploitation comedy has enough quirks to make one wonder what might have been with a better script, better director, and better actors. [PG-13]▼▐

New Interns, The (1964) **123m.** **½ D: John Rich. Michael Callan, Dean Jones, Telly Savalas, Inger Stevens, George Segal, Greg Morris, Stefanie Powers, Lee Patrick, Barbara Eden. Follow-up to THE INTERNS contains unusual hospital soap opera with better than average cast and a nifty party sequence.

New in Town (2009) **C-97m.** *½ D: Jonas Elmer. Renée Zellweger, Harry Connick, Jr., Siobhan Fallon Hogan, J. K. Simmons, Frances Conroy, Mike O'Brien, Ferron Guerreiro, James Durham, Barbara James Smith. Hopelessly formulaic romantic comedy finds tough-as-nails businesswoman Zellweger sent by a multinational company to a small town to shut down the local factory. After butting heads with the union organizer (laconically played by Connick, Jr.) she predictably falls in love and sets out to find a way to save the plant. Familiar approach of NEW IN TOWN is about as old hat as they come. [PG]▐

New Jack City (1991) **C-97m.** ** D: Mario Van Peebles. Wesley Snipes, Ice T, Allen Payne, Chris Rock, Mario Van Peebles, Judd Nelson, Michael Michele, Bill Nunn, Russell Wong, Vanessa Williams, Nick Ashford, Thalmus Rasulala. N.Y.C. police detective hires two maverick ex-cops to bring down a Napoleonic drug lord who's made his fortune selling crack (and whose role model, apparently, is the Al Pacino character in SCARFACE!). Lots of emotional energy, and strong performances, but its clearly stated anti-drug message is clouded by overblown melodrama—and several climaxes too many. [R]▼●▐

New Jersey Drive (1995) **C-95m.** ** D: Nick Gomez. Sharron Corley, Gabriel Casseus, Saul Stein, Gwen McGee, Andre Moore, Donald Adeosun Faison. Two teenagers are drawn into the underground world of carjacking in Newark, N.J., and soon find the full weight of the local police force coming down around them. Spike Lee executive-produced this gritty, well-meaning drama; unfortunately, it never shifts into high gear. Corley (in his film debut) once lived the life he portrays on-screen. [R] ▼●▐

New Kids, The (1985) **C-90m.** ** D: Sean Cunningham. Shannon Presby, Lori Loughlin, James Spader, John Philbin, Eric Stoltz. Unexciting thriller about a brother and sister (Presby, Loughlin), two nice kids who are harassed by meanie Spader and his cronies. There's no gratuitous gore, but there are also no real chills. [PG]▼●▐

New Kind of Love, A (1963) **C-110m.** **½ D: Melville Shavelson. Paul Newman, Joanne Woodward, Thelma Ritter, Eva Gabor, Maurice Chevalier, George Tobias, Marvin Kaplan, Robert Clary. Silly but enjoyable fluff with sportswriter Newman and fashion buyer Woodward tangling, and then falling in love, in Paris. The stars really put this one over; Chevalier appears as himself, title song sung by Frank Sinatra. ▼▐

New Land, The (1972-Swedish) **C-161m.**

***½ D: Jan Troell. Max von Sydow, Liv Ullmann, Eddie Axberg, Hans Alfredson, Monica Zetterlund, Per Oscarsson. Sequel to THE EMIGRANTS follows same characters as they settle in Minnesota, up to the ends of their lives. Superior performances, photography, many stirring scenes. A real winner; both films have been edited together for TV, dubbed in English, and presented as THE EMIGRANT SAGA. See also THE OX. [PG]▼●

New Leaf, A (1971) **C-102m.** **½ D: Elaine May. Walter Matthau, Elaine May, Jack Weston, George Rose, William Redfield, James Coco, Graham Jarvis, Doris Roberts, Renee Taylor, David Doyle. Amusing comedy of destitute Matthau planning to marry and murder klutzy May in order to inherit her fortune. Many funny moments, and May is terrific, but it's wildly uneven. Director/writer/star May disavowed finished film, which was reedited by others. [G]▼

New Life, A (1988) **C-104m.** **½ D: Alan Alda. Alan Alda, Ann-Margret, Hal Linden, Veronica Hamel, John Shea, Mary Kay Place, Beatrice Alda. Pleasant but pat comedy about a middle-aged couple's trials and tribulations after divorcing. Alda (sporting a beard and curly hair) also wrote the script. [PG-13]▼●

Newman's Law (1974) **C-98m.** *½ D: Richard Heffron. George Peppard, Roger Robinson, Eugene Roche, Gordon Pinsent, Louis Zorich, Abe Vigoda. Honest cop Peppard, bounced from the force for alleged corruption, investigates the case on his own. Dreary and predictable. [PG]▼

New Moon (1940) **105m.** **½ D: Robert Z. Leonard. Jeanette MacDonald, Nelson Eddy, Mary Boland, George Zucco, H. B. Warner, Grant Mitchell, Stanley Fields. Nelson and Jeanette in old Louisiana, falling in love, singing "One Kiss," "Softly as in a Morning Sunrise," "Lover Come Back to Me," "Stout-Hearted Men." Oscar Hammerstein–Sigmund Romberg score sung before in 1930 filming with Lawrence Tibbett and Grace Moore.▼●

New Moon (2009) **C-130m.** **½ D: Chris Weitz. Kristen Stewart, Robert Pattinson, Taylor Lautner, Ashley Greene, Rachelle Lefevre, Billy Burke, Peter Facinelli, Nikki Reed, Kellan Lutz, Jackson Rathbone, Anna Kendrick, Michael Sheen, Graham Greene, Christian Serratos, Michael Welch, Jamie Campbell Bower, Elizabeth Reaser, Gil Birmingham, Dakota Fanning. Second installment in the TWILIGHT series. After Bella's ill-fated 18th birthday party, the Cullens leave the town of Forks to keep her out of danger. But when she discovers that Edward's image appears every time she's in peril, Bella takes more and more risks, hoping to bring him back. This leads her to her childhood friend Jacob Black (Lautner),

who has secrets of his own. This installment of the series serves mainly as a transitional chapter, introducing us to the Volturi clan as well as werewolves. With forlorn stares, plot twists, and a love triangle, this is catnip to the series' fervent fans. Followed by ECLIPSE. Super 35. [PG-13]▶

New Orleans (1947) **89m.** **½ D: Arthur Lubin. Arturo de Córdova, Dorothy Patrick, Billie Holiday, Louis Armstrong, Woody Herman & Band, Meade Lux Lewis, other jazz stars. Hackneyed fictionalization of the birth of jazz, spanning 40 years, but there's plenty of good music. Holiday (cast as a maid!) does "Do You Know What It Means to Miss New Orleans" with Armstrong and all-star band, and it's sublime. Shelley Winters appears briefly as de Córdova's secretary.▼▶

New Rose Hotel (1999) **C-92m.** *½ D: Abel Ferrara. Christopher Walken, Willem Dafoe, Asia Argento, Yoshitaka Amano, Annabella Sciorra, Gretchen Mol, John Lurie, Ryuichi Sakamoto. Ludicrously steamy sleaze in which a pair of industrial spies (Walken, Dafoe) attempt to entice a brilliant geneticist (Amano) into switching firms by hiring a hooker (Argento) to seduce him. Meant to be a moody morality tale, but comes off silly and pompous. Based on a short story by sci-fi/cyberpunk writer William Gibson. Shot in 1997. [R] ▼▶

Newsfront (1978-Australian) **C-106m.** *** D: Phillip Noyce. Bill Hunter, Gerard Kennedy, Angela Punch, Wendy Hughes, Chris Haywood, John Ewart, Bryan Brown. Enjoyable, well-crafted tale of newsreel filmmakers—centering on dedicated cameraman Hunter—is a valentine to the movie newsreel industry. Among highlights are actual late 1940s and 1950s newsreel footage, nicely integrated into scenario. Cut by 6m. for initial U.S. release. [PG]▼●▶

Newsies (1992) **C-125m.** *½ D: Kenny Ortega. Christian Bale, Bill Pullman, Robert Duvall, Ann-Margret, Michael Lerner, Kevin Tighe, Charles Cioffi, David Moscow, Luke Edwards, Max Casella. Or, *Howard the Paperboy*. Ambitious musical about the 1899 strike by urchin peddlers of Pulitzer's *New York World* and William Randolph Hearst's *Journal*. Done in by lackluster score, and cramped production numbers that seem cheap despite the film's hefty production budget. Duvall, looking like one of the Smith Brothers, plays Pulitzer; Ann-Margret needlessly pads film's bloated running time as musical performer who inexplicably befriends the lads. Score by Alan Menken and Jack Feldman. Directing debut for choreographer Ortega. Panavision. [PG]▼●▶

Newton Boys, The (1998) **C-113m.** ** D: Richard Linklater. Matthew McConaughey, Ethan Hawke, Skeet Ulrich, Vincent D'Onofrio, Julianna Margulies, Dwight

Yoakam, Chloe Webb, Bo Hopkins. Lackadaisical true-life saga of four Texas brothers who robbed banks across the country from 1919 to 1924 and lived to tell about it. Gen-X auteur Linklater is largely unsuccessful at making a period actioner; indifferent pacing and superficial characterizations make this "The Mild Bunch." Best performance comes from Yoakam as a meek safecracking expert. Terrific honkytonk score by a group called Bad Livers (!); if you stick it out, the end credits feature interview footage of the real Newton Boys that's more entertaining than anything that preceded it. Panavision. [PG-13] ▼●▶

New Waterford Girl (2000-Canadian) C-97m. **½ D: Allan Moyle. Liane Balaban, Tara Spencer-Nairn, Nicholas Campbell, Mary Walsh, Mark McKinney, Andrew McCarthy, Cathy Moriarty. Agreeable but uneven account of dreamy 15-year-old Mooney Pottie (Balaban), who has artistic aspirations and yearns for a life in Paris, New York, or Barcelona . . . all of which makes her an odd duck to the natives in her provincial Nova Scotia hometown. On the money when zeroing in on Mooney and her frustrations, but the scenario often meanders, and some of the comic moments fall flat. U.S. version runs 90m. ▼▶

New Wave SEE: **Nouvelle Vague**

New World, The (2005) C-149m. **½ D: Terrence Malick. Colin Farrell, Christopher Plummer, Q'Orianka Kilcher, Christian Bale, August Schellenberg, Wes Studi, David Thewlis, Yorick van Wageningen, Ben Mendelsohn, Raoul Trujillo, Brian F. O'Byrne, Irene Bedard, John Savage, Noah Taylor, Jonathan Pryce, Ben Chaplin, Eddie Marsan, Roger Rees. Ambitious film about the settlement of Jamestown, Virginia, in 1607 and how Captain John Smith's relationship with a local chief's favorite daughter, Pocahontas, changes the dynamics between the natives and the new arrivals from Britain. Writer-director Malick's third film in 30 years is exquisitely detailed, with a vivid sense of time and place and a wonderfully fresh performance by 15-year-old Kilcher as Pocahontas . . . but it's still a bit like watching paint dry. At least it's beautiful paint. James Horner makes great use of Wagner themes in his score. Cut to 135m. after its initial release; longer version runs 172m. Panavision. [PG-13]▶

New Year's Day (1989) C-89m. **½ D: Henry Jaglom. Henry Jaglom, Gwen Welles, Maggie Jakobson, Melanie Winter, David Duchovny, Milos Forman, Michael Emil, Tracy Reiner. Another personal, hit-and-miss film from Jaglom, who plays a writer attempting to reclaim the N.Y.C. apartment he's sublet to Jakobson, Winter, and Welles. Typically, there is much talk about relationships and sex (among other subjects); some of it illuminating, much of it pretentious.

Odd casting: filmmaker Forman as the apartment house janitor. [R] ▼▶

New York Confidential (1955) 87m. **½ D: Russell Rouse. Broderick Crawford, Richard Conte, Marilyn Maxwell, Anne Bancroft, J. Carrol Naish, Onslow Stevens, Barry Kelley, Mike Mazurki, Celia Lovsky. Supposed "inside" story of an N.Y.C. mob family, told in semi-documentary style, doesn't wear well. ▶

New York, I Love You (2009) C-104m. ** D: Jiang Wen, Mira Nair, Shunji Iwai, Yvan Attal, Brett Ratner, Allen Hughes, Shekhar Kapur, Natalie Portman, Fatih Akin, Joshua Marston, Randy Balsmeyer. Hayden Christensen, Andy Garcia, Rachel Bilson, Natalie Portman, Irrfan Khan, Orlando Bloom, Christina Ricci, Maggie Q, Ethan Hawke, Chris Cooper, Robin Wright Penn, Anton Yelchin, James Caan, Olivia Thirlby, Blake Lively, Drea de Matteo, Bradley Cooper, Julie Christie, John Hurt, Shia LaBeouf, Taylor Geare, Carlos Acosta, Jacinda Barrett, Ugur Yücel, Shu Qi, Burt Young, Eli Wallach, Cloris Leachman, Emilie Ohana, Eva Amurri, Justin Bartha. Lackluster follow-up to PARIS JE T'AIME offers a range of episodes set in N.Y.C., mostly dealing with chance encounters. Most of them are slight and boring; these vignettes about the city that never sleeps just may put you to sleep. The few noteworthy pieces include Ratner's clever take on a 17-year-old (Yelchin) and his unusual prom date (Thirlby) and Portman's touching snapshot of a little girl (Geare) and her devoted caregiver (Acosta). Writers include some of the directors plus Israel Horovitz and Anthony Minghella. Two additional segments, by Scarlett Johansson (featuring Kevin Bacon) and Andrey Zvyagintsev (featuring Nicholas Purcell, Carla Gugino, and Goran Visnjic), are DVD extras. [R]▶

New York Minute (2004) C-91m. **½ D: Dennie Gordon. Ashley Olsen, Mary-Kate Olsen, Eugene Levy, Andy Richter, Riley Smith, Jared Padalecki, Dr. Drew Pinsky, Darrell Hammond, Andrea Martin, Jack Osbourne. Twin sisters have grown apart—one's an uptight super-student, the other a class-cutting slob—but they come together during an adventurous day in N.Y.C. as a would-be spy attempts to kidnap one of them. You get pretty much what you'd expect from this innocuous Olsen vehicle; Levy plays an overzealous truant officer on the trail of his prize prey, Mary-Kate. [PG] ▼▶

New York New York (1977) C-164m. *½ D: Martin Scorsese. Robert De Niro, Liza Minnelli, Lionel Stander, Georgie Auld, Mary Kay Place, George Memmoli, Barry Primus, Dick Miller, Diahnne Abbott. Elaborate but off-putting musical drama loosely based on THE MAN I LOVE; saxophonist De Niro and vocalist Minnelli love and fight with each other right through the Big

Band era. Some people consider this film extraordinary, but we're not among them; kudos, though, to production designer Boris Leven, music arranger Ralph Burns, and the Kander-Ebb title song. Initially released at 153m., then cut to 137m., and finally reissued in 1981 at current length with splashy "Happy Endings" number (featuring Larry Kert) added. [PG] ▼●◗

New York Stories (1989) **C-123m. **½** D: Martin Scorsese, Francis Coppola, Woody Allen. Nick Nolte, Rosanna Arquette, Steve Buscemi, Peter Gabriel, Deborah Harry, Heather McComb, Talia Shire, Giancarlo Giannini, Don Novello, Chris Elliott, Carole Bouquet, Woody Allen, Mia Farrow, Mae Questel, Julie Kavner, Mayor Edward I. Koch; Adrien Brody, Illeana Douglas, Kirsten Dunst. Three-part anthology film: Scorsese's is an obvious, heavy-handed tale of a macho artist (Nolte) and his assistant/lover (Arquette) who wants to fly the coop. Coppola's is a cute but pointless variation on the old children's book *Eloise* about a little rich girl who lives in a N.Y.C. hotel while her parents globetrot. Finally, we get to the good stuff, with Allen in great form as a man literally haunted by his nagging mother (Questel, a howl). [PG] ▼●◗

Next (2007) **C-96m. **½** D: Lee Tamahori. Nicolas Cage, Julianne Moore, Jessica Biel, Thomas Kretschmann, Tory Kittles, Jose Zuniga, Jim Beaver, Jason Butler Harner, Michael Trucco, Peter Falk. Grade-B action film that somehow attracted A-list stars. Moore is an aggressive FBI agent pursuing a clairvoyant Vegas lounge magician who she is convinced is the only one who can foil a terrorist plot to nuke L.A. What, David Copperfield had another gig? Cage gamely plays this stuff with a straight face, while the normally reliable Moore looks decidedly uncomfortable. Based on the Philip K. Dick story "The Golden Man." HD Widescreen. [PG-13] ◗

Next Best Thing, The (2000) **C-108m.** BOMB D: John Schlesinger. Madonna, Rupert Everett, Benjamin Bratt, Michael Vartan, Josef Sommer, Lynn Redgrave, Malcolm Stumpf, Neil Patrick Harris, Illeana Douglas. Awful soap opera about yoga instructor having a child with her best friend, who's gay, which works fine until she falls in love with another man. Unconvincing, even condescending at times, despite its self-satisfied script. Everett keeps telling Madonna how beautiful she is, but it takes late '40s-style Joan Crawford lighting to try to put that over. Super 35. [PG-13] ▼●◗

Next Day Air (2009) **C-84m. **½** D: Benny Boom. Donald Faison, Mike Epps, Wood Harris, Omari Hardwick, Emilio Rivera, Darius McCrary, Cisco Reyes, Yasmin Deliz, Mos Def, Debbie Allen, Lobo Sebastian, Malik Barnhardt. When delivery man Faison, perpetually high on weed, unwittingly delivers a large box full of cocaine to the wrong apartment, two inept criminals decide to cash in on this surprise gift while the intended recipient and his girlfriend frantically try to track it down. Farcical premise works in spite of director Boom's efforts to insert pointless violence via quick flashbacks that are jarringly out of place. A game cast keeps it watchable. [R] ◗

Next Friday (2000) **C-92m. *½** D: Steve Carr. Ice Cube, Mike Epps, Justin Pierce, John Witherspoon, Don "D.C." Curry, Jacob Vargas, Lobo Sebastian, Rolando Molina, Lisa Rodriguez, Tommy "Tiny" Lister, Jr. Slacker/stoner (Cube) finds that his problems are just beginning when, to escape the wrath of bully Lister, he is dispatched from the 'hood to his uncle and cousin in the 'burbs. Shrill, stupid sequel to FRIDAY is a sloppy pastiche of crude comic skits filled with lame stereotypes. Cube also scripted. Followed by FRIDAY AFTER NEXT. [R] ▼●◗

Next Karate Kid, The (1994) **C-104m. ** D: Christopher Cain. Noriyuki "Pat" Morita, Hilary Swank, Michael Ironside, Constance Towers, Chris Conrad. Harmless, formulaic KARATE KID sequel (fourth in the series) with a twist: the "kid" is now a girl (Swank), an alienated teen who is taught self-esteem and martial arts by the benevolent Mr. Miyagi (Morita). [PG] ▼●◗

Next Man, The (1976) **C-108m. *** D: Richard C. Sarafian. Sean Connery, Cornelia Sharpe, Albert Paulsen, Adolfo Celi, Charles Cioffi. Good melodrama in which scenery (N.Y.C., Bavaria, London, Morocco, etc.) and violence are blended to tell of international hit lady Sharpe falling in love with Saudi Arabian ambassador Connery as he tries to arrange peace with Palestine. Video titles: DOUBLE HIT and THE ARAB CONSPIRACY. [R] ▼◗

Next of Kin (1989) **C-108m. *½** D: John Irvin. Patrick Swayze, Liam Neeson, Adam Baldwin, Helen Hunt, Andreas Katsulas, Bill Paxton, Ben Stiller, Michael J. Pollard. Chicago cop Swayze, of Appalachian descent, takes on Mr. Mob with the help of backwoods brother Neeson. High-concept, low-rent star vehicle. Would *you* stay in a hotel managed by Pollard? [R] ▼●◗

Next One, The (1984) **C-105m. ** D: Nico Mastorakis. Keir Dullea, Adrienne Barbeau, Jeremy Licht, Peter Hobbs. Dullea, a Christ-like visitor from the future, washes up on a Greek island where widow Barbeau, living with her young son, falls in love with him. Mediocre sci-fi strains for significance. Filmed in 1981. Aka THE TIME TRAVELLER. ▼◗

Next Stop, Greenwich Village (1976) **C-109m. *** D: Paul Mazursky. Lenny Baker, Shelley Winters, Ellen Greene, Christopher Walken, Lou Jacobi, Mike Kellin, Lois Smith, Dori Brenner, Antonio Fargas, Jeff Goldblum. Comic, poignant film about

Brooklyn boy Baker who moves to Greenwich Village in 1953 hoping to become an actor. Wonderful period atmosphere and characterizations; Winters is excellent as Baker's domineering mother. Look fast for Bill Murray in a bar. Semiautobiographical script by Mazursky. [R]▼▷

Next Stop Wonderland (1998) **C-96m.** *** D: Brad Anderson. Hope Davis, Alan Gelfant, Holland Taylor, Jose Zuniga, Phil (Philip Seymour) Hoffman, Robert Klein, Roger Rees. Unabashedly old-fashioned romantic comedy about a recently jilted nurse (Davis) whose love life takes a new turn when her meddling mother (Taylor, fun as ever) secretly places a personals ad for her. Somewhere amidst a sea of overeager bachelors is her Mr. Right (Gelfant), but their lives seem to intersect without so much as a meeting. Indie spin on SLEEPLESS IN SEATTLE has silly subplots but is bolstered by a wintry Boston locale, charm to spare, and a wonderfully bittersweet performance from Davis. [R]▼▷●

Next Three Days, The (2010-U.S.-French) **C-133m.** **½ D: Paul Haggis. Russell Crowe, Elizabeth Banks, Brian Dennehy, Liam Neeson, Lennie James, Olivia Wilde, Ty Simpkins, Daniel Stern, Helen Carey, Kevin Corrigan, RZA, Jason Beghe, Aisha Hines. College professor (Crowe) teaches himself how to pull off a prison break—mostly by surfing the Internet and interviewing a notorious ex-con (Neeson, in a striking cameo)—in order to free his increasingly distraught wife (Banks) three years after she's convicted of killing her boss. Generally well-acted thriller occasionally strains credibility and fails to fully exploit some intriguing plot elements. But writer-director Haggis often generates suspense and offers an exciting high-speed getaway in his Americanized remake of the 2008 French thriller POUR ELLE. Super 35. [PG-13]▷

Next Voice You Hear . . . , The (1950) **83m.** **½ D: William Wellman. James Whitmore, Nancy Davis (Reagan), Lillian Bronson, Jeff Corey, Gary Gray. The voice of God is heard nightly on the radio (but not by the audience) and has a profound impact on average American Whitmore, his wife and son. Ambitious if not terribly successful message film produced by Dore Schary. ▼▷

Niagara (1953) **C-89m.** *** D: Henry Hathaway. Marilyn Monroe, Joseph Cotten, Jean Peters, Casey Adams (Max Showalter), Don Wilson, Richard Allan. Black murder tale of couple staying at Niagara Falls, the wife planning to kill husband. Produced and cowritten by Charles Brackett; good location work. ▼▷●

Niagara, Niagara (1998) **C-96m.** *½ D: Bob Gosse. Robin Tunney, Henry Thomas, Michael Parks, Stephen Lang, John MacKay. A teenage girl with Tourette Syndrome meets her soulmate while they're both shoplifting. Any film that launches a "romance" on that note provides ample warning for viewers who dare to continue. Tunney is unflinching in her performance as the gratingly foul-mouthed girl in this notably unpleasant film that adds a novel spin to lovers-on-the-lam cinema. [R] ▼

Nice Girl Like Me, A (1969-British) **C-91m.** ** D: Desmond Davis. Barbara Ferris, Harry Andrews, Gladys Cooper, Bill Hinnant, James Villiers. Orphaned Ferris accidentally becomes impregnated twice by different men, is looked after by caretaker Andrews, whom she really loves. Appealing, silly and predictable. [M/PG]▼

Nice Girls Don't Explode (1987) **C-92m.** ** D: Chuck Martinez. Barbara Harris, Michelle Meyrink, William O'Leary, Wallace Shawn, James Nardini. Silly comedy (with a memorable title) about a girl who causes things to explode, especially when she gets amorous. Harris and Meyrink, as mother and daughter who share this curse, give it their best, but the sparks don't ignite. [PG]▼●

Nice Little Bank That Should Be Robbed, A (1958) **87m.** ** D: Henry Levin. Tom Ewell, Mickey Rooney, Mickey Shaughnessy, Dina Merrill. Cast is game, but story is pure cornball about goofy crooks using their gains to buy a racehorse. CinemaScope.

Nicholas and Alexandra (1971-British) **C-183m.** **½ D: Franklin Schaffner. Michael Jayston, Janet Suzman, Tom Baker, Harry Andrews, Jack Hawkins, Laurence Olivier, Michael Redgrave, Alexander Knox, Curt Jurgens, Irene Worth, John Wood, Brian Cox, Ian Holm. Lavishly filmed (with Oscar-winning art direction-set decoration and costumes), well-acted chronicle of Russian leaders, and revolution that turned their world upside down. Sure and steady, but eventually tedious, despite cameos by Olivier et al. Panavision. [PG]▼▷●

Nicholas Nickleby (1947-British) **108m.** *** D: Alberto Cavalcanti. Derek Bond, Cedric Hardwicke, Alfred Drayton, Bernard Miles, Sally Ann Howes, Mary Merrall, Sybil Thorndike, Cathleen Nesbitt. Dickens's classic tale of young man's struggle to protect his family from scheming uncle and a cruel world is vividly brought to life. Can't compare with the Royal Shakespeare Company's 8½-hour stage version—but still quite good. Some American prints run 95m. ▼

Nicholas Nickleby (2002) **C-132m.** *** D: Douglas McGrath. Charlie Hunnam, Jamie Bell, Christopher Plummer, Jim Broadbent, Romola Garai, Tom Courtenay, Stella Gonet, Timothy Spall, Anne Hathaway, Juliet Stevenson, Nathan Lane, Barry Humphries, Alan Cumming, Edward Fox, Sophie Thompson. Dickens' colorful story of a young man trying to make his way after the death of his father is good, old-fashioned entertainment, with Hunnam an appealing hero, Bell a poignant sidekick, Plummer an unrepentant villain (Nicholas' heartless uncle), and the best character actors in England filling other key roles. Most inspired casting: American Lane and Dame Edna (Humphries) as the kindhearted owners of a traveling theater troupe. Super 35. [PG]▼▶

Nick & Norah's Infinite Playlist (2008) C-90m. **½ D: Peter Sollett. Michael Cera, Kat Dennings, Aaron Yoo, Rafi Gavron, Ari Graynor, Alexis Dziena, Zachary Booth, Jay Baruchel, Seth Meyers, Kevin Corrigan, John Cho, Eddie Kaye Thomas, Frankie Faison, Devendra Banhart. Heartsick N.J. high schooler Cera still carries a torch for Dziena but can't pretend he isn't attracted to Dennings, whom he chances to meet during a night on the town in N.Y.C. Alternates between sweet, sincere moments and self-conscious artificiality; at its best capturing the atmosphere of the City at night. Aimed squarely at a teenage audience. Based on a novel by Rachel Cohn and David Levithan. [PG-13]▶

Nick Carter series SEE: *Leonard Maltin's Classic Movie Guide*

Nickel Mountain (1985) C-88m. **½ D: Drew Denbaum. Michael Cole, Heather Langenkamp, Patrick Cassidy, Brian Kerwin, Grace Zabriskie, Don Beddoe, Ed Lauter. Warm drama of unwed teenage mother growing up in rural America, befriended by pathetic older man. Winning performance by Langenkamp. Adapted from John Gardner's novel; filmed in 1983.▼

Nickelodeon (1976) C-121m. *** D: Peter Bogdanovich. Ryan O'Neal, Burt Reynolds, Tatum O'Neal, Brian Keith, Stella Stevens, John Ritter, Jane Hitchcock, Harry Carey, Jr. Heartfelt valentine to early days of moviemaking, with O'Neal literally stumbling into his job as director, Reynolds an overnight screen hero. Based on reminiscences of such veterans as Raoul Walsh and Allan Dwan, film unfortunately loses steam halfway through. Entertaining on the whole, sparked by fine cast; script by Bogdanovich and W. D. Richter. Director's version runs 5m. longer in b&w. [PG]▶

Nickel Ride, The (1975) C-99m. ** D: Robert Mulligan. Jason Miller, Linda Haynes, Victor French, John Hillerman, Bo Hopkins. Uneven and generally obscure little drama about a syndicate contact man (Miller) who keeps keys to L.A. warehouses used by dealers in stolen goods. Panavision. [PG]

Nick of Time (1995) C-89m. **½ D: John Badham. Johnny Depp, Christopher Walken, Charles S. Dutton, Courtney Chase, Marsha Mason, Roma Maffia, Peter Strauss, Gloria Reuben, Bill Smitrovich, G. D. Spradlin. Businessman arrives in L.A. with his young daughter and within moments, she's taken hostage while he's instructed to commit murder! Watchable suspense yarn draws you in, but hurls credibility roadblocks in your path at every turn. A game cast gives it 100 percent. Attempt to create heightened suspense by playing out the story in "real time" (with endless closeups of clocks) doesn't pay off at all. [R]▼▶

Nico-Icon (1995-German) C/B&W-67m. *** D: Susanne Ofteringer. Fascinating documentary about a compelling, sadly tragic subject: Christa Päffgen, the beautiful but self-destructive German-born model and singer who re-created herself as Nico, one of Andy Warhol's "Superstars." Nico was no candidate for Mother-of-the-Year: she was a heroin addict who initiated her own son into using the drug! Warhol's interview, along with one of Nico filmed two years before her death in 1988, are among the highpoints. Lou Reed, Jackson Browne, and Paul Morrissey are among those seen on-camera in this trenchant documentary. ▼▶

Nicotina (2003-Mexican) C-93m. ** D: Hugo Rodríguez. Diego Luna, Marta Belaústegui, Lucas Crespi, Jesús Ochoa, Rafael Inclán, Rosa María Bianchi, Daniel Giménez Cacho, Carmen Madrid. So-so crime caper/black comedy finds nerdy guy involved with Russian mobsters after he mistakenly delivers the wrong computer disk, throwing several characters' lives into turmoil. Gimmicky movie shot (mostly) in real time also deals with every aspect of cigarette addiction imaginable. Unfortunately nothing else about this film could be described as smokin'. [R]▶

Night, The SEE: **La Notte**

Night and Day (1946) C-128m. ** D: Michael Curtiz. Cary Grant, Alexis Smith, Monty Woolley, Ginny Simms, Jane Wyman, Eve Arden, Mary Martin, Victor Francen, Alan Hale, Dorothy Malone. Music only worthy aspect of fabricated biography of songwriter Cole Porter, stiffly played by Grant, who even sings "You're The Top." Martin re-creates "My Heart Belongs to Daddy" in film's highlight. Look fast for Mel Tormé as a drummer. An altogether different perspective on Porter may be found in DE-LOVELY. ▼▶

Night and the City (1950) 101m. **½ D: Jules Dassin. Richard Widmark, Gene Tierney, Googie Withers, Hugh Marlowe, Francis L. Sullivan, Herbert Lom, Mike Mazurki, Kay Kendall. Interesting film noir portrait of assorted losers in the netherworld of London, focusing on a young American hustler (Widmark) who's desperate to succeed. Marvelous showcase for Sullivan as an oily nightclub owner. Filmed in England. Remade in 1992.▼▶

Night and the City (1992) C-98m. **½ D: Irwin Winkler. Robert De Niro, Jessica Lange, Cliff Gorman, Alan King, Jack Warden, Eli

Wallach, Barry Primus, Gene Kirkwood, Pedro Sanchez. De Niro is dynamic as always, playing a hustler who tries promoting a boxing match—setting himself up for personal and professional disaster at every turn. Colorful N.Y.C. ambience and solid cast combat the utter predictability of the story. Screenplay by Richard Price (who also plays a doctor), based on the 1950 film and its source novel by Gerald Kersh. [R]▼●

Night at the Golden Eagle (2002) C-87m. *½ D: Adam Rifkin. Donnie Montemarano, Vinny Argiro, Natasha Lyonne, Ann Magnuson, Vinnie Jones, Fayard Nicholas, Sam Moore, Kitten Natividad. Grim, distasteful melodrama set at an L.A. skid-row hotel, mostly during one hot night. Despite some good performances, the film is unconvincing and uninvolving. Stylized cinematography features coarse, solarized color. James Caan appears unbilled. Super 35. [R]▼▶

Night at the Museum (2006) C-108m. *** D: Shawn Levy. Ben Stiller, Carla Gugino, Dick Van Dyke, Mickey Rooney, Bill Cobbs, Jake Cherry, Ricky Gervais, Robin Williams, Steve Coogan, Kim Raver, Patrick Gallagher, Paul Rudd. Divorced dad (and perpetual screwup) Stiller can't afford to disappoint his son again. Desperate for a job, he tries out as night watchman at Manhattan's Museum of Natural History, unaware that the exhibits come to life every night and cause all sorts of havoc. Engaging fantasy for kids, based on Milan Trenc's book, artfully employs an arsenal of special effects; the imaginative story just happens to involve famous figures in world history. Stiller has a funny scene with a woman at an employment agency—nicely played by his mom, Anne Meara. Owen Wilson appears unbilled. Followed by a sequel. Super 35. [PG]▶

Night at the Museum: Battle of the Smithsonian (2009) C-104m. ** D: Shawn Levy. Ben Stiller, Amy Adams, Owen Wilson, Hank Azaria, Robin Williams, Christopher Guest, Alain Chabat, Ricky Gervais, Steve Coogan, Bill Hader, Jon Bernthal, Jay Baruchel, Craig Robinson, Clint Howard. With a setup that makes the word "contrived" seem mild, onetime security guard Stiller—now inexplicably a TV inventor/pitchman—comes to the rescue of his old friends, the exhibits at the Museum of Natural History, when they're shipped to cold storage underneath the Smithsonian in Washington, D.C. Hilarity ensues (it says here). Lazy writing and silly, self-indulgent ideas fill this moneyed sequel—but if you're under 10 years old it will probably play just fine. There are some funny moments, and Azaria is a hoot as the Pharaoh who sounds like movies' original Im-ho-tep. Jonah Hill appears unbilled along with surprise guests. Super 35. [PG]▶

Night at the Opera, A (1935) 92m. **** D: Sam Wood. Groucho, Chico, Harpo Marx, Kitty Carlisle, Allan Jones, Walter Woolf King, Margaret Dumont, Sigfried Rumann. The Marx Brothers invade the world of opera with devastating results. Arguably their finest film (a close race with DUCK SOUP), with tuneful music and appealing romance neatly interwoven. One priceless comedy bit follows another: the stateroom scene, the Party of the First Part contract, etc. This is as good as it gets.▼●▶

Night at the Roxbury, A (1998) C-82m. *½ D: John Fortenberry. Will Ferrell, Chris Kattan, Molly Shannon, Dan Hedaya, Loni Anderson, Elisa Donovan, Gigi Rice, Richard Grieco, Dwayne Hickman, Colin Quinn, Michael Clarke Duncan. The uncool Butabi Brothers from *Saturday Night Live* get (rather than rate) their feature film debut: a limp comedy about their attempt to wile themselves into the town's trendiest nightspot. Talk about the last days of disco; five minutes of material gets stretched into nearly an hour and a half. The two stars also scripted. Chazz Palminteri has a cameo. Grieco completists should be aware that he plays himself. [PG-13]▼●▶

Night Before, The (1988) C-85m. ** D: Thom Eberhardt. Keanu Reeves, Lori Loughlin, Theresa Saldana, Trinidad Silva, Suzanne Snyder, Morgan Lofting, Gwil Richards, Michael Greene. Mild (and all-too-familiar) comic misadventures, as a high-school nerd tries to remember what happened to him the previous night on the way to the prom. [PG-13]▼▶

Nightbreed (1990-U.S.-Canadian) C-99m. **½ D: Clive Barker. Craig Sheffer, Anne Bobby, David Cronenberg, Charles Haid, Hugh Quarshie, Hugh Ross, Doug Bradley, Catherine Chevalier, Bob Sessions, Malcolm Smith, Oliver Parker, John Agar. Mistaken for a serial killer, Sheffer is killed at the gates of mysterious Midian, "where the monsters go." He returns from the dead to join the monsters there, confusing girlfriend Bobby and enticing his psychiatrist Cronenberg, the real killer. Intelligent, imaginative horror epic, but as adapted by Barker from his novel *Cabal*, the complicated film never becomes fully involving. Eye-popping apocalyptic climax. [R]▼●▶

Night Caller (1975-French-Italian) C-91m. ** D: Henri Verneuil. Jean-Paul Belmondo, Charles Denner, Adalberto-Maria Meril, Lea Massari, Rosy Varte. Detective Belmondo tackles both a bank robbery case and an obscene phone caller who murders women at the end of the line. Action but little else. [R]

Night Call Nurses (1972) C-85m. ** D: Jonathan Kaplan. Patti Byrne, Alana Collins, Mittie Lawrence, Dick Miller, Dennis Dugan, Stack Pierce. Kaplan's feature debut is typical drive-in sex comedy; light-hearted and fast-paced, with good comic performances by Dugan and the ubiquitous Miller. Third in Roger Corman-produced series; followed by THE YOUNG NURSES. [R]▼●

Nightcap SEE: **Merci Pour le Chocolat**

Night Catches Us (2010) **C-90m.** ★★★ D: Tanya Hamilton. Kerry Washington, Anthony Mackie, Jamie Hector, Wendell Pierce, Ron Simons, Kevin C. Walls, Tariq Trotter. With racial tensions still flaring in 1976 Philadelphia, drifter Mackie returns home, under a mysterious cloud, into the remnants of wounding Black Panther personal history. The same thoughts weigh as heavily upon the lawyer for whom he harbors deeps feelings (Washington). Subject matter portends a melodrama, and we're shown here and there that Mackie's character does know how to handle himself in barroom altercations, and with Washington's punk cousin. Overall treatment, however, is uncommonly contemplative, a movie whose characterizations and evocative use of neighborhood locations sneak up on you. Written by first-time director Hamilton. [R]▶

Nightcomers, The (1972-British) **C-96m.** ★★ D: Michael Winner. Marlon Brando, Stephanie Beacham, Thora Hird, Harry Andrews, Verna Harvey, Christopher Ellis, Anna Palk. Poor direction hurts attempt to chronicle what happened to the children in Henry James' *Turn of the Screw* before original story began. [R]▼●❶

Night Creature (1978) **C-83m.** BOMB D: Lee Madden. Donald Pleasence, Nancy Kwan, Ross Hagen, Lesly Fine, Jennifer Rhodes. Macho writer Pleasence lives on Xanadu-like island retreat near Thailand, but a prowling leopard is giving him the jitters. Low-grade thriller, minus the thrills. Aka OUT OF THE DARKNESS. [PG]▼●

Night Crossing (1981-British) **C-106m.** ★★½ D: Delbert Mann. John Hurt, Jane Alexander, Glynnis O'Connor, Doug McKeon, Beau Bridges, Ian Bannen, Klaus Lowitsch, Kay Walsh. Unexceptional though well-cast and not unexciting tale of two families' escape from East Berlin via hot-air balloon. A Walt Disney production, based on a true story. [PG]▼●

Night Digger, The (1971-British) **C-100m.** ★★★ D: Alastair Reid. Patricia Neal, Pamela Brown, Nicholas Clay, Jean Anderson, Graham Crowden, Yootha Joyce. Odd, usually effective psychological thriller adapted from Joy Cowley novel by Roald Dahl. With the unexpected arrival of young handyman, sad relationship between two country women takes turn for the better, until they discover what he does on off-hours. Excellent performances, fine Bernard Herrmann score. Aka THE ROAD BUILDER. [R]❶

Night Evelyn Came Out of the Grave, The (1971-Italian) **C-90m.** ★½ D: Emilio Miraglia. Anthony Steffen, Marina Malfatti, Rod Murdock, Giacomo Rossi-Stuart, Umberto Raho. Dreadful horror whodunit about British lord released from psychiatric clinic following wife's death, who begins to suspect she is still alive when her crypt is discovered empty. Techniscope. [R]▼●

Nightfall (1957) **78m.** ★★★ D: Jacques Tourneur. Aldo Ray, Brian Keith, Anne Bancroft, Jocelyn Brando, James Gregory, Frank Albertson, Rudy Bond. Ray plays an innocent man who's being hunted by an insurance investigator and two deadly holdup men who think he has their money. Rock-solid cast in a taut thriller written by Stirling Silliphant, from a novel by David Goodis. Great location work in Los Angeles and snowy Utah by cinematographer Burnett Guffey. ▼●

Nightfall (1988) **C-82m.** BOMB D: Paul Mayersberg. David Birney, Sarah Douglas, Alexis Kanner, Andra Millian, Charles Hayward, Susie Lindeman, Starr Andreeff. Hopelessly muddled adaptation of Isaac Asimov's classic short story about an alien world in a three-star solar system whose inhabitants face the coming darkness of nightfall (occurring only once every 1000 years) with abject terror. Birney is miscast in this cheesy production. Remade in 2000 as ISAAC ASIMOV'S NIGHTFALL. [PG-13]▼

Night Falls on Manhattan (1997) **C-113m.** ★★½ D: Sidney Lumet. Andy Garcia, Richard Dreyfuss, Lena Olin, Ian Holm, Ron Leibman, James Gandolfini, Colm Feore, Shiek Mahmud-Bey, Paul Guilfoyle. Cop turned lawyer joins the D.A.'s staff in N.Y.C. and rises to the top by prosecuting a headline-making case in which his father, a veteran detective, was shot. Then he has to deal with the stickier issue of police corruption, which hits awfully close to home. Intense and watchable saga (adapted by Lumet from Robert Daley's novel *Tainted Evidence*) suffers from one major flaw: its central character's naïveté. He's constantly shocked by what we in the audience already know—or have guessed. Leibman is dynamite as the bombastic D.A. [R]▼●

Night Flier, The (1998) **C-99m.** ★★½ D: Mark Pavia. Miguel Ferrer, Julie Entwisle, Dan Monahan, Merton H. Moss. Black-hearted tabloid reporter meets his match when he tracks a mysterious bloodsucking serial killer who flies a black Cessna plane from crime scene to crime scene. Genuinely creepy mood is bolstered by Ferrer's enjoyably hissable heavy. Not-bad directorial debut for Pavia until the film's final third, which descends into typical gorefest shtick. Originally shown on cable, then released in theaters. Aka STEPHEN KING'S THE NIGHT FLIER. [R]▼●

Night Flight From Moscow (1973-French-Italian-West German) **C-113m.** ★★½ D: Henri Verneuil. Yul Brynner, Henry Fonda, Dirk Bogarde, Philippe Noiret, Virna Lisi, Farley Granger, Robert Alda, Marie Dubois, Elga Andersen. Espionage thriller about the defection of Russian diplomat Brynner is compromised by the middling screenplay adapted from Pierre Nord's cloak-and-dagger novel *Le 13e Suicide*. Originally titled THE SERPENT. Panavision. [PG]▼❶

Nightforce (1987) **C-82m.** *½ D: Lawrence D. Foldes. Linda Blair, James Van Patten, Richard Lynch, Chad McQueen, Dean R. Miller, James Marcel, Claudia Udy, Bruce Fisher, Cameron Mitchell. Cornball action film has Blair and fellow youngsters organizing a commando mission to Central America to free a kidnapped daughter of a U. S. senator. [R]▼

Night Full of Rain, A (1978-Italian) **C-104m.** ** D: Lina Wertmuller. Giancarlo Giannini, Candice Bergen, Allison Tucker, Jill Eikenberry, Michael Tucker, Anne Byrne. Wertmuller's first English language effort (shot in Rome and San Francisco) is unsatisfying fantasy drama about relationship between journalist Giannini and feminist wife Bergen, who's quite good. Full title: THE END OF THE WORLD IN OUR USUAL BED IN A NIGHT FULL OF RAIN. [R]▼❶

Night Game (1989) **C-95m.** *½ D: Peter Masterson. Roy Scheider, Karen Young, Richard Bradford, Paul Gleason, Carlin Glynn. Texas police detective goes after a serial killer. What a shame to find good actors and a talented director wasting their time with such third-rate material. [R]▼●

Night Games (1980) **C-100m.** *½ D: Roger Vadim. Cindy Pickett, Joanna Cassidy, Barry Primus, Paul Jenkins, Gene Davis. Frigid housewife will make it only with guy who shows up at night in a bird suit. Vadim may be kidding, but it's tough to tell. [R]▼

Night Has a Thousand Eyes (1948) **80m.** **½ D: John Farrow. Edward G. Robinson, Gail Russell, John Lund, Virginia Bruce, William Demarest. Intriguing story of magician who has uncanny power to predict the future; script is corny at times. Based on a story by Cornell Woolrich.

Nighthawks (1981) **C-99m.** *** D: Bruce Malmuth. Sylvester Stallone, Billy Dee Williams, Lindsay Wagner, Persis Khambatta, Nigel Davenport, Rutger Hauer, Joe Spinell, Catherine Mary Stewart. Exciting story of two N.Y.C. street cops reassigned to special unit that's tracking a ruthless international terrorist (Hauer). On target from the first scene to the fade-out, with plenty of hair-raising moments along the way. [R]▼●❶

Night in Casablanca, A (1946) **85m.** *** D: Archie Mayo. Groucho, Harpo, Chico Marx, Lisette Verea, Charles Drake, Lois Collier, Dan Seymour, Sig Ruman. No classic, but many funny sequences in latter-day Marx outing, ferreting out Nazi spies in Casablanca hotel.▼❶

Nightingale Sang in Berkeley Square, A (1979) **C-102m.** **½ D: Ralph Thomas. Richard Jordan, David Niven, Oliver To-

bias, Elke Sommer, Gloria Grahame, Hugh Griffith, Richard Johnson. American ex-con Jordan, released from a British prison, is coerced into taking part in an elaborate bank heist masterminded by Niven. Grahame, seen briefly as Jordan's brassy mom, is a joy to watch in one of her last roles. Video titles: THE BIG SCAM and THE MAYFAIR BANK CAPER.▼❶

Night in Heaven, A (1983) **C-80m.** ** D: John G. Avildsen. Lesley Ann Warren, Christopher Atkins, Robert Logan, Carrie Snodgress, Deborah Rush, Sandra Beall, Alix Elias, Denny Terrio, Andy Garcia. Teacher Warren lets her friends drag her to a male strip joint, where the star attraction (Atkins) is a student she's flunking. Off-beat romantic drama penned by Joan Tewkesbury had real possibilities, but many of them were apparently left on the cutting room floor (note brief running time). Still worth a peek for fine performance by Warren. [R]▼❶

Night in the Life of Jimmy Reardon, A (1988) **C-90m.** **½ D: William Richert. River Phoenix, Ann Magnuson, Meredith Salenger, Ione Skye, Louanne, Matthew L. Perry. Richert's film of his own youthful novel (*Aren't You Even Gonna Kiss Me Goodbye?*) doesn't work overall . . . but it has something. Phoenix is a high school Romeo preparing for a fall from grace when his more affluent friends prepare to leave for ritzier colleges; Magnuson's cameo (as an amorous family friend) is a standout, but other performances fall short. Handsomely photographed by John Connor. [R]▼●❶

Night Is My Future (1948-Swedish) **87m.** **½ D: Ingmar Bergman. Mai Zetterling, Birger Malmsten, Olof Winnerstrand, Naima Wifstrand, Hilda Borgstrom. Somber, brooding tale of young Malmsten, blinded while in military service; he struggles for self-respect, and is befriended by housemaid Zetterling. Early, minor Bergman. Aka MUSIC IN DARKNESS. ▼

Night is the Phantom SEE: **Whip and the Body, The**

Nightkill (1980-German) **C-97m.** **½ D: Ted Post. Jaclyn Smith, Mike Connors, James Franciscus, Robert Mitchum, Fritz Weaver, Sybil Danning. Confused suspense drama involving a love triangle that ends in murder and a cat-and-mouse game between a wealthy widow and a mysterious investigator. Filmed on location in Arizona by a German company. ▼

Night Listener, The (2006) **C-81m.** ** D: Patrick Stettner. Robin Williams, Toni Collette, Bobby Cannavale, Rory Culkin, Joe Morton, John Cullum, Sandra Oh, Becky Ann Baker. A radio host who spins stories drawn from his experiences responds to a young fan in a series of phone calls, but soon begins to suspect that something is not right with the boy and his overprotective mother. The nascent intrigue in this adaptation of Armistead Maupin's novel never bears fruit here; a gloomy, unsatisfying film that thwarts a talented cast. Maupin cowrote the film. [R]◗

Nightmare (1956) 89m. **½ D: Maxwell Shane. Edward G. Robinson, Kevin McCarthy, Connie Russell, Virginia Christine, Rhys Williams, Meade "Lux" Lewis, Billy May. Location filming in New Orleans is a major asset of this moody psychological drama about musician McCarthy, who has an all-too-real nightmare in which he commits murder. Robinson sparks the proceedings as a crafty homicide detective. Remake of FEAR IN THE NIGHT, based on a story by William Irish (Cornell Woolrich).

Nightmare Alley (1947) 111m. ***½ D: Edmund Goulding. Tyrone Power, Joan Blondell, Coleen Gray, Helen Walker, Taylor Holmes, Mike Mazurki, Ian Keith, Julia Dean. Morbid but fascinating story of carnival heel Power entangled with mind-reading Blondell, blackmailing psychiatrist Walker, other assorted sideshow weirdos in highly original melodrama. Compelling look at carny life. Jules Furthman scripted, from William Lindsay Gresham's novel.◗

Nightmare Before Christmas, The (1993) C-75m. *** D: Henry Selick. Voices of Danny Elfman, Chris Sarandon, Catherine O'Hara, William Hickey, Glenn Shadix, Paul Reubens, Ken Page. Highly imaginative, stop-motion animation feature about Jack Skellington, the Pumpkin King, who tires of the old routine in Halloween Town and becomes enamored of Christmas instead—unaware that his brand of Grand Guignol and the wintry holiday don't really go together. Constantly surprising visuals and character delineation mesh with Danny Elfman's lively score (he also provides Jack's beautiful singing voice). Produced by Tim Burton, who concocted the story and many of the designs years earlier. Converted to 3-D in 2006 reissue. [PG]▼◗

Nightmare in Blood (1976) C-89m. **½ D: John Stanley. Jerry Walter, Dan Caldwell, Barrie Youngfellow, Kathleen Quinlan, Kerwin Mathews. Horror film actor visiting fan convention turns out to be a real vampire after all; low-budget spoof made in San Francisco will appeal particularly to horror buffs for its many in-jokes. Techniscope. [R] ▼◗

Nightmare in Wax (1969) C-91m. ** D: Bud Townsend. Cameron Mitchell, Anne Helm, Scott Brady, Berry Kroeger, Victoria Carroll. Paraphrase of HOUSE OF WAX has Mitchell as former movie makeup man whose wax museum is full of actors "missing" from the studio. [M]▼◗

Nightmare of Terror SEE: **Demons of the Mind**

Nightmare on Elm Street, A (1984) C-92m. **½ D: Wes Craven. John Saxon,

Ronee Blakley, Heather Langenkamp, Amanda Wyss, Nick Corri, Johnny Depp, Charles Fleischer, Robert Englund. Several teenagers discover they're all having nightmares about the same character, scarfaced Fred Krueger—a kind of ghost who can enter their dreams at will, and kill them in macabre ways. It's up to surviving teen Nancy (Langenkamp) to try to stop him. Imaginative premise given routine treatment, but this box-office smash led to a handful of sequels and a TV series, *Freddy's Nightmares.* Remade in 2010. [R]▼◗

Nightmare on Elm Street, A (2010) C-95m. **½ D: Samuel Bayer. Jackie Earle Haley, Kyle Gallner, Rooney Mara, Katie Cassidy, Thomas Dekker, Kellan Lutz, Clancy Brown, Connie Britton. Surprisingly well-crafted remake of Wes Craven's seminal 1984 shocker about a scar-faced, razor-clawed bogeyman who haunts the dreams of suburban teens he intends to slay. Haley does a passable job of subbing for Robert Englund as Fred Krueger, the wisecracking, teen-shredding villain of the piece, and the scriptwriters add a few genuinely clever touches while updating the plot. Fans of the '84 version may be amused by several visual "quotes" from Craven's original. Panavision. [R]◗

Nightmare on Elm Street Part 2, A: Freddy's Revenge (1985) C-84m. ** D: Jack Sholder. Mark Patton, Kim Myers, Robert Rusler, Clu Gulager, Hope Lange, Marshall Bell, Sydney Walsh, Robert Englund. Reworking of first film's story (set five years later) has teenage boy plagued by dreams of demonic Freddy, who is intent on taking over both his mind *and* body . . . so he can kill all the neighborhood teens. Gruesome special effects dominate this slasher saga. [R]▼◗

Nightmare on Elm Street 3, A: Dream Warriors (1987) C-96m. *** D: Chuck Russell. Heather Langenkamp, Patricia Arquette, Larry Fishburne, Priscilla Pointer, Craig Wasson, Robert Englund, Brooke Bundy, Rodney Eastman, John Saxon, Dick Cavett, Zsa Zsa Gabor. When troubled teens in a psychiatric hospital begin to be visited in their dreams by the chuckling, murderous shade of Freddy Krueger, Nancy (Langenkamp), the survivor of the first film and now a psychiatrist, helps another doctor and the frightened teens battle Freddy. Well written and imaginatively directed, this is the best of the Elm Street films, and boasts some of the most startling effects as well. [R]▼◗

Nightmare on Elm Street 4, A: The Dream Master (1988) C-92m. ** D: Renny Harlin. Robert Englund, Rodney Eastman, Danny Hassel, Andras Jones, Tuesday Knight, Toy Newkirk, Ken Sagoes, Brooke Theiss, Lisa Wilcox, Brooke Bundy. Revived by flaming dog urine (!), Freddy Krueger finally kills all the children of those who originally burned him to death, and looks for new teens to terrorize, but he's opposed by a "dream master," his spiritual opposite. Series was showing its age by this point, with extravagant effects, a thin story, and far too many wisecracks. A 1989 sequel and TV series followed. [R] ▼○●

Nightmare on Elm Street, A: The Dream Child (1989) C-89m. *½ D: Stephen Hopkins. Robert Englund, Lisa Wilcox, Kelly Jo Minter, Erika Anderson, Whitby Hertford, Danny Hassel. Fifth in the NIGHTMARE series, with everyone except Englund just going through the paces. Here, scarred, dream-haunting Freddy Krueger (Englund) uses the unborn child of Wilcox to strike at her friends. As usual, special effects are a highlight but don't save the film from being a bore. Followed by FREDDY'S DEAD: THE FINAL NIGHTMARE. [R] ▼○●

Nightmares (1983) C-99m. ** D: Joseph Sargent. Cristina Raines, Timothy James, William Sanderson, Emilio Estevez, Moon Zappa, Lance Henriksen, Robin Gammell, Richard Masur, Veronica Cartwright, Bridgette Andersen, Albert Hague. Four-part film (originally made for TV) with *Twilight Zone* aspirations but uninspired writing, and mostly predictable outcomes. Hasn't anyone read O. Henry lately? Themes range from a knife-wielding loony on the loose to a kid who becomes obsessed with beating a video arcade game. [R] ▼▶

Nightmaster SEE: **Watch the Shadows Dance**

'Night, Mother (1986) C-96m. ** D: Tom Moore. Sissy Spacek, Anne Bancroft. Unhappy young woman who lives with her mother decides to commit suicide; her mother spends the night trying to talk her out of it. Well acted, directed, and edited, but still just a photographed stage drama, missing the electricity of a live performance . . . and without the element of doubt about its conclusion that marked Marsha Norman's Pulitzer Prize–winning play. [PG-13] ▼○●

Night Moves (1975) C-99m. ***½ D: Arthur Penn. Gene Hackman, Jennifer Warren, Susan Clark, Edward Binns, Harris Yulin, Kenneth Mars, James Woods, Melanie Griffith, Dennis Dugan, Max Gail. L.A. detective Hackman puts aside his marital woes to track nymphet Griffith to Florida Keys. Complicated but underrated psychological suspenser by Alan Sharp leads to stunning climax. [R] ▼○●

Night Must Fall (1937) 117m. *** D: Richard Thorpe. Robert Montgomery, Rosalind Russell, Dame May Whitty, Alan Marshal, Kathleen Harrison, E. E. Clive, Beryl Mercer. Famous film of Emlyn Williams' suspenseful play. Young woman (Russell) slowly learns identity of mysterious brutal killer terrorizing the countryside. Montgomery has showy role in sometimes stagy but generally effective film, with outstanding aid from Russell and Whitty.

Screenplay by John Van Druten. Remade in 1964. ▼▶

Night Must Fall (1964-British) 105m. **½ D: Karel Reisz. Albert Finney, Susan Hampshire, Mona Washbourne, Sheila Hancock, Michael Medwin, Joe Gladwin, Martin Wyldeck. Cerebral attempt to match flair of original, this remake is too obvious and theatrical for any credibility. Reisz and Finney produced.

Night My Number Came Up, The (1955-British) 94m. **** D: Leslie Norman. Michael Redgrave, Sheila Sim, Alexander Knox, Denholm Elliott, Ursula Jeans, Michael Hordern, George Rose, Alfie Bass. First-rate suspense film will have you holding your breath as it recounts tale of routine military flight, the fate of which may or may not depend on a prophetic dream. Screenplay by R. C. Sherriff, from an article by Victor Goddard.▼

Night Nurse (1931) 72m. *** D: William Wellman. Barbara Stanwyck, Ben Lyon, Joan Blondell, Clark Gable, Charlotte Merriam, Charles Winninger. Excellent, hardbitten tale of nurse (Stanwyck) who can't ignore strange goings-on in home where she works. Blondell adds zingy support; one of Gable's most impressive early appearances. Still potent today. ▼○●

Night of Dark Shadows (1971) C-97m. BOMB D: Dan Curtis. David Selby, Lara Parker, Kate Jackson, Grayson Hall, John Karlen, Nancy Barrett. Ripoff exploitation film bears little resemblance to popular TV serial in predictable yawner about ghosts and reincarnation in New England. Followup to HOUSE OF DARK SHADOWS lacks everything that made first one so good. [PG] ▼○

Night of Love, A SEE: **Manifesto**

Night of the Big Heat SEE: **Island of the Burning Doomed**

Night of the Blood Monster (1970-Spanish-Italian-West German) C-84m. *½ D: Jess Frank (Jesus Franco). Christopher Lee, Maria Schell, Leo Genn, Maria Rohm, Margaret Lee. Lee is fine as Judge Jeffreys, a brutal magistrate presiding over "Bloody Assizes" after the Monmouth Rebellion against King James II, but movie itself is tedious and grisly. Aka THE BLOODY JUDGE. CinemaScope. [PG]▶

Night of the Comet (1984) C-94m. **½ D: Thom Eberhardt. Catherine Mary Stewart, Kelli Maroney, Robert Beltran, Geoffrey Lewis, Mary Woronov, Sharon Farrell, Michael Bowen. World comes to an end, leaving only a couple of California valley girls behind! Smart satire, with clever and occasionally chilling moments, but plays all its cards too soon. [PG-13] ▼▶

Night of the Demon SEE: **Curse of the Demon**

Night of the Demons (1987) C-89m. *½ D: Kevin S. Tenney. Cathy Podewell, Alvin

Alexis, William Gallo, Mimi Kinkade, Linnea Quigley, Lance Fenton. On Halloween night, wouldn't you know it, some Typical Teenagers pick the wrong possessed mortuary to party in. Everything about this amateurish movie is gratuitous, including the movie itself. Good makeup, though . . . especially the prosthetics on Quigley! Aka HALLOWEEN PARTY. Followed by two sequels. Remade in 2010. [R]▼●❍

Night of the Eagle SEE: **Burn, Witch, Burn!**

Night of the Following Day, The (1969) **C-93m.** **½ D: Hubert Cornfield. Marlon Brando, Richard Boone, Rita Moreno, Pamela Franklin, Jess Hahn, Gerard Buhr. Good cast makes this sordid tale of young girl's kidnapping somewhat more interesting than it should be; pretty rough in spots. Filmed in France. [R]▼❍

Night of the Generals, The (1967-British) **C-148m.** *½ D: Anatole Litvak. Peter O'Toole, Omar Sharif, Tom Courtenay, Donald Pleasence, Joanna Pettet, Christopher Plummer, John Gregson, Philippe Noiret. A WW2 whodunit, film has potential but gets lost in murky script, lifeless performances. A dud. Panavision. ▼❍

Night of the Ghouls SEE: **Revenge of the Dead**

Night of the Grizzly, The (1966) **C-102m.** **½ D: Joseph Pevney. Clint Walker, Martha Hyer, Keenan Wynn, Nancy Kulp, Ron Ely, Regis Toomey, Jack Elam. Acceptable Western of rancher Walker overcoming all obstacles, even a persistent vicious bear, to Western life. Techniscope.▼

Night of the Hunter, The (1955) **93m.** ***½ D: Charles Laughton. Robert Mitchum, Shelley Winters, Lillian Gish, Evelyn Varden, Peter Graves, James Gleason, Billy Chapin, Sally Jane Bruce. Atmospheric allegory of innocence, evil, and hypocrisy, with psychotic religious fanatic Mitchum chasing homeless children for money stolen by their father. Mitchum is marvelously menacing, matched by Gish as wise matron who takes in the kids. Starkly directed by Laughton; his only film behind the camera. Screenplay credited to James Agee, from the Davis Grubb novel. Remade as a TVM in 1991 with Richard Chamberlain.▼❍

Night of the Iguana, The (1964) **118m.** *** D: John Huston. Richard Burton, Deborah Kerr, Ava Gardner, Sue Lyon, Skip Ward, Grayson Hall, Cyril Delevanti. Plodding tale based on Tennessee Williams play; alcoholic former clergyman Burton, a bus-tour guide in Mexico, is involved with Kerr, Gardner, and Lyon. Dorothy Jeakins won an Oscar for her costumes. Also shown in computer-colored version. ▼❍

Night of the Juggler (1980) **C-101m.** *½ D: Robert Butler. James Brolin, Cliff Gor-

man, Richard Castellano, Abby Bluestone, Linda G. Miller, Julie Carmen, Barton Heyman, Mandy Patinkin. A sickie mistakenly kidnaps the daughter of an ex-cop (Brolin), who then leads a city-wide rampage to get her back. Fast-paced but wildly implausible movie paints a notably ugly portrait of N.Y.C. and its people. [R]▼

Night of the Laughing Dead SEE: **Crazy House** (1973)

Night of the Lepus (1972) **C-88m.** *½ D: William F. Claxton. Stuart Whitman, Janet Leigh, Rory Calhoun, DeForest Kelley, Paul Fix, Melanie Fullerton. Rabbits weighing 150 pounds and standing four feet high terrorize the countryside; National Guard, not Elmer Fudd, comes to the rescue. [PG]❍

Night of the Living Dead (1968) **96m.** ***½ D: George A. Romero. Duane Jones, Judith O'Dea, Russell Streiner, Karl Hardman, Keith Wayne. Romero's first feature is the touchstone modern horror film: seven people barricade themselves inside a farmhouse while an army of flesh-eating zombies roams the countryside. Once considered the *ne plus ultra* of gore, film is less stomach-churning by today's standards, yet its essential power to chill remains undiminished despite scores of imitations. Shoestring production values merely add to authentic feel. Don't watch this alone! Remade in 1990 and 2006. Sequel: DAWN OF THE DEAD. Also shown in computer-colored version. Beware "30th Anniversary Edition" with new footage, dubbing, and music. ▼❍

Night of the Living Dead (1990) **C-96m.** ** D: Tom Savini. Tony Todd, Patricia Tallman, Tom Towles, McKee Anderson, William Butler, Katie Finnerman. Until near the end, this is a scene-for-scene remake of the disturbing original; it's in color, with a tougher heroine and more potent violence, but it has almost none of the impact of the first version. Makeup expert Savini's direction can't overcome the extreme familiarity of the material. Romero scripted, none too well. [R]▼❍

Night of the Living Dead 3D (2006) **C-80m.** BOMB D: Jeff Broadstreet. Brianna Brown, Joshua DesRoches, Johanna Black, Greg Travis, Ken Ward, Sid Haig. Pointless remake of the 1968 shocker that even 3-D couldn't salvage in its theatrical presentation. A brother and sister drive to a cemetery where their aunt is supposed to be buried; instead, they encounter a pack of flesh-eating zombies, and all hell breaks loose. Undernourished low-budget horror outing foolishly includes scenes of George Romero's original (seen on television), as if to underscore the gulf that separates the two films. [R]❍

Night of the Shooting Stars, The (1982-Italian) **C-106m.** ***½ D: Paolo and Vittorio Taviani. Omero Antonutti, Margarita Lozano, Claudio Bigagil, Massimo Bonetti, Norma Martel. Extraordinarily touching, involving, richly textured drama of a group of Tuscan villagers during WW2, in final days before liberation by Americans. With simple, lyrical images, the filmmakers unravel this life-affirming story of war's absurdities—and hope, survival. [R]▼●)

Night on Earth (1991) **C-128m.** ******* D: Jim Jarmusch. Winona Ryder, Gena Rowlands, Giancarlo Esposito, Armin Mueller-Stahl, Rosie Perez, Isaach De Bankolé, Beatrice Dalle, Roberto Benigni, Paolo Bonacelli, Matti Pellonpaa. Exhilirating five-part slice-of-life, each story unraveling at the same time in L.A., N.Y.C., Paris, Rome, and Helsinki. All are set in taxis, and spotlight brief but eloquent encounters between cab driver and passenger. The best of many highlights: the scene in which black Brooklynite Esposito and East German refugee Mueller-Stahl reveal to each other their names. [R]▼●)

Night Passage (1957) **C-90m.** ******* D: James Neilson. James Stewart, Audie Murphy, Dan Duryea, Brandon de Wilde, Dianne Foster. Sound Western of Stewart working for railroad, brother Murphy belonging to gang planning to rob train payroll; exciting climactic shoot-out. Technirama.)

Night Patrol (1985) **C-82m.** BOMB D: Jackie Kong. Linda Blair, Pat Paulsen, Jaye P. Morgan, Jack Riley, Billy Barty, Murray Langston, Pat Morita, Andrew (Dice) Clay. Threadbare rip-off of POLICE ACADEMY combines Barty's flatulence with crude one-liners. See if you can figure out why the opening sequence has subtitles. [R]▼●)

Night People (1954) **C-93m.** ******* D: Nunnally Johnson. Gregory Peck, Broderick Crawford, Anita Bjork, Rita Gam, Walter Abel, Buddy Ebsen, Max Showalter (Casey Adams), Jill Esmond, Peter Van Eyck. Keen Cold War time capsule, filmed on location in Berlin, finds intelligence officer Peck badgered by pushy fat-cat Crawford to somehow spring the latter's corpsman son, who's been kidnapped by Russians and whisked away into their German zone. In her one Hollywood movie Bjork (of MISS JULIE fame) is an East German spy with some personal history with Peck, whose casting here is tailor-made. Baseball fans may be tickled at the scene where Ebsen listens to a real Yankees broadcast of the era, announced by Mel Allen. CinemaScope.

Night Porter, The (1974-Italian) **C-115m.** ****** D: Liliana Cavani. Dirk Bogarde, Charlotte Rampling, Philippe Leroy, Gabriele Ferzetti, Isa Miranda. Sleazy, bizarre drama, set in 1957, about a sado-masochistic relationship between an ex-Nazi and the woman

he used to abuse sexually in a concentration camp. [R]▼●)

Night Shadows (1984) **C-99m.** ****** D: John (Bud) Cardos. Wings Hauser, Bo Hopkins, Lee Montgomery, Jennifer Warren, Jody Medford, Cary Guffey. Yet another tale of toxic waste creating monsters that terrorize small Southern town. Same old stuff, with inferior special effects and makeup. Aka MUTANT. [R]▼)

Night Shift (1982) **C-105m.** ******* D: Ron Howard. Henry Winkler, Michael Keaton, Shelley Long, Gina Hecht, Pat Corley, Bobby DiCicco, Nita Talbot, Richard Belzer, Charles Fleischer, Shannen Doherty. A nebbish takes a night job at the city morgue, seeking peace and quiet, but his new assistant draws him into wild scheme to start a prostitution business! Delightful, good-natured comedy (despite seamy subject matter) written with verve by Lowell Ganz and Babaloo Mandel. (Soundtrack features Rod Stewart singing "That's What Friends Are For," years before it became a hit.) Winkler has never been better; Keaton's smash debut performance made him an instant star. Is this a great country or what? Look for Kevin Costner as an extra. [R]▼●)

Nights in Rodanthe (2008) **C-96m.** ****½** D: George C. Wolfe. Richard Gere, Diane Lane, Scott Glenn, Christopher Meloni, Viola Davis, Mae Whitman. Busy mother of two, still smarting from her husband's infidelity, agrees to look after her best friend's seashore bed-and-breakfast inn in Rodanthe, on the outer banks of North Carolina. Her only guest is a handsome doctor who's come there to settle some unfinished business. Before long the man and woman—both in need of nurturing—fall in love. Utterly contrived setup for an agreeable-enough romantic drama adapted from Nicholas Sparks' novel. Gere and Lane are well matched. James Franco appears unbilled. Filmmaking debut for renowned theater director Wolfe. Super 35. [PG-13])

Nights of Cabiria (1957-Italian) **117m.** ******** D: Federico Fellini. Giulietta Masina, Francois Perier, Amedeo Nazzari, Franca Marzi, Dorian Gray. Masina is a joy as waifish prostitute dreaming of rich, wonderful life but always finding sorrow. Basis for Broadway musical and film SWEET CHARITY. One of Fellini's best, and a most deserving Oscar winner as Best Foreign Film. Restored in 1998 to put back a 7m. sequence Fellini was forced to cut after the premiere.▼)

Night Stalker, The (1987) **C-89m.** ****** D: Max Kleven. Charles Napier, Michelle Reese, Katherine Kelly Lang, Robert Viharo, Robert Zdar, Joey Gian, Leila Carlin, Gary Crosby, James Louis Watkins, Ola Ray, Tally Chanel, Joan Chen. Napier steps out impressively from supporting roles to star as a down and out L.A. cop who goes after a serial killer preying on prostitutes. Standard B movie was made in 1985. [R]▼)

Night Sun (1990-Italian-French-German) **C-112m.** *** D: Paolo and Vittorio Taviani. Julian Sands, Charlotte Gainsbourg, Nastassja Kinski, Massimo Bonetti, Margarita Lozano, Rudiger Vogler. Evocative film about an idealistic, sensitive young man (Sands), who wishes to find inner peace in a world of temptation. Based on the Tolstoi story "Father Sergius"; Sands' voice is dubbed into Italian by Giancarlo Giannini. Technovision.▼)

Night the Lights Went Out in Georgia, The (1981) **C-120m.** **½ D: Ronald F. Maxwell. Kristy McNichol, Mark Hamill, Dennis Quaid, Sunny Johnson, Don Stroud, Arlen Dean Snyder. Kristy, the more ambitious half of brother-sister country music duo, tries in vain to keep sibling Quaid out of romantic scrapes. Poor beginning and conclusion somewhat redeemed by rather appealing middle. Inspired by title-named hit record. [PG]▼

Night They Raided Minsky's, The (1968) **C-99m.** *** D: William Friedkin. Jason Robards, Britt Ekland, Norman Wisdom, Forrest Tucker, Harry Andrews, Joseph Wiseman, Denholm Elliott, Elliott Gould, Jack Burns, Bert Lahr; narrated by Rudy Vallee. Flavorful period-piece about Amish girl (Ekland) who comes to N.Y.C., gets involved with burlesque comic Robards and accidentally invents the striptease. Many nice backstage and onstage moments. Abruptness of Lahr's role is due to his death during filming. Produced and cowritten by Norman Lear. [M/PG]▼)

Night Tide (1963) **84m.** **½ D: Curtis Harrington. Dennis Hopper, Linda Lawson, Gavin Muir, Luana Anders, Marjorie Eaton, Tom Dillon, H. E. West, Cameron. Lonely sailor Hopper falls for Lawson, who works as a mermaid at the Santa Monica pier, but learns she may be a killer—and a descendant of the sirens. Odd, dreamy little drama is strangely compelling, though not a horror film, as often promoted. Written by the director.▼●)

Night to Remember, A (1958-British) **123m.** **** D: Roy (Ward) Baker. Kenneth More, David McCallum, Jill Dixon, Laurence Naismith, Frank Lawton, Honor Blackman, Alec McCowen, George Rose. Meticulously produced documentary-style account of sinking of the "unsinkable" passenger liner *Titanic.* Superb combination of disaster spectacle and emotional byplay; a notable contrast to Hollywood's *Titanic* films. Vivid adaptation by Eric Ambler of Walter Lord's book. ▼●)

Night Train (1940) SEE: **Night Train to Munich**

Night Train to Munich (1940-British) **93m.** *** D: Carol Reed. Rex Harrison, Margaret Lockwood, Paul Von Hernried (Henreid), Basil Radford, Naunton Wayne, Felix Aylmer, Roland Culver. Expert Hitchcockian thriller about British intelligence agent Harrison trying to rescue Czech scientist who escaped from the Nazis to London only to be kidnapped back to Berlin. Stylishly photographed (by Otto Kanturek), sharply scripted by Frank Launder and Sidney Gilliat, who also wrote Hitchcock's THE LADY VANISHES (which introduced the comic characters reprised here by Radford and Wayne). Based on Gordon Wellesley's novel *Report on a Fugitive.* ▼●)

Night Train to Venice (1995-German) **C-98m.** BOMB D: Carlo U. Quinterio. Hugh Grant, Tahnee Welch, Malcolm McDowell, Kristina Soderbaum, Rachel Rice. Upon completing a book on neo-Nazis, writer Grant travels to Venice to meet with a publisher—and is followed (and menaced) by skinheads. If you're looking for a boyishly charming Grant, look elsewhere; he's a dull dolt in this trashy film, made in 1993 and passed over for theatrical release. [R]▼●

Night Unto Night (1949) **85m.** ** D: Don Siegel. Ronald Reagan, Viveca Lindfors, Broderick Crawford, Rosemary DeCamp, Osa Massen, Art Baker, Craig Stevens. Somber, unconvincing film about relationship of dying scientist and mentally disturbed widow. Finished in 1947 and shelved for two years. Reagan's performance isn't bad, but script is against him. ▶

Night Visitor, The (1970) **C-106m.** **½ D: Laslo Benedek. Max von Sydow, Liv Ullmann, Trevor Howard, Per Oscarsson, Rupert Davies, Andrew Keir. An inmate plots to escape from an asylum for the criminally insane for one night, to avenge himself on people who put him away. Heavy in detail, but interesting. Filmed in Denmark and Sweden. [PG] ▼)

Night Visitor (1989) **C-94m.** ** D: Rupert Hitzig. Derek Rydall, Allen Garfield, Teresa Vander Woude, Elliott Gould, Michael J. Pollard, Brooke Bundy, Richard Roundtree, Shannon Tweed. Teenage Rydall discovers his most hated teacher (Garfield) is a Satanist and serial killer of prostitutes; when no one believes him, he turns to retired cop Gould for help. Silly, unconvincing blend of teenage comedy and thriller, helped by good performances. [R]▼)

Night Walker, The (1964) **86m.** *** D: William Castle. Barbara Stanwyck, Robert Taylor, Lloyd Bochner, Rochelle Hudson, Judi Meredith, Hayden Rorke. One of the better Castle horror films has Stanwyck as wealthy widow discovering cause of recurring dreams about lost husband. Effective psychological thriller with good cast, unusual script by Robert Bloch. Title on-screen is WILLIAM CASTLE'S THE NIGHT WALKER. ▼

Night Warning (1982) **C-94m.** **½ D: William Asher. Jimmy McNichol, Susan Tyrrell, Bo Svenson, Marcia Lewis, Julia Duffy, William (Bill) Paxton. Explosive, tour-de-force acting by Tyrrell distinguishes this formula horror film. She's a sexually repressed aunt, overly protective of her nephew McNichol, who finally turns to murder. Aka BUTCHER BAKER NIGHTMARE MAKER. [R] ▼●

Night Watch (1973-British) **C-105m.** **½ D: Brian G. Hutton. Elizabeth Taylor, Laurence Harvey, Billie Whitelaw, Robert Lang, Tony Britton. Woman (Taylor) believes she has witnessed a murder, but cannot prove it. Tired plot based on Lucille Fletcher play. [PG] ▼

Nightwatch (1998) **C-101m.** **½ D: Ole Bornedal. Nick Nolte, Patricia Arquette, Ewan McGregor, Josh Brolin, Lauren Graham, Alix Koromzay, Lonny Chapman, John C. Reilly, Brad Dourif. McGregor hires on as a part-time night watchman in spooky morgue, while a serial killer is on a city-wide rampage. Arquette is his girlfriend, Brolin his daredevil buddy, and Nolte the police inspector on the case. Remake of writer-director Bornedal's own 1995 Danish hit, NATTEVAGTEN, is stylishly creepy, but weighs down in the final third. And remember: Don't let that door close. Super 35. [R] ▼●

Night Watch (2004-Russian) **C-114m.** ** D: Timur Bekmambetov. Konstantin Khabensky, Vladimir Menshov, Valeri Zolotukhin, Mariya Poroshina, Galina Tyunina, Yuri Kutsenko. Russian horror/sci-fi drama focuses on the "Others," a group that divided into forces of darkness and light centuries ago after signing a truce agreeing that the "dark" would control the night and the "light" would patrol the day. Now, in Moscow, the dark Others are out in force in the form of vampires and must be kept in check. Clearly shows the influence of American popcorn fare, with impressive special effects. Doesn't measure up to similar Hollywood product but makes a game attempt to play in the same sandbox. Followed by DAY WATCH. [R] ●

Night We Never Met, The (1993) **C-99m.** ** D: Warren Light. Matthew Broderick, Annabella Sciorra, Kevin Anderson, Louise Lasser, Jeanne Tripplehorn, Justine Bateman, Michael Mantell, Christine Baranski, Doris Roberts, Dominic Chianese, Garry Shandling, Ranjit Chowdhry, Katharine Houghton, Tim Guinee. Disappointing romantic comedy in which about-to-be-married yuppie Anderson time-shares his rent-controlled N.Y.C. apartment with Broderick and Sciorra; all are strangers, and use the pad on alternate days. [R] ▼●

Nightwing (1979) **C-105m.** *½ D: Arthur Hiller. Nick Mancuso, David Warner, Kathryn Harrold, Stephen Macht, Strother Martin, Pat Corley. Warner is an oddball who comes to Arizona to kill vampire bats in their caves. Well . . . it's a living. From a Martin Cruz Smith novel. [PG] ▼●

Nijinsky (1980-British) **C-125m.** **½ D: Herbert Ross. Alan Bates, George De La Pena, Leslie Browne, Ronald Pickup, Alan Badel, Colin Blakely, Ronald Lacey, Carla Fracci, Jeremy Irons, Janet Suzman, Sian Phillips. Handsome but disappointing chronicle of the homosexual relationship between the legendary dancer Nijinsky (De La Pena) and Ballet Russe impresario Sergei Diaghilev (Bates). Worthy subject matter defeated by soap-opera scenario, allegedly inauthentic characterizations. Fine performance by Bates, superb one by Badel as a wealthy patron. Irons' film debut. [R] ▼

Nijinsky: The Diaries of Vaslav Nijinsky (2001-Australian-German-Swedish-Dutch) **C-95m.** *** D: Paul Cox. Narrated by Derek Jacobi. Striking, sumptuous meshing of words and images in which Nijinsky's diary—written in 1919, as he suffered a mental breakdown—is pictorialized by Cox while read off-camera by Jacobi. The great dancer's words express his deepest feelings and fears, yet the accompanying images are so beautiful that the film may be appreciated for its visuals alone. Cox used a similar approach in VINCENT. ▼●

Nil by Mouth (1997-British) **C-128m.** *** D: Gary Oldman. Ray Winstone, Kathy Burke, Charlie Creed-Miles, Laila Morse, Edna Dore, Chrissie Coterill, Jon Morrison. First-time director Oldman also scripted this gritty, in-your-face, cinéma vérité–style portrait of a desperate, dysfunctional family in working-class South London, focusing on an unhappily married couple (Winstone, Burke). Often difficult to watch with its unrelenting rage, despair, and (domestic) violence, but it's heartfelt and well acted (particularly by Burke). [R] ▼●

Nim's Island (2008-U.S.-Australian) **C-96m.** *** D: Jennifer Flackett, Mark Levin. Abigail Breslin, Jodie Foster, Gerard Butler. Wonderfully imaginative family film, from Wendy Orr's novel about a father and daughter who live on an isolated island in the South Pacific. When he gets lost at sea, the only person who responds to her is her favorite adventure-book author—an agoraphobic woman who's made her acquaintance via e-mail. Ingenious visual presentation, with likable performances from all three stars, including Foster in a rare comedic role. Super 35. [PG] ●

Nina Takes a Lover (1994) **C-100m.** ** D: Alan Jacobs. Laura San Giacomo, Paul Rhys, Michael O'Keefe, Cristi Conaway, Fisher Stevens. Nina's husband is out of town for a few weeks, and on the spur of the moment she takes a lover—a Welsh artist. If this is what "woman's pictures" have come to in the '90s, heaven help the genre. Stevens steals every scene he's in—and gives the film its only injection of life—as Nina's friend's lover. [R] ▼●)

9 (2009) **C-79m.** **½ D: Shane Acker. Voices of Elijah Wood, John C. Reilly, Jennifer Connelly, Christopher Plummer, Crispin Glover, Martin Landau, Fred Tatasciore, Alan Oppenheimer. In a bleak future world, a handful of creatures battle monsterlike machines, but one plucky survivor—numbered 9—refuses to accept defeat. Animated science-fiction yarn is imaginatively designed and well staged, but never becomes emotionally engaging as its too-familiar story plays out. Based on Acker's student Academy Award–winning short of the same name. [PG-13] ❱

Nine (2009) **C/B&W-118m.** *** D: Rob Marshall. Daniel Day-Lewis, Marion Cotillard, Penélope Cruz, Judi Dench, Fergie, Kate Hudson, Nicole Kidman, Sophia Loren, Ricky Tognazzi. Fabled (and pampered) Italian film director has run dry of ideas, though he's under the gun to start a new picture. Then the various women in his life, including his mother, his neglected wife, and his mistress, appear to him in a series of dreamlike musical vignettes and fire his imagination. Lavish adaptation of Maury Yeston and Arthur Kopit's 1982 Broadway show, inspired by Fellini's 8½, is a stylish treat, featuring some fabulous women, John Myhre's stunning production design, Dion Beebe's rich cinematography, and three newly minted Yeston songs. There are even scenes of Rome's famous Cinecittà studios, where Fellini made his masterworks. Screenplay by Michael Tolkin and Anthony Minghella. Super 35. [PG-13] ❱

Nine ½ Weeks (1986) **C-113m.** *½ D: Adrian Lyne. Mickey Rourke, Kim Basinger, Margaret Whitton, David Margulies, Christine Baranski, Dwight Weist, Roderick Cook. Saga of an obsessive sexual relationship; uninvolving and unerotic, not to mention degrading. Promises sexual fireworks, but all it delivers is a big tease (some explicit material was cut prior to release). Video version is more explicit, though not so much as European version. Followed by several direct-to-video sequels. [R] ▼●)

Nine Lives (2005) **C-112m.** ***½ D: Rodrigo García. Glenn Close, Robin Wright Penn, Holly Hunter, Sissy Spacek, Kathy Baker, Amy Brenneman, Elpidia Carrillo, Dakota Fanning, Lisa Gay Hamilton, Molly Parker, Mary Kay Place, Amanda Seyfried, Stephen Dillane, William Fichtner, Jason Isaacs, Joe Mantegna, Ian McShane, Sydney Tamiia Poitier, Aidan Quinn, Miguel Sandoval. Exquisitely acted, perceptively told vignettes about nine women, of all kinds, at emotional crossroads in their lives, from a teenage girl who feels trapped by her needy parents to a woman trying to suppress her turbulent emotions while incarcerated. Each segment is a perfect short story (written by the director), enacted in real time in one continuous camera shot, amazingly executed (on film, not digital video) by cinematographer Xavier Pérez Grobet. [R] ❱

Nine Lives of Fritz the Cat, The (1974) **C-76m.** **½ D: Robert Taylor. Voices of Skip Hinnant, Reva Rose, Bob Holt, Robert Ridgely, Pat Harrington. Animated sequel to X-rated original finds Fritz in the '70s, now on welfare with a nagging wife. He smokes pot for escape, and imagines himself in eight other lives—including being an astronaut, as an orderly to Adolf Hitler, and an aide to President Kissinger(!). Not as bold (or as memorable) as the first film, but certainly lively, with some funny moments. [R] ▼❱

Nine Months (1995) **C-103m.** ** D: Chris Columbus. Hugh Grant, Julianne Moore, Jeff Goldblum, Tom Arnold, Joan Cusack, Robin Williams, Ashley Johnson, Emily Yancy, Kristin Davis. Farcical tale of a couple whose blissful five-year relationship is blindsided by unexpected pregnancy: He simply can't deal with it. Slick Hollywood concoction tries to coast on Grant's boyish charm and Moore's radiant beauty, with Arnold adding bombastic comedy relief. But utter predictability and oafish silliness drain it dry. Williams' pair of scenes as a nervous, malaprop-spouting Russian obstetrician are definite high point. Based on popular 1994 French movie, NEUF MOIS. Panavision. [PG-13] ▼●)

$9.99 (2009-Australian-Israeli) **C-78m.** *** D: Tatia Rosenthal. Voices of Geoffrey Rush, Anthony LaPaglia, Samuel Johnson, Claudia Karvan, Joel Edgerton, Barry Otto, Leeanna Walsman. Several seriocomic stories are woven together involving inhabitants of a Sydney apartment complex who are searching for meaning in their lives and finding it in unique ways. Most interesting story revolves around lonely widower (Otto) who allows a burnt-out guardian angel (Rush) to share his flat. Title refers to one young resident who finds happiness in a paperback book, called *The Meaning of Life*, purchased for $9.99. Clever screenplay cowritten by director Rosenthal with acclaimed Israeli writer Etgar Keret, based on his short stories. Stop-motion animated film is decidedly not suitable for children. [R] ❱

Nine Queens (2000-Argentinian) **C-114m.** *** D: Fabián Bielinsky. Ricardo Darín, Gastón Pauls, Leticia Brédice, Tomas Fonzi, Celia Juarez. Entertaining Mamet-style thriller about a young con man who teams up with an old pro in present-day economically depressed Buenos Aires to try to sell a forged set of rare stamps . . . but one of them may be trying to double-cross the other. Serpentine story will keep you guessing until the end, and has a refreshing sense of humor. Written by the director, in his feature debut. Remade as CRIMINAL. [R]▼▶

Nines, The (2007) **C-99m.** **½ D: John August. Ryan Reynolds, Hope Davis, Melissa McCarthy, Elle Fanning, Dahlia Salem, David Denman, Octavia Spencer, Ben Falcone. Reynolds plays a Hollywood star with a dysfunctional private life . . . and a TV series producer . . . and a video-game inventor/family man in this triptych in which the three parts intriguingly overlap. Writer August (who similarly explored multiple-viewpoint narrative in GO) makes his feature-directing debut with this offbeat drama that boasts a number of interesting characters while providing a showcase for Reynolds. [R]▶

976-Evil (1989) **C-89m.** **½ D: Robert Englund. Stephen Geoffreys, Patrick O'Bryan, Sandy Dennis, Jim Metzler, Maria Rubell, Robert Picardo, Lezlie Deane, J.J. Cohen, Darren Burrows. Snappy CARRIE-like outsider's-revenge horror flick. Introverted teenager Geoffreys calls 976 number that provides him with satanic powers. Story is confusing, and script too jokey, but as often as not, it delivers the goods. Directorial debut for Englund, aka Freddy Krueger of the NIGHTMARE ON ELM STREET series. [R]▼▶

9 Songs (2005-British) **C-71m.** *½ D: Michael Winterbottom. Kieran O'Brien, Margo Stilley. A British geologist and an American student hook up in London; in between attending rock concerts, they indulge in sex. That's the sum total of this ponderous, erotic drama featuring realistic, graphically depicted sex. Means to be profound, but the result is profoundly boring. Alternate version runs 64m. ▶

1918 (1984) **C-94m.** **½ D: Ken Harrison. William Converse-Roberts, Hallie Foote, Matthew Broderick, Rochelle Oliver, Michael Higgins, Jeannie McCarthy, Bill McGhee, Horton Foote, Jr. Stagy, PBSy Horton Foote drama concerns the catastrophic late teens influenza epidemic that hit America—and its tragic effect on a small Texas town. Will probably be seen to best advantage on the small screen; Hallie Foote (the playwright's daughter) is excellent as a woman (based on her own real-life grandmother) whose husband and infant are both stricken. Produced for *American Playhouse*; followed by prequels ON VALENTINE'S DAY and CONVICTS. 1918 and ON VALENTINE'S DAY were telecast as STORY OF A MARRIAGE.▼▶

1984 (1956-British) **91m.** *** D: Michael Anderson. Edmond O'Brien, Michael Redgrave, Jan Sterling, David Kossoff, Mervyn Johns, Donald Pleasence. Thought-provoking version of George Orwell's futuristic novel. Lovers O'Brien and Sterling trapped in all-powerful state, try valiantly to rebel against "Big Brother." Remade in 1984.▼

Nineteen Eighty-Four (1984-British) **C-115m.** *** D: Michael Radford. John Hurt, Richard Burton, Suzanna Hamilton, Cyril Cusack, Gregor Fisher, James Walker, Phyllis Logan. Appropriately grim, well-cast version of the Orwell classic, with Hurt as the government functionary who illegally falls in love, Hamilton as his bedmate, and Burton—excellent in his final feature—as the party official who somehow seems human even when feeding his victims' faces to the rats. Superior to the 1956 version, though the oppressive gloominess of the second half does wear you down. Seedily impressive production design. [R]▼▶

1941 (1979) **C-118m.** **½ D: Steven Spielberg. Dan Aykroyd, Ned Beatty, John Belushi, Treat Williams, Nancy Allen, Robert Stack, Tim Matheson, Toshiro Mifune, Christopher Lee, Warren Oates, Bobby DiCicco, Dianne Kay, Murray Hamilton, Lorraine Gary, Slim Pickens, Eddie Deezen, John Candy, many others. Gargantuan comedy from the bigger-is-funnier school of filmmaking. Some excellent vignettes and dazzling special effects in freewheeling story of war panic in L.A. following Pearl Harbor attack, but on the whole suffers from overkill. Written by Bob Gale and Robert Zemeckis. Alternate version runs 146m. Panavision. [PG]▼▶

1900 (1976-Italian-French-German) **C-311m.** **½ D: Bernardo Bertolucci. Robert De Niro, Gérard Depardieu, Donald Sutherland, Burt Lancaster, Dominique Sanda, Stefania Sandrelli, Sterling Hayden. Sweepingly sexy, violent Bertolucci epic, with rapturous Vittorio Storaro cinematography, begins with the same-day birth of sons respectively sired by a landowner and a laborer who works his estate. The rest runs the gamut of 20th-century political bases, starting with the respective fascistic and socialistic leanings these two friendly protagonists develop on their road to middle age. Chain-sawed down to 243m. for an initial U.S. release that pleased no one, this flawed, one-of-a-kind epic of great sweep, humanity, and power doesn't seem fully realized even at its original running time. Yet aiming for the fences, it reaches them often enough to have become one of its era's most notable cult movies. [NC-17—edited from original R rating]▼▶

Nineteen Nineteen (1985-British) **C/B& W-99m.** ***½ D: Hugh Brody. Paul Scofield, Maria Schell, Frank Finlay, Diana Quick, Clare Higgins, Colin Firth. Scofield and Schell are former patients of Sigmund Freud, who come together years later to reminisce and remember. Slow and boring, wasting talents of a fine cast.

1990: The Bronx Warriors (1983-Italian) **C-84m.** BOMB D: Enzo G. Castellari. Vic Morrow, Christopher Connelly, Fred Williamson, Mark Gregory, Stefania Girolami. Bronx gang leaders vs. nasty corporation agent Morrow. Gregory plays a character named Trash, which is the best way to describe this movie. Filmed in the Bronx and Rome. Sequel: ESCAPE FROM THE BRONX. Panavision. [R]▼▶

1969 (1988) **C-93m.** ** D: Ernest Thompson. Robert Downey, Jr., Kiefer Sutherland, Bruce Dern, Mariette Hartley, Joanna Cassidy, Winona Ryder. Sutherland is terrific as a sensitive antiwar youth, and Hartley fine as his understanding mother, in this story of troubled times and troubled lives. But playwright Thompson's earnest directorial debut is disconnected and ultimately disappointing. [R] ▼●▶

Nine to Five (1980) **C-110m.** **½ D: Colin Higgins. Jane Fonda, Lily Tomlin, Dolly Parton, Dabney Coleman, Sterling Hayden, Elizabeth Wilson, Henry Jones, Lawrence Pressman, Marian Mercer. Three savvy secretaries have to contend with a doltish boss—and inadvertently find their chance to take revenge. The first half of this comedy is dynamite, culminating in Tomlin's Disneyesque fantasy of murdering the slavedriver, but film takes a disastrous turn, losing its bearings and momentum. Appealing performances by the star trio help make up for the ultimate silliness. Parton's first film. Later a TV series and a stage musical. [PG]▼●▶

95 Miles to Go (2006) **C-77m.** *½ D: Tom Caltabiano. Ray Romano, Tom Caltabiano. If you've ever wondered whether *Everybody Loves Raymond*'s easygoing star comedian has a cranky, neurotic side off-camera, this movie's for you. Romano and his pal/warm-up act Tom Caltabiano (a *Raymond* TV writer) drive from gig to gig through Florida and Georgia while an intern captures their mundane adventure on video. There's a certain fascination in a multimillionaire stressing over having to foot his buddy's room-service meal, but this comes across mostly as a vanity project for Caltabiano (who coproduced with Romano); the nadir: Ray gets indigestion. [R]

99 and 44/100% Dead (1974) **C-98m.** BOMB D: John Frankenheimer. Richard Harris, Chuck Connors, Edmond O'Brien, Bradford Dillman, Ann Turkel. Idiotic, poorly made gangster melodrama with satirical overtones: hit man Harris is hired by mobster O'Brien to knock off rival Dillman. The pits. Panavision. [PG]▼

99 River Street (1953) **83m.** *** D: Phil Karlson. John Payne, Evelyn Keyes, Brad Dexter, Peggie Castle, Ian Wolfe, Frank Faylen. Rugged crime caper with Payne caught up in tawdry surroundings, trying to prove himself innocent of murder charge. Unpretentious film really packs a punch. ▶

99 Women (1969-Spanish-German-British-Italian) **C-90m.** *½ D: Jess Franco. Maria Schell, Luciana Paluzzi, Mercedes McCambridge, Herbert Lom. Absurd drama about lesbianism in women's prison. Aka ISLE OF LOST WOMEN. X-rated and unrated versions available. SuperScope. [R] ▼▶

92 in the Shade (1975) **C-93m.** *** D: Thomas McGuane. Peter Fonda, Warren Oates, Margot Kidder, Burgess Meredith, Harry Dean Stanton, Sylvia Miles, Elizabeth Ashley, William Hickey, Louise Latham. National Book Award–nominated novel about rival fishing boat captains in Florida Keys; directed by the author. Wildly uneven but well cast and frequently hilarious. [R]▼

Ninja Assassin (2009-German-British) **C-99m.** *½ D: James McTeigue. Rain, Naomie Harris, Ben Miles, Rick Yune, Shô Kosugi, Randall Duk Kim. Rain, trained since childhood by the villainous Ozunu clan to be a killer ninja, breaks away after the murder of his sweetheart and plots bloody revenge. Enter Harris, a special agent who's investigating the clan. Nauseatingly gory martial arts mishmash. Super 35. [R]▶

Ninja III—The Domination (1984) **C-95m.** **½ D: Sam Firstenberg. Lucinda Dickey, Jordan Bennett, Sho Kosugi, David Chung. Follow-up to REVENGE OF THE NINJA about an evil Ninja, "killed" by the police, who forces his spirit on innocent Dickey. Lots of action; good of its type. [R]▼

Ninotchka (1939) **110m.** ***½ D: Ernst Lubitsch. Greta Garbo, Melvyn Douglas, Ina Claire, Bela Lugosi, Sig Ruman, Felix Bressart, Alexander Granach, Richard Carle. Amid much outdated sociological banter, a lighthearted Garbo still shines. Lubitsch's comedy pegged on tale of cold Russian agent Garbo coming to Paris, falling in love with gay-blade Douglas. Supporting cast shows fine comedy flair. Script by Billy Wilder, Charles Brackett, and Walter Reisch was basis for Broadway musical and film SILK STOCKINGS.▼●▶

Ninth Configuration, The (1980) **C-118m.** ***½ D: William Peter Blatty. Stacy Keach, Scott Wilson, Jason Miller, Ed Flanders, Neville Brand, Moses Gunn, George Di Cenzo, Robert Loggia, Tom Atkins, Alejandro Rey, Joe Spinell, Steve Sandor. In old castle used by U.S. government as asylum, new head shrink Keach quickly proves to be nuttier than any of the patients. Hilarious yet thought-provoking, with endlessly quotable dialogue and an amazing barroom fight scene. Blatty also produced and adapted his novel *Twinkle, Twinkle, Killer Kane* (this film's title at one point). Myriad versions run anywhere from 99m. to 140m.; above time is Blatty's cut, and rating applies to this version only. Panavision. [R]▼●▶

Ninth Day, The (2004-German) **C-93m.** *** D: Volker Schlöndorff. Ulrich Matthes, August Diehl, Bibiana Beglau, Germain Wagner, Götz Burger, Michael König, Hilmar Thate. Catholic priest (Matthes), incarcerated in Dachau during WW2, is given nine days' leave and returns to his home in Luxembourg, where the Nazis attempt to use him as a political pawn. Stark, riveting drama about a principled, deeply religious man who maintains his integrity, humanity, and spirituality under the most trying circumstances. The sheer horror of Dachau is vividly etched. Loosely based on the prison diary of Father Jean Bernard.◗

Ninth Gate, The (1999-French-Spanish-U.S.) **C-133m. **** D: Roman Polanski. Johnny Depp, Frank Langella, Lena Olin, Emmanuelle Seigner, Barbara Jefford, Jack Taylor, José Lopez Rodero, James Russo. Mercenary N.Y.C. rare-book sleuth Depp combs Europe for an ancient demonic tome. Part mystery, part travelogue, with traces of Polanski's sardonic wit, but can't hold a satanic candle to his 1968 ROSEMARY'S BABY. One scene is strikingly similar to a sequence in Kubrick's EYES WIDE SHUT. Also shown at 127m. Super 35. [R]▼◗

Nixon (1995) **C-190m. ***** D: Oliver Stone. Anthony Hopkins, Joan Allen, Powers Boothe, Ed Harris, Bob Hoskins, E. G. Marshall, David Paymer, David Hyde Pierce, Paul Sorvino, Mary Steenburgen, J. T. Walsh, James Woods, Brian Bedford, Kevin Dunn, Fyvush Finkel, Annabeth Gish, Tony Goldwyn, Larry Hagman, Ed Herrmann, Madeline Kahn, Saul Rubinek, Tony Lo Bianco, Corey Carrier, Tony Plana, Dan Hedaya, Michael Chiklis, John C. McGinley, John Diehl, Robert Beltran, Joanna Going, George Plimpton, Donna Dixon, James Karen. Controversial, fragmented portrait of the U.S. politician and president, presented as a driven man beset by deep-rooted insecurities. Younger viewers might have a hard time keeping track of the players, and may fall prey to director-cowriter Stone's expected, and outrageous, historical inventions. Overlong, to be sure, but still compelling, with Hopkins' persuasive lead performance, and an array of fine supporting players, especially Allen as Pat Nixon. Extended director's cut has 28m. added. Panavision. [R]▼◗●

No Big Deal (1983) **C-86m. **½** D: Robert Charlton. Kevin Dillon, Christopher Gartin, Mary Joan Negro, Jane Krakowski, Tammy Grimes, Sylvia Miles. Fair drama about troubled, alienated, streetwise teen Dillon and his attempt to fit in with his peers. A decent effort at portraying adolescent problems, but the result is a bit too pat. Interestingly, Miles is cast as a strict, bureaucratic school principal.▼◗

No Blade of Grass (1970) **C-97m. *½** D: Cornel Wilde. Nigel Davenport, Jean Wallace, John Hamill, Lynne Frederick, Patrick Holt, Anthony May. Sober-sided film trying to drive home ecology message is just an update of films like PANIC IN YEAR ZERO, with family fleeing virus-stricken London for Scottish countryside, facing panic and attack along the way. Based on John Christopher's popular novel. Panavision. [R]

Nobody Knows (2004-Japanese) **C-141m. ***** D: Hirokazu Kore-eda. Yûya Yagira, Ayu Kitaura, Hiei Kimura, Momoko Shimizu, Hanae Kan, You. Overlong but emotionally engaging drama based on a true 1988 story of four young children left home alone in Tokyo by their mother, who simply disappears. Deliberate pacing may challenge impatient viewers, but film's simplicity and almost complete focus on the kids hit the mark. Kore-eda shot this chronologically over a period of one year. Twelve-year-old Yagira became the youngest ever to receive the Best Actor prize at the Cannes Film Festival for his nuanced performance as a boy who takes on responsibilities far beyond his years. [PG-13]◗

Nobody Loves Me (1994-German) **C-104m. **½** D: Doris Dörrie. Maria Schrader, Pierre Sanoussi-Bliss, Michael von Au, Elisabeth Trissenaar, Peggy Parnass. Quirky oddity about the trials of Fanny Fink (Schrader), a death-obsessed airport security officer who is turning 30. She says she doesn't need a man, but is nonetheless desperate to find one. Her gay next-door neighbor (and kindred spirit) tells her she will soon be meeting the love of her life. Not without interest but too often as flaky and unglued as its main character.

Nobody Runs Forever SEE: **High Commissioner, The**

Nobody's Fault SEE: **Little Dorrit**

Nobody's Fool (1986) **C-107m. **½** D: Evelyn Purcell. Rosanna Arquette, Eric Roberts, Mare Winningham, Jim Youngs, Louise Fletcher, Gwen Welles, Stephen Tobolowsky, Charlie Barnett, Lewis Arquette. Innocuous romantic comedy by Beth Henley about a flaky waitress in a small Southwestern town who's become an outcast (after having a baby out of wedlock), and only begins to find herself when she meets Roberts, who's passing through town. Very modest film that benefits from a relaxed and unmannered performance by Roberts. [PG-13]▼◗●

Nobody's Fool (1994) **C-110m. ***½** D: Robert Benton. Paul Newman, Jessica Tandy, Bruce Willis, Melanie Griffith, Dylan Walsh, Pruitt Taylor Vince, Gene Saks, Josef Sommer, Philip Seymour Hoffman, Philip Bosco. Picaresque look at a small-town ne'er-do-well and his extended (dysfunctional) family of cronies; after turning his back on his real family years ago, he now finds himself spending time with his grown-up son and his young grandson. An irresistibly appealing Newman is surrounded by wonderful actors in this charmingly unpredictable character study—including Willis, as his friendly nemesis.

Benton scripted, from Richard Russo's novel. Elizabeth Wilson appears unbilled as Newman's ex-wife. [R]▼●▶

Nobody's Perfect (1968) **C-103m.** **½ D: Alan Rafkin. Doug McClure, Nancy Kwan, James Whitmore, David Hartman, Gary Vinson. Witless military service comedy involving pat shenanigans of U.S. submarine based in Japan, with every predictable gimmick thrown in. Techniscope.

Nobody's Perfect (1989-Swiss-U.S.) **C-91m.** **½ D: Robert Kaylor. Chad Lowe, Gail O'Grady, Patrick Breen, Kim Flowers, Eric Bruskotter, Robert Vaughn. Shy guy at a new college wants to make friends with an attractive girl, but is too tongue-tied, so at a friend's urging, disguises himself as a girl and ends up his target's roommate. Little comedy based on the last line of SOME LIKE IT HOT is predictable but entertaining. [PG-13]▼●▶

Nobody's Perfekt (1981) **C-95m.** BOMB D: Peter Bonerz. Gabe Kaplan, Alex Karras, Robert Klein, Susan Clark, Paul Stewart, Alex Rocco, Peter Bonerz. Entirely unfunny comedy, made in Miami, about three misfits who decide to fight City Hall when their car is totalled in a pothole and—because of a loophole—they can't sue. Klein does awful imitations of James Cagney and Bette Davis. An inauspicious theatrical directing debut for Bonerz. [PG]▼▶

No Country for Old Men (2007) **C-122m.** ***½ D: Joel Coen, Ethan Coen. Tommy Lee Jones, Javier Bardem, Josh Brolin, Woody Harrelson, Kelly Macdonald, Garret Dillahunt, Tess Harper, Barry Corbin, Stephen Root, Rodger Boyce, Ana Reeder, Beth Grant, Gene Jones. Crackling tale of three men whose lives intersect in the early 1980s: a brutal, psychopathic killer (Bardem) on the loose, an ordinary guy (Brolin) who seizes a chance to get rich quick, and a laconic West Texas sheriff (Jones) who doesn't care for the way civilization is crumbling before his very eyes. Creating tension from the first moments onward (and without the use of music), the Coens' adaptation of Cormac McCarthy's novel is a brooding tale of fate set against a stark backdrop . . . but not without irony and humor. Set on fire by Bardem's Academy Award–winning performance; brilliantly photographed by Roger Deakins. Also won Oscars for Best Picture, Best Director(s), and Best Adapted Screenplay. Super 35. [R]▶

No Deposit, No Return (1976) **C-112m.** **½ D: Norman Tokar. David Niven, Darren McGavin, Don Knotts, Herschel Bernardi, Barbara Feldon, Brad Savage, Kim Richards, Charlie Martin Smith, Vic Tayback, John Williams. Two neglected kids stage their own bogus kidnapping to stir up attention and enable them to join their mother in Hong Kong. OK Disney slapstick comedy. [G]▼▶

No Down Payment (1957) **105m.** *** D: Martin Ritt. Joanne Woodward, Jeffrey Hunter, Sheree North, Tony Randall, Cameron Mitchell, Patricia Owens, Barbara Rush, Pat Wingle. Topical suburban soaper of intertwining problems of several young married couples. CinemaScope.

No Drums, No Bugles (1971) **C-85m.** **½ D: Clyde Ware. Martin Sheen. Nicely done drama, based on West Virginia legend about conscientious objector during Civil War who spends three years in a cave rather than fight. Good acting by Sheen, who's the only one on screen for most of film. Techniscope. [G]▼

Noel (2004) **C-96m.** **½ D: Chazz Palminteri. Penélope Cruz, Susan Sarandon, Paul Walker, Alan Arkin, Marcus Thomas, Chazz Palminteri, Chantal Lonergan, Erika Rosenbaum. Ambitious tearjerker about the interactions of fearful, vulnerable friends, lovers, coworkers, and strangers on Christmas Eve: a lonely book editor (Sarandon) whose mother is suffering from Alzheimer's, a cop (Walker) whose irrational jealousy is stifling his Sophia Loren–esque fiancée (Cruz), and a heartbroken waiter (Arkin) with a strange reincarnation fantasy. Gets better as it goes along, as it zeros in on issues relating to acceptance and reconciliation. Robin Williams appears unbilled in a pivotal role. Super 35. [PG]▶

No End in Sight (2007) **C-102m.** **** D: Charles Ferguson. Narrated by Campbell Scott. Masterful screen equivalent of the myriad books that share on-the-record accounts from former military/policy players to explain how the Bush administration leaped before it looked in 2003 before invading Iraq. A standout in what is already a litany of Iraq-quagmire documentaries. The interviewees—many still bewildered by how their former superiors arrogantly brushed off or ignored experts with political/geographic/linguistic experience in the region—are photographed in like fashion to comparably dramatic effect, compounding the power of what they have to say.▶

No Escape (1994) **C-118m.** ** D: Martin Campbell. Ray Liotta, Lance Henriksen, Stuart Wilson, Kevin Dillon, Ian McNeice, Michael Lerner, Ernie Hudson. Odd mix of high tech and MOST DANGEROUS GAME finds Liotta in a maximum security prison (year 2022) before escaping to a jungle colony where isolated inmates are left to die. Not the worst of its grungy ilk, but too protracted. Wilson is amusing as a key nemesis. Arriscope. [R]▼●▶

No Good Deed (2003-U.S.-German) **C-97m.** ** D: Bob Rafelson. Samuel L. Jackson, Milla Jovovich, Stellan Skarsgård, Doug Hutchison, Joss Ackland, Grace Zabriskie, Jonathan Higgins. Sorry attempt to update a Dashiell Hammett story ("The House on Turk Street") with Jackson as a cop who stumbles into the hideout of a criminal gang and becomes their prisoner as they plan a daring heist. Nothing rings true here. [R]▼▶

No Greater Love (1959-Japanese) **208m.** ***½ D: Masaki Kobayashi. Tatsuya Nakadai, Michiyo Aratama, Ineko Arima, Chikage Awashima, Keiji Sada, Sô Yamamura, Akira Ishihama, Eitarô Ozawa, Shinji Nambara. South Manchuria, 1943: Kaji (Nakadai), a humane, married Japanese steel company employee who is about to be conscripted into the military, is assigned to supervise a rural ore-mining operation whose workers are Chinese POWs. Stirring epic mirrors age-old enmity between Japanese, Chinese, and Koreans while offering a deeply felt portrait of a man who must play a deadly balancing act as he struggles to maintain his values. Scripted by Kobayashi and Zenzo Matsuyama, based on a six-volume novel by Jumpei Gomikawa. Aka THE HUMAN CONDITION I; followed by THE ROAD TO ETERNITY and A SOLDIER'S PRAYER. Grandscope. ▶

No Highway in the Sky (1951) **98m.** *** D: Henry Koster. James Stewart, Marlene Dietrich, Glynis Johns, Jack Hawkins, Janette Scott, Elizabeth Allan, Ronald Squire, Niall MacGinnis, Kenneth More, Maurice Denham, Wilfrid Hyde-White. Offbeat, engrossing drama with Stewart as an engineer who desperately tries to convince others that aircraft can suffer from metal fatigue, and should be grounded after a given time. Dietrich is a glamorous passenger on the fateful flight. Based on a novel by Nevil Shute. Made in England, where it was released as NO HIGHWAY.▼

No Holds Barred (1989) **C-91m.** ** D: Thomas J. Wright. Hulk Hogan, Joan Severance, Kurt Fuller, Tiny Lister, Mark Pellegrino, Jesse (The Body) Ventura, Bill Henderson. For those who can't get enough of Hulk Hogan, he appears here as a TV wrestling star who must defend himself after refusing a greedy businessman's offer to switch networks. Aimed squarely at the legion of Hulkster fans. [PG-13]▼●

Noise (2008) **C-91m.** **½ D: Henry Bean. Tim Robbins, Bridget Moynahan, William Hurt, Margarita Levieva, Gabrielle Brennan, Maria Ballesteros, William Baldwin, Colleen Camp. A New Yorker, driven to distraction by the incessant noise of car alarms, starts vandalizing the cars and disabling the devices—in the guise of The Rectifier—but his vigilante tactics become so obsessive they disrupt his entire life. Darkly funny, thoughtful musing on righteous anger and the absurdity of modern life, though it can't sustain its momentum from start to finish. Written by the director. ▶

Noises Off (1992) **C-104m.** **½ D: Peter Bogdanovich. Carol Burnett, Michael Caine, Denholm Elliott, Julie Hagerty, Marilu Henner, Mark Linn-Baker, Christo-

pher Reeve, John Ritter, Nicollette Sheridan. Energetic filming of Michael Frayn's play, a clever variation on a traditional British sex farce—with the added dimension of behind-the-scenes tumult among the acting troupe. This kind of door-slamming comedy doesn't ever work on film—but Bogdanovich comes closer than anyone ever has before, with the help of a willing cast. [PG-13]▼●

No Looking Back (1980) SEE: **Out of the Blue** (1980)

No Looking Back (1998) **C-96m.** ** D: Edward Burns. Lauren Holly, Edward Burns, Jon Bon Jovi, Blythe Danner, Connie Britton. Working-class romantic triangle provides nice lead role for Holly as waitress with an OK but dead-end life with boyfriend Bon Jovi, thrown off balance by return of old sweetheart Burns. Attractive cast can't overcome a very slight story; the strong soundtrack overpowers the script. [R] ▼●

Nomad (2005-Kazakhstan-French) **C-110m.** ** D: Sergei Bodrov, Ivan Passer. Kuno Becker, Jay Hernandez, Jason Scott Lee, Mark Dacascos; voice of Bai Ling. On the barren steppes of 18th-century Kazakhstan, while rival tribes battle for sovereignty, mystic warrior Oraz (Lee) rescues an infant descended from Genghis Khan who is destined to unite the nation as "Mansur" (GOAL!'s Becker). Historical epic has vicious sabers-on-horseback duels and good production design (real human extras—no CGI!) but plodding storytelling. Reputedly rocky production also had a third filmmaker: Talgat Temenov, who in this dubbed 2007 U.S. release is billed as "Local Director." Original Kazakh-language version runs 112m. AKA: NOMAD: THE WARRIOR. Super 35. [R]▶

Nomads (1986) **C-95m.** *½ D: John McTiernan. Lesley-Anne Down, Pierce Brosnan, Adam Ant, Anna-Maria Monticelli, Hector Mercado, Mary Woronov. Doctor (Down) treats an apparent madman, then undergoes a hallucinatory rerun of his recent experiences: he's a French anthropologist who's come to L.A. and has been drawn to a band of strange street people. Potentially interesting idea for a half-hour *Twilight Zone* but pretty deadly as a feature. Unpleasant, too. [R]▼●

No Man of Her Own (1932) **85m.** **½ D: Wesley Ruggles. Clark Gable, Carole Lombard, Dorothy Mackaill, Grant Mitchell, Elizabeth Patterson, Lillian Harmer, George Barbier. Snappy story of heel reformed by good girl, noteworthy for only co-starring of Gable and Lombard (then not married).▼●

No Man of Her Own (1950) **98m.** **½ D: Mitchell Leisen. Barbara Stanwyck, John Lund, Jane Cowl, Phyllis Thaxter, Richard Denning, Milburn Stone. Turgid drama based on Cornell Woolrich tale of Stanwyck assuming another's identity, later being blackmailed by ex-boyfriend. Remade in 1982 as I MARRIED A SHADOW and in 1996 as MRS. WINTERBOURNE.

No Man's Land (1985-French-Swiss) **C-110m.** ******* D: Alain Tanner. Hugues Quester, Myriam Mezieres, Jean-Philippe Ecoffey, Betty Berr, Marie-Luce Felber. Sober, provocative account of several characters involved with smuggling contraband across the French-Swiss border, focusing on their motivations and disillusionment. May be effectively contrasted to Tanner's earlier JONAH WHO WILL BE 25 IN THE YEAR 2000.

No Man's Land (1987) **C-106m.** ****** D: Peter Werner. Charlie Sheen, D. B. Sweeney, Lara Harris, Randy Quaid, Bill Duke, R. D. Call, M. Emmet Walsh. Rookie cop goes undercover to trap a wealthy young auto buff who operates a hot car ring, finds he likes his target, the target's sister, *and* stealing Porsches. Good premise largely botched. [R]▼●◗

No Man's Land (2001-Bosnian) **C-97m.** *****½** D: Danis Tanović. Brancko Djurić, Rene Bitorajac, Filip Šovagović, Georges Siatidis, Katrin Cartlidge, Simon Callow, Serge-Henri Valcke. Riveting seriocomic war parable about two soldiers, one Bosnian and one Serb, who are trapped together with another unfortunate man in a foxhole between enemy lines in 1993. As a result, no one is willing to take responsibility for their welfare or rescue, including the United Nations forces. Debuting writer-director Tanović manages to take a difficult, even remote subject and personalize it—with the welcome addition of dark humor—in this terrific film. Oscar winner for Best Foreign Language Film. Super 35. [R] ▼◗

No Mercy (1986) **C-105m.** ***½** D: Richard Pearce. Richard Gere, Kim Basinger, Jeroen Krabbé, George Dzundza, Gary Basaraba, William Atherton, Ray Sharkey. Chicago cop Gere storms into Louisiana Bayou country seeking the killer of his partner, falls for Cajun beauty Basinger—who's been "sold" to the kingpin perpetrator of the murder. Even mindless melodramas have to make sense, at least on their own terms; this one's pretty ridiculous. The two sexy stars don't really click. [R]▼●◗

No Name on the Bullet (1959) **C-77m.** ******* D: Jack Arnold. Audie Murphy, Charles Drake, Joan Evans, Virginia Grey, Warren Stevens, Edgar Stehli, R. G. Armstrong, Willis Bouchey, Karl Swenson, Charles Watts, Jerry Paris, Whit Bissell. A quiet, cultured gunman (Murphy, in a fine performance) rides into a small town to kill someone, though no one but he knows who his target is. Guilt and paranoia create their own victims. Slow, philosophical, and intelligent, this is the best of sci-fi director Arnold's several Westerns. CinemaScope.▼◗

None But the Brave (1965) **C-105m.** ****½** D: Frank Sinatra. Frank Sinatra, Clint Walker, Tommy Sands, Tony Bill, Brad Dexter. Taut war drama focusing on crew of cracked-up plane and Japanese army patrol who make peace on a remote island during WW2. Panavision.▼●◗

None But the Lonely Heart (1944) **113m.** ****½** D: Clifford Odets. Cary Grant, Ethel Barrymore, Barry Fitzgerald, Jane Wyatt, Dan Duryea, George Coulouris, June Duprez. Odets' moody drama of a Cockney drifter features one of Grant's most ambitious performances, and some fine moments, but suffers from censorship restrictions of the time, and misplaced WW2 rhetoric. Barrymore won Supporting Actress Oscar as Grant's dying mother. Also shown in computer-colored version.▼●◗

None Shall Escape (1944) **85m.** ******* D: Andre de Toth. Marsha Hunt, Alexander Knox, Henry Travers, Richard Crane, Dorothy Morris, Eric Rolf, Ruth Nelson, Kurt Kreuger. Trial of Nazi officer reviews his savage career, in taut drama that retains quite a punch. Released before, but set after, the end of WW2.

No Nukes (1980) **C-103m.** ******* D: Julian Schlossberg, Danny Goldberg, Anthony Potenza. Jackson Browne, Crosby, Stills & Nash, The Doobie Brothers, John Hall, Gil Scott-Heron, Bonnie Raitt, Carly Simon, Bruce Springsteen, James Taylor, Jesse Colin Young, Jane Fonda. Super Springsteen joins several appealing, if long in the tooth, fellow rock stars to protest nuclear power. Pleasant, if not very magnetic, concert filmdocumentary does boast chillingly hilarious clip from pro-nuke "Big Picture" episode from early '50s. Aka THE MUSE CONCERT: NO NUKES. [PG] ▼

Noose Hangs High, The (1948) **77m.** ****½** D: Charles Barton. Bud Abbott, Lou Costello, Joseph Calleia, Leon Errol, Cathy Downs, Mike Mazurki, Fritz Feld. Mistaken identity leads to complications with the boys robbed of a large sum of money; typical A&C, bolstered by presence of Errol. Highlight: "Mudder and Fodder."▼◗

Nora Prentiss (1947) **111m.** ****½** D: Vincent Sherman. Ann Sheridan, Kent Smith, Bruce Bennett, Robert Alda, Rosemary DeCamp, John Ridgely, Robert Arthur, Wanda Hendrix. Proper married doctor Smith falls for kicked-around singer Sheridan, leading to plenty of complications. Entertaining, albeit predictable, drama.◗

Nora's Will (2008-Mexican) **C-92m.** ******* D: Mariana Chenillo. Fernando Luján, Cecilia Suárez, Ari Brickman, Angelina Peláez, Enrique Arreola, Juan Carlos Colombo, Max Kerlow, Verónica Langer, Martín LaSalle, Silvia Mariscal. Matriarch of a family commits suicide in her high-rise apartment just before Passover, having left all the makings for a traditional dinner behind. Her sardonic ex-husband discovers the body and, because the holiday prevents her from being buried in a timely manner, endures an endless parade of people through the apartment over the next five days—with the corpse present in the bedroom. Droll, often poignant comedy-drama about family dynamics and religious hypocrisy is bracing in its originality and perfectly cast. Impressive debut feature for writer-director Chenillo. Aka FIVE DAYS WITHOUT NORA.

Norbit (2007) **C-102m.** *½ D: Brian Robbins. Eddie Murphy, Thandie Newton, Terry Crews, Clifton Powell, Cuba Gooding, Jr., Mighty Rasta, Eddie Griffin, Katt Williams, Marlon Wayans. As in COMING TO AMERICA and the NUTTY PROFESSOR vehicles Murphy plays several characters: Norbit, a meek young man brought up by Chinese restaurant owner Mr. Wong and stuck in a terrifying marriage with the hideously overweight Rasputia. All three are in search of a script. Murphy shows his comedic range but is let down by the material, which includes all the fat jokes the writers (including Murphy and his brother Charles) could come up with. Prophetic ad line for the movie asked, "Have You Ever Made a Really Big Mistake?" [PG-13]█

No Reservations (2007) **C-104m.** *** D: Scott Hicks. Catherine Zeta-Jones, Aaron Eckhart, Abigail Breslin, Patricia Clarkson, Jenny Wade, Bob Balaban, Brian F. O'Byrne, Lily Rabe, John McMartin, Celia Weston. Light, frothy comedy-drama about a career-minded N.Y.C. chef who faces two simultaneous challenges: becoming the guardian of her 9-year-old niece (Breslin) and fending off competition in her restaurant kitchen from a talented sous chef (Eckhart) who develops amorous feelings toward her. Attractive stars help keep this soufflé from falling. Remake of the 2002 German film MOSTLY MARTHA. Super 35. [PG]█

Normal Life (1996) **C-102m.** *** D: John McNaughton. Luke Perry, Ashley Judd, Darwin Moxey, Tom Towles, Penelope Milford. Fascinating true-crime story of a straight-arrow suburban cop who becomes the classic enabler to a drug-addicted shopaholic wife, leading him to a successful run as a bank robber! Perry and (especially) Judd are terrific in this downbeat, straightforward, morbidly compelling tale of twisted love. Made for theatrical release, debuted on cable TV. [R]▼●█

Norman . . . Is That You? (1976) **C-91m.** ** D: George Schlatter. Redd Foxx, Pearl Bailey, Dennis Dugan, Michael Warren, Tamara Dobson, Vernee Watson, Jayne Meadows. Leering comedy based on flop Broadway show and revamped with black stars: Foxx is distraught when he discovers his son is gay and determines to "straighten him out." Shot on videotape. [PG]▼

Norman Loves Rose (1982-Australian) **C-98m.** **½ D: Henri Safran. Carol Kane, Tony Owen, Warren Mitchell, Myra de

Groot, David Downer. OK comedy of teenager Owen enamored with sister-in-law Kane. She becomes pregnant, and who is the father? [R]▼

Norma Rae (1979) **C-113m.** *** D: Martin Ritt. Sally Field, Ron Leibman, Beau Bridges, Pat Hingle, Barbara Baxley, Gail Strickland, Lonny Chapman, Noble Willingham, Grace Zabriskie. Field is excellent in Oscar-winning performance as real-life poor Southern textile worker gradually won over toward unionization by N.Y.C. labor organizer. Entertaining, though not entirely believable; haunting theme "It Goes Like It Goes," sung by Jennifer Warnes, also won an Oscar. Panavision. [PG]▼●█

No Room for the Groom (1952) **82m.** **½ D: Douglas Sirk. Tony Curtis, Piper Laurie, Spring Byington, Don DeFore, Jack Kelly. Harmless shenanigans of ex-G.I. Curtis returning home to find it filled with in-laws.

Norseman, The (1978) **C-90m.** *½ D: Charles B. Pierce. Lee Majors, Cornel Wilde, Mel Ferrer, Jack Elam, Chris Connelly, Kathleen Freeman, Susie Coelho (Bono), Denny Miller. Stodgy period adventure casts Majors as 11th-century Viking prince who sails to North America in search of his father, a Norse king abducted by Indians. Panavision. [PG]▼

North (1994) **C-88m.** *½ D: Rob Reiner. Elijah Wood, Bruce Willis, Jason Alexander, Julia Louis-Dreyfus, Dan Aykroyd, Reba McEntire, Kathy Bates, Abe Vigoda, John Ritter, Faith Ford, Richard Belzer, Jon Lovitz, Alan Arkin, Alan Rachins, Matthew McCurley, Alexander Godunov, Kelly McGillis, Rosalind Chao, Ben Stein, Scarlett Johansson. Eleven-year-old boy who's convinced his folks don't appreciate him goes to court and wins the right to choose new parents, then travels the world to find the ideal mom and dad. Wrong-headed movie never connects, and leads to an unemotional and predictable finale. Reiner co-scripted with Alan Zweibel, on whose novel this was based. [PG]▼●

North Avenue Irregulars, The (1979) **C-99m.** **½ D: Bruce Bilson. Edward Herrmann, Barbara Harris, Susan Clark, Karen Valentine, Michael Constantine, Cloris Leachman, Patsy Kelly, Virginia Capers. Young priest (Herrmann) enlists churchgoing ladies for crime-fighting brigade; innocuous Disney comedy starts well but reverts to formula, including obligatory car pile-up finale. Fine actresses like Harris, Clark, and Leachman wasted. [G]▼

North by Northwest (1959) **C-136m.** **** D: Alfred Hitchcock. Cary Grant, Eva Marie Saint, James Mason, Leo G. Carroll, Martin Landau, Jessie Royce Landis, Philip Ober, Adam Williams, Josephine Hutchinson, Edward Platt. Quintessential Hitchcock comedy-thriller, with bewildered ad-man Grant chased cross country by both spies (who think he's a double agent) and the police (who think he's an assassin). One memorable scene after another, including now-legendary crop-dusting and Mount Rushmore sequences; one of the all-time great entertainments. Witty script by Ernest Lehman, exciting score by Bernard Herrmann. VistaVision. ▼●▌

North Country (2005) **C-126m.** ** D: Niki Caro. Charlize Theron, Frances McDormand, Woody Harrelson, Sissy Spacek, Sean Bean, Richard Jenkins, Jeremy Renner, Michelle Monaghan, Rusty Schwimmer, Jillian Armenante, Xander Berkeley. Single mom with two kids goes to work in a Minnesota mine in 1989, where the sexual harassment is intense, but no other women want to rock the boat and risk their jobs. Dramatization of a landmark real-life case has good performances (especially Theron's), but it's no NORMA RAE: too pat, too obvious, and too long. Super 35. [R]▌

North Dallas Forty (1979) **C-118m.** ***½ D: Ted Kotcheff. Nick Nolte, Mac Davis, Charles Durning, Dayle Haddon, G. D. Spradlin, Bo Svenson, Steve Forrest, John Matuszak, Dabney Coleman. Seriocomic version of Peter Gent's best-seller about labor abuse in the National Football League is the best gridiron film ever made and one of the best on any sport. Boasts Super Bowl–level performances for the most part. Scripted by its producer (Frank Yablans), director, and author. Panavision. [R]▼●▌

Northern Lights (1979) **90m.** ***½ D: John Hanson, Rob Nilsson. Robert Behling, Susan Lynch, Joe Spano, Henry Martinson, Marianne Astrom-DeFina, Ray Ness, Helen Ness. Incisive, unforgettable Americana about the struggles of farmers in pre-WW1 North Dakota, with Behling attempting to organize populist Nonpartisan League. Fine first feature for Hanson and Nilsson. ▼▌

Northern Pursuit (1943) **94m.** **½ D: Raoul Walsh. Errol Flynn, Julie Bishop, Helmut Dantine, John Ridgely, Gene Lockhart, Tom Tully. Flynn, a Mountie of German descent, pretends to have Nazi sympathies in order to learn the objectives of Nazis operating in Canada, in this standard but slickly done drama. ▼▌

Northfork (2003) **C-103m.** ** D: Michael Polish. Nick Nolte, James Woods, Anthony Edwards, Daryl Hannah, Peter Coyote, Duel Farnes, Mark Polish, Josh Barker, Graham Beckel, Jon Gries, Ben Foster, Robin Sachs, Marshall Bell, Kyle MacLachlan, Claire Forlani. Third in the Polish Brothers' Northwest "trilogy" (following TWIN FALLS, IDAHO and JACKPOT) is an allegory about the shuttering of a Montana town in 1955 to make way for a dam. Fascinating at first, but both precious and pretentious as angels and otherworldly characters take center stage; even the imagery, though

striking, becomes heavy-handed after a while. Woods also coexecutive produced. Panavision. [PG-13]▼▌

North Sea Hijack SEE: **ffolkes**

North Shore (1987) **C-96m.** ** D: William Phelps. Matt Adler, Nia Peeples, John Philbin, Gerry Lopez, Cristina Raines, Gregory Harrison. The top young surfer in Arizona (think about it) pits himself against the famed title Oahu waves, as well as the family of the native Hawaiian local he loves. Exceptional surfing photography carries a generally dippy script only so far. [PG]▼▌

North Star, The (1943) **105m.** **½ D: Lewis Milestone. Anne Baxter, Dana Andrews, Walter Huston, Ann Harding, Erich von Stroheim, Jane Withers, Farley Granger, Walter Brennan. Dramatic battle sequences in WW2 Russia marred by uninteresting stretches until German von Stroheim matches wits with village leader Huston. Good performances all around; script by Lillian Hellman. Later edited to 82m. to deemphasize the good Russians and retitled ARMORED ATTACK. Also shown in computer-colored version. ▼▌

North to Alaska (1960) **C-122m.** *** D: Henry Hathaway. John Wayne, Stewart Granger, Ernie Kovacs, Fabian, Capucine, Mickey Shaughnessy, Joe Sawyer, John Qualen. Fast-moving actioner with delightful tongue-in-cheek approach; prospectors Wayne and Granger have their hands full dealing with latter's kid brother Fabian, con artist Kovacs, and gold-digging (in the other sense) Capucine. CinemaScope. ▼●▌

North West Frontier SEE: **Flame Over India**

North West Mounted Police (1940) **C-125m.** **½ D: Cecil B. DeMille. Gary Cooper, Madeleine Carroll, Preston Foster, Paulette Goddard, Robert Preston, George Bancroft, Akim Tamiroff, Lon Chaney, Jr., Robert Ryan. DeMille at his most ridiculous, with Cooper as Dusty Rivers, Goddard a fiery half-breed in love with Preston, Lynne Overman as Scottish philosopher in superficial tale of Texas Ranger searching for fugitive in Canada. Much of outdoor action filmed on obviously indoor sets.

Northwest Passage (Book I—Rogers' Rangers) (1940) **C-125m.** ***½ D: King Vidor. Spencer Tracy, Robert Young, Walter Brennan, Ruth Hussey, Nat Pendleton, Robert Barrat, Addison Richards. Gritty, evocative filming of Kenneth Roberts' book about Rogers' Rangers and their stoic leader (Tracy), enduring hardships and frustrations while opening up new territory in Colonial America. Young and Brennan are greenhorns who learn hard knocks under taskmaster Tracy. The river-fording sequence is a knockout. ▼●▌

Norwood (1970) **C-96m.** ** D: Jack Haley, Jr. Glen Campbell, Kim Darby, Joe Namath,

Carol Lynley, Pat Hingle, Tisha Sterling, Dom DeLuise, Billy Curtis. Ex-Marine Campbell hits the road for series of unrelated adventures with service buddy Namath, a midget, a Greenwich Village girl, a shiftless brother-in-law, a dancing chicken, and a young girl with whom he falls in love. Easy to take, but pointless. Look for Cass Daley and Jack Haley (the director's father) in a brief appearance. [G]

Nosferatu (1922-German) **94m. ***½** D: F. W. Murnau. Max Schreck, Alexander Granach, Gustav von Wangenheim, Greta Schroeder. Early film version of *Dracula* is brilliantly eerie, full of imaginative touches that none of the later films quite recaptured. Schreck's vampire is also the ugliest in film history. The making of this film is dramatized in SHADOW OF THE VAMPIRE. Remade in 1979. ▼●▮

Nosferatu the Vampyre (1979-West German) **C-107m. ***½** D: Werner Herzog. Klaus Kinski, Isabelle Adjani, Bruno Ganz, Roland Topor. Spooky, funny, reverent remake of F. W. Murnau's vampire masterpiece should please Dracula fans of all persuasions. Kinski is magnificent as the good Count, and Adjani's classic beauty is utilized to the hilt. English-language version, which runs 96m., also exists. [PG] ▼●▮

No Small Affair (1984) **C-102m. ** D: Jerry Schatzberg. Jon Cryer, Demi Moore, George Wendt, Peter Frechette, Elizabeth Daily, Ann Wedgeworth, Jeffrey Tambor, Tim Robbins, Jennifer Tilly, Rick Ducommun, Tate Donovan. Self-possessed, smartassy, but virginal teenager becomes obsessed with an "older woman"—struggling rock singer Moore—and will do just about anything to make her like him. Some good moments here and there, but basically unappealing characters torpedo its chances. [R] ▼●▮

Nostalghia (1983-Italian-Russian) **C/B& W-126m. ***½** D: Andrei Tarkovsky. Oleg Yankovsky, Erland Josephson, Domiziana Giordano, Laura Del Marchi, Delia Boccardo, Patrizia Terreno. Deeply personal, stunningly directed tale of a Russian poet (Yankovsky) and his beautiful translator (Giordano) who are trekking across Italy, inquiring into the life of a long-dead composer. The poet is so immersed in himself that he barely can communicate with those around him; then he meets a recluse (Josephson) who is certain that the end of the world is near. A provocative, insightful epic, lovingly rendered by one of the cinema's true poets. ▼●▮

Nostradamus (1994-British-German) **C-118m. ** D: Roger Christian. Tchéky Karyo, F. Murray Abraham, Rutger Hauer, Amanda Plummer, Julia Ormond, Anthony Higgins. Cornball biographical drama about the fabled 16th-century astrologer-physician (Karyo), who is seen prophesizing everything from Hitler's rise to the

Kennedy assassination—all the while retaining his allure for the females of his own time. Best watched when in a silly mood. [R] ▼●

No Strings Attached (2011) **C-110m. **½** D: Ivan Reitman. Natalie Portman, Ashton Kutcher, Kevin Kline, Cary Elwes, Greta Gerwig, Lake Bell, Olivia Thirlby, Chris "Ludacris" Bridges, Jake Johnson, Mindy Kaling, Talia Balsam, Ophelia Lovibond, Ben Lawson, Tim Matheson, Guy Branum, Abby Elliott, Gary David Goldberg, Nasim Pedrad. Portman and Kutcher, who first met as adolescents, run into each other as grown-ups and are immediately attracted to one another, but she doesn't want to be in a relationship. Instead, she asks if he'd be willing to agree to be sex partners and nothing more. Naturally, he says yes, and just as naturally, we know it isn't going to last. Slick, well-cast film has women talking frankly about sex, which gives a fresh coat of paint to this otherwise predictable romantic comedy, buoyed by attractive stars and colorful supporting characters. Reitman appears briefly as a director. [R] ▮

No Such Thing (2002-U.S.-Icelandic-German) **C-102m. *½** D: Hal Hartley. Robert John Burke, Julie Christie, Sarah Polley, Helen Mirren, Ilene Bergelson, Helgi Bjornsson. Good cast is completely wasted in this embarrassing takeoff on *Beauty and the Beast*. A young TV journalist is sent to follow up an investigative news story on a murderous monsterlike creature in Iceland after the original news crew disappears. Hartley goes astray here, with pretensions beyond anything he actually manages to get on the screen. Christie works far too infrequently to turn up in psychobabble such as this. [R] ▮

No Surrender (1985-British-Canadian) **C-103m. **½** D: Peter K. Smith. Michael Angelis, Ray McAnally, Avis Bunnage, James Ellis, Bernard Hill, Mark Mulholland, Joanne Whalley, Michael Ripper, Elvis Costello. Interesting parable of modern British society and its problems, set in a remote Liverpool nightclub where two warring sets of old folks come into conflict, paralleling the troubles in Northern Ireland. Ambitious script by Alan Bleasdale tries to cover too much ground, but McAnally stands out as ruthless Loyalist gunman. [R] ▮

Not Another Teen Movie (2001) **C-89m. *½** D: Joel Gallen. Chyler Leigh, Chris Evans, Jaime Pressly, Mia Kirshner, Eric Christian Olsen, Deon Richmond, Eric Jungmann, Ron Lester, Randy Quaid, Paul Gleason, Ed Lauter, Mr. T, Molly Ringwald. On a wager, a high school hunk (Evans) sets out to woo a rebellious plain Jane named Janey (Leigh) and transform her into a prom queen. Barely funny parody lifts plotlines, characters, and entire scenes from a variety of recent films. Loaded with in-jokes, sight gags, and (quite literally) bathroom humor, but the results are tepid at best. Alternate version runs 101m. [R]▼▶

Not as a Stranger (1955) **135m. *** D:** Stanley Kramer. Olivia de Havilland, Frank Sinatra, Robert Mitchum, Charles Bickford, Gloria Grahame, Broderick Crawford, Lee Marvin, Lon Chaney, Henry (Harry) Morgan, Virginia Christine, Jerry Paris. Morton Thompson novel of Mitchum marrying nurse de Havilland who supports him through medical school despite oft-strained relationship. Glossy tribute to medical profession contains excellent performances by all. Producer Kramer's directorial debut.▼▶

Not Easily Broken (2009) **C-99m. **½ D:** Bill Duke. Morris Chestnut, Taraji P. Henson, Maeve Quinlan, Kevin Hart, Eddie Cibrian, Jenifer Lewis, Wood Harris, Albert Hall, Niecy Nash. Although there's enough soap operatics to fill a Douglas Sirk '50s melodrama, this sincere story of a troubled marriage still manages to engage. When Henson is hurt in an auto accident it puts added pressure on her already wobbly relationship with well-meaning husband Chestnut. Adding to their woes is his budding "friendship" with her white physical therapist and her teenage son, and constant interference from Henson's live-in mother. With a rare, male point of view and fine acting by the leads, this recognizable human drama overcomes a rather pedantic plotline to make its points. Based on the novel by T. D. Jakes, who shows up in a brief cameo. [PG-13]▶

Notebook, The (2004) **C-124m. *** D:** Nick Cassavetes.RyanGosling,RachelMcAdams, James Garner, Gena Rowlands, James Marsden, Kevin Connolly, Joan Allen, Sam Shepard, David Thornton, Jamie Anne Brown, Heather Wahlquist, Obba Babatundé. Emotional, richly romantic drama told in flashback, as Garner reads nursing home patient Rowlands the star-crossed love story of a boy and girl. Eventually, the modern story and the vintage one intertwine. A rare, no-holds-barred portrait of love and passion without cynicism or "ironic distance." Gosling and McAdams are exceptionally good. Based on the novel by Nicholas Sparks. J-D-C Scope. [PG-13] ▼▶

No-Tell Hotel, The SEE: **Rosebud Beach Hotel, The**

Notes From Underground (1995) **C-88m. *** D:** Gary Walkow. Henry Czerny, Sheryl Lee. Biting adaptation of the Dostoyevsky novella features a soul-baring performance by Czerny as Underground Man: a sarcastic loner-loser who is at once miserable and proud, brutal and deeply human. At the crux of the narrative is his recollection of a dinner, where his presence was unwanted, and his attempt to connect with a prostitute (Lee). Difficult to watch, at times, because of its stinging insights and emotional truths, but well worth the effort.▼▶

Notes on a Scandal (2006-U.S.-British) **C-91m. ***½ D:** Richard Eyre. Judi Dench, Cate Blanchett, Bill Nighy, Andrew Simpson, Phil Davis, Michael Maloney, Juno Temple, Julia McKenzie. Fascinating drama about a spinster teacher (Dench) who adopts the new art instructor (Blanchett) at her school as a friend, which is more of a burden than the emotionally vulnerable younger woman can possibly realize. When Blanchett has a fling with one of her students, the stage is set for high drama on all fronts. Playwright Patrick Marber (*Closer*) adapted Zoë Heller's novel *What Was She Thinking?: Notes on a Scandal*, which was inspired by the real-life case of Mary Kay Letourneau. Sensational performances by both stars (and Nighy, as Blanchett's husband). [R]▶

Not for Publication (1984-U.S.-British) **C-88m. ** D:** Paul Bartel. Nancy Allen, David Naughton, Laurence Luckinbill, Alice Ghostley, Richard Paul, Barry Dennen, Cork Hubbert, Paul Bartel. Unsuccessful attempt to replicate an old-fashioned screwball comedy. Allen leads double life as the star reporter of a sleazy N.Y.C. tabloid and a worker in the reelection campaign of oddball mayor Luckinbill. Along the way shy photographer Naughton falls for her. [R]▼▶

Nothing but a Man (1964) **92m. ***½ D:** Michael Roemer. Ivan Dixon, Abbey Lincoln, Julius Harris, Gloria Foster, Martin Priest, Leonard Parker, Yaphet Kotto, Stanley Greene. Quietly powerful look at blacks in the South, with Dixon as a railroad worker who tries to settle down for the first time in his life with schoolteacher Lincoln, and has to deal with a level of prejudice—and self-denial—he's never faced before. Perceptive and honest, this film manages to make its points without melodrama. A small gem. Look for Esther Rolle and Moses Gunn in small roles.▼●▶

Nothing but the Best (1964-British) **C-99m. ***½ D:** Clive Donner. Alan Bates, Denholm Elliott, Harry Andrews, Millicent Martin, Pauline Delany. Biting look at social-climbing playboy Bates who commits murder to get ahead in the world. Written by Frederic Raphael.

Nothing but the Night (1972-British) **C-90m. *½ D:** Peter Sasdy. Christopher Lee, Peter Cushing, Diana Dors, Georgia Brown, Keith Barron, Fulton Mackay, Gwyneth Strong. Uninvolving supernatural thriller about a cult that attempts immortality by projecting their personalities into the bodies of children. Filmed by Lee's production banner in a failed attempt to encourage more serious genre films. Aka THE DEVIL'S UNDEAD and THE RESURRECTION SYNDICATE. [PG]▼

Nothing But the Truth (2008) **C-107m. *** D:** Rod Lurie. Kate Beckinsale, Matt Dillon, Vera Farmiga, Edie Falco, Alan Alda, David Schwimmer, Noah Wyle,

Angela Bassett, Courtney B. Vance, Peter Coyote, Jamey Sheridan. Washington reporter Beckinsale "outs" a CIA agent (Farmiga), who happens to be a fellow mom at her daughter's school. She's willing to go to jail to protect her source, and does, but can't anticipate how great a toll it will take on her life and her family. Potent topical drama inspired by the Judith Miller–Valerie Plame affair of 2005 deals with intriguing, personal facets of a situation that's usually explored only for the principle involved. The punch line packs a wallop. Famed First Amendment attorney Floyd Abrams, who argued for *The New York Times*' Miller in court, is very good here as the trial judge. Written by the director. Super 35. [R]▶

Nothing but Trouble (1991) **C-93m.** BOMB D: Dan Aykroyd. Chevy Chase, Dan Aykroyd, John Candy, Demi Moore, Taylor Negron, Bertila Damas, Valri Bromfield. Chase and Moore, off on a weekend, get nabbed for speeding in a hellhole town under the complete domination of ancient judge Aykroyd (unrecognizable under mounds of makeup); rest of film deals with their attempted escape. Stupefyingly unwatchable; Aykroyd's directorial debut (he also wrote it). And yes, his nose *is* supposed to look like a penis. Watch for Tupac Shakur as a "digital underground member." [PG-13] ▼●▶

Nothing in Common (1986) **C-118m.** ** D: Garry Marshall. Tom Hanks, Jackie Gleason, Eva Marie Saint, Hector Elizondo, Barry Corbin, Bess Armstrong, Sela Ward, John Kapelos, Jane Morris, Dan Castellaneta, Tracy Reiner. Interminably long, highly uneven comedy-drama about a perpetual adolescent who's forced to deal with his aging, unloving father when his mom leaves him flat. Some poignant, relevant conclusions about love and responsibility (and some funny shots at the advertising business) are undermined by overlength and meandering nature of film. Hanks is excellent; Gleason is abrasive (in his last film appearance). Later a TV series. Super 35. [PG] ▼●▶

Nothing Lasts Forever (1984) **C/B&W-82m.** **½ D: Tom Schiller. Zach Galligan, Apollonia van Ravenstein, Lauren Tom, Dan Aykroyd, Imogene Coca, Eddie Fisher, Sam Jaffe, Paul Rogers, Mort Sahl, Bill Murray, Anita Ellis. Strange, occasionally entertaining comedy of aspiring artist Galligan's experiences in a N.Y.C. of the future—and also on a trip to the moon. A most unusual cast; much better seen than described. Written by first-time director Schiller, produced by Lorne Michaels, both of TV's *Saturday Night Live*. [PG]

Nothing Like the Holidays (2008) **C-98m.** *** D: Alfredo De Villa. Alfred Molina, Elizabeth Peña, Freddy Rodríguez, Luis Guzmán, Jay Hernandez, John Leguizamo, Debra Messing, Vanessa Ferlito, Melonie Diaz. Christmas brings a Puerto Rican family together in the Humboldt Park section of Chicago. One of the three grown children (Rodríguez) has just returned from active duty in Iraq, while various rivalries, unfinished business, and a mystery surrounding the patriarch (Molina) create emotional tumult in the household. Familiar setup yields a satisfying holiday concoction with comedy, drama, and sentimentality all part of the mix—and an exceptionally good cast to carry it off. Super 35. [PG-13] ▶

Nothing Personal (1980-U.S.-Canadian) **C-97m.** *½ D: George Bloomfield. Donald Sutherland, Suzanne Somers, Lawrence Dane, Roscoe Lee Browne, Dabney Coleman, Saul Rubinek, Catherine O'Hara, John Dehner, Chief Dan George. Sutherland is a professor attempting to stop a corporation from slaughtering baby seals, Somers a lawyer who helps him. Inane romantic comedy. Look for appearances by Craig Russell, Tony Rosato, Joe Flaherty, and Eugene Levy. [PG]▼

Nothing Sacred (1937) **C-75m.** ***½ D: William Wellman. Carole Lombard, Fredric March, Walter Connolly, Charles Winninger, Sig Rumann, Frank Fay. Classic comedy about hotshot reporter (March) who exploits Vermont girl's "imminent" death from radium poisoning for headline value in N.Y.C. Ben Hecht's cynical script vividly enacted by March and Lombard (at her best). Gershwinesque music score by Oscar Levant. Trivia note: Connolly's character is named Oliver Stone! Later a Broadway musical called *Hazel Flagg*. Remade as LIVING IT UP. ▼●

Nothing to Lose (1997) **C-97m.** **½ D: Steve Oedekerk. Martin Lawrence, Tim Robbins, John C. McGinley, Giancarlo Esposito, Kelly Preston, Michael McKean, Rebecca Gayheart, Samaria Graham, Irma P. Hall, Steve Oedekerk. Stunned to find his wife in bed with his boss, Robbins drives away in a daze—only to be carjacked by out-of-work Lawrence. Having nothing to lose, Robbins roars off into the desert with his surprised passenger; this being a buddy comedy, they try to help each other out. OK comedy, with a likable cast, is undercut by predictability (and not exploiting the premise for its full comic value). [R]▼●▶

No Time for Comedy (1940) **98m.** **½ D: William Keighley. James Stewart, Rosalind Russell, Genevieve Tobin, Charles Ruggles, Allyn Joslyn, Louise Beavers. Slick but dated adaptation of S. N. Behrman play about actress who tries to keep her playwright-husband from taking himself too seriously. Smoothly done but artificial. Aka GUY WITH A GRIN.

No Time for Sergeants (1958) **119m.** ***½ D: Mervyn LeRoy. Andy Griffith, Myron McCormick, Nick Adams, Murray Hamilton, Don Knotts. Funny military comedy based on Ira Levin's Broadway play (which got its start as a 1955 *U.S. Steel Hour* TV play). Griffith and McCormick repeat roles as hayseed inducted into service and his harried sergeant. Griffith's best comedy, with good support from Adams, and, in a small role as a noncommissioned officer, Knotts. Script by John Lee Mahin. Followed years later by a TV series. ▼O◗

Not of This Earth (1988) **C-80m. ** D:** Jim Wynorski. Traci Lords, Arthur Roberts, Lenny Juliano, Ace Mask, Roger Lodge. Strictly standard remake of the 1957 Roger Corman quickie, in which Roberts comes to earth in search of blood to replenish his dying planet's population. Film's chief interest is the casting of ex-porn queen Lords as a nurse. [R] ▼O◗

Not One Less (1999-Chinese) **C-106m. ** D:** Zhang Yimou. Wei Minzhi, Zhang Huike, Tian Zhenda, Gao Enman, Sun Zhimei. A young student (Wei) is asked to act as teacher to her near-peers in a rural Chinese village after the regular schoolmaster leaves for a month to tend to his ailing mother. The stipulation: She must not permit any dropouts if she wants to earn an extra 10 yuan in pay. Based-on-fact story results in a notably slight exercise for China's top filmmaker. The actors are non-professionals, and show it, in lifeless and repetitive scenes. [G] ▼◗

Not on the Lips (2003-French-Swiss) **C-117m. *** D:** Alain Resnais. Sabine Azéma, Isabelle Nanty, Audrey Tautou, Pierre Arditi, Darry Cowl, Jalil Lespert, Daniel Prévost, Lambert Wilson. Charming musical farce is set in 1925 and involves various well-heeled Parisians and their affairs of the heart. Enjoyable trifle is as light as a soufflé, and features some gentle lampooning of pompous Americans and the era's art movements. Songs are effortlessly integrated into the action, and the actors often address the camera with observations that fit right into the flow of the story. Adapted from a 1925 Andre Bardé–Maurice Yvain operetta that was filmed before in 1931. ▼◗

Notorious (1946) **101m. ***½ D:** Alfred Hitchcock. Cary Grant, Ingrid Bergman, Claude Rains, Louis Calhern, Leopoldine Konstantin, Reinhold Schunzel, Moroni Olsen. Top-notch espionage tale by Ben Hecht, set in post-WW2 South America, with Ingrid marrying spy Rains to aid U.S. and agent Grant. Frank, tense, well acted, with amazingly suspenseful climax (and one memorably passionate love scene). Remade for cable TV in 1992. ▼O◗

Notorious (2009) **C-122m. ** D:** George Tillman, Jr. Jamal Woolard, Angela Bassett, Derek Luke, Anthony Mackie, Naturi Naughton, Antonique Smith, Aunjanue Ellis, John Ventimiglia. Overlong biopic of mysteriously assassinated-at-24 Brooklyn rap artist Biggie Smalls (aka The Notorious B.I.G.) has the authorized feel that inevitably comes with a movie listing Smalls' mother (played here by Bassett) and Sean Combs (Luke) as producers. Movie reaps sporadic snap

from the dynamic performance of Woolard as the sometimes awkward, overweight kid and onetime drug dealer sired by a religious mom, which allegedly led to tension between spiritual living and the flashy pleasures that money and available women can bring. Movie opened theatrically on the Martin Luther King birthday weekend—a stretch. Christopher Jordan Wallace, the real-life son of Biggie and Faith Evans, plays his father as a boy. Super 35. [R] ◗

Notorious Bettie Page, The (2006) **C/B&W-90m. *** D:** Mary Harron. Gretchen Mol, Chris Bauer, Jared Harris, Sarah Paulson, Cara Seymour, David Strathairn, Lili Taylor, John Cullum, Matt McGrath, Austin Pendleton, Norman Reedus, Dallas Roberts, Victor Slezak, Jonathan Woodward, Max Casella. Absorbing biopic about a nice, churchgoing girl from Nashville who rebounds from several ugly encounters with men, heads to N.Y.C. in the 1940s, and becomes a pinup icon. Her naiveté is contrasted with the sometimes-sordid world in which she works, posing for bondage photos and movies, which eventually run afoul of a U.S. Senate crackdown on smut. Mol is a pluperfect Page in this laid-back film that captures its era (and its mores) quite nicely. [R] ◗

Notorious C.H.O. (2002) **C-95m. *** D:** Lorene Machado. Margaret Cho. Lively, entertaining concert film not only presents Cho's hilarious one-woman show, as performed in Seattle, but takes us backstage and even introduces us to Margaret's mother, who figures so prominently in her monologues. A good follow-up to I'M THE ONE THAT I WANT, with more of Cho's uncensored comedy, tackling sexual and gender issues for an audience packed with fans. ▼◗

Notorious Landlady, The (1962) **123m. **½ D:** Richard Quine. Kim Novak, Jack Lemmon, Fred Astaire, Lionel Jeffries, Estelle Winwood, Maxwell Reed. Lemmon entranced by houseowner Novak, decides to find out if she really did kill her husband; set in London. Offbeat comedy-mystery written by Blake Edwards and Larry Gelbart. ◗

Not Quite Jerusalem SEE: **Not Quite Paradise**

Not Quite Paradise (1985-British) **C-105m. **½ D:** Lewis Gilbert. Joanna Pacula, Sam Robards, Todd Graff, Kevin McNally, Selina Cadell, Kate Ingram, Libby Morris. Love on a kibbutz; pleasant, low-key story of volunteers from the U.S., England, and other nations adjusting to the hard life on an Israeli farm, where Yank Robards falls in love with sabra Pacula. Not much oomph but an OK, old-fashioned romance. Originally titled: NOT QUITE JERUSALEM. [R] ▼◗

Notre Musique (2004-French-Swiss) **C-80m. **½ D:** Jean-Luc Godard. Sarah Adler, Nade Dieu, Rony Kramer, Simon Eine, Jean-Christophe Bouvet, Jean-Luc Godard. Maddening yet fascinating Godardian foray into the effect of violence on the human spirit, divided into three sections: "Hell," "Purgatory," and "Heaven." There's plenty of theoretical chatter in the skimpy narrative, set at a literary conference in war-ravaged Sarajevo whose attendees include Godard himself and a young Israeli journalist who is researching an article about a place "where reconciliation is possible." Godard contrasts footage of real-life brutality with the violence staged in Hollywood movies to entertain the masses. ▼▶

Notting Hill (1999-British) **C-123m.** *** D: Roger Michell. Julia Roberts, Hugh Grant, Hugh Bonneville, Emma Chambers, James Dreyfus, Rhys Ifans, Tim McInnerny, Gina McKee, Emily Mortimer. Bemused London bookshop owner chances to meet world-famous movie star, and sparks fly . . . but their budding relationship is bumpier than either could imagine. Enjoyable romantic comedy is a complete contrivance, but so smoothly done, and so engagingly performed, that you don't much mind. Written by Richard Curtis, whose script for FOUR WEDDINGS AND A FUNERAL made Grant a star. Alec Baldwin and Matthew Modine appear unbilled. Super 35. [PG-13] ▼●▶

Not Wanted (1949) **94m.** **½ D: Elmer Clifton. Sally Forrest, Keefe Brasselle, Leo Penn, Dorothy Adams. Well-intentioned account of unwed mother seeking affection and understanding; produced and coscripted by Ida Lupino (who also apparently directed most of the film). Later expanded with unrelated material (including childbirth footage) and released as an exploitation film, THE WRONG RUT (aka SHAME and STREETS OF SIN). ▼▶

Not With My Wife You Don't! (1966) **C-118m.** **½ D: Norman Panama. Tony Curtis, Virna Lisi, George C. Scott, Carroll O'Connor, Richard Eastham. Trivial fluff about air force officer Curtis and bored wife Lisi; pointless and aimless, but attractive to the eye. ▼▶

Not Without My Daughter (1991) **C-114m.** *** D: Brian Gilbert. Sally Field, Alfred Molina, Sheila Rosenthal, Roshan Seth, Sarah Badel, Mony Rey, Georges Corraface. American woman accompanies her Iranian-born husband on a visit to his homeland. Once there, he decides to stay, and she learns (to her horror) that in Iran she has no rights, as a wife or as a woman, so she must find a way to flee the country with her daughter. Absorbing film based on real-life experience of Betty Mahmoody; the drama works because Field is so believable, and because her husband is not portrayed as a one-dimensional monster. Filmed in Israel. [PG-13] ▼●▶

Nouvelle Vague (1990-French-Swiss) **C-88m.** **½ D: Jean-Luc Godard. Alain Delon, Domiziana Giordano, Roland Amstutz, Laurence Cote, Christophe Odent. Delon and Giordano are cast as a handsome, ultra-rich, powerful couple; the narrative focuses on sexual and political issues that run through all of Godard's films. This one's strictly a matter of taste—and one's tolerance for latter-day Godard. Aka NEW WAVE. ▼

November (2005) **C-78m.** ** D: Greg Harrison. Courteney Cox, James Le Gros, Michael Ealy, Nora Dunn, Nick Offerman, Anne Archer, Matthew Carey, Robert Wu. Artsy indie about a traumatized woman whose boyfriend has been murdered in a convenience-store robbery. A month later, he telephones her . . . or maybe not. Cox (bleakly deglamorized) passes through denial, despair, and acceptance as she, her mom (Archer), and her shrink (Dunn) try to figure out if she's psychic, psychotic, or merely overmedicated. Bloody and befuddling foray is derivative of both BLOWUP and RUN LOLA RUN. Slow end-title crawl extends a slight film barely over an hour long. The director also edited. [R] ▶

Novocaine (2001) **C-95m.** ** D: David Atkins. Steve Martin, Helena Bonham Carter, Laura Dern, Elias Koteas, Scott Caan, Keith David, Lynne Thigpen. Successful dentist who's about to marry his hygienist is fatally attracted to a new female patient, and makes one misstep that quickly snowballs into Big Trouble. Mix of film noir and black comedy starts off well, but becomes distinctly unpleasant, despite some clever twists and good performances. Kevin Bacon appears unbilled. [R] ▼▶

Now About These Women SEE: **All These Women**

Now and Forever (1983-Australian) **C-93m.** ** D: Adrian Carr. Cheryl Ladd, Robert Coleby, Carmen Duncan, Christine Amor, Aileen Britton. Chic Ladd's husband is unfaithful, then is falsely accused of rape and sent to jail. This puts quite a strain on their marriage. Based on Danielle Steel's novel. If you like Harlequin romances . . . Panavision. [R] ▼●▶

Now and Then (1995) **C-96m.** **½ D: Lesli Linka Glatter. Christina Ricci, Thora Birch, Gaby Hoffman, Ashleigh Aston Moore, Demi Moore, Melanie Griffith, Rosie O'Donnell, Rita Wilson, Willa Glen, Bonnie Hunt, Janeane Garofalo, Lolita Davidovich, Cloris Leachman, Hank Azaria. Essentially a distaff version of STAND BY ME in which we get to know four friends during their last summer of adolescence in 1970. The film is bookended by sequences of the friends reminiscing at a baby shower 20 years later. Nicely done, but covers awfully familiar territory; strongest asset is the lovely performances of its young stars. Moore also produced. Brendan Fraser appears unbilled. [PG-13] ▼●▶

No Way Out (1950) **106m.** *** D: Joseph L. Mankiewicz. Richard Widmark, Linda Darnell, Stephen McNally, Sidney Poitier,

Ruby Dee, Ossie Davis, Bill Walker. Violent tale of racial hatred involving bigot Widmark, who has gangster pals avenge his brother's death by creating race riots. Once-provocative film is still engrossing but seems a bit artificial at times. Film debuts of Poitier and Davis. ▼▶

No Way Out (1987) C-116m. *** D: Roger Donaldson. Kevin Costner, Gene Hackman, Sean Young, Will Patton, Howard Duff, George Dzundza, Jason Bernard, Iman, Fred Dalton Thompson, David Paymer. Taut melodramatic thriller about a murder and cover-up within the inner circles of the federal government. Young is tantalizingly sexy as the woman involved with both CIA liaison Costner and Secretary of Defense Hackman. Hard to tell at first that this is a remake of THE BIG CLOCK, but it is—except for a ludicrous (and totally unnecessary) "twist" ending. Script by Robert Garland, who also produced. Super 35. [R] ▼●]

No Way to Treat a Lady (1968) C-108m. ***½ D: Jack Smight. Rod Steiger, Lee Remick, George Segal, Eileen Heckart, Murray Hamilton, Michael Dunn, Barbara Baxley, Ruth White, Doris Roberts, David Doyle. Delicious blend of romantic comedy and murder, with Steiger as flamboyant ladykiller, Segal as "Mo Brummel," cop on his trail, Remick as Segal's new ladyfriend who could be next victim. Script by John Gay, from the William Goldman novel. ▼▶

Nowhere (1997) C-85m. ** D: Gregg Araki. James Duval, Rachel True, Nathan Bexton, Christina Applegate, Chiara Mastroianni, Debi Mazar, Kathleen Robertson, Jordan Ladd, Sarah Lassez, Guillermo Diaz, Jeremy Jordan, Alan Boyce, Jaason Simmons, Ryan Phillippe, Heather Graham, Scott Caan, John Ritter, Beverly D'Angelo, Denise Richards, Rose McGowan, Mena Suvari. CALIGULA for the CLUELESS set. A herd of oversexed L.A. teens searches for true love in the wasteland of SoCal. Pop visual design and eclectic cast make for some twisted fun, although the director's taste for gallows humor and brutal violence isn't for everyone. Various pop culture celebrities turn up in cameos. [R] ▼●

Nowhere Boy (2009-British-Canadian) C-99m. *** D: Sam Taylor-Wood. Aaron Johnson, Kristin Scott Thomas, Anne-Marie Duff, David Morrissey, David Threlfall, Thomas Brodie Sangster, Josh Bolt, Sam Bell, Ophelia Lovibond. In 1950s Liverpool, a teenaged John Lennon experiences growing pains. Having been raised by his tightly wound aunt (Scott Thomas), he now meets the mother (Duff) who abandoned him as a child and is drawn to the outgoing woman without really knowing what happened back then. Meanwhile, his budding interest in music leads him to start a band. Poignant story is beautifully played and never throws

foreshadowing of later history in our face. Panavision. [R] ▶

Nowhere in Africa (2001-German) C-135m. **** D: Caroline Link. Juliane Köhler, Merab Ninidze, Matthias Habich, Sidede Onyulo, Karoline Eckertz, Lea Kurka. A Jewish family manages to get out of Germany in 1938, just in the nick of time, and moves to Kenya, where they must rebuild their lives from the ground up. A sweeping, subtly powerful drama that manages to tell its story from three separate points of view—the husband, wife, and daughter—as each one forges an individual relationship with a strange, new environment. Director Link adapted the autobiographical novel by Stefanie Zweig, and presents the story with compassion and a keen eye for detail. Oscar winner for Best Foreign Language Film. Arriscope. ▼▶

Nowhere to Hide (1987-Canadian) C-90m. ** D: Mario Azzopardi. Amy Madigan, Daniel Hugh Kelly, Robin MacEachern, Michael Ironside, John Colicos. Obvious thriller with Madigan cast as the wife of Marine Kelly. He's killed while investigating suspicious helicopter crashes . . . and she becomes a target. Madigan is much better than the material. [R] ▼

Nowhere to Run (1993) C-95m. *½ D: Robert Harmon. Jean-Claude Van Damme, Rosanna Arquette, Kieran Culkin, Ted Levine, Joss Ackland, Tiffany Taubman. Embarrassingly awful Van Damme vehicle, in which he's an escaped con who comes to the aid of widow-in-distress Arquette and her two kids. Based on a story by Joe Eszterhas and Richard Marquand; Eszterhas also scripted. [R] ▼●]

Now, Voyager (1942) 117m. ***½ D: Irving Rapper. Bette Davis, Paul Henreid, Claude Rains, Gladys Cooper, Bonita Granville, John Loder, Ilka Chase, Lee Patrick, Mary Wickes, Janis Wilson. Vintage, first-class soaper with Bette as sheltered spinster brought out of her shell by psychiatrist Rains, falling in love with suave Henreid, helping shy girl Wilson. All this set to beautiful, Oscar-winning Max Steiner music makes for top entertainment of this kind. Olive Higgins Prouty's best-seller was adapted by Casey Robinson. ▼●]

Now You See Him, Now You Don't (1972) C-88m. **½ D: Robert Butler. Kurt Russell, Cesar Romero, Joe Flynn, Jim Backus, William Windom, Michael McGreevy, Ed Begley, Jr. Follow-up to THE COMPUTER WORE TENNIS SHOES has student Russell inventing an invisible spray, which of course is coveted by a gang of crooks. Some good special effects in this so-so Disney comedy. [G] ▼▶

Nuclear Run SEE: **Chain Reaction** (1980)
Nuclear Terror SEE: **Golden Rendezvous**
Nude Bomb, The (1980) C-94m. **½ D: Clive Donner. Don Adams, Andrea Howard, Vittorio Gassman, Dana Elcar, Pamela

Hensley, Sylvia Kristel, Robert Karvelas, Norman Lloyd, Rhonda Fleming, Joey Forman. Secret Agent 86 from 1960s *Get Smart* sitcom returns in feature-length spoof about a madman whose bombs will destroy the world's clothing; coscripter Bill Dana has a funny bit as fashion designer Jonathan Levinson Siegel. Agreeable time-filler. Shown on TV as THE RETURN OF MAXWELL SMART. Followed by the TV movie GET SMART, AGAIN! [PG]▼●)

Nudo di Donna (1981-Italian-French) C-105m. *** D: Nino Manfredi. Nino Manfredi, Eleonora Giorgi, Jean-Pierre Cassel, Georges Wilson. Suffering marital problems with wife of 16 years (Giorgi), Manfredi becomes infatuated with a nude rearview photo and takes up with its model, who looks just like his wife! Stunning location photography in Venice and a solid cast highlight this social comedy.▼●

Number One (1969) C-105m. *½ D: Tom Gries. Charlton Heston, Jessica Walter, Bruce Dern, John Randolph, Diana Muldaur. Heston turns in his loincloth for a jockstrap in this ludicrous drama about a New Orleans Saints quarterback who's fighting advancing age; interesting subject matter deserves better treatment. [M/PG]

Number One With a Bullet (1987) C-101m. **½ D: Jack Smight. Robert Carradine, Billy Dee Williams, Valerie Bertinelli, Peter Graves, Doris Roberts, Bobby Di Cicco. Carradine and Williams do well in this otherwise standard actioner, cast as a pair of "odd couple" detectives out to dethrone a drug kingpin. [R]▼

Number Seventeen (1932-British) 63m. *** D: Alfred Hitchcock. Leon M. Lion, Anne Grey, John Stuart, Donald Calthrop, Barry Jones, Garry Marsh. Entertaining comedy-thriller has tramp Lion stumbling upon a jewel thieves' hideout. Exciting chase sequence involves a train and bus (though the "special effects" are pretty obvious). Screenplay by Hitchcock.▼)

Number 23, The (2007) C-97m. ** D: Joel Schumacher. Jim Carrey, Virginia Madsen, Logan Lerman, Danny Huston, Rhona Mitra, Michelle Arthur, Lynn Collins, Mark Pellegrino, Ed Lauter. City dog catcher reads a book that messes with his mind—because it seems to resemble his own life, it makes him obsess about the number 23 and drives him to believe he's going to murder his wife. Utterly unconvincing thriller, especially when it finally gets around to tying up its loose ends. Visual stylistics are devoid of meaning here. Bud Cort appears unbilled. Unrated version runs 100m. Panavision. [R])

Numéro Deux (1975-French) C-88m. **½ D: Jean-Luc Godard. Sandrine Battistella, Pierre Dudry, Alexandre Rignault, Rachel Stefanopoli. Fascinating but self-conscious and confusing aural and visual smorgasbord detailing the effects of capitalism on a modern family. Shot on videotape. ▼

Nuns on the Run (1990-British) C-90m. **½ D: Jonathan Lynn. Eric Idle, Robbie Coltrane, Camille Coduri, Janet Suzman, Doris Hare, Lila Kaye, Robert Patterson. Genial farce about two career henchmen, fed up with their violent young boss, who try to make a score for themselves but bungle the job and hide out in a convent, disguised as nuns. Idle and Coltrane are great, and the film is genuinely funny at times—enough to forgive its periodic lulls. Written by director Lynn. [PG-13]▼●

Nun's Story, The (1959) C-149m. ***½ D: Fred Zinnemann. Audrey Hepburn, Peter Finch, Edith Evans, Peggy Ashcroft, Dean Jagger, Mildred Dunnock. Tasteful filming of Kathryn Hulme book, with Hepburn the nun who serves in Belgian Congo and later leaves convent. Colleen Dewhurst, as a homicidal patient, is electrifying. Screenplay by Robert Anderson. ▼●

Nunzio (1978) C-87m. **½ D: Paul Williams. David Proval, James Andronica, Tovah Feldshuh, Morgana King, Vincent Russo, Theresa Saldana, Monica Lewis. Retarded Brooklyn grocery delivery boy Proval imagines he's Superman, falls in love with bakery assistant Feldshuh. Mild story enhanced by Proval's fine performance; script by Andronica, who plays his tough but loving brother. [R]

Nurse Betty (2000) C-109m. ***½ D: Neil LaBute. Morgan Freeman, Renée Zellweger, Chris Rock, Greg Kinnear, Aaron Eckhart, Tia Texada, Crispin Glover, Pruitt Taylor Vince, Allison Janney, Kathleen Wilhoite, Sheila Kelley. Strikingly original, darkly comic (and perfectly cast) tale of sweet waitress whose fondness for a soap-opera actor turns to obsession after she witnesses a traumatic event. Screenwriters John C. Richards and James Flamberg create wonderfully surprising twists and turns—including some harsh moments of violence—yet tie everything up at the end. Super 35. [R]▼)

Nurse Sherri SEE: **Beyond the Living**

Nutcracker, The (1993) C-92m. ** D: Emile Ardolino. Darci Kistler, Damian Woetzel, Kyra Nichols, Bart Robinson Cook, Macaulay Culkin, Jessica Lynn Cohen; narrated by Kevin Kline. Much-too-stagy version of the famed, beloved ballet, set on Christmas Eve and telling the story of a little girl (Cohen) who finds herself in a fantasy-world of oversized toys. Culkin (the film's star attraction) is nothing special as the Nutcracker Prince. Adapted by Peter Martins, from the New York City Ballet production. Aka GEORGE BALANCHINE'S THE NUTCRACKER. [G]▼●

Nutcracker in 3D, The (2010-British-Hungarian) C-107m. BOMB D: Andrei Konchalovsky. Elle Fanning, Nathan Lane,

Frances de la Tour, John Turturro, Richard E. Grant, Yulia Visotskaya, Aaron Michael Drozin, Charlie Rowe, Shirley Henderson. Woeful, what-were-they-thinking musical mess shoves E.T.A. Hoffmann's 1816 gothic fairy tale into 1920s Vienna, presumably to name-drop Freud and center-stage a singing Einstein (Lane's "Everything is Relative" is among several wretched Tchaikovsky pastiches). Wide-eyed Fanning escapes unscathed, but Turturro's grotesque Rat King suggests Dana Carvey doing Phil Spector. Intermittently beautiful but generally atrocious mishmash pilfers George Lucas, steampunk, and the Ice Capades, and was shot in 2007. 3-D. [PG]

Nutcracker Prince, The (1990-Canadian) **C-75m.** *½ D: Paul Schibli. Voices of Kiefer Sutherland, Megan Follows, Peter O'Toole, Mike McDonald, Peter Boretski, Phyllis Diller. Young girl dreams of aiding toy soldiers in battle against evil Mouse King in this flat reworking of the classic story, set to Tchaikovsky music. Slow-paced low-budget animated feature based on the E.T.A. Hoffmann book *The Nutcracker and the Mouse King*; a Disney wannabe that simply isn't. [G] ▼●

Nutcracker, The Motion Picture (1986) **C-89m.** **½ D: Carroll Ballard. Hugh Bigney, Vanessa Sharp, Patricia Barker, Wade Walthall, Russell Burnett, voice of Julie Harris. Much of this version of *The Nutcracker*, performed by the Pacific Northwest Ballet, is like a music video: quick cutting and close-ups of legs, faces, and elbows. Very annoying. But the Tchaikovsky music is, of course, wonderful, as are Maurice Sendak's sets and costumes. [G] ▼●

Nuts (1987) **C-116m.** *** D: Martin Ritt. Barbra Streisand, Richard Dreyfuss, Maureen Stapleton, Eli Wallach, Robert Webber, James Whitmore, Karl Malden, Leslie Nielsen, William Prince, Hayley Taylor Block. Compelling drama about a belligerent woman assigned a Legal Aid lawyer who must fight for her right to stand trial for manslaughter, when both the state and her own parents insist that she's not in her right mind. Peerless cast of pros, and nimble staging by Ritt, manage to make you forget that this was a stage play, until the climax, when Streisand delivers a lengthy monologue—in loving close-up (she also produced). Tom Topor adapted his play, with Darryl Ponicsan and Alvin Sargent. Streisand also composed the score. [R] ▼●

Nutty Professor, The (1963) **C-107m.** *** D: Jerry Lewis. Jerry Lewis, Stella Stevens, Del Moore, Kathleen Freeman, Med Flory, Howard Morris, Elvia Allman, Henry Gibson. Jerry's wildest (and most narcissistic) comedy casts him as chipmunk-faced college professor who does Jekyll-and-Hyde transformation into swaggering Buddy Love (whom some have interpreted as a

Dean Martin caricature). More interesting than funny, although "Alaskan Polar Bear Heater" routine with Buddy Lester is a riot; Lewis buffs regard this as his masterpiece. Remade in 1996. ▼●

Nutty Professor, The (1996) **C-95m.** *** D: Tom Shadyac. Eddie Murphy, Jada Pinkett, James Coburn, Dave Chappelle, Larry Miller, John Ales. Sherman Klump is a sweet stumblebum of a science professor who's grossly overweight; when he meets a beautiful teaching assistant, he's motivated to try his lab experiments with DNA restructuring on himself and he's transformed into a thin, testosterone-overloaded superstud. Eddie is appealing and convincing as the prof, and hilarious as his alter ego; through camera magic (and the eye-popping, Osear-winning makeup by Rick Baker and David Leroy Anderson) he also plays almost every member of his family! One ingredient Jerry Lewis never thought of: enough flatulence jokes to last ten lifetimes. Followed by a sequel. [PG-13] ▼●

Nutty Professor II: The Klumps (2000) **C-106m.** ** D: Peter Segal. Eddie Murphy, Janet Jackson, Larry Miller, John Ales, Melinda McGraw, Anna Maria Horsford, Richard Gant, Chris Elliott, Kathleen Freeman. Professor Sherman Klump can't marry his sweetheart (Jackson) until he can get control of his demonic inner voice: the crass Buddy Love. Slimmest possible excuse for a sequel, though Murphy is brilliant as five members of the Klump family. The comic material is thunderously crude, however, and quickly runs out of steam. Director's cut runs 109m. [PG-13] ▼▶

O (2001) **C-95m.** *** D: Tim Blake Nelson. Mekhi Phifer, Josh Hartnett, Julia Stiles, Martin Sheen, Rain Phoenix, Elden Henson, John Heard, Andrew Keegan. Potent modern-day adaptation of Shakespeare's *Othello*, with Hartnett as the neglected son of a driven prep school basketball coach who turns his anger toward star player Phifer. Contemporary setting allows screenwriter Brad Kaaya to deal with teen angst, racism—and violence—while following the Bard's timeless story of jealousy and deceit. Fine performances all around. Completed in 1999, film's release was postponed because of real-life school shootings. [R] ▼▶

Oak, The (1992-French-Romanian) **C-105m.** *** D: Lucian Pintilie. Maia Morgenstern, Razvan Vasilescu, Victor Rebenguic, Dorel Visan. Schoolteacher Morgenstern sets out on a journey of self-discovery after her father (a former secret-police honcho) dies. Fascinating allegory–road movie mirroring the downfall of Communism in Romania. A highly personal film, strikingly directed by Pintilie, who also scripted. ▼

Objective, Burma! (1945) **142m.** ***½ D:

Raoul Walsh. Errol Flynn, William Prince, James Brown, George Tobias, Henry Hull, Warner Anderson. Zestful WW2 action film with Flynn and company as paratroopers invading Burma to wipe out important Japanese post; top excitement. Screenplay by Ranald MacDougall and Lester Cole. Reworked as DISTANT DRUMS, also directed by Walsh. Some prints cut to 127m. Also shown in computer-colored version. ▼●▌

Object of Beauty, The (1991) **C-97m.** **½ D: Michael Lindsay-Hogg. John Malkovich, Andie MacDowell, Lolita Davidovich, Rudi Davies, Joss Ackland, Bill Paterson, Ricci Harnett, Peter Riegert. Jet-set couple, who thrive on living beyond their means, find themselves stranded in a London hotel and decide to unload her coveted Henry Moore artifact—the one that may have been stolen by the hotel's newly hired deaf-mute maid. Definitely offbeat, but never really gets going; just enough style to keep it afloat, and the leads are well cast. [R] ▼▌

Object of My Affection, The (1998) **C-112m.** *** D: Nicholas Hytner. Jennifer Aniston, Paul Rudd, Alan Alda, Nigel Hawthorne, John Pankow, Tim Daly, Allison Janney, Steve Zahn, Amo Gulinello, Bruce Altman, Joan Copeland. Young woman invites a gay schoolteacher who's just been dumped by his boyfriend to move into her spare room. They enjoy each other's company so much that she proposes a long-term, nonsexual "arrangement." Appealing actors carry this longish, serpentine, unconventional romantic comedy, written by Wendy Wasserstein, from the novel by Stephen McCauley . . . though the supporting actors (Alda, Janney, Hawthorne) threaten to steal it from the stars. [R] ▼●▌

Oblomov (1980-Russian) **C-146m.** ***½ D: Nikita Mikhalkov. Oleg Tabakov, Yuri Bogatryev, Elena Soloyei, Andrei Popov. Thirtyish civil servant and absentee landlord, nicely played by Tabakov, retires to a listless existence in bed. Lyrical adaptation of Ivan Goncharov's 1858 novel; flashback sequences of Oblomov as a boy in his mother's arms are wonderful. Outstanding cinematography. Aka A FEW DAYS IN THE LIFE OF I. I. OBLOMOV. ▼▌

Oblong Box, The (1969-British) **C-91m.** ** D: Gordon Hessler. Vincent Price, Christopher Lee, Alastair Williamson, Hilary Dwyer, Peter Arne, Maxwell Shaw, Sally Geeson. Price plays British aristocrat tormented by disfigured brother who's out for revenge after briefly being buried alive. Hammy performances, long drawn-out narrative, lackluster direction. [M] ▼●▌

O Brother, Where Art Thou? (2000) **C-107m.** ***½ D: Joel Coen. George Clooney, John Turturro, Tim Blake Nelson, Holly Hunter, Charles Durning, John Goodman, Michael Badalucco, Stephen Root, Daniel von Bargen. Three escaped convicts share a series of adventures, and inadvertently become a singing sensation performing "old-timey" music in 1930s Mississippi. Delightfully eccentric adaptation of Homer's *The Odyssey*, full of clever ideas, irresistible music, and sharp dialogue. Screenplay by Ethan and Joel Coen; the title is derived from Preston Sturges' SULLIVAN'S TRAVELS. Innovative use of color by cinematographer Roger Deakins. Super 35. [PG-13] ▼▌

Observe and Report (2009) **C-86m.** *½ D: Jody Hill. Seth Rogen, Ray Liotta, Anna Faris, Michael Peña, Celia Weston, Dan Bakkedahl, Collette Wolfe, John Yuan, Matthew Yuan, Patton Oswalt, Danny McBride, Aziz Ansari. Delusional, bipolar mall cop Rogen decides to be all that he can be, by dating the cosmetics salesgirl he covets (Faris) and joining the local police department, if they'll have him. Flagrantly, proudly perverse comedy produced in an alternate universe where the ravings of a nutcase are considered funny. Or, a queasy drama about a loser who doesn't realize how ill suited he is to exist alongside "normal" people. Or, both. Super 35. [R] ▌

Obsessed (1989-Canadian) **C-100m.** **½ D: Robin Spry. Kerrie Keane, Daniel Pilon, Saul Rubinek, Lynne Griffin, Alan Thicke, Colleen Dewhurst. Good but slightly meandering drama pitting Keane against Rubinek, the thoughtless hit-and-run driver who killed her son. Well cast and engrossing, marred slightly by tendency toward sensationalism. [PG-13] ▼●

Obsessed (2009) **C-105m.** ** D: Steve Shill. Idris Elba, Beyoncé Knowles, Ali Larter, Bruce McGill, Jerry O'Connell, Christine Lahti, Matthew Humphreys. Elba is a top executive at a financial services company who makes the mistake of being courteous to the smoking-hot new office temp (Larter). With his beautiful wife (Knowles) busy at home with their young baby, Elba's life becomes nightmarish, as the manipulative Larter plays out her own version of FATAL ATTRACTION. Predictably unsurprising genre thriller has its share of loopy logic, and isn't helped by a surprisingly mediocre performance from Elba. Not a whole lot to obsess over here. Super 35. [PG-13] ▌

Obsession (1949) SEE: **Hidden Room, The**

Obsession (1976) **C-98m.** **½ D: Brian De Palma. Cliff Robertson, Genevieve Bujold, John Lithgow, Sylvia Kuumba Williams, Wanda Blackman. Viewers who don't remember Hitchcock's VERTIGO might enjoy this rehash by De Palma and writer Paul Schrader. Robertson loses his wife and child to kidnappers, then miraculously finds wife "reborn" in another woman. Holds up until denouement. Superb Bernard Herrmann score. Panavision. [PG] ▼●▌

Obsession (1980) SEE: **Circle of Two**

O.C. and Stiggs (1987) **C-109m.** ** D: Robert Altman. Daniel H. Jenkins, Neill

Barry, Paul Dooley, Jane Curtin, Jon Cryer, Ray Walston, Louis Nye, Tina Louise, Martin Mull, Dennis Hopper, Melvin Van Peebles. Quirky (even by Altman standards) film recounts title teens' summer adventures, which consist mainly of making life miserable for the Schwab family and the cutthroat insurance agent father (Dooley) who cut off Stiggs' grandfather's old-age policy. Not without its moments and Altman weirdos—including Hopper as a drug- and gun-dealing vet, Louise as the sexy school nurse, and Curtin as the drunken Schwab matriarch—but ultimately incoherent. Sat on the shelf for several years. Super 35. [R]▼❂

Oceans (2010-U.S.-French-Spanish) C-84m. *** D: Jacques Perrin, Jacques Cluzaud. Narrated by Pierce Brosnan. Eye-popping survey of life underwater around the world, capturing amazing sights and even sounds. The result of four years of filming using state-of-the-art camerawork, this family-friendly documentary shows rare species, migratory rituals, and much, much more. Like EARTH, this is an American adaptation of a 2009 French documentary by the Disney company, edited from 102m., with new narration and a closing song sung by Joe Jonas. Super 35. [G]❂

Ocean's Eleven (1960) C-127m. **½ D: Lewis Milestone. Frank Sinatra, Dean Martin, Sammy Davis, Jr., Peter Lawford, Angie Dickinson, Richard Conte, Cesar Romero, Patrice Wymore, Joey Bishop, Akim Tamiroff, Henry Silva, Ilka Chase, Norman Fell. Fanciful crime comedy about 11-man team headed by Danny Ocean (Sinatra) attempting to rob five Vegas casinos simultaneously. Entire Rat Pack's in it, but no one does much, including some surprise guests. There is a clever twist ending, though. Remade in 2001. Panavision. ▼❂

Ocean's Eleven (2001) C-116m. ** D: Steven Soderbergh. George Clooney, Matt Damon, Andy Garcia, Brad Pitt, Julia Roberts, Casey Affleck, Scott Caan, Elliott Gould, Eddie Jemison, Bernie Mac, Shaobo Qin, Carl Reiner. Remarkably lifeless caper film, based in name only on the 1960 Rat Pack film, with ex-con Clooney masterminding a major Las Vegas heist and gathering ten other "specialists" to pull it off. It also turns out that his victim, casino mogul Garcia, is keeping company with Clooney's ex-wife (Roberts). There's nothing in the script to elicit interest in any of these characters, who succeed only in being "cool." The real standout is old pro Reiner! Cameos include Angie Dickinson and Henry Silva, of the 1960 cast. Don Cheadle appears unbilled. Followed by two sequels. Super 35. [PG-13]▼❂

Ocean's Thirteen (2007) C-122m. ** D: Steven Soderbergh. George Clooney, Brad Pitt, Matt Damon, Al Pacino, Andy Garcia,

Don Cheadle, Bernie Mac, Ellen Barkin, Casey Affleck, Scott Caan, Carl Reiner, Elliott Gould, Eddie Jemison, Shaobo Qin, Vincent Cassel, David Paymer, Julian Sands, Eddie Izzard, Bob Einstein. Suave con man Danny Ocean reunites his crew one more time to pull off one more elaborate heist at a casino, whose ruthless owner (Pacino) double-crossed Danny's mentor (Gould). Another smart-alecky exercise in the art of cool, this breezy caper is so lightweight it threatens to evaporate before your eyes, but the addition of a snarling Pacino to the cast adds some gravitas to the glossy proceedings. Super 35. [PG-13]❂

Ocean's Twelve (2004) C-125m. *½ D: Steven Soderbergh. George Clooney, Brad Pitt, Matt Damon, Julia Roberts, Catherine Zeta-Jones, Andy Garcia, Don Cheadle, Bernie Mac, Casey Affleck, Scott Caan, Vincent Cassel, Eddie Jemison, Shaobo Qin, Carl Reiner, Elliott Gould, Robbie Coltrane, Eddie Izzard, Cherry Jones, Jeroen Krabbé, Jared Harris. Sorry sequel has casino boss Garcia demanding that Ocean (Clooney) and his gang repay the money they stole from him . . . so they go to Europe to plan a heist or two. Lots of talk (meant to be cool but mostly incoherent) and little action, plus in-jokes and guest-star cameos to show how much fun everyone had making the film. Bruce Willis, Albert Finney, and Topher Grace appear unbilled. Followed by OCEAN'S THIRTEEN. Super 35. [PG-13]▼❂

Octagon, The (1980) C-103m. ** D: Eric Karson. Chuck Norris, Karen Carlson, Lee Van Cleef, Art Hindle, Jack Carter. OK Kung Fu drama with Norris taking on all comers when hired by Carlson for protection from Ninja assassins. Fair of its kind, with above-average production values. [R] ▼❂

October (1928-Russian) 103m. *** D: Sergei Eisenstein, Grigori Alexandrov. Nikandrov, N. Popov, Boris Livanov. Brilliant reconstruction of the Russian Revolution contains some of Eisenstein's most striking use of montage, though most impressive sequences—such as the masterful massacre around the bridges of St. Petersburg—are in the film's first half. Based on John Reed's *Ten Days That Shook the World*, the film's alternate title. ▼❂

October Man, The (1947-British) 98m. *** D: Roy (Ward) Baker. John Mills, Joan Greenwood, Edward Chapman, Joyce Carey, Kay Walsh, Felix Aylmer, Juliet Mills. Stranger with history of mental disorders is suspected of murder and must prove innocence, even to himself. Strong character study and good local atmosphere enhance suspenseful mystery written by Eric Ambler. British running time 110m.▼

October Sky (1999) C-107m. ***½ D: Joe Johnston. Jake Gyllenhaal, Chris Cooper, Laura Dern, Chris Owen, William Lee Scott,

Chad Lindberg, Natalie Canerday, Scott Miles. Sincere, heartwarming drama based on the true story of Homer Hickam, Jr. (Gyllenhaal), who grew up in an insular West Virginia coal-mining town. When he sees *Sputnik* soaring across the nighttime sky in 1957, he becomes obsessed with the idea of building his own rocket and enlists his friends to share the dream . . . against the wishes of his father, a harsh man who's the mine foreman. Rich performances, well-drawn characters, and an old-fashioned sense of can-do American spirit make this something special. Written by Lewis Colick from Hickam's book *Rocket Boys*. Panavision. [PG]▼●)

Octopussy (1983-British) **C-130m.** ***½ D: John Glen. Roger Moore, Maud Adams, Louis Jourdan, Kristina Wayborn, Kabir Bedi, Steven Berkoff, Desmond Llewelyn, Vijay Amritraj, Lois Maxwell. Grand escapist fare as Moore, growing nicely into the role of James Bond, matches wits with a handful of nemeses, including title-named character (Adams), whose motives—and modus operandi—are more than a bit vague. Film throws in everything but the kitchen sink for the sake of an entertaining show. Panavision. [PG]▼●)

Odd Angry Shot, The (1979-Australian) **C-92m.** **½ D: Tom Jeffrey. John Hargreaves, Graham Kennedy, Bryan Brown, John Jarratt. Interesting film about a group of Australian professional soldiers stationed in Vietnam. Personal drama emphasized more than combat in poignant, sometimes broadly comic work about soldiers dealing with a war they don't think is really theirs.▼

Oddball Hall (1990) **C-87m.** ** D: Jackson Hunsicker. Don Ameche, Burgess Meredith, Bill Maynard, Tullio Moneta, Tiny Skefile. Four jewel thieves hole up in an African town, posing as members of a fraternal order called The Oddballs, and waiting to collect on a heist they pulled off years ago; a simpleminded native comes along seeking their help, and they mistake him for an Oddball chieftain. Simplistic farce is good-natured but heavy-handed; the only thing missing is laughs. [PG]▼●

Odd Birds (1985) **C-90m.** **½ D: Jeanne Collachia. Michael Moriarty, Donna Lai Ming Lew, Nancy Lee, Bruce Gray, Karen Maruyama, Scott Crawford. Awkward direction and uneven performances defeat this sensitive drama about a dreamy teenager with braces who yearns for a career as an actress, and her friendship with compassionate but disillusioned brother-teacher Moriarty. Nice feel for the way real teen girls acted back in 1965, and for the pain of being 15 and shy.▼

Odd Couple, The (1968) **C-105m.** *** D: Gene Saks. Jack Lemmon, Walter Matthau, John Fiedler, Herb Edelman, Monica Evans, Carole Shelley. Film version of Neil Simon stage hit about two divorced men living together, sloppy Oscar (Matthau) and fussy Felix (Lemmon). Lemmon's realistic performance makes character melancholy instead of funny; other surefire comic sequences remain intact. Later developed into two TV series. Followed by a sequel. Panavision. ▼●)

Odd Couple II, The (1998) **C-96m.** *½ D: Howard Deutch. Jack Lemmon, Walter Matthau, Christine Baranski, Barnard Hughes, Jonathan Silverman, Jean Smart, Lisa Waltz, Mary Beth Peil, Jay O. Sanders, Rex Linn, Alice Ghostley, Florence Stanley, Estelle Harris, Amy Yasbeck. Neil Simon wrote this sorry sequel reuniting Felix and Oscar after 17 years when their children announce their impending marriage. The two cronies meet up in L.A., get lost while driving to the ceremony, and find themselves in a series of escalating mishaps. Sporadically funny one-liners can't save this tired film. A real shame. Officially titled NEIL SIMON'S THE ODD COUPLE II. Super 35. [PG-13]▼●)

Odd Job, The (1978-British) **C-86m.** **½ D: Peter Medak. Graham Chapman, David Jason, Diana Quick, Simon Williams, Edward Hardwicke. British update of timeworn premise (used as early as 1916 by Douglas Fairbanks in FLIRTING WITH FATE): an unhappy man, jilted by his wife, hires a hit man to murder her, then has a change of heart . . . but convincing the hired killer is a formidable challenge! Coscripted by Bernard McKenna and Chapman, of Monty Python fame.▼

Odd Jobs (1984) **C-88m.** ** D: Mark Story. Paul Reiser, Robert Townsend, Scott McGinnis, Paul Provenza, Julianne Phillips, Leon Askin, Richard Dean Anderson. Lame comedy about five college students working for a moving company over the summer. Radio personality Don Imus has a cameo. [PG-13]▼)

Odd Man Out (1947-British) **115m.** **** D: Carol Reed. James Mason, Robert Newton, Kathleen Ryan, Robert Beatty, Cyril Cusack, F.J. McCormick, William Hartnell, Fay Compton, Denis O'Dea, Dan O'Herlihy. Incredibly suspenseful tale of Irish rebel leader hunted by police after daring robbery. Watch this one! Scripted by R. C. Sherriff and F. L. Green, from the latter's novel. Remade as THE LOST MAN. ▼●)

Odd Obsession (1959-Japanese) **C-96m.** **½ D: Kon Ichikawa. Machiko Kyo, Ganjiro Nakamura, Tatsuya Nakadai, Junko Kano. Elderly, vain Nakamura tempts beautiful wife (Kyo) into an affair with his young doctor (Nakadai). Uneven soap opera; a few bright moments, but disappointing overall. Original running time 107m. Remade in Italy in 1984 as THE KEY, which is also this film's alternative title (a literal translation of the Japanese title, KAGI). Daieiscope.▼

Odds Against Tomorrow (1959) **95m.** *******
D: Robert Wise. Harry Belafonte, Robert Ryan, Shelley Winters, Ed Begley, Gloria Grahame. A smorgasbord trio of "types" plots to rob an upstate N.Y. bank, but one of them (Belafonte) is black and another (Ryan) is a racist—one of those prime sociopath portrayals on which the actor held the patent. Tough, brutal, and a window to Wise's versatility, half a dozen years before he directed THE SOUND OF MUSIC. John Lewis did the jazz score, and familiar faces turn up in small parts, including Wayne Rogers, Robert Earl Jones, Zohra Lampert, and a young Cicely Tyson as a bartender. Written by Nelson Gidding and Abraham Polonsky (who was blacklisted at the time and properly credited years later). ▼▶

Odessa File, The (1974-British) **C-128m.** ****½** D: Ronald Neame. Jon Voight, Maximilian Schell, Maria Schell, Mary Tamm, Derek Jacobi, Klaus Lowitsch. Voight carries this plodding adaptation of the Frederick Forsyth best-seller, set in 1963, about a German journalist who tracks down former Nazis. OK time killer, no more. Music score by Andrew Lloyd Webber. Panavision. [PG] ▼●▶

Ode to Billy Joe (1976) **C-108m.** ****** D: Max Baer. Robby Benson, Glynnis O'Connor, Joan Hotchkis, Sandy McPeak, James Best, Terence Goodman. Bobbie Gentry's 1967 song hit provides basis for standard rural romance that grows progressively ridiculous. Benson and O'Connor, reunited after JEREMY, still have appeal. [PG] ▼▶

Odyssey of the Pacific (1981-Canadian-French) **C-100m.** ****** D: Fernando Arrabal. Mickey Rooney, Monique Mercure, Jean-Louis Roux, Guy Hoffman. Slight tale of Rooney, a retired train engineer living near an abandoned railway station, befriending a trio of homeless youngsters. Originally titled THE EMPEROR OF PERU. ▼

Oedipus Rex (1967-Italian) **C-110m.** ****½** D: Pier Paolo Pasolini. Franco Citti, Silvana Mangano, Alida Valli, Carmelo Bene, Julian Beck. Pictorially arresting but dull, disappointing adaptation of Sophocles' *Oedipus Rex* and *Oedipus at Colonus*, with Citti, as Oedipus, murdering his father and marrying his mother. Presented in both contemporary and historical settings; that's Pasolini himself as the High Priest. ▼●▶

Oedipus the King (1968-British) **C-97m.** ****½** D: Philip Saville. Christopher Plummer, Orson Welles, Lilli Palmer, Richard Johnson, Cyril Cusack, Roger Livesey, Donald Sutherland. Film version of Sophocles play is OK for students who have a test on it the next day, but others won't appreciate this version. Static, despite that cast. [G]

Off Beat (1986) **C-92m.** ****** D: Michael Dinner. Judge Reinhold, Meg Tilly, Cleavant Derricks, Joe Mantegna, Jacques D'Amboise, James Tolkan, Amy Wright, John Turturro, Anthony Zerbe, Julie Bovasso, Fred Gwynne, Harvey Keitel, Austin Pendleton, Penn Jillette, Bill Sadler, Christopher Noth. Library worker Reinhold, filling in for policeman friend at rehearsal for a dance recital, falls in love with female cop. Modest comedy works hard to live up to its name but comes up short. Reinhold and Tilly are so low-key, they almost disappear! Great cast can't save it. Written by playwright Mark Medoff (who plays Sgt. Tiegher). [PG] ▼▶

Offence, The (1973-British) **C-112m.** *******
D: Sidney Lumet. Sean Connery, Trevor Howard, Vivien Merchant, Ian Bannen, Derek Newark. Intense drama about how London detective Connery's frustrations cause him to beat a suspect to death; a fine performance by Connery. [R] ▼▶

Officer and a Gentleman, An (1982) **C-125m.** ****½** D: Taylor Hackford. Richard Gere, Debra Winger, David Keith, Louis Gossett, Jr., Robert Loggia, Lisa Blount, Lisa Eilbacher, Victor French, Grace Zabriskie, David Caruso. Two misfits seek direction in their dead-end lives—he by enrolling in Naval Officer Candidate School, she by trying to snag him as a husband. Four-letter words and steamy sex scenes can't camouflage a well-worn Hollywood formula script—with virtually every plot point telegraphed ahead of time! Made agreeable by an appealing cast, though even Gossett's Oscar-winning performance as a drill instructor is just a reprise of earlier work like Jack Webb's in THE D.I. Film's love song, "Up Where We Belong," also won an Oscar. [R] ▼●▶

Office Space (1999) **C-89m.** ****** D: Mike Judge. Ron Livingston, Jennifer Aniston, David Herman, Ajay Naidu, Diedrich Bader, Stephen Root, Gary Cole, Richard Riehle. Fitfully funny satire of office life in modern-day corporate America, with Livingston as a computer programmer who hates his job and eventually finds a way to express his disdain for his company—and his boss (Cole). Dry and undernourished, though there are some laughs along the way. Nevertheless, the film has acquired a huge following in the years since its original release. Live-action writing and directing debut for Judge, creator of the animated TV series *Beavis and Butt-head* and *King of the Hill*. [R] ▼●▶

Official Story, The (1985-Argentina) **C-113m.** ******** D: Luis Puenzo. Norma Aleandro, Hector Alterio, Analia Castro, Chunchuna Villafane. Aleandro is exceptional as woman who lives the good life, sheltered from political turmoil that surrounds her in Argentina . . . until she begins to suspect that her adopted daughter may have been the offspring of a political prisoner. One of those rare films that manages to make a strong political statement in the midst of a crackling good story. Hard to believe it was director Puenzo's first feature film (he also scripted with Aida Bortnik). Oscar winner as Best Foreign Language Film. A knockout.▼O●

Off Limits (1988) **C-102m.** *½ D: Christopher Crowe. Willem Dafoe, Gregory Hines, Fred Ward, Amanda Pays, Scott Glenn, Kay Tong Lim, David Alan Grier, Keith David. Sluggish, predictable, unusually sordid melodrama about two pros in the U.S. Army's Criminal Investigation Detachment (CID) who track down the ghoul murdering Vietnamese hookers in 1968 Saigon. Dafoe's goo-goo eyes at nun Pays are good for a few unintentional chuckles; if you can't guess the murderer, get a new hobby. [R]▼O●

Offside (2006-Iranian) **C-93m.** ***½ D: Jafar Panahi. Sima Mobarak Shahi, Safar Samandar, Shayesteh Irani, M. Kheyrabadi, Ida Sadeghi. A group of Iranian girls disguise themselves as men in order to attend a soccer game in which their national team is competing for the World Cup. In real time, the film shows their arrest and their interactions with their captors and each other. Extraordinarily well-acted film that humorously and movingly demonstrates the struggles of a group of people eager to break free from the shackles of a conservative government's values. Not surprisingly, it was banned in Iran. [PG]●

Offspring, The (1986) **C-99m.** *½ D: Jeff Burr. Vincent Price, Clu Gulager, Terry Kiser, Harry Caesar, Cameron Mitchell, Rosalind Cash, Susan Tyrrell, Martine Beswick, Angelo Rossitto, Lawrence Tierney. Small-town historian Price spins a quartet of horror tales, each of which took place in his hamlet. None is worth listening to. Helluva cast, however. Aka FROM A WHISPER TO A SCREAM. [R]▼O●

Off the Black (2006) **C-90m.** **½ D: James Ponsoldt. Nick Nolte, Trevor Morgan, Sonia Feigelson, Sally Kirkland, Rosemarie DeWitt, Timothy Hutton, Noah Fleiss, Michael Higgins, Jonathan Tchaikovsky. Nolte plays a boozing, aging baseball coach who develops a relationship with a young player whom he convinces to pose as his son for an upcoming high school reunion. Slight, character-driven story gives Nolte a prime acting opportunity and he hits it out of the park. The chemistry between him and Morgan is tangible. Super 35. [R]●

Off the Map (2004) **C-111m.** ***½ D: Campbell Scott. Joan Allen, Sam Elliott, Valentina de Angelis, J.K. Simmons, Jim True-Frost, Amy Brenneman. Beautifully realized story, set in the 1970s, about an individualistic, self-reliant New Mexico family dealing with a precocious adolescent daughter, a father who's fallen into a stupor of depression, and the arrival of an agent from the Internal Revenue Service.

Never simplistic or superficial, filled with interesting characters, telling visual and verbal detail, and wonderful performances, including young de Angelis in her film debut. Slowly paced film rewards the viewer for being patient. Joan Ackermann adapted her stage play. [PG-13]●

Of Gods and Men (2010-French) **C-120m.** ***½ D: Xavier Beauvois. Lambert Wilson, Michael Lonsdale, Olivier Rabourdin, Philippe Laudenbach, Jacques Herlin, Loïc Pichon, Xavier Maly, Jean-Marie Frin, Abdelhafid Metalsi. In 1996, the Trappist monks at a monastery in Algeria who tend to the needs of the local villagers find themselves ensnared in political strife, of which they want no part. Whether to flee to safety from terrorists (and the Army) or stay and continue their good works becomes the pressing question—and gets right to the root of the brothers' beliefs. A most unusual meditation on faith in the context of the "real world," with exceptional performances by Wilson and the entire ensemble. Beauvois scripted with Etienne Comar; based on a real-life incident. Techniscope. [PG-13]●

Of Human Bondage (1934) **88m.** *** D: John Cromwell. Leslie Howard, Bette Davis, Frances Dee, Kay Johnson, Reginald Denny, Alan Hale, Reginald Owen. Smoothly filmed, well-acted version of W. Somerset Maugham's story of doctor Howard's strange infatuation with a vulgar waitress (Davis). Many find Davis' performance overdone, but by any standards it's powerfully impressive, and put her on the map in Hollywood. Howard, lovely Johnson, others are superb. Remade in 1946 and 1964. Also shown in computer-colored version.▼O●

Of Human Bondage (1946) **105m.** ** D: Edmund Goulding. Paul Henreid, Eleanor Parker, Alexis Smith, Edmund Gwenn, Janis Paige, Patric Knowles, Henry Stephenson, Marten Lamont, Isobel Elsom, Una O'Connor. Henreid and Parker give it the old college try but are fatally miscast in this bowdlerized adaptation of Somerset Maugham's steamy novel about the sado-masochistic relationship between a club-footed artist/medical student and a sluttish waitress. Plush production can't compensate for the dearth of erotic heat, which was plentiful in the 1934 Bette Davis version.

Of Human Bondage (1964-British) **98m.** ** D: Ken Hughes. Kim Novak, Laurence Harvey, Siobhan McKenna, Robert Morley, Roger Livesey, Nanette Newman, Brenda Fricker. Third and least successful filming of Maugham novel of doctor's passion for lowbrow waitress, marred by miscasting and general superficiality.▼

Of Life and Love (1957-Italian) **103m.** **½ D: Aldo Fabrizi, Luchino Visconti, Mario Soldati, Giorgio Pastina. Anna Magnani, Walter Chiari, Natale Cirino, Turi Pandolfini, Myriam Bru, Lucia Bose. Four satisfactory episodes, three of which are based on Pirandello tales; fourth is actual event in Magnani's life ("The Lapdog"). Actually distilled from two Italian episodic features from 1953 and 1954.

Of Love and Shadows (1994-Spanish-Argentinian) **C-109m.** *½ D: Betty Kaplan. Antonio Banderas, Jennifer Connelly, Stefania Sandrelli, Diego Wallraft, Camillo Gallardo. Young fashion journalist meets a mysterious photographer and—well, more than just film develops. Adapted from an Isabel Allende novel, this love story set against the backdrop of a Chilean military dictatorship in 1973 is a complete misfire. Convoluted plot makes little sense, and there's no chemistry between the attractive leads. [R] ▼●

Of Mice and Men (1939) **107m.** **** D: Lewis Milestone. Lon Chaney, Jr., Burgess Meredith, Betty Field, Charles Bickford, Bob Steele, Noah Beery, Jr. Chaney gives best performance of his career as feeble-brained Lennie who, with migrant-worker Meredith, tries to live peacefully on ranch. John Steinbeck's morality tale remains intact in sensitive screen version. The film's action begins *before* the main title credits—an arty innovation for 1939. Script by Eugene Solow. Music by Aaron Copland. Remade in 1992 and for TV in 1968 and 1981. ▼●

Of Mice and Men (1992) **C-110m.** *** D: Gary Sinise. John Malkovich, Gary Sinise, Alexis Arquette, Sherilyn Fenn, Joe Morton, Richard Riehle, Casey Siemaszko, John Terry, Ray Walston, Noble Willingham. More than respectable rendering of the Steinbeck warhorse, with Malkovich and Sinise respectively cast as Lennie and George—the sweet simpleton and his weary protector. Rescued from mothballs (and high school English) by the subtext of today's homeless; robust performances and impressive sun-baked look (photographed by Kenneth MacMillan) make it worthwhile. Screenplay by Horton Foote. [PG-13] ▼●

Of Time and the City (2008-British) **C/B&W-74m.** ***½ D: Terence Davies. Profoundly personal memory piece about Davies' coming-of-age in Liverpool, his fascination with the cinema, his cynicism about British royalty and his own Catholicism, and dealing with his homosexual feelings. He also ruminates on how one ages and processes the passage of time. Loaded with footage of Liverpool, accompanied by period music and poetic narration. Beautifully done, and tremendously moving. ●

Of Unknown Origin (1983-Canadian) **C-88m.** ** D: George Pan Cosmatos. Peter Weller, Jennifer Dale, Lawrence Dane, Kenneth Welsh, Louis Del Grande, Shannon Tweed. N.Y.C. businessman, bacheloring it temporarily, is driven to distraction by a giant rodent on the loose in his apartment.

Slightly better than simultaneously released rat-themed DEADLY EYES. [R] ▼●

Ogre, The (1996-German-French-British) **C-117m.** **½ D: Volker Schlöndorff. John Malkovich, Gottfried John, Armin Mueller-Stahl, Marianne Sägebrecht, Volker Spengler, Heino Ferch, Dieter Laser. Seriocomic anti-Nazi parable is not nearly as good as Schlöndorff's classic THE TIN DRUM, but it's an interesting (if heavy-handed), horrific fairy tale about a childlike Frenchman (a miscast Malkovich) who willingly goes to work for the Nazis after being captured during the war and is used to "recruit" German children to join the army. Super 35. ▼●

Oh, Alfie SEE: **Alfie Darling**

O Happy Day SEE: **Seventeen and Anxious**

O'Hara's Wife (1982) **C-87m.** **½ D: William S. Bartman. Edward Asner, Mariette Hartley, Jodie Foster, Perry Lang, Tom Bosley, Ray Walston, Allen Williams, Mary Jo Catlett, Richard Schaal, Nehemiah Persoff. Only Asner is aware of the presence of wife Hartley, who's a ghost. Earnest but forgettable. [PG] ▼●

Oh Dad, Poor Dad, Mama's Hung You in the Closet and I'm Feeling So Sad (1967) **C-86m.** **½ D: Richard Quine. Rosalind Russell, Robert Morse, Barbara Harris, Hugh Griffith, Jonathan Winters, Lionel Jeffries, Cyril Delevanti. Impressive cast tries to sustain black comedy about overpossessive widow (Russell) and weirdo son (Morse) taking vacation on tropical island accompanied by coffin of her late husband. From the Arthur Kopit play. ▼

O. Henry's Full House (1952) **117m.** **½ D: Henry Hathaway, Howard Hawks, Henry King, Henry Koster, Jean Negulesco. Fred Allen, Anne Baxter, Charles Laughton, Marilyn Monroe, Gregory Ratoff, Jeanne Crain, Oscar Levant, Jean Peters, Richard Widmark, Farley Granger. Five seriocomic stories by O. Henry, introduced by John Steinbeck: "The Clarion Call," "Last Leaf," "Ransom of Red Chief," "Gift of the Magi," and "Cop and the Anthem." Dated overall but still has some effective moments. ●

Oh, God! (1977) **C-98m.** *** D: Carl Reiner. George Burns, John Denver, Teri Garr, Paul Sorvino, George Furth, Ralph Bellamy, Barnard Hughes, David Ogden Stiers. God appears in person of Burns to summon Denver as His messenger, to tell the world that He's alive and well. Film eschews cheap jokes to build a credible story with warm performances and upbeat message. Followed by a pair of sequels. [PG] ▼●

Oh God! Book II (1980) **C-94m.** *½ D: Gilbert Cates. George Burns, Suzanne Pleshette, David Birney, Louanne, Howard Duff, Hans Conried, Wilfrid Hyde-White, Conrad Janis. Burns returns as title character; here, he enlists a child (Louanne) to remind the world that God is not dead. Contrived sequel with just a trickle of laughs; Pleshette, as usual, is wasted. [PG]▼◗

Oh, God! You Devil (1984) **C-96m.** ✶✶ D: Paul Bogart. George Burns, Ted Wass, Ron Silver, Roxanne Hart, Eugene Roche, Robert Desiderio, James.Cromwell. Third go-round for Burns gives him dual role of God *and* the Devil, with Wass as struggling songwriter and performer who sells his soul for success. Good cast and good-natured attitude can't overcome blandness and predictability of this comedy. Written by Andrew Bergman. [PG]▼◗◗

Oh, Heavenly Dog! (1980) **C-103m.** ✶✶½ D: Joe Camp. Chevy Chase, Benji, Jane Seymour, Omar Sharif, Donnelly Rhodes, Robert Morley, Alan Sues. Private eye Chase returns to earth in the form of a dog to solve his own murder. Benji (in his third film) is as adorable as ever as Chase's alter ego. Filmed in England. Followed by BENJI THE HUNTED. [PG]▼◗

Oh in Ohio, The (2006) **C-88m.** ✶✶½ D: Billy Kent. Parker Posey, Paul Rudd, Danny DeVito, Mischa Barton, Miranda Bailey, Liza Minnelli, Keith David, Robert John Burke. Cleveland high school science teacher feels like less than a man since his wife has never experienced an orgasm. He finally seeks satisfaction elsewhere, and so does she—with the help of a vibrator that soon becomes her best friend. Engaging, amusing adult comedy meanders more than it should but has its fair share of funny moments and likable characters. Heather Graham appears unbilled. [R]◗

Oh, Men! Oh, Women! (1957) **C-90m.** ✶✶½ D: Nunnally Johnson. Ginger Rogers, David Niven, Dan Dailey, Barbara Rush, Tony Randall. Often bouncy sex farce revolving around psychiatrist and his assorted patients. Randall's feature debut. CinemaScope.

O'Horten (2008-Norwegian-German-French) **C-90m.** ✶✶✶ D: Bent Hamer. Bård Owe, Ghita Nørby, Espen Skjønberg, Henny Moan, Bjørn Floberg, Kai Remlov, Per Jansen. Railroad engineer Odd Horten (Owe) is forced into retirement, which is troubling for a simple man who's devoted his whole life to the routine of his job. His newfound freedom—even his attempt to attend a farewell party—leads him into a series of mild misadventures in the snowy landscape of Norway. Benign, low-key comedy (with dramatic undertones) is not for viewers seeking excitement or compelling narrative storytelling . . . but if you appreciate offbeat humor and quiet charm you'll find much to savor here. Written by the director, who achieved the same droll results in his KITCHEN STORIES. [PG-13]◗

Oh! What a Lovely War (1969-British) **C-139m.** ✶✶½ D: Richard Attenborough. Laurence Olivier, John Gielgud, Ralph Richardson, Michael Redgrave, John Mills, Vanessa Redgrave, Dirk Bogarde, Susannah York, Maggie Smith, Jack Hawkins, Kenneth More, Corin Redgrave, Jane Seymour. Actor Attenborough's directing debut; impressive but cumbersome series of vignettes on WW1, ranging from colorful musical numbers to poignant human sidelights. Adapted from stage show. Beautifully designed, wildly cinematic, but too drawn-out to make maximum antiwar impact. Panavision. [G]◗

Oh, Woe Is Me SEE: **Hèlas Pour Moi**

Oil (1977-Italian) **C-95m.** BOMB D: Mircea Dragan. Stuart Whitman, Woody Strode, Ray Milland, George Dinica, William Berger, Tony Kendall. A Sahara oilfield ablaze. After the 28th shot of the fire, you'll be ready to douse your TV set.▼

Oklahoma! (1955) **C-145m.** ✶✶✶½ D: Fred Zinnemann. Gordon MacRae, Shirley Jones, Charlotte Greenwood, Rod Steiger, Gloria Grahame, Eddie Albert, James Whitmore, Gene Nelson, Barbara Lawrence, Jay C. Flippen. Expansive film version of Rodgers and Hammerstein's landmark 1943 Broadway musical, filled with timeless songs (and the beautiful voices of MacRae and Jones to sing them) . . . plus a fine supporting cast led by incomparable Grahame as Ado Annie. Enough fine ingredients to make up for overlength of film. Songs include "Oh, What a Beautiful Mornin' " and showstopping title tune. This was filmed in two versions, one in Todd-AO and the other in CinemaScope (made from entirely separate "takes"). Both appear on DVD. ▼◗◗

Oklahoma Crude (1973) **C-108m.** ✶✶✶ D: Stanley Kramer. George C. Scott, Faye Dunaway, John Mills, Jack Palance, Harvey Jason, Woodrow Parfrey. Old-fashioned, nonthink entertainment. Strong-willed, man-hating Dunaway determined to defend lone oil well from pressures of Palance, who represents big oil trust, hires drifter Scott to help her. Scott gives brilliant comic performance in mildly enjoyable film. Panavision. [PG]▼

Oklahoma Kid, The (1939) **80m.** ✶✶✶ D: Lloyd Bacon. James Cagney, Humphrey Bogart, Rosemary Lane, Donald Crisp, Harvey Stephens, Charles Middleton, Ward Bond. Cagney's the hero, Bogey's the villain in this sturdy Western about a cowboy seeking redress for the lynching of his father. Classic scene has Cagney singing "I Don't Want to Play in Your Yard."▼●

Old Acquaintance (1943) **110m.** ✶✶✶ D: Vincent Sherman. Bette Davis, Miriam Hopkins, Gig Young, John Loder, Dolores Moran, Phillip Reed, Roscoe Karns, Anne Revere. Well-matched stars of THE OLD MAID are reunited as childhood friends who evolve personal and professional rivalry that lasts 20 years. Davis is noble and Hopkins is bitchy in this entertaining film. John Van Druten and Lenore Coffee scripted, from the former's play. Remade as RICH AND FAMOUS.◗

Oldboy (2003-Korean) **C-120m.** ****½** D: Chan-wook Park. Min-shik Choi, Ji-tae Yu, Hye-Jeong Kang, Dae-han Ji, Dal-su Oh, Byeong-ok Kim. A man, mysteriously imprisoned in a hotel room for 15 years, has only five days after release to find his captor and exact revenge. Extremely violent and unpleasant—check out the live octopus this poor guy has to digest in the sushi bar scene; however, Park's action-packed opus will appeal to his faithful fans. Production values are top grade for this genre. Winner of the Grand Prize at the 2004 Cannes Film Festival. Super 35. [R]▶

Old Boyfriends (1979) **C-103m.** BOMB D: Joan Tewkesbury. Talia Shire, Richard Jordan, Keith Carradine, John Belushi, John Houseman, Buck Henry. Distressing botch of an intriguing idea about woman who seeks out her former lovers in an attempt to analyze her past. Shire is too lightweight to carry the acting load, and Belushi is totally wasted. Written by Paul and Leonard Schrader. [R]▼●

Old Curiosity Shop, The SEE: **Mr. Quilp**

Old Dark House, The (1932) **71m.** *****½** D: James Whale. Boris Karloff, Melvyn Douglas, Charles Laughton, Gloria Stuart, Lilian Bond, Ernest Thesiger, Raymond Massey, Eva Moore. Outstanding melodrama (with tongue-in-cheek) gathers stranded travelers in mysterious Welsh household, where brutish butler Karloff is just one of many strange characters. A real gem, based on J. B. Priestley's *Benighted;* screenplay by Benn W. Levy and R. C. Sherriff. Remade in England in 1963. ▼●▶

Old Dark House, The (1963-British) **C-86m.** ****½** D: William Castle. Tom Poston, Robert Morley, Janette Scott, Joyce Grenfell, Mervyn Johns, Fenella Fielding, Peter Bull. Uneven blend of comedy and chiller, with Poston at loose ends in eerie mansion. Released theatrically in b&w. Check out the 1932 version instead.▶

Old Dogs (2009) **C-88m.** ****** D: Walt Becker. John Travolta, Robin Williams, Kelly Preston, Seth Green, Conner Rayburn, Ella Bleu Travolta, Lori Loughlin, Matt Dillon, Bernie Mac, Ann-Margret, Rita Wilson, Amy Sedaris. Hoped-for sparks from the teaming of Travolta and Williams never materialize as the pair play business partners whose big Japanese deal is disrupted when they unexpectedly inherit 7-year-old twins. The stars seem to be having a better time than the audience. Only the youngest kids are going to find this slapstick material (including Green's antics with a lovestruck gorilla) very funny. Notable only as the debut for Travolta's daughter Ella Bleu and Mac's final film appearance. Luis Guzmán, Dax Shepard, and Justin Long appear unbilled. [PG]▶

Old Dracula (1974-British) **C-89m.** ***½** D: Clive Donner. David Niven, Teresa Graves, Peter Bayliss, Jennie Linden, Linda Hayden. Niven somehow maintains his dignity in this one-joke Dracula spoof that has him extracting samples from the necks of various Playboy Bunnies in search of correct blood type to resurrect his departed wife. British title: VAMPIRA. [PG]▶

Old Enough (1984) **C-91m.** ****½** D: Marisa Silver. Sarah Boyd, Rainbow Harvest, Neill Barry, Danny Aiello, Susan Kingsley, Roxanne Hart, Fran Brill, Alyssa Milano, Anne Pitoniak. Two adolescent girls from wildly diverse socioeconomic backgrounds forge a tenuous friendship, then try to keep it going through thick and thin. Boyd (the rich one) has infinitely more screen appeal than counterpart Harvest, which further undercuts an already too-mild comedy. Funny subplot about sexy hairdresser who lives in Harvest's building. Written by first-time director Silver. [PG]▼

Oldest Profession, The (1967-French-German-Italian) **C-97m.** ***½** D: Franco Indovina, Mauro Bolognini, Philippe De Broca, Michel Pfleghar, Claude Autant-Lara, Jean-Luc Godard. Elsa Martinelli, Jeanne Moreau, Raquel Welch, Anna Karina, France Anglade, Jean-Pierre Léaud. Totally unfunny six-part story of prostitution through the ages. Original French running time: 115m. ▼●

Old Explorers (1990) **C-100m.** ****** D: William Pohland. Jose Ferrer, James Whitmore, Jeffrey Gadbois, Caroline Kaiser, William Warfield, Christopher Pohland, Storm Richardson, Dominique Berrand. Two elderly pals—Ferrer and Whitmore—get together once a week to spin tales and embark on flights of fancy. Imagining themselves as famed adventurers (usually African explorer Henry Stanley or Troy archaeologist Henry Schliemann), they recount fictional quests for lost treasures and safaris to mythical lands. Extremely slow pace robs this interesting idea of its potential. [PG]▼

Old Fashioned Way, The (1934) **71m.** *****½** D: William Beaudine. W. C. Fields, Judith Allen, Joe Morrison, Baby LeRoy, Jack Mulhall, Oscar Apfel. Fields is in fine form managing troupe of old-time melodrama *The Drunkard,* encountering various troubles as they travel from town to town. Baby LeRoy has memorable scene throwing W. C.'s watch into a jar of molasses; also contains Fields' classic juggling routine.▶

Old Gringo (1989) **C-119m.** ******* D: Luis Puenzo. Jane Fonda, Gregory Peck, Jimmy Smits, Patricio Contreras, Jenny Gago, Jim Metzler, Gabriela Roel, Anne Pitoniak, Pedro Armendariz, Jr. A youngish spinster, a fiery young Mexican general, and an aging American writer, Ambrose Bierce, cross paths amid the tumult of Pancho Villa's revolution in 1913. Intense, epic-scale drama has its share of flaws, but its rich atmosphere and superlative star performances make it well worth seeing. Director Puenzo and Aida Bortnik wrote the screenplay, from Carlos Fuentes' novel. [R] ▼●◗

Old Heidelberg SEE: **Student Prince in Old Heidelberg, The**

Old Joy (2006) **C-76m.** *** D: Kelly Reichardt. Will Oldham, Daniel London, Tanya Smith. Two old friends who haven't seen each other for a while set off for a weekend camping trip in Oregon. One (Oldham) is somewhat settled and about to become a father; the other (London) is an aging hippie, still drifting through life. At first their conversations only accentuate how much they've grown apart, but as they reach their destination, the serenity of the setting takes hold. Subtle, graceful mood piece about friendship and the way our environment affects who we are and how we live. Reichardt scripted with Jonathan Raymond (whose original short story was inspired by the photographs of Justine Kurland). ◗

Old Lady Who Walked in the Sea, The (1995-French) **C-95m.** *** D: Laurent Heynemann. Jeanne Moreau, Michel Serrault, Luc Thuillier, Geraldine Danon. Moreau's star presence sparks this entertaining, often outrageous comedy, in which she plays a veteran swindler-hustler-blackmailer named Lady M—an aged, wrinkled version of Barbara Stanwyck's LADY EVE—who becomes the mentor of a good-looking but unrefined young beach boy (Thuillier). Serrault is excellent as always as Moreau's longtime partner-in-crime.

Old Maid, The (1939) **95m.** *** D: Edmund Goulding. Bette Davis, Miriam Hopkins, George Brent, Jane Bryan, Donald Crisp, Louise Fazenda, James Stephenson, William Lundigan, Jerome Cowan, Rand Brooks, DeWolf (William) Hopper. Soap opera par excellence based on Zoe Akins play and Edith Wharton novel about rivalry and sacrifice in the Old South, focusing on cousins Davis and Hopkins. Builds to an unusually poignant finale. Exquisitely designed and detailed production. ▼●◗

Old Man and the Sea, The (1958) **C-86m.** *** D: John Sturges. Spencer Tracy, Felipe Pazos, Harry Bellaver. Well-intentioned but uneven parable of aging fisherman's daily battle with the elements. Tracy is the whole film, making the most of Hemingway's unfilmic story; Dimitri Tiomkin's expressive score won an Oscar. Remade as a TVM in 1990 with Anthony Quinn. ▼●◗

Old Mother Riley Meets the Vampire SEE: **Mother Riley Meets the Vampire**

Old School (2003) **C-90m.** **½ D: Todd Phillips. Luke Wilson, Will Ferrell, Vince Vaughn, Jeremy Piven, Ellen Pompeo, Juliette Lewis, Leah Remini, Perrey Reeves, Craig Kilborn, Harve Presnell, Snoop Dogg, Elisha Cuthbert, Artie Lange, Robert (Rob) Corddry. Three 30-something pals try to rekindle their youth by opening an "unofficial" fraternity house. That's the hook for this amusing film that never quite takes off, leaving most of the laughs to individual moments involving Ferrell and Vaughn. Andy Dick and Seann William Scott turn up, presumably as a favor to their ROAD TRIP director. Super 35. [R] ▼◗

Old Yeller (1957) **C-83m.** *** D: Robert Stevenson. Dorothy McGuire, Fess Parker, Tommy Kirk, Kevin Corcoran, Jeff York, Beverly Washburn, Chuck Connors. Disney's first film about a boy and his dog, from Fred Gipson's popular novel, is still one of the best. Atmospheric re-creation of farm life in 1869 Texas, where Kirk becomes attached to a yellow hunting dog. Sequel: SAVAGE SAM. ▼●◗

Oleanna (1994) **C-89m.** ** D: David Mamet. William H. Macy, Debra Eisenstadt. Maddeningly uneven two-character drama about a frustrated, self-involved male professor whose connection with a troubled, vulnerable female student leads to dire consequences. Potentially dynamic material suffers from too much staginess and dramatic obviousness. Scripted by Mamet, based on his play. ▼●◗

Oliver! (1968-British) **C-153m.** ***½ D: Carol Reed. Ron Moody, Oliver Reed, Shani Wallis, Mark Lester, Jack Wild, Harry Secombe, Hugh Griffith, Sheila White. Fine film of Lionel Bart's hit stage musical of Dickens' *Oliver Twist* about young boy (Lester) swept into gang of youthful thieves led by scurrilous Fagin (Moody). Colorful atmosphere; rousing score including "Consider Yourself," "As Long as He Needs Me." Six Oscars including Best Picture, Director, Art Direction, Scoring (John Green), and a special prize to Onna White for her spirited choreography. Panavision. [G] ▼●◗

Oliver & Company (1988) **C-72m.** **½ D: George Scribner. Voices of Joey Lawrence, Billy Joel, Cheech Marin, Richard Mulligan, Roscoe Lee Browne, Sheryl Lee Ralph, Dom DeLuise, Taurean Blacque, Robert Loggia, Bette Midler, Natalie Gregory. Free adaptation of Dickens' *Oliver Twist* in the cartoon world: homeless kitten falls in with the jaunty Dodger and his canine pals, who work for Fagin, a human nebbish in debt to the heartless Sikes. Dodger (Joel) has the film's best song, "Why Should I Worry?"—but an excitable Chihuahua voiced by Marin provides the biggest laughs. Disney's grittiest (grungiest?) animated feature is no classic, but it's likeable enough. [G] ▼●◗

Oliver's Story (1978) **C-92m.** *½ D: John Korty. Ryan O'Neal, Candice Bergen, Nicola Pagett, Edward Binns, Ray Milland, Swoosie Kurtz, Charles Haid, Kenneth McMillan, Josef Sommer. Vapid sequel to LOVE STORY pits money against money this time around, as O'Neal romances heiress to Bonwit Teller fortune. [PG] ▼◗

Oliver Twist (1948-British) **116m. ****** D: David Lean. Alec Guinness, Robert Newton, John Howard Davies, Kay Walsh, Francis L. Sullivan, Anthony Newley, Henry Stephenson. Superlative realization of Dickens tale of ill-treated London waif involved with arch-fiend Fagin (Guinness) and his youthful gang, headed by the Artful Dodger (Newley). Later musicalized as OLIVER! Original British running time: 116m.▼●▶

Oliver Twist (2005-British-French-Czech-Italian) **C-130m. ***** D: Roman Polanski. Ben Kingsley, Barney Clark, Leanne Rowe, Mark Strong, Jamie Foreman, Harry Eden, Edward Hardwicke, Ian McNeice, Gillian Hanna, Alun Armstrong. Stark, literate adaptation (by Ronald Harwood) of the Charles Dickens classic, spotlighting young, orphaned Oliver (Clark) and his escapades among the criminal element of Victorian London. Polanski offers a sobering portrait of the muck and grime that engulf the poor in any era. Well done, but still no match for David Lean's 1948 masterpiece. Super 35. [PG-13]▶

Olivier Olivier (1992-French) **C-110m. ***½** D: Agnieszka Holland. Francois Cluzet, Brigitte Rouan, Jean-Francois Stevenin, Gregoire Colin, Marina Golovine, Emmanuel Morozof, Faye Gatteau, Frederick Quiring. Exceptional, fact-based account of a country couple whose young son mysteriously disappears. Six years later he "reappears," but is no longer the special child who was a joy to his family; now he's a Parisian street hustler who claims to have forgotten his childhood. A fascinating film, with characters who prove to be far more intricate than they first appear. Holland also scripted. [R]▼●

Olly, Olly, Oxen Free (1978) **C-83m. **** D: Richard A. Colla. Katharine Hepburn, Kevin McKenzie, Dennis Dimster, Peter Kilman. Hepburn plays a colorful junk dealer who befriends two young boys and helps them realize their dream of hot-air ballooning. Kate's always worth watching, but except for airborne scenes, this film is nothing special. Aka THE GREAT BALLOON ADVENTURE. [G]▼▶

O Lucky Man! (1973-British) **C-178m. ****** D: Lindsay Anderson. Malcolm McDowell, Rachel Roberts, Arthur Lowe, Ralph Richardson, Alan Price, Lindsay Anderson, Helen Mirren, Mona Washbourne. Mammoth allegory with surrealistic flavor about young coffee salesman who pushes his way to the top only to fall and rise again. Brilliant performances (several actors have multiple roles) throughout; incredible score by Alan Price. Written by David Sherwin. [R]▼●▶

Olympia (1936-German) **220m. ****** D: Leni Riefenstahl. Two-part record of the 1936 Berlin Olympics, highlighted by truly eyepopping cinematography, camera movement and editing. Of course, it's all supposed to be a glorification of the Nazi state. Various edited versions exist (some of which omit all footage of Hitler, who appears throughout the original print).▼▶

Omar Khayyam (1957) **C-101m. **½** D: William Dieterle. Cornel Wilde, Debra Paget, John Derek, Raymond Massey, Michael Rennie, Yma Sumac, Sebastian Cabot. Childish but spirited costumer set in medieval Persia; cast defeated by juvenile script. VistaVision.▼

Omega Code, The (1999) **C-99m. *½** D: Rob Marcarelli. Casper Van Dien, Michael York, Catherine Oxenberg, Michael Ironside, Jan Triska, Gregory Wagrowski. TV motivational guru Van Dien gets involved with wealthy businessman York, whose eventual plans to dominate the world are tied in with secret messages encoded in the Torah. Financed by televangelist Paul Crouch of the Trinity Broadcasting Network, film did grass-roots box-office business until rank-and-file filmgoers saw it for what it was: glorified direct-to-video cheese. Followed in 2001 by MEGIDDO. [PG-13]▼▶

Omega Man, The (1971) **C-98m. **½** D: Boris Sagal. Charlton Heston, Rosalind Cash, Anthony Zerbe, Paul Koslo, Lincoln Kilpatrick, Eric Laneuville. Visually striking but unsatisfying second filming of Richard Matheson's sci-fi thriller *I Am Legend.* Heston is under siege by a race of zombies spawned by apocalyptic germ warfare. Heston is superior to Vincent Price (who had role in THE LAST MAN ON EARTH). Remade once again as I AM LEGEND. Panavision. [PG]▼●▶

Omen, The (1976) **C-111m. **½** D: Richard Donner. Gregory Peck, Lee Remick, Billie Whitelaw, David Warner, Harvey Stephens, Patrick Troughton. Effective but sensationalistic horror piece on the coming of the "Antichrist," personified in young son of Peck and Remick, Americans living in England. Discreet use of gore and a now-famous decapitation, for those who like that kind of thing. Jerry Goldsmith's score won an Oscar. Leo McKern appears unbilled. Followed by three sequels beginning with DAMIEN—OMEN II. Remade in 2006. Panavision. [R]▼●▶

Omen, The (2006) **C-110m. **** D: John Moore. Julia Stiles, Liev Schreiber, Mia Farrow, David Thewlis, Pete Postlethwaite, Michael Gambon, Seamus Davey-Fitzpatrick, Giovanni Lombardo Radice, Marshall Cupp, Amy Huck. Plodding remake finds a stone-faced Schreiber in Gregory Peck's role of an American diplomat who substitutes an orphan for his own stillborn baby without telling his wife, slowly coming to the realization that the child is the Antichrist. Virtually identical copy of the 1976 horror hit (David Seltzer wrote the script for both versions), this polished but pointless retread merely adds gory

CGI effects and tasteless references to 9/11, Hurricane Katrina, and other contemporary disasters. Farrow contributes the few genuinely scary moments as Damien's demonic nanny. [R] ◗

On a Clear Day (2005-British) **C-99m.** *** D: Gaby Dellal. Peter Mullan, Brenda Blethyn, Jamie Sives, Billy Boyd, Sean McGinley, Ron Cook, Jodhi May, Benedict Wong, Anne-Marie Timoney. A bluff working man in his 50s, just fired from the shipyard where he's worked for 36 years, comes up with a crazy scheme to swim the English Channel. Haunted by the death of one son, distant from his other boy, this adventure becomes a metaphor for everyone around him to take charge of their lives. A little obvious in its message (and more than a bit reminiscent of THE FULL MONTY), but well done. Mullan is perfect in the lead. [PG-13] ◗

On a Clear Day You Can See Forever (1970) **C-129m.** **½ D: Vincente Minnelli. Barbra Streisand, Yves Montand, Bob Newhart, Larry Blyden, Simon Oakland, Jack Nicholson. Colorful entertainment from Alan Jay Lerner–Burton Lane show about girl (Streisand) whose psychiatrist (Montand) discovers that she lived a former life, in 19th-century England. Sumptuous flashback scenes outclass fragmented modern-day plot, much of it apparently left on cutting-room floor. Glossy but never involving. Panavision. [G] ▼◗

On Any Sunday (1971) **C-91m.** *** D: Bruce Brown. Steve McQueen, Mert Lawwill, Malcolm Smith. Fine documentary on many aspects of motorcycling by Bruce Brown of ENDLESS SUMMER fame. Followed by a sequel. Followed in 2000 by ON ANY SUNDAY REVISITED. [G] ▼◗

On Any Sunday II (1981) **C-90m.** ** D: Ed Forsyth, Don Shoemaker. Undistinguished sequel to ON ANY SUNDAY, documenting the exploits of championship motorcyclists. For cycle fans only. [PG] ▼◗

Once (2007-Irish) **C-86m.** *** D: John Carney. Glen Hansard, Markéta Irglová. Dublin busker (Hansard) performs his own compositions every night and attracts the attention of a like-minded woman (Irglová) who's also quite talented. The songs they sing—on the street, in rehearsal, and in recording studios—reflect the development of their relationship over one week's time. Disarming, intimate, and utterly winning, this plays more like a cinéma vérité romance than a musical, yet that's what it is. Hansard and Irglová actually composed all the songs they perform; they won Best Original Song Oscar for "Falling Slowly." [R] ◗

Once Around (1991) **C-115m.** **½ D: Lasse Hallström. Richard Dreyfuss, Holly Hunter, Danny Aiello, Gena Rowlands, Laura San Giacomo, Roxann Hart, Danton Stone, Tim Guinee, Greg Germann, Griffin Dunne. Repressed Bostonian Hunter is swept off her feet by amorous (and ob-

noxious) supersalesman Dreyfuss, who immediately alienates her close-knit family and puts her in the center of an emotional tug-of-war. Malia Scotch Marmo's script embraces both offbeat romantic comedy and intense family drama, some of it extremely moving, some of it off-base. As an acting showcase, however, it's superb. Coproduced by costar Dunne; Hallström's U.S. directorial debut. [R] ▼◗

Once Bitten (1985) **C-93m.** BOMB D: Howard Storm. Lauren Hutton, Jim Carrey, Karen Kopins, Cleavon Little, Thomas Ballatore, Skip Lackey. Inept comedy about vampiress (Hutton) who intrudes on amorous pursuits of some teenagers because she needs the blood of a virgin to maintain her youthful glow. Pretty anemic; Carrey is very restrained. [PG-13] ▼◗

Once Fallen (2010) **C-92m.** *½ D: Ash Adams. Brian Presley, Taraji P. Henson, Ed Harris, Amy Madigan, Peter Weller, Ash Adams, Chad Lindberg, Sharon Gless, Alison Eastwood, Peter Greene, Keegan Thomas, Rance Howard, Steve Railsback, Antonio Fargas. Hackneyed, high-testosterone account of Presley, who's completing a prison stretch on a drug rap. Upon his release, he returns to his blue-collar California harbor town, where he's drawn into a racially tinged drug war. Just awful, despite the pedigree of its cast. Adams also scripted. Released direct to DVD in the U.S. [R] ◗

Once in Paris . . . (1978) **C-100m.** *** D: Frank D. Gilroy. Wayne Rogers, Gayle Hunnicutt, Jack Lenoir, Clement Harari, Tanya Lopert, Doris Roberts. Gilroy wrote this charming tale of Hollywood screenwriter who goes to Paris to work on script, falls in love instead. Lovely location filming; Lenoir steals the film as Rogers' all-knowing chauffeur (which he actually was prior to this picture). [PG] ▼

Once in the Life (2000) **C-107m.** ** D: Laurence Fishburne. Laurence Fishburne, Titus Welliver, Eamonn Walker, Dominic Chianese, Jr., Paul Calderon, Gregory Hines, Annabella Sciorra, Michael Paul Chan, Andres "Dres" Titus. Well-acted but wearisome look at N.Y.C. drug dealers and a crisis that tests friendship against the pressures of "the life," from which there is no escape. Fishburne's directing debut; he also scripted, from his one-act play *Riff Raff.* [R] ▼◗

Once Is Not Enough SEE: **Jacqueline Susann's Once Is Not Enough**

Once Upon a Crime (1992) **C-94m.** *½ D: Eugene Levy. John Candy, James Belushi, Cybill Shepherd, Sean Young, Richard Lewis, Ornella Muti, Giancarlo Giannini, George Hamilton, Joss Ackland, Elsa Martinelli. One of the loudest—and dumbest—comedies of the early '90s, about a group of strangers traveling through Europe who get mixed up with a murder and a missing dachshund. The real crime is the waste of a good cast. Directed by *SCTV* performer Levy. Based on a forgettable 1964 film, AND SUDDENLY IT'S MURDER! [PG]▼●)

Once Upon a Forest (1993) **C-80m.** ** D: Charles Grosvenor. Voices of Michael Crawford, Ben Vereen, Ellen Blain, Ben Gregory, Paige Gosney, Elizabeth Moss, Janet Waldo, Susan Silo. Pro-social animated tale of young "furlings" who leave their forest home to find a cure for a friend who's become ill breathing fumes from a chemical spill. Environmental message is imparted in a steady story with typically cute characters, but there's nothing terribly compelling about the film. [G] ▼●)

Once Upon a Honeymoon (1942) **117m.** **½ D: Leo McCarey. Ginger Rogers, Cary Grant, Walter Slezak, Albert Dekker, Albert Basserman, Ferike Boros, Harry Shannon, Hans Conried. Strange but intriguing curio with status-seeking ex-burlesque queen Rogers marrying secret Nazi bigwig Slezak . . . and radio commentator Grant coming to her rescue. Some boring stretches do it in; however, the scenes in which the star duo are mistaken for Jews and almost sent to a concentration camp are fascinating.▼●)

Once Upon a Time in America (1984) **C-139m.** *** D: Sergio Leone. Robert De Niro, James Woods, Elizabeth McGovern, Tuesday Weld, Larry Rapp, William Forsythe, James Hayden, Treat Williams, Darlanne Fleugel, Burt Young, Joe Pesci, Danny Aiello, Jennifer Connelly, Brian Bloom, James Russo, T. Scott Coffey. Long, engrossing homage to the gangster film, following the rise and fall of Jewish childhood pals on N.Y.C.'s Lower East Side. Shorn of 88m. for U.S. release, story ceases to make sense at several points, and characters appear and disappear with amazing suddenness. Even so, Leone's feel for this genre, compelling performances by De Niro and Woods, and stunning art direction make this well worth watching. Based on Harry Grey's novel *The Hoods.* Connelly's feature film debut. Complete 227m. version is quite a different film—and not without flaws of its own. (Even this long version is minus several minutes of violent footage—notably from a key rape sequence—which exist in European prints.) Director's cut runs 229m. Originally released in U.S. at 139m. [R] ▼●)

Once Upon a Time in China (1991-Hong Kong) **C-134m.** *** D: Tsui Hark. Jet Li, Yuen Biao, Rosamund Kwan, Kent Cheung, Jacky Cheung, Yan Yee-Kwan. Jet Li became a Hong Kong superstar in this influential martial-arts epic about legendary 19th-century Chinese folk hero Wong Fei Hung (the subject of over 100 Chinese movies, including Jackie Chan's DRUNKEN MASTER), a Confucian healer and kung fu master who clashes with Western interlopers as well as local criminal gangs. Crude

dialogue and silly comic relief take backseat to superbly choreographed fight sequences showcasing Li's balletic, gravity-defying skills, notably in climactic duel utilizing giant ladders. Also released in a 100m. dubbed version. Followed by five sequels. Panavision. [R] ▼)

Once Upon a Time in Mexico (2003) **C-101m.** ** D: Robert Rodriguez. Antonio Banderas, Salma Hayek, Johnny Depp, Mickey Rourke, Eva Mendes, Danny Trejo, Enrique Iglesias, Marco Leonardi, Cheech Marin, Ruben Blades, Willem Dafoe, Gerardo Vigil, Pedro Armendáriz. Rodriguez brings back the guitar-toting gunfighter character from EL MARIACHI, reprised by Banderas in DESPERADO, with a bigger budget (for stuntmen and explosions, one presumes) but not much else. Incoherent script has Banderas involved in a coup d'état, but so many characters are double-crossing each other it's hard to keep track (or care), although Depp is fun to watch as a corrupt CIA agent. Shot on high-definition video by Rodriguez, who also wrote, scored, edited, production designed, and supervised the special effects! HD 24P Widescreen. [R] ▼)

Once Upon a Time in the Midlands (2002-British) **C-104m.** **½ D: Shane Meadows. Robert Carlyle, Rhys Ifans, Kathy Burke, Shirley Henderson, Ricky Tomlinson, Finn Atkins. Goofy homage to spaghetti Westerns set in contemporary working-class England. Volatile criminal Jimmy (Carlyle) returns home to win back his estranged girlfriend and their daughter, but they've moved on. Often laugh-out-loud funny and performed by a pitch-perfect cast, but eventually runs out of ideas. Final chapter in Meadows' so-called Midlands trilogy, following TWENTYFOURSEVEN and A ROOM FOR ROMEO BRASS. Super 35. [R]▼)

Once Upon a Time in the West (1968-U.S.-Italian) **C-165m.** ***½ D: Sergio Leone. Charles Bronson, Henry Fonda, Claudia Cardinale, Jason Robards, Gabriele Ferzetti, Paolo Stoppa, Frank Wolff, Jack Elam, Woody Strode, Lionel Stander, Keenan Wynn. Leone's follow-up to his "Dollars" trilogy is languid, operatic masterpiece. Plot, admittedly lifted from JOHNNY GUITAR, has landowner Cardinale waiting for the railroad to come through, unaware she's been targeted by hired killer Fonda (brilliantly cast as one of the coldest villains in screen history). Exciting, funny, and reverent, with now-classic score by Ennio Morricone; not to be missed. Story by Leone, Bernardo Bertolucci, and Dario Argento. Beware chopped-up 140m. version. Techniscope. [M/PG] ▼●)

Once Upon a Time . . . When We Were Colored (1996) **C-111m.** **½ D: Tim Reid. Al Freeman, Jr., Phylicia Rashad, Paula Kelly, Leon, Richard Roundtree, Salli Richardson, Isaac Hayes, Polly Bergen. Well-meaning saga of a boy's childhood in a tight-knit black community on the Mississippi Delta, spanning the 1940s to the early '60s. Sometimes suffers from schmaltz and heavyhanded symbolism, but there are some lovely moments. Freeman and Roundtree are standouts. [PG]▼●)

Once Were Warriors (1994-New Zealand) C-103m. ***½ D: Lee Tamahori. Rena Owen, Temuera Morrison, Mamaengaroa Kerr-Bell, Julian (Sonny) Arahanga, Taungaroa Emile, Clifford Curtis. Shattering drama about a poor, urbanized Maori family, and the wife's growing realization that she can no longer endure her "macho" husband's abuse—both physical and psychological. Striking and powerful film marks Tamahori's directing debut; trenchant script by Riwia Brown, based on Alan Duff's novel, a best-seller in New Zealand. Not to be missed. Followed by WHAT BECOMES OF THE BROKEN HEARTED. [R]▼●)

Once You Kiss a Stranger (1969) C-106m. BOMB D: Robert Sparr. Paul Burke, Carol Lynley, Martha Hyer, Peter Lind Hayes, Philip Carey, Stephen McNally, Whit Bissell. Thinly disguised remake of STRANGERS ON A TRAIN, with Lynley as nut who pulls golfer Burke into bizarre "reciprocal murder" scheme. Slick but empty-headed, laughable. [M/PG]▐

On Dangerous Ground (1952) 82m. *** D: Nicholas Ray. Ida Lupino, Robert Ryan, Ward Bond, Charles Kemper, Anthony Ross, Ed Begley, Ian Wolfe, Cleo Moore, Olive Carey. Effective mood-piece with hardened city cop Ryan softened by blind girl Lupino, whose brother is involved in rural manhunt. Bernard Herrmann's score was reportedly his favorite work. Produced by John Houseman. ▼●)

On Deadly Ground (1994) C-101m. *½ D: Steven Seagal. Steven Seagal, Michael Caine, Joan Chen, John C. McGinley, R. Lee Ermey, Shari Shattuck, Billy Bob Thornton. After the critical/popular success of UNDER SIEGE, Seagal was allowed to direct this fast-fader about the raping of Alaska's interior by an oil company run by evil Caine. Spiritual mumbo-jumbo halfway through looks like an outtake from THE DOORS, and the star's anticlimactic final speech (after the obligatory wrist-snapping) had fans bolting for the exits. Caine looks as if he's undergone cosmetic surgery by Dwight Frye. Clairmont-Scope. [R]▼●)

Ondine (2010-Irish-U.S.) C-104m. *** D: Neil Jordan. Colin Farrell, Alicja Bachleda, Alison Barry, Stephen Rea, Tony Curran, Emil Hostina, Dervla Kirwan. Down-on-his-luck Irish fisherman (Farrell), recovering from a misspent life of alcoholism, hauls a drowned maiden (Bachleda) caught in his net aboard his ship. Miraculously, she is revived, but has lost her memory. She remains a mystery even as her life becomes intertwined with Farrell and his verbally rambunctious young

daughter (Barry), who is convinced that Bachleda is a mythical fairy-tale creature—a selkie—come to life. Writer-director Jordan deftly mixes dark reality into this fantasy-like saga. Diverting sequences between Farrell and Jordan regular Rea are a treat; newcomer Barry is a natural. [PG-13]▐

One, The (2001) C-87m. *½ D: James Wong. Jet Li, Carla Gugino, Delroy Lindo, Jason Statham, James Morrison, Dylan Bruno, Richard Steinmetz. Loud, wooden martial arts actioner plays like a video game. Li stars as a villain who's been rampaging through parallel universes, killing his alter egos and absorbing their energy; his last remaining opponent is a nice-guy L.A. lawman. The climactic showdown is all too predictable. Super 35. [PG-13]▼▐

One and Only, The (1978) C-98m. **½ D: Carl Reiner. Henry Winkler, Kim Darby, Gene Saks, Herve Villechaize, Harold Gould, William Daniels, Polly Holliday, Ed Begley, Jr., Brandon Cruz, Charles Frank, Mary Woronov. Winkler as a brash college kid determined to make it in show biz, but winds up a flamboyant wrestler. Some truly funny moments build to gradual disenchantment with his basically obnoxious character. Written by Steve Gordon. [PG]▼▐

One and Only, Genuine, Original Family Band, The (1968) C-117m. **½ D: Michael O'Herlihy. Walter Brennan, Buddy Ebsen, Lesley Ann Warren, John Davidson, Janet Blair, Kurt Russell. Musical family becomes involved in 1888 Presidential campaign; innocuous Disney entertainment with forgettable songs by the Sherman Brothers. Goldie (billed as Goldie Jeanne) Hawn debuts in tiny part as giggling dancer. [G]▼●)

One Crazy Summer (1986) C-93m. ** D: Savage Steve Holland. John Cusack, Demi Moore, Joel Murray, Curtis Armstrong, Bobcat Goldthwait, Tom Villard, William Hickey, Joe Flaherty, Jeremy Piven. Holland's follow-up to BETTER OFF DEAD is another loosely connected comedy (styled like a cartoon) about a teenage misfit spending summer on Nantucket Island in New England. Some good sight gags and bright moments but no story or real characterizations to hang on to. [PG]▼●)

One Cup of Coffee SEE: **Pastime**

One Dark Night (1983) C-89m. *½ D: Tom McLoughlin. Meg Tilly, Robin Evans, Leslie Speights, Elizabeth Daily, Adam West. Teenagers spend the night in a mausoleum. You've seen it all before, and you don't want to see it again. [PG]▼

One Day in September (1999-U.S.-British) C/B&W-92m. *** D: Kevin Macdonald. Narrated by Michael Douglas. Compelling, if slick, Oscar-winning documentary recollection of the 1972 Munich Olympics, during which Palestinian terrorists took hostage a group of Israeli athletes, with tragic consequences. The event comes alive via footage and interviews (including one with the lone surviving terrorist), but style sometimes outweighs substance, as when heavy metal rock music accompanies images of the hostages' blood-soaked corpses. [R]▼●)

One Day in the Life of Ivan Denisovich (1971-British-Norwegian) **C-100m. **½ D**: Casper Wrede. Tom Courtenay, Espen Skjonberg, James Maxwell, Alfred Burke, Eric Thompson. Another instance where a novel was just too difficult to film; Alexander Solzhenitsyn's story of a prisoner in Siberian labor camp only occasionally works on the screen. Good photography by Sven Nykvist; script by Ronald Harwood. [G]▼●

One Deadly Summer (1983-French) **C-133m. *** D**: Jean Becker. Isabelle Adjani, Alain Souchon, Francois Cluzet, Manuel Gelin, Jenny Cleve, Suzanne Flon, Michel Galabru, Maria Machado. Overlong but engrossing drama with astonishing performance by Adjani as young sexpot whose disturbed behavior masks elaborate revenge plan. Extremely well acted, especially by Souchon as her likable beau and Flon as his deaf aunt, but Adjani's character is just too obnoxious to warrant much sympathy. Sebastien Japrisot's screenplay (from his novel) retains unusual device of having several characters take turns narrating. [R]▼▶

One Down Two to Go (1983) **C-84m.** BOMB D: Fred Williamson. Fred Williamson, Jim Brown, Jim Kelly, Richard Roundtree, Paula Sills, Laura Loftus, Tom Signorelli, Joe Spinell. Kung fu tournament promoter Roundtree is ripped off, and Williamson, Brown, and Kelly go into action. Bottom-of-the-barrel blaxploitation actioner. [R]▼▶

one eight seven (1997) **C-119m. **½ D**: Kevin Reynolds. Samuel L. Jackson, John Heard, Kelly Rowan, Clifton Gonzalez Gonzalez, Karina Arroyave, Jonah Rooney. N.Y.C. high school teacher Jackson is stabbed by a student, and relocates to L.A.'s San Fernando Valley. But conditions at the school there are equally rough, and soon some of his students turn up dead. Pretentious treatment of a genuine problem: violence in American schools. A corny, obvious script doesn't help, but the fine acting from all concerned does. Title refers to California state penal code for murder. [R]▼●▶

One-Eyed Jacks (1961) **C-141m. *** D**: Marlon Brando. Marlon Brando, Karl Malden, Pina Pellicer, Katy Jurado, Ben Johnson, Slim Pickens, Timothy Carey, Elisha Cook, Jr., Margarita Cordova. Fascinating but flawed psychological Western with outlaw Brando seeking revenge on former friend Malden, now a sheriff. Visually striking, and a rich character study, but overlong. Brando's only directorial effort. VistaVision.▼●▶

One False Move (1992) **C-105m. *** D**: Carl Franklin. Bill Paxton, Cynda Williams,

Billy Bob Thornton, Michael Beach, Jim Metzler, Earl Billings, Natalie Canerday, Robert Ginnaven, Robert Anthony Bell, Kevin Hunter. Savvy L.A. cops end up in Dirt Road, Ark., awaiting three squabbling killers who are wanted for a grisly drug ripoff. Exceptionally trim—a nasty story (with a good romantic twist) methodically tracking its way toward an impending blood bath. Thornton scripted with Tom Epperson. [R]▼●▶

One Fine Day (1996) **C-108m. *** D**: Michael Hoffman. Michelle Pfeiffer, George Clooney, Mae Whitman, Alex D. Linz, Charles Durning, Jon Robin Baitz, Ellen Greene, Joe Grifasi, Pete Hamill, Anna Maria Horsford, Sheila Kelley, Robert Klein, Amanda Peet, Bitty Schram, Holland Taylor, Rachel York. A rarity in the '90s: a genuinely nice movie about two harried and self-absorbed New Yorkers who meet by chance while taking care of their young children during an impossibly hectic career day. He's a hotshot newspaper columnist, she's with an architectural firm. Cute, funny romantic comedy will surely strike many chords with parents. Pfeiffer (never more likeable) also produced. [PG]▼●▶

One Flew Over the Cuckoo's Nest (1975) **C-133m. **** D**: Milos Forman. Jack Nicholson, Louise Fletcher, Brad Dourif, William Redfield, Michael Berryman, Peter Brocco, Will Sampson, Danny DeVito, Christopher Lloyd, Scatman Crothers, Vincent Schiavelli, Sydney Lassick, Louisa Moritz. Ken Kesey's story is a triumph of the human spirit; a feisty misfit (Nicholson) enters an insane asylum and inspires his fellow patients to assert themselves, to the chagrin of strong-willed head nurse (Fletcher). The first film since IT HAPPENED ONE NIGHT to win all five top Oscars: Best Picture, Actor, Actress, Director, Screenplay (Lawrence Hauben, Bo Goldman). Lloyd's film debut. [R]▼●▶

One for the Book SEE: **Voice of the Turtle, The**

One From the Heart (1982) **C-99m. ** D**: Francis Coppola. Frederic Forrest, Teri Garr, Raul Julia, Nastassia Kinski, Lainie Kazan, Harry Dean Stanton, Allen Goorwitz (Garfield), Luana Anders. Lavishly produced but practically plotless romantic comedy about a couple (Forrest, Garr) who quarrel, then seek out other partners (Kinski, Julia). Dean Tavoularis' stylized Las Vegas set and the cinematography by Vittorio Storaro and Ronald V. Garcia are astonishing! Unfortunately, pretty images do not a film make. Tom Waits songs fill the soundtrack while the actors play out one of Coppola's most surreal entertainments. A must for the curious—others beware. Look sharp for Rebecca De Mornay as a restaurant patron. Originally 107m., completely recut by Coppola in 2003, incorporating 7m. of previously unused footage. [R]▼○▮

Onegin (1999-British) **C-106m.** ******* D: Martha Fiennes. Ralph Fiennes, Liv Tyler, Toby Stephens, Lena Headey, Martin Donovan, Alun Armstrong, Harriet Walter, Irene Worth, Jason Watkins, Francesca Annis. Visually beautiful, sensitively directed love story, set in 1820s St. Petersburg and based on Pushkin's *Eugene Onegin,* about an aristocratic bachelor who inherits a country estate and becomes involved in a paradoxical relationship with a daughter of his new neighbor. Many nice, subtle touches, though Tyler is miscast. Director Martha is the sister of Ralph (who also executive-produced); brother Magnus Fiennes composed the music and sister Sophie Fiennes has a cameo.▼▮

One Girl's Confession (1953) **74m.** ****** D: Hugo Haas. Cleo Moore, Hugo Haas, Glenn Langan, Russ Conway. Waitress Cleo steals from her ill-tempered boss, then serves jail sentence knowing the loot is waiting for her. Typical Hugo Haas production, with intriguing premise but flimsy development. Moore is presented as untouchable—but our first look at her is in an alluring low-cut bathing suit. Thanks, Hugo.▮

One Good Cop (1991) **C-114m.** ****** D: Heywood Gould. Michael Keaton, Rene Russo, Anthony LaPaglia, Kevin Conway, Rachel Ticotin, Tony Plana, Benjamin Bratt, Charlaine Woodard. Superficial look at dedicated N.Y.C. cop (and happily married man) who—faced with the prospect of fatherhood—is forced to examine his goals and his morality. Mix of urban grittiness and heart-tugging sentiment doesn't work, especially with its many convenient dramatic turns and shortcuts. Those three little girls *are* adorable, though. [R]▼○▮

One Hour Photo (2002) **C-96m.** *****½** D: Mark Romanek. Robin Williams, Connie Nielsen, Michael Vartan, Gary Cole, Dylan Smith, Eriq LaSalle, Erin Daniels. Suburban family leaves its snapshots with Sy, "the Photo Guy," a friendly fellow at the local chain store, little dreaming that Sy has become obsessed with them. Impressive feature by music video veteran Romanek (who also wrote the original screenplay), built on the sturdy foundation of Williams' persuasive and finely tuned performance. [R]▼▮

One Hour With You (1932) **80m.** *****½** D: Ernst Lubitsch, George Cukor. Maurice Chevalier, Jeanette MacDonald, Genevieve Tobin, Roland Young, Charlie Ruggles. Chic romance of happily married couple upset by arrival of flirtatious Tobin. Chevalier is delightful as always, talking (and singing) directly to the camera. Remake of Lubitsch's 1924 THE MARRIAGE CIRCLE; started by Cukor, completed by Lubitsch with Cukor as his assistant.○▮

One Hundred and One Dalmatians (1961) **C-79m.** ******* D: Wolfgang Reitherman, Hamilton Luske, Clyde Geronimi. Voices of Rod Taylor, Lisa Davis, Cate Bauer, Ben Wright, Fred Warlock, J. Pat O'Malley, Betty Lou Gerson. Likable, low-key Disney cartoon feature set in England, about the theft and recovery of some adorable dalmatian puppies by a flamboyant villain-ess named Cruella De Vil. The story's told from a doggy point-of-view, which is just one ingredient of the film's great appeal. Followed 42 years later by a direct-to-video sequel. Remade in 1996. Later a Broadway musical. ▼○▮

101 Dalmatians (1996) **C-103m.** ****½** D: Stephen Herek. Glenn Close, Jeff Daniels, Joely Richardson, Joan Plowright, Hugh Laurie, Mark Williams, John Shrapnel. Remake of the Disney animated favorite starts out charmingly well, with Daniels and Richardson a perfect pair (along with their dogs Pongo and Perdita), and Close a flamboyantly funny Cruella De Vil. But once the dalmatian puppies are stolen and Cruella's bumbling henchmen take over, this John Hughes script becomes yet another heavy-handed HOME ALONE retread, full of mechanical slapstick gags. Followed by a sequel. Panavision. [G] ▼○▮

One Hundred and One Nights (1995-French-British) **C-101m.** ******* D: Agnès Varda. Michel Piccoli, Marcello Mastroianni, Henri Garcin, Julie Gayet, Mathieu Demy, Emmanuel Salinger. Playful valentine to the cinema, brimming with ideas and clever homages to films and filmmakers. Piccoli stars as Simon Cinéma, a 100-year-old living symbol of film history. An array of international film personalities briefly appear, including Anouk Aimée, Fanny Ardant, Jean-Paul Belmondo, Alain Delon, Catherine Deneuve, Robert De Niro, Gérard Depardieu, Harrison Ford, Gina Lollobrigida, Jeanne Moreau, and Hanna Schygulla. Among the highlights: Piccoli and Depardieu amusingly recall their various cinematic death scenes, and Deneuve and a French-speaking De Niro picturesquely float on a boat in a lake. Full title is ONE HUNDRED AND ONE NIGHTS OF SIMON CINÉMA. ▼▮

102 Dalmatians (2000) **C-100m.** ****** D: Kevin Lima. Glenn Close, Gérard Depardieu, Ioan Gruffudd, Alice Evans, Tim McInnerny, Ben Crompton, Carol Macready, Ian Richardson, Timothy West; voice of Eric Idle. Excruciatingly shrill Disney sequel about the further adventures of Cruella De Vil (Close) as she continues her evil quest to acquire a Dalmatian-skin coat, this time with the help of a nefarious fur designer (Depardieu). Close's high-camp performance and wardrobe are fun for a while, and young children are sure to take to all those adorable puppies, but the results are spotty at best. [G]▼▶

One Hundred Men and a Girl (1937) **84m.** ***½ D: Henry Koster. Deanna Durbin, Leopold Stokowski, Adolphe Menjou, Alice Brady, Eugene Pallette, Mischa Auer, Frank Jenks, Billy Gilbert. Superior blend of music and comedy as Deanna pesters conductor Stokowski to give work to her unemployed father and musician friends. Brimming with charm— and beautiful music, with Charles Previn's score earning an Oscar.▼●

100 Rifles (1969) **C-110m. ** D: Tom Gries. Jim Brown, Raquel Welch, Burt Reynolds, Fernando Lamas, Dan O'Herlihy, Hans Gudegast (Eric Braeden). Overripe Western saga has deputy Brown going after Reynolds, fleeing with shipment of guns into Mexico, but meeting and falling for guerrilla leader Welch. Reynolds easily steals film. [PG]▼▶

127 Hours (2010-U.S.-British) **C-94m.** *** D: Danny Boyle. James Franco, Amber Tamblyn, Kate Mara, Clémence Poésy, Kate Burton, Lizzy Caplan, Sean A. Bott, Treat Williams. True story of Aron Ralston, a free spirit who set out on a mountain-biking adventure in 2003 without telling anyone where he was going. He slipped down a crevice, followed by a boulder that pinned his arm in place against a rock wall. The film follows his five-day struggle to survive, using inventive storytelling devices, including his video camera, memory flashbacks, and even hallucinations. Franco gives a fearless and emotionally engaging performance in this unusual film from Boyle, who also co-wrote the script with Simon Beaufoy and drew on others from his SLUMDOG MILLIONAIRE team, including composer A. R. Rahman. Squeamish viewers may want to avert their eyes during one key scene. [R]▶

One Is a Lonely Number (1972) **C-97m.** *** D: Mel Stuart. Trish Van Devere, Monte Markham, Janet Leigh, Melvyn Douglas, Jane Elliott, Jonathan Lippe. Sympathetic performance by Van Devere helps this better-than-usual soaper about life of an attractive divorcee; good supporting work by Douglas and Leigh. [PG]

One Last Thing . . . (2006) **C-93m. ** D: Alex Steyermark. Cynthia Nixon, Michael Angarano, Sunny Mabrey, Nelust Wyclef Jean, Matt Bush, Gideon Glick, Johnny Messner, Gina Gershon. Inoffensive but artificial comedy-drama about a 16-year-old boy who's dying and announces his official wish: to spend a weekend alone with his fantasy woman, a supermodel whose bikini poster adorns his bedroom wall. Some likable performances keep this from becoming saccharine, but can't invest it with any form of reality. Ethan Hawke appears unbilled.▶

One Little Indian (1973) **C-90m. **½ D:

Bernard McEveety. James Garner, Vera Miles, Clay O'Brien, Pat Hingle, Andrew Prine, Jodie Foster. Garner is AWOL cavalry corporal escaping through desert with young Indian boy and a camel. Unusual Disney comedy-drama. [G]▼▶

One Magic Christmas (1985) **C-88m.** *** D: Phillip Borsos. Mary Steenburgen, Gary Basaraba, Harry Dean Stanton, Arthur Hill, Elizabeth Harnois, Robbie Magwood, Michelle Meyrink, Elias Koteas, Jan Rubes, Sarah Polley, Graham Jarvis. Wife and mom enduring hard times has lost the Christmas spirit, but Santa Claus and guardian angel conspire with her daughter to show her the light. Entertaining Disney family fare, though pretty serious at times . . . and Stanton is the unlikeliest guardian angel in movie history! Made in Canada. [G]▼●

One Man Force (1989) **C-89m. ** D: Dale Trevillion. John Matuszak, Ronny Cox, Charles Napier, Sharon Farrell, Sam Jones, Richard Lynch, Stacey Q. Formula action vehicle for former football player Matuszak, who plays an L.A. cop who goes off the deep end when drug dealers murder his partner. Matuszak died suddenly before this film's release. [R]▼●

One Man Jury (1978) **C-104m. **½ D: Charles Martin. Jack Palance, Christopher Mitchum, Pamela Shoop, Angel Tompkins, Joe Spinell, Cara Williams. DIRTY HARRY rip-off with Palance as vigilante cop who administers his own brand of violent justice on some particularly repulsive felons. [R]▼

One Man's Hero (1999) **C-121m. **½ D: Lance Hool. Tom Berenger, Daniela Romo, Stephen Tobolowsky, Joaquim de Almeida, Mark Moses, James Gammon, Patrick Bergin. When his men are sent to prison just before the outbreak of the Mexican-American war, Berenger attempts to free them and is attacked by the U.S. Army. The fleeing squadron is then captured by guerrilla forces, but they form a bond and decide to fight together. Obviously a labor of love for star/producer Berenger, and based on a true story, but more earnest than exciting. Super 35. [R]▼▶

One Million B.C. (1940) **80m. **½ D: Hal Roach, Hal Roach, Jr. Victor Mature, Carole Landis, Lon Chaney, Jr., John Hubbard, Mamo Clark, Jean Porter. Bizarre caveman saga told in flashback is real curio, made on a big scale. Excellent special effects— from prehistoric monsters to an erupting volcano—which have turned up as stock footage in countless cheapies. Longtime rumors that D. W. Griffith directed parts are not true. Remade in 1966 as ONE MILLION YEARS B.C.

One Million Years B.C. (1966-British) **C-100m. **½ D: Don Chaffey. Raquel Welch, John Richardson, Percy Herbert, Robert

Brown, Martine Beswick. Hammer remake of 1940 prehistoric adventure boosted fur-bikinied Welch to stardom; watchable saga with spectacular Ray Harryhausen dinosaurs and percussive score by Mario Nascimbene.▼●▶

One Missed Call (2008-U.S.-Japanese-German) **C-87m.** BOMB D: Eric Valette. Shannyn Sossamon, Edward Burns, Azura Skye, Ana Claudia Talancón, Ray Wise, Johnny Lewis, Jason Beghe, Margaret Cho, Meagan Good. What if you received a message on your cell phone from your future self, with the date and time of your death? No need to stay awake nights wondering, as this film lets you know how some college students deal with just such a predicament. Another Americanized remake of a Japanese horror film (Takashi Miike's CHAKUSHIN ARI) with a good cast wasted. So bad that the title invites pithy putdowns; it's just too easy. [PG-13]▶

One More Saturday Night (1986) **C-95m.** BOMB D: Dennis Klein. Tom Davis, Al Franken, Moira Harris, Frank Howard, Bess Meyer, Dave Reynolds. Unfunny comedy written by and starring the nerdy duo from TV's *Saturday Night Live.* Unlike one of their TV skits, this feature, about various goings-on during a Saturday evening in Minnesota, runs an hour and a half. Forget it. [R]▼●

One More Time (1970) **C-93m.** *½ D: Jerry Lewis. Peter Lawford, Sammy Davis, Jr., Esther Anderson, Maggie Wright. Sequel to SALT AND PEPPER is even worse, with Sammy essentially imitating Jerry Lewis (who directed) as he and Lawford struggle to survive after losing their nightclub—and Lawford assumes his twin brother's identity. Excruciatingly bad; of interest as the only feature Lewis ever directed in which he didn't star. [PG]▶

One More Train to Rob (1971) **C-108m.** **½ D: Andrew V. McLaglen. George Peppard, Diana Muldaur, John Vernon, France Nuyen, Steve Sandor. Peppard seeks revenge on former robbery partner who sent him to jail. Unremarkable Western has some flavor, nice supporting cast of familiar faces. [PG]

One Night at McCool's (2001) **C-100m.** ** D: Harald Zwart. Liv Tyler, Matt Dillon, John Goodman, Paul Reiser, Michael Douglas, Reba McEntire, Richard Jenkins, Andrew Silverstein (Andrew Dice Clay), Leo Rossi, Eric Schaeffer. One-note black comedy about three men obsessed with a beautiful vixen (Tyler)—one poor sucker who sees her for what she is, one who worships her as a goddess, and one who's only interested in kinky sex. Some funny moments, but mostly obvious and repetitive. [R]▼▶

One Night in the Tropics (1940) **82m.** **½ D: A. Edward Sutherland. Allan Jones,

Nancy Kelly, Bud Abbott, Lou Costello, Robert Cummings, Leo Carrillo, Mary Boland. Ambitious but unmemorable musical with songs by Jerome Kern, Oscar Hammerstein and Dorothy Fields, from Earl Derr Biggers' gimmicky story *Love Insurance* (filmed before in 1919 and 1924). Abbott and Costello, in film debut, have secondary roles to Jones-Kelly-Cummings love triangle, but get to do a portion of their "Who's on First?" routine.▼▶

One Night Stand (1997) **C-103m.** ** D: Mike Figgis. Wesley Snipes, Nastassja Kinski, Kyle MacLachlan, Ming-Na Wen, Robert Downey, Jr., John Calley, Glenn Plummer, Amanda Donohoe, John Ratzenberger, Julian Sands, Thomas Haden Church, Donovan Leitch, Ione Skye, Xander Berkeley. Flashy but empty drama about a TV commercials director (Snipes) caught up in a plastic, unfeeling world, whose life is in for quite a jolt upon renewing a friendship with seriously ill Downey and having a chance encounter with Kinski. Figgis turns up as a hotel clerk. [R] ▼●▶

One Night With the King (2006) **C-122m.** **½ D: Michael O. Sajbel. Tiffany Dupont, Luke Goss, John Rhys-Davies, John Noble, Tommy "Tiny" Lister, James Callis, Jonah Lotan, Peter O'Toole, Omar Sharif. Old Testament romantic thriller about a Jewish orphan forced to hide her heritage when she's chosen as queen to Persian king Xerxes. Large-scale, rich-looking production, shot in India, is packed with tasty biblical intrigue and treachery. But it also features bad acting and dialogue, both High British and Valley Girl, with Dupont like totally wrong as a woman torn between love and loyalty. Previously filmed as ESTHER AND THE KING. O'Toole is seen for barely 30 seconds as the prophet Samuel. [PG]▶

...... One of Our Aircraft Is Missing (1942-British) **106m.** ***½ D: Michael Powell, Emeric Pressburger. Godfrey Tearle, Eric Portman, Hugh Williams, Bernard Miles, Hugh Burden, Emrys Jones, Googie Withers, Joyce Redman, Pamela Brown, Peter Ustinov, Hay Petrie, Roland Culver, Robert Helpmann, John Longden. Thoughtful study of RAF bomber crew who bail out over the Netherlands and seek to return to England. Powell and Pressburger scripted, from the latter's story. Powell makes an appearance as a dispatcher. Some U.S. prints run 82m.▼▶

One of Our Dinosaurs Is Missing (1975) **C-93m.** BOMB D: Robert Stevenson. Peter Ustinov, Helen Hayes, Clive Revill, Derek Nimmo, Joan Sims. The Disney studio's answer to insomnia, a boring film about spy with secret formula hidden in dinosaur bone, and a group of nannies determined to retrieve stolen skeleton. Filmed in England. [G]▼

One on One (1977) **C-98m.** ******* D: Lamont Johnson. Robby Benson, Annette O'Toole, G. D. Spradlin, Gail Strickland, Melanie Griffith. Benson cowrote this sincere, upbeat film about naive basketball player who tries to buck corrupt world of college athletics, and sadistic coach Spradlin. Director Johnson plays Benson's alumni big brother. [PG]▼◗

One Plus One SEE: **Sympathy for the Devil**

One Sings, the Other Doesn't (1977-French) **C-105m.** ****** D: Agnès Varda. Therese Liotard, Valerie Mairesse, Ali Raffi, Robert Dadies, Francis Lemaire. Simplistic, sugar-coated feminist story paralleling the lives of two women from the early '60s to 1976. An honest attempt to examine the meaning of womanhood, but awfully superficial.▼

One Summer Love (1976) **C-98m.** ****** D: Gilbert Cates. Beau Bridges, Susan Sarandon, Mildred Dunnock, Ann Wedgeworth, Michael B. Miller, Linda Miller. Ambitious but muddled drama of Bridges, just out of a mental hospital, attempting to trace his family; Sarandon, who sells candy in a movie theater, takes a liking to him. Screenplay by N. Richard Nash; originally released as DRAGONFLY. [PG]▼

1001 Arabian Nights (1959) **C-75m.** ****½** D: Jack Kinney. Voices of Jim Backus, Kathryn Grant (Crosby), Dwayne Hickman, Hans Conried, Herschel Bernardi, Alan Reed. Elaborate updating of Arabian Nights tales featuring nearsighted Mr. Magoo has a nice score, pleasing animation.▼

1,000 Eyes of Dr. Mabuse, The (1960-West German-French-Italian) **105m.** ******* D: Fritz Lang. Dawn Addams, Peter van Eyck, Gert Frobe, Wolfgang Preiss, Werner Peters, Andrea Checchi. Fast-paced, witty thriller, intricately plotted but crystal clear: using the secrets of the original Dr. Mabuse, a modern-day criminal genius blackmails the wealthy, resorting to murder as necessary. Lang's last film as director, marking a strong return to form. Beware of alternate versions still in circulation: THE SECRET OF DR. MABUSE and THE DIABOLICAL DR. MABUSE. ▼◗

One Touch of Venus (1948) **81m.** ****½** D: William A. Seiter. Ava Gardner, Robert Walker, Dick Haymes, Eve Arden, Olga San Juan, Tom Conway. Young man in love with department-store window statue of Venus doesn't know what to do when she magically comes to life. Amusing, but misses the bull's-eye, despite its having been a hit on Broadway. Lovely Kurt Weill–Ogden Nash score includes "Speak Low." Also shown in computer-colored version. ▼◗

One Tough Cop (1998) **C-94m.** ***½** D: Bruno Barreto. Stephen Baldwin, Chris Penn, Gina Gershon, Mike McGlone, Paul Guilfoyle, Amy Irving, Victor Slezak, Luis Guzman. Baldwin is miscast as renegade 1980s N.Y.P.D. detective Bo Dietl who, in this hackneyed, highly fictionalized account of his exploits—based on his "autobiographical novel"—stands up to the nasty Feds when they pressure him to rat out his boyhood best friend, who's now a mob boss. Filled with graphic violence and four-letter words. [R]▼◗◗

One-Trick Pony (1980) **C-98m.** ****** D: Robert M. Young. Paul Simon, Blair Brown, Rip Torn, Joan Hackett, Mare Winningham, Allen Goorwitz (Garfield), Lou Reed, The B-52's, Harry Shearer, The Lovin' Spoonful, Sam and Dave, Tiny Tim. Aging rock star tries to salvage marriage while trying to weather changes in audience tastes. Good premise, impressive supporting cast undermined by haphazard construction, lack of Simon's appeal as a leading man. Scripted and scored by Simon; one of those Hare Krishnas is Daniel Stern. [R]▼◗◗

One True Thing (1998) **C-127m.** *****½** D: Carl Franklin. Meryl Streep, Renée Zellweger, William Hurt, Tom Everett Scott, Lauren Graham, Nicky Katt, James Eckhouse, Gerrit Graham, Diana Canova. Exceptional, moving family drama about a young woman forced to temporarily move back in with her parents and come to terms with both her mother (an expert homemaker to whom she's never related) and her literary lion of a father (whom she's always idolized). Superb acting and the constant ring of truth distinguish this adaptation by Karen Croner of Anna Quindlen's best-selling novel. [R]▼◗◗

One, Two, Three (1961) **108m.** ******** D: Billy Wilder. James Cagney, Arlene Francis, Horst Buchholz, Pamela Tiffin, Lilo Pulver, Howard St. John, Hans Lothar, Leon Askin, Red Buttons. Hilarious Wilder comedy about Coke executive in contemporary West Berlin freaking out when the boss's visiting daughter secretly weds a Communist. Cagney is a marvel to watch in this machine-gun-paced comedy, his last film appearance until 1981's RAGTIME. Andre Previn's score makes inspired use of Khachaturian's "Sabre Dance." The script, by Wilder and I.A.L. Diamond, was inspired by a Ferenc Molnar one-act play. Panavision. ▼◗◗

One Way Passage (1932) **69m.** *****½** D: Tay Garnett. Kay Francis, William Powell, Aline MacMahon, Warren Hymer, Frank McHugh, Herbert Mundin. Tender shipboard romance of fugitive Powell and fatally ill Francis, splendidly acted, with good support by MacMahon and McHugh as con artists. Robert Lord won an Oscar for his original story. Remade as 'TIL WE MEET AGAIN. ◗

One Wild Moment (1977-French) **C-88m.** ****** D: Claude Berri. Jean-Pierre Marielle, Victor Lanoux, Agnes Soral, Christine

Dejoux, Martine Sarcey. Lightweight, unsatisfying sex farce about two middle-aged buddies (Marielle, Lanoux) who vacation with their sexy teen daughters (Soral, Dejoux). Not nearly as clever as other Berri comedies. Remade as BLAME IT ON RIO. Panavision. [R]▼

One Woman or Two (1985-French) **C-97m.** *½ D: Daniel Vigne. Gérard Depardieu, Sigourney Weaver, Dr. Ruth Westheimer, Michel Aumont, Zabou. Paleontologist Depardieu discovers the fossil remains of the first Frenchwoman; crass ad exec Weaver is intent on exploiting this to hype perfume. An utterly silly BRINGING UP BABY derivation, with its two stars wasted. [PG-13]▼

One Woman's Story SEE: **Passionate Friends, The**

On Golden Pond (1981) **C-109m.** *** D: Mark Rydell. Katharine Hepburn, Henry Fonda, Jane Fonda, Doug McKeon, Dabney Coleman, William Lanteau. Fonda, in his last feature, is no less than brilliant as crochety retired professor Norman Thayer, Jr., angry at being 80 years old and scared of losing his faculties. Hepburn fine as his devoted, all-knowing wife who shares his summers at Maine lakefront home; Jane is his alienated daughter. Sometimes simplistic comedy-drama, scripted by Ernest Thompson from his play, gets a heavy dose of Star Quality. Fonda, Hepburn, and writer Thompson all won Academy Awards for their work. Remade for TV in 2001. [PG]▼●)

On Guard (1997-French-German) **C-128m.** *** D: Philippe de Broca. Daniel Auteuil, Fabrice Luchini, Vincent Perez, Marie Gillain, Yann Collette, Jean-François Stévenin, Didier Pain, Philippe Noiret. A faithful swordsman rescues an infant princess from the grasp of her sinister relative; the baby's father was also the swordsman's mentor. Deliciously old-fashioned popcorn movie full of derring-do, and set in the France of Louis XIV. Auteuil is well cast as the hero; Errol Flynn would be proud. Originally titled LE BOSSU, and filmed several times before. Opened in the U.S. in 2002. Panavision. ▼)

On Her Majesty's Secret Service (1969-British) **C-140m.** ***½ D: Peter R. Hunt. George Lazenby, Diana Rigg, Gabriele Ferzetti, Telly Savalas, Bernard Lee, Lois Maxwell, Desmond Llewelyn, Catharina Von Schell (Catherine Schell), Bessie Love, Joanna Lumley. Usual globe-hopping Bond vs. Blofeld plot with novel twist: agent Bond ends up marrying Italian contessa (Rigg)! Lazenby, first non-Connery Bond, is OK, but incredible action sequences take first chair; some 007 fans consider this the best of the series. Panavision. [M/PG]▼●)

Onibaba (1964-Japanese) **103m.** *** D: Kaneto Shindô. Nobuko Otowa, Jitsuko Yoshimura, Kei Sato, Jukichi Uno. In

war-torn medieval Japan, a widow and her mother-in-law ambush and kill soldiers to sell their armor, until the younger woman falls for one of them. Visceral, erotic, and genuinely creepy folk tale is not for the squeamish, but is expertly made, highlighted by stunning Tohoscope cinematography. ▼)

Onion Field, The (1979) **C-127m.** *** D: Harold Becker. John Savage, James Woods, Franklyn Seales, Ted Danson, Ronny Cox, Dianne Hull, Christopher Lloyd, Priscilla Pointer, Pat Corley. Heart-wrenching true story about a cop who cracks up after witnessing his partner's murder and fleeing; adapted by author Joseph Wambaugh without any studio interference. Well acted and impassioned, but never quite peaks. [R]▼●)

—Only Angels Have Wings (1939) **121m.** ***½ D: Howard Hawks. Cary Grant, Jean Arthur, Richard Barthelmess, Rita Hayworth, Thomas Mitchell, Sig Ruman, John Carroll, Allyn Joslyn, Noah Beery, Jr. Quintessential Howard Hawks movie, full of idealized men and women (and what men and women!) in this look at relationships among mail pilots stationed in South America—and how things heat up when a showgirl (Arthur) is tossed into the stew. An important star-boosting showcase for Hayworth, too. Jules Furthman scripted, from a story by Hawks. ▼)

Only Game in Town, The (1970) **C-113m.** *** D: George Stevens. Elizabeth Taylor, Warren Beatty, Charles Braswell, Hank Henry, Olga Valery. Romance of chorus girl and gambler takes place in Las Vegas, but was shot in Paris and suffers for it; restriction of action to indoor scenes slows pace of this pleasant adaptation of Frank D. Gilroy's play. Beatty is excellent. Stevens' final film. [M/PG]▼

Only the Best SEE: **I Can Get It for You Wholesale**

Only the French Can SEE: **French Cancan**

Only the Lonely (1991) **C-102m.** *** D: Chris Columbus. John Candy, Maureen O'Hara, Ally Sheedy, James Belushi, Anthony Quinn, Kevin Dunn, Milo O'Shea, Bert Remsen, Joe V. Greco, Macaulay Culkin, Kieran Culkin. Chicago cop, who still lives with his mom, falls in love—and has to overcome both his mother's resistance and his feelings of guilt over leaving her. Sweet, sentimental update of MARTY shines with performances that are right on-target, including O'Hara's first since 1973's THE RED PONY. [PG-13]▼●)

Only the Strong (1993) **C-96m.** ** D: Sheldon Lettich. Mark Dacascos, Stacey Travis, Geoffrey Lewis, Paco Christian Prieto, Todd Susman, Jeffrey Anderson Gunter. Ex–Green Beret, his old Miami high school now threatened by a drug lord, turns a dozen of the joint's worst malcontents into crimebusters by teaching them a rhythmic, Brazilian form of martial arts called capoeira. Real-life martial arts champ Dacascos is appealing in a can't-act kind of way. Dopey but inoffensive; at its best in potently choreographed fight scenes. [PG-13]▼●)

Only Thrill, The (1998) C-108m. *½ D: Peter Masterson. Diane Keaton, Sam Shepard, Diane Lane, Robert Patrick, Tate Donovan, Sharon Lawrence, Stacey Travis. A fine cast can't save this drab tearjerker about the thwarted affair between a widowed seamstress and a small-town Texas shopkeeper that begins in 1966, spans three decades, and begins to repeat itself when their grown children fall in love. Stagy, contrived, and never plausible, with some hilariously unconvincing old-age wigs and makeup effects. [R]▼▼

Only When I Larf (1968-British) C-104m. **½ D: Basil Dearden. Richard Attenborough, David Hemmings, Alexandra Stewart, Nicholas Pennell. Fun con-game film finds three confidence men scheming to sell militant African diplomat scrap metal in ammunition cases. [G]

Only When I Laugh (1981) C-120m. *** D: Glenn Jordan. Marsha Mason, Kristy McNichol, James Coco, Joan Hackett, David Dukes, John Bennett Perry, Kevin Bacon. Bittersweet Neil Simon comedy about alcoholic actress Mason struggling to stay off the bottle and her relationship with teenaged daughter McNichol. Fine performances by the leads, superior ones by Coco as a gay failed actor and Hackett as an aging Park Avenue beauty. Loosely based on his play *The Gingerbread Lady*. [R]▼●

Only You (1992) C-85m. ** D: Betty Thomas. Andrew McCarthy, Kelly Preston, Helen Hunt, Daniel Roebuck, Denny Dillon, Kid Creole and The Coconuts. McCarthy, dumped by his dishy girlfriend-of-the-moment, meets sexy Preston and winds up taking her on his vacation jaunt to an idyllic beach resort . . . but are looks really everything? Pleasant-enough romantic comedy, with a capable and attractive cast, gets just too predictable to sustain itself. Reni Santoni appears unbilled. Released direct to video. Clairmont-Scope. [PG-13]▼●

Only You (1994) C-108m. *** D: Norman Jewison. Marisa Tomei, Robert Downey, Jr., Bonnie Hunt, Joaquim De Almeida, Fisher Stevens, Billy Zane, Adam LeFevre, John Benjamin Hickey, Siobhan Fallon, Phyllis Newman. Likable confection about a young woman who spends her whole life searching for her perfect mate—whose name was conjured up in childhood on a Ouija board; fate and happenstance bring her to Europe to meet her "other half." Tomei's earnest and appealing performance makes the far-fetched story work. Director Jewi-

son provides a dreamy travelogue of Italy (photographed by Sven Nykvist, no less) as her backdrop. Like so many contemporary romantic comedies, this one invokes an earlier one (ROMAN HOLIDAY) to justify its existence. [PG]▼●)

On Moonlight Bay (1951) C-95m. **½ D: Roy Del Ruth. Doris Day, Gordon MacRae, Billy Gray, Mary Wickes, Leon Ames, Rosemary DeCamp. Turn-of-the-20th-century, folksy musical based on Booth Tarkington's *Penrod* stories with tomboy (Day) and next door neighbor (MacRae) the wholesome young lovers. Sequel: BY THE LIGHT OF THE SILVERY MOON. ▼●)

On My Own (1992-Italian-Canadian-Australian) C-93m. ***½ D: Antonio Tibaldi. Judy Davis, Matthew Ferguson, David McIlwraith, Nicolas Van Burek, Michele Melega, Colin Fox, Jan Rubes. Complex, deeply felt, hauntingly powerful coming-of-age drama about 15-year-old Ferguson, who attends a boys' prep school. His parents are divorced; he's physically and emotionally distanced from his father, and learns that his mother (Davis, who is superb) is a schizophrenic. The scenario details how he is affected by her illness, her personality, and her fate.▼

On My Way to the Crusades, I Met a Girl Who . . . (1968-Italian) C-93m. BOMB D: Pasquale Festa Campanile. Tony Curtis, Monica Vitti, Hugh Griffith, John Richardson, Ivo Garrani, Nino Castelnuovo. Weak comedy about Vitti's chastity belt was held back from release for a long time, and no wonder. Aka THE CHASTITY BELT. [R]

On Our Merry Way (1948) 107m. ** D: King Vidor, Leslie Fenton. Burgess Meredith, Paulette Goddard, Henry Fonda, James Stewart, Fred MacMurray, William Demarest, Dorothy Lamour, Victor Moore, Harry James, Eduardo Ciannelli, Dorothy Ford, Hugh Herbert. Silly multi-episode comedy, with a buoyant Meredith posing as an inquiring reporter and asking people what impact a baby has had on their life. Strained slapstick throughout. Protracted sequence, with Stewart and Fonda as laconic musician pals, was written by John O'Hara. Aka A MIRACLE CAN HAPPEN. ▼)

On the Avenue (1937) 89m. *** D: Roy Del Ruth. Dick Powell, Madeleine Carroll, Alice Faye, Ritz Brothers, Alan Mowbray, Billy Gilbert, Cora Witherspoon, Joan Davis, Sig Rumann. Tasteful, intelligent musical of socialite Carroll getting involved with stage star Powell. One good Irving Berlin song after another: "I've Got My Love To Keep Me Warm," "This Year's Kisses," "Let's Go Slumming," "The Girl on the Police Gazette."▼)

On the Beach (1959) 133m. **** D: Stanley Kramer. Gregory Peck, Ava Gardner, Fred

Astaire, Anthony Perkins, Donna Anderson, John Tate, Guy Doleman. Thoughtful version of Nevil Shute's novel about Australians awaiting effects of nuclear fallout from explosion that has depopulated the rest of the world. Good performances by all, including Astaire in his first dramatic role. Screenplay by John Paxton. Remade for cable TV in 2000. ▼○)

On the Double (1961) C-92m. *** D: Melville Shavelson. Danny Kaye, Dana Wynter, Wilfrid Hyde-White, Margaret Rutherford, Diana Dors. Danny's resemblance to English general makes him valuable as a WW2 spy. At one point he does a Marlene Dietrich imitation! Repeats dual-identity gimmick from Kaye's earlier ON THE RIVIERA with equally entertaining results. Panavision.)

On the Edge (1985) C-92m. ** D: Rob Nilsson. Bruce Dern, Bill Bailey, Jim Haynie, John Marley, Pam Grier. Well-meaning but predictable, ultimately disappointing tale of middle-aged Dern, who attempts to redeem his life by competing in a grueling footrace. Available in unrated version. [PG-13]▼)

On the Line (2001) C-85m. *½ D: Eric Bross. Lance Bass, Joey Fatone, Emmanuelle Chriqui, Dave Foley, Jerry Stiller, GQ (Gregory Qayium), James Bulliard, Tamala Jones, Richie Sambora, Dan Montgomery, Al Green. Nice guy meets a cute girl on the Chicago el, fails to get her name or phone number, then mounts a campaign to find her. Intended to showcase *NSYNC's Bass, who's likable enough, but this is a simplistic five-minute concept stretched to feature length. (In fact, it's a remake of a short subject by the same writers.) Bass' onscreen friends (including *NSYNC's Fatone) are obnoxious; even Stiller and Foley flounder with unfunny material. Justin Timberlake appears unbilled. [PG] ▼)

On the Nickel (1980) C-96m. **½ D: Ralph Waite. Donald Moffat, Ralph Waite, Penelope Allen, Hal Williams, Jack Kehoe. Odd, sentimental film about bums Moffat and Waite and their experiences on L.A.'s skid row. Directed, scripted, and produced by Waite, light years away from *The Waltons*. [R]▼

On the Right Track (1981) C-98m. **½ D: Lee Philips. Gary Coleman, Lisa Eilbacher, Michael Lembeck, Norman Fell, Maureen Stapleton, Bill Russell, Herb Edelman. Coleman is a lovable 10-year-old shoeshine boy who lives out of a train station locker and predicts horserace winners like the hero of THREE MEN ON A HORSE; Stapleton is on hand as a bag lady. Coleman's theatrical starring debut is hardly feature-film material. [PG]▼

On the Riviera (1951) C-90m. *** D: Walter Lang. Danny Kaye, Gene Tierney,

Corinne Calvet, Marcel Dalio, Jean Murat. Bouncy musicomedy with Danny in dual role as entertainer and French military hero. "Ballin' the Jack," other songs in lively film. Gwen Verdon is one of chorus girls. Remake of Maurice Chevalier's FOLIES BERGÈRE and also THAT NIGHT IN RIO.)

On the Road Again SEE: **Honeysuckle Rose**

On the Ropes (1999) C-94m. ***½ D: Nanette Burstein, Brett Morgen. Compelling documentary about a former boxer named Harry Keitt who works with young people at a Brooklyn gym, hoping to give them focus and purpose as well as a possible career after they're showcased at the Golden Gloves. The film follows three of his protégés—a promising young woman who's been dealt a bad hand, a cocky young man who thinks he knows the answers, and a real comer who's too easily seduced by the lure of fame and fortune. Rich, real, often heartbreaking . . . a must-see. ▼)

On the Town (1949) C-98m. **** D: Gene Kelly, Stanley Donen. Gene Kelly, Frank Sinatra, Vera-Ellen, Betty Garrett, Ann Miller, Jules Munshin, Alice Pearce, Florence Bates. Three sailors have 24 hours to take in the sights and sounds of N.Y.C. Exuberant MGM musical, innovatively shot on location all over the City, isn't much in terms of plot and discards some of the best songs from the Betty Comden–Adolph Green–Leonard Bernstein show on which it's based . . . but it's still terrific entertainment. Highlight: "New York, New York." Oscar winner for Roger Edens and Lennie Hayton's musical scoring. An impressive directing debut for Kelly and Donen. ▼○)

On the Waterfront (1954) 108m. **** D: Elia Kazan. Marlon Brando, Karl Malden, Lee J. Cobb, Rod Steiger, Pat Henning, Eva Marie Saint, Leif Erickson, Tony Galento, John Hamilton, Nehemiah Persoff. Budd Schulberg's unflinching account of N.Y.C. harbor unions (suggested by articles by Malcolm Johnson), with Brando unforgettable as misfit, Steiger his crafty brother, Cobb his waterfront boss, and Saint the girl he loves. That classic scene in the back of a taxicab is just as moving as ever. Winner of eight Oscars: Best Picture, Director, Actor (Brando), Supporting Actress (Saint), Story & Screenplay, Cinematography (Boris Kaufman), Art Direction-Set Decoration (Richard Day), and Editing (Gene Milford). Leonard Bernstein's music is another major asset. Film debuts of Saint, Martin Balsam, Fred Gwynne, and Pat Hingle. Adapted as a Broadway show decades later. ▼○)

On the Yard (1979) C-102m. ** D: Raphael D. Silver. John Heard, Thomas D. Waites, Mike Kellin, Richard Bright, Joe Grifasi, Lane Smith. Convict Heard makes a fatal mistake by mixing it up with jailhouse kingpin Waites. So-so prison picture seems hardly worth the effort, though Kellin is memorable as an aging loser trying to get paroled. [R] ▼

On Valentine's Day (1986) **C-106m.** **½ D: Ken Harrison. William Converse-Roberts, Hallie Foote, Michael Higgins, Steven Hill, Rochelle Oliver, Richard Jenkins, Carol Goodheart, Horton Foote, Jr., Matthew Broderick. Literate but unmemorable account of the various goings-on in a small Texas town in 1917. Interesting characterizations, good performances, but doesn't add up to much. Semiautobiographical screenplay by Horton Foote. Followed by CONVICTS; both are prequels to **1918**. Produced for PBS' *American Playhouse,* where it was telecast (along with **1918**) as STORY OF A MARRIAGE. [PG] ▼ ▶

Open City (1945-Italian) **105m.** **** D: Roberto Rossellini. Aldo Fabrizi, Anna Magnani, Marcello Pagliero, Maria Michi, Vito Annicchiarico, Nando Bruno, Harry Feist. Classic Rossellini account of Italian underground movement during Nazi occupation of Rome; powerful moviemaking gem with excellent performances from a memorable cast. Cowritten by Rossellini, Federico Fellini, and Sergio Amidei. Aka ROME, OPEN CITY. The first in Rossellini's war trilogy. Followed by PAISAN and GERMANY YEAR ZERO. ▼ ▶

Open Doors (1990-Italian) **C-109m.** *** D: Gianni Amelio. Gian Maria Volonte, Ennio Fantastichini, Renzo Giovampietro, Renato Carpentieri, Tuccio Musumeci. Stimulating drama about jurist Volonte, presiding over a murder trial in Fascist Italy. A thoughtful look at the personal implications of judging others, of what it means to condemn another to death even if he is obviously guilty. It also focuses on the need to probe for truth and justice in spite of political repression. [R] ▼

Opening Night (1977) **C-144m.** *** D: John Cassavetes. Gena Rowlands, John Cassavetes, Ben Gazzara, Joan Blondell, Paul Stewart, Zohra Lampert. Fascinating if you appreciate Cassavetes' style (he also wrote it); interminable if you don't. Rowlands is an actress facing a midlife crisis triggered by the death of an adoring fan while her play is trying out in New Haven. Blondell fine as the sympathetic authoress, Cassavetes himself no less interesting as Rowlands' costar. Look for Peter Falk, Peter Bogdanovich, and Seymour Cassel. ▼ ▶

Open Range (2003) **C-138m.** *** D: Kevin Costner. Robert Duvall, Kevin Costner, Annette Bening, Michael Gambon, Michael Jeter, Diego Luna, James Russo, Abraham Benrubi, Dean McDermott, Kim Coates, Cliff Saunders. In 1882, some cattle drivers run afoul of a local despot who's declared war on "freegrazers." Instead of moving on, the highly moral Duvall and partner Costner decide to stay and fight for what's right. The story is as simple as a Roy Rogers B movie, writ large, and while some of the dialogue tends toward declarations, it's a classical Western, carefully crafted and moving at a deliberate pace as it follows all of the genre's rituals. Duvall is a pleasure to watch. Production design and use of the Alberta landscape are first-rate. Based on a novel, *The Open Range Men,* by Lauran Paine. Super 35. [R] ▼ ▶

Open Road, The (2009) **C-90m.** **½ D: Michael Meredith. Jeff Bridges, Justin Timberlake, Kate Mara, Harry Dean Stanton, Lyle Lovett, Mary Steenburgen, Ted Danson. During their cross-country road trip to visit his ailing mom, a discontented minor-league ballplayer (Timberlake) reluctantly reunites with his long-estranged father (Bridges), a retired baseball luminary who's never scored many points as husband or parent. Predictable but involving dramedy benefits from vivid lead performance by Bridges as a rascally wastrel, Timberlake's understated turn as his resentful son, and some quietly affecting scenes. The writer-director is son of famed football player Don Meredith. [PG-13] ▶

Open Season (1974-Spanish) **C-103m.** BOMB D: Peter Collinson. Peter Fonda, John Phillip Law, Richard Lynch, William Holden, Cornelia Sharpe. Sordid mixture of violence and sex as three Vietnam War buddies hunt humans. Video title: RECON GAME. Panavision. [R] ▼

Open Season (1996) **C-97m.** *** D: Robert Wuhl. Robert Wuhl, Rod Taylor, Helen Shaver, Gailard Sartain, Maggie Han, Steven C. White, Timothy Arrington, Barry Flatman, Dina Merrill, Saul Rubinek, Tom Selleck, Alan Thicke, Jimmie Walker, Joe Piscopo. Smart, funny satire of television and our competitive society. Wuhl plays a nerdy but straight-arrow worker bee at a ratings company who through personal integrity and candor has a knack for getting himself into trouble; then he stumbles into a job in public broadcasting. Fine supporting cast, including Taylor in a pungent performance as a messianic programming chief. Filmed in 1993. [R] ▼ ●

Open Season (2006) **C-86m.** **½ D: Jill Culton, Roger Allers. Voices of Martin Lawrence, Ashton Kutcher, Gary Sinise, Debra Messing, Billy Connolly, Jon Favreau, Georgia Engel, Jane Krakowski, Gordon Tootoosis, Patrick Warburton. A grizzly bear lives a pampered existence with a female park ranger who's adopted him until a hyperactive mule deer comes into his life. When he's returned to the woods his only goal is to get back to his comfy home . . . but it isn't going to be easy. Expressive characters, great comedy timing, and entertaining voice work get this off to a great start, but the simple story stretches out longer than it should. Followed by three DVD sequels. 3-D. [PG]█

Open Water (2004) C-80m. *** D: Chris Kentis. Blanchard Ryan, Daniel Travis. Young couple gets away from the stress of daily life with a last-minute vacation south of the border. After a scuba expedition they're somehow left behind by their excursion boat and must find a way to survive on their own, in the middle of the ocean, without food or water, surrounded by sharks. Intense drama eschews Hollywood clichés for a perceptive study of chance, fate, and emotions stripped raw. Debut feature for writer-director-editor-cocinematographer Kentis. His wife, Laura Lau, produced and also did camerawork. Followed by an in-name-only direct-to-video sequel. [R]▼❶

Open Your Eyes (1998-Spanish-French-Italian) C-119m. *½ D: Alejandro Amenábar. Penélope Cruz, Eduardo Noriega, Chete Lera, Fele Martínez, Najwa Nimri. A handsome young man falls in love, but his jealous former girlfriend deals him a cruel blow. Murky psychological thriller bounces from present-day reality to a nightmarish vision of the past and present. The hero becomes a tortured soul, but why do we in the audience have to suffer too? Original title: ABRE LOS OJOS. Remade in 2001 as VANILLA SKY. [R]▼❶

Operation Condor SEE: **Armour of God 2: Operation Condor**

Operation Crossbow (1965) C-116m. ***½ D: Michael Anderson. George Peppard, Sophia Loren, Trevor Howard, Tom Courtenay, Jeremy Kemp, Anthony Quayle, John Mills, Sylvia Syms, Richard Todd, Lilli Palmer. Fine "impossible mission" tale of small band of commandos out to destroy Nazi secret missile stronghold during WW2. Sensational ending, and the pyrotechnics are dazzling. Scripted by Robert Imrie (Emeric Pressburger), Derry Quinn, and Ray Rigby. Retitled THE GREAT SPY MISSION. Panavision.▼❶❶

Operation Daybreak (1975) C-102m. **½ D: Lewis Gilbert. Timothy Bottoms, Martin Shaw, Joss Ackland, Nicola Pagett, Anthony Andrews, Anton Diffring. Well-made but uninspiring account of Czech underground's attempt to assassinate Reinhard "Hangman" Heydrich, Hitler's right-hand man, during WW2. Retitled PRICE OF FREEDOM. [PG]▼❶

Operation Double 007 SEE: **Operation Kid Brother**

Operation Dumbo Drop (1995) C-107m. **½ D: Simon Wincer. Danny Glover, Ray Liotta, Denis Leary, Doug E. Doug, Corin Nemec, Dinh Thien Le, Tcheky Karyo, Hoang Ly, James Hong. In the midst of the Vietnam War, a new, by-the-book captain (Liotta) arrives in a strategic village to take the place of Glover, but finds himself on an

unlikely adventure to replace the hamlet's all-important elephant. Surprisingly flat until the climax, when things finally pick up. Also an odd choice of setting and subject for a Disney family film . . . which explains the lack of swearing and the toning-down of Leary's conniving character. Panavision. [PG]▼❶❶

Operation Kid Brother (1967-Italian) C-104m. *½ D: Alberto De Martino. Neil Connery, Daniela Bianchi, Adolfo Celi, Bernard Lee, Anthony Dawson, Lois Maxwell. Screen debut of Sean Connery's brother in James Bond spinoff is a disaster, in tale of master criminal (Celi)'s plan to blackmail Allied governments into controlling half of world's gold supply. Aka: OPERATION DOUBLE 007; video title: SECRET AGENT 00. Techniscope.▼

Operation M SEE: **Hell's Bloody Devils**

Operation Mad Ball (1957) 105m. ** D: Richard Quine. Jack Lemmon, Kathryn Grant (Crosby), Mickey Rooney, Ernie Kovacs, Arthur O'Connell, James Darren, Roger Smith. Weak service comedy about crafty soldiers planning wild party off base. Dull stretches, few gags. O'Connell comes off better than supposed comedians in film.❶

Operation Overthrow SEE: **Power Play**

Operation Pacific (1951) 111m. *** D: George Waggner. John Wayne, Patricia Neal, Ward Bond, Scott Forbes. Overzealous submariner Wayne is ultradedicated to his navy command; the WW2 action scenes are taut, and Neal makes a believable love interest.▼❶

Operation Petticoat (1959) C-124m. ***½ D: Blake Edwards. Cary Grant, Tony Curtis, Dina Merrill, Gene Evans, Arthur O'Connell, Richard Sargent, Virginia Gregg, Robert F. Simon, Gavin MacLeod, Madlyn Rhue, Marion Ross, Nicky Blair. Hilarious comedy about submarine captain Grant who's determined to make his injured ship seaworthy again, and con artist Curtis who wheels and deals to reach that goal. Some truly memorable gags; Grant and Curtis are a dynamite team in this happy film. Remade for TV in 1977.▼❶❶

Operation St. Peter's (1967-Italian) C-100m. ** D: Lucio Fulci. Edward G. Robinson, Lando Buzzanca, Jean-Claude Brialy. Average heist film with a twist: attempt to steal Michelangelo's Pietà from Vatican—it's tough to fence. Techniscope. [G]

Operation Thunderbolt (1977) C-125m. *** D: Menahem Golan. Yehoram Gaon, Klaus Kinski, Assaf Dayan, Shai K. Ophir, Sybil Danning. Stunning retelling of the famed raid by Israeli commandos on July 4, 1976, to rescue 104 hijacked passengers from a plane at Entebbe in Uganda. The stamp of official Israeli approval given this film and dedicated performances by a basically Israeli cast make this one outshine both star-laden American-made dramatizations, RAID ON ENTEBBE and VICTORY AT ENTEBBE. [PG]▼▶

Opium Connection, The SEE: **Poppy Is Also a Flower, The**

Opportunists, The (2000) C-89m. ** D: Myles Connell. Christopher Walken, Peter McDonald, Cyndi Lauper, Vera Farmiga, Donal Logue, Jose Zuniga, Tom Noonan, Anne Pitoniak, Kate Burton. Walken plays a perpetual screw-up who's persuaded to participate in a robbery that's a "sure thing" ... even though he served time for his last attempt. Low-key to the point of catatonia, this formulaic yarn gets its only juice from Walken; Lauper is good as his independent-minded girlfriend. [R]

Opportunity Knocks (1990) C-105m. **½ D: Donald Petrie. Dana Carvey, Robert Loggia, Todd Graff, Julia Campbell, Milo O'Shea, James Tolkan, Doris Belack, Sally Gracie, Del Close. Innocuous comedy about a con artist who assumes someone else's identity and falls into a plum job with a bathroom-fixture tycoon, who happens to have a cute daughter. First starring showcase for *Saturday Night Live* comic Carvey lets him do his dialect shticks, but never catches fire. [PG-13]▼▶)

Opposite of Sex, The (1998) C-105m. *** D: Don Roos. Christina Ricci, Martin Donovan, Lisa Kudrow, Lyle Lovett, Johnny Galecki, William Scott Lee, Ivan Sergei. Bold, clever black comedy about a truculent 16-year-old girl who runs away from home to stay with her gay half-brother, willfully disrupts his relationships, and sets his life into a spin. Writer-director Roos creates a gallery of unusual and interesting characters, but it's a tie who has the smartest, funniest lines—Ricci, as the smart-alecky heroine/narrator, or Kudrow, as the brother's sour confidante. Not for all tastes. [R]▼▶

Opposite Sex, The (1956) C-117m. *** D: David Miller. June Allyson, Joan Collins, Dolores Gray, Ann Sheridan, Ann Miller, Leslie Nielsen, Jeff Richards, Agnes Moorehead, Charlotte Greenwood, Joan Blondell, Sam Levene, Alice Pearce, Barbara Jo Allen (Vera Vague), Carolyn Jones, Alan Marshal, Dick Shawn, Jim Backus, Harry James, Art Mooney, Dean Jones. Well-heeled musical remake of Clare Boothe Luce's THE WOMEN has stellar cast, but still pales next to brittle original (Shearer, Crawford, Russell, etc.). Major difference: music and men appear in this expanded version. CinemaScope.▼▶

Opposite Sex (And How to Live With Them), The (1993) C-86m. BOMB D: Matthew Meshekoff. Arye Gross, Courteney Cox, Kevin Pollak, Julie Brown, Mitchell Ryan, Phil Bruns, Mitzi McCall, B. J. Ward, Jack Carter, Kimberlin Brown, Kimber Sissons, Andrea Evans. Painfully

strained comedy about courtship rituals between a Jewish jock male and a WASP female with hoity-toity friends. Complete with annoying first-person, eyes-into-the-camera chat-ups to us by all four leads. Sat on the shelf, unreleased, roughly dating back to the Polk Administration. [R]▼▶

Optimists, The (1973-British) C-110m. *** D: Anthony Simmons. Peter Sellers, Donna Mullane, John Chaffey, David Daker. Entertaining comedy-drama of London busker (street entertainer) Sellers and the two tough little kids he takes in hand. Songs by Lionel Bart include effective "Sometimes." Alternate version runs 94m. Aka THE OPTIMISTS OF NINE ELMS. [PG]▶

Orange County (2002) C-81m. ** D: Jake Kasdan. Colin Hanks, Jack Black, Catherine O'Hara, Schuyler Fisk, John Lithgow, Harold Ramis, Jane Adams, Garry Marshall, Dana Ivey, Chevy Chase, Lily Tomlin, George Murdock, Leslie Mann. Southern California teen forsakes his fun-in-the-sun life to become a writer, hoping to be accepted at Stanford University, but his wildly dysfunctional family (including a perpetually stoned brother) keeps getting in the way. Lumpy, goofball comedy suddenly turns serious and sincere toward the end—to no great effect. Written by Mike White, who also appears briefly. Kevin Kline and Ben Stiller are unbilled. [PG-13]▼▶

Orca (1977) C-92m. ** D: Michael Anderson. Richard Harris, Charlotte Rampling, Will Sampson, Peter Hooten, Bo Derek, Keenan Wynn, Robert Carradine. Killer whale avenges himself on bounty hunter Harris and crew for killing pregnant mate. For undiscriminating action fans whose idea of entertainment is watching Bo getting her leg bitten off. Panavision. [PG] ▼▶

Orchestra Conductor, The (1980-Polish) C-101m. ** D: Andrzej Wajda. John Gielgud, Krystyna Janda, Andrzej Seweryn, Jan Ciercierski. Uneven drama about aged Polish conductor Gielgud returning to his hometown. Excellent cast is defeated by a superficially philosophical script. Video title: THE CONDUCTOR.▼

Orchestra Rehearsal (1979-Italian) C-72m. **½ D: Federico Fellini. Baldwin Baas, Clara Colosimo, Elizabeth Lubi, Ronoldo Bonacchi, Ferdinando Villella. Heavy-handed allegory that examines an orchestra as microcosm of troubled world; occasional moments of wit and insight, but overall a disappointment. Made for Italian television. Music by Nino Rota. [R] ▼▶

Orchestra Wives (1942) 98m. **½ D: Archie Mayo. George Montgomery, Ann Rutherford, Glenn Miller and his Band, Lynn Bari, Carole Landis, Cesar Romero, Virginia Gilmore, Mary Beth Hughes, The Nicholas Brothers, Jackie Gleason, Henry (Harry)

Morgan. Hokey storyline (with hotshot trumpeter Montgomery impetuously marrying moony-eyed fan Rutherford) serves as a nice showcase for Miller's band, and features such hits as "Serenade in Blue," "At Last," and "I've Got a Gal in Kalamazoo," featuring Tex Beneke, The Modernaires, and a snazzy dance routine by The Nicholas Brothers. That's young Jackie Gleason as the band's bass player . . . and look fast for Dale Evans as Rutherford's soda-fountain pal. ▼●▮

Ordeal by Innocence (1984) C-87m. *½ D: Desmond Davis. Donald Sutherland, Faye Dunaway, Christopher Plummer, Sarah Miles, Ian McShane, Diana Quick, Annette Crosbie. Agatha Christie mystery has American Sutherland as amateur sleuth in 1950s English hamlet. Cast wasted, logic absent in utterly pointless film. Score by Dave Brubeck. Made in England. [PG-13] ▼●

Order, The (2003) C-102m. *½ D: Brian Helgeland. Heath Ledger, Shannyn Sossamon, Mark Addy, Benno Fürmann, Peter Weller, Francesco Carnelutti, Mattia Sbragia, Giulia Lombardi. Young priest Ledger is sent to Rome to probe the mysterious death of his mentor and discovers an ancient Catholic ritual involving "Sin Eaters," an order of immortal renegade priests who consume people's sins. Boring, bloody, and often risible EXORCIST wannabe; another directing misfire for Oscar-winning screenwriter Helgeland. Super 35. [R] ▼▮

Order of Death SEE: **Corrupt**

Order of Myths, The (2008) C-78m. *** D: Margaret Brown. Mobile, Alabama, hosts the oldest Mardi Gras in the U.S.—but to this day there are two parallel celebrations, one white and one black. Filmmaker Brown (who grew up there) explores the history of the city and reveals how age-old events still resonate there, even as eager participants gear up for the biggest event(s) of the year. A disarming and revealing slice of life that proves regionalism is alive and well in America. ▮

Ordet (1955-Danish) 125m. **** D: Carl Dreyer. Henrik Malberg, Emil Hass Christensen, Preben Lerdorff Rye. Two rural families, at odds with each other over religious differences, are forced to come to grips with their children's love for each other. Arguably Dreyer's greatest film, but certainly the movies' final word on the struggle between conventional Christianity and more personalized religious faith. Truly awe-inspiring, with a never-to-be-forgotten climactic scene. Based on a play by Kaj Munk, filmed before in 1943. ▼▮

Ordinary Decent Criminal (2000-U.S.-Irish-British) C-94m. *½ D: Thaddeus O'Sullivan. Kevin Spacey, Linda Fiorentino, Helen Baxendale, Stephen Dillane, Peter Mullan, David Hayman, Patrick Malahide, Gerard McSorley, Colin Farrell. Smug Irish criminal Spacey likes to steal and takes pleasure not only in outwitting the police but in humiliating them as well. The main character is so arrogant and unlikable that it isn't fun to watch him taunt authority. Fiorentino and Spacey fumble with their brogues in this otherwise forgettable film. Loosely based on the life of Martin Cahill, whose story was told in 1998's THE GENERAL. Super 35. [R] ▼▮

Ordinary People (1980) C-123m. **** D: Robert Redford. Donald Sutherland, Mary Tyler Moore, Judd Hirsch, Timothy Hutton, M. Emmet Walsh, Elizabeth McGovern, Dinah Manoff, James B. Sikking. Superb adaptation of Judith Guest's novel about a well-to-do family's deterioration after the death of the eldest son, told mostly from the point of view of his guilt-ridden younger brother. Intelligent, meticulously crafted film, an impressive directorial debut for Redford, who won an Academy Award, and young Hutton, who took the Best Supporting Actor prize. Other Oscars for screenwriter Alvin Sargent and for Best Picture of the Year. McGovern's film debut. [R] ▼●▮

Organization, The (1971) C-107m. *** D: Don Medford. Sidney Poitier, Barbara McNair, Sheree North, Gerald S. O'Loughlin, Raul Julia, Fred Beir, Allen Garfield, Ron O'Neal, Dan Travanty (Daniel J. Travanti), Max Gail. Poitier, in his third and final appearance as Virgil Tibbs (from IN THE HEAT OF THE NIGHT), tries to bust open a major dope-smuggling operation. Exciting chase sequences, realistic ending. [PG] ▼▮

Organizer, The (1963-Italian) 126m. *** D: Mario Monicelli. Marcello Mastroianni, Annie Girardot, Renato Salvatori, Bernard Blier. Serious look at labor union efforts in Italy, with Mastroianni giving low-keyed performance in title role. ▼

Orgazmo (1997) C-90m. **½ D: Trey Parker. Trey Parker, Dian Bachar, Robyn Lynne Raab, Michael Dean Jacobs, Ron Jeremy, Andrew W. Kemler, David Dunn, Matt Stone. Surprisingly slick—and undeniably funny—low-budget farce about a young Mormon on a mission who winds up being recruited to star in a porno movie being shot in L.A. Written by Parker, and featuring his pal Stone (together, the creators of *South Park*); raunchy and offensive, but also surprisingly conventional in its storytelling. Unrated 95m. version also available. [NC-17] ▼▮

Oriental Dream SEE: **Kismet** (1944)

Original Fabulous Adventures of Baron Munchausen, The SEE: **Fabulous Baron Munchausen, The**

Original Gangstas (1996) C-98m. ** D: Larry Cohen. Fred Williamson, Jim Brown, Pam Grier, Paul Winfield, Isabel Sanford, Oscar Brown, Jr., Paul Roundtree, Ron O'Neal, Christopher B. Duncan, Eddie Bo Smith, Jr., Dru Down, Robert Forster,

Charles Napier, Wings Hauser. Fast-paced but very violent action thriller marks a return to the blaxploitation films of the '70s, reuniting many of the genre's top stars. When a gang shoots the father of a former bad boy turned good guy, he enlists the services of his ex-buddies to rid the town of this new urban terror. Serviceable but hardly inspired; it's still fun to see these actors doing what comes naturally. [R]▼●▶

Original Kings of Comedy, The (2000) **C-117m.** **½ D: Spike Lee. Steve Harvey, D. L. Hughley, Cedric The Entertainer, Bernie Mac. Lee's straightforward filmization of a concert in Charlotte, N.C., by four leading black stand-up comics. Uncensored, funny riffs abound, mostly on the differences between blacks and whites, but the film could've benefited from some tightening. Harvey is hands down most hilarious, whether spoofing TITANIC or praising the virtues of old-school '70s soul music. [R]▼▶

Original Sin (2001-U.S.-French) **C-112m.** *½ D: Michael Cristofer. Angelina Jolie, Antonio Banderas, Thomas Jane, Pedro Armendariz, Gregory Itzin, Allison Mackie, Joan Pringle, Cordelia Richards, Jack Thompson, James Haven. Overdone, laughably bad adaptation of the Cornell Woolrich novel *Waltz Into Darkness* (previously filmed by François Truffaut as MISSISSIPPI MERMAID). Banderas plays a rich Cuban at the beginning of the 20th century who discovers his young bride isn't exactly what he thought. Of interest only for steamy sex scenes between Jolie and Banderas. Also available in unrated version. Super 35. [R]▼▶

Orlando (1992-British-Russian-French-Italian-Dutch) **C-93m.** *** D: Sally Potter. Tilda Swinton, Billy Zane, Lothaire Bluteau, John Wood, Charlotte Valandrey, Heathcote Williams, Quentin Crisp, Peter Eyre, Ned Sherrin, Jimmy Somerville. Well, it's certainly unique: the story of someone who lives four hundred years (Swinton, in a stunning performance)—first as a man, and later as a woman—evolving from a young nobleman in the era of Queen Elizabeth I (Quentin Crisp portrays the monarch!) to a highly sensitized contemporary woman of the 20th century. Set in, on, and around various continents, time frames, and locales, this adaptation of Virginia Woolf's 1928 book (scripted by the director) is highly recommended for fans of the offbeat. Swinton's young daughter, Jessica, portrays Orlando's daughter at the finale. [PG-13]▼●▶

Orphan (2009-U.S.-French-German) **C-123m.** **½ D: Jaume Collet-Serra. Vera Farmiga, Peter Sarsgaard, Isabelle Fuhrman, CCH Pounder, Jimmy Bennett, Margo Martindale. Formulaic "bad seed"-type horror movie still manages to offer up plenty of creepy Grand Guignol moments

and sports a genuine you-won't-see-it-coming twist that sets this apart from others in the overworn genre. Well-to-do couple adopts a Russian orphan, but then seem clueless as havoc slowly starts to break loose and the little darling isn't what they bargained for. Some of this goes way over the top, yet remains a guilty pleasure for genre fans. [R]▶

Orphanage, The (2007-Mexican-Spanish) **C-106m.** *** D: Juan Antonio Bayona. Belén Rueda, Fernando Cayo, Roger Príncep, Montserrat Carulla, Andrés Gertrúdix, Edgar Vivar, Geraldine Chaplin. A woman and her husband move into the seaside mansion where she spent part of her childhood when it was an orphanage. Their loving (adopted) son Simon has always had "imaginary" friends, but in this strange new environment "they" turn violent and abduct the boy. Gothic shocker builds suspense and terror in classical fashion, as this densely plotted story unfolds—with unusual parallels to James Barrie's *Peter Pan*. Bayona's directorial debut; coproduced by Guillermo del Toro. Panavision. [R]▶

Orphans (1987) **C-120m.** **½ D: Alan J. Pakula. Albert Finney, Matthew Modine, Kevin Anderson. Young punk brings a well-heeled drunk home one night, planning to fleece him, but soon learns that his "victim" is no dummy; in fact, he quickly takes over the lives of the hot-tempered mugger and his slow-witted younger brother. Lyle Kessler's script (from his own play) fails to adapt its stage conventions to the new medium . . . but the performances are so powerful, and the material so emotional, that it's still worthwhile. Besides, Finney can do no wrong. [R]▼●▶

Orpheus (1950-French) **95m.** *** D: Jean Cocteau. Jean Marais, Francois Perier, Maria Casarés, Marie Dea, Juliette Greco, Roger Blin. Compelling cinematic allegory set in modern times with poet Marais encountering Princess of Death, exploring their mutual fascination. Heavy-handed at times, but still quite special. Remade by Jacques Demy as PARKING. Original French running time: 112m. Original French title: ORPHÉE. ▼▶

Osama (2003-Afghani-Dutch-Irish-Japanese-Iranian) **C-82m.** ***½ D: Siddiq Barmak. Marina Golbahari, Arif Herati, Zubaida Sahar, Mohamad Nader Khadjeh, Hamida Refah, Khwaja Nader. When the repressive Taliban regime shuts down the small Afghan hospital at which a 12-year-old girl assists her widowed mother, any chance of eking out a living is cut off. Women are now forbidden to go outdoors unescorted by a male relative, so the child is disguised as a boy named Osama; then the real dangers begin. Harrowing drama achieves poignancy and power through its straightforward depiction of one person's destiny. Written, edited, and coproduced by the director. First film made in Afghanistan after the fall of the Taliban; in fact, the first film made since the Taliban rose to power and destroyed the Afghan film industry. [PG-13] ▼▶

Oscar, The (1966) **C-119m.** **½ D: Russell Rouse. Stephen Boyd, Elke Sommer, Eleanor Parker, Milton Berle, Joseph Cotten, Jill St. John, Ernest Borgnine, Edie Adams, Tony Bennett, Jean Hale. Shiny tinsel view of Hollywood and those competing for Academy Awards; Parker as love-hungry talent agent comes off best. Loosely based on Richard Sale novel, with many guest stars thrown in. Some of the dialogue is so bad it's laughable.▼

Oscar (1991) **C-109m.** **½ D: John Landis. Sylvester Stallone, Ornella Muti, Don Ameche, Peter Riegert, Tim Curry, Vincent Spano, Marisa Tomei, Eddie Bracken, Linda Gray, Chazz Palminteri, Kurtwood Smith, Yvonne De Carlo, Ken Howard, William Atherton, Martin Ferrero, Harry Shearer, Richard Romanus, Kirk Douglas. Stallone is surprisingly enjoyable in a comic change-of-pace, playing 1930s gangster Angelo "Snaps" Provolone, who's trying to go straight, despite the domestic and financial chaos that surrounds him. Farcical comedy, complete with mistaken identities and slamming doors, offers showcases for Palminteri as Snaps' henchman, Curry as a priggish speech teacher, Bracken as a stuttering stoolie, and Shearer and Ferrero as the Finuccis but never quite takes wing. Based on a French play, filmed before in 1967 with Louis de Funes. [PG] ▼●|

Oscar and Lucinda (1997-Australian) **C-132m.** **½ D: Gillian Armstrong. Ralph Fiennes, Cate Blanchett, Ciarán Hinds, Tom Wilkinson, Josephine Byrnes, Richard Roxburgh, Billie Brown. Odd romance of two Australian misfits in the mid 1800s: scarred and tormented clergyman's son Fiennes and independent Victorian heiress Blanchett, both of whom are gambling fanatics. The wager of their lives becomes surreal, as an iron-and-glass church is transported by sea and overland into the wilderness. Eccentricity upstages romance and passion in this adaptation of Peter Carey's novel. Reminiscent of Herzog's FITZCARRALDO. Panavision. [R] ▼●|

Osmosis Jones (2001) **C-95m.** ** D: Bobby Farrelly, Peter Farrelly; animation directors Piet Kroon, Tom Sito. Bill Murray, Elena Franklin, Molly Shannon, Chris Elliott; voices of Chris Rock, Laurence Fishburne, David Hyde Pierce, Ron Howard, Brandy Norwood, William Shatner, Kid Rock, Ben Stein. A slovenly zoo attendant who neglects his daughter takes even worse care of his body; inside his system, a maverick blood cell named Osmosis disobeys orders and tries to defeat an invading virus. Ingenious, well-designed animated film, full of clever ideas

about the workings of the human body, is all but undone by a live-action framing story about Bill Murray's character, who is simply disgusting. Clairmont-Scope. [PG] ▼▶

Ossessione (1942-Italian) **140m.** ***½ D: Luchino Visconti. Massimo Girotti, Clara Calamai, Juan deLanda, Elio Marcuzzo. Visconti's first feature triggered the great era of Italian neorealism, transplanting James Cain's *The Postman Always Rings Twice* quite successfully to Fascist Italy; however, as an unauthorized version of the book, it was not permitted to be shown in the U.S. until 1975. Heavy going at times, but fascinating nonetheless. Filmed earlier in France, twice later in the U.S. ▼▶

Osterman Weekend, The (1983) **C-102m.** **½ D: Sam Peckinpah. Rutger Hauer, John Hurt, Craig T. Nelson, Dennis Hopper, Chris Sarandon, Meg Foster, Helen Shaver, Cassie Yates, Burt Lancaster. Intriguing, sometimes confusing adaptation of Robert Ludlum thriller about a controversial talk-show host who's recruited by the CIA to expose some friends who are supposedly Soviet agents. Consistently interesting but aloof and cold, despite a top-notch cast. Peckinpah's final film. [R] ▼●|

Otello (1986-Italian) **C-120m.** ***½ D: Franco Zeffirelli. Placido Domingo, Katia Ricciarelli, Justino Diaz, Petra Malakova, Urbano Barberini. Beautifully filmed version of the Verdi opera, with Domingo in fine voice in the title role; he is more than ably assisted by Ricciarelli as wife Desdemona and Diaz as the evil, manipulative Iago. Nearly flawless in all respects; a must for opera buffs. [PG] ▼●|

Othello (1952-Italian) **92m.** ***½ D: Orson Welles. Orson Welles, Micheal MacLiammoir, Suzanne Cloutier, Robert Coote, Michael Lawrence, Fay Compton, Doris Dowling. Riveting, strikingly directed version of the Shakespeare play with Welles in the title role, lied to by Iago (MacLiammoir) into thinking that wife Desdemona (Cloutier) has been unfaithful. Shot, incredibly, between 1949 and 1952, because of budget difficulties; one of the most fascinating (and underrated) attempts at Shakespeare ever filmed. Joseph Cotten appears as a Senator, Joan Fontaine as a Page. Reconstructed (with its music score rerecorded) for 1992 reissue. Aka THE TRAGEDY OF OTHELLO: THE MOOR OF VENICE. ▼●|

Othello (1965-British) **C-166m.** **** D: Stuart Burge. Laurence Olivier, Frank Finlay, Maggie Smith, Joyce Redman, Derek Jacobi, Edward Hardwicke, Mike Gambon, John McEnery. Brilliant transferral to the screen of Shakespeare's immortal story of the Moor of Venice. Burge directed the filming, Olivier staged the production. Panavision. ▼▶

Othello (1995-U.S.-British) **C-125m.** ***

D: Oliver Parker. Laurence Fishburne, Kenneth Branagh, Irène Jacob, Nathaniel Parker, Michael Maloney, Anna Patrick, Nicholas Farrell, Indra Ove, Michael Sheen, Pierre Vaneck, Gabriele Ferzetti, Andre Oumansky, Philip Locke, John Savident. Though not as brilliantly cinematic as Welles' version, Parker's film may be more accessible to modern audiences, as the dialogue is delivered in a naturalistic fashion. Fishburne is very good in the title role, bringing out the warrior Moor's essential innocence and passion, but Branagh is brilliant as the witty, scheming Iago; Jacob, as Desdemona, is less satisfactory. Overall, an intelligent, respectable adaptation. [R] ▼●

Other, The (1972) **C-100m.** *** D: Robert Mulligan. Uta Hagen, Diana Muldaur, Chris Udvarnoky, Martin Udvarnoky, Norma Connolly, Victor French, Portia Nelson, John Ritter. Eerie tale of supernatural, with twin brothers representing good and evil. Stark, chilling mood tale adapted by Thomas Tryon from his novel. [PG] ▼▶

Other Boleyn Girl, The (2008-U.S.-British) **C-114m.** **½ D: Justin Chadwick. Natalie Portman, Scarlett Johansson, Eric Bana, Kristin Scott Thomas, Mark Rylance, David Morrissey, Jim Sturgess, Benedict Cumberbatch, Oliver Coleman, Ana Torrent, Eddie Redmayne, Juno Temple. Impoverished family's scheme to curry favor with England's King Henry VIII by foisting their daughter Anne (Portman) on him backfires when he shows more interest in her sister Mary (Johansson) . . . at least, at first. Absorbing historical drama is extremely well acted, with Bana an uncharacteristically subdued Henry VIII, but looks cheap at times and lacks a certain punch. Peter Morgan streamlined Philippa Gregory's best-selling novel, which also was filmed in 2003 for British TV. Andrew Garfield is listed in the final credit roll, but does not appear in the film. [PG-13]▶

Other Guys, The (2010) **C-107m.** **½ D: Adam McKay. Will Ferrell, Mark Wahlberg, Eva Mendes, Michael Keaton, Steve Coogan, Ray Stevenson, Samuel L. Jackson, Dwayne Johnson, Rob Riggle, Damon Wayans, Jr., Bobby Cannavale. When two freewheeling supercops (Jackson, Johnson) literally fall in the line of duty, far less stellar NYPD detectives—a desk-bound pencil pusher (Ferrell) and a trigger-happy hothead (Wahlberg)—take over a case involving a Wall Street Ponzi schemer (Coogan). Robustly played farce is a fairly entertaining parody and a textbook example of an over-the-top, buddy-cop action-comedy. Wahlberg and Ferrell are well mismatched, and Mendes gets some big laughs as the latter's improbably gorgeous wife. Famous faces turn up in cameo roles; Ice-T narrates, unbilled. Unrated version runs 116m. Super 35. [PG-13] ▶

Other Man, The (2008-U.S.-British) **C-88m.** **½ D: Richard Eyre. Liam Neeson, Antonio Banderas, Laura Linney, Romola Garai. Successful shoe designer (Linney) drops hints, to successful software developer husband (Neeson), that her eye might be wandering. Neeson later discovers that his wife may indeed be having an affair and sets out, with murder in his heart, on a journey to unearth the truth. Stars are in fine form, but the would-be film noir becomes a lukewarm soap opera. Adapted from a story by Bernhard Schlink. Panavision. [R] ▶

Other People's Money (1991) **C-101m.** **½ D: Norman Jewison. Danny DeVito, Gregory Peck, Penelope Ann Miller, Piper Laurie, Dean Jones, Tom Aldredge, R. D. Call. Ruthless Wall Street predator known as Larry the Liquidator sets his sights on acquiring—and destroying—the New England wire and cable company run in traditional and familial style by Peck . . . but he doesn't count on having to battle a lawyer as smart (or as appealing) as Miller, who just happens to be Peck's daughter. A great vehicle for DeVito, though lacking the bite (and the ethnicity) of Jerry Sterner's off-Broadway play. Slick and engaging, but never really satisfying. [R] ▼●

Others, The (2001-Spanish-U.S.) **C-101m.** *** D: Alejandro Amenábar. Nicole Kidman, Fionnula Flanagan, Christopher Eccleston, Elaine Cassidy, Eric Sykes, Alakina Mann, James Bentley, Renée Asherson. Engrossing ghost story set on the Channel Islands in 1945. A troubled woman whose husband has never returned from the war tries to maintain her creepy old house while protecting—or is it overprotecting?—her two young children. A new household staff may be part of the solution, or just another manifestation of the problem. In the tradition of THE HAUNTING (1963), this eerie film builds tension by showing virtually nothing, but firing our imagination. Written by the director. [PG-13] ▼

Other Side of Heaven, The (2001) **C-113m.** **½ D: Mitch Davis. Christopher Gorham, Anne Hathaway, Joe Folau, Miriama Smith, Nathaniel Lees. Old-fashioned, heartfelt saga based on the life of John Groberg, a dedicated young man who leaves his fiancée in the 1940s to bring religious teachings to the people of Tonga in the South Pacific. Corny and two-dimensional at times, but the film's sincerity ultimately wins out. Although the protagonist is a missionary for the Mormon church, the film does not proselytize. [PG] ▼

Other Side of Midnight, The (1977) **C-165m.** BOMB D: Charles Jarrott. Marie-France Pisier, John Beck, Susan Sarandon, Raf Vallone, Clu Gulager, Christian Marquand, Michael Lerner, Howard Hesseman. Trashy Sidney Sheldon novel gets the treatment it deserves in ponderous story, set from 1939–1947, about a woman who parlays her body into film stardom. Dull, as opposed to lively, drek. [R] ▼▶

Other Side of Paradise, The SEE: **Foxtrot**

Other Side of the Bed, The (2002-Spanish) **C-109m.** *** D: Emilio Martínez-Lázaro. Ernesto Alterio, Paz Vega, Guillermo Toledo, Natalia Verbeke, Alberto San Juan, María Esteve, Ramón Barea, Nathalie Poza. The gnarled sex lives of two couples unravel and then come together again in this colorful musical, a big hit in Spain. Everyone talks a lot and sings about sex, both straight and gay. Frolicsome, with dance numbers and (mild) sex scenes galore. It's fairly pointless but good-natured fun. Super 35. [R] ▼▶

Other Side of the Mountain, The (1975) **C-101m.** **½ D: Larry Peerce. Marilyn Hassett, Beau Bridges, Belinda J. Montgomery, Nan Martin, William Bryant, Dabney Coleman, Dori Brenner, Griffin Dunne. Pleasantly performed but undistinguished true-life tragedy about skier Jill Kinmont, once a shoo-in for the Olympics until a sporting accident left her paralyzed from the shoulders down. Followed by 1978 sequel. [PG] ▼▶

Other Side of the Mountain Part 2, The (1978) **C-100m.** **½ D: Larry Peerce. Marilyn Hassett, Timothy Bottoms, Nan Martin, Belinda J. Montgomery, Gretchen Corbett, William Bryant. Smooth continuation of story of crippled skier Jill Kinmont (Hassett), who finds true love with trucker Bottoms. Timothy's real-life father James plays his dad in this film. [PG] ▼▶

Other Sister, The (1999) **C-129m.** **½ D: Garry Marshall. Juliette Lewis, Diane Keaton, Tom Skerritt, Giovanni Ribisi, Poppy Montgomery, Sarah Paulson, Linda Thorson, Juliet Mills, Hector Elizondo. Sentimental but unfocused film about a mentally challenged girl and her first attempts to free herself from a smothering mother. Appealing performances by Lewis and Ribisi (as her boyfriend) help make up for the wandering nature of the screenplay, though it would be hard not to shed a tear by the end. Super 35. [PG-13] ▼▶○

Other Woman, The (2009) **C-102m.** **½ D: Don Roos. Natalie Portman, Scott Cohen, Charlie Tahan, Lauren Ambrose, Lisa Kudrow, Michael Cristofer, Debra Monk, Elizabeth Marvel, Anthony Rapp. A second wife struggles with Major Issues about her philandering father, the new husband's ex, and a puzzling 8-year-old stepson, in Portman's go as an unhappy Manhattanite. Director's adaptation of "Bad Mom" blogger Ayelet Waldman's 2006 novel *Love and Other Impossible Pursuits* explains how everyone got here . . . and a surprise near the end suggests where they're going. Persuasively acted and not bad, but bland. [R] ▶

Otley (1969-British) **C-90m.** ** D: Dick Clement. Tom Courtenay, Romy Schneider, Alan Badel, James Villiers, Leonard Rossiter, Fiona Lewis, Freddie Jones, Ronald Lacey. Static spy spoof about petty thief and beautiful secret agent is helped a bit by Courtenay and Schneider, but otherwise has little to recommend it. [M/PG] ▶

Our Brand Is Crisis (2005) **C-87m.** *** D: Rachel Boynton. Savvy documentary offers a revealing exploration of "foreign policy for profit," spotlighting the manner in which consulting firms market political candidates across the globe. The emphasis is on a U.S.-based firm (one of whose partners is James Carville) hired to help a less-than-forthcoming candidate win a presidential election in Brazil. While its message isn't new, the film is a worthy companion piece to such classics of the genre as THE WAR ROOM. ▶

Our Family Wedding (2010) **C-90m.** *½ D: Rick Famuyiwa. Forest Whitaker, America Ferrera, Carlos Mencia, Regina Hall, Lance Gross, Diana-Maria Riva, Lupe Ontiveros, Charlie Murphy, Shannyn Sossamon, Anna Maria Horsford, Tonita Castro. One Latino and one African-American father lead a family feud over the upcoming wedding of their kids, with all the expected hijinks. Overly hysterical and thuddingly unfunny farce throws in every stereotype in the book. Whitaker looks like he wandered onto the wrong set. You know it's bad when a goat gets all the laughs. Super 35. [PG-13] ▶

Our Hitler (1980-German) **C-420m.** ** D: Hans-Jurgen Syberberg. Heinz Schubert, Peter Kern, Hellmut Lange, Rainer von Artenfels, Martin Sperr. Frightfully pretentious, stage-influenced 7-hour rationalization of Hitler's rise to power would probably play better if shown in four parts, as it was on German TV. A stimulating intellectual exercise for some, a laxative for most; distributed in the U.S. by Francis Ford Coppola. ▶

Our Hospitality (1923) **74m.** **** D: Buster Keaton, Jack Blystone. Buster Keaton, Natalie Talmadge, Joe Keaton, Joe Roberts. Buster goes to the South to claim a family inheritance, and falls in love with the daughter of a longtime rival clan. Sublime silent comedy, one of Buster's best, with a genuinely hair-raising finale. Incidentally, Buster married his leading lady in real life. ▼▶○

Our Lady of the Assassins (2000-French-Spanish) **C-101m.** **½ D: Barbet Schroeder. Germán Jaramillo, Anderson Ballesteros, Juan David Restrepo, Manuel Busquets, Wilmar Agudelo, Juan Carlos Álvarez. A middle-aged writer returns to his birthplace of Medellín, Colombia, and begins an affair with a teenaged boy from the streets in the midst of the city's social and moral chaos. Fascinating subject matter, well filmed by

Schroeder (in high-definition video). Undeniably powerful at times, but the points about a culture of death are repeated so often that it all loses steam by the end. Screenplay by Fernando Vallejo, based on his novel. [R]▼◗

Our Man Flint (1966) C-107m. **½ D: Daniel Mann. James Coburn, Lee J. Cobb, Gila Golan, Edward Mulhare, Benson Fong, Gianna Serra. One of the countless James Bond spoofs, this saga of the man from Z.O.W.I.E. starts briskly, becomes forced after a while. Coburn makes a zesty hero, Golan an attractive decoration; look for James Brolin as a technician. Followed by a sequel (IN LIKE FLINT) and a TVM in 1976. CinemaScope. ▼◗◖

Our Man in Havana (1960-British) **107m.** **½ D: Carol Reed. Alec Guinness, Burl Ives, Maureen O'Hara, Ernie Kovacs, Noel Coward, Ralph Richardson, Jo Morrow. Weak satirical spy spoof, adapted by Graham Greene from his novel. Guinness is vacuum cleaner salesman who becomes British secret agent in Cuba. CinemaScope.◗

Our Mother's House (1967-British) C-105m. *** D: Jack Clayton. Dirk Bogarde, Margaret Brooks, Louis Sheldon-Williams, John Gugolka, Pamela Franklin, Mark Lester. Children's scheme to carry on normally when their mother dies works well until their worthless father shows up. Fine performances from all in offbeat film.

Our Time (1974) C-88m. **½ D: Peter Hyams. Pamela Sue Martin, Parker Stevenson, Betsy Slade, George O'Hanlon, Jr., Karen Balkin. Nice nostalgic tale of young love, set in a Massachusetts girls' school in 1955. Bad color photography mars otherwise effective comedic and dramatic elements. [PG]▼◗

Our Town (1940) **90m.** ***½ D: Sam Wood. William Holden, Martha Scott, Frank Craven, Fay Bainter, Beulah Bondi, Thomas Mitchell, Guy Kibbee, Stuart Erwin. Sensitive adaptation of Thornton Wilder's Pulitzer Prize–winning play about small New England town with human drama and conflict in every family. Splendid score by Aaron Copland and production design by William Cameron Menzies. Screenplay by Wilder, Harry Chandlee, and Frank Craven. Craven, Doro Merande, Arthur Allen, and Scott (in her film debut) re-create their Broadway roles.▼◗

Our Vines Have Tender Grapes (1945) **105m.** ***½ D: Roy Rowland. Edward G. Robinson, Margaret O'Brien, James Craig, Frances Gifford, Agnes Moorehead, Jackie "Butch" Jenkins, Morris Carnovsky. Sensitive portrayal of American life in Wisconsin town with uncharacteristic Robinson as O'Brien's kind, understanding Norwegian father. Screenplay by Dalton Trumbo from George Victor Martin's novel. ▼◗

Outback (1971-U.S.-Australian) **C-114m.**

*** D: Ted Kotcheff. Gary Bond, Donald Pleasence, Chips Rafferty, Sylvia Kay, Jack Thompson. Intriguing film about sensitive schoolteacher whose personality disintegrates after interaction with rough, primitive men in Australian outback. Alternate version runs 99m. Unlikely to be endorsed by Australian tourist commission. Original title: WAKE IN FRIGHT. [R]

Outbreak (1995) **C-127m.** **½ D: Wolfgang Petersen. Dustin Hoffman, Rene Russo, Morgan Freeman, Kevin Spacey, Cuba Gooding, Jr., Donald Sutherland, Patrick Dempsey, Zakes Mokae, Dale Dye, Jim Antonio, Lance Kerwin. Crusading military research medico Hoffman must stop a deadly virus that's somehow made its way from Africa to the U.S.—little dreaming that his Army superiors have an agenda of their own. Dynamite suspense thriller with a surprising sense of humor goes almost completely awry in the second half, turning Hoffman into a kind of superhero and everyone else into a caricature or stick figure. What a shame! J.T. Walsh appears unbilled. [R]▼◗◖

Outcast, The (1962-Japanese) **118m.** ***½ D: Kon Ichikawa. Raizo Ichikawa, Shiho Fujimura, Hiroyuki Nagato, Rentaro Mikuni. Schoolteacher Ichikawa hides his identity as member of an outcast class until a writer he greatly respects is murdered. Intense drama is well made, fascinating.

Outcast of the Islands (1951-British) **102m.** *** D: Carol Reed. Ralph Richardson, Trevor Howard, Robert Morley, Wendy Hiller, Kerima, George Coulouris, Wilfrid Hyde-White. Compelling adaptation of Joseph Conrad story set on Malayan island, where a desperate, misguided man turns to crime and soon becomes the object of massive manhunt. Screenplay by William Fairchild. Good job all around. Some prints run 94m.

Out Cold (1989) **C-89m.** ** D: Malcolm Mowbray. John Lithgow, Teri Garr, Randy Quaid, Bruce McGill, Lisa Blount, Alan Blumenfeld, Morgan Paull, Barbara Rhoades, Tom Byrd, Fran Ryan. Lithgow plays a meek butcher who wrongly believes he has killed his partner after discovering him frozen to death in the freezer. A wonderfully adept cast tries to pull off this black comedy, but the script knocks their efforts out cold. Aka STIFFS. [R]▼◗◖

Out Cold (2001) **C-89m.** *½ D: Brendan Malloy, Emmett Malloy. Jason London, Lee Majors, A.J. Cook, Willie Garson, Caroline Dhavernas, Derek Hamilton, Flex Alexander, Zach Galifianakis, Victoria Silvstedt. Clichés and all-around idiocy dominate this crude updating of a 1960s beach-party movie. A seedy Alaska ski resort is a haven for brainless snowboarding stoners, but a greedy land developer (Majors) wants to transform it into an upscale vacation spot. [PG-13]▼◗

Outfit, The (1973) **C-103m.** **½ D: John Flynn. Robert Duvall, Karen Black, Joe Don Baker, Robert Ryan, Timothy Carey, Richard Jaeckel, Sheree North, Marie Windsor, Jane Greer, Henry Jones, Joanna Cassidy, Elisha Cook, Jr., Anita O'Day. Engagingly trashy mob melodrama, with ex-con Duvall tackling the syndicate responsible for his brother's death. Solid supporting cast helps. Based on a novel by Donald E. Westlake (writing as Richard Stark). [PG] ▼❚

Out for Justice (1991) **C-91m.** ** D: John Flynn. Steven Seagal, William Forsythe, Jerry Orbach, Jo Champa, Shareen Mitchell, Sal Richards, Gina Gershon, Jay Acovone, Dominic Chianese, Julianna Margulies, John Leguizamo. As if he doesn't have enough trouble snapping wrists when he stops by his scum-infested deli, cop Seagal's main target is childhood buddy Forsythe—from the old Brooklyn neighborhood. Some may consider this one a Seagal stretch, but don't warm up the AFI Lifetime Achievement Award just yet. Super 35. [R] ▼●❙

Outland (1981) **C-109m.** **½ D: Peter Hyams. Sean Connery, Peter Boyle, Frances Sternhagen, James B. Sikking, Kika Markham, Clarke Peters, John Ratzenberger. HIGH NOON on Jupiter's volcanic moon Io, as 21st-century marshal Connery discovers that this outer-space mining planet is riddled with corruption—and he's the only one willing to do anything about it. Slickly made, but predictable and unpleasant in tone. Script by director Hyams. Panavision. [R] ▼●❙

Outlaw, The (1943) **116m.** *** D: Howard Hughes. Jane Russell, Jack Buetel, Walter Huston, Thomas Mitchell, Mimi Aguglia, Joe Sawyer. Notorious "sex Western" (and Russell's ballyhooed screen debut) is actually compelling—if offbeat—story of Billy the Kid, with principal honors going to Huston as Doc Holliday. Filmed in 1941 and directed mostly by Howard Hawks, though Hughes' interest in Russell's bosom is more than evident. Some prints run 95m. and 103m. ▼●❙

Outlaw Blues (1977) **C-100m.** *** D: Richard T. Heffron. Peter Fonda, Susan Saint James, John Crawford, James Callahan, Michael Lerner. Ex-convict Fonda is promoted into a country star by back-up singer Saint James, to the consternation of star Callahan, who had stolen Fonda's song. Saint James is good in her first major movie role; the picture is fun when it isn't too silly. [PG] ▼❙

Outlaw Gun SEE: **Minute to Pray, a Second to Die, A**

Outlaw Josey Wales, The (1976) **C-135m.** **½ D: Clint Eastwood. Clint Eastwood, Chief Dan George, Sondra Locke, Bill McKinney, John Vernon, Paula Trueman, Sam Bottoms, Richard Farnsworth. Long, violent Western begins near the end of the Civil War; Eastwood is a peaceful farmer who turns vigilante when Union soldiers murder his family. He in turn has a price on his head, propelling cat-and-mouse chase odyssey. Clint took over direction from Philip Kaufman, who also cowrote the screenplay. Followed by THE RETURN OF JOSEY WALES—without Eastwood. Panavision. [PG] ▼●❙

Outlaw of Gor (1989) **C-89m.** *½ D: John "Bud" Cardos. Urbano Barberini, Jack Palance, Rebecca Ferrati, Donna Denton, Nigel Chipps, Russel Savadier. Worthless sequel to GOR (which wasn't any good in the first place). Earthman hero is magically transported back to the barbaric planet Gor, where he's soon branded an assassin by evil priest Palance and wicked queen Denton. Lots of swords, no sorcery. Based on the John Norman novel. Filmed in 1987. [PG-13] ▼

Outlaws Is Coming, The (1965) **89m.** **½ D: Norman Maurer. The Three Stooges, Adam West, Nancy Kovack, Mort Mills, Don Lamond, Emil Sitka, Joe Bolton, Henry Gibson. The Stooges' last feature is one of their best, with some sharp satire and good Western atmosphere as the boys, their cowardly friend (West), and Annie Oakley (Kovack) combat an army of gunslingers and a genteel crook. Local TV kiddie-show hosts cast as outlaws, Gibson as a hip Indian. ▼❙

Out of Africa (1985) **C-161m.** ***½ D: Sydney Pollack. Meryl Streep, Robert Redford, Klaus Maria Brandauer, Michael Kitchen, Malick Bowens, Joseph Thiaka, Stephen Kinyanjui, Michael Gough, Suzanna Hamilton, Rachel Kempson, Graham Crowden. Exquisite, intelligent romantic drama based on life of Karen Blixen, who married for convenience, moved from Denmark to Nairobi, and fell in love with a British adventurer and idealist (before gaining latter-day fame as author Isak Dinesen). Pollack's film brilliantly captures time and place, with superb performances by Streep and Brandauer, sumptuous photography by David Watkin, and a rich score by John Barry. Film's only fault is overlength— and biggest challenge is asking us to accept Redford as an Englishman. Oscars include Best Picture, Director, Screenplay (Kurt Luedtke, who synthesized five books into one seamless script), Cinematography, and Music Score. [PG] ▼●❙

Out of Bounds (1986) **C-93m.** *½ D: Richard Tuggle. Anthony Michael Hall, Jenny Wright, Jeff Kober, Glynn Turman, Raymond J. Barry, Pepe Serna, Meat Loaf. Iowa farm kid comes to L.A. and within 24 hours is hunted by the police (for murders he didn't commit) and a scuzzy drug dealer (whose stash he mistakenly took from the airport). Outlandish teen thriller might be retitled OUT OF BRAINS. [R] ▼●

Out of It (1969) **95m.** **½ D: Paul Williams. Barry Gordon, Jon Voight, Lada Edmund, Jr., Gretchen Corbett, Peter Grad. Generally amusing film about high school intellectual (Gordon) bucking high school athlete (Voight). A throwback to the days when life was an *Archie* comic book. [M/PG]

Out of Season (1975-British) **C-90m.** ** D: Alan Bridges. Vanessa Redgrave, Cliff Robertson, Susan George, Edward Evans, Frank Jarvis. Mood-triangle affair: dark stranger returns to English seaside resort 20 years after affair with woman who now has grown daughter. Hints of incest and unresolved ending. Aka WINTER RATES. [R]▼

Out of Sight (1966) **C-87m.** *½ D: Lennie Weinrib. Jonathan Daly, Karen Jensen, Robert Pine, Carole Shelayne, Gary Lewis and The Playboys, The Turtles, Freddie and The Dreamers, Dobie Gray. A butler and a blonde band together to halt a spy organization's conspiracy against rock groups. Idiotic combination beach party–spy movie that fails in both departments. Techniscope.

Out of Sight (1998) **C-122m.** **½ D: Steven Soderbergh. George Clooney, Jennifer Lopez, Ving Rhames, Steve Zahn, Dennis Farina, Albert Brooks, Don Cheadle, Catherine Keener, Nancy Allen, Viola Davis, Isaiah Washington. Career criminal Clooney busts out of Florida prison and uses federal agent Lopez as a shield; though they go separate ways, they've obviously fallen in love and have a need to reconnect, despite their conflicting views of the law. Interesting Elmore Leonard crime caper (adapted by Scott Frank), with a heavy dose of humor, has an appealing cast but needs a shot of adrenaline. Michael Keaton and Samuel L. Jackson appear unbilled. [R] ▼●)

Out of the Blue (1980) **C-94m.** **½ D: Dennis Hopper. Linda Manz, Sharon Farrell, Dennis Hopper, Raymond Burr, Don Gordon. Manz, daughter of ex-biker Hopper and junkie Farrell, cannot cope with the problems of her elders, with tragic results. Taut, low-key drama; could be retitled "Child of Easy Rider." TV title: NO LOOKING BACK. [R]▼

Out of the Dark (1988) **C-89m.** **½ D: Michael Schroeder. Cameron Dye, Lynn Danielson, Tracey Walter, Silvana Gallardo, Karen Black, Bud Cort, Starr Andreeff, Geoffrey Lewis, Paul Bartel, Divine, Lainie Kazan, Tab Hunter. A clown-masked killer murders the employees of an L.A. telephone sex-talk service, one by one. Good cast and sense of humor relieve heavy-handed visual approach to the material. [R]▼●)

Out of the Darkness (1978) SEE: **Night Creature**

Out of the Fog (1941) **93m.** *** D: Anatole Litvak. Ida Lupino, John Garfield, Thomas Mitchell, Eddie Albert, George Tobias, Leo Gorcey, John Qualen, Aline MacMahon. Fine filmization of Irwin Shaw play *The Gentle People*, with racketeer Garfield terrorizing Brooklyn fishermen Qualen and Mitchell—and falling in love with the latter's daughter (Lupino). Scripted by Robert Rossen, Jerry Wald, and Richard Macauley.◗

Out of the Frying Pan SEE: **Young and Willing**

Out of the Past (1947) **97m.** ***½ D: Jacques Tourneur. Robert Mitchum, Jane Greer, Kirk Douglas, Rhonda Fleming, Richard Webb, Steve Brodie, Virginia Huston, Paul Valentine, Dickie Moore. Mitchum finds he can't escape former life when one-time employer (gangster Douglas) and lover (Greer) entangle him in web of murder and double-dealings. Classic example of 1940s film noir, with dialogue a particular standout. Script by Geoffrey Homes (Daniel Mainwaring), from his novel *Build My Gallows High*. Remade as AGAINST ALL ODDS. Also shown in computer-colored version.▼●)

Out of Time (2003) **C-105m.** ** D: Carl Franklin. Denzel Washington, Eva Mendes, Sanaa Lathan, Dean Cain, John Billingsley, Robert Baker, Alex Carter, Nora Dunn. Chief of police in a small Florida town has been playing around with a married vixen—and becomes a key suspect when foul play rears its head. Every move he makes to cover his tracks only puts him in greater jeopardy, especially when his ex-wife, detective Mendes, is assigned to the case. This film noir wannabe would have been told effortlessly in the 1940s and '50s but seems heavy-handed and overly contrived here. Lathan is a fine femme fatale but Washington is the last person you'd cast as a patsy. Super 35. [PG-13] ▼)

Out of Towners, The (1970) **C-97m.** *½ D: Arthur Hiller. Jack Lemmon, Sandy Dennis, Sandy Baron, Anne Meara, Ann Prentiss, Graham Jarvis, Ron Carey, Phil Bruns, Carlos Montalban, Billy Dee Williams, Paul Dooley, Dolph Sweet, Robert Walden, Richard Libertini. Excruciating Neil Simon script about stupidly stubborn Lemmon and wife Dennis having everything imaginable go wrong on trip to N.Y.C. More harrowing than funny, with curiously unsympathetic leading characters. Remade in 1999. [G] ▼●)

Out-of-Towners, The (1999) **C-92m.** **½ D: Sam Weisman. Goldie Hawn, Steve Martin, Mark McKinney, John Cleese, Gregory Jbara, Ernie Sabella, Josh Mostel, Joe Grifasi, John Pizzarelli. It's one calamity after another when a middle-aged Ohio couple travels to N.Y.C. so he can go on a job interview. Less abrasive and farcical than Neil Simon's 1970 original, this has its fair share of laughs, with Cleese well cast as a haughty hotel manager . . . but it's Martin's fine performance that really stands out. That's Hawn's real-life son (Oliver

Hudson) in the film's opening scenes. [PG-13] ▼●◗

Out on a Limb (1992) **C-93m. BOMB** D: Francis Veber. Matthew Broderick, Jeffrey Jones, Heidi Kling, John C. Reilly, Marian Mercer, Larry Hankin. Obnoxious comedy with Broderick cast as a yuppie who comes to the aid of his kid sister in a small town inhabited by one too many screwballs. As illogical as it is crude, and desperately unfunny. [PG] ▼●

Outrage (1950) **75m. **½** D: Ida Lupino. Mala Powers, Tod Andrews, Robert Clarke, Raymond Bond, Lillian Hamilton, Hal March, Jerry Paris. Innocent young Powers is sexually molested, and then further victimized by her gossipy, narrow-minded neighbors. The scenario's sugary optimism—specifically relating to a sympathetic preacher—is much too pat, but Lupino (who also coscripted) deserves an A for effort in tackling a then-touchy theme.

Outrage, The (1964) **97m. **½** D: Martin Ritt. Paul Newman, Edward G. Robinson, Claire Bloom, Laurence Harvey, William Shatner, Albert Salmi. Western remake of RASHOMON is pretentious fizzle, with Newman hamming it as Mexican bandit who allegedly rapes Bloom while husband Harvey stands by. Robinson as philosophical narrator is best thing about film. Also shown in computer-colored version. Panavision. ▼◗

Outrage (1993-Italian-Spanish) **C-108m. *½** D: Carlos Saura. Francesca Neri, Antonio Banderas, Lali Ramon, Walter Vidarte, Coque Malla, Achero Manas, Rodrigo Valverde. When reporter Banderas falls for circus performer Neri, they have a brief fling at happiness. Unfortunately, a (predictable) rape scene, which is horrifyingly graphic, and a subsequent shooting spree relegate this to the ranks of only diehard Banderas fans. Panavision. [R] ▼●◗

Outrageous! (1977-Canadian) **C-100m. *** D: Richard Benner. Craig Russell, Hollis McLaren, Richert Easley, Allan Moyle, Helen Shaver. Excellent comedy-drama about a very odd couple: gay hairdresser and a pregnant mental patient. McLaren's effective emoting is outshone by female impersonator Russell's flamboyant playing and imitations of Garland, Davis, Bankhead, etc. Followed ten years later by TOO OUTRAGEOUS! [R] ▼◗

Outrageous Fortune (1987) **C-100m. *** D: Arthur Hiller. Bette Midler, Shelley Long, Peter Coyote, Robert Prosky, John Schuck, George Carlin, Anthony Heald, Ji-Tu Cumbuka, Chris McDonald, Robert Pastorelli. Raucously funny tale of a female odd couple who learn they were both having a fling with the same man, after he apparently dies in a mysterious explosion . . . then things *really* get going! Bright script by Leslie Dixon is a perfect showcase for Midler and Long. [R] ▼●◗

Outside Chance of Maximilian Glick, The (1988-Canadian) **C-96m. *** D: Allan A. Goldstein. Saul Rubinek, Jan Rubes, Noam Zylberman, Susan Douglas Rubes, Fairuza Balk, Nigel Bennet. Pleasing tale of bright 12-year-old Zylberman, growing up in a small Canadian town in the early 1960s, who's caught between his own dreams and desires and his family's traditional Jewish values. Despite its cop-out ending, this intelligent little comedy-drama is perfect fare for preteens. [G] ▼

Outside Man, The (1973) **C-104m. *** D: Jacques Deray. Jean-Louis Trintignant, Ann-Margret, Angie Dickinson, Roy Scheider, Michel Constantin, Georgia Engel, Ted de Corsia, John Hillerman, Alex Rocco, Talia Shire. Okay French-American actioner, made in L.A., as interesting for its cast as its offbeat quality. Hired killer Trintignant kills gang boss Ted de Corsia, then must elude Scheider, who's out to eliminate him. Ann-Margret's plunging neckline and a shootout around de Corsia's bier (he's embalmed in a sitting position) are worth looking at, also Engel's dumb housewife. [PG] ▼

Outside Ozona (1998) **C-100m. ** D: J.S. Cardone. Robert Forster, Sherilyn Fenn, Kevin Pollak, Penelope Ann Miller, David Paymer, Meat Loaf, Swoosie Kurtz, Taj Mahal, Lois Red Elk. Various characters' lives intersect during an eventful day and evening as a long-dormant serial killer begins to strike again, a radio d.j. vents his frustrations on the air, and several others take to the road. Only fitfully interesting, despite a good cast. [R] ▼

Outside Providence (1999) **C-103m. **½** D: Michael Corrente. Shawn Hatosy, Jon Abrahams, Alec Baldwin, George Wendt, Tommy Bone, Jonathan Brandis, Jack Ferver, Adam Lavorgna, Jesse Leach, Gabriel Mann, Kristen Shorten, Amy Smart, Richard Jenkins. Unremarkable coming-of-age saga set in 1970s New England, with Hatosy as a rowdy blue-collar teen who winds up going away to prep school and falling in love. Notable mainly for casting of Baldwin as an Archie Bunker type, at which he's only marginally convincing. Screenplay by Corrente and Bobby and Peter Farrelly (based on the latter's novel). [R] ▼◗

Outsider, The (1961) **108m. *** D: Delbert Mann. Tony Curtis, James Franciscus, Bruce Bennett, Gregory Walcott, Vivian Nathan. Thoughtful biopic with Curtis giving one of his best performances as a reluctant American hero: Ira Hamilton Hayes, the Pima Indian who was one of the marines to raise the U.S. flag at Iwo Jima. Hayes' plight is also recounted in FLAGS OF OUR FATHERS.

Outsider, The (1979) **C-128m. *** D: Tony Luraschi. Craig Wasson, Patricia Quinn, Sterling Hayden, Niall Toibin, Elizabeth Begley, T. P. McKenna, Frank Grimes. A young American raised on his grandfather's stories of fighting "the Tans" in Ireland goes there to join the IRA—and is used for political and public-relations purposes. No-frills narrative, authentic and interesting, filmed on location. Script by director Luraschi. [R]

Outsiders, The (1983) **C-91m.** **½ D: Francis Coppola. C. Thomas Howell, Matt Dillon, Ralph Macchio, Patrick Swayze, Rob Lowe, Diane Lane, Emilio Estevez, Tom Cruise, Leif Garrett, Tom Waits, Sofia Coppola. Florid, highly stylized treatment of S. E. Hinton's best-selling book about troubled teenagers in '60s Oklahoma, as seen through the eyes of a boy (Howell) who likes poetry and *Gone With the Wind*. Ambitious film evokes GWTW and '50s melodramas (right down to overstated music score by Carmine Coppola), but never quite connects, despite some powerful moments. Hinton makes a cameo appearance as a nurse. Revised by Coppola in 2005 as THE OUTSIDERS: THE COMPLETE NOVEL (114m., PG-13), with a new opening and wrapup, plus Elvis-leaning pop replacing the score. This version is definitely improved but still stumbles midway through. Followed by another Coppola-Hinton project, RUMBLE FISH. Later a TV series. Panavision. [PG] ▼●◗

Outside the Law (2010-Algerian-French-Belgian-Italian) **C/B&W-139m.** *** D: Rachid Bouchareb. Jamel Debbouze, Roschdy Zem, Sami Bouajila, Chafia Boudraa, Bernard Blancan, Sabrina Seyvecou, Assaad Bouab. Following WW2, Algerians—many of whom fought for France—demand their independence, but the French respond with bullets in the streets of Sétif. This inspires some of them to adopt radical, even terrorist, methods to achieve their goal over the next twenty years. Director and cowriter Bouchareb personalizes the story by focusing on three brothers, each quite different in outlook. Potent follow-up to the filmmaker's WW2 saga INDIGÈNES/DAYS OF GLORY was labeled propaganda by some, but there's no denying its dramatic power. ◗

Out to Sea (1997) **C-106m.** ** D: Martha Coolidge. Jack Lemmon, Walter Matthau, Dyan Cannon, Brent Spiner, Gloria De Haven, Elaine Stritch, Hal Linden, Donald O'Connor, Edward Mulhare, Rue McClanahan, Alexandra Powers, Sean O'Brien, Estelle Harris. A chronic con man fools his pal into joining him for a Caribbean cruise—neglecting to inform him that he's signed them both on as dance hosts. The two likable stars are cast adrift with a boatload of talented costars—and a stupid script that should have been deep-sixed before they ever set sail. O'Connor's final film. [PG-13] ▼●◗

Overboard (1987) **C-112m.** *** D: Garry Marshall. Goldie Hawn, Kurt Russell, Edward Herrmann, Katherine Helmond, Michael Hagerty, Roddy McDowall. Cute comedy about a spoiled heiress who falls off her yacht, suffers amnesia, and is "claimed" at the hospital by her supposed husband, a rough-hewn carpenter with a pack of unruly kids. Lightweight and good-natured, with appealing performances by the star duo. McDowall also served as executive producer; director Marshall has a cameo as a drummer, and Hector Elizondo does an unbilled bit as skipper of a garbage scow. [PG] ▼●◗

Over Her Dead Body (1990) SEE: **Enid Is Sleeping**

Over Her Dead Body (2008) **C-95m.** *½ D: Jeff Lowell. Eva Longoria Parker, Paul Rudd, Lake Bell, Jason Biggs, Lindsay Sloane, Stephen Root. Killed in a freak accident on her wedding day (by a decorative ice sculpture), a would-be bride returns as a ghostly presence one year later to prevent her fiancé from finding happiness with another woman. Longoria Parker must have been more desperate than the "Housewife" she plays on TV to think this would make a good starring vehicle. Derivative and forgettable; BLITHE SPIRIT it ain't. Panavision. [PG-13] ◗

Overnight Delivery (1998) **C-87m.** **½ D: Jason Bloom. Paul Rudd, Christine Taylor, Reese Witherspoon, Sarah Silverman, Buffy Sedlachek, Richard Cody, Gary Wolf, Larry Drake. As Valentine's Day approaches, Rudd thinks he's caught girlfriend Taylor cheating on him. Witherspoon urges him to send a disgusting breakup letter, but when he learns his girlfriend was faithful after all, he has to find some way to keep the letter from winding up in her hands. Predictable but cute comedy; Witherspoon is adorable. Made in 1996; released direct to video. Super 35. [PG-13] ▼●◗

Over the Brooklyn Bridge (1984) **C-106m.** ** D: Menahem Golan. Elliott Gould, Margaux Hemingway, Sid Caesar, Burt Young, Shelley Winters, Carol Kane. Brooklyn Jewish restaurant owner Gould wants to borrow money from uncle Caesar to open a fancy Manhattan eatery, but the family objects to his Catholic girlfriend (Hemingway). Some good supporting players (especially Caesar) cannot save this stupid comedy. That's Sarah Michelle Gellar playing Young's daughter. Aka MY DARLING SHIKSA. [R] ▼

Over the Edge (1979) **C-95m.** ***½ D: Jonathan Kaplan. Michael Kramer, Pamela Ludwig, Matt Dillon, Vincent Spano, Tom Fergus, Andy Romano, Ellen Geer, Lane Smith, Harry Northup. Powerful, disturbing chronicle of alienated youth in a suburban planned community; 14-year-old rebels without causes who play with guns, deal and abuse drugs, taunt cops, chug whiskey till they're blotto. Perceptive script by Charlie Haas and Tim Hunter; stunning music score by Sol Kaplan; taut direction. A winner. Dillon's film debut. [PG]▼▶

Over the Hedge (2006) **C-84m.** ******* D: Tim Johnson, Karey Kirkpatrick. Voices of Bruce Willis, Garry Shandling, Steve Carell, Wanda Sykes, William Shatner, Nick Nolte, Thomas Haden Church, Allison Janney, Eugene Levy, Catherine O'Hara, Avril Lavigne, Omid Djalili. Funny CG-animated feature about a crafty, selfish raccoon who dupes a group of hibernating forest animals into helping him replace a winter's stash of food he stole from a mean ol' bear. Simple storyline is fleshed out with funny gags, action set pieces, and character moments. Our favorite critter: Verne the turtle leader, voiced by Shandling. Based on the comic strip by Michael Fry and T. Lewis. [PG]▶

Over the Top (1987) **C-93m.** BOMB D: Menahem Golan. Sylvester Stallone, Robert Loggia, Susan Blakely, Rick Zumwalt, David Mendenhall, Chris McCarty, Terry Funk. Mawkish, heavy-handed variation on THE CHAMP, with Stallone competing with his fat-cat father-in-law for the custody (and affection) of his son. It all climaxes at an arm-wrestling championship in Las Vegas. Stallone tries to underplay (speaking so quietly that you often can't hear what he's saying), but when push comes to shove, he *will* drive his truck through a living room! Panavision. [PG] ▼▶

Owl and the Pussycat, The (1970) **C-95m.** ******* D: Herbert Ross. Barbra Streisand, George Segal, Robert Klein, Allen Garfield, Roz Kelly. Hit Broadway comedy about semi-illiterate prostitute and stuffy intellectual sometimes substitutes bombast for wit, but the laughs are there. The Streisand-Segal pairing really works; adapted by Buck Henry from Bill Manoff's play. Originally released at 98m. Panavision. [PG]▼▶

Owning Mahowny (2003-Canadian-British) **C-105m.** *******½ D: Richard Kwietniowski. Philip Seymour Hoffman, Minnie Driver, Maury Chaykin, John Hurt, Sonja Smits, Ian Tracey, Roger Dunn. Nerdy assistant bank manager in Toronto manipulates bank funds to feed his gambling addiction. His patient girlfriend tries to give him space, while an Atlantic City casino manager tries to "read" this enigmatic new high-roller. Fascinating look at both the banking and gaming industries, based on a true story from the early 1980s. Every character, no matter how small, is interestingly written and colorfully played. A great showcase for the gifted Hoffman. Maurice Chauvet adapted Gary Ross' best-selling book *Stung.* Super 35. [R]▼▶

Ox, The (1991-Swedish) **C-91m.** ******* D: Sven Nykvist. Stellan Skarsgard, Ewa Froling, Lennart Hjulstrom, Max von Sydow, Liv Ullmann, Erland Josephson. Acclaimed cinematographer Nykvist directed and co-scripted this stark, compelling chronicle of a desperately poor family's struggle for survival in famine-ravaged Sweden during the mid-1800s. Based on a true story; the plight of their countrymen who chose to leave Sweden and settle in the U.S. is depicted in Jan Troell's THE EMIGRANTS and THE NEW LAND (which also starred von Sydow and Ullmann).▼

Ox-Bow Incident, The (1943) **75m.** ******** D: William A. Wellman. Henry Fonda, Dana Andrews, Mary Beth Hughes, Anthony Quinn, William Eythe, Henry (Harry) Morgan, Jane Darwell, Frank Conroy, Harry Davenport. The irony and terror of mob rule are vividly depicted in this unforgettable drama about a lynch mob taking the law into its own hands, despite protests of some level-headed onlookers. Based on Walter Van Tilburg Clark's book; superb script by Lamar Trotti.▼▶

Oxford Blues (1984) **C-97m.** ******½ D: Robert Boris. Rob Lowe, Ally Sheedy, Julian Sands, Amanda Pays, Michael Gough, Aubrey Morris, Gail Strickland, Alan Howard, Cary Elwes. Lightweight remake of A YANK AT OXFORD, with rough-edged Lowe pursuing titled beauty Pays while building "character" on the rowing team. Boris' wildly inconsistent script is salvaged by engaging performances. [PG-13] ▼▶

Pacific Heights (1990) **C-102m.** ******½ D: John Schlesinger. Melanie Griffith, Matthew Modine, Michael Keaton, Mako, Nobu McCarthy, Laurie Metcalf, Carl Lumbly, Dorian Harewood, Luca Bercovici, Sheila McCarthy, Dan Hedaya, Miriam Margolyes, Nicholas Pryor. Young couple purchases a Victorian home in San Francisco, fixes it up and rents out two of its apartments, unaware that one of their tenants is a nut case. Likable and reasonably credible, but too often obvious—and never really bothers to explain Keaton's bizarre, destructive behavior. Cleverest touch: making Modine the weaker and Griffith the stronger of the twosome. Beverly D'Angelo appears unbilled in key supporting role . . . and Melanie's mom, Tippi Hedren, plays a Beverly Hills matron. [R]▼▶

Pacifier, The (2005) **C-91m.** ****** D: Adam Shankman. Vin Diesel, Lauren Graham, Faith Ford, Brittany Snow, Max Thieriot, Chris Potter, Carol Kane, Brad Garrett, Morgan York, Tate Donovan, Scott Thompson. Rugged Navy SEAL Diesel is handed his toughest assignment yet: babysitting five rowdy kids while their mother tries to unravel a mystery left behind by her late husband, a scientist working for the government. Some sweet moments are smothered by heavy-handed slapstick in this strained family comedy, this generation's answer to KINDERGAR-TEN COP. Panavision. [PG]▼▶

Pack, The (1977) C-99m. **½ D: Robert Clouse. Joe Don Baker, Hope Alexander-Willis, Richard B. Shull, R. G. Armstrong, Ned Wertimer, Bibi Besch. Predictable but well-made story of resort islanders terrorized by abandoned dogs who have become a bloodthirsty pack. Aka THE LONG, DARK NIGHT. [R]▼

Package, The (1989) C-108m. ** D: Andrew Davis. Gene Hackman, Joanna Cassidy, Tommy Lee Jones, John Heard, Dennis Franz, Pam Grier, Kevin Crowley, Reni Santoni, Ike Pappas, Thalmus Rasulala. Slack political paranoia thriller with Hackman as a career Army sergeant who learns he's been used as a pawn in a conspiracy plot engineered by Russian and American military dissidents. Hackman is always worth watching, but the story loses ground (and credibility) just when it ought to be peaking. [R]▼▶

Pad and How to Use It, The (1966) C-86m. **½ D: Brian Hutton. Brian Bedford, Julie Sommars, James Farentino, Edy Williams. Peter Shaffer play *The Private Ear* is basis for sex romp involving Bedford's attempt to become Sommars' lover.

Paddy (1970-Irish) C-97m. ** D: Daniel Haller. Milo O'Shea, Des Cave, Dearbhla Molloy, Judy Cornwell, Donal LeBlanc. Irish lover Cave tries to juggle varied sexual encounters with uninspired home life in ordinary comedy-drama. [PG]▼

Padre Padrone (1977-Italian) C-114m. ** D: Vittorio and Paolo Taviani. Omero Antonutti, Saverio Marconi, Marcella Michelangeli, Fabrizio Forte. Sad, illiterate Sardinian boy, brutalized by his peasant father, still grows up to master Greek and Latin and graduate college. Even sadder still, uninvolving and curiously forgettable. Based on an autobiographical book by Gavino Ledda.▼▶

Pagemaster, The (1994) C-75m. ** D: Maurice Hunt (animation), Joe Johnston (live action). Macaulay Culkin, Christopher Lloyd, Ed Begley, Jr., Mel Harris; voices of Patrick Stewart, Whoopi Goldberg, Frank Welker, Leonard Nimoy. Phobically nervous young boy seeks shelter from a storm in the local library, and is transported to an animated world by living books who represent Adventure, Fantasy, and Horror. Uninspired, often boring cartoon feature (with live-action framework) resembles a TV special more than a movie. Heavy-handed message about the wonder of books might better be told by a book itself. [G]▼▶

Page Turner, The (2006-French) C-85m. **½ D: Denis Dercourt. Catherine Frot, Déborah François, Pascal Greggory, Xavier de Guillebon, Christine Citti, Clotilde Mollet, Jacques Bonnaffé. A 10-year-old girl who's devoted herself to becoming a piano prodigy auditions for a prestigious music conservatory, but is distracted by the president of the jury. Ten years later she insinuates herself into the same woman's home, earns the family's trust, and prepares to exact revenge. Absorbing and well acted but loses its grip as it heads toward its inevitable denouement.▶

Paid in Full (2002) C-97m. ** D: Charles Stone III. Wood Harris, Mekhi Phifer, Kevin Carroll, Esai Morales, Chi McBride, Cam'ron, Elise Neal, Regina Hall. Dry-cleaning delivery boy becomes the king of crack dealing in '80s Harlem. Cautionary tale has style and a propulsive old-school soundtrack but suffers from too-familiar scripting (although based on a true story). Rappers Busy Bee and Doug E. Fresh appear as themselves. Movie takes its title from a rap by Eric B. and Rakim. [R]▼▶

Pain in the A——, A (1974-French-Italian) C-90m. *** D: Edouard Molinaro. Lino Ventura, Jacques Brel, Caroline Cellier, Nino Castelnuovo, Jean-Pierre Darras. Very funny black comedy about the chance meeting of a hit man trying to make good on a contract and a pathetic would-be suicide who's likely to mess up the job. Wonderful performances by Ventura and Brel in adaptation of Francis Veber's stage hit, later Americanized as BUDDY BUDDY. [PG]▼

Painted Veil, The (1934) 83m. **½ D: Richard Boleslawski. Greta Garbo, Herbert Marshall, George Brent, Warner Oland, Jean Hersholt, Cecilia Parker, Keye Luke. Set in mysterious Orient, film tells Somerset Maugham's story of unfaithful wife mending her ways. Mundane script uplifted by Garbo's personality, supported by Marshall as her husband, Brent as her lover. Remade in 1957 (as THE SEVENTH SIN) and in 2006. ▼▶

Painted Veil, The (2006-U.S.-Chinese) C-125m. ***½ D: John Curran. Naomi Watts, Edward Norton, Liev Schreiber, Toby Jones, Diana Rigg, Anthony Wong, Sally Hawkins. In 1920s London, a socially backward bacteriologist impulsively asks an attractive woman to marry him, and she agrees. When he learns that she's been having an affair, he forces her to accompany him to a remote outpost in China where there's been an outbreak of cholera. Although intended as punishment, this experience gradually changes and deepens their relationship. Beautifully filmed (by Stuart Dryburgh) on location in China, this finely tuned drama becomes a deeply moving love story. Watts has never been better; she and Norton coproduced. Excellent score by Alexandre Desplat. Ron Nyswaner adapted the W. Somerset Maugham novel; filmed before in 1934 and 1957 (as THE SEVENTH SIN). Panavision. [PG-13]▶

Paint It Black (1989) C-101m. ** D:

Tim Hunter. Rick Rossovich, Sally Kirkland, Martin Landau, Julie Carmen, Doug Savant, Peter Frechette, Jason Bernard. Meandering, disappointing thriller with Rossovich a sculptor who's ripped off by his lover, art dealer Kirkland, then victimized by weirdo Savant. Never released theatrically. [R]▼●●

Paint Your Wagon (1969) **C-166m.** *** D: Joshua Logan. Lee Marvin, Clint Eastwood, Jean Seberg, Harve Presnell, Ray Walston, Tom Ligon, Alan Dexter. Splashy, expensive musical from Lerner-Loewe play about gold-rush days in No-Name City, California, where prospectors Marvin and Eastwood share one wife (Seberg) whom they bought at auction. Pure entertainment; witty, often risqué script (by Paddy Chayefsky!). Presnell outshines cast of nonsingers with "They Call the Wind Maria." Marvin, however, vocalizes his rendition of "Wand'rin' Star." Beware of shorter prints. Panavision. [M]▼●●

Paisan (1946-Italian) **90m.** ***½ D: Roberto Rossellini. Carmela Sazio, Gar Moore, Bill Tubbs, Harriet White, Maria Michi, Robert van Loon, Dale Edmonds, Carla Pisacane, Dots Johnson. Early Rossellini classic, largely improvised by a mostly nonprofessional cast. Six vignettes depict life in Italy during WW2; best has American nurse White searching for her lover in battle-torn Florence. Written by Rossellini and Federico Fellini; Giulietta Masina has a bit part. Italian running time 115m. The second in Rossellini's war trilogy, following OPEN CITY and followed by GERMANY YEAR ZERO. ▼❚

Pajama Game, The (1957) **C-101m.** ***½ D: George Abbott, Stanley Donen. Doris Day, John Raitt, Carol Haney, Eddie Foy, Jr., Barbara Nichols, Reta Shaw. Adaptation of the Broadway musical hit—with much of its original cast intact—virtually defines the word "exuberance." Day is a joy as the head of a factory grievance committee who unexpectedly falls in love with the new foreman (Raitt, in his only starring film). Richard Adler and Jerry Ross' songs include "Hey, There." Dancer Haney stands out in her "Steam Heat" feature and in the energetic "Once a Year Day" picnic number. Choreography by Bob Fosse. ▼●●

Pajama Party (1964) **C-85m.** ** D: Don Weis. Tommy Kirk, Annette Funicello, Dorothy Lamour, Elsa Lanchester, Harvey Lembeck, Jody McCrea, Buster Keaton, Susan Hart, Donna Loren. Fourth BEACH PARTY movie moves indoors, changes director and star (although Frankie Avalon and Don Rickles do have cameos). Kirk plays Martian teenager who drops in and is understandably perplexed. Just fair, though it's always nice to see Keaton at work. Teri Garr is one of the dancers buried in the sand.

Went back outside for BEACH BLANKET BINGO. Panavision. ▼❚

Paleface, The (1948) **C-91m.** *** D: Norman Z. McLeod. Bob Hope, Jane Russell, Robert Armstrong, Iris Adrian, Robert (Bobby) Watson. Enjoyable comedy-Western, a spoof of THE VIRGINIAN, has timid Bob backed up by sharpshooting Russell in gunfighting encounters; Oscar-winning song "Buttons and Bows." Remade as THE SHAKIEST GUN IN THE WEST. Sequel: SON OF PALEFACE. ▼●●

Pale Rider (1985) **C-113m.** ** D: Clint Eastwood. Clint Eastwood, Michael Moriarty, Carrie Snodgress, Christopher Penn, Richard Dysart, Sydney Penny, Richard Kiel, Doug McGrath, John Russell. Eastwood Western starts out just fine, the saga of a Good Stranger coming to the aid of some struggling miners, but winds up draggy, pretentious, and dull—with so much cloning of SHANE as to be preposterous. Well crafted, but attempts to be mythical come off as heavy-handed and ridiculous. Panavision. [R]▼●●

Palindromes (2005) **C-100m.** ** D: Todd Solondz. Ellen Barkin, Stephen Adly-Guirgis, Jennifer Jason Leigh, Emani Sledge, Valerie Shusterov, Hannah Freiman, Rachel Corr, Will Denton, Sharon Wilkins, Shayna Levine, Debra Monk, Richard Masur, Matthew Faber, Walter Bobbie. Meditation on social hypocrisy—tackling such issues as pregnancy and abortion—follows an adolescent girl who doesn't want to give up her baby and runs away from home. That the "girl" is played by a variety of actresses of different sizes, shapes, and races is just one aspect of this *very* strange (yet often striking) film, which writer-director Solondz positions as a follow-up to WELCOME TO THE DOLLHOUSE. ❚

Pal Joey (1957) **C-111m.** *** D: George Sidney. Rita Hayworth, Frank Sinatra, Kim Novak, Barbara Nichols, Hank Henry, Bobby Sherwood. Sinatra is in peak form as a cocky nightclub singer who makes a move on every "dame" he meets—including innocent showgirl Novak—but meets his Waterloo when wealthy, demanding Hayworth agrees to bankroll his dream of running his own club. Almost complete rewrite of the 1940 Broadway show based on John O'Hara's short stories, but entertaining just the same, with a great Rodgers and Hart score including "Bewitched, Bothered, and Bewildered" (with sanitized lyrics), "The Lady Is a Tramp." Look fast for Robert Reed. ▼●●

Pallbearer, The (1996) **C-97m.** **½ D: Matt Reeves. David Schwimmer, Gwyneth Paltrow, Barbara Hershey, Michael Rapaport, Toni Collette, Carol Kane, Michael Vartan, Bitty Schram, Jean DeBaer. *Friends* star Schwimmer's first film vehicle: a nerd is recruited to be a pallbearer for a "friend" he can't quite remember. Soon he's involved with the dead fellow's sexy mother (Hershey), even while pursuing a girl he had a crush on in high school (Paltrow). Protracted story is alternately touching and infuriating, as it slowly covers well-worn territory, with occasional moments of poignancy. Schwimmer's character is alarmingly one-note. [PG-13]▼●)

Palm Beach Story, The (1942) 87m. ***½ D: Preston Sturges. Claudette Colbert, Joel McCrea, Rudy Vallee, Mary Astor, Sig Arno, Robert Dudley, William Demarest, Jack Norton, Franklin Pangborn, Jimmy Conlin. Hilarious screwball comedy with Claudette running away from hubby McCrea, landing in Palm Beach with nutty millionairess Astor and her bumbling brother Vallee; overflowing with Sturges madness—from the mystifying title sequence to the arrival of the Ale & Quail Club (not to mention the Wienie King!). ▼●)

Palmetto (1998-U.S.-German) C-113m. **½ D: Volker Schlöndorff. Woody Harrelson, Elisabeth Shue, Gina Gershon, Rolf Hoppe, Michael Rapaport, Chloe Sevigny, Tom Wright. An exercise in formula film noir with embittered Florida ex-newspaperman Harrelson—just out of jail—a none-too-bright patsy for crafty (and sexy) Shue, who hires him to help her stage a phony kidnaping. Stylish and steamy, with lots of twists and turns . . . but follows a much too familiar pattern. Based on the vintage novel *Just Another Sucker* by James Hadley Chase. Super 35. [R]▼●)

Palm Springs Weekend (1963) C-100m. **½ D: Norman Taurog. Troy Donahue, Connie Stevens, Stefanie Powers, Robert Conrad, Ty Hardin, Jack Weston, Andrew Duggan, Carole Cook, Jerry Van Dyke, Billy Mumy. Cast tries to play teenagers; yarn of group on a spree in resort town is mostly predictable.▼●)

Palombella Rossa (1989-Italian) C-87m. **½ D: Nanni Moretti. Nanni Moretti, Mariella Valentini, Silvio Orlando, Alfonso Santagata, Claudio Morganti, Asia Argento. Off-the-wall satire about the choices, both political and personal, one makes in life. The hero is Michele (Moretti), a comical communist politician/water polo player; most of the film is set during a competition in which Michele constantly debates the merits of his politics. A representative introduction to one of Italy's most popular comic actor–directors. ▼)

Palookaville (1996) C-92m. *** D: Alan Taylor. William Forsythe, Vincent Gallo, Adam Trese, Frances McDormand, Robert LuPone, Lisa Gay Hamilton, Kim Dickens, Bridgit Ryan. Charming, whimsical look at a trio of lifelong friends and their amateur foray into the world of petty crime. Set in New Jersey, this comically poignant tale

has everyday characters, struggling to survive, who get themselves into some genuinely suspenseful situations. A real sleeper, inspired by the Italian film BIG DEAL ON MADONNA STREET. [R]▼●)

Panama Hattie (1942) 79m. **½ D: Norman Z. McLeod. Ann Sothern, Red Skelton, Rags Ragland, Ben Blue, Marsha Hunt, Virginia O'Brien, Alan Mowbray, Lena Horne, Dan Dailey, Carl Esmond. Cole Porter's Broadway musical (which starred Ethel Merman) about nightclub owner in Panama falls flat on screen. Porter's score mostly absent, but Lena sings "Just One of Those Things," and sprightly Sothern sings "I've Still Got My Health."▼

Pancho Villa (1972-Spanish) C-92m. ** D: Eugenio Martin. Telly Savalas, Clint Walker, Anne Francis, Chuck Connors, Angel del Pozo, Luis Davila. Noisy but dull period piece has Savalas chewing up scenery in title role, Walker playing gun-runner on his payroll, and Connors as polo-playing military martinet. Hang on, though, for smashing climax as two trains collide head-on. [PG]▼●)

Pandemonium (1982) C-82m. ** D: Alfred Sole. Tom Smothers, Carol Kane, Miles Chapin, Debralee Scott, Candy Azzara, Marc McClure, Judge Reinhold, Paul Reubens (Pee-wee Herman); guest stars, Tab Hunter, Donald O'Connor, Eve Arden, Eileen Brennan. Sporadically funny spoof of slasher films, set in a school for cheerleaders. Some clever ideas (in keeping with Canadian origin of many of those films, hero Smothers is a Mountie), but too often just forced. Panavision. [PG]▼

Pandora and the Flying Dutchman (1951-British) C-123m. ** D: Albert Lewin. James Mason, Ava Gardner, Nigel Patrick, Sheila Sim, Harold Warrender, Marius Goring, Pamela Kellino (Mason). Sorry to say, a big Technicolor bore, one of writer-director Lewin's misfires, about a woman who destroys the lives of all the men around her; then mystical, otherworldly Mason materializes. Intriguing but unconvincing tale, inspired by the legend of The Flying Dutchman, a man cursed to live for all eternity until he can find a woman capable of loving him. Only real attribute is Gardner's breathtaking beauty.▼●)

Pandora's Box (1929-German) 133m. **** D: G. W. Pabst. Louise Brooks, Fritz Kortner, Franz (Francis) Lederer, Carl Goetz. Hypnotic silent film stars legendary Brooks as flower girl who becomes protégée—then wife—of editor, with bizarre and unexpected consequences. Striking sexuality and drama, with Brooks an unforgettable Lulu. Scripters Pabst and Laszlo Wajda adapted two plays by Frank Wedekind. ▼)

Pandorum (2009-German-U.S.) C-108m. *½ D: Christian Alvart. Dennis Quaid, Ben Foster, Cam Gigandet, Antje Traue, Cung

Le, Eddie Rouse, Norman Reedus, André M. Hennicke. Twenty-second-century astronauts Quaid and Foster awake from hyper-sleep aboard a spacecraft with no memory of why they are there and discover something deadly is also along for the ride. Dreary, highly derivative sci-fi horror thriller may put *you* into hyper-sleep; it consists mainly of long crawls through dark corridors and quick flashes of familiar-looking alien creatures. Super 35. [R] ❿

Panga SEE: **Curse III: Blood Sacrifice**
Panic (2000) **C-88m.** **½ D: Henry Bromell. William H. Macy, Donald Sutherland, Neve Campbell, Tracey Ullman, John Ritter, Barbara Bain, David Dorfman. A hit man with a guilty conscience undergoes therapy and, feeling estranged from his own family, takes up with a sexy younger woman. Sort of. Low-key black comedy with Freudian overtones is fresh and interesting but never quite pays off. Excellent performances all around. Writer-director Bromell cut his teeth in episodic TV (*Homicide, Northern Exposure*). U.S. debut on cable TV. Panavision. [R] ❤❿
Panic in Needle Park, The (1971) **C-110m.** ***½ D: Jerry Schatzberg. Al Pacino, Kitty Winn, Alan Vint, Richard Bright, Kiel Martin, Michael McClanathan, Warren Finnerty, Marcia Jean Kurtz, Raul Julia, Joe Santos, Paul Sorvino. Easily the best of many drug-abuse films made in the early 1970s. Spunky small-time crook and decent young girl get hooked on heroin and go straight downhill. Pacino and Winn are tremendous. Screenplay by Joan Didion and John Gregory Dunne, from James Mills' book; produced by Dominick Dunne. [PG—edited from original R rating] ❤●❿
Panic in the City (1968) **C-97m.** ** D: Eddie Davis. Howard Duff, Linda Cristal, Stephen McNally, Nehemiah Persoff, Anne Jeffreys, Oscar Beregi, Dennis Hopper. Blah thriller with federal agent Duff attempting to prevent some commie swine from setting off an atomic bomb in L.A. Watch for Mike Farrell as a hospital radiologist. ❤❿
Panic in the Streets (1950) **93m.** ***½ D: Elia Kazan. Richard Widmark, Paul Douglas, Barbara Bel Geddes, (Walter) Jack Palance, Zero Mostel. Taut drama involving gangsters, one of whom is a carrier of pneumonic plague, and the manhunt to find him. Makes fine use of New Orleans locale; Edward and Edna Anhalt won an Oscar for their story. Screenplay by Richard Murphy. ❤●❿
Panic in Year Zero! (1962) **95m.** **½ D: Ray Milland. Ray Milland, Jean Hagen, Frankie Avalon, Mary Mitchel, Joan Freeman, Richard Garland. Intriguing film about L.A. family that escapes atomic bomb explosion to find a situation of every-man-for-himself. Loud, tinny music spoils much of film's effectiveness. CinemaScope. ●❿

Panic on the Trans-Siberian Express SEE: **Horror Express**
Panic Room (2002) **C-112m.** *** D: David Fincher. Jodie Foster, Forest Whitaker, Jared Leto, Dwight Yoakam, Kristen Stewart, Ann Magnuson, Ian Buchanan, Patrick Bauchau. Solid thriller wastes no time putting Foster and daughter in peril—trapped in a steel-encased "safe room"—inside their new Manhattan brownstone. Three creepy thieves invade the house in search of money that's hidden (where else?) in that very room. Suspenseful from the word go, this entertaining film leads to a disappointingly conventional, violent finale. Written by David Koepp; excellent score by Howard Shore. Super 35. [R] ❤❿
Pan's Labyrinth (2006-Spanish-Mexican) **C-119m.** ***½ D: Guillermo del Toro. Sergi López, Maribel Verdú, Ivana Baquero, Álex Angulo, Doug Jones, Ariadna Gil, Manolo Solo, Roger Casamajor. A dark fairy tale plays out against the backdrop of 1944 Spain. A monstrous Fascist captain (López) determines to flush out soldiers of the resistance, as his pregnant wife arrives at his countryside headquarters with her young daughter. The girl (Baquero) escapes the brutality of her new environment by drifting into a fantasy world where she is given challenging tasks to perform by a mysterious faun. Unique fable blends fantasy and fearsome violence, ultimately merging the two stories together. Superbly realized, this is a rare film that invites repeated viewings to absorb all that writer-director del Toro has put into it. Oscar winner for Cinematography (Guillermo Navarro), Makeup (David Martí, Montse Ribé), and Art Direction (Eugenio Caballero, Pilar Revuelta). Coproduced by Alfonso Cuarón. Original Spanish title: EL LABIRINTO DEL FAUNO. [R] ❿
Panther (1995) **C-124m.** ** D: Mario Van Peebles. Kadeem Hardison, Bokeem Woodbine, Joe Don Baker, Courtney B. Vance, Tyrin Turner, Marcus Chong, Anthony Griffith, Bobby Brown, Nefertiti, James Russo, Jenifer Lewis, Chris Rock, Roger Guenveur Smith, Michael Wincott, Richard Dysart, M. Emmet Walsh, Dick Gregory, Jerry Rubin, James LeGros, Robert Culp, Mario Van Peebles. Despite its impressive cast, an annoyingly simple-minded and (no pun intended) whitewashed account of the militant Black Panthers, who had had their fill of the everyday oppression against Black America and began confronting authority during the Vietnam era, becoming pivotal countercultural figures. Fascinating, politically loaded subject matter yearns for a more complex, intelligent cinematic rendering. Scripted by the director's dad, Melvin, based on his novel. [R] ❤●
Paparazzi (2004) **C-84m.** BOMB D: Paul

Abascal. Cole Hauser, Robin Tunney, Dennis Farina, Daniel Baldwin, Tom Hollander, Kevin Gage, Blake Bryan, Tom Sizemore. Hot action-movie actor and all-around nice guy (Hauser) turns real ugly when the paparazzi—and one slimy photog in particular (Sizemore)—start hounding him and his family. Odious, self-righteous revenge thriller. Chris Rock has a cameo as a pizza delivery man. Matthew McConaughey and Vince Vaughn appear as themselves. Mel Gibson coproduced and is seen briefly as a man in anger management therapy. Super 35. [PG-13] ▼▶

Papa's Delicate Condition (1963) **C-98m.** **½ D: George Marshall. Jackie Gleason, Glynis Johns, Charlie Ruggles, Laurel Goodwin, Charles Lane, Elisha Cook, Juanita Moore, Murray Hamilton. Amusing nostalgia of Corinne Griffith's childhood; Gleason dominates everything as tipsy father; set in 1900s. Oscar-winning song, "Call Me Irresponsible." ▼▶

Paper, The (1994) **C-112m.** **½ D: Ron Howard. Michael Keaton, Glenn Close, Robert Duvall, Marisa Tomei, Randy Quaid, Jason Robards, Jason Alexander, Spalding Gray, Catherine O'Hara, Lynne Thigpen, Jack Kehoe, Roma Maffia, Clint Howard, Geoffrey Owens, William Prince, Augusta Dabney, Bruce Altman. Twenty-four hours in the life of a N.Y. newspaper and its harried editors, who are trying to manage their troubled private lives against the unyielding demands of a deadline (and a few small questions about ethics). Over-the-top, far-fetched, downright silly at times, but so adrenalized—barely stopping to take a breath—that it's fun to watch just the same. Many N.Y. journalists appear in cameo roles. Music by Randy Newman. [R] ▼▶

Paperback Hero (1973-Canadian) **C-94m.** **½ D: Peter Pearson. Keir Dullea, Elizabeth Ashley, John Beck, Dayle Haddon. Local hockey hero/womanizer leads fantasy life as town gunslinger. Interesting and well acted, but ultimately a misfire. [R] ▼

Paperback Romance (1994-Australian) **C-93m.** ** D: Ben Lewin. Gia Carides, Anthony LaPaglia, Rebecca Gibney, Robyn Nevin, Jacek Koman. Paper-thin black comedy about a disabled romance novelist (Carides) who breaks her leg while stalking handsome, roguish jeweler LaPaglia. Thus, he doesn't realize that she's handicapped; she tells him she was in a skiing accident. Would-be spoof of schmaltzy novels substitutes slapstick violence for actual laughs. The stars are a real-life couple, but seem mismated in this film. [R] ▼▶

Paper Chase, The (1973) **C-111m.** ***½ D: James Bridges. Timothy Bottoms, Lindsay Wagner, John Houseman, Graham Beckel, Edward Herrmann, Craig Richard Nelson, James Naughton, Bob Lydiard, David Clennon, Lenny Baker. Near-classic comedy-drama about pressures of freshman year at Harvard Law School; Bottoms' obsession with tyrannical professor Kingsfield (Houseman) becomes even more complicated when he discovers his girl friend is Kingsfield's daughter! Splendidly adapted by Bridges from the John Jay Osborn, Jr., novel, with wonderful Gordon Willis photography and peerless acting, led by Houseman's Oscar-winning performance in the role that made him a "star" (and which he continued in the subsequent TV series). Panavision. [PG] ▼▶

Paper Heart (2009) **C-88m.** ** D: Nicholas Jasenovec. Charlyne Yi, Michael Cera, Jake Johnson, Demetri Martin, Seth Rogen, Brendan Paul, Martin Starr. Combining elements of documentary-style filmmaking with a comedic narrative, offbeat stand-up comic Yi sets out to make a movie about the meaning of love. She interviews several people on the subject while getting involved with the true object of her affection, actor Cera. As reality clashes with her own fantasies, we're never sure what's real. This interesting experiment never catches fire and seems more a conceit than a movie; Yi and Cera forget to let the audience in on the joke. [PG-13] ▶

Paperhouse (1988-British) **C-94m.** *** D: Bernard Rose. Charlotte Burke, Elliott Spiers, Glenne Headly, Ben Cross, Gemma Jones, Sarah Newbold. Insightful fantasy drama of girl on the verge of puberty who has vivid dreams that both reflect her own life and seem to be affecting the life of a boy she has never met—while awake. Tense, even frightening, psychologically valid and well acted . . . but not to every taste. Feature debut of music-video director Rose. [PG-13] ▼▶

Paper Lion (1968) **C-107m.** *** D: Alex March. Alan Alda, Lauren Hutton, Alex Karras, David Doyle, Ann Turkel, John Gordy, Roger Brown, Sugar Ray Robinson. Funny film, loosely based on George Plimpton's book, about that writer's experiences when he becomes honorary member of Detroit Lions football team. Even nonfootball fans should enjoy this one, especially scenes with Karras (then a member of the team). Look for Roy Scheider in small role. Techniscope. [G] ▼▶

Paper Man (2010) **C-111m.** ** D: Michele Mulroney, Kieran Mulroney. Jeff Daniels, Emma Stone, Lisa Kudrow, Ryan Reynolds, Kieran Culkin, Hunter Parrish, Chris Parnell, Arabella Field. Daniels and Kudrow rent a house in the Hamptons where he can supposedly write his second novel, but he is a bundle of neuroses, a fragile soul who can't write a single sentence. What's more, he still has an imaginary friend, a superhero called Captain Excellent (Reynolds). Only a budding, unconventional friendship with an introverted high school girl (Stone) gives him any comfort. Odd, sometimes off-putting film has excellent performances but doesn't add up. Written by the first-time directors. [R]🅓

Paper Mask (1991-British) C-105m. *** D: Christopher Morahan. Paul McGann, Amanda Donohoe, Frederick Treves, Tom Wilkinson, Barbara Leigh-Hunt, Jimmy Yuill. Taut chiller is a darkly cynical look at the medical profession. McGann plays a lowly hospital orderly who takes on the identity of a doctor who's been killed in a car crash and gets a job the deceased had applied for in a busy emergency room. Alternately tense, horrifying, and hilarious. [R]▼

Paper Moon (1973) 102m. **** D: Peter Bogdanovich. Ryan O'Neal, Tatum O'Neal, Madeline Kahn, John Hillerman, P. J. Johnson, Burton Gilliam, Randy Quaid. Unbeatable entertainment, harking back to Damon Runyonesque 1930s, as con man O'Neal unwillingly latches onto young girl (his real-life daughter) who's pretty sharp herself. Tatum made her film debut here, and won an Oscar for her scene-stealing work; Kahn is fun, too, as Trixie Delight. Script by Alvin Sargent from Joe David Brown's *Addie Pray*. Later a TV series. [PG]▼●🅓

Paper Tiger (1975-British) C-99m. ** D: Ken Annakin. David Niven, Toshiro Mifune, Hardy Kruger, Ando, Ivan Desny, Ronald Fraser. Lackluster tale of a plucky kidnapped lad (Ando) and his English tutor (Niven). Since the boy is the son of Japanese ambassador Mifune, Niven sees the chance to act out his many tales of heroism that have impressed the youngster. Tepid action involving political terrorism and Disney-style cuteness muck up the proceedings entirely. Panavision. [PG]▼

Papillon (1973) C-150m. *** D: Franklin J. Schaffner. Steve McQueen, Dustin Hoffman, Victor Jory, Don Gordon, Anthony Zerbe, George Coulouris, Robert Deman, Bill Mumy, Gregory Sierra. Henri Charrière—"the butterfly"—(McQueen) is determined to escape from Devil's Island, despite the odds, in this exciting adventure yarn. Extreme length and graphic realism work against its total success. Script by Dalton Trumbo and Lorenzo Semple, Jr., from Charrière's best-selling book; that's Trumbo cast as the Commandant. Music by Jerry Goldsmith. Cut to 132m. after original release. Panavision. [PG—originally rated R]▼●🅓

Paprika (2006-Japanese) C-90m. *** D: Satoshi Kon. Voices of Megumi Hayashibara, Tôru Furuya, Kôuichi Yamadera, Katsunosuke Hori, Toru Emori, Akio O™htsuka. Vivid psychedelic images highlight this Japanese anime in which machines invade and record people's dreams. Their creator is a colorless doctor with a freewheeling alter ego named Paprika who also dives into the subconscious. When one of the machines is stolen in order to turn these dreams into nightmares, the Doctor/Paprika must find a way to harness the technology and rein it in. Based on a novel by Yasutaka Tsutsui. With its imaginative visuals, this is a trip worth taking. [R]🅓

Parade (1974-French-Swedish) C-85m. ** D: Jacques Tati. Jacques Tati, Karl Kossmayr, Pia Colombo. Disappointing final feature from the beloved French comic, combining assorted provincial circus acts with Tati himself performing mime routines. The result is a curio for sure, solely of interest for fans of Tati. Shot mostly on video. Originally made for television.▼●

Paradine Case, The (1948) 116m. **½ D: Alfred Hitchcock. Gregory Peck, (Alida) Valli, Ann Todd, Charles Laughton, Charles Coburn, Ethel Barrymore, Louis Jourdan, Leo G. Carroll, John Williams. Talk, talk, talk in complicated, stagy courtroom drama, set in England. Below par for Hitchcock; producer David O. Selznick also wrote the script. Originally 132m., then cut to 125m. and finally 116m.▼🅓

Paradise (1982) C-100m. *½ D: Stuart Gillard. Willie Aames, Phoebe Cates, Tuvia Tavi, Richard Curnock, Neil Vipond, Aviva Marks. Silly BLUE LAGOON rip-off, with Aames and Cates discovering sex while stranded in the desert. Both, however, do look good sans clothes. [R]▼

Paradise (1991) C-110m. *** D: Mary Agnes Donoghue. Melanie Griffith, Don Johnson, Elijah Wood, Thora Birch, Sheila McCarthy, Eve Gordon, Louise Latham. Poignant and appealing story of a boy (Wood) who's sent to friends of his mother's in a quiet country town for the summer; there he's befriended by a precocious girl (Birch), and tries to learn what makes the married couple he's staying with so cold to one another. Idyllic film takes perhaps too much time to reach its (inevitable) climax, but offers many lovely moments. Birch is a standout. Directorial debut for screenwriter Donoghue, who adapted the 1988 French film LE GRAND CHEMIN (THE GRAND HIGHWAY). [PG-13] ▼●

Paradise Alley (1978) C-109m. *½ D: Sylvester Stallone. Sylvester Stallone, Lee Canalito, Armand Assante, Frank McRae, Anne Archer, Kevin Conway, Joyce Ingalls, Tom Waits, Ray Sharkey. Sly made his directorial debut with this Damon Runyonesque story of three none-too-bright brothers from the N.Y.C. tenements, one of whom hopes to make it big as a wrestler. Some nice moments lost in comic-book-level dramatics. Director Stallone clearly admires his star (he also croons the title song!). [PG]▼●🅓

Paradise, Hawaiian Style (1966) C-91m.

**½ D: Michael Moore. Elvis Presley, Suzanna Leigh, James Shigeta, Donna Butterworth, Marianna Hill, Irene Tsu, Julie Parrish, Philip Ahn, Mary Treen. Rehash of Presley's earlier BLUE HAWAII, with Elvis a pilot who runs a charter service while romancing local dolls. Attractive fluff.▼❶

Paradise Now (2005-Palestinian-Dutch-German-French) **C-90m. ***½** D: Hany Abu-Assad. Kais Nashef, Ali Suliman, Lubna Azabal, Amer Hlehel, Hiam Abbass, Ashraf Barhoum. Gripping drama of two young men living in the Palestine territory who try to reconcile their lives with family and friends; in 24 hours they will perpetrate a suicide-bombing mission in Tel Aviv. Events do not play out as planned, but we in the audience are all too aware of the literal time bomb ticking every minute. An exceptional film laced with humor and humanity. Written by the director and Bero Beyer. Super 35. [PG-13]❶

Paradise Road (1997-U.S.-Australian) **C-115m. **½** D: Bruce Beresford. Glenn Close, Pauline Collins, Cate Blanchett, Frances McDormand, Julianna Margulies, Jennifer Ehle, Elizabeth Spriggs, Tessa Humphries, Wendy Hughes, Susie Porter, Sab Shimono. Beresford scripted and researched this heartfelt (though cliché-ridden) based-on-fact account of a band of women who become united as they are held in a Japanese POW camp in Sumatra during WW2; they form a symphonic chorus and create beautiful harmony amid their misery. Not without many dramatically effective moments, but done in by repetition and predictability. Panavision. [R]▼❶

Parallax View, The (1974) **C-102m. ***½** D: Alan J. Pakula. Warren Beatty, Paula Prentiss, William Daniels, Walter McGinn, Hume Cronyn, Anthony Zerbe, Kenneth Mars. Director-photographer-production designer team later responsible for ALL THE PRESIDENT'S MEN gives this political thriller a brilliant "look" as reporter Beatty investigates a senator's assassination. Frightening story unfolds with each piece of evidence he uncovers. Gripping to the very end. Panavision. [R]▼❶

Paranoid Park (2007-U.S.-French) **C-84m. **½** D: Gus Van Sant. Gabe Nevins, Jake Miller, Dan Liu, Taylor Momsen, Lauren McKinney, Grace Carter. Portland, Oregon, teenager Nevins seems barely interested in his pretty girlfriend or much of anything else, other than skateboarding with his best friend. He finally starts to care when police investigate a death in an industrial area near a popular skate park. Film is similarly laid-back and artsy (parents are mostly unseen, like a *Peanuts* comic strip, and as in Van Sant's ELEPHANT, shower scenes pop up), with its long passages playing out of sequential order. This may endear it to fans of the director; others won't see

the point of it all. Based on a novel by Blake Nelson. [R]❶

Paranormal Activity (2009) **C-86m. ***** D: Oren Peli. Katie Featherston, Micah Sloat, Mark Fredrichs. Young man eagerly sets up a video camera to film the interior of his girlfriend's San Diego house over several days, hoping to catch shots of reported supernatural activities. They both get more than they hoped for. Presented without credits as though it really is amateur footage, this shoestring ($15,000) horror thriller was an enormous hit, one of the most profitable movies in terms of investment ever made. Though generally understated, it's often extremely tense and sometimes shocking. The actors are completely believable as the characters who bear their names. Followed by a sequel. [R]❶

Paranormal Activity 2 (2010) **C-86m. **½** D: Tod Williams. Sprague Grayden, Brian Boland, Molly Ephraim, Katie Featherston, Micah Sloat, Vivis Cortez. Married couple moves into a suburban house with their baby, ignoring the warnings of their cook, who claims the house is dangerous. They soon discover this for themselves. Story is again seen entirely through footage supposedly shot by security cameras; the shocks still work, but in this sequel to the 2009 hit everything seems familiar and artificial. For no clear reason, the story is set prior to events in the first movie. Unrated version runs 91m. [R]❶

Parasite (1982) **C-85m.** BOMB D: Charles Band. Robert Glaudini, Demi Moore, Luca Bercovici, James Davidson, Al Fann, Cherie Currie, Vivian Blaine. In repressive near-future, scientist who's developed voracious parasites flees with one inside him and (surprise, surprise) it gets loose. Set in the California desert, with several revolting sequences copied from ALIEN. Filmed in 3-D, with blood and parasites thrust at the viewer. StereoScope. 3-D. [R]▼❶

Parasite Murders, The SEE: **They Came From Within**

Pardners (1956) **C-90m. **½** D: Norman Taurog. Dean Martin, Jerry Lewis, Lori Nelson, Jackie Loughery, John Baragrey, Agnes Moorehead, Jeff Morrow, Lon Chaney, Jr. Ironically titled M&L vehicle (they were already on the road to their breakup) is pleasant remake of RHYTHM ON THE RANGE, with Jerry as Manhattan millionaire who cleans up Western town in his own inimitable fashion. Written by Sidney Sheldon. VistaVision.▼❶

Pardon Mon Affaire (1977-French) **C-105m. ***** D: Yves Robert. Jean Rochefort, Claude Brasseur, Guy Bedos, Victor Lanoux, Daniele Delorme, Anny Duperey. Sprightly comedy about efforts of happily married Rochefort to meet and court a dazzling model he spots in a parking garage. Another enjoyable French farce from director Robert. Sequel: WE WILL ALL MEET IN PARADISE. Later Americanized as THE WOMAN IN RED. [PG]▼●

Pardon Mon Affaire, Too SEE: **We Will All Meet in Paradise**

Pardon My Sarong (1942) 84m. *** D: Erle C. Kenton. Lou Costello, Bud Abbott, Lionel Atwill, Virginia Bruce, Robert Paige, William Demarest, Leif Erickson, Samuel S. Hinds, Nan Wynn, Four Ink Spots, Tip, Tap, Toe. A&C in good form as bus drivers who end up on tropical island, involved with notorious jewel thieves. ▼▶

Parenthood (1989) C-124m. ***½ D: Ron Howard. Steve Martin, Mary Steenburgen, Dianne Wiest, Jason Robards, Rick Moranis, Tom Hulce, Martha Plimpton, Keanu Reeves, Harley Kozak, Dennis Dugan, Leaf (Joaquin) Phoenix, Paul Linke. Insightful multi-character comedy about the trials and tribulations of parenthood, as seen from several points of view within the same large family. Warm, winning, and truthful; Martin is ideal in the lead, and surrounded by a perfect ensemble. Screenplay by Lowell Ganz and Babaloo Mandel (from a story they concocted with fellow parent Ron Howard). Later became two separate (1990, 2010) TV series. [PG-13]▼●▶

Parents (1989) C-82m. ** D: Bob Balaban. Randy Quaid, Mary Beth Hurt, Sandy Dennis, Bryan Madorsky, Juno Mills-Cockell, Kathryn Grody, Deborah Rush, Graham Jarvis. Coal-black horror comedy set in the 1950s centers on a young boy who worries about where his highly conformist parents get all that meat they eat . . . and what goes on down in the basement. Well acted but thinly plotted; a good sense of visual style and amusing production design can't keep it afloat. Feature directing debut for actor Balaban. [R]▼●▶

Parent Trap, The (1961) C-124m. *** D: David Swift. Hayley Mills, Maureen O'Hara, Brian Keith, Charlie Ruggles, Una Merkel, Leo G. Carroll, Joanna Barnes, Cathleen Nesbitt, Nancy Kulp, Frank DeVol. Hayley plays twins who've never met until their divorced parents send them to the same summer camp; after initial rivalry they join forces to reunite their mom and dad. Attempt to mix slapstick and sophistication doesn't work, but overall it's fun. Erich Kastner's story filmed before as 1954 British film TWICE UPON A TIME. Hayley starred—as mom—in 1986 and 1989 TV sequels. Remade in 1998. ▼●▶

Parent Trap, The (1998) C-128m. *** D: Nancy Myers. Lindsay Lohan, Dennis Quaid, Natasha Richardson, Elaine Hendrix, Lisa Ann Walter, Simon Kunz, Polly Holliday, Maggie Wheeler, Ronnie Stevens. Delightful remake of the 1961 Disney hit about 11-year-old girls who've been raised separately, meet each other for the first time at summer camp, and contrive to bring their parents back together—though Mom lives in London and Dad in California's Napa Valley. Nicely updated to the 1990s without losing the appeal of the original. Joanna Barnes, who played the "other woman" in the 1961 movie, appears here as that character's mother. Lohan's film debut. [PG]▼●▶

Paris Blues (1961) 98m. *** D: Martin Ritt. Paul Newman, Joanne Woodward, Diahann Carroll, Sidney Poitier, Louis Armstrong, Serge Reggiani. Film improves with each viewing; offbeat account of musicians Newman and Poitier in Left Bank Paris, romancing tourists Woodward and Carroll. Great Duke Ellington score, including explosive "Battle Royal" number; a must for jazz fans.▼

Paris Does Strange Things SEE: **Elena and Her Men**

Paris Holiday (1958) C-100m. **½ D: Gerd Oswald. Bob Hope, Fernandel, Anita Ekberg, Martha Hyer, Preston Sturges. Mixture of French and American farce humor makes for uneven entertainment, with Hope in France to buy a new screenplay. Features writer-director Sturges in a small acting role. Technirama. ▼▶

Paris Is Burning (1990) C-78m. ***½ D: Jennie Livingston. Funny, revealing, and compact documentary about N.Y.C. "drag balls"—in which black and Latino men don "vogue-ing" disguises as everything from flamboyant queens to businessmen or members of the military. Fresh and uncondescending, with a powerful element of tragedy near the end. ▼●▶

Paris je t'aime (2006-French) C-120m. **½ D: Bruno Podalydès, Gurinder Chadha, Gus Van Sant, Joel and Ethan Coen, Walter Salles and Daniela Thomas, Christopher Doyle, Isabel Coixet, Nobuhiro Suwa, Sylvain Chomet, Alfonso Cuarón, Richard LaGravenese, Olivier Assayas, Olivier Schmitz, Wes Craven, Tom Tykwer, Gérard Depardieu and Frédéric Auburtin, Alexander Payne. Florence Muller, Bruno Podalydès, Leïla Bekhti, Marianne Faithfull, Steve Buscemi, Catalina Sandino Moreno, Barbet Schroeder, Sergio Castellitto, Miranda Richardson, Leonor Watling, Juliette Binoche, Willem Dafoe, Hippolyte Girardot, Paul Putner, Nick Nolte, Ludivine Sagnier, Bob Hoskins, Fanny Ardant, Maggie Gyllenhaal, Lionel Dray, Aïssa Maïga, Elijah Wood, Olga Kurylenko, Emily Mortimer, Rufus Sewell, Natalie Portman, Melchior Beslon, Ben Gazzara, Gena Rowlands, Margo Martindale. Series of "little romances" set in 18 distinct Parisian neighborhoods. Altogether it doesn't amount to much, but a handful of the vignettes are well told and amusing: Craven's graveyard set piece with Mortimer and Sewell, who are about to marry; the Coens' funny skit with

Buscemi as an innocent bystander in the Paris Metro; a bittersweet slice of life with Rowlands and Gazzara (written by Rowlands); Payne's musing on loneliness with a perfectly cast Martindale. Followed by NEW YORK, I LOVE YOU. [R]▶

Paris, Texas (1984-French-German-British) C-150m. **½ D: Wim Wenders. Harry Dean Stanton, Nastassja Kinski, Dean Stockwell, Aurore Clement, Hunter Carson, Bernhard Wicki. Man who's been lost for years tries to put his life back together—and win back his wife and son. Oblique, self-satisfied, and slow, like most of Sam Shepard's writing, but distinguished by fine performances and rich Southwestern atmosphere by Wenders and cinematographer Robby Müller. This won raves from many critics, so it may be a matter of personal taste. [R]▼O▶

Paris 36 (2008-French-German-Czech) C-120m. *** D: Christophe Barratier. Gérard Jugnot, Clovis Cornillac, Nora Arnezeder, Kad Merad, Pierre Richard, Bernard-Pierre Donnadieu, Maxence Perrin, François Morel. Atmospheric, beautifully crafted musical salutes the romantic ideal of 1930s Paris just as politics and WW2 are about to change it forever. Three workers try to save the local vaudeville theater, and their jobs, by buying it and reinventing the aging palace as an entertainment mecca. As in LES CHORISTES, Barratier blends coldhearted reality and stylish musical sequences. And don't miss the Busby Berkeley tribute. French title: FAUBOURG 36. Panavision. [PG-13]▶

Paris Trout (1991) C-100m. ***½ D: Stephen Gyllenhaal. Dennis Hopper, Barbara Hershey, Ed Harris, Ray McKinnon, Tina Lifford, Darnita Henry, Eric Ware. Jarring drama, set in the late 1940s, about the mind and soul of an unrepentant racist, with Hopper (never better) as a Southerner who kills a 12-year-old black girl and cannot comprehend how he can be condemned for his action. Probing, bristling script by Pete Dexter, based on his National Book Award–winning novel. This debuted in the U.S. on cable TV. [R]▼●

Paris Was Made for Lovers SEE: **Time for Loving, A**

Paris—When It Sizzles (1964) C-110m. *½ D: Richard Quine. William Holden, Audrey Hepburn, Noel Coward, Gregoire Aslan. Labored, unfunny comedy defeats a game cast, in story of screenwriter and secretary who act out movie fantasies in order to finish script. Paris locations, cameos by Marlene Dietrich and other stars don't help. Remake of Julien Duvivier's LA FÊTE À HENRIETTE (1952). ▼▶

Park Row (1952) 83m. *** D: Samuel Fuller. Gene Evans, Mary Welch, Herbert Heyes, Tina Rome, Forrest Taylor. Good, tough little film with newsman Evans starting his own paper, rivaling newspaper mag-

nate Welch in 1880s N.Y.C. Written by the director, a former newspaperman.▶

Parrish (1961) C-140m. *½ D: Delmer Daves. Claudette Colbert, Troy Donahue, Karl Malden, Dean Jagger, Connie Stevens, Diane McBain, Sharon Hugueny, Sylvia Miles, Madeleine Sherwood. Slurpy soaper is so bad that at times it's funny; emotionless Donahue lives with his mother (Colbert, in her last theatrical film) on Jagger's tobacco plantation and falls in love with three girls there. Malden overplays tyrannical tobacco czar to the nth degree. Carroll O'Connor and Vincent Gardenia have small roles.▼▶

Parting Glances (1986) C-90m. **½ D: Bill Sherwood. John Bolger, Richard Ganoung, Steve Buscemi, Adam Nathan, Patrick Tull, Kathy Kinney. Two longtime gay roommates spend their final 24 hours together before one leaves N.Y.C. on a job transfer. Earnest, intelligent drama is OK within its modest framework; subsidiary characters—one of them dying of AIDS (and played by Buscemi, in an eye-opening performance)—are more compelling than the two protagonists. This was Sherwood's only feature; he died of AIDS in 1990.▼▶

Partners (1982) C-98m. BOMB D: James Burrows. Ryan O'Neal, John Hurt, Kenneth McMillan, Robyn Douglass, Jay Robinson, Denise Galik, Rick Jason. Foolish, offensive parody of CRUISING, with straight cop O'Neal impersonating homosexual while investigating gay murder. Hurt is wasted as O'Neal's partner, who really is gay. Screenplay by Francis (LA CAGE AUX FOLLES) Veber. Undistinguished feature debut for TV comedy director Burrows. [R]▼▶

Parts: The Clonus Horror (1978) C-90m. ** D: Robert S. Fiveson. Tim Donnelly, Dick Sargent, Peter Graves, Paulette Breen, David Hooks, Keenan Wynn. Cleanly made programmer about an insidious government plan to start cloning the population. Watchable but uninspired. Video title: THE CLONUS HORROR. [R]▼▶

Part 2, Sounder (1976) C-98m. ***½ D: William A. Graham. Harold Sylvester, Ebony Wright, Taj Mahal, Annazette Chase, Darryl Young. Excellent follow-up to SOUNDER, retaining the dignity and human values in the continuing tale of a proud family of Depression-era Southern sharecroppers. [G]

Part 2, Walking Tall (1975) C-109m. ** D: Earl Bellamy. Bo Svenson, Luke Askew, Robert DoQui, Bruce Glover, Richard Jaeckel, Noah Beery, Jr. Tepid follow-up to ultraviolent movie about club-swinging Tennessee Sheriff Buford Pusser. Svenson now takes the role of the one-man crusader against organized crime, but makes him come off like a standard TV hero rather than a real-life character. Aka WALKING TALL,

PART TWO. Sequel: FINAL CHAPTER—
WALKING TALL. [PG]▼▶

Party, The (1968) **C-99m.** **★★★** D: Blake
Edwards. Peter Sellers, Claudine Longet,
Marge Champion, Denny Miller, Gavin
MacLeod, Steve Franken, Carol Wayne.
Side-splitting gags highlight loosely struc-
tured film about chic Hollywood party at-
tended by bumbling Indian actor (Sellers).
Doesn't hold up to the very end, but has
some memorable set pieces. Panavision.
▼▶●

Party Girl (1958) **C-99m.** **★★★** D: Nicholas
Ray. Robert Taylor, Cyd Charisse, Lee J.
Cobb, John Ireland, Kent Smith. Crooked
lawyer (Taylor) and showgirl (Charisse)
try to break free from early 1930s Chicago
mob life. Charisse has a couple of torrid
dance numbers; Ray's stylish treatment
has won this film a following. Tony Martin
(the star's husband) sings the title song.
CinemaScope. ▼▶●

Party Girl (1995) **C-98m.** **★★½** D: Daisy
von Scherler Mayer. Parker Posey, Omar
Townsend, Sasha von Scherler, Guillermo
Diaz, Anthony DeSando, Donna Mitchell,
Liev Schreiber, Nicole Bobbitt. Slim, low-
budget film is fun, with Posey perfectly cast
as a young N.Y.C. career woman without a
career. Deciding she should be doing something more with her life than just throwing
wild parties, she seeks job fulfillment (with
admittedly no skills), and the N.Y. Public Library system will never be the same
again. Posey is trendy and insouciant, likable and hilarious, and supporting cast
scores as well—including the director's
mother as Posey's godmother. Best bit: the
Dewey Decimal Record-Spinning System!
Later a TV series. [R]▼▶●

Party Monster (2003) **C-98m.** **★½** D: Fenton Bailey, Randy Barbato. Macaulay Culkin,
Seth Green, Wilson Cruz, Chloë Sevigny,
Natasha Lyonne, Diana Scarwid, Dylan Mc-
Dermott, Marilyn Manson, Mia Kirshner,
Wilmer Valderrama, John Stamos. Culkin
gives a mannered, thoroughly annoying performance in an adult "comeback" vehicle—
his first film in 9 years—about Michael Alig, a
real-life club kid who became king of N.Y.C.'s
drug-fueled nightlife in the late '80s and early
'90s before he was arrested for murder. There
may be an interesting cautionary tale to be
told about the era (indeed, the directors made
a 1998 documentary with the same title), but
this amateurish, shot-on-video excursion into
trendy depravity certainly isn't it. [R] ▼▶

Party's Over, The (1966-British) **94m.** **★★**
D: Guy Hamilton. Oliver Reed, Ann Lynn,
Clifford David, Louise Sorel, Eddie Albert.
Sordid drama of wealthy American girl
becoming involved with group of aimless
London youths, with tragic results.

Pascali's Island (1988-British) **C-104m.**
★★½ D: James Dearden. Ben Kingsley,
Charles Dance, Helen Mirren, George
Murcell, Sheila Allen, Nadim Sawalha. A
largely ignored Turkish spy for the collapsing Ottoman Empire forms a duplicitous alliance with a mysterious Brit to rob the Greek
island of Nisi of an archeological treasure.
Well-acted drama isn't wholly successful,
but it certainly holds your interest. Scripted
by the director. [PG-13]▼●

Passage, The (1979-British) **C-99m.** **★½** D:
J. Lee Thompson. Anthony Quinn, James
Mason, Malcolm McDowell, Patricia Neal,
Kay Lenz, Christopher Lee, Paul Clemens,
Michael Lonsdale, Marcel Bozzuffi. Trashy
WW2 story of Basque guide Quinn helping
chemist Mason and his family escape over
the Pyrenees with Nazi fanatic McDowell
in hot pursuit. McDowell's campy performance must be seen to be disbelieved. Technovision. [R]

Passage to India, A (1984-British) **C-163m.**
★★★ D: David Lean. Judy Davis, Victor Banerjee, Peggy Ashcroft, James Fox, Alec
Guinness, Nigel Havers, Richard Wilson,
Antonia Pemberton, Michael Culver, Art
Malik, Saeed Jaffrey. Meticulous adaptation of E. M. Forster novel set in the late
1920s, about an East/West culture clash, as
a young, headstrong British woman goes
to India for the first time, accompanied by
the mother of her fiancé. Not a great movie,
but so rich in flavor, nuance, and the sheer
expressiveness of *film* that it offers great
satisfaction, despite its shortcomings (and
extreme length). Ashcroft won Best Supporting Actress Oscar for her fine performance as Mrs. Moore. Maurice Jarre also
got an Oscar for his anachronistic score.
Lean's last film. [PG]▼●

Passage to Marseille (1944) **110m.** **★★½** D:
Michael Curtiz. Humphrey Bogart, Claude
Rains, Michele Morgan, Philip Dorn,
Sydney Greenstreet, Peter Lorre, George
Tobias, Helmut Dantine, John Loder, Vic-
tor Francen, Vladimir Sokoloff, Edward
(Eduardo) Ciannelli, Hans Conried. WW2
Devil's Island escape film marred by
flashback-within-flashback confusion. Not
a bad war film, just too talky; a disappoint-
ment considering the cast. Also shown in
computer-colored version. ▼▶●

Passed Away (1992) **C-96m.** **★★½** D: Charlie Peters. Bob Hoskins, Jack Warden, William Petersen, Helen Lloyd Breed, Maureen
Stapleton, Pamela Reed, Tim Curry, Peter
Riegert, Blair Brown, Patrick Breen, Nancy
Travis, Teri Polo, Frances McDormand.
Likable if lightweight black comedy about
the death of a patriarch (Warden) and how it
affects the various members of his colorful
family. Pleasantly offbeat, with a very appealing cast, though Hoskins is never quite
convincing as an American. Peters also
scripted. [PG-13]▼

Passenger, The (1975-Italian) **C-126m.**
★★½ D: Michelangelo Antonioni. Jack
Nicholson, Maria Schneider, Jenny Runa-

cre, Ian Hendry, Steven Berkoff, Ambrose Bia. Enigmatic narrative about dissatisfied TV reporter on assignment in Africa who exchanges identities with an Englishman who has died suddenly in a hotel room. Some found this brilliant; judge for yourself. Original PG-rated U.S. version runs 118m. [PG-13]▼●]

Passenger 57 (1992) C-84m. **½ D: Kevin Hooks. Wesley Snipes, Bruce Payne, Tom Sizemore, Alex Datcher, Bruce Greenwood, Robert Hooks, Elizabeth Hurley, Michael Horse, Ernie Lively. Snipes is a crack anti-terrorist expert planning early retirement when he is thrust into the middle of an airline hijacking perpetrated by vile arch-criminal (Payne). Watchable action fare has a few too many coincidences but delivers both on the ground and in the air, thanks largely to the two charismatic opponents. Costar Robert Hooks, who plays FBI agent Henderson, is the director's father. Panavision and J-D-C Scope. [R] ▼●]

Passengers (2008) C-93m. ** D: Rodrigo García. Anne Hathaway, Patrick Wilson, David Morse, Andre Braugher, Clea DuVall, Dianne Wiest, William B. Davis. Grief therapist Hathaway, counseling a batch of oddly argumentative plane crash survivors, develops a special interest in euphoric stockbroker Wilson. When her patients start vanishing from the sessions, she suspects the airline of a murderous cover-up, but . . . Scareless, suspenseless, only mildly intriguing romantic thriller is a middling muddle of conspiracy paranoia, otherworldliness, and kissing. Not recommended for those with a fear of flying. Super 35. [PG-13]▐]

Passing of Evil, The SEE: **Grasshopper, The**

Passion (1982-French-Swiss) C-87m. **½ D: Jean-Luc Godard. Isabelle Huppert, Hanna Schygulla, Michel Piccoli, Jerzy Radziwilowicz, Laszlo Szabo. Characters named Isabelle, Hanna, Michel, Jerzy, and Laszlo are connected with the making of a film called PASSION, which seems to be more the visualization of a Rembrandt or Delacroix than an actual movie. Meanwhile, the extras are treated like cattle, and the moviemaking art is tainted by commerce. Truffaut's DAY FOR NIGHT celebrates the joy of filmmaking; this is, in its own way, an anti-movie. [R]▼▐

Passionada (2003) C-108m. ** D: Dan Ireland. Jason Isaacs, Sofia Milos, Emmy Rossum, Theresa Russell, Seymour Cassel, Lupe Ontiveros, Chris Tardio. Flavorful but unmemorable romantic comedy about three generations of women in a close-knit Portuguese fishing town in Massachusetts. The attractive Milos plays a recent widow reluctantly drawn into romance with a handsome Britisher who neglects to tell her certain things about himself. Easy on the eyes, and to be commended for focusing on love among adult characters (a rarity nowadays), but little more than a quick diversion. Panavision. [PG-13]▼▐

Passionate Friends, The (1949-British) 91m. **½ D: David Lean. Ann Todd, Trevor Howard, Claude Rains, Betty Ann Davies, Isabel Dean, Wilfrid Hyde-White. Predictable love triangle among the upper classes, enhanced by strong cast and Lean's craftsmanship. Based on H. G. Wells novel. Originally released in U.S. as ONE WOMAN'S STORY. ▼▐

Passionate Stranger, The SEE: **Novel Affair, A**

Passione d'Amore (1981-Italian-French) C-118m. **½ D: Ettore Scola. Bernard Giraudeau, Laura Antonelli, Valerie D'Obici, Jean-Louis Trintignant, Massimo Girotti, Bernard Blier. Hideous D'Obici pursues handsome cavalry officer Giraudeau, who's in love with gorgeous Antonelli. Intriguing Beauty and the Beast story is not completely convincing—and far from Scola's best work. Later musicalized for Broadway by Stephen Sondheim, as *Passion.* Aka PASSION OF LOVE.▼

Passion Fish (1992) C-135m. *** D: John Sayles. Mary McDonnell, Alfre Woodard, David Strathairn, Vondie Curtis-Hall, Angela Bassett, Nora Dunn, Sheila Kelley, Mary Portser, Maggie Renzi. Bitchy soap opera actress is paralyzed in an accident, and returns to her family home in Louisiana where she can be miserable to her heart's content—until her newest nurse/companion (Woodard) stands up to her. Funny, affecting, and satisfying entertainment—if a wee bit long. McDonnell's natural aloofness is put to perfect use by writer-director Sayles, who's given her the part of a lifetime. [R]▼●]

Passion Flower Hotel, The SEE: **Boarding School**

Passion in the Desert (1998-British) C-93m. **½ D: Lavinia Currier. Ben Daniels, Michel Piccoli, Paul Meston, Kenneth Collard, Nadi Odeh, Auda Mohammed Badoul. Unusual drama, from Balzac novella, of French army captain (Daniels) and a painter in his charge (Piccoli) who get stranded in the Egyptian desert during 1798 Napoleonic campaign. The officer eventually comes face-to-face with a leopard, and their unorthodox relationship forms the crux of this story. Impressively crafted (cinematographer Alexei Rodionov also shot ORLANDO), though not for all tastes. Shot in 1995. [PG-13]▼▐

Passion of Anna, The (1969-Swedish) C-101m. ***½ D: Ingmar Bergman. Liv Ullmann, Bibi Andersson, Max von Sydow, Erland Josephson, Erik Hell. Stark drama, beautifully acted, about von Sydow, living alone on a barely populated island, and relationship with widow Ullmann, architect

Josephson, and wife Andersson. Superior cinematography by Sven Nykvist. Original title was simply—and more accurately—A PASSION. [R]▼◗

Passion of Beatrice, The SEE: **Beatrice**
Passion of Evil, The SEE: **Grasshopper, The**
Passion of Joan of Arc, The (1928-French) 117m. **** D: Carl Theodor Dreyer. Maria Falconetti, Eugene Sylvain, Maurice Schutz. Joan of Arc's inquisition, trial, and burning at the stake; the scenario is based on transcript of historical trial. Masterfully directed, with groundbreaking use of close-ups; Falconetti glows in the title role. Photographed by Rudolph Maté.▼◗
Passion of Love SEE: **Passion d'Amore**
Passion of Mind (2000) C-105m. ** D: Alain Berliner. Demi Moore, Stellan Skarsgård, William Fichtner, Sinead Cusack, Peter Riegert. Romantic piffle about a woman who's either a Provence widow who dreams she's a glamorous New York literary agent . . . or vice versa. Matters are complicated when she falls in love with two very different men. Indie vehicle for Moore is sleek and watchable but plays like an International Foods Coffee version of THE DOUBLE LIFE OF VERONIQUE. Also similar to JULIA AND JULIA, although in this version scripter Ron Bass actually bothers to solve the mystery. Panavision. [R]▼◗
Passion of the Christ, The (2004) C-126m. **½ D: Mel Gibson. Jim Caviezel, Monica Bellucci, Claudia Gerini, Maia Morgenstern, Sergio Rubini, Mattia Sbragia, Hristo Naumov Shopov, Luca De Dominicis. Chronicle of the last 12 hours in the life of Jesus Christ dwells, in excruciating detail, on his suffering (or "Passion"). Despite its direct and often powerful approach, the near-obsessive visceral display—which was absolutely director-cowriter Gibson's intention—becomes narrow and repetitive, particularly since it is virtually devoid of any historical context. Also, the use of subtitled Latin and Aramaic languages does not make the narrative seem any more authentic than other sincere interpretations of this story. However, a film that speaks so strongly to those who share its beliefs is difficult to judge objectively. Panavision. [R]▼◗
Passion Play (1983) SEE: **Love Letters** (1983)
Passion Play (2011) C-94m. *½ D: Mitch Glazer. Mickey Rourke, Megan Fox, Bill Murray, Kelly Lynch, Rhys Ifans, Rory Cochrane. Jumbled noir-ish fantasy involving a once celebrated jazz trumpeter (Rourke) who now plays in a strip club. After barely avoiding being killed, he stumbles upon a carnival and becomes obsessed with Lily the Bird Girl (Fox), its main attraction, who really has wings. Murray is game, playing a hood named Happy, but even he

can't add much to this barely watchable, instantly forgettable mess. A less than auspicious directorial debut for screenwriter Glazer. Super 35. [R]◗

Passions SEE: **Grasshopper, The**
Passport to Pimlico (1949-British) 85m. ***½ D: Henry Cornelius. Stanley Holloway, Margaret Rutherford, Betty Warren, Hermione Baddeley, Barbara Murray, Basil Radford, Naunton Wayne, Paul Dupuis, Michael Hordern. Salty farce of ancient treaty enabling small group of Brits to form their own bounded territory in the middle of London. Screenplay by Cornelius and T.E.B. Clarke.▼◗
Pass the Ammo (1988) C-97m. BOMB D: David Beaird. Bill Paxton, Linda Kozlowski, Tim Curry, Annie Potts, Dennis Burkley, Glenn Withrow, Anthony Geary, Richard Paul. Shrill, heavy-handed spoof of televangelists that blunts its satiric edge by making its "heroes" (a young couple out to rob the church) so thoroughly disreputable. This subject cries for a better comedy. [R]▼◗
Past Caring (1985-British) C-77m. ** D: Richard Eyre. Denholm Elliott, Emlyn Williams, Connie Booth, Joan Greenwood, Dave Atkins. Tepid, disappointing tale of roguish Elliott, approaching old age, who finds himself incarcerated in a home for senile senior citizens. Williams scores as an elderly homosexual bent on reliving his youth.
Pastime (1991) C-94m. **½ D: Robin B. Armstrong. William Russ, Glenn Plummer, Scott Plank, Noble Willingham, Jeffrey Tambor, Dierdre O'Connell, Ricky Paull Goldin. Quiet character study set in the world of minor-league baseball, circa 1957, focusing on a 41-year-old relief pitcher whose platitudes and gung-ho attitude alienate him from his younger, cockier teammates. Well-acted but drowsy little film does manage to catch the ambience of small-time baseball. Real-life major-league greats Ernie Banks, Bob Feller, Harmon Killebrew, Bill Mazeroski, Don Newcombe, and Duke Snider appear in minor roles. Film's climax shot at now-demolished Comiskey Park in Chicago. Aka ONE CUP OF COFFEE. [PG]▼◗●
Past Midnight (1992) C-100m. **½ D: Jan Eliasberg. Rutger Hauer, Natasha Richardson, Clancy Brown, Guy Boyd, Ernie Lively, Tom Wright, Paul Giamatti. Romantic thriller of social worker becoming obsessed with her paroled killer client. Hauer (who's Dutch) and Richardson (who's British) sport pretty fair American accents playing two Oregonians. A theatrical film that premiered on cable TV instead. [R]▼●
Pat and Mike (1952) 95m. *** D: George Cukor. Spencer Tracy, Katharine Hepburn, Aldo Ray, William Ching, Jim Backus, Carl ("Alfalfa") Switzer, Charles Buchinski

(Bronson), William Self, Chuck Connors. Hepburn is Pat, top female athlete; Tracy is Mike, her manager, in pleasing comedy, not up to duo's other films. Ray is good as thick-witted sports star. Written by Ruth Gordon and Garson Kanin; many sports notables appear briefly. Also shown in computer-colored version. ▼○◕

Patch Adams (1998) **C-115m.** **½ D: Tom Shadyac. Robin Williams, Daniel London, Monica Potter, Philip Seymour Hoffman, Bob Gunton, Josef Sommer, Irma P. Hall, Frances Lee McCain, Harve Presnell, Peter Coyote, Michael Jeter, Harold Gould, Ellen Albertini Dow, Richard Kiley, Barry Sha-baka Henley. Pleasant movie based on the true story of a man who wants desperately to be a doctor and help people but rejects the sober protocol of medical school in favor of clowning and making a personal connection with patients. A natural role for Williams if there ever was one but the story, heroes, and villains are all set up a little too obviously for us to derive real satisfaction at the end. Panavision. [PG-13] ▼○◕

Patch of Blue, A (1965) **105m.** *** D: Guy Green. Sidney Poitier, Shelley Winters, Elizabeth Hartman, Wallace Ford, Ivan Dixon, John Qualen, Elisabeth Fraser. Sensitive drama of blind girl (Hartman) falling in love with black man (Poitier); well acted, not too sticky. Winters won Oscar as Hartman's harridan mother. Panavision. ▼○◕

Paternity (1981) **C-94m.** *½ D: David Steinberg. Burt Reynolds, Beverly D'Angelo, Norman Fell, Paul Dooley, Elizabeth Ashley, Lauren Hutton, Juanita Moore, Mike Kellin. Bachelor Burt, the manager of Madison Square Garden, yearns to be a papa, so he hires waitress-music student D'Angelo as surrogate mother. Predictable comedy with lethargic performances. Actor-comic Steinberg's directorial debut. [PG] ▼○

Pat Garrett & Billy the Kid (1973) **C-122m.** **½ D: Sam Peckinpah. James Coburn, Kris Kristofferson, Richard Jaeckel, Katy Jurado, Chill Wills, Jason Robards, Bob Dylan, Rita Coolidge, Jack Elam, R. G. Armstrong, Slim Pickens, Harry Dean Stanton, L. Q. Jones, Barry Sullivan, Elisha Cook, Jr. Revisionist look at Sheriff Garrett (Coburn) and his pursuit of ex-crony Billy the Kid (Kristofferson) is an interesting failure, largely because there isn't enough contrast in the two low-key lead performances. First released in a studio-butchered 106m. version, then revised in 1988 at 122m. A third version (assembled by Paul Seydor for the 2006 DVD) was trimmed back to 115m., reinstating some '73 footage removed in '88. Casual moviegoers may prefer the 2006 version, a balance of tightness and coherency with fleeting bursts of greatness . . . but angry purists will argue forever over the inclusion of Dylan's lyrics to "Knockin' on Heaven's Door" over a major death scene. Panavision. [R] ▼○◕

Pather Panchali (1955-Indian) **112m.** ***½ D: Satyajit Ray. Kanu Banerji, Karuna Banerji, Subir Banerji, Runki Banerji, Uma Das Gupta, Chunibala Devi. Unrelenting study of a poverty-stricken Indian family in Bengal. Grippingly realistic, with Karuna and Subir Banerji outstanding as the mother and her young son Apu. Ray's feature debut and the first of his "Apu" trilogy. Music by Ravi Shankar. ▼○

Pathfinder (1988-Norwegian) **C-88m.** ***½ D: Nils Gaup. Mikkel Gaup, Nils Utsi, Svein Scharffenberg, Helgi Skulason, Sara Marit Gaup, Sverre Porsanger. A teenage boy agrees to lead a group of cutthroats to the hiding place of his fellow villagers, but takes them on a wild goose chase instead. Stunning realization of an ancient folk tale from Lapland is the first film ever made in the Lapp language—and a whale of an adventure, too. Remade in 2007. Panavision. ▼

Pathfinder (2007) **C-99m.** *½ D: Marcus Nispel. Karl Urban, Russell Means, Moon Bloodgood, Clancy Brown, Jay Tavare, Nathaniel Arcand, Ralf Moeller, Kevin Loring. Young Norse boy is left behind after Vikings fight some local Indians. Fifteen years pass as he is brought up by the tribe and then must lead them in a new battle when the bloodthirsty Norsemen return and start slaughtering everyone in their way. Ultra-violent tale puts action ahead of accuracy and doesn't seem to have much of a point other than to show inventive ways heads can be lopped off. Grainy cinematography doesn't help this B movie trying to pass itself off as something more. Gruesome stuff well worth missing. Based on the 1988 Norwegian film. Unrated version runs 107m. Super 35. [R]◕

Pathology (2008) **C-93m.** *½ D: Marc Schoelermann. Milo Ventimiglia, Michael Weston, Alyssa Milano, Lauren Lee Smith, Johnny Whitworth, John de Lancie, Keir O'Donnell, Buddy Lewis, Larry Drake, Dan Callahan, Mei Melançon. Take FLAT-LINERS, add a little SAW, throw in David Cronenberg's CRASH and you have the recipe for this graphic, woefully inadequate horror oddity. A brilliant young pathology intern is sucked into a world of drugs and bizarre sexual practices when his new colleagues enlist his help to commit "perfect murders." Even genre fans might cringe at the slice-and-dice antics and kinky sex. Super 35. [R]◕

Paths of Glory (1957) **86m.** **** D: Stanley Kubrick. Kirk Douglas, Ralph Meeker, Adolphe Menjou, George Macready, Wayne Morris, Richard Anderson, Timothy Carey, Suzanne Christian, Bert Freed. During WW1, French general Macready orders his men on a suicidal charge;

when they fail, he picks three soldiers to be tried and executed for cowardice. Shattering study of the insanity of war has grown even more profound with the years; stunningly acted and directed. Calder Willingham, Jim Thompson, and Kubrick adapted Humphrey Cobb's novel—based on fact. ▼●)

Patrick (1978-Australian) **C-96m.** *½ D: Richard Franklin. Susan Penhaligon, Robert Helpmann, Robert Thompson, Rod Mullinar, Bruce Barry, Julia Blake. Patrick's in a comatose state after violently murdering his mum, but his psychokinetic powers are still intact, as the hospital staff soon discovers in this tacky thriller. [PG] ▼▶

Patriot, The (1986) **C-88m.** *½ D: Frank Harris. Gregg Henry, Simone Griffeth, Michael J. Pollard, Jeff Conaway, Leslie Nielsen, Stack Pierce, Glenn Withrow. Underwater action dominates this low-key action film. Dishonorably discharged Henry is recruited to retrieve a stolen nuclear warhead and redeem himself. [R] ▼●)

Patriot, The (1998) **C-90m.** BOMB D: Dean Semler. Steven Seagal, Gailard Sartain, L.Q. Jones, Camilla Belle, Dan Beene, Ron Andrews. A paunchy, sleepy-eyed Seagal plays a peaceful, bespectacled, pony-tailed Rocky Mountain doctor who's kind to kids, animals, and local Native Americans, but will snap your spine and shove the stem of a wine glass into your skull if he has to. Of course, he's the perfect man to combat a neo-Nazi militia using chemical warfare. Rock bottom, irresponsible star vehicle dumbs down and bloodies up serious subject matter for the yahoo crowd. Premiered in the U.S. on cable. Panavision. [R] ▼▶

Patriot, The (2000) **C-164m.** *** D: Roland Emmerich. Mel Gibson, Heath Ledger, Joely Richardson, Chris Cooper, Jason Isaacs, Tom Wilkinson, Donal Logue, Rene Auberjonois, Tchéky Karyo, Adam Baldwin, Trevor Morgan. A former hero of the French and Indian Wars, widowed with seven children, refuses to fight in the Continental Army in 1776; he's seen the horror of war firsthand and wants to protect his family. But after his eldest son enlists, fate and circumstance force him into the fray. Gibson gives a charismatic performance in this entertaining, old-fashioned period saga, exquisitely filmed (by Caleb Deschanel) in South Carolina. But Robert Rodat's script and Emmerich's direction are too often heavy-handed, especially in their cartoonish treatment of "bad guy" Isaacs. Also available in 175m. version. Super 35. [R] ▼▶

Patriot Games (1992) **C-116m.** *** D: Phillip Noyce. Harrison Ford, Anne Archer, Patrick Bergin, Thora Birch, Sean Bean, Richard Harris, James Earl Jones, James Fox, Samuel L. Jackson, Polly Walker. Edge-of-the-seat thriller has ex-CIA agent Jack Ryan (Ford) intervening in a terrorist attack—inspiring an Irish radical (Bean) to swear

vengeance on him and his family. Ford's an ideal hero in this adaptation of Tom Clancy's book, with Archer and Birch rounding out the kind of family you want to root for—and do. Only the climactic chase doesn't ring true. Alec Baldwin previously played Ryan in THE HUNT FOR RED OCTOBER. Followed by CLEAR AND PRESENT DANGER. Panavision. [R] ▼●)

Patsy, The (1964) **C-101m.** ** D: Jerry Lewis. Jerry Lewis, Ina Balin, Everett Sloane, Keenan Wynn, Peter Lorre, John Carradine, Neil Hamilton, Nancy Kulp. When a top comedian is killed in a plane crash, his sycophants try to groom a bellhop (guess who?) into taking his place. Forced, unfunny combination of humor and pathos, much inferior to somewhat similar ERRAND BOY. Lorre's last film. ▼●)

Patterns (1956) **83m.** ***½ D: Fielder Cook. Van Heflin, Everett Sloane, Ed Begley, Beatrice Straight, Elizabeth Wilson. Trenchant, masterfully acted drama of greed and abuse of power in corporate America, about an all-powerful company head (Sloane) who makes life miserable for humanistic underling Begley. Much better than the similar EXECUTIVE SUITE. Scripted by Rod Serling from his 1956 *Kraft TV Theatre* production (which also starred Sloane and Begley). ▼▶

Patton (1970) **C-169m.** **** D: Franklin Schaffner. George C. Scott, Karl Malden, Stephen Young, Michael Strong, Frank Latimore, James Edwards, Lawrence Dobkin, Michael Bates, Tim Considine. Milestone in screen biographies; Scott unforgettable as eccentric, brilliant General George Patton, whose temper often interferes with his command during WW2. Malden equally impressive as General Omar Bradley in intelligently written, finely wrought biographical war drama. Winner of seven Oscars, including Best Picture, Actor, Director, Screenplay (Francis Ford Coppola and Edmund H. North). Scott reprised the role 16 years later in a TVM, THE LAST DAYS OF PATTON. Dimension-150. [M/PG] ▼●)

Patty Hearst (1988) **C-108m.** *½ D: Paul Schrader. Natasha Richardson, William Forsythe, Ving Rhames, Dana Delany, Frances Fisher, Jodi Long, Olivia Barash. Stillborn dramatization of the newspaper heiress's kidnapping and subsequent brainwashing by the Symbionese Liberation Army. Film never recovers from a deadly opening half hour that attempts to convey, from victim's point of view, the effects of highly orchestrated psychological torture. Richardson makes a strong impression, despite having almost nothing to work with. Screenplay by Nicholas Kazan. [R] ▼●)

Paul (2011-U.S.-French-British) **C-104m.** *** D: Greg Mottola. Simon Pegg, Nick Frost, Kristen Wiig, John Carroll Lynch, Jason Bateman, Jeffrey Tambor, Jane Lynch, Sigourney Weaver, Bill Hader, Joe Lo Truglio, Blythe Danner, David Koechner; voice of Seth Rogen. Two British pals, nerds to the core, set out in a Winnebago to tour famous UFO sites in the U.S. Southwest. Things change drastically when they pick up a little green man from space named Paul (voiced by Rogen). He's been a government captive for 60 years and wants to go home. They're pursued by various agents as they try to get the friendly but sharp-tongued, media-savvy Paul to his rendezvous. Funny, likable fusion of science fiction and road comedy with everyone in good form. Paul seems so real you forget he's a visual effect. There's also a funny, appropriate voice cameo. Written by Pegg and Frost. Super 35. [R] ▶

Paul and Michelle (1974-British) **C-103m.** BOMB D: Lewis Gilbert. Sean Bury, Anicee Alvina, Keir Dullea, Catherine Allegret, Ronald Lewis. Why anyone would even *want* a sequel to FRIENDS requires investigation; further antics of those lovable teeny-boppers have about as much bearing on real life as anything Dullea encountered while going through the 2001 space-warp. [R] ▼

Paul Blart: Mall Cop (2009) **C-91m.** ** D: Steve Carr. Kevin James, Jayma Mays, Keir O'Donnell, Bobby Cannavale, Stephen Rannazzisi, Shirley Knight, Adam Ferrara, Raini Rodriguez, Gary Valentine. Hapless, overweight N.J. mall security guard—who's developed a crush on a cute girl who works at a sales kiosk—steps up to bat when a wily bad guy and his team take over the mall. Straightforward vehicle for the likable James (who cowrote the script) hasn't that many laughs but is innocuous enough to amuse kids and undemanding adults. [PG] ▌

Paulie (1998) **C-91m.** *** D: John Roberts. Gena Rowlands, Tony Shalhoub, Cheech Marin, Bruce Davison, Trini Alvarado, Jay Mohr, Buddy Hackett, Hallie Kate Eisenberg, Matt Craven, Bill Cobbs. Satisfying, enjoyable family film. A caged parrot in the basement of a scientific institution relates his colorful life story—passing from one owner to the next—to a friendly (and lonely) janitor. A sweet-natured film that dares not to be stupid; adults should enjoy it along with their kids. Mohr, who plays the sleazy Benny, is also the voice of Paulie. Written by Laurie Craig. [PG] ▼●

Pauline & Paulette (2001-Belgian-French-Dutch) **C-78m.** ***½ D: Lieven Debrauwer. Dora van der Groen, Ann Petersen, Julienne De Bruyn, Rosemarie Bergmans, Idwig Stephane. Charming, sentimental look at two sisters, the mentally retarded Pauline (van der Groen), and Paulette (Petersen), a charismatic fabric shop owner and amateur opera diva whom Pauline idolizes. When

fate brings the two together under one roof, Paulette tries to shove Pauline out of her life. Winner of five Belgian Plateau Awards, the film features outstanding performances by two legendary Belgian actresses and marks the feature debut of cowriter/director Debrauwer. [PG] ▼▌

Pauline at the Beach (1983-French) **C-94m.** *** D: Eric Rohmer. Amanda Langlet, Arielle Dombasle, Pascal Greggory, Feodor Atkine, Simon de la Brosse, Rosette. Witty, entertaining comedy of morals and manners that contrasts the hypocrisy of adult relationships and the straightforwardness of young people, as seen when a teenage girl (Langlet) spends the summer with her sexy, self-possessed older cousin (Dombasle). The third of Rohmer's "Comedies and Proverbs" series. [R] ▼●

Pavilion of Women (2001-Chinese) **C-119m.** *½ D: Yim Ho. Luo Yan, Willem Dafoe, Shek Sau, John Cho, Yi Ding, Koh Chieng Mun, Anita Loo. Lumbering epic set in 1938 China about free love vs. feudalism. A faithful wife falls for an American priest while her son longs for his father's new concubine. Has the distinction of being the first adaptation of a Pearl S. Buck novel to feature an Asian cast, but its lush production values can't compensate for a soapy script and flat performances. Try not to giggle when a lustful Yan and Dafoe go for a literal roll in the hay. Shot on location in China. [R] ▼▌

Pawnbroker, The (1965) **116m.** **** D: Sidney Lumet. Rod Steiger, Geraldine Fitzgerald, Brock Peters, Jaime Sanchez, Thelma Oliver, Juano Hernandez, Raymond St. Jacques. Important, engrossing film; Steiger is excellent as Sol Nazerman, a Jewish pawnbroker in Harlem who lives in a sheltered world with haunting memories of Nazi prison camps. Notable editing by Ralph Rosenblum and music by Quincy Jones. Edward Lewis Wallant's novel was adapted by David Friedkin and Morton Fine. ▼●

Payback (1999) **C-102m.** *½ D: Brian Helgeland. Mel Gibson, Gregg Henry, Maria Bello, Deborah Kara Unger, David Paymer, Bill Duke, Jack Conley, William Devane, Kris Kristofferson, John Glover, Lucy Alexis Liu. A slick robber is double-crossed and becomes so determined to exact revenge on his betrayer (Henry) and the crime syndicate to which he belongs that he takes on all comers, no matter how great the odds. Brutal story grows more ridiculous with each new plot turn. Based on *The Hunter,* the same Richard Stark (Donald E. Westlake) novel as POINT BLANK. James Coburn appears unbilled. Director's cut runs 90m. Super 35. [R] ▼●

Paycheck (2003) **C-119m.** **½ D: John Woo. Ben Affleck, Uma Thurman, Aaron Eckhart, Paul Giamatti, Colm Feore, Joe

[1064]

Morton, Michael C. Hall. Computer whiz Affleck makes big bucks by regularly solving top-secret problems for companies, then having his memory of the entire operation erased. But when he tackles his biggest job yet, for a giant corporation run by Eckhart, things don't go as planned. As Affleck seeks revenge—and answers—after having three years' worth of memory wiped out, the story line grows more and more outlandish. Slick, entertaining-enough escapism if you're not too demanding. Based on a Philip K. Dick story. Super 35. [PG-13] ▼▶

Payday (1973) **C-103m.** ***½ D: Daryl Duke. Rip Torn, Ahna Capri, Elayne Heilveil, Cliff Emmich, Michael C. Gwynne. Acerbic, colorful portrait of life on the road with a smug, self-centered country music star, a hellion who counts on his manager to "fix" any problems that crop up along the way. Biting, original screenplay by Don Carpenter. One of those prototypical early-1970s movies that make modern American cinema seem bland. [R] ▼▶

Pay It Forward (2000) **C-122m.** ** D: Mimi Leder. Kevin Spacey, Helen Hunt, Haley Joel Osment, Jay Mohr, James Caviezel, Jon Bon Jovi, Angie Dickinson. A teacher assigns his students to do something to change the world, which inspires Osment to help three people, unselfishly. His mom, a single parent with a drinking problem, doesn't understand her son's actions until she meets the teacher—and a romance is kindled. Well-meaning film doesn't deliver on its very real promise; the conclusion is especially unsatisfying. Osment is exceptional. Based on a novel by Catherine Ryan Hyde. [PG-13] ▼▶

Payment on Demand (1951) **90m.** *** D: Curtis Bernhardt. Bette Davis, Barry Sullivan, Peggie Castle, Jane Cowl, Kent Taylor, Betty Lynn, John Sutton, Frances Dee, Otto Kruger. Well-handled chronicle of Davis-Sullivan marriage, highlighting events which lead to divorce. ▶

PCU (1994) **C-80m.** ** D: Hart Bochner. Jeremy Piven, Chris Young, David Spade, Megan Ward, Jon Favreau, Jessica Walter, Sarah Trigger, Jake Busey, George Clinton and Parliament Funkadelic. Political correctness is out of control at Port Chester University which leads to the inevitable clash between a cadre of overly militant student groups and a coed group of dormies who revel in their political incorrectness. This campus comedy gets failing grades. [PG-13] ▼●▶

Peaceful Warrior (2006-U.S.-German) **C-120m.** **½ D: Victor Salva. Nick Nolte, Scott Mechlowicz, Amy Smart, Tim DeKay, Paul Wesley, Ashton Holmes, Agnes Bruckner, Bart Conner, Ray Wise. An arrogant Berkeley gymnast with an eye on the Olympics crashes his motorcycle, ruining his leg and his life. Coached and rewired by a grizzled—and maddeningly nameless—

service station mechanic-cum-guru, he learns to overcome himself and live in the Now. Metaphysical KARATE KID is a faithful adaptation of Dan Millman's 1980 semiautobiographical novel, but it's unapologetically crammed with platitudes. Not a movie for people who like things explained. Panavision. [PG-13] ▶

Peacemaker (1990) **C-90m.** ** D: Kevin S. Tenney. Robert Forster, Lance Edwards, Hilary Shepard, Robert Davi, Bert Remsen. Yet another alien cop after alien villain movie, pitting Forster against Edwards, with novel twist: both claim to be the cop, causing Earthwoman Shepard any number of problems. Lots of stunts and action, but also lots of absolutely awful wisecracks. Written by the director. [R] ▼●

Peacemaker, The (1997) **C-123m.** **½ D: Mimi Leder. George Clooney, Nicole Kidman, Armin Mueller-Stahl, Marcel Iures, Alexander Baluev, Rene Medvesek, Gary Werntz, Randall Batinkoff, Michael Boatman. A nuclear explosion in Russia—which turns out to be a terrorist act—triggers immediate response by a U.S. government troubleshooter team led by an inexperienced Kidman and a cocky, shoot-from-the-hip field agent (Clooney). Good action scenes are set in the midst of a confusing, barely believable yarn, which yields diminishing results as one climax after another piles up. Super 35. [R] ▼●▶

Peacock (2010) **C-91m.** *½ D: Michael Lander. Cillian Murphy, Ellen Page, Susan Sarandon, Josh Lucas, Bill Pullman, Graham Beckel, Keith Carradine. Strange, nearly hermetic bank clerk in the small town of Peacock, Nebraska, hides a dark secret: He lives a double life, going to work every day, then transforming himself into his late mother within the confines of his house. But when he's accidentally seen in his female guise one day the townspeople assume "she" is the young man's wife—and respond to her as they never have to him. Tedious (and obvious) drama grows more tiresome as it goes along. No wonder this went direct to DVD. [PG-13] ▶

Pearl Harbor (2001) **C-183m.** **½ D: Michael Bay. Ben Affleck, Josh Hartnett, Kate Beckinsale, Cuba Gooding, Jr., Alec Baldwin, Jon Voight, Mako, Tom Sizemore, Dan Aykroyd, Colm Feore, James King, Ewen Bremner, William Lee Scott, Michael Shannon, Catherine Kellner, Cary-Hiroyuki Tagawa, Scott Wilson, Jennifer Garner. Part old-fashioned silver-screen romance, part boys' adventure, part massive re-creation of December 7, 1941: a big Hollywood movie. Occasional silliness and anticlimactic rendering of Doolittle's raid on Tokyo are offset by thrilling (and horrifying) depiction of the infamous bombing attack on Pearl. Oscar winner for Sound Editing. R-rated director's cut runs 184m. Panavision. [PG-13] ▼▶

Pebble and the Penguin, The (1995-U.S.-Irish) **C-74m.** *½ No director credited. Voices of Martin Short, James Belushi, Tim Curry, Annie Golden, Angelyne Ball, B.J. Ward, Hamilton Camp, Will Ryan; narrated by Shani Wallis. Nice-guy penguin ends up on an aquatic globe-trotting odyssey with a gruff sidekick named Rocko, all for the love of a lady who's coveted by an evil penguin rival. Some movies have the smell of doom all over them; this animated feature for kids from the Don Bluth studio (with songs by Barry Manilow) is one of them. [G] ▼●🅻

Pecker (1998) **C-87m.** *** D: John Waters. Edward Furlong, Christina Ricci, Lili Taylor, Mary Kay Place, Martha Plimpton, Brendan Sexton III, Patricia Hearst, Jean Schertler, Bess Armstrong, Mink Stole. Pecker (Furlong) is a happy-go-lucky guy who loves taking pictures of life as he sees it. When a N.Y.C. art gallery owner "discovers" his work and he's embraced by the art scene, he loses his anonymity and many of his most cherished friendships. Another slice of Baltimore life from Waters, perhaps his cheeriest yet, with doggedly likable characters in some of the unlikeliest settings. [R] ▼●🅻

Pedestrian, The (1974-German) **C-97m.** ***½ D: Maximilian Schell. Gustav Rudolf Sellner, Peter Hall, Maximilian Schell, Gila von Weitershausen. Excellent award-winner examines death and guilt, when successful industrialist Sellner is revealed to have been a Nazi officer who participated in the slaughter of a Greek village. Veteran actresses Elisabeth Bergner, Françoise Rosay, Lil Dagover and Peggy Ashcroft appear in one scene. [PG] ▼

Peeper (1975) **C-87m.** *½ D: Peter Hyams. Michael Caine, Natalie Wood, Kitty Winn, Thayer David, Liam Dunn, Dorothy Adams. Tepid take-off of '40s detective dramas with Caine becoming involved with a weird family while trying to locate the long-lost daughter of his client. Best bit: the opening credits, recited by Bogart impersonator Guy Marks. Aka FAT CHANCE. Panavision. [PG]🅳

Peeping Tom (1960-British) **C-101m.** *** D: Michael Powell. Carl Boehm, Moira Shearer, Anna Massey, Maxine Audley, Brenda Bruce, Martin Miller. Sensational film—denounced in 1960—went on to develop a fervent following; personal feelings will dictate your reaction to story of psychopathic murderer who photographs his victims at the moment of death. Originally released in the U.S. at 86m. Director Powell plays the father of Boehm in the home-movie sequences. ▼●🅻

Peep World (2011) **C-79m.** *½ D: Barry W. Blaustein. Michael C. Hall, Sarah Silverman, Rainn Wilson, Ben Schwartz, Judy Greer, Taraji P. Henson, Ron Rifkin, Kate Mara, Lesley Ann Warren, Alicia Witt, Stephen Tobolowsky; narrated by Lewis Black. On the day of his 70th birthday dinner, we meet the offspring of a much-unloved patriarch (Rifkin). Three siblings feel they have been betrayed by their youngest brother (Schwartz), who has written a best-selling novel based on the family's dirty laundry. Impressive cast is wasted in this obvious, obnoxious comedy. HD Widescreen. 🅳

Pee-wee's Big Adventure (1985) **C-90m.** **½ D: Tim Burton. Pee-wee Herman (Paul Reubens), Elizabeth Daily, Mark Holton, Diane Salinger, Tony Bill, Cassandra Peterson, James Brolin, Morgan Fairchild, Jan Hooks, Phil Hartman. A live-action cartoon (directed by former animator Burton) featuring the cartoonish Pee-wee, a nine-year-old boy in a grown-up's body. Some real laughs and clever ideas as Pee-wee searches for his stolen bicycle, but not enough to sustain a feature-length film. Best sequence: the tour of the Alamo. Wonderful music by Danny Elfman. [PG] ▼●🅻

Peggy Sue Got Married (1986) **C-104m.** **½ D: Francis Coppola. Kathleen Turner, Nicolas Cage, Barry Miller, Catherine Hicks, Joan Allen, Kevin J. O'Connor, Jim Carrey, Lisa Jane Persky, Barbara Harris, Don Murray, Maureen O'Sullivan, Leon Ames, Helen Hunt, John Carradine, Sofia Coppola, Sachi Parker. 43-year-old woman, on the verge of divorce, magically travels back in time to her senior year in high school and has to deal with (among other things) her boyfriend and future husband. Turner's radiant star power bolsters this pleasant, often wistful film, whose script leaves far too many plot threads dangling. Cage's annoying performance as the boyfriend is another debit. [PG-13] ▼●🅻

Peking Opera Blues (1986-Hong Kong) **C-104m.** ***½ D: Tsui Hark. Lin Ching-Hsia, Sally Yeh, Cherie Chung, Mark Cheng, Po-chih Leong. Marvelously entertaining adventure yarn, set in 1913 China, which follows three women who become entangled with revolutionary guerrillas. Dazzling mix of comedy, drama, action, and incredible stunts, all set at a breathless pace by Hark. Proves you can make 'em like they used to, but not (perhaps) in America. ▼🅻

Pelican Brief, The (1993) **C-141m.** *** D: Alan J. Pakula. Julia Roberts, Denzel Washington, Sam Shepard, John Heard, Tony Goldwyn, James B. Sikking, William Atherton, Robert Culp, Stanley Tucci, Hume Cronyn, John Lithgow, Anthony Heald, Cynthia Nixon, Jake Weber. Entertaining thriller based on John Grisham's best-selling book about a law student whose theory (or brief) about the conspiracy behind the assassination of two Supreme Court justices places her in jeopardy. The only person who can help her: investigative reporter Washington. Well cast (with Julia a perfect pick for the lead) and well crafted, though the suspense starts to peter out toward the finish. Panavision. [PG-13]▼●▶

Pelle the Conqueror (1988-Danish-Swedish) **C-150m.** ***½ D: Bille August. Max von Sydow, Pelle Hvenegaard, Erik Paaske, Kristina Törnqvist, Morten Jorgensen. Wonderful 19th-century drama about a humble old widower (von Sydow) and his young son Pelle (Hvenegaard), Swedish immigrants in Denmark. They are simple folk with simple, modest dreams, yet they must valiantly struggle for survival in a world rife with everyday cruelties and injustices. The life-sustaining closeness between father and son is especially poignant. Martin Andersen Nexo's four-volume novel (only a fraction of which is depicted here) was adapted by the director. Oscar winner as Best Foreign Film. [PG-13]▼●▶

Pendulum (1969) **C-106m.** **½ D: George Schaefer. George Peppard, Jean Seberg, Richard Kiley, Charles McGraw, Madeleine Sherwood, Robert F. Lyons, Marj Dusay, Isabel Sanford, Dana Elcar. Half-baked whodunit has intriguing aspects but leaves too many loose ends, as police captain Peppard is suddenly accused of murder. Smoothly done, with flashy role for Sherwood as mother of young criminal, good score by Walter Scharf, but no great shakes. [M]▼●

Penelope (1966) **C-97m.** *½ D: Arthur Hiller. Natalie Wood, Ian Bannen, Dick Shawn, Peter Falk, Jonathan Winters, Lila Kedrova, Lou Jacobi, Jerome Cowan. Neglected Nat robs her husband's bank of $60,000 in this quite unfunny comedy; Winters' bit lasts only three minutes. Panavision.

Penelope (2008-U.S.-British) **C-103m.** *** D: Mark Palansky. Christina Ricci, James McAvoy, Catherine O'Hara, Peter Dinklage, Richard E. Grant, Reese Witherspoon, Simon Woods, Ronni Ancona, Russell Brand. Modern-day fairy tale about a girl who—due to an ancient family curse—is born with a pig snout for a nose. Her mother—afraid of scandal and humiliation—raises her in isolation. Now, at age 28, she interviews prospective husbands, who will receive a handsome dowry if they can stand looking at Penelope. Slim but funny and sweet, for noncynics and the young at heart. Clearly filmed in England with a mixed cast of Americans and Brits doing U.S. accents. Witherspoon (who coproduced) has a small role as a street-savvy woman who befriends Penelope. Super 35. [PG]▶

Penitentiary (1979) **C-99m.** **½ D: Jamaa Fanaka. Leon Isaac Kennedy, Thommy Pollard, Hazel Spears, Badja Djola, Gloria Delaney, Chuck Mitchell. Predictable but impassioned prison film, produced, directed and written by Fanaka, about a young black man (Kennedy) wrongly accused and imprisoned who improves his lot by boxing. Hard-hitting look at corruption, violence and homosexuality of daily prison life. Followed by several sequels. [R]▼▶

Penitentiary II (1982) **C-103m.** BOMB D: Jamaa Fanaka. Leon Isaac Kennedy, Ernie Hudson, Mr. T., Glynn Turman, Peggy Blow, Malik Carter, Cephaus Jaxon, Marvin Jones. Atrocious, disappointing sequel, with Kennedy back in prison and the ring. Leon Isaac plays "Too Sweet," the villain's name is "Half Dead," the viewer is "Ripped Off." [R]▼▶

Penitentiary III (1987) **C-91m.** *½ D: Jamaa Fanaka. Leon Isaac Kennedy, Anthony Geary, Steve Antin, Ric Mancini, Kessler Raymond, Jim Bailey. An improvement over number II—but that's not saying very much. Here, Kennedy is back in jail, where both warden and mob kingpin want him for their boxing teams. Silly and mindless time killer. [R]▼

Penn & Teller Get Killed (1989) **C-90m.** ** D: Arthur Penn. Penn Jillette, Teller, Caitlin Clarke, David Patrick Kelly, Jon Cryer, Christopher Durang, Leonardo Cimino, Celia McGuire. The bad boys of magic, guesting on a nationally televised talk show, touch off gore galore when partner Penn speculates how much fun life might be if some viewer would attempt to kill him. Barely released effort does have the courage of some sicko comic convictions. [R]▼●

Pennies From Heaven (1981) **C-107m.** *** D: Herbert Ross. Steve Martin, Bernadette Peters, Christopher Walken, Jessica Harper, Vernel Bagneris, John McMartin, Jay Garner, Tommy Rall. A unique, remarkable film, parts of which are greater than the whole. Dennis Potter adapted his own British TV miniseries about a sheet-music salesman during the Depression whose restless, unhappy life is sharply contrasted with cheery songs of the day. Stunning 1930s-style musical numbers (set to original recordings) clash with bleak, Edward Hopper–esque vision of the period. The mixture is intellectually provocative, but troubling as entertainment. Beautifully photographed by Gordon Willis and designed by Ken Adam. [R]▼●

Penny Serenade (1941) **118m.** ***½ D: George Stevens. Irene Dunne, Cary Grant, Beulah Bondi, Edgar Buchanan, Ann Doran, Eva Lee Kuney. Quintessential soap opera, with Dunne and Grant as couple who adopt baby after their unborn baby dies. A wonderful tearjerker; scripted by Morrie Ryskind, from Martha Cheavens' story. Also shown in computer-colored version. ▼●

People Against O'Hara, The (1951) **102m.** **½ D: John Sturges. Spencer Tracy, Pat O'Brien, Diana Lynn, John Hodiak, Eduardo Ciannelli, Jay C. Flippen, James Arness, Arthur Shields, William Campbell. Middling drama, with Tracy a noted criminal lawyer who repents for unethical behavior during a case. Look fast for Charles Bronson as one of Campbell's brothers.●

People I Know (2003) **C-95m.** *½ D: Dan Algrant. Al Pacino, Ryan O'Neal, Kim Basinger, Téa Leoni, Richard Schiff, Robert Klein, Bill Nunn, Mark Webber, Paulina Porizkova, Andrew Davoli, David Marshall Grant, Jon Hendricks. Tedious portrait of a once-powerful N.Y.C. press agent who's operating on fumes, with one remaining client, movie star O'Neal, who has him do his dirty work. Story lurches into unexpected territory as Pacino steps on the wrong toes in a world where high-level politics and show business collide. Even Pacino can't bring life to this film. Scripted by playwright Jon Robin Baitz. Completed in 2001. [R]▶

People Next Door, The (1970) **C-93m.** ** D: David Greene. Deborah Winters, Eli Wallach, Julie Harris, Stephen McHattie, Hal Holbrook, Cloris Leachman, Rue McClanahan, Nehemiah Persoff. JP Miller's adaptation of his TV play has dated pretty badly; Wallach and Harris' hand-wringing concern over their junkie teenage daughter now seems stiff, and Winters' overacting just the opposite. Good cast and intentions, but there are many other, better films on the topic. [R]▼

People That Time Forgot, The (1977-British) **C-90m.** **½ D: Kevin Connor. Patrick Wayne, Doug McClure, Sarah Douglas, Dana Gillespie, Thorley Walters, Shane Rimmer. OK sequel to THE LAND THAT TIME FORGOT. Wayne leads a party back to mysterious island in 1919 to find friend McClure, lost three years before. Based on Edgar Rice Burroughs' book, film has some pretty fierce monsters, though special effects are erratic. [PG]▼▶

People Under the Stairs, The (1991) **C-102m.** *½ D: Wes Craven. Brandon Adams, Everett McGill, Wendy Robie, A. J. Langer, Ving Rhames, Sean Whalen. Hoping to help his ailing mother and prevent their eviction from a ghetto slum, 13-year-old Adams finds himself trapped in the bizarre home of their insane, murderous landlords, McGill and Robie. Very strange horror movie (with occasional comedy touches) turns out to be a social parable about the exploitation of the Have-Nots by the Haves. Ambitious but extremely uneven. [R]▼●▶

People Vs. Larry Flynt, The (1996) **C-127m.** ***½ D: Milos Forman. Woody Harrelson, Courtney Love, Edward Norton, Brett Harrelson, Donna Hanover, James Cromwell, Crispin Glover, Vincent Schiavelli, James Carville, Richard Paul, Oliver Reed, Miles Chapin. Engrossing saga of an unlikely American "hero": controversial, self-proclaimed smut peddler Larry Flynt, who starts *Hustler* magazine in the 1970s and quickly discovers that he must fight for freedom of speech in order to keep it on the news-

stands. Harrelson is perfect as the mercurial, unpredictable publisher, Love is just right as his loyal but unconventional wife, and Norton is excellent as his long-suffering lawyer. Climactic showdown at the Supreme Court is a dramatic powerhouse. Screenplay by Scott Alexander and Larry Karaszewski. The real Flynt appears briefly as a Cincinnati judge. Panavision. [R]▼●▶

People Will Talk (1951) **110m.** ***½ D: Joseph L. Mankiewicz. Cary Grant, Jeanne Crain, Finlay Currie, Walter Slezak, Hume Cronyn, Sidney Blackmer, Margaret Hamilton. Genuinely offbeat, absorbing comedy-drama of philosophical doctor Grant, who insists on treating his patients as human beings; a small-minded colleague (Cronyn) is intimidated by his radical approach to doctoring and sets out to defame him. Fine cast in talky but most worthwhile film, which features obvious parallels to the then-current HUAC investigation and McCarthy witchhunt.▼▶

Pepe (1960) **C-157m.** BOMB D: George Sidney. Cantinflas, Dan Dailey, Shirley Jones, 35 guest stars. Incredibly long, pointless film wastes talents of Cantinflas and many, many others (Edward G. Robinson, Maurice Chevalier, etc.). This one's only if you're desperate. Originally released at 195m. CinemaScope.

Pepe Le Moko (1937-French) **95m.** **** D: Julien Duvivier. Jean Gabin, Mireille Balin, Gabriel Gabrio, Lucas Gridoux. Gabin is magnetic (in role that brought him international prominence) as gangster who eludes capture in Casbah section of Algiers, until he is lured out of hiding by a beautiful woman. Exquisitely photographed and directed; faithfully remade the following year as ALGIERS, later musicalized as CASBAH. 9m. originally cut from U.S. release have now been restored. ▼▶

Pepi, Luci, Bom (1980-Spanish) **C-80m.** *½ D: Pedro Almodóvar. Carmen Maura, Felix Rotaeta, Olvido Gara, Eva Siva. Almodóvar's initial feature is the story of Pepi (Maura), an heiress/rape victim who becomes an advertising executive; meanwhile, housewife Luci (Siva), whose husband had raped Pepi, leaves him and commences a lesbian relationship with Bom (Gara), a rock singer. Raunchy and outrageous, but poorly made and devoid of laughs. Aka PEPI, LUCI, BOM AND THE OTHER GIRLS and PEPI, LUCI, BOM AND OTHER GIRLS LIKE MOM.▼

Peppermint Soda (1977-French) **C-97m.** *** D: Diane Kurys. Eleanore Klarwein, Odile Michel, Coralie Clement, Marie-Veronique Maurin. Sensitive, keenly realized autobiographical (by Kurys, who also scripted) examination of early adolescence, complete with disciplinarian teacher, parents' divorce, menstrual cramps, first love. Followed by COCKTAIL MOLOTOV;

same theme reworked by Kurys 13 years later in C'EST LA VIE. [PG]▼

Percy (1971-British) **C-100m.** *½ D: Ralph Thomas. Hywel Bennett, Denholm Elliott, Elke Sommer, Britt Ekland, Cyd Hayman, Janet Key. Bennett receives the world's first penis transplant and, curious, sets out to learn about its previous owner. Some interesting points could've been made, but Thomas apparently thought he was making a *Carry On* film; too bad. Followed by PERCY'S PROGRESS. [R]▼❱

Percy Jackson & the Olympians: The Lightning Thief (2010-U.S.-Canadian) **C-119m.** ** D: Chris Columbus. Logan Lerman, Brandon T. Jackson, Alexandra Daddario, Jake Abel, Sean Bean, Pierce Brosnan, Steve Coogan, Rosario Dawson, Melina Kanakaredes, Catherine Keener, Kevin McKidd, Joe Pantoliano, Uma Thurman. High school student Percy Jackson (Lerman), living in the present day, is in for quite a shock as he learns that he is the son of Poseidon. He's also a demigod, and Zeus accuses him of pilfering a lighting bolt. Jumbled, plot-heavy *Harry Potter*-ish adventure based on *The Lightning Thief*, a novel in Rick Riordan's *Percy Jackson & the Olympians* series. Preteen fans of the books may be disappointed that Percy's age has been upped from 12 to 17. Super 35. [PG]❱

Percy's Progress SEE: **It's Not the Size That Counts**

Perez Family, The (1995) **C-112m.** **½ D: Mira Nair. Marisa Tomei, Anjelica Huston, Alfred Molina, Chazz Palminteri, Trini Alvarado, Celia Cruz, Diego Wallraff, Angela Lanza, Ranjit Chowdhry, Ellen Cleghorne, Jose Felipe Padron, Lazaro Perez, Vincent Gallo. Cuban plantation owner, imprisoned for 20 years, is finally released in 1980 and allowed to join the boat migration to Florida, where he yearns to see his wife and daughter; along the way he meets a fiery young woman who has no ties but longs for a better life in America. Meandering comedy-drama has some pleasant and poignant moments, but never quite takes off. Strongest asset: Tomei's strong, sexy (and convincing) performance. Adapted by Robin Swicord from Christine Bell's novel. [R]▼❶❱

Perfect (1985) **C-120m.** *½ D: James Bridges. John Travolta, Jamie Lee Curtis, Jann Wenner, Anne De Salvo, Stefan Gierasch, Laraine Newman, Marilu Henner, David Paymer. *Rolling Stone* reporter Travolta is writing an exposé of L.A. health clubs but finds himself attracted to aerobics instructor Curtis, whom he's about to trash in print. A smug, overlong, misguided, miscast movie, with hints of intelligent intentions; written by Bridges and reporter Aaron Latham. Real-life *Rolling Stone* editor Wenner plays himself. Wait till you hear

John and Jamie Lee expound on Emersonian values! Panavision. [R]▼●❱

Perfect Couple, A (1979) **C-110m.** *** D: Robert Altman. Paul Dooley, Marta Heflin, Titos Vandis, Belita Moreno, Henry Gibson, Dimitra Arliss, Alan Nicholls, Ted Neeley. Offbeat but endearing romantic comedy about unlikely match-up (by computer dating) of straitlaced Dooley, under the thumb of his overbearing father, and singer Heflin, whose life is wrapped up with her familial rock group. Enjoyable music by Neeley's *ad hoc* group Keepin' 'em Off the Streets. [PG]❱

Perfect Friday (1970-British) **94m.** *** D: Peter Hall. Stanley Baker, Ursula Andress, David Warner, Patience Collier, T.P. McKenna. Staid bank employee Baker decides to break loose, and plans daring heist, with beautiful Andress and her oddball husband Warner in cahoots. Entertaining caper movie with some delicious twists. [R]

Perfect Furlough, The (1958) **C-93m.** **½ D: Blake Edwards. Tony Curtis, Janet Leigh, Keenan Wynn, Linda Cristal, Elaine Stritch, King Donovan, Troy Donahue. Diverting comedy of soldier Curtis winning trip to France, romancing military psychiatrist Leigh. CinemaScope.▼❱

Perfect Getaway, A (2009) **C-97m.** *** D: David Twohy. Steve Zahn, Timothy Olyphant, Milla Jovovich, Kiele Sanchez, Marley Shelton, Chris Hemsworth. Honeymooning couple Zahn and Jovovich decide to hike a scenic but difficult trail on Kauai. With some misgivings, they join hitchhikers Olyphant and Sanchez, and also encounter a more experienced third couple. However, news of a murderous pair of visitors to Hawaii soon leads everyone to suspect everyone else. Well-made, unpretentious thriller delivers the goods with plenty of laughs, scares, and surprises. Mostly shot in Puerto Rico rather than Hawaii; wherever, the scenery is gorgeous, almost a character itself. Also available in unrated 108m. version. Super 35. [R]❱

Perfect Holiday, The (2007) **C-96m.** ** D: Lance Rivera. Morris Chestnut, Gabrielle Union, Queen Latifah, Terrence Howard, Malik Hammond, Charlie Murphy, Khail Bryant, Faizon Love. Lightweight romantic comedy with fantasy overtones, about a divorced mom (Union) whose young daughter (Bryant) helps her connect with Mr. Right—a would-be songwriter (Chestnut) working as a department-store Santa—just in time for Christmas. Murphy (Eddie's real-life brother) is a hoot as Union's ex-husband, a flamboyant rap singer. Super 35. [PG]❱

Perfectly Normal (1990-Canadian-British) **C-106m.** ** D: Yves Simoneau. Robbie Coltrane, Michael Riley, Deborah Duchene, Kenneth Welsh, Eugene Lipinski.

Slight, peculiar comedy about "perfectly normal" guy (Riley) who meets obnoxious restaurateur (Coltrane) with a shady past. Using Riley's inheritance, they open an Italian bistro where the waiters sing opera. Mild farce is too sluggish and awkward. Cowritten by Lipinski. Inventive photography by Alain Dostie. Video version runs 106m. [R]▼

Perfect Man, The (2005) C-100m. BOMB D: Mark Rosman. Hilary Duff, Heather Locklear, Chris Noth, Mike O'Malley, Caroline Rhea, Carson Kressley, Dennis DeYoung, Aria Wallace, Vanessa Lengies, Ben Feldman. With a cast of TV stalwarts, including teen pop star Duff, this treacly romantic comedy may find an audience on the small screen, but even the most undemanding viewer might prefer having dental work to sitting through this not-so-perfect movie. Hackneyed plot finds Duff inventing the so-called perfect guy for her loser-in-love mom. When the plan works, she has to produce the mythical hunk and, well, let the hi-jinks begin! [PG]▼🄿

Perfect Murder, A (1998) C-105m. *** D: Andrew Davis. Michael Douglas, Gwyneth Paltrow, Viggo Mortensen, David Suchet, Sarita Choudhury, Constance Towers, Novella Nelson. Entertaining suspense yarn which adds a few interesting twists to DIAL M FOR MURDER. Douglas is the cold-blooded husband who hires someone to kill his wife—but this time, the man he hires is her lover! The stars are perfectly cast, and the story unfolds in slick and skillful fashion. Paltrow is a perfect '90s stand-in for Grace Kelly. [R]▼🄾🄳

Perfect Score, The (2004) C-97m. ** D: Brian Robbins. Chris Evans, Erika Christensen, Bryan Greenberg, Scarlett Johansson, Darius Miles, Leonardo Nam, Matthew Lillard. A perfect heist is the plan hatched by six high school seniors looking to steal the answers to the upcoming SAT. How fortunate the corporate headquarters of the Educational Testing Service is located in their hometown! John Hughes' films of the '80s did teen-angst comedy better, although ringleader Evans underplays admirably. Real-life NBA star Miles has a role that mirrors his own career. [PG-13]▼🄿

Perfect Storm, The (2000) C-129m. **½ D: Wolfgang Petersen. George Clooney, Mark Wahlberg, John C. Reilly, Diane Lane, William Fichtner, John Hawkes, Allen Payne, Mary Elizabeth Mastrantonio, Karen Allen, Cherry Jones, Bob Gunton, Christopher McDonald, Michael Ironside. Hard-luck skipper of a Gloucester, Mass., fishing boat rousts his crew on short notice to go for a big haul . . . just as three brutal storms converge off the coast. Adaptation of Sebastian Junger's best-selling book inspired by the real-life 1991 "storm of the century" is drenched with special effects

and noisy, exciting seagoing action, but its characters and story points are bathed in cliché. Panavision. [PG-13]▼🄿

Perfect Stranger (2007) C-109m. ** D: James Foley. Halle Berry, Bruce Willis, Giovanni Ribisi, Richard Portnow, Gary Dourdan, Florencia Lozano, Nicki Aycox, Kathleen Chalfant, Gordon MacDonald, Daniella Van Graas, Paula Miranda, Patti D'Arbanville, Clea Lewis. Muckraking undercover reporter Berry, frustrated by a setback on a major story, takes on a more personal investigation after a girlhood friend of hers is murdered. Her high-tech pal Ribisi helps trace e-mails that point to high-profile ad exec Willis as a likely suspect, so Berry gets a job working for him, hoping to get close. She does. Slick thriller gets sicker as it goes along, leading up to a revelation you can't see coming—because it doesn't make much sense. The camera makes love to Berry in this one. Super 35. [R]🄿

Perfect Strangers (1945) SEE: **Vacation From Marriage**

Perfect Weapon, The (1991) C-85m. *½ D: Mark DiSalle. Jeff Speakman, John Dye, Mako, James Hong, Mariska Hargitay, Dante Basco, Seth Sakai. The Korean mob makes a very stupid move: they kill the Asian mentor of an American "weapon" with revenge on his mind. Indistinguishable from other martial-arts/vengeance sagas, which is certainly the least of its problems; to keep things simple, Speakman's character (a loner) is named Jeff. [R]▼🄾

Perfect World, A (1993) C-137m. ** D: Clint Eastwood. Kevin Costner, Clint Eastwood, Laura Dern, T. J. Lowther, Keith Szarabajka, Leo Burmester, Paul Hewitt, Bradley Whitford, Ray McKinnon, Jennifer Griffin, Bruce McGill. A prison escapee (Costner) in 1963 Texas takes young boy along with him as hostage, though they quickly build a relationship; meanwhile, an iconoclastic Texas Ranger (Eastwood) tries to pick up the convict's trail. Something new in screen entertainment: A manhunt movie with no urgency and no suspense. In its place are some interesting character vignettes and a lot of moral ambiguity. Costner, however, is commanding, in an unusually forceful performance. Panavision. [PG-13]▼🄾🄳

Performance (1970-British) C-105m. *** D: Donald Cammell, Nicolas Roeg. James Fox, Mick Jagger, Anita Pallenberg, Michele Breton, Ann Sidney, John Burdon. Psychological melodrama about criminal on the lam hiding out with rock performer, and how their lives intertwine. Not for all tastes, but a bizarre and unique film; Jagger's performance of "Memo from Turner" a highlight. [R—edited from original X rating]▼🄾🄳

Perfumed Nightmare, The (1977-Filipino) C-93m. ***½ D: Kidlat Tahimik. Kidlat Tahimik, Dolores Santamaria, Georgette Baudry, Katrin Muller, Harmut Lerch. Surreal, whimsical, thoroughly original fable of an idealistic young Filipino (played by the director), fascinated by American culture and technology, and his awakening to the disadvantages of "progress" while in Paris. Crammed with striking images and a dazzling soundtrack.▼

Perfume: The Story of a Murderer (2006-German-French-Spanish) **C-147m.** **½ D: Tom Tykwer. Ben Whishaw, Dustin Hoffman, Alan Rickman, Rachel Hurd-Wood, Karoline Herfurth, David Calder, Simon Chandler, Sian Thomas, Jessica Schwarz, Corinna Harfouch; narrated by John Hurt. In 18th-century France, a mistreated foundling has a wretched childhood. As an adult his amazing sense of smell leads him to work for an Italian perfumer (Hoffman), then to strange adventures as he obsessively tries to create the ultimate scent. Unfortunately, this requires the murders of a series of women for their aromatic essence. Strange not-quite-horror movie manages to be both passionate and remote, engrossing and uninvolving, as the lead character is impossible to identify with. Lavishly produced. From a novel by Patrick Süskind. Super 35. [R]❿

Perils of Gwendoline in the Land of the Yik Yak, The (1984-French) **C-88m.** BOMB D: Just Jaeckin. Tawny Kitaen, Brent Huff, Zabou, Bernadette Lafont, Jean Rougerie. Idiotic adaptation of erotic French comic strip, seemingly a RAIDERS OF THE LOST ARK spoof, with virginal Kitaen searching for her long-lost dad. Lots of nudity, little else. Alternate director's cut, called GWENDOLINE, runs 105m. Panavision. [R]▼●❿

Perils of Pauline, The (1947) **C-96m.** *** D: George Marshall. Betty Hutton, John Lund, Constance Collier, Billy de Wolfe, William Demarest. Lively, entertaining musical-comedy purports to be biography of silent-screen heroine Pearl White, but isn't; energetic Hutton, good Frank Loesser songs, colorful atmosphere, and presence of silent-film veterans make up for it . . . until sappy denouement.▼❿

Perils of Pauline, The (1967) **C-99m.** ** D: Herbert Leonard, Joshua Shelley. Pamela Austin, Pat Boone, Terry-Thomas, Edward Everett Horton, Hamilton Camp. Cutesy expanded TV pilot. Boone travels the globe seeking childhood sweetheart Austin; overlong, mainly for kids.

Period of Adjustment (1962) **112m.** *** D: George Roy Hill. Tony Franciosa, Jane Fonda, Jim Hutton, Lois Nettleton, John McGiver, Jack Albertson. Newlyweds (Fonda and Hutton) try to help troubled marriage of Nettleton and Franciosa, in this heartwarming comedy based on a Tennessee Williams play. Engaging performers make the most of both comic and tender moments.▼

Permanent Midnight (1998) **C-85m.** **½ D: David Veloz. Ben Stiller, Elizabeth Hurley, Maria Bello, Owen Wilson, Lourdes Benedicto, Peter Greene, Cheryl Ladd, Fred Willard, Charles Fleischer, Janeane Garofalo, Connie Nielsen, Sandra Oh. Adequate film of TV writer Jerry Stahl's drug-abuse–packed memoirs, showing how—for a while—he was able to maintain professional productivity while making a fool of himself at parties and acting irresponsibly toward the British woman he marries (Hurley) so she can obtain a U.S. visa. Bello plays the hotel bedmate to whom he unloads his past in the subplot that frames the story, and Stahl himself appears as a doctor. Inevitably episodic. [R]▼●❿

Permanent Record (1988) **C-91m.** *** D: Marisa Silver. Alan Boyce, Keanu Reeves, Michelle Meyrink, Jennifer Rubin, Pamela Gidley, Michael Elgart, Richard Bradford, Barry Corbin, Kathy Baker. Teen drama packs a wallop in tale of model student Boyce whose unexpected suicide throws high school classmates and officials into turmoil: if he went that route, who's safe? Subtle treatment by Silver of a pressing social problem, aided by excellent cast, especially Reeves as Boyce's underachieving pal. [PG-13]▼●❿

Permission to Kill (1975-British) **C-96m.** *** D: Cyril Frankel. Dirk Bogarde, Ava Gardner, Bekim Fehmiu, Timothy Dalton, Frederic Forrest. Fascinating exposé of spying as dirty business. Bogarde, spy chief of "Western Intelligence Liaison," tries to prevent Fehmiu, head of "National Freedom Party" from returning to his dictator-controlled country. Beautiful, exciting production. Panavision. [PG]▼

Perrier's Bounty (2010-Irish-English) **C-88m.** *** D: Ian FitzGibbon. Cillian Murphy, Jim Broadbent, Jodie Whittaker, Brendan Gleeson, Liam Cunningham, Brendan Coyle, Padraic Delaney, Michael McElhatton; voice of Gabriel Byrne. Harmless miscreant Murphy is in heaps of trouble when he winds up owing a large wad of cash to big-time hood Perrier (Gleeson). Things go from worse to worser when his dying father (Broadbent) arrives unannounced to make amends with his estranged son and gets involved. Dark humor cleverly softens the intensity of violent acts, which—one is ashamed to admit—generate a lot of laughs. Entire ensemble shines.❿

Perry Mason series SEE: *Leonard Maltin's Classic Movie Guide*

Persecution (1974-British) **C-92m.** *½ D: Don Chaffey. Lana Turner, Trevor Howard, Ralph Bates, Olga Georges-Picot. Overwrought, disjointed thriller with Lana as monstrous cat-loving mother of Bates, whom she torments his entire life. Slow, unpleasant, and unintentionally hilarious. Aka THE TERROR OF SHEBA and THE GRAVEYARD. [PG]▼

Persepolis (2007-French-U.S.) **C/B&W-95m.** ***½ D: Marjane Satrapi, Vincent Paronnaud. Voices of Catherine Deneuve, Chiara Mastroianni, Danielle Darrieux, Simon Abkarian, Gabrielle Lopes, François Jerosme. Remarkable animated feature from Satrapi's autobiographical graphic novels about growing up in Iran under the shah's regime in the 1970s (from a child's-eye point of view), then enduring the dehumanizing effect subsequent governments have on a comfortable way of life. Handsomely stylized film uses animation as few artists ever have to tell a highly personal story; starkly dramatic yet also disarmingly funny. One of a kind. English-language version features the voices of Deneuve, Mastroianni, Gena Rowlands, Sean Penn, and Iggy Pop. [PG-13]▶

Persona (1966-Swedish) **81m.** ***½ D: Ingmar Bergman. Bibi Andersson, Liv Ullmann, Margaretha Krook, Gunnar Bjornstrand. Actress Ullmann withdraws and becomes mute, is cared for by nurse Andersson; their minds and personalities switch. Haunting, poetic, for discerning viewers; also shown at 85m. and 90m.▼●

Personal Best (1982) **C-124m.** ***½ D: Robert Towne. Mariel Hemingway, Scott Glenn, Patrice Donnelly, Kenny Moore, Jim Moody, Larry Pennell. Athletes Hemingway and Donnelly have lesbian relationship while training for the 1980 Olympics. Annoying direction—too many close-ups of feet—but scores touchdowns galore when dealing with feelings, and women's relationship to manipulative coach Glenn. Perceptive, sensitive performance by Hemingway. Directing debut for top screenwriter Towne. [R]▼▶

Personal Services (1987-British) **C-105m.** **½ D: Terry Jones. Julie Walters, Alec McCowen, Danny Schiller, Shirley Stelfox, Victoria Hardcastle, Tim Woodward, Dave Atkins. Naive working woman stumbles into a career as a madam, and becomes bolder as business prospers. Bittersweet comedy, based on the real experiences of Cynthia Payne, is unabashedly adult, but uneven in tone. Benefits from a terrific performance by Walters. Written by David Leland. Payne's earlier years are dramatized in WISH YOU WERE HERE. [R]▼●▶

Personals, The (1981) **C-88m.** *** D: Peter Markle. Bill Schoppert, Karen Landry, Paul Eiding, Michael Laskin, Vickie Dakil. Sweet, lovable—but also honest, realistic—little comedy about what happens when recently divorced, slightly balding Schoppert places a personal ad. Perhaps a bit too much extraneous footage, but still it works nicely, and "Shelly" is a riot. Filmed independently, in Minneapolis. [PG]▼

Personal Velocity (2002) **C-86m.** *** D: Rebecca Miller. Kyra Sedgwick, Parker Posey, Fairuza Balk, David Warshofsky, Brian Tarantina, Tim Guinee, Wallace Shawn, Joel De La Fuente, Ron Leibman, Ben Shenk-

man, Lou Taylor Pucci, Seth Gilliam, David Patrick Kelly, Patti D'Arbanville; narrated by John Ventimiglia. Three vignettes about women at turning points in their lives: Sedgwick has to decide whether or not to walk out on an abusive marriage; Posey puts her marriage at risk while advancing her career; Balk chooses to help an aimless young man, but pays a price for her concern. Miller (daughter of playwright Arthur) adapted her own short stories for this insightful and satisfying film; shot on digital video. [R]▼▶

Persuasion (1995-British-U.S.-French) **C-107m.** *** D: Roger Michell. Amanda Root, Ciarán Hinds, Susan Fleetwood, Corin Redgrave, Fiona Shaw, John Woodvine, Phoebe Nicholls, Samuel West, Sophie Thompson, Judy Cornwell, Felicity Dean. A young woman has never recovered from her break with a dashing but impoverished sailor whom she was advised to turn away. Seven years later, they meet again in the midst of a tumultuous period in which her family tries to adjust to poverty. A lovingly crafted, beautifully acted adaptation of Jane Austen, this film demands patience but provides ample rewards. Impeccable yet understated period detail brings early-19th-century England to life. Made for British TV. [PG]▼●▶

Pest, The (1997) **C-82m.** *½ D: Paul Miller. John Leguizamo, Jeffrey Jones, Edoardo Ballerini, Freddy Rodriguez, Tammy Townsend, Joe Morton, Aries Spears. In a manic performance that makes Jim Carrey look like Ben Kingsley, Leguizamo plays a con artist with a unique talent for transforming himself into just about every type of persona. Soon he finds himself pursued by a variety of whacked-out bad guys. Poor showcase for star/cowriter Leguizamo. [PG-13]▼●

Pete Kelly's Blues (1955) **C-95m.** ** D: Jack Webb. Jack Webb, Janet Leigh, Edmond O'Brien, Peggy Lee, Andy Devine, Lee Marvin, Ella Fitzgerald, Martin Milner, Than Wyenn, Herb Ellis, Jayne Mansfield. Tedious roaring '20s yarn about a cornet player at a Kansas City speakeasy who tries to shield himself and his band from bootlegger/mobster O'Brien. Webb is strictly one-note here, as actor and director, but the candy-colored production design and the music are strong assets. Lee is notable in a rare dramatic role. Based on Webb's flop radio series, which he later revived for TV. CinemaScope. ▼●

Pete 'n' Tillie (1972) **C-100m.** **½ D: Martin Ritt. Walter Matthau, Carol Burnett, Geraldine Page, Barry Nelson, Rene Auberjonois, Lee H. Montgomery, Henry Jones, Kent Smith. Slick comedy-drama has its moments as wry bachelor Matthau laconically woos and marries Burnett. Later turn to melodrama doesn't work, however, and supporting characters Page and Auberjonois don't make sense. Enough good points for innocuous entertainment; adapted by Julius J. Epstein from Peter de Vries' *Witch's Milk*. Panavision. [PG]▼❶

Peter Pan (1953) C-77m. *** D: Hamilton Luske, Clyde Geronimi, Wilfred Jackson. Voices of Bobby Driscoll, Kathryn Beaumont, Hans Conried, Bill Thompson, Heather Angel, Paul Collins, Candy Candido, Tom Conway. Delightful Walt Disney cartoon feature of the classic James M. Barrie story, with Peter leading Wendy, Michael, and John Darling to Neverland, where they do battle with Captain Hook and his band of pirates. Musical highlight: "You Can Fly," as the children sail over the city of London. Followed in 2002 by RETURN TO NEVER LAND. ▼❶

Peter Pan (2003-U.S.-Australian) C-113m. ** D: P.J. Hogan. Jason Isaacs, Jeremy Sumpter, Rachel Hurd-Wood, Richard Briers, Olivia Williams, Lynn Redgrave, Ludivine Sagnier, Geoffrey Palmer, Harry Newell, Freddie Popplewell; narrated by Saffron Burrows. Handsomely filmed adaptation of the James M. Barrie classic about the boy who won't grow up. Starts off promisingly, but adds new ideas that don't necessarily benefit the story (do we really need to see Captain Hook's severed arm?), and winds up plodding instead of soaring. Kids who've never experienced the magic of earlier stage, film, and TV productions may think this is fine—but they don't know what they're missing. Panavision. [PG] ▼❶

Peter Rabbit and Tales of Beatrix Potter (1971-British) C-90m. ***½ D: Reginald Mills. Beautiful ballet film with Royal Ballet Company tells the adventures of several creatures that live by the pond; interesting version of Beatrix Potter tales. British title: TALES OF BEATRIX POTTER. [G]▼❶

Peter's Friends (1992-British) C-100m. ***½ D: Kenneth Branagh. Kenneth Branagh, Emma Thompson, Rita Rudner, Stephen Fry, Hugh Laurie, Imelda Staunton, Alphonsia Emmanuel, Tony Slattery, Alex Lowe, Richard Briers. A collegiate musical troupe's weekend reunion, after ten years, sparks feelings of love, envy, anger, and self-doubt. Glibly described as a British BIG CHILL, it stands on its own, filled with honest humor, heartache, and finely etched performances. Thompson is a standout as the group nerd, and Rudner (who also wrote this with real-life husband Martin Bergman) is very funny as a self-absorbed Hollywood star. Thompson's mother, actress Phyllida Law, turns in a fine performance as the housekeeper. ▼❶

Pete's Dragon (1977) C-134m. ** D: Don Chaffey. Helen Reddy, Jim Dale, Mickey Rooney, Red Buttons, Shelley Winters, Sean Marshall, Jane Kean, Jim Backus, Jeff Conaway; voice of Charlie Callas. Heavyhanded Disney musical about orphaned boy and his only friend, a protective dragon. Endearing animated "monster" almost makes up for the live actors' tiresome mugging. Another try for MARY POPPINS magic that doesn't come close. Some prints run 121m.; the 1985 reissue was further cut to 104m. [G]▼❶

Pete's Meteor (1998-Irish) C-103m. *½ D: Joe O'Byrne. Brenda Fricker, Alfred Molina, Mike Myers, John Kavanagh, Ian Costello, Dervla Kirwan, Gavin Dowdall. Myers plays a dramatic part (with an Irish brogue) in this peculiar, poorly written movie about three orphaned kids being raised by their grandmother. When a meteor lands in their backyard, they think it's been sent by their parents from the heavens, so they object when nerdy scientist Molina claims it for study. The film's central character, the oldest boy (Costello), is so off-putting that he makes watching the film a trial. Released direct to video in 2002. [R] ▼❶

Petrified Forest, The (1936) 83m. ***½ D: Archie Mayo. Leslie Howard, Bette Davis, Dick Foran, Humphrey Bogart, Genevieve Tobin, Charley Grapewin, Porter Hall. Solid adaptation of Robert Sherwood play, focusing on ironic survival of the physically fit in civilized world. Bogart is Duke Mantee, escaped gangster, who holds writer Howard, dreamer Davis, and others hostage at roadside restaurant in Arizona. Stagy, but extremely well acted and surprisingly fresh. Howard and Bogart re-create their Broadway roles. Scripted by Charles Kenyon and Delmer Daves. Remade as ESCAPE IN THE DESERT. Also shown in computer-colored version.▼❶

Petroleum Girls SEE: **Legend of Frenchie King, The**

Pet Sematary (1989) C-102m. BOMB D: Mary Lambert. Dale Midkiff, Fred Gwynne, Denise Crosby, Brad Greenquist, Michael Lombard, Blaze Berdahl, Miko Hughes. Couple is shocked to discover that danger lurks for their kids just outside a newly purchased rural home; aside from a spooked adjacent pet cemetery, they somehow failed to notice that semis roar down their frontyard highway every 90 seconds or so. A box-office hit whose contempt for its audience is sensed even by undiscriminating moviegoers. Stephen King, who has a cameo as a minister, scripted from his own best-seller. Followed by a sequel. [R]▼❶

Pet Sematary II (1992) C-100m. BOMB D: Mary Lambert. Edward Furlong, Anthony Edwards, Clancy Brown, Jared Rushton, Darlanne Fluegel, Sarah Trigger, Lisa Waltz, Jason McGuire. The son of an accidentally killed horror-movie actress discovers the pet cemetery that brings the dead back to life, causing the same kind of gore and horror as in the first film. Brown is a hoot as a resurrected sheriff, but the movie is mean-spirited and gruesome, much worse than the original BOMB! [R]▼◐)

Petty Girl, The (1950) **C-87m.** **½ D: Henry Levin. Robert Cummings, Joan Caulfield, Elsa Lanchester, Melville Cooper, Mary Wickes, Tippi Hedren. Mild comedy of pin-up artist George Petty (Cummings) falling for prudish Caulfield; Lanchester steals every scene she's in.

Petulia (1968) **C-105m.** **** D: Richard Lester. Julie Christie, George C. Scott, Richard Chamberlain, Shirley Knight, Arthur Hill, Joseph Cotten, Pippa Scott, Kathleen Widdoes, Richard Dysart, Austin Pendleton, Rene Auberjonois, The Grateful Dead, Big Brother and the Holding Company. Brilliant film, set against mid-'60s San Francisco scene, about recently divorced doctor and his relationship with unhappily married kook. Terrific acting, especially by Scott and Knight, in one of decade's top films; script by Lawrence B. Marcus. From John Haase's novel *Me and the Arch Kook Petulia.* [R]▼▮

Peyton Place (1957) **C-157m.** ***½ D: Mark Robson. Lana Turner, Hope Lange, Arthur Kennedy, Lloyd Nolan, Lee Philips, Terry Moore, Russ Tamblyn, Betty Field, David Nelson, Mildred Dunnock, Diane Varsi, Barry Coe, Leon Ames, Lorne Greene. Grace Metalious's once-notorious novel receives Grade A filming. Soap opera of life behind closed doors in a small New England town boasts strong cast, fine Franz Waxman score. Original running time: 162m. Sequel: RETURN TO PEYTON PLACE. Later a hit TV series. CinemaScope.▼◐)

Phantasm (1979) **C-87m.** *½ D: Don Coscarelli. Michael Baldwin, Bill Thornbury, Reggie Bannister, Kathy Lester, Angus Scrimm. Two dull brothers take on a flying object that punctures skulls and a creepy cemetery worker whose ties are so thin he belongs playing "Louie, Louie" at a 1964 prom. Followed by three sequels. [R]▼◐)

Phantasm II (1988) **C-90m.** *½ D: Don Coscarelli. James Le Gros, Reggie Bannister, Angus Scrimm, Paula Irvine, Samantha Phillips, Kenneth Tigar. Bigger-budgeted sequel to the 1979 cult success is similar—psychic teenagers experiencing recurring nightmarish visions of The Tall Man (Scrimm)—only with more graphic and unrelenting gore. [R]▼◐)

Phantasm III (1994) **C-91m.** *½ D: Don Coscarelli. Reggie Bannister, A. Michael Baldwin, Angus Scrimm, Bill Thornbury, Gloria Lynne Henry, Kevin Connors, Cindy Ambuehl, John Chandler, Brooks Gardner. More flying silver spheres, cannibal gnomes, stolen bodies, explosions, and The Tall Man—still doesn't make much sense. The end is especially unsatisfying, with limp humor, unnecessary sex scenes, and amateurish acting. Followed by another video sequel. [R]▼◐)

Phantom, The (1996-U.S.-Australian) **C-101m.** ** D: Simon Wincer. Billy Zane, Kristy Swanson, Treat Williams, Catherine Zeta Jones, James Remar, Cary-Hiroyuki Tagawa, Casey Siemaszko, Samantha Eggar, Patrick McGoohan. Lead-footed emulation of Saturday matinee serials, using Lee Falk's masked comic-strip hero ("the ghost who walks"), who starred in a bona fide serial in 1943. His longtime attempt to vanquish a society of evil puts him face-to-face with megalomaniac Xander Drax (a campy Williams). Well-meaning INDIANA JONES wannabe has no energy and offers large-scale stunts without knowing how to stage them! Panavision. [PG] ▼◐)

Phantom Lady (1944) **87m.** ***½ D: Robert Siodmak. Ella Raines, Franchot Tone, Alan Curtis, Thomas Gomez, Elisha Cook, Jr., Fay Helm, Andrew Tombes, Regis Toomey. First-rate suspense yarn of innocent man (Curtis) framed for murder of his wife. Secretary Raines seeks real killer with help of Curtis' best friend (Tone) and detective (Gomez). Sexual innuendo in drumming scene with Cook is simply astonishing—the solo was reportedly dubbed by Buddy Rich. Based on a Cornell Woolrich novel; screenplay by Bernard C. Schoenfeld. ▼

Phantom of Liberty, The (1974-French) **C-104m.** ***½ D: Luis Buñuel. Jean-Claude Brialy, Adolfo Celi, Michel Piccoli, Monica Vitti. A dreamlike comedy of irony, composed of surreal, randomly connected anecdotes. Highlighted is a dinner party, in which the openness of eating and the privacy of defecating are reversed, and a sequence in which adults fret over a young girl's disappearance—even though she remains present all along. [R]▼◐)

Phantom of Terror, The SEE: **Bird With the Crystal Plumage, The**

Phantom of the Opera, The (1925) **98m.** ***½ D: Rupert Julian. Lon Chaney, Mary Philbin, Norman Kerry, Snitz Edwards, Gibson Gowland. Classic melodrama with Chaney as the tortured composer who lives in the catacombs under the Paris Opera House, and kidnaps young Philbin as his singing protégée. Famous unmasking scene still packs a jolt, and the Bal Masque is especially impressive in two-color Technicolor. One of Chaney's finest hours. Most prints are of the 1929 reissue version, but the original is available on DVD; running times vary. Remade several times, and transformed into a Broadway musical.▼◐)

Phantom of the Opera (1943) **C-92m.** *** D: Arthur Lubin. Claude Rains, Susanna Foster, Nelson Eddy, Edgar Barrier, Jane Farrar, Miles Mander, J. Edward Bromberg, Hume Cronyn, Fritz Leiber, Leo Carrillo, Steven Geray, Fritz Feld. First talkie version of venerable melodrama often has more opera than Phantom, but Rains gives fine, sympathetic performance as disfigured composer worshipping young soprano Foster. Oscar winner for Cinematography (Hal Mohr and W. Howard Greene) and Art Direction.▼O)

Phantom of the Opera, The (1962-British) **C-84m. **** D: Terence Fisher. Herbert Lom, Heather Sears, Thorley Walters, Edward DeSouza, Michael Gough, Miles Malleson. Lom stars in this third screen version of the story. It's more elaborate than most Hammer horror films, but also more plodding, with only occasional moments of terror. ▼O)

Phantom of the Opera, The (1989) **C-90m. *½** D: Dwight H. Little. Robert Englund, Jill Schoelen, Alex Hyde-White, Bill Nighy, Stephanie Lawrence, Terence Harvey. Good-looking but gory, slow-moving remake, shot in Budapest but set in London. Changes to Gaston Leroux's novel are no improvements; instead of a mask, the Phantom stitches dead flesh onto his scarred face and has made a deal with the devil. He's still killing people to advance the career of a chosen singer. No chandelier, either. Englund ("Freddy Krueger") ranges from effective to hammy as the Phantom. [R]▼O)

Phantom of the Opera, The (1999-Italian) **C-99m. **** D: Dario Argento. Julian Sands, Asia Argento, Andrea Di Stefano, Nadia Rinaldi, Coralina Cataldi Tassoni, Istvan Bubik. Argento's gory and erotic take on the classic tale with Sands as the mysterious phantom, who, in this version, is abandoned in the sewer below the opera house as an infant and raised by a loving family of rats! The director's daughter plays the beautiful young singer with whom he becomes obsessed. Disappointingly routine and unimaginative, with only a few of the director's expected flamboyant flourishes. [R]▼D

Phantom of the Opera, The (2004-British) **C-142m. **½** D: Joel Schumacher. Gerard Butler, Emmy Rossum, Patrick Wilson, Miranda Richardson, Minnie Driver, Simon Callow, Ciarán Hinds. Overproduced adaptation of Andrew Lloyd Webber's stage musical with unnecessary additions: a superfluous flashback framing device and a "backstory" for the Phantom. The singing is fine, Rossum positively glows as Christine, major numbers like "The Music of the Night" are beautifully done, but Webber and Schumacher subscribe to the "more is more" school of entertainment, alas. Panavision. [PG-13]▼D

Phantom of the Paradise (1974) **C-92m. **** D: Brian De Palma. Paul Williams, William Finley, Jessica Harper, George Memmoli, Gerrit Graham. Effective rock version of . . . OPERA, with Finley out for revenge against producer (Williams, miscast but not bad) who stole his songs. A flop in its time—it was sold as a spoof—but now finding a cult; ironically, many of the "weird" rock performers (including Graham as "Beef") seem pretty tame alongside some of today's artists. Williams also composed the score, and Sissy Spacek was the set decorator! [PG]▼O)

Phantom of the Rue Morgue (1954) **C-84m. **** D: Roy Del Ruth. Karl Malden, Claude Dauphin, Patricia Medina, Steve Forrest, Allyn Ann McLerie, Erin O'Brien-Moore. Remake of MURDERS IN THE RUE MORGUE suffers from Malden's hamminess in the equivalent of Lugosi's role, plus little real atmosphere. On the other hand, there *is* Merv Griffin as a college student! 3-D.▼

Phantoms (1998) **C-95m. **½** D: Joe Chappelle. Peter O'Toole, Joanna Going, Rose McGowan, Liev Schreiber, Ben Affleck, Clifton Powell, Nicky Katt. Sisters are frightened to find a Rocky Mountain town totally deserted, except for a few dead bodies; sheriff Affleck shows up to help, followed by scientist O'Toole. The answer is a mysterious underground monster from the beginning of time: intelligent, deadly, and amorphous. Not-bad thriller with good performances, astute use of locations, and some suspenseful scenes. Adapted from his own novel by Dean R. Koontz. Aka DEAN KOONTZ'S PHANTOMS. [R]▼O)

Phantom Tollbooth, The (1969) **C-90m. **** D: Chuck Jones, Abe Levitow (animation); David Monahan (live-action). Butch Patrick; voices of Hans Conried, Mel Blanc, Candy Candido, June Foray, Les Tremayne, Daws Butler. Unusual animated feature (the first for both Jones and MGM), based on Norton Juster's book about bored little boy who enters strange world where letters and numbers are at war. A bit sophisticated for the Saturday matinee crowd, and the songs are pretty icky, but still quite worthwhile, especially for Jones fans. [G]▼O)

Phar Lap (1983-Australian) **C-108m. **** D: Simon Wincer. Tom Burlinson, Martin Vaughan, Judy Morris, Ron Leibman, Celia de Burgh, Vincent Ball. Entertaining chronicle of champion New Zealand–born racehorse Phar Lap, who suddenly and mysteriously died in 1933 in America. Nicely directed and acted; Down Under, the story is now a legend. Reedited for U.S. release from original 118m. Panavision. [PG]▼

Phase IV (1974) **C-86m. **½** D: Saul Bass. Nigel Davenport, Lynne Frederick, Michael Murphy, Alan Gifford, Helen Horton, Robert Henderson. Feature directing debut of famed title-maker Bass is visually stunning but rather incomprehensible science fiction about colony of super-intelligent ants (normal-sized, for a change) running rampant at a lonely scientific outpost. Difficult, but not without its rewards. [PG] ▼O)

Phat Beach (1996) **C-99m. **** D: Doug Ellin. Jermaine "Huggy" Hopkins, Brian Hooks, Eric Fleeks, Alma Collins, Claudia

Kaleem, Jennifer Lucienne, Coolio, Gregg D. Vance, Tre Black, Tiny "Zeus" Lister, Jr. A wannabe writer (Hopkins) dreams of meeting the perfect girl at the beach, so he heads off to the surf with his best friend. Hopkins' earnest, charming performance saves this from being a typical hit-the-beach and hit-on-the-girls film. Coolio and Y?N-Vee perform on-screen. [R] ▼●)

Phat Girlz (2006) **C-99m.** *½ D: Nnegest Likké. Mo'Nique, Jimmy Jean-Louis, Godfrey, Kendra C. Johnson, Jack Noseworthy, Joyful Drake, Eric Roberts. Self-indulgent, sloppily made comedy about a full-figured wannabe fashion designer (Mo'Nique). As she struggles to deal with her issues in a weight-conscious culture, she is pursued by a hunky Nigerian doctor who is attracted to plus-sized women. Supposedly well-intentioned exploration of the importance of accepting who you are and how you look is shrill, one-note, and wallows in nastiness. [PG-13]❻

Phenix City Story, The (1955) **100m.** *** D: Phil Karlson. John McIntire, Richard Kiley, Kathryn Grant (Crosby), Edward Andrews, Lenka Peterson, Biff McGuire, James Edwards. Fast-paced exposé film, compactly told, with realistic production, fine performances as lawyer returns to corrupt hometown, tries to do something about it. Sometimes shown without 13m. prologue. ❻

Phenomena SEE: **Creepers**

Phenomenon (1996) **C-124m.** ** D: Jon Turteltaub. John Travolta, Kyra Sedgwick, Forest Whitaker, Robert Duvall, Jeffrey DeMunn, Brent Spiner, Richard Kiley, Tony Genaro, Sean O'Bryan, Ellen Geer. Intriguing, humanistic story has ordinary-guy Travolta struck by a bolt of light that transforms him into a genius . . . a "blessing" that turns out to be a curse. Unfortunately, it heads nowhere and takes its sweet time getting there. Beautiful Northern California setting and lovely Thomas Newman score support Travolta's empathic performance . . . all for naught. Long, slow, and squishy in the center. Remade for TV in 2003 but titled PHENOMENON II. Panavision. [PG] ▼●)

PHFFFT (1954) **91m.** *** D: Mark Robson. Judy Holliday, Jack Lemmon, Jack Carson, Kim Novak, Donald Curtis. Saucy sex romp by George Axelrod, with Holliday and Lemmon discovering that they were better off before they divorced. ▼)

Philadelphia (1993) **C-119m.** **½ D: Jonathan Demme. Tom Hanks, Denzel Washington, Jason Robards, Mary Steenburgen, Antonio Banderas, Ron Vawter, Robert Ridgely, Charles Napier, Lisa Summerour, Joanne Woodward, Roger Corman, John Bedford Lloyd, Anna Deavere Smith, Tracey Walter, Obba Babatunde, Kathryn Witt, Bradley Whitford, Chandra Wilson. Up-and-coming lawyer Hanks is battling AIDS; when he's fired from his prosperous Main Line Philadelphia law firm (for trumped-up reasons), he decides to bring suit. The only lawyer who'll take his case: ambulance-chaser Washington, who doesn't like Hanks. Well-meaning, mainstream look at AIDS and American homophobia succeeds as a tract but falls short as drama. Hanks is terrific in an Oscar-winning performance, but we don't know anything about him, or his lover (Banderas); his Norman Rockwellian family is (alas) too good to be true. That's the Rev. Robert Castle (subject of Demme's documentary COUSIN BOBBY) as Hanks' father. Bruce Springsteen also won an Oscar for Best Song, "Streets of Philadelphia." [PG-13] ▼●)

Philadelphia Experiment, The (1984) **C-102m.** **½ D: Stewart Raffill. Michael Paré, Nancy Allen, Eric Christmas, Bobby Di Cicco, Kene Holliday. Sailor on WW2 ship falls through a hole in time and winds up in 1984. Just entertaining enough to cover production flaws and some gaping story holes. Followed by a sequel. [PG] ▼●)

Philadelphia, Here I Come (1975) **C-95m.** **½ D: John Quested. Donal McCann, Des Cave, Siobhan McKenna, Eamon Kelly, Fidelma Murphy, Liam Redmond. Brian Friel adapted his stage play about a young man and his alter ego who debate whether or not he should leave his dreary Irish home town and join an aunt in Philadelphia, U.S.A. Filmed on location; fine performances. ▼)

Philadelphia Story, The (1940) **112m.** **** D: George Cukor. Cary Grant, Katharine Hepburn, James Stewart, Ruth Hussey, John Howard, Roland Young, John Halliday, Virginia Weidler, Mary Nash, Henry Daniell, Hillary Brooke. Talky but brilliant adaptation of Philip Barry's hit Broadway comedy about society girl who yearns for down-to-earth romance; Grant is her ex-husband, Stewart a fast-talking (!) reporter who falls in love with her. Entire cast is excellent, but Stewart really shines in his offbeat, Academy Award-winning role. Donald Ogden Stewart's script also earned an Oscar. Later musicalized as HIGH SOCIETY. Also shown in computer-colored version. ▼●)

Philo Vance series SEE: *Leonard Maltin's Classic Movie Guide*

Phobia (1980-Canadian) **C-90m.** BOMB D: John Huston. Paul Michael Glaser, Susan Hogan, John Colicos, David Bolt, Patricia Collins, David Eisner. Absolutely terrible film about psychiatrist whose patients, suffering from various phobias, are being murdered one by one. Relentlessly stupid, illogical, and unpleasant. [R] ▼

Phoebe in Wonderland (2008) **C-96m.** *** D: Daniel Barnz. Elle Fanning, Felicity Huffman, Patricia Clarkson, Bill Pullman, Campbell Scott, Bailee Madison, Austin

Williams, Teala Dunn, Maddie Corman. Young girl seems to live in her own world, but finds a safe haven acting in a school production of *Alice in Wonderland* for an artsy drama teacher (Clarkson). At the same time, her mother (Huffman) is torn between trying to finish a thesis on *Alice* and committing to parenting. Ambitious drama plumbs some remarkably deep emotions, especially for a film with a 9-year-old leading lady (Fanning, who's amazing). Excellent score by Christophe Beck. Super 35. [PG-13]▮

Phoenix (1997) **C-107m.** ** D: Danny Cannon. Ray Liotta, Anjelica Huston, Anthony LaPaglia, Daniel Baldwin, Jeremy Piven, Kari Wuhrer, Xander Berkeley, Tom Noonan, Giancarlo Esposito, Giovanni Ribisi, Brittany Murphy. Gambling-addicted Arizona cop Liotta, deeply in debt to a bookie, hatches a heist with his three corrupt cop buddies to rip off a local loan shark, but naturally things unravel in typical B-movie fashion. Stylishly made neo-noir boasts a superior cast but is sunk by repellent characters and a depressingly derivative, postmodern Tarantino-esque script. Premiered on cable a year before 1998 theatrical release. Panavision. [R]▼▶

Phone Booth (2003) **C-80m.** *½ D: Joel Schumacher. Colin Farrell, Kiefer Sutherland, Forest Whitaker, Radha Mitchell, Katie Holmes, Richard T. Jones, Keith Nobbs, Josh Pais, Tia Texada, Paula Jai Parker. Farrell gives a tour de force performance in this extremely annoying film about a pushy, street hustler–style publicist who picks up a phone on 8th Avenue in Manhattan and finds himself trapped there—literally and psychologically—by a maniacal caller. Larry Cohen's story makes no sense whatsoever, so the film's only value is as an exercise, and on that level it runs out of steam pretty quickly. Ben Foster appears unbilled. Super 35. [R]▼▶

Phone Call From a Stranger (1952) **96m.** *** D: Jean Negulesco. Bette Davis, Shelley Winters, Gary Merrill, Michael Rennie, Keenan Wynn, Evelyn Varden, Warren Stevens, Beatrice Straight, Craig Stevens. Engrossing narrative of Merrill, survivor of a plane crash, visiting families of various victims. ▼▶

Phynx, The (1970) **C-92m.** BOMB D: Lee H. Katzin. A. Michael Miller, Ray Chippeway, Dennis Larden, Lonny Stevens, Lou Antonio, Mike Kellin, Joan Blondell, George Tobias, Richard Pryor. A way-off-base satire about a rock group (Miller, Chippeway, Larden, Stevens) recruited to spy behind Iron Curtain and the kidnapping of America's pop-culture heroes (in cameos, Leo Gorcey, Huntz Hall, Guy Lombardo, Joe Louis, Johnny Weissmuller, Col. Sanders, Ruby Keeler, Xavier Cugat, Dick Clark, George Jessel, and many others). Diehards

may want to see some of these stars, but it's hardly worth it. [M/PG]

Physical Evidence (1989) **C-99m.** *½ D: Michael Crichton. Burt Reynolds, Theresa Russell, Ned Beatty, Kay Lenz, Ted McGinley, Tom O'Brien. Boring drama with Reynolds going through the paces as a tough cop who's been suspended from the force, and is now the prime suspect in a murder case. Russell is badly miscast as a public defender who takes up his cause. [R]▼▶

π (1998) 85m. **½ D: Darren Aronofsky. Sean Gullette, Mark Margolis, Ben Shenkman, Pamela Hart, Stephen Pearlman, Ajay Naidu. An obsessed math genius thinks the orderliness of numbers may be able to conquer the stock market or determine God's identity, yet his own disordered life finds him at the brink of madness. Filmed in inky 16mm black and white for around $60,000, this attention-getter is a true original. Well acted by a no-name cast and, we hope, a harbinger of things to come from filmmaker Aronofsky. Cowritten by the director, Eric Watson, and leading actor Gullette. [R]▼▶

Piaf—The Early Years (1974-U.S.-French) **C-104m.** **½ D: Guy Casaril. Brigitte Ariel, Pascale Christophe, Guy Trejan, Pierre Vernier, Jacques Duby, Anouk Ferjac. Maddeningly uneven depiction of the early life and career of the legendary singer. Fascinating subject matter, good Ariel performance and great music, but melodramatic and sloppily directed. Based on the best-selling book by Simone Berteaut, Piaf's half-sister (played here by Christophe). Unreleased in America until 1982. [PG]

Pianist, The (2002-French-German-Polish-British) **C-148m.** ***½ D: Roman Polanski. Adrien Brody, Thomas Kretschmann, Frank Finlay, Maureen Lipman, Emilia Fox, Ed Stoppard, Julia Rayner, Jessica Kate Meyer, Ruth Platt. Emotionally draining story of Polish pianist Wladyslaw Szpilman and his too-fantastic-to-be-anything-but-true life during WW2, beginning in Warsaw during 1939. Devastating in its portrayal of casual Nazi atrocities, but overwhelming in its depiction of survival against all rational obstacles. Brody is splendid as Szpilman, a difficult and essentially passive role. Director Polanski revisits personal memories of his own life with this film. Screenplay by Ronald Harwood, based on Szpilman's memoirs, published in 1946. Oscar winner for Best Director, Actor (Brody), and Adapted Screenplay. [R]▼▶

Piano, The (1993-New Zealand-French) **C-121m.** ***½ D: Jane Campion. Holly Hunter, Harvey Keitel, Sam Neill, Anna Paquin, Kerry Walker, Geneviève Lemon, Tungia Baker, Ian Mune. Haunting, unpredictable tale of love and sex told from a woman's point of view. In the late 19th century, a

Scottish woman, her illegitimate daughter (Paquin), and her beloved piano arrive in remote New Zealand for an arranged marriage to farmer Neill. Then headstrong Hunter (who has been mute since childhood) strikes a bargain with moody neighbor Keitel (a Maori convert) involving the piano that leads to eye-opening consequences for the entire community. Writer-director Campion has fashioned a highly original fable, showing the tragedy and triumph erotic passion can bring to one's daily life. Hunter and Paquin both won Oscars for their performances, Campion for her screenplay. [R] ▼●◖

Piano Teacher, The (2001-French-Austrian) C-130m. ***½ D: Michael Haneke. Isabelle Huppert, Benoît Magimel, Annie Girardot, Anna Sigalevitch, Susanne Lothar. Magnificent, and decidedly adult, study of a middle-aged musician's psyche and her disturbing personal and professional relationships. Huppert has the role of her career as a woman with unusual views on intimacy and sex; costar Magimel matches her intensity. Harrowing and haunting, but not entirely humorless. Scripted by the director, from Elfriede Jelinek's 1983 novel. ▼◖

Picasso Mystery, The SEE: **Mystery of Picasso, The**

Picasso Summer, The (1969) C-90m. *½ D: Serge Bourguignon. Albert Finney, Yvette Mimieux. Boring, rambling tale of young couple so enamored by paintings that they take European vacation to find Picasso himself. Animated sequence midway can stand on its own. Based on the Ray Bradbury story. [M/PG] ◖

Picasso Trigger (1989) C-99m. ** D: Andy Sidaris. Steve Bond, Dona Speir, John Aprea, Hope Marie Carlton, Harold Diamond, Roberta Vasquez, Guich Koock, Bruce Penhall. Harmless, low-budget James Bond–like thriller with U.S. agent Bond tracking assassin Aprea, who uses fish (from a painting he admires) as his emblem. Sequel to HARD TICKET TO HAWAII and MALIBU EXPRESS has usual mix of action and T&A, and some peculiar gadgets (a killer crutch?). [R] ▼◖

Picking up the Pieces (2000) C-95m. ** D: Alfonso Arau. Woody Allen, Maria Grazia Cucinotta, Cheech Marin, David Schwimmer, Kiefer Sutherland, Alfonso Arau, Sharon Stone, Andy Dick, Fran Drescher, Joseph Gordon-Levitt, Elliott Gould, Lupe Ontiveros, Lou Diamond Phillips, Pepe Serna, Kathy Kinney, Tony Plana, Richard Sarafian, Danny de la Paz, Mia Maestro. A butcher who's hacked his wife into pieces flees to a New Mexico town, where the woman's hand becomes a focal point of worship—and ballyhoo. Whimsical black comedy in an almost total misfire, but the stellar cast maintains interest. Made for theaters but U.S. debut was on cable. Univision. ▼◖

Pickle, The (1993) C/B&W-103m. *½ D:

Paul Mazursky. Danny Aiello, Dyan Cannon, Clotilde Courau, Shelley Winters, Barry Miller, Jerry Stiller, Chris Penn, Little Richard, Jodi Long, Rebecca Miller, Stephen Tobolowsky, Caroline Aaron, Ally Sheedy, Spalding Gray, Griffin Dunne, Isabella Rossellini, Dudley Moore, Donald Trump. Misfire about an aging, self-involved film director (Aiello) who's in desperate need of a hit, and whose most recent credit is a sci-fi epic about an overgrown pickle. *The Turkey* would be a more apt title for this opus, scripted by Mazursky, who also has a cameo. [R] ▼●◖

Pickpocket (1959-French) **75m.** ***½ D: Robert Bresson. Martin Lasalle, Marika Green, Kassagi, Pierre Leymarie, Jean Pélégri, Dolly Scal, Pierre Étaix. A petty thief finds himself inexorably attracted to a life of crime and spurns a woman's love to become a professional pickpocket. One of Bresson's great films, a brilliantly shot and edited minimalist portrait of the criminal as an existentialist. Paul Schrader borrowed the moving finale for the end of AMERICAN GIGOLO. ▼◖

Pick-up Artist, The (1987) C-81m. *½ D: James Toback. Molly Ringwald, Robert Downey (Jr.), Dennis Hopper, Danny Aiello, Mildred Dunnock, Harvey Keitel, Brian Hamill, Vanessa Williams, Victoria Jackson, Polly Draper, Robert Towne, Lorraine Brac- co, Bob Gunton. Womanizing youth meets his match when he falls for the daughter of a boozy gambler in hock to the mob. Standard Toback lowlifes integrated into a conventionally romantic framework. Dismal, dour, and deadeningly dull. [PG-13] ▼●◖

Pickup on 101 (1972) C-93m. ** D: John Florea. Jack Albertson, Lesley Ann Warren, Martin Sheen, Michael Ontkean, Hal Baylor, George Chandler. Coed who wants to be liberated hits the road with rock musician and friendly hobo in this inoffensive melodrama. Video title: WHERE THE EAGLE FLIES. [PG] ▼

Pickup on South Street (1953) **80m.** ***½ D: Samuel Fuller. Richard Widmark, Jean Peters, Thelma Ritter, Richard Kiley, Murvyn Vye, Milburn Stone. Pickpocket Widmark inadvertently acquires top-secret microfilm, and becomes target for espionage agents. Tough, brutal, well-made film, with superb performance by Ritter as street peddler who also sells information. Story by Dwight Taylor; screenplay by the director. Remade as THE CAPE TOWN AFFAIR. ▼◖

Pickwick Papers, The (1952-British) **109m.** *** D: Noel Langley. James Hayter, James Donald, Hermione Baddeley, Kathleen Harrison, Hermione Gingold, Joyce Grenfell, Alexander Gauge, Lionel Murton, Nigel Patrick, Harry Fowler, Donald Wolfit. Flavorful adaptation of Dickens' classic about observations of English society by members of the Pickwick Club. ▼❶

Picnic (1955) **C-115m.** ***½ D: Joshua Logan. William Holden, Rosalind Russell, Kim Novak, Betty Field, Cliff Robertson, Arthur O'Connell, Verna Felton, Susan Strasberg, Nick Adams, Phyllis Newman, Elizabeth W. Wilson. Excellent film of William Inge's Pulitzer Prize–winning play about drifter (Holden) who stops over in Kansas, stealing alluring Novak from his old buddy Robertson (making his film debut). Russell and O'Connell almost walk away with the film in second leads, and supporting roles are expertly filled; adapted by Daniel Taradash. Remade in 2000 for TV. CinemaScope. ▼❶

Picnic at Hanging Rock (1975-Australian) **C-110m.** *** D: Peter Weir. Rachel Roberts, Dominic Guard, Helen Morse, Jacki Weaver, Vivean Gray, Margaret Nelson, Anne (Louise) Lambert. Moody, atmospheric film set in 1900 about three schoolgirls and their teacher who mysteriously disappear during an outing one sunny day. Eerie and richly textured by director Weir; based on a novel by Joan Lindsay. Reedited by Weir in 1998; that version is about 7m. shorter. [PG]▼❶

Picture Bride (1994-Japanese) **C-95m.** *** D: Kayo Hatta. Youki Kudoh, Akira Takayama, Tamlyn Tomita, Cary-Hiroyuki Togawa, Toshiro Mifune. A young Japanese woman trying to leave her unhappy past behind travels to Hawaii in the early 1900s as a "picture bride," but soon finds that her new married life is a lot different than she imagined it would be. Slow-moving but engrossing study of the pioneer spirit in Hawaii. Mifune has a nice cameo as a silent-film narrator. [PG-13] ▼❶

Picture Mommy Dead (1966) **C-88m.** **½ D: Bert I. Gordon. Don Ameche, Martha Hyer, Zsa Zsa Gabor, Signe Hasso, Susan Gordon. Hokey melodrama with Hyer newly married to Ameche, battling stepdaughter Gordon, possessed by late mother's spirit.▼

Picture of Dorian Gray, The (1945) **110m.** ***½ D: Albert Lewin. George Sanders, Hurd Hatfield, Donna Reed, Angela Lansbury, Peter Lawford, Lowell Gilmore; narrated by Cedric Hardwicke. Haunting Oscar Wilde story of man whose painting ages while he retains youth. Young Lansbury is poignant, singing "The Little Yellow Bird" (and her real-life mother Moyna MacGill is the Duchess). Sanders leaves indelible impression as elegant heavy. Several color inserts throughout the film. Harry Stradling's cinematography won an Oscar. Remade in 1970 and 2009 as DORIAN GRAY and for TV in 1974, with Nigel Davenport. ▼❶

Picture Perfect (1997) **C-100m.** *** D: Glenn Gordon Caron. Jennifer Aniston, Jay Mohr, Kevin Bacon, Olympia Dukakis, Illeana Douglas, Kevin Dunn, Faith Prince,

Anne Twomey. Cute starring vehicle for Aniston, as an up-and-comer in the advertising world who invents a fiancé to become more the kind of person her boss wants working for him. Then she has to hire a guy to act the part at a business dinner, and things get complicated. Barely credible romantic comedy is little more than an excuse to showcase Aniston's appeal—but quite watchable on that basis. [PG-13]▼❶

Picture Show Man, The (1977-Australian) **C-99m.** ** D: John Power. Rod Taylor, John Meillon, John Ewart, Harold Hopkins, Patrick Cargill, Judy Morris. Meandering tale of a traveling showman in 1920s Australia who brings moving pictures to small towns throughout the country. A lovely idea (based on the memoirs of Lyle Penn) that has moments of charm and period atmosphere, but no story, and not much energy. Top-billed Taylor (an Aussie by birth) appears sporadically as Meillon's rival—from Texas! [PG]

Picture This: The Times of Peter Bogdanovich in Archer City, Texas (1992) **C-57m.** *** D: George Hickenlooper. Absorbing documentary about filmmaker Bogdanovich's return to the scene of his first great success, THE LAST PICTURE SHOW, to make a sequel, TEXASVILLE. Cybill Shepherd, Jeff Bridges, Timothy and Sam Bottoms, Polly Platt, Randy Quaid, and others recall how the first film affected their lives (including some surprisingly candid revelations)—and townspeople compare Larry McMurtry's locally based fiction to their perception of the truth. ▼❶

Piece of the Action, A (1977) **C-135m.** **½ D: Sidney Poitier. Sidney Poitier, Bill Cosby, James Earl Jones, Denise Nicholas, Hope Clark, Tracy Reed, Titos Vandis, Ja'net DuBois. Third Poitier-Cosby teaming casts them as con men obliged to help social worker set ghetto kids on the right track. Typical comic crime material offset by serious, preachy moments. [PG] ▼❶

Pieces of April (2003) **C-80m.** **½ D: Peter Hedges. Katie Holmes, Patricia Clarkson, Derek Luke, Oliver Platt, Alison Pill, John Gallagher, Jr., Sean Hayes, SisQo, Lillias White, Isiah Whitlock. Young woman living in a N.Y.C. apartment with her new boyfriend attempts to prepare Thanksgiving dinner for her dysfunctional family, but it's debatable as to who's more nervous about the impending get-together. Quirky and funny, as you'd expect from the writer of WHAT'S EATING GILBERT GRAPE and coscenarist of ABOUT A BOY, here making his feature directing debut, though the broader comedy doesn't always work alongside the simpler, more truthful moments. Clarkson is a standout as the flaky mother whose illness has made her even more mercurial than usual. [PG-13] ▼❶

Pied Piper, The (1972-British) **C-90m.**

***½ D: Jacques Demy. Donovan, Donald Pleasence, Michael Hordern, Jack Wild, Diana Dors, John Hurt. Chilling story of piper who rids evil hamlet of rats. While originally conceived as children's tale, director Demy succeeds in weaving grimy portrait of the Middle Ages. [G]🅳

Pie in the Sky (1996) C-95m. ** D: Bryan Gordon. Josh Charles, Anne Heche, John Goodman, Christine Lahti, Peter Riegert, Bob Balaban, Christine Ebersole, Wil Wheaton, Dey Young. Comedy about a helicopter traffic reporter who has as many problems sorting out his love life as he does with freeway gridlock. Romantic tale boasts an attractive (and impressive) cast that it almost completely wastes, although Heche is a wonderfully affecting leading lady. Perfect video fodder for your next traffic jam. [R]▼●🅳

Pie in the Sky: The Brigid Berlin Story (2000) C/B&W-76m. *** D: Shelly Dunn Fremont, Vincent Fremont. Absorbing documentary about the life and times of Brigid Berlin (aka Brigid Polk), the daughter of conservative Republican American aristocracy—her father was president of the Hearst Corporation—who became an Andy Warhol superstar in the 1960s. Revealing portrait of a rebellious daughter, obsessed with food and cleanliness, who becomes her parents' worst nightmare. Archival footage and recorded telephone conversations between Brigid and her disgusted patrician mother are fascinating. Among the talking heads are John Waters, Paul Morrissey, and (most intriguingly) Patty Hearst.▼🅳

Pierrepoint (2005-British) C-95m. *** D: Adrian Shergold. Timothy Spall, Juliet Stevenson, Eddie Marsan, Cavan Clerkin, Christopher Fulford, Ian Shaw, Maggie Ollerenshaw. Potent drama based on the life of Albert Pierrepoint, the most efficient hangman in England, from the 1930s to the 1950s. He views his work as a job and remains dispassionate—up to a point. Exceptional showcase for Spall, who imbues his character with a wide range of colors. Originally shown at film festivals as THE LAST HANGMAN. [R]🅳

Pierrot le Fou (1965-French-Italian) C-110m. *** D: Jean-Luc Godard. Jean-Paul Belmondo, Anna Karina, Dirk Sanders, Raymond Devus, Samuel Fuller, Jean-Pierre Léaud. Belmondo and Karina run away together to the South of France; he is leaving his rich wife, she is escaping her involvement with gangsters. Complex, confusing, but engrossing drama, which exudes an intriguing sense of spontaneity. Allegedly shot without a script; also shown at 90m. and 95m. Techniscope.▼●🅳

Piglet's Big Movie (2003) C-75m. **½ D: Francis Glebas. Voices of John Fielder, Jim Cummings, Andre Stojka, Kath Soucie, Peter Cullen, Tom Wheatley. Winnie the Pooh

and his pals set off in search of a depressed Piglet who has wandered into the woods believing he is too small to be of use to his friends. Leisurely paced animated feature based on A. A. Milne's Pooh characters is moderately entertaining for young audiences and tolerable enough for their parents. Laid-back theatrical release, produced by Disney's direct-to-video division, comes to life during song sequences written and sung by Carly Simon. [G]▼🅳

Pigskin Parade (1936) 93m. *** D: David Butler. Stuart Erwin, Patsy Kelly, Jack Haley, Johnny Downs, Betty Grable, Arline Judge, Dixie Dunbar, Judy Garland, Anthony (Tony) Martin, Elisha Cook, Jr., Grady Sutton, The Yacht Club Boys. Entertaining college football musicomedy with Erwin the hayseed who becomes a gridiron hero, Kelly the coach's wife who knows more about the game than the coach (Haley). Cook appears as an anarchy-spouting campus radical! Garland plays Erwin's kid sister, in her feature debut, and she swings "It's Love I'm After." Alan Ladd appears as a student, and sings with The Yacht Club Boys.▼●

Pillow Book, The (1996-British-Dutch-French) C-126m. **½ D: Peter Greenaway. Vivian Wu, Ewan McGregor, Yoshi Oida, Ken Ogata, Hideko Yoshida, Judy Ongg, Ken Mitsuishi. Sensual, if dramatically exasperating, convolution about a young woman (Wu) who seeks revenge for wrongs perpetrated against her calligrapher father, who painted elaborate words and characters on her body during an unconventional childhood. Gorgeously shot by Sacha Vierny, film belatedly hits its stride with its heroine's romance with a doomed lover (McGregor), only to fade fatally during a grueling final half hour. Wu, though, is extraordinary, both as a character and a photographic subject. Super 35.▼🅳

Pillow Talk (1959) C-102m. ***½ D: Michael Gordon. Doris Day, Rock Hudson, Tony Randall, Thelma Ritter, Nick Adams, Julia Meade, Allen Jenkins, Lee Patrick, William Schallert, Frances Sternhagen. Rock pursues Doris, with interference from Randall and sideline witticisms from Ritter. Imaginative sex comedy has two stars sharing a party line without knowing each other's identity. Fast-moving; plush sets, gorgeous fashions. Oscar-winning story and screenplay by Stanley Shapiro, Russell Rouse, Clarence Greene, and Maurice Richlin. CinemaScope. ▼●🅳

Pilot, The (1979) C-99m. ** D: Cliff Robertson. Cliff Robertson, Diane Baker, Frank Converse, Dana Andrews, Milo O'Shea, Ed Binns, Gordon MacRae. Airline pilot who flies at the end of a bottle discovers that his world is collapsing. Predictable drama given a boost by Walter Lassally's spectacular aerial photography and John Addison's soaring (and seemingly misplaced) score. Video title: DANGER IN THE SKIES. Panavision. [PG]▼

Pineapple Express (2008) **C/B&W-112m.** **½ D: David Gordon Green. Seth Rogen, James Franco, Gary Cole, Rosie Perez, Danny McBride, Kevin Corrigan, Craig Robinson, Amber Heard, Ed Begley, Jr., Nora Dunn, John Krasinski, James Remar. Good-natured slacker (Rogen) witnesses a murder committed by a local druglord (Cole) and clumsily leaves a joint at the scene that can be traced back to its dealer (Franco). This impels Rogen and Franco to take it on the lam, pursued by two violent goons. Audacious comedy not only revives the pothead movie but goes on to spoof violent action films—in surprisingly vivid ways. Uneven but often ridiculously funny, with Franco scoring a bull's-eye as the ultimate stoner. Written by Rogen and Evan Goldberg, from a story they cowrote with producer Judd Apatow. Unrated version runs 118m. Super 35. [R]▶

Piñero (2001) **C/B&W-103m.** **½ D: Leon Ichaso. Benjamin Bratt, Giancarlo Esposito, Talisa Soto, Nelson Vasquez, Michael Irby, Michael Wright, Rita Moreno, Jaime Sanchez, Mandy Patinkin, Oscar Colon, Miriam Cruz, Robert Klein, Griffin Dunne. Kinetic, nonlinear biography of "Nuyorican" writer-poet Miguel Piñero, who used his prison experience to powerful effect in the award-winning play *Short Eyes* in the 1970s, but couldn't shake his drug habit or chronic irresponsibility. Bratt is magnetic and persuasive, but we still don't understand what made Piñero so self-destructive. Film's coproducer, Fisher Stevens, appears briefly. [R]▼▶

Pink Cadillac (1989) **C-122m.** ** D: Buddy Van Horn. Clint Eastwood, Bernadette Peters, Timothy Carhart, Tiffany Gail Robinson, Angela Louise Robinson, John Dennis Johnston, Geoffrey Lewis, William Hickey, James (Jim) Carrey. Harmless but off-the-cuff throwaway comedy about a bail-bond bounty hunter who helps the wife of his latest target rescue her kidnapped baby from the neo-Nazi associates of her weakling husband. No Edsel, but at two hours, seriously in need of a tuneup. Eastwood's uncharacteristically broad performance does more for the film than the film does for him. [PG-13]▼▶

Pink Floyd—The Wall (1982-British) **C-99m.** **½ D: Alan Parker. Bob Geldof, Christine Hargreaves, James Laurenson, Eleanor David, Bob Hoskins. Visualization of Pink Floyd's somber best-selling album, about a rock star's mental breakdown, is perhaps the longest rock video to date, and certainly the most depressing. Many of the images are hypnotic, but self-indulgence, and a relentlessly downbeat theme, erode one's interest after a while. Striking ani-mated sequences by Gerald Scarfe, who also designed the film. Aka THE WALL. Panavision. [R]▼▶

Pink Jungle, The (1968) **C-104m.** **½ D: Delbert Mann. James Garner, Eva Renzi, George Kennedy, Nigel Green, Michael Ansara, George Rose. Offbeat blend of comedy and adventure with photographer Garner and model Renzi involved in diamond smuggling in South America. Film shifts gears too often, but provides light-hearted entertainment. Techniscope.▼

Pink Panther, The (1964) **C-113m.** ***½ D: Blake Edwards. Peter Sellers, David Niven, Capucine, Robert Wagner, Claudia Cardinale, Brenda DeBanzie, John LeMesurier, Fran Jeffries. Delightful caper comedy introduced bumbling Inspector Clouseau to the world (as well as the cartoon character featured in the opening titles), so obsessed with catching notorious jewel thief "The Phantom" that he isn't aware his quarry is also his wife's lover! Loaded with great slapstick and especially clever chase sequence; beautiful European locations, memorable score by Henry Mancini. Remade in 2006. Followed by A SHOT IN THE DARK. Technirama.▼▶

Pink Panther, The (2006) **C-93m.** ** D: Shawn Levy. Steve Martin, Kevin Kline, Beyoncé Knowles, Jean Reno, Emily Mortimer, Henry Czerny, Roger Rees, Kristin Chenoweth. As maladroit, oblivious French *flic* Inspector Clouseau, Steve Martin won't make anyone forget Peter Sellers. Plot doesn't amount to much: the Pink Panther diamond is lifted off the body of a soccer star in front of thousands of spectators. Still, at moments, the movie and Martin deliver the goods (the star also cowrote the script). What's lacking is the wacky grace and clever timing of Blake Edwards. There are a few surprise cameos, however. Followed by a sequel. [PG]▶

Pink Panther 2, The (2009) **C-92m.** *½ D: Harald Zwart. Steve Martin, John Cleese, Jean Reno, Emily Mortimer, Andy Garcia, Alfred Molina, Yuki Matsuzaki, Aishwarya Rai Bachchan, Lily Tomlin, Jeremy Irons, Johnny Hallyday. Second outing in Martin's updating of Blake Edwards' Inspector Clouseau character is burdened by so much cement whimsy that you'd almost guess its comic stylings were directed by *Ethan* Edwards from THE SEARCHERS. Fatigued farce deals with high-stakes serial thievery that begins with someone stealing the Magna Carta and eventually involves the Pope. Mortimer offers a sweet, light touch as Clouseau's unconfident not-quite-girlfriend, but most of the fine supporting cast is wasted. Cleese replaces Kevin Kline as Clouseau's beleaguered superior, Dreyfus. Martin coscripted. [PG]▶

Pink Panther Strikes Again, The (1976-British) **C-103m.** ***½ D: Blake Edwards.

Peter Sellers, Herbert Lom, Colin Blakely, Leonard Rossiter, Lesley-Anne Down, Burt Kwouk, Andre Maranne. Fifth PINK PANTHER is one of the funniest. Sellers' former boss (Lom) goes crazy, threatens to destroy the world with a ray-gun he has commandeered. Sellers' hilarious Inspector Clouseau is backed up by better-than-usual gags—with the usual number of pain-and-destruction jokes thrown in for good measure. Omar Sharif appears unbilled. Sequel: REVENGE OF THE PINK PANTHER. Panavision. [PG]▼●▶

Pinky (1949) **102m.** ******* D: Elia Kazan. Jeanne Crain, Ethel Barrymore, Ethel Waters, Nina Mae McKinney, William Lundigan. Pioneer racial drama of black girl passing for white, returning to Southern home; still has impact, with fine support from Mmes Waters and Barrymore.▼▶

Pinocchio (1940) **C-88m.** ******** D: Ben Sharpsteen, Hamilton Luske. Voices of Dickie Jones, Christian Rub, Cliff Edwards, Evelyn Venable, Walter Catlett, Frankie Darro. Walt Disney's brilliant, timeless animated cartoon feature, based on the Collodi story about an inquisitive, tale-spinning wooden puppet who wants more than anything else to become a real boy. Technically dazzling, emotionally rich, with unforgettable characters and some of the scariest scenes ever put on film (Lampwick's transformation into a jackass, the chase with Monstro the whale). A joy, no matter how many times you see it. Songs include Oscar-winning "When You Wish Upon a Star."▼●▶

Pinocchio (2002-Italian) **C-108m.** ***½** D: Roberto Benigni. Roberto Benigni, Nicoletta Braschi, Mino Bellei, Carlo Giuffré, Peppe Barra, Franco Javarone, Max Cavallari. A carved wooden puppet comes to life as a mischievous boy who can't resist temptation of any kind. Benigni's interpretation of the beloved 1885 story by Carlo Collodi emerges as a test of one's tolerance for the bombastic comic actor. This was a big hit in Italy . . . but then, so was Mussolini. U.S. version was cut to 100m. and dubbed with Breckin Meyer (as Benigni) and a host of stars (Glenn Close, Queen Latifah, Eddie Griffin, Cheech Marin, John Cleese, Eric Idle, Regis Philbin, James Belushi, Topher Grace, David Suchet). Italian title: THE ADVENTURES OF PINOCCHIO. Panavision. [G]▼▶

Pinocchio and the Emperor of the Night (1987) **C-87m.** ****** D: Hal Sutherland. Voices of Edward Asner, Tom Bosley, Lana Beeson, Linda Gary, Jonathan Harris, James Earl Jones, Ricky Lee Jones, Don Knotts, William Windom. Uninspired continuation of the Pinocchio story: now a real boy, Pinocchio is guided by "Gee Whillikers," a wooden bug come to life, and they enjoy many adventures which parallel the

Disney classic. Fully animated by Filmation Studios, but an embarrassment next to the 1940 gem. [G]▼●

Pipe Dreams (1976) **C-89m.** ****½** D: Stephen Verona. Gladys Knight, Barry Hankerson, Bruce French, Sherry Bain, Wayne Tippit, Altovise Davis, Sally Kirkland. Singing star Knight makes acting debut in highly dramatic story set against Alaskan pipeline. Excellent location shooting. Soundtrack filled with songs by Knight and her group, the Pips. [PG]▼

Pippi Longstocking (1997-Swedish-Canadian) **C-77m.** ****½** D: Clive Smith. Voices of Catherine O'Hara, Dave Thomas, Wayne Robson, Gordon Pinsent, Melissa Altro. Faithful animated version of Astrid Lindgren's story about the world's strongest girl, Miss Pippilotta Delicatessa Windowshade Mackrelmint Efraimsdottir Longstocking, age 9, as she encounters school, friends, the circus, and burglars, all for the first time. Nelvana studio's bright artwork and the script's cheerful characterizations will please fans, but the songs are dreary. Followed by a direct-to-video sequel. [G]▼▶

Piranha (1978) **C-92m.** ******* D: Joe Dante. Bradford Dillman, Heather Menzies, Kevin McCarthy, Keenan Wynn, Dick Miller, Barbara Steele, Belinda Balaski, Bruce Gordon, Paul Bartel. Fast-paced, funny spoof of JAWS and countless 1950s sci-fi films; in-jokes and campy supporting cast will make it particular fun for film buffs. Written by John Sayles (who also plays a small role). Followed by a sequel. Remade (in name only) in 2010. [R]▼▶

Piranha (2010) **C-88m.** ****** D: Alexandre Aja. Ving Rhames, Elisabeth Shue, Christopher Lloyd, Jerry O'Connell, Adam Scott, Ricardo Chavira, Steven R. McQueen, Cody Longo, Kelly Brook, Jessica Szohr, Dina Meyer, Eli Roth, Richard Dreyfuss. An earthquake opens a fissure beneath an Arizona resort lake, freeing thousands of extra-large, famished prehistoric piranhas. It's spring break, with hundreds of often-naked college students engaged in sex, fun, and games . . . so, dinner is served. Not really a remake of PIRANHA (1978), this is 20,000 leagues more violent and gory, with people losing flesh and body parts to the hungry fishies. Tongue-in-cheek tone makes it a bit easier to watch for those who aren't gore fans, though it's not as clever as the original. Dreyfuss appears briefly as an ichthyologist named Matt (wink wink, nudge nudge). Advertised as PIRANHA 3-D. Panavision. [3-D] [R]▶

Piranha Part Two: The Spawning (1981-Italian-U.S.) **C-95m.** ***½** D: James Cameron. Tricia O'Neil, Steve Marachuk, Lance Henriksen, Ricky G. Paul, Ted Richert, Leslie Graves. A sequel in name only, this silly horror film is set at a Club Med–type resort where human mating ritu-

[1082]

als are interrupted by the spawning ritual of mutated flying fish crossed with grunions, which are oversize, deadly killers. You'd have to be psychic to have spotted any talent from director Cameron in this debut picture. [R]▼●◗

Pirate, The (1948) **C-102m.** *** **D:** Vincente Minnelli. Judy Garland, Gene Kelly, Walter Slezak, Gladys Cooper, Reginald Owen, George Zucco, The Nicholas Brothers. Judy thinks circus clown Kelly is really Caribbean pirate; lavish costuming, dancing and Cole Porter songs (including "Be a Clown") bolster stagy plot. Kelly's dances are exhilarating, as usual. Based on S. N. Behrman play.▼●◗

Pirate Movie, The (1982-Australian) **C-99m.** BOMB **D:** Ken Annakin. Kristy McNichol, Christopher Atkins, Ted Hamilton, Bill Kerr, Maggie Kirkpatrick, Garry McDonald. Appalling "update" of Gilbert & Sullivan's *The Pirates of Penzance* not only trashes the original but fails on its own paltry terms—as a teenybopper comedy with bubblegum music. Parodies (and steals from) so many other films it should have been called THE RIP-OFF MOVIE. [PG]▼◗

Pirate Radio (2009-British-French-U.S.-German) **C-111m.** ** **D:** Richard Curtis. Philip Seymour Hoffman, Bill Nighy, Rhys Ifans, Kenneth Branagh, Nick Frost, Tom Sturridge, Talulah Riley, Rhys Darby, Chris O'Dowd, Gemma Arterton, Jack Davenport, January Jones, Emma Thompson. Rock 'n' roll is in full bloom in the U.K. during the 1960s but the BBC barely plays it, so pirate radio stations flourish, like the (fictional) Radio Rock, which broadcasts from an old fishing trawler at sea. It's staffed by a colorful bunch of oddballs including a super-cool dude known as The Count (Hoffman, in a likable comedic performance). Unfortunately, once the film sets its premise it goes nowhere. Good cast and a soundtrack full of oldies can only help so much. Written by the director. Original British title: THE BOAT THAT ROCKED, running 129m. Super 35. [R]◗

Pirates (1986-French-Tunisian) **C-124m.** **½ **D:** Roman Polanski. Walter Matthau, Damien Thomas, Richard Pearson, Cris Campion, Charlotte Lewis, Olu Jacobs, Roy Kinnear, Ferdy Mayne, Tony Peck. Rich-looking, robust pirate comedy, filmed on a grand scale (in widescreen), with plenty of broad comedy, a delightful performance by Matthau, a rousing score by Philippe Sarde . . . and a certain lack of story. It's still fun. Panavision. [PG-13]▼

Pirates of Penzance, The (1983) **C-112m.** *** **D:** Wilford Leach. Kevin Kline, Angela Lansbury, Linda Ronstadt, George Rose, Rex Smith, Tony Azito. Joseph Papp's hit stage revival of the Gilbert and Sullivan perennial is transferred to film with the original cast (plus Lansbury) and director— who

decided to make no bones about its theatricality! Not for G&S purists, perhaps, but fun. Splendid production design by Elliot Scott. Panavision. [G]▼●◗

Pirates of the Caribbean: At World's End (2007) **C-168m.** *½ **D:** Gore Verbinski. Johnny Depp, Geoffrey Rush, Orlando Bloom, Keira Knightley, Jack Davenport, Bill Nighy, Jonathan Pryce, Lee Arenberg, Mackenzie Crook, Stellan Skarsgård, Chow Yun-Fat, Naomie Harris, Keith Richards. Seven leagues of boredom. Will (Bloom), Elizabeth (Knightley), and a resurrected Capt. Barbossa (Rush) unite to rescue Jack (Depp) from Davy Jones' locker and embark on an epic battle against Jones and the evil East India Trading Company. Convoluted and interminable sequel is just another soulless "product," offering precious little joie de vivre or entertainment, despite the almost nonstop action. Even the Rolling Stones' Richards as Depp's even more grungy father can't liven things up. Super 35. [PG-13]◗

Pirates of the Caribbean: Dead Man's Chest (2006) **C-151m.** ** **D:** Gore Verbinski. Johnny Depp, Orlando Bloom, Keira Knightley, Stellan Skarsgård, Bill Nighy, Jack Davenport, Mackenzie Crook, Lee Arenberg, Kevin R. McNally, Jonathan Pryce, Naomie Harris. Will Turner (Bloom) is sent to find Capt. Jack Sparrow (Depp) and retrieve a valuable compass he uses, for reasons much too complicated to explain here. Davy Jones (Nighy) is also on the prowl for Sparrow with the crew of his ghostly ship and its pirates-in-purgatory. Lumbering sequel has no real tale to tell and drains the charm out of its three lead characters, who were so much fun to watch in the first movie. Some good action/stunt set pieces can't compensate for this cheerless, seemingly endless voyage. Geoffrey Rush appears unbilled. Oscar winner for Visual Effects. Super 35. [PG-13]◗

Pirates of the Caribbean: On Stranger Tides (2011) **C-137m.** ** **D:** Rob Marshall. Johnny Depp, Penélope Cruz, Geoffrey Rush, Ian McShane, Kevin R. McNally, Sam Claflin, Astrid Bergès-Frisbey, Stephen Graham, Keith Richards, Richard Griffiths, Roger Allam, Judi Dench. Capt. Jack Sparrow (Depp, broader than ever) finds himself on a ship with Blackbeard (McShane) and his daughter (Cruz), with whom he has a checkered history, sailing in search of Ponce de Leon's Fountain of Youth. Meanwhile, Capt. Barbossa (Rush) is piloting his own vessel on the exact same course. Among the perils they face: a host of alluring but vicious mermaids. More of the same, with a convoluted, often incomprehensible story designed to string a series of large-scale action set pieces together. Not so much a movie as a consumer product. 3-D HD Widescreen. [PG-13]◗

Pirates of the Caribbean: The Curse of the Black Pearl (2003) **C-143m.** **½ **D:** Gore

Verbinski. Johnny Depp, Geoffrey Rush, Orlando Bloom, Keira Knightley, Jonathan Pryce, Jack Davenport, Kevin R. McNally, Zoe Saldana. Besotted pirate Jack Sparrow attempts to regain control of his ship, the *Black Pearl*, in spite of a ghostly curse that's been placed on its crew. Stylishly designed and shot, with rollicking performances, this depends more on special effects than the fabled stunt work of classic pirate films (although there's a nice homage to THE CRIMSON PIRATE). Fans of the original Disneyland attraction will also enjoy the references that dot the film . . . but there's no reason for it to be quite so long or plot-heavy. Followed by three sequels. Super 35. [PG-13]▼▶

Pirates Who Don't Do Anything: A VeggieTales Movie, The (2008) C-85m. **½ D: Mike Nawrocki. Voices of Phil Vischer, Mike Nawrocki, Cam Clarke, Yuri Lowenthal, Alan Lee, Cydney Trent. Elliot (aka Larry the Cucumber), Sedgewick (aka Mr. Lunt), and George (aka Pa Grape) are employees of a dinner theater who dream of putting on a show about pirates, then find themselves magically transported to the 17th century, becoming pirates on a mission to rescue a royal family from an evil tyrant. Well-made but lackluster animated feature may entertain small children with slapstick action and corny puns. Christian messages and themes are more muted than in other *VeggieTales* stories. [G]▶

Pit and the Pendulum (1961) C-80m. ***½ D: Roger Corman. Vincent Price, John Kerr, Barbara Steele, Luana Anders, Antony Carbone. Slick horror tale set right after Spanish Inquisition. Price thinks he is his late father, the most vicious torturer during bloody inquisition. Beautifully staged; watch out for that incredible pendulum . . . and bear with slow first half. The second of Corman's Poe adaptations, scripted by Richard Matheson. Panavision. ▼▶

Pit and the Pendulum, The (1991) C-97m. *** D: Stuart Gordon. Lance Henriksen, Rona De Ricci, Jonathan Fuller, Frances Bay, Mark Margolis, Jeffrey Combs, Oliver Reed. In 1492, Torquemada (Henriksen), Spain's Grand Inquisitor, is haunted by his lust for a baker's wife accused of witchcraft. Strong, well-researched script (by Dennis Paoli) owes little to Poe, but is vividly realized by Gordon; graphic scenes of torture are appropriate here, and Henriksen's intense performance is mesmerizing. The best film to come from the folks at Full Moon. Shot in Spain. Available in an unrated version. [R]▼▶●

Pitch Black (2000-U.S.-Australian) C-107m. ** D: David Twohy. Radha Mitchell, Vin Diesel, Cole Hauser, Keith David, Lewis Fitz-Gerald, Claudia Black, Rhiana Griffith. Ambitious but formulaic sci-fi/horror film set in the future, with a motley planeload of passengers crash-landing on a remote planet. Not only do they have to contend with a violent, amoral ex-con (the imposing Diesel) in their midst, but an unknown terror that's magnified by the threat of total darkness. Some exciting scenes and effects, but weighed down by a feeling of déjà vu. Also available in unrated director's cut. Followed by THE CHRONICLES OF RIDDICK. Super 35. [R]▼▶

Pitfall (1948) **84m.** *** D: Andre de Toth. Dick Powell, Lizabeth Scott, Jane Wyatt, Raymond Burr, John Litel, Byron Barr. Married man's brief extramarital fling may cost him his job and marriage. Intriguing film noir look at the American dream gone sour, typefied by Powell's character, who's got a house, a little boy, and a perfect wife—but feels bored and stifled.▼●

Pit Stop (1969) **92m.** **½ D: Jack Hill. Brian Donlevy, Richard Davalos, Ellen McRae (Burstyn), Sid Haig, Beverly Washburn, George Washburn. Surprisingly entertaining micro-budget drive-in fare about rivalry on the stock-car racing circuit, with some genuinely hair-raising footage during figure-eight races.▼▶

Pittsburgh (1942) **90m.** ** D: Lewis Seiler. Marlene Dietrich, John Wayne, Randolph Scott, Frank Craven, Louise Allbritton, Thomas Gomez, Shemp Howard. Big John loves the coal and steel business more than he does Marlene, which leaves field open for rival Scott. Slow-moving.▼▶

Pixote (1981-Brazilian) **C-127m.** **** D: Hector Babenco. Fernando Ramos da Silva, Marilia Pera, Jorge Juliano, Gilberto Moura, Jose Nilson dos Santos, Edilson Lino. Chilling drama about an abandoned 10-year-old street criminal who pimps, sniffs glue, and murders three people before the finale. Haunting performance by the baby-faced da Silva; Pera equally superb as a prostitute. Extraordinarily graphic film is not for the squeamish.▼▶

Pizza Triangle, The (1970-Italian) **C-99m.** **½ D: Ettore Scola. Marcello Mastroianni, Monica Vitti, Giancarlo Giannini. Scene-stealing stars compete in this flamboyant black comedy of two guys both in love with flower seller Vitti. Colorful photography by Carlo Di Palma. Aka A DRAMA OF JEALOUSY. Panavision. [R]

P.J. (1968) **C-109m.** ** D: John Guillermin. George Peppard, Raymond Burr, Gayle Hunnicutt, Brock Peters, Wilfrid Hyde-White, Coleen Gray, Susan Saint James. Private-eye takes job bodyguarding tycoon's mistress. OK for those who'll sit through any film of this genre, but no big deal. Techniscope.

P.K. and the Kid (1982) **C-89m.** ** D: Lou Lombardo. Paul Le Mat, Molly Ringwald, Alex Rocco, Fionnula Flanagan, Charles Hallahan, Bert Remsen, Esther Rolle, Leigh Hamilton. Stillborn tale of arm wrestling (made several years before the Sylvester Stallone classic OVER THE TOP, but released afterward) teams strong-wristed Le Mat with runaway teen Ringwald on the road to nowhere. With that cast and a mood resembling Le Mat's MELVIN AND HOWARD, this should have been more interesting. [PG-13]▼●

Place Called Glory, A (1966-German) **C-92m.** ** D: Ralph Gideon (Sheldon Reynolds). Lex Barker, Pierre Brice, Marianne Koch, Jorge Rigaud. German-made Western about a lawless town's annual celebration, which includes a duel between two duped gunslingers. Bizarre, yet interesting, but hurt by poor dubbing. Techniscope.▼

Place for Lovers, A (1968-Italian-French) **C-90m.** BOMB D: Vittorio De Sica. Faye Dunaway, Marcello Mastroianni, Caroline Mortimer, Karin Engh. One well-known critic called this "the most godawful piece of pseudo romantic slop I've ever seen!" Love story about American fashion designer and Italian engineer marks career low points for all concerned. [R]

Place in the Sun, A (1951) **122m.** *** D: George Stevens. Montgomery Clift, Elizabeth Taylor, Shelley Winters, Keefe Brasselle, Raymond Burr, Anne Revere. Ambitious remake of Theodore Dreiser's AN AMERICAN TRAGEDY derives most of its power from Clift's brilliant performance, almost matched by Winters as plain girl who loses him to alluring Taylor. Depiction of the idle rich, and American morals, seems outdated, and Burr's scenes as fiery D.A. are downright absurd. Everyone gets A for effort; six Oscars included Best Direction, Screenplay (Michael Wilson, Harry Brown), Score (Franz Waxman), Cinematography (William C. Mellor), Film Editing, and Costume Design.▼●

Places in the Heart (1984) **C-111m.** *** D: Robert Benton. Sally Field, Lindsay Crouse, Ed Harris, Amy Madigan, John Malkovich, Danny Glover, Terry O'Quinn, Bert Remsen, Ray Baker. Writer-director Benton's affectionate look at life in his hometown, Waxahachie, Texas, during the Depression 1930s. A bit too calculated and predictable, but Field is so good (as a young widow determined to survive as a cotton farmer), and film is so well made (beautifully shot by Nestor Almendros), it's hard not to like. Field won Best Actress Oscar for her performance as did Benton for his original screenplay. [PG]▼●

Place Vendôme (1998-French) **C-117m.** *** D: Nicole Garcia. Catherine Deneuve, Jean-Pierre Bacri, Emmanuelle Seigner, Jacques Dutronc, Bernard Fresson, François Berléand. When the director of a jewelry store dies, his alcoholic wife (Deneuve) becomes involved with stolen diamonds and links to past betrayal and love. Quiet, very deliberately paced story works both as low-

key thriller and character study, anchored by Deneuve's excellent lead performance. Widescreen.▼●

Plague, The (1991-French-British-Argentine) **C-105m.** *½ D: Luis Puenzo. William Hurt, Sandrine Bonnaire, Jean-Marc Barr, Robert Duvall, Raul Julia, Victoria Tennant. Obvious, muddled adaptation (by director Puenzo) of the Albert Camus novel, focusing on a dedicated doctor (Hurt), a French TV reporter (Bonnaire) and cameraman (Barr), and various other characters whose lives become intertwined during a deadly plague in a South American city. A major disappointment. Never released theatrically in the U.S. [R]▼●

Plague Dogs, The (1982) **C-86m.** *** D: Martin Rosen. Voices of John Hurt, James Bolam, Christopher Benjamin, Judy Geeson, Barbara Leigh-Hunt, Nigel Hawthorne, Patrick Stewart. Unusual animated adventure, adapted from Richard Adams's novel about a pair of dogs who escape from animal experimentation lab and are hunted down like criminals. A bit slow-moving but beautifully animated; a poignant plea for animal rights. For adults and older children only. A follow-up to WATERSHIP DOWN from same producer-director.▼●

Plague of the Zombies, The (1966-British) **C-90m.** **½ D: John Gilling. Andre Morell, Diane Clare, Brook Williams, Jacqueline Pearce, John Carson. Beautiful low-key photography and direction in fairly tense story of voodoo cult in Cornish village. Minor but effective Hammer horror.▼●●

Plainsman, The (1936) **113m.** *** D: Cecil B. DeMille. Gary Cooper, Jean Arthur, James Ellison, Charles Bickford, Porter Hall, Victor Varconi, Helen Burgess, John Miljan, Gabby Hayes, Paul Harvey, Frank McGlynn, Sr. Typical DeMille hokum, a big, outlandish Western which somehow manages to involve Wild Bill Hickok, Calamity Jane, Buffalo Bill, George Custer and Abraham Lincoln in adventure of evil Bickford selling guns to the Indians. About as authentic as BLAZING SADDLES, but who cares—it's still good fun. Look for Anthony Quinn as a Cheyenne warrior. Remade in 1966.▼●●

Plainsman, The (1966) **C-92m.** *½ D: David Lowell Rich. Don Murray, Guy Stockwell, Abby Dalton, Bradford Dillman, Leslie Nielsen. Static remake of the Cooper-Arthur vehicle is dull even on its own.

Plan B (1997) **C-102m.** **½ D: Gary Leva. Jon Cryer, Lisa Darr, Lance Guest, Mark Mathiesen, Sara Mornell. Amiable low-budget film about a group of friends, their romantic snafus, and the roadblocks they encounter in reaching their goals—to become a published novelist, to find the perfect guy, to get that big break as an actor, to conceive a child. Likable performances, reasonably credible situations and dialogue, but there are at least three endings. [R]▼

Planes, Trains & Automobiles (1987) **C-93m.** **½ D: John Hughes. Steve Martin, John Candy, Laila Robins, Michael McKean, Kevin Bacon, Dylan Baker, William Windom, Edie McClurg, Ben Stein. Bittersweet farce about a businessman trying to get home for Thanksgiving who encounters disaster at every turn and has to share most of it with a lout who becomes his steadfast companion. Martin mostly plays straight to the overbearing Candy, but writer-director Hughes refuses to make either one a caricature—which keeps this amiable film teetering between slapstick shenanigans and compassionate comedy. Hurt by an awful music score. [R]▼●)

Planet 51 (2009-U.S.-British-Spanish) **C-91m.** *½ D: Jorge Blanco, Javier Abad. Voices of Dwayne Johnson, Jessica Biel, Justin Long, Gary Oldman, Seann William Scott, John Cleese, Freddie Benedict, Alan Marriott. E.T. in reverse: animated comedy about an Earth astronaut who explores an alien planet populated by green-skinned natives who live and act, in every way, like stereotypical American suburbanites of the 1950s. One-joke idea, stretched to feature length, isn't compelling enough for adults or funny enough for older kids, though abundant slapstick action may entertain the small ones. Dialogue is clichéd and repeated references to other science-fiction movies get tiring. Explore elsewhere. Digital Widescreen. [PG]❱

Planet of Blood (1966) **C-81m.** **½ D: Curtis Harrington. John Saxon, Basil Rathbone, Judi Meredith, Dennis Hopper, Florence Marly. Eerie space opera (utilizing effects footage cribbed from a big-budget Russian film) about a space vampire brought to Earth. Best thing is the bizarre climax, if you can wait that long. Originally titled QUEEN OF BLOOD.▼●)

Planet of Horrors SEE: **Galaxy of Terror**

Planet of the Apes (1968) **C-112m.** ***½ D: Franklin J. Schaffner. Charlton Heston, Roddy McDowall, Kim Hunter, Maurice Evans, James Whitmore, James Daly, Linda Harrison. Intriguing, near-classic sci-fi. Heston leads a group of surviving astronauts in shocking future world where apes are masters, humans slaves. Only liabilities: somewhat familiar plot, self-conscious humor; otherwise, a must-see. Michael Wilson and Rod Serling scripted from Pierre Boulle's novel, spawning four sequels and two TV series. Won a special Oscar for makeup created by John Chambers. Remade in 2001. Panavision. [G]▼●)

Planet of the Apes (2001) **C-120m.** **½ D: Tim Burton. Mark Wahlberg, Tim Roth, Helena Bonham Carter, Michael Clarke Duncan, Paul Giamatti, Estella Warren,

Cary-Hiroyuki Tagawa, David Warner, Kris Kristofferson, Glenn Shadix, Lisa Marie. Entertaining if forgettable rethink of the 1968 film, as an astronaut crash-lands on a strange planet ruled by apes, where humans are slaves and regarded as scum. One ape, the daughter of a prominent senator, thinks otherwise, and even agrees to help Wahlberg escape. A good yarn with great production design and impressive makeup by Rick Baker. Finale, with Rod Serling overtones, is the major letdown. Charlton Heston is arresting in his unbilled appearance, and Linda Harrison (also from the original cast) appears briefly. Panavision. [PG-13] ▼❱

Planet of the Vampires (1965-Italian) **C-86m.** **½ D: Mario Bava. Barry Sullivan, Norma Bengell, Angel Aranda, Evi Marandi, Fernando Villena. Eerily photographed, atmospheric science-fantasy of spaceship looking for missing comrades on misty planet where strange power controls their minds. Shown on TV as THE DEMON PLANET.▼●)

Plan 9 From Outer Space (1959) **79m.** BOMB D: Edward D. Wood, Jr. Gregory Walcott, Tom Keene, Duke Moore, Mona McKinnon, Dudley Manlove, Joanna Lee, Tor Johnson, Lyle Talbot, Bela Lugosi, Vampira, Criswell. Hailed as the worst movie ever made; certainly one of the funniest. Pompous aliens believe they can conquer Earth by resurrecting corpses from a San Fernando Valley cemetery. Lugosi died after two days' shooting in 1956; his remaining scenes were played by a taller, younger man holding a cape over his face! So mesmerizingly awful it actually improves (so to speak) with each viewing. And remember: it's all based on sworn testimony! Followed by REVENGE OF THE DEAD.▼●)

Planter's Wife SEE: **Outpost in Malaya**

Platinum Blonde (1931) **90m.** *** D: Frank Capra. Jean Harlow, Loretta Young, Robert Williams, Louise Closser Hale, Donald Dillaway, Walter Catlett. Snappy comedy about wisecracking reporter who marries wealthy girl (Harlow) but can't stand confinement of life among high society. Despite engaging presence of Harlow and Young, it's Williams' show all the way.▼❱

Platoon (1986) **C-120m.** ***½ D: Oliver Stone. Tom Berenger, Willem Dafoe, Charlie Sheen, Forest Whitaker, Francesco Quinn, John C. McGinley, Richard Edson, Kevin Dillon, Reggie Johnson, Keith David, Johnny Depp. Penetrating first-person account of life on the line as a young soldier in the Vietnam War. Harrowingly realistic and completely convincing, though the motives and reactions of its main character (played by Sheen, based on writer-director Stone) are hard to relate to—leaving this otherwise excellent film with a certain degree of aloofness. Academy Award winner for Best Picture, Director, Film Editing (Claire Simpson), and Sound. [R]▼●▶

Platoon Leader (1988) **C-100m.** BOMB D: Aaron Norris. Michael Dudikoff, Robert F. Lyons, Michael De Lorenzo, Rick Fitts, Jesse Dabson. Obnoxious, bloody PLATOON rip-off, about a group of American GIs battling the commies in Southeast Asia. Director Norris is the brother of Chuck. [R]▼●

Playboys, The (1992) **C-110m.** **½ D: Gillies MacKinnon. Albert Finney, Aidan Quinn, Robin Wright, Milo O'Shea, Alan Devlin, Niamh Cusack, Ian McElhinney, Niall Buggy, Adrian Dunbar. A young woman scandalizes her provincial Irish village in the 1950s by having a child out of wedlock, and refusing to name the father; the arrival of a traveling dramatic troupe stirs things up even more. Flavorful but heavy-handed tale; good performances can only do so much with a script that's so predictable. [PG-13]▼●▶

Play Dirty (1968-British) **C-117m.** *** D: Andre de Toth. Michael Caine, Nigel Davenport, Nigel Green, Harry Andrews, Aly Ben Ayed. British army captain leads group of ex-cons into the North African campaign in WW2; film invites comparison with THE DIRTY DOZEN and holds its own quite well. Panavision. [M/PG]▶

Player, The (1992) **C-123m.** *** D: Robert Altman. Tim Robbins, Greta Scacchi, Fred Ward, Whoopi Goldberg, Peter Gallagher, Brion James, Cynthia Stevenson, Vincent D'Onofrio, Dean Stockwell, Richard E. Grant, Dina Merrill, Sydney Pollack, Lyle Lovett, Randall Batinkoff, Jeremy Piven, Gina Gershon. Sharp black comedy about a paranoid young movie executive (Robbins) who is threatened by a disgruntled screenwriter—until he begins taking the law into his own hands. Biting examination of Hollywood greed and power, with eternal renegade Altman near the top of his form (especially during the eight-minute opening tracking shot). Hilarious performances, scores of star cameos (several by Altman alumni like Elliott Gould, Lily Tomlin, Sally Kellerman, and Cher), *many* inside jokes . . . but a bit too much plot. Adapted by Michael Tolkin from his novel; Tolkin and his lookalike brother, Stephen, also appear as a pair of writers who meet with Robbins. [R]▼●▶

Players (1979) **C-120m.** BOMB D: Anthony Harvey. Ali MacGraw, Dean-Paul Martin, Maximilian Schell, Pancho Gonzalez, Steve Guttenberg, Melissa Prophet. Aspiring tennis pro has to choose between forehand and foreplay when he falls for a "kept" woman. There's something wrong with any movie where Pancho Gonzalez gives the best performance. [PG]▼

Players (1980) SEE: **Club, The**

Players Club, The (1998) **C-104m.** ** D: Ice Cube. LisaRaye, Bernie Mac, Monica Calhoun, A. J. Johnson, Ice Cube, Alex Thomas, Faizon Love, Charles O. Murphy, Adele Givens, Chrystale Wilson, Terrence Howard, Larry McCoy, Dick Anthony Williams, Tiny Lister, Jamie Foxx, John Amos, Michael Clarke Duncan. A college journalism major looks back on the sleazy events that took place during her long employment at a black strip club, among them the lurid apartment parties that took place on the side. Not a bad hook, but the film is done in by its seen-it-all-before limitations and pedestrian script. Cube also wrote the screenplay. [R]▼●

Playgirl After Dark SEE: **Too Hot to Handle** (1960)

Playgirl Gang SEE: **Switchblade Sisters**

Playing by Heart (1998) **C-120m.** ** D: Willard Carroll. Sean Connery, Gena Rowlands, Gillian Anderson, Angelina Jolie, Madeleine Stowe, Anthony Edwards, Ryan Phillippe, Dennis Quaid, Ellen Burstyn, Jay Mohr, Michael Emerson, Jon Stewart, Patricia Clarkson, Nastassja Kinski, Daniel von Bargen, Amanda Peet. Talky film—with its heart in the right place—about a handful of L.A. men and women and their fouled-up relationships, ranging from an older couple whose marriage is strained by an illness and a long-ago affair, to a woman who comes to terms with her son for the first time as he lies in a hospital bed dying of AIDS. Attractive, well-cast, but dreary multistory mosaic, written by director Carroll. Panavision. [R] ▼●▶

Playing for Keeps (1986) **C-102m.** *½ D: Bob Weinstein, Harvey Weinstein. Daniel Jordano, Matthew Penn, Leon W. Grant, Mary B. Ward, Marisa Tomei, Jimmy Baio, Harold Gould. After finishing high school, a group of friends band together to save a run-down hotel from a greedy developer in an unfriendly town. A youth comedy from the '80s that's aged; worth seeing only for a young Marisa Tomei. Also notable as the only directorial effort by the founders and honchos of Miramax. Beware of the frequently used montage! [PG-13] ▼▶

Playing God (1997) **C-93m.** *½ D: Andy Wilson. David Duchovny, Timothy Hutton, Angelina Jolie, Michael Massee, Peter Stormare, Gary Dourdan, John Hawkes, Andrew Tiernan. Preposterous story of drug-addicted ex-surgeon Duchovny hired by gangster Hutton to be the personal emergency physician for his shot-up and slashed cronies. The improvised medical treatment is so completely laughable, it upstages the absurdity of the story line. Why this movie was ever made is truly a case for *The X-Files*. [R]▼●▶

Play It Again, Sam (1972) **C-87m.** ***½ D: Herbert Ross. Woody Allen, Diane Keaton, Tony Roberts, Jerry Lacy, Susan Anspach, Jennifer Salt, Joy Bang, Viva. Delightful adaptation of Woody's own play about film buff coached by the ghost of Bogart in fumbling attempts to impress girls after his wife divorces him. More "conventional" than other early Allen films, but just as funny. [PG]▼●)

Play It As It Lays (1972) C-99m. **½ D: Frank Perry. Tuesday Weld, Anthony Perkins, Tammy Grimes, Adam Roarke, Ruth Ford, Eddie Firestone. Film version of Joan Didion's best-seller about neglected wife of self-centered film director is helped by Weld-Perkins casting. Story is believable enough, but rambles inconclusively. Look for Tyne Daly as a journalist. [R]

Play It to the Bone (1999) C-124m. **½ D: Ron Shelton. Woody Harrelson, Antonio Banderas, Lolita Davidovich, Tom Sizemore, Lucy Liu, Robert Wagner, Richard Masur, Willie Garson, Cylk Cozart, Aida Turturro, Jack Carter. Two boxer friends are hired as last-minute substitutes on a primo Las Vegas fight card, and express their doubts and fears while driving from L.A. to Vegas with their mutual ex-girlfriend. Relaxed pace of Shelton's script challenges the viewer to stay interested through the long road trip up to the stormy and eventful fight and its aftermath. Many sports and show-business celebrities appear as themselves. Panavision. [R]▼●)

Play Misty for Me (1971) C-102m. *** D: Clint Eastwood. Clint Eastwood, Jessica Walter, Donna Mills, John Larch, Irene Hervey, Jack Ging, Johnny Otis, Cannonball Adderley Quintet. Well-done shocker of late night radio D.J. stalked by homicidal ex-fan Walter. Eastwood's first film as director; *his* frequent director, Don Siegel, plays Murphy the bartender. [R]▼●)

Play Time (1967-French) C-124m. **** D: Jacques Tati. Jacques Tati, Barbara Dennek, Jacqueline Lecomte, Valerie Camille, Léon Doyen. M. Hulot (Tati) wanders through an unrecognizable modern Paris of steel and glass skyscrapers. Sight and sound gags abound in this superbly constructed film, the various episodes of which are linked by Hulot's trying to keep an appointment. Art Buchwald provided dialogue for English-speaking scenes. Alternate version runs 155m. 70mm Widescreen. ▼●)

Plaza Suite (1971) C-115m. *** D: Arthur Hiller. Walter Matthau, Maureen Stapleton, Barbara Harris, Lee Grant, Louise Sorel. One of Neil Simon's funniest plays well adapted to screen. Three separate stories about people staying in certain room at famed N.Y.C. hotel, with Matthau in all three vignettes. Best one is the last, with Matthau as flustered father of a reluctant bride. [PG]▼●)

Pleasantville (1998) C/B&W-123m. **½ D: Gary Ross. Tobey Maguire, Jeff Daniels, Joan Allen, William H. Macy, J. T. Walsh, Reese Witherspoon, Don Knotts, Jane Kaczmarek, Paul Walker. A brother and sister are magically transported into their TV set and the black-and-white world of a '50s sitcom called *Pleasantville*, where ev-

erything is swell. Soon, they infiltrate this perfect environment with their worldly sensibilities, and the façade is easily cracked. Excellent performances and a striking visual design (the black-and-white world and its people slowly acquire color) spark this satire, which bites off more than it can chew, becoming slow and somber. Anyway, hooray for Don Knotts! Directing debut for screenwriter Ross. [PG-13] ▼●)

Please Don't Eat the Daisies (1960) C-111m. *** D: Charles Walters. Doris Day, David Niven, Janis Paige, Spring Byington, Richard Haydn, Patsy Kelly, Jack Weston, Margaret Lindsay. Bright film based on Jean Kerr's stories about a drama critic and his family. Doris sings title song; her kids are very amusing, as are Byington (the mother-in-law), Kelly (housekeeper), and especially Paige as a temperamental star. Later a TV series. CinemaScope.▼●)

Please Give (2010) C-90m. ***½ D: Nicole Holofcener. Catherine Keener, Amanda Peet, Oliver Platt, Rebecca Hall, Sarah Steele, Ann Guilbert, Lois Smith, Thomas Ian Nicholas, Sarah Vowell, Josh Pais. Keener and Platt make a good team, as husband and wife, parents of a teenage girl, and owners of a used furniture store in Manhattan. But she is consumed by guilt: There are homeless people on the street, and she feels like a predator buying goods from the children of recently deceased people. Then there's their sour, elderly neighbor, whose apartment they hope to buy. Wonderfully observant look at human nature and life in the city; writer-director Holofcener is generous toward all of her realistically flawed characters. The cast couldn't be better, but Guilbert is a standout as an old woman who's incapable of a kind word or thought. Super 16. [R])

Pleasure of His Company, The (1961) C-115m. ***½ D: George Seaton. Fred Astaire, Lilli Palmer, Debbie Reynolds, Tab Hunter, Gary Merrill, Charlie Ruggles. Delightful fluff, from Samuel Taylor and Cornelia Otis Skinner's play about charming ex-husband who comes to visit, enchanting his daughter and hounding his wife's new husband. Entire cast in rare form. Taylor also scripted.

Pleasure Seekers, The (1964) C-107m. **½ D: Jean Negulesco. Ann-Margret, Pamela Tiffin, Tony Franciosa, Carol Lynley, Gene Tierney, Brian Keith, Gardner McKay, Isobel Elsom. Glossy, semi-musical remake of THREE COINS IN THE FOUNTAIN (by same director) about three girls seeking fun and romance in Spain. CinemaScope.

Pledge, The (2001) C-124m. *** D: Sean Penn. Jack Nicholson, Robin Wright Penn, Benicio Del Toro, Vanessa Redgrave, Tom Noonan, Patricia Clarkson, Michael O'Keefe, Aaron Eckhart, Costas Mandylor, Helen Mirren, Mickey Rourke, Sam Shepard, Lois Smith, Harry Dean Stanton, Pauline Roberts. Nevada police detective, on the day of his retirement, becomes involved in the case of a little girl's murder and promises her parents that he will bring the killer to justice. Another great Nicholson performance anchors this fine-tuned film, which sidesteps formula in favor of nuance. Based on a novel by Friedrich Durrenmatt. Filmed twice before in Germany (in 1958 as IT HAPPENED IN BROAD DAYLIGHT and as a 1997 TV movie) and in England (in 1995 as THE COLD LIGHT OF DAY). J-D-C Scope. [R]▼▼

Plenty (1985) **C-124m.** **½ D: Fred Schepisi. Meryl Streep, Charles Dance, Tracey Ullman, John Gielgud, Sting, Ian McKellen, Sam Neill, Burt Kwouk, Hugh Laurie. Filmization of David Hare's play about a British woman who (like Britain itself) experiences her finest hours during WW2, working for the underground . . . and never finds fulfillment or satisfaction the rest of her life. Superlative performances (Gielgud is a particular delight as aging career diplomat) and moments of insight and wit can't overcome the fact that central character played by Streep is so tedious. Schepisi makes excellent use of widescreen. Panavision. [R] ▼●

Plot Against Harry, The (1989) **80m.** *** D: Michael Roemer. Martin Priest, Ben Lang, Maxine Woods, Henry Nemo, Jacques Taylor, Jean Leslie, Ellen Herbert, Sandra Kazan. Amusing, perceptive slice of N.Y.C. life about an aging racketeer, just sprung from prison, who finds the old order changing, and his life coming apart at the seams. Sad-faced Priest is perfectly cast in this modest, location-filmed production, which was shot in 1969 but never released—until film-festival showings in 1989 won critical acclaim and a distributor.▼▼

Plots With a View SEE: **Undertaking Betty**

Plough and the Stars, The (1936) **78m.** ** D: John Ford. Barbara Stanwyck, Preston Foster, Barry Fitzgerald, Una O'Connor, J. M. Kerrigan, Bonita Granville, Arthur Shields. Dreary, theatrical filmization of Sean O'Casey's play with Foster as Irish revolutionary leader and Stanwyck as long-suffering wife who fears for his life; script by Dudley Nichols.

Ploughman's Lunch, The (1983-British) **C-100m.** *** D: Richard Eyre. Jonathan Pryce, Tim Curry, Rosemary Harris, Frank Finlay, Charlie Dore. Complex, cynical condemnation of British manners, morals and politics, centering on the activities of thoroughly self-centered radio reporter Pryce and others during the Falklands war. Quite perceptive, within the confines of its viewpoint. [R]▼▼

Plucking the Daisy SEE: **Please! Mr. Balzac**

Plumber, The (1980-Australian) **C-76m.** *** D: Peter Weir. Judy Morris, Ivar Kants, Robert Coleby, Candy Raymond. Obnoxious plumber tears apart bathroom of unwilling tenants; film's single joke is stretched no further than it will go in slight but amusing black comedy made for Australian television.▼

Plunkett & Macleane (1999-British) **C-102m.** *** D: Jake Scott. Robert Carlyle, Jonny Lee Miller, Liv Tyler, Michael Gambon, Alan Cumming, Ken Stott, Claire Rushbrook. Rousing action-adventure about two of England's most notorious 18th-century highwaymen. Plays like BUTCH CASSIDY, with anachronistic hipster humor and a bumping techno score from Craig Armstrong. Don't think too hard about this flashy import; just sit back and enjoy the ride. As a bisexual dandy, Cumming cuts quite a swath. The debuting director is Ridley Scott's son. Super 35. [R]▼▼

Plymouth Adventure (1952) **C-105m.** **½ D: Clarence Brown. Spencer Tracy, Gene Tierney, Van Johnson, Leo Genn, Dawn Addams, Lloyd Bridges, Barry Jones. Superficial soap opera, glossily done, of the cynical captain of the *Mayflower* (Tracy) and the settlers who sailed from England to New England in the 17th century. This won an Oscar for its special effects.▼▼

Pocahontas (1995) **C-82m.** *** D: Mike Gabriel, Eric Goldberg. Voices of Irene Bedard, Judy Kuhn, Mel Gibson, David Ogden Stiers, John Kassir, Russell Means, Christian Bale, Linda Hunt, Billy Connolly, Frank Welker, Michelle St. John, James Apaumut Fall. More serious in tone than most Disney cartoon features, this one tells of the brave and free-spirited woman who defied her father—and her tribe—by falling in love with Capt. John Smith, part of a plundering party from England. Entertaining if not particularly memorable, with Pocahontas a strong and appealing character, and her sidekicks, Meeko (a raccoon) and Flit (a hummingbird), providing delightful comedy relief. Songs by Alan Menken and Stephen Schwartz include one standout, "Colors of the Wind." Both that song and Menken's music score won Oscars. Special edition DVD includes one additional song and runs 84m. Followed by a direct-to-video sequel. [G]▼●

Pocketful of Miracles (1961) **C-136m.** **½ D: Frank Capra. Bette Davis, Glenn Ford, Hope Lange, Arthur O'Connell, Thomas Mitchell, Peter Falk, Edward Everett Horton, Ann-Margret, Mickey Shaughnessy, David Brian, Sheldon Leonard, Barton MacLane, John Litel, Jerome Cowan, Fritz Feld, Jack Elam, Ellen Corby. Capra's final film, a remake of his 1933 LADY FOR A DAY, is just as sentimental, but doesn't work as well. Bette is Apple Annie, a Damon Runyon character; Ford is Dave the Dude, the racketeer who turns her into a lady. Ann-Margret is appealing in her first film. Panavision. ▼●▶

Pocket Money (1972) **C-102m.** **½ D: Stuart Rosenberg. Paul Newman, Lee Marvin, Strother Martin, Christine Belford, Kelly Jean Peters, Fred Graham, Wayne Rogers, Hector Elizondo, Richard Farnsworth. Debt-ridden cowboy and shifty pal get mixed up with crooked cattleman in modern-day Western. Strangely tepid comedy is helped by good Laszlo Kovacs photography, nice bit by Peters. Marvin's car is the damnedest thing you'll ever see. Screenplay by Terrence Malick. [PG] ▼●

Poetic Justice (1993) **C-110m.** ** D: John Singleton. Janet Jackson, Tupac Shakur, Regina King, Joe Torry, Maya Angelou, Tyra Ferrell, Roger Guenveur Smith, Q-Tip, Tone Loc, Billy Zane, Lori Petty. Ambitious but fatally pretentious saga of a melancholy South Central L.A. beautician (Jackson), who has retreated from the world after her boyfriend's murder; mailman Shakur attempts to break through to her, with predictable results. Implausibly, the poetry this otherwise ordinary woman composes actually is the work of Maya Angelou (who appears on-screen as June). Jackson is OK in her screen debut. [R] ▼●

Point Blank (1967) **C-92m.** ***½ D: John Boorman. Lee Marvin, Angie Dickinson, Keenan Wynn, Carroll O'Connor, Lloyd Bochner, Michael Strong, John Vernon. Marvin, shot and left for dead by unfaithful wife and mobster boyfriend, gets revenge two years later. Taut thriller, ignored in 1967, but now regarded as a top film of the decade. Based on the novel *The Hunter* by Donald E. Westlake (writing as Richard Stark). Remade as PAYBACK in 1999. Panavision. ▼●▶

Point Break (1991) **C-122m.** **½ D: Kathryn Bigelow. Patrick Swayze, Keanu Reeves, Gary Busey, Lori Petty, John McGinley, James LeGros, John Philbin, Sydney Walsh, Vincent Klyn, Julian Reyes, Tom Sizemore. Maverick FBI agent Reeves is sent undercover into Southern California's surfing community to investigate a baffling series of perfect bank robberies. Incredible, mind-numbing plotline redeemed by great surfing and skydiving scenes. Assured, fast-moving direction by Bigelow keeps this movie hanging five, if not ten . . . though Swayze is in desperate need of a hair stylist here. Super 35. [R] ▼●▶

Point of No Return (1993) **C-109m.** *½ D: John Badham. Bridget Fonda, Gabriel Byrne, Dermot Mulroney, Anne Bancroft, Harvey Keitel, Miguel Ferrer, Olivia d'Abo, Richard Romanus, Lorraine Toussaint, Geoffrey Lewis, Calvin Levels. An awful, slicked-up Hollywoodization of LA FEMME NIKITA, with punkish criminal Fonda recruited by the U.S. government

to shoot up a chi-chi Washington restaurant (with the *Washington Post* nowhere in sight). Not a genuine emotion to be found until Mulroney shows up; even then, not many more. Panavision. [R] ▼●▶

Point Zero SEE: **Ski Bum, The**

Poison (1991) **C-85m.** *** D: Todd Haynes. Edith Meeks, Larry Maxwell, Susan Norman, Scott Renderer, James Lyons. Jarring, disturbing film about what it means to be different, to be alienated from the mainstream, consisting of three skillfully interwoven stories: a mock documentary about a seven-year-old who's shot and killed his father, and summarily disappeared; a 1950s sci-fi movie parody, in which a brilliant scientist ingests some serum and becomes disfigured; and the chronicle of a gay thief who arrives at a prison. Scripted by Haynes, and inspired by the writings of Jean Genet. [NC-17] ▼●▶

Poison Ivy (1992) **C-89m.** ** D: Katt Shea Ruben. Drew Barrymore, Sara Gilbert, Tom Skerritt, Cheryl Ladd, Leonardo DiCaprio. Blah melodrama about a sluttish teen (Barrymore, who is well cast), and the insidious influence she has on the members of a wealthy, troubled family: shy Gilbert, her alcoholic dad (Skerritt) and dying mom (Ladd), and even the pet pooch. More subtlety and character development would have helped. Followed by four DVD sequels. [R] ▼●▶

Pokémon: The First Movie (1998-Japanese) **C-75m.** *½ D: Kuniniko Yuyama, Michael Haigney. Voices of Veronica Taylor, Philip Bartlett, Rachel Lillis, Eric Stuart, Addie Blaustein. Kids' video game/ TV show/card game phenomenon hits the big screen with OK story about a mutated Pokémon clone, Mewtwo, who plans to take over the world. Not very exciting, with barely adequate animation, but kids probably won't mind. Subtitle on-screen is MEWTWO STRIKES BACK. Followed by four sequels. [G] ▼▶

Pokémon the Movie 2000 (2000-Japanese-U.S.) **C-85m.** *½ D: Kuniniko Yuyama, Michael Haigney. Voices of Veronica Taylor, Rachel Lillis, Addie Blaustein, Eric Stuart, Ed Paul. Sequel to hit movie is subtitled THE POWER OF ONE. Once again, young Ash and his pals face off against a powerful enemy, a super-scientific Pokémon collector (and his CGI flying fortress) who unleashes a flying pokémenace. Lots of thunderbolts and effects animation, but no one to root for. You can skip the opening short, PIKACHU'S RESCUE ADVENTURE. [G] ▼▶

Pokémon 3: The Movie (2001-Japanese-U.S.) **C-90m.** ** D: Kuniniko Yuyama, Michael Haigney. Voices of Veronica Taylor, Eric Stuart, Rachael Lillis, Addie Blaustein, Ikue Otani. Most coherent and colorful of the Pokémon movies (admittedly, a small compliment). This time "unknown" Pokémon kidnap a mother and father, and use their small daughter to paralyze a town and challenge our young heroes Ash, Brock, and Misty. Preceded by a short episode with little Pikachu and his Poké-pals getting lost in the big city. Subtitled: SPELL OF THE UNKNOWN. Followed by POKÉMON 4EVER, then, in 2003, POKÉMON HEROES. [G] ▼◗

Polar Express, The (2004) **C-100m.** **½ D: Robert Zemeckis. Tom Hanks, Michael Jeter, Peter Scolari, Nona Gaye, Eddie Deezen, Charles Fleischer, Steven Tyler; voice of Daryl Sabara. Boy who desperately wants to see Santa Claus with his own eyes on a snowy Christmas Eve gets more than he bargained for when he boards a railroad train that stops right in front of his house. Expansion of Chris Van Allsburg's beautifully illustrated children's book (set in the 1950s Midwest) retains a feeling of wonder as the boy and newfound friends journey to the North Pole. "Performance Capture" digital animation renders all the characters slightly unreal—the kids look like they're wearing dentures—but aside from enabling Tom Hanks to play five roles it doesn't seem to have been worth all the bother. Still an entertaining-enough adventure for children. Nice songs by Glen Ballard and Alan Silvestri mix with vintage holiday favorites. 3-D Digital Widescreen. [G] ▼◗

Pola X (1999-French-Swiss-German-Japanese) **C-129m.** ** D: Léos Carax. Guillaume Depardieu, Katerina Golubeva, Catherine Deneuve, Laurent Lucas, Patachou, Petruta Catana, Mihaella Silaghi. Young aristocrat (Depardieu), the author of a cult novel, is engaged to a sweet, beautiful woman, but then a second woman enters his life. She is crazed, semi-coherent, and claims to be his half sister. This psychological portrait is an exploration of obsession, identity, and madness, but is way overlong and oozes pretension. Ambitious, but awfully hard to sit through. Based on an obscure Herman Melville novel, *Pierre, or the Ambiguities.* ▼◗

Police (1984-French) **C-113m.** **½ D: Maurice Pialat. Gérard Depardieu, Sophie Marceau, Richard Anconina, Pascale Rocard, Sandrine Bonnaire. Taut but repetitive drama about the thin line separating cop and criminal. Depardieu is a brutal, sex-obsessed, love-starved policeman attempting to break up a drug ring; he becomes involved with tough young Marceau, one of the dealers. ▼

Police Academy (1984) **C-95m.** **½ D: Hugh Wilson. Steve Guttenberg, G. W. Bailey, George Gaynes, Kim Cattrall, Bubba Smith, Michael Winslow, Andrew Rubin, David Graf, Bruce Mahler, Leslie Easterbrook, Georgina Spelvin. Generally good-natured comedy (with typical '80s doses of sexism and tastelessness) about a group of weirdos and misfits who enroll in big-city police academy. Winslow's comic sound effects are perfect antidote for slow spots in script. Followed by far too many sequels, a TV series, and an animated TV series. [R] ▼◗

Police Academy 2: Their First Assignment (1985) **C-87m.** BOMB D: Jerry Paris. Steve Guttenberg, Bubba Smith, David Graf, Michael Winslow, Bruce Mahler, Marion Ramsey, Colleen Camp, Howard Hesseman, Art Metrano, George Gaynes, Ed Herlihy. Dreadful follow-up to 1984 hit (with different writers and director responsible). There are *Dragnet* episodes with more laughs than this movie. [PG-13] ▼◗

Police Academy 3: Back in Training (1986) **C-82m.** *½ D: Jerry Paris. Steve Guttenberg, Bubba Smith, David Graf, Michael Winslow, Marion Ramsey, Leslie Easterbrook, Art Metrano, Tim Kazurinsky, Bobcat Goldthwait, George Gaynes, Shawn Weatherly. An improvement over #2, but that's not saying much: just another collection of pea-brained gags and amateurish performances. [PG] ▼◗

Police Academy 4: Citizens on Patrol (1987) **C-87m.** BOMB D: Jim Drake. Steve Guttenberg, Bubba Smith, Michael Winslow, David Graf, Tim Kazurinsky, Sharon Stone, Leslie Easterbrook, Marion Ramsey, Lance Kinsey, G. W. Bailey, Bobcat Goldthwait, George Gaynes, Billie Bird. More of the same, only worse. [PG] ▼◗

Police Academy 5: Assignment Miami Beach (1988) **C-90m.** BOMB D: Alan Myerson. Bubba Smith, George Gaynes, G.W. Bailey, David Graf, Michael Winslow, Leslie Easterbrook, Marion Ramsey, Janet Jones, Matt McCoy. Gaynes is in Miami to receive an award before his mandatory retirement; arch-rival Bailey comes along to gum up the works. Fourth attempt to improve on imperfection is no charm; what can you say about a sequel that Steve Guttenberg won't even appear in? [PG] ▼◗

Police Academy 6: City Under Siege (1989) **C-83m.** BOMB D: Peter Bonerz. Bubba Smith, David Graf, Michael Winslow, Leslie Easterbrook, Marion Ramsey, Lance Kinsey, Matt McCoy, Bruce Mahler, G.W. Bailey, George Gaynes, Kenneth Mars, Gerrit Graham. Those wacky cops are back to solve a crime wave perpetrated by a trio that makes The Three Stooges look like Nobel laureates. This entry is only—repeat *only*—for those who thought POLICE ACADEMY 5 was robbed at Oscar time. [PG] ▼◗

Police Academy VII: Mission to Moscow (1994) **C-83m.** BOMB D: Alan Metter. G. W. Bailey, George Gaynes, Michael Winslow, David Graf, Leslie Easterbrook, Claire Forlani, Ron Perlman, Christopher Lee, Charlie Schlatter. They waited five years to make another chapter in this mindless series. It wasn't worth the wait. [PG] ▼●)

Police, Adjective (2009-Romanian) **C-115m. *** D:** Corneliu Porumboiu. Dragos Bucur, Vlad Ivanov, Ion Stoica, Irina Saulescu, Marian Ghenea, Cosmin Selesi. Bucur, a cop with a conscience, serves on a police force run by lazy, petty bureaucrats. He's tailing a high school drug user, and fears that following the letter of a law that might soon be changed will ruin the boy's life. Pointed, deliberately paced portrait of stone-cold bureaucracy and how it stifles one's sense of right and wrong. One scene, involving the use of a dictionary, is positively riveting.▶

Police Force SEE: **Police Story** (1985)
Police Story (1985-Hong Kong) **C-89m. *** D:** Jackie Chan. Jackie Chan, Bridget Lin, Maggie Cheung, Cho Yuen, Bill Tung, Kenneth Tong. Lightning-paced kung fu comedy about cop Chan, a one-man police force attempting to get the goods on some thugs. Crammed with incredible stuntwork; a real popcorn movie that's perfect for fans of the genre. Aka JACKIE CHAN'S POLICE STORY and POLICE FORCE. Followed by three sequels. CinemaScope. ▼●)
Police Story Part 2 (1988-Hong Kong) **C-90m. ** D:** Jackie Chan. Jackie Chan, Maggie Cheung, Bill Thung, Lam Kowk-Hung, Crystal Kwok, Choh Yuen, Henny Ho. This sequel is a slight step down for Chan as his Hong Kong cop tries to stop a wave of bomb threats. Some awesome stunts and fine comic touches, but not as well constructed as its predecessor. Followed by a third installment. Technovision.▼●)
Police Story III: Supercop (1992-Hong Kong) **C-96m. **½ D:** Stanley Tong. Jackie Chan, Michelle (Yeoah) Khan, Maggie Cheung, Yuen Wah, Bill Tung Piu, Ken Tsang. Third in series benefits greatly from presence of Khan, a fine action star in her own right. The two stars play cops teaming up against drug smugglers. Highlights include Khan jumping a motorcycle onto a moving train and Chan dangling from a careening helicopter. Plot slows down at times, but climactic action sequences make up for it. 1996 U.S. release version cut to 91m. and redubbed in English with a new music score. Aka SUPERCOP. Followed by POLICE STORY IV: CRIME STORY. Technovision. [R]▼●)
Polish Wedding (1998) **C-101m. *** D:** Theresa Connelly. Gabriel Byrne, Lena Olin, Claire Danes, Mili Avital, Daniel Lapaine, Rade Serbedzija, Adam Trese, Ramsey Krull, Steven Petrarca. Picaresque slice of life about a Polish-American family in Detroit. The mother of the household (Olin) is an incredible life force who is fiercely proud of her family; her husband (Byrne) has long since resigned himself to

a passive role. But their daughter (Danes) is eager to experience life—perhaps too eager. First time writer-director Connelly perfectly captures the look and feel of this unusual family and the suburban atmosphere in which they live. [PG-13]▼●)
Pollock (2000) **C-117m. ***½ D:** Ed Harris. Ed Harris, Marcia Gay Harden, Amy Madigan, Jennifer Connelly, Val Kilmer, Jeffrey Tambor, Bud Cort, John Heard, Stephanie Seymour, Tom Bower, Sada Thompson. Vivid portrait of a tortured soul, groundbreaking modern artist Jackson Pollock, superbly played by Harris, with Harden in an Oscar-winning performance as Lee Krasner, who forsook her own career to shepherd his and become his wife. First-time director Harris manages to capture the wonder of a genius at work. Difficult but rewarding. Screenplay by Barbara Turner and Susan J. Emshwiller, from the book *Jackson Pollock: An American Saga* by Steven Naifeh and Gregory White Smith. [R]▼▌
Pollyanna (1960) **C-134m. ***½ D:** David Swift. Hayley Mills, Jane Wyman, Richard Egan, Karl Malden, Nancy Olson, Adolphe Menjou, Donald Crisp, Agnes Moorehead. Disney's treatment of Eleanor Porter story is first-rate, as "the glad girl" spreads cheer to misanthropes of a New England town, including her own Aunt Polly (Wyman). Fine direction and script by Swift, excellent performances all around. Mills was awarded a special Oscar for Outstanding Juvenile Performance. First filmed in 1920 with Mary Pickford. Remade for TV in 1989 as POLLY.▼●)
Poltergeist (1982) **C-114m. ***½ D:** Tobe Hooper. Craig T. Nelson, JoBeth Williams, Beatrice Straight, Dominique Dunne, Oliver Robins, Heather O'Rourke, Zelda Rubinstein, Richard Lawson, James Karen. A young family finds its home invaded by unfriendly spirits, who "kidnap" their 5-year-old girl! Sensationally scary ghost story co-written and co-produced by Steven Spielberg. Paced like a roller-coaster ride, with dazzling special effects—and a refreshing sense of humor. Followed by two sequels. J-D-C Scope. [PG]▼●)
Poltergeist II (1986) **C-91m. **½ D:** Brian Gibson. JoBeth Williams, Craig T. Nelson, Heather O'Rourke, Oliver Robins, Zelda Rubinstein, Will Sampson, Julian Beck, Geraldine Fitzgerald. The Freeling family is terrorized again by otherworld creatures. Another pointless sequel made palatable by some jolting state-of-the-art special effects and a still-very-likable family. Be warned that an actor receives billing as The Vomit Creature. Panavision. [PG-13]▼●)
Poltergeist III (1988) **C-97m. ** D:** Gary Sherman. Tom Skerritt, Nancy Allen, Heather O'Rourke, Zelda Rubinstein, Lara Flynn Boyle, Kip Wentz, Richard Fire. O'Rourke moves in with uncle Skerritt and aunt Allen—

and is still pursued by strange, evil forces. Undistinguished and occasionally plodding; eerily, young O'Rourke died four months before the film's release. [PG-13] ▼●)

Polyester (1981) **C-86m.** **½ D: John Waters. Divine, Tab Hunter, Edith Massey, Mary Garlington, Ken King, David Samson, Mink Stole, Stiv Bators. Waters' first mainstream feature is wacky middle-class satire; housewife Francine Fishpaw (Divine), driven to the brink by nightmarish husband, children, and mother, is "rescued" by handsome drive-in owner Todd Tomorrow (Hunter). Less offensive than Waters' underground films, but still not for all tastes; Vincent Peranio's sets are hilariously hideous. Released in "Odorama"—with audience members given scratch-and-sniff cards. [R] ▼●)

Pom-Pom Girls, The (1976) **C-90m.** ** D: Joseph Ruben. Robert Carradine, Jennifer Ashley, Lisa Reeves, Michael Mullins, Bill Adler. Comedy about spoiled suburban teenagers who celebrate their senior year having food fights, making love in the back of vans, and stealing a fire truck. Routinely good-natured mayhem. [PG— edited from original R rating] ▼)

Pompatus of Love, The (1996) **C-99m.** ** D: Richard Schenkman. Jon Cryer, Adrian Pasdar, Tim Guinee, Adam Oliensis, Mia Sara, Kristin Scott Thomas, Arabella Field, Paige Turco, Dana Wheeler-Nicholson, Kristen Wilson, Michael McKean, Fisher Stevens, Jennifer Tilly, Roscoe Lee Browne, Jenny McCarthy. Yet another smug and talky ensemble comedy about self-absorbed guys struggling with life and love in the '90s. Though it's an obvious labor of love for cowriters Schenkman, Cryer, and Oliensis, it's just a passable example of a deadly subgenre. Title takes its name from a song lyric in "The Joker," which is sung here by the original artist, Steve Miller, and also by Sheryl Crow. [R] ▼●)

Pom Wonderful Presents: The Greatest Movie Ever Sold SEE: **Greatest Movie Ever Sold, The**

Ponette (1996-French) **C-97m.** **½ D: Jacques Doillon. Victoire Thivisol, Matiaz Bureau Caton, Delphine Schiltz, Xavier Beauvois, Claire Nebout, Marie Trintignant. Heart-rending, if unfulfilling, tale of a 4-year-old (Thivisol) who survives a car accident in which her mother is killed. Poignant look at the death of a parent, as the young girl tries to understand and cope with her mom's absence. Doillon, who also scripted, truly captures life through the eyes of a child, but there's more emotion than substance, and the ending is a cop-out. Thivisol's amazingly naturalistic performance is the film's greatest strength. ▼●)

Pontiac Moon (1994) **C-108m.** *½ D: Peter Medak. Ted Danson, Mary Steenburgen, Ryan Todd, Eric Schweig, Cathy Moriarty, Max Gail, Lisa Jane Persky, J. C. Quinn, John Schuck, Don Swayze. Eccentric pop (Danson) takes 11-year-old son on dusty road trip to coincide with Apollo XI moon landing in July 1969. Think agoraphobic mom (Steenburgen) will finally have the guts to leave the house and follow them? 11-year-olds may like this. Panavision. [PG-13] ▼●)

Pony Express (1953) **C-101m.** *** D: Jerry Hopper. Charlton Heston, Rhonda Fleming, Jan Sterling, Forrest Tucker. Exuberant action Western (set in 1860s) of the founding of mail routes westward, involving historical figures Buffalo Bill and Wild Bill Hickok. ▼

Pony Express Rider (1976) **C-100m.** *** D: Robert Totten. Stewart Petersen, Henry Wilcoxon, Buck Taylor, Maureen McCormick, Joan Caulfield, Ken Curtis, Slim Pickens, Dub Taylor, Jack Elam. Good family outing with Peterson joining Pony Express in 1861 to help find the man whom he believes has killed his father. [G] ▼)

Ponyo (2008-Japanese) **C-103m.** *** D: Hayao Miyazaki. Voices of Tina Fey, Noah Cyrus, Frankie Jonas, Matt Damon, Liam Neeson, Cate Blanchett, Lily Tomlin, Betty White, Cloris Leachman, Laraine Newman. Young goldfish transforms into a little girl and, despite her father's instructions, leaves the ocean to explore the world on land, becoming involved with a 5-year-old boy and his mother. Miyazaki reworks the premise of THE LITTLE MERMAID, creating a wildly imaginative, often surreal anime feature aimed at children. Miyazaki masterfully combines elements of traditional Asian folklore and Japanese cultural attitudes with a strong pro-environment message to create a strange but uniquely satisfying animated experience. Original Japanese title translates as: PONYO ON THE CLIFF BY THE SEA. Pixar supervised this U.S. release version. [G] ●)

Pooh's Heffalump Movie (2005) **C-67m.** **½ D: Frank Nissen. Voices of Jim Cummings, John Fiedler, Kath Soucie, Nikita Hopkins, Ken Sansom, Peter Cullen, Brenda Blethyn, Kyle Stanger. Depending on what you bring to it, Disney's trek back to A. A. Milne's Hundred Acre Wood will either be charmingly unpretentious in a minor key or a lost opportunity. Short running time helps, in any event, as the Wood crew takes off to find the supposedly frightening heffalump, which is actually a baby-Dumbo type named Lumpy and no threat at all to finder Roo (who's also a tot). Movie preaches tolerance to 4- and 5-year-olds, close to the age peak of the target audience. Features songs by Carly Simon. Followed by a direct-to-video sequel. [G] ▼)

Pool, The (2008) **C-104m.** *** D: Chris Smith. Venkatesh Chavan, Jhangir Badshah, Ayesha Mohan, Nana Patekar. Two impoverished young boys fend for themselves on the streets of Panjim, India, doing odd jobs to survive, but one of them (Chavan) has higher aspirations: he's admired the serene swimming pool at an estate on the hill overlooking the city. He tells his friend he's going to swim in it—not by sneaking in, but by invitation. Disarmingly simple film draws on the real lives and personalities of its youthful stars (nonprofessionals working with documentary filmmaker Smith) as its warmly humanistic story unfolds. A sleeper well worth discovering.

Poolhall Junkies (2003) **C-94m.** ** D: Mars Callahan. Chazz Palminteri, Rick Schroder, Rod Steiger, Michael Rosenbaum, Mars Callahan, Alison Eastwood, Christopher Walken, Anson Mount, Peter Mark Richman, Glenn Plummer, Peter Dobson, Ernie Reyes, Jr. Callahan cowrote, directed, and stars in this highly forgettable film about a promising pool player who wants to go pro, but is steered instead toward a life of hustling by his mentor (Palminteri). The rest of the "story" is a mess, with no real focus and poorly delineated characters. Walken (yet again) provides the film's brightest moments as a wealthy man who takes an interest in Callahan. Completed in 2001. [R]▼)

Poor Cow (1967-British) **C-104m.** **½ D: Kenneth Loach. Carol White, Terence Stamp, John Bindon, Kate Williams, Queenie Watts, Malcolm McDowell. OK drama about working-class loners, centering on promiscuous White's relationship with husband (Bindon), a thief, and his best friend (Stamp), whom she really loves. McDowell's film debut; Loach's feature directorial debut.

Poor Little Rich Girl (1936) **72m.** ***½ D: Irving Cummings. Shirley Temple, Alice Faye, Jack Haley, Gloria Stuart, Michael Whalen, Jane Darwell, Claude Gillingwater, Henry Armetta. One of Shirley's best films, a top musical on any terms, with Temple running away from home, joining vaudeville team of Haley and Faye, winning over crusty Gillingwater, eventually joining her father (Whalen) and lovely Stuart. Best of all is closing "Military Man" number. Also shown in computer-colored version.▼●

Pootie Tang (2001) **C-81m.** BOMB D: Louis C.K. Lance Crouther, Chris Rock, Jennifer Coolidge, Robert Vaughn, Wanda Sykes. Jumbled junk, spun off from skits on Rock's HBO show, finds Crouther's "folk hero" compromised by evil mogul Vaughn, who wants to exploit Pootie's sacred rep by getting him to hawk unhealthy products. Without extended credit sequences and painful interludes featuring Bob Costas in faux interviews, this would barely run an hour and small change. Rock plays two roles: a hanger-on and Pootie's laborer dad, killed by a gorilla in a steel-mill mishap. (Don't ask—and don't watch.) [PG-13]▼)

Pop & Me (2000) **C-92m.** **½ D: Chris Roe. Heartwarming—if slick—documentary of 29-year-old Roe's six-month journey around the world with his dad, Richard, interviewing fathers and sons across the globe (including a random encounter in Monaco with Julian Lennon, who comes clean about his famous genes) and learning about their own relationship in the process. Real-life male weepie is perfect Father's Day fare. [PG-13]▼)

Popcorn (1991) **C-93m.** ** D: Mark Herrier. Jill Schoelen, Tom Villard, Dee Wallace Stone, Tony Roberts, Ray Walston, Elliott Hurst, Yvette Solar, Derek Rydall, Malcolm Danare, Bruce Glover. Film students put on a round-the-clock fundraiser of schlocky '50s horror pics—and who should be haunting the premises and projection booth but a ghoulish psychopathic killer? Amusing idea, awkwardly executed, though there are some knowing re-creations of vintage b&w B's. Stone, Roberts, and Walston must have been hired for about a day's shooting apiece. [R] ▼●)

Pope Joan (1972-British) **C-132m.** BOMB D: Michael Anderson. Liv Ullmann, Keir Dullea, Robert Beatty, Jeremy Kemp, Olivia de Havilland, Patrick Magee, Maximilian Schell, Trevor Howard, Franco Nero, Nigel Havers, Lesley-Anne Down, Andre Morell. Dim story of woman who, disguised as man, works her way up to the papacy, only to be destroyed when revealed. Performers seem to be embarrassed, as well they should; screenplay by John Briley. Also shown in 112m. version. Reissued as THE DEVIL'S IMPOSTOR, with much material cut. Panavision. [PG])

Pope Must Die, The (1991-British) **C-97m.** **½ D: Peter Richardson. Robbie Coltrane, Beverly D'Angelo, Herbert Lom, Alex Rocco, Paul Bartel, Salvatore Cascio, Balthazar Getty, Peter Richardson, Robert Stephens, Annette Crosbie. So-so satire with Coltrane an honest small-town priest who, via computer error, becomes the new pontiff and finds himself in conflict with cardinal Rocco and mobster Lom. Occasionally clever but goes overboard once too often, descending into outright silliness. Controversy over the title in U.S. release caused its distributor to rename it THE POPE MUST DIET(!) [R]▼●

Pope of Greenwich Village, The (1984) **C-120m.** *** D: Stuart Rosenberg. Eric Roberts, Mickey Rourke, Daryl Hannah, Geraldine Page, Kenneth McMillan, Tony Musante, M. Emmet Walsh, Burt Young, Jack Kehoe, Philip Bosco, Val Avery, Joe Grifasi. Richly textured, sharply observant film about a young hustler in N.Y.C.'s Little Italy and his inability to separate himself from a cousin (Roberts) who's a perpetual screw-up. Not so much a story as a collection of character studies; Page stands out in great supporting cast, as harridan mother of crooked cop. Based on Vincent Patrick's novel. [R]▼●◗

Popeye (1980) **C-114m.** BOMB D: Robert Altman. Robin Williams, Shelley Duvall, Ray Walston, Paul Smith, Paul Dooley, Richard Libertini, Wesley Ivan Hurt, Linda Hunt. The beloved sailorman (Williams, in his starring debut) boards a sinking ship in this astonishingly boring movie. A game cast does its best with Jules Feiffer's unfunny script, Altman's cluttered staging, and some alleged songs by Harry Nilsson. Tune in an old Max Fleischer cartoon instead. Technovision. [PG]▼●◗

Popi (1969) **C-115m.** *** D: Arthur Hiller. Alan Arkin, Rita Moreno, Miguel Alejandro, Ruben Figueroa. Charming story of poverty in the ghetto, focusing on one man's often zany antics in securing better life for his children. Odd ending for far-fetched story. [G]▼◗

Poppy Is Also a Flower, The (1966) **C-100m.** BOMB D: Terence Young. Senta Berger, Stephen Boyd, E. G. Marshall, Trevor Howard, Eli Wallach, Marcello Mastroianni, Angie Dickinson, Rita Hayworth, Yul Brynner, Trini Lopez, Gilbert Roland, Bessie Love. Incredibly bad anti-drug feature from story by Ian Fleming, originally produced as United Nations project for TV. Acting is downright poor at times. Though never referred to that way, title actually appears on-screen as POPPIES ARE ALSO FLOWERS. Aka THE OPIUM CONNECTION.▼◗

Popsy Pop SEE: **Butterfly Affair, The**

Porco Rosso (1992-Japanese) **C-93m.** *** D: Hayao Miyazaki. Voices of Michael Keaton, Cary Elwes, Kimberly Williams, Susan Egan, David Ogden Stiers, Brad Garrett, Phil Proctor, Laraine Newman. A great WW1 aviator, mysteriously transformed into a pig (!), is coaxed into an aerial duel by an American sky pirate. If the plot sounds strange, don't be fooled: this anime feature is Miyazaki's most character-driven film, with plot and dialogue skewing more toward adults than children. Several spectacular air warfare sequences are dazzling highlights. This English-language version, supervised by Pixar, was released in 2005. ▼◗

Porgy and Bess (1959) **C-138m.** **½ D: Otto Preminger. Sidney Poitier, Dorothy Dandridge, Pearl Bailey, Sammy Davis, Jr., Brock Peters, Diahann Carroll, Ivan Dixon, Clarence Muse. Classic Gershwin folk opera about love, dreams, and jealousy among poor folk of Catfish Row; a bit stiff, but full of incredible music: "Summertime," "It Ain't Necessarily So," "I Got Plenty of Nothin'." Davis shines as Sportin' Life. Music arrangers Andre Previn and Ken Darby won Oscars. Final film of producer Samuel Goldwyn. Todd-AO.

Pork Chop Hill (1959) **97m.** *** D: Lewis Milestone. Gregory Peck, Harry Guardino, Rip Torn, George Peppard, James Edwards, Bob Steele, George Shibata, Biff Elliot, Woody Strode, Robert Blake, Norman Fell, Martin Landau, Bert Remsen, (Harry) Dean Stanton, Gavin MacLeod. Gritty Korean War combat film about the taking of a seemingly worthless hill, and the political (and communications) problems that interfere with lieutenant Peck's efforts to get the job done. Impressive cast of stars-to-be. Based on a true story.▼●◗

Porky's (1981-Canadian) **C-94m.** **½ D: Bob Clark. Dan Monahan, Mark Herrier, Wyatt Knight, Roger Wilson, Kim Cattrall, Scott Colomby, Kaki Hunter, Nancy Parsons, Alex Karras, Susan Clark. A lusty, fun-loving bunch of high school guys in South Florida circa 1954 discover that sex is great, revenge is sweet, and Jews are OK after all. Some belly laughs. This raunchy, low-budget comedy made a fortune—and spawned two sequels. [R]▼●◗

Porky's II: The Next Day (1983-Canadian) **C-95m.** *½ D: Bob Clark. Dan Monahan, Wyatt Knight, Mark Herrier, Roger Wilson, Kaki Hunter, Scott Colomby, Nancy Parsons, Edward Winter. In-name-only sequel has same cast of kids in new (and tamer) set of escapades—with no coherency, and not even the raunchiness that made the first film so popular. Sequel: PORKY'S REVENGE. [R]▼●◗

Porky's Revenge (1985) **C-91m.** BOMB D: James Komack. Dan Monahan, Wyatt Knight, Tony Ganios, Kaki Hunter, Mark Herrier, Scott Colomby. Will the gang throw the big high school basketball game or won't they? Beware of high-school seniors with post-collegiate hairlines; these guys are starting to look older than the mid-'50s Bowery Boys. This *Revenge* is preferable to Montezuma's—but not by much. [R]▼●◗

Porridge SEE: **Doing Time**

Portnoy's Complaint (1972) **C-101m.** BOMB D: Ernest Lehman. Richard Benjamin, Karen Black, Lee Grant, Jack Somack, Jeannie Berlin, Jill Clayburgh. Karen Black's excellent portrayal of "The Monkey" is buried in otherwise incredibly inept filmization of Philip Roth's novel about a not exactly warm relationship between Jewish boy and his mother. Terrible directorial debut by famed screenwriter Lehman. Panavision. [R]◗

Portrait in Black (1960) **C-112m.** **½ D: Michael Gordon. Lana Turner, Anthony Quinn, Sandra Dee, John Saxon, Richard Basehart, Lloyd Nolan, Ray Walston, Anna May Wong. Average murder/blackmail mystery filled with gaping holes that producer Ross Hunter tried to hide with glamorous decor and offbeat casting.▼◗

Portrait of a Hitman (1977) **C-86m.** BOMB D: Allan A. Buckhantz. Jack

Palance, Richard Roundtree, Rod Steiger, Bo Svenson, Ann Turkel, Philip Ahn. Gangster Steiger hires "sensitive" hit man Palance to kill Svenson, but there are complications: Svenson is a pal who once saved Palance's life, and both of them are in love with Turkel. B movie has ragged structure that makes it seem like an unfinished feature. Originally titled JIM BUCK.▼

Portrait of a Lady, The (1996-British) C-144m. ** D: Jane Campion. Nicole Kidman, John Malkovich, Barbara Hershey, Mary-Louise Parker, Martin Donovan, Shelley Winters, Richard E. Grant, Shelley Duvall, Christian Bale, Viggo Mortensen, John Gielgud. Long, often boring, and strikingly ineffectual adaptation of Henry James' novel about a young American woman, determined to live an independent life in Europe during the late 1800s. For reasons never made clear in the film, she decides to marry a man who turns out to be a spiteful, manipulative rotter. Good performances and handsome production can't overcome the dreariness of the material. A very odd, "Campionesque" prologue attempts to set a contemporary tone for what is to follow. Super 35. [PG-13]▼●〕

Portrait of Jennie (1948) 86m. *** D: William Dieterle. Jennifer Jones, Joseph Cotten, Ethel Barrymore, Lillian Gish, Cecil Kellaway, David Wayne, Albert Sharpe, Henry Hull, Florence Bates, Felix Bressart. Strange otherworldly girl (Jones) inspires penniless artist Cotten. David O. Selznick craftsmanship and a fine cast work wonders with foolish story based on the Robert Nathan novella. Originally released with last reel tinted green and final shot in Technicolor; the special effects earned an Academy Award.▼〕

Portrait of the Artist as a Young Man, A (1979) C-98m. *** D: Joseph Strick. Bosco Hogan, T. P. McKenna, John Gielgud, Rosaleen Linehan, Maureen Potter, Niall Buggy, Brian Murray. Literate adaptation (by Judith Rascoe) of James Joyce's legendary first novel; it focuses on Stephen Dedalus (Hogan), who questions his faith as he reaches manhood in turn-of-the-20th-century Dublin. McKenna, Linehan, and Potter play, respectively, Simon and May Dedalus, and Dante; in ULYSSES, which Strick made a dozen years before, they appeared as Buck Mulligan, Nurse Callan, and Josie Breen respectively. Filmed in Ireland. ▼〕

Poseidon (2006) C-99m. ** D: Wolfgang Petersen. Josh Lucas, Kurt Russell, Richard Dreyfuss, Jacinda Barrett, Emmy Rossum, Mía Maestro, Jimmy Bennett, Mike Vogel, Andre Braugher, Kevin Dillon, Freddy Rodriguez, Fergie. When a "rogue wave" overturns a luxury ocean liner, a random group of passengers bands together to find a way to escape—and survive. Who will

live? Who will die? Who will care? Well-paced remake of the 1972 hit has everything money can buy, and the requisite moments of suspense and action, but its characters are flat and uninteresting. Super 35. [PG-13]〕

Poseidon Adventure, The (1972) C-117m. *** D: Ronald Neame. Gene Hackman, Ernest Borgnine, Red Buttons, Carol Lynley, Roddy McDowall, Stella Stevens, Shelley Winters, Jack Albertson, Leslie Nielsen, Pamela Sue Martin, Arthur O'Connell, Eric Shea. Mindless but engrossing, highly charged entertainment—the vanguard of the decade's "disaster film" genre. Luxury cruise ship capsized by tidal wave, leaving small band of survivors to make way to top (bottom) of ship and hopefully escape. Introductory sequences are laughably bad, but one soon gets caught up in the story and ignores script's weaknesses. Oscar-winning song: "The Morning After"; also earned a special Oscar for special effects. Sequel: BEYOND THE POSEIDON ADVENTURE. Remade in 2006 and for TV in 2005. Panavision. [PG]▼●〕

Posse (1975) C-94m. *** D: Kirk Douglas. Kirk Douglas, Bruce Dern, Bo Hopkins, James Stacy, Luke Askew, David Canary, Alfonso Arau, Katherine Woodville, Beth Brickell. Watergate-era Western about a lawman (Douglas) who captures a notorious outlaw (Dern), hoping it will help propel him into public office . . . but the cunning criminal undermines the marshal's reputation and the loyalty of his posse. Entertaining (if not exactly subtle) revisionist yarn. Panavision. [PG] ▼●〕

Posse (1993-U.S.-British) C-109m. ** D: Mario Van Peebles. Mario Van Peebles, Stephen Baldwin, Charles Lane, Tiny Lister, Jr., Big Daddy Kane, Billy Zane, Blair Underwood, Melvin Van Peebles, Salli Richardson, Tone Loc, Pam Grier, Vesta Williams, Isaac Hayes, Robert Hooks, Richard Jordan, Paul Bartel, Stephen J. Cannell, Nipsey Russell, Reginald VelJohnson, Woody Strode, Aaron Neville, Warrington and Reginald Hudlin. Noisy, violent, but politically correct Western about a mostly black posse who do battle with a pompous, racist colonel, and a vicious white sheriff who wants to take over a peaceful black frontier settlement. Game attempt at a new take on the Old West, but at its core it's thoroughly conventional. Followed by a video sequel, LOS LOCOS: POSSE RIDES AGAIN. Panavision. [R]▼●〕

Possessed (1931) 76m. *** D: Clarence Brown. Joan Crawford, Clark Gable, Wallace Ford, Skeets Gallagher, John Miljan. Factory girl Crawford becomes the mistress of Park Avenue lawyer Gable. Fascinating feminist drama, crammed with symbolism and featuring a radiant Crawford. Outrageous pre-Code script by Lenore Coffee.▼〕

Possessed (1947) 108m. *** D: Curtis

Bernhardt. Joan Crawford, Van Heflin, Raymond Massey, Geraldine Brooks, Stanley Ridges. Crawford gives fine performance in intelligent study of woman whose subtle mental problems lead to ruin. Heflin and Massey are the men in her life; Brooks, as Massey's daughter, is radiant in her film debut. Also shown in computer-colored version. ▼○●

Possession (1981-French-West German) **C-127m.** *½ D: Andrzej Zulawski. Isabelle Adjani, Sam Neill, Heinz Bennent, Margit Carstensen, Michael Hogben. Adjani "creates" a monster, to the consternation of husband Neill, lover Bennent—and the viewer. Confusing drama of murder, horror, intrigue, though it's all attractively directed. Filmed in English; hacked down to 81m. for American release. [R] ▼●

Possession (2002) **C-119m.** ** D: Neil LaBute. Gwyneth Paltrow, Aaron Eckhart, Jeremy Northam, Jennifer Ehle, Trevor Eve, Toby Stephens, Anna Massey, Graham Crowden, Lena Headey, Tom Hollander. Two modern-day academics—an impulsive American man and a cool British woman—become unlikely partners in ferreting out a mystery about a renowned romantic poet of the mid-1800s. The period story is beautifully acted and staged, but the modern story is just the opposite—full of ludicrous dialogue and arch, affected performances. Based on a novel by A. S. Byatt. Super 35. [PG-13] ▼●

Possession (2010-U.S.-British) **C-86m.** *½ D: Joel Bergvall, Simon Sandquist. Sarah Michelle Gellar, Lee Pace, Michael Landes, Tuva Novotny, Chelah Horsdal. Gellar has a sweet, loving spouse and a crude, volatile brother-in-law. A car accident renders both men comatose; only the brother-in-law awakens . . . and claims to be Gellar's hubby. What's a girl to do? Lame chiller attempts to create an air of desperation and paranoia, but fails dismally. Remake of the 2002 South Korean film JUNGDOK (ADDICTED). Completed in 2007; released direct to DVD in the U.S. [PG-13] ●

Possession of Joel Delaney, The (1972) **C-105m.** *** D: Waris Hussein. Shirley MacLaine, Perry King, Lisa Kohane, David Elliott, Michael Hordern, Miriam Colon, Lovelady Powell. Uneven but satisfying mix of horror and social commentary with unsympathetic, affluent Manhattanite MacLaine threatened by mysterious transformations of her brother Joel (King). Offbeat throughout. [R] ▼●

Possession of Nurse Sherri, The SEE: **Beyond the Living**

Postcards From the Edge (1990) **C-101m.** ***½ D: Mike Nichols. Meryl Streep, Shirley MacLaine, Dennis Quaid, Gene Hackman, Richard Dreyfuss, Rob Reiner, Mary Wickes, Conrad Bain, Annette Bening, Simon Callow, Gary Morton, CCH Pounder, Sidney Armus, Robin Bartlett, Anthony Heald, Dana Ivey, Oliver Platt, Michael Ontkean, J.D. Souther. Brilliantly cinematic rendering of Carrie Fisher's novel about a young woman falling prey to drugs while trying to pursue an acting career—in the shadow of a famous show-business mother. Vividly real, bitingly funny. MacLaine and Streep both have show-stopping musical numbers. Fisher wrote the screenplay. [R] ▼○●

Post Grad (2009) **C-88m.** *½ D: Vicky Jenson. Alexis Bledel, Zach Gilford, Michael Keaton, Jane Lynch, Carol Burnett, Bobby Coleman, Rodrigo Santoro, Catherine Reitman, J. K. Simmons. Book-loving college graduate Bledel has a career in publishing all mapped out until her dream editor job is filled by a rival. Suddenly, she's living at home with her wacky family and forced to endure rounds of job interviews. Bland, inert comedy-drama, with a puppy-love subplot, strains to entertain. Keaton plays the eccentric but softhearted dad; Burnett, as the dotty grandmother, is not at her best. [PG-13] ●

Postman, The (1994-Italian-French) **C-113m.** ***½ D: Michael Radford. Massimo Troisi, Philippe Noiret, Maria Grazia Cucinotta, Linda Moretti, Renato Scarpa. A moving film detailing the friendship between exiled Chilean poet Pablo Neruda and the simple Italian man who delivers his mail every day. International talents combined to tell a universal story of how one person can affect another, no matter how different their life experiences may be. Noiret is masterful as always, and Troisi is understated and unforgettable in his final film role; he died of heart disease just 12 hours after the movie finished shooting. Oscar winner for Original Dramatic Score (Luis Bacalov). Original title: IL POSTINO. ▼○●

Postman, The (1997) **C-177m.** *½ D: Kevin Costner. Kevin Costner, Will Patton, Larenz Tate, Olivia Williams, James Russo, Daniel Von Bargen, Tom Petty, Scott Bairstow, Roberta Maxwell, Joe Santos, Peggy Lipton, Giovanni Ribisi, Shawn Hatosy. Long, boring, pretentious allegory about an itinerant performer in the post-apocalyptic future who passes himself off as a U.S. mail carrier. In that guise, he personifies hope for several isolated communities who've been beaten down by the cruel tactics of a demagogue (Patton, in a one-note performance). A well-meaning (but complete) misfire. That's Costner's son in the film's final shot; one daughter plays a mail carrier, the other sings "America the Beautiful." Mary Stuart Masterson appears unbilled. Panavision. [R] ▼○●

Postman Always Rings Twice, The (1946) **113m.** **** D: Tay Garnett. Lana Turner, John Garfield, Cecil Kellaway, Hume Cronyn, Audrey Totter, Leon Ames, Alan Reed, Wally Cassell. Garfield and Turner ignite the screen in this bristling drama of lovers whose problems just begin when they do away with her husband (Kellaway). Despite complaints of changes in James M. Cain's original story (mostly for censorship purposes), the film packs a real punch and outshines the more explicit 1981 remake. Harry Ruskin and Niven Busch scripted (from Cain's novel). Filmed twice before, in France and Italy. Also shown in computer-colored version. ▼○◗

Postman Always Rings Twice, The (1981) **C-123m.** *½ D: Bob Rafelson. Jack Nicholson, Jessica Lange, John Colicos, Michael Lerner, Christopher Lloyd, John P. Ryan, Anjelica Huston. Exceedingly unpleasant adaptation of James M. Cain's Depression-era novel about a drifter and a sensual young woman who conspire to free her from her loveless marriage. David Mamet's screenplay may be more faithful to Cain than the 1946 version, but who cares? Despite its much-touted sex scenes (more violent than erotic), it's dreary and forgettable. Moodily photographed by Sven Nykvist. [R] ▼○◗

Pourquoi Pas! SEE: Why Not!

Powaqqatsi (1988) **C-97m.** **½ D: Godfrey Reggio. Follow-up to KOYAANISQATSI is a visual collage in which scenes of various cultures around the world are edited together to show how Third World societies have been exploited. Beautifully photographed, but the result is somehow shallow—much like a coffee-table picture book—and not nearly as impressive as its predecessor. Music is again by Philip Glass. Followed by NAQOYQATSI. [G] ▼◗

Powder (1995) **C-111m.** ** D: Victor Salva. Mary Steenburgen, Sean Patrick Flanery, Lance Henriksen, Jeff Goldblum, Brandon Smith, Bradford Tatum, Susan Tyrrell, Missy Crider, Ray Wise. Rural teen Flanery, whose skin is ghostly white and whose nickname is Powder, is the local pariah; he's scary, shy, brilliant, and seems to have electromagnetic powers (and an odd relationship to lightning storms). Suddenly he's thrust into dealing with people and prejudices for the first time in his life. Combines a zillion 1950s and 1960s B-movie themes (including reform school) into a contemporary fable. Earnest, but doesn't add up to very much. [PG-13] ▼○◗

Power, The (1968) **C-109m.** *** D: Byron Haskin. George Hamilton, Suzanne Pleshette, Richard Carlson, Yvonne De Carlo, Earl Holliman, Gary Merrill, Ken Murray, Barbara Nichols, Arthur O'Connell, Nehemiah Persoff, Aldo Ray, Michael Rennie. Research team discovers one of their number is an evil super-genius with powerful ESP abilities who starts killing the others one by one. Can Hamilton identify the man with the power before the villain kills him too? Could you ever doubt George Hamilton? Good, underrated George Pal production. Panavision. ○◗

Power (1986) **C-111m.** *½ D: Sidney Lumet. Richard Gere, Julie Christie, Gene Hackman, Kate Capshaw, Denzel Washington, E. G. Marshall, Beatrice Straight, Fritz Weaver, Michael Learned, J. T. Walsh, E. Katherine Kerr, Matt Salinger. Slick, sanctimonious story of ruthless political media manipulator (Gere) who, it turns out, isn't as smart as he thinks he is. Subject isn't headline news anymore, but this movie treats it that way. Downright embarrassing at times. [R] ▼○◗

Power and the Glory, The (1933) **76m.** *** D: William K. Howard. Spencer Tracy, Colleen Moore, Ralph Morgan, Helen Vinson. Considered by many a precursor to CITIZEN KANE, Preston Sturges' script tells rags-to-riches story of callous industrialist (Tracy) in flashback. Silent-star Moore gives sensitive performance as Tracy's wife.

Power of One, The (1992) **C-111m.** ** D: John G. Avildsen. Stephen Dorff, Armin Mueller-Stahl, Morgan Freeman, John Gielgud, Fay Masterson, Marius Weyers, Tracy Brooks Swope, John Osborne, Daniel Craig. Precisely what you'd expect when the director of ROCKY and THE KARATE KID tackles a movie about apartheid. Rahrah mawkishness tells of a white South African lad who promotes integration by getting into the boxing ring with his oppressed black buddies. Offensive trivialization of a great subject, but at least the first half offers Freeman and Mueller-Stahl as the youth's mentors; when they're written out of the script in hour two, film becomes an ordeal to watch. [PG-13] ▼○◗

Power Play (1978-Canadian-British) **C-102m.** *½ D: Martyn Burke. Peter O'Toole, David Hemmings, Donald Pleasence, Barry Morse, Jon Granik. Story of a military coup in a country that looks vaguely European but where everybody sounds British or Canadian. Flat, unsuspenseful drama. Aka OPERATION OVERTHROW. ▼◗

Powerpuff Girls, The (2002) **C-74m.** ** D: Craig McCracken. Voices of Catherine Cavadini, Tara Strong, E. G. Daily, Roger L. Jackson, Tom Kane, Tom Kenny, Jennifer Hale. Heavy-handed expansion of the clever (and cleverly designed) animated TV series about three little girls, created by a well-meaning scientist, who have superhuman powers . . . and the evil, power-hungry Mojo Jojo, who tries to take over their city and terrorize its citizens. Fun ingredients of the series give way to violence and mayhem here. A Jimmy Durante caricature is an all-too-brief novelty. Preceded by a funny *Dexter's Laboratory* short subject. [PG] ▼◗

P.O.W.: Prisoners of War SEE: **Secret of Blood Island, The**

P.O.W. The Escape (1986) **C-90m.** *½ D:

Gideon Amir. David Carradine, Charles R. Floyd, Mako, Steve James, Phil Brock. Mindless, one-dimensional RAMBO variation, about some American P.O.W.s, headed by Col. Carradine, who battle their way to freedom as Saigon falls to the Commies. Formerly titled BEHIND ENEMY LINES. [R] ▼●

Powwow Highway (1989-British) **C-90m.** *** D: Jonathan Wacks. Gary Farmer, A Martinez, Amanda Wyss, Joanelle Romero, Sam Vlahos, Wayne Waterman, Margo Kane, Graham Greene, Wes Studi. Big, amiable Cheyenne, on a "medicine" journey to New Mexico in a beat-up Buick, gives a lift to a lifelong friend, an Indian activist. Not a totally successful film, but unusual and satisfying, with a standout performance by Farmer, an immensely likable actor who makes his character both endearing and ennobling. [R] ▼▌

Practical Magic (1998) **C-104m.** ** D: Griffin Dunne. Sandra Bullock, Nicole Kidman, Aidan Quinn, Stockard Channing, Dianne Wiest, Chloe Webb, Goran Visnjic, Evan Rachel Wood, Alexandra Artrip, Mark Feuerstein. Two sisters grow up under the curse of their ancestor (a woman hanged as a witch): any man whom they truly love is doomed. Free-spirited Kidman ignores the threat and leaves their New England home. Bullock lives with her witchly aunts, all too aware of the prophecy . . . until circumstance brings the sisters back together to work some magic of their own. Extremely likable stars make this watchable, but it's a lumpy brew. Based on a book by Alice Hoffman. Super 35. [PG-13] ▼●▌

Practice Makes Perfect (1978-French) **C-104m.** *** D: Philippe de Broca. Jean Rochefort, Nicole Garcia, Annie Girardot, Danielle Darrieux, Catherine Alric, Lila Kedrova, Jean Desailly. Funny, knowing comedy about bored, self-centered concert pianist, supposedly living ideal life, eventually receiving his retribution. Rochefort is perfectly cast as engaging womanizer. ▼

Prairie Home Companion, A (2006) **C-105m.** *** D: Robert Altman. Meryl Streep, Garrison Keillor, Kevin Kline, Lily Tomlin, Lindsay Lohan, Woody Harrelson, John C. Reilly, Virginia Madsen, Tommy Lee Jones, Maya Rudolph, Marylouise Burke, L. Q. Jones, Tim Russell, Sue Scott, Tom Keith, The Guy's All-Star Shoe Band. The extended family involved in an old-fashioned radio variety show gathers for a final performance in this bit of whimsy inspired by Keillor's real-life public radio program of the same name. Characters drift in and out, with vignettes ranging from surreal to slapstick, in a perfect melding of Keillor's humor and Altman's signature staging of ensemble scenes that seem both effortless and spontaneous. Fans will enjoy seeing

performers and musicians who appear regularly on the weekly radio show. Keillor's first screenplay; Altman's final film. HD Widescreen. [PG-13]▐

Prancer (1989) **C-102m.** *** D: John Hancock. Sam Elliott, Rebecca Harrell, Cloris Leachman, Rutanya Alda, Abe Vigoda, Ariana Richards, Michael Constantine. Eight-year-old farm girl Harrell, who marches to her own beat—and whose widowed father (Elliott) is knuckling under to financial pressure—nurses a wounded reindeer she believes is one of Santa's own. While it occasionally is a bit too obvious and cute, it's a charming fantasy about a child's undying devotion to an animal. Followed by a direct-to-video sequel. [G] ▼●▌

Prayer for the Dying, A (1987-British-U.S.) **C-107m.** *½ D: Mike Hodges. Mickey Rourke, Bob Hoskins, Alan Bates, Sammi Davis, Christopher Fulford, Liam Neeson, Alison Doody. Ponderous adaptation of Jack Higgins' novel about an IRA hit man (Rourke, with a dubious Irish accent) who can't escape his chosen calling, even when he tries to. Hoskins is badly miscast as a priest who becomes entangled with Rourke, while Bates chews it up as a flamboyant racketeer who doubles as a mortician. Heavy going all the way. [R]▼●▌

Prayer of the Rollerboys (1991) **C-94m.** **½ D: Rick King. Corey Haim, Patricia Arquette, Christopher Collet, Julius Harris, Devin Clark, Mark Pellegrino, Morgan Weisser, Jake Dengel, J.C. Quinn. To save his kid brother, orphan Haim goes undercover and joins the Rollerboys, a gang of high-powered, racist-fascist punks whose leader (Collet) might be the great-grandson of Hitler. Set in a future America in which anarchy and homelessness reign; provocative idea weakened by needlessly excessive violence—and a painfully predictable ending. [R]▼●▌

Preacher's Wife, The (1996) **C-125m.** **½ D: Penny Marshall. Denzel Washington, Whitney Houston, Courtney B. Vance, Gregory Hines, Jennifer Lewis, Lionel Richie, Justin Pierre Edmund, Shari Headley, Cissy Houston, Paul Bates, Loretta Devine, Toukie Smith. Appropriately old-fashioned remake of 1947's THE BISHOP'S WIFE concerns a semi-addled angel sent down here to assist a personally and professionally troubled clergyman only to become smitten with the latter's lovely spouse. Much too leisurely and long, but a notable showcase for its stars, and a rare contemporary Christmas movie to recapture the spirit of vintage holiday classics. With Houston as the wife, the gospel numbers have zing. [PG]▼●▌

Preaching to the Choir (2006) **C-103m.** *½ D: Charles Randolph-Wright. Billoah Greene, Darien Sills-Evans, Novella Nelson, Eartha Kitt, Janine Green, Patti LaBelle, Adewale Akinnuoye-Agbaje, Marva

Hicks, Tichina Arnold, Tim Reid, Ben Vereen. Amateurish movie aspires to be rousing entertainment but fails to rouse you out of your slumber in between gospel numbers. Almost nonexistent plot deals with the lifelong rivalry of two brothers, one a rap star named Zulu, the other a Harlem Baptist preacher. When Zulu's life is threatened due to bad business dealings, their divergent paths cross in this hip-hop spiritual comedy-musical. Nice to see Kitt still getting work, however. [PG-13] ▶

Precious (based on the novel 'Push' by Sapphire) (2009) **C-109m.** *** D: Lee Daniels. Gabourey Sidibe, Mo'Nique, Paula Patton, Mariah Carey, Sherri Shepherd, Lenny Kravitz, Kimberly Russell, Bill Sage. In 1987 Harlem, obese 16-year-old Precious (Sidibe) seems to be sleepwalking through life; it's the only way she can deal with the horrifying reality that engulfs her. Pregnant, again, by her father, she is abused at home by her monstrously cruel, layabout mother (Mo'Nique). Then she is transferred to a classroom where a caring teacher (Patton) begins to change her outlook. Raw adaptation of Sapphire's novel boasts unforgettable performances by newcomer Sidibe and stand-up comic Mo'Nique (who won an Oscar) . . . though Patton's character seems pat and less than credible. Geoffrey Fletcher's screenplay also won an Academy Award. Super 35. [R] ▶

Predator (1987) **C-107m.** *** D: John McTiernan. Arnold Schwarzenegger, Carl Weathers, Elpidia Carrillo, Bill Duke, Jesse Ventura, Sonny Landham, Richard Chaves, R.G. Armstrong, Shane Black, Kevin Peter Hall. Schwarzenegger and his super-SWAT-team-for-hire are assigned by the U.S. to a delicate rescue mission in South American jungle . . . but Arnold and his men soon find themselves battling a faceless, ferocious enemy that's picking them off one by one. Solid, suspenseful action film takes time getting started, but emerges a grabber. Followed by a sequel. [R] ▼●

Predator 2 (1990) **C-108m.** **½ D: Stephen Hopkins. Danny Glover, Gary Busey, Ruben Blades, Maria Conchita Alonso, Bill Paxton, Kevin Peter Hall, Robert Davi, Adam Baldwin, Kent McCord, Calvin Lockhart. Fast-paced (if too derivative) sequel, minus Arnold. This time, cop Glover and cronies take on the title alien in 1997 L.A. Good production design and lots of hit-'em-across-the-face action, but don't look for anything resembling inventive dialogue or character development. Then again, you wouldn't expect either from a film with Morton Downey, Jr., in its cast. Followed by ALIEN VS. PREDATOR. [R] ▼●

Predators (2010) **C-107m.** **½ D: Nimród Antal. Adrien Brody, Topher Grace, Alice Braga, Walton Goggins, Oleg Taktarov, Laurence Fishburne, Danny Trejo, Louis Ozawa Changchien, Mahershalalhashbaz Ali. A group of trained soldiers wakes up as they are parachuted into a jungle environment that turns out to be another planet. As these strangers grimly work together they realize they are prey imported for those familiar Predators to hunt down, with the help of alien hunting "dogs." MOST DANGEROUS GAME–type premise is given standard treatment; reasonably entertaining but very rote. Brody makes a surprisingly effective action hero. Mostly filmed in Hawaii. HD Widescreen. [R] ▶

Prefontaine (1997) **C-106m.** ** D: Steve James. Jared Leto, R. Lee Ermey, Ed O'Neill, Amy Locane, Lindsay Crouse, Laurel Holloman, Breckin Meyer, Brian McGovern, Kurtwood Smith. Peter Anthony Jacobs. Steve Prefontaine, an athlete from Coos Bay, Oregon, attends college, where he excels in running, eventually going to the Munich Olympics. Well-intentioned but TV-movie-like biopic fails to reveal why the runner is remembered today. Seems endless, but well acted. Story also told in WITHOUT LIMITS. [PG-13] ▼●

Prehistoric Women (1967-British) **C-91m.** *½ D: Michael Carreras. Michael Latimer, Martine Beswick, Edina Ronay, Carol White, John Raglan, Stephanie Randall, Steven Berkoff. Idiotic Hammer adventure in which Great White Hunter stumbles into lost Amazon civilization where blondes have been enslaved by brunettes. Honest! Nevertheless, this does have a cult following, due to Beswick's commanding, sensual performance as the tribe's leader. Released in Britain as SLAVE GIRLS, at 74m. CinemaScope. ▼●

Prehistoric World SEE: **Teenage Cave Man**

Prehysteria (1993) **C-86m.** **½ D: Albert Band, Charles Band. Brett Cullen, Colleen Morris, Samantha Mills, Austin O'Brien, Tony Longo, Stuart Fratkin, Stephen Lee. A family of raisin farmers (!) tries to protect five unusual critters their dog has hatched from eggs she stole from a greedy entrepreneur. An idea that will enchant children of all ages—pet dinosaurs the size of cats—overcomes a routine script. Followed by two sequels. From Full Moon. [PG] ▼●

Prelude to a Kiss (1992) **C-106m.** **½ D: Norman René. Alec Baldwin, Meg Ryan, Kathy Bates, Ned Beatty, Patty Duke, Sydney Walker, Stanley Tucci, Richard Riehle, Rocky Carroll, Annie Golden. It's love at first sight for Baldwin and Ryan, and soon they're wed—but on their honeymoon, he gets the strange feeling she's not the person he fell in love with. Winningly acted romantic comedy turns very, very odd, with a plot twist that's hard to swallow, and even harder to find endearing. A game attempt by all, including featured character actor Walker. Craig Lucas adapted his own play, with Baldwin re-creating his original N.Y. stage role and Walker repeating the part he played on tour. [PG-13]**▼○◑**

Prelude to Murder SEE: **Dressed to Kill** (1946)

Premature Burial, The (1962) **C-81m.** ** D: Roger Corman. Ray Milland, Hazel Court, Richard Ney, Heather Angel, Alan Napier, John Dierkes. Title tells the story in another of Corman's Poe adaptations, with Milland oddly cast as medical student with phobia of accidental entombment. Lavish (for this series), but not one of director's best. Panavision.**▼○◑**

Premonition, The (1976) **C-94m.** ** D: Robert Allen Schnitzer. Sharon Farrell, Richard Lynch, Jeff Corey, Ellen Barber, Edward Bell. Muddled script works against eerie atmosphere in this supernatural tale that stresses parapsychology as clue to young girl's disappearance. Mediocre results. Filmed in Mississippi. [PG]**▼◑**

Premonition (2007) **C-97m.** ** D: Mennan Yapo. Sandra Bullock, Julian McMahon, Nia Long, Kate Nelligan, Courtney Taylor Burness, Shyann McClure, Amber Valletta, Peter Stormare, Jude Ciccolella. Bullock is a standard-issue perfect housewife and mother who suddenly seems to be experiencing another reality: she awakens to alternating universes every other day or so. Can she convince everyone that husband McMahon is in peril—or is she just losing her mind? Whatever Hitchcock could have done with this genre thriller is not apparent here, and neither Bullock nor the script are up to the task. Super 35. [PG-13]**◑**

President's Analyst, The (1967) **C-103m.** **** D: Theodore J. Flicker. James Coburn, Godfrey Cambridge, Severn Darden, Joan Delaney, Pat Harrington, Will Geer, William Daniels. Totally nutty, brilliantly maneuvered satire of many sacred cows, as Coburn is pursued by half the government when he quits title job. The ending is a beauty. Screenplay by the director. Beware edited video version. Panavision.**▼○◑**

Presidio, The (1988) **C-97m.** **½ D: Peter Hyams. Sean Connery, Mark Harmon, Meg Ryan, Jack Warden, Mark Blum, Dana Gladstone, Jenette Goldstein, Don Calfa. San Francisco cop Harmon investigates a murder that took place on local military base, and clashes with an old nemesis, the presidio's chief provost Connery—whose daughter he's attracted to. Strictly formula stuff, though slickly done, with some good S.F. chase scenes. Panavision. [R]**▼○◑**

Press for Time (1966-British) **C-102m.** ** D: Robert Asher. Norman Wisdom, Angela Browne, Derek Bond, Derek Francis. Bumbling son of a commoner is sent by his government minister granddad to work as a reporter on a provincial newspaper. Wisdom has fun doing three roles; infectious musical score by Mike Vickers.**◑**

Prestige, The (2006) **C-130m.** ** D: Christopher Nolan. Hugh Jackman, Christian Bale, Michael Caine, Piper Perabo, Rebecca Hall, Scarlett Johansson, David Bowie, Andy Serkis, Roger Rees, Ricky Jay, Edward Hibbert, Daniel Davis, Christopher Neame. Airless, cheerless story of two magicians in London at the turn of the 20th century and how their rivalry develops into an unhealthy obsession. Somehow Nolan (who coscripted with his brother Jonathan, from Christopher Priest's novel) has managed to make a film about magic and illusion without a sense of wonder—or a drop of humor. Panavision. [PG-13]**◑**

Presumed Innocent (1990) **C-127m.** *** D: Alan J. Pakula. Harrison Ford, Brian Dennehy, Raul Julia, Bonnie Bedelia, Paul Winfield, Greta Scacchi, John Spencer, Joe Grifasi, Tom Mardirosian, Anna Maria Horsford, Sab Shimono, Christine Estabrook, Michael Tolan, Jeffrey Wright. Solid, well-cast screen version of Scott Turow's crackling best-seller about a prosecutor assigned to investigate the murder of a sexy assistant prosecutor with whom he'd had an affair. Soon, he's charged with the murder himself! Slow going at times, film misses its potential for greatness but still delivers many powerful moments. Screenplay by Pakula and Frank Pierson. [R] **▼○◑**

Prêt-à-Porter SEE: **Ready to Wear**

Pretty Baby (1978) **C-109m.** **½ D: Louis Malle. Keith Carradine, Susan Sarandon, Brooke Shields, Antonio Fargas, Frances Faye, Gerrit Graham, Mae Mercer, Diana Scarwid, Barbara Steele. Malle's first American film is beautifully mounted but distressingly low-keyed story of marriage between a 12-year-old New Orleans prostitute and an older photographer, set around time of WW1. Shields is striking in title role, but Carradine is pretty lifeless. Designed and cowritten (with Malle) by Polly Platt; photographed by Sven Nykvist. [R]**▼○◑**

Pretty in Pink (1986) **C-96m.** *** D: Howard Deutch. Molly Ringwald, Jon Cryer, Andrew McCarthy, Harry Dean Stanton, Annie Potts, James Spader, Alexa Kenin, Andrew "Dice" Clay, Margaret Colin, Gina Gershon, Dweezil Zappa, Kristy Swanson. A high school have-not finds herself in a quandary when one of the "richies" asks her out; her fellow outcast and fanatical devotee (Cryer) isn't too happy, either. Credible look at growing pains by writer-producer John Hughes, nicely acted, if a bit slow and self-serious. Stanton, as Molly's dad, has never been so tender on screen! [PG-13]**▼○◑**

Prettykill (1987) **C-95m.** BOMB D: George Kaczender. David Birney, Season Hubley, Susannah York, Yaphet Kotto, Suzanne Snyder, Sarah Polley. Noxious exploitation film about down on his luck cop and his girlfriend/hooker enmeshed in a case of a slasher who preys on prostitutes. Snyder gives an overwrought performance as a sweet young thing with a dual personality (she lapses into her southern fried incestuous father's voice at times!). [R]▼●

Pretty Maids All in a Row (1971) C-92m. *** D: Roger Vadim. Rock Hudson, Angie Dickinson, Telly Savalas, John David Carson, Roddy McDowall, James Doohan, Keenan Wynn, Amy (Aimee) Eccles, Barbara Leigh. Silly but enjoyable black comedy; high school guidance-counselor/coach Hudson advises frustrated Carson in sexual matters, while school is plagued with murders of pretty female students. Written and produced by Gene Roddenberry. [R]▼▶

Pretty Persuasion (2005) C-110m. *½ D: Marcos Siega. Evan Rachel Wood, Ron Livingston, James Woods, Jane Krakowski, Elisabeth Harnois, Telly Blair, Danny Comden, Robert Joy, Jaime King, Michael Hitchcock. Superficial, self-satisfied snipe at privileged Beverly Hills kids and their messed-up parents, as seen through an unenlightening portrait of a teenage psychopath (Evan Rachel Wood) who destroys everyone with whom she comes into contact. Glib, just like Woods' portrayal of the girl's scummy, bigoted father. There's no one to root for in this poisonous cast of characters. Panavision. [R]▶

Pretty Poison (1968) C-89m. *** D: Noel Black. Anthony Perkins, Tuesday Weld, Beverly Garland, John Randolph, Dick O'Neill. Oddball arsonist. Perkins enlists aid of sexy high-schooler Weld for scheme he's hatching, but soon discovers that she's got stranger notions than he does! Bright screenplay by Lorenzo Semple, Jr. (from Stephen Geller's novel, *She Let Him Continue*), sparked by Weld's vivid performance. [R]▼▶

Pretty Village, Pretty Flame (1996-Yugoslavian) C-125m. *** D: Srdjan Dragojevic. Dragan Bjelogrlic, Nikola Pejakovic, Velimir Bata Zivojinovic, Dragan Maksimovic. Biting allegorical anti-war drama about two young men, one Muslim, the other Serbian, who came of age together as best pals (depicted in poignant flashbacks) and now find themselves on opposite sides in the Bosnian civil war—and inexorably heading toward a confrontation. ▼▶

Pretty Woman (1990) C-117m. *** D: Garry Marshall. Richard Gere, Julia Roberts, Ralph Bellamy, Jason Alexander, Laura San Giacomo, Hector Elizondo, Alex Hyde-White, Elinor Donahue, Larry Miller, Jane Morris. Surprisingly successful variation on an old formula: wealthy, cold-blooded business tycoon Gere chances to meet Hollywood Boulevard hooker Roberts. He hires her to be his companion for a week, spruces her up, and—well, you can figure out the rest. Light, charming, and

thoroughly entertaining, with Roberts a delight in a star-making role. Director's cut runs 124m. [R]▼●▶

Prey for Rock & Roll (2003) C-103m. **½ D: Alex Steyermark. Gina Gershon, Drea de Matteo, Marc Blucas, Shelly Cole, Ivan Martin, Lori Petty, Sandra Seacat, Ashley Drane, Shakara Ledard, Eddie Driscoll, Texas Terri. All-femme grunge band fights hard for its big break while enduring unrelenting personal tragedies. Star-producer Gershon's feral, strikingly tattooed performance grounds the otherwise predictably gritty proceedings. Based on an autobiographical play by West Coast musician-artist Cheri Lovedog. [R]▼▶

Price Above Rubies, A (1998) C-117m. **½ D: Boaz Yakin. Renée Zellweger, Christopher Eccleston, Glenn Fitzgerald, Allen Payne, Julianna Margulies, Kathleen Chalfant, Edie Falco, John Randolph, Kim Hunter, Phyllis Newman. An unhappy Hasidic housewife in N.Y.C. yearns for sexual liberation and the freedom to pursue a career. This had critics divided, but offers a truly three-dimensional heroine, and Zellweger is convincing. Worth a look for those who seek mature, alternative fare. [R]▼▶

Priceless (2006-French) C-106m. *** D: Pierre Salvadori. Audrey Tautou, Gad Elmaleh, Marie-Christine Adam, Vernon Dobtcheff, Jacques Spiesser. Charming comedy set in the south of France, where a beautiful gold digger (Tautou) mistakes a bartender (Elmaleh) for a wealthy hotel guest and sleeps with him. When her sugar daddy finds out, he dumps her, and the guileless Elmaleh learns that he hasn't a chance with Tautou because he's a poor working stiff. Amusing and surprising twists follow in this entertaining yarn, which gives us a vicarious taste of how the super-rich enjoy the good life in Biarritz. Panavision. [PG-13]▶

Priceless Beauty (1988-Italian) C-97m. ** D: Charles Finch. Christopher Lambert, Diane Lane, Francesco Quinn, J. C. Quinn, Claudia Ohana, Monica Scattini, Joaquin D'Almeida. Reclusive former rock star, consumed by guilt over his brother's death, finds a magic lamp in the ocean and inside it a beautiful genie who tries to rebuild his self-esteem and capacity to love. Mediocre romance (starring then-real-life husband and wife Lambert and Lane) struggles to be whimsical. [R]▼●

Price of Freedom, The SEE: **Operation Daybreak**

Price of Glory (2000) C-118m. **½ 'D: Carlos Avila. Jimmy Smits, Jon Seda, Clifton Collins, Jr. (Clifton Gonzales Gonzales), Maria del Mar, Sal Lopez, Louis Mandylor, John Verea, Paul Rodriguez, Ron Perlman. Boxing saga centered around a Latino family with Smits pushing his three sons toward a success that eluded him in his fighting days. Earnest performances, and some good action in the ring, but plays like a TV movie. [PG-13] ▼▶

Price of Milk, The (2000-New Zealand) **C-87m.** ** D: Harry Sinclair. Danielle Cormack, Karl Urban, Willa O'Neill, Michael Lawrence, Rangi Motu. On a New Zealand dairy farm, a happy bride-to-be starts doubting her loving fiancé. Things get even weirder when she accidentally crashes her car into an old Maori woman who survives without a scratch. For a while this daffy fairy tale plays like a cross between Buñuel and the Brothers Grimm but doesn't sustain itself. Guaranteed to test your whimsy quotient. Featuring a lush soundtrack by the Moscow Symphony Orchestra. Super 35. [PG-13] ▼▶

Price of Sugar, The (2007) **C-90m.** **½ D: Bill Haney. Narrated by Paul Newman. Interesting if overlong documentary offers an admiring portrait of Father Christopher Hartley, a priest who champions Haitian workers employed on sugar plantations in the Dominican Republic. Hartley comes across as equal parts compassionate saint and smooth operator as he challenges a system that sustains a repressive form of virtual slavery. Newman's measured narration is effectively understated.▶

Prick Up Your Ears (1987-British) **C-108m.** *** D: Stephen Frears. Gary Oldman, Alfred Molina, Vanessa Redgrave, Wallace Shawn, Julie Walters, James Grant, Frances Barber, Lindsay Duncan, Janet Dale. Chillingly realistic and evocative look at young British playwright Joe Orton, who was murdered by his longtime lover Kenneth Halliwell in 1967. Stunning performances by Oldman (as Orton), Molina (as the tormented Halliwell), and Redgrave (as Orton's agent) make up for some lags in Alan Bennett's script. Unflinching look at homosexuality in England during the '50s and '60s (when it was a crime), but film offers no insight into Orton's great theatrical success. [R] ▼▶

Pride (2007) **C-104m.** **½ D: Sunu Gonera. Terrence Howard, Bernie Mac, Kimberly Elise, Tom Arnold, Brandon Fobbs, Alphonso McAuley, Regine Nehy, Nate Parker, Kevin Phillips, Scott Reeves, Evan Ross, Gary Anthony Sturgis. Howard plays real-life Philadelphia swim coach Jim Ellis, who in the 1970s tried to turn around the lives of some inner-city teenagers. Straightforward sports biopic has few surprises but keeps the clichés and preaching to a minimum. Howard (who coexecutive produced) and Mac make charismatic leads. Evan Ross, who plays Reggie, is the son of Diana Ross. Super 35. [PG]▶

Pride and Glory (2008) **C-129m.** **½ D: Gavin O'Connor. Edward Norton, Colin Farrell, Jon Voight, Noah Emmerich, Jennifer Ehle, John Ortiz, Shea Whigham, Frank Grillo, Lake Bell, Rick Gonzalez, Wayne Duvall, Carmen Ejogo, Ramon Rodriguez. Saga of a N.Y.C. police family that's strained to the breaking point. Norton, assigned to a special task force investigating the slaughter of four cops, discovers that his brother (Emmerich) and brother-in-law (Farrell) were complicit. No earth-shattering surprises in this brutal film, which plays out ritualistically, like an opera, but the drama is still potent and the performances first-rate. Voight is especially good as the family patriarch. [R]▶

Pride and Prejudice (1940) **118m.** **** D: Robert Z. Leonard. Greer Garson, Laurence Olivier, Edna May Oliver, Edmund Gwenn, Mary Boland, Maureen O'Sullivan, Karen Morley, Melville Cooper, E. E. Clive, Ann Rutherford, Marsha Hunt. Outstanding adaptation of Jane Austen's novel about five husband-hunting sisters in 19th-century England. Excellent cast, fine period flavor in classic comedy of manners; Aldous Huxley was one of the screenwriters. Cedric Gibbons and Paul Groesse's art direction deservedly earned an Oscar. Also shown in computer-colored version.▼▶

Pride & Prejudice (2005-British) **C-128m.** *** D: Joe Wright. Keira Knightley, Matthew Macfadyen, Brenda Blethyn, Donald Sutherland, Tom Hollander, Judi Dench, Rosamund Pike, Jena Malone, Kelly Reilly, Simon Woods, Penelope Wilton, Rupert Friend, Carey Mulligan. Vibrant version of Jane Austen's novel about five sisters whose mother is desperate to see them married off, and the reaction of Elizabeth, the most independent-minded of the bunch, to a man she initially despises. Purists will wince at liberties taken, but director Wright and screenwriter Deborah Moggach have fashioned a lively romance with an earthy atmosphere not usually found in such adaptations. Cast is tops, with Knightley enchanting as Elizabeth, Macfadyen an estimable Mr. Darcy. Ending revised for U.S. release. Super 35. [PG] ▼▶

Pride and the Passion, The (1957) **C-132m.** **½ D: Stanley Kramer. Cary Grant, Frank Sinatra, Sophia Loren, Theodore Bikel, John Wengraf. Miscast actioner involving capture of huge cannon by British naval officer (Grant) in 19th-century Spain. Spectacle scenes—filmed on location—are impressive; but most of the film is ridiculous. From the C.S. Forester novel. VistaVision.▼▶

Pride of St. Louis, The (1952) **93m.** **½ D: Harmon Jones. Dan Dailey, Joanne Dru, Richard Crenna, Hugh Sanders, Richard Hylton, James Brown. Dailey does well in this otherwise formula biography of brash, colorful Hall of Fame pitcher Dizzy Dean. Watch for Chet Huntley as a baseball broadcaster.▼

Pride of the Marines (1945) **119m.** ***½ D: Delmer Daves. John Garfield, Eleanor Parker, Dane Clark, John Ridgely, Rosemary DeCamp, Ann Doran, Ann Todd,

Warren Douglas. Solid acting by Warner Bros. stock company enhances true account of Marine blinded during Japanese attack, with Garfield as injured Al Schmid, Clark as sympathetic buddy. Screenplay by Albert Maltz.▶

Pride of the Yankees, The (1942) 127m. **** D: Sam Wood. Gary Cooper, Teresa Wright, Babe Ruth, Walter Brennan, Dan Duryea, Ludwig Stossel, Addison Richards, Hardie Albright. Superb biography of baseball star Lou Gehrig, with Cooper giving excellent performance; fine support from Wright as devoted wife. Truly memorable final sequence. Script by Jo Swerling and Herman J. Mankiewicz, with Oscar-winning editing by Daniel Mandell. Also shown in computer-colored version.▼○▶

Priest (1994-British) C-97m. ***½ D: Antonia Bird. Linus Roache, Tom Wilkinson, Cathy Tyson, Robert Carlyle, James Ellis, Lesley Sharp, Robert Pugh, Christine Tremarco, Paul Barber, Rio Fanning. Provocative drama about a man of the cloth who finds himself caught between sacred vows and his own personal beliefs, in particular his closeted homosexuality. Deft blend of melodrama and tract that manages to deal with homosexuality, abuse, incest, and the politics of the Church with incisive results—and even a dark sense of humor. Flawlessly acted. Written by Jimmy McGovern. Originally shown at 105m. and trimmed for U.S. release. [R]▼○▶

Priest (2011) C-87m. **½ D: Scott Stewart. Paul Bettany, Karl Urban, Cam Gigandet, Maggie Q, Lily Collins, Brad Dourif, Stephen Moyer, Christopher Plummer, Mädchen Amick. Director and star of LEGION reunite for an equally absurd but more exciting fantasy-thriller with religious overtones. In a postapocalyptic world ruled by the Catholic Church, an ages-old war between humans and humongous vampires has been settled by lethally efficient clerical warriors. But when rogue bloodsuckers kidnap his niece, Priest (Bettany) comes out of forced retirement to save her from a fate worse than death. Violent action-adventure borrows imagery and plot elements from THE SEARCHERS and other classic Westerns, and is all the more enjoyable as a guilty pleasure for not slipping into self-conscious campiness. Based on a Korean graphic novel series. 3-D Panavision. [PG-13]

Priest of Love (1981-British) C-125m. *** D: Christopher Miles. Ian McKellen, Janet Suzman, Ava Gardner, Penelope Keith, Jorge Rivero, John Gielgud, Sarah Miles. Literate account of the last years of D. H. Lawrence (McKellen)—"the one who writes the dirty books"—highlighted by his relationship with his wife (Suzman) and the publication of *Lady Chatterley's Lover*. Slow moving but rewarding; 11 years earlier, Miles directed the screen version

of Lawrence's THE VIRGIN AND THE GYPSY. [R]▼▶

Priest's Wife, The (1971-Italian-French) C-106m. *½ D: Dino Risi. Sophia Loren, Marcello Mastroianni, Venantino Venantini, Jacques Stany, Pippo Starnazza, Augusto Mastrantoni. Barely entertaining mixture of drama and humor with Loren as disillusioned singer who thinks she can convince priest (Mastroianni) to obtain release from his vow of celibacy and marry her. Weightier handling of subject matter can be heard on radio talk shows; film seems designed merely as vehicle for two stars. [PG]▶

Primal Fear (1996) C-129m. *** D: Gregory Hoblit. Richard Gere, Laura Linney, John Mahoney, Alfre Woodard, Frances McDormand, Edward Norton, Terry O'Quinn, Andre Braugher, Steven Bauer, Joe Spano, Tony Plana, Stanley Anderson, Maura Tierney, Jon Seda. Hotshot Chicago attorney defends an altar boy accused of brutally murdering a much-loved archbishop—even though all evidence seems to point to the young man's guilt. Gere gives a solid performance in one of his very best roles, as a cocky lawyer who—for once—doesn't have all the answers. Newcomer Norton is also very impressive. Film loses some of its impact by going on too long and by following unrelated story tangents. Still, an intelligent, absorbing drama. [R]▼○▶

Primary Colors (1998) C-143m. ***½ D: Mike Nichols. John Travolta, Emma Thompson, Kathy Bates, Adrian Lester, Billy Bob Thornton, Maura Tierney, Larry Hagman, Diane Ladd, Paul Guilfoyle, Caroline Aaron, Rob Reiner, Ben Jones, Mykelti Williamson, Bonnie Bartlett, Tony Shalhoub, Allison Janney. Dynamic adaptation of political roman à clef by Anonymous (Joe Klein) about a Southern governor's Presidential race—and an idealistic staffer (Lester) who sees in him both a true believer in people power and an insatiable womanizer who'll do anything to cover his tracks. Travolta is extraordinarily good in a Bill Clinton–esque characterization, and Nichols has cast every part around him with an unerring eye. Bates is a powerhouse as Travolta's longtime political conscience and troubleshooter. Smart, funny, foul-mouthed screenplay by Elaine May. Super 35. [R]▼○▶

Prime (2005) C-105m. **½ D: Ben Younger. Meryl Streep, Uma Thurman, Bryan Greenberg, Jon Abrahams, Zak Orth, Annie Parisse, Doris Belack, Jerry Adler. A newly divorced 37-year-old woman embarks on a relationship with a 23-year-old man, unaware that he is the son of her longtime therapist. Cute comedy has funny and romantic moments, but never quite catches fire. Bolstered by the performances of Streep and especially Thurman, who has never been looser or more appealing on-screen. Written by the director. [PG-13]▼▶

Prime Cut (1972) **C-86m.** ******* D: Michael Ritchie. Lee Marvin, Gene Hackman, Angel Tompkins, Gregory Walcott, Sissy Spacek, Janit Baldwin. Mob hijinks at a Kansas City slaughterhouse inspire well-cast, fast-moving, tongue-in-cheek trash that fans of sleazy crime melodramas should love. Spacek's first film. Panavision. [R]▼●)

Prime Gig, The (2001) **C-97m.** ****** D: Gregory Mosher. Vince Vaughn, Julia Ormond, Ed Harris, Rory Cochrane, Wallace Shawn, Stephen Tobolowsky, George Wendt, Jeannetta Arnette. Successful telemarketer Vaughn is recruited by Harris for his boiler-room operation and becomes romantically involved with Ormond. Interesting look at scam artists, but Vaughn's ambivalent character flattens the film's dramatic tension instead of heightening it. Good performances help. U.S. debut on cable TV. Panavision. [R]▼●)

Prime of Miss Jean Brodie, The (1969) **C-116m.** *****½** D: Ronald Neame. Maggie Smith, Robert Stephens, Pamela Franklin, Gordon Jackson, Celia Johnson, Jane Carr. Oscar-winning showcase for Smith as eccentric teacher in Edinburgh school who wields a spellbinding influence on her "girls." Remarkable character study, adapted by Jay Presson Allen from stage version of Muriel Spark's novel; filmed on location. Smith and Stephens were then real-life husband and wife. Later remade as a TV miniseries. [M/PG]▼●)

Primer (2004) **C-78m.** ******* D: Shane Carruth. Shane Carruth, David Sullivan, Casey Gooden, Anand Upadhyaya, Carrie Crawford. Quirky, original sci-fi thriller about a couple of young corporate engineers (Carruth, Sullivan) whose lives are altered when they accidentally invent a time-travel contraption. Shot on a budget of 35¢ (actually $7,000), and loaded with ideas and imagination; occasionally bogs down in technical jargon, but still well worth watching—and pondering. Carruth also scripted, produced, edited, wrote the score, and was cocinematographer. [PG-13]▮)

Primeval (2007) **C-93m.** ****** D: Michael Katleman. Dominic Purcell, Brooke Langton, Orlando Jones, Jürgen Prochnow, Gideon Emery, Gabriel Malema, Linda Mpondo. American reporters reluctantly trek to Africa to capture a huge man-eating crocodile the locals call Gustave, and become embroiled in a local war. Peculiar blend of JAWS and a BLOOD DIAMOND–like subplot has its moments, but is mostly routine, with herky-jerky editing in the frequent action scenes. Loosely based on real events. Super 35. [R]▮)

Primrose Path (1940) **93m.** ****½** D: Gregory La Cava. Ginger Rogers, Joel McCrea, Marjorie Rambeau, Miles Mander, Henry Travers. Girl from wrong side of the tracks falls in love with ambitious young McCrea; starts engagingly, drifts into dreary soap opera and melodramatics. Rambeau is excellent as Ginger's prostitute mother.▼●)

Prince & Me, The (2004) **C-111m.** ****½** D: Martha Coolidge. Julia Stiles, Luke Mably, Ben Miller, Miranda Richardson, James Fox, Eliza Bennett, Alberta Watson, John Bourgeois. Wisconsin farm girl with big plans is attracted to a handsome exchange student who stumbles into her life . . . little dreaming that he is the Prince of Denmark. Amiable modern-day fairy tale goes on longer than it should given its formulaic nature, but the two leads are engaging and attractive. Followed by two DVD sequels. [PG] ▼●)

Prince and the Great Race SEE: **Bush Christmas**

Prince and the Pauper, The (1937) **120m.** *****½** D: William Keighley. Errol Flynn, Billy and Bobby Mauch, Claude Rains, Alan Hale, Montagu Love, Henry Stephenson, Barton MacLane. Rousing filmization of Mark Twain's story of young look-alikes, one a mistreated urchin, the other a prince, exchanging places. Top-billed Flynn, cast as the boys' rescuer, doesn't appear until around the midway point. Great music score by Erich Wolfgang Korngold. Remade as CROSSED SWORDS. Also available in computer-colored version.▼●)

Prince and the Pauper, The (1978) SEE: **Crossed Swords**

Prince and the Showgirl, The (1957) **C-117m.** ****½** D: Laurence Olivier. Marilyn Monroe, Laurence Olivier, Sybil Thorndike. Jeremy Spenser, Richard Wattis. Thoughtful but slow-moving comedy of saucy American showgirl Monroe being romanced by Prince Regent of Carpathia (Olivier) during the 1911 coronation of George V. Filmed in England, with delightful performances by Monroe and Olivier. Script by Terence Rattigan from his play *The Sleeping Prince.*▼●)

Prince Jack (1984) **C-100m.** ****** D: Bert Lovitt. Robert Hogan, James F. Kelly, Kenneth Mars, Lloyd Nolan, Cameron Mitchell, Robert Guillaume, Theodore Bikel, Jim Backus, Dana Andrews. Yet another chronicle of life among the Kennedys, here focusing mainly on the men and their personalities. Superficial at best.▼

Prince of Darkness (1987) **C-110m.** BOMB D: John Carpenter. Donald Pleasence, Lisa Blount, Jameson Parker, Victor Wong, Dennis Dun, Susan Blanchard, Anne Howard, Alice Cooper. The anti-God entombs wayward son Satan in a cannister of glop in an abandoned L.A. church; it's up to priest Pleasence and the grad students of prof Wong to clean up the mess. Not for nothing is the religious sect involved called "Brotherhood of Sleep." Panavision. [R] ▼●)

Prince of Egypt, The (1998) **C-97m.** ****½** D: Brenda Chapman, Steve Hickner, Simon Wells. Voices of Val Kilmer, Ralph Fiennes, Michelle Pfeiffer, Sandra Bullock, Jeff Goldblum, Danny Glover, Patrick Stewart, Helen Mirren, Steve Martin, Martin Short.

Animated retelling of the story of Moses features some of the most spectacular animation in the history of the medium, dramatic staging, and an ambitious song score by Stephen Schwartz . . . but the parts are greater than the whole, and the story drags at times. An impressive achievement, but liable to test the endurance of young children. Features Oscar-winning song "When You Believe." Followed on video by JOSEPH: KING OF DREAMS. [PG]▼●◗

Prince of Foxes (1949) **107m. **½** D: Henry King. Tyrone Power, Wanda Hendrix, Orson Welles, Marina Berti, Everett Sloane, Katina Paxinou. Lavish, incredibly handsome costume epic of Renaissance-era Italy (filmed on location), with adventurer Power defying all-powerful Cesare Borgia. Story elements—from Samuel Shellabarger novel—don't match impact of Leon Shamroy's sumptuous cinematography.◗

Prince of Pennsylvania, The (1988) **C-87m. **½** D: Ron Nyswaner. Fred Ward, Keanu Reeves, Bonnie Bedelia, Amy Madigan, Jeff Hayenga, Tracey Ellis. Extremely quirky character comedy of free spirit Reeves (with a strange half-Mohawk hairdo) "finding" himself while battling with his equally wacko dad (Ward, in a marvelous performance). Madigan is excellent as the older woman whom Reeves romances; in-joke has her dressing up in a Freddy Krueger mask for a fake kidnapping. Writer Nyswaner (SMITHEREENS) turns director; many striking scenes unfortunately fail to grip as a whole. [R]▼●◗

Prince of Persia: The Sands of Time (2010) **C-116m. **** D: Mike Newell. Jake Gyllenhaal, Gemma Arterton, Ben Kingsley, Alfred Molina, Steve Toussaint, Toby Kebbell, Richard Coyle, Ronald Pickup, Reece Ritchie. Convoluted juvenile adventure yarn about an adopted prince who is unfairly accused of betrayal (and worse), and finds his fate intertwined with that of a Persian princess. Only she understands the power of a precious dagger that can turn back the sands of time. The actors are gung-ho but the story is obvious and overlong; action scenes are shot in such a way that you can't really see the stunts, just their implications. As for visual effects, quantity doesn't equal quality. Based on a video game by Jordan Mechner, who gets story credit here. Super 35. [PG-13]◗

Prince of Players (1955) **C-102m. **½** D: Philip Dunne. Richard Burton, Maggie McNamara, Raymond Massey, Charles Bickford, John Derek, Eva Le Gallienne, Mae Marsh, Sarah Padden. Burton is 19th-century actor Edwin Booth, embroiled in more offstage drama than on. Shakespearean excerpts thrown in; well performed by earnest cast. Derek plays John Wilkes Booth. Script by Moss Hart. CinemaScope.

Prince of the City (1981) **C-167m. *** D: Sidney Lumet. Treat Williams, Jerry Orbach, Richard Foronjy, Don Billett, Kenny Marino, Carmine Caridi, Bob Balaban, James Tolkan, Lindsay Crouse, Matthew Laurance, Lee Richardson, Lane Smith, Peter Michael Goetz, Lance Henriksen. Emotionally powerful story (which unfortunately is true) about a cop in a N.Y.C. special investigations unit who blows the whistle on department corruption but finds himself more a victim than a hero. Standout performances by Williams, fellow cop Orbach, weasely prosecutor Tolkan, but film's extreme length hurts overall impact; there are more details than really necessary to tell the story. Script by Lumet and Jay Presson Allen. [R]▼●◗

Prince of Tides, The (1991) **C-132m. *** D: Barbra Streisand. Nick Nolte, Barbra Streisand, Blythe Danner, Kate Nelligan, Jeroen Krabbé, Melinda Dillon, George Carlin, Jason Gould, Brad Sullivan. Nolte is both compelling and believable as a man who keeps a lifetime of harrowing memories bottled up inside—until he's forced to spill them to a psychiatrist in order to help save his suicidal sister. How much you like (or believe) Streisand's performance as the doctor may affect your feelings about the film, but she's certainly managed to tell a good story, rich in emotion. Gould (son of Streisand and Elliott Gould) plays Barbra's teenage son. Screenplay by Pat Conroy and Becky Johnston, from Conroy's sprawling novel. [R]▼●◗

Princess and the Frog, The (2009) **C-95m. *** D: John Musker, Ron Clements. Voices of Anika Noni Rose, Bruno Campos, Keith David, Michael-Leon Wooley, Jennifer Cody, Jim Cummings, Jenifer Lewis, Oprah Winfrey, Terrence Howard, John Goodman. In a black neighborhood of 1920s New Orleans, young Tiana learns that only hard work can make her dreams a reality. Then she meets visiting Prince Naveen, who's transformed into a frog and seeks her kiss. Briskly paced gumbo of a story draws on rich Louisiana culture, and every musical number has a unique design and sound. Randy Newman's flavorful songs punctuate this fairy tale, turned inside out by hip, irreverent humor—and Naveen's hilarious dialogue. (He's the first Disney prince who's funny.) Disney's return to hand-drawn animation hews to a familiar formula but makes it work. [G]◗

Princess and the Warrior, The (2000-German) **C-130m. ** D: Tom Tykwer. Franka Potente, Benno Furmann, Joachim Krol, Marita Breuer, Jurgen Tarrach, Lars Rudolph. Odd, off-putting fable about a nurse in a psychiatric hospital who has a fateful encounter with a deeply troubled ex-soldier and can't get him out of her mind. Long, slow, sometimes downright silly. Film's occasional arresting images linger long after the story's illogicality is forgotten. Tykwer also scripted and collaborated on the highly effective score. Super 35. [R]▼◗

Princess Bride, The (1987) **C-98m.** **½
D: Rob Reiner. Cary Elwes, Mandy
Patinkin, Chris Sarandon, Christopher
Guest, Wallace Shawn, Andre the Giant,
Fred Savage, Robin Wright, Peter Falk,
Peter Cook, Carol Kane, Billy Crystal, Mel
Smith. Revisionist fairy tale/adventure about
a beautiful young woman and her one true
love, who must find and rescue her after a
long separation. Some wonderful scenes
and character vignettes are periodically
undermined by a tendency toward comic
shtick (as in Crystal's cameo appearance)
and occasional incoherency (as in the opening scenes with Castilian-tongued Patinkin
and marble-mouthed Andre the Giant). Best
of all: the swashbuckling sequences. Bonus
for old-movie buffs: watching Guest, as Count
Rugen, imitate Henry Daniell (from THE
SEA HAWK). Screenplay by William Goldman, from his novel. [PG]▼●◗

Princess Caraboo (1994–U.S.-British) **C-
96m.** *** D: Michael Austin. Phoebe Cates,
Jim Broadbent, Wendy Hughes, Kevin
Kline, John Lithgow, Stephen Rea, Peter
Eyre, Jacqueline Pearce, Roger Lloyd Pack,
John Wells, John Lynch. Pleasing fairy tale–
like yarn about young "mystery woman"
Cates who is believed to be a princess from
a distant land, and is taken in by a well-
meaning British lady (Hughes) in the early
1800s. Based on a true story, believe it or
not; handsomely made, acted with gusto by
a first-rate cast. Ideal family entertainment.
Photographed by the great Freddie Francis.
[PG]▼●◗

Princess Diaries, The (2001) **C-115m.** *½
D: Garry Marshall. Julie Andrews, Anne
Hathaway, Hector Elizondo, Heather Matarazzo, Mandy Moore, Caroline Goodall,
Robert Schwartzman, Erik Von Detten, Patrick Flueger, Sandra Oh, Mindy Burbano.
High school oddball/ugly duckling learns
she's a princess from her royal grandmother
and blossoms under extensive tutelage
(and eyebrow plucking). Cute premise is
squandered by a script that goes in a hundred directions—none of them remotely
genuine—and never seems to end. Hathaway is appealing, Andrews' touch of class
is more than welcome, but the film is an ordeal. Larry Miller appears unbilled. Based
on a novel by Meg Cabot. Followed by a
sequel. [G]▼◗

**Princess Diaries 2: Royal Engagement,
The** (2004) **C-115m.** *½ D: Garry Mar-
shall. Anne Hathaway, Julie Andrews,
Hector Elizondo, Heather Matarazzo, John
Rhys-Davies, Chris Pine, Callum Blue,
Kathleen Marshall, Raven Symone, Tom
Poston, Larry Miller, Caroline Goodall,
Spencer Breslin, Elinor Donahue, Paul
Williams. Unnecessary sequel to the 2001
hit has our plucky princess set to rule the
kingdom of Genovia only to find, thanks to
one of the film's many gimmicks, she must
be married to assume the throne. A series of
sitcom scenarios played out over two hours.
Brightened by the presence of Andrews and
a game supporting cast. [G]▼◗

Princess Ka'iulani (2010-British-U.S.) **C-
97m.** ** D: Marc Forby. Q'orianka Kilcher,
Barry Pepper, Shaun Evans, Jimmy Yuill,
Will Patton, Julian Glover, Tamzin Merchant, Leo Anderson Akana, Ocean Kaow-
ili. In the late 1800s, the young princess of
Hawaii (whose father is Scottish) returns to
her homeland after being educated in England, to try to keep the island kingdom from
being annexed by the U.S. Fascinating true-
life story is told in an earnest but uninspired
manner, although Kilcher is well cast in the
title role. Super 35.◗

Princess Mononoke (1997-Japanese) **C-
133m.** ***½ D: Hayao Miyazaki. Voices
of Billy Crudup, Claire Danes, Minnie
Driver, Billy Bob Thornton, Gillian Anderson, Jada Pinkett Smith. Extraordinary animated fable, full of astonishing sights; while
the story is difficult to follow at times, it's
worth the effort. Wounded by a dying boar-
god, a young man tries to get help from a
forest spirit. He's aided by a girl who lives
with wolf-gods, and opposed by a shrewd
woman who is devoted to technology.
Writer-director Miyazaki largely created his
own mythology, and raises worthy questions
about mankind's place in the natural world.
Complex, thoughtful animated movie aimed
at adults rather than children. [PG-13]▼◗

Princess of Montpensier, The (2010-
French-German) **C-139m.** ***½ D: Bertrand Tavernier. Mélanie Thierry, Lambert
Wilson, Gaspard Ulliel, Grégoire Leprince-
Ringuet, Raphaël Personnaz, Michel
Vuillermoz, Philippe Magnan, Florence
Thomassin. While war wages between Cath-
olics and Huguenots in 16th-century France,
a stunningly beautiful young woman (Thierry) fancies her cousin but is forced by her
father to marry a prince she's never met. Also
playing a central role is an older count (Wilson), a warrior-turned-pacifist who becomes
her friend and tutor and who not so secretly
loves her. Longish but richly absorbing
drama of shifting emotions and duty versus
desire is well acted by one and all. Tavernier
makes this period piece vivid and contemporary; Bruno de Keyzer's camerawork is
exceptional, and the locations are perfectly
chosen. Based on a novella by Madame de la
Fayette. Panavision.

Princess Yang Kwei Fei (1955-Japanese)
C-91m. **** D: Kenji Mizoguchi. Machiko
Kyo, Masayuki Mori, So Yamamura, Eitaro
Shindo, Sakae Ozawa. Emperor Mori takes
country girl Kyo as his concubine. He is
forced out of power by his greedy family:
she is killed, and he worships her statue.
Breathtakingly beautiful, poetic love story/
fable/tragedy.▼

Prince Valiant (1954) **C-100m.** **½ D:

Henry Hathaway. James Mason, Janet Leigh, Robert Wagner, Debra Paget, Sterling Hayden, Victor McLaglen, Donald Crisp, Brian Aherne. Hal Foster's famed comic-strip character is the hero of this cardboard costumer decked out in 20th Century-Fox splendor, battling and loving in Middle Ages England. Script by Dudley Nichols. CinemaScope.▼●

Prince Who Was a Thief, The (1951) **C-88m.** **½ D: Rudolph Maté. Tony Curtis, Piper Laurie, Everett Sloane, Jeff Corey, Betty Garde. Juvenile costumer with Curtis fighting to regain his rightful seat on the throne; sparked by enthusiastic performances.

Principal, The (1987) **C-109m.** ** D: Christopher Cain. James Belushi, Louis Gossett, Jr., Rae Dawn Chong, Michael Wright, J.J. Cohen, Esai Morales, Troy Winbush. Following some drunken vandalism on his estranged spouse's car, schoolteacher Belushi is "promoted" to top job at the district's most crime-ridden school. Unlikely mix of comedy and drama benefits from likable performances and a reasonably tense HIGH NOON finale between Belushi and the school's leading thug. [R]▼●]

Priscilla, Queen of the Desert SEE: Adventures of Priscilla, Queen of the Desert, The

Prison (1988) **C-102m.** ** D: Renny Harlin. Lane Smith, Viggo Mortensen, Chelsea Field, Andre De Shields, Lincoln Kilpatrick, Ivan Kane. The spirit of a prisoner who was executed 20 years ago seeks revenge on his one-time guard—who's now the warden (Smith). OK special effects and location atmosphere are strongest assets of this cliched horror film. [R]▼●

Prisoner, The (1955-British) **91m.** *** D: Peter Glenville. Alec Guinness, Jack Hawkins, Raymond Huntley, Wilfrid Lawson. Grim account of cardinal in Iron Curtain country undergoing grueling interrogation. Guinness-Hawkins interplay is superb.▼●

Prisoner of Paradise (2003-Canadian-British-German-U.S.) **C/B&W-96m.** ***½ D: Malcolm Clarke, Stuart Sender. Narrated by Ian Holm. Fascinating documentary about Kurt Gerron, a popular German performer and filmmaker of the 1920s and '30s (best remembered as the nightclub owner in THE BLUE ANGEL) who stayed in Europe too long and wound up at the "model" concentration camp in Theresienstadt, where he was commissioned to make one final motion picture—for the Nazis. Extraordinary footage from the period is augmented by a handful of equally compelling interviews with surviving friends and colleagues.●

Prisoner of Second Avenue, The (1975) **C-105m.** ***½ D: Melvin Frank. Jack Lemmon, Anne Bancroft, Gene Saks, Elizabeth Wilson, Florence Stanley, M. Emmet Walsh. Neil Simon walks a tightrope between comedy and melancholia, and never falls, thanks to warm performances by Lemmon, as suddenly unemployed executive who has a nervous breakdown, and Bancroft, as his understanding wife. Look for Sylvester Stallone as an alleged pickpocket, F. Murray Abraham as a cabbie. Panavision. [PG]▼●

Prisoner of Shark Island, The (1936) **95m.** ***½ D: John Ford. Warner Baxter, Gloria Stuart, Claude Gillingwater, John Carradine, Harry Carey, Arthur Byron, Ernest Whitman, Francis McDonald. Excellent film based on true story of Dr. Samuel Mudd, who treated John Wilkes Booth's broken leg after Lincoln assassination and was sentenced to life imprisonment. Gripping story; Baxter superb, Carradine memorable as villainous sergeant, Whitman fine as Baxter's black comrade. Scripted by Nunnally Johnson. Remade as HELLGATE and the TV movie THE ORDEAL OF DR. MUDD.●

Prisoner of the Mountains (1996-Russian) **C-98m.** ***½ D: Sergei Bodrov. Oleg Menshikov, Sergei Bodrov, Jr., Jemal Sikharulidze, Susanna Mekhralieva, Alexei Jharkov. Simple, devastating account of two Russian soldiers captured by Chechen rebels and held in an impoverished mountaintop village. Film is based on a Tolstoy story, but seems more pertinent in its present-day setting. Director's son portrays the younger of the two prisoners, an impressionable soldier barely out of school. Catch this one. ▼●

Prisoner of War (1954) **80m.** ** D: Andrew Marton. Ronald Reagan, Steve Forrest, Dewey Martin, Oscar Homolka, Robert Horton, Paul Stewart, Harry Morgan, Stephen Bekassy, Darryl Hickman, Jerry Paris. G.I. Reagan parachutes into North Korea to observe the manner in which the Commies are brainwashing American POWs. By-the-numbers Korean War drama, primarily of interest as a reflection of its era.

Prisoner of Zenda, The (1937) **101m.** **** D: John Cromwell. Ronald Colman, Madeleine Carroll, Douglas Fairbanks, Jr., C. Aubrey Smith, Raymond Massey, Mary Astor, David Niven, Montagu Love, Alexander D'Arcy. Lavish costume romance/adventure with excellent casting; Colman is forced to substitute for lookalike cousin, King of Ruritanian country, but commoner Colman falls in love with regal Carroll. Fairbanks nearly steals the show as villainous Rupert of Hentzau. Screenplay by John L. Balderston, from Anthony Hope's novel. Previously filmed in 1914 and 1922, then again in 1952 and 1979. Also shown in computer-colored version.▼●]

Prisoner of Zenda, The (1952) **C-101m.** **½ D: Richard Thorpe. Stewart Granger, Deborah Kerr, Jane Greer, Louis Calhern, Lewis Stone, James Mason, Robert Douglas, Robert Coote. Plush but uninspired remake of the Anthony Hope novel, chronicling the swashbuckling adventures of Granger, a dead ringer for a small European country's king. Stick with the Ronald Colman version; this one copies it scene for scene.**▼●)**

Prisoner of Zenda, The (1979) **C-108m.** BOMB D: Richard Quine. Peter Sellers, Lynne Frederick, Lionel Jeffries, Elke Sommer, Gregory Sierra, Jeremy Kemp, Catherine Schell. Famous swashbuckler is played for laughs, but there aren't any. A return to the kind of picture that helped to destroy Sellers' career. [PG]▼

Prisoners of the Sun (1991-Australian) **C-109m.** *** D: Stephen Wallace. Bryan Brown, George Takei, Terry O'Quinn, John Bach, Toshi Shioya, John Clarke, Deborah Unger, Russell Crowe. Gritty, gripping post-WW2 drama, set on an Indonesian island where the Japanese had established a POW camp for Australian flyers. The war has ended, and truth-seeking military lawyer Brown must deal with bureaucracy, politics, and clashing cultures as he sets out to prosecute different Japanese charged with mistreating and murdering POWs. Incisive, well-acted tale. Aka BLOOD OATH. [R] ▼●)

Private Affairs of Bel Ami, The (1947) **112m.** ***½ D: Albert Lewin. George Sanders, Angela Lansbury, Ann Dvorak, Frances Dee, Albert Basserman, Warren William, John Carradine. Delicious, literate adaptation (by Lewin) of Guy de Maupassant's "story of a rogue." Sanders, who gets ahead by using his charm on prominent women, denies himself the real love of Lansbury. Fine performances; beautifully photographed by Russell Metty.▼

Private Benjamin (1980) **C-110m.** *** D: Howard Zieff. Goldie Hawn, Eileen Brennan, Armand Assante, Robert Webber, Sam Wanamaker, Barbara Barrie, Mary Kay Place, Harry Dean Stanton, Albert Brooks, Hal Williams, P. J. Soles, Sally Kirkland, Richard Herd, Gretchen Wyler, Craig T. Nelson. A bubbleheaded Jewish American Princess enlists in the Army, and after a disastrous initiation finds direction and self-esteem for the first time in her life. Entertaining comedy with more substance than one might expect; Goldie is terrific in this tailor-made vehicle (which she produced). Later a TV series. [R] ▼●)

Private Confessions (1997-Swedish) **C-127m.** *** D: Liv Ullmann. Pernilla August, Max von Sydow, Samuel Froler, Anita Bjork, Vibeke Falk, Thomas Hanzon. Intimate, compassionate autobiographical drama (an extension of THE BEST INTENTIONS) scripted by Ingmar Bergman, which further examines the stormy relationship between his parents: a strict, detached Lutheran minister (Froler) and a dynamic, restless woman caught in an unhappy marriage (August). Von Sydow brilliantly plays a fatherly priest. An exploration of religion, faith, and loneliness. Edited from a Swedish TV miniseries.▼

Private Duty Nurses (1971) **C-80m.** BOMB D: George Armitage. Kathy Cannon, Joyce Williams, Pegi Boucher, Joseph Kaufmann, Herbert Jefferson, Jr., Paul Hampton, Paul Gleason. Second of Roger Corman's five "nurse" pictures is the worst. Glum and humorless, it spends more time on then-new waterbeds than in the hospital; dull cast doesn't help. Followed by NIGHT CALL NURSES. [R] ▼)

Private Eyes, The (1980) **C-91m.** **½ D: Lang Elliott. Tim Conway, Don Knotts, Trisha Noble, Bernard Fox, John Fujioka, Fred Stuthman. Conway and Knotts are bumbling Scotland Yard sleuths—and Abbott and Costello incarnate—in this silly, well-mounted murder-in-an-old-dark-house mystery. One of the better Conway-Knotts comedies. [PG]▼●)

Private Fears in Public Places SEE: **Coeurs**

Private Files of J. Edgar Hoover, The (1977) **C-112m.** **½ D: Larry Cohen. Broderick Crawford, Dan Dailey, Jose Ferrer, Rip Torn, Michael Parks, Raymond St. Jacques, Ronee Blakley, Celeste Holm, Howard da Silva, June Havoc, John Marley, Andrew Duggan, Lloyd Nolan. Sleazy bio of former FBI chief makes for great camp with its all-star lineup of real-life politicians—not to mention that cast! [PG]▼)

Private Function, A (1985-British) **C-93m.** **½ D: Malcolm Mowbray. Michael Palin, Maggie Smith, Liz Smith, Denholm Elliott, Richard Griffiths, John Normington, Bill Paterson, Peter Postlethwaite. Droll, very British comedy by Alan Bennett set in post-WW2 England, where food rationing is still in force and a contraband pig becomes the center of attention. Often funny, but also cynical and cruel. Smith is hilarious as the social-climbing wife of milquetoasty podiatrist Palin. Later a stage musical. [R]▼)

Private Lessons (1981) **C-87m.** *½ D: Alan Myerson. Sylvia Kristel, Howard Hesseman, Eric Brown, Pamela Bryant, Ed Begley, Jr., Crispin Glover. Male adolescent from wealthy family finds sexual delight with the maid, unaware that she has other plans for him. Surprise box-office hit is pretty mild piece of sleaze. Written by humorist Dan Greenburg (who also appears as a desk clerk). Followed by an in-name-only sequel 13 years later. [R]▼●)

Private Life of Henry VIII, The (1933-British) **97m.** **** D: Alexander Korda. Charles Laughton, Binnie Barnes, Robert

Donat, Elsa Lanchester, Merle Oberon, Miles Mander, Wendy Barrie, John Loder. Sweeping historical chronicle of 16th-century English monarch, magnificently captured by Oscar-winning Laughton in a multifaceted performance. Lanchester fine as Anne of Cleves, with top supporting cast. Also shown in computer-colored version. ▼●◗

Private Life of Sherlock Holmes, The (1970) C-125m. ***½ D: Billy Wilder. Robert Stephens, Colin Blakely, Genevieve Page, Irene Handl, Stanley Holloway, Christopher Lee, Clive Revill. Atypical but extremely personal Wilder film takes melancholy look at famed sleuth. Acting, photography, and score are tops in neglected film whose reputation should soar in future years. Intended as a 3½-hour film; some deleted material can be seen on the DVD. Made in England. Panavision. [PG] ▼●◗

Private Lives of Elizabeth and Essex, The (1939) C-106m. ***½ D: Michael Curtiz. Bette Davis, Errol Flynn, Olivia de Havilland, Donald Crisp, Alan Hale, Vincent Price, Henry Stephenson, Henry Daniell, James Stephenson, Ralph Forbes, Robert Warwick, Leo G. Carroll. Colorful, elaborate costume drama with outstanding performance by Davis as queen whose love for dashing Flynn is thwarted. Not authentic history, but good drama. Norman Reilly Raine and Aeneas MacKenzie adapted Maxwell Anderson's play *Elizabeth the Queen*. Adult film debut of Nanette Fabray (Fabares). Aka ELIZABETH THE QUEEN. ▼◗

Private Lives of Pippa Lee, The (2009) C-98m. *** D: Rebecca Miller. Robin Wright Penn, Alan Arkin, Maria Bello, Blake Lively, Monica Bellucci, Julianne Moore, Keanu Reeves, Winona Ryder, Robin Weigert, Ryan McDonald, Tim Guinee, Zoe Kazan, Mike Binder, Shirley Knight. Suburban comic drama about a once-wild free spirit who now leads a predictable and unfulfilling life as her much older husband forces her to move with him into a retirement community. Writer-director Miller's film cross-cuts between flashbacks to the earlier, more vibrant Pippa (Lively) and the frustrated housewife she's become without knowing what hit her. As the mature Pippa, Penn has never been better, torn between loyalty to her unsupportive husband and reinvigorated by Reeves' sensitive soul next door. A small gem of independent filmmaking. Miller's aunt, actress Joan Copeland, appears as a piano player. [R] ◗

Private Navy of Sgt. O'Farrell, The (1968) C-92m. BOMB D: Frank Tashlin. Bob Hope, Phyllis Diller, Jeffrey Hunter, Gina Lollobrigida, Mylene Demongeot, John Myhers, Mako. Hope tries to import some beautiful nurses to improve his men's morale, gets Diller instead. Of the many terrible Hope comedies of the 1960s, this may be the worst. Unfunny and offensive. [G] ▼◗

Private Parts (1972) C-87m. *** D: Paul Bartel. Ann Ruymen, Lucille Benson, Laurie Main, John Ventantonio. Truly perverse black-comedic suspense film about runaway teenage girl staying at her aunt's strange hotel where occupants are extremely weird. There's a series of murders but the focus is more on sexual eccentricities including voyeurism, narcissism, and transvestism. If Andy Warhol's CHELSEA GIRLS had been codirected by Alfred Hitchcock and John Waters it would come close to this directorial debut by Bartel. Clearly not for every taste. [R] ▼◗

Private Parts (1997) C-109m. *** D: Betty Thomas. Howard Stern, Robin Quivers, Mary McCormack, Fred Norris, Paul Giamatti, Gary Dell'Abate, Jackie Martling, Carol Alt, "Stuttering John" Melendez, Allison Janney, Michael Murphy, Reni Santoni, Edie Falco. Horatio Alger–like saga of radio phenomenon Howard Stern, who only achieves success on the air when he starts giving vent to his most outrageous ideas. This pits him against one station management after another. Highly entertaining, even to non-Stern listeners, and evidence that (as Stern has said all along) he's actually an ordinary guy; the rest is a performance. Stern's real-life wife (at the time) plays an NBC switchboard operator. [R] ▼●◗

Private Property (2007-French-Belgian-Luxembourg) C-95m. *** D: Joachim Lafosse. Isabelle Huppert, Jérémie Renier, Yannick Renier, Kris Cuppens, Raphaëlle Lubansu, Patrick Descamps. Huppert, bitterly divorced, lives in a large Belgian farmhouse with her slacker twin sons, and is openly sexual in their presence. Emotions flare when she decides to sell the house and open a bed-and-breakfast. Edgy study of extreme dysfunction is provocative and features Huppert as yet another character who is psychologically unhinged. ◗

Private Resort (1985) C-85m. BOMB D: George Bowers. Rob Morrow, Johnny Depp, Hector Elizondo, Dody Goodman, Tony Azito, Emily Longstreth, Karyn O' Bryan, Hilary Shapiro, Michael Bowen, Andrew (Dice) Clay. Imbecilic sex comedy about a couple of young fellows on the make at a resort hotel. Notable only for its two up-and-coming stars. [R] ▼●◗

Private School (1983) C-97m. BOMB D: Noel Black. Phoebe Cates, Betsy Russell, Matthew Modine, Michael Zorek, Fran Ryan, Julie Payne, Ray Walston, Sylvia Kristel. Raunchy teenage hijinks at a girls' school, with ample nudity but no brains in sight. Even voyeurs might have a hard time sloshing through this heavy-handed, amateurish "comedy." [R] ▼●◗

Privates on Parade (1982-British) **C-100m.** ****½** D: Michael Blakemore. John Cleese, Denis Quilley, Nicola Pagett, Patrick Pearson, Michael Elphick. Uneven adaptation of Peter Nichols' British play about SADUSEA (Song And Dance Unit, South East Asia), based in Singapore in the late '40s. Quilley is an aging queen who directs and stars in their camp shows, Cleese his thick-witted commander. Some funny musical numbers mix awkwardly with satire—and unexpected drama. [R] ▼◗❍◗

Privilege (1967-British) **C-101m.** ******* D: Peter Watkins. Paul Jones, Jean Shrimpton, Marc London, Max Bacon, Jeremy Child. Overambitious yet effective account of 1970s England where all-powerful welfare state manipulates masses through such media as pop singers. Jones is good as disillusioned teen-age idol. ◗

Prize, The (1963) **C-136m.** ******* D: Mark Robson. Paul Newman, Elke Sommer, Edward G. Robinson, Diane Baker, Kevin McCarthy, Micheline Presle, Leo G. Carroll. Irving Wallace novel is mere stepping stone for glossy spy yarn set in Stockholm, involving participants in Nobel Prize ceremony. Newman and Sommer make handsome leads; Robinson has dual role. Fast-moving fun; script by Ernest Lehman. Panavision. ▼◗

Prize Fighter, The (1979) **C-99m.** ****** D: Michael Preece. Tim Conway, Don Knotts, David Wayne, Robin Clarke, Cisse Cameron, Mary Ellen O'Neill. If you like Knotts and Conway, you'll probably get through this lame, kiddie-oriented comedy about a dumb boxer and his smart-aleck manager, set in the 1930s. [PG] ▼◗

Prize Winner of Defiance, Ohio, The (2005) **C-99m.** ******* D: Jane Anderson. Julianne Moore, Woody Harrelson, Laura Dern, Trevor Morgan, Ellary Porterfield, Simon Reynolds, Nora Dunn. Midwestern woman raises ten kids in the 1950s, repeatedly keeping the wolf from the door by winning slogan contests. Not a slice of rosy-hued Americana but a pointed, often heart-rending look at a woman with indomitable spirit who kept her family together in spite of her loose-cannon, ne'er-do-well husband and the condescending attitude of the men around her. Moore is completely believable as the can-do supermom; Harrelson is equally good as her loving but self-destructive spouse. Anderson adapted Terry Ryan's memoir. [PG-13] ◗

Prizzi's Honor (1985) **C-129m.** *****½** D: John Huston. Jack Nicholson, Kathleen Turner, Anjelica Huston, Robert Loggia, William Hickey, John Randolph, Lee Richardson, Michael Lombard, Lawrence Tierney, Joseph Ruskin, Stanley Tucci. Delicious, very offbeat black comedy about a slow-witted hit man from a close-knit Mafia family who gets more than he bargained for when he falls in love with Turner. Nicholson is a joy to watch, matched by a superlative cast (Randolph is a treat as his father). Huston wrings every drop of irony from Richard Condon and Janet Roach's wry screenplay (based on Condon's novel). Beautifully photographed by Andrzej Bartkowiak. Anjelica Huston won Best Supporting Actress Oscar for her sly performance, directed by her father. ▼◗❍◗

Problem Child (1990) **C-81m.** ***½** D: Dennis Dugan. John Ritter, Michael Oliver, Jack Warden, Amy Yasbeck, Gilbert Gottfried, Michael Richards. Botched comic twist on THE BAD SEED has Ritter as an unlucky father who adopts devil-child Oliver. A promising opening leads nowhere as bad performances and crude jokes prevail. Followed by a sequel, a TV movie, and an animated TV series. [PG] ▼◗❍◗

Problem Child 2 (1991) **C-91m.** ***½** D: Brian Levant. John Ritter, Michael Oliver, Jack Warden, Laraine Newman, Amy Yasbeck, Ivyann Schwan, Gilbert Gottfried, Paul Willson, Charlene Tilton, James Tolkan, Martha Quinn. The sequel no one asked for has Ritter adopting a second demon-child, this one female and hell-bent to give her stepbrother a run for his money. Any parent who lets an impressionable child watch this stuff ought to have his or her head examined! Followed by a 1995 TVM sequel. [PG-13] ▼◗❍◗

Prodigal, The (1955) **C-114m.** ****½** D: Richard Thorpe. Lana Turner, Edmund Purdom, James Mitchell, Louis Calhern, Audrey Dalton, Neville Brand, Taina Elg, Cecil Kellaway, Henry Daniell, Walter Hampden, Joseph Wiseman. Juvenile biblical semi-spectacle, with Turner the evil goddess of love corrupting Purdom; glossy MGM vehicle. CinemaScope. ▼◗❍◗

Producers, The (1968) **C-88m.** *****½** D: Mel Brooks. Zero Mostel, Gene Wilder, Kenneth Mars, Dick Shawn, Lee Meredith, Christopher Hewett, Andreas Voutsinas, Estelle Winwood, Renee Taylor, Bill Hickey. Classic piece of insanity stars incomparable Mostel as hard-luck Broadway producer Max Bialystock, who cons meek accountant Wilder into helping him with outrageous scheme: selling 25,000% of a play that's certain to flop, then heading to Rio with the excess cash. One of those rare films that gets funnier with each viewing, highlighted by legendary "Springtime for Hitler" production number. Brooks' first feature earned him an Oscar for his screenplay. Listen for his voice dubbed into "Springtime for Hitler." Later a Broadway musical, which, in turn, was filmed in 2005. ▼◗❍◗

Producers, The (2005) **C-129m.** ****** D: Susan Stroman. Nathan Lane, Matthew Broderick, Uma Thurman, Will Ferrell,

Gary Beach, Roger Bart, Eileen Essell, David Huddleston, Jon Lovitz, Michael McKean, Richard Kind, Debra Monk, Andrea Martin, Brad Oscar. Broadway's worst producer teams up with a naïve bookkeeper to make money by producing a surefire flop, *Springtime for Hitler*. Valuable as a reproduction of the 2001 Broadway musical with its stars Lane, Broderick, Beach, Bart (and in a bit part, Oscar), but suffers as the stage show did by padding Brooks' original 1968 screenplay and softening some of its perverse, politically incorrect flavor. First-time film director Stroman tries to achieve a Broadway feeling, but the result is an odd hybrid of a stage performance and a movie. If you do watch this, stay through the closing credits. Brooks also dubs the same line in the "Springtime for Hitler" number that he did in the 1968 version. Panavision. [PG-13]▶

Professional, The (1994-U.S.-French) C-109m. ** D: Luc Besson. Jean Reno, Gary Oldman, Natalie Portman, Danny Aiello, Ellen Greene. Hit man (Reno) allies with alienated young girl (Portman, in her film debut) and together they battle thugs and cops in N.Y.C. Well-directed U.S. debut for Frenchman Besson (LA FEMME NIKITA) suffers from overly familiar, artificial situations and a bizarre, scenery-chewing performance from Oldman. This was rereleased in France in 1996 as LEON: VERSION INTEGRALE, with 26m. of additional footage. That version is also on DVD. Technovision. [R]▼●)

Professional Gun, A SEE: **Mercenary, The**

Professionals, The (1966) C-117m. *** D: Richard Brooks. Lee Marvin, Robert Ryan, Woody Strode, Burt Lancaster, Jack Palance, Ralph Bellamy, Claudia Cardinale. Bellamy employs four soldiers-of-fortune to rescue his wife from Mexican varmint Palance. Far-fetched story, but real action, taut excitement throughout; beautifully photographed by Conrad Hall. Panavision. ▼●)

Profile of Terror SEE: **Sadist, The**

Profumo di Donna SEE: **Scent of a Woman** (1974)

Program, The (1993) C-114m. ** D: David S. Ward. James Caan, Halle Berry, Omar Epps, Craig Sheffer, Kristy Swanson, Abraham Benrubi, Duane Davis, Andrew Bryniarski, Joey Lauren Adams. Ambitious but seriously flawed attempt to examine the problems of college football players, and expose abuses in contemporary university sports programs. Few of the characters are sympathetic, so it's difficult to care about them or their plight. Notorious for studio deletion, after the film's opening weeks, of a sequence involving jocks lying in the middle of a busy street to prove their manliness. This came after one teenager was killed, and

others seriously injured, allegedly imitating the sequence. [R]▼●)

Project A (1983-Hong Kong) C-106m. *** D: Jackie Chan. Jackie Chan, Yuen Biao, Samo Hung, Dick Wei, Isabella Wong. Turn-of-the-century adventure finds Chan in the Hong Kong coast guard battling pirates, teaming up with cop Yuen and thief Samo. Fantastic action comedy, with many moments reminiscent of Chan's hero, Buster Keaton. The bicycle chase is a highlight. Considered by some to be Chan's best film. Followed by a sequel. Technovision. ▼)

Project A, Part II (1987-Hong Kong) C-108m. *** D: Jackie Chan. Jackie Chan, Maggie Cheung, David Lam, Rosamund Kwan, Carina Lau, Bill Tung Pui. Terrific sequel has Jackie dodging vengeful pirates from the first film while fighting corrupt officials. Nice mix of farce and jaw-dropping action. Chan re-creates one of Buster Keaton's most famous stunts at the end of the film. Technovision. ▼)

Projected Man, The (1967-British) C-77m. ** D: Ian Curteis. Bryant Haliday, Mary Peach, Norman Wooland, Ronald Allen, Derek Farr. Using a teleportation machine something like that in all the FLY movies, scientist accidentally disfigures himself and gains the touch of death. Not bad but unoriginal. Techniscope.

Projectionist, The (1971) C-85m. **½ D: Harry Hurwitz. Chuck McCann, Ina Balin, Rodney Dangerfield, Jara Kohout, Harry Hurwitz, Robert Staats. Independently made film has ups and downs, but many pearly moments in story of daydreaming projectionist McCann who envisions himself a superhero, Captain Flash. Many film clips imaginatively used; best of all is coming-attractions trailer for the end of the world. [PG]▼)

Project X (1968) C-97m. **½ D: William Castle. Christopher George, Greta Baldwin, Henry Jones, Monte Markham, Phillip Pine, Harold Gould. Offbeat but ultimately unconvincing mixture of time travel, biological warfare, and psychology in tale of future Earth civilization searching for secret germ formula. Their amnesiac secret agent has it; how to get it?

Project X (1987) C-108m. **½ D: Jonathan Kaplan. Matthew Broderick, Helen Hunt, Bill Sadler, Johnny Ray McGhee, Jonathan Stark, Robin Gammell, Stephen Lang, Jean Smart, Dick Miller. Young military foul-up is assigned to top secret lab where he works with chimps—and soon becomes enraged at the tests they're being subjected to. Watchable but patently predictable story, with a finale vaguely reminiscent of a 1960s Disney comedy. The chimps (especially Willie, in the role of Virgil) are great, however. [PG]▼●)

Prom (2011) C-103m. *** D: Joe Nussbaum. Aimee Teegarden, Thomas McDonell, De'Vaughn Nixon, Kylie Bunbury, Danielle Campbell, Yin Chang, Jared Kusnitz, Nolan Sotillo, Cameron Monaghan, Joe Adler, Janelle Ortiz, Jonathan Keltz, Nicholas Braun, Raini Rodriguez, Christine Elise McCarthy, Dean Norris, Faith Ford, Amy Pietz, Jere Burns. Sincere, upbeat Disney movie about high school seniors preparing for that rite of passage, the prom. A "Little Miss Perfect" (Teegarden) is supervising every detail, but doesn't yet have a date herself, while a bad-boy biker (McDonell) is forced to help her with decorations as a kind of detention punishment. Many other characters and story threads are neatly woven together in a film that refreshingly takes teenagers and their emotions seriously. Parents can also watch this without cringing. [PG] 🄳

Promise, The (1979) **C-98m.** BOMB D: Gilbert Cates. Kathleen Quinlan, Stephen Collins, Beatrice Straight, Laurence Luckinbill, William Prince. Boy loves girl. Girl loses face in car accident. Boy thinks girl dead. Girl gets new face from plastic surgeon. Boy falls for old girl's new face. Viewer runs screaming from room. Panavision. [PG]▼

Promise, The (1994-German-French-Swiss) **C-119m.** *** D: Margarethe von Trotta. Corinna Harfouch, Meret Becker, August Zirner, Anian Zollner, Pierre Besson, Hans Kremer. Pointed account of star-crossed German lovers, covering a 30-year time span, beginning with their separation while trying to escape from East to West in 1961. Their relationship mirrors German history during this period and serves as a metaphor for a divided, and then reunified, nation. Another provocative, politically savvy drama from von Trotta. [R]▼

Promise, The (2005-Chinese-U.S.) **C-102m.** **½ D: Chen Kaige. Dong-Kun Jang, Hiroyuki Sanada, Cecilia Cheung, Nicholas Tse, Ye Liu, Hong Chen, Cheng Qian. Odd mixture of fantasy-romance and martial arts. A goddess offers a young girl (orphaned by a war) a life of wealth and happiness, but she will lose every man she falls in love with unless a spell can be reversed that would make the dead return and snow fall in the spring. Not as easy as it sounds! Extravagantly pictorial fable (stunningly photographed by Peter Pau) melds lofty romance with high-flying martial arts, though it is often marred by cheesy computer-generated effects and chucklesome overacting. A major box-office hit in Asia. Original running time 128m. Super 35. [PG-13]🄳

Promise at Dawn (1970-U.S.-French) **C-101m.** **½ D: Jules Dassin. Melina Mercouri, Assaf Dayan, Francois Raffoul, Despo, Fernand Gravey, Perlo Vita (Jules Dassin). Seventh teaming of Mercouri and husband Dassin, who produced, directed, wrote, and also does a bit role as Russian silent-film star Ivan Mousjoukine. It's mostly Mercouri's show, an uneven but well-acted chronicle of the life of writer Romain Gary and his resourceful actress mother. Dayan is good as the young adult Gary. [PG]▼

Promised Land (1988) **C-101m.** **½ D: Michael Hoffman. Jason Gedrick, Kiefer Sutherland, Meg Ryan, Tracy Pollan, Googy Gress, Deborah Richter, Sondra Seacat. Uneven but moody little sleeper, set in the rural Northwest, about two casual high school acquaintances whose lives intersect tragically a couple of years after graduation. Ryan is a standout as a tattooed, rod-packing high school hellcat. Aka YOUNG HEARTS. [R]▼🔴

Promise Her Anything (1966) **C-98m.** **½ D: Arthur Hiller. Warren Beatty, Leslie Caron, Bob Cummings, Hermione Gingold, Lionel Stander, Keenan Wynn. Limp premise of blue-moviemaker (Beatty) taking care of neighbor Caron's baby. Filmed in England but supposed to be Greenwich Village; screenplay by William Peter Blatty. Look for Bessie Love as a pet shop customer, Donald Sutherland as a baby's father.▼

Promises (2001) **C-100m.** ***½ D: Justine Shapiro, B.Z. Goldberg, Carlos Bolado. Observant, deeply humanistic documentary records the lives of seven Israeli and Palestinian children residing in and around Jerusalem. They live only minutes apart, yet their worlds and worldviews are vastly different. The highlight: Jewish twin boys travel to a refugee camp and spend a day playing with their Palestinian counterparts. Here, the shared humanity of all the children—which transcends religious and cultural differences—shines through.▼🄳

Promises in the Dark (1979) **C-115m.** **½ D: Jerome Hellman. Marsha Mason, Ned Beatty, Susan Clark, Michael Brandon, Kathleen Beller, Paul Clemens, Donald Moffat. Unrelievedly depressing (though well-made) film about young girl (Beller) dying of cancer, and her compassionate doctor (Mason). Directorial debut of producer Hellman. [PG]▼🄳

Prom Night (1980-Canadian) **C-91m.** ** D: Paul Lynch. Leslie Nielsen, Jamie Lee Curtis, Casey Stevens, Antoinette Bower, Robert Silverman. Killer menaces teens who were responsible for the death of a little girl six years earlier. Not the worst of its type, but that's nothing to brag about. Remade in name only in 2008. Followed by several sequels. [R]▼🔴

Prom Night II SEE: **Hello Mary Lou: Prom Night II**

Prom Night (2008) **C-88m.** **½ D: Nelson McCormick. Brittany Snow, Scott Porter, Jessica Stroup, Dana Davis, Collins Pennie, Kelly Blatz, James Ransone, Brianne Davis, Idris Elba, Mary Mara, Ming (Ming-Na) Wen, Jessalyn Gilsig, Linden

[1113]

Ashby, Johnathon Schaech. Three years after a homicidally obsessive teacher (Schaech) murdered her family, a lovely high-schooler (Snow) is stalked by an unwanted admirer on the night of her senior prom. A nominal remake of the post-HALLOWEEN slasher film, this better-than-average teen-skewing thriller relies on minimal graphic violence to sustain suspense. Super 35. [PG-13]▶

Promotion, The (2008) C-85m. ** D: Steven Conrad. Seann William Scott, John C. Reilly, Jenna Fischer, Lili Taylor, Bobby Cannavale, Fred Armisen, Gil Bellows, Jason Bateman. Assistant supermarket manager Scott is aiming for a big promotion when a competitor (Reilly) arrives, seemingly out of nowhere—but actually from Canada. Low-key comedy with serious undertones examines the working-class American dream gone somewhat sour. Bateman has one funny scene as an activities director at a company retreat. Directorial debut for screenwriter Conrad. Panavision. [R]▶

Proof (1992-Australian) C-91m. ***½ D: Jocelyn Moorhouse. Hugo Weaving, Genevieve Picot, Russell Crowe, Heather Mitchell, Jeffrey Walker, Frank Gallacher. A blind cynic who impulsively shoots photographs of everything is perversely manipulated by the housekeeper who'd like to bed him; into their circle comes a far less complex dishwasher, who puts a fresh spin on their sicko games. Assuredly made film is effectively cold, cut to the bone and reminiscent of THE SERVANT. Moorhouse also scripted. [R]▼●▶

Proof (2005) C-99m. *** D: John Madden. Gwyneth Paltrow, Anthony Hopkins, Jake Gyllenhaal, Hope Davis, Roshan Seth. A woman who cared for her father—a brilliant mathematician and professor who went crazy—during the last years of his life now questions her own sanity. Her meddlesome sister wants her to move out of the family home and distance herself from the past, while one of her father's protégés is digging through his papers to find any hidden gems (or proofs) among his work. David Auburn's challenging, provocative, and cerebral play (a Pulitzer Prize winner) is well translated to film by director Madden, with fine performances all around; adapted by Auburn and Rebecca Miller. Super 35. [PG-13]▶

Proof of Life (2000) C-136m. **½ D: Taylor Hackford. Meg Ryan, Russell Crowe, David Morse, Pamela Reed, David Caruso, Anthony Heald, Stanley Anderson, Gottfried John, Alun Armstrong, Michael Kitchen, Margo Martindale. Entertaining if all-too-familiar soap-opera/thriller set in Latin America. Hostage-negotiator-for-hire Crowe comes to the assistance of frantic wife Ryan when her idealistic engineer husband is kidnapped by a cutthroat band of political ideologues-turned-drug lords.

Caruso almost steals the film as a fellow negotiator. Super 35. [R]▼▶

Prophecy (1979) C-95m. *½ D: John Frankenheimer. Talia Shire, Robert Foxworth, Armand Assante, Richard Dysart, Victoria Racimo. Classical musician and her doctor husband fight off what appears to be a giant salami in upstate Maine after mercury poisoning turns animals into huge mutants and worse. Ridiculous horror film is good for a few laughs. Panavision. [PG]▼▶

Prophecy, The (1995) C-93m. ** D: Gregory Widen. Christopher Walken, Elias Koteas, Virginia Madsen, Eric Stoltz, Viggo Mortensen, Amanda Plummer. Seminarian Koteas abandons the church during his own ordination to become . . . a homicide cop. Soon he's investigating why Stoltz has murdered an eyeless hermaphrodite with the physiological profile of an aborted fetus. There's either too much mumbo or too much jumbo in this oddball horror pic. Give it perverse points, though, for managing to work in a Korean War subplot and for casting Walken as the Angel Gabriel. Followed by too many direct-to-video sequels. Super 35. [R]▼●▶

Prophet, A (2009-French-Italian) C-149m. ***½ D: Jacques Audiard. Tahar Rahim, Niels Arestrup, Adel Bencherif, Reda Kateb, Hichem Yacoubi, Jean-Philippe Ricci, Gilles Cohen. Quiet, 19-year-old Malik (Rahim) is sent to prison, where his mixed heritage (Corsican and Arab) draws attention from both factions. The Corsican prison kingpin (powerfully portrayed by Arestrup) forces him to commit a terrible crime, which haunts him—and binds him to the man who rules the roost. But unbeknownst to anyone, the seemingly passive Malik soaks up knowledge at every opportunity, and uses his newfound smarts to orchestrate some "business" of his own. Provocative, often grueling, graphically violent drama with a disarming performance by Rahim, who changes right before our eyes. Written by director Audiard and Thomas Bidegain, from an unproduced screenplay by Abdel Raouf Dafri and Nicolas Peufaillit. Super 35. [R]▶

Proposal, The (2009) C-108m. *** D: Anne Fletcher. Sandra Bullock, Ryan Reynolds, Craig T. Nelson, Mary Steenburgen, Betty White, Denis O'Hare, Malin Akerman, Oscar Nuñez, Aasif Mandvi, Michael Nouri. Entertaining romantic comedy about N.Y.C. publishing exec Bullock, a cold-blooded boss, who blackmails her assistant (Reynolds) into marrying her so she won't be deported to Canada. The stakes change when he brings her home to meet his loving family in Alaska. Built on a formula, to be sure, but neatly handled by a tip-top cast. Offers some laugh-out-loud moments, which is more than most modern romantic comedies can say. Hawk Scope. [PG-13]▶

Proposition, The (1998) **C-110m.** ** D: Lesli Linka Glatter. Kenneth Branagh, William Hurt, Madeleine Stowe, Blythe Danner, Robert Loggia, Neil Patrick Harris, Josef Sommer. Heavy-handed soap opera set in the 1930s gives Branagh a thankless role as a priest with more ties than one could ever imagine to wealthy Boston bigwig Hurt who can't give his wife the one thing he wants most: a child. A fine cast flounders with purple paperback fodder; sputteringly silly at times. [R]▼●

Proposition, The (2005-Australian-British) **C-104m.** ** D: John Hillcoat. Guy Pearce, Ray Winstone, Emily Watson, Danny Huston, John Hurt, David Wenham, Noah Taylor, David Gulpilil, Leah Purcell, Richard Wilson. Determined to bring law and order to a wild Australia in the 1880s, British officer Winstone makes a Devil's bargain with Pearce: he can save his life, and that of his dimwitted younger sibling, if he will kill his older brother, who raped and murdered a pregnant woman. Austere, violent, and relentlessly harsh, like the time and place it portrays. Nick Cave's screenplay challenges the viewer to find humanity amidst the *sturm und drang*; it ain't easy. Super 35. [R]▶

Proprietor, The (1996) **C-113m.** ** D: Ismail Merchant. Jeanne Moreau, Sean Young, Sam Waterston, Austin Pendleton, Josh Hamilton, Nell Carter, Christopher Cazenove, Pierre Vaneck, Jean-Pierre Aumont, Marc Tissot. Wildly uneven story set in Paris and N.Y.C. finds author Moreau exploring two distinct cultures, past and present life experiences, and relationships old and new as she examines the meaning of her life and the importance of memories. It's always nice to see Moreau in a major role, but this muddled vehicle isn't worthy of her. Rare directorial effort for producer Merchant. Super 35. [R]▼●

Prospero's Books (1991-British-Dutch) **C-129m.** **½ D: Peter Greenaway. John Gielgud, Michael Clark, Michel Blanc, Erland Josephson, Isabelle Pasco, Tom Bell. Original, daring but unsatisfactory adaptation of Shakespeare's *The Tempest*, with almost all of the dialogue spoken by 87-year-old Gielgud (in the role of Prospero); the other actors are little more than extras, and there's a mindboggling amount of nudity. Crammed with stunning, layered imagery, beautiful production design and cinematography—which tend to lessen the impact of the dialogue. Enjoyment will depend on your tolerance for Greenaway's approach to the material. [R]▶

Protector, The (1985-U.S.-Hong Kong) **C-91m.** *½ D: James Glickenhaus. Jackie Chan, Danny Aiello, Sandy Alexander, Roy Chiao, Bill Wallace. Dismal attempt to bring Chan to the American market as a N.Y.C. cop(!). Leaden directing, cold tone, and lack of comedy smother Chan's gifts; his frustrations with this film led him to

make the vastly superior POLICE STORY. ▼▶

Protector, The (2005-Thai) **C-81m.** ** D: Prachya Pinkaew. Tony Jaa, Petchtai Wongkamlao, Bongkoj Khongmalai, Nathan Jones, Johnny Nguyen, Xing Jing, Damian De Montemas. Wrongheaded mix of a kung fu movie and a boy-and-his-dog story, this cheap-looking import from Thailand gets sappy when a young martial arts fighter has his beloved elephant stolen by thugs and shipped to Australia. Following the bad guys there, he hooks up with a Thai-born Australian detective and does battle with evil gangs and others in an effort to retrieve his little Dumbo. Jaa, an international star, offers dazzling footwork, but that can't make up for the sorry script. Original running time 108m. [R]▶

Protocol (1984) **C-96m.** ** D: Herbert Ross. Goldie Hawn, Chris Sarandon, Richard Romanus, Andre Gregory, Gail Strickland, Cliff De Young, Keith Szarabajka, Ed Begley, Jr., James Staley, Kenneth Mars, Jean Smart, Joel Brooks, Daphne Maxwell, Amanda Bearse. Kenneth McMillan. Or, Goldie Goes to Washington: a contrived comedy vehicle for Hawn as inadvertent heroine (and overnight celebrity) who's rewarded with do-nothing government job . . . but soon becomes a pawn for dealing with Middle Eastern potentate. Some funny moments give way to obvious satire and a hard-to-swallow finish in which Goldie makes like Capra's Mr. Smith. [PG]▼●▶

Proud and Profane, The (1956) **111m.** **½ D: George Seaton. William Holden, Deborah Kerr, Thelma Ritter, Dewey Martin, William Redfield, Ross Bagdasarian, Marion Ross. Spotty WW2 romance with grieving war widow Kerr joining the Red Cross, becoming involved with cynical officer Holden. Ritter, as usual, steals the film as a tough but compassionate Red Cross worker. VistaVision.

Proud Rebel, The (1958) **C-103m.** *** D: Michael Curtiz. Alan Ladd, Olivia de Havilland, Dean Jagger, David Ladd, Cecil Kellaway, Henry Hull, John Carradine, (Harry) Dean Stanton. Well-presented post–Civil War study of two-fisted Southerner Ladd seeking medical help for mute son (played by Ladd's real-life son); de Havilland is the woman who tames him. ▼●▶

Providence (1977-British) **C-104m.** ** D: Alain Resnais. Dirk Bogarde, John Gielgud, Ellen Burstyn, David Warner, Elaine Stritch. Odd fantasy marked director Resnais' English-language debut. Writer Gielgud tries to complete his last novel, juxtaposes imagined thoughts about his family with real-life encounters. Muddled drama by David Mercer; interesting Miklos Rozsa score. [R]▼

Prowler, The (1951) **92m.** ***½ D: Joseph Losey. Van Heflin, Evelyn Keyes, John Maxwell, Katharine Warren. Stark, sinuous film noir about a (literal) bad cop (Heflin) who seduces a vulnerable married woman. Opens with a bang and never lets up. Unusually nasty and utterly unpredictable. Striking camerawork (by Arthur Miller) and production design. Screenplay by Dalton Trumbo, who was blacklisted at the time and received no credit, though he is heard as the voice of Keyes' husband on the radio. ◗

Prowler, The (1981) C-88m. *½ D: Joseph Zito. Vicki Dawson, Christopher Goutman, Cindy Weintraub, Farley Granger, John Seitz. WW2 veteran kills ex-girlfriend and her new amour with a pitchfork, then suddenly resumes his murderous ways 35 years later. Illogically plotted, with grue-some special effects by Tom Savini. [R] ▼●

Prozac Nation (2005-U.S.-German) C-95m. ** D: Erik Skjoldbjaerg. Christina Ricci, Jason Biggs, Anne Heche, Michelle Williams, Jonathan Rhys-Meyers, Jessica Lange, Nicholas Campbell, Jesse Moss, Zoe Miller, Sheila Paterson. Ricci's raw, intensely emotional performance partly redeems this off-putting adaptation of Elizabeth Wurtzel's best-selling memoir about a Harvard student's downward spiral into drugs and clinical depression in the mid-1980s. Well-intentioned but relentless downer of a film never really makes us care about the unsympathetic heroine's plight. Completed in 2001, released to video in the U.S. four years later! Lou Reed has a cameo as himself. [R]◗

Prudence and the Pill (1968-British) C-98m. **½ D: Fielder Cook, Ronald Neame. Deborah Kerr, David Niven, Robert Coote, Irina Demick, Joyce Redman, Judy Geeson, Keith Michell. Labored comedy treatment of modern sexual mores. Niven thinks he can patch up his in-name-only marriage by substituting aspirin for his wife's birth control pills. Good cast and performances, but weak script. [R]

p.s. (2004) C-97m. ** D: Dylan Kidd. Laura Linney, Topher Grace, Gabriel Byrne, Marcia Gay Harden, Paul Rudd, Lois Smith. Thirtysomething Columbia University admissions officer Linney is stuck in a rut, until she comes into contact with a brash prospective student (Grace) who eerily resembles an old, long-deceased boyfriend. Linney and Harden are always watchable, but the characters are caricatures and much of the dialogue is artificial, even unintentionally funny. Coscripted by Kidd and Helen Schulman, based on her novel. [R] ▼●

P.S. I Love You (2007) C-126m. **½ D: Richard LaGravenese. Hilary Swank, Gerard Butler, Kathy Bates, Lisa Kudrow, Gina Gershon, James Marsters, Harry Connick, Jr., Jeffrey Dean Morgan. After her young husband develops a brain tumor and dies, a grieving widow starts receiving a series of letters from him instructing her how to get on without him. Since Butler succumbs before the opening credits you can rest assured their courtship and marriage are going to be told completely in flashbacks. Director and cowriter LaGravenese makes this a pleasant ride most of the way, even for reluctant male viewers. [PG-13]◗

Psychic, The (1978-Italian) C-89m. BOMB D: Lucio Fulci. Jennifer O'Neill, Gabriele Ferzetti, Marc Porel, Gianni Garko, Evelyn Stewart. O'Neill has frightening premonitions of deaths in this low-grade thriller. Aka SEVEN NOTES IN BLACK. [R] ▼▼

Psychic Killer (1975) C-90m. BOMB D: Raymond Danton. Jim Hutton, Julie Adams, Paul Burke, Aldo Ray, Neville Brand, Whit Bissell. Ugly, violent shocker of mental institute patient who acquires psychic powers to revenge himself on those who wronged him. Lots of cameos: Rod Cameron, Nehemiah Persoff, Della Reese, others. [PG]▼●

Psycho (1960) 109m. **** D: Alfred Hitchcock. Anthony Perkins, Janet Leigh, Vera Miles, John Gavin, Martin Balsam, John McIntire, Lurene Tuttle, Simon Oakland, John Anderson, Mort Mills, Frank Albertson, Patricia Hitchcock. The Master's most notorious film is still terrifying after all these years, as larcenous Leigh picks the wrong place to spend a night: The Bates Motel (12 cabins, 12 vacancies . . . and 12 showers), run by a peculiar young man and his crotchety old "mother." Hitchcock's murder set pieces are so potent, they can galvanize (and frighten) even a viewer who's seen them before! Bernard Herrmann's legendary (and endlessly imitated) score adds much to the excitement. Script by Joseph Stefano from the Robert Bloch novel. Followed by three sequels (the last for cable TV) and a TV movie (BATES MOTEL) decades later, and remade in 1998. ▼●◗

Psycho (1998) C-109m. BOMB D: Gus Van Sant. Vince Vaughn, Anne Heche, Julianne Moore, Viggo Mortensen, William H. Macy, Robert Forster, Philip Baker Hall, Anne Haney, Chad Everett, Rance Howard, Rita Wilson, James Remar, James LeGros. Slow, stilted, completely pointless scene-for-scene remake of the Hitchcock classic (with a few awkward new touches to taint its claim as an exact replica). The result is an insult, rather than a tribute, to a landmark film. [R] ▼●◗

Psycho II (1983) C-113m. **½ D: Richard Franklin. Anthony Perkins, Vera Miles, Meg Tilly, Robert Loggia, Dennis Franz, Hugh Gillin. Surprisingly good sequel, with Perkins in a wonderfully canny reprise of his role as Norman Bates—now being released from asylum, supposedly rehabilitated, returning to his mother's creaky old mansion. Director Franklin builds some terrific suspense scenes, but finally goes for graphic violence toward the end, and tacks on a silly conclusion, undermining an otherwise first-rate shocker. [R] ▼●◗

[1116]

Psycho III (1986) **C-96m.** *½ D: Anthony Perkins. Anthony Perkins, Diana Scarwid, Jeff Fahey, Roberta Maxwell, Hugh Gillin, Lee Garlington. Pointless sequel plays Norman Bates strictly for laughs, but maintains a slasher-film mentality. No suspense, just some gratuitous blood and unpleasantness. Perkins' directorial debut. Good night, Norman. Followed by a TV movie prequel in 1990. [R]▼●◖

Psycho a Go-Go! SEE: **Blood of Ghastly Horror**

Psycho Beach Party (2000-U.S.-Australian) **C-95m.** ** D: Robert Lee King. Lauren Ambrose, Thomas Gibson, Nicholas Brendon, Matt Keeslar, Andrew Levitas, Amy Adams, Nick Cornish, Charles Busch, Kathleen Robertson, Beth Broderick, Kimberley Davies. Campy spoof of beach movies mixes '50s values with '70s slasher films and is only partly successful. Teenage heroine Ambrose seems virtuous but harbors multiple personalities. Busch adapted his 1987 off-Broadway hit but film version seems forced and overlong. ▼◖

Psycho-Circus (1967-British-West German) **C-65m.** **½ D: John Moxey. Christopher Lee, Heinz Drache, Margaret Lee, Suzy Kendall, Leo Genn, Cecil Parker, Klaus Kinski. Confused (due to distributor cuts) Edgar Wallace–based story of murderer stalking odd assortment of characters in big top. Is it hooded Gregor the lion-tamer? Short running time gives film old-style serial-type pacing. Original title: CIRCUS OF FEAR.▼◖

Psycho Killers SEE: **Mania**

Psychomania (1973-British) **C-95m.** **½ D: Don Sharp. George Sanders, Nicky Henson, Mary Larkin, Patrick Holt, Beryl Reid. Pact with Devil brings British motorcycle gang back from the grave. Lots of weird violence as undead bikers blaze a kamikaze trail of destruction across prepunk England. Screenplay by Julian Halevy. Aka THE DEATH WHEELERS. ▼◖

Psychopath, The (1966-British) **C-83m.** *** D: Freddie Francis. Patrick Wymark, Margaret Johnston, John Standing, Judy Huxtable. A demented killer leaves dolls as his calling card at the scene of the murders; well-made thriller from Robert Bloch script. Techniscope.

Psycho Sisters SEE: **So Evil, My Sister**

Psychotic SEE: **Driver's Seat, The**

Psych-Out (1968) **C-82m.** **½ D: Richard Rush. Susan Strasberg, Jack Nicholson, Adam Roarke, Dean Stockwell, Max Julien, Bruce Dern, Henry Jaglom, The Strawberry Alarm Clock, The Seeds, Garry Marshall. Deaf runaway Strasberg comes to Haight-Ashbury looking for missing brother Dern, falls in with rock band led by ponytailed Nicholson. Any serious intentions have long since vanished; gloriously goofy dialogue ("Warren's freakin' out at the gallery!") and psychedelic Laszlo Kovacs camerawork make this—depending on your age and sensibilities—either amusing nostalgia or a campy embarrassment. Produced by Dick Clark!▼●◖

P.S. Your Cat is Dead! (2003) **C-92m.** *½ D: Steve Guttenberg. Steve Guttenberg, Lombardo Boyar, Cynthia Watros, Shirley Knight, A. J. Benza, Paul Dillon, Tom Wright. Screen version of James Kirkwood's 1972 novel and 1975 play is obviously a labor of love for debuting director Guttenberg, but some things are better left on the page. Dated premise has down-on-his-luck actor slowly "coming out" to a burglar in a home invasion that has life-changing repercussions for all involved. Claustrophobic, one-set film features stereotypes that seem badly dated. The only character we can work up any sympathy for is the cat, which is never seen.▼◖

PT 109 (1963) **C-140m.** ** D: Leslie H. Martinson. Cliff Robertson, Ty Hardin, James Gregory, James Gregory, Robert Culp, Grant Williams, Lew Gallo, Errol John, Michael Pate, Robert Blake, Biff Elliot, Norman Fell. Gung-ho WW2 action yarn based on President John F. Kennedy's experiences in the Pacific as a PT boat captain. Very much of its time; it was released in June of the year JFK died. Panavision.▼●◖

PT Raiders SEE: **Ship That Died of Shame, The**

P2 (2007) **C-98m.** *½ D: Franck Khalfoun. Rachel Nichols, Wes Bentley, Philip Akin, Stephanie Moore, Miranda Edwards. Derivative thriller is more PU than P2, taking a well-worn psycho-on-the-loose plot and setting it in an underground N.Y.C. office garage on Christmas Eve. Workaholic woman is the last to leave and finds herself stuck with a creepy psychotic security guard. He proceeds to terrorize her as she is forced to run around wearing a wet white slip for most of the movie. Follows a bloody path to its inevitable conclusion. Super 35. [R]◖

Puberty Blues (1981-Australian) **C-86m.** **½ D: Bruce Beresford. Neil Schofield, Jad Capelja, Geoff Rhoe, Tony Hughes, Sandy Paul. Teenage growing pains, told (refreshingly) from the girls' point of view; simple, honest, but somewhat familiar. Based on a best-selling Australian book by two former surfing groupies. Panavision. [R]▼

Public Access (1992) **C-86m.** **½ D: Bryan Singer. Ron Marquette, Dina Brooks, Burt Williams, Larry Maxwell, Charles Kavanaugh, Brandon Boyce. Eerie tale of a stranger who starts his own cable-TV call-in show, ostensibly to investigate what's wrong with "our town." Debut for THE USUAL SUSPECTS director Singer is a suspenseful, disquieting film marred by a total lack of motivation for the main character. Fine music score by John Ottman, who also edited the picture. [R]▼●◖

Public Enemies (2009) **C-140m.** **½ D:

Michael Mann. Johnny Depp, Christian Bale, Marion Cotillard, Jason Clarke, Rory Cochrane, Billy Crudup, Stephen Dorff, Stephen Lang, John Ortiz, Giovanni Ribisi, David Wenham, Peter Gerety, Shawn Hatosy, James Russo, Channing Tatum, Carey Mulligan, Casey Siemaszko, Lili Taylor, Leelee Sobieski, Emilie de Ravin, Diana Krall. Ambitious examination of famed Depression-era bank robber John Dillinger (Depp) and Melvin Purvis (Bale), the G-man whom J. Edgar Hoover assigned to bring him down. Stylishly made, as expected from director-cowriter Mann (and shot in high definition digital video), but also emotionally distant, with stabs at social and cultural meaning—particularly Dillinger's celebrity-consciousness—that do not make up for lack of characterizations and an imbalance between Depp's magnetic presence and Bale's (presumably deliberate) one-note portrayal. Cotillard shines as Dillinger's girlfriend Billie Frechette. HD Widescreen. [R] ▶

Public Enemy, The (1931) 84m. ***½ D: William Wellman. James Cagney, Jean Harlow, Eddie Woods, Beryl Mercer, Donald Cook, Joan Blondell, Mae Clarke. Prohibition gangster's rise and fall put Cagney on the map, and deservedly so; he makes up for film's occasional flaws and dated notions. Still pretty powerful, this is the one where Cagney smashes a grapefruit in Clarke's face. Screened for decades at 82m., restored to full length for DVD. ▼●)

Public Eye, The (1972-British) C-95m. **½ D: Carol Reed. Mia Farrow, Topol, Michael Jayston, Margaret Rawlings, Annette Crosbie, Dudley Foster. Stuffy husband hires private-eye to watch his wife, but the sleuth falls for her. Fair expansion of Peter Shaffer's play. Farrow is good, but Topol's grin is flashed once too often. Panavision. [G]

Public Eye, The (1992) C-99m. **½ D: Howard Franklin. Joe Pesci, Barbara Hershey, Stanley Tucci, Jerry Adler, Jared Harris, Dominic Chianese, Richard Foronjy, Richard Riehle, Gerry Becler, Bob Gunton, Del Close, Nick Tate. Intriguing mood piece with a perfect Pesci role: a 1940s photographer who roams the streets of N.Y.C. at night in search of dramatic photo opportunities. An encounter with beautiful Hershey leads only to trouble, however. Great atmosphere and style are undone by an ungainly script and an unconvincing romantic subplot. Script by director Franklin, inspired by famed real-life photographer Weegee, some of whose shots are used in the film. [R] ▼●)

Puccini for Beginners (2007) C-82m. *** D: Maria Maggenti. Elizabeth Reaser, Justin Kirk, Gretchen Mol, Jennifer Dundas, Julianne Nicholson, Tina Benko. Clever, contemporary romantic comedy about a woman who has a tendency to drive her girlfriends away whenever the prospect of commitment enters the picture. Then quite by chance she finds herself simultaneously attracted to a guy and a girl, little dreaming that they are a couple that's just broken up. Inventive and funny, with appealing performances. Written by the director. ▶

Pufnstuf (1970) C-98m. **½ D: Hollingsworth Morse. Jack Wild, Billie Hayes, Martha Raye, "Mama" Cass Elliott, Billy Barty, Angelo Rossitto, Johnny Silver. OK theatrical feature based on Sid and Marty Krofft's TV series *H.R. Pufnstuf*, with Wild as young boy brought by a magic flute to Oz-like kingdom ruled by bumbling witches. Fine for kids; Hayes is fun as "Witchiepoo." [G] ▼

Pulp (1972) C-95m. *** D: Michael Hodges. Michael Caine, Mickey Rooney, Lionel Stander, Lizabeth Scott, Nadia Cassini, Al Lettieri, Dennis Price. Rooney, a retired expatriate Hollywood actor, hires paperback writer Caine to ghost his autobiography. Uneven, but good fun and well acted, especially by Rooney. [PG] ▼▶

Pulp Fiction (1994) C-154m. ***½ D: Quentin Tarantino. John Travolta, Samuel L. Jackson, Uma Thurman, Harvey Keitel, Tim Roth, Amanda Plummer, Maria de Medeiros, Ving Rhames, Eric Stoltz, Rosanna Arquette, Christopher Walken, Bruce Willis. Audacious, outrageous look at honor among lowlifes, told in a somewhat radical style overlapping a handful of separate stories. Jackson and Travolta are magnetic as a pair of hit men who have philosophical debates on a regular basis; Willis is compelling as a crooked boxer whose plan to take it on the lam hits a few detours. (In fact, there are no slackers in this cast.) This voluble, violent, pumped-up movie isn't for every taste—certainly not for the squeamish—but it's got more vitality than almost any other film of 1994. Tarantino is featured on-screen as Jimmie of Toluca Lake. Roger Avary gets costory credit with Tarantino (they won the Original Screenplay Oscar). Panavision. [R] ▼●)

Pulse (1988) C-91m. **½ D: Paul Golding. Joey Lawrence, Cliff De Young, Roxanne Hart, Charles Tyner, Myron Healey. What's got into the appliances in the home of Lawrence and his family? Scary, tense film, written by the director, a cut above the usual sci-fi/horror thriller but seriously damaged by a lack of any explanation for its outrageous premise (a living, evil short circuit). Excellent special effects. [PG-13] ▼●)

Pulse (2001-Japanese) C-118m. *** D: Kiyoshi Kurosawa. Haruhiko Katô, Kumiko Aso, Koyuki, Kurume Arisaka, Masatoshi Matsuo. A group of college students in Japan install an Internet program that invokes murderous ghosts. Plot seemed less hackneyed when it premiered in Japan four years before

[1118]

hitting U.S. screens; it remains significantly more original than American Internet-related horror films. Kurosawa effectively focuses on the fear and melancholy resulting from the urban isolation that the Internet promotes. A bit overlong and redundant, but philosophical, atmospheric, genuinely scary horror films are few and far between. Aka KAIRO and THE CIRCUIT.▶

Pulse (2006) **C-87m.** *½ D: Jim Sonzero. Kristen Bell, Ian Somerhalder, Christina Milian, Rick Gonzalez, Jonathan Tucker, Samm Levine, Ron Rifkin. Ghostly creatures emerge from computers and other machines to drain the will to live (or something) from human victims, driving them to suicide or turning them into soot. This naturally leads to the collapse of civilization. Unexpectedly epic-minded horror movie is occasionally eerie, but more often dull and nearly incomprehensible. Cowritten by Wes Craven. Remake of 2001 Japanese film. Unrated version runs 90m. Followed by two DVD sequels. Super 35. [PG-13]▶

Pumping Iron (1977) **C-85m.** *** D: George Butler, Robert Fiore. Arnold Schwarzenegger, Louis Ferrigno, Matty and Victoria Ferrigno, Mike Katz. Fascinating documentary about men's bodybuilding, centering on Schwarzenegger and his pursuit of yet another Mr. Olympia title. Schwarzenegger exudes charm and registers strong screen presence; his main rival is Ferrigno, pre-*Incredible Hulk*. Followed by a distaff sequel. [PG]▼●

Pumping Iron II: The Women (1985) **C-107 min.** *** D: George Butler. Poutylipped sexpot Rachel McLish, manlike Australian Bev Francis, and two dozen more female bodybuilders compete in a Vegas nonevent where winners are offered a choice of "cash, check, or chips." Funny, if suspiciously stagy look at the profession buoyed by some hilariously incompetent judges and an "in it for the money" emcee job by smiling George Plimpton.▼●

Pumpkin (2002) **C-121m.** BOMB D: Adam Larson Broder, Tony R. Abrams. Christina Ricci, Hank Harris, Brenda Blethyn, Dominique Swain, Marisa Coughlan, Sam Ball, Harry Lennix, Nina Foch, Caroline Aaron, Lisa Banes, Julio Oscar Mechoso, Amy Adams. A dippy, pampered college girl, caught up in sorority life, finds herself attracted to a disabled boy who's been brought to campus as a "special" athlete. Oddball film wants to have it both ways, making fun of its characters (and sentimental movies in general), then trying to tug at our heartstrings. Strange, to say the least—and interminable. [R]▼●

Pumpkin Eater, The (1964-British) **110m.** *** D: Jack Clayton. Anne Bancroft, Peter Finch, James Mason, Cedric Hardwicke, Alan Webb, Richard Johnson, Maggie Smith, Eric Porter. Intelligent if overlong drama chronicling the plight of the mother of eight children, who discovers her third husband has been unfaithful. Fine performances all around, with Bancroft a standout. Script by Harold Pinter, from the Penelope Mortimer novel.▼▶

Pumpkinhead (1988) **C-86m.** **½ D: Stan Winston. Lance Henriksen, Jeff East, John DiAquino, Kimberly Ross, Joel Hoffman, Cynthia Bain, Kerry Remsen, Florence Schauffler, Buck Flower, Tom Woodruff, Jr. Makeup expert Winston made his directorial debut with this interesting horror film set in the backwoods. When his young son is accidentally killed by "city folk," a storekeeper unleashes a powerful, fiendish demon on the interlopers. When he changes his mind, he finds he has no more control over the monstrous killer. Slides into the routine at times, but a nice try. Followed by two direct-to-video sequels. [R]▼●

Pump Up the Volume (1990) **C-100m.** **½ D: Allan Moyle. Christian Slater, Ellen Greene, Annie Ross, Samantha Mathis, Scott Paulin, Lala, Cheryl Pollak, Mimi Kennedy, Seth Green. Slater is terrific as Hard Harry, a high school kid by day who runs a pirate radio station by night, stirring up passions among his young listeners and enraging the adult population in the process. Though uneven, this does have some pertinent things to say that you don't always find in a youth-appeal film. [R]▼●

Punch-Drunk Love (2002) **C-95m.** ** D: Paul Thomas Anderson. Adam Sandler, Emily Watson, Philip Seymour Hoffman, Luis Guzman, Mary Lynn Rajskub. A paralyzingly asocial, dysfunctional man encounters a woman who is smitten with him and isn't sure how to respond. An ill-timed phone-sex call only complicates his life. Anderson's cockeyed, fairy-tale version of a romantic comedy is extremely strange, off-putting, and weird for the sake of being weird, though its leading actors certainly can't be faulted. (Sandler, discarding his goofball persona, is quite good.) Anderson's audaciousness is intriguing at first, but like his choice of music on the soundtrack, awfully hard to take. Panavision. [R]▼▶

Punchline (1988) **C-128m.** *** D: David Seltzer. Sally Field, Tom Hanks, John Goodman, Mark Rydell, Kim Greist, Pam Matteson, Taylor Negron, Barry Neikrug, Mac Robbins, Max Alexander, Paul Kozlowski, Barry Sobel, Damon Wayans. Well-written, well-cast movie about aspiring stand-up comics, focusing on brash young Hanks, who's got real talent but also a knack for pushing people away, and Field, a housewife and mom who feels driven to become a comedienne. Seltzer's serious script is compassionate and believable and manages to avoid clichés and easy answers. Field and (especially) Hanks are first-rate; actor-turned-director Rydell is perfect as the unctuous nightclub owner/entrepreneur. Director Paul Mazursky also appears in the opening scene. [R]▼●[

Punisher, The (1989-U.S.-Australian) **C-92m.** ** D: Mark Goldblatt. Dolph Lundgren, Louis Gossett, Jr., Jeroen Krabbé, Kim Miyori, Nancy Everhard, Brian Rooney, Bryan Marshall, Barry Otto, Zoshka Mizak. A cop whose family was wiped out by gangsters retaliates: *he* wipes out gangsters (125 in five years, and still counting). Cop Gossett and, especially, gangster Krabbé come close to rising above silly script, adapted from a Marvel Comics character created by Gerry Conway. Went straight to video in U.S. two years after being made. Shot in Australia but set in U.S. Remade in 2004. [R]▼●[

Punisher, The (2004) **C-124m.** BOMB D: Jonathan Hensleigh. Thomas Jane, John Travolta, Rebecca Romijn-Stamos, Will Patton, Roy Scheider, Laura Harring, Ben Foster, Samantha Mathis, James Carpinello, Eddie Jemison, John Pinette. Excruciating adaptation of the Marvel comic book about a retired FBI agent (Jane) who seeks revenge on the mobster (Travolta) and his circle who slaughtered his family. Formulaic idea is powered by repeated scenes of sadism and torture, with ham-handed performances as icing on the cake. Unbelievable, in every sense of the word. Filmed before with Dolph Lundgren. Alternate version runs 140m. Followed by PUNISHER: WAR ZONE. Super 35. [R]▼[

Puppetmaster (1989) **C-90m.** *½ D: David Schmoller. Paul LeMat, Irene Miracle, Matt Roe, William Hickey, Kathryn O'Reilly, Robin Frates, Merrya Small. Psychics drawn to a remote hotel find a malignant associate has committed suicide. They're then stalked by five living puppets left there in 1939 by famous, mystical puppeteer Toulon (Hickey)—plus another menace. Clumsy, talky script helped by (too scant) special effects by David Allen Productions. Followed by several sequels. [R]▼●[

Puppet Master II (1990) **C-90m.** ** D: David Allen. Elizabeth Maclellan, Collin Bernsen, Steve Welles, Gregory Webb, Charlie Spradling, Jeff Weston, Nita Talbot. The living puppets bring Toulon, inexplicably costumed as the Invisible Man, back from the dead; then, seeking brains for his life-giving elixir, they terrorize a group of paranormal researchers investigating the old hotel. Slow-paced thriller is an inauspicious directorial debut for effects maestro Allen. [R]▼●[

Puppet Master III: Toulon's Revenge (1991) **C-86m.** ** D: David De Coteau. Guy Rolfe, Richard Lynch, Ian Abercrom-

bie, Kristopher Logan, Aron Eisenberg, Walter Gotell, Sarah Douglas, Matthew Faison, Michelle Bauer. The mild best in this low-budget series (so far) is set in Nazi Germany, pitting the kindly old creator of living puppets (Rolfe) against Nazis who want to create an army of zombies. Minor but OK little thriller. [R]▼●[

Puppet Masters, The (1994) **C-109m.** **½ D: Stuart Orme. Donald Sutherland, Eric Thal, Julie Warner, Keith David, Will Patton, Richard Belzer, Tom Mason, Yaphet Kotto. U.S. security agency, headed by shrewd, sardonic Sutherland, discovers that the Midwest has been invaded by alien parasites who control the actions of human beings. Good script and performances are hampered by unimaginative direction. Movie imitations of Robert A. Heinlein's classic 1950 sci-fi novel took the edge off this official adaptation before it reached the screen. Aka ROBERT A. HEINLEIN'S THE PUPPET MASTERS. Panavision. [R]▼●[

Puppetoon Movie, The (1987) **C-80m.** **½ No director credited. Arnold Leibovit compiled this collage of George Pal's animated short subjects from the 1930s and '40s. Some of them (JOHN HENRY AND THE INKY-POO, TUBBY THE TUBA, JASPER IN A JAM) are terrific, but they're better seen one or two at a time. Still, there's some delightful entertainment here.▼●[

Purchase Price, The (1932) **68m.** ** D: William A. Wellman. Barbara Stanwyck, George Brent, Lyle Talbot, Hardie Albright, David Landau, Murray Kinnell, Leila Bennett, Dawn O'Day (Anne Shirley). Pre-Code Warner Bros. film about nightclub singer Stanwyck, who's seen and done it all, taking it on the lam and becoming—of all things—a mail-order bride for a naive North Dakota farmer. Starts out snappy, winds up silly, though Stanwyck is always worth watching.▼[

Pure Country (1992) **C-112m.** ** D: Christopher Cain. George Strait, Lesley Ann Warren, Isabel Glasser, Kyle Chandler, John Doe, Rory Calhoun, Molly McClure. Tuckered-out country star revisits his rural roots, falls for a redheaded rodeo aspirant who doesn't realize who he is. Strait showcase is mostly pure tedium, though film picks up some in hour two with the appearance of Glasser and (as her pop) cowboy vet Calhoun. [PG]▼●[

Pure Formality, A (1994-Italian-French) **C-108m.** ** D: Giuseppe Tornatore. Gérard Depardieu, Roman Polanski, Sergio Rubini, Nicola DiPinto, Paolo Lombardi. Police inspector Polanski, investigating a just-committed murder, interrogates world-famous novelist Depardieu, who can't remember what he was doing that afternoon. Maddeningly tedious film is shot in widescreen but mostly confined to a dark, leaky room; directed to the hilt. Not quite what you expect from the maker of CINEMA PARADISO. Panavision. [PG-13] ▼●

Pure Hell of St. Trinian's, The (1960-British) 94m. ** D: Frank Launder. Cecil Parker, Joyce Grenfell, George Cole, Thorley Walters. Absence of Alastair Sim from series lessens glow; outrageous girls' school is visited by sheik seeking harem. ▼

Pure Luck (1991) C-96m. ** D: Nadia Tass. Martin Short, Danny Glover, Sheila Kelley, Sam Wanamaker, Scott Wilson, Harry Shearer. A business magnate's accident-prone daughter disappears while vacationing in Mexico, and the father sends detective Glover to find her—accompanied by a man as unlucky as the woman he's out to find. Short's perpetual pratfalls are good for a few laughs, but otherwise this is pretty weak. American remake of French farce LE CHEVRE. [PG] ▼●▶

Purlie Victorious SEE: **Gone Are The Days**

Purple Hearts (1984) C-115m. ** D: Sidney J. Furie. Cheryl Ladd, Ken Wahl, Stephen Lee, David Harris, Lane Smith, Annie McEnroe, Paul McCrane, James Whitmore, Jr., Lee Ermey. Navy medic falls in love with feisty nurse in Vietnam. What starts out as good bread-and-butter story gets worse as it goes along toward silly conclusion. Overlong, to boot. Panavision. [R] ▼▶

Purple Noon (1960-French-Italian) C-118m. *** D: René Clement. Alain Delon, Marie Laforet, Maurice Ronet, Frank Latimore, Ave Ninchi. Marvelously photographed (in southern Italy, by Henri Decaë), tautly directed suspenser about Delon, who envies playboy-friend Ronet and schemes to murder him and assume his identity. Based on Patricia Highsmith's *The Talented Mr. Ripley.* That's Romy Schneider among the friends stopping by cafe in opening scene. Remade as THE TALENTED MR. RIPLEY; also see THE AMERICAN FRIEND and RIPLEY'S GAME. ▼●▶

Purple People Eater (1988) C-87m. *½ D: Linda Shayne. Ned Beatty, Shelley Winters, Neil (Patrick) Harris, Peggy Lipton, Chubby Checker, Little Richard, James Houghton, Thora Birch, Molly Cheek. Corny, unimaginative (if harmless) children's picture based on the famous novelty song hit of 1958, with the title character (looking like a kid in a Halloween costume) coming to Earth to form a rock band with neighborhood teens. The song's original writer-performer, Sheb Wooley, appears as a trapeze teacher. [PG] ▼●

Purple Plain, The (1954-British) C-102m. *** D: Robert Parrish. Gregory Peck, Win Min Than, Bernard Lee, Maurice Denham, Brenda De Banzie, Lyndon Brook. Absorbing Eric Ambler–scripted drama of love,

loss, and survival during WW2, charting the plight of disaffected pilot Peck, whose wife was killed on the night of their wedding during a London air raid. ▶

Purple Rain (1984) C-111m. **½ D: Albert Magnoli. Prince, Apollonia Kotero, Morris Day, Olga Karlatos, Clarence Williams III, Jerome Benton, Billy Sparks, The Revolution, The Time. Prince's film debut is about a young Minneapolis black who struggles to gain acceptance for his own brand of futuristic (and sexy) rock music . . . but it's *not* autobiographical. Right. Dynamic concert sequences are undercut by soppy storyline and sexist, unappealing characters—especially Prince's. Oscar-winning song score includes title tune, "When Doves Cry." [R] ▼●▶

Purple Rose of Cairo, The (1985) C-82m. ***½ D: Woody Allen. Mia Farrow, Jeff Daniels, Danny Aiello, Dianne Wiest, Van Johnson, Zoe Caldwell, John Wood, Milo O'Shea, Edward Herrmann, Karen Akers, Deborah Rush, Michael Tucker, Glenne Headly. Bittersweet comedy-fantasy about a Depression-era movie fan whose latest idol walks right off the screen and into her life! Farrow and Daniels' wonderful performances help offset the cold cleverness of Allen's script. The finale is a heartbreaker. [PG] ▼●▶

Purple Taxi, The (1977-French-Italian-Irish) C-107m. *½ D: Yves Boisset. Charlotte Rampling, Philippe Noiret, Agostina Belli, Peter Ustinov, Fred Astaire, Edward Albert. Confusing, overblown drama about expatriates in Ireland, with Astaire miscast as eccentric doctor who drives title vehicle. Based on Michel Deon's best-selling novel. Originally 120m. [R] ▼

Pursued (1947) 101m. *** D: Raoul Walsh. Teresa Wright, Robert Mitchum, Judith Anderson, Dean Jagger, Alan Hale, Harry Carey, Jr., John Rodney. Grim, passionate Western noir, a family saga of love, hate, revenge, and a hint of incest. Mitchum is an orphan raised by Anderson; he falls in love with foster sister Wright, complicated by his having killed her murderous brother. Stunning photography by James Wong Howe. ▼●▶

Pursuit of D. B. Cooper, The (1981) C-100m. ** D: Roger Spottiswoode. Robert Duvall, Treat Williams, Kathryn Harrold, Ed Flanders, Paul Gleason, R. G. Armstrong. What may have happened to the "legendary" D. B. Cooper (Williams, in a disappointing performance), who hijacked a plane in 1972 and bailed out with $200,000, never to be heard from again. Who cares? Lackluster comedy-chase story, with Duvall wasted as one of Cooper's pursuers. Film was plagued with problems, multiple directors, hastily refilmed ending—and it shows. [PG] ▼●

Pursuit of Happiness, The (1971) C-98m.

*** D: Robert Mulligan. Michael Sarrazin, Barbara Hershey, Robert Klein, Sada Thompson, Arthur Hill, E. G. Marshall, Barnard Hughes, Rue McClanahan. Director Mulligan has made lots of overrated films, but never got enough credit for this sympathetic tale of young man sent to jail more for his attitude in court than any particular offense. Good performances. Watch for William Devane, Charles Durning. [PG]▼◗

Pursuit of Happyness, The (2006) C-117m. *** D: Gabriele Muccino. Will Smith, Thandie Newton, Jaden Christopher Syre Smith, Brian Howe, James Karen, Dan Castellaneta, Kurt Fuller. Chris Gardner's life in San Francisco is falling apart in the early 1980s: his marriage is running on fumes, his income from selling medical equipment is meager, and before long he's out on the street with his 5-year-old son. The opportunity to turn his life around with an unpaid internship at a major brokerage firm presents itself, but it means living day to day, hour to hour, under almost unbearable stress. Smith gives a powerful, empathetic performance in this remarkable true story of a man who refuses to give up, though his all-too-believable ordeal is often difficult to watch. Super 35. [PG-13]◗

Pursuit of the Graf Spee (1956-British) C-119m. **½ D: Michael Powell, Emeric Pressburger. John Gregson, Anthony Quayle, Peter Finch, Ian Hunter, Bernard Lee, Patrick Macnee, Christopher Lee. Taut documentary-style account of WW2 chase of German warship by British forces. Original title: THE BATTLE OF THE RIVER PLATE. VistaVision.▼

Push (2009) C-111m. *½ D: Paul McGuigan. Chris Evans, Dakota Fanning, Djimon Hounsou, Camilla Belle, Cliff Curtis, Ming-Na, Neil Jackson, Maggie Siff. Hiding out in a seamy Hong Kong, American expatriates Evans and a miniskirted Fanning join forces to battle an evil U.S. agency led by Hounsou and his goons. Now pay attention: Evans is a "mover" (with telekinetic powers), Fanning is a "watcher" (more like a "sketcher" who interprets the future on a sketch pad), while Evans' girlfriend Belle and Hounsou are "pushers" (mind controllers). Belle has escaped a government lab with a potent serum everyone is after, which leads to plenty of action. Outrageously abstruse script; almost worth seeing for Fanning's pint-sized Lizabeth Scott homage. Super 35. [PG-13]◗

Pushing Hands (1992-U.S.-Taiwanese) C-100m. *** D: Ang Lee. Sihung Lung, Lai Wang, Bo Z. Wang, Deb Snyder, Haan Lee, Emily Liu. Cultures clash and a family is strained to the breaking point when a Chinese-American brings his father, a tai chi master who speaks no English, to live with his American wife and son in a N.Y.C.

suburb. Writer-director Lee's first feature is (like his later work) a keenly observed slice of life, with both humor and humanity. Lung, who plays the father, took similar roles in Lee's follow-up films, THE WEDDING BANQUET and EAT DRINK MAN WOMAN.▼◗

Pushing Tin (1999) C-124m. **½ D: Mike Newell. John Cusack, Billy Bob Thornton, Cate Blanchett, Angelina Jolie, Jake Weber, Vicki Lewis. Seriocomic slice of life about the high-pressure world of air-traffic controllers. Best-of-the-best Cusack gets caught in a macho competition with the new guy, Zen cowboy Thornton. MASH-like ensemble film starts off extremely well, with strong performances and snappy repartee, but crash-lands in its second half, becoming a dull domestic romantic comedy about Cusack trying to win back his estranged wife. Blanchett's quite good in an underwritten role as a Longuyland housewife. First feature script by *Cheers* creators Glen and Les Charles. Super 35. [R]▼◗

Pushover (1954) 88m. **½ D: Richard Quine. Fred MacMurray, Kim Novak, Phil Carey, Dorothy Malone, E. G. Marshall. MacMurray is cop who falls in love with Novak, moll of a bank heist artist; he plots with her to rob the robber, and complications ensue. Good cast covers familiar ground. ▼◗

Putney Swope (1969) C/B&W-85m. *** D: Robert Downey. Arnold Johnson, Pepi Hermine, Ruth Hermine, Allen Garfield, Antonio Fargas. Hilarious, but dated, story of blacks taking over Madison Avenue ad agency, instituting considerable changes. Best bit: series of commercial spoofs. Fargas, as The Arab, steals the film. Actor billed as "Mel Brooks" is not the Brooks we know and love. [R]▼◗

Puzzle of a Downfall Child (1970) C-104m. ** D: Jerry Schatzberg. Faye Dunaway, Barry Primus, Viveca Lindfors, Barry Morse, Roy Scheider, Barbara Carrera. Puzzling is the word for this confusing story of fashion model trying to put together the pieces of her unhappy life. [R]

Pygmalion (1938-British) 95m. **** D: Anthony Asquith, Leslie Howard. Leslie Howard, Wendy Hiller, Wilfrid Lawson, Marie Lohr, David Tree. Superlative filmization of the witty G. B. Shaw play which became MY FAIR LADY. Howard excels as the professor, with Hiller his Cockney pupil. Shaw's screenplay won an Oscar, as did its adaptation by Ian Dalrymple, Cecil Lewis, and W. P. Lipscomb. Edited by David Lean.▼◗

Pyrates (1991) C-95m. BOMB D: Noah Stern. Kevin Bacon, Kyra Sedgwick, Bruce Martyn Payne, Kristin Dattilo, Buckley Norris. Photography student Bacon and cellist Sedgwick meet, and the sex between them is so intense that they literally start fires. Crudely scripted, ineptly directed; see this only if you're interested in Bacon and Sedgwick's buns. (In real life they're husband and wife.) Set in Chicago, this film gives new meaning to the term "Windy City." [R]▼

Pyro (1964-Spanish) **C-99m. **½ D:** Julio Coll. Barry Sullivan, Martha Hyer, Sherry Moreland, Soledad Miranda. Strange chiller of man burned in fire seeking revenge on ex-girlfriend who started it.▼○●

Pyromaniac's Love Story, A (1995) **C-94m. ** D:** Joshua Brand. William Baldwin, John Leguizamo, Sadie Frost, Erika Eleniak, Michael Lerner, Joan Plowright, Armin Mueller-Stahl, Mike Starr, Julio Oscar Mechoso. A bakery burns to the ground, the work of an unknown arsonist, and the act evokes such unique emotions among a varied group of romantics that just about everyone claims responsibility for the deed—except the real culprit. Minor attempt at generating the same loopy romantic spirit as films like MOONSTRUCK. Feature directing debut for Brand, who co-created the TV series *St. Elsewhere* and *Northern Exposure.* [PG]▼○●

Pyx, The (1973-Canadian) **C-111m. ***½ D:** Harvey Hart. Karen Black, Christopher Plummer, Donald Pilon, Lee Broker, Yvette Brind'Amour. Excellent blend of horror, science-fiction, and detective thriller with a mystical theme. Police sergeant Plummer investigates prostitute Black's death, finds a devil cult, numerous decadent suspects, and a new twist on Catholic guilt. Aka THE HOOKER CULT MURDERS. Panavision. [R]▼●

Q (1982) **C-93m. *** D:** Larry Cohen. David Carradine, Michael Moriarty, Richard Roundtree, Candy Clark, John Capodice, James Dixon, Malachy McCourt. Through plot tissue that discourages elaboration, a prehistoric Aztec deity finds itself flying out of its nest atop a Manhattan skyscraper to rip the heads off rooftop sunbathers and other assorted victims; somehow, all this is integrated into a standard N.Y.C. cop story. Spirited, occasionally hilarious trash sparked by Moriarty's eccentric performance as the loser who knows where the beast resides and intends to cash in on it. Aka THE WINGED SERPENT. [R]▼○●

Q & A (1990) **C-132m. ** D:** Sidney Lumet. Nick Nolte, Timothy Hutton, Armand Assante, Patrick O'Neal, Lee Richardson, Luis Guzman, Charles Dutton, Jenny Lumet, Paul Calderon, Leonard Cimino. Wet-behind-the-ears Assistant D.A. (Hutton) is assigned to investigate an incident in which veteran street cop Nolte killed a Puerto Rican druggie . . . and soon finds himself waist-deep in corruption. Gritty, graphic, well-acted story gets slower as it goes along, dragging toward an increasingly predictable conclusion. Lu-

met scripted from Edwin Torres' novel. Ruben Blades' "Don't Double-Cross The Ones You Love" is surely the worst movie song of the '90s. [R]▼○●

Quackers SEE: **Loose Shoes**

Quackser Fortune Has a Cousin in the Bronx (1970-Irish) **C-90m. ***½ D:** Waris Hussein. Gene Wilder, Margot Kidder, Eileen Colgen, Seamus Ford. Delightfully offbeat love story. Quackser Fortune follows the horses around Dublin selling their manure for gardening. The day the horses are replaced by cars he falls in love with an American coed. Original in every way. Screenplay by Gabriel Walsh. Reissued as FUN LOVING. [PG]▼○●

Quadrophenia (1979-British) **C-115m. ***½ D:** Franc Roddam. Phil Daniels, Mark Wingett, Philip Davis, Leslie Ash, Garry Cooper, Sting. Superior mixture of early '60s "Angry Young Man" drama and rock movie tells of teenage gang battles between Mods and Rockers on the English seaside. A real sleeper. Inspired by The Who's record album. Sting makes an impressive acting debut. [R]▼○●

Quai des Orfèvres (1947-French) **106m. ***½ D:** Henri-Georges Clouzot. Louis Jouvet, Suzy Delair, Bernard Blier, Simone Renant, Charles Dullin, Henri Arius, Pierre Larquey. When a wealthy "dirty old man" is murdered, there is no shortage of suspects. A police procedural layered with telling character portraits, from a poor simp (Blier) who's suspicious of his coquettish wife, a music-hall singer (Delair), to a dour police detective (Jouvet). Clouzot's staging of key scenes—an argument during a musical rehearsal, a long scene in the back of a theater while chorus girls are dancing—is masterful, as is the overall look of this b&w gem. Title refers to the location of Paris' police headquarters. Originally shown in the U.S. as JENNY LAMOUR.▼●

Quality Street (1937) **84m. *** D:** George Stevens. Katharine Hepburn, Franchot Tone, Fay Bainter, Eric Blore, Cora Witherspoon, Estelle Winwood, Bonita Granville, Joan Fontaine, William Bakewell. Hepburn is radiant in delicate adaptation of James Barrie's whimsical play: "old maid" masquerades as her own niece in order to win back the love of a man who hasn't seen her in 10 years. Filmed before in 1927, with Marion Davies.▼○●

Quantum of Solace (2008-U.S.-British) **C-106m. **½ D:** Marc Forster. Daniel Craig, Olga Kurylenko, Mathieu Amalric, Judi Dench, Giancarlo Giannini, Gemma Arterton, Jeffrey Wright. In this direct sequel to CASINO ROYALE (2006), a brooding James Bond hunts down the man who caused the woman he loved to betray him. In so doing he uncovers a vast conspiracy led by business mogul Amalric, who's plotting to gain control of a prized natural resource. 007 has been reshaped for a BOURNE audience, turning the formerly suave, witty spy into a one-man demolition derby. Hyperactive editing renders much of the action senseless, though admittedly the film remains watchable throughout. Super 35. [PG-13]❚

Quarantine (2008) **C-89m.** **½ D: John Erick Dowdle. Jennifer Carpenter, Jay Hernandez, Johnathon Schaech, Columbus Short, Greg Germann, Steve Harris, Dania Ramirez, Doug Jones, Denis O'Hare, Bernard White, Rade Sherbedgia, Marin Hinkle. TV news crew, shadowing an L.A. fire brigade on the graveyard shift, answers a routine call that quickly escalates into horrific violence. Forcibly locked inside an apartment building, all fall victim one by one to a plague of bloody madness. New twist on the living dead is well-acted scary stuff, but this remake of the 2007 Spanish thriller [REC], nauseatingly experienced entirely through a shaky video lens, desperately calls for Dramamine. Followed by a DVD sequel. [R]❚

Quare Fellow, The (1962-Irish) **85m.** ***½ D: Arthur Dreifuss. Patrick McGoohan, Sylvia Syms, Walter Macken, Dermot Kelly, Jack Cunningham, Hilton Edwards. Irish-made adaptation of Brendan Behan play deals with new prison guard, well played by McGoohan, who changes mind about capital punishment. Finely acted; excellent script by director Dreifuss.❚

Quarrel, The (1991-Canadian) **C-88m.** **½ D: Eli Cohen. R. H. Thompson, Saul Rubinek. A pair of former friends, both Jews, meet by accident and pass the day discussing the implications of the Holocaust and how it has altered their lives. Provocative subject matter, based on a story by Chaim Grade, but the result is as static as it is thoughtful.▼❚

Quartet (1981-British-French) **C-101m.** *** D: James Ivory. Alan Bates, Maggie Smith, Isabelle Adjani, Anthony Higgins, Pierre Clementi, Daniel Mesguich, Virginie Thevenet, Suzanne Flon. Adjani is taken in by Bohemian Bates and victimized wife Smith when her husband (Higgins) is imprisoned; Bates seduces her into becoming his lover. Expertly acted drama of decadence and change; based on a book by Jean Rhys. [R]▼❚

Quatermass and the Pit: Five Million Years to Earth (1967-British) **98m.** *** D: Roy Ward Baker. James Donald, Barbara Shelley, Andrew Keir, Julian Glover, Maurice Good, Duncan Lamont. Workers unearth spaceship and remains of alien crew in modern-day London. Good cast, great script complications, and suspense in fine example of what can be done on a meager budget. Only subject matter will turn some viewers off. Superior to the earlier QUATERMASS films, known in the U.S. as THE CREEPING UNKNOWN and ENEMY FROM SPACE. Followed by THE QUATERMASS CONCLUSION. ▼●❚

Quatermass Conclusion, The (1980-British) **C-107m.** **½ D: Piers Haggard. John Mills, Simon MacCorkindale, Barbara Kellerman, Margaret Tyzack, Brewster Mason. Mills is fine as heroic Professor Bernard Quatermass (of earlier screen and television adventures) in this entertaining though poorly produced sci-fi adventure. He comes to the rescue when a death beam from outer space evaporates the world's young. Made for British TV. Original title: QUATERMASS.▼

Quatermass 2: Enemy from Space (1957-British) **84m.** *** D: Val Guest. Brian Donlevy, Michael Ripper, Sidney James, Bryan Forbes, John Longden, Vera Day, William Franklin. Even better than the original, THE QUATERMASS XPERIMENT: THE CREEPING UNKNOWN, this tense, scary science-fiction thriller concerns a secret alien invasion and BODY SNATCHERS-like takeovers of human beings. Donlevy is stern as Prof. Quatermass. Followed by QUATERMASS AND THE PIT: FIVE MILLION YEARS TO EARTH.▼●❚

Quatermass Xperiment, The: The Creeping Unknown (1955-British) **82m.** *** D: Val Guest. Brian Donlevy, Margia Dean, Jack Warner, Richard Wordsworth. A spaceship returns to Earth with only one man left on board; infested by an alien entity, he gradually transforms into a hideous monster. Tense, imaginative, adult; well acted by all concerned. Based on hit BBC-TV serial by Nigel Kneale. Followed by three sequels, beginning with QUATERMASS 2: ENEMY FROM SPACE. ▼❚

Queen, The (2006-British-French-Italian-U.S.) **C-101m.** ***½ D: Stephen Frears. Helen Mirren, Michael Sheen, James Cromwell, Helen McCrory, Alex Jennings, Roger Allam, Sylvia Syms, Mark Bazeley. Intriguing look inside the private life of England's royal family as Queen Elizabeth II contends with the death of Princess Diana, while her new, "modernist" Prime Minister, Tony Blair (Sheen), tries to persuade her that her stoic silence is out of step with the public's grief. Perceptive, persuasive, witty, and poignant, Peter Morgan's script humanizes the public figures it portrays, while actual TV news footage sets the stage for the events being dramatized. Mirren's flawless, Oscar-winning performance sets a standard met by all of her costars. Evocative and imaginative score by Alexandre Desplat. A follow-up to Frears' and Morgan's British TV movie THE DEAL (2003), in which Sheen first played Blair. [PG-13]❚

Queen Bee (1955) **95m.** *** D: Ranald MacDougall. Joan Crawford, Barry Sullivan, Betsy Palmer, John Ireland, Fay Wray, Tim Hovey. Crawford in title role has field-day maneuvering the lives of all in her

Southern mansion, with husband Sullivan providing the final ironic twist. ▼◗

Queen Christina (1933) 97m. **** D: Rouben Mamoulian. Greta Garbo, John Gilbert, Ian Keith, Lewis Stone, C. Aubrey Smith, Gustav von Seyffertitz, Reginald Owen. Probably Garbo's best film, with a haunting performance by the radiant star as 17th-century Swedish queen who relinquishes her throne for her lover, Gilbert. Garbo and Gilbert's love scenes together are truly memorable, as is the famous final shot. Don't miss this one. ▼◗●

Queen Margot (1994-French-German-Italian) C-143m. ***½ D: Patrice Chéreau. Isabelle Adjani, Daniel Auteuil, Jean-Hugues Anglade, Vincent Perez, Virna Lisi, Jean-Claude Brialy, Dominique Blanc, Pascal Greggory, Claudio Amendola, Miguel Bosé, Asia Argento, Barbet Schroeder. Enormous production, based on a Dumas novel, of the events surrounding notorious St. Bartholomew's Day massacre in 16th-century France. Young Margot (Adjani) is forced to marry Henri de Navarre (Auteuil) by her scheming mother, Catherine de Medici (Lisi), with unexpected and terrible consequences. Excellent film (produced by Claude Berri) boasts strong performances in every role, sumptuous decor, and surprisingly erotic love scenes. Intricate, intelligent and often moving epic. Scripted by Daniele Thompson and director Chéreau. Previously filmed in 1954, with Jeanne Moreau. Original French version runs 166m. [R] ▼◗●

Queen of Blood SEE: **Planet of Blood**

Queen of Hearts (1989-British) C-112m. ***½ D: Jon Amiel. Vittorio Duse, Joseph Long, Anita Zagaria, Eileen Way, Vittorio Amandola, Ian Hawkes, Tat Whalley. Extraordinary and unusual film, better seen than described, about an Italian couple who lead a pleasantly quixotic life in England running a family café. Tony Grisoni's original screenplay embraces elements of romance, humor, melodrama, mysticism, and fantasy in a heady mix. Remarkable first feature for director Amiel, who did *The Singing Detective* for British TV. [PG] ▼◗

Queen of Outer Space (1958) C-79m. ** D: Edward Bernds. Zsa Zsa Gabor, Eric Fleming, Laurie Mitchell, Patrick Waltz, Paul Birch, Lisa Davis, Dave Willock. Manned rocketship from Earth is abducted to Venus, where the planet is ruled entirely by women. Silly, to say the least, but at least some of the laughs were intentional. Zsa Zsa, incidentally, does *not* play the title character! CinemaScope. ▼◗

Queen of Spades, The (1949-British) 95m. ***½ D: Thorold Dickinson. Anton Walbrook, Edith Evans, Ronald Howard, Mary Jerrold, Yvonne Mitchell, Anthony Dawson. Exquisite production of an unusual, macabre Alexander Pushkin story about an impoverished Russian officer (Walbrook, in

a rich performance) who will do anything to learn the mystical secret of winning at cards known only by an imperious old woman (Evans). Brilliant use of chiaroscuro lighting and atmosphere in this sleeper set in 1806. ▼◗

Queen of the Damned (2002-Australian-U.S.) C-101m. **½ D: Michael Rymer. Stuart Townsend, Aaliyah, Marguerite Moreau, Vincent Perez, Paul McGann, Lena Olin, Christian Manon. Vampire Lestat awakens after a long deep sleep and goes public in the world of rock music, where he seems to blend in perfectly! But his posturing angers the man who "made" him, intrigues a young woman who's drawn to his world, and lines him up as the perfect mate for the queen of the undead (played by pop-music star Aaliyah, who died before the film's release). Dopey but amusing. Based on one of Anne Rice's *The Vampire Chronicles* novels. Panavision. [R] ▼◗

Queens Logic (1991) C-112m. **½ D: Steve Rash. Kevin Bacon, Linda Fiorentino, John Malkovich, Joe Mantegna, Ken Olin, Tony Spiridakis, Tom Waits, Chloe Webb, Jamie Lee Curtis, J. J. Johnson, Kelly Bishop, Ed Marinaro. Title refers not to royalty, but to the N.Y.C. borough. Robust performances half-spark a BIG CHILL–type reunion pic, as old pals and their mates reunite for a wedding. Actor Spiridakis penned the so-so script. Unusually fine rock-oldie score helps. [R] ▼◗●

Queen to Play (2009-French-German) C-101m. *** D: Caroline Bottaro. Sandrine Bonnaire, Kevin Kline, Francis Renaud, Jennifer Beals, Valérie Lagrange, Alexandra Gentil, Alice Pol, Didier Ferrari. A house-cleaner at a vacation inn on a small French island becomes intrigued with the game of chess after watching two elegant guests playing it on their balcony. Her growing obsession with the game threatens to drive a wedge between her and her working-class husband—especially when she convinces another of her clients, a dour American expat (Kline), to help her improve her skills. Charming story of a woman's inner journey toward self-confidence, adapted from Bertina Henrichs' novel by the director. Bonnaire is a joy to watch. Original French title: JOUEUSE. ◗

Quemada! SEE: **Burn!**

Querelle (1982-German) C-120m. BOMB D: Rainer Werner Fassbinder. Brad Davis, Franco Nero, Jeanne Moreau, Gunther Kaufmann, Hanno Poschl. Or, "A Guy in Every Port." Davis is the French sailor whose venture into an infamous whorehouse in Brest permits him to discover his true homosexual nature. Fassbinder's final film was rejected even by his admirers; gamy but slickly produced adaptation of Jean Genet novel induces boredom and giggles in equal measure. Technovision. [R] ▼◗

Quest, The (1986-Australian) C-93m. *½ D: Brian Trenchard-Smith. Henry Thomas, Tony Barry, Rachel Friend, Tamsin West, Dennis Miller, Katya Manning. Abortive Australian attempt to capitalize on young Thomas' success as the star of E.T.; here he plays a precocious child who, along with a couple of pals, visits an aboriginal burial ground where a Loch Ness–style monster lives. Competent but uninteresting. [PG] ▼

Quest, The (1996) C-95m. **½ D: Jean-Claude Van Damme. Jean-Claude Van Damme, Roger Moore, James Remar, Jack McGee, Janet Gunn, Aki Aleong, Louis Mandylor. Epic martial-arts story with high-kicking Van Damme as N.Y.C. pickpocket whose efforts to elude the police lead him to the Far East and into the most exclusive and prestigious fight in the "world." Besides Jean-Claude, film features 15 of the world's greatest martial arts champions. A passable but uninspired directing debut for the star, who also gets story credit. Super 35. [PG-13]▼●)

Quest for Camelot (1998) C-85m. **½ D: Frederick Du Chau. Voices of Jessalyn Gilsig, Cary Elwes, Gary Oldman, Eric Idle, Don Rickles, Jane Seymour, Celine Dion, Bryan White, Pierce Brosnan, Gabriel Byrne, Jaleel White, Bronson Pinchot, John Gielgud. Pretty good Disney-derivative cartoon, about the plucky daughter of a slain knight who wants to follow in her father's footsteps—and does just that when King Arthur's sword, Excalibur, is stolen. Too dark and violent for very young kids, but agreeable enough. Familiar story path, with romance, songs, and comic relief. [G] ▼●)

Quest for Fire (1981-French-Canadian) C-97m. ***½ D: Jean-Jacques Annaud. Everett McGill, Rae Dawn Chong, Ron Perlman, Nameer El Kadi. Peaceful tribe living 80,000 years ago is attacked by apes and wolves and loses its fire, essential for survival. They don't know how to make fire, so three of their own trek off to find it again. Not the epic intended, but still funny, tense, touching—and fascinating. Special languages devised by Anthony Burgess, and body languages and gestures by Desmond Morris; the makeup earned an Academy Award. Filmed in Kenya, Scotland, Iceland, and Canada. Panavision. [R]▼●)

Quest for Love (1971-British) C-90m. *** D: Ralph Thomas. Tom Bell, Joan Collins, Denholm Elliott, Laurence Naismith, Lyn Ashley, Juliet Harmer, Neil McCallum, Simon Ward. Intriguing sci-fi story of man who accidentally passes into another dimension on Earth almost identical to ours, with some strange differences. Based on John Wyndham's short story.▼

Quick and the Dead, The (1995) C-105m. ** D: Sam Raimi. Sharon Stone, Gene Hackman, Russell Crowe, Leonardo DiCaprio, Tobin Bell, Roberts Blossom, Kevin Conway, Keith David, Lance Henriksen, Pat Hingle, Gary Sinise, Olivia Burnette, Fay Masterson, Bruce Campbell. Female stranger comes to the town of Redemption to enter its annual quick-draw competition; her real motive is to seek revenge on the town's evil boss, Herod (Hackman), for what he did to her family years ago. Sluggish Western tries to turn Stone into The Man With No Name, but even on a parody level, it doesn't work; endless closeups of her beautiful face reveal nothing. One would expect more razzle-dazzle from director Raimi. Woody Strode appears briefly as a coffin maker in the opening scene; this was his final film. [R]▼●)

Quick Change (1990) C-88m. *** D: Howard Franklin, Bill Murray. Bill Murray, Geena Davis, Randy Quaid, Jason Robards, Bob Elliott, Philip Bosco, Phil Hartman, Kurtwood Smith, Jamey Sheridan, Kathryn Grody, Stanley Tucci, Tony Shalhoub. Very low-key but funny outing for Murray as a malcontent who stages a clever bank robbery—disguised as a clown—but can't seem to get out of N.Y.C. with his accomplices, Davis and Quaid. It's possible that only New Yorkers will truly appreciate the anti-City sentiments (and often hilarious vignettes) that permeate the film. Jay Cronley's novel was previously filmed in 1985 as HOLD-UP, with Jean-Paul Belmondo. [R]▼●)

Quick, Let's Get Married (1971) C-96m. BOMB D: William Dieterle. Ginger Rogers, Ray Milland, Barbara Eden, Michael Ansara, Walter Abel, Elliott Gould. Bordello madam Rogers and adventurer Milland perpetrate "miracle" hoax on gullible prostitute (Eden). Gould makes inauspicious film debut as deaf mute. This embarrassment was filmed in 1964. Aka SEVEN DIFFERENT WAYS.

Quicksand (2002-British-French-German) C-93m. **½ D: John Mackenzie. Michael Keaton, Michael Caine, Judith Godrèche, Rade Serbedzija, Matthew Marsh, Xander Berkeley, Kathleen Wilhoite, Rachel Ferjani. U.S. bank executive Keaton is in Nice to investigate a movie company's finances and instead becomes a fugitive accused of murder. Caine plays an egocentric movie star caught up in the plot. Modestly entertaining thriller with good locations; Caine is amusing as the aging idol. Released direct to video in the U.S. [R] ▼)

Quicksilver (1986) C-106m. *½ D: Tom Donnelly. Kevin Bacon, Jami Gertz, Paul Rodriguez, Rudy Ramos, Andrew Smith, Gerald S. O'Loughlin, Larry Fishburne, Louis Anderson. The lives of big-city bicycle messengers (confusingly shot in three *different* cities), and one white-collar dropout in particular. Low-gear all the way. [PG]▼●◗

Quid Pro Quo (2008) **C-82m.** **✱✱** D: Carlos Brooks. Nick Stahl, Vera Farmiga, Jacob Pitts, Aimee Mullins, James Frain, Kate Burton, Jessica Hecht, Dylan Bruno, Pablo Schreiber. Paraplegic radio personality Stahl begins a highly charged relationship with a mystery woman (Farmiga) who's obsessed with losing the ability to walk. Idiosyncratic exploration of memory and guilt is ambitious but slow moving, and not satisfying dramatically. [R]◗

Quiet, The (2005) **C-96m.** *½ D: Jamie Babbit. Elisha Cuthbert, Camilla Belle, Edie Falco, Martin Donovan, Shawn Ashmore, Katy Mixon, David Gallagher, Shannon Marie Woodward. Dull, weird, and pointless story of a deaf girl, orphaned by the death of her father, who moves in with her godparents and their scheming daughter. She soon discovers the whole crew is harboring secrets and acting stranger than the Addams Family. Film doesn't know if it wants to be a psychological thriller, a lesbian drama, a dysfunctional family story, or a teen movie. HD Widescreen. [R]◗

Quiet American, The (1958) **120m.** **✱½** D: Joseph L. Mankiewicz. Audie Murphy, Michael Redgrave, Claude Dauphin, Giorgia Moll, Bruce Cabot. Sanitized version of the Graham Greene novel, with the book's "un-American" feeling eliminated; naive American Murphy arrives in Saigon with his own plan to settle country's conflicts. More a murder mystery than the political thriller intended. Remade in 2002. ◗

Quiet American, The (2002-Australian-U.S.) **C-101m.** **✱✱✱** D: Phillip Noyce. Michael Caine, Brendan Fraser, Do Thi Hai Yen, Rade Sherbedgia, Tzi Ma, Robert Stanton, Holmes Osborne, Pham Thi Mai Hoa, Quang Hai, Ferdinand Hoang. Remake of Graham Greene's novel about a love triangle, set in 1952 Saigon, between a cynical British journalist, his young Vietnamese mistress, and an American who is not all that he seems to be. Handsomely mounted, with excellent performances by Caine and Fraser, but the central romance and political details—more faithful to Greene than Joseph L. Mankiewicz's 1958 version—are surprisingly uninvolving. Super 35. [R] ▼◗

Quiet Days in Hollywood (1996-German-U.S.) **C-91m.** BOMB D: Josef Rusnak. Bill Cusack, Peter Dobson, Meta Golding, Chad Lowe, Stephen Mailer, Daryl ("Chill") Mitchell, Hilary Swank, Natasha Gregson Wagner, Jake Busey. Messy mishmash of loosely connected vignettes linking various L.A. characters (from waitress to showbiz exec, movie star to junkie), all of whom have sex on the brain. Of interest for the presence of Swank, as a pop culture-obsessed hooker. Aka THE WAY WE ARE. [R]▼◗

Quiet Earth, The (1985-New Zealand) **C-100m.** **✱✱½** D: Geoff Murphy. Bruno Lawrence, Alison Routledge, Peter Smith. Intriguing (and extremely good-looking) end-of-the-world saga; not entirely successful but well worth a look. [R]▼◗

Quiet Man, The (1952) **C-129m.** **✱✱✱✱** D: John Ford. John Wayne, Maureen O'Hara, Barry Fitzgerald, Victor McLaglen, Mildred Natwick, Arthur Shields, Ward Bond, Ken Curtis, Mae Marsh, Jack MacGowran, Sean McClory, Francis Ford. American boxer Wayne returns to his native Ireland and falls in love with a spirited lass (O'Hara) —but has to deal with local customs (including the payment of a dowry) and the young woman's bullheaded brother (McLaglen). Boisterous blarney, with beautiful Technicolor scenery, and equally beautiful music by Victor Young. This film was clearly a labor of love for Ford and his Irish-American stars. Maurice Walsh's story was scripted by Frank Nugent. Oscar winner for Best Director and Cinematography (Winton C. Hoch and Archie Stout).▼◗

Quiet Room, The (1996-Australian) **C-91m.** **✱✱✱½** D: Rolf de Heer. Celine O'Leary, Paul Blackwell, Chloe Ferguson, Phoebe Ferguson. Revealing and compelling portrait of the disintegration of a marriage as seen completely through the eyes and mind of a seven-year-old girl. Writer-director de Heer vividly captures the truth about the experience through the self-imposed silence of a wise child who clearly sees through adult evasiveness and lies. [PG]▼

Quigley Down Under (1990) **C-119m.** **✱✱✱** D: Simon Wincer. Tom Selleck, Laura San Giacomo, Alan Rickman, Chris Haywood, Ron Haddrick, Tony Bonner, Jerome Ehlers, Conor McDermottroe, Roger Ward, Ben Mendelsohn. Selleck is excellent as a self-assured sharpshooter who travels to Australia to work for despotic land baron Rickman—and takes an instant dislike to him, spawning a deadly game of cat-and-mouse in which only one will be left alive. Expertly filmed on exquisite locations, with its good qualities outweighing occasional dips in interest. Panavision. [PG-13]▼●◗

Quiller Memorandum, The (1966-British) **C-105m.** **✱✱✱** D: Michael Anderson. George Segal, Alec Guinness, Max von Sydow, Senta Berger, George Sanders, Robert Helpmann, Robert Flemyng. Good Harold Pinter script about American secret agent who investigates neo-Nazi movement in modern-day Berlin. A relief from most spy films of the '60s. Based on novel *The Berlin Memorandum* by Elleston Trevor (using pseudonym Adam Hall). Panavision. ▼◗

Quills (2000) **C-123m.** **✱✱½** D: Philip Kaufman. Geoffrey Rush, Kate Winslet, Joaquin Phoenix, Michael Caine, Billie Whitelaw, Patrick Malahide, Amelia Warner. The Marquis de Sade (Rush, in a delicious performance) is imprisoned in a French asylum, and a laundress (Winslet) smuggles his notorious manuscripts to an eager publisher. When this proves to be an embarrassment to Napoleon, a brutal doctor (Caine) is dispatched to keep him in line. Handsome, witty, and ribald . . . then it turns grim and nasty, leaving a bad taste behind. Doug Wright adapted his play. [R] ▼❚

Quinceañera (2006) **C-90m.** *** D: Richard Glatzer, Wash Westmoreland. Emily Rios, Jesse Garcia, Chalo González, J. R. Cruz, Araceli Guzmán-Rico, Jesus Castaños-Chima, David W. Ross, Jason L. Wood. Disarming slice-of-life set in L.A.'s Echo Park community, where a 14-year-old girl about to have her traditional rite-of-passage party can't explain how she got pregnant . . . and her uncompromising father (a neighborhood pastor) doesn't believe she's innocent. Meanwhile her cousin, already a family outcast, takes up with an upscale gay couple that's moved into the changing neighborhood. González all but steals the film as the beatific uncle. Writing-directing partners Glatzer and Westmoreland were inspired by real-life events in their community. HD Widescreen. [R]❚

Quintet (1979) **C-110m.** ** D: Robert Altman. Paul Newman, Bibi Andersson, Fernando Rey, Vittorio Gassman, Nina Van Pallandt, Brigitte Fossey, David Langton. Pretentious, unappealing story about cut-throat game of survival in a frozen city of the future. Not as puzzling as it is ponderous. [R] ▼❚

Quiz Show (1994) **C-130m.** ***½ D: Robert Redford. John Turturro, Rob Morrow, Ralph Fiennes, Paul Scofield, David Paymer, Hank Azaria, Christopher McDonald, Johann Carlo, Elizabeth Wilson, Allan Rich, Mira Sorvino, George Martin, Paul Guilfoyle, Griffin Dunne, Timothy Busfield, Jack Gilpin, Bruce Altman, Carole Shelley, Illeana Douglas, Calista Flockhart. Engrossing story of the TV quiz show scandal of the late 1950s, focusing on a hotheaded sore loser (Turturro, in a sensational performance) and his successor on *Twenty-One*: instant hero Charles Van Doren (Fiennes), scion of a socially prominent, intellectual family. Overlength is its only weakness—but it never ceases to be real (if not always exactly truthful). Scofield is a joy to watch as the elder Van Doren, and director Martin Scorsese is well cast as the cold-blooded sponsor of the show. That's film director Barry Levinson as TV host Dave Garroway; look sharp for an un-billed Ethan Hawke in a Columbia University classroom. [PG-13]▼❶

Quo Vadis (1951) **C-171m.** *** D: Mervyn LeRoy. Robert Taylor, Deborah Kerr, Peter Ustinov, Leo Genn, Patricia Laffan, Finlay Currie, Abraham Sofaer, Buddy Baer. Gargantuan MGM adaptation of Henryk Sienkiewicz' novel set during the reign of Nero;

Roman soldier Taylor has to figure out how to romance Christian Kerr without both of them ending up as lunch for the lions. Meticulous production includes fine location shooting and Miklos Rozsa score based on music of the era. Remade for Italian TV in 1985. ▼❶

Rabbit Hole (2010) **C-91m.** *** D: John Cameron Mitchell. Nicole Kidman, Aaron Eckhart, Dianne Wiest, Tammy Blanchard, Miles Teller, Sandra Oh, Giancarlo Esposito, Jon Tenney, Patricia Kalember. Honest, moving portrait of how a couple deals with grief after the death of their young son. The husband and wife can't seem to connect emotionally following their trauma, as each one tries to find a way to move on. Superior acting makes this well worth seeing, despite the somber subject matter. David Lindsay-Abaire adapted his Pulitzer Prize–winning Broadway play. [PG-13] ❶

Rabbit-Proof Fence (2002-Australian-British) **C-94m.** *** D: Phillip Noyce. Everlyn Sampi, Tianna Sansbury, Laura Monaghan, David Gulpilil, Kenneth Branagh, Deborah Mailman, Jason Clarke, Ningali Lawford, Myarn Lawford. Amazing true story set in 1931 Australia, as three half-caste aboriginal girls are taken from their mothers—as the law dictates—and transferred to a camp 1,500 miles away, where they will be Anglicized and trained for domestic work. When they escape and head home, the bureaucrat who's in charge of aborigines (Branagh) does everything in his power to capture them, but he doesn't reckon on their cunning and determination. Told with restraint, this emotional story is underplayed, but the final real-life footage packs a punch. Music by Peter Gabriel. Super 35. [PG]▼❶

Rabbit, Run (1970) **C-94m.** ** D: Jack Smight. James Caan, Carrie Snodgress, Anjanette Comer, Jack Albertson, Melodie Johnson, Henry Jones, Carmen Matthews, Nydia Westman, Josephine Hutchinson, Ken Kercheval, Arthur Hill. Brilliant cast, brilliant book (by John Updike), but dull film about former high school athlete who finds that life is tougher than being on the playing field. Panavision. [R] ❶

Rabbit Test (1978) **C-86m.** **½ D: Joan Rivers. Billy Crystal, Alex Rocco, Joan Prather, Doris Roberts, George Gobel, Imogene Coca, Paul Lynde. Rivers' only film to date is like low-budget Mel Brooks: wacky comedy surrounding slim plot about first pregnant man. Some wild ideas, mostly in bad taste. Many guest-star cameos (including Rivers as a nurse). [PG]▼❶

Rabid (1977-Canadian) **C-90m.** **½ D: David Cronenberg. Marilyn Chambers, Frank Moore, Joe Silver, Patricia Gage, Susan Roman. Motorcyclist Chambers has plastic surgery after an accident, develops an insatiable hankering for human blood.

Good of its type; well directed by cult favorite Cronenberg. Porn star Chambers removes her clothes—but nothing more. [R]**▼▶**

Race for the Yankee Zephyr (1981-Australian-New Zealand) **C-108m. ** D:** David Hemmings. Ken Wahl, Lesley Ann Warren, Donald Pleasence, George Peppard, Bruno Lawrence. Addle-brained drama about good guys Wahl and Pleasence and nemesis Peppard attempting to recover $50 million in gold from DC-3 wrecked during WW2. Video title: TREASURE OF THE YANKEE ZEPHYR. Panavision. [PG]**▼▶**

Race for Your Life, Charlie Brown (1977) **C-75m. **½ D:** Bill Melendez. Voices of Duncan Watson, Greg Felton, Stuart Brotman, Gail Davis, Liam Martin. Third animated feature based on Charles Schulz's *Peanuts* comic strip is set in summer camp, highlighted by treacherous raft race. Mildly entertaining, but lacks punch. [G]**▼●**

Racers, The (1955) **C-87m. **½ D:** Henry Hathaway. Kirk Douglas, Bella Darvi, Gilbert Roland, Lee J. Cobb, Cesar Romero, Katy Jurado. Hackneyed sports-car racing yarn, not salvaged by Douglas' dynamics or European location shooting. CinemaScope.**▼**

Race the Sun (1996) **C-105m. ** D:** Charles T. Kanganis. Halle Berry, James Belushi, Kevin Tighe, Bill Hunter, Eliza Dushku, J. Moki Cho, Casey Affleck, Steve Zahn. An idealistic teacher (Berry) and gruff mechanic (Belushi) team up to mentor eight poverty-stricken kids who build a solar-powered car and take it to a racing competition across Australia. Clichés abound in this "feel-good" film, and the leads are annoying, but the kids are charming (in particular, Cho). Exotic locales help. Written by Barry Morrow (RAIN MAN). [PG]**▼**

Race to Witch Mountain (2009) **C-99m. **½ D:** Andy Fickman. Dwayne Johnson, Alexander Ludwig, AnnaSophia Robb, Carla Gugino, Ciarán Hinds, Tom Everett Scott, Cheech Marin, Garry Marshall. Speedy but routine revamping of Disney's 1970s not-quite franchise (ESCAPE TO WITCH MOUNTAIN, RETURN FROM WITCH MOUNTAIN, and some made-for-TV remakes in the 1990s) begins with the artist previously known as The Rock driving a cab in Vegas. Then, it quickly evolves into a yarn of flying saucers, teen space aliens, a cute astrophysicist, a government heavy who actually is overweight, underworld thugs, a country bar band, mouthy dweebs at a sci-fi convention . . . and, oh yeah, Witch Mountain. Affable (if forgettable) entertainment for kids. Kim Richards and Ike Eisenmann, who starred in the 1970s films, make cameo appearances. Super 35. [PG]**▶**

Race With the Devil (1975) **C-88m. **½ D:** Jack Starrett. Peter Fonda, Warren Oates,

Loretta Swit, Lara Parker, R. G. Armstrong. Two vacationing couples are pursued by local Satanists after witnessing a human sacrifice. It takes quite a human sacrifice to sit through this hybrid car-chase/horror film. [PG]**▼▶**

Rachel and the Stranger (1948) **79m. *** D:** Norman Foster. Loretta Young, William Holden, Robert Mitchum, Tom Tully, Sara Haden, Gary Gray. Charming pioneer love story of a farmer (Holden), his indentured servant wife (Young), and the farmer's wandering minstrel friend (Mitchum) who visits their homestead. Three attractive stars at their prime. Originally reviewed at 93m. Also shown in computer-colored version.**▼●**

Rachel Getting Married (2008) **C-113m. *** D:** Jonathan Demme. Anne Hathaway, Rosemarie DeWitt, Bill Irwin, Debra Winger, Tunde Adebimpe, Mather Zickel, Anisa George, Anna Deavere Smith. Emotionally charged drama, shot like a cinéma vérité documentary, about a troubled young woman (Hathaway) who's temporarily sprung from a rehab facility in order to attend her sister's wedding at the family's home . . . but Hathaway is a raw nerve who sets off sparks willy-nilly, repeatedly undermining her sister (DeWitt) and her long-suffering father (Irwin). She also has unfinished business with her divorced mother (Winger). Superb performances mitigate against the sometimes annoying ambiance, but it's all masterfully orchestrated by Demme, who finds the resonance in the debut screenplay of Jenny Lumet (Sidney's daughter). [R]**▶**

Rachel Papers, The (1989-British) **C-95m. **½ D:** Damian Harris. Dexter Fletcher, Ione Skye, Jonathan Pryce, James Spader, Bill Paterson, Lesley Sharp, Michael Gambon. Young Britisher relentlessly pursues an American girl, with the help of his computer. Skye shines (in a role similar to the one she had in SAY ANYTHING . . .) but this is really a showcase for Fletcher. Sporadically charming, adapted by first-time director Harris from Martin Amis' novel. [R]**▼▶**

Rachel, Rachel (1968) **C-101m. ***½ D:** Paul Newman. Joanne Woodward, James Olson, Kate Harrington, Estelle Parsons, Donald Moffat, Terry Kiser. Beautifully sensitive, mature film about spinster schoolteacher trying to come out of her shell. Woodward is superb; husband Newman's directorial debut. Screenplay by Stewart Stern, from a novel by Margaret Laurence. [R]**▼▶**

Rachel River (1987) **C-90m. **½ D:** Sandy Smolan. Zeljko Ivanek, Pamela Reed, Craig T. Nelson, James Olson, Alan North, Viveca Lindfors, Jo Henderson, Jon De Vries, Richard Jenkins. Occasionally contrived but mostly intelligent chronicle of Reed, a rural Minnesota mother and radio journalist, and the various people who inhabit her town. Thoughtful performances overcome the occasional insipidness. Screenplay by Judith Guest; a PBS *American Playhouse* theatrical production. [PG-13]▼

Racing Stripes (2005) **C-84m.** *½ D: Frederik Du Chau. Bruce Greenwood, Hayden Panettiere, M. Emmet Walsh, Wendie Malick; voices of Frankie Muniz, Whoopi Goldberg, Dustin Hoffman, Mandy Moore, Snoop Dogg, Jeff Foxworthy, Joe Pantoliano, Fred Dalton Thompson, David Spade, Michael Clarke Duncan, Steve Harvey, Joshua Jackson. A zebra falls off a truck and ends up in the rural household of widowed Greenwood and his adolescent daughter (Panettiere), who longs to race him. Barnyard animals speak, BABE-style, which gives work to a condo-mixer cast of voice-over talent, including Spade as a feces-craving horsefly named "Scuzz." To quote Gig Young in THEY SHOOT HORSES, DON'T THEY?, "Yowza!" [PG] ▼ ▶

Racing With the Moon (1984) **C-108m.** *** D: Richard Benjamin. Sean Penn, Elizabeth McGovern, Nicolas Cage, John Karlen, Rutanya Alda, Carol Kane, Crispin Glover, Michael Madsen, Dana Carvey. Teenage romance set in small California town just as the young man is about to go off to fight in WW2. Appealing stars and loving eye for 1940s detail make up for slow pace. That bowling alley is a gem! [PG] ▼ ▶ ●

Rack, The (1956) **100m.** *** D: Arnold Laven. Paul Newman, Wendell Corey, Walter Pidgeon, Edmond O'Brien, Anne Francis, Lee Marvin, Cloris Leachman. Newman is pensively convincing as Korean War veteran—brainwashed as a P.O.W. —now on trial for treason, with Pidgeon as his overbearing father and Francis his friend. Slick production adapted from Rod Serling teleplay. Robert Blake, Dean Jones, and Rod Taylor have small roles.▶

Racket, The (1928) **83m.** **½ D: Lewis Milestone. Thomas Meighan, Louis Wolheim, Marie Prevost, Pat Collins, Henry Sedley, George (E.) Stone, Sam De Grasse, Skeets Gallagher. A steely-eyed police captain and a tough-as-nails crime boss play cat and mouse, each determined to do the other in, in Bartlett Cormack's adaptation of his Broadway play, which foreshadows the gangster films of the early 1930s. A handful of potent scenes, well shot and staged, stand out in an otherwise routine silent film. Produced by Howard Hughes. Remade in 1951.

Racket Busters (1938) **71m.** ** D: Lloyd Bacon. George Brent, Humphrey Bogart, Gloria Dickson, Allen Jenkins, Walter Abel, Henry O'Neill, Penny Singleton. Mobster Bogie's going to take over the trucking business, but Brent doesn't want to cooperate. Standard programmer moves along well; cowritten by Robert Rossen.

Rad (1986) **C-91m.** BOMB D: Hal Needham. Bill Allen, Bart Connor, Lori Laughlin, Talia Shire, Jack Weston, Ray Walston. Allen is supposed to take his SATs, but wouldn't you know it, there's a big BMX race on the same Saturday? "Rad" is short for *radical*—as in "Radical, man"—which this trash definitely is not: Didn't we see this same plot in late '50s hot-rod and late '70s roller-disco movies? [PG] ▼ ●

Radio (2003) **C-109m.** ** D: Mike Tollin. Cuba Gooding, Jr., Ed Harris, Debra Winger, Alfre Woodard, S. Epatha Merkerson, Brent Sexton, Chris Mulkey, Sarah Drew. South Carolina high school football coach takes an interest in a mentally challenged young man who's been mistreated by some of the football players. Nicknamed Radio, he blossoms under the coach's influence, but some people in his close-knit community don't cotton to this relationship. Although "inspired" by a true story, the film feels pat and hollow, despite good performances by Gooding and Harris. Brief footage of the real coach and his protégé at the very end of the film has more meaning—and impact—than anything in the movie itself. [PG] ▼ ▶

Radioactive Dreams (1986) **C-98m.** ** D: Albert Pyun. John Stockwell, Michael Dudikoff, Lisa Blount, George Kennedy, Don Murray, Michele Little. So-so post-apocalypse drama about Stockwell and Dudikoff, who've come to maturity in a bomb shelter. They've read all of Raymond Chandler's Philip Marlowe books and have taken on the private eye's personality. Nicely filmed, but it doesn't hold up. [R] ▼ ●

Radio Days (1987) **C-85m.** *** D: Woody Allen. Mia Farrow, Seth Green, Julie Kavner, Josh Mostel, Michael Tucker, Dianne Wiest, Wallace Shawn, Tito Puente, Danny Aiello, Jeff Daniels, Tony Roberts, Diane Keaton, Kitty Carlisle Hart, Kenneth Mars, Mercedes Ruehl, Rebecca Schaeffer, Todd Field, Larry David. Richly nostalgic reminiscence (narrated by Woody) about growing up in 1940s Queens, mixing family vignettes with incidents about radio performers from that medium's golden age. The narrative never really jells, though it's always enjoyable to watch . . . especially with Allen's eye for detail and ear for dialogue. Beautifully photographed by Carlo Di Palma and designed by Santo Loquasto; filled with wonderful vintage music. Look sharp for William H. Macy. [PG] ▼ ▶ ●

Radio Flyer (1992) **C-120m.** ** D: Richard Donner. Lorraine Bracco, John Heard, Elijah Wood, Joseph Mazzello, Adam Baldwin, Ben Johnson. Two young, devoted brothers must find a way to survive their mother's marriage to an abusive drunk; their salvation is escape into a secret world, where they hatch a master plan for their

Radio Flyer wagon. Spielberg-like view of childhood seems to suggest fantasy as a solution to child abuse! Despite moving performances from the two boys, this concept just doesn't work. Tom Hanks appears unbilled. Panavision. [PG-13]▼●▶

Radio Inside (1994) **C-91m.** **½ D: Jeffrey Bell. William McNamara, Elisabeth Shue, Dylan Walsh, Ilse Earl, Pee Wee Love, Ara Madzounian, Steve Zurk. A young man, trying to cope with the death of his father and his own aimlessness, goes to live with his brother and soon falls for the brother's girlfriend. Gentle tale with some good performances, especially by McNamara. ▼●

Radioland Murders (1994) **C-112m.** *½ D: Mel Smith. Brian Benben, Mary Stuart Masterson, Ned Beatty, Scott Michael Campbell, Brion James, Michael Lerner, Michael McKean, Jeffrey Tambor, Stephen Tobolowsky, Christopher Lloyd, Larry Miller, Anita Morris, Corbin Bernsen, Bobcat Goldthwait, Robert Walden, Rosemary Clooney, Dylan Baker, Billy Barty, Tracy Byrd, Candy Clark, Anne De Salvo, Jennifer Dundas, Bo Hopkins, Robert Klein, Harvey Korman, Joey Lawrence, Peter MacNicol, Jack Sheldon. Frenetic, wearisome farce about backstage murders on opening night of a Chicago radio network in 1939. Many talented performers are given nothing to do. Executive producer George Lucas apparently concocted this story years earlier. Arriscope. [PG]▼●▶

Radio On (1979-British) **101m.** **½ D: Chris Petit. David Beames, Lisa Kreuzer, Sting. Downbeat, rambling story of disc jockey who travels across Britain because of the mysterious circumstances of his brother's recent death. Written and directed by Petit, disciple of German director Wim Wenders (film's associate producer); plot is only hinted at in this meditation on the bleakness of modern life.▶

Ra Expeditions, The (1971-Norwegian) **C-93m.** *** D: Lennart Ehrenborg. Narrated by Thor Heyerdahl and Roscoe Lee Browne. Exciting documentary about modern adventurer Heyerdahl's determination to cross the Atlantic in a papyrus boat, to prove theory that such a voyage was made thousands of years ago. Fine follow-up to KON-TIKI. [G]

Rafferty and the Gold Dust Twins (1975) **C-92m.** **½ D: Dick Richards. Alan Arkin, Sally Kellerman, Mackenzie Phillips, Alex Rocco, Charlie Martin Smith, Harry Dean Stanton. Appealing but aimless film about a pair of women who force nebbish Arkin to drive them to New Orleans from L.A. Retitled RAFFERTY AND THE HIGHWAY HUSTLERS for TV. Panavision. [R]▼

Rage (1966-U.S.-Mexican) **C-103m.** *½ D: Gilberto Gazcon. Glenn Ford, Stella Stevens, David Reynoso, Armando Silvestre,

Ariadna Welter. Overstated drama of misanthropic doctor Ford who contracts rabies and races clock across Mexican desert to get help.

Rage (1972) **C-104m.** ** D: George C. Scott. George C. Scott, Richard Basehart, Martin Sheen, Barnard Hughes, Nicolas Beauvy, Paul Stevens. When peaceful rancher Scott's young son is killed by chemical testing, he seeks revenge on those responsible for accident. Good photography, but Scott's transition from nice guy to killer isn't convincing. Scott's directorial debut. Panavision. [PG]▼▶

Rage: Carrie 2, The (1999) **C-104m.** ** D: Katt Shea. Emily Bergl, Jason London, Dylan Bruno, J. Smith-Cameron, Amy Irving, Zachery Ty Bryan, John Doe, Gordon Clapp, Rachel Blanchard, Mena Suvari. Years after CARRIE, another teenaged outsider in the same town is picked on by cruel fellow students, and again unleashes her telekinetic powers in climactic revenge. Well-acted but routine movie clumsily linked to the original. Irving's character, the only one from the original, is synthetically injected into the plot. [R]▼●▶

Rage in Harlem, A (1991) **C-115m.** **½ D: Bill Duke. Forest Whitaker, Gregory Hines, Robin Givens, Danny Glover, Zakes Mokae, Badja Djola, John Toles-Bey, Ron Taylor, Stack Pierce, George Wallace, T. K. Carter, Willard E. Pugh, Samm-Art Williams, Tyler Collins, Screamin' Jay Hawkins. Smooth operator from Mississippi (Givens) comes to Harlem to unload a stash of gold, and hooks up with a naive, nerdy mama's boy (Whitaker) who sees himself as her protector. Earnest attempt to recreate author Chester Himes' 1950s Harlem milieu doesn't quite come together in spite of some good performances. Can't hold a candle to COTTON COMES TO HARLEM (though the cop characters Gravedigger Jones and Coffin Ed reappear in this story). [R]▼●▶

Rage in Heaven (1941) **83m.** ** D: W. S. Van Dyke II. Robert Montgomery, Ingrid Bergman, George Sanders, Lucile Watson, Oscar Homolka, Philip Merivale, Matthew Boulton. Disappointing adaptation of James Hilton novel about mentally disturbed steel mill owner who plots unusual murder-revenge scheme; set in England.

Raggedy Ann and Andy (1977) **C-85m.** *½ D: Richard Williams. Voices of Didi Conn, Mark Baker, Fred Stuthman, Joe Silver. Slow-moving, uninvolving children's cartoon with endless songs by Joe Raposo that stop action dead in its tracks. Appealing characters with nowhere to go; only highlight is Camel with Wrinkled Knees singing "Song Blue." Panavision. [G]▼

Raggedy Man (1981) **C-94m.** *** D: Jack Fisk. Sissy Spacek, Eric Roberts, William Sanderson, Tracey Walter, Sam Shepard,

Henry Thomas, Carey Hollis, Jr. A young divorced woman with two children tries to forge a life for herself and her family in a small Texas town during WW2. Absorbing slice-of-life Americana with a misconceived melodramatic finale. Directorial debut for art director Fisk, who's Spacek's husband. [PG]▼●▶

Raging Bull (1980) **C/B&W-128m.** **** D: Martin Scorsese. Robert De Niro, Cathy Moriarty, Joe Pesci, Frank Vincent, Nicholas Colasanto, Theresa Saldana, John Turturro. Extraordinarily compelling look at prizefighter Jake La Motta, whose leading opponent outside the ring was always himself. That such an unappealing man could inspire so vivid a portrait is a tribute to the collaboration of Scorsese, De Niro, and writers Paul Schrader and Mardik Martin. There's not a false note in characterization or period detail. De Niro and editor Thelma Schoonmaker won richly deserved Academy Awards. [R]▼●▶

Raging Moon, The SEE: **Long Ago Tomorrow**

Ragman's Daughter, The (1972-British) **C-94m.** *** D: Harold Becker. Simon Rouse, Victoria Tennant, Patrick O'Connell, Leslie Sands. Stylishly filmed kitchen-sink drama written by Alan Sillitoe. Rouse is a young thief who falls in love with beautiful Tennant. Becker's first feature.

Ragtime (1981) **C-155m.** *** D: Milos Forman. James Cagney, Elizabeth McGovern, Howard E. Rollins, Jr., Mary Steenburgen, James Olson, Brad Dourif, Kenneth McMillan, Mandy Patinkin, Donald O'Connor, Pat O'Brien, Debbie Allen, Moses Gunn, Norman Mailer, Jeff Daniels, John Ratzenberger, Samuel L. Jackson, Fran Drescher, Michael Jeter. E. L. Doctorow's semifictional mosaic of 1906 America is glorious until Michael Weller's script narrows its focus to just one story thread: a black man's fanatical pursuit of justice. While the initial momentum is lost, there's still much to enjoy: fine performances (including Cagney's last in a theatrical film, after a 20-year hiatus), and Randy Newman's delightful score. Jeff Daniels' film debut. Later a Broadway musical. Todd-AO 35. [PG]▼●▶

Raiders of the Lost Ark (1981) **C-115m.** **** D: Steven Spielberg. Harrison Ford, Karen Allen, Wolf Kahler, Paul Freeman, Ronald Lacey, John Rhys-Davies, Denholm Elliott, Anthony Higgins, Alfred Molina. A roller-coaster ride of a movie, rekindling the spirit of Saturday matinee serials but outdoing them for genuine thrills and chills. Ford plays Indiana Jones, an archaeologist-adventurer who goes globe-trotting in search of a unique religious artifact and runs into bloodcurdling danger every step of the way. Perhaps a bit too much at times, but why carp? Conceived by Spielberg and George Lucas, with Philip Kaufman;

scripted by Lawrence Kasdan. Visual effects, editing, sound effects editing, and art direction–set decoration all earned Oscars. Followed by three INDIANA JONES films and TV series *The Young Indiana Jones Chronicles.* Panavision. [PG]▼●▶

Raid on Rommel (1971) **C-99m.** *½ D: Henry Hathaway. Richard Burton, John Colicos, Clinton Greyn, Wolfgang Preiss. Poor excuse to utilize old desert footage (mostly from TOBRUK) and new faces in worn-out WW2 actioner. Techniscope. [PG]▼●▶

Railroaded! (1947) **72m.** *** D: Anthony Mann. John Ireland, Sheila Ryan, Hugh Beaumont, Ed Kelly, Jane Randolph, Keefe Brasselle. Another tight, well-made, low-budget film noir by Anthony Mann. Ireland is a ruthless gangster who framed Ryan's brother for murder; Beaumont is a cop searching for answers. ▼●▶

Rails & Ties (2007) **C-101m.** *** D: Alison Eastwood. Kevin Bacon, Marcia Gay Harden, Miles Heizer, Marin Hinkle, Eugene Byrd, Bonnie Root, Margo Martindale. Railroad engineer (Bacon) runs his train into a woman who has driven her car onto the tracks. She wanted to commit suicide, but her 10-year-old son, left to fend for himself, seeks out the engineer, whom he blames for his mother's demise. Instead he finds a safe haven with Bacon's loving wife (Harden). Utterly contrived story is made tangible and moving by sensitive handling and a sure-footed cast. Directing debut for actress Eastwood, Clint's daughter; her brother Kyle Eastwood co-composed the score. Panavision. [PG-13]▶

Railway Children, The (1970-British) **C-109m.** *** D: Lionel Jeffries. Dinah Sheridan, Bernard Cribbins, William Mervyn, Iain Cuthbertson, Jenny Agutter, Gary Warren. Charming story of youthful trio whose one goal is to clear their father of false espionage prison sentence. Lovely Yorkshire locales add to overall effectiveness. From the novel by E. Nesbit. [G]▼▶

Rain (1932) **93m.** **½ D: Lewis Milestone. Joan Crawford, Walter Huston, William Gargan, Guy Kibbee, Walter Catlett, Beulah Bondi. Considered a flop in 1932, this version of Maugham's story looks better today. Crawford is good as South Seas island trollop confronted by fire-and-brimstone preacher Huston. Director Milestone does gymnastics with camera during stagier scenes; an interesting antique. Previously filmed as SADIE THOMPSON, then again as DIRTY GERTIE FROM HARLEM U.S.A. and MISS SADIE THOMPSON. Some prints run 77m.▼▶

Rain (2001-New Zealand) **C-92m.** **½ D: Christine Jeffs. Alicia Fulford-Wierzbicki, Sarah Peirse, Marton Csokas, Alistair Browning, Aaron Murphy. Interesting mood piece about an adolescent girl trying to find her way as her parents grow apart during a sea-side summer in the early 1970s. Knowing look at a young girl's sexual awakening while she noses into her mother's infidelity. Keenly observed drama will be too low key for some tastes; a sudden burst of melodrama toward the end is jarring. Jeffs adapted Kirsty Gunn's novel. ▼❍

Rainbow, The (1989-British) **C-104m.** **½ D: Ken Russell. Sammi Davis, Amanda Donohoe, Paul McGann, Christopher Gable, David Hemmings, Glenda Jackson. Director Russell's most restrained film in years (a relative term) is a prequel to his hit adaptation of D.H. Lawrence's *Women in Love*, with Davis as a sheltered young schoolteacher who's taken under the wing (sexually and otherwise) of worldly Donohoe. Many beautiful and striking moments don't quite jell, but still worth watching. Jackson appears as the mother of the character she played in WOMEN IN LOVE. [R] ▼●

Rainbow Thief, The (1990) **C-92m.** *½ D: Alexandro Jodorowsky. Peter O'Toole, Omar Sharif, Christopher Lee, Jude Alderson, Jane Chaplan. Impenetrable parable about an eccentric prince (and heir to a fortune) who lives underground, aided and abetted by a colorful thief. There may be some point to all of this, but it would require too much time to figure out. There's a reason this film never made it to theaters, despite its cast and director. ▼

Rainbow Warrior (1994-U.S.-New Zealand) **C-93m.** *½ D: Michael Tuchner. Jon Voight, Sam Neill, Bruno Lawrence, Kerry Fox, John Callen, Stacey Pickren. True story of 1985 bombing of a Greenpeace boat in New Zealand and the ensuing investigation. Complex tale of international conflict/intrigue is uninvolving. Neill gives a standout performance as a police superintendent. [PG] ▼●

Raining Stones (1993-British) **C-90m.** *** D: Kenneth Loach. Bruce Jones, Julie Brown, Ricky Tomlinson, Tom Hickey, Gemma Phoenix. Riveting drama focusing on a struggling out-of-work laborer (Jones) in grimy Manchester, England, a good Catholic who does whatever he can to scrape together enough money to support his wife and daughter. When faced with purchasing his child's communion dress, he unknowingly borrows its cost from a vicious, usurious loan shark. With telling irony, Loach vividly captures the frustrations and anger of honest workingfolk. ▼❍

Rainmaker, The (1956) **C-121m.** *** D: Joseph Anthony. Burt Lancaster, Katharine Hepburn, Wendell Corey, Lloyd Bridges, Earl Holliman, Cameron Prud'homme, Wallace Ford. Lancaster is in top form as a charismatic con man who offers hope to a Southwestern town beset by drought, and a woman whose life is at a crossroads. Hep-

burn is wonderful. N. Richard Nash play was later musicalized on Broadway as *110 in the Shade*. VistaVision. ▼●❍

Rainmaker, The (1997) **C-135m.** *** D: Francis Ford Coppola. Matt Damon, Danny DeVito, Claire Danes, Jon Voight, Mickey Rourke, Mary Kay Place, Danny Glover, Teresa Wright, Johnny Whitworth, Dean Stockwell, Virginia Madsen, Roy Scheider, Randy Travis, Andrew Shue. Solid, sure-footed adaptation of John Grisham's best-seller about an idealistic lawyer, fresh from school, who goes to work for a shameless ambulance-chaser, but focuses on the case most important to him: exposing an insurance company's refusal to pay a claim for a young man who is dying of leukemia. Cast to perfection, and filmed on location in Memphis . . . the finale, though, seems curiously subdued. Officially titled JOHN GRISHAM'S THE RAINMAKER. Panavision. [PG-13] ▼●

Rain Man (1988) **C-133m.** *** D: Barry Levinson. Dustin Hoffman, Tom Cruise, Valeria Golino, Jerry Molen, Jack Murdock, Michael D. Roberts, Bonnie Hunt. Young, self-centered hotshot goes home to the Midwest for his father's funeral, and learns not only that he's been cut out of his inheritance, but that he has a grown brother who's autistic, and who's been kept in an institution for most of his life. The balance of the film details the growing relationship between the two men. Top-drawer performances from Hoffman, as the idiot savant, and Cruise, as his selfish sibling, make this a must-see, even though the story meanders and becomes predictable. Director Levinson is the psychiatrist near the end. Winner of Oscars for Best Picture, Director, Actor (Hoffman), and Screenplay (Ronald Bass and Barry Morrow). [R] ▼●

Rain People, The (1969) **C-102m.** *** D: Francis Ford Coppola. James Caan, Shirley Knight, Robert Duvall, Marya Zimmet, Tom Aldredge, Laurie Crewes. Pregnant Long Island housewife, unable to take married life, flees husband and picks up simple-minded football player on the road. Strong acting and direction triumph over weak script in film whose subject matter was years ahead of its time. [R] ▼❍

Rains Came, The (1939) **104m.** **½ D: Clarence Brown. Myrna Loy, Tyrone Power, George Brent, Brenda Joyce, Nigel Bruce, Maria Ouspenskaya, Joseph Schildkraut, Mary Nash, Jane Darwell, Marjorie Rambeau, Henry Travers, H. B. Warner, Laura Hope Crews. Louis Bromfield novel reduced to Hollywood hokum, with married socialite Loy setting out to seduce dedicated Indian surgeon Power. Outstanding earthquake and flood scenes; the special effects earned an Academy Award. Remade as THE RAINS OF RANCHIPUR. ▼❍

Rains of Ranchipur, The (1955) **C-104m.**

**½ D: Jean Negulesco. Lana Turner, Richard Burton, Fred MacMurray, Joan Caulfield, Michael Rennie, Eugenie Leontovich. Superficial remake of THE RAINS CAME; story of wife of Englishman having affair with Hindu doctor. CinemaScope.

Raintree County (1957) **C-168m.** *** D: Edward Dmytryk. Elizabeth Taylor, Montgomery Clift, Eva Marie Saint, Lee Marvin, Nigel Patrick, Rod Taylor, Agnes Moorehead, Walter Abel, DeForest Kelley. Humongous MGM attempt to outdo GWTW, with Clift as a small-town Hoosier who makes the mistake of marrying Southern belle Taylor before the outbreak of the Civil War. Solid acting and memorable Johnny Green score help compensate for rambling, over-long script; Clift was disfigured in near-fatal car accident during production, and his performance understandably suffers for it. Roadshow version runs 183m. MGM Camera 65.▼●

Rain Without Thunder (1992) **C-86m.** *** D: Gary Bennett. Betty Buckley, Jeff Daniels, Frederic Forrest, Graham Greene, Linda Hunt, Carolyn McCormick, Austin Pendleton, Alyssa Rallo, Ali Thomas, Steve Zahn, Robert Earl Jones. Unique futuristic drama, told in documentary style and set in an America in which abortion is illegal. Young Thomas is incarcerated for aborting her pregnancy, and her mother (Buckley) is also put behind bars, convicted under New York State's new Unborn Child Kidnapping Act. Chilling (and politically loaded) tale. [PG-13] ▼

Raise the Red Lantern (1991-China-Taiwan-Hong Kong) **C-125m.** **** D: Zhang Yimou. Gong Li, Ma Jingwu, He Caifei, Cao Cuifeng, Jin Shuyuan, Kong Lin, Ding Weimin, Cui Zhihgang. Striking look at the life of a young concubine in 1920s China, as university-educated girl (Gong Li) is sent to feudal nobleman's palatial home to become his newest wife. The relationships between her and her predecessors—all of whom live on the premises—and the interaction among the women, the servants, and their master are brilliantly played out. An extraordinary view of sex, loyalty, intrigue, and female bonding. Deliberately paced, but worth watching for the changes in emotion that register on actress Gong Li's face alone. Screenplay by Ni Zhen, from a novel by Su Tong.▼●

Raise the Titanic (1980-British) **C-112m.** *½ D: Jerry Jameson. Jason Robards, Richard Jordan, David Selby, Anne Archer, Alec Guinness, J. D. Cannon. Long, dull adaptation of Clive Cussler's best-seller about intrigue leading to the biggest salvage job of all time. Silly plotting and laughable dialogue undermine excitement of climactic ship-raising. Technovision. [PG]▼●

Raise Your Voice (2004) **C-106m.** ** D: Sean McNamara. Hilary Duff, Rita Wilson, David Keith, Jason Ritter, Oliver James, Rebecca De Mornay, John Corbett, James Avery. Arizona teen with an overprotective father gets accepted at an esteemed L.A. music conservatory for the summer. Upon arrival, absolutely nothing surprising ever happens (unfriendly roommate, cool young professor, bitchy rival for the cute British classmate . . .). Did we mention the climactic recital? Duff's fans may enjoy this; others have been warned. Super 35. [PG] ▼●

Raising Arizona (1987) **C-92m.** ***½ D: Joel Coen. Nicolas Cage, Holly Hunter, Trey Wilson, John Goodman, William Forsythe, Sam McMurray, Frances McDormand, Randall (Tex) Cobb, M. Emmet Walsh. Formidably flaky comedy about an odd couple (chronic convenience-store robber Cage and former law-enforcement officer Hunter) who decide to kidnap one of a set of quintuplets, since they can't have a child of their own. Aggressively wacked-out sense of humor may not be for all tastes, but it's a heady mix of irony and slapstick. Look out for those chase scenes! Written by Ethan and Joel Coen; spry cinematography by Barry Sonnenfeld and music by Carter Burwell. [PG-13]▼●

Raising Cain (1992) **C-95m.** ** D: Brian De Palma. John Lithgow, Lolita Davidovich, Steven Bauer, Frances Sternhagen, Gregg Henry, Tom Bower, Mel Harris, Teri Austin, Gabrielle Carteris, Barton Heyman. Lithgow is the whole show here—literally—with more roles than you can count in this over-the-top thriller about a pair of twin brothers who'll stop at nothing to procure children for their father's scientific experiments. Tongue-in-cheek De Palma exercise (with nods to Hitchcock, Welles, and Michael Powell) is laced with satire, but the chills—and chuckles—don't add up to much. Not for the faint-hearted. [R]▼●

Raising Helen (2004) **C-119m.** **½ D: Garry Marshall. Kate Hudson, John Corbett, Joan Cusack, Hayden Panettiere, Spencer Breslin, Abigail Breslin, Helen Mirren, Sakina Jaffrey, Kevin Kilner, Felicity Huffman, Amber Valletta, Joseph Mazzello, Paris Hilton, Bernie Hiller. A busy, single executive assistant to a demanding boss inherits three children when her sister dies. Totally unprepared and inexperienced (unlike her other sister, quintessential homemaker Cusack), she tries to cope with sudden motherhood while making a living. Hudson is well cast in this sentimental slice of Hollywood hokum; it's pleasant but all too pat. Larry Miller and Hector Elizondo appear unbilled. [PG-13]▼●

Raising Victor Vargas (2003) **C-88m.** *** D: Peter Sollett. Victor Rasuk, Judy Marte, Donna Maldonado, Wilfree Vasquez, Altagracia Guzman. Disarmingly intimate portrait of a self-styled teenage stud on N.Y.C.'s Lower East Side who pursues a snobby girl with such tenacity that he wears down her resistance. A richly detailed slice of life, filmed with such intimacy (often in tight close-up) that you'd swear the conversations were overheard instead of staged. Writer-director Sollett does wonders with a mostly nonprofessional cast. Expanded remake of Sollett's short subject FIVE FEET AND RISING. Remarkably photographed by Tim Orr (GEORGE WASHINGTON). [R]▼▶️

Raisin in the Sun, A (1961) **128m. ****** D: Daniel Petrie. Sidney Poitier, Claudia McNeil, Ruby Dee, Diana Sands, Ivan Dixon, John Fiedler, Louis Gossett. Lorraine Hansberry play receives perceptive handling by outstanding cast in drama of black Chicago family's attempts to find sense in their constrained existence. Remade for TV in 1989 and in 2008. ▼●▶️

Rally 'Round the Flag, Boys! (1958) **C-106m. **½** D: Leo McCarey. Paul Newman, Joanne Woodward, Joan Collins, Jack Carson, Dwayne Hickman, Tuesday Weld, Gale Gordon. Disappointing film of Max Shulman's book about small community in uproar over projected missile base. CinemaScope.▶️

Rambling Rose (1991) **C-112m. **** D: Martha Coolidge. Laura Dern, Robert Duvall, Diane Ladd, Lukas Haas, John Heard, Kevin Conway, Robert J. Burke, Lisa Jakub, Evan Lockwood. Evocative tale set in 1930s Georgia, with Dern as an oversexed lost soul of a girl who comes to work for a genteel family headed by Duvall and Ladd. Colorful, nicely detailed, and well acted, with many pleasant surprises along the way. Ladd and Dern were the first real-life mother and daughter to be nominated for Oscars in the same year. Screenplay by Calder Willingham from his autobiographical novel. [R]▼●▶️

Rambo (2008-U.S.-German) **C-91m. *½** D: Sylvester Stallone. Sylvester Stallone, Julie Benz, Matthew Marsden, Graham McTavish, Rey Gallegos, Jake La Botz, Paul Schulze, Ken Howard. Stallone is a bit long in the tooth to be reprising his Rambo character, but here he is in the series' fourth installment (and first in two decades). This time around, everybody's favorite whacked-out Vietnam veteran–action hero emerges from a peaceful retirement in Thailand to rescue some captured missionaries and doctors in Myanmar (Burma). Needlessly bloody and unintentionally laughable. Stallone also coscripted. Alternate version runs 100m. Super 35. [R]▶️

Rambo: First Blood Part II (1985) **C-95m. *** D: George P. Cosmatos. Sylvester Stallone, Richard Crenna, Charles Napier, Julia Nickson, Steven Berkoff, Martin Kove. Comic-book action saga of one-man army who goes to Cambodia in search of American MIAs and finds he's been duped

by Uncle Sam. Never boring but incredibly dumb; if one were to take it seriously, it would also be offensive, as it exploits real-life frustrations of MIA families and Vietnam vets. Followed by RAMBO III. Panavision. [R]▼●▶️

Rambo III (1988) **C-101m. **½** D: Peter Macdonald. Sylvester Stallone, Richard Crenna, Marc de Jonge, Kurtwood Smith, Spiros Focas, Sasson Gabai. A definite improvement over PART II, this one remains firmly footed in the genre of Idiot Action Movies, as our brawny hero goes behind Russian-dominated battle lines in Afghanistan to rescue his friend and former superior (Crenna) from a prison fortress. Lots of explosions to keep things lively—and some (unintentionally?) hilarious dialogue too. Followed 20 years later by RAMBO. J-D-C Scope. [R]▼●▶️

Ramona and Beezus (2010) **C-103m. *** D: Elizabeth Allen. Joey King, Selena Gomez, John Corbett, Bridget Moynahan, Ginnifer Goodwin, Josh Duhamel, Jason Spevack, Sandra Oh. Based on Beverly Cleary's beloved children's books, this might have been called *Leave It to Beezus*, but it's Ramona who resembles a female version of Beaver Cleaver. Economic problems force dad out of his job, inspiring Ramona to embark on a series of moneymaking ideas, much to the chagrin of her older sister, Beezus. CGI sequences in which she engages in her own fantasy world fall flat, but the adorable King makes this work for the young girls to whom it is targeted. Super 35. [G]▶️

Rampage (1963) **C-98m. **½** D: Phil Karlson. Robert Mitchum, Elsa Martinelli, Jack Hawkins, Sabu, Cely Carillo, Emile Genest. German gamehunter (Hawkins), his mistress (Martinelli), and hunting guide (Mitchum) form love triangle, with men battling for Elsa. Elmer Bernstein's score is memorable.▶️

Rampage (1992) **C-97m. *** D: William Friedkin. Michael Biehn, Alex McArthur, Nicholas Campbell, Deborah van Valkenburgh, John Harkins, Art La Fleur, Billy Green Bush, Royce D. Applegate, Grace Zabriskie, Carlos Palomino, Andy Romano. A prosecutor has to prove that a serial killer's unspeakably heinous crimes were the product of a legally sane mind. Very rough, not for the squeamish, and not for too many others, either. Shot in 1987. McArthur is exceptionally creepy as the killer. [R]▼●

Rampage at Apache Wells (1966-German) **C-90m. *** D: Harold Philipps. Stewart Granger, Pierre Brice, Macha Meril, Harold Leipnitz. Granger stars as Old Shatterhand, who fights for rights of Indians taken in by crooked white men. Adequate acting but atrocious dubbing. Ultrascope.

Ramparts of Clay (1971-French-Algerian) **C-85m. *** D: Jean-Louis Bertucelli. Leila Schenna. Intriguing film about Tunisian woman, disillusioned with her way of life, who becomes involved with strike between a wealthy company and poor villagers. Very strong for patient, critical viewers; for others, boredom. [PG] ▼▶

Rampo (1994-Japanese) **C-100m.** *** D: Kazuyoshi Okuyama. Naoto Takenaka, Michiko Hada, Masahiro Motoki, Mikijiro Hira. Japanese mystery writer Edogawa Rampo hears of a bizarre murder that is eerily close to the plot of one of his banned murder thrillers. When he meets the widow of the murdered man, he discovers her to be exactly like his fictional heroine. This elegant and lush film was reshot (more than 60 percent new footage) after producer Okuyama was dissatisfied with first director Rentaro Mayuzumi's efforts. Aka THE MYSTERY OF RAMPO. [R] ▼▶

Ran (1985-Japanese-French) **C-161m.** ***½ D: Akira Kurosawa. Tatsuya Nakadai, Akira Terao, Jinpachi Nezu, Daisuke Ryu, Mieko Harada, Peter, Hisashi Igawa. Beautifully filmed adaptation of Shakespeare's *King Lear*, with Nakadai as a warlord who turns over his domain to his eldest son, inducing a power struggle by his two younger sons. Slowly paced and overly expository at the start, epic picks up with two superb battle scenes. Harada is excellent in supporting role as the most evil of women, getting her just desserts in violent fashion. Oscar winner for Costume Design. [R] ▼●▶

Rancho Deluxe (1975) **C-93m.** ***½ D: Frank Perry. Jeff Bridges, Sam Waterston, Elizabeth Ashley, Charlene Dallas, Clifton James, Slim Pickens, Harry Dean Stanton, Richard Bright, Patti D'Arbanville. Off-beat present-day comedy centers on two casual cattle rustlers; cult favorite written by Thomas McGuane (92 IN THE SHADE), with music by Jimmy Buffett (who also appears in the film). [R] ▼●▶

Rancho Notorious (1952) **C-89m.** *** D: Fritz Lang. Marlene Dietrich, Arthur Kennedy, Mel Ferrer, Lloyd Gough, Gloria Henry, William Frawley, Jack Elam, George Reeves. Entertaining, unusual Western with Kennedy looking for murderer of his sweetheart, ending up at Marlene's bandit hideout. Colorful characters spice up routine story by Daniel Taradash. ▼●▶

Random Harvest (1942) **126m.** ***½ D: Mervyn LeRoy. Ronald Colman, Greer Garson, Philip Dorn, Susan Peters, Henry Travers, Reginald Owen, Bramwell Fletcher, Margaret Wycherly, Ann Richards. Colman is left an amnesiac after WW1, and saved from life in a mental institution by vivacious music-hall entertainer Garson. James Hilton novel given supremely entertaining MGM treatment, with Colman and Garson at their best. Screenplay by Claudine West, George Froeschel, and Arthur Wimperis. ▼●▶

Random Hearts (1999) **C-133m.** *½ D:

Sydney Pollack. Harrison Ford, Kristin Scott Thomas, Charles S. Dutton, Bonnie Hunt, Dennis Haysbert, Sydney Pollack, Paul Guilfoyle, Peter Coyote, Bill Cobbs, Richard Jenkins, Edie Falco. Sub-par political movie, sub-par D.C. cop movie and sub-par romance get bludgeoned into one in this critical/commercial flop about a police sergeant and congresswoman who discover that their mates—recently killed in the same airliner crash—were having an affair. Gloomy, lugubrious, heavily altered adaptation of Warren Adler's novel suffers from one of the rare constipated Ford performances. Every once in a while it wakes up long enough to remember it's an Internal Affairs movie and that a few heads have to be bashed. [R] ▼▶

Rango (2011) **C-107m.** ** D: Gore Verbinski. Voices of Johnny Depp, Isla Fisher, Abigail Breslin, Ned Beatty, Alfred Molina, Bill Nighy, Stephen Root, Harry Dean Stanton, Timothy Olyphant, Ray Winstone. A loopy pet lizard who's used to amusing himself with the inanimate objects with whom he shares an aquarium finds himself stranded in the Mojave Desert. Wandering into a desolate town, he adopts the persona of a Western hero and becomes the local sheriff and potential savior. Depp's amusing, off-the-wall verbal riffs and a modern spin on Western mythology make this fun for a while, until the story runs dry (in every sense of the word). Staging is impressive, thanks to visual consultant Roger Deakins, but the character design emphasizes realistic desert creatures, bringing a new level of ugliness to mainstream animation. Digital Widescreen. [PG] ▶

Ransom! (1956) **109m.** **½ D: Alex Segal. Glenn Ford, Donna Reed, Leslie Nielsen, Juano Hernandez, Alexander Scourby, Juanita Moore, Robert Keith. Brooding narrative of business tycoon Ford's efforts to rescue his son who's been kidnapped. Remade in 1996.

Ransom (1975) SEE: **Terrorists, The**

Ransom (1977) **C-90m.** **½ D: Richard Compton. Oliver Reed, Deborah Raffin, Stuart Whitman, Jim Mitchum, John Ireland, Paul Koslo. Pretty good programmer about a town's efforts to catch a killer. Originally titled ASSAULT ON PARADISE, then MANIAC. ▼

Ransom (1996) **C-120m.** *** D: Ron Howard. Mel Gibson, Rene Russo, Gary Sinise, Delroy Lindo, Lili Taylor, Brawley Nolte, Liev Schreiber, Evan Handler, Donnie Wahlberg, Dan Hedaya. Gripping thriller about a ragged team of kidnappers who snatch the son of a self-made millionaire; soon, what should have been a standard kidnap-and-ransom transaction becomes a dangerous game of cat and mouse between the tycoon and the cocky ringleader. Plenty of twists and turns in this remake of the

1956 film of the same name. That's Nick Nolte's son as the victim. Coscenarist Richard Price appears briefly as Sinise's partner in an early scene. [R]▼●◗

Rapa Nui (1994) **C-107m.** *½ D: Kevin Reynolds. Jason Scott Lee, Esai Morales, Sandrine Holt, Zac Wallace, George Henare, Eru Potaka-Dewes. Lumbering, highly romanticized saga of Easter Island ("Rapa Nui"), the remote southern Pacific outpost whose mammoth human-faced statues have long baffled historians. Set in 1680, prior to Dutch colonization, with hero Lee (of the Long Ear tribe) and villain Morales (of the Short Ears) as rivals since boyhood, now facing civil war. Climactic endurance test—a grueling race on land and sea—resembles one of those splashy MTV "sports" events. Panavision. [R]▼●

Rape of Europa, The (2006) **C/B&W-117m.** *** D: Richard Berge, Nicole Newnham, Bonni Cohen; narrated by Joan Allen. Fascinating documentary compels attention and interest as an examination of Adolf Hitler's obsession with claiming Europe's art masterworks during WW2. Filmmakers celebrate incidents of ingenious heroism—notably the bold removal and concealment of Louvre treasures in France just prior to the German Occupation—and recount the remarkable efforts of the Monuments Men, a unit of U.S. Army specialists charged with locating and recovering art seized by the Nazis. Inspired by an authoritative book of the same title by Lynn H. Nicholas.◗

Rape of Malaya SEE: **Town Like Alice, A**

Rapid Fire (1992) **C-95m.** ** D: Dwight H. Little. Brandon Lee, Powers Boothe, Nick Mancuso, Raymond J. Barry, Kate Hodge, Tzi Ma, Tony Longo, Michael Paul Chan, Dustin Nguyen, John Vickery. Showcase for Bruce Lee's handsome son is more like ENTER THE LIZARD, though its script is freewheeling enough to include stopoffs in a nude modeling class, an abandoned bowling alley, and Beijing's Tiananmen Square. A bounty of bullets, but the only love scene backs its standard gauzy navel-'n'-nipple expedition with a strident guitar and an unfortunately named tune: "I Can't Find My Way." Mancuso's amusing bad guy is a standout. [R]▼●◗

Rappin' (1985) **C-92m.** ** D: Joel Silberg. Mario Van Peebles, Tasia Valenza, Charles Flohe, Leo O'Brien, Eriq La Salle, Richie Abanes, Kadeem Hardison, Harry Goz. Just what the world needs, another breakdancing–rap music musical. This one chronicles the plight of breakdancer/ex-con Van Peebles and his conflicts with street gangster Flohe and contractor Goz. [PG]▼◗

Rapture, The (1991) **C-102m.** *** D: Michael Tolkin. Mimi Rogers, Patrick Bauchau, David Duchovny, Kimberly Cullum, Will Patton, James Le Gros. Beautiful, hedonistic young woman with droning,

dead-end job opts for super-Fundamentalist religious fanaticism. Singular drama about one woman's literal ascension to heaven features swinging group sex, one genuinely shocking maternal act, and a straight-faced cameo by at least one Horseman of the Apocalypse. Not for every taste, this much-debated film truly rushes in where virtually no others have dared to tread. Scripted by first-time director Tolkin. Rogers gives a four-barrelled performance. [R]▼●◗

Rare Breed, The (1966) **C-108m.** *** D: Andrew V. McLaglen. James Stewart, Maureen O'Hara, Brian Keith, Juliet Mills, Jack Elam, Ben Johnson, Don Galloway. Cowhand Stewart is changed by British O'Hara's conviction that her Hereford bull, new to Texas, will produce better cattle. Keith (in red wig and beard) has a grand time as a Scottish rancher. Odd part-comedy Western on the unusual subject of improving cattle breeds. Hampered only by too much obvious studio shooting. Panavision. ▼◗

Rascal (1969) **C-85m.** **½ D: Norman Tokar. Steve Forrest, Bill Mumy, Pamela Toll, Bettye Ackerman, Elsa Lanchester, Henry Jones. Disney adaptation of Sterling North's well-regarded autobiographical novel about his boyhood friendship with raccoon; reworked to Disney formula, with pleasant but predictable results. [G] ▼

Rashevski's Tango (2003-Belgian-French) **C-99m.** *** D: Sam Garbarski. Hippolyte Girardot, Ludmila Mikaël, Michel Jonasz, Daniel Mesguich, Nathan Cogan, Jonathan Zaccaï, Tania Garbarski, Rudi Rosenberg, Selma Kouchy, Moscu Alcalay. The death of a matriarch spurs this portrait of a family, living in Belgium, whose various members—three generations strong—deal with their Jewish heritage in vastly different ways, alternately serious, poignant, ironic, and absurd. As the background of this culturally dysfunctional clan is gradually revealed, we come to understand why they act the way they do. Provocative and original, with deft dramatic and comedic touches. Cowritten by the director.◗

Rashomon (1950-Japanese) **88m.** **** D: Akira Kurosawa. Toshiro Mifune, Machiko Kyo, Masayuki Mori, Takashi Shimura. Kurosawa's first huge international success is superlative study of truth and human nature; four people involved in a rape-murder tell varying accounts of what happened. The film's very title has become part of our language. Oscar winner as Best Foreign Film. Remade as THE OUTRAGE.▼●◗

Rasputin (1985-Russian) **C-107m.** *** D: Elem Klimov. Alexei Petrenko, Anatoly Romashin, Velta Linei, Alice Freindlikh. Complex, impressive drama with Petrenko appropriately (and at times brilliantly) oily as the famed mad monk. A good film which might have been great if so many hands had not tinkered with it. It allegedly was completed in 1977, screened at the Moscow Film Festival in 1981 (at 148m.), and barred from the West until 1985. Sovscope.▼

Rasputin and the Empress (1932) **123m.** *** D: Richard Boleslavsky. John, Ethel, and Lionel Barrymore, Ralph Morgan, Diana Wynyard, Tad Alexander, C. Henry Gordon, Edward Arnold, Jean Parker. Good drama that should have been great, with all three Barrymores in colorful roles, unfolding story of mad monk's plotting against Russia. Contrary to expectations, it's Lionel, not John, who plays Rasputin. The three Barrymores' only film together; Ethel's talkie debut. Wynyard's first film.▼O▶

Rasputin—the Mad Monk (1966-British) **C-92m.** ** D: Don Sharp. Christopher Lee, Barbara Shelley, Richard Pasco, Francis Matthews. Confused historical drama of "monk" who actually controlled Russia before Revolution. Script uncommonly bad; Lee's performance manages to redeem film. CinemaScope.▼O▶

Ratatouille (2007) **C-111m.** ***½ D: Brad Bird. Voices of Patton Oswalt, Ian Holm, Lou Romano, Brian Dennehy, Peter Sohn, Peter O'Toole, Brad Garrett, Janeane Garofalo, Will Arnett, James Remar, John Ratzenberger, Brad Bird. Animated charmer about Remy, a highly cultivated rat with a genius for cooking, who is separated from his family in the French countryside and lands in a Parisian restaurant. There he teams up with a lowly kitchen assistant to become the toast of the town. A few longueurs in the story are compensated by stunning evocation of character and environment; director-writer Bird and Pixar's meticulous attention to detail make this a feast for the eyes. Fine voice work, with Oswalt an endearing Remy and O'Toole a treat as formidable food critic Anton Ego. Oscar winner for Best Animated Feature Film. PixarVision. [G]▶

Ratboy (1986) **C-105m.** *½ D: Sondra Locke. Sondra Locke, Robert Townsend, Christopher Hewett, Larry Hankin, Gerrit Graham, Louie Anderson. Window dresser Locke stumbles across a half-man, half-rat—then tries to parlay him into show-biz success. Locke's directorial debut is technically competent, but film plays like an E.T./ELEPHANT MAN derivation that's no longer fresh. Barely released. [PG-13]▼

Ratcatcher (1999-British) **C-93m.** **½ D: Lynne Ramsay. William Eadie, Tommy Flanagan, Mandy Matthews, Michelle Stewart, Lynne Ramsay, Jr., Leanne Mullen. Impressive feature writing-directing debut for Ramsay, who spins an oddly whimsical tale against the bleakest of backdrops, a dirt-poor Scottish neighborhood. A 12-year-old boy is accidentally involved in another lad's death; suppressing this knowledge adds to his existing anxieties, living with a drunken dad and a worn-down mother. Distinctive but terribly downbeat.▼▶

Rat Race, The (1960) **C-105m.** *** D: Robert Mulligan. Tony Curtis, Debbie Reynolds, Jack Oakie, Kay Medford, Don Rickles, Joe Bushkin. Comedy-drama of would-be musician (Curtis) and dancer (Reynolds) coming to N.Y.C., platonically sharing an apartment, and falling in love. Nice comic cameos by Oakie and Medford. Script by Garson Kanin, from his play.

Rat Race (2001) **C-112m.** **½ D: Jerry Zucker. Whoopi Goldberg, Jon Lovitz, Rowan Atkinson, Cuba Gooding, Jr., John Cleese, Kathy Najimy, Breckin Meyer, Amy Smart, Seth Green, Vince Vieluf, Lanai Chapman, Paul Rodriguez, Wayne Knight, Dave Thomas, Kathy Bates, Dean Cain. Game attempt to recapture the spirit of IT'S A MAD MAD MAD MAD WORLD, with Las Vegas casino owner Cleese enticing a group of disparate people to participate in a race: the first to get to a New Mexico railroad depot locker will claim two million dollars. Not every comic detour pays off, but there are many laugh-out-loud gags and inspired moments (especially with Atkinson and Lovitz). Panavision. [PG-13]▼▶

Rats, The SEE: **Deadly Eyes**

Rat's Tale, A (1997-German) **C-89m.** ** D: Michael F. Huse. Lauren Hutton, Beverly D'Angelo, Jerry Stiller, Josef Ostendorf; voices of Dee Bradley Baker, Lynsey Bartilson. A colony of rats living underground in N.Y.C. is threatened by a greedy developer who wants to tear down their wharf—and in the meantime is using a toxic pesticide. Furry marionettes star in this English-language version of a German film with a handful of live actors and occasional special effects. Amusing for young children, but its pacing and European sensibility may not suit some fidgety viewers. Based on the award-winning book by Tor Seidler. [G]▼O

Ravagers (1979) **C-91m.** BOMB D: Richard Compton. Richard Harris, Ann Turkel, Ernest Borgnine, Art Carney, Anthony James, Woody Strode, Alana Hamilton. This instant tax loss finds Harris searching for civilization in 1991 after most human life has been wiped out. Instead, he finds Borgnine. Panavision. [PG]

Raven, The (1935) **62m.** *** D: Louis Friedlander (Lew Landers). Karloff (Boris Karloff), Bela Lugosi, Irene Ware, Lester Matthews, Samuel S. Hinds. Momentous teaming of horror greats with Lugosi as doctor with Poe obsession, Karloff a victim of his wicked schemes. Hinds is subjected to torture from "The Pit and the Pendulum" in film's climax. Great fun throughout. ▼O▶

Raven, The (1943-French) SEE: **Le Corbeau**

Raven, The (1963) **C-86m.** *** D: Roger Corman. Vincent Price, Boris Karloff, Peter Lorre, Hazel Court, Jack Nicholson, Olive Sturgess. Funny horror satire finds magicians Price and Lorre challenging power-hungry colleague Karloff. Climactic sorcerer's duel is a highlight. Screenplay by Richard Matheson, "inspired" by the Poe poem. Panavision.▼●◗

Ravenous (1999) **C-98m. **½ D: Antonia Bird. Guy Pearce, Robert Carlyle, Jeffrey Jones, David Arquette, Jeremy Davies, John Spencer, Stephen Spinella, Neal McDonough, Joseph Running Fox, Sheila Tousey. In 1847, cavalry officer Pearce is sent to a remote California fort, where a stranger (Carlyle) stumbles out of the wintry darkness with a horrifying tale of cannibalism, a tale that isn't over yet . . . Unique blend of comedy, Western, horror, and satire is, obviously, not for every "taste." Grisly and off-putting, but ambitious and intelligent as well. Super 35. [R]▼●◗

Raw Deal (1948) **78m. *** D: Anthony Mann. Dennis O'Keefe, Claire Trevor, Marsha Hunt, Raymond Burr, John Ireland. Beautifully made, hard-boiled story of O'Keefe escaping from jail and taking out revenge on slimy Burr, who framed him; what's more, he gets caught between love of two women. Tough and convincing, with Burr a sadistic heavy.▼●◗

Raw Deal (1986) **C-97m. *½ D: John Irvin. Arnold Schwarzenegger, Kathryn Harrold, Darren McGavin, Sam Wanamaker, Paul Shenar, Steven Hill, Joe Regalbuto, Robert Davi, Ed Lauter, Blanche Baker. Stupid action movie about brawny ex-Fed who helps an old pal clean some dirty laundry—and bust a major crime ring. Sense of humor helps . . . but not enough. J-D-C Scope. [R]▼●◗

Raw Edge, The SEE: **Babysitter, The** (1975)

Rawhide (1951) **86m. *** D: Henry Hathaway. Tyrone Power, Susan Hayward, Hugh Marlowe, Dean Jagger, Edgar Buchanan, Jack Elam, George Tobias, Jeff Corey. Taut Western saga about a motley gang of no-goods holding Power and Hayward prisoner at a stagecoach way station. Straightforward and unspectacular but well done, with a crackerjack cast and striking use of Lone Pine locations. Remake of 1935 gangster saga SHOW THEM NO MERCY! ▼◗

Raw Meat (1972-British) **C-87m. **½ D: Gary Sherman. Donald Pleasence, David Ladd, Sharon Gurney, Christopher Lee, Norman Rossington, Clive Swift. Entertaining though overdone horror tale of descendants of people trapped in an abandoned underground tunnel preying as cannibals on modern-day London travelers. Good atmosphere; filmed at the Russell Square station. Originally titled DEATH LINE. [R]◗

Ray (2004) **C-153m. *** D: Taylor Hackford. Jamie Foxx, Kerry Washington, Regina King, Clifton Powell, Aunjanue Ellis, Harry Lennix, Terrence Dashon Howard, Larenz Tate, Bokeem Woodbine, Sharon Warren, Curtis Armstrong, Richard Schiff, C. J. Sanders, David Krumholtz. The genuinely remarkable story of Ray Charles is told within the framework of a conventional Hollywood biopic, anchored by flashbacks to emotional touchstones in Charles' boyhood and spiked by his sensational record hits. Foxx is uncannily perfect (lip-synching Charles' recordings), and the women (Washington as his wife, Ellis as his first vocalist and mistress, King as her replacement—the first Raelette—and Warren as his mother) are superb. Won two Oscars, for Best Actor and Sound Mixing. [PG-13]▼◗

Razorback (1984-Australian) **C-95m.** BOMB D: Russell Mulcahy. Gregory Harrison, Arkie Whiteley, Bill Kerr, Chris Haywood. Ludicrous horror film about a giant pig terrorizing the Australian countryside. Inauspicious feature debut by music video director Mulcahy. Panavision. [R]▼

Razor's Edge, The (1946) **146m. ***½ D: Edmund Goulding. Tyrone Power, Gene Tierney, John Payne. Anne Baxter, Clifton Webb, Herbert Marshall, Lucile Watson, Frank Latimore. Slick adaptation of Maugham's philosophical novel, with Marshall as the author, Power as hero seeking true meaning of life, Baxter in Oscar-winning role as a dipsomaniac, Elsa Lanchester sparkling in bit as social secretary. Screenplay by Lamar Trotti. Long but engrossing; remade in 1984.▼●◗

Razor's Edge, The (1984) **C-128m. **½ D: John Byrum. Bill Murray, Theresa Russell, Catherine Hicks, Denholm Elliott, James Keach, Peter Vaughan, Brian Doyle-Murray, Saeed Jaffrey. Ambitious, if anachronistic, remake of 1946 film with enough plot for *five* movies. Young American survives WW1 and begins to question meaning of his life—while his closest friends go through personal crises of their own. It's hard to read much spiritual thought on Murray's deadpan face, but he gives it a good try (and cowrote script with director Byrum). Russell comes off best in the showy role previously played by Anne Baxter. Warts and all, it's still an interesting film. J-D-C Scope. [PG-13]▼●◗

Reader, The (2008-U.S.-British-German) **C-124m. ***½ D: Stephen Daldry. Kate Winslet, Ralph Fiennes, David Kross, Lena Olin, Bruno Ganz, Matthias Habich, Susanne Lothar, Karoline Herfurth, Alexandra Maria Lara, Volker Bruch, Burghart Klaussner. In 1950s Germany, a naïve 15-year-old boy (Kross) has a chance encounter with an older woman who becomes his lover; later he learns that she was a guard at a concentration camp. The relationship still colors his life, as we see in modern-day scenes with Fiennes as the boy grown up.

David Hare adapted Bernhard Schlink's semi-autobiographical novel that tackles the moral dilemmas facing the generation of Germans who grew up in the years following WW2. Meticulously made and utterly fascinating. Winslet won Best Actress Oscar for her performance. Striking score by Nico Muhly. [R]❿

Read My Lips (2001-French) **C-115m.** ✳✳✳ D: Jacques Audiard. Vincent Cassel, Emmanuelle Devos, Olivier Gourmet, Olivier Perrier, Olivia Bonamy, Bernard Alane. A partially deaf, ignored female office worker hires a thuggish ex-con as her assistant and they become partners in crime. Fetishistic psychosexual heist thriller doesn't have a likable character in the mix but is so full of unexpected twists and turns you'll get hooked. Cassel and Devos are frighteningly good as the kinky outcasts. Audiard also cowrote. Super 35. [R]▼❿

Ready to Rumble (2000) **C-106m.** ✳½ D: Brian Robbins. David Arquette, Oliver Platt, Scott Caan, Bill Goldberg, Rose McGowan, Joe Pantoliano, Martin Landau, Diamond Dallas Page, Caroline Rhea. Lowbrow time-waster about simpleminded wrestling addicts Arquette and Caan, who believe the "sport" is for real, and try to help salvage the career of their disgraced favorite wrestler (Platt, embarrassingly miscast). Our "heroes" are portable-toilet maintenance workers, which allows for plenty of bathroom humor. Made in conjunction with WCW (World Championship Wrestling); a number of its stars appear in cameos. [PG-13]▼❿

Ready to Wear (Prêt-à-Porter) (1994) **C-133m.** BOMB D: Robert Altman. Marcello Mastroianni, Sophia Loren, Kim Basinger, Julia Roberts, Tim Robbins, Anouk Aimée, Stephen Rea, Forest Whitaker, Lauren Bacall, Linda Hunt, Sally Kellerman, Tracey Ullman, Danny Aiello, Teri Garr, Rupert Everett, Richard E. Grant, Lili Taylor, Jean-Pierre Cassel, Jean Rochefort, Michel Blanc, Lyle Lovett, François Cluzet, Sam Robards, Ute Lemper, Chiara Mastroianni, Harry Belafonte, Cher. Mind-numbingly awful Altman collage about the fashion industry as it descends on Paris for the annual runway shows. No plot, no momentum, no point to any of this; a particularly egregious waste of Loren and Mastroianni (who reprise the striptease from YESTERDAY, TODAY AND TOMORROW). Most telling comment is made within the film itself: characters keep stepping in dog poop. Super 35. [R]▼❿

Real Blonde, The (1998) **C-105m.** ✳✳½ D: Tom DiCillo. Matthew Modine, Catherine Keener, Daryl Hannah, Maxwell Caulfield, Elizabeth Berkley, Marlo Thomas, Bridgette Wilson, Kathleen Turner, Christopher Lloyd, Dave Chappelle, Daniel Von Bargen, Denis Leary, Buck Henry, Steve Buscemi, Alexandra Wentworth. N.Y.C. slice-of-life about a wannabe actor and his girlfriend, a makeup artist to a top fashion model. Attempts to tackle such issues as illusion vs. reality, superficiality, sexual role-playing and the worlds of modeling and soap operas. A mixed bag with good individual scenes and performances. How well you respond may depend on your tolerance for Modine's character, who's a jerk. [R]▼❿

Real Cancun, The (2003) **C-96m.** ✳✳½ D: Rick De Oliveira. Reality TV in movie form: a diverse group of young people are chosen to spend spring break at a Mexican resort, and cameras observe their interaction (and massive intake of liquor). One straight-arrow, non-drinking boy becomes the film's focal point. Slickly produced and edited, the results are surprisingly entertaining, although parents may want to shoot themselves—or their kids—after seeing it. Produced by the creators of *The Real World*, Mary-Ellis Bunim and Jonathan Murray. [R]▼❿

Real Genius (1985) **C-104m.** ✳✳½ D: Martha Coolidge. Val Kilmer, Gabe Jarret, Michelle Meyrink, William Atherton, Jonathan Gries, Patti D'Arbanville. Idealistic whiz-kid is recruited by self-styled genius (Atherton) to join his college think tank—only to find that its members are being exploited, co-opted, and generally burned out. Potentially clever satire turns into just another youth/revenge comedy with caricatures instead of characters. Panavision. [PG]▼❿

Reality Bites (1994) **C-99m.** ✳✳½ D: Ben Stiller. Winona Ryder, Ethan Hawke, Ben Stiller, Janeane Garofalo, Steve Zahn, Swoosie Kurtz, Joe Don Baker, John Mahoney, Harry O'Reilly, Susan Norfleet, David Pirner, Keith David, Kevin Pollak, Karen Duffy, David Spade, Renée Zellweger. An incisive examination of Generation X, whose young people are confused, and repelled by the world being handed to them; on the other hand, a traditional love triangle, with Ryder trying to choose between straight-arrow Stiller and laid-back superdude Hawke (who's so cool he doesn't unwrap a candy bar before biting off a piece). Generally well done, with Ryder especially appealing, and Garofalo a standout as her best friend. Debuting director Stiller features his mom, Anne Meara, as a newspaperwoman, and his sister, Amy, as Ryder's "Psychic Phone Partner." Written by Helen Childress (who has a bit as a waitress). Jeanne Tripplehorn has unbilled cameo. [PG-13]▼❿

Real Life (1979) **C-99m.** ✳✳½ D: Albert Brooks. Albert Brooks, Charles Grodin, Frances Lee McCain, J. A. Preston, Matthew Tobin. Writer-director-comedian Brooks' first feature doesn't sustain its comic premise as well as his hilarious short subjects, but still presents the world's greatest put-on artist in a compatible vehicle, as a shifty opportunist who sets out to make a filmed record of a typical American family. Written by Brooks, Monica Johnson, and Harry Shearer. Cowriter Shearer plays the helmeted cameraman Pete and James L. Brooks appears as a driving instructor. [PG]▼●

Real McCoy, The (1993) **C-106m.** *½ D: Russell Mulcahy. Kim Basinger, Val Kilmer, Terence Stamp, Gailard Sartain, Zach English, Raynor Scheine. Lame, completely inept caper film with Basinger cast as a cat burglar/ex-con who wants to go straight, but is forced into pulling off one last heist when her son is kidnapped. [PG-13]▼●

Real Men (1987) **C-96m.** *½ D: Dennis Feldman. James Belushi, John Ritter, Barbara Barrie, Bill Morey, Iva Andersen, Mark Herrier. Unfunny spy satire with CIA agent Belushi recruiting reluctant Ritter as a courier. Barely released to theaters, and with good reason. [PG-13] ▼●

Real Women Have Curves (2002) **C-86m.** ** D: Patricia Cardoso. America Ferrera, Lupe Ontiveros, Ingrid Oliu, George Lopez, Brian Sites, Soledad St. Hilaire, Jorge Cervera, Jr., Felipe De Alba. Quiet character study of a Mexican-American teenage girl about to graduate from high school and the life decisions she must make. Ontiveros is excellent as a domineering, neurotic mother, and Ferrera is good as the young woman in transition, but the film tries to deal with too much at once and becomes muddled and unfocused. [PG-13]▼●

Re-Animator (1985) **C-86m.** *** D: Stuart Gordon. Jeffrey Combs, Bruce Abbott, Barbara Crampton, Robert Sampson, David Gale. Knockout horror thriller and black comedy about H. P. Lovecraft's character Herbert West (Combs), an uppity young medical student who develops a serum to bring the dead back to life. Debut film director Gordon goes entertainingly over the line, especially in an off-color scene involving heroine Crampton and a lustful severed head. Major defect: Richard Band's music score, which is too reminiscent of Bernard Herrmann's classic PSYCHO sound track. *Lengthened* (and toned down) by Gordon for video. Followed by BRIDE OF RE-ANIMATOR. [R was surrendered] ▼●

Reaping, The (2007) **C-96m.** *½ D: Stephen Hopkins. Hilary Swank, David Morrissey, Idris Elba, AnnaSophia Robb, Stephen Rea, William Ragsdale, John McConnell. Dopey supernatural "thriller" finds Swank as a disillusioned former missionary who tries to discredit unexplained biblical phenomena. She comes upon a town where the river has turned bloodred and is being inundated with what appear to be the "ten plagues" of the Old Testament. Well-worn premise and indifferent acting sink this enterprise before we can even ask, "What the devil is going

on here?" or more important, "Who cares?" Super 35. [R]●

Reap the Wild Wind (1942) **C-124m.** *** D: Cecil B. DeMille. Ray Milland, John Wayne, Paulette Goddard, Raymond Massey, Robert Preston, Susan Hayward, Charles Bickford, Hedda Hopper, Louise Beavers, Martha O'Driscoll, Lynne Overman. Brawling DeMille hokum of 19th-century salvagers in Florida, with Goddard as fiery Southern belle, Milland and Wayne fighting for her, Massey as odious villain. Exciting underwater scenes, with the special effects earning an Oscar. Milland good in off-beat characterization.▼●

Rear Window (1954) **C-112m.** **** D: Alfred Hitchcock. James Stewart, Grace Kelly, Wendell Corey, Thelma Ritter, Raymond Burr, Judith Evelyn, Ross Bagdasarian. One of Hitchcock's most stylish thrillers has photographer Stewart confined to wheelchair in his apartment, using binoculars to pass the time "spying" on courtyard neighbors, and discovering a possible murder. Inventive Cornell Woolrich story adapted by John Michael Hayes. Stewart, society girlfriend Kelly, and no-nonsense nurse Ritter make a wonderful trio. Remade for TV in 1998 with Christopher Reeve. ▼●

Reason to Live, a Reason to Die, A (1974-Italian-French-German-Spanish) **C-92m.** ** D: Tonino Valerii. James Coburn, Telly Savalas, Bud Spencer, Robert Burton. Union Colonel Coburn and seven condemned men attempt to recapture a Missouri fort from brutal Confederate Major Savalas. So-so Western, aka MASSACRE AT FORT HOLMAN. Technoscope. [PG]▼

Rebecca (1940) **130m.** **** D: Alfred Hitchcock. Laurence Olivier, Joan Fontaine, George Sanders, Judith Anderson, Nigel Bruce, Reginald Denny, C. Aubrey Smith, Gladys Cooper, Florence Bates, Leo G. Carroll, Melville Cooper. Hitchcock's first American film is sumptuous David O. Selznick production of Daphne du Maurier novel of girl who marries British nobleman but lives in shadow of his former wife. Stunning performances by Fontaine and Anderson; haunting score by Franz Waxman. Screenplay by Robert E. Sherwood and Joan Harrison. Academy Award winner for Best Picture and Cinematography (George Barnes).▼●

Rebecca of Sunnybrook Farm (1938) **80m.** **½ D: Allan Dwan. Shirley Temple, Randolph Scott, Jack Haley, Gloria Stuart, Phyllis Brooks, Helen Westley, Slim Summerville, William Demarest. Contrived but entertaining, with surefire elements from earlier Temple movies tossed into simple story of Scott trying to make Shirley a radio star. No relation to Kate Douglas Wiggin's famous story. Also shown in computer-colored version.▼●

Rebel (1974) **C-80m.** *½ D: Robert Allen Schnitzer. Antony Page, Sylvester E. Stallone, Rebecca Grimes, Henry G. Sanders. Tiresome, justifiably obscure time-capsule featuring Stallone, pre–ROCKY stardom, as an alienated political radical (an interesting contrast to Rambo). Original title: NO PLACE TO HIDE. [PG]▼

Rebel (1985-Australian) **C-91m.** ** D: Michael Jenkins. Matt Dillon, Debbie Byrne, Bryan Brown, Bill Hunter, Ray Barrett, Julie Nihill, Kim Deacon. Odd mixture of drama and music in this tale of traumatized AWOL American GI Dillon, who attaches himself to Sydney cabaret performer Byrne during WW2. Plenty of flash and style, little substance; and Dillon is fatally miscast. Panavision. [R]▼●

Rebel Rousers (1970) **C-78m.** **½ D: Martin B. Cohen. Cameron Mitchell, Jack Nicholson, Bruce Dern, Diane Ladd, (Harry) Dean Stanton. Architect Mitchell isn't pleased when Dern holds drag-race to see who will "win" Mitchell's pregnant girlfriend. Nicholson, decked out in outrageous striped pants, steals the show in this amusing time capsule. Filmed in 1967. Aka REBEL WARRIORS. [R]▼●

Rebel Warriors SEE: **Rebel Rousers**

Rebel Without a Cause (1955) **C-111m.** **** D: Nicholas Ray. James Dean, Natalie Wood, Sal Mineo, Jim Backus, Ann Doran, William Hopper, Rochelle Hudson, Corey Allen, Edward Platt, Dennis Hopper, Nick Adams. This portrait of youthful alienation spoke to a whole generation and remains wrenchingly powerful, despite some dated elements. The yearning for self-esteem, the barrier to communication with parents, the comfort found in friendships, all beautifully realized by director Ray, screenwriter Stewart Stern, and a fine cast (far too many of whom met early ends). This was Dean's seminal performance and an equally impressive showcase for young Mineo. CinemaScope.▼●▮

Rebound (2005) **C-87m.** *½ D: Steve Carr. Martin Lawrence, Wendy Raquel Robinson, Breckin Meyer, Horatio Sanz, Oren Williams, Patrick Warburton, Megan Mullally, Eddy Martin, Steven Christopher Parker, Laura Kightlinger. Hotshot but disgraced college basketball coach gets a chance at redemption by guiding the ragtag hoopsters at the middle school he attended years ago. Slick, minimally humorous vehicle for coexecutive producer/star Lawrence is beyond predictable. Tragically, teenaged costar Tara Correa, who plays "Big Mac" in her film debut, was killed just three months after this film's release. [PG]▼▮

[°REC] (2007-Spanish) **C-78m.** *** D: Jaume Balagueró, Paco Plaza. Manuela Velasco, Ferran Terraza, Jorge-Yamam Serrano, Pablo Rosso, David Vert, Vicente Gil. An all-night news team's camcorder

focuses on a fire station call to a Barcelona apartment building that is suddenly sealed tight by officials, exposing everyone inside to a virulent contagion. Icky mayhem reigns in a mucho scary thriller that slaps a gutsy you-are-there spin on zombie flicks. Diluted U.S. remake QUARANTINE lacks this original's tap root, a startling religious rationale. A portion of the cast returns in [°REC] 2. [R]▮

Recess: School's Out (2001) **C-84m.** *½ D: Chuck Sheetz. Voices of James Woods, Andy Lawrence, Pam Segall, Dabney Coleman, Melissa Joan Hart, Jason Davis, April Winchell, Peter MacNicol, Ashley Johnson. Disney's Saturday-morning TV cartoon expanded to feature length, with no additional production values. Young T.J. and the *Recess* gang spend their summer vacation investigating some shady characters who have taken over the school building and are constructing a strange ray gun. Psychedelic end title sequence featuring Robert Goulet singing "Green Tambourine" is the creative highlight of the picture. [G]▼▮

Reckless (1984) **C-90m.** **½ D: James Foley. Aidan Quinn, Daryl Hannah, Kenneth McMillan, Cliff DeYoung, Lois Smith, Adam Baldwin, Dan Hedaya, Jennifer Grey. Rebellious teenager from wrong side of tracks takes up with straight-arrow coed, who finds in him a sense of danger and excitement missing from her comfortable existence. Nothing here we haven't seen in 1950s films about alienated youth—except for some very contemporary sex scenes—done with sincerity and a pulsing rock soundtrack. Quinn's film debut. [R]▼●

Reckless (1995) **C-92m.** *½ D: Norman Rene. Mia Farrow, Scott Glenn, Mary-Louise Parker, Tony Goldwyn, Stephen Dorff, Eileen Brennan, Giancarlo Esposito. It's Christmas Eve, and a ditsy, seemingly happy wife (Farrow) is informed by her suddenly remorseful husband that he has taken out a contract on her life. A potentially clever spoof of middle-class marital relations and phony holiday cheer quickly descends into a meandering, thoroughly ridiculous comedy-of-the-absurd. Farrow's character babbles on incessantly; it's no wonder she drives men—as well as the audience—crazy. Adapted by Craig Lucas from his play. [PG-13]▼

Reckless Kelly (1993-Australian-U.S.) **C-94m.** ** D: Yahoo Serious. Yahoo Serious, Melora Hardin, Alexei Sayle, Hugo Weaving, Kathleen Freeman, John Pinette. Modern descendant of Australia's legendary Robin Hood–like outlaw Ned Kelly (who travels around on a sputtering, klunky motorcycle) goes to L.A. to raise money to save his family's island hideout, and gets mixed up with moviemakers. Engagingly silly at the start, with some very funny sight gags, but increasingly tiresome as it moves stateside. Serious also directed, cowrote, and (according to the credits) performed his own stunts. Super 35. [PG]▼

Reckless Moment, The (1949) **82m.** ***½ D: Max Opuls (Ophuls). James Mason, Joan Bennett, Geraldine Brooks, Henry O'Neill, Shepperd Strudwick. Mason blackmails protective mother Bennett, whose teenage daughter has been involved in a man's death. Noir-ish melodrama is also a slyly subversive look at a "typical" American family. Henry Garson and R. W. Soderberg adapted Elizabeth S. Holding's novel *The Blank Wall*. Remade as THE DEEP END. ▼

Reckoning, The (1969-British) **C-111m.** **½ D: Jack Gold. Nicol Williamson, Rachel Roberts, Paul Rogers, Ann Bell. Contrived, latter day "angry young man" film, with Williamson (excellent as usual) as brooding businessman incapable of living in harmony with society, out to avenge long-ago slight to his father. [R]▶

Reckoning, The (2003-British-Spanish) **C-112m.** **½ D: Paul McGuigan. Paul Bettany, Willem Dafoe, Simon McBurney, Gina McKee, Brian Cox, Tom Hardy, Stuart Wells, Matthew Macfadyen, Jared Harris, Vincent Cassel. A priest in 1380 England runs for his life after committing a crime and joins a troupe of traveling actors. The newest village on their journey is reeling from a notorious murder, which inspires the troupe and fires the priest's need for redemption. Interesting story leaves its principal villain (Cassel) offscreen far too long, but benefits from Bettany's strong performance. Super 35. [R]▼▶

Recon Game SEE: **Open Season** (1974)

Recruit, The (2003) **C-105m.** **½ D: Roger Donaldson. Al Pacino, Colin Farrell, Bridget Moynahan, Gabriel Macht, Karl Pruner, Eugene Lipinski. College computer whiz is recruited to join the CIA by veteran Pacino, who warns him that no one is to be trusted and nothing is as it seems—especially during his intense training period at The Farm in Langley, Virginia. Good story with endless twists and moments of nail-biting excitement, pumped up by dynamic star performances . . . but the final story turn is so unexpected, and so unlikely, that it comes as a letdown. Super 35. [PG-13] ▼▶

Red (1994-Swiss-French-Polish) **C-99m.** *** D: Krzysztof Kieslowski. Irène Jacob, Jean-Louis Trintignant, Frederique Feder, Jean-Pierre Lorit, Juliette Binoche, Julie Delpy, Benoit Regent, Zbigniew Zamachowski. Final film in Kieslowski's "Three Colors" trilogy which, like BLUE and WHITE, can stand alone with its self-contained story. Fashion model Jacob meets embittered, retired judge Trintignant by accident, then develops relationship with him and enters his cloistered, secret world. Set in Geneva, this is a tale of several intertwining lives: a look at communication—and lack of same—in modern society. Acclaimed,

but not for all tastes. This final chapter is subtitled "Fraternity."▼▶

Red (2008) **C-93m.** ** D: Trygve Allister Diesen, Lucky McKee. Brian Cox, Tom Sizemore, Robert Englund, Amanda Plummer, Noel Fisher, Kyle Gallner, Shiloh Fernandez, Richard Riehle, Kim Dickens. Three punk teens harass middle-aged Cox, and one of them shoots and kills his beloved dog. Starts off promisingly as a morality tale but deteriorates into an obvious, violent revenge saga. Cox is a quietly powerful presence. Based on a book by Jack Ketchum. [R]

Red (2010) **C-111m.** **½ D: Robert Schwentke. Bruce Willis, Morgan Freeman, John Malkovich, Helen Mirren, Karl Urban, Mary-Louise Parker, Brian Cox, Julian McMahon, Richard Dreyfuss, Ernest Borgnine, Rebecca Pidgeon, James Remar. Having survived an assassination attempt, retired CIA op Willis travels the country to recruit other former agents (who are "retired, extremely dangerous") and combat a government conspiracy. He abducts a woman (Parker) he's gotten to like over the phone—she processes his pension checks—and takes her along on this bullet-ridden adventure. Based on the graphic novel by Warren Ellis and Cully Hamner, this should have been a slam dunk, but never quite takes off—and goes on far too long. Still, it's fun to watch the veteran cast at work. Super 35. [PG-13] ▶

Redacted (2007) **C-90m.** *½ D: Brian De Palma. Patrick Carroll, Rob Devaney, Daniel Stewart Sherman, Izzy Diaz, Mike Figueroa, Ty Jones, Qazi Freihat, Kel O'Neill. Misguided attempt by De Palma (who made CASUALTIES OF WAR on a much bigger scale) to tell stories of the Iraq war through the eyes of various media outlets. The focus is on a group of out-of-control U.S. soldiers who eventually rape and murder a teenage girl with cameras rolling. Unsavory aspects of the story overwhelm it, while the uniformly amateurish acting completely defeats whatever message was intended. [R]▶

Red and the Black, The SEE: **Le Rouge et le Noir**

Red Badge of Courage, The (1951) **69m.** ***½ D: John Huston. Audie Murphy, Bill Mauldin, Douglas Dick, Royal Dano, John Dierkes, Arthur Hunnicutt, Tim Durant, Andy Devine. Narrated by James Whitmore. Yankee soldier Murphy flees under fire and is guilt stricken over his apparent lack of courage. Stephen Crane's Civil War novel receives both epic and personal treatment by director Huston. Sweeping battle scenes and some truly frightening Rebel cavalry charges highlight this study of the fine line between cowardice and bravery. Many memorable vignettes: scene of Yankee general promising to share supper with half a dozen *different* platoons after the upcoming battle is a classic. Heavily re-edited after oddly negative previews; the film's troubled production is recounted in Lillian Ross' book *Picture*. Remade for TV in 1974.▼❚

Red Ball Express (1952) **83m.** **½ D: Budd Boetticher. Jeff Chandler, Alex Nicol, Charles Drake, Hugh O'Brian, Jack Kelly, Jacqueline Duval, Sidney Poitier, Jack Warden. Pretty good WW2 story about real-life truck convoy that was hurriedly created to bring supplies to Patton's Army deep inside German-held territory in France. Screenplay by John Michael Hayes.▼

Red Beard (1965-Japanese) **185m.** **½ D: Akira Kurosawa. Toshiro Mifune, Yuzo Kayama, Yoshio Tsuchiya, Reiko Dan, Kyoko Kagawa, Terumi Niki. Tough but kind doctor Mifune takes intern Kayama under his wing in charity clinic. Unoriginal drama is also way overlong. Tohoscope.▼❍❚

Redbelt (2008) **C-99m.** *** D: David Mamet. Chiwetel Ejiofor, Alice Braga, Tim Allen, Emily Mortimer, Rodrigo Santoro, Joe Mantegna, Ricky Jay, David Paymer, Max Martini, Rebecca Pidgeon, Ray Mancini, Jose Pablo Cantillo, John Machado, J. J. Johnston, Jack Wallace. Absorbing drama about a jiu-jitsu instructor (Ejiofor) whose devotion to the purity of martial arts is put to the test when he's swept into a world of corruption involving fight promoters, a movie star, and his sleazy producer. Striking if densely plotted storyline takes place in a typically unique Mamet environment. Ejiofor is terrific as usual. Super 35. [R]❚

Red Circle, The SEE: **Le Cercle Rouge**

Red Cliff (2008/2009-Chinese) **C-288m.** *** D: John Woo. Tony Leung, Takeshi Kaneshiro, Fengyi Zhang, Chen Chang, Wei Zhao, Chiling Lin, Jun Hu, Shidou Nakamura. Most expensive film in the history of mainland China documents a famous battle from A.D. 208 that has been lauded in lore for centuries. As a general in northern China runs herd over the ineffectual emperor, rebel leaders in the south (one old, one young, neither top-flight) combine resources, including their respective military advisors (Leung, Kaneshiro). Woo adapts his kinetic staging of violent action to a series of incredible, epic-scale battle scenes, but never forgets the human drama propelling the story. Original five-hour, two-part film (a smash hit in Asia) was cut in half for U.S. release to 148m. and pieced together with voice-over narration and spoon-feeding titles. Super 35. ❚

Red Corner (1997) **C-122m.** **½ D: Jon Avnet. Richard Gere, Bai Ling, Bradley Whitford, Byron Mann, Peter Donat, Robert Stanton, Tsai Chin, James Hong, Tzi Ma. American lawyer, representing cable/satellite TV interests in China, is framed for murdering a sexy model with whom he slept one night. His chances for justice are slim until the female lawyer assigned to his case (Ling) is bold enough to help him

fight the system and figure out who's really behind this crime. Repetition and elements of illogic and predictability weaken an otherwise interesting yarn. [R]▼❍❚

Red Danube, The (1949) **119m.** **½ D: George Sidney. Walter Pidgeon, Ethel Barrymore, Peter Lawford, Angela Lansbury, Janet Leigh. Louis Calhern, Francis L. Sullivan. Meandering drama of ballerina Leigh pursued by Russian agents, aided by amorous Lawford; heavy-handed at times.

Red Dawn (1984) **C-114m.** *½ D: John Milius. Patrick Swayze, C. Thomas Howell, Lea Thompson, Charlie Sheen, Powers Boothe, Ben Johnson, Harry Dean Stanton, Jennifer Grey. Small-town teens become guerrilla fighters when Commies invade U.S. Good premise gunned down by purple prose and posturing—not to mention violence. [PG-13]▼❍❚

Red Desert (1964-French-Italian) **C-118m.** ** D: Michelangelo Antonioni. Monica Vitti, Richard Harris, Rita Renoir, Carlo Chionetti. Vague, boring tale of Vitti alienated from her surroundings and on the verge of madness. Antonioni's first color film does have its followers. ▼❍❚

Red Doors (2006) **C-91m.** ** D: Georgia Lee. Jacqueline Kim, Freda Foh Shen, Kathy Shao-Lin Lee, Elaine Kao, Mia Riverton, Sebastian Stan, Jayce Bartok, Rossif Sutherland, Tzi Ma. Quirky slice of life about a suburban Chinese-American family; the mother is stereotypically flighty, the father is suicidal, saddened by the passage of time, and each daughter is in the process of ending or beginning a relationship. Well-intentioned but sketchy meditation on the different paths individuals take to find happiness. What is meant to be funny and endearing often comes off as slight and silly. [R]❚

Red Dragon (1986) SEE: **Manhunter**

Red Dragon (2002) **C-124m.** ** D: Brett Ratner. Anthony Hopkins, Edward Norton, Ralph Fiennes, Harvey Keitel, Emily Watson, Mary-Louise Parker, Philip Seymour Hoffman, Anthony Heald, Bill Duke, Ken Leung, Stanley Anderson, Azura Skye, Frankie Faison, John Rubinstein, Lalo Schifrin. Needless remake of MANHUNTER, based on Thomas Harris' novel. FBI agent (Norton) captures Hannibal Lecter, then is forced to consult with the carnivorous inmate as he tries to find a crafty serial killer. Slick production, with an exceptionally good cast, can't disguise a potboiler script that's all too obvious. (Gee, do you think the bad guy will go after Norton's *family*?) Screenplay by Ted Tally, who also adapted THE SILENCE OF THE LAMBS. Frank Whaley and Mary Beth Hurt appear unbilled; Ellen Burstyn's voice is uncredited. Panavision. [R]▼❚

Red Dust (1932) **83m.** ***½ D: Victor Fleming. Clark Gable, Jean Harlow, Mary Astor, Donald Crisp, Gene Raymond, Tully Marshall, Willie Fung. Robust romance of

Indochina rubber worker Gable, his floozie gal Harlow, and visiting Astor, who is married to Raymond, but falls for Gable. Harlow has fine comic touch. Tart script by John Lee Mahin. Remade as MOGAMBO. Also shown in computer-colored version. ▼●

Red Dust (2004-British-South African) C-111m. **½ D: Tom Hooper. Hilary Swank, Chiwetel Ejiofor, Jamie Bartlett, Nomhlé Nkyonyeni, Ian Roberts, Greg Latter, Mawonga Dominic Tyawa, Marius Weyers. An apartheid drama with a twist: apartheid has ended, and N.Y. lawyer Swank returns to her native South Africa to represent a rising black politician (Ejiofor) who was beaten and tortured while in custody years earlier. Somber drama, based on a novel by Gillian Slovo, explores the possibility of and need for forgiveness in order to heal South Africa's wounds. Well meaning but lacks dramatic spark and fire. Panavision. [R]▶

Red Eye (2005) C-85m. *** D: Wes Craven. Rachel McAdams, Cillian Murphy, Brian Cox, Jayma Mays, Jack Scalia, Robert Pine. Craven returns to form with this tight, knowingly hokey thriller that actually thrills while maintaining a sense of humor about itself. McAdams exudes star quality as a hotel manager on an early morning flight terrorized by the deliciously evil Murphy. Part of the fun is experiencing how masterfully the director manipulates the audience using familiar conventions. Panavision. [PG-13]▼▶

Red Firecracker, Green Firecracker (1994-Hong Kong) C-116m. *** D: He Ping. Hing Jing, Wu Gang, Zhao Xiaorui, Gao Yang. Evocative, romantic tale, beautifully directed and photographed and set in the early 20th century. The heroine is a young woman (Jing) who wears men's clothes and successfully operates her family's fireworks manufacturing business. Her priorities begin to change when she is attracted to a good-looking, wandering artist (Gang). [R]▼●

Red-Headed Stranger (1986) C-105m. *½ Đ: William Wittliff. Willie Nelson, Morgan Fairchild, Katharine Ross, Royal Dano, Sonny Carl Davis. Limp drama, screenwriter Wittliff's directorial debut, about a preacher (Nelson), his wayward wife (Fairchild, in an awful performance), a "good woman" (Ross), and some hooligans that have overridden his town. Adapted from Willie's 1975 album . . . and proof that hit records don't necessarily make good movies. Shot in 1984. [R]▼●

Red-Headed Woman (1932) 79m. *** D: Jack Conway. Jean Harlow, Chester Morris, Una Merkel, Lewis Stone, May Robson, Leila Hyams, Charles Boyer. Harlow has never been sexier than in this precensorship story (by Anita Loos) of a gold-digging secretary who sets out to corral her married boss (Morris). ▼●▶

Red Heat (1988) C-106m. *½ D: Walter

Hill. Arnold Schwarzenegger, James Belushi, Peter Boyle, Ed O'Ross, Larry Fishburne, Gina Gershon, Richard Bright, Oleg Vidov, Pruitt Taylor Vince. Grim-faced Soviet cop tracks a scummy Russian drug dealer to Chicago, where he's partnered with belligerent Belushi from the Chicago P.D. Cheerless, foul-mouthed action film with two of the least appealing characters imaginable as the good guys. This was the first American production allowed to shoot scenes in Moscow's Red Square (. . . but *why*?). [R]▼●▶

Red Hill (2010-Australian) C-97m. ** D: Patrick Hughes. Ryan Kwanten, Steve Bisley, Tom E. (Tommy) Lewis, Claire van der Boom, Christopher Davis, Kevin Harrington, Richard Sutherland, Cliff Ellen, Eddie Baroo. Newly transferred police constable Kwanten is looking forward to keeping the peace in a small rural outpost. His pregnant wife needs the quiet, and he's suffering from a crisis of confidence after freezing in the middle of a violent altercation. His first day on the job turns chaotic when a ferocious felon escapes from a nearby prison. As the manhunt proceeds, Kwanten realizes all is not as it appears and it's unclear who the bad guys really are. Plenty of atmosphere, but this revenge thriller never makes the grade. [R]▶

Redline (2007) C-95m. BOMB D: Andy Cheng. Nadia Bjorlin, Eddie Griffin, Angus Macfadyen, Tim Matheson, Nathan Phillips, Jesse Johnson, Denyce Lawton. Real estate developer Daniel Sadek financed, cowrote, produced, and provided his exotic car collection for this slow and curious FAST AND THE FURIOUS wannabe. Gorgeous woman who happens to be an ace driver gets caught up in the world of illegal drag racing competitions in which filthy-rich men with nothing better to do wager big bucks on the outcome. When she's not pushing the pedal to the metal, she fronts a band singing lyrics like, "I want to be your car so you can ride me tonight." Steer clear of this one. Super 35. [PG-13]▶

Red Line 7000 (1965) C-110m. **½ D: Howard Hawks. James Caan, Laura Devon, Gail Hire, Charlene Holt, John Robert Crawford, Marianna Hill, James Ward, Norman Alden, George Takei. Attempt by director Hawks to do same kind of expert adventure pic he'd done for 40 years is sabotaged by overly complex script and indifferent acting, but is a faster and less pretentious racing-car drama than GRAND PRIX. Originally ran 127m. ▼●

Red Planet (2000) C-106m. ** D: Antony Hoffman. Val Kilmer, Carrie-Anne Moss, Tom Sizemore, Benjamin Bratt, Simon Baker, Terence Stamp. Utterly ordinary sci-fi saga about a mission to Mars in the year 2050. No-nonsense commander Moss is left alone on her ship while her contentious crew checks on a terraforming project

[1145]

on Mars to create food and oxygen. Looks good, but covers awfully familiar dramatic turf. Panavision. [PG-13] ▼▶

Red Planet Mars (1952) **87m.** **½ D: Harry Horner. Peter Graves, Andrea King, Marvin Miller, Herbert Berghof, House Peters, Jr., Vince Barnett. Outrageous sci-fi of scientist deciphering messages from Mars which turn out to be from God. Hilariously ludicrous anti-Communist propaganda (*Red* Planet Mars, get it?). ▼●

Red Pony, The (1949) **C-89m.** *** D: Lewis Milestone. Myrna Loy, Robert Mitchum, Peter Miles, Louis Calhern, Shepperd Strudwick, Margaret Hamilton, Beau Bridges. John Steinbeck adapted his own stories into this warmhearted screenplay about a farm boy who learns about responsibility when he's given his own pony. Keen observations of family dynamics (with Calhern a delight as Loy's garrulous father) make this a standout, along with Tony Gaudio's Technicolor camerawork and a justly famous score by Aaron Copland. Remade for TV in 1973. ▼●▶

Red Riding Hood (2011) **C-100m.** *½ D: Catherine Hardwicke. Amanda Seyfried, Gary Oldman, Billy Burke, Shiloh Fernandez, Max Irons, Virginia Madsen, Lukas Haas, Julie Christie. A village on the edge of a deep, dark forest lives in perpetual fear of attacks by a vicious wolf. Then an exorcist of sorts (Oldman) turns up to lend his expertise and conducts a witch hunt that's almost as vicious as the animal's assaults. Tedious, heavy-handed film provides purported answers to questions no one cares to know about the story of Red Riding Hood. It also tries, and fails, to bring TWILIGHT-like sizzle to a love triangle that may or may not involve a werewolf. Super 35. [PG-13] ▶

Red Riding: The Year of Our Lord 1974 (2009-British) **C-106m.** **½ D: Julian Jarrold. Andrew Garfield, Sean Bean, Warren Clarke, Rebecca Hall, Eddie Marsan, David Morrissey, Peter Mullan, Cara Seymour, John Henshaw, Anthony Flanagan, Sean Harris, Tony Mooney. Tyro newspaper reporter Garfield returns to his hometown in Yorkshire and becomes convinced that there's more to the recent abduction of a 10-year-old girl than anyone—including the local police—is willing to admit. First of an ambitious but downbeat trilogy adapted by Tony Grisoni from David Peace's novels, inspired by the Yorkshire Ripper case. Intriguing, well made, but grim; it's hard to accept Garfield's dogged naivete given our ability to see what's happening when he cannot. Story grows even seamier in subsequent installments. Made for British TV. ▶

Red Riding: The Year of Our Lord 1980 (2009-British) **C-97m.** **½ D: James Marsh. Paddy Considine, Jim Carter, Warren Clarke, Sean Harris, David Morrissey,

Peter Mullan, Maxine Peake, Tony Pitts, Lesley Sharp, David Calder, Ron Cook, Julia Ford, James Fox, Joseph Mawle, Nicholas Woodeson, Andrew Garfield, Eddie Marsan, Tony Mooney. As the Yorkshire Ripper continues his heinous crimes, respected Manchester police officer Considine is assigned to take charge of the case—but he's got pressing personal problems, and the local cops are loath to cooperate with him. Digs deeper into the well of corruption that permeates the case, and the frustrating dead ends that face an honest investigator. Vividly captures the look and feel of its period, while anticipating what will occur in the final installment of the trilogy. As in the first segment, the impediments facing the protagonist seem painfully obvious. Richly detailed but dismal in the extreme. Made for British TV. Techniscope. ▶

Red Riding: The Year of Our Lord 1983 (2009-British) **C-105m.** ** D: Anand Tucker. Mark Addy, David Morrissey, Jim Carter, Warren Clarke, Daniel Mays, Peter Mullan, Saskia Reeves, Sean Bean, Shaun Dooley, Gerard Kearns, Cara Seymour, Robert Sheehan, Lisa Howard, Chris Walker, Sean Harris, Tony Mooney, Andrew Garfield, John Henshaw. A ragtag lawyer (Addy) is persuaded to take on the case of the man who's serving time for the crimes of the Yorkshire Ripper—although even detective Morrissey begins to doubt the man's guilt when yet another girl is abducted. Ultimately the whole repellent story is revealed, giving the viewer a chance to feel as if he's been dragged face-first through a sewer. Executed at the highest level of filmmaking skill, but to what end? Made for British TV. HD Widescreen. ▶

Red River (1948) **133m.** **** D: Howard Hawks. John Wayne, Montgomery Clift, Walter Brennan, Joanne Dru, John Ireland, Noah Beery, Jr., Paul Fix, Coleen Gray, Harry Carey, Jr., Harry Carey, Sr., Chief Yowlachie, Hank Worden. One of the greatest American adventures is really a Western MUTINY ON THE BOUNTY: Clift (in his first film) rebels against tyrannical guardian Wayne (brilliant in an unsympathetic role) during crucial cattle drive. Spellbinding photography by Russell Harlan, rousing Dimitri Tiomkin score; an absolute must. Alternate 125m. version uses Brennan's narration in place of diary pages, which Hawks preferred. Screenplay by Borden Chase and Charles Schnee, from Chase's *Saturday Evening Post* story. If you blink, you'll miss Shelley Winters dancing around a campfire. Remade for TV in 1988 with James Arness. ▼●▶

Red Road (2006-British-Scottish-Danish) **C-113m.** *** D: Andrea Arnold. Kate Dickie, Tony Curran, Martin Compston, Natalie Press, Andrew Armour. A woman who works as a security officer in Glasgow, intently surveying a bank of video monitors for criminal activity, recognizes a man she thought was gone from her life, then contrives a way to meet him. Why? And will the answer to that question explain why she is so emotionally remote? Intriguing drama takes its time playing out but never loses its hold on the audience. Arnold's feature directing debut is the first of three films to be made based on characters created by Anders Thomas Jensen and Lone Scherfig. Coproduced by Lars von Trier's Zentropa Entertainments5.◗

Red Rock West (1993) **C-98m.** **★★★** D: John Dahl. Nicolas Cage, Dennis Hopper, Lara Flynn Boyle, Timothy Carhart, J.T. Walsh, Dan Shor, Dwight Yoakam. Rock-solid little thriller, crammed with twists, turns and suspense, about honest, unemployed Cage, who's mistaken for a contract killer hired to do in seductive, adulterous Boyle. Nothing that occurs is logical or probable, but the film is so good (and so funny) that you are willing to go along for the ride. Hopper aficionados will savor his performance as "Lyle, from Dallas," the smarmiest of psychos, who is the real hit man. This debuted on cable TV. [R]▼●◗

Reds (1981) **C-200m.** **★★★** D: Warren Beatty. Warren Beatty, Diane Keaton, Edward Herrmann, Jerzy Kosinski, Jack Nicholson, Paul Sorvino, Maureen Stapleton, Nicolas Coster, Gene Hackman, William Daniels, Max Wright, M. Emmet Walsh, Ian Wolfe, Bessie Love, George Plimpton, Dolph Sweet, Josef Sommer. Sprawling, ambitious film about American idealist/journalist John Reed's involvement with Communism, the Russian Revolution, and a willful, free-thinking woman named Louise Bryant. Provocative political saga is diffused, and overcome at times, by surprisingly conventional, often sappy approach to the love story (climaxed by Bryant's Little Eva–like journey to Russia over the ice floes). Interesting but wildly overpraised film won Oscars for Beatty as Best Director (he also produced and coscripted), Stapleton as Best Supporting Actress, Vittorio Storaro for Best Cinematography. [PG]▼●◗

Red Scorpion (1989) **C-102m.** BOMB D: Joseph Zito. Dolph Lundgren, M. Emmet Walsh, Al White, T.P. McKenna, Carmen Argenziano, Brion James, Regopstann. Bottom-of-the-barrel actioner with Lundgren a Soviet officer sent to Africa to murder a rebel leader. Followed by direct-to-video sequel. [R] ▼●◗

Red Shoes, The (1948-British) **C-133m.** **★★★★** D: Michael Powell, Emeric Pressburger. Anton Walbrook, Marius Goring, Moira Shearer, Robert Helpmann, Leonide Massine, Albert Basserman, Ludmilla Tcherina, Esmond Knight. A superb, stylized fairy tale. Young ballerina is torn between two creative, possessive men, one a strug-

gling composer, the other an autocratic dance impresario. Landmark film for its integration of dance in storytelling, and a perennial favorite of balletomanes. Brian Easdale's score and Hein Heckroth and Arthur Lawson's art direction-set decoration won Oscars, and Jack Cardiff's cinematography *should* have. Shearer is exquisite in movie debut.▼●◗

Red Sky at Morning (1970) **C-112m.** **★★★** D: James Goldstone. Richard Thomas, Catherine Burns, Desi Arnaz, Jr., Richard Crenna, Claire Bloom, John Colicos, Harry Guardino, Strother Martin, Nehemiah Persoff. Unspectacular but pleasing adaptation of Richard Bradford's novel about adolescence in New Mexico during WW2. Comparable to SUMMER OF '42, and in many ways better; Thomas is superb. [PG]

Red Sonja (1985) **C-89m.** *½ D: Richard Fleischer. Brigitte Nielsen, Arnold Schwarzenegger, Sandahl Bergman, Paul Smith, Ernie Reyes, Jr., Ronald Lacey, Pat Roach. Spectacularly silly sword-and-sorcery saga with female lead, based on pulp writings of Robert E. Howard (of CONAN fame). Might amuse juvenile viewers, but only point of interest for adults is deciding who gives the worse performance, Nielsen or villainess Bergman. Schwarzenegger has a brief guest spot. Technovision. [PG-13]▼●◗

Red Sorghum (1987-Chinese) **C-91m.** ***½ D: Zhang Yimou. Gong Li, Jiang Wen, Liu Ji, Teng Rijun, Qian Ming. Evocative, beautifully filmed combination drama/black comedy/fairy tale/epic which chronicles a most untraditional union between a pair of rural lovers during the 1920s. The years pass, a new decade arrives, and with it come Japanese invaders. A triumph for director Yimou. CinemaScope.▼

Red Sun (1972-Italian-French-Spanish) **C-112m.** ** D: Terence Young. Charles Bronson, Ursula Andress, Toshiro Mifune, Alain Delon, Capucine. East meets West in this odd story of samurai warrior pursuing valuable Japanese sword stolen from train crossing American West. Intriguing elements, and refreshingly tongue-in-cheek, but a misfire. [PG]▼◗

Red Tent, The (1971-Italian-Russian) **C-121m.** *** D: Mickail K. Kalatozov. Sean Connery, Claudia Cardinale, Hardy Kruger, Peter Finch, Massimo Girotti, Luigi Vannucchi, Mario Adorf. Top-notch adventure saga for kids and adults alike, based on true story of explorer General Nobile (Finch) whose 1928 Arctic expedition turns into disaster. Exciting scenes of survival against elements, dramatic rescue, marred by awkward flashback framework. Connery appears only in a few scenes. [G]▼●◗

Red Tide, The SEE: **Blood Tide**

Red Tomahawk (1967) **C-82m.** *½ D: R. G. Springsteen. Howard Keel, Joan Caulfield, Broderick Crawford, Scott Brady, Wendell Corey, Richard Arlen, Tom Drake, Ben Cooper, Donald Barry. Captain Keel saves town from Sioux in routine Western with many likable performers in the cast.

Red Violin, The (1998-Canadian-Italian) **C-131m. **** D: François Girard. Carlo Cecchi, Irene Grazioli, Jean-Luc Bideau, Jason Flemyng, Greta Scacchi, Sylvia Chang, Samuel L. Jackson, Colm Feore, Monique Mercure, Don McKellar, Sandra Oh. Multi-episode film follows the fate of a cursed violin from 17th-century Italy to 18th-century Vienna, 19th-century England, 20th-century China and present-day Montreal. The stories are mostly downbeat and/or frustrating, and the wrapup segment with appraiser Jackson is hard to swallow. Colorful locales and intriguing premises maintain minimal interest throughout. McKellar, who plays Jackson's cohort in the final episode, also coscripted with the director. Oscar-winning score by John Corigliano.▼◗

Reefer Madness (1936) **67m.** BOMB D: Louis Gasnier. Dave O'Brien, Dorothy Short, Warren McCollum, Lillian Miles, Carleton Young, Thelma White. The granddaddy of all "Worst" movies; one of that era's many low-budget "Warning!" films depicts (in now-hilarious fashion) how one puff of pot can lead clean-cut teenagers down the road to insanity and death. Miles' frenzied piano solo is a highlight, but in this more enlightened age, overall effect is a little sad. Later a stage musical, which was filmed for cable TV in 2005. Originally titled THE BURNING QUESTION, then TELL YOUR CHILDREN; beware shorter prints. Also shown in computer-colored version.▼◗

Reel Paradise (2005) **C-111m. **½** D: Steve James. Famed film exhibitor John Pierson and wife-partner Janet spend a year on Fiji's remote Taveuni showing free films to the locals—from classics to JACKASS: THE MOVIE, though their precocious son thinks JACKASS *is* a classic. Not in the same league as James' earlier documentaries (HOOP DREAMS, STEVIE), yet its meanderings aren't without interest. The family absorbs as much of the local (anti– New York) culture as the culture absorbs from the movies. Must viewing for buffs, in any event. [R]◗

Ref, The (1994) **C-93m. **½** D: Ted Demme. Denis Leary, Judy Davis, Kevin Spacey, Robert J. Steinmiller, Jr., Glynis Johns, Raymond J. Barry, Richard Bright, Christine Baranski, Bill Raymond, Bob Ridgely, B. D. Wong. A cocky cat burglar on the lam holds a squabbling yuppie couple hostage on Christmas Eve and quickly learns he's gotten himself into a no-win situation. This caustic comedy is meatier than you might expect, with top-notch per-

formances by Spacey and Davis, but it gets unexpectedly serious—then silly and illogical. Still worth a look. Director Demme is Jonathan's nephew. [R]▼◗

Reflecting Skin, The (1990-British-Canadian) **C-95m. **½** D: Philip Ridley. Viggo Mortensen, Lindsay Duncan, Jeremy Cooper, Sheila Moore, Duncan Fraser, David Longworth. Weird, jarring chiller, set in rural Idaho in the early '50s, about a boy (Cooper) who's convinced that the young widow who lives next door is a vampire. He's especially distraught when his older brother becomes her lover. Offbeat to say the least, and not for all tastes, but still worth a look.▼◗

Reflection of Fear, A (1973) **C-89m. **½** D: William A. Fraker. Robert Shaw, Mary Ure, Sally Kellerman, Sondra Locke, Signe Hasso. Muddled story of beautiful girl who becomes the crucial link in chain of violence and murder. [PG]◗

Reflections in a Golden Eye (1967) **C-108m. **½** D: John Huston. Elizabeth Taylor, Marlon Brando, Brian Keith, Julie Harris, Robert Forster, Zorro David. Kinky version of Carson McCullers' novel about homosexual army officer in the South. Not really very good, but cast, subject matter, and Huston's pretentious handling make it fascinating on a minor level. Panavision. ▼◗

Reform School Girls (1986) **C-94m. *½** D: Tom DeSimone. Linda Carol, Wendy O. Williams, Pat Ast, Sybil Danning, Charlotte McGinnis, Sherri Stoner, Denise Gordy, Tiffany Schwartz. Comic strip–styled spoof of women's prison films offers some knowing winks (director DeSimone also made 1982's THE CONCRETE JUNGLE), but the level of exaggeration is a turnoff, such as imagining veteran rock singer Williams as a teenager. Carol is the innocent young girl learning the ropes in prison, while chubby Ast, an Andy Warhol film graduate, was born to play a prison matron—yet even her campy acting becomes monotonous. [R]▼◗

Regarding Henry (1991) **C-107m. **** D: Mike Nichols. Harrison Ford, Annette Bening, Bill Nunn, Mikki Allen, Donald Moffat, Nancy Marchand, Elizabeth Wilson, Robin Bartlett, John Leguizamo. High-powered lawyer suffers brain injury and has to start his life all over again—learning to walk, talk, and ultimately, return to his family and job. Potentially interesting story is given polished presentation, but is so placid, and so unrealistic—even trivializing the recovery process—it never achieves any emotional impact. [PG-13]▼◗

Regeneration (1997-British-Canadian) **C-96m. **½** D: Gillies MacKinnon. Jonathan Pryce, James Wilby, Jonny Lee Miller, Stuart Bunce, David Hayman, Tanya Allen, John Neville, James McAvoy. Famed WW1 poet and decorated British war hero Siegfried Sassoon is declared mentally unstable and sent to a military psychiatric hospital after publishing a denouncement of the war. Strong acting and superb cinematography enhance this talky, stagy adaptation of Pat Barker's prize-winning novel. Pryce is exceptional as an army doctor who tries to heal the soldiers' wounded psyches. Aka BEHIND THE LINES. [R]▼◗

Reggae Sunsplash (1980-German-Jamaican) **C-107m.** **½ D: Stefan Paul. Bob Marley, Peter Tosh, Third World, Burning Spear. OK documentary, filmed at the '79 Sunsplash II Festival in Montego Bay, benefits from commanding presences of Marley and company.▼

Reign of Fire (2002-British-Irish-U.S.) **C-101m.** ** D: Rob Bowman. Christian Bale, Matthew McConaughey, Izabella Scorupco, Gerard Butler, Scott James Moutter, David Kennedy, Alexander Siddig, Ned Dennehy, Alice Krige. Bleak tale takes place, for the most part, in the year 2020, when the world has been decimated by fire-breathing dragons. One enclave, holed up in a British castle, tries desperately to survive; then along comes an American military man with a mission (McConaughey) and his troops, who favor an aggressive rather than passive approach. It's hard to care about anyone in this dour story. Panavision. [PG-13]▼◗

Reign of Terror (1949) **89m.** *** D: Anthony Mann. Robert Cummings, Arlene Dahl, Richard Hart, Richard Basehart, Arnold Moss, Beulah Bondi. Vivid costume drama set during French Revolution, with valuable diary eluding both sides of battle. Moss is particularly good as the elegantly, eloquently evil Foucher. Stunningly photographed by John Alton; every shot is a painting! Aka THE BLACK BOOK. ▼◗

Reign Over Me (2007) **C-128m.** **½ D: Mike Binder. Adam Sandler, Don Cheadle, Jada Pinkett Smith, Liv Tyler, Saffron Burrows, Donald Sutherland, Robert Klein, Melinda Dillon, Mike Binder, Jonathan Banks, Rae Allen. Prosperous N.Y.C. dentist (Cheadle) spots his old college roommate (Sandler) on the street one day and presses him for a reunion. It turns out that Sandler has become an inscrutable, obsessive-compulsive hermit since his wife and daughters died on one of the ill-fated flights on 9/11. Writer-director Binder (who plays Sugarman) tries to cover too much ground, cluttering the central story with superfluous characters and trying to create a parallel character portrait for Cheadle ... but Sandler's dramatic performance is genuinely impressive. HD Widescreen. [R]◗

Reincarnation of Peter Proud, The (1975) **C-104m.** **½ D: J. Lee Thompson. Michael Sarrazin, Jennifer O'Neill, Margot Kidder, Cornelia Sharpe, Paul Hecht, Tony Stephano. The soul of a man murdered years before roosts inside Sarrazin, in moderately gripping version of Max Ehrlich's book, adapted by the author. [R]▼◗

Reindeer Games (2000) **C-104m.** *½ D: John Frankenheimer. Ben Affleck, Gary Sinise, Charlize Theron, Dennis Farina, James Frain, Donal Logue, Danny Trejo, Isaac Hayes, Gordon Tootoosis, Clarence Williams III, Ashton Kutcher. After five years in prison, a car thief assumes the identity of his cell-mate and takes up with his comrade's gorgeous pen-pal girlfriend. Soon he finds himself in a quicksand pit of crime. Ridiculous story isn't believable for one minute, especially with the shallow performances of its usually capable cast (who all seem to be playing "grown-up" parts from an old movie script). Also available in 124m. director's cut. Super 35. [R]▼◗

Reivers, The (1969) **C-107m.** ***½ D: Mark Rydell. Steve McQueen, Sharon Farrell, Will Geer, Michael Constantine, Rupert Crosse, Mitch Vogel, Lonny Chapman, Juano Hernandez, Clifton James, Ruth White, Dub Taylor, Allyn Ann McLerie, Diane Ladd; narrated by Burgess Meredith. Picaresque film from Faulkner novel about young boy (Vogel) in 1905 Mississippi who takes off for adventurous automobile trip with devil-may-care McQueen and buddy Crosse. Completely winning Americana, full of colorful episodes, equally colorful characters. Screenplay by Irving Ravetch (who also produced) and Harriet Frank, Jr. Panavision. [M]◗

Relative Values (2000-British) **C-88m.** ** D: Eric Styles. Julie Andrews, Edward Atterton, Jeanne Tripplehorn, William Baldwin, Sophie Thompson, Colin Firth, Stephen Fry. The mother of an English aristocrat schemes to break up his engagement to a sexy Hollywood movie star in this bland adaptation of Noel Coward's drawing-room comedy. The cast is game, headed by Andrews in her first big-screen role in almost a decade, but the direction is unimaginative and the farcical plot (hinging on 1950s British class distinctions) makes much ado about very little. U.S. debut on cable TV. [PG]▼◗

Relentless (1989) **C-93m.** *½ D: William Lustig. Judd Nelson, Robert Loggia, Leo Rossi, Meg Foster, Patrick O'Bryan, Ken Lerner, Mindy Seeger, Angel Tompkins. Nelson gives his one memorable performance to date, as a serial killer. Otherwise thoroughly routine, and that goes double for the finale. Followed by three sequels, beginning with DEAD ON: RELENTLESS II. [R]▼◗

Relic, The (1997) **C-110m.** **½ D: Peter Hyams. Penelope Ann Miller, Tom Sizemore, Linda Hunt, James Whitmore, Clayton Rohner, Chi Muoi Lo, Thomas Ryan, Robert Lesser, Lewis Van Bergen, Constance Towers, John Kapelos, Audra Lindley. As a big natural history museum hosts a glittering reception, a monster runs amok in the shadows. Yes, it's "ALIEN in a museum," but not bad. The monster, done both "live" and by computer graphics, is especially impressive, but the explanation for it is laughable. Panavision. [R] ▼●▶

Religulous (2008) **C-101m.** **½ D: Larry Charles. Documentary (of sorts) follows talk show host/comedian/devout atheist Bill Maher's quest to expose the lies and contradictions inherent in organized religion. Provocative, often entertaining film provides some valid insights but never cuts deep enough, content to score laughs off easy interview targets (as well as snippets from Hollywood movies) and becoming as didactic as the religious fundamentalism it abhors. [R]▶

Reluctant Astronaut, The (1967) **C-101m.** ** D: Edward Montagne. Don Knotts, Leslie Nielsen, Joan Freeman, Arthur O'Connell, Jesse White. Featherweight comedy dealing with hicksville alumnus Knotts becoming title figure; predictable and often not even childishly humorous. For kids only. ▼●▶

Reluctant Debutante, The (1958) **C-94m.** **½ D: Vincente Minnelli. Rex Harrison, Kay Kendall, John Saxon, Sandra Dee, Angela Lansbury. Bright drawing-room comedy which Harrison, Kendall, and Lansbury make worthwhile: British parents must present their Americanized daughter to society. Harrison and Kendall were real-life husband and wife at the time. Remade as WHAT A GIRL WANTS. CinemaScope. ▼●▶

Reluctant Saint, The (1962-U.S.-Italian) **105m.** **½ D: Edward Dmytryk. Maximilian Schell, Ricardo Montalban, Lea Padovani, Akim Tamiroff, Harold Goldblatt, Mark Damon. Loosely biographical account of St. Joseph of Cupertino, a 17th-century Franciscan whose modest upbringing and simple intellect would never have foretold the religious life he would lead (or the great number of miracles he would perform). Unusual fare; worth a look.▶

Remains of the Day, The (1993) **C-135m.** ***½ D: James Ivory. Anthony Hopkins, Emma Thompson, James Fox, Christopher Reeve, Peter Vaughan, Hugh Grant, Michael Lonsdale, Tim Pigott-Smith, Patrick Godfrey. HOWARDS END leads are reunited as servants at a baronial English country home—Hopkins a self-sacrificing butler who serves with the utmost discretion, and Thompson an efficient and bright head housekeeper. The two collide over work—and especially over overtures of romance. Looming over these personal stories is the (fascinating) larger tale of the misguided lord of the manor (Fox), who is excitedly making alliances with Nazi sympathizers. Kazuo Ishiguro's novel was adapted by Ruth Prawer Jhabvala, and though film can't quite dispel its literary origin, even almost-great Merchant-Ivory is better than

most anything else around. Super 35. [PG] ▼●▶

Rembrandt (1936-British) **84m.** ***½ D: Alexander Korda. Charles Laughton, Elsa Lanchester, Gertrude Lawrence, Edward Chapman, Roger Livesey, Raymond Huntley, John Clements, Marius Goring, Abraham Sofaer. Handsome bio of Dutch painter, full of visual tableaux and sparked by Laughton's excellent performance. One of Gertrude Lawrence's rare film appearances. ▼●▶

Remember Me (2010) **C-112m.** *** D: Allen Coulter. Robert Pattinson, Emilie de Ravin, Pierce Brosnan, Chris Cooper, Lena Olin, Tate Ellington, Ruby Jerins, Kate Burton. Emotionally wounded son (Pattinson) of an aloof Wall Street lawyer (Brosnan) gets a shot at redemptive love with a lovely classmate (de Ravin) who has endured a devastating tragedy. That's really all you should know before seeing this unusually affecting yet understated drama, which builds to a surprising, and surprisingly potent, finale. Martha Plimpton appears unbilled. [PG-13] ▶

Remember Me, My Love (2003-Italian) **C-125m.** **½ D: Gabriele Muccino. Fabrizio Bentivoglio, Laura Morante, Nicoletta Romanoff, Monica Bellucci, Silvio Muccino, Gabriele Lavia, Enrico Silvestrin. Italian domestic drama centered on life, loves, and longings of a family in emotional crisis. The father carries on with a former flame, the daughter wants to be a scantily clad star on a sleazy TV show, the wife wants to resume her dormant acting career, etc. Soapy and overheated at times, but human qualities come through in this sometimes touching story from the director of the superior THE LAST KISS. Super 35. ▼▶

Remember My Name (1978) **C-96m.** *** D: Alan Rudolph. Geraldine Chaplin, Anthony Perkins, Moses Gunn, Berry Berenson, Jeff Goldblum, Timothy Thomerson, Alfre Woodard, Dennis Franz. Dreamlike film presents fragmented story of woman returning from prison, determined to disrupt her ex-husband's new life. Moody, provocative film definitely not for all tastes; striking blues vocals on soundtrack by Alberta Hunter. Produced by Robert Altman. Woodard's film debut. [R]

Remember the Night (1940) **94m.** ***½ D: Mitchell Leisen. Barbara Stanwyck, Fred MacMurray, Beulah Bondi, Elizabeth Patterson, Sterling Holloway. Beautifully made, sentimental story of prosecutor MacMurray falling in love with shoplifter Stanwyck during Christmas court recess; builds masterfully as it creates a very special mood. Script by Preston Sturges. ▼▶

Remember the Titans (2000) **C-113m.** *** D: Boaz Yakin. Denzel Washington, Will Patton, Donald Faison, Wood Harris, Ryan Hurst, Ethan Suplee, Nicole Ari Parker, Hayden Panettiere, Kip Pardue,

Craig Kirkwood, Kate Bosworth, Ryan Gosling. Corny but crowd-pleasing tale of a black man who's named to replace a well-respected football coach at a Virginia high school in the early 1970s . . . and how that coach gets his team to break down racial barriers and work together. Pat and manipulative, but still effective thanks in large part to the power of Washington's performance. Based on a true story. Director's cut runs 120m. Panavision. [PG]▼❍

Remo Williams: The Adventure Begins . . . (1985) C-121m. **½ D: Guy Hamilton. Fred Ward, Joel Grey, Wilford Brimley, J. A. Preston, George Coe, Charles Cioffi, Kate Mulgrew, Michael Pataki, William Hickey. Bubble-gum action-adventure yarn based on the popular *Destroyer* books by Richard Sapir and Warren Murphy, with Ward a N.Y.C. cop recruited by secret society out to avenge society's wrongs (motto: "Thou shalt not get away with it") . . . then he's trained for job by inscrutable Korean Sinanju master (Grey). Comes close to scoring bull's-eye but misfires too many times—and goes on too long. [PG-13]▼❍●

Renaissance (2006-French-British-Luxembourg) C/B&W-105m. **½ D: Christian Volckman. Voices of Daniel Craig, Catherine McCormack, Romola Garai, Jonathan Pryce, Ian Holm. The imagery is the star of this noir-ish animated action yarn set in Paris in 2054; the storyline, which is difficult to follow, involves a cop who sets out to find a kidnapped genetics researcher who apparently has pieced together the "protocol for immortality." The motion-capture animation is stark and occasionally stunning, making the film look like a graphic novel come to life . . . but after a while it grows tiresome, as the visuals outweigh the story and characterizations. Super 35. [R]●

Renaissance Man (1994) C-129m. **½ D: Penny Marshall. Danny DeVito, Gregory Hines, James Remar, Cliff Robertson, Lillo Brancato, Jr., Stacey Dash, Kadeem Hardison, Richard T. Jones, Khalil Kain, Peter Simmons, Greg Sporleder, Mark Wahlberg, Ben Wright, Ed Begley, Jr., Isabella Hoffmann. A man whose life and career have hit a stone wall gets hired to teach some of the Army's least intelligent recruits some basics of reading. Overlong, overtly corny "feel-good" movie, bolstered by sincere and persuasive performances. Also stands as the kindest portrait of the U.S. Army in recent history. Aka BY THE BOOK. [PG-13]▼❍●

Renaldo and Clara (1978) C-292m. BOMB. D: Bob Dylan. Bob Dylan, Sara Dylan, Sam Shepard, Ronee Blakley, Ronnie Hawkins, Joni Mitchell, Harry Dean Stanton, Arlo Guthrie, Bob Neuwirth, Joan Baez, Allen Ginsberg, Mick Ronson, Roberta Flack. Self-important, poorly made fictionalized account of Dylan's *Rolling Thunder Revue.* Dylan plays Renaldo; his wife Sara is Clara. Pretentious and obnoxious. Dylan later cut it to 122m.; what's left is mostly concert footage, but it doesn't help much. Sam Shepard's first film. [R]

Rendez-vous (1985-French) C-82m. *** D: André Téchiné. Juliette Binoche, Lambert Wilson, Wadeck Stanczak, Jean-Louis Trintignant, Olimpia Carlisi, Dominique Lavanant. Stylish melodrama perceptively investigates the borderline between play-acting and real life as stage actress (Binoche) becomes involved with obsessive live-sex show star Wilson and his mentor, a renowned director (Trintignant). Morbid mood and extreme sex scenes may repel some audiences; stunning widescreen cinematography by Renato Berta. CinemaScope.▼❍●

Rendezvous in Paris (1996-French) C-100m. ***½ D: Eric Rohmer. Clara Bellar, Antoine Basler, Aurore Rauscher, Serge Renko, Michael Kraft, Benedicte Loyen. Three thoroughly enchanting tales of love, trust and ambivalence, set in the lush urban landscape of Paris. Whether it be a young woman deciding if her boyfriend can be trusted, an "almost" affair between an engaged female student and another man, or a joyless painter and his potentially amorous encounters, these tales are simply told, with a complexity just below the surface that completely captivates.▼

Rendition (2007) C-122m. ** D: Gavin Hood. Jake Gyllenhaal, Reese Witherspoon, Meryl Streep, Alan Arkin, Peter Sarsgaard, Omar Metwally, Igal (Yigal) Naor, Zineb Oukach, Moa Khouas, J. K. Simmons, Bob Gunton. Gyllenhaal, a C.I.A. analyst in North Africa, is troubled by the U.S. government's clandestine interrogation (torture) methods—especially since the foreign-born alleged terrorist "rendered" here looks to be an upstanding American citizen. Witherspoon plays the (thankless) smaller role of the suspect's anxious wife back home. Meanwhile, a Third World Romeo-and-Juliet love story takes up an inordinate amount of screen time. Topical action film tries to be both cerebral and exciting, but the central theme gets buried. U.S. filmmaking debut for Hood, South African director of the Oscar-winning TSOTSI. Super 35. [R]●

Renegade Girls SEE: **Caged Heat**

Renegades (1989) C-106m. ** D: Jack Sholder. Kiefer Sutherland, Lou Diamond Phillips, Jami Gertz, Rob Knepper, Bill Smitrovich, Floyd Westerman. An undercover cop and a Lakota Indian put aside their differences to team up and chase down a criminal who's done them both wrong. Yet another buddy/cop movie which is just an excuse to keep stuntmen gainfully employed . . . though it does give Sutherland and Phillips a chance to use the gunslinging technique they learned in YOUNG GUNS. [R]▼●◐

Rennie's Landing SEE: **Stealing Time**

Reno 911!: Miami (2007) **C-84m.** *½ D: Robert Ben Garant. Carlos Alazraqui, Mary Birdsong, Robert Ben Garant, Kerri Kenney-Silver, Thomas Lennon, Wendy McLendon-Covey, Niecy Nash, Cedric Yarbrough. If you've heard of Comedy Central's inept crew of cops and are curious to see if they might be the subject for your coming Master's or Ph.D. thesis, this off-the-cuff feature (without the cable commercials that keep their bits aptly bite-sized) will serve as an intro. The Reno sheriff's department, in Miami for a convention, is called upon to protect the city when the regular cops are quarantined amid a bioterrorism attack. Slapdash film never saw a fat joke or masturbation joke it didn't like, though cameos by Paul Rudd and especially Dwayne (The Rock) Johnson are funnier than most of the rest. Coproduced by Danny DeVito, who also appears. Unrated version also available. [R]▐

Rent (2005) **C-135m.** **½ D: Chris Columbus. Anthony Rapp, Adam Pascal, Rosario Dawson, Jesse L. Martin, Wilson Jermaine Heredia, Idina Menzel, Tracie Thoms, Taye Diggs, Sarah Silverman, Anna Deavere Smith. Close friends in N.Y.C.'s East Village are being evicted from their apartment, and as their lives are further complicated (by crisscrossing relationships, AIDS, drugs, and other ills) they cling to one another for support. Long-awaited film version of Jonathan Larson's 1996 Pulitzer Prize–winning musical play, a modern spin on *La Boheme*. Preserves the performances of many original cast members and has some vibrant musical moments, but can't make up its mind if it's a real movie (though toward the end there are fade-outs at the close of scenes!). Attempts to "open up" the play fall flat, and second half drags. A mixed bag. Super 35. [PG-13]▐

Rent-a-Cop (1988) **C-96m.** BOMB D: Jerry London. Burt Reynolds, Liza Minnelli, James Remar, Richard Masur, Dionne Warwick, Bernie Casey, Robby Benson, Michael Rooker. Chicago dick Reynolds is suspended after his botched hotel drug bust leaves half a dozen dead; Minnelli's eyewitness hooker helps him track down the bullet-happy killer responsible. Burt seems fatigued but is at least easier to take than his costar's lounge-act prostie. [R]▼●◐

Rentadick (1972-British) **C-94m.** ** D: Jim Clark. James Booth, Julie Ege, Ronald Fraser, Donald Sinden, Michael Bentine, Richard Briers, Spike Milligan. Out of the nether-land between *The Goon Show* and *Monty Python* comes this romp written by Python pals John Cleese and Graham Chapman, spoofing formula private-eye flicks. An experimental nerve gas that paralyzes from the waist down has been stolen and

Rentadick, Inc. is hired to track down the culprits.▼

Rent-a-Kid (1995-U.S.-Canadian) **C-89m.** **½ D: Stuart Gillard. Leslie Nielsen, Christopher Lloyd, Matt McCoy, Sherry Miller, Amos Crawley, Cody Jones, Tabitha Lupien, Tony Rosato. When the head of an orphanage takes a vacation, dad Nielsen takes over with a scheme to raise money by renting out children. While predictable, this silly premise is surprisingly and sensitively realized when three children are rented by a hip '90s couple thinking about adopting. A decent family film. [G]▼●

Rented Lips (1987) **C-82m.** ** D: Robert Downey. Martin Mull, Dick Shawn, Jennifer Tilly, Robert Downey, Jr., Mel Welles, Shelley Berman, Edy Williams, June Lockhart, Kenneth Mars, Eileen Brennan, Pat McCormick, Michael Horse. Uneven comedy, written and produced by Mull, about a pair of down-on-their-luck educational filmmakers (with films like "Aluminum, Your Shiny Friend" to their credit) who become involved with a porno film crew. Cast of old pros and familiar faces helps. [R]▼

Repentance (1987-Russian) **C-155m.** ** D: Tengiz Abuladze. Avtandil Makharadze, Zeinab Botsvadze, Ketevan Abuladze, Edisher Giorgobiani, Kakhi Kavsadze. A beloved city father dies, but why is his body mysteriously—and continuously—exhumed? This allegory about small town smallmindedness and political repression offers a critical look at the Stalin era, but the result bogs down into a talkfest, and is much too obvious and boring. Completed in 1984; the final part of a trilogy, following THE PLEA (1968) and THE WISHING TREE (1977). [PG]▼●◐

Replacement Killers, The (1998) **C-86m.** **½ D: Antoine Fuqua. Chow Yun-Fat, Mira Sorvino, Michael Rooker, Jürgen Prochnow, Kenneth Tsang, Til Schweiger. Chow's American debut is a disappointingly routine action yarn about a hired assassin who—after failing to kill a cop, as ordered—becomes a target himself. Not bad, but nothing special; hardly a star-making vehicle for this established Hong Kong favorite. Unrated version runs 96m. Super 35. [R] ▼●◐

Replacements, The (2000) **C-118m.** ** D: Howard Deutch. Keanu Reeves, Gene Hackman, Brooke Langton, Orlando Jones, Jon Favreau, Jack Warden, Rhys Ifans, Michael Jace, Faizon Love, Brett Cullen. Silly, by-the-numbers sports comedy about a bunch of has-beens, eccentrics, and losers who are recruited by coach Hackman as replacement players in the wake of a pro-football strike. Tired and obvious. If you really want to see Hackman play a coach, rent the basketball drama HOOSIERS. [PG-13]▼▐

Repo Man (1984) **C-92m.** **½ D: Alex Cox. Emilio Estevez, Harry Dean Stanton, Vonetta McGee, Olivia Barash, Sy Richardson, Tracey Walter, Susan Barnes, Fox Harris, The Circle Jerks. Instant cult-movie about a new-wave punk who takes a job repossessing cars. Mixes social satire and science-fiction with engaging results, though a little of this film goes a long way. Stanton is perfect as a career repo man who shows Estevez the ropes. [R] ▼●]

Repo Men (2010) **C-111m.** ** D: Miguel Sapochnik. Jude Law, Forest Whitaker, Alice Braga, Liev Schreiber, Carice van Houten, Chandler Canterbury, RZA, Liza Lapira. Set in a future where prized human organs can be purchased on credit, the plot revolves around Law as a no-nonsense organ repo man who suddenly has the tables turned and finds himself hunted when he can't pay the bills for a heart transplant. Intriguing premise with strong social implications is given uninspired execution and fails to make its point. Law and Whitaker have good chemistry but cast is wasted on a script that must have looked better on paper. Eric Garcia coscripted from his novel *The Repossession Mambo.* Alternate version runs 120m. Hawk Scope. [R]]

Report to the Commissioner (1975) **C-112m.** **½ D: Milton Katselas. Michael Moriarty, Yaphet Kotto, Susan Blakely, Hector Elizondo, Tony King, Michael McGuire, Dana Elcar, Robert Balaban, William Devane, Stephen Elliott, Richard Gere, Vic Tayback, Sonny Grosso. Rookie cop Moriarty accidentally kills undercover cop Blakely and becomes embroiled in department-wide cover-up. Brutal melodrama ranges from realistic to overblown; taut but not always convincing. Script by Abby Mann and Ernest Tidyman. Gere's film debut. [PG] ▼▮

Repossessed (1990) **C-84m.** *½ D: Bob Logan. Linda Blair, Ned Beatty, Leslie Nielsen, Anthony Starke, Lana Schwab, Thom J. Sharp. AIRPLANE-style spoof of THE EXORCIST, with Blair herself as a housewife possessed anew by the same demon she was rid of as a child. Too few gags, too many targets, and a poor finale. Blair and Nielsen (as the exorcist) are good. Written by director Logan. [PG-13] ▼●]

Repo! The Genetic Opera (2008) **C-98m.** *** D: Darren Lynn Bousman. Anthony Stewart Head, Alexa Vega, Paul Sorvino, Sarah Brightman, Terrance Zdunich, Bill Moseley, Ogre, Paris Hilton, Joan Jett. In the year 2056 a population desperate for organ replacements turns to Big Brother–ish corporation GeneCo and its despotic leader Rotti Largo (Sorvino) to survive. Largo has blackmailed his onetime romantic rival (Head) into becoming a "repo man," harvesting organs as he struggles to shield his teenage daughter (Vega) from the grim world outside her home. Imaginative rock opera with horror movie trappings and comic-book storytelling blended into the mix. Story doesn't hold up to the very end but it's still a wild ride. Based on a stage piece by Darren Smith and Terrance Zdunich (who also appears as the singing narrator). [R] ▮

Reprieve SEE: **Convicts 4**

Reprise (2006-Norwegian-Swedish) **C-107m.** **½ D: Joachim Trier. Espen Klouman Høiner, Anders Danielsen Lie, Christian Rubeck, Odd Magnus Williamson, Pål Stokka, Viktoria Winge, Silje Hagen. Visually kinetic saga of two self-absorbed boyhood friends who share a passion for an elusive Norwegian author and aspire to become successful novelists themselves. How they deal with success and failure, socially and professionally, and how fate deals with them (as intoned by an omnipresent narrator) is the crux of this bold, nonlinear feature inspired, it would seem, by JULES AND JIM. This received critical acclaim in some circles but it's hard to care about these characters. Feature debut for director and cowriter Trier. [R] ▮

Reptile, The (1966-British) **C-90m.** *** D: John Gilling. Noel Willman, Jennifer Daniels, Ray Barrett, Jacqueline Pearce. Hammer chiller about village girl with strange power to change into snake. Excellent direction, sympathetic characterizations. ▼●]

Repulsion (1965-British) **105m.** **** D: Roman Polanski. Catherine Deneuve, Ian Hendry, John Fraser, Patrick Wymark, Yvonne Furneaux, James Villiers. Polanski's first English-language film is excellent psychological shocker depicting mental deterioration of sexually repressed girl left alone in her sister's apartment for several days. Hasn't lost a bit of its impact; will leave you feeling uneasy for days afterward. Screenplay by Polanski and Gerard Brach. ▼●]

Requiem for a Dream (2000) **C-102m.** ** D: Darren Aronofsky. Ellen Burstyn, Jared Leto, Jennifer Connelly, Marlon Wayans, Christopher McDonald, Louise Lasser, Keith David, Sean Gullette. While a young man slides deeper into a life of drugs, his mother, living on her own in a Brooklyn apartment, drifts into a dream world after getting hooked on diet pills. Burstyn is great, and Aronofsky uses attention-getting visuals to tell his story, but his characters' descent into hell is difficult to watch (to say the least). You'd expect no less from a collaboration between Aronofsky and Hubert Selby, Jr.; it's based on the latter's novel. Perhaps the only film to ever credit a Refrigerator Puppeteer! Originally shown in unrated version. [R] ▼▮

Requiem for a Heavyweight (1962) **100m.** *** D: Ralph Nelson. Anthony Quinn, Jackie Gleason, Mickey Rooney, Julie Harris, Nancy Cushman, Madame Spivy, Cassius Clay (Muhammad Ali). Grim account of fighter (Quinn) whose ring career is over, forcing him into corruption and degradation. His sleazy manager Gleason, sympathetic trainer Rooney, and Harris as unrealistic

social worker are all fine. Adapted by Rod Serling from his great teleplay; original running time 87m. ▼❖
Requiem for Dominic (1990-Austrian) **C-90m.** **½ D: Robert Dornhelm. Felix Mitterer, Viktoria Schubert, August Schmolzer, Angelica Schutz, Antonia Rados, Nikolas Vogel. True story about Romanian-born Austrian who returns to his homeland to be with his best friend, who's now accused of committing 80 murders. Set at the beginning of the anti-Communist movement in late 1989. Sometimes powerful, highly political film; director Dornhelm was a childhood friend of the accused man depicted in the story. ▼●
Rescue, The (1986) SEE: **Let's Get Harry**
Rescue Dawn (2007) **C-126m.** *** D: Werner Herzog. Christian Bale, Steve Zahn, Jeremy Davies, Galen Yuen, Abhijati "Meuk" Jusakul, Chaiyan "Lek" Chunsuttiwat. Gripping reworking of Herzog's 1997 documentary LITTLE DIETER NEEDS TO FLY, about Dieter Dengler (Bale), a German-born American who came of age in the Black Forest during WW2 and experienced firsthand the destruction of his hometown by American warplanes. Dengler later emigrated to the U.S., became a fighter pilot, and was shot down in 1965 during a top-secret bombing raid over Laos. His obsession to fly results in his being tortured and abused as a prisoner of war. An edge-of-your-seat POW story, this also serves as a commentary about the U.S. involvement in Vietnam. [PG-13]❙
Rescuers, The (1977) **C-76m.** *** D: Wolfgang Reitherman, John Lounsbery, Art Stevens. Voices of Bob Newhart, Eva Gabor, Geraldine Page, Joe Flynn, Jeanette Nolan, Pat Buttram, Jim Jordan, John McIntire. Engaging, well-plotted Disney animated feature about Bernard and Bianca, members of the all-mouse Rescue Aid Society, and their efforts to save a little girl who's been kidnaped. Highlighted by some great supporting characters, including Orville the Albatross (voiced by radio's Fibber McGee, Jim Jordan), Evinrude the dragonfly, and the villainess Madame Medusa. Followed by a sequel. [G]▼●❙
Rescuers Down Under, The (1990) **C-74m.** *** D: Hendel Butoy, Mike Gabriel. Voices of Bob Newhart, Eva Gabor, George C. Scott, John Candy, Tristan Rogers, Adam Ryen, Frank Welker. Entertaining—if plotty—sequel to the 1977 Disney animated feature, with amorous mice Bernard and Bianca, the unlikely agents from the Rescue Aid Society, traveling to Australia to help a young boy in trouble. Animation buffs will notice considerable computer-assisted animation, especially the villain's demon tractor. [G]▼●❙
Reservation Road (2007) **C-102m.** **½ D: Terry George. Joaquin Phoenix, Mark Ruffalo, Jennifer Connelly, Mira Sorvino, Elle

Fanning, John Slattery. A perpetual screwup (Ruffalo) who craves his young son's love and respect swerves on a Connecticut road one evening and strikes a boy dead right in front of his family—then drives away before anyone can identify him. Balance of the story explores the anguish of the bereaved parents—and the driver's overpowering, paralyzing guilt. Intelligent, well-acted adaptation of John Burnham Schwartz's novel (which he wrote with George) . . . but emotionally demanding and tough to watch. [R]❙
Reservoir Dogs (1992) **C-99m.** *** D: Quentin Tarantino. Harvey Keitel, Tim Roth, Michael Madsen, Chris Penn, Steve Buscemi, Lawrence Tierney, Randy Brooks, Kirk Baltz, Eddie Bunker, Quentin Tarantino; voice of Steven Wright. Precocious "shock" debut from writer-director-costar Tarantino echoes THE ASPHALT JUNGLE and THE KILLING: Post-mortem dissection of a fatally bungled jewel robbery boasts at least one unwatchably graphic torture scene and the 1992 movie year's No. 1 mortality rate. Flashy—maybe *too* flashy—but fundamentally a story well told; nearly every performance is better than expected, with Tierney in his best role since the '40s. Super 35. [R]▼●❙
Resident, The (2011-British-U.S.) **C-91m.** BOMB D: Antti J. Jokinen. Hilary Swank, Jeffrey Dean Morgan, Lee Pace, Christopher Lee, Aunjanue Ellis. Unsure of herself after a romantic breakup, ER doctor Swank moves into a too-economical-to-be-true Brooklyn loft after the building's young coowner takes a liking to her. Soon, while she's at work, he's using her electric toothbrush, masturbating in her bathtub, and all the other standard Fred Mertz landlord stuff. Appallingly derivative stinker, barely released, goes through the usual litany of psychotic moves before screech-halt ending on a dime. It's incredible that any double Oscar winner would ever wind up headlining a movie like this. Even Luise Rainer never had it so bad. [R] ❙
Resident Evil (2002-German-U.S.-French) **C-100m.** *½ D: Paul Anderson. Milla Jovovich, Michelle Rodriguez, Eric Mabius, James Purefoy, Colin Salmon, Martin Crewes. Bloody, barely coherent high-tech horror film involving commandos who infiltrate The Hive, a top-secret underground research lab. Their mission: to battle a supercomputer gone awry and a mutant virus that has transformed the lab's workers into flesh-eating zombies. This time killer recalls a host of other horror films, from ALIEN to DAWN OF THE DEAD. Based on a popular video game. Followed by three sequels and a direct-to-DVD CGI feature. [R]▼❙
Resident Evil: Afterlife (2010-British-German-French-Canadian) **C-97m.** ** D: Paul W. S. Anderson. Milla Jovovich, Ali Larter, Wentworth Miller, Kim Coates,

Shawn Roberts, Sergio Peris-Mencheta, Spencer Locke, Boris Kodjoe. Fourth theatrical feature in the series finds super-powered heroine Alice (Jovovich) fleeing Canada and arriving in L.A., taking shelter in a high-rise with a few other survivors of the global apocalypse. They need to escape to a ship nearby, but thousands of cannibal-istic zombies are struggling to reach them. It is what it is: a high-tech, well-produced entry in a series based on a video game. Devotees may enjoy it more than others, who, in the unlikely event they watch, will find it repetitious, unimaginative, and rou-tine. 3-D HD Widescreen. [R] ◐

Resident Evil: Apocalypse (2004-German-French-British) **C-94m.** BOMB D: Alexan-der Witt. Milla Jovovich, Sienna Guillory, Oded Fehr, Jared Harris, Thomas Kretsch-mann, Sophie Vavasseur, Mike Epps, Iain Glen. Tiresome follow-up to RESIDENT EVIL plays more like a remake as the T-virus strikes again. As a result, the undead are out and about preying on the uninfected population of Raccoon City. Jovovich agrees to find a scientist's daughter on the condition that he will lead them out of town before a nuclear bomb is dropped. Only for fanatics of the video game. Super 35. [R] ▼◐

Resident Evil: Extinction (2007-Canadian-British) **C-94m.** ** D: Russell Mulcahy. Milla Jovovich, Oded Fehr, Ali Larter, Iain Glen, Ashanti, Mike Epps. Third episode in sci-fi franchise finds the biogenetically en-hanced Alice (Jovovich) aiding a dwindling group of non-zombies in a wasteland over-run with virus-infected flesh-eaters. Routine postapocalyptic action-adventure, recalling many ROAD WARRIOR knock-offs of the 1980s. Super 35. [R]◐

Respiro (2002-Italian-French) **C-90m.** *** D: Emanuele Crialese. Valeria Golino, Vincenzo Amato, Francesco Casisa, Ve-ronica D'Agostino, Filippo Pucillo, Muzzi Loffredo. Thoughtful, colorful account of a peasant family in a small Italian fish-ing village, focusing on an earthy, moody wife-mother (Golino); her family thinks she has a mental problem, but perhaps her dead-end lifestyle is to blame for her act-ing out. Memorable finale caps this com-pelling drama about individuals who are trapped and stifled by their environment. [PG-13]▼▶

Restoration (1995) **C-117m.** *** D: Mi-chael Hoffman. Robert Downey, Jr., Sam Neill, David Thewlis, Polly Walker, Meg Ryan, Ian McKellen, Hugh Grant, Hugh Mc-Diarmid. In 1600s England, a young doctor torn between duty and debauchery opts for the latter when he becomes a court favorite of King Charles II and a dummy bridegroom for one of the king's mistresses. Vivid period piece with contemporary parallels depends on Downey to draw us in—and he's excel-lent. Opulent production and an earnest cast

buoy this film through its metamorphosis from costume romp to social drama, though it does sag during the second half. Oscar win-ner for Art Direction and Costume Design. Filmed in England and Wales. [R]▼◐

Restrepo (2010) **C-93m.** ***½ D: Tim Hetherington, Sebastian Junger. Riveting documentary captures the spirit and indi-vidual personalities of a U.S. platoon dur-ing its 14-month tour of duty battling the Taliban in Afghanistan. The soldiers share a common humanity; as their stories are told, a question arises: What is being accom-plished here? Restrepo is the surname of one of the platoon members, a 20-year-old medic who was killed in action early in the deployment. Codirector Hetherington was later killed in Libya. [R]◐

Resurrecting the Champ (2007) **C-111m.** *** D: Rod Lurie. Samuel L. Jackson, Josh Hartnett, Kathryn Morris, Alan Alda, Teri Hatcher, David Paymer, Peter Coyote, Harry J. Lennix. Engrossing drama, loosely based on fact, about a discontented Denver sportswriter who gets a career boost by profiling a onetime heavyweight contender now barely scraping by as a homeless drunk. Movie intelligently deals with is-sues of personal and professional integrity, with vivid character turns by Alda, Hatcher, and Coyote, but the main event is Jackson's knockout performance as a bloodied-but-unbowed ex-boxer whose story may be too good to be true. Super 35. [PG-13]◐

Resurrection (1980) **C-103m.** ***½ D: Daniel Petrie. Ellen Burstyn, Sam Shepard, Richard Farnsworth, Roberts Blossom, Clifford David, Pamela Payton-Wright, Eva LeGallienne, Lane Smith. Beautifully realized story (by Lewis John Carlino) about a woman who returns to life from the brink of death with amazing healing pow-ers. Burstyn's moving performance is the centerpiece of a wonderful and underrated film. [PG]▼◐

Resurrection Syndicate, The SEE: **Noth-ing but the Night**

Return, The (1980) **C-91m.** BOMB D: Greydon Clark. Jan-Michael Vincent, Cybill Shepherd, Martin Landau, Raymond Burr, Neville Brand, Brad Rearden, Vincent Schi-avelli. Deadeningly dull story of a "close encounter" and how it affects two children and an old man in a small New Mexico town. Inept from start to finish. Retitled THE ALIEN'S RETURN.▼

Return, The (2003-Russian) **C-105m.** *** D: Andreï Zvyagintsev. Vladimir Garin, Ivan Dobronravov, Natalia Vdovina, Konstantin Lavronenko, Galina Petrova. A father who has been away for 12 years mysteriously reappears and takes his two sons to a remote island, where the supposed vacation turns into a test of their manhood and maturity. Absorbing and strikingly well made, this is a coming-of-age story like no other. Despite its clear Russian roots, the film deals with universal themes. ▼▶

Return, The (2006) **C-85m.** *½ D: Asif Kapadia. Sarah Michelle Gellar, Peter O'Brien, Adam Scott, Kate Beahan, J. C. MacKenzie, Erinn Allison, Sam Shepard. Young woman with a self-mutilation disorder, haunted by a waking dream she's had since age 11, digs into her rural roots to decipher enigmatic visions of bloody murder. Constantly thwarted by tight-lipped townspeople, she discovers that La Salle, Texas, seems to be the next town over from Silent Hill. To say more would spoil the total lack of surprise in this would-be supernatural thriller. Shepard (as the girl's father) tries to ground the film, but both he and Gellar are wasted. Super 35. [PG-13] ▶

Returner (2002-Japanese) **C-117m.** **½ D: Takashi Yamazaki. Takeshi Kaneshiro, Anne Suzuki, Goro Kishitani, Kirin Kiki, Yukio Okamoto, Mitsuro Murata, Kisuke Iida. Winsome young time traveler from 2084 tries to alter her war-ravaged future, helped only by a cool, all-but-invincible Tokyo hit man. The plot—a remix of TERMINATOR, THE MATRIX, THE ABYSS, even E.T.—is buoyed by fine CGI, plenty of gunplay and kickboxing, and two engaging, energetic lead characters. Longish and familiar, but fun. [R] ▼▶

Return From the Past (1967) **C-84m.** BOMB D: David L. Hewitt. Lon Chaney, John Carradine, Rochelle Hudson, Roger Gentry. Veteran stars wasted in utter monstrosity; five tales of supernatural told here are five too many. Original titles: GALLERY OF HORROR, DR. TERROR'S GALLERY OF HORRORS, THE BLOOD SUCKERS. Totalvision. ▼▶

Return From Witch Mountain (1978) **C-95m.** *** D: John Hough. Bette Davis, Christopher Lee, Kim Richards, Ike Eisenmann, Denver Pyle, Jack Soo, Dick Bakalyan. Sequel to ESCAPE TO WITCH MOUNTAIN has Davis and Lee kidnapping Eisenmann, hoping to put his special powers to evil use. Good fun from Disney. Followed three decades later by RACE TO WITCH MOUNTAIN. [G] ▼▶

Return of a Man Called Horse, The (1976) **C-129m.** *** D: Irvin Kershner. Richard Harris, Gale Sondergaard, Geoffrey Lewis, Bill Lucking, Jorge Luke, Enrique Lucero. Excellent sequel has Harris returning from England to right wrongs done the Yellow Hand Sioux by whites. Sun Vow ceremony now performed by dozen braves. Magnificent score by Laurence Rosenthal; followed by TRIUMPHS OF A MAN CALLED HORSE. Panavision. [PG] ▼▶

Return of Captain Invincible, The (1983-Australian-U.S) **C-90m.** **½ D: Philippe Mora. Alan Arkin, Christopher Lee, Kate Fitzpatrick, Michael Pate. Bizarre, campy

comedy about drunken, derelict ex-superhero persuaded to come out of retirement sounds better than it works. Oddly placed musical numbers seem to aim for ROCKY HORROR ambiance. Aka LEGEND IN LEOTARDS. Panavision. [PG] ▼▶

Return of Count Yorga, The (1971) **C-97m.** **½ D: Bob Kelljan. Robert Quarry, Mariette Hartley, Roger Perry, Yvonne Wilder. The Count goes out for more blood, wreaking havoc on nearby orphanage. [PG] ▼▶

Return of Doctor X, The (1939) **62m.** ** D: Vincent Sherman. Humphrey Bogart, Rosemary Lane, Dennis Morgan, John Litel, Huntz Hall, Wayne Morris. Only Bogart as a creepy lab assistant makes this low-grade sci-fi yarn worth viewing. Despite the title, not a sequel to DOCTOR X. ▶

Return of Frank James, The (1940) **C-92m.** *** D: Fritz Lang. Henry Fonda, Gene Tierney, Jackie Cooper, Henry Hull, John Carradine, J. Edward Bromberg, Donald Meek. Fonda reprises role from 1939 JESSE JAMES in story of attempt to avenge his brother Jesse's death; colorful production was Tierney's film debut. ▼▶

Return of Martin Guerre, The (1982-French) **C-111m.** *** D: Daniel Vigne. Gérard Depardieu, Nathalie Baye, Roger Planchon, Maurice Jacquemont, Bernard Pierre Donnadieu. Blockbuster art house hit, based on fact, about a 16th-century peasant who returns to his wife and family a much better person than the misfit he was seven years earlier; could it be that he's really an impostor? No artistic groundbreaker, but a solid romance and history lesson, well acted by the two leads. Alternate version runs 123m. Remade in 1993 as SOMMERSBY. ▼▶

Return of Maxwell Smart, The SEE: Nude Bomb, The

Return of Sabata, The (1972-Italian-Spanish) **C-106m.** *½ D: Frank Kramer (Gianfranco Parolini). Lee Van Cleef, Reiner Schone, Annabelle Incontrera, Jacqueline Alexandre, Pedro Sanchez (Ignazio Spalla). Last of the spaghetti Western series—and not a moment too soon—finds Van Cleef chasing down some baddies who bilked him out of $5,000. Techniscope. [PG] ▼▶

Return of Superfly, The (1990) **C-95m.** *½ D: Sig Shore. Nathan Purdee, Margaret Avery, Leonard Thomas, Christopher Curry, David Groh, Samuel L. Jackson. Belated (and unnecessary) sequel with Purdee replacing Ron O'Neal as Priest; he's now an ex-drug dealer who goes up against his vicious, violent former cronies. Only interest is Curtis Mayfield's reworking of his original SUPERFLY score to incorporate rap music. [R] ▼

Return of Swamp Thing, The (1989) **C-88m.** *½ D: Jim Wynorski. Dick Durock, Heather Locklear, Louis Jourdan, Sarah

Douglas, Daniel Taylor. The vegetable man superhero learns that mad scientist Jourdan, who's been blending people with animals, has similar designs on his chirpy stepdaughter Locklear. Oafish spoof sequel to straight original can't find a style and wastes time with two unfunny little boys. The comic books are much better. [PG-13]▼●)

Return of the Dragon (1973-Hong Kong) **C-91m.** **½ D: Bruce Lee. Bruce Lee, Chuck Norris, Nora Miao. Country hick Lee visits relatives who run Chinese restaurant in Italy and helps fight off gangsters trying to take over. Many fine comic and action sequences, including final battle with Chuck Norris in Roman Colosseum. This was made before (but released after) ENTER THE DRAGON, which was Lee's final completed film. Aka WAY OF THE DRAGON. Widescreen. [R]▼●)

Return of the Fly (1959) **80m.** **½ D: Edward L. Bernds. Vincent Price, Brett Halsey, David Frankham, John Sutton, Dan Seymour, Danielle De Metz. Adequate sequel to THE FLY proves "like father, like son." Youth attempts to reconstruct his late father's teleportation machine and likewise gets scrambled with an insect. Followed six years later by CURSE OF THE FLY. CinemaScope.▼●)

Return of the Jedi (1983) **C-131m.** ***½ D: Richard Marquand. Mark Hamill, Harrison Ford, Carrie Fisher, Billy Dee Williams, Anthony Daniels, Peter Mayhew, Sebastian Shaw, Ian McDiarmid, David Prowse, Alec Guinness, Kenny Baker, Denis Lawson, Warwick Davis; voices of James Earl Jones, Frank Oz. Third installment in the STAR WARS saga is a sheer delight, following the destiny of Luke Skywalker as his comrades reunite to combat a powerful Death Star. Some routine performances are compensated for by ingenious new characters and Oscar-winning special effects. More sentimental and episodic than its predecessors, but carried out in the best tradition of Saturday matinee serials, from which it draws its inspiration. Full title on-screen is: STAR WARS EPISODE VI: RETURN OF THE JEDI. Special edition released in 1997 features enhanced effects and 4m. of additional footage. Followed by two Ewok adventures for TV and the prequel STAR WARS EPISODE I: THE PHANTOM MENACE. J-D-C Scope. [PG] ▼●)

Return of the Killer Tomatoes! (1988) **C-99m.** *½ D: John De Bello. Anthony Starke, George Clooney, Karen Mistal, Steve Lundquist, Charlie Jones, John Astin. Sequel to ATTACK OF THE KILLER TOMATOES!, this is a mild improvement. In a tomato-fearing world, mad scientist Astin is turning tomatoes into people and vice-versa; our hero falls for an attractive one-time tomato. Long, silly, but has its moments. Notable for early screen appearance

by Clooney. Followed by KILLER TOMATOES STRIKE BACK. [PG]▼●)

Return of the Living Dead, The (1985) **C-90m.** ** D: Dan O'Bannon. Clu Gulager, James Karen, Don Calfa, Thom Mathews, Beverly Randolph, John Philbin. What starts out as a spoof of George Romero's zombie films (with wonderful comic performance by Karen as supervisor of medical warehouse) loses its footing when the tone, and the violence, turn serious. Directing debut for sci-fi screenwriter O'Bannon. Followed by two sequels and two direct-to-video sequels. [R]▼●)

Return of the Living Dead Part II (1988) **C-89m.** ** D: Ken Wiederhorn. James Karen, Thom Mathews, Michael Kenworthy, Marsha Dietlein, Dana Ashbrook, Suzanne Snyder. Awkward title identifies this as a sequel not to the George Romero zombie classics but rather the 1985 comedy offshoot. Inquisitive kids release deadly gas from a misplaced military canister, causing corpses from a nearby cemetery to rise and wreak havoc. [R]▼●)

Return of the Living Dead III (1993) **C-97m.** **½ D: Brian Yuzna. Mindy Clarke, J. Trevor Edmond, Kent McCord, Sarah Douglas, James T. Callahan, Mike Moroff, Sal Lopez. A very different approach from the first two entries results in a serious thriller about a teenager who uses the zombie gas to resurrect his girlfriend, with horrendous results. An intelligent, gruesomely imaginative, and tragic love story, but it doesn't know when to quit. [R]▼●)

Return of the Magnificent Seven SEE: **Return of the Seven**

Return of the Musketeers, The (1989-British-French-Spanish) **C-101m.** **½ D: Richard Lester. Michael York, Oliver Reed, Frank Finlay, C. Thomas Howell, Kim Cattrall, Richard Chamberlain, Philippe Noiret, Roy Kinnear, Geraldine Chaplin, Christopher Lee, Eusebio Lazaro, Jean-Pierre Cassel, Billy Connolly. Twenty years after the death of Milady de Winter, d'Artagnan (York) tries to reunite the remaining musketeers to save Queen Anne from the machinations of the devious Cardinal Mazarin (deliciously played by Noiret). Lester's follow-up to his two '70s classics is only partially successful, straining for a jaunty charm that just isn't there, but actually gets better as it goes along. Released directly to cable-TV in the U.S. in 1991. Sadly, Roy Kinnear, who played Planchet in all three films, died in an equestrian accident during production. Based on the Alexandre Dumas novel *Twenty Years Later.* [PG]▼●)

Return of the Pink Panther, The (1975-British) **C-113m.** **½ D: Blake Edwards. Peter Sellers, Christopher Plummer, Catherine Schell, Herbert Lom, Burt Kwouk, Peter Arne, Gregoire Aslan, Andre Maranne, Victor

Spinetti. Fourth PANTHER film, and first with Sellers since A SHOT IN THE DARK. Inspector Clouseau is a superb comedy character, but director-writer Edwards thinks big, violent gags are funny. Best part of this diamond-heist farce is the opening title, animated by Richard Williams and Ken Harris. Immediate sequel—THE PINK PANTHER STRIKES AGAIN—is much better. Panavision. [G] ▼●◗

Return of the Secaucus Seven (1980) C-106m. *** D: John Sayles. Mark Arnott, Gordon Clapp, Maggie Cousineau, Adam Lefevre, Bruce MacDonald, Jean Passanante, Maggie Renzi, David Strathairn. A simple low-budget film about a weekend reunion of good friends who shared the '60s radical college life and have since gone in different directions. Credible, winning performances (including one by director-writer Sayles, as Howie) enhance a script that seems to tell the story of an entire generation. Filmed with then unknown actors for a reported budget of $60,000! An interesting precursor to THE BIG CHILL. [R] ▼◗

Return of the Seven (1966) C-96m. ** D: Burt Kennedy. Yul Brynner, Robert Fuller, Warren Oates, Jordan Christopher, Claude Akins, Emilio Fernandez. The gang has reformed for more protection in this drab sequel to THE MAGNIFICENT SEVEN; it was a lot more fun when Eli Wallach was the heavy. Followed by GUNS OF THE MAGNIFICENT SEVEN. Aka RETURN OF THE MAGNIFICENT SEVEN. Panavision. ▼●◗

Return of the Soldier, The (1981-British) C-101m. ** D: Alan Bridges. Alan Bates, Julie Christie, Glenda Jackson, Ann-Margret, Ian Holm, Frank Finlay. A shell-shocked soldier comes home from WW1 with no memory of the last 20 years, but feels a vague dissatisfaction with his life, as personified by wife Christie. Top cast in this adaptation of Rebecca West's first novel, but it's slow going, and ultimately not that interesting. ▼◗

Return of the Street Fighter (1974-Japanese) C-76m. ** D: Shigehiro Ozawa. Shinichi "Sonny" Chiba, Yoko Ichiji, Masafumi Suzuki, Donald Nakajima, Milton Ishibashi. After refusing to carry out a hit for the mob, Chiba is targeted for execution himself. First sequel in the series is just a routine continuation of the original—a mélange of hilariously bad dubbing and brutal martial arts action—highlighted by a vicious fight in a steam bath. Followed by THE STREET FIGHTER'S LAST REVENGE. Actionscope. [R] ▼●◗

Return of the Tall Blond Man With One Black Shoe, The (1974-French) C-84m. **½ D: Yves Robert. Pierre Richard, Mireille Darc, Michel Duchaussoy, Jean Rochefort, Jean Carmet. Sequel to the 1972

hit reunites the principals for a lesser if still entertaining sendup of the spy game. Spy chief Rochefort wants violinist Richard killed, but the tall blond avoids danger without even realizing what's happening. Nice shots of Rio and a fairly deft James Bond takeoff help offset slow buildup. ▼

Return of the Texas Chainsaw Massacre SEE: Texas Chainsaw Massacre: The Next Generation

Return of the Vampire, The (1943) 69m. ** D: Lew Landers. Bela Lugosi, Frieda Inescort, Nina Foch, Roland Varno, Miles Mander, Matt Willis. Lugosi plays a vampire in wartorn London (with a werewolf assistant!) in limp attempt to capitalize on previous success as Dracula. Final scene is memorable, though. ▼●◗

Return to Boggy Creek (1977) C-87m. ** D: Tom Moore. Dawn Wells, Dana Plato. More sightings of monsters in this sequel to THE LEGEND OF BOGGY CREEK, but this time two children are involved. G-rated nonsense may intrigue young viewers. Followed by THE BARBARIC BEAST OF BOGGY CREEK PART II, which is actually the third Boggy Creek film. [G] ▼

Return to Macon County (1975) C-90m. *½ D: Richard Compton. Don Johnson, Nick Nolte, Robin Mattson, Robert Viharo, Eugene Daniels, Matt Greene. Unworthy follow-up to MACON COUNTY LINE, as youngsters get mixed up in drag races, sex, the law, violence and murder, in about that order. Nolte's first film. [PG] ▼

Return to Me (2000) C-116m. *** D: Bonnie Hunt. David Duchovny, Minnie Driver, Carroll O'Connor, Robert Loggia, Bonnie Hunt, David Alan Grier, Joely Richardson, James Belushi, Eddie Jones, William Bronder. Thoroughly engaging romantic comedy-drama about a man who loses his wife, then chances to meet a woman whose life has been saved by a heart transplant. Sincere performances by the leads and a joyous ensemble (including O'Connor as Driver's Irish grandfather and Loggia as her Italian uncle) make this heartwarmer a pleasure to watch. Impressive feature directing debut for Hunt, who costars and wrote the script with Don Lake (who plays the hair transplant man). [PG] ▼◗

Return to Never Land (2002) C-72m. **½ D: Robin Budd. Voices of Harriet Owen, Blayne Weaver, Corey Burton, Jeff Bennett, Kath Soucie, Dan Castellaneta, Spencer Breslin, Russi Taylor, Roger Rees, Clive Revill. Sequel to Disney's PETER PAN is set in wartorn London, where Wendy's sober daughter Jane is kidnapped by Captain Hook and whisked away to Never Land. Peter Pan comes to her rescue and must restore her sense of childhood imagination in order to fly her home. Minor-league Disney feature was produced by the TV animation department for video release, but deemed worthy of theatrical showings instead. OK but strictly for kids. [G]▼▶

Return to Oz (1985) C-110m. ** D: Walter Murch. Nicol Williamson, Jean Marsh, Fairuza Balk, Piper Laurie, Matt Clark. Distressingly downbeat sequel to THE WIZARD OF OZ, with Dorothy fleeing a spooky sanitarium in Kansas to return to her beloved land—only to find evil rulers now in charge. Many colorful characters, but few engender any warmth or feeling. Best moments involve Will Vinton's Claymation effects, where rock faces come to life. Best sequence: final showdown with the Nome King. Inauspicious directing debut for celebrated sound technician Murch (who cowrote script). [PG]▼▶▶

Return to Paradise (1998) C-109m. **½ D: Joseph Ruben. Vince Vaughn, Anne Heche, Joaquin Phoenix, David Conrad, Jada Pinkett Smith, Vera Farmiga. Two years after a wild, carefree trip to Malaysia, a woman tracks down two young men in N.Y.C. and tells them that if they don't return, the friend they made during their trip will be hanged for possession of hashish that really belonged to them. A rare contemporary film about responsibility, and a crisis of conscience, is weakened by the introduction of a love story. Still interesting, however, with strong performances all around. Remake of the 1990 French film FORCE MAJEURE. Super 35. [R]▼▶▶

Return to Peyton Place (1961) C-122m. ** D: Jose Ferrer. Carol Lynley, Jeff Chandler, Eleanor Parker, Mary Astor, Robert Sterling, Luciana Paluzzi, Brett Halsey, Gunnar Hellstrom, Tuesday Weld, Bob Crane. Muddled follow-up to PEYTON PLACE suffers from faulty direction, and, save for stalwarts Astor and Parker, miscasting. Followed by TV movie MURDER IN PEYTON PLACE. CinemaScope. ▼▶

Return to Salem's Lot, A (1987) C-96m. ** D: Larry Cohen. Michael Moriarty, Ricky Addison Reed, Samuel Fuller, Andrew Duggan, Evelyn Keyes, Jill Gatsby, June Havoc, Ronee Blakley, James Dixon, David Holbrook, Tara Reid. Anthropologist Moriarty, trying to befriend his estranged son, is lured to a small Maine town where the populace—almost all vampires—want him to write their history. Typically cheap, oddball Cohen film, which he cowrote, has little to do with Stephen King's novel or the TV movie based on it. [R]▼▶

Return to Snowy River (1988-Australian) C-97m. **½ D: Geoff Burrowes. Tom Burlinson, Sigrid Thornton, Brian Dennehy, Nicholas Eadie, Bryan Marshall. Follow-up to THE MAN FROM SNOWY RIVER is not nearly as good. Young Burlinson must again prove his worth as he battles villainous Eadie, who's become engaged to his beloved (Thornton). All those shots of galloping horses, however, are still eye-popping. Panavision. [PG]▼▶▶

Return to the Blue Lagoon (1991) C-100m. BOMB D: William A. Graham. Brian Krause, Milla Jovovich, Lisa Pelikan, Garette Patrick Ratliff, Courtney Barilla. The two-year-old son of LAGOON 1's deceased parents is rescued by a ship carrying a widow and her year-old daughter; circumstances (read: cholera) force the trio onto another tropical island, so the kids can eventually partake in PG-13 prurience. [PG-13]▼▶▶

Return to the Lost World (1994-Canadian) C-99m. *½ D: Timothy Bond. John Rhys-Davies, David Warner, Eric McCormack, Nathania Stanford, Darren Peter Mercer, Tamara Gorski. In this sequel to THE LOST WORLD (1993), shot at the same time in 1991, bad Belgians begin to exploit The Lost World, so Challenger and friends come to the rescue. Long, weary sequel has even fewer dinosaurs than the first film, if that's possible. An insult to Conan Doyle. Good performances by Rhys-Davies and Warner are lost in this world. [PG]▼▶

Return to Treasure Island (1954-Australian) SEE: **Long John Silver**

Reuben, Reuben (1983) C-101m. *** D: Robert Ellis Miller. Tom Conti, Kelly McGillis, Roberts Blossom, Cynthia Harris, E. Katherine Kerr, Joel Fabiani, Kara Wilson, Lois Smith. Boozy Scottish poet (an amalgam of Dylan Thomas and Brendan Behan) sponges off hospitable women in New England college town—then falls in love with beautiful young student McGillis (in her film debut). Deliciously witty script by Julius J. Epstein (adapted from writings of Peter DeVries) and fine performances help offset general feeling of anachronism about the film . . . and a curious finale. [R]▼

Reunion (1989-French-German-British) C-110m. *** D: Jerry Schatzberg. Jason Robards, Christian Anholt, Samuel West, Alexander Trauner, Françoise Fabian, Maureen Kerwin, Barbara Jefford. Elderly Jewish man journeys back to Stuttgart, Germany, to seek out boyhood friend he hasn't seen since leaving for the U.S. in 1933. Much of the film is told in flashback, with Anholt giving a fine performance as high-school–age Robards, and West equally good as his Aryan chum. Screenplay by Harold Pinter; veteran art director Trauner, who designed the film, has a small role as a porter. Panavision. [PG-13]▼

Reunion in France (1942) 104m. ** D: Jules Dassin. Joan Crawford, John Wayne, Philip Dorn, Reginald Owen, Albert Bassermann, John Carradine, Henry Daniell. Glossy romance, with Frenchwoman Crawford believing fiancé Dorn is a Nazi collaborator; she hides (and falls for) American flyer Wayne. Propaganda ele-

ments date badly. Watch for Ava Gardner as a salesgirl. ▼▶
Revenge (1971-British) SEE: **Inn of the Frightened People**
Revenge (1979) SEE: **Blood Feud**
Revenge (1986) **C-100m.** BOMB D: Christopher Lewis. Patrick Wayne, John Carradine, Bennie Lee McGowan. Boring, filmed sequel to the videotaped horror opus BLOOD CULT details the further goings-on of a Tulsa, Oklahoma, devilworship cult led this time by (who else?) Carradine, that preys on students for human sacrifices. Strictly for fans of mindless violence; never released theatrically. Director Lewis is (gulp!) Loretta Young's son. [R]▼▶
Revenge (1990) **C-124m.** *½ D: Tony Scott. Kevin Costner, Anthony Quinn, Madeleine Stowe, Sally Kirkland, Tomas Milian, Joaquin Martinez, James Gammon, Miguel Ferrer, Joe Santos, John Leguizamo. Navy pilot Costner (yes, Tony—we *know* you directed TOP GUN) visits power-broker pal Quinn at his posh Mexican estate; soon he and Stowe (Quinn's young Mrs.) are enjoying a closet quickie, in both senses of the term. Ponderous mix of the slick and the sordid died at the box office; the second half—source of the film's title—is especially tough to endure. Director's cut runs 100m. Panavision. [R]▼●▶
Revenge of Dracula, The SEE: **Dracula vs. Frankenstein** (1971)
Revenge of Frankenstein, The (1958-British) **C-91m.** *** D: Terence Fisher. Peter Cushing, Francis Matthews, Eunice Gayson, Michael Gwynn, Lionel Jeffries, John Welsh. Sequel to THE CURSE OF FRANKENSTEIN is quite effective with the good doctor still making a new body from others, ably assisted by hunchback dwarf and young medical student. Thoughtprovoking script has fine atmosphere, especially in color. Followed by THE EVIL OF FRANKENSTEIN. ▼●▶
Revenge of the Creature (1955) **82m.** ** D: Jack Arnold. John Agar, Lori Nelson, John Bromfield, Nestor Paiva, Robert B. Williams. OK sequel to CREATURE FROM THE BLACK LAGOON destroys much of that film's mystery and terror by removing Gill Man from Amazonian home and placing him in Florida oceanarium. Clint Eastwood has his first screen role as lab technician. 3-D. ▼●▶
Revenge of the Nerds (1984) **C-90m.** ** D: Jeff Kanew. Robert Carradine, Anthony Edwards, Timothy Busfield, Andrew Cassese, Curtis Armstrong, Larry B. Scott, Julie Montgomery, Michelle Meyrink, Ted McGinley, Matt Salinger, John Goodman, Bernie Casey, Jamie (James) Cromwell. Geeky college freshmen, tired of being humiliated by the campus jocks and coed cuties, form their own fraternity, leading to

all-out war. As raunchy teen comedies go, not bad, helped by two leads' likable performances. Followed by several sequels. [R]▼●▶
Revenge of the Nerds II: Nerds in Paradise (1987) **C-98m.** *½ D: Joe Roth. Robert Carradine, Curtis Armstrong, Larry B. Scott, Timothy Busfield, Courtney Thorne-Smith, Andrew Cassese, Donald Gibb, Ed Lauter, Anthony Edwards, Jamie (James) Cromwell. Sequel, set at a fraternity gathering in Ft. Lauderdale, is strictly by-the-numbers; once again the geeky "heroes" manage to triumph over their beefier (but not brainier) college counterparts . . . but this is a lot less fun than the original. Edwards, Carradine's costar in the first picture, makes a token appearance. Followed by 1992 TV sequel. [PG-13]▼●▶
Revenge of the Ninja (1983) **C-88m.** ** D: Sam Firstenberg. Sho Kosugi, Keith Vitali, Virgil Frye, Arthur Roberts, Mario Gallo. Good ninja Kosugi takes on evil ninja Roberts, a heroin smuggler/kidnapper/killer. Kung fu aficionados should enjoy it, otherwise beware. A follow-up to ENTER THE NINJA, followed by NINJA III—THE DOMINATION. [R]▼▶
Revenge of the Pink Panther (1978) **C-99m.** ** D: Blake Edwards. Peter Sellers, Herbert Lom, Robert Webber, Dyan Cannon, Burt Kwouk, Robert Loggia, Paul Stewart, Andre Maranne, Graham Stark, Ferdy Mayne. Sellers' final go-round as bumbling Inspector Clouseau is one of the dullest, until a bright wrap-up in Hong Kong with some good sight gags and plenty of spark from Cannon. The "plot" has Clouseau supposedly murdered, allowing him to find "killer" incognito. Followed by TRAIL OF THE PINK PANTHER. Panavision. [PG]▼●▶
Revenge of Ukeno-Jo, The SEE: **Actor's Revenge, An**
Revengers, The (1972) **C-112m.** BOMB D: Daniel Mann. William Holden, Ernest Borgnine, Susan Hayward, Woody Strode, Roger Hanin, Rene Koldehoff. Rancher goes after those who massacred his family. Hayward (in her final theatrical feature) is the only good thing about this terrible Western. Panavision. [PG]
Revengers' Comedies, The SEE: **Sweet Revenge** (1999)
Reversal of Fortune (1990) **C-120m.** ***½ D: Barbet Schroeder. Glenn Close, Jeremy Irons, Ron Silver, Annabella Sciorra, Uta Hagen, Fisher Stevens, Jack Gilpin, Christine Baranski, Stephen Mailer, Felicity Huffman. Tantalizing and complex film, embracing drama and very black comedy, sparked by Irons' devastating Oscarwinning performance as the aristocratic, enigmatic Claus von Bülow, who was accused of attempting to murder his socialite wife Sunny. Silver is perfectly cast as real-

life Harvard law professor Alan Dershowitz, who agreed to take on the challenge
of reversing the jury's decision. Teasingly
ambiguous, and one of the most strikingly structured narrative films ever made.
Scripted by Nicholas Kazan from Dershowitz's book. Julie Hagerty has small, unbilled
role. [R]▼●▶

Revolution (1985) **C-123m.** BOMB
D: Hugh Hudson. Al Pacino, Donald
Sutherland, Nastassja Kinski, Joan Plowright, Dave King, Annie Lennox, Steven
Berkoff, Jesse Birdsall, Graham Greene,
Robbie Coltrane. Only a half-dozen or so
movies have dealt more than superficially
with the Revolutionary War; thanks to
this megabomb, it may be 2776 until we
get another one. Pacino, two centuries
too contemporary to be convincing, is
the trapper whose boat and son are conscripted by the Continental Army; Kinski
is the headstrong rebel from a family of
Tories. Ludicrous script and acting sink
some splendid production values. Reedited by Hudson, with new narration by
Pacino, in 2009; this version runs 115m.
Super 35. [PG] ▼●▶

Revolutionary, The (1970) **C-100m.** ***
D: Paul Williams. Jon Voight, Jennifer Salt,
Seymour Cassel, Robert Duvall. Tight,
well-written study of a college youth who
slowly gets drawn into role of political revolutionary with near-tragic results. Hans Kon-
ing adapted his novel. [PG]▼

Revolutionary Road (2008-U.S.-British)
C-119m. **½ D: Sam Mendes. Leonardo
DiCaprio, Kate Winslet, Kathy Bates,
Michael Shannon, Kathryn Hahn, David
Harbour, Dylan Baker, Richard Easton,
Zoe Kazan, Jay O. Sanders, Max Casella.
Intense adaptation of Richard Yates' novel
about a young couple whose love cannot
overcome a feeling of discontent creeping
into their supposedly ideal existence in the
suburbs of N.Y.C. in the 1950s. Gloomy, to
say the least. Superior acting by the entire
ensemble (including the two stars, reunited
for the first time since TITANIC in 1997)
and meticulous craftsmanship can't compensate for lack of character development
that one might find in the book. And where
do the couple's kids disappear to all the
time? Super 35. [R]▶

Revolution Will Not Be Televised, The
(2002-Irish-Dutch-U.S.-German-Finni
sh-British) **C-74m.** ***½ D: Kim Bartley,
Donnacha O'Briain. A European film crew
on location in Caracas is amazed to find
itself amidst a violent uprising that temporarily ousts Venezuelan President Hugo
Chavez. Sharp editing and pointed narration
strongly suggest covert U.S. involvement
in the attempted coup of the charismatic
Chavez, who is always center stage in this
surprisingly enjoyable documentary. Sound
bites contributed by Colin Powell, George

Tenet, and Jesse Helms. Aka CHAVEZ: IN-
SIDE THE COUP.

Revolver (2005-British-French) **C-115m.**
** D: Guy Ritchie. Jason Statham, Ray Liotta, Vincent Pastore, André Benjamin, Terence Maynard, Francesca Annis, Andrew
Howard, Mark Strong. Gambler spends
seven years in prison perfecting his game;
when he gets out he defeats (and humili-
ates) a casino boss, who puts out a hit on
him. Two strangers come to his aid and
the ultimate con is on—but who's conning
who? So confusing it would take a book
called *Revolver for Dummies* to figure it out.
Ritchie throws in all the visual gimmicks he
can. After a dismal reception in England, he
recut the film for long-delayed U.S. release
in 2007, to no avail. Super 35. [R]▶

Rhapsody (1954) **C-115m.** **½ D: Charles
Vidor. Elizabeth Taylor, Vittorio Gassman,
John Ericson, Louis Calhern, Michael
Chekhov. Three-cornered romance
among rich Taylor, violinist Gassman,
and pianist Ericson: melodic interludes
bolster this soap opera. Script by Fay and
Michael Kanin.▼▶

Rhapsody in August (1991-Japanese)
C-98m. **½ D: Akira Kurosawa. Sachiko
Murase, Richard Gere, Hisashi Igawa,
Narumi Kayashima. Thoughtful but (by his
standards) minor Kurosawa, about the painful memories of a Japanese grandmother
who recalls the bombing of Nagasaki at the
end of WW2. Gere, in a glorified cameo,
doesn't seem too out of place as a Japanese-
American member of the old woman's extended clan. The director manages a few
memorable visual touches, but talky film
never quite recovers from its nearly static
opening. [PG]▼●▶

Rhapsody in Blue (1945) **139m.** *** D:
Irving Rapper. Robert Alda, Joan Leslie,
Alexis Smith, Oscar Levant, Charles Coburn, Julie Bishop, Albert Basserman, Morris Carnovsky, Herbert Rudley, Rosemary
DeCamp, Paul Whiteman, Hazel Scott, Al
Jolson. Hollywood biography of George
Gershwin is largely pulp fiction, but comes
off better than most other composer biopics,
capturing Gershwin's enthusiasm for his
work, and some of his inner conflicts. Highlight is virtually complete performance of
title work.▼●

Rhinestone (1984) **C-111m.** *½ D: Bob
Clark. Sylvester Stallone, Dolly Parton,
Richard Farnsworth, Ron Leibman, Tim
Thomerson. Parton bets that she can turn
anyone into a country singer—even N.Y.C.
cabdriver Stallone. Contrived, cornball comedy with acres of unfunny dialogue. Panavision. [PG]▼●▶

Rhinoceros (1974) **C-101m.** BOMB D:
Tom O'Horgan. Zero Mostel, Gene Wilder,
Karen Black, Robert Weil, Joe Silver, Marilyn Chris. Eugene Ionesco entry in "Theater
of the Absurd" makes sorry transition from

stage to screen as clerk Wilder refuses to conform by turning into a pachyderm. The performers try. An American Film Theater Production. [PG]▼◐

Rhythm Romance SEE: **Some Like It Hot** (1939)

Rhythm Thief (1995) 88m. **½ D: Matthew Harrison. Jason Andrews, Eddie Daniels, Kevin Corrigan, Kimberly Flynn, Sean Hagerty, Mark Alfred, Christopher Cooke, Bob McGrath. At once intriguing and pretentious ultra-low-budget portrait of aloof but agonized Andrews, who lives on N.Y.C.'s grimy Lower East Side and earns his keep by selling tapes of illicitly recorded rock music. Original and provocative at times, but too often revels in its artiness. Filmed in 11 days, for $11,000.◗

Rich and Famous (1981) C-117m. ** D: George Cukor. Jacqueline Bisset, Candice Bergen, David Selby, Hart Bochner, Steven Hill, Meg Ryan, Matt Lattanzi, Michael Brandon. Muddled, misguided remake of OLD ACQUAINTANCE, with Bisset and Bergen as women who maintain a stormy friendship for more than 20 years, despite rivalries in love and career. Idiotic dialogue and Bisset's sexual ruminations weaken what should have been a strong contemporary version of John Van Druten's story. Bisset's company produced. Among guests at Malibu party are Marsha Hunt, Christopher Isherwood, and Roger Vadim; later party offers glimpses of Ray Bradbury, Nina Foch, and Frances Bergen (Candice's mother). Cukor's last film; Meg Ryan's first. [R]▼◐◗

Rich and Strange (1931-British) 83m. **½ D: Alfred Hitchcock. Henry Kendall, Joan Barry, Betty Amann, Percy Marmont, Elsie Randolph. Kendall and Barry, married and bored are given money and travel around the world; he has affair with a "princess," while she becomes romantically attached to an explorer. Fragmented, offbeat drama (until the finale).▼◐◗

Richard Pryor . . . Here & Now (1983) C-83m. *½ D: Richard Pryor. The comedian's fourth concert film is his least satisfying to date, though hecklers in the audience are as much to blame as any defects in Pryor's material. Some amusing bits on drunks and dopeheads, plus some biting digs at the Reagan White House. Filmed on Bourbon Street in New Orleans. [R]▼◐◗

Richard Pryor Is Back Live in Concert (1979) C-78m. ** D: Jeff Margolis. Pryor's still funny, but much of the material is ripped off from RICHARD PRYOR—LIVE IN CONCERT, released earlier that year.

Richard Pryor—Live in Concert (1979) C-78m. *** D: Jeff Margolis. Pryor on race, sex, machismo, death, filmed in performance in Long Beach, California. The comedian, uncensored, is at his raunchy best.▼◐◗

Richard Pryor Live on the Sunset Strip (1982) C-82m. **½ D: Joe Layton. Pryor on Africa, sex, lawyers, his wife, sex, Italian mobsters, more sex, and—inevitably—freebasing. Some of it's funny, some isn't, but the audience is always shown doubled over with laughter. [R]▼◐◗

Richard's Things (1980-British) C-104m. ** D: Anthony Harvey. Liv Ullmann, Amanda Redman, Tim Pigott-Smith, Elizabeth Spriggs, David Markham. Widow Ullmann is seduced by her late husband's girlfriend. Dreary drama, with a catatonic performance by Liv. Screenplay by Frederic Raphael, based on his novel. Made for British TV. [R]▼

Richard III (1955-British) C-155m. ***½ D: Laurence Olivier. Laurence Olivier, John Gielgud, Ralph Richardson, Claire Bloom, Alec Clunes, Cedric Hardwicke, Stanley Baker, Pamela Brown, Michael Gough. Elaborate if stagy version of Shakespeare's chronicle of ambitious 15th-century British king and his court intrigues. Some prints run 139m. VistaVision.▼◐◗

Richard III (1995-U.S.-British) C-104m. *** D: Richard Loncraine. Ian McKellen, Annette Bening, Jim Broadbent, Robert Downey, Jr., Nigel Hawthorne, Kristin Scott Thomas, Maggie Smith, John Wood, Jim Carter, Adrian Dunbar, Edward Hardwicke, Tim McInnerny, Bill Paterson, Donald Sumpter, Dominic West. Ingenious resetting of Shakespeare's drama of multiple murders and political intrigue in 1930s England, during a Fascist coup. McKellen dominates the screen as the devil incarnate, with a persona for every occasion. Visually compelling, often shocking (with glamour, sex, drugs, and violence), and yet doesn't fully capture the power of McKellen's (and Richard Eyre's) stage production, on which it is based. Super 35. [R]▼◐◗

Rich Girl (1991) C-96m. **½ D: Joel Bender. Jill Schoelen, Don Michael Paul, Sean Kanan, Ron Karabatsos, Paul Gleason, Bentley Mitchum. Extremely mild time-filler about "poor little rich girl" Schoelen leaving her life of ease in her daddy's Bel-Air mansion and trying to make it on her own, eventually hooking up with a blue-collar rock singer. [R]▼◐

Richie Rich (1994) C-95m. **½ D: Donald Petrie. Macaulay Culkin, John Larroquette, Edward Herrmann, Jonathan Hyde, Christine Ebersole, Stephi Lineburg, Michael McShane, Chelcie Ross, Ben Stein. Amusing kids' film with Culkin as the comic-book character Richie Rich, the world's wealthiest boy—which naturally makes him the target of a scheming bad guy (Larroquette). Hyde is excellent as the boy's very proper valet/companion, and Herrmann and Ebersole are endearing as Richie's parents. Avoids some of the formulaic crudity of John Hughes movies, but weakens during the protracted action finale. Followed by a direct-to-video sequel. [PG]▼●▶

Rich in Love (1993) C-105m. **½ D: Bruce Beresford. Albert Finney, Jill Clayburgh, Kathryn Erbe, Kyle MacLachlan, Piper Laurie, Ethan Hawke, Suzy Amis, Alfre Woodard. The people behind DRIVING MISS DAISY have taken Josephine Humphreys' novel and tried hard to weave another evocative Southern tale; they don't really succeed, but there are many fine moments. Film centers on teenager (Erbe, in an award-calibre performance) trying to hold her extended family together; among the members are her idle father (another great Finney portrayal), absent mother, and nutty sister. Beautiful touches both in script and visualization are offset by unfocused, meandering story. [PG-13]▼●▶

Rich Kids (1979) C-101m. *** D: Robert M. Young. Trini Alvarado, Jeremy Levy, John Lithgow, Kathryn Walker, David Selby, Terry Kiser, Paul Dooley, Olympia Dukakis, Jill Eikenberry. Alvarado and Levy are upper class N.Y.C. kids who become best friends as her parents are dissolving their marriage. Effect of divorce is focal point for this fine acting showcase, which also makes good use of N.Y.C. locations. Produced by Robert Altman. [PG]▼

Rich Man's Wife, The (1996) C-94m. BOMB D: Amy Holden Jones. Halle Berry, Christopher McDonald, Clive Owen, Peter Greene, Charles Hallahan, Frankie Faison, Clea Lewis. Abandoned Berry somehow gets picked up by a shady character following a vacation tiff with her husband. This leads to a murder-blackmail situation conceived by a filmmaker who's seen STRANGERS ON A TRAIN one too many times. Lots of unintentional yuks, but nothing else to recommend this D.O.A. release. [R]▼●▶

Richthofen and Brown SEE: **Von Richthofen and Brown**

Ricochet (1991) C-97m. ** D: Russell Mulcahy. Denzel Washington, John Lithgow, Ice T, Kevin Pollak, Lindsay Wagner, Mary Ellen Trainor, Josh Evans, Victoria Dillard, John Amos. Street cop (Washington) becomes a citywide hero when he brings down bad-guy Lithgow—little dreaming that the psycho spends every waking moment in prison planning his revenge. Slick, well-cast, occasionally ugly urban thriller grows more tiresome and predictable as it goes along. Panavision. [R]▼●▶

Ricochets (1986-Israeli) C-90m. *** D: Eli Cohen. Roni Pincovich, Shaul Mizrahi, Alon Aboutboul, Dudu Ben-Ze'ev, Boaz Ofri. Gritty, uncompromising look at a group of Israeli soldiers living and dying in occupied Lebanon, focusing on the experiences of one young officer. Made as an Israeli Army training film and shot on location; nevertheless, an eloquent anti-war drama.

Riddle of the Sands, The (1979-British) C-102m. ** D: Tony Maylam. Simon MacCorkindale, Michael York, Jenny Agutter, Alan Badel, Jurgen Andersen, Olga Lowe, Wolf Kahler. Sailing off the coast of Germany in 1901, yachtsman MacCorkindale stumbles onto what seems to be a plan to invade England, and summons old chum York to help him out. Erskine Childers' novel is considered the prototype of the modern spy thriller, but this adaptation is just too slow and stiff to be really effective. Good to look at, though. Released in the U.S. in 1984. Panavision.▼

Ride a Wild Pony (1976-Australian) C-91m. *** D: Don Chaffey. Michael Craig, John Meillon, Robert Bettles, Eva Griffith, Graham Rouse. Genial, atmospheric Disney story about an irresistible pony and the two children—son of poor farm family and crippled rich girl—who vie for its love and ownership. Sentimental tale adapted from James Aldridge's *A Sporting Proposition.* [G]▼

Ride Beyond Vengeance (1966) C-100m. **½ D: Bernard McEveety. Chuck Connors, Michael Rennie, Kathryn Hays, Joan Blondell, Gloria Grahame, Gary Merrill, Bill Bixby, James MacArthur, Claude Akins, Paul Fix, Ruth Warrick, Arthur O'Connell, Frank Gorshin, Jamie Farr. Good supporting cast makes the most of stereotyped roles in flashback account of Connors' sundry encounters with outlaws.▶

Ride 'Em Cowboy (1942) 86m. **½ D: Arthur Lubin. Bud Abbott, Lou Costello, Dick Foran, Anne Gwynne, Johnny Mack Brown, Ella Fitzgerald, Douglass Dumbrille. Good combination of Western, comedy, and musical in A&C vehicle, with Ella and the Merry Macs singing tunes including "A Tisket A Tasket," Foran crooning "I'll Remember April."▼●▶

Ride in the Whirlwind (1965) C-83m. **½ D: Monte Hellman. Cameron Mitchell, Jack Nicholson, Tom Filer, Millie Perkins, Katherine Squire, Rupert Crosse, Harry Dean Stanton. Nicholson coproduced and wrote the screenplay for this offbeat Western about three cowboys who find themselves wrongly pursued as outlaws. Neither as arty nor as intriguing as THE SHOOTING, which was filmed simultaneously.▼●▶

Ride Lonesome (1959) C-73m. *** D: Budd Boetticher. Randolph Scott, Karen Steele, Pernell Roberts, James Best, Lee Van Cleef, James Coburn. Typically interesting Boetticher chamber-Western (with a Burt Kennedy script) about a tight-lipped bounty hunter who acquires unwanted companions while bringing in a wanted criminal. Unusually good supporting cast, including Coburn in his film debut. CinemaScope.▶

Rider on the Rain (1970-French) C-115m. ***½ D: René Clement. Charles Bronson, Marlene Jobert, Jill Ireland, Annie Cordy.

Chilling suspense piece about mysterious man who winds up using Jobert as accomplice when she discovers what he is up to. Best sequence: long, rainy prologue. Story and screenplay by Sebastien Japrisot. [PG]▼〉

Riders of the Storm (1986-British) **C-92m.** *½ D: Maurice Phillips. Dennis Hopper, Michael J. Pollard, Eugene Lipinski, James Aubrey, Nigel Pegram. Unsatisfactory chronicle of Vietnam vets who run a pirate television station and jam right-wing broadcasts; they attempt to sabotage the campaign of a female presidential candidate who is not to their liking. Bright premise, thoroughly stale result. Originally titled THE AMERICAN WAY, at 105m. [R]▼●

Ride the High Country (1962) **C-94m.** **** D: Sam Peckinpah. Randolph Scott, Joel McCrea, Mariette Hartley, Ron Starr, Edgar Buchanan, R. G. Armstrong, Warren Oates, John Anderson, L. Q. Jones, James Drury. Literate, magnificent Western about two aged gunfighter pals who reflect on the paths their lives have taken while guarding gold shipment. Considered by some to be Peckinpah's finest film; breathtaking widescreen photography (by Lucien Ballard) and scenery, and flawless performances, with Buchanan notable as a drunken judge. Written by N. B. Stone, Jr. Hartley's first film, Scott's last. CinemaScope.▼●

Ride the Pink Horse (1947) **101m.** ***½ D: Robert Montgomery. Robert Montgomery, Wanda Hendrix, Thomas Gomez, Andrea King, Fred Clark, Art Smith, Rita Conde, Grandon Rhodes. Strong film noir of Montgomery coming to small New Mexican town during fiesta to blackmail gangster Clark, but romantic Hendrix and FBI agent Smith keep getting in his way. Taut script by Ben Hecht and Charles Lederer (from the Dorothy B. Hughes novel); super performance by Gomez as friendly carny. Remade for TV as THE HANGED MAN (1964).

Ride to Glory SEE: **Deserter, The**

Ride to Hangman's Tree, The (1967) **C-90m.** **½ D: Al Rafkin. Jack Lord, James Farentino, Don Galloway, Melodie Johnson, Richard Anderson, Robert Yuro. Formula Universal backlot Western, of outlaws in old West.

Ride with the Devil (1999) **C-134m.** **½ D: Ang Lee. Skeet Ulrich, Tobey Maguire, James Caviezel, Jonathan Rhys Meyers, Simon Baker, Jeffrey Wright, Jewel, Tom Wilkinson, Jonathan Brandis, Tom Guiry, Mark Ruffalo. A different take on the Civil War, focusing on the Bushwhackers, Southern guerrilla forces made up largely of young men who stage daring raids on Union farms and towns along the Kansas/Missouri border. Interesting subject matter is diffused by overlong, sometimes unfocused treatment, though the time and place

are well drawn. Pop singer Jewel makes an impressive acting debut. Alternate version runs 160m. 2.35 Research PLC. [R]▼〉

Ridicule (1996-French) **C-102m.** *** D: Patrice Leconte. Charles Berling, Jean Rochefort, Fanny Ardant, Judith Godreche, Bernard Giraudeau. Spirited tale of an earnest young landowner who tries to obtain an audience with King Louis XVI in order to get grant money for swamp drainage. He soon discovers that the only way to be presented at court is to display a ready (and preferably savage) wit—which, to everyone's surprise, he is willing and able to do. Fine performances in this unusual and original period piece. Panavision. [R]▼●〉

Riding Alone for Thousands of Miles (2005-Hong Kong-Chinese-Japanese) **C-108m.** ***½ D: Zhang Yimou. Ken Takakura, Shinobu Terajima, Kiichi Nakai, Li Jiamin, Qiu Lin, Jiang Wen, Yang Zhenbo. Deceptively simple, profoundly moving tale of elderly Takakura, a Japanese fisherman who does not express himself easily and is long estranged from his son. Upon learning his offspring is terminally ill, he heads to China to follow through on his son's attempt to film a rural mask-opera singer, which proves to be no easy task. Wise, poignant film offers a tailor-made role for Takakura, best known for playing Yakuza movie gangsters and loners. [PG]〉

Riding Giants (2004) **C-101m.** ***½ D: Stacy Peralta. Superior examination of surf culture and the desire to confront the biggest waves imaginable. Effective interviews with legends like Greg Noll illuminate the quest for the ultimate ride and make it palatable to people who might think some of these guys are just nuts. Remarkable new sequences are interspersed with vintage footage for an experience that lifts this well above other surfing documentaries. The director of DOGTOWN AND Z-BOYS outdoes himself with this epic look at the big waves and their conquerors. [PG-13]〉

Riding High (1950) **112m.** **½ D: Frank Capra. Bing Crosby, Coleen Gray, Charles Bickford, Margaret Hamilton, Frances Gifford, James Gleason, Raymond Walburn, William Demarest, Ward Bond, Clarence Muse, Percy Kilbride, Gene Lockhart, Douglass Dumbrille, Harry Davenport, Charles Lane, Frankie Darro. Musical remake of BROADWAY BILL follows it so closely that stock footage with some of the actors in their original parts is included from 1934 film. Crosby is racehorse owner whose nag has yet to come through. OK songs, Capra touch make this pleasing if unmemorable entertainment. Oliver Hardy is fun in rare solo appearance. Joe Frisco appears as himself.▼●〉

Riding in Cars With Boys (2001) **C-122m.** ** D: Penny Marshall. Drew Barrymore,

Steve Zahn, Brittany Murphy, James Woods, Adam Garcia, Lorraine Bracco, Sara Gilbert, Desmond Harrington, Peter Facinelli, Rosie Perez, Maggie Gyllenhaal. Well-acted but uneven film inspired by Beverly Donofrio's memoir of a working-class adolescence in 1960s Connecticut, and having her dreams of college—and a writing career—sidetracked by having a baby and marrying Mr. Wrong. Barrymore (always watchable, even as an unsympathetic character) and a strong cast almost succeed in covering the many holes in the script—but ultimately cannot. [PG-13] ▼▶

Riding the Bullet (2004-U.S.-Canadian-German) **C-98m. *½** D: Mick Garris. Jonathan Jackson, Erika Christensen, David Arquette, Cliff Robertson, Barbara Hershey, Barry W. Levy, Matt Frewer, Jeff Ballard. While hitchhiking across Maine on Halloween night in 1969 to visit his ill mother, a death-obsessed college student experiences sinister hallucinations and is picked up by a man who may be the Grim Reaper himself. Gory, cliché-ridden snoozefest based on Stephen King's "e-book" story is for the author's hard-core fans only, though it plays like a parody of his work. Aka STEPHEN KING'S RIDING THE BULLET. [R] ▼▶

Riding the Rails (1997) **C-75m. ***½** D: Michael Uys, Lexy Lovell. Acclaimed documentary about the thousands of young people who left home to hop freight trains during the Great Depression—some seeking adventure, some hoping to make a living, some with nowhere else to go. Fascinating interviews with octogenarian survivors of that school of hard knocks; debunks most of the "romance" of hobo life. ▼▶

Riff Raff (1991-British) **C-96m. ***** D: Ken Loach. Robert Carlyle, Emer McCourt, Ricky Tomlinson, Jimmy Coleman, George Moss, David Finch. Probing, bitingly funny comedy about the ongoing struggle between the classes in England, examining the plight of a blue-collar type (Carlyle), newly arrived in London, who signs on at a construction site. Some of the regional accents and dialects are so indecipherable that subtitles have been added! Screenplay by Bill Jesse, an ex-construction worker. ▼

Rififi (1955-French) **115m. ****** D: Jules Dassin. Jean Servais, Carl Mohner, Magali Noel, Robert Manuel, Perlo Vita (Jules Dassin). The granddaddy of all caper/heist movies, centering on quartet of French jewel thieves who find each other more dangerous than the cops. The burglary sequence itself is famous for being in complete silence. Scripted by director Dassin, Rene Wheeler, and Auguste LeBreton, from LeBreton's novel. ▼▶

Right At Your Door (2007) **C-96m. **½** D: Chris Gorak. Mary McCormack, Rory Cochrane, Tony Perez, Scotty Noyd, Jr., Max Kasch, Jon Huertas. When a dirty bomb is unleashed in L.A., panic ensues and a man must quarantine his home to prevent contamination. As the crisis escalates he becomes increasingly worried about locating his wife, who is AWOL from her office. Seems almost like a stage play or a *Twilight Zone* episode that has been stretched to feature length. Though overlong this modest film builds tension throughout, since its premise is (sad to say) so plausible. [R] ▶

Righteous Kill (2008) **C-100m. **** D: Jon Avnet. Robert De Niro, Al Pacino, Carla Gugino, Curtis (50 Cent) Jackson, Donnie Wahlberg, Brian Dennehy, John Leguizamo, Trilby Glover, Melissa Leo, Oleg Taktarov, Barry Primus, Rob Dyrdek, Alan Rosenberg. Overly busy whodunit storyline follows manhunt to identify a serial killer who only murders sleazy types "who deserve it," and whose m.o. suggests that he may be a cop. Pairing of De Niro and Pacino as longtime partners on the NYPD gives this film its raison d'être; their commanding presence and effortless teamwork make this movie watchable. Super 35. [R] ▶

Right Hand Man, The (1987-Australian) **C-100m. **½** D: Di Drew. Rupert Everett, Hugo Weaving, Catherine McClements, Arthur Dignam, Jennifer Claire. Well-made but only occasionally involving drama about the various troubles of aristocrat Everett, and what happens when he hires stagecoach driver Weaving. Has its moments, but ultimately peters out. [R] ▼▶

Right Stuff, The (1983) **C-193m. ***** D: Philip Kaufman. Sam Shepard, Scott Glenn, Ed Harris, Dennis Quaid, Fred Ward, Barbara Hershey, Kim Stanley, Veronica Cartwright, Kathy Baker, Pamela Reed, Donald Moffat, Levon Helm, Scott Wilson, David Clennon, William Russ, Jeff Goldblum, Harry Shearer. Offbeat look at the birth of America's space program and the first astronauts, adapted from Tom Wolfe's best-selling book, and tethered to the story of iconoclastic test pilot Chuck Yeager. Writer-director Kaufman draws all his characters as cartoons (including Lyndon Johnson) except for the pilots—and puts thrillingly realistic recreations of space flights against broadly caricatured scenes on Earth. A real curio of a film, with some astonishing performances, exhilarating moments, but a curious overall air of detachment. Long, but never boring. Winner of four Oscars, including Best Editing, Sound, and Original Score (Bill Conti). The real Chuck Yeager has a cameo role as a bartender. [PG] ▼●

Rikki and Pete (1988-Australian) **C-107m. **½** D: Nadia Tass. Stephen Kearney, Nina Landis, Tetchie Agbayani, Bill Hunter, Bruno Lawrence, Bruce Spence, Dorothy Allison. Pete is a misfit with a penchant for gimmicky inventions, Rikki is his sister who's still trying to find herself; together they flee to a remote mining village where their lives take some unexpected turns. Follow-up to MALCOLM by the same writing-directing team (Tass and writer/cinematographer David Parker) hasn't the same sweetness or consistency, but it's admirably quirky, and Parker's Rube Goldberg–ish devices are fun. [R]▼●)

Ring, The (2002) C-115m. ** D: Gore Verbinski. Naomi Watts, Martin Henderson, David Dorfman, Brian Cox, Jane Alexander, Lindsay Frost, Pauley Perrette, Amber Tamblyn, Sara Rue, Daveigh Chase, Adam Brody. Teenage friends watch a videotape that supposedly causes the viewer to die. (Wouldn't you?) The aunt of one victim, newspaper reporter Watts, determines to find out the truth about the tape and its origins. Opens with a bang, but drags us on a long, winding (and ultimately pointless) investigative path before reaching its silly conclusion. Based on the Japanese movie hit RINGU. Followed by a sequel. [PG-13] ▼)

Ring Two, The (2005) C-111m. **½ D: Hideo Nakata. Naomi Watts, Simon Baker, David Dorfman, Elizabeth Perkins, Gary Cole, Sissy Spacek, Ryan Merriman. Fleeing Seattle for the small town of Astoria, Oregon, Watts discovers that the coldhearted ghost of a loveless child is still after her and her son, as well as anyone else hanging around. Slow and overlong, but often delivers the spooky goods, and director Nakata—who made the Japanese RINGU—uses misty Pacific Northwest locations well. Entire cast is good, especially young Dorfman, but not everything makes sense. This is *not* a remake of the Japanese sequel to RINGU. Unrated version also available. [PG-13] ▼)

Ringer, The (2005) C-94m. **½ D: Barry W. Blaustein. Johnny Knoxville, Brian Cox, Katherine Heigl, Geoffrey Arend, Edward Barbanell, Bill Chott, Leonard Flowers, Jed Rees. What if a guy, strapped for money, went in on a scheme to pass himself off as a drooling, mentally challenged adult so he can enter (and rig) the Special Olympics? Give the filmmakers (including the Farrelly Brothers, who produced) credit for pulling this off and delivering a film with smiles and heart. Knoxville puts his *Jackass* persona on hold, working alongside actual Special Olympics participants, who naturally get the last laugh. A generally entertaining, and surprising, comedy. Super 35. [PG-13] ●

Ringmaster (1998) C-90m. *½ D: Neil Abramson. Jerry Springer, Jaime Pressly, William McNamara, Molly Hagan, Michael Dudikoff, Ashley Holbrook, Michael Jai White. A mom and daughter share a husband/stepfather in a trailer park, but instead of duking it out in secret, they ap-

ply to vent their spleens on Springer's TV show, sharing adjacent hotel accommodations with other profiled subjects. Surprisingly well acted under the circumstances, this otherwise listless junk lacks focus and is thoroughly done in by Springer's sanctimoniousness. Tries to do for the host's career what PRIVATE PARTS did for Howard Stern's and can't even pull off that modest feat. [R]▼●)

Ring of Bright Water (1969-British) C-107m. *** D: Jack Couffer. Bill Travers, Virginia McKenna, Peter Jeffrey, Jameson Clark, Helena Gloag. Fine children's film should be a treat for adults, too; modest story of man's love for his pet otter is intelligently and believably told. Nice acting and photography. [G]▼)

Ringu (1998-Japanese) C-95m. *** D: Hideo Nakata. Nanako Matsushima, Miki Nakatani, Hiroyuki Sanada, Yuko Takeuchi, Hitomi Sato, Yoichi Numata. After the mysterious death of her niece, a reporter investigates—and views—a "cursed" videotape that purportedly kills all those who watch it exactly seven days later. Stark cinematic technique suits this subtle, unsettling, and genuinely spooky psychological thriller, in the best tradition of metaphysical Japanese ghost stories, which builds a relentless sense of mounting dread. Based on a novel by Kôji Suzuki ("the Stephen King of Japan"), this became a phenomenon in Asia, inspiring two sequels, a prequel, a Korean version and an American remake, THE RING. ▼)

Rio (2011) C-96m. *** D: Carlos Saldanha. Voices of Anne Hathaway, Jesse Eisenberg, Jemaine Clement, Jamie Foxx, Leslie Mann, Tracy Morgan, will.i.am, George Lopez, Rodrigo Santoro, Jake T. Austin, Jane Lynch, Wanda Sykes, Carlos Ponce, Judah Friedlander. Brightly colored cartoon confection about a blue macaw taken from Brazil as an infant and raised in—of all places—Minnesota. Then a naturalist tells his loving owner that if they don't bring him back to Brazil and mate him with the one remaining female, he'll be the last of his species. Lighthearted, fast-paced adventure yarn is strictly formulaic but pulses with the sights and sounds of Brazil and energetic voice work. Eisenberg is fun to listen to in a first-rate comedic performance. 3-D Digital Widescreen. [G] ●

Rio Bravo (1959) C-141m. ***½ D: Howard Hawks. John Wayne, Dean Martin, Ricky Nelson, Angie Dickinson, Walter Brennan, Ward Bond, John Russell, Claude Akins, Bob Steele. Sheriff Wayne tries to prevent a killer with connections from escaping from the town jail, with only a drunken Dino, leggy Angie, gimpy Brennan, and lockjawed Ricky to help him. Quintessential Hawks Western, patronized by reviewers at the time of its release, is now regarded as an American classic; overlong, but great fun. Written by Leigh Brackett and Jules Furthman. Followed by EL DORADO; sort of remade as ASSAULT ON PRECINCT 13.▼●]

Rio Conchos (1964) **C-107m. *** D:** Gordon Douglas. Richard Boone, Stuart Whitman, Tony Franciosa, Edmond O'Brien, Jim Brown. Post–Civil War Texas is the setting for this action-filled Western centering around a shipment of stolen rifles, and Boone taking on Franciosa. Brown is notable in his film debut, and there's a zesty performance by O'Brien. CinemaScope.▼]

Rio Grande (1950) **105m. *** D:** John Ford. John Wayne, Maureen O'Hara, Ben Johnson, Harry Carey, Jr., Victor McLaglen, Claude Jarman, Jr., Chill Wills, J. Carrol Naish, Grant Withers, Pat Wayne. The last of director Ford's Cavalry trilogy (following FORT APACHE and SHE WORE A YELLOW RIBBON), and the most underrated: a vivid look at the gentlemanly spirit of the Cavalry during post–Civil War days . . . and the difficult relationship between an estranged father (commander Wayne) and his son (new recruit Jarman). Beautifully shot by Bert Glennon and Archie Stout, with lovely theme by Victor Young, songs by Sons of the Pioneers (including Ken Curtis). Also shown in computer-colored version.▼

Rio Lobo (1970) **C-114m. *** D:** Howard Hawks. John Wayne, Jorge Rivero, Jennifer O'Neill, Jack Elam, Chris Mitchum, Mike Henry, Susana Dosamantes, Victor French, Sherry Lansing, Bill Williams, David Huddleston, Jim Davis, Robert Donner. Hawks' final film is a lighthearted Western in the RIO BRAVO mold, with the Duke as ex-Union colonel out to settle some old scores. Youthful costars are weak, but stays on track thanks to snappy dialogue, crisp action, and riotous performance by Elam as shotgun-toting old looney. Future Paramount studio head Lansing's last film as an actress; George Plimpton has a one-line bit that served as the basis of a TV special. [G]▼●]

Rio Rita (1942) **91m. **½ D:** S. Sylvan Simon. Bud Abbott, Lou Costello, Kathryn Grayson, John Carroll, Tom Conway, Barry Nelson. Vintage Broadway musical brought up to date, with Nazis invading Western ranch where Bud and Lou work; some good music helps this one. Previously filmed in 1929 with Wheeler and Woolsey.▼●]

Riot (1969) **C-97m. **½ D:** Buzz Kulik. Jim Brown, Gene Hackman, Ben Carruthers, Mike Kellin, Gerald O'Loughlin. Unsurprising film about convicts Hackman and Brown planning a prison break; violent, for its time. [PG—edited from original R rating]▼

Riot in Cell Block 11 (1954) **80m. *** D:** Don Siegel. Neville Brand, Emile Meyer, Frank Faylen, Leo Gordon, Robert Osterloh. Realistic, powerful prison drama still packs a punch. Among the contemporary themes in this 1954 film is "media manipulation," with prisoners trying to use press for leverage.▼

Riot on Sunset Strip (1967) **C-85m. *½ D:** Arthur Dreifuss. Aldo Ray, Mimsy Farmer, Michael Evans, Laurie Mock, Tim Rooney, Bill Baldwin. Weak exploitation of real-life mid-'60s riots on the Strip concerns cop Ray's enraged response when his daughter gets involved with drugs and hippies.❚

Ripley's Game (2003-Italian-British) **C-110m. **½ D:** Liliana Cavani. John Malkovich, Dougray Scott, Ray Winstone, Lena Headey, Chiara Caselli. Tom Ripley, now living as a gentleman of leisure in Italy, sets up a benign neighbor (Scott) to become an assassin because of a thuggish associate's need for a killer who can't be traced. Malkovich is fine, though his Ripley isn't as intriguing or ambiguous as he's portrayed in PURPLE NOON or THE TALENTED MR. RIPLEY. Starts well but eventually becomes a much-too-conventional thriller. Filmed on colorful Italian and German locations. Patricia Highsmith's novel was made before as THE AMERICAN FRIEND. U.S. debut on cable TV. [R]▼❚

Ripped Off (1971-Italian) **C-83m. **½ D:** Franco Prosperi. Robert Blake, Ernest Borgnine, Gabriele Ferzetti, Catherine Spaak, Tomas Milian. Boxer Blake, framed for the murder of his corrupt manager, is hounded by detective Borgnine and protected by victim's daughter (Spaak). OK of its type; aka THE BOXER, MURDER IN THE RING, and COUNTER PUNCH. [R]▼❚

Rise and Fall of Legs Diamond, The (1960) **101m. *** D:** Budd Boetticher. Ray Danton, Karen Steele, Elaine Stewart, Jesse White, Simon Oakland, Robert Lowery, Warren Oates. Snappy chronicle of Depression-days gangster, well balanced between action gun battles and Danton's romancing flashy dolls (like young Dyan Cannon). Outstanding photography by Lucien Ballard.▼❚

Rise: Blood Hunter (2007-U.S.-New Zealand) **C-94m. BOMB D:** Sebastian Gutierrez. Lucy Liu, Michael Chiklis, James D'Arcy, Carla Gugino, Elden Henson, Julio Oscar Mechoso, Simon Rex, Allan Rich, Fran Kranz, Mako, Marilyn Manson, Nick Lachey, Robert Forster. Reporter Liu, investigating a potentially hot story, stumbles onto a cult of murderous vampires. Slick but staggeringly dumb, with a near-incoherent storyline; Liu wears a constant scowl, and Forster cameos as "Lloyd from Fresno." Unrated version runs 122m. [R]❚

Rise of Louis XIV, The (1966-French) **C-100m. *** D:** Roberto Rossellini. Jean-Marie Patte, Raymond Jourdan, Silvagni, Katharina Renn, Dominique Vincent,

Pierre Barrat. Attractive, but somewhat pedantic effort to show colorful court of not-quite straitlaced Louis XIV. Objective, almost documentary-like, but final effect is uninvolving. Made for French TV. Aka THE TAKING OF POWER BY LOUIS XIV. ▼❒

Rising of the Moon, The (1957-Irish) 81m. **½ D: John Ford. Introduced by Tyrone Power. Cyril Cusack, Maureen Connell, Noel Purcell, Frank Lawton, Jimmy O'Dea. Trio of flavorful stories about Irish life: "Majesty of the Law," "A Minute's Wait," "1921," as performed by Dublin's renowned Abbey Players.

Rising Sun (1993) C-129m. **½ D: Philip Kaufman. Sean Connery, Wesley Snipes, Harvey Keitel, Cary-Hiroyuki Tagawa, Kevin Anderson, Mako, Ray Wise, Stan Egi, Stan Shaw, Tia Carrere, Steve Buscemi. L.A. cop Snipes and Japan expert Connery investigate a homicide case that implicates a powerful Japanese corporation and a U.S. senator. Stripped-down version of Michael Crichton's detailed and controversial novel (adapted by Crichton and Kaufman) is alternately compelling, confusing, obvious, and silly, with credibility strained to the breaking point. [R] ▼●❒

Risky Business (1983) C-96m. *** D: Paul Brickman. Tom Cruise, Rebecca De Mornay, Curtis Armstrong, Bronson Pinchot, Raphael Sbarge, Joe Pantoliano, Nicholas Pryor, Janet Carroll, Richard Masur, Kevin Anderson, Megan Mullally. Piquant, original comedy about a reticent teenager who goes a bit wild while his parents are out of town, and becomes involved—in more ways than one—with a prostitute. Brickman's darkly satiric script is balanced by Cruise's utterly likable (and believable) performance in the lead. [R] ▼●❒

Rita, Sue and Bob Too (1986-British) C-95m. *** D: Alan Clarke. Siobhan Finneran, Michelle Holmes, George Costigan, Lesley Sharp, Willie Ross, Patti Nicholls, Kulvinder Ghir. Rita and Sue, two plain-looking, slightly overweight working class teens, babysit for Bob and his frigid wife . . . and soon, Rita, Sue and Bob are making three-way whoopee. A shamelessly funny, profane, well-acted sleeper that's definitely not for all tastes. Some of the sex scenes—particularly those in Bob's car—are a riot. [R] ▼●

Rite, The (1969-Swedish) 76m. *** D: Ingmar Bergman. Ingrid Thulin, Gunnar Bjornstrand, Anders Ek, Erik Hell. Penetrating four-character drama, crammed with symbolism, about a trio of actors—a woman, her husband, and her lover—who have been accused of performing a provocative mime act in public, and come before a judge. Strange, disturbing, sexually frank, and uniquely Bergmanesque, with an anti-censorship point of view. Starkly directed and photographed (by Sven Nykvist); a showcase for all four performers. This was Bergman's first film for television. ▼

Rite, The (2011) C-114m. ** D: Mikael Håfström. Anthony Hopkins, Colin O'Donoghue, Alice Braga, Ciarán Hinds, Toby Jones, Rutger Hauer, Marta Gastini. Young man (O'Donoghue) becomes a novitiate priest for the education, but while studying at the Vatican he's assigned to work with Hopkins, a matter-of-fact specialist in exorcism. The priest invites his guest to witness an exorcism—and later begins to show signs of demonic possession himself. Though this takes a serious approach to the subject, from a Catholic point of view, it's not likely to convince many. Hopkins is good, but the movie seems trivial and is short on horror content, with the demonic activity mostly in the last third. Panavision. [PG-13] ❒

Rites of Summer SEE: **White Water Summer**

Ritual (2006) C-106m. ** D: Avi Nesher. Jennifer Grey, Craig Sheffer, Daniel Lapaine, Kristen Wilson, Gabriel Casseus, Tim Curry, Dorothy Cunningham, Carl Bradshaw. Dr. Grey doesn't realize what she's getting herself into when she heads for Jamaica to care for a young man who's convinced he's turning into a zombie. Lame remake of I WALKED WITH A ZOMBIE is tolerable only when sticking to the plot, which isn't often enough. Stephen Tobolowsky appears unbilled. Filmed in 2001, released direct to DVD five years later! Aka TALES FROM THE CRYPT PRESENTS RITUAL. [R]❒

Rituals (1978-Canadian) C-100m. *½ D: Peter Carter. Hal Holbrook, Lawrence Dane, Robin Gammell, Ken James, Gary Reineke. Ripoff of DELIVERANCE with Holbrook and four fellow M.D.s terrorized during wilderness vacation. Unpleasant, to say the least. Reissued as THE CREEPER. [R]▼

Ritz, The (1976) C-91m. **½ D: Richard Lester. Jack Weston, Rita Moreno, Jerry Stiller, Kaye Ballard, F. Murray Abraham, Treat Williams, Paul Price, George Coulouris, Bessie Love, John Ratzenberger. Brisk filming of Terrence McNally's farce about a schnook fleeing his murderous brother-in-law by hiding in gay baths suffers from feeling that it's all a photographed stage performance. Moreno is memorable recreating her Tony-winning role as no-talent entertainer Googie Gomez. Filmed in England. [R]▼●❒

Rivals (1972) C-103m. **½ D: Krishna Shah. Robert Klein, Joan Hackett, Scott Jacoby. A remarriage forces young child to try and murder the new rival for his mother's affections. Offbeat, to say the least. [R]▼

River, The (1951-Indian) C-99m. **** D: Jean Renoir. Patricia Walters, Nora Swinburne, Arthur Shields, Radha, Adrienne Corri, Esmond Knight; narrated by June

Hillman. Immensely moving, lyrical adaptation of Rumer Godden novel about English children growing up in Bengal. One of the great color films, a total triumph for cinematographer Claude and director Jean Renoir. Scripted by Godden and Renoir.▼●]

River, The (1984) C-122m. **½ D: Mark Rydell. Sissy Spacek, Mel Gibson, Shane Bailey, Becky Jo Lynch, Scott Glenn, Don Hood, Billy Green Bush, James Tolkan. Close-knit family struggles to make good on their farm, which is constantly threatened by river that flows alongside. Spacek's a perfect farm woman (and mother) but Gibson's character is so coldly stubborn that it's hard to empathize. Beautifully shot by Vilmos Zsigmond. [PG-13]▼●]

River Niger, The (1976) C-105m. *** D: Krishna Shah. James Earl Jones, Cicely Tyson, Glynn Turman, Lou Gossett, Roger E. Mosley, Jonelle Allen. Intelligent, moving story (based on 1972 Tony Award– winning play) of black family trying to come to terms with the world and themselves. Touching and convincing. [R]▼]

River of Darkness SEE: Eureka (1983)

River of Death (1989) C-111m. *½ D: Steve Carver. Michael Dudikoff, Donald Pleasence, Herbert Lom, Cynthia Erland, Robert Vaughn, L. Q. Jones, Sarah Maur Thorp. Complicated jungle yarn involving a lost city, mad Nazi scientist Vaughn, vengeful Nazi war criminal Pleasence, hero Dudikoff, and the usual hangers-on. Absurd adventure from Alistair MacLean's novel. [R]▼●]

River of No Return (1954) C-91m. **½ D: Otto Preminger. Robert Mitchum, Marilyn Monroe, Rory Calhoun, Tommy Rettig, Murvyn Vye, Douglas Spencer. Mitchum rescues Calhoun and Monroe from leaky raft; Calhoun returns the favor by stealing his horse and abandoning them (and Mitchum's young son) to hostile Indians. Dialogue leaves a lot to be desired, but it's worth watching Mitchum and Monroe at her most beautiful—not to mention some gorgeous locations (seen to best advantage in CinemaScope).▼●]

River Rat, The (1984) C-93m. **½ D: Tom Rickman. Tommy Lee Jones, Nancy Lea Owen, Brian Dennehy, Martha Plimpton. Occasionally perceptive drama about ex-con Jones, falsely imprisoned for murder, and his arrival home after 13 years in the slammer. Works best when focusing on his relationship with his 12-year-old daughter (Plimpton), but spins out of control when dealing with a search for hidden money. Directorial debut for screenwriter Rickman (COAL MINER'S DAUGHTER). [PG]▼●]

River Runs Through It, A (1992) C-123m. **½ D: Robert Redford. Craig Sheffer, Brad Pitt, Tom Skerritt, Emily Lloyd, Brenda Blethyn, Edie McClurg, Stephen Shellen, Vann Gravage, Nicole Burdette, Susan

Traylor, Joseph Gordon-Levitt; narration (uncredited) by Robert Redford. A preacher (Skerritt) teaches his sons about life, grace, and love through the art of fly-fishing in their native Montana, but as the boys grow up and follow very different paths they find that fishing is the one bond that still draws them together. Respectful adaptation of Norman Maclean's autobiographical novella. Beautifully filmed in Montana, with Oscar-winning cinematography by Philippe Rousselot . . . but the pace is deliberate, the emotions muted, and the result is a bit sleepy at times. [PG]▼●]

River's Edge (1986) C-99m. *** D: Tim Hunter. Crispin Glover, Keanu Reeves, Ione Skye Leitch, Roxana Zal, Daniel Roebuck, Tom Bower, Constance Forslund, Leo Rossi, Jim Metzler, Dennis Hopper. Gripping story of teenagers who don't know how to react when one of their friends murders a girl from their clique and leaves her body along the riverbank. Absorbing, if not perfect, study of contemporary kids and their feelings of alienation from grown-ups, from society, and from responsibility . . . with a wild performance by Glover as their self-styled ringleader. Best of all is Hopper, perfectly cast as a leftover biker and druggie who can't relate to the kids' lack of values. Disturbing and thought-provoking—all the more so when you learn that the story was based on a real-life incident! [R]▼●]

River Wild, The (1994) C-108m. *** D: Curtis Hanson. Meryl Streep, Kevin Bacon, David Strathairn, Joseph Mazzello, John C. Reilly, Elizabeth Hoffman, Victor H. Galloway, Benjamin Bratt. Exciting, well-wrought adventure yarn about a woman taking her young son and nearly estranged husband on a whitewater raft ride—and falling prey to a pair of bad guys on the lam. Streep's complete credibility, as a wife, mom, and rafting expert, keeps this afloat, along with good performances and vivid action scenes. Panavision. [PG-13]▼●]

Rize (2005) C-86m. **½ D: David LaChapelle. Enlightening documentary examines the evolution of Krumping, an energetic hip-hop-derived style of dancing that emerged from the 1992 L.A. riots. Profiles some of the leaders of this movement and spotlights some of their competitive dance-offs, also revealing the often abysmal, dysfunctional home lives that generate a yearning for self-expression and release. A crowd pleaser at several film festivals. Feature debut for well-regarded photographer and music video director LaChapelle, who expanded this from a short called KRUMPED that debuted at Sundance in 2004. [PG-13]▼●]

Road, The (2009) C-111m. *** D: John Hillcoat. Viggo Mortensen, Kodi Smit-McPhee, Charlize Theron, Robert Duvall, Guy Pearce, Molly Parker, Michael Kenneth Williams, Garret Dillahunt. Wrenchingly difficult movie, adapted from Cormac McCarthy's best-selling novel, about a father's determination to protect his young son and prepare him to survive in a grim, postapocalyptic world. Bleak, to be sure, but compelling, with a great performance by Mortensen—and an impressive one by Smit-McPhee as the boy. Super 35. [R] ◗

Road Builder, The SEE: **Night Digger, The**

Roadgames (1981-Australian) **C-100m.** **½ D: Richard Franklin. Stacy Keach, Jamie Lee Curtis, Marion Edward, Grant Page, Bill Stacey. Adequate thriller about truckdriver Keach pursuing a murderer. Curtis is a hitchhiker he picks up. Not bad. Director Franklin, an avowed Hitchcock disciple, went on to make PSYCHO II. Panavision. [PG] ▼◗

Road Home, The (1999-China) **C/B&W-89m.** **½ D: Zhang Yimou. Zhang Ziyi, Sun Honglei, Zheng Hao, Zhao Yuelin, Li Bin, Chang Guifa, Sung Wencheng, Liu Qi. A businessman returns to his rural native village upon the death of his father and recalls how his parents met: his father came to the village as the new schoolteacher, and his mother was instantly smitten. A pleasant but minor film for a great filmmaker, buoyed by an appealing performance by Zhang Ziyi (playing the mother as a girl). Panavision. [G] ▼◗

Road House (1948) **95m.** *** D: Jean Negulesco. Ida Lupino, Cornel Wilde, Celeste Holm, Richard Widmark, O. Z. Whitehead, Robert Karnes. Psychotic roadhouse owner Widmark deludes himself into thinking he "owns" singer Lupino; when she falls for his childhood friend and employee (Wilde), sparks fly in this entertaining melodrama. Ida even gets to sing, introducing the standard "Again." ▼◗

Road House (1989) **C-114m.** *½ D: Rowdy Herrington. Patrick Swayze, Kelly Lynch, Sam Elliott, Ben Gazzara, Marshall Teague, Kevin Tighe, Kathleen Wilhoite, The Jeff Healey Band. Bouncer Swayze—an N.Y.U. philosophy major, no less—is hired to clean house at a hellhole Midwest saloon and tangles with local kingpin Gazzara. One broken limb won't suffice when 27 will do; brain-dead yahoo fare is fun for a while. Followed by a direct-to-video sequel. Panavision. [R] ▼◗

Roadhouse 66 (1984) **C-96m.** *½ D: John Mark Robinson. Willem Dafoe, Judge Reinhold, Kaaren Lee, Kate Vernon, Stephen Elliot, Alan Autry. Predictable, paper-thin nonsense about upper-class Reinhold and hitchhiker Dafoe and their troubles in a small Arizona town after their car breaks down. Pretty boring stuff. [R] ▼◗

Roadie (1980) **C-105m.** *½ D: Alan Rudolph. Meat Loaf, Kaki Hunter, Art Carney, Gailard Sartain, Alice Cooper, Blondie, Roy Orbison, Hank Williams, Jr., Ramblin' Jack Elliot. Fat roadie (Loaf) and skinny aspiring groupie (Hunter) spend nearly two hours of screen time trying to meet Cooper. Talented director Rudolph turns into a Hal Needham clone with loud, excruciatingly dopey comedy. [PG] ▼◗

Road Killers, The (1995) **C-89m.** **½ D: Deran Sarafian. Christopher Lambert, Craig Sheffer, David Arquette, Josh Brolin, Michelle Forbes, Joseph Gordon-Levitt, Adrienne Shelly. HOT RODS TO HELL redux, updated to the dysfunctional '90s: a group of vacationers (led by stone-faced Lambert), on a road trip through the Nevada desert, are terrorized by a gang of psychos (led by Sheffer in a hilarious hippie wig). Enjoyably trashy drive-in fodder—but since there are no more drive-ins, this one went straight to video. Filmed in 1993 under the title ROADFLOWER. Panavision. [R] ▼◗

Roadside Prophets (1992) **C-96m.** *** D: Abbe Wool. John Doe, Adam Horovitz, David Carradine, John Cusack, Bill Cobbs, Jennifer Balgobin, David Anthony Marshall, Stephen Tobolowsky, Timothy Leary, Arlo Guthrie, Ellie Raab, Don Cheadle. Construction worker Doe, whose best friend is his motorcycle, rides from L.A. to seek the "legendary" city of El Dorado in Nevada. His purpose: to dispose of the ashes of an acquaintance, who died while playing a video game. Along the way he gains a traveling companion (Horovitz) and meets various characters who are leftovers from the 1960s counterculture. A bit too self-consciously hip but a wry, potent look at modern-day alienation and how yesterday's pop culture becomes today's nostalgia. [R] ▼●◗

Road to Bali (1952) **C-90m.** *** D: Hal Walker. Bob Hope, Dorothy Lamour, Bing Crosby, Murvyn Vye, Ralph Moody. Only color ROAD film has lush trappings, many guest stars and good laughs, as Bob and Bing save Dorothy from evil princess and jungle perils. Carolyn Jones has a bit. ▼◗

Road to Corinthe, The (1967-French-Greek-Italian) **C-97m.** *** D: Claude Chabrol. Jean Seberg, Maurice Ronet, Christian Marquand, Michel Bouquet, Saro Urzi, Claude Chabrol, Romain Gary. Sly spy spoof about the wife of a NATO agent in Greece who's framed for his murder and goes on the run to catch the real killer. Meanwhile, she's also trying to find out who's smuggling black boxes into the country that are jamming American radar installations. James Bond/Hitchcock pastiche works as both an entertaining espionage thriller and a surreal satire of the genre. Originally released in the U.S. in an 85m. version called WHO'S GOT THE BLACK BOX? ▼◗

Road to El Dorado, The (2000) **C-89m.** **

D: Eric "Bibo" Bergeron, Don Paul. Voices of Kevin Kline, Kenneth Branagh, Rosie Perez, Armand Assante, Edward James Olmos, Jim Cummings. Two con-artist pals in the 16th century find themselves on an accidental journey to the legendary city of gold with a map in their hands. Beautifully designed and staged, but relentlessly mediocre, with one-note humor and forgettable Elton John–Tim Rice songs. Great animation doesn't matter if you don't care about the characters. [PG]▼▶

Road to Eternity, The (1959-Japanese) 183m. ***½ D: Masaki Kobayashi. Tatsuya Nakadai, Michiyo Aratama, Kokinji Katsura, Jun Tatara, Michio Minami, Ryohei Uchida, Kei Sato, Kenjiro Uemura, Keiji Sada, Minoru Chiaki. In this second in Kobayashi's three-part epic (following NO GREATER LOVE and succeeded by A SOLDIER'S PRAYER), military conscript Kaji (Nakadai) is seen in training and eventually in battle. While surrounded by hostility and violence, he strains to preserve his humanity. Highlights include Kaji's poignant one-night reunion with his wife (Aratama) and an unforgettable final, extended battle sequence. Scripted by Kobayashi and Zenzo Matsuyama, based on a six-volume novel by Jumpei Gomikawa. Aka THE HUMAN CONDITION II. Grandscope. ▶

Road to Guantanamo, The (2006-British) C-95m. *** D: Michael Winterbottom, Mat Whitecross. Riz Ahmed, Farhad Harun, Waqar Siddiqui, Arfan Usman, Shahid Iqbal, Sher Khan, Jason Salkey, James Buller. Four British Pakistanis—young men who have returned to Karachi on a lark—find that the country of their childhood is no more. While touring in neighboring Afghanistan, they're mistaken for Taliban fighters and become prisoners of war, ending up at the notorious Cuban prison for weeks, then months, then years. Unusual political thriller poses as a documentary, complete with interviews with the "survivors." Harrowing film blames America for its unnecessary military intervention in the Middle East and fictionally shows some tragic repercussions of Bush and Blair's steadfastness. [R]▶

Road to Hong Kong, The (1962) 91m. **½ D: Norman Panama. Bob Hope, Bing Crosby, Joan Collins, Dorothy Lamour, Robert Morley, Walter Gotell, Peter Sellers. Final ROAD picture was the first in a decade, and while it's fun it lacks the carefree spirit of its predecessors; Bob and Bing are con men who become involved in international intrigue—and space travel! Sellers has a hilarious cameo; Lamour appears briefly as herself. Look fast for the Bob Crosby Band. Filmed in England. ▼▶

Road to Morocco (1942) 83m. *** D: David Butler. Bing Crosby, Dorothy Lamour, Bob Hope, Dona Drake, Anthony Quinn,

Vladimir Sokoloff, Monte Blue, Yvonne De Carlo. Typically funny ROAD picture, with Bing selling Bob to slave-trader in mysterious Morocco, both going after princess Lamour. Bing sings "Moonlight Becomes You."▼▶

Road to Nashville (1967) C-110m. *½ D: Robert Patrick. Marty Robbins, Doodles Weaver, Connie Smith, Richard Arlen. Inept promoter tries to line up talent for Country-Western jamboree. The music's not bad when the plot gets out of the way. Techniscope.▼▶

Road to Perdition (2002) C-117m. ***½ D: Sam Mendes. Tom Hanks, Paul Newman, Jude Law, Jennifer Jason Leigh, Stanley Tucci, Daniel Craig, Tyler Hoechlin, Liam Aiken, Dylan Baker, Ciarán Hinds. A Midwestern hit man finds himself in an untenable situation with his surrogate father, a powerful underworld boss, and flees to Chicago with his wide-eyed 12-year-old son during the depths of the Great Depression. A good yarn played out on a grand scale, with dynamic performances, impressive production design by Dennis Gassner, Oscar-winning cinematography by Conrad L. Hall, and the emotional pull of a story about fathers and sons. Further enhanced by Thomas Newman's beautiful score. Screenplay by David Self, from the graphic novel by Max Allan Collins, illustrated by Richard Piers Rayner. Super 35. [R]▼▶

Road to Rio (1947) 100m. *** D: Norman Z. McLeod. Bing Crosby, Bob Hope, Dorothy Lamour, Gale Sondergaard, Frank Faylen, The Wiere Brothers. Bob and Bing are musicians trying to wrest Dorothy from sinister aunt Sondergaard. Very funny outing in series. Songs: "But Beautiful," "You Don't Have to Know the Language," sung with guests The Andrews Sisters.▼▶

Road to Salina (1971-French-Italian) C-96m. **½ D: Georges Lautner. Mimsy Farmer, Robert Walker, Rita Hayworth, Ed Begley, Bruce Pecheur. Enjoyably trashy tale about wanderer who returns to his mother's diner and spends much time making love with a girl who might be his sister. And if that isn't kinky enough for you, Rita does the frug with Ed Begley! Panavision. [R]▼

Road to Singapore (1940) 84m. **½ D: Victor Schertzinger. Bing Crosby, Dorothy Lamour, Bob Hope, Charles Coburn, Judith Barrett, Anthony Quinn, Jerry Colonna, Monte Blue, Arthur Q. Bryan. Bing and Bob swear off women, hiding out in Singapore; then they meet saronged Lamour. First ROAD film is not the best, but still fun. ▼▶

Road to Utopia (1946) 90m. *** D: Hal Walker. Bing Crosby, Bob Hope, Dorothy Lamour, Hillary Brooke, Douglass Dumbrille, Jack LaRue, Jim Thorpe. Bob and Bing in the Klondike with usual quota of gags, supplemented by talking animals, Dorothy's song "Personality," Robert Benchley's dry commentary.▼●)

Road to Wellville, The (1994) **C-117m.** ★★ D: Alan Parker. Anthony Hopkins, Bridget Fonda, Matthew Broderick, John Cusack, Dana Carvey, Michael Lerner, Colm Meaney, John Neville, Lara Flynn Boyle, Traci Lind, Camryn Manheim, Norbert Weisser, Carole Shelley. Disappointing adaptation of T. Coraghessan Boyle's comic novel, following the plight of a couple (Fonda, Broderick) after they converge on a turn-of-the-century spa operated in Battle Creek, Michigan, by health zealot John W. Kellogg (the real-life inventor of corn flakes). Maddeningly uneven, with plot threads constantly being picked up and dropped. Carvey is especially wasted as Kellogg's oddball son. Only Hopkins' delightful, over-the-top performance as John W. makes this worth watching. [R] ▼●)

Road to Zanzibar (1941) **92m.** ★★½ D: Victor Schertzinger. Bing Crosby, Bob Hope, Dorothy Lamour, Una Merkel, Eric Blore. Weaker ROAD series entry, still amusing, with Bob and Bing circus performers traveling through jungle with Lamour and Merkel, looking for diamond mine. ▼●)

Road Trip (2000) **C-91m.** ★★★ D: Todd Phillips. Breckin Meyer, Seann William Scott, Amy Smart, Paulo Costanzo, DJ Qualls, Rachel Blanchard, Anthony Rapp, Fred Ward, Tom Green, Andy Dick, Horatio Sanz. A college student in upstate N.Y. has to head off an incriminating videotape accidentally sent to his girlfriend in Austin, Texas . . . so he and three others set off on a frantic road trip. Likable teen comedy has the requisite number of gross-out gags and female nudity to please its intended audience . . . but by any standards, it's pretty funny. Hollywood directing debut for Phillips, who made the documentary FRAT HOUSE. Also available in unrated version. Followed by a DVD sequel. [R] ▼●

Road Warrior, The (1981-Australian) **C-94m.** ★★★½ D: George Miller. Mel Gibson, Bruce Spence, Vernon Wells, Mike Preston, Virginia Hey, Emil Minty, Kjell Nilsson. Sequel to MAD MAX finds Max, now a loner, reluctantly helping tiny oil-producing community defend itself against band of depraved crazies thirsty for precious fuel. Far less original script-wise, but trend-setting visual design and some of the most unbelievable car stunts ever filmed make this equal to, if not better than, the first one. Original title: MAD MAX 2; followed by MAD MAX BEYOND THUNDERDOME. Panavision. [R] ▼●)

Roar (1981) **C-102m.** ★★ D: Noel Marshall. Tippi Hedren, Noel Marshall, John Marshall, Melanie Griffith, Jerry Marshall, Kyalo Mativo. Accident-ridden produc-

tion that took 11 years and $17 million for Hedren and husband Marshall to finish. Comedy-adventure about wife and children visiting eccentric scientist husband in jungle after being separated for years is also pro-preservation-of-African-wildlife statement. Nice try, but no cigar. Of additional interest today for early appearance of Hedren's daughter Griffith. Panavision. [PG]

Roaring Timber SEE: **Come and Get It**

Roaring Twenties, The (1939) **104m.** ★★★ D: Raoul Walsh. James Cagney, Priscilla Lane, Humphrey Bogart, Gladys George, Jeffrey Lynn, Frank McHugh, Joe Sawyer. Army buddies Cagney, Bogart, and Lynn find their lives intertwining dramatically after WW1 ends. Cagney becomes big-time prohibition racketeer in largely hackneyed script punched across by fine cast, vivid direction. Also shown in computer-colored version. ▼●)

Robbery (1967-British) **C-114m.** ★★★ D: Peter Yates. Stanley Baker, Joanna Pettet, James Booth, Frank Finlay, Barry Foster, William Marlowe. Another study of the British Royal Mail robbery; few surprises, but generally exciting, well handled. ▼

Robe, The (1953) **C-135m.** ★★½ D: Henry Koster. Richard Burton, Jean Simmons, Victor Mature, Michael Rennie, Richard Boone, Jay Robinson, Dawn Addams, Dean Jagger, Jeff Morrow, Ernest Thesiger. Earnest but episodic costume drama from Lloyd C. Douglas novel about Roman centurion who presides over Christ's crucifixion. Burton's Oscar-nominated performance seems stiff and superficial today, while Mature (as his slave Demetrius) comes off quite well! Famed as first movie in CinemaScope, though it was simultaneously shot "flat." Sequel: DEMETRIUS AND THE GLADIATORS. ▼●)

Roberta (1935) **106m.** ★★★ D: William A. Seiter. Irene Dunne, Fred Astaire, Ginger Rogers, Randolph Scott, Helen Westley, Claire Dodd, Victor Varconi, Candy Candido. The story of this famous Jerome Kern–Otto Harbach musical creaks and groans, but "supporting" characters Astaire and Rogers make up for it in their exuberant dance numbers. You can try counting how many times Scott says "swell," or try to spot young Lucille Ball in fashion-show sequence to get through the rest. Songs include "I Won't Dance," "Lovely to Look At," "Smoke Gets in Your Eyes," and "Yesterdays." Based on the Alice Duer Miller novel *Gowns By Roberta*. Remade as LOVELY TO LOOK AT.▼●)

Robert A. Heinlein's The Puppet Masters SEE: **Puppet Masters, The**

Robert et Robert (1978-French) **C-105m.** ★★★ D: Claude Lelouch. Charles Denner, Jacques Villeret, Jean-Claude Brialy, Macha Meril, Germaine Montero, Regine. Winning comedy about a friendship between two lonely bachelors named Robert, one an eccentric, impatient cab driver, the other a shy, indecisive apprentice traffic cop. Villeret really scores as the latter.▼

Robin and Marian (1976) **C-112m.** **½ D: Richard Lester. Sean Connery, Audrey Hepburn, Robert Shaw, Richard Harris, Nicol Williamson, Denholm Elliott, Kenneth Haigh, Ian Holm, Ronnie Barker, Victoria Abril. Middle-aged Robin Hood returns to Sherwood Forest after years in exile, rekindles romance with Maid Marian and faces final challenge against arch-enemy Sheriff of Nottingham. Arid, uninvolving film strips beloved characters of all their magic. "Revisionist" script by James Goldman. [PG]▼●)

Robin and the 7 Hoods (1964) **C-123m.** *** D: Gordon Douglas. Frank Sinatra, Dean Martin, Sammy Davis, Jr., Bing Crosby, Peter Falk, Barbara Rush, Victor Buono, Sig Ruman, Allen Jenkins, Hans Conried, Jack LaRue, Edward G. Robinson. Rat Pack's final fling is amusing transposition of the merrie legend to 1928 Chicago, with gangleader Sinatra surprised to find he's something of a local hero. No classic, but good-looking and easy to take; Crosby is adroit as gang's elder statesman. Cahn-Van Heusen songs include "My Kind of Town," "Style," "Mr. Booze." Produced in 2010 as a stage musical. Panavision.▼●)

Robin Hood (1973) **C-83m.** **½ D: Wolfgang Reitherman. Voices of Brian Bedford, Phil Harris, Monica Evans, Peter Ustinov, Terry-Thomas, Andy Devine, Roger Miller, Pat Buttram, George Lindsey, Carole Shelley. Undistinguished Disney cartoon feature is pleasant enough for kids, but lacks story strength (and heart). Animals fill traditional Robin Hood roles, with Phil Harris' Little John a virtual reprise of his Baloo the Bear from THE JUNGLE BOOK. Disney's live-action THE STORY OF ROBIN HOOD AND HIS MERRIE MEN was much better. [G]▼●)

Robin Hood (2010-U.S.-British) **C-140m.** *** D: Ridley Scott. Russell Crowe, Cate Blanchett, Max von Sydow, William Hurt, Mark Strong, Oscar Isaac, Danny Huston, Eileen Atkins, Mark Addy, Matthew Macfadyen, Kevin Durand, Scott Grimes, Alan Doyle, Douglas Hodge, Léa Seydoux. Gritty, large-scale historical adventure might be called THE MAN WHO WOULD BE ROBIN HOOD, as it dramatizes events leading up to the creation of the legendary outlaw. Crowe is solid as ever as a loyal soldier of King Richard the Lionheart who discovers that his fate lies in Nottingham. There he encounters a widowed Marian (Blanchett) and her father (von Sydow, in a terrific turn), who holds the key to Robin's past—and his fateful future. Epic in scale, masterfully crafted, this saga goes on a bit too long—and its seaside battle climax seems to belong in another movie—but it's still entertaining. Alternate version runs 156m. Super 35. [PG-13]▼●)

Robin Hood: Men in Tights (1993) **C-102m.** **½ D: Mel Brooks. Cary Elwes, Richard Lewis, Roger Rees, Amy Yasbeck, David Chappelle, Mark Blankfield, Tracey Ullman, Eric Allan Kramer, Megan Cavanagh, Mel Brooks, Dom DeLuise, Dick Van Patten, Matthew Porretta, Isaac Hayes, Robert Ridgely, Chuck McCann, Clive Revill. Disappointingly mild Brooks parody with Elwes as the hero of Sherwood Forest, and Rees a hilarious Sheriff of Rottingham. (Brooks himself plays Rabbi Tuchman, a variation on Friar Tuck.) Laughs come in fits and starts, but the film has no momentum and no memorable set pieces. Cameos by Brooks regulars help a bit; DeLuise is hilarious as The Godfather. [PG-13]▼●)

Robin Hood: Prince of Thieves (1991) **C-138m.** *** D: Kevin Reynolds. Kevin Costner, Morgan Freeman, Mary Elizabeth Mastrantonio, Christian Slater, Alan Rickman, Geraldine McEwan, Michael McShane, Brian Blessed, Michael Wincott, Nick Brimble, Jack Wild. A Robin Hood for the '90s, light years removed from the romantic vision of Errol Flynn . . . but this gritty, pumped-up version can stand on its own, if you're willing to stick with it through a lumpy first hour, and can accept a very American Costner in the lead. Rough, tough, and rousing at times, with Rickman's off-the-wall approach to the Sheriff of Nottingham a real surprise. Extended edition runs 150m. [PG-13]▼●)

Robinson Crusoe (1952) SEE: **Adventures of Robinson Crusoe**

Robinson Crusoe (1998) **C-91m.** *½ D: Rod K. Hardy, George Miller. Pierce Brosnan, William Takaku, Polly Walker, Ian Hart, James Frain, Damian Lewis. Flat retelling of the Defoe classic with Brosnan playing the shipwrecked survivor. Visually appealing, and the actors try, but film lacks an emotional punch. Brosnan's real-life son Sean plays a cabin boy. Shot in 1994; never released theatrically in the U.S. Full onscreen title is DANIEL DEFOE'S ROBINSON CRUSOE. [PG-13]▼)

Robinson Crusoeland SEE: **Utopia**

Robinson Crusoe on Mars (1964) **C-109m.** **½ D: Byron Haskin. Paul Mantee, Vic Lundin, Adam West. Surprisingly agreeable reworking of the classic Defoe story, with Mantee as stranded astronaut, at first accompanied only by a monkey. "Friday" turns out to be a similarly trapped alien. Beautifully shot in Death Valley by Winton C. Hoch; film's intimate nature helps it play better on TV screens than most widescreen space films. Techniscope.▼●)

RoboCop (1987) **C-103m.** *** D: Paul Verhoeven. Peter Weller, Nancy Allen, Daniel O'Herlihy, Ronny Cox, Kurtwood Smith, Miguel Ferrer, Robert DoQui, Ray Wise,

Felton Perry, Paul McCrane, Del Zamora. The setting: Detroit, in the near future. A cop who dies in the line of duty is transformed into an ultrasophisticated cyborg by the corporation which now runs the police department. Only hitch: this "perfect" cop still seeks revenge on the sadistic creeps who killed him. Sharp, slick, slam-bang action entertainment, with fantastic stop-motion animation supervised by Phil Tippett (ED 209 is a wow!) . . . but its view of life in the future is unremittingly bleak and ugly. Followed by two sequels, an animated and a live-action TV series. Also shown in unrated version. [R]▼●)

RoboCop 2 (1990) **C-118m.** *½ D: Irvin Kershner. Peter Weller, Nancy Allen, Daniel O'Herlihy, Belinda Bauer, Tom Noonan, Gabriel Damon, Felton Perry, Robert DoQui, Willard Pugh, Patricia Charbonneau. Appallingly (and unnecessarily) mean, ugly sequel in which coldblooded corporation czar O'Herlihy and drug kingpin Noonan threaten to end Robo's existence—while the laboratory whizzes cook up a bigger, "better" cyborg cop to take his place. Offensively violent and humorless. Phil Tippett's stop-motion animation is the film's only asset. [R] ▼●)

RoboCop 3 (1993) **C-105m.** ** D: Fred Dekker. Robert John Burke, Nancy Allen, Rip Torn, John Castle, Jill Hennessy, CCH Pounder, Mako, Robert DoQui, Remy Ryan, Bruce Locke. When the evil corporation OCP uses a policelike group to force impoverished Detroit citizens out of their homes, Robocop (Burke) steals the force and joins the rebellion. The script (by Frank Miller and the director) is smug but crude; though it lacks the first sequel's violence, it's also short on spectacle. Filmed in 1991. [PG-13]▼●)

Robo Man SEE: Who?

Robot Carnival (1987-Japanese) **C-91m.** *** D: Katsuhiro Otomo, Atsuko Fukushima, Kouji Morimoto, Kiroyuki Kitazume, Mao Lamdo, Hidetoshi Ohmori, Yasuomi Umetsu, Hiroyuki Kitakubo, Takashi Nakamura. Nine animators collaborated to create eight short stories on the subject of robots: there's comic book fantasy, romance, comedy, and spectacle. Not all the stories hit the bull's-eye, but the best are quite good: "Presence," about a man falling in love with his female robot, and "Nightmare," in which a drunk awakens to find his city overrun by mechanical creatures. ▼●

Robot Monster (1953) **63m.** BOMB D: Phil Tucker. George Nader, Gregory Moffett, Claudia Barrett, Selena Royle, John Mylong. Gorilla in diving helmet wipes out entire Earth population save one family and Nader, then spends most of film's running time lumbering around Bronson Canyon trying to find them. One of the genuine legends of Hollywood: embarrassingly, hilariously awful . . . and dig that bubble machine with the TV antenna! Originally in 3-D (except for the dinosaur

stock footage from ONE MILLION B.C. and LOST CONTINENT). 3-D. ▼●)

Robots (2005) **C-90m.** **½ D: Chris Wedge. Voices of Ewan McGregor, Halle Berry, Robin Williams, Greg Kinnear, Mel Brooks, Drew Carey, Jim Broadbent, Amanda Bynes, Stanley Tucci, Dianne Wiest, Paul Giamatti, Jennifer Coolidge, Dan Hedaya, James Earl Jones, Natasha Lyonne. Naive son of a humble dishwasher sets off for Robot City to pursue his dream of being an inventor; there he learns that his hero, industrialist Bigweld, has been usurped by a greedy capitalist who intends to make older robots obsolete. Inventive CG-animated film has dazzling production design (by children's book author-illustrator William Joyce, who also coproduced); the script is less magical, with an alarming number of *derrière* jokes, but still entertaining, with a lively voice cast, including various celebrity cameos. [PG] ▼)

Rob Roy (1995-U.S.-Scottish) **C-139m.** *** D: Michael Caton-Jones. Liam Neeson, Jessica Lange, John Hurt, Tim Roth, Eric Stoltz, Andrew Keir, Brian Cox, Brian McCardie, Gilbert Martin, Vicki Masson. Absorbing tale of Rob Roy MacGregor, a lowborn man of high ideals in early 1700s Scotland who refuses to sacrifice his integrity to save his skin—or his family's. Beautiful scenery and rugged action (including several sword fights) complement an intelligent script. Deliberately paced, with solid performances from Neeson and Lange, and a delicious, scene-stealing turn by Roth as a smarmy bad guy. Never quite rousing but always entertaining. J-D-C Scope. [R]▼●)

Rocco and His Brothers (1960-Italian) **180m.** ***½ D: Luchino Visconti. Alain Delon, Renato Salvatori, Annie Girardot, Katina Paxinou, Claudia Cardinale, Roger Hanin, Suzy Delair. Sweeping chronicle of familial loyalty and the tainting of innocence, chronicling the plight of idealistic, saintly Rocco (Delon) after he and his mother and brothers leave their rural southern Italian community and settle in Milan. Stunningly photographed by Giuseppe Rotunno. Restored to its original running time in 1991; beware many shorter, visually inferior versions. ▼●)

Rock, The (1996) **C-136m.** ** D: Michael Bay. Sean Connery, Nicolas Cage, Ed Harris, Michael Biehn, William Forsythe, David Morse, John Spencer, John C. McGinley, Tony Todd, Bokeem Woodbine, Danny Nucci, Vanessa Marcil, Anthony Clark, Claire Forlani. Big, loud, often dumb action/suspense yarn about a disgruntled Marine general who takes over Alcatraz, threatening to obliterate San Francisco with high-tech poison gas. Enter FBI biochemist Cage and long-imprisoned British agent Connery—the only man who ever escaped from The Rock—

to lead a rescue team onto the island. Plenty of kinetic action and destruction, as well as contrivances and story holes. David Marshall Grant appears unbilled. Super 35. [R]▼●◖

Rock-a-Bye Baby (1958) C-103m. *** D: Frank Tashlin. Jerry Lewis, Marilyn Maxwell, Connie Stevens, Baccaloni, Reginald Gardiner, James Gleason, Hans Conried. Good-natured schnook Jerry becomes full-time baby-sitter for movie sex-siren Maxwell, who doesn't want her public to know she's had triplets. Loose remake of Preston Sturges's THE MIRACLE OF MORGAN'S CREEK, with many funny moments. That's Lewis' son Gary playing Jerry as a boy in the musical flashback sequence. VistaVision.▼

Rock-a-Doodle (1992) C-77m. ** D: Don Bluth. Voices of Glen Campbell, Christopher Plummer, Phil Harris, Sandy Duncan, Eddie Deezen, Charles Nelson Reilly, Sorrell Booke, Ellen Greene, Toby Scott Granger. A cocky cock heads for Vegas after suffering a severe blow to his ego, finds success as a nightclub superstar in the Elvis mode. Kiddie cartoon is missing the essential components to make it more than passable entertainment for six-year-olds. [G]▼●◖

Rock & Rule (1983) C-85m. **½ D: Clive A. Smith. Voices of Don Francks, Paul Le Mat, Susan Roman, Sam Langevin, Catherine O'Hara. Animated rock fable, with innovative, often dazzling visuals and a solid score (featuring Lou Reed, Debbie Harry, Cheap Trick, Earth, Wind and Fire, Iggy Pop, and others) . . . but story leaves something to be desired. A triumph of technique for Canada's Nelvana animation studio, and certainly worth a look. [PG]▼●◖

Rock Around the Clock (1956) 77m. ** D: Fred F. Sears. Bill Haley and His Comets, The Platters, Tony Martinez and His Band, Freddie Bell and His Bellboys, Alan Freed, Johnny Johnston. Premise is slim (unknown band brought to N.Y.C. where they become famous) but picture is now a time-capsule look at the emergence of rock 'n' roll. Bill Haley and the Comets perform "See You Later Alligator," "Razzle Dazzle," and the title song; the Platters chip in with "Only You" and "The Great Pretender." Remade as TWIST AROUND THE CLOCK.▼◖

Rocker, The (2008) C-102m. **½ D: Peter Cattaneo. Rainn Wilson, Christina Applegate, Teddy Geiger, Josh Gad, Emma Stone, Jeff Garlin, Jane Lynch, Jason Sudeikis, Will Arnett, Howard Hesseman, Fred Armisen, Bradley Cooper, Lonny Ross, Jonathan Glaser, Jane Krakowski, Pete Best. Drummer of about-to-be-famous heavy metal band is unceremoniously dumped in favor of record company exec's nephew. After 20 years of wallowing in anonymity he hooks up with some kick-ass high school rockers. Starts off abysmally, improves as

it goes along, but then there's that formulaic, barely credible finale. Gets much of its mileage from Wilson's amusing Jack Black imitation. [PG-13]▼◖

Rockers (1978-Jamaican) C-100m. *** D: Theodoros Bafaloukos. Leroy Wallace. Richard Hall, Monica Craig, Marjorie Norman, Jacob Miller. Winningly funky though predictable comedy/drama about Rastafarian drummer Wallace's efforts to earn money and crack open the music establishment. Superior reggae score featuring Peter Tosh, Bunny Wailer, Burning Spear, Third World and Gregory Isaacs.▼

Rocketeer, The (1991) C-108m. **½ D: Joe Johnston. Bill Campbell, Jennifer Connelly, Alan Arkin, Timothy Dalton, Paul Sorvino, Terry O'Quinn, Ed Lauter, James Handy, Tiny Ron, Melora Hardin. Campbell plays a rough-and-ready 1930s pilot who stumbles onto a sought-after secret weapon: an air-pack that turns him into a rocket-man. Film captures the look of the '30s, as well as the gee-whiz innocence of Saturday matinee serials, but it's talky—and takes too much time to get where it's going. Dalton has fun as a villain patterned after Errol Flynn. Film buffs will get a kick out of the Rondo Hatton–esque bad guy (courtesy of makeup whiz Rick Baker). Panavision. [PG]▼◖

Rocket Gibraltar (1988) C-100m. *** D: Daniel Petrie. Burt Lancaster, Suzy Amis, Patricia Clarkson, Frances Conroy, Sinead Cusack, John Glover, George Martin, Bill Pullman, Kevin Spacey, Macaulay Culkin. A family gathers to celebrate patriarch Lancaster's 77th birthday; his grown-up children love him but don't really understand what he's going through, while his grandchildren make a more emotional connection to the old man . . . and vow to carry out his unusual final wish. Lancaster's presence gives the film authority, and a talented ensemble lends credibility to Amos Poe's script. Culkin is wonderful as Lancaster's canny five-year-old grandson. Filmed at beautiful locations on Long Island. [PG]▼◖

RocketMan (1997) C-94m. BOMB D: Stuart Gillard. Harland Williams, Jessica Lundy, William Sadler, Jeffrey DeMunn, James Pickens, Jr., Beau Bridges, Peter Onorati. Goofball computer expert Williams is the only possible choice to replace an ailing crewman on the first manned expedition to Mars. Predictable "comic" complications ensue, including painfully overstated farting-in-a-spacesuit jokes. Apparently, someone felt Williams was both hilarious and endearing, but we beg to differ. [PG]▼●◖

Rocket Science (2007) C-101m. ** D: Jeffrey Blitz. Reece Daniel Thompson, Anna Kendrick, Nicholas D'Agosto, Vincent Piazza, Margo Martindale, Aaron Yoo, Josh Kay, Steve Park, Denis O'Hare, Lisbeth Bartlett, Jonah Hill. Highly idiosyncratic (and unfocused) coming-of-age saga about a stuttering high school student who's persuaded to join the debate team by a beautiful girl who offers to mentor him. Pointed, often poignant observations about under- and overachievers dot this unpredictable film, which has its supporters. Scripted by first-time feature director Blitz, who made the hit documentary SPELLBOUND. [R]🄳

Rockets Galore SEE: **Mad Little Island**

Rocketship X-M (1950) **77m. **½** D: Kurt Neumann. Lloyd Bridges, Osa Massen, Hugh O'Brian, John Emery, Noah Beery, Jr. Slightly better than average production of spaceship to moon that is thrown off-course to Mars. Nice photography, good acting. Video version contains new special effects shot in 1976.▼●🄳

Rocket to the Moon SEE: **Cat-Women of the Moon**

Rocking Horse Winner, The (1949-British) **91m. ***½** D: Anthony Pelissier. Valerie Hobson, John Howard Davies, John Mills, Ronald Squire, Hugh Sinclair, Charles Goldner, Susan Richards. Truly unique, fascinating drama based on D. H. Lawrence story; small boy has knack for picking racetrack winners, but complications set in before long. Beautifully done. Screenplay by the director.▼🄳

Rock My World (2002-Canadian) **C-106m. **½** D: Sidney J. Furie. Peter O'Toole, Joan Plowright, Alicia Silverstone, Jaimz Woolvett, Keram Malicki-Sánchez, Christopher Bolton, Lochlyn Munro. Not-bad comedy set in England (but shot and financed in Canada) went straight to video in the U.S. but is far more engaging than its theatrical fate would indicate. An aristocratic British couple rent their country mansion to a rock band and wind up posing as the butler and cook when the motley crew finally shows up. Watching the interplay develop between these very different generations and cultures is fun and the music is surprisingly catchy. Plowright and O'Toole elevate this lightweight material, making for a couple of harmless hours in front of the telly. Aka GLOBAL HERESY. [R] 🄳

RocknRolla (2008-U.S.-British) **C-114m. **½** D: Guy Ritchie. Gerard Butler, Tom Wilkinson, Thandie Newton, Mark Strong, Idris Elba, Tom Hardy, Karel Roden, Toby Kebbell, Jeremy Piven, Chris "Ludacris" Bridges, Jimi Mistry, Gemma Arterton. Jack-of-all-trades Butler and partner Elba borrow money from crime kingpin Wilkinson to clinch a deal, which sets off a dominolike series of events involving a Russian speculator (Roden), his slick accountant (Newton), and assorted other colorful characters. Clever, intricate tapestry of criminal activity with a lethal sense of humor. Writer-director Ritchie tries to re-create a vintage Ritchie movie; less spontaneous and more deliberate than his breakthrough films, but still enjoyable. HD Widescreen. [R]🄳

Rock 'n' Roll High School (1979) **C-93m. *** D: Allan Arkush. P. J. Soles, Vincent Van Patten, Clint Howard, Dey Young, The Ramones, Mary Woronov, Paul Bartel, Alix Elias. A 1950s movie gone berserk. A rock-crazy teenager marshals her fellow students to rebel against the repression of new principal Miss Togar. An irresistible, high-energy comedy set to a nonstop soundtrack of Ramones music (and a few oldies). Soles is wonderful as the group's number one fan, Riff Randell. The songs include "Teenage Lobotomy," "Blitzkrieg Bop," "I Wanna Be Sedated," and "Sheena Is a Punk Rocker." Followed by ROCK 'N' ROLL HIGH SCHOOL FOREVER. [PG]▼●🄳

Rock, Pretty Baby (1956) **89m. ** D: Richard Bartlett. Sal Mineo, John Saxon, Luana Patten, Edward C. Platt, Fay Wray, Rod McKuen, Shelley Fabares, George "Foghorn" Winslow. Prototype of rock 'n' roll entries of 1950s revolving around high school rock group's effort to win big-time musical contest.▼

Rock Rock Rock! (1956) **83m. ** D: Will Price. Tuesday Weld, Teddy Randazzo, Alan Freed, Frankie Lymon and The Teenagers, The Moonglows, Chuck Berry, The Flamingos, Johnny Burnette Trio, LaVern Baker, Cirino and The Bowties. Weld, in her film debut and barely out of her training bra, must raise $30 to buy a strapless evening dress for a prom! Filmed on a budget of $6.95—and it shows. But the rock 'n' rollers, particularly Chuck Berry, are lively. Lymon and The Teenagers sing "I'm Not a Juvenile Delinquent." Weld's singing voice was dubbed by Connie Francis. One of the teens is young Valerie Harper.▼🄳

Rockshow (1980-British) **C-105m. **½** No director credited. Paul McCartney, Linda McCartney, Jimmy McCulloch, Joe English, Denny Laine. Adequate concert film of Paul McCartney and Wings on tour. Effect of Dolby sound recording will be lost on the small screen. [G]▼

Rock Star (2001) **C-106m. **½** D: Stephen Herek. Mark Wahlberg, Jennifer Aniston, Jason Flemyng, Timothy Olyphant, Timothy Spall, Dominic West, Stephan Jenkins, Jason Bonham, Heidi Mark, Dagmara Dominczyk, Rachel Hunter. In the early 1980s, a wide-eyed young man fronts a band that slavishly imitates his favorite heavy-metal group, and then gets an offer to take their lead singer's place. It seems too good to be true, and he comes to learn that it is, but that lesson is obvious to us early on. Simplistic storyline undermines sincere, likable performances by Wahlberg and Aniston (as his girlfriend and manager). Super 35. [R]▼🄳

Rockula (1990) **C-87m. *½** D: Luca Bercovici. Dean Cameron, Tawny Fere, Susan Tyrrell, Bo Diddley, Thomas Dolby, Toni

Basil. Teen vampire Cameron is unable to lose his virginity because of a centuries-old curse. Pretty stale stuff; of interest only for—but not redeemed by—the presence of Diddley. [PG-13]▼●

Rocky (1976) **C-119m.** ***½ D: John G. Avildsen. Sylvester Stallone, Talia Shire, Burt Young, Carl Weathers, Burgess Meredith, Thayer David. This story of a two-bit fighter who gets his "million-to-one shot" for fame, and self-respect, in a championship bout is impossible to dislike, even though it's just an old B movie brought up to date. Knowing that the film was a similar do-or-die project for writer-star Stallone added to its good vibes. Oscar winner for Best Picture, Director, Editing (Richard Halsey, Scott Conrad). Followed by five sequels. [PG]▼●)

Rocky II (1979) **C-119m.** *** D: Sylvester Stallone. Sylvester Stallone, Talia Shire, Burt Young, Carl Weathers, Burgess Meredith. Officially a sequel, this slightly silly film is more of a rehash, but the climactic bout (and buildup to it) hits home. [PG]▼●)

Rocky III (1982) **C-99m.** **½ D: Sylvester Stallone. Sylvester Stallone, Talia Shire, Burt Young, Burgess Meredith, Carl Weathers, Mr. T. Here, the Italian Stallion is trained by Apollo Creed after being dethroned by obnoxious Clubber Lang (Mr. T). Stallone's got a winning formula, but enough already. [PG]▼●)

Rocky IV (1985) **C-91m.** **½ D: Sylvester Stallone. Sylvester Stallone, Dolph Lundgren, Carl Weathers, Talia Shire, Burt Young, Brigitte Nielsen, Michael Pataki, James Brown. Totally artificial (and unnecessary) sequel has Rocky doin' what a man's gotta do—avenging a friend's demise and fighting for the U.S.A. (and world peace) against a superhuman Russian champ. Still, Stallone knows how to press all the right buttons, especially in a great training montage. [PG]▼●)

Rocky V (1990) **C-104m.** ** D: John G. Avildsen. Sylvester Stallone, Talia Shire, Burt Young, Sage Stallone, Burgess Meredith, Tommy Morrison, Richard Gant. The one-time champ has hit rock bottom (again). He winds up in his old neighborhood, broke and ostracized (again). He trains a young boxer who turns ingrate, and in spite of his own brain damage (from the fight in ROCKY IV) is willing to risk everything on another bout. Again. You pays your money, and you gets what you expects in this Stallone screenplay, but the thrill is gone. Stallone's real-life son plays Rocky, Jr. Followed by ROCKY BALBOA. [PG-13]▼●)

Rocky Balboa (2006) **C-102m.** **½ D: Sylvester Stallone. Sylvester Stallone, Burt Young, Milo Ventimiglia, Geraldine Hughes, James Fráncis Kelly III, Tony Burton, A. J.

Benza, Henry G. Sanders, Antonio Tarver. Title character, now a 60-ish widower and restaurant owner who's alienated from his corporate yuppie son (Ventimiglia), decides to reenter the ring one last time (unless, of course, screenwriter Stallone concocts yet another sequel) to battle the current heavyweight champ. Not as bad as it might have been, even though it strains credibility; contrived, to be sure, but also curiously endearing. A number of ESPN-type TV personalities appear as themselves. Super 35. [PG]❘)

Rocky Horror Picture Show, The (1975-British) **C-95m.** *** D: Jim Sharman. Tim Curry, Susan Sarandon, Barry Bostwick, Richard O'Brien, Jonathan Adams, Meatloaf, Little Nell (Campbell), Charles Gray, Patricia Quinn. Outrageously kinky horror movie spoof, spiced with sex, transvestism, and rock music, about a straight couple, Janet and Brad (Sarandon, Bostwick), stranded in an old dark house full of weirdos from Transylvania. Music and lyrics by O'Brien; songs include "Time Warp," "Dammit Janet," and "Wild and Untamed Thing." British running time: 100m. Followed by SHOCK TREATMENT. [R]▼●)

Rodan (1956-Japanese) **C-70m.** ** D: Ishiro Honda. Kenji Sawara, Yumi Shirakawa, Akihiko Hirata, Akio Kobori. Colossal pterodactyl hatches in mine, later goes on destructive rampage in Fukuoka. Colorful comic book stuff, all too typical of Toho Studios' monster formula.▼●)

Roger & Me (1989) **C-87m.** ***½ D: Michael Moore. Inspired, darkly ironic documentary-style film about one man's attempts to track down General Motors chairman Roger Smith, to show him what his factory closing did to the town of Flint, Michigan, where 30,000 jobs were lost. Filmmaker/narrator Moore cemented his reputation with this irresistible blend of documentary and humorous essay in this unique piece of Americana. Followed in 1992 by Moore's 24m. short, PETS OR MEAT: THE RETURN TO FLINT. [R]▼●)

Roger Dodger (2002) **C-104m.** **½ D: Dylan Kidd. Campbell Scott, Jesse Eisenberg, Isabella Rossellini, Elizabeth Berkley, Jennifer Beals, Ben Shenkman, Mina Badie, Chris Stack. Arsenic-drenched portrait of a misanthrope who fancies himself a lady-killer and decides to show his impressionable teenage nephew the ropes in N.Y.C. Scott's performance is a tour de force from his first moment on-screen, and he's in fine company with his self-assured female costars, but director Kidd's relentless, self-consciously clever script leaves an unpleasant aftertaste. [R]▼❘)

Role Models (2008-U.S.-German) **C-99m.** **½ D: David Wain. Seann William Scott, Paul Rudd, Christopher Mintz-Plasse, Bobb'e

J. Thompson, Elizabeth Banks, Jane Lynch, Ken Marino, Kerri Kenney-Silver, Ken Jeong, David Wain. While Scott is content to work as a mascot for an energy drink, his coworker Rudd feels as if he's stuck in a rut. When the two get in trouble with the law, they are given the choice of doing community service by mentoring kids or going to prison. For the sake of society, they should have chosen the hoosegow. Admittedly formulaic and juvenile, relying heavily on dirty jokes; a talented cast helps mask the film's shortcomings. Lynch is a standout. Unrated version runs 101m. [R]🔲

Roll Bounce (2005) **C-112m.** **½ D: Malcolm D. Lee. Bow Wow, Chi McBride, Mike Epps, Wesley Jonathan, Kellita Smith, Meagan Good, Nick Cannon, Jurnee Smollett, Wayne Brady, Tim Kazurinsky. A group of skate-loving teenagers on Chicago's South Side have to prove themselves to the snobs on the other side of town when their local skating rink closes, all while facing the joys and pains of growing up. As fad-based coming-of-age movies go, this is a notch or two below SATURDAY NIGHT FEVER and an improvement over ROLLER BOOGIE. Despite clichés, its '70s atmosphere, energetically filmed roller-skating sequences, and surprisingly engaging characters make it an entertaining diversion. Super 35. [PG-13]🔲

Rollerball (1975) **C-122m.** **½ D: Norman Jewison. James Caan, John Houseman, Maud Adams, John Beck, Moses Gunn, Ralph Richardson. Great-looking but disappointing drama of the 21st century; Caan is the champ at a violent sport in a society where violence has been outlawed. Filmed in Munich and London, adapted by William Harrison from his story *Roller Ball Murders*. Remade in 2002. [R]🔻⭕🔲

Rollerball (2002-U.S.-German-Japanese) **C-98m.** *½ D: John McTiernan. Chris Klein, Jean Reno, LL Cool J, Rebecca Romijn-Stamos, Naveen Andrews, Oleg Taktarov, David Hemblen, Paul Heyman. Reckless Klein follows his high school football teammate (LL Cool J) to a Middle Eastern country to play rollerball, a violent arena game that's more a circus than a sport. Somehow neither one of them figures out that the game's entrepreneur (Reno) will literally kill for good TV ratings. Remake of a not-so-hot movie manages to be even worse than the original. Laughably dumb. Video version is rated R. Panavision. [PG-13]🔻🔲

Roller Boogie (1979) **C-103m.** BOMB D: Mark L. Lester. Linda Blair, Jim Bray, Beverly Garland, Roger Perry, Mark Goddard, Sean McClory. Blair, Bray, and friends join forces to thwart evil Goddard from closing local roller skating rink. Made to cash in on roller-disco fad, with amateurish script and performances. [PG]🔻🔲

Rollercoaster (1977) **C-119m.** ** D: James Goldstone. George Segal, Richard Widmark, Timothy Bottoms, Henry Fonda, Harry Guardino, Susan Strasberg, Helen Hunt, Dorothy Tristan, Craig Wasson, William Prince, Robert Quarry. Silly disaster-type film almost redeemed by Segal's winning performance as civic inspector who tries to nail extortionist (Bottoms) before he sabotages another amusement park. Overlong, but at least home viewers won't have to watch it in "Sensurround." Hunt's film debut. Panavision. [PG]🔻⭕🔲

Rolling Thunder (1977) **C-99m.** ** D: John Flynn. William Devane, Tommy Lee Jones, Linda Haynes, James Best, Dabney Coleman, Lisa Richards, Luke Askew. Devane comes home after eight years as P.O.W. in Vietnam, sees his family murdered, and cold-bloodedly goes for revenge. Intriguing aspects of story (by Paul Schrader) and main characters thrown off-course by graphic violence and vigilante melodramatics. [R]🔻⭕🔲

Rollover (1981) **C-118m.** *½ D: Alan J. Pakula. Jane Fonda, Kris Kristofferson, Hume Cronyn, Josef Sommer, Bob Gunton, Martha Plimpton. Laughably pretentious, barely comprehensible drama about petrochemical heiress (and former film star) Fonda, banker-troubleshooter Kristofferson, and their high-financial dealings. Cronyn excels as a cunning banker. A rare example of financial science fiction. [R]🔻🔲

Romance (1999-French) **C-97m.** *½ D: Catherine Breillat. Caroline Ducey, Sagamore Stévenin, François Berléand, Rocco Siffredi, Reza Habouhossen. Notorious French film from writer-director Breillat about a woman who, rejected by her lover, goes on a sexual odyssey that leads her down some very strange paths. Novelty of a sexual film from a woman's point of view quickly wears off; it's startlingly explicit but strangely unerotic—and, more important, dull. Alternate 84m. video version is rated R. 🔻🔲

Romance & Cigarettes (2007) **C-106m.** **½ D: John Turturro. James Gandolfini, Susan Sarandon, Kate Winslet, Steve Buscemi, Bobby Cannavale, Mandy Moore, Mary-Louise Parker, Christopher Walken, Aida Turturro, Barbara Sukowa, Elaine Stritch, Eddie Izzard, Amy Sedaris, Cady Huffman, Tonya Pinkins, David Thornton. Bawdy, highly personal movie from writer-coproducer-director Turturro is an urban musical-romance-comedy-drama, unlike anything you've ever seen. Blue-collar couple Gandolfini and Sarandon are going through one hell of a midlife crisis, thanks to Gandolfini's adultery. Cast belts out songs, karaoke-style (from Tom Jones to Bruce Springsteen). Wildly uneven but endearing love letter to Queens, N.Y. A must for Kate Winslet completists. Panavision. [R]🔲

Romance of a Horsethief (1971-U.S.-Yugoslavian) **C-100m.** *½ D: Abraham

Polonsky. Yul Brynner, Eli Wallach, Jane Birkin, Oliver Tobias, Lainie Kazan, David Opatoshu. Wily Jewish horsetraders scheme to outwit Cossack captain Brynner and his men, in a Polish village circa 1904. A heartfelt endeavor for director Polonsky and actor-screenwriter Opatoshu that just doesn't come off. [PG]▼▶

Romance on the High Seas (1948) **C-99m.** *** D: Michael Curtiz. Jack Carson, Janis Paige, Don DeFore, Doris Day, Oscar Levant, S. Z. Sakall, Fortunio Bonanova, Eric Blore, Franklin Pangborn. Sparkling, trivial romantic musical set on an ocean voyage, with Doris' star-making feature film debut, singing "It's Magic," "Put 'em in a Box." Easygoing fun.▼◉▶

Romancing the Stone (1984) **C-105m.** *** D: Robert Zemeckis. Kathleen Turner, Michael Douglas, Danny DeVito, Zack Norman, Alfonso Arau, Manuel Ojeda. Very likable high-adventure hokum about mousy writer of romantic fiction who finds herself up to her neck in trouble in Colombia, with only a feisty American soldier-of-fortune as her ally. Silly story never stops moving—with some terrific action and stunts—but it's Turner's enormously appealing performance that really makes the film worthwhile. Sequel: THE JEWEL OF THE NILE. Panavision. [PG]▼◉▶

Roman de Gare (2007-French) **C-104m.** *** D: Claude Lelouch. Fanny Ardant, Dominique Pinon, Audrey Dana, Myriam Boyer, Michele Bernier, Boris Ventura Diaz. Lelouch returns to the style and sophistication of earlier film successes with this entertaining cinematic puzzle in which things and people are not always what they seem to be. Plotlines converge, involving the relationship between a novelist and her ghostwriter and a hairdresser and a stranger who could be a serial killer—or not. Magic, illusion, and lies are at the core of this elegant mystery, which mixes humor and intrigue in equal doses. In order to keep us guessing, Lelouch cast two unknowns in leading roles. HD Widescreen. [R]

Roman Holiday (1953) **119m.** ***½ D: William Wyler. Audrey Hepburn, Gregory Peck, Eddie Albert, Tullio Carminati. Hepburn got first break and an Oscar as princess, yearning for normal life, who runs away from palace, has romance with reporter Peck. Screenplay by John Dighton and Ian McLellan Hunter, from an Oscar-winning story (written by blacklisted Dalton Trumbo and credited for almost 40 years to Hunter, who acted as his "front"). Utterly charming. Remade for TV in 1987 with Catherine Oxenberg and Tom Conti. ▼◉▶

Roman Spring of Mrs. Stone, The (1961) **C-104m.** *** D: Jose Quintero. Vivien Leigh, Warren Beatty, Lotte Lenya, Jill St. John, Jeremy Spenser, Coral Browne, Cleo Laine, Bessie Love, Jean Marsh. Middle-aged actress retreats to Rome, buying a fling at romance from gigolo Beatty. Lenya, as Leigh's waspish friend, comes off best. Adapted from Tennessee Williams novella. Remade for cable TV in 2003.▼▶

Romantic Comedy (1983) **C-103m.** *½ D: Arthur Hiller. Dudley Moore, Mary Steenburgen, Frances Sternhagen, Janet Eilber, Robyn Douglass, Ron Leibman. Faithful adaptation of Bernard Slade's paper-thin play looks even worse on screen, despite a perfect cast. Moore is a playwright who tries to stifle his feelings for his female writing partner over many years' time. Title sounds suspiciously like a generic product—like Canned Peas or Toilet Tissue. Hold out for brand names. [PG]▼▶

Romantic Englishwoman, The (1975-British) **C-115m.** ***½ D: Joseph Losey. Michael Caine, Glenda Jackson, Helmut Berger, Beatrice Romand, Kate Nelligan, Nathalie Delon, Michel Lonsdale. Caine, a successful novelist married to Jackson, invites Berger into their home to generate material for a screenplay he's writing. Underrated comedy-drama by Tom Stoppard and Thomas Wiseman from Wiseman's novel; stylish and believable. [R]▼▶

Romantics, The (2010) **C-95m.** ** D: Galt Niederhoffer. Katie Holmes, Anna Paquin, Josh Duhamel, Malin Akerman, Jeremy Strong, Candice Bergen, Adam Brody, Elijah Wood, Rebecca Lawrence, Dianna Agron, Will Hutchins. College friends reunite for a wedding, though no one quite understands why Duhamel suddenly proposed to Paquin when he was seriously involved with Holmes for such a long time . . . or why Holmes agreed to be Paquin's maid of honor. Well-acted drama may leave you asking the same questions, and more; it's intriguing but unsatisfying because we don't know enough about the characters (or even why they've remained friends). First-time director Niederhoffer adapted her novel. [PG-13]▶

Rome Adventure (1962) **C-119m.** *** D: Delmer Daves. Troy Donahue, Angie Dickinson, Rossano Brazzi, Suzanne Pleshette, Constance Ford, Chad Everett, Al Hirt, Hampton Fancher. Plush soaper with Pleshette as schoolteacher on Roman fling to find romance, torn between roué (Brazzi) and architect (Donahue). As Troy's mistress, Dickinson has some rare repartee. Lush Max Steiner score. Donahue and Pleshette married two years later.▼◉▶

Romeo and Juliet (1936) **126m.** ***½ D: George Cukor. Norma Shearer, Leslie Howard, John Barrymore, Edna May Oliver, Basil Rathbone, C. Aubrey Smith, Andy Devine, Reginald Denny, Ralph Forbes. Well-acted, lavish production of Shakespeare's play about ill-fated lovers. Howard and Shearer are so good that one can forget they are too old for the roles. Not the great film it might have been, but a very good one.**▼●)**

Romeo and Juliet (1954-British) **C-140m.** *** D: Renato Castellani. Laurence Harvey, Susan Shentall, Flora Robson, Mervyn Johns, Bill Travers, Sebastian Cabot; introduced by John Gielgud. Sumptuously photographed in Italy, this pleasing version of Shakespeare's tragedy has the virtue of good casting.**▼●)**

Romeo and Juliet (1966-British) **C-126m.** **½ D: Paul Czinner. Margot Fonteyn, Rudolf Nureyev, David Blair, Desmond Doyle, Julia Farron, Michael Somes. Anyone interested in dance will want to see this filmed record of the Royal Ballet production, but actually, it doesn't adapt very well to film; zoom lens is poor substitute for immediacy of live performance.**▼)**

Romeo and Juliet (1968-British-Italian) **C-138m.** ***½ D: Franco Zeffirelli. Leonard Whiting, Olivia Hussey, Milo O'Shea, Michael York, John McEnery, Pat Heywood, Robert Stephens; narrated by Laurence Olivier. One of the best cinematic versions of Shakespeare's immortal tale of two young lovers kept apart by their families. Unique for its casting leads who were only 17 and 15, respectively, this exquisitely photographed film (by Pasquale de Santis, who won an Oscar) has a hauntingly beautiful musical score by Nino Rota and Oscar-winning costumes by Danilo Donati. [PG—edited from original G rating]**▼●)**

Romeo & Juliet (1996) **C-120m.** **½ D: Baz Luhrmann. Claire Danes, Leonardo DiCaprio, Brian Dennehy, John Leguizamo, Pete Postlethwaite, Paul Sorvino, Christina Pickles, Vondie Curtis Hall, M. Emmet Walsh, Miriam Margolyes, Diane Venora, Harold Perrineau, Paul Rudd. Arrestingly original, post-modern MTV-style '90s version of Shakespeare's tragic love story, set in Miami. The words are all authentic, the images dizzyingly clever, but the conceit wears thin after a while. What keeps it alive is the earnestness of the two youthful leads, whose passion for one another is tangible and appealing. Postlethwaite also scores strongly as Friar Lawrence. Officially titled—with no apparent irony—WILLIAM SHAKESPEARE'S ROMEO & JULIET. Panavision. [PG-13]**▼●)**

Romeo Is Bleeding (1993) **C-108m.** **½ D: Peter Medak. Gary Oldman, Lena Olin, Annabella Sciorra, Juliette Lewis, Roy Scheider, David Proval, Will Patton, Larry Joshua, James Cromwell, Julia Migenes, Dennis Farina, Ron Perlman. Nasty, hopped-up contemporary film noir about a crooked cop who's ordered by a crime-family kingpin to bump off a sexy hit woman. Film's standout virtue—and it's a doozy—is Olin's robust performance as a sadistic dominatrix who ends up strangling her assailant between her thighs and tying him down to electrified bedsprings. Outlandish, sometimes funny, but confuses overcooked with hard-boiled. [R]**▼●)**

Romeo Must Die (2000) **C-115m.** **½ D: Andrzej Bartkowiak. Jet Li, Aaliyah, Delroy Lindo, Henry O, Isaiah Washington, Russell Wong, DMX, D.B. Woodside, Anthony Anderson. If there's a Romeo, there must be a Juliet, and this Oakland-set bone-crusher deals with two warring gang families (one African-American, one Chinese) whose straight-and-narrow offspring want no part of the inevitable mayhem. Martial arts star Li's English-language starring debut has toned down the brutality to fashion a movie of slightly broader appeal. OK but overelaborate and overlong. Directorial debut for renowned cinematographer Bartkowiak. Super 35. [R] **▼)**

Rome, Open City SEE: **Open City**

Romero (1989) **C-102m.** *** D: John Duigan. Raul Julia, Richard Jordan, Ana Alicia, Eddie Velez, Alejandro Bracho, Tony Plana, Lucy Reina, Harold Gould, Al Ruscio, Robert Viharo. Absorbing biography of El Salvador's Archbishop Oscar Romero, chronicling his transformation from passive cleric to eloquent defender of his church and people. Thoughtfully directed with a good script by John Sacret Young and a quietly powerful performance by Julia. The initial feature film financed by officials of the United States Roman Catholic Church. [PG-13]**▼●)**

Romper Stomper (1992-Australian) **C-92m.** *** D: Geoffrey Wright. Russell Crowe, Daniel Pollock, Jacqueline McKenzie, Alex Scott, Leigh Russell, Daniel Wyllie, James McKenna. Lashing out at Asians in their neighborhood, a gang of white supremacist Melbourne skinheads is gradually reduced to a handful. Well-observed story is extremely tense, with strong doses of violence and sex. Reminiscent of A CLOCKWORK ORANGE, Wright's feature debut is vividly directed and well acted, but whittling the story down to a sexual triangle is a letdown. Very successful (and controversial) in its native Australia.**▼●)**

Romulus, My Father (2007-Australian) **C-104m.** **½ D: Richard Roxburgh. Eric Bana, Franka Potente, Marton Csokas, Kodi Smit-McPhee, Russell Dykstra, Jacek Koman, Alethea McGrath. A close-knit community of immigrants in Victoria gets too close, as a jealous Romanian husband goes mental while his German wife is AWOL with another bloke, their little boy tossed and torn among them all. 1960s melodrama is visually beautiful and convincingly acted, with assured direction by Roxburgh (in the actor's debut behind the camera) . . . but this abusive, violent gut-wrencher is often too much to bear. Adapted from Raimond Gaita's 1998 memoir. [R]**)**

Romy and Michele's High School Re-

union (1997) **C-91m.** **½ D: David Mirkin. Mira Sorvino, Lisa Kudrow, Janeane Garofalo, Alan Cumming, Julia Campbell, Mia Cottet, Kristin Bauer, Camryn Manheim. Best-friend airheads decide to attend their 10-year high school reunion in Tucson…then realize that they'd better put on airs if they're going to impress all the A-list snobs who used to make their lives a living hell. Flighty comedy has lulls to match its laughs, but benefits from airtight performances by the two gaudy, likable leads. Followed by a made-for-TV prequel. [R]▼●)

Ronin (1998) **C-121m.** ** D: John Frankenheimer. Robert De Niro, Jean Reno, Natascha McElhone, Stellan Skarsgård, Jonathan Pryce, Sean Bean, Skipp Sudduth, Michael (Michel) Lonsdale, Jan Triska, Katarina Witt. A group of mercenaries is brought together in France to secure a mysterious package for a high-powered client—but a double-cross leads to a guessing game of whom can be trusted. Great car chases (from the director of GRAND PRIX) are the only draw in this otherwise flat, self-serious espionage yarn. Dialogue about Japanese Ronin doesn't even apply to these characters! Cowriter Richard Weisz is in fact David Mamet. Super 35. [R]▼●)

Rooftops (1989) **C-95m.** *½ D: Robert Wise. Jason Gedrick, Troy Beyer, Eddie Velez, Tisha Campbell, Alexis Cruz, Allen Payne. Routine urban B musical about a teenage white male, his forbidden Hispanic girlfriend, drug pushers, and a form of "combat dancing"—the last employing martial-arts footwork, but without the bone crushing. Sole distinction: that it was directed by veteran Wise, who won an Oscar for the thematically similar WEST SIDE STORY. [R]▼●)

Rookie, The (1990) **C-121m.** *½ D: Clint Eastwood. Clint Eastwood, Charlie Sheen, Raul Julia, Sonia Braga, Tom Skerritt, Lara Flynn Boyle, Pepe Serna, Mara Corday. Formula filmmaking that even bored its intended audience. Cop Eastwood chews stogies for breakfast, while new partner Sheen is a rich kid who (from evidence supplied here) apparently enjoys collecting facial contusions. Still, there's one good freeway crackup, the you-asked-for-it teaming of Julia and Braga as Germans, and the sight of handcuffed Clint performing under extreme pressure to Braga's bondage rape of him. (Maybe she saw TIGHTROPE.) Panavision. [R]▼●)

Rookie, The (2002) **C-127m.** *** D: John Lee Hancock. Dennis Quaid, Rachel Griffiths, Jay Hernandez, Beth Grant, Angus T. Jones, Brian Cox, Rick Gonzalez, Royce D. Applegate. High school teacher/baseball coach inspires his ragtag team to win, and they in turn egg him on to follow his longtime dream of pitching in the major leagues. Upbeat, feel-good movie about following your dreams and tying up loose ends in your life. Based on the true story of Jim Morris, who appears briefly as an umpire. Panavision. [G]▼)

Rookie of the Year (1993) **C-103m.** *** D: Daniel Stern. Thomas Ian Nicholas, Gary Busey, Albert Hall, Amy Morton, Dan Hedaya, Bruce Altman, Eddie Bracken, Daniel Stern, Robert Gorman. Amiable film for kids about a boy who, after breaking his arm, turns out to have an incredible fastball pitch, which earns him a spot as the new star pitcher for the Chicago Cubs. Benign (almost to a fault), sometimes broad comedy/fantasy has a paper-thin plot, but makes all the right moves to entertain the youthful audience it's aiming for. First-time feature director Stern gives himself the silliest part in the film, as a dimwitted pitching coach. John Candy appears unbilled as an excitable Cubs broadcaster. Similar in premise to a 1954 film, ROOGIE'S BUMP. [PG]▼●)

Room at the Top (1959-British) **118m.** **** D: Jack Clayton. Laurence Harvey, Simone Signoret, Heather Sears, Hermione Baddeley, Donald Wolfit, Ambrosine Philpotts, Donald Houston, Wendy Craig. Brilliant drama of ambitious Harvey determined to rise in the hierarchy of the factory that employs him; complications arise when he becomes involved with older, unhappily married Signoret. Trenchant and powerful adaptation of John Braine novel won Oscars for Signoret and screenwriter Neil Paterson. Followed by LIFE AT THE TOP and MAN AT THE TOP.▼●)

Room for Romeo Brass, A (2000-British) **C-90m.** *** D: Shane Meadows. Paddy Considine, Andrew Shim, Frank Harper, Ladene Hall, Vicky McClure, Ben Marshall, Julia Ford, James Higgins, Bob Hoskins, Darren O. Campbell. Poignant and scary story of Romeo and Gavin, two 12-year-old boys whose friendship is put to the test when they meet a childlike man with a violent temper who becomes obsessed with Romeo's older sister. Unique mix of coming-of-age dramedy and psychological suspense is buoyed by Meadows' sensitive direction and an intense De Niro–esque performance from Considine in his debut film. Second part of Meadows' Midlands trilogy (TWENTYFOURSEVEN, ONCE UPON A TIME IN THE MIDLANDS). [R]

Roommate, The (2011) **C-91m.** BOMB D: Christian E. Christiansen. Leighton Meester, Minka Kelly, Cam Gigandet, Alyson Michalka, Danneel Harris, Frances Fisher, Tomas Arana, Billy Zane. Young woman (Kelly) moves into her dorm at an L.A. college. At first, she likes her shy, somewhat disturbed roommate (Meester), but soon discovers the young woman has become frighteningly attached to her. Trivial, trite would-be thriller shamelessly copies SINGLE WHITE FEMALE. You've seen this before, and done much better. Super 35. [PG-13] **▶**

Roommates (1995) **C-108m.** ****½** D: Peter Yates. Peter Falk, D. B. Sweeney, Julianne Moore, Ellen Burstyn, Jan Rubes, Frankie Faison, Noah Fleiss, Joyce Reehling, Ernie Sabella, William H. Macy. A movie best described as "nice," about a crotchety, working-class Polish immigrant who raises his grandson when the boy is orphaned, and remains a dominant figure in his life even after the young man is married and a father himself. Falk is in fine form in this mildly entertaining story, based on coscreenwriter Max Apple's own experiences. [PG] **▼▶**

Room Service (1938) **78m.** ******* D: William A. Seiter. Groucho, Chico and Harpo Marx, Lucille Ball, Ann Miller, Frank Albertson, Donald MacBride. Broadway farce about destitute producers trying to keep their play afloat—and avoid being evicted from their hotel room—is transformed by scenarist Morrie Ryskind into a vehicle for the Marx Bros. More conventional than their earlier outings, but still has a lot of funny material (and, thankfully, no intrusive songs). Remade as a musical, STEP LIVELY. MacBride reprises his Broadway role as the hothead trying to evict his brothers. Also shown in computer-colored version. **▼▶**

Room with a View, A (1986-British) **C-115m.** ******* D: James Ivory. Maggie Smith, Helena Bonham Carter, Denholm Elliott, Julian Sands, Daniel Day-Lewis, Simon Callow, Judi Dench, Rosemary Leach, Rupert Graves. Elegant and witty adaptation of E. M. Forster novel about British manners and mores, and a young woman's awakening experiences during a trip (chaperoned, of course) to Florence. Splendid performances, fine attention to detail; only fault is its deliberate pace, which allows interest level to lag from time to time. Won Oscars for screenplay adaptation (Ruth Prawer Jhabvala), art direction, and costume design. **▼▶**

Rooster Cogburn (1975) **C-107m.** ****** D: Stuart Millar. John Wayne, Katharine Hepburn, Anthony Zerbe, Strother Martin, Richard Jordan, John McIntire, Richard Farnsworth. Reprising Wayne's character from TRUE GRIT and teaming him with Hepburn was an obvious attempt to spark an AFRICAN QUEEN–type hit, but starpower is all this film has going for it. Dull story has unlikely duo going after men who murdered Kate's father. Panavision. [PG] **▼▶**

Roosters (1993) **C-95m.** ***½** D: Robert M. Young. Edward James Olmos, Sonia Braga, Maria Conchita Alonso, Danny Nucci, Sarah Lassez. Leaden-paced drama of irresponsible ex-con Olmos, who's consumed by his machismo, and what happens when he returns to his family in the rural South-

west. Uninvolving and at times downright boring, despite all of the characters' simmering emotions. An *American Playhouse* coproduction. [R] **▼▶**

Roots of Heaven, The (1958) **C-131m.** ****½** D: John Huston. Errol Flynn, Juliette Greco, Trevor Howard, Eddie Albert, Orson Welles, Herbert Lom, Paul Lukas. Turgid melodramatics set in Africa, with conglomerate cast philosophizing over sanctity of elephants; loosely based on Romain Gary novel. CinemaScope.

Rope (1948) **C-80m.** ******* D: Alfred Hitchcock. James Stewart, John Dall, Farley Granger, Cedric Hardwicke, Joan Chandler, Constance Collier, Douglas Dick. Two young men kill prep-school pal, just for the thrill of it, and challenge themselves by inviting friends and family to their apartment afterward—with the body hidden on the premises. Hitchcock's first color film was shot in ten-minute takes to provide a seamless flow of movement, but it remains today what it was then: an interesting, highly theatrical experiment. Inspired by the real-life Leopold-Loeb murder case, which later was depicted in COMPULSION and SWOON. Patrick Hamilton's play was adapted by Hume Cronyn and scripted by Arthur Laurents. **▼▶**

Rope of Sand (1949) **104m.** ******* D: William Dieterle. Burt Lancaster, Paul Henreid, Corinne Calvet, Claude Rains, Peter Lorre, Sam Jaffe, John Bromfield, Mike Mazurki. Sturdy cast in adventure tale of smooth thief trying to regain treasure he hid away, with various parties interfering. **▶**

Rory O'Shea Was Here (2004-Irish-British-French) **C-104m.** ****½** D: Damien O'Donnell. James McAvoy, Steven Robertson, Romola Garai, Gerard McSorley, Tom Hickey, Brenda Fricker, Alan King, Ruth McCabe, Anna Healy. Sensitive, seriocomic Irish drama about a bad-boy quadriplegic (McAvoy) living in a home for the disabled, who befriends a young man with cerebral palsy and convinces him that they should get their own apartment. They're assisted by an unlikely and beautiful young female caretaker (Garai). The leads (especially Garai) are all terrific in this tearjerker, but they can't quite transcend the familiar CUCKOO'S NEST trappings. Original U.K. title: INSIDE I'M DANCING. Panavision. [R] **▶**

Rosalie Goes Shopping (1989-German) **C-94m.** ******* D: Percy Adlon. Marianne Sägebrecht, Brad Davis, Judge Reinhold, William Harlander, Erika Blumberger, Patricia Zehentmayr, Alex Winter. Bavarian-born Sägebrecht has settled with American husband Davis in Stuttgart, Arkansas, and they have more children than you can count; she's become obsessed with spending money and having possessions, and devises an ingenious plan to beat the bill collector. Delightfully loopy comedy (written by the director, Eleanor Adlon and Christopher Dorherty). [PG]▼

Rosa Luxemburg (1986-German) **C-116m.** ***½ D: Margarethe von Trotta. Barbara Sukowa, Daniel Olbrychski, Otto Sander, Adelheid Arndt, Jurgen Holtz, Doris Schade. Sukowa offers a towering performance in this compelling, multileveled biography of the dedicated, idealistic democratic socialist/pacifist/humanist who played a prominent role in German politics in the early years of the century. Extremely provocative and well directed.▼

Rosary Murders, The (1987) **C-101m.** ** D: Fred Walton. Donald Sutherland, Charles Durning, Belinda Bauer, Josef Sommer, James Murtaugh, John Danelle, Addison Powell, Kathleen Tolan. Mass killer of Motown priests and nuns confesses to Sutherland, who obviously can't inform the cops. Despite a script cowritten by Elmore Leonard, Sutherland's performance is the sole reward. Starts promisingly but soon fizzles. Filmed on location in Detroit. See I CONFESS instead. [R]▼●

Rose, The (1979) **C-134m.** ** D: Mark Rydell. Bette Midler, Alan Bates, Frederic Forrest, Harry Dean Stanton, Barry Primus, David Keith. Spin-off of the Janis Joplin saga equates show biz with hell, then concentrates on giving the audience too much of the latter. Midler (in her starring debut) and Forrest deliver dynamic performances, but film leaves a lot to be desired. Impressive photography by Vilmos Zsigmond. [R]▼●❘

Rose and the Sword, The SEE: **Flesh + Blood** (1985)

Rosebud (1975) **C-126m.** BOMB D: Otto Preminger. Peter O'Toole, Richard Attenborough, Cliff Gorman, Claude Dauphin, John V. Lindsay, Peter Lawford, Raf Vallone, Isabelle Huppert, Kim Cattrall. Nadir for director Preminger and usually competent performers. Arab terrorists kill crew of yacht "Rosebud" and kidnap five wealthy young ladies aboard. O'Toole and Attenborough (to say nothing of former N.Y.C. Mayor Lindsay) are embarrassingly bad. Panavision. [PG]▼

Rosebud Beach Hotel, The (1984) **C-87m.** *½ D: Harry Hurwitz. Colleen Camp, Peter Scolari, Christopher Lee, Fran Drescher, Monique Gabrielle, Eddie Deezen, Chuck McCann. Idiotic, fifth-rate comedy about buffoon Scolari, who with girlfriend Camp operates a resort hotel and hires happy hookers as bellgirls. Camp's bright presence raises the rating of this from BOMB. Originally titled THE BIG LOBBY; aka THE NO-TELL HOTEL. [R]▼●

Rose Garden, The (1989-U.S.-West German) **C-111m.** **½ D: Fons Rademakers. Liv Ullmann, Maximilian Schell, Peter Fonda, Jan Niklas, Kurt Hubner. Attorney Ullmann defends Schell on charges of at-tacking an elderly man whom he recognized as the commandant of a Nazi concentration camp in which his family was killed. Story is earnest and compassionate but uninspired; benefits from fine performances by Ullmann and an almost unrecognizable Schell. [PG-13]▼●

Roseland (1977) **C-103m.** *** D: James Ivory. Teresa Wright, Lou Jacobi, Geraldine Chaplin, Helen Gallagher, Joan Copeland, Christopher Walken, Lilia Skala, David Thomas. Trilogy set in N.Y.C.'s venerable Roseland Ballroom examines bittersweet lives of people who gravitate there. First story is weakest, but other two are absorbing and beautifully performed, with Copeland and Skala as standouts. [PG]▼●

Rose-Marie (1936) **110m.** *** D: W. S. Van Dyke II. Jeanette MacDonald, Nelson Eddy, Reginald Owen, Allan Jones, James Stewart, Alan Mowbray, Gilda Gray. Don't expect the original operetta: story has opera star Jeanette searching for fugitive brother Stewart, as Mountie Nelson pursues the same man. The two fall in love, sing "Indian Love Call," among others. David Niven appears briefly as Jeanette's unsuccessful suitor. Retitled INDIAN LOVE CALL; previously filmed in 1928, then again in 1954.▼●

Rose Marie (1954) **C-115m.** **½ D: Mervyn LeRoy. Ann Blyth, Howard Keel, Fernando Lamas, Bert Lahr, Marjorie Main, Joan Taylor, Ray Collins. More faithful to original operetta than 1936 version, but not as much fun. Mountie-Keel tries to "civilize" tomboy Blyth, but falls in love with her instead. Adventurer Lamas completes the triangle. Lahr sings "I'm the Mountie Who Never Got His Man" in comic highlight. CinemaScope.●❘

Rosemary's Baby (1968) **C-136m.** **** D: Roman Polanski. Mia Farrow, John Cassavetes, Ruth Gordon, Sidney Blackmer, Maurice Evans, Ralph Bellamy, Elisha Cook, Jr., Patsy Kelly, Charles Grodin. Classic modern-day thriller by Ira Levin, perfectly realized by writer-director Polanski: Farrow is unsuspecting young wife whose husband becomes involved with Satanists and their diabolical plans. Listen closely for Tony Curtis' voice in a phone conversation. Gordon won Best Supporting Actress Oscar. Followed by a made-for-TV sequel, LOOK WHAT'S HAPPENED TO ROSEMARY'S BABY (1976, aka ROSEMARY'S BABY II). [R] ▼●❘

Rosemary's Disciples SEE: **Necromancy**

Rosencrantz & Guildenstern Are Dead (1990) **C-118m.** ** D: Tom Stoppard. Gary Oldman, Tim Roth, Richard Dreyfuss, Joanna Roth, Iain Glen, Donald Sumpter, Joanna Miles, Ian Richardson. Oldman and Roth are engaging as the puckish incidental characters from *Hamlet* who wander into a series of (mostly verbal) adventures in and around the royal castle. Full of delicious wordplay and some imaginative visual ideas, but there's a basic lifelessness to this film, proving that it should have remained on stage. Playwright Stoppard's feature film directing debut, an adaptation of his own play. [PG] ▼●◗

Rosenstrasse (2003-German) **C-136m.** ** D: Margarethe von Trotta. Katja Riemann, Maria Schrader, Martin Feifel, Jürgen Vogel, Jutta Lampe, Doris Schade, Fedja van Huêt, Carola Regnier. Schrader, a Jewish New Yorker, travels to Germany to meet the elderly woman who sheltered her mother during WW2. Worthy film brings to light a long-forgotten act of heroism against Nazi tyranny, when Aryan women mounted a protest in Berlin after the SS arrested their Jewish husbands—but the result plays like a soap opera. A major disappointment. Super 35. [PG-13] ▶◗

Rose Tattoo, The (1955) **117m.** ***½ D: Daniel Mann. Anna Magnani, Burt Lancaster, Marisa Pavan, Ben Cooper, Virginia Grey, Jo Van Fleet. Magnani shines in Oscar-winning role as earthy, deluded widow in Gulf Coast city who's romanced by rambunctious truck driver Lancaster. Flavorful adaptation of Tennessee Williams play; cinematographer James Wong Howe also won an Oscar. VistaVision. ▼◗◗

Rosetta (1999-Belgian-French) **C-95m.** ** D: Luc Dardenne, Jean-Pierre Dardenne. Emilie Dequenne, Fabrizio Rongione, Anne Yernaux, Olivier Gourmet, Florian Delain. Unrelenting, cinema vérité-style portrait of a teenaged girl who is desperate to escape the harshness of her life. She gets a job, but has no idea how to deal with the world around her—except for the desperate survival techniques she has taught herself. With its hand-held camera and fly-on-the-wall storytelling approach, the film paints a vivid picture, but it's tough to watch, and tougher still to pierce the emotional shell of its main character. Top prize-winner at the Cannes Film Festival. [R] ▼

Rosewood (1997) **C-142m.** **½ D: John Singleton. Jon Voight, Ving Rhames, Don Cheadle, Bruce McGill, Loren Dean, Esther Rolle, Michael Rooker, Elise Neal, Catherine Kellner. Fact-based story of two neighboring Florida towns, circa 1922–23, and the festering racism that threatens to explode into violence and destroy a law-abiding black community in the process. Rhames (in his biggest role to date) is an outsider who rallies the protest. Well acted and crafted, but turns overly melodramatic. Undoubtedly the most repugnant depiction of Southern "rednecks" since DELIVERANCE. Panavision. [R] ▼●◗

Rosie! (1967) **C-98m.** *** D: David Lowell Rich. Rosalind Russell, Sandra Dee, Brian Aherne, Audrey Meadows, James Farentino, Vanessa Brown, Leslie Nielsen,

Margaret Hamilton. One of Russell's best late-career performances as madcap grandmother, whose children want her money now. Based on a play by Ruth Gordon. Techniscope.

Rough Cut (1980) **C-112m.** **½ D: Donald Siegel. Burt Reynolds, Lesley-Anne Down, David Niven, Timothy West, Patrick Magee, Al Matthews, Joss Ackland, Roland Culver. Handsome but uneven romantic caper uses its stars' charm and chemistry to offset weaknesses in script. World-class jewel thief Reynolds falls in love with beautiful woman who's been set up to snag him for Scotland Yard. Filmed in England and Holland. Troubled David Merrick production went through four directors, and scripter Larry Gelbart used a pseudonym; hastily refilmed ending is chief giveaway. [PG] ▼●

Rough Magic (1995-French-British) **C-104m.** ** D: Clare Peploe. Bridget Fonda, Russell Crowe, Jim Broadbent, D. W. Moffett, Kenneth Mars, Paul Rodriguez, Andy Romano, Richard Schiff, Euva Anderson, Michael Ensign. Odd little road movie, with Fonda a magician's assistant in 1950s L.A. who hides out in Mexico with several men in pursuit. Thrust of story concerns "miracle elixirs," a Mayan shaman (female), and farcical situations south of the border. An uneasy mix of genres, faintly reminiscent of THE BIG STEAL. [PG-13] ▼◗

Rough Night in Jericho (1967) **C-97m.** ** D: Arnold Laven. Dean Martin, George Peppard, Jean Simmons, John McIntire, Slim Pickens, Don Galloway. Gory Western casts Martin as total villain who owns the town. Attractive cast can't fight clichés. Techniscope. ▼◗

Rounders, The (1965) **C-85m.** **½ D: Burt Kennedy. Glenn Ford, Henry Fonda, Sue Ane Langdon, Hope Holiday, Chill Wills, Edgar Buchanan, Kathleen Freeman. Agreeable comedy-Western from Max Evans' novel about two cowboys and an ornery horse was one of the sleepers of its year; nothing much happens, but cast and scenery make it a pleasant way to kill an hour-and-a-half. Panavision. ▼◗

Rounders (1998) **C-121m.** **½ D: John Dahl. Matt Damon, Edward Norton, Gretchen Mol, John Turturro, John Malkovich, Famke Janssen, Martin Landau, Michael Rispoli, Josh Mostel, Tom Aldredge, Michael Lombard, Mal Z. Lawrence. Young poker whiz (Damon) tries to give up the game and focus on being a law student. When his longtime pal—aptly nicknamed Worm (Norton)—is released from prison, he soon finds himself caught up again in the allure of high-stakes games, not because he likes to gamble, but because he knows how good he is. Provocative, interesting, but never entirely engaging—with enough card-playing jargon to last a lifetime. Super 35. [R] ▼●◗

Round Midnight (1986-U.S.-French) **C-131m.** ***½ D: Bertrand Tavernier. Dexter Gordon, François Cluzet, Gabrielle Haker, Sandra Reaves-Phillips, Lonette McKee, Herbie Hancock, Bobby Hutcherson, Wayne Shorter, John Berry, Martin Scorsese, Philippe Noiret. A boozy American jazzman working in 1950s Paris is virtually adopted by a fan, and their unusual relationship causes them both to thrive. A loving homage to jazz musicians and their world (inspired by the lives of Bud Powell and Lester Young), with a once-in-a-lifetime performance by real-life tenor-sax great Gordon. Music director—and Oscar winner—Herbie Hancock and his colleagues not only create great jazz right on-screen but also help establish a perfect ambiance. Written by Tavernier and David Rayfiel; designed by premier art director Alexandre Trauner. Panavision. [R]▼●)

Roustabout (1964) **C-101m.** **½ D: John Rich. Elvis Presley, Barbara Stanwyck, Leif Erickson, Joan Freeman, Sue Ane Langdon. Elvis is a free-wheeling singer who joins Stanwyck's carnival, learns the meaning of hard work and true love. Stanwyck and supporting cast make this a pleasing Presley songer, with "Little Egypt" his one outstanding tune. Raquel Welch has a bit, and Teri Garr is one of the dancers. Techniscope.▼)

Rover, The (1967) **C-103m.** *½ D: Terence Young. Anthony Quinn, Rosanna Schiaffino, Rita Hayworth, Richard Johnson, Ivo Garrani, Mino Doro. Quinn stars as 18th-century pirate whose escape from French authorities is sidetracked by relationship with innocent, feeble-minded girl. Plodding film from Joseph Conrad story; made in Italy, barely released here.▼

Rover Dangerfield (1991) **C-74m.** **½ D: Jim George, Bob Seeley. Voices of Rodney Dangerfield, Susan Boyd, Ronnie Schell, Ned Luke, Shawn Southwick, Dana Hill. A wisecracking dog thrives on his life in Las Vegas, until fate sends him to a farm in the middle of nowheresville. The idea of Dangerfield-style one-liners being spoken by a cartoon dog is fun for a while, but the film wavers uneasily between adult and juvenile appeal. Animation fans should check out the incredible opening shot. Dangerfield wrote, produced, and even contributed lyrics to the songs. [G]▼●)

Rowdyman, The (1971-Canadian) **C-95m.** **½ D: Peter Carter. Gordon Pinsent, Frank Converse, Will Geer, Linda Goranson, Ted Henley. Pinsent is the whole show in this occasionally intriguing but ultimately superficial drama about a hard-living womanizer and his fate after accidentally causing the death of a childhood pal. Filmed in Newfoundland; Pinsent also scripted.

Roxanne (1987) **C-107m.** **½ D: Fred Schepisi. Steve Martin, Daryl Hannah, Rick Rossovich, Shelley Duvall, John Kapelos, Fred Willard, Max Alexander, Michael J. Pollard, Damon Wayans, Matt Lattanzi, Kevin Nealon. Martin fashioned this update of *Cyrano de Bergerac* as a vehicle for himself, with Hannah as the object of his affection and Rossovich as the empty-headed hunk for whom he "fronts." Extremely likable and sweet-natured romantic comedy set in a sleepy ski town. Peters out somewhere along the line, unfortunately. Panavision. [PG]▼●)

Roxie Hart (1942) **75m.** **½ D: William Wellman. Ginger Rogers, Adolphe Menjou, George Montgomery, Lynne Overman, Nigel Bruce, Phil Silvers, Spring Byington, Iris Adrian, George Chandler. Fast-moving spoof of Roaring '20s, with Ginger as publicity-seeking dancer on trial for murder, Menjou her overdramatic lawyer. Hilarious antics make up for dry spells; scripted and produced by Nunnally Johnson. Previously filmed in 1927 as CHICAGO, also the title of the later Broadway and movie musical. ▼)

Royal Flash (1975-British) **C-98m.** *** D: Richard Lester. Malcolm McDowell, Alan Bates, Florinda Bolkan, Oliver Reed, Britt Ekland, Lionel Jeffries, Tom Bell, Alastair Sim, Michael Hordern, Joss Ackland, Christopher Cazenove, Bob Hoskins. Comic swashbuckler with McDowell forced to impersonate a Prussian nobleman and marry Ekland. Zippy Lester entry with a fine cast; script by George MacDonald Fraser, from his novel. [PG]▼)

Royal Hunt of the Sun, The (1969-British) **C-118m.** *** D: Irving Lerner. Robert Shaw, Christopher Plummer, Nigel Davenport, Michael Craig, Leonard Whiting, James Donald. Colorful tale of Spanish explorer Pizzaro and his quest for gold in South America; from acclaimed stage play by Peter Shaffer, adapted by Philip Yordan. Franscope. [G]▼)

Royal Scandal, A (1945) **94m.** **½ D: Ernst Lubitsch, Otto Preminger. Tallulah Bankhead, Charles Coburn, Anne Baxter, William Eythe, Vincent Price, Mischa Auer. Comedy of manners about Catherine the Great of Russia promoting favored soldier Eythe to high rank; started by Lubitsch, "finished" by Preminger. Remake of Lubitsch's 1924 FORBIDDEN PARADISE.

Royal Tenenbaums, The (2001) **C-108m.** **½ D: Wes Anderson. Gene Hackman, Anjelica Huston, Gwyneth Paltrow, Ben Stiller, Owen Wilson, Luke Wilson, Bill Murray, Danny Glover, Seymour Cassel; narrated by Alec Baldwin. Ne'er-do-well Hackman abandoned his wife and three genius children long ago, but now feels the need to make up for lost time—especially since he's flat broke. Rambling comedy has the same likable, eccentric qualities as the filmmakers' BOTTLE ROCKET and

RUSHMORE and benefits from Hackman's savvy performance, but strains for effect and essentially has no story. Written by Anderson and Owen Wilson. Panavision. [R]▼●

Royal Wedding (1951) **C-93m.** ******* D: Stanley Donen. Fred Astaire, Jane Powell, Peter Lawford, Sarah Churchill, Keenan Wynn, Albert Sharpe. Pleasant MGM musical (written by Alan Jay Lerner) about brother and sister team who take their show to London at the time of Queen Elizabeth II's wedding, and find romance of their own. Highlights: Astaire's dancing on the ceiling and partnering with a hat-rack, and his dynamite duet with Powell, "How Could You Believe Me When I Said I Loved You (When You Know I've Been a Liar All My Life)?" Burton Lane/ Alan Jay Lerner score also includes "Too Late Now." Donen's first solo directing credit.▼●

R.P.M. (1970) **C-97m.** ***½** D: Stanley Kramer. Anthony Quinn, Ann-Margret, Gary Lockwood, Paul Winfield, Graham Jarvis, Alan Hewitt. Old-fashioned liberal Quinn becomes head of university, then authorizes a police bust of radicals to save institution (*Revolutions* Per Minute, get it?). Inept Erich Segal script, equally bad Kramer direction give film certain camp value, but otherwise, look out. [R]▼●

Rubber (2010-French) **C-82m.** ****½** D: Quentin Dupieux. Stephen Spinella, Jack Plotnick, Wings Hauser, Roxane Mesquida, Ethan Cohn, Charley Koontz, Daniel Quinn. After a sheriff explains that the movie we're watching has "no reason" to exist, we're shown the tale of a discarded automobile tire that comes to life and develops the power to blow stuff up real good. Some spectators watch things from a distance, with binoculars provided by their host; they have paid to see the movie, which is real. Got that? Clever, one-of-a-kind English-language parody of monster movies set in the Southwestern U.S. is consistently watchable and wryly amusing, but the sheer weirdness of it all is its main attraction. A cult film aborning? [R]◗

Rubin and Ed (1992) **C-92m.** ***½** D: Trent Harris. Crispin Glover, Howard Hesseman, Karen Black, Michael Green, Brittney Lewis. Weird odyssey of two men on a mission to bury a frozen cat. This is one road movie Hope and Crosby never thought of—with good reason. Glover once made an infamous appearance on David Letterman's TV show playing the same character he does here. Letterman kicked him off the show; you can simply stop watching. [PG-13]▼

Ruby (1977) **C-84m.** ****½** D: Curtis Harrington. Piper Laurie, Stuart Whitman, Roger Davis, Janit Baldwin, Crystin Sinclaire, Paul Kent. Complex plot has longdead gangster's spirit possessing deaf-mute girl, sending her on a killing spree at drive-in theater (which specializes in horror movies) run by ex-gang members. A few moments, comic and horrific, stand out in generally uneven supernatural thriller. Some prints run 85m, with a hastily added epilogue. That version is credited to pseudonymous director Allen Smithee. [R]▼●

Ruby (1992) **C-110m.** ****½** D: John Mackenzie. Danny Aiello, Sherilyn Fenn, Arliss Howard, Tobin Bell, David Duchovny, Richard Sarafian, Joe Cortese, Marc Lawrence. OK speculation about the life and motives of lowlife Jack Ruby, the mob errand boy, FBI informant, and nightclub owner who killed JFK assassin Lee Harvey Oswald. Aiello is good and period recreations are adequate, but film suffers from too many lawyer-dictated characterizations (Frank Sinatra becomes singer "Tony Montana"). [R]▼●

Ruby & Quentin (2003-French-Italian) **C-84m.** ******* D: Francis Veber. Gérard Depardieu, Jean Reno, Jean-Pierre Malo, Richard Berry, André Dussollier, Ticky Holgado, Léonor Varela, Aurélien Recoing, Michel Aumont. A hard-boiled criminal (Reno) won't crack under police pressure, so they "sic" their secret weapon on him: a congenital idiot who could drive anyone crazy. Typically funny Veber farce, with a surprisingly thin Depardieu playing the grinning idiot for all it's worth. Aka TAIS-TOI! Technovision.

Ruby Gentry (1952) **82m.** ****½** D: King Vidor. Jennifer Jones, Charlton Heston, Karl Malden, Josephine Hutchinson. Turgid, meandering account of easy-virtue Southerner Jones marrying wealthy Malden to spite Heston, the man she loves.▼●

Ruby in Paradise (1993) **C-115m.** ******* D: Victor Nunez. Ashley Judd, Todd Field, Bentley Mitchum, Allison Dean, Dorothy Lyman. Fine independent effort about a young woman who leaves her Tennessee home for a new life in the beach community of Panama City in West Florida. Though too often self-consciously "poetic," this is a refreshingly low-key character study with none of the easy emotional payoffs of typical Hollywood films. The acting is fine, with Judd (sister of singer Wynonna) outstanding in the lead role. Director Nunez also wrote the screenplay. [R]▼

Ruby's Dream SEE: **Dear Mr. Wonderful**

Ruckus (1982) **C-91m.** ****** D: Max Kleven. Dirk Benedict, Linda Blair, Ben Johnson, Matt Clark, Richard Farnsworth. Slick but ordinary drive-in fare about a shell-shocked Vietnam vet who becomes object of massive manhunt in sleepy Alabama town. Same basic story as later FIRST BLOOD, but less pretentious. [PG]▼

Rude Awakening (1989) **C-100m.** ***½** D: Aaron Russo, David Greenwalt. Cheech Marin, Eric Roberts, Julie Hagerty, Robert Carradine, Buck Henry, Louise Lasser,

Cindy Williams, Andrea Martin, Cliff DeYoung. "Cheech and Roberts" lacks zing as a comedy-team concept; so does hippie-dippy political farce about a pair of long-haired '60s burnouts who return to N.Y.C. after 20 years in a Central American commune. Henry scrapes up a few chuckles in his only scene. [R]▼●

Rude Boy (1980-British) **C-133m.** ***
D: Jack Hazan, David Mingay. The Clash, Ray Gange, John Green, Barry Baker, Terry McQuade, Caroline Coon. Angry young rebel Gange is hired by the punk rock group The Clash as a roadie. Gritty, realistic, documentary-like character study; excellent concert footage. Punk rock fans will not be disappointed: others, beware. Most U.S. prints run 120m. [R]▼▶

Rudolph the Red-nosed Reindeer: The Movie (1998) **C-83m.** ** D: Bill Kowalchuk. Voices of John Goodman, Eric Idle, Bob Newhart, Debbie Reynolds, Richard Simmons, Whoopi Goldberg. Old-fashioned, innocuous animated feature about that reindeer with the very shiny nose is aimed at very young children and adds some new plot twists and characters to the old story, including a fox (Idle), a polar bear (Newhart) and an evil ice queen (Goldberg). The animation is rudimentary, but the movie is a gentle antidote to the plethora of hyperkinetic contemporary cartoons. [G]▼▶

Rudo y Cursi (2008-Mexican) **C-102m.** *** D: Carlos Cuarón. Gael García Bernal, Diego Luna, Guillermo Francella, Dolores Heredia, Adriana Paz, Jessica Mas. Two brothers (García Bernal and Luna) from a rural village in Mexico are recruited by an oily agent/promoter to play professional soccer in Mexico City. How these competitive, none-too-bright siblings deal with sudden fame, fortune, and a myriad of temptations is all part of the fun. Broadly entertaining comedy turns traditional rags-to-riches stories (and morality plays) inside out, and serves as a great showcase for its two dynamic stars, reunited with the cowriter of their breakout hit, Y TU MAMÁ TAMBIÉN. P.S. Rudo means tough; Cursi means corny. [R]▐

Rudy (1993) **C-112m.** *** D: David Anspaugh. Sean Astin, Ned Beatty, Robert Prosky, Charles S. Dutton, Lili Taylor, Jon Favreau, Jason Miller, Vincent (Vince) Vaughn. Rock-solid, immensely entertaining based-on-fact account of Rudy Ruettiger (Astin), a working-class boy intent on realizing his dream of playing football at old Notre Dame—despite his uninspiring academic record and unimposing athletic ability. Few surprises, but it's well acted (with special kudos to Dutton), and a real crowd-pleaser. Director Anspaugh and screenwriter Angelo Pizzo previously worked together on HOOSIERS. [PG]▼●

Rudyard Kipling's The Jungle Book (1994) **C-110m.** **½ D: Stephen Sommers.

Jason Scott Lee, Cary Elwes, Lena Headey, Sam Neill, John Cleese, Jason Flemyng, Stefan Kalipha, Ron Donachie. Agreeably old-fashioned "boys adventure"-style adaptation of Kipling's stories produced under the Disney banner (but with few Disney touches). Lee is simply terrific as Mowgli, the boy raised in the Indian jungle who's brought back to "civilization" by the daughter of a British regiment officer. Sumptuously filmed, with an exciting climax involving a lost city filled with treasure, but somehow never as compelling as it ought to be. Panavision. [PG]▼●

Rudyard Kipling's The Second Jungle Book: Mowgli & Baloo (1997) **C-88m.** *½ D: Duncan McLachlan. James Williams, Bill Campbell, Roddy McDowall, David Paul Francis, Gulshan Grover, Dyrk Ashton. Bland, unimaginative story of a jungle boy pursued by a circus animal procurer, saved again and again by his animal friends. Some stereotypical characters border on racism; a family film that could give "wholesome" a bad name. Hard to believe Kipling would want his name on it. Filmed in Sri Lanka. Technovision. [PG]▼●

Ruggles of Red Gap (1935) **92m.** **** D: Leo McCarey. Charles Laughton, Mary Boland, Charlie Ruggles, ZaSu Pitts, Roland Young, Leila Hyams. Laughton is marvelous as butler won in poker game by uncouth but amiable westerner Ruggles and socially ambitious wife Boland; ZaSu is spinster he falls in love with. A completely winning movie. Harry Leon Wilson's story was filmed before in 1918 and 1923, then remade as FANCY PANTS.▼●

Rugrats Go Wild (2003) **C-80m.** ** D: Norton Virgien, John Eng. Voices of E.G. Daily, Christine Cavanaugh, Kath Soucie, Lacey Chabert, Tim Curry, Bruce Willis, Chrissie Hynde, Nancy Cartwright, Cheryl Chase, Tara Strong, Melanie Chartoff, Jack Riley, Tress MacNeille, Michael Bell, Flea, LL Cool J. Headache-inducing hybrid of two popular animated TV series, *Rugrats* and *The Wild Thornberrys*, as the cast of the former washes ashore on an island where the naturalists of the latter show have set up camp. Unimaginative feature plays like a distended TV episode, and not a terribly good one at that. Chief novelty is Willis providing the voice of Spike the dog, who normally doesn't talk. Digital Widescreen. [PG]▼▶

Rugrats in Paris: The Movie (2000) **C-78m.** *** D: Stig Bergqvist, Paul Demeyer. Voices of E.G. Daily, Christine Cavanaugh, Cheryl Chase, Kath Soucie, Jack Riley, Melanie Chartoff, Susan Sarandon, Michael Bell, John Lithgow, Debbie Reynolds, Casey Kasem, Tim Curry, Dan Castellaneta. Funny follow-up to THE RUGRATS MOVIE is sharper in every department. The babies join their folks in Paris and rescue Chuckie's widower dad from marrying an evil Euro-theme-park executive. Animation and settings are colorful, story is both funny and sentimental, and Sarandon stands out as the egocentric Coco La Bouche. Followed by RUGRATS GO WILD. [G]▼▶

Rugrats Movie, The (1998) C-79m. **½ D: Norton Virgien, Igor Kovalyov. Voices of E.G. Daily, Christine Cavanaugh, Kath Soucie, Cheryl Chase, Tara Charendoff, Melanie Chartoff, Jack Riley, Joe Alaskey, Phil Proctor, Michael Bell, Tress MacNeille, Busta Rhymes, Tim Curry, Whoopi Goldberg, David Spàde, Margaret Cho. Theatrical spinoff of the popular TV cartoon puts Tommy and his infant friends into a nonstop adventure, which begins with the arrival of a new baby brother and escalates as the kids get lost in the woods. Clever and funny, with some likable songs, though even at 79m. it seems padded . . . and loud. Followed by RUGRATS IN PARIS: THE MOVIE. [G] ▼▶

Ruins, The (2008) C-90m. ** D: Carter Smith. Jonathan Tucker, Jena Malone, Shawn Ashmore, Laura Ramsey, Joe Anderson, Dimitri Baveas, Sergio Calderón. LITTLE SHOP OF HORRORS meets THE DESCENT as two young couples on vacation in Mexico decide to add a little culture to their trip by exploring an off-the-map Mayan ruin with their new European friends. Little do they know that the ruins are hidden for a very good reason. Gory scenes will have you squirming in your seat, although watching the characters take themselves too seriously is more funny than scary. Adapted by Scott B. Smith from his novel. Unrated version runs 93m. Panavision. [R]

Rules of Attraction, The (2002) C-110m. BOMB D: Roger Avary. James Van Der Beek, Ian Somerhalder, Shannyn Sossamon, Jessica Biel, Kip Pardue, Thomas Ian Nicholas, Kate Bosworth, Jay Baruchel, Fred Savage, Eric Stoltz, Clifton Collins, Jr., Faye Dunaway, Swoosie Kurtz, Clare Kramer. Repellent look at amoral college kids whose sole interests are sex, drugs, and booze. The scummiest of them all is Sean Bateman (Van Der Beek), who falls in love with the one woman he can't have (Sossamon). Writer-director Avary, Quentin Tarantino's partner in crime on PULP FICTION, uses a take-no-prisoners approach to Bret Easton Ellis' book, a prequel to *American Psycho.* Yuccchhhh. [R] ▼▶

Rules of Engagement (2000) C-127m. **½ D: William Friedkin. Tommy Lee Jones, Samuel L. Jackson, Guy Pearce, Ben Kingsley, Bruce Greenwood, Blair Underwood, Philip Baker Hall, Anne Archer, Dale Dye. Held responsible for a Middle East embassy massacre in which scores of civilians (and so-called civilians) were killed, Marine officer Jackson calls upon just-retired colleague Jones to defend him in a court-martial after he's left out to dry. Watchable but sometimes silly melodrama finds time for a client-defendant fistfight, and offers a

truly novel movie villain: a dastardly government official. Story's punchline has no punch. Panavision. [R]▼▶

Rules of the Game, The (1939-French) 106m. **** D: Jean Renoir. Marcel Dalio, Nora Gregor, Mila Parély, Jean Renoir, Gaston Modot, Roland Toutain, Paulette Dubost, Julien Carette, Odette Talazac. Sublime, endlessly imitated film about romantic intrigues at a French country estate, both upstairs and downstairs. Renoir, who costars as Octave, uses the façade of light comedy to satirize (and skewer) the bourgeoisie—their follies, rituals, and class distinctions—as Europe was about to go up in flames. His light touch and extraordinarily fluid staging and camerawork are what make the film still seem so poignant, funny, and fresh. Vilified on its initial release, it was severely cut, then rediscovered decades later and justly hailed as a masterpiece. Reconstructed in the 1960s. ▼▶

Ruling Class, The (1972-British) C-154m. ***½ D: Peter Medak. Peter O'Toole, Alastair Sim, Arthur Lowe, Harry Andrews, Coral Browne, Michael Bryant, Carolyn Seymour, Nigel Green, William Mervyn, James Villiers. Hilarious, irreverent black comedy by Peter Barnes about heir to British lordship (O'Toole) who thinks he's Jesus Christ. Overflowing with crazy ideas, people bursting into song, boisterously funny characterizations, and one-and-only Sim as befuddled bishop. Some prints run 130m; the "uncut" version released in 1983 runs 141m. [PG]▼▶

Rumble Fish (1983) 94m. ** D: Francis Coppola. Matt Dillon, Mickey Rourke, Diane Lane, Dennis Hopper, Diana Scarwid, Vincent Spano, Nicolas Cage, Christopher Penn, Larry Fishburne, Tom Waits, Sofia Coppola. Ambitious mood piece from S. E. Hinton's young-adult novel about alienated teenager who lives in the shadow of his older brother. Emotionally intense but muddled and aloof; highly stylized, in looks (filmed mostly in black & white) and sounds (with impressionistic music score by Stewart Copeland). Dillon's third Hinton film, Coppola's second (following THE OUTSIDERS). [R]▼▶

Rumble in the Bronx (1996-U.S.-Hong Kong) C-89m. **½ D: Stanley Tong. Jackie Chan, Anita Mui, Bill Tung, Francoise Yip, Marc Akerstream, Garvin Cross, Morgan Lam, Kris Lord. Jackie visits his uncle in America, and agrees to help the woman who's buying the uncle's market to fend off a local gang. Chan's breakthrough film for the U.S. market is slim on story (and even slimmer on credibility). From the '60s-style dubbing to the characterizations, everything is tacky but Jackie; still, he's so engaging he makes up for all the rest, with a nonstop array of eye-popping stunts. The skyline of Vancouver makes a shabby and rather silly substitute for the Bronx. Edited for U.S. release. Technovision. [R] ▼●◗

Rumor has it . . . (2005-U.S.-German) C-97m. *½ D: Rob Reiner. Jennifer Aniston, Kevin Costner, Shirley MacLaine, Mark Ruffalo, Richard Jenkins, Christopher McDonald, Mena Suvari. While home for her sister's wedding, Aniston becomes convinced that her late mother, grandmother MacLaine, and future techno-magnate Costner inspired the Charles Webb novel that became THE GRADUATE. Premise is icky (Aniston goes on a fling with a guy she initially thought was her father!) without being pointed. MacLaine gives it a shot with acerbic but unfunny rejoinders. If THE GRADUATE didn't still "live," this would be pretty close to grave robbing. Kathy Bates appears unbilled. [PG-13]◗

Rumor of Angels, A (2002) C-95m. **½ D: Peter O'Fallon. Vanessa Redgrave, Ray Liotta, Catherine McCormack, Trevor Morgan, Ron Livingston, George Coe, Michelle Grace. Twelve-year-old boy spending the summer in Maine with his too-busy father and stepmother forms a bond with an odd-seeming older lady who helps him unlock traumatic events in his life, and vice-versa. Nice, sweet story that took nearly 20 years to get made plays a little too much like a Hallmark Hall of Fame TV movie but simply soars whenever Redgrave is on-screen, as she takes somewhat familiar material and lifts it up several notches, making this definitely worth a look. Hawk-Scope. [PG-13] ▼◗

Rumpelstiltskin (1987) C-84m. ** D: David Irving. Amy Irving, Billy Barty, Clive Revill, Priscilla Pointer, John Moulder-Brown, Robert Symonds. Threadbare musical adaptation of the Grimms' fairy tale, with Irving and Barty well cast in the leads. Likely to bore even the small-fry. Filmed in Israel, this was a family affair: writer-director Irving is Amy's brother, and Pointer (who plays the Queen) is her mother. [G] ▼◗

Run (1990) C-91m. **½ D: Geoff Burrowes. Patrick Dempsey, Kelly Preston, Ken Pogue, Alan C. Peterson, Marc Strange, Christopher Lawford. Law student becomes the object of a citywide chase when he accidentally kills the loutish son of the town's Mr. Hood while blowing time in a gambling club. Sheer speed compensates for lack of distinction. Dempsey's "what-me-worry?" quotient is relatively subdued. Not to be confused with Kurosawa's RAN. [R] ▼●

Runaway (1984) C-100m. ** D: Michael Crichton. Tom Selleck, Cynthia Rhodes, Gene Simmons, Kirstie Alley, Stan Shaw, Joey Cramer, G. W. Bailey. Futuristic comic-book nonsense that actually takes itself seriously. Selleck plays a cop who specializes in tracking down robots that have gone "bad." Simmons (from rock group KISS) is ultra-bad-guy who uses robots and other high-tech

devices to carry out his evil deeds. Special effects are good, but characters are cold and story is for the birds. Panavision. [PG] ▼●◗

Runaway Bride (1999) C-116m. *** D: Garry Marshall. Julia Roberts, Richard Gere, Joan Cusack, Hector Elizondo, Rita Wilson, Paul Dooley, Christopher Meloni, Donal Logue, Sela Ward. Slick romantic comedy about a newspaper columnist who becomes intrigued by a small-town Maryland woman who repeatedly leaves grooms at the altar. Reteaming of the stars and director of PRETTY WOMAN delivers the goods, with Gere in particular more engaging than he's ever been onscreen. Super 35. [PG] ▼●◗

Runaway Jury (2003) C-127m. *** D: Gary Fleder. John Cusack, Gene Hackman, Dustin Hoffman, Rachel Weisz, Bruce Davison, Bruce McGill, Jeremy Piven, Nick Searcy, Jennifer Beals, Bill Nunn, Nora Dunn, Stanley Anderson, Cliff Curtis, Joanna Going, Leland Orser, Orlando Jones, Celia Weston. Entertaining if longish adaptation of John Grisham's novel about a New Orleans lawyer (Hoffman) whose client is suing a major gun manufacturer, claiming culpability for her husband's murder. A cold-blooded jury consultant (Hackman) is working the other side, and there's a wild card, juror Cusack, who seems to have his own agenda. Finale doesn't have the emotional punch it should, but it's such a treat to watch these actors at work it almost doesn't matter. Dylan McDermott and Luis Guzman appear unbilled. Super 35. [PG-13] ▼◗

Runaways, The (2010) C-106m. *** D: Floria Sigismondi. Kristen Stewart, Dakota Fanning, Michael Shannon, Alia Shawkat, Scout Taylor-Compton, Riley Keough, Stella Maeve, Tatum O'Neal, Brett Cullen, Keir O'Donnell, Johnny Lewis, Peggy Stewart. In 1975, 17-year-old wannabe musician Joan Jett is teamed with 15-year-old blond Cherie Currie and several other females to form an all-girl band called The Runaways. The mastermind behind the group is a savvy but slimy Kim Fowley (Shannon), who sends them out on tour, unchaperoned, which leads the girls to indulge in every imaginable excess. Although the genre is well worn, this telling seems genuine and fresh; Fanning and Shannon are exceptionally good. Based on Currie's book, and produced by Jett, this tells their version of the saga. Impressive feature debut for Sigismondi, who also scripted. Super 35. [R]

Runaway Train (1985) C-111m. *** D: Andrei Konchalovsky. Jon Voight, Eric Roberts, Rebecca De Mornay, Kyle Heffner, John P. Ryan, T. K. Carter, Kenneth McMillan, Stacey Pickren. A rare bird, this film: an existential action movie! Hardened criminal and young accomplice escape from prison and hide out on a train that's barreling through Alaska without an engineer. Tough, violent, with hair-raising action footage and a superb characterization by Voight in his most atypical role to date. Based on a screenplay by Akira Kurosawa. [R]▼●)

Rundown, The (2003) C-104m. **½ D: Peter Berg. The Rock, Seann William Scott, Rosario Dawson, Christopher Walken, Ewen Bremner, Jon Gries, William Lucking, Ernie Reyes, Jr., Stuart Wilson. The Rock is a "retrieval expert" for a loan shark but wants to get out of the business and open a restaurant; first he has to bring back his boss's wayward son from some hellhole in the Amazon jungle. There he gets mixed up in a treasure hunt and runs afoul of an evil mine owner (Walken, playing another one of his patented eccentric slimeballs). This cheerfully derivative adventure is mindlessly entertaining but might have been better with a less campy approach and fewer slo-mo body-slammin' fights and stunts. There's an amusing cameo in the opening scene. Super 35. [PG-13] ▼●

Runestone, The (1992) C-105m. ** D: Willard Carroll. Peter Riegert, Joan Severance, William Hickey, Tim Ryan, Chris Young, Alexander Godunov, Mitchell Laurence, Lawrence Tierney, Dawan Scott. An ancient stone, buried in North America by Norsemen, is unearthed, and promptly turns an archaeologist into an elaborate but unconvincing monster, who slaughters a lot of people with no apparent goal in mind. Handsome production has some interesting moments, but the routine plot weighs it down. Adapted by the director from the novella by Mark E. Rogers. [R]▼●

Run Fatboy Run (2007-U.S.-British) C-100m. *** D: David Schwimmer. Simon Pegg, Thandie Newton, Hank Azaria, Dylan Moran, Matthew Fenton, Harish Patel, Simon Day, India de Beaufort, Ruth Sheen. Lovable loser leaves his pregnant fiancée at the altar. Five years later he realizes the error of his ways and tries to win her back from her slick new boyfriend—or at least earn her respect—by impulsively deciding to compete in a London marathon for which he's ill-prepared. Pegg (who wrote this with Michael Ian Black) somehow takes this familiar material, punctuated with the most obvious gags, and makes it work. Feature directing debut for *Friends* star Schwimmer. Super 35. [PG-13]▐

Run for Cover (1955) C-93m. **½ D: Nicholas Ray. James Cagney, Viveca Lindfors, John Derek, Jean Hersholt, Ernest Borgnine. Offbeat Western has ex-con Cagney becoming sheriff, while his embittered young companion (Derek) grows restive and antagonistic. Interesting touches cannot overcome familiar storyline. Retitled: COLORADO. VistaVision.

Run Lola Run (1998-German) C-88m. **½ D: Tom Tykwer. Franka Potente, Moritz Bleibtreu, Herbert Knaup, Armin Rohde, Joachim Król, Nina Petri. Hyperkinetic, flashy concept film about a young woman who tries to save her boyfriend, who botched a drug deal, by finding 100,000 marks in 20 minutes' time. Style definitely outranks substance in this visually arresting film, which presents three different scenarios of what might happen, but it's wearying after a while. [R]▼▐

Runner Stumbles, The (1979) C-99m. *½ D: Stanley Kramer. Dick Van Dyke, Kathleen Quinlan, Maureen Stapleton, Ray Bolger, Tammy Grimes, Beau Bridges. Sober adaptation of Milan Stitt's Broadway play, based on true story of small-town priest accused of murdering young nun for whom he'd shown unusual affection. Aloof and unconvincing, with Van Dyke unbearably stiff as the clergyman. [PG]▼

Running (1979-Canadian) C-103m. *½ D: Steven Hilliard Stern. Michael Douglas, Susan Anspach, Lawrence Dane, Eugene Levy, Charles Shamata. Douglas—32, out of work and father of two daughters—wants to run in the Olympics. A few yocks in this absurdly melodramatic jock drama, but not enough of them. [PG]

Running Brave (1983-Canadian) C-105m. **½ D: D. S. Everett (Donald Shebib). Robby Benson, Pat Hingle, Claudia Cron, Jeff McCracken, August Schellenberg, Graham Greene. Story of real-life Olympic champion Billy Mills, who left the Sioux reservation to find his destiny as a runner—and win a gold medal at the 1964 Tokyo Olympics. Modestly entertaining, but too corny and simplistic. [PG]▼●

Running Free (2000) C-82m. ** D: Sergei Bodrov. Chase Moore, Jan Decleir, Arie Verveen, Maria Geelbooi; narration by Lukas Haas. Anemic kiddie flick about a lonely foal who befriends a plucky orphan in the South African desert; a reminder that good horse movies are a rare breed. Exotic cinematography can't make up for awkward narration and editing, not to mention a less-than-rousing storyline. Bodrov's first English-language film is a real comedown from PRISONER OF THE MOUNTAINS. Produced by Jean-Jacques Annaud (THE BEAR), who also wrote the story. Super 35. [G]▼▐

Running Man, The (1987) C-100m. **½ D: Paul Michael Glaser. Arnold Schwarzenegger, Maria Conchita Alonso, Yaphet Kotto, Jim Brown, Richard Dawson, Jesse Ventura, Mick Fleetwood, Dweezil Zappa. It's 2019, and the U.S. is a totalitarian state; framed mass murderer Arnie is ordered to take part in a *Most Dangerous Game*–type TV show where convicted felons get their one chance for freedom. Relentlessly trashy picture gets big boost from Dawson's sleazy portrayal of the game-show host. Based on a novel by Richard Bachman (Stephen King). [R]▼●)

[1190]

Running on Empty (1988) C-116m. ***½ D: Sidney Lumet. Christine Lahti, River Phoenix, Judd Hirsch, Martha Plimpton, Jonas Arby, Ed Crowley, L.M. Kit Carson, Steven Hill, Augusta Dabney. Intense, moving story of onetime student radicals who are still on the run from the FBI after 17 years—now with two kids in tow, whose lives are stifled for the sake of sheer survival. Quiet and believable throughout, with superior performances by all. Written by Naomi Foner. [PG-13]▼●

Running Scared (1986) C-106m. **½ D: Peter Hyams. Gregory Hines, Billy Crystal, Steven Bauer, Darlanne Fluegel, Joe Pantoliano, Dan Hedaya, Jonathan Gries, Tracy Reed, Jimmy Smits. Two longtime Chicago street cops (who act more like Dead End Kids) decide maybe it's time to retire—but there's one more scuzzbag to track down first. Crystal lights up the screen, and there's a great car chase on the Chicago El tracks, but otherwise this is pretty blah. Panavision. [R]▼●

Running Scared (2006-U.S.-Canadian-German) C-122m. *½ D: Wayne Kramer. Paul Walker, Cameron Bright, Vera Farmiga, Karel Roden, Chazz Palminteri, Johnny Messner. When the thuggish Russian meth dealer next door is shot by his physically abused stepson (Bright), Mob flunky Walker must retrieve the missing gun or sleep with some Jersey fishes. The 10-year-old boy is then subjected to more acts of violence and scenes of depravity—some completely gratuitous—than most movies are ever asked to handle. Not without style, but violent and sordid. Super 35. [R]●

Running Time (1997) 70m. *** D: Josh Becker. Bruce Campbell, Jeremy Roberts, Anita Barone, Stan Davis, Gordon Jennison, Art LeFleur. Smart, classical heist-gone-wrong thriller made in the all-in-one-take method of ROPE. Shot entirely on real locations in the L.A. area, in gritty black and white. Well acted, suspenseful, both realistic and romantic.▼▶

Running Wild (1973) C-103m. *** D: Robert McCahon. Lloyd Bridges, Dina Merrill, Pat Hingle, Morgan Woodward, Gilbert Roland, Lonny Chapman, R. G. Armstrong. Good family-oriented drama about a news photographer (Merrill) who protests treatment of wild horses while doing a story in Colorado. Beautiful scenery complements solid script. [G]▼

Running with Scissors (2006) C-121m. ** D: Ryan Murphy. Annette Bening, Gwyneth Paltrow, Jill Clayburgh, Brian Cox, Joseph Fiennes, Evan Rachel Wood, Alec Baldwin, Joseph Cross, Gabrielle Union, Kristin Chenoweth, Dagmara Dominczyk, Beth Grant, Colleen Camp, Patrick Wilson. Highly uneven adaptation of Augusten Burroughs' bestselling memoir about growing up crazy—with a flamboyant, theatrical mother and a bizarre surrogate family headed by a crackpot psychiatrist (Cox). After a sharp, funny opening it turns dark, twisted, and claustrophobic. Use of '70s/'80s pop recordings in the foreground (rather than the background) of the soundtrack is distracting, to say the least. Great performance piece for Bening, as the self-absorbed mom, and Clayburgh, as Cox's addled but good-hearted wife. Feature debut for writer-director Murphy, creator of TV's *Nip/Tuck*. Super 35. [R]▶

Run of the Arrow (1957) C-86m. **½ D: Samuel Fuller. Rod Steiger, Sarita Montiel, Brian Keith, Ralph Meeker, Jay C. Flippen, Charles Bronson, Olive Carey, Colonel Tim McCoy. Confederate soldier (played by Steiger with a broad Irish brogue!) cannot accept surrender to the North, aligns himself instead with Sioux Indians after submitting to a grueling test of endurance. Intriguing if not entirely satisfying, with choppy continuity. Angie Dickinson reportedly dubbed Montiel's voice. Video title: HOT LEAD. RKO-Scope.▼

Run of the Country, The (1995-U.S.-British) C-109m. ** D: Peter Yates. Albert Finney, Matt Keeslar, Victoria Smurfit, Anthony Brophy, David Kelly, Dearbhla Molloy, Carole Nimmons, Vinnie McCabe, Clark Trevor. OK, plot-heavy, Irish family drama about the testy relationship between a widowed cop and his university-aged son who eventually gets involved with a woman who threatens dad's plans. Film takes half its length to decide what it wants to be about. Super 35. [R]▼●

Run Silent Run Deep (1958) 93m. *** D: Robert Wise. Clark Gable, Burt Lancaster, Jack Warden, Brad Dexter, Nick Cravat, Mary LaRoche, Don Rickles, Eddie Foy III. Battle of wills between officers Gable and Lancaster on WW2 submarine is basis for interesting drama. Script by John Gay, from a novel by Commander Edward L. Beach. One of the great WW2 "sub" pictures.▼▶

Run, Stranger, Run SEE: **Happy Mother's Day Love, George**

Runteldat (2002) C-103m. ** D: David Raynr. Martin Lawrence returns to his stand-up beginnings in this comedy concert, filmed in Washington, D.C. He announces he intends to deal with his life problems (drugs, etc.), but largely avoids accepting responsibility. Despite the rolling-in-the-aisles response of the audience, it's only occasionally funny; it lacks focus and a sense of purpose. ("Runteldat" seems to mean "run tell that," though its application is unclear.) Full title on-screen is MARTIN LAWRENCE LIVE: RUNTELDAT. [R]▼▶

Run Wild, Run Free (1969-British) C-100m. **½ D: Richard C. Sarafian. John

Mills, Mark Lester, Sylvia Syms, Gordon Jackson, Bernard Miles, Fiona Fullerton. Good cast helps leisurely, but better-than-usual children's film about young mute and his love for a white colt; nice subdued photography by Wilkie Cooper. [G]

Rush (1991) **C-120m.** ** D: Lili Fini Zanuck. Jason Patric, Jennifer Jason Leigh, Sam Elliott, Max Perlich, Gregg Allman, Tony Frank, William Sadler. Gritty adaptation of Kim Wozencraft's novel about a young woman recruited to be an undercover narc in 1970s Texas, joining a man who's already a bit too strung out to be completely effective. First-time director Zanuck skillfully creates an oppressively seedy atmosphere, but can't compensate for the fact that the story—if not the entire premise—of the film is unconvincing. Patric's performance is a standout, ditto Eric Clapton's striking score. [R] ▼●)

Rush Hour (1998) **C-98m.** *** D: Brett Ratner. Jackie Chan, Chris Tucker, Elizabeth Peña, Tom Wilkinson, Philip Baker Hall, Mark Rolston, Tzi Ma, Rex Linn, Chris Penn, Ken Leung, Barry Shabaka Henley. Enjoyable action no-brainer with Hong Kong detective Chan coming to L.A. to help his friend, the Chinese consul, rescue his kidnapped daughter. The FBI doesn't want an outsider on the case, however, so they give him to cocky L.A. cop Tucker to baby-sit. Combination of buddy movie, fish-out-of-water comedy, and urban action thriller works well if you don't demand a lot of logic. Followed by two sequels. Panavision. [PG-13] ▼●)

Rush Hour 2 (2001) **C-90m.** **½ D: Brett Ratner. Jackie Chan, Chris Tucker, John Lone, Zhang Ziyi, Roselyn Sanchez, Harris Yulin, Alan King, Kenneth Tsang, Jeremy Piven, Saul Rubinek. Sequel coasts on the formula—and goodwill—of the original, with the stars' personalities carrying a wafer-thin plot. Tucker vacations in Hong Kong and gets involved with Chan's investigation of a crimelord (Lone), which leads them to L.A. and Las Vegas. Some good stunt sequences sprinkled in among the comedy. Don Cheadle appears unbilled. Panavision. [PG-13] ▼▶

Rush Hour 3 (2007) **C-91m.** **½ D: Brett Ratner. Chris Tucker, Jackie Chan, Max von Sydow, Hiroyuki Sanada, Youki Kudoh, Yvan Attal, Noémie Lenoir, Jingchu Zhang, Tzi Ma, Dana Ivey, Julie Depardieu, Henry O. An ambassador is gunned down in L.A. while Chan is guarding him. Tucker (now directing traffic) insists on joining him on a trek to Paris to uncover the plot behind this assassination, which is linked to the deadly Chinese Triads. Chan's agile antics and likability and Tucker's machinegun bursts of dialogue mesh well for a third time, though it all becomes outlandishly silly by the climax. Philip Baker Hall and

Roman Polanski (!) appear unbilled. Panavision. [PG-13] ▶

Rushmore (1998) **C-93m.** ***½ D: Wes Anderson. Jason Schwartzman, Bill Murray, Olivia Williams, Seymour Cassel, Brian Cox, Mason Gamble, Sara Tanaka, Stephen McCole, Connie Nielsen, Luke Wilson, Andrew Wilson. The saga of a bona fide oddball who thrives on life at Rushmore prep school in Houston, but complicates his life by falling in love with a first-grade teacher (Williams) and befriending a local tycoon (Murray) who feels a kinship with this young iconoclast. A genuine original, full of keen observational humor and detail, with characters that always ring true. Remarkable debut performance by Schwartzman (son of Talia Shire), and a perfect showcase for Murray. Written by Anderson and Owen Wilson. Panavision. [R] ▼●)

Russia House, The (1990) **C-123m.** ** D: Fred Schepisi. Sean Connery, Michelle Pfeiffer, Roy Scheider, James Fox, Klaus Maria Brandauer, John Mahoney, Michael Kitchen, J. T. Walsh, Ken Russell, David Threlfall, Ian McNeice, Christopher Lawford. John le Carré yarn (adapted by Tom Stoppard) contends that the business of spying is alive and well—in spite of *glasnost*. Connery plays a British publisher drawn into espionage by a Soviet woman (Pfeiffer), who acts as emissary for a volatile friend. Alternately tedious and intriguing, but it never catches fire. Fox is a standout as a British intelligence officer. Technovision. [R] ▼●)

Russian Ark (2002-Russian-German) **C-95m.** *** D: Alexander Sokurov. Sergei Dreiden, Maria Kuznetsova, Leonid Mozgovoy, David Giorgobiani, Alexander Chaban, Maxim Sergeyev. Remarkable technical tour de force is the first feature-length film shot in one single take, a steadicam shot moving through more than 30 rooms of St. Petersburg's Hermitage museum (with some 2,000 extras), as director Sokurov tries to tie three centuries of Russian history together. The result is an almost surreal journey through the ages. A must-see for anyone interested in cinema's seemingly limitless possibilities. ▼▶

Russian Roulette (1975) **C-93m.** **½ D: Lou Lombardo. George Segal, Cristina Raines, Bo Brundin, Denholm Elliott, Gordon Jackson, Peter Donat, Louise Fletcher, Val Avery. Assassins threaten to kill Soviet premier Kosygin during his trip to Vancouver; Segal is assigned to capture elusive troublemaker thought to be the hit-man in this violent, unsatisfying thriller. Filmed in Canada. [PG] ▼

Russians Are Coming The Russians Are Coming, The (1966) **C-126m.** **½ D: Norman Jewison. Carl Reiner, Eva Marie Saint, Alan Arkin, Brian Keith, Jonathan Winters, Paul Ford, Theodore Bikel, Tessie O'Shea, John Phillip Law, Ben Blue, Andrea Dromm, Dick Schaal, Parker Fennelly, Doro Merande, Johnnie Whitaker, Michael J. Pollard. Popular comedy about Russian submarine that lands off New England coast was incredibly overrated in 1966; now it's merely a TV sitcom saved by pretty photography and good comic bits by Arkin and Winters. Script by William Rose from Nathaniel Benchley's novel *The Off-Islanders*. Alan Arkin's starring film debut. Panavision. ▼○●

Russicum SEE: **Third Solution, The**

Russkies (1987) **C-99m.** *½ D: Rick Rosenthal. Whip Hubley, Leaf (Joaquin) Phoenix, Peter Billingsley, Stefan DeSalle, Susan Walters, Patrick Kilpatrick, Vic Polizos, Charles Frank, Susan Blanchard, Carole King, Summer Phoenix. Feeble reworking of THE RUSSIANS ARE COMING, THE RUSSIANS ARE COMING about Soviet sailor Hubley, washed ashore in Florida, and the trio of youngsters who befriend him. Well meaning in its message of fellowship, but slight. [PG]▼○●

Rustlers' Rhapsody (1985) **C-88m.** ** D: Hugh Wilson. Tom Berenger, G. W. Bailey, Marilu Henner, Andy Griffith, Fernando Rey, Sela Ward, Patrick Wayne. Good-natured but only sporadically funny send-up of Saturday matinee Westerns. If the old cowboy movies were this dull, they never would have survived. [PG]▼○●

Rust Never Sleeps (1979) **C-103m.** *** D: Bernard Shakey (Neil Young). Ragged-out but rousing record of Neil Young in concert, with 16 well-performed tunes by rockdom's most lovable downer. My My, Hey, Hey. [PG]▼●

Ruthless (1948) **104m.** *** D: Edgar G. Ulmer. Zachary Scott, Louis Hayward, Diana Lynn, Sydney Greenstreet, Lucille Bremer, Martha Vickers, Edith Barrett, Dennis Hoey, Raymond Burr. Ulmer's engrossing, fascinating take on CITIZEN KANE, with Scott stepping on one and all as he rises in the world of high finance. Greenstreet is especially good as a Southern tycoon. ●

Ruthless Four, The (1968-Italian-German) **C-96m.** *** D: Giorgio Capitani. Van Heflin, Gilbert Roland, George Hilton, Klaus Kinski, Sarah Ross. Good Western about the complicated relationships of four dubious partners in a Nevada gold mine. Apart from the action, it's a pleasure just to watch Heflin and Roland. Aka EVERY MAN FOR HIMSELF, EACH ONE FOR HIMSELF, and SAM COOPER'S GOLD. Techniscope. [M/PG]▼●

Ruthless People (1986) **C-93m.** **½ D: Jim Abrahams, David Zucker, Jerry Zucker. Danny DeVito, Bette Midler, Judge Reinhold, Helen Slater, Anita Morris, Bill Pullman, William G. Schilling, Art Evans. Wealthy DeVito plans to murder his obnoxious wife—unaware that at that moment she's being kidnapped, and equally unaware that his paramour plans to take *him* for his dough. Clever farce written by Dale Launer has lots of laughs, bright performances, but turns sour: these really *are* unpleasant people! [R]▼○●

RV (2006) **C-96m.** **½ D: Barry Sonnenfeld. Robin Williams, Jeff Daniels, Cheryl Hines, Kristin Chenoweth, Joanna "JoJo" Levesque, Josh Hutcherson, Will Arnett, Tony Hale. Beleaguered husband and dad takes his fractured family on a camping trip in an unwieldy recreational vehicle—and tries to sneak in some work for his demanding boss on the q.t. Obvious in every way but still pretty funny at times. Daniels and Chenoweth are a hoot as a dense down-home couple that Williams and family encounter on the road and can't get rid of. Super 35. [PG]●

Ryan's Daughter (1970-British) **C-194m.** **½ D: David Lean. Robert Mitchum, Trevor Howard, Sarah Miles, Christopher Jones, John Mills, Leo McKern, Barry Foster. Simple love story blown up to gargantuan proportions in western coastal Ireland, where young girl (Miles) marries simple, plodding schoolteacher (Mitchum) and has affair with British soldier (Jones) stationed in town. Elephantine production overpowers Robert Bolt's thin story, admittedly beautiful scenes dwarfing what plot there is. Mills won Oscar in supporting role as the town idiot, as did—most deservedly—cinematographer Freddie Young. Re-edited after film's debut; original running time 206m. Super Panavision 70. [PG]▼●

Sabata (1969-Italian-Spanish) **C-107m.** ** D: Frank Kramer (Gianfranco Parolini). Lee Van Cleef, William Berger, Franco Ressel, Linda Veras, Pedro Sanchez (Ignazio Spalla). First of three spaghetti Westerns is the best, though that isn't saying much. Van Cleef plays a gambler hired by a trio of nasty businessmen to steal $100,000. Needless to say, the transaction becomes trickier than they expected. Sequel: ADIOS, SABATA. Techniscope. [PG]●

Sabotage (1936-British) **76m.** *** D: Alfred Hitchcock. Sylvia Sidney, Oscar Homolka, John Loder, Desmond Tester, Joyce Barbour. Elaborately detailed thriller about woman who suspects that her kindly husband (Homolka), a movie theater manager, is keeping something from her. Full of intriguing Hitchcock touches. Based on Joseph Conrad's *Secret Agent*, originally retitled A WOMAN ALONE for the U.S. ▼○●

Saboteur (1942) **108m.** *** D: Alfred Hitchcock. Robert Cummings, Priscilla Lane, Norman Lloyd, Otto Kruger, Alan Baxter, Alma Kruger, Dorothy Peterson, Vaughan Glaser. Extremely offbeat wartime Hitchcock yarn about a munitions worker who's falsely accused of sabotage and forced to take it on the lam. Full of quirky touches, unusual supporting characters, and some outstanding set pieces, including famous Statue of Liberty finale . . . though actual story resolution is unfortunately abrupt. Screenplay by Peter Viertel, Joan Harrison, and Dorothy Parker.▼●)

Saboteur, Code Name Morituri, The SEE: **Morituri**

Sabrina (1954) 113m. ***½ D: Billy Wilder. Humphrey Bogart, Audrey Hepburn, William Holden, John Williams, Francis X. Bushman, Martha Hyer, Nancy Kulp. Samuel Taylor's play *Sabrina Fair* is good vehicle for Hepburn as chauffeur's daughter romanced by aging tycoon Bogart to keep her from his playboy brother (Holden). Offbeat casting works in this fun film. Screenplay by Ernest Lehman, Billy Wilder, and Taylor. Remade in 1995.▼●)

Sabrina (1995) C-127m. *** D: Sydney Pollack. Harrison Ford, Julia Ormond, Greg Kinnear, Nancy Marchand, John Wood, Richard Crenna, Angie Dickinson, Lauren Holly, Dana Ivey, Miriam Colon, Elizabeth Franz, Fanny Ardant, Paul Giamatti. Enjoyable (if overlong) remake of the 1954 movie about a chauffeur's daughter with a lifelong crush on the handsome younger brother in the wealthy household where her father works. When he finally shows some interest in her, his older sibling tries to woo her away—for strictly business reasons. Credible cast (including Kinnear in an impressive film debut), sure-handed direction and a very funny script by Barbara Benedek and David Rayfiel. The Paris scenes are especially lovely. [PG] ▼●)

Sacco and Vanzetti (1971-French-Italian) C-120m. *½ D: Giuliano Montaldo. Gian Maria Volonte, Riccardo Cucciolla, Milo O'Shea, Cyril Cusack, Rosanna Fratello, Geoffrey Keen. Classic tale of American miscarriage of justice cries for cinematic treatment, but this version makes South Braintree, Massachusetts, look like a town in a Clint Eastwood spaghetti Western. Joan Baez sings title song. [PG]▼)

Sacred Ground (1983) C-100m. **½ D: Charles B. Pierce. Tim McIntire, Jack Elam, Serene Hedin, Mindi Miller, Eloy Phil Casados, L. Q. Jones. Fair drama of turmoil resulting when mountain man McIntire, his Apache wife and baby settle on holy Paiute burial ground. [PG]▼)

Sacred Hearts (1985-British) C-95m. **½ D: Barbara Rennie. Anna Massey, Katrin Cartlidge, Oona Kirsch, Fiona Shaw, Anne Dyson, Gerard Murphy, Murray Melvin. Repressive, tyrannical Sister Thomas (Massey) ignores the questions, feelings, and fears of her young charges in a convent as the bombs explode around them in WW2 Britain. Sometimes quietly stimulating but also slow and predictable; occasional bits of humor help.❑)

Sacrifice, The (1986-Swedish-French)

C-145m. **½ D: Andrei Tarkovsky. Erland Josephson, Susan Fleetwood, Valerie Mairesse, Allan Edwall, Gundun Gisladottir. A cataclysmic event occurs during the birthday festivities of intellectual Josephson, who as a result becomes compelled to perform an act of faith. Slow, overly intense, but beautifully filmed (by Sven Nykvist) examination of the need for, and lack of, spirituality in modern society. Decidedly not for all tastes. Tarkovsky's final film. [PG] ▼●)

Saddest Music in the World, The (2004-Canadian) C/B&W-99m. ** D: Guy Maddin. Mark McKinney, Isabella Rossellini, Maria de Madeiros, David Fox, Ross McMillan, Darcy Fehr. Deliriously bizarre film pays homage to 1930s moviemaking with a twisted sensibility: Rossellini (in a platinum wig) plays the legless boss of a popular brewery that sponsors an international competition to find the saddest music in the world. The big-money prize inspires cutthroat competition from all the competing countries. Intentionally blurs the line between melodrama and camp, with dreamlike images and ideas typical of Maddin's work. [R] ▼)

Sadie McKee (1934) 92m. *** D: Clarence Brown. Joan Crawford, Franchot Tone, Gene Raymond, Edward Arnold, Esther Ralston, Leo G. Carroll, Akim Tamiroff, Gene Austin. Solidly entertaining film follows serpentine story of working-girl Crawford and the three men in her life: smooth-talking Raymond, tipsy millionaire Arnold, earnest employer Tone. Beautifully paced, handsomely filmed. Song: "All I Do Is Dream of You," plus amusing rendition of "After You've Gone" by Austin, Candy Candido.▼●)

Sad Sack, The (1957) 98m. ** D: George Marshall. Jerry Lewis, Phyllis Kirk, David Wayne, Peter Lorre, Gene Evans, Mary Treen. Disjointed comedy vaguely based on George Baker comic strip of Army misfit. Lorre appears as Arab in last part of film. VistaVision▼

Safe (1995) C-119m. **½ D: Todd Haynes. Julianne Moore, Xander Berkeley, Peter Friedman, James Le Gros, Mary Carver, Jessica Harper, Brandon Cruz. Well-to-do L.A. housewife becomes allergic to her own environment when almost overnight everyday household chemicals and substances turn into toxins. Intriguing allegorical approach to society's ills—based on a factual case—never really jells, and second half, set at a New Mexico retreat, grows tiresome. Notable mainly for Moore's terrific performance. [R]▼●)

Safe at Home! (1962) 83m. **½ D: Walter Doniger. Mickey Mantle, Roger Maris, William Frawley, Patricia Barry, Don Collier, Bryan Russell. Kid is pressured into lying to Little League pals about friendship with M&M. The stoic poetry of Jack Webb's acting pales beside that of Maris' in this kiddie time-capsule; leads, cameos by Whitey Ford and

Ralph Houk make it a must for Yankee fans . . . if no one else. ▼❶

Safe Conduct (2002-French) **C-163m.** ***½ D: Bertrand Tavernier. Jacques Gamblin, Denis Podalydès, Christian Berkel, Marie Gillain, Charlotte Kady, Marie Desgranges, Maria Pitarresi, Thierry Gibault. Long, ambitious, and heroic film about two men who struggle to maintain their integrity while working in the French film industry during WW2, under the supervision of the Germans. Real names and incidents are used in this panoramic and surprisingly humorous story of courage and absurdity in a time of cowardice and crisis. Written by Tavernier and Jean Cosmos, based on the recollections of Jean Aurenche and Jean Devaivre. Super 35. ▼❶

Safe Men (1998) **C-99m.** **½ D: John Hamburg. Sam Rockwell, Steve Zahn, Michael Lerner, Harvey Fierstein, Mark Ruffalo, Josh Pais, Paul Giamatti, Christina Kirk, Allen Swift. Amusing if flyweight low-budget comedy about a couple of guys—who've never made good at anything—who are mistaken for ace safecrackers by small-time hood Lerner, who puts them to work. Colorful characterizations by Lerner, Fierstein, and Giamatti add zip to this offbeat concoction set in Providence, R.I. Feature debut for writer-director Hamburg. [R] ▼●❶

Safe Passage (1994) **C-98m.** ** D: Robert Allan Ackerman. Susan Sarandon, Sam Shepard, Nick Stahl, Marcia Gay Harden, Robert Sean Leonard, Sean Astin, Matt Keeslar, Jeffrey DeMunn, Philip Bosco, Jason London, Rutanya Alda. Self-consciously predictable, TV movie-ish portrait of a dysfunctional family, with Sarandon (solid as usual) as a woman, estranged from her husband, who's placed her life on hold while raising seven sons. The family pulls together when it learns that one of the boys may have been killed. [PG-13] ▼●❶

Safe Place, A (1971) **C-94m.** ** D: Henry Jaglom. Tuesday Weld, Jack Nicholson, Orson Welles, Philip Proctor, Gwen Welles. Spaced-out, water-logged fantasy of weird girl who lives in dream world where she can never grow up. [PG] ❶

Safety Last (1923) **78m.** *** D: Fred Newmeyer, Sam Taylor. Harold Lloyd, Mildred Davis, Bill Strothers, Noah Young. Crackerjack silent comedy about go-getter Harold determined to make good in the big city includes his justly famous building-climbing sequence—still hair-raising after all these years. ▼❶

Safety of Objects, The (2003) **C-120m.** **½ D: Rose Troche. Glenn Close, Dermot Mulroney, Jessica Campbell, Patricia Clarkson, Joshua Jackson, Moira Kelly, Robert Klein, Timothy Olyphant, Mary Kay Place, Kristen Stewart, Alex House. Ambitious adaptation (by Troche) of A. M. Homes' collection of short stories about suburban families

whose lives are linked by one tragic incident. Close is a mother clinging to her son, who's on life support; Mulroney has run out on his job but can't tell his family; Place is a restless wife and mother who fancies a fling. Superior acting gives this uneven film a built-in level of interest, but as the pieces of its puzzle come together they don't create a satisfying whole. Shot in 2001. Super 35. [R] ▼❶

Saga of Gosta Berling, The SEE: **Atonement of Gosta Berling, The**

Saga of the Viking Women and Their Voyage to the Waters of the Great Sea Serpent, The SEE: **Viking Women and the Sea Serpent**

Sahara (1943) **97m.** ***½ D: Zoltan Korda. Humphrey Bogart, Bruce Bennett, J. Carrol Naish, Lloyd Bridges, Rex Ingram, Richard Nugent, Dan Duryea, Kurt Kreuger. Excellent actioner of British-American unit stranded in Sahara desert in the path of Nazi infantry; Bogie's the sergeant, with fine support by Naish and Ingram. Based on the 1937 Russian film THE THIRTEEN (and reminiscent of THE LOST PATROL); also made as NINE MEN and LAST OF THE COMANCHES; imitated many other times. Remade for cable-TV in 1995 with James Belushi. ▼●❶

Sahara (1984) **C-104m.** *½ D: Andrew V. McLaglen. Brooke Shields, Lambert Wilson, Horst Buchholz, John Rhys-Davies, Ronald Lacey, John Mills, Steve Forrest, Perry Lang, Cliff Potts. Tacky modern variation on THE PERILS OF PAULINE with Brooke filling in for her late father in free-for-all auto race across North African desert in the 1920s, being kidnapped by handsome desert sheik. Any resemblance to a good movie is just a mirage. J-D-C Scope. [PG] ▼

Sahara (2005-U.S.-British-Spanish-German) **C-127m.** **½ D: Breck Eisner. Matthew McConaughey, Penélope Cruz, Steve Zahn, William H. Macy, Delroy Lindo, Lambert Wilson, Glynn Turman, Rainn Wilson. Dirk Pitt (McConaughey) and his lifelong ex–Navy SEAL pal Al (Zahn) set off in search of a Civil War ironclad that they believe made its way to the River Niger. Along the way they're joined by a World Health Organization doctor who's trying to contain a possible plague in the country of Mali, where all three discover they're facing formidable opposition. Old-fashioned high adventure adapted from one of Clive Cussler's popular Pitt novels has lots of action but an inconsistent tone and too much plot. Super 35. [PG-13] ▼❶

Sailor Beware (1951) **108m.** *** D: Hal Walker. Dean Martin, Jerry Lewis, Corinne Calvet, Marion Marshall, Robert Strauss, Vince Edwards; guest, Betty Hutton. Hilarious adventures of Martin & Lewis in the Navy. Induction scenes, boxing sequence are highlights in one of the team's funniest outings. James Dean can be glimpsed in the boxing scene. Remake of THE FLEET'S IN.▶

Sailor From Gibraltar, The (1967-British) 89m. ** D: Tony Richardson. Jeanne Moreau, Ian Bannen, Vanessa Redgrave, Zia Mohyeddin, Hugh Griffith, Orson Welles, Umberto Orsini, Eleanor Bron, John Hurt. Uneven adaptation of Marguerite Duras' novel has Moreau (who even gets to warble a song) as the mythical nymphomaniac wandering the seas in search of reunion with her dream sailor. Boasts an intriguing cast, but Richardson's handheld camera and other 1960s techniques have badly dated.

Sailor Who Fell From Grace With the Sea, The (1976-British) C-104m. *** D: Lewis John Carlino. Sarah Miles, Kris Kristofferson, Jonathan Kahn, Margo Cunningham, Earl Rhodes. A troubled, impressionable boy tries to deal with his widowed mother's love affair with an amiable sailor, and falls under the influence of a morbid young friend. Passionate love scenes and a bizarre ending highlight this unusual film, beautifully shot by Douglas Slocombe on English seacoast locations. Adapted by the director from a novel by Yukio Mishima. Panavision. [R]▼▶

Saint, The series SEE: *Leonard Maltin's Classic Movie Guide*

Saint, The (1997) C-116m. ** D: Phillip Noyce. Val Kilmer, Elisabeth Shue, Rade Serbedzija, Valery Nikolaev, Henry Goodman, Alun Armstrong, Emily Mortimer. Spy for hire and master of disguises Simon Templar agrees to steal a fusion formula for a controversial Russian leader—but falls in love with the beautiful professor who cooked up the recipe. Fanciful, globe-trotting action adventure is fun at first but throws credibility out the window early on, and only gets dumber. And how many endings are we supposed to sit through? Bears little resemblance to Leslie Charteris' hero. Listen for the voice on the radio in the final scene, if you make it that far. Panavision. [PG-13]▼●▶

Saint Ex (1995-British) C/B&W-86m. *** D: Anand Tucker. Bruno Ganz, Miranda Richardson, Janet McTeer, Ken Stott, Brid Brennan, Eleanor Bron, Katrin Cartlidge, Anna Calder-Marshall. A self-described "work of imagination," poetic and surreal, freely inspired by the life of Antoine de Saint-Exupéry. Not your standard screen biography, as the dramatic narrative is interspersed with interviews of real people who knew the famed aviator and author of *The Little Prince*. A telling and heartfelt tale of a fascinating man. Richardson plays the spirited and independent-minded woman who is the love of his life. [PG]▼

Saint Jack (1979) C-112m. *** D: Peter Bogdanovich. Ben Gazzara, Denholm El-

liott, James Villiers, Joss Ackland, Rodney Bewes, George Lazenby, Lisa Lu, Peter Bogdanovich. Absorbing character study of an amiable, ambitious pimp who thrives in Singapore during early 1970s. Fine performances from Gazzara and Elliott, excellent use of location milieu. From a Paul Theroux novel. [R]▼▶

Saint Joan (1957) 110m. ** D: Otto Preminger. Jean Seberg, Richard Widmark, Richard Todd, Anton Walbrook, John Gielgud, Felix Aylmer, Harry Andrews, Barry Jones, Finlay Currie, Bernard Miles, Margot Grahame. Big-scale filming of Shaw's play sounded large that when released; some good acting, but Seberg (who won her first film role after a nationwide search) not suited to film's tempo, throws production askew. Script by Graham Greene. Full title on-screen is BERNARD SHAW'S SAINT JOAN. Also shown in computer-colored version. ▼●

Saint John of Las Vegas (2010) C-85m. BOMB D: Hue Rhodes. Steve Buscemi, Romany Malco, Sarah Silverman, Peter Dinklage, Emmanuelle Chriqui, Tim Blake Nelson, John Cho, Jessi Garcia, Danny Trejo. Doggedly unfunny deadpan comedy, supposedly "inspired" by Dante's *Inferno*, about the tedious misadventures of a compulsive gambler (Buscemi) who reluctantly returns to Las Vegas during his first assignment as an insurance fraud investigator. If Joel and Ethan Coen had no talent whatsoever, their movies might look and sound like this. Super 35. [R]▶

Saint of Fort Washington, The (1993) C-108m. ** D: Tim Hunter. Matt Dillon, Danny Glover, Rick Aviles, Nina Siemaszko, Ving Rhames, Joe Seneca. Sincere but undistinguished portrayal of N.Y.C.'s homeless, with Glover showing the ropes to new friend Dillon, a mentally impaired youth who snaps photographic studies without any film in his camera. Despite impressive location footage and a downbeat conclusion, this (barely released) film seems slick and old-Hollywood. [R]▼●▶

Saint Ralph (2005-Canadian) C-98m. *** D: Michael McGowan. Adam Butcher, Campbell Scott, Jennifer Tilly, Gordon Pinsent, Shauna MacDonald, Tamara Hope, Frank Crudele, Michael Kanev. In Hamilton, Ontario, ambitious 14-year-old Catholic schooler Ralph Walker (Butcher) sets his sights on winning the 1954 Boston Marathon, hoping to awaken his comatose mother through the miracle of his victory. Neither snow nor sleet nor a sternly disapproving headmaster can knock him off track. Scott and Tilly are outstanding as his skeptical but supportive coaches in this comic, touching, pint-sized CHARIOTS OF FIRE. Based on a true story; written by the director. [PG-13]▶

Salaam Bombay! (1988-Indian-British) C-113m. *** D: Mira Nair. Shafiq Syed,

Sarfuddin Quarrassi, Raju Barnad, Raghubir Yadav, Aneeta Kanwar. Gut-wrenching chronicle of young country boy Syed and his various experiences among the street hustlers, drug peddlers, and prostitutes of Bombay. Unravels as a novel, with a gallery of vividly drawn supporting characters. Fine feature debut for director Nair.▼●❶

Salamander, The (1981-U.S.-British-Italian) **C-101m.** *½ D: Peter Zinner. Franco Nero, Anthony Quinn, Martin Balsam, Sybil Danning, Christopher Lee, Cleavon Little, Paul Smith, Claudia Cardinale, Eli Wallach. Colonel Nero attempts to prevent a fascist coup d'etat in Italy. A cornball script sinks this potentially intriguing drama, from a Morris West novel.▼❶

Salo, or The 120 Days of Sodom (1975-Italian) **C-117m.** BOMB D: Pier Paolo Pasolini. Paolo Bonacelli, Giorgio Cataldi, Umberto P. Quinavalle, Aldo Valletti, Caterina Boratto. Controversial, disturbing adaptation of de Sade's novel, set during WW2 in Italy, where Fascist rulers brutalize and degrade adolescents. Sadism, scatology, and debauchery galore; Pasolini, whose last film this is, wallows in his own sensationalism.▼❶

Salome (1953) **C-103m.** **½ D: William Dieterle. Rita Hayworth, Stewart Granger, Charles Laughton, Judith Anderson, Cedric Hardwicke, Maurice Schwartz. Great cast struggles with unintentionally funny script in biblical drama of illustrious dancer who offers herself to spare John the Baptist. Filmed before with Nazimova in 1923.▼❶

Salome's Last Dance (1988-British) **C-90m.** **½ D: Ken Russell. Glenda Jackson, Stratford Johns, Nickolas Grace, Imogen Millais-Scott, Douglas Hodge. As Oscar Wilde lounges in a brothel (the same one where his subsequent arrest would lead to his downfall), the proprietor stages a production of the playwright's title work, with Salome, Herod, John the Baptist and Co. all strutting their stuff. Typical Russell litmus test for one's tolerance of the outrageous, but wittier and less oppressive than some of the director's other historical pageants. Grace's weak Wilde aside, the actors do remarkably well under the circumstances. [R]▼❶

Salon, The (2007) **C-99m.** ** D: Mark Brown. Vivica A. Fox, Darrin Henson, Kym Whitley, Dondre Whitfield, D'Angelo Wilson, Monica Calhoun, Taral Hicks, Garrett Morris, Brooke Burns, Terrence Howard. Preachy variation on BARBERSHOP about the employees of an inner-city Baltimore women's hair salon. While servicing their customers they gossip, complain, and argue; then they learn the government wants to demolish the shop and replace it with a municipal parking lot. Not so much a movie as a soapbox for its characters, too many of them stereotypes; the street wino is particu-

larly annoying. Fox coproduced; Brown, who also scripted, was the cowriter of BARBERSHOP. Based on Shelly Garrett's play *Beauty Shop.* [PG-13]❶

Salsa (1988) **C-97m.** ** D: Boaz Davidson. Robby Rosa, Rodney Harvey, Magali Alvarado, Miranda Garrison, Moon Orona, Angela Alvarado, Celia Cruz, Tito Puente. All flash and no substance in this DIRTY DANCING–inspired feature-length music video with a Latin beat. Rosa (of the pop group Menudo) stars as a young auto repairman who'd much rather be shaking his body to salsa. Main problem: Where's the script? [PG]▼❶

Salt (2010) **C-100m.** **½ D: Phillip Noyce. Angelina Jolie, Liev Schreiber, Chiwetel Ejiofor, Daniel Olbrychski, Andre Braugher, August Diehl, Daniel Pearce, Hunt Block. Tough, experienced CIA operative, now holding down a desk job in Washington, D.C., is accused of being a Russian "sleeper agent"—brainwashed from girlhood to act against the U.S. at a given time—and takes it on the lam. Is she innocent or guilty? We're not quite sure as she leads her fellow agents on a breathless chase. Jolie's sincerity and physicality make her a perfect fit for this part, and the film moves like a bullet—which is good, because if you think about it too much, it doesn't make a lot of sense. Great stunt work and action scenes make this mindless fun. Alternate versions run 101m. and 104m. Super 35. [PG-13]❶

Salt & Pepper (1968-British) **C-101m.** **½ D: Richard Donner. Sammy Davis, Jr., Peter Lawford, Michael Bates, Ilona Rodgers, John LeMesurier. Soho nightclub owners find trouble when two baddies turn up at their club. Contrived, broad comedy. Sequel: ONE MORE TIME. [G]❶

Salt of the Earth (1953) **94m.** ***½ D: Herbert Biberman. Juan Chacon, Rosaura Revueltas, Will Geer, Mervin Williams, Frank Talavera, Clinton Jencks, Virginia Jencks. Earnest film about Latino mine workers in New Mexico who go on strike—in spite of the tremendous hardships it causes. This film is particularly impressive considering its history—made under difficult conditions (and on a shoestring), with many nonprofessional actors, by blacklisted filmmakers. Produced by Paul Jarrico and written by Michael Wilson, two of Hollywood's more prominent blacklistees.▼❶

Salton Sea, The (2002) **C-103m.** *½ D: D.J. Caruso. Val Kilmer, Vincent D'Onofrio, Adam Goldberg, Luis Guzman, Doug Hutchison, Anthony LaPaglia, Glenn Plummer, Peter Sarsgaard, Deborah Kara Unger, Chandra West, B.D. Wong, R. Lee Ermey, Shirley Knight, Meat Loaf, Danny Trejo. Dreadful film noir–ish thriller with Kilmer as a druggie who's actually a rat for the LAPD . . . or is he? Cluttered story about chance and revenge has more scummy characters than any audience should have to encounter in one movie. [R]▼❚

Salute of the Jugger SEE: **Blood of Heroes, The**

Salut l'Artiste (1974-French) C-102m. *** D: Yves Robert. Marcello Mastroianni, Jean Rochefort, Françoise Fabian, Carla Gravina. Light comedy about second-rate actors Mastroianni and Rochefort; the former scampers about while going nowhere; the latter opts out for an ad executive job. Amusing, with first-rate cast and performances.▼

Salvador (1986) C-123m. **½ D: Oliver Stone. James Woods, James Belushi, Michael Murphy, John Savage, Elpedia Carrillo, Tony Plana, Colby Chester, Cindy (Cynthia) Gibb, John Doe. Uneven but compelling drama based on real experiences of journalist Richard Boyle in strife-ridden El Salvador in 1980–81. Effective propaganda, often potent drama; it takes time to grab hold because lead characters Woods and Belushi are such incredible sleazeballs. Woods' dynamic performance makes up for a lot; his first visit to confession in 32 years is a memorably funny scene. Screenplay by Boyle himself and director Stone. [R]▼❚❚

Salvation! (1987) C-80m. *½ D: Beth B. Stephen McHattie, Dominique Davalos, Exene Cervenka, Viggo Mortensen, Rockets Redglare, Billy Bastani. Satire of false TV evangelist (McHattie) who gets involved in a sex incident, was released right after the Jim & Tammy Bakker scandal. Unfortunately, underground filmmaker Beth B directs in the manner of an incoherent music video, swamping McHattie's convincing central performance (resembling a young John Carradine). [R]▼

Salzburg Connection, The (1972) C-92m. *½ D: Lee H. Katzin. Barry Newman, Anna Karina, Klaus Maria Brandauer, Karen Jensen, Joe Maross, Wolfgang Preiss. Terrible film version of Helen MacInnes' bestseller about American lawyer on vacation in Salzburg who gets mixed up with spies; irritating use of slow-motion and freeze-frame gimmicks. Brandauer's debut and only film appearance until MEPHISTO. [PG]▼

Same Old Song (1997-French-Swiss-British) C-120m. *** D: Alain Resnais. Pierre Arditi, Sabine Azema, Jean-Pierre Bacri, Andre Dussollier, Agnes Jaoui, Lambert Wilson, Jane Birkin. Resnais adds a distinctly personal sensibility to this intricately plotted, tongue-in-cheek confection about a group of overindulgent middle-class Parisians who constantly break into lip-synched song as a way of expressing themselves. Bacri and Jaoui scripted this affectionate homage to Dennis Potter (THE SINGING DETECTIVE, PENNIES FROM HEAVEN). Winner of seven César awards.▼❚

Same Time, Next Year (1978) C-117m. *** D: Robert Mulligan. Ellen Burstyn, Alan Alda. Bernard Slade's two-character Broadway play makes pleasing film, with Alda and Burstyn as adulterous couple who share one weekend a year for 26 years; warm, human comedy-drama reflects changes in American life and attitudes since early '50s in likable fashion. [PG]▼❚❚

Sam Marlowe, Private Eye SEE: **Man with Bogart's Face, The**

Sammy and Rosie Get Laid (1987-British) C-100m. ** D: Stephen Frears. Shashi Kapoor, Claire Bloom, Ayub Khan Din, Frances Barber, Roland Gift, Wendy Gazelle, Suzette Llewellyn. The curious lives of a couple with an open sexual relationship are thrown into disarray by the arrival of his father, a powerful reactionary political figure from India who cannot understand their lifestyle—or what has happened to the traditional British way of life he used to enjoy. Disturbing but monotonous look at social and sexual anarchy in England, written by Hanif Kureishi, who previously collaborated with director Frears on MY BEAUTIFUL LAUNDRETTE.▼❚

Sammy Going South SEE: **Boy Ten Feet Tall, A**

Samson and Delilah (1949) C-128m. *** D: Cecil B. DeMille. Victor Mature, Hedy Lamarr, George Sanders, Angela Lansbury, Henry Wilcoxon, Olive Deering, Fay Holden, Russell (Russ) Tamblyn, George Reeves, Tom Tyler, Fritz Leiber, Mike Mazurki. With expected DeMille touches, this remains a tremendously entertaining film. Mature is surprisingly good as Samson, though his famous fight with lion is hopelessly phony; also difficult to swallow idea of Lansbury being Lamarr's *older* sister. Sanders supplies biggest surprise by underplaying his role as the Saran. This won Oscars for its Art Direction-Set Decoration and Costumes. Remade for TV in 1984 (with Mature as Samson's father) and 1996.▼❚

Sam's Son (1984) C-104m. ** D: Michael Landon. Eli Wallach, Anne Jackson, Timothy Patrick Murphy, Hallie Todd, Alan Hayes, Jonna Lee, Michael Landon. Landon wrote, directed, and appears briefly in this autobiographical saga about an underdog kid, who's a champion javelin thrower, and his loving but frustrated father, who never got to pursue his dreams. Wallach's performance as the father is major asset of this sometimes syrupy film. [PG]▼❚

Sam's Song (1969) C-92m. *½ D: Jordan Leondopoulos (John Shade, John C. Broderick). Robert De Niro, Jennifer Warren, Jered Mickey, Martin Kelley, Viva. Dreary film about film editor's weekend with friends on Long Island, interesting only for early De Niro performance. Extensive reshooting includes new characters played by Lisa Blount and Sybil Danning; film was reissued in 1979 as THE SWAP. Video title: LINE OF FIRE. [R]▼◗

Samurai Cowboy (1993-Canadian) **C-101m.** **½ D: Michael Keusch. Hiromigo Go, Catherine Mary Stewart, Matt McCoy, Conchata Ferrell, Robert Conrad. A Japanese businessman, enthralled with classic American Western movies, buys a ranch in Montana and attempts to live his dream of becoming a cowboy. Although hampered by a predictable plot and many formula characters, Japanese pop star Go's ingratiating performance enhances this likable tale.▼

Samurai Rebellion (1967-Japanese) **121m.** *** D: Masaki Kobayashi. Toshirô Mifune, Yôko Tsukasa, Go Kato, Shigeru Kôyama, Masao Mishima, Michiko Otsuka, Tatsuya Nakadai. A feudal lord banishes a dishonored concubine from his castle, commanding her to marry a retired swordsman's son. They wed, fall in love, and have a child. Two years later, when the master wants her back, the family stubbornly challenges his order. What had been a romance kindled by courtly intrigue now mutates into a righteously angry defiance that can end only one way. This was the director's first work outside the studio system and his only collaboration with Mifune. Tohoscope.◗

Sam Whiskey (1969) **C-96m.** ** D: Arnold Laven. Burt Reynolds, Clint Walker, Ossie Davis, Angie Dickinson, Rick Davis, William Schallert, Woodrow Parfrey. Modestly mounted, uninteresting Western wasting talents of good cast. Schemer Whiskey coerced into organizing heist of golden bullion. For Western aficionados and Reynolds addicts only. [M/PG]◗

San Antonio (1945) **C-111m.** *** D: David Butler. Errol Flynn, Alexis Smith, S. Z. Sakall, Victor Francen, Florence Bates, John Litel, Paul Kelly. Elaborate Western has predictable plot but good production values as good guy Flynn tangles with villains romancing singer Smith. Screenplay by *The Searchers* novelist Alan LeMay and W. R. Burnett.▼◗

Sanctuary (1961) **100m.** ** D: Tony Richardson. Lee Remick, Yves Montand, Bradford Dillman, Harry Townes, Odetta, Howard St. John, Jean Carson, Reta Shaw, Strother Martin. Flat melodrama about a Southern governor's daughter (Remick) and her plight after she's raped by bootlegger Montand. Awkward adaptation (by James Poe) of William Faulkner's novels *Sanctuary* (previously filmed as THE STORY OF TEMPLE DRAKE) and *Requiem for a Nun*, and Ruth Ford's stage adaptation of the latter. CinemaScope.

Sanctum (2011-U.S.-Australian) **C-103m.** **½ D: Alister Grierson. Richard Roxburgh, Ioan Gruffudd, Rhys Wakefield, Alice Parkinson, Dan Wyllie, Christopher Baker, Allison Cratchley. Crass billionaire

backer (Gruffudd) of a daring cave expedition in New Guinea brings his girlfriend along and joins the feisty, fearless explorer (Roxburgh) who's leading the odyssey—little dreaming they'll all be trapped underground with only a slim chance of survival. The characters are painted in the broadest strokes (in keeping with producer James Cameron's m.o.), but the underwater action is consistently exciting—and convincing. Makes excellent use of 3-D. 3-D. [R]◗

Sanders (1963-British) **C-83m.** ** D: Lawrence Huntington. Richard Todd, Marianne Koch, Albert Lieven, Vivi Bach, Jeremy Lloyd. Loose adaptation of Edgar Wallace novel *Sanders of the River* follows police inspector's investigation of murder in an African hospital and discovery of hidden silver mine. British title DEATH DRUMS ALONG THE RIVER. Todd repeated role of Harry Sanders in 1964 COAST OF SKELETONS. Techniscope.

Sanders of the River (1935-British) **98m.** *** D: Zoltan Korda. Paul Robeson, Leslie Banks, Nina Mae McKinney, Robert Cochran, Martin Walker. Dated adventure story (by Edgar Wallace) about river patrol officer maintains interest today, particularly for Robeson's strong presence and African location shooting. A fascinating relic of the sun-never-sets school of British imperialism. Sanders character revived in 1960s' SANDERS (DEATH DRUMS ALONG THE RIVER) and COAST OF SKELETONS.▼◗

Sandlot, The (1993) **C-101m.** **½ D: David Mickey Evans. Tom Guiry, Mike Vitar, Patrick Renna, Chauncey Leopardi, Marty York, Brandon Adams, Denis Leary, Karen Allen, James Earl Jones, Maury Wills, Art La Fleur. Innocuous film for kids about a '60s sandlot baseball team, their acceptance of the new kid on the block, and their ongoing battle with a ferocious neighboring dog. No real insight or resonance here (and incredibly condescending, heavy-handed narration)—but a pleasant enough time-filler for younger viewers. Arliss Howard and Brooke Adams appear unbilled. Followed by two direct-to-video sequels. J-D-C Scope. [PG]▼◗

Sand Pebbles, The (1966) **C-179m.** *** D: Robert Wise. Steve McQueen, Richard Attenborough, Richard Crenna, Candice Bergen, Mako, Marayat Andriane, Simon Oakland, Larry Gates, Gavin MacLeod. McQueen gives one of his finest performances as cynical sailor on U.S. gunboat cruising China's Yangtze River in 1926. Long but generally compelling drama mixes traditional action and romance with some pointed notions about American imperialism (and a few parallels to Vietnam). Splendidly photographed by Joseph MacDonald. Panavision.▼◗

Sandpiper, The (1965) **C-116m.** **½ D:

Vincente Minnelli. Elizabeth Taylor, Richard Burton, Eva Marie Saint, Charles Bronson, Robert Webber, Torin Thatcher, Morgan Mason, Tom Drake. Ordinary triangle love affair. Beatnik Taylor in love with Burton, who is married to Saint. Nothing new, but beautiful California Big Sur settings help; so does Oscar-winning theme, "The Shadow of Your Smile." Written by Dalton Trumbo and Michael Wilson. Panavision.▼●▶

Sandpit Generals, The SEE: **Wild Pack, The**

Sandra (1965-Italian) **100m. **½ D: Luchino Visconti. Claudia Cardinale, Jean Sorel, Michael Craig, Marie Bell, Renzo Ricci, Amalia Troiani. A small-town Italian beauty returns home with her American husband to attend a ceremony in memory of her Jewish father, who died in a concentration camp, setting off a series of emotional entanglements with her unfaithful mother and incestuous brother. Well acted but awfully soapy and melodramatic for Visconti.

Sands of Beersheba (1966) **90m. ** D: Alexander Ramati. Diane Baker, David Opatoshu, Tom Bell, Paul Stassino. Sluggish account of the Arab-Israeli conflict, involving a non-Jewish American whose fiancé died in the 1948 Palestinian war, an Israeli gunrunner, a Jew-hating Arab terrorist, and the latter's father who's tired of all the bloodshed. The issues remain compelling, but the film is mostly a bore.▼

Sands of Iwo Jima (1949) **110m. *** D: Allan Dwan. John Wayne, John Agar, Adele Mara, Forrest Tucker, Arthur Franz, Julie Bishop, Richard Jaeckel, Wally Cassell, Richard Webb. Enormously popular WW2 saga, with Wayne in one of his best roles as a tough Marine top-sergeant. Story and characters are pretty two-dimensional, and a bit worn from having been copied so many times since, but it's still good entertainment; use of authentic combat footage is striking. Wayne's first Oscar-nominated performance. The three surviving Marine vets who raised the American flag on Mt. Suribachi have small parts. Also shown in computer-colored version.▼●▶

San Francisco (1936) **115m. ***½ D: W. S. Van Dyke II. Clark Gable, Jeanette MacDonald, Spencer Tracy, Jack Holt, Jessie Ralph, Ted Healy, Shirley Ross, Al Shean. Top-grade entertainment with extremely lavish production. Jeanette overdoes it a bit as the belle of San Francisco, but the music, Tracy's performance, and earthquake climax are still fine. Originally had footage of Golden Gate Bridge under construction; other rhythmically edited shots of S.F. were changed for later reissue. Script by Anita Loos. Also shown in computer-colored version.▼●▶

Sanjuro (1962-Japanese) **96m. *** D: Akira Kurosawa. Toshiro Mifune, Tatsuya Nakadai, Takashi Shimura, Yuzo Kayama, Reiko Dan. Sequel to YOJIMBO has shabby, wandering samurai Mifune aiding nine bumbling younger warriors in exposing corruption among the elders of their clan. Satirical comic-book actioner features a typically deadpan Mifune performance. Tohoscope.▼●▶

San Quentin (1937) **70m. **½ D: Lloyd Bacon. Pat O'Brien, Humphrey Bogart, Ann Sheridan, Veda Ann Borg, Barton MacLane. Warner Bros. formula prison film; convict Bogart's sister (Sheridan) loves O'Brien, who's captain of the guards. MacLane is memorable as tough prison guard.▶

Sansho the Bailiff (1954-Japanese) **125m. **** D: Kenji Mizoguchi. Kinuyo Tanaka, Kisho Hanayagi, Kyoko Kagawa, Eitaro Shindo, Ichiro Sugai. Epic, poetic drama of 11th-century Japan, focusing on the tribulations of a family. Kindly father, a provincial governor, is exiled; children (Hanayagi, Kagawa) become slaves; mother (Tanaka) is sold as a prostitute. Haunting, with stunning direction and cinematography (by Kazuo Miyagawa). Original running time 130m. Aka THE BAILIFF.▼●▶

Santa Claus (1985) **C-112m. **½ D: Jeannot Szwarc. Dudley Moore, John Lithgow, David Huddleston, Burgess Meredith, Judy Cornwell, Jeffrey Kramer, Christian Fitzpatrick, Carrie Kei Heim. Story of how Santa came to be starts out so wonderfully—with eye-filling looks at his North Pole toy factory, reindeer, and sleigh—that it's too bad the rest of the film (with contemporary tale of humbug kid and greedy toy magnate) can't measure up. Still entertaining, just a bit less magical than it should have been. Referred to as SANTA CLAUS: THE MOVIE everywhere but on-screen! J-D-C Scope. [PG]▼●▶

Santa Claus Conquers the Martians (1964) **C-80m. BOMB D: Nicholas Webster. John Call, Leonard Hicks, Vincent Beck, Donna Conforti. Absurd low-budget fantasy (with a Milton Delugg score!) about Santa and two Earth children being abducted to Mars to help solve some of their domestic problems—like kids watching too much TV. One of the Martian tykes is Pia Zadora! Aka SANTA CLAUS DEFEATS THE ALIENS.▼▶

Santa Clause, The (1994) **C-97m. *** D: John Pasquin. Tim Allen, Judge Reinhold, Wendy Crewson, Eric Lloyd, David Krumholtz, Peter Boyle, Larry Brandenburg, Mary Gross, Paige Tamada. Neglectful divorced dad inadvertently frightens Santa off his roof and, when he puts on the deceased St. Nick's suit, begins to turn into Santa Claus himself—first on the outside, and then, more significantly, on the inside. Clever script by Steve Rudnick and Leo Benevenuti takes a potential one-joke idea and develops it in interesting and unexpected ways, effectively infusing heart and sentiment into its 1990s sensibility. Impressive screen debut for Allen. Followed by two sequels. [PG]▼●▶

Santa Clause 2, The (2002) **C-104m.** *** D: Michael Lembeck. Tim Allen, Elizabeth Mitchell, David Krumholtz, Eric Lloyd, Judge Reinhold, Wendy Crewson, Spencer Breslin, Liliana Mumy, Art LaFleur, Aisha Tyler, Kevin Pollak, Jay Thomas, Michael Dorn, Molly Shannon. Sequel finds the human-turned-Santa learning that unless he finds a wife, he'll cease to exist. Revisiting his former home, he falls in love with the unlikeliest candidate—and in the process helps straighten out his troubled teenage son. Sweet, noncynical Disney film is played with conviction and charm; good family entertainment. [G]▼▶

Santa Clause 3: The Escape Clause, The (2006) **C-98m.** ** D: Michael Lembeck. Tim Allen, Martin Short, Elizabeth Mitchell, Eric Lloyd, Judge Reinhold, Wendy Crewson, Alan Arkin, Spencer Breslin, Liliana Mumy, Ann-Margret, Abigail Breslin, Art LaFleur, Aisha Tyler, Kevin Pollak, Jay Thomas, Peter Boyle, Zach Mills. Third time's not the charm for this Disney series, as Santa (Allen) is forced to bring his earthly in-laws (Arkin and Ann-Margret) to the North Pole for a visit without revealing his identity, while jealous Jack Frost (Short) tries to hijack Christmas for his own greedy purposes. All this negativity doesn't make for much fun. Allen coproduced. [G]▶

Santa Fe Satan SEE: **Catch My Soul**

Santa Fe Trail (1940) **110m.** ** D: Michael Curtiz. Errol Flynn, Olivia de Havilland, Raymond Massey, Ronald Reagan, Alan Hale, Guinn ("Big Boy") Williams, William Lundigan, Ward Bond, Van Heflin, Gene Reynolds, John Litel, Charles Middleton. Lopsided picture can't make up its mind about anything: what side it's taking, what it wants to focus on, etc. Worthless as history, but amid the rubble are some good action scenes as Jeb Stuart (Flynn) and cohorts go after John Brown (Massey). Reagan plays Flynn's West Point classmate and romantic rival, George Armstrong Custer(!). Also shown in computer-colored version.▼●▶

Santa Sangre (1989-Italian-Mexican) **C-121m.** ** D: Alejandro Jodorowsky. Axel Jodorowsky, Blanca Guerra, Sabrina Dennison, Guy Stockwell, Thelma Tixou, Adan Jodorowsky, Faviola Elenka Tapia. Grotesque story about an entertainer whose act consists of performing as the arms for his armless mother; he's also an unwilling murderer. Made in luxurious color with dreamy art direction, this lacks the intellectual charge of Jodorowsky's earlier films. Filmed in English. [Shown both in NC-17 and R-rated versions]▼●▶

Santee (1973) **C-93m.** ** D: Gary Nelson.

Glenn Ford, Michael Burns, Dana Wynter, Jay Silverheels, Harry Townes, John Larch, Robert Wilke, Robert Donner. Bounty hunter Ford, whose boy has been murdered, adopts son of outlaw he has just killed. OK Western. [PG]▼▶

Saraband (2003-Swedish) **C-107m.** *** D: Ingmar Bergman. Liv Ullmann, Erland Josephson, Börje Ahlstedt, Julia Dufvenius. Ullmann and Josephson return as Marianne and Johan, the dysfunctional couple they created so unforgettably in SCENES FROM A MARRIAGE, reunited thirty years after their divorce and involved in family turmoil. A prominent subplot involving Johan's son and granddaughter is less effective, but it's a joy to see the two stars together; their scenes have the rich, deep emotional complexity that characterizes Bergman's best films. Another quibble: the antiseptic digital cinematography leaves one yearning for the raw quality that 16mm afforded its predecessor. Originally made for Swedish television. Bergman's final film as director. [R]▶

Sarafina! (1992-U.S.-British-French) **C-115m.** **½ D: Darrell James Roodt. Whoopi Goldberg, Leleti Khumalo, Miriam Makeba, John Kani, Mbongeni Ngema. Wobbly film version of the anti-apartheid musical stage hit about a young South African black girl inspired by teacher Goldberg, who's courting trouble by deviating from the curriculum mandated by the white power structure. Arguably the most violent musical ever (taking what was abstract on stage and literalizing it), a key indication of the film's uncertain style. [PG-13]▼●▶

Sarah Silverman: Jesus Is Magic (2005) **C-70m.** **½ D: Liam Lynch. Sarah Silverman, Brian Posehn, Bob Odenkirk, Laura Silverman, Steve Agee. If all of the world's invisible social tensions coalesced into a cheerfully offensive, politically incorrect comedian with a surprisingly cute voice, you'd have Sarah Silverman. It's hard to know what to make of such a creature, but one thing seems certain: by joking about taboo issues that many choose to ignore (9/11, the Holocaust, Jesus, Jewishness, AIDS, race, and sex), she forces the audience to think about them. Often-hilarious concert film is needlessly interrupted by several poorly produced musical numbers.▶

Saratoga (1937) **94m.** **½ D: Jack Conway. Clark Gable, Jean Harlow, Lionel Barrymore, Frank Morgan, Walter Pidgeon, Una Merkel, Cliff Edwards, George Zucco, Hattie MacDaniel, Margaret Hamilton. Harlow's last film—she died during production—has stand-in Mary Dees doing many scenes, but comes off pretty well, with Jean as granddaughter of horse-breeder Barrymore, Gable an influential bookie.▼●

Saratoga Trunk (1945) **135m.** *½ D: Sam Wood. Gary Cooper, Ingrid Bergman, Flora Robson, Jerry Austin, John Warburton, Florence Bates. Elaborate but miscast, overlong version of Edna Ferber's novel of New Orleans vixen Bergman and cowboy Cooper. Unbearable at times. Made in 1943.▼❶

Satan Bug, The (1965) **C-114m. ***½** D: John Sturges. George Maharis, Richard Basehart, Anne Francis, Dana Andrews, Edward Asner, Frank Sutton, John Larkin, Henry Beckman. Overlooked little suspense gem, loosely based on Alistair MacLean novel, detailing nerve-racking chase after lunatic who's stolen flasks containing horribly lethal virus from government lab. Taut script (by Edward Anhalt and James Clavell) and direction, stunning photography by Robert Surtees. Panavision.▼❶

Satanic Rites of Dracula, The SEE: **Count Dracula and His Vampire Bride**

Satan Met a Lady (1936) **75m. **** D: William Dieterle. Bette Davis, Warren William, Alison Skipworth, Arthur Treacher, Winifred Shaw, Marie Wilson, Porter Hall. Dashiell Hammett's *Maltese Falcon* incognito; far below 1941 remake. William is private eye, Davis the mysterious client, Skipworth the strange woman searching for priceless artifact (here, a ram's horn). Filmed in 1931 and 1941 as THE MALTESE FALCON.▼❶

Satan Never Sleeps (1962) **C-126m. **** D: Leo McCarey. William Holden, Clifton Webb, France Nuyen, Athene Seyler, Martin Benson, Edith Sharpe. Dreary goings-on of two priests holding fast when Communist China invades their territory. McCarey's last film. CinemaScope.❶

Satan's Cheerleaders (1977) **C-92m. **** D: Greydon Clark. Kerry Sherman, John Ireland, Yvonne DeCarlo, Jacqueline Cole, Jack Kruschen, John Carradine, Sydney Chaplin. Amusing drive-in fodder about a busload of high school cheerleaders who fall into clutches of a demonic cult. Humor and a cast full of old pros help, but this film is too tame to be really effective. [R]▼❶

Satan's Claw SEE: **Blood on Satan's Claw, The**

Satan's Harvest (1970) **C-104m. *** D: Douglas K. Stone (George Montgomery). George Montgomery, Tippi Hedren, Matt Monro, Davy Kaye, Brian O'Shaughnessy. American detective Montgomery inherits South African ranch and discovers it to be headquarters for a drug smuggling operation. Colorful scenery, tepid story.▼

Satan's Playthings SEE: **In the Devil's Garden**

Satan's Sadists (1970) **C-88m.** BOMB D: Al Adamson. Russ Tamblyn, Scott Brady, Kent Taylor, John Cardos, Greydon Clark, Regina Carrol, William Bonner. Renegade cyclists on the loose down the highway. Change the channel. [R]▼❶

Satan's Skin SEE: **Blood on Satan's Claw, The**

Satisfaction (1988) **C-92m.** BOMB D: Joan Freeman. Justine Bateman, Liam Neeson, Trini Alvarado, Britta Phillips, Julia Roberts, Scott Coffey. Bubble-gum theatrical release about a four-girl/one-guy garage band that gets its first break rocking in a wealthy summer resort town. With the entire band shacked up in a single room, figure out where sole male member Coffey sleeps—or *how* he sleeps. Duds like this were more fun in the 1950s. Retitled GIRLS OF SUMMER. [PG-13]▼❶

Saturday Night and Sunday Morning (1960-British) **90m. ***½** D: Karel Reisz. Albert Finney, Shirley Anne Field, Rachel Roberts, Norman Rossington. Grim yet refreshing look at angry young man, who in a burst of nonconformity alters the lives of girlfriends Field and Roberts. Superbly enacted. Script by Alan Sillitoe, from his novel. One of the first and best of Britain's "angry young men" dramas of the '60s.▼❶

Saturday Night Fever (1977) **C-119m. **** D: John Badham. John Travolta, Karen Lynn Gorney, Barry Miller, Joseph Cali, Paul Pape, Donna Pescow, Julie Bovasso, Denny Dillon, Robert Costanza, Fran Drescher. Travolta's first starring film is thoughtful study of Brooklyn youth who finds only meaning in his life when dancing at local disco. Film pulses to dynamic Bee Gees music score ("Night Fever," "How Deep Is Your Love," "Staying Alive," etc). Plethora of street language may offend some, but not in "alternate" 108m. PG-rated version, where dialogue and certain scenes have been changed or dropped entirely. Later a Broadway musical. Sequel: STAYING ALIVE. [R]▼❶

Saturday's Children (1940) **101m. **½** D: Vincent Sherman. John Garfield, Anne Shirley, Claude Rains, Lee Patrick, George Tobias, Roscoe Karns, Dennie Moore, Elisabeth Risdon. N.Y.C.-based story of poor, hardworking Shirley, her dreamer-boyfriend Garfield, and what happens when they marry. Rains steals film as Shirley's sacrificing father. Based on Maxwell Anderson play previously filmed in 1929 and (as MAYBE IT'S LOVE) in 1935.

Saturday the 14th (1981) **C-75m. *½** D: Howard R. Cohen. Richard Benjamin, Paula Prentiss, Severn Darden, Jeffrey Tambor, Kari Michaelson, Kevin Brando, Rosemary DeCamp. Limp horror film parody, with Benjamin and Prentiss moving into a weird house and dealing with an assortment of menacing types. A follow-up came along seven years later. [PG]▼❶

Saturday the 14th Strikes Back (1988) **C-78m.** BOMB D: Howard R. Cohen. Jason Presson, Ray Walston, Avery Schreiber, Patty McCormack, Julianne McNamara, Rhonda Aldrich, Leo V. Gordon. Follow-up to 1981 turkey is even worse, if that seems imaginable: a schlocky, amateurish spoof of horror films with a bevy of monsters attacking Presson on his birthday. [PG]▼🄳

Saturn 3 (1980-British) **C-88m.** ** D: Stanley Donen. Farrah Fawcett, Kirk Douglas, Harvey Keitel, Douglas Lambert. Flashy but empty-headed outer-space opus, with Douglas and Fawcett menaced by Keitel and his sex-starved robot Hector; good-looking package with nothing inside. [R]▼🄾🄳

Savage Attraction SEE: **Hostage** (1983)

Savage Eye, The (1960) **68m.** *** D: Ben Maddow, Sidney Meyers, Joseph Strick. Barbara Baxley, Herschel Bernardi, Gary Merrill, Jean Hidey. Documentary-style drama of divorcee Baxley trying to start life anew in L.A.; contrived but intriguing.▼🄳

Savage Grace (2008) **C-97m.** *½ D: Tom Kalin. Julianne Moore, Stephen Dillane, Eddie Redmayne, Elena Anaya, Unax Ugalde, Belén Rueda, Hugh Dancy. Creepy chronicle of socially ambitious Barbara Daly's marriage to arrogant Brooks Baekeland, the Bakelite plastics heir, and their troubled relationship with their son Tony. Six vignettes, set in various locations around the globe, span the years 1946 to 1972—though no one seems to age except the boy. Off-putting portrait of a decadent life offers no illumination or reward for watching. Based on the book by Natalie Robins and Steven M. L. Aronson.🄳

Savage Innocents, The (1960-Italian-French-British) **C-110m.** **½ D: Nicholas Ray. Anthony Quinn, Yoko Tani, Peter O'Toole, Marie Yang. Striking but uneven film about conflict of civilization vs. simple ways of Eskimo people. Quinn gives remarkable performance as native Eskimo; beautiful documentary-type location photography combined with studio work. O'Toole's voice is dubbed. Super Technirama 70.

Savage Is Loose, The (1974) **C-114m.** BOMB D: George C. Scott. George C. Scott, Trish Van Devere, John David Carson, Lee H. Montgomery. Scott produced, directed, starred in and even distributed this farrago about the eventual incest between mother and son after they, along with dad, have been stranded on an island for years. Not very stimulating. Panavision. [R]▼

Savage Messiah (1972-British) **C-100m.** *** D: Ken Russell. Dorothy Tutin, Scott Antony, Helen Mirren, Lindsay Kemp, Peter Vaughan. Thoughtful, if intense chronicle of the platonic affair between sculptor Henri Gaudier-Brzeska (Antony), who died in WW1 at age 24, and Sophie Brzeska (Tutin). A convincing, impressive "portrait of an artist as a young man." [R]▼🄳

Savage Nights (1992-French) **C-126m.** *** D: Cyril Collard. Cyril Collard, Romane Bohringer, Carlos Lopez, Corine Blue, Claude Winter, Maria Schneider. Rude, socially irresponsible, in-your-face AIDS movie with raw, subjective power. Collard,

who in real life succumbed to the disease just three days before his film swept France's César Awards, plays a bisexual moviemaker/ musician who reacts to his biological death warrant by sleeping around unprotected with sassy teenager Bohringer and rugby player Lopez, who are both messed up on their own. Occasionally ugly, but can't be dismissed. Imagine these characters taking over the Dean, Wood, and Mineo roles in REBEL WITHOUT A CAUSE.▼

Savage Pampas (1966-Spanish) **C-100m.** ** D: Hugo Fregonese. Robert Taylor, Ron Randell, Ty Hardin, Rosenda Monteros. Remake of 1946 Argentinian film PAMPA BARBARA. Taylor is rugged army captain combating outlaw Randell whose gang is made up of army deserters. Adequate actioner. Superpanorama 70.▼🄳

Savages, The (2007) **C-113m.** ***½ D: Tamara Jenkins. Laura Linney, Philip Seymour Hoffman, Philip Bosco, Peter Friedman, David Zayas, Gbenga Akinnagbe, Cara Seymour, Margo Martindale, Debra Monk. A brother and sister who aren't especially close must come together when their long-estranged father is left alone, in need of constant care. In dealing with this sudden challenge they also have to contend with unfinished business in their own relationship. He's a serious-minded theater professor with a hard outer shell; she's a neurotic would-be playwright who's still trying to find her way in life. Three great actors— Linney, Hoffman, and Bosco—sink their teeth into Jenkins' beautifully nuanced, heart-rending screenplay. [R]🄳

Savage Seven, The (1968) **C-96m.** *½ D: Richard Rush. Robert Walker, Jr., Larry Bishop, Adam Roarke, Max Julien, Duane Eddy, Joanna Frank, Penny Marshall. Below-par motorcycle melodrama that lives up to its title but nothing else.▼

Savannah Smiles (1982) **C-107m.** **½ D: Pierre DeMoro. Mark Miller, Donovan Scott, Bridgette Andersen, Peter Graves, Chris Robinson, Michael Parks. A rich little girl (Andersen) runs away from home and reforms criminals. Fair morality tale for kids, written by leading actor Miller. [PG]▼🄾🄳

Saved! (2004) **C-92m.** **½ D: Brian Dannelly. Jena Malone, Mandy Moore, Macaulay Culkin, Patrick Fugit, Heather Matarazzo, Eva Amurri, Martin Donovan, Mary-Louise Parker, Chad Faust, Valerie Bertinelli. Malone plays a senior at a Christian high school who has never questioned her faith, until her boyfriend tells her he thinks he's gay. When her prayer-inspired solution to the problem makes her an outcast, she sees her friends (especially class leader Moore) and even her mother in a brand-new light. Satire of religious hypocrisy by first-time feature director Dannelly and cowriter Michael Urban loses its footing after a promising start but benefits from a talented ensemble. Later a stage musical. [PG-13]▼◗

Save the Last Dance (2001) **C-105m. **½** D: Thomas Carter. Julia Stiles, Sean Patrick Thomas, Kerry Washington, Fredro Starr, Terry Kinney, Bianca Lawson, Vince Green, Garland Whitt. By-the-numbers tale of whitebread teen Stiles, a wannabe professional ballerina, who moves to Chicago to live with her estranged jazz musician father after her mother's death. She becomes involved with Thomas, and discovers the liberating force of hip-hop. Attractive performances elevate this clichéd teen culture/romantic drama. [PG-13]▼◗

Save the Tiger (1973) **C-101m. **** D: John G. Avildsen. Jack Lemmon, Jack Gilford, Laurie Heineman, Norman Burton, Patricia Smith, Thayer David, Lara Parker. Pretentious Steve Shagan script about dress manufacturer trying to reconcile hero-worship of his childhood with degradations he submits himself to in business world. Film purports to be totally honest, but phoniness comes through; David has best scenes as professional arsonist. Lemmon won Best Actor Oscar. [R]▼◗◖

Saving Face (2005) **C-97m. ***** D: Alice Wu. Michelle Krusiec, Joan Chen, Lynn Chen, Jin Wang, Guang Lan Koh, Jessica Hecht, Ato Essandoh, David Shih, Brian Yang. Entertaining, well-observed comedy about Chinese-American doctor Krusiec (who can't admit that she's a lesbian) and her tradition-bound mother Joan Chen (who won't explain how she's gotten pregnant at the age of 48). Romantic and cultural complications abound in this heartfelt and genuinely funny film, an impressive debut feature for writer-director Wu. [R]◗

Saving Grace (1986) **C-112m. **½** D: Robert M. Young. Tom Conti, Fernando Rey, Erland Josephson, Giancarlo Giannini, Donald Hewlett, Edward James Olmos, Patricia Mauceri. Youthful Pope Conti, overwhelmed by meaningless duties and a general feeling of uselessness, sneaks incognito out of the Vatican and into a small Italian village that has lost its spirit. If you're going to spin a whopper like this, don't pace it so slowly that the audience has too much time to ponder the improbabilities. Technovision. [PG]▼◗

Saving Grace (2000-British) **C-93m. **½** D: Nigel Cole. Brenda Blethyn, Craig Ferguson, Martin Clunes, Tchéky Karyo, Jamie Foreman, Bill Bailey, Valerie Edmond, Leslie Phillips, Phyllida Law. A newly impoverished widow with a green thumb is prevailed upon by her gardener to use her skills to grow marijuana, with surprising results. Impish comedy is great fun until the climax, when it becomes silly and loses all connection to reality. Ferguson (who plays the gardener) cowrote and coproduced. Super 35. [R]▼◗

Saving Private Ryan (1998) **C-169m.**

***½ D: Steven Spielberg. Tom Hanks, Edward Burns, Tom Sizemore, Jeremy Davies, Vin Diesel, Adam Goldberg, Barry Pepper, Giovanni Ribisi, Matt Damon, Dennis Farina, Ted Danson, Harve Presnell, Dale Dye, Bryan Cranston, David Wohl, Paul Giamatti, Ryan Hurst, Harrison Young. Trenchant WW2 drama about an Army captain (Hanks) assigned to take his squad of seven men into France, locate a private whose three brothers have been killed in combat . . . and give him a ticket home. Conventional elements in the script are balanced by a genuinely complex examination of heroism in the field, and overpowered by the most realistic, relentlessly harrowing battle footage ever committed to a fiction film. Spielberg (aided immeasurably by cameraman Janusz Kaminski and a superb creative team) has created the ultimate vision of war as hell on earth. Oscars include Best Director, Cinematography, Editing (Michael Kahn). [R]▼◗◖

Saving Shiloh (2006) **C-90m. **** D: Sandy Tung. Scott Wilson, Gerald McRaney, Jason Dolley, Ann Dowd, Kyle Chavarria, Jordan Garrett, Taylor Momsen, Bonnie Bartlett, Kari. Third in the SHILOH series finds McRaney replacing Michael Moriarty, along with a new young lead (Dolley) and a new dog. This time the cute beagle and his human friend learn more about their curmudgeon of a neighbor Judd (Wilson) while collecting clues to solve a murder. Same pleasant-natured entertainment as the first two films, but not as good as its intentions. [PG]◗

Saving Silverman (2001) **C-91m. **½** D: Dennis Dugan. Jason Biggs, Amanda Peet, Steve Zahn, Jack Black, Amanda Detmer, R. Lee Ermey, Neil Diamond. Dreadful exercise in Farrelly-esque gross-out fare about two dudes (Black, Zahn) who kidnap their best pal's bitchy girlfriend to prevent him from getting married. Funny premise is botched by violent slapstick and an unrelenting mean streak. A giddy wrap-up featuring Neil Diamond, in his first screen appearance since THE JAZZ SINGER (1980), barely redeems this from complete BOMB-dom. R-rated version also available. Super 35. [PG-13]▼◗

Savior, The (1998) **C-103m. ***** D: Peter Antonijevic. Dennis Quaid, Nastassja Kinski, Stellan Skarsgård, Sergej Trifunovic, Natasa Ninkovic. Earnest drama about a man who, after a personal tragedy, joins the Foreign Legion and winds up as a cold-blooded fighting machine. But when he comes upon a young woman about to give birth in Bosnia, he takes care of her and soon becomes emotionally attached to both the mother and infant. Quaid is excellent. Super 35. [R]▼◗◖

Saw (2004) **C-103m. ***** D: James Wan. Cary Elwes, Danny Glover, Monica Potter,

Leigh Whannell, Michael Emerson, Tobin Bell, Ken Leung, Makenzie Vega, Shawnee Smith, Dina Meyer. Two strangers (Elwes, Whannell) awaken to find themselves held prisoner by an unknown maniac in an abandoned warehouse bathroom. The psychopath enjoys devising gruesome torture games for unsuspecting victims, while cops Glover and Leung seek to end his sadistic crime spree. Unpleasant but intense, effective thriller in the SE7EN vein. Scripted by Whannell from a story he devised with the director. Timid or squeamish viewers may not want to watch this alone . . . or ever. Followed by six sequels. [R] ▼▶

Saw II (2005) **C-93m.** **½ D: Darren Lynn Bousman. Donnie Wahlberg, Shawnee Smith, Tobin Bell, Franky G, Glenn Plummer, Dina Meyer, Emmanuelle Vaugier, Beverley Mitchell, Erik Knudsen, Tim Burd. Sadistic sequel finds fiendish mastermind "Jigsaw" holding a group of strangers captive in a spooky, booby-trapped house. Plenty of gore for fans, as the victims race the clock while a lethal gas fills their lungs. Wahlberg is the lead cop on the case, but can he match wits with this twisted madman? Unrated edition is 95m. [R] ▼▶

Saw III (2006) **C-108m.** ** D: Darren Lynn Bousman. Tobin Bell, Shawnee Smith, Angus Macfadyen, Bahar Soomekh, Mpho Koaho, Dina Meyer, Barry Flatman, Lyriq Bent, J. LaRose, Costas Mandylor, Alan Van Sprang, Donnie Wahlberg. The blade has begun to dull on this franchise as a feeble Jigsaw (Bell) uses his protégée (Smith) to carry out his master plan of torturing the privileged. At the same time, they have kidnapped a brain surgeon and are forcing her to try to save his sorry carcass. Weak story and acting help sink this: Soomekh's performance as the medic is horrid (and not in the good sense). Unrated version runs 113m. "Director's Cut" runs 120m. [R] ▶

Saw IV (2007) **C-92m.** **½ D: Darren Lynn Bousman. Tobin Bell, Costas Mandylor, Scott Patterson, Betsy Russell, Lyriq Bent, Athena Karkanis, Justin Louis, Simon Reynolds, Donnie Wahlberg, Angus Macfadyen, Shawnee Smith, Bahar Soomekh, Dina Meyer. Jigsaw is dead, but his ingenious torture devices mysteriously continue, with law enforcement agents Mandylor and Patterson on the trail. We also learn how and why a successful architectural engineer morphed into this Satan. Decent rebound from its lackluster predecessor, this entry is less claustrophobic than usual, though many performances are typically subpar—which is almost part of the perverse appeal. [R] ▶

Saw V (2008) **C-92m.** *½ D: David Hackl. Tobin Bell, Costas Mandylor, Scott Patterson, Betsy Russell, Mark Rolston, Julie Benz, Carlo Rota, Mike Butters, Meagan Good, Greg Bryk, Donnie Wahlberg, Danny Glover. Rival law enforcement investigators Mandylor (about as expressive as a mummy) and Patterson (still grimly ultra-determined) try to thwart the never-ending killings of Jigsaw, who, for a corpse, has plenty of screen time in this deadly dull fifth installment. The now-standard "strangers imprisoned in a dank warehouse maze of torture games" subplot is weaker than ever (even the gross-out factor is, relatively speaking, quite tame). This entry is almost a total buzz-killer. Unrated version runs 96m. [R] ▶

Saw VI (2009) **C-91m.** ** D: Kevin Greutert. Tobin Bell, Costas Mandylor, Betsy Russell, Mark Rolston, Peter Outerbridge, Shawnee Smith, Athena Karkanis, Samantha Lemole, Caroline Cave, George Newbern, Darius McCrary, James Van Patten. Series entry boasts the topicality of watching mortgage scammers and coldhearted health-care bureaucrats suffer and die. That's about the only fresh blood here, although this is an improvement over its dreadful predecessor. Bad-cop Mandylor tries to stay one step ahead of the FBI's investigation—but the unending series of Jigsaw's (Bell) instructional videotapes from the grave is preposterous, and the filmmakers appear to have run out of ideas for sadistic torture devices. Series veterans Scott Patterson and Angus Macfadyen can be glimpsed fleetingly, both unbilled. [R] ▶

Saw 3D (2010) **C-90m.** **½ D: Kevin Greutert. Tobin Bell, Costas Mandylor, Betsy Russell, Cary Elwes, Sean Patrick Flanery, Chad Donella, Gina Holden, Laurence Anthony, Dean Armstrong, James Van Patten. It's being touted as the final chapter (though it would have been more helpful to just bill it as SAW VII), and while predictably far from great, this is an OK entry in the low-budget torture series. Monster cop Mandylor and Jigsaw's widow (Russell) continue to thrust and parry, but the plot pivots on newcomer Flanery as a firebrand profiting from his notoriety as a former victim. As usual, only hardcore fans will care. The three-dimensional thrills aren't. 3-D. [R] ▶

Sawdust and Tinsel (1953-Swedish) **92m.** **** D: Ingmar Bergman. Harriet Andersson, Ake Gronberg, Anders Ek, Gudrun Brost, Hasse Ekman, Annika Tretow. Sparks fly in this beautiful, allegorical film set in a small-time circus and focusing on the relationship between circus owner Gronberg and his oversexed mistress (Andersson). A key credit in Bergman's developing maturity as a filmmaker. Aka THE NAKED NIGHT. ▼●

Say Amen, Somebody (1982) **C-100m.** **** D: George T. Nierenberg. Willie Mae Ford Smith, Thomas A. Dorsey, Sallie Martin, The Barrett Sisters, The O'Neal Brothers. Wonderful documentary about gospel music and two of its shining stars,

"Mother" Willie Mae Ford Smith and "Professor" Thomas Dorsey, that brings us into their lives as well as their careers and demonstrates the power of music sung from the heart. A genuine treat. [G]▼●◗

Say Anything . . . (1989) **C-100m.** *** D: Cameron Crowe. John Cusack, Ione Skye, John Mahoney, Lili Taylor, Amy Brooks, Pamela Segall, Jason Gould, Loren Dean, Jeremy Piven, Bebe Neuwirth, Eric Stoltz, Chynna Phillips, Joanna Frank. Satisfying teenage comedy-drama about a self-assured loner who goes after the Class Brain, and finds her surprisingly human. Amusing, endearing, and refreshingly original; written by first-time director Crowe. Cusack's real-life sister Joan plays his sister here, and Lois Chiles has a cameo as Skye's mother; both appear unbilled. [PG-13]▼●◗

Say Hello to Yesterday (1971-British) **C-91m.** *½ D: Alvin Rakoff. Jean Simmons, Leonard Whiting, Evelyn Laye, John Lee, Jack Woolgar, Constance Chapman. Ridiculous plot concerning 4Q-year-old Simmons' affair with 22-year-old Whiting. Symbolic touches by director Rakoff further shroud purpose of film. [PG]▼

Say It Isn't So (2001) **C-96m.** *½ D: James B. Rogers. Heather Graham, Chris Klein, Orlando Jones, Sally Field, Richard Jenkins, John Rothman, Brent Briscoe, Sarah Silverman. Agreeably unambitious Klein falls for the new hairdresser in town (Graham)—only to learn, after mutually satisfying sexual activity, that she's his sister. Even the Farrelly Brothers' names in the credits—as producers—couldn't keep this gross-out comedy from flopping. Film is only for those who want to experience Field as they've never seen or even imagined before; the crude humor extends even to her. [R]▼◗

Sayonara (1957) **C-147m.** ***½ D: Joshua Logan. Marlon Brando, Ricardo Montalban, Miiko Taka, Miyoshi Umeki, Red Buttons, Martha Scott, James Garner. Romantic James Michener tale of Korean War pilot Brando falling in love with Japanese entertainer Taka; extremely well acted, with Oscar-winning support from Buttons and Umeki, and statuettes also going to the art direction–set decoration. Theme song by Irving Berlin. Paul Osborn wrote the screenplay. Technirama.▼●◗

Scalawag (1973) **C-93m.** *½ D: Kirk Douglas. Kirk Douglas, Mark Lester, Don Stroud, Neville Brand, Lesley-Anne Down, Phil Brown, Danny DeVito; voice of Mel Blanc. TREASURE ISLAND goes West in this weak adaptation, with a hammy Kirk as one-legged cutthroat; songs turn up when you least expect them. Filmed in Yugoslavia. [G]

Scalphunters, The (1968) **C-102m.** **½ D: Sydney Pollack. Burt Lancaster, Shelley Winters, Ossie Davis, Telly Savalas, Armando Silvestre, Nick Cravat, Dabney Coleman. Western comedy about a fur trapper

and his highly educated slave has its moments, but isn't funny enough, nor exciting enough, nor pointed enough to qualify as all-out success. Cast helps. Panavision.▼◗

Scam (1993) **C-101m.** ** D: John Flynn. Christopher Walken, Lorraine Bracco, Miguel Ferrer, Martin Donovan, Daniel Von Bargen. Con artist Bracco and greedy ex-fed Walken form a stormy alliance to scam a bundle in underworld cash. This would-be erotic thriller was made for theatrical release but premiered on cable. [R]▼

Scamp, The SEE: **Strange Affection**

Scandal (1989) **C-106m.** *** D: Michael Caton-Jones. John Hurt, Joanne Whalley-Kilmer, Bridget Fonda, Ian McKellen, Leslie Phillips, Britt Ekland, Daniel Massey, Roland Gift, Jeroen Krabbé. Absorbing look at the people behind Britain's incredible government-sex scandal of the early '60s, with Whalley-Kilmer just right as impressionable showgirl Christine Keeler, and Hurt outstanding as Stephen Ward, the social gadfly and sexual provocateur who introduces Keeler to Cabinet Minister John Profumo (whose wife, incidentally, was a former film star, Valerie Hobson). Fascinating and credible; a good job by first-time director Michael Caton-Jones. Screenplay by Michael Thomas. Original 114m. British version was trimmed to avoid an X-rating in the U.S. Both versions are available on video. [R]▼●◗

Scandal in Paris, A (1946) **106m.** *** D: Douglas Sirk. George Sanders, Carole Landis, Akim Tamiroff, Signe Hasso, Gene Lockhart, Alan Napier, Alma Kruger. Stylish (though studio-bound) 18th-century story based on the memoirs of the notorious Frenchman Eugene Vidocq, whose life of crime reaches a crossroads when he encounters a young woman who idolizes him. Witty script was tailor-made for Sanders. Aka THIEVES' HOLIDAY.▼◗

Scandalous (1984) **C-94m.** ** D: Rob Cohen. Robert Hays, John Gielgud, Pamela Stephenson, Jim Dale, M. Emmet Walsh, Bow Wow Wow. Featherbrained farce about investigative TV reporter who runs afoul of team of con artists as he tries to extricate himself from murder charge. Alternately stupid and obnoxious, with Gielgud presumably having fun as a disguise-happy sharpster. [PG]▼◗

Scandalous John (1971) **C-113m.** *** D: Robert Butler. Brian Keith, Michele Carey, Rick Lenz, Harry Morgan, Simon Oakland, Alfonso Arau, Bill Williams, Bruce Glover, John Ritter, Iris Adrian. Spirited Disney comedy-Western chronicling what happens when elderly, lovably ornery rancher Keith refuses to sell his land to a developer. Keith's crafty performance as a modern-day Don Quixote gives this one a lift. Panavision. [G]▼◗

Scandal Sheet (1952) **82m.** *** D: Phil Karlson. Broderick Crawford, Donna Reed,

John Derek, Rosemary DeCamp, Henry O'Neill, Henry (Harry) Morgan. Engrossing melodrama about an ambitious editor who accidentally kills his ex-wife, then finds his ace reporters investigating the story. Based on a Samuel Fuller novel. ▶

Scanner Cop (1994-Canadian-U.S.) **C-94m.** **½ D: Pierre David. Daniel Quinn, Darlanne Fluegel, Richard Grove, Mark Rolston, Richard Lynch, Hilary Shepard, James Horan, Gary Hudson, Luca Bercovici, Brion James. Rookie Quinn, a powerful telepath (scanner) since childhood, uses his powers, which might destroy him, to track a renegade scientist who's causing ordinary people to kill cops. Despite logic and acting lapses, an entertaining entry—and welcome change of direction—in the SCANNERS series. [R] ▼●

Scanner Cop II: Volkin's Revenge SEE: **Scanners: The Showdown**

Scanner Darkly, A (2006) **C-100m.** *** D: Richard Linklater. Keanu Reeves, Robert Downey, Jr., Woody Harrelson, Winona Ryder, Rory Cochrane, Melody Chase, Sean Allen, Natasha Valdez, Chamblee Ferguson. In a run-down future, three aging slackers share an Orange County tract house: surfer dude Harrelson, armed and paranoid Downey, and tire jockey Reeves, who's got a narc . . . he's a narc. Every day he dons a scramble suit to hide his ID and ferret out bad guys who peddle brain-rotting Substance D. Bleak cautionary tale about loss of self, rendered in eye-popping rotoscoped animation that dimensionalizes deluded abusers who are way more than dazed and confused. Adapted by Linklater from Philip K. Dick's novel. [R] ▶

Scanners (1981-Canadian) **C-102m.** **½ D: David Cronenberg. Jennifer O'Neill, Stephen Lack, Patrick McGoohan, Lawrence Dane, Charles Shamata. Title refers to superbrains who can read minds and cause others' heads to explode; here, a "good" scanner helps doctors track down a bad one. Rather plodding treatment of interesting idea, aided somewhat by great (if yucky) special effects. Followed by several sequels. [R] ▼●▶

Scanners II: The New Order (1991-Canadian) **C-105m.** ** D: Christian Duguay. David Hewlett, Deborah Raffin, Yvan Ponton, Isabelle Mejias, Tom Butler, Raoul Trujillo. Would-be despotic police officer conspires with scientist to trap "scanners" (people with strong ESP abilities), but complications arise when they confront a scanner with principles. OK for what it is. David Cronenberg had no connection with this sequel to his 1981 film. [R] ▼●

Scanners III: The Takeover (1992-Canadian) **C-101m.** BOMB D: Christian Duguay. Liliana Komorowska, Valerie Valois, Daniel Pilon, Collin Fox, Claire Cellucci, Michael Copeman, Steve Parrish.

A new drug turns good "scanners" bad, and makes Komorowska into yet another telekinetic megalomaniac. Poorly acted, badly written, plodding trifle reduces evil to mere cruelty, and Cronenberg's original ideas to absurdity. Awful. [R] ▼●

Scanners: The Showdown (1994) **C-95m.** **½ D: Steve Barnett. Daniel Quinn, Patrick Kilpatrick, Khrystyne Haje, Stephen Mendel, Robert Forster, Brenda Swanson, Jerry Potter, Jewel Shepard. Evil scanner Kilpatrick returns to L.A. with a new power—he can suck the life out of other scanners—and a lust for revenge on scanner cop Quinn, who sent him to prison. Effective, entertaining sequel to SCANNER COP delivers its goods with solid B-movie skill. Aka SCANNER COP II: VOLKIN'S REVENGE. [R] ▼●

Scapegoat, The (1959-British) **92m.** **½ D: Robert Hamer. Alec Guinness, Bette Davis, Nicole Maurey, Irene Worth, Peter Bull, Pamela Brown, Geoffrey Keen. Decent acting rescues a fuzzy script. French gentleman murders his wife, tries to involve his British lookalike in scheme. Davis has small but impressive role as the guilty Guinness' dope-ridden mother. Adapted by Hamer and Gore Vidal from a Daphne du Maurier novel.

Scaramouche (1952) **C-118m.** ***½ D: George Sidney. Stewart Granger, Eleanor Parker, Janet Leigh, Mel Ferrer, Henry Wilcoxon, Lewis Stone, Richard Anderson, Robert Coote. Excellent cast in rousing adaptation of Sabatini novel of illustrious ne'er-do-well who sets out to avenge friend's death, set in 18th-century France. Impeccably done. Highlight is climactic sword duel—the longest in swashbuckling history. Screenplay by Ronald Millar and George Froeschel. Filmed before in 1923. ▼●▶

Scarecrow (1973) **C-115m.** *** D: Jerry Schatzberg. Gene Hackman, Al Pacino, Dorothy Tristan, Eileen Brennan, Ann Wedgeworth, Richard Lynch. Drifter Hackman, who wants to start car-wash business, meets drifter Pacino, who has abandoned his wife. Moody, not altogether successful tale benefits from top performances and photography (by Vilmos Zsigmond), plus good use of locations. Panavision. [R] ▼●▶

Scared Stiff (1953) **108m.** **½ D: George Marshall. Dean Martin, Jerry Lewis, Lizabeth Scott, Carmen Miranda, Dorothy Malone. Usual Martin and Lewis hijinks with duo on spooky Caribbean island inherited by Scott. Remake of Bob Hope's THE GHOST BREAKERS. ▼●▶

Scarface (1932) **90m.** ***½ D: Howard Hawks. Paul Muni, Ann Dvorak, George Raft, Boris Karloff, Karen Morley, Vince Barnett, Osgood Perkins, C. Henry Gordon. Powerful gangster film is the most potent of the 1930s, with Muni delivering emotionally charged performance as Caponelike mobster with more than just a soft spot for his sister (Dvorak). Raw, harsh, and brimming with unsubtle symbolism; five writers include Ben Hecht and W. R. Burnett. Filmed in 1931, release delayed by censors. The full title is SCARFACE, THE SHAME OF THE NATION. Remade in 1983.▼●▶

Scarface (1983) **C-170m.** *½ D: Brian De Palma. Al Pacino, Steven Bauer, Michelle Pfeiffer, Mary Elizabeth Mastrantonio, Robert Loggia, Miriam Colon, F. Murray Abraham, Paul Shenar, Harris Yulin. 1932 gangster movie updated by making lead character a Cuban refugee in Miami, and changing profession from bootlegging to drug-dealing . . . but this film wallows in excess and unpleasantness for nearly *three hours,* and offers no new insights except that crime doesn't pay. At least the 1932 movie *moved.* Even so, this has become a pop-culture phenomenon, with Pacino's Tony Montana an underdog hero! Screenplay by Oliver Stone. Panavision. [R] ▼●▶

Scarlet Blade, The SEE: **Crimson Blade, The**

Scarlet Claw, The (1944) **74m.** ***½ D: Roy William Neill. Basil Rathbone, Nigel Bruce, Gerald Hamer, Arthur Hohl, Miles Mander, Ian Wolfe, Paul Cavanagh, Kay Harding. The ominous marshes of a French-Canadian village provide the setting for gruesome mutilation murders in this excellent *Sherlock Holmes* mystery, moodily photographed by George Robinson. Clearly the best of the series. ▼▶

Scarlet Diva (2001-Italian) **C-91m.** *½ D: Asia Argento. Asia Argento, Jean Shepard, Vera Gemma, Fabio Camilli. Lurid, pretentious navel-gazing from the actress daughter of Italian horror-meister Dario Argento. All about a 26-year-old drug-fueled pregnant starlet who travels from N.Y.C. to L.A. to Amsterdam in search of her American lover, only to be pursued by men and women who will stop at nothing to rape her. Cult film's biggest revelation is how willing the smoldering Argento is to get naked.▌

Scarlet Empress, The (1934) **110m.** *** D: Josef von Sternberg. Marlene Dietrich, John Lodge, Louise Dresser, Sam Jaffe, C. Aubrey Smith, Edward Van Sloan. Von Sternberg tells the story of Catherine the Great and her rise to power in uniquely ornate fashion, with stunning lighting and camerawork and fiery Russian music. It's a visual orgy; dramatically uneven, but cinematically fascinating. ▼▶

Scarlet Letter, The (1973-German) **C-90m.** *** D: Wim Wenders. Senta Berger, Lou Castel, Hans-Christian Blech, Yella Rottlander, Yelina Samarina, William Layton. Absorbing version of the oft-filmed Hawthorne classic, with Berger as Hester Prynne, Blech as Roger Prynne, and Castel as Rev. Dimmesdale. While it lacks the

spontaneity of Wenders' other early films, there is much to ponder and relish here: in particular, Wenders' portrayal of the immigrant New England settlers. Remade in 1995. Filmed in Spain.▼

Scarlet Letter, The (1995) **C-135m.** BOMB D: Roland Joffé. Demi Moore, Gary Oldman, Robert Duvall, Joan Plowright, Robert Prosky, Edward Hardwicke, Roy Dotrice, Dana Ivey, George Aguilar, Amy Wright, Diane Salinger, Eric Schweig; voice of Jodhi May. Hokey adaptation of Nathaniel Hawthorne's classic novel throws in everything from witch hunts to Indian attacks to a controversial happy ending—all to no avail. Moore is woefully miscast as Hester Prynne (though she sure fills a Puritan frock), Oldman gives a histrionic performance, while Duvall is simply incomprehensible. "Erotic" love scenes are especially embarrassing, in soft focus with phallic candles and a chirpy Disney bird (credited as Rudy the Robin) who sings for sexual freedom! J-D-C Scope. [R] ▼●▶

Scarlet Pimpernel, The (1935-British) **95m.** ***½ D: Harold Young. Leslie Howard, Merle Oberon, Raymond Massey, Nigel Bruce, Bramwell Fletcher, Anthony Bushell, Joan Gardner, Melville Cooper. Excellent costumer with Howard leading double life, aiding innocent victims of French revolution while posing as foppish member of British society. Baroness Orczy's novel was scripted by Robert E. Sherwood, Sam Berman, Arthur Wimperis, and Lajos Biro; produced by Alexander Korda. Remade as THE ELUSIVE PIMPERNEL, and for TV in 1982. Also shown in computer-colored version. ▼●▶

Scarlet Street (1945) **103m.** *** D: Fritz Lang. Edward G. Robinson, Joan Bennett, Dan Duryea, Margaret Lindsay, Rosalind Ivan. Meek, henpecked Robinson is pulled into world of crime and deception by seductive Bennett and her manipulative boyfriend Duryea. Stars and director of THE WOMAN IN THE WINDOW keep it interesting, but don't match earlier film. Dudley Nichols adapted this remake of Jean Renoir's LA CHIENNE. Also shown in computer-colored version. ▼▶

Scars of Dracula (1970-British) **C-94m.** *** D: Roy Ward Baker. Christopher Lee, Dennis Waterman, Jenny Hanley, Christopher Matthews, Wendy Hamilton. Good fang work as young couple tangles with Dracula in search of the young man's missing brother. Last of Hammer's period *Draculas*; followed by DRACULA A.D. 1972. [R] ▼●▶

Scary Movie (2000) **C-88m.** **½ D: Keenen Ivory Wayans. Jon Abrahams, Carmen Electra, Shannon Elizabeth, Anna Faris, Kurt Fuller, Regina Hall, Lochlyn Munro, Cheri Oteri, Dave Sheridan, Marlon Wayans, Shawn Wayans, Rick Ducommun, David L. Lander. L-o-o-o-o-o-w-brow spoof of the

SCREAM trilogy and TV hits of the late '90s. Ribald, raunchy, and raucous, with gags that would embarrass a frat boy; the fact that the MPAA gave this an R surprised even Hollywood. Costars Shawn and Marlon were among the six writers; director Keenen has a small part. Followed by three sequels. Super 35. [R]▼▶

Scary Movie 2 (2001) **C-82m.** *½ D: Keenen Ivory Wayans. Shawn Wayans, Marlon Wayans, Anna Faris, Regina Hall, Chris Masterson, Kathleen Robertson, Chris Elliott, James Woods, Tim Curry, Tori Spelling, David Cross, Natasha Lyonne, Andy Richter, Veronica Cartwright; voice of Vitamin C. Distressingly flat, unentertaining sequel finds Faris and friends invited to spend weekend as an experiment in haunted mansion. Filmmakers must have felt that one crummy remake of THE HAUNTING just wasn't enough. [R]▼▶

Scary Movie 3 (2003) **C-84m.** ** D: David Zucker. Anna Faris, Charlie Sheen, Simon Rex, Leslie Nielsen, Regina Hall, Camryn Manheim, Anthony Anderson, Queen Latifah, Jeremy Piven, Eddie Griffin, Pamela Anderson, Jenny McCarthy, George Carlin, Darrell Hammond, Denise Richards, D.L. Hughley, Drew Mikuska, Jianna Ballard. An improvement over the second installment—what wouldn't be?—as SIGNS, THE RING, and 8 MILE are all spoofed. Faris, now a TV reporter, and Hall are the only returning cast members (though they play new characters, if anyone's keeping track). Scattershot laughs, as you'd expect from the director and cowriter of AIRPLANE! and NAKED GUN (Nielsen appears here as the president of the U.S.) but hardly inspired. Many pop culture figures appear in cameos. Unrated version also available. [PG-13]▼▶

Scary Movie 4 (2006) **C-83m.** ** D: David Zucker. Anna Faris, Regina Hall, Craig Bierko, Leslie Nielsen, Charlie Sheen, Bill Pullman, Carmen Electra, Anthony Anderson, Cloris Leachman, Chris Elliott, Molly Shannon, Michael Madsen, Simon Rex, Kevin Hart, Shaquille O'Neal, Dr. Phil McGraw, James Earl Jones. This time the parodists pair Faris (sending up THE GRUDGE) and Bierko (spoofing Tom Cruise in WAR OF THE WORLDS) with THE VILLAGE, SAW, and a dollop of BROKEBACK MOUNTAIN. Hall is back as Faris' (extraneous) sidekick and Nielsen returns briefly as the U.S. President. Mining adolescent "comedy" from recent movie hits is wearing awfully thin. [PG-13]▮

Scavenger Hunt (1979) **C-117m.** BOMB D: Michael Schultz. Richard Benjamin, James Coco, Scatman Crothers, Ruth Gordon, Cloris Leachman, Cleavon Little, Roddy McDowall, Robert Morley, Richard Mulligan, Tony Randall, Dirk Benedict, Willie Aames, Stephanie Faracy, Meat Loaf, Carol Wayne, Arnold Schwarzeneg-

ger. Vincent Price dies, and his relatives and servants are practically forced to kill each other for his inheritance by collecting commodes, wild animals, etc. in an allotted time. Hard to believe a comedy with so much talent could misfire so greatly, but it does; only Mulligan manages to get some laughs. [PG]▼

Scene of the Crime (1986-French) **C-90m.** *** D: André Téchiné. Catherine Deneuve, Danielle Darrieux, Wadeck Stanczak, Nicholas Giraudi, Victor Lanoux, Jean Bousquet, Claire Nebout. Stylish, Chabrol-like drama about an unhappy young boy (Giraudi), his equally unhappy mother (Deneuve), and what results when escaped convict Stanczak invades their lives. Entertaining, perceptive, if occasionally uneven examination of repression and desperation.▼▶

Scenes From a Mall (1991) **C-87m.** ** D: Paul Mazursky. Bette Midler, Woody Allen, Bill Irwin, Daren Firestone, Rebecca Nickels, Paul Mazursky. Affluent L.A. couple, celebrating their anniversary, spend the day together at a mall, where various revelations cause their marriage to unravel. Bette and Woody make a terrific couple, but after a promising start the seriocomic script takes some strange turns and leaves reality behind. Fans of the stars should take a look, but this one ranks as a major disappointment. [R]▼●▶

Scenes From a Marriage (1973-Swedish) **C-168m.** **** D: Ingmar Bergman. Liv Ullmann, Erland Josephson, Bibi Andersson, Jan Malmsjo, Anita Wall. Passionate, probing and honest look at a marriage, its disintegration, and the relationship that follows. Ullmann and Josephson are remarkable throughout this intimate and often painful portrait, originally made as six TV episodes and edited into feature-length by writer-director Bergman. The characters are seen 30 years later in SARABAND. Original version runs 299m. [PG]▼▶

Scenes From the Class Struggle in Beverly Hills (1989) **C-102m.** *½ D: Paul Bartel. Jacqueline Bisset, Ray Sharkey, Mary Woronov, Robert Beltran, Ed Begley, Jr., Wallace Shawn, Arnetia Walker, Paul Bartel, Paul Mazursky, Rebecca Schaeffer. Bizarre, scattershot sex romp with various characters of various classes playing musical beds in Beverly Hills. Tries to be outrageous and irreverent while satirizing L.A. types and lifestyles, but mostly inane, veering uncomfortably between drama and farce. The best thing about this is its title. [R]▼●

Scent of a Woman (1974-Italian) **C-104m.** *** D: Dino Risi. Vittorio Gassman, Alessandro Momo, Agostina Belli. Blind, arrogant army captain Gassman galavants through Italy, sensing the presence of attractive women along the way; hapless private Momo is his guide on this fateful trip. Gassman shines in this sharply observed black comedy-drama, based on a novel by Giovanni Arpino. Remade in the U.S. in 1992. Original Italian title: PROFUMO DI DONNA. [R]▼▶

Scent of a Woman (1992) **C-157m.** **½ D: Martin Brest. Al Pacino, Chris O'Donnell, James Rebhorn, Gabrielle Anwar, Philip S. (Seymour) Hoffman, Richard Venture, Bradley Whitford, Rochelle Oliver, Frances Conroy. Timid prep school student earns much-needed money on a long weekend taking a job as companion to crusty, blind, hard-drinking ex-Army colonel—little dreaming the colonel has his own agenda. Enjoyable (if barely believable) story galvanized by Pacino's bravura, Oscar-winning performance. Bo Goldman's script is seriously weakened by a story appendage that plays like leftover material from DEAD PO-ETS SOCIETY. Based on the 1974 Italian film PROFUMO DI DONNA. [R] ▼●▶

Scent of Green Papaya, The (1993-French-Vietnamese) **C-104m.** *** D: Hung Tran Anh. Tran Nu Yen-Khe, Lu Man San, Truong Thi Loc, Nguyen Anh Hoa, Vuong Hoa Hoi. Thoughtful, carefully observed drama about a ten-year-old servant girl who comes to work in a Saigon household in 1951; the scenario details her relationships with the various household members and concludes a decade later with her growing into a beautiful young woman. Unhurried in its execution and filled with lingering shots, the film is as captivating as its title.▼●▶

Schindler's List (1993) **C/B&W-195m.** **** D: Steven Spielberg. Liam Neeson, Ben Kingsley, Ralph Fiennes, Caroline Goodall, Jonathan Sagalle, Embeth Davidtz, Malgoscha Gebel, Shmulik Levy, Mark Ivanir, Beatrice Macola. Staggering adaptation of Thomas Keneally's best-seller about the real-life Catholic war profiteer who initially flourished by sucking up to the Nazis, but eventually went broke saving the lives of more than 1,000 Polish Jews by employing them in his factory, manufacturing crockery for the German army. Filmed almost entirely on location in Poland, in gritty b&w, but with a pace to match the most frenzied Spielberg works, this looks and feels like nothing Hollywood has ever made before. The three central characters rate—and receive—unforgettable performances: Neeson, who's towering as Oskar Schindler; Kingsley, superb as his Jewish accountant (and conscience); and Fiennes, who's frightening as the odious Nazi commandant. Outstanding screenplay by Steven Zaillian and cinematography by Janusz Kaminski. Spielberg's most intense and personal film to date. Seven Oscars include Best Picture, Director, Adapted Screenplay, Art Direction, Cinematography, Editing, and Original Score (John Williams). [R] ▼●▶

Schizopolis (1997) **C-99m.** *** D: Steven Soderbergh. Steven Soderbergh, Betsy Brantley, David Jensen. Giddy mélange of surrealism, satire, silliness, and old-fashioned underground filmmaking written, directed by, and starring Soderbergh. A broad-ranging jab at modern society and its ills, its tone is arch, its technique one of non sequiturs, and its audience likely to be small. But if you latch onto it early enough, you may find (as we did) that it's fun—and funny—to watch.▼▶

Schlock (1971) **C-80m.** **½ D: John Landis. Saul Kahan, Joseph Piantadosi, Eliza Garrett, John Landis. Landis' first film is enjoyable spoof of B horror flicks; director (in gorilla suit by Rick Baker) plays missing link on the loose in small town. Many in-jokes for film buffs. Aka THE BANANA MONSTER. [PG]▼▶

School Daze (1988) **C-114m.** **½ D: Spike Lee. Larry Fishburne, Giancarlo Esposito, Tisha Campbell, Kyme, Joe Seneca, Art Evans, Ellen Holly, Ossie Davis, Bill Nunn, Branford Marsalis, Kadeem Hardison, Spike Lee, Darryl M. Bell, Joie Lee, Tyra Ferrell, Jasmine Guy, Gregg Burge, Kasi Lemmons, Samuel L. Jackson, Phyllis Hyman. Comedy-cum-fantasy about life on a black college campus in the South, where one self-serious student activist fights a lonely battle not only against the administration, but the pervasive mindlessness of his fellow students, most of whom are wrapped up in fraternity and sorority nonsense. Writer-director-costar Lee offers much entertainment and some provocative ideas, though he doesn't follow up on his initial premise until the anticlimactic final scene. [R]▼●▶

School for Scoundrels (1960-British) **94m.** *** D: Robert Hamer. Ian Carmichael, Terry-Thomas, Janette Scott, Alastair Sim, Dennis Price, Peter Jones, Edward Chapman. Wimpy Carmichael, about to lose the girl of his dreams to pushy Thomas, attends the title institute, where he learns "one-upmanship" and "gamesmanship." Clever, funny, veddy British satire. Full title on-screen is SCHOOL FOR SCOUNDRELS OR HOW TO WIN WITHOUT ACTUALLY CHEATING. Remade in 2006. ▼▶

School for Scoundrels (2006) **C-101m.** ** D: Todd Phillips. Billy Bob Thornton, Jon Heder, Jacinda Barrett, Michael Clarke Duncan, Luis Guzmán, David Cross, Horatio Sanz, Sarah Silverman, Matt Walsh, Todd Louiso, Dan Fogler, Bob Stephenson, Ben Stiller, Jim Parsons. Nerdy guy who lets people step all over him is recruited by a mysterious entrepreneur who runs a class for worms in need of turning. But our would-be hero isn't prepared for his "teacher" to start playing dirty tricks on him. Most contemporary comedies are too crude for our taste, but this one is terminally bland and never takes off as it repeatedly promises to do. Remake of the 1960 British comedy. Unrated version runs 107m. Panavision. [PG-13]▐

School of Flesh, The (1998-French) **C-107m.** **½ D: Benoit Jacquot. Isabelle Huppert, Vincent Martinez, Vincent Lindon, Marthe Keller, François Berléand, Danièle Dubroux, Bernard LeCoq. The always-watchable Huppert plays a well-to-do 40-ish woman who, against her better judgment, falls into an obsessive relationship with a young stud (Martinez) whom she meets at a bar in Paris. Candid examination of relationships is unmemorable, but benefits from star charisma. Based on the novel by Yukio Mishima. Panavision. [R]▼▐

School of Rock, The (2003) **C-108m.** ***½ D: Richard Linklater. Jack Black, Joan Cusack, Mike White, Sarah Silverman, Joey Gaydos, Jr., Maryam Hassan, Kevin Clark, Rebecca Brown, Robert Tsai, Caitlin Hale, Aleisha Allen, Miranda Cosgrove, Amy Sedaris. Perpetual screw-up Black, who fancies himself a hard-core rocker, pretends to be roommate White and takes a substitute-teaching job at a tony private school. There he finds the raw material for his dream band: a roomful of musically talented kids. Writer-costar White tailored this script for Black, who's simply perfect. Cusack is hilarious as his uptight principal. Delightful comedy hits all the right notes—for audiences of all ages. Frank Whaley appears unbilled. [PG-13]▼▐

School That Ate My Brain, The SEE: **Zombie High**

School Ties (1992) **C-107m.** **½ D: Robert Mandel. Brendan Fraser, Matt Damon, Chris O'Donnell, Randall Batinkoff, Andrew Lowery, Cole Hauser, Amy Locane, Zeljko Ivanek, Kevin Tighe, Ed Lauter, Peter Donat, Michael Higgins, Ben Affleck, Anthony Rapp. In the 1950s, a Jewish student (well played by Fraser) with working-class roots wins a football scholarship to a snooty prep school, where he's victimized by anti-Semitism. Youth-oriented film tackles an important subject, but it's strained and obvious. [PG-13]▼●▐

Science of Sleep, The (2006-French-Italian) **C-105m.** **½ D: Michel Gondry. Gael García Bernal, Charlotte Gainsbourg, Alain Chabat, Miou-Miou, Pierre Vaneck, Emma de Caunes, Aurélia Petit. Bernal's charismatic performance (in English) anchors this fanciful film about a childlike man who lives in a constant state of confusion about what's real and what's happening in his dreams. When he falls in love with his attractive next-door neighbor, his anxiety about their uncertain relationship blurs the line even more. Gondry's script meanders, but his constantly imaginative visual touches help to compensate. [R]▐

Scissors (1991) **C-105m.** ** D: Frank De Felitta. Sharon Stone, Steve Railsback, Ronny Cox, Michelle Phillips. Sexually traumatized Stone is driven mad—à la GASLIGHT—by objects that seemingly come to life in her apartment. Unfortunately, Stone is forced to carry off these histrionics in a generally lifeless, slow-moving production. Interesting idea could have been better executed (no pun intended). [R]▼●

Scooby-Doo (2002) **C-87m.** ** D: Raja Gosnell. Freddie Prinze, Jr., Sarah Michelle Gellar, Matthew Lillard, Linda Cardellini, Rowan Atkinson, Miguel A. Nunez, Jr., Isla Fisher, Sugar Ray. Hanna-Barbera's TV cartoon canine gets the big-screen treatment as Scooby and pals try to solve a mystery on Spooky Island. Flat comic whodunit with a computer-generated title character; a mild diversion for kids and older fans of the vintage series. Followed by a sequel. Also followed by a direct-to-DVD prequel, SCOOBY-DOO! THE MYSTERY BEGINS. [PG]▼●

Scooby Doo 2 Monsters Unleashed (2004) **C-91m.** ** D: Raja Gosnell. Freddie Prinze, Jr., Sarah Michelle Gellar, Matthew Lillard, Linda Cardellini, Seth Green, Alicia Silverstone, Peter Boyle, Tim Blake Nelson. It is what it is. [PG]▼●

Scoop (2006-British-U.S.) **C-96m.** *** D: Woody Allen. Woody Allen, Scarlett Johansson, Hugh Jackman, Ian McShane, Romola Garai, Fenella Woolgar, Charles Dance, John Standing, Richard Johnson, Anthony Head, Julian Glover, Margaret Tyzack. Larkish comedy-fantasy-mystery plays like an afterpiece to MATCH POINT, also set in London. A famous reporter returns from the dead to tip off college journalist Johansson that wealthy, well-connected Jackman may be a serial killer. She enlists the help of stage magician Allen to get close to Jackman and break the case. Endearingly silly and off the cuff, but you may have to be a Woodyphile to truly enjoy it. Allen is in good comic form as a walking show-business cliché. [PG-13]▐

Scorchy (1976) **C-99m.** *½ D: Hikmet Avedis. Connie Stevens, Cesare Danova, William Smith, Marlene Schmidt, Normann Burton, Joyce Jameson, Greg Evigan. Tawdry actioner with Stevens as Seattle undercover cop who sets out to bust high-level drug ring. Plenty of action and gore. [R]▼

Score, The (2001) **C-120m.** *** D: Frank Oz. Robert De Niro, Edward Norton, Marlon Brando, Angela Bassett, Gary Farmer, Paul Soles, Jamie Harrold. A master thief who lives a double life as a Montreal jazz club owner decides to pull one more job, then settle down, but an eager young cohort spells trouble from the start. Deliberate, almost laconic in its pacing, this caper never loses its grip. Worth watching for the cast alone; Brando, in his final screen role, is great fun in a colorful performance as De Niro's client/fence. Jazz singers Cassandra Wilson and Mose Allison appear briefly. Panavision. [R] ▼▶

Scorpio (1973) **C-114m.** **½ D: Michael Winner. Burt Lancaster, Alain Delon, Gayle Hunnicutt, Paul Scofield, John Colicos, J. D. Cannon, Joanne Linville. Tough espionage film of CIA agent in trouble, and hired killer who wants to go straight but finds himself caught in the system. Good action, dialogue amid familiar trappings. [PG] ▼●▶

Scorpion King, The (2002) **C-88m.** **½ D: Chuck Russell. The Rock (Dwayne Johnson), Kelly Hu, Steven Brand, Michael Clarke Duncan, Grant Heslov, Peter Facinelli, Ralf Moeller, Bernard Hill, Roger Rees. Follow-up to the two MUMMY movies features wrestler The Rock as a warrior who accepts the task of assassinating a desert despot (Brand). An entertaining old-fashioned B movie writ large, with nonstop action, special effects, muscular heroes, and beautiful women. The Rock is quite good as an action star, but even at this running time the story seems padded out. Followed by a DVD sequel. Super 35. [PG-13] ▼▶

Scotland, Pa. (2002) **C-103m.** **½ D: Billy Morrissette. James LeGros, Maura Tierney, Christopher Walken, Kevin Corrigan, James Rebhorn, Tom Guiry, Amy Smart, Andy Dick, Timothy Speed Levitch, Geoff Dunsworth. Joe McBeth (LeGros) is stuck in a go-nowhere fast-food job in 1970s Pennsylvania, until his wife hatches a scheme to murder the boss and climb the ladder of success. Modern-day *Macbeth* has many clever ideas, enthusiastic performances and ingenious production design, but runs out of steam as the story grows dark and nasty. Walken is a welcome comedic presence as Inspector McDuff. Written by debuting director Morrissette; Tierney is his wife. [R] ▼▶

Scott Joplin (1977) **C-96m.** **½ D: Jeremy Paul Kagan. Billy Dee Williams, Clifton Davis, Godfrey Cambridge, Art Carney, Seymour Cassel, Eubie Blake, Margaret Avery, Sam Fuller. Well-made, colorful but downbeat life story of famed ragtime composer. Made for TV, then given fitful theatrical release. Best sequence: the barrel-house piano "duel." [PG] ▼▶

Scott of the Antarctic (1948-British) **C-110m.** **½ D: Charles Frend. John Mills, Derek Bond, Harold Warrender, James Robertson Justice, Reginald Beckwith, Kenneth More, John Gregson, Christopher Lee. Unrelenting docudrama of determined British explorer Robert Falcon Scott (Mills), highlighting the details of his last expedition to the South Pole. This saga of bravery and endurance features an especially moving finale. Music by Vaughan Williams, who

later used part of this score in his seventh symphony. ▼▶

Scott Pilgrim vs. the World (2010-U.S.-British) **C-112m.** **½ D: Edgar Wright. Michael Cera, Mary Elizabeth Winstead, Kieran Culkin, Chris Evans, Anna Kendrick, Brie Larson, Alison Pill, Aubrey Plaza, Brandon Routh, Jason Schwartzman, Johnny Simmons, Mark Webber, Mae Whitman, Ellen Wong. Utterly ordinary Scott Pilgrim (Cera) is dating a high school girl when he encounters the woman of his dreams (Winstead). Suddenly, nothing else matters—despite her warnings that she comes with baggage: namely, seven deadly "exes." Lively, clever, funky adaptation of Bryan Lee O'Malley's graphic novels makes use of video-game graphics and iconography, which is great fun—for a while. Result is like an *Archie* comic book on steroids. Likable actors keep it real enough to balance the hyperactive stylistic flourishes, but the novelty wears off before the movie is over. Clifton Collins Jr. and Thomas Jane appear unbilled. Super 35/ Panavision. [PG-13] ▶

Scoundrel in White SEE: **High Heels** (1972)

Scout, The (1994) **C-107m.** ** D: Michael Ritchie. Albert Brooks, Brendan Fraser, Dianne Wiest, Anne Twomey, Lane Smith, Michael Rapaport, Barry Shabaka Henley, Tony Bennett, George Steinbrenner, Marcia Rodd. Woefully disappointing baseball yarn, with Brooks as a hard-luck N.Y. Yankees scout who finds a powerhouse pitcher and batter . . . with some serious psychological problems. Funny at first, with Brooks in good form; then takes a sharp left turn toward drama and never recovers. Brooks cowrote the final screenplay (based on an article by Roger Angell) with partner Monica Johnson. Many ballplayers and sportscasters appear as themselves. [PG-13] ▼●▶

Scream (1996) **C-110m.** *** D: Wes Craven. Neve Campbell, Skeet Ulrich, Drew Barrymore, Rose McGowan, Matthew Lillard, Jamie Kennedy, Courteney Cox, David Arquette, Liev Schreiber, Linda Blair. Murderer, obsessed with horror movies, begins slaughtering teens in a small city just a year after Campbell's mother was murdered—and the killer seems to be targeting people she knows. Well-drawn characters, suspenseful situations, several plot twists and entertaining movie references highlight this snappy horror thriller, one of Craven's best. Henry Winkler appears unbilled. Followed by three sequels. Panavision. [R] ▼●▶

Scream 2 (1997) **C-120m.** **½ D: Wes Craven. David Arquette, Neve Campbell, Courteney Cox, Sarah Michelle Gellar, Jamie Kennedy, Laurie Metcalf, Elise Neal, Jerry O'Connell, Timothy Olyphant, Jada Pinkett, Liev Schreiber, Lewis Arquette, Duane Martin, Rebecca Gayheart, Portia de Rossi, Omar

Epps, David Warner, Heather Graham, Kevin Williamson. Valiant survivor Campbell is in college when STAB, a movie based on the murder spree depicted in SCREAM, is released—and more murders begin. As good a sequel as the filmmakers could have done; it's only the climactic showdown that disappoints. As in the first film, there are plenty of slashes and scares, as well as humor. Panavision. [R]▼●❍

Scream 3 (2000) **C-116m.** **½ D: Wes Craven. David Arquette, Neve Campbell, Courteney Cox Arquette, Patrick Dempsey, Scott Foley, Lance Henriksen, Matt Keeslar, Jenny McCarthy, Emily Mortimer, Parker Posey, Deon Richmond, Patrick Warburton, Liev Schreiber, Jamie Kennedy, Kelly Rutherford, Josh Pais, Heather Matarazzo, Roger Corman. "Finale" of the SCREAM trilogy, set in Hollywood on the soundstages of STAB 3: RETURN TO WOODSBORO. Several actors (Posey, Keeslar, etc.) play "stars" who are portraying your SCREAM favorites. Wonder who's trying to slice them up, one by one? Fun for fans, with some choice cameos. Panavision. [R]▼●

Scream 4 (2011) **C-111m.** ** D: Wes Craven. Neve Campbell, Courteney Cox, David Arquette, Emma Roberts, Hayden Panettiere, Rory Culkin, Nico Tortorella, Mary McDonnell, Lucy Hale, Erik Knudsen, Mariellé Jaffe, Anthony Anderson, Adam Brody, Alison Brie, Anna Paquin, Kristen Bell, Marley Shelton, Shenae Grimes, Brittany Robertson. Set ten years after the earlier trilogy, we're back in Woodsboro, where we meet Campbell's teenaged cousin (Roberts) and her pretty partying pals just as Campbell has returned to town as a published author. Is anyone surprised that Ghostface has come back home as well to terrorize the MP3 generation? There's little here to get bloody excited about—and the self-aware genre ironies are wearing thin. It's pretty much all downhill following the iteration of those renowned slasher prologue sequences. Panavision. [R]

Scream and Scream Again (1970-British) **C-95m.** **½ D: Gordon Hessler. Vincent Price, Christopher Lee, Peter Cushing, Judy Huxtable, Alfred Marks, Peter Sallis. Distinguished cast does their darnedest to enliven (no pun intended) tired, confusing plot concerning mad scientist's organ/limbs experiments and race of emotionless beings he creates. [M/PG]▼●❍

Scream, Blacula, Scream! (1973) **C-95m.** ** D: Bob Kelljan. William Marshall, Don Mitchell, Pam Grier, Michael Conrad, Richard Lawson. Poor sequel to BLACULA finds black vampire recalled from eternal rest and forced to go out and nibble again in contemporary black U.S. [PG]▼●

Screamers (1995-Canadian) **C-107m.** **½ D: Christian Duguay. Peter Weller, Roy Dupuis, Jennifer Rubin, Andy Lauer, Charles Powell, Ron White, Michael Caloz, Liliana Komorowska. 2078: War has devastated a distant planet; the few human survivors are pitted against "Screamers," self-evolving robots programed to kill. Now the Screamers are able to look exactly like human beings. Intelligent sci-fi action thriller is undermined by a bad ending. Cowritten by Dan O'Bannon; based on the short story "Second Variety" by Philip K. Dick. Followed by a DVD sequel 14 years larter. [R]▼●

Screaming Mimi (1958) **79m.** ** D: Gerd Oswald. Anita Ekberg, Phil Carey, Harry Townes, Gypsy Rose Lee, Romney Brent, Red Norvo. Lurid low-budget melodrama about a woman who cracks up after being assaulted, takes a job as exotic dancer in Lee's nightclub but remains under the influence of a possessive psychiatrist. Strange, kinky film that sounds more interesting than it really is.●

Screwed (2000) **C-82m.** BOMB D: Scott Alexander, Larry Karaszewski. Norm Macdonald, Dave Chappelle, Elaine Stritch, Danny DeVito, Daniel Benzali, Sherman Hemsley, Sarah Silverman. Title describes your inevitable state if you waste just two minutes watching this woeful attempt to revive screwball slapstick. Chauffeur Macdonald works for a stingy baking tycoon (Stritch) who won't even buy him a uniform—so he decides to kidnap her attack-mode pet dog and hold it for ransom. Movie tries everything—even making DeVito a mortician who's also vice-president of Jack Lord's fan club—but fizzles for the duration. Directing debut for the writers of ED WOOD and THE PEOPLE VS. LARRY FLYNT. [PG-13]▼❍

Screw Loose (1999-Italian) **C-85m.** ** D: Ezio Greggio. Ezio Greggio, Mel Brooks, Julie Condra, Gianfranco Barra, Randi Ingerman. Heavy-handed farce about an inept businessman who promises his dying father that he'll find the American who saved his life during WW2. Brooks hams it up, but the results are only sporadically funny. Shot in both English- and Italian-language versions. [R]▼❍

Scrooge (1935-British) **78m.** **½ D: Henry Edwards. Sir Seymour Hicks, Donald Calthrop, Robert Cochran, Mary Glynne, Oscar Asche, Maurice Evans. Faithful adaptation of *A Christmas Carol*, with an impressive Sir Seymour (who also cowrote the script) as Scrooge. Dickens' era brought colorfully to life.▼❍

Scrooge (1970-British) **C-118m.** *** D: Ronald Neame. Albert Finney, Alec Guinness, Edith Evans, Kenneth More, Laurence Naismith, Michael Medwin, David Collings, Gordon Jackson, Roy Kinnear, Kay Walsh. Handsome musicalization of Dickens' *A Christmas Carol*, with Finney genially hamming it up in the title role and Guinness a surprisingly fey Marley's Ghost.

Leslie Bricusse's score is pretty forgettable, save effervescent "Thank You Very Much"; lovely sets by Terry Marsh and evocative title design by Ronald Searle. Panavision. [G]▼●)

Scrooged (1988) **C-101m.** ** D: Richard Donner. Bill Murray, Karen Allen, John Forsythe, John Glover, Bobcat Goldthwait, David Johansen (Buster Poindexter), Carol Kane, Robert Mitchum, Nicholas Phillips, Michael J. Pollard, Alfre Woodard, Mabel King, John Murray, Brian Doyle-Murray. Ostensibly a hip, funny rereading of Dickens' *A Christmas Carol*, with Murray as a venal TV executive. The laughs are mild and widely scattered, and toward the end the film seems to want us to take its brotherhood message seriously. Or does it? Features a variety of "guest stars." [PG-13] ▼●)

Scrubbers (1982-British) **C-90m.** ** D: Mai Zetterling. Chrissie Cotterill, Amanda York, Elizabeth Edmonds, Kate Ingram, Kathy Burke. Life in a teenage girls' borstal (reform school), complete with heartbreak, cruelty, lesbianism, suicide. Harrowing but repetitious, and the hows and whys of the girls' anger is never explored. [R]▼

Scum (1979-British) **C-98m.** **½ D: Alan Clarke. Ray Winstone, Mick Ford, John Judd, Phil Daniels, John Blundell, Ray Burdis, Julian Firth. The horrors of a borstal (British reform school). Harrowing but familiar; the accents are almost unintelligible. An earlier TV version was commissioned, then banned by the BBC. Alternate version runs 78m. [R]▼)

Seabiscuit (2003) **C-140m.** *** D: Gary Ross. Tobey Maguire, Jeff Bridges, Chris Cooper, Elizabeth Banks, Gary Stevens, William H. Macy, Kingston DuCoeur, Eddie Jones, Ed Lauter, Michael O'Neill, Royce D. Applegate, Annie Corley, Sam Bottoms; narrated by David McCullough. Astonishing true story of three men whom fate drew together in the depths of the Great Depression: a go-getting entrepreneur with a hole in his life (Bridges), an overweight jockey who's led a hardscrabble existence (Maguire), and a loner with a gift for training horses (Cooper), even a down-and-out nag like Seabiscuit. Writer-director Ross' distillation of Laura Hillenbrand's bestselling book makes all the right moves, then keeps selling the story as if it needed to be driven across. Still a beautifully crafted film. Super 35. [PG-13] ▼)

Sea Chase, The (1955) **C-117m.** **½ D: John Farrow. John Wayne, Lana Turner, Tab Hunter, David Farrar, Lyle Bettger, James Arness, Claude Akins. Strange WW2 film, with Wayne as German (!) captain of fugitive ship with unusual cargo, assorted crew, plus passenger/girlfriend Turner. CinemaScope.▼●)

Sea Gull, The (1968-British) **C-141m.** **½ D: Sidney Lumet. James Mason, Vanessa Redgrave, Simone Signoret, David Warner, Harry Andrews, Eileen Herlie, Denholm Elliott. Tasteful but reverentially slow-moving transcription of Chekhov play. Signoret's accent becomes rather disconcerting among British players, all trying to be 19th-century Russians. [G]

Sea Gypsies, The (1978) **C-101m.** *** D: Stewart Raffill. Robert Logan, Heather Rattray, Mikki Jamison-Olsen, Shannon Saylor, Cjon Damitri Patterson. Nice family adventure has Logan sailing round the world with daughters, journalist Jamison-Olsen, and little stowaway Patterson, learning to survive when shipwrecked in Alaska. Fine location filming. [G]▼

Sea Hawk, The (1940) **127m.** **** D: Michael Curtiz. Errol Flynn, Brenda Marshall, Claude Rains, Donald Crisp, Flora Robson, Alan Hale, Henry Daniell, Una O'Connor, Gilbert Roland, Edgar Buchanan. Top-notch combination of classy Warner Bros. costumer and Flynn at his dashing best in adventure on the high seas; lively balance of piracy, romance, and swordplay, handsomely photographed and staged, with rousing Erich Wolfgang Korngold score. Has nothing to do with the Sabatini novel, which was filmed faithfully in 1924. Restored for video, with additional final scene intended for British audiences, in which Queen Elizabeth I offers morale-building war-time message. Beware of shorter prints. Also shown in computer-colored version.▼●)

Sea Inside, The (2004-Spanish-French-Italian) **C-125m.** ***½ D: Alejandro Almenábar. Javier Bardem, Belén Rueda, Lola Dueñas, Mabel Rivera, Celso Bugallo, Clara Segura. A man who has lived as a quadriplegic for 28 years battles for the right to die, but his family—and even a lawyer who agrees to represent him—goes through a variety of emotions about his struggle and its possible outcome. Imaginatively told, with an extraordinary performance by Bardem. Oscar winner for Best Foreign Language Film. Scripted by the director and Mateo Gil, based on the life of Ramón Sampedro. Super 35. [PG-13]❱)

Sea Killer SEE: **Beyond the Reef**

Seance on a Wet Afternoon (1964-British) **115m.** **** D: Bryan Forbes. Kim Stanley, Richard Attenborough, Patrick Magee, Nanette Newman, Judith Donner, Gerald Sim, Maria Kazan, Margaret Lacey. Gripping drama of crazed medium Stanley involving husband Attenborough in shady project. Brilliant acting, direction in this must-see film. Forbes adapted Mark McShane's novel and coproduced the film with Attenborough. Remade in Japan in 2000 as SÉANCE. ▼)

Sea of Grass, The (1947) 131m. **½ D: Elia Kazan. Katharine Hepburn, Spencer Tracy, Melvyn Douglas, Phyllis Thaxter, Robert Walker, Edgar Buchanan, Harry Carey. Plodding drama from Conrad Richter story of farmer-rancher feud over New Mexico grasslands. Walker stands out in hardworking but unsuccessful cast.▼❶

Sea of Love (1989) C-112m. ***½ D: Harold Becker. Al Pacino, Ellen Barkin, John Goodman, Michael Rooker, William Hickey, Richard Jenkins, Christine Estabrook, Barbara Baxley, Patricia Barry, Samuel L. Jackson, Jacqueline Brookes, John Spencer. Streetwise cop, going through mid-life crisis, falls in love with a suspect while investigating a serial murder case. Tough, smart, sexy urban thriller with a dynamite script by Richard Price, a perfect role for Pacino, and a steamy showcase for Barkin. [R]▼❶

Sea of Sand SEE: **Desert Patrol**

Search, The (1948) 105m. **** D: Fred Zinnemann. Montgomery Clift, Ivan Jandl, Aline MacMahon, Jarmila Novotna, Wendell Corey. Poignant drama of American soldier Clift caring for concentration camp survivor Jandl in postwar Berlin, while the boy's mother desperately searches all Displaced Person's Camps for him. Beautifully acted and directed; won a Best Story Academy Award for Richard Schweizer and David Wechsler and a special prize for Jandl for outstanding juvenile performance. Also shown in computer-colored version.▼❶

Search and Destroy (1981) C-93m. ** D: William Fruet. Perry King, Tisa Farrow, Don Stroud, Park Jong Soo, George Kennedy. Undistinguished actioner about former South Vietnamese official Soo seeking revenge against American G.I.s King and Stroud. Filmed in 1978. [PG]▼❶

Search and Destroy (1995) C-90m. *½ D: David Salle. Griffin Dunne, Illeana Douglas, Dennis Hopper, Christopher Walken, John Turturro, Rosanna Arquette, Ethan Hawke, Martin Scorsese. A badly-in-hock worm on the outer limits of show biz schemes to obtain financing for his dream movie project, an adaptation of the pop-psychologist rantings of a men's-movement guru. Despite a black-comedy dream cast and participation by executive producer Scorsese (who directed the thematically comparable THE KING OF COMEDY), this diffuse film grows progressively out of control before collapsing entirely. Directorial debut for N.Y. artist Salle. [R] ▼❶

Searchers, The (1956) C-119m. **** D: John Ford. John Wayne, Jeffrey Hunter, Vera Miles, Ward Bond, Natalie Wood, John Qualen, Harry Carey, Jr., Olive Carey, Antonio Moreno, Henry Brandon, Hank Worden, Ken Curtis, Lana Wood, Dorothy Jordan, Pat Wayne. Superb Western saga of Wayne's relentless search for niece (Wood) kidnapped by Indians, spanning many years. Color, scenery, photography all splendid, with moving, insightful Frank Nugent script to match (based on Alan LeMay's novel). And who could ever forget that final shot? Remade and imitated many times since (CARAVANS, WINTERHAWK, GRAYEAGLE, etc.). VistaVision. ▼❶

Search for One-Eyed Jimmy, The (1996) C-82m. *½ D: Sam Henry Kass. John Turturro, Samuel L. Jackson, Steve Buscemi, Michael Badalucco, Ray "Boom Boom" Mancini, Anne Meara, Jennifer Beals, Nicholas Turturro, Aida Turturro, Holt McCallany, Sam Rockwell, Tony Sirico. Oddball story of a documentary filmmaker, fresh out of college, who returns to his old Brooklyn neighborhood and finds cinematic inspiration as his camera follows the trail of a missing local lowlife. Funny premise, fine cast, but never lives up to its promise. A must for Turturro fans, however, as most of the family turns up here. Filmed in 1993. [R]▼●

Search for Signs of Inteligent Life in the Universe, The (1991) C-120m. *** D: John Bailey. Clever re-creation of Lily Tomlin's 1985 one-woman Broadway show. Her characterizations run the gamut from bag lady (narrating the proceedings) to teen punk to New Age Woman, with much of the material in a feminist vein. Written by longtime Tomlin collaborator Jane Wagner. (The title is misspelled on purpose.) See also LILY TOMLIN, a 1986 documentary chronicling Tomlin and Wagner's preparation for the show. [PG-13] ▼❶

Search for the Mother Lode: The Last Great Treasure SEE: **Mother Lode**

Searching for Bobby Fischer (1993) C-110m. ***½ D: Steven Zaillian. Joe Mantegna, Max Pomeranc, Joan Allen, Ben Kingsley, Laurence Fishburne, Michael Nirenberg, Robert Stephens, David Paymer, William H. Macy, Dan Hedaya, Anthony Heald, Josh Mostel, Tony Shalhoub, Austin Pendleton. Compelling, surefooted drama, based on a true story: A father discovers that his 7-year-old son has a genius for chess, and enters him in competition, losing sight of what this does to the boy's psyche—and his pure enjoyment of the game. Poignant, heart-rending at times (especially for any parent) and exceptionally well done. Screenplay by first-time director Zaillian, from the book by Fred Waitzkin, who's the real-life chess whiz's father. [PG] ▼❶

Sea Serpent, The (1986-Spanish) C-92m. *½ D: Gregory Greens. Timothy Bottoms, Taryn Power, Jared Martin, Ray Milland, Gerard Tichy, Carole James. In order to clear his name, discredited captain Bottoms searches for sea monster that has been roused from the deep by A-bomb tests. Childish sci-fi with a monster depicted by puppets! Shot in 1984. Milland's last film. ▼

Season of Dreams SEE: **Stacking**

Season of the Witch (2011) **C-95m.** *½ D: Dominic Sena. Nicolas Cage, Ron Perlman, Stephen Campbell Moore, Claire Foy, Stephen Graham, Ulrich Thomsen, Christopher Lee, Brian F. O'Byrne. After 12 years of warfare in the Crusades, two dispirited knights head home across Europe, but first stop in a village where witches were executed. They are persuaded to transport a suspected witch to a distant monastery where a sacred document is stored that can deal with her. Troubles, both natural and supernatural, follow, of course. Slow, sullen, and grim-looking, with bursts of action and effects, but it all adds up to very little. Super 35. [PG-13] ▶

Sea Wall, The SEE: **This Angry Age**

Sea Wolf, The (1941) **90m.** ***½ D: Michael Curtiz. Edward G. Robinson, John Garfield, Ida Lupino, Alexander Knox, Gene Lockhart, Barry Fitzgerald, Stanley Ridges. Bristling Jack London tale of brutal but intellectual sea captain Robinson battling wits with accidental passenger Knox, as brash seaman Garfield and fugitive Lupino try to escape. Script by Robert Rossen. Originally released at 100m. Remade many times (BARRICADE, WOLF LARSEN, etc.), as well as several silent versions. Also shown in computer-colored version. ▼

Sea Wolves, The (1980-British-U.S.) **C-120m.** *** D: Andrew V. McLaglen. Gregory Peck, Roger Moore, David Niven, Trevor Howard, Barbara Kellerman, Patrick Macnee. You may have to be over 30 to like this true story of a retired British cavalry unit undertaking an espionage operation in WW2, but it's both action filled and funny. The target: a German radio transmitter on a ship in an Indian port. Moore can't shake his Bond image, and Peck struggles with his British accent, so nothing is to be taken very seriously. Script by Reginald Rose. [PG] ▼▶

Sebastian (1968-British) **C-100m.** **½ D: David Greene. Dirk Bogarde, Susannah York, Lilli Palmer, John Gielgud, Margaret Johnston, Nigel Davenport. Flashy but cluttered espionage film of counterintelligence agent Bogarde, who deciphers codes for England, becoming enmeshed in international battle of wits. Intriguing, colorful, but a bit trying; look for Donald Sutherland in a small role. ▼

Second Best (1994-British-U.S.) **C-105m.** *** D: Chris Menges. William Hurt, John Hurt, Chris Cleary Miles, Keith Allen, Jane Horrocks, Prunella Scales, Alan Cumming, Jodhi May. Pensive drama with Hurt excellent in an unusual role: an unmarried, terminally shy, 42-year-old postmaster in

a small Welsh town who attempts to adopt a deeply troubled 10-year-old boy (Miles). [PG-13] ▼●

Second Chance (1953) **C-81m.** **½ D: Rudolph Maté. Robert Mitchum, Linda Darnell, Jack Palance, Reginald Sheffield, Roy Roberts, Dan Seymour, Fortunio Bonanova, Milburn Stone. Two runaways—gambler's girlfriend Darnell and tainted prizefighter Mitchum—fall in love in Mexico. Complications arise when Palance arrives with orders to kill Darnell. OK melodrama. 3-D. ▼●▶

Second Chorus (1940) **83m.** ** D: H. C. Potter. Fred Astaire, Paulette Goddard, Artie Shaw and His Orchestra, Charles Butterworth, Burgess Meredith. Routine musical comedy with Astaire and Meredith as musicians who want to join Shaw's band; they both have designs on Goddard. Not enough music and hardly any dancing, but what's there is fun. Fred and Paulette dance to "(I Ain't Hep to That Step but I'll) Dig It." ▼▶

Second Coming of Suzanne, The (1974) **C-90m.** *½ D: Michael Barry. Sondra Locke, Paul Sand, Jared Martin, Richard Dreyfuss, Gene Barry, Penelope Spheeris. Pretentious time capsule about an egocentric counterculture filmmaker (Martin) who recruits the title character (Locke) to star in his latest epic, a re-creation of the story of Christ! At its very best, this is very bad Fellini; writer-director Barry is the son of Gene (who executive-produced). Strictly for Dreyfuss completists. Aka SUZANNE. ▼▶

Second-Hand Hearts (1981) **C-102m.** BOMB D: Hal Ashby. Robert Blake, Barbara Harris, Collin Boone, Amber Rose Gold, Bert Remsen, Shirley Stoler. Blake, beer-bellied and jowly, is Loyal Muke (rhymes with Puke), middle-aged drifter, who married Dinette Dusty (Harris) while in a drunken stupor. Pointless, confusing, overblown, a comedy that is embarrassingly unfunny. Even the usually reliable Harris can't salvage this mess. Filmed in 1979 as THE HAMSTER OF HAPPINESS. [PG]

Secondhand Lions (2003) **C-107m.** *** D: Tim McCanlies. Michael Caine, Robert Duvall, Haley Joel Osment, Kyra Sedgwick, Nicky Katt, Michael O'Neill, Deirdre O'Connell, Emmanuelle Vaugier, Josh Lucas, Adrian Pasdar. A negligent mother deposits her son with his eccentric great-uncles, who live as recluses on a quiet Texas property. The boy soon discovers that there's more to his new guardians than meets the eye, especially when Caine starts spinning tales about their globe-trotting adventures as young men. Likable, old-fashioned fairy-tale yarn is elevated by the sheer presence of its two veteran stars, and young Osment, who holds his own alongside them. If you buy into this, you'll forgive its flaws. Written by the director. Super 35. [PG] ▼▶

Second Jungle Book: Mowgli & Baloo, The SEE: **Rudyard Kipling's The Second Jungle Book: Mowgli & Baloo**

Seconds (1966) **106m.** ***½ D: John Frankenheimer. Rock Hudson, Salome Jens, John Randolph, Will Geer, Jeff Corey, Murray Hamilton, Wesley Addy. Frustrated middle-aged businessman is transformed into new identity (Hudson) but finds himself at odds with old and new life conflicts. Fascinating from start to finish, with good performances, striking camerawork by James Wong Howe; script by Lewis John Carlino. On video only in the original European version which features just over 1m. of additional footage. ▼▶

Second Sight (1989) **C-84m.** BOMB D: Joel Zwick. John Larroquette, Bronson Pinchot, Bess Armstrong, Stuart Pankin, John Schuck, James Tolkan, William Prince, Christine Estabrook, Cornelia Guest. Superpsychic Pinchot and an otherworldly entity assist ex-cop Larroquette's Second Sight Detective Agency; if that's not enough, there's a cute-'n'-perky nun as love interest! No psychic was needed to gauge how long this one would last in theaters. [PG] ▼▶

Second Thoughts (1983) **C-98m.** BOMB D: Lawrence Turman. Lucie Arnaz, Craig Wasson, Ken Howard, Anne Schedeen, Arthur Rosenberg, Peggy McCay. Dreary, laughably unrealistic account of lawyer Arnaz divorcing banker Howard and, to her regret, taking up with idealistic Wasson, who is still living in the 1960s. [PG] ▼

Secret Admirer (1985) **C-98m.** **½ D: David Greenwalt. C. Thomas Howell, Lori Loughlin, Kelly Preston, Dee Wallace Stone, Cliff De Young, Leigh Taylor-Young, Fred Ward, Casey Siemaszko, Corey Haim. Comedy of errors about an unsigned love letter that causes chain of confusion among some teenagers *and* their parents. Cute farce with some appealing performers, but surrenders to the obvious too often. Nice score by Jan Hammer. [R] ▼▶

Secret Agent (1936-British) **86m.** **½ D: Alfred Hitchcock. John Gielgud, Madeleine Carroll, Robert Young, Peter Lorre, Percy Marmont, Lilli Palmer. Strange blend of comedy and thriller elements which don't quite mesh; Carroll and Gielgud are secret agents who pose as man and wife while on assignment in Switzerland to kill enemy spy. One of Hitchcock's oddest films. ▼▶

Secret Agent, The (1996-British) **C-95m.** BOMB D: Christopher Hampton. Bob Hoskins, Patricia Arquette, Gérard Depardieu, George Spelvin, Jim Broadbent, Christian Bale, Eddie Izzard, Elizabeth Spriggs, Julian Wadham, Peter Vaughan. Stultifying adaptation of the Joseph Conrad novel about Verloc (Hoskins), an anarchist who actually is a secret agent for the Russian government in late 19th-century London; his wife (Arquette) has no idea of his activities. Guaranteed to drive you to slumber land despite its cast (including an unbilled Robin Williams). Aka JOSEPH CONRAD'S THE SECRET AGENT. [R] ▼▶

Secret Agent 00 SEE: **Operation Kid Brother**

Secretariat (2010) **C-123m.** *** D: Randall Wallace. Diane Lane, John Malkovich, Scott Glenn, James Cromwell, Dylan Walsh, Dylan Baker, Margo Martindale, Fred Dalton Thompson, Nelsan Ellis, Kevin Connolly, Eric Lange, Nestor Serrano, AJ Michalka. Entertaining story of the legendary racehorse and the woman who steered his success, Penny Chenery, a housewife and mother who strode into the man's world of horse breeding and training in Virginia in 1969 and wouldn't take no for an answer. Lane is ideal and is surrounded by well-drawn, well-cast characters in Mike Rich's finely tuned screenplay. Designed to be a crowd-pleaser, with exciting and impressive race scenes shot by Dean Semler. Super 35/HD Widescreen. [PG] ▶

Secretary (2002) **C-112m.** *** D: Steven Shainberg. James Spader, Maggie Gyllenhaal, Jeremy Davies, Patrick Bauchau, Stephen McHattie, Oz Perkins, Jessica Tuck, Amy Locane, Lesley Ann Warren. Intriguing black comedy about the relationship between a young woman, recently released from a mental institution, and her new boss, a lawyer who thrives on sadomasochism. Often fascinating exploration of obsessive (some might say sick) behavior and two people's struggle to find common ground. Goes astray toward the end, but still a bold and provocative film, with superb performances by Gyllenhaal and Spader. [R] ▼▶

Secret Beyond the Door (1948) **98m.** ** D: Fritz Lang. Joan Bennett, Michael Redgrave, Anne Revere, Barbara O'Neil, Natalie Schafer. Tedious Lang misfire along lines of Hitchcock's SUSPICION, with Bennett believing her husband is a demented murderer. ▼

Secret Ceremony (1968-British) **C-109m.** ***½ D: Joseph Losey. Elizabeth Taylor, Mia Farrow, Robert Mitchum, Pamela Brown, Peggy Ashcroft. Farrow resembles Taylor's dead daughter, Taylor resembles Farrow's dead mother, and their meeting has strange results. Excellent psychological drama. [R] ▼

Secret Friends (1992-U.S.-British) **C-97m.** BOMB D: Dennis Potter. Alan Bates, Gina Bellman, Frances Barber, Tony Doyle, Joanna David, Colin Jeavons, Ian McNeice, Davyd Harries. Amnesiac Bates is a deeply disturbed, guilt-ridden, and jealous man whose young, sexy wife (Bellman) is a constant pain to him. Film, set in part on long train journey, gives new meaning to the term "jumping back and forth in time"; result is appalling, incomprehensible mishmash. Only film to be directed by esteemed writer Dennis Potter, suggested by his novel *Ticket to Ride*. Buffs may enjoy McNeice and Harries as throwbacks to Basil Radford and Naunton Wayne.

Secret Garden, The (1949) **92m. *** D: Fred M. Wilcox. Margaret O'Brien, Herbert Marshall, Dean Stockwell, Gladys Cooper, Elsa Lanchester. Young girl who comes to live at run-down Victorian estate finds abandoned garden, devotes herself to it and eventually changes the lives of everyone living there. Vividly atmospheric film with some color sequences. Based on the classic children's book by Frances Hodgson Burnett. Remade as a TV movie in 1987 and as a feature in 1993, as well as a Broadway musical.▼

Secret Garden, The (1993) **C-101m. *** D: Agnieszka Holland. Kate Maberly, Heydon Prowse, Andrew Knott, Maggie Smith, Laura Crossley, John Lynch, Walter Sparrow, Irène Jacob. Handsome remake of the children's classic, with Maberly as the 10-year-old orphan who restores an abandoned garden in her uncle's eerie Victorian manor. Well crafted, but doesn't sustain the drama of its story as well as the 1949 version. Francis Ford Coppola was executive producer. [G]▼●)

Secret Honor (1984) **C-90m. ***½** D: Robert Altman. Philip Baker Hall. Richard Nixon, with a Chivas Regal assist, paces around his study in a near-psychotic rail against Hiss, Castro, Ike, Kissinger, and anyone named Kennedy. Hall's one-man stage show is fluidly filmed and outrageously conceived—a titillating one-of-a-kind for anyone who rooted for Khrushchev in the Kitchen Debates. Aka LORDS OF TREASON.▼)

Secret in Their Eyes, The (2009-Argentinean-Spanish) **C-130m. *** D: Juan José Campanella. Ricardo Darín, Soledad Villamil, Guillermo Francella, Pablo Rago, Javier Godino, José Luis Gioia. Retired criminal-court employee visits his longtime colleague, now a judge, for whom he's always had deep feelings, to tell her that he plans to write about a case they worked on 25 years ago. The rape and murder of a beautiful young woman had troubling consequences for them both—but they've never discussed it. Multifaceted drama alternates between the past and present, combining murder mystery, love story, character study, and pointed criticism of Argentina's corrupt judicial system in the 1970s. Smart, witty, sinuous storytelling, adapted from Eduardo Sacheri's novel by the author and director Campanella. Oscar winner for Best Foreign Language Film. HD Widescreen. [R]●

Secret Life of an American Wife, The

(1968) **C-92m. *** D: George Axelrod. Walter Matthau, Anne Jackson, Patrick O'Neal, Edy Williams, Richard Bull, Paul Napier. Talky, generally unfunny farce about neglected wife who decides to pose as a call girl with one of her husband's clients—a screen lover (Matthau). Disappointing next to the writer-director's hilarious LORD LOVE A DUCK. [R]▼

Secret Life of Bees, The (2008) **C-110m. *** D: Gina Prince-Bythewood. Queen Latifah, Dakota Fanning, Jennifer Hudson, Alicia Keys, Sophie Okonedo, Paul Bettany, Nate Parker, Tristan Wilds, Hilarie Burton. Emotional journey set in the deep South of 1964. An unloved girl flees from her abusive father, with her black housekeeper in tow, and finds refuge in the home of a warmhearted woman (Latifah) who lives with her two sisters and operates a thriving business manufacturing honey. Here the two lost souls discover an oasis that almost makes them forget the brutality they've left behind—until ugliness rears its head once more. Sue Monk Kidd's novel is vividly brought to life by writer-director Prince-Bythewood and an ideal cast. Panavision. [PG-13]●

Secret Life of Walter Mitty, The (1947) **C-110m. **½** D: Norman Z. McLeod. Danny Kaye, Virginia Mayo, Boris Karloff, Fay Bainter, Ann Rutherford, Florence Bates, Thurston Hall. Formula comedy casts Danny as milquetoast who dreams of manly glory. Not much Thurber here, but daydream sequences are lots of fun, and so is Kaye's famous "Anatole of Paris" patter number. Young Robert Altman, smiling and smoking a cigarette, appears as an extra in a nightclub scene with Kaye.▼●)

Secret Life of Words, The (2005-Spanish) **C-115m. *** D: Isabel Coixet. Sarah Polley, Tim Robbins, Javier Cámara, Sverre Anker Ousdal, Eddie Marsan, Julie Christie, Daniel Mays, Leonor Watling. An emotionally remote young woman who works robotically at a factory job is ordered to take a vacation by her boss. Instead, she volunteers to serve as nurse to a severe-burn victim (Robbins) on an oil rig. The insular, isolated life on the rig—which has only a skeleton crew in the wake of a terrible accident—suits her fine, but her patient persists in trying to get her to open up. Intriguing character study with a great performance by Polley and agreeable sketches of the motley characters who work on the rig. Written by the director.●

Secret Lives of Dentists, The (2002) **C-105m. *** D: Alan Rudolph. Campbell Scott, Hope Davis, Denis Leary, Robin Tunney, Jon Patrick Walker, Kevin Carroll, Kate Clinton, Lydia Jordan, Cassidy Hinkle. Intelligent, absorbing scenes from a marriage about a suburban dentist couple with three daughters. Scott suspects his wife is having an affair, and his decision not to confront her results in his summoning up visions of his most difficult patient (Leary). Benefits from two terrific lead performances and wry direction from Rudolph. Only sign of halitosis: a little Leary, as Scott's ranting, chain-smoking id, goes a long way. Based on the Jane Smiley novella *The Age of Grief*, adapted by playwright Craig Lucas. [R] ▼◗

Secret of Dorian Gray, The SEE: **Dorian Gray**

Secret of Dr. Mabuse, The SEE: **1,000 Eyes of Dr. Mabuse, The**

Secret of Kells, The (2009-Irish-French-Belgian) **C-75m.** ******* D: Tomm Moore. Voices of Brendan Gleeson, Evan McGuire, Christen Mooney, Liam Hourican, Mick Lally, Michael McGrath. Set in a 9th-century Irish monastery, this stylish and compelling animated feature about the creation of the legendary illuminated Book of Kells is told through the eyes of young Brendan, the abbot's nephew. While the abbot oversees construction of a wall to keep Viking invaders at bay, Brendan assists the Book's master illustrator by venturing into the woods for berries to make ink. There he encounters life-or-death situations—and a magical fairy intent on protecting her forest. Visual tour-de-force produced in traditional hand-drawn form, aimed at older children and adults. Surprised Hollywood by coming "out of nowhere" to earn a much-deserved Oscar nomination.◗

Secret of My Success, The (1987) **C-110m.** ****½** D: Herbert Ross. Michael J. Fox, Helen Slater, Richard Jordan, Margaret Whitton, John Pankow, Fred Gwynne, Elizabeth Franz, Christopher Durang, Mercedes Ruehl. Naive but bright, ambitious young man from the sticks hustles his way into the corporate world of N.Y.C., deftly juggling the various complications he encounters. Likable comedy goes on too long, gets most of its juice from Fox's energetic and appealing performance. [PG-13] ▼◗

Secret of NIMH, The (1982) **C-82m.** ****½** D: Don Bluth. Voices of Elizabeth Hartman, Derek Jacobi, Dom DeLuise, John Carradine, Peter Strauss. When her family homestead is threatened, a young widowed mouse seeks help, and comes upon a secret society of superintelligent rats. Well-animated adaptation of Robert C. O'Brien's prize-winning children's book, but not as involving, or as well paced, as it ought to be. First feature from Don Bluth Productions, the studio founded by a group of former Disney artists. Shannen Doherty is the voice of one of the mice children. Followed by a direct-to-video sequel. [G]▼◗

Secret of Roan Inish, The (1994) **C-102m.** ******* D: John Sayles. Jeni Courtney, Eileen Colgan, Mick Lally, Richard Sheridan, John Lynch. Gentle, charming tale of a girl who is sent to live with her grandparents on the west coast of Ireland and discovers the myths and magic that have affected her

family. A "small" story to be sure, but it gradually works its spell on you, with an admirably unsentimental tone (perfectly embodied in solemn young Courtney), moody cinematography from Haskell Wexler, and remarkable "performances" from the seals and gulls that populate the film. Adapted from Rosalie Frye's novella *The Secret of Ron Mor Skerry* by director Sayles, who also edited. [PG] ▼◗

Secret of Santa Vittoria, The (1969) **C-140m.** ****½** D: Stanley Kramer. Anthony Quinn, Anna Magnani, Virna Lisi, Hardy Kruger, Sergio Franchi, Renato Rascel, Eduardo Ciannelli, Giancarlo Giannini, Valentina Cortese. Entertaining comedy from Robert Crichton's novel of Italian town which hides a million bottles of wine from occupying Germans in WW2. Story wanders, however, with needless subplots that make it overlong. Kruger excellent as civilized German officer. Panavision. [M/PG]▼◗

Secret of the Grain, The (2007-French) **C-154m.** ******* D: Abdellatif Kechiche. Habib Boufares, Hafsia Herzi, Faridah Benkhetache, Abdelhamid Aktouche, Bouraouïa Marzouk, Hatika Karaoui, Alice Houri. Robust, often startlingly realistic slice of life about a Tunisian immigrant who's laid off from his longtime job at a French shipyard. We meet his large, boisterous family, including his ex-wife (who's a wonderful cook), his longtime mistress, and her loving, self-possessed daughter. Through their conversations, arguments, and everyday encounters we assemble a richly detailed portrait of one man's legacy to his real and extended family—and where they stand in modern French society—as everyone pitches in to help him turn an abandoned freighter into a restaurant. Overlong but rewarding. Written by the director.◗

Secret of the Red Orchid, The SEE: **Puzzle of the Red Orchid, The**

Secret Places (1985-British) **C-96m.** ****½** D: Zelda Barron. Marie-Theres Relin, Tara MacGowran, Claudine Auger, Jenny Agutter, Cassie Stuart, Ann-Marie Gwatkin. Two schoolgirls from very different backgrounds form a friendship that leads to heartbreak on the eve of WW2; set in small English village. Warm, often moving film that somehow falls short. Lead roles are well played by Relin (daughter of Maria Schell) and MacGowran (daughter of Jack MacGowran). [PG]▼

Secret Policeman's Other Ball, The (1982-British) **C-91m.** ******* D: Julien Temple, Roger Graef. John Cleese, Peter Cook, Michael Palin, Graham Chapman, Terry Jones, Pete Townshend, Sting, Phil Collins, Eric Clapton, Jeff Beck, Eleanor Bron, Pamela Stephenson, Alexei Sayle. Poorly photographed but entertaining distillation of two concerts (in 1979 and 1981) organized as fund-raisers for Amnesty International. Almost as much music as comedy, but several funny bits by Cook and the Python boys stand out, including hilarious "Cheese Shop" routine. [R]▼◗

Secret Rapture (1993-British) **C-96m.** ** D: Howard Davies. Juliet Stevenson, Joanne Whalley-Kilmer, Penelope Wilton, Neil Pearson, Alan Howard, Robert Stephens. Disappointing psychological thriller about vulnerable Stevenson, who was extremely close to her just-deceased father, and who must contend with her shrill, tyrannical sister (Wilton). Good cast flounders in David Hare's one-note script (based on his play); much of its bite regarding greed and business-as-usual amorality in Thatcherite England has been toned down. [R]▼●

Secrets (1971) **C-86m.** *½ D: Philip Saville. Jacqueline Bisset, Per Oscarsson, Shirley Knight Hopkins, Robert Powell, Tarka Kings, Martin C. Thurley. A husband, wife, and daughter all have sexual experiences during the course of a day, which must remain secrets. Dull, somewhat pretentious film notable only for nude Bisset in passionate lovemaking scene. Released in 1978. [R]▼

Secrets & Lies (1996-British) **C-142m.** ***½ D: Mike Leigh. Brenda Blethyn, Marianne Jean-Baptiste, Timothy Spall, Phyllis Logan, Claire Rushbrook, Elizabeth Berrington, Michele Austin, Alison Steadman. Another of filmmaker Leigh's compelling portraits of ordinary people and the sometimes extraordinary circumstances of their lives; here, a young black woman goes in search of her birth parents and discovers that her mother is a working-class white woman. Emotionally wrenching at times, but also endearingly funny. Superlative performances spark this long, deliberately paced, but rewarding slice of life. [R]▼●◗

Secrets of Women (1952-Swedish) **114m.** *** D: Ingmar Bergman. Anita Bjork, Karl-Arne Holmsten, Jarl Kulle, Maj-Britt Nilsson, Birger Malmsten, Eva Dahlbeck, Gunnar Bjornstrand. Episodic early Bergman drama about several women in a summer house who confide about their relationships with their men. Final sequence, with Dahlbeck and Bjornstrand trapped in an elevator, is most fascinating.▼

Secret Things (2002-French) **C-112m.** *½ D: Jean-Claude Brisseau. Coralie Revel, Sabrina Seyvecou, Roger Mirmont, Fabrice Deville, Blandine Bury, Olivier Soler, Viviane Théophildès. A jaded exotic dancer befriends a shy young woman and both use their seductive powers to rise in the business world, with unforeseen consequences. Laughably pretentious treatise on love, voyeurism, and sexual politics grows more ludicrous as it goes on and, despite copious nudity, is never as shocking or as probing as it thinks it is.◗

Secret War of Harry Frigg, The (1968) **C-110m.** ** D: Jack Smight. Paul Newman, Sylva Koscina, Andrew Duggan, Tom Bosley, John Williams, Vito Scotti, James Gregory. Noncom soldier selected to free five generals held captive during WW2 in this slick but inane comedy, one of Newman's few real losers. Techniscope.▼◗

Secret Weapon SEE: **Sherlock Holmes and the Secret Weapon**

Secret Window (2004) **C-95m.** ** D: David Koepp. Johnny Depp, John Turturro, Maria Bello, Timothy Hutton, Charles S. Dutton, Len Cariou, Joan Haney. A creepy stranger knocks on the door of a writer's rural lakeside house and accuses him of plagiarizing one of his stories. As the man's threats grow more ominous, the writer begins to wonder if he's going crazy—which also concerns his ex-wife and the local sheriff. Writer-director Koepp's adaptation of a Stephen King novella repeatedly teases the audience but offers very little suspense. The ending isn't much of a revelation, and even the significance of the title is trifling. Depp's presence is the film's major asset. Super 35. [PG-13]▼◗

Secret Yearnings SEE: **Good Luck, Miss Wyckoff**

Secuestro Express (2005-Venezuelan) **C-86m.** ** D: Jonathan Jakubowicz. Mía Maestro, Rubén Blades, Carlos Julio Molina, Pedro Perez, Carlos Madera, Jean Paul Leroux. Tarantinoesque film focuses on a young upper-middle-class couple kidnapped in broad daylight by three thugs who demand a ransom from the girl's wealthy father. As they are taken on a wild ride through the bowels of modern-day Caracas, they attempt to turn the tables on their abductors. If motion sickness is a problem, it might be wise to skip this frenetic, fast-paced picture. Jakubowicz shoots this like a video game, squandering an opportunity to say something serious about an ongoing crisis in many countries. [R]◗

Seducers, The SEE: **Death Game**

Seducing Dr. Lewis (2003-Canadian) **C-108m.** **½ D: Jean-François Pouliot. Raymond Bouchard, Dominic Michon-Dagenais, Guy-Daniel Tremblay, Nadia Droun, Rita Lafontaine, Roc LaFortune, Réal Bossé, Guy Vaillancourt. Start with LOCAL HERO, throw in a little THE FULL MONTY, mix with WAKING NED DEVINE and you have the recipe for this harmless comic tale of a small fishing village promised a much-desired new factory if they can lure a full-time M.D. to their town. Filled with the usual assortment of oddballs one finds in this type of film; the setting, Québec's Harrington Harbour Island, is gorgeous. Original French title: LA GRANDE SÉDUCTION.▼◗

Seduction, The (1982) **C-104m.** BOMB D: David Schmoeller. Morgan Fairchild,

Michael Sarrazin, Vince Edwards, Andrew Stevens, Colleen Camp, Wendy Smith Howard. A flashy L.A. TV newswoman is terrorized by a persistent fan. Preposterous, derivative film is neither suspenseful nor titillating, despite its title and sexy star (in her first movie vehicle). Super 35. [R]▼❶

Seduction of Joe Tynan, The (1979) **C-107m. **½ D:** Jerry Schatzberg. Alan Alda, Barbara Harris, Meryl Streep, Rip Torn, Charles Kimbrough, Melvyn Douglas. Earnest but shallow drama (written by Alda) about young senator who faces moral dilemmas while climbing political ladder in Washington. Ludicrous resolution really hurts film as a whole. [R]▼❶

Seduction of Mimi, The (1972-Italian) **C-89m. *** D:** Lina Wertmuller. Giancarlo Giannini, Mariangela Melato, Agostina Belli, Elena Fiore. Mimi is actually a man (Giannini) whose stubbornness and stupidity get him into trouble politically and sexually. Climactic scene where he tries to make love to an impossibly obese woman is unforgettable. Entertaining film was later Americanized as WHICH WAY IS UP? Released in the U.S. in 1974. [R]▼

Seed of Chucky (2004) **C-87m. ** D:** Don Mancini. Jennifer Tilly, Hannah Spearritt, John Waters, Redman, Keith-Lee Castle, Steve Lawton, Jason Flemyng, Tony Gardner; voices of Billy Boyd, Brad Dourjf. Fifth in the CHILD'S PLAY puppet-horror franchise is the silliest yet, as Hollywood decides to make a movie based on the (now-deceased) Chucky and Tiffany legend. Son Glen (voiced by LORD OF THE RINGS star Boyd) gets wind of it and comes to L.A. to bring his parents back to life, and they wreak havoc on the production. Tilly plays herself, taking no prisoners in an over-the-top self-portrait that garners the movie's only real laughs. Series creator-writer Mancini directs for the first time and might want to hand himself a better script next time. [R] ▼❶

Seeing Other People (2004) **C-90m. *** D:** Wally Wolodarsky. Jay Mohr, Julianne Nicholson, Lauren Graham, Bryan Cranston, Josh Charles, Jonathan Davis, Matt Davis, Andy Richter, Helen Slater, Liz Phair, Alex Borstein, Mimi Rogers. Small-scale but smart, funny comedy, set in L.A., about a happy couple on the verge of getting married when she decides they ought to have sexual experiences with other people before they tie the knot. Well cast and well written by the director and Maya Forbes, sitcom veterans who are married in real life. Super 35. [R] ▼❶

Seeker: The Dark is Rising, The (2007) **C-99m. ** D:** David L. Cunningham. Alexander Ludwig, Ian McShane, Frances Conroy, Christopher Eccleston, Gregory Smith, Amelia Warner, James Cosmo, Wendy Crewson. Youngsters may appreciate this formulaic fantasy-adventure, based on Susan Cooper's novel, about a plucky adolescent (Ludwig) who learns on his 14th birthday that he's destined to save the human race from the forces of darkness. Adults are more likely to dismiss this action-packed yet oddly uninvolving trifle as a knockoff of the HARRY POTTER films. Super 35. [PG]❶

Seems Like Old Times (1980) **C-102m. *** D:** Jay Sandrich. Goldie Hawn, Chevy Chase, Charles Grodin, Robert Guillaume, Harold Gould, George Grizzard, Yvonne Wilder, T. K. Carter. Neil Simon's homage to 1930s screwball farces is quite enjoyable, with Goldie as a good-hearted lawyer whose ex-husband (Chase) disrupts her life and threatens the career of her new spouse (Grodin). Funny lines and situations all the way up to pointless finale. Feature debut of TV comedy director Sandrich. [PG]▼❶

See No Evil (1971-British) **C-89m. *** D:** Richard Fleischer. Mia Farrow, Dorothy Alison, Robin Bailey, Diane Grayson, Lila Kaye. Terrifying chiller by Brian Clemens; blind girl slowly discovers that her uncle's entire family has been murdered and that the killer is silently stalking her. Watch out for the boots. British title: BLIND TERROR. [PG]▼❶

See No Evil (2006) **C-83m. *½ D:** Gregory Dark. Kane, Christina Vidal, Michael J. Pagan, Samantha Noble, Steven Vidler. Formulaic slasher pic aimed at genre fans with an insatiable appetite for eye gouging and flesh ripping. World Wrestling Entertainment superstar Kane (real name: Glen Jacobs) is suitably humongous as a hulking psycho who annihilates overage juvenile delinquents in a gone-to-seed hotel. [R]❶

See No Evil, Hear No Evil (1989) **C-103m. ** D:** Arthur Hiller. Richard Pryor, Gene Wilder, Joan Severance, Kevin Spacey, Kirsten Childs, Alan North, Anthony Zerbe. Wilder and Pryor are reteamed in this stupid comedy about a deaf man and a blind man who inadvertently become murder suspects and take it on the lam, hoping to catch the real killers. Five writers (including Wilder) are credited for this labored, foul-mouthed comedy; two such talented stars deserve better. [R]▼❶

See Spot Run (2001) **C-94m. *½ D:** John Whitesell. David Arquette, Michael Clarke Duncan, Leslie Bibb, Paul Sorvino, Joe Viterelli, Angus T. Jones, Steven R. Schirripa, Anthony Anderson. A bumbling mailman and his would-be girlfriend's son adopt a runaway dog that turns out to be an FBI agent targeted for assassination by mobster Sorvino. Clumsy slapstick comedy for kids has only a few funny moments and a main character who's an imbecile. This represents the combined efforts of five writers! [PG]▼❶

See You in the Morning (1989) **C-119m. ** D:** Alan J. Pakula. Jeff Bridges, Alice Krige, Farrah Fawcett, Linda Lavin, Drew Barrymore, Lukas Haas, David Dukes, Frances Sternhagen, Theodore Bikel, George Hearn, Macaulay Culkin, Robin Bartlett. Bridges and Krige follow a bumpy road to a second marriage (for both of them), trying to erase bad memories and lingering problems . . . and having to win over each other's children. Overall intelligence, warmth, and gentility cannot overcome a certain patness (and forced cuteness) in director Pakula's script—or the greater problem of not knowing when to wrap things up. [PG-13]**▼●◗**

Seize the Day (1986) C-93m. ***½ D: Fielder Cook. Robin Williams, Joseph Wiseman, Jerry Stiller, Glenne Headly. Williams is outstanding as Tommy Wilhelm, pushing 40 and a failure by society's standards, who's broke, much abused, and desperate for love. Wiseman and Stiller offer fine support as his coldhearted father and a con man he naively trusts. A small masterpiece, like the Saul Bellow novel on which it's based, with a faithful screenplay by Ronald Ribman. Plenty of familiar faces in small roles: Tony Roberts, Richard Shull, John Fiedler, Jo Van Fleet, William Hickey, Eileen Heckart, many others.**▼●◗**

Seizure (1974-Canadian) C-93m. ** D: Oliver Stone. Jonathan Frid, Martine Beswick, Christina Pickles, Joe Sirola, Herve Villechaize, Mary Woronov, Troy Donahue. Stone's directorial debut is stylish but incoherent shocker in which novelist Frid, his family and friends are forced to play games of death by trio of evil weirdos who may or may not be his nightmares come to life. [PG]**▼◗**

Selena (1997) C-130m. **½ D: Gregory Nava. Jennifer Lopez, Edward James Olmos, Jon Seda, Constance Marie, Jacob Vargas, Lupe Ontiveros, Jackie Guerra, Rebecca Lee Meza. Glossy, congenially corny biography of the spirited young Tejano singer whose dreams of showbiz fame were cut short by her murder (just as she was about to win success as a cross-over performer). Lopez offers a dynamic, star-making turn as Selena and Olmos also scores as her loving but possessive father. Ironically, the film does more to solidify Selena's celebrity than she was able to accomplish in her short lifetime. Super 35. [PG]**▼●◗**

Seminole (1953) C-87m. **½ D: Budd Boetticher. Rock Hudson, Barbara Hale, Anthony Quinn, Richard Carlson, Hugh O'Brian, Russell Johnson, Lee Marvin, James Best. Capable cast in unusual drama about earnest cavalry lieutenant Hudson trying to help Indian tribe's efforts to remain free of white man law.

Semi-Pro (2008) C-91m. ** D: Kent Alterman. Will Ferrell, Woody Harrelson, André Benjamin, Maura Tierney, Andrew Daly, Will Arnett, Andy Richter, Rob Corddry, Jackie Earle Haley, David Koechner, Kristen Wiig, Ed Helms, Patti LaBelle, Tim Meadows. Retro-'70s comedy about a one-hit wonder disco crooner (Ferrell)

who buys a struggling Detroit basketball team. Installing himself as player, owner, and chief promoter, he attempts to make the team NBA-worthy with a little help from a fading vet hoopster (Harrelson) and a raw-talented up-and-comer (Benjamin). Profane, silly movie tries to do for basketball what SLAP SHOT did for hockey . . . but Ferrell's shtick is wearing thin by now. Super 35. [R]**◗**

Semi-Tough (1977) C-108m. *** D: Michael Ritchie. Burt Reynolds, Kris Kristofferson, Jill Clayburgh, Robert Preston, Bert Convy, Lotte Lenya, Roger E. Mosley, Richard Masur, Carl Weathers, Brian Dennehy, Ron Silver. Easygoing comedy about two football stars and their mutual girlfriend wanders too much to hit any major targets but has some funny moments. Reynolds' charm makes up for film's other deficiencies. Adapted from Dan Jenkins' novel by Ring Lardner, Jr. (who took his name off the credits) and Walter Bernstein. Later a brief TV series. [R]**▼●◗**

Sender, The (1982-British) C-91m. *** D: Roger Christian. Kathryn Harrold, Zeljko Ivanek, Shirley Knight, Paul Freeman, Sean Hewitt, Harry Ditson. Solid thriller about telepathic, suicidal Ivanek, unable to control his powers, who transfers his nightmares to psychiatrist Harrold and causes havoc in a hospital. Very good of its type. [R]**▼●◗**

Send Me No Flowers (1964) C-100m. *** D: Norman Jewison. Rock Hudson, Doris Day, Tony Randall, Clint Walker, Paul Lynde, Hal March, Edward Andrews, Patricia Barry. Hypochondriac Rock, convinced he has a short time to live, has Randall find new husband for wife Doris. Funny script by Julius J. Epstein; Lynde is a riot as aggressive cemetery plot salesman.**▼●◗**

Seniors, The (1978) C-87m. ** D: Rod Amateau. Jeffrey Byron, Gary Imhof, Dennis Quaid, Lou Richards, Priscilla Barnes, Alan Reed, Edward Andrews, Robert Emhardt, Alan Hewitt. Four collegians open a bogus sex clinic, which mushrooms into a multimillion-dollar business. Alternately silly and satirical, with some innocuous nudity thrown in. Veteran character actors help a great deal. Written by Stanley (PILLOW TALK) Shapiro. Video title: THE SENIOR. [R]**▼◗**

Sense and Sensibility (1995) C-135m. ***½ D: Ang Lee. Emma Thompson, Alan Rickman, Kate Winslet, Hugh Grant, James Fleet, Harriet Walter, Gemma Jones, Elizabeth Spriggs, Robert Hardy, Greg Wise, Imelda Staunton, Imogen Stubbs, Hugh Laurie, Emilie François, Tom Wilkinson. Vivid, contemporary reading of Jane Austen's novel about two newly impoverished sisters—one impulsive and flirtatious, the other repeatedly thwarted and forced to suppress her feelings of love. Perfectly cast and performed, a spirited and moving look at social mores and how disparate personalities dealt with them in early 19th-century England. Thompson won an Oscar for Best Screenplay Adaptation. [PG]▼●▶

Senseless (1998) **C-93m.** ** D: Penelope Spheeris. Marlon Wayans, David Spade, Matthew Lillard, Rip Torn, Brad Dourif, Tamara Taylor, Richard McGonagle. Embroiled in cutthroat competition for a job, college business major gets a dose of one-upmanship when he agrees to take an injection of sense-enhancing "green stuff" as part of a campus lab experiment. Beware those side effects, and beware a comedy in which guinea pig Wayans outmugs even another Marlon (Brando—when he played mad Dr. Moreau). Torn is amusing as the kind of corporate smoothie he can now play in his sleep. [R]▼●▶

Sense of Loss, A (1972-U.S.-Swiss) **C/B&W-135m.** *** D: Marcel Ophuls. Thoughtful documentary about the continuing, never-ending political conflict—and violence—in Northern Ireland. Not up to Ophuls' previous film, THE SORROW AND THE PITY, but still heartbreaking in its most powerful moments.▼

Senso (1954-Italian) **C-115m.** **½ D: Luchino Visconti. Alida Valli, Farley Granger, Massimo Girotti, Heinz Moog. Carefully paced study of human emotions, chronicling the relationship between earthy, materialistic Austrian officer Granger and his aristocratic Italian mistress (Valli). An intriguing union of the neorealism of Visconti's earlier work and the lush romanticism often found in his later films. Retitled WANTON CONTESSA. English-language version, titled THE WANTON COUNTESS, features dialogue by Tennessee Williams and Paul Bowles!▼▶

Sensuous Nurse, The (1976-Italian) **C-78m.** *½ D: Nello Rossati. Ursula Andress, Jack Palance, Duilio Del Prete, Luciana Paluzzi, Lino Toffolo, Mario Pisu. Voluptuous Ursula hires on to help hasten the demise of a wealthy vintner with a heart condition by keeping his pulse racing in this smarmy sex comedy. Ursula does look great in the nude, however. [R]▼▶

Sentinel, The (1977) **C-93m.** ** D: Michael Winner. Cristina Raines, Ava Gardner, Chris Sarandon, Burgess Meredith, Sylvia Miles, Jose Ferrer, Arthur Kennedy, John Carradine, Christopher Walken, Eli Wallach, Jerry Orbach, Jeff Goldblum, Beverly D'Angelo, Martin Balsam, William Hickey, Tom Berenger. Slick but empty-headed shocker about N.Y.C. fashion model who rents Brooklyn Heights brownstone, finds it's full of demons and she's to be the next sentinel guarding the gateway to Hell. Good cast makes it somewhat endurable, but climax is awfully yucky. Freely based on Jeffrey Konvitz' best-seller. [R]▼▶

Sentinel, The (2006) **C-107m.** **½ D: Clark Johnson. Michael Douglas, Kiefer Sutherland, Eva Longoria, Kim Basinger, Martin Donovan, Ritchie Coster, Blair Brown, David Rasche, Paul Calderon, Gloria Reuben. Decorated Secret Service Agent—who's having an affair with the First Lady—is blackmailed, which leads another agent (and onetime friend) to believe he's the "inside man" suspected of conspiring to kill the President. Slick action-thriller is lively and entertaining until a crucial moment three-quarters of the way through, when it goes flat and credibility becomes a serious issue. Director Johnson has a small but significant role as one of Douglas' fellow agents. Super 35. [PG-13]▶

Separate Lies (2005-British) **C-87m.** *** D: Julian Fellowes. Tom Wilkinson, Emily Watson, Rupert Everett, Hermione Norris, John Warnaby, Richenda Carey, Linda Bassett, John Neville. The lives of a well-heeled barrister (Wilkinson) and his wife (Watson) are disrupted upon the arrival in their community of good-looking, patronizing Everett. Adding to the mix is a hit-and-run accident in which their housekeeper's husband is killed. Razor-sharp drama explores the reasons why people lie to themselves and to those closest to them, and puts forth the notion that there is turmoil in even the most seemingly placid lives. The three leads—particularly Wilkinson—are in fine form. First-time director Fellowes scripted, from Nigel Balchin's 1951 novel *A Way Through the Wood.* [R]▶

Separate Lives (1995) **C-102m.** *½ D: David Madden. Linda Hamilton, James Belushi, Vera Miles, Elisabeth Moss, Drew Snyder. Limp psychosexual thriller has detective (Belushi) on the trail of a murderer who's killing the patients of his sexy group therapist (Hamilton)—while she's convinced she's committing them herself. Predictable and bland. [R]▼

Separate Peace, A (1972) **C-104m.** BOMB D: Larry Peerce. John Heyl, Parker Stevenson, William Roerick, Peter Brush, Victor Bevine, Scott Bradbury. Supposedly sensitive story of two roommates in a 1940s prep school, taken from John Knowles' overrated novel, is enough to make anyone gag. Story is morbid, acting amateurish, and direction has no feeling at all for the period. A total bummer. Remade for cable TV in 2003. [PG]▼

Separate Tables (1958) **99m.** **** D: Delbert Mann. Burt Lancaster, Rita Hayworth, David Niven, Deborah Kerr, Wendy Hiller, Gladys Cooper, Cathleen Nesbitt, Rod Taylor, Felix Aylmer. Terence Rattigan's pair of romantic playlets set at English seaside resort are reworked here into superb drama in the GRAND HOTEL vein; Lancaster and Hayworth are divorced couple trying to make another go of it, Hiller is his timid mistress,

Niven a supposed war hero, Kerr a lonely spinster dominated by mother Cooper. Bouquets all around, especially to Oscar winners Niven and Hiller. Screenplay by Rattigan and John Gay.▼○▶

Separate Ways (1981) **C-92m.** ** D: Howard Avedis. Karen Black, Tony LoBianco, Arlene Golonka, David Naughton, Jack Carter, Sharon Farrell, William Windom, Robert Fuller, Noah Hathaway, Sybil Danning. Low-budget U.S. answer to A MAN AND A WOMAN has former race-car driver LoBianco suffering marital problems with wife Black, exacerbated by her one-night stand with younger man Naughton. Good cast is wasted. [R]▼▶

September (1987) **C-82m.** ** D: Woody Allen. Denholm Elliott, Mia Farrow, Elaine Stritch, Sam Waterston, Jack Warden, Dianne Wiest. Six people vent their angst during a weekend in the country. Intelligent and well acted, but after a while it dawns on you that there's no earthly reason to be interested in these people and their whining. Stritch is a standout as Mia's flamboyant mom, and it's hard to completely dislike a film that plugs jazz pianist Art Tatum so vigorously. Set in Vermont but filmed completely on a soundstage. Writer-director Allen fared better with his earlier drama, INTERIORS. [PG]▼○▶

September Dawn (2007) **C-111m.** **½ D: Christopher Cain. Jon Voight, Trent Ford, Tamara Hope, Jon Gries, Huntley Ritter, Krisinda Cain, Shaun Johnston, Lolita Davidovich, Terence Stamp. Fictionalized *Romeo and Juliet*–style love story about a Mormon boy and a Christian girl in 1857 Utah set against the backdrop of a controversial, real-life (if little-known) incident in which 120 men, women, and children from her wagon train are ruthlessly murdered. Film places blame for the massacre on Mormon leaders, including Brigham Young (Stamp), although this is vehemently denied by the church. Low-budget (but handsome-looking) drama blends facts with Hollywood speculation to create a fairly compelling tale. Director Cain coscripted; his son Dean has a cameo as Joseph Smith. [R]▶

September 30, 1955 (1978) **C-101m.** **½ D: James Bridges. Richard Thomas, Susan Tyrrell, Deborah Benson, Lisa Blount. Thomas Hulce, Dennis Quaid, Dennis Christopher. Arkansas undergrad, well played by Thomas, goes off his nut when James Dean dies, with tragic results for a girl friend. Original, if excessively uneven drama, is worth consideration for being one of the few films to deal at all seriously with the movie star mystique. Original title: 9/30/55. [PG]▼●

Seraphim Falls (2007) **C-115m.** *** D: David Von Ancken. Pierce Brosnan, Liam Neeson, Michael Wincott, John Robinson, Ed Lauter, Robert Baker, Jimmi Simpson,

Nate Mooney, Anjelica Huston, Kevin J. O'Connor, Shannon Zeller, Xander Berkeley, Angie Harmon, Wes Studi, Tom Noonan. Beautifully photographed (by John Toll) widescreen Western set a few years after the Civil War about a colonel who embarks on a search for a man with whom he must settle a score. Entertaining to see Neeson as a man on a mission and Brosnan using his ingenuity to avoid capture in the wide-open wilderness. Testosterone-heavy scenario is entirely watchable and offers solid roles to its two stars. Panavision. [R]▶

Séraphine (2008-French-Belgian) **C-126m.** ***½ D: Martin Provost. Yolande Moreau, Ulrich Tukur, Anne Bennent, Geneviève Mnich, Adélaïde Leroux, Nico Rogner. On the eve of WW1, a prominent German art collector on sabbatical in rural France is stunned to discover his dowdy, hardscrabble cleaning lady can paint like an angel. Reverent, restrained dual biopic of modern primitive master Séraphine de Senlis and her patron Wilhelm Uhde is an ardently devout portrait of the bliss and the madness that fuel the creative soul. Astute sense of time, place, and character sustains the film over decades. Written by Provost and Marc Abdelnour.▶

Serendipity (2001) **C-91m.** *** D: Peter Chelsom. John Cusack, Kate Beckinsale, Jeremy Piven, Molly Shannon, Eugene Levy, John Corbett, Bridget Moynahan, Lucy Gordon. A chance meeting in N.Y.C. leads to a romantic evening for Cusack and Beckinsale, but she chooses to leave it to fate to decide if they should ever see each other again. Several years later, on the eve of his wedding, Cusack decides he simply must find her. Endearing romantic comedy with appealing stars and wonderful support from Piven and Levy. Buck Henry appears unbilled. [PG-13]▼▶

Serenity (2005) **C-119m.** **½ D: Joss Whedon. Nathan Fillion, Gina Torres, Alan Tudyk, Morena Baccarin, Adam Baldwin, Jewel Staite, Sean Maher, Summer Glau, Ron Glass, Chiwetel Ejiofor, David Krumholtz, Sarah Paulson, Michael Hitchcock. Five hundred years in the future, a mercenary and his crew on the ragtag airship *Serenity* battle the powerful Alliance and try to deprogram a teenage girl whose telepathic powers have been turned to the dark side. Whedon gives fans of his canceled 2002 TV series *Firefly* a chance to round out its unfinished story, while providing a self-contained continuity for newcomers. A sort of low-rent STAR WARS with Fillion as the Han Solo–ish antihero, this feature has spunk and spirit but goes on too long. Super 35. [PG-13]▼▶

Sergeant, The (1968) **C-107m.** ** D: John Flynn. Rod Steiger, John Phillip Law, Ludmila Mikael, Frank Latimore, Elliott Sullivan. Predictable drama, set in France, about homosexual Army sergeant Steiger and his desire for handsome private Law. Director

Flynn has nice eye for detail, but overall, film doesn't make much of an impression. [R]◗

Sergeant Rutledge (1960) **C-111m.** ✱✱✱ D: John Ford. Jeffrey Hunter, Woody Strode, Constance Towers, Billie Burke, Carleton Young, Juano Hernandez, Willis Bouchey, Mae Marsh, Hank Worden, Jack Pennick. Arresting story of a black U.S. cavalryman on trial for rape and murder; his story is pieced together in flashback during his court-martial. Unusual subject matter for its time, solidly presented by Ford (with some occasionally awkward comic relief). Strode is commanding in the central role.▼◗

Sergeant Ryker (1968) **C-85m.** ✱✱½ D: Buzz Kulik. Lee Marvin, Bradford Dillman, Vera Miles, Peter Graves, Lloyd Nolan, Murray Hamilton. Adapted from TV film *The Case Against Sergeant Ryker*, story concerns court-martial of Marvin in title role, an Army sergeant during Korean War suspected of being a traitor; Miles is his wife and Dillman the dynamic defense attorney. Aka TORN BETWEEN TWO VALUES.▼

Sergeant Steiner SEE: **Breakthrough** (1978)

Sergeants 3 (1962) **C-112m.** ✱✱½ D: John Sturges. Frank Sinatra, Dean Martin, Sammy Davis, Jr., Peter Lawford, Joey Bishop, Ruta Lee, Henry Silva. Second reworking of GUNGA DIN is amusing, but not up to 1939 original. This time it's out West with the Rat Pack as cavalry sergeants. Davis can't eclipse Sam Jaffe as Gunga Din, though. Panavision.◗

Sergeant York (1941) **134m.** ✱✱✱½ D: Howard Hawks. Gary Cooper, Walter Brennan, Joan Leslie, George Tobias, Stanley Ridges, Margaret Wycherly, Ward Bond, Noah Beery, Jr., June Lockhart. Excellent story of pacifist Alvin York (Cooper) drafted during WW1, realizing purpose of fighting and becoming hero. Oscar-winning performance by Cooper in fine, intelligent film, balancing segments of rural America with battle scenes. John Huston was one of the writers. Also available in computer-colored version.▼◗

Serial (1980) **C-86m.** ✱✱✱ D: Bill Persky. Martin Mull, Tuesday Weld, Sally Kellerman, Bill Macy, Tom Smothers, Christopher Lee, Peter Bonerz, Jennifer McAlister, Nita Talbot, Stacey Nelkin, Barbara Rhoades, Pamela Bellwood. Trenchant satire on Marin County, Cal., and its residents' obsession with various freakish fads, sexual trends, and psychological mumbo-jumbo, with a Frank Capra–esque finale. Mull (in his first starring role) plays the only sane one in the bunch. Adapted from Cyra McFadden's column and book. [R]▼◗

Serial Mom (1994) **C-93m.** ✱✱½ D: John Waters. Kathleen Turner, Sam Waterston, Ricki Lake, Matthew Lillard, Scott Wesley Morgan, Walt MacPherson, Justin Whalin, Patricia Dunnock, Mink Stole, Mary Jo Catlett, Traci Lords, Patricia Hearst, Suzanne Somers. Beaming, cheerful Turner is the perfect mom to her suburban family; she's also a serial killer, bumping off anyone who offends her sense of family values. The main target of this movie's satirical barbs are those who would turn murderers into media heroes, but it takes plenty of other potshots along the way. Blander than most of Waters' films, this works only intermittently, despite a knockout performance from Turner. [R]▼◗

Series 7: The Contenders (2001) **C-88m.** ✱✱½ D: Daniel Minahan. Brooke Smith, Glenn Fitzgerald, Marylouise Burke, Michael Kaycheck, Richard Venture, Merritt Wever, Donna Hanover, Angelina Phillips. Imagine a *Survivor*-type show where the contestants literally have to kill each other! That's the premise of this jet-black satire of reality TV. It's all a bit too ironic and postmodern for its own good, but it's still fun, in a sick vein, especially when we follow Dawn (Smith, who's terrific), the reigning champion with ten kills who happens to be pregnant and about to burst! [R]▼

Serious Man, A (2009-U.S.-French-British) **C-105m.** ✱✱½ D: Ethan Coen, Joel Coen. Michael Stuhlbarg, Richard Kind, Fred Melamed, Sari Lennick, Adam Arkin, Aaron Wolff, Jessica McManus, Amy Landecker, George Wyner, Katherine Borowitz, Yelena Shmulenson, Fyvush Finkel, Simon Helberg, Michael Lerner. Quixotic, existential, highly detailed black comedy about a Jewish man in a Midwestern suburban town in 1967 whose life falls apart, piece by piece—beginning with his wife telling him she's leaving. (This is preceded by a portentous prologue, in Yiddish.) The Coens draw on their own Midwestern Jewish upbringing for this grimly amusing fable, so anyone who grew up in a similar environment will easily relate. But one is forced to ask the same question as the film's protagonist: What does it all mean? (Other than "life's a bitch, then you die.") [R] ◗

Serious Moonlight (2009) **C-84m.** ✱✱ D: Cheryl Hines. Meg Ryan, Tim (Timothy) Hutton, Kristen Bell, Justin Long. Spurned wife takes action against her philandering husband by duct-taping him to a toilet seat in their bathroom, convinced that in time she can win back his love. Things don't go as planned. Oddball black comedy starts on a promising note but doesn't end that way, though the cast is game. Final screenplay by actress-filmmaker Adrienne Shelly; Hines' feature directing debut. [R] ◗

Serpent, The SEE: **Night Flight From Moscow**

Serpent and the Rainbow, The (1988) **C-98m.** ✱✱ D: Wes Craven. Bill Pullman, Cathy Tyson, Zakes Mokae, Paul Winfield, Brent Jennings, Theresa Merritt, Michael Gough. Ambitious (by Craven standards) but gratuitous chiller about a real-life anthropologist's experiences with black magic and voodoo in Haiti. Well done, but wallows in its atmosphere and special effects; however, Craven fans will boost the rating by a star. Based on the book by Wade Davis. [R] ▼●)

Serpent's Egg, The (1978-German-U.S.) **C-120m.** *½ D: Ingmar Bergman. Liv Ullmann, David Carradine, Gert Frobe, Heinz Bennent, Glynn Turman, James Whitmore. Smorgasbord of depravities makes story of Jewish trapeze artist in pre-WW2 Germany an overwhelmingly unpleasant movie experience. Sven Nykvist's camerawork is brilliant as usual, but Cårradine is fatally miscast. [R] ▼●

Serpico (1973) **C-129m.** ***½ D: Sidney Lumet. Al Pacino, John Randolph, Jack Kehoe, Biff McGuire, Barbara Eda-Young, Cornelia Sharpe, Tony Roberts, James Tolkan, Lewis J. Stadlen, M. Emmet Walsh, F. Murray Abraham, Kenneth McMillan. Tough, exciting filmization of Peter Maas book based on true-life accounts of N.Y.C. undercover cop whose nonconformism—and exposure of department corruption—isolate him from the force. Screenplay by Waldo Salt and Norman Wexler. Look for Judd Hirsch as a cop. Followed by a TV movie and short-lived series. [R] ▼●)

Servant, The (1963-British) **115m.** ***½ D: Joseph Losey. Dirk Bogarde, James Fox, Sarah Miles, Wendy Craig, Catherine Lacey, Patrick Magee. Insidious story of moral degradation as corrupt manservant Bogarde becomes master of employer Fox; superb study of brooding decadence. Scripted by Harold Pinter. ▼▶

Serving Sara (2002) **C-99m.** ** D: Reginald Hudlin. Matthew Perry, Elizabeth Hurley, Bruce Campbell, Cedric the Entertainer, Vincent Pastore, Amy Adams, Joe Viterelli, Terry Crews, Jerry Stiller. Lackluster comedy about a N.Y.C. process server who makes a deal with his "mark" to find her philandering husband and serve *him* with *her* divorce papers—in return for half of her take. This takes them on a bumpy road to Texas. It's a long way from IT HAPPENED ONE NIGHT. Mike Judge appears unbilled as a motel clerk. [PG-13] ▼▶

Sesame Street Presents Follow That Bird (1985) **C-88m.** **½ D: Ken Kwapis. Caroll Spinney, Jim Henson, Frank Oz, Paul Bartel, Sandra Bernhard, John Candy, Chevy Chase, Joe Flaherty, Waylon Jennings, Dave Thomas. Sweet, simple film about Sesame Street's beloved Big Bird, who's placed in foster home but tries to hitchhike back to Sesame Street. Aimed solely at young children, who should enjoy it—though for adults nothing can top Oscar the Grouch's opening anthem. Cute songs throughout. [G] ▼●)

Session 9 (2001) **C-100m.** ** D: Brad Anderson. David Caruso, Peter Mullan, Brendan Sexton III, Stephen Gevedon, Paul Guilfoyle, Josh Lucas. A ragtag asbestos-removal team's new job site is an immense, abandoned insane asylum. Since the crew doesn't get along well from the get-go, just imagine the teasing, taunting, and tensions unleashed in the dark corridors day after day. Genuinely spooky film unfortunately suffers from underdeveloped characters. Written by the director and costar Gevedon. Claustrophobics beware. HD 24P Widescreen. [R] ▼▶

Session With the Committee, A (1969) **C-90m.** **½ D: Del Jack. Peter Bonerz, Barbara Bosson, Garry Goodrow, Carl Gottlieb, Jessica Myerson, Christopher Ross, Melvin Stewart, Don Sturdy (Howard Hesseman). Filmed collection of live skits by L.A. comic troupe isn't exactly "pure" cinema, but has the same appeal as a good comedy record album. Plenty of laughs. [PG] ▼

Set It Off (1996) **C-121m.** ** D: F. Gary Gray. Jada Pinkett, Queen Latifah, Vivica A. Fox, Kimberly Elise, Blair Underwood, John C. McGinley, Anna Maria Horsford, Ella Joyce, Charlie Robinson, Chaz Lamar Shepard, Dr. Dre. Four black women from the L.A. projects decide to beat the system by robbing banks, and end up testing their friendship to deadly ends. Frustrating, overdirected film wants to be a hard-edged urban drama but relies on pyrotechnics and car chases for impact. Even worse is an unnecessary romantic subplot between Pinkett and suave banker Underwood. Latifah's powerhouse performance as a gun-toting lesbian gives the film a much needed jolt of realism. Super 35. [R] ▼●)

Set-Up, The (1949) **72m.** ***½ D: Robert Wise. Robert Ryan, Audrey Totter, George Tobias, Alan Baxter, James Edwards, Wallace Ford. Gutsy account of washed-up fighter refusing to give up or go crooked; Ryan has never been better. Art Cohn's pungent screenplay was inspired by a narrative poem(!) by Joseph Moncure March. Photographed by Milton Krasner. Played out in real time—as you'll see by the clock shown in opening and closing shots. ▼●)

Seven (1979) **C-100m.** ** D: Andy Sidaris. William Smith, Barbara Leigh, Guich Koock, Art Metrano, Martin Kove, Richard Le Pore, Susan Kiger. Brawny Smith is hired by U.S. intelligence to destroy Hawaiian crime syndicate, which he does with enthusiastic team of "specialists." Violent, sexy, tongue-in-cheek action yarn includes the "shooting the swordsman" gag later immortalized in RAIDERS OF THE LOST ARK. [R] ▼

Se7en (1995) **C-127m.** *** D: David Fincher. Brad Pitt, Morgan Freeman, Kevin Spacey, Gwyneth Paltrow, Richard Roundtree, R. Lee Ermey, John C. McGinley, Julie Araskog, Mark Boone Junior, John Cassini, Reginald E. Cathey, Peter Crombie, Hawthorne James, Michael Massee, Leland Orser, Richard Portnow. Dedicated detective (Freeman) breaks in his replacement (Pitt) during his last week before retiring—then stumbles onto the trail of a serial killer who's out to punish perpetrators of the seven deadly sins. Exceptionally well-crafted, intelligently written, and well-acted thriller . . . but also extremely unsettling, almost oppressive at times. Not much violence per se, but the film seems to wallow in the depths of human depravity it so passionately decries. Super 35. [R] ▼●❶

Seven Alone (1975) **C-96m.** **½ D: Earl Bellamy. Dewey Martin, Aldo Ray, Anne Collings, Dean Smith, Stewart Petersen. OK family-wilderness picture on true story of seven children who make perilous 2,000 mile trek West during the 1800s after their parents die en route. [G] ▼❶

Seven Beauties (1976-Italian) **C-115m.** **** D: Lina Wertmuller. Giancarlo Giannini, Fernando Rey, Shirley Stoler, Elena Fiore, Enzo Vitale. Director-writer Wertmuller's masterpiece follows a small-time Casanova through the horrors of WW2 battle and imprisonment in a concentration camp, where he learns to survive—at any cost. Giannini is superb in this harrowing, unforgettable film. [R] ▼❶

Seven Brides for Seven Brothers (1954) **C-103m.** **** D: Stanley Donen. Howard Keel, Jane Powell, Jeff Richards, Russ Tamblyn, Tommy Rall, Virginia Gibson, Julie Newmeyer (Newmar), Ruta Kilmonis (Lee), Matt Mattox. Rollicking musical perfectly integrates song, dance, and story: Keel's decision to get himself a wife (Powell) inspires his rowdy brothers to follow suit. Tuneful Johnny Mercer–Gene DePaul score (with Oscar-winning musical direction by Adolph Deutsch and Saul Chaplin), but it's Michael Kidd's energetic dance numbers that really stand out, with rare screen work by dancers Jacques D'Amboise and Marc Platt. The barn-raising sequence is an absolute knockout. Screenplay by Albert Hackett, Frances Goodrich, and Dorothy Kingsley, from a Stephen Vincent Benet story. Later a TV series and a Broadway musical. CinemaScope. ▼●❶

Seven Brothers Meet Dracula, The (1974-British-Hong Kong) **C-72m.** ** D: Roy Ward Baker. Peter Cushing, David Chiang, Julie Ege, Robin Stewart, Shih Szu, John Forbes-Robertson. Vampire hunter Van Helsing (Cushing) is in China in the late 19th century to vanquish Dracula with the help of some karate-chopping assistants. Odd blend of Kung Fu action, supernatural, and Dracula themes reportedly worked better in original 89m. version called LEGEND OF THE 7 GOLDEN VAMPIRES. Aka SEVEN GOLDEN VAMPIRES—THE LAST WARNING! Panavision. [R] ▼●❶

7 Capital Sins (1961-French-Italian) **113m.** ** D: Jean-Luc Godard, Roger Vadim, Sylvaine Dhomme, Edouard Molinaro, Philippe De Broca, Claude Chabrol, Jacques Demy. Marie-Jose Nat, Dominique Paturel, Jean-Marc Tennberg, Perrette Pradier. Potpourri of directors and talents play out modern parables concerning anger, envy, gluttony, greed, laziness, lust, and pride. Aka SEVEN DEADLY SINS and LES SEPT PECHES CAPITAUX. Dyaliscope. ▼

Seven Chances (1925) **56m.** ***½ D: Buster Keaton. Buster Keaton, T. Roy Barnes, Snitz Edwards, Ruth Dwyer, Frankie Raymond, Jules Cowles. Buster will inherit a fortune if he's married by 7:00 that evening; a miscommunication with his girlfriend leads to his pursuit by thousands of would-be brides. The highlight: a furious chase down a hill in which Buster dodges dozens of oversized boulders! One of Keaton's silent gems. That's young Jean Arthur as a switchboard operator who turns down Buster's marriage proposal. Remade as THE BACHELOR (1999). ▼●❶

Seven Days in May (1964) **118m.** *** D: John Frankenheimer. Burt Lancaster, Kirk Douglas, Fredric March, Ava Gardner, Edmond O'Brien, Martin Balsam, George Macready, Whit Bissell, Hugh Marlowe. Absorbing, believable story of military scheme to overthrow the government. Fine cast includes Lancaster as the general planning the coup and Douglas as the colonel who discovers the plot, March as U.S. President; intelligent suspense in Rod Serling screenplay from Fletcher Knebel and Charles W. Bailey novel. John Houseman made his screen acting debut in small but crucial role. Remade for cable as THE ENEMY WITHIN. ▼●❶

Seven Days to Noon (1950-British) **93m.** **** D: John Boulting. Barry Jones, Olive Sloane, Andre Morell, Sheila Manahan, Hugh Cross, Joan Hickson. Superbly paced thriller (from Paul Dehn and James Bernard's Oscar-winning story) about scientist threatening to explode atomic bomb in London if his demands are not met. Screenplay by Roy Boulting and Frank Harvey.

Seven Different Ways SEE: **Quick, Let's Get Married**

7 Faces of Dr. Lao (1964) **C-100m.** *** D: George Pal. Tony Randall, Barbara Eden, Arthur O'Connell, John Ericson, Kevin Tate, Argentina Brunetti, Noah Beery, Jr., Minerva Urecal, John Qualen, Lee Patrick. Engaging fantasy of Western town brought to its senses by parables performed by mysterious traveling circus; tour de force for Randall, who plays six roles. William Tuttle won special Oscar for makeup creations. Based on Charles G. Finney's novel *The Circus of Dr. Lao.* ▼●❶

Seven Golden Vampires—The Last Warning! SEE: **Seven Brothers Meet Dracula, The**

Seven Graves for Rogan SEE: **Time to Die, A** (1983) ▼

Seven Hours to Judgment (1988) **C-89m.**

** D: Beau Bridges. Beau Bridges, Ron Leibman, Julianne Phillips, Reggie Johnson, Al Freeman, Jr. Bridges directs himself in an earnest but farfetched revenge saga as the hapless judge whom nut case Leibman feels had been too lenient with the minority punks who killed Leibman's wife; Ron retaliates by kidnapping Beau's beautiful spouse (Phillips) and setting Bridges on a survival quest in a tough part of town. [R]▼●]

Seven Little Foys, The (1955) **C-95m.** *** D: Melville Shavelson. Bob Hope, Milly Vitale, George Tobias, Billy Gray, James Cagney. Pleasant biography of vaudevillian Eddie Foy and his performing family. Hope lively in lead role, Cagney guests as George M. Cohan; their table-top dance duet is the movie's high point. VistaVision.▼]

Seven Men From Now (1956) **C-78m.** *** D: Budd Boetticher. Randolph Scott, Gail Russell, Lee Marvin, Walter Reed, John Larch, Donald Barry. Scott tracks down seven bandits who held up Wells Fargo station and killed his wife. Solid Western, first of seven from the Scott-Boetticher team, with a script by Burt Kennedy. Marvin is terrific.]

Seven Minutes, The (1971) **C-116m.** **½ D: Russ Meyer. Wayne Maunder, Marianne McAndrew, Philip Carey, Yvonne De Carlo, Jay C. Flippen, Edy Williams, John Carradine, Harold J. Stone. Host of fine character actors fail to save laughable adaptation of Irving Wallace's best-seller about pornography trial; interesting mainly as Meyer's only "straight" film. Look for Tom Selleck as a publisher. [PG—edited from original R rating]

Seven Notes in Black SEE: **Psychic, The**

Seven-Per-Cent Solution, The (1976) **C-113m.** *** D: Herbert Ross. Nicol Williamson, Alan Arkin, Vanessa Redgrave, Robert Duvall, Laurence Olivier, Joel Grey, Samantha Eggar, Jeremy Kemp, Charles Gray, Regine. Sherlock Holmes meets Sigmund Freud in this handsome, entertaining film adapted by Nicholas Meyer from his novel. Shifts gears from serious drama to tongue-in-cheek adventure, but stays on target all the way. Nice score by John Addison. [PG]▼●]

Seven Pounds (2008) **C-123m.** *½ D: Gabriele Muccino. Will Smith, Rosario Dawson, Michael Ealy, Barry Pepper, Woody Harrelson, Elpidia Carrillo, Robinne Lee, Bill Smitrovich, Joe Nunez, Tim Kelleher, Gina Hecht. IRS agent calls on various people to determine if they're worthy of the good deeds he intends to perform on their behalf. But why? Enervating film withholds the answers so long that it's difficult to engage with Smith's tortured protagonist. As the answers become clear the film is more off-putting than ever. Strange

vehicle for the popular star. Super 35. [PG-13]]

Seven Samurai (1954-Japanese) **141m.** **** D: Akira Kurosawa. Toshiro Mifune, Takashi Shimura, Yoshio Inaba, Ko Kimura, Seiji Miyaguchi, Minoru Chiaki. Classic film about 16th-century Japanese village which hires professional warriors to fend off bandits. Kurosawa's "far-east Western" has served as model for many films since, including American remake THE MAGNIFICENT SEVEN (a title once given this film for U.S. release). The complete 208m. version is even *more* impressive for its humanity as well as its powerful action sequences.▼●]

Seven Sinners (1940) **87m.** *** D: Tay Garnett. Marlene Dietrich, John Wayne, Albert Dekker, Broderick Crawford, Anna Lee, Mischa Auer, Billy Gilbert. Alluring Dietrich makes Wayne forget about the Navy for a while in this engaging actionlove story with excellent supporting cast. Remade as SOUTH SEA SINNER.▼●]

17 Again (2009) **C-102m.** **½ D: Burr Steers. Zac Efron, Matthew Perry, Leslie Mann, Thomas Lennon, Melora Hardin, Sterling Knight, Michelle Trachtenberg, Hunter Parrish, Jim Gaffigan, Nicole Sullivan, Margaret Cho. Twenty years after a life-altering decision, a former high school basketball star (Perry) is given the opportunity to become a teenager again in order to change his future—and his lousy marriage. Efron's nuanced, intriguing performance (and a talented cast) make this otherwise predictable and uneven film enjoyable. Super 35. [PG-13]]

1776 (1972) **C-141m.** *** D: Peter H. Hunt. William Daniels, Howard da Silva, Ken Howard, Donald Madden, Ron Holgate, David Ford, Blythe Danner, Roy Poole, Virginia Vestoff, John Cullum. America's first Congress in struggle for independence from Britain provides framework for this unique musical by Sherman Edwards and Peter Stone. Almost all of the original Broadway cast remain, with Daniels as John Adams and da Silva as Benjamin Franklin leading the pack. Laserdisc version ran 176m., incorporating footage director Hunt was forced to cut from original release; he then supervised a revised edition for DVD running 166m. Panavision. [G]▼●]

Seventh Coin, The (1992) **C-95m.** *½ D: Dror Soref. Alexandra Powers, Navin Chowdhry, Peter O'Toole, John Rhys-Davies, Ally Walker, Julius Washington, Nicholas Kallsen. Teen-oriented action-adventure film lacking action and adventure. O'Toole, believing he's King Herod reincarnated, pursues two youths who have a precious coin which belonged to Herod. O'Toole looks and acts waxen. Remember: reading is fun. [PG-13]▼●]

Seventh Continent, The (1989-Austrian) **C-104m.** ***½ D: Michael Haneke. Birgit Doll, Dieter Berner, Leni Tanzer, Udo Samel, Silvia Fenz, Robert Dietl, Elisabeth Rath, Georges Kern, Georg Friedrich. Haneke's theatrical feature debut as writer-director is a disturbing account of middle-class malaise, following the lives of an ordinary (albeit emotionally disconnected) family: a husband, wife, and their young daughter. Starkly directed with Haneke initially, and revealingly, filming his actors' hands, feet, and torsos—but not their faces. Each sequence is short and abrupt, and ends in a blackout. Final extended sequence is positively devastating . . . and it's all based on a true story! First in a trilogy, followed by BENNY'S VIDEO and 71 FRAGMENTS OF A CHRONOLOGY OF CHANCE.◖

Seventh Cross, The (1944) **110m.** *** D: Fred Zinnemann. Spencer Tracy, Signe Hasso, Hume Cronyn, Jessica Tandy, Herbert Rudley, Felix Bressart, Ray Collins, Alexander Granach, Agnes Moorehead, George Macready, Steven Geray, Kaaren Verne, George Zucco. Seven men escape from Nazi concentration camp and are pursued by the Gestapo. Exciting film makes strong statement about a cynic who regains hope when others risk their lives to save him. Tandy and Cronyn's first film together. An early winner for Zinnemann.▼

7th Dawn, The (1964-British) **C-123m.** *½ D: Lewis Gilbert. William Holden, Susannah York, Capucine, Tetsuro Tamba, Michael Goodliffe. Dreary tale of personal and political conflict among WW2 allies—now adversaries—in postwar Malaya.▼◖

7th Heaven (1927) **119m.** **½ D: Frank Borzage. Janet Gaynor, Charles Farrell, Ben Bard, David Butler, Marie Mosquini, Albert Gran. One of the most famous screen romances of all time does not hold up as perfectly as one would like; Gaynor won first Academy Award as Diane, mistreated Paris waif redeemed and revived by cocky sewer-worker Chico (Farrell). His performance weakens film, as does terrible war subplot and finale. Still interesting, though; beautifully filmed, with lovely theme "Diane." Gaynor received her Oscar for this film, SUNRISE, and STREET ANGEL. Also won Oscars for Screenplay (Benjamin Glazer) and Director. Remade in 1937.▼◖

Seventh Heaven (1937) **102m.** ** D: Henry King. Simone Simon, James Stewart, Jean Hersholt, Gregory Ratoff, Gale Sondergaard, J. Edward Bromberg, John Qualen. Stewart is miscast as a cocky Parisian street cleaner but still gives a good performance in this remake of the 1927 silent classic, with Simon appropriately waiflike as his true love, Diane. Starts well but soon becomes claustrophobic, and lacks the lyrical quality of the silent.

Seven Thieves (1960) **102m.** ***½ D: Henry Hathaway. Edward G. Robinson, Rod Steiger, Joan Collins, Eli Wallach, Alexander Scourby, Michael Dante, Berry Kroeger, Sebastian Cabot. Taut caper of well-planned Monte Carlo heist, with excellent cast giving credibility to far-fetched premise. CinemaScope.▼

Seventh Seal, The (1957-Sweden) **96m.** **** D: Ingmar Bergman. Max von Sydow, Gunnar Bjornstrand, Nils Poppe, Bibi Andersson, Bengt Ekerot. Sydow, a disillusioned knight on his way back from the Crusades, tries to solve the mysteries of life while playing chess game with Death, who has offered him a short reprieve. Spellbinding, one-of-a-kind masterpiece helped gain Bergman international acclaim.▼◖◗

Seventh Sign, The (1988) **C-98m.** *½ D: Carl Schultz. Demi Moore, Michael Biehn, Jürgen Prochnow, Peter Friedman, Manny Jacobs, John Taylor, Lee Garlington, Akosua Busia, John Heard, Ian Buchanan. Pregnant Moore is convinced it's apocalypse now and that boarder Prochnow wants her baby for his end-of-the-world machinations. Could be; look out for dead ocean life, icy deserts, and rivers running with blood. Supernatural grab bag is directed with all the zeal one brings to a documentary on stock portfolios; result has an extraordinarily high "oh, come on" quotient. Panavision. [R]▼◖◗

Seventh Sin, The (1957) **94m.** **½ D: Ronald Neame. Eleanor Parker, Bill Travers, Françoise Rosay, George Sanders, Jean-Pierre Aumont, Ellen Corby. Remake of W. Somerset Maugham's THE PAINTED VEIL has virtue of Parker's earnest performance as adulterous wife of a doctor who redeems herself during an epidemic; set in Hong Kong and inner China. CinemaScope.

Seventh Veil, The (1945-British) **95m.** ***½ D: Compton Bennett. James Mason, Ann Todd, Herbert Lom, Hugh McDermott, Albert Lieven. Superb psychological drama of pianist Todd, left as ward to her neurotic cousin Mason. Psychiatrist Lom uses hypnosis to enable Todd to regain her professional and personal sanity. All three stars are first-rate in one of the key British films of the 1940s. Muriel and Sydney Box's screenplay won an Oscar.▼◗

Seventh Victim, The (1943) **71m.** *** D: Mark Robson. Tom Conway, Kim Hunter, Jean Brooks, Evelyn Brent, Elizabeth Russell, Hugh Beaumont, Erford Gage, Isabel Jewell, Barbara Hale. Offbeat Val Lewton chiller of innocent Hunter stumbling onto N.Y.C. group of devil-worshipers. Genuinely eerie.▼◗

7th Voyage of Sinbad, The (1958) **C-87m.** ***½ D: Nathan Juran. Kerwin Mathews, Kathryn Grant (Crosby), Richard Eyer, Torin Thatcher. Top-notch adventure/ fantasy pits hero Sinbad against unscrupulous magician (Thatcher) who has reduced Princess Grant to miniature size. Good pacing, eye-popping special effects by Ray Harryhausen (including famed duel with skeleton), music score by Bernard Herrmann. A winner all the way. ▼●⦆

71 Fragments of a Chronology of Chance (1994-Austrian-German) **C-95m.** ✻✻✻ D: Michael Haneke. Gabriel Cosmin Urdes, Lukas Miko, Otto Grünmandl, Anne Bennent, Udo Samel, Branko Samarovski, Claudia Martini, Georg Friedrich. Chilling, challenging tapestry-like portrait of isolated, alienated people whose lives are presented in snippets, including a scruffy runaway boy, a sullen orphaned girl, a solitary old man, and an unhappily married couple. Mixed in are TV news reports involving violence and conflict across the globe, and Michael Jackson being accused of child abuse. Not unexpectedly, these "fragments" are bookended by a tragedy. A celluloid treatise on the manner in which TV numbs the senses. Third in a trilogy, written by the director, following THE SEVENTH CONTINENT and BENNY'S VIDEO.⦆

Seven-Ups, The (1973) **C-103m.** ✻✻½ D: Philip D'Antoni. Roy Scheider, Tony LoBianco, Bill Hickman, Richard Lynch, Victor Arnold. THE FRENCH CONNECTION producer directed this unofficial sequel, with Scheider scoring as a tough cop. Action outweighs plot, and car chase is one of the best yet filmed. Shot in N.Y.C. [PG] ▼●⦆

Seven Waves Away SEE: **Abandon Ship**

7 Women (1966) **C-87m.** ✻✻ D: John Ford. Anne Bancroft, Sue Lyon, Margaret Leighton, Flora Robson, Mildred Dunnock, Anna Lee, Betty Field, Eddie Albert, Mike Mazurki, Woody Strode. Flat soaper of dedicated missionaries in China in 1935, menaced by warrior cutthroats. Despite cast and director, a dull film. Ford's last feature. Panavision.●

Seven Year Itch, The (1955) **C-105m.** ✻✻✻ D: Billy Wilder. Marilyn Monroe, Tommy (Tom) Ewell, Evelyn Keyes, Sonny Tufts, Victor Moore, Oscar Homolka, Carolyn Jones, Doro Merande, Robert Strauss. While Ewell's wife is vacationing in the country, wide-eyed Tom fantasizes about the sexpot who moves in upstairs. This film entered the ranks of pop culture when Marilyn stepped on a subway grating wearing a billowy white skirt . . . but writer-director Wilder had to skirt censorship issues in adapting George Axelrod's Broadway play, and the results are much tamer than the original (though still entertaining). Marilyn is delightful. Clever titles by Saul Bass. CinemaScope. ▼●⦆

Seven Years in Tibet (1997) **C-136m.** ✻✻✻ D: Jean-Jacques Annaud. Brad Pitt, David Thewlis, B. D. Wong, Mako, Danny Den-

zongpa, Victor Wong, Jamyang Jamtsho Wangchuk. Long but absorbing tale of Austrian mountaineer/adventurer Heinrich Harrer, whose attempt to scale a formidable Himalayan mountain peak in 1939 is interrupted by WW2—and whose subsequent adventures bring him to Tibet and the holy city of Llasa, normally closed to outsiders. There he meets and is befriended by the 14-year-old Dalai Lama. Pitt is excellent as Harrer, a difficult character because he is selfish and arrogant—until he learns humility in Tibet. Magnificently filmed. Panavision. [PG-13] ▼●⦆

Severance (2006-British-German) **C-96m.** ✻✻✻ D: Christopher Smith. Toby Stephens, Danny Dyer, Laura Harris, Tim McInnerny, Claudie Blakley, Andy Nyman, Babou Ceesay, David Gilliam, Matthew Baker. A group of British sales employees of a multinational weapons firm are traveling by chartered bus to a remote Eastern European location for a company retreat. Very quickly, however, all plans are off as the bickering bunch is stranded in one very scary forest. With its sly wit and violent mayhem this corporate-slasher film scores by updating an age-old movie staple with diverting flair. [R]⦆

Severed Head, A (1971-British) **C-96m.** ✻✻✻ D: Dick Clement. Ian Holm, Lee Remick, Richard Attenborough, Claire Bloom, Clive Revill, Jennie Linden. Sophisticated sex comedy-drama seemed out of step with the youthful '70s, looks better today; vintner Holm is expected to keep a stiff upper lip while wife Remick has an open affair with her shrink (Attenborough). Sharp performances, thoughtful adaptation of the Iris Murdoch novel by Frederic Raphael. [R]⦆

Sex and Death 101 (2007) **C-117m.** ✻✻½ D: Daniel Waters. Simon Baker, Winona Ryder, Leslie Bibb, Mindy Cohn, Julie Bowen, Neil Flynn, Patton Oswalt, Frances Fisher. All heck breaks loose when a glitch in the earth's computer hard drive informs a young man (Baker), via e-mail, of his past and future sexual exploits. Problem is, he's engaged to be wed and his fiancée's name is nowhere near the end of the list. What's a fellow to do? Thrown into this fantastical comic stew is a femme fatale serial killer (Ryder) bent on revenge against any male crossing her path. Rely on suspending disbelief for this one; mindless but pleasant enough. [R]⦆

Sex and Lucía (2001-Spanish) **C-128m.** ✻✻½ D: Julio Medem. Paz Vega, Tristán Ulloa, Najwa Nimri, Daniel Freire, Elena Anaya, Javier Cámara. Sizzling Spanish import about a young waitress seeking solace on a Mediterranean island after the loss of her boyfriend, a writer. During her stay she rediscovers herself and uncovers a past relationship. Worth seeing just for Vega's dazzling presence. At times too metaphysical but mostly just . . . well, physical. This film played unrated in theaters to avoid an inevitable NC-17. HD 24P Widescreen. ▼◗

Sex and the City (2008) **C-145m.** ✲✲✲ D: Michael Patrick King. Sarah Jessica Parker, Kim Cattrall, Kristin Davis, Cynthia Nixon, Chris Noth, Candice Bergen, Jennifer Hudson, David Eigenberg, Evan Handler, Jason Lewis, Mario Cantone, Joanna Gleason, Malcolm Gets, Gilles Marini. Exuberant follow-up to Darren Star's hit TV series about four inseparable gal pals. Their leader—and our narrator—Carrie Bradshaw (Parker) is about to do the unthinkable and marry her longtime lover, Mr. Big (Noth), but the best laid plans . . . Funny, insightful, and sexually candid, this entertaining movie puts a 21st-century spin on female friendship in middle age. Hudson is a welcome addition as a new assistant who has the same dreams and aspirations Parker did when she first came to N.Y.C. Written by the director, a series veteran; based on the book by Candace Bushnell. Alternate version runs 157m. Followed by a sequel. Super 35. [R]◗

Sex and the City 2 (2010) **C-146m.** ✲✲½ D: Michael Patrick King. Sarah Jessica Parker, Kristin Davis, Cynthia Nixon, Kim Cattrall, Chris Noth, John Corbett, David Eigenberg, Evan Handler, Jason Lewis, Willie Garson, Mario Cantone, Liza Minnelli. In this sequel to the 2008 hit, three of the female friends are married and two have kids, so writer-director King has to manufacture crises for each of them. Then Cattrall scores an all-expenses-paid trip to Abu Dhabi, where the women have a grand adventure, far from family and obligations. Filled with eye candy, this episodic, broadly played, ridiculously long outing with the gal pals should please their loyal fans, even if it's wildly uneven. Several celebrities make cameo appearances—and homage is paid to b&w movie classics. [R]◗

Sex and the Other Man (1996) **C-89m.** ✲½ D: Karl Slovin. Stanley Tucci, Kari Wuhrer, Ron Eldard. Impotent Eldard discovers his sex-starved girlfriend (Wuhrer) about to hop into bed with her yuppie wimp boss (Tucci), and promptly goes bonkers. Good cast flounders in this poorly scripted, sloppily directed psychodrama. [R]▼◗▐

Sex and the Single Girl (1964) **C-114m.** ✲✲½ D: Richard Quine. Natalie Wood, Tony Curtis, Lauren Bacall, Henry Fonda, Mel Ferrer, Fran Jeffries, Edward Everett Horton, Larry Storch, Stubby Kaye, Count Basie and Orchestra. Helen Gurley Brown's book shoved aside, title used to exploit fairly amusing tale of smut-magazine editor Curtis wooing notorious female psychologist Wood. Bacall and Fonda wrap it up as a battling married couple. Coscripted by Joseph Heller. ▼◗▐

Sex Drive (2008) **C-109m.** ✲½ D: Sean Anders. Josh Zuckerman, Clark Duke, Amanda Crew, James Marsden, Seth Green, David Koechner, Brian Posehn, Alice Greczyn, Katrina Bowden. High school senior Zuckerman finally has the chance to lose his virginity to a girl he met on the Internet. He and his best friends (Duke, Crew) embark on a road trip to meet up with the girl and make all of his dreams come true—or so he thinks. Crude, predictable gags and situations abound, though the cast does its best. Unrated version runs 129m. [R]◗

Sex, Drugs, Rock & Roll (1991) **C-96m.** ✲✲½ D: John McNaughton. Eric Bogosian. Industrial-strength performance film of Bogosian's one-man stage show, locking us in a room with ten insufferables it would be a pleasure to avoid. Keenly observed, though, with Bogosian a brilliant mimic; film should benefit from at-home showings, enabling viewers to absorb as much or little as they want in a single sitting. [R]▼

Sex Is Comedy (2002-French-Portuguese) **C-92m.** ✲✲ D: Catherine Breillat. Anne Parillaud, Grégoire Colin, Roxane Mesquida, Ashley Wanninger, Dominique Colladant, Bart Binnema. Turgid semi-autobiographical account of a filmmaker (Parillaud) and the problems she encounters while shooting a difficult sex scene with two performers who loathe each other. Mesquida, who plays the actress, appeared in a similar sequence in Breillat's FAT GIRL; this film is an offshoot. Off-putting, barefaced Breillat ego trip, but still of interest as a peek into the filmmaking process, showing how a tyrannical, insecure director attempts to control her actors. [R] ▼◗

Sex Kittens Go to College (1960) **94m.** BOMB D: Albert Zugsmith. Mamie Van Doren, Tuesday Weld, Mijanou Bardot (Brigitte's sister), Louis Nye, Martin Milner, Mickey Shaughnessy, Pamela Mason, (Norman) "Woo Woo" Grabowski, Jackie Coogan, John Carradine. Priceless title and cast fail to deliver in shockingly unfunny comedy; new head of college science department (Mamie, working very hard to convince us she's a genius) turns out to be an ex-stripper. Finding a movie with worse direction would be almost as impossible as finding another movie with a night club jazz combo fronted by Conway Twitty! Don't say you weren't warned. Aka THE BEAUTY AND THE ROBOT.

sex, lies, and videotape (1989) **C-100m.** ✲✲✲ D: Steven Soderbergh. James Spader, Andie MacDowell, Peter Gallagher, Laura San Giacomo. A selfish, successful lawyer—whose wife has turned frigid and whose sister-in-law has become his lover—welcomes an old college friend for a visit, little dreaming the effect he'll have on all of them. This intriguing, exceptionally well-acted first feature for writer-director Soderbergh took top prize at the Cannes Film Festival; its deliberate pace and talky nature are reminiscent of an Eric Rohmer film—and like one of his, it's not to everyone's taste. [R] ▼●)

Sextette (1978) **C-91m.** BOMB D: Ken Hughes. Mae West, Tony Curtis, Ringo Starr, Dom DeLuise, Timothy Dalton, George Hamilton, Alice Cooper, Keith Moon, Rona Barrett, Walter Pidgeon, George Raft. Astonishing is the only word for this comedy about a Hollywood glamor queen whose many ex-husbands keep popping up during her latest honeymoon. Naturally there's curiosity value in seeing octogenarian Mae still strutting her stuff, but it wears out pretty fast. Her last movie, based on her play *Sex*. [PG] ▼)

Sexy Beast (2001-British-Spanish) **C-88m.** **½ D: Jonathan Glazer. Ray Winstone, Ben Kingsley, Ian McShane, Amanda Redman, Cavan Kendall, Julianne White, Álvaro Monje, James Fox. A retired British gangster, living the good life in Spain, is visited by a vicious hood who wants him to work one more job. Stylish, brutal, modern-day gangster yarn has good performances—including a bravura turn by Kingsley as the ferocious visitor—but leaves a bad aftertaste. Super 35. [R] ▼)

S.F.W. (1995) **C-92m.** BOMB D: Jefery Levy. Stephen Dorff, Reese Witherspoon, Jake Busey, Joey Lauren Adams, Pamela Gidley, David Barry Gray, Jack Noseworthy, Richard Portnow, Annie McEnroe, Natasha (Gregson) Wagner, Tobey Maguire, Gary Coleman. Self-described "seriocomedy about terrorism, beer, and talk shows" centers on a surly young rebel who becomes a nationwide hero after being held hostage for 36 days by convenience-store terrorists. Woefully self-deluding in terms of its own importance, strident film at least provides the catch phrase to summarize its worth: title stems from anti-hero Dorff's constant spouting of "S.F.W." (So [expletive] What?). [R] ▼)

Sgt. Bilko (1996) **C-94m.** *** D: Jonathan Lynn. Steve Martin, Dan Aykroyd, Phil Hartman, Glenne Headly, Daryl Mitchell, Max Casella, Eric Edwards, Dan Ferro, John Marshall Jones, Brian Ortiz, Pamela Segall, Catherine Silvers, Chris Rock, Richard Herd, Travis Tritt. Master Sergeant Ernie Bilko has a moneymaking scheme for every occasion at Fort Baxter, Kansas. His superior, Col. Hall (Aykroyd), looks the other way until the sergeant's long-ago nemesis Major Thorn (Hartman) turns up and seeks revenge. Amiable recycling of the classic 1950s Nat Hiken TV comedy series, which starred Phil Silvers; that's his daughter Catherine as the owlish, uptight Pentagon auditor. Martin remains a first-rate

farceur and is surrounded by a highly capable comedy cast. Super 35. [PG] ▼●)

Sgt. Pepper's Lonely Hearts Club Band (1978) **C-111m.** *½ D: Michael Schultz. Peter Frampton, The Bee Gees, George Burns, Frankie Howerd, Donald Pleasence, Sandy Farina, Dianne Steinberg, Billy Preston, Steve Martin, Earth, Wind & Fire. Attempt to link songs from The Beatles' classic album into some sort of storyline just doesn't work; sequences range from tolerable to embarrassing. As to The Bee Gees' acting talent, if you can't say something nice . . . Panavision. [PG] ▼●)

Shack Out on 101 (1955) **80m.** *** D: Edward Dein. Terry Moore, Frank Lovejoy, Lee Marvin, Keenan Wynn, Whit Bissell. Lee Marvin *is* Slob in this trash classic about the efforts of hash slinger Moore to combat Communism while juggling the lecherous advances of nearly all her co-stars. Absolutely one of a kind, with most of the action taking place on a single shabby set (Wynn's beanery). ▼

Shades of Fear (1993-British) **C-92m.** ** D: Beeban Kidron. Rakie Ayola, John Hurt, Jonathan Pryce, Vanessa Redgrave, Dorothy Tutin. Flat, disappointing drama about a young woman (Ayola) who aspires to become a pilot and the various characters who cross her path as she sails for England. Scripted by Jeanette Winterson, who wrote the far superior ORANGES ARE NOT THE ONLY FRUIT, the British telefilm which helped establish Kidron's reputation. Original title: GREAT MOMENTS IN AVIATION. [R] ▼)

Shadey (1985-British) **C-106m.** **½ D: Philip Saville. Antony Sher, Billie Whitelaw, Patrick Macnee, Lesley Ash, Larry Lamb, Bernard Hepton, Katherine Helmond. Occasionally funny but mostly uninvolving comedy-fantasy-thriller about the title character (Sher), who is able to transmit to film visions from his mind. He wants to use his ability only for peaceful purposes—yet he also needs money for a sex-change operation. Helmond's role is best, that of a hilariously unpredictable, looney Lady. ▼

Shadow, The (1994) **C-108m.** **½ D: Russell Mulcahy. Alec Baldwin, John Lone, Penelope Ann Miller, Peter Boyle, Ian McKellen, Tim Curry, Jonathan Winters, Sab Shimono, Andre Gregory, James Hong, Arsenio "Sonny" Trinidad, Joseph Maher, John Kapelos, Max Wright, Ethan Phillips, Larry Joshua. Lamont Cranston, having lived a life of moral degradation, is "reborn" as a singleminded crimefighter with the ability to cloud men's minds. This adaptation of the venerable pulp novels and beloved radio show (brought to the screen before in the late 1930s, and in a 1940 serial) comes frustratingly close to working, but fails. Cranston is both inscrutable and uninteresting. Great production design and wonderful effects get lost in a movie that keeps the viewer at arm's length throughout. And what a waste of a great supporting cast! [PG-13]▼●◗

Shadowboxer (2006) **C-93m.** **✱✱✱** D: Lee Daniels. Helen Mirren, Cuba Gooding, Jr., Stephen Dorff, Vanessa Ferlito, Joseph Gordon-Levitt, Macy Gray, Mo'Nique. Hit woman Mirren and her partner Gooding have an unusual personal and professional relationship, but he's unprepared for her to make the decision she does when confronted with an assignment that calls for her to shoot a pregnant young woman. The two stars are at their very best in this highly offbeat, brutally violent sleeper, best taken as stylized storytelling and not as a slice of real life. Panavision. [R]◗

Shadow Conspiracy (1997) **C-103m.** BOMB D: George P. Cosmatos. Charlie Sheen, Donald Sutherland, Linda Hamilton, Stephen Lang, Ben Gazzara, Nicholas Turturro, Sam Waterston, Charles Cioffi, Theodore Bikel, Gore Vidal, Terry O'Quinn, Paul Gleason, Penny Fuller. White House whiz kid Sheen learns of a sinister conspiracy in the highest levels of the government, but soon becomes a target of the sinister killer himself. Painfully obvious, wearily derivative, and driven by ludicrous coincidences. Panavision. [R]▼●

Shadowlands (1985-British) **C-90m.** **✱✱✱** D: Norman Stone. Joss Ackland, Claire Bloom, David Waller, Rupert Baderman, Rhys Hopkins. Poignant, wise, quietly rewarding drama about British writer C. S. Lewis (Ackland), a confirmed bachelor, and how he is changed when he falls in love with American divorcée Bloom. Lovely performances by the stars; exceptional award-caliber script by William Nicholson, who later turned this into a stage play. Aka C. S. LEWIS: THROUGH THE SHADOWLANDS. Remade in 1993. ▼

Shadowlands (1993-British) **C-130m.** **✱✱✱½** D: Richard Attenborough. Anthony Hopkins, Debra Winger, Edward Hardwicke, Michael Denison, Joseph Mazzello, John Wood, Robert Flemyng, Peter Howell, Peter Firth. Absorbing tale of British writer C. S. Lewis (*The Lion, The Witch and the Wardrobe*) whose comfortable if rigid life as an Oxford don in the 1950s is shaken by his meeting with a forthright American poet, Joy Gresham. Intelligent and moving, with Hopkins in peak form and Winger his match; the supporting actors are equally good. Filmed on location at Oxford. Adapted by William Nicholson from his 1985 television script and subsequent play. Panavision. [PG]▼●◗

Shadow Magic (2000-Chinese-German) **C-** 115m. **✱✱✱** D: Ann Hu. Jared Harris, Xia Yu, Xing Yufei, Liu Peiqi, Lu Liping. In what could be called CHINESE PARADISO, the earliest days of China's film industry are portrayed in this story of a traveling

Englishman. His show, called "shadow magic," causes wonder and conflict all around as it turns the camera's eye on people who see themselves and their country in a way they never have before. Delightful look at early-20th-century China and the culture-bridging effect only movies seem to achieve. Feature debut for N.Y.-based director Hu. [PG]▼

Shadow of a Doubt (1943) **108m.** **✱✱✱½** D: Alfred Hitchcock. Teresa Wright, Joseph Cotten, Macdonald Carey, Patricia Collinge, Henry Travers, Wallace Ford, Hume Cronyn. Perceptive Americana intertwined with story of young girl who slowly comes to realize her beloved Uncle Charley is really the Merry Widow murderer; Cronyn steals film as nosy pulp-story fan, in his film debut. Scripted by Thornton Wilder, Alma Reville, and Sally Benson from Gordon McDonell's story. Remade in 1958 (as STEP DOWN TO TERROR) and for TV in 1991. ▼●◗

Shadow of the Thin Man (1941) **97m.** **✱✱✱** D: W. S. Van Dyke II. William Powell, Myrna Loy, Barry Nelson, Donna Reed, Sam Levene, Alan Baxter. Nick and Nora probe murder at a race track and run into the usual assortment of shady characters in this agreeable fourth entry in the series, notable for famed future acting teacher Stella Adler in a rare film role (as a gambler's moll). Look fast for Ava Gardner walking by a car at the race track.

Shadow of the Vampire (2000-U.S.-British) **C-93m.** **✱✱✱½** D: E. Elias Merhige. John Malkovich, Willem Dafoe, Cary Elwes, John Aden Gillet (Aden Gillett), Eddie Izzard, Udo Kier, Catherine McCormack. Colorful and amusing fiction about the making of F.W. Murnau's classically creepy German silent film NOSFERATU. Malkovich is good as always as the fastidious filmmaker; Dafoe is exceptional as Max Schreck, an actor (or is he?) cast as the vampire. Film has a unique look and feel. Screenplay by Steven Katz. Super 35. [R]▼◗

Shadow of the Wolf (1993-Canadian-French) **C-112m.** **✱✱** D: Jacques Dorfman. Lou Diamond Phillips, Toshiro Mifune, Jennifer Tilly, Bernard-Pierre Donnadieu, Donald Sutherland. Overwrought adventure epic set in the Arctic, in which a murder sets the stage for an Eskimo couple's battle against the overwhelming odds of nature and fate. Based on the best-selling Canadian novel *Agaguk*, this film looks expensive—and is—but despite the talent in front of the camera and behind it (including Oscar-winning cinematographer Billy Williams), the scenery easily upstages the drama. Super 35. [PG-13]▼●

Shadow on the Wall (1950) **84m.** **✱✱✱** D: Patrick Jackson. Ann Sothern, Zachary Scott, Gigi Perreau, Nancy Davis (Reagan), Kristine Miller, John McIntire, Barbara Billingsley. Clever noir-ish melodrama with young Perreau traumatized when she witnesses the murder of her adulterous stepmother. Davis has one of her best roles as a psychiatrist.

Shadow Play (1986) C-95m. *½ D: Susan Shadburne. Dee Wallace Stone, Cloris Leachman, Ron Kuhlman, Barry Laws, Al Strobel. Tepid chiller about playwright Stone, and the psychological problems she's been facing since her lover's demise. Very minor fare. [R]▼

Shadows (1960) 87m. *** D: John Cassavetes. Hugh Hurd, Lelia Goldoni, Ben Carruthers, Anthony Ray, Rupert Crosse, Tom Allen (Reese). Cassavetes' first film as director, an improvisational, groundbreaking, independently made effort about a light-skinned black girl (Goldoni) who becomes involved with a Caucasian (Ray). Formless, crude, but strikingly realistic, with great use of N.Y.C. locations. Look fast for Cassavetes, Gena Rowlands, Seymour Cassel, and Bobby Darin. ▼●)

Shadows and Fog (1992) 86m. ** D: Woody Allen. Woody Allen, Kathy Bates, John Cusack, Mia Farrow, Jodie Foster, Fred Gwynne, Julie Kavner, Madonna, John Malkovich, Kenneth Mars, Kate Nelligan, Donald Pleasence, Lily Tomlin, Philip Bosco, Robert Joy, Wallace Shawn, Kurtwood Smith, Josef Sommer, David Ogden Stiers, John C. Reilly, W. (William) H. Macy. A Kafkaesque nightmare, shrouded in fog, is Woody-ized with only mildly comic results. A strangler who strikes at night terrorizes a city—and a nebbish who's caught between conspiratorial factions in the town. A galaxy of stars pop up in cameo roles, which is more a distraction than an asset. [PG-13] ▼●)

Shadows of the Peacock SEE: **Echoes of Paradise**

Shadows Run Black (1986) C-89m. *½ D: Howard Heard. William J. Kulzer, Elizabeth Trosper, Shea Porter, George J. Engelson, Dianne Hinkler. Routine slasher film about cop tracking supposed vigilante killer who is preying on a high school ring dealing in drugs and prostitution. An early role for Kevin Costner. Filmed in 1981. ▼)

Shadowzone (1990) C-89m. ** D: J. S. Cardone. David Beecroft, Louise Fletcher, Shawn Weatherly, James Hong, Miguel Nunez, Lu Leonard, Frederick Flynn. Experiments in human sleep have unlocked a path to another dimension, and a monster invades an isolated underground government lab in Nevada. Basically just another ALIEN imitation, but it's reasonably suspenseful, well produced on a low budget. Written by the director. ▼●)

Shadrach (1998) C-86m. *** D: Susanna Styron. Andie MacDowell, Harvey Keitel, John Franklin Sawyer, Monica Bugajski, Scott Terra, Darrell Larson, Deborah Hedwall, Daniel Treat; narrated by Martin Sheen. Nicely realized film set in Virginia

in 1935. A 99-year-old former slave walks hundreds of miles to the ramshackle property now owned by Keitel and MacDowell so he can die on the land where he was born. Though he's a stranger—and a strange presence indeed—the family feels compelled to help him. Kudos to first-time director Styron; the film is adapted from a short story by her father William. [PG-13] ▼

Shaft (1971) C-100m. *** D: Gordon Parks. Richard Roundtree, Moses Gunn, Charles Cioffi, Christopher St. John, Drew Bundini Brown, Gwenn Mitchell, Lawrence Pressman, Antonio Fargas. Slick, upbeat entertainment has Ernest Tidyman's black private-eye John Shaft hired to find kidnapped daughter of Harlem ganglord. Heavy doses of sex and violence professionally packaged by director Parks. Isaac Hayes' theme won Oscar. Followed by two sequels and a TV series. Remade (very loosely) in 2000. [R]▼●)

Shaft (2000) C-98m. *** D: John Singleton. Samuel L. Jackson, Vanessa Williams, Jeffrey Wright, Christian Bale, Busta Rhymes, Dan Hedaya, Toni Collette, Richard Roundtree, Ruben Santiago-Hudson, Josef Sommer, Lynne Thigpen, Philip Bosco, Pat Hingle, Mekhi Phifer. Fiercely independent N.Y.C. detective (nephew of same-named John Shaft, played by Roundtree) allows personal feelings to affect his behavior in dealing with a smug, racist criminal (Bale) and a Dominican drug lord (Wright). Jackson cuts a dashing figure in Armani, Isaac Hayes's theme song still resonates, but there's no sex in this slick update of the 1971 crime thriller. Gordon Parks, who made the original SHAFT, has a cameo. Super 35. [R]▼)

Shaft in Africa (1973) C-112m. *** D: John Guillermin. Richard Roundtree, Frank Finlay, Vonetta McGee, Neda Arneric, Cy Grant, Jacques Marin. Strong action vehicle for Roundtree finds detective Shaft forced into helping African nation stop latter-day slave trading. Extremely tough and violent. Script by Stirling Silliphant. Panavision. [R] ▼)

Shaft's Big Score! (1972) C-104m. *** D: Gordon Parks. Richard Roundtree, Moses Gunn, Drew Bundini Brown, Joseph Mascolo, Kathy Imrie, Wally Taylor, Joe Santos. Dynamic sequel to SHAFT (reteaming director Parks and writer Ernest Tidyman) has private eye Roundtree running afoul of the underworld as he investigates a friend's murder. Sexy, violent, with hair-raising chase finale; Parks also did the music. Panavision. [R]▼)

Shag (1988) C-98m. **½ D: Zelda Barron. Phoebe Cates, Scott Coffey, Bridget Fonda, Annabeth Gish, Page Hannah, Robert Rusler, Tyrone Power, Jr., Jeff Yagher, Carrie Hamilton, Shirley Anne Field. Southern belle high-school grad Cates is about to get married, so her three girlfriends decide to take her on a "last fling" weekend to Myrtle Beach. Pleasant outing set in 1963 with an unusually appealing and talented young cast. [PG]▼**O)**

Shaggy D.A., The (1976) **C-91m.** *** D: Robert Stevenson. Dean Jones, Suzanne Pleshette, Tim Conway, Keenan Wynn, Jo Anne Worley, Dick Van Patten. Sequel to Disney's SHAGGY DOG is winning slapstick romp, with Jones as helpless victim of transformations. Cast is peppered with a score of movie veterans in supporting and bit parts. Followed by THE RETURN OF THE SHAGGY DOG. [G]▼**O)**

Shaggy Dog, The (1959) **104m.** **½ D: Charles Barton. Fred MacMurray, Jean Hagen, Tommy Kirk, Annette Funicello, Tim Considine, Kevin Corcoran, Cecil Kellaway, Alexander Scourby. Disney's first slapstick comedy has fine fantasy premise (a boy who turns into a sheepdog through ancient spell) but sluggish script. Some good gags, but not up to later Disney standard. Jack Albertson has bit part as reporter. Sequels: THE SHAGGY D.A. and a 1987 TV movie, THE RETURN OF THE SHAGGY DOG. Remade in 2006 and for TV in 1994. Also shown in computer-colored version. ▼**O)**

Shaggy Dog, The (2006) **C-98m.** ** D: Brian Robbins. Tim Allen, Robert Downey, Jr., Kristin Davis, Danny Glover, Spencer Breslin, Zena Grey, Jane Curtin, Philip Baker Hall, Craig Kilborn, Laura Kight-linger. Deputy D.A. Allen is so wrapped up in his work he's lost touch with his wife and kids; then a bite from a mystical Tibetan sheepdog turns him into a canine! Five writers created this needlessly complicated remake of the 1959 Disney comedy and its 1976 sequel, THE SHAGGY D.A. Takes a long time to get to the Funny Stuff, and never pays off as well as it should. Adults will bemoan the waste of talent; kids may be less judgmental. Super 35. [PG]**D**

Shaka Zulu SEE: **Mark of the Hawk, The**

Shakedown (1950) **80m.** **½ D: Joseph Pevney. Howard Duff, Peggy Dow, Brian Donlevy, Bruce Bennett, Peggie Castle, Anne Vernon, Lawrence Tierney. Fast-paced but familiar chronicle of ambitious photographer Duff, who uses any and all means—starting with blackmail—to get ahead. Look for Rock Hudson as a doorman.

Shakedown (1988) **C-90m.** *** D: James Glickenhaus. Peter Weller, Sam Elliott, Patricia Charbonneau, Blanche Baker, Antonio Fargas, Richard Brooks, Tom Waits, Kathryn Rossetter, Paul Bartel, John C. McGinley. Entertaining actioner with public defender Weller and undercover cop Elliott combining forces to rid N.Y.C. of drugs and corruption. Good of its kind, with oodles of sensational stuntwork to compensate for the dearth of originality. [R]▼**O)**

Shake Hands With the Devil (1959) **110m.** ***½ D: Michael Anderson. James Cagney, Don Murray, Dana Wynter, Glynis Johns, Michael Redgrave, Cyril Cusack, Sybil Thorndike, Richard Harris. Gripping drama of war-torn Ireland in 1920s, with American student trying to stay aloof, but, drawn by circumstances, he joins rebel army led by iron-willed Cagney. Strikingly filmed on location.▼

Shake, Rattle and Rock (1956) **72m.** ** D: Edward L. Cahn. Touch (Mike) Connors, Lisa Gaye, Sterling Holloway, Fats Domino, Joe Turner, Tommy Charles, Margaret Dumont, Raymond Hatton. Sub-par 1950s rock film with standard plot about adults trying to put the lid on kids' music, benefitting from presences of Domino, Turner, and veteran character actors. Partially remade in 1994 for cable TV.▼

Shaker Run (1985-New Zealand) **C-90m.** ** D: Bruce Morrison. Cliff Robertson, Leif Garrett, Lisa Harrow, Shane Briant, Ian Mune, Peter Rowell, Peter Hayden, Bruce Phillips. Robertson adds character to this otherwise predictable (and implausible) car chase drama. He's a crusty American stunt driver, touring in New Zealand, who unknowingly becomes involved in a plot to transport a stolen virus. ▼**O)**

Shakespeare in Love (1998) **C-122m.** ***½ D: John Madden. Joseph Fiennes, Gwyneth Paltrow, Geoffrey Rush, Judi Dench, Simon Callow, Colin Firth, Imelda Staunton, Ben Affleck, Tom Wilkinson, Martin Clunes, Antony Sher. Spirited, entertaining speculation about a love affair that inspired Will Shakespeare (Fiennes) to write *Romeo and Juliet*. Witty, sensual, and peopled with colorful characters. Climactic performance in the 16th-century theater is as vivid a re-creation of theatergoing in Shakespeare's time as anyone could hope for. Screenplay by Marc Norman and Tom Stoppard. Rupert Everett appears unbilled as Christopher Marlowe. Winner of seven Oscars including Best Picture, Screenplay, Actress (Paltrow), Supporting Actress (Dench), Costumes (Sandy Powell), Score (Stephen Warbeck). Super 35. [R] ▼**O)**

Shakespeare Wallah (1965-Indian) **115m.** *** D: James Ivory. Shashi Kapoor, Felicity Kendal, Geoffrey Kendal, Laura Liddell, Madhur Jaffrey, Utpal Dutt. Playboy Kapoor, who has an actress-mistress, romances Felicity Kendal, a member of a two-bit English theatrical company touring Shakespeare in India. Simple, poignant drama.▼

Shakes the Clown (1991) **C-83m.** BOMB D: Bobcat Goldthwait. Bobcat Goldthwait, Julie Brown, Blake Clark, Adam Sandler, Tom Kenny, Sydney Lassick, Paul Dooley, Florence Henderson, Tim Kazurinsky, La Wanda Page, Robin Williams. Excruciating would-be-comic mishmash about an alcoholic clown (Goldthwait) whose slowly disintegrating "career" virtually collapses when he's framed on a murder rap. Aimless, crude, and headache-inducing, not even salvaged by Williams' brief, unbilled appearance as a mime teacher. Not the cultish black comedy one would like it to be. Goldthwait also scripted. [R]▼●▶

Shakiest Gun in the West, The (1968) C-101m. **½ D: Alan Rafkin. Don Knotts, Barbara Rhoades, Jackie Coogan, Donald Barry, Ruth McDevitt, Frank McGrath. Remake of Bob Hope's THE PALEFACE provides Knotts with one of his better vehicles, as Philadelphia dentist who finds himself out West, tangled up with gunslingers and beautiful Rhoades. Techniscope. ▼●▶

Shalako (1968-British) C-113m. *½ D: Edward Dmytryk. Sean Connery, Brigitte Bardot, Stephen Boyd, Jack Hawkins, Peter Van Eyck, Honor Blackman, Woody Strode, Alexander Knox, Valerie French. European aristocrats on hunting tour of New Mexico during 1880s are menaced by Apaches. Supposed potent casting of Connery and Bardot can't revive slow-moving Western, based on a Louis L'Amour novel. Franscope. [M/PG]▼▶

Shalimar (1978-Indian) C-85m. *½ D: Krishna Shah. Rex Harrison, Sylvia Miles, John Saxon, Dharmendra, Zenat Aman, Shammi Kapoor. Wily Harrison invites the world's greatest thieves to try and steal the world's most valuable ruby from his custody—at the risk of their lives. This was filmed in both English and Hindi-language versions, but the results were so dull that the English print never made it to theaters. Video title: DEADLY THIEF. ▼▶

Shallow Grave (1994-Scottish) C-94m. *** D: Danny Boyle. Kerry Fox, Christopher Eccleston, Ewan McGregor, Ken Stott, Keith Allen, Colin McCredie. Three Edinburgh roommates—a sardonic trio with an iconoclastic worldview—take in a boarder. When they find him dead, and a suitcase full of money in his possession, their worst instincts rise to the surface and involve them in a snowballing scheme to keep the cash. Razor-sharp thriller from screenwriter John Hodge and first-time feature director Boyle is as cold as ice (and too mean-spirited for some tastes) but fascinating at the same time. A Scottish variation on BLOOD SIMPLE with stylistic ties to that flamboyant film. [R]▼●▶

Shallow Hal (2001) C-114m. ** D: Bobby Farrelly, Peter Farrelly. Gwyneth Paltrow, Jack Black, Jason Alexander, Joe Viterelli, Rene Kirby, Bruce McGill, Tony Robbins, Susan Ward, Zen Gesner, Brooke Burns, Rob Moran. Would-be stud Black pursues women strictly for their looks, until self-help guru Robbins hypnotizes him to see only their inner beauty. Thus, an obese Paltrow looks slim and beautiful in his eyes,

and he falls madly in love with her. Lumbering attempt at a message movie from the creators of DUMB & DUMBER, with too few laughs—and too much hypocrisy—to score as either comedy or morality tale. [PG-13]▼▶

Shall We Dance (1937) 116m. ***½ D: Mark Sandrich. Fred Astaire, Ginger Rogers, Eric Blore, Edward Everett Horton, Ann Shoemaker, Jerome Cowan, Harriet Hoctor. Lesser Astaire-Rogers is still top musical, with Gershwin's "Let's Call The Whole Thing Off," "They All Laughed," and "They Can't Take That Away From Me" holding together flimsy plot about dance team pretending to be wed. ▼●▶

Shall We Dance? (1996-Japanese) C-118m. ***½ D: Masayuki Suo. Koji Yakusho, Tamiyo Kusakari, Naoto Takenaka, Eriko Watanabe, Akira Emoto, Yu Tokui, Hiromasa Taguchi, Reikô Kusamura. Beautifully realized film of middle-aged businessman (Yakusho), who secretly yearns to break out of the rigid conformity of his daily life, encountering the world of ballroom dance. Deliberately paced and laced with humor, with a game cast. Ballerina-turned-actress Kusakari matches Yakusho's fine performance. Written by the director. Remade in 2004. [PG]▼●▶

Shall We Dance (2004) C-106m. **½ D: Peter Chelsom. Richard Gere, Jennifer Lopez, Susan Sarandon, Stanley Tucci, Bobby Cannavale, Lisa Ann Walter, Omar Benson Miller, Anita Gillette, Richard Jenkins, Nick Cannon. Adequate remake of the Japanese hit with Gere as a Chicago lawyer who's devoted to his family but immersed in the banality of everyday life; on an impulse, he begins taking ballroom dancing lessons with sultry Lopez. Likable enough, but far too predictable; lacks the heart and soul of the original. [PG-13]▼▶

Shame (1949) SEE: **Not Wanted**

Shame (1962) SEE: **Intruder, The** (1962)

Shame (1968-Swedish) 103m. **** D: Ingmar Bergman. Liv Ullmann, Max von Sydow, Gunnar Bjornstrand, Sigge Furst, Birgitta Valberg, Hans Alfredson. Powerful, brilliantly acted drama (written by the director) examines how married concert violinists are morally challenged by a civil war that rages across their island. One of Bergman's best. [R]▼▶

Shame (1988-Australian) C-90m. ** D: Steve Jodrell. Deborra-Lee Furness, Tony Barry, Simone Buchanan, Gillian Jones, Peter Aanensen, Margaret Ford. Unusual, watchable, but not terribly successful feminist revenge piece, as femme motorcyclist/lawyer takes on a village of goons who look the other way when a gang of teen boys rapes a 16-year-old girl. Strange mix of genres—biker movie, neo-Western, and more—but no MAD MAX. Remade for U.S. TV. [R]▼●

Shame of the Jungle (1975-French-Belgian)

C-73m. *½ D: Picha, Boris Szulzinger. Voices of Johnny Weissmuller, Jr., John Belushi, Bill Murray, Brian Doyle-Murray, Christopher Guest, Andrew Duncan. Raunchy cartoon spoof of Tarzan films, created by Belgian cartoonist Picha, then Americanized for U.S. release in 1979 by *Saturday Night Live* writers Anne Beatts and Michael O'Donoghue, with stars of that show providing voices. Crass, unfunny, and unattractive, despite a promising start. Original French-language version ran 85m. [R—edited from original X rating]▼

Shaming, The SEE: **Good Luck, Miss Wyckoff**

Shampoo (1975) **C-109m.** **½ D: Hal Ashby. Warren Beatty, Julie Christie, Goldie Hawn, Lee Grant, Jack Warden, Tony Bill, Carrie Fisher, Howard Hesseman. Muddy satire of morals and mores in Southern California, centered around restless hairdresser and his demanding female customers. Some bright moments lost in dreary comedy-drama by Beatty and Robert Towne. Fisher's film debut; Grant won Best Supporting Actress Oscar. [R]▼●)

Shamus (1973) **C-106m.** *** D: Buzz Kulik. Burt Reynolds, Dyan Cannon, Giorgio Tozzi, John Ryan, Joe Santos. Exciting but mindless story of offbeat private-eye trying to crack bizarre case while recovering from numerous beatings, jumpings, and other heroic exploits. [PG]▼●)

Shane (1953) **C-118m.** **** D: George Stevens. Alan Ladd, Jean Arthur, Van Heflin, (Walter) Jack Palance, Brandon de Wilde, Ben Johnson, Edgar Buchanan, Emile Meyer, Elisha Cook, Jr. Former gunfighter Ladd comes to defense of homesteaders and is idolized by their son. Palance is unforgettable in role of creepy hired gunslinger. Classic Western is splendid in every way. Breathtaking cinematography by Loyal Griggs won an Oscar. Screenplay by A. B. Guthrie, Jr., from the Jack Schaefer novel. Arthur's final film. Shot in 1951. Later a brief TV series. ▼●)

Shanghai Express (1932) **80m.** *** D: Josef von Sternberg. Marlene Dietrich, Anna May Wong, Warner Oland, Clive Brook, Eugene Pallette, Louise Closser Hale. Dated but prime Dietrich vehicle, grandly photographed by Lee Garmes (who won an Oscar). Marlene is Shanghai Lily, Brook her old flame, Oland a cruel war lord, Wong a spunky partisan, in Jules Furthman–scripted yarn of train ride through China during civil warfare. Remade as PEKING EXPRESS.▼●

Shanghai Gesture, The (1941) **98m.** ** D: Josef von Sternberg. Gene Tierney, Walter Huston, Victor Mature, Ona Munson, Maria Ouspenskaya, Phyllis Brooks, Albert Bassermann, Eric Blore, Mike Mazurki. Slow, overblown drama of Huston discovering daughter Tierney in Asian gambling setup. Intriguing direction somehow never makes it. The mural is by artist (and actor) Keye Luke!▼●)

Shanghai Knights (2003) **C-114m.** ** D: David Dobkin. Jackie Chan, Owen Wilson, Aaron Johnson, Thomas Fisher, Aidan Gillen, Fann Wong, Donnie Yen, Gemma Jones. Inane follow-up to SHANGHAI NOON sends Chan and Wilson to 1887 London to recover a precious royal seal that Chan's father was guarding in the Forbidden City of China. The star teaming is no longer fresh, the story is as phony as the bogus Victorian settings, and the comedy is strained throughout this manufactured sequel. Chan's action scenes are the only bright spots. Panavision. [PG-13] ▼)

Shanghai Noon (2000) **C-110m.** **½ D: Tom Dey. Jackie Chan, Owen Wilson, Lucy Liu, Brandon Merrill, Roger Yuan, Rafael Baez, Walton Goggins, Xander Berkeley, Jason Connery. In 1881, a faithful servant to Chinese princess follows her from the Forbidden City to Nevada, where she's been taken by kidnappers; along the way he forms a thorny partnership with a slick outlaw who's got the gift of gab. Enjoyable if uneven Western comedy gets better as it goes along and Chan goes into action; still no match for Jackie's Asian starring vehicles. Followed by SHANGHAI KNIGHTS. Panavision. [PG-13]▼)

Shanghai Surprise (1986) **C-97m.** BOMB D: Jim Goddard. Sean Penn, Madonna, Paul Freeman, Richard Griffiths, Philip Sayer, Clyde Kusatsu, Kay Tong Lim. Missionary Madonna hires adventurer Penn (her then real-life husband) to capture a cache of stolen opium (for medicinal purposes only) in 1937 China. It's all stupefyingly dull. As one critic noted, it's tough for Penn to succeed in the grand adventure movie tradition when the screen legend he most reminds you of here is Ratso Rizzo. Coexecutive producer George Harrison, who appears briefly as a nightclub singer, wrote the songs. [PG-13]▼●)

Shanghai Triad (1995-Chinese-French) **C-109m.** *** D: Zhang Yimou. Gong Li, Li Baotian, Li Suejian, Shun Chun, Wang Xiao Xiao. Absorbing tale of Chinese underworld in the 1930s, focusing on a boy who's hired to be the silent servant of a pampered nightclub queen—the mistress of one of Shanghai's gangland bosses. An intriguing companion piece to American gangster movies, and another dazzling showcase for leading lady Gong Li. [R]▼●)

Shanks (1974) **C-93m.** *** D: William Castle. Marcel Marceau, Tsilla Chelton, Philippe Clay, Cindy Eilbacher, Helena Kallianiotes, Larry Bishop. One of the strangest movies ever made: mute puppeteer Marceau is given device by dying inventor (also Marceau) which can animate dead bodies. Relatively little dialogue in this bizarre horror-fantasy; alternately amusing and disturbing, with unique performances by three top mimes. A real curio for director Castle, who makes a cameo appearance. This was his final film. [PG]

Shaolin Soccer (2001-Hong Kong) **C-111m.** ****** D: Stephen Chow. Stephen Chow, Vicki Zhao, Ng Mang Tat, Patrick Tse Yin, Cecilia Cheung, Karen Mok, Vincent Kok, Li Hui. Injured soccer player discovers a down-and-out kung fu master (Chow) with a strong kick and decides to build a team around him. His goal: to beat the team coached by the man who caused his lameness so many years ago. Marriage of underdog story with martial arts and special effects was a huge comedy hit in Hong Kong for writer-director-star Chow, but loses something in translation, playing like a souped-up SON OF FLUBBER. Opened in Hong Kong at 97m., then expanded by Chow. [PG-13]◗

Shape of Things, The (2003) **C-97m.** ****½** D: Neil LaBute. Rachel Weisz, Paul Rudd, Gretchen Mol, Frederick Weller. Nerdy college student falls in love with a feisty art major who persuades him to improve his appearance. Their relationship also has an impact on his best friends, who have just gotten engaged. LaBute adapted his stage play (with its original N.Y. cast), which starts with a surprisingly light tone and then, inevitably, turns sour. The story's "lesson" is flawed at best, exposing only LaBute's certainty about the foulness of human nature. Panavision. [R]▼◗

Shape of Things to Come, The (1979-Canadian) **C-95m.** ***½** D: George McCowan. Jack Palance, Carol Lynley, John Ireland, Barry Morse, Nicholas Campbell, Eddie Benton. Lackluster, low-budget remake of H. G. Wells story has nothing in common with 1936 THINGS TO COME, as few survivors of Earth's destruction are now living in peril on the moon. Diehard sci-fi fans may want to take a look, but it's hardly worth the trouble. [PG]◗

Shark! (1969-U.S.-Mexican) **C-92m.** ****** D: Samuel Fuller. Burt Reynolds, Barry Sullivan, Arthur Kennedy, Silvia Pinal, Enrique Lucero, Charles Berriochoa. Tired drama of adventurers diving for shark-guarded treasure earned some infamy when a stunt diver was killed by one of the beasts. Fuller disowned this production, which was taken out of his hands and re-edited. Reissued as MAN-EATER. [R—edited from original M rating]▼◗

Shark Boy of Bora Bora SEE: **Beyond the Reef**

Sharks' Treasure (1975) **C-95m.** ****** D: Cornel Wilde. Cornel Wilde, Yaphet Kotto, John Nellson, Cliff Osmond, David Canary, David Gilliam. Old-fashioned adventure yarn about diving for sunken treasure in the Caribbean is peppered with physical-fitness messages from director-writer-star Wilde. [PG]▼

Shark Tale (2004) **C-90m.** ******* D: Vicky Jenson, Bibo Bergeron, Rob Letterman. Voices of Will Smith, Robert De Niro, Renée Zellweger, Jack Black, Angelina Jolie, Martin Scorsese, Peter Falk, Michael Imperioli, Vincent Pastore, Doug E. Doug, Ziggy Marley. Amusing underwater CG animated feature about a cocky street character (bearing Smith's voice and persona) who has big dreams and spins equally big lies. After saving the life of a fishy godfather's wimpy son, the two improbable allies find themselves in hot water—in more ways than one. Formulaic, but still fun, with enough clever ideas to amuse parents as well as kids. Film buffs will enjoy Sykes, a puffer fish who has Scorsese's eyebrows as well as his voice. [PG]▼◗

Sharky's Machine (1981) **C-119m.** ****** D: Burt Reynolds. Burt Reynolds, Rachel Ward, Vittorio Gassman, Brian Keith, Charles Durning, Bernie Casey, Henry Silva, Earl Holliman, Richard Libertini, John Fiedler, Darryl Hickman, Hari Rhodes. Jarring, loud, and extremely bloody actioner; vice cop Reynolds' vendetta against underworld honcho Gassman intensifies after he falls for one of his $1000-a-night hookers (Ward). Action scenes are competently staged, but you'll eventually become numbed by all the sleaze; film's weirdest aspect is its mainstream jazz score. Based on the William Diehl novel, but won't fool anyone who's ever seen LAURA. [R]▼◗◗

Shatter SEE: **Call Him Mr. Shatter**

Shattered (1972) SEE: **Something to Hide**

Shattered (1991) **C-98m.** ****½** D: Wolfgang Petersen. Tom Berenger, Bob Hoskins, Greta Scacchi, Joanne Whalley-Kilmer, Corbin Bernsen, Theodore Bikel. Man survives catastrophic car accident, but as an amnesiac; trying to piece his life back together, he uncovers growing evidence that things were not quite right even before the crash. Extremely well-made Hitchcock-like thriller comes closer to hitting the mark than most such pretenders, but still falls short. Implausibilities undo a capable cast. [R]▼◗◗

Shattered (2007-U.S.-British) **C-95m.** BOMB D: Mike Barker. Pierce Brosnan, Gerard Butler, Maria Bello, Claudette Mink, Callum Keith Rennie, Peter Keleghan. The perfect couple (Butler and Bello) have their lives turned upside down when their young daughter is kidnapped by sadistic Brosnan. They are then put through a series of twisted tests of love, trust, and betrayal to keep their child alive. Dull and pointless. [R]◗

Shattered Glass (2003) **C-94m.** ****½** D: Billy Ray. Hayden Christensen, Peter Sarsgaard, Chloë Sevigny, Rosario Dawson, Melanie Lynskey, Steve Zahn, Hank Azaria, Mark Blum, Ted Kotcheff. Reporter Stephen Glass endears himself to his colleagues at *The New Republic* magazine as he writes a series of colorful, amusing feature stories . . . until a rival discovers serious discrepancies in one of his pieces, and editor Chuck Lane (Sarsgaard) is forced to confront Glass' credibility. Based on a now-famous journalistic scandal from 1998, this well-made, entertaining film should have been a knockout, but the missing ingredient is a three-dimensional main character: Glass remains a cipher. Directing debut for screenwriter Ray. Super 35. [PG-13] ▼ ◗

Shaun of the Dead (2004-British) **C-97m.** *** D: Edgar Wright. Simon Pegg, Kate Ashfield, Lucy Davis, Nick Frost, Dylan Moran, Bill Nighy, Penelope Wilton, Jessica Stevenson, Rafe Spall. Engaging comedy about a young working stiff (Pegg) who slowly—very slowly—begins to realize that London has been overrun by the walking dead. His only ally is his no-account roommate, his only thought, to rescue his girlfriend (who just broke up with him) and his mum. Clever and funny, whether you're a fan of the zombie genre or not. From the team responsible for the British TV series *Spaced*. Written by the director and leading actor Pegg. Super 35. [R] ▼ ◗

Shawshank Redemption, The (1994) **C-142m.** **½ D: Frank Darabont. Tim Robbins, Morgan Freeman, Bob Gunton, William Sadler, Clancy Brown, Gil Bellows, James Whitmore, Mark Rolston, Jeffrey DeMunn, Paul McCrane. Straight-arrow banker Robbins is railroaded for a double murder and sent to prison for life in the late 1940s. Fellow lifer Freeman and his buddies eventually come to admire Robbins' moral code—and his ability to get things done, in spite of a heinous warden and brutal prison guard. Widely praised film is well crafted but terribly overlong, and (like much of Stephen King's non-horror writing) hollow and predictable. First-time feature director Darabont adapted King's novella *Rita Hayworth and Shawshank Redemption*. [R] ▼ ◗

She (1935) **95m.** *** D: Irving Pichel, Lansing C. Holden. Helen Gahagan, Randolph Scott, Helen Mack, Nigel Bruce, Gustav von Seyffertitz. Escapist adventure on a grand scale, from H. Rider Haggard's story of expedition seeking Flame of Eternal Life, which has been given to one all-powerful woman. Gahagan's cold personality is major drawback, but film is still fun, with outstanding Max Steiner score. Some prints run 89m. Previously filmed in 1917 and 1926, remade several times. Also available in computer-colored version. ◗

She (1965-British) **C-106m.** **½ D: Robert Day. Ursula Andress, John Richardson, Peter Cushing, Bernard Cribbins, Christopher Lee, Andre Morell. Effective refilming of H. Rider Haggard's fantasy of love-starved eternal queen, seeking the reincarnation of her long-dead lover. The two leads certainly are attractive. Followed by

THE VENGEANCE OF SHE. Hammerscope. ▼ ◗ ◗

She (1985-Italian) **C-106m.** BOMB D: Avi Nesher. Sandahl Bergman, David Goss, Quin Kessler, Harrison Muller, Elena Wiedermann, Gordon Mitchell. Bottom-of-the-barrel remake, loosely based on the H. Rider Haggard novel, chronicling the various adventures of the title character (Bergman). Shot in 1982. ▼

Sheba, Baby (1975) **C-89m.** ** D: William Girdler. Pam Grier, Austin Stoker, D'Urville Martin, Rudy Challenger, Dick Merrifield. Middling black action-melodrama with Grier as female private eye trying to help father and friend save their loan business. Less sex and violence than usual, but weak script and amateurish acting. [PG] ▼

She-Beast, The (1966-Italian-Yugoslavian) **C-74m.** *½ D: Michael Reeves. Barbara Steele, John Karlsen, Ian Ogilvy, Mel Welles, Jay Riley, Richard Watson. A witch killed by Transylvanian villagers in 18th century comes back to life as modern, attractive English girl on her honeymoon. Really tacky, though it has some laughs. Cromoscope. ▼ ◗

She-Creature, The (1956) **77m.** ** D: Edward L. Cahn. Marla English, Tom Conway, Chester Morris, Ron Randell, Frieda Inescort, Cathy Downs, El Brendel, Jack Mulhall, Frank Jenks. Bizarre blend of CREATURE FROM THE BLACK LAGOON and THE SEARCH FOR BRIDEY MURPHY. Evil hypnotist uses mesmerized assistant to call back the murderous ghost of the sea creature of which she is a reincarnation. Slow and preposterous but effectively moody, with one of Paul Blaisdell's more memorable monsters, which he also plays. Really odd cast. Remade as CREATURE OF DESTRUCTION and again for cable in 2001. ◗

She Dances Alone (1981-U.S.-Austrian) **C-87m.** *** D: Robert Dornhelm. Kyra Nijinsky, Bud Cort, Patrick Dupond, Sauncey Le Sueur, Max von Sydow. Engrossing blend of reality and fiction, with Cort a director attempting to make a documentary about the late, legendary dancer Vaslav Nijinsky, starring Nijinsky's plump, aging, single-minded daughter Kyra. Her overwhelming presence dominates this strikingly unusual film. Von Sydow appears as himself, and that's his voice reading Nijinsky's diary.

She-Devil (1989) **C-99m.** ** D: Susan Seidelman. Meryl Streep, Roseanne Barr, Ed Begley, Jr., Linda Hunt, Sylvia Miles, Elizabeth Peters, Bryan Larkin, A Martinez. When her slimeball husband walks out on her, unliberated housewife Barr sets out to methodically destroy his life—while creating one for herself. Extremely disappointing comedy offers no surprises and no irony; what it has is a magnificent comedic performance by Streep as the glamorous, self-absorbed romance novelist who lures Roseanne's husband away. Based on Fay Weldon's novel *The Life and Loves of a She-Devil,* which spawned a British miniseries. [PG-13]▼●)

She Done Him Wrong (1933) 66m. **** D: Lowell Sherman. Mae West, Cary Grant, Gilbert Roland, Noah Beery, Rochelle Hudson, Rafaela Ottiano, Louise Beavers. West repeats her stage role of Diamond Lil in Gay 90s spoof. Grant is invited by Mae to come up and see her sometime—he does, fireworks result. Mae sings "Frankie and Johnny" and "Easy Rider" in her best film, which she coscripted from her Broadway hit.▼●)

Sheena (1984) C-117m. BOMB D: John Guillermin. Tanya Roberts, Ted Wass, Donovan Scott, Elizabeth of Toro. Tanya looks great as the queen of jungle jiggle, but Mother Nature forgot to endow her with a script. Supposed to be campy, but it's just plain awful. Panavision. [PG]▼●)

Sheepman, The (1958) C-85m. *** D: George Marshall. Glenn Ford, Shirley MacLaine, Leslie Nielsen, Mickey Shaughnessy, Edgar Buchanan. Modest, entertaining comedy-Western with Ford battling Nielsen for sheep herds and MacLaine, though not always in that order. Shaughnessy is typically amusing. Written by genre vets William Bowers and James Edward Grant. CinemaScope. ●)

She Gets What She Wants SEE: **Slap Her, She's French**

She Hate Me (2004) C-138m. **½ D: Spike Lee. Anthony Mackie, Kerry Washington, Ellen Barkin, Monica Bellucci, Jim Brown, Ossie Davis, Jamel Debbouze, Brian Dennehy, Woody Harrelson, Bai Ling, Lonette McKee, Paula Jai Parker, Q-Tip, John Turturro, Chiwetel Ejiofor, Sarita Choudhury, Joie Lee. Bright exec at a pharmaceuticals firm blows the whistle on his crooked bosses, only to find himself the scapegoat for their shenanigans. Strapped for money, he accepts his ex-fiancée's cold-cash offer to impregnate her and her lesbian lover. Only Spike Lee could have concocted this mishmash of sexual comedy, social commentary, and polemics. Some good scenes and funny moments are offset by heavy-handedness and speechifying. Co-writer Michael Genet appears as Mackie's brother. [R]▼●)

Sheik, The (1921) 80m. *** D: George Melford. Rudolph Valentino, Agnes Ayres, Adolphe Menjou, Walter Long, Lucien Littlefield, George Waggner. Ayres, a "civilized" woman, falls completely under the spell of desert chieftain Valentino. The silent film that helped create the Valentino legend is hokey and campy, but still entertaining. It's easy to see why women went crazy for the Latin star. Racist/imperialist angle of the story is

equally fascinating. Followed by SON OF THE SHEIK.▼)

Sheila Levine Is Dead and Living in New York (1975) C-113m. BOMB D: Sidney J. Furie. Jeannie Berlin, Roy Scheider, Rebecca Dianna Smith, Janet Brandt, Sid Melton. Dead is right. Gail Parent's sardonically funny novel about a Jewish American Princess trying to make good in N.Y.C. becomes an unbelievably bad movie, that just goes on and on. Panavision. [PG]

Sheltering Sky, The (1990) C-137m. ** D: Bernardo Bertolucci. Debra Winger, John Malkovich, Campbell Scott, Jill Bennett, Timothy Spall, Eric Vu-An, Sotigui Koyate, Paul Bowles. Infuriatingly long, dense story of a married American couple who travel to North Africa in the late 1940s, with a friend in tow, hoping for some sort of adventure to spark their odd, repressed relationship. Paul Bowles' novels are often referred to as unfilmable, and this is certainly proof of that. Vividly atmospheric, well acted, and sexually explicit, but this is a journey you may not want to take. Bowles narrates and appears on-screen as mysterious man in bar. [R]▼●)

Shenandoah (1965) C-105m. *** D: Andrew V. McLaglen. James Stewart, Doug McClure, Glenn Corbett, Patrick Wayne, Rosemary Forsyth, Katharine Ross, Tim McIntire, Paul Fix, Denver Pyle, George Kennedy, James Best, Harry Carey, Jr., Dabbs Greer, Strother Martin. Rousing, well-acted saga of Virginia widower indifferent to War between the States until his family is involved. Sentimental drama captures heartbreak of America's Civil War. Basis for later Broadway musical. Ross's film debut.▼●)

Shepherd of the Hills, The (1941) C-98m. *** D: Henry Hathaway. John Wayne, Betty Field, Harry Carey, Beulah Bondi, James Barton, Samuel S. Hinds, Marjorie Main, Ward Bond, Marc Lawrence, John Qualen. Beautifully mounted production of Harold Bell Wright story about Ozark mountain folk, and a man who lives his life in the shadow of a curse: the promise to kill the man who abandoned his mother. Wayne is excellent, and surrounded by fine character actors, with unusual roles for Lawrence and Main. Fuzzy Knight sings a sentimental song ("Happy Hunting Ground") as he did in the not dissimilar THE TRAIL OF THE LONESOME PINE. Exquisitely shot by Charles Lang, Jr., and W. Howard Greene; filmed before in 1919 and 1928, then remade in 1963.▼)

Sheriff of Fractured Jaw, The (1959-British) C-103m. **½ D: Raoul Walsh. Kenneth More, Jayne Mansfield, Henry Hull, William Campbell, Bruce Cabot, Robert Morley. Innocuous Western spoof with Englishman More handed job of sheriff in war-torn town, which he handles surprisingly well. CinemaScope.▼)

Sherlock Holmes series SEE: *Leonard Maltin's Classic Movie Guide*

Sherlock Holmes (1932) **68m.** **½ D: William K. Howard. Clive Brook, Ernest Torrence, Miriam Jordan, Alan Mowbray, Herbert Mundin, Reginald Owen. Genteel, stylish approach to Holmes, set in modern-day London; pleasing but subdued. Torrence is a most enjoyable Moriarty.

Sherlock Holmes (2009) **C-128m.** ** D: Guy Ritchie. Robert Downey, Jr., Jude Law, Rachel McAdams, Mark Strong, Eddie Marsan, Kelly Reilly, James Fox. Murky, noisy, overproduced claptrap about the world-famous detective (and martial arts specialist, we learn here), whose partner Dr. Watson is about to leave Baker St. to get married. Then Holmes is pulled into a baffling case involving the evil Lord Blackwood (Strong) and his longtime love, the duplicitous Irene Adler (McAdams). Annoying in the extreme—and unintelligible at times—the film gets better in the second half as an actual story emerges, but the overuse of Ritchie-branded editing and CGI effects is deadening. [PG-13] ▶

Sherlock Holmes and the Secret Weapon (1942) **68m.** *** D: Roy William Neill. Basil Rathbone, Nigel Bruce, Lionel Atwill, Kaaren Verne, William Post, Jr., Dennis Hoey, Mary Gordon, Holmes Herbert. Holmes is hired to protect the inventor of a new bombsight from the deadly clutches of Moriarty (Atwill). Exciting entry with Hoey scoring as the comically maladroit Inspector Lestrade. Also shown in computer-colored version. ▼●▶

Sherlock Holmes and the Spider Woman SEE: **Spider Woman, The**

Sherlock Holmes and the Voice of Terror (1942) **65m.** **½ D: John Rawlins. Basil Rathbone, Nigel Bruce, Evelyn Ankers, Reginald Denny, Thomas Gomez, Henry Daniell, Montagu Love. First entry in the Universal Rathbone-Bruce series is probably the least impressive, but still enjoyable once you accept the premise of Victorian Holmes (with a particularly risible haircut) battling Nazi saboteurs in WW2 England. Excellent supporting performances by Gomez (in his film debut) and Ankers. Aka VOICE OF TERROR. ▼●▶

Sherlock Holmes and the Woman in Green SEE: **Woman in Green, The**

Sherlock Holmes Faces Death (1943) **68m.** *** D: Roy William Neill. Basil Rathbone, Nigel Bruce, Hillary Brooke, Milburn Stone, Arthur Margetson, Halliwell Hobbes, Dennis Hoey. The deductive master and his blundering companion check into a mansion for convalescing war officers where a series of murders occurs. Very amusing entry replete with a strange clock tower, a subterranean crypt, and a human chessboard. Look for Peter Lawford in a bit as a sailor. ▼●▶

Sherlock Holmes in Washington (1943) **71m.** **½ D: Roy William Neill. Basil Rathbone, Nigel Bruce, Marjorie Lord, Henry Daniell, George Zucco, John Archer, Gavin Muir. Holmes and Watson are off to D.C. in search of some hidden microfilm in this cheeky entry notable for its strong WW2 propaganda content and Watson's fascination with American bubble-gum. ▼▶

Sherlock Holmes' Smarter Brother SEE: **Adventure of Sherlock Holmes' Smarter Brother, The**

Sherlock, Jr. (1924) **45m.** **** D: Buster Keaton. Buster Keaton, Kathryn McGuire, Ward Crane, Joseph Keaton, Erwin Connolly. Keaton reached his pinnacle with this brilliant and hilarious story of a hapless projectionist who walks right into the screen and takes part in the imaginary detective drama unfolding. Sublime study of film and fantasy, which has undoubtedly influenced countless filmmakers such as Woody Allen, Jacques Rivette, even Buñuel. ▼●▶

Sherman's March (1986) **C-157m.** **** D: Ross McElwee. Totally unique documentary odyssey, as romantic sadsack McElwee retraces the title Civil War trek while simultaneously examining the mystique of Southern womanhood. Overlong by a half hour, but the flesh-and-blood subjects end up getting to you the way people in real life do; CRIMES OF THE HEART suffers terribly by comparison. Hilarious subplot involving Burt Reynolds. Followed by sequel, TIME INDEFINITE. ▼▶

SherryBaby (2006) **C-96m.** *** D: Laurie Collyer. Maggie Gyllenhaal, Brad William Henke, Sam Bottoms, Kate Burton, Giancarlo Esposito, Ryan Simpkins, Danny Trejo, Rio Hackford. Compelling film about a recent parolee trying to connect with her young daughter, who's now in the custody of her brother and sister-in-law. Character study of a tough, drug-addicted woman who's trying to make her way back into a society just waiting for her to relapse and return to prison. Scenes with her parole officer (Esposito) are particularly powerful as Gyllenhaal proves she is one of her generation's finest actresses. Worth watching for her superb, gut-wrenching performance. Written by the director. [R] ▶

She's All That (1999) **C-96m.** **½ D: Robert Iscove. Freddie Prinze, Jr., Rachael Leigh Cook, Matthew Lillard, Paul Walker, Jodi Lyn O'Keefe, Kevin Pollak, Anna Paquin, Kieran Culkin, Elden Henson, Usher Raymond, Kimberly "Lil Kim" Jones, Tim Matheson, Debbi Morgan, Alexis Arquette, Clea DuVall, Chris Owen. High school hunk who's just been dumped by his bitchy but popular girlfriend accepts a bet that he can turn a geeky girl into prom queen. Naturally, he falls in love for real . . . and of course, the geeky girl (Cook) is already quite pretty. Fairly innocuous, predictable teen fare with a likable cast. Sarah Michelle Gellar appears unbilled. [PG-13]▼●❸

She's Gotta Have It (1986) **C/B&W-84m.** *** D: Spike Lee. Tracy Camilla Johns, Tommy Redmond Hicks, John Canada Terrell, Spike Lee, Raye Dowell, Bill Lee, S. Epatha Merkerson. Breezy, funky film about a sexy, independent black woman and the three "macho" men who compete for her undivided attention. The acting is far from smooth; film's streetwise charm compensates. Breakthrough film for writer-director Lee, who also appears as the iconoclastic Mars; his father, Bill Lee, wrote the music score. One charming sequence is filmed in color. [R]▼●❸

She's Having a Baby (1988) **C-106m.** **½ D: John Hughes. Kevin Bacon, Elizabeth McGovern, Alec Baldwin, Isabel Lorca, William Windom, Cathryn Damon, Holland Taylor, James Ray, Dennis Dugan, John Ashton, Edie McClurg, Paul Gleason, Lili Taylor. Trials and tribulations of a young couple as they embark on marriage, domestic life, and impending parenthood, as told by the young husband, who feels trapped from the start and questions the meaning of it all. Likable enough comedy-drama grows monotonous after a while; the stars are very appealing, however. Many famous faces appear at the finale. [PG-13]▼●❸

She's Out of Control (1989) **C-95m.** *½ D: Stan Dragoti. Tony Danza, Catherine Hicks, Wallace Shawn, Dick O'Neill, Ami Dolenz, Laura Mooney, Derek McGrath, Dana Ashbrook, Matthew Perry. Superficial expanded sitcom with Danza offering a one-note performance as a widower suffering anxiety pangs over the budding sexuality of daughter Dolenz (whose real-life dad is ex-Monkee Micky). This one seems as if it was spit out of a computer. [PG]▼●❸

She's Out of My League (2010) **C-104m.** **½ D: Jim Field Smith. Jay Baruchel, Alice Eve, T. J. Miller, Mike Vogel, Nate Torrence, Krysten Ritter, Geoff Stultz, Lindsay Sloane, Kyle Bornheimer, Jessica St. Clair, Debra Jo Rupp, Adam LeFevre. Teen comedy about a nerdy kid with low self-esteem who meets the girl of his dreams but screws it up due to lack of confidence—and bad advice from his wacky family and friends. Slightly better than average for the genre, the film benefits from smart casting (including the likable Baruchel in the lead) and a limit on the kind of gross-out humor in which these things usually wallow. Super 35. [R]❸

She's So Lovely (1997-French-U.S.) **C-97m.** *** D: Nick Cassavetes. Sean Penn, Robin Wright Penn, John Travolta, Harry Dean Stanton, Debi Mazar, James Gandolfini, Gena Rowlands, Burt Young, Chloe Webb. An errant husband's latest rage sends him to a mental hospital. Meanwhile, his slightly mad wife remarries, gets her life in order, and raises three children. When husband number one is released ten years later, he sees no reason why he and his ex shouldn't pick up just where they left off. This edgy, extremely well acted comedy-drama could only have been written by John Cassavetes, and it was; his son directed, and his widow (Rowlands) appears in a small role. 2.35 Research PLC. [R]▼●❸

She's the Man (2006) **C-105m.** ** D: Andy Fickman. Amanda Bynes, Channing Tatum, Laura Ramsey, Robert Hoffman, Alex Breckenridge, Jonathan Sadowski, Julie Hagerty, Vinnie Jones, David Cross. Shallow time-killer with the appealing Bynes. Farcical to a fault, this umpteenth cross-dressing story finds the new girl on campus disguising herself as her AWOL brother in order to get closer to the "cool" jock who lusts after the best-looking girl in school. Cast looks like they just jumped off the cover of *Tiger Beat*. Screenplay credit reads "inspired by *Twelfth Night* by William Shakespeare," but unfortunately this film is to Shakespeare what Paris Hilton is to Meryl Streep. Or, no great Shakes. [PG-13]❸

She's the One (1996) **C-96m.** **½ D: Edward Burns. Edward Burns, Jennifer Aniston, Cameron Diaz, John Mahoney, Maxine Bahns, Mike McGlone, Leslie Mann, Anita Gillette, Frank Vincent, Amanda Peet. Amusing comedy about a guy, still smarting from catching his fiancée cheating on him three years ago, who marries on impulse, while his cocky married brother turns out to be a philanderer. Winning performances, funny lines and situations abound, though it starts to go flat toward the finale. Writer-director Burns' second film, following THE BROTHERS McMULLEN. Original songs written and performed by Tom Petty. [R]▼●❸

She Wore a Yellow Ribbon (1949) **C-103m.** ***½ D: John Ford. John Wayne, Joanne Dru, John Agar, Ben Johnson, Harry Carey, Jr., Victor McLaglen, Mildred Natwick, George O'Brien, Arthur Shields, Francis Ford, Noble Johnson, Tom Tyler. Director Ford's stock company in fine form. Wayne excellent as cavalry officer about to retire, unwilling to walk out on impending war with Indians. Beautifully filmed in color by Oscar-winning Winton C. Hoch, but a bit top-heavy with climaxes. Second of Ford's cavalry trilogy; followed by RIO GRANDE. ▼●❸

Shillingbury Blowers, The (1980-British) **C-82m.** *½ D: Val Guest. Trevor Howard, Robin Nedwell, Diane Keen, Jack Douglas, Sam Kydd, John LeMesurier. Dated trifle about cantankerous Howard and cronies resisting attempts by young Nedwell to improve the band in an Olde English village.

Shiloh (1997) **C-93m.** ** D: Dale Rosenbloom. Blake Heron, Michael Moriarty, Scott Wilson, Ann Dowd, J. Madison Wright, Rod

Steiger, Bonnie Bartlett, Frannie. A beagle, training to be a hunting dog, runs away from its cruel owner and meets up with a lonely preteen. Not your usual boy-and-his-dog tale (no one falls down a mine shaft), it chronicles Heron's attempts to buy the dog from its master. Good cast, solid family values, but lumbering story never picks up. Followed by two sequels. [PG]▼O◗

Shiloh 2: Shiloh Season (1999) **C-96m. ★★** D: Sandy Tung. Michael Moriarty, Zachary Browne, Scott Wilson, Rod Steiger, Bonnie Bartlett, Ann Dowd, Frannie. The boy and his dog return in this sequel which deals with why people are bad and whether they can change. More life lessons explored by a game cast, but the story plods. Followed by SAVING SHILOH. [PG]▼◗

shinbone alley (1971) **C-86m. ★★½** D: John D. Wilson, David Detiege. Voices of Eddie Bracken, Carol Channing, John Carradine, Alan Reed, Sr. Genuinely odd animated feature based on a Broadway musical (by Joe Darion and Mel Brooks) about Don Marquis's famous characters of archy, the lovesick, philosophical cockroach, and mehitabel, the object of his affection, a hedonistic cat. Episodic, to say the least, with some witty and tuneful moments, and great vocal performances by Bracken and Channing. Not really for kids. Aka ARCHY AND MEHITABEL. [G]▼◗

Shine (1996-Australian) **C-105m. ★★★½** D: Scott Hicks. Geoffrey Rush, Armin Mueller-Stahl, Noah Taylor, Alex Rafalowicz, Sonia Todd, Lynn Redgrave, John Gielgud, Nicholas Bell, Googie Withers. Young piano prodigy is pushed to the breaking point by his smothering father. As a dysfunctional adult, he eventually finds peace in the very thing that drove him to the edge: his music. He also finds love for the first time in his life. Arresting film based on the true story of David Helfgott, with a great cast, led by an astonishing Rush in his Oscar-winning performance. [PG-13]▼O◗

Shine a Light (2008) **C/B&W-122m. ★★★½** D: Martin Scorsese. Mick Jagger, Keith Richards, Charlie Watts, Ronnie Wood. Having documented legends like The Band and Bob Dylan, Scorsese takes on the "greatest rock band ever." Capturing a 2006 Rolling Stones concert in the rather intimate setting of N.Y.C.'s Beacon Theatre, the director places his cameras seemingly everywhere (manned by Robert Richardson's team of A-list cinematographers) and brilliantly captures the raw energy of this legendary band. A unique view of the masters of one medium from the master of another; if it doesn't thrill baby boomers then they can't get no satisfaction from any filmed rock concert. [PG-13]◗

Shiner (2001-British) **C-99m. ★★** D: John Irvin. Michael Caine, Martin Landau, Frances Barber, Claire Rushbrook, Frank Harper,

Andy Serkis, Matthew Marsden, Gary Lewis. Obvious yarn, with echoes of *King Lear*, about a seedy London promoter who manages to stage a major boxing bout for his son—only to see his dream of glory, and almost everything else he holds dear, crumble to bits. Caine is always interesting to watch, but this is just a potboiler. Released direct to video in U.S. J-D-C Scope. [R]▼◗

Shining, The (1980) **C-142m. ★★** D: Stanley Kubrick. Jack Nicholson, Shelley Duvall, Danny Lloyd, Scatman Crothers, Barry Nelson, Joe Turkel, Anne Jackson. Intriguing but ineffectual adaptation of Stephen King's thriller about a man who becomes off-season caretaker at isolated resort hotel—and almost immediately begins to lose his mind. Nicholson goes off the wall so quickly there's no time to get involved in his plight. Some eerie scenes, to be sure, but the film goes on forever. Cut by Kubrick after premiering at 146m. Remade for TV in 1997. [R]▼O◗

Shining Star (1975) **C-100m. *½** D: Sig Shore. Harvey Keitel, Ed Nelson, Cynthia Bostick, Bert Parks, Jimmy Boyd, Michael Dante. Low key yarn about mob-dominated recording company. Poor sound and photography. Saved—barely—by intriguing look behind the scenes of music business. Music by Earth, Wind and Fire. Originally titled THAT'S THE WAY OF THE WORLD.▼◗

Shining Through (1992) **C-127m. ★★½** D: David Seltzer. Michael Douglas, Melanie Griffith, Liam Neeson, Joely Richardson, John Gielgud, Francis Guinan, Patrick Winczewski, Sylvia Syms. Overlong, overbaked spy drama/romance set in WW2, with a very appealing Griffith as an outspoken young woman who falls in love with her boss (Douglas), and convinces him to let her take a dangerous assignment in Berlin—though she has no espionage experience except what she's seen in movies. Lavish production and empathic performance by Griffith make this palatable—but the story gets more implausible as it reaches its climax. Based on the novel by Susan Isaacs. Panavision. [R]▼O◗

Ship Ahoy (1942) **95m. ★★½** D: Edward Buzzell. Eleanor Powell, Red Skelton, Virginia O'Brien, Bert Lahr, John Emery, Tommy Dorsey Orchestra, Frank Sinatra, Jo Stafford. Nonsensical plot of Skelton thinking U.S. agent is working for Axis; shipboard yarn has some salty dancing and singing, good Dorsey numbers featuring drummer Buddy Rich.▼◗

Ship of Fools (1965) **149m. ★★★★** D: Stanley Kramer. Vivien Leigh, Oskar Werner, Simone Signoret, Jose Ferrer, Lee Marvin, Jose Greco, George Segal, Elizabeth Ashley, Michael Dunn, Charles Korvin, Lilia Skala. GRAND HOTEL at sea in pre-WW2 days. Superb cast including Leigh, in her last film, as disillusioned divorcée, Werner and

Signoret as illicit lovers, Marvin as punchy baseball player. Penetrating drama, when not a soaper. Script by Abby Mann from Katherine Anne Porter's novel; won Oscars for Cinematography (Ernest Laszlo) and Art Direction. ▼●▮

Shipping News, The (2001) C-111m. *** D: Lasse Hallström. Kevin Spacey, Julianne Moore, Judi Dench, Cate Blanchett, Pete Postlethwaite, Scott Glenn, Rhys Ifans, Gordon Pinsent, Jason Behr, Larry Pine, Jeannetta Arnette, Marc Lawrence. A man beaten down by life is brought—by circumstance—to his ancestral home of Newfoundland, where he begins to gain confidence in himself as the skeletons in his family closet emerge. An unbeatable cast brings this sympathetic adaptation of E. Annie Proulx's Pulitzer Prize-winning novel to life; the setting contributes as much as the actors. Super 35. [R] ▼▮

Ship That Died of Shame, The (1955-British) 91m. *** D: Basil Dearden. Richard Attenborough, George Baker, Bill Owen, Virginia McKenna, Roland Culver, Bernard Lee, Ralph Truman. Crew of British gunboat reteams after WW2 and uses the same vessel for smuggling purposes, until "it" begins to rebel at their increasingly grimy exploits. Fine cast in offbeat drama. Retitled PT RAIDERS and cut to 78m. ▮

Shipwrecked (1990-Norwegian) C-91m. *** D: Nils Gaup. Stian Smestad, Gabriel Byrne, Louisa Haigh, Trond Munch, Bjorn Sundquist, Eva Von Hanno, Kjell Stormoen. Young Smestad signs on a South Seas voyage as cabin boy; just before pirate/passenger Byrne is about to take over the ship, a hurricane strands the lad on the very island where Byrne's treasure booty is hidden. Enjoyable pirate yarn with an exciting HOME ALONE–like finish when Smestad booby-traps the island against the invading pirates. A Disney release. Panavision. [PG] ▼●▮

Shiri (1999-Korean) C-125m. *** D: Je-gyu Kang. Suk-kyu Han, Min-sik Choi, Kang-ho Song, Yun-jin Kim. G-men partners, one of them a groom-to-be, race to stop a chameleon assassin from blowing up Seoul in the name of reunification. This imitation John Woo actioner offers the usual excessively bloody violence, sentimental melodrama, noisy gunplay, and laser-bright visuals, but its credibility is elevated by fiercely charged political motivations. A major Asian box-office hit. [R] ▼▮

Shirley Valentine (1989-U.S.-British) C-108m. *** D: Lewis Gilbert. Pauline Collins, Tom Conti, Alison Steadman, Julia McKenzie, Joanna Lumley, Bernard Hill, Sylvia Syms. Collins repeats her London and Broadway stage triumphs in the role of a saucy, middle-aged, married woman who feels that life has passed her by—until she gets the opportunity to travel to Greece, sans husband. Collins' endearing performance (much of it

talking directly to the audience) makes this a must, smoothing over lulls in Willy Russell's adaptation of his own stage play. The same team made EDUCATING RITA. [R] ▼●▮

Shivers SEE: **They Came From Within**

Shoah (1985-French) C-503m. **** D: Claude Lanzmann. Remarkable documentary, shown in two parts, each lasting about four and a half hours, chronicling the memories of those who lived through the Holocaust—both victims and oppressors. Lanzmann's persistent interview approach hammers away at details in order to intensify our cumulative response . . . and we begin to see exactly how the unthinkable became a reality. A unique and eloquent film. ▼▮

Shock (1979) SEE: **Beyond the Door II**

Shock Corridor (1963) C/B&W-101m. *** D: Samuel Fuller. Peter Breck, Constance Towers, Gene Evans, James Best, Hari Rhodes. Journalist Breck gets admitted to mental institution to unmask murderer, but soon goes crazy himself. Powerful melodrama with raw, emotional impact. Fuller also produced and wrote the script; imaginative photography by Stanley Cortez. Three sequences are in color. ▼●▮

Shocked SEE: **Mesmerized**

Shocker (1989) C-110m. BOMB D: Wes Craven. Michael Murphy, Peter Berg, Cami Cooper, Mitch Pileggi, Sam Scarber, Heather Langenkamp, Theodore Raimi, Richard Brooks, Dr. Timothy Leary. Teenager Berg, son of policeman Murphy, is psychically linked to mass murderer, but when the killer is executed, his spirit is free to inhabit a series of victims. Writer-director Craven attempted to create a new Freddy Krueger with this misbegotten farago, a waste of excellent special effects and some good ideas. [R] ▼●▮

Shockproof (1949) 79m. *** D: Douglas Sirk. Cornel Wilde, Patricia Knight, John Baragrey, Esther Minciotti, Howard St. John. Parole officer Wilde is lured into love affair with parolee Knight which threatens to destroy him. Stylish film noir, cowritten by Samuel Fuller, which unfortunately cops out at the end. ▮

Shock to the System, A (1990) C-91m. **½ D: Jan Egleson. Michael Caine, Elizabeth McGovern, Peter Riegert, Swoosie Kurtz, Will Patton, Jenny Wright, John McMartin, Barbara Baxley. Caine adds luster to this so-so black comedy as a harried ad executive who discovers how easy it is to kill anyone in his way after he's passed over for a promotion. Has its moments as a topical look at greed, corporate-style, but could have been far more pointed and involving. [R] ▼●▮

Shock Treatment (1964) 94m. ** D: Denis Sanders. Stuart Whitman, Carol Lynley, Roddy McDowall, Lauren Bacall, Olive Deering, Ossie Davis, Donald Buka, Bert Freed, Douglass Dumbrille. Out-of-work actor (Whitman) goes undercover at state mental asylum to discover whereabouts of murderer McDowall's supposed million-dollar stash. Odd, unsatisfying melodrama. CinemaScope.

Shock Treatment (1981) C-94m. *½ D: Jim Sharman. Jessica Harper, Cliff De Young, Richard O'Brien, Patricia Quinn, Charles Gray, Ruby Wax, Nell Campbell. Dreary, disappointing spin-off from THE ROCKY HORROR PICTURE SHOW, with same director and many cast members. Brad and Janet (played here by De Young and Harper) find themselves contestants (or more appropriately, prisoners) on a TV game show—spoofed far more successfully in MELVIN AND HOWARD. [PG]▼▍

Shock Waves (1975) C-86m. ** D: Ken Wiederhorn. Peter Cushing, Brooke Adams, John Carradine, Fred Buch, Jack Davidson, Luke Halpin. On an island near Florida, pleasure boaters encounter a recluse (Cushing), who turns out to be the creator and guardian of underwater Nazi zombies, left over from WW2. Oddball, partly effective low-budgeter. Adams' film debut. Aka DEATH CORPS. [PG]▼▍

Shoeshine (1946-Italian) 93m. **** D: Vittorio De Sica. Rinaldo Smerdoni, Franco Interlenghi, Anniello Mele, Bruno Ortensi, Pacifico Astrologo. A brilliant, haunting neorealist drama about two youngsters struggling to survive in war-scarred Italy; they become involved with black marketeering and are sent to reform school. This deservedly won a special Oscar—before Best Foreign Film prizes were awarded.▼▍

Shoes of the Fisherman, The (1968) C-157m. ** D: Michael Anderson. Anthony Quinn, Laurence Olivier, Oskar Werner, David Janssen, Vittorio De Sica, Leo McKern, John Gielgud, Barbara Jefford. Pope Quinn, a Russian who spent 20 years as a political prisoner in Siberia, tries to fend off atomic war plus starvation in Red China for half a film while correspondent Janssen tries to patch up his petty marital problems the rest of the time. Fine cast is wasted in slapdash film version of Morris L. West's best-seller, dully directed by Anderson. Panavision. [G]▼●▍

Shogun Assassin (1981-Japanese-U.S.) C-86m. ***½ D: Kenji Misumi, Robert Houston. Tomisaburo Wakayama, Masahiro Tomikawa, voices of Lamont Johnson, Marshall Efron. Coherent film brilliantly edited out of two different features in Japanese *Sword of Vengeance* series about samurai warrior who travels across countryside pushing his young son in a baby cart, stopping only to get involved in inordinate amounts of combat. Americanized version, narrated by child, is absolutely stunning visual ballet of violence and bloodletting. Sort of a sequel to LIGHTNING SWORDS OF DEATH. Panavision. [R]▼●▍

Shogun Assassin II SEE: **Lightning Swords of Death**

Shoot (1976-Canadian) C-98m. BOMB D: Harvey Hart. Cliff Robertson, Ernest Borgnine, Henry Silva, James Blendick, Larry Reynolds, Les Carlson, Kate Reid, Helen Shaver. There's a faint echo of DELIVERANCE in this ludicrous tale of gun-happy pals who allow the shooting of one hunter to escalate into warfare. Supposedly anti-gun, the film is also apparently anti-entertainment. [R]▼

Shoot 'Em Up (2007) C-86m. *½ D: Michael Davis. Clive Owen, Paul Giamatti, Monica Bellucci, Stephen McHattie, Greg Bryk, Daniel Pilon, Ramona Pringle, Julian Richings, Tony Munch. Mystery man (Owen) who has an uncanny knack for killing people with sharp carrots (!) delivers a woman's baby during a shootout, then protects the infant from a crazed hit man (Giamatti) with the help of a lactating hooker (Bellucci). All of this somehow is tied into a bone marrow–harvesting scheme involving a corrupt presidential candidate. Insane plot is matched by cartoonish, over-the-top action, tongue-in-cheek gore, and ridiculous stylistics that try to make John Woo look like Ozu. Despite the game efforts of the slumming cast, this sleazy film leaves a bad aftertaste. Super 35. [R]▍

Shooter (2007) C-124m. **½ D: Antoine Fuqua. Mark Wahlberg, Michael Peña, Danny Glover, Kate Mara, Elias Koteas, Rhona Mitra, Ned Beatty, Jonathan Walker, Justin Louis, Tate Donovan, Rade Sherbedgia, Levon Helm, Lane Garrison. Highly trained military marksman (Wahlberg) lives in seclusion since a terrible incident that occurred on duty three years earlier. Now he's approached by a government official (Glover) to help prevent a presidential assassination plot by figuring out all the angles. But things don't go as planned, and Wahlberg is forced to become a one-man army. Good action-thriller overplays its hand and becomes ludicrous in the final act. The "bad guys" act so broadly you'd think they were playing in a Roy Rogers Western. Based on Stephen Hunter's novel *Point of Impact*. Panavision. [R]▍

Shooting, The (1967) C-82m. *** D: Monte Hellman. Millie Perkins, Jack Nicholson, Will Hutchins, Warren Oates. Cryptic, unconventional Western with deceptively familiar revenge "story." Ultimately powerful film, with offbeat performance by Nicholson as a hired gun . . . and an incredible, unexpected finale. Filmed simultaneously with RIDE IN THE WHIRLWIND.▼●▍

Shooting Fish (1997-British) C-93m. **½ D: Stefan Schwartz. Dan Futterman, Stuart Townsend, Kate Beckinsale, Claire Cox, Dominic Mafham, Nickolas Grace, Peter Capaldi, Annette Crosbie, Jane Lapotaire, Phyllis Logan. Smooth-talking American con artist and British techno-geek team up in London to scam the rich; the catch is they may or may not be "giving to the poor" as they claim. Beckinsale is the innocent but brainy temp who assists them. Amiably frantic farce in the spirit of 1960s Swinging London caper comedies is lightweight fun. Original British running time 112m. Super 35. [PG] ▼●]

Shooting Party, The (1984-British) **C-98m.** **★★★½** D: Alan Bridges. James Mason, Dorothy Tutin, Edward Fox, Cheryl Campbell, John Gielgud, Gordon Jackson, Aharon Ipale, Rupert Frazer, Robert Hardy, Judi Bowker. Rewarding film about varied personalities, intrigues, and conflicts that crisscross during weekend shooting party in 1913. Mason, the weekend's host, presides over all with grace, wit, and understanding. A telling look at class structure and class consciousness; screenplay by Julian Bond from Isabel Colegate's novel. ▼]

Shootist, The (1976) **C-99m.** **★★★½** D: Don Siegel. John Wayne, Lauren Bacall, Ron Howard, James Stewart, Richard Boone, Hugh O'Brian, Harry Morgan, Rick Lenz, John Carradine, Sheree North, Scatman Crothers. Intelligent story about a legendary gunfighter who learns he has cancer and tries to die in peace, but cannot escape his reputation. A fitting (and poignant) valedictory to Wayne's career. Miles Hood Swarthout and Scott Hale adapted Glendon Swarthout's novel. [PG] ▼●]

Shoot Loud, Louder ... I Don't Understand (1966-Italian) **C-100m.** **★★** D: Eduardo De Filippo. Marcello Mastroianni, Raquel Welch, Guido Alberti, Leopoldo Trieste. Surrealistic but flat film in which Mastroianni plays antique dealer whose life suddenly becomes very complex. Panoramica. ▼]

Shoot Out (1971) **C-95m.** **★★** D: Henry Hathaway. Gregory Peck, Pat Quinn, Robert F. Lyons, Susan Tyrrell, Jeff Corey, James Gregory, Rita Gam, Dawn Lyn. Same producer, director and screenwriter of TRUE GRIT in another Western about cowboy and little girl. Formula doesn't work; in spite of title, film has too much talk and not enough action. [PG] ▼]

Shoot the Moon (1982) **C-123m.** **★★★** D: Alan Parker. Albert Finney, Diane Keaton, Karen Allen, Peter Weller, Dana Hill, Viveka Davis, Tracey Gold, Tina Yothers, Leora Dana. Highly charged, emotional drama about the breakup of a marriage. The insights and emotional touchstones of Bo Goldman's script—and superlative acting—help make up for strange gaps of logic and credibility. We learn precious little about what makes the central characters tick; director Parker gives us picture-postcard views of Marin County, California, instead. [R] ▼●]

Shoot the Piano Player (1960-French) **81m.** **★★★★** D: François Truffaut. Charles Aznavour, Marie Dubois, Nicole Berger, Michele Mercier, Albert Remy. Atmospheric early Truffaut gem. Aznavour is marvelous

as a former concert pianist who traded in his fame and now plays in rundown Parisian cafe. His ambitious girlfriend wants him to resume his career, but he gets involved with gangsters and murder instead. This film, more than any other, reflects the influence of Hollywood low-budget melodramas on Truffaut and his cinematic style. Dyaliscope. ▼●]

Shoot to Kill (1988) **C-110m.** **★★½** D: Roger Spottiswoode. Sidney Poitier, Tom Berenger, Kirstie Alley, Clancy Brown, Richard Masur, Andrew Robinson, Kevin Scannell, Frederick Coffin. Big-city cop (Poitier) is forced to team up with stubborn mountain guide (Berenger) to go into the wilds of the Pacific Northwest in search of a hunting party being led by the guide's girlfriend (Alley)—and infiltrated by a ruthless killer whom Poitier is determined to capture. Slick but highly improbable tale strains credibility, but keeps its grip thanks mostly to a riveting Poitier (his first starring role in ten years). Super 35. [R] ▼●]

Shop Around the Corner, The (1940) **97m.** **★★★½** D: Ernst Lubitsch. Margaret Sullavan, James Stewart, Frank Morgan, Joseph Schildkraut, Sara Haden, Felix Bressart, William Tracy, Charles Smith. The ultimate in sheer charm, a graceful period comedy about coworkers in a Budapest notions shop who don't realize that they are lonelyhearts penpals. Superbly scripted by Samson Raphaelson, from Nikolaus Laszlo's play *Parfumerie*. Later musicalized as IN THE GOOD OLD SUMMERTIME, brought to Broadway as *She Loves Me*, remade as YOU'VE GOT MAIL. Also shown in computer-colored version. ▼●]

Shopgirl (2005-U.S.-British) **C-116m.** **★★★** D: Anand Tucker. Steve Martin, Claire Danes, Jason Schwartzman, Bridgette Wilson-Sampras, Sam Bottoms, Frances Conroy, Rebecca Pidgeon. Stylish romantic comedy about a young woman, recently transplanted to L.A., who finds herself wooed in very different ways by a wealthy older businessman and a slobby young guy. Unique meditation on loneliness and the yearning for physical and emotional contact—adapted by Martin from his own novella—is witty, philosophical, and melancholy, though more than a bit self-conscious. Danes is marvelous in the title role. Martin also coproduced. Panavision. [R]]

Shop on Main Street, The (1965-Czech) **128m.** **★★★★** D: Jan Kadar, Elmar Klos. Josef Kroner, Ida Kaminska, Han Slivkova, Frantisek Holly, Martin Gregor. Potent, poignant drama set in WW2 Czechoslovakia, where an old Jewish woman loses her small button shop, and depends on man who takes it over to shield her from further persecution. Oscar winner as Best Foreign Film. Originally titled THE SHOP ON HIGH STREET. ▼●]

Shopping (1994-British) **C-106m.** *½ D: Paul (W. S.) Anderson. Sadie Frost, Jude Law, Sean Bean, Jonathan Pryce, Sean Pertwee, Marianne Faithfull, Eamonn Walker, Jason Isaacs, Fraser James. Looking fresh-faced early in his career, Law bolts out of the pokey in a semi-futuristic Brit milieu to get back into his former trade: hijacking, looting, and crashing cars through storefront windows. Grubby anomaly in Anderson's more fantasy-prone later career was somewhat controversial at the time, with its portrayal of nihilistic violence by low-I.Q. punks who have less redeeming social value than napalm. Now, it's just one more ho-hummer that looks like a thousand other screechy-wheel melodramas of the day. Frost plays the comparably straighter accomplice who tries getting Law to give it up. Later in real life, the stars married and had three children, which will give you something to think about during the dramatic vacuum. [R] ▶

Shopworn Angel, The (1938) **85m.** *** D: H. C. Potter. Margaret Sullavan, James Stewart, Walter Pidgeon, Hattie McDaniel, Sam Levene, Nat Pendleton. Stewart and Sullavan are always a fine pair, even in this fairly routine soaper. Naive soldier falls in love with loose-moraled actress, who gradually softens under his influence. Beautifully done, including Slavko Vorkapich's masterful opening WW1 montage. Remake of 1929 film with Gary Cooper and Nancy Carroll; filmed again as THAT KIND OF WOMAN.▼▶

Shortbus (2006) **C-102m.** **½ D: John Cameron Mitchell. Sook-Yin Lee, Paul Dawson, Lindsay Beamish, PJ DeBoy, Raphael Barker, Peter Stickles, Jay Brannan, Justin Bond, Alan Mandell, Adam Hardman, Ray Rivas. Married couples, gay couples, lonely singles, transsexuals, and others just off the street hang at a N.Y.C. club, Shortbus, in order to overcome their unique (to say the least) sexual problems. Amidst all the orgies and couplings (and that's real sex going on) there's a surprising emotional undertone. The actors are all appealing, but be warned: with its full-frontal, almost nonstop sexual content, this is not for everyone. Released without a rating in order to avoid an NC-17 tag. Written by the director.▶

Short Circuit (1986) **C-98m.** **½ D: John Badham. Ally Sheedy, Steve Guttenberg, Fisher Stevens, G. W. Bailey, Austin Pendleton, Brian McNamara, voice of Tim Blaney. State-of-the-art robot develops a mind of its own and decides that it doesn't want to go "home" to weapons company from which it escaped. Sheedy is cute as the animal-lover who becomes enamored of "No. 5," the equally cute robot. E. T. clone is good fodder for kids but too formula-bound for our taste. Followed by a sequel. Panavision. [PG]▼▶

Short Circuit 2 (1988) **C-110m.** ** D: Kenneth Johnson. Fisher Stevens, Michael McKean, Cynthia Gibb, Jack Weston, Dee McCaffrey, David Hemblen, voice of Tim Blaney. Innocuous (but overlong) sequel has malaprop-prone Stevens and No. 5 (now called Johnny Five) out on their own, falling in with would-be toymaker McKean and bad-guy Weston. Okay for kids, with some chuckles for adults here and there. [PG]▼▶

Short Cuts (1993) **C-189m.** **½ D: Robert Altman. Andie MacDowell, Bruce Davison, Jack Lemmon, Julianne Moore, Matthew Modine, Anne Archer, Fred Ward, Jennifer Jason Leigh, Chris Penn, Lili Taylor, Robert Downey, Jr., Madeleine Stowe, Tim Robbins, Lily Tomlin, Tom Waits, Frances McDormand, Peter Gallagher, Annie Ross, Lori Singer, Lyle Lovett, Buck Henry, Huey Lewis, Robert DoQui, Darnell Williams, Michael Beach, Charles Rocket, Dirk Blocker. Mordant mosaic of unpleasant, unhappy lives in Southern California, adapted from the short stories of Raymond Carver. Altman paints on another oversized canvas, with a series of marginally interconnected vignettes about various couples, parents, lovers, and friends (from a phone-sex purveyor who feeds her baby while plying her trade to a children's party clown seized by melancholia) . . . played by a virtual who's who of contemporary talent. As a feat—a directorial achievement—it's something to behold and admire, but as entertainment it's less rewarding. One of the stories depicted here is expanded and retold in JINDABYNE. Super 35. [R]▼▶

Shortcut to Happiness (2007) **C-106m.** BOMB D: Harry Kirkpatrick (Alec Baldwin). Anthony Hopkins, Alec Baldwin, Jennifer Love Hewitt, Dan Aykroyd, Kim Cattrall, Barry Miller, Amy Poehler, Mike Doyle, Gregg Bello, Bobby Cannavale, Darrell Hammond. In modern-day N.Y.C., failed writer Jabez Stone (Baldwin) sells his soul to the Devil (Hewitt) for fame and fortune. But when the Devil later demands her own, Stone turns to publisher Daniel Webster (Hopkins) to defend him in the Devil's courtroom. Misbegotten, overproduced revision of Stephen Vincent Benet's classic fable "The Devil and Daniel Webster" was filmed in 2001, disowned by debuting director Baldwin, and barely released years later. Painfully dull, hard to sit through even on television. A genuine disaster. Filmed before in 1941 as THE DEVIL AND DANIEL WEBSTER. [PG-13]

Short Eyes (1977) **C-104m.** ***½ D: Robert M. Young. Bruce Davison, Jose Perez, Nathan George, Don Blakely, Shawn Elliott, Curtis Mayfield, Freddy Fender. Raw, uncompromisingly powerful story of men in prison, from Miguel Pinero's highly acclaimed play. Utterly realistic film was

[1247]

shot at N.Y.C.'s now-shuttered Men's House of Detention, known as The Tombs. Title is prison slang for child molester (played by Davison). Scripted by Pinero, who also appears as GoGo. Retitled: SLAMMER. [R]▼◗

Short Fuse SEE: Good to Go

Shorts (2009-U.S.-United Arab Emirates) C-89m. **½ D: Robert Rodriguez. Jimmy Bennett, Jake Short, Kat Dennings, James Spader, Jon Cryer, Leslie Mann, William H. Macy, Trevor Gagnon, Jolie Vanier, Devon Gearhart, Rebel Rodriguez, Leo Howard. Tween comedy about schoolboy pals, the dastardly multinational corporation that employs their parents (with hulking headquarters amusingly situated in the midst of their suburban housing tract), and a magical rainbow stone. Rodriguez's concoction, replete with monsters, will appeal to young audiences but is typically weak in its cardboard depictions of most adults . . . and even some of the kids. Chapters unfold in a nonchronological order, for no discernible reason. [PG]◗

Short Time (1990) C-97m. **½ D: Gregg Champion. Dabney Coleman, Matt Frewer, Teri Garr, Barry Corbin, Joe Pantoliano, Xander Berkeley, Rob Roy, Jak-Erik Eriksen. Street-cop Coleman thinks he has a short time to live, and decides to get himself killed on the job so his wife and son will be taken care of financially. Incredible action stunts commingle uneasily with touches of sentiment in this middling comedy; Coleman is so good he almost pulls it off single-handedly. [PG-13]▼◗

Shot at Glory, A (2002) C-115m. **½ D: Michael Corrente. Robert Duvall, Michael Keaton, Ally McCoist, Brian Cox, Kirsty Mitchell, Cole Hauser, Morag Hood, Libby Langdon. In Scotland, the coach of a second-string soccer team (Duvall, with authentic burr) hopes his returning son-in-law, a superstar player, will take his team to the top, but the two are estranged and the team's American owner wants to take it to Ireland. Handsomely shot on Scottish locations, and well acted, but predictability—and too many off-the-field entanglements—make it hard to care what happens. Released in the UK in 2001. Panavision. [R]▼◗

Shot in the Dark, A (1964) C-101m. **** D: Blake Edwards. Peter Sellers, Elke Sommer, George Sanders, Herbert Lom, Tracy Reed, Burt Kwouk, Graham Stark, Andre Maranne, Turk Thrust (Bryan Forbes). Second Inspector Clouseau comedy is far and away the funniest, with the great detective convinced gorgeous Sommer is innocent of murder despite all evidence to the contrary. Gaspingly hilarious farce never slows down for a second, with memorable scene in a nudist colony. Script by Edwards and William Peter Blatty; fine Henry Mancini

score. Series debuts of Lom, Kwouk, Stark, and Maranne; last Clouseau film (excluding 1968's INSPECTOR CLOUSEAU, made by other hands) until THE RETURN OF THE PINK PANTHER in 1975. Panavision.▼◗◗

Shout, The (1978-British) C-87m. **½ D: Jerzy Skolimowski. Alan Bates, Susannah York, John Hurt, Robert Stephens, Tim Curry. Well-filmed but obscure yarn about an off-his-nut wanderer who dominates the household of a young married couple. Title refers to his aboriginal ability to kill by *shouting*. Worth a look on a slow evening. [R]▼

Shout (1991) C-89m. BOMB D: Jeffrey Hornaday. John Travolta, James Walters, Heather Graham, Richard Jordan, Linda Fiorentino, Scott Coffey, Glenn Quinn, Frank von Zerneck, Michael Bacall. Preposterous '50s twaddle about the birth of rock 'n' roll, with Travolta as a fugitive hired as music teacher and bandmaster at an ill-defined Texas school for wayward youths. Prisoner Walters and warden's daughter Graham are the kissy-facers who form a forbidden alliance. WHEEZE would have been a better title for this turkey. Film debut of Gwyneth Paltrow. [PG-13] ▼◗◗

Shout at the Devil (1976-British) C-119m. **½ D: Peter R. Hunt. Lee Marvin, Roger Moore, Barbara Parkins, Ian Holm, Rene Kolldehoff. Plot-heavy action nonsense, set in Mozambique, about a poacher, his daughter and an expatriate Englishman who eventually set out to blow up a German battle cruiser at the outset of WW1. Occasionally fun but overlong. Original British running-time: 144m. Panavision. [PG]▼◗

Show, The (1995) C/B&W-90m. **½ D: Brian Robbins. Craig Mack, Dr. Dre, Naughty by Nature, Run-DMC, Slick Rick, Snoop Doggy Dogg, Tha Dogg Pound. Spotty concert and backstage documentary still has enough to satisfy fans of rap and hip-hop, contrasting the younger breed—a couple of whom have had serious scrapes with the law—with the wizened old-breed performers like LL Cool J and members of Run-DMC. Film's non-linear structure comes off as more haphazard than creative. [R]▼◗◗

Show Boat (1936) 113m. *** D: James Whale. Irene Dunne, Allan Jones, Helen Morgan, Paul Robeson, Charles Winninger, Hattie McDaniel. Entertaining treatment of Jerome Kern–Oscar Hammerstein II musical (filmed before in 1929) mixes music, sentiment, and melodrama, with enough great moments to make up for the rest: Robeson doing "Old Man River," Morgan singing her unforgettable "Bill," etc. Originally an Edna Ferber novel; Hammerstein also wrote the screenplay. Filmed again in 1951.▼◗

Show Boat (1951) C-107m. *** D: George Sidney. Kathryn Grayson, Ava Gardner, Howard Keel, Joe E. Brown, Marge and

Gower Champion, Robert Sterling, Agnes Moorehead, Leif Erickson, William Warfield. MGM's Technicolor valentine to this old-fashioned musical about life on a Mississippi show boat; acted with sincerity, stylishly shot and staged. Gardner makes a beautiful and poignant Julie. Timeless Jerome Kern–Oscar Hammerstein II songs include "Bill" (lyrics by P. G. Wodehouse), "Can't Help Lovin' That Man," "Make Believe," "Old Man River." ▼●)

Showdown (1966) SEE: **Tramplers, The**

Showdown (1973) **C-99m.** **½ D: George Seaton. Rock Hudson, Dean Martin, Susan Clark, Donald Moffat, John McLiam, Ed Begley, Jr. Two friends in love with the same woman go their separate ways, until Hudson (now a sheriff) is forced to hunt down Martin (now a robber). Agreeable but unexceptional Western yarn was Seaton's final film. Todd-AO 35. [PG]▼

Showdown at Williams Creek (1991-Canadian) **C-97m.** *** D: Allan Kroeker. Tom Burlinson, Donnelly Rhodes, Michelle Thrush, John Pyper Ferguson, Alex Bruhanski, Raymond Burr. Compelling allegory of racism, exploitation, greed, and survival in the Northwest Territory during the 19th century. The scenario, which unravels in flashback, details the journey of Irishman Burlinson from British army officer to scruffy "squaw man" on trial for murder. Based on actual events. [R]▼▶

Showdown in Little Tokyo (1991) **C-76m.** BOMB D: Mark L. Lester. Dolph Lundgren, Brandon Lee, Carey-Hiroyuki Tagawa, Tia Carrere, Toshiro Obata. Knuckleheaded martial-arts actioner, with Lundgren and Lee (the son of Bruce Lee) going up against Japanese mobsters. Poorly directed, acted, and (especially) scripted. [R]▼▶

Shower (1999-Chinese) **C-92m.** ***½ D: Zhang Yang. Pu Cun Xin, Zhu Xu, Jiang Wu, He Zheng. Bittersweet, thoroughly winning tale of a businessman (Pu) who pays a visit to his father, the operator of a public bathhouse that's about to be torn down and replaced by a high-rise; the old man also looks after his sweet but slow-witted younger son. Zhang effectively contrasts the fast pace of modern life with the value of tradition, as symbolized by the taking of a fast, impersonal shower vs. luxuriating in a bath. [PG-13]▼▶

Showgirls (1995) **C-131m.** BOMB D: Paul Verhoeven. Elizabeth Berkley, Kyle MacLachlan, Gina Gershon, Glenn Plummer, Robert Davi, Alan Rachins, Gina Ravera, Lin Tucci, Greg Travis, Patrick Bristow. Stupefyingly awful movie—whose creators swear to have made it with serious intentions—about a young, hotheaded drifter who hitches her way to Vegas, becomes a "lap dancer," and then a full-fledged showgirl, discovering that sex and career moves are hopelessly intertwined.

Part soft-core porn, part hokey backstage drama, full of howlingly hilarious dialogue. Berkley sets the tone for her performance in an early scene in which she expresses fury by vigorously spewing ketchup over her french fries. Written by Joe Eszterhas. Released on video in alternate R-rated format with 61 seconds cut, and 20 seconds of footage altered by using different camera angles. Super 35. [NC-17]▼●)

Show of Force, A (1990) **C-93m.** ** D: Bruno Barreto. Amy Irving, Robert Duvall, Andy Garcia, Lou Diamond Phillips, Kevin Spacey, Joe Campanella, Erik Estrada, Priscilla Pointer, Hattie Winston. Oddly stagnant political thriller about Puerto Rico's 1978 version of Watergate. Irving plays a local TV reporter convinced that the F.B.I. set up and killed two political radicals to earn voting support for the current governor. Garcia's role is a glorified cameo; Phillips is surprisingly effective as a flamboyant villain. [R]▼●)

Showtime (2002) **C-95m.** ** D: Tom Dey. Robert De Niro, Eddie Murphy, Rene Russo, Pedro Damián, Mos Def, Frankie R. Faison, William Shatner, Nestor Serrano, Kadeem Hardison. Veteran L.A. cop De Niro is punished for his reckless ways by being assigned to work on a new reality TV show with Murphy, an eager but inexperienced partner (who's also a wannabe actor). What starts out as a satire of TV cop shows and movies eventually becomes the very thing it's spoofing. The stars have almost nothing to work with here. The star's daughter, Drena De Niro, plays Russo's assistant. Super 35. [PG-13]▼▶

Shrek (2001) **C-88m.** *** D: Andrew Adamson, Vicky Jenson. Voices of Mike Myers, Eddie Murphy, Cameron Diaz, John Lithgow, Vincent Cassel, Jim Cummings, Kathleen Freeman. An antisocial troll is joined by a talkative donkey as he goes on a quest to save a beautiful princess. Funny spoof of fairy-tale sagas with some good laughs, not all of them aimed at children. Computer-animated fable mixes heightened reality with fanciful designs; from Pacific Data Images, the folks who made ANTZ. Based on a children's book by William Steig. Alternate version runs 91m. Winner of the first Oscar for Best Animated Feature. Followed by a 3-D short, three sequels, a holiday TV special, *Shrek the Halls*, and a Broadway musical. [PG] ▼▶

Shrek 2 (2004) **C-88m.** **½ D: Andrew Adamson, Kelly Asbury, Conrad Vernon. Voices of Mike Myers, Eddie Murphy, Cameron Diaz, Julie Andrews, John Cleese, Antonio Banderas, Rupert Everett, Jennifer Saunders, Conrad Vernon, Larry King, Joan Rivers. Sequel to the 2001 megahit tries to devise enough story to justify another feature, with middling results. Newlyweds Shrek and Fiona visit her parents, who don't know their daughter has married an ogre. Then a crafty Fairy Godmother does everything in her power to split up the couple so her son, Prince Charming, can claim Fiona as his bride. Skillfully made, but pointless and short on laughs; Banderas comes off best as a Zorro-like Puss in Boots. [PG]▼◖

Shrek the Third (2007) **C-93m.** ** D: Chris Miller. Voices of Mike Myers, Eddie Murphy, Cameron Diaz, Antonio Banderas, Julie Andrews, John Cleese, Rupert Everett, Eric Idle, Justin Timberlake, Seth Rogen, Larry King, John Krasinski, Ian McShane, Cheri Oteri, Regis Philbin, Amy Poehler, Maya Rudolph, Amy Sedaris. When the king of Far Far Away dies, it's up to the big green ogre to take his place, but he doesn't want the job. So he, Donkey, and Puss in Boots go off in search of the only other heir to the throne. Third trip to the well finds the water stale and filled with silt . . . but kids may still be entertained. [PG]◖

Shrek Forever After (2010) **C-93m.** ** D: Mike Mitchell. Voices of Mike Myers, Eddie Murphy, Cameron Diaz, Antonio Banderas, Walt Dohrn, Jane Lynch, Craig Robinson, Julie Andrews, John Cleese, Jon Hamm. Shrek finds himself bored with family life and longs for his earlier days as a fearsome ogre. Enter evil Rumpelstiltskin, who makes Shrek an offer he cannot refuse, sending him into an alternate universe where events of the first three films never happened. There, Stiltskin is a tyrannical king, Donkey is a slave, Puss is an overweight slob, and Fiona is a warrior princess leading the resistance. A notch better than the third film, and kids may enjoy the slapstick and the familiar characters, but the freshness and cleverness are now far, far away. Advertised as "The Final Chapter"; one can only hope it is. Numerous celebrities voice small parts. 3-D Digital Widescreen. [PG]◖

Shrieking, The SEE: **Hex**

Shrimp on the Barbie, The (1990) **C-86m.** *½ D: Alan Smithee. Cheech Marin, Emma Samms, Vernon Wells, Terence Cooper, Jeanette Cronin, Carole Davis. Marin goes Down Under, gets a job as waiter in a Mexican restaurant, winds up posing as the fiancé of a wealthy heiress to thwart her powerful father. Cheech shows some charm, but you know something's up when the director takes his name off the project. Shot in New Zealand. Video version runs 87m., and is rated R. [PG-13]▼◉◖

Shrink (2009) **C-105m.** *½ D: Jonas Pate. Kevin Spacey, Mark Webber, Keke Palmer, Saffron Burrows, Jack Huston, Pell James, Dallas Roberts, Laura Ramsey, Jesse Plemons, Robert Loggia, Gore Vidal. Paper-thin slice of life about a celebrity L.A. psychiatrist (Spacey) whose life is coming apart. Means to be a thoughtful exploration of the shallowness of contemporary Hollywood, but the result is meandering and the ending is not at all credible. Robin Williams and Griffin Dunne appear unbilled. [R]◖

Shrunken Heads (1994) **C-86m.** **½ D: Richard Elfman. Aeryk Egan, Becky Herbst, A. J. Damato, Bo Sharon, Darris Love, Bodhi Elfman, Meg Foster, Julius Harris. Clever special effects enliven this run-of-the-mill Full Moon horror-comedy in which Haitian voodoo master Harris revives three murdered kids, who seek revenge against the trash responsible for their deaths. Title music composed by the director's brother, Danny Elfman. [R]▼◉

Shutter (2008) **C-85m.** ** D: Masayuki Ochiai. Joshua Jackson, Rachael Taylor, Megumi Okina, David Denman, John Hensley, Maya Hazen, James Kyson Lee. Young married couple is shocked when they find ghostly images on a roll of film they develop. Soon they are haunted by the spirit of a Japanese girl the husband may have known before. Original 2004 film was a huge hit in its native Thailand; this remake is set in Japan with American stars, and a Japanese cast and director. Attempt to duplicate the success of movies like THE GRUDGE and THE RING is defeated by mundane plotting and dopey dialogue. Alternate version runs 90m. [PG-13]◖

Shuttered Room, The (1967-British) **C-99m.** **½ D: David Greene. Gig Young, Carol Lynley, Oliver Reed, Flora Robson. Young couple inherit old house in New England, threatened by local toughs and unseen presence. Good cast deserves better material; even revelation is tame. Based on an August Derleth–H. P. Lovecraft story. Video title: BLOOD ISLAND.▼◖

Shutter Island (2010) **C-138m.** ** D: Martin Scorsese. Leonardo DiCaprio, Mark Ruffalo, Ben Kingsley, Michelle Williams, Emily Mortimer, Max von Sydow, Patricia Clarkson, Jackie Earle Haley, Ted Levine, John Carroll Lynch, Elias Koteas. In 1954, federal marshal DiCaprio and his new partner (Ruffalo) take a ferry to a remote island, off the coast of Boston, to investigate the disappearance of a violent patient from an asylum for the criminally insane. The place is creepy and its staff is secretive and strange, which only makes things worse for DiCaprio, who has a personal agenda. Nothing is what it seems in this portentous production, and the "big reveal" may well make the whole thing pointless. With Scorsese behind the lens (and a gold-plated roster of collaborators on both sides of the camera), it's hard to dismiss—but it doesn't rate much as entertainment. Based on a novel by Dennis Lehane. Super 35. [R]◖

Shut Up & Sing (2006) **C-93m.** *** D: Barbara Kopple, Cecilia Peck. Fascinating documentary on the flare-up that occurred near the beginning of the Iraq war when superstar country group The Dixie Chicks told a foreign concert audience they were ashamed to be from the same state as President George W. Bush. With cameras seemingly following the trio 24 hours a day, we see the repercussions the statement had on their lives and careers. Remarkable not only for its political content but as a primer on how a show-business career is made and marketed. Like very few movies of its ilk, this one shows us the "Chicks" machine at work with an image transformation played out in extreme close-up. Backstage drama is melded with several fine concert sequences. [R]◗

Shy People (1987) **C-118m.** **½ D: Andrei Konchalovsky. Jill Clayburgh, Barbara Hershey, Martha Plimpton, Mare Winningham, Merritt Butrick, John Philbin, Don Swayze, Pruitt Taylor Vince. N.Y.C. photo-journalist Clayburgh ventures into the Louisiana bayous (dragging along rebellious daughter Plimpton and a totally inappropriate wardrobe) to research a *Cosmopolitan* article on a *very* distant branch of her family. Hodgepodge film is implausible, melodramatic, ridiculous—and fascinating. Recommended chiefly for Hershey's riveting performance (as the head of the backwoods clan), and for cinematographer Chris Menges' remarkable opening shot of Manhattan. J-D-C Scope. [R]▼◗

Sibling, The SEE: **So Evil, My Sister**

Sibling Rivalry (1990) **C-88m.** ** D: Carl Reiner. Kirstie Alley, Bill Pullman, Carrie Fisher, Jami Gertz, Scott Bakula, Sam Elliott, Ed O'Neill, Frances Sternhagen, John Randolph, Paul Benedict, Bill Macy, Matthew Laurance. Black comedy about a repressed woman, stuck in a tedious marriage; at the urging of her sister, she has a fling with a chance acquaintance—who dies after an afternoon of mad, passionate sex. And that's just the *beginning* of the story. Some clever ideas get bogged down in this heavy-handed film. [PG-13]▼◗●

Sicilian, The (1987) **C-115m.** BOMB D: Michael Cimino. Christopher Lambert, Terence Stamp, Barbara Sukowa, Giulia Boschi, Joss Ackland, John Turturro, Richard Bauer, Ray McAnally, Barry Miller, Joe Regalbuto, Aldo Ray. Militantly lugubrious bio of Salvatore Giuliano, who took on Church, State, and Mafia in an attempt to promote Sicily's secession from Italy in the late 1940s. Gore Vidal contributed to the screenplay, credited to Steve Shagan. The 146-minute director's cut (**) is available on cassette and actually seems shorter, thanks to more coherency and Sukowa's strengthened role. Neither version, though, can overcome two chief liabilities: Cimino's missing sense of humor and Lambert's laughably stone-faced performance. Title figure was previously the subject of Francesco Rosi's 1962 SALVATORE GIULIANO. J-D-C Scope. [R]▼◗●

Sicilian Clan, The (1969-French) **C-121m.** *** D: Henri Verneuil. Jean Gabin, Alain Delon, Lino Ventura, Irina Demick, Amedeo Nazzari, Sydney Chaplin. Gangland family's plans for jewel heist grow increasingly complex; crime caper on grandiose scale, totally implausible but great fun. Gabin is smooth head of clan, Delon a young ambitious thief hired for the occasion. Panavision. [PG]

Sicko (2007) **C-123m.** ***½ D: Michael Moore. Provocative exposé of American health care is alternately entertaining and infuriating, focusing less on the uninsured than on people who have supposed coverage. Moore lets various victims of the system speak for themselves, then enters the picture to show us how other countries deal with the issue. In a heart-rending climax he takes some of his interviewees to Cuba, of all places, where they receive not only care but compassion. Moore makes no pretense of fairness, objectivity, or thoroughness—but still strikes home in what may be his best film to date. [PG-13]◗

Sid and Nancy (1986) **C-111m.** *** D: Alex Cox. Gary Oldman, Chloe Webb, Drew Schofield, David Hayman, Debby Bishop, Tony London, Perry Benson, Gloria LeRoy, Courtney Love. Harrowing look at the bizarre, self-destructive, and curiously compelling relationship between British punk rock singer Sid Vicious (of The Sex Pistols) and American groupie Nancy Spungen in the 1970s. Director Cox achieves a masterful level of docu-realism, then laces it with allegorical dream images, with striking results. At the core of the film are two remarkable performances, by Oldman and Webb, who don't seem to be performing at all: they *are* Sid and Nancy. A downer, to be sure, but fascinating. [R] ▼◗

Siddhartha (1973) **C-95m.** **½ D: Conrad Rooks. Shashi Kapoor, Simi Garewal, Romesh Shama, Pinchoo Kapoor, Zul Vellani, Amrik Singh. Uneven version of Hermann Hesse novel follows Indian as he leaves family to find more exciting life. Too arty, but on-location photography by Sven Nykvist (Ingmar Bergman's cinematographer) is often dazzling. Panavision. [R] ▼◗

Sidecar Racers (1975-Australian) **C-100m.** ** D: Earl Bellamy. Ben Murphy, Wendy Hughes, John Clayton, Peter Graves, John Meillon, John Derum. Murphy becomes a champion sidecar racer; the usual. [PG]

Side Out (1990) **C-100m.** *½ D: Peter Israelson. C. Thomas Howell, Peter Horton, Courtney Thorne-Smith, Harley Jane Kozak, Christopher Rydell, Terry Kiser, Randy Stoklos, Sinjin Smith, Kathy Ireland. College kid comes to Southern California for a summer job evicting tenants for his sleazy uncle but instead winds up joining with one of his intended victims for the ultimate beach volleyball match. Sand, surf, and sun are the sole highlights of this no-brainer which purports to be the first major studio film about volleyball. What's next? Badminton? [PG-13]▼●❘

Side Street (1949) 83m. *** D: Anthony Mann. Farley Granger, Cathy O'Donnell, James Craig, Paul Kelly, Edmon Ryan, Paul Harvey, Jean Hagen, Charles McGraw, Adele Jergens, Harry Bellaver, Whit Bissell. Story of part-time postman Granger impulsively stealing a wad of money, and finding himself involved with gangsters and murder, is bolstered by striking N.Y.C. locations and stark cinematography by Joseph Ruttenberg. The chase finale is a highlight.❘

Sidewalks of London (1938-British) 84m. *** D: Tim Whelan. Charles Laughton, Vivien Leigh, Rex Harrison, Tyrone Guthrie, Larry Adler. Laughton is superb as a busker (street entertainer), with Leigh almost matching him as his protegée, who uses and abuses all in her quest for success as a stage star (a character not unlike Scarlett O'Hara!). Top entertainment . . . until that ill-conceived final sequence. Original British title: ST. MARTIN'S LANE.▼❘

Sidewalks of New York (2001) C-107m. **½ D: Edward Burns. Edward Burns, Rosario Dawson, Heather Graham, Stanley Tucci, David Krumholtz, Dennis Farina, Brittany Murphy, Callie Thorne, Aida Turturro. Generally funny comedy about the romantic entanglements of a group of New Yorkers, some likable and others self-absorbed. Has an unmistakable Woody Allen–ish feel, but Burns' script is no match for Allen. Graham blatantly imitates Diane Keaton's Annie Hall; her character is even named Annie. Tucci is on target as a smarmy, philandering dentist. [R]▼❘

Sidewalk Stories (1989) 97m. *** D: Charles Lane. Charles Lane, Nicole Alysia, Sandye Wilson, Darnell Williams, Trula Hoosier. Charming, Chaplinesque fantasy that, in its own modest way, boldly comments on the plight of the homeless in America. Lane stars as a homeless man struggling for survival on the streets of Greenwich Village who finds himself caring for a cute toddler whose father has been stabbed by muggers. There's almost no dialogue; Marc Marder's evocative score adds immeasurably to the film's mood. Don't miss this sweet, gentle sleeper. [R]

Sideways (2004) C-126m. ***½ D: Alexander Payne. Paul Giamatti, Thomas Haden Church, Virginia Madsen, Sandra Oh, Marylouise Burke, Jessica Hecht. Giamatti gives another great—and thoroughly natural, totally believable—performance as a would-be author, passionate oenophile, and social misfit who takes a college pal off for a week in California wine country before he gets married. Along the way, this odd couple meets two attractive women who seem to return

their interest. Told with wit, truth, compassion, and the eye for detail that marks all of Payne's work. Oscar-winning screenplay by Payne and Jim Taylor, adapted from Rex Pickett's previously unpublished novel. [R]▼❘

Sidney Sheldon's Bloodline SEE: **Bloodline**

Siege, The (1998) C-116m. *** D: Edward Zwick. Denzel Washington, Annette Bening, Bruce Willis, Tony Shalhoub, Sami Bouajila, Ahmed Ben Larby, Liana Pai, Mark Valley, Jack Gwaltney, David Proval, Lance Reddick. Terrorists set off bombs all over N.Y.C., crippling the city and leading to the imposition of martial law—including concentration camps for all Arabs, foreigners and citizens alike. Soon the general in charge (a cardboard Willis) is behaving like a tyrant, clashing with FBI man Washington and CIA agent Bening (both excellent). Well made and suspenseful. Super 35. [R]▼●❘

Siegfried SEE: **Die Nibelungen**

Siesta (1987) C-97m. *½ D: Mary Lambert. Ellen Barkin, Gabriel Byrne, Jodie Foster, Martin Sheen, Grace Jones, Julian Sands, Isabella Rossellini. Sky diver Barkin ends up disheveled and semi-nude in Spain (by way of Death Valley); her subsequent odyssey has something to do with murder (which may actually be a fantasy) and a taxi driver with rusty teeth who keeps trying to rape her. So-called experimental film is a throwback to some of the more incomprehensible efforts of the 1960s. Music score by Miles Davis. Barkin and Byrne later married in real life. [R]▼●

Signal 7 (1983) C-92m. **½ D: Rob Nilsson. Bill Ackridge, Dan Leegant, Bob Elross, Hagit Farber, John Tidwell, Herb Mills. Touching and revealing but rambling stream-of-consciousness tale of middle-aged cabdrivers—their camaraderie, illusions, desperation. Ambitious but uneven; dedicated, appropriately, to John Cassavetes. Shot on video then transferred to 16mm. for theatrical release.▼❘

Sign of the Cross, The (1932) 124m. **½ D: Cecil B. DeMille. Fredric March, Elissa Landi, Claudette Colbert, Charles Laughton, Ian Keith, Vivian Tobin, Nat Pendleton, Joe Bonomo. Well-meaning but heavy-handed account of Christians seeking religious freedom in Rome under Emperor Nero. Very slow going, despite fine work by March as Marcus Superbus, Laughton as Nero, and especially Colbert as alluring Poppaea. Reissued in 1944 at 118m. with many cuts of sexy and sadistic scenes, and a nine-minute WW2 prologue added.▼❘

Sign of the Pagan (1954) C-92m. **½ D: Douglas Sirk. Jeff Chandler, Jack Palance, Ludmilla Tcherina, Rita Gam, Jeff Morrow, Alexander Scourby. Uneven script hampers story of Attila the Hun threatening Rome;

Sirk's stylish direction helps somewhat. CinemaScope.

Sign o' the Times (1987) **C-85m.** ******* D: Prince. Prince, Sheila E., Sheena Easton, Dr. Fink, Miko Weaver, Levi Seacer, Jr., Wally Safford, Gregory Allen Brooks, Boni Boyer. Mostly punchy Prince concert film, shot in Rotterdam and Minnesota, features 13 numbers, some overhead photography and lots of bump and grind from both sexes. Stolen to some degree by star drummer Sheila E.; otherwise "live" film features Sheena Easton's rock video "U Got the Look." [PG-13]▼❶

Signs (2002) **C-106m.** ****½** D: M. Night Shyamalan. Mel Gibson, Joaquin Phoenix, Cherry Jones, Rory Culkin, Abigail Breslin, Patricia Kalember. A minister who's lost his way after the death of his wife discovers strange crop signs outside his home and soon finds his family threatened. Creepy movie about ultra-close encounters with invading aliens is thwarted by its own ambitions to tackle even bigger subjects like faith, fate, and the order of the universe. When it dwells on those matters it's downright silly at times, but when it sticks to the scary stuff it makes you jump. Written by the director, who also plays Ray. [PG-13] ▼❶

Signs & Wonders (2000-French-U.S.) **C-108m.** ******* D: Jonathan Nossiter. Stellan Skarsgård, Charlotte Rampling, Deborah Kara Unger, Dimitris Katalifos, Ashley Remy. Unusual drama about a crumbling American marriage in Athens, Greece. After having an extramarital affair, a husband becomes blindly determined to win back his wife, even though she's now romantically involved with a Greek political activist. Plays like an art-house sociopolitical FATAL ATTRACTION with multiple stalkers, but it's worth sticking with thanks to an intelligent script and intense performances from Rampling and Skarsgård as a couple on the brink. [R]▼❶

Signs of Life (1989) **C-91m.** ****½** D: John David Coles. Arthur Kennedy, Kevin J. O'Connor, Vincent Phillip D'Onofrio, Michael Lewis, Beau Bridges, Kate Reid, Kathy Bates, Mary-Louise Parker, Georgia Engel. A generations-old boat-building business in Maine closes its doors, and the people, young and old, who've spent their lives working there try to figure out what to do next. An ideal showcase for Kennedy (in his first film in ten years) and a talented cast, but superlative acting cannot completely make up for an air of familiarity in Mark Malone's script. A PBS *American Playhouse* production. [PG-13]▼●

Silas Marner (1985-British) **C-92m.** *****½** D: Giles Foster. Ben Kingsley, Jenny Agutter, Patrick Ryecart, Jonathan Coy, Freddie Jones, Frederick Treves, Angela Pleasence. Solid, marvelously detailed version of the George Eliot novel with Kingsley quite moving as the title character, a weaver who becomes a recluse after he's falsely accused of thievery and sent into exile. Reworked in 1994 as A SIMPLE TWIST OF FATE. ▼❶

Silence, The (1963-Swedish) **95m.** *****½** D: Ingmar Bergman. Ingrid Thulin, Gunnel Lindblom, Håkan Jahnberb, Birger Malmsten. Stark, forceful symbolic narrative of two sisters who stop at a hotel in a North European city. One sister (Thulin) is a frustrated lesbian with no future, the other (Lindblom) a free-loving mother of a 10-year-old boy. The last in Bergman's trilogy on faith, following THROUGH A GLASS DARKLY and WINTER LIGHT.▼●❶

Silence (1974) **C-88m.** ****½** D: John Korty. Will Geer, Ellen Geer, Richard Kelton, Ian Geer Flanders, Craig Kelly. Outdoor drama of autistic boy Flanders lost in the wilderness is a Geer family affair, interestingly done. Aka CRAZY JACK AND THE BOY. [G]▼

Silence of the Hams, The (1994) **C-81m.** BOMB D: Ezio Greggio. Dom DeLuise, Billy Zane, Joanna Pacula, Charlene Tilton, Martin Balsam, Stuart Pankin, John Astin, Phyllis Diller, Bubba Smith, Larry Storch, Rip Taylor, Shelley Winters. Zane is a rookie FBI agent on the trail of a serial killer; DeLuise is the psychotic criminal he turns to for help. Lame comedy in the AIRPLANE! tradition spoofs THE SILENCE OF THE LAMBS and PSYCHO. Film buffs might want to note cameos by such directors as Joe Dante and John Carpenter. Others might want to avoid the movie altogether. [R]▼●

Silence of the Lambs, The (1991) **C-118m.** *****½** D: Jonathan Demme. Jodie Foster, Anthony Hopkins, Scott Glenn, Ted Levine, Anthony Heald, Brooke Smith, Diane Baker, Kasi Lemmons, Charles Napier, Tracey Walter, Roger Corman, Chris Isaak. FBI trainee Foster is recruited to attempt to get through to a brilliant psychotic criminal, "Hannibal the Cannibal" Lecter (Hopkins), in the hope that he may help catch a serial killer. Almost unbearably intense, brilliantly acted (by Foster and Hopkins), and cannily put together—though the subject material is at times repellent. Based on the Thomas Harris best-seller; the Hannibal character appeared in a previous Harris adaptation, MANHUNTER. Oscar winner for Best Picture, Actor (Hopkins), Actress (Foster), Director, and Adapted Screenplay (Ted Tally). Followed 10 years later by HANNIBAL. [R]▼●❶

Silence of the North (1981-Canadian) **C-94m.** ****** D: Allan Winton King. Ellen Burstyn, Tom Skerritt, Gordon Pinsent, Jennifer McKinney, Donna Dobrijevic, Colin Fox. OK drama of independent-minded Burstyn surviving in the Canadian wilderness. Beautiful scenery; based on a true story. Panavision. [PG]▼

Silencers, The (1966) **C-102m.** ****½** D: Phil Karlson. Dean Martin, Stella Stevens, Daliah Lavi, Victor Buono, Robert Webber, James Gregory, Arthur O'Connell, Cyd Charisse, Roger C. Carmel, Nancy Kovack. Donald Hamilton's secret agent Matt Helm is pulled out of "retirement" to combat Buono's efforts to destroy a U.S. atomic testing site. First of four theatrical Helms is far and away the best, with Stevens just wonderful as well-meaning klutz. Sequel: MURDERERS' ROW.▼●)

Silent Assassins (1988) **C-92m.** ****½** D: Lee Doo-yong, Scott Thomas. Sam J. Jones, Linda Blair, Jun Chong, Phillip Rhee, Bill Erwin, Gustav Vintas, Mako, Rebecca Ferratti, Stuart Damon. Well-made actioner has commando Jones whip into action when a scientist is kidnapped by baddies for his secret biological-warfare formula. His helpers, Chong and Rhee, doubled as film's producers and fight choreographers.▼

Silent Enemy, The (1958-British) **92m.** ****½** D: William Fairchild. Laurence Harvey, Dawn Addams, John Clements, Michael Craig. British Naval frogmen, headed by Harvey, are assigned to combat enemy counterpart during WW2; underwater sequences well handled, with some pre-THUNDERBALL gimmicks.▼

Silent Fall (1994) **C-100m.** ***½** D: Bruce Beresford. Richard Dreyfuss, Linda Hamilton, John Lithgow, J.T. Walsh, Ben Faulkner, Liv Tyler. When an autistic youngster (Faulkner) is the only witness to his parents' bloody double murder, controversial shrink Dreyfuss tries to unlock the boy's mind in an attempt to crack the case. Murky all the way, and predictable *nearly* all the way, except for an ill-advised "light" wrap-up that'll make you take a loud fall out of your seat. Barely released. [R]▼●)

Silent Hill (2006-U.S.-French) **C-127m.** ***½** D: Christophe Gans. Radha Mitchell, Sean Bean, Laurie Holden, Alice Krige, Deborah Kara Unger, Kim Coates, Tanya Allen, Jodelle Ferland, Colleen Williams. Don't check this movie for parenting tips. When her little girl starts drawing strange images and uttering the words "silent hill" as she sleepwalks through recurring nightmares, the mother actually finds the obscure place on a map and drives her daughter straight into the fog-laden, deserted ghost town it has become. Another video game becomes a hokey excuse for a two-hour-plus horror movie. Dialogue is so laughable it might be advisable to watch SILENT HILL with the sound turned off. Super 35. [R]▼

Silent Movie (1976) **C-86m.** ****½** D: Mel Brooks. Mel Brooks, Marty Feldman, Dom DeLuise, Bernadette Peters, Sid Caesar, Harold Gould, Ron Carey, guests Burt Reynolds, James Caan, Liza Minnelli, Paul Newman, Anne Bancroft, Marcel Marceau, Harry Ritz. Disappointing attempt to revive silent com-

edy, with Brooks as movie producer hoping for comeback. Blackout gags range from very funny to misfire. Results are only mild instead of the knockout they should have been. [PG]▼●)

Silent Night, Bloody Night (1973) **C-87m.** ****** D: Theodore Gershuny. Patrick O'Neal, James Patterson, Mary Woronov, Astrid Heeren, John Carradine, Walter Abel. Uneven low-budgeter about escaped killer from insane asylum terrorizing small New England town, and inhabitants of mysterious old mansion that's up for sale. [R]▼▼

Silent Night, Deadly Night (1984) **C-79m.** BOMB D: Charles E. Sellier, Jr. Lilyan Chauvan, Gilmer McCormick, Toni Nero, Robert Brian Wilson, Britt Leach. Controversial—and worthless—splatter movie about a psychotic (Wilson), dressed in a Santa suit, who commits brutal ax-murders. Theaters that played this film were picketed; what next—the Easter Bunny as a child molester? "Uncut and uncensored" DVD runs 85m. Followed by four sequels! [R]▼●)

Silent Night, Deadly Night Part II (1987) **C-88m.** BOMB D: Lee Harry. Eric Freeman, James L. Newman, Elizabeth Kaitan. Embarrassing (and unnecessary) follow-up to the Santa Claus-killer film has hero's younger brother continuing the psychotic carnage. About half the footage here is lifted from the original film (including a memorable scene featuring Linnea Quigley); new scenes are perfunctory. [R]▼●)

Silent Night, Deadly Night III—Better Watch Out! (1989) **C-91m.** ****** D: Monte Hellman. Samantha Scully, Bill Moseley, Richard Beymer, Robert Culp, Eric Da Re, Laura Herring. Shrewdly made sequel pits now grown killer from Part II against young blind woman linked to him by ESP. Well made, with touches of black comedy, but still only a slasher movie, less gruesome than most. Santa Claus is not the heavy this time—he's a victim. [R]▼●)

Silent Night, Deadly Night 4 (1990) **C-90m.** ***½** D: Brian Yuzna. Maud Adams, Tommy Hinkley, Allyce Beasley, Clint Howard, Neith Hunter, Jeanne Bates, Laurel Lockhart. Investigating a strange death, a young woman would-be reporter becomes involved with witches, large bugs, worms, and Clint Howard. Though intelligent, it's gratuitously gruesome, dull, poorly acted, and bizarrely anti-feminist. Christmas elements are completely superfluous. Actual title on-screen is INITIATION: SILENT NIGHT, DEADLY NIGHT 4. [R]▼●)

Silent Night, Deadly Night 5: The Toymaker (1991) **C-90m.** ****** D: Martin Kitrosser. Jane Higginson, William Thone, Tracy Fraim, Mickey Rooney, Brian Bremer, Neith Hunter, Clint Howard. Toys are out to kill a little boy at Christmastime, but who's responsible? Drunken toymaker Petto (Rooney) or his odd son Pino? (The names are clumsy clues.) Overplotted but OK horror thriller with a lot of sex. No plot connection to earlier films in series. [R] ▼●)

Silent Night, Evil Night SEE: **Black Christmas**

Silent Partner, The (1978-Canadian) C-103m. *** D: Daryl Duke. Elliott Gould, Christopher Plummer, Susannah York, Celine Lomez, Michael Kirby, Ken Pogue, John Candy. Offbeat film about crafty bank teller Gould playing cat-and-mouse with psychotic robber Plummer. Well directed, with fine eye for detail, but bursts of graphic violence are jarring. Nice score by Oscar Peterson. Screenplay by Curtis Hanson. [R] ▼●)

Silent Rage (1982) C-105m. *½ D: Michael Miller. Chuck Norris, Ron Silver, Steven Keats, Toni Kalem, William Finley, Brian Libby, Stephen Furst. Small-town Texas sheriff Norris versus sickie killer Libby, a Frankenstein-like creation of science. Ho-hum. [R] ▼●)

Silent Running (1971) C-89m. *** D: Douglas Trumbull. Bruce Dern, Cliff Potts, Ron Rifkin, Jesse Vint. Space-age ecology tale of botanist's fight on space station to keep Earth's final vegetation samples from being destroyed. Interesting film marked directorial debut of special effects whiz Trumbull (2001, CLOSE ENCOUNTERS). Script by Deric Washburn, Michael Cimino, and Steven Bochco; unusual score by Peter Schickele. [G] ▼●)

Silent Scream (1980) C-87m. *½ D: Denny Harris. Rebecca Balding, Cameron Mitchell, Avery Schreiber, Barbara Steele, Yvonne De Carlo. Another illogical, obvious kids-caught-in-eerie-old-house melodrama. Some scares, but who cares? [R] ▼●

Silent Tongue (1994) C-98m. BOMB D: Sam Shepard. Richard Harris, Alan Bates, River Phoenix, Dermot Mulroney, Sheila Tousey, Jeri Arredondo, Tantoo Cardinal, Bill Irwin, David Shiner, The Red Clay Ramblers. While his son goes delirious in the New Mexico prairie, dragging around the corpse of his halfbreed bride, Harris tries to negotiate a deal for her sister from medicine show proprietor Bates (who sired both girls). If you wonder how a movie with this cast could remain on the shelf for two years, proceed at your own peril. Phoenix's penultimate film (released after his death), though it gives him nothing to do. Shepard also wrote the script. Panavision. [PG-13] ▼●)

Silent World, The (1956-French) C-86m. *** D: Jacques-Yves Cousteau, Louis Malle. Frederic Duman, Albert Falco, Jacques-Yves Cousteau. Academy Award-winning documentary account of an expedition above and—most memorably—below the sea's surface by Captain Cousteau and his divers and crew. Beautifully photographed; Malle's first film.

Silk (2007-Canadian-Italian-Japanese) C-109m. ** D: François Girard. Michael Pitt, Keira Knightley, Kôji Yakusho, Alfred Molina, Sei Ashina, Kenneth Welsh. Beautiful but bland period piece, based on popular novel by Alessandro Baricco, about a 19th-century French merchant (Pitt) who falls for a mysterious local beauty (Ashina) while bargaining for silkworms in Japan. Unfortunately, he has a loving wife (Knightley) at home, so nothing good comes of this. Molina adds a bit of life to ponderous proceedings as the merchant's roguish boss, but that's not quite enough. Super 35. [R] ●

Silk Road, The (1992-Chinese-Japanese) C-126m. **½ D: Junya Sato. Koichi Sato, Toshiyuki Nishida, Tsunehiko Watase, Daijiro Harada, Takahiro Tamura. Extravagant but hokey, overly melodramatic epic set in 11th-century China, about a young man (Koichi Sato) who becomes involved in various adventures and falls in love with a princess. The much-hyped battle scenes are nicely done, but fall short next to those in other films (for example, Kurosawa's KAGEMUSHA and RAN). [PG-13] ▼●

Silk Stockings (1957) C-117m. *** D: Rouben Mamoulian. Fred Astaire, Cyd Charisse, Janis Paige, Peter Lorre, George Tobias, Jules Munshin, Joseph Buloff, Barrie Chase. Words, music, dance blend perfectly in stylish remake of Garbo's NINOTCHKA. This time Charisse is cold Russian on Paris mission, Astaire the movie producer man-about-town who warms her up. Score by Cole Porter includes "All of You" and "Stereophonic Sound"; Mamoulian's final film. CinemaScope. ▼●)

Silkwood (1983) C-128m. *** D: Mike Nichols. Meryl Streep, Kurt Russell, Cher, Craig T. Nelson, Diana Scarwid, Fred Ward, Ron Silver, Charles Hallahan, Josef Sommer, Sudie Bond, Henderson Forsythe, E. Katherine Kerr, Bruce McGill, David Strathairn, M. Emmet Walsh, Ray Baker, Tess Harper, Anthony Heald. Superb performances, and vivid dramatization of workaday life in an Oklahoma nuclear-parts factory, give strength to a flawed film. Streep is outstanding as real-life Karen Silkwood, but anyone who followed news story knows how this film will end, and that places a special burden on such a long, slowly paced film. Script by Nora Ephron and Alice Arlen. [R] ▼●)

Silverado (1985) C-132m. *** D: Lawrence Kasdan. Kevin Kline, Scott Glenn, Kevin Costner, Danny Glover, John Cleese, Rosanna Arquette, Brian Dennehy, Linda Hunt, Jeff Goldblum, Ray Baker, Joe Seneca, Lynn Whitfield, Jeff Fahey, Richard Jenkins, Sheb Wooley, James Gammon. Sprawling, well-made Western about four unlikely comrades who join forces against some very bad guys. First major Hollywood Western in a long time is no classic but offers ample entertainment by throwing in everything but the kitchen sink—and never stops moving. Just don't think about it too hard. Script by Mark and Lawrence Kasdan, fine score by Bruce Broughton. Super Techniscope. [PG-13]▼●)

Silver Bears (1978) **C-113m.** ******* D: Ivan Passer. Michael Caine, Cybill Shepherd, Louis Jourdan, Martin Balsam, Stephane Audran, Tommy Smothers, David Warner, Charles Gray, Jay Leno. Entertaining comedy better suited to TV than theater screens; fine cast in story of high-level chicanery in world silver market. Adapted from Paul Erdman's novel by Peter Stone; filmed in Switzerland and Morocco. Technovision. [PG]▼

Silver Bullet (1985) **C-95m.** ****** D: Daniel Attias. Corey Haim, Gary Busey, Megan Follows, Everett McGill, Terry O'Quinn, Robin Groves, Leon Russom, Bill Smitrovich, Lawrence Tierney; voice of Tovah Feldshuh. What can it be that's terrorizing a small town by the light of the full moon? The answer is a werewolf, but it takes the folks in this movie a long time to figure that out. Well-acted but often stupid and unbelievable horror tale from Stephen King's novelette *Cycle of the Werewolf.* Aka STEPHEN KING'S SILVER BULLET. J-D-C Scope. [R]▼●)

Silver Chalice, The (1954) **C-144m.** ****** D: Victor Saville. Virginia Mayo, Pier Angeli, Jack Palance, Paul Newman, Walter Hampden, Joseph Wiseman, Alexander Scourby, Lorne Greene, E. G. Marshall, Natalie Wood. Newman's screen debut is undistinguished in story of Greek who designs framework for cup used at Last Supper. This is the film Newman once apologized for in a famous Hollywood trade ad. From the Thomas Costain novel; Greene's first film, too. CinemaScope.▼●)

Silver City (1951) **C-90m.** ****** D: Byron Haskin. Edmond O'Brien, Yvonne De Carlo, Richard Arlen, Gladys George, Barry Fitzgerald. Capable cast is above this mishmash set in the mining area of the West, with usual rivalry over gals and ore.

Silver City (1984-Australian) **C-110m.** ****½** D: Sophie Turkiewicz. Gosia Dobrowolska, Ivar Kants, Anna Jemison, Steve Bisley, Debra Lawrence. Fair soaper about love affair between Polish immigrants Dobrowolska and Kants in 1940s Australia. The catch: He is married to her close friend. Panavision. [PG]▼

Silver City (2004) **C-124m.** ****½** D: John Sayles. Chris Cooper, Danny Huston, Richard Dreyfuss, Maria Bello, James Gammon, Daryl Hannah, Kris Kristofferson, Mary Kay Place, Tim Roth, Thora Birch, David Clennon, Miguel Ferrer, Michael Murphy, Billy Zane, Alma Delfina, Sal López, Luis Saguar, Ralph Waite. Ensemble piece about a reporter-turned-investigator who's hired to

see who might be trying to sabotage the gubernatorial campaign of Colorado's favored son. A film noir–ish mystery is the framework for Sayles' attack on political corruption, corporate greed, and the apathy and resignation of a generation that once tried to change the world. Cooper does a slyly funny impression of Pres. George W. Bush, with a perfectly cast Murphy as his kingmaker dad. Plottier than it needs to be, and fairly obvious, but still entertaining and relevant. [R]▼)

Silver Dream Racer (1980-British) **C-111m.** ***½** D: David Wickes. David Essex, Beau Bridges, Cristina Raines, Clarke Peters, Harry H. Corbett, Diane Keen, Lee Montague, Sheila White. Hackneyed drama chronicling the trials of garage-mechanic-turned-motorcyclist Essex as he strives to win the Big Race. Essex wrote and performed music score as well. Panavision. [PG]▼)

Silver Lode (1954) **C-80m.** ****½** D: Allan Dwan. John Payne, Lizabeth Scott, Dan Duryea, Dolores Moran, Emile Meyer, Harry Carey, Jr., Morris Ankrum, Stuart Whitman, Alan Hale, Jr. A Western town's respected citizen (Payne) is accused of thievery and murder on his wedding day by a slimy U.S. "marshal" (Duryea). So-so melodrama is a fascinating relic of its era as both a HIGH NOON variation and an obvious allegory of HUAC/McCarthyist hypocrisy. The action unfolds on July 4, and the villain is named "McCarty"!▼)

Silver River (1948) **110m.** ***½** D: Raoul Walsh. Errol Flynn, Ann Sheridan, Thomas Mitchell, Bruce Bennett, Tom D'Andrea, Barton MacLane, Monte Blue. Mediocre Flynn vehicle: Ann and Errol marry out West, he becomes corrupt.▼

Silver Streak (1976) **C-113m.** ******* D: Arthur Hiller. Gene Wilder, Jill Clayburgh, Richard Pryor, Patrick McGoohan, Ned Beatty, Ray Walston, Scatman Crothers, Clifton James, Richard Kiel, Fred Willard. Nutty blend of comedy, romance, action and suspense as mild-mannered editor Wilder becomes involved in murder plot on cross-country train ride. Switch from comedy to violence is sometimes jarring, but on the whole a highly entertaining picture. One of the best Wilder/Pryor pairings. Imitation Hitchcock written by Colin Higgins. [PG]▼●)

Simian Line, The (2001) **C-106m.** ****½** D: Linda Yellen. Lynn Redgrave, Jamey Sheridan, Harry Connick, Jr., Cindy Crawford, Samantha Mathis, William Hurt, Tyne Daly, Eric Stoltz, Dylan Bruno, Monica Keena, Jeremy Zelig. Small-scale film intertwines four couples' lives at crossroads: Redgrave is insecure about her relationship with her much-younger lover (Connick, Jr.), especially when a young couple moves in next door. What's more, her house is haunted by ghosts of long ago (Mathis, Hurt). Highly uneven, with the mystical elements the weakest, but marked by fine performances from Redgrave, Connick, and a surprisingly good Crawford. [R]▶

Simon (1980) **C-97m.** **½ D: Marshall Brickman. Alan Arkin, Madeline Kahn, Austin Pendleton, Judy Graubart, William Finley, Fred Gwynne, Adolph Green. Uneven comedy about psychology professor (Arkin) who's brainwashed by group of think-tank weirdos to believe he's come from another planet. There's a cruel edge to the humor, and signs of a serious film trying to break out, in screenwriter Brickman's directorial debut. [PG]▼

Simon Birch (1998) **C-113m.** *** D: Mark Steven Johnson. Ian Michael Smith, Joseph Mazzello, Ashley Judd, Oliver Platt, David Strathairn, Dana Ivey, Beatrice Winde, Jan Hooks, Jim Carrey. Fable set in the early 1960s about a young boy with arrested growth (real-life 11-year-old Smith) who believes he's part of God's plan, and is destined to be a hero. That destiny is hard to discern in his sad, often frustrated life; the bright spot is his friendship with Mazzello, who's also an outsider as a bastard child in a small town. Well-made tearjerker loosely adapted from John Irving's novel *A Prayer for Owen Meany*; manipulative, borderline mushy at times, but very well done. [PG]▼◐▶

S1MØNE (2002) **C-117m.** ** D: Andrew Niccol. Al Pacino, Catherine Keener, Winona Ryder, Evan Rachel Wood, Jay Mohr, Pruitt Taylor Vince, Jason Schwartzman, Stanley Anderson, Rachel Roberts. One-joke idea about a desperate filmmaker who, fed up with temperamental stars, creates his new discovery on a computer—and then can't get anyone to believe she doesn't exist. Alas, no one in the film is real, which makes it hard to accept, even as satire. There are echoes of FROM NOON TILL THREE, MEET JOHN DOE, even THE RETURN OF MARTIN GUERRE . . . but to no effect. From the writer of THE TRUMAN SHOW. Elias Koteas and Rebecca Romijn-Stamos appear unbilled. Panavision. [PG-13]▼▶

Simon Magus (2000-German-British) **C-105m.** ** D: Ben Hopkins. Noah Taylor, Embeth Davidtz, Rutger Hauer, Ian Holm, Stuart Townsend, Sean McGinley, Terence Rigby, Amanda Ryan. Shunned by his Jewish community because of his claims that he has the ability to put a "curse" on crops and often talks to the Devil, Simon (Taylor) becomes the unlikely key player in the local tug-of-war to bring a railway station to a backwater village in the 1800s. Minor, offbeat directing debut for Hopkins; memorable only for a quirky lead performance by the talented Taylor and some fine supporting players.

Simon of the Desert (1965-Mexican) **45m.** **** D: Luis Buñuel. Claudio Brook, Silvia Pinal, Hortensia Santovena, Enrique Alvarez Felix. Hilarious parable about a bearded ascetic who plops himself atop a pillar to communicate with God better. Could only have been made by one filmmaker; even by Buñuel's standards, the ending of this one is pretty wild. ▼▶

Simon Sez (1999) **C-85m.** BOMB D: Kevin Elders. Dennis Rodman, Xin-Xin Xiong, Dane Cook, Natalia Cigliuti, Filip Nicolic, Emma Sjoberg. Absolutely dreadful actioner with Rodman—the NBA's most famous cross-dressing power forward—playing a James Bond–like Interpol agent who sets out to rescue a kidnapped heiress. Bottom of the barrel in all departments. [PG-13]▼▶

Simpatico (1999) **C-106m.** ** D: Matthew Warchus. Nick Nolte, Jeff Bridges, Sharon Stone, Catherine Keener, Albert Finney, Shawn Hatosy, Kimberly Williams, Liam Waite. Bridges is a Kentucky millionaire horseman whose life comes apart when he hears from a boyhood pal (Nolte) who threatens to expose their dark, longtime secret. Film's overheated tone seems unwarranted by the material itself, but it's great fun watching old-pro Finney. Based on a play by Sam Shepard. [R]▼▶

Simple Men (1992) **C-105m.** *** D: Hal Hartley. Robert Burke, William Sage, Karen Sillas, Elina Löwensohn, Martin Donovan, Mark Chandler Bailey. Original, ingratiating tale of brothers Burke and Sage, who set out in search of their fugitive father, a former Brooklyn Dodgers all-star shortstop who, in the 1960s, became a bomb-throwing anarchist. Infused with a wry sense of humor and consistent offbeat tilt, but the emotions underneath are genuine, and that's what makes the film so endearing. A PBS *American Playhouse* coproduction. [R]▼◐▶

Simple Plan, A (1998) **C-121m.** **½ D: Sam Raimi. Bill Paxton, Billy Bob Thornton, Bridget Fonda, Brent Briscoe, Gary Cole, Chelcie Ross, Jack Walsh, Becky Ann Baker. Wintry tale of three men—a family man, his slow-witted brother, and the latter's redneck pal—who stumble onto a cache of money in a downed airplane. Their decision to keep the cash quickly snowballs into a whirlpool of tension that leads to other crimes. Thornton's exceptional performance makes the film worth seeing, but the story—and its mild-mannered characters' sudden transformation—simply doesn't ring true. Adapted by Scott B. Smith from his novel. [R]▼◐▶

Simple Story, A (1978-French) **C-110m.** *** D: Claude Sautet. Romy Schneider, Bruno Cremer, Claude Brasseur, Arlette Bonnard. Fortyish laborer examines her life after aborting a child and dropping her lover. Schneider gives one of her best performances in this graceful drama.▼

Simple Twist of Fate, A (1994) **C-106m.** **½ D: Gillies MacKinnon. Steve Martin, Gabriel Byrne, Catherine O'Hara, Stephen

[1257]

Baldwin, Laura Linney, Byron Jennings, Michael des Barres, Ed Grady, Kristoffer Tabori, Anne Heche. Circumstances drive a man to become a recluse and a miser, until an orphaned toddler wanders into his life. Martin produced, wrote, and starred in this adaptation of George Eliot's novel *Silas Marner,* an odd choice of material that yields an interesting if never quite arresting story. Some of the most entertaining moments are also the most incongruous, when the sober-faced lead character suddenly— and unexpectedly—becomes funny, à la Steve Martin. [PG-13]▼●◗

Simple Wish, A (1997) **C-89m.** **½ D: Michael Ritchie. Martin Short, Mara Wilson, Kathleen Turner, Robert Pastorelli, Amanda Plummer, Francis Capra, Ruby Dee, Teri Garr. Amusing family film about a bungling male fairy godmother who tries to help a little girl whose wish is to see her father get a part in a new musical play. Short and Wilson are fun, Turner is over the top as a wicked witch, and the special effects are good . . . though the film never quite takes off. Highlight for grownups is the bogus Andrew Lloyd Webber–ish musical play *Two Cities* which figures in the plot. (Director Ritchie wrote the songs with Lucy Simon.) [PG]▼●◗

Simply Irresistible (1999) **C-96m.** ** D: Mark Tarlov. Sarah Michelle Gellar, Sean Patrick Flanery, Patricia Clarkson, Dylan Baker, Christopher Durang, Larry Gilliard, Jr., Betty Buckley, Amanda Peet. Old-fashioned, overcooked romantic comedy-fantasy about a talentless chef (Gellar) struggling to keep her late mother's restaurant afloat, who is transformed by a magical crab (!) into a master cook whose concoctions seem to have special powers. Along the way, she becomes romantically involved with an executive (Flanery) who is setting up a gourmet restaurant. Occasionally likable, but far too predictable. Super 35. [PG-13] ▼●◗

Simpsons Movie, The (2007) **C-87m.** ***。 D: David Silverman. Voices of Dan Castellaneta, Julie Kavner, Nancy Cartwright, Yeardley Smith, Hank Azaria, Harry Shearer, Marcia Wallace, Tress MacNeille, Pamela Hayden, A. (Albert) Brooks, Joe Mantegna, Tom Hanks. Springfield is quarantined under a huge dome by the EPA (and President Schwarzenegger), and eventually marked for destruction, after Homer causes an environmental disaster by dumping a massive amount of poop from his pet pig into the local lake. Can he save the town and win back the affection of his fed-up family? Long-running TV cartoon's debut on the big—and ultrawide—screen is entertaining, albeit not as sharply satirical as the best episodes of the series. Digital Widescreen. [PG-13]◗

Sin, The SEE: **Good Luck, Miss Wyckoff**
Sinbad and the Eye of the Tiger

(1977-British) **C-113m.** *½ D: Sam Wanamaker. Patrick Wayne, Jane Seymour, Taryn Power, Margaret Whiting, Patrick Troughton. Dreary followup to GOLDEN VOYAGE OF SINBAD has unusually hackneyed script (even for this kind of film), disappointing Ray Harryhausen effects, and goes on forever. For patient kids only. Taryn is Tyrone Power's daughter. [G]▼●◗

Sinbad: Legend of the Seven Seas (2003) **C-86m.** *** D: Tim Johnson, Patrick Gilmore. Voices of Brad Pitt, Catherine Zeta-Jones, Michelle Pfeiffer, Joseph Fiennes, Dennis Haysbert, Timothy West, Adriano Giannini. Entertaining animated blend of adventure, fantasy, comedy, and romance as bad-boy Sinbad takes on a noble mission to save his boyhood pal, the prince—whose fiancée tags along for the ride. Pitt and Zeta-Jones play bantering, bickering romantic leads with great verve, even if it's hard to forget whose voices we're listening to. Pfeiffer is also fun as Eris, the goddess of chaos. Slick production needlessly injects computer-generated monsters into the already good-looking 2-D world it's created. [PG]▼◗

Sinbad the Sailor (1947) **C-117m.** *** D: Richard Wallace. Douglas Fairbanks, Jr., Maureen O'Hara, Anthony Quinn, Walter Slezak, George Tobias, Jane Greer, Mike Mazurki, Sheldon Leonard. Tongue-in-cheek swashbuckler, with lavish color production. Great fun.▼◗

Since You Went Away (1944) **172m.** ***½ D: John Cromwell. Claudette Colbert, Jennifer Jones, Joseph Cotten, Shirley Temple, Monty Woolley, Hattie McDaniel, Agnes Moorehead, Craig Stevens, Keenan Wynn, Nazimova, Robert Walker, Lionel Barrymore. Tear-jerker supreme with Colbert at her valiant best. Story of family suffering through WW2 with many tragedies and complications dates a bit, but still is very smooth film. Producer David O. Selznick wrote the screenplay, from Margaret Buell Wilder's book. Beautifully photographed by Lee Garmes and Stanley Cortez. Max Steiner's score won an Oscar. Film debuts of Guy Madison (then an actual sailor, in the role of sailor Harold Smith) and John Derek (an extra).▼◗

Sin City (2005) **C-124m.** *½ D: Frank Miller, Robert Rodriguez. Bruce Willis, Clive Owen, Jessica Alba, Benicio Del Toro, Rosario Dawson, Jaime King, Brittany Murphy, Mickey Rourke, Carla Gugino, Elijah Wood, Devon Aoki, Alexis Bledel, Powers Boothe, Michael Clarke Duncan, Josh Hartnett, Rutger Hauer, Michael Madsen, Nick Stahl, Nicky Katt, Marley Shelton. Vignettes, both short and long, from Frank Miller's graphic novels about a violent, corrupt city full of hard-boiled characters (and naked women) are brought to life in a computer-enhanced film noir world. Stylish, audacious, but completely artificial; the initial excitement of watching these images soon dies off but the film refuses to do the same. Miller fans and adolescent boys will probably rate this much higher. Quentin Tarantino is billed as Special Guest Director. On-screen title is FRANK MILLER'S SIN CITY. Alternate version runs 147m. HD 24P Widescreen. [R]▼◗

Sinful Davey (1969-British) **C-95m.** **½ D: John Huston. John Hurt, Pamela Franklin, Nigel Davenport, Ronald Fraser, Robert Morley, Fidelma Murphy, Maxine Audley, Brenda Fricker. Tale of 19th-century Scottish highwayman and his love for a "nice" girl is rather ordinary, but does have pleasant performance by Franklin. Based on a true story. Anjelica Huston has a bit part. Panavision. [M/PG]

Sinful Life, A (1989) **C-90m.** ** D: William Schreiner. Anita Morris, Rick Overton, Dennis Christopher, Mark Rolston, Cynthia Szigeti, Blair Tefkin, Cynthia Songe. Very offbeat comedy (filmed on a low, low budget) about a former Sonny and Cher dancer named Claire Vin Blanc who fights to keep her rather *unusual* child, Baby, from being removed to a more "respectable" environment. Not for everyone, but it does give Morris a great vehicle for her comedic talent. Based on the play *Just Like the Pom Pom Girls,* originally presented by L.A.'s Groundlings comedy troupe. [R]▼◗

Sing (1989) **C-97m.** BOMB D: Richard Baskin. Lorraine Bracco, Peter Dobson, Jessica Steen, Louise Lasser, George DiCenzo, Patti LaBelle, Cuba Gooding, Jr. Title refers to a true-life, decades-old tradition—a song-dance competition (or "Sing") between seniors and underclassmen in Brooklyn high schools. Script (by Dean Pitchford) is decades old, too: B-movie clichés about a rebel, a "nice" girl, an understanding teacher, and jelly-spined administrators all locking horns during pageant rehearsals. Threatens to go over the brink throughout . . . and eventually does. [PG-13]▼◗

Singapore, Singapore (1968-French) **C-103m.** ** D: Bernard Toublanc Michel. Sean Flynn, Marika Green, Terry Downes, Marc Michel, Peter Gayford, Denis Berry. So-so espionage tale interesting primarily for Flynn (Errol's son) playing a CIA agent looking into the disappearance of a number of Marines in Singapore. Based on Jean Bruce's novel. Aka FIVE ASHORE IN SINGAPORE.

Sing, Baby, Sing (1936) **87m.** *** D: Sidney Lanfield. Alice Faye, Adolphe Menjou, Gregory Ratoff, Ted Healy, Patsy Kelly, Tony Martin. Pleasant musicomedy stolen by Menjou as John Barrymore prototype involved with publicity-seeking Faye. Songs: "When Did You Leave Heaven?," "You Turned the Tables on Me," title tune. The Ritz Brothers are quite good in their feature-film debut.

Sing Boy Sing (1958) **90m.** ** D: Henry Ephron. Tommy Sands, Lili Gentle, Edmond O'Brien, John McIntire, Nick Adams, Diane Jergens, Josephine Hutchinson, Jerry Paris, Regis Toomey. A teen idol and Elvis Presley clone (Sands) is manipulated by his cold-hearted manager (O'Brien) and kept apart from his roots. Muddled relic of its era, which purports to expose the evils of rock 'n' roll and showbiz (in between Sands' endless musical numbers). Sands' film debut; based on 1957 TV play *The Singin' Idol.* CinemaScope.

Singing Detective, The (2003) **C-109m.** **½ D: Keith Gordon. Robert Downey, Jr., Robin Wright Penn, Mel Gibson, Jeremy Northam, Katie Holmes, Carla Gugino, Adrien Brody, Jon Polito, Saul Rubinek, Alfre Woodard, Amy Aquino. A writer who's hospitalized with a horrific skin condition fantasizes about his gumshoe alter ego and hallucinates a series of musical numbers that relate to his problems, both real and imagined. The late Dennis Potter reconceived his brilliant 1986 British miniseries as an American-based feature film, and changed the time period from the 1940s to the 1950s, but in compressing (and even lightening the tone of) the material he lost some of its impact. The results are uneven, though still often striking. Gibson also coproduced. Super 35. [R]▼◗

Singing Nun, The (1966) **C-98m.** ** D: Henry Koster. Debbie Reynolds, Ricardo Montalban, Greer Garson, Agnes Moorehead, Chad Everett, Katharine Ross, Ed Sullivan, Juanita Moore, Tom Drake. Syrupy comic-book stuff based on real-life Belgian nun whose devotion is split between religious work and making hit records. Panavision. ▼◗

Singin' in The Rain (1952) **C-102m.** **** D: Gene Kelly, Stanley Donen. Gene Kelly, Debbie Reynolds, Donald O'Connor, Jean Hagen, Cyd Charisse, Millard Mitchell, Douglas Fowley, Madge Blake, Rita Moreno. Perhaps the greatest movie musical of all time, fashioned by Betty Comden and Adolph Green from a catalogue of Arthur Freed–Nacio Herb Brown songs. The setting is Hollywood during the transition to talkies, with Hagen giving the performance of a lifetime as Kelly's silent screen costar, whose voice could shatter glass. Kelly's title number, O'Connor's "Make 'Em Laugh," are just two highlights in a film packed with gems. Later a Broadway musical. ▼◗

Single Girl, A (1995-French) **C-90m.** ***½ D: Benoit Jacquot. Virginie Ledoyen, Benoit Magimel, Dominique Valadie, Vera Briole, Michel Bompoil, Jean-Cretien Sibertin-Blanc. Bright, scintillating slice-of-life, told in real time, about a young woman (Ledoyen) whose personal life is complicated to say the least, and who must contend with additional pressures in her new job as a room-service waitress

[1259]

in a fancy hotel. Exudes the freshness and spontaneity of the early French New Wave; 19-year-old Ledoyen (who seems like Anna Karina reborn) offers a star-making performance.▼❶

Single Handed SEE: **Sailor of the King**

Single Man, A (2009) **C/B&W-99m.** ★★★ D: Tom Ford. Colin Firth, Julianne Moore, Nicholas Hoult, Matthew Goode, Jon Kortajarena, Paulette Lamori, Ryan Simpkins, Ginnifer Goodwin, Lee Pace. We follow closeted homosexual college professor Firth through one seemingly ordinary day in 1962—but behind his preternaturally calm demeanor there is great turbulence. After 8 years of grieving over the loss of his life partner, he can't find a reason to go on; the well-meaning ramblings of his one, alcoholic, friend (Moore) aren't enough. Flawlessly detailed visualization of Christopher Isherwood's landmark novel benefits from a superb performance by Firth, but its resolute restraint also keeps it a bit aloof at times. Impressive directorial debut for fashion designer Ford, who also coscripted. Jon Hamm does an uncredited voiceover. Super 35. [R]❶

Single Room Furnished (1968) **C-93m.** *½ D: Matteo Ottaviano (Matt Cimber). Jayne Mansfield, Dorothy Keller, Fabian Dean, Billy M. Greene, Martin Horsey, Walter Gregg. Pathetic woman, twice impregnated and thrice deserted, decides to become prostitute. Mansfield's last film, released after her death, opens with Walter Winchell tribute and degenerates as she attempts to display serious acting talent.▼❶

Singles (1992) **C-99m.** ★★½ D: Cameron Crowe. Bridget Fonda, Matt Dillon, Campbell Scott, Kyra Sedgwick, Sheila Kelley, Jim True, Bill Pullman, James Le Gros, Devon Raymond, Camilo Gallardo, Ally Walker, Jeremy Piven, Paul Giamatti, Tim Burton. Life in the Seattle singles scene; it ain't easy. Lively seriocomedy with some appealing performances (especially by Scott and Sedgwick), but never as solid—or as insightful—as you hope it will be. Film has music, setting, and style galore, but also a rather uneven script. Eric Stoltz (who has appeared in all of the director's films), Tom Skerritt, and Peter Horton have amusing cameos. [PG-13]▼❶

Single White Female (1992) **C-107m.** ★★½ D: Barbet Schroeder. Bridget Fonda, Jennifer Jason Leigh, Steven Weber, Peter Friedman, Stephen Tobolowsky, Frances Bay, Rene Estevez, Ken Tobey. Self-employed N.Y. career woman (Fonda), her engagement kaput, ends up sharing her dream apartment with the Roommate from Hell. PERSONA meets Roman Polanski's entire oeuvre in well-acted thriller that's terrific for about an hour—until standard slasher-pic silliness sets in. Screendom's first psychological probing to wrap up with a Chrissie Hynde vocal. Based on John Lutz novel *SWF Seeks Same.* Followed by a direct-to-video sequel. [R]▼❶

Sinister Invasion (1971-Mexican-U.S.) **C-90m.** BOMB D: Jack Hill, Juan Ibanez. Boris Karloff, Enrique Guzman, Christa Linder, Maura Monti, Yerye Beirute, Sergio Kleiner. 19th-century scientist Karloff's experiments accidentally summon aliens who dominate a local Ripper-like killer. Cheap, flaccid, ugly film, one of four Karloff worked on simultaneously in 1968; unfortunately this was his last film work. Aka INCREDIBLE INVASION, INVASION SINIESTRA, and ALIEN TERROR.▼

Sink the Bismarck! (1960-British) **97m.** ★★★ D: Lewis Gilbert. Kenneth More, Dana Wynter, Carl Mohner, Laurence Naismith, Geoffrey Keen, Karel Stepanek, Michael Hordern. Good WW2 film based on fact. Exciting sea battles as British navy starts deadly hunt for famed German war vessel. Script by Edmund H. North. CinemaScope.▼❶

Sinners' Holiday (1947) SEE: **Christmas Eve**

Sin Nombre (2009-U.S.-Mexican) **C-96m.** ★★★ D: Cary Joji Fukunaga. Paulina Gaitan, Edgar Flores, Kristyan Ferrer, Tenoch Huerta Mejía, Diana García, Luis Fernando Peña, Héctor Jiménez. Vivid, painfully believable drama about a Honduran girl who reluctantly joins her father and uncle in boarding a train for Mexico as the first step toward emigrating to the U.S. Meanwhile, a Mexican gang member whose leader has betrayed his trust joins the trek, though he knows he's a marked man. Borders on melodrama, with almost Shakespearean overtones yet palpably real every step of the way. Impressive feature debut for writer-director Fukunaga. Super 35. [R]❶

Sin Noticias de Dios SEE: **Don't Tempt Me**

Sin of Harold Diddlebock, The (1947) **90m.** ★★½ D: Preston Sturges. Harold Lloyd, Frances Ramsden, Jimmy Conlin, Raymond Walburn, Edgar Kennedy, Arline Judge, Lionel Stander, Rudy Vallee. Fascinating idea of updating Lloyd's 1920s character to show what's happened to that go-getter doesn't fulfill its promise. Aimless comedy can't top opening sequence from THE FRESHMAN (1925), despite enthusiasm of fine cast. Reedited to 79m. and reissued in 1950 as MAD WEDNESDAY.▼❶

Sins of Lola Montes, The SEE: **Lola Montes**

Sins of Rachel Cade, The (1961) **C-124m.** ★★½ D: Gordon Douglas. Angie Dickinson, Peter Finch, Roger Moore, Woody Strode, Rafer Johnson, Juano Hernandez, Mary Wickes, Scatman Crothers. Turgid melodrama set in Belgian Congo with Dickinson a missionary nurse involved in romance and native conflicts.❶

Sioux City (1994) **C-102m.** ★★½ D: Lou Diamond Phillips. Lou Diamond Phillips, Salli Richardson, Melinda Dillon, Lise

Cutter, Apesanahkwat, Gary Farmer, Ralph Waite, Tantoo Cardinal, Adam Roarke. Overworked doctor Phillips, Lakota Indian by birth but adopted as a child by an affluent Jewish couple, goes on vacation and returns to the reservation where he was born; there, he learns of the death of his real mother, faces anti-Indian sentiment, and ultimately confronts the mysteries of his past. Sensitively handled drama is engrossing and suspenseful until the ridiculous finale. [PG-13]▼●)

Sirens (1994-Australian-British) **C-94m.** *** D: John Duigan. Hugh Grant, Tara Fitzgerald, Sam Neill, Elle Macpherson, Portia de Rossi, Kate Fischer, Pamela Rabe, Ben Mendelsohn, John Polson. Piquant social comedy about a young, liberal British minister and his wife who drop in on scandalous Australian artist Norman Lindsay (Neill), and find themselves seduced (somewhat) by his libertarian ways—and his three gorgeous, free-thinking models, who have no qualms about posing nude. Some may be attracted by the prospect of seeing supermodel Macpherson naked, but she also delivers a good performance. Droll and imaginative work by writer-director Duigan (who also appears onscreen as the earnest minister). Artist Lindsay was portrayed by James Mason in the 1969 film AGE OF CONSENT. [R]▼●)

Sir Henry at Rawlinson End (1980-British) **72m.** **½ D: Steve Roberts. Trevor Howard, Patrick Magee, Denise Coffey, J. G. Devlin, Sheila Reid, Harry Fowler. Howard is fine as an eccentric, alcoholic aristocrat who attempts to exorcise a family spirit from his domain. Strange but entertaining, and veddy British.

Sirocco (1951) **98m.** **½ D: Curtis Bernhardt. Humphrey Bogart, Marta Toren, Lee J. Cobb, Everett Sloane, Gerald Mohr, Zero Mostel, Nick Dennis, Onslow Stevens, Ludwig Donath, Harry Guardino, Jeff Corey. Bogart's company produced this slick if superficial paraphrase of CASABLANCA with Bogie as a gunrunner who's the unofficial boss of Damascus in 1925, vying with French military officer Cobb for the affections of Toren. A strong supporting cast adds flavor. ▼●)

Sister Act (1992) **C-100m.** *** D: Emile Ardolino. Whoopi Goldberg, Maggie Smith, Harvey Keitel, Bill Nunn, Kathy Najimy, Wendy Makkena, Mary Wickes, Robert Miranda, Richard Portnow, Joseph Maher. A Reno lounge singer, targeted for murder by her mobster boyfriend, hides out in a convent—where she shakes things up as the new choir director. Crowd-pleasing comedy, cannily written (by Joseph Howard, aka Paul Rudnick) and directed, with a plum part for Whoopi—though veteran character actress Wickes has many of the funniest lines. Followed by a sequel and a Broadway musical. [PG]▼●)

Sister Act 2: Back in the Habit (1993) **C-106m.** **½ D: Bill Duke. Whoopi Goldberg, Maggie Smith, Kathy Najimy, Barnard Hughes, Mary Wickes, James Coburn, Michael Jeter, Wendy Makkena, Sheryl Lee Ralph, Robert Pastorelli, Thomas Gottschalk, Jennifer Love Hewitt. Affable piffle unconvincingly finds Goldberg back with the nuns, coaching students in a choral competition as heavy Coburn plots to close their school. Though someone involved apparently saw THE BELLS OF ST. MARY'S a few too many times, needless sequel does send you out with a smile, thanks to a smashing musical finale and an end-credit sequence that's the best thing in the picture. Very slow going at first. [PG]▼●)

Sisterhood of the Traveling Pants, The (2005) **C-119m.** *** D: Ken Kwapis. Amber Tamblyn, Alexis Bledel, America Ferrera, Blake Lively, Jenna Boyd, Bradley Whitford, Nancy Travis, Rachel Ticotin, Mike Vogel, Leonardo Nam. Story follows four best friends spending their first summer apart from one another and sharing a magical pair of jeans. Despite being of various shapes and sizes, each of them fits perfectly into the pants, and as every girl has her turn with them, life-changing events occur. Sweet but not sappy; the four leads give excellent performances in a charming coming-of-age tale. Based on the popular young-adult book by Ann Brashares. Followed by a sequel. Panavision. [PG]▼●)

Sisterhood of the Traveling Pants 2, The (2008) **C-111m.** *** D: Sanaa Hamri. Amber Tamblyn, Alexis Bledel, America Ferrera, Blake Lively, Rachel Nichols, Tom Wisdom, Rachel Ticotin, Leonardo Nam, Michael Rady, Shohreh Aghdashloo, Blythe Danner. The four pals are now in college and their friendship has been strained, so when summer arrives they go their separate ways, no longer dependent on each other—and the fabled pair of jeans—to see them through, or so they think. Simple, straightforward sequel nearly matches the spirit and charm of the original, and even returns to picture-postcard Greece; the four appealing actresses are in fine form. Kyle MacLachlan appears unbilled. [PG-13]▶)

Sister in Law, The (1974) **C-85m.** ** D: Joseph Ruben. John Savage, W. G. McMillan, Anne Saxon, Meredith Baer, Jon Oppenheim, Tom Mahoney. Interesting curio has Savage becoming involved with destructive title character as his brother's dupe in drug-smuggling. Hurt by needlessly negative finale. Savage also composed the score and sings several folk ballads pleasantly. [R]▼●)

Sister Kenny (1946) **116m.** ***½ D: Dudley Nichols. Rosalind Russell, Alexander Knox, Dean Jagger, Philip Merivale, Beulah Bondi, Dorothy Peterson. Russell shines in title role, as Australian nurse who initiated treatment for polio. Engrossing drama is among the better Hollywood biopics.

Scripted by Nichols, Knox, and Mary Mc-Carthy, from Elizabeth Kenny's autobiography *And They Shall Walk*.▼●

Sister My Sister (1994-British) **C-102m.** *** D: Nancy Meckler. Julie Walters, Joely Richardson, Jodhi May, Sophie Thursfield. Compelling psychological drama about a dour madame (Walters), obsessed with her respectability, who controls her ungainly daughter (Thursfield) and two maids (Richardson, May); the latter are sisters who share a complicated emotional—and sexual—bond. Strains among the characters build, leading to emotional fireworks. A based-on-fact story that served as the basis of Jean Genet's *The Maids*. [R]▼▶

Sisters, The (1938) **98m.** *** D: Anatole Litvak. Errol Flynn, Bette Davis, Anita Louise, Ian Hunter, Donald Crisp, Beulah Bondi, Jane Bryan, Lee Patrick, Mayo Methot, Laura Hope Crews, Dick Foran, Henry Travers, Patric Knowles, Alan Hale. Davis, Louise, and Bryan are sisters whose marital problems are traced in this lavish film; Bette's got the most trouble, of course, with unreliable husband Flynn in San Francisco, 1905.▼

Sisters (1973) **C-93m.** *** D: Brian De Palma. Margot Kidder, Jennifer Salt, Charles Durning, Barnard Hughes, William Finley, Mary Davenport, Olympia Dukakis. De Palma's first venture into Hitchcock territory, about separated Siamese twins (Kidder), one of whom is a homicidal maniac, and the reporter (Salt) who—shades of REAR WINDOW—thinks she witnessed one of the slayings. Eerie, gory, tremendously suspenseful, with one of Bernard Herrmann's most chilling scores. Remade for DVD in 2007. [R]▼▶

Sisters, The (2005) **C-113m.** *½ D: Arthur Allan Seidelman. Maria Bello, Elizabeth Banks, Erika Christensen, Stephen Culp, Tony Goldwyn, Mary Stuart Masterson, Eric McCormack, Alessandro Nivola, Chris O'Donnell, Rip Torn, Greg Foote. Chekhov's play *Three Sisters* "inspired" an American version (by Richard Alfieri), which has now inspired this deadly film about four siblings who just can't seem to get along. Talk about your dysfunctional families! The Russian setting of the original has been replaced by a faculty lounge in a N.Y.C. university, where endless chunks of verbose dialogue are hurled at one another by a starry, if uneven, cast. Most of the drivel uttered by this assemblage of academics wouldn't get a passing grade. [R]▶

Sister, Sister (1987) **C-91m.** *½ D: Bill Condon. Eric Stoltz, Jennifer Jason Leigh, Judith Ivey, Dennis Lipscomb, Anne Pitoniak, Benjamin Moulton. Leigh and Ivey are title siblings, two women with myriad problems and repressions. They've converted their parents' mansion into a dreary guest house . . . one which you will not want to visit. Thoroughly unappealing. Super 35. [R]▼●

Sisters, or the Balance of Happiness

(1979-German) **C-95m.** **½ D: Margarethe von Trotta. Jutta Lampe, Gudrun Gabriel, Jessica Fruh, Rainer Delventhal, Konstantin Wecker. Slow but not unrewarding psychological study of the complex relationship between two sisters; one, a successful executive secretary, is supporting the other, a graduate student in biology.▼▶

Sister Streetfighter (1975-Japanese) **C-81m.** *½ D: Kazuhiko Yamaguchi. Etsuko "Sue" Shiomi, Mie "May" Hayakawa, Hiroshi "Harry" Kondo, Shinichi "Sonny" Chiba, Sanae Obori, Tatsuya Nanjo. Shiomi kicks some major butt when her spy brother is captured by drug runners in Hong Kong. The most outlandishly campy and cartoonish of the STREET FIGHTER series, this is a crudely made concoction of sex and sadism, with Chiba only appearing in a few scenes. Actionscope. [R]▼●

Sita Sings the Blues (2009) **C-81m.** *** D: Nina Paley. Voices of Reena Shah, Sanjiv Jhaveri, Aseem Chhabra, Bhavana Nagulapally, Manish Acharya, Nina Paley. Animator Paley tells an autobiographical tale of how she was dumped by her husband and contrasts it with the epic Indian saga called the Ramayana. Three Indian shadow-puppet figures comment on the proceedings (not unlike *Mystery Science Theater 3000*), all of which is punctuated by the story's Hindu heroine breaking into song—in the appealing voice of 1920s pop singer Annette Hanshaw. Unusual mélange of elements, including highly appealing visual design, makes this a disarming experience, and a unique animated feature.▶

Sitting Ducks (1980) **C-90m.** *** D: Henry Jaglom. Michael Emil, Zack Norman, Patrice Townsend, Irene Forrest, Richard Romanus, Henry Jaglom. Energetic, funny sleeper about timid Syndicate accountant Emil and womanizing pal Norman, who take a day's collections and rip off the Mob. Emil and Norman have comedy team potential as the bickering buddies, Townsend (then Mrs. Jaglom) is luscious as a woman they pick up. Lots of belly laughs. [R]▼▶

Sitting Pretty (1948) **84m.** ***½ D: Walter Lang. Robert Young, Maureen O'Hara, Clifton Webb, Richard Haydn, Louise Allbritton, Ed Begley. Webb is perfect as self-centered genius who accepts job as full-time babysitter in gossip-laden suburban town. Highly entertaining, followed by the MR. BELVEDERE comedies.▼

Sitting Target (1972-British) **C-93m.** *½ D: Douglas Hickox. Oliver Reed, Jill St. John, Ian McShane, Edward Woodward, Frank Finlay, Freddie Jones. Reed breaks out of prison to settle two scores—one of them with his cheating wife (St. John). Violent, generally unpleasant film. [R]

Situation, The (2007) **C-106m.** ** D: Philip Haas. Connie Nielsen, Damian Lewis, Mido Hamada, Saïd Amadis, Nasser Memarzia, Mahmoud El Lozy, John Slattery, Tom McCarthy, Driss Roukh. American journalist (Nielsen) covers the war in Iraq and juggles romantic involvements with a U.S. intelligence officer (Lewis) and an Iraqi photographer (Hamada). Lackluster attempt to involve us in a love triangle while portraying various points of view about the "situation" in Iraq. First screenplay by journalist Wendell Steavenson isn't nearly as interesting as the many documentaries covering the subject.▶

Six Bridges to Cross (1955) **96m.** *** D: Joseph Pevney. Tony Curtis, Julia (Julie) Adams, George Nader, Sal Mineo, Jay C. Flippen, Jan Merlin. Entertaining film about a cop's longtime relationship with a juvenile delinquent who grows up to be a high-class crook. Based on the infamous Brink's truck robbery; filmed on location in Boston. Mineo's film debut. Title song sung by Sammy Davis, Jr.

Six Days Seven Nights (1998) **C-101m.** *** D: Ivan Reitman. Harrison Ford, Anne Heche, David Schwimmer, Jacqueline Obradors, Temuera Morrison, Allison Janney, Douglas Weston, Danny Trejo, Taj Mahal. Entertaining romantic comedy about a N.Y.C. career woman who's forced to interrupt an idyllic tropical vacation with her boyfriend for a business side trip. Then her charter plane crash-lands, and she's stranded on a deserted island with her pilot—who's not exactly her type (and vice versa). An obvious setup is played out with great verve by the stars. Ford is especially loose and funny. Panavision. [PG-13]▼●①

Six Degrees of Separation (1993) **C-111m.** *** D: Fred Schepisi. Stockard Channing, Will Smith, Donald Sutherland, Ian McKellen, Mary Beth Hurt, Bruce Davison, Richard Masur, Anthony Michael Hall, Heather Graham, Eric Thal, Anthony Rapp, Osgood Perkins, Catherine Kellner, Jeffrey Abrams, Kitty Carlisle Hart. Stylish, opened-up adaptation by John Guare of his stage success about a handsome con man who convinces well-off, gullible New Yorkers that he is Sidney Poitier's son. Impressively acted film flows smoothly in its first two acts, before the satire gives way to chest-thumping tragedy. Dominant virtue is the widescreen snap Schepisi gives to the N.Y. settings, both indoors and out. Based on a true incident. Many N.Y.C. society types pop up in cameos. Super 35. [R]▼

Six of a Kind (1934) **62m.** *** D: Leo McCarey. W. C. Fields, George Burns, Gracie Allen, Charlie Ruggles, Mary Boland, Alison Skipworth. George and Gracie drive Mary and Charlie crazy traveling westward on vacation; Fields as pool-playing sheriff adds to confusion. Zany, wonderful nonsense.▼①

Six Pack (1982) **C-110m.** ** D: Daniel Petrie. Kenny Rogers, Diane Lane, Erin Gray, Barry Corbin, Terry Kiser, Bob Hannah,

Anthony Michael Hall. Stock car driver more or less inherits six orphans whose idea of good clean fun is stripping down someone else's auto. Not as bad as it sounds, but it won't make your day, either; Rogers' theatrical debut. [PG]▼①

Six-Pack Annie (1975) **C-88m.** *** D: Graydon F. David. Lindsay Bloom, Jana Bellan, Ray Danton, Joe Higgins, Stubby Kaye, Louisa Moritz, Richard Kennedy, Doodles Weaver, Bruce Boxleitner, Pedro Gonzalez-Gonzalez, Sid Melton. Minor drive-in classic has busty Bloom as a young girl who goes to Miami to become a hooker to raise money to save her mom's failing diner. Includes a very funny bit by Kennedy as a drunk Texan. [R]

16 Blocks (2006-U.S.-German) **C-102m.** *** D: Richard Donner. Bruce Willis, Mos Def, David Morse, Jenna Stern, Casey Sander, Cylk Cozart, David Zayas, Robert Racki. A burnt-out N.Y.C. cop is given the no-brainer job of escorting a witness from lockup to the courthouse, but their 16-block journey is interrupted by assassins who want the witness dead. It turns out there are no clear-cut good guys or bad guys in this suspenseful yarn laced with incisive character snapshots and the irresistible ingredient of a man in need of redemption. Action scenes are pulse-pounding, and the performances first-rate. Super 35. [PG-13]▶

Sixteen Candles (1984) **C-93m.** ** D: John Hughes. Molly Ringwald, Anthony Michael Hall, Michael Schoeffling, Paul Dooley, Justin Henry, Gedde Watanabe, Blanche Baker, Carlin Glynn, Edward Andrews, Billie Bird, Carole Cook, Max Showalter, John Cusack, Joan Cusack, Jami Gertz, Beth Ringwald, Haviland Morris. A girl turns 16 and dreams of finding Mr. Right—little dreaming that he's already got his eye on her. Observant, potentially winning comedy cluttered up with cheap jokes and offensive material. Redeemed somewhat by Ringwald's charming performance and Hall's engaging portrayal of a would-be hustler. [PG]▼①

6th Day, The (2000) **C-124m.** *** D: Roger Spottiswoode. Arnold Schwarzenegger, Tony Goldwyn, Michael Rapaport, Robert Duvall, Michael Rooker, Sarah Wynter, Wendy Crewson, Ken Pogue, Christopher Lawford. Interesting sci-fi premise set in the near future, when cloning animals is common but cloning human beings is illegal. After ordering a hit on helicopter pilot Schwarzenegger, megalomaniac tycoon Goldwyn has a "copy" made; instead, there are two Arnolds on the loose, seeking revenge. Entertaining if overly plotty film benefits from a sharp sense of humor. Super 35. [PG-13]▼①

Sixth Man, The (1997) **C-107m.** *½ D: Randall Miller. Marlon Wayans, Kadeem Hardison, Kevin Dunn, Michael Michele, David Paymer, Gary Jones. Disney couldn't stop at remaking ANGELS IN THE OUT-

FIELD and THE ABSENT MINDED PROFESSOR: they had to combine them, in this cloying fantasy about a dead college basketball star who spurs his brother (Wayans) and their team to gravity-defying court feats. Your brain will need a liberal application of Ben-Gay after being pummeled by the idiocy of this foul-mouthed comedy. Wayans mugs outrageously, but he had to do *something*. [PG-13] ▼●)

Sixth Sense, The (1999) **C-107m.** ***½ D: M. Night Shyamalan. Bruce Willis, Toni Collette, Haley Joel Osment, Olivia Williams, Donnie Wahlberg, Glenn Fitzgerald, Mischa Barton. Exceptional thriller about a dedicated child psychologist who faces his greatest challenge in reaching—and understanding—a young boy who spends his life paralyzed by fear, because he lives in a world of ghosts. Young Osment is extraordinarily good; the film is sinuous and creepy without being manipulative. Writer-director Shyamalan also has a cameo as a doctor. [PG-13] ▼)

Sixty Six (2006-British) **C-95m.** *** D: Paul Weiland. Helena Bonham Carter, Eddie Marsan, Gregg Sulkin, Peter Serafinowicz, Catherine Tate, Stephen Rea, Ben Newton, Richard Katz, Geraldine Somerville. A misfit lad with an eccentric family relates the misadventures leading up to his bar mitzvah in 1966—the same year England played Germany in the World Cup. Billed, rather disarmingly, as "a true-ish story" based on director Weiland's experiences. Slight but endearingly funny, wellcast comedy of recognition. [PG-13]❭

Six Weeks (1982) **C-107m.** ** D: Tony Bill. Dudley Moore, Mary Tyler Moore, Katherine Healy, Shannon Wilcox, Bill Calvert, Joe Regalbuto. Curiously unmoving tearjerker about a politician who meets a precocious young girl who's dying of leukemia, and becomes involved with her mother. Genteel, well acted (Dudley is absolutely charming) but hollow; the characters just don't ring true. Healy, in real life, is an award-winning ballerina. Dudley also composed the score. [PG] ▼●

Six Wives of Henry Lefay, The (2010) **C-95m.** *½ D: Howard Michael Gould. Tim Allen, Barbara Barrie, Elisha Cuthbert, Jenna Dewan, Jenna Elfman, Edward Herrmann, Chris Klein, Andie MacDowell, S. Epatha Merkerson, Larry Miller, Eric Christian Olsen, Lindsay Sloane, Paz Vega. At a beach resort, oft-married Allen complains about his life, cites his regrets, and then dies in a parasailing accident. His daughter, mother, and wives (present and past) gather for his funeral, where there are plenty of surprises in store. Lame time waster veers from stale, offensive humor to eye-rolling pathos, and too many of the characters are downright annoying. Released direct to DVD in the U.S. [PG-13]❭

Sizzle Beach, U.S.A. (1986) **C-93m.** BOMB D: Richard Brander. Terry Congie, Leslie Brander, Roselyn Royce, Kevin Costner. Ultra-low-budget beach-bimbo junk, of interest solely as the first film appearance of Costner. Made in 1974. [R]▼●❭

Skateboard (1977) **C-97m.** ** D: George Gage. Allen Garfield, Kathleen Lloyd, Leif Garrett, Richard Van Der Wyk, Tony Alva, Antony Carbone. In trouble with his bookie, Garfield organizes local skateboarders into moneymaking team. Good premise given lackluster treatment. [PG] ▼❭

Skatetown, U.S.A. (1979) **C-98m.** *½ D: William A. Levey. Scott Baio, Flip Wilson, Ron Palillo, Ruth Buzzi, Dave Mason, Greg Bradford, Kelly Lang, Billy Barty, Dorothy Stratten. Comedy-fantasy for the light of heart and slow of brain, with occasionally amusing comedy bits spicing plotless look at the ultimate roller-disco palace. Film's only real distinction is that it's better than ROLLER BOOGIE. Film debut of Patrick Swayze. [PG]

Skeeter (1994) **C-91m.** **½ D: Clark Brandon. Tracy Griffith, Jim Youngs, Charles Napier, Jay Robinson, William Sanderson, Eloy Casados, John Putch, Saxon Trainor, Stacy Edwards, Michael J. Pollard, Buck Flower. Mysterious deaths around a dwindling desert community are traced to toxic waste and the crow-sized mosquitoes it has spawned. Good acting and imaginative, inventive direction result in a funny little thriller that almost overcomes its routine story. ▼●❭

Skeleton Key, The (2005) **C-104m.** ** D: Iain Softley. Kate Hudson, Gena Rowlands, John Hurt, Peter Sarsgaard, Joy Bryant, Maxine Barnett. New Orleans nursing student Hudson gets a job at a decrepit house in the bayous where she cares for mute, paralyzed Hurt and takes orders from his domineering sister Rowlands. Using a key that opens every door, she finds hoodoo (not voodoo) paraphernalia in the attic, and mysterious events follow. Well produced and occasionally suspenseful, but populated with unpleasant characters and a story that develops too slowly. Another in a long line of horror thrillers aimed at a female audience. Panavision. [PG-13]▼❭

Sketches of Frank Gehry (2006) **C-83m.** *** D: Sydney Pollack. Highly personal portrait of the innovative architect, seen through the eyes of his longtime friend filmmaker Pollack. We get to see the artist at work, collaborating with his team, at home in the space he designed, and hear his life story in his own words—and those of various friends, colleagues, and patrons, ranging from Philip Johnson to Dennis Hopper. Because Gehry is candid and at ease with Pollack, the film is both entertaining and illuminating. [PG-13]❭

Ski Bum, The (1971) **C-136m.** BOMB D:

Bruce Clark. Zalman King, Charlotte Rampling, Joseph Mell, Dimitra Arliss, Anna Karen. Deservedly obscure film version of Romain Gary's novel about a ski bum who goes establishment, winds up a pawn in a shady business deal. Aka POINT ZERO. [R] ▼

Skidoo (1968) **C-98m. **½ D:** Otto Preminger. Jackie Gleason, Carol Channing, Frankie Avalon, Fred Clark, Michael Constantine, Frank Gorshin, John Phillip Law, Peter Lawford, Burgess Meredith, George Raft, Cesar Romero, Mickey Rooney, Groucho Marx, Austin Pendleton. Avalon plays an up-and-coming gangster, Groucho a mob kingpin named "God," and every single credit to the film is sung. Consequently, about one in a thousand will have the temperament to like this; everyone else will sit there dumbstruck. Music score by Harry Nilsson. Groucho's final film. Panavision. [M]▶

Ski Fever (1969) **C-98m. *½ D:** Curt Siodmak. Martin Milner, Claudia Martin, Vivi Bach, Dietmar Schoenherr, Toni Sailor, Dorit Dom. American ski instructor giving lessons in Austria to finance his education is unpleasantly surprised to learn his duties include entertaining guests after hours. Why complain when most of them are good-looking girls? Claudia is Dean Martin's daughter. [M]

Skin (2009 - South African - British) **C-102m. ***½ D:** Anthony Fabian. Sophie Okonedo, Sam Neill, Alice Krige, Tony Kgoroge, Ella Ramangwane, Faniswa Yisa, Hannes Brummer. Heart-rending true story of Sandra Laing (Okonedo), a black child of white parents, and how that anomaly affects her life in apartheid South Africa during the 1960s, '70s, and '80s. Her father, shopkeeper Neill, insists that the government declare her legally white, failing to recognize that she will still be ostracized—and may even feel more at home with black people. Astonishing saga spans 30 years and features great performances by Okonedo, Neill, and Krige (as Sandra's mother). Written by Helen Crawley, Jessie Keyt, and Helena Kriel, from a story by Fabian; based on Judith Stone's book *When She Was White*. [PG-13]▶

Skin Deep (1989) **C-101m. **½ D:** Blake Edwards. John Ritter, Vincent Gardenia, Alyson Reed, Joel Brooks, Julianne Phillips, Chelsea Field, Nina Foch, Denise Crosby, Michael Kidd, Sheryl Lee Ralph. Successful L.A. writer can't keep his hedonistic life on track—not with diversions around like wine (he's an alcoholic), women (he's insatiable), and song (Cole Porter's a favorite). Spotty, often obvious comedy from writer-director Edwards does have some real laughs—and some unforgettable condoms. Panavision. [R]▼●

Skin Game, The (1931-British) **86m. ** D:** Alfred Hitchcock. Edmund Gwenn, Jill Esmond, John Longden, C. V. France, Helen Haye, Phyllis Konstam. Gwenn adds the only spark of life to this dull adaptation of the Galsworthy play about rivalry between neighboring landowners. Hitchcock claims he didn't make it by choice, and one can believe it considering the many long, static dialogue scenes; very atypical of the Master.▼

Skin Game (1971) **C-102m. ***½ D:** Paul Bogart. James Garner, Louis Gossett, Susan Clark, Brenda Sykes, Edward Asner, Andrew Duggan. Exceptional comedy about Garner and Gossett running con-game posing as master and slave in pre–Civil War era. Serious undertones enhance this offbeat, entertaining film; Clark delightful as female con-artist who joins duo. Scripter "Pierre Marton" is Peter Stone. Remade for TV by Burt Kennedy as SIDEKICKS in 1974. Panavision. [PG]▼▶

Skins (2002) **C-87m. ***½ D:** Chris Eyre. Graham Greene, Eric Schweig, Gary Farmer, Noah Watts, Lois Red Elk, Michelle Thrush, Nathaniel Arcand, Chaske Spencer. Deeply emotional film about two Oglala Sioux brothers, raised in the dirt-poor region of Wounded Knee; one becomes a policeman, the other a hopeless, embarrassing drunk, but the bond between them remains strong. A moving story of love, guilt, and accountability. The film's polemics are woven into an absorbing, personal story, and distinguished by two exceptional lead performances. Adapted from Adrian C. Louis' novel by Jennifer D. Lyne. [R] ▼▶

Skinwalkers (2007-U.S.-Canadian-German) **C-110m. *½ D:** James Isaac. Jason Behr, Elias Koteas, Rhona Mitra, Kim Coates, Natassia Malthe, Matthew Knight, Sarah Carter, Tom Jackson, Rogue Johnston, Barbara Gordon, Shawn Roberts, Wendy Crewson. Twelve-year-old Knight and his mother are unaware that the other members of their family are "good" werewolves who protect them. They battle a band of "bad" werewolves who are determined to kill the boy, and the result is yet another hackneyed horror movie. Super 35. [PG-13]▶

Ski Party (1965) **C-90m. ** D:** Alan Rafkin. Frankie Avalon, Dwayne Hickman, Deborah Walley, Yvonne Craig, Robert Q. Lewis, Bobbi Shaw, Aron Kincaid. BEACH PARTY gang puts on some clothes in this one, but the shenanigans are the same. Guest star Lesley Gore sings "Sunshine, Lollipops and Rainbows." James Brown sings "I Got You." Panavision.▶

Skipped Parts (2000) **C-93m. ** D:** Tamra Davis. Jennifer Jason Leigh, Mischa Barton, Bug Hall, R. Lee Ermey, Angela Featherstone, Peggy Lipton, Brad Renfro, Michael Greyeyes, Drew Barrymore. In 1963, a despotic Southern millionaire sends his slutty daughter and her son packing for Wyoming, where they try to fit in—and he learns the facts of life from a girl who befriends him.

All-too-familiar territory gets uneven treatment; adapted by Tim Sandlin from his novel. Barrymore appears in several scenes as Hall's dream girl. Released direct to video. Widescreen. [R] ▼▶

Skull, The (1965-British) **C-83m.** **½ D: Freddie Francis. Peter Cushing, Patrick Wymark, Christopher Lee, Nigel Green, Jill Bennett, Michael Gough, George Coulouris, Patrick Magee. Good cast lends needed support to questionable script (based on a Robert Bloch story) of skull of Marquis de Sade that has mysterious powers. Techniscope. ▼▶

Skullduggery (1970) **C-105m.** *½ D: Gordon Douglas. Burt Reynolds, Susan Clark, Roger C. Carmel, Chips Rafferty, Edward Fox, Wilfrid Hyde-White, Pat Suzuki, Rhys Williams. In New Guinea, Reynolds and Clark find gentle ape people called the Tropi; their humanity has to be proved in court to keep them from being slaughtered by developers. Unusual but unsuccessful story whose author had his name removed from the credits. Panavision. [M/PG]▼

Skulls, The (2000) **C-106m.** BOMB° D: Rob Cohen. Joshua Jackson, Paul Walker, Hill Harper, Leslie Bibb, Christopher McDonald, William Petersen, Craig T. Nelson, Steve Harris, Malin Akerman. Quickly termed THE NUMBSKULLS, this Ivy League groaner deals with an unnamed university (it might be Yale because it's not Slippery Rock) and the power-mad chicanery of its secret organization. Insipid acting, dialogue and situations abound, with the film asking us to believe that a treacherous act could be covered up when it's been videotaped and a couple dozen well-connected high-rollers know about it. Followed by two direct-to-video sequels. [PG-13]▼▶

Sky Bandits (1986-British) **C-92m.** BOMB D: Zoran Perisic. Scott McGinnis, Jeff Osterhage, Ronald Lacey. McGinnis and Osterhage are a poor man's BUTCH CASSIDY AND THE SUNDANCE KID in this dreary adventure of two Western buddies' aerial exploits during WWI. Poorly cast and has nothing to offer but high-flying special effects, designed by director Perisic (who made Chris Reeve "fly" in SUPERMAN). [PG]

Sky Blue (2003-Korean) **C-86m.** **½ D: Moon-Saeng Kim. Voices of David Naughton, Kirk Thornton, Catherine Cavadini. Decades after a catastrophic worldwide environmental disaster, wealthy city-dwelling survivors go to war with the working-class outsiders over the mining of an energy source, which is also a deadly pollutant. Korean-made sci-fi anime feature is a dazzling visual tour-de-force, filled with violent action and impressive animation, but is less successful as an ecological cautionary tale.

Sky Captain and the World of Tomorrow (2004-U.S.-British-Italian) **C-107m.** ** D:

Kerry Conran. Gwyneth Paltrow, Jude Law, Angelina Jolie, Giovanni Ribisi, Michael Gambon, Bai Ling, Omid Djalili. Elaborate homage to Saturday matinee serials and their vision of the future, set in 1939. Law is a hero for hire, Paltrow a plucky reporter and ex-girlfriend, Ribisi his sidekick, and Jolie an exotic captain of an amphibious squadron. All the settings were rendered on a computer (designed by writer-director Conran) and look great, but they only underscore the film's artificiality. Those old serials were energetic; this film is inert. Ribisi and Jolie seem to be having the most fun. The late Laurence Olivier appears on a giant screen, reminiscent of the Wizard of Oz. Law coproduced. [PG] ▼

Sky High (2005) **C-100m.** **½ D: Mike Mitchell. Michael Angarano, Kurt Russell, Kelly Preston, Danielle Panabaker, Kevin Heffernan, Lynda Carter, Mary Elizabeth Winstead, Bruce Campbell, Dave Foley, Kevin McDonald, Steven Strait, Dee-Jay Daniels, Nicholas Braun, Kelly Vitz, Will Harris, Cloris Leachman. Teenaged son of two superheroes, The Commander and Jetstream, feels he can never measure up—especially when on his first day at Sky High he's forced to admit that unlike his classmates, he hasn't yet acquired any super powers. Benign film for kids is well acted but doesn't have much pizzazz, despite the clever concept and visual effects. Carter is amusingly cast as high school principal Powers. Super 35. [PG]▶

Skyjacked (1972) **C-100m.** **½ D: John Guillermin. Charlton Heston, Yvette Mimieux, James Brolin, Claude Akins, Jeanne Crain, Susan Dey, Roosevelt Grier, Mariette Hartley, Walter Pidgeon, Ken Swofford, Leslie Uggams, Mike Henry, John Hillerman. Commercial flight hijacked to Russia. Entertaining for first half, even exciting; second half deteriorates. Good cast will distract some from tedium elsewhere. Retitled: SKY TERROR. Panavision. [PG]●▶

Skylark (1941) **94m.** ***½ D: Mark Sandrich. Claudette Colbert, Ray Milland, Brian Aherne, Binnie Barnes, Walter Abel, Ernest Cossart, Grant Mitchell. Sophisticated romance with Aherne trying to take Claudette away from business-minded husband Milland. Stars are at their peak in this smooth adaptation of Samson Raphaelson play.

Skyline (2010) **C-94m.** BOMB D: The Brothers Strause. Eric Balfour, Scottie Thompson, Brittany Daniel, Crystal Reed, Neil Hopkins, David Zayas, Donald Faison. After a long night of hearty partying, acquaintances awaken to find spacecraft of extraterrestrial invaders hovering in the sky outside their luxury penthouse. Nothing good comes of this. Lame sci-fi thriller pilfers from INDEPENDENCE DAY, TRANSFORMERS, and several other superior films, but the end result resembles nothing so much as a direct-to-video pot-boiler. Even the special effects aren't all that special. Super 35. [PG-13] ▶

Sky Pirates (1986-Australian) **C-86m.** *½ D: Colin Eggleston. John Hargreaves, Meredith Phillips, Max Phipps, Bill Hunter, Simon Chilvers, Alex Scott. Yet another RAIDERS–INDIANA JONES variation, about an aircraft that crashes through a time warp, a search for a special stone, and other assorted nonsense. Boring and confusing, but Hargreaves earns an A for effort. Panavision. [PG-13]▼

Sky Riders (1976) **C-93m.** *** D: Douglas Hickox. James Coburn, Susannah York, Robert Culp, Charles Aznavour, Harry Andrews, John Beck. Lively thriller about a political kidnapping, highlighted by spectacular sequences of hang-gliding. The aerial derring-do and the magnificent Greek scenery make this one worth sitting through. Todd-AO 35. [PG]▼

Skyscraper Wilderness SEE: **Big City** (1937)

Sky's the Limit, The (1943) **89m.** *** D: Edward H. Griffith. Fred Astaire, Joan Leslie, Robert Benchley, Robert Ryan, Elizabeth Patterson, Marjorie Gateson. Fred's a flier on leave who meets photographer Leslie; Benchley's dinner speech, Astaire's "One For My Baby" and "My Shining Hour" make this worthwhile.▼●

Sky Terror SEE: **Skyjacked**

Sky West and Crooked SEE: **Gypsy Girl**

Slacker (1991) **C-97m.** *** D: Richard Linklater. Weird, unique social satire about various contemporary drop-outs in Austin, Texas, who—like the beatniks of the '50s and hippies of the '60s—have formed their own subculture. They're loaded with thoughts and ideas, none of which they seem capable of acting upon. Shot in a free-form style, and featuring a large cast of nonprofessional actors. That's writer-director Linklater as the young man in the taxi. [R]▼●▶

Slackers (2002) **C-87m.** BOMB D: Dewey Nicks. Jason Schwartzman, Devon Sawa, Jason Segel, Michael Maronna, James King, Laura Prepon, Joe Flaherty, Mamie Van Doren. Three college buddies have cheated their way to senior year, but when nerdy Schwartzman discovers their secret, he blackmails them into setting him up with campus beauty King. Repellent excuse for a comedy, even by 21st-century teen-movie standards. A couple of surprise movie-star cameos add nothing to the mix, though Van Doren's scene is memorable—for all the wrong reasons. [R]▼▶

Slam (1998) **C-103m.** ***½ D: Marc Levin. Saul Williams, Sonja Sohn, Bonz Malone, Beau Sia, Lawrence Wilson. Extraordinary fly-on-the-wall filmmaking technique makes this story of a D.C. ghetto victim seem absolutely real from start to

finish. Sent to prison, he has an awakening there and realizes that he cannot endure, or condone, the endless cycle of violence in his community, and uses his gift for poetry as an outlet. Cowritten by its leading actors (Williams, Sohn, Malone) with Levin and Richard Stratton. [R]▼●▶

Slamdance (1987) **C-100m.** BOMB D: Wayne Wang. Tom Hulce, Mary Elizabeth Mastrantonio, Virginia Madsen, Harry Dean Stanton, Millie Perkins, Don Opper, Adam Ant, John Doe. Underground cartoonist/painter Hulce, devoted to his ex-wife and young child, is framed—apparently by the entire population of L.A.—for the murder of party girl Madsen. Weird, without compensating originality. Lifeless melodrama deals only peripherally with the "club" scene; there is as much slamdancing in PYGMALION. [R]▼●▶

Slam Dunk Ernest (1995) **C-92m.** *½ D: John Cherry. Jim Varney, Cylk Cozart, Miguel A. Nunez, Jr., Lester Barrie, Colin Lawrence, Richard Leacock, Jay Brazeau, Lossen Chambers, Kareem Abdul-Jabbar. Likable dolt Ernest P. Worrell wants to play basketball with his coworkers; they let him play benchwarmer instead, until a pair of magic shoes transforms him into a hoop star. Secondary characters are more interesting than Varney in this direct-to-video release. For Ernest fans only. Followed by ERNEST IN THE ARMY. [PG]▼▶

Slammer SEE: **Short Eyes**

Slams, The (1973) **C-97m.** ** D: Jonathan Kaplan. Jim Brown, Judy Pace, Roland "Bob" Harris, Frank de Kova, Ted Cassidy. Mindless actioner has Brown in L.A. prison after stashing away a heroin cache and $1.5 million. Halfway through, comedy takes over for a fast pickup. [R]

Slap Her, She's French (2002-German-U.S.) **C-93m.** ** D: Melanie Mayron. Piper Perabo, Jane McGregor, Trent Ford, Michael McKean, Julie White, Brandon Smith, Jesse James. Ambitious Texas teen (McGregor) whose dream is to host *Good Morning America* decides it would be a good move to take in a foreign-exchange student—but the French girl (Perabo) who comes to live with her family is not the meek young thing she pretends to be. Heavy-handed comedy with little to recommend it except McGregor's energetic performance as the picture-perfect heroine. Aka SHE GETS WHAT SHE WANTS. [PG-13]▶

Slappy and the Stinkers (1998) **C-78m.** BOMB D: Barnet Kellman. B. D. Wong, Bronson Pinchot, Jennifer Coolidge, Joseph Ashton, Gary LeRoi Gray, David Dukes, Sam McMurray. Inane story of a group of completely, irresponsibly unsupervised nerdy seven-year-olds rescuing a sea lion against his will. Along the way they torture the head of their boarding school with their antics. A totally unfunny comedy, and a waste of talent on both sides of the camera. [PG]▼●

Slap Shot (1977) **C-122m.** **★★★** D: George Roy Hill. Paul Newman, Michael Ontkean, Lindsay Crouse, Jennifer Warren, Melinda Dillon, Strother Martin, Jerry Houser, Swoosie Kurtz, (M.) Emmet Walsh, Kathryn Walker, Paul Dooley. Newman is star of bush-league hockey team that's going nowhere until they decide to play dirty. Uneven but raucously funny at times, with very satisfying wrapup. Andrew Duncan is hilarious as local sports broadcaster; barbed (and very profane) script by Nancy Dowd. Followed by two DVD sequels. [R]▼●

Slapstick (Of Another Kind) (1984) **C-82m.** **★½** D: Steven Paul. Jerry Lewis, Madeline Kahn, Marty Feldman, Jim Backus, John Abbott, Pat Morita, Samuel Fuller, Merv Griffin, Steven Paul; voice of Orson Welles. Lewis and Kahn give birth to enormous, deformed twins (also Lewis and Kahn) who are in reality alien messengers capable of solving the world's problems—as long as they're not separated. Given that cast and a Kurt Vonnegut novel as source material, you'd think there'd be no way to screw it up, but writer/producer/ director/ costar Paul manages; some funny things do survive (Fuller and the elder Lewis come off best), but overall, pretty appalling. Filmed in 1982. [PG]▼●

Slate, Wyn & Me (1987-Australian) **C-90m.** **★★** D: Don McLennan. Sigrid Thornton, Simon Burke, Martin Sacks, Tommy Lewis, Lesley Baker. Meandering drama of brothers Burke and Sacks, who rob a bank, kill a cop . . . and kidnap Thornton, who witnesses their crime. Potentially intriguing tale falls flat after twenty minutes. Panavision. [R]▼

Slattery's Hurricane (1949) **83m.** **★★½** D: Andre de Toth. Richard Widmark, Linda Darnell, Veronica Lake, John Russell, Gary Merrill. Weather pilot Widmark, in midst of storm, thinks back on his life; Darnell and Lake are his two loves. Interesting idea; coscripted by Herman Wouk, who later expanded it into a novel.

Slaughter (1972) **C-92m.** **★★** D: Jack Starrett. Jim Brown, Stella Stevens, Rip Torn, Don Gordon, Cameron Mitchell, Marlene Clark, Robert Phillips. Stevens and Torn are far too good for this violent tripe about ex–Green Beret Brown who goes after syndicate after it kills his parents. Sequel: SLAUGHTER'S BIG RIP-OFF. Todd-AO 35. [R]▼●

Slaughterhouse-Five (1972) **C-104m.** **★★★** D: George Roy Hill. Michael Sacks, Ron Leibman, Eugene Roche, Sharon Gans, Valerie Perrine, John Dehner, Holly Near, Perry King. Sometimes draggy, sometimes on-target, sprawling view of life through eyes of one Billy Pilgrim, professional nobody who becomes "unstuck" in time.

Big-budget adaptation of Kurt Vonnegut's bizarre fantasy novel is hard going for those unfamiliar with author's point of view, gains through repeat viewings. [R]▼●)

Slaughter in San Francisco (1981-Hong Kong) **C-87m.** BOMB D: William Lowe. Don Wong, Chuck Norris, Sylvia Channing, Robert Jones, Dan Ivan. Former cop Wong seeks vengeance on murderer of his partner; Norris, in a supporting role, is the bad guy. Shoddy production will disappoint chop-socky genre buffs. Filmed in 1973; released to take advantage of Norris' subsequent popularity. Aka KARATE COP and CHUCK NORRIS VS. THE KARATE COP. Widescreen. [R]▼

Slaughter's Big Rip-Off (1973) **C-93m.** **★½** D: Gordon Douglas. Jim Brown, Ed McMahon, Brock Peters, Don Stroud, Gloria Hendry, Dick Anthony Williams, Art Metrano. Slaughter's still playing cat and mouse with the Mob in this dreary actioner; McMahon gives his role as the Syndicate head better than it deserves. Todd-AO 35. [R]▼●

Slave Girls SEE: **Prehistoric Women**

Slave of the Cannibal God (1978-Italian) **C-93m.** **★½** D: Sergio Martino. Ursula Andress, Stacy Keach, Claudio Cassinelli, Antonio Marsina, Franco Fantasia. Too-glamorous Andress captured by natives and painted in preparation for sacrifice in a scene virtually identical to that directed by ex-husband John Derek for current wife Bo years later in TARZAN, THE APE MAN. Aka MOUNTAIN OF THE CANNIBAL GOD. Techniscope. [R]▼●

Slavers (1978-German) **C-102m.** **★★** D: Jurgen Goslar. Trevor Howard, Ron Ely, Britt Ekland, Jurgen Goslar, Ray Milland, Ken Gampu, Cameron Mitchell. Pulp-fiction stuff about slave trading in Africa during the 19th century. Good cast saddled with second-rate script. [R]▼

Slaves (1969) **C-110m.** **★½** D: Herbert J. Biberman. Stephen Boyd, Dionne Warwick, Ossie Davis, Marilyn Clark, Gale Sondergaard, Shepperd Strudwick, Nancy Coleman, Julius Harris, David Huddleston. Strange cast in revisionist drama about Kentucky slave Davis standing up for his rights; might have meant something in the '60s, but now it's just laughable, with Boyd properly embarrassed as Simon Legree–type "Massa." Notable only as Sondergaard's first film after 20-year blacklist, courtesy director-cowriter (and husband) Biberman.

Slaves of New York (1989) **C-125m.** **★½** D: James Ivory. Bernadette Peters, Adam Coleman Howard, Chris Sarandon, Mary Beth Hurt, Nick Corri, Madeleine Potter, Mercedes Ruehl, Betty Comden, Steve Buscemi, Michael Schoeffling, Tammy Grimes, Charles McCaughan, Anthony LaPaglia. Misguided filming of Tama Janowitz's bestselling collection of stories, set among the too-hip-for-words denizens of N.Y.C.'s downtown art world. As the central character, the talented Peters seems all wrong: too intelligent to spend most of the film being humiliated by her boyfriend (Howard). Overlong and unfocused. Janowitz (who plays Abby) scripted. [R]▼●▮

Slayground (1984-British) **C-89m.** *½ D: Terry Bedford. Peter Coyote, Billie Whitelaw, Philip Sayer, Bill Luhr, Mel Smith. Dreary actioner about robber Coyote on the lam from a hired killer. Whitelaw in particular is wasted as an amusement park owner. Based on a novel by Donald E. Westlake, writing as Richard Stark. [R]▮

SLC Punk! (1999-U.S.-Australian) **C-97m.** **½ D: James Merendino. Matthew Lillard, Michael Goorjian, Annabeth Gish, Jennifer Lien, Christopher McDonald, Devon Sawa, Adam Pascal, Til Schweiger. Seriocomic coming of ager about punk rocker Stevo and his best pal, Heroin Bob, whose pursuit of "total chaos" is at odds with living in conservative Salt Lake City, Utah, circa 1985. Writer-director Merendino has real affection for the punk scene, but it would've worked better without overused gimmick of having the lead character talk directly to the camera. Charismatic performance from Lillard. Panavision. [R]▼▮

Sleazy Uncle, The (1991-Italian) **C-105m.** **½ D: Franco Brusati. Vittorio Gassman, Giancarlo Giannini, Andrea Ferreol, Stefania Sandrelli, Beatrice Palme. Playfully lecherous uncle (Gassman) is forced to seek temporary asylum with his rich, repressed nephew (Giannini). Predictably, uncle Gassman's outrageous antics—which range from seducing Giannini's mistress and passing out his blood-test certificates to all the ladies ("for your security") —result in setting Giannini's placid life on its ear. A little too laid back to achieve the farcical comedy attempted here.▼

Sleeper (1973) **C-88m.** ***½ D: Woody Allen. Woody Allen, Diane Keaton, John Beck, Mary Gregory, Don Keefer, John McLiam. Woody turns to slapstick in this engagingly silly tale of a man who's frozen in 1973 and awakened 200 years later. Typical Allen combination of great jokes and duds, with more sight-gags than usual and energetic score by the Preservation Hall Jazz Band. Screenplay by Allen and Marshall Brickman. [PG]▼●▮

Sleepers (1996) **C-147m.** **½ D: Barry Levinson. Kevin Bacon, Robert De Niro, Dustin Hoffman, Jason Patric, Brad Pitt, Minnie Driver, Brad Renfro, Bruno Kirby, Vittorio Gassman, Billy Crudup, Ron Eldard, Terry Kinney, John Slattery, Aida Turturro. Absorbing tale of young friends in N.Y.C.'s Hell's Kitchen who wind up in reform school, where they endure a living hell at the hands of sadistic guards. Later in life, one of them (now working for the D.A.) sows the seeds for revenge. Based on Lorenzo Carcaterra's purportedly nonfiction book, the movie grabs and holds you but never quite convinces; the resolution is too pat. Strong performances. Super 35. [R]▼●▮

Sleeping Beauty (1959) **C-75m.** *** D: Clyde Geronimi. Voices of Mary Costa, Bill Shirley, Eleanor Audley, Verna Felton, Barbara Jo Allen (Vera Vague), Barbara Luddy. Walt Disney's most expensive and elaborate animated feature (at the time) is actually a simple, straightforward telling of the classic fairy tale, with music adapted from Tchaikovsky, and such memorable characters as Flora, Fauna, and Merryweather (the three good fairies) and the evil witch Maleficent. Highlight: the final, fiery confrontation between Maleficent and Prince Phillip. Strikingly designed (in widescreen) by artist Eyvind Earle. Super Technirama 70. ▼●▮

Sleeping Car, The (1990) **C-87m.** ** D: Douglas Curtis. David Naughton, Judie Aronson, Kevin McCarthy, Jeff Conaway, Ernestine Mercer, John Carl Buechler, Dani Minnick. Good-looking but heavily overstated horror film pitting Naughton and friends against a vicious ghost haunting an old railway sleeping car, now used as an apartment. [R]▼●

Sleeping Car Murder, The (1965-French) **90m.** *** D: Costa-Gavras. Simone Signoret, Yves Montand, Pierre Mondy, Jean-Louis Trintignant, Jacques Perrin, Michel Piccoli, Catherine Allegret, Charles Denner. Quick-paced, atmospheric police-chasing-mad-killer movie. Nice photography by Jean Tournier; original action good but dubbing hurts. Based on a Sebastien Japrisot novel. Costa-Gavras' directorial debut. CinemaScope.

Sleeping Dogs (1977-New Zealand) **C-107m.** ** D: Roger Donaldson. Sam Neill, Ian Mune, Warren Oates, Nevan Rowe, Donna Akersten, Ian Watkin, Bill Julliff, Clyde Scott. Muddled thriller about apolitical loner Neill unable to remain aloof from repressive government and revolutionaries during workers' strike. Fascinating concept defeated by confusing direction, illogical plot development, insufficiently defined characters. Michael Seresin's top-notch cinematography helps. The first New Zealand film ever to open in the U.S.▼▮

Sleeping Tiger, The (1954-British) **89m.** *** D: Victor Hanbury (Joseph Losey). Alexis Smith, Dirk Bogarde, Alexander Knox, Hugh Griffith, Patricia McCarron, Billie Whitelaw. Well-done drama with Knox a psychiatrist who takes low-life criminal Bogarde into his home, much to the consternation of his wife (Smith, in one of her best roles); the result is sexual and emotional fireworks. Losey's first film made outside the U.S., where he was blacklisted; this accounts for the pseudonym.▼▮

Sleeping With the Enemy (1991) **C-98m.**
**** D: Joseph Ruben. Julia Roberts, Patrick Bergin, Kevin Anderson, Elizabeth Lawrence, Kyle Secor, Claudette Nevins. Practically suspense-less thriller about a young woman who flees from her brutal husband and tries to start life anew in Iowa. Unabashed star vehicle for Roberts (complete with "cute" montage set to the oldie "Brown-Eyed Girl") is relentlessly predictable. [R] ▼●)

Sleepless in Seattle (1993) **C-104m.** ***
D: Nora Ephron. Tom Hanks, Meg Ryan, Bill Pullman, Ross Malinger, Rosie O'Donnell, Rob Reiner, Gaby Hoffmann, Victor Garber, Rita Wilson, Barbara Garrick, Carey Lowell, Calvin Trillin, Dana Ivey, David Hyde Pierce. Woman who's just gotten engaged hears a widower on a call-in radio show talking about his departed wife and becomes obsessed with meeting him, convinced that he may be her destiny. Sweet romantic comedy, with perfectly cast stars, though its repeated allusions to the old tearjerker AN AFFAIR TO REMEMBER make you wonder if the only way to generate old-fashioned romance in a '90s movie is to invoke a product of Hollywood's Golden Age. Coscripted by Ephron. [PG] ▼●)

Sleep, My Love (1948) **97m.** *** D: Douglas Sirk. Claudette Colbert, Robert Cummings, Don Ameche, Hazel Brooks, Rita Johnson, George Coulouris, Keye Luke, Raymond Burr, Ralph Morgan. Entertaining melodrama with adulterous Ameche trying to drive wealthy wife Colbert crazy; her new acquaintance (Cummings) becomes interested in her plight. Leo Rosten coscripted, based on his novel. "Presented" by Mary Pickford.

Sleepover (2004) **C-89m.** ** D: Joe Nussbaum. Alexa Vega, Mika Boorem, Jane Lynch, Sam Huntington, Sara Paxton, Brie Larson, Scout Taylor-Compton, Douglas Smith, Jeff Garlin, Steve Carell. OK, where have we seen this before? Young girls about to become high school freshmen embark on an all-night scavenger hunt to beat their more popular rivals, but of course the real victory is what they learn about themselves in the process. Mind-numbing fluff for anyone but its target audience. [PG] ▼)

Sleepwalkers (1992) **C-91m.** **½ D: Mick Garris. Brian Krause, Mädchen Amick, Alice Krige, Jim Haynie, Cindy Pickett, Lyman Ward, Ron Perlman, Dan Martin, Glenn Shadix. A mother-and-son pair of "sleepwalkers" move to a Norman Rockwell–ish Midwestern town, looking for prey. The shape-changing Sleepwalkers live on the life force of teenage virgins, but the target this time (Amick) is one tough cookie. Stephen King's script is thinly plotted and confusing, but the movie is directed with flair and a nicely twisted sense of humor. Excellent effects. Cameos by Joe Dante, John Landis,

Clive Barker, Tobe Hooper, and King himself, as well as an unbilled one by Mark Hamill. Aka STEPHEN KING'S "SLEEPWALKERS." [R] ▼●)

Sleepwalking (2008-U.S.-Canadian) **C-101m.** ** D: William Maher. Nick Stahl, AnnaSophia Robb, Charlize Theron, Dennis Hopper, Woody Harrelson, Deborra-Lee Furness, Mathew St. Patrick. Theron is a struggling single mother (and poor role model) to a preteen daughter in a rural town. After they move in with her younger brother (Stahl) things get even worse. Balance of story features the bonding of uncle and niece, eking out a life in town and on the road until, eventually, the source of much of the family's pain is revealed. Unsurprisingly melodrama lays it on thick. Coproducer Theron's screen time is limited; Stahl is quite moving as an invisible member of working-class society. Super 35. [R] ▼

Sleep With Me (1994) **C-86m.** ** D: Rory Kelly. Craig Sheffer, Eric Stoltz, Meg Tilly, Todd Field, Thomas Gibson, Parker Posey, Adrienne Shelly, Susan Traylor, Tegan West, June Lockhart, Quentin Tarantino, Joey Lauren Adams. Forgettable three-sided romance; as Stoltz and Tilly are about to be married, their best friend (Sheffer) declares his love for her. A self-indulgent study of self-absorption. Scripted by six writers, each of whom contributed a different section of the film. The one standout scene has Tarantino explaining his unique theory about the subtext of TOP GUN. [R] ▼●)

Sleepy Hollow (1999) **C-105m.** ** D: Tim Burton. Johnny Depp, Christina Ricci, Miranda Richardson, Michael Gambon, Casper Van Dien, Jeffrey Jones, Richard Griffiths, Ian McDiarmid, Michael Gough, Christopher Walken, Marc Pickering, Lisa Marie, Christopher Lee, Alun Armstrong. Convoluted and unsatisfying script defeats a good-looking revision of the Washington Irving classic. Depp is fun as a bumbling constable who tries to use scientific methods to figure out a series of killings in New York's Hudson Valley. Burton must have had fun figuring out how many different ways he could show beheadings . . . yet the film is anything but scary. Oscar-winning Art Direction by Rick Heinrichs and Peter Young. Martin Landau appears unbilled. [R] ▼●)

Slender Thread, The (1965) **98m.** **½ D: Sydney Pollack. Sidney Poitier, Anne Bancroft, Telly Savalas, Steven Hill, Edward Asner, Dabney Coleman. Interchange between stars is the whole film in an interesting idea that doesn't fulfill potential. Bancroft takes overdose of sleeping pills and calls crisis clinic for help; college student volunteer Poitier tries to keep her on phone while rescue is organized. Filmed on location in Seattle; written by Stirling Silliphant, music by Quincy Jones. Pollack's directorial debut. ▼

Sleuth (1972) **C-138m.** ******** D: Joseph L. Mankiewicz. Laurence Olivier, Michael Caine. Lighthearted mystery tour de force for two stars, adapted by Anthony Shaffer from his hit play about games-playing mystery writer Olivier leading his wife's lover (Caine) into diabolical trap. But who gets the last laugh on whom? Delicious from start to finish; remarkable production design by Ken Adam. Mankiewicz's last film. Remade in 2007. [PG] ▼●)

Sleuth (2007) **C-86m.** BOMB D: Kenneth Branagh. Michael Caine, Jude Law. Fabulously successful mystery novelist invites a young man who's been carrying on with his wife to his home, where he hopes to entrap him—both physically and psychologically. Reinvention of Anthony Shaffer's play (filmed in 1972 with Caine—as the younger character—and Laurence Olivier) by Harold Pinter has had every ounce of entertainment drained from it. Unbelievably bad, especially given the talent involved. Pinter appears as a talk-show guest on Caine's television set. Panavision. [R]▶

Sliding Doors (1998-U.S.-British) **C-108m.** ****½** D: Peter Howitt. Gwyneth Paltrow, John Hannah, John Lynch, Jeanne Tripplehorn, Zara Turner, Douglas McFerran, Paul Brightwell, Virginia McKenna. Likable romantic comedy explores—in parallel scenes—what happens when Paltrow catches her boyfriend sleeping with another woman, and what would have happened if she'd missed her train and not walked in at that moment. The doltish boyfriend (Lynch) and his extremely bitchy paramour (Tripplehorn) are overstated, unsympathetic characters who bring down the otherwise bright proceedings. Paltrow, sporting a British accent, is delightful; so is Scotsman Hannah. Writing and directing debut for Howitt. [PG-13] ▼●)

Slight Case of Murder, A (1938) **85m.** *****½** D: Lloyd Bacon. Edward G. Robinson, Jane Bryan, Allen Jenkins, Ruth Donnelly, Willard Parker, John Litel, Edward Brophy, Harold Huber, Bobby Jordan, Margaret Hamilton. Robinson's in peak comedy form as gangster who goes straight when Prohibition ends. This hilarious adaptation of a play by Damon Runyon and Howard Lindsay has brewer Robinson going bankrupt in a rented summer house filled with characters and corpses. Remake: STOP, YOU'RE KILLING ME.▶

Slightly Scarlet (1956) **C-99m.** ****½** D: Allan Dwan. John Payne, Arlene Dahl, Rhonda Fleming, Kent Taylor, Ted de Corsia, Lance Fuller. Effective study (from a James M. Cain novel) of big-city corruption; Payne involved with dynamic sister duo (Fleming, Dahl). Arlene steals the show as tipsy ex-con sister. SuperScope.▼▶

Sling Blade (1996) **C-134m.** *****½** D: Billy Bob Thornton. Billy Bob Thornton, Dwight Yoakam, J. T. Walsh, John Ritter,

Lucas Black, Natalie Canerday, James Hampton, Robert Duvall, Rick Dial, Jim Jarmusch. Fascinating portrait of a mentally deficient man sprung from prison 20 years after killing his mother and her boyfriend; now he attempts to blend into "real life," helped by a boy who befriends him. Incredibly controlled performance by Thornton (who also wrote and directed) anchors this long but rewarding tale, which leads to a somewhat inevitable finale. Young Black is exceptional as Thornton's new friend, country singer Yoakam is first-rate as a short-fused bully, and Ritter is terrific in a most unusual part. Oscar winner for Best Screenplay Adaptation; based on the short film SOME CALL IT A SLING BLADE. [R]▼●)

Slingshot, The (1993-Swedish) **C-102m.** ****½** D: Ake Sandgren. Jesper Salen, Stellan Skarsgård, Basia Frydman, Niclas OØlund, Ernst-Hugo Järegård. Odd childhood remembrance, from 78-year-old Roland Schutt's autobiographical novel, about a 10-year-old outcast in 1920s Sweden: Mom's a Russian Jew, Dad's a socialist, and young Roland (Selen) fashions slingshots from the condoms sold by mother on the black market. Perhaps tries to pack too much material into one film, but this was a great success in Sweden. [R] ▼●

Slipper and the Rose, The (1976-British) **C-146m.** ******* D: Bryan Forbes. Richard Chamberlain, Gemma Craven, Annette Crosbie, Michael Hordern, Margaret Lockwood, Christopher Gable, Kenneth More, Edith Evans. Bright musical version of Cinderella in which everyone (including veteran British actors) sings and dances; Craven is delightful as Cindy. Songs by the Sherman Brothers. Good fun. Panavision. [G]▼▶

Slipping-Down Life, A (2004) **C-111m.** ****** D: Toni Kalem. Lili Taylor, Guy Pearce, John Hawkes, Sara Rue, Irma P. Hall, Tom Bower, Shawnee Smith, Veronica Cartwright, Marshall Bell, Bruno Kirby, Clea DuVall. Introverted young woman becomes obsessed with an iconoclastic singer-songwriter, and even carves his name on her forehead. Somehow this sparks an actual relationship between the two social misfits. Taylor's radiant performance is the main attraction here; otherwise, Kalem's adaptation of Anne Tyler's Southern Gothic novel is slow going. Pearce does his own singing, which is pretty good. Filmed in 1998. [R]▼▶

Slip Slide Adventures SEE: **Water Babies, The**

Slipstream (1989-British) **C-92m.** ****** D: Steven M. Lisberger. Bill Paxton, Bob Peck, Mark Hamill, Kitty Aldridge, Eleanor David, F. Murray Abraham, Ben Kingsley, Robbie Coltrane. In the future, nature has rebelled, sending people scurrying to live in valleys away from the high-speed slipstream (high winds) that dominates the planet. Unfortunately this unusual setting has little to do with standard story of adventurer Paxton, who swipes a captive from tough bounty hunter Hamill (delivering a top-notch performance). Just as story should be building to a peak, it lurches into clumsy satire. This big-scale production never made it to theaters in the U.S. [PG-13]▼O❍

Slipstream (2007) **C-96m.** BOMB D: Anthony Hopkins. Anthony Hopkins, Stella Arroyave, John Turturro, Christian Slater, Jeffrey Tambor, Michael Clarke Duncan, Fionnula Flanagan, Camryn Manheim, S. Epatha Merkerson, Christopher Lawford, Kevin McCarthy. Self-consciously "experimental" miasma from writer-director-actor-composer Hopkins and his real-life spouse Arroyave—who costars as Gina—is only for the terminally curious. Hopkins plays a screenwriter who seems to be losing his grip on reality and is summoned to the Mojave Desert, where a movie shoot is going very awry. Moments of coherence are undermined by whiplash-inducing editing of Hopkins' feverdream screenplay. HD Widescreen. [R]❍

Slither (1973) **C-97m.** *** D: Howard Zieff. James Caan, Peter Boyle, Sally Kellerman, Louise Lasser, Allen Garfield, Richard B. Shull. Engaging film is essentially a massive shaggy dog joke; colorful gallery of characters engaged in hunt for elusive cache of money. Perhaps a bit too airy, but perfect TV fare. [PG]▼❍

Slither (2006-U.S.-Canadian) **C-95m.** *** D: James Gunn. Nathan Fillion, Elizabeth Banks, Michael Rooker, Gregg Henry, Tania Saulnier, Brenda James, Don Thompson, Jenna Fischer, Rob Zombie, Lloyd Kaufman. Zombie movie connoisseurs will relish this gory, gross—and expertly devised—horror-comedy involving a meteorite that lands near a small town and discharges a slimy, flesh-eating extraterrestrial. Crammed with equal doses of scares and chuckles; writer-director Gunn, who penned the remake of DAWN OF THE DEAD, references a slew of earlier films, from the original INVASION OF THE BODY SNATCHERS and THE BLOB to vintage David Cronenberg and John Carpenter. [R]❍

Sliver (1993) **C-109m.** ** D: Phillip Noyce. Sharon Stone, William Baldwin, Tom Berenger, Polly Walker, Colleen Camp, Amanda Forman, Martin Landau, CCH Pounder, Nina Foch, Keene Curtis, Nicholas Pryor. Lonely Stone moves into a tall, slender, and luxurious Manhattan apartment building with a history of unusual deaths. Writer Berenger pursues her, though she's more interested in Baldwin; however, she soon comes to suspect one of the two is a killer. Robert Evans' handsomely produced sex-and-murder mystery (emphasis on sex) was severely damaged by reshooting (which changed identity of the killer), but Joe Eszterhas' script was already

pretentious and exploitive. From Ira Levin's novel. Alternate unrated version runs 107m. Panavision. [R]▼❍

Slow Burn (2007) **C-93m.** ** D: Wayne Beach. Ray Liotta, LL Cool J (James Todd Smith), Mekhi Phifer, Jolene Blalock, Chiwetel Ejiofor, Taye Diggs, Guy Torry, Bruce McGill, Frank Schorpion, Fisher Stevens, Donny Falsetti, Barbara Alexander. Confusing drama centers around a district attorney who gets caught up in a gang-related investigation, an interrogation with a shady street-smart leader, and a confrontation with a manipulative but attractive assistant D.A., among others. As Liotta tries to piece together the puzzle the movie collapses under the weight of its disjointed story. Despite a good cast, this weak attempt at film noir doesn't make much sense. Completed in 2005. [R]❍

Slow Dancing in the Big City (1978) **C-101m.** *½ D: John G. Avildsen. Paul Sorvino, Anne Ditchburn, Nicolas Coster, Anita Dangler, Hector Jaime Mercado. Straightfaced romantic absurdity about Jimmy Breslin-like columnist who falls for ailing ballerina who has been told she should no longer dance; he also befriends a little Hispanic orphan/junkie. Shameless climax will fry your brain cells with its bathos. [PG]

Slugger's Wife, The (1985) **C-105m.** *½ D: Hal Ashby. Michael O'Keefe, Rebecca De Mornay, Martin Ritt, Randy Quaid, Cleavant Derricks, Lisa Langlois, Loudon Wainwright III. Remarkably unappealing Neil Simon original about a boorish baseball star who falls in love with a singer. Dull and disjointed, full of mediocre music—in short, a mess! The team's manager is played by film director (and former actor) Martin Ritt. [PG-13]▼❍

Slumber Party '57 (1977) **C-89m.** BOMB D: William A. Levey. Noelle North, Bridget Hollman, Debra Winger, Mary Ann Appleseth, Rainbeaux Smith, Rafael Campos, Will Hutchins, Joyce Jillson, Joe E. Ross. Smutty, sloppily made schlock about a group of girls who swap tales about their sexual initiations, which are recreated in flashback. Of interest only for the appearance of Winger, in her film debut. [R]▼❍

Slumber Party Massacre (1982) **C-78m.** *½ D: Amy Jones. Michele Michaels, Robin Stille, Michael Villela, Andre Honore, Debra Deliso, Gina Mari. Girls have overnight party, boys clown around, crazed killer does them all in. The screenplay, incredibly, is by feminist author Rita Mae Brown. If it's supposed to be a parody, it's about as clever as *Hogan's Heroes.* Followed by two sequels. [R]▼❍

Slumdog Millionaire (2008-British-U.S.) **C-120m.** **** D: Danny Boyle. Dev Patel, Freida Pinto, Madhur Mittal, Anil Kapoor, Irrfan Khan, Tanay Hemant Chheda, Tanvi Ganesh Lonkar, Ashutosh Lobo Gajiwala,

Ayush Mahesh Khedekar, Rubina Ali, Azharuddin Mohammed Ismail. Young man about to win a fortune on India's version of the game show *Who Wants to Be a Millionaire?* is accused of cheating. Then in flashbacks we learn how his tumultuous, often tortured experiences as an orphan on the streets of Bombay have enabled him to relate to and answer all of the questions on the show. Through a cascade of images and sounds director Boyle immerses us in his character's world and takes us along on this remarkable, often painful, life journey, moving from darkness to light for a truly joyful finale. Simon Beaufoy wrote the screenplay, inspired by the novel *Q&A* by Vikas Swarup. Winner of eight Oscars: Best Picture, Director, Adapted Screenplay, Cinematography (Anthony Dod Mantle), Editing (Chris Dickens), Sound, Score (A. R. Rahman), and Song ("Jai-Ho"). Super 35. [R]▶

Slums of Beverly Hills (1998) C-91m. *** D: Tamara Jenkins. Natasha Lyonne, Alan Arkin, Marisa Tomei, Kevin Corrigan, Jessica Walter, Carl Reiner, Rita Moreno, Eli Marienthal, David Krumholtz, Mena Suvari. Keenly observed, semi-autobiographical slice-of-life from novice director-writer Jenkins, set in the 1970s, about the Abramowitz clan, "Jewish Joads" who move from one low-rent living space to another as the poorest inhabitants of the title municipality. The focus is on Lyonne, the only sane person in a sweetly insane environment, as she attempts to deal with her sexual awakening. Razor-sharp and right on the money. [R]▼●▶

Small Back Room, The (1949-British) 106m. ***½ D: Michael Powell, Emeric Pressburger. David Farrar, Jack Hawkins, Kathleen Byron, Anthony Bushell, Michael Gough, Leslie Banks, Robert Morley, Cyril Cusack, Renee Asherson. Mature, powerful story of crippled munitions expert Farrar, who's frustrated by his infirmity and mindless government bureaucracy during WW2. Robert Morley appears unbilled. Original U.S. title: HOUR OF GLORY.▼▶

Small Change (1976-French) C-104m. **** D: François Truffaut. Geory Desmouceaux, Philippe Goldman, Claudio Deluca, Frank Deluca, Richard Golfier, Laurent Devlaeminck. Thoroughly charming, intelligent film examines the lives of young children—their joys, sorrows, frustrations, adventures—in a small French village. Wise, perceptive, and witty. [PG]▼●▶

Small Circle of Friends, A (1980) C-112m. BOMB D: Rob Cohen. Brad Davis, Karen Allen, Jameson Parker, Shelley Long, John Friedrich, Gary Springer. Cloyingly cute by-the-numbers treatment of '60s campus turmoil as an apparently moronic *ménage à trois* tries to make it through Harvard. Almost makes one long for R.P.M. [R]▼●▶

Smallest Show on Earth, The (1957-British) 80m. *** D: Basil Dearden. Bill Travers, Virginia McKenna, Margaret Rutherford, Peter Sellers, Bernard Miles, Leslie Phillips. Charming, often hilarious comedy about a couple who inherit a run-down movie house and its three equally run-down attendants (Sellers, Rutherford, Miles). Lovely scene in which the three veterans express their love for silent films.▼▶

Small Faces (1995-Scottish-English) C-108m. ***½ D: Gillies MacKinnon. Iain Robertson, Joseph McFadden, J. S. Duffy, Laura Fraser, Garry Sweeney, Clare Higgins, Kevin McKidd, Mark McConnochie. Grim look at a working-class family of three boys in 1968 Glasgow, focusing on the youngest (Robertson), barely a teenager, and his indoctrination into gang warfare. Straightforward and powerful. Written by the director and his brother, Billy MacKinnon. [R]▼●

Small Soldiers (1998) C-99m. **½ D: Joe Dante. Kirsten Dunst, Gregory Smith, Jay Mohr, Phil Hartman, Kevin Dunn, Denis Leary, David Cross, Ann Magnuson, Wendy Schaal, Dick Miller, Robert Picardo; voices of Tommy Lee Jones, Frank Langella, Ernest Borgnine, Jim Brown, Bruce Dern, George Kennedy, Clint Walker, Christopher Guest, Michael McKean, Harry Shearer, Sarah Michelle Gellar, Christina Ricci. Overeager toy marketer puts military microchips into new combat figures; all hell breaks loose as they declare war on their "enemy" toys. Good premise is weakened by a predictable script. Computer animation is terrific, and director Dante throws in bonuses for film buffs—using cast members from THE DIRTY DOZEN and THIS IS SPINAL TAP as voices, adopting the BRIDE OF FRANKENSTEIN music at a key moment. Hartman's final film. Super 35. [PG-13]▼●▶

Small Time Crooks (2000) C-94m. **½ D: Woody Allen. Woody· Allen, Tracey Ullman, Hugh Grant, Elaine May, Michael Rapaport, Jon Lovitz, Tony Darrow, Elaine Stritch, George Grizzard. Unusually lightweight comedy from Allen about an ex-con dishwasher who convinces his wife (Ullman) to invest their life's savings in a scheme to rob a bank. Instead, their "front" for the robbery, a cookie store, becomes a success, and wealth goes to her head. Slight, often unfocused, but entertaining, with enjoyable performances and a rare screen appearance by May. [PG]▼▶

Small Town Girl (1953) C-93m. **½ D: Leslie Kardos. Jane Powell, Farley Granger, Ann Miller, S. Z. Sakall, Billie Burke, Bobby Van, Robert Keith, Nat King Cole, Fay Wray. Bland MGM musical pairing playboy Granger and apple-pie Powell, who meet when he's thrown in jail by her father for speeding through town. Van's human pogo-stick number and Miller's "I've Gotta Hear That Beat," with Busby Berkeley's disembodied orchestra, are highlights. ▼●▮

Small Town in Texas, A (1976) **C-95m.** ** D: Jack Starrett. Timothy Bottoms, Susan George, Bo Hopkins, Art Hindle, Morgan Woodward, John Karlen. Bottoms seeks revenge against heinous sheriff Hopkins, who framed him on a drug charge and has stolen his wife (George). Not bad, but you know what to expect. Techniscope. [PG]▼

Small Voices (2003-Filipino) **C-109m.** **½ D: Gil Portes. Alessandra de Rossi, Dexter Doria, Gina Alajar, Amy Austria, Bryan Homecillo, Pierro Rodriguez. A new teacher in a remote elementary school, not much older than her charges, attempts to organize a student chorus despite opposition from impoverished parents and a disinterested faculty. Nothing startlingly new here, but fact-based film succeeds as a heart-rending and heartwarming tale, with storytelling that's earnest to a fault.

Smart Alec (1986) **C-88m.** ** D: Jim Wilson. Ben Glass, Natasha Kautsky, Antony Alda, Lucinda Crosby, Kerry Remsen, Orson Bean, David Hedison, Bill Henderson, Zsa Zsa Gabor. Dull, silly (but not inaccurate) account of pint-sized eccentric Glass, an aspiring filmmaker, and his repeated frustrations as he attempts to finance his movie. Kautsky is most attractive as the model he covets as his leading lady. Aka THE MOVIE MAKER. ▼

Smart People (2008) **C-95m.** **½ D: Noam Murro. Dennis Quaid, Sarah Jessica Parker, Thomas Haden Church, Ellen Page, Ashton Holmes, Christine Lahti. Curmudgeonly English lit professor Quaid, a widower, presides over a dysfunctional household including his supersmart teenage daughter, an alienated son, and (lately) an adopted brother who acts like an overage adolescent. Then he strikes up a hesitant relationship with a former student who's now a physician. Bittersweet comedy-drama isn't uninteresting but the script feels undernourished. Super 35. [R]▮

Smashing the Crime Syndicate SEE: **Hell's Bloody Devils**

Smashing Time (1967-British) **96m.** **½ D: Desmond Davis. Rita Tushingham, Lynn Redgrave, Michael York, Anna Quayle, Ian Carmichael. Two girls come to London to crash big-time. Spoof of trendy fashion/show biz world tries to turn Redgrave and Tushingham into Laurel and Hardy, with middling results. Slapstick scenes only mildly funny. ▼▮

Smash Palace (1981-New Zealand) **C-100m.** *** D: Roger Donaldson. Bruno Lawrence, Anna Jemison, Greer Robson, Keith Aberdein, Desmond Kelly. Lawrence is more interested in his cars than wife Jemison, who craves attention and affection. Sometimes confusing and overly melodramatic, but still worthwhile—particularly when focusing on their 7-year-old daughter (Robson). ▼●▮

Smash-up Alley (1972) **C-83m.** ** D: Edward J. Lakso. Darren McGavin, Richard Petty, Kathie Browne, Noah Beery, Jr., Pierre Jalbert, L. Q. Jones. Stock-car racer Petty plays himself, McGavin is his father, Lee, in this forgettable chronicle of their careers. Aficionados of the sport may enjoy it, however. Aka 43: THE PETTY STORY. [G]▼▮

Smash-up: The Story of a Woman (1947) **103m.** *** D: Stuart Heisler. Susan Hayward, Lee Bowman, Marsha Hunt, Eddie Albert, Carl Esmond, Carleton Young. Hayward is excellent as an insecure nightclub singer who gives up her career when she weds soon-to-be radio star Bowman . . . and finds herself helplessly mired in alcoholism. This was Hayward's breakthrough role after a decade in Hollywood, and it deservedly earned her her first Oscar nomination. Taut script by John Howard Lawson, from an original story by Dorothy Parker and Frank Cavett.▼▮

Smile (1975) **C-113m.** ***½ D: Michael Ritchie. Bruce Dern, Barbara Feldon, Michael Kidd, Geoffrey Lewis, Nicholas Pryor, Colleen Camp, Joan Prather, Annette O'Toole, Melanie Griffith, Maria O'Brien. Hilarious, perceptive satire centering around the behind-the-scenes activity at a California "Young American Miss" beauty pageant, presented as a symbol for the emptiness of American middle-class existence. One of the unsung films of the 1970s, written by Jerry Belson; Kidd is terrific as the contest's career-slumped choreographer. Later a Broadway musical. [PG] ▼●▮

Smile (2005) **C-107m.** ** D: Jeffrey Kramer. Sean Astin, Mika Boorem, Beau Bridges, Yi Ding, Linda Hamilton, Cheri Oteri, Essie Shure, Jonathon Trent, Erik von Detten. Wildly uneven but well-meaning film (inspired by director Kramer's daughter) about a girl who leaves the comforts of Malibu High to travel to China as part of the Doctor's Gift program (which receives some proceeds from the film's profits). There she meets a facially deformed girl from a small village and helps to make her "smile" again. Poorly structured screenplay spends nearly an hour setting up the main action and dwells endlessly on an unnecessary subplot about the young high schooler's virginity. Reminiscent of a preachy after-school special. [PG-13]▮

Smile Like Yours, A (1997) **C-98m.** BOMB D: Keith Samples. Greg Kinnear, Lauren Holly, Joan Cusack, Jay Thomas, France Nuyen, Christopher McDonald, Donald Moffat, Shirley MacLaine, Ben Stein.

He's an engineer, she designs perfumes, and together they cannot conceive a child. The maladroit comic result is so strange that it turns into its year's definitive "what were they thinking of?" movie. That's '60s star Nuyen wielding fertility instruments straight from the Chamber of Horrors. Super 35. [R]▼●◗

Smiles of a Summer Night (1955-Swedish) **108m.** **** D: Ingmar Bergman. Ulla Jacobsson, Eva Dahlbeck, Margit Carlquist, Harriet Andersson, Gunnar Bjornstrand, Jarl Kulle. One of the finest romantic comedies ever made, a witty treatise on manners, mores, and sex during a weekend at a country estate in the late 19th century. Inspired the Broadway musical and subsequent film A LITTLE NIGHT MUSIC (as well as Woody Allen's A MIDSUMMER NIGHT'S SEX COMEDY).▼●◗

Smiley Face (2007-U.S.-German) **C-84m.** *½ D: Gregg Araki. Anna Faris, Danny Masterson, Adam Brody, Rick Hoffman, Jane Lynch, John Krasinski, Marion Ross, Michael Hitchcock, John Cho, Danny Trejo. Loser goes from A to Z when she devours her roomie's maryjane-spiked cupcakes, propelling this slacker into an episodic series of pot-fueled misadventures. But this colorful, technically adept comedy simply isn't funny; a big disappointment from onetime indie wunderkind Araki. Roscoe Lee Browne narrates, as himself. Scott "Carrot Top" Thompson has a three-second cameo. [R]◗

Smiling Fish and Goat On Fire (2000) **C-90m.** *½ D: Kevin Jordan. Derick Martini, Steven Martini, Christa Miller, Bill Henderson, Rosemarie Addeo. Two L.A. brothers finally grow up when they meet their true loves. Made on a shoestring budget of $40,000, this practically plotless film may have been a labor of love but it's awfully low octane. Subplot about an 80-year-old black man who worked on Paul Robeson movies feels totally extraneous, though Henderson is good in the role. Title relates to the brothers' nicknames given to them by their half–Native American grandmother. [R]▼◗

Smiling Lieutenant, The (1931) **88m.** *** D: Ernst Lubitsch. Maurice Chevalier, Claudette Colbert, Miriam Hopkins, Charlie Ruggles, George Barbier, Hugh O'Connell, Elizabeth Patterson. Utterly charming Lubitsch confection about a Viennese lieutenant who's forced to marry the naive, mousy Princess of Flausenthurm (Hopkins) when in fact he's in love with violinist Colbert. Pretty racy for its time. Highlight: the leading ladies singing "Jazz Up Your Lingerie." Based on the operetta *The Waltz Dream,* which was filmed under that title in Germany in 1928.●◗

Smilla's Sense of Snow (1997-German-Swedish-Danish) **C-121m.** ** D: Bille August. Julia Ormond, Gabriel Byrne, Richard Harris, Robert Loggia, Vanessa Redgrave,

Jim Broadbent, Peter Capaldi, Tom Wilkinson. Disappointing adaptation of Peter Hoeg's novel, with Ormond as an alienated woman who is devastated by death of neighboring Inuit boy—and obsessed with uncovering details of his possible murder. Part soul-searching saga, action story, romance, and medical thriller . . . and none of it gels. Admittedly a great woman's role, but it gets muddled in the execution. Panavision. [R]▼●◗

Smith! (1969) **C-112m.** *** D: Michael O'Herlihy. Glenn Ford, Nancy Olson, Dean Jagger, Keenan Wynn, Warren Oates, Chief Dan George. Offbeat Disney drama of stubborn, pro-Indian farmer Ford who steps forward to help Indian accused of murder. Well done, with good characterizations, but low-key qualities soften impact. [G]▼◗

Smithereens (1982) **C-90m.** ***½ D: Susan Seidelman. Susan Berman, Brad Rinn (Rijn), Richard Hell, Roger Jett, Nada Despotovitch, Kitty Summerall, Christopher Noth. Gritty little character study of selfish, self-assured, rootless hustler Berman, and her vague dreams of success as a punk-rock band manager. Solid characterizations and simple, fluid direction; the sequence with the hooker and her chicken salad sandwich is memorable. [R]▼●◗

Smoke (1995) **C-112m.** *** D: Wayne Wang. William Hurt, Harvey Keitel, Stockard Channing, Harold Perrineau, Jr., Forest Whitaker, Victor Argo, Erica Gimpel, Clarice Taylor, Giancarlo Esposito, Ashley Judd. A tapestry of lives that intertwine around a Brooklyn smoke shop; key figures include the philosophical manager (Keitel), a burnt-out novelist (Hurt), a worldly wise teenager (Perrineau) whom Hurt more or less adopts, and the boy's actual father (Whitaker), whom he hasn't seen since infancy. Another of Wang's low-key, barely-there narratives that won't enchant every viewer, but does offer considerable pleasure. The actors are compelling and credible; several cast members appear in a second film, BLUE IN THE FACE. Written by Paul Auster. [R]▼●◗

Smoke Signals (1998) **C-88m.** **½ D: Chris Eyre. Adam Beach, Evan Adams, Irene Bedard, Gary Farmer, Tantoo Cardinal, Cody Lightning, Simon Baker, Michelle St. John, Tom Skerritt, Cynthia Geary. Two Coeur d'Alene Indians—tough, brooding Beach and likable, nerdy Adams—travel from their Idaho reservation to Phoenix to retrieve the remains of the former's dead father, and discover some truths about themselves along the way. Amusing, quirky road movie offers a refreshing Native American point of view, but is too schematic in setting up relationships and themes. However, it does have the memorable chant "John Wayne's Teeth." [PG-13]▼●◗

Smokey and the Bandit (1977) **C-96m.**

*** D: Hal Needham. Burt Reynolds, Sally Field, Jackie Gleason, Jerry Reed, Mike Henry, Paul Williams, Pat McCormick. Box-office smash is one long comedy chase, as bootlegger Reynolds outraces Sheriff Gleason for nearly the entire film. Directorial debut of ace stuntman Needham is (expectedly) brimming with stunts. About as subtle as The Three Stooges, but a classic compared to the sequels and countless rip-offs which followed. [PG] ▼●)

Smokey and the Bandit II (1980) **C-104m.** *½ D: Hal Needham. Burt Reynolds, Jackie Gleason, Jerry Reed, Dom DeLuise, Sally Field, Paul Williams, Pat McCormick, John Anderson. Strange sequel to 1977 hit has Bandit and friends agreeing to truck a pregnant elephant to Texas. Unfortunately, film has hardly any action, and its main character is portrayed as an embittered egomaniac. Some laughs, but not enough to overcome these obstacles. [PG] ▼●)

Smokey and the Bandit Part 3 (1983) **C-88m.** BOMB D: Dick Lowry. Jackie Gleason, Jerry Reed, Colleen Camp, Paul Williams, Pat McCormick, Mike Henry, Burt Reynolds. Desperate attempt to wring more laughs from this formula, with Gleason as a flustered red-neck sheriff and Reed as his latest nemesis. Originally filmed as SMOKEY IS THE BANDIT, with Gleason playing *both* roles; when preview audiences were confused, the film was reshot with Reed replacing the "second" Gleason. Panavision. [PG] ▼●)

Smokey Bites the Dust (1981) **C-85m.** BOMB D: Charles B. Griffith. Jimmy McNichol, Janet Julian, Walter Barnes, Patrick Campbell, Kari Lizer, John Blyth Barrymore. Young McNichol kidnaps homecoming queen, much to the consternation of her sheriff father. Poor excuse for a movie, with all its car-chase action bodily lifted from such earlier films as EAT MY DUST, GRAND THEFT AUTO, THUNDER AND LIGHTNING, and MOVING VIOLATION. [PG] ▼)

Smokin' Aces (2007) **C-109m.** *½ D: Joe Carnahan. Jeremy Piven, Ryan Reynolds, Alicia Keys, Peter Berg, Jason Bateman, Ben Affleck, Andy Garcia, Ray Liotta, Common, Martin Henderson, Taraji P. Henson, Chris Pine, Nestor Carbonell, Curtis Armstrong, Alex Rocco, David Proval, Wayne Newton. Good cast can't save this unwieldy patchwork of farce, action, and drama. Piven is a Vegas entertainer about to inform on the mob who is tracked by a horde of assassins, bounty hunters, and unsavory characters. Keys is solid in her screen debut as one of the bounty hunters, but the story is a mess and director Carnahan seems to be in love with ludicrous, over-the-top violence. Matthew Fox is unrecognizable in a cameo as a security person. Followed by a direct-to-DVD sequel. Super 35. [R] ▶)

Smoky (1946) **C-87m.** *** D: Louis King. Fred MacMurray, Anne Baxter, Burl Ives, Bruce Cabot, Esther Dale, Roy Roberts. First-rate family film from Will James story of man's devotion to his horse. Previously filmed in 1933, then again in 1966.

Smoky (1966) **C-103m.** ** D: George Sherman. Fess Parker, Diana Hyland, Katy Jurado, Hoyt Axton, Chuck Roberson. Third version of the Will James horse opera about especially independent horse named Smoky who knows what he wants.

Smooth Talk (1985) **C-92m.** **½ D: Joyce Chopra. Treat Williams, Laura Dern, Mary Kay Place, Levon Helm, Elizabeth Berridge. Disarmingly realistic depiction of teenage girl's growing pains and family relations takes sharp left turn when Williams enters as mysterious (and alluring) stranger . . . and all but deadens rest of the film. Worth seeing if only for Dern's fine performance. Impressive feature debut for documentary director Chopra; script by Tom Cole from a Joyce Carol Oates short story. Originally made for PBS' *American Playhouse*. [PG-13]▼●)

Smorgasbord SEE: **Cracking Up**

Smother (2008) **C-92m.** *½ D: Vince Di Meglio. Diane Keaton, Dax Shepard, Liv Tyler, Ken Howard, Jerry Lambert, Selma Stern, Mike White. Cringe-inducing sitcom-style movie about a 60-ish eccentric who leaves her husband and moves in with her carpet-salesman son and his schoolmarm spouse. Ensuing meddling and misunderstandings over the course of a painfully miserable week are almost totally funny-free with way too many third-act Serious Scenes. Keaton makes a valiant but futile effort. [PG-13]▐

Snake Eyes (1998) **C-99m.** ** D: Brian De Palma. Nicolas Cage, Gary Sinise, Carla Gugino, Stan Shaw, Kevin Dunn, Mike Starr. Slick, corrupt Atlantic City cop finds himself in the midst of a multi-level conspiracy after a shooting at a heavyweight prizefight. Slick, kinetic filmmaking technique (by De Palma and cinematographer Stephen H. Burum) can only carry this unappealing story so far. By the finale, it's hard to care much about anyone—or anything—in the picture. Panavision. [R] ▼●)

Snake People (1970-Mexican-U.S.) **C-90m.** BOMB D: Jhon Ibanez (Juan Ibanez and Jack Hill). Boris Karloff, Julissa, Charles (Carlos) East, Ralph Bertrand, Tongolele. Police captain tries to investigate an island where voodoo, LSD, and snake-worshipers run rampant. Ludicrous horror film wastes Karloff's talent. One of the last four films Karloff made; he shot his scenes in 1968. Original title: ISLE OF THE SNAKE PEOPLE. Aka CULT OF THE DEAD. ▼)

Snake Pit, The (1948) **108m.** ***½ D: Anatole Litvak. Olivia de Havilland, Mark

Stevens, Leo Genn, Celeste Holm, Glenn Langan, Helen Craig, Leif Erickson, Beulah Bondi, Lee Patrick, Natalie Schafer, Ruth Donnelly, Frank Conroy, Minna Gombell, Ann Doran, Betsy Blair, Isabel Jewell. One of the first films to deal intelligently with mental breakdowns and the painstakingly slow recovery process. Gripping film set in mental institution lacks original shock value but still packs a good punch, with de Havilland superb. Screenplay by Frank Partos and Millen Brand, from the Mary Jane Ward novel. ▼●◗

Snakes on a Plane (2006) C-105m. **½ D: David R. Ellis. Samuel L. Jackson, Julianna Margulies, Nathan Phillips, Rachel Blanchard, Flex Alexander, Kenan Thompson, Lin Shaye, David Koechner, Bobby Cannavale, Todd Louiso. It isn't like the old days when you called the box office to see what was playing and the response was, "PHFFFT" or "ZOTZ!" Here you know what you're getting, and for the lovers having taboo sex in the overly cramped jet lavatory, it's a lot more than chafed behinds. Why? Because an indicted thug tries to silence a witness by crashing an entire passenger plane through hissing means. You can bet FBI agent Jackson has conflicting ideas about this. The premise is fun, but a premise is just about all there is. Super 35. [R]◗

Snapper, The (1993-British) C-95m. *** D: Stephen Frears. Colm Meaney, Tina Kellegher, Ruth McCabe, Colm O'Byrne, Eanna Macliam, Ciara Duffy, Joanne Gerrard, Peter Rowen, Fionnula Murphy, Karen Woodley, Pat Laffan, Brendan Gleeson. Wonderful adaptation of Roddy Doyle's novel about a working-class Irish family, and the teenage daughter who finds herself pregnant—with the circumstances too embarrassing to discuss. Vivid, funny, and believable, sparked by good performances—especially Meaney as the bewildered (but basically good-hearted) father; he also appeared earlier in THE COMMITMENTS, the first of Doyle's Barrytown trilogy. Followed by THE VAN. [R]▼●◗

Snatch. (2000) C-102m. *** D: Guy Ritchie. Benicio Del Toro, Dennis Farina, Vinnie Jones, Brad Pitt, Rade Sherbedgia, Jason Statham, Alan Ford, Mike Reid, Robbie Gee, Lennie James, Stephen Graham, Jason Flemyng. Writer-director Ritchie's follow-up to LOCK, STOCK AND TWO SMOKING BARRELS is a similarly energized, violent farce about sleazy underworld types (involved in everything from a diamond heist to a bare-knuckle boxing match) whose agendas—and bodies—collide. Populated by characters with names like Franky Four Fingers. Pitt is amusing as a garble-mouthed Irish gypsy fighter. Fresh, funny, and full of punch. [R]▼●◗

Sneakers (1992) C-126m. **½ D: Phil Alden Robinson. Robert Redford, Dan

Aykroyd, Ben Kingsley, Mary McDonnell, River Phoenix, Sidney Poitier, David Strathairn, Timothy Busfield, George Hearn, Stephen Tobolowsky, James Earl Jones. High-tech caper yarn about an offbeat security team that takes on a dangerous assignment to steal a "black box" containing volatile security secrets. Redford is in fine form in a lighthearted leading-man role, and his "team" is fun, but why does this story take so long to unravel—and why does it jettison every shred of believability toward the end? [PG-13]▼●◗

Sniper, The (1952) 87m. *** D: Edward Dmytryk. Adolphe Menjou, Arthur Franz, Marie Windsor, Richard Kiley, Mabel Paige. Excellent, realistically filmed drama of mentally deranged sniper (Franz) who can't help himself from killing unsuspecting women. Fine performances by all. ◗

Sniper (1993) C-98m. ** D: Luis Llosa. Tom Berenger, Billy Zane, J.T. Walsh, Aden Young, Ken Radley, Dale Dye, Richard Lineback. A tough Marine sergeant and a green Olympics marksman team up in the Panamanian jungle to eliminate a rebel honcho and his drug lord bankroller. Plodding film is as life affirming as a broken septic tank, and about as useful; the slow-motion bullet trajectories are a little livelier than the actors. Followed by three direct-to-video sequels. [R]▼●◗

Snoopy Come Home (1972) C-70m. *** D: Bill Melendez. Voices of Chad Webber, David Carey, Stephen Shea, Bill Melendez. Charming *Peanuts* feature (the second) centering around Snoopy, the world's most independent pooch. [G]▼●◗

Snow Angels (2008) C-106m. ** D: David Gordon Green. Kate Beckinsale, Sam Rockwell, Michael Angarano, Deborah Allen, Jeannetta Arnette, Griffin Dunne, Peter Blais, Brian Downey, Nicky Katt, Amy Sedaris, Olivia Thirlby, Tom Noonan. Life in a small American town is examined in this adaptation of Stewart O'Nan's best seller about the intersecting fates of a young man, his ex-babysitter, her soon-to-be ex-husband, and their daughter. Played out against a snowy, frigid backdrop that serves to underscore the depressing story being told. Acting is first-rate but film only sporadically makes you care about these people. Super 35. [R]◗

Snowball Express (1972) C-99m. ** D: Norman Tokar. Dean Jones, Nancy Olson, Harry Morgan, Keenan Wynn, Johnny Whitaker, Michael McGreevey. Jones plays N.Y. accountant who inherits battered hotel in Rockies and tries to convert it into ski lodge. Slapstick ski chase is highlight of formula Disney comedy. [G]▼◗

Snow Cake (2006-British-Canadian) C-113m. *** D: Marc Evans. Alan Rickman, Sigourney Weaver, Carrie-Anne Moss, Emily Hampshire, James Allodi, Callum Keith

Rennie, David Fox, Jayne Eastwood. Solitary middle-aged man with a troubled past picks up a young female hitchhiker while driving across Canada; the out-of-left-field event that happens next profoundly affects the rest of the story and the lives of all its characters. Quirky, thoughtful drama is refreshing for its profound humanity. Weaver is tremendous as the hitchhiker's autistic mother.▐

Snow Creature, The (1954) **70m.** *½ D: W. Lee Wilder. Paul Langton, Leslie Denison, Teru Shimada, Rollin Moriyama. Yeti brought back from Himalayas languishes in customs while officials wrangle over whether it is cargo or a passenger. Dull film at least has virtue of being made for adults, though only kids may like it now.▼▐

Snow Day (2000) **C-89m.** ** D: Chris Koch. Chris Elliott, Mark Webber, Jean Smart, Schuyler Fisk, Iggy Pop, Pam Grier, Chevy Chase, John Schneider, Zena Grey, Emmanuelle Chriqui, Connor Matheus, J. Adam Brown. A late-season snowstorm closes upstate N.Y. schools, allowing for plot threads spotlighting local weatherman Chase and two of his children: an adolescent boy who is smitten with his dream girl, and his kid sister, who takes on comically sadistic snowplow driver Elliott. Predictable family film, a Nickelodeon production. Fisk (who plays Webber's tomboyish pal) is the daughter of Sissy Spacek. [PG]▼▐

Snow Dogs (2002) **C-99m.** ** D: Brian Levant. Cuba Gooding, Jr., James Coburn, Sisqó, Nichelle Nichols, M. Emmet Walsh, Graham Greene, Brian Doyle-Murray, Joanna Bacalso, Jean-Michel Paré. Miami dentist goes to Alaska for the reading of his mother's will and is persuaded to follow his destiny by learning to race her team of sled dogs. Clumsy Disney film is aimed at kids who only respond to the broadest kind of comedy. Gooding may set a new record for the most times a leading man falls down in one movie! [PG]▼▐

Snow Falling on Cedars (1999) **C-126m.** ** D: Scott Hicks. Ethan Hawke, James Cromwell, Richard Jenkins, James Rebhorn, Sam Shepard, Eric Thal, Max von Sydow, Youki Kudoh, Rick Yune, Jan Rubes, Celia Weston, Max Wright, Z¥eljko Ivanek, Daniel von Bargen. Ambitious but unsuccessful adaptation of David Guterson's best-selling novel. Flashback-laden story skips from the 1930s to the 1950s on an island in the Pacific Northwest where a boy falls in love with a Japanese-American girl. Equal parts murder mystery, forbidden romance, history lesson (about racial prejudice), and courtroom drama. Hawke is dull, but von Sydow livens things up as an aged but clever attorney. Self-consciously arty photography by Robert Richardson. Panavision. [PG-13]▼▐▶

Snow Job (1972) **C-90m.** *½ D: George Englund. Jean-Claude Killy, Danielle Gaubert, Cliff Potts, Vittorio De Sica. Heist film involving the taking of $250,000 in loot. Although professional skier Killy is appropriate star for film set against the Alps, he can't act; neither can the beautiful Gaubert. Panavision. [PG]

Snows of Kilimanjaro, The (1952) **C-117m.** *** D: Henry King. Gregory Peck, Susan Hayward, Ava Gardner, Hildegarde Neff, Leo G. Carroll. Peck finds his forte as renowned writer critically injured while on safari in Africa, trying to decide if he found any meaning to his past; based on Hemingway story.▼▐▶

Snow White and the Seven Dwarfs (1937) **C-83m.** **** D: David Hand. Voices of Adriana Caselotti, Harry Stockwell, Lucille LaVerne, Scotty Mattraw, Roy Atwell, Pinto Colvig, Otis Harlan, Billy Gilbert, Moroni Olsen. Walt Disney's groundbreaking animated feature film—the first of its kind—is still in a class by itself, a warm and joyful rendition of the classic fairy tale, enhanced by the vivid personalities of the seven dwarfs. Only a real-life Grumpy could fail to love it. Songs include "Whistle While You Work," "Heigh Ho," and "Some Day My Prince Will Come."▼▐▶

Snow White and the Three Stooges (1961) **C-107m.** BOMB D: Walter Lang. Three Stooges, Patricia Medina, Carol Heiss, Buddy Baer, Guy Rolfe, Edgar Barrier. Big mistake with skating star Heiss as Snow White, Three Stooges as . . . the Three Stooges. Comics aren't given much to do, despite title; rest of film is rather stodgy. Even kids won't be thrilled with it. CinemaScope.▼▐

Snow White: A Tale of Terror (1997-U.S.-British) **C-101m.** *** D: Michael Cohn. Sigourney Weaver, Sam Neill, Gil Bellows, Taryn Davis, Brian Glover, David Conrad, Monica Keena. We're not in Disneyland here, kiddies. Extremely dark, rather bloody, live-action version of the Brothers Grimm fairy tale and an exercise in Gothic horror, with over-the-top Weaver as the evil stepmother. Filmed on location in various castles in the Czech Republic and in Prague Government Park, doubling for the Black Forest. Great (if sadistic) fun. Made for theaters; debuted on cable in U.S. Aka THE GRIMM BROTHERS' SNOW WHITE. ▼▐▶

Snow White in the Land of Doom SEE: **Happily Ever After**

Soapdish (1991) **C-95m.** ** D: Michael Hoffman. Sally Field, Kevin Kline, Robert Downey, Jr., Cathy Moriarty, Whoopi Goldberg, Elisabeth Shue, Carrie Fisher, Garry Marshall, Teri Hatcher, Paul Johansson, Costas Mandylor, Stephen Nichols, Kathy Najimy, Ben Stein. Farcical comedy about a soap opera queen who's losing her grip—

on the show, and her life. Field and Kline are a treat to watch playing larger-than-life characters, but Whoopi is wasted, Downey is miscast, and the script (by Robert Harling and Andrew Bergman) thinks "frantic" equals "funny." Any one scene in TOOTSIE tops this hands down. Leeza Gibbons' best film work to date; John Tesh also appears. [PG-13]▼●◗

S.O.B. (1981) **C-121m.** **½ D: Blake Edwards. Julie Andrews, William Holden, Richard Mulligan, Robert Preston, Robert Vaughn, Loretta Swit, Larry Hagman, Marisa Berenson, Robert Webber, Stuart Margolin, Craig Stevens, Shelley Winters, Rosanna Arquette, Jennifer Edwards, Robert Loggia, John Pleshette, Larry Storch, Gene Nelson, Joe Penny, Corbin Bernsen. A producer hatches a scheme to turn his latest turkey into a hit: juice it up with pornography and have his wife-star (Andrews) bare her breasts. A glib satire on modern-day Movieland (and writer-director Edwards' revenge for Hollywood's treatment of him in the early '70s) throws in everything from black humor to slapstick, with wildly uneven results. Holden's last film. Panavision. [R]▼●◗

So big! (1932) **80m.** ** D: William A. Wellman. Barbara Stanwyck, George Brent, Dickie Moore, Guy Kibbee, Bette Davis, Mae Madison, Hardie Albright, Alan Hale. Disappointing adaptation of Edna Ferber's saga of an orphaned girl who becomes a schoolteacher in the midst of a farming community and raises her son to aspire to big things. Abrupt continuity and sudden aging of its lead character keep this from amounting to very much. Stanwyck and Davis are both in the final scene—but never appear on screen together! Filmed before in 1925, remade in 1953.

So Big (1953) **101m.** *** D: Robert Wise. Jane Wyman, Sterling Hayden, Nancy Olson, Steve Forrest, Martha Hyer, Tommy Rettig. Superficial but engrossing Edna Ferber soaper/saga about teacher who brings up son to be self-sufficient. Filmed before in 1925 and 1932.

Social Network, The (2010) **C-120m.** **** D: David Fincher. Jesse Eisenberg, Andrew Garfield, Justin Timberlake, Armie Hammer, Max Minghella, Josh Pence, Brenda Song, Rashida Jones, John Getz, David Selby, Denise Grayson, Douglas Urbanski, Rooney Mara, Joseph Mazzello, Dakota Johnson. The saga of how a socially awkward, mentally agile Harvard student named Mark Zuckerberg (Eisenberg) created the phenomenally popular Facebook—after being dumped by his girlfriend—is traced in this fascinating film. Told from several points of view, derived from lawsuits filed against Zuckerberg by his onetime friend and partner (Garfield) and two students who claimed he appropriated their idea (both played by Hammer). Vivid, immediate, and whip smart, thanks to Aaron Sorkin's Oscar-winning screenplay, based on Ben Mezrich's nonfiction book *The Accidental Billionaires*, and Fincher's blazing treatment of it. How close it is to the truth we'll never know—but it certainly makes a great story, and a cautionary tale for our times about the push-pull of business and friendship. Also won Oscars for Editing (Kirk Baxter, Angus Wall) and Score (Trent Reznor and Atticus Ross). HD Widescreen. [PG-13]◗

So Close (2002-Hong Kong) **C-111m.** **½ D: Cory Yuen. Shu Qi, Zhao Wei, Karen Mok, Song Seung Hun, Michael Wai, Yasuaki Kurata, Derek Wan. Two sisters, ostensibly ultra-tech computer surveillance operators, are secretly—gasp!!—assassins decimating a murderously corrupt corporation suit by suit. Fighting tooth and nail with gun and sword, they're countered by a clever policewoman similarly well versed in martial arts. Super-flashy action set pieces far outplay the draggy interpersonals in this chop-socky CHARLIE'S ANGELS wannabe. [R]▼◗

So Dear to My Heart (1949) **C-84m.** ***½ D: Harold Schuster. Burl Ives, Beulah Bondi, Bobby Driscoll, Luana Patten, Harry Carey. Warm, nostalgic Disney film about young boy's determination to raise a black sheep and bring him to State Fair competition. Brimming with period charm and atmosphere; several animated sequences, too. Songs include "Lavender Blue (Dilly Dilly)." Screenplay by John Tucker Battle, from Sterling North's book *Midnight and Jeremiah*. ▼◗

Sodom and Gomorrah (1962-Italian) **C-154m.** **½ D: Robert Aldrich. Stewart Granger, Pier Angeli, Stanley Baker, Anouk Aimée, Rossana Podesta. Lavish retelling of life in biblical twin cities of sin. Strong cast, vivid scenes of vice, gore, and God's wrath, make this overly long tale of ancient Hebrews fairly entertaining.▼●

So Evil, My Sister (1972) **C-76m.** ** D: Reginald LeBorg. Susan Strasberg, Faith Domergue, Sydney Chaplin, Charles Knox Robinson, Steve Mitchell, Kathleen Freeman, John Howard. Gothic B-movie thriller with veteran cast has Strasberg and Domergue as sisters playing cat-and-mouse with the police who are investigating the mysterious death of Strasberg's husband. Several clever twists in the final reel are worth waiting for. Retitled PSYCHO SISTERS. Video title: THE SIBLING. [R]▼

Sofie (1992-Danish-Norwegian-Swedish) **C-146m.** **½ D: Liv Ullmann. Karen-Lise Mynster, Erland Josephson, Ghita Norby, Jesper Christensen, Torben Zeller, Stig Hoffmeyer. Ullman's directorial debut (which she also coscripted) is a thoughtful but uneven, Bergmanesque tale of a young Jew in late 19th-century Copenhagen who is unable to break free of family tradition, ruining her one chance at true love. Beautifully detailed but episodic (especially in its second half) and overlong. Mynster offers an effectively subtle performance as Sofie.▼❸

So Fine (1981) **C-91m.** ******* D: Andrew Bergman. Ryan O'Neal, Jack Warden, Mariangela Melato, Richard Kiel, Fred Gwynne, Mike Kellin, David Rounds. Wacky comedy about professor-son of a N.Y.C. garment manufacturer who is dragooned into the business and inadvertently succeeds with an idea for see-through jeans. Film goes off in unexpected directions— some of them surprisingly silly—but remains funny most of the time. Writer Bergman's directorial debut. [R]▼●❶

Soft Beds, Hard Battles SEE: **Undercovers Hero**

Soft Fruit (2000-Australian-U.S.) **C-101m.** ****** D: Christina Andreef. Jeanie Drynan, Linal Haft, Russell Dykstra, Genevieve Lemon, Sacha Horler, Alicia Talbot. Four grown children—three sisters and a brother who's just gotten out of jail—return home to be with their mother, who's dying of liver cancer. Amiable enough mix of comedy and drama about an oddball family doesn't add up to much. Scripted by the director. [R]▼

Soft Skin, The (1964-French) **120m.** ******* D: François Truffaut. Françoise Dorleac, Jean Desailly, Nelly Benedetti. Moody tale of married businessman drawn into tragic affair with beautiful airline stewardess; smooth direction uplifts basic plot.▼●❶

So I Married an Axe Murderer (1993) **C-93m.** ****½** D: Thomas Schlamme. Mike Myers, Nancy Travis, Anthony LaPaglia, Amanda Plummer, Brenda Fricker, Debi Mazar, Matt Doherty. A guy who's always avoided commitment by finding absurd reasons to break up with his girlfriends finally meets Miss Right—and then comes to believe that she's a notorious axe murderess! Myers is ingratiating and funny (especially in a second role as his own contrary Scottish father) but the film never shifts into high gear. Cameos by such familiar comic personalities as Charles Grodin, Steven Wright, Phil Hartman, and Michael Richards seem mostly gratuitous. Alan Arkin appears unbilled. [PG-13]▼●❶

Solarbabies (1986) **C-94m.** BOMB D: Alan Johnson. Richard Jordan, Jami Gertz, Jason Patric, Lukas Haas, Charles Durning, Peter DeLuise, Adrian Pasdar, Sarah Douglas, Frank Converse, Terrence Mann, Kelly Bishop. Futuristic teen junk has Gertz and her mostly male cohorts imprisoned by Nazi-like Jordan inside a fortress; the group plots an escape with the help of "Bohdi" —an ancient mystical force. Appallingly bad stinker from (Mel) Brooksfilm that barely got released. J-D-C Scope. [PG-13]▼●❶

Solar Crisis (1990-U.S.-Japanese) **C-112m.** ****½** D: Alan Smithee (Richard Sarafian). Tim Matheson, Charlton Heston, Peter Boyle, Annabel Schofield, Corin Nemec, Jack Palance, Tetsuya Bessho, Dorian Harewood, Brenda Bakke. Futuristic sci-fi thriller with Matheson leading a save-the-planet mission to the sun to prevent a solar flare from destroying the earth. Fine special effects, quality acting, and suspenseful story in space, marred by earth antics of bad boy Boyle who (preposterously) wants to sabotage the mission. Panavision. [PG-13]▼●❶

Solaris (1972-Russian) **C-165m.** *****½** D: Andrei Tarkovsky. Natalya Bondarchuk, Donatas Banionis, Yuri Yarvet, Anatoly Solonitsin. Mind-bending, metaphysical sci-fi about a psychologist who's sent to a space station to investigate mysterious deaths and discovers supernatural phenomena. Slow moving and occasionally pretentious, but hypnotic once one adjusts, and an undoubted tour de force by Tarkovsky, who also cowrote the screenplay. Remade in 2002. Sovscope.▼●❶

Solaris (2002) **C-99m.** ****** D: Steven Soderbergh. George Clooney, Natascha McElhone, Jeremy Davies, Viola Davis, Ulrich Tukur. In the near future, psychologist Clooney is summoned to a space station where the crew has been acting strange, to say the least. There he meets an eerie replica of his dead wife! Ice-cold adaptation (by Soderbergh) of Stanislaw Lem's science-fiction novel, distinguished by Philip Messina's striking production design and a strong performance by Clooney. All that's missing is the ability to care about his character. Filmed before in 1972. Panavision. [PG-13]▼❶

Solas (2000-Spanish) **C-98m.** ******* D: Benito Zambrano. Ana Fernández, María Galiana, Carlos Alvarez-Novoa. A trio of lonely people—an embittered, alcoholic woman, her provincial mother, and a kind-hearted neighbor widower—get a second chance at life in this poignant film. All three lead performances are terrific, and despite a somewhat rushed wrap-up, the film earns our affections honestly. As much a tribute to unconventional families as Almodóvar's ALL ABOUT MY MOTHER.▼❶

Soldier, The (1982) **C-96m.** ***½** D: James Glickenhaus. Ken Wahl, Klaus Kinski, William Prince, Alberta Watson, Jeremiah Sullivan. CIA superagent Wahl takes on Russian terrorists who have planted a plutonium bomb in a Saudi Arabian oil field. Clichéd, violent drama. [R]▼

Soldier (1998) **C-98m.** ****** D: Paul Anderson. Kurt Russell, Jason Scott Lee, Connie Nielsen, Sean Pertwee, Michael Chiklis, Gary Busey, Jason Isaacs, Jared Thorne, Taylor Thorne. In the near future, Russell, raised to be a soldier, is declared obsolete, thought dead, and dumped on a planet used as a garbage heap. He's befriended by people who crash-landed there some time before; then his old fighting partners show up to "cleanse" the planet. Russell is good, but the movie is derivative, the "science" ludicrous, and the outcome highly predictable. *Please* come back, Shane. Panavision. [R] ▼●◖

Soldier Blue (1970) **C-112m.** *½ D: Ralph Nelson. Candice Bergen, Peter Strauss, Donald Pleasence, John Anderson, Jorge Rivero, Dana Elcar, James Hampton. Well-meant attempt to dramatize U.S. mistreatment of the Indians (and perhaps equate it with Vietnam) wasn't very good then and hasn't improved; bulk of the film is still cutesy romance between two survivors of Indian attack, climaxed by cavalry's slaughter of entire village in sequence that remains almost unwatchable. Panavision. [PG—edited from original R rating] ▼●◖

Soldier in Skirts SEE: **Triple Echo**
Soldier in the Rain (1963) **88m.** *** D: Ralph Nelson. Jackie Gleason, Steve McQueen, Tuesday Weld, Tony Bill, Tom Poston, Ed Nelson, John Hubbard, Adam West. Strange film wavers from sentimental drama to high comedy. Gleason is swinging sergeant, McQueen his fervent admirer. Script by Blake Edwards and Maurice Richlin from William Goldman's novel. ▼◖

Soldier of Fortune (1955) **C-96m.** *** D: Edward Dmytryk. Clark Gable, Susan Hayward, Michael Rennie, Gene Barry, Tom Tully, Alex D'Arcy, Anna Sten. Gable is hired to find Susan's husband (Barry) held captive in Hong Kong. Rennie is good as police chief. Scripted by Ernest K. Gann, from his novel. CinemaScope. ▼◖

Soldier of Orange (1979-Dutch) **C-165m.** ***½ D: Paul Verhoeven. Rutger Hauer, Jeroen Krabbé, Peter Faber, Derek De Lint, Eddy Habbema, Susan Penhaligon, Edward Fox. The lives of six wealthy, carefree Dutch university students are irrevocably altered when the Germans occupy their homeland in 1940. Superior drama, with Hauer coming into his own as a handsome aristocrat who becomes involved in the Resistance. Based on autobiographical novel by Erik Hazelhoff. [R] ▼●◖

Soldier's Daughter Never Cries, A (1998) **C-127m.** **½ D: James Ivory. Kris Kristofferson, Barbara Hershey, Leelee Sobieski, Jesse Bradford, Anthony Roth Costanzo, Dominique Blanc, Jane Birkin. Picaresque story of an expatriate American family living in Paris during the '60s and '70s, and what happens when they move back home. Kristofferson is excellent as a macho novelist, and Sobieski and Bradford are equally good as his kids, who are going through various teenage crises, but the film loses its grip when it shifts to America and becomes much more mundane. Based on an autobio-

graphical novel by Kaylie Jones, whose father was author James Jones. [R] ▼●◖

Soldiers of Fortune SEE: **You Can't Win 'Em All**
Soldier's Prayer, A (1961-Japanese) **196m.** ***½ D: Masaki Kobayashi. Tatsuya Nakadai, Yusuke Kawazu, Tamao Nakamura, Chishu Ryu, Taketoshi Naitô, Reiko Hitomi, Kyôko Kishida, Fujio Suga. Final installment of Kobayashi's three-part rumination on the horrors of WW2 (after NO GREATER LOVE and THE ROAD TO ETERNITY) is set in the waning days of the conflict. Here, Kaji (Nakadai) and other soldiers and civilians struggle to stay alive in the desolate Manchurian countryside. Meanwhile, Kaji wonders if his beloved wife is still living, and if he will ever find her. The finale is haunting . . . and fitting. Scripted by Kobayashi, Zenzo Matsuyama, and Koichi Inagaki, based on a six-volume novel by Jumpei Gomikawa. Aka THE HUMAN CONDITION III. Grandscope. ◖

Soldier's Story, A (1984) **C-101m.** ***½ D: Norman Jewison. Howard E. Rollins, Jr., Adolph Caesar, Dennis Lipscomb, Art Evans, Denzel Washington, Larry Riley, David Alan Grier, Robert Townsend, Patti LaBelle, Wings Hauser, Trey Wilson. Electrifying drama by Charles Fuller from his Pulitzer Prize–winning play (featuring most of original Negro Ensemble Company cast) about murder of a black officer at Southern military post in the 1940s. A solid whodunit plus a probing look at racism within black ranks. It was inspired by Herman Melville's *Billy Budd.* Can't completely escape its stage origins but still a riveting film. [PG] ▼●◖

Soldier's Tale, A (1988) **C-94m.** **½ D: Larry Parr. Gabriel Byrne, Marianne Basler, Judge Reinhold, Paul Wyett. Poignant, thought-provoking WW2 story of a beautiful woman accused of being a German collaborator by the French resistance. Byrne plays a British soldier who tries to protect her. Reinhold is on screen for all of three minutes. [R] ▼●◖

Soldiers Three (1951) **87m.** *** D: Tay Garnett. Stewart Granger, Walter Pidgeon, David Niven, Robert Newton, Cyril Cusack, Greta Gynt, Robert Coote, Dan O'Herlihy. Boisterous action-adventure with light touch; GUNGA DIN–esque story has three soldiering comrades in and out of spats with each other as they battle in 19th-century India. Loosely based on stories by Rudyard Kipling.

Solid Gold Cadillac, The (1956) **99m.** *** D: Richard Quine. Judy Holliday, Paul Douglas, Fred Clark, John Williams, Arthur O'Connell, Hiram Sherman, Neva Patterson, Ray Collins; narrated by George Burns. Dazzling Judy in entertaining comedy of small stockholder in large company becoming corporate heroine by trying to oust crooked board of directors. George S. Kaufman–Howard Teichman play adapted by Abe Burrows. Jean Louis earned an Oscar for the costumes. Last scene in color. ▼▶

Solitary Man (2010) **C-90m.** **★★★** D: Brian Koppelman, David Levien. Michael Douglas, Susan Sarandon, Danny DeVito, Mary-Louise Parker, Jenna Fischer, Jesse Eisenberg, Imogen Poots, Richard Schiff, Ben Shenkman, David Costabile, Anastasia Griffith. Douglas married his college sweetheart and built an empire of car dealerships . . . but something went wrong along the way and he lost his moral compass. Now he's at the end of his rope, with his gift of gab his only remaining resource. When he accompanies his current lady friend's daughter to scout out a college, he tries to impart his worldly wisdom to a nerdy student (Eisenberg). Provocative character study of a louse, played with charismatic bravado by Douglas, who's surrounded by good actors in similarly three-dimensional roles. Olivia Thirlby appears unbilled. Written by codirector Koppelman. Super 35. [R]▶

Sol Madrid (1968) **C-90m.** **★★½** D: Brian G. Hutton. David McCallum, Stella Stevens, Telly Savalas, Ricardo Montalban, Rip Torn, Pat Hingle, Paul Lukas, Michael Ansara. Old-fashioned but solid thriller about police, Mafia, and running heroin from Mexico. Panavision.

Solo (1996-U.S.-Mexican) **C-94m.** **★★** D: Norberto Barba. Mario Van Peebles, William Sadler, Adrien Brody, Seidy Lopez, Abraham J. Verduzco, Barry Corbin. Solo is an android who has a crisis of conscience when he directly disobeys an order that would result in the murder of innocent people. This sets him on a collision course with his creators, particularly a sadistic colonel. Standard action for nondiscerning fans of the genre. Van Peebles is actually quite appealing in the lead. Super 35. [PG-13] ▼▶

Sólo Con Tu Pareja (1991-Mexican) **C-94m.** **★★★** D: Alfonso Cuarón. Daniel Giménez Cacho, Claudia Ramírez, Luis de Icaza, Astrid Hadad, Dobrina Liubomirova, Isabel Benet. A womanizing Mexico City copywriter gets his comeuppance when he is falsely diagnosed as being H.I.V. positive, thanks to a spurned nurse who was one of his many conquests. Cowritten with his brother Carlos, Cuarón's feature debut (not released in the U.S. until 2006) is a breezily dark sex comedy in the early-Almodóvar style, strikingly shot by the director's regular cinematographer, Emmanuel Lubezki. Aka LOVE IN THE TIME OF HYSTERIA.▶

Soloist, The (2009-U.S.-British-French) **C-117m.** **★★½** D: Joe Wright. Jamie Foxx, Robert Downey, Jr., Catherine Keener, Tom Hollander, Lisa Gay Hamilton, Nelsan Ellis, Rachael Harris, Stephen Root, Lorraine Toussaint. *Los Angeles Times* columnist Steve Lopez (Downey) writes a piece about street musician Nathaniel Ayers (Foxx), whose men-

tal illness has defeated his natural talent. He feels compelled to help Ayers but doesn't comprehend the magnitude of the man's problems, or how tough it is to be responsible for another human being. True story offers moments of soaring emotions (most of them inspired by Beethoven music), contrasted against the squalor of homelessness in downtown L.A. To its credit this isn't a glib, feel-good movie—but on the other hand it's painfully difficult to watch. Panavision. [PG-13] ▶

Solomon and Gaenor (1999-British) **C-100m.** **★★½** D: Paul Morrison. Ioan Gruffudd, Nia Roberts, Sue Jones-Davies, William Thomas, Mark Lewis Jones, Maureen Lipman, David Horovitch. Heartfelt, albeit predictable, Romeo and Juliet–style love story, set in poverty-stricken 1911 Wales, about a forbidden romance between Roberts, the offspring of rigid churchgoers, and Gruffudd, a Jewish fabric peddler who hides his religion from his lover and her clan. [R]▼▶

Solomon and Sheba (1959) **C-139m.** **★★★** D: King Vidor. Yul Brynner, Gina Lollobrigida, George Sanders, Marisa Pavan, John Crawford, Alejandro Rey, Harry Andrews. Splashy spectacle with alluring Gina and stoic Brynner frolicking in biblical days. Tyrone Power died during filming in Spain, was replaced by Brynner who refilmed Power's early scenes. Some long shots still show Power, not Brynner. Vidor's final film as director. Also shown at 120m. Super Technirama 70. ▼▶

So Long at the Fair (1950-British) **90m.** **★★★** D: Terence Fisher, Anthony Darnborough. Jean Simmons, Dirk Bogarde, David Tomlinson, Honor Blackman, Cathleen Nesbitt, Felix Aylmer, Andre Morell, Betty Warren. Atmospheric drama set during 1889 Paris Exposition with English woman searching for brother who's mysteriously vanished. Absorbing, well-made rendering of a famous "urban legend" tale that retains every bit of its eerie allure.

Somebody Killed Her Husband (1978) **C-97m.** **★½** D: Lamont Johnson. Farrah Fawcett-Majors, Jeff Bridges, John Wood, Tammy Grimes, John Glover, Patricia Elliott. First starring feature for the ex-Charlie's Angel was redubbed "Somebody Killed Her Career" by industry wags, but in any case, this tepid comedy-mystery-romance written by Reginald Rose has little to recommend it. Filmed in Manhattan. [PG]

Somebody to Love (1995-French) **C-103m.** **★★½** D: Alexandre Rockwell. Rosie Perez, Harvey Keitel, Anthony Quinn, Michael DeLorenzo, Steve Buscemi, Samuel Fuller, Stanley Tucci, Steven Randazzo, Sam Rockwell. Occasionally inspired but mostly meandering slice-of-life with Perez giving her all as a spirited taxi dancer who has moved from Brooklyn to L.A. in the hope of making it big in showbiz. Keitel is her middle-aged has-been actor/lover, DeLorenzo the young man who falls for her and tries to impress her by becoming involved with mobster Quinn. Buscemi is outstanding as a transvestite taxi dancer. Watch for Quentin Tarantino as a bartender, Lelia Goldoni as a waitress. [R]▼●]

Somebody Up There Likes Me (1956) **113m. ***½** D: Robert Wise. Paul Newman, Pier Angeli, Everett Sloane, Eileen Heckart, Sal Mineo, Joseph Buloff, Robert Loggia, Steve McQueen, Dean Jones. Top biography of boxer Rocky Graziano's rise from N.Y.C. sidewalks to arena success with fine performance by Newman. Script by Ernest Lehman; cinematographer Joseph Ruttenberg won an Oscar. ▼●]

Some Call It Loving (1973) **C-103m.** BOMB D: James B. Harris. Zalman King, Carol White, Tisa Farrow, Richard Pryor. Slow, pretentious fantasy transplanting the story of Sleeping Beauty (played by Farrow, Mia's younger sister) to modern California. As her Prince Charming, King gives a sleepwalking nonperformance. Pryor's vulgar turn as a pathetic graffiti artist/wino clashes with the rest of the picture. [R]▼

Some Came Running (1958) **C-136m. *** D: Vincente Minnelli. Frank Sinatra, Dean Martin, Shirley MacLaine, Martha Hyer, Arthur Kennedy, Nancy Gates. Slick adaptation of James Jones' novel about disillusionment in a small midwestern town in the late 1940s; more character study than narrative. MacLaine is especially good as luckless floozie who's stuck on Sinatra; Elmer Bernstein's music score also a standout. CinemaScope. ▼●]

Some Girls (1988) **C-94m. ** D: Michael Hoffman. Patrick Dempsey, Jennifer Connelly, Sheila Kelley, Andre Gregory, Florinda Bolkan, Lila Kedrova. Odd little comedy about American college student Dempsey and the various complications when he spends Christmas in Quebec City with girlfriend Connelly's family. Gregory rises above the material as Connelly's eccentric father. [R]▼]

Some Girls Do (1969-British) **C-93m. **½** D: Ralph Thomas. Richard Johnson, Daliah Lavi, Beba Loncar, Robert Morley, Sydne Rome, James Villiers. Brisk thriller involving Bulldog Drummond (played with a lack of dash by Johnson) vs. long-time archenemy Carl Peterson (Villiers), who is trying to sabotage Britain's supersonic plane plans. Morley is a delight as an eccentric teacher of high cuisine. Sequel to DEADLIER THAN THE MALE (1967). [G]

Some Kind of a Nut (1969) **C-89m.** BOMB D: Garson Kanin. Dick Van Dyke, Angie Dickinson, Rosemary Forsyth, Zohra Lampert, Elliott Reid, Pippa Scott. Banker Van Dyke loses his job when he grows a beard. Pathetic "contemporary" comedy dates more than Kanin's films of the '30s and '40s. [M/PG]

Some Kind of Hero (1982) **C-97m. ** D: Michael Pressman. Richard Pryor, Margot Kidder, Ray Sharkey, Ronny Cox, Lynne Moody, Olivia Cole, Paul Benjamin. Pryor rises above uneven, poorly directed comedy-drama about Vietnam veteran who's in for a few surprises when he returns home after six years as a POW. Based on a James Kirkwood novel. [R]▼●]

Some Kind of Wonderful (1987) **C-93m. **½** D: Howard Deutch. Eric Stoltz, Lea Thompson, Mary Stuart Masterson, Craig Sheffer, John Ashton, Elias Koteas, Molly Hagan, Candace Cameron, Chynna Phillips, Scott Coffey. Adorable tomboy Masterson loves Stoltz, but it takes him the entire film to realize she is better for him than the flashier Thompson. Deutch and producer John Hughes have, in effect, done a sex-switch remake of their own PRETTY IN PINK; the OK result has strong performances by both female leads, and surprises by not making Thompson a snooty bitch. [PG-13]▼●]

Some Like It Hot (1939) **65m. **½** D: George Archainbaud. Bob Hope, Shirley Ross, Una Merkel, Gene Krupa, Rufe Davis, Bernard Nedell, Richard Denning, Frank Sully, Jack (J. Scott) Smart. Sideshow owner Hope repeatedly takes advantage of Ross to keep his show afloat. Pleasant enough comedy-drama based on a Gene Fowler–Ben Hecht play (filmed in 1934 as SHOOT THE WORKS), though we never understand why Ross puts up with Hope's wayward ways. Krupa's numbers are mediocre but the film introduces "The Lady's in Love With You." Retitled RHYTHM ROMANCE. ▼

Some Like It Hot (1959) **119m. **** D: Billy Wilder. Jack Lemmon, Tony Curtis, Marilyn Monroe, Joe E. Brown, George Raft, Pat O'Brien, Nehemiah Persoff, Joan Shawlee, Mike Mazurki. Legendary comedy by Wilder and I.A.L. Diamond about two musicians who witness the St. Valentine's Day Massacre and try to elude their pursuers by joining an all-girl band heading for Miami. Sensational from start to finish, with dazzling performances by Lemmon and Curtis, a memorably comic turn by Monroe as Sugar Kane, and Oscar-winning costumes by Orry-Kelly. Brown has film's now-classic closing line. Based on a 1935 French movie, FANFARE D'AMOUR. Basis for hit Broadway musical *Sugar.* ▼●]

Some May Live (1967) **105m. ** D: Vernon Sewell. Joseph Cotten, Martha Hyer, Peter Cushing, John Ronane. Unexciting suspenser set in contemporary Saigon with Cotten a U.S. Intelligence officer setting a trap for the espionage agent within his department. Retitled: IN SAIGON, SOME MAY LIVE.

Some Mother's Son (1996-U.S.-British-Irish) **C-112m. **½** D: Terry George. Helen Mirren, Fionnula Flanagan, Aidan Gillen, David O'Hara, John Lynch, Tim Woodward. Respectable but muted true-life story about a hunger strike staged by a jailed IRA member in the early 1980s, with Mirren a prisoner's mom who becomes involved in the struggle upon realizing that she doesn't really have a choice. No match for IN THE NAME OF THE FATHER, which treated comparable subject matter far more passionately. Coproduced by Jim Sheridan; associate-produced by Mirren. [R]▼●◗

Someone Behind the Door (1971-French) **C-97m.** ** D: Nicolas Gessner. Charles Bronson, Anthony Perkins, Jill Ireland, Henri Garcin, Adriano Magestretti. Neuropsychiatrist (Perkins) turns an amnesiac murderer (Bronson) into his tool for revenge on his philandering wife; farfetched melodrama. [PG]▼●◗

Someone Else's America (1996-British-French) **C-96m.** **½ D: Goran Paskaljevic. Tom Conti, Maria Casares, Miki Manojlovic, Sergei Trifunovic, Zorka Manojlovic. Spanish immigrant moves his blind mother to Brooklyn in hopes of pursuing the American dream. His efforts to make it in the Land of the Free are often amusing, and well observed by Belgrade-born Paskaljevic. Slight but charming character study that speaks a universal language. Casares is well remembered for such earlier films as ORPHEUS and THE TESTAMENT OF ORPHEUS. [R]▼

Someone Like You (2001) **C-97m.** ** D: Tony Goldwyn. Ashley Judd, Hugh Jackman, Greg Kinnear, Marisa Tomei, Ellen Barkin, Catherine Dent, Peter Friedman. Dumped by her coworker boyfriend (Kinnear), a TV talent booker (Judd) becomes obsessed with her own "new cow theory," that men leave women like bulls go through herds of cows. She's so consumed she doesn't realize she's falling for her hunky roommate (Jackman). Starts brightly with appealing performances but quickly turns formulaic, leading to a lame finale. Based on the novel *Animal Husbandry* by Laura Zigman. Blink and you'll miss a cameo by Ashley's mom, Naomi Judd, as a makeup artist. [PG-13]▼◗

Someone to Love (1987) **C-111m.** **½ D: Henry Jaglom. Henry Jaglom, Andrea Marcovicci, Sally Kellerman, Orson Welles, Michael Emil, Oja Kodar, Dave Frishberg, Stephen Bishop, Ronee Blakley, Kathryn Harrold, Monte Hellman, Jeremy Kagan, Miles Kreuger. Jaglom is Danny, a filmmaker who's seeking "someone to love." He throws a Valentine's Day party where he questions various friends on the subject . . . and films their responses. Welles, in his last screen appearance, is on hand to offer various insights and profundities, and they're the best thing in this alternately boring and interesting experiment. [R]▼●◗

Someone to Watch Over Me (1987) **C-106m.** *** D: Ridley Scott. Tom Berenger, Mimi Rogers, Lorraine Bracco, Jerry Orbach, John Rubinstein, Andreas Katsulas, Tony DiBenedetto, James Moriarty. Happily married N.Y.C. cop becomes infatu-

ated with the wealthy and beautiful woman he's assigned to protect from a death threat. Solid romantic thriller, compassionately and believably told; director Scott's warmest film to date (and just as stylish as ever). [R]▼●◗

Somersault (2004-Australian) **C-106m.** *** D: Cate Shortland. Abbie Cornish, Sam Worthington, Lynette Curran, Nathaniel Dean, Erik Thomson, Leah Purcell, Hollie Andrew, Olivia Pigeot. Raw, razor-sharp drama depicting the plight of an alluring adolescent runaway (Cornish), a child in a woman's body who is lusted after by men, though too young and inexperienced to be aware of her sexual power. Impressive debut feature for writer-director Shortland, with Cornish offering a vivid, award-caliber performance.◗

Somers Town (2008-British) **C/B&W-71m.** *½ D: Shane Meadows. Piotr Jagiello, Thomas Turgoose, Ireneusz Czop, Elisa Lasowski, Perry Benson, Kate Dickie, Huggy Leaver. Two teenage boys forge a strange and unlikely friendship in Somers Town, near London. Tomo (Turgoose, who starred in Meadows' THIS IS ENGLAND) is a troublesome runaway from Nottingham; Marek (Jagiello) is a Polish immigrant living with his father, who works on the railways. The boys are both infatuated with the same girl (Lasowski) and spend their time arguing over who loves her more and showering her with childish gifts and devotion. Meadows' films usually focus on life in (or people from) the Midlands, and are mostly appreciated by locals and those who know the area. If you're not an Anglophile you may find this slow and/or depressing.◗

something big (1971) **C-108m.** BOMB D: Andrew V. McLaglen. Dean Martin, Brian Keith, Honor Blackman, Carol White, Ben Johnson, Albert Salmi, Paul Fix, Denver Pyle. Repellent "comedy"-Western detailing long-running feud between outlaw Martin and cavalry colonel Keith; "happy ending" consists of Dino robbing a stagecoach and mowing down hundreds of Mexicans with a gatling gun—all to a peppy Marvin Hamlisch score. Blecch. [PG]

Something Borrowed (2011) **C-112m.** **½ D: Luke Greenfield. Ginnifer Goodwin, Kate Hudson, Colin Egglesfield, John Krasinski, Steve Howey, Ashley Williams, Jill Eikenberry, Geoff Pierson. Agreeable screen adaptation of Emily Giffin novel is romantic fluff, served by a likable young cast. Hudson plays against type as a party girl who becomes engaged to a handsome lawyer who also happens to be the secret law school crush of lifelong best friend Goodwin. Complications arise when the latter shacks up with him one night, then tries to keep it secret. There's nothing new here, but director Greenfield keeps things fairly fresh and engaging. Krasinski is a comic standout as Goodwin's pal. [PG-13]

Something for Everyone (1970) **C-112m.**

**½ D: Harold Prince. Angela Lansbury, Michael York, Anthony Corlan, Heidelinde Weis, Eva-Maria Meineke, Jane Carr. Very black comedy about amoral, bisexual young man (York) who manipulates staff and family of impoverished Countess (Lansbury) to his advantage. Intriguing but needlessly protracted story; Broadway director Prince's first film, made in Bavaria. [R]▼

Something Is Out There SEE: **Day of the Animals**

Something New (2006) **C-99m.** *** D: Sanaa Hamri. Sanaa Lathan, Simon Baker, Mike Epps, Donald Faison, Blair Underwood, Wendy Raquel Robinson, Alfre Woodard, Golden Brooks, Taraji P. Henson, Earl Billings, John Ratzenberger. Hardworking black career woman finds herself attracted to a white landscape architect—in spite of her better judgment and the disapproval of friends and family. Veteran TV writer-producer Kriss Turner offers a fresh take on romantic comedy and prejudice, presenting an honest picture of successful blacks who still have battles to fight on a daily basis. Pokes fun at stereotyping on both sides of the racial fence. Lathan and Baker couldn't be more appealing. [PG-13]▐

Something of Value (1957) **113m.** *** D: Richard Brooks. Rock Hudson, Dana Wynter, Sidney Poitier, Wendy Hiller, Frederick O'Neal. Robert Ruark's novel transformed to screen, sharply detailing brutal Mau Mau warfare in Kenya. Hudson and Poitier fine as British colonial farmer and his childhood friend; Hiller memorable as widow struggling to retain dignity and spirit.▼▐

Something's Gotta Give (2003) **C-128m.** *** D: Nancy Meyers. Jack Nicholson, Diane Keaton, Keanu Reeves, Frances McDormand, Amanda Peet, Jon Favreau, Paul Michael Glaser, Rachel Ticotin. A self-styled Lothario with a penchant for younger women heads to his current girlfriend's weekend home, only to find her mother there; to his own amazement, he finds himself attracted to her, even as she is pursued by a much younger man. Entertaining comedy for (and about) grown-ups with delightful performances by the two leads. Written by the director. Stay through the credits to hear Jack sing "La Vie en Rose." [PG-13] ▼▐

Something Short of Paradise (1979) **C-91m.** ** D: David Helpern, Jr. Susan Sarandon, David Steinberg, Jean-Pierre Aumont, Marilyn Sokol, Joe Grifasi, Robert Hitt. Aptly titled romantic comedy pairs movie theater manager Steinberg and magazine writer Sarandon, but offers little; Steinberg's character is particularly obnoxious in this blatant ANNIE HALL rip-off. Film buffs will enjoy main-title sequence comprised of old movie ads. [PG]▼▐

Something Special (1986) **C-93m.** *** D: Paul Schneider. Pamela Segall, Patty Duke, Eric Gurry, John Glover, Mary Tanner, Seth Green, Jeb Ellis-Brown, John David Cullum, Corey Parker. Cute, original, generally pleasing little comedy-drama-fantasy about a 14-year-old girl (Segall, in a spunky performance) who wants to become a male—and has her wish granted. Bogs down when the adults are around, but it's still perfect fare for older kids. A shorter version, with tamer language, runs 86m. Original title: WILLY MILLY. Aka I WAS A TEENAGE BOY. [PG-13]▼●

Something to Hide (1972-British) **C-100m.** *½ D: Alastair Reid. Peter Finch, Shelley Winters, Colin Blakely, Linda Hayden, John Stride. All-out marital fighting match between memorably overwrought Winters and Finch deteriorates into unconvincing melodrama concerning pregnant trollop Hayden and Finch's eventual mental breakdown. Unpleasant. Retitled: SHATTERED.▼

Something to Live For (1952) **89m.** **½ D: George Stevens. Joan Fontaine, Ray Milland, Teresa Wright, Douglas Dick, Rudy Lee. Turgid melodrama trying to be another THE LOST WEEKEND. Fontaine is alcoholic in love with Milland, but he's married.

Something to Talk About (1995) **C-106m.** **½ D: Lasse Hallström. Julia Roberts, Dennis Quaid, Robert Duvall, Gena Rowlands, Kyra Sedgwick, Brett Cullen, Haley Aull, Muse Watson, Anne Shropshire. A somewhat scattered Southern woman discovers her husband is playing around and tries to cut him off, but strong ties—and his involvement in the family business (a prosperous horse farm)—make it hard to do. The cast is amiable, the film is good looking, but Callie Khouri's screenplay is unfocused and never gives us a handle on Roberts' character. Sedgwick gets a license to steal (scenes, that is), with all the funniest lines in the picture. David Huddleston appears unbilled. [R] ▼●▐

Something Wicked This Way Comes (1983) **C-94m.** **½ D: Jack Clayton. Jason Robards, Jonathan Pryce, Diane Ladd, Pam Grier, Royal Dano, Shawn Carson, Vidal Peterson, Mary Grace Canfield, James Stacy; narrated by Arthur Hill. A mysterious carnival pitches its tent outside an idyllic American town in the early part of the century and fulfills the dreams of its citizens—for a heavy price. Told from a young boy's point of view, film has affecting moments, but never really hits its stride, with the ultimate "revelation" about Mr. Dark and his carnival no surprise at all. Disappointing Disney production of Ray Bradbury's classic story, scripted by the author. [PG]▼●

Something Wild (1961) **112m.** **½ D: Jack Garfein. Carroll Baker, Ralph Meeker, Mildred Dunnock, Martin Kosleck, Jean Stapleton. Bizarre study of rape victim Baker falling in love with would-be attacker Meeker, coming to rational understanding with mother Dunnock. N.Y.C. location scenes perk melodramatic soaper.

Something Wild (1986) **C-113m.** ** D: Jonathan Demme. Jeff Daniels, Melanie Griffith, Ray Liotta, Margaret Colin, Tracey Walter, Dana Preu, Jack Gilpin. Straight-arrow businessman Daniels goes for a joyride with a flaky, sexy girl he chances to meet, and in the course of a couple of days she turns his life inside out. Many surprising twists and turns as this film veers from kooky comedy to violent melodrama, but end result isn't satisfying, especially with tacked-on happy ending. Filmmakers John Waters and John Sayles have amusing cameos as a used-car salesman and a motorcycle cop, respectively. [R] ▼●〖

Sometimes a Great Notion (1971) **C-114m.** ** D: Paul Newman. Paul Newman, Henry Fonda, Lee Remick, Michael Sarrazin, Richard Jaeckel, Linda Lawson. Disappointing film version of Ken Kesey's mammoth novel about modern-day loggers in Oregon. Jaeckel's performance is outstanding and movie has one great scene involving a drowning, but otherwise film is a letdown. Retitled NEVER GIVE A INCH (the family's motto) for TV. Panavision. [PG] ▼●〖

Somewhere (2010-U.S.-Italian-French-Japanese) **C-97m.** *½ D: Sofia Coppola. Stephen Dorff, Elle Fanning, Chris Pontius, Ellie Kemper. Stultifying slice of someone else's life—in this case, an indolent, pampered movie actor (Dorff) who lives a life of luxury and ease at the Chateau Marmont Hotel in L.A., doing whatever he's told to and little more. Then his ex-wife charges him with taking care of their 11-year-old daughter, to whom he's been an absentee parent so far. Writer-director Coppola authentically captures the actor's world and the atmosphere of the fabled Hollywood haunt where he lives, but it all adds up to . . . nothing. (Spoiler alert: The actor comes to realize that his life is empty!) Michelle Monaghan and Benicio Del Toro add verisimilitude in cameo roles. [R] 〖

Somewhere I'll Find You (1942) **108m.** **½ D: Wesley Ruggles. Clark Gable, Lana Turner, Robert Sterling, Patricia Dane, Reginald Owen, Lee Patrick, Charles Dingle, Sara Haden, Rags Ragland, Van Johnson, Leonid Kinskey, Grady Sutton, Keye Luke. Turner and Gable are improbable as WW2 war correspondents, but their love scenes between battles are most convincing. Film debut of Keenan Wynn. ▼〖

Somewhere in the Night (1946) **108m.** **½ D: Joseph L. Mankiewicz. John Hodiak, Nancy Guild, Lloyd Nolan, Richard Conte, Josephine Hutchinson, Fritz Kortner, Sheldon Leonard, Whit Bissell, Jeff Corey, Henry (Harry) Morgan. Satisfactory drama of amnesiac Hodiak trying to discover his true identity and getting mixed up

with mobsters and murder; not up to later Mankiewicz efforts.〖

Somewhere in Time (1980) **C-103m.** *½ D: Jeannot Szwarc. Christopher Reeve, Jane Seymour, Christopher Plummer, Teresa Wright, Bill Erwin, George Voskovec, Tim Kazurinsky, W. (William) H. Macy, George Wendt. Superficial tearjerker about unhappy playwright Reeve who falls in love with a 70-year-old photograph of an actress (Seymour), then wills himself back in time to meet her. Stilted dialogue, corny situations, pretty scenery (on Mackinac Island). Script by Richard Matheson from his novel *Bid Time Return*. [PG] ▼●〖

Somewhere Tomorrow (1983) **C-87m.** *** D: Robert Wiemer. Sarah Jessica Parker, Nancy Addison, Tom Shea, Rick Weber, Paul Bates, James Congdon. Offbeat drama about fatherless teen who, after seeing TOPPER on TV and bumping her head, meets the ghost of a boy who's been killed in a plane crash. Not without flaws, but still charming and moving. [PG] ▼〖

Sommersby (1993-U.S.-French) **C-113m.** **½ D: Jon Amiel. Richard Gere, Jodie Foster, Bill Pullman, James Earl Jones, William Windom, Brett Kelley, Richard Hamilton, Maury Chaykin, Lanny Flaherty, Frankie Faison, Wendell Wellman, Clarice Taylor, Ronald Lee Ermey. Gere returns to his home in the postwar South, after six years' imprisonment during the Civil War, but his wife can't quite believe he's the same man she married. Sumptuously designed and photographed (in Virginia), this is the kind of film that takes you to another time and place, but despite strong performances, the characters remain aloof—and so does their plight. Executive produced by Gere. Remake of the French hit THE RETURN OF MARTIN GUERRE. Panavision. [PG-13] ▼●〖

Son, The (2002-Belgian-French) **C-100m.** ***½ D: Jean-Pierre Dardenne, Luc Dardenne. Olivier Gourmet, Morgan Marinne, Isabella Soupart, Rémy Renaud, Nassim Hassani. Quiet, methodical man teaches carpentry to boys who have just been released from prison or reform school, but he takes special interest in one teenager. The reason is revealed to us gradually, like everything else in this exceptional film. A powerful study of repressed emotions and the reality behind pent-up thoughts of revenge and closure. The Dardennes make brilliant use of handheld camera and natural locations to give the film a tangible sense of reality; naturalistic performances complete the picture. ▼〖

Sonatine (1994-Japanese) **C-94m.** *** D: Takeshi Kitano. Beat Takeshi, Tetsu Watanabe, Aya Kokumai, Masanobu Katsumura, Susumu Terashima. Well-observed portrait of a middle-aged gangster who's looking to his future when he's asked to settle a dispute between two warring factions of yakuza on Okinawa. Writer-director-star Kitano (who acts under the name of Beat Takeshi) isn't timid about depicting violence, but he does it with style. [R] ▼●▶

Songcatcher (2001) **C-105m.** **★★★★** D: Maggie Greenwald. Janet McTeer, Aidan Quinn, Pat Carroll, Jane Adams, Gregory Cook, Iris DeMent, E. Katherine Kerr, Emmy Rossum, David Patrick Kelly, Taj Mahal. Beautifully rendered tale of an independent-minded musicologist (McTeer) who collects folk songs in Appalachia in the early 20th century. Carroll is wonderful as the earth mother. Written by the director. [PG-13] ▼▶

Song for Martin, A (2001-Danish-German-Swedish) **C-118m.** **★★½** D: Bille August. Sven Wollter, Viveka Seldahl, Reine Brynolfsson, Linda Källgren, Lisa Werlinder, Peter Engman, Klas Dahlstedt, Lo Wahl, Kristina Törnqvist. A woman begins a new life when she marries a famous composer, then struggles as he succumbs to Alzheimer's disease. Sensitive drama with fine performances, but also a long, diligent haul to a foregone conclusion with the inescapable effect of a TV movie. ▼▶

Song Is Born, A (1948) **C-113m.** **★★½** D: Howard Hawks. Danny Kaye, Virginia Mayo, Hugh Herbert, Steve Cochran, Felix Bressart; guest stars Benny Goodman, Louis Armstrong, Charlie Barnet, Lionel Hampton, Tommy Dorsey. A group of dowdy intellectuals need to learn about jazz to write an intelligent entry for their upcoming encyclopedia. Watered-down remake of BALL OF FIRE (also directed by Hawks) does give Danny some good material, and enables a formidable array of jazz greats to do their stuff (including Benny Goodman, made up as one of the bookish profs). ▼●

Song of Bernadette, The (1943) **156m.** **★★★½** D: Henry King. Jennifer Jones, William Eythe, Charles Bickford, Vincent Price, Lee J. Cobb, Anne Revere, Gladys Cooper. Overlong but excellent story of religious French girl in 1800s who sees great vision, incurs local wrath because of it. George Seaton adapted Franz Werfel's bestselling novel. Four Oscars include Best Actress, Cinematography (Arthur Miller), Score (Alfred Newman). That's Linda Darnell, unbilled, as the Virgin Mary. ▼●▶

Song of Love (1947) **119m.** **★★½** D: Clarence Brown. Katharine Hepburn, Paul Henreid, Robert Walker, Henry Daniell, Leo G. Carroll, Gigi Perreau, Tala Birell, Henry Stephenson. Classy production but slow-moving story of Clara Schuman (Hepburn), her composer husband (Henreid), and good friend Brahms (Walker). ▼▶

Song of Norway (1970) **C-142m.** BOMB D: Andrew L. Stone. Florence Henderson, Toralv Maurstad, Christina Schollin,

Frank Porretta, Edward G. Robinson, Harry Secombe, Robert Morley, Oscar Homolka. A poor biography of composer Edvard Grieg, with weak and abridged versions of his best music. Beautiful to look at, but a dud. Super Panavision 70. [G] ▼

Song of Songs, The (1933) **90m.** **★★½** D: Rouben Mamoulian. Marlene Dietrich, Brian Aherne, Lionel Atwill, Alison Skipworth, Hardie Albright, Helen Freeman. Naïve country girl Dietrich falls in love with sculptor Aherne, for whom she poses in the nude . . . but Atwill, a wealthy reprobate, manages to marry her. Humdrum story made worthwhile by good performances. Dietrich is luminous in her first Hollywood film *not* directed by Josef von Sternberg. ▼▶

Song of the Islands (1942) **C-75m.** **★★★** D: Walter Lang. Betty Grable, Victor Mature, Jack Oakie, Thomas Mitchell, Hilo Hattie, George Barbier, Billy Gilbert. Mature (with sidekick Oakie) visits idyllic Pacific island and falls in love with Grable, but romance is hindered by feuding between their fathers. Buoyant Technicolor fluff, full of engagingly silly songs by Mack Gordon and Harry Owens. ▼●

Song of the South (1946) **C-94m.** **★★★½** D: Wilfred Jackson (animation), Harve Foster (live-action). Ruth Warrick, James Baskett, Bobby Driscoll, Luana Patten, Lucile Watson, Hattie McDaniel, Glenn Leedy. Lonely, misunderstood little boy, living on a plantation in the Old South, finds his only happiness in the tales spun by Uncle Remus. Sentimental but moving story serves as framework for three terrific Disney cartoon sequences featuring Brer Rabbit, Brer Fox, and Brer Bear (based on writings of Joel Chandler Harris). Superb blend of live-action and animation, sincere performances (Baskett earned a special Academy Award for his), and tuneful songs including Oscar-winning "Zip a Dee Doo Dah" make this a treat. Available only on Japanese import laserdisc.●

Song of the Thin Man (1947) **86m.** **★★½** D: Edward Buzzell. William Powell, Myrna Loy, Keenan Wynn, Dean Stockwell, Philip Reed, Patricia Morison, Gloria Grahame, Jayne Meadows, Don Taylor, Leon Ames. Nick and Nora search for clues to a murder in the dark and mysterious atmosphere of N.Y.C. jazz clubs. Eleven-year-old Stockwell portrays Nick, Jr., in this sixth and final series entry, still amiable and entertaining thanks to the stars' chemistry. ▼●

Song Remains the Same, The (1976) **C-136m.** **★★** D: Peter Clifton, Joe Massot. Amateurish mixture of fantasy sequences and documentary footage from Led Zeppelin's 1973 tour is for fans only. Even without the stereo sound, film will still clean out all eight sinus cavities. [PG] ▼▶

Song to Remember, A (1945) **C-113m.**

**½ D: Charles Vidor. Cornel Wilde, Paul Muni, Merle Oberon, Stephen Bekassy, Nina Foch, George Coulouris, Sig Arno. Colorful but superficial biography of Chopin (Wilde) with exaggerated Muni as his mentor, lovely Oberon as George Sand; good music, frail plot. ▼●)

Song Without End (1960) **C-141m.** **½ D: Charles Vidor. Dirk Bogarde, Capucine, Genevieve Page, Patricia Morison, Ivan Desny, Martita Hunt, Lou Jacobi. Beautiful music (scoring won an Oscar) submerged by dramatics of composer Franz Liszt's life. Bogarde tries; settings are lavish. Vidor died during filming, George Cukor completed picture. CinemaScope. ▼●)

Songwriter (1984) **C-94m.** **½ D: Alan Rudolph. Willie Nelson, Kris Kristofferson, Melinda Dillon, Rip Torn, Lesley Ann Warren, Mickey Raphael, Rhonda Dotson, Richard C. Sarafian. Loose, friendly, rambling film about a couple of country singers—one of whom (Nelson) has become an entrepreneur but calls on his old partner Kris to help him outwit a greedy backer (played by film director Sarafian). Doesn't add up to much but certainly pleasant to watch, with top supporting cast and lots of music. [R] ▼●)

Son In Law (1993) **C-95m.** ** D: Steve Rash. Pauly Shore, Carla Gugino, Lane Smith, Cindy Pickett, Mason Adams, Patrick Renna, Dennis Burkley, Dan Gauthier. Liberated college freshman brings her dorm's biggest goof home to the family farm over Thanksgiving break, passing him off as her fiancé to discourage a hometown lout from proposing. Exactly what you would expect, even more so when Shore teaches squaredancers the funky chicken. Even on his best days Pauly Shore is an acquired taste, but at least the film isn't mean-spirited. Gugino has an infectious cackle. Brendan Fraser appears unbilled. [PG-13] ▼●)

Sonny (2002) **C-110m.** **½ D: Nicolas Cage. James Franco, Brenda Blethyn, Mena Suvari, Harry Dean Stanton, Scott Caan, Seymour Cassel, Brenda Vaccaro. Just out of the army and looking for work, Franco's Sonny is reluctant to return to mom Blethyn's family business: working out of a New Orleans brothel. But though he fancies recent live-in Suvari, his natural talent as a male stud is too impressive to ignore . . . especially when so many other doors are slammed in his face. Overheated but compelling Southern Gothic tale gives Stanton his best role in years as a mysterious, melancholy hang-around friend, and Vaccaro a variation on her role in MIDNIGHT COWBOY. Look for a semi-disguised Cage in one late barroom scene. This marks the actor's feature directing debut. [R] ▼)

Sonny and Jed (1973-Italian) **C-98m.** ** D: Sergio Corbucci. Tomas Milian, Telly Savalas, Susan George, Rosanna Janni, Laura Betti. Lighthearted spaghetti Western that teams escaped convict, pillaging his way across Mexico, with free-spirited gal who wants to be an outlaw. Shiny-domed Telly is determined lawman dogging their every move. Techniscope. [R] ▼

Sonny Boy (1990) **C-98m.** BOMB D: Robert Martin Carroll. David Carradine, Paul L. Smith, Brad Dourif, Conrad Janis, Sydney Lassick, Alexandra Powers, Michael Griffin. Repulsive, socially unredeemable waste of celluloid detailing gruesome upbringing of abused "sonny boy" who's kidnapped by wacko couple Smith and his "wife" Carradine (who plays the role in full drag). Filmed for no apparent reason except to offend and appall. Panavision. [R] ▼●)

Son of a Gunfighter (1966-Spanish) **C-92m.** *½ D: Paul Landres. Russ Tamblyn, Kieron Moore, James Philbrook, Fernando Rey. Title tells all in oater peppered with Anglo-Saxon actors and bits of the Old West. CinemaScope.

Son of Blob SEE: **Beware! The Blob**

Son of Darkness: To Die For II (1991) **C-95m.** ** D: David F. Price. Rosalind Allen, Michael Praed, Scott Jacoby, Steve Bond, Amanda Wyss, Remy O'Neill, Devin Corrie Sims. Busy plot: Vlad Tepesh is now Dr. Max Schreck, at a hospital in the mountains, in pursuit of heroine who has unknowingly adopted his half-vampire baby. Beautifully shot, and tries to be romantic—but it's routine. [R] ▼

Son of Dracula (1943) **78m.** *** D: Robert Siodmak. Lon Chaney, Jr., Robert Paige, Louise Allbritton, Evelyn Ankers, Frank Craven, J. Edward Bromberg, Samuel S. Hinds. Mysterious gentleman named Alucard turns up in the Deep South to sample the local cuisine. One of Universal's most atmospheric chillers, with crisp acting, fine effects . . . and an unexpected finale. ▼●)

Son of Dracula (1974-British) **C-90m.** *½ D: Freddie Francis. Harry Nilsson, Ringo Starr, Rosanna Lee, Freddie Jones, Dennis Price, Skip Martin. Offbeat but uninspired rock horror pic with seven tunes by Nilsson, who plays the title character. Ringo produced. Retitled: YOUNG DRACULA. [PG]

Son of Flubber (1963) **100m.** **½ D: Robert Stevenson. Fred MacMurray, Nancy Olson, Keenan Wynn, Tommy Kirk, Elliott Reid, Joanna Moore, Leon Ames, Ed Wynn, Charlie Ruggles, Paul Lynde, Jack Albertson. Silly, disjointed sequel to THE ABSENT MINDED PROFESSOR has new inventions—flubbergas, dry rain—and appropriate slapstick highlights, to compensate for uneven script. Helped, too, by cast full of old pros, especially Lynde as smug sportscaster. ▼●)

Son of Frankenstein (1939) **99m.** *** D: Rowland V. Lee. Basil Rathbone, Boris Karloff, Bela Lugosi, Lionel Atwill, Josephine Hutchinson, Edgar Norton, Donnie Dunagan. Third in the series (after BRIDE) finds late doctor's son (Rathbone) attempting to clear family name by making the Monster "good." He should live so long. Lavishly made shocker is gripping and eerie, if a bit talky, with wonderfully bizarre sets by Jack Otterson and Lugosi's finest performance as evil, broken-necked blacksmith Ygor. Karloff's last appearance as the Monster. Look fast for Ward Bond(!) as a constable guarding Castle Frankenstein from angry villagers late in film. Sequel: THE GHOST OF FRANKENSTEIN.▼●)

Son of Fury (1942) 98m. *** D: John Cromwell. Tyrone Power, Gene Tierney, George Sanders, Frances Farmer, Roddy McDowall, Kay Johnson, John Carradine, Elsa Lanchester, Harry Davenport, Dudley Digges, Ethel Griffies. Good costumer about aristocratic Sanders abusing nephew Power, who flees to desert isle to plan revenge; Tierney's on the island, too. Remade as TREASURE OF THE GOLDEN CONDOR.▼)

Son of Godzilla (1967-Japanese) C-86m. *½ D: Jun Fukuda. Tadao Takashima, Akira Kubo, Bibari Maeda, Akihiko Hirata, Kenji Sahara. Godzilla and son are threatened by giant mantises and a huge spider in this good-natured monster rally, but where's Mrs. Godzilla when you really need her? Some of the same footage later seen in GODZILLA'S REVENGE. Tohoscope.▼)

Son of Kong, The (1933) 70m. **½ D: Ernest B. Schoedsack. Robert Armstrong, Helen Mack, Victor Wong, John Marston, Frank Reicher, Lee Kohlmar. Disappointing sequel to KING KONG, hurriedly put together—and it shows. Armstrong is back as Carl Denham, who retraces his steps from the first film and discovers Kong's cute li'l offspring. Mostly comedic film has some good moments, and Willis O'Brien's effects are still superb.▼●)

Son of Lassie (1945) C-102m. **½ D: S. Sylvan Simon. Peter Lawford, Donald Crisp, June Lockhart, Nigel Bruce, William Severn, Leon Ames, Fay Helm, Donald Curtis, Nils Asther, Helen Koford (Terry Moore). War-themed sequel to popular LASSIE COME HOME with Lawford and Lockhart playing adult roles of McDowall and Taylor. Crisp and Bruce are now training dogs for the war effort and Lassie's son (both roles played here by talented collie Pal) accompanies pilot Lawford to Nazi-occupied Norway.▼)

Son of Monte Cristo, The (1940) 102m. *** D: Rowland V. Lee. Louis Hayward, Joan Bennett, George Sanders, Florence Bates, Lionel Royce, Montagu Love, Ian Wolfe, Clayton Moore, Ralph Byrd, Rand Brooks, Henry Brandon. Nothing new in big-scale swashbuckler, but very well done

with Hayward battling Sanders and vying for Bennett's hand. ▼●)

Son of Paleface (1952) C-95m. ***½ D: Frank Tashlin. Bob Hope, Jane Russell, Roy Rogers, Douglass Dumbrille, Bill Williams, Harry Von Zell, Iron Eyes Cody. One of Hope's best; same basic set-up as THE PALEFACE, but the presence of Rogers gives this one a satirical punch the original doesn't have. Full of director-cowriter Tashlin's cartoonlike gags; the scene where Hope and Trigger share the same bed is an unheralded comedy classic.▼●)

Son of Rambow (2008-British-French) C-95m. *** D: Garth Jennings. Bill Milner, Will Poulter, Jules Sitruk, Jessica Stevenson, Neil Dudgeon, Ed Westwick. The setting is England in the early 1980s. A lonely, fatherless boy (Milner) whose family is part of a strict religious sect finds an exhilarating outlet for his vivid imagination: making home movies with an unlikely new friend, a cheeky miscreant (Poulter) who happens to have a video camera. Together they emulate the adventures of Sylvester Stallone's Rambo character from FIRST BLOOD. Endearingly eccentric view of the pain and wonder of boyhood from the Hammer & Tongs production team, with a larky music score by Joby Talbot. Panavision. [PG-13]●)

Son of Satan SEE: **Whip and the Body, The**

Son of Sinbad (1955) C-88m. *½ D: Ted Tetzlaff. Dale Robertson, Sally Forrest, Lili St. Cyr, Vincent Price. Limp Arabian Nights adventure has Sinbad, captured by caliph, forced to perform wonders to win freedom and save Baghdad from evil Tamerlane. Look fast for Kim Novak as one of the ladies garbed in full-length hooded capes. 3-D SuperScope. ▼

Son of Spartacus SEE: **Slave, The**

Son of the Bride (2001-Argentinian-Spanish) C-124m. *** D: Juan José Campanella. Ricardo Darín, Héctor Alterio, Norma Aleandro, Eduardo Blanco, Natalia Verbeke, Gimena Nóbile. Health crisis forces 40ish man to deal with the past and face his future in a new, mature way he once never dreamed possible. Sophisticated, warm, funny and altogether engaging film puts a human focus on troubled Argentina in a manner audiences anywhere in the world can respond to. Touching film reunites THE OFFICIAL STORY's Aleandro and Alterio in a wedding that's hard to forget. Darín is splendid. Well worth seeing. [R] ▼)

Son of the Mask (2005) C-95m. BOMB D: Lawrence Guterman. Jamie Kennedy, Alan Cumming, Bob Hoskins, Ben Stein, Traylor Howard, Steven Wright, Kal Penn. Kennedy isn't ready to be a father but conceives a baby anyway, wearing a supernatural mask. It, in turn, is coveted by a Norse god's son (Cumming, in another of his leftover Paul

Reubens roles). The god himself is played by Hoskins, in layers of makeup, and by this time the creaks are louder than anything in THE SON OF THE SHEIK. So-called sequel to THE MASK (1994) is raucous without mercy, and burdened by a charmless cast; it has to plunder Chuck Jones' cartoon ONE FROGGY EVENING to glean even a few good moments. [PG] ▼●)

Son of the Pink Panther (1993) **C-93m.** *½ D: Blake Edwards. Roberto Benigni, Herbert Lom, Claudia Cardinale, Burt Kwouk, Debrah Farentino, Robert Davi, Graham Stark, Jennifer Edwards, Anton Rodgers. Feeble attempt to revive the series, with Benigni as the son of inept Inspector Clouseau, on the trail of a kidnapped princess (Farentino) with plenty of misfired sight gags along the way. Lom, Kwouk, and Stark reprise their roles from past entries, and Benigni's enthusiasm helps, but Peter Sellers is sorely missed. Opening animation/live-action credits with Bobby McFerrin's version of the Panther theme is best part of film. Panavision. [PG] ▼●)

Son of the Shark (1993-French) **C-88m.** ***½ D: Agnes Merlet. Ludovic Vandendaele, Erick Da Silva, Sandrine Blancke, Maxime Leroux. Harrowing, sobering fact-based slice-of-life about two out-of-control pre-teen brothers (Vandendaele and Da Silva, in dazzling performances), who've been abandoned by their mother and abused by their father. One minute they are childlike, the next they are hoodlums who terrorize their hometown. They are neither romanticized nor depicted as villains or victims; the point is that there is no adult around to nurture their good instincts. A grimly realistic film, gutwrenching and heartbreaking. Panavision. ▼

Son of the Sheik, The (1926) **72m.** *** D: George Fitzmaurice. Rudolph Valentino, Vilma Banky, Agnes Ayres, Karl Dane, Bull Montana. Sequel to THE SHEIK contains flavorful account of desert leader who falls in love with dancing-girl Banky. Handsomely mounted silent film is first-rate adventure/romance, with tongue slightly in cheek. Valentino plays a dual role in this, his last film. ▼●)

Sons and Lovers (1960-British) **103m.** ***½ D: Jack Cardiff. Trevor Howard, Dean Stockwell, Wendy Hiller, Mary Ure, Heather Sears, William Lucas, Donald Pleasence, Ernest Thesiger. Grim D. H. Lawrence story of sensitive youth Stockwell egged on by mother to make something of his life, away from coalmining town and drunken father Howard. Script by Gavin Lambert and T.E.B. Clarke. Freddie Francis' rich cinematography won an Oscar. CinemaScope.

Sons of Katie Elder, The (1965) **C-122m.** *** D: Henry Hathaway. John Wayne, Dean Martin, Martha Hyer, Michael Anderson,

Jr., Earl Holliman, Jeremy Slate, James Gregory, George Kennedy, Paul Fix, Dennis Hopper, John Litel, Strother Martin. Typical Western with Duke, Holliman, Anderson, and Martin the rowdy sons of frontier woman Katie Elder, who set out to learn why she died broke. Film marked return to big screen for Wayne after first highly publicized cancer operation. Lively fun. Music score by Elmer Bernstein. Panavision. ▼●)

Sons of the Desert (1933) **69m.** ***½ D: William A. Seiter. Stan Laurel, Oliver Hardy, Charley Chase, Mae Busch, Dorothy Christy, Lucien Littlefield. L&H's best feature film; duo sneaks off to fraternal convention without telling the wives; then the fun begins, with Chase as hilariously obnoxious conventioneer. Also shown in computer-colored version. ▼●)

Son's Room, The (2001-Italian-French) **C-87m.** *** D: Nanni Moretti. Nanni Moretti, Laura Morante, Jasmine Trinca, Giuseppe Sanfelice, Silvio Orlando, Claudia Della Seta, Stefano Accorsi, Sofia Vigliar. Quietly moving examination of a family torn apart by sudden tragedy. Moretti plays a mild-mannered analyst whose well-ordered life threatens to crumble under the pressure. Subtle, perceptive, and moving. Moretti also coscripted. ▼

Sophie's Choice (1982) **C-157m.** **½ D: Alan J. Pakula. Meryl Streep, Kevin Kline, Peter MacNicol, Rita Karin, Stephen D. Newman, Josh Mostel; narrated by Josef Sommer. Streep's Oscar-winning performance is the centerpiece (and raison d'être) for this slavishly faithful, but deadeningly slow-moving, adaptation of William Styron's book about a Polish woman's attempt to justify her existence in America after surviving a living hell during WW2. Nestor Almendros' camera is in love with Streep, but her stunning characterization can't carry the film alone. [R] ▼●)

Sophie Scholl: The Final Days (2005-German) **C-117m.** ***½ D: Marc Rothemund. Julia Jentsch, Fabian Hinrichs, Gerald Alexander Held, Johanna Gastdorf, André Hennicke, Florian Stetter. Gripping true story set in 1943 Munich, based in part on newly discovered documents and testimonials. Siblings Hans and Sophie Scholl, members of the White Rose student resistance movement, are arrested after distributing anti-Nazi leaflets. Film follows Sophie's verbal sparring with a Gestapo interrogator intent on breaking her spirit . . . but Sophie is an intellectual of unusual poise. Impressive filmmaking, focusing on words and ideas, made more vivid by the spare, drab settings. Sophie's story has been told in other films, including THE WHITE ROSE. Written by Fred Breinersdorfer. ●)

Sophie's Place SEE: **Crooks and Coronets**
So Proudly We Hail! (1943) **126m.** *** D:

Mark Sandrich. Claudette Colbert, Paulette Goddard, Veronica Lake, George Reeves, Sonny Tufts, Barbara Britton, Walter Abel. Flag-waving soaper of nurses in WW2 Pacific, headed by Colbert. Versatile cast, action scenes, and teary romancing combine well in this woman's service story. Dated but still entertaining. ▼▶

Sorcerer (1977) **C-122m. **½** D: William Friedkin. Roy Scheider, Bruno Cremer, Francisco Rabal, Amidou, Ramon Bieri, Peter Capell. Four fugitives in seedy Latin American town try to buy freedom by driving trucks of nitroglycerine over bumpy roads to help put out oil fire. Expensive remake of THE WAGES OF FEAR never really catches hold in spite of a few astounding scenes. Strange electronic score by Tangerine Dream. [PG]▼●▶

Sorcerers, The (1967-British) **C-87m. **½** D: Michael Reeves. Boris Karloff, Catherine Lacey, Ian Ogilvy, Elizabeth Ercy, Susan George. Interesting but flawed low-budgeter. Husband-and-wife scientist team attempt to perfect domination-of-will techniques, persuade young man (Ogilvy) to join experiments. Downhill from there.▼

Sorcerer's Apprentice, The (2010) **C-109m. **½** D: Jon Turteltaub. Nicolas Cage, Jay Baruchel, Alfred Molina, Teresa Palmer, Monica Bellucci, Toby Kebbell, Omar Benson Miller, Alice Krige. Nerdy college science student Baruchel learns that a weird encounter he experienced at the age of 10 wasn't a one-time occurrence. Master sorcerer Cage has discovered that the boy is the "chosen one" to fend off the destruction of mankind by a sorceress who's been locked up for eons. Formulaic but enjoyable-enough mix of large-scale action and humor from the folks who brought you NATIONAL TREASURE, ostensibly inspired by the famous sequence in Disney's FANTASIA. Wittiest part of the film is the inventive use of Manhattan locations, from Wall Street to a ledge on the Chrysler Building. Super 35. [PG] ▶

Sordid Lives (2001) **C-111m. BOMB** D: Del Shores. Olivia Newton-John, Beau Bridges, Delta Burke, Bonnie Bedelia, Beth Grant, Ann Walker, Kirk Geiger, Leslie Jordan. More hick hijinks from writer-director Shores (author of DADDY'S DYIN' . . . WHO'S GOT THE WILL?) about an eccentric Texas family dealing with a variety of repressed emotions when their matriarch dies. Horribly filmed, endless parade of ear-piercing trailer-trash clichés and "meaningful" moments that are embarrassing. The performances, alas, match the subtlety of the writing. Shores adapted his own play. Now has a cult following.▼●

Sorority Boys (2002) **C-94m. *½** D: Wallace Wolodarsky. Barry Watson, Harland Williams, Michael Rosenbaum, Melissa Sagemiller, Heather Matarazzo, Kathryn Stockwood, James Daughton, Stephen Furst, Mark Metcalf, Peter Scolari, Wendie Jo Sperber, John Vernon. Crude comedy about three sexist frat boys forced into passing themselves off as women and taking refuge in a sorority house. A more appropriate title would be SOME LIKE IT STUPID. Aging baby boomers will note the presence in the cast of several aging graduates of ANIMAL HOUSE. [R]▼▶

Sorority Row (2009) **C-91m. *½** D: Stewart Hendler. Briana Evigan, Leah Pipes, Margo Harshman, Rumer Willis, Jamie Chung, Matt O'Leary, Julian Morris, Debra Gordon, Carrie Fisher, Audrina Patridge. A group of sorority girls have no idea what they're getting into when they decide to play a prank on one of their sisters' cheating boyfriends. Complete with beautiful half-naked girls, sex, and blood, this typical "scary movie" doesn't make any attempt to be original. Remake of 1983's THE HOUSE ON SORORITY ROW. [R]

Sorrento Beach SEE: **Hotel Sorrento**

Sorrow and the Pity, The (1970-Swiss) **260m. ****** D: Marcel Ophuls. Incredibly ambitious documentary about France's performance during WW2 is a total success. Film never becomes dull, in spite of four-and-a-half-hour length, even though bulk of footage is devoted to interviews with those who lived through the Nazi threat. A truly great film. 1999 reissue runs 249m. [PG]▼▶

Sorrowful Jones (1949) **88m. **½** D: Sidney Lanfield. Bob Hope, Lucille Ball, William Demarest, Mary Jane Saunders, Bruce Cabot, Thomas Gomez. Average racetrack comedy, actually a remake of LITTLE MISS MARKER and hardly as good. Remade as 40 POUNDS OF TROUBLE and again as LITTLE MISS MARKER in 1980. ▼●▶

Sorry, Haters (2006) **C-86m. *** D: Jeff Stanzler. Robin Wright Penn, Abdellatif Kechiche, Sandra Oh, Aasif Mandvi, Élodie Bouchez, Fred Durst, Josh Hamilton. Hot-button film about a Muslim cabdriver in Manhattan who becomes involved with a passenger, an emotionally distraught businesswoman. Topical thriller attempts to deal with tensions and prejudices in post-9/11 N.Y.C. Good performances help, but Stanzler's script goes wildly askew.▶

Sorry, Wrong Number (1948) **89m. *** D: Anatole Litvak. Barbara Stanwyck, Burt Lancaster, Ann Richards, Wendell Corey, Ed Begley, Leif Erickson, William Conrad. Overly complicated adaptation of famous radio thriller, but still a tense study of woman overhearing murder plan on telephone, discovering she's to be the victim. Stanwyck won an Oscar nomination for her bravura performance; adapted—or rather, expanded—by Lucille Fletcher, from her radio drama (which starred Agnes Moorehead). Remade for cable TV in 1989 with Loni Anderson.▼◗

Sotto, Sotto (1984-Italian) **C-105m.** **½ D: Lina Wertmuller. Enrico Montesano, Veronica Lario, Luisa de Santis, Massimo Wertmuller. Obvious, but not unentertaining, tale of Lario, who finds herself attracted to longtime best friend de Santis; her husband (Montesano), a sexist animal with a fragile ego, then goes comically berserk. Incidentally, actor Wertmuller is the director's nephew. [R]▼

Soul Food (1997) **C-114m.** *** D: George Tillman, Jr. Vanessa L. Williams, Vivica A. Fox, Nia Long, Brandon Hammond, Michael Beach, Mekhi Phifer, Irma P. Hall. When Chicago-based black matriarch Hall, the glue that holds her family together, falls ill, grandson Hammond does his best to step in. A rare '90s movie about family values that really works. Excellent ensemble cast in a poignant story that is honest and heartwarming. [R]▼◗

Soul Kitchen (2009-German-French) **C-100m.** **½ D: Fatih Akin. Adam Bousdoukos, Moritz Bleibtreu, Birol Ünel, Dorka Gryllus, Pheline Roggan, Anna Bederke, Wötan Wilke Möhring. In Hamburg, well-meaning but hopelessly disorganized Zinos (Bousdoukos) runs a funky neighborhood restaurant called Soul Kitchen. When he decides to follow his girlfriend to Shanghai he signs over ownership to his irresponsible brother (Bleibtreu), unaware that an old schoolmate is determined to buy the restaurant and tear it down. Enjoyable fluff strays toward farce at times but remains likable because we develop rooting interest for the harried hero. Bousdoukos cowrote the screenplay with director Akin.◗

Soul Man (1986) **C-101m.** ** D: Steve Miner. C. Thomas Howell, Arye Gross, Rae Dawn Chong, James Earl Jones, Melora Hardin, Leslie Nielsen, James B. Sikking, Max Wright, Jeff Altman, Julia Louis-Dreyfus, Ron Reagan. Young man desperate to go to Harvard Law School masquerades as a black in order to get minority scholarship. Slick but distressingly superficial; if this is the 1980s version of social satire, we're all in trouble. [PG-13]▼◗

Soul Men (2008) **C-103m.** **½ D: Malcolm D. Lee. Samuel L. Jackson, Bernie Mac, Sharon Leal, Sean Hayes, Adam Herschman, Affion Crockett, Jennifer Coolidge, John Legend, Isaac Hayes. Death of a Motown-type singing star inspires onetime backup singer Mac to locate his estranged partner (Jackson) and persuade him to travel cross-country to perform at a memorial concert at the Apollo Theater in Harlem. Road trip/reunion/buddy comedy is pretty thin but it's still fun to watch Jackson and Mac together, especially when they sing and put on their performance moves. Ends with

footage that pays tribute to Isaac Hayes and especially Mac, both of whom died before the film's release. Super 35. [R]◗

Soul of Nigger Charley, The (1973) **C-104m.** *½ D: Larry Spangler. Fred Williamson, D'Urville Martin, Denise Nicholas, Pedro Armendariz, Jr., Richard Farnsworth. Weak sequel to LEGEND OF NIGGER CHARLEY finds Charley trying to free slaves held captive by former Confederate Army officer in Mexico. Panavision. [R]

Soul Plane (2004) **C-86m.** *½ D: Jessy Terrero. Tom Arnold, Kevin Hart, Method Man, K. D. Aubert, Godfrey, Brian Hooks, D. L. Hughley, Arielle Kebbel, Mo'Nique, Ryan Pinkston, Missi Pyle, Sommore, Sofia Vergara, Gary Anthony Williams, John Witherspoon, Snoop Dogg. Young man who's always loved planes wins one hundred million dollars in a lawsuit and starts his own all-black airline. Arnold and his all-white family wind up on the first flight. Slight plot supports a nonstop string of (largely L.A.-centric) jokes, some of them funny, most of them vulgar, many of them bouncing off, if not reinforcing, stereotypes of black culture. How much you laugh is strictly a matter of personal taste. At least it's short. Unrated version runs 92m. [R] ▼◗

Souls at Sea (1937) **92m.** *** D: Henry Hathaway. Gary Cooper, George Raft, Frances Dee, Olympe Bradna, Henry Wilcoxon, Harry Carey, Robert Cummings, Joseph Schildkraut, George Zucco, Virginia Weidler. Fine actioner with Cooper and Raft struggling to save lives during ship tragedy; Cooper wrongly accused of irresponsibility. The stars make a good team here.▼

Souls for Sale SEE: **Confessions of an Opium Eater**

Soul Surfer (2011) **C-106m.** *** D: Sean McNamara. AnnaSophia Robb, Dennis Quaid, Helen Hunt, Lorraine Nicholson, Carrie Underwood, Craig T. Nelson, Ross Thomas, Kevin Sorbo, Sonya Balmores (Chung), David Chokachi. Inspiring true story of Bethany Hamilton, teenaged Hawaiian surfing whiz whose right arm was bitten off by a shark. Film chronicles the horrific accident's aftermath and Hamilton's determination to get back into competition. Gorgeous Kauai locations and cinematography make this a must for surf enthusiasts, but it's the remarkable pluck, drive, and faith of its main character that make it worthwhile overall. Robb captures Hamilton's spirit and believably hangs ten on those big waves. Pop star Underwood makes an OK acting debut as a church group leader. Nicholson, who plays best friend Alana, is the daughter of Jack Nicholson. Super 35. [PG]◗

Soul Survivors (2001) **C-85m.** BOMB D: Steve Carpenter. Melissa Sagemiller, Casey Affleck, Wes Bentley, Eliza Dushku, Angela Featherstone, Luke Wilson. A young woman and her three friends have one last night of celebration before going their separate ways for college. Unfortunately, something goes *terribly* wrong. Supernatural, horror, teensploitation, reality/fantasy grab bag set to pulsing music, this movie shamelessly steals ideas from good movies—and bad ones too. So-called "Killer Cut" is rated R. [PG-13] ▼▶

Soul to Soul (1971) **C-95m.** *** D: Denis Sanders. Wilson Pickett, Ike and Tina Turner, Santana, Roberta Flack, Les McCann, Willie Bobo, Eddie Harris, The Staple Singers. Good documentary of American soul, jazz and gospel performers in a concert commemorating the 14th anniversary of Ghanaian independence. Pickett is in top form singing "Funky Broadway" and "Land of 1,000 Dances." [G] ▼▶

Sound and the Fury, The (1959) **C-115m.** **½ D: Martin Ritt. Yul Brynner, Joanne Woodward, Margaret Leighton, Stuart Whitman, Ethel Waters, Jack Warden, Albert Dekker. Strange adaptation of William Faulkner novel becomes plodding tale of girl seeking independence from strict family rule in the South. CinemaScope.

Sound Barrier, The SEE: **Breaking the Sound Barrier**

Sounder (1972) **C-105m.** **** D: Martin Ritt. Cicely Tyson, Paul Winfield, Kevin Hooks, Carmen Mathews, Taj Mahal, James Best, Janet MacLachlan. Beautiful film, romanticizing in a positive sense experiences of black sharecropper family in 1930s —and the maturation of young Hooks. Full of fine performances that make characters utterly real. Mahal also composed the score. Screenplay by Lonnie Elder III from William Armstrong's novel. Remade for TV in 2003. Sequel: PART 2, SOUNDER. Panavision. [G] ▼▶●

Sounder, Part Two SEE: **Part 2, Sounder**

Sound of Music, The (1965) **C-174m.** ***½ D: Robert Wise. Julie Andrews, Christopher Plummer, Eleanor Parker, Peggy Wood, Richard Haydn, Anna Lee, Portia Nelson, Norma Varden, Marni Nixon. The children: Charmian Carr, Nicolas Hammond, Heather Menzies, Duane Chase, Angela Cartwright, Debbie Turner, Kym Karath. Call it corn if you like, but blockbuster Rodgers & Hammerstein musical based on Austria's real-life Von Trapp family, who fled their homeland in 1938 to escape from Nazi rule, pleased more people than practically any other film in history. Fine music, beautiful scenery help offset coy aspects of script. Five Oscars include Best Picture, Director, Score Adaptation (Irwin Kostal), Editing (William Reynolds). Screenplay by Ernest Lehman, based on the Howard Lindsay–Russel Crouse Broadway show. Songs include "Do Re Mi," "Climb Ev'ry Mountain" and title tune. Todd-AO ▼▶●

Sound of Thunder, A (2005-U.S.-German-Czech) **C-103m.** *½ D: Peter Hyams. Edward Burns, Catherine McCormack, Ben Kingsley, Jemima Rooper, David Oyelowo, Wilfried Hochholdinger, August Zirner, Corey Johnson. In Chicago, 2055, a company takes expeditions back in time to hunt dinosaurs. Precautions are taken, but (of course) something goes wrong, and a tiny change in the past sends alterations down through time that our heroes try to set right. Misguided expansion of Ray Bradbury short story with mediocre effects and a confusing script. It's easy to see why this remained on the shelf so long. Filmed in 2002. Panavision. [PG-13]▶

Sound of Trumpets, The SEE: **Il Posto**

Soupçon (1979-French) **C-93m.** **½ D: Jean-Charles Tacchella. Jean Carmet, Marie Dubois, Alain Doutey, Rachel Jenevein, Jose Laccioni. Middle-aged couple (Carmet, Dubois) decide to separate after a quarter century of marriage. Spirited and attractively played, but still forgettable; a disappointment from the director of COUSIN, COUSINE.

Soup for One (1982) **C-87m.** **½ D: Jonathan Kaufer. Saul Rubinek, Marcia Strassman, Gerrit Graham, Teddy Pendergrass, Richard Libertini, Andrea Martin, Lewis J. Stadlen. Sometimes winning but uneven account of single New Yorker Rubinek searching for his dream girl. The cast is game; solid work by 26-year-old director Kaufer. [R]▼

Source, The (1999) **C-88m.** *** D: Chuck Workman. Pop-style documentary on the Beat movement, drawing on archival footage of Jack Kerouac plus fresh material on William Burroughs and Allen Ginsberg. Audience-friendly rather than scholarly, this lively film serves as an excellent primer on this seminal movement in American culture. Key poems by Kerouac, Burroughs, and Ginsberg are performed on-camera by a well-chosen Johnny Depp, Dennis Hopper, and John Turturro, respectively. ▼▶

Source Code (2011) **C-94m.** **½ D: Duncan Jones. Jake Gyllenhaal, Michelle Monaghan, Vera Farmiga, Jeffrey Wright, Brent Skagford, Cas Anvar, Michael Arden, Craig Thomas, Russell Peters, James A. Woods. Gyllenhaal awakens on a Chicago commuter train in a stranger's body, sitting opposite his supposed girlfriend. After the train is hit by a firebomb, he learns that he is a soldier who has been transported into someone else's body in order to investigate the bombing and discover its perpetrator. But every time he returns for a replay of the same action, he becomes more emotionally engaged. Pretty good movie based on an intriguing concept, though it adds more layers of complexity than truly necessary, especially toward the end. [PG-13]▶

Sour Grapes (1998) **C-92m.** **½ D: Larry David. Steven Weber, Craig Bierko, Matt

Keeslar, Karen Sillas, Robyn Peterman, Viola Harris, Jennifer Leigh Warren. Bierko hits a $400,000 slot machine jackpot at a casino; Weber, his doctor cousin, thinks he's due half the loot because he loaned him the necessary quarters. Occasionally very funny, the movie is undermined by overemphatic "comedy" acting, unsympathetic characters, and a sitcom approach. Writer-director David cocreated *Seinfeld,* which explains both the good and the bad stuff here. [R]▼●◗

South Central (1992) **C-99m.** **½ D: Steve Anderson. Glenn Plummer, Byron Keith Minns, LaRita Shelby, Carl Lumbly, Lexie D. Bingham, Christian Coleman. Sobering, well-meaning drama of life and desperation in inner-city L.A. is similar in theme to (but not nearly as effective as) BOYZ N THE HOOD. Plummer is aces as an embattled street-gang veteran who undergoes an odyssey of transformation, and determines to spare his young son (Coleman) from the ravages of gang life. Anderson scripted, based on the novel *Crips* by L.A. schoolteacher Donald Bakeer. The executive producer was Oliver Stone. [R]▼●◗

Southern Comfort (1981) **C-106m.** ** D: Walter Hill. Keith Carradine, Powers Boothe, Fred Ward, Franklyn Seales, T. K. Carter, Lewis Smith, Les Lannom, Peter Coyote, Brion James. Macho National Guardsmen patronize Cajuns in the Louisiana swamp, much to their regret. Survival-of-the-fittest yarn is an intellectually muddled, Grade B DELIVERANCE, despite its crisp direction. [R]▼●◗

Southerner, The (1945) **91m.** **** D: Jean Renoir. Zachary Scott, Betty Field, Beulah Bondi, J. Carrol Naish, Norman Lloyd, Bunny Sunshine, Jay Gilpin, Estelle Taylor, Percy Kilbride, Blanche Yurka. Superb drama of family struggling to make farmland self-supporting against serious odds. Renoir adapted George Sessions Perry's novel *Hold Autumn in Your Hand.* ▼◗

Southern Star, The (1969-British-French-U.S.) **C-102m.** **½ D: Sidney Hayers. George Segal, Ursula Andress, Orson Welles, Ian Hendry, Harry Andrews, Michel Constantin. Uneven combination comedy-adventure detailing multiparty chase for possession of unusually large diamond boasts beautiful locations in Senegal, Africa, but not much else. Based on a Jules Verne novel. Techniscope. [M/PG]◗

Southern Yankee, A (1948) **90m.** *** D: Edward Sedgwick. Red Skelton, Brian Donlevy, Arlene Dahl, George Coulouris, Lloyd Gough, John Ireland, Charles Dingle, Joyce Compton. Hilarious Skelton comedy set during Civil War with Red a bumbling Yankee spy down South. Reminiscent of silent comedies, since Buster Keaton devised many of the film's gags.▼

Southland Tales (2007) **C-144m.** *½ D: Richard Kelly. Dwayne Johnson, Seann William Scott, Sarah Michelle Gellar, Mandy Moore, Justin Timberlake, Nora Dunn, John Larroquette, Bai Ling, Jon Lovitz, Cheri Oteri, Amy Poehler, Lou Taylor Pucci, Miranda Richardson, Wallace Shawn, Holmes Osborne, Kevin Smith, Christopher Lambert, Janeane Garofolo, Beth Grant, Zelda Rubinstein, Curtis Armstrong, Will Sasso. Impressive cast is wasted in an overlong, overwrought wallow set in 2008 Southern California 3 years after a disastrous nuclear attack on Texas has turned America into a police state. Focuses on several people trying to survive in this postapocalyptic environment, including a B-action-film actor, a porn star turned TV commentator, and an L.A. police officer on a journey of self-discovery when his personality is split in two. Even more convoluted and disjointed than it sounds. Super 35. [R]●◗

South of Heaven West of Hell (2000) **C-127m.** ** D: Dwight Yoakam. Dwight Yoakam, Vince Vaughn, Billy Bob Thornton, Bridget Fonda, Peter Fonda, Paul Reubens, Bud Cort, Bo Hopkins, Matt Clark, Noble Willingham, Scott Wilson, Luke Askew, Michael Jeter, Joe Ely, Warren Zevon. Standard Western plot of redemption pits marshal Yoakam against his former "foster family" of outlaws, led by Bible-toting patriarch Askew. Cowriter/director/composer/star Yoakam overreached in this overlong story, and seems to have given his large cast free rein. Executive produced by Buck Owens. Runs 100m. on VHS. Panavision. [R]▼◗

South Pacific (1958) **C-151m.** **½ D: Joshua Logan. Rossano Brazzi, Mitzi Gaynor, John Kerr, Ray Walston, Juanita Hall, France Nuyen, Tom Laughlin, voice of Giorgio Tozzi. Disappointing filmization of great Rodgers & Hammerstein show; adaptation of James Michener's moving vignettes about WW2 life on Pacific island needs dynamic personalities to make it catch fire, and they aren't here. Even location filming is lackluster. Adequate but hardly memorable. Songs include "Some Enchanted Evening," "There Is Nothing Like a Dame." Among the sailors and servicemen you'll spot John Gabriel, Ron Ely, Doug McClure, and James Stacy. Originally shown at 171m. Remade in 2001 for TV. Todd-AO. ▼●◗

South Park Bigger Longer & Uncut (1999) **C-81m.** *** D: Trey Parker. Voices of Trey Parker, Matt Stone, Mary Kay Bergman, Isaac Hayes, George Clooney, Brent Spiner, Minnie Driver, Dave Foley, Eric Idle, Mike Judge, Nick Rhodes, Stewart Copeland. The pint-sized, animated kids of South Park, Colorado, are so fond of the new R-rated Terrance and Phillip movie that they start imitating its rude dialogue. This inspires the parents of South Park to mount a campaign against the movie's stars—and homeland, Canada. Sharp, funny (and yes, foul-mouthed) satire, based on the irreverent TV series; sparked by great songs by Parker and Marc Shaiman. [R]▼●)

Soylent Green (1973) **C-100m.** ** D: Richard Fleischer. Charlton Heston, Edward G. Robinson, Leigh Taylor-Young, Chuck Connors, Joseph Cotten, Brock Peters, Paula Kelly, Whit Bissell, Mike Henry, Dick Van Patten. Well-intentioned but cardboard adaptation of Harry Harrison's science-fiction classic *Make Room! Make Room!* In the year 2022, Manhattan has become an overcrowded hellhole; cop Heston, investigating murder of bigwig, stumbles onto explosive government secret (which you'll figure out long before he does). Robinson is splendid in his final film; title refers to a precious foodstuff made of soybeans and lentils. Panavision. [PG]▼●)

Spaceballs (1987) **C-96m.** **½ D: Mel Brooks. Mel Brooks, John Candy, Rick Moranis, Bill Pullman, Daphne Zuniga, Dick Van Patten, George Wyner, Michael Winslow, Lorene Yarnell, John Hurt, Ronny Graham, Rhonda Shear; voices of Joan Rivers, Dom DeLuise. Likably silly parody of STAR WARS (years after the fact) is basically a collection of jokes, both verbal and visual. Enough of them are funny to make for pleasant, if not hilarious, fare. Surprisingly innocuous for Brooks and Co., with Mel tackling two roles, including the diminutive Yogurt. Followed by an animated series. Super 35. [PG] ▼●)

SpaceCamp (1986) **C-107m.** ** D: Harry Winer. Kate Capshaw, Lea Thompson, Kelly Preston, Larry B. Scott, Leaf (Joaquin) Phoenix, Tate Donovan, Tom Skerritt, Barry Primus, Terry O'Quinn, Or, BRATS IN SPACE, the story of some kids who wouldn't rate at McDonald's College of Hamburger Knowledge, but somehow get chosen to train at NASA summer camp— and accidentally get launched into space. There's a cute robot, but other special effects are way below par. [PG]▼●)

Space Chimps (2008) **C-81m.** *½ D: Kirk DeMicco. Voices of Andy Samberg, Cheryl Hines, Jeff Daniels, Kristin Chenoweth, Kenan Thompson, Jane Lynch, Stanley Tucci, Patrick Warburton, Zack Shada, Omid Abtahi. Lame, unfunny animated tale has freewheeling Ham III, grandson of the first chimp astronaut, sent into space along with two other dimwitted simians on a mission to eliminate the evil leader of another planet. Paint-by-numbers CGI animation is flat and the lifeless script is full of hoary gags. Followed by a DVD sequel. Digital Widescreen. [G]▌

Space Cowboys (2000) **C-129m.** **½ D: Clint Eastwood. Clint Eastwood, Tommy Lee Jones, Donald Sutherland, James Garner, Marcia Gay Harden, James Cromwell, Blair Brown, William Devane, Loren Dean, Courtney B. Vance, Rade Sherbedgia, Barbara Babcock, Jon Hamm. Amiable yarn about onetime hotshot Air Force pilots who are recruited by NASA—in desperation—to rescue a Russian satellite built with now-obsolete technology only they can comprehend. Barely believable but good-natured fun, especially for fans of the stars. Panavision. [PG-13]▼●)

Spaced Invaders (1990) **C-102m.** *½ D: Patrick Read Johnson. Douglas Barr, Royal Dano, Ariana Richards, J. J. Anderson, Gregg Berger, Kevin Thompson, Jimmy Briscoe. Martians, out to "kick some Earthling butt," fly into a Mayberry-type burg after mistaking a Halloween rebroadcast of Orson Welles' *War of the Worlds* for legitimate invasion orders. Have you ever noticed that Welles couldn't get financing for decades, but movies like this keep getting made? Criminally overlong. [PG]▼●)

Spacehunter: Adventures in the Forbidden Zone (1983-Canadian) **C-90m.** *½ D: Lamont Johnson. Peter Strauss, Molly Ringwald, Ernie Hudson, Andrea Marcovicci. Title character roams a planet's barren wasteland in order to rescue three damsels in distress, who are being held captive by a vicious mutant called Overdog. Boring and obnoxious, even in 3-D. Panavision. [PG]▼●)

Space Jam (1996) **C-87m.** *** D: Joe Pytka. Bugs Bunny, Michael Jordan, Wayne Knight, Theresa Randle, Larry Bird, Charles Barkley, Patrick Ewing, Muggsy Bogues, Larry Johnson, Patricia Heaton, Dan Castellaneta; voices of Danny DeVito, Billy West, Dee Bradley Baker, Bob Bergen, Bill Farmer, June Foray. A "high-concept" movie that actually works: basketball superstar Jordan is sucked into Looney Tune Land to help Bugs Bunny, Daffy Duck, Porky Pig and Co. square off against a group of space invaders in a do-or-die basketball game. Jordan is very engaging, the vintage characters perform admirably (although whoever "airbrushed" them had a heavy hand), and the computer-generated special effects are a collective knockout. Bill Murray appears unbilled, and many sports figures appear as themselves. [PG] ▼●)

Spaceman in King Arthur's Court, A SEE: **Unidentified Flying Oddball**
Space Mission of the Lost Planet SEE: **Vampire Men of the Lost Planet**
Space Rage (1985) **C-77m.** BOMB D: Conrad Palmisano. Richard Farnsworth, Michael Paré, John Laughlin, Lee Purcell, Lewis Van Bergen, William Windom. Meek space Western is set on a prison planet. Farnsworth is ex-cop who straps on his laser beam six-shooter to teach Paré and the

other outlaws a lesson; he should've turned the laser on this bomb instead! [R]▼

Space Raiders (1983) **C-82m.** ** D: Howard R. Cohen. Vince Edwards, David Mendenhall, Patsy Pease, Thom Christopher, Luca Bercovici, Dick Miller. This toothless adventure is another Roger Corman–produced space opera using special effects footage and music from BATTLE BEYOND THE STARS. Acceptable genre fare for the undemanding viewer. [PG]▼

Spaceship SEE: **Creature Wasn't Nice, The**
Space Travellers SEE: **Marooned**
Space Vampires SEE: **Astro-Zombies, The**

Spanglish (2004) **C-131m.** ** D: James L. Brooks. Adam Sandler, Téa Leoni, Paz Vega, Cloris Leachman, Shelbie Bruce, Sarah Steele, Ian Hyland, Thomas Haden Church. Strong-minded Mexican woman goes to work for a well-to-do L.A. family, causing reverberations within that dysfunctional clan—and changing the life of her impressionable young daughter. Sandler gives a mushy performance as the father/husband (a star chef, though we never get a sense of his mastery in the kitchen), while Leoni is stunningly strident as his wife. There are nuggets—a good scene here, a moment of sharp observation there—in writer-director Brooks' script, but mostly it's a mess. [PG-13] ▼▶

Spanish Prisoner, The (1998) **C-112m.** **½ D: David Mamet. Campbell Scott, Steve Martin, Rebecca Pidgeon, Ben Gazzara, Ricky Jay, Felicity Huffman, Ed O'Neill, J. J. Johnston. Naïve young man, who's developed a secret and highly valuable program for a high-tech company, is concerned that he won't be properly compensated and thus is easy prey for those who would steal the secret. *Too* easy, if you ask us, and that's the problem with this ice-cold but intriguing Mamet screenplay: we didn't buy it at crucial points in its serpentine story. Scott and Martin are excellent; leading lady Pidgeon is Mrs. Mamet. [PG] ▼▶●

Spanking the Monkey (1994) **C-106m.** **½ D: David O. Russell. Jeremy Davies, Alberta Watson, Benjamin Hendrickson, Carla Gallo, Matthew Puckett, Judette Jones. Just your average black comedy about masturbation and incest: Bright teenager is told by his traveling-salesman father that he must sacrifice a prestigious summer internship to stay home and tend to his bedridden mother. The intimacy of having to take care of her every need soon leads to unexpected behavior. Debuting writer-director Russell shows assuredness and maintains credibility throughout (thanks, too, to bull's-eye performances), but the tone of the film wavers uncomfortably from comedy to drama. A film festival sleeper and audience favorite. ▼▶●

Sparkle (1976) **C-100m.** **½ D: Sam O'Steen. Philip M. (Michael) Thomas, Irene Cara, Lonette McKee, Dwan Smith, Mary Alice, Dorian Harewood, Tony King. Rise of singing group not unlike The Supremes suffers from cliché overdose, but benefits from slick filmmaking, good musical numbers (by Curtis Mayfield), vivid performance by McKee. Worth comparing to later (and similar) Broadway musical *Dreamgirls.* [PG]▼▶

Spartacus (1960) **C-184m.** ***½ D: Stanley Kubrick. Kirk Douglas, Laurence Olivier, Jean Simmons, Tony Curtis, Charles Laughton, Peter Ustinov, John Gavin, Nina Foch, Herbert Lom, John Ireland, Charles McGraw, Woody Strode, Joanna Barnes. Epic-scale saga with Douglas as a rebellious slave who leads a crusade for freedom against the forces of the Roman Empire. Overlength (particularly in fully restored version released in 1991) and some dramatic weaknesses are offset by Alex North's magnificent score, staggering battle scenes, and the delicious performances of Olivier, Laughton, and especially Ustinov, who won a Best Supporting Actor Oscar for his scene-stealing work. Oscars also went to Art Direction, Costume Design, and Russell Metty's Cinematography. Screenplay by Dalton Trumbo from the Howard Fast novel. Cut for 1967 reissue. In restored print, Anthony Hopkins dubbed Olivier's voice for notorious bathing scene with Curtis. Remade for cable TV in 2004. Super Technirama 70.▼▶●

Spartan (2004) **C-107m.** ** D: David Mamet. Val Kilmer, Derek Luke, William H. Macy, Ed O'Neill, Kristen Bell, Saïd Taghmaoui, Linda Kimbrough, Tia Texada, Clark Gregg, J.J. Johnston, Natalia Nogulich, Matt Malloy, Alexandra Kerry. A military operations specialist accustomed to following orders finds himself in unfamiliar territory when he has to think for himself—and use his initiative—to rescue the kidnapped daughter of the President of the U.S. Writer-director Mamet gives us a leading character who's so off-putting, in a plot so convoluted, that when there's finally some tension and excitement toward the end it's too little, too late. David Paymer appears unbilled. Super 35. [R]▼▶

Spasms (1983-Canadian) **C-87m.** BOMB D: William Fruet. Peter Fonda, Oliver Reed, Kerrie Keane, Al Waxman, Marilyn Lightstone. Reed has a telepathic—or, should we say, telepathetic—connection with a deadly serpent. Grade Z junk; filmed in 1981. Aka DEATH BITE. [R]▼▶

Spawn (1997) **C-97m.** ** D: Mark A. Z. Dippé. John Leguizamo, Michael Jai White, Martin Sheen, Theresa Randle, D. B. Sweeney, Nicol Williamson, Melinda Clarke, Miko Hughes. Government assassin White is killed by evil boss Sheen and goes to Hell, where a demon endows him with great powers and returns him to Earth. Despite the efforts of infernal clown Leguizamo, he becomes a hero. Baroque visual style is film's major virtue, but that can't overcome the many faults, including a boring, familiar, and illogical plot. Love that cape, though. From Todd McFarlane's comic book. Director's cut, rated R, has over a minute of additional footage. [PG-13]▼●)

Speaking Parts (1989-Canadian) **C-92m.** *** D: Atom Egoyan. Michael McManus, Arsinée Khanjian, Gabrielle Rose, Tony Nardi, David Hemblen, Patricia Collins, Gerard Parkes. Fascinating account of laundry worker Khanjian and her fixation on aspiring actor McManus, who finds himself in an unusual relationship with screenwriter Rose. Sinuous story about three lost souls whose lives intersect, in person and on video. Very much of a piece with writer-director Egoyan's other work.▼●)

Special (2008) **C-81m.** **½ D: Hal Haberman, Jeremy Passmore. Michael Rapaport, Paul Blackthorne, Josh Peck, Robert Baker, Jack Kehler, Alexandra Holden, Ian Bohen, Christopher Darga. Shy social misfit signs up for a clinical drug-testing program and becomes convinced that the pill he's taking has given him super powers, just like his comic-book heroes. Slight, small-scale film has surprisingly good visual effects and stunt work, but its real strength is Rapaport's convincing performance in the lead. Written by the directors, making their feature-film debuts. Released in the U.K. in 2006. [R]▌

Special Agent (1935) **78m.** **½ D: William Keighley. Bette Davis, George Brent, Ricardo Cortez, Jack LaRue, Henry O'Neill. Programmer about Brent using Davis to get low-down on racketeer Cortez.

Special Day, A (1977-Italian-Canadian) **C-106m.** **½ D: Ettore Scola. Sophia Loren, Marcello Mastroianni, John Vernon, Françoise Berd, Nicole Magny. Two lonely people chance to meet on an eventful day in 1938; Loren is frumpy housewife, Mastroianni a troubled homosexual. Fine performances bolster this pleasant but trifling film.▼●)

Special Delivery (1976) **C-99m.** *** D: Paul Wendkos. Bo Svenson, Cybill Shepherd, Michael Gwynne, Tom Atkins, Sorrell Booke, Jeff Goldblum, Vic Tayback, Deidre Hall, Gerrit Graham. Diverting comedy-action caper has Vietnam vets led by Svenson robbing a bank. When only Svenson escapes, he has to contend with nutty artist Shepherd (who's quite good) and killers after he stuffs the loot into a mailbox. Aka DANGEROUS BREAK. [PG]▼

Special Effects (1984) **C-93m.** **½ D: Larry Cohen. Zoe Tamerlis, Eric Bogosian, Brad Rijn, Kevin O'Connor, Bill Oland. Intriguing but uneven tale of a down-on-his-luck director who films the murder of a young actress, and commences making a movie about his deed. He even finds someone to star in his epic who resembles his victim; both are played by Tamerlis. [R]▼●)

Specialist, The (1975) **C-93m.** ** D: Hikmet Avedis. Ahna Capri, John Anderson, Adam West, Alvy Moore, Christiane Schmidtmer, Marlene Schmidt. Campy exploitation film has Capri well cast as a zaftig female version of usual macho killer-for-hire. Writer-producer Schmidt (director Avedis' wife) plays West's wife. [R]▼▌

Specialist, The (1994) **C-109m.** ** D: Luis Llosa. Sylvester Stallone, Sharon Stone, James Woods, Rod Steiger, Eric Roberts, Mario Ernesto Sanchez. Explosives expert and freelance hit man Stallone, sullenly suffering angst over his CIA activities, is approached by Stone, who wants him to kill Roberts, the man who murdered her parents years earlier. But Stallone has been targeted by kinetic bad guy Woods and Cuban gangster Steiger, Roberts' father (who sounds like Ricky Ricardo and looks like Fred Mertz). Woods, in a funny, dynamic performance, breezily walks off with the movie. And he's welcome to it. Some good stunts and good work by Stone help keep it watchable. [R]▼●)

Specials, The (2000) **C-82m.** ** D: Craig Mazin. Rob Lowe, Jamie Kennedy, Thomas Haden Church, Paget Brewster, Judy Greer, Jordan Ladd, Sean Gunn, John Doe, Kelly Coffield, James Gunn, Barry Del Sherman, Melissa Joan Hart. A squad of L.A. superheroes loses morale when their lucrative action-figure deal goes awry. Wacko comic cheapie isn't just a MYSTERY MEN retread, but never quite comes together despite game cast and flashes of wit. Funniest character is Minute Man; nobody gets his name right even though his superpower is that he can shrink. [R]▼▌

Special Section (1975-French) **C-110m.** ** D: Costa-Gavras. Louis Seigner, Michel Lonsdale, Jacques Perrin, Bruno Cremer, Pierre Dux, Henri Serre. Overlong, excessively wordy drama of true happening in occupied Paris in 1941. Four expendables are tried and ceremonially condemned for the murder of a young German naval cadet. Some interest. [PG]

Special Treatment (1980-Yugoslavian) **C-94m.** *** D: Goran Paskaljevic. Ljuba Tadic, Dusica Zegarac, Danilo Stojkovic, Milena Dravic, Petar Kralj. Fanatical doctor Tadic brings a group of alcoholics he's been treating to a brewery to show off his skills as a healer; of course, his charges don't remain sober for long. Strange, deadpan comedy is occasionally slow but mostly funny.

Species (1995) **C-111m.** **½ D: Roger Donaldson. Ben Kingsley, Michael Madsen, Forest Whitaker, Natasha Henstridge, Alfred Molina, Marg Helgenberger, Whip Hubley, Michelle Williams, Jordan Lund. DNA-tampering scientists at a Utah facility ultimately get theirs after creating a murderous creature, complete with tentacles, who's packaged like a blond centerfold. Fast and not without entertainment value, but don't look at yourself in the mirror too closely if you end up defending it. Direction is somewhat sturdier than the script, which has its share of (we think) unintentional howlers. Followed by three sequels; the latter two are direct-to-video. Panavision. [R]▼O**)**

Species II (1998) **C-95m.** BOMB D: Peter Medak. Natasha Henstridge, Michael Madsen, Marg Helgenberger, Mykelti Williamson, Justin Lazard, James Cromwell, George Dzundza, Richard Belzer. The first man on Mars gets infested with alien DNA, and begins raping women who immediately, and fatally, give birth. Elsewhere, scientists have re-created the half-alien woman from the first film, hoping she'll be nice this time. Compared to this clunker, the first looks like a collaboration between Arthur C. Clarke and Ray Bradbury. Peter Boyle appears unbilled. [R]▼O**)**

Speechless (1994) **C-98m.** **½ D: Ron Underwood. Michael Keaton, Geena Davis, Christopher Reeve, Bonnie Bedelia, Ernie Hudson, Charles Martin Smith, Gailard Sartain, Ray Baker, Mitchell Ryan, Harry Shearer, Steven Wright. Keaton and Davis fall in love, unaware that they work as speechwriters for opposing political candidates in a tough New Mexico senate race. Cheerful contemporary comedy, with amusing digs at politics and the news media. How well you tolerate the ups and downs of the script and its protracted climax will depend on your fondness for the two stars. [PG-13]▼O**)**

Speed (1994) **C-116m.** ***½ D: Jan De Bont. Keanu Reeves, Dennis Hopper, Sandra Bullock, Jeff Daniels, Joe Morton, Alan Ruck, Glenn Plummer, Richard Lineback. Incredibly kinetic, supercharged action yarn about an elite SWAT-team cop (Reeves) who's targeted by a psycho/mastermind (Hopper), and led onto an L.A. city bus that's triggered to explode. If you're going to make a nonstop action movie, this is the way to do it—with expert pacing, eye-popping stunts and special effects, and characters who make sense. A bull's-eye! Oscar winner for Best Sound and Sound Effects Editing. Followed by a sequel. Panavision. [R]▼O**)**

Speed 2: Cruise Control (1997) **C-121m.** BOMB D: Jan De Bont. Sandra Bullock, Jason Patric, Willem Dafoe, Temuera Morrison, Brian McCardie, Christine Firkins, Colleen Camp, Lois Chiles, Jeremy Hotz, Bo Svenson, Glenn Plummer, Tim Conway. Mind-numbingly stupid action yarn opens with a chase scene that makes no sense, and never improves. Bullock (whose character here is especially annoying) agrees to go on a Caribbean cruise with boyfriend Patric, an L.A.P.D. officer. When madman Dafoe takes control of the ship, Patric feels it's his duty to try and stop him. Did anyone read the script before signing on for this one? Panavision. [PG-13]▼O**)**

Speed Racer (2008) **C-129m.** ** D: The Wachowski Brothers. Emile Hirsch, Christina Ricci, Susan Sarandon, John Goodman, Matthew Fox, Roger Allam, Paulie Litt, Benno Fürmann, Hiroyuki Sanada, Rain, Richard Roundtree, Kick Gurry. Driving fast cars is all Speed Racer (Hirsch) cares about—even after a crash takes his older brother's life. A ruthless corporate giant wants to sponsor him, but his heart is still with his Pop's independent racing team. High-octane, CGI-crazy update of Tatsuo Yoshida's 1960s TV series but a thimbleful of story but takes more than two hours to tell! Racing scenes are video games writ large, so unreal there's no emotion attached to them. HD Widescreen. [PG]**)**

Speedtrap (1977) **C-98m.** ** D: Earl Bellamy. Joe Don Baker, Tyne Daly, Richard Jaeckel, Robert Loggia, Morgan Woodward, Timothy Carey. Private eye Baker is called in by the cops to trap an elusive car thief, and teamed with policewoman Daly. Good cast and predictable screeching tires can't save muddled script. [PG]▼

Speedway (1968) **C-94m.** ** D: Norman Taurog. Elvis Presley, Nancy Sinatra, Bill Bixby, Gale Gordon. Routine Presley tuner with Elvis starring as a bighearted stockcar racer and Sinatra along for the ride as a tax inspector. Richard Petty, Cale Yarborough and other real-life auto racers are featured. Panavision.▼O**)**

Speed Zone! (1989) **C-95m.** *½ D: Jim Drake. Peter Boyle, Donna Dixon, John Candy, Eugene Levy, Tim Matheson, The Smothers Brothers, Matt Frewer, Joe Flaherty, Shari Belafonte, Art Hindle, John Schneider, Jamie Farr, Lee Van Cleef, Michael Spinks, Brooke Shields, Alyssa Milano, Carl Lewis. Yet another variation on the CANNONBALL RUN cross-country road race, with Boyle as a sheriff who's determined to stop the race before it begins. Pointless, derivative, and unfunny, a particular waste of such talents as Candy, Levy, and Flaherty. You know you're in trouble when Brooke Shields gives the funniest performance in the film! [PG]▼O**)**

Spellbinder (1988) **C-99m.** ** D: Janet Greek. Timothy Daly, Kelly Preston, Rick Rossovich, Diana Bellamy, Audra Lindley, Cary-Hiroyuki Tagawa, Anthony Crivello, Roderick Cook, Stefan Gierasch. L.A. lawyer falls for a mysterious beauty, slowly learns she's a witch, a member of a coven that wants her back as a sacrifice. A whybother? occult thriller: slick, empty, and extremely predictable. [R]▼

Spellbound (1945) **111m.** ***½ D: Alfred Hitchcock. Ingrid Bergman, Gregory Peck, Leo G. Carroll, John Emery, Michael Chekhov, Wallace Ford, Rhonda Fleming, Bill Goodwin, Regis Toomey. Absorbing tale of psychiatrist Bergman trying to uncover Peck's hangups; Dali dream sequences, innovative (and Oscar-winning) Miklos Rozsa score help Hitchcock create another unique film. Based on novel *The House of Dr. Edwardes* by Francis Beeding; screenplay by Ben Hecht. In original theatrical prints, a key gunshot was shown in color.▼●▶

Spellbound (2003) **C-97m.** ***½ D: Jeffrey Blitz. Terrific documentary that follows eight very different young contestants who participate in the 1999 National Spelling Bee. An enormously entertaining and often pointed examination of ideas about success and the American dream, with the final spelling duel as riveting as anything to be found in a fiction film. [G] ▼▶

Spencer's Mountain (1963) **C-119m.** ** D: Delmer Daves. Henry Fonda, Maureen O'Hara, James MacArthur, Donald Crisp, Wally Cox, Veronica Cartwright, Victor French. Mawkish sudser about Wyoming landowner Fonda who keeps promising to build another family house. Good cast stuck with inferior script. Based on the Earl Hamner, Jr. novel; later developed into *The Waltons.* Panavision.▼●▶

Spent (2000) **C-91m.** ** D: Gil Cates, Jr. Jason London, Charlie Spradling, Phill Lewis, Erin Beaux, James Parks, Richmond Arquette, Barbara Barrie, Gilbert Cates, Rain Phoenix, Margaret Cho. Ambitious but unconvincing portrait of addiction, deception, and denial, centering on a hopeless young movie industry wannabe whose chronic gambling is getting out of hand. He's surrounded by troubled souls, including a roommate (Parks) who refuses to acknowledge his sexual preference and a girlfriend (Spradling) who's an alcoholic. Aka $PENT. ▼▶

Spetters (1980-Dutch) **C-115m.** *** D: Paul Verhoeven. Hans van Tongeren, Toon Agterberg, Renee Soutendijk, Maarten Spanjer, Marianne Boyer, Rutger Hauer. Adolescent shenanigans and dreams in Holland; teenagers sleep around and race their motorcycles while idolizing race champ Hauer. Graphically sexual, with crisp direction by Verhoeven; luscious Soutendijk scores as an ambitious hash-slinger. [R] ▼●▶

Sphere (1998) **C-133m.** *½ D: Barry Levinson. Dustin Hoffman, Sharon Stone, Samuel L. Jackson, Peter Coyote, Liev Schreiber, Queen Latifah. Failed sci-fi saga (from Michael Crichton novel) about a group of scientists from different disciplines who are brought to a super-secret underwater site where the U.S. Navy has discovered a mysterious wreckage. What does it signify? Where did it come from and when? Intriguing set-up leads nowhere, with increasingly stupid behavior from the principals and ridiculous chapter headings that lend supposed import to each new sequence. A bust. Super 35. [PG-13]▼●▶

Sphinx (1981) **C-117m.** *½ D: Franklin J. Schaffner. Lesley-Anne Down, Frank Langella, Maurice Ronet, John Gielgud, Martin Benson, John Rhys-Davies. Harried Egyptologist Down continuously eludes death as she searches for a mystery tomb. Awful script, mummylike performances, impressive Egyptian scenery. Adapted by John Byrum from Robin Cook novel. Panavision. [PG] ▼▶

Spice World (1997-British) **C-92m.** **½ D: Bob Spiers. The Spice Girls (Mel B, Emma, Mel C, Geri, Victoria), Richard E. Grant, Alan Cumming, Roger Moore, George Wendt, Claire Rushbrook, Mark McKinney, Richard O'Brien, Barry Humphries, Jason Flemyng, Naoki Mori, Meat Loaf, Bill Paterson, Jools Holland, Stephen Fry, Richard Briers, Hugh Laurie. A fantasy look at several days in the lives of the pop phenomenon The Spice Girls and their existence with road manager Grant, leading up to a concert at Albert Hall in London. Amusing, vapid, sometimes silly but lively vignettes featuring the five flashy females who took the pop world by storm in the late '90s. Cameos by Elton John, Bob Hoskins, Bob Geldof, Elvis Costello, The Dream Boys, Jonathan Ross, and Jennifer Saunders. [PG]▼●▶

Spider, The (1958) SEE: **Earth vs the Spider**

Spider (2002-Canadian-British) **C-90m.** ** D: David Cronenberg. Ralph Fiennes, Miranda Richardson, Gabriel Byrne, Bradley Hall, Lynn Redgrave, John Neville, Gary Reineke. Intriguing but relentlessly downbeat film about a seriously disturbed man paralyzed by memories of his childhood with an abusive father and a hardworking, well-meaning mother. We discover the source of his misery through flashbacks, but as the pieces come together they're not terribly surprising. Richardson's artful handling of multiple roles is the film's major asset, and Fiennes is good as usual. Scripted by Patrick McGrath, from his novel. [R]▼▶

Spider-Man (2002) **C-121m.** **½ D: Sam Raimi. Tobey Maguire, Willem Dafoe, Kirsten Dunst, James Franco, Cliff Robertson, Rosemary Harris, J. K. Simmons, Gerry Becker, Bill Nunn. Big-budget Hollywood version of a Saturday matinee serial: High school nerd who's never had the nerve to speak to the beautiful girl next door is bitten by a spider and mutates into Spider-Man, crime fighter. Slick entertainment, with Maguire a likable Peter Parker, but the cartoony effects distance (rather than involve) us in his springy moments of action, and the story runs out of gas long before two hours are up. Lucy Lawless, Randy Savage, Bruce Campbell, and Stan Lee make brief appearances. Based on characters created for Marvel Comics by Lee and Steve Ditko. Followed by two sequels. [PG-13] ▼▶

Spider-Man 2 (2004) **C-127m.** ***½ D: Sam Raimi. Tobey Maguire, Kirsten Dunst, James Franco, Alfred Molina, Rosemary Harris, J. K. Simmons, Donna Murphy, Daniel Gillies, Dylan Baker, Bill Nunn, Willem Dafoe, Cliff Robertson, Bruce Campbell. A brilliant scientist (the always masterful Molina) loses control of his latest experiment, turns into the maniacal Dr. Octopus (or Doc Ock)—and blames Spider-Man for his tragic failure. Possibly the best comic-book movie ever made, rich in emotion as well as big, exciting action sequences. What's more, its visual effects are far superior to those in the first SPIDER-MAN movie. Screenplay by Alvin Sargent, based on screen story by Alfred Gough, Miles Millar, and Michael Chabon. Oscar winner for Visual Effects. Alternate version runs 136m. Super 35. [PG-13] ▼❶

Spider-Man 3 (2007) **C-139m.** ** D: Sam Raimi. Tobey Maguire, Kirsten Dunst, James Franco, Thomas Haden Church, Topher Grace, Bryce Dallas Howard, Rosemary Harris, J. K. Simmons, James Cromwell, Theresa Russell, Dylan Baker, Bill Nunn, Bruce Campbell, Elizabeth Banks, Ted Raimi, Willem Dafoe, Cliff Robertson. All the worst qualities of a manufactured sequel converge here: dorky Peter Parker's relationship with Mary Jane goes on the rocks (so it can be fixed), villainous Harry Osborn turns good while Spider-Man, infected by an alien fungus, turns bad, an escaped convict is molecularly transformed into Sandman (to provide another menace), and Peter acquires a ruthless rival at the *Daily Bugle* (for even more villainy). Slickly made but often boring and ineffectual, leading up to a climax where—surprise!—Spidey cries real tears. Special effects can't save an inferior script. Super 35. [PG-13]❶

Spider's Stratagem, The (1970-Italian) **C-100m.** *** D: Bernardo Bertolucci. Giulio Brogi, Alida Valli, Tino Scotti, Pippo Campanini, Franco Giovanelli. Young man visits the provincial town where his anti-Fascist father was assassinated 30 years earlier, is rejected by the populace at every turn. Exceedingly atmospheric puzzler, from a Jorge Luis Borges short story, boasts some of the most beautiful color cinematography (by Vittorio Storaro) in memory.▼

Spiderwick Chronicles, The (2008) **C-97m.** *** D: Mark Waters. Freddie Highmore, Mary-Louise Parker, Nick Nolte, Sarah Bolger, Andrew McCarthy, Joan Plowright, David Strathairn; voices of Seth Rogen, Martin Short. Newly divorced woman and her three kids move to a spooky old family mansion where ghostly spirits prevail. Then Jared, the most sensitive of the kids (Highmore), unearths a long-hidden book, a "field guide" compiled by their great-great-uncle Arthur Spiderwick,

which contains the secrets of the fairies and goblins that surround them—and places the entire family in great peril. Highly imaginative, emotionally satisfying fantasy-adventure adapted from Tony DiTerlizzi and Holly Black's books. The special effects are impressive but always in the service of the story. Super 35. [PG]❶

Spider Woman, The (1944) **62m.** *** D: Roy William Neill. Basil Rathbone, Nigel Bruce, Gale Sondergaard, Dennis Hoey, Mary Gordon, Arthur Hohl, Alec Craig. A mysterious villainess is responsible for a series of deaths in which the victims are driven to suicide after being bit by poisonous spiders. Rip-roaring entry with thrills to spare; one of the best in the Sherlock Holmes series.▼❶

Spies Like Us (1985) **C-109m.** *** D: John Landis. Chevy Chase, Dan Aykroyd, Steve Forrest, Donna Dixon, Bruce Davison, William Prince, Bernie Casey, Tom Hatten, Matt Frewer. Chase and Aykroyd become government spies—never dreaming that they've been set up as decoys. Engagingly silly comedy patterned after the Hope-Crosby ROAD pictures, with at least one pertinent cameo appearance and minor roles filled by a number of film directors (Michael Apted, Constantin Costa-Gavras, Joel Coen, Sam Raimi, Martin Brest, Bob Swaim, Terry Gilliam, Ray Harryhausen). Written by Aykroyd, Lowell Ganz, and Babaloo Mandel, from a story by Aykroyd and Dave Thomas. [PG]▼●❶

Spike of Bensonhurst (1988) **C-91m.** ** D: Paul Morrissey. Sasha Mitchell, Ernest Borgnine, Anne DeSalvo, Sylvia Miles, Geraldine Smith, Maria Patillo, Talisa Soto. Blah Mafia comedy with Mitchell as an ambitious Brooklyn street kid who dreams of becoming a boxing champ—and finds himself in trouble when he courts the daughter of the local mob boss (Borgnine). Ethnic stereotypes abound. [R]▼●

Spikes Gang, The (1974) **C-96m.** *½ D: Richard Fleischer. Lee Marvin, Ron Howard, Charlie Martin Smith, Arthur Hunnicutt, Noah Beery, Gary Grimes. Veteran gunfighter turns a trio of runaway boys into bank robbers; old-hat storyline has humor, but not much else. [PG]❶

Spinal Tap SEE: **This Is Spinal Tap**

Spinning Into Butter (2009) **C-86m.** ** D: Mark Brokaw. Sarah Jessica Parker, Mykelti Williamson, Beau Bridges, Miranda Richardson, James Rebhorn, Victor Rasuk, Paul James, Peter Friedman, Becky Ann Baker, Richard Riehle, Enver Gjokaj. African-American student (James), newly enrolled at a small New England university famous for its liberalism, is harassed by a shadowy racist, and a dean (Parker) finds herself in the eye of the ensuing storm. Well-intentioned film means to examine race relations, politics, and bureaucracy within the walls of academia, but the result is flat and deeply flawed. [R] ▮

Spinout (1966) **C-90m.** **½ D: Norman Taurog. Elvis Presley, Shelley Fabares, Diane McBain, Deborah Walley, Cecil Kellaway, Una Merkel, Warren Berlinger, Carl Betz. Typical Presley vehicle finds the singer racing autos and wooing the girls. Elvis' songs ("Beach Shack," "Adam and Evil," "Smorgasbord") are far from his best. Panavision. ▼●▮

Spiral Road, The (1962) **C-145m.** *½ D: Robert Mulligan. Rock Hudson, Burl Ives, Gena Rowlands, Geoffrey Keen, Will Kuluva, Neva Patterson. Jan de Hartog's novel about love, leprosy, and lunacy in Java makes for an interminable moviegoing experience. Hudson at his most wooden, Mulligan's direction at its most impersonal. ▮

Spiral Staircase, The (1946) **83m.** ***½ D: Robert Siodmak. Dorothy McGuire, George Brent, Ethel Barrymore, Kent Smith, Rhonda Fleming, Gordon Oliver, Elsa Lanchester, Rhys Williams, Sara Allgood. Superb Hitchcock-like thriller with unforgettable performance by McGuire as mute servant in eerie household which may be harboring a killer. Well scripted by Mel Dinelli, adapting Ethel Lina White's novel *Some Must Watch.* Remade in 1975. ▼●▮

Spiral Staircase, The (1975-British) **C-89m.** ** D: Peter Collinson. Jacqueline Bisset, Christopher Plummer, Sam Wanamaker, Mildred Dunnock, Gayle Hunnicutt, John Phillip Law, Elaine Stritch. Stellar cast gives Ethel Lina White's mystery novel *Some Must Watch* another go in a somewhat mechanical fashion that can't touch the 1946 version. ▼

Spirit, The (2008) **C-108m.** *½ D: Frank Miller. Gabriel Macht, Eva Mendes, Scarlett Johansson, Samuel L. Jackson, Sarah Paulson, Dan Lauria, Paz Vega, Eric Balfour, Jaime King, Louis Lombardi. Graphic novelist Miller's first solo foray into directing (after collaborating on SIN CITY) is an awkward, annoyingly illogical live-action adaptation of Will Eisner's celebrated comic strip about a deceased cop who returns to life as a masked vigilante. The storyline is a mishmash, the direction is clunky, and you may well cringe at the sight of Jackson (as The Octopus, the Spirit's arch-nemesis) decked out in Nazi regalia. Miller and Eisner fans will be sorely disappointed. Miller also scripted. HD Widescreen. [PG-13] ▮

Spirited Away (2001-Japanese) **C-125m.** ***½ D: Hayao Miyazaki. Voices of Daveigh Chase, Jason Marsden, Suzanne Pleshette, Michael Chiklis, Lauren Holly, John Ratzenberger, Tara Strong. While moving to a new home in the suburbs, a sullen, easily frightened 10-year-old and her parents discover a hillside tunnel that leads into an enchanted world. Japanese animation maestro Miyazaki's abiding interest in the supernatural and the inner lives of children (especially little girls) is in full flower here. A wondrous work of art with an astonishing array of gorgeous images and fantastically imagined creatures, this won an Oscar for Best Animated Film. The English dubbing, produced by TOY STORY director John Lasseter, is outstanding. [PG] ▼▮

Spirit Is Willing, The (1967) **C-100m.** *½ D: William Castle. Sid Caesar, Vera Miles, Barry Gordon, John McGiver, Cass Daley, Mary Wickes, Jesse White, Harvey Lembeck, Jay C. Flippen, Jill Townsend, John Astin, Doodles Weaver. Some good comedy performers are thrown away in stupid comedy about Caesar and family's summer house that happens to be haunted; based on Nathaniel Benchley's *The Visitors.*

Spirit of 76, The (1991) **C-82m.** *½ D: Lucas Reiner. David Cassidy, Olivia d'Abo, Geoff Hoyle, Leif Garrett, Jeff McDonald, Steve McDonald, Barbara Bain, Julie Brown, Tommy Chong, Iron Eyes Cody, Devo, Carl Reiner, Rob Reiner, Moon Zappa. Three time-travelers from 2176 trying to find the true basis of America think they've arrived in 1776, but it's really 1976. Limp spoof of the 1970s simply catalogues the fads, styles, and fashions. Director and cowriter Reiner is Carl's son, Rob's brother. Sofia Coppola did the costumes. [PG-13] ▼▮

Spirit of St. Louis, The (1957) **C-138m.** *** D: Billy Wilder. James Stewart, Patricia Smith, Murray Hamilton, Marc Connelly. Long but inventive presentation of Lindbergh's flight across the Atlantic is mainly a tour de force by Stewart, backed by good Franz Waxman music score. CinemaScope. ▼●▮

Spirit of the Beehive (1973-Spanish) **C-95m.** ***½ D: Victor Erice. Fernando Fernan Gomez, Teresa Gimpera, Ana Torrent, Isabel Telleria. Torrent is unforgettable as a lonely little village girl who sees Boris Karloff's FRANKENSTEIN in the town hall and becomes entranced by the monster. Her sister convinces her the monster is still alive, and she treks off into the countryside to find him. Delicate and haunting, a masterful piece of filmmaking. ▼▮

Spirit of the Dead SEE: **Asphyx, The**

Spirits of the Dead (1968-French-Italian) **C-117m.** ***½ D: Roger Vadim, Louis Malle, Federico Fellini. Brigitte Bardot, Alain Delon, Jane Fonda, Terence Stamp, Peter Fonda, James Robertson Justice. Narrated by Vincent Price. Three separate Poe tales, impossible to describe, delightful to watch, done with skill and flair by three top directors. [R] ▼●▮

Spirit: Stallion of the Cimarron (2002) **C-83m.** *** D: Kelly Asbury, Lorna Cook. Voices of Matt Damon, James Cromwell, Daniel Studi. Autobiography of a wild horse who loves running free through the vast expanse of the West, until he's captured and brought to a U.S. cavalry fort. There he meets his one human friend, a Lakota Indian. Beautifully designed, with superior animation (the horse characters all express themselves in pantomime) and many exciting moments; fine, vigorous family fare. Songs by Bryan Adams. Digital widescreen. [G] ▼●

Spitfire (1934) 88m. ** D: John Cromwell. Katharine Hepburn, Robert Young, Ralph Bellamy, Martha Sleeper, Sara Haden, Sidney Toler, High Ghere (Bob Burns). Bizarre, boring melodrama with Hepburn sorely miscast in one of her oddest roles: Trigger, a spirited, single-minded but superstition-laden Ozark tomboy who attracts married engineer Young. This one's only for the curious. ▼▶

Spitfire (1942-British) 117m. *** D: Leslie Howard. Leslie Howard, David Niven, Rosamund John, Roland Culver, Anne Firth, David Horne, J. H. Roberts, Derrick de Marney, Bernard Miles, Patricia Medina. Howard plays R.J. Mitchell, who developed the ace fighting-plane Spitfire which later became one of the Allies' most valuable WW2 assets. Good biographical drama. Howard's last screen appearance. Original title: THE FIRST OF THE FEW. U.S. version cut to 90m. ▼▶

Spitfire Grill, The (1996) C-116m. **½ D: Lee David Zlotoff. Alison Elliott, Ellen Burstyn, Marcia Gay Harden, Will Patton, Kieran Mulroney, Gailard Sartain. Ex-convict Elliott arrives in the small, gossip-driven town of Gilead, Maine, and goes to work for Burstyn at the title-named restaurant, hoping to rebuild her life. Sincere, well-acted story goes awry toward the end with contrivance and melodrama; still, Elliott and Burstyn give memorable performances. Written by the director. Later an off-Broadway musical. [PG-13] ▼●▶

Splash (1984) C-111m. *** D: Ron Howard. Daryl Hannah, Tom Hanks, John Candy, Eugene Levy, Dody Goodman, Richard B. Shull, Shecky Greene, Howard Morris. Entertaining comedy about a man who falls in love with a mermaid, who's played to perfection by Hannah. Buoyant cast, winning gags make this a lot of fun, despite a tendency toward overlength. Script by Lowell Ganz, Babaloo Mandel, and Bruce Jay Friedman. Followed by a TV movie sequel in 1988. [PG] ▼●

Splendor (1999) C-93m. **½ D: Gregg Araki. Kathleen Robertson, Johnathon Schaech, Matt Keeslar, Kelly Macdonald, Eric Mabius. Amusing modern-day romantic comedy with a twist: a willing heroine can't decide between two handsome guys she meets the same evening, so she winds up living with both of them. After such a spiky start, it's too bad it winds up being

so conventional . . . but the spirits are high and the cast is engaging. Almost benign for filmmaker Araki. [R] ▼▶

Splendor in the Grass (1961) C-124m. *** D: Elia Kazan. Natalie Wood, Warren Beatty, Pat Hingle, Audrey Christie, Sean Garrison, Sandy Dennis, Phyllis Diller, Barbara Loden, Zohra Lampert, Gary Lockwood. Sentimental sudser by William Inge (who won an Oscar) about emotionally broken girl (Wood) rebuilding her life; set in late 1920s Midwest. Film debuts of Beatty, Dennis, and Diller; look for Inge as the minister. Remade for TV in 1981. ▼●

Splice (2010-U.S.-Canadian-French) C-104m. **½ D: Vincenzo Natali. Adrien Brody, Sarah Polley, Delphine Chanéac, Brandon McGibbon, Simona Maicanescu, David Hewlett, Abigail Chu. Two dynamic young scientists who create small, drug-producing artificial life forms for a pharmaceutical company are rejected in their bid to create one using human genes. They work secretly and create a semi-human, rapidly developing infant they name "Dren." Continuing their research in a private location, they are entranced and repelled by what Dren is becoming—and she is entranced by them. Intelligently written and well acted, this begins well but becomes too much a standard horror film in the last couple of reels. Excellent effects. [R] ▶

Split, The (1968) C-91m. *½ D: Gordon Flemyng. Jim Brown, Diahann Carroll, Julie Harris, Ernest Borgnine, Gene Hackman, Jack Klugman, Warren Oates, James Whitmore, Donald Sutherland. Cast is good, but it's no match for routine, clichéd story of plot to rob L.A. Coliseum during a Rams game. Only for those who love caper movies. Panavision. [R]

Split Decisions (1988) C-95m. ** D: David Drury. Gene Hackman, Craig Sheffer, Jeff Fahey, Jennifer Beals, John McLiam, Eddie Velez, Carmine Caridi, James Tolkan. Violent family drama set amidst the world of boxing and three generations of prizefighters. Basically just another ROCKY ripoff, but Hackman, in a supporting role, stands out as usual. [R] ▼●▶

Split Image (1982) C-111m. *** D: Ted Kotcheff. Michael O'Keefe, Karen Allen, Peter Fonda, James Woods, Elizabeth Ashley, Brian Dennehy, Ronnie Scribner, Pamela Ludwig, Michael Sacks, Peter Horton. Solid drama of nice middle-class boy (superbly played by O'Keefe) who falls for Allen and is brainwashed into joining a cult headed by Fonda. Top performances by Dennehy as O'Keefe's father, Woods as a deprogrammer. Panavision. [R] ▼

Split Second (1992-U.S.-British) C-90m. *½ D: Tony Maylam. Rutger Hauer, Kim Cattrall, Neil Duncan, Alun Armstrong, Pete Postlethwaite, Ian Drury, Robert

Eaton, Michael J. Pollard. In London's near future, tough cop Hauer is after the serial killer who murdered his partner and is saddled with new partner Duncan. The murderer is an ALIEN-like monster, the plot mushes together fantasy and sci-fi elements, and the movie is a derivative, tedious mess. Won't someone rescue Hauer from this kind of junk? [R]▼●〗

Splitting Heirs (1993-U.S.-British) **C-86m.** ** D: Robert Young. Rick Moranis, Eric Idle, Barbara Hershey, Catherine Zeta Jones, John Cleese, Sadie Frost, Stratford Johns. A loser (Idle) learns he's really a duke and tries to reclaim his title from the bogus heir (Moranis). Strained comedy in the Monty Python tradition, filled with puns, sight gags, and silliness—only some of which is funny. Idle executive produced and coscripted. [PG-13]▼●〗

Spoiled Children (1977-French) **C-113m.** *** D: Bertrand Tavernier. Michel Piccoli, Christine Pascal, Michel Aumont, Gerard Jugnot, Arlette Bonnard, Georges Riquier, Gerard Zimmerman. Enticing, penetrating tale which examines, among other issues, the particular problems faced by artists— in this case, a famous but blocked writer-director (Piccoli) who becomes involved with a younger woman (Pascal) and in a tenants' battle with his apartment building's abusive landlord. Fine performances. The semi-autobiographical script was penned by Tavernier with Pascal and Charlotte Dubreuil. ▼

Spoilers, The (1942) **87m.** **½ D: Ray Enright. Marlene Dietrich, Randolph Scott, John Wayne, Margaret Lindsay, Harry Carey, Richard Barthelmess. Retelling of famous Yukon tale has good cast but thuds out as average Western, with Dietrich as stereotyped saloon gal. Previously filmed in 1914, 1923, and 1930, then again in 1955.▼●〗

Spoilers, The (1955) **C-84m.** **½ D: Jesse Hibbs. Anne Baxter, Jeff Chandler, Rory Calhoun, Barbara Britton, Raymond Walburn. Fifth filming of Rex Beach's Klondike actioner; elaborate fight scene, better than ever.

Spoken Word (2010) **C-116m.** **½ D: Victor Nuñez. Kuno Becker, Rubén Blades, Miguel Sandoval, Persia White, Antonio Elias, Monique Gabriela Curnen, Maurice Compte. A star (Becker) of the West Coast spoken word/slam poetry scene returns to his hometown in New Mexico to be with his dying father (Blades), but falls back into his old self-destructive life of drugs and crime. Earnest, well-acted family drama from veteran indie filmmaker Nuñez suffers from a predictable script and a plodding pace. 〗

SpongeBob SquarePants Movie, The (2004) **C-87m.** *** D: Stephen Hillenburg. Voices of Tom Kenny, Bill Fagerbakke, Clancy Brown, Rodger Bumpass, Mr. Law-rence, Alec Baldwin, Scarlett Johansson, Jeffrey Tambor. Popular (and absorbent) TV cartoon character hits the big screen as he and starfish pal Patrick search for King Neptune's crown, which has been stolen by the nefarious Plankton as part of his diabolical Plan Z. The animation may just be serviceable, but the story and overall mood are unapologetically contagiously goofy, and filled with moments of inspired silliness. Stay through the end credits. David Hasselhoff appears (naturally) as himself. [PG] ▼〗

Spontaneous Combustion (1990) **C-97m.** *½ D: Tobe Hooper. Brad Dourif, Cynthia Bain, Jon Cypher, William Prince, Dey Young, Melinda Dillon, Dale Dye, Dick Butkus, John Landis. Paranoia fuels this misfired horror thriller dealing with spontaneous human combustion, allegedly a reality. Here, however, the blazing deaths are due to the FIRESTARTER-like mental powers of Dourif, the result of yet another evil government experiment. Badly paced and ludicrous. Cowritten by the director. [R]▼●〗

Spook Who Sat By the Door, The (1973) **C-102m.** *½ D: Ivan Dixon. Lawrence Cook, Paula Kelly, Janet League, J. A. Preston, Paul Butler. Cook, token black in the CIA, uses his knowledge to organize bands of teenaged guerrillas to bring whitey to his knees. Offbeat but offensive, and way too talky for cheap action fare. [PG]▼〗

Spot SEE: **Dogpound Shuffle**

Spread (2009) **C-97m.** **½ D: David Mackenzie. Ashton Kutcher, Anne Heche, Margarita Levieva, Sebastian Stan, Rachel Blanchard, Eric Balfour, Hart Bochner, Sonia Rockwell, Maria Conchita Alonso. SHAMPOO wannabe with Kutcher as a street-smart gigolo who moves in on his willing new prey (Heche), a successful older woman who knows the score and keeps him anyway. While Kutcher carries on behind her back, he finds the life of a kept man may not be all it's cracked up to be. Entertaining, if sleazy, comedy-drama with a Hollywood setting benefits from good performances by Kutcher and especially Heche. [R]〗

Spring and Port Wine (1970-British) **C-101m.** *** D: Peter Hammond. James Mason, Susan George, Diana Coupland, Marjorie Rhodes, Arthur Lowe. Unpretentious little gem about the generation gap in a lower-middle-class English family. Mason has one of his better later roles as the strict patriarch.

Spring Break (1983) **C-101m.** BOMB D: Sean S. Cunningham. David Knell, Steve Bassett, Perry Lang, Paul Land, Richard B. Shull, Corinne Alphen. Life among the party-animals who trek to Fort Lauderdale during Easter vacation. Where are Frankie and Annette when you really need them? [R]▼●〗

Spring Forward (2000) **C-110m.** ***½ D:

Tom Gilroy. Ned Beatty, Liev Schreiber, Campbell Scott, Ian Hart, Peri Gilpin, Bill Raymond, Catherine Kellner, Hallee Hirsh. Quietly powerful chamber piece about a Connecticut parks maintenance man and his new helper, a young hothead just out of prison. Perceptive drama in which each vignette reveals another layer of the characters' personalities as their friendship deepens from one season to the next. Beatty and Schreiber are simply great. Feature-film writing and directing debut for actor/playwright/theater director Gilroy. [R]▼▶

Spring Parade (1940) **89m.** *** D: Henry Koster. Deanna Durbin, Robert Cummings, Mischa Auer, Henry Stephenson, Butch and Buddy, Anne Gwynne. Delightful Austrian fluff with Durbin romancing Cummings, working for baker S. Z. Sakall, dancing with wacky Auer, and singing, of course.▶

Spring, Summer, Fall, Winter . . . and Spring (2003-Korean-German) **C-103m.** ***½ D: Kim Ki-duk. Oh Yeong-su, Kim Ki-duk, Kim Young-min, Seo Jae-kyeong, Ha Yeo-jin, Kim Jong-ho. Exquisite, deceptively simple account of the evolving connection between an aging monk and his protégé (who is played by five actors, one of whom is writer-director Kim). Set in a small, floating monastery on a rural mountain lake, the scenario is presented in five sections that correspond to the seasons and portray the younger monk's coming-of-age. Poetic allegory of human behavior and the meaning of spirituality features luminous cinematography by Baek Dong-hyeon. [R] ▼▶

Springtime in the Rockies (1942) **C-91m.** *** D: Irving Cummings. Betty Grable, John Payne, Carmen Miranda, Cesar Romero, Charlotte Greenwood, Edward Everett Horton, Jackie Gleason. Near-definitive 1940s Fox musical: Grable at her prettiest, Miranda at her silliest (doing a Brazilian "Chattanooga Choo Choo"), Technicolor at its lushest, and Harry James and His Band at their best, with Helen Forrest introducing "I Had the Craziest Dream." The "plot"—about a bickering Broadway duo—is neither too tiresome nor too intrusive. Good fun all the way. ▼●

Sprung (1997) **C-105m.** *½ D: Rusty Cundieff. Tisha Campbell, Rusty Cundieff, Paula Jai Parker, Joe Torry, John Witherspoon, Jennifer Lee, Clarence Williams III, Isabel Sanford, Sherman Hemsley. Forgettable and hopelessly predictable plot about a young couple who try planning the perfect wedding for their friends. Unbelievable situations, incredibly hokey sentiment overcome this amateurish attempt at creating a '90s screwball comedy. Preston Sturges is probably spinning in his grave. [R] ▼●

Spun (2003) **C-96m.** BOMB D: Jonas Åkerlund. Jason Schwartzman, John Leguizamo, Brittany Murphy, Mena Suvari, Patrick Fugit, Peter Stormare, Alexis Arquette, Deborah Harry, Eric Roberts, Mickey Rourke. Schwartzman enters a whole new world when he meets junkie Murphy at the home of dealer Leguizamo. Music-video–style treatment of the drug culture is nonjudgmental, but so scummy that it's hard to find anything redeeming about the characters or the film itself. But if you really want to see Suvari sitting on the toilet, this is the movie for you! Score by Billy Corgan, who also appears in a cameo along with Ron Jeremy, Tony Kaye, China Chow, and Rob Halford. [R]▼▶

Spy Game (2001-U.S.-German) **C-127m.** ** D: Tony Scott. Robert Redford, Brad Pitt, Catherine McCormack, Stephen Dillane, Larry Bryggman, Marianne Jean-Baptiste, David Hemmings, Charlotte Rampling. As he's about to retire from the CIA, Redford learns that his onetime protégé is being held by a hostile government and determines to save him—which, due to political complications, is not the Agency's priority. The men's relationship is then traced in an ultimately wearying parade of flashbacks. Redford and Pitt are in fine form and work well together, but the movie rambles, and Scott's hyperactive visual style (replete with meaningless helicopter shots) cannot compensate. Panavision. [R]▼▶

Spy Hard (1996) **C-81m.** ** D: Rick Friedberg. Leslie Nielsen, Nicollette Sheridan, Charles Durning, Marcia Gay Harden, Barry Bostwick, Andy Griffith, John Ales, Elya Baskin, Mason Gamble, Carlos Lauchu, Stephanie Romanov, Clyde Kusatsu, Julie Brown, Eddie Deezen, Julie Payne, Thom Sharp. Mild James Bond spoof with Nielsen as Agent WD-40, locking horns with master criminal General Rancor (Griffith). Steady stream of gags (ribbing everything from HOME ALONE to TRUE LIES), mostly silly, sometimes funny, too often sloppy or misfired. Nielsen is much better than the material. Many familiar faces in surprise cameos. Best of all: Weird Al Yankovic's title sequence and song. Nielsen also coexecutive-produced. [PG-13]▼●

Spy in Black, The (1939-British) **82m.** *** D: Michael Powell. Conrad Veidt, Sebastian Shaw, Valerie Hobson, Marius Goring, June Duprez, Helen Haye, Cyril Raymond, Hay Petrie. Intriguing espionage melodrama set in WW1 Scotland with Veidt as German naval officer/spy and Hobson a charming double agent. Nice surprise twists in story, with bittersweet romance worked in. That's Bernard Miles as the desk clerk in the opening scene. Scripted by Emeric Pressburger and Roland Pertwee; first collaboration of Powell and Pressburger. Original U.S. title: U-BOAT 29.▼●

Spy Kids (2001) **C-86m.** *** D: Robert

Rodriguez. Antonio Banderas, Carla Gugino, Alexa Vega, Daryl Sabara, Alan Cumming, Tony Shalhoub, Teri Hatcher, Cheech Marin, Robert Patrick, George Clooney. A brother and sister discover that their parents are secret agents when Mom and Dad are kidnapped and they must come to the rescue. High-flying, high-tech fantasy adventure has enough humor and imagination to entertain both parents and kids, with delightful performances by Banderas and Cumming. Two neat songs by Danny Elfman add to the fun. A rare family film that's cool without being crude. Rodriguez also scripted and edited. Followed by two sequels. [PG]▼▶

Spy Kids 2: The Island of Lost Dreams (2002) **C-99m.** *** D: Robert Rodriguez. Antonio Banderas, Carla Gugino, Alexa Vega, Daryl Sabara, Emily Osment, Matt O'Leary, Mike Judge, Ricardo Montalban, Holland Taylor, Christopher McDonald, Danny Trejo, Cheech Marin, Steve Buscemi, Alan Cumming, Bill Paxton, Tony Shalhoub. Entertaining sequel focuses more on the kids, and their new, pint-sized competitors in the junior spy game, as they try to unlock the secret of a mysterious island. Banderas has some very funny moments as the prideful dad who also has to suffer from the meddling of his know-it-all in-laws (perfectly played by Taylor and Montalban). Rodriguez again provides a panoply of outlandish special-effects creatures—with a nice nod to Ray Harryhausen. [PG]▼▶

Spy Kids 3-D: Game Over (2003) **C-89m.** **½ D: Robert Rodriguez. Antonio Banderas, Carla Gugino, Alexa Vega, Daryl Sabara, Ricardo Montalban, Holland Taylor, Sylvester Stallone, Mike Judge, Matt O'Leary, Emily Osment, Cheech Marin, Courtney Jines, Bobby Edner, Ryan James Pinkston. Juni (Sabara) is recruited by the President of the U.S. to rescue his sister from the virtual-reality world created by the sinister Toymaker (Stallone). Helter-skelter story is a thin, if amiable, excuse for the kids to go through their paces in a video-game environment. Stallone has fun with multiple identities, and there are cameos by former series costars (George Clooney, Tony Shalhoub, Alan Cumming, Steve Buscemi, Danny Trejo, Bill Paxton) as well as Salma Hayek and Elijah Wood. The parents barely appear in this one, but grandfather Montalban is genuinely heroic. Rodriguez wrote, edited, photographed, coproduced, did the music and production design, and was co-visual effects supervisor. 3-D. [PG]▼▶

Spy Next Door, The (2010) **C-94m.** *½ D: Brian Levant. Jackie Chan, Amber Valletta, Madeline Carroll, Will Shadley, Alina Foley, George Lopez, Billy Ray Cyrus, Katharine Boecher. Moronic kiddie comedy has Chan as Bob Ho (!), a former CIA spy who ends up taking care of his new girlfriend's three kids, who aren't exactly fond of him.

When complications arise, Ho's old Russian foes descend upon the house, putting him, the kids, and his new romantic life in jeopardy. Silly slapstick and Chan-anigans are so broad that the movie never comes up for air. Although this kind of formula comedy has worked for other action stars, it seems a waste of Chan's talent. [PG]▶

S*P*Y*S (1974) **C-87m.** BOMB D: Irvin Kershner. Donald Sutherland, Elliott Gould, Zouzou, Joss Ackland, Shane Rimmer, Vladek Sheybal. Sutherland-Gould teaming fails to regenerate MASH electricity in a good director's worst film. Laughless CIA spoof about the defection of a Russian dancer is unworthy of anyone's time. [PG]▼▶

Spy Who Came In from the Cold, The (1965) **112m.** ***½ D: Martin Ritt. Richard Burton, Claire Bloom, Oskar Werner, Peter Van Eyck, George Voskovec, Sam Wanamaker, Cyril Cusack, Michael Hordern, Bernard Lee. John le Carré's potent account of a Cold War spy's existence—minus glamorous trappings of movie cliché. Burton is excellent as embittered agent at the end of his career. Scripted by Paul Dehn and Guy Trosper.▼●▶

Spy Who Loved Me, The (1977) **C-125m.** ***½ D: Lewis Gilbert. Roger Moore, Barbara Bach, Curt Jurgens, Richard Kiel, Caroline Munro, Bernard Lee, Lois Maxwell, Desmond Llewelyn. Rousing, lavishly produced James Bond adventure with wily 007 joining forces with a seductive Russian agent to quash arch-villain Stromberg's (Jurgens) plans for world destruction. At his best doing battle with a persistent steel-toothed goon, menacingly played by seven-foot-two-inch Kiel. Grand fun for one and all; Carly Simon sings Marvin Hamlisch's theme, "Nobody Does It Better." Panavision. [PG]▼●▶

Spy with a Cold Nose, The (1966-British) **C-93m.** ** D: Daniel Petrie. Laurence Harvey, Daliah Lavi, Lionel Jeffries, Eric Portman, Denholm Elliott, Colin Blakely, Paul Ford. Spoof on secret agent movies. British agents plant bug in bulldog Disraeli, gift to Russian ambassador. Cast tries to keep story afloat.▼

Spy With My Face, The (1966) **C-88m.** **½ D: John Newland. Robert Vaughn, Senta Berger, David McCallum, Leo G. Carroll. Another expanded *Man From U.N.C.L.E.* TV series entry, with Vaughn matching wits with his double (working for foreign powers); Berger is the enemy femme fatale.

Squanto: A Warrior's Tale (1994) **C-101m.** *** D: Xavier Koller. Adam Beach, Mandy Patinkin, Michael Gambon, Nathaniel Parker, Eric Schweig, Donal Donnelly, Stuart Pankin, Alex Norton, Irene Bedard. Thoughtful, painstakingly observed Disney yarn which follows the plight of a 17th-century American Indian (Beach) who is abducted by British traders and taken back to England. At the scenario's core are Squanto's conflicts with (and spiritual similarities to) some reclusive monks. A film to be savored by children and adults alike. [PG]▼●◖

Square, The (2008-Australian) **C-105m.** **½ D: Nash Edgerton. David Roberts, Claire van der Boom, Joel Edgerton, Anthony Hayes, Lucy Bell, Kieran Darcy-Smith, Brendan Donoghue, Lisa Bailey, Bill Hunter. An adulterous couple (Roberts, van der Boom) plans to steal her husband's secret stash of money, then run away together . . . but one thing after another goes wrong, pulling Roberts into an escalating series of soul-sucking crimes. Modern-day film noir is well plotted and executed, but the actors lack charisma and the movie has no heart. Cowritten by Joel Edgerton, who plays Billy, and directed by his brother. Super 35. [R]◖

Square Dance (1987) **C-112m.** **½ D: Daniel Petrie. Jason Robards, Jane Alexander, Winona Ryder, Rob Lowe, Deborah Richter, Guich Koock. Top-notch performances bolster this much too leisurely look at a Texas teenage girl's coming of age, as she leaves her dour grandfather's farm to be with her feisty mom in Fort Worth. Alexander (who coproduced with fellow actor Charles Haid) is a standout as the mother; Lowe effects a real change of pace playing a retarded man befriended by Ryder. Shown on TV as HOME IS WHERE THE HEART IS. [PG-13]▼●◖

Squeeze, The (1980-Italian) **C-100m.** *½ D: Anthony M. Dawson (Antonio Margheriti). Lee Van Cleef, Karen Black, Edward Albert, Lionel Stander, Robert Alda, Angelo Infanti. Good cast wasted in humdrum caper film about a retired thief (Van Cleef) breaking open one last safe. Filmed in N.Y.C. [R]▼◖

Squeeze, The (1987) **C-101m.** BOMB D: Roger Young. Michael Keaton, Rae Dawn Chong, Liane Langland, Leslie Bevis, John Davidson, Meat Loaf, Ronald Guttman. Dreadful comedy, almost completely devoid of laughs, with Keaton as a con man who gets involved in murder and mayhem. Davidson plays a slick but corrupt TV lottery host. [PG-13]▼●

Squeeze (1997) **C-89m.** ** D: Robert Patton-Spruill. Tyrone Burton, Eddie Cutanda, Phuong Van Duong, Geoffrey Rhue, Russell G. Jones, Leigh Williams. Three Boston ghetto youths are caught between the violent gang and drug life on the streets and a promise of hope and a better life found in their local youth center. The conflict the teens go through is well played out with terrific performances, especially Burton's, but the dialogue is sometimes stilted and the ending too pat. Great visual style; shot on location in Boston in 1995. [R]▼◖

Squid and the Whale, The (2005) **C-88m.** ***½ D: Noah Baumbach. Jeff Daniels, Laura Linney, Jesse Eisenberg, Owen Kline, Anna Paquin, William Baldwin. Intimate look at a family coming apart at the seams in 1980s Brooklyn. The two boys, aged 12 and 16, don't know what to make of the rift in their parents' relationship: he's a self-absorbed novelist, given to opinionated pronouncements and fierce competition; she's a loving mother who's coming into her own as a writer. Youthful angst and the dissolution of a relationship have seldom been better portrayed. Searing, semiautobiographical drama written by Baumbach. Everyone is good, but Daniels scores a knockout. Young Kline is the son of Kevin Kline and Phoebe Cates. [R]◖

Squirm (1976) **C-92m.** *** D: Jeff Lieberman. Don Scardino, Patricia Pearcy, R. A. Dow, Jean Sullivan, Peter MacLean. Above-average horror outing builds to good shock sequences: when power line falls to the ground on rainy Georgia night, it drives large, slimy sandworms from the ground, which terrorize small town. [PG—edited from original R rating]▼◖

Squizzy Taylor (1982-Australian) **C-89m.** *** D: Kevin Dobson. David Atkins, Jacki Weaver, Alan Cassell, Michael Long, Kim Lewis, Steve Bisley. Atkins shines as the title character, a famous gangster in 1920s Melbourne. Enjoyable, with the era colorfully re-created.▼

Sssssss (1973) **C-99m.** *** D: Bernard L. Kowalski. Strother Martin, Dirk Benedict, Heather Menzies, Richard B. Shull, Tim O'Connor, Jack Ging. Well-done horror tale of doctor who finds a way of transforming man into King Cobra. Exceptional job by makeup master John Chambers. [PG]▼◖

Stacey (1973) **C-79m.** *½ D: Andy Sidaris. Anne Randall, Alan Landers, James Westmoreland, Cristina Raines, Anitra Ford, Marjorie Bennett. Voluptuous former Playmate Randall stars as near-superwoman private eye on absurdly complex case involving murder, blackmail, and a Moonie-like cult. Very sexy and violent, but not very good, with grating, obnoxious score by jazz veteran Don Randi. Aka STACEY AND HER GANGBUSTERS. [R]▼

Stacking (1987) **C-109m.** ** D: Martin Rosen. Christine Lahti, Frederic Forrest, Megan Follows, Jason Gedrick, Ray Baker, Peter Coyote, James Gammon, Kaiulani Lee, Jacqueline Brookes, Irene Daily. Some fine performers (and performances) are wasted in this boring, ever so obvious account of the various experiences and troubles of a young teen (Follows), growing up in the rural West in the early 1950s. More or less a clone of the far superior DESERT BLOOM. Originally titled SEASON OF DREAMS. [PG]▼●

Stacy's Knights (1983) **C-95m.** **½ D: Jim Wilson.** Andra Millian, Kevin Costner, Eve Lilith, Mike Reynolds, Garth Howard, Ed Semenza. Millian is Plain Jane struck with blackjack gambling fever who recruits a squad of sharpies to break a casino after her young mentor (Costner) is killed by the casino's goons. Unexciting B-movie offers insight into the world of professional gambling and features a flavorful performance by Costner in his first leading role. (Wilson and screenwriter Michael Blake later reteamed with Costner to make DANCES WITH WOLVES.) [PG] ▼ ●

Stage Beauty (2004-U.S.-British-German) **C-105m.** **½ D: Richard Eyre.** Billy Crudup, Claire Danes, Rupert Everett, Tom Wilkinson, Ben Chaplin, Hugh Bonneville, Richard Griffiths, Edward Fox, Zoë Tapper. In 17th-century England, the most beautiful and celebrated actress on the stage is a man, Ned Kynaston (Crudup). When the whimsical King Charles II repeals the ban forbidding women from acting, Kynaston is not just unemployable: he is crushed. Colorful, well-crafted period piece doesn't completely convince us that its central character (and his sexual confusion) is all that interesting. Screenplay by Jeffrey Hatcher, from his play *Compleat Female Stage Beauty*. Super 35. [R] ▼ ●

Stagecoach (1939) **96m.** **** D: John Ford. Claire Trevor, John Wayne, Andy Devine, John Carradine, Thomas Mitchell, Louise Platt, George Bancroft, Donald Meek, Berton Churchill, Tim Holt, Tom Tyler, Chris-Pin Martin, Francis Ford, Jack Pennick. One of the great American films, and a landmark in the maturing of the Western, balancing character study (as disparate passengers travel together on the same stagecoach) and peerless action (in a lengthy Indian attack, featuring Yakima Canutt's famous stuntwork). Also the film that propelled John Wayne to genuine stardom. Mitchell won an Oscar as the drunken doctor, as did the music score. Script by Dudley Nichols, from Ernest Haycox's story "Stage to Lordsburg" (whose plot is reminiscent of Guy de Maupassant's *Boule de Suif*). Filmed in Ford's beloved Monument Valley on the Arizona-Utah border. Remade in 1966 and as a TVM in 1986. Also shown in computer-colored version. ▼ ● ●

Stagecoach (1966) **C-115m.** **½ D: Gordon Douglas.** Ann-Margret, Alex Cord, Red Buttons, Michael Connors, Bing Crosby, Bob Cummings, Van Heflin, Slim Pickens, Stefanie Powers, Keenan Wynn. Colorful, star-studded Western is OK, but can't hold a candle to the 1939 masterpiece. Overlong, with only occasional action scenes to liven it up. Wayne Newton sings the title song! CinemaScope.

Stage Door (1937) **90m.** **** D: Gregory La Cava. Katharine Hepburn, Ginger Rogers, Adolphe Menjou, Andrea Leeds, Gail Patrick, Constance Collier, Lucille Ball, Eve Arden, Ann Miller, Ralph Forbes, Franklin Pangborn, Jack Carson. Theatrical boarding house is setting for wonderful film, from Edna Ferber–George S. Kaufman play. Dynamite cast includes Hepburn as rich girl trying to succeed on her own, Menjou as propositioning producer, Leeds as hypersensitive actress, and several stars-to-be: Lucille Ball, Ann Miller, and Eve Arden. Scripted by Morrie Ryskind and Anthony Veiller. ▼ ● ●

Stage Door Canteen (1943) **132m.** **½ D: Frank Borzage.** Cheryl Walker, William Terry, Marjorie Riordan, Lon McCallister, Margaret Early, Michael Harrison (Sunset Carson). Wartime story of romance between soldier and hostess at N.Y.C.'s fabled canteen is filled with cameos, walk-ons, speeches, and musical numbers by an incredible battery of stars, including Katharine Hepburn, Harpo Marx, Paul Muni, Helen Hayes, Benny Goodman, Count Basie, Edgar Bergen. Many prints run 93m. ▼ ● ●

Stage Fright (1950) **110m.** **½ D: Alfred Hitchcock.** Marlene Dietrich, Jane Wyman, Michael Wilding, Richard Todd, Kay Walsh, Alastair Sim, Joyce Grenfell, Sybil Thorndike, Patricia Hitchcock. Drama student Wyman turns undercover sleuth when actress' husband is murdered; some exciting moments, but the Master misses on this one. Filmed in London with delightful British supporting cast; Marlene sings "The Laziest Gal in Town." ▼ ● ●

Stage Struck (1958) **C-95m.** **½ D: Sidney Lumet.** Henry Fonda, Susan Strasberg, Joan Greenwood, Christopher Plummer, Herbert Marshall. Faded remake of MORNING GLORY retelling the ascent of Broadway-bound actress. Supporting cast hampered by unconvincing Strasberg in lead role and by unreal theater world atmosphere. ▼ ●

Staircase (1969-British) **C-100m.** ** D: Stanley Donen. Richard Burton, Rex Harrison, Cathleen Nesbitt, Beatrix Lehmann. Shock value of Burton and Harrison as a gay couple was all this film had going for it in 1969, and nothing has changed since then, except heightened sophistication of audiences. A curio, to be sure. Dudley Moore composed the score. Panavision. [R]

Stairway to Heaven SEE: **Matter of Life and Death, A**

Stakeout (1987) **C-115m.** *** D: John Badham. Richard Dreyfuss, Emilio Estevez, Aidan Quinn, Madeleine Stowe, Dan Lauria, Forest Whitaker, Ian Tracey, Earl Billings. While working with his partner on a stakeout, cop Dreyfuss falls in love with the woman he's supposed to be watching. Wildly improbable, and ultimately down-

[1307]

right silly, but entertaining throughout, thanks to sharp dialogue and performances, and some big laughs. Dreyfuss and Estevez make a great team. Written by Jim Kouf. Followed by a sequel, ANOTHER STAKEOUT. [R]▼●◗

Stakeout on Dope Street (1958) **83m.** *½ D: Irvin Kershner. Yale Wexler, Jonathan Haze, Morris Miller, Abby Dalton, Herschel Bernardi. Trio of youths discover cache of heroin, believing their futures will now be uncomplicated; good premise poorly executed.

Stalag 17 (1953) **120m.** **** D: Billy Wilder. William Holden, Don Taylor, Otto Preminger, Robert Strauss, Harvey Lembeck, Richard Erdman, Peter Graves, Neville Brand, Sig Ruman, Ross Bagdasarian, Gil Stratton, Jr. The pinnacle of all WW2 POW films. Holden (in Oscar-winning performance) is super-cynical sergeant suspected of being Nazi spy. Wilder brilliantly blends drama with comedy to show monotonous, anxiety-ridden life of POWs. Wonderful comic relief by Strauss and Lembeck (repeating their Broadway roles), plus superb turn by Preminger as Nazi camp commander. Scripted by Wilder and Edwin Blum, from Donald Bevan and Edmund Trzcinski's play. ▼●◗

Stalker (1979-Russian) **C/B&W-160m.** *** D: Andrei Tarkovsky. Alexander Kaidanovsky, Nikolai Grinko, Anatoli Solonitsin, Alice Friendlich. Stark, eerie, cerebral story of title character, who guides intellectuals Grinko and Solonitsin through the "Zone," a mysterious, forbidden wasteland. Very slow but well acted and rewarding. ▼◗

Stalking Moon, The (1969) **C-109m.** ** D: Robert Mulligan. Gregory Peck, Eva Marie Saint, Robert Forster, Noland Clay, Russell Thorson, Frank Silvera. Army scout helps white woman who has lived with the Apaches to escape with her young half-breed son, while boy's father comes after them. Potentially interesting Western is both slick and dull; nice photography by Charles Lang. Panavision. [G]▼◗

Stand Alone (1985) **C-90m.** ** D: Alan Beattie. Charles Durning, Pam Grier, James Keach, Bert Remsen, Barbara Sammeth, Lu Leonard, Luis Contreras. Vigilante opus has miscast Durning as a war vet who goes after Latino thugs who are preying on his neighborhood. Grier is wasted in a goody-two-shoes role. Spectacle of overweight Durning running around in action scenes is unintentionally funny. [R]▼

Stand and Deliver (1987) **C-105m.** ***½ D: Ramon Menendez. Edward James Olmos, Lou Diamond Phillips, Rosana de Soto, Andy Garcia, Will Gotay, Ingrid Oliu, Virginia Paris, Mark Eliot. Olmos gives a tour-de-force performance in this outstanding drama as a tough, demanding teacher who inspires his East L.A. barrio students to pass

an Advanced Placement Calculus Test . . . and that's only the beginning of the story. Based on fact, with a screenplay by director Menendez and Tom Musca. This *American Playhouse* feature is a triumph for all concerned. [PG]▼●◗

Standard Operating Procedure (2008) **C-116m.** *** D: Errol Morris. Documentarian Morris follows up his Oscar-winning THE FOG OF WAR with this disturbing examination of the wartime scandal at Iraq's Abu Ghraib, the site of human torture and abuse of Iraqi prisoners by a group of American soldiers. Participants indicted themselves by recording all their atrocities with video and still cameras (although Morris also stages reenactments). Effective doc also features several interviews with the military personnel who took part. Resembles nothing so much as a horror film. Beware of extremely graphic images and re-creations that may be too stomach-churning for some viewers. [R]◗

Standard Time SEE: **Anything But Love**

Stand by Me (1986) **C-87m.** *** D: Rob Reiner. Wil Wheaton, River Phoenix, Corey Feldman, Jerry O'Connell, Kiefer Sutherland, Casey Siemaszko, John Cusack, Richard Dreyfuss. Affectionate Americana looking back at boyhood friendship and adventures in the 1950s (and narrated by Dreyfuss, representing author Stephen King, whose novella "The Body" is the basis for this film). Irresistible and wholly believable performances from all four youthful leads. Only complaint: the high volume of four-letter words, decidedly not characteristic of the 1950s. [R]▼●◗

Stander (2003-Canadian-German-South African) **C-116m.** *** D: Bronwen Hughes. Thomas Jane, Ashley Taylor, David O'Hara, Dexter Fletcher, Deborah Kara Unger, Marius Weyers. True account of South African police captain Andre Stander who, frustrated with his unwilling involvement in apartheid, becomes a notorious criminal, leading the Stander Gang on a string of daily robberies in the early '80s. Gripping story well told, with a strong performance by Jane in the title role. This might seem like hokum if it weren't based on a true story. [R] ▼◗

Stand-In (1937) **91m.** *** D: Tay Garnett. Leslie Howard, Humphrey Bogart, Joan Blondell, Alan Mowbray, Marla Shelton, C. Henry Gordon, Jack Carson. Enjoyable spoof of Hollywood, with stuffy banker Howard sent to assess dwindling fortunes of Colossal Pictures, becoming involved with perky stand-in Blondell and mercurial producer Bogart to save company from ruin. Sags in second half. ▼◗

Standing in the Shadows of Motown (2002) **C-108m.** *** D: Paul Justman. Narrated by Andre Braugher. Entertaining documentary about the unsung musicians (known as The Funk Brothers) who helped to create the Motown sound in the 1950s, '60s, and '70s, and played on countless hit records. Newly staged concert sequences with contemporary singers like Joan Osborne, Meshell Ndegeocello, Ben Harper, Bootsy Collins, Montell Jordan, and Chaka Khan are intercut with interviews of the still-vibrant players. Dramatic re-creations of remembered moments are weak, but the music is irresistible. Based on Allan Slutsky's book. [PG] ▼●

Stand Up and Be Counted (1972) C-99m. *½ D: Jackie Cooper. Jacqueline Bisset, Stella Stevens, Steve Lawrence, Gary Lockwood, Lee Purcell, Loretta Swit, Hector Elizondo. Touted as first film about Women's Lib; writer Bisset returns to home town, first becomes aware of abuses women must endure. Cardboard all the way; only standout is Stevens' comic performance. Script by Bernard Slade. [PG]

Stand Up and Cheer! (1934) 69m. ** D: Hamilton MacFadden. Warner Baxter, Madge Evans, James Dunn, Sylvia Froos, John Boles, Shirley Temple, Ralph Morgan, Aunt Jemima, Mitchell and Durant, Nick (Dick) Foran, Nigel Bruce, Stepin Fetchit. Dismal musical fantasy about big-time show producer Baxter being named Secretary of Amusement by the President, to chase the country's Depression blues. Tough sledding until Shirley Temple shows up with Dunn to perform "Baby Take a Bow" (which helped make her a star). Originally released at 80m. Also shown in computer-colored version. ▼●

Stanley (1972) C-106m. ** D: William Grefe. Chris Robinson, Alex Rocco, Susan Carroll, Steve Alaimo, Mark Harris, Paul Avery. Classic depiction of the Vietnam veteran as a one-dimensional psycho: Robinson cannot relate to any other human being; his only friends are poisonous snakes, which he uses to gain revenge on anyone who mistreats him. WILLARD with snakes instead of rats. [PG] ▼●

Stanley & Iris (1990) C-104m. **½ D: Martin Ritt. Jane Fonda, Robert De Niro, Swoosie Kurtz, Martha Plimpton, Harley Cross, Jamey Sheridan, Feodor Chaliapin, Zohra Lampert, Loretta Devine, Julie Garfield. Beleaguered working-class Fonda, still grieving over the loss of her husband eight months before, chances to meet De Niro, a loner who harbors a terrible secret—he can't read. She winds up tutoring him, and they circle each other warily before deciding if they're in love. Story is flat and underdeveloped, but the screen presence and charm of two great stars make it worth watching. Panavision. [PG-13] ▼●●

Stanley and Livingstone (1939) 101m. *** D: Henry King. Spencer Tracy, Nancy Kelly, Richard Greene, Walter

Brennan, Charles Coburn, Cedric Hardwicke, Henry Hull, Henry Travers, Miles Mander. Elaborate production with Tracy as determined reporter who searches turn-of-the-20th-century Africa for missing missionary (Hardwicke). Entertaining drama with beautifully understated performance by Tracy. ▼

Star, The (1952) 89m. ***½ D: Stuart Heisler. Bette Davis, Sterling Hayden, Natalie Wood, Warner Anderson, Minor Watson, June Travis. An Oscar-winning actress tries to deal with the fact that her career is over, her money is gone, and she must find some way to put her life together. Modest film, shot on locations all around L.A., has many moments of truth (and a typically compelling performance by Davis) to make up for its excesses. ▼●

Star! (1968) C-176m. **½ D: Robert Wise. Julie Andrews, Richard Crenna, Michael Craig, Daniel Massey, Robert Reed, Bruce Forsyth, Beryl Reid, Jenny Agutter, Tony LoBianco, Conrad Bain, Roy Scheider, Bernard Fox. Razzle-dazzle biography of stage star Gertrude Lawrence never rings true, but does have mammoth production numbers worth seeing (especially in color). Julie tries, but never comes across; Massey is amusing if affected as Noel Coward (his real-life godfather). After box office flop, film was trimmed to 120m. and retitled THOSE WERE THE HAPPY TIMES. Todd-AO. [G] ▼●

Star Chamber, The (1983) C-109m. **½ D: Peter Hyams. Michael Douglas, Hal Holbrook, Yaphet Kotto, Sharon Gless, James B. Sikking, Joe Regalbuto, Don Calfa, DeWayne Jessie, Jack Kehoe. Young judge, frustrated by having to turn rapists and murderers free because of legal technicalities, is drawn into a secret judicial society. Well done, but too predictable, and ultimately too unbelievable, to really score. Panavision. [R] ▼●

Starcrash (1979-Italian) C-92m. *½ D: Lewis Coates (Luigi Cozzi). Marjoe Gortner, Caroline Munro, Christopher Plummer, David Hasselhoff, Robert Tessier, Joe Spinell, voice of Hamilton Camp. Grinning Gortner and sexy Munro are recruited to save the universe from destruction by bad-guy Spinell. Moronic sci-fi movie with variable special effects; unless you're a Munro fan, it's only good for a few laughs, nothing more. Aka FEMALE SPACE INVADERS. [PG] ▼●

Stardom (1999-Canadian-French) C-100m. *** D: Denys Arcand. Jessica Paré, Dan Aykroyd, Charles Berling, Thomas Gibson, Frank Langella, Robert Lepage, Patrick Huard. Trenchant look at our media culture as an attractive young Canadian hockey player (Paré) is transformed into a model and then a celebrity. Dead-on satire seen through the "eyes" of superficial TV shows that cover the celebrity beat. Arcand scripted with J. Jacob Potashnik. [R]▼▶

Stardust (1975-British) **C-107m.** ***½ D: Michael Apted. David Essex, Adam Faith, Larry Hagman, Keith Moon, Dave Edmunds, Ines Des Longchamps, Edd Byrnes. Powerful sequel to THAT'LL BE THE DAY follows amazing rise and fall of Beatles-like rock group and its lead singer (Essex). Candid, provocative, and utterly believable. [R]

Stardust (2007) **C-125m.** *** D: Matthew Vaughn. Claire Danes, Michelle Pfeiffer, Robert De Niro, Charlie Cox, Sienna Miller, Ricky Gervais, Jason Flemyng, Rupert Everett, Peter O'Toole, Mark Strong, David Kelly; narrated by Ian McKellen. To prove his love for the fairest maiden in the land (Miller), our wide-eyed young hero (Cox) ventures into the forbidden kingdom of Stormhold to bring back a fallen star. The star has taken human form, however, and is being sought by others in the kingdom whose motives are not so pure—including a malevolent witch (played with gusto by Pfeiffer). Wondrously imaginative fantasy yarn, adapted from Neil Gaiman's novel, creates a world all its own and is dotted with colorful characters, but goes on far too long. Panavision. [PG-13]▶

Stardust Memories (1980) **91m.** *** D: Woody Allen. Woody Allen, Charlotte Rampling, Jessica Harper, Marie-Christine Barrault, Tony Roberts, Daniel Stern, Amy Wright. Woody plays a character not unlike himself who's persuaded to attend a film-seminar weekend, at which he's hounded by fans, favor-seekers, groupies, studio executives, relatives, and lovers. Pointed, seriocomic look at fame and success—though many viewers found it simply narcissistic. Look sharp for Sharon Stone on passing train; Louise Lasser and Laraine Newman appear unbilled. [PG]▼▶

Star 80 (1983) **C-102m.** *½ D: Bob Fosse. Mariel Hemingway, Eric Roberts, Cliff Robertson, Carroll Baker, Roger Rees, David Clennon, Josh Mostel, Sidney Miller, Jordan Christopher, Keenen Ivory Wayans, Stuart Damon, Ernest Thompson. Straightforward telling of a lurid tale: innocent Dorothy Stratten's mental seduction by small-time hustler Paul Snider, who promoted her career as a *Playboy* centerfold and movie starlet, then murdered her in a rage of jealousy. Extremely well-crafted, well-acted movie that leaves viewer with nothing but a feeling of voyeurism—and no redeeming insights. Fosse's final film. See also TV movie version DEATH OF A CENTERFOLD. [R]▼▶

Stargate (1994-French-U.S.) **C-119m.** **½ D: Roland Emmerich. Kurt Russell, James Spader, Viveca Lindfors, Jaye Davidson, Alexis Cruz, Mili Avital, Leon Rippy, John Diehl, Carlos Lauchu, Djimon (Hounsou), French Stewart, Rae Allen, Richard Kind. A scholar of ancient languages and hieroglyphics (Spader) is recruited to help the military penetrate the mystery of a stone gateway which, in fact, leads to other planets in our universe. Interesting odyssey, impressively mounted and jammed with visual effects, but loses its way dramatically. Davidson (of CRYING GAME fame) is featured as a sort of fey Ming the Merciless. Followed by a made-for-TV movie, a TV series, and a DVD movie. Alternate version runs 128m. Panavision. [PG-13]▼▶

Starhops (1978) **C-92m.** ** D: Barbara Peeters. Dorothy Buhrman, Sterling Frazier, Jillian Kesner, Peter Paul Liapis, Paul Ryan, Anthony Mannino, Dick Miller. Ultra-low-budget formula film about three car hops who try to salvage a failing drive-in. Not bad of its type; screenplay by Stephanie Rothman. [R]▼

Star Is Born, A (1937) **C-111m.** ***½ D: William Wellman. Fredric March, Janet Gaynor, Adolphe Menjou, May Robson, Andy Devine, Lionel Stander, Franklin Pangborn. Two remakes haven't dimmed the glow of this drama about a self-destructive actor and the young movie hopeful he marries. March and Gaynor are at their best and 1930s flavor (captured in early Technicolor) is a plus; screenplay by Dorothy Parker, Alan Campbell, and Robert Carson was inspired in part by 1932 film WHAT PRICE HOLLYWOOD? Won an Oscar for Carson and director Wellman's original story and a special Oscar for W. Howard Greene's cinematography.▼▶

Star Is Born, A (1954) **C-170m.** **** D: George Cukor. Judy Garland, James Mason, Charles Bickford, Jack Carson, Tom Noonan. Powerful semi-musical remake of the 1937 classic, with Garland and Mason at their peaks as doomed Hollywood star couple, she on the way up, he down. Incisive script by Moss Hart; great Harold Arlen–Ira Gershwin songs include spellbinding "The Man That Got Away" and the showstopping "Born in a Trunk" sequence by Leonard Gershe. Badly cut to 154m. after premiere engagements of 181m.; restored in 1983 to present length using still photos to cover missing bits of footage. CinemaScope.▼▶

Star Is Born, A (1976) **C-140m.** **½ D: Frank Pierson. Barbra Streisand, Kris Kristofferson, Gary Busey, Oliver Clark, Paul Mazursky, Marta Heflin, M.G. Kelly, Sally Kirkland, Robert Englund. By-now familiar story is given an unconvincing treatment, with change of setting to the world of rock music. Only comes to life during Streisand's vibrant numbers, which transcend script and surrounding drama; she and Paul Williams won an Oscar for song "Evergreen."

Screenplay by Pierson, Joan Didion, and John Gregory Dunne. ▼●❶

Star Kid (1998) C-101m. ** D: Manny Coto. Joseph Mazzello, Joey Simmrin, Danny Masterson, Richard Gilliland, Corinne Bohrer, Ashlee Levitch. A lonely boy finds a "cyborsuit"—superpowered alien armor—in a junkyard, and has fun trying it out. Comic book–like but occasionally entertaining. [PG]▼●❶

Star Knight (1986-Spanish) C-90m. *½ D: Fernando Colomo. Klaus Kinski, Harvey Keitel, Fernando Rey, Maria Lamor, Miguel Bosè. Infantile fantasy about a spaceship that lands in a Spanish lake in medieval times and is thought to be a dragon. Keitel (Bronx accent intact) is the only cast member who isn't dubbed. OK special effects. Originally titled: THE KNIGHT OF THE DRAGON.▼●❶

Starlight Hotel (1987-New Zealand) C-93m. *** D: Sam Pillsbury. Peter Phelps, Greer Robson, Marshall Napier, The Wizard, Alice Fraser, Patrick Smyth. Nice little film about the exploits of troubled teen Robson and psychologically scarred WW1 vet Phelps. A friendly film about a most unlikely friendship. Warrick Attewell's cinematography is a standout. [PG] ▼●

Starlight Slaughter SEE: **Eaten Alive!**

Star Maker, The (1995-Italian) C-117m. ** D: Giuseppe Tornatore. Sergio Castellitto, Tiziana Bodato, Franco Scaldati, Leopoldo Trieste, Clelia Rondinella, Tano Cimarosa, Jane Alexander. CINEMA PARADISO's Tornatore offers up the flip side of that beloved film in this period piece about a self-described talent scout who tours Sicily selling screen tests and the pipe dream of a movie career to naive locals who fall prey to his sales pitch. Maybe PARADISO is just too tough an act to follow, but this one doesn't even come close. Tornatore coscripted, from his story. Panavision. [R] ▼●❶

Starman (1984) C-115m. **½ D: John Carpenter. Jeff Bridges, Karen Allen, Charles Martin Smith, Richard Jaeckel. Extremely pleasant, genteel sci-fi about alien who lands on earth, abducts young widow to help him travel cross-country so he can rendezvous with spaceship. Her toughest problem: he's made himself look just like her late husband, and she finds herself attracted to him. Familiar, derivative storyline is given solid boost by two lead performances. Later a TV series. Panavision. [PG]▼●❶

Star Maps (1997) C-95m. **½ D: Miguel Arteta. Douglas Spain, Efrain Figueroa, Kandeyce Jorden, Martha Velez, Lysa Flores. Occasionally potent but uneven allegorical drama about an 18-year-old with movie-star aspirations who returns from Mexico to L.A. and goes to work for his father as a male prostitute in a ring which is

fronted by the selling of "star maps" of celebrity homes. Done in by its preachy tone and lack of depth. [R]▼●

Stars and Bars (1988) C-94m. BOMB D: Pat O'Connor. Daniel Day-Lewis, Harry Dean Stanton, Martha Plimpton, Matthew Cowles, Joan Cusack, Maury Chaykin, Deirdre O'Connell, Will Patton, Steven Wright, Keith David, Laurie Metcalf, Glenne Headly, Spalding Gray, Rockets Redglare. A complete misfire, with Day-Lewis thoroughly wasted as a British art expert who treks to America to purchase a Renoir, and instead tangles with hick Stanton and other assorted eccentrics. Overbaked, unfunny, and embarrassing. [R]▼●

Stars Fell on Henrietta, The (1995) C-110m. **½ D: James Keach. Robert Duvall, Aidan Quinn, Frances Fisher, Brian Dennehy, Lexi Randall, Kaytlyn Knowles, Billy Bob Thornton, Victor Wong, Paul Lazar, Spencer Garrett, Park Overall, Dylan Baker. Old-fashioned (and a tad contrived) folktale set in the Depression-era Texas dust bowl stars Duvall as a wily old oil prospector who charms a cotton farmer and his wife into believing their land is a valuable rig. Suffers mainly from overlength. A real labor of love from the people at Malpaso, Clint Eastwood's production company. Expert casting and superb contributions from cinematographer Bruce Surtees and production designer Henry Bumstead (plus a lush score by David Benoit) keep things enjoyable. That's director Keach's wife Jane Seymour in the opening saloon shot, and Fisher and Eastwood's daughter as Mary. Panavision. [PG]▼●❶

Starship Invasions (1977-Canadian) C-87m. *½ D: Ed Hunt. Robert Vaughn, Christopher Lee, Daniel Pilon, Helen Shaver, Henry Ramer. Abducted by good aliens to help battle bad aliens who are trying to take over earth, UFO expert Vaughn helps save the day with his pocket calculator. Good cast wasted in film boasting the worst special effects since PLAN 9 FROM OUTER SPACE. [PG]▼●

Starship Troopers (1997) C-129m. *** D: Paul Verhoeven. Casper Van Dien, Dina Meyer, Denise Richards, Jake Busey, Neil Patrick Harris, Clancy Brown, Seth Gilliam, Patrick Muldoon, Michael Ironside, Rue McClanahan. A gung-ho WW2 movie transplanted to the future, when high school kids are encouraged to become "citizens" by enlisting in the army and serving the state. Little do they dream that they'll be engaged in a full-scale war against marauding insects. With Verhoeven at the helm, you know this won't be subtle, but it's so sharp, energetic, and (at times) funny that it transcends being a "giant bug" movie. Not for the squeamish, with its graphic dismemberment of humans and insects, but robust entertainment just the same. Based on the novel by Robert A. Heinlein. The incredible creature animation was supervised by Phil Tippett. Tippett directed the 2004 sequel, which debuted on cable TV. A second sequel was released direct to DVD. [R] ▼●◖

Stars in My Crown (1950) **89m.** ***½ D: Jacques Tourneur. Joel McCrea, Ellen Drew, James Mitchell, Dean Stockwell, Alan Hale, Lewis Stone, Ed Begley, Amanda Blake, James Arness, Juano Hernandez; narrated by Marshall Thompson. Gentle, moving story of a quiet but persuasive minister in rural 19th-century America; episodic film creates warm feeling for characters and setting. Prime Americana from Joe David Brown's popular novel. Also interesting for pre-*Gunsmoke* casting of Arness and Blake. ▼◖

Starsky & Hutch (2004) **C-100m.** **½ D: Todd Phillips. Ben Stiller, Owen Wilson, Vince Vaughn, Juliette Lewis, Snoop Dogg, Fred Williamson, Amy Smart, Carmen Electra, Jason Bateman, Chris Penn, Brande Roderick, Molly Sims. Comedic take on the 1970s TV cop show pairs straight-arrow cop with a new partner who's more of a slacker. Their goal: nailing slick drug dealer Vaughn. Stiller and Wilson do what Stiller and Wilson usually do; Snoop Dogg is the freshest member of the cast as Huggy Bear, the local mover and shaker. Plenty of '70s music and fashions on hand; the only thing missing is laughs. Even some star cameos are bungled. Will Ferrell appears unbilled. Panavision. [PG-13] ▼◖

Stars Look Down, The (1939-British) **110m.** **** D: Carol Reed. Michael Redgrave, Margaret Lockwood, Edward Rigby, Emlyn Williams, Nancy Price, Cecil Parker, Linden Travers. Classic adaptation of A. J. Cronin's novel (coscripted by the author) about English coal miners struggling against dangerous working conditions, and Redgrave as a collier's son who intends to run for office. Gripping all the way. ▼◖

Star Spangled Girl (1971) **C-92m.** *½ D: Jerry Paris. Sandy Duncan, Tony Roberts, Todd Susman, Elizabeth Allen. Very unfunny Neil Simon comedy about the saccharine-sweet girl-next-door who falls in with two ultraradical campus newspaper editors. [G] ▼◖

Star Spangled Rhythm (1942) **99m.** *** D: George Marshall. Bing Crosby, Ray Milland, Bob Hope, Veronica Lake, Dorothy Lamour, Susan Hayward, Dick Powell, Mary Martin, Alan Ladd, Paulette Goddard, Cecil B. DeMille, Arthur Treacher, Preston Sturges, Eddie Anderson, Robert Preston, William Bendix, many others. Paramount's silly but agreeable star-packed WW2 extravaganza, filled with songs and sketches. There's a slight plot, about a studio switchboard operator (Betty Hutton) and gate guard (Victor Moore); the latter has told his son (Eddie Bracken), a sailor, that he's the studio's boss. Better numbers include "(That

Old) Black Magic," "Time to Hit the Road to Dreamland." ▼●◖

Starstruck (1982-Australian) **C-95m.** *** D: Gillian Armstrong. Jo Kennedy, Ross O'Donovan, Pat Evison, Margo Lee, Max Cullen, John O'May, Geoffrey Rush. Bright little musical comedy about a teenage boy who's determined to promote his cousin to singing stardom as a new-wave rocker . . . no matter what it takes. Amiable tongue-in-cheek outing pokes fun at Hollywood musicals and media hype. Original Australian running time 102m. [PG] ▼●◖

Starter for 10 (2006-U.S.-British) **C-95m.** **½ D: Tom Vaughan. James McAvoy, Alice Eve, Rebecca Hall, Catherine Tate, Dominic Cooper, Benedict Cumberbatch, Charles Dance, Lindsay Duncan. Working-class boy with a thirst for knowledge manages to get into college in the mid-1980s, where he finds he still has a lot to learn about dealing with real-life issues like friendship, loyalty, and the opposite sex. Pleasant if bland and derivative, until the final act. David Nicholls adapted his novel. [PG-13] ◖

Starting Out in the Evening (2007) **C-110m.** ***½ D: Andrew Wagner. Frank Langella, Lauren Ambrose, Lili Taylor, Adrian Lester, Jessica Hecht, Michael Cumpsty, Joel West. Aging, widowed literary lion is approached by a grad student who's writing a thesis about him. He attempts to rebuff her but she ingratiates herself, becomes important to him—and in the process, opens up old emotional wounds. Meanwhile, his 40-ish daughter (Taylor) tries to get her life on track. Mature, nuanced drama is anchored by Langella's masterful performance, complemented by director Wagner's keen, almost tactile, observations of a fast-fading Manhattan milieu. Wagner and Fred Parnes adapted Brian Morton's novel. Impressively photographed by Harlan Bosmajian. [PG-13] ◖

Starting Over (1979) **C-106m.** *** D: Alan J. Pakula. Burt Reynolds, Jill Clayburgh, Candice Bergen, Charles Durning, Frances Sternhagen, Austin Pendleton, Mary Kay Place, Wallace Shawn, Daniel Stern, Anne De Salvo, Charles Kimbrough. Likable comedy about divorced man who falls in love but can't erase feelings for his ex-wife; top performances but unfortunately, story goes awry toward conclusion for a lackluster turn of events and denouement. Scripted by James L. Brooks, from the Dan Wakefield novel. Look quickly for Kevin Bacon as a young husband. [R] ▼◖

Star Trek (2009) **C-126m.** ***½ D: J. J. Abrams. Chris Pine, Zachary Quinto, Leonard Nimoy, Eric Bana, Bruce Greenwood, Karl Urban, Zoë Saldana, Simon Pegg, John Cho, Anton Yelchin, Ben Cross, Winona Ryder, Chris Hemsworth, Jennifer Morrison, Faran Tahir, Clifton Collins, Jr., Tyler Perry. Energetic, inventive prequel to

Gene Roddenberry's landmark TV series imagines how the crew of the U.S.S. *Enterprise* came together—and how a fiery, rule-breaking James T. Kirk (Pine) and a half-Vulcan, half-human Spock (Quinto) became lifelong friends. Opens with a big action sequence, then Roberto Orci and Alex Kurtzman's screenplay carefully develops its characters and their relationships, never allowing visual effects to overpower the content. Nimoy makes a welcome return as the older Spock. Soaring score by Michael Giacchino. Oscar winner for Best Makeup (Barney Burman, Mindy Hall, Joel Harlow). Panavision. [PG-13] ❘

Star Trek: First Contact (1996) **C-110m.** *** D: Jonathan Frakes. Patrick Stewart, Jonathan Frakes, Brent Spiner, LeVar Burton, Michael Dorn, Gates McFadden, Marina Sirtis, Alfre Woodard, James Cromwell, Alice Krige, Robert Picardo. Capt. Picard lives his worst nightmare as the villainous Borg (who almost overtook him in a two-part TV episode) land on earth with domination their goal. The solution: the crew travels back in time to 2063 to make sure a cockeyed scientist (Cromwell) fulfills his role in history with a precedent-setting rocket flight. Story goes on a bit, following two concurrent threads, but series fans will have no complaints. Krige is a standout as the seductive Borg Queen. Feature directing debut for Frakes, better known as Riker. Panavision. [PG-13] ▼●❘

Star Trek Generations (1994) **C-118m.** *** D: David Carson. Patrick Stewart, William Shatner, Malcolm McDowell, Jonathan Frakes, Brent Spiner, LeVar Burton, Michael Dorn, Gates McFadden, Marina Sirtis, James Doohan, Walter Koenig, Barbara March, Gwyneth Walsh, Alan Ruck. The old guard gives way to the new, as Capt. Kirk (Shatner) passes the baton to a new Starfleet commander, Capt. Picard (Stewart). Episodic adventure yarn plays like an elongated segment of the *Next Generation* TV series; not inspired, perhaps, but entertaining just the same, with some impressive special effects. Oddly enough, the weakest segment is the climactic teaming of Picard and Kirk, which seems like a leftover from an old Saturday matinee serial. Whoopi Goldberg appears unbilled as Guinan. Panavision. [PG] ▼●❘

Star Trek: Insurrection (1998) **C-103m.** *** D: Jonathan Frakes. Patrick Stewart, Jonathan Frakes, Brent Spiner, LeVar Burton, Michael Dorn, Gates McFadden, Marina Sirtis, F. Murray Abraham, Donna Murphy, Anthony Zerbe, Gregg Henry, Daniel Hugh Kelly. Good entry in the long-running series has the crew befriending the eternally youthful residents of a Shangri-La–like planet whose existence is threatened by the vengeful Ru'afo (Abraham). Picard (Stewart) even has a dalliance with one of the women there

(Murphy). Reliably entertaining for *Star Trek* fans. Panavision. [PG] ▼●❘

Star Trek: Nemesis (2002) **C-117m.** *** D: Stuart Baird. Patrick Stewart, Jonathan Frakes, Brent Spiner, LeVar Burton, Michael Dorn, Marina Sirtis, Gates McFadden, Tom Hardy, Ron Perlman, Shannon Cochran, Dina Meyer, Jude Ciccolella, Kate Mulgrew, Wil Wheaton. Satisfying if formulaic series entry has Riker and Troi celebrating their marriage when the *Enterprise* crew is confronted with a dual challenge: facing a villain who is an evil clone of Captain Picard and examining an adversarial prototype of the android Data. Entertaining, though the conclusion is never in doubt; Stewart's commanding performance anchors the film. Spiner gets cos-tory credit—and sings a few bars of "Blue Skies." Whoopi Goldberg appears unbilled. Panavision. [PG-13] ▼❘

Star Trek—The Motion Picture (1979) **C-132m.** **½ D: Robert Wise. William Shatner, Leonard Nimoy, DeForest Kelley, Stephen Collins, Persis Khambatta, James Doohan, Nichelle Nichols, Walter Koenig, George Takei, Majel Barrett, Grace Lee Whitney, Mark Lenard. The crew of the *Enterprise* is reunited to combat a lethal force field headed toward Earth. Slow, talky, and derivative, somewhat redeemed by terrific special effects and majestic Jerry Goldsmith score; still, mainly for purists. Video version—generally considered an improvement—runs 143m. Director's edition released in 2002 is 136m. and rated PG. Followed by many sequels—and several new TV series! Panavision. [G] ▼●❘

Star Trek II: The Wrath of Khan (1982) **C-113m.** *** D: Nicholas Meyer. William Shatner, Leonard Nimoy, DeForest Kelley, Ricardo Montalban, James Doohan, Walter Koenig, George Takei, Nichelle Nichols, Kirstie Alley, Bibi Besch, Merritt Butrick, Paul Winfield. Kirk and the *Enterprise* crew must do battle with the nefarious villain of 1967's "Space Seed" episode. A bit hokey and pretentious at times, but a likable adventure overall, with nice touches of warmth and humor. Director's edition runs 116m. Originally released without the "II" in its title. Panavision. [PG] ▼●❘

Star Trek III: The Search for Spock (1984) **C-105m.** *** D: Leonard Nimoy. William Shatner, DeForest Kelley, James Doohan, George Takei, Walter Koenig, Nichelle Nichols, Christopher Lloyd, Robin Curtis, Merritt Butrick, Mark Lenard, Dame Judith Anderson, James B. Sikking, John Larroquette, Robert Hooks, Miguel Ferrer, Leonard Nimoy. Picking up where #2 left off, Kirk reassembles his crew and shang-hais the *Enterprise* to try and rescue Spock while both he and the rapidly destructing Genesis Planet are endangered by a Klingon warship (led by Lloyd, in an ineffectual performance). Subdued sci-fi outing very much in keeping with tone of the original TV series. Panavision. [PG]▼●)

Star Trek IV: The Voyage Home (1986) **C-119m.** ***½ D: Leonard Nimoy. William Shatner, Leonard Nimoy, DeForest Kelley, James Doohan, George Takei, Walter Koenig, Nichelle Nichols, Jane Wyatt, Catherine Hicks, Mark Lenard, Robin Curtis, Robert Ellenstein, John Schuck, Brock Peters. The *Enterprise* crew takes a sharp left turn toward comedy in this uncharacteristic—and very entertaining—movie. Story has the familiar characters time-traveling back to the 20th century in order to save the Earth of the future, with the help of some humpback whales. Sheer novelty of the comic tone excuses some forays into the obvious; it's all in fun. Panavision. [PG]▼●)

Star Trek V: The Final Frontier (1989) **C-106m.** ** D: William Shatner. William Shatner, Leonard Nimoy, DeForest Kelley, James Doohan, Walter Koenig, Nichelle Nichols, George Takei, David Warner, Laurence Luckinbill, Charles Cooper. The *Enterprise* crew takes off on an emergency mission when an apparent madman takes over a distant planet and holds its interstellar ambassadors hostage; his motives, however, turn out to be anything but terrorist. Dramatically shaky trek starts off with a case of the cutes, and gets worse before it (finally) gets better. A weak entry in the series. Shatner's feature-film directing debut; he also shares story credit. Panavision. [PG]▼●)

Star Trek VI: The Undiscovered Country (1991) **C-109m.** *** D: Nicholas Meyer. William Shatner, Leonard Nimoy, DeForest Kelley, James Doohan, Walter Koenig, Nichelle Nichols, George Takei, Kim Cattrall, Christopher Plummer, Mark Lenard, Grace Lee Whitney, Brock Peters, Kurtwood Smith, Rosana DeSoto, David Warner, Iman, John Schuck, Michael Dorn, Christian Slater. The *Enterprise* crew is assigned to negotiate truce with Klingon leaders, only to fall prey to a trap set by one of his renegade cohorts (Plummer, in a deliciously flamboyant performance). Entertaining saga cowritten by director Meyer. Nimoy helped concoct the story and also executive produced. Video version has 2m. of additional footage. Super 35. [PG]▼●)

Start the Revolution Without Me (1970) **C-91m.** *** D: Bud Yorkin. Gene Wilder, Donald Sutherland, Hugh Griffith, Jack MacGowran, Billie Whitelaw, Victor Spinetti, Ewa Aulin, Orson Welles. Madcap comedy involving two sets of mismatched twins who meet just before French Revolution. Somewhat ignored in 1970, now has a deserved cult following; the cast, especially Wilder, is hilarious. [PG]▼●)

Startup.com (2001) **C-103m.** ***½ D: Chris Hegedus, Jehane Noujaim. Riveting cinéma vérité–style documentary about two boyhood friends—one a computer whiz, the other a business brain—who join forces to start an online service. The enterprise is fraught with all the pitfalls that plague contemporary business—from fund-raising to ethical issues. The filmmakers followed their subjects for more than a year to create this incredibly dramatic and resonant film, a cautionary tale for our time. Produced by D.A. Pennebaker. [R]▼)

Star Wars (1977) **C-121m.** ***½ D: George Lucas. Mark Hamill, Harrison Ford, Carrie Fisher, Peter Cushing, Alec Guinness, Anthony Daniels, Kenny Baker; voice of James Earl Jones (as Darth Vader). Elaborate, imaginative update of Flash Gordon incredibly became one of the most popular films of all time. It's a hip homage to B-movie ethics and heroism in the space age, as a callow youth (Hamill) becomes an interplanetary hero with the help of some human and robot friends. R2-D2 and C-3P0 steal the show. Won seven Oscars for various technical achievements and John Williams' rousing score. Full title onscreen (on re-release prints) is STAR WARS EPISODE IV: A NEW HOPE. Followed by THE EMPIRE STRIKES BACK and RETURN OF THE JEDI. Special Edition released in 1997 features souped-up special effects and about 4m. of new footage. Panavision. [PG]▼●)

Star Wars Episode I: The Phantom Menace (1999) **C-133m.** *** D: George Lucas. Liam Neeson, Ewan McGregor, Natalie Portman, Jake Lloyd, Samuel L. Jackson, Frank Oz, Pernilla August, Terence Stamp, Ian McDiarmid, Hugh Quarshie, Ray Park, Ahmed Best, Brian Blessed, Sofia Coppola, Keira Knightley. Qui-Gon Jinn (Neeson) and his protégé Obi-Wan Kenobi (McGregor) try to negotiate peace but find themselves in the midst of war instead; while attempting to protect the Queen of Naboo (Portman), they stop over on the planet Tatooine, where they encounter young Anakin Skywalker (Lloyd), who clearly has a special gift. The beginning of Lucas' epic saga resembles his first STAR WARS film in both story and tone, with quantum leaps forward in special effects—including computer-generated characters (like comic-relief character Jar Jar Binks) who seem astonishingly real. Not a lot of heart, but certainly a lot of fun in Saturday matinee serial fashion. Followed by a sequel. Arriscope. [PG]▼)

Star Wars Episode II: Attack of the Clones (2002) **C-143m.** ** D: George Lucas. Ewan McGregor, Natalie Portman, Hayden Christensen, Christopher Lee, Samuel L. Jackson, Frank Oz, Ian McDiarmid, Pernilla August, Rose Byrne, Temuera Morrison, Jimmy Smits, Jack Thompson, Ahmed Best, Anthony Daniels, Kenny Baker. Ten years after Episode I, Anakin Skywalker is beginning to resent his father figure, Obi-Wan Kenobi, and finds himself falling in love with Padmé, the former queen. Lavish production showcases an overlong story that serves mainly as a transition between Episodes I and III in this ongoing saga. Wooden characterizations and dialogue don't help . . . but the computer-generated Yoda is terrific, and the coliseum action sequence (an homage to Ray Harryhausen) is a knockout. HD 24P Widescreen. [PG]▼◗

Star Wars Episode III: Revenge of the Sith (2005) **C-140m.** *** D: George Lucas. Ewan McGregor, Natalie Portman, Hayden Christensen, Ian McDiarmid, Samuel L. Jackson, Christopher Lee, Jimmy Smits, Frank Oz, Peter Mayhew, Temuera Morrison, Ahmed Best, Kenny Baker, Anthony Daniels, Keisha Castle-Hughes; voice of James Earl Jones. The *Star Wars* saga comes full circle as Anakin Skywalker (Christensen), in a desperate attempt to protect his wife, Padmé Amidala (Portman), succumbs to a persuasive Chancellor Palpatine and embraces the dark side of the Force. Long, uneven, but meticulously crafted entry in the six-part story has some of the same faults as its immediate predecessors, but delivers an emotional wallop as it brings the "prequel trilogy" to a conclusion. Yoda dominates every scene he's in—and gives the best performance in the film! HD 24P Widescreen. [PG-13]◗

Star Wars: The Clone Wars SEE: **Clone Wars, The**

State and Main (2000) **C-105m.** *** D: David Mamet. Alec Baldwin, William H. Macy, Philip Seymour Hoffman, Sarah Jessica Parker, Rebecca Pidgeon, Charles Durning, Patti LuPone, David Paymer, Julia Stiles, Ricky Jay, Michael Higgins, Clark Gregg, J. J. Johnston, John Krasinski. Writer-director Mamet has fun depicting the adventures of a desperate film crew that moves into—and takes over—a small New England town. The observations are perceptive, and the performances delicious (especially Macy as the director who can talk anybody into anything), though it may strike some that Mamet has chosen too easy a target. [R]▼◗

State Fair (1933) **96m.** *** D: Henry King. Janet Gaynor, Will Rogers, Lew Ayres, Sally Eilers, Norman Foster, Louise Dresser, Victor Jory, Frank Craven. Not just a Rogers vehicle, but slice of life '30s-style as farm family gets ready for annual outing to state fair: Mom's entering bake-off contest, Dad the pig contest, son and daughter looking for first love. Great atmosphere, good performances. Phil Stong's novel has been remade twice (so far!).

State Fair (1945) **C-100m.** *** D: Walter Lang. Jeanne Crain, Dana Andrews, Dick Haymes, Vivian Blaine, Charles Winninger, Fay Bainter, Donald Meek, Frank McHugh, Percy Kilbride. Remake of the 1933 film is bright, engaging musical of family's adventures at Iowa State Fair; colorful, with fine Rodgers and Hammerstein songs (their only

film score), including "That's for Me," "Grand Night for Singing," Oscar-winning "It Might As Well Be Spring." Retitled IT HAPPENED ONE SUMMER for TV. ▼◗◗

State Fair (1962) **C-118m.** BOMB D: Jose Ferrer. Pat Boone, Bobby Darin, Pamela Tiffin, Ann-Margret, Alice Faye, Tom Ewell, Wally Cox. Remake of sprightly 1945 musical is pretty bad. Faye came out of retirement to play Tiffin's mother—a bad mistake. Ewell even sings to a pig! Third-rate Americana. CinemaScope.▼◗

Statement, The (2003-Canadian-French-British) **C-120m.** *½ D: Norman Jewison. Michael Caine, Tilda Swinton, Jeremy Northam, Noam Jenkins, Charlotte Rampling, Matt Craven, Alan Bates, John Neville, Ciarán Hinds, David De Keyser, William Hutt. Woefully artificial rendering of Brian Moore's novel about a French Nazi collaborator who kills seven Jews in 1944 and spends the next five decades in hiding—with the help of the Catholic church. In 1992, a judge (Swinton) is handed the political hot potato of finding and prosecuting him, but he proves to be as elusive as ever. While based on historical truths, there isn't a convincing moment, despite a good cast and location filming in France. Written by Ronald Harwood. [R]▼◗

State of Grace (1990) **C-134m.** **½ D: Phil Joanou. Sean Penn, Ed Harris, Gary Oldman, Robin Wright, John Turturro, Burgess Meredith, John C. Reilly. Three strong actors play Irish-American mobsters (inspired by real-life gang, the Westies) contending with the police, the Mafia, and Yuppie gentrification in N.Y.C.'s Hell's Kitchen (a neighborhood now known as Clinton!). Combination of moody stylishness and extreme violence nearly succeeds, but script is more meandering than incisive. This is basically Cagney terrain with a Scorsese-De Niro spin; Oldman and especially Harris sear the screen. [R]▼◗◗

State of Play (2009-U.S.-British-French) **C-127m.** **½ D: Kevin Macdonald. Russell Crowe, Ben Affleck, Rachel McAdams, Helen Mirren, Robin Wright Penn, Jason Bateman, Jeff Daniels, Michael Berresse, Harry Lennix, Josh Mostel, Michael Weston, Barry Shabaka Henley, Viola Davis. Colorful, old-school D.C. newspaper reporter Crowe tries to link two seemingly unrelated murders, then a third (involving a female aide to hotshot Congressman Affleck—who happens to be Crowe's old roommate) seems to indicate that there's a larger conspiracy afoot. Meanwhile Crowe is paired up with blogger McAdams, who's never done on-the-ground reporting before. Engrossing, well-cast thriller is also a paean to the dying newspaper business—but drops the ball at the finale, which simply isn't satisfying. Adapted from the acclaimed 2003 BBC miniseries. Panavision. [PG-13]◗

State of Siege (1973-French) **C-120m.** ***

[1315]

D: Costa-Gavras. Yves Montand, Renato Salvatori, O. E. Hasse, Jacques Weber, Jean-Luc Bideau, Evangeline Peterson. Highly controversial film, based on fact, about political assassination in Uruguay; interesting, but way too one-sided to be truly effective.▼

State of the Union (1948) **124m.** ***½ D: Frank Capra. Spencer Tracy, Katharine Hepburn, Angela Lansbury, Van Johnson, Adolphe Menjou, Lewis Stone, Raymond Walburn, Margaret Hamilton, Carl ("Alfalfa") Switzer, Charles Lane, Tor Johnson. Contemporary as ever, this literate comedy-drama (adapted from the Howard Lindsay–Russel Crouse play) casts Tracy as an industrialist who struggles to keep his integrity as he's swallowed into the political machinery of running for President. Hepburn is his wife and conscience, Lansbury a power-hungry millionairess backing the campaign, Van Johnson the sardonic campaign manager. Great entertainment.▼○❙

State of Things, The (1982-German) **120m.** *** D: Wim Wenders. Allen Goorwitz (Garfield), Samuel Fuller, Paul Getty III, Roger Corman, Patrick Bauchau. Fascinating if uneven mystery from Wenders, centering on what happens as a film crew attempts to complete a remake of Corman's THE DAY THE WORLD ENDED on location in Portugal. Interesting as a peek behind the scenes at the filmmaking process, and as an homage to Corman.▼◗

State Property (2002) **C-88m.** BOMB D: Abdul Malik Abbott. Beanie Sigel, Jay-Z, Damon Dash, Memphis Bleek, Omillio Sparks, Brother Newz, Oschino, Sundy Carter, Dee Lee, Tyran "Ty-Ty" Smith. Violent junk about the rise (and inevitable fall) of a cocky, brutal gangsta, a Philadelphia drug lord named Beans (Sigel). The characters endlessly utter the "f" and "n" words, and are as demeaning and stereotypical as those played decades earlier by Stepin Fetchit. [R]▼❙

Stateside (2004-U.S.-German) **C-97m.** ** D: Reverge Anselmo. Rachael Leigh Cook, Jonathan Tucker, Agnes Bruckner, Val Kilmer, Joe Mantegna, Daniel Franzese, Carrie Fisher, Diane Venora, Ed Begley, Jr., Paul Le Mat, Joanne Pankow, George DiCenzo. Ill-fated love story between a young Marine and a schizophrenic musician who's confined to a mental hospital. Though family and friends try to keep these two messed-up kids apart, it doesn't always work out that way. Strange, disjointed romance has lots of loose ends with nothing tying them together. Impressive cast members appear mostly in misbegotten cameos. Kilmer is a hoot as the D.I.; look for an unbilled Penny Marshall as a lieutenant. Super 35. [R]▼❙

Static (1985) **C-93m.** **½ D: Mark Romanek. Keith Gordon, Amanda Plummer, Bob Gunton, Barton Heyman, Lily Knight, Jane Hoffman. Annoyingly uneven

comedy-drama about a strange young man (Gordon) and his rather unusual invention, a TV which can supposedly tune in to heaven. Sometimes genuinely touching and funny, but long stretches are deadening and dull. Gunton steals the film with his expert performance as a hilariously paranoid street evangelist. Written by leading actor Gordon and director Romanek. [R]▼○❙

Station, The (1990-Italian) **C-92m.** *** D: Sergio Rubini. Sergio Rubini, Margherita Buy, Ennio Fantastichini. Engrossing comedy-drama, with director Rubini starring as an unpretentious rural railroad clerk. His peaceful life is disrupted by the arrival of a beautiful woman on the lam from her brutal boyfriend. The manner in which the three characters interrelate forms the crux of this engaging, allegorical sleeper.▼

Station Agent, The (2003) **C-88m.** *** D: Tom McCarthy. Peter Dinklage, Patricia Clarkson, Bobby Cannavale, Raven Goodwin, Paul Benjamin, Michelle Williams, Richard Kind, Josh Pais, John Slattery. Refreshingly original indie about three lonely people who become friends in a quiet lakefront N.J. town: a dwarf who inherits (and moves into) a decrepit railroad depot, a young hotshot who operates the food wagon outside, and a divorced woman who's trying to get over some emotional hurdles. A small, observant, eminently satisfying film. Writer and first-time director McCarthy tailored the leading roles for these three actors. [R]▼❙

Stationmaster's Wife, The (1977-German) **C-111m.** **½ D: Rainer Werner Fassbinder. Kurt Raab, Elisabeth Trissenaar, Gustal Bayrhammer, Bernhard Helfrich, Udo Kier, Volker Spengler. Studied, stylized look at a beautiful woman's affairs and manipulation of her husband in pre-Hitler Germany. Some telling moments, and fine performances, but awfully slow going. Made for German television at 200m. Released theatrically in U.S. in 1983.▼❙

Station West (1948) **80m.** *** D: Sidney Lanfield. Dick Powell, Jane Greer, Tom Powers, Steve Brodie, Gordon Oliver, Raymond Burr, Agnes Moorehead, Burl Ives, Guinn Williams, Regis Toomey. Entertaining adaptation of Luke Short story about undercover military intelligence officer Powell stirring up trouble in Western town to find who's behind series of gold robberies. Script (by Frank Fenton and Winston Miller) has sharp dialogue throughout. Originally released at 92m. Also shown in computer-colored version.▼

Statue, The (1970-British) **C-84m.** BOMB D: Rod Amateau. David Niven, Virna Lisi, Robert Vaughn, Ann Bell, John Cleese, David Mills. Poor comedy concerning 20-foot statue (replica of Niven) with enormous male organ. [R]▼

Statutory Affair SEE: **Lola** (1969)

Stavisky . . . (1974-French-Italian) **C-**

118m. ***½ D: Alain Resnais. Jean-Paul Belmondo, Charles Boyer, François Périer, Anny Duperey, Michel Lonsdale, Roberto Bisacco, Claude Rich, Gérard Depardieu. Stylish bio of French swindler of the early 1930s; pleasant cast, lavish photography (by Sacha Vierny), fine Stephen Sondheim score. Screenplay by Jorge Semprun. [PG]▼▶

Stay (2005) **C-99m.** ** D: Marc Forster. Ewan McGregor, Naomi Watts, Ryan Gosling, Janeane Garofalo, B. D. Wong, Bob Hoskins, Kate Burton, Michael Gaston, Mark Margolis, Elizabeth Reaser, Amy Sedaris, Isaach De Bankolé. Shrink McGregor becomes psychologically unhinged as he takes on a new patient, a deeply disturbed, suicidal college student. Ambitious film plays with concepts of time, reality, and the meaning of sanity and insanity, as dead people come alive and the past, present, and future blend . . . but it's all a jumble, despite some arresting visuals. A disappointment from Forster (MONSTER'S BALL, FINDING NEVERLAND). You might add the Brooklyn Bridge to the cast list. Super 35. [R]▶

Stay Alive (2006) **C-85m.** ** D: William Brent Bell. Jon Foster, Samaire Armstrong, Frankie Muniz, Sophia Bush, Adam Goldberg, Jimmi Simpson, Milo Ventimiglia. Hard-core video gamers test an underground horror survival title, only to die gruesomely, one by one, exactly like their digital avatars. The culprit: 17th-century Hungarian "Blood Countess" Elizabeth Báthory, who haunts the game and hunts its players. Startling juxtaposition of real life and realm life is the New Orleans–set thriller's sole thrill, but it's a good one. As for the dramaturgy, Báthory—even if undead—should sue for defamation. Alternate version runs 101m. Super 35. [PG-13]▶

Stay As You Are (1978-French) **C-95m.** *½ D: Alberto Lattuada. Marcello Mastroianni, Nastassia Kinski, Francisco Rabal, Monica Randal, Giuliana Calandra. Yawner with a twist: Kinski, the teenaged romance of middle-aged Mastroianni, may be his illegitimate daughter. For those who want to see Kinski during her nymphet stage; others beware.▼

Stay Away, Joe (1968) **C-102m.** *½ D: Peter Tewksbury. Elvis Presley, Burgess Meredith, Joan Blondell, Katy Jurado, Thomas Gomez, Henry Jones, L. Q. Jones. Bad film, even for Presley, about contemporary Indians. Reinforces stereotypes, fails to entertain. Panavision. [M/PG]▼▶

Stay Hungry (1976) **C-103m.** *** D: Bob Rafelson. Jeff Bridges, Sally Field, Arnold Schwarzenegger, R. G. Armstrong, Robert Englund, Helena Kallianiotes, Roger Mosley, Scatman Crothers, Fannie Flagg, Joanna Cassidy, Richard Gilliland, Ed Begley, Jr., John David Carson, Joe Spinell. Charles Gaines novel about body-building in the "New South" is eccentric mixture of comedy and drama, but many fine scenes; happy performances from Field and Schwarzenegger make it worthwhile. [R]▼▶

Staying Alive (1983) **C-96m.** ** D: Sylvester Stallone. John Travolta, Cynthia Rhodes, Finola Hughes, Steve Inwood, Julie Bovasso, Frank Stallone. Sequel to SATURDAY NIGHT FEVER is fashioned by director/cowriter Stallone into a ROCKY-type vehicle for Travolta, who juggles two women in his life while trying to score as a dancer on Broadway. Broadway show finale, *Satan's Alley* (billed, with amazing accuracy, as a musical trip through Hell) is a camp classic, but neither the script nor the music (mostly by Sly's brother Frank) are in a class with the original 1977 film. Look closely for Patrick Swayze as a fellow terpsichorean. [PG]▼▶

Staying Together (1989) **C-91m.** **½ D: Lee Grant. Sean Astin, Stockard Channing, Melinda Dillon, Jim Haynie, Levon Helm, Dinah Manoff, Dermot Mulroney, Tim Quill, Keith Szarabajka, Daphne Zuniga. Close-knit small-town family, with three boys on the verge of manhood, gets pulled in all directions. Pat comedy-drama has one too many subplots, though entire cast is good. [R]▼▶

Stay Tuned (1992) **C-87m.** *½ D: Peter Hyams. John Ritter, Pam Dawber, Jeffrey Jones, Eugene Levy, David Tom, Heather McComb, Bob Dishy, Joyce Gordon, Erik King, Salt 'n Pepa. Terminal couch potato Ritter unwittingly makes a pact with Devilish Jones, and finds himself and his wife sucked into a TV world in which they're part of the shows, from wrestling to private-eye mysteries. Promising premise goes nowhere in this dismal comedy; the only chuckles come from quick spoofs of TV titles, and the only segment that works is an animated cartoon supervised by the great Chuck Jones. Panavision. [PG]▼▶

Steagle, The (1971) **C-90m.** ** D: Paul Sylbert. Richard Benjamin, Chill Wills, Cloris Leachman, Jean Allison, Susan Tyrrell. Missile crisis causes professor to go berserk and try living in lifestyles that previously were mental fantasies. Farfetched. [R]▼▶

Steal Big, Steal Little (1995) **C-135m.** ** D: Andrew Davis. Andy Garcia, Alan Arkin, Rachel Ticotin, Joe Pantoliano, Holland Taylor, Ally Walker, David Ogden Stiers, Charles Rocket, Richard Bradford, Kevin McCarthy. Amiable mess of a movie with plot strands going in all directions; a real shame, too, because there's a nice feel to this modern fable about twin brothers, separated in childhood, who take different paths in life. One greedily pursues money and power, the other grows up with a free-spirited share-the-wealth ideal. Garcia has never been more engaging. Set and shot in Santa Barbara, California. [PG-13]▼▶

Stealing Beauty (1996-French-Italian-British-U.S.) **C-119m.** *** D: Bernardo Bertolucci. Jeremy Irons, Liv Tyler, Joseph Fiennes, Sinead Cusack, Rachel Weisz, Stefania Sandrelli, Jean Marais, D. W. Moffett, Donal McCann, Jason Flemyng. 19-year-old American girl spends the summer at a villa in Tuscany filled with wildly divergent characters and discovers her own independence as she affects the lives of all those around her. Bertolucci returns to his Italian roots for this charming contemporary story. Tyler is a star in the making here, and Irons is touching as a dying man who finds renewed life from this young visitor. Bertolucci coscripted, from his story. Super 35. [R] ▼●)

Stealing Harvard (2002) **C-83m.** *½ D: Bruce McCulloch. Tom Green, Jason Lee, Leslie Mann, Megan Mullally, Dennis Farina, Tammy Blanchard, Richard Jenkins, Chris Penn, John C. McGinley, Seymour Cassel, Linda Cardellini. Engaged Lee's $30,000 nest egg goes poof when he's rudely reminded of a years-ago offer to put trailer-dwelling niece Blanchard through school. Now, she's become Harvard material, and it's up to Lee's pal Green to help him come up with the cash. "Tom Green" and "Harvard" should never appear on the same marquee, though not every movie can get Farina (as Lee's future in-law) into a dress. He makes it look almost as off-the-rack as this script. [PG-13] ▼▶)

Stealing Heaven (1988-British-Yugoslavian) **C-115m.** *** D: Clive Donner. Kim Thomson, Derek de Lint, Denholm Elliott, Mark Jax, Bernard Hepton, Kenneth Cranham, Angela Pleasence, Rachel Kempson. Beautifully photographed (if somewhat anachronistic) period piece about the real-life 12th-century lovers Abelard and Héloise. Intelligent treatment even incorporates discussions of theology in the context of this passionate romance. Threatened with an X rating, film was trimmed to 108m. for U.S. release; both versions available on video. [R] ▼●

Stealing Home (1988) **C-98m.** **½ D: Steven Kampmann, Will Aldis. Mark Harmon, Jodie Foster, William McNamara, Blair Brown, Harold Ramis, Jonathan Silverman, Richard Jenkins, John Shea, Ted Ross, Helen Hunt, Thatcher Goodwin, Yvette Croskey. Has-been baseball player is summoned home to take care of the ashes of an old friend, who killed herself. Story flashes back to his relationship with her at several ages. Earnest but pat, semi-autobiographical script (by the directors) is helped immeasurably by Foster's wise, outstanding performance as the late friend, a troubled free spirit. [PG-13] ▼●)

Stealing Time (2003) **C-99m.** *½ D: Marc Fusco. Charlotte Ayanna, Ethan Embry, Peter Facinelli, Scott Foley, Jennifer Garner, Paul Dooley. Well-meaning but muddled account of four recent college graduates, all anxious to start their real-world lives, who deal with their frustrations as they attempt to realize their dreams. Then one of them learns he is terminally ill. Tries desperately to be philosophical and poignant but then, confusingly and annoyingly, morphs into a caper film . . . a bad one at that! Aka RENNIE'S LANDING. [R] ▶)

Stealth (2005) **C-121m.** ** D: Rob Cohen. Josh Lucas, Jessica Biel, Jamie Foxx, Sam Shepard, Richard Roxburgh, Joe Morton, Ian Bliss, Ebon Moss-Bachrach; voice of Wentworth Miller. It's TOP GUN with HAL-9000 as a pilot. Hotshot Navy pilots Lucas, Biel, and Foxx are presented with the fourth member of their team: a plane that flies itself, so smart it has a personality. When the aircraft ventures beyond its programming, highly predictable crises ensue. Expensive action thriller with lots of effects but hollow characters. Panavision. [PG-13] ▼▶

Steal This Movie (2000) **C-111m.** ** D: Robert Greenwald. Vincent D'Onofrio, Janeane Garofalo, Jeanne Tripplehorn, Kevin Pollak, Donal Logue, Kevin Corrigan, Troy Garity, Joyce Gordon, Bernard Kay, Michael Cera. One-dimensional portrait of celebrated 1960s/70s political activist Abbie Hoffman, founder of the Yippie movement, who spent years hiding out from the Feds. D'Onofrio (who coexecutive produced) is good, but the film is disappointingly superficial. Garofalo and Tripplehorn are well cast as the women in Hoffman's life. Garity plays his real-life father, Tom Hayden. [R] ▼▶

Steamboat Bill, Jr. (1928) **71m.** *** D: Charles F. Riesner. Buster Keaton, Ernest Torrence, Marion Byron, Tom Lewis, Tom McGuire. Buster plays a milquetoast who must prove his manhood to steamboat captain father (Torrence). Not one of Keaton's best silents, but there are great moments, and classic, eye-popping cyclone finale. ▼●)

Steamboat 'Round the Bend (1935) **96m.** *** D: John Ford. Will Rogers, Anne Shirley, Irvin S. Cobb, Eugene Pallette, Berton Churchill, John McGuire, Stepin Fetchit, Francis Ford, Pardner Jones, Charles Middleton. Enjoyable Ford/Rogers period piece of steamboat captain (Rogers) who pilots a ramshackle floating waxworks museum, from which he also dispenses highly alcoholic cure-all medicine. Shirley is particularly good as swamp girl taken in by Rogers. Churchill shines in comic role of river prophet "The New Moses." Climactic steamboat race is a gem. Released posthumously after Rogers' tragic death. ▶)

Steamboy (2004-Japanese) **C-126m.** **½ D: Katsuhiro Ōtomo. Voices of Anna Paquin, Alfred Molina, Patrick Stewart, Kari Wahlgren. Set in Victorian England, this elaborate, overlong anime feature by the director of AKIRA runs out of steam (no pun intended) midway through. Youngster Ray Steam is entrusted with a "steam ball," an

[1318]

incredible source of energy at the heart of a feud between his power-mad father and ec-centric reclusive grandfather. It all comes to a head during action-packed climax, when father's gargantuan Steam Tower runs amok through London. Too much talk, not enough action, though there are compelling visuals, elaborate production design, and first-rate animation. Original version (available in sub-titled form) runs 140m. [PG-13]▮

Steaming (1985-British) **C-95m.** **½ D: Joseph Losey. Vanessa Redgrave, Sarah Miles, Diana Dors, Patti Love, Brenda Bruce, Felicity Dean, Sally Sagoe. Disap-pointing adaptation of the Nell Dunn play, about the interactions of a group of women in a run-down London steam bath. Not all that bad, really, with collectively above-average performances, but sorely lacks the humor that made it work so well on stage. Director Losey's last film, and Dors' as well. [R]▼

Steel (1980) **C-99m.** **½ D: Steve Carver. Lee Majors, Jennifer O'Neill, Art Carney, George Kennedy, Harris Yulin, Terry Kiser, Richard Lynch, Roger Mosley, Albert Salmi, R. G. Armstrong. Fast-moving, en-tertaining time-killer about construction workers struggling to complete a skyscraper on schedule. Filmed in Lexington, Ky. Aka LOOK DOWN AND DIE and MEN OF STEEL. [PG]▼

Steel (1997) **C-97m.** *½ D: Kenneth John-son. Shaquille O'Neal, Annabeth Gish, Judd Nelson, Richard Roundtree, Irma P. Hall, Ray J., Charles Napier. Film version of DC Com-ics' "Steel" with basketball great Shaq in the title role, as a tall superhero with a heart of gold, wearing a funny metal suit and doing battle with stereotypical enemies of modern civilization. As endearing as Shaq can be, he should definitely *not* give up his day job. [PG-13] ▼●

Steel Dawn (1987) **C-100m.** ** D: Lance Hool. Patrick Swayze, Lisa Niemi, Christo-pher Neame, Brion James, Anthony Zerbe, John Fujioka, Brett Hool. Futuristic rehash of SHANE has Swayze as the mysteri-ous warrior who ends up protecting pretty farmer Niemi (his real-life wife) and her cute son against evil Zerbe and his hench-men. Filmed on attractive desert locations in southern Africa, this failed to extend Swayze's meteoric success in DIRTY DANCING. [R]▼●

Steele Justice (1987) **C-95m.** ** D: Robert Boris. Martin Kove, Sela Ward, Ronny Cox, Bernie Casey, Joseph Campanella, Soon-Teck Oh, Jan Gan Boyd, Robert Kim, Peter Kwong, Shannon Tweed, Sarah Douglas. Howlingly absurd action-revenge yarn with beefy Vietnam vet Kove investigating the murder of a Vietnamese friend and his family in L.A., and going after former Viet general who's now a drug lord in America. Nagging doubts persist—do the filmmak-ers intend this to be so funny?—but Kove's

impromptu wound-cauterizing scene makes it all worthwhile. [R]▼●

Steel Helmet, The (1951) **84m.** ***½ D: Samuel Fuller. Gene Evans, Robert Hutton, Steve Brodie, James Edwards, Richard Loo, Sid Melton. Evans is a gutsy American ser-geant caught in dizzying turn of events in early days of Korean war; solid melodrama written by Fuller, with surprisingly contemporary view of war itself.▼

Steel Magnolias (1989) **C-118m.** *** D: Her-bert Ross. Sally Field, Dolly Parton, Shirley MacLaine, Daryl Hannah, Olympia Dukakis, Julia Roberts, Tom Skerritt, Sam Shepard, Dy-lan McDermott, Kevin J. O'Connor, Bill Mc-Cutcheon, Ann Wedgeworth, Janine Turner. Slick comedy-drama about several years in the lives of the women who congregate at Parton's beauty parlor in a small Louisiana town. No TERMS OF ENDEARMENT, but does provide solid entertainment. Written by Robert Harling, who expanded his own one-set play for the screen (and plays the minister here). Super 35. [PG]▼●

Steelyard Blues (1973) **C-93m.** *** D: Alan Myerson. Jane Fonda, Donald Suther-land, Peter Boyle, Garry Goodrow, How-ard Hesseman, John Savage. Entertaining comic concoction by David S. Ward about band of misfits who become involved in nutty project of rejuvenating abandoned airplane. Amiably antiestablishment film highlights Boyle as an ingenious fantasist named Eagle. [PG]▼▮

Stella (1990) **C-109m.** ** D: John Erman. Bette Midler, John Goodman, Trini Al-varado, Stephen Collins, Marsha Mason, Eileen Brennan, Linda Hart, Ben Stiller, William McNamara. Update of the peren-nial soaper STELLA DALLAS goes with the times on only one plot element: in this version, Stella *doesn't* marry the father of her child. Tolerable for a while, but hope-lessly anachronistic. [PG-13] ▼●

Stella Dallas (1937) **106m.** *** D: King Vidor. Barbara Stanwyck, John Boles, Anne Shirley, Barbara O'Neil, Alan Hale, Tim Holt, Marjorie Main. Definitive soap opera (from Olive Higgins Prouty's novel) of woman who sacrifices everything for her daughter; Stanwyck gives one of her finest performances. Tearjerking score by Alfred Newman. Filmed before in 1925; remade in 1990 as STELLA. ▼●

St. Elmo's Fire (1985) **C-108m.** **½ D: Joel Schumacher. Rob Lowe, Demi Moore, Andrew McCarthy, Judd Nelson, Ally Sheedy, Emilio Estevez, Mare Winning-ham, Martin Balsam, Jon Cutler, Joyce Van Patten, Andie MacDowell, Blake Clark, Matthew Laurance, Anna Maria Horsford. Slick vehicle for some charismatic young actors, as recent college grads having a hard time coping with Real Life. Invites com-parison to THE BREAKFAST CLUB and THE BIG CHILL, but these "young adults" are pretty immature, and so is the film, written by director Schumacher. Panavision. [R]▼●◗

Step Brothers (2008) **C-98m.** ** D: Adam McKay. Will Ferrell, John C. Reilly, Richard Jenkins, Mary Steenburgen, Kathryn Hahn, Adam Scott, Seth Rogen, Horatio Sanz, Andrea Savage, Lurie Poston, Elizabeth Yozamp. Ferrell and Reilly are 40-year-olds still living at home with their single parents; they suddenly become stepbrothers when their respective mom and dad meet each other, marry, and move in together—all before the opening credits! Crux of the film has them trying to adjust to each other while being threatened with eviction. Dumb comedy milks its premise for some occasional laughs. Unrated version runs 105m. Super 35. [R]◗

Stepfather, The (1987) **C-98m.** *** D: Joseph Ruben. Terry O'Quinn, Jill Schoelen, Shelley Hack, Stephen Shellen, Charles Lanyer. Engrossing thriller has well-cast O'Quinn as a meek-looking guy desperately seeking to have the perfect little family. He turns out to be a psycho who marries widows and eventually erupts into violence. Thoughtful screenplay by Donald E. Westlake and taut direction by Ruben highlight this sleeper. Story by Westlake, Carolyn Lefcourt, and Brian Garfield. Followed by two sequels; remade in 2009. [R]▼●◗

Stepfather, The (2009) **C-102m.** ** D: Nelson McCormick. Dylan Walsh, Sela Ward, Penn Badgley, Amber Heard, Sherry Stringfield, Paige Turco, Jon Tenney, Nancy Linehan Charles. Competent remake of the 1987 thriller about a psychopath who marries unsuspecting women, then murders them and their children begs the question, "Why remake this?" It ain't Hitchcock, so rehashing this sordid tale seems pointless. For undiscriminating fans of suburban horror it has the requisite scares and a fairly effective lead in Walsh. Super 35. [PG-13]◗

Stepfather II (1989) **C-86m.** *½ D: Jeff Burr. Terry O'Quinn, Meg Foster, Jonathan Brandis, Caroline Williams, Mitchell Laurance, Henry Brown, Leon Martell, Renata Scott. Mad family killer O'Quinn escapes from the booby hatch, sets himself up in suburbia as a marriage counselor, and starts courting a potential new wife (Foster). Inferior sequel is completely devoid of suspense and looks cheap, but O'Quinn still manages to deliver a good performance. [R]▼●◗

Stepford Wives, The (1975) **C-115m.** *** D: Bryan Forbes. Katharine Ross, Paula Prentiss, Peter Masterson, Nanette Newman, Patrick O'Neal, Tina Louise, Dee Wallace, William Prince. Effective chiller finds suburban housewives Ross and Prentiss trying to understand perpetually blissful state of the women of Stepford, Connecticut. Script by William Goldman from Ira Levin's best-seller. Seven-year-old Mary Stuart Masterson makes her film debut

(playing the daughter of real-life dad Peter Masterson). Followed by three inferior TV sequels (REVENGE OF THE STEPFORD WIVES, THE STEPFORD CHILDREN, and THE STEPFORD HUSBANDS) and a 2004 remake. [PG]▼●◗

Stepford Wives, The (2004) **C-93m.** ** D: Frank Oz. Nicole Kidman, Matthew Broderick, Bette Midler, Glenn Close, Christopher Walken, Roger Bart, David Marshall Grant, Jon Lovitz, Faith Hill, Mike White. Recently fired workaholic TV exec Kidman moves with husband Broderick and their kids to a Connecticut community where everything seems perfect—a little *too* perfect—especially the docile housewives. Misguided remake of the 1975 movie substitutes broad comedy for the eeriness that made the original (based on Ira Levin's novel) so effective. What's more, the concept was fresh back then; now the term "Stepford wife" has entered the vernacular and there's no suspense at all. Written by Paul Rudnick. [PG-13]▼◗

Stephanie Daley (2007) **C-92m.** *** D: Hilary Brougher. Tilda Swinton, Amber Tamblyn, Timothy Hutton, Denis O'Hare, Jim Gaffigan, Deirdre O'Connell, Halley Feiffer, Kel O'Neill, Melissa Leo, Caitlin Van Zandt, Novella Nelson. When a 16-year-old girl is accused of killing her newborn baby during a ski trip, forensic psychologist Swinton—who's about to have her first child—is hired to determine whether the teenager was fully aware of what she did. As Tamblyn recounts her experiences, Swinton attempts to come to terms with her fears about her own pregnancy. Provocative and satisfying drama, written by director Brougher, explores two women at different stages of their lives. The acting is superior. [R]◗

Stephen King's Cat's Eye SEE: **Cat's Eye**
Stephen King's Graveyard Shift SEE: **Graveyard Shift**
Stephen King's Riding the Bullet SEE: **Riding the Bullet**
Stephen King's Silver Bullet SEE: **Silver Bullet**
Stephen King's "Sleepwalkers" SEE: **Sleepwalkers**
Stephen King's The Night Flier SEE: **Night Flier, The**
Stephen King's Thinner SEE: **Thinner**

Step Into Liquid (2003) **C-88m.** *** D: Dana Brown. Entertaining, eye-catching surfer documentary in which a bevy of beautiful bodies—a who's who of contemporary surfers—hit the waves at locations around the globe. Director is the son of Bruce Brown, who explored the subject in THE ENDLESS SUMMER and THE ENDLESS SUMMER II. ◗

Step Lively (1944) **88m.** *** D: Tim Whelan. Frank Sinatra, George Murphy, Adolphe Menjou, Gloria DeHaven, Eugene Pallette, Anne Jeffreys, Walter Slezak.

Brisk musical remake of ROOM SERVICE with producer Murphy wheeling and dealing to get his show produced. Engagingly frantic, with sharp dialogue, funny contribution by Slezak as the hotel manager. If you blink you'll miss (brunette) Dorothy Malone as switchboard operator in lobby. ▼▶

Stepmom (1998) **C-125m.** **✶✶** D: Chris Columbus. Susan Sarandon, Julia Roberts, Ed Harris, Jena Malone, Liam Aiken, Lynn Whitfield. Slick, big-studio, all-star treatment of life after divorce. Sarandon plays a woman who objects to the presence of her ex's girlfriend in her children's lives. Glossy melodrama with occasional touches of humor; the leads outshine the mawkish material. Panavision. [PG-13] ▼●▶

Stepmother, The (1971) **C-94m.** **✶½** D: Hikmet Avedis. Alejandro Rey, John Anderson, Katherine Justice, John D. Garfield, Marlene Schmidt, Claudia Jennings, Duncan McLeod. Rey is okay as anti-hero of this cheapie murder-suspenser in the Hitchcock mold. John Garfield's son is unimpressive in support. Aka IMPULSION. [R] ▼

Steppenwolf (1974) **C-105m.** **✶✶½** D: Fred Haines. Max von Sydow, Dominique Sanda, Pierre Clementi, Carla Romanelli, Alfred Bailloux. Literal adaptation of Herman Hesse's unfilmable novel about a misanthropic writer and an enigmatic young woman. Visually jazzy, rarely boring, but a dead end. [R] ▼●▶

Stepping Out (1991) **C-106m.** **✶✶** D: Lewis Gilbert. Liza Minnelli, Shelley Winters, Bill Irwin, Ellen Greene, Julie Walters, Robyn Stevan, Jane Krakowski, Sheila McCarthy, Andrea Martin, Carol Woods, Nora Dunn. Harmless blue-haired musical soaper about a smorgasbord group of Buffalo tap-dancing aspirants who bicker under Minnelli's tutelage. Richard Harris (not the actor) adapted his play, glitzed up by director Gilbert. There's a gratuitous show-stopping piece at the end for Liza-watchers, while Winters has some genuinely affecting moments as the piano accompanist. [PG] ▼●

Step Up (2006) **C-103m.** **✶✶** D: Anne Fletcher. Channing Tatum, Jenna Dewan, Rachel Griffiths, Mario, Drew Sidora, Damaine Radcliff, De'Shawn Washington, Heavy D, Isaiah Washington. Monosyllabic urban punk with some major dance moves—but little else—is busted vandalizing a school of the arts, earning 200 hours of community service as a janitor at the scene of the crime. There he falls for a student ballerina and initiates an adagio both in and out of the rehearsal hall. Teen musical culminates with the Big Show, combining hip-hop with ballet, like Eminem *en pointe*. Director-choreographer Fletcher also plays the dance teacher, whose style suggests Martha Graham trying to breakdance. Followed by two sequels. J-D-C Scope. [PG-13] ▶

Step Up 2 the Streets (2008) **C-98m.** **✶✶** D: Jon M. Chu. Briana Evigan, Robert Hoffman, Adam G. Sevani, Cassie Ventura, Danielle Polanco, Will Kemp, Channing Tatum. Troublesome tomboy Evigan (daughter of TV star Greg) enrolls at a performing arts school, where she assembles a dance crew made up of fellow outcasts, hoping to compete in an underground dance battle called the Streets. Story takes a distant backseat to the incredible dancing, culminating in an exciting finale. Tatum's brief cameo is the only connection to STEP UP. Followed by STEP UP 3D. Super 35. [PG-13] ▶

Step Up 3D (2010) **C-97m.** **✶✶½** D: Jon M. Chu. Rick Malambri, Adam G. Sevani, Sharni Vinson, Alyson Stoner, Keith Stallworth, Kendra Andrews, Stephen "tWitch" Boss, Joe Slaughter, Kathy Najimy. Two friends (Malambri and Vinson) embark on college life at N.Y.U., but he is distracted by the street dance scene and starts spending all his time and energy at a warehouse that serves as haven, home, and creative workshop all in one. Corny storyline is energized by dance numbers, including high-energy competitive dance-offs, a nifty tango, and an exuberant three-minute Fred & Ginger–inspired set piece on a Manhattan brownstone block. Aimed at Disneyfied teenage girls and designed to show off 3-D, which it does with great zest. 3-D. [PG-13] ▶

Sterile Cuckoo, The (1969) **C-107m.** **✶✶✶** D: Alan J. Pakula. Liza Minnelli, Wendell Burton, Tim McIntire. Lonely Pookie Adams (Minnelli) forces herself on shy freshman Burton, who's impelled to pay attention. Winning look at young love and sensitive feelings gives Liza a stand-out role, with Burton equally fine as naive boy who eventually outgrows her. Dory Previn's song "Come Saturday Morning" is featured. Producer Pakula's directorial debut. Based on a novel by John Nichols. [PG] ▼●

Stevie (1978-British) **C-102m.** **✶✶✶** D: Robert Enders. Glenda Jackson, Mona Washbourne, Alec McCowen, Trevor Howard. Film version of Hugh Whitemore's London stage play about British poetess Stevie Smith (Jackson), who lives with her maiden aunt (Washbourne). Finely wrought character study; excellent performances. [PG] ▼

Stevie (2003) **C-145m.** **✶✶✶½** D: Steve James. Documentary from HOOP DREAMS director is just as powerful in its own way. Filmed over an extended period, it's a poignant portrait of a rural Illinois trouble magnet to whom James, in earlier times, was an official Big Brother. Now the youth is awaiting sentencing for an alleged offense far more serious than his usual scrapes: sexually abusing his 8-year-old cousin. Best scene reunites Stevie with the first, and most loving, of his many foster-home parents (some of whom abused *him*). This is really a movie that leaves you wondering, "What if . . . ?"▶

St. Helens (1981) **C-90m.** **½ D: Ernest Pintoff. Art Carney, David Huffman, Cassie Yates, Ron O'Neal, Bill McKinney, Albert Salmi. Mount St. Helens is about to erupt, and old codger Carney (named Harry Truman!) refuses to leave his home. Not too bad, with a fine Carney performance; based on a true story. [PG]▼▶

Stick (1985) **C-109m.** *½ D: Burt Reynolds. Burt Reynolds, Candice Bergen, George Segal, Charles Durning, Jose Perez, Richard Lawson, Alex Rocco, Tricia Leigh Fisher, Dar Robinson. Incredibly boring underworld melodrama about an ex-con who sets out to avenge the death of an old buddy and finds himself knee-deep in ugly drug dealers. Originally set for release in 1984, then pulled back for some reshooting, which apparently didn't help. Based on an Elmore Leonard novel. [R]▼●

Stick It (2006) **C-105m.** ** D: Jessica Bendinger. Jeff Bridges, Missy Peregrym, Vanessa Lengies, Nikki SooHoo, Maddy Curley, Kellan Lutz, John Patrick Amedori, Jon Gries, Gia Carides, Polly Holliday, Julie Warner, Annie Corley. The writer of BRING IT ON makes her directing debut with this story of competition, dirty tricks, and behind-the-scenes juice in the world of teenage gymnastics. Peregrym is a washout with personal problems who walked away from a championship and now has nowhere to go but back to training with Bridges. Diffuse screenplay (by Bendinger) strays in too many directions and stumbles to a ho-hum finish. [PG-13]▶

Sticky Fingers (1988) **C-97m.** ** D: Catlin Adams. Helen Slater, Melanie Mayron, Danitra Vance, Eileen Brennan, Carol Kane, Loretta Devine, Stephen McHattie, Christopher Guest, Gwen Welles. Dippy roommates find themselves the custodians of a suitcase full of drug money, which they proceed to "borrow" and spend. Earnest attempt at wacky, female-slanted comedy goes completely askew. Likable stars and a high energy level can't keep it afloat. Scripted by director Adams and costar Mayron. [PG-13]▼●

Stiffs SEE: **Out Cold** (1989)

Stiff Upper Lips (1998-British) **C-94m.** ** D: Gary Sinyor. Peter Ustinov, Prunella Scales, Georgina Cates, Samuel West, Sean Pertwee, Robert Portal, Brian Glover, Frank Finlay. A high-born young woman falls in love with a handsome peasant. Anemic spoof of Merchant-Ivory films and the type of fodder that turns up on *Masterpiece Theatre*. Some easy laughs here and there, but as parodies go this one is second-rate.▼▶

Stigmata (1999) **C-103m.** *½ D: Rupert Wainwright. Patricia Arquette, Gabriel Byrne, Jonathan Pryce, Nia Long, Thomas Kopache, Rade Sherbedgia (Serbedzija), Enrico Colantoni, Dick Latessa, Portia de

Rossi. A lotta *Sturm,* a lotta *Drang,* but not much else in this EXORCIST derivation about a young woman who quite suddenly suffers from bloody attacks (à la stigmata) and hallucinations . . . and the Vatican scientist/priest who comes to investigate. Loud, flamboyant (with meaningless closeups of coffee pouring, an egg frying, etc.), but hopeless. Super 35. [R]▼▶

Stiletto (1969) **C-98m.** *½ D: Bernard Kowalski. Alex Cord, Britt Ekland, Patrick O'Neal, Joseph Wiseman, Barbara McNair, Roy Scheider, Charles Durning, M. Emmett Walsh. Weak Mafia melodrama about handsome killer who lives like a playboy, kills for money. Repercussions abound when he decides to quit his job. From the Harold Robbins novel. Look fast for Raul Julia in a party scene. [R]▼

Still Breathing (1998) **C-108m.** **½ D: James F. Robinson. Brendan Fraser, Joanna Going, Celeste Holm, Ann Magnuson, Lou Rawls, Angus MacFadyen, Toby Huss, Paolo Seganti, Michael McKean, Junior Brown, The Jim Cullum Jazz Band. One of those supposedly "magical" romances, in which two complete opposites (San Antonio puppeteer/dreamer Fraser and L.A. con artist/cynic Going) eventually find each other. Two fine lead performances help lift this above the routine and keep it from being overly syrupy. [PG-13]▼▶

Still Crazy (1998-U.S.-British) **C-97m.** *** D: Brian Gibson. Stephen Rea, Billy Connolly, Jimmy Nail, Timothy Spall, Bill Nighy, Juliet Aubrey, Helena Bergstrom, Bruce Robinson, Rachael Stirling. Amiable film about the reunion of a 1970s rock band called Strange Fruit and its star-crossed musicians, whose resentments and peccadilloes are still fresh after 20 years. Built on a surefire foundation, the story has just enough twists to keep you guessing where it's going and a gallery of enjoyable performances. Bonus: the music is actually good. [R]▼●

Still of the Night (1982) **C-91m.** ** D: Robert Benton. Roy Scheider, Meryl Streep, Jessica Tandy, Joe Grifasi, Sara Botsford, Josef Sommer. Yet another disappointing homage to Hitchcock in this tale of a psychiatrist attracted to a woman who may or may not have murdered one of his patients. A cold film with more plot holes than one would care to count. [PG]▼▶

Still Smokin' (1983) **C-91m.** BOMB D: Thomas Chong. Cheech Marin, Thomas Chong, Hansman In't Veld, Carol Van Herwijnen, Shirleen Stroker, Susan Hahn. Rock bottom. Not even the most forgiving C & C fans can justify this nonmovie that climaxes a scant plot involving an Amsterdam film festival with twenty minutes of laughless concert footage. An unreleaseable film that somehow made it to theaters—for five-day runs. [R]▼●

Sting, The (1973) **C-129m.** ***½ D:

George Roy Hill. Paul Newman, Robert Redford, Robert Shaw, Charles Durning, Ray Walston, Eileen Brennan, Harold Gould, Dana Elcar, Jack Kehoe, Dimitra Arliss, Charles Dierkop, Sally Kirkland. Two small-time Chicago con men try to put "the sting" on a high-roller from N.Y.C. (Shaw) after he has one of their pals killed. This long but entertaining film won seven Oscars, including Best Picture, Director, and Screenplay (David S. Ward), and sparked national revival of Scott Joplin's ragtime music (arranged here by Oscar winner Marvin Hamlisch). Sequel: THE STING II. [PG] ▼●)

Sting II, The (1983) C-102m. *½ D: Jeremy Paul Kagan. Jackie Gleason, Mac Davis, Teri Garr, Karl Malden, Oliver Reed, Bert Remsen. Even as recent sequels go, this tardy follow-up to the Oscar winner is pretty limp. Gleason and Davis (in Newman's and Redford's roles!) rig a boxing match designed to shaft Malden, with Reed (in Shaw's role) as an unknowing cog in the scheme. Despite the male milieu, only Garr delivers a lively performance. Oddly, David S. Ward wrote this one, too. [PG] ▼●)

Stingray (1978) C-100m. *½ D: Richard Taylor. Sherry Jackson, Christopher Mitchum, Bill Watson, Les Lannom, Sondra Theodore, Bert Hinchman. Low-grade mix of action, blood, and comedy as Mitchum and Lannom buy a Stingray, unaware that it's filled with stolen loot and dope, prompting pursuit by murderous Jackson. Filmed in and around St. Louis. Aka ABIGAIL: WANTED. [PG]▼

Stir (1980-Australian) C-100m. ***½ D: Stephen Wallace. Bryan Brown, Max Phipps, Dennis Miller, Michael Gow, Phil Motherwell, Gary Waddell. Harrowing tale of life in prison, focusing on the jailors' brutality and culminating in riots and destruction. Excellent performances by all, particularly Brown; a memorable first feature for Wallace. Screenplay by Ben Jewson, based on first-hand experience.

Stir Crazy (1980) C-111m. *** D: Sidney Poitier. Gene Wilder, Richard Pryor, Georg Stanford Brown, JoBeth Williams, Miguelangel Suarez, Craig T. Nelson, Barry Corbin, Erland van Lidth de Jeude, Lee Purcell. Broadly funny film about two yoyos who bungle their way into prison. No great shakes in terms of script or direction; just a lot of good laughs. Screenplay by Bruce Jay Friedman; lively score by Tom Scott. Later a brief TV series. [R]▼●)

Stir of Echoes (1999) C-99m. **½ D: David Koepp. Kevin Bacon, Kathryn Erbe, Kevin Dunn, Illeana Douglas, Liza Weil, Conor O'Farrell, Jenny Morrison, Zachary David Cope. Working-class Chicagoan undergoes hypnosis for a lark and suddenly finds himself haunted by visions and premonitions— just like his five-year-old son, who sees ghosts. Intriguing film plays with our emo-

tions and becomes increasingly unpleasant as it goes along. Koepp adapted Richard Matheson's novel. Followed by a direct-to-DVD sequel. [R] ▼●)

Stitches (1985) C-89m. BOMB D: Alan Smithee (Rod Holcomb). Parker Stevenson, Geoffrey Lewis, Brian Tochi, Robin Dearden, Eddie Albert. Derivative comedy about medical students' hijinks is not titillating or funny enough to be diverting. Director Holcomb had his name removed from the credits after film was doctored during postproduction. [R]▼

St. Ives (1976) C-93m. ** D: J. Lee Thompson. Charles Bronson, John Houseman, Jacqueline Bisset, Harry Guardino, Maximilian Schell, Harris Yulin, Dana Elcar, Elisha Cook, Michael Lerner, Daniel J. Travanti. Muddled yarn about would-be writer Bronson who becomes a pawn for wealthy conniver Houseman and his beautiful associate (Bisset) and finds himself involved in murder. Glossy but stupid. Look for Jeff Goldblum and Robert Englund as hoods. [PG]▼

St. Louis Blues (1958) 93m. ** D: Allen Reisner. Nat "King" Cole, Eartha Kitt, Ruby Dee, Pearl Bailey, Juano Hernandez, Cab Calloway, Ella Fitzgerald, Mahalia Jackson. Treacly dramatics interspersed with outstanding musical performances in this so-called biography of W. C. Handy (Cole, in his lone starring role), who composed the title tune. Billy Preston plays Handy as a boy. VistaVision.

St. Martin's Lane SEE: **Sidewalks of London**

Stolen (2010) C-91m. ** D: Anders Anderson. Josh Lucas, Jon Hamm, Rhona Mitra, James Van Der Beek, Jessica Chastain, Joanna Cassidy, Jimmy Bennett, Morena Baccarin, Rick Gomez, Michael Cudlitz, Beth Grant. Parallel sagas of two young boys disappearing while under their respective fathers' care (Hamm, Lucas), weaving back and forth between 1958 and the present day. Somber tone, well-executed art direction, and even huge chunks of plot call to mind THE LOVELY BONES, minus the fantasia-like other world. But this tragedy, while giving it a good go, comes across like an advanced actors' exercise rather than a satisfying story. [R] ▶

Stolen Children (1992-Italian-French) C-112m. ***½ D: Gianni Amelio. Enrico Lo Verso, Valentina Scalici, Giuseppe Ieracitano, Florence Darel, Marina Golovine. A sister and brother are dragged across half of Italy after their no-good mother is arrested; they've been neglected, and the girl knows more about the business of prostitution than any 11-year-old should. Young military man Lo Verso, charged with transporting these unwanted wards of the state, grows to care about them. Stunning, simple film (a multi-award winner in Europe) harks back to the Italian Neo-realist school, with three unbeatable performances. Scripted by Sandro Petraglia, Stefano Rulli, and the director. Original title: IL LADRO DI BAMBINI. ▼

Stolen Hours (1963) C-100m. **½ D: Daniel Petrie. Susan Hayward, Michael Craig, Diane Baker, Edward Judd, Paul Rogers. Hayward takes Bette Davis' DARK VICTORY, transplants it to contemporary England, in tale of woman with fatal illness trying to get as much out of life as she can. Original is far superior in all departments. ▼❿

Stolen Kisses (1968-French) C-87m. **** D: François Truffaut. Jean-Pierre Léaud, Delphine Seyrig, Michel Lonsdale, Claude Jade, Harry Max, Daniel Ceccaldi. This alternately touching and hilarious film about an inept but likable jerk-of-all-trades is possibly Truffaut's best movie and one of the best treatments of young love ever put on the screen. Third in his Antoine Doinel series, followed by BED AND BOARD. [R]▼❿

Stolen Life, A (1946) 107m. **½ D: Curtis Bernhardt. Bette Davis, Glenn Ford, Dane Clark, Walter Brennan, Charlie Ruggles, Bruce Bennett, Peggy Knudsen. A twin takes her sister's place as wife of the man they both love in this slick but far-fetched soaper with Bette in dual role; remake of 1939 film with Elisabeth Bergner. Only movie produced by Davis.▼❿

Stolen Summer (2002) C-90m. **½ D: Pete Jones. Aidan Quinn, Bonnie Hunt, Kevin Pollak, Eddie Kaye Thomas, Mike Weinberg, Adi Stein, Brian Dennehy. Catholic boy in Chicago whose teacher keeps warning him that he's headed for Hell decides to do something to earn himself a place in Heaven: converting a Jew to Christianity. Child's-eye story of faith and tolerance set in the 1970s is simple and sincere; it wears its heart on its sleeve but dares to swim against the tide of cynicism. Produced by Ben Affleck and Matt Damon as part of their "Project Greenlight" endeavor to give struggling filmmakers a chance. [PG]▼❿

Stomp the Yard (2007) C-114m. **½ D: Sylvain White. Columbus Short, Meagan Good, Ne-Yo, Darrin Henson, Brian J. White, Laz Alonso, Valarie Pettiford, Harry Lennix, Chris Brown. DIRTY DANCING meets BOYZ N THE HOOD in this energetic musical drama in which a South L.A. youth discovers talent for an old tradition when he starts "stepping" after transferring to an Atlanta college. In doing so he becomes the focus of a major competition between dueling fraternities. Story has a nice message but it's Short's high "stepping" style that carries the day—and the film. Followed by a DVD sequel. Super 35. [PG-13]❿

Stone (2010) C-105m. ** D: John Curran. Robert De Niro, Edward Norton, Milla Jovovich, Frances Conroy, Enver Gjokaj, Pepper Binkley. Long-term convict Norton

tries playing mind games with prison parole officer De Niro, who's got problems of his own. Then Norton sics his sexy wife (Jovovich) on De Niro and the situation grows even more complicated. Somber drama offers no characters one can care about—except perhaps Conroy, as De Niro's long-suffering wife, who has turned to religion and alcohol! Super 35. [R]❿

Stone Angel, The (2008-Canadian-British) C-115m. ** D: Kari Skogland. Ellen Burstyn, Christine Horne, Cole Hauser, Wings Hauser, Ellen Page, Kevin Zegers, Dylan Baker, Luke Kirby. Multigenerational tale based on a beloved 1964 Canadian novel casts Burstyn as a proud, stubborn 90-year-old who evades her son's plan to put her in a nursing home, instead heading up north to relive memories (in flashback) of her youth and marriage to a gruff husband (played at different ages by father and son Wings and Cole Hauser). Sheer scope of the story, spanning several decades, eludes writer-director Skogland, who employs a rushed TV cutting style that truncates whatever pleasures were found in Margaret Laurence's book. Burstyn is in fine form. Super 35. [R]❿

Stone Boy, The (1984) C-93m. ***½ D: Chris Cain. Robert Duvall, Jason Presson, Glenn Close, Frederic Forrest, Wilford Brimley, Gail Youngs, Cindy Fisher, Linda Hamilton, Dean Cain. Tragedy sends a simple farming family into shock, and leaves the youngest boy to sort out his problems on his own. Perceptive and poignant look at the way people react to serious situations in real life, with a gallery of outstanding performances. May be too slow and introspective for some viewers' taste. Film debut of Cain (the director's stepson). [PG]▼❿

Stone Cold (1991) C-90m. *½ D: Craig R. Baxley. Brian Bosworth, Lance Henriksen, William Forsythe, Arabella Holzbog, Sam McMurray. Football's "Boz" infiltrates a gang of Mississippi bikers whose extortion antics have caught the attention of both the Feds *and* the Mob. Only some amazing stunts save this silliness from the BOMB scrap heap. Written and executive produced by Walter Doniger, who once directed Mantle and Maris in SAFE AT HOME! [R]▼❶❿

Stone Cold Dead (1980-Canadian) C-97m. **½ D: George Mendeluk. Richard Crenna, Paul Williams, Linda Sorenson, Belinda J. Montgomery, Charles Shamata, George Chuvalo. Cop Crenna versus mobster Williams. Compact little drama. [R]▼

Stoned (2006-British) C-102m. *½ D: Stephen Woolley. Leo Gregory, Paddy Considine, David Morrissey, Ben Whishaw, Monet Mazur, Tuva Novotny, Amelia Warner. Movie alleges that debauched and deposed Rolling Stones guitarist Brian Jones didn't just drown in his swimming pool but was drowned by his builder-turned-gofer. Mick Jagger, Keith Richards, and Anita Pallenberg are among the supporting characters. This can't miss, you say? It does. For a biopic about early Brit rock see BACKBEAT, and for one about star resentment, see AUTO FOCUS. Focus is the problem here, or lack of it. And a movie about the Stones that's missing Stones music is a fuzzy-brained concept to begin with.▶

Stone Killer, The (1973) **C-95m.** **½ D: Michael Winner. Charles Bronson, Martin Balsam, David Sheiner, Norman Fell, Ralph Waite. Good action in thriller about hardheaded cop trying to unravel chain of mystery that leads to elaborate plan using Vietnam vets to stage underworld massacre. Well made but pretty violent. [R]▼●

Stone Reader (2003) **C-128m.** *** D: Mark Moskowitz. Filmmaker Moskowitz, an avid reader, revisits a 1972 novel called *The Stones of Summer* and determines to find out what ever happened to its author, Dow Mossman, who never published again despite strong reviews for his debut book. In his search he talks to literary critics, teachers, writers, and fellow readers, not just about the elusive Mossman but about the nature of books and how they affect their readers. An offbeat but fascinating odyssey, especially for book lovers. [PG-13]▼▶

Stonewall (1995-U.S.-British) **C-99m.** **½ D: Nigel Finch. Guillermo Diaz, Fred Weller, Brendan Corbalis, Bruce MacVittie, Luis Guzman, Duane Boutte, Matthew Faber. Historic look-back at the 1969 Greenwich Village bar riot that sparked the gay rights movement, told as a fictitious personal story about a young Puerto Rican drag queen (the terrific Diaz) who becomes politically conscious when he falls in love with an idealistic midwestern hippie. Important subject matter deserved better, bigger-budgeted film, but this is still an effective portrait of discrimination. Director Finch died of AIDS shortly after the film was completed. Isaiah Washington has a bit part as a cop. [R]▼●▶

Stoning of Soraya M., The (2009) **C-114m.** *** D: Cyrus Nowrasteh. Shohreh Aghdashloo, Jim Caviezel, Mozhan Marnò, Navid Negahban, David Diaan, Ali Pourtash, Vida Ghahremani. Chilling drama based on French-Iranian Freidoune Sahebjam's book about a real-life incident from 1986. Caviezel plays the journalist whose car breaks down in a small Iranian village, where a desperate woman (Aghdashloo) tells him the story of what just happened to her niece. We then learn how two evil men—and others without backbone—allowed an entire community to turn on an innocent woman and punish her by the ancient ritual of stoning. Plays like melodrama at times, but it's all true. Aghdashloo's solid presence anchors the film. Super 35. [R]▶

Stony Island (1978) **C-97m.** *** D: Andrew Davis. Richard Davis, Edward Stony Robinson, Ronnie Barron, George Englund, Gene Barge, Susanna Hoffs, Rae Dawn Chong. Independent feature, filmed in Chicago, about an integrated group of youthful rhythm and blues performers and the death of an older black musician, nicely played by Barge. Fine music sequences and use of urban locations make up for lack of character and story development. Aka MY MAIN MAN FROM STONY ISLAND. [PG]

Stooge, The (1953) **100m.** **½ D: Norman Taurog. Dean Martin, Jerry Lewis, Polly Bergen, Eddie Mayehoff, Marion Marshall. Egocentric singer (Martin) learns the hard way just how important his stooge (Lewis) is to his success. Martin & Lewis go dramatic with middling results. Completed in 1951, not released for two years.▼▶

Stoogemania (1985) **C-83m.** *½ D: Chuck Workman. Josh Mostel, Melanie Chartoff, Sid Caesar, Josh Miner, Thom Sharp. Wellmeaning but completely unfunny tale of one Howard F. Howard, whose passion for The Three Stooges has overtaken his life. Incorporates real footage of the Stooges, and while most of it is far from their best, it's still vastly superior to the new material in this feature. For those who care, some of the Stooge footage is computer-colored. [PG]▼

Stoolie, The (1974) **C-90m.** **½ D: John G. Avildsen. Jackie Mason, Dan Frazer, Marcia Jean Kurtz, Anne Marie. Flawed but interesting little film, with Mason as a paid police informer who absconds to Miami with $7,500 in an attempt to "retire."▼▶

Stop-Loss (2008) **C-112m.** *** D: Kimberly Peirce. Ryan Phillippe, Abbie Cornish, Channing Tatum, Joseph Gordon-Levitt, Ciarán Hinds, Timothy Olyphant, Victor Rasuk, Rob Brown, Mamie Gummer, Josef Sommer, Linda Emond, Alex Frost, Laurie Metcalf. After losing some of his men in a bloody ambush in Iraq, Army staff sergeant Phillippe and other members of his squadron return home to Texas and find readjusting to "normal" life to be difficult—if not impossible. Then Phillippe is told that instead of being mustered out he's been "stop-lossed," set for another tour of duty overseas. Moving story of young men torn apart (literally and figuratively) by a brutal war and a hypocritical military agenda. Veers toward melodrama at times, but it still has the ring of truth. [R]▶

Stop Making Sense (1984) **C-88m.** **** D: Jonathan Demme. Brilliantly conceived, shot, edited, and performed Talking Heads concert film benefits from the presence of a major filmmaker behind the camera, as well as the imagination of lead singer/mastermind David Byrne. One of the greatest rock movies ever made; video version runs 99m. and contains three extra tunes.▼▶

Stop! or My Mom Will Shoot (1992) **C-**

87m. *½ D: Roger Spottiswoode. Sylvester Stallone, Estelle Getty, JoBeth Williams, Roger Rees, Martin Ferrero, Gailard Sartain, Dennis Burkley, Ving Rhames. Cop Stallone is joined by his loud-mouthed, gun-toting mamma (Getty), and they erase crime from the streets of L.A. One-joke action-comedy which quickly wears thin; Getty's character, meant to be funny, comes off as thoroughly obnoxious. [PG] ▼●)

Stop the World—I Want to Get Off (1966-British) **C-98m. **½** D: Philip Saville. Tony Tanner, Millicent Martin, Leila Croft, Valerie Croft. One of producer Bill Sargent's photographed stage presentations, this one preserves Anthony Newley and Leslie Bricusse's allegorical musical about an everyman named Littlechap and his bouts with life and success. A bit heavy-handed, though the score includes "What Kind Of Fool Am I?" Opens in b&w, then changes to color. Remade as SAMMY STOPS THE WORLD. ▼●

Stop, You're Killing Me (1952) **C-86m. **** D: Roy Del Ruth. Broderick Crawford, Claire Trevor, Virginia Gibson, Sheldon Leonard, Margaret Dumont. Mild froth based on Damon Runyon story of racketeer Crawford going legitimate. Remake of A SLIGHT CASE OF MURDER.

Stormbreaker SEE: **Alex Rider, Operation Stormbreaker**

Storm Center (1956) **85m. *½** D: Daniel Taradash. Bette Davis, Brian Keith, Kim Hunter, Paul Kelly. Librarian becomes center of controversy over censorship and Communism. Not even Davis can uplift clichés. An inauspicious directorial debut by veteran screenwriter Taradash.❚

Storm Warning (1951) **93m. **½** D: Stuart Heisler. Ginger Rogers, Ronald Reagan, Doris Day, Steve Cochran, Hugh Sanders, Lloyd Gough, Ned Glass. Feverish but engrossing story of a woman who discovers that her sister (Day) has married a loutish Ku Klux Klansman. Good cast, with Reagan in one of his better roles as a crusading D.A.; cowritten by Richard Brooks.❚

Stormy Monday (1988-British) **C-93m. **** D: Mike Figgis. Melanie Griffith, Tommy Lee Jones, Sting, Sean Bean, James Cosmo, Mark Long, Brian Lewis. Extremely stylish film noir about the convergence of four characters in the economically depressed city of Newcastle, where Sting runs a jazz club, and a ruthless American businessman (Jones) hopes to make a killing in redevelopment. More atmosphere than story here, and told at a very deliberate pace, but strong performances by all four leads and striking visual ideas by writer-director Figgis (and cinematographer Roger Deakins) definitely compensate. Figgis is also credited with the music score. [R] ▼●)

Stormy Weather (1943) **77m. **½** D:

Andrew L. Stone. Lena Horne, Bill (Bojangles) Robinson, Cab Calloway and His Band, Katherine Dunham, Fats Waller, Dooley Wilson, The Nicholas Brothers. This musical offers a legendary lineup of black performers, with Lena singing title song, Fats performing "Ain't Misbehavin'," others doing what they do best. Only problem: a silly storyline that improbably pairs Bojangles and Horne romantically. ▼●)

Story of Adele H, The (1975-French) **C-97m. **½** D: François Truffaut. Isabelle Adjani, Bruce Robinson, Sylvia Marriott, Reubin Dorey, Joseph Blatchley, M. White. Understated drama of young woman (the daughter of author Victor Hugo) obsessed with a soldier who does not return her love. Adjani's performance is excellent, but film is curiously unmoving. Shot in simultaneous English and French-language versions. [PG] ▼●)

Story of Alexander Graham Bell, The (1939) **97m. **** D: Irving Cummings. Don Ameche, Loretta Young, Henry Fonda, Charles Coburn, Spring Byington, Gene Lockhart, Polly Ann Young. Ameche overacts at times in his famous title role, but entertaining version of inventor is given plush 20th Century-Fox presentation.▼

Story of a Love Story (1973-French) **C-110m. **½** D: John Frankenheimer. Alan Bates, Dominique Sanda, Evans Evans, Lea Massari, Michel Auclair, Laurence De Monaghan. Writer Bates has an extramarital affair with Sanda—or is it his imagination? Interesting premise, middling result. Originally titled IMPOSSIBLE OBJECT; never released theatrically.▼

Story of a Marriage, The SEE: **On Valentine's Day** and **1918**

Story of a Three Day Pass, The (1967-French) **87m. **** D: Melvin Van Peebles. Harry Baird, Nicole Berger, Christian Marin, Pierre Doris. Flawed but impressive film about affair between black American soldier and white French girl. Also on tape as LA PERMISSION. ▼▮

Story of a Woman (1970) **C-90m. *½** D: Leonardo Bercovici. Bibi Andersson, Robert Stack, James Farentino, Annie Girardot, Didi Perego, Mario Nascimbene. Turgid tale of pianist who tries to remain faithful to her husband, even though she's still hung up on old flame; Bibi is wasted. [R]

Story of Boys and Girls, The (1991-Italian) **C-92m. **** D: Pupi Avati. Lucretia della Rovere, Davide Bechini, Valeria Bruni Tadeschi, Lina Bernardi, Anna Bonaiuto, Alessandro Haber, Enrico Maria Modungo. A country beauty invites her fiancé's elegant Bolognese family to a 20-course banquet in Italy's Emilia Romagna farmland in 1936. Easygoing, keenly observed comedy of culture clashing, whose subliminal effect isn't completely apparent until the film's conclusion. Have a snack handy.▼

Story of Esther Costello, The (1957-British) **103m.** **½ D: David Miller. Joan Crawford, Rossano Brazzi, Heather Sears, Lee Patterson, Fay Compton, Bessie Love, Ron Randell. Socialite rehabilitates impoverished blind and deaf girl and promotes charity fund in her name. Interesting look at charity hucksttering but melodrama is overwrought and often unintentionally funny.▼

Story of G.I. Joe, The (1945) **109m.** ***½ D: William Wellman. Burgess Meredith, Robert Mitchum, Freddie Steele, Wally Cassell, Jimmy Lloyd. Meredith is superb as war correspondent Ernie Pyle living with Yank soldiers on front lines to report their stories; Mitchum's first outstanding film role as soldier. Full title: ERNIE PYLE'S STORY OF G.I. JOE. ▼▶

Story of Gilbert and Sullivan, The SEE: **Great Gilbert and Sullivan, The**

Story of Gosta Berling, The SEE: **Atonement of Gosta Berling, The**

Story of Louis Pasteur, The (1936) **85m.** ***½ D: William Dieterle. Paul Muni, Josephine Hutchinson, Anita Louise, Donald Woods, Fritz Leiber, Porter Hall, Akim Tamiroff. The achievements of the famous French scientist are chronicled in this engrossing film. Muni gives Oscar-winning performance; writers Sheridan Gibney and Pierre Collings also won.▼▶

Story of Mankind, The (1957) **C-100m.** ** D: Irwin Allen. Ronald Colman, Cedric Hardwicke, Vincent Price; guest stars Hedy Lamarr, Groucho, Harpo, Chico Marx, Virginia Mayo, Agnes Moorehead, Francis X. Bushman, Charles Coburn, Marie Windsor, John Carradine, Dennis Hopper. Ambitious in concept, laughable in juvenile results. Henrik Van Loon book of highlights of man's history becomes string of clichéd costume episodes, badly cast, and packed with stock footage; the Marxes don't even appear together! Colman's last film.▶

Story of Piera, The (1983-Italian-French) **C-105m.** ** D: Marco Ferreri. Isabelle Huppert, Hanna Schygulla, Marcello Mastroianni, Bettina Gruhn, Tanya Lopert. Odd chronicle of the lifelong relationship between nutty, sensuous Schygulla and her daughter (Gruhn as a pre-teen, then Huppert). Ferreri presents a liberated alternative for relating as a wife, mother, daughter, woman; however, the result is mostly rambling, boring.

Story of Qiu Ju, The (1992-Chinese) **C-100m.** ***½ D: Zhang Yimou. Gong Li, Lei Lao Sheng, Liu Pei Qi, Ge Zhi Jun, Ye Jun, Yang Liu Xia. Exceptional drama about a naive but determined Chinese farm woman (Li), who demands to receive an explanation and simple apology after her husband is beaten up by the obstinate chief of her village. This deft, ironic story of a woman's search for justice examines government bureaucracy and how regulations and rules often have little to do with the real needs of people. [PG]▼●▶

Story of Robin Hood and His Merrie Men, The (1952) **C-83m.** *** D: Ken Annakin. Richard Todd, Joan Rice, Peter Finch, James Hayter, James Robertson Justice, Martita Hunt, Hubert Gregg, Michael Hordern. Zesty, colorful retelling of the familiar story, filmed in England by Walt Disney with excellent cast. Not as personality oriented as other versions, but just as good in its own way.▼●▶

Story of Ruth, The (1960) **C-132m.** **½ D: Henry Koster. Elana Eden, Stuart Whitman, Tom Tryon, Peggy Wood, Viveca Lindfors, Jeff Morrow. Static biblical non-epic retelling story of woman renouncing her "gods" when she discovers true faith. CinemaScope.▼▶

Story of Seabiscuit, The (1949) **C-93m.** ** D: David Butler. Shirley Temple, Barry Fitzgerald, Lon McCallister, Rosemary DeCamp, Donald MacBride, Pierre Watkin. Technicolor hokum with Fitzgerald as the toora-loora trainer who convinces Charles S. Howard (Watkin) that the title horse has real possibilities. Temple is Fitzgerald's niece, whose brother was killed in a racing accident. Never a great film, this is now rendered meaningless (if not downright ludicrous) by Laura Hillenbrand's book and the 2003 adaptation, SEABISCUIT. ▼▶

Story of the Weeping Camel, The (2004-German-Mongolian) **C-87m.** ***½ D: Byambasuren Davaa, Luigi Falorni. Fascinating docudrama about a family of shepherds in a remote part of Mongolia's Gobi Desert who assist their camel herd in giving birth. When one of the animals has a difficult delivery she rejects the colt, forcing the family to resort to a traditional ritual and find a musician who can get the camel to nurse her baby. Masterfully filmed, using real people in real situations, even though it's a "story" being enacted by its participants. [PG]▶

Story of Three Loves, The (1953) **C-122m.** *** D: Vincente Minnelli, Gottfried Reinhardt. Pier Angeli, Moira Shearer, Ethel Barrymore, Kirk Douglas, Farley Granger, Leslie Caron, James Mason, Agnes Moorehead, Zsa Zsa Gabor. Bittersweet trio of love stories, told as flashbacks involving passengers on ocean liner.▶

Story of Us, The (1999) **C-95m.** ** D: Rob Reiner. Bruce Willis, Michelle Pfeiffer, Tim Matheson, Rob Reiner, Rita Wilson, Julie Hagerty, Jayne Meadows, Tom Poston, Betty White, Red Buttons. A couple on the verge of splitting reflect on their 15-year marriage—and try to understand where it went wrong. Sympathetic portrayal of married life has likable performances on its side, but its moments of keen observation are too often undercut by annoying, sitcom-style dialogue that bears no relation to real life. Paul Reiser appears unbilled. [R]▼●)

Story of Vernon & Irene Castle, The (1939) **93m.** *** D: H. C. Potter. Fred Astaire, Ginger Rogers, Edna May Oliver, Walter Brennan, Lew Fields. Fred and Ginger take an unusual turn, downplaying their usual breezy comedy to portray America's hugely popular early-20th-century husband-and-wife dance team. Many fine period dance numbers and songs. This was the last Astaire–Rogers film until THE BARKLEYS OF BROADWAY ten years later. Incidentally, that's young Marge Champion (then known as Marjorie Belcher) as Irene's girlfriend.▼●)

Story of Will Rogers, The (1952) **C-109m.** *** D: Michael Curtiz. Will Rogers, Jr., Jane Wyman, Carl Benton Reid, James Gleason, Mary Wickes, Eddie Cantor. One of few show biz biographies that rings true, with Rogers Jr. faithfully portraying his father, rodeo star turned humorist; Wyman is his loving wife, Cantor appears as himself.)

Story of Women (1988-French) **C-110m.** *** D: Claude Chabrol. Isabelle Huppert, Francois Cluzet, Marie Trintignant, Nils Tavernier, Louis Ducreux. Huppert gives one of her best performances as a woman who builds a thriving career as an abortionist in Vichy France—and becomes the last of her sex to be guillotined in her country. Ironic, fact-based story provides Chabrol with one of his best subjects; the director is in top form here. ▼)

Story on Page One, The (1959) **123m.** *** D: Clifford Odets. Rita Hayworth, Anthony Franciosa, Gig Young, Mildred Dunnock, Hugh Griffith, Sanford Meisner, Robert Burton. Lovers Hayworth and Young are accused of killing Rita's husband, hire Franciosa to represent them in court. Odets' stark film has high tension and sincere performances, although Dunnock's Mama portrayal is a bit much. CinemaScope.

Storytelling (2002) **C-88m.** ** D: Todd Solondz. Selma Blair, Leo Fitzpatrick, Aleksa Palladino, Robert Wisdom, Noah Fleiss, Paul Giamatti, John Goodman, Julie Hagerty, Lupe Ontiveros, Jonathan Osser, Franka Potente, Steve Railsback, Xander Berkeley, Crista Moore. Two-part film offers some wry observations about everyday cruelty in typical Solondz fashion, but little resonance. In "Fiction," writing student Blair breaks off with her disabled boyfriend/college classmate and sleeps with her angry black teacher. In "Non-Fiction," a blowhard would-be documentary filmmaker chronicles a typical affluent suburban N.J. family, little suspecting the drama that's unfolding right under his nose. Film's conclusion leaves us wanting. [R]▼)

Storyville (1992) **C-112m.** *½ D: Mark Frost. James Spader, Joanne Whalley-Kilmer, Jason Robards, Piper Laurie, Charlotte Lewis, Michael Warren, Michael Parks, Chuck McCann, Charles Haid, Chino Fats Williams, Woody Strode, Jeff Perry. Young, obscenely wealthy Louisiana congressional candidate Spader discovers skeletons deeply hidden in his family's closet. Good performances can't save this muddled and obtuse contemporary drama; the murder, mayhem, and mistresses are more than anyone will care about. [R]▼●)

Stowaway (1936) **86m.** **½ D: William A. Seiter. Robert Young, Alice Faye, Shirley Temple, Eugene Pallette, Helen Westley, Arthur Treacher. Predictable yet engaging shipboard story with Faye and Young romancing, Temple the incurably curious child. Shirley even speaks Chinese! Also shown in computer-colored version.▼)

Straight on Till Morning (1972-British) **C-96m.** ** D: Peter Collinson. Rita Tushingham, Shane Briant, Tom Bell, Annie Ross, Claire Kelly. Offbeat thriller, but not terribly effective. Naive Tushingham journeys from Liverpool to London to find a willing male to impregnate her, meets ladykiller Briant. The title, if you don't know, is derived from *Peter Pan.* Video titles: TILL DAWN DO US PART and DRESSED FOR DEATH. [R]▼)

Straight Out of Brooklyn (1991) **C-91m.** **½ D: Matty Rich. George T. Odom, Ann D. Sanders, Lawrence Gilliard, Jr., Barbara Sanon, Reana E. Drummond, Mark Malone. Sobering look at a working-class black family's dead-end existence in the housing projects of Brooklyn, N.Y., and a young man's foolish scheme to turn their lives around. Ambitious and interesting first feature for teenaged writer-director Rich (who also appears on-screen as the talkative Larry). Extremely rough-edged, but redeemed by some fine performances— and searing emotions. [R]▼●)

Straight Story, The (1999) **C-111m.** ***½ D: David Lynch. Richard Farnsworth, Sissy Spacek, Harry Dean Stanton, Jane Galloway Heit, Everett McGill, Jennifer Edwards-Hughes. Wonderful, deceptively simple slice of Americana (based on a true story) about a 73-year-old Iowa man who drives a lawnmower some 300 miles to see his ailing brother, with whom he hasn't spoken in a decade. Its measured pace and episodic quality may not appeal to everyone, but its charm and belief in the basic decency of people make it very special indeed. Farnsworth shines in the leading role. Director Lynch's most benign film. Written by Mary Sweeney and John Roach. Panavision. [G]▼)

Straight Talk (1992) **C-91m.** *½ D: Barnet Kellman. Dolly Parton, James Woods, Griffin Dunne, Michael Madsen, Deirdre O'Connell, John Sayles, Teri Hatcher, Spalding Gray, Jerry Orbach, Philip Bosco, Charles Fleischer, Jay Thomas, Jane Lynch. New-in-town Dolly is mistaken for the just-hired psychologist at a Chicago radio station, but is a hit on the air with her down-home advice. About as credible as Parton's romance with costar Woods, who despite his billing was completely missing from the film's coming attraction. [PG]▼●◗

Straight Through the Heart (1983-German) **C-91m.** ******* D: Doris Dörrie. Beate Jensen, Sepp Bierbichler, Gabrielle Litty, Nuran Filiz. Highly original, sharply observed tale of a rather peculiar young girl (nicely played by Jensen) and her relationship with divorced, lonely, middle-aged dentist Bierbichler. An impressive initial feature from Dörrie (the director of MEN . . .).

Straight Time (1978) **C-114m.** ******* D: Ulu Grosbard. Dustin Hoffman, Theresa Russell, Harry Dean Stanton, Gary Busey, M. Emmet Walsh, Sandy Baron, Kathy Bates, Rita Taggart. Hoffman knocks heads with slimy parole officer Walsh following his release from prison and begins a downward slide. Engrossing if not particularly distinguished melodrama gets a real shot in the arm from terrific supporting performances. Hoffman started directing the film himself, then turned it over to Grosbard. Based on the novel *No Beast So Fierce* by Edward Bunker, who also appears in film as Mickey. [R]▼◗

Straight to Hell (1987) **C-86m.** BOMB D: Alex Cox. Sy Richardson, Joe Strummer, Dick Rude, Courtney Love, Dennis Hopper, Elvis Costello, Grace Jones, Jim Jarmusch, The Pogues. "Self-indulgent" is an understated way of describing this spaghetti Western spoof, written by cult director Cox and costar Rude. Has the insistent air of a hip in-joke, except that it isn't funny. In fact, it's *awful*. Expanded and rereleased to art houses and DVD in 2010 as STRAIGHT TO HELL RETURNS at 91m. [R]▼◗

Strait-Jacket (1964) **89m.** ****½** D: William Castle. Joan Crawford, Diane Baker, Leif Erickson, Anthony Hayes, Howard St. John, Rochelle Hudson, George Kennedy. Crawford served 20 years for axe murders; now, living peacefully with daughter Baker, murders start again and she's suspected. Crawford's strong portrayal makes this one of best in the BABY JANE genre of older-star shockers; script by Robert Bloch. The first person to be decapitated is Lee Majors, in his unbilled screen debut. And stick around to see the Columbia Pictures logo at the end. ▼●◗

Stranded (1987) **C-80m.** ****** D: Tex Fuller. Ione Skye, Joe Morton, Maureen O'Sullivan, Susan Barnes, Cameron Dye, Michael Greene, Brendan Hughes. A couple of effective moments cannot uplift this unrewarding sci-fi entry about aliens who come to earth, taking teen Skye and grandmother O'Sullivan hostage. [PG-13]▼●

Strange Affair, The (1968-British) **C-106m.** ****½** D: David Greene. Michael York,

Jeremy Kemp, Susan George, Jack Watson, Nigel Davenport, George A. Cooper, Barry Fantoni. Pretty good police melodrama about young recruit York's dallying with sexy hippie and superior Kemp's failure to get needed conviction; George steals the show in one of her first film appearances. Techniscope. [R]

Strange Affair of Uncle Harry, The (1945) **80m.** ******* D: Robert Siodmak. George Sanders, Geraldine Fitzgerald, Ella Raines, Sara Allgood, Moyna MacGill, Samuel S. Hinds. Engrossing melodrama about mild-mannered Sanders falling in love, but unable to break from grip of domineering sister (Fitzgerald). Vivid, if not always believable, with unfortunate ending demanded by 1940s censorship. Produced by longtime Hitchcock associate Joan Harrison. Originally titled UNCLE HARRY.▼●

Strange Bedfellows (1965) **C-98m.** ****½** D: Melvin Frank. Rock Hudson, Gina Lollobrigida, Gig Young, Terry-Thomas, Nancy Kulp. Hudson ambles through another marital mix-up comedy, this one with fiery Gina and lots of slapstick. Mild entertainment; filmed in London. ▼◗

Strange Behavior (1981-New Zealand) **C-98m.** ****** D: Michael Laughlin. Michael Murphy, Louise Fletcher, Dan Shor, Fiona Lewis, Arthur Dignam, Scott Brady, Charles Lane. This shocker about grisly murders in a small Midwestern town (shot in New Zealand!) got inexplicably good reviews in many quarters. You may rightly wonder what all the shouting was about. Originally titled DEAD KIDS. Panavision. [R]▼◗

Strange Brew (1983) **C-90m.** ****½** D: Dave Thomas, Rick Moranis. Dave Thomas, Rick Moranis, Max von Sydow, Paul Dooley, Lynne Griffin; voice of Mel Blanc. Uneven but likably goofy film about Bob and Doug, the beer-guzzling McKenzie Brothers introduced on the *SCTV* show. Lags at times, but keeps coming up with funny scenes, especially when playing with the conventions of moviemaking. The stars also directed and cowrote the film, the first in Hoserama. Loosely based on, believe it or not, *Hamlet*. Moranis and Thomas later did variations on these characters—as moose—in BROTHER BEAR. [PG]▼●

Strange Cargo (1940) **113m.** ******* D: Frank Borzage. Joan Crawford, Clark Gable, Ian Hunter, Peter Lorre, Albert Dekker, Paul Lukas, Eduardo Ciannelli. Intriguing allegorical film of prisoners escaping from Devil's Island with Christ-like presence of Hunter. Not for all tastes, but there are fine, realistic performances and flavorful Franz Waxman score.▼◗

Strange Case of Madeleine SEE: **Madeleine**

Strange Days (1995) **C-122m.** ****½** D: Kathryn Bigelow. Ralph Fiennes, Angela Bassett, Juliette Lewis, Tom Sizemore, Michael Wincott, Vincent D'Onofrio, Glenn Plummer, Brigitte Bako, Richard Edson, William Fichtner, Josef Sommer, Chris Douridas, Todd Graff. Dazzling but uneasy mixture of futuristic action and social relevance. Fiennes is a hustler selling mental recordings of real-life experiences, to which some become addicted; then he stumbles into a murky murder conspiracy involving his clients. Bombastic and overambitious, but manages to capture, in fits, the addictive thrill of virtual reality. (An interracial romance between Fiennes and Bassett doesn't ring true in the end.) Cowritten by Jay Cocks and James Cameron. Super 35. [R] ▼●)

Strange Door, The (1951) 81m. *½ D: Joseph Pevney. Charles Laughton, Boris Karloff, Sally Forrest, Richard Stapley, Michael Pate, Alan Napier, Paul Cavanagh. Laughton camps it up in this heavy-handed, obvious adaptation of a Robert Louis Stevenson story about a sadistic squire and his nefarious schemes. Karloff has a thankless role as a servant named Voltan. ▼●)

Strange Fascination (1952) 80m. ** D: Hugo Haas. Hugo Haas, Cleo Moore, Mona Barrie, Rick Vallin, Karen Sharpe. A concert pianist's career—and luck—fall apart because of his obsessive love for a young blonde. Starts interestingly but descends into hollow melodrama. Produced, directed, and written by Haas.

Strange Illusion (1945) 80m. ** D: Edgar G. Ulmer. James Lydon, Sally Eilers, Warren William, Regis Toomey. Intriguing but unconvincing melodrama, a B-movie update of *Hamlet*, with teenaged Lydon having doubts about smooth-talker (William) who's wooing his widowed mother (Eilers). Typically bizarre Ulmer touches in this low-budget quickie. ▼)

Strange Impersonation (1946) 68m. *** D: Anthony Mann. Brenda Marshall, William Gargan, Hillary Brooke, George Chandler, Ruth Ford, H. B. Warner, Lyle Talbot. Marshall gives a first-rate performance in this grade-B film noir about a research scientist whose face is horribly disfigured in a so-called accident. Plastic surgery enables her to unravel the mystery behind that incident and seek revenge. Perhaps the definitive Hillary Brooke movie. ▼)

Strange Interlude (1932) 110m. *** D: Robert Z. Leonard. Norma Shearer, Clark Gable, May Robson, Maureen O'Sullivan, Robert Young, Ralph Morgan, Henry B. Walthall, Alexander Kirkland. Talky Eugene O'Neill play becomes marathon of inner thoughts revealed only to audience in chronicle of Gable, Shearer, et al. growing old without resolving their problems. Engrossing film, with Shearer at her radiant best. ▼)

Strange Invaders (1983) C-94m. **½ D:

Michael Laughlin. Paul LeMat, Nancy Allen, Diana Scarwid, Michael Lerner, Louise Fletcher, Wallace Shawn, Fiona Lewis, Kenneth Tobey, June Lockhart. Affectionate spoof of '50s sci-fi films (with a touch of '80s New Wave), about a Midwestern town overtaken by aliens. Has a wonderful feel to it but suffers from weak writing and lethargic pacing. Evocative score by John Addison. Panavision. [PG] ▼●)

Strange Love of Martha Ivers, The (1946) 116m. *** D: Lewis Milestone. Barbara Stanwyck, Kirk Douglas, Lizabeth Scott, Van Heflin, Judith Anderson, Darryl Hickman. Gripping melodrama, with Stanwyck bound to her husband by crime she committed long ago. Douglas' film debut. ▼●)

Strange One, The (1957) 100m. *** D: Jack Garfein. Ben Gazzara, George Peppard, Pat Hingle, Mark Richman, Geoffrey Horne, James Olson. Bizarre military school account of far-out Gazzara's peculiar hold over various underclassmen. Remarkably frank version of Calder Willingham's *End as a Man*, scripted by the author; also filmed as SORORITY GIRL. Film debuts of Gazzara and Peppard. Released on DVD in 2009 with added footage that had been deleted prior to the theatrical release. ▼)

Strange Planet (1999-Australian) C-92m. ** D: Emma-Kate Croghan. Claudia Karvan, Naomi Watts, Alice Garner, Tom Long, Aaron Jeffery, Felix Williamson, Hugo Weaving, Rebecca Frith. Scattershot account of a year in the lives of three twentysomething female friends and three equivalent males. Attempts to offer a profound take on the transitory nature of relationships among contemporary young people, but the result is superficial. Notable for Watts' eye-opening performance as the most sensitive of the women. ▼)

Stranger, The (1946) 95m. *** D: Orson Welles. Orson Welles, Loretta Young, Edward G. Robinson, Richard Long, Martha Wentworth. Fine study of escaped Nazi war criminal Welles sedately living in small Connecticut town, about to marry unsuspecting Young. Robinson nicely understates role as federal agent out to get him. Also shown in computer-colored version. ▼●)

Stranger, The (1967-Italian-French) C-105m. ***½ D: Luchino Visconti. Marcello Mastroianni, Anna Karina, Bernard Blier, Georges Wilson, Bruno Cremer. Excellent adaptation of Albert Camus' existential novel about a man who feels completely isolated from society. Mastroianni is perfectly cast in lead.

Stranger, The (1987-U.S.-Argentine) C-88m. **½ D: Adolfo Aristarain. Bonnie Bedelia, Peter Riegert, Barry Primus, David Spielberg, Marcos Woinski. Clever if occasionally shallow thriller about Bedelia, who observes killings . . . and gets amnesia while the culprits are out to get her. Fairly entertaining most of the way, but could have been much better. Filmed in Buenos Aires. [R]▼

Stranger, The (1994) SEE: **Kabloonak**

Stranger Among Us, A (1992) **C-109m.** **½ D: Sidney Lumet. Melanie Griffith, Eric Thal, John Pankow, Tracy Pollan, Lee Richardson, Mia Sara, Jamey Sheridan, Jake Weber, James Gandolfini, Burtt Harris. N.Y.C. cop Griffith goes to live among Brooklyn's Hasidic community of religious Jews in order to find the "insider" who murdered one of them. Intriguing at first, but the story gets stalled along the way and never gets back on track, especially in the farfetched finale. Griffith is surprisingly credible as a policewoman. [PG-13]▼●]

Stranger and the Gunfighter, The (1976-Italian-Hong Kong) **C-107m.** **½ D: Anthony Dawson (Antonio Margheriti). Lee Van Cleef, Lo Lieh, Patty Shepard, Julian Ugarte, Karen Yeh. Lively, low-grade tongue-in-cheek actioner has hard-drinking cowboy joining forces with kung fu expert to recover missing fortune, with portions of the map tattooed on the posteriors of assorted lovelies. Amusing mix of spaghetti Western and karate thriller. Panavision. [PG]▼●

Stranger at My Door (1956) **85m.** **½ D: William Witney. Macdonald Carey, Patricia Medina, Skip Homeier, Louis Jean Heydt, Stephen Wootton, Slim Pickens. Offbeat Western about clergyman jeopardizing his family's safety when he tries to reform an outlaw. Solid performances in this original script by Barry Shipman. Highlighted by some truly remarkable scenes with an untamed horse.

Stranger in the House SEE: **Black Christmas**

Stranger in Town, A (1966-Italian-U.S.) **C-86m.** *½ D: Vance Lewis (Luigi Vanza). Tony Anthony, Frank Wolff, Yolanda Modio, Gia Sandri. Poor imitation of Sergio Leone Western finds Anthony blood-bathing a murderous bandit into submission. Sequel: THE STRANGER RETURNS. [R]

Stranger Is Watching, A (1982) **C-92m.** ** D: Sean S. Cunningham. Kate Mulgrew, Rip Torn, James Naughton, Shawn Von Schreiber, Barbara Baxley, Stephen Joyce. Psychopath Torn kidnaps TV newscaster Mulgrew and young Von Schreiber, holding them hostage in catacombs beneath Grand Central Station. Convoluted thriller from the director of FRIDAY THE 13TH. [R]▼●

Stranger on the Prowl (1953-Italian) **82m.** **½ D: Joseph Losey. Paul Muni, Vittorio Manunta, Joan Lorring, Aldo Silvani. Murky drama of Muni a fugitive on the run who tries to set a young would-be crook straight.

Stranger on the Third Floor (1940) **64m.**

*** D: Boris Ingster. Peter Lorre, John McGuire, Margaret Tallichet, Charles Waldron, Elisha Cook, Jr. Reporter's testimony has convicted Cook in brutal murder case, but the newspaperman has second thoughts. Excellent sleeper, with one nightmare montage that's a knockout.▼●]

Stranger Returns, The (1968-U.S.-Italian) **C-90m.** BOMB D: Vance Lewis (Luigi Vanza). Tony Anthony, Dan Vadis, Daniele Vargas, Marco Gugielmi, Jill Banner. Sequel to A STRANGER IN TOWN has Anthony chasing solid gold stagecoach full of thieves. Worthless. [R]

Strangers (1953) SEE: **Voyage in Italy**

Strangers, The (2008) **C-90m.** ** D: Bryan Bertino. Liv Tyler, Scott Speedman, Glenn Howerton. Couple about to embark on a road trip spend the night at his father's cabin deep in the woods. A knock on the door in the middle of the night is the first step into a nightmarish experience in which they are emotionally and physically tormented by three masked figures who offer no explanation for their attacks. Not terribly scary, in spite of insistent bursts of music and loud effects on the soundtrack . . . but even worse, it's pointless. Super 35. [R]▶

Strangers in Good Company (1991-Canadian) **C-100m.** *** D: Cynthia Scott. Alice Diablo, Constance Garneau, Winifred Holden, Cissy Meddings, Mary Meigs, Catherine Roche, Michelle Sweeney, Beth Webber. Slow-paced but rewarding study of a group of women temporarily stuck in the Canadian wilderness when their bus breaks down. All the actresses play themselves in this unusual film from the National Film Board of Canada. It's mainly talk, as we learn about the hopes and sorrows of women who share their feelings during an interlude in their lives. [PG]▼▶

Strangers in the Night (1944) **56m.** **½ D: Anthony Mann. William Terry, Virginia Grey, Helene Thimig, Edith Barrett, Anne O'Neal. An eccentric old woman harbors a dark secret in her hilltop home on the California coast, and lures a wounded soldier (just back from combat) there on the promise of meeting her beautiful daughter. Intriguing story idea gets silly by the end, but it's still a pretty good B, full of the shadowy staging favored by young director Mann.

Strangers Kiss (1984) **C-94m.** **½ D: Matthew Chapman. Peter Coyote, Victoria Tennant, Blaine Novak, Dan Shor, Richard Romanus, Linda Kerridge. Interesting, offbeat little film about the making of a low-budget movie, circa 1955, and the off-camera relationship between lead actors Novak and Tennant. Novak also cowrote screenplay with director Chapman, inspired by Stanley Kubrick's KILLER'S KISS. [R]▼

Strangers on a Train (1951) **101m.** ★★★★
D: Alfred Hitchcock. Farley Granger, Ruth
Roman, Robert Walker, Leo G. Carroll,
Patricia Hitchcock, Marion Lorne. Walker
gives his finest performance as psychopath
involved with tennis star Granger in "exchange murders." Lorne is unforgettable
as doting mother; so is merry-go-round
climax. First-class Hitchcock, based on a
Patricia Highsmith novel and coscripted
by Raymond Chandler. Remade as ONCE
YOU KISS A STRANGER and the inspiration for THROW MOMMA FROM THE
TRAIN. British version of film, now available, runs almost two minutes longer, has
a different ending and franker dialogue in
the first scene where Granger and Walker
meet. ▼●◗

Stranger's Return, The (1933) **89m.** ★★★½
D: King Vidor. Lionel Barrymore, Miriam
Hopkins, Franchot Tone, Stuart Erwin, Irene
Hervey, Beulah Bondi. A young woman, recently separated from her husband, leaves
the city to stay at her grandfather's farm.
Here she finds her roots, as well as a kindred
spirit in neighboring farmer Tone, a college
graduate. Why this rich, mature, beautifully
made film isn't better known is a mystery.
Phil Stong helped adapt his own novel for
director Vidor.

Strangers When We Meet (1960) **C-117m.**
★★½ D: Richard Quine. Kirk Douglas, Kim
Novak, Ernie Kovacs, Barbara Rush, Wal-
ter Matthau, Virginia Bruce, Kent Smith.
Expensive soaper with attractive stars; both
are married, but fall in love with each other.
Script by Evan Hunter, from his novel.
CinemaScope. ▼◗

Strangers With Candy (2006) **C-86m.**
★★½ D: Paul Dinello. Amy Sedaris, Stephen Colbert, Paul Dinello, Dan Hedaya,
Deborah Rush, Ian Holm, Elizabeth Harnois, Joseph Cross, Kristen Johnston,
Justin Theroux, Chandra Wilson. Jerri
Blank (Sedaris), a 47-year-old juvenile
delinquent, gets out of prison and returns
to high school. Prequel to the cult TV comedy show feels like a half-hour episode
stretched to feature length, and the formula
wears thin. Still, writer-performers Sedaris, Colbert, and Dinello create a satisfying amount of genuinely tasteless hilarity
as they inject the proceedings with their
bizarre sensibilities and off-kilter comic
timing. A number of famous faces appear
in cameo roles. [R]◗

Stranger Than Fiction (2006) **C-113m.**
★★★ D: Marc Forster. Will Ferrell, Maggie
Gyllenhaal, Emma Thompson, Dustin Hoffman, Queen Latifah, Tony Hale, Tom Hulce,
Linda Hunt, Kristin Chenoweth. Buttoned-
down IRS auditor (Ferrell) suddenly becomes
aware that his life is being narrated—but
only he can hear the woman's voice. Then
the author (Thompson), who's been suffering from writer's block, discovers that

the character she's created is real, and she
holds his life in her hands. Clever concept
by writer Zach Helm is fully realized by a
fine cast and creative visual interpretation
by Forster. Ferrell is good in a seriocomic
role. Super 35. [PG-13]◗

Stranger Than Paradise (1984) **90m.** ★★★
D: Jim Jarmusch. John Lurie, Eszter Balint, Richard Edson, Cecillia Stark. Simple
story of a nondescript young man, his doltish best friend, and his 16-year-old female
cousin who comes to America from Hungary. Critically acclaimed comedy-road
movie is, at its worst, a bit slow; at its best,
original, ingratiating, and extremely funny.
Independently filmed and developed from a
30m. short. Screenplay by Jarmusch, music
by Lurie. [R]▼●◗

Strange Shadows in An Empty Room
(1977) **C-99m.** ★½ D: Martin Herbert (Alberto DeMartino). Stuart Whitman, John
Saxon, Martin Landau, Tisa Farrow, Gayle
Hunnicutt, Carole Laure. Far-fetched,
violent film has police detective Whitman
searching for his sister's murderer. Tawdry
stuff; filmed in Montreal as BLAZING
MAGNUMS (a far more appropriate title).
Panavision. [R]▼

Strange Vengeance of Rosalie, The (1972)
C-107m. ★★ D: Jack Starrett. Bonnie Bedelia, Ken Howard, Anthony Zerbe. Offbeat
story of Indian girl who holds man captive
in rambling house. Far-fetched tale goes
way off-base. [PG]

Strange Wilderness (2008) **C-85m.** BOMB
D: Fred Wolf. Steve Zahn, Allen Covert,
Jonah Hill, Kevin Heffernan, Peter Dante,
Ashley Scott, Harry Hamlin, Robert Patrick, Joe Don Baker, Justin Long, Jeff Garlin, Ernest Borgnine, Blake Clark, Oliver
Hudson. Painfully unfunny farce about
producers of a ratings-challenged wildlife
TV series who desperately seek Bigfoot in
the wilds of Ecuador. You can't help feeling
embarrassed for Zahn, as the clueless host,
when a wild turkey chomps on his private
parts and won't let go. Shelved for nearly
two years before a fleeting theatrical run.
Panavision. [R]◗

Strange Woman, The (1946) **100m.** ★★½
D: Edgar G. Ulmer. Hedy Lamarr, George
Sanders, Louis Hayward, Gene Lockhart,
Hillary Brooke. Lamarr offers one of her
best performances as a shrewish young
woman in 19th-century Maine who affects
the lives of three very different men. Nicely
directed by Ulmer; a rare instance in which
he was allowed a Grade-A cast. ▼◗

Strapless (1989-British) **C-103m.** ★★½
D: David Hare. Blair Brown, Bruno Ganz,
Bridget Fonda, Hugh Laurie, Alan Howard, Billy Roch, Camille Coduri, Alexandra Pigg, Michael Gough, Gary O'Brien.
American doctor Brown, living and working in London, hits 40 and finds herself at
a crossroads, just as her 25-year-old sister

arrives for an extended vacation. Brown is fine, and Fonda completely winning in this studied, sometimes ponderous story of the need to face emotions head-on, no matter where they may lead. [R] ▼●)

Strategic Air Command (1955) **C-114m.** ****½** D: Anthony Mann. James Stewart, June Allyson, Frank Lovejoy, Barry Sullivan, Bruce Bennett, Rosemary DeCamp. Film only gets off the ground when Stewart does, as baseball player recalled to air force duty; Allyson is his sugary wife. VistaVision.▼●

Stratton Story, The (1949) **106m.** *****½** D: Sam Wood. James Stewart, June Allyson, Frank Morgan, Agnes Moorehead, Bill Williams, Jimmy Dykes, Bill Dickey. Stewart is fine as Monty Stratton, the baseball player whose loss of one leg did not halt his career; well played by good cast, including ballplayers Dykes and Dickey. Oscar winner for story (Douglas Morrow); screenplay by Morrow and Guy Trosper. Also shown in computer-colored version.▼)

Strawberry and Chocolate (1994-Cuban) **C-110m.** ****½** D: Tomas Gutierrez Alea, Juan Carlos Tabio. Jorge Perugorria, Vladimir Cruz, Mirta Ibarra, Francisco Gattorono, Marilyn Solaya. Entertaining and sympathetic account of the unlikely friendship between David, a heterosexual and devoted Communist who knows nothing of the arts (and is depressed over being dumped by his girlfriend), and homosexual, cultured Diego, who's full of life and doesn't care much for politics. Controversial in its home country, but notable too as the first Cuban film ever nominated for a Best Foreign Film Oscar. [R] ▼●)

Strawberry Blonde, The (1941) **97m.** ******* D: Raoul Walsh. James Cagney, Olivia de Havilland, Rita Hayworth, Alan Hale, Jack Carson, George Tobias, Una O'Connor, George Reeves. Cagney's dynamic in entertaining turn-of-the-century story of dentist infatuated with gold-digger Hayworth, and his subsequent marriage to de Havilland. Remade in 1948 as ONE SUNDAY AFTERNOON, the title of the 1933 Gary Cooper film of which *this* is a remake.▼)

Strawberry Statement, The (1970) **C-103m.** ****** D: Stuart Hagmann. Bruce Davison, Kim Darby, Bob Balaban, James Kunen, Jeannie Berlin, Bud Cort, David Dukes, James Coco, Bert Remsen. Cluttered adaptation of James Kunen's book about Columbia University's riots tries to be too many things at once—comedy, social commentary, musical. Good performances. Script by Israel Horovitz (who also plays Dr. Benton). [R]▼

Straw Dogs (1971) **C-113m.** *****½** D: Sam Peckinpah. Dustin Hoffman, Susan George, Peter Vaughan, T. P. McKenna, Peter Arne.

One of the most controversial violence-themed films of its day. Hoffman portrays American mathematician whose pacifism is put to supreme test when he and British wife George move to isolated village and are menaced by local hooligans. Screenplay by Peckinpah and David Zelag Goodman from Gordon Williams' novel *The Siege of Trenchers Farm*. David Warner appears unbilled. Filmed in England. Original running time: 118m. [R] ▼●)

Stray Dog (1949-Japanese) **122m.** ******** D: Akira Kurosawa. Toshiro Mifune, Takashi Shimura, Keiko Awaji. Classic Japanese film noir, most effective as a look at life in post-WW2 Tokyo. Mifune does well as a detective whose gun is stolen; he sets out on an odyssey to reclaim his weapon, and to seek out a killer. Although not as well known as RASHOMON, this film is just as important to career of Kurosawa and the growth of Japanese cinema.▼●)

Strayed (2003-French) **C-95m.** ******* D: André Téchiné. Emmanuelle Béart, Gaspard Ulliel, Grégoire Leprince-Ringuet, Clémence Meyer, Jean Fornerod, Samuel Labarthe. In 1940, as the Nazis advance into Paris, a bourgeois widow (Béart) and her two children flee to the countryside, where they meet a resourceful, illiterate 17-year-old (Ulliel), who teaches them how to survive and further affects their lives. Intense drama offers an intimate account of the chaos of war and how it affects both individuals and families. ▼)

Streamers (1983) **C-118m.** ******* D: Robert Altman. Matthew Modine, Michael Wright, Mitchell Lichtenstein, David Alan Grier, Guy Boyd, George Dzundza. A couple of days in an army barracks at the dawn of America's involvement in Vietnam becomes a parable about manhood, death and relationships between the races. Overlong and depressing but still worthwhile, with fine performances in meaty roles. Screenplay by David Rabe, from his play. [R]▼●

Streetcar Named Desire, A (1951) **122m.** ******** D: Elia Kazan. Marlon Brando, Vivien Leigh, Kim Hunter, Karl Malden. Stunning production of Tennessee Williams' play, with Brando as the animalistic Stanley Kowalski and Leigh as his wistful, neurotic sister-in-law, Blanche Dubois, pressed together in a grim New Orleans tenement. Oscars went to Leigh, Hunter, and Malden for their flawless performances, as well as for the art direction-set decoration—but it's Brando who left an indelible mark on audiences. Highly influential jazz score by Alex North. Rereleased in 1993 with 4m. of footage that was censored in 1951, playing up the sexual tension between Blanche and Stanley and Stella's carnal attraction to her husband. Remade twice for TV.▼●)

Street Fight SEE: Coonskin

Street Fighter, The (1974-Japanese) **C-**

91m. **½ D: Shigehiro Ozawa. Sonny Chiba, Gerald Yamada, Doris Nakajima, Tony Cetera, Teijo Shikeharo. Japan's answer to Bruce Lee, Shinichi "Sonny" Chiba, who takes on both the Mafia and Yakuza in this cult film notable for the level of its bone-crunching, blood-spurting violence. Staged with more skill than most kung fu epics, the plentiful fight scenes required four action directors. Title sequence for U.S. version designed by Jack Sholder, who later directed THE HIDDEN. Originally rated X, then re-rated R after being cut to 75m. Unrated version released on video. Followed by RETURN OF THE STREET FIGHTER. Actionscope. [X]▼●◗

Street Fighter (1994) C-97m. BOMB D: Steven E. de Souza. Jean-Claude Van Damme, Raul Julia, Ming-Na Wen, Damian Chapa, Kylie Minogue, Simon Callow, Roshan Seth, Wes Studi, Andrew Bryniarski, Adrian Cronauer. "Allied Nations" commando Van Damme and his action team battle high-tech warlord Julia (looking depressingly gaunt in his final theatrical film) who's holding hostages ransom for $20 billion, and conducting mutation experiments in his mad-scientist lab. Callow, a costar of FOUR WEDDINGS AND A FUNERAL, plays a prissy A.N. undersecretary in the worst movie to date inspired by a video game. Plays more like FOUR HUNDRED FUNERALS AND NO SEX. Followed by STREET FIGHTER II: THE ANIMATED MOVIE and a 2009 sequel. Super 35. [PG-13]▼●◗

Street Fighter's Last Revenge, The (1974-Japanese) C-79m. ** D: Shigehiro Ozawa. Shinichi "Sonny" Chiba, Etsuko "Sue" Shiomi, Masafumi Suzuki, Frankie Black, Reiko Ike, Willy Dosey. Chiba swears vengeance on the mob after doing a job for them and getting double-crossed when it's payoff time. Third entry in the ultraviolent series offers more of the same, although Chiba is fashioned as a Bondian secret agent type this time around. Highlight: a character gets knocked into a coffin and sent through a crematory! Followed by SISTER STREET-FIGHTER. Actionscope. [R]▼●◗

Street Fighter: The Legend of Chun-Li (2009-U.S.-Japanese-Canadian) C-96m. BOMB D: Andrzej Bartkowiak. Kristin Kreuk, Chris Klein, Neal McDonough, Michael Clarke Duncan, Robin Shou, Moon Bloodgood, Edmund Chen, Josie Ho. Pointless new film version of the popular video game series finds pretty martial arts–trained Asian-American Chun-Li (Kreuk) spurred into action in Bangkok after her father is kidnapped. She uses all her wiles to snuff out the main bad guy, local crime lord McDonough, and his henchmen, led by the imposing Duncan. The 1987 game inspired a 1994 film version, which is CITIZEN KANE compared to this inept action vehicle,

where even the centerpiece fight sequences are lamely choreographed and hopelessly contrived. When Interpol agent Klein yells, "Bomb! Get out now!" it would be wise to heed his advice. Super 35. [PG-13]◗

Street Gang SEE: **Vigilante**

Street Justice (1989) C-94m. *½ D: Richard S. Sarafian. Michael Ontkean, Joanna Kerns, Catherine Bach, J.D. Cannon, Jeanette Nolan, Richard Cox, William Windom, Sandra Currie. Standard Western plot transposed to modern city setting: loner hero cleans up corrupt town dominated by ruthless, wealthy family. Slow, unconvincing, and instantly forgettable. [R]▼

Street Kings (2008) C-108m. ** D: David Ayer. Keanu Reeves, Forest Whitaker, Hugh Laurie, Chris Evans, Martha Higareda, Cedric "The Entertainer" Kyles, Jay Mohr, John Corbett, Terry Crews, Naomie Harris, Common, Cle Sloan, The Game, Amaury Nolasco, Daryl Gates. Violent L.A. police (i.e., racial) drama makes old Joseph Wambaugh fodder seem positively quaint: Reeves is a very tough, alcoholic psycho-cop who is at the center of numerous gang/revenge/corruption/internal affairs maneuvers/conspiracies. Action-packed and somewhat entertaining (James Ellroy concocted the story and coscripted), but awfully far-fetched. Reeves seems to put more sweat into portraying emotional depth than into chasing bad guys. Followed by a direct-to-DVD sequel. Super 35. [R]◗

Street of Shame (1956-Japanese) 96m. ***½ D: Kenji Mizoguchi. Machiko Kyô, Ayako Wakao, Aiko Mimasu, Michiyo Kogure. The stories of various prostitutes in Dreamland, a Tokyo brothel, are sensitively handled in Mizoguchi's last completed film. Kyô is particularly memorable as a tough, cynical lady of the night; her scene with her father is a highlight.▼◗

Street of Sorrow, The SEE: **Joyless Street, The**

Streets (1990) C-86m. **½ D: Katt Shea Ruben. Christina Applegate, David Mendenhall, Eb Lottimer, Patrick Richword, Alan Stock, Alexander Folk, Mel Castelo, Kay Lenz. Serious, well-made story of runaways living in Venice, California, is compromised by concurrent story of psychotic cop who's a serial killer of prostitutes. Applegate is excellent as illiterate heroine. Understated but shockingly violent at times. [R]▼

Street Scene (1931) 80m. ***½ D: King Vidor. Sylvia Sidney, William Collier, Jr., David Landau, Estelle Taylor, Walter Miller, Beulah Bondi. Heartbreakingly realistic account of life in N.Y. tenements, and younger generation's desperation to get out. Elmer Rice's Pulitzer Prize–winning play (adapted by him) enhanced by fine performances, George Barnes' striking camerawork, Alfred Newman's classic music score.▼◗

Street Smart (1987) **C-97m.** ****½** D: Jerry Schatzberg. Christopher Reeve, Kathy Baker, Mimi Rogers, Morgan Freeman, Jay Patterson, Andre Gregory, Anna Maria Horsford. Out-of-favor writer for a slick Manhattan magazine pitches a high-profile study of N.Y.C pimpdom; unable to find a cooperative subject, he fakes the story, which boomerangs when the D.A. concludes the story is about a real-life murder suspect. Intriguing idea, based on screenwriter David Freeman's own experience at *New York* magazine, but just misses; powerhouse performances by pimp Freeman and hooker Baker make up for Reeve's blandness in the lead. [R]▼●❶

Streets of Fire (1984) **C-93m.** ******* D: Walter Hill. Michael Paré, Diane Lane, Rick Moranis, Amy Madigan, Willem Dafoe, Deborah Van Valkenburgh, Richard Lawson, Rick Rossovich, Bill Paxton, Lee Ving, Robert Townsend, Elizabeth Daily, Marine Jahan, Ed Begley, Jr., Olivia Brown, Matthew Laurance, The Blasters. Female rock star is kidnapped by sadistic bikers, and her embittered ex-boyfriend agrees to bring her back—for a price. This "rock 'n' roll fable" is actually a 1950s B movie brought up to date with pulsating rock score (principally by Ry Cooder), state-of-the-art visuals, and a refusal to take itself too seriously. Unfortunately, near the climax the glitter gives out and we're left with the story—which can't carry film to a really satisfying conclusion. Stunningly photographed (mostly on a soundstage, believe it or not) by Andrew Laszlo. [PG]▼●❶

Streets of Gold (1986) **C-95m.** ****½** D: Joe Roth. Klaus Maria Brandauer, Adrian Pasdar, Wesley Snipes, Angela Molina, Elya Baskin, Rainbow Harvest, John Mahoney. Former Russian boxing champ, now a dishwasher in Brooklyn, trains two street kids for U.S. boxing team—hoping to beat his former Russian coach. Well-meaning "feelgood" movie along ROCKY lines; utterly ordinary but for Brandauer's performance. [R]▼●

Streets of Sin SEE: **Not Wanted**

Streetwalkin' (1984) **C-85m.** BOMB D: Joan Freeman. Melissa Leo, Dale Midkiff, Antonio Fargas, Julie Newmar, Leon Robinson, Annie Golden. Ultra-slick, sleazy, hopelessly predictable trash about hooker-with-a-heart-of-gold and her sadistic, unbelievably stupid pimp. [R]▼●

Strictly Ballroom (1992-Australian) **C-94m.** ******* D: Baz Luhrmann. Paul Mercurio, Tara Morice, Bill Hunter, Barry Otto, Pat Thompson, Gia Carides, Peter Whitford, John Hannan. Spirited, allegorical musical about a young, competitive ballroom dancer (Mercurio) who outrages his mother, and the "establishment," by insisting on dancing his own provocative steps; he takes on a new ugly-duckling partner (Morice) who blooms

under his tutelage. This crowd-pleaser sacrifices credibility for caricature but despite its rough edges emerges a winner. [PG]▼●❶

Strictly Business (1991) **C-83m.** ****** D: Kevin Hooks. Tommy Davidson, Joseph C. Phillips, Anne Marie Johnson, David Marshall Grant, Halle Berry, Jon Cypher, Sam (Samuel L.) Jackson, Kim Coles, James McDaniel, Paul Provenza, Annie Golden, Sam Rockwell. Corporate man-on-the-move with a "yuppie-plus" girlfriend falls for pretty show-biz hopeful, then enlists the aid of an indolent mailroom employee to loosen up his act, and increase his funk quotient. Silly, simplistic comedy. Director Hooks appears in a small role. [PG-13]▼●❶

Strike! (1998) SEE: **All I Wanna Do**

Strike (2007-German-Polish) **C/B&W-104m.** ****½** D: Volker Schlöndorff. Katharina Thalbach, Andrzej Chyra, Dominique Horwitz, Andrzej Grabowski, Dariusz Kowalski, Krzysztof Kiersznowski, Ewa Telega. Fact-based account of Agnieszka Kowalska (Thalbach), a relentless, tough-minded Gdansk dockworker whose struggle for workers' rights resulted in the birth of Poland's Solidarity movement. The character is a stand-in for Anna Walentynowicz, a colleague of Lech Walesa (Chyra) during the formation of Solidarity. Dramatically uneven, but still effective in showing how individual acts of conscience occasionally lead to enormous social or cultural change.❶

Strikebound (1983-Australian) **C-100m.** ******* D: Richard Lowenstein. Chris Haywood, Carol Burns, Hugh Keays-Byrne, Rob Steele, Nik Forster. Documentarylike chronicle, based on actual incidents, of a miners' strike in the Australian coal fields during the 1930s, culminating with the workers—many of them Communist Party members—barricading themselves in their mine. Seems a bit romanticized but still taut, perceptive, and extremely well made.

Strike It Rich (1990-British) **C-87m.** ***½** D: James Scott. Robert Lindsay, Molly Ringwald, John Gielgud, Max Wall, Simon de la Brosse. Second film version of Graham Greene novella *Loser Takes All,* about an obscure conglomerate accountant talked into honeymooning beyond his means in Monte Carlo following a chance encounter with the firm's Grand Old Man. The leads in DRIVING MISS DAISY have more sexual chemistry than postnuptial Lindsay and Ringwald; sole compensations are Gielgud and '50s production design. [PG]▼●❶

Strike Up the Band (1940) **120m.** ****½** D: Busby Berkeley. Mickey Rooney, Judy Garland, Paul Whiteman, June Preisser, William Tracy, Larry Nunn, Margaret Early, Ann Shoemaker. Rooney is leader of high school band hoping to compete in Paul Whiteman's nationwide radio contest. Typical Mickey-Judy fare, with good songs:

"Our Love Affair" and an extended finale featuring the Gershwins' title tune. George Pal contributes a unique segment featuring a symphony performed by animated pieces of fruit (an idea apparently hatched by Vincente Minnelli). ▼◐●

Striking Distance (1993) **C-101m.** **✫ D:** Rowdy Herrington. Bruce Willis, Sarah Jessica Parker, Dennis Farina, Tom Sizemore, Brion James, Robert Pastorelli, Timothy Busfield, John Mahoney, Andre Braugher, Jodi Long. Slick but empty, overly familiar thriller about maverick Pittsburgh river cop Willis, who bucks the status quo within his department, and becomes a pawn in a case involving a serial killer. [R] ▼◐●

Stripes (1981) **C-105m.** **✫½ D:** Ivan Reitman. Bill Murray, Harold Ramis, Warren Oates, P. J. Soles, Sean Young, John Candy, John Larroquette, Judge Reinhold, Timothy Busfield, Bill Paxton. Loser Murray joins the Army in this predictable service comedy, which somehow pulled in millions at the box office. Sometimes funny, but eminently forgettable. Ramis, who plays Murray's buddy, also coscripted. Brief appearances by Joe Flaherty and Dave Thomas. Extended edition runs 122m. [R] ▼◐●

Stripped to Kill (1987) **C-88m.** **✫½ D:** Katt Shea Ruben. Kay Lenz, Greg Evigan, Norman Fell, Pia Kamakahi, Tracey Crowder, Debby Nassar. Who's killing the classy strippers of L.A.? It's up to policewoman Lenz to find out, by posing as a stripper herself. Stylish, inventive Roger Corman B production hampered by too many strip numbers. Followed by a 1989 sequel. [R] ▼●

Stripper, The (1963) **95m.** **✫½ D:** Franklin Schaffner. Joanne Woodward, Richard Beymer, Claire Trevor, Carol Lynley, Robert Webber, Gypsy Rose Lee, Louis Nye, Michael J. Pollard. Aging stripper falls in love with teen-age boy in this OK filmization of William Inge's play *A Loss of Roses.* Director Schaffner's first movie. CinemaScope. ▼

Striptease (1996) **C-115m.** BOMB D: Andrew Bergman. Demi Moore, Armand Assante, Burt Reynolds, Ving Rhames, Robert Patrick, Paul Guilfoyle, Rumer Willis, Frances Fisher. Unspeakably dreary—not to mention dreadful—movie (based on Carl Hiaasen's novel) about a woman who's lost custody of her young daughter to her sleazeball ex-husband and becomes a stripper in order to raise money fast for a court appeal. Then she becomes entangled with a horny congressman. Not funny enough, or dramatic enough, or sexy enough, or bad enough, to qualify as entertainment in *any* category. That's Moore's real-life daughter playing her little girl. Unrated video version includes 2m. of additional footage. [R] ▼◐●

Stroke of Midnight (1991) **C-91m.** **✫½ D:** Tom Clegg. Rob Lowe, Jennifer Grey, Andrea Ferreol, Elizabeth Vitali, Rebecca Potok, Sacha Brignet. Direct-to-video dud about completely self-absorbed fashion mogul Lowe's search for a "new face" to represent his line of clothes; of course, he's barely aware of aspiring shoe designer Grey, who works for him. Poorly executed Cinderella yarn—replete with magic shoes. Unfortunately, there's no magic in this movie. [PG] ▼●

Stroker Ace (1983) **C-96m.** BOMB D: Hal Needham. Burt Reynolds, Ned Beatty, Jim Nabors, Loni Anderson, Parker Stevenson, Bubba Smith, John Byner, Frank O. Hill. One of Burt's worst has him as champion race-car driver and pea-brain who delights in tormenting his sponsor (Beatty) and leering at buxom Anderson. Lame "good old boy" hijinks, punctuated with TV stock footage of race-car crackups! Note: Jim Nabors sings, too. [PG] ▼●

Stromboli (1949-Italian) **81m.** **✫½ D:** Roberto Rossellini. Ingrid Bergman, Mario Vitale, Renzo Cesana, Mario Sponza. Rambling dreariness with refugee Bergman marrying fisherman Vitale; even an erupting volcano doesn't jar this plodding film, which was boycotted in the U.S. because Bergman had left her husband (Petter Lindstrom) for Rossellini. Original 107m. version is now available, but is little improvement over U.S. release (which was edited by Alfred Werker and has a different ending). ▼

Stronger Than the Sun (1980-British) **C-101m.** **✫✫✫ D:** Michael Apted. Francesca Annis, Tom Bell. Annis is excellent as a nuclear power plant worker who attempts to expose a radioactive leak. Timely drama bears a striking resemblance to the Karen Silkwood story.

Strongest Man in the World, The (1975) **C-92m.** **✫✫ D:** Vincent McEveety. Kurt Russell, Joe Flynn, Eve Arden, Cesar Romero, Phil Silvers, Dick Van Patten, Harold Gould, James Gregory. Third of Disney's cookie-cutter student comedies with Russell and pals again discovering a magic formula—this one for super-strength—and battling crooks who want to get their hands on it. Good opening and closing, but even kids may find it draggy midway through. [G] ▼●

Strong Man, The (1926) **78m.** **✫✫✫ D:** Frank Capra. Harry Langdon, Priscilla Bonner, Gertrude Astor, Brooks Benedict, Arthur Thalasso, Robert McKim, William V. Mong. Baby-faced Langdon's best movie (and Capra's feature-film debut) casts him as a Belgian WW1 veteran who comes to America in search of the girl he corresponded with during the war. Many fine set pieces make this a memorable comedy; the star never fared as well again. ▼◐●

Strong Medicine (1979) **C-84m.** **✫✫½ D:** Richard Foreman. Kate Mannheim, Scotty Snyder, Bill Raymond, Harry Roskolenko, Ron Vawter, Carol Kane, Raul Julia, Buck

Henry, Wallace Shawn. Alternately fascinating, boring, surreal chronicle of the various activities and adventures of a mad, manic, eccentric woman. Foreman is an innovative theater director; ultimately, this film is an acquired taste.

Stroszek (1977-German) **C-108m.** *******
D: Werner Herzog. Bruno S., Eva Mattes, Clemens Scheitz. Berlin street singer and former mental patient Bruno S. joins with whore (Mattes) and aging eccentric (Scheitz) to travel to the gold-paved streets of America the promised-land—which turns out to be dreary, rural Wisconsin. Most effective as tragicomic, ultimately bitter ridicule of American society.▼▶

St. Trinian's (2007-British) **C-101m.** *½
D: Oliver Parker, Barnaby Thompson. Rupert Everett, Colin Firth, Lena Headey, Jodie Whittaker, Russell Brand, Anna Chancellor, Stephen Fry, Celia Imrie, Toby Jones, Caterina Murino, Fenella Woolgar, Talulah Riley, Mischa Barton, Gemma Arterton, Juno Temple, Lucy Punch, Nathaniel Parker. Painfully unfunny updating of the venerable series, with near bankrupt (financially and otherwise) St. Trinian's school ineptly managed by an oddball headmistress; Everett (in drag) plays Miss Fritton, as well as her shady brother. The students are either sluttish or sadistic; no outsider is spared their pranks, not even England's new Education Minister (Firth). Paging Alastair Sim. Followed by a sequel. [PG-13]▶

Stuart Little (1999) **C-92m.** ******* D: Rob Minkoff. Geena Davis, Hugh Laurie, Jonathan Lipnicki, Jeffrey Jones, Julia Sweeney, Allyce Beasley, Brian Doyle-Murray, Dabney Coleman, Estelle Getty; voices of Michael J. Fox, Nathan Lane, Chazz Palminteri, Jennifer Tilly, Bruno Kirby, David Alan Grier, Steve Zahn. Cute family film loosely based on E. B. White's much-loved book about a mouse, adopted by a human family, who falls prey to the plotting of a jealous housecat. Sincere human performances and remarkable computer animation of Stuart make this entertaining for young and old alike. Followed by a sequel and a direct-to-video animated feature. [PG]▼▶

Stuart Little 2 (2002) **C-72m.** **½ D: Rob Minkoff. Geena Davis, Hugh Laurie, Jonathan Lipnicki; voices of Michael J. Fox, Nathan Lane, Melanie Griffith, James Woods, Steve Zahn. Stuart is feeling a bit lonely until he rescues a bird named Margalo from an attacking falcon and takes her into the Little home. Not much of a story here—more a series of vignettes—but the characters are appealing, the animation is skillful, and Lane's dialogue as Snowbell the cat is hilarious, all of which makes up for the film's shortcomings. Good entertainment for kids. [PG]▼▶

Stuart Saves His Family (1995) **C-95m.**

** D: Harold Ramis. Al Franken, Laura San Giacomo, Vincent D'Onofrio, Shirley Knight, Harris Yulin, Lesley Boone, John Link Graney, Julia Sweeney. Feature-film vehicle for Stuart Smalley, writer-performer Franken's endearingly dippy self-affirmation advocate from *Saturday Night Live* TV skits ("I'm good enough, I'm smart enough, and doggone it, people *like* me"). Unfortunately, this purported comedy about Stuart's attempts to wrest himself from his dysfunctional family (and the blight caused by his alcoholic father) becomes deadly serious! [PG-13] ▼▶

Stuck (2008-U.S.-Canadian) **C-85m.** *******
D: Stuart Gordon. Stephen Rea, Mena Suvari, Russell Hornsby, Rukiya Bernard, Carolyn Purdy-Gordon. Often shockingly hilarious black comedy, loosely based on a notorious real-life incident, about a down-sized white-collar drone (Rea) who has a close encounter with an oncoming car, then remains painfully stuck in the windshield while left to die in a garage by the monstrously self-absorbed driver (Suvari). As Rea struggles to survive the mishap (and Suvari's attempts to finish him off), this ingeniously nasty small-budget indie slyly suggests that the last best hope for a hard-luck loser is to be placed in a situation where there's nothing left to lose. [R]▶

Stuck on You (2003) **C-118m.** *½ D: Bobby Farrelly, Peter Farrelly. Matt Damon, Greg Kinnear, Eva Mendes, Cher, Wen Yann Shih, Pat Crawford Brown, Ray "Rocket" Valliere, Seymour Cassel, Michael Callan, Griffin Dunne, Rhona Mitra, Jessica Cauffiel. Inscrutable Farrelly Brothers comedy about conjoined twins, one of whom yearns to pursue an acting career in Hollywood. This *rara avis* is a one-joke movie where even the one joke isn't very good. As usual, the filmmakers make fun of people with disabilities and warmly embrace them at the same time. Various celebrities appear in cameos, most notably Meryl Streep. Super 35. [PG-13] ▼▶

Stud, The (1978-British) **C-95m.** BOMB D: Quentin Masters. Joan Collins, Oliver Tobias, Sue Lloyd, Mark Burns, Walter Gotell, Emma Jacobs. A waiter works his way up in the world (so to speak) by sleeping with the boss' wife. Idiotic softcore porn written by Jackie Collins (Joan's sister). Followed by THE BITCH. [R]▼▶

Student Bodies (1981) **C-86m.** *½ D: Mickey Rose. Kristen Riter, Matthew Goldsby, Richard Brando, Joe Flood, Joe Talarowski. Spoof of HALLOWEEN-type pictures has a promising start, then simply falls apart; ending is particularly bad. Plagued by production problems, as indicated by producing credit for the ubiquitous and nonexistent Allen Smithee (Michael Ritchie here). [R]▼▶

Student Nurses, The (1970) **C-89m.** **½

[1337]

D: Stephanie Rothman. Elaine Giftos, Karen Carlson, Brioni Farrell, Barbara Leigh, Reni Santoni, Richard Rust. First of five "nurse" movies produced by Roger Corman is easily the best, with good cast, comparatively thoughtful script (cowritten by Rothman), along with expected sex and action; most interesting subplot concerns guilt by young activist nurse after she accidentally shoots a cop. Followed by PRIVATE DUTY NURSES. [R]▼●)

Student Prince, The (1954) C-107m. **½ D: Richard Thorpe. Ann Blyth, Edmund Purdom, John Ericson, Louis Calhern, Edmund Gwenn. Romberg music, dubbed voice of Mario Lanza chief assets in venerable operetta about heir to throne sent to Heidelberg for one last fling, where he falls in love with barmaid Blyth. Filmed before (sans music) in 1919 and 1927. CinemaScope.▼●)

Student Prince in Old Heidelberg, The (1927) 105m. **** D: Ernst Lubitsch. Ramon Novarro, Norma Shearer, Jean Hersholt, Gustav von Seyffertitz, Philippe de Lacy, Edgar Norton, George K. Arthur, Edythe Chapman. Silent version of Sigmund Romberg's famed operetta has youthful prince Novarro breaking out of his cloistered life—for the first time—and attending Heidelberg University, where he falls in love with a commoner, pretty barmaid Shearer. This is Lubitsch at his best, an absolute delight from start to finish, and truly the kind of charmer "they just don't make anymore." Also known as OLD HEIDELBERG. Previously filmed in 1919; remade (with music) in 1954.▼●)

Student Teachers, The (1973) C-79m. **½ D: Jonathan Kaplan. Susan Damante, Brooke Mills, Bob Harris, John Cramer, Dick Miller, Don Steele, Robert Phillips, Charles Dierkop. Antics at Valley High School, with both feminist and "alternate learning center" concepts mixed into the usual sexploitation package. Freewheeling direction by Kaplan; followed by SUMMER SCHOOL TEACHERS. [R]▼

Studs Lonigan (1960) 95m. **½ D: Irving Lerner. Christopher Knight, Frank Gorshin, Venetia Stevenson, Carolyn Craig, Jack Nicholson, Dick Foran. Interesting if not altogether successful adaptation of James T. Farrell's "notorious" novel about a restless, sexually active young man (Knight) in 1920s Chicago. Good period atmosphere, but script makes unfortunate compromises with 1960 taste and censorship. Nicholson is one of Studs' cronies; Foran is impressive as Studs' father. Scripted and produced by Philip Yordan. Basis for a 1979 TV miniseries.▼●)

Study in Terror, A (1965-British) C-94m. *** D: James Hill. John Neville, Donald Houston, Georgia Brown, John Fraser, Anthony Quayle, Barbara Windsor, Robert Morley, Cecil Parker, Frank Finlay, Kay Walsh, Judi Dench. Compact little thriller pits Sherlock Holmes against Jack the Ripper; violent, well paced, and well cast. For another version of Holmes vs. the Ripper, see MURDER BY DECREE.▼●)

Stuff, The (1985) C-93m. **½ D: Larry Cohen. Michael Moriarty, Andrea Marcovicci, Garrett Morris, Paul Sorvino, Scott Bloom, Danny Aiello, James Dixon, Alexander Scourby, Russell Nype, Brian Bloom, Rutanya Alda. The new dessert sensation that's sweeping the country turns out to be deadly stuff indeed. Typically slapdash Larry Cohen production has some engaging performances, and the spirit of silly '50s science-fiction films, but doesn't always come off—as horror *or* comedy. It *does* have its moments, however—and a bunch of familiar "Commercial Spokes-persons." [R]▼●)

Stunt Man, The (1980) C-129m. **** D: Richard Rush. Peter O'Toole, Steve Railsback, Barbara Hershey, Chuck Bail, Allen Goorwitz (Garfield), Adam Roarke, Alex Rocco, Sharon Farrell, Philip Bruns. An outrageous black comedy in which reality and make-believe blur. Fugitive Railsback stumbles onto a movie set, where he accidentally causes the death of their ace stunt man; director O'Toole offers to hide him from the police—if he'll replace the stunt man. Crammed with first-rate action and sly wit, plus a mesmerizing performance by O'Toole as the Christ-like Eli Cross. Attention must be paid, but the rewards are more than ample. Dazzlingly scripted (by Lawrence B. Marcus from Paul Brodeur's novel) and directed; amusing score by Dominic Frontiere. Filmed in 1978. [R]▼●)

Stunts (1977) C-89m. **½ D: Mark L. Lester. Robert Forster, Fiona Lewis, Joanna Cassidy, Darrell Fetty, Bruce Glover, James Luisi. When a stunt man dies while making a film, his brother (Forster) takes his place in order to probe the "accident." Engaging B movie with terrific action scenes and a wild helicopter-and-car finale. Retitled WHO IS KILLING THE STUNTMEN? [PG]▼●)

Stupids, The (1996) C-94m. **½ D: John Landis. Tom Arnold, Jessica Lundy, Bug Hall, Alex McKenna, Mark Metcalf, Matt Keeslar, Frankie Faison, Christopher Lee, Jenny McCarthy. Likably goofy film for kids about a lunkhead family that somehow gets involved in espionage and an illegal weapons scheme. The cast is ideal, straight-facedly portraying these well-meaning morons (from the children's books by James Marshall and Harry Allard); the tone of the film is admirably consistent and often quite funny. As usual Landis features cameos by other directors, including Robert Wise, Gillo Pontecorvo, Costa-Gavras,

Atom Egoyan, Norman Jewison, and David Cronenberg. And yes, that's Captain Kangaroo (Bob Keeshan) as the museum curator. Remember, trust in the Lloyd. [PG]▼●◗

St. Valentine's Day Massacre, The (1967) C-100m. **½ D: Roger Corman. Jason Robards, Jr., George Segal, Ralph Meeker, Jean Hale, Clint Ritchie, Frank Silvera, Joseph Campanella, Bruce Dern. This had the makings of a good film, but they blew it, with Robards (as Al Capone) and Segal (doing a Jimmy Cagney imitation) overacting as they've never done before. So much shooting throughout film that final massacre seems tame by comparison. Many familiar faces appear throughout: Harold Stone, Kurt Krueger, Milton Frome, Mickey Deems, John Agar, Reed Hadley, Alex D'Arcy, etc. Pay close attention and you'll see Jack Nicholson, too! Panavision.▼

Sub-A-Dub-Dub SEE: **Hello Down There**

Subject Was Roses, The (1968) C-107m. *** D: Ulu Grosbard. Patricia Neal, Jack Albertson, Martin Sheen, Don Saxon, Elaine Williams, Grant Gordon. Frank D. Gilroy's Pulitzer Prize–winning play about young veteran's strained relationship with his parents makes a generally good film. This was Neal's first film after her near fatal stroke. Sheen and Oscar winner Albertson recreated their Broadway roles. Gilroy adapted his own play for the screen. [G]▼◗

Submarine (2011-British) C-97m. *** D: Richard Ayoade. Craig Roberts, Yasmin Paige, Sally Hawkins, Noah Taylor, Paddy Considine. In Wales, a self-conscious 15-year-old boy tells us about his life as he tries to salvage his uptight parents' strained relationship and pursues a freethinking female schoolmate who might become his first real girlfriend. Low-key but witty coming-of-age story adapted from Joe Dunthorne's novel by first-time feature director Ayoade. Hawkins and Taylor are amusing as the clueless parents. Ben Stiller (who coexecutive produced) appears unbilled. [R]◗

Submarine Patrol (1938) 95m. **½ D: John Ford. Richard Greene, Nancy Kelly, Preston Foster, George Bancroft, Slim Summerville, John Carradine, J. Farrell MacDonald, Maxie Rosenbloom, Jack Pennick, Elisha Cook, Jr. Routine actioner with tough captain Foster revitalizing beat-up Splinter Fleet ship and demoralized crew for duty in WW1.

Submarine X-1 (1968-British) C-89m. **½ D: William Graham. James Caan, Rupert Davies, David Summer, William Dysart, Norman Bowler. After losing submarine in battle with German ship, naval officer Caan gets second chance in daring raid with midget subs. Standard WW2 fare. [G]◗

Subspecies (1991) C-90m. ** D: Ted Nicolaou. Michael Watson, Laura Tate, Anders Hove, Michelle McBride, Irina Movila, Ivan J. Rado, Angus Scrimm. Nasty vampire is after some American girls but has to contend with his good-vampire brother. Actually shot in Transylvania on picturesque locations, but the director has no idea how to set up shock scenes. Followed by four sequels. [R]▼●◗

Substance of Fire, The (1996) C-101m. *** D: Daniel Sullivan. Ron Rifkin, Tony Goldwyn, Timothy Hutton, Sarah Jessica Parker, Lee Grant, Eric Bogosian, Elizabeth Franz, Gil Bellows, Roger Rees, Ronny Graham, Adolph Green, George Morfogen, Debra Monk, Viola Davis. Literate, intelligent adaptation of Jon Robin Baitz' Off-Broadway play about a brilliant but inordinately arrogant—and deeply troubled—Holocaust survivor (Rifkin). Now a book publisher, he's obsessed with publishing an extensive history of Nazi medical experiments, rather than a potentially lucrative novel that may save his company from financial ruin. Not surprisingly, he has alienated his three grown children. Extremely well acted, especially by Rifkin (who created his role onstage). Baitz scripted. [R]▼◗

Substitute, The (1996) C-114m. ** D: Robert Mandel. Tom Berenger, Diane Venora, Ernie Hudson, Glenn Plummer, William Forsythe, Richard Brooks, Cliff De Young. The CIA goes to high school in this preposterous but entertaining action story of agent Berenger who substitutes for teacher/girlfriend Venora when her leg is broken by a gang member. When he's not disciplining students, this substitute is busy exposing and fighting drug smugglers. Mindless diversion. Followed by three sequels. [R]▼●◗

Subterfuge (1968-British) C-92m. ** D: Peter Graham Scott. Gene Barry, Joan Collins, Richard Todd, Suzanna Leigh, Michael Rennie. American agent Barry is forced into helping British Intelligence in this routine espionage drama.▼

Subterraneans, The (1960) C-89m. **½ D: Ranald MacDougall. Leslie Caron, George Peppard, Janice Rule, Roddy McDowall, Anne Seymour, Jim Hutton, Scott Marlowe. Glossy, superficial study of life and love among the beatniks, with pure cornball stereotype performances; MGM was not the studio for this one. Script by Robert Thom, from the Jack Kerouac novel. Music by Andre Previn, who also appears on screen along with such jazz artists as Gerry Mulligan, Carmen McRae, Art Pepper, Art Farmer, Shelly Manne. CinemaScope.

Suburban Commando (1991) C-90m. **½ D: Burt Kennedy. Hulk Hogan (Terry Bollea), Christopher Lloyd, Shelley Duvall, Larry Miller, William Ball, JoAnn Dearing, Jack Elam, Roy Dotrice, Michael

Faustino, Elizabeth Moss. Engaging film for kids about outer-space warrior who comes to earth for some r&r, and gets involved in the lives of a somewhat stressed-out suburban family. Hogan is surprisingly likable as a vigilante/crusader in this comic vehicle which he coexecutive-produced. [PG]▼●〗

Suburbans, The (1999) **C-90m.** *½ D: Donal Lardner Ward. Donal Lardner Ward, Amy Brenneman, Craig Bierko, Will Ferrell, Jennifer Love Hewitt, Tony Guma, Bridgette Wilson, Ben Stiller, Jerry Stiller, Robert Loggia. Pointless trifle about a one-hit-wonder band from the 1980s attempting to revitalize their career. Not even the Stillers can make it work. [R]▼▼〗

Suburbia (1983) SEE: **Wild Side, The**

subUrbia (1996) **C-118m.** **½ D: Richard Linklater. Giovanni Ribisi, Steve Zahn, Amie Carey, Samia Shoaib, Ajay Naidu, Nicky Katt, Jayce Bartok, Parker Posey, Dina Spybey. Knowing, laced-in-acid son-of-SLACKER, depicting a group of aimless, alienated 20-year-olds who hang out in a generic suburban parking lot, where various frictions and jealousies emerge—especially upon the appearance of one of their old pals, who has become a rock star. Collectively well acted and pungently scripted by Eric Bogosian (based on his play), though its stage origins weigh it down a bit. [R]▼●

Subway (1985-French) **C-104m.** ** D: Luc Besson. Isabelle Adjani, Christopher Lambert, Richard Bohringer, Michel Galabru, Jean-Hugues Anglade. Dripping in new wave style and attitude, this (literally) underground fable, set in the Paris métro, where various lives intertwine, is utterly aimless and pointless. Intrigues and amuses at first, and then just runs out of steam. Technovision. [R]▼●〗

Subway to the Stars (1987-Brazilian) **C-103m.** **½ D: Carlos Diegues. Guilherme Fontes, Milton Goncalves, Taumaturgo Ferreira, Ze Trindade, Ana Beatriz Wiltgen. Gritty, grim account of young sax player and his experiences as he roams the back streets of Rio in search of his missing girlfriend. Has its moments of insight, but overall too meandering. [R]▼

Success (1979) SEE: **American Success Company, The**

Success Is the Best Revenge (1984-British) **C-90m.** **½ D: Jerzy Skolimowski. Michael York, Joanna Szerbic, Michael Lyndon, George Skolimowski, Michel Piccoli, Anouk Aimée, John Hurt. Intriguing if uneven yarn about a Polish director (York) in exile in London and his rebellious teen son (Lyndon), who is anxious to explore his heritage. Skolimowski—himself an exile—explores the meaning of living in a country other than one's own, but he fared better with previous film, MOONLIGHTING.▼●

Such a Gorgeous Kid Like Me (1972-French) **C-98m.** ***½ D: François Truffaut. Bernadette Lafont, Claude Brasseur, Charles Denner, Guy Marchand, Philippe Léotard. Delightful black comedy of female murderer who relates her sordid past to criminology student, gradually entices him just as she did her former "victims." Lafont ideal in leading role. [R]

Such Good Friends (1971) **C-100m.** *** D: Otto Preminger. Dyan Cannon, James Coco, Jennifer O'Neill, Ken Howard, Nina Foch, Laurence Luckinbill, Louise Lasser, Burgess Meredith, Sam Levene. Tart black comedy about man going to hospital, prompting wife (Cannon) to reexamine their relationship and learn about his romantic sideline activities. Fine ensemble acting buoys acidly funny script (by Elaine May, who used a pseudonym); from the Lois Gould novel. [R]〗

Sucker Punch (2011) **C-110m.** ** D: Zack Snyder. Emily Browning, Abbie Cornish, Jena Malone, Vanessa Hudgens, Jamie Chung, Carla Gugino, Oscar Isaac, Jon Hamm, Scott Glenn. Abused girl (Browning) is wrongly committed to a corrupt insane asylum, where she bonds with four other captive young women and finds freedom in her fantasies, in which she and the others are kick-ass superheroines. Genuinely weird, broadly played, comic-bookish film is all style, with little substance that isn't laughable. Will it inspire or empower downtrodden adolescent girls . . . or will it just make them want to play video games? Alternate R-rated version runs 127m. Super 35. [PG-13]〗

Sudden Death (1995) **C-110m.** *½ D: Peter Hyams. Jean-Claude Van Damme, Powers Boothe, Raymond J. Barry, Whittni Wright, Ross Malinger, Dorian Harewood, Paul Mochnick, Kate McNeil, Michael Gaston, Audra Lindley. Sardonic mastermind Boothe holds the Vice President hostage in a private box during Stanley Cup hockey playoffs in Pittsburgh, demanding a few billion, or he'll blow up the whole arena. But fire inspector Van Damme is on the job, and Boothe has unwisely captured our hero's daughter . . . DIE HARD clone bludgeons credulity to death early on, and the movie never recovers, despite plenty of action and effects. Panavision. [R]▼●

Sudden Fear (1952) **110m.** *** D: David Miller. Joan Crawford, Jack Palance, Gloria Grahame, Bruce Bennett, Touch (Mike) Connors, Virginia Huston. Wealthy playwright Crawford discovers new husband Palance (an actor whom she once fired) is planning to kill her; she uses her writing skills to concoct a scheme to make him trip himself up. Solid suspense thriller with many neat twists.▼●〗

Sudden Impact (1983) **C-117m.** **½ D:

Clint Eastwood. Clint Eastwood, Sondra Locke, Pat Hingle, Bradford Dillman, Paul Drake, Jack Thibeau, Albert Popwell. Fourth DIRTY HARRY vehicle relies on durable formula, as maverick cop gives us vicarious pleasure of doing in society's scum, but this entry is longer, and sillier, than need be. Locke plays a woman taking out murderous revenge on men (and one lesbian!) who raped her and her sister years ago. Michael V. Gazzo appears unbilled. Followed by THE DEAD POOL. Panavision. [R]▼●◗

Suddenly (1954) 77m. ***½ D: Lewis Allen. Frank Sinatra, Sterling Hayden, James Gleason, Nancy Gates, Willis Bouchey, Kim Charney, Paul Frees, Christopher Dark, Charles Smith. Sinatra leads trio of paid assassins who take over house in small town where the President will pass on his way to a fishing trip. White-knuckle thriller, written by Richard Sale, with Sinatra excellent in thoroughly detestable role; rest of cast equally fine. "Suddenly," incidentally, is the name of the town. Also shown in computer-colored version.▼●◗

Suddenly, Last Summer (1959) 114m. ***½ D: Joseph L. Mankiewicz. Elizabeth Taylor, Katharine Hepburn, Montgomery Clift, Mercedes McCambridge, Albert Dekker. Fascinating if talky (though cleaned-up) Tennessee Williams yarn about wealthy Southern matriarch (Hepburn), her supposedly mad niece (Taylor) and a neurosurgeon (Clift); grandly acted. Adaptation by Gore Vidal. Remade for TV in 1992 with Maggie Smith.▼●◗

Sudden Terror (1970-British) C-95m. ** D: John Hough. Mark Lester, Lionel Jeffries, Susan George, Tony Bonner, Jeremy Kemp. Adequate variation on boy-who-cried-wolf theme: prankish youngster witnesses murder of visiting dignitary, but can't convince others. Almost ruined by self-conscious direction. Originally titled EYEWITNESS. [PG] ▼◗

Suez (1938) 104m. *** D: Allan Dwan. Tyrone Power, Loretta Young, Annabella, Henry Stephenson, Maurice Moscovich, Joseph Schildkraut, Sidney Blackmer, J. Edward Bromberg, Sig Ruman, Nigel Bruce, Miles Mander, George Zucco, Leon Ames. Power is 19th-century French architect (and dreamer) Ferdinand de Lesseps, who pursues a single-minded goal of building the Suez Canal; his real problem is choosing between aristocratic Loretta and down-to-earth Annabella. Entertaining and elaborate hokum which apparently bears no resemblance to history. Power and Annabella later wed in real life.

Sugar (2009) C-118m. *** D: Anna Boden, Ryan Fleck. Algenis Perez Soto, Rayniel Rufino, Andre Holland, Michael Gaston, Jaime Tirelli, José Rijo, Ann Whitney, Richard Bull, Ellary Porterfield. Illuminat-

ing portrait of a 19-year-old baseball player from the Dominican Republic nicknamed Sugar (Perez Soto), who leaves his family and friends to come to America, where he is assigned to a team in Iowa as his first step toward the major leagues. A poignant look at cultural disorientation, this leisurely, very low-key character study isn't really a sports movie—although it does offer a revealing look at the business end of American baseball. Real-life Dominican-born major leaguer Rijo plays Alvarez. Second feature for the writing-directing team that made HALF NELSON. Super 35. [R] ◗

Sugar and Spice (2001) C-81m. ** D: Francine McDougall. Marley Shelton, James Marsden, Mena Suvari, Marla Sokoloff, Rachel Blanchard, Melissa George, Alexandra Holden, Sara Marsh, Sean Young. Five high school cheerleader pals rally around their squad captain when she becomes pregnant (by the school's new hotshot quarterback) . . . and stage a robbery in order to help her out. Only mildly amusing, though the cast is enthusiastic, and Marsden is fun as an egocentric doofus. Alternate version runs 84m. Super 35. [PG-13]▼◗

Sugarbaby (1985-German) C-87m. **½ D: Percy Adlon. Marianne Sägebrecht, Eisi Gulp. It's love at first sight for chubby mortuary attendant Sägebrecht and subway-train driver Gulp in this droll romantic satire. Players and story are offbeat, but the avant-garde lighting effects and camera movements by cinematographer Johanna Heer become annoying. Remade as BABY-CAKES for American TV.▼

Sugar Cane Alley (1984-French) C-107m. ***½ D: Euzhan Palcy. Darling Legitimus, Garry Cadenat, Routa Seck, Joby Bernabe, Francisco Charles. Beautifully made, heartfelt drama about an 11-year-old boy and his all-sacrificing grandmother, surviving in a Martinique shantytown during the 1930s. Rich, memorable characterizations; a humanist drama of the highest order. [PG]▼●◗

Sugar Hill (1974) C-91m. ** D: Paul Maslansky. Marki Bey, Robert Quarry, Don Pedro Colley, Richard Lawson, Betty Anne Rees, Zara Cully. Bey stars as "Sugar" Hill, who avenges the mob's rubout of her fiancé, conjuring up black zombies from the grave. Outlandish blend of blaxploitation, revenge, and voodoo/ horror elements. [PG]▼

Sugar Hill (1994) C-123m. ** D: Leon Ichaso. Wesley Snipes, Michael Wright, Theresa Randle, Clarence Williams III, Abe Vigoda, Larry Joshua, Ernie Hudson, Leslie Uggams, Khandi Alexander, Raymond Serra, Joe Dallesandro, Vondie Curtis-Hall. So-what crime melodrama featuring Snipes and Wright as Roemello and Raynathan Skuggs, drug-dealing siblings in Harlem. Unlike the more zealous Raynathan, the solitary, soulful Roemello yearns for a career change. Shades of SUPERFLY! Dense and preposterous; you'll be as bored with the film as Roemello is with his life. [R]▼●)

Sugarland Express, The (1974) **C-109m.** ***½ D: Steven Spielberg. Goldie Hawn, Ben Johnson, Michael Sacks, William Atherton, Steve Kanaly, Louise Latham. Perfect entertainment, based on fact, about a young fugitive couple fleeing to Sugarland, Texas, to reclaim their son (whom they refuse to give up for adoption), and the cops who pursue them throughout Texas. Spielberg's first theatrical feature, written by Hal Barwood and Matthew Robbins. Panavision. [PG]▼●)

Sugar Town (1999-U.S.-British) **C-92m.** *** D: Allison Anders, Kurt Voss. Ally Sheedy, Rosanna Arquette, John Taylor, Jade Gordon, Michael Des Barres, Larry Klein, Beverly D'Angelo, Vincent Berry, Richmond Arquette, Lucinda Jenney, Martin Kemp. Amusing mosaic of L.A. life featuring a handful of characters whose lives dovetail: a music-world wannabe who'll do anything to get ahead, an uptight single woman who attracts the wrong guys like a magnet, and a band made up of washed-up '80s rock stars, to name a few. Slight, made on a shoestring, but sharp and well observed; good cast includes a number of real-life musicians. Written by the directors. [R]▼

Suicide Kings (1998) **C-106m.** **½ D: Peter O'Fallon. Christopher Walken, Denis Leary, Henry Thomas, Sean Patrick Flanery, Jay Mohr, Jeremy Sisto, Johnny Galecki, Laura San Giacomo, Laura Harris, Cliff De Young, Brad Garrett. Intriguing premise: a group of spoiled rich kids abduct a smooth underworld character and hold him hostage to gain leverage in the kidnaping of Thomas' sister. But during one long night, the mobster (Walken, in fine form) sizes up his captors and plays on their weaknesses. Well-thought-out chamber piece, with some good story twists and first-rate performances; too bad the wrapup isn't as strong as the rest of the film. [R]▼●)

Sullivans, The (1944) **111m.** *** D: Lloyd Bacon. Anne Baxter, Thomas Mitchell, Selena Royle, Ward Bond, Bobby Driscoll, Addison Richards. Homey, patriotic but fictionalized story of the real-life Sullivan brothers of Waterloo, Iowa, who fought together in WW2. Knowing the outcome of this story makes it very sad to watch. The Sullivans are played by Edward Ryan, John Campbell, James Cardwell, John Alvin, and George Offerman, Jr. Aka THE FIGHTING SULLIVANS. ▼)

Sullivan's Travels (1942) **90m.** **** D: Preston Sturges. Joel McCrea, Veronica Lake, Robert Warwick, William Demarest, Margaret Hayes, Porter Hall, Eric Blore, Robert Greig, Jimmy Conlin, Al Bridge,

Franklin Pangborn. Tired of making fluff, movie director McCrea decides to do a "serious" film, O BROTHER, WHERE ART THOU?; to research it, he sets out with 10¢ in his pocket to experience life in "the real world." Slapstick and sorrow blend seamlessly in this landmark Hollywood satire, which grows more pertinent with each passing year. A unique achievement for writer-director Sturges. ▼●)

Summer (1986-French) **96m.** ***½ D: Eric Rohmer. Marie Riviere, Lisa Heredia, Vincent Gauthier, Beatrice Romand, Carita. Sensitive but whiny Riviere, abandoned by friends on the eve of a group vacation, goes it alone with initially lonely results. Seemingly more improvised than the other Rohmers, this demands viewer patience and some tolerance of Riviere's "difficult" personality, but patience is rewarded. Finale is quite moving, in what emerges as one of the director's better efforts, from his series "Comedies and Proverbs." Original French title: LE RAYON VERT. [R]▼●)

Summer and Smoke (1961) **C-118m.** ***½ D: Peter Glenville. Geraldine Page, Laurence Harvey, Una Merkel, John McIntire, Pamela Tiffin, Rita Moreno, Thomas Gomez, Earl Holliman, Casey Adams (Max Showalter), Lee Patrick. Spinster Page is in love with young doctor Harvey, but he's understandably not interested; vivid adaptation of Tennessee Williams play, set in 1916 in small Mississippi town, with torrid performances making up for frequent staginess. Atmospheric score by Elmer Bernstein. Panavision.▼●)

Summer Camp Nightmare (1987) **C-87m.** *½ D: Bert L. Dragin. Chuck Connors, Charles Stratton, Adam Carl, Harold Pruett, Melissa Brennan, Tom Fridley, Nancy Calabrese. Synthetic update of LORD OF THE FLIES has young Fascist Stratton staging a small-scale revolution by having kids take over two adjoining summer camps, imprisoning the adults. Stratton good in difficult role, but plot gimmicks fail to convince, especially the kids' quickie descent into barbarism. Based on William Butler's novel *The Butterfly Revolution.* [PG-13]▼●

Summer Catch (2001) **C-104m.** ** D: Mike Tollin. Freddie Prinze, Jr., Jessica Biel, Matthew Lillard, Brian Dennehy, Fred Ward, Jason Gedrick, Brittany Murphy, Bruce Davison, Marc Blucas, Wilmer Valderrama. Substandard comedy/romance/coming-of-age story set in Cape Cod, with underprivileged baseball player Prinze falling for local rich girl, then having to deal with her snobby father, while tending his budding career. Takes itself too seriously, though Lillard adds welcome comedy relief. Beverly D'Angelo and John C. McGinley appear unbilled. [PG-13] ▼)

Summer City (1976-Australian) **C-83m.** ** D: Christopher Fraser. John Jarratt, Mel

Gibson, Phil Avalon, Steve Bisley, James Elliot, Debbie Forman. Slight, low-budget rock 'n roll road movie detailing the escapades of four buddies who head out of Sydney for a surfing weekend. The shy, quiet one is played by Mel Gibson—it's his screen debut. Aka COAST OF TERROR. ▼▐

Summer Fling SEE: **Last of the High Kings, The**

Summer Heat (1987) C-90m. ** D: Michie Gleason. Lori Singer, Anthony Edwards, Bruce Abbott, Kathy Bates, Clu Gulager. How soon will sultry farm wife Singer, neglected by husband Edwards, succumb to the charms of hired hand Abbott? Not long enough for you to want to sit through this bore. Summer Heat, indeed . . . [R] ▼●

Summer Holiday (1948) C-92m. **½ D: Rouben Mamoulian. Mickey Rooney, Walter Huston, Frank Morgan, Agnes Moorehead, Butch Jenkins, Selena Royle, Marilyn Maxwell, Gloria De Haven, Anne Francis. Lavish musical remake of AH, WILDERNESS! with Rooney (who played the younger brother in 1935) as the young man coming of age. Extremely good-looking film, with exquisite use of Technicolor, but dramatically unexceptional—and not nearly as good as the earlier film. This version was made in 1946. ▼●▐

Summer Holiday (1963-British) C-107m. ** D: Peter Yates. Cliff Richard, Lauri Peters, David Kossoff, Ron Moody, The Shadows, Melvyn Hayes, Una Stubbs, Teddy Green, Jeremy Bulloch. Richard, Hayes, Green, and Bulloch travel through Europe on a bus in this silly but cheerful musical; inauspicious directorial debut by Yates. CinemaScope. ▐

Summer Hours (2008-French) C-102m. ***½ D: Olivier Assayas. Juliette Binoche, Charles Berling, Jérémie Renier, Edith Scob, Dominique Reymond, Valérie Bonneton, Isabelle Sadoyan, Kyle Eastwood. Perceptive look at a French family and what happens when the matriarch passes away, leaving her three grown children to decide what to do with her country home and its many valuable possessions. A meditation on the changing face of family life in the 21st century and the value of things—in intrinsic, sentimental, and financial terms. Intimate, utterly believable, and quite moving. Written by the director. ▐

Summer House, The (1993-British) C-82m. *** D: Waris Hussein. Jeanne Moreau, Joan Plowright, Julie Walters, Lena Headey, David Threlfall, Maggie Steed, John Wood, Catherine Schell. An actors' field day, as flamboyant Moreau comes to stay with her girlhood friend Walters (now a frumpy housewife in 1950s Croydon) when her strangely reticent daughter is about to be married—to the twit next door. Plowright is wonderful as the idiot-groom's aged mother; her scenes with Moreau are a real treat. Based on the novel *The Clothes in the Wardrobe* by Alice Thomas Ellis. Made for British television. ▼●

Summer in Genoa, A (2008-British-Italian) C-93m. *** D: Michael Winterbottom. Colin Firth, Catherine Keener, Willa Holland, Perla Haney-Jardine, Hope Davis, Margherita Romeo, Alessandro Giuggioli. Chicago widower moves abroad with his daughters for a year's sabbatical to soothe their shared grief. Once there, the older girl (Holland) wallows in peer-pressure pleasures, while the little one (Haney-Jardine) drowns in guilt over causing the car crash that killed her mother (Davis) . . . even as the mom's ghost tries to console her. Meanwhile, an expatriate Harvard alumna (Keener) and an alluring graduate student (Romeo) wait in the wings. A subdued Firth captains this melancholy voyage of discovery about going on but never forgetting. Released direct to DVD in the U.S. Aka GENOVA. [R] ▐

Summer Interlude SEE: **Illicit Interlude**

Summer Love (1958) 85m. ** D: Charles Haas. John Saxon, Molly Bee, Rod McKuen, Judi Meredith, Jill St. John, George Winslow, Fay Wray, Edward Platt, Shelley Fabares, Troy Donahue. Sequel to ROCK, PRETTY BABY has Saxon et al. hired to perform at summer resort camp; perky performances.

Summer Lovers (1982) C-98m. ** D: Randal Kleiser. Peter Gallagher, Daryl Hannah, Valerie Quennessen, Barbara Rush, Carole Cook. This one's a matter of tolerance: Any movie that makes you think seriously about having a ménage à trois on a Greek island can't be all bad, but here's a film that's on an even lower intellectual level than you'd *expect* from the director of THE BLUE LAGOON. Bouncy rock soundtrack. [R] ▼●

Summer Magic (1963) C-110m. **½ D: James Neilson. Hayley Mills, Burl Ives, Dorothy McGuire, Deborah Walley, Eddie Hodges, Una Merkel. Disney's rehash of MOTHER CAREY'S CHICKENS has McGuire as widow who raises family on a shoestring in rambling Maine house. Burl sings "The Ugly Bug Ball." Pleasant but forgettable. ▼▐

Summer Night, with Greek Profile, Almond Eyes and Scent of Basil (1987-Italian) C-94m. *½ D: Lina Wertmuller. Mariangela Melato, Michele Placido, Roberto Herlipzka, Massimo Wertmuller. Melato's presence, in a sexual cat-and-mouse tale, might lead one to expect another SWEPT AWAY, but this is light years removed: a relentlessly heavy-handed comedy about a rich, sexy Italian capitalist who abducts a notorious terrorist and tries to give him a taste of his own medicine . . . until she finds herself attracted to him. This "night" seems like it will never end! ▼▐

Summer of '42 (1971) C-102m. *** D:

Robert Mulligan, Jennifer O'Neill, Gary Grimes, Jerry Houser, Oliver Conant, Katherine Allentuck, Christopher Norris, Lou Frizell. Enticing if unprofound nostalgia by Herman Raucher about teenager Grimes with crush on young war bride O'Neill. Captures 1940s flavor, adolescent boyhood, quite nicely. Michel Legrand won an Oscar for the score. Followed by CLASS OF '44. [PG—originally rated R] ▼●◗

Summer of Sam (1999) **C-142m.** ** D: Spike Lee. John Leguizamo, Adrien Brody, Mira Sorvino, Jennifer Esposito, Anthony LaPaglia, Ben Gazzara, Bebe Neuwirth, Patti LuPone, Mike Starr, Michael Rispoli, John Savage, Michael Badalucco, Jimmy Breslin, Spike Lee. Mosaic of Italian-American characters living in the Bronx during the steamy summer of 1977, when the serial killer known as Son of Sam terrorized N.Y.C., firing both passions and paranoia. Interesting, mostly unpleasant slice of life/period piece goes on much too long . . . and gets pretty sleazy. Cowriters Michael Imperioli and Victor Colicchio appear as Midnight and Chickie, respectively. [R] ▼◗

Summer of '64 SEE: **Girls on the Beach, The**

Summer Place, A (1959) **C-130m.** *** D: Delmer Daves. Richard Egan, Dorothy McGuire, Sandra Dee, Arthur Kennedy, Troy Donahue, Constance Ford, Beulah Bondi. Lushly photographed (by Harry Stradling) soaper of adultery and teenage love at resort house on Maine coast. Excellent Max Steiner score (the theme was a big hit); based on the Sloan Wilson novel. ▼●◗

Summerplay SEE: **Illicit Interlude**

Summer Rental (1985) **C-88m.** **½ D: Carl Reiner. John Candy, Karen Austin, Richard Crenna, Rip Torn, John Larroquette, Richard Herd, Lois Hamilton, Carmine Caridi. Breezy, low-key comedy about a working stiff's refusal to let some arrogant fat cats spoil his family's vacation in Florida. Candy proves he can be endearing in a realistic characterization—and still be funny. [PG] ▼●◗

Summer School (1987) **C-98m.** **½ D: Carl Reiner. Mark Harmon, Kirstie Alley, Robin Thomas, Dean Cameron, Gary Riley, Shawnee Smith, Courtney Thorne-Smith. Harmon is delinquent high school teacher forced to spend his vacation trying to educate group of delinquent students. Not bad as these films go: decent acting, OK pacing, some good laughs . . . with extra chuckles for fans of TEXAS CHAINSAW MASSACRE and those movie-critic TV shows. Director Reiner has a cameo as Harmon's predecessor. [PG-13] ▼●◗

Summer School Teachers (1975) **C-87m.** ** D: Barbara Peeters. Candice Rialson, Pat Anderson, Rhonda Leigh-Hopkins, Dick Miller. Well-paced, episodic film of three girls' romantic adventures while teaching high school. A followup to THE STUDENT TEACHERS. [R] ▼

Summer Stock (1950) **C-109m.** *** D: Charles Walters, Judy Garland, Gene Kelly, Eddie Bracken, Marjorie Main, Gloria De Haven, Phil Silvers, Hans Conried. Kelly's theater troupe takes over Judy's farm, she gets show biz bug. Thin plot, breezy Judy, frantic Silvers, chipper De Haven. Judy sings "Get Happy," Kelly dances on newspapers. ▼●◗

Summer Storm (1944) **106m.** ** D: Douglas Sirk. George Sanders, Linda Darnell, Edward Everett Horton, Anna Lee, Hugo Haas, Sig Ruman. Darnell gives one of her best performances as a peasant who victimizes every man she meets. Dreary adaptation of Chekhov's "The Shooting Party" enlivened by Horton as an amoral Russian count. ◗

Summer Story, A (1988-British) **C-95m.** *** D: Piers Haggard. Imogen Stubbs, James Wilby, Ken Colley, Sophie Ward, Susannah York, Jerome Flynn. Beautifully made romantic drama, circa 1902, set and filmed entirely in rural southwestern England. Young London lawyer Wilby and farm girl Stubbs fall deeply in love; he soon must make decisions of the mind and heart that could change their lives forever. The two leads are superb. Penelope Mortimer adapted John Galsworthy's story "The Apple Tree." [PG-13] ▼

Summertime (1955) **C-99m.** ***½ D: David Lean. Katharine Hepburn, Rossano Brazzi, Isa Miranda, Darren McGavin, Mari Aldon, Andre Morell. Lilting film of spinster vacationing in Venice, falling in love with married man. Hepburn's sensitive portrayal is one of her best. Screenplay by Lean and H.E. Bates, from Arthur Laurents' play *The Time of the Cuckoo.* Beautifully filmed on location by Jack Hildyard. ▼●◗

Summertime Killer (1973-French-Italian-Spanish) **C-109m.** ** D: Antonio Isasi. Karl Malden, Christopher Mitchum, Raf Vallone, Claudine Auger, Olivia Hussey. Varied cast in OK revenge meller about a man pursuing his father's murderers. Lots of action, if not much continuity. [PG] ▼

Summertree (1971) **C-88m.** ** D: Anthony Newley. Michael Douglas, Jack Warden, Brenda Vaccaro, Barbara Bel Geddes, Kirk Callaway, Bill Vint, Rob Reiner. Highly acclaimed (if overrated) off-Broadway play by Ron Cowen fails as a film; Douglas plays a young music student who clashes with parents over Vietnam War. [PG] ▼◗

Summer Wishes, Winter Dreams (1973) **C-93m.** *** D: Gilbert Cates. Joanne Woodward, Martin Balsam, Sylvia Sidney, Dori Brenner, Ron Rickards. Sensitive character study of frigid woman (Woodward) obsessed by her childhood, upset by her own aloofness towards others; Balsam equally good as understanding husband. [PG]▼▶

Summer With Monika (1953-Swedish) **96m.** ***½ D: Ingmar Bergman. Harriet Andersson, Lars Ekborg, John Harryson, Georg Skarstedt, Dagmar Ebbesen, Ake Gronberg. A brief affair between two working-class youngsters, aggressive Andersson and boyish Ekborg, results in the birth of their baby and marriage. Simple storyline has been filmed before and since, but rarely with such sensitivity. Video title: MONIKA.▼

Sum of All Fears, The (2002) **C-124m.** **½ D: Phil Alden Robinson. Ben Affleck, Morgan Freeman, James Cromwell, Liev Schreiber, Alan Bates, Bridget Moynahan, Philip Baker Hall, Ron Rifkin, Bruce McGill, Ciarán Hinds, Marie Matiko, Colm Feore, Josef Sommer, Michael Byrne. Follow-up to CLEAR AND PRESENT DANGER with Affleck taking over from Harrison Ford as Jack Ryan. Convoluted tale has a fascist using the new president of Russia to draw the U.S. into war, in an attempt to destroy both countries and establish a united Europe as the new world power. Tries to have it both ways, with a story rooted in reality—but hinging on coincidences and improbabilities. Affleck acquits himself adequately as Tom Clancy's CIA agent hero, surrounded here by a top-notch cast. Panavision. [PG-13]▼▶

Sum of Us, The (1994-Australian) **C/B &W-99m.** **½ D: Kevin Dowling, Geoff Burton. Jack Thompson, Russell Crowe, John Polson, Deborah Kennedy, Mitch Mathews, Joss Moroney, Julie Herbert. Sincere tale about the relationship between a young, gay man (Crowe) and his devoted, widowed father (Thompson), who is refreshingly tolerant of his son's lifestyle. Two solid performances help put this one over, but it's almost undone by the annoying device of having the characters speak to the camera. Scripted by David Stevens, based on his play. ▼▶

Sun Also Rises, The (1957) **C-129m.** *** D: Henry King. Tyrone Power, Ava Gardner, Mel Ferrer, Errol Flynn, Eddie Albert, Gregory Ratoff, Juliette Greco, Marcel Dalio, Henry Daniell, Robert Evans. Hemingway story of expatriates in Parisian 1920s has slow stretches; worthwhile for outstanding cast, especially Flynn as a souse. European and Mexican locations add flavor to tale of search for self-identity. Remade (poorly) for TV in 1984. CinemaScope.▶

Sunburn (1979) **C-94m.** **½ D: Richard C. Sarafian. Farrah Fawcett-Majors, Charles Grodin, Art Carney, Joan Collins, Alejandro Rey, William Daniels. Insurance investigator Grodin has Farrah pose as his wife in order to crack a murder/suicide case in Acapulco. Sloppily made film benefits from appealing performances. Eleanor Parker, Keenan Wynn, and John Hillerman get co-starring billing but barely appear at all. [PG]▼

Sunchaser (1996) **C-122m.** *½ D: Michael Cimino. Woody Harrelson, Jon Seda, Anne Bancroft, Alexandra Tydings, Matt Mulhern, Talisa Soto, Richard Bauer, Lawrence Pressman, Harry Carey, Jr., Brett Harrelson. Brilliant but insensitive doctor Harrelson is taken captive by sensitive but dying gang banger Seda, and is forced to drive into the Southwest in search of a lake of spiritual renewal. Misbegotten mess tries to touch all trendy bases, scrambling American Indian mysticism, "New Age" theories and buddy-movie clichés into the format of a road movie. Harrelson and Seda are good, Bancroft is wasted. Panavision. [R]▼▶

Sunday (1997) **C-93m.** *** D: Jonathan Nossiter. David Suchet, Lisa Harrow, Jared Harris, Larry Pine, Joe Grifasi, Arnold Barkus. Moving drama of a former corporate executive—now homeless—crossing paths in Queens, N.Y., with an out-of-work actress. What unfolds is essentially a two-character story of middle-aged romance, with harsh reminders of "real life" all around. Suchet and Harrow make flawless leads, though film is admittedly not for all tastes.▼▶

Sunday Bloody Sunday (1971-British) **C-110m.** *** D: John Schlesinger. Glenda Jackson, Peter Finch, Murray Head, Peggy Ashcroft, Tony Britton, Maurice Denham, Vivian Pickles, Frank Windsor, Bessie Love, Jon Finch. Glenda loves Murray, but Peter loves Murray, too. Murray loves both, in very good, adult script by Penelope Gilliatt. Schlesinger's direction less forceful than usual, also less effective. Head's bland portrayal offsets brilliant work by Jackson and Finch. A mixed bag. Look for Daniel Day-Lewis as a young vandal. [R]▼▶

Sunday in New York (1963) **C-105m.** *** D: Peter Tewksbury. Cliff Robertson, Jane Fonda, Rod Taylor, Robert Culp, Jim Backus. Entire cast bubbles in this Norman Krasna sex romp of virginal Fonda discovering N.Y.C. and love. Peter Nero's score is perky.▶

Sunday in the Country, A (1984-French) **C-94m.** ***½ D: Bertrand Tavernier. Louis Ducreux, Sabine Azema, Michel Aumont, Genevieve Mnich, Monique Chaumette, Claude Winter. An elderly widowed French impressionist who never quite made the grade indulges in title gathering with offspring who never quite fulfilled his expectations. Painterly, lovingly acted drama owes not a little to Jean Renoir's A DAY IN THE COUNTRY and is no less affecting for that. Among the best imports of the mid-1980s. [G]▼▶

Sunday Lovers (1980) **C-127m.** *½ D: Bryan Forbes, Edouard Molinaro, Dino Risi, Gene Wilder. Roger Moore, Lynn Redgrave, Priscilla Barnes, Lino Ventura, Robert Webber, Ugo Tognazzi, Sylva Koscina, Gene Wilder, Kathleen Quinlan. Love and sex in four countries. British segment, with Moore, is old-hat farce. French vignette, with Ventura, is intriguing but doesn't go anywhere. Italian skit is broadly funny at times. American contribution, written by, directed by, and starring Wilder, is a pretentious fable of a sanitarium patient, and embarrassingly bad. [R]

Sundays and Cybele (1962-French) **110m.** ***½ D: Serge Bourguignon. Hardy Kruger, Nicole Courcel, Patricia Gozzi, Daniel Ivernel. Intelligently told account of shell-shocked Kruger finding source of communication with the world via orphaned waif Gozzi, with tragic results. Splendidly realized, Oscar winner as Best Foreign Language Film. Filmed in Franscope.▼

Sunday's Children (1992-Swedish) **C-118m.** *** D: Daniel Bergman. Henrik Linnros, Thommy Berggren, Lena Endre, Jakob Leygraf, Malin Ek, Birgitta Valberg, Borje Ahlstedt. Bergman (son of Ingmar) expertly directs his father's evocative, autobiographical script about a young boy called Pu (Linnros) and his connection to his minister father and other family members; also depicted is the adult Pu's disquieting relationship with his elderly dad. A deeply personal film; Bergman's family history also is explored in FANNY AND ALEXANDER, THE BEST INTENTIONS, and PRIVATE CONFESSIONS.▼

Sunday Too Far Away (1975-Australian) **C-95m.** *** D: Ken Hannam. Jack Thompson, John Ewart, Reg Lye. The rivalries and problems of macho sheep shearers, focusing on gutsy Thompson, a champion of his trade. Simple and solid.▼

Sunday Woman, The (1976-Italian) **C-110m.** *** D: Luigi Comencini. Marcello Mastroianni, Jacqueline Bisset, Jean-Louis Trintignant, Aldo Reggiani, Pino Caruso. Detective Mastroianni investigates murder among idle rich in Torino, falls in love with wealthy Bisset. Good whodunit makes interesting observation about social structure. [R]

Sundowners, The (1950) **C-83m.** **½ D: George Templeton. Robert Preston, Cathy Downs, Robert Sterling, John Barrymore, Jr., Jack Elam, Chill Wills. Preston shines in this Western about brothers on opposite sides of the law. Filmed in Texas; written by Alan LeMay (*The Searchers*).▼

Sundowners, The (1960) **C-133m.** **** D: Fred Zinnemann. Deborah Kerr, Robert Mitchum, Peter Ustinov, Glynis Johns, Dina Merrill, Chips Rafferty, Michael Anderson, Jr., Lola Brooks, Wylie Watson, Mervyn Johns. First-rate film of Australian family who travel to allow the husband to shear sheep at various ranches. Entire cast excellent, Kerr especially fine. Isobel Lennart adapted Jon Cleary's novel. Wonderfully filmed on location by Jack Hildyard. ▼●)

Sundown, the Vampire in Retreat (1991) **C-104m.** ** D: Anthony Hickox. David Carradine, Morgan Brittany, Bruce Campbell, Jim Metzler, Maxwell Caulfield, Deborah Foreman, M. Emmet Walsh, John Ireland, John Hancock, Dabbs Greer, Bert Remsen. Overplotted vampire comedy-drama set in present-day American West, as a family happens upon a town populated by bloodsuckers trying—but failing—to "go straight." Unpleasantly smug, with nothing to be smug about. Panavision.▼)

Sunflower (1969-Italian) **C-101m.** ** D: Vittorio De Sica. Sophia Loren, Marcello Mastroianni, Ludmilla Savelyeva, Anna Carena. Weak love story of woman who searches for her lost lover. Sophia is wasted in this soppy tale. Original title: I GIRASOLI. [G]▼)

Sunnyside (1979) **C-100m.** *½ D: Timothy Galfas. Joey Travolta, John Lansing, Stacey Pickren, Andrew Rubin, Michael Tucci, Talia Balsam, Joan Darling. John Travolta's brother made bid for stardom in this cliché-ridden picture about a street kid who wants to end local gang warfare and leave that life behind. Sorry, Joey. [R]▼

Sunrise (1927) **94m.** **** D: F. W. Murnau. George O'Brien, Janet Gaynor, Bodil Rosing, Margaret Livingston, J. Farrell MacDonald. Exquisite silent film is just as powerful today as when it was made, telling simple story of farmer who plans to murder his wife, led on by another woman. Triumph of direction, camerawork, art direction, and performances, all hauntingly beautiful. Screenplay by Carl Mayer, from Hermann Suderman's story. Cinematographers Karl Struss and Charles Rosher won Oscars, as did the film for "artistic quality of production." Gaynor also won Best Actress Oscar (shared for her performances in 7TH HEAVEN and STREET ANGEL). Remade in Germany as THE JOURNEY TO TILSIT. Full title on-screen is SUNRISE A SONG OF TWO HUMANS. ▼●)

Sunrise at Campobello (1960) **C-143m.** *** D: Vincent J. Donehue. Ralph Bellamy, Greer Garson, Hume Cronyn, Jean Hagen, Ann Shoemaker, Alan Bunce, Tim Considine, Zina Bethune, Frank Ferguson, Lyle Talbot. Sincere story of President Franklin Delano Roosevelt, his battles in politics and valiant struggle against polio. Well acted; Bellamy (re-creating his Tony-winning stage role) and Garson *are* the Roosevelts. Script by Dore Schary, from his hit play. ▼●)

Sunset (1988) **C-107m.** *½ D: Blake Edwards. Bruce Willis, James Garner, Malcolm McDowell, Mariel Hemingway, Jennifer Edwards, Kathleen Quinlan, Patricia Hodge, Richard Bradford, M. Emmet Walsh, Joe Dallesandro. Cowboy star Tom Mix (Willis) joins forces with legendary marshal Wyatt Earp (Garner) to solve a serpentine whodunit involving the seamier side of Tinseltown. Appallingly abysmal murder-mystery set in late 1920s Hollywood; unpleasant and unbelievable from the word go. Willis registers zero playing one of movie's most magnetic stars, while Garner saves this piece of junk from being a total BOMB with his effortless charisma. Panavision. [R]▼●◗

Sunset Blvd. (1950) **110m.** **** D: Billy Wilder. Gloria Swanson, William Holden, Erich von Stroheim, Nancy Olson, Fred Clark, Jack Webb, Hedda Hopper, Buster Keaton, Cecil B. DeMille, Anna Q. Nilsson. Legendary Hollywood black comedy about faded silent-film star Norma Desmond (Swanson), living in the past with butler (von Stroheim), who shelters hack screenwriter (Holden) as boyfriend. Bitter, funny, fascinating; Gloria's tour de force. Oscar winner for Best Screenplay (Wilder, Charles Brackett, D. M. Marshman, Jr.), Score (Franz Waxman), and Art Direction–Set Decoration. Later a Broadway musical.▼●◗

Sunset Park (1996) **C-99m.** **½ D: Steve Gomer. Rhea Perlman, Fredro Starr, Carol Kane, Terrence Dashon Howard, Camille Saviola, De'Aundre Bonds, James Harris, Anthony Hall. Feisty N.Y.C. teacher Perlman, hoping to make enough money to retire to St. Croix, becomes the coach of an all-black high school basketball team. The premise is contrived, and the Great Teacher story is a cliché by now, but the acting is good and the characters well drawn. Perlman's husband Danny DeVito was one of the producers. [R]▼●◗

Sunshine (1999-Hungarian-British-German-Canadian) **C-182m.** ** D: Istvan Szabo. Ralph Fiennes, Rosemary Harris, Rachel Weisz, Jennifer Ehle, Molly Parker, Deborah (Kara) Unger, James Frain, John Neville, Miriam Margolyes, David De Keyser, William Hurt, Bill Paterson. Ambitious but trite, rambling soap opera chronicling a Hungarian-Jewish family over three generations, beginning in mid-19th century. Fiennes plays three roles; the middle one, a world-champion fencer and self-hating Jew, is the most intriguing. Themes are worthy, but results are obvious and overwrought. Scripted by Szabo and Israel Horovitz. [R]▼◗

Sunshine (2007-U.S.-British) **C-107m.** **½ D: Danny Boyle. Cillian Murphy, Chris Evans, Rose Byrne, Michelle Yeoh, Hiroyuki Sanada, Cliff Curtis, Troy Garity, Benedict Wong, Mark Strong; voice of Chipo Chung. Intriguing sci-fi story set in 2057, almost entirely on sophisticated spaceship *Icarus II* as it travels toward our imperiled sun. Brilliant, multicultural crew faces unforeseen dilemmas, crises, and some heated (and entertaining) personality clashes. Frequent collaborators Boyle and screenwriter Alex Garland have concocted a cinematic voyage that initially impresses

but falters toward a far-fetched denouement. Hawk-Scope. [R]◗

Sunshine Boys, The (1975) **C-111m.** *** D: Herbert Ross. Walter Matthau, George Burns, Richard Benjamin, Lee Meredith, Carol Arthur, Howard Hesseman, Ron Rifkin, Fritz Feld, Jack Bernardi, F. Murray Abraham. Two cranky ex-vaudevillians are persuaded to reteam for a TV special in this popular Neil Simon comedy, from his Broadway play. Some of the "humor" is abrasive, but Matthau and Oscar-winning Burns are masters at work. This was George's first starring film role since HONOLULU in 1939. Remade for TV in 1997. [PG] ▼●◗

Sunshine Cleaning (2009) **C-91m.** *** D: Christine Jeffs. Amy Adams, Emily Blunt, Alan Arkin, Jason Spevack, Steve Zahn, Mary Lynn Rajskub, Clifton Collins, Jr., Eric Christian Olsen, Paul Dooley, Kevin Chapman, Judith Jones. In Albuquerque, N.M., struggling single mom Adams starts a business mopping up crime scenes— though she has no experience in this highly specialized field—and recruits her slacker sister (Blunt) to help out. Likable comedy-drama about siblings whose lives have been shaped and shadowed by the early death of their mother. The two stars are perfectly cast and aided by a handpicked ensemble. Impressive debut script by Megan Holley. Super 35. [R] ◗

Sun Shines Bright, The (1953) **90m.** *** D: John Ford. Charles Winninger, Arleen Whelan, John Russell, Stepin Fetchit, Milburn Stone, Russell Simpson, Francis Ford, Grant Withers, Slim Pickens, Mae Marsh, Jane Darwell, Clarence Muse, Jack Pennick, Patrick Wayne. This was director Ford's favorite film, a picaresque remake of JUDGE PRIEST with Winninger involved in political contest in small Southern town. Fine array of Ford regulars in character roles. Video and TV version is 100m. print prepared by Ford but never released.▼

Sunshine State (2002) **C-141m.** *** D: John Sayles. Edie Falco, Jane Alexander, Ralph Waite, Angela Bassett, James McDaniel, Mary Alice, Bill Cobbs, Gordon Clapp, Mary Steenburgen, Timothy Hutton, Tom Wright, Marc Blucas, Perry Lang, Miguel Ferrer, Charlayne Woodard, Clifton James, Alan King. Rich, Saylesian slice of life set on a Florida island where longtime residents, from both the black and white communities, are forced to deal with "progress" as developers see nothing but dollar signs. A mosaic of character studies, brought to life by wonderful actors. [PG-13] ▼◗

Sun Valley Serenade (1941) **86m.** *** D: H. Bruce Humberstone. Sonja Henie, John Payne, Glenn Miller and His Orchestra, Milton Berle, Lynn Bari, Joan Davis, Dorothy Dandridge, The Nicholas Brothers. Light musicomedy with Henie a war refugee, Payne her foster parent, traveling with the Miller band and manager Berle to Sun Valley. Songs: "It Happened In Sun Valley," "In the Mood," "Chattanooga Choo-Choo," "I Know Why (And So Do You)." ▼●

Super, The (1991) **C-86m.** *½ D: Rod Daniel. Joe Pesci, Vincent Gardenia, Madolyn Smith-Osborne, Ruben Blades, Stacey Travis, Carole Shelley, Paul Benjamin, Kenny Blank. N.Y.C. slumlord Pesci is forced to move in with his tenants. A worthy idea, and Pesci is watchable as always, but the execution is all wrong: the scenario disastrously veers to comedy when it shouldn't, and the sentimental elements are utterly unbelievable. [R] ▼●●

Super (2011) **C-96m.** *½ D: James Gunn. Rainn Wilson, Ellen Page, Liv Tyler, Kevin Bacon, Michael Rooker, Nathan Fillion, Linda Cardellini, William Katt. Unable to cope with his wife (Tyler) relapsing into drugs and leaving him for a dealer (Bacon), a self-proclaimed loser (Wilson) decides that the only way to save her—and the rest of society—from sinking into despair is to become a superhero. What starts out as something relatable becomes extremely dark, upsetting, and needlessly violent. We never really root for our hero or care if he succeeds. His sidekick (Page) is pretty much the film's saving grace, as she brings comedy and heart to this otherwise soulless mess. ●

Superbabies: Baby Geniuses 2 (2004) **C-88m.** BOMB D: Bob Clark. Jon Voight, Justin Chatwin, Scott Baio, Vanessa Angel, Skyler Shaye, Gerry Fitzgerald, Leo Fitzgerald, Myles Fitzgerald, Whoopi Goldberg. Sequel to BABY GENIUSES casts Voight as a media mogul out to brainwash children via a tot-aimed TV network. He wants to use them to take over the world, but a band of tykes catches on and sets out to stop him. Gimmick has kids speaking to each other, thanks to creepy computer-generated lip movement. Crude humor makes this not just bad but insulting. Super 35. [PG] ▼●

Superbad (2007) **C-112m.** *** D: Greg Mottola. Jonah Hill, Michael Cera, Christopher Mintz-Plasse, Bill Hader, Seth Rogen, Martha MacIsaac, Emma Stone, Aviva, Joe Lo Truglio, Kevin Corrigan. Nerdy friends Hill and Cera are desperate to have girlfriends—and maybe sex itself—before going to college. They get the chance when they're invited to a party by a hot girl from their high school, but naturally, complications arise. Raunchy comedy features an almost endless torrent of vulgar (and very funny) language . . . but it's also an apt, occasionally even sensitive study of young, confused desires and the inevitable embarrassments that go along with them. Screenplay by Rogen and Evan Goldberg; coproduced by Judd Apatow. 119m. unrated version also available. [R] ●

Superchick (1973) **C-94m.** ** D: Ed Forsyth. Joyce Jillson, Louis Quinn, Thomas Reardon,

Tony Young, John Carradine, Uschi Digard, Mary Gavin (Candy Samples). Silly but harmless drive-in fodder has Jillson (better known as an astrologer) as blonde, free-loving stewardess (juggling boyfriends in several cities) who's so desirable she adopts a mousey brunette disguise to get her work done. [R] ▼●

Supercop SEE: **Police Story III: Supercop**

Super Cops, The (1974) **C-94m.** ***½ D: Gordon Parks. Ron Leibman, David Selby, Sheila Frazier, Pat Hingle, Dan Frazer. Fast, funny, tough telling of the exploits of the Batman and Robin team of David Greenberg (Leibman) and Robert Hantz (Selby) who used unorthodox methods to stop the drug market in Brooklyn's black Bedford-Stuyvesant area. Filmed on location, with Greenberg and Hantz in bits. [PG]

Supercross (2005) **C-80m.** *½ D: Steve Boyum. Steve Howey, Mike Vogel, Cameron Richardson, Sophia Bush, Aaron Carter, Channing Tatum, Robert Patrick, Robert Carradine. Also known as SUPERCROSS THE MOVIE (for those who need things spelled out), this film presents a thin plot about two disparate brothers who are suddenly thrust into the world of hyper-competitive uber-bike championships after the mysterious death of their father. One of the boys is sponsored, which allows plenty of opportunity to hawk everything from motor oil to tires. Product placement never had it so good. A lame-brained ESPN program passing for a movie. [PG-13] ●

Superdad (1974) **C-96m.** BOMB D: Vincent McEveety. Bob Crane, Kurt Russell, Barbara Rush, Joe Flynn, Kathleen Cody, Dick Van Patten, Joby Baker, B. Kirby, Jr. (Bruno Kirby), Ed Begley, Jr. Disney generation gap comedy is superbad. Crane competes with daughter's fiancé in effort to prove future son-in-law worthy. [G] ▼●

Superdude SEE: **Hangup**

Super 8 (2011) **C-112m.** ***½ D: J. J. Abrams. Kyle Chandler, Elle Fanning, Joel Courtney, Gabriel Basso, Noah Emmerich, Ron Eldard, Riley Griffiths, Ryan Lee, Zach Mills, Dan Castellaneta, Glynn Turman, Michael Hitchcock, AJ Michalka, Jessica Tuck; voice of Bruce Greenwood. Small-town boy (newcomer Courtney), still reeling from his mother's death, joins his pals to make a horror movie. One night the amateur filmmakers chance to witness a catastrophic train wreck. When strange occurrences follow, along with an invasion of secretive military forces, the kids figure out what's going on long before the grown-ups have a clue. Writer-director Abrams' homage to Steven Spielberg movies like CLOSE ENCOUNTERS OF THE THIRD KIND and E.T. THE EXTRA-TERRESTRIAL, actually produced by Spielberg and appropriately set in 1979, has the kind of heart and passion missing from many contemporary blockbusters, along with storytelling savvy and state-of-the-art visual effects. Thoroughly entertaining. Panavision. [PG-13]

Superfly (1972) **C-96m.** ******* D: Gordon Parks Jr. Ron O'Neal, Carl Lee, Sheila Frazier, Julius W. Harris, Charles McGregor. Morally dubious but undeniably exciting tale of Harlem drug dealer out for the last killing before he quits the business. Film was accused of glorifying drug pushers. Benefits from excellent Curtis Mayfield score. Sequels: SUPERFLY T.N.T. and THE RETURN OF SUPERFLY. [R]▼▶

Superfly T.N.T. (1973) **C-87m.** BOMB D: Ron O'Neal. Ron O'Neal, Roscoe Lee Browne, Sheila Frazier, Robert Guillaume, Jacques Sernas, William Berger, Roy Bosier. Confused, sloppily constructed and executed B film about black ex-drug pusher, dissatisfied with idyllic existence in Europe, deciding to aid official from African country (Browne). Followed years later by THE RETURN OF SUPERFLY. [R]▼

Super Fuzz (1981-U.S.-Italian) **C-94m.** *½ D: Sergio Corbucci. Terence Hill, Ernest Borgnine, Joanne Dru, Marc Lawrence, Julie Gordon, Lee Sandman. Rookie Miami cop Hill is exposed to radiation, gains superpowers and takes on mobster Lawrence. Pretty poor, including the special effects. Also known as SUPERSNOOPER. Originally 106m. [PG]▼▶

Supergirl (1984-British) **C-114m.** *½ D: Jeannot Szwarc. Faye Dunaway, Helen Slater, Peter O'Toole, Peter Cook, Brenda Vaccaro, Mia Farrow, Simon Ward, Marc McClure, Hart Bochner, Maureen Teefy, Matt Frewer. This comic-book movie is a superdrag: long, dull, heavy-handed. Slater is cute but bland in title role; Dunaway is a predictably campy villainess. Also available in 138m. director's cut and 124m. European version. Panavision. [PG]▼▶●

Supergrass, The (1985-British) **C-105m.** ** D: Peter Richardson. Adrian Edmondson, Jennifer Saunders, Peter Richardson, Dawn French, Keith Allen, Nigel Planer, Robbie Coltrane. To impress a girl, Edmondson innocently brags that he's a big-time drug dealer—much to his regret. Inoffensive comedy. [R]▼

Superhero Movie (2008) **C-82m.** ** D: Craig Mazin. Drake Bell, Sara Paxton, Christopher McDonald, Leslie Nielsen, Kevin Hart, Marion Ross, Brent Spiner, Robert Joy, Jeffrey Tambor, Nicole Sullivan, Tracy Morgan, Simon Rex, Dan Castellaneta, Pamela Anderson, Keith David, Regina Hall, Craig Bierko, John Getz, Charlene Tilton, Robert Hays, Li'l Kim. After being bitten by a genetically altered dragonfly, high school outcast Bell develops super powers. Like Spider-Man, he makes himself a suit and attempts to save the world, only to be confronted by a villain named The Hourglass (McDonald). Parodying films from BATMAN BEGINS to FANTASTIC FOUR,

this spoof's low-grade humor may make you cringe at times but it does provide some laughs—amidst a barrage of flatulence jokes and pop-culture references. Alternate version runs 86m. [PG-13]▶

Superman (1978) **C-143m.** ***½ D: Richard Donner. Christopher Reeve, Margot Kidder, Marlon Brando, Gene Hackman, Ned Beatty, Jackie Cooper, Marc McClure, Glenn Ford, Valerie Perrine, Phyllis Thaxter, Jeff East, Trevor Howard, Susannah York, Maria Schell, Terence Stamp, Sarah Douglas, Harry Andrews, Lise Hilboldt, Larry Hagman, John Ratzenberger. Dynamic, grandly entertaining saga of the Man of Steel, tracing his life from Krypton to Smallville to Metropolis, mixing equal parts sincerity, special effects (which earned a special Oscar), and send-up. Great fun. The network TV version added 49m. of outtakes—including cameos by Noel Neill and Kirk Alyn as Lois Lane's parents. Advertised as SUPERMAN—THE MOVIE. 2001 video release runs 151m. Followed by three sequels. Panavision. [PG]▼▶●

Superman II (1981) **C-127m.** *** D: Richard Lester. Christopher Reeve, Margot Kidder, Gene Hackman, Ned Beatty, Jackie Cooper, Valerie Perrine, Susannah York, Clifton James, E. G. Marshall, Marc McClure, Terence Stamp, Sarah Douglas, Jack O'Halloran. Screw the Superman legend, forget logic, and full speed ahead: that's the attitude of this flashy sequel, wherein three villains from Krypton, with powers just like Superman's, threaten the Earth—while Lois Lane and the Man of Steel fall in love. Full of great effects and entertainingly played, but lacking the sense of awe and wonder of the original film, adding cruelty and violence instead. Released in Europe in 1980. In 2006, Richard Donner supervised a recut, using footage he shot before the producers replaced him with Lester. Overall story is the same, but there are many different scenes, including some with Brando. The tone of this version is at once less comic and more epic. Panavision. [PG] ▼▶●

Superman III (1983) **C-123m.** *½ D: Richard Lester. Christopher Reeve, Richard Pryor, Annette O'Toole, Jackie Cooper, Marc McClure, Annie Ross, Pamela Stephenson, Robert Vaughn, Margot Kidder. Appalling sequel trashes everything that Superman is all about for the sake of cheap laughs and a costarring role for Pryor, as computer operator who unwittingly gives villainous Vaughn a chance to conquer the Man of Steel. Director Lester's opening slapstick ballet is a funny set piece, but doesn't belong in this movie. Panavision. [PG]▼▶●

Superman IV: The Quest for Peace (1987) **C-90m.** ** D: Sidney J. Furie. Christopher Reeve, Gene Hackman, Jackie Cooper, Marc McClure, Jon Cryer, Sam Wanamaker, Mark Pillow, Mariel Hemingway, Margot Kidder, Jim Broadbent. Superman does his bit for world peace by ridding the globe of nuclear weapons—which inspires Lex Luthor to become a black-market arms profiteer. He also challenges Superman by creating Nuclear Man. Disappointing fantasy adventure is pretty ordinary, with second-rate special effects. Sincere performances help a lot. Reeve receives costory credit on this one (along with 2nd unit directing). J-D-C Scope. [PG] ▼●❚

Superman and the Mole-Men (1951) 58m. ** D: Lee Sholem. George Reeves, Phyllis Coates, Jeff Corey, Walter Reed, J. Farrell MacDonald, Stanley Andrews. Reporters Clark Kent and Lois Lane go to small town to see the world's deepest oil well; instead, they discover that "mole-men" have climbed out of the well, from their home at the center of Earth. This very low-budget feature served as a pilot for the long-running TV series *Adventures of Superman*, but it's more serious (and less fun) than the subsequent show—and we don't even get to see Superman fly! But it's still great to watch Reeves as the Man of Steel. Edited down and retitled "The Unknown People" to run as a TV *Superman* two-parter. ▼●❚

Superman Returns (2006) C-154m. *** D: Bryan Singer. Brandon Routh, Kate Bosworth, Kevin Spacey, James Marsden, Frank Langella, Eva Marie Saint, Parker Posey, Kal Penn, Sam Huntington, James Karen, Peta Wilson, Jack Larson, Noel Neill. Superman has disappeared for five years. Now he returns to Earth, only to find that Lois Lane has given birth to a child—and Lex Luthor is a free man. Traditionalist's view of the Man of Steel emphasizes romance and keeps campiness to a minimum. Newcomer Routh is an appealing Superman *and* Clark Kent. Fun to watch until the third act, which drags. Through movie magic Marlon Brando reappears as Superman's father, Jor-El, in footage derived from 1978's SUPERMAN. Part 3-D HD Widescreen. [PG-13]❚

Super Mario Bros. (1993) C-104m. *½ D: Rocky Morton, Annabel Jankel. Bob Hoskins, John Leguizamo, Dennis Hopper, Samantha Mathis, Fisher Stevens, Richard Edson, Fiona Shaw, Lance Henriksen. Super, indeed! This overblown, effects-laden turkey chronicles the convoluted story of the title boys from Brooklyn (Hoskins, Leguizamo), plumber-siblings who go up against the villainous King Koopa (Hopper), a semi-human dinosaur who instigates the kidnapping of Daisy (Mathis), a princess who possesses a magical meteorite fragment. This listless film has far less appeal than the video game that inspired it. [PG] ▼●❚

Supernaturals, The (1986) C-85m. BOMB D: Armand Mastroianni. Maxwell Caulfield, Talia Balsam, Bradford Bancroft, LeVar Burton, Bobby DiCicco, Scott Jacoby, Nichelle Nichols. Ludicrous fantasy has butch drill sergeant Nichols (better known as Lt. Uhura on *Star Trek*) leading young troops on maneuvers, accidentally stumbling on Rebel ghosts from the Civil War who

are seeking revenge. Boring tale has the production values of a home movie; never released theatrically. [R] ▼

Supernova (2000) C-90m. *½ D: Thomas Lee. James Spader, Angela Bassett, Lou Diamond Phillips, Robert Forster, Robin Tunney, Peter Facinelli. Alan Smithee gets competition that neither he nor the industry needs; Lee is a pseudonym for director Walter Hill, who took his name off this costly but listlessly derivative space adventure. Story deals with a hospital ship rescuing a battered freighter that has sent out a distress call in "black hole" territory. Spader and Phillips are so pumped up that you wonder where they're getting the celestial weight-room time. Video version is rated R. Super 35. [PG-13] ▼●❚

Super Size Me (2004) C-100m. *** D: Morgan Spurlock. Arresting "personal documentary" in the Michael Moore vein: Spurlock decides to monitor the results of eating three meals a day for a month at McDonald's. Even his doctors are surprised by the effect on his system. In fact, the film is about much more than a wacky experiment; it's a wide-ranging indictment of Americans' poor eating habits, corporate (and even civic) complicity in our fast-food culture, and the alarming epidemic of obesity that has resulted. Surprisingly entertaining and informative. Alternate PG version also available. [PG-13] ▼❚

Supersnooper SEE: **Super Fuzz**

Superstar (1999) C-81m. *½ D: Bruce McCulloch. Molly Shannon, Will Ferrell, Elaine Hendrix, Tom Green, Harland Williams, Mark McKinney, Glynis Johns, Emmy Laybourne. One-note comedy in which Shannon re-creates her *Saturday Night Live* character of Mary Katherine Gallagher, a dorky, self-deluded Irish Catholic schoolgirl who wears the unsexiest white underwear, dreams of fame, and pursues the most popular boy in class (Ferrell). Little improvement over such *SNL*-derived feature films as IT'S PAT and A NIGHT AT THE ROXBURY. [PG-13] ▼●❚

Superstar: The Life and Times of Andy Warhol (1991) C-87m. *** D: Chuck Workman. Tom Wolfe, Sylvia Miles, David Hockney, Taylor Mead, Dennis Hopper, and a Campbell's Soup spokesman are just some of the many who offer comment on N.Y.C.'s life of the party—and if Workman can't find much old footage of his subject conjugating nouns and verbs, it may not exist. Inevitably entertaining, though Warhol seems no less enigmatic at the conclusion. ▼❚

Super Troopers (2002) C-103m. **½ D: Jay Chandrasekhar. Jay Chandrasekhar, Brian Cox, Daniel von Bargen, Marisa Coughlan, Jim Gaffigan, Erik Stolhanske, Steve Lemme, Kevin Heffernan, Paul Soter. A bumbling group of Vermont state troopers get a second chance to save their jobs from being taken over by the local police when they stumble onto a drug ring. Gleefully raunchy comedy is just a string of gags but a lot of them surprisingly hit. First Hollywood feature from comedy troupe Broken Lizard plays like an anarchic cross between the Farrellys and Monty Python. [R]▼❙

Support Your Local Gunfighter (1971) C-92m. *** D: Burt Kennedy. James Garner, Suzanne Pleshette, Jack Elam, Harry Morgan, John Dehner, Joan Blondell, Dub Taylor, Ellen Corby, Henry Jones, Marie Windsor, Dick Curtis, Chuck Connors, Grady Sutton. Engaging comedy-Western, not a sequel to SHERIFF despite director and cast. Con artist Garner tries to profit from mining dispute by passing off bumbling Elam as notorious gunslinger. Seemingly endless list of character actors adds sparkle, with Elam giving his most side-splitting performance as "Swifty" Morgan; his final line is a gem. [G]▼❙

Support Your Local Sheriff! (1969) C-93m. ***½ D: Burt Kennedy. James Garner, Joan Hackett, Walter Brennan, Harry Morgan, Jack Elam, Bruce Dern, Henry Jones, Gene Evans. Delightful Western parody in which no-fisted Garner tames lawless town by using his wits, breaking all the rules—and kicking virtually every Western cliché in the pants. Brennan is wonderful spoofing his Old Man Clanton character from MY DARLING CLEMENTINE, but Hackett's wealthy klutz, Elam's inept deputy, and Dern's bratty killer are also fine. Written and produced by William Bowers. [G]▼○❙

Suppose They Gave a War and Nobody Came? (1970) C-113m. **½ D: Hy Averback. Tony Curtis, Brian Keith, Ernest Borgnine, Suzanne Pleshette, Ivan Dixon, Bradford Dillman, Tom Ewell, Don Ameche, Arthur O'Connell, John Fiedler. Awful title obscures surprisingly strong satire about strained relations between redneck town and nearby Army base eventually reaching the breaking point. No real "good guys" in this unusual film; not without flaws, but certainly worth a look. Later ripped off by TANK. [M/PG]▼❙

Sure Fire (1993) C-86m. *** D: Jon Jost. Tom Blair, Kristi Hager, Robert Ernst, Kate Dezina, Philip R. Brown. Provocative tale of smug, hot-shot entrepreneur (Blair), who concocts a scheme to build summer houses in Utah for city-dwelling Californians. Another impressive, visually arresting feature from acclaimed independent filmmaker Jost. ▼❙

Sure Thing, The (1985) C-94m. **½ D: Rob Reiner. John Cusack, Daphne Zuniga, Anthony Edwards, Boyd Gaines, Tim Robbins, Lisa Jane Persky, Viveca Lindfors, Nicollette Sheridan. Amusing film updates IT HAPPENED ONE NIGHT as two college students who don't get along find themselves traveling cross-country together. Utterly predictable, but cute. [PG-13]▼○❙

Surfer, Dude (2008) C-86m. **½ D: S. R. Bindler. Matthew McConaughey, Alexie Gilmore, Scott Glenn, Jeffrey Nordling, Ramon Rodriguez, Zachary Knighton, Nathan Phillips, Todd Stashwick, Sarah Wright, Willie Nelson, Woody Harrelson, K. D. Aubert. Celebrity "surfer dude" (a perfectly cast McConaughey), who's an old-style purist, returns to Malibu, where a sleazy promoter is determined to sign him for a reality TV show. Meant to be a caustic denunciation of commercialism and the lack of privacy in a nothing-is-sacred culture, but the result is formulaic and only intermittently successful. ❙

Surf Ninjas (1993) C-86m. BOMB D: Neal Israel. Ernie Reyes, Jr., Rob Schneider, Nicolas Cowan, Leslie Nielsen, Tone Loc, Ernie Reyes, Sr., Keone Young, Kelly Hu, John Karlen. Fast-talking Southern California surf dudes travel to a distant Asian kingdom to regain their throne as lost crown princes. Are you following this so far? If you care what happens next, this may be your kind of movie. [PG]▼○❙

Surf's Up (2007) C-85m. *** D: Ash Brannon, Chris Buck. Voices of Shia LaBeouf, Jeff Bridges, Zooey Deschanel, James Woods, Jon Heder, Diedrich Bader, Mario Cantone. A surfing penguin from Shiverpool, Antarctica, heads to a sunny tropical island to compete in a championship contest. Cleverly made in the style of a behind-the-scenes documentary, this charming animated comedy boasts striking visuals (the big-wave surfing sequences are knockouts) and a funky, laid-back quality. Bridges' performance as Geek is perfectly in tune with all of this. [PG]▼

Surf II (1984) C-91m. *½ D: Randall Badat. Eddie Deezen, Linda Kerridge, Cleavon Little, Peter Isaacksen, Lyle Waggoner, Eric Stoltz, Morgan Paull, Ruth Buzzi, Carol Wayne, Terry Kiser. Creditable cast washes ashore in '80s spoof of '70s gore films and '60s surfer films (with appropriate oldies on the soundtrack). Deezen's always good for a few laughs, but the film's best joke is its title: there never was a SURF I. [R]▼

Surprise Package (1960-British) 100m. **½ D: Stanley Donen. Yul Brynner, Mitzi Gaynor, Barry Foster, Eric Pohlmann, Noel Coward, George Coulouris. Versatile Brynner tries screwball comedy, not doing too badly as devil-may-care gambler planning big-time robbery; Gaynor is sprightly leading lady. Script by Harry Kurnitz, from the Art Buchwald novel. ▼❙

Surrender (1987) C-95m. ** D: Jerry Belson. Sally Field, Michael Caine, Steve Guttenberg, Peter Boyle, Jackie Cooper, Julie Kavner, Louise Lasser, Iman, Christian Clemenson. Attractive cast injects little energy into this tired, familiar comedy about confused Field, oft-married Caine, and their complicated courtship. Even Caine's charm cannot save it. Scripted by the director. [PG]▼●

Surrogate, The (1984-Canadian) **C-95m.**
**½ D: Don Carmody. Art Hindle, Carole
Laure, Shannon Tweed, Michael Ironside,
Jim Bailey, Marilyn Lightstone, Jackie Burroughs. Clever whodunit has handsome
couple (Tweed and Hindle) reluctantly turning
to sex surrogate Laure to help with their marital problems. Solid Canadian cast punches
home contrived script in which nearly every
character (including top female impersonator
Bailey, as Tweed's best friend) appears to be a
psychotic suspect. [R]▼

Surrogates (2009) **C-89m.** *** D: Jonathan Mostow. Bruce Willis, Radha Mitchell, Rosamund Pike, Boris Kodjoe, James
Francis Ginty, James Cromwell, Ving
Rhames, Jack Noseworthy. Smart science-
fiction tale set in the near future when
people allow attractive, realistic robots to
experience life for them. Crime is practically nonexistent—until a wave of killings
wipes out not just the surrogates but their
"controllers" as well. FBI agents Willis
and Mitchell investigate, while Willis tries
to persuade his wife to abandon her surrogate and repair their damaged relationship.
Slick entertainment has some provocative
ideas behind it. Based on a graphic novel
by Robert Venditti and Brett Weldele. Super 35. [PG-13] ◗

Surveillance (2008-U.S.-German-Cana-
dian) **C-97m.** BOMB D: Jennifer Lynch.
Julia Ormond, Bill Pullman, Pell James,
Ryan Simpkins, Cheri Oteri, Michael Ironside, French Stewart, Kent Harper, Caroline
Aaron, Gill Gayle, Hugh Dillon. Federal
agents Ormond and Pullman, investigating
a grisly crime in a rural stretch of America,
meet resistance from the lunk-headed local
cops and an odd array of witnesses. Odious,
one-note RASHOMON-like hodgepodge is
poorly directed and scripted. Lynch's first
feature since 1993's BOXING HELENA;
her father, David Lynch, executive produced. Super 35. [R] ◗

Survival of the Dead (2010-U.S.-Cana-
dian) **C-90m.** ** D: George A. Romero.
Alan Van Sprang, Kenneth Welsh, Kathleen
Munroe, Devon Bostick, Richard Fitzpatrick, Athena Karkanis, Stefano Di Matteo.
Another Romero visit to an America overrun with cannibalistic walking corpses.
This time a small paramilitary group hopes
to evade the chaos by going to an island off
the Delaware Coast, but conflict between
the two very Irish patriarchs that control
the place over how to treat the numerous re-
animated corpses means only more chaos.
Less nihilistic than others in the series,
with stronger characterizations and good
cinematography, but it's really just more of
the same. Won't someone give Romero the
money to do another kind of movie? Aka
GEORGE A. ROMERO'S SURVIVAL OF
THE DEAD. HD Widescreen. [R] ◗

Survival Run (1980) **C-90m.** *½ D: Larry

Spiegel. Peter Graves, Ray Milland, Vin-
cent Van Patten, Pedro Armendariz, Jr.,
Alan Conrad. Graves, Milland, and com-
pany stalk teenagers stranded in the desert.
The object is murder; the film is dreadful.
[R]▼

Survive! (1976-Mexican) **C-86m.** *½ D:
Rene Cardona (Sr.). Pablo Ferrel, Hugo
Stiglitz, Luz Maria Aguilar, Fernando Lar-
ranga, Norma Lazareno. Survivors of a South
American plane crash are forced to cannibal-
ize each other in order to stay alive. Based on
a true incident, but do you really care? Same
story retold in U.S. film ALIVE. [R]◗

Surviving Christmas (2004) **C-92m.**
BOMB D: Mike Mitchell. Ben Affleck,
James Gandolfini, Christina Applegate,
Catherine O'Hara, Josh Zuckerman, Bill
Macy, Jennifer Morrison, Udo Kier, Steph-
anie Faracy, Stephen Root, David Selby.
Self-involved businessman (Affleck) with-
out domestic ties suddenly yearns for an
ideal family Christmas . . . so he purchases
kin for the holidays. Scrooge is proven right
with this awful, lowbrow mess of a comedy.
[PG-13] ▼◗

Surviving Picasso (1996) **C-125m.** *** D:
James Ivory. Anthony Hopkins, Natascha
McElhone, Julianne Moore, Joss Ackland,
Joan Plowright, Peter Eyre, Jane Lapotaire,
Joseph Maher, Diane Venora, Bob Peck, Peter Gerety, Dominic West, Susannah Harker,
Dennis Boutsikaris. Pablo Picasso uses
women, then tosses them away, but a young
artist ventures into a relationship with him
just the same, certain that this time it will
be different. McElhone makes an impressive film debut as the willing "victim," but
it's Hopkins' charismatic performance as
the ego-driven artist that makes this worth
seeing. One must be willing to accept a lack
of European accents—and the absence of
genuine Picasso art. [R]▼●◗

Surviving the Game (1994) **C-96m.** *½
D: Ernest Dickerson. Rutger Hauer, Ice-T,
Gary Busey, F. Murray Abraham, Charles
S. Dutton, John C. McGinley, Jeff Corey.
Only the absence of Maria Conchita Alonso
keeps this umpteenth variation of THE
MOST DANGEROUS GAME from having
the definitive schlock action cast, as destitute Ice-T is unwittingly hired to perform
vague duties at a secluded woodsy resort,
only to learn he's the prey of high-roller
hunters. Sub-routine chase pic is Confusion
City all the way; it's difficult to believe that
the same plot could be recycled less than
a year after John Woo's far more stylish
HARD TARGET. [R]▼●◗

Survivors, The (1983) **C-102m.** ** D:
Michael Ritchie. Walter Matthau, Robin
Williams, Jerry Reed, James Wainwright,
Kristen Vigard, Anne Pitoniak, John Goodman. Two disparate men lose their jobs
and find their lives intertwined when they
identify a robber and are told that they'll

be "fixed." One (Williams) decides to arm himself to the teeth in this combination black comedy and social satire. Likable stars do their best with scattershot script credited to Michael Leeson. [R]▼●▶

Susana (1951-Mexican) **82m.** **½ D: Luis Buñuel. Rosita Quintana, Fernando Soler, Victor Manuel Mendoza, Matilde Palou. A voluptuous orphan of the storm, engagingly played by Quintana, undermines the loving fabric of the family that rescues her. Well handled and staged by Buñuel, until the cop-out finale.▼▶

Susan and God (1940) **115m.** **½ D: George Cukor. Joan Crawford, Fredric March, Ruth Hussey, John Carroll, Rita Hayworth, Nigel Bruce, Bruce Cabot, Rose Hobart, Rita Quigley, Marjorie Main, Gloria De Haven. Crawford is satisfying as woman whose religious devotion loses her the love of her family. Gertrude Lawrence fared better on stage. Screenplay by Anita Loos, based on Rachel Crothers' play.▼▶

Susan Lenox: Her Fall and Rise (1931) **76m.** **½ D: Robert Z. Leonard. Greta Garbo, Clark Gable, Jean Hersholt, John Miljan, Alan Hale. A young woman flees from her loutish father—who wants to marry her off—and finds refuge with Gable, but circumstances keep them apart until the final clinch. Contrived melodrama made compelling by the ever-mesmerizing Garbo. ▼▶

Susannah of the Mounties (1939) **78m.** **½ D: William A. Seiter. Shirley Temple, Randolph Scott, Margaret Lockwood, J. Farrell MacDonald, Moroni Olsen, Victor Jory. Mountie Scott raises orphan Shirley in this predictable but entertaining Temple vehicle. Also shown in computer-colored version.▼▶

Susan Slade (1961) **C-116m.** **½ D: Delmer Daves. Troy Donahue, Dorothy McGuire, Connie Stevens, Lloyd Nolan, Brian Aherne, Bert Convy, Kent Smith. Slick soaper, beautifully photographed by Lucien Ballard. McGuire pretends to be mother of daughter's (Stevens) illegitimate child. Donahue is Connie's true love.▶

Susan Slept Here (1954) **C-98m.** **½ D: Frank Tashlin. Dick Powell, Debbie Reynolds, Anne Francis, Glenda Farrell, Alvy Moore. Screenwriter Powell agrees to look after high-spirited delinquent Reynolds in this "cute" sex comedy, which has the distinction of being the only film in history ever narrated by an Oscar statuette!▼●▶

Suspect, The (1944) **85m.** ***½ D: Robert Siodmak. Charles Laughton, Ella Raines, Dean Harens, Molly Lamont, Henry Daniell, Rosalind Ivan. Superb, Hitchcock-like thriller of henpecked London tobacconist Laughton planning to get his wife out of the way so he can pursue lovely Raines.

Suspect (1987) **C-121m.** *** D: Peter Yates. Cher, Dennis Quaid, Liam Neeson, John Mahoney, Joe Mantegna, Philip Bosco, E. Katherine Kerr. Dedicated public defender (Cher) battles a nearly hopeless case, representing a deaf derelict accused of murder, with the unexpected help of one of her jurors (Quaid). Entertaining film manages to override its many implausibilities, with Cher turning in a fine and utterly believable performance. [R]▼●▶

Suspect Zero (2004) **C-99m.** ** D: E. Elias Merhige. Aaron Eckhart, Ben Kingsley, Carrie-Anne Moss, Harry Lennix, William Mapother. Troubled FBI agent (Eckhart), just transferred to the New Mexico office, suspects that the man they're trying to track down for a string of disappearances and murders is not exactly what he seems. Complex premise, reminiscent at times of RED DRAGON, with striking visual style, is hindered by the oppressive nature of the material and the fact that there's no one to care about. [R]▼▶

Suspended Animation (2003) **C-114m.** *½ D: John D. Hancock. Alex McArthur, Laura Esterman, Sage Allen, Rebecca Harrell, Fred Meyers, Maria Cina, Jeff Puckett. Hollywood animation filmmaker on a winter vacation is held captive, MISERY-style, by a pair of crazed sisters. He escapes and returns to Malibu, obsessed with the (now supposedly dead) women who caused his ordeal. Well produced, but the story is unpleasant and suffers from a rotten ending. Most of the characters lack appeal, though Esterman is quite good as one of the sisters. [R]▼▶

Suspicion (1941) **99m.** ***½ D: Alfred Hitchcock. Cary Grant, Joan Fontaine, Cedric Hardwicke, Nigel Bruce, Dame May Whitty, Isabel Jeans, Heather Angel, Leo G. Carroll. Fontaine won Oscar for portraying wife who believes husband Grant is trying to kill her. Suspenser is helped by Bruce as Cary's pal, but finale (imposed by the Production Code) leaves viewer flat. Scripted by Samson Raphaelson, Joan Harrison, and Alma Reville (Hitchcock's wife), from *Before the Fact* by Francis Iles (Anthony Berkeley). Remade as a TVM in 1987. Also shown in computer-colored version.▼●▶

Suspiria (1977-Italian) **C-98m.** *** D: Dario Argento. Jessica Harper, Stefania Casini, Joan Bennett, Alida Valli, Flavio Bucci, Udo Kier. Terrifying tale of American student (Harper) attending European ballet school that turns out to be a witches' coven. Often dumb plot is enriched and overcome by brilliant camerawork, atmosphere, music score and performance (by Argento and rock group Goblin). Originally cut to 92m. for U.S. release. Followed by INFERNO. Technovision. [R]▼●▶

Suture (1993) **93m.** *** D: Scott McGehee, David Siegel. Dennis Haysbert, Mel Harris, Dina Merrill, Sab Shimono, Michael Harris, David Graf, Fran Ryan, John

Ingle. Unique, off-the-wall tale of Vincent (Michael Harris), who is suspected of murdering his father; he hatches a scheme to fake his own death, substituting the body of his estranged half-brother, Clay (Haysbert), as his corpse. Although these men remark on their uncanny physical resemblance, Vincent is white and Clay is black: a joke which only the audience is in on. A novel and perceptive film about identity. An impressive debut for writer-director-producer duo McGehee and Siegel. Super 35. ▼●)

Suzanne SEE: **Second Coming of Suzanne, The**

Svengali (1931) 82m. *** D: Archie Mayo. John Barrymore, Marian Marsh, Donald Crisp, Carmel Myers, Bramwell Fletcher, Luis Alberni. Absorbing tale of artist's obsession with young girl, Trilby, who becomes singing artist under his hypnotic spell. Prime Barrymore in interesting production with bizarre Paris sets by Anton Grot, memorable visual effects. Followed by THE MAD GENIUS. ▼●)

Svengali (1954-British) C-82m. **½ D: Noel Langley. Hildegarde Neff, Donald Wolfit, Terence Morgan, Noel Purcell, Alfie Bass. Lacks flair of earlier version of du Maurier's novel about mesmerizing teacher and his actress-pupil Trilby. Robert Newton, originally cast as Svengali, quit in mid-production but can still be seen in some long shots. ▼▶

Swamp Thing (1982) C-91m. **½ D: Wes Craven. Louis Jourdan, Adrienne Barbeau, Ray Wise, David Hess, Nicholas Worth. Research scientist continues to love Barbeau from afar even after a chemical turns him into walking vegetation. This was better as a DC comic, though Jourdan's villainous camping in this sweet-natured monster pic is almost on a level with Vincent Price's standard routine. Followed by THE RETURN OF SWAMP THING and a cable TV series. [PG] ▼●)

Swamp Water (1941) 90m. **½ D: Jean Renoir. Dana Andrews, Walter Brennan, Anne Baxter, Walter Huston, Virginia Gilmore, John Carradine, Ward Bond, Guinn ("Big Boy") Williams, Eugene Pallette, Joe Sawyer, Mary Howard. Renoir's first American film is moody but erratic thriller set in the Okefenokee. Trapper Andrews finds fugitive Brennan hiding in the swamp, tries to clear him of murder rap without letting on that he knows the man's whereabouts. Powerhouse cast, handsome production, weakened by cornball dialogue and miscasting of Brennan. Remade as LURE OF THE WILDERNESS.

Swan, The (1956) C-112m. *** D: Charles Vidor. Grace Kelly, Alec Guinness, Louis Jourdan, Agnes Moorehead, Jessie Royce Landis, Brian Aherne, Leo G. Carroll, Estelle Winwood. Mild Molnar comedy of

manners has attractive cast but not much sparkle. Jourdan good as Kelly's suitor, but she's promised to prince Guinness. Filmed before in 1925 and (as ONE ROMANTIC NIGHT) in 1930. CinemaScope. ▼●)

Swann in Love (1984-French) C-110m. **½ D: Volker Schlöndorff. Jeremy Irons, Ornella Muti, Alain Delon, Fanny Ardant, Marie-Christine Barrault, Nathalie Juvet. Lavish but lifeless telescoping of Proust's *Remembrance of Things Past* with Irons surprisingly stiff as French aristocrat obsessed with scandalous, lower-class Muti in 1885 Paris. Redeemed somewhat by the latter and Delon (as a homosexual baron), a sexy under-the-covers love scene, and Sven Nykvist photography. [R] ▼▶

Swan Princess, The (1994) C-90m. ** D: Richard Rich. Voices of Jack Palance, Howard McGillin, Michelle Nicastro, Liz Callaway, John Cleese, Steven Wright, Sandy Duncan. Charmless, by-the-numbers animated fantasy about Prince Derek and Princess Odette, who seem fated to wed; barriers arise when they quarrel, and a sorcerer transforms the princess into a swan. Partially based on the fable that inspired *Swan Lake.* Too imitative of Disney's BEAUTY AND THE BEAST for its own good. In fact, the film was made by former Disney animators. Followed by two sequels. [G] ▼●)

Swap, The SEE: **Sam's Song**

Swarm, The (1978) C-116m. BOMB D: Irwin Allen. Michael Caine, Katharine Ross, Richard Widmark, Henry Fonda, Richard Chamberlain, Olivia de Havilland, Fred MacMurray, Ben Johnson, Lee Grant, Jose Ferrer, Patty Duke Astin, Slim Pickens, Bradford Dillman. This formula disaster film from Irwin Allen portrays killer bee invasion with no sting at all; succeeds only in wasting a lot of talented actors. For masochists only: runs even longer (156m.) on DVD. Panavision. [PG] ▼●)

Swashbuckler (1976) C-101m. BOMB D: James Goldstone. Robert Shaw, James Earl Jones, Peter Boyle, Genevieve Bujold, Beau Bridges, Geoffrey Holder, Avery Schreiber, Anjelica Huston. Poorly constructed, bubble-headed picture—laced with kinky PG sex scenes—would make Errol Flynn turn over in his grave. Incredible waste of talent. Panavision. [PG] ▼●)

Swastika Savages SEE: **Hell's Bloody Devils**

S.W.A.T. (2003) C-116m. **½ D: Clark Johnson. Samuel L. Jackson, Colin Farrell, Michelle Rodriguez, James Todd Smith aka LL Cool J, Josh Charles, Jeremy Renner, Brian Van Holt, Olivier Martinez. Slick, if not especially original, cops-and-robbers action yarn about maverick L.A.P.D. sergeant Jackson being hired to train an elite S.W.A.T. team. He deliberately recruits the force's misfits and square pegs, who meet their match in a wily French criminal (Martinez). The pulsating music is wall-to-wall, and the action, while not always brilliantly staged, is just good enough. Steve Forrest, star of the vintage TV series of the same name, has a cameo. A hip-hop song sung over the closing credits is called "Samuel Jackson." Followed by a direct-to-DVD sequel. Super 35. [PG-13] ▼❚

Sweeney Todd, The Demon Barber of Fleet Street (1936-British) **68m.** ** D: George King. Tod Slaughter, Bruce Seton, Stella Rho, Eve Lister, Ben Soutten, D.J. Williams. Not many chills in this adaptation of the George Dibdin-Pitt play (later one of the sources for the Broadway musical *Sweeney Todd* by Stephen Sondheim and Hugh Wheeler), but it does contain a quintessential eye-rolling performance by Britain's master of grand guignol, Tod Slaughter, playing the sadistic barber who dumps his customers into the cellar and turns them into meat pies. Photographed by Ronald Neame. Not released in the U.S. until 1939. ▼❚

Sweeney Todd: The Demon Barber of Fleet Street (2007) **C-117m.** *** D: Tim Burton. Johnny Depp, Helena Bonham Carter, Alan Rickman, Timothy Spall, Sacha Baron Cohen, Jayne Wisener, Jamie Campbell Bower, Edward Sanders, Laura Michelle Kelly. Stylized adaptation of the legendary Stephen Sondheim–Hugh Wheeler musical about a barber seeking revenge against 19th-century London society because of the judge who unjustly imprisoned him— and stole his wife and young daughter. Burton's naturally morbid sensibilities mesh well with Sondheim's dark, brooding score. The result—whose textual changes will certainly pain Broadway purists—may not be as powerful as the original, but it actually works as a *film*. Depp and Bonham Carter (who, like the entire cast, do their own singing) bring gravity and wit to their roles, and the physical production is grimly spectacular. Oscar winner for Best Art Direction (Dante Ferretti and Francesca Lo Schiavo). Not for the squeamish. [R] ❚

Sweet and Lowdown (1999) **C-95m.** **½ D: Woody Allen. Sean Penn, Samantha Morton, Uma Thurman, Brian Markinson, Anthony LaPaglia, James Urbaniak, Gretchen Mol, John Waters, Brad Garrett. A Woody Allen diversion about a fictional jazz guitarist of the 1930s, Emmet Ray (brilliantly played by Penn), who's a musical genius but a rotten human being. Morton is a standout as a naive (and mute) woman with whom he has an unlikely relationship. Music is great, period flavor impeccable, but the story wanders. Howard Alden doubles Penn's guitar playing. Allen appears on-screen as one of the experts recalling Emmet Ray's career. [PG-13] ▼❚

Sweet Bird of Youth (1962) **C-120m.** ***½ D: Richard Brooks. Paul Newman, Geraldine Page, Shirley Knight, Ed Begley, Rip Torn, Mildred Dunnock, Madeleine Sherwood, Philip Abbott, Corey Allen. Tennessee Williams' play, cleaned up for the movies, still is powerful drama. Newman returns to Southern town with dissipated movie queen Page, causing corrupt town "boss" Begley (who won an Oscar) to have him fixed proper. Glossy production with cast on top of material. Scripted by Brooks. Newman, Page, Sherwood, and Torn reprised their Broadway performances. Remade for TV in 1989 with Elizabeth Taylor. CinemaScope. ▼❶❚

Sweet Body of Deborah, The (1969-Italian-French) **C-105m.** BOMB D: Romolo Guerrieri. Carroll Baker, Jean Sorel, Evelyn Stewart, Luigi Pistilli, Michel Bardinet. Convoluted soaper about murder, suicide, blackmail, and other sordid goings-on. This "body" really sags. Techniscope. [R]

Sweet Candy SEE: **Candy Stripe Nurses**
Sweet Charity (1969) **C-153m.** *** D: Bob Fosse. Shirley MacLaine, John McMartin, Ricardo Montalban, Sammy Davis, Jr., Chita Rivera, Paula Kelly, Stubby Kaye, Ben Vereen, Lee Roy Reams. Fine, overlooked adaptation of the Broadway musical written by Neil Simon, and based on Fellini's NIGHTS OF CABIRIA, about prostitute-with-heart-of-gold who falls in love with naive young man who doesn't know about her "work." Cy Coleman–Dorothy Fields score includes "Big Spender," "If They Could See Me Now," rousing "Rhythm of Life." Script by Peter Stone. Fosse's debut as film director. Look for Bud Cort and Kristoffer Tabori as flower children. Also shown in 145 and 147m. versions—one with a happy ending, one not! Panavision. [G] ▼❶❚

Sweet Country (1986) **C-150m.** BOMB D: Michael Cacoyannis. Jane Alexander, Franco Nero, Carole Laure, Joanna Pettet, Irene Papas, Randy Quaid, Jean-Pierre Aumont. Grueling, heavy-handed drama of a family's reactions to the 1973 Chilean revolution. Notable for idiotic miscasting (Laure and Pettet as Papas' daughters; Quaid as a lip-smacking, lecherous soldier named Raoul). Quite a comedown for ZORBA THE GREEK director Cacoyannis, who includes tasteless sexploitation footage for good measure. Filmed in Greece. [R] ▼❶

Sweet Dreams (1985) **C-115m.** **½ D: Karel Reisz. Jessica Lange, Ed Harris, Ann Wedgeworth, David Clennon, James Staley, Gary Basaraba, John Goodman, P.J. Soles. Flavorful look at 1950s country singing star Patsy Cline can't escape déjà vu from so many other show-biz biopics. Focuses mainly on Cline's marriage to ne'er-do-well Harris, which also has a too-familiar ring. Made worthwhile by truly fine performances (including Wedgeworth as Patsy's mother) and a lot of wonderful music (Lange lip-syncs to Cline's original recordings). [PG-13]▼●◗

Sweetest Thing, The (2002) **C-84m.** **½ D: Roger Kumble. Cameron Diaz, Christina Applegate, Selma Blair, Thomas Jane, Jason Bateman, Parker Posey, Georgia Engel. Loopy comedy—scripted by *South Park* writer and standup comic Nancy M. Pimental—tracks the misadventures of three oversexed girlfriends who make Betty and Veronica seem like eggheads. Attempt to put good-looking women into the kind of raunchy comedy usually associated with guys is wildly uneven, but hard to dislike. Johnathon Schaech (Applegate's real-life husband) appears unbilled. [R]▼◗

Sweethearts (1938) **C-114m.** **½ D: W. S. Van Dyke II. Jeanette MacDonald, Nelson Eddy, Frank Morgan, Florence Rice, Ray Bolger, Mischa Auer. Enjoyable but overlong; Nelson and Jeanette are stage stars of Victor Herbert operetta who are manipulated by their producer (Morgan) into having a marital spat. Handsome color production filled with Herbert melodies. Cinematographer Oliver Marsh won an Oscar.▼●◗

Sweet Hearts Dance (1988) **C-101m.** **½ D: Robert Greenwald. Don Johnson, Susan Sarandon, Jeff Daniels, Elizabeth Perkins, Kate Reid, Justin Henry, Holly Marie Combs, Heather Coleman. Comedy-drama, set in a small Vermont town, about the breakup of a marriage between two high-school sweethearts—just as their longtime friend is embarking on a serious relationship. Engaging cast, led by Johnson in a very appealing performance, but after a while you wish the two lead characters would just get on with it. Written by Ernest Thompson. [R]▼●◗

Sweet Hereafter, The (1997-Canadian) **C-110m.** *** D: Atom Egoyan. Ian Holm, Sarah Polley, Bruce Greenwood, Tom McCamus, Arsinée Khanjian, Alberta Watson, Gabrielle Rose, Maury Chaykin, David Hemblen. Tenacious lawyer comes to a Canadian town that's been shattered by a schoolbus accident in which many of its children were killed. He tries to convince the parents to hire him to sue whoever may be responsible—if, indeed, anyone is. Meanwhile, he tries to deal with his fragmented relationship with his own drug-addicted daughter. Egoyan brings his quiet, elliptical approach to Russell Banks' novel and creates a haunting film that's hard to forget . . . though not for every taste. Holm is simply superb. Panavision. [R]▼●◗

Sweet Home Alabama (2002) **C-109m.** ** D: Andy Tennant. Reese Witherspoon, Josh Lucas, Patrick Dempsey, Candice Bergen, Mary Kay Place, Fred Ward, Jean Smart, Ethan Embry, Melanie Lynskey, Courtney Gains, Mary Lynn Rajskub, Dakota Fanning. Rising N.Y.C. fashion designer is engaged to the mayor's son—but returns home to Alabama to get her estranged husband to sign their divorce papers, which he's put off for seven years. Once there she feels pangs of homesickness and an unexplainable attraction to her slothful ex. Lazy romantic comedy doesn't bother to flesh out any of its characters or explain their motivations; even as fluff, it falls short. Only Witherspoon's sunny presence keeps this one afloat. Super 35. [PG-13] ▼◗

Sweetie (1989-Australian) **C-97m.** **½ D: Jane Campion. Genevieve Lemon, Karen Colston, Tom Lycos, Jon Darling, Dorothy Barry. New Zealander Campion's offbeat account of an unbalanced, demanding young woman (Lemon), and her relationship with her weak, obsessive sister (Colston) and her parents. Some brilliant directorial touches, but too many sequences simply don't work. Unsettling, occasionally depressing, and not for all tastes. [R]▼●◗

Sweet Kill SEE: **Arousers, The**

Sweet Land (2005) **C-110m.** ***½ D: Ali Selim. Elizabeth Reaser, Tim Guinee, Alan Cumming, John Heard, Alex Kingston, Ned Beatty, Lois Smith, Patrick Heusinger, Stephen Pelinski, Paul Sand. Beautifully realized depiction of rural post-WW1 Minnesota and the German mail-order bride who causes a stir in the close-knit Norwegian community. Reaser is exceptional, but whole cast shines (including Smith, 50 years after her film debut in EAST OF EDEN) in this moving drama of immigration, love, and hardship. Scripted by the director; based on Will Weaver's short story "A Gravestone Made of Wheat." [PG]◗

Sweet Liberty (1986) **C-107m.** ** D: Alan Alda. Alan Alda, Michael Caine, Michelle Pfeiffer, Bob Hoskins, Lise Hilboldt, Lillian Gish, Saul Rubinek, Lois Chiles. Amiable but aimless comedy of college professor who becomes involved with a movie troupe as his historical novel is filmed. Ingratiating cast maintains some level of interest, with funny turns by Caine as a cocky leading man and Hoskins as an eager-to-please screenwriter. But deep down inside, it's really shallow. [PG]▼●◗

Sweet Lies (1986) **C-96m.** *½ D: Nathalie Delon. Treat Williams, Joanna Pacula, Julianne Phillips, Laura Manszky, Norbert Weisser, Bernard Fresson. Boring romantic comedy with Williams sorely miscast as an insurance-company detective involved in sexual shenanigans with a trio of women while on assignment in Paris. [R]▼

Sweet Lorraine (1987) **C-91m.** *** D: Steve Gomer. Maureen Stapleton, Trini Alvarado, Lee Richardson, John Bedford Lloyd, Giancarlo Esposito, Edith (Edie) Falco, Todd Graff, Evan Handler, Freddie Roman. The Lorraine is a cozy little Catskill hotel that's way past its prime; Stapleton is its proprietress, Alvarado her granddaughter who spends a summer working in its kitchen. There's a wealth of atmosphere and some sturdy characterizations in this warm, friendly, very personal slice-of-life sleeper. [PG-13]▼▶

Sweet Love, Bitter (1967) **92m.** **½ D: Herbert Danska. Dick Gregory, Don Murray, Diane Varsi, Robert Hooks, John Randolph. Intriguing film about the unlikely friendship between a great jazz musician (Gregory) who's seen better days and a college professor who's hit the skids (Murray). Loosely based on the life of jazz legend Charlie "Bird" Parker; dated in some ways, but also a fascinating artifact of its time. Its comments on race relations are still as potent as ever.▼

Sweet Nothing (1996) **C-90m.** ** D: Gary Winick. Michael Imperioli, Mira Sorvino, Paul Calderon, Lisa Langford. Tragic story of a family affected by the horrors of drugs. Father looking to make a better life for his wife and kids gets in way over his head in the seedy world of crack, becoming both a user and a seller. Grim film offers unappealing characters and storyline, showing the harrowing effects of drug addiction on innocent lives. Made in 1993, before Sorvino's Oscarwinning turn in MIGHTY APHRODITE, but released (just barely) after. [R]▼

Sweet November (1968) **C-114m.** **½ D: Robert Ellis Miller. Sandy Dennis, Anthony Newley, Theodore Bikel, Burr DeBenning, Sandy Baron, Marj Dusay, Martin West. Kooky Dennis takes a new lover every month, helping insecure men find confidence, then sending them away; her plans go awry when one of them (Newley) insists on marrying her. Some touching moments in this likable (if implausible) comedy-drama by Herman Raucher. Remade in 2001.▼▶

Sweet November (2001) **C-119m.** **½ D: Pat O'Connor. Keanu Reeves, Charlize Theron, Jason Isaacs, Greg Germann, Liam Aiken, Lauren Graham, Frank Langella, Ray Baker, Robert Joy. Kooky San Francisco woman persuades uptight, careerdriven man to spend one month with her so she can transform him into more of a human being . . . as she has for many guys before him. Harmless fluff is neither spontaneous nor convincing enough, though Reeves and Theron give it their best shot. Remake of the 1968 movie. [PG-13]▼▶

Sweet Revenge (1977) **C-90m.** BOMB D: Jerry Schatzberg. Stockard Channing, Sam Waterston, Franklin Ajaye, Richard Doughty. Public defender Waterston falls in love with a car thief (Channing) in this turkey, originally called DANDY, THE ALL-AMERICAN GIRL. Panavision. [PG]

Sweet Revenge(1999-British-French-U.S.) **C-90m.** ** D: Malcolm Mowbray. Sam Neill, Helena Bonham Carter, Kristin Scott Thomas, Liz Smith, Rupert Graves, Martin Clunes, Steve Coogan, Charlotte Coleman, John Wood. Two suicidal souls vow to avenge the people who wronged them in this twist on STRANGERS ON A TRAIN. Quirky comedy has moments, but too few, though the lead actors seem to delight in this (uneven) blend of slapstick and mayhem. Based on the plays by Alan Ayckbourn. U.S. debut on cable TV. Original British title: THE REVENGERS' COMEDIES. [PG-13]▼▶

Sweet Ride, The (1968) **C-110m.** *½ D: Harvey Hart. Tony Franciosa, Michael Sarrazin, Jacqueline Bisset, Bob Denver, Michael Wilding, Michele Carey, Warren Stevens. Absurd claptrap about a tennis bum, a surfer, and a beautiful girl; some of the Malibu scenery is nice. Panavision. [R]

Sweet Rosie O'Grady (1943) **C-74m.** **½ D: Irving Cummings. Betty Grable, Robert Young, Adolphe Menjou, Reginald Gardiner, Virginia Grey, Phil Regan. Pleasant musical of ex-burlesque star and exposé reporter. Menjou steals film as editor of *Police Gazette*. Previously filmed as LOVE IS NEWS; remade again as THAT WONDERFUL URGE.

Sweet 16 (1981) **C-90m.** ** D: Jim Sotos. Bo Hopkins, Susan Strasberg, Don Stroud, Dana Kimmell, Aleisa Shirley, Don Shanks, Steve Antin, Logan Clarke, Patrick Macnee, Michael Pataki, Larry Storch, Henry Wilcoxon, Sharon Farrell. Standard terror film (with good cast) set in Texas about a rash of murders occurring as Shirley's 16th birthday approaches. Identity of the vengeful murderer is quite predictable; integration of a racial prejudice (persecuting Indians) subplot doesn't work. Hopkins plays his slightly slow-witted Southern sheriff role for the umpteenth time. [R]▼

Sweet Sixteen (2002-British-German-Spanish) **C-106m.** *** D: Ken Loach. Martin Compston, Annmarie Fulton, William Ruane, Michelle Abercromby, Michelle Coulter, Gary McCormack, Tommy McKee. Another gritty, grimly realistic slice of life from Loach, this one about 15-year-old Liam (Compston), a career-criminal-intraining, and his dysfunctional Glasgow family; he loves (and is protective of) his mother, who is completing a stretch in the pen. Occasionally rambles, but still a sobering look at the forces that contribute to a young man's dead-end existence. The dialogue is laced with profanity, and the Scottish accents are so thick that the film is English-subtitled.▼▶

Sweet Smell of Success (1957) **96m.** ***½ D: Alexander Mackendrick. Burt Lancaster, Tony Curtis, Marty Milner, Sam Levene, Barbara Nichols, Susan Harrison, Joe Frisco, Chico Hamilton Quintet. Searing Clifford Odets–Ernest Lehman script about ruthless, all-powerful columnist J. J. Hunsecker (Lancaster) and a smarmy press agent (Curtis) who'll do *anything* to curry his favor. Vivid performances, fine jazz score by Elmer Bernstein, outstanding camerawork by James Wong Howe that perfectly captures N.Y.C. nightlife. Later a Broadway musical. ▼●▮

Sweet Sweetback's Baad Asssss Song (1971) **C-97m.** *** D: Melvin Van Peebles. Melvin Van Peebles, Rhetta Hughes, Simon Chuckster, John Amos. Van Peebles produced, directed, financed, wrote, scored, and stars in this angry, violent, reverse-racist blaxploitation drama as a superstud who runs, runs, runs from the police. Visually exciting, surprisingly effective. Controversial (and X-rated) when first released. Van Peebles' son Mario chronicled the making of this film in BAADASSSSS! [R] ▼●▮

Sweet Talker (1990-Australian) **C-88m.** **½ D: Michael Jenkins. Bryan Brown, Karen Allen, Chris Haywood, Bill Kerr, Bruce Spence, Bruce Myles, Paul Chubb, Peter Hehir, Justin Rosniak. Amiable if thoroughly familiar tale of a con man who comes to a remote Australian coastal town to sell his bill of goods, falls in love, and has second thoughts about going through with the con. Pleasant, picturesque, and predictable. Brown cowrote the story. [PG] ▼●▮

Sweet Violent Tony SEE: Cuba Crossing
Sweet William (1980-British) **C-92m.** **½ D: Claude Whatham. Sam Waterston, Jenny Agutter, Anna Massey, Geraldine James, Daphne Oxenford, Rachel Bell, Arthur Lowe, Tim Pigott-Smith. Waterston is charming as an erratic ALFIE-like bigamist who seduces Agutter in this OK entertainment. [R] ▼▮

Swept Away (2002-British) **C-89m.** ** D: Guy Ritchie. Madonna, Adriano Giannini, Jeanne Tripplehorn, Bruce Greenwood, Elizabeth Banks, David Thornton, Michael Beattie, Yorgo Voyagis. Tame remake of Lina Wertmuller's fiery SWEPT AWAY . . . with Giannini doing a creditable job in the part created by his father, and Madonna (directed by her real-life husband) giving one of her better performances as the spoiled rich bitch who's cast away with him on a deserted island. Ill-advised music-video–style sequences only remind us that it *is* Madonna, which doesn't help us believe in her character. Not a disgrace, as media coverage indicated, but utterly unmemorable. [R] ▼▮

Swept Away . . . by an unusual destiny in the blue sea of August (1974-Italian) **C-116m.** **** D: Lina Wertmuller. Giancarlo Giannini, Mariangela Melato. A slovenly sailor is cast adrift on an island with his employer, a rich, selfish woman. Cut off from society, he reverses their roles, stripping her of pride and vanity, and controlling her completely. This fascinating and provocative adult film put writer-director Wertmuller on the map in this country. Remade in 2002. [R] ▼●▮

Swept From the Sea (1998-U.S.-British) **C-114m.** ** D: Beeban Kidron. Rachel Weisz, Vincent Perez, Ian McKellen, Kathy Bates, Joss Ackland, Tony Haygarth, Zoë Wanamaker, Tom Bell. Nineteenth-century melodrama of a silent servant girl who falls in love with the sole survivor of a shipwreck, a Ukrainian emigrant. This tragic romance is the talk of the entire disapproving town. Gorgeous scenery and storms galore can't save this sluggish, shallow film "inspired by" the haunting Joseph Conrad novel *Amy Foster*. Super 35. [PG-13] ▼●▮

Swimfan (2002) **C-86m.** ** D: John Polson. Jesse Bradford, Erika Christensen, Shiri Appleby, Kate Burton, Clayne Crawford, Jason Ritter, Kia Joy Goodwin, Dan Hedaya, Michael Higgins. Waterlogged teenage version of FATAL ATTRACTION with Christensen as a new girl in town who sets her sights on high school swimming champion Bradford—who already has a girlfriend—and doesn't take rejection well. Even as a formula film this falls short, becoming outlandish, with laughable plot turns and dialogue. J-D-C Scope. [PG-13] ▼▮

Swimmer, The (1968) **C-94m.** ***½ D: Frank Perry. Burt Lancaster, Janet Landgard, Janice Rule, Tony Bickley, Marge Champion, Bill Fiore, Kim Hunter, Joan Rivers. Middle-aged man swims from pool to pool on journey home during hot afternoon; each pool evokes past moments and events. Fascinating, vastly underrated film adapted from John Cheever short story; Lancaster is superb, and location filming in Connecticut perfectly captures mood. Script by Eleanor Perry. [M/PG] ▼●▮

Swimming Pool (2003-French-British) **C-102m.** **½ D: François Ozon. Charlotte Rampling, Ludivine Sagnier, Charles Dance, Marc Fayolle, Jean-Marie Lamour, Mireille Mossé. A creatively and emotionally blocked mystery writer (Rampling) vacations in her editor's French villa, then the editor's sexy, uninhibited daughter (Sagnier) shows up, leading to unexpected consequences for both of them. Intriguing psychological character study develops a sinuous, tantalizing mood, then turns to literal melodrama and never quite recovers. Rampling and Sagnier are very good—and very sexy. Unrated version also available. [R] ▼▮

Swimming to Cambodia (1987) **C-87m.** *** D: Jonathan Demme. Spalding Gray talks for nearly an hour and a half—about life in general, and about his experiences in Cambodia, where he spent some time while appearing in a minor role in THE KILLING FIELDS. There is no reason why a lengthy monologue should become such a fascinating film—but it does, thanks to Gray's storytelling skills, and Demme's artful (and subtle) direction. An unusual and rewarding experience. Followed by MONSTER IN A BOX. ▼▮

Swimming Upstream (2003-Australian)

C-97m. ** D: Russell Mulcahy. Geoffrey Rush, Judy Davis, Jesse Spencer, Tim Draxl, Deborah Kennedy, David Hoflin, Craig Horner, Brittany Byrnes, Mitchell Dellevergin. Fact-based story of two Australian teenage swimmers and their working-class family. In the 1950s, a piano-playing mama's boy (Spencer) is coaxed by his boorish father into striving for glory in the pool. Then Dad unfathomably pushes his other son (Draxl) to rival his sibling in increasingly competitive races. Rush and Davis predictably shine as the parents in an abusive marriage, but film is overly melodramatic. Scripted and coexecutive produced by Anthony Fingleton, from the memoir he coauthored with his sister, Diane. Original Australian running time 114m. [PG-13] ▼▶

Swimming With Sharks (1994) **C-93m.** ** D: George Huang. Kevin Spacey, Frank Whaley, Michelle Forbes, Benicio Del Toro, Jerry Levine, T. E. Russell, Roy Dotrice. Young man signs on as the new assistant to venal Hollywood exec Buddy Ackerman and learns new facets of the word "abusive"... until the day he exacts revenge on his tormentor. Dark, "inside" comedy is a one-joke idea (written by first-time director Huang, who—not surprisingly—toiled as an underling in the film biz), but Spacey's performance as the modern-day monster is galvanizing. He alone makes the film worth seeing. Incidentally, Spacey also coproduced the picture. [R] ▼●

Swim Team (1979) **C-92m** *½ D: James Polakoff. James Daughton, Stephen Furst, Richard Young, Jenny Neumann, guest star Buster Crabbe. Can the Whalers reverse their seven-year losing streak as a swim team? Can you sit through this terrible movie to find out? [PG] ▼

Swindle, The (1955-Italian) **92m.** **½ D: Federico Fellini. Broderick Crawford, Giulietta Masina, Richard Basehart, Franco Fabrizi. Absorbing Fellini tale, which he coscripted, about a trio of small-time crooks who go about fleecing peasants in Italy, each planning for a better life. The spotlight is on the eldest, a world-weary loser nicely played by Crawford. Not among the director's best; still an intriguing portrait of hope and desperation. Aka THE SWINDLERS. Original title: IL BIDONE. ▼

Swindle, The (1997-French) **C-101m.** *** D: Claude Chabrol. Isabelle Huppert, Michel Serrault, François Cluzet, Jean-François Balmer, Jackie Berroyer. Absorbing comedy/caper film with Huppert and Serrault perfectly cast as a pair of con artists who may or may not be scheming to cheat each other. The crux of the story is set at a Swiss dentists' convention, where Huppert hooks up with enigmatic Cluzet. Slick, engaging entertainment. ▼▶

Swinger, The (1966) **C-81m.** ** D: George Sidney. Ann-Margret, Tony Franciosa, Robert

Coote, Horace McMahon, Nydia Westman. Brassy, artificial yarn of good-girl Ann-Margret posing as swinger to impress girlie magazine editor Franciosa.

Swingers (1996) **C-96m.** **½ D: Doug Liman. Jon Favreau, Vince Vaughn, Ron Livingston, Patrick Van Horn, Alex Desert, Deena Martin, Katherine Kendall, Brooke Langton, Heather Graham. Slight but entertaining look at single life in L.A. from a guy's point of view. Main character is a comedian who broke up with his girlfriend six months earlier and hasn't yet gotten over her. Some pointed jabs at L.A. life distinguish this contemporary urban tale, a kind of hip update of AMERICAN GRAFFITI. Leading actor Favreau wrote the script; director Liman also photographed it. [R] ▼●▶

Swing High, Swing Low (1937) **95m.** ** D: Mitchell Leisen. Carole Lombard, Fred MacMurray, Charles Butterworth, Jean Dixon, Dorothy Lamour, Harvey Stephens, Anthony Quinn. Musical drama with cornball plot of musician MacMurray's rise and fall. Redeemed somewhat by good cast, glossy production. From the stage play *Burlesque,* made before as THE DANCE OF LIFE and remade as WHEN MY BABY SMILES AT ME. ▼▶

Swing Kids (1993) **C-112m.** ** D: Thomas Carter. Robert Sean Leonard, Christian Bale, Frank Whaley, Barbara Hershey, Tushka Bergen, David Tom, Julia Stemberger, Jayce Bartok, Noah Wyle. This year's NEWSIES, and poor Bale is in both. Transparent Yank actors struggle through a THREE COMRADES kind of yarn about the Nazi persecution of German teens who openly embrace American swing music—taboo, because it employs so many black musicians. Singularly weird enough to carry a mild fascination, but it's the kind of film that needs daring flamboyance to have a prayer of coming off. Eye-massaging production design by Allan Cameron. Kenneth Branagh appears unbilled in a key role as a Nazi. [PG-13] ▼●▶

Swing Shift (1984) **C-100m.** ** D: Jonathan Demme. Goldie Hawn, Kurt Russell, Christine Lahti, Ed Harris, Fred Ward, Sudie Bond, Holly Hunter, Patty Maloney, Roger Corman, Belinda Carlisle. Misfired attempt to fashion fictional story around real-life situation of housewives who became factory workers during WW2. All the women are interesting (especially Lahti, in a wonderful performance), but the men are shallow and poorly defined—and consequently, so is the film. Pseudonymous screenplay credit for "Rob Morton" masks several top writers, with half-an-hour reportedly shot by another director at producer Hawn's insistence. [PG] ▼●▶

Swing Time (1936) **103m.** **** D: George Stevens. Fred Astaire, Ginger Rogers, Victor Moore, Helen Broderick, Eric Blore, Betty Furness. One of the best Astaire-Rogers films, with stars as dance team whose romance is hampered by Fred's engagement to girl back home (Furness). Fine support by Moore and Broderick, unforgettable Jerome Kern–Dorothy Fields songs "A Fine Romance," "Pick Yourself Up." Oscar-winning "The Way You Look Tonight." Astaire's Bojangles production number is a screen classic.▼●）

Swing Vote (2008) **C-119m.** *** D: Joshua Michael Stern. Kevin Costner, Kelsey Grammer, Paula Patton, Dennis Hopper, Nathan Lane, Stanley Tucci, Madeline Carroll, George Lopez, Mare Winningham, Judge Reinhold. Sharp, funny, relevant comedy about a quirk of fate that leaves the determination of a U.S. presidential campaign in the hands of one not-so-solid citizen—an irresponsible, beer-swilling single dad (Costner). His young daughter takes the situation much more seriously than he does, especially as a media circus mushrooms around them . . . and he gradually undergoes an awakening. Genuinely Capraesque movie has a terrific cast that makes the most of the screenplay by director Stern and Jason Richman. Many newscasters and celebrities appear in cameos. Worth comparing to THE GREAT MAN VOTES (1939). Super 35. [PG-13]）

Swiss Conspiracy, The (1975-U.S.-German) **C-88m.** ** D: Jack Arnold. David Janssen, Senta Berger, John Ireland, John Saxon, Elke Sommer, Ray Milland, Anton Diffring. Confusing cat-and-mouse intrigue set in Switzerland, where Janssen is hired to protect valued bank customers with large secret accounts. [PG]▼）

Swiss Family Robinson (1940) **93m.** *** D: Edward Ludwig. Thomas Mitchell, Edna Best, Freddie Bartholomew, Tim Holt, Terry Kilburn. Mitchell decides to move family to Australia for a purer life, but shipwreck strands them on a remote island where his three spoiled sons learn honest values. Excellent adaptation of Johann Wyss book boasts impressive special effects, strong performances, and much darker elements than the later Disney version. Uncredited opening narration by Orson Welles. ▼

Swiss Family Robinson (1960) **C-128m.** ***½ D: Ken Annakin. John Mills, Dorothy McGuire, James MacArthur, Janet Munro, Sessue Hayakawa, Tommy Kirk, Kevin Corcoran. Rollicking entertainment Disney-style, with shipwrecked family building island paradise, neatly dispatching Hayakawa and his pirate band. Pure escapism, larger than life. Panavision.▼●）

Swiss Miss (1938) **72m.** ** D: John Blystone. Stan Laurel, Oliver Hardy, Della Lind, Walter Woolf King, Eric Blore, Adia Kuznetzoff, Charles Judels. Contrived romantic story with music tries hard to submerge L&H, but Stan and Ollie's scenes save film, especially when Ollie serenades his true love with Stan playing tuba.▼

Switch (1991) **C-104m.** *½ D: Blake Edwards. Ellen Barkin, Jimmy Smits, JoBeth Williams, Lorraine Bracco, Tony Roberts, Perry King, Bruce Martyn Payne, Catherine Keener, Téa Leoni. Inferior ripoff of GOODBYE, CHARLIE about a philandering male who's shot by a vindictive conquest and returns to earth as a woman. Old-hat premise with precious few opportunities to exploit Edwards' flair for cartoonish physical humor. Barkin is sole saving grace, far better than anything else in the film. Panavision. [R]▼●）

Switch, The (2010) **C-101m.** ** D: Josh Gordon, Will Speck. Jennifer Aniston, Jason Bateman, Patrick Wilson, Jeff Goldblum, Juliette Lewis, Jason Jones, Todd Louiso. N.Y.C. career woman Aniston decides it's time to have a baby and seeks out a sperm donor, to the chagrin of her neurotic best friend (Bateman), who can't get himself to admit that he's in love with her. He drunkenly substitutes his own sperm for the donor's—and doesn't remember doing it, at first. Flat, connect-the-dots romantic comedy squanders a talented cast . . . although the kid who plays Aniston's son (Thomas Robinson) is cute. Based on Jeffrey Eugenides' short story "Baster." Super 35. [PG-13]）

Switchback (1997) **C-121m.** **½ D: Jeb Stuart. Dennis Quaid, Danny Glover, R. Lee Ermey, Jared Leto, Ted Levine. DIE HARD/FUGITIVE screenwriter Stuart debuts as director of this thriller about the kidnapping of an FBI agent's son, and the pursuit of the serial killer who has him. Preposterous plot devices are overshadowed by excellent cast. You really care what happens to these people. Panavision. [R]▼●）

Switchblade Sisters (1975) **C-91m.** ** D: Jack Hill. Robbie Lee, Joanne Nail, Monica Gayle, Kitty Bruce, Marlene Clark, Michael Miller. Pretty good cheapie about a female gang, although feminism clearly takes a back seat to action. Predates the cycle of gang films by four years; Bruce is Lenny's daughter. Originally released as THE JEZEBELS (the gang's name); reissued as PLAYGIRL GANG. [R]▼●）

Switching Channels (1988) **C-105m.** *** D: Ted Kotcheff. Kathleen Turner, Burt Reynolds, Christopher Reeve, Ned Beatty, Henry Gibson, George Newbern, Al Waxman, Ken James, Joe Silver, Charles Kimbrough, Tony Rosato. TV reporter Turner tries to quit her job to marry wealthy Reeve, but her boss (and ex-husband) Reynolds isn't going to give her up so easily. Surprisingly good remake of THE FRONT PAGE/HIS GIRL FRIDAY updated to the satellite-television era, but less effective in its use of satire and occasional melodrama than its classic predecessors. All three stars are terrific. [PG]▼●◑

Swoon (1992) **92m.** ******* D: Tom Kalin. Daniel Schlachet, Craig Chester, Ron Vawter, Michael Kirby, Michael Stumm, Valda Z. Drabla, Natalie Stanford. Impressive low-budget stunt of a movie about Chicago's legendary Leopold-Loeb "thrill" killing, with added subtext about the climate of homophobia that figured in the jury's reaction to one of the century's most heinous crimes. Daring and original (though with severe dramatic limitations) and a fascinating companion piece to Hollywood's ROPE and COMPULSION; moody use of black-and-white.▼●◑

Sword and the Rose, The (1953) **C-93m.** *****½** D: Ken Annakin. Richard Todd, Glynis Johns, Jameš Robertson Justice, Michael Gough, Jane Barrett. Colorful filming of *When Knighthood Was in Flower,* with Johns as Mary Tudor, who uses wiles and power to kindle romance with Todd—but runs afoul of villainous Duke (Gough). Rich period flavor, fine performance by Justice as King Henry VIII. Filmed in England by Walt Disney.▼●

Sword and the Sorcerer, The (1982) **C-100m.** ****** D: Albert Pyun. Lee Horsley, Kathleen Beller, Simon MacCorkindale, George Maharis, Richard Lynch, Richard Moll, Robert Tessier, Nina Van Pallandt, Anna Bjorn, Jeff Corey. Aided by resurrected warlock Maharis, nasty Lynch enslaves the kingdom, and it's up to sword-swinging Horsley to save the day. Strictly second-rate in scripting, acting, and production, with just enough bloodletting to please undemanding fans of this kind of stuff. [R]▼●◑

Swordfish (2001) **C-99m.** ****½** D: Dominic Sena. John Travolta, Hugh Jackman, Halle Berry, Don Cheadle, Vinnie Jones, Sam Shepard, Drea de Matteo, Rudolf Martin, Zach Grenier. Notorious computer hacker Jackman is shanghaied by master criminal Travolta to do his bidding in this action-crime caper, framed in flashback. Some terrific post-MATRIX action moments and stunt set pieces are the only saving grace, as it becomes silly and unreasonably far-fetched. Derivation of the title is never fully explained, but we'd like to think it's from the Marx Brothers' HORSE FEATHERS. Panavision. [R]▼❿

Sword in the Stone, The (1963) **C-75m.** ****½** D: Wolfgang Reitherman. Voices of Ricky Sorenson, Sebastian Cabot, Karl Swenson, Junius Matthews. One of Disney's weakest animated features follows a young boy named Wart, who is destined to become King Arthur—with the considerable help of Merlin the Magician. Mildly entertaining and fast moving, but dialogue heavy, and full of "modern" references that remove much of the magic and wonder from T. H.

White's story. Highlight: wizard's duel between Merlin and Madame Mim. ▼●◑

Sword of Lancelot (1963-British) **C-116m.** ****½** D: Cornel Wilde. Cornel Wilde, Jean Wallace, Brian Aherne, George Baker. Camelot comes alive, minus music, with profuse action and splendid scenery. Some may find Wilde's approach too juvenile, overly sincere, and Aherne a bit too cavalier. Originally titled LANCELOT AND GUINEVERE. Panavision.▼❿

Sword of the Ninja SEE: **Challenge, The** (1982)

Sword of The Valiant (1985-British) **C-101m.** ****** D: Stephen Weeks. Miles O'Keeffe, Cyrielle Claire, Leigh Lawson, Sean Connery, Trevor Howard, Peter Cushing, Ronald Lacey, Lila Kedrova, John Rhys-Davies. Connery (as the Green Knight) may only be on-screen for a few scenes, but he adds zest to this lumbering account of a chivalrous young squire (a wooden O'Keeffe) who must solve a riddle in one year or die. Remake of GAWAIN AND THE GREEN KNIGHT by the same filmmakers . . . and not much of an improvement! Filmed in 1982. J-D-C Scope. [PG]▼❿

Sydney SEE: **Hard Eight**

Sydney White (2007) **C-108m.** ****** D: Joe Nussbaum. Amanda Bynes, Sara Paxton, Matt Long, John Schneider, Jack Carpenter, Jeremy Howard, Crystal Hunt. Contemporary take on *Snow White and the Seven Dwarfs.* Freshman Bynes is rejected from her deceased mother's sorority by its president (Paxton), who's also the most popular girl on campus. The outcast is then taken in by an unofficial fraternity consisting of seven "dorks." Soon she finds herself challenging her own university's elitist Greek system, increasing her popularity and finding her very own Prince Charming. Harmless, somewhat amusing, but best suited to loyal fans of Bynes. Super 35. [PG-13]❿

Sylvester (1985) **C-102m.** ****** D: Tim Hunter. Richard Farnsworth, Melissa Gilbert, Michael Schoeffling, Constance Towers, Pete Kowanko, Arliss Howard, James Gammon. Seemingly surefire story of a girl and her horse can't clear the hurdles because lead character isn't terribly likable. Some nice riding sequences but uneven narrative (by Carol Sobieski) weighs it down. [PG]▼●◑

Sylvia (1965) **115m.** ****½** D: Gordon Douglas. Carroll Baker, George Maharis, Joanne Dru, Peter Lawford, Viveca Lindfors, Edmond O'Brien, Aldo Ray, Ann Sothern. Baker's prelude to HARLOW is much better, despite overuse of flashbacks and rambling episodes; she plays a bad girl turned good with melodrama unfolding as detective Maharis investigates her life.

Sylvia (1985-New Zealand) **C-98m.** ******* D: Michael Firth. Eleanor David, Nigel Terry, Tom Wilkinson, Mary Regan, Joseph George, Eileen Glover. David gives a strong performance as famed educator Sylvia Ashton-Warner, who struggled in the early 1940s to buck New Zealand's educational establishment with innovative reading methods for Maori children. Adapted from her works *Teacher* and *I Passed This Way*. Shirley MacLaine's otherwise unbearable TWO LOVES, based on an Ashton-Warner semiautobiographical story, makes an interesting cross reference. [PG]▼

Sylvia (2003-British) **C-105m.** *** D: Christine Jeffs. Gwyneth Paltrow, Daniel Craig, Jared Harris, Blythe Danner, Michael Gambon, Amira Casar. Incisive portrait of Sylvia Plath, the celebrated American poet of the 1950s and '60s, whose life was intermittently lifted out of a suicidal fog by her love for British poet Edward "Ted" Hughes. Not destined to be a feel-good film, this relies largely on Paltrow to give the character color and shading, and she does. Danner, Paltrow's real-life mother, plays her mother here. Super 35. [R] ▼▶

Sylvia Scarlett (1935) **94m.** *** D: George Cukor. Katharine Hepburn, Cary Grant, Brian Aherne, Edmund Gwenn, Natalie Paley, Dennie Moore. Offbeat, charming comedy-drama; Hepburn and ne'er-do-well father Gwenn take to the road when he gets in trouble. She disguises as a boy as they travel with Cockney Grant in touring show. Most unusual film made interesting by performances of Hepburn and Grant in their first film together. Also shown in computer-colored version. ▼●

Sympathy for Delicious (2011) **C-96m.** ** D: Mark Ruffalo. Mark Ruffalo, Christopher Thornton, Juliette Lewis, Orlando Bloom, Laura Linney, Noah Emmerich, James Karen, John Carroll Lynch, Dov Tiefenbach. Thornton, a real-life paraplegic, wrote this oddball drama about a man in a wheelchair, living near L.A.'s Skid Row, who accidentally discovers that he can heal people with his hands. The only one he can't help is himself. A priest (Ruffalo) encourages him to use his powers to help the unfortunate, and then starts to exploit him, so Thornton—who works as a D.J. under the name Delicious D—hooks up with a rock band and goes on the road. Interesting for a while but terribly unfocused; worst of all, it's hard to care or root for Thornton's misanthropic character. Ruffalo's directorial debut. ▶

Sympathy for Mr. Vengeance (2002-Korean) **C-121m.** **½ D: Park Chan-wook. Song Kang-ho, Shin Ha-gyun, Bae Du-na, Im Ji-eun, Han Bo-bae, Kim Se-dong, Lee Dae-yeon. A deaf-mute's harebrained kidnapping plot to pay for a kidney transplant for his dying sister spins out of control into a bloody cycle of retribution. First of the director's "revenge trilogy" is a stylish blend of surreal imagery, pitch-black humor, narrative confusion, and stomach-turning violence. Superbly made, but morally dubious and not for the squeamish. Followed by OLDBOY and LADY VENGEANCE. Original running time 129m. Super 35. [R]▶

Sympathy for the Devil (1970-French) **C-92m.** ** D: Jean-Luc Godard. Muddled documentary which utilizes the Rolling Stones as a catchall for interspersed study of revolution. Godard's cut, titled ONE PLUS ONE and running somewhat longer, is still extant. ▼●▶

Synanon (1965) **107m.** **½ D: Richard Quine. Chuck Connors, Stella Stevens, Alex Cord, Richard Conte, Eartha Kitt, Edmond O'Brien, Chanin Hale, Alejandro Rey. Potentially powerful study of dope-addiction treatment via the Synanon House methods bogs down in pat romantic tale with stereotyped performances. ▶

Synecdoche, New York (2008) **C-124m.** ** D: Charlie Kaufman. Philip Seymour Hoffman, Samantha Morton, Michelle Williams, Catherine Keener, Emily Watson, Dianne Wiest, Jennifer Jason Leigh, Hope Davis, Tom Noonan. A tormented stage director whose private life is disintegrating channels his frustrations into a massive theatrical project. Screenwriter Kaufman (in his directorial debut) incorporates many of his darkly comic, non-sequitur trademarks at first, then grows melancholy and downbeat as his hero confronts the futility of his quest to understand what his life is all about. Clever and original but wearying, not unlike its main character. The cast is uniformly fine. Super 35. [R]▶

Syriana (2005) **C-128m.** ***½ D: Stephen Gaghan. George Clooney, Matt Damon, Jeffrey Wright, Chris Cooper, William Hurt, Mazhar Munir, Tim Blake Nelson, Amanda Peet, Christopher Plummer, Alexander Siddig, David Clennon, Robert Foxworth, Max Minghella, Jamey Sheridan, Nicky Henson, Jayne Atkinson, Viola Davis. Complex, intriguing drama follows multiple storylines involving characters who affect and are affected by the politics of the Middle East, U.S. oil interests, and government corruption on all sides. "Labyrinthine" doesn't begin to describe this, a rare political thriller with smarts and a conscience; extremely well made, with a terrific cast. Gaghan's script was "suggested" by Robert Baer's book *See No Evil*. Clooney won a Supporting Actor Oscar. Super 35. [R]▶

Syrian Bride, The (2004-Israeli-French-German) **C-97m.** ***½ D: Eran Riklis. Hiyam Abbass, Makram J. Khoury, Clara Khoury, Ashraf Barhoum, Eyad Sheety, Evelyne Kaplun, Julie-Anne Roth. Contemplative, multilayered exploration of the state of the Middle East, centering on events preceding an arranged marriage between a Syrian television actor and a Druze from the Golan Heights; the nuptials will result in the bride's permanent separation from her family. This compassionate film is loaded with recognizable, fully fleshed-out characters, and deals insightfully with feelings and issues both personal and political. Written by the director and Suha Arraf. Super 35. **)**

System, The SEE: **Girl-Getters, The**

Table for Five (1983) **C-122m.** ******* D: Robert Lieberman. Jon Voight, Richard Crenna, Marie-Christine Barrault, Millie Perkins, Roxana Zal, Robby Kiger, Son Hoang Bui, Kevin Costner. Solid (and unabashed) tearjerker with Voight as a divorced man who tries to make up for being an absentee father by taking his three children on a cruise to Europe—little dreaming how tough an experience it will turn out to be. Curl up and have a good cry. [PG]**▼●)**

Taboo (1999-Japanese) **C-100m.** ******* D: Nagisa Oshima. Beat Takeshi (Takeshi Kitano), Ryuhei Matsuda, Shinji Takeda, Tadanobu Asano, Koji Matoba, Masato Ibu. The austere atmosphere of a mid-19th-century samurai warrior academy is rattled to its core upon the arrival of a new student (Matsuda), a multitalented young fighter who also is effeminate and flirtatious. Provocative drama explores the essence of machismo and the nature of sexuality in a repressed society. Originally titled GOHATTO.**▼)**

Tabu—A Story of the South Seas (1931) **82m.** *****½** D: F.W. Murnau. Anna Chevalier, Matahi, Hitu, Jean, Jules, Kong Ah. Fascinating melding of ethnographic documentary and narrative, about pearl fisherman Matahi and his ill-fated love for young Chevalier, who's been deemed by the gods as taboo to all men. Shot in Tahiti in 1929, produced and scripted by Murnau and Robert Flaherty; the latter left the project in mid-production because of differences in opinion with Murnau—who died in a car accident just prior to the film's premiere. Floyd Crosby's cinematography won an Academy Award.**▼●)**

Tadpole (2002) **C-78m.** ******* D: Gary Winick. Sigourney Weaver, John Ritter, Bebe Neuwirth, Aaron Stanford, Robert Iler, Adam LeFevre, Ron Rifkin, Kate Mara. A fresh comic look at a younger-man-older-woman relationship. Stanford hits just the right note as a self-possessed, preppie high school student who rejects the youth and naiveté of girls his age—because he's got a crush on his worldly stepmother (Weaver). Clever comedy set in N.Y.C., with touches of French farce, is short and sweet. Shot on digital video. [PG-13]**▼)**

Taffin (1988-British) **C-96m.** ****** D: Francis Megahy. Pierce Brosnan, Ray McAnally, Alison Doody, Jeremy Child, Patrick Bergin. Dull thriller about a bill collector (an uncharismatic Brosnan) and his exploits as he takes on some shady businessmen

attempting to build a chemical plant in an Irish village. [R]**▼●)**

Tag: The Assassination Game (1982) **C-92m.** ****** D: Nick Castle. Robert Carradine, Linda Hamilton, Kristine De Bell, Bruce Abbott, Michael Winslow, Frazer Smith. A role-playing game, played by college students with toy guns, turns deadly when one player (Abbott) becomes unhinged and substitutes real bullets. Short on sense and suspense, with some unintended laughs along the way. Aka EVERYBODY GETS IT IN THE END. [PG]**▼**

Tailor of Panama, The (2001-U.S.-Irish) **C-109m.** ****½** D: John Boorman. Pierce Brosnan, Geoffrey Rush, Jamie Lee Curtis, Catherine McCormack, Brendan Gleeson, Leonor Varela, Harold Pinter, Mark Margolis, Daniel Radcliffe. A rotter from the British secret service is relocated to Panama City, where he aligns himself with a well-connected (but double-dealing) tailor to get the lay of the land. Genuinely nasty espionage tale/character study is novel at first but eventually becomes off-putting. Rush is extremely good. John le Carré adapted his book with director Boorman and Andrew Davies. Panavision. [R]**▼)**

Tai-Pan (1986) **C-127m.** ***½** D: Daryl Duke. Bryan Brown, Joan Chen, John Stanton, Tim Guinee, Bill Leadbitter, Russell Wong, Kyra Sedgwick, Bert Remsen, Janine Turner. Spectacularly silly adventure yarn based on James Clavell's sprawling novel about 19th-century trade baron who establishes his headquarters in Hong Kong. So much story is telescoped, and so many accents are poor and plot points handled with sledgehammer subtlety that there's nothing left to do but treat the whole thing as a goof—or skip it altogether. Actually filmed in China, if that matters. J-D-C Scope. [R]**▼●)**

Tais-Toi! SEE: **Ruby & Quentin**

Take, The (1974) **C-93m.** ****** D: Robert Hartford-Davis. Billy Dee Williams, Eddie Albert, Vic Morrow, Frankie Avalon, Albert Salmi. Tepid action pic concerns police lieutenant Williams' efforts to stop syndicate chief Morrow while accepting bribe money on the side. Surprisingly neat cameo by Avalon as a cheap crook. [PG]**)**

Take a Girl Like You (1970-U.S.-British) **C-101m.** ****½** D: Jonathan Miller. Hayley Mills, Oliver Reed, Noel Harrison, Sheila Hancock, John Bird, Aimi MacDonald, Ronald Lacey, Penelope Keith. Hayley's a young schoolteacher intent on staying virginal until her wedding day. Reed and Harrison are intent on proving otherwise. Pleasant fare with good cast. Based on a Kingsley Amis novel. [R]**▼**

Take a Hard Ride (1975) **C-109m.** ****** D: Anthony Dawson (Antonio Margheriti). Jim Brown, Lee Van Cleef, Fred Williamson, Catherine Spaak, Jim Kelly, Dana Andrews, Barry Sullivan, Harry Carey, Jr.

Oddball Western filmed in Canary Islands. Brown must carry large bankroll across Mexican border, attracts a colorful band of "comrades" for his journey, runs afoul of bandit Van Cleef. Good personalities wasted in blah script. [PG]▼▶

Take a Letter, Darling (1942) 93m. *** D: Mitchell Leisen. Rosalind Russell, Fred MacMurray, Constance Moore, Robert Benchley, Macdonald Carey, Dooley Wilson, Cecil Kellaway. Witty repartee as advertising exec Roz hires MacMurray as secretary, but relationship doesn't end there. Benchley is wry as Russell's game-playing business partner.

Take Down (1978) C-107m. *** D: Kieth Merrill. Edward Herrmann, Kathleen Lloyd, Lorenzo Lamas, Maureen McCormick, Nick Beauvy, Kevin Hooks, Stephen Furst. Serio-comic look at high school wrestling, focusing on rebellious student Lamas and reluctant coach Herrmann. Well done.▼

Take Her, She's Mine (1963) C-98m. ** D: Henry Koster. James Stewart, Sandra Dee, Audrey Meadows, Robert Morley, Philippe Forquet, John McGiver, Bob Denver, Irene Tsu. Obvious family comedy with Stewart the harried father of wild teenage daughter Dee. Predictable gags don't help. Script by Nunnally Johnson, from the Broadway hit by Phoebe and Henry Ephron; later ripped off by THE IMPOSSIBLE YEARS. Look for James Brolin in airport scene. CinemaScope.

Take Me Home Tonight (2011) C-97m. ** D: Michael Dowse. Topher Grace, Anna Faris, Dan Fogler, Teresa Palmer, Chris Pratt, Michael Biehn, Michelle Trachtenberg, Angie Everhart, Bob Odenkirk, Ginnifer Goodwin, Lucy Punch, Michael Ian Black, Demetri Martin. Grace has just graduated from MIT but can't get his act together; when he runs into his high school crush (Palmer) he pretends to be a success in the world of high finance. He maintains the charade at a wild party that night that also brings his twin sister, best friend, and school rivals together. Purported homage to '80s comedies (from a story cowritten by Grace) hasn't much "period" feel, and while it's innocuous enough it's also highly derivative. Super 35. [R]▶

Take Me Out to the Ball Game (1949) C-93m. *** D: Busby Berkeley. Frank Sinatra, Esther Williams, Gene Kelly, Betty Garrett, Edward Arnold, Jules Munshin, Richard Lane, Tom Dugan. Contrived but colorful musical set in 1906, with Williams taking over Sinatra and Kelly's baseball team. "O'Brien to Ryan to Goldberg" and Kelly's "The Hat My Father Wore on St. Patrick's Day" are musical highlights. Reworking of THEY LEARNED ABOUT WOMEN (1930). ▼▶)

Take Me to Town (1953) C-81m. **½ D: Douglas Sirk. Ann Sheridan, Sterling Hayden, Philip Reed, Lee Patrick, Lane Chandler, Lee Aaker. Unpretentious Americana of saloon singer Sheridan on the lam, finding love with widowed preacher Hayden and his three children.

Taken (2008-French) C-91m. ** D: Pierre Morel. Liam Neeson, Maggie Grace, Famke Janssen, Xander Berkeley, Leland Orser, Jon Gries, David Warshofsky, Katie Cassidy, Holly Valance. Former CIA op Neeson has given up his career to make up for being an absentee father to his now-teenaged daughter. When she's abducted while visiting Paris he springs into action, using all his "special skills" to find her, even if it requires leaving a trail of carnage in his wake. Slick, visceral, and never dull, this action yarn starts well but becomes utterly preposterous. Cowritten and produced by Luc Besson. Unrated version runs 93m. Super 35. [PG-13]▶

Takers (2010) C-107m. **½ D: John Luessenhop. Matt Dillon, Paul Walker, Idris Elba, Jay Hernandez, Michael Ealy, Tip "T.I." Harris, Chris Brown, Hayden Christensen, Marianne Jean-Baptiste, Steve Harris, Johnathon Schaech, Glynn Turman, Nick (Nicholas) Turturro, Zoe Saldana. Familiar but flashy thriller charts parallel progressions of high-living, risk-taking criminals plotting an armored-car robbery and a hard-bitten cop (Dillon) doggedly following their trail from an earlier heist. Exciting set pieces, including a fast and furious foot chase through downtown L.A., and some intriguing character touches help maintain interest. Mildly disappointing ending plays like a last-minute rewrite aimed at leaving door open for a sequel. HD Widescreen. [PG-13]▶

Take the High Ground! (1953) C-101m. *** D: Richard Brooks. Richard Widmark, Karl Malden, Elaine Stewart, Steve Forrest, Carleton Carpenter, Russ Tamblyn, Jerome Courtland. Taut account of infantry basic training with on-location filming at Fort Bliss, Texas, helping.

Take the Lead (2006) C-117m. *½ D: Liz Friedlander. Antonio Banderas, Rob Brown, Alfre Woodard, Yaya DaCosta, John Ortiz, Laura Benanti, Jonathan Malen. Hackneyed cross between *Dancing With the Stars* and TO SIR, WITH LOVE, not to mention other big-hearted teacher-in-the-ghetto films . . . yet it's based on a true story. Kinda. Dance instructor Pierre Dulaine (Banderas) comes to an inner-city high school to teach its most hardened kids ballroom dancing. Before you can say Lambada, he's got gangbangers cha-cha-cha-ing like hip-hop reincarnations of Fred and Ginger. Some of the dancing is good, but the storytelling is stale. Dulaine inspired the far more engaging documentary MAD HOT BALLROOM. [PG-13]▶

Take the Money and Run (1969) C-85m. *** D: Woody Allen. Woody Allen, Janet

Margolin, Marcel Hillaire, Jacquelyn Hyde; narrator, Jackson Beck. Woody's first film as director/writer/star is full of funny ideas, telling documentary-style, life story of compulsive thief. Nonstop parade of jokes; some work, some don't, but the ones that *do* are a riot! Louise Lasser seen briefly. [M/PG]▼●〇

Take This Job and Shove It (1981) **C-100m. **½** D: Gus Trikonis. Robert Hays, Art Carney, Barbara Hershey, David Keith, Tim Thomerson, Martin Mull, Eddie Albert, Penelope Milford. Hays returns to his hometown with orders from his conglomerate to modernize an old-fashioned brewery . . . but being with his old cronies, and one-time girlfriend, effects a change of attitude. Unpretentious film named after '70s hit record by Johnny Paycheck has Capraesque flavor at times, but eventually settles for obvious formula schtick. [PG]▼〇

Taking Care of Business (1990) **C-107m. **½** D: Arthur Hiller. James Belushi, Charles Grodin, Anne DeSalvo, Loryn Locklin, Stephen Elliott, Hector Elizondo, Veronica Hamel, Mako, Gates McFadden, John de Lancie, Terrence McNally. At the outset of a weekend business trip, Grodin loses his pocket organizer, which holds the keys to his very existence; escaped convict Belushi finds the combination wallet and appointment book, and assumes Grodin's identity for an eventful weekend. Cute comedy, with Belushi's most appealing role to date . . . but goes on a bit too long. [R]▼〇

Taking Lives (2004) **C-103m. *** D: D.J. Caruso. Angelina Jolie, Ethan Hawke, Kiefer Sutherland, Gena Rowlands, Olivier Martinez, Tchéky Karyo, Jean-Hugues Anglade, Paul Dano, Marie-Josée Croze. Tough thriller gives Jolie a perfect part as a cool, collected FBI profiler who's called to Montreal to help solve the latest in a series of brutal murders. Her utter professionalism may be compromised by her attraction to eyewitness Hawke. Not for the squeamish, this film offers surprises, genuine shocks, and of course some red herrings to keep you off-balance. Jon Bokenkamp adapted Michael Pye's novel. Director's cut runs 109m. Super 35. [R]▼〇

Taking of Beverly Hills, The (1991) **C-118m. ** D: Sidney J. Furie. Ken Wahl, Matt Frewer, Harley Jane Kozak, Robert Davi, Lee Ving James, Branscombe Richmond, Lyman Ward, Michael Bowen, William Prince, Ken Swofford, George Wyner. The owner of L.A.'s pro football team masterminds a false toxic spill, which allows his flunkies to loot the estates of Beverly Hills' rich-and-famous while the owners are temporarily whisked away to shelter. Quarterback Wahl ends up *literally* lobbing a few bombs in this speedy stupidity, which languished unreleased for well over a year.

Look for Pamela Anderson as a cheerleader. Panavision. [R]▼●

Taking Off (1971) **C-93m. ***½** D: Milos Forman. Lynn Carlin, Buck Henry, Linnea Heacock, Audra Lindley, Paul Benedict, Georgia Engel, Vincent Schiavelli, The Ike and Tina Turner Revue. Forman's first American film is beguilingly funny look at American life-styles from two generations' points of view, centering on runaway girl (Heacock) who drives parents (Carlin, Henry) into new experiences of their own. Screenplay by Forman, John Guare, Jean-Claude Carrière, and John Klein. Among the auditioning singers are Carly Simon, Jessica Harper, and Bobo (Kathy) Bates. [R]

Taking of Pelham One Two Three, The (1974) **C-104m. ***½** D: Joseph Sargent. Walter Matthau, Robert Shaw, Martin Balsam, Hector Elizondo, Earl Hindman, Dick O'Neill, Jerry Stiller, Tony Roberts, Lee Wallace, Doris Roberts, Kenneth McMillan, Julius Harris, James Broderick, Sal Viscuso. Ruthless Shaw and three cohorts hijack N.Y.C. subway train, hold passengers for one million in cash—to be delivered *in one hour!* Outstanding thriller, laced with cynical comedy, bursts with heart-stopping excitement, terrific performances, and first-rate editing. Crackerjack Peter Stone screenplay greatly improves John Godey's best-seller; pulsating score by David Shire. Remade for TV in 1998 and theatrically in 2009. Panavision. [R]▼●〇

Taking of Pelham 1 2 3, The (2009) **C-106m. **½** D: Tony Scott. Denzel Washington, John Travolta, James Gandolfini, John Turturro, Luis Guzmán, Michael Rispoli, Frank Wood, Ramon Rodriguez, John Benjamin Hickey, Aunjanue Ellis, Gary Basaraba. Wily madman (Travolta) hijacks a N.Y.C. subway train and communicates his demands to a transit authority rep (Washington) who just happens to field his call—and becomes deeply entwined in the citywide crisis. Interesting for a while, then becomes needlessly complicated and cluttered (unlike the sharply written 1974 original), with logic discarded completely by the time it winds down. Travolta is quite good, however. Super 35. [R]〇

Taking of Power by Louis XIV, The SEE: **Rise of Louis XIV, The**

Taking Sides (2002-French-German-British) **C-108m. ** D: István Szabó. Harvey Keitel, Stellan Skarsgård, Moritz Bleibtreu, Birgit Minichmayr, Ulrich Tukur, Oleg Tabakov, R. Lee Ermey. Disappointing film based on the life of Wilhelm Furtwängler, conductor of the Berlin Philharmonic during the Nazi era who was investigated in postwar Germany. Ronald Harwood adapted his play, exploring the dilemma of artists in a time of political upheaval and turmoil, but it's too stagy to really work as a film. Uninspired direction by Szabó, who dealt with similar themes in the superior MEPHISTO. **▼◗**

Taking Woodstock (2009) **C-120m. **½** D: Ang Lee. Demetri Martin, Emile Hirsch, Imelda Staunton, Henry Goodman, Liev Schreiber, Jonathan Groff, Eugene Levy, Mamie Gummer, Richard Thomas, Jeffrey Dean Morgan, Kelli Garner, Paul Dano, Edward Hibbert. Vivid re-creation of events leading up to the once-in-a-lifetime Woodstock music festival in the summer of 1969. Martin plays Elliot Tiber, whose parents own a run-down motel that becomes the nerve center of the operation . . . but as the film drags on and focuses more on him than the event, it loses its impetus and strays off course. Worth seeing for some wonderful scenes and performances but something of a disappointment. [R] ◗

Talented Mr. Ripley, The (1999) **C-139m. **½** D: Anthony Minghella. Matt Damon, Gwyneth Paltrow, Jude Law, Cate Blanchett, Philip Seymour Hoffman, Jack Davenport, James Rebhorn, Sergio Rubini, Philip Baker Hall, Celia Weston, Lisa Eichhorn. An unscrupulous (and penniless) young man accepts a job from an American millionaire to find his wastrel son in Italy and convince him to come home. Instead, Tom Ripley (Damon) befriends the young man and aspires to live his carefree life . . . at any price. Two-thirds of a really good movie; Minghella's free adaptation of Patricia Highsmith's novel goes adrift toward the end. Attractive cast and gorgeous views of Italy compensate. Worth comparing to earlier version of same story, PURPLE NOON. Dennis Hopper plays Tom Ripley in THE AMERICAN FRIEND. John Malkovich assumes the role in RIPLEY'S GAME. [R] ▼◗

Talent for Loving, A (1969) **C-110m. **** D: Richard Quine. Richard Widmark, Topol, Cesar Romero, Genevieve Page, Judd Hamilton, Caroline Munro. Rambunctious Western concerning a professional gambler trapped into marrying within rich Mexican family cursed by the Aztecs with a talent for loving. From Richard Condon's novel. Video title: GUN CRAZY. [PG] ▼

Talent for the Game (1991) **C-91m. **½** D: Robert M. Young. Edward James Olmos, Lorraine Bracco, Jamey Sheridan, Terry Kinney, Jeffrey Corbett. Cliché-ridden story of California Angels baseball scout Olmos, who discovers a superior pitching talent on an Idaho farm. Kinney is slimy as a billionaire who buys the team. This struck out in its scant theatrical release and went right to the showers—er, the video shelves. [PG] ▼◗

Tale of Africa, A SEE: **Afurika Monogatari**

Tale of a Vampire (1992-British-Japanese) **C-93m. **½** D: Shimako Sato. Julian Sands, Suzanna Hamilton, Kenneth Cranham, Mar-

ian Diamond, Michael Kenton. London: Lonely vampire Sands becomes attracted to librarian Hamilton, who resembles his lost love . . . but mysterious Cranham is keeping an eye on both of them. Horror thriller emphasizes romance; it's good looking and well acted, but ponderous and pretentious. [R] ▼

Tale of Despereaux, The (2008) **C-93m. **** D: Sam Fell, Robert Stevenhagen. Voices of Matthew Broderick, Sigourney Weaver, Emma Watson, Dustin Hoffman, Robbie Coltrane, Christopher Lloyd, Kevin Kline, Tracey Ullman, Richard Jenkins, Frank Langella, William H. Macy, Stanley Tucci, Frances Conroy, Ciarán Hinds. Unusually brave little mouse embarks on an adventure that changes the lives of an unhappy rat, a homely servant girl, and a princess. Visually attractive, but a confusing and slowly paced animated film with little of interest for grown-ups. Even the all-star voice cast sounds bored. Based on the book by Kate DiCamillo. Digital Widescreen. [G] ◗

Tale of Springtime, A (1989-French) **C-112m. **** D: Eric Rohmer. Anne Teyssedre, Hugues Quester, Florence Darel, Eloise Bennett, Sophie Robin. Typically refreshing, perceptive Rohmer concoction, about high school philosophy teacher Teyssedre; she meets and befriends young Darel, who tries to match her up with her father. Not his best work, but a little Rohmer goes a long way. The first of the filmmaker's "Tales of the Four Seasons," followed by A TALE OF WINTER. ▼◗

Tale of Two Cities, A (1935) **128m. ***** D: Jack Conway. Ronald Colman, Elizabeth Allan, Edna May Oliver, Reginald Owen, Basil Rathbone, Blanche Yurka, Isabel Jewell, Walter Catlett, Henry B. Walthall, H. B. Warner, Donald Woods. Dickens' panorama of the 1780s French Revolution becomes an MGM blockbuster, with Colman as carefree lawyer awakened to responsibility, aiding victims of the Reign of Terror. Stage star Blanche Yurka creates a memorable Mme. Defarge in her film debut. Tremendous cast in a truly lavish production. Written for the screen by W. P. Lipscomb and S. N. Behrman. Also shown in computer-colored version. ▼◗

Tale of Two Cities, A (1958-British) **117m. **** D: Ralph Thomas. Dirk Bogarde, Dorothy Tutin, Cecil Parker, Stephen Murray, Athene Seyler, Christopher Lee, Donald Pleasence, Ian Bannen. Faithful retelling of Dickens story in this well-made British production, with Bogarde a good Sydney Carton. Remade again for TV in 1980. ▼

Tale of Winter, A (1992-French) **C-114m. **½** D: Eric Rohmer. Charlotte Véry, Frédéric Van Den Driessche, Michel Voletti, Hervé Furic, Ava Loraschi, Christiane Desbois. Hairdresser Véry has an affair with an itinerant cook at a beachside resort. They lose touch, and she has his child. She's romanced by two very different suitors, but can't decide upon the one with whom to settle. Bittersweet allegory about not accepting second-best in love; however, it's difficult to sympathize with Véry's flaky character. The second of Rohmer's "Tales of the Four Seasons."▼

Tales From the Crypt (1972-British) **C-92m.** **½ D: Freddie Francis. Ralph Richardson, Peter Cushing, Joan Collins, Richard Greene, Patrick Magee, Ian Hendry, Nigel Patrick. Five stories of terror involving deceit, mayhem, and a few well-timed laughs. Nothing extraordinary, however; based on the old E. C. comics. Followed by VAULT OF HORROR. [PG]▼▶

Tales From the Crypt, Part II SEE: **Vault of Horror**

Tales From the Crypt Presents Bordello of Blood SEE: **Bordello of Blood**

Tales From the Crypt Presents Demon Knight (1995) **C-92m.** ** D: Ernest Dickerson. Billy Zane, William Sadler, Jada Pinkett, Brenda Bakke, CCH Pounder, Thomas Haden Church, Charles Fleischer, Dick Miller. Tepid terror tale of a dashing demon and avenging angel vying for the souls of a band of outsiders (town drunkard, lonely prostitute, etc.). Tries for tongue-in-cheek humor but only supplies some gross-out gore and a fair share of t&a. Based on the HBO TV series. [R]▼▶

Tales From the Crypt Presents Ritual SEE: **Ritual**

Tales From the Darkside: The Movie (1990) **C-93m.** ** D: John Harrison. Deborah Harry, Matthew Lawrence, Christian Slater, Robert Sedgwick, Julianne Moore, David Johansen (Buster Poindexter), William Hickey, James Remar, Rae Dawn Chong, Robert Klein, Steve Buscemi. Boy imprisoned by suburban cannibal Harry tells her three horror stories—about a walking mummy, a supernatural cat, and a vow made to a gargoyle—to stave off being served as a main course. Good production values, but the stories are tepid; only the third one, by Michael McDowell, has a kick (the first two are by Arthur Conan Doyle and Stephen King). Connection to TV series of the same name is tenuous at best. [R]▼▶

Tales From the Hood (1995) **C-98m.** *** D: Rusty Cundieff. Corbin Bernsen, Lamont Bentley, De'Aundre Bonds, Rosalind Cash, Rusty Cundieff, Anthony Griffith, David Alan Grier, Brandon Hammond, Wings Hauser, Sam Monroe, Paula Jai Parker, Joe Torry, Clarence Williams III, Tom Wright. Four horror stories with African-American themes are told to three black hoodlums by a bizarre mortician (Williams). The first (a walking corpse) and the third (vengeful dolls) are standard plots with a racial twist, but the second (boy terrorized by monster

at his door) and the fourth (gang member subjected to behavior modification) are something different. Good direction, colorful acting, and nifty effects put this above average for horror anthologies of any color. Spike Lee was the executive producer. [R]▼▶

Tales of Beatrix Potter SEE: **Peter Rabbit and Tales of Beatrix Potter**

Tales of Hoffmann, The (1951-British) **C-127m.** **½ D: Michael Powell, Emeric Pressburger. Moira Shearer, Robert Rounseville, Leonide Massine, Robert Helpmann, Pamela Brown. Jacques Offenbach's fantasy opera of student who engages in bizarre dreams, revealing three states of his life. Striking and offbeat film, not for all tastes. Beware of 118m. prints. Famous score conducted by Sir Thomas Beecham. ▼▶

Tales of Manhattan (1942) **118m.** *** D: Julien Duvivier. Charles Boyer, Rita Hayworth, Henry Fonda, Ginger Rogers, Charles Laughton, Edward G. Robinson, Ethel Waters, Paul Robeson, Eddie "Rochester" Anderson, Thomas Mitchell, Cesar Romero, George Sanders. Charming film about the effect a dress tailcoat has on its various owners; five episodes, alternately amusing, poignant, ironic. Our favorite: down-and-out Robinson attending 25th class reunion. Pictorially stylish throughout; photographed by Joseph Walker. Video version has 9m. W. C. Fields episode deleted from original theatrical release.▼

Tales of Ordinary Madness (1983-Italian) **C-107m.** *½ D: Marco Ferreri. Ben Gazzara, Ornella Muti, Susan Tyrrell, Tanya Lopert, Roy Brocksmith. Pretentious swill about poet Gazzara who boozes endlessly and meets the oddest assortment of women. Gazzara, and especially Tyrrell, have never been worse. Based on stories by Charles Bukowski.▼▶

Tales of Terror (1962) **C-90m.** *** D: Roger Corman. Vincent Price, Peter Lorre, Basil Rathbone, Debra Paget, Maggie Pierce, Leona Gage, Joyce Jameson. Four Edgar Allan Poe stories distilled by Richard Matheson into three-part film, with Lorre's comic performance as vengeful husband walling up adulterous wife the standout. Price appears in all three segments. Notable for its odd widescreen and color effects. Panavision.▼▶

Tales That Witness Madness (1973-British) **C-90m.** *½ D: Freddie Francis. Kim Novak, Georgia Brown, Joan Collins, Jack Hawkins, Donald Houston, Peter McEnery, Suzy Kendall, Donald Pleasence. Absurd collection of four lame *Twilight Zone*–like stories. A waste of time and talent. [R]▼

Talion SEE: **Eye for an Eye, An** (1966)

Talk About a Stranger (1952) **65m.** *** D: David Bradley. George Murphy, Nancy

Davis (Reagan), Billy Gray, Kurt Kasznar, Lewis Stone. A lonely boy tries to prove reclusive neighbor Kasznar killed his dog. Good use of California orchard locations, well-judged direction, and John Alton's moody photography result in a fine little B that deserves to be better known.

Talkin' Dirty After Dark (1991) **C-86m.** *½ D: Topper Carew. Martin Lawrence, John Witherspoon, Phyllis Yvonne Stickney, Jedda Jones, "Tiny" Lister, Jr., Darryl Sivad. A night in the life of a black L.A. comedy club, on-stage and off; broad (to say the least), energetically vulgar, and poorly made. [R] ▼●)

Talking Picture, A (2003-Portuguese-French-Italian) **C-95m.** *** D: Manoel de Oliveira. Leonor Silveira, Filipa de Almeida, John Malkovich, Irene Papas, Catherine Deneuve, Stefania Sandrelli, Luís Miguel Cintra. Unique, compelling exercise in cinematic philosophizing by 95-year-old master de Oliveira. A history teacher sails to Bombay with her precocious young daughter, showing her some of the world's great sights and explaining the wars that have been fought over them. Along the way, the solicitous ship's captain (Malkovich) leads a high-minded conversation with three striking women from different countries who discuss their views of modern civilization. Unexpected turn of events makes de Oliveira's ultimate point about the state of the world post 9/11. ▶

Talk of Angels (1998) **C-96m.** **½ D: Nick Hamm. Polly Walker, Frances McDormand, Vincent Perez, Franco Nero, Marisa Paredes, Penelope Cruz, Rossy de Palma. An Irish governess for a wealthy Spanish family falls in love with their married anarchist son. Strong supporting cast and sumptuous period detail can't quite make up for lackluster script and lethargic lead performances from Walker and Perez. McDormand is good in a small role as a repressed lesbian. [PG-13] ▼●)

Talk of the Town, The (1942) **118m.** **** D: George Stevens. Jean Arthur, Ronald Colman, Cary Grant, Glenda Farrell, Edgar Buchanan, Charles Dingle, Rex Ingram, Emma Dunn, Tom Tyler, Lloyd Bridges. Intelligent comedy with brilliant cast; fugitive Grant hides out with unsuspecting professor Colman and landlady Arthur, and tries to convince legal-minded Colman there's a human side to all laws. Splendid film written by Irwin Shaw and Sidney Buchman. ▼●)

Talk Radio (1988) **C-110m.** **½ D: Oliver Stone. Eric Bogosian, Alec Baldwin, Ellen Greene, Leslie Hope, John C. McGinley, John Pankow, Michael Wincott. Eric Bogosian's one-set play (written with Ted Savinar) is fleshed out for this feature film about an abrasive talk-show host who puts

down his many callers but can't get his own life together. Well acted, extremely well shot and directed, but one's enjoyment may depend on one's tolerance for this kind of talk-radio host. Stone and Bogosian collaborated on the screenplay, which also incorporated elements of Steven Singular's book *Talked to Death: The Life and Murder of Alan Berg*. [R] ▼●)

Talk to Her (2002-Spanish) **C-112m.** **** D: Pedro Almodóvar. Javier Cámara, Darío Grandinetti, Leonor Watling, Rosario Flores, Geraldine Chaplin, Mariola Fuentes. One-of-a-kind film about two comatose women and the men who love them, in very different ways. Superb, haunting meditation on love, desire, and loneliness could only have been made by Almodóvar. A silent-film segment is outrageous and unforgettable. Sad, funny, shocking, beautifully filmed and acted. A masterpiece. Almodóvar won an Oscar for Best Original Screenplay. Panavision. [R] ▼)

Talk to Me (2007) **C-118m.** **½ D: Kasi Lemmons. Don Cheadle, Chiwetel Ejiofor, Cedric the Entertainer, Taraji P. Henson, Mike Epps, Vondie Curtis Hall, Martin Sheen. Cocky convict "Petey" Greene tries to parlay his stint as a prison d.j. into a bona fide radio career in Washington, D.C., during the turbulent 1960s. Buttoned-down radio exec Ejiofor resists him at first and then realizes he can hitch his wagon to this budding star. "Inspired by" real-life characters, screenplay follows current events and changing times, but loses its focus—and momentum—along the way, though Cheadle's electrifying performance makes this worth seeing. Super 35. [R]▶

Talladega Nights: The Ballad of Ricky Bobby (2006) **C-108m.** ** D: Adam McKay. Will Ferrell, John C. Reilly, Sacha Baron Cohen, Gary Cole, Michael Clarke Duncan, Leslie Bibb, Jane Lynch, Amy Adams, Andy Richter, Molly Shannon, Greg Germann, David Koechner, Pat Hingle, Rob Riggle, Jack McBrayer. Silly saga of a boy who's always wanted to "go fast" and finally gets his chance, but as a NASCAR champion his ego expands to the size of the Goodyear blimp. Broad comedy has a big following, but Ferrell (who coscripted with McKay) keeps hitting the same notes—and yes, he runs around in his underwear. Various celebrities and race-car personalities appear as themselves. Unrated version runs 121m. Super 35. [PG-13]▶

Tall Blond Man With One Black Shoe, The (1972-French) **C-90m.** *** D: Yves Robert. Pierre Richard, Bernard Blier, Jean Rochefort, Mireille Darc, Jean Carmet. Engaging French farce with rival secret agents making life a shambles for the Tall Blond Man (Richard) who's been innocently pegged a spy. Followed by RETURN OF . . . in 1974 and an American remake

(THE MAN WITH ONE RED SHOE) in 1985. [PG]▼

Tall Guy, The (1989-British) **C-90m.** **½ D: Mel Smith. Jeff Goldblum, Emma Thompson, Rowan Atkinson, Emil Wolk, Geraldine James, Kim Thomson, Anna Massey. Quirky comedy of downtrodden American actor living in London, playing second banana to a vile star comedian (Atkinson) in a West End revue. Love, allergies, naked strangers, and the lead in a wickedly inspired musical version of *The Elephant Man* ensue. Goldblum is great in this spotty satire. Screenplay by Richard Curtis. [R]▼●▶

Tall in the Saddle (1944) **87m.** *** D: Edwin L. Marin. John Wayne, Ella Raines, Ward Bond, Gabby Hayes, Elisabeth Risdon, Raymond Hatton, Paul Fix, Audrey Long. Fast-paced, entertaining Western with Wayne a cowhand who becomes involved in affairs of rancher Raines. Also shown in computer-colored version.▼●▶

Tall Men, The (1955) **C-122m.** ** D: Raoul Walsh. Clark Gable, Jane Russell, Robert Ryan, Cameron Mitchell, Juan Garcia, Harry Shannon, Emile Meyer, Mae Marsh. Large-scale Western with Gable and Mitchell as ex-Rebels who sign on for Ryan's cattle drive, and in short order all three are fighting Indians, blizzards, and each other (over Russell, of course). Pretty dull. CinemaScope.▼▶

Tall Story (1960) **91m.** **½ D: Joshua Logan. Anthony Perkins, Jane Fonda, Ray Walston, Marc Connelly, Anne Jackson, Murray Hamilton, Elizabeth Patterson, Bob Wright, Bart Burns, Gary Lockwood. Fast-moving froth about man-hungry coed Fonda (in film debut) falling in love with college basketball star Perkins. Based on Howard Lindsay–Russel Crouse play.▼●

Tall T, The (1957) **C-78m.** *** D: Budd Boetticher. Randolph Scott, Richard Boone, Maureen O'Sullivan, Henry Silva, Skip Homeier, John Hubbard, Arthur Hunnicutt. Scott becomes involved with kidnapped O'Sullivan, and tries to undermine unity of outlaw gang holding them prisoner. Solid Western all the way, scripted by Burt Kennedy from an Elmore Leonard story.▼▶

Tall Tale (1995) **C-96m.** ** D: Jeremiah Chechik. Patrick Swayze, Oliver Platt, Roger Aaron Brown, Nick Stahl, Scott Glenn, Stephen Lang, Jared Harris, Catherine O'Hara, Moira Harris, Joseph Grifasi, John P. Ryan, Scott Wilson. Misfired revisionist take on tall-tale heroes Pecos Bill, Paul Bunyan, John Henry, and Calamity Jane, who (in an extended dream sequence) enter the life of an unhappy young boy whose farmer father is being threatened by an evil land developer. Follows a *Wizard of Oz* story structure, but its dark, neurotic tone obliterates the occasional moments of wonder. O'Hara has little more than a cameo as Calamity Jane; Burgess

Meredith and William H. Macy appear unbilled. Panavision. [PG]▼●▶

Tall Target, The (1951) **78m.** *** D: Anthony Mann. Dick Powell, Paula Raymond, Adolphe Menjou, Marshall Thompson, Ruby Dee, Will Geer, Leif Erickson. Gripping film noir–ish suspense as detective Powell follows tip that Abraham Lincoln is going to be assassinated during 1861 train ride. Interestingly, Powell's character is named John Kennedy!▶

Tamango (1957-French) **C-98m.** *** D: John Berry. Dorothy Dandridge, Curt Jurgens, Jean Servais, Roger Hanin, Guy Mairesse, Alex Cressan. Stirring historical drama in which newly enslaved black African Cressan stirs revolt while being transported to Cuba aboard a slave ship. Dandridge is excellent in the complex role of a slave who is ship captain Jurgens' mistress. Way ahead of its time, and ripe for rediscovery. Based on a novelette by Prosper Merimée. CinemaScope.▼

Tamara Drewe (2010-British) **C-111m.** *** D: Stephen Frears. Gemma Arterton, Roger Allam, Bill Camp, Dominic Cooper, Luke Evans, Tamsin Greig, Jessica Barden, Charlotte Christie. Young woman returns to her hometown in Dorset, having had a notable nose job, intending to sell her family home; instead, she inspires a chain reaction of sexual adventures. Her youthful boyfriend is now a handyman with lingering feelings for her. A couple uses their B&B as a writers' retreat, and the lord of the manor (a self-absorbed, best-selling author) has eyes for her as well. Then there are two mischievous teenage girls who feel left out. . . . Constantly surprising lark of a film is based on Posy Simmonds' graphic novel, which in turn was inspired by Thomas Hardy's *Far From the Madding Crowd*. Well cast and filmed on a beautiful location. HD Widescreen. [R]▶

Tamarind Seed, The (1974) **C-123m.** *** D: Blake Edwards. Julie Andrews, Omar Sharif, Anthony Quayle, Daniel O'Herlihy, Sylvia Sims, Oscar Homolka. Well-mounted espionage/romance story set in London, Paris, and Barbados; shows what a capable director can do with sappy material. Panavision. [PG]▼

Taming of the Shrew, The (1967-U.S.-Italian) **C-126m.** ***½ D: Franco Zeffirelli. Elizabeth Taylor, Richard Burton, Vernon Dobtcheff, Michael Hordern, Natasha Pyne, Michael York, Cyril Cusack, Alan Webb, Victor Spinetti. Colorful version of Shakespeare's romp is well served by Richard and Elizabeth, good supporting cast, lovely photography, and fine musical score by Nino Rota. Shakespeare purists may object, but Zeffirelli has succeeded in making a film instead of a photographed stage play. Scripted by Suso Cecchi d'Amico, Paul Dehn, and Zeffirelli. Panavision. ▼●▶

T.A.M.I. Show, The (1964) **100m.** ***
D: Steve Binder. The Rolling Stones, James Brown, Chuck Berry, Marvin Gaye, The Supremes, Jan and Dean, Gerry & The Pacemakers, Smokey Robinson & The Miracles, Lesley Gore, Billy J. Kramer & The Dakotas. Historic rock and r&b concert at the Santa Monica Civic Auditorium was covered by television cameras and kinescoped onto film by whiz-kid Binder. Invaluable document of music history, with great early Mick Jagger and electrifying footwork by Brown. (Two of those go-go dancers are Teri Garr and Toni Basil!) Originally 113m., with Beach Boys sequence that was later cut (although they're still visible in the finale). Title stands for Teenage Awards Music International. Followed by THE BIG T.N.T. SHOW; see also THAT WAS ROCK.▼❶

Tam Lin SEE: **Ballad of Tam Lin, The**
Tammy and the Bachelor (1957) **C-89m.** *** D: Joseph Pevney. Debbie Reynolds, Walter Brennan, Leslie Nielsen, Mala Powers, Fay Wray, Sidney Blackmer, Mildred Natwick, Louise Beavers. Unpretentious if cutesy romantic corn of country girl Reynolds falling in love with pilot Nielsen whom she's nursed back to health after plane crash. Followed by two sequels and a TV series. CinemaScope.▼❶

Tammy and the Doctor (1963) **C-88m.** **½ D: Harry Keller. Sandra Dee, Peter Fonda, Macdonald Carey, Beulah Bondi, Margaret Lindsay, Reginald Owen, Adam West. Sugary fluff involving homespun Tammy (Dee) courted by a doctor (Fonda, in his film debut); supporting cast adds touching cameos.▼❶

Tammy and the Millionaire (1967) **C-87m.** ** D: Sidney Miller, Ezra Stone, Leslie Goodwins. Debbie Watson, Frank McGrath, Denver Pyle, George Furth, Donald Woods, Dorothy Green. Four episodes of the TV series spliced into low-grade feature, diluting the fuzzy folksy charm of backwoods girl trying to better the world.

Tammy Tell Me True (1961) **C-97m.** ** D: Harry Keller. Sandra Dee, John Gavin, Virginia Grey, Beulah Bondi, Cecil Kellaway, Edgar Buchanan. Tired romance of girl coming to college for first time, makes name for herself by helping dean of women. Script and acting very uneven.❶

Tampopo (1986-Japanese) **C-114m.** ***½ D: Juzo Itami. Ken Watanabe, Tsutomu Yamazaki, Nobuko Miyamoto, Koji Yakusho. Funny, original comedy-satire about one of everybody's favorite subjects: food. The scenario, which unravels as a series of vignettes, concerns a truck driver who helps a widow make her noodle shop a viable business. A clever, irreverent delight.▼❶

T&A Academy SEE: **H.O.T.S.**
Tangled (2010) **C-100m.** ***½ D: Byron Howard, Nathan Greno. Voices of Mandy Moore, Zachary Levi, Donna Murphy, Ron Perlman, Jeffrey Tambor, Brad Garrett, M. C. Gainey, Paul F. Tompkins, Richard Kiel. Bewitching Disney animated musical reinvention of the Rapunzel fairy tale with a feisty heroine, a selfish captor who poses as her mother, and a cocky hero named Flynn Rider who unwittingly comes to her rescue. Manages to layer hip, contemporary humor and well-staged action scenes onto the classic story without sacrificing sincerity or rooting interest, recalling the best Disney animated features of yore. Sparked by two great supporting characters who never utter a word: an expressive horse named Maximus and Rapunzel's chameleon friend Pascal. Screenplay by Dan Fogelman; songs by Alan Menken and Glenn Slater. 3-D. [PG] ❶

Tango (1998-Argentinian-Spanish) **C-114m.** *** D: Carlos Saura. Miguel Angel Solà, Cecilia Narova, Mia Maestro, Juan Carlos Copes, Julio Bocca, Juan Luis Galiardo. Mesmerizing film, not unlike Saura's earlier CARMEN, in which the planning of a performance blurs the line between drama and real life. A middle-aged choreographer plans an ambitious tango piece, which (to the dismay of his backers) will also trace the recent history of Argentina. He also becomes involved with his leading dancer, until now the girlfriend of his principal backer. Long, but full of incredible moments and superlative dance numbers; sinuously photographed by Vittorio Storaro. Univision. [PG-13]▼❶

Tango & Cash (1989) **C-98m.** ** D: Andrei Konchalovsky. Sylvester Stallone, Kurt Russell, Teri Hatcher, Jack Palance, Brion James, James Hong, Marc Alaimo. Rumored $55 million budget must have gone for male hairstyling in congenitally derivative narc caper about two competitive cops who take on Mr. Big. Surprisingly tolerable, though, with a nifty prison break sequence and a pleasingly relaxed Stallone. Panavision. [R]▼❶

Tango Bar (1988-Puerto Rican-Argentinian) **C-90m.** *** D: Marcos Zurinaga. Raul Julia, Valeria Lynch, Ruben Juarez. Perceptive, entertaining "political musical" about a tango dancer who left Argentina when the military coup occurred and is now reunited with her longtime partner Julia after ten years in exile. Serves as both an anthology of the tango and a tale of Argentina's recent political history. Crammed with clips of film and TV personalities, from Fred Astaire to Fred Flintstone, doing the tango.▼

Tango Lesson, The (1997-U.S.-French-Argentinean) **C/B&W-101m.** *** D: Sally Potter. Sally Potter, Pablo Veron, Carlos Copello, Olga Besio, Caroline Iotti, Gustavo Naveira. A middle-aged British filmmaker named Sally (played by Potter) promises to cast in a movie a distinguished

Argentinean tango dancer named Pablo (Veron, who is the same) if he only will give her dance lessons. Film charts their evolving relationship. Striking, provocative (not to mention highly risky and deeply personal) film which blends fiction and reality. Nicely photographed (mostly in black-and-white) by Robby Müller. [PG]▼

Tank (1984) C-113m. ** D: Marvin Chomsky. James Garner, G.D. Spradlin, C. Thomas Howell, Shirley Jones, Jenilee Harrison, James Cromwell, Dorian Harewood. One-dimensional rehash of SUPPOSE THEY GAVE A WAR AND NOBODY CAME? turns that film's shades of gray into simplistic good-guy/bad-guy story. Teenage son of career military man is wrongfully jailed by vindictive redneck sheriff; Dad goes to rescue him with the help of his own Sherman tank. Odd to find Garner in such a cornball movie. [PG]▼●)

Tank Girl (1995) C-104m. ** D: Rachel Talalay. Lori Petty, Ice-T, Naomi Watts, Don Harvey, Jeff Kober, Reg E. Cathey, Scott Coffey, Malcolm McDowell, Ann Cusack, Brian Wimmer, Iggy Pop, James Hong. In the waterless future of 2033, tough, smart-mouthed survivor Petty joins forces with mutated kangaroos to combat evil McDowell, who schemes to corner the world's water. Aggressively trendy, self-consciously hip, with animated interludes and attitude to spare, this might have worked had it been well directed—but it's not. Petty is a lot of fun, though. Based on the British comic book. Super 35. [R]▼●

Tao of Steve, The (2000) C-90m. *** D: Jenniphr Goodman. Donal Logue, Greer Goodman, Kimo Wills, Ayelet Kaznelson, David Aaron Baker, Nina Jaroslaw. Likable comedy about layabout Dex (Logue), a self-styled ladies' man who follows the Tao of Steve, a code for being cool. Having the knack of bedding women at will, Dex is flustered when he actually falls in love with one. Smart and original, anchored by Logue's engaging performance. Leading lady Goodman cowrote the screenplay with director Goodman, who's also her sister, and Duncan North, the model for Dex. [R]▼)

Tap (1989) C-110m. *** D: Nick Castle. Gregory Hines, Suzzanne Douglas, Sammy Davis, Jr., Savion Glover, Joe Morton, Dick Anthony Williams, Terrence McNally, Sandman Sims, Bunny Briggs, Steve Condos, Jimmy Slyde, Pat Rico, Arthur Duncan, Harold Nicholas, Etta James. Slight, old-fashioned but engaging story of a man who shuns his tap-dancing heritage for the good life and easy money he can make pulling jewel robberies . . . until the call of the tap is just too strong. A loving tribute to tap, with some clever contemporary touches by writer-director Castle (whose same-named

father was a top choreographer). Hines has never been better; Davis is a standout as Little Mo (in his final feature film), and the challenge dance with old-time hoofers is a special treat. [PG-13]▼●)

Tape (2001) C-86m. *** D: Richard Linklater. Ethan Hawke, Uma Thurman, Robert Sean Leonard. Highly effective three-character, one-set piece takes place in a dingy hotel room, and focuses on the interaction of a hyper, ill-mannered slacker–drug dealer (Hawke), his old school friend (Leonard), who has become a filmmaker, and a woman they once knew but have not seen in years (Thurman). Scripted by Stephen Belber, based on his play, and shot on digital video. [R] ▼)

Tapeheads (1988) C-97m. ** D: Bill Fishman. John Cusack, Tim Robbins, Doug McClure, Connie Stevens, Clu Gulager, Mary Crosby, Katy Boyer, Lyle Alzado, Jessica Walter, Susan Tyrrell, Junior Walker, Sam Moore. Energetic but pretentious and silly account of Cusack and Robbins' escapades and adventures as they try to make it in the L.A. music world. Too clever for its own good. Robbins coscripted and wrote the song "Repave America," which later turned up in his film BOB ROBERTS. [R]▼●)

Taps (1981) C-126m. **½ D: Harold Becker. Timothy Hutton, George C. Scott, Ronny Cox, Sean Penn, Tom Cruise, Brendan Ward. Hutton leads fellow students in armed takeover of their military academy, hoping their "clout" will keep it from being torn down. Earnest performances help carry this film, which plays all its cards too soon, leaving a lot of dead space before its predictable outcome. Penn's film debut. [PG]▼)

Tarantula (1955) 80m. *** D: Jack Arnold. John Agar, Mara Corday, Leo G. Carroll, Nestor Paiva, Ross Elliott, Eddie Parker. Scientist Carroll's new growth formula works a little *too* well, and pretty soon there's a humongous spider chewing up the countryside. One of the best giant-insect films, with fast pacing, convincing special effects, and interesting subplot detailing formula's effect on humans. That's Clint Eastwood as the jet squadron leader in final sequence.▼●)

Taras Bulba (1962) C-122m. **½ D: J. Lee Thompson. Tony Curtis, Yul Brynner, Christine Kaufmann, Sam Wanamaker, George Macready. Cardboard costumer of 16th-century Ukraine, centering on Cossack life and fighting. Nice photography (on location in Argentina) by Joe MacDonald and fine musical score by Franz Waxman. The Gogol novel was previously filmed in 1936 in France (TARASS BOULBA) and in 1939 in England (THE REBEL SON). Remade in Russia in 2009. Panavision.▼●)

Target (1985) C-117m. ** D: Arthur Penn. Gene Hackman, Matt Dillon, Gayle Hunnicutt, Victoria Fyodorova, Josef Sommer, Guy Boyd, Herbert Berghof. Ordinary guy and his teenage son are suddenly plunged into world of international intrigue when wife/mom is kidnapped while vacationing in Paris. Some good action scenes help, but story is so farfetched, key scenes so badly written, and film so overlong that it has to count as a misfire. Reteaming of Hackman and director Penn certainly promised better. [R]▼●)

Target (1995-Indian) **C-122m.** ******* D: Sandip Ray. Om Puri, Mohan Agashe, Anian Srivastava, Baroon Champa Chakravarty. Intimate story of working-class life in India, directed by the son of Satyajit Ray from his late father's screenplay. A *gangato,* a hunter of the lowest caste (Puri), is hired by a rich and nasty landowner (Agashe) to lead his next safari. The hunter has to live with the landowner's oppressed peasants, and before long he rebels. Stunning countryside locations shot by Barun Raha, who worked on the elder Ray's last three films.

Target Earth (1954) **75m.** ****½** D: Sherman Rose. Richard Denning, Virginia Grey, Kathleen Crowley, Richard Reeves, Whit Bissell, Robert Roark, Steve Pendleton. People in deserted city trapped by invading robot force. Competently acted movie starts off beautifully but bogs down too soon. ▼●)

Target: Embassy SEE: **Embassy**

Target: Harry (1969) **C-81m.** ***½** D: Henry Neill (Roger Corman). Vic Morrow, Suzanne Pleshette, Victor Buono, Cesar Romero, Stanley Holloway, Charlotte Rampling, Michael Ansara, Ahna Capri. Humdrum redoing of THE MALTESE FALCON, with the three stars mirroring Bogart, Astor, and Greenstreet. Originally shot for TV. Aka HOW TO MAKE IT. [R]

Target of an Assassin (1976-South African) **C-102m.** ****** D: Peter Collinson. Anthony Quinn, John Phillip Law, Simon Sabela, Marius Weyers, Sandra Prinsloo. Fairish thriller story about two men who conspire against black African leader—one, a paid assassin, the other a desperate down-and-outer who kidnaps him for ransom. Original title: TIGERS DON'T CRY; aka THE LONG SHOT, AFRICAN RAGE, and FATAL ASSASSIN. [PG]▼)

Targets (1968) **C-90m.** *****½** D: Peter Bogdanovich. Boris Karloff, Tim O'Kelly, Nancy Hsueh, James Brown, Sandy Baron, Arthur Peterson, Peter Bogdanovich. Karloff (as more or less himself) intends to retire, claiming his films can't compete with the horrors of everyday life; meanwhile, O'Kelly proves it by going out and shooting everybody in sight. Bogdanovich's first feature is incredibly suspenseful, with sweat-inducing climax at drive-in theatre; excellent photography by Laszlo Kovacs. Some prints still have brief gun-control pro-

logue, which was added after Robert Kennedy's assassination. That's Mike Farrell as victim in phone booth. [R]▼)

Tarnation (2004) **C-88m.** ****½** D: Jonathan Caouette. Alternately fascinating, frustrating, and uncomfortable to watch, this nakedly personal cinematic diary of a young gay filmmaker's challenge living with a mentally ill mother documents his entire life from photos, Super 8 films, answering-machine messages, clippings, and scraps to piece together the extraordinary puzzle of a difficult youth. Caouette's eventual redemption makes the journey worthwhile, though it's still more a therapy session than a documentary. Primitively edited using Apple computer's iMovie program. Caouette claims the film was made for $218, but you could have fooled us; it looks as if it could have cost twice that! (In truth, many thousands of dollars in music and clip clearances were required to release the movie.) ▼)

Tarnished Angels, The (1958) **91m.** *****½** D: Douglas Sirk. Rock Hudson, Dorothy Malone, Robert Stack, Jack Carson, Robert Middleton, Troy Donahue, William Schallert. Compelling adaptation of William Faulkner's fatalistic drama *Pylon,* set in 1930s, with Hudson as newspaperman drawn to barnstorming pilot Stack—his curious life-style and ethics, his put-upon wife, and his frustrated mechanic. CinemaScope. ▼)

Tartars, The (1961-Italian) **C-83m.** ****** D: Richard Thorpe. Orson Welles, Victor Mature, Folco Lulli, Liana Orfei. Welles' performance as Burundai, head of Tartar invasion of Volga River, plus appearance of Mature, are only distinguishing features of otherwise routine spectacle. Totalscope.

Tarzan series SEE: *Leonard Maltin's Classic Movie Guide*

Tarzan (1999) **C-88m.** ******* D: Kevin Lima, Chris Buck. Voices of Tony Goldwyn, Minnie Driver, Glenn Close, Rosie O'Donnell, Brian Blessed, Nigel Hawthorne, Lance Henriksen, Wayne Knight. Vibrant animated Disney take on Edgar Rice Burroughs' classic character, with brilliant staging, terrific songs (by Phil Collins), and likable characters (especially Jane, colorfully and amusingly voiced by Driver). Storyline, involving a greedy, hot-headed hunter, almost seems too conventional—and predictable—for all the visual innovations and superior efforts that surround it. Oscar winner for Best Song, "You'll Be in My Heart." Followed by a direct-to-video sequel and a TV series. Later a Broadway musical. [G]▼)

Tarzan and His Mate (1934) **105m.** *****½** D: Cedric Gibbons, Jack Conway. Johnny Weissmuller, Maureen O'Sullivan, Neil Hamilton, Paul Cavanagh, Forrester Harvey. Jane's jilted fiance (Hamilton) returns to the jungle with a rapacious ivory poacher (Cavanagh) and tries to get Tarzan to lead them to the elephant graveyard, but the native couple is having too much fun swinging. Opulent, action-packed entry codirected by MGM's famed art director Gibbons, and notable for pre-Code sexual candor and a distinct lack of clothes. Beware 95m. prints. ▼●◗

Tarzan and the Amazons (1945) **76m.** **½ D: Kurt Neumann. Johnny Weissmuller, Brenda Joyce, Johnny Sheffield, Henry Stephenson, Maria Ouspenskaya, Barton MacLane. Archeologists seeking to plunder Amazon treasures have to deal with Tarzan first in this amusing nonsense highlighted by the diminutive Ouspenskaya as the Amazon Queen! ◗

Tarzan and the Great River (1967) **C-99m.** *½ D: Robert Day. Mike Henry, Jan Murray, Manuel Padilla, Jr., Diana Millay, Rafer Johnson. Childish entry about an Amazonian despot, although borscht-belt comedian Murray is good for a few (unintentional) laughs. Location filming in South America adds little. Panavision. ◗

Tarzan and the Green Goddess (1938) **72m.** *½ D: Edward Kull. Herman Brix (Bruce Bennett), Ula Holt, Frank Baker, Don Castello, Lewis Sargent. More juvenile jungle escapades, with an educated Ape Man. Derived from 1935's THE NEW ADVENTURES OF TARZAN serial, produced by Edgar Rice Burroughs' own company and filmed on location in Guatemala. Contains footage not used in serial. ▼◗

Tarzan and the Huntress (1947) **72m.** ** D: Kurt Neumann. Johnny Weissmuller, Brenda Joyce, Johnny Sheffield, Patricia Morison, Barton MacLane. Familiar bungle in the jungle has Tarzan fighting a zoologist (Morison) who's trying to make off with a menagerie. Weissmuller was tired by this time, and so were the plots. ◗

Tarzan and the Jungle Boy (1968) **C-99m.** *½ D: Robert Day. Mike Henry, Alizia Gur, Ronald Gans, Rafer Johnson, Ed Johnson, Steven Bond. A tedious search for the son of a drowned geologist, though Henry isn't bad as the Ape Man. Panavision. ◗

Tarzan and the Leopard Woman (1946) **72m.** ** D: Kurt Neumann. Johnny Weissmuller, Brenda Joyce, Johnny Sheffield, Acquanetta, Edgar Barrier, Tommy Cook. Tarzan and Boy take on a murder cult, and almost pay with their lives. The series was becoming increasingly silly, though it's still fun by Saturday matinee standards. ◗

Tarzan and the Lost City (1998-Australian-U.S.-German) **C-105m.** *½ D: Carl Schenkel. Casper Van Dien, Jane March, Steven Waddington, Winston Ntshona, Rapulana Seiphemo, Ian Roberts. Tarzan returns to Africa on eve of his wedding to Jane; she follows, and together they fight off mercenaries trying to plunder the "mythic city" of Opar. Lousy film—even by jungle

adventure standards. Van Dien equates jaw-clenching with acting, and he must be the shortest Lord of the Apes on record. Oddly, the producer of this also made the classy GREYSTOKE. Super 35. [PG] ▼●◗

Tarzan and the Lost Safari (1957-British) **C-84m.** ** D: H. Bruce Humberstone. Gordon Scott, Yolande Donlan, Robert Beatty, Betta St. John, Wilfrid Hyde-White, George Couloris. Color and widescreen spruce up this entry about the passengers of a plane that crashes in the jungle, who are pursued by savage Oparians. But Tarzan still speaks in monosyllables, and the story is pretty slow going. RKO-Scope. ◗

Tarzan and the Mermaids (1948) **68m.** **½ D: Robert Florey. Johnny Weissmuller, Brenda Joyce, Linda Christian, John Lanenz, George Zucco, Fernando Wagner. Tarzan comes to the aid of a native (stunning Christian) who's being forced to wed a phony island "God" (Wagner) by evil high priest Zucco. Outlandish, often campy outing filmed in Mexico. Weissmuller hung up his loincloth after this. ◗

Tarzan and the She-Devil (1953) **76m.** *½ D: Kurt Neumann. Lex Barker, Joyce MacKenzie, Raymond Burr, Monique Van Vooren, Tom Conway. Boring hokum about ivory poachers led by seductive Van Vooren. Barker's last appearance as Tarzan. Burr is an exceptionally good heavy. ◗

Tarzan and the Slave Girl (1950) **74m.** ** D: Lee Sholem. Lex Barker, Vanessa Brown, Robert Alda, Hurd Hatfield, Arthur Shields, Anthony Caruso, Denise Darcel. When a tribe of lion worshippers kidnaps Jane (Brown) and alluring half-breed Darcel, it's Tarzan, Cheetah, and friends to the rescue. ◗

Tarzan and the Trappers (1958) **74m.** *½ D: Charles Haas, Sandy Howard. Gordon Scott, Eve Brent, Rickie Sorensen, Leslie Bradley. Cheaply made hokum about evil white hunters on an expedition to find a lost city filled with treasure. Edited together from three episodes of a Tarzan TV series that never got off the ground. ▼◗

Tarzan and the Valley of Gold (1966) **C-90m.** **½ D: Robert Day. Mike Henry, David Opatoshu, Manuel Padilla, Jr., Nancy Kovack, Don Megowan. Ex-football star Henry takes over the loincloth (after doffing his suit and tie!) in a hunt for kidnapers and jewel thieves. This Tarzan-for-the-60's is pretty good, if you can accept the Ape Man as a jungle James Bond. Excellent location filming in Mexico. Panavision. ◗

Tarzan Escapes (1936) **89m.** *** D: Richard Thorpe. Johnny Weissmuller, Maureen O'Sullivan, John Buckler, Benita Hume, William Henry, Herbert Mundin. Graphically violent (for its time), and energetically directed, this entertaining entry has Tarzan captured by a hunter who wants to put him on exhibition in England. This film was completely reshot and reworked when the original version proved too potent and blood-curdling for preview audiences; as a result there are some plot holes in what might have been the best Tarzan movie of all.▼●◗

Tarzan Finds a Son! (1939) 90m. *** D: Richard Thorpe. Johnny Weissmuller, Maureen O'Sullivan, Johnny Sheffield, Ian Hunter, Frieda Inescort, Laraine Day, Henry Wilcoxon. The jungle lovers find a child whose parents were killed in a plane crash and fight his greedy relatives to adopt him in this diverting entry. This was to be O'Sullivan's final appearance as Jane, but the end was reshot so she could return (in TARZAN'S SECRET TREASURE).▼●◗

Tarzan Goes to India (1962-British) C-86m. **½ D: John Guillermin. Jock Mahoney, Mark Dana, Simi, Leo Gordon, Jai. At the request of a dying maharajah, Tarzan tries to save a herd of elephants imperiled by the construction of a dam. Location shooting helps. CinemaScope.◗

Tarzan of the Apes (1918) 55m. **½ D: Scott Sidney. Elmo Lincoln, Enid Markey, True Boardman, Kathleen Kirkham, Gordon Griffith. The very first Tarzan film is a surprisingly watchable and straightforward telling of the Greystoke tale, though Lincoln looks like he's about 50 years old, with a beer belly to boot.▼◗

Tarzan's Deadly Silence (1970) C-99m. *½ D: Robert L. Friend, Lawrence Dobkin. Ron Ely, Manuel Padilla, Jr., Jock Mahoney, Woody Strode, Gregorio Acosta. A maniacal soldier plans to capture an African village with his private army; a two-part TV episode released as a feature. [G]

Tarzan's Desert Mystery (1943) 70m. **½ D: William Thiele. Johnny Weissmuller, Nancy Kelly, Johnny Sheffield, Otto Kruger, Joseph Sawyer, Lloyd Corrigan, Robert Lowery. Tarzan vs. Nazis, take two, with some evil Arabs and prehistoric creatures (including a giant spider) thrown in for good measure.◗

Tarzan's Fight for Life (1958) C-86m. ** D: H. Bruce Humberstone. Gordon Scott, Eve Brent, Rickie Sorensen, Jil Jarmyn, James Edwards, Woody Strode. The jungle do-gooder helps a medic fight superstitious natives and a conniving witch doctor. Cheesy series entry with the cast stomping around a studio jungle set.◗

Tarzan's Greatest Adventure (1959-British) C-88m. *** D: John Guillermin. Gordon Scott, Anthony Quayle, Sara Shane, Niall MacGinnis, Scilla Gabel, Sean Connery. Honorable attempt to upgrade the series' quality, with Tarzan on the trail of diamond-hunting scoundrels (including a young Connery). A superior action yarn shot on location in Africa, more adult than most of its predecessors.

Tarzan has a much expanded vocabulary in this one.

Tarzan's Hidden Jungle (1955) 73m. ** D: Harold Schuster. Gordon Scott, Vera Miles, Peter Van Eyck, Jack Elam, Rex Ingram. Scott's debut as Tarzan is a competent, if unexciting, outing focusing on his battle with evil hunter Elam who tries to butcher half the animal kingdom.◗

Tarzan's Jungle Rebellion (1970) C-92m. *½ D: William Witney. Ron Ely, Manuel Padilla, Jr., Ulla Stromstedt, Sam Jaffe, William Marshall, Lloyd Haynes. Compilation of a two-part episode from the NBC TV series is substandard in all departments. [G]

Tarzan's Magic Fountain (1949) 73m. **½ D: Lee Sholem. Lex Barker, Brenda Joyce, Evelyn Ankers, Albert Dekker, Alan Napier, Charles Drake, Henry Brandon. Barker's first series entry, and one of his most endurable, as Tarzan finds a secret valley where nobody ages—unless they leave. (Sound a bit like LOST HORIZON?) Too bad the rest of the Barker films weren't as good. Elmo Lincoln, the screen's first Tarzan, has a bit part.◗

Tarzan's New York Adventure (1942) 72m. **½ D: Richard Thorpe. Johnny Weissmuller, Maureen O'Sullivan, Johnny Sheffield, Virginia Grey, Charles Bickford, Paul Kelly, Russell Hicks, Chill Wills. When Boy is snatched from the jungle by nasty circus owners, Tarzan swings into action across the seas and over the Brooklyn Bridge to retrieve him. Seems pretty original until you realize that KING KONG was made a decade earlier! Still, an amusing entry; Tarzan's first encounter with indoor plumbing is truly memorable. O'Sullivan's final appearance in the series. ▼●◗

Tarzan's Peril (1951) 79m. **½ D: Byron Haskin. Lex Barker, Virginia Huston, George Macready, Douglas Fowley, Dorothy Dandridge, Alan Napier. White gunrunners out to get Tarzan try to stir up trouble between warring tribes in this fairly respectable entry with an interesting supporting cast. Dandridge is excellent, if wasted in a small role.◗

Tarzan's Revenge (1938) 70m. ** D: D. Ross Lederman. Glenn Morris, Eleanor Holm, George Barbier, C. Henry Gordon, Hedda Hopper, George Meeker. Olympic decathlon champ Morris cavorts capably enough in this adventure about an evil African ruler who covets perky Holm (a champion swimmer herself). No other Tarzan film had the Ape Man off screen for such long stretches, however.▼◗

Tarzan's Savage Fury (1952) 80m. ** D: Cyril Endfield. Lex Barker, Dorothy Hart, Patric Knowles, Charles Korvin, Tommy Carlton. Slackly handled entry about diamond thieves who trick Tarzan into being their guide.◗

Tarzan's Secret Treasure (1941) 81m. **½ D: Richard Thorpe. Johnny Weissmuller, Maureen O'Sullivan, Johnny Sheffield, Reginald Owen, Barry Fitzgerald, Tom Conway. Melodramatic entry about greedy gold seekers who try to dupe Tarzan into helping them. Tarzan and Jane's treehouse has become pretty elaborate by now.▼●▶

Tarzan's Three Challenges (1963) C-92m. **½ D: Robert Day. Jock Mahoney, Woody Strode, Ricky Der, Tsuruko Kobayashi, Earl Cameron. Tarzan protects a young heir to the throne in Thailand from his malevolent uncle in this picturesque entry that includes a wicked machete fight. The athletic Mahoney became deathly ill while filming in India—which is all too obvious from his dramatic weight loss during the course of the picture. Dyaliscope.▶

Tarzan the Ape Man (1932) 99m. *** D: W. S. Van Dyke. Johnny Weissmuller, Maureen O'Sullivan, C. Aubrey Smith, Neil Hamilton, Doris Lloyd. British gentry meets jungle savagery when the daughter of an English hunter is captured by Tarzan and decides she prefers his primal charms to those of her upper-crust fiancé. The original Weissmuller-MGM *Tarzan* entry is a little starchy, but still holds up thanks to a plush production and vivid atmosphere (with jungle footage provided by TRADER HORN). Also shown in a computer-colored version.▼●▶

Tarzan, the Ape Man (1959) C-82m. BOMB D: Joseph Newman. Denny Miller, Joanna Barnes, Cesare Danova, Robert Douglas, Thomas Yangha. Take one blond UCLA basketball star (Miller), the production values of a pep rally, steal Johnny Weissmuller's famous yell and (tinted) footage of him swinging through the trees, add a pseudo African jazz score by Shorty Rogers, and you get a cheesy, inept effort by MGM to reuse safari footage from KING SOLOMON'S MINES for the umpteenth time.

Tarzan, the Ape Man (1981) C-112m. BOMB D: John Derek. Bo Derek, Richard Harris, Miles O'Keeffe, John Phillip Law, Wilfrid Hyde-White. Deranged "remake" of original Tarzan film lacks action, humor, and charm—and nearly forced editors of this book to devise a rating lower than BOMB. Forget about Weissmuller comparisons: O'Keeffe makes *Elmo Lincoln* look like Edwin Booth. [R]▼●▶

Tarzan the Fearless (1933) 85m. *½ D: Robert Hill. Buster Crabbe, Jacqueline Wells (Julie Bishop), E. Alyn Warren, Edward Woods, Philo McCullough, Matthew Betz, Frank Lackteen, Mischa Auer. Feature version of a crude serial about a scientific expedition to find the lost city of Zar. Crabbe's Tarzan is even more tightlipped than Weissmuller's.▼▶

Tarzan the Magnificent (1960-British)

C-88m. *** D: Robert Day. Gordon Scott, Jock Mahoney, Betta St. John, John Carradine, Alexandra Stewart, Lionel Jeffries, Earl Cameron. Tarzan captures a murderer and faces numerous perils trying to escort him to the police through the jungle. Similarly mature follow-up to TARZAN'S GREATEST ADVENTURE, with a strong supporting cast. Ironically, villain Mahoney would take over the lead role from Scott in the next entry.▶

Tarzan Triumphs (1943) 78m. *** D: William Thiele. Johnny Weissmuller, Frances Gifford, Johnny Sheffield, Stanley Ridges, Sig Ruman. First of the series made by RKO features stunning Gifford (who earlier starred as Edgar Rice Burroughs' JUNGLE GIRL in a Republic serial) as the princess of a lost city invaded by Nazi paratroopers. WW2 propaganda all the way, with Tarzan an incongruous participant, but still an entertaining and energetic programmer. Cheetah's curtain-closing bit with the Nazis' short-wave radio is not to be missed.▶

Task Force (1949) 116m. **½ D: Delmer Daves. Gary Cooper, Jane Wyatt, Wayne Morris, Walter Brennan, Julie London, Bruce Bennett, Stanley Ridges, Jack Holt. Well-made but unremarkable story of a Naval officer's career, tracing aircraft carrier development. Originally shown with some scenes in color.▼▶

Taste of Cherry (1997-Iranian) C-98m. ***½ D: Abbas Kiarostami. Homayon Ershadi, Abdolrahman Bagheri, Afshin Khorshid Bakhtiari, Safar Ali Moradi. Fascinating film about a brooding man who rides around Tehran in a Range Rover trying to find someone who will accept a generous fee to bury him after he commits suicide. The man's encounters with several diverse candidates flesh out his haunting and original story, which disappoints only at the very end. A contemplation of humanity quite unlike any other captured on film. Written by the director. [PG]▼▶

Taste of Fear SEE: **Scream of Fear**

Taste of Honey, A (1961-British) 100m. ***½ D: Tony Richardson. Rita Tushingham, Robert Stephens, Dora Bryan, Murray Melvin, Paul Danquah. Homely young girl who has affair with black sailor and becomes pregnant is cared for by homosexual friend. Shelagh Delaney's London and Broadway stage hit is poignant and uncompromising film with fine, sensitive performances. Screenplay by Delaney and Richardson.▼

Taste of Others, The (2000-French) C-112m. *** D: Agnes Jaoui. Jean-Pierre Bacri, Anne Alvaro, Agnes Jaoui, Gerard Lanvin, Christiane Millet, Brigitte Catillon, Alain Chabat. Sharply observed romantic comedy that offers food for thought on the passions and yearnings of contemporary middle-aged men and women, spotlighting a wealthy, ill-mannered—and married—businessman (Bacri) who is drawn to a vain, attractive actress (Alvaro); a secondary relationship involves the businessman's bodyguard (Lanvin) and a barmaid (Jaoui). Bacri and Jaoui scripted; they're married in real life. Super 35. ▼◗

Taste the Blood of Dracula (1970-British) C-95m. **½ D: Peter Sasdy. Christopher Lee, Geoffrey Keen, Gwen Watford, Linda Hayden, Roy Kinnear, Ralph Bates. Fourth in Hammer series (after DRACULA HAS RISEN FROM THE GRAVE) with Lee as famed vampire out to avenge death of Black Magic wizard by affluent thrill seekers in Victorian England. Not bad, but what was point of having Dracula in film? Beginning and end best parts. Sequel: SCARS OF DRACULA. [PG] ▼◗

Tatie Danielle (1991-French) C-110m. *** D: Etienne Chatiliez. Tsilla Chelton, Catherine Jacob, Isabelle Nanty, Neige Dolsky, Eric Prat, Laurence Fevrier. Chelton plays an elderly, extremely unpleasant and manipulative widow who wreaks havoc on the people caring for her as she mourns the loss of her husband. Another delight from the director of LIFE IS A LONG QUIET RIVER, but this time the comedy is a good deal blacker. Renowned stage actress Chelton is wonderful as a woman so mean the movie's ads proclaimed her "the *real* Terminator." ▼●

Tattered Dress, The (1957) 93m. **½ D: Jack Arnold. Jeff Chandler, Jeanne Crain, Jack Carson, Gail Russell, George Tobias, Philip Reed. Slowly paced but watchable account of lawyer Chandler defending society man accused of murder; Crain is his sympathetic wife. CinemaScope.

Tattoo (1981) C-103m. *½ D: Bob Brooks. Bruce Dern, Maud Adams, Leonard Frey, Rikke Borge, John Getz, Peter Iachangelo. Mentally ill tattoo-artist Dern kidnaps fashion model Adams so he can use her body as a canvas. Improbable, sleazy melodrama; screenplay by Joyce Buñuel (Luis's daughter-in-law) from a story by director Brooks. [R] ▼

Taxi! (1932) 70m. **½ D: Roy Del Ruth. James Cagney, Loretta Young, George E. Stone, Dorothy Burgess, Guy Kibbee, Leila Bennett, Cotton Club Orchestra. Hokey but colorful Depression melodrama of warring N.Y.C. cab drivers, with Cagney fine as a hotheaded hack. Yes, that's George Raft as his dance-contest rival. Nothing can top Jimmy's opening bit in Yiddish!

Taxi (2004) C-97m. *½ D: Tim Story. Queen Latifah, Jimmy Fallon, Henry Simmons, Jennifer Esposito, Gisele Bündchen, Ann-Margret, Ana Cristina De Oliveira, Christian Kane, John Krasinski. Hotshot cabbie teams up with an incompetent hot-dog cop in this weak action-comedy. Latifah and

Fallon are strangers-turned-buddies out to catch a team of bank robbers (who happen to look like supermodels). Not a good showcase for the Queen or for former *Saturday Night Live* member Fallon. Produced by Luc Besson, based on the 1998 French film of the same name, which he wrote and coproduced. Extended version runs 112m. Super 35. [PG-13] ▼◗

Taxi Blues (1990-Russian-French) C-110m. ***½ D: Pavel Lounguine. Piotr Mamonov, Piotr Zaitchenko, Vladimir Kachpour, Natalia Koliakanova, Hal Singer. Controversial, laced-in-acid tragicomedy chronicling the relationship between a brutish, narrow-minded Moscow cabdriver and an alcoholic Jewish musician: characters who become symbols of the Old and New Russia. Lounguine deservedly earned the best director prize at the Cannes Film Festival for this important, provocative film. ▼◗

Taxi Driver (1976) C-113m. ** D: Martin Scorsese. Robert De Niro, Cybill Shepherd, Harvey Keitel, Peter Boyle, Jodie Foster, Albert Brooks, Leonard Harris, Joe Spinell, Martin Scorsese. To some, Scorsese and writer Paul Schrader's perception of hell—as a crazed taxi driver's vision of N.Y.C.—was brilliant. To us, this gory, cold-blooded story of sick man's lurid descent into violence is ugly and unredeeming. (It's undeniably influential to a generation of filmmakers; some scenes and images have become iconic.) Judge for yourself. Searing performances and Bernard Herrmann's final music score are among film's few virtues. [R] ▼◗

Taxing Woman, A (1987-Japanese) C-126m. ***½ D: Juzo Itami. Nobuko Miyamoto, Tsutomu Yamazaki. Disarming contemporary comedy about a tireless, single-minded investigator for the Japanese Revenue Service, and her confrontation with a hotshot businessman who thinks he knows all the angles when it comes to cheating the government. Somewhat overlong, but delightful, with a winning performance by Miyamoto (writer-director Itami's wife) in the lead. Followed by a sequel. ▼●◗

Taxing Woman's Return, A (1988-Japanese) C-127m. *** D: Juzo Itami. Nobuko Miyamoto, Rentaro Mikuni, Masahiko Tsugawa, Tetsuro Tamba, Toru Masuoka, Takeya Nakamura, Hosei Komatsu, Mihoko Shibata. Miyamoto "returns" as the dedicated tax investigator; here, she takes on a gaggle of industrialists, politicians, mobsters, and other assorted hypocrites who've conspired to grossly inflate Tokyo's real estate values. On-the-mark satire is as pointed and knowing as it is funny. ▼◗

Taxi to the Dark Side (2007) C-106m. ***½ D: Alex Gibney. Historically important, imperatively queasy documentary begins with the 2002 detention, torture, and death of an Afghanistan taxi driver in American custody at Bagram prison—despite scant evidence of his linkage to al-Qaeda or the Taliban (he was never, in fact, charged). From here, it's noted, there was a predictably scant leap to further prisoner abuses at Guantanamo Bay and Abu Ghraib that rocked the world. A wide array of interviewees includes guards, fellow prisoners, reporters, Bush administration personnel, and more. Masterful achievement took the Oscar for Best Documentary. [R]▶

Taxman, The (1999) **C-100m.** ** D: Avi Nesher. Joe Pantoliano, Robert Townsend, Wade Dominguez, Michael Chiklis, Elizabeth Berkley, Fisher Stevens, Casey Siemaszko, Mike Starr. Investigator for the N.Y. state tax office becomes obsessed with a trail he's certain leads to big-time criminal activities involving Russian immigrants in Brighton Beach. Rare leading role for Pantoliano, who's in fine form, but story lags and characters are not fully drawn. Based on a true story written by a former tax investigator. [R]▼▶

Taza, Son of Cochise (1954) **C-79m.** **½ D: Douglas Sirk. Rock Hudson, Barbara Rush, Gregg Palmer, Bart Roberts (Rex Reason), Morris Ankrum, Joe Sawyer. Actually two sons: one wants to live peacefully with the white man, the other thinks Geronimo has a better idea. Sirk's only Western is uneven follow-up to BROKEN ARROW—with Jeff Chandler popping in just long enough to die—but sweeping action scenes and sympathetic treatment of Indians help. 3-D.▶

Tea and Sympathy (1956) **C-122m.** *** D: Vincente Minnelli. Deborah Kerr, John Kerr, Leif Erickson, Edward Andrews, Darryl Hickman, Dean Jones, Norma Crane. Glossy but well-acted version of Robert Anderson play about prep school boy's affair with a teacher's wife, skirting homosexual issues. Both Kerrs give sensitive portrayals; they and Erickson re-create their Broadway roles. Scripted by the playwright. CinemaScope.▼▶

Teacher, The (1974) **C-98m.** ** D: Hikmet Avedis. Angel Tompkins, Jay North, Anthony James, Marlene Schmidt, Sivi Aberg, Barry Atwater, Med Flory. Trashy but enjoyable film has "older" woman Tompkins introducing North (TV's *Dennis the Menace* all grown up) to sex, while a psychopathic killer (James) threatens both their lives. John Cassavetes' and Gena Rowlands' mommies have cute cameos as disapproving bystanders in a restaurant scene. [R]▼▶

Teachers (1984) **C-106m.** ** D: Arthur Hiller. Nick Nolte, JoBeth Williams, Judd Hirsch, Ralph Macchio, Lee Grant, Richard Mulligan, Allen Garfield, Royal Dano, Laura Dern, Morgan Freeman, William Schallert, Crispin Glover, Zohra Lampert, Art Metrano. "Outrageous" blend of comedy-drama set in urban high school (and filmed in Columbus, Ohio). Seemingly patterned after Paddy

Chayefsky's THE HOSPITAL and NETWORK but nowhere near as good. Slick, well cast, but dramatically disjointed and obvious at every turn. [R]▼▶

Teacher's Pet (1958) **120m.** *** D: George Seaton. Clark Gable, Doris Day, Gig Young, Mamie Van Doren, Nick Adams, Charles Lane. Self-educated city editor Gable clashes with journalism teacher Day in this airy, amusing comedy. Young is memorable as Doris' intellectual boyfriend. Written by Fay and Michael Kanin. VistaVision. ▼▶

Teacher's Pet (2004) **C-73m.** *** D: Timothy Björklund. Voices of Nathan Lane, Kelsey Grammer, Shaun Fleming, Debra Jo Rupp, David Ogden Stiers, Jerry Stiller, Paul Reubens, Megan Mullally, Rob Paulsen, Wallace Shawn, Estelle Harris, Jay Thomas. Lightning-paced, irreverently funny film based on the Disney animated TV series about a dog who disguises himself as a boy in order to attend school with his master. They're separated during summer vacation, until Pet sees a mad doctor on TV who says he can transform an animal into a human being—permanently. Lane, Grammer, and company sing some clever new songs written by the show's creators. Designed by Gary Baseman in a style somewhere between underground comics and pop art. Officially titled DISNEY'S TEACHER'S PET. [PG]▼▶

Teaching Mrs. Tingle (1999) **C-95m.** *½ D: Kevin Williamson. Helen Mirren, Katie Holmes, Barry Watson, Marisa Coughlan, Liz Stauber, Jeffrey Tambor, Michael McKean, Molly Ringwald, Vivica A. Fox. When they confront a coldhearted teacher who can destroy their college dreams, three high school students accidentally knock her out, then tie her to her bed in order to talk her into changing her ways. Preposterous premise is devoid of story, interest or suspense, with only Mirren's icy, sarcastic performance to recommend it. Williamson (making his directing debut) scripted, but this is a far cry from SCREAM. Lesley Ann Warren appears unbilled. [PG-13]▼▶

Tea for Two (1950) **C-98m.** **½ D: David Butler. Doris Day, Gordon MacRae, Gene Nelson, Patrice Wymore, Eve Arden, Billy De Wolfe, S. Z. Sakall, Bill Goodwin, Virginia Gibson. Pleasant but unexceptional musical very loosely based on the stage play *No, No, Nanette* (which was filmed before in 1930 and 1940). Day bets uncle Sakall she can answer no to every question for the length of a weekend—in order to win her chance to star in a Broadway show.▼▶

Teahouse of the August Moon, The (1956) **C-123m.** ***½ D: Daniel Mann. Marlon Brando, Glenn Ford, Machiko Kyo, Eddie Albert, Paul Ford, Henry (Harry) Morgan. Outstanding comedy scripted by John Patrick from his hit play of Army officers involved with Americanization of post-WW2 Okinawa. A warm and memorable film.

Paul Ford recreates his Broadway role and nearly steals the show. Based on book by Vern J. Sneider. CinemaScope.▼◖❶

Team America World Police (2004) C-96m. *½ D: Trey Parker. Voices of Trey Parker, Matt Stone. Blundering (if well-meaning) squad of Americans fight terrorism around the world but meet their match in North Korean leader Kim Jung Il. The *South Park* boys run aground in a pointless film enacted by marionettes (a spoof of Gerry Anderson's *Thunderbirds* series of old). Unlike their sharp, on-target TV scripts and previous films, this one repeatedly swings and misses at such easy targets as politically outspoken actors. Even the songs are uninspired. Heavy-handed, sour, and, worst of all, not funny. One scene of wild puppet sex will probably rate an asterisk in film histories. Unrated version runs 98m. Super 35. [R] ▼❶

Tears of the Black Tiger (2000-Thailand) C-109m. **½ D: Wisit Sasanatieng. Chart-chai Ngamsan, Stella Malucchi, Supakorn Kitsuwon, Arawat Ruangvuth, Sombatl, Pairoj Jaisingha. Boy from the wrong side of the tracks falls in love with an upper-class girl; he grows up to be a notorious bandit called the Black Tiger, while her father plans to marry her off to the policeman in charge of capturing Tiger and his gang. Campy, candy-colored, and very bloody, this Thai cowboy soap opera with songs pays homage to classic Westerns (mostly Spaghetti) and the highly stylized films of Seijun Suzuki. Fun for a while, but its extreme artificiality becomes self-conscious and exhausting. Alternate version runs 101m.❶

Tears of the Sun (2003) C-118m. *** D: Antoine Fuqua. Bruce Willis, Monica Bellucci, Cole Hauser, Eamonn Walker, Nick Chinlund, Fionnula Flanagan, Malick Bowens, Tom Skerritt, Chad Smith. Stoic Navy SEAL commander Willis and his squadron are sent to evacuate a female doctor from a Nigerian village, but she opens his eyes to the terrorism the people around her have been subjected to. Eventually Willis must decide whether to help. Well-made action film bears a message that doing the right thing isn't a political decision but a humanist one. Undermined more than once by awkward dialogue and miscasting of the very sexy Bellucci. Director's "extended" cut runs 146m. Panavision. [R] ▼❶

Tea with Mussolini (1999-Italian-British) C-117m. *** D: Franco Zeffirelli. Cher, Maggie Smith, Judi Dench, Joan Plowright, Lily Tomlin, Baird Wallace, Charlie Lucas, Massimo Ghini, Paolo Seganti, Paul Checquer. A boy whose mother has died and whose father has all but abandoned him is raised by a group of eccentric British women in 1930s Florence. The coming of war has great impact on the women—known as the Scorpioni—and their flamboyant American counterparts in the artsy expatriate community, but cannot sever ties between the young man and his "surrogate mothers." Entertaining if not always focused comedy-drama based on director Zeffirelli's own experiences as a youth; co-scripted by John Mortimer. [PG] ▼❶

Ted & Venus (1991) C-100m. *½ D: Bud Cort. Bud Cort, James Brolin, Kim Adams, Carol Kane, Rhea Perlman, Woody Harrelson, Martin Mull, Timothy Leary, Cassandra Peterson, Gena Rowlands. Cort's directing debut is a hard-to-take tale of an obnoxious Southern California misfit who relentlessly pursues his "dream woman." Cameos by familiar faces add little to this modest production. [R] ▼❶

Teddy Bears' Picnic (2002) C-80m. BOMB D: Harry Shearer. John Michael Higgins, Ming-Na, Henry Gibson, David Rasche, Robert Mandan, Morgan Fairchild, Michael McKean, Harry Shearer, Justin Kirk, George Wendt, Kenneth Mars, Bob Einstein, John O'Hurley, Howard Hesseman, Fred Willard, Annabelle Gurwitch, Joyce Hyser, Kurtwood Smith, Larry Miller. Wretched botch by actor/writer/director/producer Shearer ostensibly satirizing northern California rustic retreat of the rich and powerful (here called Zambesi Glen). Real disappointment considering the comic talent involved. Alan Thicke and Peter Marshall play themselves. ▼❶

Teenage Cave Man (1958) 66m. ** D: Roger Corman. Robert Vaughn, Darrah Marshall, Leslie Bradley, Frank De Kova. Vaughn, light years away from THE YOUNG PHILADELPHIANS or S.O.B., is the title character, a prehistoric adolescent hankering for greener pastures, in this AIP quickie with predictable "surprise" ending. Superama. ▼❶

Teenage Doll (1957) 68m. ** D: Roger Corman. June Kenney, Fay Spain, Richard Devon, Dorothy Neumann. Title dish (Kenney) doesn't want to spend school nights at home in her room, gets involved with punk peers. This above-average sleazy B won't obscure memory of Dreyer and Ozu, but is true to its era. ▼❶

Teenage Dream SEE: **Flying**

Teen-age Millionaire (1961) C/B&W-84m. BOMB D: Lawrence Doheny. Jimmy Clanton, ZaSu Pitts, Rocky Graziano, Diane Jergens, Chubby Checker, Jackie Wilson, Dion, Marv Johnson, Bill Black, Jack Larson, Vicki Spencer, Sid Gould, Maurice Gosfield. Deadening musical about teenager Clanton, with a huge inheritance, who becomes a pop star. The rock acts are unusually and annoyingly tame here.

Teenage Mutant Ninja Turtles (1990) C-93m. ** D: Steve Barron. Judith Hoag, Elias Koteas, Sam Rockwell; voices of Robbie Rist, Kevin Clash, Brian Tochi, David McCharen, Corey Feldman. Four mutated turtles who live in the sewers of N.Y.C. with their ninja master (an oversized rat from Japan) befriend a plucky TV reporter and help crack an insidious crime wave. The wacked-out comic book creation of Kevin Eastman and Peter Laird (which led to a hit animated TV series) should have inspired a much better movie. Badly written, flatly directed, and murky-looking, it jump-starts every now and then—but not often enough. Strongest asset is the design and articulation of the Turtles by Jim Henson's Creature Shop. Followed by three sequels. [PG] ▼●)

Teenage Mutant Ninja Turtles II: The Secret of the Ooze (1991) **C-88m.** *½ D: Michael Pressman. Paige Turco, David Warner, Ernie Reyes, Jr., Michelan Sisti, Leif Tilden, Kenn Troum, Mark Caso, Kevin Clash, Raymond Serra, Vanilla Ice. The evil Shredder finds one remaining container of the ooze that caused the turtles to mutate in the first place. Brainless sequel aims lower than first film, and strips the half-shell heroes of any personality (even having them call each other by nicknames—Raf instead of Raphael, Donny instead of Donatello). Appearance by Vanilla Ice, performing a ninja turtle rap song, is the nadir. [PG]

Teenage Mutant Ninja Turtles III (1993) **C-96m.** ** D: Stuart Gillard. Elias Koteas, Paige Turco, Stuart Wilson, Sab Shimono, Vivian Wu, Mark Caso, Matt Hill, Jim Raposa, David Fraser, James Murray. The guys bolt the sewer for feudal Japan to help rebel villagers conquer an evil lord. SEVEN SAMURAI it ain't (nor Russ Meyer's THE SEVEN MINUTES, either), but those who still care will find a more mellowed-out Turtles saga, complete with a lecture by Raphael on the dangers of violence. Like totally Woodstock, dude! [PG] ▼●)

Teenage Psycho Meets Bloody Mary, The SEE: **Incredibly Strange Creatures Who Stopped Living and Became Mixed-Up Zombies, The**

Teen-age Rebel (1956) **94m.** **½ D: Edmund Goulding. Ginger Rogers, Michael Rennie, Betty Lou Keim, Mildred Natwick, Rusty Swope, Warren Berlinger, Lilli Gentle, Louise Beavers, Irene Hervey. Pat yet provocative film of divorcée Rogers, now remarried, trying to reestablish understanding with her daughter. CinemaScope.

Teenagers From Outer Space (1959) **86m.** BOMB D: Tom Graeff. David Love, Dawn Anderson, Harvey B. Dunn, Bryant Grant, Tom Lockyear (Tom Graeff). Ridiculous sci-fi about alien youths who bring monster to Earth, shown as the shadow of a lobster! Very, very cheap; but still a camp classic. Besides directing and playing a small part, Graeff wrote, produced, photographed, and edited! ▼)

Teenage Zombies (1957) **73m.** BOMB D: Jerry Warren. Don Sullivan, Katherine Victor, Steve Conte, Paul Pepper, Bri Murphy, Mitzi Albertson. Victor captures teenagers snooping around her island, imprisons them for experiments. Typically awful Warren

horror film with long stretches in which nothing happens . . . and incidentally, no teenage zombies! Remade as FRANKENSTEIN ISLAND. ▼)

Teen Witch (1989) **C-105m.** ** D: Dorian Walker. Robyn Lively, Dan Gauthier, Joshua Miller, Dick Sargent, Zelda Rubinstein, Lisa Fuller, Shelley Berman. Teen comedy with a moral, about a girl who, one week before her sixteenth birthday, learns that she's a descendant of some bona fide Salem witches . . . and uses her newfound magical powers to snare a football hero as boyfriend. Some nice ideas, but mostly falls flat. Berman is funny as a stuffy English teacher who becomes a victim of the teenage witch's black magic. [PG-13] ▼)

Teen Wolf (1985) **C-91m.** ** D: Rod Daniel. Michael J. Fox, James Hampton, Scott Paulin, Susan Ursitti, Jerry Levine, Jim MacKrell. Teenager with usual growing pains discovers that he's also a were wolf—and that this finally makes him popular at school. Pleasant at best, but anemic comedy has nowhere to go. Best moments come from TV comedy writer-producer (and former comic) Jay Tarses as Fox's athletic coach. Followed by an animated TV series and TEEN WOLF TOO. [PG] ▼●)

Teen Wolf Too (1987) **C-95m.** BOMB D: Christopher Leitch. Jason Bateman, Kim Darby, John Astin, Paul Sand, James Hampton, Mark Holton. Limp comedy, chronicling the adventures of the Teen Wolf's cousin (Bateman), makes the original seem like Preston Sturges in his prime. Excruciating. [PG] ▼)

Teeth (2008) **C-88m.** **½ D: Mitchell Lichtenstein. Jess Weixler, John Hensley, Josh Pais, Hale Appleman, Ashley Springer, Vivienne Benesch, Lenny von Dohlen, Nicole Swahn, Julia Garro, Adam Wagner. Dawn (Weixler) is an active church member and helps guide young people around her to remain abstinent until marriage. However, as she is faced with her own budding sexuality, she discovers that she isn't like the other girls; she has something known as *vagina dentata*. Kitschy and not for the faint of heart. The ultimate in female empowerment, though it may leave some men scarred for life. The director is the son of artist Roy Lichtenstein. [R])

Telefon (1977) **C-102m.** *** D: Don Siegel. Charles Bronson, Lee Remick, Donald Pleasence, Tyne Daly, Patrick Magee, Alan Badel, Sheree North. Slick espionage thriller from Walter Wager's ingenious novel; Bronson is Russian agent sent to stop crazy defector from triggering hypnotized spies to commit sabotage throughout U.S. Daly is terrific as wisecracking computer expert. Script by Stirling Silliphant and original director Peter Hyams. [PG] ▼)

Telephone, The (1988) **C-82m.** BOMB

D: Rip Torn. Whoopi Goldberg, Severn Darden, Amy Wright, Elliott Gould, John Heard. Goldberg may have hit rock bottom with this clinker in which she's cast as an out-of-work actress with major psychological problems. The star sued to prevent this version from being released. Terrible script by Harry Nilsson and Terry Southern. Hang up on this wrong number. Actor Torn's directing debut. [R]▼●

Telling Lies in America (1997) **C-101m.** *** D: Guy Ferland. Kevin Bacon, Brad Renfro, Maximilian Schell, Calista Flockhart, Paul Dooley, Jonathan Rhys Myers, Luke Wilson. Evocative and well-done Joe Eszterhas-scripted memoir, set in Cleveland during the early 1960s, about a Hungarian-born teen (Renfro), an outsider trying to find his place in pre-Beatles rock 'n' roll America. Bacon is the standout here, offering an award-calibre performance as the boy's mentor, a slick, payola-taking disc jockey. Super 35. [PG-13]▼●❋

Tell It to the Judge (1949) **87m** **½ D: Norman Foster. Rosalind Russell, Robert Cummings, Gig Young, Marie McDonald, Harry Davenport, Douglass Dumbrille. Flyweight marital farce with Russell and Cummings in and out of love every ten minutes; enjoyable if you like the stars.▼

Tell Me a Riddle (1980) **C-90m** **½ D: Lee Grant. Melvyn Douglas, Lila Kedrova, Brooke Adams, Dolores Dorn, Bob Elross, Joan Harris, Zalman King. Thoughtful but static filmization of Tillie Olsen's novella chronicling the relationship between a dying woman and her husband of 40 years. Well acted by Douglas and Kedrova; Grant's first feature as director. That's Peter Coyote as the young Douglas. [PG]▼❋

Tell Me Lies (1968-British) **C-118m.** ** D: Peter Brook. Glenda Jackson, The Royal Shakespeare Company, Kingsley Amis, Stokely Carmichael, Paul Scofield. Strange, unsuccessful combination of songs, skits, and newsreel footage attacking U.S. involvement in Vietnam wasn't even liked by doves. Interesting now merely as historical document.

Tell Me That You Love Me, Junie Moon (1970) **C-112m.** ***½ D: Otto Preminger. Liza Minnelli, Ken Howard, Robert Moore, James Coco, Kay Thompson, Fred Williamson, Nancy Marchand, Anne Revere. Moving story of three misfits who decide to live together: facially scarred Minnelli, epileptic Howard, wheelchair-bound homosexual Moore. Moments of comedy, melodrama, compassion expertly blended by Preminger in one of his best films; adapted from her novel by Marjorie Kellogg. [PG]

Tell No One (2006-French) **C-131m.** *** D: Guillaume Canet. François Cluzet, André Dussollier, Marie-Josée Croze, Kristin Scott Thomas, Nathalie Baye, François Berléand, Jean Rochefort, Gilles Lellouche, Marina Hands, Philippe Lefebvre, Olivier Marchal. The police have never stopped being suspicious of pediatrician Cluzet since the mysterious death of his wife eight years ago—even though he was cleared—so when a new body is dug up near the crime scene he becomes their leading suspect. At the same time, he is given reason to believe his wife may be alive after all. Complex but exciting thriller is packed with plot twists and action, expertly handled by actor-turned-director Canet, who coscripted this adaptation of Harlan Coben's American novel (and appears briefly in flashbacks as the sleazy Philippe Neuville). Super 35. ❙

Tell-Tale Heart, The (1960-British) **81m.** **½ D: Ernest Morris. Laurence Payne, Adrienne Corri, Dermot Walsh, Selma Vaz Dias. Atmospheric Edgar Allan Poe yarn about a meek librarian who becomes obsessed, sexually and otherwise, with his pretty new neighbor—but she shows more of an interest in his charming and good-looking best friend.▼❙

Tell Them Willie Boy Is Here (1969) **C-96m.** *** D: Abraham Polonsky. Robert Redford, Katharine Ross, Robert Blake, Susan Clark, Barry Sullivan, Charles McGraw, John Vernon. Massive manhunt for Indian who killed in self-defense pretends to be more important than it is, but is so well crafted the preaching can be overlooked. Moodily photographed by Conrad Hall. The blacklisted Polonsky's first film since FORCE OF EVIL 21 years before. Panavision. [PG—originally rated M]▼●❙

Temp, The (1993) **C-96m.** ** D: Tom Holland. Timothy Hutton, Lara Flynn Boyle, Faye Dunaway, Dwight Schultz, Oliver Platt, Steven Weber, Colleen Flynn, Scott Coffey, Dakin Matthews. Another "(Fill in the blank) From Hell" movie— this one suggesting what Eve Harrington might have been like with a psychotic streak and a penchant for office work instead of backstage-Broadway groupiedom. Surprisingly bearable until office casualties sparked by schemer Boyle's temporary employment become way too silly. [R]▼●❙

Tempest (1982) **C-140m.** ** D: Paul Mazursky. John Cassavetes, Gena Rowlands, Susan Sarandon, Vittorio Gassman, Raul Julia, Molly Ringwald, Sam Robards, Paul Stewart. Aimless comedy, loosely based on Shakespeare's play, has Cassavetes as a N.Y.C. architect who tries to solve his midlife crisis by moving to a Greek island with his teenage daughter. Appealing cast, beautiful scenery, some engaging scenes . . . but they don't quite add up. [PG]▼❙

Tempest, The (2010) **C-110m.** *½ D: Julie Taymor. Helen Mirren, Russell Brand, Felicity Jones, Reeve Carney, David Strathairn, Tom Conti, Alan Cumming, Chris Cooper, Ben Whishaw, Djimon Hounsou, Alfred

Molina. Taymor's ambitious take on the Shakespeare classic pulls a gender switch, turning Prospero into Prospera, the deposed wizard who is banished to an island, where she engages in a power struggle for survival. In the hands of Mirren the character is still able to conjure up some intriguing magic. Unfortunately, this misguided adaptation is wildly uneven, needlessly convoluted, and filled with CGI effects, which reduce it to a lot of thunder and lightning. Fine actors are game at navigating the language, but Mirren is the only one who makes a strong impression. Super 35. [PG-13] ▶

Tempter, The (1974-Italian) **C-96m.** BOMB D: Alberto de Martino. Carla Gravina, Mel Ferrer, Arthur Kennedy, George Coulouris, Alida Valli, Umberto Orsini. Frenzied but pointless rip-off of THE EXORCIST with Gravina as Ferrer's demonized daughter. Blecch. Aka THE ANTICHRIST. [R] ▼▶

Temptress Moon (1996-Hong Kong-Chinese) **C-127m.** ** D: Chen Kaige. Gong Li, Leslie Cheung, Zhou Yemang, Kevin Lin, He Saifei, Zhang Shi. Elaborate epic, set in and around Shanghai in the 1920s, about the long and involved relationship between a boy and girl raised together in an ancestral palace—and their renewed relationship in adult life after the former becomes an underworld character. There's opium, blackmail, implied incest, you name it—but joyless cohesion that the U.S. distributor had to affix the equivalent of a baseball scoreboard at the movie's beginning so that audiences would know what was happening. [R] ▼▶

10 (1979) **C-122m.** ** D: Blake Edwards. Dudley Moore, Julie Andrews, Bo Derek, Robert Webber, Dee Wallace, Sam Jones, Brian Dennehy, Max Showalter, Don Calfa, Nedra Volz, James Noble, Doug Sheehan. Middle-aged songwriter finds himself hung up on sex, especially when he sets eyes on beautiful Derek. Blake Edwards' idea of a real sophisticated movie; sporadically funny but tiresome, glib, and pompous. Panavision. [R] ▼▶

Ten, The (2007) **C-96m.** BOMB D: David Wain. Paul Rudd, Famke Janssen, Winona Ryder, Jessica Alba, Adam Brody, Gretchen Mol, Justin Theroux, A. D. Miles, Oliver Platt, Ken Marino, Rob Corddry, Kerri Kenney-Silver, Liev Schreiber, Ron Silver, Bobby Cannavale, Thomas Lennon, Robert Ben Garant, Jason Sudeikis, Janeane Garofalo, Jon Hamm. Smugly unfunny collection of go-nowhere skits relating to the Ten Commandments, hosted by Rudd (the film's co-producer), who plays an unhappily married man. Many talented performers are stuck on the same sinking ship, steered by Wain and Marino of *The State*. This breaks the Eleventh Commandment: Thou Shalt Not Make a Crummy Movie. [R] ▶

Tenacious D: The Pick of Destiny (2006) **C-92m.** **½ D: Liam Lynch. Jack Black, Kyle Gass, J. R. (Jason) Reed, Ronnie James Dio, Paul F. Tompkins, Troy Gentile, Dave Grohl, Amy Adams. Wacky fantasy-comedy about the formation of Black and Gass' singing team Tenacious D and their search for a magical guitar pick. Broad, silly, with an animated segment and occasional gag cameos. Lightly likable throughout, but probably best left to fans of the act. Gentile is almost eerie in his replication of Black as a boy. [R] ▶

Tenant, The (1976-French-U.S.) **C-125m.** ***½ D: Roman Polanski. Roman Polanski, Isabelle Adjani, Melvyn Douglas, Jo Van Fleet, Shelley Winters, Bernard Fresson, Lila Kedrova, Claude Dauphin. Unique, bizarrely cast horror film about a timid clerk who rents an apartment whose previous inhabitant attempted suicide. Critically drubbed upon release but a latter-day cult item. Fine photography by Sven Nykvist. [R] ▼▶

Tenants, The (2006) **C-97m.** ** D: Danny Green. Dylan McDermott, Snoop Dogg, Rose Byrne, Seymour Cassel, Niki J. Crawford, Aldis Hodge. Grim drama, set in Brooklyn during the early 1970s, about a liberal—and very naïve—Jewish writer who is the lone resident of a graffiti-strewn tenement. As he obsessively pounds away on his typewriter, attempting to complete a book, he befriends a Jekyll-and-Hyde–like black man, a wannabe novelist who is at once friendly and uncompromisingly hostile. Intriguing story is based on a novel by Bernard Malamud, but what might have been a potent exploration of race relations is ponderous and melodramatic. [R] ▶

Ten Canoes (2006-Australian-Italian) **C/ B&W-92m.** *** D: Rolf de Heer, Peter Djigirr. Crusoe Kurddal, Jamie Dayindi Gulpilil Dalaithngu, Richard Birrinbirrin, Peter Minygululu, Frances Djulibing; narrated by David Gulpilil Ridjimiraril Dalaithngu. Absorbing, beautifully filmed two-part story. The first, shot in b&w, involves an Aborigine tribesman who covets one of the wives of his older brother; the second, in color, illustrates a story he is told that mirrors his yearning. First feature made in an Aboriginal language, executed with the assistance of the Ramingining people, many of whom appear on-screen. Super 35. ▶

Ten Commandments, The (1923) **146m.** *** D: Cecil B. DeMille. Theodore Roberts, Charles de Roche, Estelle Taylor, Richard Dix, Rod La Rocque, Leatrice Joy, Nita Naldi, Agnes Ayres. Biblical story, told in compact form (but on a gargantuan scale—with several scenes in two-color Technicolor) is only first portion of this silent film. The rest is a modern-day parable involving two brothers, one a saint, the other a sinner—and it's anything but subtle. Still, it's good entertainment in the best DeMille style. Remade in 1956, for TV in 2006, and as an animated feature in 2007.▼❍

Ten Commandments, The (1956) C-220m. **** D: Cecil B. DeMille. Charlton Heston, Yul Brynner, Anne Baxter, Edward G. Robinson, Yvonne De Carlo, Debra Paget, John Derek, Cedric Hardwicke, H.B. Warner, Henry Wilcoxon, Nina Foch, Martha Scott, Judith Anderson, Vincent Price, John Carradine, Woodrow (Woody) Strode. Vivid storytelling at its best. Biblical epic follows Moses' life from birth and abandonment through manhood, slavery, and trials in leading the Jews out of Egypt. Few subtleties in DeMille's second handling of this tale (first filmed in 1923) but few lulls, either. Parting of the Red Sea, writing of the holy tablets are unforgettable highlights. Oscar-winning special effects. VistaVision.▼❍❍

Ten Days That Shook the World SEE: **October**

Ten Days Wonder (1972-French) C-101m. **½ D: Claude Chabrol. Orson Welles, Anthony Perkins, Marlene Jobert, Michel Piccoli, Guido Alberti. Ellery Queen meets Claude Chabrol in erratic but moody mystery concerning Perkins' love affair with stepmother Jobert. Film doesn't work, but is often fascinating to watch. [PG]▼❍

Tender Comrade (1943) C-102m. **½ D: Edward Dmytryk. Ginger Rogers, Robert Ryan, Ruth Hussey, Patricia Collinge, Mady Christians, Kim Hunter, Jane Darwell. Rogers and friends live communally while their men are out fighting the war, a situation that caused this Dmytryk-Dalton Trumbo collaboration to be labeled as Communist propaganda by HUAC in later years. Some unbearable—and ironically, pro-American—speechifying, but occasionally fascinating as social history.▼

Tender Flesh SEE: **Welcome to Arrow Beach**

Tender Is the Night (1962) C-146m. **½ D: Henry King. Jennifer Jones, Jason Robards, Jr., Joan Fontaine, Tom Ewell, Jill St. John, Paul Lukas. Sluggish, unflavorful version of F. Scott Fitzgerald novel with Jones unsatisfactory as mentally unstable wife of psychiatrist Robards; Fontaine is her chic sister; set in 1920s Europe. CinemaScope.

Tender Mercies (1983) C-92m. *** D: Bruce Beresford. Robert Duvall, Tess Harper, Allan Hubbard, Betty Buckley, Ellen Barkin, Wilford Brimley, Lenny Von Dohlen, Paul Gleason. Winning but extremely low-key film about a country singer who finds the inspiration to put his life back together when he meets an attractive young widow and her little boy. Duvall's Oscar-winning performance is the real attraction here, though the whole cast is excellent; Hor-

ton Foote's screenplay (also an Oscar winner) is not so much a story as a series of vignettes. Incidentally, Duvall wrote two of his own songs for the film. [PG]▼❍

Tenderness (2009) C-101m. *½ D: John Polson. Russell Crowe, Jon Foster, Sophie Traub, Arija Bareikis, Alexis Dziena, Michael Kelly, Vivienne Benesch, Tanya Clarke, Laura Dern. Annoyingly uneven psychological drama, based on a Robert Cormier novel, in which flirtatious, alienated teen Traub attempts to connect with Foster, who's murdered his parents and has just been released from juvenile detention. Although top-billed, Crowe plays a secondary role as a semiretired cop who's convinced that Foster is a serial killer. There are plot holes galore here, and the revelations at the finale just don't add up. Panavision. [R]❍

Tender Scoundrel (1966-French-Italian) C-94m. *½ D: Jean Becker. Jean-Paul Belmondo, Nadja Tiller, Robert Morley, Genevieve Page. Dumb story of delightful rogue and ladies' man who is constantly on the hustle. Techniscope.

Tender Trap, The (1955) C-111m. **½ D: Charles Walters. Frank Sinatra, Debbie Reynolds, Celeste Holm, David Wayne, Carolyn Jones, Lola Albright, Tom Helmore, James Drury. Silly romp of swinging, set-in-his-ways N.Y.C. bachelor Sinatra, who meets his match in determined, marriage-minded Reynolds. A real time capsule of 1950s attitudes toward men, women, and sex. Impeccable support from Holm and Wayne; memorable Cahn–Van Heusen title tune. Julius J. Epstein adapted the Max Shulman and Robert Paul Smith play. CinemaScope. ▼❍

Tenebrae SEE: **Unsane**

Ten From Your Show of Shows (1973) 92m. **** D: Max Liebman. Sid Caesar, Imogene Coca, Carl Reiner, Howard Morris, Louis Nye. Incomparable collection from early '50s TV show displaying comic genius of four stars, working with classic material by Mel Brooks, among others. Ten skits include FROM HERE TO ETERNITY spoof, silent-movie sendup, Swiss clock, and final, unbearably funny takeoff on *This Is Your Life*. A must. [G]▼

10 Items or Less (2006) C-82m. **½ D: Brad Silberling. Morgan Freeman, Paz Vega, Bobby Cannavale, Anne Dudek, Kumar Pallana, Leonardo Nam, Jennifer Echols, Jonah Hill, Jim Parsons, Danny DeVito, Rhea Perlman. Slight but disarming character study of a movie actor who goes to a supermarket to research a role and winds up spending the day with checker Vega. Something of a lark for writer-director Silberling and actor-producer Freeman, who's seldom given a chance to be this lighthearted on-screen. His charm and charisma (and some sly in-jokes about Hollywood) make this worth seeing. [R]❍

Ten Little Indians (1966-British) **92m.** **½ D: George Pollock. Hugh O'Brian, Shirley Eaton, Fabian, Leo Genn, Stanley Holloway, Wilfrid Hyde-White, Daliah Lavi, Dennis Price. Fair remake of Agatha Christie's whodunit AND THEN THERE WERE NONE, with suspects trapped in remote Alpine mansion. Originally released with gimmick of murder-minute for audience to guess killer. Remade again in 1975 and 1989.▼❶

Ten Little Indians (1975-British) **C-98m.** *½ D: Peter Collinson. Oliver Reed, Elke Sommer, Herbert Lom, Richard Attenborough, Charles Aznavour, Stephane Audran, Gert Frobe, Adolfo Celi; voice of Orson Welles. Third rendering of Agatha Christie whodunit, set this time in Iran. Great plot cannot survive such tired retelling. [PG]▼

Ten Little Indians (1989) **C-98m.** BOMB D: Alan Birkinshaw. Donald Pleasence, Frank Stallone, Sarah Maur Thorp, Brenda Vaccaro, Herbert Lom, Warren Berlinger, Paul L. Smith, Moira Lister. Producer Harry Alan Towers' *third* redo of the Christie classic is his worst yet. This time he isolates an uninteresting cast in an African safari camp in the 1930s, and boringly plods through this once-intriguing, now-weary plot. [PG]▼❶

Tennessee's Partner (1955) **C-87m.** **½ D: Allan Dwan. John Payne, Rhonda Fleming, Ronald Reagan, Coleen Gray, Morris Ankrum. Offbeat little Western with Payne excellent in an unusual "heel" characterization, Reagan accidentally becoming his pal. Based on a Bret Harte story. Filmed in SuperScope.▼❶

Ten North Frederick (1958) **102m.** *** D: Philip Dunne. Gary Cooper, Diane Varsi, Suzy Parker, Geraldine Fitzgerald, Tom Tully, Ray Stricklyn, Stuart Whitman, Barbara Nichols. Grasping wife (Fitzgerald) prods her husband (Cooper) into big-time politics, with disastrous results. He finds personal solace in love affair with much younger woman (Parker). Good performances in somewhat soapy adaptation of John O'Hara novel. CinemaScope.▼

10 Rillington Place (1971-British) **C-111m.** *** D: Richard Fleischer. Richard Attenborough, Judy Geeson, John Hurt, Pat Heywood, Andre Morell. Low-key presentation of famous John Christie–Timothy Evans murder case that rocked Great Britain in the early 1950s. No overt editorializing but psychological undertone exists; outstanding performances by entire cast and location filming inseparable with film's total effect. [PG]▼❶

Ten Seconds to Hell (1959-U.S.-British) **93m.** **½ D: Robert Aldrich. Jeff Chandler, Jack Palance, Martine Carol, Robert Cornthwaite, Dave Willock, Wesley Addy. Chandler and Palance are almost believable as Germans involved in defusing bombs in Berlin, while competing for Carol's affection. Also shown in computer-colored version.

Tentacles (1977-Italian) **C-90m.** *½ D: Oliver Hellman (Ovidio Assonitis). John Huston, Shelley Winters, Henry Fonda, Bo Hopkins, Delia Boccardo, Cesare Danova. Giant octopus threatens a seaside community in this rip-off of JAWS. Some unexpected casting and the spectacle of having killer whales emerge the heroes save the picture from total decay. Technovision. [PG]▼❶

Ten Tall Men (1951) **C-97m.** **½ D: Willis Goldbeck. Burt Lancaster, Jody Lawrance, Gilbert Roland, Kieron Moore. Tongue-in-cheek Foreign Legion tale, with dynamic Lancaster pushing the action along.

Tenth Avenue Angel (1948) **74m.** BOMB D: Roy Rowland. Margaret O'Brien, Angela Lansbury, George Murphy, Phyllis Thaxter, Warner Anderson, Rhys Williams, Barry Nelson, Connie Gilchrist. Capable cast is lost in terrible, syrupy script about 8-year-old tenement girl O'Brien, her attachment to ex-con Murphy, and how she learns various, obvious lessons about faith. Filmed in 1946.

10 Things I Hate About You (1999) **C-97m.** **½ D: Gil Junger. Heath Ledger, Julia Stiles, Joseph Gordon-Levitt, Larisa Oleynik, David Krumholtz, Andrew Keegan, Susan May Pratt, Larry Miller, Daryl "Chill" Mitchell, Allison Janney, David Leisure, Letters to Cleo, Save Ferris. Overprotective dad rules that his pretty, popular daughter Bianca can only date when his hostile older daughter Katerina does. Several guys interested in Bianca therefore hire someone to pursue her doggedly unfriendly sister. Cute teen-comedy takeoff of *The Taming of the Shrew* set at Padua High School. Janney is great fun as Ms. Perky. Followed by a TV series. [PG-13]▼❶

10:30 PM Summer (1966-U.S.-Spanish) **C-85m.** ** D: Jules Dassin. Melina Mercouri, Romy Schneider, Peter Finch, Julián Mateos, Isabel Maria Pérez, Beatriz Savón. A couple traveling in a foreign country encounters problems and complications in their relationship. Largely unknown, all but forgotten Dassin film made in Spain is typical of similarly pretentious and mostly incoherent '60s fare. Mercouri is watchable as always; her scenes with Schneider pop off the screen. Scripted by Dassin and Marguerite Duras, from her novel.❶

10,000 BC (2008) **C-109m.** ** D: Roland Emmerich. Steven Strait, Camilla Belle, Cliff Curtis, Joel Virgel, Affif Ben Badra, Mo Zinal, Nathanael Baring, Mona Hammond, Marco Khan; narrated by Omar Sharif. Tale of prehistoric life follows a small group who leave their tribe of mammoth hunters in an effort to rescue others captured by slavers. This leads them to a pre-Egyptian city of ruthless pyramid-builders and much adventure. Earnest, well produced on rugged locations with occasionally good effects, but for the most part as ludicrous as other films of this type. Features cinema's first superfluous saber-tooth tiger. Super 35. [PG-13]◗

Ten Thousand Bedrooms (1957) **C-114m.** ** D: Richard Thorpe. Dean Martin, Anna Maria Alberghetti, Eva Bartok, Dewey Martin, Walter Slezak, Paul Henreid, Jules Munshin, Marcel Dalio, Dean Jones. Dean's first film without Jerry Lewis seemed to spell doom for his career; it's a lightweight but overlong musical romance with Dino as a playboy hotel-manager in Rome. Cinema-Scope. ◗

Tenth Victim, The (1965-Italian) **C-92m.** *** D: Elio Petri. Marcello Mastroianni, Ursula Andress, Elsa Martinelli, Salvo Randone, Massimo Serato. Cult sci-fi of futuristic society where violence is channeled into legalized murder hunts. Here, Ursula hunts Marcello. Intriguing idea, well done. Based on Robert Sheckley's story "The Seventh Victim." ▼◗

Ten 'til Noon (2007) **C-88m.** **½ D: Scott Storm. Alfonso Freeman, Rick D. Wasserman, Rayne Guest, Jenya Lano, Thomas Kopache, Daniel Hagen, Dylan Kussman, Jennifer Hill, George Williams, Daniel Nathan Spector, Jason Hamer, Paul J. Alessi. Low-rent, Tarantinoesque crime thriller with a gimmick. A man is awakened by a gun-wielding assassin who tells him he's going to die in 10 minutes. We then live the same tense 10 minutes with a series of interlocking characters. The conclusion isn't as satisfying as the buildup, but Paul Osborne's script has some clever ideas. [R]◗

Ten to Midnight (1983) **C-100m.** ** D: J. Lee Thompson. Charles Bronson, Andrew Stevens, Gene Davis, Lisa Eilbacher, Wilford Brimley, Geoffrey Lewis. Handsome psycho-killer does his woman-killing in the nude, but runs afoul of police detective Bronson, whose daughter he terrorizes. Kicked off the force for falsifying evidence against the killer, Bronson goes on his usual Death Wish rampage. Ultraviolent, kinkier-than-average Bronson vehicle. [R] ▼◗

Tenue de Soirée SEE: **Ménage**

Tenure (2009-U.S.-British) **C-89m.** ** D: Mike Million. Luke Wilson, David Koechner, Gretchen Mol, Sasha Alexander, William Bogert, Rosemarie DeWitt, Michael Cudlitz, Hilary Pingle, Andrew Daly, Bob Gunton. College professor Wilson is desperate to earn tenure but can't seem to please his stuffy superiors. Meant to be a spot-on parody of pressure, politics, and pomposity in academia, but the result is inane and predictable, despite the likable presence of Wilson and Mol (playing a rival tenure-track instructor). Released direct to DVD. Super 35. [R]◗

Teorema (1968-Italian) **C-98m.** ** D: Pier Paolo Pasolini. Terence Stamp, Silvana Mangano, Massimo Girotti, Anna Wiazemsky, Laura Betti, Andres Jose Cruz. Pointed but obvious, occasionally hokey political/ sexual fable, with Stamp cast as a young stranger who may be Christ—or Satan. He leaves an irrevocable impression on a bourgeois family by sleeping with its every member. Reworked as DALLAS DOLL, with Sandra Bernhard in the Stamp role! ▼◗

Tequila Sunrise (1988) **C-116m.** **½ D: Robert Towne. Mel Gibson, Michelle Pfeiffer, Kurt Russell, Raul Julia, J.T. Walsh, Arliss Howard, Ann Magnuson, Arye Gross. Lifelong friends, one a supposedly retired drug dealer, the other a fast-rising L.A. cop, are forced to confront each other, both in business and in vying for the affections of a sleek restaurant owner. All three leads exude considerable charisma, but after a snappy start the script leads them nowhere. Veteran director Budd Boetticher plays a judge. Disappointing result for writer-director Towne. [R]▼◗

Teresa (1951) **102m.** ** D: Fred Zinnemann. Pier Angeli, John Ericson, Patricia Collinge, Richard Bishop, Peggy Ann Garner, Ralph Meeker, Bill Mauldin, Edward Binns, Rod Steiger. Ambitious but slow-moving psychological drama of a sensitive young man (Ericson), saddled with a mother from hell, who meets and marries a sweet young Italian (Angeli) while fighting in Italy during WW2. Steiger plays a psychiatrist in his screen debut. See if you can spot Lee Marvin as a GI on board the ship returning to the U.S.

Teresa's Tattoo (1993) **C-95m.** BOMB D: Julie Cypher. C. Thomas Howell, Nancy McKeon, Lou Diamond Phillips, Casey Siemaszko, Jonathan Silverman, Adrienne Shelly, Diedrich Bader, Anthony Clark, Tippi Hedren, k.d. lang, Joe Pantoliano, Mary Kay Place, Mare Winningham, Nanette Fabray, Majel Barrett. Moronic kidnappers' equally moronic hostage accidentally drowns, and guess who's her double? A brainy doctoral candidate in applied mathematics. The laughs are nil in this alleged comedy, with a name cast going slumming. Melissa Etheridge (who did the original songs) appears as a hooker. Kiefer Sutherland appears unbilled as a cop. [R]▼

Terminal, The (2004) **C-128m.** *** D: Steven Spielberg. Tom Hanks, Catherine Zeta-Jones, Stanley Tucci, Chi McBride, Diego Luna, Barry Shabaka Henley, Kumar Pallana, Zoë Saldana, Eddie Jones, Jude Ciccolella, Michael Nouri, Benny Golson. Good-hearted man from Eastern Europe lands at Kennedy Airport just as turmoil in his country causes his passport to be suspended. As a result, he's forced to live inside the airport, where he makes friends and becomes the bête noire of uptight security official Tucci. Spielberg takes a page from Frank Capra's LADY FOR A DAY and asks us to accept a sweet, optimistic fable—not easy for some people to do in this day and age. [PG-13] ▼❶

Terminal Bliss (1992) **91m.** **½ D: Jordan Alan. Timothy Owen, Luke Perry, Estee Chandler. Modern teen-angst drama of disaffected rich kids as they betray each other, seduce one another's girlfriends, act self-indulgent, and seem bored by life. Major attraction here is *Beverly Hills 90210* heartthrob Perry—though he poses no major threat to James Dean. Made in 1987. [R] ▼●

Terminal Choice (1985-Canadian) **C-97m.** *½ D: Sheldon Larry. Joe Spano, Diane Venora, David McCallum, Robert Joy, Don Francks, Nicholas Campbell, Ellen Barkin. Deadly doings at a hospital; good cast wasted in this unsavory thriller. Also known as DEATHBED. [R] ▼

Terminal Island (1973) **C-88m.** *½ D: Stephanie Rothman. Phyllis Elizabeth Davis, Don Marshall, Barbara Leigh, Sean Kenney, Roger Mosley, Tom Selleck, Jo Morrow. Cynical exploitation film about futuristic offshore California penal colony where murderers are sent in lieu of abolished death penalty. Reissued a decade later to capitalize on the presence of several future stars, including *Magnum P.I.*'s Selleck and Mosley. [R] ▼❶

Terminal Man, The (1974) **C-107m.** *** D: Mike Hodges. George Segal, Joan Hackett, Richard A. Dysart, Jill Clayburgh, Donald Moffat, Matt Clark, James (B.) Sikking, Ian Wolfe, Steve Kanaly, Lee DeBroux. Cold but engrossing thriller has computer scientist Segal coming under influence of computers in his brain which cause violence. Well acted; based on the Michael Crichton novel. [PG]

Terminal Station SEE: **Indiscretion of an American Wife**

Terminal Velocity (1994) **C-103m.** *** D: Deran Sarafian. Charlie Sheen, Nastassja Kinski, James Gandolfini, Christopher McDonald, Gary Bullock, Melvin Van Peebles, Hans R. Howes. Hotshot skydiving instructor Sheen is horrified when, on her first jump, his student Kinski plummets to her death—or does she? While trying to prove what really happened, he's plunged into intrigue, danger, and romance. Fast paced and witty, this is a bright variation on Hitchcock themes that, blessedly, never pretends to take itself very seriously. Sheen is miscast, but Kinski is terrific; so are the action scenes. Panavision. [PG-13] ▼❶

Terminator, The (1984) **C-108m.** ***½

D: James Cameron. Arnold Schwarzenegger, Michael Biehn, Linda Hamilton, Paul Winfield, Lance Henriksen, Rick Rossovich, Earl Boen, Dick Miller, Bill Paxton. A cyborg is sent here from the future to kill a seemingly innocent woman. Schwarzenegger is perfectly cast as violence-prone robot who cannot be stopped. Terrific action picture never lets up for a minute—a model for others to follow. Director Cameron cowrote with producer Gale Anne Hurd (inspired by the works of Harlan Ellison). Followed by three sequels and a TV series spinoff. [R] ▼●❶

Terminator 2: Judgment Day (1991) **C-136m.** **½ D: James Cameron. Arnold Schwarzenegger, Linda Hamilton, Edward Furlong, Robert Patrick, Earl Boen, Joe Morton, S. Epatha Merkerson, Castulo Guerra, Danny Cooksey, Jenette Goldstein, Xander Berkeley. A "kinder, gentler" cyborg from the future returns, this time to protect the soon-to-be savior of humanity from destruction by a *rival* terminator. Box-office smash has special effects to knock your socks off (especially the "liquid metal"), and action to spare, but like so many sequels, lacks the freshness of the first film and gives us no one to root for. Oscar winner for Best Makeup, Sound, Sound Effects Editing, and Visual Effects. Some versions feature additional footage. Super 35. [R] ▼●❶

Terminator 3: Rise of the Machines (2003) **C-109m.** *** D: Jonathan Mostow. Arnold Schwarzenegger, Nick Stahl, Claire Danes, David Andrews, Kristanna Loken, Mark Famiglietti, Christopher Lawford. A sleek, sexy new terminator (Loken) returns to kill a now-grown-up John Connor (Stahl), but a T-101 (Schwarzenegger) is on her trail. Not as innovative as the original, or as overblown as the sequel, this one simply entertains, with lots of large-scale action and special effects. Its weakest moments: trying to play off Arnold's "I'll be back" catchlines. Stan Winston's robotic creations are as impressive as ever. Super 35. [R] ▼❶

Terminator Salvation (2009) **C-114m.** *** D: McG. Christian Bale, Sam Worthington, Anton Yelchin, Moon Bloodgood, Bryce Dallas Howard, Common, Jane Alexander, Helena Bonham Carter, Jadagrace berry, Michael Ironside, Ivan Gvera, Terry Crews; voice of Linda Hamilton. In the year 2018 a handful of surviving humans wage war with the machines that rule the planet, run by a network known as Skynet. John Connor (Bale) is part of the armed resistance trying to destroy this army of terminators—but he doesn't know what to make of a superstrong stranger (Worthington) who shows up with no memory of where he came from. Viscerally exciting (if sometimes ear-splitting) blend of action and science fiction has visual effects to spare but boils down to an epic battle between the good guys and the bad. Available director's cut runs 118m. Super 35. [PG-13] ▶

Termini Station (1989-Canadian) **C-105m.** ** D: Allan King. Colleen Dewhurst, Megan Follows, Gordon Clapp, Debra McGrath, Leon Pownall, Elliott Smith, Norma Dell'Agnese, Hanna Lee. Dreary, unenlightening portrait of an angst-ridden family: the father was killed in what may have been a suicide, the mother has become an alcoholic, the son a self-absorbed heel, the daughter a grim-faced prostitute. Tennis, anyone?▼

Term of Trial (1962-British) **113m.** **½ D: Peter Glenville. Laurence Olivier, Simone Signoret, Sarah Miles, Terence Stamp, Roland Culver, Hugh Griffith. Talky story of schoolmaster charged with assault by young Miles, and subsequent trial's effect on Olivier's wife, Signoret. Despite fine cast, a wearisome film. Miles' film debut. ▶

Terms of Endearment (1983) **C-132m.** **** D: James L. Brooks. Shirley MacLaine, Debra Winger, Jack Nicholson, John Lithgow, Jeff Daniels, Lisa Hart Carroll, Danny DeVito. Wonderful mix of humor and heartache follows the relationship of a mother and daughter over the years. Consistently offbeat and unpredictable, with exceptional performances by all three stars; first-time director Brooks also wrote the screenplay from Larry McMurtry's novel. Won Oscars for MacLaine, Nicholson, Screenplay, Director, and Best Picture. Sequel: THE EVENING STAR. [PG] ▼●▶

Terribly Happy (2008-Danish) **C-100m.** *** D: Henrik Ruben Genz. Jakob Cedergren, Lene Maria Christensen, Kim Bodnia, Lars Brygmann, Anders Hove, Jens Jørn Spottag. Emotionally depleted detective, temporarily reassigned to a southern Danish township, encounters an unhappy wife who quickly opens up to him, which is the opposite reaction of the rest of the community. In fact, the entire town is caught in the vise-like hold of one local man's violent disposition . . . or so it seems. Nicely plotted, well-executed thriller grips at one's guts with a disquieting intensity that rarely lets up. Adapted from an Erling Jepsen novel by director Genz and Dunja Gry Jensen. Super 35. ▶

Terror, The (1963) **C-81m.** **½ D: Roger Corman. Boris Karloff, Jack Nicholson, Sandra Knight, Dick Miller. Engaging chiller nonsense with Karloff the mysterious owner of a castle where eerie deeds occur; set on Baltic coast in 1800s. This is the legendary Corman quickie for which all of Karloff's scenes were shot in less than three days as the sets (from THE RAVEN) were being torn down around them! Vistascope.▼

Terror at Red Wolf Inn SEE: **Terror House**

Terror at the Opera (1987-Italian) **C-107m.** **½ D: Dario Argento. Cristina Marsillach,

Ian Charleson, Urbano Barberini, Daria Nicolodi, Corallina G. Tassoni. Horror opus about a young diva who's being stalked by a madman. As customary with Argento, this is stylish but nonsensical, with some over-the-top gore, backed up by a screeching rock score and insane camera calisthenics. Also available in unrated version. Aka OPERA. Super 35. [R]▼▶

Terror Beneath the Sea (1970-Japanese) **C-85m.** *½ D: Hajimo Sato. Peggy Neal, Andrew Hughes, Shinichi (Sonny) Chiba, Mike Daneen, Eric Nielson. Mad scientist creates monsters from human prisoners in an underwater city. The usual.▼▶

Terror By Night (1946) **60m.** **½ D: Roy William Neill. Basil Rathbone, Nigel Bruce, Alan Mowbray, Dennis Hoey, Renee Godfrey, Mary Forbes. Sherlock Holmes dodges death at every turn while guarding a priceless diamond on a bullet-train en route from London to Edinburgh. Lesser, later entry does give Mowbray a fine supporting role. Also shown in computer-colored version.▼●▶

Terror Castle SEE: **Horror Castle**

Terror From Under the House SEE: **Inn of the Frightened People**

Terror Hospital SEE: **Beyond the Living**

Terror House (1972) **C-98m.** *½ D: Bud Townsend. Linda Gillin, Arthur Space, John Neilson, Mary Jackson, Michael Macready. A young woman gets more than she bargained for when she wins a "vacation" trip to an old mansion. Predates other cannibalism efforts, and doesn't take itself that seriously—but still not very good. Aka CLUB DEAD, THE FOLKS AT RED WOLF INN, and TERROR AT RED WOLF INN. Some prints run 83m. Video title: TERROR ON THE MENU. [PG—edited from original R rating]▼▶

Terror in a Texas Town (1958) **80m.** **½ D: Joseph H. Lewis. Sterling Hayden, Sebastian Cabot, Carol Kelly, Eugene Martin, Ned Young, Victor Millan. Offbeat Western drama about Scandinavian whaler (Hayden) who comes to his father's farm in Texas, finds town terrorized by Cabot, who's forcing everyone to sell their oil-rich land. Incredible final showdown.▼▶

Terror in the Aisles (1984) **C/B&W-85m.** *½ D: Andrew J. Kuehn. Nancy Allen, Donald Pleasence. Endless collage of film clips from almost 75 terror movies, from ALIEN to WAIT UNTIL DARK, with the kitchen sink in between. There's silly commentary from Allen and Pleasence, sitting in a simulated movie house, and just too much footage for it all to make any sense. For diehard genre addicts only. [R]▼

Terror in the Wax Museum (1973) **C-93m.** *½ D: Georg Fenady. Ray Milland, Broderick Crawford, Elsa Lanchester, Maurice Evans, Shani Wallis, John Carradine, Louis Hayward, Patric Knowles,

Mark Edwards. Low-grade murder mystery takes little advantage of wax museum horror potential; a good cast wasted. If you look closely you can see the "wax figures" moving. [PG] ▼

Terror in Toyland SEE: **You Better Watch Out**

Terrorist, The (1999-Indian) **C-95m.** *** D: Santosh Sivan. Ayesha Dharkar, Parmeshwaran, Vishnu Vardhan, Bhanu Prakash, K. Krishna, Sonu Sisupal, Vishwas. Contemplative, multilayered portrait of the title character (Dharkar), a 19-year-old fighter in a guerilla war against an unnamed enemy who is recruited as a suicide bomber. Her mission is to assassinate a politician, and it is guaranteed to end in her death. The film's strength is that she is depicted insightfully, as a human being, rather than as a one-dimensional villain or heroine. Well worth seeing. ▼ ▶

Terrorists, The (1975-British) **C-97m.** *½ D: Caspar Wrede. Sean Connery, Ian McShane, Jeffrey Wickham, Isabel Dean, John Quentin. Muddled thriller about political terrorism and airline hijacking is indifferently acted by Connery and McShane, amateurishly directed, and tediously unspooled. Pity, because premise is sound and photography (by Sven Nykvist) is smashing. Original British title: RANSOM. Filmed in Norway. [PG] ▼ ▶

Terrornauts, The (1967-British) **C-75m.** *½ D: Montgomery Tully. Simon Oates, Zena Marshall, Charles Hawtrey, Patricia Hayes, Stanley Meadows, Max Adrian. Alien forces kidnap an entire building on Earth, people and all. Based on Murray Leinster's novel *The Wailing Asteroid,* this sci-fi film is hampered by low budget. ▼

Terror of Dr. Hichcock SEE: **Horrible Dr. Hichcock, The**

Terror of Frankenstein (1975-Swedish-Irish) **C-91m.** *** D: Calvin Floyd. Leon Vitali, Per Oscarsson, Nicholas Clay, Stacey Dorning, Jan Ohlsson. Literate, well-made adaptation of the classic story, definitely worth a look for horror buffs. This is the most faithful of all film versions of Mary Shelley's novel. Original title: VICTOR FRANKENSTEIN. ▼ ▶

Terror of Mechagodzilla (1975-Japanese) **C-83m.** *½ D: Ishiro Honda. K. Sasaki, Tomoko Ai, Akihiko Hirata, Kenji Sahara. Mechagodzilla is restored by villains and sent to destroy Godzilla again, aided by the remote-controlled Titanosaurus. Colorful and full of brawling monsters. Tohoscope. ▼ ▶

Terror of Sheba, The SEE: **Persecution**

Terror of Tiny Town, The (1938) **63m.** *½ D: Sam Newfield. Billy Curtis, Yvonne Moray, Little Billy, John Bambury. If you're looking for a midget musical Western, look no further. A typical sagebrush plot is enacted (pretty badly) by a cast of little people, and the indelible impression is that of characters sauntering into the saloon *under* those swinging doors! ▼ ▶

Terror on the Menu SEE: **Terror House**

Terror's Advocate (2007-French) **C-137m.** *** D: Barbet Schroeder. Forceful, unsettling documentary chronicling the life of Jacques Vergès, a lawyer who fought for the Free French during WW2 and later became notorious for defending such war criminals and terrorists as Klaus Barbie, Slobodan Milosevic, and Carlos the Jackal. He also wed one of his clients: Djamila Bouhired, an Algerian who planted bombs during the French-Algerian war. Schroeder poses some provocative questions about his subject's convictions and motivations. Does he have a political agenda, or is he merely an egomaniac? ▶

Terror Train (1980-Canadian) **C-97m.** ** D: Roger Spottiswoode. Ben Johnson, Jamie Lee Curtis, Hart Bochner, David Copperfield, Derek Mackinnon, D. D. Winters (Vanity), Timothy Weber. Fraternity hires a train for a night-long graduation costume party only to have an ex-member, emotionally scarred by an initiation prank, come aboard, disguised and uninvited, to seek revenge. Stylish photography—by John (A CLOCKWORK ORANGE) Alcott, of all people—and novelty of killer donning the costume of each successive victim lift this above most of the others in this disreputable genre. [R] ▼ ● ▶

TerrorVision (1986) **C-85m.** BOMB D: Ted Nicolaou. Diane Franklin, Mary Woronov, Gerrit Graham, Chad Allen, Bert Remsen, Alejandro Rey, Randi Brooks, Sonny Carl Davis. Inept direction and overacting sink this cartoonish tale of a family and friends' reactions when a monster from outer space emerges from their TV set. Watch the old *Outer Limits* episode instead. [R] ▼

Terror Within, The (1988) **C-88m.** ** D: Thierry Notz. Andrew Stevens, Starr Andreeff, Terri Treas, George Kennedy, John LaFayette, Tommy Hinkley. Grim horror/sci-fi concoction set after plague has wiped out 99 percent of humanity. An underground medical center is attacked by hybrid monsters born of human women and bent on creating more of the same. Low-budget Roger Corman production is a cross between ALIEN and THE DAY THE WORLD ENDED, with a routine, predictable plot. Followed by a sequel. [R] ▼ ▶

Terror Within II, The (1992) **C-89m.** *½ D: Andrew Stevens. Andrew Stevens, Stella Stevens, Chick Vennera, R. Lee Ermey, Burton "Bubba" Gilliam, Clare Hoak. More monsters vs. more scientists in underground bunker after catastrophic plague. Debuting director (and star) Stevens, looking like Rambo, fogs the cheap sets and shows a few good ideas, but his own absurd story sinks it all. That's his mom in a costarring part. [R]▼

Tess (1979-French-British) **C-170m.** ***½ D: Roman Polanski. Nastassia Kinski, Peter Firth, John Bett, Tom Chadbon, Rosemary Martin, Leigh Lawson, Sylvia Coleridge. Handsome, evocative adaptation of Thomas Hardy's *Tess of the D'Urbervilles,* with Kinski in her star-making performance as the strong-willed girl from a poor family whose fortunes rise and fall when she is foisted onto polite society. Long but engrossing. Oscar winner for Cinematography, Costume Design, and Art Direction. Panavision. [PG]▼●

Tess of the Storm Country (1960) **C-84m.** **½ D: Paul Guilfoyle. Diane Baker, Jack Ging, Lee Philips, Archie Duncan, Nancy Valentine, Bert Remsen, Wallace Ford. Leisurely reworking of Grace Miller White novel set in Pennsylvania Dutch country. Here, Tess (Baker) becomes immersed in a dispute between farmers, Mennonites, and chemical plant operators who are polluting the environment. Previously filmed in 1914, 1922, and 1932. CinemaScope.

Testament (1983) **C-89m.** ***½ D: Lynne Littman. Jane Alexander, William Devane, Roxana Zal, Ross Harris, Lukas Haas, Philip Anglim, Lilia Skala, Leon Ames, Rebecca De Mornay, Lurene Tuttle, Kevin Costner. Admirably understated drama about a small town contending with nuclear holocaust, focusing on one tight-knit family. Restrained and effective, with a heartrending performance by Alexander. Screenplay by John Sacret Young, from a story by Carol Amen. Originally made for PBS' *American Playhouse.* [PG]▼●

Testament of Dr. Mabuse, The (1933-German) **121m.** ***½ D: Fritz Lang. Rudolf Klein-Rogge, Otto Wernicke, Gustav Diessl, Karl Meixner. Criminal mastermind controls his underworld empire even while confined to an insane asylum! Fabled character from Lang's silent-film epic returns in less stylized but no less entertaining crime story—which even incorporates supernatural elements. Film was a subject of controversy during Nazi era. Lang returned to this character once more for THE 1,000 EYES OF DR. MABUSE in 1960, but other hands remade this script in 1962. Aka THE LAST WILL OF DR. MABUSE. Some prints run 75m. Retitled THE CRIMES OF DR. MABUSE.▼●

Testament of Orpheus, The (1959-French) **80m.** ***½ D: Jean Cocteau. Jean Cocteau, Edouard Dermit, Henri Cremieux, Jean-Pierre Léaud, Alice Saprich, Françoise Christophe, Yul Brynner, Daniel Gélin, Maria Casares, François Perier, Charles Aznavour, Pablo Picasso, Luis Miguel Dominguin, Lucia Bosé, Jean Marais, Brigitte Bardot, Roger Vadim, Claudine Auger. Cocteau's deeply personalized farewell is

a catalogue of his philosophies and phantasies. Occasionally too artsy, his reverie has no storyline per se, just a succession of astonishingly dreamy images with a seemingly impossible cast. A few moments are in startling color. Third in his Orphic Trilogy after THE BLOOD OF A POET and ORPHEUS. Full title on-screen is THE TESTAMENT OF ORPHEUS OR DO NOT ASK ME WHY. ▼●

Testimony (1987-British) **C/B&W-157m.** ** D: Tony Palmer. Ben Kingsley, Terence Rigby, Ronald Pickup, John Shrapnel, Sherry Baines, Robert Stephens, Murray Melvin, Robert Urquhart. Ambitious, overlong biopic of composer Dmitri Shostakovich focuses on his political problems in the Soviet Union. Kingsley brings depth to the leading role, and Nic Knowland provides fabulous widescreen camerawork in b&w (with flashes of color), but these attributes cannot overcome a turgid narrative. Panavision.●

Test of Love, A (1984-Australian) **C-93m.** *** D: Gil Brealey. Angela Punch McGregor, Drew Forsythe, Wallas Eaton, Simon Chilvers, Liddy Clark, Tina Arhondis. Moving, inspirational, if a bit too predictable story of a young teacher (Punch McGregor), and her attempts to reach a disabled girl (Arhondis, whose performance is truly wonderful). Based on a true story; originally titled ANNIE'S COMING OUT. [PG]▼

Test Pilot (1938) **118m.** *** D: Victor Fleming. Clark Gable, Myrna Loy, Spencer Tracy, Lionel Barrymore, Samuel S. Hinds, Marjorie Main, Gloria Holden, Louis Jean Heydt. Blend of romantic comedy and drama doesn't always work, but with those stars it's well worth watching. Tracy steals film as Gable's mechanic/pal in story of daredevils who try out new aircraft. Based on a Frank "Spig" Wead story.▼

Tetro (2009-U.S.-Argentinean-Spanish-Italian) **127m.** **½ D: Francis Ford Coppola. Vincent Gallo, Alden Ehrenreich, Maribel Verdú, Klaus Maria Brandauer, Carmen Maura, Rodrigo De La Serna, Leticia Brédice. Newcomer Ehrenreich gives an impressive performance as a naïve 17-year-old who grows up fast when he goes to Buenos Aires to reunite with his estranged older stepbrother (Gallo), a once-promising writer who fled from the family and their domineering orchestra-conductor father (Brandauer) ten years earlier. Visually striking (shot mainly in lustrous black-and-white) but overlong, and occasionally overwrought, coming-of-age tale, written by Coppola and loosely inspired by his own family. HD Widescreen. [R]● .

Tex (1982) **C-103m.** *** D: Tim Hunter. Matt Dillon, Jim Metzler, Meg Tilly, Bill McKinney, Frances Lee McCain, Ben Johnson, Emilio Estevez, Jack Thibeau.

First of S. E. Hinton's young-adult best sellers to reach the screen (via the Disney company) is an understated but likable tale of a boy whose mother has died, whose father is away, whose brother is trying to raise him with no money and little patience . . . and whose self-esteem is nil. Straightforward little drama. Hinton has a cameo as a teacher. [PG]▼●)

Texas (1941) **93m.** *** D: George Marshall. William Holden, Glenn Ford, Claire Trevor, George Bancroft, Edgar Buchanan. High-level Western of two friends, one a rustler (Holden), the other a cattleman (Ford), competing for Trevor's affection.▼

Texas Across the River (1966) **C-101m.** *** D: Michael Gordon. Dean Martin, Alain Delon, Joey Bishop, Rosemary Forsyth, Peter Graves, Tina Marquand (Aumont), Andrew Prine, Michael Ansara, Dick (Richard) Farnsworth. Diverting takeoff on cowboy-and-Indian films, with Bishop hilarious as a deadpan Indian and Marquand cute as a young Indian maiden. Techniscope.▼●

Texas Carnival (1951) **C-77m.** ** D: Charles Walters. Esther Williams, Howard Keel, Red Skelton, Ann Miller, Keenan Wynn, Tom Tully, Red Norvo. Emptier than usual, this flabby MGM musical about penniless carny mistaken for millionaire leaves fine cast high and dry with no fresh material.▼●

Texas Chain Saw Massacre, The (1974) **C-83m.** *** D: Tobe Hooper. Marilyn Burns, Gunnar Hansen, Edwin Neal, Allen Danzinger, Paul A. Partain, William Vail. Travelers in rural Texas encounter crazed family of bizarros who have a committed though unusual sense of what cuts of meat you need for good barbecue. Sweat-inducing, claustrophobic, unrelenting suspense-comic-horror film. Classic and influential—and nowhere nearly as violent as it's reputed to be. Narrated by an unbilled John Larroquette. Remade in 2003. Followed by three sequels. [R]▼●)

Texas Chainsaw Massacre, The (2003) **C-98m.** *½ D: Marcus Nispel. Jessica Biel, Jonathan Tucker, Erica Leerhsen, Mike Vogel, Eric Balfour, Andrew Bryniarski, R. Lee Ermey, David Dorfman; narrated by John Larroquette. Teenagers in Texas are attacked by an inbred family of cannibals. This remake is intense but completely lacks the leavening sense of humor that enhanced the original. Once it kicks into gear, it's brutally unrelenting toward its unappealing characters—and the audience. Followed by the "prequel" THE TEXAS CHAINSAW MASSACRE: THE BEGINNING. [R]▼)

Texas Chainsaw Massacre 2, The (1986) **C-95m.** BOMB D: Tobe Hooper. Dennis Hopper, Caroline Williams, Bill Johnson, Jim Siedow, Bill Moseley. Hooper returns with a mind-numbing, pretentious sequel. Hopper plays a nutty ex-Texas Ranger obsessed with revenge against the crazed family of Texas cannibals, while deejay Williams is simply looking to save her own skin when the cannibals go after her following a broadcast that angers them. Frenetic overacting and unfunny attempts at black humor sink this mess. Followed by LEATHERFACE: TEXAS CHAINSAW MASSACRE III. [R]▼●

Texas Chainsaw Massacre: The Beginning, The (2006) **C-91m.** *½ D: Jonathan Liebesman. Jordana Brewster, Taylor Handley, Diora Baird, Matthew Bomer, Lee Tergesen, R. Lee Ermey, Andrew Bryniarski; narrated by John Larroquette. When the ideas for endless sequels wear out, bring on the prequels! This one creates a backstory for the chainsaw-wielding Leatherface, set in the 1970s. Two teen brothers and their girlfriends go on a final fling before shipping off to Vietnam, get caught up in the infamous house of horrors and face-lifts after a car accident brings them to the attention of the evil local sheriff. There is nothing to suggest the '70s period; it's all about graphic violence. This is one "beginning" whose ending can't come quickly enough. Unrated version runs 96m. Super 35. [R]▶

Texas Chainsaw Massacre: The Next Generation (1997) **C-84m.** *½ D: Kim Henkel. Renée Zellweger, Matthew McConaughey, Robert Jacks, Tonie Perenski, Lisa Newmyer, Tyler Cone, John Harrison. More Texas teenagers are menaced by a backwoods family of murderous maniacs. Though a semi-remake of the first film, it's nowhere near as interesting or scary—no chainsaws, no cannibalism. Writer-director Henkel tries for profundity at the end and blows it, but it's clear why Zellweger and the scenery-devouring McConaughey went on to bigger things. Aka RETURN OF THE TEXAS CHAINSAW MASSACRE; that version runs 94m. [R]▼▶

Texas Detour (1978) **C-92m.** ** D: Hikmet Avedis. Patrick Wayne, Mitch Vogel, Lindsay Bloom, R. G. Armstrong, Priscilla Barnes, Cameron Mitchell. Typical low-grade action picture about a macho stunt driver. [R]▼

Texas Lady (1955) **C-86m.** ** D: Tim Whelan. Claudette Colbert, Barry Sullivan, Greg Walcott, Horace McMahon, John Litel. Genteel oater with Colbert lovely as crusading newspaper editor in old West. Mediocre script. SuperScope.▼

Texas Rangers, The (1936) **95m.** *** D: King Vidor. Fred MacMurray, Jack Oakie, Jean Parker, Lloyd Nolan, Edward Ellis. Fine, elaborate Western of three comrades who split up; MacMurray and Oakie become rangers, Nolan an outlaw. Remade as STREETS OF LAREDO; sequel: THE TEXAS RANGERS RIDE AGAIN.▼▶

Texas Rangers, The (1951) **C-74m.** **½ D: Phil Karlson. George Montgomery, Gale Storm, Jerome Courtland, Noah Beery, Jr. Aimless Western involving Texas law enforcers against gang of outlaws. ▼

Texas Rangers, The (2001) **C-90m.** **½ D: Steve Miner. James Van Der Beek, Dylan McDermott, Usher Raymond, Ashton Kutcher, Robert Patrick, Rachael Leigh Cook, Alfred Molina, Tom Skerritt, Leonor Varela, Randy Travis, Matt Keeslar, Jon Abrahams, Vincent Spano, Oded Fehr, Joe Spano. Young man joins the recently formed Texas Rangers to avenge the death of his family and becomes an aide to the unit's enigmatic leader (McDermott). Beautifully mounted widescreen Western isn't bad, but its story is superficial and derivative. Of the young stars, Van Der Beek fares best, while Molina has fun as a sneering villain. This sat on the shelf for almost two years. Panavision. [PG-13]▼▶

Texasville (1990) **C-123m.** **½ D: Peter Bogdanovich. Jeff Bridges, Cybill Shepherd, Annie Potts, Timothy Bottoms, Cloris Leachman, Randy Quaid, Eileen Brennan, William McNamara, Angie Bolling. Mildly diverting sequel to THE LAST PICTURE SHOW, from Larry McMurtry's novel, revealing that time has turned a number of the leading characters into Texas caricatures. No real plot to speak of, just a series of vignettes, some better than others. Potts stands out as Bridges' brassy wife, with Shepherd trying to assert the seriousness of her underwritten role by wearing no makeup and looking as bad (realistic?) as possible in every single shot. [R]▼▶●

Texican, The (1966) **C-91m.** ** D: Lesley Selander. Audie Murphy, Broderick Crawford, Diana Lorys, Luz Marquez, Antonio Casas, Antonio Perel. Routine Spanish-made Western pits ex-lawman Murphy against ruthless frontier town boss Crawford. Techniscope.▼▶

Thank God It's Friday (1978) **C-90m.** BOMB D: Robert Klane. Donna Summer, Valerie Landsburg, Terri Nunn, Chick Vennera, Ray Vitte, Jeff Goldblum, Paul Jabara, Debra Winger, Andrea Howard, The Commodores (with Lionel Richie). Perhaps the worst film ever to have won some kind of Oscar (for Summer's hit song, "Last Dance"), this one-night-in-the-life-of-a-disco comedy is about as monotonous and uninventive as disco music itself. [PG]▼▶

Thanks a Million (1935) **87m.** *** D: Roy Del Ruth. Dick Powell, Ann Dvorak, Fred Allen, Patsy Kelly, Alan Dinehart, Margaret Irving, Paul Whiteman and Orchestra, Yacht Club Boys. Very entertaining musical of crooner Powell running for governor, with help of wisecracking manager Allen, sweetheart Dvorak, and blustery politician Raymond Walburn. Good fun, with several breezy tunes and specialties by Whiteman

and Yacht Club Boys. Script by Nunnally Johnson. Remade as IF I'M LUCKY.

Thank You All Very Much (1969-British) **C-105m.** *** D: Waris Hussein. Sandy Dennis, Ian McKellen, Eleanor Bron, John Standing. Absorbing study of unwed mother who decides to have her baby. Realistic and touching. Original British title: A TOUCH OF LOVE. [M/PG]

Thank You for Smoking (2006) **C-92m.** *** D: Jason Reitman. Aaron Eckhart, Maria Bello, Adam Brody, Katie Holmes, Cameron Bright, Robert Duvall, William H. Macy, Rob Lowe, David Koechner, Sam Elliott, J. K. Simmons, Kim Dickens. Spot-on satire of American culture and the phenomenon of spinmeisters, focusing on Nick Naylor (Eckhart, in a dynamic performance), who's the unapologetic spokesman for the tobacco industry in Washington, D.C. A trip to California gives the divorced dad a chance to spend time with (and explain himself to) his inquisitive and impressionable son. Impressive feature debut for director Reitman (son of Ivan), who also adapted Christopher Buckley's book. Panavision. [R]◗

Thank Your Lucky Stars (1943) **127m.** *** D: David Butler. Eddie Cantor, Dennis Morgan, Joan Leslie; guest stars Humphrey Bogart, Bette Davis, Olivia de Havilland, Errol Flynn, John Garfield, Ida Lupino, Ann Sheridan, etc. Very lame plot (Cantor plays both himself and lookalike cabbie) frames all-star Warner Bros. show, with Davis singing "They're Either Too Young Or Too Old," Flynn delightfully performing "That's What You Jolly Well Get," other staid stars breaking loose. ▼▶●

That Certain Age (1938) **101m.** **½ D: Edward Ludwig. Deanna Durbin, Melvyn Douglas, Jackie Cooper, Irene Rich, Nancy Carroll, John Halliday, Jack Searl. Deanna develops crush on her parents' houseguest, sophisticated Douglas, leaving boyfriend Cooper out in the cold—and saddled with responsibility for putting on amateur show. Silly script made bearable by stars. ▼▶

That Certain Feeling (1956) **C-103m.** BOMB D: Norman Panama, Melvin Frank. Bob Hope, Eva Marie Saint, George Sanders, Pearl Bailey, Al Capp, Jerry Mathers. Incredibly bad Hope comedy with Bob as neurotic cartoonist; Sanders gives only life to stale film. Pearl sings title song. VistaVision.

That Certain Woman (1937) **93m.** **½ D: Edmund Goulding. Bette Davis, Henry Fonda, Ian Hunter, Donald Crisp, Anita Louise, Minor Watson, Sidney Toler. Remake of Goulding's early talkie THE TRESPASSER (with Gloria Swanson) features Bette as a gangster's widow who's trying to start life afresh and finds herself in a romantic triangle with weak-willed playboy Fonda and lawyer Hunter. Well-acted soaper.▼▶

That Championship Season (1982) C-110m. ** D: Jason Miller. Bruce Dern, Stacy Keach, Robert Mitchum, Martin Sheen, Paul Sorvino, Arthur Franz. Disappointing adaptation of Miller's Pulitzer Prize–winning play (which took 10 years to reach the screen), about the 24th annual reunion of a high school basketball squad and their paternalistic coach. Whatever made it work on stage is missing here; the movie never catches fire, and its characters come off more as caricatures. Remade for TV in 1999. [R]▼❂

That Cold Day in the Park (1969) C-113m. *½ D: Robert Altman. Sandy Dennis, Michael Burns, Susanne Benton, John Garfield, Jr., Luana Anders, Michael Murphy. Strange, plodding film with frustrated spinster taking in young man she sees in the park. What follows is bizarre and unmoving; a far cry from Altman's later work. Filmed in Canada. [R]▼

That Darn Cat! (1965) C-116m. *** D: Robert Stevenson. Hayley Mills, Dean Jones, Dorothy Provine, Roddy McDowall, Neville Brand, Elsa Lanchester, William Demarest, Frank Gorshin, Ed Wynn. Long but entertaining suspense comedy from Disney, about a cat that leads FBI man Jones on trail of kidnapped woman. Slapstick scenes and character vignettes highlight this colorful film. Remade in 1997. ▼❂

That Darn Cat (1997) C-89m. *½ D: Bob Spiers. Christina Ricci, Doug E. Doug, Dean Jones, George Dzundza, Peter Boyle, Michael McKean, Bess Armstrong, Dyan Cannon, John Ratzenberger, Megan Cavanagh, Estelle Parsons, Rebecca Schull. Remake of the 1965 film follows basically the same plot, but without the same results; every change is for the worse. Even the cat is boring. Director Spiers hammers every joke flat, so his talented cast is helpless, though Ricci and McKean have some good moments. Doug is funny, but seems to come from a different, broader movie. [PG] ▼❂

That Evening Sun (2009) C-109m. *** D: Scott Teems. Hal Holbrook, Raymond McKinnon, Walton Goggins, Mia Wasikowska, Carrie Preston, Barry Corbin, Dixie Carter. Stubborn 80-year-old man walks out of the nursing home where he's been sent to live and returns to his Tennessee farm, only to find it occupied by a "white trash" family. He refuses to see the land he built up in the hands of a man he considers a no-account. Modest but nicely detailed Southern character piece is elevated by Holbrook's commanding presence. Adapted from a William Gay short story by the director. [PG-13]❂

That Forsyte Woman (1949) C-114m. **½ D: Compton Bennett. Errol Flynn, Greer Garson, Walter Pidgeon, Robert Young, Janet Leigh, Harry Davenport. Rather superficial adaptation of John Galsworthy novel of a faithless woman (Garson) who finds herself attracted to her niece's fiancé; good-looking, but no match for the later BBC-TV series *The Forsyte Saga.* ▼❂

That Funny Feeling (1965) C-93m. **½ D: Richard Thorpe. Sandra Dee, Bobby Darin, Donald O'Connor, Nita Talbot, Larry Storch, Leo G. Carroll, Robert Strauss. Funny only if you adore Darin and Dee, and even then story of footloose playboy and maid who pretends she lives in his apartment wears thin.▼

That Hagen Girl (1947) 83m. **½ D: Peter Godfrey. Ronald Reagan, Shirley Temple, Rory Calhoun, Lois Maxwell, Dorothy Peterson, Charles Kemper, Conrad Janis, Penny Edwards, Jean Porter, Harry Davenport. Obvious but fascinating time capsule about small-town small-mindedness, with teen Temple ostracized because gossips think she's illegitimate. Of interest for the casting of Temple and Reagan (playing a lawyer who supposedly is Shirley's father), and as a portrait of a time in which illegitimate children were victimized because of the circumstances of their births.

That Hamilton Woman (1941) 128m. *** D: Alexander Korda. Vivien Leigh, Laurence Olivier, Alan Mowbray, Sara Allgood, Gladys Cooper, Henry Wilcoxon, Heather Angel, Halliwell Hobbes, Gilbert Emery. Olivier and Leigh—both breathtakingly beautiful—enact ill-fated historical romance of Lord Admiral Nelson and Lady Emma Hamilton in American-made film intended to spur pro-British feelings before the U.S. entered WW2. Vincent Korda's sets are incredibly opulent. P.S. This was Winston Churchill's favorite movie. Aka LADY HAMILTON. ▼❂

That Kind of Woman (1959) 92m. *** D: Sidney Lumet. Sophia Loren, Tab Hunter, George Sanders, Jack Warden, Keenan Wynn, Barbara Nichols. WW2 soldier Hunter and dishy Loren are attracted to each other on a train, but she's the mistress of elegant fatcat Sanders. Surprisingly adult comedy-drama for its era; excellent performances from all but Hunter, and even he's better than usual. Well shot by Boris Kaufman. Remake of THE SHOPWORN ANGEL, scripted by Walter Bernstein. Look for young Bea Arthur as a WAC. VistaVision.

That Lady (1955) C-100m. **½ D: Terence Young. Olivia de Havilland, Gilbert Roland, Paul Scofield, Dennis Price, Christopher Lee. Unemotional costumer set in 16th-century Spain, with de Havilland a widowed noblewoman involved in court intrigue. Scofield's film debut. CinemaScope.

That Lady in Ermine (1948) C-89m. **½ D: Ernst Lubitsch. Betty Grable, Douglas

Fairbanks, Jr., Cesar Romero, Walter Abel, Reginald Gardiner, Harry Davenport. Entertaining if overblown musical of mythical European kingdom where Grable is a just-married princess; her ancestors magically come to life as Fairbanks' conquering army descends on her castle. Lubitsch died during production, which was completed by Otto Preminger. Script by Samson Raphaelson.

That'll Be the Day (1974-British) **C-90m.** *** D: Claude Whatham. David Essex, Ringo Starr, Rosemary Leach, James Booth, Billy Fury, Keith Moon. Compelling story traces British working-class youth (Essex) from adolescence to early adulthood in the 1950s, as his growing frustrations find their eventual outlet in rock music. First half of dynamic story, continued in STARDUST, where character's resemblance to John Lennon crystallizes. [PG]▼●]

That Lucky Touch (1975-British) **C-93m.** *½ D: Christopher Miles. Roger Moore, Susannah York, Shelley Winters, Lee J. Cobb, Jean-Pierre Cassel, Raf Vallone, Sydne Rome, Donald Sinden. Tepid romantic farce with Moore cast as an arms dealer; York is the feisty journalist who conflicts with him. Moore sleepwalks through this. Of note only as Cobb's last movie (and he's the best thing in it). [PG]▼

That Man Bolt (1973) **C-105m.** ** D: Henry Levin, David Lowell Rich. Fred Williamson, Byron Webster, Teresa Graves, Jack Ging, Miko Mayama. Scenic actioner, filmed in Hong Kong, Las Vegas and L.A., mixes kung fu, some comedy and two songs by Graves. Plot has Williamson as international courier of syndicate money. [R]▼]

That Man From Rio (1964-French) **C-114m.** *** D: Philippe De Broca. Jean-Paul Belmondo. Françoise Dorleac, Jean Servais, Adolfo Celi, Simone Renant. Engaging spoof of Bond-type movies features Belmondo as hero, chasing double-crosser and thief in search for Brazilian treasure. Nice cinematography by Edmond Séchan complements fast-moving script. Enjoyed great international success and spawned many imitations.▼

That Night (1992) **C-90m.** ** D: Craig Bolotin. Juliette Lewis, C. Thomas Howell, Eliza Dushku, Helen Shaver, J. Smith-Cameron, John Dossett, Katherine Heigl. Young suburban girl (Dushku) worships fiery teen Lewis, who embarks on an ill-fated romance with sensitive bad-boy Howell. Disappointing view of adolescent angst and a child's initial experience with grown-up emotions; about as subtle as a blaring boom-box. [PG-13]▼●

That Night in Rio (1941) **C-90m.** **½ D: Irving Cummings. Alice Faye, Don Ameche, Carmen Miranda, S. Z. Sakall, J. Carrol Naish, Curt Bois, Leonid Kinsky, Frank Puglia. Standard 20th Century-Fox

musical of mistaken identities, uses Miranda to best advantage; Maria Montez has a tiny role. Filmed before as FOLIES BERGÈRE and again as ON THE RIVIERA. ◗

That Obscure Object of Desire (1977-Spanish-French) **C-103m.** *** D: Luis Buñuel. Fernando Rey, Carole Bouquet, Angela Molina, Julien Bertheau, Andre Weber. Buñuel's last film is as audacious as any of his classics; wealthy sadomasochist Rey falls hard for a young maid, and she's only too happy to make him "suffer." Buñuel's bizarrest stroke is having Bouquet and Molina alternate playing the girl! Shot in French, with Rey dubbed by Michel Piccoli. Based on a Pierre Louys novel; filmed several times, most notably as THE DEVIL IS A WOMAN (1935). [R]▼●]

That Old Feeling (1997) **C-105m.** **½ D: Carl Reiner. Bette Midler, Dennis Farina, Paula Marshall, Gail O'Grady, David Rasche, Jamie Denton, Danny Nucci. Silly but likable comedy about long-feuding exspouses who meet after 12 years at their daughter's wedding—and to their own shock and amazement, start having an affair. This seems to have a ricochet effect on everyone around them, in French farce fashion. Not the most believable movie ever made, but it's fun; Midler and Farina make a great couple. [PG-13]▼●]

That's Dancing! (1985) **C/B&W-105m.** **½ D: Jack Haley, Jr. Narrated and hosted by Gene Kelly, Sammy Davis, Jr., Mikhail Baryshnikov, Liza Minnelli, Ray Bolger. Too many mediocre selections, flat introductions by five guest hosts . . . but there's still much to enjoy in this dance compilation, from Fred and Ginger's "Pick Yourself Up" to WEST SIDE STORY. Added curio: a Bolger number cut from THE WIZARD OF OZ. 1980s selections that end the film seem lumbering and ludicrous compared to the marvels of movement that precede them. Part Widescreen. [G]▼●]

That's Entertainment! (1974) **C-132m.** **** D: Jack Haley, Jr. Hosted by Fred Astaire, Bing Crosby, Gene Kelly, Peter Lawford, Liza Minnelli, Donald O'Connor, Debbie Reynolds, Mickey Rooney, Frank Sinatra, James Stewart, Elizabeth Taylor. Stars host nostalgia bash with scenes from nearly 100 MGM musicals. There are many cherished moments with the above-named stars plus unexpectedly delightful numbers with Esther Williams, Clark Gable (singing and dancing!), Jimmy Durante, and Eleanor Powell, whose challenge dance with Astaire is unforgettable. Only complaint: why shorten the final AMERICAN IN PARIS ballet? Followed by two sequels. Part Widescreen. [G]▼●]

That's Entertainment, Part II (1976) **C-133m.** ***½ D: Gene Kelly. Fred Astaire and Gene Kelly host this inevitable sequel and do some engaging song-and-dance work. Film hasn't cohesion or momentum of its predecessor, but the material is irresistible. This time, comedy and drama are included along with musical numbers—Tracy and Hepburn, Marx Brothers, etc. Most imaginative segment of all is wonderful title sequence by Saul Bass. Cut to 126m. after initial showings. Part Widescreen. [G]▼●●

That's Entertainment! III (1994) C-108m. ***½ D: Bud Friedgen, Michael J. Sheridan. June Allyson, Cyd Charisse, Lena Horne, Howard Keel, Gene Kelly, Ann Miller, Debbie Reynolds, Mickey Rooney, Esther Williams. Yet another collection of marvelous musical moments from the MGM library, spiked by some never-before-seen footage eliminated from the finished films, including a discarded Fred Astaire dance routine (shown in split-screen with its retake), Judy Garland singing Irving Berlin's "Mr. Monotony," Cyd Charisse and Joan Crawford singing and dancing to the same prerecorded number, Lena Horne singing "Ain't It the Truth" from CABIN IN THE SKY, and much, much more. Video release has expanded versions of some numbers cut for the theatrical print. Part Widescreen. [G]▼●●

That Sinking Feeling (1979-Scottish) C-92m. *** D: Bill Forsyth. Robert Buchanan, John Hughes, Billy Greenlees, Gordon John Sinclair, Janette Rankin. Forsyth's initial feature is a witty little comedy about a gang of bored teens unable to find work in dreary Glasgow. Their leader comes up with a scheme to boost their morale: pilfering sinks from a warehouse. Released in U.S. after the success of Forsyth's subsequent films (GREGORY'S GIRL, LOCAL HERO). [PG]▼●

That's Life! (1986) C-102m. *** D: Blake Edwards. Jack Lemmon, Julie Andrews, Sally Kellerman, Robert Loggia, Jennifer Edwards, Rob Knepper, Matt Lattanzi, Chris Lemmon, Cynthia Sikes, Emma Walton, Felicia Farr. Deeply felt observation of an affluent family and its members' personal crises— including Lemmon's anxiety over turning 60 and his loving wife's fear that she may have cancer. Far from perfect, but mostly believable and quite moving. Filmed at Edwards' and wife Andrews' actual Malibu home, with most of their (and Lemmon's) real-life family on-screen . . . including at least one pet! Panavision. [PG-13]▼●●

That's My Boy (1951) 98m. ** D: Hal Walker. Dean Martin, Jerry Lewis, Marion Marshall, Eddie Mayehoff, Ruth Hussey, Polly Bergen, John McIntire. Ex-football star Mayehoff wants klutzy son Lewis to follow in his footsteps, induces Martin to coach him. Supposed comic idea is played straight, with very few laughs, maudlin situations . . . yet it was considered quite funny

in 1951 when M&L were in their heyday. Later a TV series.●

That's The Way of the World SEE: **Shining Star**

that thing you do! (1996) C-110m. *** D: Tom Hanks. Tom Everett Scott, Johnathon Schaech, Steve Zahn, Ethan Embry, Liv Tyler, Tom Hanks, Charlize Theron, Bill Cobbs, Obba Babatunde, Giovanni Ribisi, Alex Rocco, Chris Isaak, Kevin Pollak, Clint Howard, Bryan Cranston, Colin Hanks. Likable yarn, set in 1964, about some young people in Erie, Pa., who form a band that, improbably, soars to success with a hit record. Sunny attitude and appealing cast make this hard to resist, even if it turns out to be a "lite" version of THE COMMITMENTS. Hanks also wrote the script and some of the songs. Hanks's wife, Rita Wilson, has an amusing cameo as a cocktail waitress, and his long-ago *Bosom Buddies* TV costar Peter Scolari plays a television host. Alternate version runs 155m. [PG]▼●●

That Touch of Mink (1962) C-99m. **½ D: Delbert Mann. Cary Grant, Doris Day, Gig Young, Audrey Meadows, John Astin, Dick Sargent. Attractive cast in silly piece of fluff with wealthy playboy Grant pursuing Day. Amusing at times, but wears thin; Astin is memorable as a creep with designs on poor Doris, and there's a clever sequence featuring Mickey Mantle, Roger Maris, Yogi Berra, and umpire Art Passarella. Panavision. ▼●●

That Uncertain Feeling (1941) 84m. *** D: Ernst Lubitsch. Merle Oberon, Melvyn Douglas, Burgess Meredith, Alan Mowbray, Olive Blakeney, Harry Davenport, Sig Rumann, Eve Arden. Chic little Lubitsch comedy about married couple with problems, and their absurd pianist friend. Stolen hands down by Meredith as the musical malcontent. Filmed before (in 1925) by Lubitsch as KISS ME AGAIN. Also shown in computer-colored version. ▼●

That Was Then, This Is Now (1985) C-100m. **½ D: Christopher Cain. Emilio Estevez, Craig Sheffer, Kim Delaney, Barbara Babcock, Jill Schoelen, Frank Howard, Larry B. Scott, Ramon Sheen, Morgan Freeman. Delinquent kid, alienated from society, clings to his relationship with adoptive brother—and freaks out when the older boy takes on a girlfriend, whom he sees as a threat. Estevez wrote the script, from S. E. Hinton's young-adult novel, but its intense emotions probably read better than they play out on screen. A variable film with some strong moments. [R]▼●●

Theater of Blood (1973-British) C-104m. *** D: Douglas Hickox. Vincent Price, Diana Rigg, Robert Morley, Ian Hendry, Harry Andrews, Coral Browne, Robert Coote, Michael Hordern, Jack Hawkins, Diana Dors, Dennis Price, Milo O'Shea. A one-joke film, albeit a great joke: hammy

Shakespearean actor Price vows revenge on critics who've blasted him, murders them one by one by recreating famous death scenes from the plays. Somewhat spoiled by incredibly gory killings; great cast has fun with it, though. [R]▼○●

Theatre of Death (1967-British) **C-90m.** **½ D: Samuel Gallu. Christopher Lee, Julian Glover, Lelia Goldoni, Jenny Till, Evelyn Laye, Ivor Dean. Vampire-like murders revolving around Paris' Grand Guignol stage sensation and its beautiful young starlet under sinister hypnotic trance. Solid, low-budget mystery-thriller benefits from believable performances. Aka BLOOD FIEND. Technicolor.▼●

Thelma & Louise (1991) **C-128m.** *** D: Ridley Scott. Susan Sarandon, Geena Davis, Harvey Keitel, Michael Madsen, Christopher McDonald, Stephen Tobolowsky, Brad Pitt, Timothy Carhart, Lucinda Jenney. Female friends leave responsibilities (as well as husband and boyfriend) behind to take a short trip, but an unexpected incident turns them into fugitives from the law. Dynamic star duo—and Callie Khouri's Oscar-winning feminist script—give this a lot of juice, though it still covers all-too-familiar road-movie territory. Panavision. [R]▼○●

Thelma Jordon SEE: **File on Thelma Jordon, The**

Thelonious Monk: Straight No Chaser (1988) **C/B&W-90m.** *** D: Charlotte Zwerin. Comprehensive documentary portrait of the legendary, innovative jazz pianist-composer, crammed with footage of Monk in performance. Much of the material was shot during the late 1960s by Christian Blackwood. Executive producer is Clint Eastwood; released the same year as the latter's Charlie Parker biography, BIRD. [PG-13]▼○●

Them! (1954) **94m.** ***½ D: Gordon Douglas. James Whitmore, Edmund Gwenn, Joan Weldon, James Arness, Onslow Stevens. First-rate '50s sci-fi about giant ant mutations running wild in the Southwest. Intelligent script (by Ted Sherdeman, from George Worthing Yates' story) extremely well directed, with memorable climax in L.A. sewers. Fess Parker has small but memorable role. Look fast for Leonard Nimoy at a teletype machine.▼○●

Them (2006-French-Romanian) **C-76m.** **½ D: David Moreau, Xavier Palud. Olivia Bonamy, Michaël Cohen, Adriana Moca, Maria Roman, Camelia Maxim. Clementine and Lucas, a schoolteacher and a writer, revel in their peaceful rural weekend far from Bucharest . . . until they're awakened by shadowy, mysterious home invaders way worse than giant ants. Simple, tense, terse two-character thriller has a cold, cold heart, and rates kudos for scant grue. But the disappointing Big Reveal is just a variation on the same-old same-old, brandishing a dull

and rusty cutting edge. Written by the directors. Digital Video Widescreen. [R]▶

Then She Found Me (2008) **C-100m.** *** D: Helen Hunt. Helen Hunt, Colin Firth, Bette Midler, Matthew Broderick, Ben Shenkman, John Benjamin Hickey, Lynn Cohen. Hunt's adoptive mother dies and her feckless husband opts out of their marriage. At her most vulnerable, and desperate to have a baby, two new people enter her life: a garrulous TV talk show host who claims to be her birth mother (Midler, who's perfect) and a wounded single father (Firth) who's attracted to her. There's nary a false move in this smart, funny, timely comedy-drama, a notable feature directorial debut for Hunt, who also helped to adapt Elinor Lipman's novel. Hunt's ob-gyn is played by author Salman Rushdie. [R]▶

Theodora Goes Wild (1936) **94m.** ***½ D: Richard Boleslawski. Irene Dunne, Melvyn Douglas, Thomas Mitchell, Thurston Hall, Rosalind Keith, Spring Byington. Dunne's first starring comedy is a delightful story about small-town woman who writes scandalous best-seller and falls in love with sophisticated New Yorker who illustrated the book. Lots of funny twists in this engaging farce, scripted by Sidney Buchman from a Mary McCarthy story.▼▶

Theodore Rex (1996) **C-91m.** *½ D: Jonathan Betuel. Whoopi Goldberg, Armin Mueller-Stahl, Juliet Landau, Bud Cort, Stephen McHattie, Richard Roundtree, Jack Riley; voices of George Newbern, Carol Kane. Set in the future, when DNA technology has led to the reanimation of dinosaurs, police officer Goldberg teams up with a talking Tyrannosaurus Rex to solve a murder. Cheesy production and low-key performances hinder this aimless tale. Children may like the cookie-loving dino. Plans for wide theatrical release were (understandably) scrubbed; it went to video instead. [PG]▼○●

Theory of Flight, The (1998-British) **C-100m.** ** D: Paul Greengrass. Helena Bonham Carter, Kenneth Branagh, Gemma Jones, Holly Aird, Ray Stevenson. A perpetual screwup who feels he has something to express but no clue how to do it is punished for his last stunt by having to perform community service. His assignment: to spend time with a brilliant but hostile young woman in a wheelchair suffering from motor neuron disease, whose one dream is to have sex. Frightfully contrived from the word go, this forced piece of whimsy never takes off, despite two gifted stars. [R]▼○

There Be Dragons (2011-U.S.-Spanish) **C-122m.** **½ D: Roland Joffé. Charlie Cox, Wes Bentley, Dougray Scott, Rodrigo Santoro, Jordi Mollá, Derek Jacobi, Golshifteh Farahani, Geraldine Chaplin, Olga Kurylenko, Unax Ugalde, Ana Torrent, Charles Dance, Lily Cole. Joffé returns to the historical style of THE MISSION in this challenging story of the conflict between two very different men during the Spanish Civil War. Contemporary journalist Scott travels to Spain to investigate the story behind a candidate for sainthood, only to find his now aging father harbors deep secrets about his own relationship to the man. Tale is told mostly in flashbacks as the complex connections unfold between Cox as a founder of the controversial Catholic sect Opus Dei and Bentley as the poor revolutionary who once attended the same seminary school. Convoluted, to be sure, but Joffé brings a passion to the material that makes it more compelling than it might be in other hands. Super 35. [PG-13]

There Goes My Baby (1994) **C-99m.** *** D: Floyd Mutrux. Dermot Mulroney, Rick Schroder, Kelli Williams, Noah Wyle, Jill Schoelen, Kristin Minter, Lucy Deakins, Seymour Cassel, Paul Gleason, Andrew Robinson, Mark Ruffalo; narrated by Anne Archer. It's 1965 and a group of high school seniors pause on the brink of Real Life. If it sounds a lot like AMERICAN GRAFFITI, you're right . . . but this film takes place in 1965, not 1962. In the interim, JFK has been assassinated, the Civil Rights movement is boiling, and Vietnam has become a divisive issue. Writer-director Mutrux effectively blends nostalgia and political awareness in this entertaining film. Made in 1990. [R] ▼●)

There Goes the Bride (1979-British) **C-88m.** BOMB D: Terence Marcel. Tom Smothers, Twiggy, Martin Balsam, Sylvia Syms, Michael Witney, Hermione Baddeley, Broderick Crawford, Phil Silvers, Jim Backus. Addle-brained father-of-the-bride Smothers throws the wedding party into a tizzy when he has a fling with 1920's-flapper model, Twiggy, whom he has conjured up and only he can see. Unfunny slapstick that comes alive for about 45 seconds when Smothers and Twiggy do an on-target, extravagantly staged Astaire-Rogers routine. Based on Ray Cooney's and John Chapman's 1974 West End farce. [PG] ▼●

There Goes the Neighborhood (1992) **C-88m.** *½ D: Bill Phillips. Jeff Daniels, Catherine O'Hara, Hector Elizondo, Rhea Perlman, Judith Ivey, Harris Yulin, Jonathan Banks, Dabney Coleman, Chazz Palminteri, Jeremy Piven, Mary Gross. Feeble comedy in which various greedy characters attempt to dig up a fortune buried in the basement of a suburban house. Strong cast deserves better material than this. [PG-13] ▼●

Theremin: An Electronic Odyssey (1993) **C/B&W-83m.** *** D: Steven M. Martin. A fascinating chronicle of the life and times of Leon Theremin, the Russian-born genius who invented the first electronic musical instrument (which was adopted by Hollywood for use in movie soundtracks during the 1940s and '50s). Music history meets political and pop-culture history in this end-

lessly surprising documentary, more interesting for the material it offers than for the brilliance of its presentation. Comic highlight: a passionate if incoherent interview with Beach Boy Brian Wilson, who used the theremin on his hit record "Good Vibrations." [PG] ▼●)

There's a Girl in My Soup (1970-British) **C-95m.** *½ D: Roy Boulting. Peter Sellers, Goldie Hawn, Tony Britton, Nicky Henson, Diana Dors, Nicola Pagett, Christopher Cazenove. Middle-aged Sellers groping for youth, woos kookie Hawn. Silly story, just a few real laughs. [R] ▼▼

There's Always Tomorrow (1956) **84m.** **½ D: Douglas Sirk. Barbara Stanwyck, Fred MacMurray, Joan Bennett, William Reynolds, Pat Crowley, Gigi Perreau, Jane Darwell. MacMurray is in a rut, at work and at home, making him particularly susceptible to old-flame Stanwyck, who comes back into his life. Sudsy but well-acted soap opera, filmed before in 1934. ▶

Therese (1986-French) **C-91m.** *** D: Alain Cavalier. Catherine Mouchet, Aurore Prieto, Sylvie Habault, Ghislane Mona, Helene Alexandridis. Stark, stylistically directed, fact-based story of a dreamy, intense 15-year-old girl (Mouchet) and her desire to become a Carmelite nun, to be wedded to Christ. Winner of six César Awards, including Best Picture. Remake of the 1938 film THÉRÈSE MARTIN. ▼▶

Thérèse Raquin (1953-French-Italian) **103m.** **½ D: Marcel Carné. Simone Signoret, Raf Vallone, Jacques Duby, Sylvie, Roland Lesaffre, Maria Pia Casilio, Marcel André, Paul Frankeur. Complications ensue when weary Signoret, saddled with a small-minded husband and a mother-in-law from hell, begins an affair with earthy truck driver Vallone. Melodrama of passion and obsession has the right pedigree—Carné and Charles Spaak adapted Émile Zola's novel—but lacks the necessary fire to make it memorable. ▶

There's No Business Like Show Business (1954) **C-117m.** **½ D: Walter Lang. Ethel Merman, Dan Dailey, Donald O'Connor, Marilyn Monroe, Johnnie Ray, Mitzi Gaynor, Hugh O'Brian, Frank McHugh. Gaudy (and seemingly interminable) hokum about a show-biz family, built around catalog of Irving Berlin songs. Entertaining if not inspired, with several expensive numbers designed to fill the wide screen. Merman and Dailey are fine, Marilyn's at her sexiest, and O'Connor is in top form throughout. Then there's Johnnie Ray deciding to become a priest. . . . CinemaScope. ▼●)

There's Something About Mary (1998) **C-119m.** ** D: Bobby Farrelly, Peter Farrelly. Cameron Diaz, Matt Dillon, Ben Stiller, Lee Evans, Chris Elliott, Lin Shaye, Jeffrey Tambor, Markie Post, Keith David, Jonathan Richman, Sarah Silverman, Richard

Jenkins, Brett Favre. Hugely popular comedy about a guy who's never stopped loving the girl he almost got to take to the high school prom—until a painful accident interfered. The ultimate in sophomoric comedy, reveling in politically incorrect gags, but it drags on for two hours. Only the very appealing Mary (Diaz) keeps it afloat. Extended version runs 130m. [R] ▼●🅓

There Was a Crooked Man . . . (1970) C-118m. ***½ D: Joseph L. Mankiewicz. Kirk Douglas, Henry Fonda, Hume Cronyn, Warren Oates, Burgess Meredith, John Randolph, Michael Blodgett, Arthur O'Connell, Martin Gabel, Alan Hale, Victor French, Barbara Rhoades, Lee Grant. Bawdy, entertaining Western-comedy-prison-film with Douglas as cocky inmate at territorial prison circa 1883 who matches wits with progressive warden Fonda towards one goal: escape. Powerhouse cast, handsome production. Written by David Newman and Robert Benton. Panavision. [R] ▼●🅓

There Will Be Blood (2007) C-158m. ***½ D: Paul Thomas Anderson. Daniel Day-Lewis, Paul Dano, Kevin J. O'Connor, Ciarán Hinds, Dillon Freasier, Sydney McCallister, David Willis, David Warshofsky, Colton Woodward. Day-Lewis dominates this riveting film as a turn-of-the-20th-century oilman who talks his way into a California community, determined to control its rich oil interests. At first we think he's just a slickster, but as layer after layer of truth is revealed we see his utter amorality. He meets his match in a local preacher (Dano) who's just as greedy and ambitious as he is. Fascinating piece, loosely based on Upton Sinclair's book *Oil!*, captures the particulars of a time and place, but it's Day-Lewis' character (with a voice borrowed from John Huston) that stands out. Chilling score by Jonny Greenwood creates a feeling of dread right from the start. Written by the director. Day-Lewis and cinematographer Robert Elswit earned Academy Awards. Panavision. [R]🅓

These Are the Damned (1963-British) 96m. **½ D: Joseph Losey. Macdonald Carey, Shirley Anne Field, Viveca Lindfors, Alexander Knox, Oliver Reed, James Villiers. Odd film chronicling American Carey's confrontation with a Teddy Boy motorcycle gang in Weymouth—after which the scenario becomes a *Twilight Zone*–like sci-fi drama! Original British title: THE DAMNED. Hammerscope. 🅓

These Three (1936) 93m. **** D: William Wyler. Miriam Hopkins, Merle Oberon, Joel McCrea, Catherine Doucet, Alma Kruger, Bonita Granville, Marcia Mae Jones, Margaret Hamilton, Walter Brennan. Penetrating drama of two young women (Oberon, Hopkins) running girls' school, ruined by lies of malicious student Granville; loosely based on Lillian Hellman's *The Children's Hour*. Superb acting by all, with Granville chillingly impressive; scripted by the playwright. Remade in 1961 by same director as THE CHILDREN'S HOUR. ▼●

These Wilder Years (1956) 91m. **½ D: Roy Rowland. James Cagney, Barbara Stanwyck, Walter Pidgeon, Betty Lou Keim, Don Dubbins, Edward Andrews, Dean Jones, Tom Laughlin. Unusual to see Cagney in this kind of soap opera, about a man who wants to find his illegitimate son and becomes involved with teenage unwed mother (Keim) through intervention of foundling home director Stanwyck. Look for young Michael Landon in pool room.

They (2002) C-89m. ** D: Robert Harmon. Laura Regan, Marc Blucas, Ethan Embry, Jon Abrahams, Dagmar Dominczyk, Jay Brazeau. Bland, predictable horror entry in which psychology student Regan is terrorized by mysterious, spiderlike creatures that thrive in the dark. Uplifted a bit by its striking finale. "Presented" by Wes Craven. Super 35. [PG-13] ▼🅓

They All Died Laughing SEE: **Jolly Bad Fellow, A**

They All Kissed the Bride (1942) 85m. **½ D: Alexander Hall. Joan Crawford, Melvyn Douglas, Roland Young, Billie Burke, Allen Jenkins. Good stars in fairly amusing film of man being arrested for kissing bride at wedding. ▼

They All Laughed (1981) C-115m. **½ D: Peter Bogdanovich. Audrey Hepburn, Ben Gazzara, John Ritter, Colleen Camp, Dorothy Stratten, Blaine Novak, Patti Hansen, George Morfogen, Sean Ferrer, Glenn Scarpelli, Elizabeth Pena. Quirky romantic comedy, long on style, short on substance, follows the adventures and amours of four private detectives. Spotlights some sharp-looking ladies, makes excellent use of N.Y.C. locations, but personal taste will have to judge its degree of success. Ferrer is the son of Hepburn and Mel Ferrer. Stratten was killed prior to film's release. [PG] ▼●🅓

They Call Me Bruce? (1982) C-88m. *½ D: Elliot Hong. Johnny Yune, Ralph Mauro, Pam Huntington, Margaux Hemingway. Unfunny, frequently obnoxious kung fu parody with Korean comedian Yune a doltish cook who is constantly mistaken for Bruce Lee. About two-thirds of the gags are based on TV commercials. Aka A FISTFUL OF CHOPSTICKS and followed by THEY STILL CALL ME BRUCE. [PG] ▼🅓

They Call Me MISTER Tibbs! (1970) C-108m. ** D: Gordon Douglas. Sidney Poitier, Barbara McNair, Martin Landau, David Sheiner, Anthony Zerbe, Jeff Corey, Ed Asner. Weak follow-up to IN THE HEAT OF THE NIGHT finds black detective Virgil Tibbs (now married and living in San Francisco) investigating murder of girl, with priest-friend Landau implicated. Followed by THE ORGANIZATION. [PG] ▼🅓

They Call Me Trinity (1971-Italian) C-

**109m. **½ D: E. B. Clucher (Enzo Barboni). Terence Hill, Bud Spencer, Farley Granger, Gisela Hahn, Stephen Zacharias, Dan Sturkie. Wild spoof of THE MAGNIFICENT SEVEN made international superstars of Hill and Spencer; they play half-brothers who try to help Mormon settlement protect itself from the inevitable band of Mexican marauders. Virtually nonstop slapstick spiced with gentle ribbing of the spaghetti Western genre; good fun. Sequel: TRINITY IS STILL MY NAME. Techniscope. [G]▼●⟩

They Came From Beyond Space (1967-British) **C-85m.** BOMB D: Freddie Francis. Robert Hutton, Jennifer Jayne, Zia Mohyeddin, Bernard Kay, Michael Gough. Hutton is free to combat spacemen because the silver plate he carries inside his skull makes him immune to their powers. Based on Joseph Millard's *The Gods Hate Kansas*. ▼⟩

They Came From Within (1975-Canadian) **C-87m.** *½ D: David Cronenberg. Paul Hampton, Joe Silver, Lynn Lowry, Allen Magicovsky, Barbara Steele, Susan Petrie. Bizarre, sexually oriented parasites run rampant through dwellers in high-rise apartment building with plenty of gory violence quick to ensue. First "major" film by cult favorite Cronenberg sets the disgusting pattern for most of his subsequent pictures. Originally titled SHIVERS, then THE PARASITE MURDERS. [R]▼●⟩

They Came to Cordura (1959) **C-123m.** **½ D: Robert Rossen. Gary Cooper, Rita Hayworth, Van Heflin, Tab Hunter, Richard Conte, Michael Callan, Dick York. Soapy oater set in 1916 Mexico. Cooper is Army officer accused of cowardice, sent to find five men worthy of Medal of Honor. Hayworth is shady lady he meets on the way. CinemaScope.▼●⟩

They Came to Rob Las Vegas (1968-Spanish-French-Italian) **C-128m.** ** D: Antonio Isasi. Gary Lockwood, Elke Sommer, Lee J. Cobb, Jack Palance. Big heist is small potatoes as armed robbers plot to intercept Vegas gambling money. Techniscope. [R]⟩

They Died With Their Boots On (1941) **138m.** *** D: Raoul Walsh. Errol Flynn, Olivia de Havilland, Arthur Kennedy, Charley Grapewin, Gene Lockhart, Anthony Quinn, Stanley Ridges, Sydney Greenstreet, Regis Toomey, Hattie McDaniel, Walter Hampden. Sweeping Hollywood version of Little Bighorn battle, with Flynn flamboyant as Custer. Fine vignettes amidst episodic buildup to exciting Last Stand climax. This being Errol and Olivia's final film together lends poignance to their farewell scene. Superb score by Max Steiner. Also shown in computer-colored version. ▼●⟩

They Drive by Night (1940) **93m.** ***½ D: Raoul Walsh. George Raft, Ann Sheridan, Ida Lupino, Humphrey Bogart, Gale Page, Alan Hale, Roscoe Karns. Marvelous melodrama of truck-driving brothers, Bogie and Raft, battling the dangers of the open road as well as a murder frame-up by Lupino. Unforgettable dialogue by Jerry Wald and Richard Macaulay. Partial reworking of BORDERTOWN. Also shown in computer-colored version.▼●⟩

They Gave Him a Gun (1937) **94m.** **½ D: W. S. Van Dyke II. Spencer Tracy, Gladys George, Franchot Tone, Edgar Dearing, Charles Trowbridge, Cliff Edwards, Mary Lou Treen. Gun-shy hayseed Tone, who was taught "thou shalt not kill," changes dramatically when he fights in WW1. Tracy is his devoted pal, who later tries to save him from a life of crime. Dramatically obvious, and falls apart with the entrance of nurse George; still, the opening montage is striking, and the war-related scenes exceptional.

They Got Me Covered (1943) **95m.** ** D: David Butler. Bob Hope, Dorothy Lamour, Lenore Aubert, Otto Preminger, Eduardo Ciannelli, Marion Martin, Donald MacBride, Walter Catlett, Donald Meek. Spy yarn (by Harry Kurnitz) set in Washington was topical at the time, awkward now; not up to Hope standards.▼●⟩

They Knew What They Wanted (1940) **96m.** *** D: Garson Kanin. Carole Lombard, Charles Laughton, William Gargan, Harry Carey, Frank Fay. Laughton and Lombard are excellent in this flawed adaptation by Robert Ardrey of Sidney Howard's play (filmed twice before). He's an Italian grape-grower in California who conducts correspondence with waitress and asks her to marry him. Fay is too sanctimonious for words as local priest. Watch for Karl Malden and Tom Ewell as rowdy guests at the pre-wedding party.▼

They Live (1988) **C-97m.** ** D: John Carpenter. Roddy Piper, Keith David, Meg Foster, George "Buck" Flower, Peter Jason, Raymond St. Jacques, Jason Robards III, Larry Franco. Lonely drifter arrives in L.A., discovers that consumerist society is being dominated by aliens, whose human disguises and subliminal advertising messages are visible only through special glasses. Satiric sci-fi adventure begins well, degenerates into standard urban action piece, not helped by awful alien makeup. Screenwriter "Frank Armitage" (working from a short story by Ray Faraday Nelson) is actually director Carpenter. Panavision. [R]▼●⟩

They Live by Night (1949) **95m.** ***½ D: Nicholas Ray. Farley Granger, Cathy O'Donnell, Howard da Silva, Jay C. Flippen, Helen Craig. Director Ray's first film is sensitive, well-made story of young lovers who are fugitives from the law. Set in 1930s, it avoids clichés and builds considerable impact instead. Based on Edward Anderson's *Thieves Like Us*, remade in 1974 under that name. Also shown in computer-colored version.▼●⟩

They Loved Life SEE: **Kanal**

They Made Me a Criminal (1939) **92m.** **½ D: Busby Berkeley. John Garfield, Claude Rains, Gloria Dickson, May Robson, Billy Halop, Huntz Hall, Leo Gorcey, Bobby Jordan, Gabriel Dell, Barbara Pepper, Ward Bond, Ann Sheridan. Garfield takes it on the lam when he thinks he's killed a reporter, stays out West with Robson and Dead End Kids. Enjoyable, with Rains miscast as a Dick Tracy type. Remake of THE LIFE OF JIMMY DOLAN. ▼●▶

They Made Me a Fugitive (1947-British) **103m.** *** D: Cavalcanti. Trevor Howard, Sally Gray, Griffith Jones, Rene Ray, Mary Merrall, Charles Farrell. Dilettante crook is double-crossed by his boss and seeks revenge while on the lam from police. Potent (yet little-known) British film noir packs a real punch, with no holds barred in terms of brutality (and refusal to provide a pat, happy ending). Strikingly photographed by Otto Heller. Look sharp and you'll spot young Peter Bull and Sebastian Cabot. Originally cut when released in U.S. as I BECAME A CRIMINAL; also trimmed for British reissue. Finally restored on video in 1999. ▼●

They Met in Bombay (1941) **93m.** **½ D: Clarence Brown. Clark Gable, Rosalind Russell, Peter Lorre, Jessie Ralph, Reginald Owen, Eduardo Ciannelli. Two jewel thieves team up in ordinary romantic comedy-actioner, spiced by Lorre as money-hungry cargo-ship captain. Look for Alan Ladd in a small role. ▼▶

They Might Be Giants (1971) **C-86m.** *** D: Anthony Harvey. Joanne Woodward, George C. Scott, Jack Gilford, Lester Rawlins, Al Lewis, Rue McClanahan, Theresa Merritt, Eugene Roche, James Tolkan, Kitty Winn, Sudie Bond, F. Murray Abraham, Paul Benedict, M. Emmet Walsh. Fun yarn of slightly daffy gentleman (Scott) who believes he is Sherlock Holmes, and his psychiatrist tagalong (Woodward) whose real name is Dr. Watson. Alternate version on DVD runs 91m. [G] ▼

They Only Kill Their Masters (1972) **C-97m.** **½ D: James Goldstone. James Garner, Katharine Ross, Hal Holbrook, Harry Guardino, June Allyson, Christopher Connelly, Tom Ewell, Peter Lawford, Edmond O'Brien, Arthur O'Connell, Ann Rutherford. Great cast in complicated modern-day whodunit set in coastal California town; tries for Dashiell Hammett feeling, doesn't quite make it. Policeman Garner tries to solve murder of pregnant woman, with formidable Doberman pinscher figuring prominently. Not bad, but a letdown. [PG] ▼▶

They Passed This Way SEE: **Four Faces West**

They're Playing With Fire (1984) **C-96m.** BOMB D: Howard (Hikmet) Avedis.

Eric Brown, Sybil Danning, Andrew Prine, Paul Clemens, K. T. Stevens. What starts off as rehash of Brown's PRIVATE LESSONS quickly turns into sick, ugly slasher film. Danning (as a college English professor!) lures Brown into helping her with a let's-kill-Mom-and-make-off-with-my-inheritance plot—except that someone else is killing everybody in sight. Not even Danning's formidable nude scenes are reason enough to sit through this slop. [R] ▼▶

They Saved Hitler's Brain (1963) **74m.** BOMB D: David Bradley. Walter Stocker, Audrey Caire, Carlos Rivas, John Holland, Dani Lynn, Marshall Reed, Nestor Paiva. Daughter of kidnapped scientist traces him to isle of Mandoras, where Nazis still flourish under the leadership of Hitler's still-living head. Unbelievably muddled plot results from intercutting 1950s studio potboiler, beautifully photographed by Stanley Cortez (MAGNIFICENT AMBERSONS) with super-cheap 1960s footage involving completely different cast. Originally titled MADMEN OF MANDORAS. ▼▶

They Shoot Horses, Don't They? (1969) **C-120m.** ***½ D: Sydney Pollack. Jane Fonda, Michael Sarrazin, Susannah York, Gig Young, Red Buttons, Bonnie Bedelia, Bruce Dern, Allyn Ann McLerie, Michael Conrad, Al Lewis, Severn Darden, Art Metrano, Paul Mantee. 1930s marathon dance becomes microcosm of life, with myriad of subplots, characters' lives intertwining. Fonda is self-destructive girl who attracts aimless Sarrazin with tragic results; Young won Oscar as oily promoter of grueling "contest." Fascinating. Based on Horace McCoy's novel; script by James Poe and Robert E. Thompson. Panavision. [M/PG] ▼●▶

They Still Call Me Bruce (1987) **C-91m.** *½ D: Johnny Yune, James Orr. Johnny Yune, David Mendenhall, Pat Paulsen, Joey Travolta, Robert Guillaume, Bethany Wright, Carl Bensen. In-name-only sequel to THEY CALL ME BRUCE has at least one thing in common with its predecessor: it's awful. This time Yune plays a Korean searching for the American GI who saved him years ago, winding up instead as a big-brother figure for orphan Mendenhall. [PG] ▼

They Went That-A-Way and That-A-Way (1978) **C-95m.** *½ D: Edward Montagne, Stuart E. McGowan. Tim Conway, Chuck McCann, Richard Kiel, Dub Taylor, Reni Santoni. Lame prison escape comedy (with script by Conway) puts Conway and McCann through lackluster routines as a road-company Laurel and Hardy. [PG] ▼▶

They Were Expendable (1945) **135m.** **** D: John Ford. Robert Montgomery, John Wayne, Donna Reed, Jack Holt, Ward Bond, Louis Jean Heydt, Marshall Thompson, Leon Ames, Cameron Mitchell, Russell Simpson, Jack Pennick, Robert Barrat, Tom Tyler. One of the finest (and most underrated) of all WW2 films, based on the true story of America's PT boat squadron in the Philippines during the early days of the war. Moving, exquisitely detailed production (photographed by Joseph August) under Ford's distinctive hand, with real-life Naval officer Montgomery a convincing lead. Screenplay by Frank "Spig" Wead. Also shown in computer-colored version. ▼●◗

They Who Dare (1953-British) **C-101m.** **✓½** D: Lewis Milestone. Dirk Bogarde, Denholm Elliott, Akim Tamiroff, Eric Pohlmann, David Peel. Effective WW2 actioner with good character delineation, tracing commando raid on German-controlled Aegean air fields.

They Won't Believe Me (1947) **95m. ✓✓✓½** D: Irving Pichel. Susan Hayward, Robert Young, Jane Greer, Rita Johnson, Tom Powers, Don Beddoe, Frank Ferguson. Fine James Cain–type melodrama about a philanderer who gets involved with three women, leading to tragedy (and a terrific twist ending). Young excels in his unsympathetic role; Johnson does wonders with her scenes as his wife. ▼●

They Won't Forget (1937) **95m. ✓✓✓✓** D: Mervyn LeRoy. Claude Rains, Gloria Dickson, Otto Kruger, Allyn Joslyn, Elisha Cook, Jr., Edward Norris. Electrifying drama begins when pretty high school student is murdered in Southern town. A man is arrested, and a big-time Northern lawyer takes the case, but everyone seems more interested in exploiting personal interests than in seeing justice triumph. No punches are pulled in this still-powerful film. Lana Turner plays the unfortunate girl, in her first important role. Script by Robert Rossen and Aben Kandel, from the book *Death in the Deep South* by Ward Greene; based on notorious 1913 incident later dramatized for TV as THE MURDER OF MARY PHAGAN. ▼◗

Thick as Thieves SEE: **Code, The** (2009)
Thief, The (1952) **85m. ✓✓½** D: Russell Rouse. Ray Milland, Rita Gam, Martin Gabel, Harry Bronson. Spy yarn set in N.Y.C. with a difference: no dialogue. Gimmick grows wearisome, script is tame. ▼◗

Thief (1981) **C-122m. ✓✓✓** D: Michael Mann. James Caan, Tuesday Weld, Willie Nelson, James Belushi, Robert Prosky, Tom Signorelli, Dennis Farina, William L. Petersen. Arresting drama about a professional thief, inventively realized by writer-director Mann (in his feature debut). Caan is excellent as the man with one drive: survival. Stylishly photographed (by Donald Thorin) and scored (by Tangerine Dream). [R] ▼●◗

Thief, The (1997-Russian) **C-94m. ✓✓✓**

D: Pavel Chukhrai. Vladimir Mashkov, Ekaterina Rednikova, Misha Philipchuk. Intimate character study set in post WW2 Russia: an abandoned single mother and her adorable 6-year-old son fall for a swarthy military officer, not knowing he's really a petty thief. A powerful tragedy, simply and beautifully told, with superlative performances from its three leads, particularly Mashkov, who exudes the sexy malevolence of a young Robert Mitchum. [R] ▼●◗

Thief and the Cobbler, The SEE: **Arabian Knight**

Thief of Bagdad, The (1924) **155m. ✓✓✓½** D: Raoul Walsh. Douglas Fairbanks, Julanne Johnston, Anna May Wong, Sojin, Snitz Edwards, Charles Belcher, Brandon Hurst. Fairbanks is unusually balletic (and ingratiating as ever) in this elaborate Arabian Nights pantomime, designed to instill a true sense of wonder. Quite long, but never dull; one of the most imaginative of all silent films, with awesome sets by William Cameron Menzies. Remade three times (so far). ▼●◗

Thief of Bagdad, The (1940-British) **C-106m. ✓✓✓✓** D: Ludwig Berger, Tim Whelan, Michael Powell. Sabu, John Justin, June Duprez, Conrad Veidt, Rex Ingram, Miles Malleson, Mary Morris. Remarkable fantasy of native boy Sabu outdoing evil magician Veidt in Arabian Nights fable with incredible Oscar-winning Technicolor photography by Georges Perinal and Osmond Borradaile, special effects, and art direction. Ingram gives splendid performance as a genie; vivid score by Miklos Rozsa. ▼●◗

Thief of Baghdad (1961-Italian) **C-90m. ✓✓** D: Arthur Lubin. Steve Reeves, Giorgia Moll, Arturo Dominici, Edy Vessel. Reeves searches for enchanted blue rose so he can marry Sultan's daughter. Nothing like Sabu version, but occasionally atmospheric. CinemaScope. ▼

Thief of Hearts (1984) **C-100m. ✓✓** D: Douglas Day Stewart. Steven Bauer, Barbara Williams, John Getz, David Caruso, Christine Ebersole, George Wendt. While ransacking a house Bauer steals woman's diaries, reads them through, and then determines to woo her—using the "secret" knowledge he's learned. Slick but curiously unappealing film written by first-time director Stewart. Reworked slightly for video, with potentially X-rated shots added. [R] ▼●◗

Thief of Paris, The (1967-French) **C-119m. ✓✓✓** D: Louis Malle. Jean-Paul Belmondo, Genevieve Bujold, Marie Dubois, Francoise Fabian, Julien Guiomar. Solid comedy-drama with personal setbacks turning Belmondo to thievery for revenge on society; soon he finds that robbery has become his whole life.

Thief Who Came to Dinner, The (1973)

C-105m. ** D: Bud Yorkin. Ryan O'Neal, Jacqueline Bisset, Warren Oates, Jill Clayburgh, Charles Cioffi, Ned Beatty, Austin Pendleton, Gregory Sierra, Michael Murphy, John Hillerman. Disappointing caper comedy (considering cast and director) about a computer expert who becomes a jewel thief in Houston's top social circles. Clayburgh (pre-stardom) has small but telling role as O'Neal's ex-wife; script by Walter Hill. [PG]▼

Thieves (1977) **C-92m.** BOMB D: John Berry. Marlo Thomas, Charles Grodin, rwin Corey, Hector Elizondo, Mercedes McCambridge, John McMartin, Gary Merrill, Ann Wedgeworth. Pretentious, boring adaptation of Herb Gardner's play about crazy couple trying to recapture their innocence in a corrupt N.Y.C. Corey (as Thomas' cabbie father) adds only life to so-called comedy. Bob Fosse has a brief role. [PG]

Thieves (1996) SEE: **Les Voleurs**

Thieves' Highway (1949) **94m.** *** D: Jules Dassin. Richard Conte, Valentina Cortese, Lee J. Cobb, Barbara Lawrence, Jack Oakie, Millard Mitchell, Joseph Pevney. Tough postwar drama of a returning vet seeking to avenge his trucker/father's treatment at the hands of a crooked fruit dealer in San Francisco. Masterfully directed; script by A. I. Bezzerides, from his novel. Only the ending seems pat.◖

Thieves' Holiday SEE: **Scandal in Paris, A**

Thieves Like Us (1974) **C-123m.** ***½ D: Robert Altman. Keith Carradine, Shelley Duvall, John Schuck, Bert Remsen, Louise Fletcher, Ann Latham, Tom Skerritt. Three misfits escape from prison camp in 1930s South, go on a crime spree; the youngest (Carradine) falls in love with a simple, uneducated girl (Duvall). Despite familiar trappings, Altman digs deep into period atmosphere and strong characterizations; this film gets better every time you look at it. Remake of THEY LIVE BY NIGHT. Scripted by Calder Willingham, Joan Tewkesbury, and Altman. [R]▼◖

Thin Air (1969-British) **C-91m.** *½ D: Gerry Levy. George Sanders, Maurice Evans, Patrick Allen, Neil Connery, Hilary Dwyer, Robert Flemyng. Parachutists keep disappearing, due to unseen forces; routine sci-fi with little to recommend it. Original British title: THE BODY STEALERS (INVASION OF THE BODY STEALERS). [G]▼

Thin Blue Line, The (1988) **C-96m.** **** D: Errol Morris. Remarkable, perhaps even landmark, documentary, as Morris sets out to prove that a convicted hitchhiker did *not* kill a Dallas policeman in 1976—and that the lowlife who fingered him (and who wound up on Death Row for a subsequent murder) did. Very subjective but totally convincing, so much so that the case was reopened after film's premiere, and the defendant was exonerated. Philip Glass' score adds to hypnotic effect. ▼◖

Thing, The (1982) **C-108m.** *½ D: John Carpenter. Kurt Russell, A. Wilford Brimley, Richard Dysart, Richard Masur, Donald Moffat, T.K. Carter, David Clennon. Remake of 1951 film about Antarctic outpost terrorized by an alien organism. More faithful to the original story, but nonstop parade of slimy, repulsive special effects turns this into a freak show and drowns most of the suspense. Panavision. [R]▼◖

Thing About My Folks, The (2005) **C-97m.** **½ D: Raymond De Felitta. Peter Falk, Paul Reiser, Olympia Dukakis, Elizabeth Perkins, Mackenzie Connolly, Lydia Jordan, Ann Dowd, Claire Beckman. Confronted with the sudden news that his father intends to divorce his mother, after decade's of marriage, Reiser takes his dad (Falk) on a road trip to take his mind off his troubles. Along the way, father and son bond for the first time, and the younger man learns a lot about what makes his old man tick. Labor-of-love project was written by Reiser with Falk in mind, and it shows: Falk gives an irresistible performance in this predictable but likable comedy-drama. [PG-13]◖

Thing Called Love, The (1993) **C-116m.** **½ D: Peter Bogdanovich. River Phoenix, Samantha Mathis, Dermot Mulroney, Sandra Bullock, K. T. Oslin, Anthony Clark, Trisha Yearwood, Barry Shabaka Henley. Ordinary drama about country singer–songwriter Mathis, who yearns to make it in Nashville, and her experiences as she strives for success. At its best when depicting the friendship and rivalry among struggling artists. Of interest mostly as one of Phoenix's last films; he's good as a sulky but talented singer who covers up his emotions. Director's cut runs 118m. [PG-13]▼◖

Thing From Another World, The (1951) **87m.** ***½ D: Christian Nyby. Kenneth Tobey, Margaret Sheridan, Robert Cornthwaite, Douglas Spencer, James Arness, Dewey Martin, William Self, George Fenneman. Classic blend of science-fiction and horror, loosely based on John W. Campbell, Jr.'s *Who Goes There?* Scientists at lonely Arctic outpost dig up alien (Arness) from the permafrost and must fight for their lives when it's accidentally thawed. Tense direction (often credited to producer Howard Hawks), excellent performances, eerie score by Dimitri Tiomkin. Screenplay by Charles Lederer. Watch out for 81m. reissue prints. Remade in 1982. Also shown in computer-colored version. ▼◖

Things Are Tough All Over (1982) **C-92m.** ** D: Tom Avildsen. Cheech Marin, Thomas Chong, Shelby Fiddis, Rikki Marin, Evelyn Guerrero. Besides their standard characterizations, the boys play two Arab brothers whose paths cross C & C's as the latter drive a ritzy car to California, one that happens to have $5 million hidden inside. Superb makeup and mimicry give evidence to the team's genuine talent, but the laughs just aren't there most of the time. Panavision. [R] ▼O◗

Things Change (1988) **C-100m.** **½ D: David Mamet. Don Ameche, Joe Mantegna, Robert Prosky, J. J. Johnson, Ricky Jay, Mike Nussbaum, Jack Wallace, Dan Conway, William H. Macy, J. T. Walsh, Felicity Huffman. Simple Italian shoemaker (Ameche) agrees to take the rap for a Chicago mob murder for a fee, but the man assigned to baby-sit him for a weekend (Mantegna) decides to take the old man on a final fling before he goes to jail. Slight, sometimes flat comic fable by Mamet and Shel Silverstein is buoyed by some wonderful vignettes and endearing performances by the stars. Ameche is a joy to watch. [PG] ▼O◗

Things to Come (1936-British) **92m.** *** D: William Cameron Menzies. Raymond Massey, Cedric Hardwicke, Ralph Richardson, Maurice Braddell, Edward Chapman, Ann Todd. Stunning visualization of H. G. Wells' depiction of the future. Massey portrays leader of new world, Richardson despotic wartime ruler. Aloof but always interesting, enhanced by Menzies' sets. Vibrant music by Arthur Bliss; Wells himself wrote the screenplay. Originally released at 108m. 1979 movie THE SHAPE OF THINGS TO COME, though taking the actual title of Wells' book, has nothing in common with this film. ▼◗

Things To Do in Denver When You're Dead (1995) **C-124m.** ** D: Gary Fleder. Andy Garcia, Gabrielle Anwar, Christopher Walken, Christopher Lloyd, William Forsythe, Treat Williams, Bill Nunn, Steve Buscemi, Jack Warden, Fairuza Balk, Bill Cobbs, Marshall Bell, Glenn Plummer, Sarah Trigger, Jenny McCarthy, Don Cheadle. Another entry in the post-Tarantino, faux-hip crime genre, with Garcia as a reformed crook who agrees to stage an assault to placate his evil, now-wheelchaired mentor Walken. Naturally the plans go horribly wrong. Stylized, violent, and absolutely empty, though Williams' psycho is his best part in years, and Buscemi's hit man has a great name: Mr. Shhh. [R] ▼O◗

Things We Lost in the Fire (2007) **C-119m.** *** D: Susanne Bier. Halle Berry, Benicio Del Toro, David Duchovny, Alison Lohman, John Carroll Lynch, Paula Newsome, Omar Benson Miller, Alexis Llewellyn, Micah Berry. When her husband dies unexpectedly, Berry reaches out to his lifelong best friend—a druggie she never wanted anything to do with. He moves into her guest room, but when he begins to take her husband's place in the eyes of her kids

she feels great resentment toward him. Interesting adult drama about grief, forgiveness, and healing, if a bit tidy in its plotting. Especially good showcase for Del Toro, who's never played such a warm, sympathetic character before. U.S. filmmaking debut for Danish director Bier. Super 35. [R] ◗

Things You Can Tell Just By Looking at Her (2001) **C-109m.** *** D: Rodrigo García. Glenn Close, Cameron Diaz, Calista Flockhart, Kathy Baker, Amy Brenneman, Valeria Golino, Holly Hunter, Matt Craven, Gregory Hines, Miguel Sandoval, Noah Fleiss, Danny Woodburn, Penelope Allen, Roma Maffia, Elpidia Carrillo. Anthology of five intersecting stories about a diverse group of women and the physical and emotional toll everyday life takes on them. Introspective, absorbing and beautifully acted, this is a "woman's picture" in the best sense. U.S. debut on cable TV. [PG-13] ▼◗

Thing With Two Heads, The (1972) **C-93m.** ** D: Lee Frost. Ray Milland, Rosey Grier, Don Marshall, Roger Perry, Chelsea Brown. Fantastic tale of bigot who finds his head transplanted onto black man's body. Played partially for laughs, which helps a little. [PG] ▼◗

Think Dirty (1970-British) **C-94m.** *½ D: Jim Clark. Marty Feldman, Shelley Berman, Judy Cornwell, Julie Ege, Patrick Cargill, Jack Watson. Leering, obnoxious comedy-fantasy with adman Feldman having to use sex to promote a cereal on TV; meanwhile, his prudish wife is mounting a campaign to purify the airwaves. Original British title: EVERY HOME SHOULD HAVE ONE. ▼

Thin Line Between Love and Hate, A (1996) **C-108m.** ** D: Martin Lawrence. Martin Lawrence, Lynn Whitfield, Regina King, Bobby Brown, Della Reese, Malinda Williams, Daryl M. Mitchell, Roger E. Mosley, Faizon Love, Tracy Morgan. There is a thin line between a movie and a vanity production as director/cowriter/executive producer/star/music supervisor Lawrence plays a young man seemingly irresistible to women. He boasts to a friend that he can bed a beautiful but hard-to-get woman they encounter, leading to a comedic FATAL ATTRACTION: she's harder to get rid of than she ever was to get! Lawrence's first foray behind the scenes is amusing only in spots. Super 35. [R] ▼O◗

The Thin Man series SEE: *Leonard Maltin's Classic Movie Guide*

Thin Man, The (1934) **93m.** **** D: W. S. Van Dyke. William Powell, Myrna Loy, Maureen O'Sullivan, Nat Pendleton, Minna Gombell, Cesar Romero, Natalie Moorhead, Edward Ellis, Porter Hall. Nick and Nora investigate the disappearance of an inventor in this classic blend of laughs and suspense which marked the first pairing of what was to become one of the movies' great romantic teams. Shot in just two weeks by director Woody "One-Shot" Van Dyke and cinematographer James Wong Howe, this has gone on to become *the* sophisticated comedy-mystery par excellence, inspiring five sequels as well as countless imitations. Frances Goodrich and Albert Hackett adapted Dashiell Hammett's novel. ▼●)

Thin Man Goes Home, The (1944) **100m.** *** D: Richard Thorpe. William Powell, Myrna Loy, Lucile Watson, Gloria De Haven, Anne Revere, Helen Vinson, Harry Davenport, Leon Ames, Donald Meek, Edward Brophy. Nick takes the family on a vacation to Sycamore Springs to visit his parents, but naturally winds up embroiled in a murder case. Leisurely entry, with even more comedy than usual. ▼●)

Thinner (1996) **C-92m.** ** D: Tom Holland. Robert John Burke, Joe Mantegna, Lucinda Jenney, Joy Lenz, Michael Constantine, Sam Freed, Kari Wuhrer, John Horton, Daniel Von Bargen. Overweight Maine lawyer Burke accidentally kills an old gypsy woman, so her even older father (Constantine) puts a curse on him; he starts losing weight, and can't stop. Though well made, with good performances and astonishingly convincing makeup by Greg Cannom, the leading characters are unsympathetic and the situation unrelentingly grim. From the novel by Stephen King (writing as "Richard Bachman"), who has his usual cameo. Aka STEPHEN KING'S THINNER (which he is). [R] ▼●)

Thin Red Line, The (1964) **99m.** *** D: Andrew Marton. Keir Dullea, Jack Warden, James Philbrook, Kieron Moore. Gritty adaptation of James Jones' novel about personal conflict during the bloody attack on Guadalcanal during WW2. Dullea is the sensitive, iconoclastic soldier and Warden is the brutal sergeant who won't leave him alone. Remade in 1998. CinemaScope. ●)

Thin Red Line, The (1998) **C-170m.** *** D: Terrence Malick. Sean Penn, Adrien Brody, Jim Caviezel, Ben Chaplin, Nick Nolte, Elias Koteas, John Cusack, Woody Harrelson, Jared Leto, Dash Mihok, Tim Blake Nelson, John C. Reilly, John Savage, George Clooney, John Travolta, Nick Stahl, Shawn Hatosy, Tom (Thomas) Jane. Ethereal, moodily philosophical interpretation of James Jones' novel (previously filmed in 1964) about the taking of Guadalcanal during WW2, sparked by intense character studies: a pacifistic soldier (Caviezel), his antagonistic sergeant (Penn), a captain who refuses to sacrifice his men without cause (Koteas), a lieutenant colonel who only wants to see results (Nolte). These powerful portraits are the glue that holds the film together when it begins to wander. Those wanderings turned many viewers off, but

the film's strengths outweigh its imperfections. Malick also scripted. Panavision. [R] ▼●)

Third Day, The (1965) **C-119m.** **½ D: Jack Smight. George Peppard, Elizabeth Ashley, Roddy McDowall, Arthur O'Connell, Mona Washbourne, Herbert Marshall, Robert Webber, Charles Drake, Sally Kellerman, Vincent Gardenia, Arte Johnson. Capable cast helps standard amnesia tale about Peppard's inability to remember events that have caused him to be accused of murder. Panavision. ●)

Third Generation, The (1979-German) **C-111m.** ***½ D: Rainer Werner Fassbinder. Eddie Constantine, Hanna Schygulla, Volker Spengler, Margit Carstensen, Bulle Ogier, Udo Kier, Hark Bohm. Pitch-black comedy about upper-middle-class German terrorists, their cops-and-robbers antics, and how they provide excuse for government oppression. Superb ensemble cast in one of Fassbinder's best films. ●)

Third Key, The (1956-British) **96m.** *** D: Charles Frend. Jack Hawkins, John Stratton, Dorothy Alison, Geoffrey Keen, Ursula Howells. Exciting story of Scotland Yard, as Inspector Hawkins and rookie sergeant (Stratton) diligently pursue safecracking incident to its surprising conclusion. Original British title: THE LONG ARM. ▼

Third Man, The (1949-British) **104m.** **** D: Carol Reed. Orson Welles, Joseph Cotten, (Alida) Valli, Trevor Howard, Bernard Lee, Wilfrid Hyde-White. Graham Greene's account of mysterious Harry Lime (Welles) in post-WW2 Vienna is a bona fide classic, with pulp-writer Cotten on a manhunt for Harry. Anton Karas' zither rendition of "The Third Man Theme" adds just the right touch; cinematographer Robert Krasker won an Oscar. Note: there are two versions of this film. The British version features introductory narration by director Reed; the American print is narrated by Cotten and runs 93m. Little of substance was actually cut, but the film was tightened somewhat by coproducer David O. Selznick. Later on radio with Welles and on TV with Michael Rennie. Also shown in computer-colored version. ▼●)

Third Man on the Mountain (1959) **C-105m.** *** D: Ken Annakin. James MacArthur, Michael Rennie, Janet Munro, James Donald, Herbert Lom, Laurence Naismith. Fine Disney adventure about Swiss boy (MacArthur) determined to climb the Matterhorn (here called the Citadel) who learns more than just mountain-climbing in his dogged pursuit. Look quickly to spot MacArthur's mother, Helen Hayes, in a cameo as tourist. ▼●)

Third Miracle, The (1999) **C-119m.** *** D: Agnieszka Holland. Ed Harris, Anne Heche, Armin Mueller-Stahl, Michael Rispoli, Charles Haid, James Gallanders, Caterina Scorsone, Barbara Sukowa. A priest who's struggling with his faith is assigned to investigate a statue of the Virgin Mary that's weeping blood; it's a direct link to a beloved woman in a working-class community whom many believe is worthy of nomination for sainthood. Consistently involving and surprising, with fine performances. Based on a novel by Richard Vetere. [R] ▼●

Third Secret, The (1964-British) **103m.**
**½ D: Charles Crichton. Stephen Boyd, Jack Hawkins, Richard Attenborough, Diane Cilento, Pamela Franklin, Paul Rogers, Alan Webb, Judi Dench. Police rule that a celebrated psychoanalyst has committed suicide. His 14-year-old daughter (Franklin) thinks otherwise, and convinces news commentator Boyd (who also was one of the doctor's patients) to investigate. Talky, episodic whodunit; Dench's screen debut. CinemaScope. ▉

Third Solution, The (1989-Italian) **C-113m.** *½ D: Pasquale Squitieri. F. Murray Abraham, Treat Williams, Danny Aiello, Rita Rusic, Robert Balchus, Rossano Brazzi, Nigel Court. Good cast is wasted in this overbaked spy melodrama, with American Williams uncovering a plot to foil the Pope's scheduled visit to the Soviet Union. Original title: RUSSICUM. Panavision. ▼●

Third Voice, The (1960) **79m.** *** D: Hubert Cornfield. Edmond O'Brien, Laraine Day, Julie London, Ralph Brooks, Roque Ybarra, Henry Delgado. Neat suspense film involving murder, impersonation, and double-crossing. CinemaScope.

Thirst (1949) SEE: **Three Strange Loves**

Thirst (1979-Australian) **C-98m.** *** D: Rod Hardy. Chantal Contouri, David Hemmings, Henry Silva, Max Phipps, Shirley Cameron. Strange, stylish, chilling tale of secret society trying to brainwash Contouri and transform her into a baroness-vampire. Minimum of plot and characterization but maximum suspense in this well-directed shocker. Panavision. [R] ▼●

Thirst (2009-U.S.-Korean) **C-134m.** ** D: Park Chan-wook. Song Kang-ho, Kim Ok-vin, Kim Hae-sook, Shin Ha-kyun. Minister with a martyr complex survives a medical procedure that should have killed him—but he now harbors a dark secret. Elevated to sainthood status by the common folk, he faces a daily struggle between the forces of good and evil. Ick factor diminishes otherwise absorbing tale. [R] ▉

Thirsty Dead, The (1975) **C-90m.** BOMB D: Terry Becker. John Considine, Jennifer Billingsley, Judith McConnell, Tani Guthrie. Guide abducts actress and friends to jungle where strange tribe drinks human blood to regain youth. Boring Philippine-made junk. Aka BLOOD HUNT. [PG] ▼●

13 SEE: **Eye of the Devil**

Thirteen (2003) **C-95m.** ***½ D: Catherine Hardwicke. Holly Hunter, Evan Rachel Wood, Nikki Reed, Jeremy Sisto,

Brady Corbet, Deborah Kara Unger, Kip Pardue, Sarah Clarke, D.W. Moffett. Searing look at life through the eyes of an impressionable teenage girl in L.A., as she's led in the wrong direction by a "popular" classmate who all but overtakes her existence. Hunter is terrific as the girl's single mom who's simply struggling to keep her head above water. Troubling but incredibly potent, and all too believable. Written by first-time director Hardwicke (a noted production designer) and Reed, who plays the "bad" girl. Hunter coexecutive produced. [R] ▉

Thirteen Chairs, The (1970-French-Italian) **C-95m.** ** D: Nicholas Gessner. Vittorio Gassman, Sharon Tate, Orson Welles, Vittorio De Sica, Terry-Thomas, Mylene Demongeot, Tim Brooke Taylor. Slight comedy about a search for 13 antique chairs, inside one of which is hidden a fortune. Of interest mainly for its cast, including Tate, who was murdered shortly after this was completed in 1969. Mel Brooks' version of this same, oft-filmed story was called THE TWELVE CHAIRS. Original title: 12 + 1. ▼

Thirteen Conversations About One Thing (2001) **C-103m.** **½ D: Jill Sprecher. Matthew McConaughey, John Turturro, Alan Arkin, Clea DuVall, Amy Irving, Barbara Sukowa, David Connolly, Tia Texada, Frankie Faison, William Wise, Shawn Elliott. Intriguing, moody film weaves a handful of seemingly disconnected stories together, all involving people whose lives are unfulfilled: college professor Turturro, insurance man Arkin, attorney McConaughey, house cleaner DuVall. Intelligent and interesting, but not as profound as it seems to think it is. Written by the director and her sister Karen Sprecher. [R] ▼●

Thirteen Days (2000) **C-145m.** *** D: Roger Donaldson. Kevin Costner, Bruce Greenwood, Steven Culp, Dylan Baker, Michael Fairman, Henry Strozier, Frank Wood, Kevin Conway, Len Cariou, Christopher Lawford, Lucinda Jenney, James Karen, Ed Lauter. Absorbing dramatization of the 1962 Cuban missile crisis, and how President John F. Kennedy dealt with the difficult decisions at hand, with hostile opposition from his military chiefs. Seen through the eyes of JFK's political advisor Kenny O'Donnell (Costner), who seems too good to be true. [PG-13] ▼▉

13 Frightened Girls (1963) **C-89m.** BOMB D: William Castle. Murray Hamilton, Joyce Taylor, Hugh Marlowe, Khigh Dhiegh. One of Castle's weirdest films (no mean feat), set in Swiss boarding school catering to daughters of diplomats; after trading bits of info they picked up from Daddy during the holidays, the girls decide to go off and do spy stuff. Castle held a worldwide talent search to find his "stars," for whom this was their first—and no doubt last—

film. A side-splitting camp classic awaiting rediscovery.▶

13 Ghosts (1960) **C/B&W-88m.** **½ D: William Castle. Charles Herbert, Donald Woods, Martin Milner, Jo Morrow, Rosemary DeCamp, Margaret Hamilton, John Van Dreelen. Typically tongue-in-cheek Castle spook opera, about nice, all-American family (with children named Buck and Medea!) that inherits a haunted house. Plenty of chills and chuckles, with Hamilton cleverly cast as sinister housekeeper. Some prints run 85m., minus footage of Castle introducing "Illusion-O"—movie patrons were given "ghost viewers" enabling them to see (or not see) the spirits. Remade in 2001. ▼●▌

Thir13en Ghosts (2001) **C-91m.** *½ D: Steve Beck. Tony Shalhoub, Embeth Davidtz, Matthew Lillard, Shannon Elizabeth, Alec Roberts, JR Bourne, Rah Digga, F. Murray Abraham. In-name-only remake of William Castle's gimmick thriller puts a widowed father, his two kids, and their housekeeper in a diabolically designed house that's one giant maze. What's more, it houses 12 troubled, violent spirits. Neither scary nor clever . . . a poor excuse for Halloween fodder. [R] ▼▌

13 Going on 30 (2004) **C-97m.** **½ D: Gary Winick. Jennifer Garner, Mark Ruffalo, Judy Greer, Christa B. Allen, Andy Serkis, Kathy Baker, Phil Reeves, Alex Black, Alexandra Kyle. A 13-year-old girl with typical adolescent problems wishes she were a grown-up and magically awakens inside a 30-year-old body. Now she has to deal with a high-powered job as a magazine editor and figure out why she's no longer friendly with her onetime soul mate, the boy who lived next door. Variation on (rip-off of?) BIG is plottier than it needs to be but is energized by the irresistible charm of Garner, in her first starring vehicle; Ruffalo is also good as her childhood pal grown up. [PG-13]▼▌

13 Rue Madeleine (1947) **95m.** *** D: Henry Hathaway. James Cagney, Annabella, Richard Conte, Frank Latimore, Walter Abel, Melville Cooper, Sam Jaffe. Gripping documentary-style WW2 story about the training of new O.S.S. operatives, their first overseas assignments, and the ferreting-out of a German enemy agent in their ranks. ▼▌

Thirteenth Floor, The (1999-U.S.-German) **C-100m.** **½ D: Josef Rusnak. Craig Bierko, Armin Mueller-Stahl, Gretchen Mol, Vincent D'Onofrio, Dennis Haysbert, Steven Schub. Scientists create a virtual-reality 1937 L.A. so realistic that even the "inhabitants" have their own minds, and don't realize they and everything around them exists only in a computer . . . then murder links the worlds of the created and the creators. Well-produced sci-fi in film noir style is interesting throughout, but too talky,

and the basic idea is familiar. Based on the novel *Simulacron-3* by Daniel F. Galouye. Previously filmed by Rainer Werner Fassbinder for German TV as WORLD ON A WIRE. Super 35. [R].▼●▌

13th Letter, The (1951) **85m.** **½ D: Otto Preminger. Linda Darnell, Charles Boyer, Michael Rennie, Constance Smith, Judith Evelyn. Interesting account of effect of series of poison pen letters on townsfolk, set in Canada. Remake of Henri Georges Clouzot's LE CORBEAU.

13th Warrior, The (1999) **C-102m.** *** D: John McTiernan. Antonio Banderas, Diane Venora, Dennis Storhoi, Vladimir Kulich, Omar Sharif. In ancient times, exiled Arabian nobleman Banderas travels with some Norsemen to their homelands, there to face possibly supernatural nighttime marauders, who eat their victims. Sturdy, action-packed adventure with horror overtones, realistic but in the heroic tradition, shot on spectacular Canadian locations. Based on Michael Crichton's novel *Eaters of the Dead,* itself inspired by true travel writings and the medieval tale of *Beowulf.* Panavision. [R]▼▌

—30— (1959) **96m.** *½ D: Jack Webb. Jack Webb, William Conrad, David Nelson, Whitney Blake, Louise Lorimer, Joe Flynn, James Bell. Hackneyed, overwritten tale of a typical night on a big-city newspaper. Conrad chews the scenery as city editor, but the script's the main villain, abetted by atrocious music score. Title, by the way, is journalists' way of indicating "the end."▼▌

30 Days of Night (2007-U.S.-New Zealand) **C-113m.** **½ D: David Slade. Josh Hartnett, Melissa George, Danny Huston, Ben Foster, Mark Boone Junior, Mark Rendall, Amber Sainsbury, Manu Bennett. Barlow, Alaska, the northernmost point in the U.S., undergoes 30 days without sun every year. The residents take it in stride, until a horde of ravenous vampires arrives one sunless day. Intensely grim, this well-crafted thriller isn't for the faint of heart, as it delivers yet another movie view of vampires. Huston is outstanding as the head bloodsucker. Based on the graphic novel by Ben Templesmith and Steve Niles (who cowrote the film). Followed by a DVD sequel. Super 35. [R]▌

35 Up (1991-British) **C/B&W-122m.** *** D: Michael Apted. Still compelling continuation of 28 UP, in which Apted again peeks in on the lives of the subjects he has been filming at seven-year intervals, beginning at age seven. A thoughtful, revealing look at lives lived, and dreams fulfilled and unfulfilled within the British class system. As with all prior entries, this was originally produced for British TV. Followed by 42 UP.▼▌

30-Foot Bride of Candy Rock, The (1959) **75m.** ** D: Sidney Miller. Lou Costello, Dorothy Provine, Gale Gordon, Charles

Lane, Jimmy Conlin, Peter Leeds. Lou Costello's only starring film without Bud Abbott is nothing much, mildly entertaining, with Provine enlarged to gigantic proportions. ▼▶

30 Is a Dangerous Age, Cynthia (1968-British) **C-85m.** **½ D: Joseph McGrath. Dudley Moore, Eddie Foy, Jr., Suzy Kendall, John Bird. Man who has frittered away his life decides that within six weeks he wants to be married and famous. Funny, but sometimes falls flat. Dudley also composed the score and cowrote the screenplay. ▼

39 Steps, The (1935-British) **87m.** **** D: Alfred Hitchcock. Robert Donat, Madeleine Carroll, Lucie Mannheim, Godfrey Tearle, Peggy Ashcroft, John Laurie, Wylie Watson. Classic Hitchcock mystery with overtones of light comedy and romance, as innocent Donat is pulled into spy-ring activities. Memorable banter between Donat and Carroll, who thinks he's a criminal, set style for sophisticated dialogue for years. John Buchan's novel was adapted by Charles Bennett and Alma Reville; additional dialogue by Ian Hay. Remade three times and later adapted to the Broadway stage. ▼▶●

39 Steps, The (1959-British) **C-93m.** **½ D: Ralph Thomas. Kenneth More, Taina Elg, Brenda de Banzie, Barry Jones, Reginald Beckwith, Sidney James, James Hayter. Young man is accidentally involved in murder and espionage and ensnares the aid of disbelieving young woman. More and Elg are delightful in this replica of 1935 classic; not nearly as good, but still entertaining. Remade in 1978 and as a BBC 2008 TVM. ▼▶

Thirty-Nine Steps, The (1978-British) **C-102m.** **½ D: Don Sharp. Robert Powell, David Warner, Eric Porter, Karen Dotrice, John Mills, George Baker. Based more on John Buchan's book than Hitchcock adaptation, remake isn't bad but lacks panache; Powell plays innocent man pursued by villains who believe he's obtained details of their plot to hatch WW1. [PG] ▼●

Thirty Seconds Over Tokyo (1944) **138m.** *** D: Mervyn LeRoy. Van Johnson, Robert Walker, Spencer Tracy, Phyllis Thaxter, Scott McKay, Robert Mitchum, Don DeFore, Stephen McNally, Louis Jean Heydt, Leon Ames, Paul Langton, Bill Williams. Exciting WW2 actioner of first American attack on Japan with sturdy cast, guest appearance by Tracy as General Doolittle. Script by Dalton Trumbo. Oscar-winning special effects. ▼●●

36 Fillette (1988-French) **C-88m.** **½ D: Catherine Breillat. Delphine Zentout, Etienne Chicot, Olivier Parniere, Jean-Pierre Léaud. Annoyingly uneven account of a restless, amply endowed 14-year-old (well played by Zentout): will she or won't she lose her virginity while on vacation at the beach with her family? Some effective moments, but the film goes nowhere. ▼▶

36 Hours (1964) **115m.** **½ D: George Seaton. James Garner, Eva Marie Saint, Rod Taylor, Werner Peters, Celia Lovsky, Alan Napier. Intriguing WW2 yarn with Garner as captured spy brainwashed into thinking the war is over begins well, but peters out fast. Taylor as German officer is interesting casting. Remade for cable TV as BREAKING POINT in 1989 with Corbin Bernsen. Also shown in computer-colored version. Panavision. ▼▶

Thirty Two Short Films About Glenn Gould (1993-Canadian) **C-93m.** **½ D: Francois Girard. Colm Feore. As the title says . . . and the result is an occasionally illuminating but much too fragmented bio of the famed reclusive concert pianist. People who know Gould talk about him, key scenes from his life are enacted and his works are performed, but it doesn't quite add up, either as documentary or biography. Girard scripted, with Don McKellar. ▼▶

30 Years of Fun (1963) **85m.** **** Compiled by Robert Youngson. Charlie Chaplin, Buster Keaton, Laurel and Hardy, Harry Langdon, Sydney Chaplin, Charley Chase, etc. Without repeating from previous films, Youngson presents hilarious silent comedy footage. Included is rare sequence of Laurel and Hardy performing together for the first time in 1921's LUCKY DOG. ▶

This Above All (1942) **110m.** **½ D: Anatole Litvak. Tyrone Power, Joan Fontaine, Thomas Mitchell, Nigel Bruce, Gladys Cooper, Sara Allgood, Phillip Merivale, Alexander Knox. Fontaine, a daughter of the English aristocracy turned WAAF, falls in love with blind date Power, a bloke in civilian clothes during wartime who's obviously haunted by a Terrible Secret. Adapted by R. C. Sherriff from Eric Knight's novel, this soap opera/flag-waver suffers from miscasting of Power (making no attempt at Englishness), Fontaine's speech making, and overgenerous running time. ▶

This Angry Age (1958-Italian-U.S.) **C-111m.** ** D: René Clement. Silvana Mangano, Anthony Perkins, Alida Valli, Richard Conte, Jo Van Fleet, Nehemiah Persoff. Ludicrous mishmash set in Indo-China with Van Fleet a stereotyped, dominating mother who's convinced that her children (Perkins and Mangano) can make their rice fields a going proposition. Originally titled THE SEA WALL. Technirama.

This Boy's Life (1993) **C-115m.** ***½ D: Michael Caton-Jones. Robert De Niro, Ellen Barkin, Leonardo DiCaprio, Jonah Blechman, Eliza Dushku, Chris Cooper, Carla Gugino, Zack Ansley, Tracey Ellis, Kathy Kinney, Gerrit Graham, Tobey Maguire. Harrowing but utterly absorbing story, set in the 1950s, of a young boy and his footloose mother who wind up living in a remote part of Washington state with a lout who both browbeats the youngster and beats him physically. Searing character study is a showcase for masterful performances (including an eye-opener for young DiCaprio), but what ultimately makes it work is learning that the story is true. Screenplay by Robert Getchell, from Tobias Wolff's memoir. Clairmont-Scope. [R] ▼●)

This Christmas (2007) C-117m. **½ D: Preston A. Whitmore II. Delroy Lindo, Idris Elba, Loretta Devine, Chris Brown, Keith Robinson, Mekhi Phifer, Regina King, Lupe Ontiveros. Pleasant holiday-themed comedy-drama, with a fine ensemble breathing fresh life into generic clichés and stock characters. When members of an extended family gather for their first Christmas reunion in four years, secrets are revealed, grievances are aired, and, of course, crises are resolved. Aptly cast as a would-be singer, Brown (a real-life R&B artist) delivers a knockout rendition of "Try a Little Tenderness" in a key scene. Written by the director. [PG-13]▶

This Could Be the Night (1957) **103m.** **½ D: Robert Wise. Jean Simmons, Paul Douglas, Anthony Franciosa, Joan Blondell, Neile Adams, ZaSu Pitts, J. Carrol Naish, Ray Anthony. Forced, frantic comedy of prim teacher Simmons working as secretary to gangster Douglas, who runs a nightclub; Franciosa is the young associate who romances her. CinemaScope.▼●

This Earth Is Mine (1959) C-125m. **½ D: Henry King. Rock Hudson, Jean Simmons, Dorothy McGuire, Claude Rains, Kent Smith, Anna Lee, Ken Scott. Disjointed soaper set in 1930s California vineyards about intertwining family romances, focusing on Hudson-Simmons love story. CinemaScope.

This Film Is Not Yet Rated (2006) C-97m. *** D: Kirby Dick. Smart, often hilarious documentary focusing on the Motion Picture Association of America's movie rating system. Intertwining interviews with former panelists, directors (including Kevin Smith, John Waters, and Atom Egoyan), and studio execs, director Dick explores the flaws in the system and accusations of censorship tactics imposed by the mysterious board. Also an engrossing detective story, as the filmmaker hires a couple of determined female private eyes who use methods Bogart would have loved in order to unmask the tight-lipped board members. Originally slapped with an NC-17, this feature was released unrated instead.▶

This Gun for Hire (1942) 80m. *** D: Frank Tuttle. Alan Ladd, Veronica Lake, Robert Preston, Laird Cregar, Tully Marshall, Marc Lawrence, Pamela Blake. Ladd came into his own as paid gunman seeking revenge on man who double-crossed him, with Lake as a fetching vis-à-vis. Script by W. R. Burnett and Albert Maltz, from Graham Greene's novel *A Gun For Sale*. Remade in 1957 (as SHORT CUT TO HELL) and for cable TV in 1991 (with Robert Wagner).▼●)

This Happy Breed (1944-British) C-110m. ***½ D: David Lean. Robert Newton, Celia Johnson, John Mills, Kay Walsh, Stanley Holloway, Amy Veness, Alison Leggatt. Splendidly acted saga follows British family from 1919 to 1939 in this adaptation of Noel Coward play. Scripted by director Lean, cinematographer Ronald Neame, and coproducer Anthony Havelock-Allan. Unbilled Laurence Olivier provides opening narration. ▼

This Happy Feeling (1958) C-92m. *** D: Blake Edwards. Debbie Reynolds, Curt Jurgens, John Saxon, Alexis Smith, Estelle Winwood, Mary Astor, Troy Donahue, Joe Flynn. Most engaging cast gives zip to simple yarn of Reynolds enthralled by actor Jurgens, but sparked by suitor Saxon; Winwood fine as eccentric housekeeper. CinemaScope.▼

This Is Elvis (1981) C/B&W-101m. **½ D: Malcolm Leo, Andrew Solt. David Scott, Paul Boensh III, Johnny Harra, Lawrence Koller, Rhonda Lyn, Debbie Edge, Larry Raspberry, Furry Lewis. Unusual examination of Elvis' life combines documentary footage with sequences of actors playing Presley at various stages of his life. The film is both fascinating and phony, an insightful portrayal of a tragic legend and yet another excuse to rake in profits by trading on his memory. Alternate versions run 144m. and 246m. [PG]▼●)

This is England (2007-British) C-103m. ***½ D: Shane Meadows. Thomas Turgoose, Stephen Graham, Jo Hartley, Joe Gilgun, Andrew Shim, Vicky McClure, Rosamund Hanson, Andrew Ellis, Perry Benson, George Newton. It's 1983 in Thatcher-era, bleak coastal England. Fatherless schoolboy Shaun (Turgoose) is a hapless 12-year-old who unexpectedly falls in with the local skinhead gang. Writer-director Meadows (TWENTYFOURSEVEN) has created a canvas of disenfranchised, nihilistic young people that rings all too true in story, performance, and tone. Result is an example of a genre that the cinema has often excelled in: the loss of childhood innocence.▶

This Is It (2009) C-111m. *** D: Kenny Ortega. Episodic but often fascinating look at rehearsals for a planned Michael Jackson concert tour. Ortega, who was directing the show, compiled this feature from a number of sources, including home-video footage. Not only provides a view of what Jackson had in store for his fans but gives us a glimpse of his work ethic and how he dealt with his colleagues. A remake of THRILLER can't top the original music video, but other elaborate, high-tech production numbers are dazzling, and a new video segment in which Jackson interacts with Humphrey Bogart, Rita Hayworth, and other vintage stars is fun. Clouded, naturally, by the realization that this talented performer died shortly after all of this was filmed. Advertised as MICHAEL JACKSON'S THIS IS IT. [PG] ▶

This Island Earth (1955) **C-86m.** ******* D: Joseph Newman. Jeff Morrow, Rex Reason, Faith Domergue, Russell Johnson, Lance Fuller, Douglas Spencer. Suspenseful, intelligent science fiction about scientists lured to mysterious project, only to find they've been recruited—or more appropriately, shanghaied—by aliens to help them defend their invasion-torn planet. Thoughtful and exciting, with excellent visuals; based on Raymond F. Jones' novel. Film is spoofed in MYSTERY SCIENCE THEATER 3000: THE MOVIE. ▼●▶

This Is My Affair (1937) **101m.** ******* D: William A. Seiter. Barbara Stanwyck, Robert Taylor, Victor McLaglen, Brian Donlevy, Sidney Blackmer, John Carradine, Sig Ruman. Exciting film of undercover man Taylor joining gang of robbers on order from President McKinley; Stanwyck is saloon singer who loves Taylor (they married in real life two years later).

This is my Father (1999-Canadian-Irish) **C-120m.** ****** D: Paul Quinn. Aidan Quinn, James Caan, Stephen Rea, John Cusack, Moya Farrelly, Jacob Tierney, Colm Meaney, Donal Donnelly, Brendan Gleeson. Burned-out Chicago schoolteacher (Caan) travels to his ancestral home in Ireland, with his teenage nephew in tow, to unlock the mystery of his father's identity. Played both in present day and flashback, the film aims high but doesn't succeed, despite good performances and period flavor. A labor of love for first-time writer-director Quinn; brother Aidan stars, brother Declan photographed it, and sister Marian appears briefly. All three brothers executive-produced. [R] ▼▶

This Is My Life (1992) **C-105m.** ****½** D: Nora Ephron. Julie Kavner, Samantha Mathis, Gaby Hoffmann, Carrie Fisher, Dan Aykroyd, Bob Nelson, Caroline Aaron, Danny Zorn, Joy Behar, Kathy Najimy. Single mom with two daughters pursues her dream of becoming a standup comic and, virtually overnight, her career takes off—leaving her girls in second place. Kavner is perfect, the girls are adorable, and the story is certainly credible—but somehow the film doesn't quite deliver. Directing debut for writer Ephron (who penned this script with sister Delia), based on Meg Wolitzer's novel *This Is Your Life*. [PG-13] ▼●

This Is Spinal Tap (1984) **C-82m.** ******* D: Rob Reiner. Michael McKean, Chris-

topher Guest, Harry Shearer, Rob Reiner, Tony Hendra, June Chadwick, R.J. Parnell, David Kaff, Fran Drescher. Admirably precise parody of a rock documentary, with Reiner as director Marty Di Bergi, who chronicles latest American tour of aging British rock group that's a working definition of the term "loser." Collaborative effort improvised by Reiner and his cast of colleagues; cunning satire through and through, though not always terribly funny. Our favorite bit: the amplifier that goes to "11." Many familiar faces appear in cameos. P.S.: In the '90s the "fictitious" group reunited for a series of concerts and a TV special. Rereleased in 1995 with many new scenes. [R] ▼●▶

This Is the Army (1943) **C-121m.** ******* D: Michael Curtiz. George Murphy, Joan Leslie, Lt. Ronald Reagan, Sgt. Joe Louis, Kate Smith, George Tobias, Alan Hale, Charles Butterworth, Dolores Costello, Una Merkel, Stanley Ridges, Rosemary DeCamp, Frances Langford, Irving Berlin, many others. Soldiers who staged Irving Berlin's WWI musical *Yip Yip Yaphank* reunite to help mount similar WW2 effort; corny but enjoyable framework (with Warner Bros. cast) for filmed record of legendary 1940s show, a topical melange of songs and skits. P.S.: This is the film where George Murphy plays Ronald Reagan's father! ▼▶

This Land Is Mine (1943) **103m.** ****** D: Jean Renoir. Charles Laughton, Maureen O'Hara, George Sanders, Walter Slezak, Kent Smith, Una O'Connor, Philip Merivale, George Coulouris, Nancy Gates. Meek French teacher Laughton, aroused by Nazi occupation, becomes hero. Patriotic wartime film is dated and disappointing today; written by Dudley Nichols. ▼●

This Man Must Die (1969-French-Italian) **C-107m.** *****½** D: Claude Chabrol. Michel Duchaussoy, Jean Yanne, Caroline Cellier, Lorraine Rainer, Marc DiNapoli, Guy Marly. Outstanding film about man who sets out to find the person who killed his young son in hit-and-run accident and the complications which ensue. This may be the best of many fine Chabrol dramas; Yanne and Cellier are unforgettable, the cinematography (by Jean Rabier) beautiful. [PG] ▼▶

This Property Is Condemned (1966) **C-110m.** ****** D: Sydney Pollack. Natalie Wood, Robert Redford, Charles Bronson, Kate Reid, Mary Badham, Robert Blake, Alan Baxter, Dabney Coleman, Jon Provost. Often absurd film version of Tennessee Williams' one-act play has doe-eyed Wood falling for Redford, the out-of-towner staying in her mama's boardinghouse. Except for James Wong Howe's photography, this is trash without the style that often makes trash enjoyable. Francis Ford Coppola was one of the screenwriters. ▼●▶

This Rebel Age SEE: **Beat Generation, The**
This Rebel Breed (1960) **90m.** **½ D:
Richard L. Bare. Rita Moreno, Mark Damon, Gerald Mohr, Jay Novello, Eugene
Martin, Tom Gilson, Diane (Dyan) Cannon,
Al Freeman (Jr.). Above average drama
about racial tensions in a multi-ethnic high
school, with Moreno well cast as a Latina
teen involved with an Anglo boy (which
displeases her trouble-prone brother). Cannon is amusingly cast as a gang deb! Retitled THREE SHADES OF LOVE and THE
BLACK REBELS, the latter with incongruous R-rated footage added.▼▶
This Sporting Life (1963-British) **129m.**
***½ D: Lindsay Anderson. Richard Harris,
Rachel Roberts, Alan Badel, William Hartnell, Colin Blakely, Arthur Lowe. Yorkshire
coal miner "betters" himself by becoming
professional rugby player. Powerful film
(written by David Storey) about love, success, and disillusionment; also serves to
illustrate what a grueling game rugby is.
Film debut of Glenda Jackson. Originally
134m.▼▶
This Time for Keeps (1947) **C-105m.**
**½ D: Richard Thorpe. Esther Williams,
Jimmy Durante, Lauritz Melchior, Johnnie
Johnston, Xavier Cugat, Dame May Whitty,
Sharon McManus. Slight MGM musical
with Johnston falling for aquacade star Wil-
liams, neglecting to inform her that he's
engaged.▼▶
This Woman Is Dangerous (1952) **100m.**
**½ D: Felix E. Feist. Joan Crawford, Den-
nis Morgan, David Brian, Richard Webb,
Sherry Jackson. In typical tough-girl role,
Crawford finds true love after countless
mishaps, including an eye operation.▶
This World, Then the Fireworks (1997)
C-100m. ** D: Michael Oblowitz. Billy
Zane, Gina Gershon, Sheryl Lee, Rue Mc-
Clanahan, Seymour Cassel, Will Patton,
Richard Edson. Period noir drama set in the
'50s about two devoted siblings, partners
in cons and murder, who seemingly find
a way out of their miserable lives when a
repressed policewoman enters their world.
Intriguing title, nice period re-creation,
good performances, but we've been down
this road too many times before—in better
movies. Zane also coexecutive-produced.
[R]▼▶
Thomas and the Magic Railroad (2000-
U.S.-British) **C-86m.** *½ D: Britt Allcroft.
Alec Baldwin, Mara Wilson, Peter Fonda,
Didi Conn, Michael E. Rodgers, Russell
Means; voices of Eddie Glen, Colm Feore.
The world's most famous choo-choo makes
a movie boo-boo: a dull, dippy screen spin-
off for Thomas the Tank Engine, star of
the children's TV show. A foolish-looking
Baldwin inherits the conductor role origi-
nated by Ringo Starr in a story about a
threatening (loco) motive named Diesel 10.
Fonda is a dour grandpa. Grownups should

pair this with EASY RIDER on a slow
night. [G]▼▶
Thomas Crown Affair, The (1968) **C-
102m.** *** D: Norman Jewison. Steve
McQueen, Faye Dunaway, Paul Burke,
Jack Weston, Biff McGuire, Yaphet Kotto.
Glittery production complements story of
supercool millionaire McQueen who plots
perfect bank robbery, as insurance investigator Dunaway coldly determines to nab the
gentleman-thief. Perfect nonthink entertainment; dazzling use of multi-image screens
(designed by Pablo Ferro). Oscar-winning
song, "The Windmills of Your Mind," by
Michel Legrand and Alan and Marilyn
Bergman. Remade in 1999. [R] ▼●▶
Thomas Crown Affair, The (1999) **C-
112m.** **½ D: John McTiernan. Pierce
Brosnan, Rene Russo, Denis Leary, Ben Gazzara, Frankie Faison, Fritz Weaver, Charles
Keating, Mark Margolis, Faye Dunaway. A
handsome, wealthy, jet-setting industrialist
moonlights as an art thief, and delights in
playing cat-and-mouse with a beautiful insurance investigator. A distant cousin to the 1968
version (despite the presence of Dunaway, as
Brosnan's shrink), this is slick and entertaining, but everyone seems to be working a bit
too hard to make it look effortless. Brosnan
also produced. Panavision. [R]▼●▶
Thomasine & Bushrod (1974) **C-95m.**
**½ D: Gordon Parks, Jr. Max Julien,
Vonetta McGee, George Murdock, Glynn
Turman, Juanita Moore. OK mixture of
black exploitation and Western action with
comedy, as a black "Bonnie and Clyde"
team operate in 1911 Texas. Julien scripted
and co-produced, along with the classy-
looking McGee. Shot in New Mexico. [PG]
Thor (2011) **C-115m.** **½ D: Kenneth
Branagh. Chris Hemsworth, Natalie Portman, Anthony Hopkins, Tom Hiddleston,
Stellan Skarsgård, Kat Dennings, Clark
Gregg, Colm Feore, Ray Stevenson, Idris Elba, Jaimie Alexander, Rene Russo,
Tadanobu Asano, Joshua Dallas, Adriana
Barraza. Norse mythology by way of Marvel
Comics' Stan Lee and Jack Kirby: mighty
hammer-wielding Thor (Hemsworth) is
banished from the kingdom of Asgard by
his ailing father (Hopkins)—with a little
help from a jealous brother (Hiddleston)—
and sent to Earth. There he's discovered by
scientist Portman, who's been investigating
strange phenomena in the New Mexico night
sky—and finds herself attracted to the otherworldly hunk. Heavy going in the artificial-
looking Norse world, while the tone on Earth
is one of cheeky comedy. This lighthearted
material is novel and fun, but it undercuts the
story's deadly serious intentions. In short, a
mixed bag. 3-D Panavision. [PG-13]▶
Thoroughbreds Don't Cry (1937) **80m.**
**½ D: Alfred E. Green. Judy Garland,
Mickey Rooney, Ronald Sinclair, Sophie
Tucker, C. Aubrey Smith, Frankie Darro,

Henry Kolker, Helen Troy. Fairly good racetrack story with jockey Rooney involved in crooked deals, young Garland adding some songs. Mickey and Judy's first film together. ▼●)

Thoroughly Modern Millie (1967) **C-138m.** **½ D: George Roy Hill. Julie Andrews, James Fox, Mary Tyler Moore, Carol Channing, Beatrice Lillie, John Gavin, Jack Soo, Pat Morita, Philip Ahn. Up to a point this Ross Hunter attempt to recapture some of Andrews' *Boy Friend* magic is successful, but after nearly two and a half hours, one begins to yawn. 1920s farce has a fatal case of the cutes. Elmer Bernstein's score won an Oscar. Later a Broadway musical. ▼●)

Those Calloways (1965) **C-131m.** *** D: Norman Tokar. Brian Keith, Vera Miles, Brandon de Wilde, Walter Brennan, Ed Wynn, Linda Evans, Philip Abbott. Long, episodic but rewarding Disney film about an eccentric New England man (Keith) and his family, focusing on his determined efforts to use nearby lake for bird sanctuary before it's bought up by business interests. Film debut of Linda Evans. Music score by Max Steiner. ▼)

Those Daring Young Men in their Jaunty Jalopies (1969-British-Italian-French) **C-122m.** **½ D: Ken Annakin. Tony Curtis, Susan Hampshire, Terry-Thomas, Eric Sykes, Gert Frobe, Peter Cook, Dudley Moore, Jack Hawkins. Slapstick adventures of participants in 1,500-mile car race to Monte Carlo during the 1920s. Some funny scenes, but backfires a bit too often. Cut for U.S. release to 93m. Original British title: MONTE CARLO OR BUST. Panavision. [G] ▼)

Those Fantastic Flying Fools (1967) **C-95m.** **½ D: Don Sharp. Burl Ives, Troy Donahue, Gert Frobe, Terry-Thomas, Hermione Gingold, Daliah Lavi, Lionel Jeffries. Lightweight tale of Victorian England moon race, loosely adapted from Jules Verne story (previously filmed as FROM THE EARTH TO THE MOON). Original title: BLAST-OFF. Panavision. ▼)

Those Lips, Those Eyes (1980) **C-107m.** *** D: Michael Pressman. Frank Langella, Glynnis O'Connor, Thomas Hulce, Kevin McCarthy, Jerry Stiller, Herbert Berghof. Stagestruck adolescent learns about love the hard way while interning in Cleveland summer stock during the early '50s. Hulce is too nerdish in the key role, but Langella as down-on-his-luck actor, O'Connor as company's resident dish, are both quite good. A sleeper, written by David Shaber. [R] ▼)

Those Magnificent Men in Their Flying Machines (1965) **C-132m.** *** D: Ken Annakin. Stuart Whitman, Sarah Miles, James Fox, Alberto Sordi, Robert Morley, Gert Frobe, Jean-Pierre Cassel, Terry-Thomas, Irina Demick, Benny Hill, Flora

Robson, Sam Wanamaker, Gordon Jackson, Millicent Martin, Red Skelton, Tony Hancock; narrated by James Robertson Justice. Long but enjoyable film of great 1910 London-to-Paris airplane race involving international conflicts, cheating, and romance. Skelton has funny cameo in amusing prologue, tracing history of aviation. Clever title caricatures and designs by Ronald Searle. Todd-AO. ▼●)

Thousand Acres, A (1997) **C-105m.** ** D: Jocelyn Moorhouse. Michelle Pfeiffer, Jessica Lange, Jason Robards, Jennifer Jason Leigh, Colin Firth, Keith Carradine, Kevin Anderson, Pat Hingle, John Carroll Lynch, Michelle Williams, Elizabeth Moss. When a stubborn, single-minded widowed father decides to relinquish ownership of his farm to his three daughters, a family is abruptly torn apart, and long-held secrets come out of the closet. The only thing missing from this melodrama is character motivation, which presumably did exist in Jane Smiley's Pulitzer Prize–winning novel, a variation on *King Lear*. A hollow film notable only for the strong performances of the two leading women (whose companies jointly produced the film). Bob Gunton appears unbilled. [R] ▼●)

Thousand and One Nights, A (1945) **C-93m.** *** D: Alfred E. Green. Cornel Wilde, Evelyn Keyes, Phil Silvers, Adele Jergens, Dusty Anderson, Dennis Hoey, Rex Ingram. Wilde is a genial, singing Aladdin in this slice of Technicolor escapism, with Silvers as his very contemporary sidekick. Keyes is fun as the impish genie who emerges from a magic lamp. Ingram (who played the genie in THE THIEF OF BAGDAD) has a throwaway role here as a giant. Look fast for Shelley Winters. ▼

Thousand and One Nights, A (1968-Spanish) **C-86m.** ** D: Joe Lacy (Jose Maria Elorrieta). Jeff Cooper, Raf Vallone, Luciana Paluzzi, Perla Christal, Reuben Rojo. Tongue-in-cheek Arabian Nights fantasy with the familiar tapestry: a flying carpet, a handsome swordsman, a beautiful part-time genie, a sinister vizier. Not to be confused with the similarly titled Cornel Wilde movie of the '40s.

Thousand Clowns, A (1965) **118m.** ***½ D: Fred Coe. Jason Robards, Barbara Harris, Martin Balsam, Barry Gordon, Gene Saks, William Daniels. Faithful adaptation by Herb Gardner of his Broadway comedy about society dropout who's being pressured to drop in again for the sake of young nephew who lives with him. Perfectly cast, filmed in N.Y.C., with Balsam's Oscar-winning performance as Robards' brother. ▼●)

Thousand Eyes of Dr. Mabuse, The SEE: **1,000 Eyes of Dr. Mabuse, The**

Thousands Cheer (1943) **C-126m.** **½ D: George Sidney. Mickey Rooney, Judy Garland, Gene Kelly, Red Skelton, Eleanor

Powell, Ann Sothern, Lucille Ball, Virginia O'Brien, Frank Morgan, Kathryn Grayson, Lena Horne, many others. Grayson lives with officer-father John Boles at Army base, falls for hotheaded private Kelly and decides to prepare an all-star show for the soldiers. Dubious plot is an excuse for specialty acts by top MGM stars. ▼●】

Thousand Years of Good Prayers, A (2007) **C-82m.** *** D: Wayne Wang. Faye Yu, Henry O, Vida Ghahremani. Elderly Chinese man comes to visit his daughter in Spokane, Washington, but she regards his visit as something of a nuisance. While she is off at work, he strikes up a relationship with an Iranian woman he meets at the park; in spite of their language barrier, the two senior citizens are able to communicate with a candor that's absent from his relationship with his daughter. Quiet but revealing film adapted by Yiyun Li from her short story. The two lead performers are perfect.】

Thrashin' (1986) **C-90m.** ** D: David Winters. Josh Brolin, Robert Rusler, Pamela Gilday, Brooke McCarter, Brett Marx, Sherilyn Fenn. Skateboard-riding youth gangs are pitted against each other in this WEST SIDE STORY on wheels . . . minus the spirit and originality, not to mention music. [PG-13] ▼▶

Threads (1984-British) **C-110m.** *** D: Mick Jackson. Karen Meagher, Reece Dinsdale, Rita May, Nicholas Lane, Victoria O'Keefe. Britain's answer to THE DAY AFTER is a powerful, if a bit overlong, drama about effect of nuclear holocaust on working-class town of Sheffield, with the focus on a pair of families whose son and daughter are about to wed. Unrelentingly graphic and grim, sobering, and shattering—as it should be. Originally produced for British television. ▼

Threat, The (1949) **65m.** *** D: Felix Feist. Charles McGraw, Michael O'Shea, Virginia Grey, Julie Bishop, Robert Shayne, Anthony Caruso. Thug McGraw escapes prison, kidnaps cop and D.A. who put him away, plus singer he suspects of having squealed. Fast, rugged little "B" keeps action hopping until tough conclusion. ▼

Three Ages (1923) **63m.** *** D: Buster Keaton, Edward F. Cline. Buster Keaton, Margaret Leahy, Wallace Beery, Joe Roberts, Horace Morgan, Lillian Lawrence. Buster's comic observations on the pursuit of a mate in the Stone Age, the Roman Empire, and modern times. Entertaining silent comedy, with Keaton making a memorable entrance atop a dinosaur. ▼●】

¡Three Amigos! (1986) **C-105m.** ** D: John Landis. Steve Martin, Chevy Chase, Martin Short, Patrice Martinez, Alfonso Arau, Tony Plana, Joe Mantegna, Jon Lovitz, Phil Hartman. Silent film Western heroes are summoned to Mexico for what they think will be a public appearance, find out

they're really supposed to rid a village of its bandit chieftain. Smarmy one-joke comedy has its moments but not too many; buffs may be amused to note that villain Arau was one of the key bad guys in THE WILD BUNCH. Coscripter Randy Newman wrote the songs. [PG] ▼●】

3 Bad Men (1926) **92m.** ***½ D: John Ford. George O'Brien, Lou Tellegen, J. Farrell MacDonald, Tom Santschi, Frank Campeau. Three gruff outlaws become benevolent protectors of young woman whose father is killed during Western settlement period. Beautiful mixture of action, drama, comedy, and sentiment in one of Ford's best silents. An obvious variation on 3 GODFATHERS. ▼

Three Bites of the Apple (1967) **C-105m.** *½ D: Alvin Ganzer. David McCallum, Sylva Koscina, Tammy Grimes, Harvey Korman, Domenico Modugno, Aldo Fabrizi. Good scenery is only plus of flimsy comedy about McCallum's attempts to avoid heavy taxation of money he's won in a casino on the Riviera. Panavision.

Three Brothers (1980-Italian-French) **C-113m.** *** D: Francesco Rosi. Philippe Noiret, Charles Vanel, Michele Placido, Vittorio Mezzogiorno, Andrea Ferreol, Maddalena Crippa, Sara Tafuri, Marta Zoffoli. Wise, touching, but slow-moving account of three very different brothers who return to the country village of their youth for their mother's funeral. The recollections of their elderly peasant father (Vanel) and scenes with his young granddaughter (Zoffoli) are particularly moving. Adapted from Platonov's *The Third Son.* [PG] ▼】

Three Burials of Melquiades Estrada, The (2005-U.S.-French) **C-116m.** ***½ D: Tommy Lee Jones. Tommy Lee Jones, Barry Pepper, Julio César Cedillo, Dwight Yoakam, Melissa Leo, January Jones, Levon Helm. When his Mexican comrade is shot and killed and the local cops don't care, Texas cowboy Jones makes good on a promise by taking the man's dead body home, dragging along his killer for good measure. Compelling modern-day Western parable about friendship, morality, reckoning, and forgiveness. Impressive work by Jones on both sides of the camera; this marks his theatrical feature directing debut. Written by Guillermo Arriaga. Jones' daughter Victoria appears as Leticia. Panavision. [R]】

Three Caballeros, The (1945) **C-70m.** *** D: Norman Ferguson. Aurora Miranda, Carmen Molina, Dora Luz, voices of Sterling Holloway, Clarence Nash, Jose Oliveira, Joaquin Garay. Colorful Disney pastiche that followed 1940s Good Neighbor Policy by saluting Latin America, through the eyes of Donald Duck. Filled with infectious music (including "Baia," "You Belong to My Heart"), eye-popping visuals, amusing cartoon sequences, and clever combinations of live-action and animation. Donald, Jose Carioca, and Panchito perform title song in a dazzling display of cartoon wizardry. ▼●▶

Three Came Home (1950) **106m. ***½** D: Jean Negulesco. Claudette Colbert, Patric Knowles, Florence Desmond, Sessue Hayakawa, Sylvia Andrew, Phyllis Morris. Stunning performances by Colbert and Hayakawa make this a must. British and American families living on Borneo during WW2 are sent to prison camps by Japanese, but cultured officer Hayakawa takes an interest in authoress Colbert. Producer Nunnally Johnson adapted Agnes Newton Keith's autobiographical book. ▼▶

Three Cases of Murder (1955-British) **99m. **½** D: Wendy Toye, David Eady, George More O'Ferrall. Alan Badel, Hugh Pryse, John Gregson, Elizabeth Sellars, Emrys Jones, Orson Welles, Maxwell Reed, Richard Wattis; introduced by Eammon Andrews. Three offbeat murder stories; opener "In the Picture" is genuinely eerie, closer "Lord Mountdrago" (from Somerset Maugham story) has Welles in absorbing tale of a pompous British government official haunted by a rival. ▼●

Three Coins in the Fountain (1954) **C-102m. *** D: Jean Negulesco. Clifton Webb, Dorothy McGuire, Jean Peters, Louis Jourdan, Maggie McNamara, Rossano Brazzi, Cathleen Nesbitt. Splashy romance yarn made ultra-pleasing by Rome locations. Three women make wishes for romance at Fountain of Trevi, spurring several amorous adventures. Won Oscars for Milton Krasner's photography and the Jule Styne–Sammy Cahn title tune (sung by Frank Sinatra). Remade by same director as THE PLEASURE SEEKERS; reworked for TV in 1990 as COINS IN THE FOUNTAIN. CinemaScope. ▼●▶

Three Comrades (1938) **98m. ***½** D: Frank Borzage. Robert Taylor, Margaret Sullavan, Franchot Tone, Robert Young, Guy Kibbee, Lionel Atwill. Beautifully poignant film of Erich Maria Remarque's tale of post-WW1 Germany, and three lifelong friends who share a love for dying Sullavan. Excellent performances all around; coscripted by F. Scott Fitzgerald. ▼▶

Three Days of the Condor (1975) **C-117m. *** D: Sydney Pollack. Robert Redford, Faye Dunaway, Cliff Robertson, Max von Sydow, John Houseman, Carlin Glynn. Redford, a reader for U.S. intelligence office, learns more than he should, and suddenly finds himself a hunted man. Dunaway is excellent as innocent woman who shelters him. Good suspense yarn. Panavision. [R] ▼●▶

Three . . . Extremes (2004-Hong Kong-Korean-Japanese) **C-125m. **½** D: Fruit Chan, Chan Wook-Park, Takashi Miike. Miriam Yeung, Bai Ling, Tony Ka-Fai Leung, Byung-Hun Lee, Lim Won-Hee,

Kang Hye-Jeong, Kyoko Hasegawa, Atsuro Watabe. Three horror stories by Asian directors. In "Dumplings," a wealthy TV star comes to an apartment in a bad part of Hong Kong to dine on very special dumplings. In "Cut," a Korean horror-movie director is taken captive in his home by a clever stranger bent on murderous revenge. "Box" concerns a successful writer who has strange dreams of being buried in a box. First two segments are graphically gory; the third is elliptical and puzzling, but is also the best. All three stories are intelligent, intended for adults. Not for every taste, but the adventurous will find this worth checking out. The episodes were reordered for U.S. release. Followed by a sequel that was released direct-to-DVD in the U.S. [R] ▶

Three Faces of Eve, The (1957) **91m. ***½** D: Nunnally Johnson. Joanne Woodward, David Wayne, Lee J. Cobb, Nancy Kulp, Vince Edwards; narrated by Alistair Cooke. Academy Award tour de force by Woodward as young woman with multiple personalities and three separate lives. Cobb is psychiatrist who tries to cure her. Johnson also produced and wrote the screenplay. CinemaScope. ▼●▶

Three Faces West (1940) **79m. **½** D: Bernard Vorhaus. John Wayne, Sigrid Gurie, Charles Coburn, Spencer Charters, Roland Varno, Russell Simpson. Offbeat WW2-era drama about Austrian refugees heading for Oregon under Wayne's sponsorship. Gurie is hardly typical leading lady for the Duke, but film's odd mix of frontier and Nazi elements makes it worth a look. ▼▶

3:15 (1986) **C-95m. ** D: Larry Gross. Adam Baldwin, Deborah Foreman, Rene Auberjonois, Ed Lauter, Scott McGinnis, Danny De La Paz, John Scott Clough, Mario Van Peebles. Good cast in lackluster, low-budget teenage gang film, filmed in 1984. [R] ▼

Three for the Road (1987) **C-88m. *½** D: B. W. L. Norton. Charlie Sheen, Kerri Green, Alan Ruck, Sally Kellerman, Blair Tefkin, Raymond J. Barry, Alexa Hamilton. Anachronistic youth movie about the spoiled-brat daughter of a senator who travels to boarding school with Sheen and Ruck—and hits more than a few detours. Dull in the extreme. [PG] ▼●

Three for the Show (1955) **C-93m. ** D: H. C. Potter. Betty Grable, Marge and Gower Champion, Jack Lemmon, Myron McCormick. Grable's dead husband (Lemmon) turns out to be very much alive in this weak musical remake of TOO MANY HUSBANDS. Dance numbers cleverly staged for widescreen by Jack Cole. CinemaScope. ▼●▶

Three Fugitives (1989) **C-93m. **½** D: Francis Veber. Nick Nolte, Martin Short, Sarah Rowland Doroff, James Earl Jones,

Alan Ruck, Kenneth McMillan, Bruce McGill. Bumbling bank robber—who's only pulling the heist to support his little daughter—takes a hostage with him, little dreaming that the guy is a notorious holdup man who's just finished a long stretch in prison. Fast-paced farce doesn't quite hang together, despite energetic performances; Veber's first American film is a remake of his own French comedy LES FUGITIFS. [PG-13]▼●)

Three Godfathers (1936) **82m.** ★★★ D: Richard Boleslawski. Chester Morris, Lewis Stone, Walter Brennan, Irene Hervey, Willard Robertson, Sidney Toler. Little-seen and underrated version of Peter B. Kyne's story (filmed twice before) about three bad guys who adopt a foundling in the desert. Beautifully shot and warmly acted.)

3 Godfathers (1948) **C-105m.** ★★★ D: John Ford. John Wayne, Pedro Armendariz, Harry Carey, Jr., Ward Bond, Mae Marsh, Jane Darwell, Ben Johnson, Mildred Natwick. Sturdy, sentimental, sometimes beautiful rendition of Peter B. Kyne's oft-filmed saga of three bandits who "adopt" a baby born in the desert. Final scene doesn't ring true, but Ford makes up for it in balance of film. Dedicated to the director's first star, Harry Carey, Sr. Remade for TV as THE GODCHILD and as a Japanese animated feature, TOKYO GODFATHERS.▼●)

300 (2007) **C-116m.** ★★★ D: Zack Snyder. Gerard Butler, Lena Headey, Dominic West, David Wenham, Vincent Regan, Michael Fassbender, Tom Wisdom, Andrew Pleavin, Rodrigo Santoro, Stephen McHattie. Frank Miller's graphic novel becomes a living comic book, using cutting-edge computer technology. Butler is commanding as King Leonidas, who leads his elite corps of Spartans into battle against Xerxes of Persia at Thermopylae in 480 B.C. Though greatly outnumbered they use cunning, strategy, and sheer courage to hold off the invaders . . . while Leonidas' wife fights a psychological battle on the home front. Not a history lesson but an adrenaline-pumped, larger-than-life interpretation of this famous battle, drenched in comic-book blood. Super 35. [R])

300 Spartans, The (1962) **C-114m.** *½ D: Rudolph Maté. Richard Egan, Ralph Richardson, Diane Baker, Barry Coe, David Farrar, Donald Houston, Kieron Moore, Laurence Naismith. Events leading up to heroic Greek stand against the Persian Army at Thermopylae; strictly cardboard, despite Mediterranean locations filmed in widescreen by Geoffrey Unsworth. However, this did have a profound effect on Frank Miller, who later created the graphic novel *300*. CinemaScope.)

Three in the Attic (1968) **C-92m.** ★★½ D: Richard Wilson. Christopher Jones, Judy

Pace, Yvette Mimieux, Maggie Thrett. Silly tale of youth with so much style that he works three girls at once until they get wise and decide to lock him in and drain him of his potency. [R]▼

Three in the Cellar SEE: **Up in the Cellar**

Three Into Two Won't Go (1969-British) **C-93m.** ★★ D: Peter Hall. Rod Steiger, Claire Bloom, Judy Geeson, Peggy Ashcroft, Paul Rogers. Marriage of Steiger and Bloom breaks up when he becomes infatuated with sexy hitchhiker Geeson. Originally an OK drama, but Universal shot extra footage and reedited original film to 100m. for television. [R]

3-Iron (2004-South Korean-Japanese) **C-88m.** ★★★½ D: Kim Ki-duk. Lee Seung-yeon, Jae Hee, Kwon Hyuk-ho, Joo Jin-mo, Choi Jeong-ho. Eerie, captivating fable about a young transient who sneaks into and lives in houses whose inhabitants are out of town. He forms an unusual bond with a woman who is patronized and battered by her husband. Quietly powerful film with a main character who doesn't speak a word of dialogue. The title refers to his obsession with hitting golf balls. [R])

Three Kings (1999) **C-115m.** ★★★ D: David O. Russell. George Clooney, Mark Wahlberg, Ice Cube, Spike Jonze, Nora Dunn, Jamie Kennedy, Mykelti Williamson, Cliff Curtis, Said Taghmaoui, Judy Greer. At the end of the Persian Gulf War, four renegade U.S. soldiers try to pull off a heist of Kuwaiti gold, but find themselves getting involved with innocent civilians who are being targeted by Saddam Hussein—and being left to fend for themselves by a retreating United States military. A gritty, violent action film with a brain and a point of view. Scripted by the director. Super 35. [R]▼)

Three Little Girls in Blue (1946) **C-90m.** ★★★ D: H. Bruce Humberstone. June Haver, George Montgomery, Vivian Blaine, Celeste Holm, Vera-Ellen, Frank Latimore, Charles Smith. Cheerful tale of three spunky sisters out to trap wealthy husbands; familiar plot with good tunes like "You Make Me Feel So Young." A remake of THREE BLIND MICE and MOON OVER MIAMI, set in turn-of-the-20th-century Atlantic City. Holm's film debut.

Three Little Words (1950) **C-102m.** ★★★ D: Richard Thorpe. Fred Astaire, Vera-Ellen, Red Skelton, Arlene Dahl, Keenan Wynn, Gloria De Haven, Debbie Reynolds, Carleton Carpenter. Standard MGM musical about famous songwriters Kalmar and Ruby and their climb to fame; bouncy cast, fine tunes, including "Who's Sorry Now?," "Thinking of You," title song. Debbie plays Helen Kane, but the real Helen dubbed "I Wanna Be Loved by You."▼●)

Three Lives and Only One Death (1996-French-Portuguese) **C-123m.** ★★★ D: Raoul Ruiz. Marcello Mastroianni, Anna

Galiena, Marisa Paredes, Melvil Poupaud, Chiara Mastroianni, Arielle Dombasle, Feodor Atkine, Lou Castel. One of Mastroianni's last films casts him in a quartet of roles: a traveling salesman, an anthropology professor, a butler, and a wealthy industrialist. Clever, stimulating film is better seen than described, with plenty of surprises in store. Chiara Mastroianni (daughter of Marcello and Catherine Deneuve) and Poupaud play the young couple who inherit the mansion where Marcello works as a butler. ▼

Three Lives of Thomasina, The (1964) C-97m. *** D: Don Chaffey. Patrick McGoohan, Susan Hampshire, Karen Dotrice, Matthew Garber, Vincent Winter, Denis Gilmore, Laurence Naismith, Finlay Currie. Charming Disney film made in England from Paul Gallico's story about a heartless veterinarian, his daughter's devotion to her pet cat, and a mystical young woman with life-giving "powers." A winner. ▼●)

3 Men and a Baby (1987) C-102m. *** D: Leonard Nimoy. Tom Selleck, Steve Guttenberg, Ted Danson, Nancy Travis, Margaret Colin, Philip Bosco, Celeste Holm, Derek de Lint, Cynthia Harris, Lisa & Michelle Blair. Enjoyable remake of France's big hit THREE MEN AND A CRADLE, about a trio of swinging bachelor roommates who suddenly find themselves custodians of an infant. Winning performances all around help keep this buoyant comedy on-track from start to finish. Followed by 3 MEN AND A LITTLE LADY. [PG] ▼●)

Three Men and a Cradle (1985-French) C-106m. *** D: Coline Serreau. Roland Giraud, Michel Boujenah, Andre Dussolier, Philippine Leroy Beaulieu, Dominique Lavanat, Marthe Villalonga. Very entertaining comedy about three swinging bachelors who find themselves stuck with a baby, which one of them fathered. Compassionate and funny; a real charmer. A box-office sensation in France and winner of three César awards. Remade in U.S. as 3 MEN AND A BABY. [PG-13] ▼●)

3 Men and a Little Lady (1990) C-100m. **½ D: Emile Ardolino. Tom Selleck, Steve Guttenberg, Ted Danson, Nancy Travis, Robin Weisman, Christopher Cazenove, Sheila Hancock, Fiona Shaw, John Boswall, Jonathan Lynn, Sydney Walsh. Pleasant (if unexceptional) follow-up to hit comedy has the growing tyke's mother (Travis) deciding to marry British actor Cazenove, and move to England . . . forcing the three bachelor fathers to prove that the prospective husband and father is really a rotter before it's too late. [PG] ▼●)

Three Musketeers, The (1921) 118m. *** D: Fred Niblo. Douglas Fairbanks, Marguerite De La Motte, Adolphe Menjou, Barbara La Marr, Leon Barry, George Siegmann,

Eugene Pallette, Nigel de Brulier, Boyd Irwin, Mary MacLaren, Sidney Franklin, Charles Stevens. Robust period adventure with Fairbanks a hearty D'Artagnan, Alexandre Dumas' swashbuckling hero who joins the King's Musketeers, becomes pals with Athos, Porthos, and Aramis, and battles evil in the court of Louis XIII. De Brulier almost steals the film as Cardinal Richelieu. Great fun! Followed by THE IRON MASK. ▼●)

Three Musketeers, The (1935) 90m. ** D: Rowland V. Lee. Walter Abel, Paul Lukas, Ian Keith, Onslow Stevens, Ralph Forbes, Margot Grahame, Heather Angel. Dullest version of Dumas story, with Abel miscast as D'Artagnan. ▼●

Three Musketeers, The (1939) 73m. *** D: Allan Dwan. Don Ameche, The Ritz Brothers, Lionel Atwill, Binnie Barnes, Miles Mander, Gloria Stuart, Pauline Moore, John Carradine, Joseph Schildkraut. Spirited musical, generally faithful to Dumas story; Ameche flavorful as D'Artagnan, Barnes lovely as Lady DeWinter, Ritz Brothers funny substitutes for unsuspecting musketeers. ▼▶

Three Musketeers, The (1948) C-125m. **½ D: George Sidney. Lana Turner, Gene Kelly, June Allyson, Van Heflin, Angela Lansbury, Robert Coote, Frank Morgan, Vincent Price, Keenan Wynn, Gig Young. Oddball, lavish production of Dumas tale with Kelly as D'Artagnan. Occasional bright moments, but continual change of tone and Heflin's drowsy characterization as Athos bog down the action. Lana makes a stunning Lady DeWinter. ▼●)

Three Musketeers, The (1974-British) C-105m. ***½ D: Richard Lester. Oliver Reed, Raquel Welch, Richard Chamberlain, Michael York, Frank Finlay, Christopher Lee, Geraldine Chaplin, Faye Dunaway, Charlton Heston, Jean-Pierre Cassel, Roy Kinnear, Spike Milligan. Delightful tongue-in-cheek version of Dumas classic, mixing swashbuckling adventure and romance with broad slapstick. One of Raquel Welch's finest hours. Followed by THE FOUR MUSKETEERS, which was actually filmed simultaneously, and THE RETURN OF THE MUSKETEERS (1989). [PG] ▼●)

Three Musketeers, The (1993) C-105m. *** D: Stephen Herek. Charlie Sheen, Kiefer Sutherland, Chris O'Donnell, Oliver Platt, Tim Curry, Rebecca De Mornay, Gabrielle Anwar, Michael Wincott, Paul McGann, Julie Delpy, Hugh O'Conor. Once again, D'Artagnan (O'Donnell) and the Three Musketeers (Sutherland, Sheen, and Platt) meet for the first time, and cross swords with the lackeys of scheming Cardinal Richelieu. Really just "Young Swords," but it's fast paced and entertaining; lots of action, handsome Austrian locations and attractive costumes. Curry's Richelieu is broad, anachronistic—and absolutely delightful, the highlight of the film. Panavision. [PG] ▼●)

3 Needles (2006-Canadian) **C-129m.** **½ D: Thom Fitzgerald. Shawn Ashmore, Stockard Channing, Tanabadee Chokpikultong, Olympia Dukakis, Lucy Liu, Sandra Oh, Ian Roberts, Chloë Sevigny, Gary Farmer. Fitzgerald also scripted this three-part opus, which attempts to humanize the tragedy of the AIDS epidemic by portraying individuals from different cultures who become HIV-positive. The scenarios follow Chinese farmers who are infected by tainted needles as they give blood, a Montreal porn actor, and three missionaries who come to Africa to save the souls of those afflicted with the virus. Raw and poignant in its best moments, but also slow moving, unevenly paced, and not as emotionally involving as it ought to be.▶

3 Ninjas (1992) **C-87m.** ** D: Jon Turteltaub. Victor Wong, Michael Treanor, Max Elliott Slade, Chad Power, Rand Kingsley, Alan McRae, Margarita Franco, Patrick Laborteaux. Three young brothers take their hard-earned ninja skills and put them to use against big-time baddies who are out to kidnap them. Harmless Disney release borrows ideas from every kiddie hit of its era. A surprising box-office success. Followed by three sequels. [PG] ▼●)

3 Ninjas: High Noon at Mega Mountain (1998) **C-93m.** ** D: Sean McNamara. Loni Anderson, Hulk Hogan, Jim Varney, Victor Wong, Mathew Botuchis, Michael J. O'Laskey II, J. P. Roeske II, Chelsey Earlywine, Alan McRae. Latest adventures of the three would-be ninjas (with new cast members) finds them putting their prowess to work unexpectedly when Anderson and a team of commando types take over an amusement park, holding the families inside hostage. OK kids' fare. [PG] ▼)

3 Ninjas Kick Back (1994) **C-99m.** ** D: Charles T. Kanganis. Victor Wong, Max Elliott Slade, Sean Fox, Evan Bonifant, Caroline Junko King, Dustin Nguyen, Alan McRae, Margarita Franco, Jason Schombing, Angelo Tiffe, Sab Shimono, Joey Travolta. More silliness aimed straight for the sub-teen crowd, as the three brothers (two of them recast from the original film) sacrifice a championship baseball game to fly to Japan to help their grandfather, who's been targeted by an age-old rival. A few moralistic lessons are sprinkled among the slapstick and toilet humor. [PG] ▼●)

3 Ninjas Knuckle Up (1995) **C-85m.** *½ D: Simon S. Sheen. Victor Wong, Charles Napier, Michael Treanor, Max Elliott Slade, Chad Power, Crystle Lightning, Patrick Kirkpatrick. Rocky, Tum Tum, and Colt join their grandfather to help an Indian tribe whose land is being abused by a corrupt business tycoon (Napier). This artless

blend of juvenile slapstick and martial arts was filmed in 1992, *before* 3 NINJAS KICK BACK, with the youthful star trio from the first film intact, but only released (barely, at that) in 1995. Followed by 3 NINJAS: HIGH NOON AT MEGA MOUNTAIN. [PG-13] ▼●)

Three O'Clock High (1987) **C-101m.** *½ D: Phil Joanou. Casey Siemaszko, Anne Ryan, Richard Tyson, Jeffrey Tambor, Philip Baker Hall, John P. Ryan, Stacey Glick, Jonathan Wise. High school journalist is assigned to do a welcome-wagon profile on the new psycho in class, finds himself challenged by this behemoth to duke it out in the parking lot after school. Steven Spielberg protégé Joanou is to the camera what James Brown is to shoes, but it's a lot of energy expended over nothing. Siemaszko is underwhelming in the lead. [PG-13] ▼●)

Three of Hearts (1993) **C-102m.** **½ D: Yurek Bogayevicz. William Baldwin, Kelly Lynch, Sherilyn Fenn, Joe Pantoliano, Gail Strickland, Cec Verrell, Claire Callaway, Marek Johnson, Monique Mannen, Tony Amendola, Tawny Kitaen. Original little film that begins with the end of a relationship between gay couple Lynch and Fenn and goes on to have the former hire a male escort (Baldwin) to try to get her lover back. Effective first half, with a strident Lynch getting to know the cocky gigolo; unfortunately second half of film becomes a more ordinary romantic tale, with the stud falling for his prey. A conventional gangster subplot doesn't help. Still, good use of N.Y.C. locations and excellent performances by Baldwin (who's never been better) and Lynch. [R] ▼●)

Three on a Couch (1966) **C-109m.** *½ D: Jerry Lewis. Jerry Lewis, Janet Leigh, Mary Ann Mobley, Gila Golan, Leslie Parrish, James Best, Kathleen Freeman. For psychiatrist Leigh to marry him, Lewis has to play five roles; one of them is "straight" but unintentionally funny, the other four zany, but unintentionally unfunny. The women are attractive.

Three on a Match (1932) **64m.** *** D: Mervyn LeRoy. Warren William, Joan Blondell, Bette Davis, Ann Dvorak, Humphrey Bogart, Lyle Talbot, Glenda Farrell, Dawn O'Day (Anne Shirley), Edward Arnold. Fine, fast-moving (and surprisingly potent) pre-Code melodrama of three girls who renew childhood friendship, only to find suspense and tragedy. Dvorak is simply marvelous. Remade as BROADWAY MUSKETEERS. ▼●)

3 Penny Opera, The (1931-German) **112m.** ***½ D: G. W. Pabst. Rudolph Forster, Lotte Lenya, Carola Neher, Reinhold Schunzel, Fritz Rasp, Valeska Gert. Fine musical satire chronicling activities of dashing gangster Forster, his cohorts, and antagonists, with Lenya outstanding as Pirate Jenny. From Bertolt Brecht's play, with music by Kurt Weill, adapted from John Gay's *The Beggar's Opera*. Remade many times since.▼●❸

3 Ring Circus (1954) **C-103m.** ** D: Joseph Pevney. Dean Martin, Jerry Lewis, Joanne Dru, Zsa Zsa Gabor, Wallace Ford, Sig Ruman, Nick Cravat, Elsa Lanchester. So-so Martin and Lewis comedy has them as discharged servicemen up to trouble in a circus. Reissued in shorter version as JERRICO, THE WONDER CLOWN. Remade as ROUSTABOUT. VistaVision.

Three Seasons (1999) **C-113m.** *** D: Tony Bui. Don Duong, Nguyen Ngoc Hiep, Tran Manh Cuong, Harvey Keitel, Zöe Bui, Nguyen Huu Duoc. Absorbing multicharacter story about modern-day Saigon, where a poor boy struggles to survive on the streets, a bicycle-taxi driver falls in love with a prostitute, a young woman who harvests flowers tries to connect with her mysterious employer, and an American soldier (Keitel) returns to make amends for his past. In any other setting these stories might not have the resonance they do. Impressive debut for Vietnamese-American writer-director Bui. [PG-13]▼

Three Secrets (1950) **98m.** *** D: Robert Wise. Eleanor Parker, Patricia Neal, Ruth Roman, Frank Lovejoy, Leif Erickson. Sturdy melodrama; three women wait anxiously for word of which one's child survived plane crash. Remade for TV in 1999.▼

Three Shades of Love SEE: **This Rebel Breed**

Three Sisters (1970-British) **C-165m.** **** D: Laurence Olivier, John Sichel. Laurence Olivier, Joan Plowright, Alan Bates, Jeanne Watts, Louise Purnell, Derek Jacobi. Brilliant rendering of Chekhov play about three daughters of deceased Russian colonel living in provinces, circa 1900. Olivier's vibrant production is definitive screen version of this classic. Released here in 1974 by American Film Theater. [PG]▼❸

Three Smart Girls (1936) **84m.** ***½ D: Henry Koster. Deanna Durbin, Binnie Barnes, Alice Brady, Ray Milland, Barbara Read, Mischa Auer, Nan Grey, Charles Winninger. Delightful musicomedy with Deanna's feature-film debut as matchmaking girl who brings long-divided parents back together. Songs: "Someone to Care for Me," "My Heart Is Singing." Sequel: THREE SMART GIRLS GROW UP.▼●❸

Three Smart Girls Grow Up (1939) **90m.** *** D: Henry Koster. Deanna Durbin, Charles Winninger, Nan Grey, Helen Parrish, Robert Cummings, William Lundigan. Little Deanna still matchmaking for sisters, warming up stern father, singing "Because," winning over everyone in sight.▼●❸

Threesome (1994) **C-95m.** *** D: Andrew Fleming. Lara Flynn Boyle, Stephen Baldwin, Josh Charles, Alexis Arquette,

Martha Gehman. Through computer error, college student Flynn Boyle is assigned to room with two guys—shy, intellectual Charles, who may be gay, and in-your-face, sex-obsessed Baldwin—resulting in various couplings and emotional complications. Coming-of-age comedy-drama is at once intelligent and impertinent; unlike 'many other Hollywood films, it does not cop out in its examination of the issue of homosexuality. Fleming also scripted. [R]▼●❸

Three Stooges Go Around the World in a Daze, The (1963) **94m.** **½ D: Norman Maurer. Three Stooges, Jay Sheffield, Joan Freeman, Walter Burke, Peter Forster. Even those who dislike the Stooges may enjoy this funny updating of Jules Verne's tale, replete with sight gags and world travel. ▼❸

Three Stooges in Orbit, The (1962) **87m.** **½ D: Edward Bernds. The Three Stooges, Carol Christensen, Edson Stroll, Emil Sitka. Nutty scientist Sitka invents a tanklike contraption that flies and floats. The Stooges accidentally launch it and run headlong into a few Martian invaders, with usual slapstick results for younger audiences.▼❸

Three Stooges Meet Hercules, The (1962) **89m.** **½ D: Edward Bernds. The Three Stooges, Vicki Trickett, Quinn Redeker, George N. Neise. Time machine takes the Stooges back to era of Roman legions; they are trapped on galley ship, battle Cyclops, and wind up with chariot chase. Good slapstick for kids and fans. ▼❸

Three Strange Loves (1949-Swedish) **84m.** *** D: Ingmar Bergman. Eva Henning, Birger Malmsten, Birgit Tengroth, Mimi Nelson, Hasse Ekman. Interesting early Bergman drama which foreshadows much of his future work. This one explores the dynamics of a three-cornered love relationship, from a distinctly female perspective, and examines the possibility of two women having the same personality. Bergman can be seen on camera as a train passenger. Aka THIRST.▼❸

Three Strangers (1946) **92m.** ***½ D: Jean Negulesco. Sydney Greenstreet, Geraldine Fitzgerald, Peter Lorre, Joan Lorring, Robert Shayne, Marjorie Riordan. Greenstreet and Lorre team up with Fitzgerald as partners holding winning sweepstakes ticket under unusual circumstances. Bizarre John Huston–Howard Koch script makes fascinating viewing.

3 Strikes (2000) **C-82m.** *½ D: D. J. Pooh. Brian Hooks, N'Bushe Wright, Faizon Love, Starletta DuPois, George Wallace, David Alan Grier, Antonio Fargas, De'aundre Bonds, Mo'Nique, Mike Epps, Vincent Schiavelli, David Leisure, Gerald S. O'Loughlin. Alleged comedy about a newly minted ex-con (Hooks) with two felony convictions to his name; he knows that a third will land him in jail for 25 years, but he can't seem to avoid trouble. A must for fanciers of flatulence jokes and general idiocy. [R]▼◗

3:10 to Yuma (1957) **92m. ***½** D: Delmer Daves. Van Heflin, Glenn Ford, Felicia Farr, Leora Dana, Henry Jones, Richard Jaeckel, Robert Emhardt. Extremely suspenseful Western, one of the best of the 1950s. Farmer Heflin, needing the money, agrees to hold captured outlaw Ford until the train arrives, but Ford starts to psych him out. Gripping every step of the way, with memorable George Duning theme sung by Frankie Laine. Script by Halsted Welles from an Elmore Leonard story. Remade in 2007. ▼◗●

3:10 to Yuma (2007) **C-117m. ***** D: James Mangold. Russell Crowe, Christian Bale, Peter Fonda, Ben Foster, Gretchen Mol, Alan Tudyk, Logan Lerman, Dallas Roberts, Vinessa Shaw, Luce Rains, Luke Wilson. Farmer Bale, desperate for money (and for his older son's respect), agrees to help escort notorious outlaw Crowe to a train that will send him off to trial . . . but the captor counts on his gang to rescue him. Well-filmed adaptation of Elmore Leonard's story, expanded and altered from its 1957 film version. The new ending is a mixed blessing, and the story goes on longer than it needs to, but it's still very entertaining, with fine work from Bale, Fonda, and Foster, and a charismatic performance by Crowe as the bad guy who can quote from the Bible. Super 35. [R]◗

Three the Hard Way (1974) **C-93m. **½** D: Gordon Parks, Jr. Jim Brown, Fred Williamson, Jim Kelly, Sheila Frazier, Jay Robinson, Alex Rocco, Corbin Bernsen. Top black action cast in nonstop, nearly bloodless thriller of white supremist Robinson's insane plot to eliminate blacks with a serum in the water supply. Produced by Harry Bernsen (Corbin's father). [R]▼

3000 Miles to Graceland (2001) **C-125m.** BOMB D: Demian Lichtenstein. Kevin Costner, Kurt Russell, Courteney Cox, Christian Slater, Kevin Pollak, David Arquette, Jon Lovitz, Howie Long, Thomas Haden Church, Bokeem Woodbine, Ice-T, David Kaye, Paul Anka. A gang of Elvis impersonators pulls off a heist in Las Vegas. Potentially clever idea degenerates into an overlong, bloody (and bloody awful) bore. All the violence is mindless; all the plot developments are brainless. Russell actually once played Presley, in the TV movie ELVIS. Super 35. [R]▼◗

Three Times (2005-Taiwanese) **C-135m. ***** D: Hou Hsiao-Hsien. Shu Qi, Chang Chen, Mei Fang, Liao Su-jen, Di Mei, Chen Shih-shan, Lee Pei-hsuan. The universality and timelessness of love and communication are explored via three separate stories set in 1966, 1911, and 2005, and featuring the same male and female leads (playing

different characters). Although the last part is its weakest, this languid and lyrical film, which is shot in varying styles reflecting each of its time periods, is an accomplished and moving mood piece.◗

Three to Tango (1999) **C-103m. *½** D: Damon Santostefano. Matthew Perry, Neve Campbell, Dylan McDermott, Oliver Platt, Bob Balaban, Cylk Cozart, John C. McGinley, Deborah Rush. Architect Perry is given the job of spying on the mistress of his insanely jealous—and rich—client, who mistakenly thinks he is gay, until they (predictably) fall in love. Glossy comedy of mistaken sexual identity with TV-star cast manages a couple of laughs but tries so hard to get them that it hardly seems worth the effort. [PG-13]▼◗

Three Tough Guys (1974-Italian-U.S.) **C-92m. **½** D: Duccio Tessari. Lino Ventura, Fred Williamson, Isaac Hayes, Paula Kelly. Oddball but fast-moving actioner, with tough priest Ventura and ex-cop Hayes solving million-dollar bank robbery. Hayes, who also did the music, is nicely subdued as an actor. [PG]

Three Violent People (1956) **C-100m. **½** D: Rudolph Maté. Charlton Heston, Anne Baxter, Gilbert Roland, Tom Tryon, Forrest Tucker, Elaine Stritch, Bruce Bennett, Barton MacLane. Adequately paced Western set in post–Civil War Texas; Heston, returning home with bride Baxter, is forced to fight carpetbaggers and deal with wife's shady past. VistaVision.▼

Three Wishes (1995) **C-107m. **** D: Martha Coolidge. Patrick Swayze, Mary Elizabeth Mastrantonio, Joseph Mazzello, Seth Mumy, David Marshall Grant, Jay O. Sanders, Michael O'Keefe, John Diehl, Diane Venora, Colleen Camp, Bill Mumy. A mysterious man and his dog enter the life of a Korean War widow who's doing her best to raise two sons on her own. Is there more to this stranger than meets the eye? Flashback-framed '50s tale hints at fantasy but doesn't let it flow until the end—by which time it seems like an afterthought. Another purported family film that moves like molasses and dwells on the melancholy. D. B. Sweeney appears unbilled. [PG]▼◗●

3 Women (1977) **C-125m. ***½** D: Robert Altman. Sissy Spacek, Shelley Duvall, Janice Rule, Robert Fortier, Ruth Nelson, John Cromwell. Brilliant, moody, thought-provoking film about a strange young girl (Spacek) who gets a job in an old-age convalescent home and attaches herself to coworker Duvall, who fancies herself a social butterfly. Their interrelationship and involvement with a quiet, embittered woman (Rule) form the "plot." Hypnotic film for Altman fans, heavy going for others; a completely unconventional movie. Panavision. [PG]◗

3 Worlds of Gulliver, The (1960-British)

[1416]

C-100m. *** D: Jack Sher. Kerwin Mathews, Jo Morrow, June Thorburn, Lee Patterson, Gregoire Aslan, Basil Sydney, Peter Bull. Hero is washed overboard and finds himself in the Land of Lilliput . . . but that's just the beginning. Well-made adventure/fantasy designed for kids, fun for older viewers, too. Fine special effects by Ray Harryhausen, charming Bernard Herrmann score. ▼●)

Threshold (1981-Canadian) **C-97m.** *** D: Richard Pearce. Donald Sutherland, John Marley, Sharon Ackerman, Mare Winningham, Jeff Goldblum, Michael Lerner, Allan Nicholls, Paul Hecht, Robert Joy. Excellent, surprisingly low-key drama about the first artificial heart transplant, with more humanism and offbeat touches than you'd find in typical TV treatment of this sort of thing. Goldblum and Winningham score as, respectively, the biologist who invents the artificial heart and its first recipient. Unreleased in the U.S. until 1983, when Barney Clark's real-life operation made headlines. [PG] ▼

Thrill of a Romance (1945) **C-105m.** ** D: Richard Thorpe. Van Johnson, Esther Williams, Frances Gifford, Henry Travers, Spring Byington, Carleton G. Young, Lauritz Melchior, Tommy Dorsey. Slight musical-romance with sweet Williams, abandoned by her businessman husband on their honeymoon, falling for war hero Johnson. ▼)

Thrill of It All, The (1963) **C-108m.** *** D: Norman Jewison. Doris Day, James Garner, Arlene Francis, Edward Andrews, Reginald Owen, ZaSu Pitts, Elliott Reid. Enjoyable spoof of TV and commercials by Carl Reiner; good vehicle for Day as housewife-turned-TV-spokeswoman and Garner as her neglected husband. Reiner has a particularly funny series of cameos. ▼)

Throne of Blood (1957-Japanese) **108m.** **** D: Akira Kurosawa. Toshiro Mifune, Isuzu Yamada, Takashi Shimura, Minoru Chiaki. Graphic, powerful adaptation of *Macbeth* in a samurai setting. Gripping finale, with Taketoki Washizu (the Macbeth character, masterfully played by Mifune) attacked by arrows. ▼●)

Through a Glass, Darkly (1961-Swedish) **91m.** ***½ D: Ingmar Bergman. Harriet Andersson, Gunnar Bjornstrand, Max von Sydow, Lars Passgard. Four-character drama about just-released mental patient, her husband, her father, and her younger brother who spend summer together on secluded island. Moody, evocative story of insanity—well-deserved Oscar winner, one of Bergman's best. The first in the filmmaker's "faith" trilogy, followed by WINTER LIGHT and THE SILENCE. ▼●)

Throw Momma From the Train (1987) **C-88m.** **½ D: Danny DeVito. Danny DeVito, Billy Crystal, Anne Ramsey, Kim Greist, Kate Mulgrew, Branford Marsalis, Rob Reiner, Bruce Kirby. Black comedy spin-off of Hitchcock's STRANGERS ON A TRAIN, with DeVito (in an excellent performance) as a childish man who tries to persuade his writing professor (Crystal) to "exchange murders" with him so he can bump off his harridan of a mother (Ramsey, who's incredible). Uneven and not as all-out funny as you might expect from the starring duo. Director DeVito has many offbeat ideas, and cinematographer Barry Sonnenfeld (who did those wild gags in RAISING ARIZONA) leaves a distinctive stamp on this film—particularly the run-away car sequence. Written by Stu Silver. [PG-13] ▼●)

Thumbelina (1994) **C-86m.** **½ D: Don Bluth, Gary Goldman. Voices of Jodi Benson, Gary Imhoff, Gino Conforti, Barbara Cook, Will Ryan, Charo, June Foray, Kenneth Mars, Gilbert Gottfried, John Hurt, Carol Channing. Animated retelling of Hans Christian Andersen's classic fairy tale has the digit-sized heroine evading the clutches of various toads, moles, and beetles before she can proceed with her courtship with her dream lover, Prince Cornelius. Pleasant enough diversion for the small fry, with a handful of sweetly romantic songs from Barry Manilow. [G] ▼●)

Thumbsucker (2005) **C-95m.** ***½ D: Mike Mills. Lou (Taylor) Pucci, Tilda Swinton, Vincent D'Onofrio, Kelli Garner, Keanu Reeves, Benjamin Bratt, Vince Vaughn, Chase Offerle. A 17-year-old boy who still sucks his thumb struggles to find his way while grappling with the curious dynamics of his family. Perceptive, multilayered look at alienation and the challenges that face both kids and their parents. Disarmingly real, with a top-notch cast and a dynamite performance by Pucci. Impressive, stylish feature debut (in Widescreen) for graphic designer, music video and commercial director Mills, who also adapted Walter Kirn's novel. Swinton coexecutive-produced. Panavision. [R] ●)

Thumb Tripping (1972) **C-94m.** **½ D: Quentin Masters. Michael Burns, Meg Foster, Mariana Hill, Bruce Dern, Michael Conrad, Joyce Van Patten. Amusing as a period piece on the hippie era, with Burns and Foster as hitchhikers who decide to travel together and share experiences. [R] ▼

Thunder Alley (1967) **C-90m.** *½ D: Richard Rush. Annette Funicello, Fabian, Diane McBain, Warren Berlinger, Jan Murray, Maureen Arthur. Fabian's inept stockcar driving gets him suspended from racing, but unfortunately, the acting profession doesn't have the same rules. Panavision. ▼)

Thunder and Lightning (1977) **C-95m.** **½ D: Corey Allen. David Carradine, Kate Jackson, Roger C. Carmel, Sterling Holloway, Ed Barth, Ron Feinberg. Amiable moonshine picture with attractive pairing of Carradine and Jackson and lots of expected car smash-ups. [PG]▼●)

Thunderball (1965-British) **C-129m.** **½ D: Terence Young. Sean Connery, Claudine Auger, Adolfo Celi, Luciana Paluzzi, Rik Van Nutter, Martine Beswick, Bernard Lee, Lois Maxwell, Desmond Llewelyn, Roland Culver. Fourth James Bond film isn't as lively as the others. Plenty of gimmicks, and Oscar-winning special effects, as world is threatened with destruction, but film tends to bog down—especially underwater. Celi makes a formidable Bond villain. Remade eighteen years later—with Connery—as NEVER SAY NEVER AGAIN. Panavision.▼●)

Thunder Bay (1953) **C-102m.** *** D: Anthony Mann. James Stewart, Joanne Dru, Gilbert Roland, Dan Duryea, Jay C. Flippen, Henry (Harry) Morgan. Action-packed account of oil-drillers vs. Louisiana shrimp fishermen, with peppery cast.▼)

Thunder Birds (1942) **C-78m.** ** D: William Wellman. Gene Tierney, Preston Foster, John Sutton, Dame May Whitty, Reginald Denny, Jack Holt, George Barbier. Ultra-patriotic time capsule is an ode to the WW2 flyer/flying instructor. Freewheeling veteran aviator Foster and intern-turned-trainee Sutton (who's afraid of heights) compete for the affection of flirtatious Tierney.●)

Thunderbirds (2004) **C-95m.** *½ D: Jonathan Frakes. Bill Paxton, Ben Kingsley, Anthony Edwards, Genie Francis, Brady Corbet, Dominic Colenso, Ben Torgersen, Sophia Myles. Rehash of Gerry Anderson's well-remembered British TV series of the '60s (which featured marionettes) is turned for some reason into a bloated live-action "family adventure" that's as wooden as those puppets from the original show. Plot has the heroic International Rescue family stranded in outer space as they try to save the world from The Hood (Kingsley). This one was in and out of theaters faster than you could say DVD. [PG]▼)

Thunderbolt and Lightfoot (1974) **C-114m.** *** D: Michael Cimino. Clint Eastwood, Jeff Bridges, George Kennedy, Geoffrey Lewis, Catherine Bach, Gary Busey, Jack Dodson, Vic Tayback, Dub Taylor, Bill McKinney. Thief Eastwood and drifter Bridges team up with Clint's ex-partners (Kennedy and Lewis) to retrieve loot from previous robbery. Colorful, tough melodrama-comedy with good characterizations; Lewis is particularly fine, but Bridges steals the picture. Cimino's directorial debut. Panavision. [R]▼●)

Thundercloud SEE: **Colt .45**

Thunderhead—Son of Flicka (1945) **C-78m.** **½ D: Louis King. Roddy McDowall, Preston Foster, Rita Johnson, James Bell, Diana Hale, Carleton Young. Good, colorful attempt to repeat MY FRIEND FLICKA's

success; doesn't match original, but it's enjoyable. Followed by GREEN GRASS OF WYOMING.●)

Thunderheart (1992) **C-118m.** *** D: Michael Apted. Val Kilmer, Sam Shepard, Graham Greene, Fred Ward, Fred Dalton Thompson, Sheila Tousey, Chief Ted Thin Elk, John Trudell, Dennis Banks, David Crosby. Part-Sioux FBI agent Kilmer is awakened to his heritage when he's assigned to investigate a murder on an Oglala Sioux reservation. Engrossing thriller is notable for its keen attention to detail regarding Sioux customs and spirituality, and its enlightened point of view. Based on events which occurred in the 1970s at Pine Ridge Reservation in South Dakota, where the film was shot. Coproduced by Robert De Niro; before directing this, Apted made a documentary, INCIDENT AT OGLALA, about Indian activist Leonard Peltier. [R]▼●)

Thunder in the East (1953) **98m.** **½ D: Charles Vidor. Alan Ladd, Deborah Kerr, Charles Boyer, Corinne Calvet, Cecil Kellaway, John Williams. Adequate, politically loaded adventure with gunrunner Ladd caught amid tension and rebellion in rural India. Kerr and Boyer uplift the proceedings as a refined blind woman who falls for Ladd and a stubbornly pacifistic government official.

Thunder in the Sun (1959) **C-81m.** **½ D: Russell Rouse. Susan Hayward, Jeff Chandler, Jacques Bergerac, Blanche Yurka, Carl Esmond, Fortunio Bonanova. Hayward is romanced by wagon train scout Chandler and Bergerac, head of French Basque immigrants on way to California.

Thunder on the Hill (1951) **84m.** *** D: Douglas Sirk. Claudette Colbert, Ann Blyth, Robert Douglas, Anne Crawford, Gladys Cooper. Nun Colbert can't believe visitor Blyth, about to be hanged, is murderess, sets out to prove her innocent; Cooper fine as Mother Superior. Sincere, interesting drama.●)

Thunder Road (1958) **92m.** *** D: Arthur Ripley. Robert Mitchum, Gene Barry, Jacques Aubuchon, Keely Smith, James Mitchum. Rural bootlegger takes on Feds *and* the Mob in cult favorite that even today continues to play in drive-ins; for many this remains the definitive moonshine picture. Jim Mitchum makes screen debut playing Bob's *brother;* the elder Mitchum got a hit record out of the title tune, which he also wrote!▼●)

THX 1138 (1971) **C-88m.** **½ D: George Lucas. Robert Duvall, Donald Pleasence, Maggie McOmie, Don Pedro Colley, Ian Wolfe. Futuristic tale in the *1984* vein about robotlike society where sex is forbidden and everyone looks the same. Dull script (by Lucas and Walter Murch), but visually impressive; Lucas' first feature is expanded version of prize-winning featurette he made at USC. Revised by the director (with no change in running time) for 2004 reissue; that version is rated R. Techniscope. [PG]▼●◗

Tic Code, The (2000) **C-91m.** *** D: Gary Winick. Gregory Hines, Polly Draper, Christopher George Marquette, Desmond Robertson, Carlos McKinney, Dick Berk, Tony Shalhoub, Bill Nunn, Fisher Stevens, Carol Kane, Camryn Manheim. Sincere, well-made drama about a boy with Tourette Syndrome who finds release in playing jazz piano and a soul mate in musician Hines. Written by Draper, who plays the boy's mother, inspired by her experience with husband Michael Wolff, the film's composer and producer. Shot in 1997. [R]▼◗

Tickets (2005-Italian-British) **C-109m.** *** D: Ermanno Olmi, Abbas Kiarostami, Ken Loach. Carlo Delle Piane, Valeria Bruni Tedeschi, Silvana De Santis, Filippo Trojano, Martin Compston, Gary Maitland, William Ruane. Trilogy of stories by three world-renowned directors, set on a passenger train en route to Rome and connected only by some recurring characters: An elderly biochemist reflects on his life and his meeting earlier that day with an attractive young woman; a young man performing civil service to avoid military duty has to escort a general's overbearing widow; and three unruly Scottish soccer fans have a life-changing encounter with a family of Albanian refugees. Though all three segments are different in mood and style, this meditative, humorous, and poignant trip is well worth taking.◗

Ticket to Heaven (1981-Canadian) **C-107m.** *** D: Ralph L. Thomas. Nick Mancuso, Saul Rubinek, Meg Foster, Kim Cattrall, R. H. Thomson, Jennifer Dale, Guy Boyd. Mancuso, strung out from bad relationship, is seduced into becoming a "heavenly child" in a Moonie-like cult. Pointed drama is frightening in its relevancy. Mancuso is excellent, Rubinek and Thomson lend fine support as his best friend and a deprogrammer. [PG]▼◗

Ticket to Tomahawk, A (1950) **C-90m.** *** D: Richard Sale. Dan Dailey, Anne Baxter, Rory Calhoun, Walter Brennan, Charles Kemper, Connie Gilchrist, Arthur Hunnicutt, Mauritz Hugo, Chief Yowlachie, Victor Sen Yung. Engaging comedy-Western about stagecoach company that hires gunslinger Calhoun to keep dreaded railroad from running on time. Good fun; one of the chorus girls with Dailey in a musical number is Marilyn Monroe. Filmed in Colorado. ▼

Tickle Me (1965) **C-90m.** **½ D: Norman Taurog. Elvis Presley, Jocelyn Lane, Julie Adams, Jack Mullaney, Merry Anders, Connie Gilchrist. That's the only way to get any laughs out of this one: Elvis works at all-girl dude ranch singing his usual quota of songs. Written by Elwood Ullman and Edward Bernds, both of whom worked with The Three Stooges in better days. Panavision. ▼◗

Ticklish Affair, A (1963) **C-89m.** ** D: George Sidney. Shirley Jones, Gig Young, Red Buttons, Carolyn Jones, Edgar Buchanan. Amiable film of Navy commander Young falling in love with widow Jones; all it lacks is wit, sparkle, and a fresh script. Panavision.

. . . tick . . . tick . . . tick . . . (1970) **C-100m.** ** D: Ralph Nelson. Jim Brown, George Kennedy, Fredric March, Lynn Carlin, Don Stroud, Clifton James, Janet MacLachlan. Poor man's IN THE HEAT OF THE NIGHT with black man (Brown) replacing white sheriff (Kennedy) in Southern town, flaring local hostilities. March adds film's only spice as aging, cantankerous mayor. Panavision. [PG]

Tidal Wave (1975) **C-82m.** *½ D: Shiro Moriana, Andrew Meyer. Lorne Greene, Kiliu Kobayashi, Rhonda Leigh Hopkins, Hiroshi Fujioka. Laughable Americanization of big-budget (and much superior) Japanese film, SUBMERSION OF JAPAN; epic special effects dwarfed by idiotic new footage with Greene, and horrible dubbing. For diehard disaster buffs only. Panavision. [PG]▼

Tideland (2006-Canadian-British) **C-121m.** BOMB D: Terry Gilliam. Jodelle Ferland, Brendan Fletcher, Janet McTeer, Jennifer Tilly, Jeff Bridges, Dylan Taylor, Wendy Anderson, Sally Crooks. In a golden field of Johnsongrass, inside a rotting farmhouse, a very poor little girl's junkie dad dies of an overdose, like her recently deceased unstable mom. She escapes into the rabbit hole of her imagination, guided by an all too bluntly referenced volume of *Alice in Wonderland*. Wrongheaded and squirmy on every count—the child prepares her father's lethal syringe and later engages in premature sexual experimentation with a brain-damaged neighbor boy. Depressing fairy tale is monumentally awful. Adapted from the 2000 novel by Mitch Cullin. Super 35. [R]◗

Tiefland (1954-German) **98m.** **½ D: Leni Riefenstahl. Leni Riefenstahl, Franz Eichberger, Bernard Minetti, Maria Koppenhofer, Luis Rainer. Blonde, dreamy shepherd Eichberger and arrogant marquis Minetti vie for Spanish dancer Riefenstahl. Atmospheric, visually poetic drama, even though the characters lack depth. Filmed between 1942 and 1945; editing wasn't completed until 1954.▼◗

Tie Me Up! Tie Me Down! (1990-Spanish) **C-101m.** **½ D: Pedro Almodóvar. Victoria Abril, Antonio Banderas, Francisco Rabal, Loles Leon, Julieta Serrano, Maria Barranco. Mental patient kidnaps a former porn star/junkie, slaps her around some,

[1419]

then ties her to a bed; actually, he just wants to get married and have kids. Potential NOW nightmare comes off as surprisingly tame for Almodóvar, though it still has his unpredictable black humor. Thought provoking and energetically performed. Two scenes (one a loud but fairly explicit sex scene) earned this an X rating, so the distributor decided to release it unrated instead. Later rerated for video. [NC-17] ▼●❙

Tie That Binds, The (1995) **C-98m.** BOMB D: Wesley Strick. Daryl Hannah, Keith Carradine, Moira Kelly, Vincent Spano, Julia Devin, Ray Reinhardt, Barbara Tarbuck. Two psychotic fugitives terrorize the family that's legally adopted their daughter after the youngster was taken into police custody following a foiled robbery attempt. This is what audiences get for having made THE HAND THAT ROCKS THE CRADLE a hit; film (from the same studio) is sleazy, insultingly derivative, and full of dangling plot issues. Directorial debut for screenwriter Strick. [R] ▼●❙

Tiger and the Pussycat, The (1967-Italian-U.S.) **C-105m.** **½ D: Dino Risi. Ann-Margret, Vittorio Gassman, Eleanor Parker, Antonella Stani, Fiorenzo Fiorentini. Innocuous sex-comedy of middle-aged businessman Gassman unintentionally getting involved with promiscuous young Ann-Margret. Italian and American players work well together. ▼❙

Tiger and the Snow, The (2006-Italian) **C-114m.** *½ D: Roberto Benigni. Robert Benigni, Nicoletta Braschi, Jean Reno, Emilia Fox, Amid Farid, Giuseppe Battiston, Andrea Renzi, Gianfranco Varetto, Tom Waits. Life-loving Italian poetry teacher (Benigni, who else?) longs for the woman of his dream—literally. When she is injured during a trip to Baghdad, he goes there and repeatedly risks his life to save hers. Attempt by cowriter-director Benigni to create a comedy-tragedy in the LIFE IS BEAUTIFUL mold falls flat: the Iraq war is a superficial backdrop to romantic woes and his character's constant rambling becomes insufferable. Final surprise twist is laughable . . . but not in a good way. Super 35.❙

Tiger Bay (1959-British) **105m.** *** D: J. Lee Thompson. John Mills, Horst Buchholz, Hayley Mills, Yvonne Mitchell, Megs Jenkins, Anthony Dawson. Lonely Cardiff child witnesses a murder and is abducted by the Polish sailor-killer. A poignant, sensitive, and very different police chase story. Hayley steals the film in first major acting role. ▼❙

Tiger by the Tail (1968) **C-99m.** ** D: R. G. Springsteen. Christopher George, Tippi Hedren, Dean Jagger, Charo, Glenda Farrell, Lloyd Bochner, Alan Hale, Skip Homeier, R. G. Armstrong. Vietnam war hero is accused of murdering his brother and recruits his socialite girlfriend in hunt for the real killer. Overly talkative thriller. [M/PG]

Tigerland (2000) **C-109m.** *** D: Joel Schumacher. Colin Farrell, Matthew Davis, Clifton Collins, Jr., Thomas Guiry, Shea Whigham, Russell Richardson, Cole Hauser, Michael Shannon. Gritty, original take on the military, the specter of the Vietnam war, and its effect on raw recruits who train for combat duty. From Fort Polk, Louisiana, these disparate young men move on to a simulated Vietnam battlefield known as Tigerland. Farrell is excellent as an iconoclast who rocks the boat—hard—but cares about his comrades. [R] ▼❙

Tiger Makes Out, The (1967) **C-94m.** **½ D: Arthur Hiller. Eli Wallach, Anne Jackson, Bob Dishy, John Harkins, David Burns, Ruth White, Rae Allen, Charles Nelson Reilly. One-man crusader against society (Wallach) symbolically kidnaps suburban housewife (Jackson). Originally a one-act, two-character play by Murray Schisgal, his expanded screenplay loses focus, relies on vivid N.Y. locations and funny cameos by character actors. Dustin Hoffman's film debut.

Tiger of Eschnapur, The (1958-German) **C-101m.** ** D: Fritz Lang. Debra Paget, Paul Hubschmid, Walther Reyer, René Deltgen, Luciana Paluzzi. Exotic dancer Paget is desired by dastardly maharajah Reyer, but she loves architect Hubschmid; meanwhile, Reyer's subjects are plotting revolution. Slow-moving, disappointing adventure-romance of interest mostly for Lang's participation. The first of the director's Indian diptych, followed by THE INDIAN TOMB; both were originally edited down to 95m., dubbed and released as JOURNEY TO THE LOST CITY.❙

Tigers Don't Cry SEE: **Target of an Assassin**

Tiger Shark (1932) **80m.** *** D: Howard Hawks. Edward G. Robinson, Richard Arlen, Zita Johann, J. Carrol Naish, Vince Barnett. Robinson gives rich, colorful performance as Portuguese tuna fisherman who marries wayward girl out of pity, then sees her fall in love with his best friend—a plot gambit Warner Bros. reused several times (SLIM, MANPOWER, etc.). Authentically filmed amid fisheries on Monterey coast.❙

Tigers in Lipstick (1979-Italian) **C-83m.** ** D: Luigi Zampa. Ursula Andress, Laura Antonelli, Sylvia Kristel, Monica Vitti, Michele Placido, Roberto Benigni, Orazio Orlando. Veteran comedy director Zampa pilots a fun but overly tame throwback to '60s sex comedies that spotlights four beautiful actresses (individually) in seven separate segments, emphasizing aggressive women who take advantage of men. Best segment: "The Pickup," in which Antonelli is a frantic businesswoman who disrupts the life of an orchestra conductor. Originally titled: WILD BEDS. [R]▼

Tiger's Tail, The (2007-Irish-British) C-107m. *** D: John Boorman. Brendan Gleeson, Kim Cattrall, Ciarán Hinds, Sinéad Cusack, Seán McGinley, Briain Gleeson, Angeline Ball. Ruthless, self-made Irish tycoon lets nothing stand in his way as he develops new properties—although with each success, it seems, there are more poor people on the streets and less time to spend with his wife and son. Then he thinks he sees his double lurking about and becomes haunted by the doppelganger. Writer-director Boorman criticizes the state of things in Ireland in this unsubtle but provocative parable. That's Gleeson's real-life boy playing his son. [R]❚

Tiger's Tale, A (1987) C-97m. *½ D: Peter Douglas. Ann-Margret, C. Thomas Howell, Charles Durning, Kelly Preston, William Zabka, Ann Wedgeworth, James Noble, Tim Thomerson, Steven Kampmann, Angel Tompkins. Unbelievable romantic comedy about a high school senior who gets involved with his girlfriend's mother, a nurse named Rose Butts. Need we say more? Debuting writer-director Douglas (Kirk's son) has bitten off more than he can chew—or we can swallow. Ann-Margret is watchable, as always, but miscast. [R]▼●

Tiger Walks, A (1964) C-91m. **½ D: Norman Tokar. Brian Keith, Vera Miles, Pamela Franklin, Sabu, Kevin Corcoran, Peter Brown, Una Merkel, Frank McHugh, Edward Andrews, Jack Albertson. Oddball Disney film about young girl (Franklin) whose compassion for tiger which has broken away from circus stirs controversy and political wheeling-and-dealing. Surprisingly bitter portrait of small-town America. Sabu's last film.▼❚

Tiger Warsaw (1988) C-93m. *½ D: Amin Q. Chaudhri. Patrick Swayze, Piper Laurie, Lee Richardson, Mary McDonnell, Barbara Williams, Bobby DiCicco, Jenny Chrisinger, Kaye Ballard. Muddled melodrama about troubled ex-junkie Swayze and what happens when he comes home and attempts to sort out his life. Hokey and highly improbable. [R]▼●❚

Tigger Movie, The (2000) C-77m. **½ D: Jun Falkenstein. Voices of Jim Cummings, John Fiedler, Nikita Hopkins, Ken Sansom, Peter Cullen, Kath Soucie; narrated by John Hurt. Tigger, who's always boasted that "he's the only one," comes to feel the need for family, and his friends in the Hundred Acre Wood try to help him. Cute movie aimed squarely at young children; not in the same class as major Disney animated features, but serves its purpose well. Best of all are the songs by Disney veterans Richard B. and Robert M. Sherman and their imaginative staging. [G]▼❚

Tight Little Island (1949-British) 82m.

**** D: Alexander Mackendrick. Basil Radford, Joan Greenwood, James Robertson Justice, Jean Cadell, Gordon Jackson, Wylie Watson, John Gregson; narrated by Finlay Currie. Hilarious, fast-paced comedy about WW2 ship sinking while loaded with whiskey and the antics of local Scottish islanders thirsting for its cargo. A solid hit. Scripted by Compton Mackenzie, the author of the novel, who has a small role as Captain Buncher. British title: WHISKY GALORE! Followed by MAD LITTLE ISLAND.▼❚

Tightrope (1984) C-114m. **½ D: Richard Tuggle. Clint Eastwood, Geneviève Bujold, Alison Eastwood, Jennifer Beck, Dan Hedaya. New Orleans cop finds he has much in common with the sex murderer he's pursuing. Intriguing Eastwood vehicle undone by sleaziness—and darkness. [R]▼●❚

Tight Spot (1955) 97m. ** D: Phil Karlson. Ginger Rogers, Edward G. Robinson, Brian Keith, Lorne Greene, Katherine Anderson. Rogers, key witness at a N.Y.C. crime lord's upcoming trial, does a lot of high-volume BORN YESTERDAY-like verbal sparring with Keith, her police lieutenant bodyguard, in this slack crime melodrama based on a flop Broadway play. A double dose of disappointment for Eddie G. fans: His screen time is short, and he plays the uninteresting role of the prosecutor!▼

Tigrero: A Film That Was Never Made (1994-Finnish-German-Brazilian) C-75m. *** D: Mika Kaurismaki. Absorbing documentary charting director Samuel Fuller's ill-fated attempt to shoot a film in Brazil among the remote Karaja tribe in 1954. Fuller is on hand, returning to the Karaja village where he describes the events to filmmaker Jim Jarmusch and screens footage he shot four decades earlier for villagers. A must for movie-history aficionados, and cultists of Jarmusch, the Kaurismaki brothers, and (especially) Fuller.▼●❚

Till Dawn Do Us Part SEE: **Straight on Till Morning**

Till Human Voices Wake Us (2002-Australian) C-97m. ** D: Michael Petroni. Guy Pearce, Helena Bonham Carter, Frank Gallacher, Lindley Joyner, Brooke Harman, Peter Curtin, Margot Knight. A boy's idyllic summer is jolted by the accidental death of his best friend, a disabled girl. The boy grows up to be a psychiatrist and lives a solitary life until he chances to meet a vulnerable young woman. Intriguing at first, but once this lugubrious movie's central idea becomes obvious—and it does—it's a sleepy ride to the conclusion. The title comes from a T. S. Eliot poem. Super 35. [R]▼❚

Tillie and Gus (1933) 58m. ***½ D: Francis Martin. W.C. Fields, Alison Skipworth, Baby LeRoy, Edgar Kennedy, Jacqueline

Wells (Julie Bishop), Clifford Jones, Barton MacLane, Clarence Wilson. Fields and Skipworth are perfectly matched as card hustlers in this very entertaining comedy, which also pits W.C. against Baby LeRoy for the first time. Nominal plot has them helping niece Wells win a crucial riverboat race.

Tillman Story, The (2010) C-95m. ***½ D: Amir Bar-Lev. Narrated by Josh Brolin. Wrenching, and ultimately infuriating, story of college and professional football star Pat Tillman, who walked away from a lucrative career to enlist in the Army. His subsequent death in Afghanistan saddened his family, friends, and fans. Filmmaker Bar-Lev traces his parents' determination to learn the truth about how he died—and how the military, and the U.S. government, covered up the incident for the sake of "patriotic" propaganda. As frustrating as the story becomes, it does give the viewer more reason than ever to admire Pat Tillman, a modest young man of exceptional integrity. [R] ▶

Till Marriage Do Us Part (1974-Italian) C-97m. **½ D: Luigi Comencini. Laura Antonelli, Alberto Lionello, Michele Placido, Jean Rochefort, Karin Schubert. A naive young woman unable to consummate her marriage seeks and finds sexual fulfillment elsewhere. Light, forgettable farce featuring Antonelli at her sexiest. [R] ▼●

Till the Clouds Roll By (1946) C-137m. **½ D: Richard Whorf. Robert Walker, Van Heflin, Lucille Bremer, Dorothy Patrick, many guest stars including Judy Garland, Kathryn Grayson, Lena Horne, Tony Martin, Dinah Shore, Frank Sinatra, June Allyson, Angela Lansbury, Cyd Charisse, Virginia O'Brien. Soggy biography of songwriter Jerome Kern (Walker) uplifted by song numbers featuring some high-powered MGM talent. Highlights include Lansbury's "How D'Ya Like to Spoon With Me," Lena's "Why Was I Born?," Judy's "Look for the Silver Lining," and mini-production of *Show Boat.* ▼●❂

Till the End of Time (1946) 105m. *** D: Edward Dmytryk. Dorothy McGuire, Guy Madison, Robert Mitchum, Bill Williams, Tom Tully, William Gargan, Jean Porter, Ruth Nelson. Solid, sympathetic drama of three returning WW2 veterans was released months before THE BEST YEARS OF OUR LIVES; the focus is on Madison falling for troubled war widow McGuire. Screenplay by Allen Rivkin, based on Niven Busch's novel *They Dream of Home.* Title song (based on Chopin's Polonaise in A-flat Major) was a big hit. ▼●

Till There Was You (1990-U.S.-Australian) C-94m. BOMB D: John Seale. Mark Harmon, Deborah Unger, Jeroen Krabbé, Shane Briant. Saxophone player Harmon is summoned to the South Pacific island of Vanuatu by his brother, whose subsequent

murder he predictably solves, after bungee jumping with the natives! Pretty scenery can't save this one. [R] ▼

Tilt (1978) C-111m. ** D: Rudy Durand. Brooke Shields, Ken Marshall, Charles Durning, John Crawford, Gregory Walcott, Geoffrey Lewis. Meandering tale of pinball wizard Shields and musician Marshall traveling cross-country, eventually challenging champion Durning. Only value of film (aside from Durning) is dazzling point-of-view photography inside pinball machine. Recut by director Durand to 100m. [PG] ▼

'Til There Was You (1997) C-114m. ** D: Scott Winant. Jeanne Tripplehorn, Dylan McDermott, Sarah Jessica Parker, Jennifer Aniston, Craig Bierko, Nina Foch, Christine Ebersole, Michael Tucker, Steve Antin, Ken Olin, Susan Walters, Karen Allen. A man and a woman's lives mirror each other for over 20 years, and they even have several brief chance encounters. Of course, when they finally do meet, it's love at first sight. Cloying and excruciatingly overlong. It doesn't help that the actors don't really seem to believe in the material. Best moments belong to Parker as a spoiled former TV sitcom teen. [PG-13] ▼●❂

Tim (1979-Australian) C-108m. **½ D: Michael Pate. Piper Laurie, Mel Gibson, Alwyn Kurts, Pat Evison, Peter Gwynne, Deborah Kennedy. Lush, well-meaning if a bit schmaltzy chronicle of the relationship between older woman (Laurie) and younger, retarded man (nicely played by Gibson). Pate wrote the screenplay from Colleen McCullough's first novel. Remade for TV in 1996 as MARY & TIM. ▼❂

Timbuktu (1959) 91m. ** D: Jacques Tourneur. Victor Mature, Yvonne De Carlo, George Dolenz, John Dehner, Marcia Henderson, James Foxx. Mature plays adventurer involved in African story of plot to overthrow government. Script is below average; cast is uneven.

Tim Burton's Corpse Bride (2005) C-76m. **½ D: Tim Burton, Mike Johnson. Voices of Johnny Depp, Helena Bonham Carter, Emily Watson, Tracey Ullman, Paul Whitehouse, Joanna Lumley, Albert Finney, Richard E. Grant, Christopher Lee, Michael Gough, Jane Horrocks, Deep Roy, Danny Elfman. Victor Van Dort is supposed to endure an arranged marriage for his family's sake, but somehow winds up wed to a corpse who rises from her grave to be betrothed! Settings and characters are a treat for the eye and Elfman's songs suit the occasion, but the storyline is terribly disjointed in this labor-of-love feature. What's more, the classic stop-motion animation technique is so slick it looks like CG, which rather defeats the idea. [PG] ❂

Tim Burton's The Nightmare Before Christmas SEE: **Nightmare Before Christmas, The**

Time After Time (1979) **C-112m.** **½
D: Nicholas Meyer. Malcolm McDowell,
David Warner, Mary Steenburgen, Charles
Cioffi, Kent Williams, Patti D'Arbanville,
Joseph Maher, Corey Feldman, Shelley
Hack. Fanciful tale of H. G. Wells follow-
ing Jack the Ripper from Victorian England
to 1979 America in his time machine. En-
gaging premise eroded by story loopholes
and halfhearted attempts at social com-
ment. Best is Steenburgen in an appealing,
star-making performance as Wells' modern
American girlfriend. Vivid score by Miklos
Rozsa. Panavision. [PG]▼●)

Time After Time (1985-British) **C-103m.**
*** D: Bill Hays. John Gielgud, Googie
Withers, Helen Cherry, Ursula Howells,
Brenda Bruce, Freddie Jones, Fiona Walker,
Trevor Howard. Very funny comedy about
Gielgud, living on an estate with his three
elderly sisters (named April, May, and Baby
June)—their eccentricities, memories, and
what happens when they are visited by their
manipulative, long-lost cousin (Withers).
Great script by Andrew Davies, from Molly
Keane's novel; hampered only by awkward
direction.

Time and Tide (2001-Hong Kong) **C-
113m.** ** D: Tsui Hark. Nicholas Tse, Wu
Bai, Candy Lo, Cathy Chui, Anthony Wong,
Joventino Couto Remotigue, Jr. Virtually
indescribable plot about an aimless young
man who finds himself pitted against a
friend in gangland showdown is just an excuse for action. Movie's American advertising declared, "You won't be able to tell who's
shooting at who," and that's the problem: the
adrenaline-pumped action scenes by past
master Hark don't carry the weight they
should because the story is so confusing!
Fans of pure action may feel otherwise. Super 35. [R]▼●

Time Bandits (1981-British) **C-110m.** **½
D: Terry Gilliam. Sean Connery, Shelley
Duvall, John Cleese, Katherine Helmond,
Ian Holm, Michael Palin, Ralph Richardson, Peter Vaughan, David Warner, Kenny
Baker, David Rappaport. Six dwarfs, pursued by the Supreme Being (Richardson),
escort a young English schoolboy through
time. They meet Robin Hood (Cleese), Napoleon (Holm), King Agamemnon (Connery).
Imaginative, but not as funny or as thrilling
as it should be. Look for young Jim Broadbent as a TV host. Written by Gilliam and
Palin, of Monty Python fame. British running time 116m. [PG]▼●)

Timebomb (1991) **C-96m.** **½ D: Avi
Nesher. Michael Biehn, Patsy Kensit,
Tracy Scoggins, Robert Culp, Raymond
St. Jacques, Richard Jordan, Billy Blanks,
Jim Maniaci, Steven J. Oliver, Ray Mancini.
When mysterious people try to kill watch-
maker Biehn, he finds to his surprise he has
the skills to defeat them. He then kidnaps psy-
chologist Kensit to try to find out who he really

is. Intriguing premise effectively blends sci-fi
and spy elements, with good performances a
real plus, but soon the improbable overtakes
the unlikely. [R]▼●

Timecode (2000) **C-97m.** **½ D: Mike
Figgis. Saffron Burrows, Stellan Skarsgård, Jeanne Tripplehorn, Salma Hayek,
Julian Sands, Holly Hunter, Steven Weber,
Danny Huston, Leslie Mann, Alessandro
Nivola, Kyle MacLachlan, Glenne Headly.
Unique film shot digitally in four concurrent
90-minute takes follows 20-odd L.A. characters as their unhappy lives crisscross, both
personally and professionally. Sound levels
direct our attention to the most significant
quadrant at any given time. As an experiment
it's fresh and exciting; as entertainment it's
wildly uneven, although the largely improvised dialogue is at least an improvement over
THE BLAIR WITCH PROJECT. [R]▼●

Timecop (1994) **C-99m.** **½ D: Peter
Hyams. Jean-Claude Van Damme, Mia
Sara, Ron Silver, Bruce McGill, Gloria
Reuben, Scott Bellis, Jason Schombing. In
the year 2004, a new law enforcement agency
polices time-tripping criminals; top agent Van
Damme is determined to nail the ringleader
of these thugs, an evil and ambitious senator
(Silver). Thoroughly watchable adaptation of
the comic book series, but lacks the energy
and imagination to be really satisfying. Followed in 2003 by a direct-to-video sequel.
Panavision. [R]▼●

Timecrimes (2008-Spanish) **C-89m.** **½
D: Nacho Vigalondo. Karra Elejalde, Candela Fernández, Nacho Vigalondo, Bárbara
Goenaga, Ion Inciarte. An otherwise ordinary man stumbles onto a time machine
that allows him to travel an hour into the
past. This propels him into a surreal, frightening journey. Occasionally clever sci-fi
thriller is akin to a puzzle that's fun to put
together—but too many pieces just don't
fit. [R]●

Time for Drunken Horses, A (1999-Ira-
nian) **C-80m.** ***½ D: Bahman Ghobadi.
Nezhad Ekhtiar-Dini, Amaneh Ekhtiar-
Dini, Madi Ekhtiar-Dini, Ayoub Ahmadi,
Jouvin Younessi. Heartbreaking story about
a family of Kurdish orphans eking out an
existence and trying to raise money for an
operation to save their dying brother. The
everyday struggle that these children go
through just to survive is starkly, movingly
conveyed. Written by the director and shot
in his native village, with a cast of extraordinary non-professionals.▼

Time for Killing, A (1967) **C-88m.** ** D:
Phil Karlson. Glenn Ford, Inger Stevens,
George Hamilton, Paul Petersen, Max
Baer, Timothy Carey, Kenneth Tobey,
Dick Miller, (Harry) Dean Stanton. Civil
War drama pits Union captain Ford against
Confederate major Hamilton, when the lat-
ter kidnaps his bride-to-be. Director Karl-
son has done some good minor films in the

past; this isn't one of them. Look for young Harrison Ford. Also known as THE LONG RIDE HOME. Panavision.

Time for Loving, A (1971-British) **C-104m. **½ D: Christopher Miles. Mel Ferrer, Joanna Shimkus, Britt Ekland, Philippe Noiret, Susan Hampshire, Mark Burns, Lila Kedrova, Robert Dhery, Michel Legrand. Sophisticated Jean Anouilh liaison trilogy in the LA RONDE style. Sometimes called PARIS WAS MADE FOR LOVERS.

Time Guardian, The (1987-Australian) **C-105m. ** D: Brian Hannant. Tom Burlinson, Nikki Coghill, Dean Stockwell, Carrie Fisher, Tim Robertson, Peter Merrill, Wan Thye Liew, Damon Sanders. Burlinson and Fisher are sent to the 1988 Australian desert, where he teams up with geologist Coghill to battle an army of killer cyborgs from the 41st century. Confusing sci-fi adventure. Panavision. [PG]▼●

Time Indefinite (1993) **C-117m. ***½ D: Ross McElwee. Revealing, highly personal visual diary in which McElwee offers a glimpse into the dynamics of his family: the relationships between its members, the linking of the generations, and, most poignantly, the way it's affected by marriage and death. McElwee's unique cinematic sensibility adds immeasurably to this impressive follow-up to SHERMAN'S MARCH. ▼●

Time Limit (1957) **96m. *** D: Karl Malden. Richard Widmark, Richard Basehart, Dolores Michaels, June Lockhart, Carl Benton Reid, Martin Balsam, Rip Torn, Kaie Deei (Khigh Dhiegh). Imaginative direction and acting spark this courtroomer concerning the trial of American military officer suspected of collaborating with enemy while POW in North Korea. Malden's sole foray behind the camera; Widmark coproduced.

Timeline (2003) **C-116m. ** D: Richard Donner. Paul Walker, Frances O'Connor, Gerard Butler, Billy Connolly, David Thewlis, Anna Friel, Neal McDonough, Matt Craven, Ethan Embry, Michael Sheen, Lambert Wilson, Marton Csokas, Rossif Sutherland. Archeologists travel back in time to rescue Walker's father, who's gotten stuck in the 14th century in the midst of the Hundred Years' War . . . but the time machine's owner, a high-tech honcho, hasn't told them all they should know about the risks involved in their adventure. Lively, noisy, convoluted story becomes so confusing it's difficult to know who's who, let alone what's what. Based on a Michael Crichton novel. Super 35. [PG-13] ▼●

Time Lost and Time Remembered (1966-British) **91m. *** D: Desmond Davis. Sarah Miles, Cyril Cusack, Julian Glover, Sean Caffrey. Thoughtful study of Miles' unhappy marriage to older man, emphasized by visit home where she discovers new set of values. Original British title: I WAS HAPPY HERE. ▶

Time Machine, The (1960) **C-103m. *** D: George Pal. Rod Taylor, Alan Young, Yvette Mimieux, Sebastian Cabot, Tom Helmore, Whit Bissell, Doris Lloyd. H. G. Wells' fantasy reduced to comic book level, but still entertaining, with Taylor as single-minded turn-of-the-20th-century London scientist who invents time-travel device and has vivid experiences in the future. Oscar-winning special effects. Remade in 1978 (for TV) and 2002. ▼●

Time Machine, The (2002) **C-96m. **½ D: Simon Wells. Guy Pearce, Samantha Mumba, Orlando Jones, Mark Addy, Jeremy Irons, Phyllida Law, Sienna Guillory, Alan Young, Omero Mumba. Rethinking of the H. G. Wells classic has absentminded professor Pearce traveling back in time to undo a tragedy involving his fiancée, then hurtling forward into the future, where the evil Morlocks rule over the Eloi. The effects are impressive, but the story doesn't have the impact it should . . . and Pearce may not be the ideal choice for an old-fashioned hero. Directed by H. G. Wells' great-grandson! Young, who costarred in 1960, has a tiny role here. Panavision. [PG-13] ▼●

Time of Destiny, A (1988) **C-118m. ** D: Gregory Nava. William Hurt, Timothy Hutton, Melissa Leo, Stockard Channing, Megan Follows, Francisco Rabal. Major disappointment from the makers of EL NORTE. Plodding soaper, set in the WW2 era, with tragedy and revenge coming between close friends and fellow GIs Hurt and Hutton (whose performances are far from their best). Written and produced by Anna Thomas. [PG-13] ▼●

Time of Favor (2000-Israeli) **C-98m. *** D: Joseph Cedar. Aki Avni, Tinkerbell, Assi Dayan, Idan Alterman, Micha Selektar, Amnon Volf, Shimon Mimran. Religion and politics clash in this provocative melodrama-thriller, most of which unfolds in a contemporary West Bank settlement. Menachem (Avni), a soldier who commands a military unit comprised of yeshiva students, becomes involved with the rebellious daughter of a charismatic orthodox rabbi who commands that she instead wed a scholar—who happens to be Menachem's best friend. The love triangle is routine, but the film offers a powerful and timely examination of the fine line between religious devotion and fanaticism. ▼●

Time of the Gypsies (1989-Yugoslavian) **C-142m. **½ D: Emir Kusturica. Davor Dujmovic, Bora Todorovic, Ljubica Adzovic, Sinolicka Trpkova, Husnija Hasimovic. Fair chronicle of the coming of age of a naive young gypsy (Dujmovic) and his initiation into the ways of petty crime. Sometimes effective, but way overlong and in no way as magical or memorable as Kusturica's WHEN

FATHER WAS AWAY ON BUSINESS. However, he did earn the Best Director prize at the Cannes Film Festival. Shot in a Gypsy language called Romany, this may be the first film ever to require subtitles in every country in which it plays! [R]▼●

Time of Their Lives, The (1946) 82m. *** D: Charles Barton. Bud Abbott, Lou Costello, Marjorie Reynolds, Binnie Barnes, John Shelton, Gale Sondergaard, Jess Barker. Most unusual film for A&C, and one of their best. Costello and Reynolds are killed during Revolutionary times, and their ghosts haunt a country estate where (in the 20th century) Abbott and friends come to live. Imaginative, funny, and well done.▼●

Time of the Wolf (2003-French-Austrian-German) C-114m. **½ D: Michael Haneke. Isabelle Huppert, Béatrice Dalle, Patrice Chéreau, Rona Hartner, Olivier Gourmet, Maurice Bénichou, Brigitte Rouan. In the midst of cataclysmic social collapse, a family arrives at its country vacation home and plunges into a fight for survival when sudden personal tragedy strikes. About as bleak as movies get, this despairing look at a world gone mad is not for every taste, but it's never boring. Huppert is superb, as usual, wrenching in her portrayal of a mother trying to keep her family together against all odds. Written by the director. Super 35. [R]▐

Time of Your Life, The (1948) 106m. ** D: H. C. Potter. James Cagney, William Bendix, Wayne Morris, Jeanne Cagney, Broderick Crawford, Ward Bond, James Barton, Paul Draper, James Lydon, Gale Page, Richard Erdman. Uninspired version of William Saroyan's prizewinning morality play about the various characters who populate Nick's Saloon, Restaurant and Entertainment Palace, which is actually a waterfront dive. Interesting cast, but it just doesn't come together.▼●

Time Out (2001-French) C-130m. ***½ D: Laurent Cantet. Aurélien Recoing, Karin Viard, Serge Livrozet, Jean-Pierre Mangeot, Monique Mangeot, Nicolas Kalsch, Marie Cantet, Felix Cantet. Wrenching slice of social realism about a suddenly unemployed husband and father who pretends he has a new prestigious job and convinces his friends to make large investments that he pockets in order to keep up the lie. Another vivid story about the workplace and the economic food chain from Cantet (HUMAN RESOURCES). His own kids appear in the film. [PG-13]▼●

Time Regained (1999-French) C-161m. ***½ D: Raul Ruiz. Marcello Mazzarella, Catherine Deneuve, Emmanuelle Béart, Vincent Perez, John Malkovich, Pascal Greggory, Marie-France Pisier, Christian Vadim, Arielle Dombasle, Chiara Mastroianni, Elsa Zylberstein. Complex, elegant adaptation of the final volume of Proust's *Remembrance of Things Past,* with the author reflecting on his life and art while on his deathbed. Difficult to follow at times, but Ruiz creates a unique, free-floating visual and structural variation on Proust's prose that uses the film frame to examine memory, fantasy, and mortality. Sumptuous production; well acted by all. Screenplay by Ruiz and Gilles Taurand.▼▐

Timerider (1983) C-93m. ** D: William Dear. Fred Ward, Belinda Bauer, Peter Coyote, Ed Lauter, Richard Masur, Tracey Walter, L. Q. Jones. Motocross bike racer is accidentally sent back in time to the Old West, circa 1875 . . . and that's where the writers fell asleep. Good premise and cast are left hanging as film crawls downhill. Produced and cowritten by Michael Nesmith. [PG]▼●▐

Time Runner (1993-Canadian-U.S.) C-90m. BOMB D: Michael Mazo. Mark Hamill, Rae Dawn Chong, Brion James, Marc Baur, Gordon Tipple, Allen Forget, Barry W. Levy. Fleeing an exploding space station in 2022 when Earth is under attack by aliens, Hamill ends up in 1992, trying to prevent the future war. Silly, poorly plotted, badly presented. [R]▼●

Times of Harvey Milk, The (1984) C-87m. ***½ D: Robert Epstein. Narrated by Harvey Fierstein. Extremely moving documentary about Harvey Milk, the first gay supervisor elected in San Francisco; mayor George Moscone; and clean-cut, respectable supervisor Dan White, who assassinated them both. Eerie, fascinating, sad, funny; as dramatic and involving as the most carefully plotted fiction. This deservedly earned a Best Documentary Academy Award. See also MILK (2008). ▼●▐

Times Square (1980) C-111m. BOMB D: Allan Moyle. Tim Curry, Trini Alvarado, Robin Johnson, Peter Coffield, Herbert Berghof, Miguel Pinero, Elizabeth Pena. A pair of teenage runaways, one (Alvarado) upper class, the other (Johnson) "of the streets," romp around a curiously unmenacing Times Square. Illogical, unrealistic scenario, frantic direction, music score for the hard of hearing. Script by film critic Jacob Brackman. [R]▼▐

Time to Die, A (1983) C-91m. *½ D: Matt Cimber. Rex Harrison, Rod Taylor, Edward Albert, Jr., Raf Vallone, Linn Stokke. Deadening time-waster with WW2 veteran Albert seeking out the six killers of his wife. Based on a story by Mario Puzo, and filmed in 1979. Originally titled SEVEN GRAVES FOR ROGAN. [R]▼

Time to Die, A (1991) C-93m. ** D: Charles Kanganis. Traci Lords, Richard Roundtree, Jeff Conaway, Robert Miano, Jesse Thomas, Nitchie Barrett. By-the-numbers programmer with ex-porn queen Lords cast as a freelance photographer attempting to make a home for her young son.

Trouble comes her way when she finds herself and her camera in the right place at the wrong time. [R]▼●◗

Time to Kill, A (1996) **C-149m.** *** D: Joel Schumacher. Sandra Bullock, Samuel L. Jackson, Matthew McConaughey, Kevin Spacey, Brenda Fricker, Oliver Platt, Ashley Judd, Donald Sutherland, Kiefer Sutherland, Patrick McGoohan, Kurtwood Smith, Chris Cooper, Joe Seneca, Anthony Heald, Charles S. Dutton, Rae'ven Larrymore Kelly, John Diehl. First-rate adaptation of John Grisham's best-seller about a Mississippi town rocked by a black man's murder of two white-trashers who raped his 10-year-old daughter. Young attorney McConaughey (in a star-making performance) takes the man's case and finds himself in the midst of a firestorm that threatens his life and that of everyone around him. This TIME flies by, thanks to crackerjack storytelling and a well-chosen cast. M. Emmet Walsh appears unbilled. Panavision. [R] ▼●◗

Time to Leave (2005-French) **C-85m.** *** D: François Ozon. Melvil Poupaud, Jeanne Moreau, Valeria Bruni Tedeschi, Daniel Duval, Marie Rivière, Christian Sengewald, Louise-Anne Hippeau. Handsome, gay, 31-year-old fashion photographer (Poupaud), living in a world of glamour and vanity, gets a harsh dose of reality when he learns he is terminally ill. How will he spend his remaining days? How will he deal with his lover and the members of his family? Simple, deeply felt film cuts to the heart of how individuals choose to live their lives in the face of mortality. Moreau is luminous in her few scenes as the photographer's beloved grandmother. Written by the director. Panavision.◗

Time to Love and a Time to Die, A (1958) **C-132m.** *** D: Douglas Sirk. John Gavin, Lilo Pulver, Jock Mahoney, Don DeFore, Keenan Wynn, Thayer David, Dana (Jim) Hutton, Klaus Kinski. Intensely dramatic love story set against background of WW2. German soldier on furlough from battle falls in love, inevitably must return to the trenches. Well-directed version of Erich Maria Remarque novel (with the author in a small role). Hutton's film debut. CinemaScope.▼

Time to Sing, A (1968) **C-92m.** *½ D: Arthur Dreifuss. Hank Williams, Jr., Ed Begley, Shelley Fabares, Charles Robinson, D'Urville Martin, Donald Woods, Clara Ward. Down-home tale of Williams suppressing love for singing to please uncle-guardian (Begley). Script aimed at 10-year-old mentality, matched by Williams' wooden performance. Panavision. [PG]

Time Trackers (1989) **C-87m.** *½ D: Howard R. Cohen. Ned Beatty, Wil Shriner, Kathleen Beller, Bridget Hoffman, Alex Hyde-White, Lee Bergere, Robert Cornthwaite. Tepid sci-fi tale about group from the future chasing down evil genius determined to use time travel to alter history in his favor. Beatty is a 20th-century cop accidentally picked up along the way. Some laughs at the beginning, but spends far too long (most of the film in fact) in medieval England. [PG]▼

Time Traveler's Wife, The (2009) **C-107m.** **½ D: Robert Schwentke. Rachel McAdams, Eric Bana, Ron Livingston, Arliss Howard, Jane McLean, Stephen Tobolowsky. A man who travels back and forward in time—uncontrollably—meets the future love of his life when she's just a little girl. In time she grows up and falls in love with him, but their relationship is sorely challenged by his continual (and unplanned) disappearance. Melancholy romantic drama based on Audrey Niffenegger's best-selling novel (adapted by Bruce Joel Rubin, of GHOST fame) maintains an ethereal tone throughout, and the two attractive stars do a fine job . . . but the concept is difficult to fully embrace. Super 35. [PG-13]◗

Time Traveller, The SEE: **Next One, The**

Time Walker (1982) **C-83m.** BOMB D: Tom Kennedy. Ben Murphy, Nina Axelrod, Kevin Brophy, James Karen, Shari Belafonte-Harper, Antoinette Bower. Alien, buried in King Tut's tomb, is unwrapped and wreaks havoc. Low-budget junk. [PG]▼◗

Time Warp SEE: **Journey to the Center of Time**

Time Without Pity (1957-British) **88m.** *** D: Joseph Losey. Michael Redgrave, Alec McCowen, Ann Todd, Peter Cushing, Leo McKern, Renee Houston, Lois Maxwell, Joan Plowright. Tense thriller with an anti-capital punishment point-of-view, as alcoholic Redgrave has 24 hours to prove son McCowen's innocence on a murder rap. Scripted by Ben Barzman, from an Emlyn Williams play.▼◗

Tin Cup (1996) **C-133m.** ** D: Ron Shelton. Kevin Costner, Rene Russo, Don Johnson, Cheech Marin, Linda Hart, Dennis Burkley, Rex Linn. Portrait of a run-down golf pro, now operating a shabby Texas driving range, who's inspired to compete in the U.S. Open in order to impress a woman—the girlfriend of his longtime rival. Costner always wants to "go for it" instead of playing it safe. Costner and Russo are appealing, but this long, redundant comedy has alarmingly little to say, and takes its sweet time playing all 18 holes. Cowritten by director Shelton. Panavision. [R]▼●◗

Tin Drum, The (1979-German) **C-142m.** **** D: Volker Schlöndorff. David Bennent, Mario Adorf, Angela Winkler, Daniel Olbrychski, Katharina Thalbach, Heinz Bennent, Andrea Ferreol, Charles Aznavour. Mesmerizing adaptation of the Gunter Grass novel. Three-year-old Oskar (David Bennent) ceases to grow physically as the Nazis take power in Germany and beats out his anger on his drum. A "realistic fantasy" with superb acting, particularly by 12-year-old Bennent. Memorable sequence after memorable sequence; deservedly won a Best Foreign Film Academy Award. [R]▼●⟩

Tingler, The (1959) **82m.** **½ D: William Castle. Vincent Price, Judith Evelyn, Darryl Hickman, Philip Coolidge, Patricia Cutts. Preposterous but original shocker: coroner Price discovers that fear causes a creepy-crawly creature to materialize on people's spines; it can be subdued only by screaming. This is the infamous picture that got moviegoers into the spirit with vibrating gizmos under selected theater seats!—a gimmick director/producer Castle billed as "Percepto." Also noteworthy as likely the earliest film depicting an LSD trip. One critical sequence is in color.▼●⟩

Tin Men (1987) **C-112m.** **½ D: Barry Levinson. Richard Dreyfuss, Danny DeVito, Barbara Hershey, John Mahoney, Jackie Gayle, Stanley Brock, Seymour Cassel, Bruno Kirby, J.T. Walsh, Michael Tucker. Writer-director Levinson returns to DINER territory (literally—it's set in 1963 Baltimore) for a melancholy comedy-drama about a hustler (Dreyfuss) and a loser (DeVito), both in the aluminum-siding business, whose lives converge after their cars meet in an accident. Some fine comedy and pointed observations on human nature are undermined by unresolved ideas and inconsistencies in the way the characters behave. Stand-up comic Gayle is hilarious as DeVito's partner, who has *Bonanza* on the brain. [R]▼●⟩

Tin Pan Alley (1940) **94m.** *** D: Walter Lang. Alice Faye, Betty Grable, Jack Oakie, John Payne, Esther Ralston, Allen Jenkins, Nicholas Brothers, John Loder, Elisha Cook, Jr. Predictable plot of struggling pre-WW1 songwriters enlivened by Alfred Newman's Oscar-winning score and colorful numbers including "Sheik of Araby" with Billy Gilbert as sultan. Oakie is in top form. Remade as I'LL GET BY.▼

Tin Star, The (1957) **93m.** *** D: Anthony Mann. Henry Fonda, Anthony Perkins, Betsy Palmer, Neville Brand, Lee Van Cleef, John McIntire, Michel Ray. Fledgling sheriff Perkins turns to bounty hunter Fonda to help combat outlaws preying on his town; solid, well-acted Western. Scripted by Dudley Nichols. VistaVision.▼●⟩

Tintorera (1977-British-Mexican) **C-91m.** BOMB D: Rene Cardona, Jr. Susan George, Hugo Stiglitz, Andres Garcia, Fiona Lewis, Jennifer Ashley, Priscilla Barnes, Laura Lyons. Can two Mexican shark hunters find satisfaction with an assortment of vacationing beauties from England and the U.S.? That's the main issue of this listless JAWS rip-off, loaded with gore and nude scenes. [R]▼●⟩

Tiny Furniture (2010) **C-98m.** *** D: Lena Dunham. Lena Dunham, Laurie Simmons, Grace Dunham, Jemima Kirke, Alex Karpovsky, David Call, Merritt Wever. Just out of college, Aura (Dunham) moves back into her mom's combination apartment and artist's studio in Manhattan's TriBeCa neighborhood while she contemplates the next step in her life. Wry, pointed social comedy about a child-woman going through an awkward period seems utterly genuine and spontaneous; kudos to writer, director, and star Dunham and her cast mates. Dunham's real-life mother and sister play themselves. Digital Video.

Tip on a Dead Jockey (1957) **99m.** *** D: Richard Thorpe. Dorothy Malone, Robert Taylor, Gia Scala, Martin Gabel, Jack Lord. Neat account of Taylor tied in with smuggling syndicate in Madrid, romancing Malone. Good Charles Lederer adaptation of Irwin Shaw story. CinemaScope.

'Tis Autumn: The Search for Jackie Paris (2007) **C-100m.** *** D: Raymond De Felitta. Homegrown documentary about the filmmaker's fascination with jazz singer Paris—and his quest to learn what kept him from achieving real success when he was so admired by fellow musicians. Somewhat ragged cinematically, but when De Felitta captures unguarded moments with his interviewees their raw emotions sear the screen. Fascinating exploration of the many factors that make up an artist's life, for better or worse. Many notable jazz figures appear on-screen.⟩

Titan A.E. (2000) **C-95m.** ** D: Don Bluth, Gary Goldman. Voices of Matt Damon, Drew Barrymore, Bill Pullman, Janeane Garofalo, Nathan Lane, John Leguizamo, Ron Perlman, Tone-Loc. Boring animated sci-fi adventure set in the future. Young man with a chip on his shoulder learns that he's the only hope to save what's left of the human race. Basic good vs. evil outer-space saga has great visual effects but stock characters and situations—and the dullest voice performances in animation history. CinemaScope. [PG]▼⟩

Titan Find SEE: **Creature**

Titanic (1943-German) **85m.** **½ D: Herbert Selpin, Werner Klingler. Sybille Schmitz, Hans Nielsen, Karl Schönböck, Charlotte Thiele, Otto Wernicke. Little-seen German drama about the doomed ocean liner was made during WW2, so a German officer is depicted as the only brave, outspoken man on board, while the English owner pursues an "endless quest for profit." Creditable disaster film, although the script is no more inspired than later versions of the saga. Some shots were reused in A NIGHT TO REMEMBER. Banned in Germany in 1943 because the scenes of panic were considered too potent in the midst of wartime air raids.▼⟩

Titanic (1953) **98m.** *** D: Jean Negulesco.

Clifton Webb, Barbara Stanwyck, Robert Wagner, Richard Basehart, Audrey Dalton, Thelma Ritter, Brian Aherne. Hollywood-ized version of sea tragedy centers on shipboard story. Not bad, but events better told in A NIGHT TO REMEMBER . . . and more spectacularly in the 1997 film. Oscar-winning script by producer Charles Brackett, Walter Reisch, and Richard Breen. ▼●▶

Titanic (1997) **C-194m.** ***½ D: James Cameron. Leonardo DiCaprio, Kate Winslet, Billy Zane, Frances Fisher, Kathy Bates, David Warner, Danny Nucci, Victor Garber, Gloria Stuart, Bernard Hill, Bernard Fox, Jonathan Hyde, Bill Paxton, Suzy Amis. Sweeping romance set against the backdrop of the R.M.S. *Titanic*'s maiden voyage in 1912—and framed by a modern-day story of a salvager who stumbles onto a heretofore unknown survivor of the sinking (beautifully played by 1930s leading lady Stuart). Spectacular in every way, an eye-filling re-creation of the sights and sounds of the grandest ship of its time, but what keeps it afloat are the magnetic performances of the young leads. Storytelling savvy and momentum make up for some banal dialogue. Some footage of the actual *Titanic* wreckage is sprinkled into the opening sequence. Written by the director. Winner of 11 Oscars including Best Picture, Director, Visual Effects, Music (James Horner), Song ("My Heart Will Go On"), Cinematography (Russell Carpenter), Sound, and Costumes (Deborah L. Scott). Cameron revisited the ship's watery grave with his 2003 IMAX documentary GHOSTS OF THE ABYSS. Super 35. [PG-13] ▼●▶

Titanic Town (1999-British-Irish) **C-102m.** *** D: Roger Michell. Julie Walters, Ciarán Hinds, Nuala O'Neill, Elizabeth Donagy, Ciaran McMenamin, Jaz Pollock, Doreen Hepburn. Working-class Irish Catholic housewife becomes a reluctant political activist (and ostracizes herself from her own family) when her backyard becomes a battleground between the British Army and the IRA. Distinguished by its literate script, precise emotional tone, and supercharged performances from Walters and newcomer O'Neill as a sparring mother and daughter. Based on Mary Costello's autobiographical novel.

Titfield Thunderbolt, The (1953-British) **C-84m.** *** D: Charles Crichton. Stanley Holloway, George Relph, Naunton Wayne, John Gregson, Godfrey Tearle, Edie Martin, Hugh Griffith, Sid James, Jack MacGowran. Boisterous Ealing comedy about villagers who are attached to their antiquated railway line and run it themselves in competition with the local bus line. Lovely photography by Douglas Slocombe. Script by T.E.B. Clarke. ▶

Tito and Me (1992-Yugoslavian-French) **C-104m.** *** D: Goran Markovic. Dimitrie Vojnov, Lazar Ristovski, Anica Dobra, Pedrag Manojlovic. Sweet, funny comedy-reminiscence about Zoran (Vojnov), a pudgy 10-year-old growing up in Belgrade in 1954. He is obsessed with "Comrade Tito," his nation's leader, just as a love-sick teen pines over a movie or rock star; the heart of the film focuses on how Zoran comes to realize the folly of worshipping false idols. This reportedly is the last film to come out of war-torn Yugoslavia. ▼▶

Titus (1999) **C-162m.** *** D: Julie Taymor. Anthony Hopkins, Jessica Lange, Alan Cumming, Jonathan Rhys Meyers, Angus Macfadyen, Matthew Rhys, Harry Lennix, James Frain, Colm Feore, Laura Fraser, Geraldine McEwan, Osheen Jones. Potent, time-bending adaptation of Shakespeare's *Titus Andronicus*, with Hopkins as a victorious Roman general whose rigid code of honor and duty proves to be his downfall. Lange is his prisoner, Tamora, queen of the Goths, who plots revenge. Impressive work by innovative theater director Taymor, who also wrote the screenplay as an examination of violence—its cause and effect—as it relates to modern society. Lennix is a standout as Aaron, the Moor. Super 35. [R] ▼▶

T-Men (1947) **92m.** *** D: Anthony Mann. Dennis O'Keefe, Alfred Ryder, Charles McGraw, Wallace Ford, Mary Meade, June Lockhart. Semidocumentary-style story of undercover treasury agents trying to get to the bottom of counterfeit ring. Vividly exciting; director Mann and cameraman John Alton went out of their way to use unusual, effective lighting and compositions in this A-1 film. ▼●▶

TMNT (2007) **C-87m.** *½ D: Kevin Munroe. Voices of Chris Evans, Sarah Michelle Gellar, Mako, Kevin Smith, Patrick Stewart. Those TEENAGE MUTANT NINJA TURTLES (who starred in three movies of the 1990s) return, computerized this time around. The superheroes, having temporarily retired after defeating arch-nemesis Shredder, must reunite to battle a wealthy industrialist who has collected an army of ancient monsters in an effort to take over the world. CGI has been utilized effectively to create moody, comic-book-urban scenery, and the cool-looking monsters will probably appeal to kids. But bland characters and choppy, uninvolving fight scenes are likely to bore adults, including those who loved the turtles in their heyday. Digital Widescreen. [PG] ▶

T.N.T. Jackson (1974) **C-73m.** ** D: Cirio Santiago. Jeanne Bell, Stan Shaw, Pat Anderson, Ken Metcalf. OK Filipino-shot black actioner with statuesque former Playmate Bell as karate expert searching for her missing brother and kicking the hell out of anyone who gets in her way. A blaxploitation favorite, no doubt for the curious way Bell's shirts get torn off at the start of every fight scene. [R] ▼▶

Toast of New Orleans, The (1950) **C-97m.** **½ D: Norman Taurog. Kathryn Grayson,

Mario Lanza, David Niven, Rita Moreno, J. Carrol Naish. Lanza plays fisherman transformed into operatic star. Rest of cast good, and Lanza sings "Be My Love."▼●◗

Toast of New York, The (1937) **109m.** ✱✱✱ D: Rowland V. Lee. Edward Arnold, Cary Grant, Frances Farmer, Jack Oakie, Donald Meek, Clarence Kolb, Billy Gilbert, Stanley Fields. Arnold is in fine form as rags-to-riches businessman Jim Fisk in late 19th century. Grant is his partner in hokey but entertaining biographical fiction; good showcase for spirited Farmer.▼●◗

Tobacco Road (1941) **84m.** ✱✱½ D: John Ford. Charley Grapewin, Marjorie Rambeau, Gene Tierney, William Tracy, Elizabeth Patterson, Dana Andrews, Slim Summerville, Ward Bond, Grant Mitchell. Lightly entertaining but genuinely odd seriocomedy about "quaint" Georgia backwoods community; worthwhile mainly to see Grapewin repeating his stage role as cheerful ne'er-do-well Jeeter Lester. Adapted (and sanitized) by Nunnally Johnson from the long-running Broadway play by Jack Kirkland, based on Erskine Caldwell's novel.◗

To Begin Again (1982-Spanish) **C-93m.** ✱✱✱ D: Jose Luis Garci. Antonio Ferrandis, Encarna Paso, Jose Bodalo, Agustin Gonzalez, Pablo Hoyo. Distinguished—and dying—professor Ferrandis revisits Spain, where he journeys through his past and romances old flame Paso. Sweetly sentimental; Oscar winner for Best Foreign Film. [PG]

To Be or Not to Be (1942) **99m.** ✱✱✱½ D: Ernst Lubitsch. Jack Benny, Carole Lombard, Robert Stack, Lionel Atwill, Felix Bressart, Sig Ruman, Tom Dugan, Helmut Dantine, Stanley Ridges. Benny has the role of a lifetime as "that great, great actor" Joseph Tura, whose Polish theater troupe is put out of business by invading Nazis—until they become involved in espionage and find their thespian skills being put to the ultimate test. Superb black comedy scripted by Edwin Justus Mayer; the opening gag with Dugan is a gem. Lombard's final film, released after her death. Remade in 1983.▼●◗

To Be or Not to Be (1983) **C-108m.** ✱✱½ D. Alan Johnson. Mel Brooks, Anne Bancroft, Charles Durning, Tim Matheson, Jose Ferrer, James Haake, Christopher Lloyd, George Gaynes, George Wyner, Jack Riley, Lewis J. Stadlen. Remake of 1942 classic follows the original almost scene for scene, with Brooks and Bancroft—in fine comic form—as stars of Polish theater who become involved with invading Nazis. Offers more laughs than the original film, but less substance; incessant schtick undermines occasional attempts at poignancy. [PG] ▼●◗

Tobruk (1967) **C-110m.** ✱✱½ D: Arthur Hiller. Rock Hudson, George Peppard, Nigel Green, Guy Stockwell, Jack Watson, Leo Gordon, Norman Rossington, Percy Herbert, Liam Redmond. WW2 actioner of Allies trying to destroy Rommel's fuel supply in the Sahara, bogs down in pretentiousness, much social comment, etc. Gordon also wrote the screenplay. Techniscope.▼

Toby Tyler, or Ten Weeks with a Circus (1960) **C-96m.** ✱✱½ D: Charles Barton. Kevin Corcoran, Henry Calvin, Gene Sheldon, Bob Sweeney, Richard Eastham, James Drury. Likable Disney fare about a young boy who runs away to join the circus at the turn of the 20th century.▼●◗

To Catch a Spy (1971-British-French) **C-94m.** ✱½ D: Dick Clement. Kirk Douglas, Marlene Jobert, Trevor Howard, Tom Courtenay, Patrick Mower, Bernadette Lafont, Bernard Blier. Feeble comedy-mystery of events resulting when Jobert's new husband is arrested by the Russians as a spy; Douglas is a mystery man, Courtenay a bumbling British agent. Also known as CATCH ME A SPY.▼◗

To Catch a Thief (1955) **C-106m.** ✱✱✱ D: Alfred Hitchcock. Grace Kelly, Cary Grant, Jessie Royce Landis, John Williams, Charles Vanel, Brigitte Auber. The French Riviera serves as picturesque backdrop for this entertaining (if fluffy) Hitchcock caper with Grant as reformed cat burglar suspected in new wave of jewel robberies. Chic and elegant in every way—and Kelly never looked more ravishing. Script (including much-imitated fireworks scene) by John Michael Hayes; Oscar-winning photography by Robert Burks. VistaVision.▼●◗

To Commit a Murder (1967-French) **C-91m.** ✱½ D: Edouard Molinaro. Louis Jourdan, Senta Berger, Edmond O'Brien, Bernard Blier, Fabrizzio Capucci. Playboy/writer Jourdan gets involved with a plot to abduct French nuclear scientist; interesting idea poorly handled.▼

Today We Live (1933) **113m.** ✱✱ D: Howard Hawks. Joan Crawford, Gary Cooper, Robert Young, Franchot Tone, Roscoe Karns. Stilted William Faulkner story of WW1 romance and heroism; despite star-studded cast, not much. Faulkner cowrote the screenplay. Torpedo attack scenes were directed by Richard Rosson.▼

Todd Killings, The (1971) **C-93m.** ✱✱ D: Barry Shear. Robert F. Lyons, Richard Thomas, Barbara Bel Geddes, Sherry Miles, Gloria Grahame, Edward Asner, Belinda Montgomery, Meg Foster. Good cast in sleazy story of hip girl-getter Lyons actually involved in series of murders. Retitled A DANGEROUS FRIEND. Panavision. [R]▼

To Die For (1989) **C-90m.** ✱½ D: Deran Sarafian. Brendan Hughes, Sydney Walsh, Amanda Wyss, Scott Jacoby, Micah Grant, Steve Bond. Dracula legend is updated to modern-day, morally decadent L.A., but the results are strictly second-rate. Vampire "Vlad Tepish" sets his sights on sexy real-estate agent Walsh—apparently unaware that realtors in L.A. are a bloodless lot. Followed by SON OF DARKNESS: TO DIE FOR II. [R]▼●◗

To Die For (1995) **C-103m.** **½ D: Gus Van Sant. Nicole Kidman, Matt Dillon, Joaquin Phoenix, Illeana Douglas, Casey Affleck, Alison Folland, Dan Hedaya, Wayne Knight, Kurtwood Smith, Holland Taylor, Susan Traylor, Maria Tucci, David Cronenberg. Kidman is perfect as a tightly focused sicko who'll stop at nothing, including murder, to reach her goal: a TV career. Based on the real-life case that inspired Joyce Maynard's book, this black comedy seems to make all the right moves, but plays out its story with a surprising lack of irony; by the climax it has nothing more to offer. Douglas is a particular standout as Kidman's sister-in-law, who sees through her artifice from the git-go. George Segal appears unbilled, and the film's screenwriter, Buck Henry, plays a humorless schoolteacher. [R]▼●◗

To Die of Love (1972-French) **C-110m.** **½ D: André Cayatte. Annie Girardot, Bruno Pradal, François Simon, Monique Melinand, Nathalie Nell, Nicolas Dumayet. Girardot's superb performance carries true story about French schoolteacher who was driven to suicide after she was forced to abandon 16-year-old student she loved. More interesting for subject matter than for execution. [PG]

To Each His Own (1946) **122m.** *** D: Mitchell Leisen. Olivia de Havilland, John Lund, Mary Anderson, Roland Culver, Philip Terry, Griff Barnett. Well-turned soaper of unwed mother giving up baby, lavishing love on him as his "aunt" without revealing truth. Fine support by Culver as aging Olivia's beau. De Havilland won Best Actress Oscar. Lund's film debut.▼

To Elvis, With Love SEE: **Touched by Love**

To Find a Man (1972) **C-90m.** *** D: Buzz Kulik. Pamela (Sue) Martin, Darren O'Connor, Lloyd Bridges, Phyllis Newman, Tom Ewell, Tom Bosley. Solid comedy-drama about two high-schoolers' attempts to find an abortionist. Study of friendships is good, and exceedingly fine acting of youthful leads is a definite plus. [PG]

To Forget Venice (1979-Italian) **C-110m.** ** D: Franco Brusati. Erland Josephson, Mariangela Melato, Elenora Giorgi, David Pontremoli. Two pairs of homosexuals (male and female) come to grips with each other at the country estate of a dying opera star. So-so drama managed an Oscar nomination for Best Foreign Film.▼

Together? (1979-Italian) **C-100m.** *½ D: Armenia Balducci. Jacqueline Bisset, Maximilian Schell, Terence Stamp, Monica Guerritore. Bisset and neurotic lover Schell argue, eat, argue, talk about sex, argue, have sex, argue some more. And the viewer gets a migraine. Originally titled I LOVE YOU, I LOVE YOU NOT. [R]▼

Together (2000-Swedish-Swiss-Italian) C-

106m. **½ D: Lukas Moodysson. Lisa Lindgren, Michael Nyqvist, Gustaf Hammarsten, Jessica Liedberg, Ola Norell. Amusing flashback to 1975 as a group of supposedly like-minded people live as a collective under one roof. Long-suffering Goran (Hammarsten) discovers that theories of free love, harmony, and anticommercialism don't always apply in the day-to-day life at Tillsammans (Swedish for "together," the name of the commune). Likable, often perceptive social comedy; written by the director. [R]◗

Together (2002-Chinese-South Korean) **C-118m.** ***½ D: Chen Kaige. Tang Yun, Liu Peiqi, Chen Hong, Wang Zhiwen, Chen Kaige, Cheng Qiang, Zhang Qing. Crowd-pleasing story of a 13-year-old violin prodigy who is taken to Beijing by his father, who will sacrifice anything to make sure his son gets the best teacher and the greatest opportunities. In time, the boy must make his own choice between what he's being told and what he really feels. Expertly made, the story builds to an emotional crescendo—aided in no small way by its musical score. The leading actor is in fact a musical virtuoso. Director Chen (who cowrote the film with Xue Xiaolu) also costars as the well-to-do piano teacher. [PG]▼◗

Together Again (1944) **100m.** *** D: Charles Vidor. Irene Dunne, Charles Boyer, Charles Coburn, Mona Freeman, Elizabeth Patterson. Little bit of nothing carried off beautifully by Dunne, widow mayor of small town, and Boyer, suave New Yorker whom she hires to sculpt a statue of her late husband; charming comedy.◗

Together Brothers (1974) **C-94m.** **½ D: William A. Graham. Anthony Wilson, Ahmad Nurradin, Glynn Turman, Richard Yniguez, Lincoln Kilpatrick, Owen Pace. Suspense thriller with five young blacks scouring ghetto for the killer of their policeman friend. Violent treatment balanced by sensitive character studies. [PG]

Togetherness (1970) **C-103m.** ** D: Arthur Marks. George Hamilton, Peter Lawford, John Banner, Olinka Berova, Jesse White. American playboy Hamilton woos Communist athlete Berova in this dated comedy filmed in Greece. [PG]

To Gillian on Her 37th Birthday (1996) **C-92m.** *** D: Michael Pressman. Peter Gallagher, Michelle Pfeiffer, Claire Danes, Bruce Altman, Kathy Baker, Wendy Crewson, Freddie Prinze, Jr., Laurie Fortier. Straightforward tearjerker—with ample comedy leavening—about a man unable and unwilling to let go of his wife's memory two years after her sudden death; his sister-in-law fears that his inertia and melancholy threaten his teenage daughter at a crucial time in her life. Well acted all around. Based on a play by Michael Brady, adapted and coproduced by David E. Kelley (Pfeiffer's husband). [PG-13]▼●◗

To Have and Have Not (1944) **100m. ***½**
D: Howard Hawks. Humphrey Bogart, Walter Brennan, Lauren Bacall, Hoagy Carmichael, Dan Seymour, Marcel Dalio, Dolores Moran, Sheldon Leonard. Hemingway's "worst novel" forms the basis for Hawks' version of CASABLANCA: tough skipper-for-hire Bogart reluctantly becomes involved with French Resistance, less reluctantly woos even tougher Bacall (in her film debut). Their legendary love scenes make the movie, but there are also solid performances, taut action, and a couple of songs. (Andy Williams was hired to dub Bacall's singing, but that's her voice, after all.) Super dialogue by William Faulkner and Jules Furthman; remade as THE BREAKING POINT and THE GUN RUNNERS. Also shown in computer-colored version. ▼●●

To Hell and Back (1955) **C-106m. ***
D: Jesse Hibbs. Audie Murphy, Marshall Thompson, Charles Drake, Jack Kelly, Paul Picerni, Gregg Palmer, Brett Halsey, David Janssen, Art Aragon, Rand Brooks, Denver Pyle, Susan Kohner. Murphy (the most decorated soldier of WW2) stars in very good war film based on his autobiography, with excellent battle sequences depicting Murphy's often breathtaking heroic exploits. Clichés in script are overcome by Murphy and cast's easygoing delivery. CinemaScope. ▼●

Toi et Moi (2006-French) **C-94m. **½** D: Julie Lopes-Curval. Marion Cotillard, Julie Depardieu, Jonathan Zaccaï, Eric Berger, Tomer Sisley, Sergio Perris Mancheta, Chantal Lauby. Pragmatic, talented orchestra cellist (Cotillard) and her head-in-the-clouds, romance-writer sister (Depardieu) stumble about in search of everlasting love. Familiar tale charms with its quiet humor, imperfect but likable characters, and topsy-turvy, bittersweet ending. ●

To Joy (1950-Swedish) **95m. **½** D: Ingmar Bergman. Stig Olin, Maj-Britt Nilsson, John Ekman, Margit Carlquist, Victor Seastrom (Sjöström), Birger Malmsten. Early Bergman drama offers a thematic prelude of what was to come from the filmmaker. Modest, occasionally insightful chronicle of Olin and Nilsson's failing marriage. ▼●

To Kill a Clown (1972) **C-104m. **** D: George Bloomfield. Alan Alda, Blythe Danner, Heath Lamberts, Eric Clavering. Couple whose marriage is on the rocks get trapped on island off New England coast by crippled, deranged Vietnam veteran. Weird mixture of traditional chiller film elements and topical considerations. [R]▼

To Kill a Mockingbird (1962) **129m. **** D: Robert Mulligan. Gregory Peck, Mary Badham, Philip Alford, John Megna, Brock Peters, Robert Duvall, Frank Overton, Rosemary Murphy, Paul Fix, Collin Wilcox, Alice Ghostley, William Windom; narrated by Kim Stanley. In a small Alabama town in the 1930s, lawyer Atticus Finch (Peck) defends a black man (Peters) accused of raping a white woman. Their father's innate decency affects his two motherless children as they learn about life, especially about that spooky house in the neighborhood. Peck won a well-deserved Best Actor Oscar; screenwriter Horton Foote received one as well. This outstanding film only gains in stature as time passes. One of the best of the 1960s. From the semiautobiographical novel by Harper Lee. Duvall makes his screen debut as Boo Radley. Produced by Alan J. Pakula, with a memorable score by Elmer Bernstein. ▼●●

To Kill a Priest (1988-U.S.-French) **C-117m. ** D: Agnieszka Holland. Ed Harris, Christopher Lambert, David Suchet, Joss Ackland, Tim Roth, Joanne Whalley, Peter Postlethwaite, Timothy Spall, Cherie Lunghi. Well-intentioned but inept drama about ill-fated Polish priest Lambert (a character based on Father Jerzy Popieluszko, who supported the country's trade unionists and paid for his activism with his life); here he tangles with bullying secret policeman Harris. Director Holland may be a Polish exile, but the film only superficially explores the plight of her country. Panavision. [R]▼●●

Tokyo Decadence (1992-Japanese) **C-112m. **½** D: Ryu Murakami. Miho Nikaido, Tenmei Kano, Yayoi Kusama, Sayoko Amano. So-so account of the various experiences of a young, wide-eyed Tokyo hooker (Nikaido), whose specialty is sadomasochism and whose clients are upper-class businessmen. Initially works as a look at how kinky sexual desires result from take-no-prisoners attitudes in the workplace; it eventually becomes repetitive and muddled. Scripted by Murakami, based on his novel. ▼●●

Tokyo Drifter (1966-Japanese) **C-83m. ***½** D: Seijun Suzuki. Tetsuya Watari, Ryuji Kita, Hideaki Esumi, Michio Hino, Tamio Kawachi, Hideaki Nitani, Chieko Matsubara. Spectacularly stylized, tongue-in-cheek thriller about a hit man who is betrayed by his boss and takes on rival gangsters and an army of assassins. Audacious and deliriously imaginative use of color, widescreen, and sound make this Suzuki's pulp masterpiece, replete with songs, choreographed gunfights, and a parody of a Western saloon brawl. Nikkatsu-Scope. ▼●

Tokyo Joe (1949) **88m. **½** D: Stuart Heisler. Humphrey Bogart, Florence Marly, Sessue Hayakawa, Alexander Knox, Jerome Courtland. Lesser Bogart film about American in postwar Tokyo pulled into smuggling and blackmail for the sake of his ex-wife and child. ▼●●

Tokyo Olympiad (1965) **C-170m. **** D: Kon Ichikawa. Once compromised by edited versions that diminished its power, epic documentary about the 1964 Olympics is artistically mentionable in the same breath as Leni Riefenstahl's OLYMPIA—and without the Hitler baggage. Though Ichikawa had over a hundred Tohoscope cameras at his disposal, result is less a reportorial chronicle than a sensory agony/ecstasy portrayal set against panoramic crowd shots. Broad jumpers compete on a messy, muddy track and a lonely runner from Chad finds himself . . . somewhere . . . in downtown Tokyo. CinemaScope. ▼●❿

Tokyo Pop (1988) **C-99m.** **½ D: Fran Rubel Kazui. Carrie Hamilton, Yutaka Tadokoro, Taiji Tonoyama, Tetsuro Tamba, Masumi Harukawa. Trifling if occasionally amusing tale of what happens when punk rocker Hamilton treks off to Japan in search of celebrity. The West-meets-East theme has possibilities, but the result is curiously slight (despite Hamilton's winning performance). By the way, she's the daughter of Carol Burnett. [R] ▼●

Tokyo Sonata (2009-Japanese-Dutch-Hong Kong) **C-121m.** *** D: Kiyoshi Kurosawa. Teruyuki Kagawa, Kyôko Koizumi, Yû Koyanagi, Kai Inowaki, Haruka Igawa, Kanji Tsuda, Kôji Yakusho. Subtly devastating rumination on the emptiness of contemporary middle-class life, centering on a proud corporate administrator (Kagawa) who's downsized from his job but is unable to tell his loved ones. Meanwhile, his wife and sons are dealing with their own issues. Kurosawa (best known for his horror films and thrillers) effectively delineates the distances between his characters and the fragile bonds that keep them connected. [PG-13]❿

Tokyo Story (1953-Japanese) **134m.** **** D: Yasujiro Ozu. Chishu Ryu, Chieko Higashiyama, So Yamamura, Haruko Sugimura, Setsuko Hara. An elderly couple (Ryu, Higashiyama) visit their children in Tokyo, who are too busy living their lives and treat them tactlessly. Quietly powerful story of old age, the disappointments parents experience with their children, and the fears the young have of time passing. A masterpiece. Not shown in the U.S. until 1972. ▼❿

Tol'able David (1921) **94m.** ***½ D: Henry King. Richard Barthelmess, Gladys Hulette, Ernest Torrence, Warner Richmond, Walter P. Lewis. A mild-mannered boy is forced to take his brother's place delivering the mail—and dealing with a trio of heinous criminals who've moved into their rural community. Beautifully crafted Americana, shot on location in Virginia. The finale is a rip-roaring piece of movie storytelling. Remade in 1930. ▼●❿

To Live (1994-Chinese) **C-132m.** ***½ D: Zhang Yimou. Ge You, Gong Li, Niu Ben, Guo Tao, Jiang Wu, Ni Dahong, Liu Tianchi, Zhang Lu, Xiao Cong, Dong Fei. Another stirring production from director/actress team of Zhang Yimou and Gong Li, although this time the female role is less powerful, and less pivotal, than the male lead. Film follows married couple as their fortunes rise and fall, through several decades of Chinese life, from 1940s onward. Viewer gets history lesson as time passes, children grow, and freedoms are suppressed. Ge You is outstanding as simple yet unstereotypical patriarch; only flaw is that episodic story eventually develops Edna Ferber–ish soap opera quality. Based on the novel *Lifetimes* by Yu Hua. ▼●❿

To Live and Die in L.A. (1985) **C-116m.** *½ D: William Friedkin. William L. Petersen, Willem Dafoe, John Pankow, Debra Feuer, John Turturro, Darlanne Fluegel, Dean Stockwell, Robert Downey, Dwier Brown. Gritty movie equivalent of TV's *Miami Vice* makes it hard to root for anyone, since the good guys are as sleazy as the bad guys! Petersen plays hotshot Secret Service agent going after slimy counterfeiter—but for a crack federal agent he acts pretty dumb! One spectacular car chase is not enough to counteract bad taste the film leaves behind. [R] ▼●❿

To Love a Vampire SEE: **Lust for a Vampire**

Tollbooth (1994) **C-108m.** *** D: Salome Breziner. Fairuza Balk, Lenny Von Dohlen, Will Patton, Seymour Cassel, James Wilder, William Katt, Louise Fletcher. Clever, humorously macabre sleeper about a young woman (Balk) who for years has been awaiting the return of her missing father. She refuses to sleep with the man she loves (Von Dohlen) until her father shows up; the plot is set into motion when Boyfriend sets out to track down Dad. Cassel appears in two roles and offers a riveting performance as the father. ▼●

Tom and Huck (1995) **C-92m.** **½ D: Peter Hewitt. Jonathan Taylor Thomas, Brad Renfro, Eric Schweig, Charles Rocket, Amy Wright, Micheal McShane, Marian Seldes, Rachael Leigh Cook, Lanny Flaherty. Umpteenth, by-the-numbers retelling of the Mark Twain classic *The Adventures of Tom Sawyer,* with Taylor Thomas and Renfro both doing well as the title duo. Might amuse kids who are completely unfamiliar with the story. Panavision. [PG] ▼●❿

Tom and Jerry: The Movie (1992) **C-84m.** ** D: Phil Roman. Voices of Richard Kind, Dana Hill, Anndi McAfee, Charlotte Rae, Tony Jay, Henry Gibson, Rip Taylor, Michael Bell, Sydney Lassick, David L. Lander. Tom and Jerry, suddenly homeless, hook up with a little girl who's trying to escape from the clutches of a cruel guardian. Flat attempt to put the lively cat & mouse duo into a feature-length story, with more lulls than highlights, and a score that's not only unmemorable but irrelevant. Released in the U.S. in 1993. [G] ▼●❿

Tom & Viv (1994-British-U.S.) **C-125m.** **½ D: Brian Gilbert. Willem Dafoe, Miranda Richardson, Rosemary Harris, Tim Dutton, Nickolas Grace, Philip Locke. Intriguing (but only partially successful) chronicle of the relationship between poet T. S. Eliot (Dafoe) and his wife, loony socialite Vivienne Haigh-Wood (Richardson), whose psychological affliction was improperly diagnosed. Well acted by the two leads, but the drama comes in fits and starts. Lacks the necessary passion to make you care about the characters and their union. Based on a play by Michael Hastings, who coscripted. Super 35. [R] ▼●▶

Tomb of Ligeia, The (1964-British) **C-81m. *** D:** Roger Corman. Vincent Price, Elizabeth Shepherd, John Westbrook, Richard Johnson, Derek Francis. Price's late wife seems to be manifesting herself all over the place, both as a cat and in new bride Shepherd. Super-stylish chiller with superb location work. The last of Corman's eight Poe adaptations; screenplay by Robert Towne. Filmed in Widescreen Colorscope. ▼●▶

Tomboy (1985) **C-92m. BOMB D:** Herb Freed. Betsy Russell, Jerry Dinome (Gerard Christopher), Kristi Somers, Richard Erdman, Cynthia Ann Thompson. Bottom-of-the-barrel formula teenage sex tease film. Role reversal is stressed as Russell is an automotive wiz determined to outrace and win the romantic favor of handsome Dinome. [R] ▼▶

Tomb Raider SEE: **Lara Croft Tomb Raider**

Tom Brown's Schooldays (1951-British) **93m. ***½ D:** Gordon Parry. John Howard Davies, Robert Newton, Diana Wynyard, Hermione Baddeley, Kathleen Byron, James Hayter, John Charlesworth, John Forrest, Michael Hordern, Max Bygraves. Well-acted film of Victorian England school life with exceptional British cast and good direction. Noel Langley scripted, from Thomas Hughes' novel. ▼▶

Tombstone (1993) **C-128m. **½ D:** George P. Cosmatos. Kurt Russell, Val Kilmer, Michael Biehn, Powers Boothe, Robert Burke, Dana Delany, Sam Elliott, Stephen Lang, Terry O'Quinn, Joanna Pacula, Bill Paxton, Jason Priestley, Michael Rooker, Jon Tenney, Dana Wheeler Nicholson, Billy Zane, Buck Taylor, Harry Carey, Jr., Thomas Haden Church, Pedro Armendariz, Jr., Frank Stallone, Billy Bob Thornton, Charlton Heston; narrated by Robert Mitchum. Wyatt Earp (Russell) attempts to leave his violent days behind him, moving to Tombstone with his two brothers . . . but the murderous gang called The Cowboys (whose members include the Clantons) dictates otherwise. Not-bad Western saga, with a forceful performance by Russell and a likably eccentric one by Kilmer as the tubercular Doc Holliday. Delany, however, is positively goofy as Wyatt's love interest, and the story goes on way past the O.K. Corral shootout, with a series of redundant gun battles and showdowns. The real Earp's fifth cousin, Wyatt Earp, plays Billy Claiborne. Panavision. [R] ▼●▶

Tomcats (2001) **C-92m. BOMB D:**

Gregory Poirier. Jerry O'Connell, Shannon Elizabeth, Jake Busey, Horatio Sanz, Jaime Pressly, Travis Fine, Joseph D. Reitman, Bill Maher, David Ogden Stiers, Bernie Casey, Dakota Fanning. After their pal's wedding, a band of male chauvinist morons creates a "kitty" to be won by the last of their lot to avoid wedding bells. Busey, one of the two remaining bachelors, once deflowered and dumped Elizabeth; his competitor (O'Connell) schemes to get them hitched. Trashy, poorly made comic dud is strictly for the litter box. Comic nadir: the plight of the cancerous testicle. [R] ▼▶

Tom, Dick and Harry (1941) **86m. ***½ D:** Garson Kanin. Ginger Rogers, George Murphy, Alan Marshal, Burgess Meredith, Joe Cunningham, Jane Seymour, Phil Silvers. Spirited comic dilemma as wide-eyed Ginger chooses among three anxious suitors: sincere Murphy, wealthy Marshal, nonconformist Meredith. Silvers has hilarious role as obnoxious ice-cream man. Written by Paul Jarrico. Remade as THE GIRL MOST LIKELY. ▼●▶

Tom Horn (1980) **C-98m. *½ D:** William Wiard. Steve McQueen, Linda Evans, Richard Farnsworth, Billy Green Bush, Slim Pickens, Elisha Cook. McQueen's next-to-last film is beautifully shot, otherwise deadly Western about the final days of real-life Wyoming bounty hunter. See also MR. HORN, a TVM with David Carradine in the title role. Panavision. [R] ▼●▶

Tom Jones (1963-British) **C-129m. **** D:** Tony Richardson. Albert Finney, Susannah York, Hugh Griffith, Edith Evans, Joyce Redman, Diane Cilento, Joan Greenwood, David Tomlinson, Peter Bull, David Warner; narrated by Michael MacLiammoir. High-spirited adaptation of the Henry Fielding novel about a young man's misadventures and bawdy experiences in 18th-century England; rowdy, randy, and completely disarming. Academy Award winner as Best Picture, it also won Oscars for Richardson, who directed with great flair and imagination, screenwriter John Osborne, who caught the gritty flavor of the period to perfection, and composer John Addison, whose infectious score suits the picture to a tee. Film debuts of Lynn Redgrave and David Warner. Richardson cut the film by seven minutes for its 1989 reissue. ▼●▶

Tommy (1975-British) **C-111m. *** D:** Ken Russell. Roger Daltrey, Ann-Margret, Oliver Reed, Elton John, Eric Clapton, Keith Moon, Robert Powell, Tina Turner, Jack Nicholson. Energetic rendering of The Who's best-selling rock opera, with standout musical performances by Clapton, John (who sings "Pinball Wizard"), and Turner. [PG] ▼●▶

Tommy Boy (1995) **C-96m. *½ D:** Peter Segal. Chris Farley, David Spade, Brian Dennehy, Bo Derek, Dan Aykroyd, Julie Warner, Sean McCann, Zack Grenier. Just out of college, perpetual foul-up Farley returns home to work in his father's factory and witness his dad's marriage to Derek. Dad's sudden death forces Farley to try and save the business—with the help of coworker Spade. Utterly predictable comedy with scattershot laughs; Farley and Spade don't quite have the finesse of Wheeler and Woolsey. Rob Lowe appears unbilled as Derek's "son." [PG-13] ▼●◗

Tomorrow (1972) 103m. ***½ D: Joseph Anthony. Robert Duvall, Olga Bellin, Sudie Bond, Richard McConnell, Peter Masterson, William Hawley. Overlooked Faulkner story about a handyman who cares for and eventually falls in love with an abandoned pregnant woman. Bellin is excellent, Duvall astonishingly good in best-ever screen presentation of the author's work. Screenplay by Horton Foote. [PG] ▼◗

Tomorrow Is Forever (1946) 105m. *** D: Irving Pichel. Claudette Colbert, Orson Welles, George Brent, Lucile Watson, Richard Long, Natalie Wood. Weepy rehash of *Enoch Arden*, with Welles as man listed dead in WW1 returning decades later with new face to find wife Colbert remarried to Brent. Bravura work by Welles; good support by Wood as his adopted daughter. ▼

Tomorrow Never Comes (1977-Canadian-British) C-109m. ** D: Peter Collinson. Oliver Reed, Susan George, Raymond Burr, John Ireland, Stephen McHattie, Donald Pleasence. Young man goes bananas when he learns his girlfriend has been unfaithful, leading to violent standoff with police in busy resort town. Uninvolving melodrama. [PG] ▼◗

Tomorrow Never Dies (1997) C-119m. **½ D: Roger Spottiswoode. Pierce Brosnan, Jonathan Pryce, Michelle Yeoh, Teri Hatcher, Joe Don Baker, Ricky Jay, Götz Otto, Judi Dench, Desmond Llewelyn, Vincent Schiavelli, Geoffrey Palmer, Samantha Bond, Gerard Butler. James Bond goes after a megalomaniacal media magnate (Pryce) whose tentacles reach around the globe, and whose wife was a former flame of 007. Along the way, he teams up with Asian action-film star Yeoh, who proves a compatible screen companion. The action never flags, though it becomes somewhat mechanical after a while. Panavision. [PG-13] ▼●◗

Tomorrow, the World! (1944) 95m. *** D: Leslie Fenton. Fredric March, Betty Field, Agnes Moorehead, Skippy Homeier, Joan Carroll. Homeier re-creates his knockout Broadway performance as a German-raised child adopted by his American uncle, who soon discovers that the boy is a rabid Nazi with a sinister mindset. Still-potent and thoughtful drama about tolerance. Scripted by Ring Lardner, Jr., and Leopold Atlas from the play by James Gow and Armand D'Usseau. ▼◗

Tom Sawyer (1973) C-104m. *** D: Don Taylor. Johnnie Whitaker, Celeste Holm, Warren Oates, Jeff East, Jodie Foster. Well-crafted musical remake of Tom Sawyer, the boy wonder of Hannibal, Mo., and his friends Huckleberry Finn and Becky Thatcher. Songs by Richard M. and Robert B. Sherman. Panavision. [PG] ▼●◗

tom thumb (1958) C-98m. ***½ D: George Pal. Russ Tamblyn, June Thorburn, Peter Sellers, Terry-Thomas, Alan Young, Jessie Matthews, Bernard Miles. Excellent children's picture with Tamblyn as tiny tom thumb, taken in by kindly couple but exploited by villainous Terry-Thomas and henchman Sellers. Charming Puppetoons sequences, Oscar-winning special effects, perfect Peggy Lee–Sonny Burke score. Filmed in England. ▼●◗

Toni (1935-French) 90m. ***½ D: Jean Renoir. Charles Blavette, Celia Montalvan, Jenny Helia, Max Dalban. Italian quarry worker Blavette lives with Montalvan, but falls in love with farm girl Helia—who in turn is wooed away by swaggering foreman Dalban. Renoir coscripted this simple, touching drama, which he filmed in a style that influenced the Italian Neorealist movement of the 1940s. ▼

Tonight and Every Night (1945) C-92m. *** D: Victor Saville. Rita Hayworth, Janet Blair, Lee Bowman, Marc Platt, Leslie Brooks, Professor Lamberti, Florence Bates. Entertaining, brightly colored wartime musical of British theater that never misses a performance, despite bombings and personal hardships. Try spotting Shelley Winters as one of the chorines. Story of the real-life theater also chronicled in MRS. HENDERSON PRESENTS. ▼◗

Tonight at 8:30 (1952-British) C-81m. *** D: Anthony Pelissier. Valerie Hobson, Nigel Patrick, Jack Warner, Kay Walsh, Ted Ray, Martita Hunt, Stanley Holloway, Betty Ann Davies. Three Noel Coward one-act plays ideally transferred to film. Original British title: MEET ME TONIGHT.

Tonka (1958) C-97m. **½ D: Lewis R. Foster. Sal Mineo, Philip Carey, Jerome Courtland, Rafael Campos, H. M. Wynant, Joy Page. Mineo stands out in this modest Disney film about an Indian brave's attachment to a wild horse, lone "survivor" of Little Bighorn battle, which he captures and tames. Weak resolution and cut-rate version of Custer's Last Stand detract from promising story. Retitled A HORSE NAMED COMANCHE. ▼

Tony Rome (1967) C-110m. **½ D: Gordon Douglas. Frank Sinatra, Jill St. John, Richard Conte, Sue Lyon, Gena Rowlands, Simon Oakland, Jeffrey Lynn, Lloyd Bochner. Good cast in moderately diverting detective caper. Private eye Rome (Sinatra) hired by millionaire (Oakland) to find out why his daughter would wind up drunk and unconscious in low-class Miami hotel. Sequel: LADY IN CEMENT. Panavision.▼●▶

Too Beautiful for You (1989-French) C-91m. ** D: Bertrand Blier. Gérard Depardieu, Josiane Balasko, Carole Bouquet, Roland Blanche, Francois Cluzet. Car dealer Depardieu cheats on beautiful, cultured wife Bouquet; the object of his affection is his plain, pudgy temporary receptionist (Balasko). Starts off brightly, but then goes absolutely nowhere. Panavision. [R]▼▶

Too Hot to Handle (1938) 105m. *** D: Jack Conway. Clark Gable, Myrna Loy, Walter Pidgeon, Leo Carrillo, Johnny Hines, Virginia Weidler. Gable and Pidgeon are rival newsreel photographers vying for aviatrix Loy in this fast-paced action-comedy; Gable's scene faking enemy attack on China is a gem.▼▶

Too Hot to Handle (1960-British) C-92m. ** D: Terence Young. Jayne Mansfield, Leo Genn, Carl Boehm, Christopher Lee, Barbara Windsor. Seamy study of chanteuse Mansfield involved with one man too many in the nightclub circuit. Aka PLAYGIRL AFTER DARK.▼▶

Too Late Blues (1962) 100m. ** D: John Cassavetes. Bobby Darin, Stella Stevens, John Cassavetes, Rupert Crosse, Vincent Edwards, Cliff Carnell, Seymour Cassel. Somewhat pretentious drama about jazz musician Darin becoming involved with selfish Stevens. Score by David Raksin, with on-camera performances "doubled" by such jazz greats as Benny Carter, Shelly Manne, and Jimmy Rowles.

Too Late the Hero (1970) C-133m. *** D: Robert Aldrich. Michael Caine, Cliff Robertson, Henry Fonda, Ian Bannen, Harry Andrews, Denholm Elliott, Ronald Fraser. Two reluctant soldiers (Robertson, Caine) sent on suicide mission on Pacific island during WW2; turns into battle of wits between them and Japanese officer. Action-packed film builds to pulsating finale. Metroscope. [R]▼▶

Toolbox Murders, The (1978) C-93m. *½ D: Dennis Donnelly. Cameron Mitchell, Pamelyn Ferdin, Wesley Eure, Nicholas Beauvy, Aneta Corsaut, Tim Donnelly, Evelyn Guerrero. A film that delivers exactly what its title promises: graphic slayings of young women by means of various pieces of hardware. Yecch. Remade in 2005. [R]▼▶

Toolbox Murders (2005) C-94m. *½ D: Tobe Hooper. Angela Bettis, Brent Roam, Juliet Landau, Greg Travis, Marco Rodriguez, Sara Downing, Adam Gierasch, Sheri Moon, Adam Weisman, Rance Howard. A black-garbed maniac is murdering one and all in a creepy old L.A. apartment building. Will Bettis, who's just moved into this house of horrors, track him down . . . or become a victim? Decent production values do little to elevate this predictable 1970s-style gorefest, which is in fact a remake of a 1978 movie.

Released theatrically overseas in 2004, but direct-to-video in the U.S. [R]▼▶

Too Many Girls (1940) 85m. *** D: George Abbott. Lucille Ball, Richard Carlson, Eddie Bracken, Ann Miller, Hal LeRoy, Desi Arnaz, Frances Langford. Engaging Rodgers-Hart musical comedy with winning cast, sharp dialogue. Four boys are hired to keep an eye on footloose Lucy at Pottawatomie College in Stopgap, New Mexico. Stagy presentation of musical numbers seems to work fine here; Van Johnson is very noticeable as one of the chorus boys (it was his film debut, as well as Arnaz and Bracken's). Incidentally, this is where Lucy and Desi met.▼●▶

Too Many Husbands (1940) 84m. *** D: Wesley Ruggles. Jean Arthur, Fred MacMurray, Melvyn Douglas, Harry Davenport, Dorothy Peterson, Edgar Buchanan. Jean is married to Douglas when husband #1 (MacMurray), thought dead, turns up. Excellent comedy from W. Somerset Maugham's play *Home and Beauty*. Remade as THREE FOR THE SHOW.▶

Too Much Sun (1991) C-110m. *½ D: Robert Downey. Robert Downey, Jr., Laura Ernst, Jim Haynie, Eric Idle, Ralph Macchio, Andrea Martin, Leo Rossi, Howard Duff, Jennifer Rubin. Farce about competition of brother and sister to have a child first, so as to inherit a fortune from their father; trouble is they're both gay. Few laughs in this dopey comedy that didn't stay long in theaters. [R]▼▶

Too Much, Too Soon (1958) 121m. ** D: Art Napoleon. Dorothy Malone, Errol Flynn, Efrem Zimbalist, Jr., Ray Danton, Neva Patterson, Martin Milner, Murray Hamilton. But not enough, in sensationalistic tale of Diana Barrymore's decline. Flynn steals the show as John Barrymore.▶

Too Outrageous! (1987-Canadian) C-100m. **½ D: Richard Benner. Craig Russell, Hollis McLaren, David McIlwraith, Ron White, Lynne Cormack, Michael J. Reynolds. Russell shines in this disappointing sequel to OUTRAGEOUS! as female impersonator Robin Turner, who's become a smash in N.Y.C.—but will he go mainstream? Unfortunately, the scenario is too hackneyed to make you care. Best moments are his impersonations of Streisand, Mae West, etc. [R]

Too Scared to Scream (1985) C-104m. *½ D: Tony Lo Bianco. Mike Connors, Anne Archer, Leon Isaac Kennedy, Ian McShane, Ruth Ford, John Heard, Carrie Nye, Maureen O'Sullivan, Murray Hamilton. Good cast stuck in dreary film about attempts to catch a psycho killer. Filmed in 1982. [R]▼

Tooth Fairy (2010) C-101m. ** D: Michael Lembeck. Dwayne Johnson, Ashley Judd, Stephen Merchant, Ryan Sheckler, Seth MacFarlane, Julie Andrews, Brandon

T. Jackson, Chase Ellison, Billy Crystal. When an unpopular hockey player nicknamed "tooth fairy" for his habit of knocking out opponents' teeth does a bad deed to a kid, his penance is to actually *become* a tooth fairy for a week. Under the tutelage of head fairy Andrews and "gadget guy" Crystal (in a brief cameo spewing groaner Borscht Belt–style jokes), macho Johnson dons a tutu, sprouts wings, and gets his comeuppance. Uninspired screenplay and routine performances fail to make this worth even the dollar Johnson leaves under the pillow . . . though it's always nice to see Andrews. [PG] ▐

Toots (2007) **C-84m.** *** D: Kristi Jacobson. Delightful documentary about legendary N.Y.C. restaurateur Toots Shor made by his granddaughter, with the help of an oral history he recorded late in life. His unique approach to running a watering hole for celebrities and sports figures is lovingly recalled by such famous patrons as Walter Cronkite, Yogi Berra, Whitey Ford, Frank Gifford, and a host of other sports stars and journalists. A wonderfully evocative portrait of a colorful period in New York nightlife. ▐

Tootsie (1982) **C-116m.** **** D: Sydney Pollack. Dustin Hoffman, Jessica Lange, Teri Garr, Dabney Coleman, Charles Durning, Sydney Pollack, George Gaynes, Geena Davis, Estelle Getty, Christine Ebersole. Smashing comedy about an obnoxious N.Y. actor who finally lands a job—disguised as a woman—and soon finds himself a better person female than he ever was male! Farcical premise becomes totally credible thanks to razorsharp script (credited to Larry Gelbart and Murray Schisgal, from Gelbart and Don McGuire's story), fine direction, and superlative performances all around—including director Pollack's as Hoffman's harried agent. Lange won Best Supporting Actress Oscar. Bill Murray appears unbilled. Film debut of Geena Davis. Panavision. [PG] ▼●◗

Topaz (1969) **C-127m.** *** D: Alfred Hitchcock. John Forsythe, Frederick Stafford, Dany Robin, John Vernon, Karin Dor, Michel Piccoli, Philippe Noiret, Claude Jade, Roscoe Lee Browne. French Intelligence agent Stafford works with American official Forsythe to dig out info on Russia's involvement in Cuba. Whirlwind plot circles globe, maintains intrigue level; good, not great Hitchcock, scripted by Samuel Taylor from Leon Uris' best-seller. Video release includes not one but *two* alternate endings Hitchcock shot and then decided not to use! [M/PG] ▼●◗

Topaze (1933) **78m.** *** D: (Harry) D'Abbadie D'Arrast. John Barrymore, Myrna Loy, Albert Conti, Luis Alberni, Reginald Mason, Jobyna Howland. De-

lightful film adapted from Marcel Pagnol's play about an impeccably honest but naive schoolteacher in France who unwittingly becomes a dupe for wealthy baron's business scheme. Barrymore is perfect. Remade as I LIKE MONEY. ▼●

Top Banana (1954) **C-100m.** *** D: Alfred E. Green. Phil Silvers, Rose Marie, Danny Scholl, Judy Lynn, Jack Albertson, Joey Faye, Herbie Faye. Fascinating curio is literally a filmed version of Silvers' Broadway hit about a Milton Berle–like TV comic. Full of burlesque chestnuts, and filmed (believe it or not) in 3-D. Current prints run 84m., with some musical numbers deleted. ▼

Top Dog (1995) **C-87m.** *½ D: Aaron Norris. Chuck Norris, Erik Von Detten, Michele Lamar Richards, Carmine Caridi, Herta Ware, Clyde Kusatsu, Francesco Quinn, Timothy Bottoms, Reno the Dog. When terrorists threaten to blow up San Diego, heroic cop Norris is forced to collaborate with a canine partner who seems to outsmart him every step of the way. Not much plot here, and needless to say, the dog steals the show. [PG-13] ▼●◗

Top Gun (1986) **C-110m.** **½ D: Tony Scott. Tom Cruise, Kelly McGillis, Val Kilmer, Anthony Edwards, Tom Skerritt, Michael Ironside, John Stockwell, Barry Tubb, Rick Rossovich, Tim Robbins, James Tolkan, Meg Ryan, Adrian Pasdar. Young studs vie for glory, on the ground and in the air, at elite naval aviation training school. Contrived beyond belief, with dogfights that play like video games, and total lack of sexual chemistry between the two leads . . . but slickly calculated to please '80s audiences (and fans of ever-smiling Cruise). Edwards, as Cruise's sidekick, steals the show. Giorgio Moroder and Tom Whitlock won an Oscar for the song "Take My Breath Away," performed by Berlin. Super 35. [PG] ▼●◗

Top Hat (1935) **99m.** **** D: Mark Sandrich. Fred Astaire, Ginger Rogers, Edward Everett Horton, Helen Broderick, Eric Blore, Erik Rhodes. What can we say? Merely a knock-out of a musical with Astaire and Rogers at their brightest doing "Cheek to Cheek," "Isn't This a Lovely Day to Be Caught in the Rain," "Top Hat, White Tie, and Tails," and the epic "Piccolino," and other Irving Berlin songs, as the duo goes through typical mistaken-identity plot. Wonderful support from rest of cast; that's Lucille Ball as the flower shop clerk. Scripted by Dwight Taylor and Allan Scott, from a play by Alexander Farago and Aladar Laszlo. Originally 101m.; some prints are 93m. ▼●◗

Topkapi (1964) **C-120m.** **** D: Jules Dassin. Melina Mercouri, Peter Ustinov, Maximilian Schell, Robert Morley, Akim Tamiroff, Despo Diamantidou. First-rate entertainment of would-be thieves who plan perfect crime in Constantinople museum; lighthearted caper has inspired many imitations. Filmed in Istanbul, with Ustinov's delightful performance copping an Academy Award. Written by Monja Danischewsky, from Eric Ambler's novel *The Light of Day*; memorable score by Manos Hadjidakis.▼●)

To Please a Lady (1950) **91m. **½ D:** Clarence Brown. Clark Gable, Barbara Stanwyck. Adolphe Menjou, Roland Winters, Will Geer, Emory Parnell, Frank Jenks. Unremarkable love story of reporter Stanwyck and race-car driver-heel Gable. ▼▶

Top o' the Morning (1949) **100m. **½ D:** David Miller. Bing Crosby, Barry Fitzgerald, Ann Blyth, Hume Cronyn, John McIntire, Eileen Crowe. Crosby-Fitzgerald malarkey is wearing thin in this fanciful musical of Bing searching for thief hiding the Blarney Stone.

Topper (1937) **97m. ***½ D:** Norman Z. McLeod. Constance Bennett, Cary Grant, Roland Young, Billie Burke, Alan Mowbray, Eugene Pallette, Arthur Lake, Hedda Hopper. Delightful gimmick comedy with ghosts Grant and Bennett dominating life of meek Young; sparkling cast in adaptation of Thorne Smith novel, scripted by Jack Jevne, Eddie Moran, and Eric Hatch. Followed by two sequels, a TV series, and a 1979 TV remake starring Kate Jackson and Andrew Stevens. Also shown in computer-colored version (the first b&w film to be "colorized," in 1985).▼●)

Topper Returns (1941) **88m. *** D:** Roy Del Ruth. Joan Blondell, Roland Young, Carole Landis, Billie Burke, Dennis O'Keefe, Patsy Kelly, Eddie "Rochester" Anderson. Topper helps ghostly Blondell solve her own murder in the last of this series, with hilarious results. Also shown in computer-colored version. ▼●)

Topper Takes a Trip (1939) **85m. *** D:** Norman Z. McLeod. Constance Bennett, Roland Young, Billie Burke, Alan Mowbray, Verree Teasdale, Franklin Pangborn. Cary Grant is missing (except in a flashback), but rest of cast returns for repeat success as Young is frustrated on Riviera vacation by ghostess Bennett. Also shown in computer-colored version.▼

Top Secret! (1984) **C-90m. **½ D:** Jim Abrahams, David Zucker, Jerry Zucker. Val Kilmer, Lucy Gutteridge, Christopher Villiers, Jeremy Kemp, Michael Gough, Omar Sharif, Peter Cushing. Likably silly comedy from the writing-directing team that brought you AIRPLANE!, about an Elvis-like rock star who becomes embroiled in espionage work while touring East Germany—with Nazis as bad guys and French resistance fighters as allies! Lots of laughs but no real momentum—and where's the ending? [PG]▼●)

Top Secret Affair (1957) **100m. **½ D:** H. C. Potter. Susan Hayward, Kirk Douglas, Paul Stewart, Jim Backus, John Cromwell. John P. Marquand's *Melville Goodwin, U.S.A.* becomes fair comedy, with most credit going to Hayward as fiery publisher who knows all about the past of Senate appointee (Douglas). ▶

Topsy-Turvy (1999-British) **C-160m. ***½ D:** Mike Leigh. Jim Broadbent, Allan Corduner, Lesley Manville, Eleanor David, Ron Cook, Timothy Spall, Kevin McKidd, Martin Savage, Shirley Henderson, Wendy Nottingham, Charles Simon, Alison Steadman, Andy Serkis. Fascinating, intimate portrait of Gilbert and Sullivan, and the time in which they lived, focusing on their peccadilloes and personalities, and the process of turning their latest ideas into the operetta masterpiece *The Mikado*. Broadbent and Corduner are superb in the leads, and Spall makes a wonderful Mikado. Overflowing with personal and period detail (including Oscar-winning Costume Design and Makeup), this long but rewarding film gets better and better as it goes along. Their story also told in THE GREAT GILBERT AND SULLIVAN. [R]▼▶

Tora! Tora! Tora! (1970-U.S.-Japanese) **C-143m. *** D:** Richard Fleischer, Toshio Masuda, Kinji Fukasaku. Martin Balsam, Soh Yamamura, Jason Robards, Joseph Cotten, Tatsuya Mihashi, E. G. Marshall, James Whitmore, Wesley Addy, Leon Ames, George Macready. Events leading up to (well-staged) Pearl Harbor attack, from both American and Japanese points of view. Well-documented screenplay shows major and minor blundering on both sides, then recreates attack with frightening realism. Well-made film creates incredible tension. Oscar-winning special effects. Panavision. [PG]▼●)

Torch, The (1950-Mexican) **90m. ** D:** Emilio Fernandez. Paulette Goddard, Pedro Armendariz, Gilbert Roland, Walter Reed. Mexican revolutionary captures town and falls for daughter of nobility. Rare English-language effort by Mexico's top director; a shame it isn't better. Beautifully photographed by Gabriel Figueroa.▼▶

Torchlight (1984) **C-90m. ** D:** Tom Wright. Pamela Sue Martin, Steve Railsback, Ian McShane, Al Corley, Rita Taggart. Married couple Martin and Railsback's world is wrecked when he becomes a cocaine addict. Below-average morality tale: its message may be important, but its dramatics are muddled. [R]▼●

Torch Song (1953) **C-90m. **½ D:** Charles Walters. Joan Crawford, Michael Wilding, Marjorie Rambeau, Gig Young, Henry (Harry) Morgan, Dorothy Patrick, Benny Rubin, Nancy Gates. Crawford is hard as nails as a Broadway musical star who chews up people for lunch—until she meets blind pianist Wilding, who isn't cowed by her. Glossy, often hilariously clichéd drama reminds us that It's Lonely At the Top. There's one absurd musical number in which Crawford appears in blackface! Her "clumsy" dance partner in the opening number is director Walters, a former dancer and choreographer. ▼●◖

Torch Song Trilogy (1988) **C-117m.** **½ D: Paul Bogart. Anne Bancroft, Matthew Broderick, Harvey Fierstein, Brian Kerwin, Karen Young, Charles Pierce. Fierstein rewrote (and considerably compressed) his landmark Broadway play about a drag queen, and lost something in the process. Changing sensibilities in the AIDS era also affect the original material, though there are still fine moments. Fierstein reprises his stage performance as Arnold Beckoff, and Bancroft scores strongly as his mother. [R]▼●◖

Torchy Blane series SEE: *Leonard Maltin's Classic Movie Guide*

Torment (1944-Swedish) **100m.** ***½ D: Alf Sjoberg. Mai Zetterling, Stig Jarrel, Alf Kjellin, Olof Winnerstrand. Schoolboy Kjellin and girl he falls in love with (Zetterling) are hounded by sadistic teacher Jarrel. Moody and evocative, with a script by Ingmar Bergman. Also known as FRENZY. ▼◖

Tormented (1960) **75m.** BOMB D: Bert I. Gordon. Richard Carlson, Juli Reding, Susan Gordon, Lugene Sanders, Joe Turkel, Lillian Adams. Low-budget hogwash of guilt-ridden pianist dubious over his forthcoming marriage to society woman. Weak ghost story.▼◖

Torn Apart (1989) **C-96m.** **½ D: Jack Fisher. Adrian Pasdar, Cecilia Peck, Barry Primus, Machram Huri, Arnon Zadok, Margit Polak. Boy and girl grow up together and fall in love—but he's Jewish, she's Arab, and the setting is Israel. A new slant on *Romeo and Juliet* with a topical backdrop, this humanist drama has convincing performances and a timely message. Peck is the daughter of Gregory Peck. [R] ▼◖

Torn Between Two Values SEE: **Sergeant Ryker**

Torn Curtain (1966) **C-128m.** **½ D: Alfred Hitchcock. Paul Newman, Julie Andrews, Lila Kedrova, David Opatoshu, Ludwig Donath. Oddly unmoving Hitchcock Cold War thriller about American scientist (Newman) pretending to be defector. Slick but empty film. ▼●◖

Torque (2004) **C-81m.** *½ D: Joseph Kahn. Martin Henderson, Ice Cube, Monet Mazur, Adam Scott, Matt Schulze, Jaime Pressly, Jay Hernandez, Will Yun Lee, Fredro Starr, Justina Machado, Faizon Love. Ultra-cool biker returns to his home turf, where he leads two rival gangs and the FBI on a frantic chase. Music-video–style biker movie is fast and loud, but ultra-dumb, often laughable. Even Ice Cube is reduced to cliché

here. Thanks to aggressive product placement a climactic catfight turns out to be a battle between Pepsi and Mountain Dew! Super 35. [PG-13] ▼◖

Torrents of Spring (1990-Italian-French) **C-101m.** **½ D: Jerzy Skolimowski. Timothy Hutton, Natassja Kinski, Valeria Golino, William Forsythe, Urbano Barberini, Francesca De Sapio, Jacques Herlin. No disgrace, but an almost inevitably stilted film version of an Ivan Turgenev story. Russian Hutton (!), engaged to German Golino, gets roving glands for married Kinski, who's negotiating to purchase his estate. Nicely shot (with a good dual scene), but Hutton's regal bearing falls apart whenever he's asked to open his mouth. [PG-13]▼●◖

Torrid Zone (1940) **88m.** ***½ D: William Keighley. James Cagney, Ann Sheridan, Pat O'Brien, Andy Devine, Helen Vinson, Jerome Cowan, George Tobias, George Reeves. South-of-the-border comedy, action and romance with nightclub star Sheridan helping plantation owner O'Brien keep Cagney from leaving. Zesty dialogue (scripted by Richard Macauley and Jerry Wald) in this variation on THE FRONT PAGE. ●◖

Torso (1974-Italian) **C-90m.** *½ D: Sergio Martino. Suzy Kendall, Tina Aumont, John Richardson, Luc Merenda. A killer is carving up beautiful co-eds in this bloody potboiler. Uncut version runs 93m. [R]▼◖

Tortilla Flat (1942) **105m.** *** D: Victor Fleming. Spencer Tracy, Hedy Lamarr, John Garfield, Frank Morgan, Akim Tamiroff, Sheldon Leonard, Donald Meek, John Qualen, Allen Jenkins. Steinbeck's salty novel of California fishing community vividly portrayed by three top stars, stolen by Morgan as devoted dog lover. Also shown in computer-colored version.▼●◖

Tortilla Heaven (2007) **C-94m.** *½ D: Judy Hecht Dumontet. José Zúñiga, Miguel Sandoval, Olivia Hussey, Elpidia Carrillo, Alexis Cruz, Judy Herrera, Marcelo Tubert, Irene Bedard, Lupe Ontiveros, Del Zamora, George Lopez. Isidor (Zúñiga) makes the best tortillas in Falfúrrias, New Mexico, population 73. Then one day the image of Jesus miraculously appears on one of his tortillas. Anemic farce goes nowhere . . . and takes a long time getting there. [PG-13] ◖

Tortilla Soup (2001) **C-110m.** *** D: María Ripoll. Hector Elizondo, Jacqueline Obradors, Tamara Mello, Nikolai Kinski, Joel Joan, Paul Rodriguez, Elizabeth Peña, Raquel Welch, Constance Marie. Engaging remake of EAT DRINK MAN WOMAN reset in L.A., with Elizondo as a stern but loving patriarch with three quite different daughters—and a penchant for communicating through cooking. Good cast makes the most of the material; Peña is especially good as a schoolteacher who blossoms as she falls in love. [PG-13]▼◖

Torture Chamber of Baron Blood, The
SEE: **Baron Blood**

Torture Chamber of Dr. Sadism, The
(1967-German) **C-90m.** **½ D: Harald
Reinl. Christopher Lee, Lex Barker, Karin
Dor, Carl Lange, Vladimir Medar. A re-
surrected Lee seeks revenge on Barker and
Dor; after luring them to his castle they are
mentally and physically tortured. Based on
Poe's *Pit and the Pendulum*. Atmospheric,
but not for the squeamish. Aka THE
BLOOD DEMON and CASTLE OF THE
WALKING DEAD (running 75m.). Tech-
niscope. ▼●

Torture Garden (1967-British) **C-93m.**
**½ D: Freddie Francis. Jack Palance,
Burgess Meredith, Beverly Adams, Peter
Cushing, Barbara Ewing, Michael Bryant, Maurice Denham. Anthology horror
film revolving around sideshow weirdo
Dr. Diabolo (Meredith) with power to let
curious visitors see and experience their
near-future. Good cast and production, but
stories uneven; first and last tales best. Written by Robert Bloch. ▼●

Torture Zone SEE: **Fear Chamber, The**

To Sir, With Love (1967-British) **C-105m.**
***½ D: James Clavell. Sidney Poitier, Judy
Geeson, Christian Roberts, Suzy Kendall,
Faith Brook, Geoffrey Bayldon, Patricia
Routledge, Adrienne Posta, Lulu, Michael
Des Barres. Excellent film of novice teacher
Poitier assigned to roughhouse London
school, gradually earning respect from his
students. Well acted, with nice work by Brit-
ish newcomers; Lulu also sings hit title song.
Written and produced by Clavell, from
E. R. Braithwaite's novel. Followed by a
made-for-TV sequel in 1996. ▼●

To Sleep With Anger (1990) **C-102m.**
*** D: Charles Burnett. Danny Glover,
Paul Butler, Mary Alice, Carl Lumbly,
Vonetta McGee, Richard Brooks, Sheryl
Lee Ralph, Ethel Ayler, Julius Harris, Sy
Richardson, Jimmy Witherspoon. Evocative domestic drama about the effect
storyteller/trickster Glover has on the
various members of a black family. More
than just a portrait of contemporary black
society, it's a story of cultural differences
between parents and children, of how individuals learn (or don't learn) from experience, and of how there should be no place
for those who cause violence and strife.
Scripted by Burnett. Screen couple Lumbly and McGee are also married in real life.
[PG]▼●

Total Eclipse (1995-U.S.-French) **C-110m.**
BOMB D: Agnieszka Holland. Leon-
ardo DiCaprio, David Thewlis, Romane
Bohringer, Dominique Blanc, Felicie Pa-
sotti Cabarbaye, Nita Klein, James Thieree,
Christopher Hampton. Really bad film
about 19th-century French poets Arthur
Rimbaud (DiCaprio) and Paul Verlaine
(Thewlis) plays like a homosexual version

of AMADEUS. Well intentioned and based
on fact, but just awful. Hampton adapted the
script from his own play. Pick up a couple of
poetry books instead. [R] ▼●

Totally F*ed Up** (1993) **C-85m.** **½
D: Gregg Araki. James Duval, Roko Belic,
Susan Behshid, Jenee Gill, Gilbert Luna,
Lance May, Alan Boyce, Craig Gilmore.
Jarring, Godardian portrait of a group of
bored, alienated L.A. teens. They hang out
and talk about sex, relationships, and their
parents; their language is littered with such
words as "grossomatic" and "gagorama."
And . . . they're gay, so there is no shortage of venom vented against homophobia.
Not bad, but still a come-down from Araki's
breakthrough film, THE LIVING END.
Araki also scripted, edited, photographed
and coproduced. ▼●

Total Recall (1990) **C-109m.** *** D: Paul
Verhoeven. Arnold Schwarzenegger, Rachel Ticotin, Sharon Stone, Ronny Cox, Michael Ironside, Marshall Bell, Mel Johnson,
Jr. Schwarzenegger learns he's a victim of
mind-tampering in this 21st-century tale—
and once he discovers his true identity, journeys to Mars to help fight a power-hungry
madman there. Riveting yarn (based on Philip
K. Dick's short story "We Can Remember It
for You Wholesale") offers endless twists and
intriguing ideas . . . and the kind of over-the-
top violence for which director Verhoeven is
known. Dazzling, Oscar-winning special
effects throughout. Later "inspired" a cable
TV series. [R] ▼●

To the Devil a Daughter (1976-British-
German) **C-95m.** **½ D: Peter Sykes.
Richard Widmark, Christopher Lee, Honor
Blackman, Denholm Elliott, Nastassja
Kinski, Michael Goodliffe. Occult novel-
ist Widmark is enlisted to help young girl
(Kinski) who's being pursued by defrocked
priest Lee for satanic ritual. Hammer Films
adaptation of Dennis Wheatley book is well
made but lacks punch. Aka CHILD OF SA-
TAN. [R]▼●

To the Ends of the Earth (1948) **109m.**
***½ D: Robert Stevenson. Dick Powell,
Signe Hasso, Ludwig Donath, Vladimir
Sokoloff, Edgar Barrier. Fast-moving
thriller of government agent tracking down
narcotics smuggling ring has good acting
and ironic ending.

To the Victor (1948) **100m.** **½ D: Delmer
Daves. Dennis Morgan, Viveca Lindfors,
Victor Francen, Eduardo Ciannelli, Anthony Caruso, Tom D'Andrea, William
Conrad, Dorothy Malone, Joseph Buloff,
Bruce Bennett. Thought-provoking post-
WW2 drama about an apolitical black marketer (Morgan) who becomes involved with
a mystery woman (Lindfors) whose life is
in danger. Richard Brooks' script attempts
to deal with issues relating to war, peace,
morality, and responsibility, but too many
dull stretches do this in. Strikingly photo-

graphed on location in Paris and especially at Normandy's Omaha Beach.

Toto the Hero (1991-Belgian-French-German) **C-90m.** *** D: Jaco van Dormael. Michel Bouquet, Mireille Perrier, Jo De Backer, Gisela Uhlen, Peter Bohlke, Thomas Godet, Sandrine Blancke. Original, immensely clever journey through the life of a character named Thomas, who is shown (through constant cross-cutting) as a child, adult, and elderly man. The young boy imagines that he'll grow up to be Toto the Hero, a secret agent; instead, he'll have to cope with his ultimate ordinariness, his memories, and his dreams. A unique blend of comedy, tragedy, and mystery, especially notable for its discerning—and unflinching—look at childhood. Writer-director van Dormael, a former circus clown, makes his feature directing debut. [PG-13]▼●

To Trap a Spy (1966) **C-92m.** **½ D: Don Medford. Robert Vaughn, Luciana Paluzzi, Patricia Crowley, Fritz Weaver, William Marshall, Ivan Dixon, David McCallum. Adequate action/spy yarn, expanded from initial segment of *The Man From U.N.C.L.E.* TV series, with Napoleon Solo (Vaughn) attempting to thwart the assassination of an African head of state. McCallum, Vaughn's costar on the show, only appears briefly.

Touch, The (1971-U.S.-Swedish) **C-112m.** *½ D: Ingmar Bergman. Elliott Gould, Bibi Andersson, Max von Sydow, Sheila Reid. Bergman's first English-language film should be called THE TETCHED, in view of the fact that Andersson leaves doctorhusband von Sydow for boorish Gould. The two Bergman regulars are fine, but Gould is miscast and dialogue embarrassingly awkward. [R]▼

Touch (1997) **C-96m.** **½ D: Paul Schrader. Bridget Fonda, Christopher Walken, Skeet Ulrich, Tom Arnold, Gina Gershon, Lolita Davidovich, Paul Mazursky, Janeane Garofalo, John Doe, Conchata Ferrell, Mason Adams, Anthony Zerbe, LL Cool J, Tamlyn Tomita, Don Novello. Satirical fable about a young ex-monk who has the ability to effect miracle healings—while suffering stigmata: bleeding as Christ did on the cross. This causes no small furor among exploiters like Walken and fanatics like Arnold. Interesting and well cast (with Arnold a standout as the religious zealot), but awfully subdued; it's a film that leaves you wanting. Based on an Elmore Leonard novel, scripted by Schrader. [R]▼●)

Touchables, The (1968-British) **C-97m.** BOMB D: Robert Freeman. Judy Huxtable, Esther Anderson, Marilyn Richard, Kathy Simmonds. Dreary tale of four girls and a guy who try to kidnap pop singing idol. Terrible. [PG—edited from original R rating]

Touch and Die (1991) **C-108m.** BOMB D: Piernico Solinas. Renee Estevez, Martin Sheen, David Birney, Franco Nero. The Rome bureau chief of an American newspaper finds lots of bodies with their hands chopped off as he follows the trail of plutonium thieves. Sheen tries to keep real-life daughter Estevez locked in her hotel room, to keep her out of trouble (and off-screen), which may be a wise choice. Extremely confusing globe-trotting thriller. [R]▼

Touch and Go (1980-Australian) **C-92m.** ** D: Peter Maxwell. Wendy Hughes, Chantal Contouri, Carmen Duncan, Jeanie Drynan, Liddy Clark. Sexy female Robin Hoods steal for worthy causes. A well-meaning comedy-caper film that is slight and forgettable.▼

Touch and Go (1986) **C-101m.** **½ D: Robert Mandel. Michael Keaton, Maria Conchita Alonso, Ajay Naidu, Maria Tucci, Max Wright, Jere Burns, Lara Jill Miller. Self-centered hockey star becomes involved with delinquent kid and his mother. Aptly titled film has persuasive performances but unconvincing storyline. [R]▼●

Touched (1983) **C-93m.** ** D: John Flynn. Robert Hays, Kathleen Beller, Ned Beatty, Gilbert Lewis, Lyle Kessler. Uninspired, poorly scripted latter-day DAVID AND LISA with Hays and Beller escaping from mental institution and trying to build a "normal" life for themselves. Good performances, anyway. [R]▼

Touched by Love (1980) **C-95m.** **½ D: Gus Trikonis. Deborah Raffin, Diane Lane, Michael Learned, Cristina Raines, Mary Wickes, Clu Gulager, John Amos, Clive Shalom. Sentimental drama, based on nursing trainee Lena Canada's memoir, of cerebral palsy victim's pen-pal relationship with Elvis Presley. Fine performances by Lane and Raffin. Originally titled TO ELVIS, WITH LOVE. [PG]▼

Touchez Pas au Grisbi (1954-French) **94m.** ***½ D: Jacques Becker. Jean Gabin, René Dary, Jeanne Moreau, Dora Doll, Gaby Basset, Denise Clair, Michel Jourdan, Daniel Cauchy, Lino Ventura. An elegant French gangster who's pulled off a daring heist forsakes his plan to keep the loot under wraps in order to save the life of his impetuous best friend. As much an observation about a certain way of life as it is a crime thriller; unpretentious and skillfully made, with a typically commanding performance by the incomparable Gabin. Aka GRISBI. ▼)

Touching the Void (2003-British) **C-106m.** *** D: Kevin Macdonald. Nicholas Aaron, Richard Hawking, Brendan Mackey, Joe Simpson, Simon Yates. Amazing docudrama of two climbers and their perilous journey up the Siula Grande peak in the Peruvian Andes in 1985. After reaching the top they are separated upon descent; one is left for dead by his partner but miraculously survives to tell the tale. Using actors and bridging techniques of fictional action pictures, film cuts between interviews with survivors Simpson and Yates and highly accomplished re-creations to present a real-life story that has every bit of suspense, adventure, and drama any Hollywood production could aspire to. Based on the book by Simpson. ▼▶

Touch of Class, A (1973) **C-105m.** ** D: Melvin Frank. George Segal, Glenda Jackson, Paul Sorvino, Hildegard Neil, Cec Linder, K Callan, Mary Barclay. Undeniable chemistry of Segal and Jackson can only occasionally breathe life into this stale comedy about married man who intends nothing more than having a carefree affair, only to fall genuinely in love. Jackson won Best Actress Oscar. Panavision. [PG]▼▶

Touch of Evil (1958) **108m.** **** D: Orson Welles. Charlton Heston, Orson Welles, Janet Leigh, Joseph Calleia, Akim Tamiroff, Marlene Dietrich, Dennis Weaver, Valentin de Vargas, Mort Mills, Victor Milian, Joanna Moore, Zsa Zsa Gabor. Narc Heston and corrupt cop Welles tangle over murder investigation in sleazy Mexican border town, with Heston's bride Leigh the pawn of their struggle. Fantastic, justifiably famous opening shot merely commences stylistic masterpiece, dazzlingly photographed by Russell Metty. Great Latin rock score by Henry Mancini; neat unbilled cameos by Joseph Cotten, Ray Collins, and especially Mercedes McCambridge. Reconstructed according to Welles' notes in 1998, at 111m. Beware 95m. version. ▼●

Touch of Love, A SEE: **Thank You All Very Much**

Touch of Pink (2004-Canadian-British) **C-91m.** ** D: Ian Iqbal Rashid. Jimi Mistry, Kyle MacLachlan, Kristen Holden-Reid, Suleka Mathew, Brian George, Veena Sood, Raoul Bhaneja. Strained attempt to re-create the fluffy style of an early-'60s bedroom comedy that might have starred Cary Grant and Doris Day (like, say, THAT TOUCH OF MINK). The twist is that the leading man is gay, a fact he is trying to hide from his visiting mother, a devout Muslim who tries to set him up with a girl in time to attend a big family wedding. What's more, the ghost of Cary Grant appears to offer advice on life and love to our hapless hero. MacLachlan tries his best, but his impression of the peerless Grant just doesn't cut it, and neither does this well-meaning film. [R] ▼▶

Tough Enough (1983) **C-106m.** ** D: Richard Fleischer. Dennis Quaid, Carlene Watkins, Stan Shaw, Pam Grier, Warren Oates, Bruce McGill, Wilford Brimley, Fran Ryan. Numerous problems plagued production of this predictable tale of would-be Country-Western singer Quaid entering Tough Man amateur boxing competitions for exposure. Insipid ROCKY rip-off wastes good cast. Shot in 1981. [PG] ▼▶

Tough Guys (1986) **C-104m.** **½ D: Jeff Kanew. Burt Lancaster, Kirk Douglas, Charles Durning, Alexis Smith, Dana Carvey, Darlanne Fluegel, Eli Wallach, Monty Ash, Billy Barty. A couple of former crooks—who staged America's last train robbery 30 years ago—are finally sprung from prison and gamely try to adjust to 1980s life. Watching Burt and Kirk (in this tailor-made comedy) is a joy, but the film gets more childish and predictable as it goes along. Still watchable but what a shame! Panavision. [PG]▼●

Tough Guys Don't Dance (1987) **C-110m.** **½ D: Norman Mailer. Ryan O'Neal, Isabella Rossellini, Debra Sandlund, Wings Hauser, Lawrence Tierney, Penn Jillette, Frances Fisher, John Bedford Lloyd, Clarence Williams III. Genuinely odd film noir cum black-comedy adapted by Mailer from his own novel, with O'Neal as a loser who may have committed murder—but can't remember. Peopled exclusively by weird characters who speak in purple prose... but it does have its moments, and a lively performance by Tierney as O'Neal's no-nonsense father who wants to "deep-six the heads." Filmed in Provincetown, Massachusetts. [R]▼●▶

Tourist, The (2010) **C-103m.** ** D: Florian Henckel von Donnersmarck. Johnny Depp, Angelina Jolie, Paul Bettany, Timothy Dalton, Steven Berkoff, Rufus Sewell, Christian De Sica, Raoul Bova. Update of 2005 French thriller ANTHONY ZIMMER is the kind of thing Hitchcock or Donen could have pulled off in their sleep, but this frenetic mishmash only puts *us* to sleep. American tourist Depp is mending a broken heart in Venice and caught up in international intrigue, while mysterious Jolie sets him up as a decoy to avoid Russian mobsters who are after her. Complicated blend of romance and action needs a lighter touch. Chemistry is virtually nonexistent between the uncharacteristically schlumpy Depp character and the ultra-elegant Jolie, who looks every bit as stunning as the shimmering Italian scenery. As a travelogue it's *bella*; as a movie, not so hot. Panavision. [PG-13] ▶

Tourist Trap (1979) **C-85m.** *½ D: David Schmoeller. Chuck Connors, Jon Van Ness, Jocelyn Jones, Robin Sherwood, Tanya Roberts, Keith McDermott. Here's an original idea for a horror movie: those life-size dummies in Connors' "museum" are strangely lifelike, aren't they? Not so much that the idiots he lures there ever catch on. A couple of genuine scares, but mostly boring thriller. [PG]▼●

Tous les Matins du Monde (1991-French) **C-114m.** ***½ D: Alain Corneau. Jean-Pierre Marielle, Gérard Depardieu, Anne Brochet, Guillaume Depardieu, Caroline Sihol, Carole Richert, Myriam Boyer, Michel Bouquet. Exquisitely detailed historical biography examining the relationship between Sainte Colombe (Marielle), the obsessive, almost mystical 17th-century baroque composer and cellist, and his protegé, Marin Marais (Gérard Depardieu), a man of far less elevated artistic aspirations, who was a celebrated court composer at Versailles. Both stars are excellent, with Depardieu's son Guillaume effectively playing the young Marin Marais. Exemplary use of music on the soundtrack. Screenplay by the director and Pascal Quignard, based on the latter's novel. A smash hit in France, where it won seven César awards. Video title: ALL THE MORNINGS OF THE WORLD. ▼●❚

Tout Va Bien (1972-French) **C-96m.** **★★★** D: Jean-Luc Godard, Jean-Pierre Gorin. Yves Montand, Jane Fonda, Vittorio Caprioli, Élisabeth Chauvin, Castel Casti, Éric Chartier, Anne Wiazemsky. Reporter Fonda covers a crisis at a meatpacking plant whose workers are striking against their elitist bosses. She is accompanied by her husband (Montand), an ex–French New Wave screenwriter who now makes television commercials. Godard and Gorin expand the boundaries of narrative cinema while exploring the aftermath of the late-1960s "revolution" . . . and specifically, the struggle of the individual to remain political and relevant while supporting a comfortable lifestyle. Very much a snapshot of its time. ▼❚

Tovarich (1937) **98m.** **★★★** D: Anatole Litvak. Claudette Colbert, Charles Boyer, Basil Rathbone, Anita Louise, Melville Cooper, Isabel Jeans, Morris Carnovsky. Boyer and Colbert, royal Russians, flee the Revolution with court treasury but nothing for themselves; they're finally reduced to working as servants. Enjoyable but dated romantic comedy set in Paris. Based on a French play Americanized by Robert E. Sherwood.

To Walk With Lions (1999-Canadian-British-Kenyan) **C-108m.** **★★½** D: Carl Schultz. Richard Harris, John Michie, Kerry Fox, Ian Bannen, Hugh Quarshie, Honor Blackman, Geraldine Chaplin. Fact-based account of Tony Fitzjohn, an aimless young man who becomes the protégé of George Adamson (a perfectly cast Harris), the fiercely dedicated "lion man" who teaches lions born in captivity how to survive in the wild. Some of the supporting characters are underwritten, and the scenes in which the humans and lions interact are pasted together, but the film is engaging when exploring Adamson's spiritual connection to the animals. This BORN FREE follow-up did not earn a U.S. theatrical release. Super 35. [PG-13] ▼❚

Toward the Unknown (1956) **C-115m.** **★★½** D: Mervyn LeRoy. William Holden, Lloyd Nolan, Virginia Leith, Charles McGraw, James Garner, Murray Hamilton, L.Q. Jones, Paul Fix, Karen Steele. Intelligent narrative about test pilots, focusing on a tarnished air officer (Holden) eager to regain the respect of his men. Garner's film debut.❚

Towelhead (2008) **C-124m.** **★★★** D: Alan Ball. Aaron Eckhart, Toni Collette, Maria Bello, Peter Macdissi, Summer Bishil, Eugene Jones, Matt Letscher, Chase Ellison. A 13-year-old girl leaves her mercurial mother to live with her uptight, culturally conflicted Lebanese father in the suburbs of Houston, Texas. Exploring her newfound sexuality, the girl flirts with danger at every turn, inciting and inviting the attentions of next-door neighbor Eckhart. Provocative, darkly funny adult fare, intended to shock and amuse in equal measure, explores sexual abuse, cultural stereotypes, and adolescent angst, yet somehow avoids being exploitive. Bishil is perfect in a remarkable film debut. Alicia Erian's novel was adapted by first-time director Ball (who wrote AMERICAN BEAUTY). Super 35. [R]❚

Towering Inferno, The (1974) **C-165m.** **★★½** D: John Guillermin, Irwin Allen. Steve McQueen, Paul Newman, William Holden, Faye Dunaway, Fred Astaire, Susan Blakely, Richard Chamberlain, Jennifer Jones, O. J. Simpson, Robert Vaughn, Robert Wagner, Susan Flannery, Gregory Sierra, Dabney Coleman. All-star idiocy about a burning skyscraper. Purports to pay tribute to firemen but spends most of its time devising grisly ways for people to die. The pyrotechnics are gripping, but the movie is just another cold-blooded Hollywood "product." Oscar-winner for Cinematography, Editing and Song ("We May Never Love Like This Again"). Panavision. [PG] ▼●❚

Tower of Evil (1972-British) **C-85m.** BOMB D: Jim O'Connolly. Bryant Haliday, Jill Haworth, Anna Palk, Jack Watson, Mark Edwards, Derek Fowlds. One of the horrors here is a series of brutal murders masterminded by a lunatic; another one is the film itself. Reissued as HORROR ON SNAPE ISLAND. [R] ▼❚

Tower of London (1939) **92m.** **★★½** D: Rowland V. Lee. Basil Rathbone, Boris Karloff, Barbara O'Neil, Ian Hunter, Vincent Price, Nan Grey, Leo G. Carroll, John Sutton, Miles Mander, Donnie Dunagan. Muddled historical melodrama (not a horror film, as many believe), with Rathbone as unscrupulous, power-hungry Richard III and Karloff as his dutiful executioner Mord. Court intrigue leads to uninspired battle scenes. Same-named 1962 movie has little in common with this—except the historical figures. ▼❚

Tower of London (1962) **79m.** **★½** D: Roger Corman. Vincent Price, Michael Pate, Joan Freeman, Robert Brown. Price gives his all as Richard III, who dispatches all his rivals for the crown of England, but this is a far cry from Shakespeare, and not even up to par for director Corman. Has little in common with the 1939 film of the same name, in which Price played the Duke of Clarence. ▼●❚

Tower of Terror SEE: **In the Devil's Garden**

Town, The (2010) **C-125m.** ***½ D: Ben Affleck. Ben Affleck, Rebecca Hall, Jon Hamm, Jeremy Renner, Blake Lively, Pete Postlethwaite, Chris Cooper, Slaine, Owen Burke, Titus Welliver. In Charlestown, Massachusetts, it's second nature to lead a criminal life like Affleck and Renner. They and their cohorts execute a string of daring robberies, but in their latest bank hit some-one may have recognized them, so Affleck boldly approaches bank teller Hall to feel her out—and winds up becoming involved with her. A knockout of a movie with great dialogue, characterizations, and heart-pounding action, photographed by Robert Elswit. Affleck does fine work on both sides of the camera; he also coscripted with Pe-ter Craig and Aaron Stockard, from Chuck Hogan's novel *Prince of Thieves.* Unrated version runs 153m. Super 35. [R]▶

Town & Country (2001) **C-104m.** *½ D: Peter Chelsom. Warren Beatty, Diane Keaton, Goldie Hawn, Garry Shandling, Andie MacDowell, Nastassja Kinski, Jenna Elfman, Josh Hartnett, Charlton Heston, Marian Seldes, Katherine Towne. Two cou-ples celebrate their long-term marriages—just as both relationships start to come apart. A train wreck of a movie that starts out as romantic comedy, lurches into French farce, then lumbers along to a point beyond com-prehension. The cast tries its best. Cowritten by Buck Henry, who appears as a divorce lawyer. Filmed mostly in 1998. [R]▼▶

Town Called Hell, A (1971-British-Spanish) **C-95m.** BOMB D: Robert Parrish. Robert Shaw, Telly Savalas, Stella Stevens, Mar-tin Landau, Fernando Rey. A manhunt for Mexican revolutionary Shaw. The pits. Originally titled A TOWN CALLED BAS-TARD. Franscope. [R]▼▶

Town Is Quiet, The (2001-French) **C-133m.** **½ D: Robert Guédiguian. Ariane Ascaride, Jean-Pierre Darroussin, Gérard Meylan, Jacques Boudet, Christine Brücher, Jacques Pieiller. Slow-paced, dark, but inter-esting tale of life in Marseilles, a working-class French city that has seen better days—as have many of the inhabitants depicted here. Beautifully atmospheric and certainly real-istic, film demands more than many viewers may want to give; those who like gritty hu-man drama will probably find this a satisfying way to spend a couple of hours. ▼▶

Town Like Alice, A (1956-British) **107m.** **½ D: Jack Lee. Virginia McKenna, Peter Finch, Maureen Swanson, Vincent Ball. Taut WW2 tale, well acted, about Japanese oppression of female British POWs in Ma-laysia. Based on Nevil Shute's novel, later remade as TV miniseries. Retitled: RAPE OF MALAYA.▼●

Town That Dreaded Sundown, The (1977) **C-90m.** **½ D: Charles B. Pierce. Ben Johnson, Andrew Prine, Dawn Wells, Christine Ellsworth, Charles B. Pierce. OK thriller made from true story of a hooded killer who terrorized town of Texarkana in the mid-'40s. Ben Johnson's presence gives it some stature. Panavision. [R]▼

Town Without Pity (1961) **105m.** **½ D: Gottfried Reinhardt. Kirk Douglas, E. G. Marshall, Christine Kaufmann, Robert Blake, Richard Jaeckel, Frank Sutton, Bar-bara Rutting. Courtroom drama of G.I.s ac-cused of raping German girl. Decent cast, but could have been better handled. Title song, sung by Gene Pitney, was a big hit. Filmed in Germany.▼▶

To Wong Foo Thanks For Everything, Julie Newmar (1995) **C-108m.** *½ D: Bee-ban Kidron. Patrick Swayze, Wesley Snipes, John Leguizamo, Stockard Channing, Arliss Howard, Chris Penn, Melinda Dillon, Blythe Danner, Beth Grant, RuPaul, Naomi Camp-bell, Quentin Crisp, Julie Newmar. Incred-ibly tiresome tale of three self-proclaimed drag queens heading for Hollywood whose car breaks down in a small rural town. There they befriend—and enliven—the local fe-male population. Robin Williams appears in one scene, unbilled, and provides easily the film's funniest moments. [PG-13]▼●▶

Toxic Avenger, The (1985) **C-100m.** **½ D: Michael Herz, Samuel Weil. Andree Maranda, Mitchell Cohen, Jennifer Baptist, Cindy Manion, Robert Prichard, Mark Torgi, Marisa Tomei. Funny spoof about 90-pound weakling Torgi, who is transformed into a monster who only does good deeds. Not without violence and gore but still entertain-ing; recommended mostly for fans of the genre. Followed by three sequels. [R]▼●▶

Toy, The (1982) **C-99m.** *½ D: Richard Donner. Richard Pryor, Jackie Gleason, Scott Schwartz, Teresa Ganzel, Ned Beatty, Wilfrid Hyde-White, Annazette Chase. Stultifying remake of the Pierre Richard comedy LE JOUET with Pryor as penni-less writer hired by zillionaire Gleason as plaything for spoiled son Schwartz. A few good gags are lost in a sea of you-can't-buy-friends-you-gotta-earn-them lectures, not to mention dubious taste. [PG]▼●▶

Toys (1992) **C-121m.** *½ D: Barry Levin-son. Robin Williams, Michael Gambon, Joan Cusack, Robin Wright, LL Cool J, Donald O'Connor, Arthur Malet, Jack War-den, Debi Mazar, Jamie Foxx, Blake Clark, Art Metrano, Yeardley Smith. Appall-ingly bad movie about one man's lifelong dream—a whimsical toy factory—turned into a nightmare by his brother, a military martinet with outsized ambitions. This was director-cowriter Levinson's longtime pet project! Aside from Ferdinando Scarfiotti's ingenious production design (worth seeing at least for a few minutes) and some sweet moments at the outset, this is a heavy-handed mess. [PG-13]▼●▶

Toys in the Attic (1963) **90m. **½** D: George Roy Hill. Dean Martin, Geraldine Page, Yvette Mimieux, Wendy Hiller, Gene Tierney, Larry Gates, Nan Martin. Timid adaptation (by James Poe) of Lillian Hellman play about man returning home to New Orleans with childlike bride; Page and Hiller are Martin's overprotective sisters. Panavision. ▼❶

Toy Soldiers (1984) **C-91m. **** D: David Fisher. Jason Miller, Cleavon Little, Rodolfo De Anda, Terri Garber, Tracy Scoggins, Willard Pugh, Mary Beth Evans, Tim Robbins. Fast-paced but forgettable adventure has a plot resembling HIGH RISK (which also starred Little): Miller and Little help kids rescue their young friends from captivity in rebellion-torn Latin American nation. [R] ▼❶

Toy Soldiers (1991) **C-112m. **½** D: Daniel Petrie, Jr. Sean Astin, Wil Wheaton, Keith Coogan, Andrew Divoff, Louis Gossett, Jr., Denholm Elliott, T. E. Russell, George Perez, Mason Adams, R. Lee Ermey, Tracy Brooks Swope. Prep school populated by wealthy misfit kids is taken over by Colombian terrorists—who haven't counted on the youngsters' ingenuity or determination. Mindless movie takes a seemingly idiotic premise and makes it entertaining, with likable kids and Gibraltar-like Gossett as their father-figure dean. Jerry Orbach appears unbilled. [R] ▼❶●

Toy Story (1995) **C-80m. **** D: John Lasseter. Voices of Tom Hanks, Don Rickles, Jim Varney, Wallace Shawn, John Ratzenberger, Annie Potts, John Morris, Erik Von Detten, Laurie Metcalf, R. Lee Ermey. A boy's favorite toy, a cowboy doll named Woody, feels threatened (and rightly so) by the arrival of a new birthday present, a high-tech spaceman model advertised on TV. Clever, incredible-looking animated film, produced entirely on computer. A grownup story masquerading as a kid's film, this story of friendship, fickleness, and the need for acceptance features a colorful cast of characters led by Woody and his rival, Buzz Lightyear. The "acting" of the two leads—their facial expressions and body language—is as good as anything ever seen in a conventional animated cartoon. Presented by Disney, but produced by the innovative Pixar studio. Director Lasseter received a special Oscar for this animation milestone. Followed by two sequels. Converted to 3-D in 2009 for reissue. [G] ▼❶●

Toy Story 2 (1999) **C-92m. ***½** D: John Lasseter. Voices of Tom Hanks, Tim Allen, Joan Cusack, Kelsey Grammer, Don Rickles, Jim Varney, Wallace Shawn, John Ratzenberger, Annie Potts, Wayne Knight, John Morris, Laurie Metcalf, Estelle Harris, R. Lee Ermey, Jodi Benson. One of the few sequels to live up to—and top—the original: a clever and engaging tale of cowboy doll Woody falling into the hands of a sleazy toy dealer. Shows the relationship of toys and their owners in a canny but heartwarming way, with great gags, a heart-rending song, "When She Loved Me" by Randy Newman (sung by Sarah MacLachlan), and spectacular staging by the computer-animation folks at Pixar. Followed by a Buzz Lightyear TV series and video feature. Converted to 3-D in 2009 for reissue. [G] ▼❶

Toy Story 3 (2010) **C-103m. ***½** D: Lee Unkrich. Voices of Tom Hanks, Tim Allen, Joan Cusack, Ned Beatty, Don Rickles, Michael Keaton, Wallace Shawn, John Ratzenberger, Estelle Harris, Jodi Benson, Emily Hahn, Laurie Metcalf, Timothy Dalton, Kristen Schaal, Jeff Garlin, Bonnie Hunt, Whoopi Goldberg, R. Lee Ermey, Richard Kind, John Morris. Third time is still the charm for Woody, Buzz Lightyear, Jessie, and company, who all find a new home at a day-care center when their owner, Andy, prepares to go off to college. Things are going great for the toys, but things are not as ideal as they seem at first. Irresistible blend of Pixar's technical virtuosity, lovable characters, great gags, and a story that deals emotionally (and convincingly) with loss and growing up. Screenplay by Michael Arndt from a story by John Lasseter, Andrew Stanton, and director Unkrich. Oscars for Best Animated Feature and Randy Newman's song "We Belong Together." 3-D. [G] ❶

Traces of Red (1992) **C-105m. *½** D: Andy Wolk. James Belushi, Lorraine Bracco, Tony Goldwyn, William Russ, Michelle Joyner, Joe Lisi. Tawdry/silly West Palm Beach melodrama with so many suspects that its red herring line has been expanded to include blush, burgundy, and mauve. Belushi and Goldwyn are cops all but tripping over the female corpses, with Bracco a rich widow in an array of unflattering fashions. Narrated by Belushi's corpse à la SUNSET BLVD., but sorely missing anything resembling Billy Wilder's touch. [R] ▼❶

Trackdown (1976) **C-98m. **½** D: Richard T. Heffron. Jim Mitchum, Karen Lamm, Anne Archer, Erik Estrada, Cathy Lee Crosby, Vince Cannon. Montana rancher Mitchum comes to L.A. in search of his runaway sister, who's fallen into seamy street life. Not much depth but lots of action. [R]

Track of the Cat (1954) **C-102m. **** D: William Wellman. Robert Mitchum, Teresa Wright, Tab Hunter, Diana Lynn, Beulah Bondi, Philip Tonge, William Hopper, Carl ("Alfalfa") Switzer. Tennessee Williams meets American Gothic in this unusually harsh drama about a household filled with bitterness, regret, and envy, and how the hunt for a killer cougar changes the dynamics of the family. A. I. Bezzerides adapted the story by Walter Van Tilburg Clark; William Clothier's "colorless" palette and daring camera angles are the film's strongest assets. ▼❶

Track of the Vampire SEE: **Blood Bath**
Tracks (1976) **C-90m.** *½ D: Henry Jaglom.
Dennis Hopper, Taryn Power, Dean Stockwell, Topo Swope, Michael Emil, Zack Norman. Hopper escorts dead Vietnam buddy
across the country by train, eventually goes
bonkers. We've seen it before and almost
always in less muddled fashion. Emil's and
Norman's characters later got their own feature, SITTING DUCKS.▼●]
Track 29 (1988-British) **C-90m.** *½ D: Nicolas Roeg. Theresa Russell, Gary Oldman,
Christopher Lloyd, Colleen Camp, Sandra
Bernhard, Seymour Cassel, Leon Rippy,
Vance Colvig. Bizarre black comedy about
a love-starved woman, her nerdy husband
who's obsessed with model trains, and a
stranger who claims to be her long lost son!
Even allowing for the usual eccentricities of
director Roeg and writer Dennis Potter, this
is pretty weird and not terribly entertaining.
Filmed in North Carolina. [R]▼
Trade (2007-U.S.-German) **C-120m.** ** D:
Marco Kreuzpaintner. Kevin Kline, Alicia
Bachleda, Paulina Gaitan, Kathleen Gati,
Pasha D. Lychnikoff, Anthony Crivello,
Linda Emond, Zack Ward, Cesar Ramos,
Marco Pérez, Tim Reid. A 13-year-old girl
is abducted by members of a sex-trafficking
ring. As her older brother follows her trail,
he hooks up with a Texas cop (Kline) who
has his own reasons for investigating this
outfit. Downbeat drama exposes a shocking,
shameful situation, but it's maddeningly
uneven, one minute bold and powerful (especially with Polish actress Bachleda) and
the next incredibly banal. Based on a *New
York Times* article. Super 35. [R]]
Trader Horn (1931) **120m.** *** D: W. S.
Van Dyke II. Harry Carey, Edwina Booth,
Duncan Renaldo, Olive Golden (Carey),
Mutia Omoolu, C. Aubrey Smith. Early
talkie classic filmed largely in African jungles still retains plenty of excitement in tale
of veteran native dealer Carey encountering
tribal hostility. Remade in 1973.▼
Trader Horn (1973) **C-105m.** *½ D: Reza
S. Badiyi. Rod Taylor, Anne Heywood,
Jean Sorel, Don Knight, Ed Bernard, Stack
Pierce. Laughable remake of 1931 version
has Taylor famed explorer and trader of
African interior, accompanied by young
widow. Obvious use of stock footage and
the fact that cast never leaves backlot ruin
all notion of believability. [PG]
Trading Hearts (1988) **C-88m.** *½ D:
Neil Leifer. Raul Julia, Beverly D'Angelo,
Jenny Lewis, Parris Buckner. Poor baseball
romance in which precocious 11-year-old
Lewis tries to manipulate her mother
(D'Angelo), a show-biz failure, into marriage
with broken-down ballplayer Julia. Look for
former N.Y.C. mayor Ed Koch in a bit as a
Florida tourist; scripted by Frank DeFord,
who can be seen as a bartender. [PG]▼●
Trading Mom (1994) **C-82m.** *½ D: Tia

Brelis. Sissy Spacek, Anna Chlumsky,
Aaron Michael Metchik, Asher Metchik,
Maureen Stapleton, Merritt Yohnka, Andre
the Giant. Three siblings who can't stand
their mother (Spacek) cast a spell which
makes her—and all memory of her—
disappear, then go to the Mommy Market to
find a replacement mom. A flat and lifeless
tale with poor production values. Spacek has
a field day as three wildly different moms,
but a couple of humiliation scenes made us
wince. Brelis adapted the screenplay, based
on her mother's story "The Mummy Market." Filmed in 1992. [PG]▼●]
Trading Places (1983) **C-116m.** **½ D:
John Landis. Dan Aykroyd, Eddie Murphy,
Ralph Bellamy, Don Ameche, Denholm
Elliott, Jamie Lee Curtis, Paul Gleason,
Kristin Holby, Jim Belushi, Alfred Drake,
Al Franken, Tom Davis, Bill Cobbs. Fine
cast breathes life into time-worn comedy
premise (remember those Three Stooges
shorts?) testing heredity vs. environment
by switching a "have" (preppie Aykroyd)
and a "have-not" (street hustler Murphy).
Murphy, in his second film, is a comic pow-
erhouse, and makes up for director Landis'
indulgences—like a subplot involving a
horny gorilla. [R]▼●]
Traffic (1971-French) **C-89m.** ** D:
Jacques Tati. Jacques Tati, Maria Kimberly,
Marcel Fraval, H. Bostel, Tony Kneppers.
Initially enjoyable outing with M. Hulot
(Tati) trying to transport car from France to
Dutch auto show bogs down in aimless side
trips. Bright spots overwhelmed by general
lethargy. [PG]▼]
Traffic (2000) **C-147m.** *** D: Steven
Soderbergh. Michael Douglas, Catherine
Zeta-Jones, Benicio Del Toro, Don Cheadle,
Luis Guzman, Dennis Quaid, Steven Bauer,
Tomas Milian, Erika Christensen, Miguel
Ferrer, Albert Finney, Topher Grace, Benja-
min Bratt, Amy Irving, James Brolin, Clifton
Collins, Jr., D. W. Moffett, Peter Riegert,
Jacob Vargas, Rena Sofer, Viola Davis, John
Slattery. Absorbing look at U.S./Mexico drug
scene from several points of view: battle-
hardened cops on both sides of the border, the
unsuspecting wife of a wealthy drug lord, dis-
affected teenagers who seek escape, and the
man who's just been named America's drug
czar, who refuses to acknowledge the prob-
lem within his own family. Soderbergh also
photographed, under a pseudonym. Salma
Hayek appears unbilled. Loosely based on
a British TV miniseries. Oscar winner for
Best Director, Supporting Actor (Del Toro),
Adapted Screenplay (Stephen Gaghan), and
Film Editing (Stephen Mirrione). [R]▼]
Tragedy of a Ridiculous Man (1981-Italian)
C-116m. ** D: Bernardo Bertolucci. Ugo
Tognazzi, Anouk Aimée, Laura Morante,
Victor Cavallo, Ricardo Tognazzi. Disap-
pointing drama about cheese manufacturer
Tognazzi coping with son's alleged kid-

napping by political terrorists. Bertolucci seems to be commenting on modern social and familial stresses and upheavals, but his message is incredibly muddled. [PG]▼

Tragedy of Othello: The Moor of Venice, The SEE: **Othello** (1952)

Trail of the Lonesome Pine, The (1936) **C-99m.** *** D: Henry Hathaway. Sylvia Sidney, Henry Fonda, Fred MacMurray, Fred Stone, Fuzzy Knight, Beulah Bondi, Spanky McFarland, Nigel Bruce. Classic story of feuding families and changes that come about when railroad is built on their land. Still strong today, with fine performances, and Fuzzy Knight's rendition of "Melody from the Sky." First outdoor film in full Technicolor. Previously filmed in 1915.▼

Trail of the Pink Panther (1982) **C-97m.** ** D: Blake Edwards. Peter Sellers, David Niven, Herbert Lom, Richard Mulligan, Joanna Lumley, Capucine, Robert Loggia, Harvey Korman, Burt Kwouk, Graham Stark, Peter Arne. Attempt to fashion a new Pink Panther film, despite the death of series star Sellers, using previously unseen footage and new linking material. It almost works—until the seams begin to show, as reporter Lumley seeks out people who knew Clouseau for a TV story. Lom *does* have a sidesplitting scene in which he tries to eulogize his long-time nemesis—and can't stop laughing. Filmed at the same time as subsequent CURSE OF THE PINK PANTHER. Panavision. [PG]▼●◗

Train, The (1964) **133m.** **** D: John Frankenheimer. Burt Lancaster, Paul Scofield, Jeanne Moreau, Michel Simon, Suzanne Flon, Wolfgang Preiss, Albert Remy. Gripping WW2 actioner of French Resistance trying to waylay train carting French art treasures to Germany. High-powered excitement all the way.▼●◗

Training Day (2001) **C-120m.** ** D: Antoine Fuqua. Denzel Washington, Ethan Hawke, Scott Glenn, Tom Berenger, Harris Yulin, Raymond J. Barry, Cliff Curtis, Dr. Dre, Snoop Dogg, Macy Gray, Eva Mendes, Nick Chinlund. Rookie cop (Hawke) is partnered with a corrupt veteran narcotics detective (Washington) and learns more than he ever wanted to know about the mean streets of L.A. Starts off strongly, then gets dumber and dumber, abandoning credibility for melodrama, coincidences, and a cartoonlike climax. Redeemed partially by Washington's magnetic, Oscar-winning performance. Clairmont-Scope. [R]▼●◗

Train of Life (1998-French-Belgian-Dutch) **C-103m.** *** D: Radu Mihaileanu. Lionel Abelanski, Rufus, Clement Harari, Marie-Jose Nat, Agathe de la Fontaine. Energetic fable set in 1941, in which the inhabitants of a small Central European Jewish village, all too aware of their imminent demise, plot to foil the Nazis by staging their own deportation to Russia. Comedic and dramatic elements occasionally clash, and some of the subplots are inconsequential, but it still works. Released in the U.S. after LIFE IS BEAUTIFUL and JAKOB THE LIAR, but this was actually the first to go into production. Widescreen. [R]▼

Train Robbers, The (1973) **C-92m.** **½ D: Burt Kennedy. John Wayne, Ann-Margret, Rod Taylor, Ben Johnson, Christopher George, Ricardo Montalban, Bobby Vinton, Jerry Gatlin. Interesting little chamber-Western, reminiscent of Kennedy's early Randolph Scott scripts. Outlaw's widow hires Wayne and his pals to locate buried gold so she can return it and clear family name. Low-key film emphasizes character instead of action; relaxed performances, twist ending. Panavision. [PG] ▼●◗

Trainspotting (1996-British) **C-94m.** *** D: Danny Boyle. Ewan McGregor, Ewen Bremner, Jonny Lee Miller, Kevin McKidd, Robert Carlyle, Kelly Macdonald. Fascinating look at the drug underground in Edinburgh, Scotland, as seen through the eyes of McGregor, who's part of that world but still somehow able to distance himself from his friends' bizarre behavior. Alternately hilarious and harrowing, with some startling surrealistic moments, this was an enormous hit in the U.K. but suffered some backlash in the U.S. for its supposed condoning of drugs—which is simply not true. Adapted by John Hodge from Irvine Welsh's novel. [R]▼●◗

Traitor (2008) **C-114m.** **½ D: Jeffrey Nachmanoff. Don Cheadle, Guy Pearce, Neal McDonough, Saïd Taghmaoui, Jeff Daniels, Alyy Khan, Archie Panjabi, Lorena Gale. Is he or is he not a traitor to his country? Witnessing a life-altering terrorist act in his youth makes Cheadle prime turncoat material and the FBI continuously dogs his tail in an effort to find out. Straightforward espionage drama attempts to seriously explore religious fervor as it applies to acts of terrorism and suicide bombers. Documentary style makes it intelligent and realistic but not terrifically entertaining. Nachmanoff's screenplay is based on a story he cowrote with Steve Martin. Super 35. [PG-13]◗

Tramplers, The (1966-Italian) **C-105m.** ** D: Albert Band. Joseph Cotten, Gordon Scott, James Mitchum, Ilaria Occhini, Franco Nero. Foreign-made Western set in post–Civil War South, with Cotten the domineering father; all just an excuse for gunplay. Aka SHOWDOWN.▼

Trancers (1985) **C-76m.** *** D: Charles Band. Tim Thomerson, Helen Hunt, Art La Fleur, Biff Manard, Anne Seymour, Richard Herd, Richard Erdman. Comedian Thomerson is cleverly cast as a low-budget version of Harrison Ford from BLADE

RUNNER, sent back in time 300 years to 1985 L. A. to inhabit the body of one of his ancestors and change history to prevent a totalitarian state from coming into power. Sci-fi satire is most amusing and visually arresting. Also known as FUTURE COP (1985). Followed by a slew of sequels. [PG-13] ▼●]

Trancers II (1991) **C-86m.** ** D: Charles Band. Tim Thomerson, Helen Hunt, Megan Ward, Biff Manard, Richard Lynch, Martine Beswicke, Jeffrey Combs, Alyson Croft, Telma Hopkins, Art La Fleur, Barbara Crampton. A cop from the future whose mind wound up in our time in the first film finds that his job isn't through as more zombie-like Trancers are on the loose. What's more, he has to contend with two wives, one from the present, one from the future. Badly structured, but scrupulously faithful to a superior original. Too cheap for its ambitions. [R]▼●]

Trancers III (1992) **C-83m.** ** D: C. Courtney Joyner. Tim Thomerson, Melanie Smith, Andrew Robinson, Tony Pierce, Dawn Ann Billings, Helen Hunt, Megan Ward, Stephen Macht, Telma Hopkins, R. A. Mahailoff. Time travel gets a workout here: taken from 1992 to 2352, Jack Deth (Thomerson) is then sent to 2005 to destroy those pesky (and obscurely defined) Trancers at their source. The series continues to be watchable, and Robinson provides a swell villain, but the end is a mess. [R]▼●]

Transamerica (2005) **C-103m.** *** D: Duncan Tucker. Felicity Huffman, Kevin Zegers, Fionnula Flanagan, Elizabeth Peña, Graham Greene, Burt Young, Carrie Preston. A transsexual on the verge of having final surgery to become a woman learns she has a teenage son—in a N.Y.C. jail. Without revealing her identity she bails out the young hustler, and the ultimate odd couple (she is a fussbudget, he is a disaffected kid who hides his emotions) embarks on a cross-country trip. Comedy-drama of consciousness-raising and forgiveness becomes a somewhat conventional road movie but is elevated by Huffman's astonishing, nuanced performance as Bree. Debut feature for writer-director Tucker. [R]●

Transformers, The (1986) **C-86m.** BOMB D: Nelson Shin. Voices of Orson Welles, Robert Stack, Leonard Nimoy, Eric Idle, Judd Nelson, Lionel Stander. Obnoxious animated feature about the title good guys, who defend the universe against an evil planet (which has a voice of its own . . . provided by Orson Welles). Deafening rock score doesn't help. Kid-oriented, toy-centric film served as a link between seasons of the animated TV series. The characters were later reinvented for the 2007 live-action movie. [PG]▼●]

Transformers (2007) **C-143m.** **½ D: Michael Bay. Shia LaBeouf, Megan Fox, Josh Duhamel, Tyrese Gibson, Rachael Taylor, Anthony Anderson, Jon Voight, John Turturro, Michael O'Neill, Kevin Dunn, Julie White, Bernie Mac; voices of Mark Ryan, Peter Cullen, Hugo Weaving, Robert Foxworth. After buying a beat-up used car that turns into an Autobot, a nerdy teen (LaBeouf) finds himself at the center of an epic battle to save Earth from transforming alien robots—and manages to win the hottest babe in school to boot. Slam-bang actioner based on the popular series of toys is surprisingly well done for a summer blockbuster—by Michael Bay, no less—with dazzling special effects, though by the time the big climactic battle comes along we just don't care anymore. Supposed 11th-grader Fox looks more like a candidate for the Pussycat Dolls. Followed by a sequel. Panavision. [PG-13]●

Transformers: Revenge of the Fallen (2009) **C-149m.** ** D: Michael Bay. Shia LaBeouf, Megan Fox, Josh Duhamel, Tyrese Gibson, John Turturro, Ramon Rodriguez, Kevin Dunn, Rainn Wilson, Julie White, Isabel Lucas, John Benjamin Hickey, Deep Roy; voices of Hugo Weaving, John Turturro, Peter Cullen, Robert Foxworth, Michael York. LaBeouf heads off to college—apparently, he's enrolled at Hottie University—only to discover that the Transformers aren't out of his life. Power-mad Decepticons are multiplying at an alarming rate and out to destroy the planet. It's up to LaBeouf to save the Transformers . . . and Mother Earth. Bigger, louder, and longer than the first film, this swaps size and volume for a sense of fun. Packed with action, visual effects, and leering shots of foxy Fox. Panavision. [PG-13]●

Transmutations SEE: Underworld (1985)

Transporter, The (2002-French) **C-92m.** **½ D: Cory Yuen. Jason Statham, Shu Qi, François Berléand, Matt Schulze, Ric Young. Serviceable action yarn with calm, cool Statham (in his starring debut) as a driver-for-hire who'll take anything anywhere, so long as it's on his terms. When he discovers that the "package" in his trunk is a young Asian woman, he breaks his own code and frees her, involving himself in a fierce underworld brouhaha. Some terrific chase scenes staged by Hong Kong veteran Yuen (including a finale involving trucks) highlight this no-brainer. Coproduced and cowritten by Luc Besson. Followed by two sequels. Super 35. [PG-13]▼●

Transporter 2 (2005-French) **C-87m.** ** D: Louis Leterrier. Jason Statham, Alessandro Gassman, Amber Valletta, Kate Nauta, Matthew Modine, Jason Flemyng, Keith David, Hunter Clary, François Berléand. Shiny sequel about a "chauffeur" who downshifts, improvises, and kickboxes his way through Miami to rescue a little kid whose abduction sparks a more sinister plot. Bullet-headed thriller often soars with its Audis and Uzis into the half-past ludicrous, breaking speed limits and bones in spiffy action scenes by Hong Kong vet Cory Yuen (who directed the first entry). But as the bad guy dutifully reminds us, "Wit is not a requirement of the job." Coproduced and cowritten by Luc Besson. Followed by a sequel. Super 35. [PG-13]🄳

Transporter 3 (2008-French) **C-104m.** ** D: Olivier Megaton. Jason Statham, Natalya Rudakova, François Berléand, Robert Knepper, Jeroen Krabbé, Alex Kobold, David Atrakchi, Yann Sundberg. Gassed up on adrenaline, and with a bracelet bomb for cruise control, dapper driver Frank Martin delivers another package . . . this time, the abducted daughter of a beleaguered pro-environment Ukrainian statesman. Slickly lubed slot car race across Europe offers breath-holding stunt work beyond the impossible, once again staged by Cory Yuen, but this underplotted slugfest is running on fumes. Cowritten by producer Luc Besson. Super 35. [PG-13]🄳

Transsiberian (2008-Spanish-British-German-Lithuanian) **C-106m.** **½ D: Brad Anderson. Woody Harrelson, Emily Mortimer, Ben Kingsley, Kate Mara, Eduardo Noriega, Thomas Kretschmann. Mortimer (typically solid) and husband Harrelson have completed a humanitarian mission in China when they board the Trans-Siberian Express for the long train journey to Moscow. Among the backpackers and shady characters they befriend a bohemian couple (Noriega, Mara) who lead them astray in more ways than one. Stark landscapes and brutal surprises await. Uneven action-melodrama has its moments and gets a boost from Kingsley's colorful performance as a Russian cop. Super 35. [R]🄳

Transylvania 6-5000 (1985) **C-94m.** BOMB D: Rudy DeLuca. Jeff Goldblum, Joseph Bologna, Ed Begley, Jr., Carol Kane, Jeffrey Jones, John Byner, Geena Davis, Michael Richards, Norman Fell, Teresa Ganzel. Tediously unfunny horror-movie spoof that wastes a lot of talent. Shot in Yugoslavia, and should have stayed there. [PG]▼●🄳

Trap, The (1959) **C-84m.** **½ D: Norman Panama. Richard Widmark, Lee J. Cobb, Tina Louise, Earl Holliman, Carl Benton Reid, Lorne Greene. Turgid drama set in Southwest desert town, with gangsters on the lam intimidating the few townspeople.▼

Trap, The (1966-British) **C-106m.** *** D: Sidney Hayers. Rita Tushingham, Oliver Reed, Rex Sevenoaks, Barbara Chilcott, Linda Goranson. Fur trapper Reed, having missed annual wife auction after three winters in the snow, settles for orphaned mute Rita. Vivid 1890s tale, well photographed by Robert Krasker. Panavision.▼

Trapeze (1956) **C-105m.** *** D: Carol Reed. Burt Lancaster, Tony Curtis, Gina Lollobrigida, Katy Jurado, Thomas Gomez, Johnny Puleo. Moody love triangle with a European circus background; aerialists Lancaster and Curtis vie in the air and on the ground for Gina's attention. Nice aerial stunt-work by various big top professionals. CinemaScope.▼●🄳

Trapped (2002) **C-105m.** ** D: Luis Mandoki. Charlize Theron, Courtney Love, Stuart Townsend, Kevin Bacon, Pruitt Taylor Vince, Dakota Fanning, Colleen Camp. A perfect couple and their asthmatic daughter are terrorized by sleazy kidnappers: Theron is held by Bacon at home while Townsend is locked in his convention hotel room by Love. Unconvincing thriller confuses manipulation with drama. [R]▼▼

Trapped Ashes (2006-U.S.-Japanese-Canadian) **C-104m.** ** D: Sean S. Cunningham, Joe Dante, John Gaeta, Monte Hellman, Ken Russell. Jayce Bartok, Amelia Cooke, Lara Harris, Scott Lowell, Luke MacFarlane, Michèle-Barbara Pelletier, Tahmoh Penikett, Rachel Veltri, John Saxon, Henry Gibson, Dick Miller. A haunted house set on a studio tour mysteriously ensnares a motley group of visitors, who tell tales of personal terror to pass the time until they're released. Old-school horror anthology of four bookended vignettes is an affectionate (if highly grisly) homage to EC Comics and Amicus Studios, but its time has passed. Creepiest sight is helmer Russell in ghastly drag. [R]🄳

Trapped in Paradise (1994) **C-112m.** ** D: George Gallo. Nicolas Cage, Jon Lovitz, Dana Carvey, John Ashton, Mädchen Amick, Donald Moffat, Richard Jenkins, Florence Stanley, Angela Paton, Vic Manni, Frank Pesce, Sean McCann, Richard B. Shull. Two larcenous siblings just sprung from jail trick their ambivalent brother into joining them on a trip to the small town of Paradise, Pennsylvania, where there's a bank just waiting to be robbed. Trouble is, the townspeople are so darned nice it seems wrong to take advantage of them . . . especially at Christmastime. Promising idea is flattened out by vaguely drawn characters and a lack of energy. Panavision. [PG-13]▼●🄳

Trauma (1993-U.S.-Italian) **C-86m.** **½ D: Dario Argento. Christopher Rydell, Asia Argento, Laura Johnson, James Russo, Brad Dourif, Frederic Forrest, Piper Laurie. Corny theatrics and campy bloodletting effectively blend in this shocker about a traumatized teen (Asia Argento, the director's daughter) and a hooded killer who is sawing off the heads of his victims. Not a typical Argento gorefest, but the filmmaker's fans shouldn't be disappointed. Unrated video version runs 106m. Technovision. [R]▼●🄳

Traveling Executioner, The (1970) **C-95m.** *½ D: Jack Smight. Stacy Keach, Marianna Hill, Bud Cort, Graham Jarvis, James J. Sloyan. Story of a man's love for an electric chair (spiritual) and love for a woman prisoner (sexual) may or may not be intended for laughs; either way, film is dull and the usually fine Keach gives hammy performance. Panavision. [R]

Traveller (1997) **C-101m.** **½ D: Jack N. Green. Bill Paxton, Mark Wahlberg, Julianna Margulies, James Gammon, Luke Askew, Nikki Deloach, Danielle Wiener, Michael Shaner, Jo Ann Pflug. Laid-back look at a band of Irish-American gypsy con artists known as "travellers." Paxton takes on the son of an ousted "family" member as his protégé, teaching him various petty scams, and finds himself falling for one of his marks, bartender Margulies. Amiable and well acted, though it doesn't really add up to much. Paxton also coproduced. Directing debut for Clint Eastwood's longtime cinematographer Green. [R]▼●)

Travelling North (1987-Australian) **C-98m.** **½ D: Carl Schultz. Leo McKern, Julia Blake, Henri Szeps, Graham Kennedy, Michele Fawdon, Diane Craig. Irascible retiree falls in love with a divorcee, and they move to an idyllic retirement home in North Queensland, Australia . . . but their life together is clouded almost immediately when he learns he has a serious heart condition. Fine performances highlight this simple, straightforward adaptation of David Williamson's play—which, ultimately, may be a bit *too* simple and straightforward. [PG-13]▼

Travels With Anita SEE: **Lovers and Liars**

Travels With My Aunt (1972) **C-109m.** **½ D: George Cukor. Maggie Smith, Alec McCowen, Lou Gossett, Robert Stephens, Cindy Williams. Stylish adaptation of Graham Greene book about straitlaced McCowen being swept into crazy world of his aunt (Smith) who takes him all over Europe on what turns out to be shady scheme. Deliberately paced film never really gets going, leaves viewer in midair like final tossed coin. Anthony Powell earned an Oscar for his costumes. Panavision. [PG]▼●

T. R. Baskin (1971) **C-90m.** **½ D: Herbert Ross. Candice Bergen, Peter Boyle, James Caan, Marcia Rodd, Erin O'Reilly, Howard Platt. Beautiful young small-town girl tries to make it in Chicago, finds problems in the big city. Wildly uneven comedy-drama has a few nice scenes, good acting by Caan in small role. Written and produced by Peter Hyams. [PG]

Treasure Island (1934) **105m.** ***½ D: Victor Fleming. Wallace Beery, Jackie Cooper, Lewis Stone, Lionel Barrymore, Otto Kruger, Nigel Bruce, Douglass Dumbrille. Stirring adaptation of Robert Louis Stevenson pirate yarn of 18th-century England and journey to isle of hidden bounty; Beery is a boisterous Long John Silver in fine film with top production values. Only flaw is a stiff Cooper as Jim Hawkins. Also shown in computer-colored version.▼)

Treasure Island (1950) **C-96m.** ***½ D: Byron Haskin. Bobby Driscoll, Robert Newton, Basil Sydney, Walter Fitzgerald, Denis O'Dea, Ralph Truman, Finlay Currie. Vivid Disney version of Robert Louis Stevenson's classic, filmed in England, with Driscoll a fine Jim Hawkins and Newton *the* definitive Long John Silver. Changes the novel's original ending, but who's quibbling? ▼●)

Treasure Island (1972-British) **C-94m.** ** D: John Hough. Orson Welles, Kim Burfield, Walter Slezak, Lionel Stander. Weak retelling of classic tale finds very hammy Welles (who also coscripted) in the role of Long John Silver. [G]▼)

Treasure of Jamaica Reef, The (1974) **C-96m.** *½ D: Virginia Stone. Stephen Boyd, Chuck Woolery, David Ladd, Cheryl Stoppelmoor (Ladd). A search for gold buried deep in the Caribbean. Of interest only for the presence of Stoppelmoor/Ladd pre-*Charlie's Angels*. Originally titled EVIL IN THE DEEP. Todd-AO 35. [PG]▼)

Treasure of Matecumbe (1976) **C-117m.** **½ D: Vincent McEveety. Robert Foxworth, Joan Hackett, Peter Ustinov, Vic Morrow, Jane Wyatt, Johnny Doran, Billy "Pop" Attmore. Two boys with treasure map are aided in their quest by Foxworth, Hackett, and Ustinov . . . and pursued by bad-guy Morrow. Ustinov adds life to Disney film, but the "quest" seems endless. Filmed in the Florida Keys. [G]▼)

Treasure of San Gennaro, The (1966-Italian-German-French) **C-102m.** ** D: Dino Risi. Nino Manfredi, Senta Berger, Harry Guardino, Claudine Auger, Totò, Mario Adorf. American Guardino and girlfriend Berger plan to rob the treasure of Naples' patron saint, San Gennaro, in typical caper film occasionally redeemed by good comic bits. Poorly dubbed. Filmed in Panoramica.

Treasure of the Amazon, The (1985-Mexican) **C-104m.** ** D: Rene Cardona, Jr. Stuart Whitman, Emilio Fernandez, Donald Pleasence, Bradford Dillman, Ann Sidney, John Ireland, Sonia Infante. Silly adventure film has Whitman leading South American expedition to recover treasure trove of diamonds. Mucho violence. ▼)

Treasure of the Sierra Madre, The (1948) **124m.** **** D: John Huston. Humphrey Bogart, Walter Huston, Tim Holt, Bruce Bennett, Barton MacLane, Alfonso Bedoya. Excellent adaptation of B. Traven's tale of gold, greed, and human nature at its worst, with Bogart, Huston, and Holt as unlikely trio of prospectors. John Huston won Oscars for Best Direction and Screenplay, and his father Walter won as Best Supporting Actor. That's John as an American tourist near the beginning, and young Robert Blake selling lottery tickets. Also shown in computer-colored version. ▼●)

Treasure Planet (2002) **C-95m.** ****½** D: John Musker, Ron Clements. Voices of Joseph Gordon-Levitt, Brian Murray, David Hyde Pierce, Emma Thompson, Michael Wincott, Martin Short, Laurie Metcalf, Patrick McGoohan, Roscoe Lee Browne, Corey Burton. Entertaining, if uninspired (and somewhat cluttered) Disney cartoon version of *Treasure Island* in a futuristic, sci-fi setting. Jim Hawkins finds the map that leads to a distant planet where pirates hid a king's ransom, but soon learns that many people are after that treasure, including his shipmate John Silver. It's fun listening to Pierce, as an adventure-starved astrophysicist, Thompson, as a very British ship captain, and Short, as a screw-loose robot. [PG] ▼▼

Tree Grows in Brooklyn, A (1945) **128m.** ******** D: Elia Kazan. Dorothy McGuire, Joan Blondell, James Dunn, Lloyd Nolan, Peggy Ann Garner, Ted Donaldson, James Gleason, Ruth Nelson, John Alexander. Splendid, sensitive film from Betty Smith's novel about a bright young girl trying to rise above the hardships of her tenement life in turn-of-the-20th-century Brooklyn, New York. Perfect in every detail. Dunn won an Oscar as the father, an incurable pipe dreamer; Garner received a special Academy Award for her performance. Screenplay by Tess Slesinger and Frank Davis. An impressive Hollywood directorial debut by Kazan. Remade for TV in 1974 with Cliff Robertson and Diane Baker. ▼●)

Tree of Hands SEE: **Innocent Victim**

Tree of Life, The (2011) **C-138m.** ****½** D: Terrence Malick. Brad Pitt, Sean Penn, Jessica Chastain, Fiona Shaw, Irene Bedard, Jessica Fuselier, Hunter McCracken, Laramie Eppler, Tye Sheridan. A poetic meditation on the creation and continuum of life and man's place in it, focusing on a boy's upbringing in rural Texas in the 1950s. We follow him from infancy onward, as he experiences the pain, pleasure, and adventuresome curiosity of youth, while having to deal with a stern, unpredictable father (Pitt). Dotted with beautiful passages about childhood and a mother's unconditional love, but the fleeting shots of a meditative Penn, as the boy grown up, are elliptical and disconnected . . . and the shots of Earth's creation and evolution don't seem to jell with the rest of the picture. Deeply felt by writer-director Malick, but he withholds more than he shares with us in the audience. Exquisitely photographed by Emmanuel Lubezki. [PG-13]

Tree of Wooden Clogs, The (1978-Italian) **C-185m.** ******** D: Ermanno Olmi. Luigi Ornaghi, Francesca Moriggi, Omar Brignoli, Antonio Ferrari. A year in the life of a community of peasants in Northern Italy, just before the turn of the century. Simple, quietly beautiful epic; a work of art. ▼●)

Trees Lounge (1996) **C-94m.** ******* D: Steve Buscemi. Steve Buscemi, Mark Boone Junior, Chloë Sevigny, Michael Buscemi, Anthony LaPaglia, Elizabeth Bracco, Danny Baldwin, Carol Kane, Bronson Dudley, Debi Mazar, Michael Imperioli, Samuel L. Jackson, Seymour Cassel, Mimi Rogers, Steve Randazzo, Rockets Redglare. Colorful, credible slice-of-life set in and around a neighborhood bar in Long Island, N.Y., where a perpetual screw-up (Buscemi) interacts with various family members and fellow barflies. Impressive writing and directing debut for character actor Buscemi, who has a good eye and ear and creates a rich gallery of characters. [R] ▼●)

Trekkies (1999) **C-87m.** ******* D: Roger Nygard. Former *Star Trek: The Next Generation* star Denise Crosby conducts this slightly condescending documentary examining the *Trek* fan phenomenon. Many of the actors associated with *Trek* are interviewed, as well as many die-hard Trekkies of varying degrees of obsession. While some are clearly 'round the bend in their fixation on the show, most are shown to be very bright, and live happy, productive lives, even if pointed ears and Klingons figure prominently in them. Followed by a direct-to-video sequel in 2004. [PG] ▼●)

Trembling Before G-d (2001-Israeli-U.S.) **C-84m.** ******* D: Sandi Simcha Dubowski. Illuminating documentary exploring the sometimes difficult lives of ultra-Orthodox and Hasidic Jewish gays and lesbians. Film focuses on a number of people who struggle with both their religious and sexual identity in this cloistered world. Interesting, somewhat controversial, and quite different look at an unfamiliar facet of the Jewish experience. ▼▼

Tremors (1990) **C-96m.** ******* D: Ron Underwood. Kevin Bacon, Fred Ward, Finn Carter, Michael Gross, Reba McEntire, Bobby Jacoby, Charlotte Stewart, Tony Genaros, Victor Wong. Sharp, funny, and fast-paced, this is an effective updating of 1950s monster-movie themes. Bacon and Ward, amiable handymen, lead a misfit group in a desert valley battling against giant wormlike predators that burrow through the sand. Cast is good, the music appropriate, and special effects outstanding. A small winner all around. Followed by several video sequels and a TV series. [PG-13] ▼●)

Trenchcoat (1983) **C-91m.** ****** D: Michael Tuchner. Margot Kidder, Robert Hays, Daniel Faraldo, Gila von Weitershausen, David Suchet, Ronald Lacey. Another attempt by the Disney studio to change image finds amateur mystery writer Kidder on vacation in Malta, suddenly involved in real murder and international intrigue with undercover agent Hays. Forced mystery-comedy is reminiscent of the company's juvenile outings of the '50s and '60s, but has no Shaggy Dog to redeem it. [PG] ▼

Trespass (1992) **C-101m.** *** D: Walter Hill. Bill Paxton, Ice T, William Sadler, Ice Cube, Art Evans, De'Voreaux White, Bruce A. Young, Glenn Plummer, Stoney Jackson, John Toles-Bey. Two white firemen get wind that ancient treasure is buried in a slummy building, little knowing that the structure they've invaded is headquarters for a band of very tough drug pushers. Fast, furious, culturally disreputable entertainment filmed in potent cat-and-mouse style by director Hill—his most entertaining movie in years. Executive produced and written by Bob Gale and Robert Zemeckis. [R] ▼●◐

Triage (2009-Irish-French-Spanish) C-99m. ***½ D: Danis Tanovic. Colin Farrell, Paz Vega, Kelly Reilly, Jamie Sives, Branko Djuric, Juliet Stevenson, Christopher Lee. Two freelance photojournalists and best friends are covering the war in Kurdistan in 1988. One decides to return home to Dublin; after being wounded, the other (Farrell) follows him, but his troubles are just beginning. Shattering account of death and suffering during wartime; Tanovic's screenplay (based on a book by Scott Anderson) also explores the mind-set of individuals who choose to be in war zones, as well as the physical and psychological scars inflicted on war's survivors. Parts of this film just may move you to tears. Released direct to DVD in the U.S. [R] ◐

Trial (1955) **105m.** *** D: Mark Robson. Glenn Ford, Dorothy McGuire, John Hodiak, Arthur Kennedy, Katy Jurado, Rafael Campos. Intelligent filming of Don Mankiewicz novel, scripted by the author. Courtroomer involves Mexican boy accused of murder, but actually tied in with pro- vs. anti-Communist politics.

Trial, The (1962-French-Italian-German) **118m.** ***½ D: Orson Welles. Anthony Perkins, Jeanne Moreau, Romy Schneider, Elsa Martinelli, Orson Welles, Akim Tamiroff. Gripping, if a bit confusing, adaptation of Kafka novel of man in nameless country arrested for crime that is never explained to him. Not for all tastes. ▼●◐

Trial and Error (1962-British) SEE: **Dock Brief, The**

Trial and Error (1997) **C-98m.** *** D: Jonathan Lynn. Michael Richards, Jeff Daniels, Charlize Theron, Rip Torn, Alexandra Wentworth, Austin Pendleton, Lawrence Pressman, Max Casella. When button-down lawyer Daniels can't appear in court (because of a bachelor party hangover), his best friend, wannabe actor Richards, tries to help by taking his place . . . but when the case is ordered to proceed, Richards has to keep up the ruse. Smart, funny farce with terrific performances by the two leads and laugh-out-loud situations; Theron is adorable as the

young woman who catches Daniels' eye—even though he's about to marry the boss' daughter. Super 35. [PG-13] ▼●◐

Trial by Combat SEE: **Dirty Knight's Work**

Trial by Jury (1994) **C-107m.** **½ D: Heywood Gould. Joanne Whalley-Kilmer, Armand Assante, Gabriel Byrne, William Hurt, Kathleen Quinlan, Margaret Whitton, Ed Lauter, Richard Portnow, Lisa Arrindell Anderson, Jack Gwaltney, Graham Jarvis, William R. Moses, Stuart Whitman. Juror Whalley is terrorized by defendant in a murder case; meanwhile, D.A. Byrne tries to size up the jurors who'll be deciding the fate of this mobster. Improbable but still watchable, with an unusual part for Hurt as a strong-arm man. David Cronenberg appears briefly as a director. Similar premise later utilized in THE JUROR. [R] ▼●◐

Trial of Billy Jack, The (1974) **C-175m.** BOMB D: Frank Laughlin. Tom Laughlin, Delores Taylor, Victor Izay, Teresa Laughlin, William Wellman, Jr., Sacheen Littlefeather. Further adventures of Mr. Peace-through-Violence prove that Laughlin is the only actor intense enough to risk a hernia from reading lines. Laughable until final, nauseating massacre scene that renders film's constant yammering about "peace" ludicrous. Panavision. [PG] ▼◐

Trials of Oscar Wilde, The (1960-British) **C-130m.** *** D: Ken Hughes. Peter Finch, Yvonne Mitchell, John Fraser, Lionel Jeffries, Nigel Patrick, James Mason. Fascinating, well-acted chronicle of Oscar Wilde's libel suit against the Marquis of Queensberry and the tragic turn his life takes because of it. Finch is superb as the once brilliant wit; stylish widescreen photography by Ted Moore. Released at the same time as OSCAR WILDE with Robert Morley. Super Technirama 70. ▼

Tribute (1980-Canadian) **C-121m.** ** D: Bob Clark. Jack Lemmon, Robby Benson, Lee Remick, Colleen Dewhurst, John Marley, Kim Cattrall, Gale Garnett. Mawkish adaptation of Bernard Slade's play about a life-of-the-party type who's dying of cancer and wants to work out a relationship with his estranged son. Badly directed, with sledgehammer approach to sentiment. Worked much better on stage (where Lemmon created the role). Scripted by Slade. [PG] ▼●

Tribute to a Bad Man (1956) **C-95m.** *** D: Robert Wise. James Cagney, Don Dubbins, Stephen McNally, Irene Papas, Vic Morrow, Royal Dano, Lee Van Cleef. Cagney is the whole show in this Western about a resourceful, ruthless land baron using any means possible to retain his vast possessions. CinemaScope. ▼

Trick (1999) **C-89m.** **½ D: Jim Fall. Christian Campbell, John Paul Pitoc, Tori Spelling, Steve Hayes, Clinton Leupp, Brad Beyer, Lorri Bagley. Shy, aspiring Broadway composer meets the go-go boy of his dreams one night but can't find any place for them to be alone together in all of Manhattan. Lightweight gay comedy-romance set in N.Y.C.'s West Village is sweet but short on plot. Campbell (brother of Neve) is an appealing, boyish lead. [R]▼❶

Trick Baby (1973) **C-89m.** ** D: Larry Yust. Kiel Martin, Mel Stewart, Dallas Edwards Hayes, Beverly Ballard. Con-man who passes for white uses trickery to cash in on society. Usual black exploitation film. Retitled DOUBLE CON. [R]▼❶

Trick or Treat (1986) **C-97m.** ** D: Charles Martin Smith. Marc Price, Tony Fields, Lisa Orgolini, Doug Savant, Gene Simmons, Ozzy Osbourne. Hey kids, rock 'n' roll really *is* the Devil's music! Fan of recently killed rocker conjures the dead star by playing his unreleased last album backward—but finds his hero is evil and bent on the world's destruction. Clever and well made, but story becomes terribly trite. Debuting director Smith has a cameo as a high school teacher. [R]▼❶

Trick or Treats (1982) **C-91m.** BOMB D: Gary Graver. Jackelyn Giroux, David Carradine, Carrie Snodgress, Steve Railsback, Peter Jason, Paul Bartel. Giroux is too old to be convincing as a terrorized babysitter in this cheap horror spoof. Orson Welles is credited as consultant; Graver is better known as the cameraman Welles relied upon in his later film projects. [R]▼

Trigger Effect, The (1996) **C-98m.** **½ D: David Koepp. Kyle MacLachlan, Elisabeth Shue, Dermot Mulroney, Richard T. Jones, Bill Smitrovich, Michael Rooker. Maddeningly uneven apocalyptic thriller about married suburbanites and their plight in the wake of a gigantic, never-ending blackout. Intended as an examination of contemporary insensitivity and alienation, and how society might unravel in the wake of such a catastrophe, but falls apart after a solid start. The finale is especially incongruous. Feature directorial debut for screenwriter Koepp. [R]▼❶❸

Trigger Happy SEE: **Mad Dog Time**

Trinity Is STILL My Name! (1972-Italian) **C-117m.** **½ D: E. B. Clucher (Enzo Barboni). Terence Hill, Bud Spencer, Harry Carey, Jr., Jessica Dublin, Yanti Somer. Sequel to THEY CALL ME TRINITY is even funnier, as Trinity and Bambino mosey their way through a clutch of archetypal Western situations with their usual aplomb; scene in a chic French restaurant is a hoot. Later cut to 101m.; original Italian running time 124m. Aka ALL THE WAY, TRINITY. Techniscope. [G]▼❶❸

Trinity Rides Again SEE: **Boot Hill**

Trinity: Tracking For Trouble SEE: **Knock Out Cop, The**

Trio (1950-British) **88m.** *** D: Ken Annakin, Harold French. James Hayter, Kathleen Harrison, Anne Crawford, Nigel Patrick,

Jean Simmons, Michael Rennie. Following the success of QUARTET, three more diverting Somerset Maugham stories, "The Verger," "Mr. Know-all," and "Sanatorium." All beautifully acted.▼

Trip, The (1967) **C-85m.** ** D: Roger Corman. Peter Fonda, Susan Strasberg, Bruce Dern, Dennis Hopper, Salli Sachse, Dick Miller, Luana Anders, Michael Nader, Peter Bogdanovich. TV commercial director Fonda takes his first LSD trip. Definitely a relic of its era, with a screenplay by Jack Nicholson.▼❶❸

Trip, The (2011-British) **C-111m.** *** D: Michael Winterbottom. Steve Coogan, Rob Brydon, Claire Keelan, Margo Stilley, Kerry Shale. Comedic actor Coogan is invited to visit some of rural Northern England's top restaurants. He'd planned to travel with his girlfriend, but when she ducks out he's forced to ask his protégé (and friendly rival) Brydon to join him on this road trip instead. The week consists of them needling each other, comparing mimicry skills (check out their dueling Michael Caines), and taking stock of their lives, while downing a series of sumptuous meals. Largely improvised, and building on the one-upsmanship the duo first revealed in TRISTRAM SHANDY, this won't be everyone's cup of chamomile . . . but if you find the two leads amusing there's much to savor. Edited down from a 2010 TV miniseries. Ben Stiller appears unbilled.

Triple Cross (1966-French-British) **C-126m.** ** D: Terence Young. Christopher Plummer, Yul Brynner, Romy Schneider, Trevor Howard, Gert Frobe, Claudine Auger. Adequate WW2 spy yarn features Plummer as real-life British safecracker Eddie Chapman, who works both sides of the fence. A bit too long.▼❶

Triple Echo (1973-British) **C-90m.** *** D: Michael Apted. Glenda Jackson, Oliver Reed, Brian Deacon, Jenny Lee Wright. High-powered talent in sensitive story of transvestite in English countryside during WW2. Young Deacon, an army deserter, is persuaded by lonely farm woman Jackson to pose as her sister, then tough tank Sergeant Reed becomes infatuated. Retitled SOLDIER IN SKIRTS. [R]▼

Triplets of Belleville, The (2003-Canadian-Belgian-French) **C-80m.** *** D: Sylvain Chomet. Voices of Jean-Claude Donda, Michel Robin, Monica Viegas, Michèle Caucheteux. A bicycle racer falls into the clutches of the French Mafia; it's up to his grandmother-trainer and three strange old women (once a famed singing trio in the 1930s) to rescue him. This eccentric, strikingly designed, almost dialogue-free hand-drawn animated feature is a triumph for Chomet and succeeds as an homage to Jacques Tati, Buster Keaton, and Max Fleischer (whose cartoons are evoked in the prologue, which features the song "Belleville Rendez-vous"). Droll rather than funny, and often bizarre, with a disappointing finale . . . but any film that offers caricatures of Django Reinhardt and Josephine Baker has us rooting for it. [PG-13]▼◗

Tripper, The (2007) **C-93m.** **½ D: David Arquette. David Arquette, Courteney Cox, Jaime King, Thomas Jane, James Mewes, Balthazar Getty, Paul Reubens, Lukas Haas, Marsha Thomason, Richmond Arquette. A group of modern-day, drug-addled hippies at a Woodstock-like music festival are stalked by a serial killer wearing a Ronald Reagan mask and his man-eating dogs (the meanest is named Nancy). Labor of love from first-time director and cowriter Arquette (who distributed it himself) looks and feels more like a grindhouse film than GRINDHOUSE, and makes up for its meandering, redundant plot with enough gore, nudity, bizarre acid-trip sequences, and political commentary to give fans of the genre a good time. [R]◗

Trippin' (1999) **C-92m.** ** D: David Raynr (Hubbard).DeonRichmond,MaiaCampbell, Donald (Adeosun) Faison, Guy Torry, Countess Vaughn, Michael Warren. Goofy teen comedy about a Walter Mitty–esque high school senior who could win his dream girl if he started taking the future seriously. Likable cast can't compensate for clichéd material and gratuitous t&a quotient. Features a pointless cameo by Naomi Campbell. [R]▼◗

Trip to Bountiful, The (1985) **C-106m.** *** D: Peter Masterson. Geraldine Page, John Heard, Carlin Glynn, Richard Bradford, Rebecca De Mornay, Kevin Cooney. Leisurely, richly textured filmization of Horton Foote's 1953 television play (later done on Broadway) about a widow, living unhappily with her son and daughter-in-law, determined to make her way home to Bountiful, Texas, for one last look. Page won well-deserved Oscar for her heartbreaking performance, but entire cast is excellent. Fine filmmaking debut for stage director Masterson. [PG]▼●◗

Tristana (1970-French-Spanish) **C-98m.** ***½ D: Luis Buñuel. Catherine Deneuve, Fernando Rey, Franco Nero, Jesus Fernandez, Lola Gaos, Vincent Solder. Deneuve plays a young woman who goes to live with her guardian Rey after her mother dies. He falls in love with her but faces competition from Nero. One of Buñuel's most serene, serious yet perverse studies of Catholicism, old age, death, desire, and deformity. Beautifully filmed in Toledo, Spain. Released in Europe at 105m. [PG]▼●

Tristan and Isolde (1979) SEE: **Lovespell**
Tristan + Isolde (2006) **C-126m.** **½ D: Kevin Reynolds. James Franco, Sophia Myles, Rufus Sewell, David Patrick O'Hara, Henry Cavill, JB Blanc, Jamie King, Richard Dillane. Ireland and England—they just can't get along. England's Lord Marke (Sewell, rising above the material) is betrayed by adoptive son Tristan (Franco), who sneaks off for illicit trysts with his onetime Irish rescuer and Marke-betrothed Isolde (Myles); these

two youngsters just can't stop themselves. The kind of movie Hollywood could do in its sleep during the Golden Age now benefits, at least moderately, from novelty value. Franco broods too much, but Myles has regal bearing. Respectable without being exceptional in any way. Super 35. [PG-13]◗

Tristram Shandy: A Cock and Bull Story (2006-British) **C-91m.** *** D: Michael Winterbottom. Steve Coogan, Rob Brydon, Jeremy Northam, Raymond Waring, Dylan Moran, Keeley Hawes, Kelly Macdonald, Shirley Henderson, Stephen Fry, Naomie Harris, Ian Hart, Roger Allam, Gillian Anderson, Benedict Wong, Greg Wise, Ronni Ancona. Laurence Sterne's ribald, unconventional 18th-century novel *The Life and Opinions of Tristram Shandy, Gentleman* is the springboard for this very funny deconstruction of a movie in production, dealing with everything from actors' egos to location liaisons. Coogan and Brydon's straight-faced rivalry bookends the film, right through the closing credits. Score makes wonderful use of classical and contemporary source music, especially Nino Rota's theme from Fellini's AMARCORD. HD 24P Widescreen. [R]◗

Triumph of Love (2001-Italian-British) **C-107m.** ** D: Clare Peploe. Mira Sorvino, Ben Kingsley, Fiona Shaw, Jay Rodan, Ignazio Oliva, Rachael Stirling, Luis Molteni. A princess in disguise insinuates herself into the household of a philosopher who harbors tremendous resentment toward her because her father had no right to the throne. In due course, she makes the man, his handsome son, and his flighty sister all fall in love with her! Sorvino is delightful in this rendition of the 1732 play by Pierre Marivaux, but like most stage farces it doesn't really work onscreen. Peploe coscripted with husband Bernardo Bertolucci and Marilyn Goldin. [PG-13]▼◗

Triumph of the Spirit (1989) **C-121m.** *** D: Robert M. Young. Willem Dafoe, Edward James Olmos, Robert Loggia, Wendy Gazelle, Kelly Wolf, Costas Mandylor, Kario Salem. Hard-hitting, heartbreaking, based-on-fact account of Salamo Arouch (Dafoe), Greek-Jewish boxer who is deported with his family to Auschwitz during WW2. Sometimes *too* grim, but it's a story that needs to be told and remembered. Filmed on location. [R]▼◗

Triumph of the Will (1935-German) **110m.** **** D: Leni Riefenstahl. Riefenstahl's infamous documentary on Hitler's 1934 Nuremberg rallies is rightly regarded as the greatest propaganda film of all time. Fascinating and (of course) frightening to see.▼

Triumphs of a Man Called Horse (1983-U.S.-Mexican) **C-86m.** *½ D: John Hough. Richard Harris, Michael Beck, Ana De Sade, Vaughn Armstrong, Anne Seymour, Buck Taylor. Limp sequel to THE RETURN OF A MAN CALLED HORSE with Beck, as Harris' half-breed son, attempting to shelter Sioux from greedy white settlers. Fans of the two earlier HORSES will be disappointed. [PG]▼

Trixie (2000) **C-116m.** *½ D: Alan Rudolph. Emily Watson, Dermot Mulroney, Nick Nolte, Nathan Lane, Brittany Murphy, Lesley Ann Warren, Will Patton, Stephen Lang. A dimwitted young woman given to malapropisms takes a job doing undercover security at a lakeside resort, where she uncovers a shady development deal involving a local bigwig (Patton) and a bombastic senator (Nolte). Seriocomic film noir is stylized to the point where it bears no relation to any recognizable reality. In other words, a fizzle. [R]▼▶

Trog (1970-British) **C-91m.** BOMB D: Freddie Francis. Joan Crawford, Michael Gough, Kim Braden, David Griffin, John Hamill. Missing Link discovered by anthropologist Crawford naturally gets loose and does its thing. Do yours—don't watch it. Sadly, Crawford's last film. [PG]▼▶●

Trojan Eddie (1996-British-Irish) **C-105m.** **½ D: Gillies Mackinnon. Richard Harris, Stephen Rea, Brendan Gleeson, Sean McGinley, Angeline Ball, Brid Brennan. Rea is a spieler who can sell anything to anyone but whose life has otherwise been in shambles; he finds himself caught in the middle when the young wife of his thuggish boss (Harris) runs off with her lover (who is Eddie's assistant). Harris and Rea offer fine, understated performances in this odd, intriguing mood piece. ▼▶

Trojan Women, The (1972-Greek-U.S.) **C-105m.** ** D: Michael Cacoyannis. Katharine Hepburn, Irene Papas, Genevieve Bujold, Vanessa Redgrave, Patrick Magee, Brian Blessed. Euripides' tragedy about the plight of the women of Troy after its army is defeated gets a surprisingly flat (albeit faithful) rendering, although any film which brings together four such great actresses can't be totally dismissed. [PG] ▼▶

Troll (1986) **C-86m.** *½ D: John Buechler. Michael Moriarty, Shelley Hack, Noah Hathaway, Jenny Beck, Sonny Bono, June Lockhart, Anne Lockhart, Brad Hall, Julia Louis-Dreyfus. If your idea of entertainment is seeing Sonny Bono metamorphose into an apartment of foliage, this is the movie for you. Angelic tyke is possessed by a troll, who takes over her body and starts turning the neighbors into seed pods that eventually turn into new trolls. Too close to GREMLINS; some viewers may get off on hearing June Lockhart swear. Sequel: TROLL II. [PG-13]▼▶●

Troll in Central Park, A (1994) **C-76m.** ** D: Don Bluth, Gary Goldman. Voices of Dom DeLuise, Cloris Leachman, Phillip Glasser, Tawney Sunshine Glover, Hayley Mills, Jonathan Pryce, Charles Nelson Reilly. Good-hearted troll falls from favor in Troll Land and is banished to . . . N.Y.C.!

There his green thumb helps beautify Central Park and the lives of those around him, including two neglected kids. Amiable and good-looking cartoon feature will appeal mainly to the small fry. DeLuise is fun in the title role. [G]▼▶●

Tron (1982) **C-96m.** ** D: Steven Lisberger. Jeff Bridges, Bruce Boxleitner, David Warner, Cindy Morgan, Barnard Hughes, Dan Shor. A computer whiz is sucked inside a powerful computer, where he must fight for his life in a giant video-game competition. State-of-the-art special effects are stunning, but the story runs out of steam too soon, with only Bridges' charisma to keep it afloat. Disappointing Disney production. Followed by a sequel in 2010. Super Panavision 70. [PG]▼▶●

Tron Legacy (2010) **C-127m.** ** D: Joseph Kosinski. Jeff Bridges, Garrett Hedlund, Olivia Wilde, Bruce Boxleitner, Michael Sheen, James Frain, Beau Garrett. Hedlund's father, a brilliant video game designer, disappeared when he was a boy. Now a young man, Hedlund finds a way to step inside that video world, where he is reunited with his father but finds himself threatened by an evil clone. Like the original TRON, this one is full of flashy visuals, with great production and costume design, but hasn't enough story to support it. Seeing Bridges "youthified" to the age of 35 by digital means isn't magical—just weird. Hard-core gamers may be more enthusiastic. Cillian Murphy appears unbilled. 3-D HD Widescreen. [PG] ▶

Troop Beverly Hills (1989) **C-105m.** **½ D: Jeff Kanew. Shelley Long, Craig T. Nelson, Betty Thomas, Mary Gross, Stephanie Beacham, Audra Lindley, Edd Byrnes, Ami Foster, Jenny Lewis. Sometimes-amusing comedy about a spoiled, wealthy Beverly Hills housewife who leads her daughter's Girl Scout troop on unique outings on which everyone learns about self-esteem—and Gucci loafers. Predictable, but undemanding fun. [PG] ▼▶

Tropic of Cancer (1970) **C-87m.** ***½ D: Joseph Strick. Rip Torn, James Callahan, Ellen Burstyn, David Bauer, Laurence Ligneres, Phil Brown. Director Strick is generally more successful with Henry Miller than he's been with James Joyce, thanks to Torn's earthy portrayal of the loose-living expatriate author amidst a string of amorous adventures in '20s Paris. Slapdash but invigorating; Burstyn makes a strong impression in tiny role as Henry's wife. [X]▼▶

Tropic Thunder (2008) **C-106m.** **½ D: Ben Stiller. Ben Stiller, Jack Black, Robert Downey, Jr., Nick Nolte, Steve Coogan, Jay Baruchel, Danny McBride, Brandon T. Jackson, Bill Hader, Brandon Soo Hoo, Matthew McConaughey, Tom Cruise. Hollywood movie troupe heads to Vietnam to make a wartime action yarn but nothing goes quite right. How could it with star and director egos running rampant and a violent drug cartel operating in their midst? Scatter-shot comedy opens with four mock trailers that are funnier than the movie itself. Black is wasted here but Downey shines in an out-rageous turn as a white Aussie actor who's playing a black man—and never goes out of character. Cruise, in heavy makeup, plays a loathsome Jewish studio exec, which is good for a few laughs but (like so much else here) goes on too long. Cowritten by Stiller. Tobey Maguire and Kevin Pollak appear unbilled. Unrated version runs 121m. Super 35. [R]●

Tropic Zone (1953) **C-94m.** *½ D: Lewis R. Foster. Ronald Reagan, Rhonda Fleming, Estelita, Noah Beery (Jr.). Blah actioner set in South America with Reagan fighting the good cause to save a banana plantation from outlaws.

Trouble Along the Way (1953) **110m.** **½ D: Michael Curtiz. John Wayne, Donna Reed, Charles Coburn, Sherry Jackson, Marie Windsor, Tom Tully, Leif Erickson, Chuck Connors. Unusually sentimental Wayne vehicle casts him as divorced man trying to maintain custody of his daughter (Jackson); he earns back self-respect by coaching foot-ball team for small Catholic school. ▼●

Trouble at 16 SEE: **Platinum High School**
Trouble Bound (1993) **C-89m.** *½ D: Jeffrey Reiner. Michael Madsen, Patricia Arquette, Florence Stanley, Seymour Cas-sel, Billy Bob Thornton. Ex-con Madsen and "college" girl Arquette are on the run in this Mafia mess which features gamblers, drug dealers, hit people, strippers, and a corpse who talks. The two leads save this from being a total loss. [R]●

Trouble Every Day (2001-French) **C-89m.** BOMB D: Claire Denis. Vincent Gallo, Tri-cia Vessey, Beatrice Dalle, Alex Descas, Florence Loiret, Nicolas Duvauchelle. So bad it's almost funny. Atrocious French concoction deals with experiments gone terribly wrong that seem to be turning "nor-mal" people into cannibals, who give new meaning to the idea of eating after sex. One of those woebegone cinematic mistakes that make you wonder, "What were they think-ing?" Tindersticks' score and title song are so good they belong in another movie.

Trouble in Mind (1985) **C-111m.** **½ D: Alan Rudolph. Kris Kristofferson, Keith Carradine, Lori Singer, Genevieve Bujold, Joe Morton, Divine, George Kirby, John Considine. Highly stylized, highly indi-vidualistic melodrama set in the near future, with Kristofferson as idealistic ex-cop, fresh from a stretch in jail, who gets in-volved with some young innocents who've just come to the big city. Odd, unusual, with 1940s film noir feeling but so determinedly vague and unreal that it also comes off rather cold. Still, it's an eyeful, and recom-mended for fans of the offbeat and Rudolph

in particular. Title song sung by Marianne Faithful. [R]▼●

Trouble in Paradise (1932) **83m.** ****
D: Ernst Lubitsch. Miriam Hopkins, Kay Francis, Herbert Marshall, Charlie Rug-gles, Edward Everett Horton, C. Aubrey Smith, Robert Grieg, Leonid Kinskey. Sparkling Lubitsch confection about two thieves (Marshall and Hopkins) who fall in love, but find their relationship threatened when he turns on the charm to their newest (female) victim. This film is a working defi-nition of the term "sophisticated comedy." Script by Samson Raphaelson and Grover Jones.●

Trouble in the Glen (1954-British) **C-91m.** ** D: Herbert Wilcox. Margaret Lock-wood, Orson Welles, Forrest Tucker, Victor McLaglen. Scottish-based drama of feud over closing of road that has been used for a long time. Average-to-poor script benefits from Welles.▼

Troublemaker, The (1964) **80m.** ** D: Theodore Flicker. Tom Aldredge, Joan Darling, Theodore Flicker, Buck Henry, Godfrey Cambridge, Al Freeman, Jr. Ter-ribly dated, independently made comedy about a country bumpkin's adventures in N.Y.C.; interesting as an artifact of its time, made by the talented improvisational com-edy troupe known as The Premise.

Trouble Man (1972) **C-99m.** ** D: Ivan Dixon. Robert Hooks, Paul Winfield, Ralph Waite, William Smithers, Paula Kelly, Ju-lius W. Harris. Hooks is superslick black troubleshooter caught in gang warfare. Cliché-ridden script includes about four hundred killings, glorifying underworld life. Well made but tasteless. [R]●

Trouble the Water (2008) **C-96m.** *** D: Carl Deal, Tia Lessin. Harrowing and reso-nant documentary about the human toll of New Orleans' disastrous Hurricane Katrina. With remarkable footage taken during the storm by one survivor (an aspiring rapper who was eventually relocated to the Super-dome), the film tells the larger story of the hurricane through her attempts to help oth-ers. Pointing out that even a year later not much had been done to improve the lives of the storm's poorest victims, this film makes salient points about human spirit and sur-vival in the wake of complete governmental meltdown.●

Trouble With Angels, The (1966) **C-112m.** **½ D: Ida Lupino. Rosalind Russell, Hay-ley Mills, June Harding, Binnie Barnes, Mary Wickes, Gypsy Rose Lee, Camilla Sparv. Cutesy study of Pennsylvania con-vent school, with students Mills and Hard-ing driving mother superior Russell to distraction. Episodic, occasionally touch-ing comedy. Sequel: WHERE ANGELS GO . . . TROUBLE FOLLOWS.▼●

Trouble With Girls (and How to Get Into It), The (1969) **C-104m.** **½ D: Peter

Tewksbury. Elvis Presley, Marlyn Mason, Nicole Jaffe, Sheree North, Edward Andrews, John Carradine. Vincent Price, Joyce Van Patten, Dabney Coleman, John Rubinstein, Duke Snider. One of the better Presley vehicles has Elvis as manager of a Chautauqua company (medicine show) in the 1920s; nice feeling for the period. Panavision. [PG] ▼○●

Trouble With Harry, The (1955) **C-99m.** *** D: Alfred Hitchcock. Edmund Gwenn, John Forsythe, Shirley MacLaine, Mildred Natwick, Mildred Dunnock, Jerry Mathers, Royal Dano. Offbeat, often hilarious black comedy courtesy Mr. Hitchcock and scripter John Michael Hayes about bothersome corpse causing all sorts of problems for peaceful neighbors in New England community. Gwenn is fine as usual, MacLaine appealing in her first film. Beautiful autumn locations, whimsical score (his first for Hitch) by Bernard Herrmann. VistaVision. ▼○●

Trouble With Spies, The (1987) **C-91m.** BOMB D: Burt Kennedy. Donald Sutherland, Ned Beatty, Ruth Gordon, Lucy Gutteridge, Michael Hordern, Robert Morley, Gregory Sierra. Awful spy comedy about incompetent British and Soviet secret agents. Good actors wasted; this one's as bad as they come. Filmed in 1984. [PG] ▼

Trout, The (1982-French) **C-105m.** ** D: Joseph Losey. Isabelle Huppert, Jacques Spiesser, Jeanne Moreau, Jean-Pierre Cassel, Daniel Olbrychski, Alexis Smith, Craig Stevens. Elaborate but muddled account of country girl Huppert and her encounters, sexual and otherwise, in the world of high finance. Moreau is wasted as the wife of businessman Cassel; Smith and Stevens appear in cameos. Original title: LA TRUITE. Also released at 116m. [R] ▼●

Troy (2004-British-Maltese) **C-162m.** ***½ D: Wolfgang Petersen. Brad Pitt, Eric Bana, Orlando Bloom, Diane Kruger, Brian Cox, Sean Bean, Brendan Gleeson, Peter O'Toole, Rose Byrne, Saffron Burrows, Julie Christie. When callow Trojan prince Paris (Bloom) steals the beautiful Helen from under the nose of her husband, Menelaus, greedy King Agamemnon (a ferocious Cox) seizes the opportunity to declare war on Troy. Achilles (Pitt) is his greatest asset, but the almost superhuman warrior follows his own agenda. Spectacular production offers battle scenes unlike any ever staged before—both epic-scale and man-to-man—but it's the well-defined characters (and a gallery of strong performances) that make this so compelling. Impressive adaptation of Homer's *The Iliad* by David Benioff. Director's cut runs 192m. Super 35. [R] ▼●

Truce, The (1997-Italian-French-Swiss-German-British) **C-117m.** *** D: Francesco Rosi. John Turturro, Massimo Ghini, Rade Serbedzija, Stefano Dionisi, Teco Celio, Roberto Citran. Moving adaptation of Primo Levi's autobiography, which follows the author's liberation from Auschwitz and his emotional reawakening as he struggles to get home to Turin, Italy. Episodic structure dilutes some of the dramatic impact, but there are many powerful, affecting moments, and Turturro is beautifully understated. An interesting companion piece to the documentary THE LONG WAY HOME. [R] ▼●

Trucker (2009) **C-93m.** *** D: James Mottern. Michelle Monaghan, Nathan Fillion, Benjamin Bratt, Jimmy Bennett, Joey Lauren Adams, Matthew Lawrence. Monaghan is an independent woman who likes being a truck driver because she can come and go as she pleases and doesn't make long-term attachments. Then she's saddled with an 11-year-old boy, the son she abandoned as an infant when she walked out on her husband (Bratt), who's now fighting cancer. What could be formulaic and routine is richly drawn as the mother and son—who have no use for one another—gradually develop a bond. Great showcase for Monaghan. Written by the director. [R] ●

Truck Stop Women (1974) **C-88m.** **½ D: Mark Lester. Lieux Dressler, Claudia Jennings, Dennis Fimple, Jennifer Burton. Sloppy but good-natured exploitation fare about women who run truck stop as front for prostitution and truck hijacking activities. Business is so good the Mob tries to move in. Jennings is a standout in this raucous sleaze romp. Techniscope. [R] ▼

Truck Turner (1974) **C-91m.** *½ D: Jonathan Kaplan. Isaac Hayes, Yaphet Kotto, Alan Weeks, Annazette Chase, Sam Laws, Nichelle Nichols. Extremely violent black exploiter, with Hayes only distinguishing feature as a skip-tracer (a detective who hunts bail jumpers). His original score is familiar. [R] ▼●

True Believer (1989) **C-103m.** *** D: Joseph Ruben. James Woods, Robert Downey, Jr., Yuji Okumoto, Margaret Colin, Kurtwood Smith, Tom Bower, Charles Hallahan. Woods gives his usual dynamic performance as a once-idealistic lawyer, a radical hero of the '60s who's lost his scruples—until his hero-worshipping clerk (Downey) goads him into taking the near-hopeless case of an Asian-American who was apparently railroaded into prison eight years before. Contrived, but entertaining all the way. Followed by a TV series, *Eddie Dodd*. [R] ▼○●

True Colors (1991) **C-111m.** **½ D: Herbert Ross. John Cusack, James Spader, Imogen Stubbs, Mandy Patinkin, Richard Widmark, Dina Merrill, Philip Bosco, Paul Guilfoyle. Well-acted but thoroughly obvious story of friendship, ethics, and betrayal, following two law-school roommates who take different paths in life: one goes to work for the Justice Department, determined to right wrongs; the other goes into politics, looking for any angle that can get him ahead.

No surprises, thus little impact. Stubbs' British accent (in the role of senator Widmark's daughter) also gets in the way. Widmark's final film. [R] ▼●◗

True Confessions (1981) C-108m. **½ D: Ulu Grosbard. Robert De Niro, Robert Duvall, Charles Durning, Ed Flanders, Burgess Meredith, Rose Gregorio, Cyril Cusack, Kenneth McMillan, Dan Hedaya, Jeanette Nolan. Methodically slow, complex, and provocative film (adapted by John Gregory Dunne and Joan Didion from Dunne's novel) about the uneasy bond and surprising similarities between two brothers, one a hardened police detective, the other a power-wielding monsignor in the Catholic Church. A meaty but somehow unsatisfying film (based on a true case previously filmed as a TVM, WHO IS THE BLACK DAHLIA?) with two characteristically fine performances by De Niro and Duvall. [R] ▼●◗

True Crime (1999) C-127m. *** D: Clint Eastwood. Clint Eastwood, Isaiah Washington, Denis Leary, Lisa Gay Hamilton, James Woods, Bernard Hill, Diane Venora, Michael McKean, Michael Jeter, Mary McCormack, Hattie Winston, Francesca Fisher-Eastwood, Sydney Poitier, Frances Fisher, Christine Ebersole, Anthony Zerbe, William Windom, Lucy Alexis Liu. Formulaic but gripping story about a burnt-out reporter who becomes convinced that a man due to die at San Quentin that night is innocent. Bouncing back and forth between the story of the reporter—who's looking for redemption—and the stoic prisoner doesn't always work, but the suspense is undeniable. Woods is dynamite as Eastwood's sharp-tongued editor. Eastwood's wife, Dina Ruiz, ex-companion (Fisher), and young daughter all appear. [R] ▼●◗

True Grit (1969) C-128m. *** D: Henry Hathaway. John Wayne, Glen Campbell, Kim Darby, Jeremy Slate, Robert Duvall, Strother Martin, Dennis Hopper, Jeff Corey. Film version of Charles Portis's wonderful novel about an over-the-hill marshal who helps 14-year-old track down her father's killer. Not as good as the book, but Wayne's Oscar-winning performance and rousing last half hour make it fine screen entertainment. Sequel: ROOSTER COGBURN. Followed by a TV movie in 1978 with Warren Oates and Lisa Pelikan. Remade in 2010. [G—edited from original M rating] ▼●◗

True Grit (2010) C-110m. *** D: Joel Coen, Ethan Coen. Jeff Bridges, Matt Damon, Josh Brolin, Hailee Steinfeld, Barry Pepper, Dakin Matthews, Elizabeth Marvel. Remake of the 1969 hit allows Bridges to put his own stamp on the role of one-eyed marshal Rooster Cogburn originated by John Wayne. Newcomer Steinfeld plays Mattie Ross, an outlandishly precocious (and verbose) 14-year-old girl who vows to avenge her father's murder by capturing his killer (Brolin). She insists on accompanying the irresponsible Cogburn on his manhunt, in which they are joined by self-assured Texas Ranger Damon. The Coens' script calls on their love of language (much of it directly from Charles Portis' novel), while cinematographer Roger Deakins fills the screen with beautiful imagery. Entertaining, to be sure, but being as unsentimental as it is, there isn't any emotional resonance when it's all over. Super 35. [PG-13] ◗

True Identity (1991) C-93m. **½ D: Charles Lane. Lenny Henry, Frank Langella, Charles Lane, Andreas Katsulas, Michael McKean, James Earl Jones, Melvin Van Peebles. Aspiring black actor recognizes a supposedly dead mob boss on an airplane and disguises himself as an Italian-American hit man in order to save his skin. Familiar premise with a somewhat unfamiliar variation. Serves as a passable showcase for Brit wit Henry and his great gift of mimicry. [R] ▼●

True Lies (1994) C-141m. *** D: James Cameron. Arnold Schwarzenegger, Jamie Lee Curtis, Tom Arnold, Bill Paxton, Tia Carrere, Art Malik, Charlton Heston, Eliza Dushku, Grant Heslov, Jane Morris. In-your-face entertainment from the Schwarzenegger/Cameron team, with Arnold as a spy in a super-secret, high-tech government agency whose wife thinks he's just a nerdy computer salesman. With humor and action in equal doses, this film makes all the right moves—until it gets bogged down in plot (and a general putdown of women) midway through. A slam-bang action finale brings it back on-course, as credibility is gleefully tossed aside. Cameron also scripted, based on a French film, LA TOTALE. Super 35. [R] ▼●◗

True Love (1989) C-104m. *** D: Nancy Savoca. Annabella Sciorra, Ron Eldard, Aida Turturro, Roger Rignack, Star Jasper, Michael J. Wolfe, Kelly Cinnante. Refreshing, low-budget slice-of-life sleeper about an Italian wedding in the Bronx. There's tons of atmosphere, and the script (by Savoca and her husband, Richard Guay) is never condescending. Fine performances with Sciorra and Eldard perfectly cast as no-nonsense bride and immature groom. [R] ▼●◗

True Romance (1993) C-118m. **½ D: Tony Scott. Christian Slater, Patricia Arquette, Dennis Hopper, Gary Oldman, Brad Pitt, Christopher Walken, Val Kilmer, Bronson Pinchot, Michael Rapaport, Saul Rubinek, Chris Penn, Tom Sizemore, Samuel L. Jackson, James Gandolfini. A '90s twist on the young-lovers-on-the-lam genre, with hedonism, highly stylized (but potent) violence, and colorful supporting characters the main ingredients. Oldman, as a drug dealer in dreadlocks, is the standout in a first-rate cast. Hopper plays the most "normal" person in the movie! Written by Quentin Tarantino. Also available in unrated 120m. version. Panavision. [R]▼●◖

True Stories (1986) **C-89m.** ✱✱ D: David Byrne. David Byrne, John Goodman, Swoosie Kurtz, Annie McEnroe, Spalding Gray, Alix Elias, Pops Staples. Smarmy, pseudo-hip tour of modern-day Texas by Talking Heads' Byrne; is there anything easier to satirize than eccentric Lone Star crazies? Photography, likable Goodman performance, and a couple of numbers make this worth a look if you're curious; mostly, though, it's depressing. Playwright Beth Henley had a part in the screenplay. [PG]▼●◖

True Story of Jesse James, The (1957) **C-92m.** ✱✱½ D: Nicholas Ray. Robert Wagner, Jeffrey Hunter, Hope Lange, Agnes Moorehead, Alan Hale (Jr.), John Carradine, Alan Baxter, Frank Gorshin. Remake of 1939 Tyrone Power/Henry Fonda classic (JESSE JAMES) understandably lacks its star power, but there are enough offbeat Ray touches to keep things interesting (along with some stock footage from the original). Screenplay by Walter Newman. CinemaScope.◖

Truly Madly Deeply (1991-British) **C-107m.** ✱✱½ D: Anthony Minghella. Juliet Stevenson, Alan Rickman, Bill Paterson, Michael Maloney, Christopher Rozycki, Keith Bartlett, David Ryall, Stella Maris. Young woman, unable to get over the death of her musician lover, gets the shock of her life when he turns up in her apartment—a ghost, to be sure, but seemingly alive. Minghella conceived this as a vehicle for Stevenson, and that it is (though it also serves as a showcase for Rickman, in an uncharacteristic low-key role); charmingly quirky at times, but unable to sustain its offbeat premise to the very end.▼●◖

Truman Show, The (1998) **C-102m.** ✱✱½ D: Peter Weir. Jim Carrey, Laura Linney, Ed Harris, Noah Emmerich, Natascha McElhone, Holland Taylor, Brian Delate, Paul Giamatti, Harry Shearer. Truman Burbank lives a seemingly ideal existence in a tranquil seaside community. What he doesn't know is that his life is a giant 24-hour-a-day TV show, orchestrated by electronic mastermind/artist Harris in a completely controlled environment. Satire of our voyeuristic, consumer-driven society scores some points and offers Carrey a change of pace, but after the premise is established it doesn't know where to go. Perhaps that's because it's a short-story idea, not a feature film; *The Twilight Zone* used to do this kind of thing—better—in half-hour segments. [PG] ▼●◖

Trumps SEE: **Enormous Changes at the Last Minute**

Trunk to Cairo (1966-Israeli) **C-80m.** ✱½ D: Menahem Golan. Audie Murphy, George Sanders, Marianne Koch, Hans Von Bosodi, Joseph Yadin. Murphy, in rare non-Western role, plays still another secret agent in Cairo to investigate Sanders' attempt to build a rocket bound for the moon.

Trust (1991) **C-105m.** ✱✱✱ D: Hal Hartley. Adrienne Shelly, Martin Donovan, Merritt Nelson, John McKay, Edie Falco, Marko Hunt. A pregnant high-school senior is dumped by a football star who fears for his pending college scholarship. When her dad drops dead at the news, she finds a dubious savior: a bookish fellow who can't even clean a bathroom to his own dad's satisfaction. Drollness on-screen can sometimes be had cheaply, but a perfect cast is tougher to bankroll; this original has both, enough to defuse the smugness that seems to linger in its soul. [R]▼●

Trust (2011) **C-106m.** ✱✱½ D: David Schwimmer. Clive Owen, Catherine Keener, Viola Davis, Liana Liberato, Noah Emmerich, Jason Clarke, Chris Henry Coffey. The 14-year-old daughter of well-to-do suburban parents feels the pangs of first love as she strikes up a disastrous relationship on the 'net with a 35-year-old predator who poses as another teen. The crisis builds as her father starts to take matters into his own hands to keep his family together. Owen and Keener offer good performances, but the film is really a showcase for young Liberato, who socks home a portrayal of youthful desire and self-doubt with the assurance of a veteran. Effective family drama becomes overly melodramatic at times. Super 35. [R]◖

Trust Me (1989) **C-104m.** ✱✱½ D: Bobby Houston. Adam Ant, David Packer, Talia Balsam, William DeAcutis, Joyce Van Patten, Barbara Bain. Some scattershot laughs cannot sustain this satire of the art scene. Ant plays a gallery owner who will do all he can to see artist Packer dead—so the value of his work will increase. Bright idea, uneven result. [R]▼

Trust the Man (2006) **C-103m.** ✱✱ D: Bart Freundlich. David Duchovny, Julianne Moore, Billy Crudup, Maggie Gyllenhaal, Eva Mendes, Ellen Barkin, Garry Shandling, James Le Gros, Dagmara Dominczyk, Jim Gaffigan. Being the misadventures of two Manhattan couples having relationship problems. The women (mostly) have their feet on the ground, while the men are utterly infantile. Romantic comedy with echoes of vintage Woody Allen films (and a rosy view of N.Y.C.) has occasional bright spots but mostly lurches from one episode to another. Unsatisfying, to put it mildly. Bob Balaban appears unbilled. [R]◖

Truth About Cats & Dogs, The (1996) **C-97m.** ✱✱½ D: Michael Lehmann. Uma Thurman, Janeane Garofalo, Ben Chaplin, Jamie Foxx, James McCaffrey. Cute comedy about a guy who falls in love with a radio talk-show host (Garofalo) before he even meets her; she, on the other hand, is self-conscious about her looks and has her knockout neighbor, a prototypical dumb blonde (Thurman), take her place. Enjoyable romantic comedy with *Cyrano* overtones stays afloat with three engaging performances (plus one terrific dog) but stretches credibility to the limit. [PG-13] ▼●◗

Truth About Charlie, The (2002) **C-104m.** ** D: Jonathan Demme. Mark Wahlberg, Thandie Newton, Tim Robbins, Joong-Hoon Park, Ted Levine, Lisa Gay Hamilton, Christine Boisson, Stephen Dillane, Simon Abkarian, Charles Aznavour, Anna Karina, Agnès Varda, Magali Noël. Pallid remake of CHARADE, set again in Paris, has Newton as the damsel in distress, Wahlberg as her gallant new friend, and Robbins as all-too-suspicious government official. Instead of playing the story with conviction, the film distances us by calling attention to itself with dizzying camerawork, cacophonous music, and indulgent references to French New Wave cinema, including appearances by three of its leading lights (Aznavour, Karina, and Varda). Four writers are credited with complicating Peter Stone's 1963 screenplay; one of them (Peter Joshua) is a pseudonym for Stone, who earned the credit for supplying the original plot. Panavision. [PG-13] ▼◗

Truth About Spring, The (1965-British) **C-102m.** *** D: Richard Thorpe. Hayley Mills, John Mills, James MacArthur, Lionel Jeffries, Harry Andrews, Niall MacGinnis, David Tomlinson. Skipper Mills introduces daughter Hayley to first boyfriend, MacArthur, in enjoyable film geared for young viewers.

Truth or Consequences, N.M. (1997) **C-106m.** ** D: Kiefer Sutherland. Vincent Gallo, Mykelti Williamson, Kiefer Sutherland, Kevin Pollak, Kim Dickens, Grace Phillips, Max Perlich, Rod Steiger, Martin Sheen. A robbery goes awry, resulting in murder, and the four criminals take two ordinary people captive to evade Utah police. Well acted, but there's nothing at all new here, and it's pretentious to boot. Sutherland's feature debut as a director. [R] ▼●◗

Truth or Dare (1991) **C/B&W-118m.** *** D: Alek Keshishian. Madonna. Revealing backstage/performance film, very much in the mold of DON'T LOOK BACK, examines the phenomenon we know as . . . Madonna. Authorized account, iron-fist commissioned by its subject, is simultaneously candid and manipulated, but the dynamics between Madonna and members of her family (and a couple of hilarious what-me-worry cameos by her then-squeeze Warren Beatty) are compelling. An important film even if you don't care for Madonna; overlength makes the final half-hour a mild ordeal. (The video offers *additional* footage!) Video title: MADONNA TRUTH OR DARE. [R] ▼●◗

Trygon Factor, The (1967-British) **C-87m.** *½ D: Cyril Frankel. Stewart Granger, Susan Hampshire, Robert Morley, Cathleen Nesbitt, James Robertson Justice. Impossible-to-follow Scotland Yard whodunit. Centers around bizarre old English family and series of interesting murders.

Try Seventeen SEE: **All I Want**

Tsotsi (2005-South African-British) **C-94m.** ***½ D: Gavin Hood. Presley Chweneyagae, Terry Pheto, Kenneth Nkosi, Mothusi Magano, Zenzo Ngqobe, Zola, Rapulana Seiphemo, Nambitha Mpumlwana. A young, steely-eyed, amoral hoodlum who lives in a Johannesburg shantytown shoots a woman, steals her car, and then discovers her baby in the backseat. How a hardened criminal gets in touch with his own humanity is the crux of this crowd-pleasing drama, adapted by Hood from Athol Fugard's novel. The characters speak an argot made up of many languages, including English and Afrikaans, and the film is fueled by pulsating South African music. Newcomer Chweneyagae is superb in the leading role. Oscar winner as Best Foreign Language Film. Super 35.◗

Tucker: The Man and His Dream (1988) **C-111m.** ***½ D: Francis Ford Coppola. Jeff Bridges, Joan Allen, Martin Landau, Frederic Forrest, Mako, Dean Stockwell, Elias Koteas, Nina Siemaszko, Christian Slater, Corky Nemec, Marshall Bell, Don Novello, Peter Donat, Dean Goodman, Patti Austin. Smart, sassy, stylish film about Preston Tucker, who tried to build "the car of the future" in the 1940s, only to be crushed by the Big Three automakers and their political cronies. Told with great flair by Coppola (who obviously felt a kinship with the indomitable, family-minded visionary), filled with fine performances, especially Landau in a poignant characterization as Tucker's unlikely partner. Lloyd Bridges (Jeff's dad) appears unbilled as an adversarial senator. Lively score by Joe Jackson. Technovision. [PG] ▼●◗

Tuck Everlasting (1980) **C-100m.** ***½ D: Frederick King Keller. Margaret Chamberlain, Paul Flessa, Fred A. Keller, James McGuire, Sonia Raimi, Bruce D'Auria. Lovely, sweet, entertaining fable about family, invulnerable to pain, aging, and death, and the young girl who learns their secret. Perfect for children who prefer books to video games. Produced independently in upstate New York; based on Natalie Babbitt's award-winning novel. Remade in 2002. ▼

Tuck Everlasting (2002) **C-90m.** *** D: Jay Russell. Alexis Bledel, Sissy Spacek, William Hurt, Jonathan Jackson, Scott Bairstow, Ben Kingsley, Amy Irving, Victor Garber; narrated by Elisabeth Shue. Genteel adaptation of Natalie Babbitt's novel about a well-to-do teenage girl, living a cloistered life in the early 20th century, whose world is opened up by a chance meeting with a boy and his backwoods family. They have discovered the secret for eternal life, but what seems to be a blessing is in fact a kind of curse. Entertaining for young people, but lacks the dramatic punch that might have made it an even better movie. Panavision. [PG] ▼❚

Tuff Turf (1985) **C-112m.** *½ D: Fritz Kiersch. James Spader, Kim Richards, Paul Mones, Matt Clark, Claudette Nevins, Robert Downey (Jr.), Olivia Barash, Jack Mack & the Heart Attack. Old-fashioned, unrealistic troubled-teen melodrama with overtones of WEST SIDE STORY, set in a fantasy version of the San Fernando Valley. Pre-SEX, LIES AND VIDEOTAPE Spader, as preppie newcomer, is mannered, but Richards is good. [R] ▼❚❶

Tugboat Annie (1933) **87m.** **½ D: Mervyn LeRoy. Marie Dressler, Wallace Beery, Robert Young, Maureen O'Sullivan, Willard Robertson, Frankie Darro. Marie is skipper of the tugboat *Narcissus,* Beery her ne'er-do-well husband in this rambling, episodic comedy drama; inimitable stars far outclass their wobbly material. Followed by TUGBOAT ANNIE SAILS AGAIN (1940), and a 1950s TV series. ❶

Tulips (1981-Canadian) **C-92m.** *½ D: Stan Ferris. Gabe Kaplan, Bernadette Peters, Henry Gibson, Al Waxman, David Boxer. Weak romance, with Kaplan and Peters each attempting to commit suicide, then meeting and falling in love. "Stan Ferris" is a pseudonym for Mark Warren, Rex Bromfield, and Al Waxman—and the lack of directorial cohesion shows. [PG] ▼

Tully (2002) **C-102m.** **½ D: Hilary Birmingham. Anson Mount, Julianne Nicholson, Glenn Fitzgerald, Catherine Kellner, Bob Burrus, Natalie Canerday, John Diehl. Low-budget indie based on Tom McNeal's short story "What Happened to Tully," this overly talky movie manages to avoid melodrama, for the most part, with a touching story of how a woman's death affects her rancher husband and their two sons. Fine performances, especially from Mount, who has real acting chops. [R] ▼❚

Tulsa (1949) **C-90m.** *** D: Stuart Heisler. Susan Hayward, Robert Preston, Pedro Armendariz, Lloyd Gough, Chill Wills, Ed Begley, Jimmy Conlin. Bouncy drama of cattlewoman Hayward entering the wildcat oil business to avenge the death of her father, losing her values along the way as she becomes blinded by her success. ▼❚

Tumbleweeds (1925) **81m.** ***½ D: King Baggot. William S. Hart, Barbara Bedford, Lucien Littlefield, J. Gordon Russell, Richard R. Neill. One of the screen's most famous Westerns, with Hart deciding to get in on the opening of the Cherokee Strip in 1889, particularly if pretty Bedford is willing to marry him and settle there. Land rush scene is one of the great spectacles in silent films. Above running time

does not include a poignant eight-minute introduction Hart made to accompany 1939 reissue of his classic. ▼❶

Tumbleweeds (1999) **C-102m.** *** D: Gavin O'Connor. Janet McTeer, Kimberly J. Brown, Jay O. Sanders, Lois Smith, Laurel Holloman, Michael J. Pollard, Noah Emmerich, Gavin O'Connor. Exceptional performances elevate this somewhat familiar tale of a trailer-trash Southern belle with a penchant for hooking up with crummy men, dragging her young daughter along as she moves from town to town. McTeer is terrific in the lead, matched by Brown as the girl, with cowriter-director O'Connor first rate as a truck driver who comes into their lives. [PG-13] ▼❚

Tune, The (1992) **C-72m.** *** D: Bill Plympton. Offbeat, original cartoon feature from award-winning short-subject animator Plympton follows the trials and tribulations of a songwriter searching for that elusive hit. Maureen McElheron's clever songs provide the tone for a series of imaginative vignettes. Unconventional in every way (including its colored-pencil visuals, executed almost singlehandedly by Plympton) but a quiet treat, especially for animation buffs. ▼❚

Tune In Tomorrow . . . (1990) **C-102m.** **½ D: Jon Amiel. Barbara Hershey, Keanu Reeves, Peter Falk, Bill McCutcheon, Patricia Clarkson, Richard Portnow, Jerome Dempsey, Richard B. Shull. Oddball movie set in 1951 New Orleans. Reeves plays an impressionable young man who falls in love with his sexy aunt (Hershey), while falling under the spell of Falk, a wildly eccentric writer for a radio soap opera who draws on real life in ways his young protégé cannot conceive of. Funny, funky, original; not always on target, but there are inspired moments. Falk is a howl. Familiar faces appear in amusing cameos. Music by Wynton Marsalis, who also appears on camera. Based on Mario Vargas Llosa's novel *Aunt Julia and the Scriptwriter.* [PG-13] ▼❶

Tunes of Glory (1960-British) **C-106m.** **** D: Ronald Neame. Alec Guinness, John Mills, Susannah York, Kay Walsh, Dennis Price, John Fraser, Duncan Macrae, Gordon Jackson, Allan Cuthbertson. Engrossing clash of wills in peacetime Scottish Highland regiment as popular, easygoing Lt. Col. (Guinness) is replaced by stiff-necked martinet (Mills). Outstanding performances by both men, each in a role more naturally suited to the other! Impressive bagpipe-driven score by Malcolm Arnold. Scripted by James Kennaway, from his novel. York's film debut. ▼❶

Tunnel of Love, The (1958) **98m.** *** D: Gene Kelly. Doris Day, Richard Widmark, Gig Young, Gia Scala. Bright comedy of married couple Widmark and Day enduring endless red tape to adopt a child. Good cast spices adaptation of Joseph Fields–Peter de Vries play. CinemaScope. ▼●)

Tunnelvision (1976) **C-67m.** ** D: Neal Israel, Brad Swirnoff. Phil Proctor, Howard Hesseman, Ernie Anderson, Edwina Anderson, James Bacon, Gerrit Graham, Betty Thomas, Chevy Chase, Roger Bowen, Al Franken, Tom Davis, William Schallert, Laraine Newman, Ron Silver. Crude, uneven parody of what TV programming will be like in the future. Of interest only for appearances by now famous performers. [R] ▼)

Tupac: Resurrection (2003) **C-111m.** *** D: Lauren Lazin. You don't have to be a devotee of rap music to be intrigued by this introspective documentary about Tupac Shakur, the gangsta rapper who was murdered in 1996. Tupac himself narrates (his words are culled from interviews) and the result is a multidimensional portrait of the world of rap and how one complex, controversial personality is victimized by fame. Afeni Shakur, Tupac's mother, is one of the executive producers. [R] ▼)

Turbo: A Power Rangers Movie (1997-U.S.-Japanese) **C-99m.** *½ D: David Winning. Jason David Frank, Steve Cardenas, Catherine Sutherland, Johnny Yong Bosch, Nakia Burrise, Hilary Shepard Turner, Blake Foster. The Mighty Morphin Power Rangers are back in this cheesy feature, and doing battle against the evil Divatox. Kids may like the gadgets and gimmicks, but few others will. Followed by a direct-to-video sequel. [PG] ▼●)

Turbulence (1997) **C-103m.** **½ D: Robert Butler. Ray Liotta, Lauren Holly, Brendan Gleeson, Ben Cross, Rachel Ticotin, Jeffrey DeMunn, John Finn, Catherine Hicks, Hector Elizondo. As a 747 roars through a rising storm, stewardess Holly faces serial killer Liotta—alone. Though undeniably silly (a slasher movie on a plane?), this often delivers the goods through sheer brassiness, and Liotta has a high old time as the nutzoid killer. Followed by two direct-to-video sequels. Super 35. [R] ▼●)

Turistas (2006) **C-94m.** ** D: John Stockwell. Josh Duhamel, Melissa George, Olivia Wilde, Desmond Askew, Beau Garrett, Max Brown, Agles Steib, Miguel Lunardi. A group of backpacking, bikini-wearing, beer-swilling young tourists are marooned in a remote Brazilian jungle village, where they soon find organ donations are not a voluntary practice. Low-budget horror item presents its main villain as a sort of modern-day Robin Hood who takes from the rich and gives to the poor, medically speaking. Largely exploitative film does have its moments, just not too many of them. Unrated version runs 102m. Super 35. [R])

Turkey Shoot SEE: **Escape 2000**

Turk 182! (1985) **C-98m.** ** D: Bob Clark. Timothy Hutton, Robert Urich, Kim Cattrall, Robert Culp, Darren McGavin, Steven Keats, James Tolkan, Peter Boyle, Paul Sorvino, Dick O'Neill. Contrived attempt at Capra-esque comedy. Young Brooklynite turns into super-graffiti artist to protest N.Y.C.'s lack of support for his brother, an injured fireman. Hutton's brooding persona doesn't suit this comic setting. Panavision. [PG-13] ▼)

Turner & Hooch (1989) **C-97m.** ** D: Roger Spottiswoode. Tom Hanks, Mare Winningham, Craig T. Nelson, Reginald VelJohnson, Scott Paulin, J.C. Quinn, John McIntire, Beasley. Detective Hanks' only means of catching some murderers is by extracting their identity from the sole murder witness: a dog named Hooch. Hanks (who plays a neatness freak) and Hooch (a lovably ugly dog who makes a mess of everything) squeeze all the humor they can out of a paper-thin script—but even they can't make up for a bummer of an ending. [PG] ▼●)

Turning, The (1992) **C-91m.** ** D: L. A. Puopolo. Karen Allen, Raymond J. Barry, Michael Dolan, Tess Harper, Gillian Anderson. A disturbed young man arrives in his small Virginia hometown and tries to prevent his parents' divorce, which leads instead to violence. Meant to show how loveless homes can irrevocably scar children, but leaden paced and boring. [R] ▼)

Turning Point, The (1952) **85m.** **½ D: William Dieterle. William Holden, Alexis Smith, Edmond O'Brien, Ed Begley, Tom Tully, Don Porter, Ted de Corsia, Neville Brand, Carolyn Jones. Tough script by Warren Duff sparks this gritty if familiar drama. O'Brien is a crime-buster investigating big-city corruption; Holden, his boyhood friend, is a cynical reporter. Scenario was inspired by the Kefauver Committee hearings into organized crime.

Turning Point, The (1977) **C-119m.** **½ D: Herbert Ross. Anne Bancroft, Shirley MacLaine, Mikhail Baryshnikov, Leslie Browne, Tom Skerritt, Martha Scott, Marshall Thompson. Two friends who started in ballet are reunited after many years; Bancroft is now a star ballerina, MacLaine a Midwestern housewife/dance teacher whose daughter (Browne) is embarking on her own ballet career. Promising idea bogs down in clichés, with supposedly liberated treatment of women's relationships exemplified by wild catfight. Those few dance sequences presented intact give film its only value. Written by Arthur Laurents; photographed by Robert Surtees. Baryshnikov's film debut. [PG] ▼●)

Turning to Stone (1985-Canadian) **C-98m.** *** D: Eric Till. Nicky Guadagni, Shirley Douglas, Anne Anglin, Jackie Richardson, Bernard Behrens. Riveting psychological drama about Guadagni, a nice young girl who's busted for smuggling drugs, and her adjustment to unhappy realities of life behind bars. For once, a nonexploitation women's prison drama. Fine performances all around; expert script by Judith Thompson.

Turn It Up (2000) **C-87m.** *½ D: Robert Adetuyi. Pras, Ja Rule, Vondie Curtis Hall, Tamala Jones, Jason Statham. An aspiring rapper is held back by his criminal best pal and reunited with his estranged musician father. Contrived, gratuitously violent B movie manages to rip off both Jimmy Cagney and blaxploitation. In his first leading-man role, Pras (of Fugees fame) has all the charisma of a shipping crate. Not even music cameos from DJ Scribble and Faith Evans raise the pulse of this clichéd bloodbath. Turn it off! Super 35. [R]▼●

Turn of the Screw, The (1992-British-French) **C-95m.** ** D: Rusty Lemorande. Patsy Kensit, Stephane Audran, Julian Sands, Clare Szekores, Joseph England, Marianne Faithfull. Sands hires governess Kensit to look after his deceptively sweet-looking niece and nephew, who reside in a country manor. Wooden adaptation (by director Lemorande) of the Henry James masterpiece. Filmed far more successfully as THE INNOCENTS. ▼●

Turn the River (2008) **C-92m.** *** D: Chris Eigeman. Famke Janssen, Jaymie Dornan, Rip Torn, Matt Ross, Lois Smith, Marin Hinkle, Terry Kinney, John Juback, Jordan Bridges, Ari Graynor. Intimate drama about a tough cookie who ekes out a living hustling pool games for money, with some help from an old friend (Torn) who runs a billiard parlor. She also has a secret relationship with the son she gave up in infancy, who lives with his father and stepmother, and schemes to find a way they can run off together. Interesting characterizations and a great part for Janssen mark this small-scale indie; writing and directing debut for actor Eigeman, who has a small role near the end of the film. [R]●

Turtle Beach (1992-Australian) **C-85m.** BOMB D: Stephen Wallace. Greta Scacchi, Joan Chen, Jack Thompson, Art Malik, Norman Kaye, Victoria Longley, Martin Jacobs. Photojournalist/mom Scacchi ankles Australia for Malaysia to cover Chen and the Vietnamese boat people, leaving herself open to charges of parental neglect. Not so much edited as patched, and even drably shot by the great Russell Boyd. This unredeemed stinker was barely released in the U.S. [R]

Turtle Diary (1985-British) **C-97m.** *** D: John Irvin. Glenda Jackson, Ben Kingsley, Richard Johnson, Michael Gambon, Harriet Walter, Rosemary Leach, Eleanor Bron, Nigel Hawthorne. Deliciously original (if low-key) fable of two repressed people who are drawn together—and ultimately freed—by an unusual common interest: they both become concerned about the fate of captive giant turtles at the zoo. Witty, decidedly offbeat script by Harold Pinter (who does a cameo as a bookstore customer), based on Russell Hoban's novel. Johnson, who plays Jackson's jovial next-door neighbor, also produced the film. [PG]▼●

Tuvalu (2000-German) **C-87m.** *** D: Veit Helmer. Denis Lavant, Chulpan Hamatova, Philippe Clay, Terrence Gillespie, Djoko Rossich (Rosic). Gloriously odd, wildly whimsical creation, a virtually silent film with a hand-tinted look. This fairy tale takes place at a once-grand, now-crumbling bathhouse that stands in the middle of nowhere. The owner's son (Lavant) struggles to keep the operation alive, for the sake of his blind father, even as developers threaten to destroy it. A dreamlike movie filled with charm and invention, though it may be too bizarre for some viewers. Filmed in Bulgaria. CinemaScope. [R]▼●

Tuxedo, The (2002) **C-98m.** BOMB D: Kevin Donovan. Jackie Chan, Jennifer Love Hewitt, Jason Isaacs, Debi Mazar, Ritchie Coster, Romany Malco, Mia Cottet, Peter Stormare, Colin Mochrie, James Brown. Dreadful concoction casts Chan as a cabbie-turned-chauffeur who must take the place of his new boss, a dashing government spy; when he dons the secret agent's specially designed tuxedo, he acquires superhuman skills. Boneheaded movie replaces (or augments) Chan's dazzling martial arts skills with special effects; what's more, the script's t&a "humor" is a poor fit for the ever-likable star. Hewitt is incredibly obnoxious as Jackie's new partner. Bob Balaban appears unbilled. [PG-13] ▼●

TV Set, The (2007) **C-88m.** *** D: Jake Kasdan. David Duchovny, Sigourney Weaver, Ioan Gruffudd, Judy Greer, Fran Kranz, Lindsay Sloane, Justine Bateman, Lucy Davis, M. C. Gainey, Philip Baker Hall, Andrea Martin, Willie Garson, Kathryn Joosten. Duchovny plays a TV writer-producer who has created a personal, and well-regarded, script for a potential series. But casting and shooting that pilot while appeasing the "network suits" are no easy tasks if you want to hang on to your soul. Amusing if low-key satire has the feel of being made by people who know this path all too well. Written by the director. HD Widescreen. [R]●

Twelfth Night (1996-British) **C-134m.** **½ D: Trevor Nunn. Imogen Stubbs, Helena Bonham Carter, Toby Stephens, Nigel Hawthorne, Ben Kingsley, Richard E. Grant, Mel Smith, Imelda Staunton, Nicholas Farrell, Stephen Mackintosh. Shakespeare's farce gets transported here to the 1890s, with Stubbs donning male disguise in the court of a duke after she's separated from her brother in a shipwreck. For a surprising amount of its long running time, the film plays the story straight, only to loosen up some in the later scenes—particularly those involving Malvolio. Lackluster, but easy to take. Stephens (who plays Orsino) is the son of actors Maggie Smith and Robert Stephens. [PG] ▼●❙

12 (2007-Russian) **C-154m.** *** D: Nikita Mikhalkov. Sergey Makovetsky, Nikita Mikhalkov, Sergey Garmash, Valentin Gaft, Alexey Petrenko, Yuri Stoyanov, Sergey Gazarov, Mikhail Efremov, Alexey Gorbunov, Sergey Artsybashev, Victor Verzhbitsky, Roman Madianov, Alexander Adabashian, Apti Magamaev. The fate of a Chechen youth on trial for murdering his adoptive father is passionately debated by eleven jurors who want to convict him and the one holdout among the group. Mikhalkov's expanded and updated adaptation of Reginald Rose's screenplay for Sidney Lumet's 1957 classic 12 ANGRY MEN is long and talky but superbly acted. Absorbing both as drama and as a metaphor for the breakup of post-Soviet Russian society. Super 35. [PG-13]❙

Twelve and Holding (2006) **C-94m.** *** D: Michael Cuesta. Conor Donovan, Jesse Camacho, Zoe Weizenbaum, Linus Roache, Annabella Sciorra, Jeremy Renner, Jayne Atkinson, Marcia Debonis, Tom McGowan, Mark Linn-Baker, Tony Roberts, Michael Fuchs. Searing and provocative look at the painful adolescence of three friends: a boy with a twin brother trying to deal with the fallout of a family tragedy, a girl with a distracted mother who wants to assert her sexuality, and an obese boy whose attempt to reinvent himself doesn't sit well with his parents. Uncomfortably raw at times (like Cuesta's earlier film, L.I.E.) but sharply observed, with exceptional performances from the three young leads. [R]❙

12 Angry Men (1957) **95m.** **** D: Sidney Lumet. Henry Fonda, Lee J. Cobb, Ed Begley, E. G. Marshall, Jack Klugman, Jack Warden, Martin Balsam, John Fiedler, George Voskovec, Robert Webber, Edward Binns, Joseph Sweeney. Brilliant film about one man who tries to convince 11 other jurors that their hasty guilty verdict for a boy on trial should be reconsidered. Formidable cast (including several character-stars-to-be); Lumet's impressive debut film. Script by Reginald Rose, from his television play. Remade for TV in 1997 and as **12** in Russia in 2007. ▼●❙

Twelve Chairs, The (1970) **C-94m.** *** D: Mel Brooks. Ron Moody, Frank Langella, Dom DeLuise, Mel Brooks, Bridget Brice, Robert Bernal. Impoverished Russian nobleman Moody seeks one of 12 dining chairs, now scattered, with jewels sewn into seat. DeLuise hilarious as his chief rival. Unsympathetic characters hamper film's success, though mastermind Brooks still provides many laughs. Filmed in Yugoslavia; versions of this same story have been made in Hollywood, Germany, Argentina, England, and Cuba! [G]▼●❙

Twelve Monkeys (1995) **C-131m.** **½ D: Terry Gilliam. Bruce Willis, Madeleine Stowe, Brad Pitt, Christopher Plummer, Frank Gorshin, David Morse, Jon Seda. In the bleak world of the near-future, a prisoner is sent back in time to the 1990s to discover the source of a plague that killed billions and forced society to move underground. Plays with present/past/future tense in ways both clever and confusing; the kind of movie that leaves you with plenty to talk about afterward. Inspired by Chris Marker's 1962 short film, LA JETÉE. [R]▼●❙

Twelve O'Clock High (1949) **132m.** **** D: Henry King. Gregory Peck, Hugh Marlowe, Gary Merrill, Millard Mitchell, Dean Jagger, Paul Stewart. Taut WW2 story of U.S. flyers in England, an officer replaced for getting too involved with his men (Merrill) and his successor who has same problem (Peck). Jagger won Oscar in supporting role; Peck has never been better. Written by Sy Bartlett and Beirne Lay, Jr., from their novel. Later a TV series. ▼●❙

12:08 East of Bucharest (2006-Romanian) **C-89m.** *** D: Corneliu Porumboiu. Mircea Andreescu, Teo Corban, Ion Sapdaru. Smart, funny, engaging comedy finds a history teacher, a senior citizen, and a TV commentator spending the bulk of a Christmastime local broadcast debating whether a revolution actually occurred in their small town 16 years earlier. With echoes of everyone from Billy Wilder to Milos Forman, this sharply effective film deals with Romanian politics by emphasizing the human factor. Impressive feature debut for writer-director Porumboiu. ❙

12 + 1 SEE: **Thirteen Chairs, The**

12 Rounds (2009) **C-108m.** **½ D: Renny Harlin. John Cena, Aidan Gillen, Ashley Scott, Steve Harris, Brian White, Gonzalo Menendez. Utterly preposterous but enjoyably fast-paced thriller finds World Wrestling Entertainment star Cena cast as a hard-charging New Orleans cop forced into a series of beat-the-clock, life-or-death challenges by a vengeful arms dealer (Gillen) who has kidnapped the cop's sweetheart (Scott). Director Harlin keeps pedal to metal throughout, so that nothing—not even Cena's obvious limitations as an actor—ever decelerates the high-velocity spectacle. Clever use of N.O. locations (many still bearing marks of 2005's Hurricane Katrina) is a plus. Super 35. [PG-13]❙

Twentieth Century (1934) **91m.** **** D: Howard Hawks. John Barrymore, Carole Lombard, Walter Connolly, Roscoe Karns, Etienne Girardot, Ralph Forbes, Charles Levison (Lane), Edgar Kennedy. Super screwball comedy in which egomaniacal Broadway producer Barrymore makes shopgirl Lombard a star; when she leaves him, he does everything he can to woo her back on lengthy train trip. Barrymore has never been funnier, and Connolly and Karns are aces as his long-suffering cronies. Matchless script by Ben Hecht and Charles MacArthur, from their play; later a hit Broadway musical, *On the Twentieth Century.* ▼▶

Twenty Bucks (1993) C-90m. ** D: Keva Rosenfeld. Linda Hunt, Brendan Fraser, Elisabeth Shue, Steve Buscemi, Christopher Lloyd, Spalding Gray, David Rasche, George Morfogen, Concetta Tomei, Shohreh Agdashloo, Gladys Knight, William H. Macy, Diane Baker, David Schwimmer, Jeremy Piven, Kevin Kilner, Matt Frewer, Nina Siemaszko, Kamal Holloway. Intriguing concept—a $20 bill passes from hand to hand, and is briefly in the possession of a diverse group of people—but the result is slight and forgettable. Based on an unsold script written by Endre Boehm in 1935; this updated version was scripted by his son Leslie. Chloe Webb appears unbilled. [R] ▼▶

20 Dates (1999) C-88m. **½ D: Myles Berkowitz. Wannabe filmmaker Berkowitz concocts the idea of filming 20 dates—as the hook to make a movie and as a means of finding love. Contemporary comedy, told in documentary style, is original and fun to watch, with a resolution neither Berkowitz nor the audience could have foreseen. [R] ▼

28 Days (2000) C-104m. **½ D: Betty Thomas. Sandra Bullock, Viggo Mortensen, Dominic West, Diane Ladd, Elizabeth Perkins, Steve Buscemi, Alan Tudyk, Azura Skye, Michael O'Malley, Reni Santoni, Marianne Jean-Baptiste, Margo Martindale. Drunken N.Y. writer with an equally boozy boyfriend checks into rehab after an alcohol-induced accident. She gradually conforms to the program after the institution's seen-it-all patients swing their hatchets at the chip on her shoulder. After a strong beginning, film takes a quick nosedive by going for too many cheap belly-laughs. Helping to a point are generally strong performances, including Bullock's best to date. [PG-13] ▼▶

28 Days Later (2002-British-U.S.) C-112m. *** D: Danny Boyle. Cillian Murphy, Naomie Harris, Brendan Gleeson, Megan Burns, Christopher Eccleston, Noah Huntley. Truly frightening film that begins with an incident at a laboratory where animals are being used for medical research and leads to a deadly virus spreading like wildfire throughout England. Twenty-eight days later, it's up to a handful of still-healthy individuals to band together—and avoid contact with their rabid fellow humans before it's too late. Grim, uncomfortably believable, and scary as hell. Also released theatrically with alternate, more downbeat, ending. Written by Alex Garland. Followed by 28 WEEKS LATER. [R] ▼▶

28 Up (1985-British) C/B&W-133m. ***

D: Michael Apted. Unique documentary in which Apted interviews a diverse group of individuals at ages 7, 14, 21, and 28. A one-of-a-kind portrayal of dreams, aspirations, and realities; fascinating to see the subjects literally age before your eyes. Raise this rating to ***½ if viewed in separate installments—the way it was originally made for TV. Followed by 35 UP. ▼▶

28 Weeks Later (2007-British-U.S.) C-99m. ** D: Juan Carlos Fresnadillo. Robert Carlyle, Rose Byrne, Jeremy Renner, Harold Perrineau, Catherine McCormack, Mackintosh Muggleton, Imogen Poots, Idris Elba, Raymond Waring. Sequel to 28 DAYS LATER takes place in London months after the virus outbreak, as the city is ready to be repopulated under the supervision of U.S.-led NATO forces. Carlyle is reunited with his children (Muggleton, Poots) but lies to them about the fate of their mother, whom he left for dead amid a horde of flesh-eating zombies. Visceral and more graphic than the earlier film, this may satisfy bloodthirsty fans, but it grows tiresome and its metaphoric relationship to the Iraqi occupation is a one-note idea. Better than many sequels, it still suffers in comparison to the original. [R] ▶

25th Hour, The (1967-French-Italian-Yugoslavian) C-119m. ** D: Henri Verneuil. Anthony Quinn, Virna Lisi, Michael Redgrave, Gregoire Aslan, Marcel Dalio, Serge Reggiani. Story of Rumanian peasant's Nazi-enforced 8-year separation from his beautiful wife is indifferently done, in spite of capable acting by stars. Franscope.

25th Hour (2002) C-134m. **½ D: Spike Lee. Edward Norton, Philip Seymour Hoffman, Barry Pepper, Rosario Dawson, Anna Paquin, Brian Cox, Tony Siragusa, Levani Outchaneichvili, Tony Devon. A convicted Manhattan drug dealer (Norton) confronts the choices he has made in life on his last day before serving a 7-year prison sentence. Ambitious attempt to fuse intimate character studies with a larger examination of post-9/11 N.Y.C. never quite succeeds, despite powerful moments and good acting, especially by Norton and Pepper. David Benioff adapted his own novel. Super 35. [R] ▼▶

2046 (2004-Hong Kong-Chinese) C-130m. ***½ D: Wong Kar Wai. Tony Leung, Gong Li, Zhang Ziyi, Takuya Kimura, Faye Wong, Maggie Cheung, Chen Chang. A writer is penning a science-fiction novel presumably titled *2046*, which also happens to be the number of the hotel room next door to him, where many events unfold in this dense, atmospheric film about sexual relationships. In the film/novel a mysterious train takes its passengers to the year 2046 (the year China has set for the end of Hong Kong's current state of independence), but whether in the past, present, or future, the protagonist must deal with love, loss, and regret. A sinuous, romantic, elliptical film that seems to exist in a dream state. Leung plays a darker version of the character he introduced in IN THE MOOD FOR LOVE. Panavision. [R]🔲

24 Hour Party People (2002-British) C-113m. *** D: Michael Winterbottom. Steve Coogan, Lennie James, Shirley Henderson, Paddy Considine, Andy Serkis, Sean Harris, John Simm, Chris Coghill. Smart, sharp, funny, evocative film about the punk rock scene in Manchester, England, in the early 1970s, and one of its progenitors—who disarmingly tells his own story to us on camera (even commenting on the film itself). Entertaining even if you don't know much about the subject. Coogan is dynamic in the leading role. [R] ▼🔲

24 Hour Woman, The (1999) C-95m. ** D: Nancy Savoca. Rosie Perez, Marianne Jean-Baptiste, Patti LuPone, Karen Duffy, Diego Serrano, Wendell Pierce, Aida Turturro, Rosana De Soto, Chris Cooper. Producer of a morning TV show discovers she's pregnant, and begins to deal with the conflicts facing a career woman who's also trying to start a family. Meanwhile, a mother of three returns to the workforce as her new assistant. Credible and energetic, but the "lesson" it teaches is obvious from the start. A disappointment from talented filmmaker Savoca. [R]▼

TwentyFourSeven (1997-British) **96m.** *** D: Shane Meadows. Bob Hoskins, Danny Nussbaum, James Hooton, Darren Campbell, Justin Brady, Jimmy Hynd, Karl Collins, Johann Myers, Anthony Clarke. Poignant, hard-hitting little drama about an idealist 1980s burnout (Hoskins) who tries to encourage the aimless, angry young men in his working-class town by setting up a boxing club. What might have been a standard, clichéd story is uplifted by a solid script (by Meadows and Paul Fraser), good performances, and plenty of grit. The first in Meadows' so-called Midlands trilogy. Followed by A ROOM FOR ROMEO BRASS and ONCE UPON A TIME IN THE MIDLANDS. [R]▼●

20 Million Miles to Earth (1957) **82m.** *** D: Nathan Juran. William Hopper, Joan Taylor, Frank Puglia, Thomas Browne Henry, John Zaremba, Tito Vuolo, Bart Bradley (Braverman). First spaceship to Venus crashes into the sea off Sicily, with two survivors: pilot Hopper and a fast-growing Venusian monster that just wants to be left alone (but fights back when frightened). Climax takes place in the Colosseum in Rome. Intelligent script, fast pace, and exceptional special effects by Ray Harryhausen make this one of the best monster-on-the-loose movies ever. Unnamed monster is known as the "Ymir" to its fans. Also shown in a computer-colored version. ▼●🔲

Twentynine Palms (2003-French-German) C-119m. BOMB D: Bruno Dumont. Katia (Yekaterina) Golubeva, David Wissak. Smarmy, ultra-pretentious "road" picture with dialogue that sounds like it was recorded from a cell phone as a ZABRISKIE (WITHOUT A) POINT for a new generation. Photographer and his unemployed girlfriend, ostensibly scouting locales for a photo shoot, drive endlessly through the California desert, frequently stopping for sexual favors on picturesque rocky slopes or in nondescript motel rooms until their idyllic interludes turn graphically violent because . . . well, that's art. TV viewing could actually improve film as nothing much happens for chunks of time, making it ideal to watch while paying bills, sorting laundry, talking to friends or writing your memoirs. Widescreen.▼🔲

29th Street (1991) C-101m. **½ D: George Gallo. Danny Aiello, Anthony LaPaglia, Lainie Kazan, Frank Pesce, Donna Maghani, Rick Aiello, Vic Manni, Ron Karabatsos, Robert Forster, Pete Antico, Joe Franklin. ·Richly seasoned look at N.Y.C. Italian-Americans through the eyes of Frank Pesce, who sees his life as blessed with luck, even though it presents itself in strange ways; the story is told in flashback on the night of New York State's first lottery drawing. Aiello and LaPaglia are dynamite as father and son, and that's the real Frank Pesce as older brother Vito; he also cowrote the story, based on his life. Directing debut for MIDNIGHT RUN screenwriter Gallo. [R]▼●🔲

Twenty-one (1991-British) C-101m. ** D: Don Boyd. Patsy Kensit, Jack Shepherd, Patrick Ryecart, Maynard Eziashi, Rufus Sewell, Sophie Thompson. One Brit's jog around the sexual track before reaching the age of . . . guess. Her array of beaus includes one junkie, and one married jerk who openly hustles her at his own wedding. Inferior to DARLING and THE GRASSHOPPER, of an earlier generation; Kensit's first-person monologues are unusually frank but not as captivating as intended. [R]▼●

21 (2008) C-122m. **½ D: Robert Luketic. Jim Sturgess, Kevin Spacey, Kate Bosworth, Laurence Fishburne, Aaron Yoo, Liza Lapira, Jacob Pitts, Jack McGee, Josh Gad. Working-class whiz kid (Sturgess) who's wondering how he's going to pay his way through M.I.T. is recruited by professor Spacey to join his elite team: a small group of supersmart students who've learned how to count cards and beat the blackjack tables in Las Vegas. Entertaining wish-fulfillment yarn, taken from a true story, starts to deflate toward the climax when—inevitably—Sturgess goes riding for a fall. Based on Ben Mezrich's book *Bringing Down the House.* HD Widescreen. [PG-13]🔲

21 Grams (2003) C-125m. *** D: Alejandro González Iñárritu. Sean Penn, Benicio Del Toro, Naomi Watts, Charlotte Gainsbourg, Melissa Leo, Clea DuVall, Danny Huston,

Paul Calderon, Eddie Marsan. Three disparate people—an ex-con who has found religion, a woman who has lost her family, and a professor given a second chance at life—are brought together through unforeseen circumstances. Arresting drama told in fragmented, nonlinear fashion (not surprising from the creators of AMORES PERROS, director Iñárritu and writer Guillermo Arriaga) that does not quite illuminate the heavy material as much as the filmmakers would like to think. Beautifully acted by the three leads. [R] ▼▼

27 Dresses (2008) **C-106m.** ****½** D: Anne Fletcher. Katherine Heigl, James Marsden, Malin Akerman, Edward Burns, Judy Greer, Melora Hardin, Brian Kerwin. Having played the role of bridesmaid in far too many weddings, Heigl finally decides to tell her boss (Burns) that she loves him. Just then, he meets and falls in love with her beautiful sister (Akerman) and Heigl is left to plan her dream wedding for her sibling. Heigl and Marsden are fun to watch in this amiable (if conventional) film. Panavision. [PG-13]▮

20000 Leagues Under the Sea (1954) **C-127m.** ******** D: Richard Fleischer. Kirk Douglas, James Mason, Paul Lukas, Peter Lorre, Robert J. Wilke, Carleton Young. Superb Disney fantasy-adventure on grand scale, from Jules Verne's novel. 19th-century scientist Lukas and sailor Douglas get involved with power-hungry Captain Nemo (Mason) who operates futuristic submarine. Memorable action sequences, fine cast make this a winner. Won Oscars for Art Direction and Special Effects. First filmed in 1916. Remade in 1997 as both a miniseries and made-for-TV movie. CinemaScope. ▼●▮

20000 Years in Sing Sing (1933) **81m.** ******* D: Michael Curtiz. Spencer Tracy, Bette Davis, Arthur Byron, Lyle Talbot, Warren Hymer, Louis Calhern, Grant Mitchell, Sheila Terry. Still-powerful prison drama has only teaming of Tracy and Davis. He's a hardened criminal, she's his girl. Based on Warden Lewis E. Lawes' book. Remade as CASTLE ON THE HUDSON.▮

23 Paces to Baker Street (1956) **C-103m.** ******* D: Henry Hathaway. Van Johnson, Vera Miles, Cecil Parker, Patricia Laffan, Maurice Denham, Estelle Winwood. Absorbing suspenser filmed in London has blind playwright Johnson determined to thwart crime plans he has overheard. CinemaScope.

2012 (2009) **C-158m.** ****** D: Roland Emmerich. John Cusack, Chiwetel Ejiofor, Amanda Peet, Oliver Platt, Thandie Newton, Danny Glover, Woody Harrelson, Tom McCarthy, George Segal, Stephen McHattie, Patrick Bauchau, Beatrice Rosen, Johann Urb. After solar flares upset Earth's balance, tsunamis, earthquakes, and volcanoes destroy cities and decimate citizenry across the globe, seemingly in fulfillment of ancient Mayan prophecy. State-of-the-art CGI wizardry is employed to eye-popping effect in this latest apocalyptic extravaganza from the director of THE DAY AFTER TOMORROW. But the pace too often is plodding, the performances wildly uneven, and the script crammed with laughable clichés and preposterous coincidences. Despite game efforts by Harrelson, Ejiofor, and Platt, this amped-up version of a '70s disaster film offers little more than very expensive cheap thrills. HD Widescreen. [PG-13] ▮

Twice in a Lifetime (1985) **C-111m.** ******* D: Bud Yorkin. Gene Hackman, Ann-Margret, Ellen Burstyn, Amy Madigan, Ally Sheedy, Brian Dennehy, Stephen Lang, Darrell Larson. Middle-aged man falls in love with younger woman and must endure the pain he causes not only his wife but also his children—especially his oldest daughter. Realistic look at the way different people react to situation keeps this film away from cliché and predictability; superior acting, especially by Hackman, Burstyn, and Madigan (as the angry daughter) make it special. Written by Colin Welland. [R]▼●▮

Twice-Told Tales (1963) **C-119m.** ******* D: Sidney Salkow. Vincent Price, Sebastian Cabot, Mari Blanchard, Brett Halsey, Richard Denning. Episodic adaptation of Hawthorne stories has good cast, imaginative direction, and sufficient atmosphere to keep one's interest. One of the TALES is an abbreviated HOUSE OF THE SEVEN GABLES, which also starred Price in the 1940 version.▼●▮

Twice Upon a Time (1983) **C-75m.** *****½** D: John Korty, Charles Swenson. Voices of Lorenzo Music, Judith Kahan Kampmann, Marshall Efron, James Cranna, Julie Payne, Hamilton Camp, Paul Frees. Captivating, hilarious animated feature done in a pseudo–cut-out style called "Lumage." Evil bosses of the Murkworks intend to blanket the world with perpetual nightmares; only a looney (and indescribable) bunch of would-be heroes can stop them. Too complex and fast-paced for small children, but a real treat for everyone else. Never given a full theatrical release, despite having George Lucas as executive producer. [PG]▼●

Twice Upon a Yesterday (1998-Spanish-British) **C-96m.** ****** D: Maria Ripoll. Douglas Henshall, Lena Headey, Penélope Cruz, Gustavo Salmeron, Eusebio Lazaro, Mark Strong, Charlotte Coleman, Elizabeth McGovern. Scotsman Henshall torpedoes his longtime relationship with Headey through his constant philandering. Then two garbage men with magical powers enable him to go back in time and make things right. Odd, undernourished little film doesn't make the most of its premise. [R]▼▮

Twilight (1998) **C-94m.** ****½** D: Robert

Benton. Paul Newman, Susan Sarandon, Gene Hackman, Reese Witherspoon, Stockard Channing, James Garner, Giancarlo Esposito, Liev Schreiber, Margo Martindale, John Spencer, M. Emmet Walsh. Newman does a favor for old friend Hackman and finds himself waist-deep in murder and intrigue, as skeletons tumble out of the closet. Old-fashioned private-eye yarn, set in L.A. Newman is in fine form, surrounded by a great cast, but the film lacks spark, momentum, and an original point of view. Benton cowrote this with Richard Russo, but this is no match for their earlier collaboration (with Newman), NOBODY'S FOOL. [R]▼●)

Twilight (2008) **C-121m.** *** D: Catherine Hardwicke, Kristen Stewart, Robert Pattinson, Billy Burke, Peter Facinelli, Elizabeth Reaser, Cam Gigandet, Ashley Greene, Anna Kendrick, Nikki Reed, Taylor Lautner, Kellan Lutz, Jackson Rathbone, Michael Welch, Justin Chon, Jose Zuniga, Rachelle Lefevre, Edi Gathegi. Adroit adaptation of the first book in Stephenie Meyer's wildly popular series of novels about Bella (Stewart), a misfit teen who's just moved to Forks, Washington, to live with her divorced dad. There she falls under the spell of mysterious fellow student Edward Cullen (Pattinson), who turns out to be a vampire. Blending the romantic with the supernatural, and taking itself seriously at every turn, this film touches all the bases and neatly sets up its sequel: NEW MOON. Super 35. [PG-13]▌

Twilight for the Gods (1958) **C-120m.** **½ D: Joseph Pevney. Rock Hudson, Cyd Charisse, Arthur Kennedy, Leif Erickson, Charles McGraw, Ernest Truex, Richard Haydn, Wallace Ford. Ernest K. Gann book, adapted by the author, becomes turgid soaper of people on run-down vessel heading for Mexico, their trials and tribulations to survive when ship goes down.

Twilight of the Golds (1997) **C-93m.** *** D: Ross Marks. Jennifer Beals, Faye Dunaway, Brendan Fraser, Garry Marshall, Sean O'Bryan, Jon Tenney, Rosie O'Donnell. Reality-based film focuses on the ensuing turmoil after a geneticist's pregnant wife undergoes genetic testing. Thought-provoking drama, outstanding cast; Fraser is particularly captivating as gay Uncle David. Based on an off-Broadway play. Debuted on cable TV before theatrical release. [PG-13] ▼●)

Twilight People, The (1972-U.S.-Filipino) **C-84m.** BOMB D: Eddie Romero. John Ashley, Pat Woodell, Charles Macaulay, Pam Grier, Jan Merlin, Eddie Garcia. Incredibly inept rip-off of ISLAND OF LOST SOULS has former SS doctor performing hideous experiments resulting in beings half-human, half-creature. Will put insomniacs to sleep. Aka BEASTS. [PG]▼)

Twilight Saga: Eclipse SEE: **Eclipse** (2010)

Twilight Saga: New Moon, The SEE: **New Moon** (2009)

Twilight's Last Gleaming (1977-U.S.-German) **C-146m.** **½ D: Robert Aldrich. Burt Lancaster, Richard Widmark, Charles Durning, Melvyn Douglas, Paul Winfield, Burt Young, Joseph Cotten, Roscoe Lee Browne, Gerald S. O'Loughlin, Richard Jaeckel, Vera Miles, Leif Erickson, Charles McGraw, John Ratzenberger. Unstable Air Force officer seizes missile installation, threatens to start World War 3 unless U.S. comes clean on its former Vietnam policy. OK if overlong; based on Walter Wager's novel *Viper Three*. [R]▼●

Twilight Time (1983-U.S.-Yugoslavian) **C-102m.** *½ D: Goran Paskaljevic. Karl Malden, Jodi Thelen, Damien Nash, Mia Roth, Pavle Vujisic, Dragon Maksimovic. Sincere but unsuccessful film about an old man saddled with the upbringing of two grandchildren in rural Yugoslavia. Malden's performance is first-rate, but uneasy blend of American and Yugoslav elements and snail's pace all but sink it. [PG]

Twilight Zone—The Movie (1983) **C-102m.** **½ D: John Landis, Steven Spielberg, Joe Dante, George Miller. Vic Morrow, Scatman Crothers, Bill Quinn, Selma Diamond, Kathleen Quinlan, Jeremy Licht, Kevin McCarthy, William Schallert, John Lithgow, Abbe Lane, Bill Mumy, John Larroquette, narrated by Burgess Meredith. Dan Aykroyd and Albert Brooks provide entertaining prologue for four unusual tales (three actual remakes from Rod Serling's classic TV series), but none of them provides all-important moment of revelation that made the show so memorable . . . and more tellingly, none improves on the original. Best—final segment, remake of "Nightmare at 20,000 Feet," with Lithgow as terrified airline passenger, though even this episode is more explicit (and therefore less intriguing) than '60s TV version. [PG]▼●)

Twin Dragons (1992-Hong Kong) **C-89m.** *** D: Ringo Lam, Tsui Hark. Jackie Chan, Maggie Cheung, Teddy Robin (Kwan), Nina Li Chi, Alfred Cheung, Lai Ying Chow, Kirk Wong. Separated at birth, twin Jackies unexpectedly meet in Hong Kong; one's a famous conductor, the other a race car mechanic whose best friend has just been kidnapped; the twins are mentally linked, Corsican Brothers–style. Fast-paced action comedy with great stunts is one of Jackie's best vehicles, if silly at times. Reedited and redubbed for 1999 U.S. theatrical release from the 100m. original. Directors Lam and Hark have cameos, as does John Woo. Original title: SEUNG LUNG WUI. Technovision. [PG-13]▼●)

Twin Falls, Idaho (1999) **C-110m.** **½ D: Michael Polish. Michael Polish, Mark Polish, Michele Hicks, Jon Gries, Patrick Bauchau, Lesley Ann Warren, Garrett Morris, William Katt, Holly Woodlawn. Dreamy, oddball tale of Siamese twins, one of whom falls in love with a down-on-her-luck prostitute (Hicks). Surprisingly poignant film about family ties never opts for the grotesque and has a refreshing sense of deadpan humor. Ambitious debut from the Polish brothers, who wrote and costar. Only problem is overlength. [R]▼▶

Twinkle and Shine SEE: **It Happened to Jane**

Twinkle, Twinkle, Killer Kane SEE: **Ninth Configuration, The**

Twin Peaks: Fire Walk With Me (1992) C-135m. *½ D: David Lynch. Sheryl Lee, Ray Wise, Kyle MacLachlan, Mädchen Amick, Dana Ashbrook, Phoebe Augustine, David Bowie, Eric DaRe, Miguel Ferrer, Pamela Gidley, Heather Graham, Chris Isaak, Moira Kelly, Peggy Lipton, James Marshall, Jürgen Prochnow, Harry Dean Stanton, Kiefer Sutherland, Lenny Von Dohlen, Grace Zabriskie, Frank Silva, Victor Rivers, Calvin Lockhart. Prototypically weird, but also strangely indifferent, prequel to the cult TV series, chronicling the final week in the life of murdered teen Laura Palmer (Lee). Lee is rather affecting under the circumstances, but film was understandably hissed at the Cannes Film Festival and greeted by moviegoer ennui here at home. Two surreal set pieces (one in a bar, the other in a traffic jam) may make it worthwhile for Lynch completists. The director appears as FBI Bureau Chief Gordon Cole. [R]▼▶●

Twins (1988) C-112m. *** D: Ivan Reitman. Arnold Schwarzenegger, Danny DeVito, Kelly Preston, Chloe Webb, Bonnie Bartlett, Marshall Bell, Trey Wilson, Hugh O'Brian, Nehemiah Persoff, David Caruso, Maury Chaykin. Entertaining comedy about genetically designed twins (Schwarzenegger and DeVito!) who discover each other's existence at the age of 35. Effectively blends sentiment and roughhouse humor, with the two mismatched stars packing extra punch in their delightful performances. That's Heather Graham as the mom-to-be in the opening scene. [PG]▼▶●

Twins of Evil (1971-British) C-85m. **½ D: John Hough. Peter Cushing, Madeleine Collinson, Mary Collinson, Luan Peters, Dennis Price, Isobel Black, Harvey Hall. One of the twins is a vampire, but nobody can tell which is which. Engaging Hammer chiller makes inspired use of *Playboy*'s first twin playmates. Follow-up to VAMPIRE LOVERS and LUST FOR A VAMPIRE [R]▼●

Twin Town (1997-British) C-101m. ** D: Kevin Allen. Llyr Evans, Rhys Ifans, Dorien Thomas, Dougray Scott, Biddug Williams, Ronnie Williams, Rachel Scorgle. Black comedy—more nasty than funny—about brothers who seek revenge on a bigwig roofing contractor after their handyman father takes a fall. Executive-produced by the

makers of TRAINSPOTTING, this features the same brand of cheeky humor, and a rare look at life on the fringe in the U.K. (Swansea, Southwest Wales), but it stalls midway from absurd plotting and never recovers; we're left with irritating characters who have unintelligible dialects. The director cameos as a local TV host. [R]▼●

Twist, The (1976-French) C-105m. *½ D: Claude Chabrol. Bruce Dern, Stephane Audran, Ann-Margret, Sydne Rome, Jean-Pierre Cassel, Curt Jurgens, Maria Schell, Charles Aznavour. Undistinguished chronicle of the infidelities of various boring upper-class characters. Lackluster direction, with a superior cast wasted. Originally titled FOLIES BOURGEOISES, and filmed in both English and French versions.▼▶

Twist (1992-Canadian) C/B&W-78m. *** D: Ron Mann. Entertaining documentary about the early years of rock 'n' roll, culminating with the popularity of the Twist, the dance craze which swept the nation during the early 1960s. Interesting as a cultural document (showing how whites co-opted black music and styles), and great fun as a trip down memory lane.▼●▶

Twist All Night (1961) 78m. BOMB D: William Hole, Jr. Louis Prima, June Wilkinson, Sam Butera and The Witnesses, Gertrude Michael, David Whorf. Stupid comedy about Prima's attempts to keep his nightclub going; sexy Wilkinson is his girlfriend. Sometimes shown with a nine-minute color prologue, TWIST CRAZE, directed by Allan David. Aka THE CONTINENTAL TWIST.

Twist and Shout (1984-Danish) C-99m. *** D: Bille August. Adam Tonsberg, Lars Simonsen, Ulrikke Juul Bondo, Camilla Soeberg, Thomas Nielsen. Funny, endearing, pleasantly nostalgic tale of a pair of teen buddies in the era of The Beatles' heyday. One (Simonsen) is dominated by his stern, manipulative father, while the other (Tonsberg) experiences the joy and pain of love. Sequel to August's earlier ZAPPA. [R]▼▶

Twist Around the Clock (1961) 86m. ** D: Oscar Rudolph. Chubby Checker, Dion, The Marcels, Vicki Spencer, Clay Cole, John Cronin, Mary Mitchell. Agent Cronin tries to book Twist performers; of course, by the finale, the dance is the rage of America. Dion performs "The Wanderer" and "Runaround Sue." Remake of ROCK AROUND THE CLOCK.▼▶

Twisted (1992) C-82m. *½ D: Adam Holender. Lois Smith, Christian Slater, Tandy Cronyn, Brooke Tracy, Dina Merrill, Dan Ziskie, Karl Taylor, Noelle Parker, John Cunningham, J. C. Quinn. Sadistic teenage genius Slater, already a murderer, sets his sights on babysitter Smith, a recovering mental patient. Made in 1986. Talky, slow, unconvincing and extremely unpleasant. Aka TWISTED: A STEP BEYOND INSANITY. [R]▼

Twisted (2004) **C-97m.** ** D: Philip Kaufman. Ashley Judd, Samuel L. Jackson, Andy Garcia, David Strathairn, Russell Wong, Camryn Manheim, Bill Duke, Mark Pellegrino, Titus Welliver, D.W. Moffett, Richard T. Jones, Leland Orser. Hotshot San Francisco cop, an orphan who was raised by her dad's ex-partner (now the city police commissioner), earns a promotion to homicide inspector, but finds herself the chief suspect in a string of brutal murders. There's no one to root for in this collection of bruised and off-putting characters, least of all Judd (in yet another Ashley-in-jeopardy vehicle), who releases her inner demons in the worst possible ways. Veronica Cartwright appears unbilled. [R]▼▶

Twisted Obsession (1989-Spanish-French) **C-103m.** *½ D: Fernando Trueba. Jeff Goldblum, Miranda Richardson, Anemone, Daniel Ceccaldi, Dexter Fletcher, Liza Walker. Laughable, would-be erotic thriller, with Goldblum a writer in Paris who gets mixed up with a strange British director and his seductive 16-year-old sister. Pretentious, enervated Eurotrash like this gives "art" movies a bad name . . . but where else could you see Goldblum playing an irresistible stud? Originally titled THE MAD MONKEY. Panavision. [R]▼▶●

Twister (1988) **C-94m.** *½ D: Michael Almereyda. Harry Dean Stanton, Suzy Amis, Crispin Glover, Dylan McDermott, Jenny Wright, Lois Chiles. Squirrelly clan comedy assembles some unlikely siblings at the old man's mansion; try imagining Stanton as any extended group's patriarch! Film's eccentricity is more off-putting than whimsical; Amis and Glover as siblings would be a challenge to any parent's reproductive tract. Based on Mary Robison's well-regarded novel *OH!.* [PG-13]▼▶●

Twister (1996) **C-114m.** *** D: Jan De Bont. Helen Hunt, Bill Paxton, Cary Elwes, Jami Gertz, Lois Smith, Alan Ruck, Philip Seymour Hoffman, Jeremy Davies, Todd Field, Zach Grenier, Jake Busey. A wild ride of a movie, dealing with storm chasers who want to learn all they can about tornadoes—by getting inside them. The plot and characterizations are best described as lame, but the special effects are so convincing, and the storms so incredible, that they carry you along (no pun intended) from one kinetic burst to another. Great fun. Written by Michael Crichton and his wife, Anne-Marie Martin. Panavision. [PG-13]▼▶●

Twist of Sand, A (1968-British) **C-90m.** ** D: Don Chaffey. Richard Johnson, Honor Blackman, Jeremy Kemp, Peter Vaughan, Roy Dotrice. Ex-submarine commander Johnson leads crew of smugglers on expedition for diamonds in ordinary programmer.

Twitch of the Death Nerve (1971-Italian) **C-90m.** *** D: Mario Bava. Claudine Auger, Claudio Volonte, Luigi Pistilli, Leopoldo Trieste, Isa Miranda, Laura Betti. The *ne plus ultra* of Bava's colorful horror movies, this influenced such later films as HALLOWEEN and FRIDAY THE 13TH. People in an isolated house are killed one by one in gruesome, imaginative ways. Those who love Bava don't love him for his stories, but for his extraordinary mastery of cinema technique, vividly displayed here. Aka LAST HOUSE ON THE LEFT, PART II (though it has no connection with Part I), BAY OF BLOOD, and CARNAGE—with good reason. Panoramica. [R]▼▶

Two Against the World (1936) **57m.** ** D: William McGann. Humphrey Bogart, Beverly Roberts, Linda Perry, Carlyle Moore, Jr., Henry O'Neill, Claire Dodd. Remake of FIVE STAR FINAL in radio station is more contrived, not as effective. Retitled: ONE FATAL HOUR.

Two Bits (1995) **C-93m.** **½ D: James Foley. Mary Elizabeth Mastrantonio, Al Pacino, Jerry Barrone, Patrick Borriello, Andy Romano, Donna Mitchell, Mary Lou Rosato, Joe Grifasi, Joanna Merlin; narrated by Alec Baldwin. Poignant memoir of growing up in South Philadelphia during the Depression, as seen through the eyes of young Gennaro (Barrone, in his movie debut), who lives with his widowed mother and his talkative grandfather (Pacino)—who insists he's going to die any day now. Beautifully acted by the leads, written with feeling by producer Joseph Stefano, but too slow and delicate to realize its full potential. Still worth seeing for a handful of crystalline moments. Panavision. [PG-13]▼▶●

Two Brothers (2004-French-British) **C-108m.** **½ D: Jean-Jacques Annaud. Guy Pearce, Jean-Claude Dreyfus, Freddie Highmore, Philippine Leroy-Beaulieu, Moussa Maaskri, Vincent Scarito, Maï Anh Lê, Oanh Nguyen. Two Asian tiger cubs are separated; fate takes them on unpredictable paths and introduces them to humans both kind and cruel. The animal footage is much more commanding than the story in this strange, off-kilter family film that contrasts the purity of the jungle with the difficulties of "civilized" life. Moments of magisterial beauty are offset by Disney-esque animal slapstick and broadly sketched, ill-defined human characters. HD 24P Widescreen. [PG]▼▶

Two Can Play That Game (2001) **C-90m.** ** D: Mark Brown. Vivica A. Fox, Morris Chestnut, Anthony Anderson, Wendy Raquel Robinson, Tamala Jones, Bobby Brown, Mo'Nique Imes Jackson, Gabrielle Union, Ray Wise. Sassy, self-possessed business exec Fox dispenses advice to her girlfriends on a regular basis, so when her boyfriend (Chestnut) strays one night, she's ready with a foolproof 10-day plan to teach him a lesson. Fun for a while, but Fox's game playing (and talking directly to the camera) soon grows tedious. Anderson adds comic energy every time he's on screen. Film ends with a novel twist: outtakes that aren't funny. [R] ▼▶

Two Daughters (1961-Indian) **114m.** ***½ D: Satyajit Ray. Anil Chatterjee, Chandana Bannerjee, Soumitra Chatterjee, Aparna Das Gupta, Sita Mukherji. A pair of episodes, adapted from the writings of Rabindranath Tagore, one good and the other superb. The former concerns the curious relationship between a postmaster and an orphan girl; the latter is the funny, gentle chronicle of what happens when a student rejects the woman his mother has chosen for his wife, deciding instead to marry the local tomboy. Ray scripted both stories. Originally released in India as part of a trilogy, running 171m. ▼

2 Days in Paris (2007-French) **C-96m.** *** D: Julie Delpy. Julie Delpy, Adam Goldberg, Daniel Brühl, Marie Pillet, Albert Delpy. First-time director Delpy gets a boost from her own screen chemistry with costar Goldberg, as they play a N.Y.C.-based couple using travel to mend their relationship. The two end up feeling smothered in Paris-bred Delpy's apartment when they're not running into another of her former squeezes (who seem to loom around every corner). Small-scale but breezy, smart, and assured comedy milks Goldberg's increasingly funny fits of exasperation. Delpy's real-life parents play themselves. Delpy wrote, coproduced, edited, and composed the score. [R] ▶

2 Days in the Valley (1996) **C-107m.** *** D: John Herzfeld. Danny Aiello, James Spader, Eric Stoltz, Greg Cruttwell, Jeff Daniels, Teri Hatcher, Glenne Headly, Peter Horton, Marsha Mason, Paul Mazursky, Charlize Theron, Keith Carradine, Louise Fletcher, Austin Pendleton, Lawrence Tierney. Wry crime thriller with gnarled plot involving a murder for hire, a betrayed crook, his slick partner, a dogged cop, a deadly wife, and others caroming off each other in L.A.'s San Fernando Valley. Entertaining and stylish, with fine performances, but more than a little contrived. Written by the director. Panavision. [R] ▼▶

Two Deaths (1995-British) **C-102m.** ** D: Nicolas Roeg. Michael Gambon, Sonia Braga, Patrick Malahide, Ion Caramitru, Nickolas Grace. Bizarre drama about a doctor (Gambon) who has various guests in his home for an elegant dinner party while, outside, a revolution rages and the streets are filling with blood. Braga is the host's mysterious, silent housekeeper. Potentially intriguing drama is done in by its obvious symbolism and leaden pace. [R] ▼▶

Two English Girls (1971-French) **C-108m.** ***½ D: François Truffaut. Jean-Pierre Léaud, Kika Markham, Stacey Tendeter, Sylvia Marriott, Marie Mansart, Philippe Leotard. Profoundly moving tale of a young writer (Léaud), and his lengthy love affair with two sisters. Fine performances and superb Nestor Almendros cinematography; directed with great feeling by Truffaut. In 1984, he added additional footage, increasing the running time to 132m.—and this version rates ****, one of Truffaut's greatest achievements. ▼▶

Two Evil Eyes (1990-Italian) **C-115m.** *½ D: George Romero, Dario Argento. "The Facts in the Case of Mr. Valdemar": Adrienne Barbeau, Ramy Zada, Bingo O'Malley, Jeff Howell, E. G. Marshall. "The Black Cat": Harvey Keitel, Madeleine Potter, John Amos, Sally Kirkland, Kim Hunter, Holter Ford Graham, Martin Balsam. A pair of Poe stories poorly adapted by two leading horror directors. In the first, by Romero, a greedy wife and unscrupulous doctor leave a man hovering in limbo between life and death. In the second, by Argento, a self-obsessed photographer kills his mistress' black cat, then seals the woman behind a wall with another feline. The second is slightly more successful than the first. [R] ▼▶

Two-Faced Woman (1941) **94m.** **½ D: George Cukor. Greta Garbo, Melvyn Douglas, Constance Bennett, Roland Young, Robert Sterling, Ruth Gordon, Frances Carson. Garbo's last film, in which MGM tried unsuccessfully to Americanize her personality. Attempted chic comedy of errors is OK, but not what viewer expects from the divine Garbo. Constance Bennett is much more at home in proceedings, stealing the film with her hilarious performance. ▼▶

Two Faces of Dr. Jekyll, The (1960-British) **C-88m.** ** D: Terence Fisher. Paul Massie, Dawn Addams, Christopher Lee, David Kossoff, Francis De Wolff, Norma Marla. Uneven, sometimes unintentionally funny reworking of Stevenson story stresses Mr. and Mrs. relationship, plus fact that doctor himself is a weakling (and Hyde is suave and handsome!). Unfortunately, dialogue and situations are boring. Look for Oliver Reed as a bouncer. Megascope. ▼▶

Two Family House (2000) **C-107m.** *** D: Raymond De Felitta. Michael Rispoli, Kelly Macdonald, Katherine Narducci, Kevin Conway, Matt Servitto, Michele Santopietro, Louis Guss, Rosemary DeAngelis, Victor Arnold, Dominic Chianese, Richard B. Shull. Charming fable about an Italian-American ne'er-do-well who bucks his wife and family to pursue a dream of operating a bar in Staten Island during the 1950s. Along the way he becomes involved with a feisty young (and pregnant) Irish woman. Warmhearted tale written by the director, based on his own family lore; a welcome, non-clichéd look at this ethnic group. [R] ▼▶

2 Fast 2 Furious (2003) **C-108m.** **½ D: John Singleton. Paul Walker, Tyrese, Eva

Mendes, Cole Hauser, Chris "Ludacris" Bridges, James Remar, Thom Barry, Michael Ealy, Devon Aoki. All but abandoning the street-racing milieu of THE FAST AND THE FURIOUS (except for a high-energy opening sequence), this sequel takes Walker to Florida, where he's recruited as an undercover fed to help capture a drug lord who hires fast drivers. Enough action to please undiscriminating fans, but the script leaves a lot to be desired. Followed by THE FAST AND THE FURIOUS: TOKYO DRIFT. Super 35. [PG-13] ▼▶

Two Flags West (1950) **92m.** ** D: Robert Wise. Joseph Cotten, Linda Darnell, Jeff Chandler, Cornel Wilde, Dale Robertson, Jay C. Flippen, Noah Beery, Jr. Very uneven Civil War Western. Battle scenes of good quality mixed with unappealing script and weak performances.

Two for the Money (2005) **C-122m.** ** D: D. J. Caruso. Al Pacino, Matthew McConaughey, Rene Russo, Jeremy Piven, Armand Assante, Jaime King, Kevin Chapman, Carly Pope. Hotshot hustler who promotes sports gambling over phone lines recruits a former football player to join his team, and fashions him as a protégé—with many strings attached. Although "inspired by a true story," this needlessly convoluted yarn goes on too long and takes far too many detours to score. Pacino is compelling to watch, as always, but his character is alternately inscrutable and infuriating. Super 35. [R] ▼▶

Two for the Road (1967-British) **C-112m.** *** D: Stanley Donen. Audrey Hepburn, Albert Finney, Eleanor Bron, William Daniels, Claude Dauphin, Nadia Gray, Jacqueline Bisset. Beautifully acted film of bickering couple Hepburn and Finney stopping to reminisce about their 12 years of marriage, trying to work to save their happiness. Perceptive, winning film, well directed by Donen. Lovely theme by Henry Mancini; script by Frederic Raphael. Photographed by Christopher Challis, on luscious French locations. Panavision. ▼▶

Two for the Seesaw (1962) **119m.** **½ D: Robert Wise. Robert Mitchum, Shirley MacLaine, Edmon Ryan, Elisabeth Fraser. Well-acted but dated drama about the evolving relationship between two imperfect, vulnerable people: wandering Nebraska lawyer Mitchum and eccentric "born victim" MacLaine. Based on the William Gibson play. Panavision. ▼▶

2 Friends (1986-Australian) **C-76m.** **½ D: Jane Campion. Kris Bidenko, Emma Coles, Kris McQuade, Peter Hehir, Kerry Dwyer, Stephen Leeder, Deborah May, Tony Barry, Steve Bisley. Campion's debut feature, produced for Australian television, is the slice-of-life portrait of a friendship between two adolescent girls, and the subtle changes in their relationship. Not without inspired moments, but lacks the assurance of Campion's later work. The scenario unravels in reverse time, a dramatic structure that seems more gimmicky than inspired. Released in the U.S. in 1996. ▼▶

Two Gentlemen Sharing (1969-British) **C-92m.** ** D: Ted Kotcheff. Robin Phillips, Judy Geeson, Hal Frederick, Esther Anderson, Norman Rossington. Unusual story of mixed racial couples is done more with the sensational in mind than honest portrayal. [R]

Twogether (1994) **C-122m.** *½ D: Andrew Chiaramonte. Nick Cassavetes, Brenda Bakke, Damian London, Jeremy Piven, Jim Beaver. Overlong, uninvolving "relationship drama" in which a couple finds love and fights a lot, in Venice Beach, California. The bodies look good, and there are a couple of hot scenes, but there's nothing much else to recommend in this independently made feature. The leading man is John Cassavetes and Gena Rowlands' son. [R] ▼

Two Girls and a Guy (1998) **C-92m.** ** D: James Toback. Robert Downey, Jr., Heather Graham, Natasha Gregson Wagner, Angel David, Frederique Van Der Wal. Two women—each of whom believes she has found the perfect lover—discover that they're both in love with the same man. Virtually a one-set (Downey's N.Y.C. loft) film, it's well played by the three leads but remains more of an actor's dream than a movie. Manages to be fairly funny and scathing in equal parts; also contains one serious though dimly lit sex scene. Wagner is the daughter of Natalie Wood. [R] ▼▶

Two Hands (1999-Australian) **C-90m.** ** D: Gregor Jordan. Heath Ledger, Bryan Brown, Rose Byrne, Susie Porter, Steve Vidler, David Field, Tom Long, Tony Forrow, Mariel McClorey. Minor crime thriller/comedy-of-errors involving an ambitious but irresponsible young hotshot (Ledger) who becomes a courier for a Sydney mobster and screws up his first assignment. Tries to be outrageous but only intermittently succeeds; it also spotlights a hero who is impossible to root for. Released direct to DVD in the U.S. in 2005. [R] ▶

Two-Headed Spy, The (1958-British) **93m.** *** D: Andre de Toth. Jack Hawkins, Gia Scala, Alexander Knox, Felix Aylmer, Donald Pleasence, Michael Caine, Laurence Naismith. Exciting true story of British spy (Hawkins) who operated in Berlin during WW2 is loaded with heart-stopping tension and suspense. Fine performances all around; one of Caine's earliest roles.

200 Cigarettes (1999) **C-101m.** *½ D: Risa Bramon Garcia. Ben Affleck, Casey Affleck, Jennifer Albano, Dave Chappelle, Guillermo Diaz, Angela Featherstone, Janeane Garofalo, Gaby Hoffmann, Kate Hudson, Catherine Kellner, Courtney Love, Brian McCardie, Jay Mohr, Nicole Parker, Martha Plimpton, Christina Ricci, Paul

Rudd, David Johansen, Elvis Costello. It's New Year's Eve 1981, in N.Y.C.'s East Village, with an assortment of young people trying (not too hard) to reach a loft party thrown by frantic Plimpton. Merits some sort of prize for Most Obnoxious Ensemble . . . and sorely lacks a coherent script. [R]▼●▶

200 Motels (1971) **C-98m. **½** D: Frank Zappa, Tony Palmer. Frank Zappa, Mothers of Invention, Theodore Bikel, Ringo Starr, Keith Moon. Visual, aural assault disguised as movie; completely berserk, freeform film (shot on videotape in England) featuring bizarre humor of Zappa and the Mothers. Some of it ingenious, some funny, but not enough to maintain entire film. Funny, raunchy animation sequence. [R]▼●▶

Two If by Sea (1996) **C-96m. *½** D: Bill Bennett. Denis Leary, Sandra Bullock, Stephen Dillane, Yaphet Kotto, Wayne Robson, Jonathan Tucker, Mike Starr, Michael Badalucco. Alternately boring and grating comedy about a pair of low-class lovers on the lam after he's stolen a valuable painting. Leary cowrote this unsatisfying "romantic" caper which changes moods with each scene. Bullock's charm emerges unscathed. [R]▼●▶

Two Jakes, The (1990) **C-137m. ** ** D: Jack Nicholson. Jack Nicholson, Harvey Keitel, Meg Tilly, Madeleine Stowe, Eli Wallach, Ruben Blades, Frederic Forrest, David Keith, Richard Farnsworth, Tracey Walter, Joe Mantell, James Hong, Perry Lopez, Rebecca Broussard, Luana Anders. Belated sequel to CHINATOWN set in 1948 L.A., with oil having replaced water as the natural resource of choice. Jake Gittes investigates complex case of adultery and shady real estate dealings by Keitel (excellent, as the other Jake) and cheating wife Tilly. Ponderous and convoluted beyond belief (though never boring), film will make no sense to anyone who's never seen CHINATOWN; the old indecipherable plot routine that worked for THE BIG SLEEP (1946) doesn't cut it here. Faye Dunaway makes a brief (and welcome) contribution; Tom Waits appears unbilled as a policeman. Super 35. [R]▼●▶

Two-Lane Blacktop (1971) **C-101m. ***½** D: Monte Hellman. James Taylor, Warren Oates, Laurie Bird, Dennis Wilson, David Drake, Richard Ruth, Alan Vint. Cult film about race across the Southwest between a '55 Chevy and a new GTO has intense direction to compensate for low-key script; Oates' performance is about as good as you'll ever see and should have had the Oscar. Quintessential movie of its time, with aimless characters who only know one thing: the need to race their cars. Watch for Harry Dean Stanton as a hitchhiker. Techniscope. [R]▼●▶

Two Lovers (2009-U.S.-French) **C-109m. ***½** D: James Gray. Joaquin Phoenix,

Gwyneth Paltrow, Vinessa Shaw, Isabella Rossellini, Elias Koteas, Moni Moshonov, Julie Budd, Nick Gillie. Fragile young man (Phoenix) lives with his parents in a claustrophobic Brighton Beach, Brooklyn, apartment. Just after meeting a nice, "safe" woman (Shaw) who's interested in him—and happens to be the daughter of his father's new business partner—he encounters a beautiful but troubled neighbor and falls recklessly in love with her, despite the fact that she doesn't return his feelings. Intensely felt, emotionally direct drama from cowriter-director Gray invokes the spirit of vintage American and European films. Wonderfully observed, it makes great use of its locations and offers its stars a terrific showcase. HD Widescreen. [R]▶

Two Loves (1961) **C-100m. ** ** D: Charles Walters. Shirley MacLaine, Laurence Harvey, Jack Hawkins, Juano Hernandez, Nobu McCarthy. Plodding sudser set in New Zealand with spinster teacher MacLaine trying to decide between suitors Harvey and Hawkins. CinemaScope.

Two-Minute Warning (1976) **C-115m. *½** D: Larry Peerce. Charlton Heston, John Cassavetes, Martin Balsam, Beau Bridges, Marilyn Hassett, David Janssen, Jack Klugman, Gena Rowlands, Walter Pidgeon, Brock Peters, David Groh, Mitchell Ryan, Pamela Bellwood, Andy Sidaris, Vincent Baggetta, Robert Ginty. Pointless story of attempt to catch sniper in packed football stadium. Usual mélange of hackneyed characters in this contrived Hollywood product. Merv Griffin sings the national anthem! Panavision. [R]▼●▶

Two Moon Junction (1988) **C-104m. **½** D: Zalman King. Sherilyn Fenn, Richard Tyson, Louise Fletcher, Burl Ives, Kristy McNichol, Millie Perkins, Don Galloway, Herve Villechaize, Dabbs Greer, Screamin' Jay Hawkins. Or, *Sorority Girl Goes Nympho.* Well-bred Dixie beauty gets an itch south of the navel to take off with a traveling carny hunk; rich grandma Fletcher and sheriff Ives conspire to halt the union. Camp fest is just funny and sexy enough to maintain interest; McNichol has a lively cameo as a bisexual cowgirl. The title *may* be a pun. Followed by a sequel. [R]▼●▶

Two Mrs. Carrolls, The (1947) **99m. **½** D: Peter Godfrey. Humphrey Bogart, Barbara Stanwyck, Alexis Smith, Nigel Bruce, Isobel Elsom. Shrill murder drama with Bogie as psychopathic artist who paints wives as Angels of Death, then kills them; Stanwyck registers all degrees of panic as the next marital victim. Filmed in 1945. Also shown in computer-colored version. ▼▶

Two Much (1996-U.S.-Spanish) **C-118m. *½** D: Fernando Trueba. Antonio Banderas, Melanie Griffith, Daryl Hannah, Danny Aiello, Joan Cusack, Eli Wallach, Austin Pendleton, Gabino Diego, Alan Rich, Phil

Leeds, Vincent Schiavelli. Miami scam artist Banderas falls for the sister of his new finacée and pretends to be his own twin brother in order to pursue her. Would-be screwball comedy is filled with embarrassing dialogue, which cast struggles to surmount by overacting. A fiasco . . . and an unfortunate English-language debut for the director of the Oscar-winning BELLE EPOQUE. Based on a novel by Donald E. Westlake. Panavision. [PG-13]▼●]

Two Mules for Sister Sara (1970) **C-105m.** *** D: Don Siegel. Clint Eastwood, Shirley MacLaine, Manolo Fabregas, Alberto Morin, Armando Silvestre. Engaging story of drifter Eastwood helping nun MacLaine across Mexican desert, becoming wary of her un-pious nature. Beautifully shot (by Gabriel Figueroa), well-acted, good fun, marred by needlessly violent massacre climax. Albert Maltz wrote the screenplay, from a story by Budd Boetticher. Panavision. [M/PG]▼]

Two Ninas (2001) **C-90m.** **½ D: Neil Turitz. Ron Livingston, Amanda Peet, Cara Buono, Bray Poor, Linda Larkin, John Rothman, Jill Hennessy. Diverting comedy about a guy who, having reached a self-professed dead end with the opposite sex, winds up in serious relationships with two women at the same time—both of them named Nina! Made on a shoestring, but fresh and funny; written by the director. Filmed in 1998. [R]▼]

Two of a Kind (1983) **C-87m.** BOMB D: John Herzfeld. John Travolta, Olivia Newton-John, Charles Durning, Oliver Reed, Beatrice Straight, Scatman Crothers, Castulo Guerra, Ernie Hudson, Kathy Bates; voice of Gene Hackman. Puerile fantasy-romance with a script that must have been scrawled on a gum wrapper. A quartet of angels try to persuade God to give the human race another chance—using two pretty unappealing subjects (an inventor-turned-bank robber and a not-so-innocent bank teller) as guinea pigs. Just awful. [PG]▼●]

Two of Us, The (1968-French) **86m.** ***½ D: Claude Berri. Michel Simon, Alain Cohen, Luce Fabiole, Roger Carel, Paul Preboist, Charles Denner. Charming film about growing relationship between young Jewish boy sent away from WW2 Paris and blustery, anti-Semitic guardian who lives in the country. Warm, funny, beautifully acted.▼]

Two on a Guillotine (1965) **107m.** **½ D: William Conrad. Connie Stevens, Dean Jones, Cesar Romero, Parley Baer, Virginia Gregg. To receive inheritance from her late father (Romero), a stage illusionist, Connie must spend a week in his spooky mansion. Familiar plot with some scares. Panavision.

2 or 3 Things I Know About Her

(1967-French) **C-95m.** ***½ D: Jean-Luc Godard. Marina Vlady, Anny Duperey, Roger Montsoret, Jean Narboni, Juliet Berto, Claude Miller. Masterly dissection of marriage, materialism, and suburban anomie, depicting a day in the life of an attractive French housewife who goes into Paris once a week for a little casual prostitution in order to maintain her bourgeois lifestyle. Stylish and penetrating sociological study, with great photography by Raoul Coutard. Techniscope.▼]

Two People (1973) **C-100m.** **½D: Robert Wise. Peter Fonda, Lindsay Wagner, Estelle Parsons, Alan Fudge, Geoffrey Horne, Frances Sternhagen. Soapy, but oddly affecting drama about Army deserter returning home to face the consequences and fashion model with whom he falls in love. Beautiful photography by Gerald Hirschfeld and likable performance by Wagner in her first major role. [R]

Two Rode Together (1961) **C-109m.** **½ D: John Ford. James Stewart, Richard Widmark, Linda Cristal, Shirley Jones, Andy Devine, John McIntire, Mae Marsh, Henry Brandon, Anna Lee. Fair Western with Stewart as cynical marshal hired to rescue pioneers captured by the Comanches years ago; Widmark is cavalry officer who accompanies him.▼●

Two Small Bodies (1993) **C-85m.** **½ D: Beth B. Fred Ward, Suzy Amis. Suspicious, neurotic cop Ward investigates the mysterious disappearance of the two children of cocktail waitress Amis, who seems strangely ambivalent over the tragedy. Eerie, effective two-character psychodrama; however, both characters are so unlikable that the film occasionally becomes difficult to watch.▼

2001: A Space Odyssey (1968-British) **C-139m.** **** D: Stanley Kubrick. Keir Dullea, William Sylvester, Gary Lockwood, Daniel Richter; voice of HAL: Douglas Rain. A unique masterpiece, immensely influential; Kubrick starkly depicts several encounters mankind has with never-glimpsed aliens, from the dawn of Man four million years ago to the title year, when an alien artifact is found on the Moon. An expedition tracking its radio signal is launched to Jupiter, with mysterious, haunting results. A visual feast, film also boasts distinction of having put Richard Strauss into the Top 40 with "Also Sprach Zarathustra." Cut by 17 minutes after premiere, by Kubrick himself, to present length. Oscar-winning special effects. Screenplay by Arthur C. Clarke and the director, from Clarke's *The Sentinel.* Followed by 2010 in 1984. Super Panavision 70. [G]▼●]

2010 (1984) **C-114m.** *** D: Peter Hyams. Roy Scheider, John Lithgow, Helen Mirren, Bob Balaban, Keir Dullea, Madolyn Smith, Dana Elcar, Elya Baskin, Savely Kramarov; voice of Douglas Rain. Ambitious sequel to 2001: A SPACE ODYSSEY written by director Hyams from the follow-up novel by Arthur C. Clarke (who has a cameo on Washington park bench). Scheider is perfect Everyman who journeys into space on joint American-Soviet mission to solve mystery of what went wrong on original *Discovery* flight. More concrete and therefore less mystical than 2001, with an ending that's *much* too literal, but still an entertaining journey, with state-of-the-art visual effects by Richard Edlund. Panavision. [PG]▼●◗

2000 Years Later (1969) **C-80m. **** D: Bert Tenzer. Terry-Thomas, Edward Everett Horton, John Abbott, Pat Harrington, Lisa Seagram, Monti Rock III, Rudi Gernreich. Amusing story of 20th-century man exploiting a Roman soldier who comes back to life after 2000 years. [R]

Two Way Stretch (1960-British) **87m. ***** D: Robert Day. Peter Sellers, Wilfrid Hyde-White, Lionel Jeffries, Liz Fraser, Maurice Denham, Bernard Cribbins, David Lodge. Wry shenanigans of Sellers et al. as prisoners who devise a means of escaping to commit a robbery and then return to safety of their cells.▼◗

Two Weeks (2006) **C-102m. **** D: Steve Stockman. Sally Field, Ben Chaplin, Tom Cavanaugh, Julianne Nicholson, Glenn Howerton, Clea DuVall, James Murtaugh, Michael Hyatt, Susan Misner, Jenny O'Hara. Four squabbling siblings reunite at their dying mother's house but the quick stay they were expecting turns into an agonizing two weeks. It talks and walks like a *Lifetime* TV movie, uneasily blending comic moments with agonizing scenes of a cancer-ridden Field. The star is expert, as always, in a story that may feel much more comfortable on the small screen. [R]◗

Two Weeks in Another Town (1962) **C-107m. ***** D: Vincente Minnelli. Kirk Douglas, Edward G. Robinson, Cyd Charisse, George Hamilton, Claire Trevor, Daliah Lavi, Rossana Schiaffino, Constance Ford. Overly ambitious attempt to intellectualize Irwin Shaw novel, revolving around problems of people involved in moviemaking in Rome. Reunites much of the talent from THE BAD AND THE BEAUTIFUL, footage from which is used as the film-within-a-film here. CinemaScope. ▼●◗

Two Weeks in September (1967-French) **C-96m. **½** D: Serge Bourguignon. Brigitte Bardot, Laurent Terzieff, Michael Sarne, James Robertson Justice. Bardot, mistress to older man, has fling with younger lover, can't decide between the two. Location shooting in London and Scotland enhances OK story. Franscope.▼◗

Two Weeks Notice (2002) **C-101m. **½** D: Marc Lawrence. Sandra Bullock, Hugh Grant, Alicia Witt, Dana Ivey, Robert Klein, Heather Burns, David Haig, Dorian

Missick. Community activist and lawyer (Bullock) is hired by a charming, wealthy playboy (Grant) whose development project was formerly one of her targets. She winds up running his life for him, but only when she tires of that (and serves notice) does she begin to realize how much she cares about him. A contrivance from the word go, this paper-thin romantic comedy is still enjoyable because of the two stars' charming performances. [PG-13]▼◗

Two Women (1960-Italian) **99m. ****** D: Vittorio De Sica. Sophia Loren, Raf Vallone, Eleanora Brown, Jean-Paul Belmondo. Loren deservedly won Oscar for heart-rending portrayal of Italian mother who, along with young daughter, is raped by Allied Moroccan soldiers during WW2. How they survive is an intensely moving story. Screenplay by Cesare Zavattini from an Alberto Moravia novel. Loren remade this in 1989 as a two-part Italian TVM.▼●◗

Two Years Before the Mast (1946) **98m. *½** D: John Farrow. Alan Ladd, Brian Donlevy, William Bendix, Esther Fernandez, Howard da Silva, Barry Fitzgerald, Albert Dekker, Darryl Hickman. Badly scripted story of Richard Henry Dana's (Donlevy) crusade to expose mistreatment of men at sea. Da Silva is standout as tyrannical captain. Filmed in 1943. ▼

Tycoon (1947) **C-128m. **½** D: Richard Wallace. John Wayne, Laraine Day, Cedric Hardwicke, Judith Anderson, James Gleason, Anthony Quinn, Grant Withers. Wayne plays determined railroad builder in this overlong, but well-acted drama with fine cast. ▼◗

Tyler Perry's Daddy's Little Girls SEE: **Daddy's Little Girls**

Tyler Perry's Diary of a Mad Black Woman SEE: **Diary of a Mad Black Woman**

Tyler Perry's Madea Goes to Jail SEE: **Madea Goes to Jail**

Tyler Perry's Madea's Big Happy Family SEE: **Madea's Big Happy Family**

Tyler Perry's Madea's Family Reunion SEE: **Madea's Family Reunion**

Tyler Perry's Meet the Browns SEE: **Meet the Browns**

Tyler Perry's The Family That Preys SEE: **Family That Preys, The**

Tyler Perry's Why Did I Get Married? SEE: **Why Did I Get Married?**

Tyler Perry's Why Did I Get Married, Too? SEE: **Why Did I Get Married, Too?**

Tyson (2009) **C-90m. ***** D: James Toback. Emotionally punchy, predominantly talking-head portrait of onetime heavyweight champion Mike Tyson, terrifyingly invincible in his prime but shockingly beatable once he lost the fire in his belly and personal demons wore him down. Given his past fascination, in print and on-screen, with actor-athlete Jim Brown, Toback was probably the best imaginable auteur to get

Tyson to open up so dramatically and disturbingly about his three-year stretch in prison, his inability to trust, his disastrous marriage to actress Robin Givens, and his horrific public outbursts both in and out of the ring. And yet Tyson reveals a tender side that's as compelling as it is surprising. A keen companion to Barbara Kopple's 1993 documentary FALLEN CHAMP: THE UNTOLD STORY OF MIKE TYSON. [R] ▶

──────────

U-Boat 29 SEE: **Spy in Black, The**
U-571 (2000) **C-116m.** **½ D: Jonathan Mostow. Matthew McConaughey, Bill Paxton, Harvey Keitel, Jon Bon Jovi, Jake Weber, David Keith, T.C. Carson, Jack Noseworthy, Thomas Guiry, Erik Palladino, Dave Power, Will Estes. WW2 submarine crew has to find a way to board and overtake a German U-boat and bring back a crucial secret-code transmitter. It turns out to be more difficult than they expect. Agreeably old-fashioned WW2 submarine drama starts with a bang and holds interest throughout, but fizzles out at the end. Still pretty entertaining. Super 35. [PG-13] ▼●
UFOria (1986) **C-100m.** **½ D: John Binder. Cindy Williams, Harry Dean Stanton, Fred Ward, Harry Carey, Jr., Beverly Hope Atkinson. Amiable if sometimes uneasy mix of MELVIN AND HOWARD and CLOSE ENCOUNTERS OF THE THIRD KIND with Williams as a kooky grocery store cashier who believes she has received a message from outer space and will become a female Noah on UFO ark. Made in 1980, this finally found a distributor (and an audience). [PG]▼
Ugetsu (1953-Japanese) **96m.** ***½ D: Kenji Mizoguchi. Machiko Kyô, Masayuki Mori, Kinuyo Tanaka, Sakae Ozawa. Eerie ghost story set in 16th-century Japan tells of two peasants who leave their families; one seeks wealth in the city and the other wishes to become a samurai warrior. Superbly photographed by Kazuo Miyagawa. Full title UGETSU MONOGATARI.▼●
Ugly American, The (1963) **C-120m.** **½ D: George H. Englund. Marlon Brando, Sandra Church, Pat Hingle, Eiji Okada, Arthur Hill, Kukrit Pramoj, Jocelyn Brando. Brando is American ambassador to Asian country; his arrival stirs up pro-communist elements, leading to havoc. Political revelations of U.S. power struggle aren't meat for exciting film. Adapted by Stewart Stern from the William J. Lederer–Eugene Burdick book.▼▶
Ugly Dachshund, The (1966) **C-93m.** ** D: Norman Tokar. Dean Jones, Suzanne Pleshette, Charlie Ruggles, Kelly Thordsen, Parley Baer. Silly, featherweight Disney comedy about husband and wife who train their respective dogs for competition at dog show. Fun for kids, but too contrived and silly for anyone else to enjoy.▼▶

Ugly Truth, The (2009) **C-96m.** **½ D: Robert Luketic. Katherine Heigl, Gerard Butler, Bree Turner, Eric Winter, Nick Searcy, Cheryl Hines, John Michael Higgins, Kevin Connolly, Jesse D. Goins. Battle-of-the-sexes comedy gets down and dirty with a scenario about a trash-talking male chauvinist pig who gets hired by a local TV station. He has to deal with an uptight feminist producer who resents his act, but reluctantly starts taking his advice on how to land a guy. Things really haven't changed much in the 50 years since Rock Hudson and Doris Day did the same kind of comedy, minus the salty language. Fun, if forgettable, fluff. Super 35. [R] ▶
UHF (1989) **C-97m.** ** D: Jay Levey. "Weird Al" Yankovic, Victoria Jackson, Kevin McCarthy, Michael Richards, David Bowe, Stanley Brock, Anthony Geary, Trinidad Silva, Gedde Watanabe, Billy Barty, John Paragon, Fran Drescher, Sue Ane Langdon, Emo Philips. Music video parodist Yankovic's starring feature debut casts him as the manager of a small-time TV station who inadvertently hits it big with his unconventional programming ideas. Story is threadbare, but some of the spoofs of commercials, movies, and TV shows are fun. Yankovic scripted with director Levey. [PG-13]▼●
Ulee's Gold (1997) **C-111m.** *** D: Victor Nuñez. Peter Fonda, Patricia Richardson, Jessica Biel, J. Kenneth Campbell, Christine Dunford, Steven Flynn, Dewey Weber, Tom Wood, Vanessa Zima. A small gem from writer-director Nuñez about a taciturn beekeeper in northern Florida whose ordered life is disrupted when his son sends an SOS from prison. His wife is in trouble, and while Fonda has had no use for her since she abandoned her two daughters (whom he is raising) he tries to help—and gets caught in a quagmire involving his son's former partners in crime. Slow and steady, like the leading character, but rewarding, with Fonda a tower of strength in the best part he's ever had. [R] ▼●
Ultimate Gift, The (2006) **C-117m.** *½ D: Michael O. Sajbel. Drew Fuller, James Garner, Abigail Breslin, Ali Hillis, Lee Meriwether, Brian Dennehy, Bill Cobbs. A spoiled trust-fund brat finds his world turned upside down when his recently deceased grandfather leaves him a series of tasks he must accomplish in order to collect his inheritance. On his journey, he has a variety of experiences—predominantly an encounter with a young single mother and her leukemia-stricken daughter—that help him learn important life lessons about hard work, love, Christianity, and the value of money. Well-meaning film becomes sanctimonious, and its rhetorical methods are so overt (and often shameless) that it fails to charm, move, or persuade. From the novel by Jim Stovall. [PG]▶

Ultimate Solution of Grace Quigley, The SEE: **Grace Quigley**

Ultimate Warrior, The (1975) **C-94m.** **½ D: Robert Clouse. Yul Brynner, Max von Sydow, Joanna Miles, William Smith, Stephen McHattie, Lane Bradbury. Routine acting and directing spoil potentially intriguing futuristic sci-fi. In the 21st century, Brynner and von Sydow control a decreasing band of people fighting for whatever is left in N.Y.C. following ecological disasters. [R]▼❿

Ulysses (1954-Italian) **C-104m.** ** D: Mario Camerini. Kirk Douglas, Silvana Mangano, Anthony Quinn, Sylvie, Rossana Podesta. Hokey, lumbering costumer with Douglas as Ulysses, on his Odyssey home to Penelope after the Trojan War. Watch Kirk speak in dubbed Italian, then English. Seven writers are credited for this, including Ben Hecht and Irwin Shaw.▼❿

Ulysses (1967) **124m.** **½ D: Joseph Strick. Barbara Jefford, Milo O'Shea, Maurice Roeves, T. P. McKenna, Martin Dempsey, Sheila O'Sullivan. Idea of putting James Joyce's massive novel on the screen seemed daring in 1967, but now seems like a stupid stunt. Lots of good prose makes it to the screen, but end result is interesting curio, not a film. Shot on location in Ireland; Strick far more successfully filmed Joyce's A PORTRAIT OF THE ARTIST AS A YOUNG MAN in 1979. Panavision.▼❶❿

Ulzana's Raid (1972) **C-103m.** ***½ D: Robert Aldrich. Burt Lancaster, Bruce Davison, Jorge Luke, Richard Jaeckel, Joaquin Martinez, Lloyd Bochner, Karl Swenson, Richard Farnsworth. Lancaster is a savvy, straight-talking Indian scout who leads cavalry lieutenant Davison (still wet behind the ears) and his company on a discouraging pursuit of an Apache chief. Gritty Western tale written by Alan Sharp, with jarring bursts of violence. [R]▼❶❿

Umberto D (1952-Italian) **89m.** **** D: Vittorio De Sica. Carlo Battisti, Maria Pia Casilio, Lina Gennari. Ex-bureaucrat on a meager fixed pension is about to be forced out into Rome streets with only his beloved mongrel to comfort him. De Sica is said to have considered this his greatest work, and he may have been right; subplot about Battisti's relationship with an unmarried, pregnant woman is as touching as predominant storyline. Shattering, all the way up to the tear-jerking conclusion.▼❶❿

Umbrellas of Cherbourg, The (1964-French) **C-91m.** ***½ D: Jacques Demy. Catherine Deneuve, Nino Castelnuovo, Anne Vernon, Marc Michel, Ellen Farnen. Haunting music (score by Michel Legrand, lyrics by Demy) and gorgeous photography make this an outstanding romantic drama. All dialogue is sung. Followed by THE YOUNG GIRLS OF ROCHEFORT. ▼❶❿

Umbrella Woman, The SEE: **Good Wife, The**

Unaccompanied Minors (2006) **C-89m.** ** D: Paul Feig. Lewis Black, Wilmer Valderrama, Tyler James Williams, Dyllan Christopher, Brett Kelly, Gina Mantegna, Quinn Shephard, Paget Brewster, Rob Corddry, Dominique Saldana, Jessica Walter, Teri Garr, Rob Riggle, Michelle Sandler, David Koechner, Kevin McDonald, Bruce McCulloch, Mark McKinney, Kristen Wiig. Six diverse kids, all heading from one divorced parent to another, are stranded at a Midwestern airport on Christmas Eve, where they wreak havoc and make life miserable for Black, who's in charge of "passenger relations." Low-grade time-filler for kids has neither wit nor subtlety in its shallow bag of tricks. Inspired by a story by Susan Burton first heard on the NPR show *This American Life*. Super 35. [PG]❿

Unbearable Lightness of Being, The (1988) **C-171m.** **** D: Philip Kaufman. Daniel Day-Lewis, Juliette Binoche, Lena Olin, Derek de Lint, Erland Josephson, Pavel Landovsky, Donald Moffat. Extraordinarily well-made adaptation of the acclaimed novel by Milan Kundera about a young Czech doctor of the 1960s who has a way with women (lots of women) and an aversion to politics but who finds himself caught up in his country's political turmoil—and a crisis of commitment with the women in his life. Kaufman and Jean-Claude Carrière's adaptation unfolds just like a good book, taking its time but never meandering as it paints a vivid picture of the character's life and times. Sensual, intelligent, and beautifully acted by the three leads; strikingly photographed by Sven Nykvist. [R]▼❶❿

Unbecoming Age (1992) **C-93m.** **½ D: Deborah Ringel, Alfredo Ringel. Diane Salinger, John Calvin, Wallace Shawn, Colleen Camp, George Clooney, Shera Danese, Nicholas Guest, Priscilla Pointer. Salinger turns 40; depressed and bored, she blows "magic bubbles" which allow her to forget her age and recapture her youthful vigor. Cute romantic comedy–fantasy works most of the way before it runs out of steam. Video title: THE MAGIC BUBBLE. ▼❶

Unbelievable Truth, The (1990) **C-90m.** ** D: Hal Hartley. Adrienne Shelly, Robert Burke, Christopher Cooke, Julia McNeal, Mark Bailey, Gary Sauer, Katherine Mayfield, Edie Falco. Tall, mysterious man returns to his hometown after a stint in prison, causing a variety of reactions from the locals. Small, independently made black comedy may not be to everyone's taste, but it has its moments. Burke went on to replace Peter Weller as Robocop. [R]▼❶❿

Unborn, The (1991) **C-83m.** **½ D: Rodman Flender. Brooke Adams, Jeff Hayenga, James Karen, K Callan, Jane Cameron, Kathy Cameron, Kathy Griffin, Lisa Kudrow. Young wife with a history of miscarriages is convinced that mysterious doctor (Karen) has inseminated her with mutated sperm. The result: a monstrous fetus which is so tough it outlives an attempted abortion. Convincing performances place this horror tale a notch above its exploitive subject matter. 1994 sequel: THE UNBORN II. [R]▼●◗

Unborn, The (2009) C-88m. *½ D: David S. Goyer. Odette Yustman, Gary Oldman, Cam Gigandet, Meagan Good, Idris Elba, Jane Alexander, James Remar, Carla Gugino. When she isn't taking showers or scampering about in scanty underthings, Yustman desperately seeks an explanation for creepy visitations by a twin brother who died at birth. Steeped in Jewish mysticism, and featuring one of the very few on-screen exorcisms performed by a rabbi (Oldman), writer-director Goyer's low-voltage shocker is often inadvertently comical enough to qualify as camp. Even so, some viewers may be seriously offended by this supernatural drama's exploitation of the Holocaust as a plot device. Alternate version runs 89m. Panavision. [PG-13]◗

Unbreakable (2000) C-107m. ** D: M. Night Shyamalan. Bruce Willis, Samuel L. Jackson, Robin Wright Penn, Charlayne Woodard, Spencer Treat Clark, James Handy, Eamonn Walker, Leslie Stefanson. Sullen security guard Willis, on the verge of divorce, is pursued by a strange man who runs a comic-art gallery and is trying to convince him that he has extrasensory abilities. Somber, pin-drop drama from the writer-director of THE SIXTH SENSE, inspired by comic-book–style fiction, is like a shaggy-dog joke that doesn't seem worth the effort once you hear the punchline. Panavision. [PG-13]▼◗

Uncanny, The (1977-British-Canadian) C-85m. ** D: Denis Heroux. Peter Cushing, Ray Milland, Susan Penhaligon, Joan Greenwood, Alexandra Stewart, Chloe Franks, Donald Pleasence, Samantha Eggar, John Vernon. Lackluster trilogy of "super-natural" tales built around author Cushing's assertion that cats are conspiring against mankind.▼

Un Carnet de Bal (1937-French) 109m. **** D: Julien Duvivier. Marie Bell, Francoise Rosay, Louis Jouvet, Harry Baur, Pierre-Richard Willm, Raimu, Pierre Blanchar, Fernandel, Robert Lynen, Roger Legris. Wealthy widow travels to various locales, intent on looking up the former beaux who filled her dance card ("carnet de bal"). What she finds surprises her, and viewer is treated to a number of poignant vignettes (some ahead of their time) acted by the cream of 1930s France. Hugely successful, this was the inspiration for all the episodic films that followed. (Duvivier even reworked it in Hollywood in 1941 as

LYDIA.) Coscripted by the director, from his story. Music by Maurice Jaubert.

Uncertain Glory (1944) 102m. ** D: Raoul Walsh. Errol Flynn, Jean Sullivan, Paul Lukas, Lucile Watson, Faye Emerson, Douglass Dumbrille, Dennis Hoey, Sheldon Leonard. Wavering script about French criminal Flynn deciding to give his life for his country.▼◗

Uncertainty (2009) C-105m. *½ D: Scott McGehee, David Siegel. Joseph Gordon-Levitt, Lynn Collins, Assumpta Serna, Olivia Thirlby, Nelson Landrieu, Manoel Felciano, Jenn Colella. Every decision we make has its own consequences. With the flip of a coin, you could find yourself in two very different scenarios—in this case, the filmmakers contrast a domestic drama and a thriller involving the same protagonists, lovers Gordon-Levitt and Collins. Interesting concept is shot in a raw and experimental form, but the stories don't come together and the characters are never explored fully enough for us to care about the outcome. HD Widescreen.◗

Unchained (1955) 75m. ** D: Hall Bartlett. Elroy "Crazylegs" Hirsch, Barbara Hale, Chester Morris, Todd Duncan, Johnny Johnston, Peggy Knudsen, Jerry Paris. Fair drama of life at prison farm at Chino, California; highlighted by Alex North–Hy Zarek theme song: "Unchained Melody." Saxophonist Dexter Gordon is seen briefly as a musician (though his playing was dubbed by Georgie Auld).

Uncle Boonmee Who Can Recall His Past Lives (2011-Thai) C-114m. **½ D: Apichatpong Weerasethakul. Thanapat Saisaymar, Jenjira Pongpas, Sakda Kaewbuadee. Widely acclaimed film represents more of the director's carefully cultivated style with measured pacing, peaceful and magical vistas, and quirky vision. A spiritual quest for some will be frustrating to others as Weerasethakul explores religious, mystical, and metaphysical themes wrapped in dreams and memories. In a world populated with ghosts and half-human creatures, the movie seems to be recounting the final days of Boonmee's life as he prepares to enter the next realm. Ethereal art film is anything but accessible; it may not be easy to comprehend, but it's still intriguing from beginning to end. Written by the director.◗

Uncle Buck (1989) C-100m. **½ D: John Hughes. John Candy, Amy Madigan, Jean Louisa Kelly, Gaby Hoffman, Macaulay Culkin, Elaine Bromka, Garrett M. Brown, Laurie Metcalf, Jay Underwood. Ne'er-do-well bachelor Candy has to look after his brother's kids for a couple of days . . . and surprise! The perpetual foul-up turns out to be a caring and responsible uncle. Comedy with serious and sentimental strains gives Candy one of his better vehicles, though writer-director Hughes' inconsistencies keep it from scoring a bull's-eye. Followed by a TV series. [PG]▼●▶

Uncle Harry SEE: **Strange Affair of Uncle Harry, The**

Uncle Joe Shannon (1978) **C-115m.** BOMB D: Joseph C. Hanwright. Burt Young, Doug McKeon, Madge Sinclair, Jason Bernard, Bert Remsen, Allan Rich. Slobbering, self-indulgent film (written by Young) about down-and-out trumpet player and young boy who tries to resist his "charm." Several hands from ROCKY—including Young—were hoping to duplicate that film's success. Maynard Ferguson dubbed Young's trumpet licks. [PG]

Uncle Nino (2003) **C-104m.** ** D: Robert Shallcross. Joe Mantegna, Anne Archer, Pierrino Mascarino, Trevor Morgan, Gina Mantegna, Duke Doyle, Daniel Adebayo, Gary Houston, Chelcie Ross. Mascarino is the title character, a kindhearted Old World eccentric who unexpectedly visits his dysfunctional suburban American relatives and, predictably, transforms their lives. Means to be as zesty as Mama's homemade tomato sauce, but lacks originality; it plays like a well-meaning after-school TV special. This ran for a year in a Grand Rapids, Michigan, movie theater before opening nationally in 2005. Gina Mantegna is Joe's daughter. [PG]▶

Un Coeur en Hiver (1992-French) **C-105m.** ***½ D: Claude Sautet. Daniel Auteuil, Emmanuelle Béart, André Dussollier. Fascinating study of what happens when two longtime business partners in the classical music world find their "friendship" split apart by the appearance of a beautiful young woman. All three stars shine in this talky, offbeat tale of love and music (specifically Ravel). An original film, admittedly not for all tastes.▼▶

Uncommon Valor (1983) **C-105m.** **½ D: Ted Kotcheff. Gene Hackman, Robert Stack, Fred Ward, Reb Brown, Randall "Tex" Cobb, Patrick Swayze, Harold Sylvester, Tim Thomerson, Michael Dudikoff. Formula action film about a retired Army officer who gathers motley crew of Vietnam vets to invade Laos in search of his son, still Missing in Action. Solid performances make this watchable. [R]▼●▶

Unconditional Love (2003) **C-124m.** *½ D: P.J. Hogan. Kathy Bates, Rupert Everett, Meredith Eaton, Dan Aykroyd, Jonathan Pryce, Lynn Redgrave, Peter Sarsgaard, Stephanie Beacham, Richard Briers, Julie Andrews, Barry Manilow. Quirky tale about a housewife, abandoned by her husband, who's mourning the death of her favorite singer. She finds herself on a journey to England (and, of course, self-discovery), where she meets the dead crooner's secret gay lover (Everett). Nothing quite works in this disappointing mess of a movie, despite a good cast. Cowritten by the director.

Made in 2001; U.S. debut on cable TV. Panavision. [PG-13]▼▶

Unconquered (1947) **C-146m.** **½ D: Cecil B. DeMille. Gary Cooper, Paulette Goddard, Howard da Silva, Boris Karloff, Cecil Kellaway, Ward Bond, Katherine DeMille, C. Aubrey Smith, Porter Hall, Mike Mazurki. Gargantuan DeMille colonists-vs.-Indians nonsense, one of his most ludicrous films but still fun.▼

Undefeated, The (1969) **C-119m.** ** D: Andrew V. McLaglen. John Wayne, Rock Hudson, Tony Aguilar, Roman Gabriel, Bruce Cabot, Lee Meriwether, Ben Johnson, Merlin Olsen, Michael (Jan-Michael) Vincent, Harry Carey, Jr., Royal Dano, Richard Mulligan, James McEachin, Gregg Palmer, Kiel Martin. Aside from interesting Wayne-Hudson teaming and the presence of football stars Gabriel and Olsen, this routine Western has little to offer. Post-Civil War tale casts two stars as Union and Confederate colonels. Best line: "The conversation sorta dried up." Panavision. [G]▼●▶

Under Capricorn (1949-British) **C-117m.** ** D: Alfred Hitchcock. Ingrid Bergman, Joseph Cotten, Michael Wilding, Margaret Leighton, Cecil Parker. Stuffy costumer set in 19th-century Australia; Bergman is frail wife of hardened husband Cotten; Wilding comes to visit, upsetting everything. Leighton excellent in supporting role. One of Hitchcock's few duds.▼●▶

Underclassman (2005) **C-94m.** BOMB D: Marcos Siega. Nick Cannon, Shawn Ashmore, Roselyn Sanchez, Kelly Hu, Ian Gomez, Hugh Bonneville, Cheech Marin. Pause here for a Jack Webb "uh-huh": Instead of being canned when he precipitates half a mile's worth of car-chase damages, barely-literate cop Cannon is assigned to pose incognito as a student at a swanky prep school that's been victimized by a car-theft ring. Few clichés are missed, including Cannon's inevitable yen for the campus Spanish instructor (Sanchez). Script is in serious stupor, as if it has spent a month in a locked room with some of Cheech's old stash. Super 35. [PG-13]▶

Under Cover (1987) **C-94m.** *½ D: John Stockwell. David Neidorf, Jennifer Jason Leigh, Barry Corbin, Kathleen Wilhoite, David Harris. Neidorf is an out-of-town cop operating undercover with female narc Leigh to catch the drug pushers who killed another cop on the case. Best known as the pilot "Cougar" in TOP GUN, Stockwell here makes an uninspired directorial debut. [R]▼

Undercover Blues (1993) **C-89m.** ** D: Herbert Ross. Kathleen Turner, Dennis Quaid, Fiona Shaw, Stanley Tucci, Larry Miller, Obba Babatunde, Tom Arnold, Park Overall, Ralph Brown, Jan Triska, Richard Jenkins, Saul Rubinek, Dave Chappelle. Paper-thin comedy-romance-thriller about supercool married ex-spies Jeff and Jane

Blue, parents of a baby girl, who tangle with various heavies in New Orleans. Quaid and Turner are no William Powell and Myrna Loy, and this is no THIN MAN. Tucci, however, is hilarious as thug named Muerte. [PG-13] ▼●]

Undercover Brother (2002) **C-84m.** ** D: Malcolm D. Lee. Eddie Griffin, Chris Kattan, Denise Richards, Aunjanue Ellis, Dave Chappelle, Chi McBride, Neil Patrick Harris, Billy Dee Williams, Jack Noseworthy, James Brown, Robert Townsend. When an African-American general and potential presidential candidate (Williams) mysteriously announces that he's opening a fried chicken franchise, one man is chosen to find out why: a bro with a fro in the know (Griffin). Loopy comedy has some real laughs, but its gags fall flat far too often. Based on an Internet series. Not solid. [PG-13] ▼]

Undercover Man, The (1949) **85m.** *** D: Joseph H. Lewis. Glenn Ford, Nina Foch, James Whitmore, Barry Kelley, Howard St. John. Realistic drama of mob leader (loosely based on Al Capone) being hunted down by Secret Service men who hope to nail him on tax-evasion charge. Whitmore's film debut.

Undercovers Hero (1974-British) **C-95m.** BOMB D: Roy Boulting. Peter Sellers, Lila Kedrova, Curt Jurgens, Beatrice Romand, Jenny Hanley, Rex Stallings. Inept WW2 "comedy," with Sellers in six roles, including Hitler; a total dud. Made in 1973, barely released here. British title: SOFT BEDS, HARD BATTLES. [R]

Undercurrent (1946) **116m.** **½ D: Vincente Minnelli. Katharine Hepburn, Robert Taylor, Robert Mitchum, Edmund Gwenn, Marjorie Main, Jayne Meadows, Clinton Sundberg. Stale melodramatics of newly married Hepburn, whose husband (Taylor) is bitterly estranged from his brother; however, there's more to the story than she realizes. Saved only by the fine cast and usual high MGM production quality. ▼]

Underdog (2007) **C-82m.** ** D: Frederik Du Chau. Peter Dinklage, James Belushi, Patrick Warburton, Alex Neuberger, Taylor Momsen, John Slattery, Samantha Bee; voices of Jason Lee, Amy Adams, Brad Garrett. Ordinary pup is given superpowers by a mad scientist who wants to use the dog for his own evil purposes. Live-action version of the popular 1960s TV cartoon series never takes off; CGI flying effects can't make up for stock villains and subpar plotting. Contrived and inane; uninspired voice casting of Lee as Underdog doesn't help. Where is Wally Cox when we really need him? Super 35. [PG]]

Under Fire (1983) **C-128m.** ***½ D: Roger Spottiswoode. Nick Nolte, Gene Hackman, Joanna Cassidy, Ed Harris, Jean-Louis Trintignant, Richard Masur, Rene Enriquez, Hamilton Camp. First-rate political thriller about journalists on the line in

Managua, Nicaragua, 1979, how their lives intertwine, and how two of them risk their professionalism by becoming involved in the revolutionary conflict. One of those rare films that manages to combine real-life politics and realistic romance with a no-nonsense story. Trio of stars are superb; so is Jerry Goldsmith's music. Only problem: It goes on too long. Screenplay by Ron Shelton and Clayton Frohman. [R] ▼●]

Underground (1941) **95m.** *** D: Vincent Sherman. Jeffrey Lynn, Philip Dorn, Kaaren Verne, Mona Maris, Frank Reicher, Martin Kosleck. Gripping story of German underground movement, with Dorn shielding his activities from loyal soldier-brother Lynn. Kosleck is definitive Nazi swine. ▼]

Under Milk Wood (1972-British) **C-90m.** ** D: Andrew Sinclair. Richard Burton, Elizabeth Taylor, Peter O'Toole, Glynis Johns, Sian Phillips, Vivien Merchant. Rather obscure Dylan Thomas, not in terms of his work but in the film's ambitions. Beautiful images, but rather overbearing technique weighs down the acting. [PG] ▼]

Under My Skin (1950) **86m.** **½ D: Jean Negulesco. John Garfield, Micheline Presle, Luther Adler, Orley Lindgren, Noel Drayton. Pensive study of troubled, crooked jockey Garfield, attempting to reform for the sake of son Lindgren and pretty widow Presle. Based on Ernest Hemingway's *My Old Man*; remade for TV in 1979 under that title.]

Underneath (1995) **C-99m.** **½ D: Steven Soderbergh. Peter Gallagher, Alison Elliott, William Fichtner, Adam Trese, Joe Don Baker, Paul Dooley, Elisabeth Shue, Anjanette Comer, Shelley Duvall, Joe Chrest. Ne'er-do-well returns home to Austin to attend his mother's wedding, and foolishly tries to pick up the pieces of his life before he left town. Soon he's pursuing his ex-girlfriend, annoying her gangsterish boyfriend, and cooking up a robbery scheme. Remake of the film noir favorite CRISS CROSS is stylish, intriguing, but awfully low-key. A must for fans of flashbacks. Panavision. [R] ▼●]

Under Satan's Sun (1987-French) **C-97m.** *** D: Maurice Pialat. Gérard Depardieu, Sandrine Bonnaire, Maurice Pialat, Alain Artur, Yann Dedet. A very demanding and difficult film, not for all tastes but most rewarding to those who can relate to the subject: the questions, conflicts, and torments of rural priest Depardieu. Adapted from a book by Georges Bernanos, author of *Diary of a Country Priest*. Video title: UNDER THE SUN OF SATAN. ▼

Under Siege (1992) **C-102m.** **½ D: Andrew Davis. Steven Seagal, Tommy Lee Jones, Gary Busey, Erika Eleniak, Patrick O'Neal, Nick Mancuso, Andy Romano, Colm Meaney. DIE HARD at sea, with cook Seagal playing tiger-and-mouse with

[1479]

thugs plotting to steal nuclear arms from aboard a 900-foot Navy battleship. Seagal's best film to date; Jones and Busey are better villains than film deserves. Worth it just to see Steve in a chef's cap. Followed by a sequel. [R]▼●◗

Under Siege 2: Dark Territory (1995) C-100m. ** D: Geoff Murphy. Steven Seagal, Eric Bogosian, Katherine Heigl, Morris Chestnut, Everett McGill, Brenda Bakke, Peter Greene, Andy Romano, Nick Mancuso, Royce D. Applegate, Kurtwood Smith, Afifi. Bad guys take over a cross-continental train to seize control of a satellite particle-beam weapon; then they threaten to blow up the Eastern seaboard. But they didn't reckon with Casey the Cook (Seagal). Elaborately produced and well directed, but still just another connect-the-dots action thriller. [R]▼●◗

Under Suspicion (1992-U.S.-British) C-99m. ** D: Simon Moore. Liam Neeson, Laura San Giacomo, Kenneth Cranham, Alphonsia Emmanuel, Maggie O'Neill, Martin Grace, Stephen Moore. Brighton, England, 1959: Ex-cop turned seedy private eye Neeson becomes chief suspect in a murder, and must (surprise!) set out to prove his innocence. Dour-looking and sluggishly paced film is helped by Neeson, good as always, and Cranham—playing his only ally on the police force. San Giacomo is unfortunately miscast as a femme fatale, mistress of a world-renowned artist; she seems absurd in the role and entire production suffers. Panavision. [R]▼●◗

Under Suspicion (2000-U.S.-French) C-110m. **½ D: Stephen Hopkins. Gene Hackman, Morgan Freeman, Thomas Jane, Monica Bellucci, Nydia Caro, Miguel Ángel Suárez, Isabel Algaze. In Puerto Rico, police captain Freeman calls in political bigshot Hackman for questioning, but takes his time revealing that he's a suspect in a series of rapes and murders. Hopkins uses some imaginative techniques, and the two leads are excellent, as usual, but overall it's routine and familiar. Freeman and Hackman executive produced. Remake of the superior GARDE À VUE (1981). [R]▼◗

Undertaking Betty (2003-U.S.-British-German) C-94m. **½ D: Nick Hurran. Brenda Blethyn, Alfred Molina, Naomi Watts, Christopher Walken, Lee Evans, Robert Pugh, Jerry Springer, Miriam Margolyes. Intermittently funny farce involving mortician/wannabe ballroom dancer Molina, who's long had a crush on kindhearted but unhappily married Blethyn. He agrees to help stage her "demise" so she may avoid the embarrassment of divorcing her philandering husband. Walken is a riot as an oddball rival undertaker who stages outlandish themed funerals while proclaiming, "The root word of funeral is fun." Originally titled PLOTS WITH A VIEW. Super 35. [R]▶

Under the Boardwalk (1989) C-104m. *½ D: Fritz Kiersch. Richard Joseph Paul, Danielle Von Zerneck, Steve Monarque, Keith Coogan, Roxana Zal, Hunter Von Leer, Tracey Walter, Dick Miller, Sonny Bono, Elizabeth Kaitan. Surfers from the San Fernando Valley ("Vals") square off against Venice locals ("Lokes"), with Romeo-and-Juliet-like conflict of Val boy who loves Loke girl. Anemic teen picture is a major waste of time. Oddest element: jargon-spouting narrator is 20 years in the future. [R]▼●

Under the Cherry Moon (1986) 98m. *½ D: Prince. Prince, Jerome Benton, Kristin Scott Thomas, Steven Berkoff, Francesca Annis, Emmanuelle Sallet, Alexandra Stewart, Victor Spinetti. Supremely silly vanity film with Prince self-cast as American gigolo/entertainer in the south of France who has a devastating effect on women (yes, it's a science-fiction story). Stylish-looking fairy tale/fable, filmed in black & white, is a triumph of self-adoration, and overall embarrassment. Some music throughout, but in fragmented scenes. Kristin Scott Thomas' film debut. [PG-13]▼●◗

Under the Gun (1989) C-89m. ** D: James Sbardellati. Sam Jones, Vanessa Williams, John Russell, Michael Halsey, Sharon Williams, Bill McKinney, Rockne Tarkington, Don Stark, Nick Cassavetes. Cop Jones teams up with lawyer Williams to go after plutonium thief who ordered the death of Jones' brother. Acceptable but familiar odd-couple crime melodrama; at least it keeps moving. [R]▼●

Under the Hula Moon (1995) C-96m. **½ D: Jeff Celentano. Stephen Baldwin, Emily Lloyd, Christopher Penn, Musetta Vander, Pruitt Taylor Vince, Edie McClurg, Carel Stuycken, R. Lee Ermey. An escaped convict holes up with his long-estranged brother, a dreamer/schemer who lives in the desert trying to make his fortune manufacturing a revolutionary sunscreen. Baldwin and Lloyd are an endearingly loopy couple in this off-kilter comedy. Written by the director. [R]▼●

Under the Rainbow (1981) C-98m. BOMB D: Steve Rash. Chevy Chase, Carrie Fisher, Eve Arden, Joseph Maher, Adam Arkin, Mako, Pat McCormick, Billy Barty. Even by today's standards this is an astoundingly unfunny and tasteless comedy about spies, undercover agents, and midgets who cross paths in a hotel during filming of THE WIZARD OF OZ. Is this film the Wicked Witch's revenge? [PG]▼◗

Under the Roofs of Paris (1930-French) 92m. ***½ D: René Clair. Albert Prejean, Pola Illery, Gaston Modot, Edmond Greville, Paul Olivier. Mime and song, with a minimum of dialogue, tell the story in this wonderful film about two ordinary Parisians involved with the same woman.

A groundbreaking link between silent and sound cinema; Lazare Meerson's sets are outstanding. Written by Clair.▼◗

Under the Same Moon (2008-U.S.-Mexican) **C-109m.** **✱✱✱** D: Patricia Riggen. Adrian Alonso, Kate del Castillo, Eugenio Derbez, Maya Zapata, Carmen Salinas, America Ferrera, Jesse Garcia, Los Tigres del Norte. A mother is separated from her young son when they try to cross the U.S. border. After four years she's working in L.A., still hoping to save enough to bring him to America, while he's being raised by his grandmother. Circumstances cause him to make the journey on his own, and he meets both kind and cruel people along the way. Amazing performance from young Alonso anchors this movie, which flirts with cliché but scores a bull's-eye emotionally. Aka LA MISMA LUNA. [PG-13]◗

Under the Sand (2001-French) **C-95m.** **✱✱✱** D: François Ozon. Charlotte Rampling, Bruno Cremer, Jacques Nolot, Alexandra Stewart, Pierre Vernier, Andrée Tainsy. Happily married, middle-aged woman (Rampling) goes into denial after her husband mysteriously disappears while they are vacationing at the beach. This introspective, quietly powerful drama presents a vivid exploration of the psychology of heartbreak and grief. Rampling has never been better.▼◗

Under the Sun of Satan SEE: **Under Satan's Way**

Under the Tuscan Sun (2003) **C-115m.** **✱✱✱** D: Audrey Wells. Diane Lane, Sandra Oh, Raoul Bova, Lindsay Duncan, Vincent Riotta, Elden Henson, Mario Monicelli. While traveling through Tuscany, an American divorcée, still dazed by the collapse of her marriage, impulsively decides to buy a house and settle there, even though she doesn't know a soul. A perfect showcase for Lane, whose winning, empathic performance allows us to share her experiences. Everything looks and feels right in this entertaining fictionalization of Frances Mayes' best-selling memoir by director-screenwriter Wells. Jeffrey Tambor appears unbilled. [PG-13] ▼◗

Under the Volcano (1984) **C-109m.** **✱✱✱½** D: John Huston. Albert Finney, Jacqueline Bisset, Anthony Andrews, Ignacio Lopez Tarso, Katy Jurado, James Villiers. Somber but striking adaptation of Malcolm Lowry's novel about alcoholic diplomat in Mexico during the late 1930s; rich in atmosphere and texture, with a great performance by Finney. Screenplay by Guy Gallo; music by Alex North. [R]▼O◗

Under the Yum Yum Tree (1963) **C-110m.** **✱✱½** D: David Swift. Jack Lemmon, Carol Lynley, Dean Jones, Edie Adams, Imogene Coca, Paul Lynde, Robert Lansing. Obvious sex comedy owes most of its enjoyment to Lemmon as love-hungry landlord trying

to romance tenant Lynley who's living with her fiancé (Jones).▼◗

Undertow (2004) **C-107m.** **✱✱½** D: David Gordon Green. Jamie Bell, Josh Lucas, Devon Alan, Dermot Mulroney, Kristen Stewart, Shiri Appleby, Pat Healy, Bill McKinney. Two teenaged brothers live with their widowed father on a dreary pig farm in the American South; their lives are abruptly altered by the arrival of their manipulative ex-con uncle. Atmospheric but flawed drama of family secrets and jealousies; story takes too long to develop, and when it does the result is strictly standard. Coproduced by Terrence Malick. [R]▼◗

Under Two Flags (1936) **96m.** **✱✱✱** D: Frank Lloyd. Ronald Colman, Claudette Colbert, Victor McLaglen, Rosalind Russell, Gregory Ratoff, Nigel Bruce, Herbert Mundin, John Carradine, J. Edward Bromberg. Debonair legionnaire Colman is caught between two women (aristocratic Russell and camp follower Colbert), and the envy of jealous commandant McLaglen in this unbelievable but entertaining Foreign Legion story, from the book by Ouida (filmed before in 1916 and 1922). Originally ran 110m.

Underwater! (1955) **C-99m.** **✱✱** D: John Sturges. Jane Russell, Gilbert Roland, Richard Egan, Lori Nelson, Jayne Mansfield. Standard skin-diving fare, with Roland and Egan seeking out treasure in the deep. Russell in a bathing suit is the main attraction. SuperScope.▼O

Underwater Odyssey, An SEE: **Neptune Factor, The**

Underworld (1985-British) **C-100m.** **✱✱½** D: George Pavlou. Denholm Elliott, Steven Berkoff, Larry Lamb, Miranda Richardson, Art Malik, Nicola Cowper, Ingrid Pitt. Fair thriller about mutants who live underground and who kidnap pretty hooker Cowper in order to obtain from Dr. Elliott the drug that will keep them alive. Retired gunman Lamb is hired by gang boss Berkoff to rescue her. Video title: TRANSMUTATIONS. [R]▼O

Underworld (2003-British-German-Hungarian-U.S.) **C-121m.** **✱✱** D: Len Wiseman. Kate Beckinsale, Scott Speedman, Michael Sheen, Shane Brolly, Erwin Leder, Bill Nighy. In the foreboding setting of a dark city, war is raging between vampires and lycans (known to us as werewolves) . . . but bloodsucker Beckinsale finds herself attracted to, and protective of, Speedman, who doesn't realize his own lycanthropic fate. Should be fun, but it's inexplicably dull, even with razzle-dazzle action scenes and effects, and Beckinsale fails to deliver as a sexy, leather-clad vampire. Unrated version runs 134m. Followed by a prequel and a sequel. Super 35. [R] ▼◗

Underworld: Evolution (2006) **C-106m.** **✱½** D: Len Wiseman. Kate Beckinsale, Scott Speedman, Tony Curran, Derek Jacobi, Bill

Nighy, Steven Mackintosh, Shane Brolly, Brian Steele, Zita Görög, Michael Sheen. Monotonous sequel is about what you'd expect, with vampire-warrior Beckinsale and half-vampire/half-werewolf pal Speedman battling vampire Curran, who is intent on liberating his beastly, imprisoned werewolf brother. Loud, gory, and boring. Super 35. [R]▶

Underworld Informers (1963-British) **105m.** *** D: Ken Annakin. Nigel Patrick, Catherine Woodville, Margaret Whiting, Colin Blakely, Harry Andrews, Frank Finlay. Tight, taut crime tale as Scotland Yard inspector Patrick must clear his name by bringing in notorious gangland leaders. Vivid atmosphere, fine acting by all. Original British title: THE INFORMERS.

Underworld: Rise of the Lycans (2009) **C-93m.** ** D: Patrick Tatopoulos. Michael Sheen, Bill Nighy, Rhona Mitra, Steven Mackintosh, Kate Beckinsale. Prequel to UNDERWORLD (2003) and UNDERWORLD: EVOLUTION (2006) should satisfy fans—if no one else. It plays like a period swashbuckler while depicting first skirmishes in the centuries-long war between aristocratic vampires and rampaging werewolves. Series regulars Sheen (leader of the werewolves) and Nighy (lord of the vampires) are in fine form, but series devotees can debate whether Mitra (as Nighy's rebellious daughter and Sheen's secret lover) is an effective substitute for the nearly-absent Beckinsale, the leather-clad vampire-warrior in previous two UNDERWORLD monster rallies, who appears only fleetingly at the very end of this one. Super 35. [R]▶

Underworld U.S.A. (1961) **99m.** **½ D: Samuel Fuller. Cliff Robertson, Dolores Dorn, Beatrice Kay, Robert Emhardt, Larry Gates. Robertson sees his father murdered and develops lifetime obsession to get even with the mob responsible. One of director Fuller's most visually striking films; unfortunately, his script goes astray and doesn't fulfill initial promise.▼▶

Undiscovered (2005) **C-98m.** *½ D: Meiert Avis. Pell James, Steven Strait, Kip Pardue, Shannyn Sossamon, Ashlee Simpson, Carrie Fisher, Peter Weller, Fisher Stevens, Stephen Moyer. Young people trying to make it in show business have to deal with the dilemma of selling out or trying to remain true to themselves. Tired script goes nowhere, and dull dialogue can't put life into these clichés. Acclaimed music-video director Avis makes the action literally difficult to watch. Super 35. [PG-13]▼▶

Undisputed (2002) **C-94m.** *** D: Walter Hill. Wesley Snipes, Ving Rhames, Peter Falk, Michael Rooker, Jon Seda, Wes Studi, Fisher Stevens, Dayton Callie, Amy Aquino. Simple, solid (albeit by-the-numbers) boxing melodrama in which a Mike Tyson–like champ-turned-convict (Rhames), jailed on a rape charge, butts heads with the prison's

top pugilist (Snipes), a lifer doing time for murder. The two stars are excellent. Followed by two direct-to-video sequels. Super 35. [R]▼▶

Une Femme Douce (1969-French) **C-87m.** *** D: Robert Bresson. Dominique Sanda, Guy Frangin, Jane (Jeanne) Lobre. Sanda gives a remarkable performance in her film debut as a gentle soul who marries a tyrannical pawnbroker with tragic results. Bresson's first color film is a depressing but hypnotic portrait of loneliness and alienation. Based on a Dostoyevsky story.▼

Unfaithful (2002) **C-123m.** **½ D: Adrian Lyne. Richard Gere, Diane Lane, Olivier Martinez, Erik Per Sullivan, Dominic Chianese, Kate Burton, Chad Lowe, Željko Ivanek, Gary Basaraba, Margaret Colin, Michael Emerson. Devoted wife and mom Lane becomes sexually attracted to a charming Frenchman she chances to meet. Against her better judgment, she puts her marriage on the line, leaving the next move to husband Gere. Deftly directed, with careful observation of life's ordinary details, and well acted, but steers off course and drags to a doleful conclusion. Remake of Claude Chabrol's LA FEMME INFIDÈLE. [R]▼▶

Unfaithfully Yours (1948) **105m.** **** D: Preston Sturges. Rex Harrison, Linda Darnell, Rudy Vallee, Barbara Lawrence, Kurt Kreuger, Lionel Stander, Robert Greig, Edgar Kennedy, Julius Tannen, Al Bridge. Brilliant Sturges comedy of symphony conductor Harrison, who suspects his wife of infidelity and considers three courses of action (including murder) during concert. Great moments from Vallee and Kennedy; often side-splittingly funny. Remade in 1984.▼▶

Unfaithfully Yours (1984) **C-96m.** **½ D: Howard Zieff. Dudley Moore, Nastassja Kinski, Armand Assante, Albert Brooks, Cassie Yates, Richard Libertini, Richard B. Shull. Remake of Preston Sturges' wonderful film about an orchestra conductor who suspects his wife of having an affair—and plans to murder her. Pretty funny, with a perfect cast, but loses steam somewhere along the way. Certainly no match for the witty original. [PG]▼▶

Unfaithful Wife, The SEE: **La Femme Infidele**

Unfinished Business (1984-Canadian) **C-99m.** *** D: Don Owen. Isabelle Mejias, Peter Spence, Leslie Toth, Peter Kastner, Julie Biggs, Chuck Shamata. Appealing sequel to Owen's NOBODY WAVED GOODBYE. It's 20 years later: Kastner and Biggs, now divorced, have a rebellious offspring of their own, 17-year-old Mejias. Story focuses on her problems and anxieties as she approaches adulthood.

Unfinished Life, An (2005) **C-107m.** *** D: Lasse Hallström. Robert Redford, Jennifer Lopez, Morgan Freeman, Josh Lucas, Camryn Manheim, Becca Gardner, Damian

Lewis. Needing to escape from her abusive boyfriend, and with no money, Lopez and her 11-year-old daughter go to the only place they can: the Wyoming farm of her father-in-law (Redford), who still blames her for the death of his son. Also living on the farm is ranch hand Freeman, who was mauled by a bear a year earlier. Warmhearted, embracing story about family ties and the need for forgiveness. It's a treat to watch Redford and Freeman as two old codgers with an unshakable bond of friendship. Completed in 2003. Panavision. [PG-13] ▶

Unforgettable (1996) C-111m. *½ D: John Dahl. Ray Liotta, Linda Fiorentino, Peter Coyote, Christopher McDonald, Kim Cattrall, Kim Coates, David Paymer, Duncan Fraser, Caroline Elliott. Police department medical examiner who was accused of murdering his wife is obsessed with finding out the truth. When he meets a lab scientist (Fiorentino) who has discovered a way of transferring memory by injection, he experiments on himself, hoping to learn how and why his wife was killed. A solid premise (along the lines of a '50s sci-fi film) is dissipated by plodding treatment and a script that becomes ludicrous. A disappointment from director Dahl. Unendurable is more like it. [R] ▼●)

Unforgettable Summer, An (1994-French-Rumanian) C-82m. **½ D: Lucian Pintilie. Kristin Scott Thomas, Claudiu Bleont, Olga Tudorache, George Constantin, Ion Pavlescu, Marcel Iures, Razvan Vasilescu. Atmospheric 1920s tale of Rumanian military officer's wife, whose devotion to her family and concern for others causes nothing but strife. Ironic and sadly pertinent story set predominately on remote border post where peasant Bulgarians, Macedonians, and Rumanians reside amidst constant tension and turmoil. Scott Thomas is excellent. ▼●

Unforgiven, The (1960) C-125m. *** D: John Huston. Burt Lancaster, Audrey Hepburn, Audie Murphy, John Saxon, Charles Bickford, Lillian Gish, Doug McClure, Joseph Wiseman, Albert Salmi. Western set in 1850s Texas tells of two families at odds with Indians over Hepburn, whom the latter claim as one of theirs. Gish and Bickford are outstanding in stellar-cast story, with rousing Indian attack climax. Panavision. ▼●

Unforgiven (1992) C-127m. *** D: Clint Eastwood. Clint Eastwood, Gene Hackman, Morgan Freeman, Richard Harris, Jaimz Woolvett, Saul Rubinek, Frances Fisher, Anna Thomson, Anthony James. Elegiac anti-Western about a one-time mad killer, long since reformed, who comes out of "retirement" to make one more hit because he needs the money for his family. Powerful examination of morality and hypocrisy in the Old West—and the impact of killing (and being killed)—but marred by a midsection that plods. Exquisitely shot by

Jack N. Green. Oscar winner for Best Picture, Best Director, Best Supporting Actor (Hackman), Best Film Editing (Joel Cox). Panavision. [R] ▼●)

Unholy, The (1988) C-100m. ** D: Camilo Vila. Ben Cross, Hal Holbrook, Jill Carroll, William Russ, Trevor Howard, Ned Beatty, Claudia Robinson, Nicole Fortier. Ambitious horror film puts priest Cross to the test when archbishop Holbrook assigns him to cast out the devil from a New Orleans church. Veteran Philip Yordan's script (cowritten by film's designer Fernando Fonseca) is weird but unconvincing. Special effects are arresting, but highlight is Fortier as the supersexy demon. [R] ▼●

Unholy Rollers (1972) C-88m. **½ D: Vernon Zimmerman. Claudia Jennings, Louis Quinn, Betty Anne Rees, Roberta Collins. Behind-the-scenes life on roller derby circuit, Roger Corman–style; raunchy low-budgeter offers some fun. [R] ▼

Unhook the Stars (1996-French-U.S.) C-103m. *** D: Nick Cassavetes. Gena Rowlands, Marisa Tomei, Gérard Depardieu, Moira Kelly, Jake Lloyd, David Thornton, David Sherrill, Clint Howard. Wonderful showcase for Rowlands as a widow with grown children who comes to the rescue of a flaky young neighbor and looks after her little boy one day; soon the two develop a strong bond based on their genuine need for each other. Lovely film cowritten by Cassavetes, son of Rowlands and John Cassavetes. Depardieu (who coproduced the film) has the only underwritten part in the picture. [R] ▼●)

Unidentified Flying Oddball (1979) C-93m. **½ D: Russ Mayberry. Dennis Dugan, Jim Dale, Ron Moody, Kenneth More, John LeMesurier, Rodney Bewes, Shelia White. Innocuous Disney update of Mark Twain's *A Connecticut Yankee in King Arthur's Court*, with young Dugan (and a lookalike robot) catapulted back to medieval times. Retitled A SPACEMAN IN KING ARTHUR'S COURT. [G] ▼●)

Uninvited, The (1944) 98m. ***½ D: Lewis Allen. Ray Milland, Ruth Hussey, Donald Crisp, Gail Russell, Cornelia Otis Skinner, Dorothy Stickney, Barbara Everest, Alan Napier. Eerie ghost suspenser about Russell disturbed by dead mother's specter; Milland and Hussey, new owners of haunted house, try to solve mystery. No trick ending in this ingenious film, which introduced Victor Young's melody "Stella by Starlight." Spooky cinematography by Charles Lang, Jr. Scripted by Dodie Smith and Frank Partos, from Dorothy Macardle's novel. ▼●

Uninvited, The (2009) C-87m. **½ D: The Guard Brothers. Emily Browning, Elizabeth Banks, Arielle Kebbel, David Strathairn, Maya Massar, Kevin McNulty, Jesse Moss, Dean Paul Gibson. Two teenage sisters—one a waifish ex-mental patient

(Browning), the other a smart-mouthed wild child (Kebbel)—suspect the worst when, all too soon after their mother's death, their father (Strathairn) becomes romantically involved with their late mom's former nurse (Banks). Supernatural manifestations only serve to intensify their suspicions. Based on A TALE OF TWO SISTERS, a 2003 South Korean horror movie, this familiar but effectively atmospheric thriller gets a big boost from a genuinely surprising plot twist in the final reel. Directed by British siblings Charles and Thomas Guard, who bill themselves as The Guard Brothers. [PG-13]▶

Union Pacific (1939) 135m. *** D: Cecil B. DeMille. Barbara Stanwyck, Joel McCrea, Robert Preston, Akim Tamiroff, Brian Donlevy, Anthony Quinn, Lynne Overman, Evelyn Keyes, Fuzzy Knight, J. M. Kerrigan, Regis Toomey. Brawling DeMille saga about building the first transcontinental railroad; McCrea the hero, Donlevy the villain, Stanwyck (with Irish brogue!) caught between McCrea and likable troublemaker Preston. Action scenes, including spectacular train wreck, Indian attack, and subsequent cavalry rescue via railroad flat cars are highlights. ▼◐▶

Union Station (1950) 80m. **½ D: Rudolph Maté. William Holden, Nancy Olson, Barry Fitzgerald, Jan Sterling, Allene Roberts, Lyle Bettger. Dated police techniques, plus general implausibility, detract from well-made film about manhunt for kidnapper (Bettger) of young blind woman (Roberts). ▼▶

United 93 (2006-U.S.-French-British) C-111m. ***½ D: Paul Greengrass. David Alan Basche, Richard Bekins, Susan Blommaert, Ray Charleson, Christian Clemenson, Khalid Abdalla, Lewis Alsamari, David Rasche, Chip Zien, Denny Dillon, Rebecca Schull, Gregg Henry, Olivia Thirlby. Harrowing dramatization of a flight that was hijacked on September 11, 2001, as terrorists attempted to fly the plane into the Capitol in Washington, D.C. Film follows the parallel drama of how flight controllers and military personnel first realized something was wrong and then tried to deal with it. Several key people on the ground portray themselves in this impeccably crafted, emotionally charged drama, written by the director. Super 35. [R]▶

United States of Leland, The (2004) C-104m. *** D: Matthew Ryan Hoge. Don Cheadle, Ryan Gosling, Chris Klein, Jena Malone, Lena Olin, Kevin Spacey, Michelle Williams, Martin Donovan, Ann Magnuson, Kerry Washington, Sherilyn Fenn, Matt Malloy, Ron Canada. Strikingly original mood piece/morality play about a quiet teenage boy (Gosling) consumed by the unhappiness of the world. He commits an unthinkable crime that even he can't explain, and it has repercussions on everyone around him, young and old alike, who are all trying to

cope with their own problems. Told in a mosaic form, flashing back and forth in time. Written by the director. [R]▼▶

Universal Soldier (1992) C-104m. ** D: Roland Emmerich. Jean-Claude Van Damme, Dolph Lundgren, Ally Walker, Ed O'Ross, Jerry Orbach, Leon Rippy, Tico Wells, Ralph Moeller. Van Damme and Lundgren—well, it's not exactly Tracy and March in INHERIT THE WIND. Hunks are well cast as rival cyborgs (in a runaway government experiment, natch) whose human components hated each other during Vietnam. Has the requisite number of explosions. The director slyly keeps the grocery store Muzak going during Lundgren's one big emoting scene—right after he eats raw meat from a bin. Followed by a sequel and two cable sequels and a direct-to-DVD sequel: UNIVERSAL SOLDIER 3. Panavision. [R] ▼◐▶

Universal Soldier: The Return (1999) C-82m. ** D: Mic Rodgers. Jean-Claude Van Damme, Michael Jai White, Heidi Schanz, Xander Berkeley, Daniel von Bargen, Kiana Tom. The muscles from Brussels is back and must stop an out-of-control supercyborg from world domination. Derivative but not boring rehash of the original. Features two tough heroines, Schanz and ESPN fitness guru Tom, but if you're threatened by the enlightened sexual politics, there's also a gratuitous brawl at a nudie bar. In his acting debut, WCW superstar Bill Goldberg proves he has all the dramatic range of Foghorn Leghorn. [R]▼◐▶

Unknown (2006) C-85m. **½ D: Simon Brand. Jim Caviezel, Greg Kinnear, Bridget Moynahan, Joe Pantoliano, Barry Pepper, Jeremy Sisto, Peter Stormare, Chris Mulkey, Kevin Chapman, Mark Boone (Junior), Clayne Crawford, David Selby. A group of strangers wake up in a locked warehouse with a dead security guard, unaware of who they are and how they got there. Reasonably engaging, unpredictable mystery with a solid cast, but it comes across as little more than a puree of recent indie hits (MEMENTO, SAW). Simultaneously released in theaters and on cable. Super 35.▶

Unknown (2011-U.S.-German-French) C-113m. **½ D: Jaume Collet-Serra. Liam Neeson, Diane Kruger, January Jones, Aidan Quinn, Bruno Ganz, Frank Langella, Sebastian Koch. American college professor Neeson arrives in Berlin with his wife (Jones) to attend a conference on biotechnology. Before he can even check into his hotel a mishap causes him to take a taxi ride, which ends in an accident and robs him of his memory. When he regains his mental equilibrium, no one recognizes him—not even his wife. Hitchcockian story, based on a novel by French author Didier van Cauwelaert, has a great setup, a good cast, fresh Berlin locations, and a couple of nifty chase scenes, but doesn't pay off as well as it should. Passable escapism, no more. [PG-13]▶

Unknown Woman, The (2006-Italian-French) **C-118m.** *** D: Giuseppe Tornatore. Xenia Rappoport, Michele Placido, Claudia Gerini, Pierfrancesco Favino, Margherita Buy, Alessandro Haber, Piera Degli Esposti, Clara Dossena, Angela Molina. Offbeat mystery involves a Russian woman with a checkered background who insinuates herself into the ordered lives of an upwardly-mobile Italian family. Her job as a nanny to their young daughter eventually unlocks secrets about everyone. Clearly inspired by Hitchcock, Tornatore constructs a classic puzzle; the head-scratching pieces all add up to an absorbing thriller that successfully takes the CINEMA PARADISO writer-director into brand-new territory. One of Ennio Morricone's best scores in recent years.▶

Unlawful Entry (1992) **C-111m.** *** D: Jonathan Kaplan. Kurt Russell, Ray Liotta, Madeleine Stowe, Roger E. Mosley, Ken Lerner, Deborah Offner, Carmen Argenziano, Dick Miller, Djimon (Hounsou). A break-in at the home of Russell and Stowe leads to their befriending lonely LAPD officer Liotta. But the disturbed cop develops a fixation on the wife—and we're into another urban paranoia thriller. It has the genre's usual contrivances and plot holes, but it's tense and exciting, with a terrific performance by Liotta. [R]▼●▶

Unleashed (2005-French-British) **C-102m.** **½ D: Louis Leterrier. Jet Li, Morgan Freeman, Bob Hoskins, Kerry Condon, Michael Jenn, Vincent Regan, Dylan Brown, Phyllida Law. Li is kept on a leash—literally—and is raised by Glasgow gangster Hoskins since childhood to become his personal attack dog. He escapes and tries to start a new life with the aid of a blind piano tuner (Freeman), but is forced to confront his violent past. Typically slick and brutal Euro-actioner from writer-producer Luc Besson has a ludicrous premise amped up with exhilarating fight scenes choreographed by martial arts master Yuen Wo Ping. European title: DANNY THE DOG. Also available in an unrated version. Super 35. [R]▶

Unman, Wittering and Zigo (1971-British) **C-102m.** *** D: John Mackenzie. David Hemmings, Carolyn Seymour, Douglas Wilmer, Hamilton Dyce, Anthony Haygarth, Donald Gee. Nifty little sleeper with Hemmings as new boys' school teacher who is promptly informed by his class that they murdered his predecessor, and that he'd better stay in line . . . or else. Creepy, chilling mystery, loaded with twists and stylishly photographed by Geoffrey Unsworth. Title refers to the last three names on the roll . . . but Zigo is always absent. [PG]

Unmarried Woman, An (1978) **C-124m.** **** D: Paul Mazursky. Jill Clayburgh, Alan Bates, Michael Murphy, Cliff Gorman, Pat Quinn, Kelly Bishop, Lisa Lucas, Michael Tucker, Jill Eikenberry. Intelligent, compassionate look at how a woman copes when her husband walks out on her. Mazursky (who also wrote script) pulls no punches and makes no compromises—his characters are living, breathing people and his film is a gem. Clayburgh is magnificent in title role. [R]▼▶

Unreasonable Man, An (2007) **C-122m.** ***½ D: Henriette Mantel, Steve Skrovan. Fascinating, aptly titled documentary on pioneering consumer activist Ralph Nader follows a remarkable arc: from his challenge to Goliath-like General Motors as a young man out of nowhere to a presidential run in 2000 that lost him many former allies, because they think the votes he won cost Al Gore the election. Though the film ultimately comes down on its protagonist's side by a margin a little larger than the one that separated Gore and Bush, it's hard hitting both pro and con, as it should be. Lots of supportive, disillusioned, and angry voices get their due; there's even rich footage from the episode Nader hosted of *Saturday Night Live.*▶

Unsane (1982-Italian) **C-101m.** ** D: Dario Argento. Anthony Franciosa, John Saxon, Daria Nicolodi, Giuliano Gemma, Mirella D'Angelo, John Steiner. Not as interesting as most of horror stylist Argento's thrillers, story is about novelist Franciosa becoming the subject of death threats. Extremely bloody but featuring some arresting camerawork by Luciano Tovoli, who also photographed THE PASSENGER. Originally titled: TENEBRAE. Video version runs 91m. [R]▼●▶

Unsinkable Molly Brown, The (1964) **C-128m.** *** D: Charles Walters. Debbie Reynolds, Harve Presnell, Ed Begley, Jack Kruschen, Hermione Baddeley, Audrey Christie, Martita Hunt, Harvey Lembeck. Big, splashy, tuneful adaptation of Broadway musical. Debbie is energetically entertaining as backwoods girl who knows what she wants, eventually gets to be wealthiest woman in Denver in the late 1800s. Based on a true story! Meredith Willson score includes "I Ain't Down Yet," "Belly Up to the Bar, Boys." Panavision.▼●▶

Unstoppable (2010-U.S.-British) **C-98m.** ***½ D: Tony Scott. Denzel Washington, Chris Pine, Rosario Dawson, Kevin Dunn, Ethan Suplee, Kevin Corrigan, Lew Temple, Kevin Chapman. Sensationally exciting thriller, very loosely based on real-life events, recalls DIE HARD in its focus on working-class heroes in the wrong place at the right time. Veteran engineer facing forced retirement (Washington) and a first-day-on-the-job hothead (Pine) must transcend their differences and defy their superiors to halt an out-of-control, half-mile-long freight train carrying hazardous cargo through heavily populated areas. White-knuckle action sequences and stripped-to-essentials storytelling enhance the full-throttle impact. Written by Mark Bomback. Super 35. [PG-13] ▶

Unstrung Heroes (1995) C-94m. **½ D: Diane Keaton. Andie MacDowell, John Turturro, Michael Richards, Maury Chaykin, Nathan Watt, Kendra Krull, Joey Andrews, Celia Weston, Anne DeSalvo, Candice Azzara. A boy's adventures growing up in an off-center Jewish family of the early '60s with a nutty inventor father, a loving mother (who takes ill), and two highly eccentric uncles. The characters are colorful, and the performances are first-rate, but the film never quite jells. Young Watt is a real find. Freely adapted from the autobiographical book by Franz Lidz. [PG] ▼●▶

Unsuitable Job for a Woman, An (1981-British) C-94m. *** D: Christopher Petit. Pippa Guard, Billie Whitelaw, Paul Freeman, Dominic Guard, Elizabeth Spriggs. Moody, entertaining film noir thriller about a woman detective (P. Guard) and her investigation of an unusual murder case after her boss commits suicide. Based on a novel by P. D. James. ▼

Unsuspected, The (1947) 103m. **½ D: Michael Curtiz. Claude Rains, Joan Caulfield, Audrey Totter, Constance Bennett, Hurd Hatfield. Predictable melodrama with good cast; superficially charming radio star Rains has murder on his mind, with niece Caulfield the victim. ▶

Untamed (1955) C-111m. *** D: Henry King. Tyrone Power, Susan Hayward, Agnes Moorehead, Richard Egan, Rita Moreno, John Justin. Quite vivid account of Boer trek through hostile South African country, with Power romancing Hayward. CinemaScope.

Untamed Heart (1993) C-102m. **½ D: Tony Bill. Christian Slater, Marisa Tomei, Rosie Perez, Kyle Secor, Willie Carson. Multiple-hankie romantic tale about two troubled adults. Waitress Tomei can't seem to keep a boyfriend, while shy busboy Slater is a well-meaning orphan with a heart ailment. Solid production and good performances (especially from the two stars) go a long way to offset the basically hokey story. Romantics of all ages are sure to enjoy this. [PG-13] ▼●▶

Unthinkable (2010) C-89m. *½ D: Gregor Jordan. Samuel L. Jackson, Carrie-Anne Moss, Michael Sheen, Martin Donovan, Stephen Root, Gil Bellows, Brandon Routh, Holmes Osborne, Benito Martinez, Sasha Roiz. Sheen sends a video message to the government: He has placed three nuclear devices at different areas across the U.S. He is quickly caught, but interrogator Jackson will do anything in order to extract information that will lead to the bombs before they explode. How far is too far? Attempts to make Jackson's character appear

normal only succeed in making him seem even more psychotic. Other than Sheen's chameleon-like performance, there's no upside here. In fact, the whole movie is unthinkable. Released direct to DVD in the U.S. Alternate version runs 95m. [R] ▶

Until September (1984) C-95m. ** D: Richard Marquand. Karen Allen, Thierry Lhermitte, Christopher Cazenove, Marie-Christina Conti, Nitza Saul, Hutton Cobb. Temporarily stranded in Paris, Allen falls in love with handsome (and married) banker Lhermitte. Utterly predictable romantic drama. [R] ▼▶

Until the End of the World (1991) C-158m. ** D: Wim Wenders. William Hurt, Solveig Dommartin, Sam Neill, Max von Sydow, Jeanne Moreau, Rudiger Vogler, Ernie Dingo, Chick Ortega, Eddy Mitchell. In the near future, Dommartin joins Hurt on a mysterious global mission, which leads to the creation of a device that will enable blind people to see. Intended as the "ultimate road movie," but the story doesn't take off until almost halfway through, and the characters and themes remain a jumble. Even the locations (fifteen cities on four continents) can't help. There are some sparks from von Sydow, interesting high-definition TV effects, and an eclectic, all-star soundtrack, but it's still a major disappointment. [R] ▼●

Until They Sail (1957) 95m. **½ D: Robert Wise. Paul Newman, Joan Fontaine, Jean Simmons, Sandra Dee, Piper Laurie, Charles Drake, Patrick Macnee, Dean Jones. Soaper courtroom story set in WW2 New Zealand, with sisters (Fontaine, Simmons, Laurie, and Dee) involved in love, misery, and murder. From James Michener story. Dee's film debut. Eydie Gormé sings title song. CinemaScope. ▼▶

(Untitled) (2009) C-96m. *** D: Jonathan Parker. Adam Goldberg, Marley Shelton, Eion Bailey, Lucy Punch, Zak Orth, Vinnie Jones, Ptolemy Slocum, Svetlana Efremova, Michael Panes, Janet Carroll. Sound artist Goldberg, who usually defends his highly individual mode of creativity, finds himself on the other side of the art world when he becomes involved with gallery owner Shelton. Director Parker, who coauthored script with Catherine di Napoli, gives equal weight to all points of view, teasing while simultaneously taking it all seriously in this "but-is-it-art?" dramedy. Goldberg's passive performance is a hoot. [R] ▶

Untouchables, The (1987) C-119m. **** D: Brian De Palma. Kevin Costner, Sean Connery, Charles Martin Smith, Andy Garcia, Robert De Niro, Richard Bradford, Jack Kehoe, Brad Sullivan, Billy Drago, Patricia Clarkson. High-energy entertainment that packs a wallop; writer David Mamet's update of the well-remembered TV series tells how an earnest but naive federal agent named Eliot Ness learns (the hard way) to deal with both underworld crime and police corruption in Prohibition-era Chicago. Fluidly (and often flamboyantly) filmed, with powerhouse performances by Connery (in his Oscar-winning role), as a seasoned street cop, and De Niro, as a grandiose Al Capone. Climactic shoot-out, with echoes of POTEMKIN, will have you on the edge of your seat! Photographed by Stephen H. Burum, with a rich music score by Ennio Morricone. Panavision. [R] ▼●

Untraceable (2008) **C-100m.** **½ D: Gregory Hoblit. Diane Lane, Billy Burke, Colin Hanks, Joseph Cross, Mary Beth Hurt, Perla Haney-Jardine. Formulaic but effective thriller about a computer-savvy psycho who devises the ultimate killer app: On his website, he offers downstreaming video of captives tormented by torture devices that grow increasingly more painful, and eventually lethal, as voyeurs worldwide click to watch. Not for the squeamish. About as satisfying as a better-than-average episode of a TV police-procedural drama. Lane is persuasive as the FBI agent on the killer's trail. Super 35. [R] ▮

Unvanquished, The SEE: Aparajito

Unzipped (1995) **C/B&W-72m.** *** D: Douglas Keeve. Lively, if selective, documentary about N.Y. fashion designer Isaac Mizrahi, which begins with him mired in a creative slump and ends with a 1994 show that trumpets his "Eskimo line." Benefits from the ceaseless effervescence of its subject, whose oft-demonstrated tastes in movies and television extend to Bette Davis (in BABY JANE mode), Loretta Young, and his beloved Mary Tyler Moore. [R] ▼●

Up (2009) **C-96m.** ***½ D: Pete Docter. Voices of Ed Asner, Christopher Plummer, Jordan Nagai, Delroy Lindo, John Ratzenberger, Elie Docter. Wonderfully imaginative Pixar animated film about an old man who, just as life seems to be shutting him down, embarks on a great adventure, the kind he's dreamed about since he was a boy. He hoists his house in the air with balloons and heads for South America and the spot he and his wife always dreamed of visiting—accompanied by a well-meaning boy from an Explorer troop. Sweet, touching, exciting, funny, and constantly surprising, with great character design and attention to detail. Michael Giacchino's Oscar-winning score perfectly supports a wide range of emotions. Written by Docter and Bob Peterson (who codirected and supplies the voice of Dug) from their story with Tom McCarthy. Oscar winner for Best Animated Feature. 3-D. [PG] ▮

Up and Down (2004-Czech) **C-108m.** **½ D: Jan Hřebejk. Petr Forman, Emília Vášáryová, Jan Tríska, Ingrid Timková, Kristyna Liška Boková, Jiří Macháček. A couple of small-time smugglers discover an abandoned baby, triggering a series of alternately funny and tragic consequences among a disparate group of people trying to sort out life in the complicated new ways of the Czech Republic. Well-made, quirky tale spins its web against the changing social, economic, and political landscape of a country that is learning to start over. Super 35. [R] ▮

Up at the Villa (2000-U.S.-British) **C-115m.** ** D: Philip Haas. Kristin Scott Thomas, Sean Penn, Anne Bancroft, James Fox, Jeremy Davies, Derek Jacobi, Massimo Ghini. Awkward adaptation of W. Somerset Maugham novella set in 1938 Florence. Thomas takes pity on Austrian immigrant Davies and initiates one night of sex, but the young man shoots himself when she refuses to extend the relationship. Davies' dreadful performance would be enough to sink most movies by itself, but there's also a lack of chemistry between Thomas and Penn (as a roving-eyed American adventurer). As their social circle's resident gossip, Bancroft is broad enough to fit right in with the "Florence set" in the more entertaining TEA WITH MUSSOLINI. [PG-13] ▼▮

Up Close & Personal (1996) **C-124m.** *** D: Jon Avnet. Robert Redford, Michelle Pfeiffer, Stockard Channing, Joe Mantegna, Kate Nelligan, Glenn Plummer, James Rebhorn, Scott Bryce, Raymond Cruz, Dedee Pfeiffer, Miguel Sandoval, Noble Willingham, James Karen. Ambitious young woman goes to work for veteran newsman at a Miami TV station, where he shapes and prods her into a good reporter. As their personal relationship blossoms, they both know it's time for her to move on—and up the television ladder. Paraphrase of A STAR IS BORN has everything but Pfeiffer saying "This is Mrs. Norman Maine" at the end, but it still works because of the thousand-watt charisma of its leads. Screenplay by Joan Didion and John Gregory Dunne, of all people. [PG-13] ▼●

Uphill All the Way (1985) **C-86m.** BOMB D: Frank Q. Dobbs. Roy Clark, Mel Tillis, Burl Ives, Glen Campbell, Trish Van Devere, Burt Reynolds, Frank Gorshin, Sheb Wooley. Teaming of singing stars Tillis and Clark as inept robbers in the Old West probably sounded like fun on paper but emerges as a mirthless chase film. Cameo contributions of pals Reynolds and Campbell add little. [PG] ▼

Up in Arms (1944) **C-106m.** **½ D: Elliott Nugent. Danny Kaye, Dana Andrews, Constance Dowling, Dinah Shore, Louis Calhern, Lyle Talbot, Margaret Dumont, Elisha Cook, Jr. Danny's first feature film (about a hypochondriac in the Army) doesn't wear well, biggest asset being vivacious Dinah Shore; Virginia Mayo is one of the chorus girls. Only those great patter songs—including "The Lobby Number" and "Melody in 4F"—hold up. Based on *The Nervous Wreck*, filmed before in 1926 and later with Eddie Cantor as WHOOPEE!▼

Up in Central Park (1948) **88m.** ** D: William A. Seiter. Deanna Durbin, Dick Haymes, Vincent Price, Albert Sharpe, Tom Powers. Disappointing screen version of Broadway musical hit (minus many of its songs) about an Irish colleen in turn-of-the-20th-century N.Y.C. who helps expose the crooked Tammany Hall tactics of Boss Tweed (Price).▼

Up in Smoke (1978) **C-86m.** *** D: Lou Adler. Cheech Marin, Tommy Chong, Stacy Keach, Tom Skerritt, Edie Adams, Strother Martin. This silly pothead comedy breaks down all resistance with its cheerful vignettes about two dummies in search of "good grass." Nothing great, but undeniably funny; this was Cheech and Chong's first movie. Panavision. [R]▼●◗

Up in the Air (2009) **C-109m.** ***½ D: Jason Reitman. George Clooney, Vera Farmiga, Anna Kendrick, Jason Bateman, Amy Morton, Melanie Lynskey, J. K. Simmons, Sam Elliott, Danny McBride, Zach Galifianakis, Chris Lowell. Clooney, who works for a company that "handles" mass firings, has fashioned his life around constant (and efficient) travel, and distancing himself from relationships. Then two women come into his life: a young hotshot MBA (Kendrick) who thinks she has a better way of doing his job, and a savvy, sexy businesswoman (Farmiga) who becomes his sexual partner on the road. A pointed, timely, sometimes funny, sometimes rueful rumination on modern life and the way we connect or disconnect from the people around us. Brilliantly adapted by Sheldon Turner and Reitman from Walter Kirn's novel. The cast couldn't be better . . . but the people reacting to firings at various points in the film are real, not actors. [R]◗

Up in the Cellar (1970) **C-92m.** *** D: Theodore J. Flicker. Wes Stern, Joan Collins, Larry Hagman, Judy Pace. Above-average story of alluring youth who knows how to turn women on. Flicker's screenplay is exceptionally sharp. Made to cash in on success of THREE IN THE ATTIC, and was in fact retitled THREE IN THE CELLAR. [R]▼

Upper Hand, The (1966-French) **C-86m.** **½ D: Denys de la Patelliere. Jean Gabin, George Raft, Gert Frobe, Nadja Tiller. Labored international underworld yarn, with wooden performances by cast involved in gold smuggling. Franscope.

Up Periscope (1959) **C-111m.** **½ D: Gordon Douglas. James Garner, Edmond O'Brien, Andra Martin, Alan Hale, Carleton Carpenter, Frank Gifford. Garner is Navy lieutenant transferred to submarine during WW2, with usual interaction among crew as they reconnoiter Japanese held island. WarnerScope.▼●◗

Upside of Anger, The (2005) **C-118m.** *** D: Mike Binder. Joan Allen, Kevin Costner, Erika Christensen, Evan Rachel Wood, Keri Russell, Alicia Witt, Mike Binder, Dane Christensen. Allen gives another knockout performance in this absorbing slice of life about a woman whose husband walks out on her, leaving her to cope with four daughters and an enormous well of anger. Costner is quite good as an ex–baseball-player-turned-radio-personality who insinuates himself into her life. Writer-director Binder plays Costner's producer. Filmed in England, though it takes place in the U.S. Super 35. [R]◗

Upstairs and Downstairs (1959-British) **C-100m.** *** D: Ralph Thomas. Mylene Demongeot, Michael Craig, Anne Heywood, James Robertson Justice, Daniel Massey, Claudia Cardinale. Witty study of human nature: Craig married boss' daughter (Heywood) and they must entertain firm's clients. Traces chaos of party-giving and odd assortment of servants who come and go.

Up the Academy (1980) **C-88m.** ** D: Robert Downey. Ron Leibman, Wendell Brown, Ralph Macchio, Tom Citera, Tom Poston, Stacey Nelkin, Barbara Bach, Leonard Frey, Robert Downey, Jr. Crude, tasteless but occasionally lively comedy about misadventures in a boys' military school. Leibman had his name taken off credits and advertising, but film isn't *that* bad. Aka *MAD MAGAZINE* PRESENTS UP THE ACADEMY, although for cable TV release all references to *Mad* and Alfred E. Neuman were excised. Macchio's film debut. Panavision. [R]▼◗

Up the Creek (1958-British) **83m.** **½ D: Val Guest. David Tomlinson, Wilfrid Hyde-White, Peter Sellers, Vera Day, Michael Goodliffe. Broad naval spoof à la MISTER ROBERTS, which leans too much on slapstick rather than barbs; Hyde-White is best as nonplussed admiral. Previously filmed as OH, MR. PORTER. Hammerscope.▼

Up the Creek (1984) **C-95m.** ** D: Robert Butler. Tim Matheson, Jennifer Runyon, Stephen Furst, Dan Monahan, Sandy Helberg, Jeff East, Blaine Novak, James B. Sikking, John Hillerman. Silly comedy—though far from the worst of its kind—about four college losers (played by graduates of PORKY'S and ANIMAL HOUSE) who battle dastardly preppies and gung-ho military cadets to win a raft race. Plenty of skimpily clad girls, plus a genuinely funny charade scene. [R]▼●

Up the Down Staircase (1967) **C-124m.** *** D: Robert Mulligan. Sandy Dennis, Patrick Bedford, Eileen Heckart, Ruth White, Jean Stapleton, Sorrell Booke, Roy Poole, Ellen O'Mara. Film version of Bel Kaufman's bestseller about N.Y.C. public schools is too slickly handled to be taken seriously, but generally entertaining. Good acting, especially by O'Mara as pathetic student. ▼▶

Up the River (1930) **92m.** **½ D: John Ford. Spencer Tracy, Claire Luce, Warren Hymer, Humphrey Bogart, William Collier, Sr. Silly but disarmingly funny comedy about a pair of habitual convicts, played by Tracy (dynamic in his feature-film debut) and Hymer, and their efforts to help fellow inmate Bogart (in his *second* feature), who's fallen in love with female prisoner Luce. Notable for its confluence of great talents at the beginnings of their careers—but it's also fun to watch.▶

Up the Sandbox (1972) **C-97m.** **½ D: Irvin Kershner. Barbra Streisand, David Selby, Jane Hoffman, John C. Becher, Jacobo Morales, Barbara Rhoades, Stockard Channing, Isabel Sanford, Conrad Bain, Paul Dooley, Anne Ramsey. Uneasy mixture of naturalism and fantasy somewhat redeemed by Streisand's performance, some funny sequences, and genuine feeling for plight of neglected young mother in N.Y.C. [R] ▼▶

Up Tight (1968) **C-104m.** *** D: Jules Dassin. Raymond St. Jacques, Ruby Dee, Frank Silvera, Julian Mayfield, Roscoe Lee Browne, Max Julien. Tough remake of THE INFORMER, ghetto-style. Black revolutionaries betrayed by one of their own. [PG—originally rated M]

Up to His Ears (1965-French-Italian) **C-108m.** *** D: Philippe De Broca. Jean-Paul Belmondo, Ursula Andress, Maria Pacome, Valerie Lagrange, Jess Hahn. Wealthy young man decides to end his troubles by hiring a killer to do him in, then changes his mind. Energetic comedy runs hot and cold, but has many delicious moments. Beware of 94m. version.

Uptown Girls (2003) **C-93m.** **½ D: Boaz Yakin. Brittany Murphy, Dakota Fanning, Marley Shelton, Donald Faison, Jesse Spencer, Austin Pendleton, Heather Locklear, Fisher Stevens. Would-be fairy tale about the spoiled daughter of a rock star who suddenly discovers she's broke and is forced to take her first job ever—as nanny to a precocious 8-year-old girl whose mother ignores her. Murphy and Fanning are well cast and give the film its spark, but the muddled script wavers uneasily between comedy and drama, settling too often for formulaic glibness. [PG-13] ▼▶

Uptown Saturday Night (1974) **C-104m.** **½ D: Sidney Poitier. Sidney Poitier, Bill Cosby, Harry Belafonte, Calvin Lockhart, Flip Wilson, Richard Pryor, Rosalind Cash, Roscoe Lee Browne, Paula Kelly. Undeniably entertaining, this film still looks like an *Amos 'n Andy* script dusted off. Broad, silly comedy about two pals (Poitier, Cosby) who try to retrieve a stolen winning lottery ticket and get involved with an underworld kingpin (Belafonte, in an uproarious Godfather par-

ody). A pair of follow-ups: LET'S DO IT AGAIN and A PIECE OF THE ACTION. [PG] ▼▶

Up Your Alley (1989) **C-88m.** **½ D: Bob Logan. Murray Langston, Linda Blair, Bob Zany, Kevin Benton, Ruth Buzzi, Glen Vincent, Jack Hanrahan, Melissa Shear, Johnny Dark, Yakov Smirnoff. Ambitious low-budget comedy with dramatic underpinnings. Reporter Blair pretends to be homeless to write a story about cynical street person Langston, and his innocent friend Zany. Gags too often undermine sensitive and serious moments. Cowritten by director Logan and star Langston (a.k.a. The Unknown Comic). [R] ▼▶

Uranus (1991-French) **C-100m.** *** D: Claude Berri. Philippe Noiret, Gérard Depardieu, Jean-Pierre Marielle, Michel Blanc, Gérard Desarthe, Michel Galabru, Fabrice Luchini, Daniel Prevost. Communists and anti-communists, collaborators and ex-resisters lobby for power in a French village formerly held by the Nazis. Less politically ambiguous than muddled, and perhaps overplotted—but a potent showcase for some powerhouse French actors.▼

Urban Cowboy (1980) **C-135m.** *** D: James Bridges. John Travolta, Debra Winger, Scott Glenn, Madolyn Smith, Barry Corbin, Brooke Alderson, Mickey Gilley, Charlie Daniels Band, Bonnie Raitt. A young hard-hat new to Pasadena, Texas, gravitates to the incredible honky-tonk named Gilley's, with its easy women, macho ambience, and mechanical bull, perfecting an "image" of manhood that doesn't quite work out in real life. An evocative slice of life adapted from Aaron Latham's magazine story by Latham and director Bridges. Later a Broadway musical. Panavision. [PG] ▼▶

Urbania (2000) **C-103m.** *** D: Jon Shear. Dan Futterman, Alan Cumming, Matt Keeslar, Josh Hamilton, Lothaire Bluteau, Samuel Ball, Paige Sukowa, Paige Turco, Gabriel Olds. Unusual, surreal drama of a gay New Yorker trying to cope with daily life—and the meaning of life—after apparently losing his lover. Film has an enigmatic structure, a strong cast and a superb performance by Futterman. Shear's feature directing debut; he also coscripted. ▼▶

Urban Legend (1998) **C-99m.** ** D: Jamie Blanks. Jared Leto, Alicia Witt, Rebecca Gayheart, Natasha Gregson Wagner, Michael Rosenbaum, Loretta Devine, Joshua Jackson, John Neville, Robert Englund, Danielle Harris, Brad Dourif, Tara Reid. College friends are stalked by an unknown murderer, who kills them one by one in the style of famous urban legends. Clever premise is undercut by standard presentation and a truly rotten ending. Just another SCREAM clone, but a bit more entertaining than most. Followed by two sequels. Super 35. [R] ▼▶

Urban Legends: Final Cut (2000) **C-98m.** BOMB D: John Ottman. Jennifer Morrison, Matthew Davis, Hart Bochner, Loretta Devine, Eva Mendes, Joseph Lawrence, Anson Mount, Jessica Cauffiel, Anthony Anderson, Michael Bacall, Marco Hofschneider. Rivalry between student filmmakers—some with mysterious pasts— seems to lead to a series of murders. Only tenuously linked to the first film, this mostly avoids the "urban legends" premise, and also avoids being worth your time. Just another slasher movie, defanged by oversensitivity to violence and gore. Rebecca Gayheart appears unbilled. Followed by URBAN LEGENDS: BLOODY MARY. Super 35. [R]▼▶

Used Cars (1980) **C-113m.** *** D: Robert Zemeckis. Kurt Russell, Jack Warden, Gerrit Graham, Frank McRae, Deborah Harmon, Joseph P. Flaherty, David L. Lander, Michael McKean, Andrew Duncan, Wendie Jo Sperber. Outrageous comedy about used car dealer rivalry that leads to spectacular and outlandish customer-getting schemes. Hilarious script by Bob Gale and Bob Zemeckis revels in bad taste, but does it so good-naturedly it's difficult to resist. And remember, $50 never killed anybody. [R]▼▶●

Used People (1992) **C-115m.** **½ D: Beeban Kidron. Shirley MacLaine, Kathy Bates, Jessica Tandy, Marcello Mastroianni, Marcia Gay Harden, Sylvia Sidney, Joe Pantoliano, Mathew Branton, Bob Dishy, Charles Cioffi, Louis Guss, Doris Roberts. When her husband dies, a middle-aged Jewish woman (MacLaine) finds herself being courted—persistently—by an Italian man (Mastroianni) who's admired her from afar for more than 20 years! Heavily plotted family saga (adapted by actor Todd Graff from a series of his plays) offers many touching and amusing—if never quite convincing—vignettes, with an all-star lineup of actors (again, not terribly convincing, but fun to watch). [PG-13]▼▶●

Ushpizin (2004-Israeli) **C-90m.** *** D: Giddi Dar. Shuli Rand, Michal Bat-Sheva Rand, Shaul Mizrahi, Ilan Ganani, Avraham Abutboul, Yonathan Danino, Daniel Dayan. Compassionate, folksy comedy—a box-office smash in Israel—about a childless Orthodox Jewish husband and wife (played by real-life spouses) who are struggling financially as they celebrate the Sukkoth holiday with some loutish houseguests. Made by secular filmmakers in collaboration with members of Jerusalem's Orthodox community; together, they offer an insider's view of Orthodox Jewish customs while presenting characters whose experiences are universal. Shuli Rand, who plays the husband, wrote the screenplay—with the approval of his rabbi. Film's title translates to "holy guests." [PG]▶

U.S. Marshals (1998) **C-133m.** *** D: Stuart Baird. Tommy Lee Jones, Wesley Snipes, Robert Downey, Jr., Kate Nelligan, Joe Pantoliano, Irène Jacob, Daniel Roebuck, Tom Wood, Latanya Richardson, Michael Paul Chan. The take-charge marshal (Jones) from THE FUGITIVE and his team are back on the job when a criminal suspect flees after a plane carrying him and other prisoners crash-lands. The search is helped/hampered by the addition of a Federal agent (Downey, Jr.). Action thriller scarcely takes a breath; falters toward the finale and doesn't know when to quit, but still entertaining. [PG-13]▼▶

U.S.S. Teakettle SEE: **You're in the Navy Now**

Usual Suspects, The (1995) **C-105m.** **½ D: Bryan Singer. Stephen Baldwin, Gabriel Byrne, Chazz Palminteri, Kevin Pollak, Pete Postlethwaite, Kevin Spacey, Suzy Amis, Benicio Del Toro, Giancarlo Esposito, Dan Hedaya, Paul Bartel. Five criminals of slightly different stripes are busted and put in a police lineup for a crime they didn't commit. They soon discover that fate—and perhaps more earthly forces—brought them together. Terrific cast makes the most of Christopher McQuarrie's intriguing, Oscar-winning, but convoluted script. (If you think about it, the final twist negates the entire film!) Highly praised, but to our minds, too "clever" for its own good. Spacey won an Oscar as Best Supporting Actor. Super 35. [R]▼▶●

U.S. vs. John Lennon, The (2006) **C/B&W-99m.** *** D: John Scheinfeld, David Leaf. Provocative look at how the U.S. government targeted ex-Beatle John Lennon in the early 1970s because this great popularity made his anti-Vietnam stance seem to be a threat. Historical footage is linked by interviews with Yoko Ono and leading cultural icons of the era, from Angela Davis and Bobby Seale to Walter Cronkite and Senator George McGovern. Ono's obvious devotion to Lennon comes through and provides a revealing portrait of a woman who's been demonized for years. [PG-13]▶

Utilities (1981-Canadian) **C-91m.** *½ D: Harvey Hart. Robert Hays, Brooke Adams, John Marley, James Blendick, Ben Gordon, Jane Malett, Tony Rosato. Social worker Hays declares war on the gas, electric and phone companies in this undercooked satiric comedy. [PG]▼●

Utopia (1951-French) **82m.** *½ D: Leo Joannon. Stan Laurel, Oliver Hardy, Suzy Delair, Max Elloy. L&H's final film saddles the great comics with poor script and production, despite decent premise of the duo inheriting a uranium-rich island. Aka ATOLL K and ROBINSON CRUSOE-LAND. Original European running time 98m. ▼▶

Utu (1983-New Zealand) **C-104m.** *½ D: Geoff Murphy. Anzac Wallace, Bruno Lawrence, Tim Elliott, Kelly Johnson, Wi Kuki Kaa. Maori tribesman (and British army subordinate) in New Zealand goes on a ritualistic rampage after his family is wiped out in a senseless raid. Downbeat, dull, and full of stereotypical characters—without the compensating power of Australia's not dissimilar THE CHANT OF JIMMY BLACKSMITH. Original running time 118m; this review is based on the shorter U.S. version. [R]▼●

U Turn (1997) **C-125m.** ** D: Oliver Stone. Sean Penn, Nick Nolte, Jennifer Lopez, Powers Boothe, Claire Danes, Joaquin Phoenix, Billy Bob Thornton, Jon Voight, Abraham Benrubi, Julie Hagerty, Bo Hopkins, Laurie Metcalf, Liv Tyler. Young punk heading for Vegas is forced to stop in a one-horse Arizona town when his car breaks down; he quickly finds himself in a nightmare world where everything that can go wrong does. You know what you're in for when an animal is killed during the main titles; it only gets worse. A sturdy cast does its best with this predictable, savagely unpleasant pulp nonsense. [R]▼●

U2: Rattle and Hum (1988) **C/B&W-99m.** **½ D: Phil Joanou. Title Irish rock band was the late '80s' most celebrated, but scattershot documentary never really explains why to the unknowing or unconverted. Music compensates to some degree, with some of the best numbers fortunately weighted near the end; a side trip to Elvis' Graceland seems out of place. For no apparent reason, first half is in grainy b&w, second is in color. [PG-13]▼●

Utz (1992-British-German-Italian) **C-94m.** ** D: George Sluizer. Armin Mueller-Stahl, Brenda Fricker, Peter Riegert, Paul Scofield, Gaye Brown, Miriam Karlin. Good cast does its best in this overly sedate account of an elderly, dying man (Mueller-Stahl) and his lifelong obsession with collecting porcelain figurines. The point—the ultimate meaninglessness of materialism—is obvious. Scripted by Hugh Whitemore; based on Bruce Chatwin's novel.▼

Vacancy (2007) **C-80m.** **½ D: Nimród Antal. Kate Beckinsale, Luke Wilson, Frank Whaley, Ethan Embry, Scott G. Anderson, Mark Casella, David Doty. An estranged couple's car breaks down in a desolate area, forcing them to spend the night at a motel run by creepy Whaley, who looks like he'd make a good roommate for Norman Bates. They soon discover they have checked into a room with hidden cameras used to make snuff films and realize they are intended to star in the next production. Tight, economic thriller is helped by director Antal's inventive approach to basically sleazy material. Saul Bass–inspired title and end credit sequences are a highlight. Followed by DVD prequel. Super 35. [R]▶

Vacation From Marriage (1945-British) **92m.** *** D: Alexander Korda. Robert Donat, Deborah Kerr, Glynis Johns, Ann Todd, Roland Culver, Elliot Mason. Donat and Kerr sparkle in story of dull couple separated by WW2, each rejuvenated by wartime romance. Johns is perky as Kerr's military friend. Clemence Dane won an Oscar for her original story. British version, titled PERFECT STRANGERS, ran 102m.

Vagabond (1985-French) **C-105m.** ***½ D: Agnés Varda. Sandrine Bonnaire, Macha Meril, Stephane Freiss, Elaine Cortadellas, Marthe Jarnias, Yolande Moreau. Haunting drama about young drifter who wanders about hitching a ride here, sleeping there, and how those she encounters respond to her. A simple, powerful, superbly directed film about chance meetings, missed opportunities, and the price one must pay for one's choices. ▼●

Vagabond King, The (1956) **C-86m.** ** D: Michael Curtiz. Kathryn Grayson, Oreste, Rita Moreno, Cedric Hardwicke, Walter Hampden, Leslie Nielsen; narrated by Vincent Price. Bland remake of Rudolf Friml's operetta (filmed before in 1930), about poet-scoundrel François Villon. Oreste was touted as new musical star in 1956, but didn't quite make it. Story, sans music, filmed in 1927 (THE BELOVED ROGUE) and 1938 (IF I WERE KING). VistaVision.

Vagrant, The (1992-U.S.-French) **C-91m.** *½ D: Chris Walas. Bill Paxton, Michael Ironside, Marshall Bell, Mitzi Kapture, Colleen Camp, Patrika Darbo, Mark McClure, Stuart Pankin, Teddy Wilson, Derek Mark Lochran. A timid, rising executive (Paxton) buys a house where an ugly, diseased hobo has been living, then finds himself terrorized by the bum. Misfired comic satire. Executive produced by Mel Brooks. [R]▼

Valachi Papers, The (1972-Italian) **C-125m.** **½ D: Terence Young. Charles Bronson, Lino Ventura, Jill Ireland, Joseph Wiseman, Walter Chiari, Amedeo Nazzari. Sloppy but engrossing account of Mafia life as seen through eyes of famed informer Joseph Valachi (Bronson). Lots of blood. From the book by Peter Maas. [PG—edited from original R rating]▼●

Valdez Horses, The SEE: Chino

Valdez Is Coming (1971) **C-90m.** **½ D: Edwin Sherin. Burt Lancaster, Susan Clark, Jon Cypher, Barton Heyman, Richard Jordan, Frank Silvera, Hector Elizondo. OK intellectual Western with Lancaster a Mexican-American deputy sheriff forced to confront ruthless land baron after triggering local hostilities. Shot in Spain; first film for noted Broadway director Sherin. Based on a novel by Elmore Leonard. [PG]▼●

Valentin (2003-Argentinian-Dutch) **C-86m.** *** D: Alejandro Agresti. Julieta Cardinali, Carmen Maura, Jean Pierre Noher, Mex Urtizberea, Rodrigo Noya. With his womanizing father and absent mother separated, an 8-year-old "cupid," living with his grandmother, must use all his wits to solve his dysfunctional family's problems. Story set in Buenos Aires in the late 1960s is charming and slight, sort of an edgy THE COURTSHIP OF EDDIE'S FATHER with Argentinian seasoning. Noya, in the title role, avoids the kid actor "cutes" and scores with a winning performance. Writer-director Agresti also plays the imperfect dad who discovers that his son comes in handy when it comes to attracting women. [PG-13]▶

Valentine (2001) **C-126m.** *½ D: Jamie Blanks. Marley Shelton, David Boreanaz, Denise Richards, Jessica Capshaw, Jessica Cauffiel, Daniel Cosgrove, Fulvio Cecere, Johnny Whitworth, Katherine Heigl, Hedy Burress. Four gorgeous friends receive ominous valentines—and then someone starts murdering them. Could it be that geek they spurned back in junior high? Handsome but dismayingly routine retro-slasher shies away from both gore and sex. Loosely based on the novel by Tom Savage. Super 35. [R]▼▶

Valentine's Day (2010) **C-124m.** ** D: Garry Marshall. Ashton Kutcher, Jessica Alba, Jennifer Garner, Julia Roberts, Patrick Dempsey, Bradley Cooper, Anne Hathaway, Jamie Foxx, Jessica Biel, Shirley MacLaine, Queen Latifah, George Lopez, Hector Elizondo, Taylor Lautner, Taylor Swift, Kathy Bates, Eric Dane, Topher Grace, Carter Jenkins, Emma Roberts, Bryce Robinson, Larry Miller. Pastiche of (mostly) interlocking stories about men and women in L.A. celebrating and/or suffering through Valentine's Day, beginning with Kutcher popping the question to Alba—who breaks up with him—and extending to longtime marrieds MacLaine and Elizondo questioning their relationship. May set some record for the most attractive people ever packed into one movie, but the emptyheaded proceedings don't warrant this all-star lineup. MacLaine is seen in shots from her 1958 movie HOT SPELL with Warren Stevens. Joe Mantegna and director Marshall appear unbilled. [PG-13] ▶

Valentino (1951) **C-102m.** *½ D: Lewis Allen. Anthony Dexter, Eleanor Parker, Richard Carlson, Patricia Medina, Joseph Calleia, Dona Drake, Lloyd Gough, Otto Kruger. Undistinguished, superficial biography of famed star of American silent films.

Valentino (1977) **C-127m.** *½ D: Ken Russell. Rudolf Nureyev, Leslie Caron, Michelle Phillips, Carol Kane, Felicity Kendal, Seymour Cassel, Peter Vaughan, Anton Diffring. Typically excessive, visually flamboyant Ken Russell "biography" offers little insight on great screen lover, and suffers further from Nureyev's awkward performance. But any film that casts Huntz Hall as movie mogul Jesse Lasky can't be *all* bad. [R]▼▶●

Valentino Returns (1987) **C-102m.** **½ D: Peter Hoffman. Frederic Forrest, Veronica Cartwright, Barry Tubb, Jenny Wright, David Packer, Seth Isler, Miguel Ferrer. Meandering drama of young Tubb and his no-account father, frustrated mother, and his desperation to experience sex. Great atmosphere, so-so result. Set in 1950s California. Screenplay by Leonard Gardner (who plays Lyle), based on his short story. [R]▼●

Valet, The (2006-French) **C-85m.** **½ D: Francis Veber. Gad Elmaleh, Daniel Auteuil, Kristin Scott Thomas, Alice Taglioni, Richard Berry, Virginie Ledoyen, Michèle Garcia, Michel Jonasz, Dany Boon, Michel Aumont. Business tycoon Auteuil is photographed in a compromising moment with his mistress, a top model (Taglioni), so to throw his wife off his trail, he hires a nerdy parking valet (Elmaleh) to pretend to be the model's *real* boyfriend. Complications snowball for all concerned in this slick Veber farce; not one of his best but still diverting. Technovision. [PG-13]▶

Valiant (2005-U.S.-British) **C-80m.** **½ D: Gary Chapman. Voices of Ewan McGregor, Ricky Gervais, Tim Curry, Jim Broadbent, Hugh Laurie, John Cleese, John Hurt, Pip Torrens, Rik Mayall, Olivia Williams. Cute CG-animated feature about a small but plucky bird who joins the elite Royal Homing Pigeon Service working for Britain during WW2. Before they're really ready, he and other new recruits are assigned a vital mission to deliver a message without running afoul of enemy falcons. Entertaining yarn for younger kids, with smart gags to amuse adults as well (opening b&w newsreel is called BIRDS ON THE MARCH). [G]▶

Valkyrie (2008-U.S.-German) **C-120m.** **½ D: Bryan Singer. Tom Cruise, Kenneth Branagh, Bill Nighy, Tom Wilkinson, Carice van Houten, Thomas Kretschmann, Terence Stamp, Eddie Izzard, Kevin McNally, Christian Berkel, David Bamber, Tom Hollander, Ian McNeice, Christian Oliver. Cruise plays German hero Col. Claus von Stauffenberg, central figure in the daring scheme to assassinate Adolf Hitler in 1944. Pulling off the actual killing is simple compared to the infighting among the politicians and military bureaucrats who launch this conspiracy. After so many vivid WW2 movies in recent years this one rings hollow at first; finally hits its stride about halfway through the proceedings. [PG-13]▶

Valley Girl (1983) **C-95m.** **½ D: Martha Coolidge. Nicolas Cage, Deborah Foreman, Colleen Camp, Frederic Forrest, Elizabeth Daily, Lee Purcell. Refreshingly nonexploitative punker-suburbanite romance is several cuts above most contemporary teen pics, but the result is still distressingly mild. Attractive leads, amusing performances by Camp and Forrest as Foreman's hippieish parents, but film never really goes anywhere. [R]▼●

Valley of Decision, The (1945) **119m.** ★★★
D: Tay Garnett. Greer Garson, Gregory
Peck, Donald Crisp, Lionel Barrymore,
Preston Foster, Marsha Hunt, Gladys Cooper, Reginald Owen, Dan Duryea, Jessica
Tandy, Barbara Everest, Marshall Thompson, Dean Stockwell. Polished adaptation
of Marcia Davenport's novel about labor
and class struggles in 1870 Pittsburgh, and a
star-crossed relationship between a housemaid (Garson) and the son of a steel mill
owner (Peck). ▼◗

Valley of Gwangi, The (1969) **C-95m.** ★★½
D: James O'Connolly. James Franciscus,
Gila Golan, Richard Carlson, Laurence Naismith, Dennis Kilbane. Standard reworking of King Kong theme; adventurers in
Mexico stumble upon prehistoric monster,
hit on idea to display their find in a traveling
circus, make money. Script and production
have holes, but film is sparked by Ray Harryhausen special effects. Based on a story
by Willis O'Brien. ▼◗

Valley of Mystery (1967) **C-94m.** ★★ D:
Josef Leytes. Richard Egan, Peter Graves,
Joby Baker, Lois Nettleton, Harry Guardino, Julie Adams, Fernando Lamas, Leonard Nimoy. Lackluster melodrama in which
a plane crash-lands in the South American
jungle. Expanded from a TV pilot.

Valley of the Dolls (1967) **C-123m.** BOMB
D: Mark Robson. Barbara Parkins, Patty
Duke, Sharon Tate, Susan Hayward, Paul
Burke, Tony Scotti, Martin Milner, Lee
Grant, Joey Bishop, George Jessel. Scattered
unintentional laughs do not compensate for
terribly written, acted, and directed adaptation of Jacqueline Susann novel about three
young women in show biz. Author Susann
has a bit role as a reporter. Look for Richard
Dreyfuss in a quick backstage bit. Remade as
a TV movie in 1981. Panavision. ▼◗

Valley of the Eagles (1951-British) **85m.**
★★½ D: Terence Young. Jack Warner, John
McCallum, Nadia Gray, Anthony Dawson,
Mary Laura Wood, Christopher Lee, Naima
Wifstrand. Above-par chase tale of Swedish
scientist tracking down his wife and assistant who stole his research data and headed
for the north country. Filmed in Lapland.
▼

Valmont (1989-French-British) **C-137m.**
★★½ D: Milos Forman. Colin Firth, Annette
Bening, Meg Tilly, Fairuza Balk, Sian Phillips, Jeffrey Jones, Henry Thomas, Fabia
Drake, Ian McNeice. Ah, the bedhopping
of Choderlos de Laclos's *Les Liaisons Dangereuses*! Meticulous retelling of the sexual
shenanigans of 18th-century French aristocrats. Youthful cast makes this seem more
mischievous than other versions . . . but that
playfulness also softens some of its bite. Elderly Drake, who died shortly after film's
release, steals every scene she's in. Panavision. [R] ▼◗

Vamp (1986) **C-94m.** ★½ D: Richard

Wenk. Chris Makepeace, Sandy Baron,
Robert Rusler, Dedee Pfeiffer, Gedde
Watanabe, Grace Jones, Billy Drago. Fun-
loving college guys run afoul of a female
vampire in this dreary and distasteful horror
outing. Starts out promisingly, with tongue-
in-cheek, but soon drops the light touch in
favor of the kinky. [R] ▼◗

Vampira SEE: **Old Dracula**

Vampire Circus (1971-British) **C-87m.**
★★½ D: Robert Young. John Moulder
Brown, Adrienne Corri, Laurence Payne,
Thorley Walters, Lynne Frederick, David
Prowse. Very weird Hammer horror with
unique gimmick; 19th-century European circus travels from town to town for good reason:
most everyone is a vampire—including the
animals! Last-minute cuts muddled the film
considerably, but still well worth a look.
[PG—edited from original R rating]◗

Vampire in Brooklyn (1995) **C-102m.**
★★ D: Wes Craven. Eddie Murphy, Angela
Bassett, Allen Payne, Kadeem Hardison,
John Witherspoon, Zakes Mokae, Joanna
Cassidy, Simbi Khali. Sleek Caribbean
vampire Murphy, to perpetuate his race,
needs to persuade Brooklyn cop Bassett
that she's his soul mate. Oddball film has
Murphy cracking jokes, but he's thoroughly
evil; on the other hand, it's not scary enough
to work as a horror film . . . and it's overlong, to boot. [R] ▼◗

Vampire Lovers, The (1970-British)
C-88m. ★★½ D: Roy Ward Baker. Ingrid
Pitt, Pippa Steele, Madeleine Smith, Peter
Cushing, George Cole, Dawn Addams,
Kate O'Mara. Rather erotic Hammer chiller
about lesbian vampires faithfully adapted
from Sheridan Le Fanu's *Carmilla*, filmed
many times before and since. Followed by
LUST FOR A VAMPIRE and TWINS OF
EVIL. [R] ▼◗

Vampire Men of the Lost Planet (1970)
C-85m. BOMB D: Al Adamson. John Car-
radine, Robert Dix, Vicki Volante, Joey
Benson, Jennifer Bishop. Scientist traces
epidemic of vampire attacks on earth to
strange, distant planet, with the aid of stock
footage from other movies. A real mish-
mash, released theatrically as HORROR OF
THE BLOOD MONSTERS, CREATURES
OF THE PREHISTORIC PLANET, HOR-
ROR CREATURES OF THE PREHIS-
TORIC PLANET, and SPACE MISSION OF
THE LOST PLANET. [PG] ▼◗

Vampires (1998) **C-107m.** ★★ D: John
Carpenter. James Woods, Daniel Baldwin,
Sheryl Lee, Thomas Ian Griffith, Maximilian Schell, Tim Guinee, Mark Boone, Jr.,
Gregory Sierra. Under directions from the
Vatican, Woods and his team kill pesky
vampires in the Southwest, while head
vampire Griffith looks for the talisman that
will allow his kind to exist in daylight. Like
many Carpenter movies, it begins well,
then crashes in a heap by the end. Based

on the novel *Vampire$* by John Steakley. Aka JOHN CARPENTER'S VAMPIRES. Followed ·by two direct-to-video sequels. Panavision. [R] ▼●▶

Vampire's Kiss (1989) **C-96m.** **½ D: Robert Bierman. Nicolas Cage, Maria Conchita Alonso, Jennifer Beals, Elizabeth Ashley, Kasi Lemmons, Bob Lujan, Jennifer Lundy. N.Y. literary agent, Reagan-era trendy, is convinced that he's been bitten by a you-know-what. Cage's conversation-piece performance is so over the top that it's conceivable the actor was bitten in real life. Amusing at times, also tasteless, with a pointed office-harassment subplot. [R] ▼●▶

Vampires Suck (2010) **C-82m.** BOMB D: Jason Friedberg, Aaron Seltzer. Jenn Proske, Matt Lanter, Diedrich Bader, Chris Riggi, Ken Jeong, David DeLuise, Dave Foley. Spoof of vampire-themed movies in which a girl is torn between two boys and everything comes to a head at the prom. With a cast of TWILIGHT look-alikes and little else, this tired comedy is completely lacking in originality and laughs. It might have worked as a very short short. Unrated version runs 84m. [PG-13] ▶

Vampyr (1932-French-German) **73m.** *** D: Carl Theodor Dreyer. Julian West (Baron Nicolas de Gunzburg), Sybille Schmitz, Maurice Schutz, Henriette Gerard. Dreyer's stylized use of light, shadow, and camera angles takes precedence over the plot in this chilling vampire-in-a-castle tale. Based on the novella *Carmilla* by Sheridan Le Fanu; filmed several times later. Originally made in French, German, and English versions. ▼●▶

Van, The (1976) **C-92m.** *½ D: Sam Grossman. Stuart Getz, Deborah White, Danny DeVito, Harry Moses, Marcie Barkin, Bill Adler, Stephen Oliver. Shy Getz uses his fancy new van to seduce pretty girls. Innocuous idiocy of the California youth genre. Aka CHEVY VAN. [R] ▼▶

Van, The (1996-British) **C-105m.** ** D: Stephen Frears. Colm Meaney, Donal O'Kelly, Ger Ryan, Caroline Rothwell, Brendan O'Carroll, Stuart Dunn. Slight, disappointing farce in which unemployed pals attempt to bring in the bucks by operating a hamburger business out of a van. The third (and by far least impressive) of Roddy Doyle's Barrytown Trilogy, following THE COMMITMENTS and THE SNAPPER. [R] ▼●

Van Gogh (1991-French) **C-155m.** *** D: Maurice Pialat. Jacques Dutronc, Alexandra London, Gérard Sety, Bernard Le Coq, Corinne Bourdon. Highly subjective chronicle focusing on Van Gogh's final months. Unlike other films, he's clearly depicted as *not* being deranged; the result is a solid, austere work which steers clear of any sort of sensationalism or melodrama.

Dutronc offers a thoughtful lead performance. [R] ▼▶

Van Helsing (2004) **C-132m.** BOMB D: Stephen Sommers. Hugh Jackman, Kate Beckinsale, Richard Roxburgh, David Wenham, Shuler Hensley, Elena Anaya, Will Kemp, Kevin J. O'Connor, Alun Armstrong, Josie Maran, Robbie Coltrane. Working for a secret organization bent on destroying evil, Gabriel Van Helsing is sent to Transylvania for his most difficult assignment: killing Count Dracula. He also has to deal with Frankenstein's monster and The Wolf Man. After a b&w prologue that pays homage to classic Universal horror films, this noisy, interminable, videogame–like movie discards all semblance of story or characterization. Even the charismatic Jackman is rendered dull. Edward Van Sloan, R.I.P. [PG-13] ▼▶

Vanilla Sky (2001) **C-136m.** ** D: Cameron Crowe. Tom Cruise, Penélope Cruz, Cameron Diaz, Kurt Russell, Jason Lee, Noah Taylor, Timothy Spall, Tilda Swinton, Michael Shannon, Alicia Witt, Johnny Galecki. A man who seems to have it all is victimized by a jealous lover after he spends the night with an alluring—and intriguing—woman he's just met. From that moment on, his life becomes a nightmare. Remake of the Spanish OPEN YOUR EYES (which also starred Cruz) combines dreams within dreams, causing its main character to wonder what's real, and what might have been. The stars look great, and Diaz is terrific, but is there a point? Crowe scripted this unfortunate misfire. Steven Spielberg appears briefly. [R] ▼▶

Vanishing, The (1988-French-Dutch) **C-101m.** *** D: George Sluizer. Bernard-Pierre Donnadieu, Gene Bervoets, Johanna Ter Steege. Disturbing psychodrama of a man's obsession with discovering what happened to his girlfriend, who inexplicably vanishes at a vacation rest stop. The viewer, too, becomes involved as the abductor recounts his steps leading up to the crime. A thriller without blood that maintains an uneasy tension from the beginning through ·its haunting (if implausible) climax. Sluizer also directed the American remake. ▼●▶

Vanishing, The (1993) **C-110m.** ** D: George Sluizer. Jeff Bridges, Kiefer Sutherland, Nancy Travis, Sandra Bullock, Park Overall, Maggie Linderman, Lisa Eichhorn, George Hearn, Lynn Hamilton. Sutherland's girlfriend disappears at a gas station, and after three years of searching for her he's become a man obsessed. Meanwhile, her wily abductor (Bridges) considers revealing himself. Well-performed but unpleasant film can't hold a candle to Sluizer's 1988 original. [R] ▼●▶

Vanishing American, The (1955) **90m.** ** D: Joseph Kane. Scott Brady, Audrey

Totter, Forrest Tucker, Gene Lockhart, Jim Davis, Jay Silverheels. Mild, minor film about landgrabbers trying to take Navajo territory; loosely based on Zane Grey novel, filmed before in 1925.

Vanishing on 7th Street (2011) **C-91m.** ** D: Brad Anderson. Hayden Christensen, Thandie Newton, John Leguizamo, Jacob Latimore, Taylor Groothuis, Jordan Trovillion, Arthur Cartwright, Neal Huff. When an unexplained blackout strikes Detroit, causing most of the population to mysteriously vanish, a small group of survivors takes refuge in a bar as whispering shadows descend upon the darkened city. Arty, low-budget apocalyptic puzzler is moody but murky and talky, with a less-than-satisfying ending. HD Widescreen. [R] ▶️

Vanishing Point (1971) **C-99m.** ** D: Richard C. Sarafian. Barry Newman, Cleavon Little, Dean Jagger, Paul Koslo, Robert Donner, Severn Darden, Gilda Texter, Victoria Medlin. Told to drive a Dodge Challenger from Denver to San Francisco, Newman—for no apparent reason—decides to do it in 15 hours. Naturally, the cops are soon in hot pursuit, but Barry gets some help from blind d.j. Super Soul (Little). Existential chase thriller was a big drive-in hit, and remains a cult favorite, but is pretty much a disappointment. Exceptional rock score. British version, also on DVD, runs 106m. Remade for TV in 1997 with Viggo Mortensen. [PG] ▼●▶

Vanishing Prairie, The (1954) **C-75m.** *** D: James Algar. Narrated by Winston Hibler. Disney's second True-Life Adventure feature provides astonishing footage of animal life in the great plains, including the birth of a buffalo calf. Fine presentation with little Disney gimmickry; Academy Award winner. ▼▶

Vanishing Wilderness (1974) **C-93m.** *** D: Arthur Dubs, Heinz Seilmann. Cowboy actor/singer Rex Allen narrates this stunningly photographed wildlife documentary which covers virtually all of North America—from the alligators of the Everglades to the polar bears of the Arctic. Topnotch but for excessive narration and heavenly choirs punctuating each scene. [G] ▼

Vanity Fair (2004-U.S.-British) **C-141m.** **½ D: Mira Nair. Reese Witherspoon, Bob Hoskins, Rhys Ifans, Gabriel Byrne, Romola Garai, Jim Broadbent, Eileen Atkins, Geraldine McEwan, James Purefoy, Jonathan Rhys Meyers, Robert Pattinson. Good-looking production of Thackeray's novel about Becky Sharp, a poor girl who will stop at nothing to improve her position in society in 19th-century England. Generally well done, but overlong and heavy-handed at times. Witherspoon's star quality definitely buoys the proceedings. Filmed before in 1923, 1932, and 1935 (as BECKY SHARP). Super 35. [PG-13] ▼▶

Vantage Point (2008) **C-90m.** **½ D: Pete Travis. Dennis Quaid, Sigourney Weaver, Forest Whitaker, Matthew Fox, Bruce McGill, Edgar Ramirez, Saïd Taghmaoui, Ayelet Zurer, Zoe Saldana, William Hurt, James Le Gros, Eduardo Noriega, Richard T. Jones. In true RASHOMON fashion, the assassination of a U.S. President in a foreign country is told from eight different perspectives (a news crew, a tourist, a terrorist, a secret service agent, et al.). Tedious at first, with stilted dialogue and laughable B-movie histrionics threatening to sink the ambitious enterprise, but as film progresses the mystery deepens and a couple of twists make the effort pay off. Super 35. [PG-13] ▶

Van Wilder SEE: **National Lampoon's Van Wilder**

Van Wilder 2: The Rise of Taj SEE: **National Lampoon's Van Wilder 2: The Rise of Taj**

Vanya on 42nd Street (1994) **C-120m.** ***½ D: Louis Malle. Wallace Shawn, Phoebe Brand, George Gaynes, Jerry Mayer, Andre Gregory, Julianne Moore, Larry Pine, Brooke Smith, Lynn Cohen, Mahdur Jaffrey. Malle's final feature is a riveting, highly cinematic "filmed theater" piece, which examines the illusion that is the theater. Actors come to a crumbling midtown Manhattan stage to rehearse David Mamet's adaptation of Chekhov's *Uncle Vanya*; Gregory is the director, Shawn is taking the leading role (in which he is superb), and all of them remain in street clothes as the rehearsal subtly becomes the play, which intertwines with "real life." As stunningly original as Malle's MY DINNER WITH ANDRE (which also featured Shawn and Gregory). [PG] ▼●▶

Varan, the Unbelievable (1958-Japanese-U.S.) **70m.** *½ D: Ishirô Honda, Jerry Baerwitz. Myron Healey, Tsuruko Kobayashi, Kozo Nomura, Ayumi Sonoda. Typical Japanese rubber monster film except that creature defies clear definition. It's vaguely reptilian, but some insist it's a giant squirrel, since in Japanese prints it flies like a flying squirrel. Regardless, it stomps cities and scares the masses. Unbelievable is key word. Tohoscope. ▼▶

Variety Girl (1947) **97m.** **½ D: George Marshall. Mary Hatcher, Olga San Juan, DeForest Kelley, William Demarest, Frank Faylen, Frank Ferguson. Hatcher and San Juan head for Hollywood with hopes of stardom; flimsy excuse for countless Paramount guest stars, including Gary Cooper and Ray Milland. Bob Hope and Bing Crosby come off best in amusing golfing scene. Puppetoon segment in color. ▼

Variety Lights (1950-Italian) **93m.** **½ D: Federico Fellini, Alberto Lattuada. Peppino De Filippo, Carla Del Poggio,

Giulietta Masina, John Kitzmiller, Dante Maggio, Checco Durante. Fellini's first film (though codirected) is a rather ordinary tale of the lovely Del Poggio struggling through small-town music halls to become a star. Some funny and touching scenes featuring the usual Fellini eccentrics. ▼○◑

Varsity Blues (1999) C-104m. *½ D: Brian Robbins. James Van Der Beek, Jon Voight, Paul Walker, Ron Lester, Scott Caan, Ali Larter, Amy Smart. Cliché-ridden, MTV-produced high school pigskin drama about a reluctant second-string quarterback (Van Der Beek) and his nefarious steroid-distributing coach (Voight, who seems to think he's doing Eugene O'Neill). Veers between leering low comedy and heavy-handed melodrama. Lester rises above his exploitative role as an overweight lineman. [R] ▼○◑

Va Savoir (2001-French-Italian) C-150m. *** D: Jacques Rivette. Jeanne Balibar, Sergio Castellitto, Marianne Basler, Jacques Bonnaffé, Hélène de Fougerolles, Bruno Todeschini, Catherine Rouvel, Claude Berri. Laid-back comedy follows the romantic entanglements of six characters, beginning with an actress (Balibar) who has returned to Paris to star in a Pirandello play in which the script mirrors the offstage goings-on. Rich, carefully observed movie for grown-ups. [PG-13] ▼◑

Vasectomy: A Delicate Matter (1986) C-90m. BOMB D: Robert Burge. Paul Sorvino, Cassandra Edwards, Abe Vigoda, Ina Balin, June Wilkinson, William Marshall, Lorne Greene, Gary Raff. Bank executive Sorvino is the father of eight. His wife gives him an ultimatum: Get a vasectomy, or it's bye-bye sex life. Utterly inane comedy that's almost (but not quite) too stupid to be offensive. [PG-13] ▼

Vatel (2000-French-British) C-117m. *** D: Roland Joffé. Gérard Depardieu, Uma Thurman, Tim Roth, Julian Glover, Julian Sands, Timothy Spall, Arielle Dombasle, Hywel Bennett, Richard Griffiths, Murray Lachlan Young. Richly textured study of François Vatel, who works as master steward for a retired French general in 1671. When King Louis XIV comes to visit, Vatel must stage a magnificent feast and spectacle so the King will relieve his master of his debts . . . but Louis has his own agenda. Tom Stoppard adapted Jeanne Labrune's screenplay; based on a true story of court intrigue, this also serves as a contemporary parable about personal integrity. Sumptuously filmed. Super 35. [PG-13] ▼◑

Vatican Affair, The (1969-Italian) C-94m. ** D: Emilio Miraglia. Walter Pidgeon, Ira Furstenberg, Klaus Kinski, Tino Carraro. Pidgeon masterminds Vatican robbery in routine heist film. Colorscope. [M/PG]

Vault of Horror (1973-British) C-87m. **½ D: Roy Ward Baker. Daniel Massey,

Anna Massey, Terry-Thomas, Glynis Johns, Curt Jurgens, Dawn Addams, Tom Baker, Denholm Elliott, Michael Craig, Edward Judd. Five horror tales interwoven by thin connecting thread, dealing with murder, torture, bloodthirsty vampires, voodoo; adapted from old E. C. Comics. Fine cast with so-so material. Follow-up to TALES FROM THE CRYPT; reissued as TALES FROM THE CRYPT, PART II. [PG] ▼◑

Vegas Vacation (1997) C-95m. **½ D: Stephen Kessler. Chevy Chase, Beverly D'Angelo, Randy Quaid, Ethan Embry, Marisol Nichols, Miriam Flynn, Shae D'Lyn, Siegfried & Roy, Wallace Shawn, Sid Caesar, Julia Sweeney, Christie Brinkley. Just what you'd expect, as the Griswold family goes to Las Vegas, where Chase locks horns with a spiteful blackjack dealer (Shawn), D'Angelo is wooed by Wayne Newton, son Embry is mistaken for a high roller, and daughter Nichols is influenced by her cousin, an exotic dancer. Quaid steals every scene he's in. That's producer Jerry Weintraub as slick gambler Jilly from Philly. [PG] ▼○◑

Velocity SEE: **Wild Ride, The**

Velocity of Gary, The (1999) C-98m. *½ D: Dan Ireland. Salma Hayek, Vincent D'Onofrio, Thomas Jane, Chad Lindberg, Olivia d'Abo, Shawn Michael Howard, Ethan Hawke. Sloppy, stilted soap opera, set amid the N.Y.C. porno–drag queen subculture, involving a love triangle between bisexual porn actor D'Onofrio, aimless hustler Jane, and frenzied waitress Hayek. AIDS (though never named) plays a key role in the story, which labors to be hip but is only affected and muddled. Clairmont-Scope. [R] ▼◑

Velvet Goldmine (1998-U.S.-British) C-117m. **½ D: Todd Haynes. Ewan McGregor, Jonathan Rhys Meyers, Toni Collette, Christian Bale, Eddie Izzard, Emily Woof, Michael Feast. Opulent, glittery paean to early '70s glam rock (and youth-culture head movies like QUADROPHENIA and PERFORMANCE) is such a triumph of style and excess it's easy to overlook the film's clunky CITIZEN KANE narrative structure and emotionally aloof characters. Rhys Meyers is effectively snotty as a bisexual David Bowie-esque pop star, but Collette is a standout as his neglected party-girl wife. Sandy Powell's inventive, androgynous costumes are great. [R] ▼○◑

Velvet Vampire, The (1971) C-80m. ** D: Stephanie Rothman. Michael Blodgett, Celeste Yarnall, Sherry Miles, Jerry Daniels. Stylish transfer of vampire legend to western U.S. with Yarnall as sexy bloodsucker. Later reissued as CEMETERY GIRLS. [R] ▼○◑

Venetian Affair, The (1967) C-92m. ** D: Jerry Thorpe. Robert Vaughn, Elke Som-

[1496]

mer, Felicia Farr, Karl Boehm, Luciana Paluzzi, Boris Karloff, Edward Asner. Limp spy vehicle not far removed from Vaughn's *Man from U.N.C.L.E.* TV series. International intrigue isn't too intriguing in this one; Karloff is good in a supporting role. Panavision.

Venetian Woman, The (1986-Italian) **C-84m.** *** D: Mauro Bolognini. Laura Antonelli, Jason Connery, Monica Guerritore, Claudio Amendola, Annie-Belle. Disarmingly straightforward 16th-century sex comedy-drama of Connery (son of Sean Connery and Diane Cilento) arriving in Venice and juggling affairs with lovely but frustrated older women. Exquisite art direction, gorgeous Antonelli, and clever musical score by Ennio Morricone heighten this little gem. Original Italian title: LA VENEXIANA.

Vengeance of Fu Manchu, The (1967-British) **C-91m.** ** D: Jeremy Summers. Christopher Lee, Douglas Wilmer, Tsai Chin, Horst Frank, Maria Rohm, Howard Marion Crawford. Third entry in low-budget series that keeps Sax Rohmer stories in period. This time evil genius is out to destroy world police organization, and discredit arch-nemesis Nayland Smith (Wilmer) with a double. Good cast working below capabilities; lousy script. Followed by BLOOD OF FU MANCHU. ▼

Vengeance of She, The (1968-British) **C-101m.** ** D: Cliff Owen. John Richardson, Olinka Berova, Edward Judd, Colin Blakely. Not a sequel, but more like a remake of Hammer's 1965 version of Haggard's SHE; here, the spirit of Ayesha takes over young Berova. Pretty boring. [G]▼●▮

Vengeance Valley (1951) **C-83m.** ** D: Richard Thorpe. Burt Lancaster, Robert Walker, Joanne Dru, Sally Forrest, John Ireland, Carleton Carpenter, Hugh O'Brian. Sex in the West with Lancaster and Walker as battling brothers, Dru and Forrest their women. Walker plays slimy villain with gusto. ▼●▮

Vengo (2001-French-Spanish) **C-90m.** ** D: Tony Gatlif. Antonio Canales, Orestes Villasan Rodriguez, Antonio Perez Dechent, Bobote, Juan Luis Corrientes. A proud Andalusian gypsy tries to put an end to the blood feud between his family and a rival clan. Things get complicated when his mentally retarded nephew is targeted for death. Works marginally as an ode to Spanish flamenco dancing, but as a vendetta drama it's monotonous and melodramatic. Super 35.▼▮

Venice/Venice (1992) **C-108m.** ** D: Henry Jaglom. Nelly Alard, Henry Jaglom, Suzanne Bertish, Melissa Leo, Daphna Kastner, David Duchovny, Diane Salinger, Zack Norman, John Landis. Jaglom pretentiously parodies himself, playing a "maverick" American filmmaker at the Venice Film Festival; Alard is cast as a French journalist who becomes involved with him. Annoyingly self-absorbed, but occasionally effective when depicting the artificial emotion at the festival. The title refers to Venice, Italy, and Venice, California. ▼▮

Venom (1982-British) **C-98m.** ** D: Piers Haggard. Klaus Kinski, Nicol Williamson, Oliver Reed, Sarah Miles, Sterling Hayden, Cornelia Sharpe, Susan George, Michael Gough. World's deadliest snake terrorizes a London town house—in the midst of a hostage crisis. Not a horror movie, as its title would indicate, and pretty short on thrills. Unusually strong cast for such an unexceptional film. [R] ▼▮

Venom (2005) **C-86m.** *½ D: Jim Gillespie. Agnes Bruckner, Jonathan Jackson, Laura Ramsey, D. J. Cotrona, Rick Cramer, Meagan Good, Bijou Phillips, Method Man. A Creole healing woman accidentally releases supernaturally poisonous reptiles whose bites kill, then reanimate, a redneck tow-truck driver. He spends the rest of the movie decimating a small town's denizens, primarily dopey high schoolers in an old dark house on the bayou. Slavish imitation of I KNOW WHAT YOU DID LAST SUMMER—by its creators—is practically a remake (crowbar instead of fishhook) with voodoo thrown in. Standard slaughterfest is merely SNAKES ON A PLANTATION. Super 35. [R]▮

Venus (2006-British) **C-94m.** *** D: Roger Michell. Peter O'Toole, Leslie Phillips, Jodie Whittaker, Richard Griffiths, Vanessa Redgrave. O'Toole has his best film role in decades as an aged actor who forms an unlikely relationship with a friend's roughhewn 19-year-old niece. Hanif Kureishi's screenplay examines mortality and the gradations of passion in surprising ways, but it is O'Toole who makes it special, with a performance of subtlety and consummate skill that, inevitably, draws on our own knowledge of his cinematic legacy. [R]▮

Venus Beauty Institute (1999-French) **C-105m.** ** D: Tonie Marshall. Nathalie Baye, Bulle Ogier, Mathilde Seigner, Audrey Tautou, Robert Hossein, Samuel Le Bihan, Jacques Bonnaffe. Baye plays an attendant at a fashionable Paris salon whose customers believe that treatments and beauty products will make them desirable—though she herself has never found happiness. Interesting to a point but dry and superficial—though it won four César Awards, including Best Picture. That's the filmmaker's mother, Micheline Presle, playing her Aunt Maryse, alongside Emmanuelle Riva. [R]▼▮

Venus in Furs (1970-British-Italian-German) **86m.** *½ D: Jess Franco. James Darren, Barbara McNair, Maria Rohm, Klaus Kinski, Dennis Price, Margaret Lee. Musician is baffled to see a woman who had previously washed ashore in a mutilated state; poor mystery. [R]▼▮

Vera Cruz (1954) **C-94m.** ******* D: Robert Aldrich. Gary Cooper, Burt Lancaster, Denise Darcel, Cesar Romero, George Macready, Ernest Borgnine, Charles (Bronson) Buchinsky. Lumbering yet exciting Western set in 1860s Mexico with Cooper and Lancaster involved in plot to seize a stagecoach filled with Emperor Maximilian's gold. SuperScope.▼●▶

Vera Drake (2004-British-French) **C-125m.** ******* D: Mike Leigh. Imelda Staunton, Phil Davis, Peter Wight, Adrian Scarborough, Heather Craney, Daniel Mays, Alex Kelly, Sally Hawkins, Eddie Marsan, Jim Broadbent, Allan Corduner, Ruth Sheen. Vivid re-creation of English working-class life in 1950, centered on an upbeat middle-aged woman who works hard, takes good care of her family, and puts on the kettle for a fresh pot of tea to solve any problem . . . until a crisis erupts that even she can't handle so easily: her secret life as an abortionist is revealed to the authorities. Staunton is extraordinary in another of Leigh's kitchen-sink dramas that depicts a society that—for all its faults, some quite serious—was more civilized than ours. [R]▶

Verboten! (1959) **93m.** ****½** D: Samuel Fuller. James Best, Susan Cummings, Tom Pittman, Paul Dubov, Dick Kallman, Steven Geray. American soldier falls in love with embittered German girl in occupied Berlin after WW2. High-pitched drama, flamboyantly directed by Fuller.▼●▶

Verdict, The (1946) **86m.** ****½** D: Don Siegel. Peter Lorre, Sydney Greenstreet, Joan Lorring, George Coulouris, Arthur Shields, Rosalind Ivan, Holmes Herbert. Greenstreet and Lorre make the most of this "perfect crime" yarn, with Greenstreet as Scotland Yard inspector who's "retired" after he sends innocent man to gallows. Director Siegel's first feature. Remake of THE CRIME DOCTOR (1934).▶

Verdict, The (1974) SEE: **Jury of One**

Verdict, The (1982) **C-129m.** ******** D: Sidney Lumet. Paul Newman, Charlotte Rampling, Jack Warden, James Mason, Milo O'Shea, Edward Binns, Julie Bovasso, Lindsay Crouse, Roxanne Hart, James Handy. Newman gives one of his finest performances as Boston lawyer who's hit bottom, until a medical negligence case gives him a chance to restore his self-esteem—while fighting for the kind of justice he still believes in. Director Lumet uses silence as eloquently as dialogue, and turns a story with more than a few loopholes into an emotionally charged experience. Look carefully for Bruce Willis as a courtroom spectator. Screenplay by David Mamet, from Barry Reed's novel. [R]▼●▶

Verne Miller (1987) **C-92m.** BOMB D: Rod Hewitt. Scott Glenn, Barbara Stock, Thomas G. Waites, Lucinda Jenney, Sonny Carl Davis, Diane Salinger, Andrew Robinson. Dumb drama with Glenn in a one-note performance as a real-life ex–South Dakota sheriff who became a notorious gangster during the 1920s and '30s. All attitude and posturing. [R]▼●

Veronica Guerin (2003-Irish-British) **C-96m.** ****½** D: Joel Schumacher. Cate Blanchett, Gerard McSorley, Ciarán Hinds, Brenda Fricker, Barry Barnes, Joe Hanley, David Murray, Gerry O'Brien, Colin Farrell. Disappointing drama about the fearless real-life newspaper reporter who continually put herself in harm's way in order to expose the drug lords who bred so many adolescent addicts. Blanchett is as watchable as ever, but it's hard to muster (or maintain) empathy for the wantonly reckless Guerin. As a final touch, this Hollywood-produced film turns sanctimonious toward the end. Joan Allen played a fictionalized Guerin in WHEN THE SKY FALLS. Super 35. [R]▼▶

Veronika Voss (1982-German) **105m.** ******* D: Rainer Werner Fassbinder. Rosel Zech, Hilmar Thate, Cornelia Froboess, Annemarie Duringer, Doris Schade, Volker Spengler. Interesting saga of faded '40s movie star Zech, allegedly a friend of Goebbels, who ten years after the war's end is a morphine addict. Good, but not great, Fassbinder; the last of his trilogy about postwar Germany, following THE MARRIAGE OF MARIA BRAUN and LOLA. [R]▼▶

Vertical Limit (2000) **C-123m.** ****** D: Martin Campbell. Chris O'Donnell, Robin Tunney, Scott Glenn, Bill Paxton, Izabella Scorupco, Nicholas Lea, Temuera Morrison, Stuart Wilson. Over two hours of people dangling from rope over cliffs, with explosions, avalanches, and some exposition in between. O'Donnell plays a young climber who must launch a dangerous rescue mission up K2 to save his sister. Spectacular scenery (shot mostly in New Zealand) and a few good action set pieces might stop you from cutting this loose. [PG-13]▼▶

Vertical Ray of the Sun, The (2001-French-Vietnamese) **C-112m.** ****½** D: Tran Anh Hung. Tran Nu Yen Khe, Nguy Nhu Quynh, Le Khanh, Ngo Quang Hai, Chu Hung. In modern-day Hanoi, three sisters prepare a memorial banquet to honor the anniversary of both their parents' deaths. Despite the Chekhovian setup, this is another sensual tone poem with nominal plotting from the director of THE SCENT OF GREEN PAPAYA; cinematographer Mark Lee Ping-Bin shoots with hothouse radiance. Frequently intoxicating . . . but also slow-going. [PG-13]▼▶

Vertigo (1958) **C-128m.** ******** D: Alfred Hitchcock. James Stewart, Kim Novak, Barbara Bel Geddes, Tom Helmore, Henry Jones, Ellen Corby, Raymond Bailey, Lee Patrick. One of Hitchcock's most discussed films. Retired police detective Stewart, who has a fear of heights, is hired by old school chum in San Francisco to keep an eye on his wife (Novak), eventually falls in love with his quarry . . . and that's just the beginning; to reveal more would be unthinkable. Alec Coppel and Samuel Taylor scripted, from the novel *D'entre les morts* by Pierre Boileau and Thomas Narcejac. Haunting, dreamlike thriller, with riveting Bernard Herrmann score to match; a genuinely great motion picture that demands multiple viewings. VistaVision.▼●◗

Very Annie-Mary (2001-British-Welsh-French) C-105m. **½ D: Sara Sugarman. Rachel Griffiths, Jonathan Pryce, Ioan Gruffudd, Matthew Rhys, Kenneth Griffith, Ruth Madoc, Joanna Page. Alternately charming and curious concoction from writer-director Sugarman. The baker in the small Welsh town of Ogw is also the resident ladies' man and star tenor . . . but he oppresses his simple-minded daughter, who yearns to break free. Full of quirky characters and incidents, but its major assets are the performances by Griffiths, as the clumsy but good-hearted Annie-Mary, and Pryce, as her quietly diabolical father. It's hard to top that opening shot!▼◗

Very Bad Things (1998) C-100m. ** D: Peter Berg. Christian Slater, Cameron Diaz, Daniel Stern, Jeanne Tripplehorn, Jon Favreau, Jeremy Piven, Leland Orser. Black—make that *really* black—comedy about a guy who goes to Las Vegas with four pals for a bachelor party. The scene turns ugly very fast, leaving the friends to deal with a couple of crimes and raging guilt as the wedding draws nearer. Extreme, to say the least, but true to its dark mandate, which is awfully grim. Feature writing and directing debut for actor Berg. [R] ▼●◗

Very Brady Sequel, A (1996) C-89m. *** D: Arlene Sanford. Shelley Long, Gary Cole, Tim Matheson, Christopher Daniel Barnes, Christine Taylor, Paul Sutera, Jennifer Elise Cox, Henrietta Mantel, Jesse Lee, Olivia Hack, John Hillerman. With a better script than the first BRADY movie, this silly/funny follow-up has the '70s time-warp family thrown asunder when a man claiming to be Carol's first husband shows up. Further problems arise when Greg and Marsha find themselves unsettlingly attracted to one another! Full of the same double-entendre sexual gags as the first film, plus wonderful musical moments and a handful of gag cameos. [PG-13]▼●◗

Very Long Engagement, A (2004-French) C-133m. **½ D: Jean-Pierre Jeunet. Audrey Tautou, Gaspard Ulliel, Jérôme Kircher, Dominique Bettenfeld, Jodie Foster, Jean-Pierre Darroussin, Denis Lavant, Clovis Cornillac, Chantal Neuwirth, Dominique Pinon, Marion Cotillard, André Dussollier, Ticky Holgado, Jean-Paul Rouve, Julie Depardieu, Tchéky Karyo, Michel Vuillermoz, Jean-Claude Dreyfus. During WW1,

a young woman refuses to believe that her fiancé has died, despite circumstantial evidence to the contrary; she will not rest until she finds him. Full of dazzling visuals (many recreating famous French photographs) and moments of charm and humor, as well as grim depictions of war, but goes on much longer than it should. Based on the novel by Sébastien Japrisot. Super 35. [R]▼◗

Very Private Affair, A (1962-French-Italian) C-95m. ** D: Louis Malle. Brigitte Bardot, Marcello Mastroianni, Gregor von Rezzori, Eleonore Hirt, Dirk Sanders. Rather remote romantic drama in which Bardot plays a famous movie star (from Geneva) who is robbed of her privacy and retreats from the world. Mastroianni is her mom's former lover, a theater director now protecting Bardot. Flashy ending filmed against backdrop of the Spoleto Festival. Originally titled: LA VIE PRIVÉE. ▼

Very Special Favor, A (1965) C-104m. **½ D: Michael Gordon. Rock Hudson, Leslie Caron, Charles Boyer, Walter Slezak, Dick Shawn, Larry Storch, Nita Talbot, Jay Novello. Too-often blah, forced comedy of Boyer asking Hudson to romance daughter Caron.◗

Very Thought of You, The (1998-British) C-88m. *** D: Nick Hamm. Monica Potter, Joseph Fiennes, Rufus Sewell, Tom Hollander, Ray Winstone. Cute romantic comedy about an American woman who impulsively packs up and flies to England, where she simultaneously shakes up the lives of three men. Nicely done. Original British title: MARTHA, MEET FRANK, DANIEL AND LAURENCE. [PG-13]▼◗

V for Vendetta (2006-British-German-U.S.) C-132m. *** D: James McTeigue. Natalie Portman, Hugo Weaving, Stephen Rea, Stephen Fry, John Hurt, Tim Pigott-Smith, Rupert Graves, Sinéad Cusack, Eddie Marsan. In the near future, England chafes under an Orwellian government led by Hurt. Society's savior: masked rebel V (Weaving), who, invoking the spirit of Guy Fawkes, launches the movie by blowing up Old Bailey to the strains of Tchaikovsky. Portman is quite good as the man's captive, even sporting a symbolic Joan of Arc cut in the movie's second half. Uncommonly provocative for a major-studio movie, though cloaked in comic-book ambiance. Based on the Vertigo/DC Comics graphic novel by Alan Moore, illustrated by David Lloyd. Written and produced by The Wachowski Brothers. Super 35.▼◗

Vibes (1988) C-99m. ** D: Ken Kwapis. Cyndi Lauper, Jeff Goldblum, Julian Sands, Googy Gress, Peter Falk, Michael Lerner, Ramon Bieri, Elizabeth Pena, Bill McCutcheon, Karen Akers, Park Overall, Steve Buscemi. Unsatisfactory romantic adventure comedy about psychics Lauper (in her first starring role) and Goldblum, and their quest for a supposed city of gold in the mountains of Ecuador. Unfortunate misfire from comedy writers Lowell Ganz and Babaloo Mandel. [PG]▼◗

Vice Squad (1982) **C-97m. **** D: Gary A. Sherman. Season Hubley, Gary Swanson, Wings Hauser, Pepe Serna, Beverly Todd. Hooker helps Hollywood cops catch sadistic pimp who sexually mutilates other prostitutes. Both dull and sleazy, but Hauser is undeniably a great movie villain. [R]▼◗

Vice Versa (1948-British) **111m. ***** D: Peter Ustinov. Roger Livesey, Kay Walsh, David Hutcheson, Anthony Newley, James Robertson Justice, Petula Clark, Patricia Raine, Joan Young. Entertaining comedy about Victorian stockbroker Livesey and his schoolboy son Newley, who change places after wishing on a magic stone. Parts of it are silly, but much of it is inspired and hilarious. Justice is great as a hypocritical headmaster; Ustinov also wrote the script. Predates the father-son "comedies" of the 1980s.▼

Vice Versa (1988) **C-100m. ***** D: Brian Gilbert. Judge Reinhold, Fred Savage, Corinne Bohrer, Swoosie Kurtz, David Proval, Jane Kaczmarek, William Prince, Gloria Gifford, Jane Lynch. An ill-gotten mystical Thai skull enables a department store workaholic and his 11-year-old son to become each other. Not up to BIG, but better than it ought to be; Reinhold and Savage appear to be having a whale of a time in their roles. [PG]▼◗

Vicky Cristina Barcelona (2008) **C-97m. ***** D: Woody Allen. Javier Bardem, Penélope Cruz, Scarlett Johansson, Rebecca Hall, Patricia Clarkson, Kevin Dunn, Chris Messina, Zak Orth, Carrie Preston, Pablo Schreiber. While summering with family friends in Barcelona, two American girls are approached by a sexy artist who asks them to spend a weekend with him. One is outraged, the other intrigued, but what happens next is completely unpredictable. A light, funny concoction by Woody Allen filled with attractive people and equally attractive postcard scenery. Blithely entertaining, with a terrific showcase part for Cruz, who won Best Supporting Actress Oscar as Bardem's fiery ex-wife. [PG-13]◗

Victim (1961-British) **100m. ***½** D: Basil Dearden. Dirk Bogarde, Sylvia Sims, Dennis Price, Nigel Stock, Peter McEnery, Donald Churchill, Anthony Nicholls, Hilton Edwards, Norman Bird. Fine thriller with lawyer Bogarde risking reputation by trying to confront gang of blackmailers who caused death of his onetime lover. Considered daring at the time for treatment of homosexuality. Screenplay by Janet Green and John McCormick. ▼◗

Victor Frankenstein SEE: **Terror of Frankenstein**

Victors, The (1963) **156m. ***** D: Carl Foreman. George Hamilton, George Peppard, Vince Edwards, Eli Wallach, Melina Mercouri, Romy Schneider, Jeanne Moreau, Peter Fonda, Senta Berger, Elke Sommer, Albert Finney. Sprawling WW2 drama of Allied soldiers on the march through Europe, focusing on their loving and fighting. Good cast and direction overcome Foreman's ambling script. Originally released at 175m. Panavision.

Victor/Victoria (1982) **C-133m. ***½** D: Blake Edwards. Julie Andrews, James Garner, Robert Preston, Lesley Ann Warren, Alex Karras, John Rhys-Davies, Graham Stark, Peter Arne. Down-and-out singer Andrews masquerades as a man and becomes the toast of Paris cabarets in the 1930s, to the delight of her gay mentor (Preston) and the confusion of an American admirer (Garner). Sophisticated, often hilarious comedy, with Henry Mancini and Leslie Bricusse earning Oscars for their song score and adaptation. Edwards' screenplay is based on VIKTOR UND VIKTORIA, a 1933 German film (remade in 1936 as FIRST A GIRL with Jessie Matthews). Later a Broadway musical. Panavision. [PG] ▼◗

Victory (1981) **C-110m. *½** D: John Huston. Sylvester Stallone, Michael Caine, Max von Sydow, Pele, Daniel Massey, Carole Laure. POWs get a chance to escape German prison camp but stick around to finish soccer game—just as it would have happened in real life. Only Pele's celebrated kicks save this silly bore from a BOMB rating. Panavision. [PG]▼◗

Victory at Sea (1954) **108m. ***** Produced by Henry Salomon. Narrated by Alexander Scourby. Briskly edited version of popular TV documentary series, highlighting Allied fight during WW2. Excellent photography. Rousing score by Richard Rodgers and Robert Russell Bennett. ▼

Videodrome (1983-Canadian) **C-90m. **** D: David Cronenberg. James Woods, Sonja Smits, Deborah Harry, Peter Dvorsky, Les Carlson, Jack Creley, Lynne Gorman. Genuinely intriguing story premise—about pirate cable-TV programmer (Woods, in a dynamic performance) who's mesmerized by bizarre, untraceable transmissions that have hallucinatory power. Unfortunately, story gets slower—and sillier—as it goes along, with icky special effects by Rick Baker. [R]▼◗

View From the Bridge, A (1962-French) **110m. ***** D: Sidney Lumet. Raf Vallone, Maureen Stapleton, Carol Lawrence, Jean Sorel, Morris Carnovsky, Harvey Lembeck, Vincent Gardenia. Effective adaptation of Arthur Miller drama set near Brooklyn waterfront, involving dock worker Vallone's rejection of wife Stapleton and suppressed love of niece Lawrence; Sorel is smuggled-in immigrant Lawrence loves.▼

View from the Top (2003) **C-87m.** ** D: Bruno Barreto. Gwyneth Paltrow, Christina Applegate, Mark Ruffalo, Candice Bergen, Kelly Preston, Rob Lowe, Mike Myers, Chad Everett, Stephen Tobolowsky. A poor girl pursues her dream by becoming a flight attendant, with stewardess-turned-airline-owner Bergen as her role model. Eventually she has to choose between a career and the man she loves. The cast is engaging, and the fashions are fun, but this retro fairy tale plays like a bland 1960s Hollywood movie, except for Myers, whose cross-eyed comic shtick seems to belong in an entirely different film. George Kennedy appears unbilled. Super 35. [PG-13] ▼▶

View to a Kill, A (1985-British) **C-131m.** ** D: John Glen. Roger Moore, Christopher Walken, Tanya Roberts, Grace Jones, Patrick Macnee, Patrick Bauchau, Fiona Fullerton, Alison Doody, Desmond Llewelyn, Robert Brown, Lois Maxwell, Walter Gotell, Dolph Lundgren. One of the weakest James Bond films saddles 007 with a bland villain (Walken, who wants to destroy California's lucrative Silicon Valley), a monotonous villainess (Jones), and a wimpy leading lady (Roberts). And it goes on forever. Only some spectacular stunt sequences keep it alive. (Oh, yes, there's also a gorgeous Russian spy—played by Fullerton—who disappears too soon.) Moore's final appearance as 007. Panavision. [PG] ▼▶

Vigil (1984-New Zealand) **C-90m.** **½ D: Vincent Ward. Bill Kerr, Fiona Kay, Gordon Shields, Penelope Stewart, Frank Whitten. Ward's first feature is an apt predecessor to his NAVIGATOR. It's a grim, thinly scripted, but visually arresting account of how a young farm girl reacts to the arrival of a stranger upon the death of her father. ▼

Vigilante (1982) **C-90m.** BOMB D: William Lustig. Robert Forster, Fred Williamson, Richard Bright, Rutanya Alda, Willie Colon, Joe Spinell, Carol Lynley, Woody Strode. Forster is driven to join DEATH WISH–type vigilantes after his family is viciously attacked by degenerate punks. Script is full of holes, and so is some of the cast after various bloody attacks. Truly distasteful. Unrated director's cut runs 89m. Originally titled STREET GANG. Panavision. [R] ▼▶

Vigilante Force (1976) **C-89m.** **½ D: George Armitage. Kris Kristofferson, Jan-Michael Vincent, Victoria Principal, Bernadette Peters, Brad Dexter, David Doyle, Andrew Stevens. Vietnam vet Kristofferson, hired to help restore order when small California town is overrun by workers from nearby oilfields, succeeds but then takes over town himself. Minor but interesting, fast-paced film. [PG] ▶

Vigil in the Night (1940) **96m.** *** D: George Stevens. Carole Lombard, Brian Aherne, Anne Shirley, Julien Mitchell, Robert Coote, Brenda Forbes, Rhys Williams, Peter Cushing. Compelling drama of provincial hospital life in England, with outstanding work by Lombard as dedicated nurse, Shirley as her flighty sister, Aherne as doctor. Potentially corny script made credible and exciting by good cast, fine direction pulling viewer into the story. ▶

Viking Queen, The (1967-British) **C-91m.** ** D: Don Chaffey. Don Murray, Carita, Donald Houston, Andrew Keir, Adrienne Corri, Niall MacGinnis, Wilfrid Lawson. Empty-headed Hammer Films costumer of early England under Roman rule, with plenty of gore as anarchists incite a violent uprising among the people. Murray and fine British actors are lost. ▼▶

Vikings, The (1958) **C-114m.** **½ D: Richard Fleischer. Kirk Douglas, Tony Curtis, Ernest Borgnine, Janet Leigh, Alexander Knox, Frank Thring; narrated by Orson Welles. Big-name cast and on-location photography in Norway and Brittany are only standouts in routine Viking adventure, sweepingly photographed by Jack Cardiff. Technirama. ▼▶

Viking Women and the Sea Serpent (1957) **66m.** BOMB D: Roger Corman. Abby Dalton, Susan Cabot, Brad Jackson, Richard Devon, Jonathan Haze. The title ladies are held captive on an island. The original title of this Grade-Z hokum is THE SAGA OF THE VIKING WOMEN AND THEIR VOYAGE TO THE WATERS OF THE GREAT SEA SERPENT(!) By any name, it stinks. ▼

Village, The (2004) **C-109m.** *½ D: M. Night Shyamalan. Joaquin Phoenix, Adrien Brody, William Hurt, Sigourney Weaver, Bryce Dallas Howard, Brendan Gleeson, Cherry Jones, John Christopher Jones, Celia Weston, Judy Greer, Jayne Atkinson, Fran Kranz, Michael Pitt, Jesse Eisenberg, Frank Collison. Somber, straight-faced story about a sequestered community that lives a simple, ascetic life, surrounded by woods where "those we don't speak of" pose a constant threat. One young man (Phoenix) proposes venturing through the woods to "the towns" to get badly needed medicine, but the elders will not hear of it. Evolves into a self-parody at some point before becoming downright ridiculous. Impressive only as a showcase for newcomer Howard (daughter of Ron). [PG-13] ▼▶

Village of the Damned (1960-British) **78m.** *** D: Wolf Rilla. George Sanders, Barbara Shelley, Michael Gwynne, Martin Stephens, Laurence Naismith, John Phillips, Richard Vernon. Fine adaptation of John Wyndham novel (*The Midwich Cuckoos*) about blackout in English village followed by birth of strange, emotionless children.

Eerie, well-made chiller, followed by CHILDREN OF THE DAMNED. Remade in 1995. ▼●◗

Village of the Damned (1995) C-98m. **½ D: John Carpenter. Christopher Reeve, Kirstie Alley, Linda Kozlowski, Michael Paré, Mark Hamill, Meredith Salenger, Constance Forslund, Buck Flower, Thomas Dekker, Lindsey Haun. A strange mist overcomes an idyllic coastal town, causing ten women to give birth to children who turn out to be mind-controlling demons! Carpenter's remake of the 1960 film is, naturally, more explicit and more violent, with some new characters who don't make much sense (especially Alley), but the premise is still potent enough to pull you in. Panavision. [R] ▼●◗

Village of the Giants (1965) C-80m. BOMB D: Bert I. Gordon. Tommy Kirk, Johnny Crawford, Beau Bridges, Ronny Howard, Tisha Sterling, Tim Rooney, Joy Harmon. Poor special effects are just one problem with this silly film about teenagers growing to tremendous heights. Based on H. G. Wells story, refilmed by Gordon in 1976 as FOOD OF THE GODS. ▼◗

Villain (1971-British) C-98m. *½ D: Michael Tuchner. Richard Burton, Ian McShane, Nigel Davenport, Joss Ackland, Fiona Lewis, Donald Sinden, Cathleen Nesbitt. Nasty, stomach-churning melodrama about British underworld, taken from James Barlow's novel *The Burden of Proof*. Burton plays vicious homosexual thug only a mother (Nesbitt) could love. Panavision. [R]

Villain, The (1979) C-89m. ** D: Hal Needham. Kirk Douglas, Ann-Margret, Arnold Schwarzenegger, Paul Lynde, Foster Brooks, Ruth Buzzi, Jack Elam, Strother Martin. Lynde plays an Indian chief named Nervous Elk, and so it goes. Combination Western spoof/Road Runner cartoon makes CAT BALLOU look subtle, but may make you laugh if it hits you in a silly frame of mind. [PG] ▼●◗

Villa Rides! (1968) C-125m. ** D: Buzz Kulik. Yul Brynner, Robert Mitchum, Charles Bronson, Herbert Lom, Jill Ireland, Alexander Knox, Fernando Rey. Witless retelling of Villa's Mexican campaign, with broadened focus on cohort Bronson, captured pilot Mitchum. Rare chance to see Brynner with hair; screenplay by Robert Towne and Sam Peckinpah. John Ireland has an unbilled cameo near the end. Panavision. [R] ▼◗

Vincent (1987-Australian) C-99m. *** D: Paul Cox. Engrossing, thoughtfully directed documentary look at the life and letters of Vincent van Gogh. A rare and revealing celluloid examination of an artist and his creativity. The voice of John Hurt is heard as van Gogh. Cox later used a similar approach in NIJINSKY: THE DIARIES OF VASLAV NIJINSKY. Originally titled

VINCENT—THE LIFE AND DEATH OF VINCENT VAN GOGH. ▼◗

Vincent & Theo (1990-British-French-Italian-Dutch) C-138m. ***½ D: Robert Altman. Tim Roth, Paul Rhys, Johanna Ter Steege, Wladimir Yordanoff, Jip Wijngaarden, Anne Canovas, Hans Kesting, Jean-Pierre Cassel. Evocative, emotionally powerful look at the symbiotic relationship between Vincent van Gogh (Roth) and his brother Theo (Rhys). A far cry from the standard Hollywood bios of tortured artists, with typically unconventional Altman direction and excellent performances by the leads. Beautiful photography by Jean Lepine and art direction by Stephen Altman (the director's son). Originally a four-hour miniseries for European TV. [PG-13] ▼●◗

Vincent, Francois, Paul and the Others (1974-French) C-118m. **** D: Claude Sautet. Yves Montand, Michel Piccoli, Serge Reggiani, Gérard Depardieu, Stephane Audran. Melancholy, enormously satisfying life-goes-on drama about longtime male buddies who pursue their respective vocations during the week—medicine, boxing, factory ownership, etc.—then team up for food and drink on idyllic country weekends. Montand stands out in a dream French cast as a going-broke boss in perilous romantic and physical shape. ▼●

Vince Vaughn's Wild West Comedy Show: 30 Days & 30 Nights—Hollywood to the Heartland (2008) C-100m. **½ D: Ari Sandel. Vince Vaughn, Keir O'Donnell, Justin Long, Ahmed Ahmed, Peter Billingsley, John Caparulo, Bret Ernst, Sebastian Maniscalco. Vaughn leads a troupe of comics on a 30-day tour across America in documentary/concert film, which sheds light on what the middle of the country finds funny and what this band of performers learns about the U.S. A nice idea and some very funny individual bits make this a passably entertaining journey. [R]◗

Vindicator, The (1986-Canadian) C-88m. ** D: Jean Claude Lord. Terri Austin, Richard Cox, Pam Grier, Maury Chaykin, David McIlwraith. Updating of FRANKENSTEIN saga concerns infighting among scientists working on cyborg experiments. Highlights: an impressive metallic monster design by Stan Winston plus tough-girl troubleshooter role for guest star Grier. Originally titled: FRANKENSTEIN '88. [R] ▼

Violated (1984) C-88m. BOMB D: Richard Cannistraro. J. C. Quinn, John Heard, D. Balin, April Daisy White, Kaye Dowd. Dreary exploitation film about N.Y.C. businessmen who prey on young party girls. White is a rape victim befriended by cop Quinn, who goes after the big boys. Contains a brief, standout performance by Heard as a fidgety intermediary who hires Quinn as a hit man. [R] ▼

Violent City SEE: **Family, The** (1970)

Violent Enemy, The (1968-British) **C-94m.** *** D: Don Sharp. Tom Bell, Susan Hampshire, Ed Begley, Jon Laurimore, Michael Standing, Noel Purcell. Intense drama of IRA plot to blow up British power plant, and various motives involved.

Violent Men, The (1955) **C-96m.** **½ D: Rudolph Maté. Glenn Ford, Barbara Stanwyck, Edward G. Robinson, Dianne Foster, Brian Keith, May Winn, Warner Anderson, Lita Milan, Richard Jaeckel, James Westerfield, Jack Kelly. Ford is a Civil War veteran who takes up the good fight against a bitter, greedy rancher (Robinson), his scheming wife (Stanwyck), and slimy brother (Keith). Some good action sequences highlight this standard horse opera. CinemaScope. ▼●]

Violent Ones, The (1967) **C-84m.** *½ D: Fernando Lamas. Fernando Lamas, Aldo Ray, Tommy Sands, David Carradine, Lisa Gaye, Melinda Marx. Junk about lawman Lamas' problems in getting Mexican community to refrain from lynching his prisoners when they are suspected of raping and murdering Marx. ▼

Violent Saturday (1955) **C-91m.** *** D: Richard Fleischer. Victor Mature, Richard Egan, Stephen McNally, Virginia Leith, Tommy Noonan, Lee Marvin, Margaret (Maggie) Hayes, J. Carrol Naish, Sylvia Sidney, Ernest Borgnine, Brad Dexter. Effective study of repercussion on small Arizona town when bank robbers carry out a bloody holdup. CinemaScope.●

Violets Are Blue . . . (1986) **C-88m.** ** D: Jack Fisk. Sissy Spacek, Kevin Kline, Bonnie Bedelia, John Kellogg, Jim Standford, Augusta Dabney. Romantic drama about onetime high school sweethearts, reunited after many years, who try to pick up where they left off—though he's married and settled in their hometown and she's single and a globetrotting photojournalist. Pleasant, attractive, but dull. [PG-13] ▼●]

Violette (1978-French) **C-122m.** ** D: Claude Chabrol. Isabelle Huppert, Stephane Audran, Jean Carmet, Jean Francoise Garreaud, Bernadette Lafont. Slow-moving account, based on true incident of 14-year-old girl who led double life and poisoned her parents, killing her father. Huppert sleepwalks through the role, and Chabrol lacks his usual directorial flair. Full title VIOLETTE NOZIERE. [R] ▼●

V.I.P.s, The (1963-British) **C-119m.** **½ D: Anthony Asquith. Elizabeth Taylor, Richard Burton, Louis Jourdan, Margaret Rutherford, Rod Taylor, Maggie Smith, Orson Welles, Linda Christian, Elsa Martinelli, Dennis Price, David Frost, Michael Hordern, Robert Coote. Glossy GRAND HOTEL plot, set in London airport. Everyone is terribly rich and beautiful; if you like

watching terribly rich, beautiful people, fine. If not, it's all meaningless. Rutherford (who won an Oscar for this) is excellent, and so is Maggie Smith. Written by Terence Rattigan. Panavision. ▼●]

Virgin and the Gypsy, The (1970-British) **C-92m.** **½ D: Christopher Miles. Joanna Shimkus, Franco Nero, Honor Blackman, Mark Burns, Maurice Denham, Fay Compton, Kay Walsh. D. H. Lawrence's novella comes to screen as interesting, atmospheric, but unbelievable love story. Priest's daughter falls for vagabond gypsy and suffers consequences. Miles later directed Lawrence biopic, PRIEST OF LOVE. [R] ▼

Virginia City (1940) **121m.** **½ D: Michael Curtiz. Errol Flynn, Miriam Hopkins, Randolph Scott, Humphrey Bogart, Frank McHugh, Alan Hale, Guinn ("Big Boy") Williams, John Litel. Follow-up to DODGE CITY has big cast in lush Civil War Western, but tale of rebel spy Hopkins posing as dance hall girl doesn't live up to expectations; Bogart miscast as slimy Mexican bandido. ▼]

Virginian, The (1929) **90m.** **½ D: Victor Fleming. Gary Cooper, Richard Arlen, Walter Huston, Mary Brian, Chester Conklin, Eugene Pallette. Owen Wister's pioneering 1902 novel becomes stiff but interesting Western, salvaged in good climactic shootout; Huston is slimy villain, and Cooper has one of his better early roles. Famous line: "If you want to call me that, *smile*." Filmed before in 1914. Remade in 1946 and 2000 (for cable TV); also a hit TV series in the 1960s. ▼

Virginian, The (1946) **C-90m.** **½ D: Stuart Gilmore. Joel McCrea, Brian Donlevy, Sonny Tufts, Barbara Britton, Fay Bainter, Henry O'Neill, William Frawley, Vince Barnett, Paul Guilfoyle. Remake of '29 classic Western follows story closely. Good, not great, results due to story showing its age. McCrea is hero, Donlevy the villain, Tufts a good-guy-turned-bad. ▼]

Virginity Hit, The (2010) **C-90m.** *½ D: Huck Botko, Andrew Gurland. Matt Bennett, Zack Pearlman, Jacob Davich, Justin Kline, Krysta Rodriguez, Nicole Weaver. Four friends decide to document the year in which they will all lose their virginity and take a hit from a ceremonial bong. Shot using handheld cameras in mockumentary style, this movie has been compared to everything from PORKY'S to AMERICAN PIE. Interesting concept quickly loses steam because we never really connect with its lead characters. [R] ●

Virgin of Nuremburg, The SEE: **Horror Castle**

Virgin Queen, The (1955) **C-92m.** *** D: Henry Koster. Bette Davis, Richard Todd, Joan Collins, Herbert Marshall, Jay Robinson, Dan O'Herlihy, Rod Taylor. Davis is in full authority in her second portrayal of Queen

Elizabeth I, detailing her conflicts with Walter Raleigh. CinemaScope. ▼◗

Virgin Soldiers, The (1969-British) **C-96m.** *** D: John Dexter. Hywel Bennett, Nigel Patrick, Lynn Redgrave, Nigel Davenport, Rachel Kempson, Tsai Chin, Jack Shepherd, David Bowie. Smooth comedy-drama about British recruits in Singapore; title refers to their lack of experience in battle as well as in bed. Solid Carl Foreman production, adapted by John Hopkins from Leslie Thomas' novel. Followed by STAND UP, VIRGIN SOLDIERS in 1977. [R]▼

Virgin Spring, The (1960-Swedish) **88m.** *** D: Ingmar Bergman. Max von Sydow, Birgitta Valberg, Gunnel Lindblom, Birgitta Pettersson. Brooding medieval fable of a deeply religious farming family whose daughter is raped and murdered by vagrants. Fascinating, beautifully made, an Oscar winner for Best Foreign Film. Remade as—or, more appropriately, ripped off by—LAST HOUSE ON THE LEFT. ▼◗

Virgin Suicides, The (2000) **C-97m.** **½ D: Sofia Coppola. James Woods, Kathleen Turner, Kirsten Dunst, Hannah Hall, Chelse Swain, A. J. Cook, Leslie Hayman, Josh Hartnett, Michael Paré, Scott Glenn, Danny DeVito, Hayden Christensen; narrated by Giovanni Ribisi. In 1970s suburbia, four lovely sisters head toward a sorry fate as a quartet of neighborhood boys become obsessed with them. First-time writer-director Coppola adapted Jeffrey Eugenides' novel, but for all its atmosphere and good performances (especially Woods and Turner as the girls' uptight, overprotective parents) it never quite comes together. [R]▼◗

Virgin Territory (2006-Italian-British-French-Luxembourgian) **C-97m.** ** D: David Leland. Hayden Christensen, Mischa Barton, Anna Galiena, Matthew Rhys, Craig Parkinson, Tim Roth. Roguish Christensen, escaping his debtors, hides out as a deaf-mute gardener in a convent, while nasty Roth assails his beloved Barton. Randy Renaissance sex comedy, deflatingly set amidst the Black Plague, claims inspiration from Boccaccio's *Decameron*. But a pop score, lush Roberto Cavalli costumes, and even lusher historical babes sidle it closer to A KNIGHT'S TALE. Much bawd (even a pole dance!) but little wit. Written by the director. [R]◗

Viridiana (1961-Spanish) **90m.** ***½ D: Luis Buñuel. Francisco Rabal, Silvia Pinal, Fernando Rey, Margarita Lozano. Powerful psychological study of novice nun Pinal, who loses her innocence when forced by Mother Superior to visit nasty uncle Rey. Near-perfect direction by a master filmmaker; solid performances by all. ▼◗

Virtuosity (1995) **C-105m.** *½ D: Brett Leonard. Denzel Washington, Kelly Lynch, Russell Crowe, Stephen Spinella, William Forsythe, Louise Fletcher, William Ficht-

ner, Costas Mandylor, Kevin J. O'Connor, Traci Lords. In the near future, control of the police has unwisely been given over to computer-driven technology, and both the programming nerds and their cold-blooded bosses are out of control. Ex-cop and current convict Washington is the only one who can track down a computer-generated bad guy who's been "sampled" from the world's worst serial killers! Ugly, to say the least, although it's built on a foundation of some interesting ideas. Super 35. [R] ▼◗

Virus (1980-Japanese) **C-155m.** **½ D: Kinji Fukasaku. Sonny Chiba, Chuck Connors, Glenn Ford, Stephanie Faulkner, Masao Kusakari, Isao Natsuki, Stuart Gillard, Olivia Hussey, George Kennedy, Henry Silva, Bo Svenson, Cecil Linder, Robert Vaughn. Mankind is destroyed by a plague and nuclear war—except for 858 men and eight women. Beautiful sequences filmed in the Antarctic, adequate special effects, but overlong and meandering. Allegedly the biggest budgeted Japanese film to date. [PG]▼◗

virus (1999-U.S.-Japanese-German) **C-99m.** BOMB D: John Bruno. Jamie Lee Curtis, William Baldwin, Donald Sutherland, Joanna Pacula, Marshall Bell, Julio Oscar Mechoso, Sherman Augustus, Cliff Curtis. In the eye of a hurricane, the crew of a tugboat boards an abandoned Russian ship possessed by what seems to be living alien electricity. This "creature" apparently considers people just another virus to be wiped out. Drearily routine, with borrowed ideas and stereotyped characters, though Curtis and Pacula try. From the comic book created by Chuck Pfarrer. Super 35. [R]▼◗

Visioneers (2008) **C-95m.** **½ D: Jared Drake. Zach Galifianakis, Judy Greer, Mia Maestro, D. W. Moffett, Matthew Glave, Fay Masterson, Chris Coppola, Aubrey Morris, Missi Pyle, James LeGros. Chunky Everyman Galifianakis works for a bureaucratic company where productivity is emphasized, yet no one does any real work. His home life is just as deadening but, of course, he has feelings . . . and frustrations. Ambitious film occasionally works as a deft parody of contemporary corporate culture and the hollowness of modern life, but is hampered by too many boring stretches. ◗

Vision Quest (1985) **C-105m.** ** D: Harold Becker. Matthew Modine, Linda Fiorentino, Michael Schoeffling, Ronny Cox, Harold Sylvester, Roberts Blossom, Charles Hallahan, Daphne Zuniga, Forest Whitaker, Raphael Sbarge. Muddled, over-long growing-pains movie with too many familiar elements. Modine is a high-school wrestler with a philosophical bent; Fiorentino is a tough-talking older woman who turns him on. Based on a novel by Terry Davis. Madonna appears briefly onscreen singing "Crazy for You." [R]▼◗

Visions of Eight (1973) **C-110m.** ** D:

Juri Ozerov, Mai Zetterling, Arthur Penn, Michael Pfleghar, Kon Ichikawa, Milos Forman, Claude Lelouch, John Schlesinger. Seemingly good idea of having eight different directors give eight different views of 1972 Olympics results in strangely disappointing film, considering all the talent involved; with possible exception of Schlesinger's final chapter on the marathon, none of the episodes is memorable. [G] ▼

Visions of Light: The Art of Cinematography (1993-U.S.-Japanese) **C/B&W-90m.** ***½ D: Arnold Glassman, Todd McCarthy, Stuart Samuels. Contemporary lens masters (E.T.'s Allen Daviau, RAGING BULL's Michael Chapman) discuss their own work and pay tribute to pioneer cinematographers of the past (BIRTH OF A NATION's Billy Bitzer, CITIZEN KANE's Gregg Toland). More than 100 films are excerpted, from critical and commercial hits to offbeat pictures and B movies. Interestingly, many of the most absorbing and amusing anecdotes concern sixties films (IN COLD BLOOD, THE GRADUATE, ROSEMARY'S BABY), a decade full of remarkable innovation and experimentation in filmmaking. Part Widescreen. ▼●◗

Visit, The (1964-German-French-Italian) **100m.** **½ D: Bernhard Wicki. Ingrid Bergman, Anthony Quinn, Irina Demick, Paolo Stoppa, Hans-Christian Blech, Romolo Valli, Valentina Cortese, Eduardo Ciannelli. Intriguing but uneven film parable of greed and evil; wealthy Bergman returns to European home town, offering a fantastic sum to the people there if they will legitimately kill her first seducer (Quinn). Actors struggle with melodramatic script; results are interesting if not always successful. Bowdlerized version of Friedrich Durrenmatt's play. Remade in 1992 as HYÉNES. CinemaScope.

Visit, The (2000) **C-107m.** **½ D: Jordan Walker-Pearlman. Hill Harper, Obba Babatunde, Rae Dawn Chong, Billy Dee Williams, Marla Gibbs, Phylicia Rashad, Talia Shire, David Clennon, Glynn Turman, Efrain Figueroa, Amy Stiller. Prisoner dying of AIDS tries to gain redemption by connecting again with his family, which has largely ignored him during his incarceration. Based on a play (inspired in turn by a true story), film is somewhat stagy but often powerful tale of a man who comes to terms with himself and his life just as it is about to end. Fine performances by Harper and particularly Williams make this worth watching. [R]▼◗

Visiting Hours (1982-Canadian) **C-103m.** BOMB D: Jean Claude Lord. Michael Ironside, Lee Grant, Linda Purl, William Shatner, Harvey Atkin, Helen Hughes. Awful programmer, set in a hospital with demented Ironside stalking TV journalist Grant, who hopefully was well paid for this junk. [R]▼◗

Visitor, The (1979-Italian) **C-90m.** ** D: Michael J. Paradise (Giulio Paradisi). Mel Ferrer, Glenn Ford, Lance Henriksen, John Huston, Joanne Nail, Shelley Winters, Sam Peckinpah. Filmed Stateside by the BEYOND THE DOOR folks, this passable time-killer wastes a good cast in yet another OMEN rip-off; too bad Huston or Peckinpah couldn't have directed as well. Alternate version runs 108m. [R]▼◗

Visitor, The (2008) **C-100m.** ***½ D: Tom McCarthy. Richard Jenkins, Haaz Sleiman, Danai Gurira, Hiam Abbass, Marian Seldes, Michael Cumpsty, Richard Kind. Bracingly original film from the writer-director of THE STATION AGENT about a lonely widower (Jenkins) who plods along as a professor in Connecticut, but begins to embrace life anew after he chances to meet a charismatic Syrian musician (Sleiman) in Manhattan. Minimalist filmmaking at its best, a combination character study—with brilliant and nuanced performances—and commentary on the perils and pleasures of life in today's American melting pot. Alternate version runs 108m. [PG-13]◗

Visitors, The (1972) **C-88m.** BOMB D: Elia Kazan. Patrick McVey, Patricia Joyce, James Woods, Chico Martinez, Steve Railsback. Deplorable story of two Vietnam vets who, upon release from prison for sex crime, invade the house of third vet who testified at their trial. Woods' film debut. [R]▼

Visitors, The (1993-French) **C-106m.** **½ D: Jean-Marie Poiré. Jean Reno, Christian Clavier, Valérie Lemercier, Marie-Anne Chazel, Christian Bujeau, Isabelle Nanty, Gérard Séty. Rollicking time-travel saga of 12th-century knight (Reno) and his loyal-but-dim squire (Clavier) who find themselves in the contemporary French countryside, trying to make sense of their descendants, indoor plumbing, and the like. Broad hijinks should be a big hit with the kids. A smash in French cinemas, where it played as LES VISITEURS. Remade as JUST VISITING. Followed by THE CORRIDORS OF TIME: THE VISITORS II. Super 35. [R]▼●◗

Visit to a Chief's Son (1974) **C-92m.** **½ D: Lamont Johnson. Richard Mulligan, Johnny Sekka, John Philip Hogdon, Jesse Kinaru, Chief Lomoiro, Jock Anderson. OK family drama about a self-centered father and son who become humanized on an African safari. [G]

Visit to a Small Planet (1960) **85m.** **½ D: Norman Taurog. Jerry Lewis, Joan Blackman, Earl Holliman, Fred Clark, John Williams, Jerome Cowan, Lee Patrick, Gale Gordon, Buddy Rich. Gore Vidal satiric play becomes talky Lewis vehicle with Jerry the alien who comes to Earth to observe man's strange ways.

Vital Signs (1990) **C-103m.** *½ D: Marisa Silver. Adrian Pasdar, Diane Lane, Jimmy Smits, Norma Aleandro, Jack Gwaltney,

Laura San Giacomo, Jane Adams, Tim Ransom, Bradley Whitford, Lisa Jane Persky, William Devane, James Karen, Telma Hopkins. Third-year medical students experience the usual clichés: performing rounds, undercutting rivals, questioning authority, and sneaking an occasional quickie in the hospital linen closet. Watchable, but of absolutely no distinction; stick with THE NEW INTERNS, where you can at least compare the acting styles of Dean Jones and Telly Savalas. Smits effectively projects quiet authority as the surgeon instructor. [R]▼●)

Vitus (2006-Swiss) **C-123m.** ***½ D: Fredi M. Murer. Bruno Ganz, Fabrizio Borsani, Teo Gheorghiu, Julika Jenkins, Urs Jucker, Eleni Haupt, Daniel Rohr. Moving and involving family drama of a boy genius being pushed into the life of a piano prodigy by his demanding parents. Instead of following their wishes he sets off on his own course with the help of his eccentric grandfather. Story should appeal to young and old alike with its focus on what is truly important in life. Stirring musical sequences add to the many pleasures of a film as beautifully crafted as a Swiss watch. [PG]

Vivacious Lady (1938) **90m.** *** D: George Stevens. James Stewart, Ginger Rogers, James Ellison, Beulah Bondi, Charles Coburn, Frances Mercer, Grady Sutton, Jack Carson, Franklin Pangborn, Hattie McDaniel, Willie Best. Overlong but entertaining comedy of professor Stewart marrying nightclub singer Rogers, trying to break the news to his conservative family and fiancée back home. Bondi is fun in amusing variation on her usual motherly role.▼

Viva Knievel! (1977) **C-104m.** BOMB D: Gordon Douglas. Evel Knievel, Gene Kelly, Lauren Hutton, Marjoe Gortner, Red Buttons, Eric Olson, Leslie Nielsen, Cameron Mitchell, Frank Gifford, Albert Salmi, Dabney Coleman. The senses reel at this hilariously inept attempt to turn the infamous stunt driver into a movie hero. The Bad Guys plan to have Evel "accidentally" killed in Mexico, so they can use his truck to smuggle drugs back into the U.S.! Don't miss opening scene, in which Our Hero sneaks into orphanage at midnight to distribute Evel Knievel plastic model kits—whereupon one little boy miraculously throws away his crutches! Panavision. [PG]▼)

Viva Las Vegas (1964) **C-86m.** **½ D: George Sidney. Elvis Presley, Ann-Margret, Cesare Danova, William Demarest, Jack Carter. Elvis and Ann-Margret are well teamed in this popular Presley vehicle, with Elvis a race car driver. Songs include "The Lady Loves Me," "What'd I Say?," "I Need Somebody to Lean On," "Come On, Everybody," and classic title tune. Panavision.▼●)

Viva Maria! (1965-French-Italian) **C-119m.** ***½ D: Louis Malle. Brigitte Bardot, Jeanne Moreau, George Hamilton,

Gregor Von Rezzori, Paulette Dubost. Rollicking tale of two beautiful entertainers/revolutionaries in Mexico has inconsistent first half, then takes off for hilarious finish. Lots of fun. Panavision.▼)

Viva Max! (1969) **C-92m.** **½ D: Jerry Paris. Peter Ustinov, Pamela Tiffin, Jonathan Winters, John Astin, Keenan Wynn, Harry Morgan, Alice Ghostley, Kenneth Mars, Ann Morgan Guilbert, Paul Sand. Mildly amusing yarn of eccentric Mexican general recapturing Alamo, sending equally inept American militia to rout him out. Forced humor doesn't always work, but not bad; Astin is excellent as Ustinov's loyal sergeant. [G]▼

Viva Villa! (1934) **115m.** ***½ D: Jack Conway. Wallace Beery, Leo Carrillo, Fay Wray, Donald Cook, Stuart Erwin, George E. Stone, Henry B. Walthall, Joseph Schildkraut, Katherine DeMille. Viva Beery, in one of his best films as the rowdy rebel who led the fight for Madero's Mexican Republic. Ben Hecht's script plays with facts, but overall, film is entertaining.▼●

Viva Zapata! (1952) **113m.** **** D: Elia Kazan. Marlon Brando, Jean Peters, Anthony Quinn, Joseph Wiseman, Margo, Mildred Dunnock. Vibrant film about Mexican peasant's rise to a position of leadership and power. Brando is perfect in title role, Quinn equally fine in Oscar-winning performance as his brother. Script by John Steinbeck.▼●)

Vivement Dimanche! SEE: **Confidentially Yours**

Vivre Sa Vie SEE: **My Life to Live**

V.I. Warshawski (1991) **C-89m.** BOMB D: Jeff Kanew. Kathleen Turner, Jay O. Sanders, Charles Durning, Angela Goethals, Nancy Paul, Frederick Coffin, Charles McCaughan, Stephen Meadows, Wayne Knight, Stephen Root. Wretchedly scripted, directed, and photographed assemblage of characters taken from Sara Paretsky's series of novels. Turner is a tough Chicago private detective (and closet fashion plate) investigating the murder of a hockey player who'd once caught her fancy. On paper, the star and her character should have melded; slipshod production helps render this a hall-of-fame boo-boo. [R]▼●)

Voice of Terror SEE: **Sherlock Holmes and the Voice of Terror**

Voice of the Turtle, The (1947) **103m.** ***½ D: Irving Rapper. Ronald Reagan, Eleanor Parker, Eve Arden, Wayne Morris, Kent Smith. Delightful wartime comedy of what happens when dreamy young actress Parker (who's been hurt once too often in love) meets soldier-on-leave Reagan. Arden is at her peak as Parker's flighty friend. John van Druten adapted his own Broadway hit. Retitled ONE FOR THE BOOK.

Voices (1979) **C-107m.** ** D: Robert Markowitz. Michael Ontkean, Amy Irving,

Alex Rocco, Barry Miller, Herbert Berghof, Viveca Lindfors. Aspiring rock singer falls for deaf woman (well played by Irving) who, never having heard him sing, is able to return his love. Sincerely intentioned drama is ultimately compromised by Hollywood formulas. Musical score by Jimmy Webb. [PG]▼◗

Voices of Sarafina! (1989) **C-85m. ***½** D: Nigel Noble. Miriam Makeba, Mbongeni Ngema. Powerful, profound documentary of young, black South African actors performing in the Broadway musical *Sarafina*, which chronicles the involvement of black schoolchildren in the 1976 Soweto uprising. Also details their relationship with Ngema, the show's controversial writer-director. Finale, in which exiled South African singer Makeba appears backstage after a performance, is especially moving. The show itself was filmed with Whoopi Goldberg in 1992.▼

Volcano (1969) SEE: **Krakatoa, East of Java**

Volcano (1997) **C-102m. ***** D: Mick Jackson. Tommy Lee Jones, Anne Heche, Gaby Hoffmann, Don Cheadle, Jacqueline Kim, Keith David, John Corbett, Michael Rispoli, John Carroll Lynch. Strange rumblings underground in L.A. attract the attention of the head of the Office of Emergency Management (Jones) and a scientist from Cal Tech (Heche)—who discover a volcanic eruption that can't be stopped. Good, solid disaster movie with credible characters and first-rate special effects. A few sly inside jokes will add to the fun for L.A. viewers— as compensation for seeing their home turf treated so badly. [PG-13]▼◗●

Volere Volare (1991-Italian) **C-92m. **½** D: Maurizio Nichetti, Guido Manuli. Maurizio Nichetti, Angela Finocchiaro, Mariella Valentini, Patrizio Roversi, Remo Remotti, Renato Scarpa. Italian comedian and cowriter/codirector Nichetti again satirizes the frenzy and soullessness of modern life (as he did in THE ICICLE THIEF), this time playing a naive movie sound-effects technician. When he meets a woman with a hilariously naughty profession, romance blossoms—until this lover of cartoons starts turning into an animated character himself! A decidedly adult tale of childlike love, this comic spree never entirely takes flight, though its title translates as "I Want to Fly." [R]▼●

Volunteers (1985) **C-106m. *½** D: Nicholas Meyer. Tom Hanks, John Candy, Rita Wilson, Tim Thomerson, Gedde Watanabe, George Plimpton. Dismal, grimy-looking comedy about spoiled playboy who accidentally joins Peace Corps and tries running things his way in Thailand. Candy has a few good moments but not enough. Hanks and Wilson later married. [R]▼◗●

Volver (2006-Spanish) **C-121m. ***½** D: Pedro Almodóvar. Penélope Cruz, Carmen Maura, Lola Dueñas, Blanca Portillo, Yohana Cobo, Chus Lampreave, Antonio de la Torre, Carlos Blanco, Isabel Díaz, Nieves Sanz Escobar. A woman who works hard to be a good wife, mother, sister, niece, and neighbor encounters more trouble than even she is accustomed to. Her aged aunt seems to be having visions, while her sister is talking to their mother, who died in a fire years ago. Lively, colorful Almodóvar mixture of comedy, drama, emotion, and mysticism clicks with its opening shot and never lets up. The writer-director also gives Cruz an extraordinary screen showcase. Panavision. [R]◗

Von Richthofen and Brown (1971) **C-97m. **** D: Roger Corman. John Phillip Law, Barry Primus, Peter Masterson, Karen Huston, Hurd Hatfield, Robert La Tourneaux. Weak historical drama of "Red Baron" of WW1 fame and aerial dogfights with his assorted enemies. Aerial work is excellent; it's the ground work which crashes. Aka BATTLE OF THE ACES. [PG]◗

Von Ryan's Express (1965) **C-117m. **** D: Mark Robson. Frank Sinatra, Trevor Howard, Raffaella Carra, Brad Dexter, Sergio Fantoni, Edward Mulhare, James Brolin, Adolfo Celi, John Leyton, Vito Scotti. Exciting WW2 saga with Sinatra a POW colonel who leads daring escape by taking over freight train that is transporting prisoners. Strong supporting cast helps. CinemaScope.▼◗●

Voodoo Bloodbath SEE: **I Eat Your Skin**

Voyage, The (1974-Italian) **C-95m. **** D: Vittorio De Sica. Sophia Loren, Richard Burton, Ian Bannen, Barbara Pilavin, Annabella Incontera, Paolo Lena. Listless adaptation of Pirandello story about star-crossed lovers Burton and Loren, forbidden to marry and shadowed by tragedy. Attractive stars and surroundings, but a draggy film. [PG]

Voyage in Italy (1954-Italian) **97m. **** D: Roberto Rossellini. Ingrid Bergman, George Sanders, Paul Muller, Maria Mauban, Natalia Ray. Beautiful, meditative tale of married couple Bergman and Sanders trying to reconcile their faltering relationship while driving through Italy. Received dreadful reviews when first released, but was rediscovered (and labelled a masterpiece) by French filmmakers and critics. Originally released in U.S. as STRANGERS.▼

Voyage of the Damned (1976-British) **C-134m. **** D: Stuart Rosenberg. Faye Dunaway, Oskar Werner, Max von Sydow, Orson Welles, Malcolm McDowell, Lynne Frederick, James Mason, Lee Grant, Wendy Hiller, Jose Ferrer, Luther Adler, Katharine Ross, Sam Wanamaker, Denholm Elliott, Nehemiah Persoff, Julie Harris, Maria Schell, Ben Gazzara. Absorbing fact-based drama. In 1939 a ship full of German-

Jewish refugees bound for Havana, denied permission to land anywhere, was forced to return to Germany. Picture almost dissolves into separate stories, but von Sydow as ship's captain holds it together. Originally released at 158m. [PG]▼▶

Voyager (1991-German-French-Greek) **C-117m.** *** D: Volker Schlöndorff. Sam Shepard, Julie Delpy, Barbara Sukowa, Dieter Kirchlechner, Traci Lind, Deborah-Lee Furness, August Zirner, Thomas Heinze. In the 1950s, American construction engineer Shepard—an inveterate, nearly rootless traveler—meets a man with a link to his pre-WW2 student days in Europe; soon after, he encounters young German beauty Delpy and they take a romantic journey to her home in Athens. Adult tale is quite leisurely paced but well acted and directed. Long-awaited adaptation of Max Frisch's 1957 Swiss-German best-seller, *Homo Faber*; not without flaws, but more interesting and thought-provoking than most contemporary films. [PG-13]▼●

Voyage to the Beginning of the World (1997-Portuguese-French) **C-95m.** *** D: Manoel de Oliveira. Marcello Mastroianni, Jean-Yves Gautier, Leonor Silveira, Diogo Doria, Isabel de Castro, Jose Pinto, Isabel Ruth. Touching, reflective road movie from octogenarian director de Oliveira about an aged filmmaker named Manoel (Mastroianni, in his final screen role) who looks back on his life as he visits various locales from his past in the company of several colleagues. Loaded with insights about life and memory, women and sexual attraction, sinning and confessing sins, and the passage of time. Aka JOURNEY TO THE BEGINNING OF THE WORLD.▼●

Voyage to the Bottom of the Sea (1961) **C-105m.** *** D: Irwin Allen. Walter Pidgeon, Joan Fontaine, Robert Sterling, Barbara Eden, Michael Ansara, Peter Lorre, Frankie Avalon, Henry Daniell, Regis Toomey. Entertaining, colorful nonsense about conflicts aboard massive atomic submarine, with Pidgeon the domineering admiral trying to keep the Earth from being fried by a burning radiation belt. No deep thinking, just fun. Later a TV series. CinemaScope.▼●●

Voyage to the Planet of Prehistoric Women (1968) **C-80m.** *½ D: Derek Thomas (Peter Bogdanovich). Mamie Van Doren, Mary Marr, Paige Lee, Aldo Roman, Margot Hartman. Astronauts land on Venus and kill the creature worshiped by the planet's gill-women. Actually a 1962 Russian picture, PLANET OF STORMS, framed with new footage conceived (and narrated) by Bogdanovich in 1966. Still an awful movie, but of definite curio interest to film buffs. Also see next entry. ▼●

Voyage to the Prehistoric Planet (1966) **80m.** *½ D: Jonathan Sebastian (Curtis Har-

rington). Basil Rathbone, Faith Domergue, Marc Shannon, Christopher Brand. Slow, ponderous saga of an expedition to Venus in the year 2020; made up mostly of footage from handsome Russian epic PLANET OF STORMS, involving a robot, dinosaurs, other monsters, and hidden, intelligent Venusians. Rathbone's scenes were shot on the sets for PLANET OF BLOOD, made at the same time.▼●

Vulgar (2002) **C-91m.** BOMB D: Bryan Johnson. Brian Christopher O'Halloran, Jerry Lewkowitz, Matthew Maher, Ethan Suplee, Kevin Smith, Jason Mewes, Bryan Johnson. Children's party clown eking out meager existence opts to try entertaining adults as a gag, but instead is brutally attacked (and worse) by weirdos. Co-executive produced by Smith. Crap. [R]▼●

Vulture, The (1967-British-Canadian) **C-91m.** *½ D: Lawrence Huntington. Robert Hutton, Akim Tamiroff, Broderick Crawford, Diane Clark, Phillip Friend, Patrick Holt, Linda Bell. Disappointing, unsatisfying sci-fi horror with laughable mad scientist (Tamiroff) who becomes half-man, half-bird and avenges death of his ancestor. Released theatrically in b&w.▼

W (1974) **C-95m.** *½ D: Richard Quine. Twiggy, Michael Witney, Dirk Benedict, John Vernon, Eugene Roche, Alfred Ryder. Twiggy struggles through story in which sadistic Benedict, her ex-husband convicted of her supposed murder, menaces her and new husband Witney. Flamboyant but unsuccessful thriller, retitled I WANT HER DEAD. [PG]▼

W. (2008) **C-131m.** **½ D: Oliver Stone. Josh Brolin, James Cromwell, Elizabeth Banks, Richard Dreyfuss, Jeffrey Wright, Thandie Newton, Toby Jones, Ellen Burstyn, Scott Glenn, Stacy Keach, Bruce McGill, Ioan Gruffudd, Dennis Boutsikaris, Noah Wyle, Jesse Bradford, Colin Hanks, Jason Ritter, Rob Corddry, Marley Shelton. Surprisingly sympathetic look at the life of George W. Bush, who failed at everything until the age of 40 and never succeeded at pleasing his father, even after ascending to the Presidency of the United States. Brolin (as W.), Cromwell (as the elder Bush), and Dreyfuss (as Dick Cheney) stand out in a vast ensemble bringing recent history to life, but the film can't effectively cover all the things it wants to and never gets inside its central character's head. It doesn't so much end as stop. Super 35. [PG-13]▶

Wabash Avenue (1950) **C-92m.** *** D: Henry Koster. Betty Grable, Victor Mature, Phil Harris, Reginald Gardiner, James Barton, Margaret Hamilton. Bright, colorful period piece with scoundrel Mature trying to break up romance between saloon-owner Harris and his musical star, Grable. Enjoyable remake of Grable's 1943 vehicle CONEY ISLAND.

Wackiest Ship in the Army?, The (1960) C-99m. *** D: Richard Murphy. Jack Lemmon, Ricky Nelson, John Lund, Chips Rafferty, Tom Tully, Joby Baker, Warren Berlinger, Patricia Driscoll. Comedy-drama sometimes has you wondering if it's serious or not; it succeeds most of the time. Offbeat WW2 story about broken-down sailing ship used as decoy doesn't make fun of the war, for a change, and is entertaining. Later a TV series. CinemaScope. ▼●)

Wackness, The (2008) C-99m. *** D: Jonathan Levine. Ben Kingsley, Josh Peck, Famke Janssen, Olivia Thirlby, Mary-Kate Olsen, Jane Adams, Method Man, Aaron Yoo, Talia Balsam, David Wohl, Bob Dishy, Joanna Merlin. The summer of 1994 is no picnic for high school senior Peck, a gangsta wannabe who sells grass in N.Y.C. His parents are always at each other's throats and he's never had a girlfriend. A sympathetic, hippie-esque shrink (Kingsley) who trades psychiatric advice for weed says what he really needs is sex. Then Kingsley's stepdaughter (Thirlby) unexpectedly shows interest in Peck. Shrill at first but quick to warm up, Levine's well-wrought screenplay dodges coming-of-age clichés even as it covers familiar ground, and it's not afraid to be uncynical. Kingsley is incredibly good. Super 35. [R]▌

Wacko (1981) C-90m. *½ D: Greydon Clark. Joe Don Baker, Stella Stevens, George Kennedy, Jeff Altman, Anthony James, Andrew (Dice) Clay. A dedicated cop goes after the dreaded "lawnmower killer" who last terrorized a town 13 years ago. Heavy-handed spoof of HALLOWEEN-type horror films works hard for laughs but delivers very few. [R—edited from original PG rating]▼●

Waco (1966) C-85m. **½ D: R.G. Springsteen. Howard Keel, Jane Russell, Brian Donlevy, Wendell Corey, Terry Moore, John Smith, John Agar, Gene Evans, Richard Arlen, Ben Cooper, Jeff Richards. Gunfighter Keel comes to clean up town, but former girl friend Russell is now married to Reverend Corey. Nice veteran cast, but film is only for Western addicts. Techniscope.

Wages of Fear, The (1953-French-Italian) 148m. ***½ D: H. G. Clouzot. Yves Montand, Charles Vanel, Peter Van Eyck, Vera Clouzot, Folco Lulli, William Tubbs. Marvelous, gritty, and extremely suspenseful epic set in South America, chronicling the personalities of and relationships among four men involved in long-distance driving of trucks filled with nitroglycerine. Beware: many other shorter versions exist. Remade as SORCERER.▼●)

Wagner (1983-British-Hungarian-Austrian) C-300m. ** D: Tony Palmer. Richard Burton, Vanessa Redgrave, Gemma Craven,

Laszlo Galffi, John Gielgud, Ralph Richardson, Laurence Olivier, Ronald Pickup, Joan Plowright, Arthur Lowe, Franco Nero. Glossy but uninspired biography of the composer, monotonously acted by Burton. Overlong, to state the obvious. Originally a nine-hour British TV series.▼)

Wagon Master (1950) 86m. *** D: John Ford. Ben Johnson, Joanne Dru, Harry Carey, Jr., Ward Bond, Alan Mowbray, Jane Darwell, James Arness, Jim Thorpe, Russell Simpson, Hank Worden, Francis Ford. Good Ford Western about two roaming cowhands who join a Mormon wagon train heading for Utah frontier. Fine showcase for young stars Johnson and Carey. Beautifully filmed. Inspired the later *Wagon Train* TV series. Also shown in computer-colored version.▼●)

Wagons East (1994) C-106m. *½ D: Peter Markle. John Candy, Richard Lewis, John C. McGinley, Ellen Greene, Robert Picardo, Ed Lauter, Rodney A. Grant, William Sanderson, Melinda Culea, Russell Means, Charles Rocket. Candy (who died near the end of the film's production) plays an incompetent wagonmaster who leads a group of pioneers who are sick of the wild and woolly West, and have decided to head back East. Astoundingly unfunny, even sad—given knowledge of Candy's fate. [PG-13] ▼●)

Wagons Roll at Night, The (1941) 84m. **½ D: Ray Enright. Humphrey Bogart, Sylvia Sidney, Eddie Albert, Joan Leslie, Sig Ruman, Cliff Clark, Charley Foy, Frank Wilcox. KID GALAHAD in circus trappings is OK, thanks to cast: Bogie's the circus manager, Sidney his star, Albert the hayseed turned lion tamer.▼)

Wag the Dog (1997) C-97m. *** D: Barry Levinson. Robert De Niro, Dustin Hoffman, Anne Heche, Denis Leary, Willie Nelson, Andrea Martin, Kirsten Dunst, William H. Macy, Suzie Plakson, Woody Harrelson. A desperate White House team, eager to fend off impending negative publicity about the President, hires a political fixer (De Niro) who recruits a hotshot Hollywood producer (Hoffman) to stage a nonexistent war, simply to distract the public. Pungent (and unexpectedly timely) satire grows a bit self-satisfied after a while, but it's full of funny, clever scenes. Hoffman is a standout in this first-rate cast. Screenplay by David Mamet and Hilary Henkin; based on the novel *American Hero* by Larry Beinhart. Craig T. Nelson appears unbilled. [R]▼●)

Wah-Wah (2006-British-French-South African) C-99m. **½ D: Richard E. Grant. Gabriel Byrne, Miranda Richardson, Emily Watson, Julie Walters, Nicholas Hoult, Celia Imrie, Julian Wadham, Fenella Woolgar, Zachary Fox. Actor Grant's debut film as writer-director is an autobiographical story of growing up in Swaziland during the waning days of British colonial rule in the late

1960s. A boy's happy world is shattered when his mother walks out and his father takes to the bottle . . . and that's just for starters. Uneven, crammed with incident, but buoyed by outstanding performances and Grant's obvious passion for the material. His real-life daughter Olivia plays the boy's first girlfriend. First feature ever given permission to be filmed in Swaziland. Super 35. [R]❿

Waist Deep (2006) **C-96m.** ****** D: Vondie Curtis Hall. Tyrese Gibson, Meagan Good, Larenz Tate, H. Hunter Hall, Kimora Lee Simmons, The Game, Kasi Lemmons. During a virulent South L.A. heat wave, a supermarket security guard gets carjacked at a stoplight, with his son still in the backseat. It isn't a random act; it's revenge . . . but for what? Unlikeliness abounds in this by-the-numbers bullet-riddled and profane urban crime drama. Subtext weakly encourages a rally against street violence, but it's really only about running, driving, and shooting. Super 35. [R]❿

Waiting . . . (2005) **C-92m.** ***½** D: Rob McKittrick. Ryan Reynolds, Anna Faris, Justin Long, David Koechner, Luis Guzman, Chi McBride, John Francis Daley, Kaitlin Doubleday, Alanna Ubach, Dane Cook, Jordan Ladd, Wendy Malick. A day in the life of a popular chain restaurant called ShenaniganZ, where the foul-mouthed/bored/stoned/angry/horny employees amuse themselves by dishing out lewd abuse to the customers and each other. Amiable cast serves up a few crudely funny bits, but this plotless series of gross-out gags just may put you on a hunger strike. Unrated version runs 94m. Followed by a DVD sequel. [R] ▼❿

Waiting for Forever (2011) **C-94m.** ****½** D: James Keach. Rachel Bilson, Tom Sturridge, Richard Jenkins, Blythe Danner, Matthew Davis, Scott Mechlowicz, Jaime King, Nikki Blonsky, Nelson Franklin, Roz Ryan, Richard Gant. Free-spirited street performer who never got over a boyhood crush on his best friend, who is now a TV actress, returns to the small town where they grew up and pursues her all these years later. Although the character is a bit strange and could be mistaken for a stalker, Sturridge invests such purity and innocence into this smitten character we sort of buy it all in the name of true love. Odd but good-hearted independent film is worth seeing for Danner and Jenkins, who steal the show as a long-married couple facing the reality of death. [PG-13]❿

Waiting for Guffman (1997) **C-84m.** ****½** D: Christopher Guest. Christopher Guest, Eugene Levy, Fred Willard, Catherine O'Hara, Parker Posey, Lewis Arquette, Matt Keeslar, Bob Balaban, Paul Dooley, Paul Benedict, Larry Miller, Brian Doyle-Murray. Slight but amusing mock documentary about the mounting of a musical show celebrating the 150th anniversary of Blaine, Missouri. Guest plays the outlandish Corky St. Clair, who directs the town's amateur talent in a show he hopes will take him (and them) to Broadway. Engaging performers make this fun. Written by Guest and costar Levy. [R]▼❿

Waiting for Superman (2010) **C-111m.** ******* D: Davis Guggenheim. High-profile documentary examines U.S. public education and finds much to lament and many people to blame within the system—especially when it fails students who want to learn and families who encourage them. It also shows success stories involving education visionaries, dedicated teachers, and superintendents who are willing to clean house even if it means ruffling feathers. While the film generated flak for not presenting the whole picture in some cases, much of its content is hard to refute—and the images of students who don't get into better schools because they didn't win a lottery are heartbreaking. [PG]❿

Waiting for the Light (1990) **C-94m.** ****½** D: Christopher Monger. Shirley MacLaine, Teri Garr, Clancy Brown, Vincent Schiavelli, John Bedford Lloyd, Jeff McCracken, Jack McGee, Colin Baumgartner, Hillary Wolf. Shirley is the whole show in this slimly plotted comic fable as Zena, beloved great-aunt of Wolf and Baumgartner, and what happens when one of her magic tricks causes a "miracle" as Americans are panicking during the 1962 Cuban missile crisis. [PG]▼❿

Waiting for the Moon (1987) **C-85m.** ***½** D: Jill Godmilow. Linda Hunt, Linda Bassett, Bruce McGill, Jacques Boudet, Andrew McCarthy, Bernadette Lafont. Spiritless, sleep-inducing account of the complex relationship between an ailing Gertrude Stein (Bassett) and her companion, Alice B. Toklas (Hunt). Slow, occasionally confusing, and very disappointing. A PBS *American Playhouse* presentation. [PG]▼❿

Waiting to Exhale (1995) **C-121m.** ****** D: Forest Whitaker. Whitney Houston, Angela Bassett, Loretta Devine, Lela Rochon, Gregory Hines, Dennis Haysbert, Mykelti Williamson, Michael Beach, Leon, Wendell Pierce, Donald Adeosun Faison. Four black women can't seem to find decent men in their lives; this may be because most men are jerks. A cinematic equivalent to easy-listening soul radio, this grows increasingly dreary as it eases along its redundant path. Based on the popular novel by Terry McMillan. Omnipresent music supervised by Kenneth "Babyface" Edmonds. Wesley Snipes and Kelly Preston appear unbilled. [R]▼❿

Waitress! (1982) **C-93m.** BOMB D: Samuel Weil, Michael Herz. Carol Drake, June Martin, Renata Majer, Jim Harris, David Hunt, Calvert DeForest. If watching a chef spit in soup is your idea of fun, then you might find a couple of laughs in this moronic comedy set in a restaurant. [R]▼❿

Waitress (2007) **C-104m.** ***½ D: Adrienne Shelly. Keri Russell, Nathan Fillion, Cheryl Hines, Adrienne Shelly, Eddie Jemison, Jeremy Sisto, Andy Griffith. Delightful film about a woman who works at a small-town Southern diner and deals with her problems by inventing new and fanciful pies. She can't escape from her self-centered pig of a husband, especially now that she's pregnant; then she meets the handsome new ob-gyn in town. Writer-director-costar Shelly creates a tangible environment and suffuses her film with warmth, honesty, and humor. Russell is remarkably good, and Griffith is great in a plum supporting role. Sadly, Shelly died before the film's release. [PG-13]▐

Wait Until Dark (1967) **C-108m.** *** D: Terence Young. Audrey Hepburn, Alan Arkin, Richard Crenna, Efrem Zimbalist, Jr., Jack Weston, Samantha Jones. Solid shocker with Hepburn as blind woman left alone in apartment, terrorized by psychotic Arkin and henchmen looking for heroin they think is planted there. Memorable nail-biter, flashy role for Arkin; based on Frederick Knott's Broadway hit.▼●▐

Wait Until Spring, Bandini (1989-Belgian-Italian-French) **C-100m.** ** D: Dominique Deruddere. Joe Mantegna, Ornella Muti, Faye Dunaway, Michael Bacall, Daniel Wilson, Alex Vincent, Burt Young. A boy recalls turbulent times in 1920s Colorado with his father, an Italian-American bricklayer (who thinks the world owes him a living) and his long-suffering wife. Competent but unremarkable adaptation of John Fante's novel. [PG]▼

Wake in Fright SEE: Outback

Wake Island (1942) **87m.** *** D: John Farrow. Brian Donlevy, Robert Preston, Macdonald Carey, Albert Dekker, Walter Abel, Barbara Britton, William Bendix, Rod Cameron. Stirring war film of U.S.'s fight to hold Pacific island at outbreak of WW2. Nothing new here, but exciting and well done.▼▐

Wake of the Red Witch (1949) **106m.** **½ D: Edward Ludwig. John Wayne, Gail Russell, Luther Adler, Gig Young, Adele Mara, Eduard Franz, Henry Daniell, Paul Fix. Rivalry between East Indies magnate and adventuresome ship's captain over pearls and women. Film is a bit confused, but nicely photographed by Reggie Lanning. Incidentally, Wayne took the name of his production company, Batjac, from this film's shipping firm. Also shown in computer-colored version.▼●▐

Waking Life (2001) **C-99m.** **½ D: Richard Linklater. Bold, innovative film uses a striking visual style—animation based on live-action video, but heightened and enhanced rather than literalized—to depict a young man's stream-of-consciousness experiences as he discusses philosophy with a variety of people he encounters. An unusually apt melding of style and substance, this film also dares to be boring at times. Toronto Film Festival notes praised the film's ability to create "metaphysical nausea," which may or may not be a worthy goal. Ethan Hawke, Julie Delpy, and Steven Soderbergh appear in animated form. [R]▼▐

Waking Ned Devine (1998-British-French) **C-91m.** **½ D: Kirk Jones. Ian Bannen, David Kelly, Fionnula Flanagan, Susan Lynch, James Nesbitt, Maura O'Malley, Robert Hickey, Paddy Ward. Slight comedy about a tiny Irish village (pop. 52) turned asunder when one of its aged residents wins the lottery—and his neighbors try to contrive a way to share the wealth. The whimsy is laid on a bit heavily, to say the least, but it's still fun, especially with old pros like Bannen, Kelly, and Flanagan on hand. Panavision. [PG]▼●▐

Waking Sleeping Beauty (2010) **C-86m.** *** D: Don Hahn. Lively, highly personal documentary about the evolution of the Walt Disney animation studio from its low point in the late 1970s to its renaissance, from the late 1980s through the mid-1990s, resulting in THE LITTLE MERMAID, ALADDIN, BEAUTY AND THE BEAST, and THE LION KING. A revealing look at creative people and their ego-driven bosses, derived from vintage video and film footage, with audio interviews on the soundtrack, narrated by Hahn, a longtime staff producer. Its primary hero: the late lyricist Howard Ashman. A must for Disney fans and buffs. [PG]▐

Waking the Dead (2000) **C-105m.** *** D: Keith Gordon. Billy Crudup, Jennifer Connelly, Hal Holbrook, Molly Parker, Janet McTeer, Paul Hipp, Sandra Oh, Lawrence Dane, Ed Harris. Arresting film jumps back and forth in time to tell story of a straight-arrow, blue-collar young man who feels that public service is his destiny . . . but is haunted by his undying love for a free-thinking woman. Uneven but intensely emotional, and beautifully acted by Crudup and Connelly (who never had such a great part before). Robert Dillon adapted Scott Spencer's novel. [R]▼▐

Waking Up in Reno (2002) **C-91m.** *½ D: Jordan Brady. Billy Bob Thornton, Charlize Theron, Natasha Richardson, Patrick Swayze, Holmes Osborne, Chelcie Ross, Penélope Cruz, Tony Orlando. Two couples on their way to a monster-truck show in Nevada get romantically entangled in ways they will regret. Picture BOB & CAROL & TED & ALICE GO TO THE OZARKS, with *Jerry Springer Show*–type screaming and revelations. Audiences in the mood for a redneck love quadrangle may get some laughs out of this. Cowritten by Brent Briscoe, who appears as a sheriff. [R]▼▐

Walkabout (1971-Australian) **C-95m.** *** D: Nicolas Roeg. Jenny Agutter, Lucien

[1511]

John, David Gulpilil, John Meillon. Lost in the wilderness of Australia, a child (John) and an adolescent (a ravishing Agutter) rely on young aborigine Gulpilil in order to survive. Roeg, in his first solo outing as director, also beautifully photographed this mind-massaging cult favorite; lush score by John Barry. John is Roeg's son and later worked with his father using the name Luc Roeg. Expanded by 5m. for its 1996 rerelease. [PG]▼●◐

Walk, Don't Run (1966) C-114m. *** D: Charles Walters. Cary Grant, Samantha Eggar, Jim Hutton, John Standing, Miiko Taka, Ted Hartley. Enjoyable fluff about Eggar unwittingly agreeing to share her apartment with businessman Grant and athlete Hutton during the Tokyo Olympics. Stars are most agreeable in this remake of THE MORE THE MERRIER. Grant's last film as an actor. Panavision.▼●◐

Walker (1987) C-90m. BOMB D: Alex Cox. Ed Harris, Marlee Matlin, Richard Masur, René Auberjonois, Peter Boyle, Miguel Sandoval, Gerrit Graham. Juvenile, intentionally anachronistic comic history of William Walker, American soldier of fortune (previously played by Marlon Brando in BURN!) who became president of 19th-century Nicaragua thanks to an assist from Cornelius Vanderbilt. Matlin's follow-up to her Oscar is actually an inglorious cameo; the sorry screenplay is by Rudy Wurlitzer. A self-indulgent mess. [R]▼●

Walker, The (2007-U.S.-British) C-108m. ** D: Paul Schrader. Woody Harrelson, Kristin Scott Thomas, Ned Beatty, Lily Tomlin, Lauren Bacall, Mary Beth Hurt, Willem Dafoe, Moritz Bleibtreu. An escort for some of Washington D.C.'s finest society women gets caught up in a scandal-tinged murder mystery. Very dark, rarely involving drama could have been the gay flip side of Schrader's AMERICAN GIGOLO but never settles on exactly what it wants to be. Fine cast tries valiantly but Harrelson's monotonous delivery grates on the nerves after a while. Bacall is amusing in her limited screen time. Written by the director. Super 35. [R]◐

Walk Hard: The Dewey Cox Story (2007) C-96m. **½ D: Jake Kasdan. John C. Reilly, Jenna Fischer, Kristen Wiig, Raymond J. Barry, Tim Meadows, Chris Parnell, Matt Besser, Harold Ramis, Margo Martindale, David Krumholtz, John Michael Higgins, Frankie Muniz, Craig Robinson, Ed Helms, Jack McBrayer. Reilly gives a sweet, earnest performance—and does his own singing—in this uneven, sometimes hilarious comedy chronicling the rise, fall, and redemption of a legendary singer-songwriter. Spot-on spoof of biopic clichés (particularly WALK THE LINE and RAY) and various pop music styles is too often crude and juvenile. Coproduced (and cow-

ritten) by Judd Apatow. Many music stars appear in cameos. Jack Black, Paul Rudd, Justin Long, and Jason Schwartzman play The Beatles; Jane Lynch and Jonah Hill also appear unbilled. Unrated DVD runs 120m. HD Widescreen. [R]

Walking and Talking (1996) C-85m. **½ D: Nicole Holofcener. Catherine Keener, Anne Heche, Todd Field, Liev Schreiber, Kevin Corrigan, Randall Batinkoff, Joseph Siravo, Allison Janney. Two longtime best friends are closing in on thirty; that's bad enough, but when Keener learns of Heche's impending marriage, she feels happy, jealous, panicked, and desolate. Amusing look at the joy and strain of friendship (not to mention dating and therapy), with fine performances all around. [R]▼●◐

Walking Dead, The (1995) C-89m. ** D: Preston A. Whitmore II. Allen Payne, Eddie Griffin, Joe Morton, Vonte Sweet, Roger Floyd, Bernie Mac. Predominantly black Vietnam Marines have ended up serving for reasons beyond love of the Corps: better housing, lost jobs, legal flight from murder charges, impressing women. Filmmakers try to stylize both the combat and stateside scenes, but their ambitions outpace their abilities. Griffin stands out with his comic commentary throughout the film. [R]▼●

Walking Stick, The (1970-British) C-101m. **½ D: Eric Till. Samantha Eggar, David Hemmings, Emlyn Williams, Phyllis Calvert, Ferdy Mayne, Francesca Annis. Potentially interesting story of beautiful polio victim coerced into assisting her worthless lover in a robbery is just too low-key to be consistently absorbing. Eggar's performance helps. Panavision. [PG]

Walking Tall (1973) C-125m. ** D: Phil Karlson. Joe Don Baker, Elizabeth Hartman, Gene Evans, Rosemary Murphy, Noah Beery, Felton Perry. Sickeningly violent actioner about determined Southern sheriff's one-man war against corruption. Huge theatrical success, based on real-life exploits of baseball-bat–wielding Buford Pusser; muscular performance by Baker. Followed by a pair of sequels, a 1978 TVM with Brian Dennehy (A REAL AMERICAN HERO) and a series. Remade in 2004. [R]▼●◐

Walking Tall (2004) C-86m. ** D: Kevin Bray. The Rock, Johnny Knoxville, Neal McDonough, Kristen Wilson, Ashley Scott, Khleo Thomas, John Beasley, Barbara Tarbuck, Michael Bowen. The Rock returns home after eight years in the service and learns that the town is "owned" lock, stock, and barrel by an old schoolmate (McDonough) who's opened a casino. With the help of a four-by-four and a trusted friend (Knoxville) he determines to set things straight. Buford Pusser is nowhere in sight, but his vigilante break-everything-in-sight spirit lives on in this yahoo action yarn based on the 1973 hit. Followed by two direct-to-video sequels. Super 35. [PG-13]▼❶

Walking Tall—Final Chapter SEE: **Final Chapter—Walking Tall**

Walking Tall, Part Two SEE: **Part 2, Walking Tall**

Walk in the Clouds, A (1995) **C-103m.** ******* D: Alfonso Arau. Keanu Reeves, Aitana Sánchez-Gijón, Anthony Quinn, Giancarlo Giannini, Angelica Aragon, Evangelina Elizondo, Freddy Rodriguez, Debra Messing. A young man just back from WW2 overseas duty helps out a beautiful woman by pretending to be her husband, in order to smooth over the expected fireworks when her father learns she's pregnant. Of course, he not only falls in love with her but with her family and their idyllic Napa Valley homestead. Blatantly old-fashioned and romantic, even corny, with household scenes reminiscent of the director's LIKE WATER FOR CHOCOLATE. If you're willing to buy into it, it actually works—until the climax. Based on a 1942 Italian film, QUATTRO POASSI FRA LE NUVOLE. [PG-13]▼❶

Walk in the Shadow (1966-British) **93m.** ******* D: Basil Dearden. Patrick McGoohan, Janet Munro, Paul Rogers, Megs Jenkins. Fine courtroom melodrama, as emotions flare after a girl's drowning.

Walk in the Spring Rain (1970) **C-100m.** ****½** D: Guy Green. Anthony Quinn, Ingrid Bergman, Fritz Weaver, Katherine Crawford. Happily married Bergman has extramarital affair in this low-key romantic drama. One expects more from such a cast. Scripted and produced by Stirling Silliphant. Panavision. [M/PG]▼❶

Walk in the Sun, A (1945) **117m.** *****½** D: Lewis Milestone. Dana Andrews, Richard Conte, Sterling Holloway, George Tyne, John Ireland, Herbert Rudley, Norman Lloyd, Lloyd Bridges, Huntz Hall. Human aspect of war explored as American battalion attacks Nazi hideout in Italy; good character studies of men in war. Adapted by Robert Rossen from Harry Brown's novel.▼❶❶

Walk Like a Man (1987) **C-86m.** BOMB D: Melvin Frank. Howie Mandel, Christopher Lloyd, Cloris Leachman, Colleen Camp, Amy Steel, Stephen Elliott, George DiCenzo. Mandel is returned to civilization after being raised by wolves, with the expected slapstick results. Puerile comedy with a cast that deserves much better. [PG]▼❶

Walk on the Moon, A (1999) **C-107m.** ****½** D: Tony Goldwyn. Diane Lane, Liev Schreiber, Anna Paquin, Viggo Mortensen, Tovah Feldshuh, Bobby Boriello. A family spends the summer of 1969 at a bungalow colony in the Catskills, where the young wife is drawn into an affair with "the blouse man." Meanwhile, her teenage daughter is on the verge of a first love—and aching to attend a rock concert nearby called Woodstock. Well-observed script by Pamela Gray follows a fairly predictable path, but Lane is miscast as a young Jewish hausfrau. Julie Kavner's distinctive voice is unbilled. Coproduced by Dustin Hoffman. [R]▼❶❶

Walk on the Wild Side (1962) **114m.** ****½** D: Edward Dmytryk. Laurence Harvey, Capucine, Jane Fonda, Anne Baxter, Barbara Stanwyck. Lurid hodgepodge set in 1930s New Orleans, loosely based on Nelson Algren novel, of Harvey seeking lost love Capucine, now a member of bordello run by lesbian Stanwyck. Memorable titles by Saul Bass; fine score by Elmer Bernstein.▼❶

Walk Proud (1979) **C-102m.** ****** D: Robert Collins. Robby Benson, Sarah Holcomb, Domingo Ambriz, Pepe Serna, Trinidad Silva. Sincerely intentioned but not very forceful gang picture about a Chicano (Benson) who falls for a WASP beauty who goes to his high school. [PG]

Walk the Line (2005) **C-136m.** ******* D: James Mangold. Joaquin Phoenix, Reese Witherspoon, Ginnifer Goodwin, Robert Patrick, Dallas Roberts, Dan John Miller, Larry Bagby, Shelby Lynne, Tyler Hilton. Solid, straightforward biopic of Johnny Cash and the woman who, in spite of many and varied detours, was destined to be his wife, June Carter. Story follows Cash from his hardscrabble childhood and early encounter with tragedy through young manhood, musical success, and a long battle with addiction. A premier performance piece for Phoenix and Witherspoon, who are utterly convincing—and do their own singing as well. Witherspoon won a Best Actress Oscar for her work. Director Mangold wisely tells much of the story in close-ups. Shooter Jennings plays his father Waylon; coproducer James Keach has a cameo as a prison warden. Extended cut runs 153m. Super 35. [PG-13]❶

Walk to Remember, A (2002) **C-101m.** ****½** D: Adam Shankman. Mandy Moore, Shane West, Peter Coyote, Daryl Hannah, Lauren German, Clayne Crawford, Al Thompson, Paz de la Huerta. Pop star Moore does a creditable job as a high school misfit who doesn't care about being popular and lives by the ideals espoused by her widowed father, a minister in their small Southern town. Bad-boy West is attracted to her in spite of—not because of—her sincerity and soon falls under her spell. Earnest hybrid of teen movie and tearjerker, with spiritual values rarely found in this kind of film; based on Nicholas Sparks' best-selling novel. Super 35. [PG]▼❶

Walk With Love and Death, A (1969) **C-90m.** ****** D: John Huston. Anjelica Huston, Assaf Dayan, Anthony Corlan, John Hallam, Robert Lang, Michael Gough. Fine period flavor but little else of note in story of young love set against turmoil of 14th-century France. Anjelica Huston's film debut; father John has small role. [M/PG]

Wall, The (1982-British) SEE: **Pink Floyd—The Wall**

Wallace & Gromit in The Curse of the Were-Rabbit (2005-British-U.S.) **C-82m.** ******* D: Nick Park, Steve Box. Voices of Peter Sallis, Ralph Fiennes, Helena Bonham Carter, Peter Kay, Nicholas Smith, Liz Smith, Geraldine McEwan. Cheese-loving inventor Wallace and his long-suffering canine pal Gromit retain all the quirky, inventive, distinctly British humor of Park's three award-winning shorts in this delightful clay-animated feature. Our heroes play humane pest-control experts who meet their match in an oversized rabbit that terrorizes the local British gardens. Wallace also finds love in the person of Lady Campanula Tottington, who becomes his benefactor. Engagingly silly British stereotypes are played to a fare-thee-well by Sallis, Bonham Carter, Fiennes, and other voice actors. Oscar winner as Best Animated Feature. [G]▼🄳

Wall•E (2008) **C-97m.** ****½** D: Andrew Stanton. Fred Willard; voices of Ben Burtt, Elissa Knight, Jeff Garlin, John Ratzenberger, Kathy Najimy, Sigourney Weaver. On a future Earth, humans are long gone and only one robotic creature, trained to gather and compact garbage, is left: WALL•E (Waste Allocation Load Lifter Earth-Class). Then a flying robot named Eve shows up to evaluate the planet, and a smitten WALL•E follows her onto her spacecraft, which exposes him to human beings for the first time. With an irresistible main character, a dynamite opening sequence, exceptional production design and imagination, this Pixar animated film starts out great but becomes heavy-handed in its message. Nevertheless, it won the hearts of audiences—and a Best Animated Feature Academy Award. Pixarvision. [G]🄳

Walls of Glass (1985) **C-86m.** ****½** D: Scott Goldstein. Philip Bosco, Geraldine Page, Linda Thorson, Olympia Dukakis, Brian Bloom, Steven Weber, Louis Zorich, William Hickey. Intriguing if uneven character study with Bosco nicely cast as a middle-aged, sonnet-spouting N.Y.C. cab driver who hates his job and yearns for success as an actor. Occasionally slow, but still effective. [R]▼

Wall Street (1987) **C-124m.** ******* D: Oliver Stone. Michael Douglas, Charlie Sheen, Daryl Hannah, Hal Holbrook, Martin Sheen, Terence Stamp, Sean Young, Sylvia Miles, James Spader, John McGinley, Saul Rubinek, Franklin Cover, James Karen, Richard Dysart, Josh Mostel, Millie Perkins, Cecilia Peck, Grant Shaud. Young hotshot who's going nowhere in a N.Y. brokerage firm manages to buttonhole the highest roller on Wall Street (Douglas, in an Oscar-winning performance) and win his confidence—but he sells his soul, so to speak, in return for admittance to that

high-powered world of wheeling and dealing. Modern-day morality tale by cowriter-director Stone (whose father was a broker, and to whom the film is dedicated) is short on subtlety but completely absorbing, especially in the wake of the real-life "insider trading" scandal of 1986. Stone, Monique Van Vooren, and Liliane Montevecchi can be glimpsed. Stone filmed a sequel in 2010. [R]▼🄳

Wall Street: Money Never Sleeps (2010) **C-133m.** ****½** D: Oliver Stone. Michael Douglas, Shia LaBeouf, Josh Brolin, Carey Mulligan, Eli Wallach, Susan Sarandon, Frank Langella, Austin Pendleton, Sylvia Miles, John Bedford Lloyd, Vanessa Ferlito, Jason Clarke. In 2008, just before the market crashes, financial guru Gordon Gekko (Douglas) is released from prison after eight years. His estranged daughter (Mulligan) is in love with an ambitious young trader (LaBeouf), who introduces himself to the former Wall Street whiz. Gekko then helps the younger man take revenge on an arrogant investment banker (Brolin) who helped put him away—and ruined LaBeouf's mentor (Langella). The high-stakes power games are undeniably compelling in this slick production, which is filled with good performances (including 94-year-old Wallach). Too bad the ending is weak. Stone can be glimpsed and Charlie Sheen appears unbilled. Super 35. [PG-13]🄳

Walt & El Grupo (2009) **C-105m.** ******* D: Theodore Thomas. Absorbing chronicle of Walt Disney's ten-week "goodwill" sojourn to South America in 1941, accompanied by a cadre of his talented artists. Escaping a bitter labor strike at home, Disney and his team were welcome ambassadors, but also derived inspiration from the colorful sights and sounds to which they were exposed. All of this is nicely evoked through home movies, letters the travelers wrote home, and their beautiful artwork—as well as contemporary interviews with people who still remember the trip. Of particular interest to Disney aficionados. [PG]🄳

Waltz Across Texas (1982) **C-99m.** ****½** D: Ernest Day. Terry Jastrow, Anne Archer, Richard Farnsworth, Noah Beery, Mary Kay Place, Josh Taylor, Ben Piazza. Oilman Jastrow and geologist Archer fall in love. Predictable, but far from unpleasant. The leads are husband and wife off-screen; they wrote the story, coproduced the film. [PG]▼🄳

Waltz of the Toreadors (1962-British) **C-105m.** ******* D: John Guillermin. Peter Sellers, Dany Robin, Margaret Leighton, John Fraser. Jean Anouilh's saucy sex romp gets top notch handling with Sellers as the retired military officer who still can't keep his eye off the girls.▼🄳

Waltz With Bashir (2008-Israeli-French-German) **C-87m.** *****½** D: Ari Folman.

Voices of Ari Folman, Ori Sivan, Ronny Dayag, Shmuel Frankel, Prof. Zahava Solomon, Ron Ben-Yishai, Dror Harazi. War vet with selective amnesia about being a young soldier in Israel's 1982 Beirut invasion embarks on a series of investigative interviews to recapture the truth regarding his role in a Palestinian refugee massacre. Gruesome, sometimes shocking memoir of "the terrible silence of death" is eerie, surreal, and one of a kind, rendered in consistently inventive animation, neither cartoon nor documentary, yet both. Title refers to Lebanon's assassinated Christian president. [R]▶

Wanda (1971) **C-101m.** ***½ D: Barbara Loden. Barbara Loden, Michael Higgins, Charles Dosinan, Frank Jourdano. Touching, original little drama about passive woman (Loden) who takes up with two-bit thief Higgins. Well acted. [PG]▶

Wanda Nevada (1979) **C-105m.** *½ D: Peter Fonda. Peter Fonda, Brooke Shields, Fiona Lewis, Luke Askew, Ted Markland, Severn Darden, Paul Fix, Henry Fonda. Fonda wins Shields in a poker game, and they set out to prospect for gold in the Grand Canyon. If this film were any more laid-back it would be nonexistent. Peter and Henry's only film together. [PG]▼

Wanderers, The (1979) **C-113m.** ***½ D: Philip Kaufman. Ken Wahl, John Friedrich, Karen Allen, Toni Kalem, Alan Rosenberg, Linda Manz, Erland van Lidth de Jeude, Olympia Dukakis. Impressionistic look at Bronx-Italian high school life in 1963 isn't always consistent in tone, but there are dozens of privileged moments. Understandably, it's become a cult favorite. [R]▼●▶

Wannsee Conference, The (1984-German-Austrian) **C-87m.** ***½ D: Heinz Schirk. Dietrich Mattausch, Gerd Bockmann, Friedrich Beckhaus, Gunter Spoerrie, Martin Luttge, Peter Fritz. Fascinating, chilling recreation of the infamous meeting, held in a Berlin suburb in January 1942, in which Nazi bigwigs discussed implementation of the Final Solution. Participants plot the destruction of millions with a casual air, which only adds to the terror. Based on minutes taken at the conference; film's length matches the event's actual running time. Same topic covered in a TVM, CONSPIRACY.▼●

Want a Ride, Little Girl? SEE: **Impulse** (1974)

Wanted (2008) **C-110m.** *** D: Timur Bekmambetov. James McAvoy, Morgan Freeman, Angelina Jolie, Terence Stamp, Thomas Kretschmann, Common, Kristen Hager, Marc Warren, David Patrick O'Hara. Nebbishy office drone McAvoy is suddenly—and dramatically—recruited to join a secret society of assassins led by Freeman after his father (who was part of the team) is killed. Flamboyant, in-your-face action filled with innovative visual

flourishes from Russian director Bekmambetov, in his Hollywood debut. Ace-high action thriller never runs out of steam. Based on the comic books by Mark Millar and J. G. Jones. Super 35. [R]▶

Wanted: Babysitter SEE: **Babysitter, The** (1975)

Wanted: Dead or Alive (1987) **C-104m.** BOMB D: Gary Sherman. Rutger Hauer, Gene Simmons, Robert Guillaume, Mel Harris, William Russ, Susan McDonald, Jerry Hardin. Hauer plays Nick Randall, grandson of fellow bounty hunter Josh, the character Steve McQueen played in the identically named TV series. Link is mentioned, then ignored, in routine cheapo about the CIA's pursuit of an Arab terrorist. Bravura grenade-in-mouth finale. [R]▼●▶

Wanton Contessa SEE: **Senso**

Wanton Countess, The SEE: **Senso**

War, The (1994) **C-125m.** **½ D: Jon Avnet. Elijah Wood, Kevin Costner, Mare Winningham, Lexi Randall, Christine Baranski, Gary Basaraba, Raynor Scheine, Latoya Chisholm, Charlette Julius. Growing up isn't easy for a brother and sister in 1970 Mississippi; their father means well, but hasn't been stable since returning from Vietnam, and his attempts to teach them tolerance and peaceful ways are hard to absorb when they're constantly bullied by a family of mean-spirited kids who live nearby. Well-intentioned message film for young people, diluted by overlength, a lack of focus, and an overabundance of dramatic climaxes. [PG-13]▼●▶

War (2007) **C-103m.** ** D: Philip G. Atwell. Jet Li, Jason Statham, John Lone, Devon Aoki, Luis Guzmán, Saul Rubinek. While a maverick FBI agent (Statham) tries to settle an old score with an infamous hit man (Li), the killer—borrowing a page from Akira Kurosawa's YOJIMBO (and Dashiell Hammett's *Red Harvest*)—plays two rival Asian gangs against each other in a San Francisco turf war. Teaming of action stars Li and Statham raises high expectations that are frustratingly unfulfilled by a standard-issue crime drama laced with uninspired martial artistry. Super 35. [R]▶

War and Peace (1956-U.S.-Italian) **C-208m.** **½ D: King Vidor. Audrey Hepburn, Henry Fonda, Mel Ferrer, Vittorio Gassman, John Mills, Herbert Lom, Oscar Homolka, Anita Ekberg, Helmut Dantine, Barry Jones, Milly Vitale, Jeremy Brett, Wilfrid Lawson, Mai Britt. Tolstoy's sprawling novel fails to come alive in this overlong, oversimplified adaptation. Star-studded cast and spectacular battle scenes (directed by Mario Soldati) cannot compensate for clumsy script (by six writers, including Vidor) and some profound miscasting. Filmed far more successfully in 1968. VistaVision.▼●▶

War and Peace (1968-Russian) **C-373m.**

**** D: Sergei Bondarchuk. Ludmila Savelyeva, Vyacheslav Tihonov, Hira Ivanov-Golovko, Irina Gubanova, Antonia Shuranova. Sergei Bondarchuk. Even in theaters, poor English dubbing hurt this definitive film version of Tolstoy's novel. Even so, it should be seen for production values alone; a dazzling film. Oscar winner for Best Foreign Film. Originally shown in U.S. in two parts; released in the USSR in 1966–67 in four parts, totaling 507m. Sovscope 70.▼❶

War at Home, The (1996) **C-123m.** ****** D: Emilio Estevez. Emilio Estevez, Kathy Bates, Martin Sheen, Kimberly Williams, Corin Nemec, Carla Gugino, Renee Estevez. Stagey adaptation by James Duff of his own play *Homefront,* about recently returned Vietnam vet Estevez trying to move on with his life but haunted by his experience in combat. His family is unable to deal with the fact that the boy they sent off to war never came home. Great acting, especially by Bates, but good intentions outweigh results. Panavision. [R]▼❶❶

War Between Men and Women, The (1972) **C-110m.** ****½** D: Melville Shavelson. Jack Lemmon, Barbara Harris, Jason Robards, Herb Edelman, Lisa Gerritsen, Lisa Eilbacher, Severn Darden. Fans of James Thurber won't think much of this mixture of famed writer-cartoonist's material and Hollywood schmaltz, but film occasionally makes for pleasant comedy-romance. Harris comes off best. Material had previously inspired a TV series, *My World—And Welcome To It.* [PG]▼

Wardance (2007) **C-107m.** ******* D: Sean Fine, Andrea Nix Fine. Compassionate, uplifting documentary account of Ugandan orphans who only have known lives of war and strife. They reside in a DP camp, where they prepare to vie for a National Music Competition trophy. Despite their horror stories, the youngsters show astounding resilience, and the film is a primer on the power of music to elevate the spirit. Only flaw: it's a tad overlong. [PG-13]❶

War Game, The (1967-British) **47m.** ******* D: Peter Watkins. Fascinating, frightening simulated documentary, which vividly projects the aftermath of a nuclear holocaust. Originally produced for television by the BBC and British Film Institute, but deemed to be too incendiary for home audiences. It did open theatrically, and earned a Best Documentary Academy Award.▼❶

WarGames (1983) **C-110m.** ****½** D: John Badham. Matthew Broderick, Dabney Coleman, John Wood, Ally Sheedy, Barry Corbin, Juanin Clay, Maury Chaykin, Michael Madsen, John Spencer. FAIL SAFE for the Pac-Man generation: a pop movie about a computer whiz-kid who taps into government early-warning system and nearly starts WW3. Entertaining to a point,

but gets more contrived as it goes along, leading to finale straight out of an old B movie. Incidentally, it's easy to see why this was so popular with kids: most of the adults in the film are boobs. Followed by a DVD sequel in 2008. [PG]▼❶❶

War Hunt (1962) **81m.** ****½** D: Denis Sanders. John Saxon, Robert Redford, Charles Aidman, Sydney Pollack. Well-done Korean War story focusing on kill-happy soldier Saxon who tries to help an orphan boy. Redford and Pollack's film debuts.❶

War, Inc. (2008) **C-107m.** ****** D: Joshua Seftel. John Cusack, Hilary Duff, Marisa Tomei, Joan Cusack, Ben Kingsley, Dan Aykroyd, Lubomir Neikov, Ben Cross. Would-be satire of the war in Iraq features Cusack as an assassin-for-hire who takes an assignment from the former Vice President of the U.S. (Aykroyd) to rub out the oil minister of a Middle Eastern country. His "cover" is a trade show where the main distraction is the wedding of a bratty pop star (Duff). Self-satisfied poke at contemporary events has a good cast and attitude to spare but its targets are painfully obvious—and so is its approach. Cowritten by John Cusack. [R]❶

War, Italian Style (1966-Italian) **C-84m.** ****** D: Luigi Scattini. Buster Keaton, Franco and Ciccio, Martha Hyer, Fred Clark. Sloppy, meandering spy satire set in WW2 Italy, redeemed barely by Keaton's appearance. Unfortunately, this was his final film. Techniscope.

Warlock (1959) **C-121m.** ******* D: Edward Dmytryk. Richard Widmark, Henry Fonda, Anthony Quinn, Dorothy Malone, Dolores Michaels, Wallace Ford, Tom Drake, Richard Arlen, DeForest Kelley, Regis Toomey. Philosophical vigilante "sheriff" Fonda is hired to clean up the crime-infested Western town of Warlock. This sets off a complex storyline involving, among others, crippled Quinn, guilt-ridden Widmark, and embittered Malone. Literate, allegorical adult Western examines the lynch-mob mentality and the meaning of machismo. Forgotten, but worthy of rediscovery. Scripted by Robert Alan Aurthur. Cinema-Scope. ▼❶

Warlock (1991) **C-102m.** ****½** D: Steve Miner. Julian Sands, Lori Singer, Richard E. Grant, Mary Woronov, Richard Kuss, Allan Miller, Kevin O'Brien, Anna Levine, David Carpenter. A warlock escapes from 1691 Boston to 1991 L.A., with a local witch-hunter in full time-warp pursuit; object of their squabble is the Grand Grimoire, or Satan's bible. More fun might have ensued had they ended up on a dusty street with, say, Henry Fonda, but it's worth half-a-star just to see the ever-intense Grant in a rare (for him) heroic role. Released overseas in 1989. Followed by two sequels. [R] ▼❶

Warlock: The Armageddon (1993) **C-98m.** ***½** D: Anthony Hickox. Julian

Sands, Christopher Young, Paula Marshall, Steve Kahan, Charles Hallahan, R. G. Armstrong, Nicole Mercurio, Craig Hurley, Bruce Glover, Zach Galligan, Joanna Pacula. Evil warlock Sands is (literally) reborn, even though there is nothing connecting this entry with the first, other than Sands himself and his role as a wicked, flying sorcerer—this time trying to unleash his father (Satan) upon the world. Weak, jokey film has only Sands' sardonic performance and some good effects to recommend it. Followed by a direct-to-video sequel. [R]▼●❶

War Lord, The (1965) **C-123m.** **✱** D: Franklin Schaffner. Charlton Heston, Rosemary Forsyth, Richard Boone, Maurice Evans, Guy Stockwell, Niall McGinnis, James Farentino, Henry Wilcoxon, Michael Conrad. Intriguing, generally well-done adaptation of Leslie Stevens' *The Lovers,* with Heston as feudal knight invoking little-known law allowing him to have another man's bride on their wedding night. Title and medieval setting would seem to indicate sweeping spectacle . . . which this certainly isn't. Panavision.▼●❶

Warlords, The (2007-Hong Kong-Chinese) **C-113m.** **✱✱✱** D: Peter Ho-Sun Chan. Jet Li, Andy Lau, Takeshi Kaneshiro, Xu Jinglei, Guo Xiao Dong, Jacky Heung. Big-budget historical drama centering on three men from different backgrounds who become blood brothers in 19th-century China, but find their bonds of friendship tested during a civil war. Li eschews his customary martial arts heroics here, but there are plenty of large-scale action set pieces in this somber epic. Original running time: 127m. Super 35. [R]❶

Warlords of Atlantis (1978-British) **C-96m.** **✱✱½** D: Kevin Connor. Doug McClure, Peter Gilmore, Shane Rimmer, Lea Brodie, John Ratzenberger, Cyd Charisse, Daniel Massey. Monsters and mayhem abound in this palatable Saturday matinee item with McClure joining British scientists in search for underwater city.

Warlords of the 21st Century (1982) **C-91m.** **✱✱** D: Harley Cokliss. Michael Beck, Annie McEnroe, James Wainwright, John Ratzenberger, Bruno Lawrence. Routine action film set after WW3 in time of an oil shortage. Wainwright (as the ruthless, right-wing military villain) virtually repeated his role in the contemporary-set Robin Williams comedy THE SURVIVORS. Filmed in New Zealand; originally titled BATTLETRUCK. [PG]▼❶

War Lover, The (1962-British) **105m.** **✱✱½** D: Philip Leacock. Steve McQueen, Robert Wagner, Shirley Anne Field, Gary Cockrell, Michael Crawford, Al Waxman. John Hersey's thoughtful novel becomes superficial account of egocentric, psychotic WW2 pilot McQueen, who becomes unhinged when copilot Wagner begins a romantic relationship with Field. Worth seeing for McQueen's edgy, riveting presence.▼●❶

Warm December, A (1973) **C-100m.** **✱✱** D: Sidney Poitier. Sidney Poitier, Esther Anderson, Johnny Sekka, Yvette Curtis. George Baker, Earl Cameron. Story of Poitier's love for Anderson, who is dying of sickle cell anemia, isn't as sappy as it might be, but isn't particularly good, either. Anderson is attractive. Made in England. [PG]▼❶

Warm Water Under a Red Bridge (2001-Japanese) **C-114m.** **✱✱✱** D: Shohei Imamura. Koji Yakusho, Misa Shimizu, Mitsuko Baisho, Manasaku Fuwa, Isao Natsuyagi, Kazuo Kitamura. Clever, sweetly funny comedy-drama about middle-aged Yakusho, trapped and victimized by the modern rat race, who becomes involved with a beautiful—and most unusual—woman in a small fishing village. Offbeat but profound film stresses the importance of enjoying life and exercising free will.▼❶

Warning Shot (1967) **C-100m.** **✱✱✱½** D: Buzz Kulik. David Janssen, Ed Begley, Keenan Wynn, Lillian Gish, Eleanor Parker, Sam Wanamaker, Stefanie Powers, George Sanders, George Grizzard, Steve Allen, Carroll O'Connor, Joan Collins, Walter Pidgeon. Exciting action-filled melodrama about cop's attempt to clear his name after killing a supposedly innocent doctor.❶

Warning Sign (1985) **C-100m.** **✱½** D: Hal Barwood. Sam Waterston, Kathleen Quinlan, Yaphet Kotto, Jeffrey De Munn, Richard Dysart, G. W. Bailey, Jerry Hardin, Rick Rossovich, Cynthia Carle. Self-important, would-be CHINA SYNDROME about disastrous results of chemical spill at research lab that's secretly been working on germ warfare for the government. Unpleasant and ineffectual. Screenwriter Barwood's directing debut. [R]▼❶

War of the Buttons (1994-British-French-Japanese) **C-90m.** **✱✱½** D: John Roberts. Gregg Fitzgerald, John Coffey, Liam Cunningham, Johnny Murphy, Colm Meaney, Jim Bartley, Gerard Kearney, Anthony Cunningham. The children of two neighboring Irish towns gradually escalate their quarrels to outright—if painless—warfare. This pleasant comedy-drama tries to say something about war, but the point is obscured as the story begins to focus on two particular boys. Based on the 1912 Louis Pergaud novel *La Guerre des Boutons,* previously filmed in 1938 and 1962. [PG]▼●❶

War of the Colossal Beast (1958) **68m.** **✱½** D: Bert I. Gordon. Sally Fraser, Roger Pace, Dean Parkin, Russ Bender, Charles Stewart. Sequel to THE AMAZING COLOSSAL MAN finds our oversized hero alive but not well; his face is a mess, and so is his mind, leading to the inevitable low-budget rampage. Forget it. Last shot is in color. ▼●

War of the Gargantuas, The (1966-U.S.-Japanese) **C-93m.** BOMB D: Ishiro Honda. Russ Tamblyn, Kumi Mizuno, Kipp Hamilton, Yu Fujiki. Japan is menaced by a mean, green "gargantua" (humanoid giant), with a friendly brown gargantua trying to make peace. Strange, even by Japanese monster-movie standards. Tohoscope. ▼

War of the Roses, The (1989) **C-116m. **½ D: Danny DeVito. Michael Douglas, Kathleen Turner, Danny DeVito, Marianne Sägebrecht, Sean Astin, Heather Fairfield, G. D. Spradlin, Peter Donat, Dan Castellaneta, Danitra Vance. When Douglas and Turner can't agree on a property settlement in their divorce proceedings, war breaks out in (and over) their exquisitely appointed house. As a satire on yuppie materialism, this very black comedy scores a bull's-eye—for about an hour. Then it continues for nearly an hour more as the couple grows increasingly vicious and irrational, literally destroying their home. Some people loved this film (the stars *are* perfect), so obviously it's a matter of taste. DeVito's odd point of view and wild camera angles are an asset throughout. [R] ▼●

War of the Wildcats SEE: **In Old Oklahoma**

War of the Worlds, The (1953) **C-85m. ***½ D: Byron Haskin. Gene Barry, Les Tremayne, Ann Robinson, Robert Cornthwaite, Henry Brandon, Jack Kruschen; narrated by Sir Cedric Hardwicke. Vivid, frightening adaptation of H. G. Wells' novel about a Martian invasion, transplanted from 19th-century England to contemporary USA. Dramatically sound and filled with dazzling, Oscar-winning special effects; superior sci-fi, produced by George Pal. Later a TV series. Remade three times in 2005 as WAR OF THE WORLDS, H. G. WELLS' THE WAR OF THE WORLDS and H. G. WELLS' WAR OF THE WORLDS. ▼

War of the Worlds (2005) **C-116m. **½ D: Steven Spielberg. Tom Cruise, Dakota Fanning, Miranda Otto, Justin Chatwin, Tim Robbins, Rick Gonzalez, Lisa Ann Walter, Amy Ryan; narrated by Morgan Freeman. Divorced, beer-swilling New Jersey construction worker with two kids realizes that all hell is breaking loose and hits the road, hoping to dodge the chaos of an alien invasion and reach his ex-wife's family home in Boston. Update of H. G. Wells' novel never names Mars as the source of the invaders, but wastes no time getting started, throwing action and special effects sequences at the viewer almost nonstop . . . but it ends with a whimper, not a bang, muting the entire experience. Gene Barry and Ann Robinson, stars of the 1953 version, make a welcome cameo. [PG-13] ▼)

War Party (1989) **C-97m. ** D: Franc Roddam. Billy Wirth, Kevin Dillon, Tim Sampson, Jimmie Ray Weeks, M. Emmet Walsh, Dennis Banks, Kevyn Major Howard, Bill McKinney. Reenactment of a hundred-year-old battle between Blackfoot Indian tribe and U.S. Cavalry turns into the real thing once again when one white youth brings a loaded gun to the festivities. Basically an excuse for a cowboys and Indians movie, this intriguing premise becomes just another botched opportunity for Hollywood to shed light on the problems of the American Indian. [R] ▼●

Warrior, The (2001-British-French-German) **C-86m. *** D: Asif Kapadia. Irfan Khan, Puru Chibber, Anupam Shyam, Noor Mani, Damayanti Marfatia, Aino Annuddin. Minimalist fable involving the title character (Khan), one of a band of killers who slaughters innocent villagers on the order of his boss, a brutal Indian warlord. His life changes dramatically when he decides to quit his job and seek spiritual redemption. Harsh, ironic reworking of a samurai/Western morality tale, stunningly filmed in the deserts and mountains of Northwestern India. Released in the U.S. in 2005. [R] ▼)

Warrior and the Sorceress, The (1984) **C-76m. *½ D: John Broderick. David Carradine, Luke Askew, Maria Socas, Anthony DeLongis, Harry Townes, William Marin. Copycat version of both A FISTFUL OF DOLLARS and YOJIMBO transplants story of a lone fighter playing both ends against the middle to a mythical kingdom on a planet circling two suns. Lovely leading lady Socas plays the entire film topless; you also might note the very convincing makeup effects on a pretty dancer who has four breasts. [R] ▼●

Warrior Queen (1987) **C-69m.** BOMB D: Chuck Vincent. Sybil Danning, Donald Pleasence, Richard Hill, Josephine Jacqueline Jones, Tally Chanel, Stasia Micula (Samantha Fox). Ridiculous made-in-Italy exploitation film emphasizes sex in recreating the decadence of ancient Pompeii. Pleasence is at his hammy worst as the mayor whose wife (porn star Fox) has eyes for other men. Relies extensively on footage from the '60 LAST DAYS OF POMPEII for an apocalyptic climax. Unrated 79m. video version has more sex scenes. [R] ▼●

Warriors, The (1955-British) **C-85m. **½ D: Henry Levin. Errol Flynn, Joanne Dru, Peter Finch, Patrick Holt, Yvonne Furneaux, Michael Hordern, Christopher Lee. Flynn's final swashbuckler casts him as British prince protecting French conquests (and lovely Dru) from attacks by Finch and his supporters. Well made but awfully familiar. British title: THE DARK AVENGER. CinemaScope. ▼

Warriors, The (1979) **C-90m. *** D: Walter Hill. Michael Beck, James Remar,

Thomas Waites, Dorsey Wright, Brian Tyler, Deborah Van Valkenburgh, Mercedes Ruehl. Comic-book plot about N.Y.C. gang crossing rival turfs to get "home" is redeemed by lightning pace, tough action sequences, creative use of color. Notorious for the number of violent incidents it allegedly instigated in theaters, but worthy of some respect. Script by Hill and David Shaber; photographed by Andrew Laszlo. Director's cut runs 93m. [R]▼●◗

Warriors of the Wind SEE: **Nausicaä of the Valley of the Wind**

Warriors of Virtue (1997) C-103m. *½ D: Ronny Yu. Angus Macfadyen, Mario Yedidia, Marley Shelton, Jack Tate, Chao-Li Chi, Doug Jones, Michael John Anderson. Incoherent kiddie kung fu movie about an American boy (Yedidia, who's the spitting image of Elijah Wood) who gets hold of a secret Chinese manuscript that transports him to a mystical wonderland where kangaroo warriors fight against evil. Yu's English filmmaking debut is a big disappointment after his fantastical (and very adult) Hong Kong sword and sorcery epics THE BRIDE WITH WHITE HAIR, Parts 1 and 2. Macfadyen chews scenery as the villain, acting like the errant offspring of Ming the Merciless and Little Richard. Panavision. [PG]▼●◗

Warrior's Way, The (2010-New Zealand) C-100m. ** D: Sngmoo Lee. Jang Dong Gun, Geoffrey Rush, Kate Bosworth, Danny Huston, Tony Cox, Ti Lung. A legendary 19th-century Asian swordsman journeys from his homeland—with a baby in tow—to start a new life in the American West, but soon finds himself fighting a band of crazed outlaws and an army of assassins from his past. Hyper-stylized hybrid of martial arts action, samurai battles, and Spaghetti Western motifs is undeniably visually striking, but overdoes the surreal CGI effects and piles on too many action set pieces. Super 35. [R]◗

War Room, The (1993) C-95m. *** D: D. A. Pennebaker, Chris Hegedus. Compelling documentary which follows the behind-the-scenes machinations of Bill Clinton's 1992 presidential campaign. No great insights or revelations, but still an inherently interesting (and very entertaining) look at political kingmaking, done in classic cinéma vérité style. Chief political strategist James Carville (the "Ragin' Cajun") has more on-screen charisma than many Hollywood stars.▼●◗

War Wagon, The (1967) C-101m. *** D: Burt Kennedy. John Wayne, Kirk Douglas, Howard Keel, Robert Walker, Keenan Wynn, Bruce Cabot, Joanna Barnes, Bruce Dern. Amiable tongue-in-cheek Western, with ex-con Wayne seeking to settle a score with villainous Cabot by plundering his gold-laden stagecoach—with the help of Douglas (who's been hired to kill Wayne on Cabot's behalf) and a motley band of associates. Keel is hilarious as wise-cracking Indian. Panavision.▼●◗

War Within, The (2005) C-93m. **½ D: Joseph Castelo. Ayad Akhtar, Firdous Bamji, Nandana Sen, Sarita Choudhury, Charles Daniel Sandoval, Varun Sriram, John Ventimiglia, Mike McGlone. Introspective account of how a good-natured Pakistani student has been politicized and transformed into a suicide bomber. He comes to the U.S., where his eventual target is N.Y.C.'s Grand Central Station. Well-meaning attempt to explore the psychology of its main character; while the story is all too believable, it runs out of dramatic steam. Coscripted by Akhtar, Castelo, and Tom Glynn. [R]◗

War Zone, The (1999-British-Italian) C-98m. *** D: Tim Roth. Ray Winstone, Tilda Swinton, Lara Belmont, Freddie Cunliffe, Colin Farrell. Roth's directorial debut is an ultra-realistic, deeply affecting portrait of incest in a working-class British family. With devastating candor, he charts the unfolding events as 15-year-old Cunliffe suspects that his father (Winstone) is acting inappropriately with his older sister (Belmont). Sometimes difficult to watch, as Roth pulls no punches in his portrayal of this deeply troubled family. Panavision. ▼◗

Wasabi (2002-French-Japanese) C-94m. **½ D: Gérard Krawczyk. Jean Reno, Michel Muller, Ryoko Hirosue, Carole Bouquet, Ludovic Berthillot, Yan Epstein, Michel Scourneau. Minor but diverting comedy-action yarn about a cop (Reno) with a penchant for punching out people who's called to Japan. It seems the love of his life—who walked out on him 19 years ago—has died, leaving him a fortune, a daughter he never knew about, and a platoon of hit men on his trail. Reno is his usual charismatic self in a hand-tailored role, and the action is sharply staged. Written and produced by Luc Besson. Super 35. [R]▼◗

Wash, The (2001) C-96m. ** D: DJ Pooh. Snoop Dogg, Dr. Dre, George Wallace, Angell Conwell, Tommy "Tiny" Lister, Jr., Alex Thomas. With director Pooh citing Michael Schultz's CAR WASH as a direct influence, you know what you're going to get in this agreeable but ragged yarn about rent-owing roomies working at the same cleansing facility. Look for: full-figured women in bikinis sudsing up cars, an obese cop who's made fun of, and someone having intestinal problems when there are houseguests. Any movie that gives you cameos by Shaquille O'Neal, Tommy Chong, *and* Pauly Shore is going the extra mile. [R]▼◗

Washington Square (1997) C-115m. *** D: Agnieszka Holland. Jennifer Jason Leigh, Albert Finney, Ben Chaplin, Maggie

Smith, Judith Ivey, Betsy Brantley, Jennifer Garner, Peter Maloney. Spirited adaptation of the Henry James novel about the awkward, plain-Jane daughter of a wealthy, domineering doctor, who is suddenly courted by a poor but handsome fortune hunter in 19th-century N.Y.C. Like a number of celebrated period stories filmed in the 1990s, this one features a pointed contemporary feminist sensibility. Filmed before as THE HEIRESS. [PG] ▼●

Wasn't That a Time! SEE: **Weavers, The: Wasn't That a Time!**

Wasp Woman, The (1960) 66m. **½ D: Roger Corman. Susan Cabot, Fred (Anthony) Eisley, Barboura Morris, Michael Mark, William Roerick. Enjoyable Corman cheapie about cosmetics magnate Cabot, fearful of aging, using royal jelly from wasps to become young and beautiful. She also periodically turns into a wasp-monster that must kill. Minor camp classic; an unauthorized semi-remake, EVIL SPAWN, was made for video in 1987. Remade for TV in 1996. ▼●

Wassup Rockers (2006) C-111m. **½ D: Larry Clark. Jonathan Velasquez, Francisco Pedrasa, Eddie Velasquez, Yunior Usvaldo Panameno, Eddie Velazquez, Luis Rojas-Salgado, Carlos Velasco, Iris Zelaya, Laura Cellner, Jessica Steinbaum. Lighter in tone, more accessible, and less explicit than Clark's previous forays into the world of troubled youth (KIDS, BULLY, KEN PARK), this story of seven Latino skateboarders examines their lives not only in their home base of South Central L.A. but in the suburban environs of Beverly Hills. When they meet two rich white girls they find themselves skating down the streets and backyards of the wealthy in sequences that almost seem like an homage to THE SWIMMER. While raw and undisciplined, film offers an interesting perspective on class and race and serves as a showcase for a good young cast. [R]▶

Watched! (1972) C-95m. *½ D: John Parsons. Stacy Keach, Harris Yulin, Brigid Polk, Denver John Collins. Keach plays a former government lawyer who went underground, befriending dopers. Yulin is chief of the narcotics squad, using lots of surveillance filming in his war of wills with Keach. Haphazard structure of this low-budget film relies upon Keach's nearly one-man show, expressing the personal transition out of 1960s culture. [R]▼

Watcher, The (2000) C-96m. *½ D: Joe Charbanic. James Spader, Marisa Tomei, Keanu Reeves, Ernie Hudson, Chris Ellis, Robert Cicchini. The millionth serial killer movie in a decade offers little in the way of novelty (not that this would be anyone's wish). FBI agent Spader has gotten so worn out trying to track down woman-preying Reeves that he's relocated from L.A. to Chicago and put himself in the care of psychoanalyst Tomei. (Guess who ends up being victimized?)

Empty thriller directed by—surprise!—a former maker of rock videos. [R]▼▶

Watcher in the Woods, The (1980) C-84m. **½ D: John Hough. Bette Davis, Carroll Baker, David McCallum, Lynn-Holly Johnson, Kyle Richards, Ian Bannen, Richard Pasco. All-American family takes over British country house, where young Johnson is tormented by the spirit of owner Davis' long-missing daughter. Not bad, with atmospheric photography by Alan Hume, but awfully familiar. First shown with an abrupt conclusion, then with special effects sequence that made things worse, then reworked again and improved (by Vincent McEveety)—for 1981 rerelease! Original running time 100m. [PG]▼●▶

Watchers (1988-U.S.-Canadian) C-92m. *½ D: Jon Hess. Corey Haim, Michael Ironside, Barbara Williams, Lala, Duncan Fraser, Dale Wilson, Blu Mankuma. Young Haim is befriended by a super-intelligent dog (the product of military research), but soon both are pursued by a swift, deadly monster. Awful adaptation of Dean R. Koontz's novel, with a ludicrous monster. Followed by three sequels. [R]▼●▶

Watchers 2 (1990-U.S.-Canadian) C-97m. ** D: Thierry Notz. Marc Singer, Tracy Scoggins, Tom Poster, Jonathan Farwell, Mary Woronov. Singer and a super-intelligent dog are pursued by a monster who's the result of the same experimentation that created the canine. More a remake of than a sequel to WATCHERS, and a better movie, though still no world-beater. Followed by two sequels. [R]▼●▶

Watch It (1993) C-102m. *** D: Tom Flynn. Peter Gallagher, Suzy Amis, John C. McGinley, Jon Tenney, Cynthia Stevenson, Lili Taylor, Tom Sizemore, Terri Hawkes, Jordana Capra. Drifter Gallagher returns to Chicago and moves in with smarmy, womanizing cousin Tenney and his crude, immature housemates. He falls for (but cannot make a commitment to) veterinarian Amis, who's had rotten luck with men. Despite some plot implausibilities and a cop-out ending, a perceptive and ingratiating film. Flynn also scripted. [R]▼●

Watchmen (2009) C-161m. ** D: Zack Snyder. Billy Crudup, Malin Akerman, Patrick Wilson, Jeffrey Dean Morgan, Jackie Earle Haley, Matthew Goode, Carla Gugino, Matt Frewer, Stephen McHattie, Robert Wisden. Slick, superficially faithful but heavy-handed adaptation of Alan Moore and Dave Gibbons' celebrated graphic novel, set in a bleak, alternate 1985 where the newest generation of vigilante superheroes has been retired by an act of Congress. Only the very naked Dr. Manhattan (Crudup) is still at work, as he holds the power to stave off impending nuclear war—but he has been drained of his humanity and can't even relate to his girlfriend anymore. And so it goes.

Deliberately extreme violence and sexuality seem pointless in this highly stylized but overlong comic book saga. Haley's performance as Rorschach is the lone standout. Extended version runs 186m. Super 35. [R]▶❙

Watch on the Rhine (1943) **114m.** ***½ D: Herman Shumlin. Bette Davis, Paul Lukas, Geraldine Fitzgerald, Lucile Watson, Beulah Bondi, George Coulouris, Donald Woods, Henry Daniell. Fine filmization of Lillian Hellman's timely WW2 play of German Lukas and wife Davis pursued and harried by Nazi agents in Washington. Lukas gives the performance of his career, which won him an Oscar; Bette somewhat overshadowed. Script by Dashiell Hammett. ▼❙

Watch the Shadows Dance (1987-Australian-Canadian) **C-87m.** ** D: Mark Joffe. Tom Jennings, Nicole Kidman, Joanne Samuel, Vince Martin, Craig Pearce, Doug Parkinson. Low-grade actioner involving a group of students who participate in a violent fantasy war game, with predictable results. Of interest solely for the presence of Kidman, cast as one of the players. Aka NIGHTMASTER. [R]▼❙

Water (1985-British) **C-95m.** BOMB D: Dick Clement. Michael Caine, Brenda Vaccaro, Leonard Rossiter, Valerie Perrine, Jimmie Walker, Billy Connolly, Dennis Dugan. Inept comedy of errors concerns a Caribbean British colony where the local governor (Caine) juggles greedy U.S. oil interests, a comical rebellion, and other assorted looneys as a valuable mineral water is discovered. Rossiter is funny as a diplomat sent from England to calm the situation, and Maureen Lipman is terrific in a nasty caricature of Prime Minister Thatcher; Vaccaro is miscast in strained Carmen Miranda impression. Pointless cameos by Dick Shawn, Fred Gwynne, film's executive producer George Harrison, Eric Clapton, and Ringo Starr. [PG-13]▼❙

Water (2005-Canadian-Indian) **C-117m.** **½ D: Deepa Mehta. Lisa Ray, Seema Biswas, Sarala, Kulbhushan Kharbanda, Waheeda Rehman, Raghuvir Yadav, Vinay Pathak, Rishma Malik. 1930s-set drama about a group of widows living a life of poverty at a temple while struggling for independence from British Colonial rule. Tragic story focuses on one girl in particular, forced into prostitution by her superiors, who tries to have a relationship with a young man she is forbidden to see. Well-meaning, deliberately paced film sheds light on a little-known aspect of Indian life but fails to set off much dramatic spark despite exquisite filming by Toronto-based director Mehta. Super 35. [PG-13]❙

Water Babies, The (1978-British-Polish) **C-92m.** ** D: Lionel Jeffries. James Mason, Billie Whitelaw, Bernard Cribbins, Joan Greenwood, David Tomlinson, Tommy Pender, Samantha Gates. Combination live action and animated film for children, framing its fairy-tale undersea adventure with virtually unrelated story and characters in Dickensian London. Inoffensive for children, but downright boring at times. Aka SLIP SLIDE ADVENTURES.▼❙

Waterboy, The (1998) **C-88m.** *** D: Frank Coraci. Adam Sandler, Kathy Bates, Fairuza Balk, Henry Winkler, Jerry Reed, Larry Gilliard, Jr., Blake Clark, Clint Howard, Rob Schneider. Dimwitted Cajun boy, sheltered by his smothering mama (Bates), lives only to serve—as a much-abused waterboy for football teams. But when a downtrodden coach (Winkler) discovers that the waterboy can, when properly motivated, run and tackle with great force, he turns him into a football star. Likable, crowd-pleasing comedy with heart. Sandler gets strong support here from Winkler and Bates. Director Coraci plays Roberto in the closing scenes; various sports figures appear as themselves. Sandler coscripted. [PG-13]▼❙

Waterdance, The (1992) **C-106m.** *** D: Neal Jimenez, Michael Steinberg. Eric Stoltz, Wesley Snipes, William Forsythe, Helen Hunt, Elizabeth Pena, Grace Zabriskie. Fine, affecting story of a young novelist (Stoltz) who becomes paraplegic after a hiking accident and learns to adjust in a multiethnic rehabilitation center. Things haven't changed too much since THE MEN, but potentially maudlin situations are handled with directness, grace, and great humor, and the entire cast—particularly Snipes and Forsythe—is excellent. Jimenez, himself paralyzed since an accident in 1984, also wrote the screenplay. [R]▼●❙

Water for Elephants (2011) **C-120m.** **½ D: Francis Lawrence. Reese Witherspoon, Robert Pattinson, Christoph Waltz, Hal Holbrook, Paul Schneider, Jim Norton, Mark Povinelli, Richard Brake, James Frain. When his parents are killed just before his final exam, aspiring veterinarian Pattinson runs away and winds up on a circus train. He not only ingratiates himself with the troupe and its mercurial owner (Waltz), but falls in love with the owner's wife, the show's star performer (Witherspoon). Waltz's character is puzzling at best, and the love story never catches fire, but the film does offer a beautiful evocation of Depression-era America and circus life, thanks to cinematographer Rodrigo Prieto, production designer Jack Fisk, and costume designer Jacqueline West, among others. Richard LaGravenese adapted Sara Gruen's best-selling novel. Panavision. [PG-13]❙

Waterhole #3 (1967) **C-95m.** **½ D: William Graham. James Coburn, Carroll O'Connor, Margaret Blye, Claude Akins, Bruce Dern, Joan Blondell, James Whitmore. Amusing Western comedy of three confederates who rob Army of a fortune in gold and bury it in desert waterhole. Produced by Blake Edwards. Techniscope. ▼●❙

Water Horse: Legend of the Deep, The (2007-U.S.-British) **C-111m.** *** D: Jay Russell. Emily Watson, Alex Etel, Ben Chaplin, David Morrissey, Priyanka Xi, Marshall Napier, Brian Cox. The boy-and-his-pet formula gets a different spin as the pet is the mythical title character, who grows up to be the Loch Ness monster! Unusual family fare set in WW2 Scotland, where a lonely boy whose father has gone off to war finds his only real companionship in a creature who hatches from an egg he chances to find. Alternately fanciful and dark, with a winning young hero in Etel (who was so memorable in MILLIONS). Based on a book by Dick King-Smith, who also wrote the novel that became BABE. Super 35. [PG]▶

Waterland (1992-British) **C-95m.** *** D: Stephen Gyllenhaal. Jeremy Irons, Sinead Cusack, Ethan Hawke, John Heard, Grant Warnock, Lena Headey, David Morrissey, Peter Postlethwaite. Arresting film about a desperate, middle-aged high school history teacher who's led a life of emotional upheaval, and seems trapped by his past—all of which affects the way he relates to his students. Peter Prince's screenplay effectively interprets Graham Swift's seemingly unfilmable novel. Irons is ideally cast and offers a peerless performance. The director's daughter, Maggie Gyllenhaal, appears in a small role. Technovision. [R]▼●

Waterloo (1971-Italian-Russian) **C-123m.** ** D: Sergei Bondarchuk. Rod Steiger, Christopher Plummer, Orson Welles, Jack Hawkins, Virginia McKenna, Dan O'Herlihy, Michael Wilding. Cumbersome historical film centering around Napoleon's defeat at Waterloo. Tremendous action but muddled plot. The original Russian version ran nearly four hours. Panavision. [G]▼

Waterloo Bridge (1931) **81m.** *** D: James Whale. Mae Clarke, Kent Douglass (Douglass Montgomery), Doris Lloyd, Frederick Kerr, Enid Bennett, Bette Davis, Ethel Griffies. Excellent early-talkie version of Robert E. Sherwood play, a tearjerker romance with an exceptional performance by Clarke as an American chorus-girl-turned-prostitute in WW1 London. Has a pre-Code grittiness missing from its glossier, more famous 1940 remake; remade again in 1956 as GABY. One of Davis' earliest screen roles.▶

Waterloo Bridge (1940) **103m.** ***½ D: Mervyn LeRoy. Vivien Leigh, Robert Taylor, Lucile Watson, Virginia Field, Maria Ouspenskaya, C. Aubrey Smith. Sentimental love story, well-acted, of soldier and ballet dancer meeting during London air raid, falling in love instantly. Cleaned-up version of the Robert E. Sherwood play, with beautiful performance by lovely Leigh. Screenplay by S.N. Behrman, Hans Rameau, and George Froeschel. First filmed in 1931,

remade as GABY. Also shown in computer-colored version. ▼●▶

Watermelon Man (1970) **C-97m.** **½ D: Melvin Van Peebles. Godfrey Cambridge, Estelle Parsons, Howard Caine, D'Urville Martin, Kay Kimberly, Mantan Moreland, Erin Moran. Provocative serio-comedy about bigoted white man who suddenly turns black and sees his life go upside down. Worth seeing, although Herman Raucher's one-joke script makes its point and then has nowhere to go. [R] ▼●

Watership Down (1978-British) **C-92m.** ***½ D: Martin Rosen. Voices of John Hurt, Richard Briers, Ralph Richardson, Denholm Elliott, Harry Andrews, Joss Ackland; narrated by Michael Hordern. Stylish animated-cartoon from Richard Adams' best-selling book about a family of rabbits seeking a safe place to live, encountering many perils along the way; not a kiddie film. Bird character voiced by Zero Mostel provides only comic relief in this sometimes grim cartoon. Excellent score by Angela Morley and Malcolm Williamson. One of the best non-Disney animated features ever made. [PG]▼●

Waterworld (1995) **C-135m.** *** D: Kevin Reynolds. Kevin Costner, Dennis Hopper, Jeanne Tripplehorn, Tina Majorino, Michael Jeter, Sab Shimono, Robert Joy, R. D. Call, Zakes Mokae, Leonardo Cimino, Gerard Murphy, Neil Giuntoli, Jack Black. Notoriously expensive movie can't live up to its price tag but does offer great action scenes and an interesting futuristic premise. In a world engulfed by water, the drifters and scavengers are pitted against bad guys called Smokers. Costner, known as The Mariner, is a hardened (and remarkably resourceful) survivor who readies himself for the ultimate Smoker showdown with a woman and child in tow. Full of eye-popping stunts and set pieces, and anchored by Costner's forceful and physical performance. Too poky at times and not fully fleshed out at the conclusion, but still solid entertainment. [PG-13]▼●▶

Watts Monster, The SEE: **Dr. Black, Mr. Hyde**

Wattstax (1973) **C-98m.** ***½ D: Mel Stuart. Isaac Hayes, The Staple Singers, Luther Ingram, Rev. Jesse Jackson, Richard Pryor, Rufus Thomas, Carla Thomas, Bar-Kays, Kim Weston, The Emotions, Johnnie Taylor. Exciting, vibrant documentary with music, centering around L.A. community of Watts, and the black experience. Pryor's monologues are exceptionally good. Reissued in 2003 at 104m., with new footage of Hayes. [R]▶

Wavelength (1983) **C-87m.** ** D: Mike Gray. Robert Carradine, Cherie Currie, Keenan Wynn. Cheap science-fiction film about aliens on Earth and a government coverup steals liberally from earlier pictures for ideas. Best thing is a varied musical score by Tangerine Dream. [PG]▼●

Waxwork (1988) **C-97m.** *½ D: Anthony Hickox. Zach Galligan, Deborah Foreman, David Warner, Michelle Johnson, Patrick Macnee, Dana Ashbrook, Miles O'Keeffe, John Rhys-Davies. Garbled, peculiar comedy-horror thriller set in evil magician's waxwork exhibit, with apocalyptic battle between humans and most of the famous monsters of history—Dracula, Frankenstein, the Mummy, a werewolf, Phantom of the Opera, Audrey II, etc. Followed by WAXWORK II: LOST IN TIME. [R]▼●

Way Ahead, The (1944-British) **91m.** ***½ D: Carol Reed. David Niven, Stanley Holloway, James Donald, John Laurie, Leslie Dwyer, Hugh Burden, Jimmy Hanley, Billy Hartnell, Raymond Huntley, Reginald Tate, Leo Genn, Penelope Dudley Ward, Renée Asherson, Raymond Lovell, Peter Ustinov, Trevor Howard. Exhilarating wartime British film showing how disparate civilians come to work together as a fighting unit; full of spirit and charm, with an outstanding cast, and fine script by Eric Ambler and Peter Ustinov. Film debut of Trevor Howard. Originally released in the U.S. in a shortened, more serious version called THE IMMORTAL BATTALION (with an introduction by journalist Quentin Reynolds). Original British running time 116m.▼▶

Way and the Body, The SEE: **Whip and the Body, The**

Way Back, The (2011-U.S.-Abu Dhabi-Polish-Indian) **C-133m.** **½ D: Peter Weir. Jim Sturgess, Ed Harris, Colin Farrell, Saoirse Ronan, Dragos Bucur, Mark Strong, Alexandru Potocean, Sebastian Urzendowsky, Gustaf Skarsgård. Sweeping saga of multinational prisoners who break out of a Siberian internment camp in 1941 and walk 4,000 miles, through every kind of climate and terrain, to freedom in India. Episodic story is told on a vast canvas, in a grand style reminiscent of David Lean. Unfortunately, despite some genuinely exciting passages and strong performances, the film goes on too long and leads to an unsatisfying conclusion. Perhaps its most noteworthy achievement is making us believe its actors are genuinely Russian, Polish, etc. Based on Slavomir Rawicz's book *The Long Walk*, purportedly a true story (which was later disputed). [PG-13]▶

Way Down East (1920) **119m.** *** D: D. W. Griffith. Lillian Gish, Richard Barthelmess, Lowell Sherman, Burr McIntosh, Kate Bruce, Mary Hay, Creighton Hale. The ultimate stage melodrama—with a city slicker despoiling the innocence of a virginal heroine, who then must pay the price. Executed with conviction by Griffith and a fine cast, building up to famous climax with Gish drifting away on the ice floes. Often shown in shorter versions; restored to 148m. by the Museum of Modern Art in 1985. Remade in 1935.▼●

Way Home . . . , The (2002-South Korean) **C-88m.** *** D: Jeong-Hyang Lee. Kim Eul-boon, Yu Seung-ho, Min Kyung-hoon, Yim Eun-kyung, Dong Hyo-hee. Sweet fable about a demanding, fast food/video game–loving seven-year-old city boy and the culture shock he experiences after being left in the care of his mute, old-world grandmother in a rural mountain village. Simple, but never simplistic, tale of generational bonding exudes warmth and compassion without ever wallowing in sentimentality. [PG]▼▶

Wayne's World (1992) **C-95m.** ** D: Penelope Spheeris. Mike Myers, Dana Carvey, Rob Lowe, Tia Carrere, Brian Doyle-Murray, Lara Flynn Boyle, Kurt Fuller, Colleen Camp, Donna Dixon, Meat Loaf, Ed O'Neill. Hit movie based on silly skit from TV's *Saturday Night Live*. Myers and Carvey are funny as the self-styled party dudes with their own cable TV show, and leading lady Carrere is certainly a "babe," but the story has too many slow spots and muffed jokes. Even casting Lowe as a slimeball doesn't pay off—because he's still so dull. Our advice: party elsewhere. Followed by a sequel. Super 35. [PG-13] ▼●

Wayne's World 2 (1993) **C-94m.** ** D: Stephen Surjik. Mike Myers, Dana Carvey, Tia Carrere, Christopher Walken, Kim Basinger, Ralph Brown, Ed O'Neill, Harry Shearer, James Hong, Drew Barrymore, Chris Farley. The Party Boys return with Wayne organizing a Waynestock music festival, and Garth being seduced by Honey Hornée (Basinger, in a tailor-made role she plays to the hilt). Tired gags from first film run throughout, but occasional bits and cameos (especially from "the better actor") make it worthy. [PG-13]▼●

Way of the Dragon SEE: **Return of the Dragon**

Way of the Gun, The (2000) **C-119m.** ** D: Christopher McQuarrie. Ryan Phillippe, Benicio Del Toro, James Caan, Juliette Lewis, Taye Diggs, Nicky Katt, Dylan Kussman, Scott Wilson, Kristin Lehman, Geoffrey Lewis, Sarah Silverman. Two young criminals decide to kidnap a surrogate mother who's supposedly carrying the child of a millionaire, and find themselves in way over their heads. Dense, often muddled, extremely violent film has some visceral action set pieces but—in spite of some pretentious narration—no discernible point. Directing debut for THE USUAL SUSPECTS screenwriter McQuarrie. [R] ▼▶

Way Out West (1937) **65m.** ***½ D: James W. Horne. Stan Laurel, Oliver Hardy, Sharon Lynn, James Finlayson, Rosina Lawrence, Stanley Fields, Vivien Oakland. Stan and Ollie are sent to deliver mine deed to daughter of late prospector, but crooked Finlayson leads them to wrong girl. One of their best features; moves well without resorting to needless romantic subplot. Another bonus: some charming musical interludes, and the boys perform a wonderful soft-shoe dance. Also shown in computer-colored version.▼●▶

Way to the Stars, The (1945-British) **109m.** **** D: Anthony Asquith. John Mills, Michael Redgrave, Douglass Montgomery, Rosamund John, Stanley Holloway, Trevor Howard, Felix Aylmer, Bonar Colleano. Excellent drama about a British airfield and the men stationed there, focusing mainly on personal relationships in wartime. Jean Simmons appears briefly as a singer. Script by Terence Rattigan and Anatole de Grunwald. Originally released in U.S. as JOHNNY IN THE CLOUDS.▶

Way . . . Way Out (1966) **C-106m.** BOMB D: Gordon Douglas. Jerry Lewis, Connie Stevens, Robert Morley, Dennis Weaver, Howard Morris, Brian Keith, Dick Shawn, Anita Ekberg, James Brolin. One of Jerry's worst. Plot concerns comedian's trip to the moon with sexy astronaut Stevens; hopefully they took the film's negative along. CinemaScope.

Way We Are, The SEE: **Quiet Days in Hollywood**

Way West, The (1967) **C-122m.** *½ D: Andrew V. McLaglen. Kirk Douglas, Robert Mitchum, Richard Widmark, Lola Albright, Michael Witney, Stubby Kaye, Sally Field, Jack Elam. Despite cast, this version of A. B. Guthrie, Jr.'s epic novel fails completely. McLaglen's lackluster direction partially to blame, but big problem is script, which may hold all-time record for undeveloped subplots. Mitchum is good through it all; Sally Field's first feature. Panavision.▼

Way We Were, The (1973) **C-118m.** *** D: Sydney Pollack. Barbra Streisand, Robert Redford, Bradford Dillman, Murray Hamilton, Patrick O'Neal, Viveca Lindfors, Lois Chiles, Allyn Ann McLerie, Herb Edelman, James Woods, Connie Forslund, Sally Kirkland, George Gaynes, Susie Blakely, Dan Seymour. First-class love story about political activist Streisand and her opposite, Waspish Joe College–type Redford, from late '30s to early '50s. Prerelease cutting excised meatiest sequence on blacklist era in Hollywood, alas, leaving Hamilton and Lindfors with bit parts, and some confusion in last portion of plot. Still quite good, with literate Arthur Laurents script from his own novel. Marvin Hamlisch's score and title song (lyrics by Alan and Marilyn Bergman) won Oscars—and look sharp at Beverly Hills movie screening for a Hamlisch cameo. Panavision. [PG]▼●▶

W. C. Fields and Me (1976) **C-111m.** *** D: Arthur Hiller. Rod Steiger, Valerie Perrine, John Marley, Jack Cassidy, Paul Stewart, Bernadette Peters, Billy Barty. Story of comedian's romance with Carlotta Monti is a cut above most Hollywood bios, thanks to

Steiger's excellent performance, authentic atmosphere, good cast. Has little relation to the truth, but still entertaining. [PG]

We All Loved Each Other So Much (1974-Italian) **C/B&W-124m.** ***½ D: Ettore Scola. Nino Manfredi, Vittorio Gassman, Aldo Fabrizi, Stefania Sandrelli, Stefano Satta Flores, Giovanna Ralli. Spirited, wistful comedy of three friends (Gassman, Manfredi, Satta Flores) who each love Sandrelli over the course of three decades. The latter, an actress, plays a bit role in LA DOLCE VITA; the shooting of Anita Ekberg's Trevi Fountain scene is re-created, complete with Mastroianni and Fellini! A loving homage to Fellini, De Sica, and postwar Italian cinema.▼●▶

We Are Marshall (2006) **C-124m.** *** D: McG. Matthew McConaughey, Matthew Fox, David Strathairn, Anthony Mackie, Ian McShane, Kate Mara, January Jones, Kimberly Williams-Paisley, Robert Patrick, Brian Geraghty. True story of tragic November 1970 airplane crash that took the lives of the Marshall University football team, their coaches, and key boosters as they were returning from a game. Dealing with the West Virginia town's devastation and reluctance to start over again, a new coach is recruited to do just that a year later. Highly dramatic telling could have dissolved into sports movie clichés but wisely focuses on the human element and the inherent need to move on with life when it seems most challenging. McConaughey, as the new coach, Fox, as a guilt-plagued assistant coach who traded his seat on the fateful flight, and Strathairn, as the university president, are outstanding in this worthwhile film. Super 35. [PG]▶

Weather Girl (2009) **C-93m.** **½ D: Blayne Weaver. Tricia O'Kelley, Patrick J. Adams, Ryan Devlin, Kaitlin Olson, Mark Harmon, Jon Cryer, Jane Lynch, Blair Underwood, Enrico Colantoni. After an on-the-air breakup with her unfaithful anchorman boyfriend (Harmon), a newly unemployed TV weather forecaster (O'Kelley) struggles to find another job and regain her self-respect. Lightweight comedy doesn't cover any new ground, but takes a few clever detours en route to its inevitable happy ending. [R]▶

Weather Man, The (2005) **C-102m.** ***½ D: Gore Verbinski. Nicolas Cage, Michael Caine, Hope Davis, Michael Rispoli, Nicholas Hoult, Gemmenne de la Peña, Gil Bellows, Judith McConnell. Chicago TV weatherman is a local celebrity but finds his "success" hollow and even alienating. He's constantly at odds with his ex-wife, loves his kids but doesn't know how to communicate with them, and feels like an utter failure alongside his father, an award-winning novelist who's emotionally distant. Nobody plays lost souls quite like Cage, and he's perfect in this melancholy, keenly observant view of the American dream that unfolds like a good novel. Written by Steven Conrad. [R]▶

Weavers, The: Wasn't That a Time! (1982) **C-78m.** **** D: Jim Brown. Lee Hays, Pete Seeger, Fred Hellerman, Ronnie Gilbert. Simply wonderful documentary about a reunion of the much-loved folk-singing quartet of the 1940s and '50s, climaxed by footage of their Carnegie Hall concert. Irresistible film built on the foundation of Lee Hays' wit and indomitable spirit.▼●

Web of Passion (1959-French) **C-101m.** **½ D: Claude Chabrol. Madeleine Robinson, Antonella Lualdi, Jean-Paul Belmondo, Jacques Dacqmine. Non-conformist Belmondo insinuates himself into a family's graces, delighting in breaking down their standards, with murders resulting. Talky but intriguing drama. Aka LEDA and Á DOUBLE TOUR.▶

Web of the Spider (1970-Italian) **C-94m.** ** D: Anthony Dawson (Antonio Margheriti). Anthony Franciosa, Michele Mercier, Peter Carsten, Karen Field, Silvano Tranquilli. Overly familiar thriller about the skeptic who accepts a wager that he cannot survive the night alone in a haunted house. Franciosa and associates try vainly to give it a fresh twist. Previously made by the same director as CASTLE OF TERROR. Techniscope.▼▶

Wedding, A (1978) **C-125m.** **½ D: Robert Altman. Carol Burnett, Desi Arnaz, Jr., Amy Stryker, Vittorio Gassman, Geraldine Chaplin, Mia Farrow, Paul Dooley, Lillian Gish, Lauren Hutton, John Cromwell, Pat McCormick, Howard Duff, Pam Dawber, Dennis Christopher, Peggy Ann Garner, Nina Van Pallandt, Dina Merrill, John Considine, Viveca Lindfors, Dennis Franz. Unfocused look at family intrigues surrounding a nouveau riche wedding; some amusing moments and pointed characterizations, but doesn't quite jell. Panavision. [PG]▼▶

Wedding Banquet, The (1993-U.S.-Taiwanese) **C-108m.** *** D: Ang Lee. Winston Chao, May Chin, Mitchell Lichtenstein, Sihung Lung, Ah-Leh Gua, Tien Pien. Gay Taiwanese-American Chao tries to fool his parents via a fake wedding, with unexpected complications. Top-notch comedy which knowingly and poignantly examines the meaning of cultural identity and child-parent relationships. Neatly scripted by Lee, Neil Peng, and James Schamus. [R]▼●▶

Wedding Bell Blues (1996) **C-100m.** **½ D: Dana Lustig. Illeana Douglas, Paulina Porizkova, Julie Warner, John Corbett, Jonathan Penner, Charles Martin Smith, Richard Edson, Joe Urla, Stephanie Beacham, Carla Gugino, Leo Rossi, John Capodice, Victoria Jackson, Debbie Reynolds. A trio of roommates, each about to turn 30 and feeling pressure to marry, splits for Las Vegas to find quickie husbands. Attractive cast helps maintain interest in this somewhat

familiar "where-are-all-the-good-men?" saga. [R]▼●▶

Wedding Crashers (2005) **C-119m.** *** D: David Dobkin. Owen Wilson, Vince Vaughn, Christopher Walken, Rachel McAdams, Isla Fisher, Jane Seymour, Ellen Albertini Dow, Keir O'Donnell, Bradley Cooper, Ron Canada, Henry Gibson, Dwight Yoakam, Rebecca De Mornay. D.C. law partners and pals Wilson and Vaughn systematically crash weddings of all kinds in search of free food, good parties, and vulnerable women. Then, at an exclusive celebration for the daughter of a government official (Walken), Wilson falls in love with the sister of the bride. Comic complications ensue, many of them predictable, some needlessly drawn out, but this often-raunchy comedy is played with such gusto that the overall results are hilarious. Expect some fun cameos. Also available in longer unrated version. Super 35. [R]▼▶

Wedding Date, The (2005) **C-88m.** *½ D: Clare Kilner. Debra Messing, Dermot Mulroney, Amy Adams, Jack Davenport, Sarah Parish, Jeremy Sheffield, Peter Egan, Holland Taylor. Tense New Yorker Messing hires an A-list male escort (Mulroney) to accompany her to her half-sister's London wedding, all to make the ex-fiancé who dumped her jealous. The sibling has a dark side, their parents are sweet, the ex probably needs professional help, while Mulroney doesn't register much emotion at all. Given all this, it's no surprise that director Kilner has a tough time finding a consistent tone for this failed comedy. [PG-13] ▼▶

Wedding Daze (2008) **C-90m.** ** D: Michael Ian Black. Jason Biggs, Isla Fisher, Joanna Gleason, Edward Herrmann, Matt Malloy, Audra Blaser, Joe Pantoliano, Rob Corddry, Jay O. Sanders, Michael Weston, Margo Martindale, Mark Consuelos, Ebon Moss-Bachrach. Proposing to an attractive stranger (Fisher) is possibly the most rational decision Anderson (Biggs) has made recently. After she (surprisingly) says yes, they go about meeting each other's crazy family and friends. Thin, occasionally outrageous comedy may best be appreciated by dedicated fans of writer-director Black and followers of *The State* and *Stella*. Released direct to DVD in the U.S. [R]▶

Wedding Gift, The (1993-British) **C-87m.** *** D: Richard Loncraine. Julie Walters, Jim Broadbent, Thora Hird, Sian Thomas, Andrew Lancel, Anastasia Mulroney, Joanna McCallum. Spirited spin on "disease-of-the-week" stories, with marvelous performances by Walters and Broadbent as a loving couple whose sense of humor helps them deal with her mysterious and debilitating ailment. Based on the true story of a woman who decided to find her husband a new mate before she died. Alternately humorous and heart-rending; well worth a look. Based on the memoir by Denis

Longden. Made for British TV, where it was shown as WIDE-EYED AND LEGLESS. [PG-13]▼●▶

Wedding in Blood (1973-French-Italian) C-98m. **½ D: Claude Chabrol. Stephane Audran, Michel Piccoli, Claude Pieplu, Clothilde Joano, Eliana de Santis. Piccoli and Audran, each married to another, are having an affair. How soon will they murder their spouses? And get caught? Medium Chabrol. [PG]▼

Wedding in White (1972-Canadian) C-106m. *** D: William Fruet. Donald Pleasence, Carol Kane, Doris Petrie, Doug McGrath, Leo Phillips. Fine performances in sad tale of girl impregnated by brother's drunken pal during WW2 and her father's efforts to save the family's honor. Panavision. [R]▼▶

Wedding March, The (1928) 113m. **** D: Erich von Stroheim. Erich von Stroheim, Fay Wray, ZaSu Pitts, George Fawcett, Maude George, George Nicholls, Cesare Gravina. In pre-WW1 Vienna, a roguish prince (played to perfection by von Stroheim) agrees to marry for money and position to help his family, then falls in love with a poor but beautiful and crippled girl (Wray). A masterpiece, blending romance and irony, with an unforgettable finale . . . though what we see is just the first half of the film von Stroheim completed (the second no longer exists). One sequence in two-color Technicolor. ▼·

Wedding Night, The (1935) 84m. **½ D: King Vidor. Gary Cooper, Anna Sten, Ralph Bellamy, Walter Brennan, Helen Vinson, Sig Ruman. Study of romance and idealism; unbelievable love yarn but entertaining. Producer Samuel Goldwyn's third and final attempt to make Anna Sten a new Garbo.▼▶

Wedding Party, The (1969) 92m. *½ D: Cynthia Munroe, Brian De Palma, Wilford Leach. Jill Clayburgh, Charles Pfluger, Valda Satterfield, Raymond McNally, Jennifer Salt, John Braswell, Judy Thomas, Robert De Niro, William Finley. Talky, corny, boring comic oddity detailing events preceding marriage of Clayburgh and Pfluger; the bride and her family are boorish, and the groom grows ever more reluctant. Self-consciously directed; of interest only for De Palma's participation, and initial screen appearances of Clayburgh and De Niro (spelled "DeNero" in the credits). Shot in 1963, and barely released.▼▶

Wedding Planner, The (2001) C-102m. ** D: Adam Shankman. Jennifer Lopez, Matthew McConaughey, Bridgette Wilson-Sampras, Justin Chambers, Judy Greer, Alex Rocco, Joanna Gleason, Charles Kimbrough, Kevin Pollak, Fred Willard, Kathy Najimy. Lopez is a wedding planner whose fast-track lifestyle doesn't allow her time for a personal life. She finds herself attracted to a doctor (McConaughey) who is otherwise engaged, but guess who's been hired to plan his nuptials? Occasional bright moments are done in by long, deadening stretches, a serious lack of chemistry between the leads, and a predictable finale. Panavision. [PG-13]▼▶

Wedding Singer, The (1998) C-96m. *** D: Frank Coraci. Adam Sandler, Drew Barrymore, Angela Featherstone, Allen Covert, Matthew Glave, Christine Taylor, Kevin Nealon, Christina Pickles, Billy Idol. Sandler plays a genuinely sweet guy whose life is shattered when his fiancée stands him up at the altar—but finds consolation in the friendship of a waitress who he discovers is about to marry a real jerk. Sandler has never been more appealing, or Barrymore more adorable. Entertaining romantic comedy set in 1985 marred only by moments of crude dialogue that don't seem absolutely necessary. Steve Buscemi and Jon Lovitz appear unbilled. Later a Broadway musical. Unrated version runs 100m. [PG-13]▼●▶

Wednesday's Child SEE: **Family Life**

We Don't Live Here Anymore (2004) C-101m. **½ D: John Curran. Mark Ruffalo, Laura Dern, Peter Krause, Naomi Watts. Two unhappy couples become sexually intertwined while keeping secrets from each other, which isn't healthy for any of them. Well-observed, well-acted but rather one-dimensional (and depressing) slice of life set in a small New England town. Adapted from two of Andre Dubus' short stories. Super 35. [R]▼▶

Weeds (1987) C-115m. **½ D: John Hancock. Nick Nolte, Rita Taggart, Lane Smith, William Forsythe, John Toles-Bey, Joe Mantegna, Ernie Hudson, Anne Ramsey, Charlie Rich. San Quentin lifer/aspiring playwright is near-miraculously sprung from prison when a newspaper critic lobbies for his release, and goes on to form a "Barbed Wire Theatre" acting troupe of ex-cons. Odd, original mix of comedy and drama based on Rick Cluchey's real-life experiences with the San Quentin Drama Group. Earnest, well acted but never quite gels. [R]▼●

Weekend (1967-French-Italian) C-103m. ***½ D: Jean-Luc Godard. Mireille Darc, Jean Yanne, Jean-Pierre Kalfon, Valerie Lagrange, Jean-Pierre Léaud. Mind-expanding anti-Western diatribe about one woman's road to guerrillahood is among Godard's more fully realized works, with a long traffic-jam sequence that is justifiably regarded as one of the great set pieces in screen history. An essential '60s time-capsule entry.▼▶

Weekend at Bernie's (1989) C-97m. **½ D: Ted Kotcheff. Andrew McCarthy, Jonathan Silverman, Catherine Mary Stewart, Terry Kiser, Don Calfa, Louis Giambalvo. Two young hustlers, far down on the cor-

[1526]

porate ladder, win an invitation to their boss' sumptuous beach house for the weekend . . . only to find him dead upon arrival. Slim . . . but agreeably silly farce, written by Robert Klane. Followed by a sequel. [PG-13]▼●)

Weekend at Bernie's II (1993) C-89m. BOMB D: Robert Klane. Andrew McCarthy, Jonathan Silverman, Terry Kiser, Barry Bostwick, Troy Beyer, Tom Wright, Steve James. Witless sequel to a movie that didn't exactly cry out for a followup. Insurance execs McCarthy and Silverman are suspected of embezzlement, and can only save their skins with the help of their "dead body" buddy Bernie (Kiser). After this debacle, let's hope Bernie is allowed to rest in peace. [PG]▼●)

Week-end at the Waldorf (1945) 130m. *** D: Robert Z. Leonard. Ginger Rogers, Lana Turner, Walter Pidgeon, Van Johnson, Edward Arnold, Phyllis Thaxter, Keenan Wynn, Robert Benchley, Leon Ames, Porter Hall, George Zucco, Xavier Cugat. Several "typical" days in the life of the fabled Waldorf-Astoria Hotel. Ultra-glossy MGM remake of GRAND HOTEL weaves disparate characters' lives together. No resonance whatsoever, but good, slick entertainment, with Rogers and Pidgeon standing out in the attractive cast.▼●

Week-end in Havana (1941) C-80m. *** D: Walter Lang. Alice Faye, Carmen Miranda, John Payne, Cesar Romero, Cobina Wright, Jr., George Barbier, Leonid Kinskey, Sheldon Leonard, Billy Gilbert. Typically entertaining, Technicolored 20th Century-Fox musical fluff with Payne showing Faye a good time in Havana for business purposes only, but falling in love with her instead. Miranda adds her usual zest.▼●

Weekend Pass (1984) C-92m. BOMB D: Lawrence Bassoff. Patrick Hauser, D. W. Brown, Chip McAllister, Peter Ellenstein, Hilary Shapiro, Pamela G. Kay. Intolerable drive-in comedy lifts its premise from ON THE TOWN: having completed basic training, four stereotypical naval recruits set off for 72 "wild" hours in L.A. 92 minutes of mine sweeping would be more entertaining. [R]▼●)

Weekend Warriors (1986) C-85m. *½ D: Bert Convy. Chris Lemmon, Vic Tayback, Lloyd Bridges, Graham Jarvis, Daniel Greene, Marty Cohen, Brian Bradley. Low-level, sloppily made comedy about some goof-offs who join the National Guard, and their subsequent hijinks. Convy's debut as director. [R]▼

Week's Vacation, A (1980-French) C-102m. *** D: Bertrand Tavernier. Nathalie Baye, Gerard Lanvin, Michel Galabru, Philippe Noiret, Philippe Leotard. Subtle drama of schoolteacher Baye briefly escaping her problems by visiting her parents in

Lyons. Sensitive depiction of inter-personal relations is director Tavernier's strong suit. Panavision. [R]

Wee Willie Winkie (1937) 99m. *** D: John Ford. Shirley Temple, Victor McLaglen, C. Aubrey Smith, June Lang, Michael Whalen, Cesar Romero, Constance Collier, Douglas Scott. Shirley and her widowed mother come to live at a British Army outpost in India, where the moppet works hard to win over her crusty grandfather, the Colonel (Smith), and is quickly adopted by a soft-hearted sergeant (McLaglen). One of Shirley's best vehicles, "inspired" (it says here) by the Rudyard Kipling story. Beware 77m. prints. Also shown in computer-colored version.▼

Weight of Water, The (2002-French-U.S.) C-113m. ** D: Kathryn Bigelow. Catherine McCormack, Sarah Polley, Sean Penn, Josh Lucas, Elizabeth Hurley, Ciarán Hinds, Katrin Cartlidge, Vinessa Shaw. Weighty adaptation of Anita Shreve's best-seller that parallels events 100 years apart: the mysterious, brutal murder of two young women on an island off New Hampshire, and a modern-day sailing party including a photo-journalist (McCormack) who's investigating the case and her moody poet husband (Penn). The story's ultimate revelations don't bring any understanding of the contemporary characters or their problems, although the acting is certainly good. [R]▼)

Weird Science (1985) C-94m. *½ D: John Hughes. Anthony Michael Hall, Kelly LeBrock, Ilan Mitchell-Smith, Bill Paxton, Suzanne Snyder, Judie Aronson, Robert Downey (Jr.), Robert Rusler. Two nerdy teens use computer to conjure up woman of their dreams (sexy LeBrock), but writer-director Hughes doesn't follow through on his own premise! Appalling excuse for comedy; tasteless and endless, unredeemed by Hughes's sharp teenage dialogue and Hall's engaging performance. Later a cable TV series. [PG-13]▼●)

Welcome Home (1989) C-96m. ** D: Franklin J. Schaffner. Kris Kristofferson, JoBeth Williams, Sam Waterston, Brian Keith, Thomas Wilson Brown, Trey Wilson. Please, not again. Presumed dead Air Force officer Kristofferson, 17 years in Cambodia with a new wife and two children, returns home to remarried spouse number one and their teenage son. Tolerably sincere at best, embalmed at worst. Director Schaffner's final film. [R]▼

Welcome Home, Roscoe Jenkins (2008) C-114m. ** D: Malcolm D. Lee. Martin Lawrence, James Earl Jones, Margaret Avery, Joy Bryant, Cedric the Entertainer, Nicole Ari Parker, Michael Clarke Duncan, Mike Epps, Mo'Nique, Damani Roberts. Broad, witless comedy in which out-of-touch L.A. talk show host Lawrence returns to his Georgia home for a family get-together. A talented cast is wasted here. [PG-13]🔲

Welcome Home Roxy Carmichael (1990) C-98m. *½ D: Jim Abrahams. Winona Ryder, Jeff Daniels, Laila Robins, Dinah Manoff, Thomas Wilson Brown, Joan McMurtrey, Frances Fisher, Graham Beckel, Robin Thomas, Robby Kiger, Sachi Parker, Stephen Tobolowsky. Small Ohio town goes berserk anticipating return of sexy and mysterious hometown girl Roxy Carmichael, who's been away in Hollywood living a life of luxury. Teenage beatnik Ryder—moody, brilliant, alienated, intuitive, and adopted—starts fantasizing that Roxy is actually her mother. Flat, disjointed satiric comedy with Ryder the sole bright spot. [PG-13]▼●◐

Welcome Home, Soldier Boys (1972) C-91m. ** D: Richard Compton. Joe Don Baker, Paul Koslo, Alan Vint, Elliott Street, Jennifer Billingsley, Billy "Green" Bush, Geoffrey Lewis, Francine York. Sensationalistic melodrama about four ex-Green Berets who adjust to civilian life by gang-raping a girl and burning down a town. Yet another one-dimensionally violent depiction of Vietnam veterans. [R]

Welcome Stranger (1947) 107m. *** D: Elliott Nugent. Bing Crosby, Barry Fitzgerald, Joan Caulfield, Wanda Hendrix, Frank Faylen, Elizabeth Patterson. Entertaining musical of Crosby filling in for vacationing doctor in small community, getting involved with local girl. ▼▶

Welcome to Arrow Beach (1974) C-99m. ** D: Laurence Harvey. Laurence Harvey, Joanna Pettet, Stuart Whitman, John Ireland, Meg Foster, Jesse Vint, Gloria LeRoy. Harvey's final film (edited by phone from his deathbed) is strange but watchable shocker. He plays a war veteran who returns to California and kills passersby to feed his newly acquired taste for human flesh. Good cast helps, especially spellbinding Foster in an early role. Retitled: TENDER FLESH. [R]▼

Welcome to Collinwood (2002) C-86m. ** D: Anthony Russo, Joe Russo. Luis Guzman, Michael Jeter, Patricia Clarkson, Andrew Davoli, Isaiah Washington, William H. Macy, Sam Rockwell, Gabrielle Union, Jennifer Esposito, George Clooney. Remake of BIG DEAL ON MADONNA STREET set in a grimy, ethnic Cleveland suburb has flavor but no fizz. The single funniest moment replicates the highlight of the classic Italian film. Clooney (who produced the film with Steven Soderbergh) has a minor part as a safecracking expert. Written by the directors. Super 35. [R]▼▶

Welcome to 18 (1987) C-89m. ** D: Terry Carr. Courtney Thorne-Smith, Mariska Hargitay, Jo Ann Willette, Cristen Kaufman, John Putch. Tired teen titillation yarn about three girlfriends who spend their first summer out of high school experiencing life in the fast lane in Nevada. Attractive newcomers (including brunette Hargitay, daughter of Jayne Mansfield) muddle through preachy, plot-heavy nonsense. [PG-13]▼

Welcome to Hard Times (1967) C-105m. *** D: Burt Kennedy. Henry Fonda, Janice Rule, Keenan Wynn, Janis Paige, John Anderson, Aldo Ray, Warren Oates, Fay Spain, Edgar Buchanan, Lon Chaney, Jr., Elisha Cook, Jr. Intriguing, symbol-laden account of run-down Western town victimized by outlaw Ray, with Fonda finally forced to shoot it out to save what's left. Adapted by Kennedy from E. L. Doctorow novel.

Welcome to L.A. (1977) C-106m. **½ D: Alan Rudolph. Keith Carradine, Sally Kellerman, Geraldine Chaplin, Harvey Keitel, Lauren Hutton, Viveca Lindfors, Sissy Spacek, Denver Pyle, John Considine, Richard Baskin. This chronicle of lost, lonely Southern Californians who can only connect for fleeting moments between the sheets is occasionally intriguing, but pales beside some of Rudolph's later, better work. A major debit: Baskin's music, which quickly becomes monotonous. Produced by Robert Altman. [R]▼

Welcome to Mooseport (2004) C-110m. *** D: Donald Petrie. Gene Hackman, Ray Romano, Marcia Gay Harden, Maura Tierney, Christine Baranski, Fred Savage, Rip Torn, June Squibb, Wayne Robson. Easygoing hardware store owner in a Maine village where everybody knows everybody else finds himself running for mayor—and competing for the affection of his long-time girlfriend—with the cocky former President of the U.S., who's just moved to town. Amiable film offers Hackman a good comedy vehicle and Romano a tailor-made role. Edward Herrmann appears unbilled. [PG-13]▼▶

Welcome to Sarajevo (1997-British-U.S.) C-101m. *** D: Michael Winterbottom. Stephen Dillane, Woody Harrelson, Marisa Tomei, Emira Nusevic, Kerry Fox, Goran Visnjic, Emily Lloyd. Achingly realistic, unsentimental look at reporters covering the Bosnian war in Sarajevo. One British TV reporter becomes especially outraged by the plight of orphaned children and finds his casual promise to a young girl—that he will lead her to safety—being put to the test. Based on a true story, and told with a compelling blend of genuine and staged footage. Difficult to watch at times, but rewarding. Super 35. [R]▼●◐

Welcome to the Ch'tis (2008-French) C-106m. ***½ D: Dany Boon. Kad Merad, Dany Boon, Zoé Félix, Philippe Duquesne, Line Renaud, Michel Galabru, Stéphane Freiss, Guy Lecluyse, Anne Marivin, Patrick Bosso. Crowd-pleasing comedy with heart about a post-office manager, perennially cowed by his wife, who's sent to

[1528]

the French equivalent of Siberia: a northern province that his fellow Southerners have ridiculed and demonized. When he moves there (leaving his family behind) he learns that the rumors of poor weather and backward citizens are false, though he does have to acclimate to the openhearted people . . . and their very strange dialect. Great entertainment and a smash hit in France. Director-costar Boon also cowrote the screenplay. Aka WELCOME TO THE STICKS. Super 35.

Welcome to the Dollhouse (1996) **C-87m. ***½** D: Todd Solondz. Heather Matarazzo, Brendan Sexton, Jr., Daria Kalinina, Matthew Faber, Angela Pietropinto, Eric Mabius. The pain of puberty has never been portrayed so unflinchingly; smart-but-ordinary Matarazzo has to deal with her incredibly un-nurturing suburban family (which dotes on her "adorable" younger sister), and worse, the pranks and sexual threats of virtually her entire junior high school. Amid this dire lack of support and warmth is a heroine of enormous pluck and cunning. While viewer may wince as numerous unpleasant situations play out, there is also terrific satire (and guffaws) as life in the Seventh-Grade-From-Hell is depicted with dead-on clarity. Strong performances; sharply scripted by the director. [R]▼◐)

Welcome to the Rileys (2010-U.S.-British) **C-111m. ***** D: Jake Scott. James Gandolfini, Kristen Stewart, Melissa Leo, Joe Chrest, Ally Sheedy, Eisa Davis, Tiffany Coty, Lance E. Nichols. Gandolfini and Leo's marriage ground to a halt when their teenage daughter died in an auto accident years ago. When he leaves Indiana to attend a business convention in New Orleans and encounters a foulmouthed young stripper, he sees someone in need and decides it's his job to straighten out her messy life. Low-key drama may be a stretch if one takes it literally, but it works as a metaphor about people who need to reconnect with life. It's also a fine showcase for its three leading actors. [R]▐

Welcome to the Sticks SEE: **Welcome to the Ch'tis**

Welcome to Woop Woop (1997-Australian-British) **C-96m. **½** D: Stephan Elliott. Johnathon Schaech, Rod Taylor, Susie Porter, Dee Smart, Barry Humphries, Richard Moir, Paul Mercurio, Rachel Griffiths, Maggie Kirkpatrick, Tina Louise. American con artist (Schaech) flees to the Outback, where he meets a man-hungry hitchhiker who drags him off to the very remote municipality of Woop Woop. Native Australian Taylor is outrageous as Schaech's dictatorial, unbalanced, Rodgers & Hammerstein–loving father-in-law. Raucous, raunchy farce from the director of THE ADVENTURES OF PRISCILLA, QUEEN OF THE DESERT. 2.35 Research PLC. [R]▼▐

Well-Digger's Daughter, The (1941-French) **142m. ***½** D: Marcel Pagnol. Raimu, Fernandel, Josette Day, Charpin, George Grey. Naive Day is seduced and abandoned—with child—and peasant father Raimu isn't very pleased. Both touching and hilarious.▼

Wendell Baker Story, The (2007) **C-102m. *½** D: Andrew Wilson, Luke Wilson. Luke Wilson, Eva Mendes, Seymour Cassel, Eddie Griffin, Kris Kristofferson, Harry Dean Stanton, Owen Wilson, Jacob Vargas, Angela Alvarado, Buck Taylor, Azura Skye, Will Ferrell. Woebegone vanity film for writer-star-codirector Wilson, playing a cocky Texan who takes his girlfriend (Mendes) for granted until he's thrown in prison and she wises up. When he gets out he tries to go straight, working at a state home for the elderly run by a slimy crook (Owen W.). Nice supporting roles for Cassel, Stanton, and Kristofferson aren't adequate compensation for sitting through this tedious trifle. Made in 2003. Super 35. [PG-13]▐

Wendigo (2002) **C-90m. **½** D: Larry Fessenden. Patricia Clarkson, Jake Weber, Erik Per Sullivan, John Speredakos, Christopher Wynkoop. Eerie, well-made chiller in which a N.Y.C. couple (Clarkson, Weber) and their eight-year-old son (Sullivan) head off for a weekend in the country, and a car accident involving a deer sets off a disturbing chain of events. Hampered only by a formulaic ending. The title refers to a Native American spirit that plays a key role in the story. [R]▼▐

Wendy and Lucy (2008) **C-80m. *** D: Kelly Reichardt. Michelle Williams, Will Patton, John Robinson, Larry Fessenden, Will Oldham, Walter Dalton. Slice of life about a young woman on the road with her dog who gets stuck in a sleepy Oregon town. Like Reichardt's OLD JOY, this is an exercise in minimalist filmmaking—but vivid, immediate, and heartbreaking. Based on a story by coscreenwriter Jon Raymond. Williams gives an honest, finely tuned performance. [R]▐

Went to Coney Island on a Mission from God . . . Be Back by Five (2000) **C-92m. *** D: Richard Schenkman. Jon Cryer, Rick Stear, Rafael Báez, Ione Skye, Frank Whaley, Peter Gerety, Dominic Chianese. Two friends spend a day wandering around the boardwalk at Coney Island in search of a childhood pal who dropped out of sight years ago. Moving series of vignettes about dreams gone astray; Schenkman (who cowrote the script with Cryer) makes perfect use of his Coney Island locations. [R]▼▐

We of the Never Never (1983-Australian) **C-132m. *** D: Igor Auzins. Angela Punch McGregor, Arthur Dignam, Tony Barry, Tommy Lewis, Lewis Fitz-Gerald.

True story based on memoirs of first white woman to travel into Australian wilderness known as the Never Never is visually stunning but never develops narrative momentum or dramatic punch. Still, it's a pleasure to look at. Technovision. [G]▼▶

We Own the Night (2007) **C-117m.** ******* D: James Gray. Joaquin Phoenix, Mark Wahlberg, Robert Duvall, Eva Mendes, Danny Hoch, Tony Musante, Antoni Corone, Moni Moshonov, Oleg Taktarov, Alex Veadov. Phoenix, the black sheep of his family, lives the high life in 1970s N.Y.C., managing a hot Brooklyn nightclub for his Russian boss, and ignoring other criminal activities taking place under his nose. But when the same Russian family threatens his brother and father, both dedicated policemen, he's forced to take sides. Writer-director Gray offers another story of fate, writ large. Not as operatic as LITTLE ODESSA or THE YARDS but considerably more effective, with pulse-pounding action scenes. Former N.Y.C. Mayor Ed Koch plays himself! [R]▶

We're Back: A Dinosaur's Story (1993) **C-72m.** ****½** D: Dick Zondag, Ralph Zondag, Phil Nibbelink, Simon Wells. Voices of John Goodman, Charles Fleischer, Felicity Kendal, Rhea Perlman, Martin Short, Walter Cronkite, Julia Child, Kenneth Mars, Jay Leno. Amiable children's animated feature about a quartet of dinosaurs given the opportunity to visit modern-day N.Y.C., where they help two troubled kids—but fall prey to a devilish circus proprietor. Mostly fun, though slow at times, and the freakshow subplot is a bit eerie for younger kids. Executive-produced by Steven Spielberg, the same year he made another well-known film about dinosaurs. [G]▼●

We're No Angels (1955) **C-106m.** ****½** D: Michael Curtiz. Humphrey Bogart, Aldo Ray, Peter Ustinov, Joan Bennett, Basil Rathbone, Leo G. Carroll. Mild entertainment as three escapees from Devil's Island find refuge with French family and extricate them from various predicaments. Remade in 1989. VistaVision.▼▶●

We're No Angels (1989) **C-106m.** ***½** D: Neil Jordan. Robert De Niro, Sean Penn, Demi Moore, Hoyt Axton, Bruno Kirby, Ray McAnally, James Russo, Wallace Shawn, John C. Reilly. Lumbering comedy about a couple of dimwitted convicts who inadvertently escape from prison and find refuge pretending to be priests visiting a nearby shrine. De Niro, who also served as executive producer, mugs as never before, playing Leo Gorcey to Penn's Huntz Hall. Handsome production design is no compensation for a lugubrious script by David Mamet, "suggested by" the play that was filmed before in 1955. Panavision. [PG-13]▼▶●

We're Not Dressing (1934) **77m.** ******* D: Norman Taurog. Bing Crosby, Carole Lombard, George Burns, Gracie Allen, Ethel Merman, Leon Errol, Ray Milland. Musical *Admirable Crichton* with rich-girl Lombard falling in love with sailor Crosby when entourage is ship-wrecked on desert isle. Merman is man-chasing second fiddle, with Burns and Allen on tap as local expeditionists. Great fun; Bing sings "Love Thy Neighbor."▼▶

We're Not Married! (1952) **85m.** ******* D: Edmund Goulding. Ginger Rogers, Fred Allen, Victor Moore, Marilyn Monroe, Paul Douglas, David Wayne, Eve Arden, Louis Calhern, Zsa Zsa Gabor, James Gleason, Jane Darwell, Eddie Bracken, Mitzi Gaynor. Fine froth served up in several episodes as five married couples discover their weddings weren't legal. Segments vary in quality but the cast generally delivers the goods. Written and produced by Nunnally Johnson. Lee Marvin has a bit. ▼▶

Werewolf, The (1956) **83m.** ****½** D: Fred F. Sears. Steven Ritch, Don Megowan, Joyce Holden, Eleanore Tanin, Harry Lauter. A stranger in a mountain town is revealed to be a werewolf, created by unscrupulous scientists seeking a cure for radiation poisoning. Surprisingly tense, with attractive use of Big Bear Lake locations, and a good performance by Ritch.▶

Werewolf in a Girl's Dormitory (1961-Italian-Austrian) **84m.** BOMB D: Richard Benson (Paolo Heusch). Carl Schell, Barbara Lass, Curt Lowens, Maurice Marsac. Superintendent at school for problem girls doubles as a werewolf. Strictly bottom-of-the-barrel.▼▶

WereWolf of London (1935) **75m.** ****½** D: Stuart Walker. Henry Hull, Warner Oland, Valerie Hobson, Lester Matthews, Spring Byington. The first film about werewolves is dated but still effective. Scientist Hull stumbles onto curse of lycanthropy and terrorizes London as a mad killer. Oland is fun as mysterious man who warns Hull of impending doom.▼▶●

Werewolf of Washington, The (1973) **C-90m.** ***½** D: Milton Moses Ginsberg. Dean Stockwell, Biff McGuire, Clifton James, Beeson Carroll, Thayer David, Jane House, Michael Dunn. Juvenile attempt to mix Watergate horrors with the more traditional kind. For the curious only. [PG] ▼▶

Wes Craven Presents: Dracula 2000 (2000) **C-105m.** ****** D: Patrick Lussier. Jonny Lee Miller, Christopher Plummer, Justine Waddell, Gerard Butler, Colleen Fitzpatrick, Jennifer Esposito, Danny Masterson, Jeri Ryan, Lochlyn Munro, Sean Patrick Harris, Omar Epps, Shane West. Miller heads to New Orleans to save a sweet young thing from the charms of cinema's most famous bloodsucker (Butler). Perhaps the only film in history that manages to get its producer's name, lead character and release date all in the official title, this modern-day take on the vampire classic shows why some characters are best left in their own era. Has a few good moments and better performances than you might expect. Followed by two direct-to-video sequels. Super 35. [R]▼❶

Wes Craven Presents: They SEE: **They**

Wes Craven's New Nightmare (1994) C-112m. ******* D: Wes Craven. Robert Englund, Heather Langenkamp, Miko Hughes, David Newsom, Sara Risher, Robert Shaye, Wes Craven, John Saxon, Jeffrey John Davis. Actress Heather Langenkamp, having nightmares about the fictional murderer Freddy Krueger, gradually learns that the NIGHTMARE movies were protecting the world from a monstrous demon, who has taken on the persona of Freddy and is acting out the events in Wes Craven's new NIGHTMARE script as he writes them. And the script doesn't look like it will have a happy ending. . . . Langenkamp, Wes Craven, and others associated with the NIGHTMARE ON ELM STREET series play themselves in this complex, sophisticated thriller. Scary, intelligent, and witty, but it's also too long, and the last twenty minutes are a bit of a letdown. Followed by FREDDY VS. JASON. [R]▼❶❶

Westerner, The (1940) **100m.** *****½** D: William Wyler. Gary Cooper, Walter Brennan, Fred Stone, Doris Davenport, Forrest Tucker, Chill Wills, Dana Andrews, Tom Tyler, Lillian Bond. Excellent tale of land disputes getting out of hand in the old West, with Brennan's mercurial Judge Roy Bean winning him his third Oscar. Tucker's film debut. Also shown in computer-colored version.▼❶❶

Western Union (1941) **C-94m.** ******* D: Fritz Lang. Robert Young, Randolph Scott, Dean Jagger, Virginia Gilmore, John Carradine, Slim Summerville, Chill Wills, Barton MacLane. Big-scale Western, in gorgeous Technicolor, focuses on renegade attempts to thwart Western Union on the last leg of its westward expansion in the 1860s. Entertaining, if not terribly inspired.▼

We Still Kill the Old Way (1967-Italian) **C-92m.** ****** D: Elio Petri. Irene Papas, Gian Maria Volonte, Luigi Pistilli. Crimes of honor in old Sicily purport to show old-world Mafia methods; actually nothing more than a small revenge film.

West Point Story, The (1950) **107m.** ****½** D: Roy Del Ruth. James Cagney, Virginia Mayo, Doris Day, Gordon MacRae, Gene Nelson, Alan Hale, Jr., Jack Kelly, Roland Winters. Silly but watchable musical about a Broadway director staging a revue at West Point. Wait till you hear "The Military Polka." Cagney hoofs in several numbers with Day and Mayo.▼❶

West Side Story (1961) **C-151m.** ********

D: Robert Wise, Jerome Robbins. Natalie Wood, Richard Beymer, George Chakiris, Rita Moreno, Russ Tamblyn, Tucker Smith, David Winters, Tony Mordente, Simon Oakland, John Astin. Vivid film adaptation of the landmark Broadway musical, updating Romeo and Juliet story to youth-gang atmosphere of late 1950s N.Y.C. Wood and Beymer lack charisma, but everything surrounding them is great: Robbins' choreography, Leonard Bernstein–Stephen Sondheim score (including "Maria," "America," and "Something's Coming"). Script by Ernest Lehman, from Arthur Laurents' play. Winner of 10 Academy Awards including Best Picture, Direction, Supporting Actor and Actress (Chakiris, Moreno), Cinematography, Costumes, Art Direction-Set Decoration, Editing, Scoring; Robbins earned a special award for his choreography. Super Panavision 70.▼❶❶

Westward the Women (1951) **118m.** ******* D: William Wellman. Robert Taylor, Denise Darcel, Beverly Dennis, John McIntire, Hope Emerson, Lenore Lonergan, Julie Bishop, Marilyn Erskine. Intriguing Western with Taylor heading wagon train full of females bound for California to meet mail-order husbands. Based on a story by Frank Capra. Also shown in computer-colored version.▼

Westworld (1973) **C-88m.** ******* D: Michael Crichton. Richard Benjamin, Yul Brynner, James Brolin, Norman Bartold, Alan Oppenheimer, Victoria Shaw, Steve Franken. Adult vacation resort of the future offers opportunity to live in various fantasy worlds serviced by robots. Benjamin chooses old-time Western town, but begins to fear when the robots begin malfunctioning. Engaging story by Crichton; followed by FUTUREWORLD. Panavision. [PG]▼❶

Wetherby (1985-British) **C-97m.** ****½** D: David Hare. Vanessa Redgrave, Joely Richardson, Judi Dench, Ian Holm, Tim McInnerny, Suzanna Hamilton, Tom Wilkinson. Uninvited guest shows up for dinner at a Yorkshire schoolteacher's, then returns the next day to blow his brains out. Writer David Hare's first film as director has some excellent performances and occasionally biting dialogue but is far too self-consciously gloomy. Richardson, radiant as the younger Redgrave in the flashbacks, is real-life daughter of Vanessa and director Tony Richardson. [R]▼❶

We Think the World of You (1988-British) **C-94m.** ******* D: Colin Gregg. Alan Bates, Gary Oldman, Frances Barber, Liz Smith, Max Wall, Kerry Wise. In 1950s London, middle-aged Bates becomes entwined in the lives of imprisoned boyfriend Oldman's working-class family, and Oldman's pet dog in particular. Diverting comedy-drama of unrequited love, adapted by Hugh Stoddart from Joseph R. Ackerley's semiautobiographical novel. A must for animal lovers... and romantics. [PG]▼●

Wet Hot American Summer (2001) C-97m. *** D: David Wain. Janeane Garofalo, David Hyde Pierce, Michael Showalter, Marguerite Moreau, Paul Rudd, Zak Orth, Christopher Meloni, A.D. Miles, Molly Shannon, Gideon Jacobs, Bradley Cooper, Amy Poehler, Elizabeth Banks, Judah Friedlander, Ken Marino, Michael Ian Black. It's late August, 1981, on the final day of summer camp in Maine. Garofalo plays camp director trying (not too hard) to have some semblance of regimen as the counselors and campers—all of them either oversexed or undersexed—prepare to depart. Send-up of 1970s/'80s teen flicks is subversive fun, with a lot of heart amid the satire. Made by several members of MTV sketch-comedy group, The State. [R]▼▶

We Were Soldiers (2002) C-137m. ** D: Randall Wallace. Mel Gibson, Madeleine Stowe, Greg Kinnear, Sam Elliott, Chris Klein, Keri Russell, Barry Pepper, Don Duong, Ryan Hurst, Marc Blucas, Jon Hamm, Clark Gregg, Desmond Harrington, Dylan Walsh. Lt. Col. Hal Moore (Gibson) leads U.S. forces into their first battle in Vietnam in November 1965, and while the results are bloody, he inspires his men to fight with honor and promises he will leave none behind. Gibson is square jawed, almost corny (like the film itself—especially in home-front scenes), but an old-fashioned war film would have made its point without so much graphic violence. Based on the book *We Were Soldiers Once... and Young* by Moore and Joseph Galloway. Panavision. [R]▼▶

We Were Strangers (1949) 106m. *** D: John Huston. Jennifer Jones, John Garfield, Pedro Armendariz, Gilbert Roland, Ramon Novarro. Intense, intriguing political drama of Garfield and Jones joining with the Cuban underground in a plot to overthrow the government. Well directed by Huston; Garfield is fine, but Roland steals the film as one of the revolutionaries. Scripted by Huston and Peter Viertel.▶

We Will All Meet in Paradise (1977-French) C-110m. **½ D: Yves Robert. Jean Rochefort, Claude Brasseur, Guy Bedos, Victor Lanoux, Daniele Delorme, Daniel Gelin. The trials and hangups of four boyish middle-aged Frenchmen. Cheerful but slight sex comedy; follow-up to PARDON MON AFFAIRE, and not as good. Aka PARDON MON AFFAIRE, TOO. Panavision. [PG]▼

Whale Rider (2003-New Zealand) C-101m. ***½ D: Niki Caro. Keisha Castle-Hughes, Rawiri Paratene, Vicky Haughton, Cliff Curtis. Contemporary retelling of an ancient Maori legend in which a young girl must go against all odds—and tradition—to prove to her grandfather that she is a natural leader. Film's title indicates where the picture is

headed, but that doesn't diminish its inspirational tone. Powered by a thrilling debut performance by Castle-Hughes, who never strikes a false note. Shot on the East Coast of New Zealand's North Island, this is a family film in the best sense of the term, with standout cinematography and musical score. Based on the book by Witi Ihimaera. Super 35. [PG-13]▼▶

Whales of August, The (1987) C-90m. ***½ D: Lindsay Anderson. Bette Davis, Lillian Gish, Vincent Price, Ann Sothern, Harry Carey, Jr., Margaret Ladd, Tisha Sterling, Mary Steenburgen. Two elderly sisters live together in a cottage in Maine, with ever-patient Gish forced to care for blind and irascible Davis... who may be turning senile. Sothern is their ebullient friend and neighbor, Carey their veteran handyman, and Price a courtly Russian émigré who works his charms on the ladies; they're all terrific, but Gish and Davis dominate the film, a lifetime of movie memories in each classic face. An exquisitely delicate film, adapted by David Berry from his play, and beautifully directed by Anderson (in his American debut). Tisha Sterling, Sothern's real-life daughter, plays Sothern as a young woman in opening scene. Gish's and Sothern's last film.▼●▶

What SEE: **Whip and the Body, The**

What? (1973-Italian) C-112m. **½ D: Roman Polanski. Sydne Rome, Marcello Mastroianni, Hugh Griffith, Romolo Valli, Guido Alberti, Roman Polanski. Ribald comedy about gorgeous innocent who stays at mansion of eccentric millionaire and can't understand all the commotion she causes. Change-of-pace for Polanski is agreeable, if not outstanding; good cast—especially underrated Rome—keeps things bubbling. Later cut to 94m. and reissued as DIARY OF FORBIDDEN DREAMS. Todd-AO 35. [R]▼

What About Bob? (1991) C-99m. *** D: Frank Oz. Bill Murray, Richard Dreyfuss, Julie Hagerty, Charlie Korsmo, Kathryn Erbe, Tom Aldredge, Susan Willis, Roger Bowen, Fran Brill, Doris Belack. Phobic patient Murray pursues pompous psychiatrist Dreyfuss to his vacation retreat, where he ingratiates himself with the shrink's family—and drives the doctor crazy. Very funny outing, with Murray and Dreyfuss approaching the relationship of the Road Runner and the Coyote. Only at the very end does it succumb to silliness. [PG]▼●▶

What a Girl Wants (2003) C-100m. **½ D: Dennie Gordon. Amanda Bynes, Colin Firth, Kelly Preston, Eileen Atkins, Anna Chancellor, Jonathan Pryce, Oliver James, Christina Cole. Teenage girl (Bynes), raised by her bohemian mother in N.Y.C., travels to England to meet her father, a British lord, for the first time. While her arrival disrupts his campaign to run for Parliament, he wants her to stay—unlike his scheming fiancée and her snooty daughter. Cute comedy for adolescents showcases the perky TV star and an expert cast of adults. Remake of THE RELUCTANT DEBUTANTE. Super 35. [PG] ▼▐

What Alice Found (2003) C-96m. **½ D: A. Dean Bell. Judith Ivey, Bill Raymond, Emily Grace, Jane Lincoln Taylor, Justin Parkinson, Tim Hayes, Lucas Papaelias, Katheryn Winnick. Young woman without much of a future meets a seemingly friendly couple (Ivey and Raymond) at a gas station and soon becomes part of their surprising, somewhat seedy lifestyle. Best not to know too much about this extremely low-budget film and let it take you into its well-defined world of trailer trash roaming the South. Very explicit sexual situations (not to mention rough, digital camerawork) make this drama an acquired taste, but Ivey has the role of a lifetime and she runs with it. [R] ▼▐

What a Way to Go! (1964) C-111m. *** D: J. Lee Thompson. Shirley MacLaine, Paul Newman, Robert Mitchum, Dean Martin, Gene Kelly, Bob Cummings, Dick Van Dyke, Reginald Gardiner, Margaret Dumont, Fifi D'Orsay. Lavish, episodic black comedy by Betty Comden and Adolph Green stars MacLaine as jinx who marries succession of men, each of whom promptly dies, leaving her even wealthier than before. Series of movie parodies is amusing, and performances are uniformly charming, especially Newman as obsessed painter and Kelly as egotistical film star. Based on a story by Gwen Davis. One of the dancers on boat deck is Teri Garr. CinemaScope. ▐

What Became of Jack and Jill? (1972-British) C-93m. **½ D: Bill Bain. Vanessa Howard, Paul Nicholas, Mona Washbourne, Peter Copley, Peter Jeffrey. Game attempt at detailing modern day, no-holds-barred love affair twisted by intrusion of grandmother; defeated by smug script, odd point of view. [PG]

What Did You Do in the War, Daddy? (1966) C-119m. *** D: Blake Edwards. James Coburn, Dick Shawn, Sergio Fantoni, Aldo Ray, Harry Morgan, Carroll O'Connor, Leon Askin, Giovanna Ralli. A not too funny but quite pleasant film about group of misfit American soldiers trying to tame wacky Italian town into surrender. Written by William Peter Blatty; O'Connor's blustery performance led to his being cast in *All in the Family*. Panavision. ▼▐

What Doesn't Kill You (2008) C-100m. *** D: Brian Goodman. Mark Ruffalo, Ethan Hawke, Amanda Peet, Will Lyman, Brian Goodman, Donnie Wahlberg, Angela Featherstone. Two boys grow to manhood in South Boston doing errands for a local racketeer, but when one of them tries to go straight for the sake of his family he faces the greatest challenge of his life. Strong performances by Hawke and especially Ruffalo make this tough movie well worth seeing. Cowritten by Wahlberg, Paul T. Murray, and first-time director Goodman, who also costars as Pat Kelly—and lived this story. Super 35. [R] ▐

What Do You Say to a Naked Lady? (1970) C-90m. *** D: Allen Funt. Amusing risqué *Candid Camera* effort. Accent is on sex, and some of the reactions to stunts, and queries, are hilarious. Look for Richard Roundtree! [R—edited from original X rating] ▼

What Dreams May Come (1998) C-113m. BOMB D: Vincent Ward. Robin Williams, Cuba Gooding, Jr., Annabella Sciorra, Max von Sydow, Rosalind Chao, Matt Salinger, Werner Herzog, Lucinda Jenney. Off-putting gobbledygook about a man who loses his kids in a car accident, then dies himself, and tries to reach out to his loving, grieving wife on earth. Despite its pedigree (a novel by Richard Matheson, a good director and cast), this film fails to evoke any tangible emotions. It just doesn't work. Its elaborate (in fact, overelaborate) special effects won an Oscar. Super 35. [PG-13] ▼▐●

Whatever (1998) C-112m. *** D: Susan Skoog. Liza Weil, Chad Morgan, Kathryn Rossetter, Frederic Forrest, Gary Wolf, Dan Montano. Sensitive, at times disturbing, portrait of a teenage girl (Weil) coming of age circa 1981, dealing with sex, drugs, and her reckless party-girl best friend (Morgan). Has the texture of a Joyce Carol Oates short story and features a terrific performance by Weil. Written by the director. Good period soundtrack featuring Iggy Pop, Blondie, The Ramones, and The Pretenders. [R] ▼●

What Ever Happened to Aunt Alice? (1969) C-101m. *** D: Lee H. Katzin. Geraldine Page, Ruth Gordon, Rosemary Forsyth, Robert Fuller, Mildred Dunnock. Eccentric Page stays wealthy by murdering her housekeepers, stealing their savings. Gordon hires on as next "victim," trying to solve missing-persons mystery. Played to the hilt; most enjoyable. [M/PG] ▼▐

What Ever Happened to Baby Jane? (1962) 132m. ***½ D: Robert Aldrich. Bette Davis, Joan Crawford, Victor Buono, Marjorie Bennett, Anna Lee. Far-fetched, thoroughly engaging black comedy of two former movie stars; Joan's a cripple at the mercy of demented sister Baby Jane Hudson (Davis). Bette has a field day in her macabre characterization, with Buono a perfect match. Triggered a decade-long spate of older female stars in horror films. Script by Lukas Heller, from Henry Farrell's novel. Remade for TV in 1991 with Vanessa and Lynn Redgrave. ▼▐●

Whatever It Takes (2000) C-94m. ** D: David Raynr (Hubbard). James Franco, Marla Sokoloff, Jodi Lyn O'Keefe, Shane West, Aaron Paul, Richard Schiff, Julia

Sweeney. Latest screen variation on *Cyrano de Bergerac* is just one more teen-comedy-of-the-week. When dumb jock Franco can't get to first base with Sokoloff, he asks her platonic next-door neighbor (West) to intervene and supply him romantic "material." As reward, he'll set up his newfound cohort with his school-dish cousin (O'Keefe)—who, in typical bad-movie fashion, is much less attractive than the next-door gal-pal. Movie is a bust down the middle, but director Raynr has some fun around the edges. [PG-13]▼▶

Whatever Works (2009) **C-92m.** **½ D: Woody Allen. Larry David, Evan Rachel Wood, Patricia Clarkson, Ed Begley, Jr., Michael McKean, Conleth Hill, Henry Cavill, John Gallagher, Jr., Jessica Hecht, Carolyn McCormick, Christopher Evan Welch. David (of *Curb Your Enthusiasm* fame) is no actor, but he does his best as a N.Y.C. misanthrope who relates his unusual story directly to us: alone and happy to be (since he feels superior to everyone around him), he takes in a homeless waif from Mississippi (Wood) and, to his surprise, actually begins to like the simpleminded girl. Typical Allenesque fable is off-putting at first, and may remain so for those who aren't attuned to Woody Allen . . . but finds warmth and optimism by the time of the fade-out. [PG-13]▶

What Goes Up (2009) **C-107m.** ** D: Jonathan Glatzer. Steve Coogan, Hilary Duff, Molly Price, Olivia Thirlby, Josh Peck, Molly Shannon, Max Hoffman, Andrea Brooks, Ingrid Nilson, Laura Konechny. Interesting but odd, sometimes off-putting film, set in 1986, about a cynical N.Y.C. newspaper reporter who goes to New Hampshire to write about a teacher who's traveling on the NASA Space Shuttle. Instead he falls in with a group of misfit high school kids who are mourning the death of a teacher who was their champion—and hero. Well acted but it's uncertain what the point is supposed to be. [R]▶

What Happened Was . . . (1993) **C-91m.** *** D: Tom Noonan. Tom Noonan, Karen Sillas. Revealing, extremely well-acted two-character drama follows what happens to two lonely, mismatched coworkers as they experience their first date. Original film is set in real time, on one set; anyone who's ever gone on a first date will surely relate to this material. Actor Noonan also scripted and made his directorial debut with this impressive film. [R]▼▶

What Happens in Vegas (2008) **C-99m.** **½ D: Tom Vaughan. Cameron Diaz, Ashton Kutcher, Rob Corddry, Lake Bell, Jason Sudeikis, Treat Williams, Deirdre O'Connell, Michelle Krusiec, Zach Galifianakis, Queen Latifah, Dennis Farina, Dennis Miller. Super-organized Diaz, dumped by her fiancé, and irresponsible Kutcher,

fired by his father from the family business, both seek escape in Las Vegas—and wind up married to one another after a drunken evening. But dissolving the union becomes a challenge when a judge orders them to live together for six months. About what you'd expect, especially as the duo engage in dirty tricks, but as the film goes on it becomes more benign and entertaining—boosted by the two stars' engaging personalities. Super 35. [PG-13]▶

What Have I Done to Deserve This? (1985-Spanish) **C-100m.** *** D: Pedro Almodóvar. Carmen Maura, Chus Lampreave, Veronica Forque, Kiti Manver. Off-the-wall black comedy about an off-the-wall housewife (delightfully played by Maura) and her various trials and escapades. A fresh, original film, featuring a feminist heroine of classic proportions.▼▶

What Just Happened (2008) **C-104m.** *** D: Barry Levinson. Robert De Niro, Sean Penn, Catherine Keener, John Turturro, Robin Wright Penn, Stanley Tucci, Kristen Stewart, Michael Wincott, Bruce Willis. Hotshot producer De Niro attempts to maintain appearances while juggling demands of studio heads, wobbly investors, ex- (or soon to be ex-) wives and childish, tantrum-causing stars in this darkly funny tale that answers the question, "What does a producer do?" Cutting so close to the bone it could only have been scripted by one who has walked the walk, this was based on producer Art Linson's autobiographical book. Should hold special appeal for those who appreciate Hollywood's ability to take itself to task while providing a few, albeit uncomfortable, laughs. Super 35. [R]▶

What Lies Beneath (2000) **C-126m.** **½ D: Robert Zemeckis. Harrison Ford, Michelle Pfeiffer, Diana Scarwid, Miranda Otto, James Remar, Joe Morton, Amber Valletta, Wendy Crewson. Happily married woman senses the presence of a ghost in her idyllic Vermont home—could her husband have anything to do with it? Slickly made, with plenty of scares, but after a red-herring subplot is over, the ultimate story twist doesn't make sense . . . and there are at least three endings! Panavision. [PG-13]▼▶

What Love Is (2007) **C-88m.** *½ D: Mars Callahan. Cuba Gooding, Jr., Matthew Lillard, Sean Astin, Mars Callahan, Andrew Daly, Gina Gershon, Anne Heche, Tamala Jones, Shiri Appleby, Jud Tylor, Terrence "T.C." Carson. On Valentine's Day, Gooding is dumped by his live-in lover. He commiserates with four of his pals, each of whom is a stereotype; they're eventually joined by five equally one-dimensional women. This loud, trite mess of a movie appears to have been edited with a hacksaw. It holds your interest . . . but not for the right reasons. Callahan also scripted, and casts himself as the most grounded of the men;

Lillard chews the scenery as the most misogynistic. [R]▶

What Planet Are You From? (2000) C-105m. **½ D: Mike Nichols. Garry Shandling, Annette Bening, Greg Kinnear, Ben Kingsley, Linda Fiorentino, John Goodman, Richard Jenkins, Caroline Aaron, Judy Greer, Nora Dunn, Ann Cusack, Camryn Manheim, Jane Lynch, Cathy Ladman. Alien is sent to earth by his planet with the mandate to find a woman who will bear his child. The last thing the interplanetary visitor expects to experience is genuine love and caring. If you're a Shandling fan, you may cut this comedy more slack than others will; it's low-key and somewhat predictable, but surprisingly good-natured. Shandling cowrote the script. Janeane Garofalo and Sarah Silverman appear unbilled. [R]▼▶

What Price Glory (1926) 120m. *** D: Raoul Walsh. Victor McLaglen, Edmund Lowe, Dolores Del Rio, William V. Mong, Phyllis Haver, Leslie Fenton, Barry Norton. Boisterous rivalry between Capt. Flagg (McLaglen) and Sgt. Quirt (Lowe) centers on lovely Charmaine (Del Rio) when they go to France during WW1. Zesty comedy, with plenty of fireworks for lip-readers, abruptly turns grim as focus shifts to horrors of war, only to return to Flagg-Quirt hijinks for finale. Fine entertainment, from Laurence Stallings–Maxwell Anderson play; two main characters reappeared in a handful of follow-ups, none of them as good as this. Remade in 1952.▼▶

What Price Glory (1952) C-111m. **½ D: John Ford. James Cagney, Corinne Calvet, Dan Dailey, Robert Wagner, Marisa Pavan, James Gleason. Classic silent film becomes shallow Cagney-Dailey vehicle of battling Army men Flagg and Quirt in WW1 France.▼▶

What Price Hollywood? (1932) 88m. *** D: George Cukor. Constance Bennett, Lowell Sherman, Neil Hamilton, Gregory Ratoff, Brooks Benedict. Soused movie director Sherman helps waitress Bennett fulfill her ambition to become a movie star—while he sinks into alcoholic ruin. Surprisingly sharp-eyed look at Hollywood—both comic and dramatic—that served as inspiration for later A STAR IS BORN. From a story by Adela Rogers St. Johns.▼●

What's Cooking? (2000-U.S.-British) C-109m. **½ D: Gurinder Chadha. Alfre Woodard, Mercedes Ruehl, Joan Chen, Kyra Sedgwick, Julianna Margulies, Dennis Haysbert, A Martinez, Lainie Kazan, Maury Chaykin, Victor Rivers, Douglas Spain, Estelle Harris, Will Yun Lee. Mosaic of four ethnic families—black, Asian, Latino, Jewish—preparing for Thanksgiving in L.A., and dealing with a variety of domestic crises. Soapy at times, but the film has heart and occasional insights; bolstered by an excellent cast. [PG-13]▼▶

What's Eating Gilbert Grape (1993) C-117m. **½ D: Lasse Hallström. Johnny Depp, Leonardo DiCaprio, Juliette Lewis, Mary Steenburgen, Darlene Cates, Laura Harrington, Mary Kate Schellhardt, Kevin Tighe, John C. Reilly, Crispin Glover, Penelope Branning. Middling slice-of-life about a young man in a dead-end town saddled with the responsibility of caring for his retarded younger brother, and depressed by his obese mother, who hasn't left the house in seven years. You keep thinking something significant is going to happen, but nothing ever does; still, there are some poignant vignettes and first-rate performances (especially by newcomer Cates, as the mom). [PG-13]▼●

What's Good for the Goose (1969-British) C-105m. BOMB D: Menahem Golan. Norman Wisdom, Sally Geeson, Sally Bazely, Sarah Atkinson, Terence Alexander. Weak, unfunny, sex romp wherein the object is to score as often as possible. Skip it. [R]▼▶

What's Love Got to Do With It (1993) C-119m. *** D: Brian Gibson. Angela Bassett, Laurence Fishburne, Vanessa Bell Calloway, Jenifer Lewis, Rae'ven Kelly, Phyllis Yvonne Stickney, Chi (Chi McBride), Khandi Alexander, Penny Johnson, Robert Guy Miranda, Pamela Tyson, Barry Shabaka Henley. Highly charged musical bio of singer Tina Turner, who joined r&b musician Ike Turner as a naive teenager and went on to become a dynamic performer—all the while suffering various forms of abuse at home. Vivid, immediate, and persuasive (though Tina's personality is never explored, and she's painted as something of a saint), but the real attraction here is the phenomenal performances of Bassett and Fishburne as Tina and Ike. Based on *I, Tina* by Turner and Kurt Loder. [R]▼●

What's New Pussycat? (1965) C-108m. ** D: Clive Donner. Peter Sellers, Peter O'Toole, Romy Schneider, Capucine, Paula Prentiss, Woody Allen, Ursula Andress. Disturbed fashion editor O'Toole goes to psychiatrist Sellers for help with his romantic problems, but Sellers is even crazier than he. Woody Allen's first feature as actor and writer, and like many of his comedies, one sits through a lot of misfired gags to get to a few undeniable gems. Hit title song by Burt Bacharach and Hal David.▼●

What's So Bad About Feeling Good? (1968) C-94m. **½ D: George Seaton. George Peppard, Mary Tyler Moore, Dom DeLuise, John McMartin, Don Stroud, Nathaniel Frey, Susan Saint James, Charles Lane, Thelma Ritter. Amiable attempt at old-fashioned Capraesque comedy, with pixillated toucan spreading good feeling throughout N.Y.C. Doesn't hit bull's-eye, but has its moments. Written by Seaton and

Robert Pirosh. Look for Cleavon Little, Moses Gunn. Techniscope.

What's the Matter with Helen? (1971) **C-101m.** ******* D: Curtis Harrington. Debbie Reynolds, Shelley Winters, Dennis Weaver, Agnes Moorehead, Michael MacLiammoir. Campy murder tale set in 1930s. Reynolds and Winters try to erase their sordid past, start anew in Hollywood with school for talented kids. Good fun; Debbie ideal in period setting. Written by Henry Farrell. [PG]▼❍

What's the Worst That Could Happen? (2001) **C-95m.** ****½** D: Sam Weisman. Martin Lawrence, Danny DeVito, John Leguizamo, Glenne Headly, Carmen Ejogo, Bernie Mac, Larry Miller, Nora Dunn, Richard Schiff, William Fichtner, Ana Gasteyer, Siobhan Fallon. Uninspired comedy about a thief who has the tables turned on him by his latest "victim," crooked business tycoon DeVito—and swears vengeance at any cost. Good cast does what it can with a mediocre script, based on the comic crime novel by Donald E. Westlake. [PG-13]▼❍

What's Up, Doc? (1972) **C-94m.** ******* D: Peter Bogdanovich. Barbra Streisand, Ryan O'Neal, Kenneth Mars, Austin Pendleton, Madeline Kahn, Sorrell Booke, Michael Murphy, Liam Dunn, John Hillerman, M. Emmet Walsh. Modern-day screwball comedy with impish Streisand making life miserable for stuffy musicologist O'Neal and his fiancée (Kahn, in feature debut), becoming involved in mixup over stolen jewels. Great comic chase scenes highlight overpowering farce, Bogdanovich's bouquet to 1930s Hollywood (and BRINGING UP BABY in particular). Look for John Byner and Randy Quaid at the hotel banquet. [G]▼❍●

What's Up, Tiger Lily? (1966) **C-80m.** ******* Compiled by Woody Allen. Japanese version directed by Senkichi Taniguchi. Tatsuya Mihashi, Miya Hana, Eiko Wakabayashi, Tadao Nakamura, Woody Allen, China Lee. Slick Japanese imitation James Bond movie (KAGI NO KAG, or KEY OF KEYS, released in 1964) is redubbed by Allen into one long, very funny joke. The object of international intrigue is a valued egg-salad recipe, and the main characters are named Phil Moscowitz, Terri Yaki, and Suki Yaki. Music by The Lovin' Spoonful (who also appear in the film). One of the new voices is Louise Lasser. Tohoscope. ▼❍●

What the Bleep Do We Know!? (2004) **C/B&W-108m.** ****½** D: Mark Vicente, Betsy Chasse, William Arntz. Marlee Matlin, Elaine Hendrix, Barry Newman, Robert Bailey, Jr., Armin Shimerman, John Ross Bowie. Curious, ambitious narrative-documentary hybrid attempts to explore the physical, the metaphysical, and the nature of reality. As various real-life experts discuss quantum physics, a fictional photographer (Matlin) sets out to probe the essence of her being. Some surrealistic animation sequences are thrown

in for good measure. Filled with imagination, good intentions, and plenty of New Age philosophizing, this little film understandably became a word-of-mouth success. The fictional sequences don't work nearly as well as the provocative nonfiction content. Followed by a direct-to-video sequel, WHAT THE BLEEP DO WE KNOW?: DOWN THE RABBIT HOLE. Aka WHAT THE #\$*! DO WE KNOW!? ▼❍

What Time is it There? (2001-Taiwanese-French) **C-116m.** ****** D: Ming-liang Tsai. Kang-sheng Lee, Shiang-chyi Chen, Yi-ching Lu, Tien Miao, Jean-Pierre Léaud. Street vendor falls for a girl on her way to Paris and sets about changing all the clocks in his home city of Taipei to French time as he thinks only of her. Odd, extremely drawn-out premise shows off Tsai's directorial talents but at the end is a bit of a "so-what." Look for legendary Truffaut star Léaud playing himself. ▼❍

What Waits Below (1985) **C-88m.** ****** D: Don Sharp. Robert Powell, Lisa Blount, Timothy Bottoms, Richard Johnson, Anne Heywood, Liam Sullivan. Disappointing fantasy thriller of archaeologists stumbling upon a lost race of Lemurians living in South American caves. Effects aren't very special; a good cast is wasted. [PG]▼

What Women Want (2000) **C-126m.** ******* D: Nancy Meyers. Mel Gibson, Helen Hunt, Marisa Tomei, Mark Feuerstein, Lauren Holly, Ashley Johnson, Alan Alda, Judy Greer, Valerie Perrine, Delta Burke, Sarah Paulson, Ana Gasteyer, Lisa Edelstein, Loretta Devine. Entertaining comedy about a cocky, chauvinistic ad agency exec who magically acquires the ability to hear what women are thinking. He puts this to especially good use with his new superior (Hunt), whose job he was in line to get. Smart, likable film lacks only a solid punchline. Bette Midler appears unbilled. Remade in China(!) in 2010. [PG-13]▼❍

Wheeler Dealers, The (1963) **C-106m.** ******* D: Arthur Hiller. Lee Remick, James Garner, Jim Backus, Phil Harris, Shelley Berman, Chill Wills, John Astin, Louis Nye. Funny, fast-moving spoof of Texas millionaires who play with investments just for fun. Garner also catches Lee Remick along the way. Panavision. ▼❍

Wheel of Fortune SEE: **Man Betrayed, A**

Wheels of Terror SEE: **Misfit Brigade, The**

When a Man Loves a Woman (1994) **C-125m.** ****½** D: Luis Mandoki. Andy Garcia, Meg Ryan, Ellen Burstyn, Tina Majorino, Mae Whitman, Lauren Tom, Philip Seymour Hoffman, Eugene Roche, Gail Strickland. Wife and mother of two is forced to deal with the fact that she's an alcoholic . . . but her husband soon learns that he has as much to deal with as she does. Ryan gives a standout performance in this surprisingly frank exploration of the trauma this kind of disease can cause to a family. The film succeeds more as tract than entertainment, however. [R]▼●)

When a Stranger Calls (1979) **C-97m.** *½ D: Fred Walton. Carol Kane, Charles Durning, Colleen Dewhurst, Tony Beckley, Rachel Roberts, Ron O'Neal. Psycho murders two children after terrorizing their babysitter, returns seven years later to extend his crime. Unpleasant, improbable melodrama falls apart after OK opening segment. Based on a short subject called THE SITTER. Followed, over a decade later, by a TV sequel. Remade in 2006. [R]▼●)

When a Stranger Calls (2006) **C-87m.** *½ D: Simon West. Camilla Belle, Tommy Flanagan, Katie Cassidy, Tessa Thompson, Brian Geraghty, Clark Gregg, Derek De Lint; voice of Lance Henriksen. Remake of 1979 movie in which a babysitter is haunted by repeated phone calls that grow more terrifying as she realizes they are coming from within the house. More graphic and obvious than its predecessor and the 1993 TV movie follow-up WHEN A STRANGER CALLS BACK, geared to a generation that likes its horror in nonstop vivid close-ups rather than gradually revealed. Why this one-note concept has been so durable is a bigger mystery than anything in the film. What's next? WHEN A STRANGER E-MAILS? Super 35. [PG-13]❘

When Brendan Met Trudy (2000-Irish-British) **C-95m.** *** D: Kieron J. Walsh. Peter McDonald, Flora Montgomery, Marie Mullen, Pauline McLynn, Maynard Eziashi. Charming bit of blarney about a pair of misfit lovers: a straitlaced boys' school teacher and a free-spirited woman who just happens to be a cat burglar. Brendan's other love is movies, which results in some clever homages to BREATHLESS, THE SEARCHERS, and SUNSET BLVD. McDonald and Montgomery are appealing screwball leads. Written by Roddy Doyle.

When Comedy Was King (1960) **81m.** **** Compiled by Robert Youngson. Charlie Chaplin, Buster Keaton, Laurel and Hardy, Ben Turpin, Fatty Arbuckle, Wallace Beery, Gloria Swanson. Second Youngson compilation of silent comedy clips has many classic scenes. Chaplin, Keaton, L & H, Keystone Kops, Charley Chase, and others shine in this outstanding film.▼●)

When Did You Last See Your Father? (2007-British) **C-92m.** **½ D: Anand Tucker. Jim Broadbent, Colin Firth, Juliet Stevenson, Gina McKee, Matthew Beard, Sarah Lancashire, Elaine Cassidy, Carey Mulligan. Firth attends to his aged father, now a bedridden invalid, but can't help thinking about his teenage years when everything his father did caused him embarrassment—including the old man's womanizing. Well acted but bland and uninvolving. Based on Blake Morrison's best-selling memoir. Panavision. [PG-13]❘

When Dinosaurs Ruled the Earth (1970-British) **C-99m.** *** D: Val Guest. Victoria Vetri, Robin Hawdon, Patrick Allen, Drewe Henley, Imogen Hassall, Magda Konopka, Patrick Holt. Fast-paced, enjoyable prehistoric actioner with Vetri and Hawdon lovers ostracized by respective tribes. Beautiful locations, very good special effects by Jim Danforth, and honorable attempt to simulate period, although Vetri (*Playboy*'s 1968 Playmate of the Year—then known as Angela Dorian) seems to have ordered her wardrobe from Frederick's of Bedrock. Story by J. G. Ballard. Original U.S. release was cut by 3m. to earn G rating. [G]▼●)

When Do We Eat? (2006) **C-93m.** ** D: Salvador Litvak. Michael Lerner, Lesley Ann Warren, Jack Klugman, Meredith Scott Lynn, Shiri Appleby, Milli Avital, Ben Feldman, Cynda Williams. Oy vey! Misbegotten, over-the-top ethnic comedy about a disastrous Passover Seder meal has lots of dysfunction and shouting but little heart. The family gathering goes terribly awry when a troublemaking son slips a hallucinogenic drug into dad's drink, his wife invites a mysterious man for dinner, and the kids run amok. Mildly amusing at times, but so frenetically paced you may find yourself thinking, "When do we leave?" [R]❘

When Eight Bells Toll (1971-British) **C-94m.** ** D: Etienne Perier. Anthony Hopkins, Robert Morley, Nathalie Delon, Jack Hawkins, Ferdy Mayne, Corin Redgrave, Derek Bond. Alistair MacLean adapted his best-seller of gold piracy at sea, but the production lacks flash and finesse and Hopkins is too disagreeable a hero. Panavision. [PG]

When Father Was Away on Business (1985-Yugoslavian) **C-135m.** ***½ D: Emir Kusturica. Moreno D'E Bartolli, Miki Manojlovic, Mirjana Karanovic, Mustafa Nadarevic, Mira Furlan, Andrew Kopperud. Captivating story about a family's efforts to get along when the head of the household is sent to a labor camp for making an indiscreet remark. Told mostly through the eyes of a six-year-old boy (D'E Bartolli, whose concerns and flights of fancy are irresistible. Set in Sarajevo in the early 1950s. [R]▼❘

When Harry Met Sally . . . (1989) **C-95m.** ***½ D: Rob Reiner. Billy Crystal, Meg Ryan, Carrie Fisher, Bruno Kirby, Steven Ford, Lisa Jane Persky, Michelle Nicastro, Harley Kozak. Delightful Woody Allen-ish romantic comedy set in N.Y.C. about a man and woman who carve out a genuine friendship, and struggle to keep it from becoming a romantic attachment. Full of great dialogue and knowing remarks about the way men and women view each other. Screenplay by Nora Ephron (with some distinctive Billy Crystalisms throughout). Director Reiner's mother has the movie's single funniest line, at the end of the delicatessen scene. Later adapted for the stage. [R]▼●◗

When in Rome (2010) C-91m. ** D: Mark Steven Johnson. Kristen Bell, Josh Duhamel, Anjelica Huston, Danny DeVito, Will Arnett, Jon Heder, Dax Shepard, Alexis Dziena, Kate Micucci, Peggy Lipton, Luca Calvani, Keir O'Donnell, Lee Pace. Career-driven New Yorker goes to Rome for her sister's wedding, where she's attracted to a handsome American (Duhamel). But when she thinks he's lied to her she drunkenly wades into the "Fountain of Love" outside and removes four coins—casting a love spell over the men who have tossed them in. Bell is likable, but this chaotic romantic comedy is cluttered with meaningless gags and side trips. Celebrity cameos are as random as everything else; Don Johnson appears unbilled as Bell's father. Panavision. [PG-13]◗

When Lovers Meet SEE: **Lover Come Back** (1946)

When Night Is Falling (1995-Canadian) C-96m. *** D: Patricia Rozema. Pascale Bussières, Rachael Crawford, Henry Czerny, Don McKellar, Tracy Wright. Though essentially soft-focus lesbian eye-candy, this is also a tremendously entertaining retelling of the myth of Cupid and Psyche. Camille (Bussières), a professor at a Calvinist college engaged to marry a fellow teacher of religion (Czerny), falls for Petra (Crawford), an uninhibited circus performer. The scenes of cinema erotica resemble *Red Shoe Diaries* rather than Fellini, but the film's attitude is refreshingly tongue-in-cheek. (Also, both women are stunners and the story's sweet.) [R]▼▶

When Pigs Fly (1993-German-U.S.-Dutch) C-94m. **½ D: Sara Driver. Alfred Molina, Marianne Faithfull, Seymour Cassel, Rachel Bella, Maggie O'Neill, Freddie Brooks. Charming, oddball film about a hipster musician who's visited by a couple of ghostly spirits who need to settle accounts in their lives. With his help, they do, and of course, it helps him get his own act together. Supernatural comedy-drama is vague about where it's set; it was actually shot in Germany. Music by Joe Strummer; coexecutive-produced by Jim Jarmusch.▼

When the Cat's Away (1996-French) C-91m. *** D: Cédric Klapisch. Garance Clavel, Zinedine Soualem, Renée Le Calm, Olivier Py, Romain Duris. Sweet, deft look at a side of Paris rarely seen on-screen as a young woman returns from vacation to discover her cat has disappeared. She takes off on a journey through city streets not only to find her pet but, as it turns out, herself as well. A simple, welcome film about love and loneliness. [R]▼

When the Legends Die (1972) C-105m. *** D: Stuart Millar. Richard Widmark, Frederic Forrest, Luana Anders, Vito Scotti,

Herbert Nelson. Offbeat story of aging rodeo cowboy who cannot accept fact that years are creeping up on him, and young Indian he befriends. [PG]▼

When the North Wind Blows (1974) C-113m. **½ D: Stewart Raffill. Henry Brandon, Herbert Nelson, Dan Haggerty. A hermit trapper protects snow tigers in Siberia. Beautiful scenery; OK fare for children. [G]▼

When the Party's Over (1992) C-114m. **½ D: Matthew Irmas. Rae Dawn Chong, Fisher Stevens, Sandra Bullock, Elizabeth Berridge, Brian McNamara, Kris Kamm, Michael Landes, Stephen Meadows. Perceptive but seriously flawed, often confusing drama about making it in L.A., focusing on three women and a gay male who share a house and are involved in each other's lives. Chong (as a manipulative yuppie careerist) and Bullock (as a cynical feminist artist) are standouts. [R]▼●◗

When the Sky Falls (2000-Irish-U.S.) C-106m. *½ D: John Mackenzie. Joan Allen, Patrick Bergin, Liam Cunningham, Pete Postlethwaite, Kevin McNally, Jimmy Smallhorne. Allen plays a crusading Dublin journalist whose articles about drug gangs put her life in jeopardy. Dull, plot-heavy film (based on true story of reporter Veronica Guerin) has a surprising lack of emotional pull. U.S. debut on cable TV. Same story told in VERONICA GUERIN. ▼◗

When the Whales Came (1989-British) C-100m. ** D: Clive Rees. Paul Scofield, Helen Mirren, Helen Pearce, Max Rennie, David Suchet, David Threlfall, Barbara Jefford, Jeremy Kemp. Dull dud set in 1914 with Scofield, in a performance that's not among his best, cast as a deaf old hermit who loves birds; he lives alone on a remote island and is befriended by youngsters Rennie and Pearce (the latter a nonactor discovered on Britain's Scilly Isles, where film was made). [G]▼●

When Time Ran Out . . . (1980) C-121m. BOMB D: James Goldstone. Paul Newman, Jacqueline Bisset, William Holden, James Franciscus, Edward Albert, Red Buttons, Ernest Borgnine, Burgess Meredith, Valentina Cortesa, Veronica Hamel, Alex Karras, Barbara Carrera. WHEN IDEAS RAN OUT, or, THE BLUBBERING INFERNO: Irwin Allen's shameless rehash of all his disaster-movie clichés, set on a Pacific island, is a monumental bore that even a volcanic eruption cannot save. Written by Carl Foreman and Stirling Silliphant—who were presumably well paid. Video version runs 141m. Panavision. [PG] ▼◗

When We Were Kings (1996) C-92m. ***½ D: Leon Gast. Muhammad Ali, George Foreman, Don King, James Brown, B. B. King, Spike Lee, Norman Mailer, George Plimpton. Highly entertaining, Oscar-winning documentary about the classic 1974

"Rumble in the Jungle" matchup in Zaire of heavyweight champions Ali and Foreman. Film chronicles the preparations for the fight, and its postponement, enabling us to learn more about The Greatest in his prime than a more conventional account could ever tell us. Full of fascinating observations from the participants as well as contemporary observers like Mailer, Plimpton, and Lee. Gast spent 23 years trying to bring this film to fruition; it was well worth the wait. [PG]▼◐)

When Will I Be Loved (2004) **C-81m.** ** D: James Toback. Neve Campbell, Fred Weller, Dominic Chianese, Karen Allen, Barry Primus, Mike Tyson, Lori Singer, James Toback. On-the-make N.Y.C. bitch Campbell has taken up with obnoxious con man Weller and becomes involved in an IN-DECENT PROPOSAL–style scenario with Italian kazillionaire Chianese. Unlikable film is crammed with coldhearted characters who are obsessed with big bucks, sleazy sex, and endless hustling. Toback plays a Columbia University professor; Singer, Tyson, and various Toback buddies appear as themselves, and the film is book-ended by Campbell appearing nude in a shower. Super 35. [R] ▼◗

When Willie Comes Marching Home (1950) **82m.** **½ D: John Ford. Dan Dailey, Corinne Calvet, Colleen Townsend, William Demarest, Mae Marsh. Schmaltzy WW2 adventures of West Virginia youth Dailey, including interlude with French underground leader Calvet.◗

When Wolves Cry SEE: **Christmas Tree, The**

When Women Had Tails (1970-Italian) **C-110m.** *½ D: Pasquale Festa Campanile. Senta Berger, Giuliano Gemma, Frank Wolff, Lando Buzzanca, Aldo Giuffre. Cute, harmless but unfunny slapstick comedy with Berger a most attractive cavewoman. Lina Wertmuller cowrote the screenplay. Sequel: WHEN WOMEN LOST THEIR TAILS. [R] ▼

When Worlds Collide (1951) **C-81m.** *** D: Rudolph Maté. Richard Derr, Barbara Rush, Peter Hanson, Larry Keating, John Hoyt. Scientist tries to convince a doubting world that Earth is in path of rogue planet. Convince yourself this could happen and you'll have fun. Special effects (including submersion of Manhattan) won Oscar for this George Pal production. Based on the novel by Edwin Balmer and Philip Wylie. ▼◐)

When You Comin' Back, Red Ryder? (1979) **C-118m.** *½ D: Milton Katselas. Marjoe Gortner, Hal Linden, Lee Grant, Peter Firth, Candy Clark, Pat Hingle, Stephanie Faracy, Audra Lindley, Bill McKinney. Stagy, unpleasant film of Mark Medoff's play about a psycho terrorizing a disparate group of people in roadside diner.

Has its moments, but not enough to justify nearly two hours of viewing. [R]

Where Angels Fear to Tread (1991-British) **C-112m.** **½ D: Charles Sturridge. Helena Bonham Carter, Judy Davis, Rupert Graves, Giovanni Guidelli, Barbara Jefford, Helen Mirren, Thomas Wheatley, Sophie Kullman. Interesting drama of repressed and unleashed sexuality within the British upper class, based on E. M. Forster's first novel. The story follows events after British widow Mirren dallies with and weds a young Tuscan (Guidelli) while vacationing in Italy. Faithful to its source material, and the performances (particularly Bonham Carter's, as Mirren's traveling companion) are first-rate, but the presentation is less inspired than one would like.▼◐)

Where Angels Go . . . Trouble Follows (1968) **C-95m.** **½ D: James Neilson. Rosalind Russell, Stella Stevens, Binnie Barnes, Mary Wickes, Dolores Sutton, Susan Saint James, Barbara Hunter; guest stars Milton Berle, Arthur Godfrey, Van Johnson, William Lundigan, Robert Taylor. For *Flying Nun* fans only; contrived comedy follow-up to THE TROUBLE WITH ANGELS with Mother Superior Russell pitted against young, progressive nun Stevens. [G]▼◗

Where Are the Children? (1986) **C-92m.** *½ D: Bruce Malmuth. Jill Clayburgh, Max Gail, Harley Cross, Elisabeth Harnois, Elizabeth Wilson, Barnard Hughes, Frederic Forrest. Clayburgh's two children are kidnapped—just as, nine years before, her first two kids (by a previous marriage) also vanished. Creates some suspense but becomes more ludicrous as it unfolds. Despite a raging storm, the Cape Cod location is the most attractive aspect of the film. Based on Mary Higgins Clark's novel. [R]▼

Where Danger Lives (1950) **82m.** *** D: John Farrow. Robert Mitchum, Faith Domergue, Claude Rains, Maureen O'Sullivan, Charles Kemper, Ralph Dumke, Billy House, Jack Kelly. San Francisco doctor Mitchum falls for beautiful patient Domergue. When she kills her husband (Rains), she convinces the doctor that *he* did it, and the two flee for Mexico. The doctor suffers a concussion, barely able to function—and then learns the woman is insane. Another film noir with Mitchum as a duped schnook who wises up too late, this is dreamlike, almost hypnotic, with an especially dangerous *femme fatale*. Decidedly peculiar but entertaining and involving.◗

Where Does It Hurt? (1972) **C-88m.** BOMB D: Rod Amateau. Peter Sellers, Jo Ann Pflug, Rick Lenz, Harold Gould, Hope Summers, Eve Bruce, Kathleen Freeman. Abysmal, tasteless "comedy" about hospital run by corrupt Sellers, staffed by money-hungry incompetents. [R]

Where Eagles Dare (1968) **C-158m.** ***½

D: Brian G. Hutton. Richard Burton, Clint Eastwood, Mary Ure, Michael Hordern, Patrick Wymark, Robert Beatty, Ferdy Mayne, Anton Diffring, Donald Houston, Ingrid Pitt. Modern-day version of Republic serial, with slam-bang cliff-hanger action that never lets up. Burton and company assigned to free American officer held captive in German mountain castle during WW2. Terrific; script by Alistair MacLean, from his best-selling novel. Panavision. [M/PG]▼●❙

Where God Left His Shoes (2008) C-101m. **½ D: Salvatore Stabile. John Leguizamo, Leonor Varela, David Castro, Samantha M. Rose, Jerry Ferrara. Well-intentioned but rambling account of down-on-his-luck boxer Leguizamo, an ex-con and Desert Storm veteran. He and his family are evicted from their apartment and end up in a homeless shelter with Christmas just around the corner. Formulaic and longwinded, but director Stabile (who also scripted) does make excellent use of N.Y.C. locations.❙

Where in the World is Osama Bin Laden? (2008) C-93m. ** D: Morgan Spurlock. Spurlock, who made his name targeting the fast-food industry in SUPER SIZE ME, takes on the far-less-comical war on terror when concerns for the kind of world his newborn child will face thrust him into a Rambo-like quest to find and defeat 9/11 mastermind bin Laden. Broadly staged "training" sequences and man-on-the-street encounters in several Middle Eastern countries are uncomfortably played for laughs, making Spurlock's adventure seem more ego trip than serious journey. Call it Michael Moore lite. [PG-13]❙

Where It's At (1969) C-104m. **½ D: Garson Kanin. David Janssen, Robert Drivas, Rosemary Forsyth, Brenda Vaccaro, Don Rickles, Edy Williams. Pleasant but undistinguished comedy about strained relationship between Las Vegas casino owner and his Princeton-graduate son. [R]

Where Love Has Gone (1964) C-114m. **½ D: Edward Dmytryk. Bette Davis, Susan Hayward, Michael Connors, Jane Greer, Joey Heatherton, George Macready. Glossy drama of Heatherton killing mother Hayward's lover; Davis is the domineering grandmother, Greer is a sympathetic probation officer. Script by John Michael Hayes, from Harold Robbins' novel. Techniscope.▼❙

Where's Charley? (1952) C-97m. *** D: David Butler. Ray Bolger, Allyn Ann McLerie, Robert Shackleton, Mary Germaine, Horace Cooper, Margaretta Scott. Bolger recreates Broadway role in musical adaptation of CHARLEY'S AUNT, as Oxford student whose face-saving impersonation of dowdy dowager leads to endless complications. Frank Loesser score includes "Once in Love With Amy." One of the principal dancers is Jean Marsh. Filmed in England.

Where's Jack? (1969-British) C-119m. **½ D: James Clavell. Tommy Steele, Stanley Baker, Fiona Lewis, Alan Badel, Dudley Foster, Sue Lloyd, Noel Purcell. Despite good cast and production values, surprisingly unengrossing historical adventure tale of Britain's most celebrated highwayman and escape artist, Jack Sheppard (Steele), wanted by British government and notorious mercenary (Baker). [G]

Where's Marlowe? (1999) C/B&W-97m. ** D: Daniel Pyne. Miguel Ferrer, John Livingston, Dante Beze (Mos Def), John Slattery, Allison Dean, Clayton Rohner, Elizabeth Schofield, Miguel Sandoval, Bill McKinney, Heather McComb, Wendy Crewson, Lisa Jane Persky. Ambitious little film about two documentary filmmakers who latch on to a low-level L.A. private detective; while trying to chronicle his day-to-day existence, they become involved in ways they never anticipated. Some clever ideas get lost, though everyone gets an A for effort. [R]▼❙

Where's Picone? (1984-Italian) C-122m. *** D: Nanni Loy. Giancarlo Giannini, Lina Sastri, Aldo Giuffre, Clelia Rondinelli, Carlo Croccolo. Giannini is hilarious in a role tailor-made for his talent: a sleazy, two-bit, ultimately hapless conniver who must live by his wits to survive on the fringes of Neapolitan society. A biting black comedy about bureaucracy and corruption Italian-style.▼

Where's Poppa? (1970) C-82m. **½ D: Carl Reiner. George Segal, Ruth Gordon, Trish Van Devere, Ron Leibman, Rae Allen, Vincent Gardenia, Barnard Hughes, Rob Reiner, Garrett Morris, Paul Sorvino. Absurdist comedy has cult following, but grisly subject matter makes it an acquired taste; Segal plays a repressed N.Y.C. lawyer whose senile mother dominates his life. Outlandish gags involve mugging, rape, nursing homes, and other ills. Original ending was *too* potent, and changed. Script by Robert Klane, from his novel. Look for Penny Marshall as a courtroom spectator. Reissued as GOING APE. [R] ▼❙

Where the Boys Are (1960) C-99m. **½ D: Henry Levin. Dolores Hart, George Hamilton, Yvette Mimieux, Jim Hutton, Barbara Nichols, Paula Prentiss, Connie Francis, Frank Gorshin, Chill Wills. Not-bad film about teenagers during Easter vacation in Ft. Lauderdale. Connie Francis, in her first film, is pretty good, and sings the hit title tune; other young players seen to good advantage. Nichols is hilarious as usual as a flashy blonde. Ineptly remade in 1984. CinemaScope.▼●❙

Where the Boys Are '84 (1984) C-93m. BOMB D: Hy Averback. Lisa Hartman, Lorna Luft, Wendy Schaal, Lynn-Holly

Johnson, Russell Todd, Howard McGillin, Louise Sorel, Alana Stewart. Tacky remake of 1960 film about four college girls (three horny, one virginal) who descend on Ft. Lauderdale, Florida in search of cheap sex. This Allan Carr production has all the appeal of an oil slick. [R]▼

Where the Buffalo Roam (1980) **C-96m.** BOMB D: Art Linson. Peter Boyle, Bill Murray, Bruno Kirby, Rene Auberjonois, R. G. Armstrong, Rafael Campos, Leonard Frey, Mark Metcalf, Craig T. Nelson. Intended celebration of notorious "Gonzo" journalist Hunter S. Thompson will baffle those unfamiliar with his work and insult those who are. Even Neil Young's music can't save dreadful comedy. [R]▼●

Where the Bullets Fly (1966-British) **C-88m.** **½ D: John Gilling. Tom Adams, Dawn Addams, Tim Barrett, Michael Ripper. Well-paced super spy satire involving Adams tracking down special fuel formula. Sequel to THE SECOND BEST SECRET AGENT IN THE WHOLE WIDE WORLD. ▼

Where the Day Takes You (1992) **C-105m.** **½ D: Marc Rocco. Dermot Mulroney, Robert Knepper, Sean Astin, Balthazar Getty, Will Smith, James Le Gros, Ricki Lake, Lara Flynn Boyle, Peter Dobson, Kyle MacLachlan, Nancy McKeon, Adam Baldwin, Rachel Ticotin, Alyssa Milano, David Arquette, Leo Rossi, Stephen Tobolowsky, Laura San Giacomo. Alternately slick and scuzzy look at homeless L.A. street kids, as related by Mulroney (very good here) to prison psychologist San Giacomo. Wavers in quality from the reasonably compelling to the overwrought; a film that shows us junkie Astin vomiting all over himself can probably do without sappy musical montages. Christian Slater appears unbilled. [R] ▼●

Where the Eagle Flies SEE: **Pickup on 101**

Where the Green Ants Dream (1984-German) **C-100m.** **½ D: Werner Herzog. Bruce Spence, Wandjuk Marika, Roy Marika, Ray Barrett, Norman Kaye, Colleen Clifford. Rambling account of a group of wise, noble Australian aborigines who must go up against a mining company set on bulldozing their sacred land in a quest for uranium. The theme—a clash of civilizations—is characteristic of Herzog, but the result just doesn't gel. [R]▼●

Where the Heart Is (1990) **C-94m.** ** D: John Boorman. Dabney Coleman, Uma Thurman, Joanna Cassidy, Crispin Glover, Suzy Amis, Christopher Plummer, Maury Chaykin, David Hewlett. Disappointing farce about wealthy N.Y.C. demolitions expert Coleman, who decides to teach his family humility—and the value of money—by shutting them out and making them homeless. Well-intended hodgepodge that's too

outlandish to be taken seriously. Scripted by Boorman and his daughter, Telsche; some saw this as an update of the director's earlier LEO THE LAST. [R]▼●

Where the Heart Is (2000) **C-120m.** *½ D: Matt Williams. Natalie Portman, Ashley Judd, Stockard Channing, Sally Field, Joan Cusack, James Frain, Dylan Bruno. Billie Letts' novel probably made more sense than this numbingly scattershot script about an abandoned, ill-educated young woman (a miscast Portman) and the circle of friends who nurture her after she gives birth in a Wal-Mart. A near-fatal twister? The baby's kidnapping? The rocky country-western career of the baby's father? Everything here is given equal weight, and the episodic scenes pile up without any cumulative effect. Feature directing debut for the creator/producer of such hit TV sitcoms as *Roseanne* and *Home Improvement*. [PG-13]▼●

Where the Hot Wind Blows! (1958-French-Italian) **120m.** ** D: Jules Dassin. Gina Lollobrigida, Pierre Brasseur, Marcello Mastroianni, Melina Mercouri, Yves Montand, Paolo Stoppa. Sure-fire cast is wasted in pedestrian drama of hypocrisy in a small Italian town. Lollobrigida is poverty-stricken wench who falls for engineer Mastroianni; Mercouri is judge's wife in love with thug Montand's son. Aka THE LAW. ▼●

Where the Lilies Bloom (1974) **C-96m.** *** D: William A. Graham. Julie Gholson, Jan Smithers, Matthew Burril, Helen Harmon, Harry Dean Stanton, Rance Howard, Sudie Bond. Four Appalachian children carry on by themselves when their father dies—and keep the news of his death a secret, so they won't be taken away by the state. First-rate family drama scripted by Earl Hamner, Jr. and filmed on location in North Carolina. [G]▼

Where the Money Is (2000) **C-89m.** ** D: Marek Kanievska. Paul Newman, Linda Fiorentino, Dermot Mulroney, Susan Barnes, Anne Pitoniak, Bruce MacVittie. Savvy convalescent-home nurse Fiorentino senses something about her newest patient, a mute stroke victim who's just been transferred from prison. She becomes convinced that with his bank-robbing background, he can help her and her husband make some easy money. Potentially clever caper goes flat, in spite of charismatic performances by Newman and Fiorentino. A real letdown. [PG-13]▼●

Where the Red Fern Grows (1974) **C-98m.** *** D: Norman Tokar. James Whitmore, Beverly Garland, Jack Ging, Lonny Chapman, Stewart Petersen. Appealing family drama about a boy's devotion to two hunting dogs, and how his experiences teach him about responsibility and growing up. Set in 1930s Oklahoma. Based on Wilson Rawls' novel. Followed years later by a sequel. Remade in 2003. [G]▼●

Where There's Life . . . (1947) **75m.** *******
D: Sidney Lanfield. Bob Hope, Signe
Hasso, William Bendix, George Coulouris,
Vera Marshe, George Zucco, Dennis Hoey,
Harry Von Zell. Wacky comedy with fast-
talking Manhattan radio DJ Hope, just
about to be married, earmarked as new king
of Barovia, and tangling with the country's enemies, along with its top military
authority—who happens to be a woman
(Hasso). Bendix is fun as Hope's forever-
bellowing brother-in-law-to-be.▼▶

Where the River Runs Black (1986)
C-100m. ****½** D: Chris Cain. Charles
Durning, Alessandro Rabelo, Marcelo
Rabelo, Conchata Ferrell, Peter Horton,
Dana Delany. Orphaned boy raised in the
Amazon jungle is brought to civilization by
a well-meaning priest who knew his father.
Slow-moving story starts well but loses its
grip as it leaves behind mystical elements
and focuses more on child's-eye view of
good guys and bad guys. Filmed on location
in Brazil. Super 35. [PG]▼

Where the Rivers Flow North (1993) **C-
106m.** ****½** D: Jay Craven. Rip Torn, Tantoo Cardinal, Bill Raymond, Michael J.
Fox, Mark Margolis, Treat Williams, Amy
Wright. Thoughtful tale of a man who holds
out against authorities determined to buy
his Vermont property in order to erect a dam
in the late '20s. It turns out that the holdout
(Torn) has a hidden agenda, which is one
reason this story avoids becoming an idealized good guys vs. bad guys cliché. Fox appears in a supporting role as a heavy. Craven
also coscripted. ▼●▶

Where the Sidewalk Ends (1950) **95m.**
*** D: Otto Preminger. Dana Andrews,
Gene Tierney, Gary Merrill, Karl Malden,
Bert Freed, Tom Tully, Ruth Donnelly, Craig
Stevens, Neville Brand. While investigating
a homicide, brutal N.Y.C. cop (Andrews) inadvertently kills a man, then tries to conceal
his own guilt while continuing his search for
murderer. Moody crime melodrama is a good
illustration of film noir. Fine characterizations, pungent script by Ben Hecht from William Stuart's novel *Night Cry.* Oleg Cassini
(film's costume designer and Tierney's then-
husband) has a cameo.▶

Where the Spies Are (1966-British) **C-
110m.** ******* D: Val Guest. David Niven,
Françoise Dorleac, John Le Mesurier, Cyril
Cusack, Eric Pohlmann, Reginald Beckwith.
Well made mixture of dry comedy and
suspense in tale of doctor forced into spying. Good cast names enhance already fine
movie. Panavision.

Where the Truth Lies (2005-Canadian-
British) **C-117m.** ****** D: Atom Egoyan.
Kevin Bacon, Colin Firth, Alison Lohman,
Rachel Blanchard, David Hayman, Maury
Chaykin, Kristin Adams, Sonja Bennett,
Deborah Grover, Beau Starr, Don McKellar, Arsinée Khanjian, David Hemblen.
In the 1970s a young female journalist is
hired to help write the memoirs of a fading
star who was half of a popular 1950s show
business team. Her task: to uncover the
truth about a woman who was found dead
in their hotel room one fateful day. Would-
be film noir (replete with graphic sex and
nudity) is torpedoed by a lack of chemistry
between the stars and a bewilderingly bad
performance by Lohman. Egoyan adapted
Rupert Holmes' novel, in which the characters more closely resemble Dean Martin
and Jerry Lewis. Also available in R-rated
version on DVD. Panavision. ▶

Where the Wild Things Are (2009) **C-
101m.** ****½** D: Spike Jonze. Max Records,
Catherine Keener, Mark Ruffalo; voices of
James Gandolfini, Lauren Ambrose, Forest
Whitaker, Catherine O'Hara, Chris Cooper,
Paul Dano. A needy but neglected 9-year-old
boy (Records) leaves home and escapes to a
remote island, where he encounters a race
of large furry creatures who believe he is
their king. He revels in the role—until he
learns that these "wild things" are just as
emotional and unpredictable as any human
beings. Jonze and Dave Eggers adapted and
expanded Maurice Sendak's much-loved
children's book. Depiction of childhood is
disarming—almost unsettling—in its honesty, and young Records gives an astonishing performance, but the film's enchanting
high spots are punctuated by unfortunate
lulls. Still a singular achievement, with the
creatures an ingenious combination of live
performers in sophisticated body suits and
CGI facial movements. Super 35. [PG] ▶

Where Time Began (1978-Spanish) **C-
86m.** ****** D: Piquer Simon. Kenneth More,
Pep Munne, Jack Taylor. Mundane retelling
of Jules Verne's JOURNEY TO THE CEN-
TER OF THE EARTH, with predictable
parade of sea serpents, giant turtles, and
dinosaurs. Aka THE FABULOUS JOUR-
NEY TO THE CENTER OF THE EARTH.
[G]▼▶

**Where Were You When the Lights Went
Out?** (1968) **C-94m.** ***½** D: Hy Averback.
Doris Day, Robert Morse, Terry-Thomas,
Steve Allen, Lola Albright, Jim Backus,
Patrick O'Neal, Pat Paulsen, Ben Blue, Earl
Wilson. Below average Doris Day comedy
centering around the massive N.Y.C. black-
out on November 9, 1965. Panavision. [M/
PG]▼

Which Way Is Up? (1977) **C-94m.** ****½**
D: Michael Schultz. Richard Pryor, Lonette
McKee, Margaret Avery, Dolph Sweet,
Morgan Woodward. Americanization of
Lina Wertmuller's very funny THE SE-
DUCTION OF MIMI doesn't quite make
it. Pryor gets to play three roles—a cotton-
picking orange picker, a minister, and a
dirty old man—and gets the most laughs as
the latter. [R]▼▶

Which Way to the Front? (1970) **C-96m.**

BOMB D: Jerry Lewis. Jerry Lewis, John Wood, Jan Murray, Kaye Ballard, Robert Middleton, Paul Winchell, Sidney Miller, Gary Crosby. One of Jerry's worst has him a 4-F millionaire playboy who enlists other 4-Fs to fight Hitler. His last completed film until HARDLY WORKING. Co-scripted by Dick Miller. [G]▼▶

Whiffs (1975) C-91m. *½ D: Ted Post. Elliott Gould, Eddie Albert, Harry Guardino, Godfrey Cambridge, Jennifer O'Neill, Alan Manson. Gould is guinea pig for Army Chemical Corps who has outlived his usefulness . . . but the military isn't rid of him so easily. Another sorry attempt to recapture the lunacy of MASH. Panavision. [PG]▼

While She Was Out (2008-U.S.-Canadian) C-85m. **½ D: Susan Montford. Kim Basinger, Craig Sheffer, Lukas Haas, Leonard Wu. Emotionally battered suburban soccer mom (Basinger) finds more at the mall than she went shopping for—namely, bad guys led by slimeball Haas. Nicely done noirish thriller; less-is-more approach creates enough tension at the start and finish to make up for the see-it-coming middle. Basinger, who executive produced with Guillermo del Toro, is solid to the end. Based on Edward Bryant's short story. [R]

While the City Sleeps (1956) **100m.** *** D: Fritz Lang. Dana Andrews, Ida Lupino, Rhonda Fleming, George Sanders, Vincent Price, Thomas Mitchell, Sally Forrest, Howard Duff, James Craig, John Barrymore, Jr., Mae Marsh. Veteran cast and intertwining storylines keep interest in account of newspaper reporters and police on the track of a berserk killer. SuperScope.▼▶

While You Were Sleeping (1995) C-103m. **½ D: Jon Turteltaub. Sandra Bullock, Bill Pullman, Peter Gallagher, Peter Boyle, Jack Warden, Glynis Johns, Micole Mercurio, Jason Bernard, Michael Rispoli, Ally Walker, Monica Keena. Lonely Chicago transit worker saves her dream man from muggers, and when he falls into a coma she passes herself off as his fiancée; things get stickier as she's welcomed into his family, and grows close to his brother. Bullock's first starring vehicle showcases her irresistible girl-next-door appeal, but this pleasant, well-cast comedy suffers from anemia. It's a cute story, but it should have been snappier (and shorter). [PG] ▼▶

Whip and the Body, The (1963-Italian) C-91m. *** D: Mario Bava. Daliah Lavi, Christopher Lee, Tony Kendall, Isli Oberon, Harriet Medin, Luciano Pigozzi, Dean Ardow. Soon after domineering Lee returns to his castle home and resumes his sadomasochistic relationship with sister-in-law Lavi, he's murdered. But then he returns as a ghost—with a whip. Perhaps horror maestro Bava's best film, moody, beautiful and deceptively simple. Lee is excellent, despite

being dubbed. Aka SON OF SATAN, THE WAY AND THE BODY, and NIGHT IS THE PHANTOM. Beware of shorter version called WHAT.▶

Whip It (2009) C-111m. *** D: Drew Barrymore. Ellen Page, Marcia Gay Harden, Kristen Wiig, Drew Barrymore, Juliette Lewis, Daniel Stern, Landon Pigg, Alia Shawkat, Andrew Wilson, Jimmy Fallon, Zoë Bell, Eve, Ari Graynor. Texas high school girl (Page), forced to compete in beauty pageants by her dominating mother, discovers a sense of personal identity—and freedom—in a most unlikely way, by joining a roller derby team. First-time feature director Barrymore (who also appears as teammate Smashley Simpson) celebrates girl power in this engaging comedy-drama about the pains and pleasures of adolescence and mother-daughter relationships. Adapted by Shauna Cross from her novel *Derby Girl*. Panavision. [PG-13]▶

Whipped (2000) C-82m. *½ D: Peter M. Cohen. Amanda Peet, Brian Van Holt, Judah Domke, Zorie Barber, Jonathan Abrahams, Callie Thorne. Leering, obnoxious battle-of-the-sexes comedy about a trio of chauvinist pigs who all fall for the same foxy lady. Attempts to invoke the spirit of both Neil LaBute and the Farrelly Brothers but fails. All that saves this from a BOMB is the appealing Peet. [R]▼▶

Whirlpool (1949) **97m.** *** D: Otto Preminger. Gene Tierney, Richard Conte, Jose Ferrer, Charles Bickford, Barbara O'Neil, Eduard Franz, Fortunio Bonanova, Constance Collier. Ruthless con artist Ferrer uses hypnosis and his powers of persuasion to get away with various crimes, implicating innocent Tierney, who's married to bow-tied psychiatrist Conte. Mildly subversive portrait of "perfect" postwar couple and their well-ordered life going awry seems obvious today, especially Ferrer's overripe performance. Written by Ben Hecht (using pseudonym) and Andrew Solt, from Guy Endore's novel.▶

Whisky Galore! SEE: **Tight Little Island**

Whisperers, The (1966-British) **106m.** ** D: Bryan Forbes. Edith Evans, Eric Portman, Nanette Newman, Avis Bunnage, Gerald Sim, Ronald Fraser. Dame Edith is the whole show in this mediocre melodrama about dotty old lady who is sure she is being spied upon; things get worse when her scummy son and husband drop by. Too restrained to be really absorbing, but worth catching just for her performance; moody score by John Barry.▼▶

Whispers (1990-Canadian) C-96m. ** D: Douglas Jackson. Victoria Tennant, Chris Sarandon, Jean LeClerc, Peter MacNeill, Linda Sorensen, Eric Christmas. Tennant is forced to kill LeClerc when he attacks her—but he later turns up alive, puzzling police detective Sarandon. Routine, predictable thriller, though LeClerc is amusingly looney. From the best-seller by Dean R. Koontz. ▼●

Whispers in the Dark (1992) **C-102m.** **½ D: Christopher Crowe. Annabella Sciorra, Jamey Sheridan, Alan Alda, Jill Clayburgh, Anthony LaPaglia, John Leguizamo, Deborah Unger, Anthony Heald, Jacqueline Brookes. Psychiatrist Sciorra is troubled by her reaction to a female patient, but her failure to respond effectively leads to problems for both of them—and everyone around them. Intriguing, well-cast thriller goes on too long, with more twists and turns than necessary, not all of them plausible. Standout performances by LaPaglia, as a determined cop, and Alda, as Sciorra's psychiatry mentor. [R] ▼●)

Whistle at Eaton Falls, The (1951) **96m.** **½ D: Robert Siodmak. Lloyd Bridges, Dorothy Gish, Carleton Carpenter, Murray Hamilton, Anne Francis, Ernest Borgnine, Doro Merande, Arthur O'Connell. Set in New Hampshire, this documentary-style film deals with labor relation problems in a small town when new plant manager has to lay off workers. Gish is factory owner in interesting supporting role.

Whistle Blower, The (1986-British) **C-100m.** *** D: Simon Langton. Michael Caine, James Fox, Nigel Havers, Felicity Dean, John Gielgud, Gordon Jackson, Barry Foster. Deftly handled thriller about a middle-aged former intelligence officer (an effectively subtle Caine), whose linguist son has a high-security government position . . . and is a bit too bright and idealistic for his own good. A literate, multileveled story, adapted by Julian Bond from John Hale's novel. [PG] ▼●)

Whistle Down the Wind (1961-British) **99m.** ***½ D: Bryan Forbes. Hayley Mills, Alan Bates, Bernard Lee, Norman Bird, Elsie Wagstaffe. Fugitive murderer seeking refuge in a North Country barn is discovered by three children who think him to be Christ. Mills and Bates are excellent in this poignant, believable, and well-produced story of childhood innocence. Adapted from novel by Mary Hayley Bell (Hayley's mother). Forbes' directorial debut. ▼

The Whistler series SEE: *Leonard Maltin's Classic Movie Guide*

White (1993-French) **C-92m.** ***½ D: Krzysztof Kieslowski. Zbigniew Zamachowski, Julie Delpy, Janusz Gajos, Jerzy Stuhr. Second of Polish director Kieslowski's "Three Colors" trilogy based on the "liberty, equality, fraternity" symbolism of the blue, white, and red French flag. This story concerns a hapless Pole whose beautiful French wife (Delpy) is divorcing him for no longer being able to perform in bed. Full of irony and subtle wit; the best of the trilogy. Kieslowski wrote the screenplay with frequent collaborator Krzysztof

Piesiewicz. Title onscreen is THREE COLORS: WHITE. ▼●)

White Balloon, The (1995-Iranian) **C-85m.** *** D: Jafar Panahi. Aïda Mohammad-khani, Mohsen Kafili, Fereshteh Sadr Orfaj, Anna Borkowska. It's the Iranian New Year, and a young girl convinces her mother to give her money to buy a goldfish; her trip to make the purchase becomes a mini-odyssey in which she experiences wide-ranging emotions while mixing with characters who run the gamut from greedy to kind. This sweet little film offers an engaging picture of everyday humanity. ▼●

Whiteboyz (1999) **C-97m.** ** D: Marc Levin. Danny Hoch, Dash Mihok, Mark Webber, Piper Perabo, Eugene Byrd, Bonz Malone, Snoop Dogg, Dr. Dre, Fat Joe, Dread Prez, Mic Geronimo, Doug E. Fresh. Hoch is terrific as a young man named Flip who's convinced he's black on the inside, and does his best to talk like an inner-city rapper. This is especially tough for people to understand in the middle of Iowa, where he lives. Fresh and funny for a while, but soon the idea is exhausted; its dramatic climax is all too predictable. [R] ▼●

White Buffalo, The (1977) **C-97m.** ** D: J. Lee Thompson. Charles Bronson, Jack Warden, Will Sampson, Kim Novak, Clint Walker, Stuart Whitman, Slim Pickens, Cara Williams, John Carradine, Martin Kove. Wild Bill Hickok is haunted by the image of a buffalo that symbolizes his fear of death; strange, murky film, with atypical Bronson role, good support from Warden and Novak. [PG] ▼●

White Cargo (1942) **90m.** ** D: Richard Thorpe. Hedy Lamarr, Walter Pidgeon, Frank Morgan, Richard Carlson, Reginald Owen. Lamarr, in one of her best-known roles, is the seductive Tondelayo who entrances all at British plantation post in Africa, with Pidgeon the expeditionist who really falls for her. Exotic love scenes, corny plot. Previously filmed in 1929. ▼

White Chicks (2004) **C-108m.** ** D: Keenen Ivory Wayans. Shawn Wayans, Marlon Wayans, Jaime King, Frankie Faison, Lochlyn Munro, John Heard, Busy Philipps, Terry Crews, Brittany Daniel, Eddie Velez, Jessica Cauffiel, Maitland Ward, Anne Dudek, Jennifer Carpenter. Two male, maverick FBI agents go deep undercover, disguised as air-headed twin sisters, to flush out a criminal. They're black but the girls are white, and that's the central joke. Logic aside (and it certainly is), this heavy-handed comedy is a fragile excuse for the Wayans brothers to do a series of broad, silly riffs, poking fun at stereotypical white people. Unrated version runs 115m. [PG-13] ▼●

White Christmas, A (1954) **C-120m.** ** D: Michael Curtiz. Bing Crosby, Danny Kaye, Rosemary Clooney, Vera-Ellen, Dean Jagger, Mary Wickes, Sig Ruman,

Grady Sutton. Nice Irving Berlin score is unfortunately interrupted by limp plot of Army buddies Crosby and Kaye boosting popularity of winter resort run by their ex-officer Jagger. "What Can You Do with a General" stands out as Berlin's least memorable tune. Partial reworking of HOLIDAY INN, not half as good. Film first released in VistaVision. Later a Broadway musical. ▼●)

White Cliffs of Dover, The (1944) **126m.** *** D: Clarence Brown. Irene Dunne, Alan Marshal, Van Johnson, Frank Morgan, C. Aubrey Smith, Dame May Whitty, Roddy McDowall, Gladys Cooper, Peter Lawford. American Dunne marries Britisher Marshal in patriotic WW1 romancer that boasts wonderful cast (including young Elizabeth Taylor). Slick but shallow. ▼)

White Comanche (1968-Spanish) **C-90m.** *½ D: Gilbert Kay (Jose Briz). Joseph Cotten, William Shatner, Perla Cristal, Rossana Yanni. Boring time-killer detailing the conflict between twin boys whose mother is Indian and whose father is white. ▼)

White Countess, The (2005-U.S.-British-Chinese-German) **C-138m.** *** D: James Ivory. Ralph Fiennes, Natasha Richardson, Vanessa Redgrave, Lynn Redgrave, Madeleine Potter, Hiroyuki Sanada, John Wood, Madeleine Daly, Allan Corduner. Shanghai, 1936: former diplomat Fiennes, accustomed to his recent blindness, hopes to open a small, perfect bar. Impressed by exiled Russian Countess Sofia (Richardson), who has turned to prostitution to help her impoverished—and largely ungrateful—family, he wants her for his hostess. Trying to live a reduced but elegant life, he is oblivious to increasing war tensions. Good but not great Merchant-Ivory production, unfortunately their last: producer Ismail Merchant died before the film was released. Richardson works here with her mother Vanessa and aunt Lynn. [PG-13])

White Dawn, The (1974) **C-109m.** **½ D: Philip Kaufman. Warren Oates, Timothy Bottoms, Lou Gossett, Simonie Kopapik. Rambling adventure about three whalers in 1896 who become lost in the Arctic and their subsequent exploitation of the Eskimos who save them. Brilliant photography by Michael Chapman. [PG] ▼●)

White Dog (1982) **C-89m.** **½ D: Samuel Fuller. Kristy McNichol, Paul Winfield, Burl Ives, Jameson Parker, Lynn Moody, Marshall Thompson, Paul Bartel, Dick Miller, Parley Baer. Young actress takes in a white dog, unaware that it's been trained to attack black people on sight; professional animal trainer Winfield takes on challenge to *re*train him. Interesting but downbeat drama, undeserving of the controversy and preposterous charges of racism that kept it from being released. Script by director Fuller (who has a cameo as Kristy's agent)

and Curtis Hanson, loosely based on the Romain Gary novel. [PG])

White Fang (1972-Italian-Spanish-French) **C-97m.** **½ D: Lucio Fulci. Franco Nero, Vima Lisi, Fernando Rey, Rik Battaglia, Harry Carey, Jr. Scenic but needlessly violent tale of a boy and his dog in the wilds of Alaska, based on the Jack London adventure. [PG] ▼

White Fang (1991) **C-107m.** *** D: Randal Kleiser. Klaus Maria Brandauer, Ethan Hawke, Seymour Cassel, Susan Hogan, James Remar. Winning Disney version of the Jack London perennial, with Hawke a young prospector in Alaska who hooks up with Brandauer and Cassel and befriends the title wolf-dog. Fine fare for kids. Previously filmed in 1936 and 1972. Followed by a sequel. [PG] ▼●)

White Fang 2: Myth of the White Wolf (1994) **C-106m.** ** D: Ken Olin. Scott Bairstow, Charmaine Craig, Alfred Molina, Geoffrey Lewis, Al Harrington, Anthony Michael Ruivivar, Victoria Racimo, Paul Coeur. Tepid Disney follow-up to 1991 film, with young prospector Bairstow working the Alaskan gold mine of his predecessor (played in the original by Ethan Hawke) and teaming up with wolf/dog White Fang. Boy and pet then meet Haida Indian princess and become involved with her tribal village. Lumpy blend of mysticism, villainy, romance, and adventure, aimed at kids. Hawke appears unbilled. [PG] ▼●)

White Heat (1949) **114m.** ***½ D: Raoul Walsh. James Cagney, Virginia Mayo, Edmond O'Brien, Margaret Wycherly, Steve Cochran. Cagney returned to gangster films, older but forceful as ever, as psychopathic hood with mother obsession; Mayo is his neglected wife, O'Brien the cop out to get him. "Top of the World" finale is now movie legend. Written by Ivan Goff and Ben Roberts, from a Virginia Kellogg story. Also shown in computer-colored version. ▼●)

White Hunter Black Heart (1990) **C-112m.** *** D: Clint Eastwood. Clint Eastwood, Jeff Fahey, George Dzundza, Alun Armstrong, Marisa Berenson, Timothy Spall, Mel Martin. Mature, intelligent (if somewhat one-note) adaptation of Peter Viertel's 1953 novel based on his experiences during the filming of THE AFRICAN QUEEN, and his closeup observations of its macho director, John Huston. Eastwood gives an excellent performance as the contrary, self-destructive (and fictionalized) filmmaker, who becomes obsessed with bagging an elephant while on location in Africa. May not be compelling if you're not already interested in the subject, but convincingly re-creates the time and place. Scripted by Viertel, James Bridges, and Burt Kennedy. [PG] ▼●)

White Irish Drinkers (2011) **C-109m.**

½ D: John Gray. Stephen Lang, Peter Riegert, Karen Allen, Nick Thurston, Geoff Wigdor, Leslie Murphy. Predictable but often compelling drama, set in 1975 Brooklyn, about a sensitive young man (Thurston) who considers helping his criminal brother (Wigdor) rob a neighborhood theater—on the night its manager (Riegert) has invited The Rolling Stones to perform—so they can finance lives far away from their abusive alcoholic father (Lang). Well-acted indie production benefits from writer-director Gray's sympathetic appreciation for sometimes affectionate, sometimes belligerent give-and-take among working-class friends and family members. [R] **◖

White Lightning (1973) C-101m. **½ D: Joseph Sargent. Burt Reynolds, Jennifer Billingsley, Ned Beatty, Bo Hopkins, Matt Clark, Louise Latham, Diane Ladd. Formula melodrama with moonshiner Burt going after crooked sheriff who drowned his brother; pleasant cast helps this OK action pic. Young Laura Dern (Ladd's daughter) is visible throughout; it's her film debut. Sequel: GATOR. [PG] **◖**

White Line Fever (1975) C-92m. *** D: Jonathan Kaplan. Jan-Michael Vincent, Kay Lenz, Slim Pickens, L. Q. Jones, Leigh French, Don Porter, Martin Kove. A B picture that hits bull's-eye. Vincent is a young trucker who battles corruption on the road and off, with a diesel truck as his "good buddy." [PG] **▼◖**

White Lions, The (1981) C-96m. ** D: Mel Stuart. Michael York, Glynnis O'Connor, Donald Moffat, J. A. Preston, Roger E. Mosley. Slight tale of life in an African wildlife preserve with naturalist York and his family. Mainly for the kids. [PG]

White Man's Burden (1995) C-96m. **½ D: Desmond Nakano. John Travolta, Harry Belafonte, Kelly Lynch, Margaret Avery, Tom Bower, Carrie Snodgress, Andrew Lawrence, Sheryl Lee Ralph. Flawed but fascinating, politically loaded allegory, set in a fictitious America in which blacks are the wealthy, white-collar majority and whites comprise the unruly, ill-kempt lower class. Travolta plays a factory worker who is fired due to a misunderstanding and chooses to take desperate action against his former boss (Belafonte). Designed to push the buttons of viewers of both races, but Nakano (who also scripted) tends to generalize a bit too often. [R] **▼◖**

White Men Can't Jump (1992) C-114m. *** D: Ron Shelton. Wesley Snipes, Woody Harrelson, Rosie Perez, Tyra Ferrell, Cylk Cozart, Kadeem Hardison, Ernest Harden, Jr. Smart, funny, highly profane comedy about urban basketball hustlers Snipes and Harrelson. Writer-director Shelton really knows the territory, and both stars look good on the court, though the film does become slightly redundant after a point. Perez

is fun as Woody's girlfriend whose goal is to appear on *Jeopardy!* Some versions run 117m. [R] **▼◖**

White Mischief (1988-British) C-106m. *** D: Michael Radford. Sarah Miles, Joss Ackland, John Hurt, Greta Scacchi, Charles Dance, Susan Fleetwood, Jacqueline Pearce, Murray Head, Geraldine Chaplin, Trevor Howard, Hugh Grant. Elegantly kinky tale based on James Fox's book about the British colony living in Kenya's Happy Valley during early days of WW2, and true story of a husband's response to the local stud stealing his beautiful wife. Sensual and quietly bizarre, with meticulous production detail and a fine cast, headed by Scacchi at her most stunning. [R] **▼◖**

White Nights (1957-Italian) 94m. *** D: Luchino Visconti. Maria Schell, Jean Marais, Marcello Mastroianni, Clara Calamai. Shy Mastroianni comes upon mysterious Schell, who's been dumped by sailor boyfriend Marais (or so it seems). A captivating, elaborately plotted love story, and a key film in Visconti's transition away from neorealism. Based on a Dostoyevsky story. Original running time 107m. Aka LE NOTTI BIANCHE. **▼◖**

White Nights (1985) C-135m. **½ D: Taylor Hackford. Mikhail Baryshnikov, Gregory Hines, Isabella Rossellini, Jerzy Skolimowski, Helen Mirren, Geraldine Page, John Glover. Prominent ballet star who defected from Russia to U.S. finds himself back in the U.S.S.R. after a forced plane landing . . . while American expatriate tap dancer is used as bait to wear down his resistance about fleeing the country again. Baryshnikov's powerful presence (as actor and dancer) almost makes up for contrived story. Nicest surprise is surefooted performance by director Skolimowski as KGB agent. [PG-13] **▼◖**

White Noise (2005-Canadian-British) C-98m. *½ D: Geoffrey Sax. Michael Keaton, Deborah Kara Unger, Chandra West, Ian McNeice, Sarah Strange, Nicholas Elia, Mike Dopud. Despairing over the sudden death of his wife, Keaton is taken in by McNeice, who's developed the ability to see and hear messages from the dead amidst the static on his audio and video recorders. Before long, Keaton is obsessed with E.V.P. (Electronic Voice Phenomenon), to the detriment of his mental and physical well-being. Decent-enough hook for a thriller leads us up a series of blind alleys and never delivers the goods. Followed by a direct-to-DVD sequel. Super 35. [PG-13] **▼◖**

White of the Eye (1987-British) C-110m. *** D: Donald Cammell. David Keith, Cathy Moriarty, Art Evans, Alan Rosenberg, Alberta Watson, Michael Greene, Mark Hayashi. Bizarre thriller set in a small Arizona town about psycho Keith, who's (understandably) having marital squabbles with wife Moriarty. Dazzling technique recalling the experimental films of the 1960s marks this disturbing picture, a smashing return to films for director Cammell (PERFORMANCE, DEMON SEED) and Moriarty. [R]▼

White Oleander (2002) **C-109m.** ***½ D: Peter Kosminsky. Alison Lohman, Robin Wright Penn, Michelle Pfeiffer, Renée Zellweger, Billy Connolly, Svetlana Efremova, Patrick Fugit, Cole Hauser, Noah Wyle, Taryn Manning. Moving adaptation of Janet Fitch's best-selling novel about a teenage girl who tries to wrest herself from the influence of her imprisoned mother, a free-spirited artist with a cruel streak, as she moves from one foster home to another. Lohman is the focal point in this well-cast film, which miraculously manages to avoid sentimentality while spinning its unpredictable story. Impressive Hollywood feature debut for British TV and documentary director Kosminsky. Screenplay by Mary Agnes Donoghue. Incidentally, Zellweger shows Lohman footage of herself in TEXAS CHAINSAW MASSACRE: THE NEXT GENERATION. [PG-13] ▼❱

Whiteout (2009-U.S.-Canadian-French) **C-101m.** ** D: Dominic Sena. Kate Beckinsale, Gabriel Macht, Tom Skerritt, Columbus Short, Alex O'Loughlin, Shawn Doyle, Joel Keller, Jesse Todd. Good-looking but paper-thin thriller involving U.S. marshal Beckinsale, stationed in Antarctica, who struggles to exorcise her demons while investigating some gruesome killings. Even though her character is constantly in danger, Beckinsale is always perfectly coiffed; early on, she even peels off her clothes and takes a steamy shower. Only in the movies. . . . Based on a graphic novel by Greg Rucka and Steve Lieber. Super 35. [R] ❱

White Palace (1990) **C-103m.** *** D: Luis Mandoki. Susan Sarandon, James Spader, Jason Alexander, Kathy Bates, Eileen Brennan, Spiros Focas, Gina Gershon, Steven Hill, Rachel Levin (Chagall), Corey Parker, Renee Taylor, Jeremy Piven. Superficial but entertaining story of a vulnerable yuppie who's swept away by a sexy older woman . . . and then has to deal with the reality of their enormous social and ethnic differences. Sarandon is ideal in a vivid and believable performance. Reportedly, the improbable conclusion was tacked on at the last minute. Scripted by Ted Tally and Alvin Sargent, from Glenn Savan's novel. [R]▼❱❱

White Ribbon, The (2009-German) **142m.** *** D: Michael Haneke. Christian Friedel, Leonie Benesch, Ulrich Tukur, Ursina Lardi, Burghart Klaussner, Susanne Lothar. In a seemingly pastoral German village where a land baron rules community economics, and rigid religiosity prevails, a mysterious array of serious accidents spooks the collective psyche, causing everyone to ask, "What's going on?" Set in flashback shortly before the outbreak of WW1, this long but absorbing film suggests—without overreaching—how the young generation portrayed here might have become especially pliable in the years that followed. As with many Haneke films, it's what isn't said, and isn't shown, that matters most. A major asset: Christian Berger's b&w cinematography, of a quality that Ingmar Bergman or Carl Dreyer might have been proud to call their own. [R] ❱

White Rose, The (1983-German) **C-108m.** *** D: Michael Verhoeven. Lena Stolze, Martin Benrath, Wulf Kessler, Werner Stocker. Pointed, fascinating account of a group of Munich students who, in 1942, launched an anti-Nazi uprising. Based on fact; Stolze also played her character in Percy Adlon's THE FIVE LAST DAYS and later starred in Verhoeven's not-dissimilar THE NASTY GIRL.▼

White Sands (1992) **C-101m.** ** D: Roger Donaldson. Willem Dafoe, Mary Elizabeth Mastrantonio, Mickey Rourke, Sam (Samuel L.) Jackson, M. Emmet Walsh, James Rebhorn, Maura Tierney. Smalltown lawman finds a corpse, then starts snooping around into what turns out to be some dirty undercover-narc business involving the FBI. Competently performed (even by Rourke), but with little else to distinguish it from dozens of its ilk; Mastrantonio fares best as a complex society type up to her neck in drug-dealing. Mimi Rogers, Fred Dalton Thompson, and John P. Ryan appear unbilled. Panavision. [R] ▼❱

White Sheik, The (1951-Italian) **86m.** **½ D: Federico Fellini. Alberto Sordi, Brunella Bova, Leopoldo Trieste, Giulietta Masina. Fellini's first solo film as director is a minor chronicle of the adventures of a provincial couple honeymooning in Rome and the wife's involvement with a cartoon hero, The White Sheik (Sordi). Remade, more or less, as THE WORLD'S GREATEST LOVER.▼❱

White Sister, The (1933) **110m.** **½ D: Victor Fleming. Helen Hayes, Clark Gable, Lewis Stone, Louise Closser Hale, May Robson, Edward Arnold. Dated but interesting remake of 1923 silent with Lillian Gish and Ronald Colman. Hayes is woman who enters convent when she thinks her lover has been killed in the war. Fine performances offset predictable story.▼❱

White Sister (1973-Italian) **C-104m.** **½ D: Alberto Lattuada. Sophia Loren, Adriano Celentano, Fernando Rey. Strange love story of hospital Mother Superior and self-professed young Communist who helps run the wards. [R]

White Squall (1996) **C-127m.** *** D: Ridley Scott. Jeff Bridges, Caroline Goodall, John Savage, Scott Wolf, Jeremy Sisto,

Ryan Phillippe, David Lascher, Eric Michael Cole, Jason Marsden, David Selby, Julio Mechoso, Balthazar Getty, Zeljko Ivanek, Ethan (Randall) Embry, James Rebhorn. In 1960, teenage boys—many of them misfits—sign on as shipmates and students with a "floating school" skippered by hard-nosed Bridges, who wants them to learn to rely both on themselves and each other. Put down by some as a paraphrase of DEAD POETS SOCIETY, this is an involving, well-acted coming-of-age drama on its own terms. Climactic storm sequence is genuinely gripping, but the finale seems somehow tacked on. Panavision. [PG-13]▼●)

White Water Summer (1987) **C-90m.** *½ D: Jeff Bleckner. Kevin Bacon, Sean Astin, Jonathan Ward, K.C. Martel, Matt Adler, Caroline McWilliams, Charles Siebert. Feeble account of Bacon teaching city lad Astin and his pals the ways of the wilderness. Filmed in 1985 and barely released theatrically. Aka RITES OF SUMMER. Super 35. [PG]▼●)

White Wilderness (1958) **C-73m.** *** D: James Algar. Narrated by Winston Hibler. Typically good Disney True-Life feature takes a look at the Arctic region; highlight is extended sequence on lemmings and their ritualistic march off a cliff. Oscar winner as Best Documentary.▼)

White Witch Doctor (1953) **C-96m.** **½ D: Henry Hathaway. Susan Hayward, Robert Mitchum, Walter Slezak, Timothy Carey, Bakuba territory is scene of diverse interests of nurse Hayward who wants to bring modern medicine to natives and adventurers Mitchum and Slezak bent on finding hidden treasure.

White Zombie (1932) **73m.** *** D: Victor Halperin. Bela Lugosi, Madge Bellamy, Joseph Cawthorn, Robert Frazer, John Harron, Brandon Hurst, Clarence Muse. Zombie master Lugosi menaces newlyweds on Haitian sugar plantation; eerie, unique low-budget chiller. Also shown in a computer-colored version. ▼●)

Whity (1971-German) **C-95m.** *** D: Rainer Werner Fassbinder. Ron Randell, Gunter Kaufmann, Hanna Schygulla, Katrin Schaake, Harry Baer, Ulli Lommel, Tom as Blanco, Stefano Capriati, Elaine Baker, Mark Salvage, Helga Ballhaus. For Fassbinder completists comes this avant-garde horse opera filmed in Spain on the sets of Sergio Leone's spaghetti Westerns. B-movie stalwart Randell plays a sadistic rancher whose depraved family (painted in whiteface) includes a nympho wife, two sons—one a transvestite, the other mentally retarded—and a mulatto butler who's really his illegitimate son. One of a kind, brilliantly shot in widescreen by Michael Ballhaus, and featuring Fassbinder himself as a whip-wielding barroom gambler. CinemaScope. ▶)

Who? (1973-British) **C-93m.** **½ D: Jack Gold. Elliott Gould, Trevor Howard, Joseph Bova, Ed Grover, James Noble, John Lehne. Gould plays FBI agent investigating American scientist's car crash in Russia, and subsequent reappearance with a strangely restructured face. Intriguing if not completely satisfying spy/sci-fi mix. Based on the novel by Algis Budrys. Video title: ROBO MAN. [PG]▼)

Who Am I? SEE: **Jackie Chan's Who Am I?**

Who Dares Wins SEE: **Final Option, The**

Who Done It? (1942) **75m.** *** D: Erle C. Kenton. Bud Abbott, Lou Costello, Patric Knowles, Louise Allbritton, William Gargan, William Bendix, Mary Wickes, Don Porter, Thomas Gomez, Jerome Cowan, Ludwig Stossel. One of A&C's best finds the boys as would-be radio writers who pretend to be detectives when the network's president is murdered, and everyone believes them—including the killer! Great supporting cast is topped by Wickes as wise-cracking secretary and Bendix as real cop who's even dumber than Lou.▼●)

Who Do You Love (2010) **C-92m.** ** D: Jerry Zaks. Alessandro Nivola, Chi McBride, David Oyelowo, Jon Abrahams, Megalyn Echikunwoke, Marika Dominczyk, Miko DeFoor, Keb' Mo', Robert Randolph. True-life saga of Leonard Chess, son of an immigrant Chicago junk dealer who (with his brother Philip) founded a nightclub and record label that specialized in spotting and nurturing black musicians like blues greats Willie Dixon (McBride), Muddy Waters (Oyelowo), and Etta James (renamed Ivy Mills here, and played by Echikunwoke) in the late 1940s and 1950s . . . to the detriment of his marriage. Basic story is good, and so is the music, but this treatment isn't quite as rich as the one in CADILLAC RECORDS, made around the same time but released first.

Whoever Slew Auntie Roo? SEE: **Who Slew Auntie Roo?**

Who Fears the Devil SEE: **Legend of Hillbilly John, The**

Who Framed Roger Rabbit (1988) **C-103m.** ***½ D: Robert Zemeckis. Bob Hoskins, Christopher Lloyd, Joanna Cassidy, Stubby Kaye, Alan Tilvern, and the voices of Charles Fleischer, Lou Hirsch, Mel Blanc, Mae Questel, Tony Anselmo, June Foray, Wayne Allwine. Staggering special-effects comedy places down-and-out 1940s detective Hoskins on the trail of a murderer, with cartoon star Roger Rabbit (the chief suspect) at his side. Flaws in story and characterization pale alongside the incredible blend of live-action and animation, but the ultimate feat is making us believe that Roger and his cartoon colleagues actually exist. Extra fun: spotting the many cartoon stars who make cameo appearances.

Jessica Rabbit's speaking voice was done by Kathleen Turner (unbilled) and her singing voice by Amy Irving. A coproduction of the Steven Spielberg and Walt Disney companies. Animation director Richard Williams received a special Academy Award; three other Oscars included one for Special Visual Effects. [PG]▼●◗

Who Has Seen the Wind (1977-Canadian) **C-100m.** **½ D: Allan King. Brian Painchaud, Douglas Junor, Gordon Pinsent, Chapelle Jaffe, Jose Ferrer, Helen Shaver. OK chronicle of young Painchaud and Junor's life in Saskatchewan during the Depression. Ferrer is amusing as a bootlegger.▼

Who is Cletis Tout? (2002-Canadian) **C-92m.** ** D: Chris Ver Wiel. Christian Slater, Tim Allen, Richard Dreyfuss, Portia de Rossi, Billy Connolly, Peter MacNeill, Elias Zarou, RuPaul. A movie-buff hit man (Allen) encourages his captive (Slater) to tell his story as if he's pitching a script to a Hollywood producer: it's the saga of a bank heist, jailbreak, mob hit, and romance . . . but it plays like a deflated balloon. Writer-director Ver Wiel has seen a lot of movies, but can only come up with a pale imitation of a crime caper; his worst mistake is opening with a great movie scene, the finale of BREAKFAST AT TIFFANY'S. Completed in 2000. Super 35. [R] ▼◗

Who Is Harry Kellerman and Why Is He Saying Those Terrible Things About Me? (1971) **C-108m.** ** D: Ulu Grosbard. Dustin Hoffman, Barbara Harris, Jack Warden, David Burns, Gabriel Dell, Dom DeLuise, Betty Walker. Muddled comedy-drama by Herb Gardner casts Dustin as successful rock composer-singer who finds money doesn't answer all of life's questions. Harris comes along late in film to save this debacle with an outstanding performance. [PG]▼

Who Is Killing the Great Chefs of Europe? (1978) **C-112m.** *** D: Ted Kotcheff. George Segal, Jacqueline Bisset, Robert Morley, Jean-Pierre Cassel, Philippe Noiret, Jean Rochefort, Madge Ryan, Joss Ackland, Nigel Havers. Slick comedy whodunit with self-explanatory title has luscious views of European scenery and food, plus a magnificently funny role for Morley as the world's premier gourmet. Script by Peter Stone, based on Nan and Ivan Lyons' novel. [PG]▼◗

Who Is Killing the Stuntmen? SEE: **Stunts**

Who Killed Mary What's'ername? (1971) **C-90m.** **½ D: Ernie Pintoff. Red Buttons, Alice Playten, Sylvia Miles, Sam Waterston, Dick Williams, Conrad Bain. Diabetic ex-boxer sets out to find a prostitute's murderer when he becomes angered at everyone's indifference. Whodunit isn't bad, but nothing special; acting is generally good. [PG]▼

Who Killed the Electric Car? (2006) **C-92m.** *** D: Chris Paine. Narrated by Martin Sheen. Fine documentary about the mysterious death of the once-highly-touted electric car, a product that threatened to revolutionize an industry and warm the hearts of environmentalists. Instead, as this well-researched film suggests, there may have been sinister corporate forces at work behind its virtual disappearance. In addition to exploring the unplugging of a dream, Paine's potent narrative also puts a spotlight on the world's energy crisis and the urgent need for renewable sources of fuel. Fascinating and important. [PG]◗

Whole Nine Yards, The (2000) **C-99m.** **½ D: Jonathan Lynn. Bruce Willis, Matthew Perry, Rosanna Arquette, Michael Clarke Duncan, Amanda Peet, Natasha Henstridge, Kevin Pollak. Perry is broadly funny as a miserably married dentist who learns that his new neighbor is a notorious hit man. He figures to get something he wants by ratting out the gunman to his former Chicago gang . . . but quickly gets in over his head. Farcical black comedy has enough twists, turns, and laughs to overcome its basic silliness. Followed by a sequel. [R]▼●◗

Whole Shootin' Match, The (1978) **108m.** *** D: Eagle Pennell. Lou Perryman (Perry), Sonny Davis, Doris Hargrave, Eric Henshaw, David Weber, James Harrell. Relaxed, low-key portrait of two Texas good ol' boys whose many dreams and schemes never quite pan out. Short on narrative but long on atmosphere, this poster child for low-budget, regional American cinema boasts amiable—and completely believable—performances by its leading actors, and a refreshingly nonjudgmental look at their existence. A cornerstone of the indie film movement, written by Pennell and Lin Sutherland.◗

Whole Ten Yards, The (2004) **C-99m.** BOMB D: Howard Deutch. Bruce Willis, Matthew Perry, Amanda Peet, Kevin Pollak, Natasha Henstridge. The sequel for which no one was clamoring reunites the cast of THE WHOLE NINE YARDS, a pleasant-enough film, and puts them in a frantically unfunny story about Willis (who's supposedly deceased) being forced back into the crime game to help dentist Perry rescue his kidnapped wife. Or something like that. Perry falls down and bumps into everything imaginable, a valiant effort to find laughs in a script that has none to offer. That's Willis' daughter Tallulah as the foulmouthed Buttercup Scout. [PG-13] ▼◗

Whole Town's Talking, The (1935) **95m.** *** D: John Ford. Edward G. Robinson, Jean Arthur, Wallace Ford, Arthur Hohl, Edward Brophy, Arthur Byron, Donald Meek. Entertaining comedy with meek clerk Robinson a lookalike for notorious gangster; fine performances by E. G. and Arthur. Script by Jo Swerling and Robert Riskin, from a W. R. Burnett novel. Reworked as SO YOU WON'T TALK. ▼

Whole Wide World, The (1996) **C-105m.** *** D: Dan Ireland. Vincent D'Onofrio, Renée Zellweger, Ann Wedgeworth, Harve Presnell, Benjamin Mouton, Michael Corbett. Poignant, based-on-fact drama, set in Texas during the 1930s and charting the complex relationship between two independent-minded souls: pulp novelist Robert E. Howard, the obsessive, overbearing creator of Conan the Barbarian, and schoolteacher/aspiring writer Novalyne Price, upon whose memoir this is based. Their dreams and realities are vividly etched in this extremely well acted film. Clairmont-Scope. [PG]▼●)

Who'll Stop the Rain (1978) **C-126m.** *** D: Karel Reisz. Nick Nolte, Tuesday Weld, Michael Moriarty, Anthony Zerbe, Richard Masur, Ray Sharkey, David Opatoshu, Gail Strickland, Charles Haid. Robert Stone's National Book Award–winning *Dog Soldiers* suffers from excessively genteel treatment in telling its truly mean story about the smuggling of heroin from Vietnam to California. Strong performances in virtually every role. Aka DOG SOLDIERS. [R] ▼●

Wholly Moses (1980) **C-109m.** *½ D: Gary Weis. Dudley Moore, Laraine Newman, James Coco, Paul Sand, Jack Gilford, Dom DeLuise, John Houseman, Madeline Kahn, David L. Lander, Richard Pryor, John Ritter. Great cast flounders in this stale saga of "savior" Moore, who thinks God has ordained him to lead the Jews out of Egypt. Some amusing bits, notably by DeLuise; otherwise, an appalling waste. Panavision. [PG]▼●)

Whoopee Boys, The (1986) **C-88m.** BOMB D: John Byrum. Michael O'Keefe, Paul Rodriguez, Denholm Elliott, Carole Shelley, Andy Bumatai, Eddie Deezen, Marsha Warfield, Joe Spinell, Dan O' Herlihy. Awful comedy about a couple of wiseguys who try to break into Palm Beach society. Crude, to say the least. [R]▼)

Whore (1991) **C-85m.** ** D: Ken Russell. Theresa Russell, Benjamin Mouton, Antonio Fargas, Sanjay, Elizabeth Morehead, Michael Crabtree, John Diehl, Jack Nance, Tom Villard, Ginger Lynn Allen. Reinventing the Wheel: The gist of this melodrama is that streetwalking is a dead-end profession with lots of sordid characters. Russell's performance is so broad—but sometimes so funny—that it's difficult to gauge how good or bad it is. Available on video in a 92m. uncut European release, in the 85m. NC-17 version released in U.S. theaters, in an 85m. "R" version—and in the same 85m. version that's been packaged for title-shy sellers as IF YOU CAN'T SAY IT, JUST SEE IT. Hardly worth the trouble. ▼●

Who's Afraid of Virginia Woolf? (1966) **129m.** ***½ D: Mike Nichols. Elizabeth Taylor, Richard Burton, George Segal, Sandy Dennis. Two couples get together for an all-night session of bitter conversation; Burton and Taylor's finest hour (together) in searing Edward Albee drama. Taylor and Dennis won Oscars, as did Haskell Wexler's incisive b&w photography, Richard Sylbert's art direction, and Irene Sharaff's costumes. Film broke Hollywood taboos for adult material, would cause lesser furor today. Script by producer Ernest Lehman. Nichols' first film as director. ▼●)

Who Says I Can't Ride a Rainbow? (1971) **C-85m.** **½ D: Edward Mann. Jack Klugman, Norma French, Reuben Figueroa, David Mann, Morgan Freeman, Esther Rolle. Offbeat story of man who feels it is the children of the world who will determine its future. Freeman's film debut. [G]

Who's Been Sleeping in My Bed? (1963) **C-103m.** **½ D: Daniel Mann. Dean Martin, Elizabeth Montgomery, Carol Burnett, Martin Balsam, Jill St. John, Richard Conte, Louis Nye. Undemanding fluff about TV star Martin being urged altar-ward by fiancée Montgomery. Burnett, in her film debut, is his psychiatrist's nurse. Panavision.

Whose Life Is It Anyway? (1981) **C-118m.** ***½ D: John Badham. Richard Dreyfuss, John Cassavetes, Christine Lahti, Bob Balaban, Kenneth McMillan, Kaki Hunter, Janet Eilber, Thomas Carter. Searing black comedy in which sculptor Dreyfuss is paralyzed from the neck down in an auto accident, argues for his right to die. Remarkable performance by Dreyfuss, excellent ones by hospital chief of staff Cassavetes, doctor Lahti, judge McMillan, nurse trainee Hunter. From Brian Clark's hit play, with a script by the author and Reginald Rose. Panavision. [R]▼)

Who's Got the Action? (1962) **C-93m.** **½ D: Daniel Mann. Dean Martin, Lana Turner, Eddie Albert, Nita Talbot, Walter Matthau, Paul Ford, Margo, John McGiver, Jack Albertson. Strained froth of Turner combatting hubby Martin's horse-racing fever by turning bookie. Panavision. ▼

Who's Got the Black Box? SEE: **Road to Corinthe, The**

Who's Harry Crumb? (1989) **C-98m.** ** D: Paul Flaherty. John Candy, Jeffrey Jones, Annie Potts, Tim Thomerson, Barry Corbin, Shawnee Smith, Valri Bromfield, Renee Coleman, Joe Flaherty, Lyle Alzado, James Belushi, Stephen Young. Candy is ideally cast as an inept private detective attempting to unearth a kidnapper in this uneven comedy. Has some very funny moments, but too much outright silliness. [PG-13]▼●)

Who Shot Patakango? (1990) **C-102m.** ** D: Robert Brooks. David Knight, Sandra Bullock, Kevin Otto, Aaron Ingram, Brad Randall, Allison Janney. Slight, meandering account of life at a Brooklyn vocational high school in 1957, a time when blacks were moving from the South into Northern inner cities and whites had not yet fled to the suburbs. Brooks coscripted and coedited with wife Halle; he also photographed, and she produced. Aka WHO SHOT PAT? [R]▼●⊙

Who Slew Auntie Roo? (1971) **C-89m.** ** D: Curtis Harrington. Shelley Winters, Mark Lester, Chloe Franks, Ralph Richardson, Lionel Jeffries, Hugh Griffith. Sickie about daffy old lady who steers unwitting children into her lair. Made in England; intended to be a variation of *Hansel and Gretel*! Aka WHOEVER SLEW AUNTIE ROO? [PG]▼▮

Who's Minding the Mint? (1967) **C-97m.** ***½ D: Howard Morris. Jim Hutton, Dorothy Provine, Milton Berle, Joey Bishop, Bob Denver, Walter Brennan, Victor Buono, Jack Gilford, Jamie Farr, Jackie Joseph. Hilarious comedy, neglected at time of release, is tremendous fun in the classic comedy tradition, with motley gang of thieves helping U.S. Mint worker Hutton replace money he accidentally destroyed. Buono is especially funny as pompous ex-skipper.▼

Who's Minding the Store? (1963) **C-90m.** **½ D: Frank Tashlin. Jerry Lewis, Agnes Moorehead, Jill St. John, John McGiver, Ray Walston, Nancy Kulp, Francesca Bellini. Jerry Lewis vehicle with bumbling idiot (guess who?) set loose in department store. Great supporting cast in stereotyped comic foil roles, plus one good inventive bit.▼

Who's That Girl? (1987) **C-94m.** BOMB D: James Foley. Madonna, Griffin Dunne, Haviland Morris, John McMartin, Robert Swan, Drew Pillsbury, John Mills. Atrocious attempt at screwball comedy with Dunne as the hapless hero whose life is turned inside out when he's assigned to escort Madonna (just sprung from jail) out of town. Derivative film is missing just two things: charm and humor. [PG]▼●⊙

Who's That Knocking at My Door (1968) **90m.** *** D: Martin Scorsese. Zina Bethune, Harvey Keitel, Anne Collette, Lennard Kuras, Michael Scala, Harry Northup, Bill Minkin. Crude but fascinating autobiographical drama from Scorsese, his first feature, focusing on relationship between streetwise Keitel, hung up by his strict Catholic upbringing, and independent young woman (Bethune). Keitel's film debut. Also released as J.R.▼▮

Who's the Man? (1993) **C-85m.** ** D: Ted Demme. Ed Lover, Doctor Dre, Badja Djola, Cheryl "Salt" James, Jim Moody, Ice T, Andre B. Blake, Rozwill Young, Colin Quinn, Bernie Mac, Denis Leary, Kurt Loder, Richard Bright, Terrence Dashon Howard, Queen Latifah. Nonsensical airhead of a movie in which MTV rap veejays

Ed Lover and Doctor Dre play characters named Ed Lover and Doctor Dre, inept Harlem haircutters who somehow become N.Y.C. cops and battle a villainous real estate speculator. Loud, crude, and crammed with cameos by a variety of rap artists (Kriss Kross, B-Real, Humpty Hump). Not without laughs, but more valuable as an artifact of the early '90s. [R]▼●⊙

Who's Your Caddy? (2007) **C-92m.** *½ D: Don Michael Paul. Antwan Andre "Big Boi" Patton, Jeffrey Jones, Tamala Jones, Sherri Shepherd, Faizon Love, Garrett Morris. Gangsta rapper C-Note (Patton) and his posse seek membership in a snooty South Carolina country club, much to the chagrin of its condescending president (Jones). Predictably, crotches are pummeled, gas is passed, and stereotypes run amok while this flimsy farce alternates between crude slapstick and sappy sentiment. Failed bid for solo movie stardom for OutKast hip-hop artist Patton. [PG-13]▮

Who Was That Lady? (1960) **115m.** *** D: George Sidney. Tony Curtis, Dean Martin, Janet Leigh, James Whitmore, John McIntire, Barbara Nichols, Joi Lansing. Spicy shenanigans move along at lively pace as Curtis and Martin pretend to be secret agents to confuse Tony's jealous wife Leigh; script by Norman Krasna, from his play.▮

Why Did I Get Married? (2007) **C-118m.** **½ D: Tyler Perry. Janet Jackson, Tyler Perry, Sharon Leal, Malik Yoba, Jill Scott, Richard T. Jones. Appreciably more subdued than his previous films, writer-director Perry's sudsy comedy-drama plays for keeps even while it's playing for laughs as four couples swap stories and air grievances during their annual semi-therapeutic get-together at a Colorado resort. Subtlety is in short supply, but the ensemble is first-rate, and a few scenes have potent emotional impact. Followed by a sequel. [PG-13]▮

Why Did I Get Married Too? (2010) **C-121m.** *½ D: Tyler Perry. Tyler Perry, Janet Jackson, Jill Scott, Sharon Leal, Malik Yoba, Richard T. Jones, Tasha Smith, Lamman Rucker, Michael Jai White, Louis Gossett, Jr., Cicely Tyson, Valarie Pettiford. Annoying sequel to 2007 movie finds the four couples arriving in the Bahamas for their annual vacation together, where they sit around analyzing the state of their not-so wedded bliss. Things get dicey when one wife's ex-hubby unexpectedly shows up to try and break up her marriage to a younger man. Despite a talented cast, Perry's penchant for over-the-top melodrama and in-your-face comedy makes for an uneasy mix. Dwayne Johnson turns up during the closing credits to set up yet another sequel. [PG-13]▮

Why Do Fools Fall in Love (1998) **C-112m.** ** D: Gregory Nava. Halle Berry, Vivica A. Fox, Lela Rochon, Larenz Tate,

Paul Mazursky, Pamela Reed, Alexis Cruz, David Barry Gray, Miguel A. Nunez, Jr., Clifton Powell, Ben Vereen, Lane Smith. Disappointing account of ill-fated 1950s rock 'n' roller Frankie Lymon (Tate), who ended up a junkie and died of an overdose in 1968 at age 26, and the three very different women he allegedly married. Superficial, to say the least, and sometimes embarrassing. Little Richard (playing himself) enlivens the proceedings whenever he is on-screen. [R] ▼○◗

Why Has Bodhi-Dharma Left for the East? (1989-Korean) **C-135m.** *** D: Bae Yong-kyun. Yi Pan-yong, Sin Won-sop, Huang Hae-jin, Ko Su-myong, Kim Hae-yong. Meditative, mind-expanding account of an elderly, dying Zen master and his two disciples, a monk and a boy; they retire to a rural monastery, away from the "turbulence of life," where the master attempts to guide the others toward a state of enlightenment. An unusual film, not for all temperaments, but most rewarding if you can immerse yourself in its flow. Premiered theatrically in the U.S. in 1993. ▼○◗

Why Not! (1979-French) **C-93m.** *** D: Coline Serreau. Sami Frey, Christine Murillo, Mario Gonzalez, Michel Aumont, Nicole Jamet, Mathe Souverbie. Frey, Murillo, and Gonzalez, trying to leave their pasts behind, are roommates—and share the same bed. Then Frey becomes involved with Jamet. Sometimes funny and touching, but not as involving as it should be. Original title: POURQUOI PAS!

Why Shoot the Teacher? (1977-Canadian) **C-101m.** *** D: Silvio Narizzano. Bud Cort, Samantha Eggar, Chris Wiggins, Gary Reineke, John Friesen, Michael J. Reynolds. Simple, warm, enjoyable story of Cort's experiences when he takes a teaching job in a small, isolated farming town during the Depression. ▼

Why We Fight (2006-U.S.-British-Danish) **C/B&W-98m.** *** D: Eugene Jarecki. Low-key polemic (possibly too much so) takes off from Frank Capra's pugnacious WW2 documentaries and President Eisenhower's final address that famously and presciently warned of the "military-industrial complex." Film's thesis is that the brass and big munitions companies play a game of "risky synergy" and that America has to drum up wars on which the dragon it has created can gorge. A few neo-conservatives also get their say. Not a lot of revelations here, but the material and interviewees are interesting. Ever-reliable wag Gore Vidal alludes to "the United States of Amnesia." [PG-13]◗

Why Worry? (1923) **77m.** ***½ D: Fred Newmeyer, Sam Taylor. Harold Lloyd, Jobyna Ralston, John Aasen, Leo White, James Mason. Hilarious story of millionaire playboy Lloyd who stumbles into

revolution-ridden country and inadvertently becomes involved. Packed with belly-laugh sight-gags.◗

Why Would Anyone Want to Kill a Nice Girl Like You? (1969-British) **C-99m.** ** D: Don Sharp. Eva Renzi, David Buck, Peter Vaughan, Paul Hubschmid, Sophie Hardy, Kay Walsh. A young tourist on the French Riviera thinks someone is trying to kill her, but none of the local officials will believe her. Familiar storyline handled in routine fashion.

Why Would I Lie? (1980) **C-105m.** *½ D: Larry Peerce. Treat Williams, Lisa Eichhorn, Gabriel Swann, Susan Heldfond, Anne Byrne, Valerie Curtin, Jocelyn Brando, Nicolas Coster, Severn Darden. Irrational dud about compulsive liar Williams, who tries to unite Swann with ex-con mother Eichhorn. Film is also odiously reactionary; the villainess (Heldfond) is a one-dimensionally manipulative, man-hating feminist. [PG]

Wicked Dreams of Paula Schultz, The (1968) **C-113m.** BOMB D: George Marshall. Elke Sommer, Bob Crane, Werner Klemperer, Joey Forman, John Banner, Maureen Arthur. Laughless dud about beautiful East German Olympic hopeful who polevaults over Berlin Wall to freedom; unengaging cast was mostly recruited from *Hogan's Heroes.*

Wicked Lady, The (1983-British) **C-98m.** *½ D: Michael Winner. Faye Dunaway, Alan Bates, John Gielgud, Denholm Elliott, Prunella Scales, Oliver Tobias, Glynis Barber, Joan Hickson, Marina Sirtis. Remake of 1945 film about a scheming vixen who becomes a "highwayman" by night; hasn't the panache to turn its campy material into the romp it's intended to be. Heavy-handed stuff—including the periodic nudity. [R] ▼

Wicked Stepmother (1989) **C-92m.** BOMB D: Larry Cohen. Bette Davis, Barbara Carrera, Colleen Camp, David Rasche, Lionel Stander, Tom Bosley, Richard Moll, Evelyn Keyes. Complete mess, pieced together from a troubled (to say the least) production which Davis left after filming for just one week. Resulting patchwork story has Bette as a witch who marries Stander and then, for some reason, turns into Carrera. Notable only as a footnote in Davis' career; this was her final film. [PG-13]▼◗

Wicked, Wicked (1973) **C-95m.** BOMB D: Richard L. Bare. Tiffany Bolling, Scott Brady, David Bailey, Edd Byrnes. Disastrous mystery-thriller centering around series of hotel murders. Film was released in Duo-vision split-screen process with two things happening at once. Pity there was not enough material for even one. [PG]

Wicker Man, The (1973-British) **C-99m.** ***½ D: Robin Hardy. Edward Woodward, Christopher Lee, Britt Ekland, Diane Cilento, Ingrid Pitt, Lindsay Kemp. Harrowing, absorbing thriller by Anthony Shaffer; not really a horror film as many believe. Scot police sergeant Woodward comes to small island investigating disappearance of a child, discovers a society of modern pagans. Eerie and erotic, with seemingly authentic local color and folk music; a must-see. Shown only in truncated versions for many years; beware the 87m. and 95m. prints, which may still be in circulation. Remade in 2006. [R] ▼❶

Wicker Man, The (2006) **C-102m.** *½ D: Neil LaBute. Nicolas Cage, Ellen Burstyn, Kate Beahan, Frances Conroy, Molly Parker, Leelee Sobieski, Diane Delano, Aaron Eckhart, James Franco. Cop travels to an isolated island after receiving word from his ex that her child has disappeared and finds the place populated by a quietly tyrannical cult of women. Interesting (if misogynistic) reimagining of the 1973 film's concept is poorly executed: a mysterious, building dread has been replaced with the obvious presence of an evil that the hero is too dumb to figure out. Cage is sometimes hilariously hammy; only Burstyn, chillingly warm and civilized as the cult's leader, emerges unscathed. LaBute adapted Anthony Shaffer's original screenplay. Unrated 106m. version has more gore and a shortened, improved ending. Super 35. [PG-13]❶

Wicker Park (2004) **C-115m.** *½ D: Paul McGuigan. Josh Hartnett, Rose Byrne, Matthew Lillard, Diane Kruger, Christopher Cousins, Jessica Paré, Vlasta Vrana, Amy Sobol. Adman Hartnett puts his life on hold as he becomes obsessed with a woman he spies in a restaurant; he thinks she's his ex-love, who unexpectedly departed a couple of years earlier. Muddled thriller is loaded with flashbacks and plot twists, too many of which make no sense whatsoever. Remake of the French film L'APPARTEMENT (1996). Super 35. [PG-13] ▼❶

Wide Awake (1998) **C-90m.** *** D: M. Night Shyamalan. Joseph Cross, Timothy Reifsnyder, Dana Delany, Denis Leary, Robert Loggia, Rosie O'Donnell, Camryn Manheim, Dan Lauria, Julia Stiles. A 10-year-old Catholic school student has loving, affluent parents, but since the recent death of his beloved grandfather, he's been trying to figure out the meaning of life. Warm, quirky, and sensitive comedy/drama/parable. Young lead Cross and costar Loggia (as the deceased grandparent, in flashbacks) stand out in fine cast. Written by the director; shot in 1995. [PG] ▼❶❶

Wide Blue Road, The (1957-Italian) **C-99m.** ***½ D: Gillo Pontecorvo. Yves Montand, Alida Valli, Francisco Rabal, Umberto Spadaro, Peter Carsten, Federica Ranchi, Terence Hill. Moving, robust slice of life about an insular Italian fishing village and one proud, stubborn man who continues to engage in dynamite fishing (even though it's illegal), which pits him against a coast guard lieutenant—and the community. Montand was never more charismatic. Pontecorvo's debut film (which he cowrote with Franco Solinas) pays homage to neorealism but charts its own course—in breathtaking color. ▼❶

Wide-Eyed and Legless SEE: **Wedding Gift, The**

Wide Sargasso Sea (1993-U.S.-Australian) **C-100m.** ** D: John Duigan. Karina Lombard, Nathaniel Parker, Rachel Ward, Michael York, Martine Beswicke, Claudia Robinson, Rowena King, Naomi Watts. In 1840s Jamaica, free-spirited Creole Antoinette (Lombard), heiress to a declining estate, marries proper Englishman Rochester (Parker); at first entranced by her powerful sensuality, he fears losing control, and coldly turns away from her, which leads to tragedy. Though attractive, a failed attempt to build real drama out of humid tropical passions. Based on Jean Rhys' novel, this is a "prequel" to Charlotte Brontë's *Jane Eyre*. Also available in R-rated version. [NC-17] ▼❶❶

Widow of Saint-Pierre, The (2000-French) **C-108m.** **½ D: Patrice Leconte. Juliette Binoche, Daniel Auteuil, Emir Kusturica, Philippe Magnan, Michel Duchaussoy. Unusual story set in a remote French island off the coast of Canada in 1850, where a condemned murderer cannot be put to death because there is no guillotine. While waiting for one to arrive, the military commandant's wife makes the prisoner's rehabilitation her pet project. Interesting but unsatisfying morality tale, with Yugoslav director Kusturica a strong presence as the prisoner. Panavision. [R] ▼❶

Widows' Peak (1994-British) **C-101m.** **½ D: John Irvin. Joan Plowright, Mia Farrow, Natasha Richardson, Adrian Dunbar, Jim Broadbent, Britta Smith, Gerard McSorley. Fitfully amusing feminine slant on John Ford's brand of Blarney, with sadsack Farrow butting heads with flashy WW1 widow Richardson, who's moved to an Irish resort village in the mid 1920s. Inconsistent in tone, but three strong leads make it watchable. [PG] ▼❶

Wife, The (1994) **C-105m.** **½ D: Tom Noonan. Julie Hagerty, Tom Noonan, Wallace Shawn, Karen Young. Married New Age therapists Noonan and Hagerty are visited one evening by one of their patients (Shawn) and his seemingly emotionally disturbed wife (Young). Alternately pretentious and intriguing talkfest gets better as it goes along, but it's nowhere near as impressive as Noonan's previous film, WHAT HAPPENED WAS . . . . [R] ▼❶

Wifemistress (1977-Italian) **C-110m.** **½ D: Marco Vicario. Marcello Mastroianni, Laura Antonelli, Leonard Mann, Annie-Belle, Gastone Moschin, William Berger. Antonelli, repressed by philandering hus-

[1553]

band Mastroianni, sets out to explore his secret lives after he is forced into hiding and experiences her own sexual awakening. Sometimes erotic but mostly murky comedy-drama. [R]▼

Wife vs. Secretary (1936) 88m. **½ D: Clarence Brown. Clark Gable, Jean Harlow, Myrna Loy, May Robson, George Barbier, James Stewart, Hobart Cavanaugh. Perfect example of Hollywood gloss, with three topnotch stars towering over inferior material. Harlow is particularly good in tale of secretary who becomes invaluable to her boss (Gable), causing complications in both of their lives.▼)

Wigstock: The Movie (1995) C-85m. *** D: Barry Shils. Campy documentary record of Wigstock, the drag ball held in N.Y.C. each Labor Day weekend. While famous drag queens like RuPaul appear, the focus is just as much on lesser-known characters such as The Lady Bunny (Wigstock's M.C.), Mistress Formica, and, best of all, the Dueling (Tallulah) Bankheads.▼◑)

Wilbur Wants to Kill Himself (2002-British-Danish) C-109m. *** D: Lone Scherfig. Jamie Sives, Adrian Rawlins, Shirley Henderson, Lisa McKinlay, Mads Mikkelsen, Julia Davis, Susan Vidler. Winning comedy-drama about a handful of life's lost souls, set in Glasgow. Wilbur (Sives) is forever trying to do himself in, placing a terrible burden on his brother Harbour (Rawlins) to keep a constant eye on him. Then a young woman (Henderson) with a young daughter in tow comes into their lives, causing surprising changes for all of them. A quirky sense of humor diverts us at first from the film's serious goals and its good-hearted concern for every character on-screen. The director coscripted. HD 24P Widescreen. [R]▼)

Wilby Conspiracy, The (1975) C-101m. *** D: Ralph Nelson. Sidney Poitier, Michael Caine, Nicol Williamson, Prunella Gee, Persis Khambatta, Saeed Jaffrey, Rutger Hauer. Slick chase movie about black African political activist and the reluctant white companion he drags with him on cross-country flight from the law. Memories of Poitier's earlier THE DEFIANT ONES keep focusing throughout, but the two stars maintain a light touch. Sinister Williamson steals it from them both. [PG]▼)

Wild, The (2006) C-94m. ** D: Steve "Spaz" Williams. Voices of Kiefer Sutherland, James Belushi, Eddie Izzard, Janeane Garofalo, William Shatner, Richard Kind, Patrick Warburton, Laraine Newman. When his son is accidentally shipped off to the jungle, a lion and a quartet of misfit animals leave the safety of the Central Park Zoo to rescue the cub. Disney-released CG-animated feature can't decide if it's a zany comedy or a drama with heart; it winds up being neither. Shamelessly derivative of MADAGASCAR and FINDING NEMO. Highlight is stylized

opening in which the father tells his son of past battles in the jungle, including a sincere homage to earlier Disney classics. This is not destined to be one of them. [G]◑

Wild America (1997) C-106m. ** D: William Dear. Jonathan Taylor Thomas, Devon Sawa, Scott Bairstow, Frances Fisher, Jamey Sheridan, Tracey Walter, Don Stroud. Ho-hum based-on-fact account of the three adventurous Stouffer brothers, who trek across America in 1967 to film wild animals in their natural habitats. The clichéd subplots do this one in, but it's harmless enough fare for kids. The eldest brother, Marty Stouffer (Bairstow), grew up to become a noted wildlife documentary filmmaker. Danny Glover appears unbilled. Clairmont-Scope. [PG] ▼◑

Wild Angels, The (1966) C-93m. *½ D: Roger Corman. Peter Fonda, Nancy Sinatra, Bruce Dern, Diane Ladd, Buck Taylor, Norman Alden, Michael J. Pollard, Joan Shawlee, Gayle Hunnicutt, Dick Miller. Predecessor of EASY RIDER without that film's class; Charles Griffith's story of destructive motorcycle gang is OK after about 24 beers. Peter Bogdanovich worked extensively on this film: writing, editing, second unit, etc.; he also can be glimpsed in one of the rumbles. Panavision.▼)

Wild at Heart (1990) C-127m. ** D: David Lynch. Nicolas Cage, Laura Dern, Diane Ladd, Willem Dafoe, Isabella Rossellini, Harry Dean Stanton, Crispin Glover, Grace Zabriskie, J.E. Freeman, Calvin Lockhart, Marvin Kaplan, W. Morgan Sheppard, David Patrick Kelly, Freddie Jones, John Lurie, Jack Nance, Sherilyn Fenn, Sheryl Lee, Pruitt Taylor Vince. He's Elvis, she's Marilyn, they're madly in love and on the lam: they hop in her convertible and make an odyssey through Hell—or is it Oz? Diehard fans of writer-director Lynch may love this violent Southern Gothic melodrama (and there *are* great moments) but his utter absorption with ugliness makes it tough to take. Formidable performances all around, including real-life mother and daughter Ladd and Dern. Lynch based his screenplay on a novel by Barry Gifford. Rossellini's character went on to get a movie all her own, PERDITA DURANGO (1997). There, the role is played by Rosie Perez. Panavision. [R]▼◑

Wild Beds SEE: **Tigers in Lipstick**
Wild Bill (1995) C-97m. ** D: Walter Hill. Jeff Bridges, Ellen Barkin, John Hurt, Diane Lane, Keith Carradine, Christina Applegate, Bruce Dern, James Gammon, David Arquette, Marjoe Gortner, James Remar. Odd revisionist take on Wild Bill Hickok, told in episodic form that creates distance from—rather than understanding of—the legendary hell-raiser of the Old West. The title of the film really should be THE ASSASSINATION OF WILD BILL, because that's what it's all about. There *are* those opium

dreams to break the monotony . . . Barkin is fun as Calamity Jane, but other characters are superficially drawn at best. [R]▼●◗

Wild Bunch, The (1969) **C-134m.** ★★★★ D: Sam Peckinpah. William Holden, Ernest Borgnine, Robert Ryan, Edmond O'Brien, Warren Oates, Ben Johnson, Jaime Sanchez, Strother Martin, L. Q. Jones, Albert Dekker, Bo Hopkins, Emilio Fernandez, Dub Taylor. Peckinpah's best film won instant notoriety for its "beautiful" bloodletting, but seems almost restrained alongside today's films. Aging outlaws with their own code of ethics find themselves passe in 1913 and decide to retire after one final haul. Acting, dialogue, direction, score, photography, and especially editing are world class; an authentic American classic. Reissued in 1981 at 142m., with two deleted sequences restored. European theatrical version running 144m. now available on video. Panavision. [R] ▼●◗

Wildcats (1986) **C-107m.** ★★ D: Michael Ritchie. Goldie Hawn, Swoosie Kurtz, Robyn Lively, Brandy Gold, James Keach, Jan Hooks, Bruce McGill, Nipsey Russell, Mykel T. Williamson, Wesley Snipes, Woody Harrelson, M. Emmet Walsh, George Wyner, Ann Doran, Gloria Stuart, L.L. Cool J. Football-crazy phys-ed teacher Hawn finally gets her wish—to coach a varsity team—at a rough inner-city high school. Never strays from formula but manages to deliver the laughs. Entertaining. [R]▼●◗

Wild Child, The (1970-French) **85m.** ★★★ D: François Truffaut. François Truffaut, Jean-Pierre Cargol, Jean Daste, Paul Ville. Initially absorbing true story of wild boy raised alone in French woods and the doctor who tries to civilize him. Simply told, deliberately old-fashioned in technique; film loses steam half-way through. Truffaut is ideal as the doctor. Set in 1700s. [G]▼●◗

Wild Child (2008-U.S.-British-French) **C-99m.** ★★ D: Nick Moore. Emma Roberts, Natasha Richardson, Shirley Henderson, Alex Pettyfer, Nick Frost, Aidan Quinn, Juno Temple. Distaff rehash of A YANK AT OXFORD transplants spoiled Roberts from Malibu to Abbey Mount School (est. 1797) for proper British girls. There, a bad blonde teen learns how to be a better brunette woman from her patient classmates, while chasing a dreamboat who's somehow the only boy on campus. Broad and often slapsticky, this is a flashy, polished production, but void. Richardson, however, is aces as the dedicated headmistress, in her final film. [PG-13] ◗

Wild Country, The (1971) **C-100m.** ★★½ D: Robert Totten. Steve Forrest, Vera Miles, Ronny Howard, Jack Elam, Frank deKova, Morgan Woodward, Clint Howard. Standard Disney fare, adapted from Ralph Moody's *Little Britches,* about joys

and hardships faced by family which moves from Pittsburgh to Wyoming in 1880s. Magnificent scenery. [G]▼

Wild Drifter SEE: **Cockfighter**

Wild Duck, The (1983-Australian) **C-96m.** ★½ D: Henri Safran. Liv Ullmann, Jeremy Irons, Lucinda Jones, John Meillon, Arthur Dignam, Michael Pate. Dreary, disappointing adaptation of the Ibsen play, centering on two days in the lives of the Ackland (anglicized from "Ekdal") family members and updating the story by 20-odd years. The question is: Why? Performances are OK, but it's oh so slow and pretentious. [PG]▼

Wilde (1998-British) **C-115m.** ★★½ D: Brian Gilbert. Stephen Fry, Jude Law, Tom Wilkinson, Vanessa Redgrave, Jennifer Ehle, Gemma Jones, Judy Parfitt, Michael Sheen, Zoë Wanamaker, Orlando Bloom, Ioan Gruffudd. Profile of playwright/author Oscar Wilde is much gamier (to its arguable detriment) than the two 1960 biopics. Begins choppily, drags at the end, but generally compels in a long midsection that deals with events leading up to Wilde's 1895 sodomy trial and conviction. Fry bears a striking resemblance to Wilde, while Wilkinson gives another in a string of rich performances as Wilde's chief adversary, the Marquis of Queensbury. 2.35 Research PLC. [R]▼

Wilder Napalm (1993) **C-109m.** ★½ D: Glenn Gordon Caron. Debra Winger, Dennis Quaid, Arliss Howard, M. Emmet Walsh, Jim Varney. Bizarre, almost incomprehensible account of brothers Quaid and Howard, who share a rare talent: when concentrating deeply enough, they can make objects burst into flames. Winger is cast as Howard's spirited wife. It's no wonder that this barely watchable film remained unreleased for quite some time. [PG-13]▼●◗

Wilderness Family, Part 2, The SEE: **Further Adventures of the Wilderness Family, The**

Wildflowers (1999) **C-97m.** ★★½ D: Melissa Painter. Daryl Hannah, Clea DuVall, Eric Roberts, Tomas Arana, Richard Hillman, Irene Bedard, John Doe, Alan Gelfant. Introspective drama about a teen (DuVall) who grew up on a hippie commune and is looking to find herself, and her obsession with a free-spirited older woman (Hannah) who may be her mother. Slow moving at times, but extremely involving when it stays on track. Hannah coexecutive produced. [R]▼◗

Wild for Kicks (1960-British) **92m.** ★★ D: Edmond T. Greville. David Farrar, Noelle Adam, Christopher Lee, Gillian Hills, Adam Faith, Shirley Anne Field, Peter McEnery, Oliver Reed. Sultry teen Hills, with a bad attitude, resents her father's pretty new French-born wife and summarily gets into all sorts of mischief. Not very good; of interest mainly as a period piece. Original British title: BEAT GIRL. ▼ ●)

Wild Geese, The (1978-British) **C-134m.** **½ D: Andrew V. McLaglen. Richard Burton, Roger Moore, Richard Harris, Hardy Kruger, Stewart Granger, Jack Watson, Frank Finlay, Jeff Corey, Winston Ntshona. Silly but entertaining action yarn by Reginald Rose with Burton miscast as leader of mercenaries who rescue kidnapped African leader. Better (and shorter) script would have helped. Sequel followed in 1985. [R] ▼ ●)

Wild Geese II (1985-British) **C-125m.** ** D: Peter Hunt. Scott Glenn, Barbara Carrera, Edward Fox, Laurence Olivier, Robert Webber, Robert Freitag, Kenneth Haigh. Cluttered action-adventure about a much-wanted mercenary hired to spring arch-Nazi Rudolf Hess from Berlin's Spandau prison and the incidents this triggers. Uncomfortable mix of straight action and tongue-in-cheek. [R] ▼

Wild Grass (2010-French-Italian) **C-104m.** ** D: Alain Resnais. Sabine Azéma, André Dussollier, Anne Consigny, Emmanuelle Devos, Mathieu Amalric, Michel Vuillermoz, Nicolas Duvauchelle, Sara Forestier, Annie Cordy, Roger-Pierre. After purchasing a pair of shoes, a woman (Azéma) has her wallet stolen. A married man (Dussollier) finds it and becomes irrationally obsessed with her. Odd, teasing, dreamlike farce from 88-year-old Resnais is an exploration of chance and fate, and the strange, complex relationship that develops between these two characters . . . but it's curiously unsatisfying. [PG] ▶

Wild Heart, The (1950-British) **C-82m.** ** D: Michael Powell, Emeric Pressburger. Jennifer Jones, David Farrar, Cyril Cusack, Sybil Thorndike, Edward Chapman, George Cole, Hugh Griffith, Esmond Knight. Muddled tale of strange Welsh girl in late 19th century whose life is dominated by superstitions; she marries minister but is stirred by lusty squire. Beautiful location photography by Christopher Challis. Reedited from 110m. British release called GONE TO EARTH, which plays much better.

Wild Hearts Can't Be Broken (1991) **C-88m.** *** D: Steve Miner. Gabrielle Anwar, Michael Schoeffling, Cliff Robertson, Dylan Kussman, Kathleen York, Frank Renzulli. Absorbing Disney picture about real-life Sonora Webster, a strong-willed girl who joins a traveling show in the early 1930s and trains to become a "diving girl"—sitting astride a horse as it dives 40 feet into a tank of water. Simply told, and well acted, with Robertson first-rate as a road-company Buffalo Bill. Captures Depression-era flavor (and look) much better than many more ambitious and expensive films. Incidentally, no horses were subjected to high dives in the making of the film. [G] ▼ ●)

Wild Hogs (2007) **C-99m.** ** D: Walt Becker. Tim Allen, John Travolta, Martin Lawrence, William H. Macy, Ray Liotta, Marisa Tomei, Kevin Durand, M. C. Gainey, Jill Hennessy, Tichina Arnold, Stephen Tobolowsky. Four middle-aged pals whose lives have stagnated decide to take a road trip together on their Harleys and immediately get into all sorts of trouble—from camping mishaps to antagonizing a hostile biker gang. Silly, sometimes downright stupid slapstick comedy puts likable actors into the kind of sappy vehicle that Kirk Douglas and Burt Lancaster didn't make until their 70s (see—or rather, don't see—TOUGH GUYS). John C. McGinley appears unbilled, and there's a surprise cameo near the end. Super 35. [PG-13] ▶

Wild Horse Hank (1979-Canadian) **C-94m.** **½ D: Eric Till. Linda Blair, Michael Wincott, Al Waxman, Pace Bradford, Richard Crenna. Inoffensive adventure of college student Blair trying to save horses from being butchered for dog food. A bit overlong, and Blair walks through her role; still, older children may enjoy it. ▼

Wild in the Country (1961) **C-114m.** **½ D: Philip Dunne. Elvis Presley, Hope Lange, Tuesday Weld, Millie Perkins, John Ireland, Gary Lockwood. Can *you* resist Elvis in a Clifford Odets script about a back-country hothead with literary aspirations? Clichéd if earnest, but an undeniable curiosity with some good performances, Elvis' among them. That's young Christina Crawford as Lockwood's girlfriend. CinemaScope. ▼ ▶

Wild in the Sky (1972) **C-87m.** **½ D: William T. Naud. Georg Stanford Brown, Brandon de Wilde, Keenan Wynn, Tim O'Connor, James Daly, Dick Gautier, Robert Lansing. Zany idea doesn't quite come off in story of three prisoners who hijack a B-52 bomber. Written by Naud, Gautier, and Peter Marshall. Original title: BLACK JACK.

Wild in the Streets (1968) **C-97m.** **½ D: Barry Shear. Christopher Jones, Shelley Winters, Diane Varsi, Hal Holbrook, Millie Perkins, Ed Begley, Richard Pryor, Bert Freed. Dark satire about millionaire singing idol/drug pusher who is elected President after voting age is lowered to 14. Wildly overrated by some critics, film is nonetheless enjoyable on a nonthink level. [PG—originally rated R] ▼ ●)

Wild Is the Wind (1957) **114m.** **½ D: George Cukor. Anna Magnani, Anthony Quinn, Anthony Franciosa, Dolores Hart, Joseph Calleia. Turgid soaper set in the West, with Quinn marrying the sister of his dead wife, not able to separate the two. Good acting helps script along. VistaVision.

Wild Life, The (1984) **C-96m.** *½ D: Art Linson. Christopher Penn, Ilan Mitchell-Smith, Eric Stoltz, Jenny Wright, Lea Thompson, Rick Moranis, Hart Bochner,

Michael Bowen, Randy Quaid, Sherilyn Fenn, Lee Ving, Nancy Wilson, Laura Dern, Jack Kehoe, Robert Ridgely, Dean Devlin, Ben Stein. Unfunny youth comedy about straight-arrow high school grad Stoltz deciding to leave home and move into "swinging singles" apartment. Meager attempt to clone FAST TIMES AT RIDGEMONT HIGH with same writer and producer (doubling here as director), and Christopher Penn trying to ape brother Sean's flaky character—unsuccessfully. Penn's real-life dad, Leo Penn, plays his father here. [R]▼●

Wild Man Blues (1998) **C-105m.** *** D: Barbara Kopple. Oscar-winning documentarian Kopple follows Woody Allen and his companion (later wife), Soon-Yi Previn, on a 1996 European concert tour given by Allen and his New Orleans–style jazz band. A must for Woodyphiles, surprisingly revealing even in its most mundane moments; others may find it less compelling. It also helps to like the traditional, even primitive, style of music being played. [PG]▼●

Wild McCullochs, The (1975) **C-93m.** ** D: Max Baer. Forrest Tucker, Max Baer, Julie Adams, Janice Heiden, Dennis Redfield, Don Grady, William Demarest. Forgettable QUIET MAN rip-off has Tucker as self-made Texas millionaire who tries to raise his sons in his two-fisted image, with Baer eventually forced to prove he is "a man." Yawn. [PG]▼●

Wild One, The (1954) **79m.** ***½ D: Laslo Benedek. Marlon Brando, Mary Murphy, Robert Keith, Lee Marvin, Jay C. Flippen, Jerry Paris, Alvy Moore, Gil Stratton, Jr. The original motorcycle film with Brando's renowned performance as pack-leader raising Cain in small town; dated, but well worth viewing. Script by John Paxton, based on a story by Frank Rooney; produced by Stanley Kramer.▼●❚

Wild Orchid (1990) **C-111m.** BOMB D: Zalman King. Mickey Rourke, Jacqueline Bisset, Carré Otis, Assumpta Serna, Bruce Greenwood, Oleg Vidov, Milton Goncalves. Prim lawyer Otis, employed by banker Bisset, gets assaulted by Rio de Janeiro carny-time temptation: semi-public fornicators, limousine raunch, and the sight of earringed Rourke in deep bronze makeup. Notorious simulated sex scene caused a stir, but it's all for naught; this picture is enough to make any two bananas roll over in Carmen Miranda's grave. Followed by a sequel. Unrated version runs 116m. [R] ▼●❚

Wild Orchid II: Two Shades of Blue (1992) **C-107m.** BOMB D: Zalman King. Nina Siemaszko, Wendy Hughes, Tom Skerritt, Robert Davi, Brent Fraser, Christopher McDonald, Liane Curtis, Joe Dallesandro, Lydie Denier. For viewers who haven't seen ORCHID 1, the title demands a "what is it?"

question. For those who have, it's a "why is it?" question. By day, blond Siemaszko puppy-loves a high school jock—but by night, she dons a black wig in the local brothel to entertain the same unwitting dufus. Standard heavy breathing from director King, but with even more lung congestion than usual. [R]▼●❚

Wild Pack, The (1971) **C-102m.** **½ D: Hall Bartlett. Kent Lane, Tisha Sterling, John Rubinstein, Butch Patrick, Mark de Vries, Peter Nielsen. Fairly interesting drama, set in Brazil, about day-to-day life of a group of black and white orphans who steal food; film won grand prize at Moscow Film Festival. Originally titled THE SANDPIT GENERALS. Video title: THE DEFIANT. Panavision.▼

Wild Pair, The (1987) **C-88m.** *½ D: Beau Bridges. Beau Bridges, Bubba Smith, Lloyd Bridges, Gary Lockwood, Raymond St. Jacques, Danny De La Paz, Lela Rochon, Ellen Geer. Trite police thriller, with cop Smith and FBI agent Beau Bridges teaming up to bring some drug dealing racists to justice. Utterly ordinary in all departments. Bridges' first theatrical film as director. [R]▼●

Wild Parrots of Telegraph Hill, The (2005) **C-83m.** *** D: Judy Irving. In San Francisco, a flock of colorful parrots, descendants of escaped pets, make Telegraph Hill their base. Philosophical, unemployed Mark Bittner befriends the birds, naming them and feeding them. Documentary focuses more on ingratiating Bittner than on the parrots, and at the end unexpectedly reveals itself as a true-life love story. Charming, likeable film about charming, likeable birds and people; a quiet little gem, full of low-key surprises. [G]❚

Wild Party, The (1929) **76m.** **½ D: Dorothy Arzner. Clara Bow, Fredric March, Shirley O'Hara, Marceline Day, Joyce Compton, Jack Oakie. Fascinating antique about dishy new prof at all-girls' school and his on-again, off-again relationship with a sexy student who thinks college is just a lark. Absolutely awful by any objective standards, but great fun to watch. Clara's talkie debut. ▼

Wild Party, The (1975) **C-95m.** ** D: James Ivory. James Coco, Raquel Welch, Perry King, Tiffany Bolling, David Dukes, Royal Dano, Dena Dietrich. Uneven evocation of 1920s Hollywood with Coco as a Fatty Arbuckle-type comedian who throws a lavish party to try and save his failing career. Film has definite assets (notably its performances) but just doesn't come off. Based on the narrative poem by Joseph Moncure March; cut by its distributor, later restored by Ivory to 107m. [R]▼❚

Wild Racers, The (1968) **C-79m.** *½ D: Daniel Haller. Fabian, Mimsy Farmer, Judy Cornwall, David Landers. Dumb racer

Fabian loves his work and one-night stands; Farmer is his latest challenge.

Wild Reeds (1994-French) **C-110m.** ***½ D: André Téchiné. Elodie Bouchez, Gael Morel, Staphane Rideau, Frederick Gorny, Michele Moretti. Richly evocative film, set in 1962, about four young people in rural France (where the kids listen to American Top 40 songs!) coming of age and exploring their sexuality. The ideological and emotional turbulence caused by the Algerian war is felt in a quiet boarding school with the arrival of a new French-Algerian student, whose radical politics throw things into disarray. A multilayered story, masterfully directed. Winner of four César Awards including Best Picture. ▼●▮

Wild Ride, The (1960) **63m.** *½ D: Harvey Berman. Jack Nicholson, Georgianna Carter, Robert Bean. Amateurish low-budgeter about a hedonistic hot-rodder who's as casual about killing people as he is about stealing his buddy's girlfriend. Worth seeing only if you're curious about this early Nicholson performance. Revised for 2000 release as VELOCITY. ▼▮

Wild River (1960) **C-110m.** ***½ D: Elia Kazan. Montgomery Clift, Lee Remick, Jo Van Fleet, Albert Salmi, Jay C. Flippen, James Westerfield. Clift plays Tennessee Valley Authority official trying to convince elderly Van Fleet to sell her property for new projects. Kazan's exquisite evocation of 1930s Tennessee—and moving romance between Clift and Remick—give this film its strength. Bruce Dern makes his film debut in supporting role. Screenplay by Paul Osborn, from a novel by William Bradford Hine and Borden Deal. Cinema-Scope. ▮

Wildrose (1984) **C-95m.** ***½ D: John Hanson. Lisa Eichhorn, Tom Bower, Jim Cada, Cinda Jackson, Dan Nemanick, Bill Schoppert. Eichhorn excels in this vivid tale of a female iron pit worker, both strong and insecure, who must deal with the resentment of her male co-workers—as well as a romance. Filmed in Minnesota, with the landscape and its inhabitants carefully, almost lovingly, etched. ▼

Wild Rovers (1971) **C-109m.** ***½ D: Blake Edwards. William Holden, Ryan O'Neal, Karl Malden, Lynn Carlin, Tom Skerritt, Joe Don Baker, Rachel Roberts, Moses Gunn. Underrated Western about two cowpokes who become fugitives after they rob a bank on whim. Choppy script seems unimportant in light of Holden's performance, incredibly lyrical scenes. Edwards' original 136m. version has finally been restored and released, which may boost the film's maligned reputation. Panavision. [PG] ▼●▮

Wild Side, The (1983) **C-96m.** BOMB D: Penelope Spheeris. Chris Pederson, Bill Coyne, Jennifer Clay, Timothy Eric O'Brien,

Andrew Pece, Don Allen. Perfectly awful drama about alienated suburban teenagers, angry kids who cut their hair instead of growing it long and live in abandoned, rat-infested crash pad. Tries to "make a statement" while wallowing in gratuitous violence. Aka SUBURBIA. [R]▼▮

Wild Strawberries (1957-Swedish) **90m.** **** D: Ingmar Bergman. Victor Sjostrom, Ingrid Thulin, Bibi Andersson, Gunnar Bjornstrand, Folke Sundquist, Bjorn Bjelvenstam. Elderly Stockholm professor reviews the disappointments of his life, while traveling by car to receive an honorary degree. Superb use of flashbacks and brilliant performance by Sjostrom make this Bergman classic an emotional powerhouse. Still a staple of any serious filmgoer's education.▼●▮

Wild Target (2010-British) **C-98m.** *½ D: Jonathan Lynn. Bill Nighy, Emily Blunt, Rupert Grint, Rupert Everett, Eileen Atkins, Martin Freeman, Gregor Fisher. Mother-dominated hit man Nighy has reached middle age without letting romance or much else interfere with his orderly world. But oh, so gradually, he begins to fall for his latest target, an art world con woman (Blunt) he decides to let live so that the script can plunk them into the rural countryside, for no particular reason, with redhead Grint from the *Harry Potter* movies. Knocking a movie about professional killing for lacking charm may not be completely fair, but this film tries to meld affection for its characters with frequent brutality. Both normally pleasing leads are utterly defeated by the material. Remake of France's CIBLE ÉMOUVANTE (1993). Super 35. [PG-13]▮

Wild Thing (1987) **C-92m.** *½ D: Max Reid. Rob Knepper, Kathleen Quinlan, Robert Davi, Maury Chaykin, Betty Buckley. Misguided mishmash about a boy whose parents are murdered and who grows up into a "wild thing" who protects street people from the likes of arch-villain Davi. One would like to think that screenwriter John Sayles had more in mind for this fable than what turned out on screen. [PG-13] ▼

Wild Things (1998) **C-108m.** *** D: John McNaughton. Kevin Bacon, Matt Dillon, Neve Campbell, Theresa Russell, Denise Richards, Daphne Rubin-Vega, Robert Wagner, Bill Murray, Carrie Snodgress. In South Florida, high school counselor Dillon is accused of rape by rich teenage sexpot Richards *and* her tattooed trailer-trash classmate Campbell. Cop Bacon suspects there's a plot behind it, and he's right: this raunchy, entertaining neo-noir has more twists than a pretzel factory. Gorgeously photographed (by Jeffrey L. Kimball) and well played, it never takes itself too seriously. Murray is a hoot as an ambulance-chasing shyster.

Followed by three in-name-only direct-to-DVD sequels. Unrated version runs 115m. Panavision. [R]▼●◗

Wild Thornberrys Movie, The (2002) C-108m. *** D: Jeff McGrath, Cathy Malkasian. Voices of Lacey Chabert, Tom Kane, Tim Curry, Lynn Redgrave, Jodi Carlisle, Danielle Harris, Flea, Rupert Everett, Marisa Tomei, Alfre Woodard, Brock Peters, Brenda Blethyn, Obba Babatundé, Kevin Michael Richardson. Eliza Thornberry thrives on life in the African wild with her documentary-filmmaker parents, especially after she discovers she can talk to animals—but her grandmother insists she be sent to boarding school in England. Handsome, well-written feature based on the hip, funny (and environmentally conscious) TV series, with good songs by Paul Simon and Peter Gabriel. Followed by RUGRATS GO WILD. Digital Widescreen. [PG]▼◗

Wild West (1992-British) C-85m. **½ D: David Attwood. Naveen Andrews, Sarita Choudhury, Ronny Jhutti, Ravi Kapoor, Ameet Chana. A Pakistani living in a London suburb encounters typical (and not-so-typical) problems when he tries to put together a country-western band. Funny and colorful film plays on its offbeat characters and backdrop to dodge the fact that the story is actually the same old breaking-into-showbiz warhorse.▼

Wild Wild West (1999) C-107m. *½ D: Barry Sonnenfeld. Will Smith, Kevin Kline, Kenneth Branagh, Salma Hayek, Ted Levine, M. Emmett Walsh, Bai Ling, Frederique van der Wal, Musetta Vander. Rehash of 1960s TV series finds special agents James West (Smith) and inventor Artemus Gordon (Kline) on a special mission for President Grant to capture nefarious bad guy Arliss Loveless (Branagh). Overstuffed with visual gimmickry, but leaden in every way. You can hear the banter landing with a thud every few minutes. [PG-13]▼●◗

Wild, Wild Winter (1966) C-80m. ** D: Lennie Weinrib. Gary Clarke, Chris Noel, Steve Franken, Don Edmonds. Light-headed ski-slope musical froth, with guest stars Jay and The Americans, The Beau Brummels, Dick and Dee Dee. Techniscope.

Willard (1971) C-95m. ** D: Daniel Mann. Bruce Davison, Elsa Lanchester, Ernest Borgnine, Sondra Locke, Michael Dante, J. Pat O'Malley, Jody Gilbert, Joan Shawlee. Touching story of a boy and his rats captured public's fancy at the box office, but film's lack of style prevents it from being anything more than a second-rate thriller. Remade in 2003. Sequel: BEN. [PG]▼●

Willard (2003) C-100m. ** D: Glen Morgan. Crispin Glover, R. Lee Ermey, Laura Elena Harring, Jackie Burroughs. As if eating Ernest Borgnine in the '71 version weren't enough of a feast, those pesky rodents are back. Glover is the put-upon misfit who finds rats to be his only friends. Given how much the second floor of Glover's home resembles Norman Bates' digs, writer/director Morgan has obviously studied his Hitchcock. Not without style but stretched beyond all limits, film isn't quite bad enough to make you use "rats!" as an expletive. "Pleh!" is more like it. Bruce Davison, who starred in the original film, has an unbilled cameo. Super 35. [PG-13]▼◗

William Shakespeare's A Midsummer Night's Dream SEE: **Midsummer Night's Dream, A** (1999)

William Shakespeare's Romeo & Juliet SEE: **Romeo & Juliet** (1996)

William Shakespeare's The Merchant of Venice SEE: **Merchant of Venice, The**

Willie and Joe Back at the Front SEE: **Back at the Front**

Willie and Phil (1980) C-115m. *** D: Paul Mazursky. Michael Ontkean, Margot Kidder, Ray Sharkey, Jan Miner, Tom Brennan, Julie Bovasso, Louis Guss, Kathleen Maguire, Kaki Hunter, Larry Fishburne, Natalie Wood. Affectionate, perceptive, underrated retelling of JULES AND JIM. Ontkean and Sharkey meet after a screening of the Truffaut classic, become fast pals, then friends and lovers of free-spirited Kidder. A wistful tale of how chance encounters alter lives, how camaraderie between friends is everlasting, how men always do the asking but women do the deciding. [R]●

Willie Dynamite (1974) C-102m. *** D: Gilbert Moses. Roscoe Orman, Diana Sands, Thalmus Rasulala, Roger Robinson, George Murdock. Good black actioner set in N.Y.C., with Orman as a pimp out to topple big-shot Robinson, an outrageous homosexual. Sands is fine in her last film. [R]▼◗

Willow (1988) C-125m. *** D: Ron Howard. Val Kilmer, Joanne Whalley, Warwick Davis, Jean Marsh, Patricia Hayes, Billy Barty, Pat Roach, Kevin Pollak. Rollicking fantasy-adventure, from a story by George Lucas (not hard to guess, since it follows a definite STAR WARS formula) about a little person (Davis) who takes on the challenge of shepherding an abandoned baby to its place of destiny—where it will destroy the evil powers of Queen Bavmorda (Marsh). Plenty of action, humor, and eye-filling special effects, though a bit intense at times for the youngsters at whom it's targeted. Panavision. [PG]▼●◗

Will Penny (1968) C-108m. ***½ D: Tom Gries. Charlton Heston, Joan Hackett, Donald Pleasence, Lee Majors, Bruce Dern, Ben Johnson, Slim Pickens, Anthony Zerbe, Clifton James. One of the best films on the cowboy/loner ever to come out of Hollywood. Heston's character is one of great strength; supporting actors are exceptional,

Written by director Gries. Memorable score by David Raksin. ▼●)

Will Success Spoil Rock Hunter? (1957) **C-94m.** ***½ D: Frank Tashlin. Tony Randall, Jayne Mansfield, Betsy Drake, Joan Blondell, John Williams, Henry Jones, Mickey Hargitay. Guest star, Groucho Marx. Clever satire uses George Axelrod play about ad man who tries to persuade glamorous star to endorse Stay-Put Lipstick as springboard for scattershot satire on 1950s morals, television, sex, business, etc. Director-writer Tashlin in peak form. CinemaScope. ▼●)

Willy Milly SEE: **Something Special**

Willy Wonka & the Chocolate Factory (1971) **C-98m.** **½ D: Mel Stuart. Gene Wilder, Jack Albertson, Peter Ostrum, Roy Kinnear, Aubrey Woods, Michael Bollner, Ursula Reit. Adaptation of Roald Dahl's book *Charlie and the Chocolate Factory* has all the ingredients of classic fantasy. Enigmatic Wilder gives kids a tour of his mystery-shrouded candy factory, but cruel edge taints film's enjoyment. Anthony Newley–Leslie Bricusse score includes "Candy Man." Scripted by Dahl, with eye-popping sets by Harper Goff. Remade in 2005 as CHARLIE AND THE CHOCOLATE FACTORY. [G] ▼●)

Wimbledon (2004-British) **C-97m.** **½ D: Richard Loncraine. Kirsten Dunst, Paul Bettany, Sam Neill, Jon Favreau, Bernard Hill, Eleanor Bron, Austin Nichols, Robert Lindsay, Celia Imrie, James McAvoy. Old-fashioned romantic movie about two tennis champions, one past his prime (Bettany), the other a rising star (Dunst), who fall for each other while competing at the Wimbledon tournament. Bettany is endearing and his chemistry with Dunst bolsters a pleasant but predictable script. Several famous tennis stars make cameos. Super 35. [PG-13] ▼)

Win A Date With Tad Hamilton! (2004) **C-96m.** **½ D: Robert Luketic. Kate Bosworth, Topher Grace, Josh Duhamel, Ginnifer Goodwin, Nathan Lane, Sean Hayes, Gary Cole, Kathryn Hahn. Cute comedy about a starstruck girl from West Virginia who wins a date with her favorite Hollywood heartthrob, much to the dismay of her best friend (Grace), who's never had the nerve to tell her he loves her. Slight at best, but put over by a winning cast that plays it for real, with no cynicism in sight. Super 35. [PG-13] ▼)

Winchester '73 (1950) **92m.** ***½ D: Anthony Mann. James Stewart, Shelley Winters, Dan Duryea, Stephen McNally, Charles Drake, Millard Mitchell, John McIntire, Will Geer, Jay C. Flippen, Rock Hudson, Anthony (Tony) Curtis. Exceptional Western story of Stewart tracking down a man—and his stolen rifle—through series of interrelated episodes, leading to memorable shootout among rock-strewn

hills. First-rate in every way, this landmark film was largely responsible for renewed popularity of Westerns in the 1950s. Script by Robert L. Richards and Borden Chase, from a story by Stuart N. Lake. Beautifully photographed by William Daniels; remade for TV in 1967. ▼●)

Wind, The (1928) **88m.** **** D: Victor Seastrom. Lillian Gish, Lars Hanson, Montagu Love, Dorothy Cumming, Edward Earle, William Orlamond. Virgin Virginian Gish battles the elements in a barren dustbowl town—marrying on the rebound a man who disgusts her, shooting the lout who rapes her. Probably Gish's greatest vehicle—and one of the last great silents—with a splendidly staged climactic desert storm sequence. Written by Frances Marion, from Dorothy Scarborough's novel. ▼●)

Wind, The (1987) **C-92m.** BOMB D: Nico Mastorakis. Meg Foster, Wings Hauser, David McCallum, Robert Morley, Steve Railsback. Good cast is wasted in old-fashioned thriller about mystery writer Foster terrorized by Hauser in her spooky house in Greece. Unconvincing structure has hero Railsback injected artificially into the story in later reels. Released direct to video. ▼)

Wind (1992) **C-125m.** **½ D: Carroll Ballard. Matthew Modine, Jennifer Grey, Cliff Robertson, Jack Thompson, Stellan Skarsgard, Rebecca Miller, Ned Vaughn. Enjoyable if overly formulaic tale of competitive yacht racing, about young people determined to build their own craft and reclaim the America's Cup from Australia. Story takes a back seat to the sailing sequences, breathtakingly photographed by John Toll. [PG-13] ▼●)

Wind Across the Everglades (1958) **C-93m.** **½ D: Nicholas Ray. Burl Ives, Christopher Plummer, Gypsy Rose Lee, George Voskovec, Tony Galento, Emmett Kelly, Chana Eden, MacKinlay Kantor. Oddball cast in even odder story of boozy turn-of-the-20th-century Florida game warden (Plummer) who takes it upon himself to rid the area of poachers. Matchup of director Ray and writer-producer Budd Schulberg makes this a genuine curio. Peter Falk makes his film debut in a small role; rare out-of-makeup appearance by top clown Kelly. Filmed in the Everglades.

Wind and the Lion, The (1975) **C-119m.** **½ D: John Milius. Sean Connery, Candice Bergen, Brian Keith, John Huston, Geoffrey Lewis, Steve Kanaly, Vladek Sheybal. Milius brings modern sensibilities to an old-fashioned adventure-romance, with uneven results. Connery is Moroccan sheik who kidnaps American woman and her children, sparking international incident in which Teddy Roosevelt (Keith) becomes involved. Loosely based on a true incident. Panavision. [PG] ▼●)

Wind Chill (2007) **C-91m.** **½ D: Gregory

Jacobs. Emily Blunt, Ashton Holmes, Martin Donovan, Ned Bellamy, Chelan Simmons. Old-fashioned supernatural chiller in which two college students sharing a ride home for Christmas take a shortcut, break down on the side of the road, and have a series of ghostly encounters. Director Jacobs eschews CGI ghost effects for character development, good performances, and slow-building, eerily evocative scares (turning the song "Rockin' Around the Christmas Tree" into an effective harbinger of dread). Falls apart in its last third, but it's easy to forgive a movie that in its first hour actually makes your spine tingle. Super 35. [R]▶

Wind in the Willows, The (1997-British) **C-83m.** *** D: Terry Jones. Steve Coogan, Eric Idle, Terry Jones, Antony Sher, Nicol Williamson, John Cleese, Michael Palin, Bernard Hill, Julia Sawalha. Charming, veddy British adaptation of Kenneth Grahame's classic children's story in which Rat, Badger, and Mole team up to save their wealthy, reckless friend Toad from losing his estate. Benefits from creative reteaming of many Monty Python members; Jones not only wrote and directed but plays Toad with wild comic abandon. Williamson lends excellent support as the blustery Badger. James Acheson's costumes and production design are wittily on target. Kids and adults alike should enjoy this. Aka MR. TOAD'S WILD RIDE. [G]▼▶

Window, The (1949) **73m.** *** D: Ted Tetzlaff. Bobby Driscoll, Barbara Hale, Arthur Kennedy, Paul Stewart, Ruth Roman. Sleeper film less impressive now than in 1949; still good, with young Driscoll earning a special Academy Award for his performance as a little boy who witnesses a murder and is unable to convince his parents he's not lying. Parents' dialogue weakens credibility, but suspense still mounts; extremely well photographed (by William Steiner) and staged. Based on a story by Cornell Woolrich. Remade as THE BOY CRIED MURDER and CLOAK AND DAGGER (1984).▼▶

Windows (1980) **C-96m.** BOMB D: Gordon Willis. Elizabeth Ashley, Talia Shire, Joseph Cortese, Kay Medford. Homicidal lesbian Ashley is in love with mousy neighbor Shire, who is in turn in love with bland detective Cortese. Reactionary, offensive thriller whose only element of mystery is why it was ever filmed. Directing debut for gifted cinematographer Willis. [R]▼

Windrider (1986-Australian) **C-92m.** **½ D: Vincent Monton. Tom Burlinson, Nicole Kidman, Charles Tingwell, Jill Perryman, Simon Chilvers. Windsurfer Burlinson and rock star Kidman become romantically involved. Occasionally appealing, but slight and forgettable. [R]▼

Windtalkers (2002) **C-134m.** ** D: John Woo. Nicolas Cage, Adam Beach, Christian Slater, Peter Stormare, Noah Emmerich, Mark Ruffalo, Brian Van Holt, Roger Willie, Frances O'Connor, Martin Henderson. During WW2, two Marines are given the job of protecting a pair of Navajo code talkers (Beach, Willie) at all costs during the bloody battle of Saipan. Opportunity to learn about the Navajo-inspired code operation is squandered, as Cage's shell-shocked character takes center stage instead. Clichéd dialogue with homesick soldiers is the only respite from endless shots of gruesome combat violence. Director's cut runs 153m. Super 35. [R]▼▶

Wind That Shakes the Barley, The (2006-Irish-British-German-Italian-Spanish-French) **C-127m.** *** D: Kenneth Loach. Cillian Murphy, Padraic Delaney, Liam Cunningham, Orla Fitzgerald, Mary O'Riordan, Mary Murphy, Laurence Barry. Simple, powerful slice of Irish history, set in the early 1920s, dramatizes the transformation of a young doctor (Murphy) from passive citizen to Irish Republican Army guerrilla warrior. Scenario, penned by frequent Loach collaborator Paul Laverty, reflects the belief that those who are subjugated must acknowledge their plight, organize themselves, and fight their oppressors . . . no matter the personal toll.▶

Windwalker (1980) **C-108m.** **½ D: Kieth Merrill. Trevor Howard, Nick Ramus, James Remar, Serene Hedin, Dusty Iron Wing McCrea. Indian patriarch Howard returns to life to save his family from the vengeance of his son, a twin who was stolen at birth and raised by an enemy tribe. Curious casting of Howard; however, the Utah scenery is glorious in this unusual Western. Filmed in the Cheyenne and Crow languages, and subtitled. [PG]▼▶

Wind Will Carry Us, The (1999-Iranian-French) **C-118m.** *** D: Abbas Kiarostami. Behzad Dourani. An engineer from Tehran travels to a remote mountain village in Iranian Kurdistan, claiming to be an archaeologist looking for buried treasure. In reality, he is part of a film crew that is secretly planning to record a local funeral ceremony ritual surrounding a 100-year-old woman who is dying. Slow, haunting, and poetic meditation on mortality features some surprisingly humorous moments; breathtakingly filmed in the tiny village of Siah Dareh, whose residents make up most of the cast. Written by the director.▶

Windy City (1984) **C-102m.** ** D: Armyan Bernstein. John Shea, Kate Capshaw, Josh Mostel, Jim Borrelli, Jeffrey DeMunn, Lewis J. Stadlen. Promising but uneven film flashes back to last hurrah for some youthful pals whose lives haven't turned out quite as they'd hoped or planned. Writer Bernstein (making directorial debut) invades BIG CHILL/SECAUCUS 7 territory with extremely mixed results. [R]▼●

Wing Commander (1999) **C-99m.** *½ D: Chris Roberts. Freddie Prinze, Jr., Saffron Burrows, Matthew Lillard, Tchéky

Karyo, Jürgen Prochnow, David Suchet, David Warner. In a 27th-century space war between humans and aliens, the outcome turns out to depend on a single fighter pilot. Well-produced, with lots of CGI effects, but instantly forgettable trifle based on a computer game. Super 35. [PG-13]▼●)

Winged Migration (2001-French-German-Spanish-Italian-Swiss) **C-91m.** *** D: Jacques Perrin. The producer of MICROCOSMOS turns director to explore birds in flight, using revolutionary filming techniques to make us feel as if we're right alongside them (not to mention above, below, behind, and in front). The film homes in on various species as they migrate on a seasonal basis in order to survive, often spanning oceans and entire continents. Impressive and eye-opening, though without a narrative thrust one's interest can lag at times. [G]▼)

Winged Serpent, The SEE: Q

Wings (1927) **139m.** **½ D: William A. Wellman. Clara Bow, Charles "Buddy" Rogers, Richard Arlen, Jobyna Ralston, Gary Cooper, El Brendel. One of the most famous silent films is, alas, not one of the best, despite rose-colored memories. Story of two all-American boys (in love with the same girl) who enlist in the Army Air Corps during WW1 is much too thin to sustain such a long movie. What's important here are the combat flying sequences, among the best in Hollywood history. First Oscar winner as Best Picture.▼●

Wings of Courage (1995) **C-40m.** ** D: Jean-Jacques Annaud. Craig Sheffer, Elizabeth McGovern, Tom Hulce, Val Kilmer, Ken Pogue, Ron Sauve, Molly Parker. Beautiful scenery aside, this is a lumbering, boring true-life adventure in which pioneer aviator Henri Guillaumet (Sheffer) must fight for survival in the Andes after his plane is forced down while on a mail run circa 1930. Dramatically speaking, it's about as lively as a 1930s Monogram programmer. Of note as the first fiction film made in IMAX 3-D. Annaud coscripted. 3-D. [G]▼

Wings of Desire (1988-West German-French) **C/B&W-130m.** ***½ D: Wim Wenders. Bruno Ganz, Solveig Dommartin, Otto Sander, Curt Bois, Peter Falk. Haunting, lyrical, fascinating meditation/fairy tale about a pair of angels who wander through the streets of West Berlin. They observe life around them and ponder what it would be like to be human. Scripted by Wenders and Peter Handke and inspired in part by some Rainer Maria Rilke poems. A must-see. Sequel: FARAWAY, SO CLOSE! Remade as CITY OF ANGELS. [PG-13]▼●)

Wings of Eagles, The (1957) **C-110m.** **½ D: John Ford. John Wayne, Maureen O'Hara, Dan Dailey, Ward Bond, Ken Curtis, Edmund Lowe, Kenneth Tobey, Sig Ruman. Biography of Frank "Spig" Wead, pioneer WW1 aviator who later turned to screenwriting (including AIR MAIL and

THEY WERE EXPENDABLE for Ford) after an accident; first half is slapstick comedy, with no sense of period detail, then abruptly changes to drama for balance of film. Very mixed bag; film buffs will have fun watching Bond play "John Dodge," spoofing director Ford.▼)

Wings of the Dove, The (1997-British-U.S.) **C-101m.** **½ D: Iain Softley. Helena Bonham Carter, Linus Roache, Alison Elliott, Charlotte Rampling, Elizabeth McGovern, Michael Gambon, Alex Jennings. Exquisite but emotionally uneven film (from the Henry James novel) about a young woman torn between her love for a working man (Roache) and her desire for wealth and position . . . complicated by her growing friendship with a rich, guileless American woman (Elliott). Sophisticated and intelligent, but the characters' vacillations and ambiguous feelings make it difficult to empathize with anyone. Venice has never been portrayed so beautifully, or romantically. Gambon and McGovern have thankless roles. Super 35. [R]▼●)

Winner, The (1997) **C-95m.** **½ D: Alex Cox. Rebecca De Mornay, Vincent D'Onofrio, Michael Madsen, Billy Bob Thornton, Delroy Lindo, Frank Whaley, Richard Edson. When word gets out that a loner (D'Onofrio) wins consistently, every Sunday night at a low-rent Las Vegas casino, the leeches begin to gather around him, including a sexy nightclub singer, an opportunistic thief from out of town, and his own homicidal brother. Interesting fable with a first-rate cast. De Mornay also coexecutive-produced. Debuted on cable TV before theatrical run.▼●

Winner Take All (1932) **68m.** **½ D: Roy Del Ruth. James Cagney, Virginia Bruce, Marian Nixon, Guy Kibbee, Alan Mowbray, Dickie Moore. Minor but engaging Cagney vehicle with Jimmy as a thick-witted, cocky prizefighter torn between good-girl Nixon and fickle society-girl Bruce. Look fast for George Raft as night club bandleader.

Winning (1969) **C-123m.** *** D: James Goldstone. Paul Newman, Joanne Woodward, Richard Thomas, Robert Wagner, David Sheiner, Clu Gulager. Above average racing story of man who will let nothing stand in the way of track victory. Panavision. [PG]▼●)

Winning Season, The (2010) **C-103m.** *** D: James C. Strouse. Sam Rockwell, Emma Roberts, Rob Corddry, Shareeka Epps, Emily Rios, Rooney Mara, Meaghan Witri, Melanie Hinkle, Margo Martindale, Jessica Hecht. Boozy Rockwell is recruited by an old friend to coach the girls' basketball team at his Indiana high school. How he motivates the girls and molds them into a team while pulling his life back together (and reaching out to his own estranged daughter) is the crux of this lightweight, likable, well-cast film. Indiana-born novelist-filmmaker Strouse has fun playing with the obvious story formula and even includes a reference to HOOSIERS. [PG-13] ►

Winning Team, The (1952) **98m.** **½ D: Lewis Seiler. Doris Day, Ronald Reagan, Frank Lovejoy, Eve Miller, James Millican, Rusty Tamblyn. Biography of baseball pitching great Grover Cleveland Alexander focuses on his relationship with supportive wife whose "teamwork" helps Alexander through problems with alcoholism and lack of confidence. Reagan is fine as the Hall of Fame hurler and film boasts good reenactments of Alexander's legendary 1926 World Series heroics. Cameo appearances by real-life big leaguers Bob Lemon, Peanuts Lowrey, Hank Sauer, Gene Mauch, and others.▼●►

Win, Place or Steal (1975) **C-81m.** ** D: Richard Bailey. Dean Stockwell, Russ Tamblyn, Alex Karras, McLean Stevenson, Alan Oppenheimer, Kristina Holland. OK racetrack caper comedy, with Tamblyn and Karras doing a Laurel and Hardy. Aka THE BIG PAYOFF. [PG]▼

Winslow Boy, The (1948-British) **117m.** ***½ D: Anthony Asquith. Robert Donat, Margaret Leighton, Cedric Hardwicke, Francis L. Sullivan, Frank Lawton, Basil Radford, Wilfrid Hyde-White, Ernest Thesiger. Superior courtroom melodrama from Terence Rattigan's play, headed by Donat as barrister defending innocent Naval cadet (Neil North) accused of school theft. Script by Rattigan and Anatole de Grunwald. Remade in 1999.▼

Winslow Boy, The (1999) **C-110m.** *** D: David Mamet. Nigel Hawthorne, Rebecca Pidgeon, Jeremy Northam, Gemma Jones, Guy Edwards, Matthew Pidgeon, Colin Stinton, Aden Gillett. Absorbing remake of the Terence Rattigan play about a boy in 1910 England who's expelled from school for a petty theft. His father determines to clear his good name—nearly sacrificing his family in the process. As much about social mores and conventions as the case itself, this even-handed film benefits from a superlative performance by Hawthorne as the head of the Winslow household. Neil North, who plays the First Lord of the Admiralty, was the boy in the 1948 movie. [G]▼►

Winter Guest, The (1997-British-U.S.) **C-110m.** *** D: Alan Rickman. Phyllida Law, Emma Thompson, Gary Hollywood, Arlene Cockburn, Sheila Reid, Sandra Voe, Douglas Murphy, Sean Biggerstaff. A Scottish seaside town is frozen over—as is the ocean itself—on a wintry day during which four relationships are explored: a young widow and her mother, who's trying to break through her daughter's defensive shield; the widow's teenage son, who experiences his first sexual encounter; two older women whose hobby is attending funerals; and a couple of boys playing hooky. An incredibly quiet, concentrated

film—which, perhaps, goes on too long. Based on a play, coadapted by Rickman (making his feature directing debut). Law and Thompson are real-life mother and daughter. [R]▼●

Winterhawk (1976) **C-98m.** ** D: Charles B. Pierce. Michael Dante, Leif Erickson, Woody Strode, Denver Pyle, Elisha Cook Jr., L. Q. Jones, Arthur Hunnicutt, Dawn Wells. Well-meaning but overly melodramatic story of Blackfoot Indian brave (Dante) who comes to white man for smallpox serum, is attacked instead, and gets revenge by kidnapping two white youngsters. Quite violent at times. Techniscope.▼

Winter in Lisbon (1990-Spanish-French-Portuguese) **C-100m.** *½ D: Jose Antonio Zorilla. Christian Vadim, Dizzy Gillespie, Helene de Saint-Pere, Eusebio Poncela, Fernando Guillen. Disjointed, turgid account of jazz pianist Vadim and his torrid affair with deceitful de Saint-Pere. Of interest solely for Gillespie's bright presence as an aging, expatriate American jazzman.

Winter in Wartime (2008-Dutch-Belgian) **C-103m.** *** D: Martin Koolhoven. Martijn Lakemeier, Yorick van Wageningen, Jamie Campbell Bower, Raymond Thiry, Melody Klaver, Anneke Blok. A mischievous, resentful teenage boy (Lakemeier) is coming of age in a small Dutch town at the tail end of WW2. For the sake of his survival, he is encouraged to remain detached from the world around him; all that changes when he discovers and comes to the aid of a downed RAF pilot. Engrossing drama effectively portrays the horror of the Nazi occupation of the Netherlands and the choices one makes in wartime; the boy's relationship with his father, the town's mayor, is especially poignant. Based on Jan Terlouw's semiautobiographical novel. Super 35. [R]►

Winter Kills (1979) **C-97m.** **½ D: William Richert. Jeff Bridges, John Huston, Anthony Perkins, Sterling Hayden, Eli Wallach, Belinda Bauer, Richard Boone, Ralph Meeker, Dorothy Malone, Toshiro Mifune, Tomas Milian, Elizabeth Taylor. Younger brother of an assassinated U.S. President tries to solve the case, opens up several cans of political worms. A failure in 1979, it was reedited in 1983 (with original ending restored) and newly appreciated as a black comedy, which not everybody recognized the first time around. Still wildly uneven, but worth a look, if only for Huston's wonderful performance as Bridges' kingpin father. Panavision. [R]▼●

Winter Light (1963-Swedish) **80m.** ***½ D: Ingmar Bergman. Ingrid Thulin, Gunnar Bjornstrand, Max von Sydow, Gunnel Lindblom, Allan Edwall. A difficult film for non-Bergman buffs, this look at a disillusioned priest in a small village is the second of Bergman's trilogy on faith (the first, THROUGH A

GLASS DARKLY; the third, THE SILENCE). Powerful, penetrating drama. ▼●

Winter Meeting (1948) 104m. **½ D: Bretaigne Windust. Bette Davis, Janis Paige, James (Jim) Davis, John Hoyt, Florence Bates. Sluggish script of disillusioned poetess who loves embittered war hero, prevents well-acted film from achieving greater heights. Notable as only romantic lead for Jim Davis, better known for his Westerns and TV series *Dallas*. ▼

Winter of Our Dreams, The (1981-Australian) C-90m. **½ D: John Duigan. Judy Davis, Bryan Brown, Cathy Downes, Baz Luhrmann, Peter Mochrie, Mervyn Drake. Davis is fine as a lonely prostitute who becomes involved with dissatisfied bookshop-owner Brown, married to Downes. Intriguing drama is a bit disjointed, particularly near the finale. ▼

Winter Passing (2006) C-98m. *½ D: Adam Rapp. Ed Harris, Zooey Deschanel, Daniel Larson, Will Ferrell, Deirdre O'Connell, Rachel Dratch, Amy Madigan, Mandy Siegfried, Amelia Warner, Dallas Roberts, Sam Bottoms. Uninvolving misfire about an actress who is offered big bucks to produce long-lost love letters written by her reclusive novelist father to her deceased mother. When she travels back home she discovers there are new influences in his life she never knew about. Snail-paced drama can't gather dramatic momentum as talented actors fail to gel as a believable family. Normally reliable Harris chews the scenery and Deschanel mumbles. This winter takes a loooooooong time to pass. [R]●

Winter People (1989) C-110m. ** D: Ted Kotcheff. Kurt Russell, Kelly McGillis, Lloyd Bridges, Mitchell Ryan, Amelia Burnette, Eileen Ryan, Jeffrey Meek. Turgid tale of backwoods clans and a blood feud that flares up when McGillis bears a child with the wrong father. Set in the 1930s, but extremely odd by any period's standards; how it came to be made in 1989 is anyone's guess. Overwrought, to say the least. Panavision. [PG-13] ▼●

Winter Rates SEE: **Out of Season**

Winter's Bone (2010) C-100m. *** D: Debra Granik. Jennifer Lawrence, John Hawkes, Kevin Breznahan, Dale Dickey, Garret Dillahunt, Sheryl Lee. In the Ozark backwoods of Missouri, a 17-year-old girl is forced to care for her two young siblings because her mother is incompetent and her father—who cooks drugs—has run off. If he doesn't show up for a court date, the family will lose its home, so she goes in search of him, stonewalled at every turn by family and so-called friends. Unremittingly harsh story focuses on its heroine (Lawrence, in a remarkable performance), who is forced to find both inner and outer strength in order to ensure her family's survival. A fascinating glimpse into a world

most of us will never know firsthand. Granik and Anne Rosellini adapted Daniel Woodrell's novel. [R]●

Winter Solstice (2005) C-93m. *** D: Josh Sternfeld. Anthony LaPaglia, Aaron Stanford, Mark Webber, Michelle Monaghan, Allison Janney, Brendan Sexton III, Ron Livingston. Subdued but well-observed slice of life about a widower and his two sons, one of whom is itching to set off on his own. Looks, glances, and body language tell as much as dialogue in this simple film about a family still reeling from loss yet inextricably tied to one another. LaPaglia is terrific as always; he also coexecutive-produced. Debut feature for writer-director Sternfeld. [R]●

Winter's Tale, The (1968-British) C-151m. ** D: Frank Dunlop. Laurence Harvey, Jane Asher, Diana Churchill, Moira Redmond, Jim Dale. Filmed record of 1966 Edinburgh Festival presentation of Shakespeare's play is as static as a photographed stage play can be.

Win Win (2011) C-106m. ***½ D: Tom McCarthy. Paul Giamatti, Amy Ryan, Bobby Cannavale, Jeffrey Tambor, Burt Young, Melanie Lynskey, Alex Shaffer, Margo Martindale, David Thompson. Small-town N.J. lawyer, family man, and high school wrestling coach Giamatti is having trouble making ends meet. Feeling desperate, he subverts his own ethics by becoming official guardian for an elderly man in order to collect a handsome monthly fee. When the man's previously unknown grandson turns up, estranged from his druggie mother, Giamatti takes him in and the emotional stakes get higher, especially when it turns out that he's a talented wrestler. Wonderfully humane, socially relevant slice of life about flawed people just trying to get by; scripted by McCarthy (based on a story by the director and Joe Tiboni) and cast to perfection. [PG-13] ●

Wired (1989) C-108m. BOMB D: Larry Peerce. Michael Chiklis, Ray Sharkey, J. T. Walsh, Patti D'Arbanville, Lucinda Jenney, Alex Rocco, Gary Groomes, Jere Burns, Billy Preston. The film fiasco of its year, a numbingly wrongheaded adaptation of Bob Woodward's best-selling cautionary bio of John Belushi—complete with a cab-driving guardian angel (Sharkey). Chiklis looks a little like Belushi but conveys none of his comic genius in some clumsy *Saturday Night Live* re-creations. Walsh, as Woodward, is an unintentional howl with the decade's most constipated performance. Sole cast survivor: D'Arbanville as Cathy Smith, the woman who administered the star's fatal drug overdose. [R] ▼●

Wisdom (1986) C-109m. BOMB D: Emilio Estevez. Emilio Estevez, Demi Moore, Tom Skerritt, Veronica Cartwright, William Allen Young, Richard Minchenberg, Ernie Brown.

Recent grad Estevez can't find work because of a long-ago felony on his record; frustration launches him and girlfriend Moore on a cross-country series of bank heists to aid the American farmer's plight. Robert Wise assisted Estevez on the direction, which is certainly more competent than his wretched script; film has one of the most self-defeating wrapups you'll ever see. [R] ▼○)

Wise Blood (1979) **C-108m.** ***½ D: John Huston. Brad Dourif, Daniel Shor, Amy Wright, Harry Dean Stanton, Ned Beatty, Mary Nell Santacroce. Brilliant translation of Flannery O'Connor's peculiar hell-and-salvation tale. Flawless cast, led by Dourif as obsessed preacher of The Church Without Christ, inhabits Southern Gothic world as though born in it. Huston (who bills himself here as *Jhon* Huston) appears as a preacher. Screenplay by Benedict Fitzgerald. [PG] ▼)

Wise Guys (1986) **C-91m.** *½ D: Brian De Palma. Danny DeVito, Joe Piscopo, Harvey Keitel, Ray Sharkey, Dan Hedaya, Captain Lou Albano, Julie Bovasso, Patti LuPone. Whimsical black comedy (that's what we said) about two losers who work for small-time hood in Newark, N.J. When their efforts to double-cross him fail, he sets them up to kill each other. Unsuccessful change of pace for director De Palma is an almost total misfire; buoyed only by DeVito's comic energy. [R] ▼)

Wishful Thinking (1999) **C-90m.** ** D: Adam Park. Jennifer Beals, James Le Gros, Drew Barrymore, Jon Stewart, Eric Thal, Mel Gorham. A N.Y.C.-based movie about relationships, told in overlapping "chapters," as paranoiacally jealous Le Gros keeps finding ways to drive his lover (Beals) away . . . with a little help from his lovesick friend Barrymore. Makes clever use of footage from an old Steve Cochran movie. Never released theatrically. [R] ▼)

Wishmaster (1997) **C-90m.** *½ D: Robert Kurtzman. Tammy Lauren, Andrew Divoff, Chris Lemmon, Wendy Benson, Tony Crane, Kane Hodder, Tony Todd, Robert Englund, Ted Raimi. An evil djinn (genie to you) is freed from captivity in a gem and sets out to grant (backfiring) wishes while seeking Lauren, because granting *her* wishes will enable him to destroy the world . . . or something. The mythology is too complex, the story too thin, and the plentiful gore mostly gratuitous. Followed by three direct-to-video sequels. [R] ▼○)

Wish You Were Here (1987-British) **C-92m.** *** D: David Leland. Emily Lloyd, Tom Bell, Clare Clifford, Barbara Durkin, Geoffrey Hutchings, Charlotte Barker, Chloe Leland, Jesse Birdsall, Geoffrey Durham, Pat Heywood. A troubled teenage girl expresses herself by being sexually outrageous—without understanding what the consequences might be. Bittersweet film set in early 1950s England with a knockout

performance by 16-year-old Lloyd. Strong directing debut for screenwriter Leland, who based his central character on Cynthia Payne, the young madam depicted in PERSONAL SERVICES, which he wrote. [R] ▼○)

Wistful Widow of Wagon Gap, The (1947) **78m.** **½ D: Charles Barton. Bud Abbott, Lou Costello, Marjorie Main, George Cleveland, Gordon Jones, William Ching, Peter Thompson, Glenn Strange, Audrey Young. Unusual Western spoof for A&C, inspired by real-life law: Lou is accused of killing a man, and is required to take care of his wife (Main) and children (seven). He then becomes sheriff, convinced that no one will dare kill him. Some slow spots, but overall, fun. ▼)

Witchboard (1985) **C-98m.** ** D: Kevin S. Tenney. Todd Allen, Tawny Kitaen, Stephen Nicholas, Kathleen Wilhoite, Burke Byrnes, Rose Marie, Susan Nickerson. Standard low-budget horror film with a few twists. An evil spirit, contacted by means of a Ouija board (a "witchboard"), impersonates the ghost of a small boy to kill its victims. Well plotted but routinely directed and acted. Followed by a whole bunch of sequels connected only by the Ouija board. [R] ▼○)

Witchery (1989-Italian) **C-96m.** BOMB D: Martin Newlin (Fabrizio Laurenti). Linda Blair, David Hasselhoff, Catherine Hickland, Annie Ross, Hildegard Knef, Leslie Cumming, Rick Farnsworth. Competently made but ponderous, underplotted horror tale of people isolated at old hotel on island, killed one by one by vengeful witch Knef. Horror scenes emphasize torture. Uncomfortable, predictable, and boring. Filmed in Massachusetts. ▼)

Witches, The (1990-British) **C-91m.** *** D: Nicolas Roeg. Anjelica Huston, Mai Zetterling, Jasen Fisher, Rowan Atkinson, Bill Paterson, Jane Horrocks, Jenny Runacre, Brenda Blethyn. A young boy's seaside vacation turns into a nightmare when he discovers that the hotel is also hosting a convention of witches! Roald Dahl stories can be cruel, and this is no exception, but as a far-flung child's-eye fantasy it's pretty good. Zetterling is wonderful as the boy's loving grandmother; Jim Henson's Creature Shop provided the incredible-looking witches—and mice. This was Henson's final feature-film project. [PG] ▼○)

Witches' Brew (1980) **C-99m.** **½ D: Richard Shorr, Herbert L. Strock. Lana Turner, Richard Benjamin, Teri Garr, Kathryn Leigh Scott, Jordan Charney. College prof Benjamin's wife Garr resorts to witchcraft in order to further his career. Turner (in her final film) is good as the veteran witch who has selfish reasons for helping Benjamin's cause. After a dull first half, this comic remake of BURN, WITCH, BURN! finally hits its stride. Originally done as WEIRD

WOMAN. Based on the book *Conjure Wife* by Fritz Leiber. [PG]▼

Witches of Eastwick, The (1987) **C-118m.** *** D: George Miller. Jack Nicholson, Cher, Susan Sarandon, Michelle Pfeiffer, Veronica Cartwright, Richard Jenkins, Keith Jochim, Carel Struycken. Lively, colorful fantasy about three man-hungry women in picture-postcard New England town who, unaware of their witchly powers, conjure up the ultimate man: the devil. Magnetic performances and handsome production keep it entertaining throughout, though it careens wildly from sensual fantasy to black-comic farce to full-throttle horror, and ends up not making a lot of sense. Buoyed by an infectious John Williams score. Loosely based on John Updike's novel. Later a TV series and a stage musical. Panavision. [R]▼●)

Witches of Salem, The SEE: **Crucible, The** (1956)

Witchfinder General, The SEE: **Conqueror Worm**

Witching, The SEE: **Necromancy**

Witch Without a Broom, A (1968-Spanish) **C-78m.** *½ D: Joe Lacy (Jose Maria E. Lorrieta). Jeffrey Hunter, Maria Perschy, Perla Cristal, Gustavo Rojo. Jeff finds himself bewitched by a 15th-century apprentice sorceress who takes him on an odyssey from the Stone Age to a futuristic Martian jaunt. Pointless fantasy.▼

With a Friend Like Harry . . . (2000-French) **C-117m.** *** D: Dominik Moll. Laurent Lucas, Sergi Lopez, Mathilde Seigner, Sophie Guillemin. Hitchcockian thriller (in the best sense of that term) in which a chance encounter with a barely remembered high school classmate causes great consternation for a family on vacation as he insinuates himself into their lives. Wickedly funny and scary at the same time; a psychological exercise in suspense. Winner of four César Awards, including Best Actor for Lopez. Super 35. [R]▼)

With a Song in My Heart (1952) **C-117m.** *** D: Walter Lang. Susan Hayward, Rory Calhoun, David Wayne, Thelma Ritter, Robert Wagner, Una Merkel. Well-intentioned schmaltz based on events in life of singer Jane Froman with Hayward earnest as songstress struggling to make comeback after crippling plane crash. Alfred Newman won an Oscar for Scoring. Froman dubbed Hayward's singing.)

With Friends Like These . . . (1999) **C-105m.** *** D: Philip F. Messina. Robert Costanzo, Adam Arkin, Amy Madigan, David Strathairn, Laura San Giacomo, Jon Tenney, Elle Macpherson, Lauren Tom, Beverly D'Angelo, Michael McKean, Jason Alexander, Bill Murray, Martin Scorsese, Garry Marshall. Close friends who are character actors find themselves in a fiercely competitive situation when word gets out that Martin Scorsese is casting a new film on Al Capone. How much does friendship count at a time like this? Affectionate, seriocomic look at working actors, with a fine ensemble. Written by the director. Made for theaters, debuted on cable TV. [R]▼

With Honors (1994) **C-103m.** ** D: Alek Keshishian. Joe Pesci, Brendan Fraser, Moira Kelly, Patrick Dempsey, Josh Hamilton, Gore Vidal, Deborah Fortson, Marshall Hambro. Homeless Pesci trades pages for food after callow Ivy Leaguer Fraser meets him in Irene Dunne screwball style when his thesis falls through a grate into the Harvard boiler room where Pesci resides. Comedy-drama might be insulting if it had just a little more sting, but it's a fizzle almost from the beginning. [PG-13]▼●)

Withnail & I (1987-British) **C-105m.** **½ D: Bruce Robinson. Richard E. Grant, Paul McGann, Richard Griffiths, Ralph Brown, Michael Elphick. "I" is a young longhair, living in London in the last months of 1969; Withnail is his eccentric, self-absorbed roommate. Both are unemployed actors, children of their times, who endure a disastrous vacation in the country. Director Robinson wrote this autobiographical film, which has its amusing moments but eventually becomes monotonous. Best laugh: consultant credit for "Richard Starkey, M.B.E." Fellow Beatle George Harrison coexecutive-produced the film. [R]▼●)

Without a Clue (1988-British) **C-106m.** **½ D: Thom Eberhardt. Michael Caine, Ben Kingsley, Jeffrey Jones, Lysette Anthony, Paul Freeman, Nigel Davenport, Pat Keen, Peter Cook. Mild farce built on the premise that Sherlock Holmes was a fictional creation of wily Dr. John Watson, who is forced to hire a second-rate actor (Caine) to impersonate the now famous and sought-after detective. Scattered laughs, engaging performances by star duo. [PG]▼●)

Without a Paddle (2004) **C-99m.** ** D: Steven Brill. Seth Green, Matthew Lillard, Dax Shepard, Ethan Suplee, Abraham Benrubi, Rachel Blanchard, Burt Reynolds, Christina Moore, Bonnie Somerville, Ray Baker. Anemic summertime comedy about three boyhood pals who reunite to take the river journey they always promised themselves they'd take, to search for the lost treasure of D. B. Cooper. Derivative mishmash of slapstick and sentiment gets what mileage it can from its three likable stars. Reynolds' presence is surely intended to evoke memories of DELIVERANCE . . . but doesn't. Followed by a DVD sequel. Super 35. [PG-13]▼)

Without Apparent Motive (1972-French) **C-102m.** ** D: Philippe Labro. Jean-Louis Trintignant, Dominique Sanda, Sacha Distel, Carla Gravina, Paul Crauchet, Laura

Antonelli, Jean-Pierre Marielle. Powerhouse European cast can't do much for Ed McBain tale about detective Trintignant's attempts to solve series of unpredictable killings; Erich Segal plays an astrologer. [PG]

Without a Trace (1983) C-120m. **½ D: Stanley R. Jaffe. Kate Nelligan, Judd Hirsch, David Dukes, Stockard Channing, Jacqueline Brookes, Kathleen Widdoes, Caroline Aaron, Dan Lauria, W. (William) H. Macy. Story of one woman's ordeal when her six-year-old son disappears while walking to school one morning. Genteel, well-made film keeps an arm's-length emotionally, especially in Nelligan's cold portrayal of the mother. The resolution is not to be believed. Based on a real-life N.Y.C. incident that had a much different outcome. Directorial debut of producer Jaffe. [PG]▼●

Without Limits (1998) C-117m. *** D: Robert Towne. Billy Crudup, Donald Sutherland, Monica Potter, Jeremy Sisto, Matthew Lillard, Billy Burke, Dean Norris, Judith Ivey. Second screen bio of the late University of Oregon runner Steve Prefontaine is more polished than 1997's PREFONTAINE, especially in its re-creation of competition scenes. Produced by Tom Cruise, this barely released sleeper benefits from Sutherland's excellent performance as coach Bill Bowerman. Another plus: outstanding—and non-clichéd—use of period music. Super 35. [PG-13] ▼●

Without Love (1945) 111m. *** D: Harold S. Bucquet. Spencer Tracy, Katharine Hepburn, Lucille Ball, Keenan Wynn, Carl Esmond, Patricia Morison, Felix Bressart, Gloria Grahame. Tracy and Hepburn have never been livelier, but script (by Donald Ogden Stewart, from Philip Barry's play) lets them down in story of inventor and widow who marry for convenience, later fall in love. Wynn and Ball are excellent second leads. ▼●

Without Reservations (1946) 107m. *** D: Mervyn LeRoy. Claudette Colbert, John Wayne, Don DeFore, Anne Triola, Frank Puglia, Phil Brown, Thurston Hall, Louella Parsons, Dona Drake, Ruth Roman. Authoress Colbert meets perfect man to play hero in movie version of her new book: soldier Wayne. Engaging comedy-romance, with some amusing swipes at Hollywood, several surprise guest stars. Look fast for Raymond Burr during dance scene. ▼●

Without Warning! (1952) 77m. *** D: Arnold Laven. Adam Williams, Meg Randall, Edward Binns, Harlan Warde, John Maxwell, Angela Stevens, Byron Kane, Charles Tannen, Robert Shayne. Creepy character actor Williams shines in a rare starring role as a shy, lonely gardener with a penchant for plunging his shears into bottle-blonde bombshells who remind him of his former wife. Low-budget noir is a taut and

trim little crime thriller, stylishly shot by Joseph F. Biroc, which presents an evocative look at a seedy '50s L.A. and such vanished parts of the city as Chavez Ravine before it was cleared to make way for Dodger Stadium.▌

Without Warning (1980) C-89m. *½ D: Greydon Clark. Jack Palance, Cameron Mitchell, Martin Landau, Ralph Meeker, Tarah Nutter, Sue Ane Langdon, Neville Brand, Larry Storch. Very silly horror film. Alien launches carnivorous disks at various citizens. A few scattered laughs and shudders, some intense acting, and a flagrantly bad job by Landau as a militant ex-sergeant named Fred Dobbs. Aka IT CAME WITHOUT WARNING. [R]

Without You I'm Nothing (1990) C-94m. **½ D: John Boskovich. Sandra Bernhard, John Doe, Steve Antin, Lu Leonard, Ken Foree, Cynthia Bailey, Djimon Hounsou. Adaptation of Bernhard's one-woman off-Broadway show, in which she takes on a number of roles in order to examine American pop culture, and the challenge of surviving in modern society. She's definitely an acquired taste, but the material does hit its targets more often than not—especially when Sandra does her take on Diana Ross. Video version runs 89m. [R]▼●

With Six You Get Eggroll (1968) C-95m. ** D: Howard Morris. Doris Day, Brian Keith, Pat Carroll, Barbara Hershey, George Carlin, Alice Ghostley, Vic Tayback, Jamie Farr, William Christopher. Oft-told tale of a widow and widower who try to move their children under the same roof. Amiable but slow on laughs. Day's last film to date. Panavision. [G]▼●

Witless Protection (2008) C-97m. BOMB D: Charles Robert Carner. Larry the Cable Guy (Dan Whitney), Ivana Milicevic, Jenny McCarthy, Yaphet Kotto, Eric Roberts, Peter Stormare, Joe Mantegna. Another rattletrap vehicle for comic Whitney's redneck character. This time, Larry is a small-town deputy sheriff who kidnaps a beautiful government witness (Milicevic) from the crooked FBI agents assigned to "protect" her. Not just unfunny but offensive whenever good-ol'-boy Larry makes snide remarks about Arabs, Asians, or African-Americans. Stormare and Mantegna mug furiously, to little effect. [PG-13]▌

Witness (1985) C-112m. *** D: Peter Weir. Harrison Ford, Kelly McGillis, Josef Sommer, Lukas Haas, Jan Rubes, Alexander Godunov, Danny Glover, Patti LuPone, Viggo Mortensen. A big-city cop on the lam hides out on an Amish farm, where he and a young widow are attracted to each other. Entertaining film is marred by jarring shifts in tone, especially toward the end. Oscar winner for writers Earl W. Wallace, William Kelley, Pamela Wallace. [R]▼●

Witness for the Prosecution (1957) 114m.

**** D: Billy Wilder. Marlene Dietrich, Tyrone Power, Charles Laughton, Elsa Lanchester, John Williams, Henry Daniell, Una O'Connor, Ian Wolfe. Fantastically effective London courtroom suspenser from Agatha Christie play. Dietrich is peerless as wife of alleged killer (Power). Laughton at his best as defense attorney, and Lanchester delightful as his long-suffering nurse. Power's last completed film. Scripted by Wilder and Harry Kurnitz. Remade as a TVM.▼●)

Witness to Murder (1954) **83m.** *** D: Roy Rowland. Barbara Stanwyck, George Sanders, Gary Merrill, Jesse White, Claude Akins. Stanwyck sees ex-Nazi neighbor Sanders strangle a woman, but can't convince detective Merrill. However, *Sanders* believes her. . . . Unconvincing and rather shrill, but suspenseful and well acted, with striking photography (by John Alton).

Wives and Lovers (1963) **103m.** **½ D: John Rich. Janet Leigh, Van Johnson, Shelley Winters, Martha Hyer, Ray Walston, Jeremy Slate. Surface, slick entertainment; newly famous writer Johnson, wife Leigh and child move to suburbia. Literary agent Hyer on the make almost causes divorce; Winters is wise-cracking neighbor. Script by Edward Anhalt, from Jay Presson Allen's play.

Wiz, The (1978) **C-133m.** ** D: Sidney Lumet. Diana Ross, Michael Jackson, Nipsey Russell, Ted Ross, Mabel King, Theresa Merritt, Thelma Carpenter, Lena Horne, Richard Pryor. Diana Ross weeps and whines her way through modern black variation on THE WIZARD OF OZ, from the Broadway show by William F. Brown and Charlie Smalls. Some good musical numbers, fine supporting cast, but dreary finale—and drearier performance by Ross—really weigh it down. Music arranged and conducted by Quincy Jones. [G]▼●)

Wizard, The (1989) **C-99m.** ** D: Todd Holland. Fred Savage, Luke Edwards, Jenny Lewis, Beau Bridges, Christian Slater, Will Seltzer, Jackey Vinson, Wendy Phillips, Sam McMurray. A road movie for kids, with Savage, his traumatized brother Edwards, and Lewis pursued across the Southwest by various relatives and other grown-ups. Limp, overplotted comedy suffers from heavy product plugs. ROCKY-like finish, dealing with Edwards' video-game wizardry, may thrill preteens but few others. Look for Tobey Maguire in a bit part. [PG]▼●)

Wizard of Loneliness, The (1988) **C-111m.** ** D: Jenny Bowen. Lukas Haas, Lea Thompson, John Randolph, Anne Pitoniak, Dylan Baker, Lance Guest, Jeremiah Warner. Top-notch acting (especially by precocious young star Haas) fails to save a haphazardly constructed adaptation of John Nichols' novel about a youngster growing up with his grandparents in New England

during WW2. His aunt (Thompson in an unusual character role) carries a dark secret that leads to a melodramatic climax. A co-production of PBS' *American Playhouse*. [PG-13]▼●

Wizard of Oz, The (1939) **C/B&W-101m.** **** D: Victor Fleming. Judy Garland, Ray Bolger, Bert Lahr, Jack Haley, Frank Morgan, Billie Burke, Margaret Hamilton, Charley Grapewin, Clara Blandick, The Singer Midgets. A genuine American classic, based on L. Frank Baum's story of a Kansas girl who goes "Over the Rainbow" to a land of colorful characters and spirited adventure. A perfect cast in the perfect fantasy, with Harold Arlen and E. Y. Harburg's unforgettable score. Just as good the fifteenth time as it is the first time. Won Oscars for "Over the Rainbow" and Herbert Stothart's scoring, plus a special miniature award for Judy. Previously filmed in 1925; remade as THE WIZ (set in N.Y.C.), OZ (Australia), and for TV in 2005 with the Muppets. A pair of sequels: JOURNEY BACK TO OZ and RETURN TO OZ.▼●)

Wizard of Speed and Time, The (1988) **C-95m.** **½ D: Mike Jittlov. Mike Jittlov, Paige Moore, Richard Kaye, David Conrad, John Massari, Steve Brodie, Frank LaLoggia, Philip Michael Thomas. A young special-effects whiz and his pals buck the Hollywood system and try to make a movie. This completely self-referential low-budget comedy scores big points for gumption and enthusiasm, which helps make up for some amateurish qualities. Best of all are Jittlov's eye-popping, one-of-a-kind visual effects. Expanded from a popular short subject of the same name. [PG]▼●

Wizards (1977) **C-80m.** *½ D: Ralph Bakshi. Voices of Bob Holt, Jesse Wells, Richard Romanus, David Proval, Mark Hamill. Animated sci-fi tale of future world after devastation, with warring factions that conjure up Hitler's armies. Turgid, unappealing film for adults or children. [PG]▼●)

Wolf (1994) **C-122m.** *** D: Mike Nichols. Jack Nicholson, Michelle Pfeiffer, James Spader, Kate Nelligan, Christopher Plummer, Richard Jenkins, Eileen Atkins, David Hyde Pierce, Om Puri, Ron Rifkin, Prunella Scales, David Schwimmer, Allison Janney. Thoughtful, imaginative werewolf tale in a modern urban setting, with Nicholson as a genteel book editor who's bitten by a wolf—just as he's going through a personal and professional crisis. Literate, intriguing, though perhaps too slowly paced (and genteel) for rabid horror fans. Written by Jim Harrison and Wesley Strick, with makeup effects by Rick Baker. [R]▼●)

Wolf at the Door (1987-French-Danish) **C-90m.** *** D: Henning Carlsen. Donald Sutherland, Max von Sydow, Valerie Morea, Sofie Grabol, Fanny Bastin, Merete Voldstedlund. Sutherland is more subdued as Gauguin than Anthony Quinn was in LUST FOR LIFE; generally interesting bio covers the middle period of the artist's life, when he returned to Paris from Tahiti—then struggled to raise the money to go back. Arouses your interest in the subject. [R] ▼

Wolf Creek (2005-Australian) **C-99m.** *½ D: Greg McLean. John Jarratt, Cassandra Magrath, Kestie Morassi, Nathan Phillips, Gordon Poole, Guy O'Donnell. Yet another would-be BLAIR WITCH PROJECT, this even played in competition at Sundance and Cannes but isn't nearly as special as its Fest cred would indicate. Three backpacking friends are stranded in the dark, deserted, remote area of the Outback known as Wolf Creek. A seemingly friendly local truck driver offers assistance, but unfortunately he isn't that nice and tows them to . . . *terror!* Just another graphic showcase for gore and degradation. 104m. version also available. [R] ▶

Wolfen (1981) **C-115m.** *** D: Michael Wadleigh. Albert Finney, Diane Venora, Edward James Olmos, Gregory Hines, Tom Noonan, Dick O'Neill. Detective Finney tracks mysterious beasts (werewolves?) that are terrorizing N.Y.C. Surreal, allegorical mystery is satisfying—and could have been great. Hines stands out as coroner; Gerry Fisher's ingenious cinematography is also noteworthy. Based on the novel by Whitley Streiber. Panavision. [R]▼●▶

Wolf Lake (1978) **C-87m.** *½ D: Burt Kennedy. Rod Steiger, David Huffman, Robin Mattson, Jerry Hardin, Richard Herd, Paul Mantee. Dull revenge film. Steiger (intense as ever) and four old army buddies stay at hunting lodge run by Huffman, a Vietnam deserter who fled to Canada. Steiger lost his son in the Vietnam war and tries to take out his grief (violently) on Huffman, with tragic results. Also known as THE HONOR GUARD. [R]▼

Wolf Larsen (1975-Italian) **C-92m.** ** D: Giuseppi Vari. Chuck Connors, Barbara Bach, Giuseppi Pambieri. Tired new version of Jack London's SEA WOLF with Connors chewing up scenery as the sadistic sea captain. Video titles: LEGEND OF SEA WOLF and LARSEN, WOLF OF THE SEVEN SEAS.▼▶

Wolf Man, The (1941) **70m.** ***½ D: George Waggner. Lon Chaney, Jr., Evelyn Ankers, Claude Rains, Maria Ouspenskaya, Ralph Bellamy, Patric Knowles, Warren William, Bela Lugosi, Fay Helm. One of the finest horror films ever made: Larry Talbot (Chaney) is bitten by werewolf Lugosi, survives to carry the curse himself. Outstanding cast includes Rains as Chaney's oblivious father, Ankers as perplexed girl friend, Ouspenskaya as wizened gypsy woman who foretells his fate and attempts to care for him. Literate and very engross-

ing, with superb makeup by Jack Pierce, atmospheric music (re-used in many other Universal chillers) by Charles Previn and Hans J. Salter. Written by Curt Siodmak. Sequel: FRANKENSTEIN MEETS THE WOLF MAN. Remade in 2010. ▼●▶

Wolfman, The (2010) **C-102m.** **½ D: Joe Johnston. Benicio Del Toro, Anthony Hopkins, Emily Blunt, Hugo Weaving, Art Malik, Geraldine Chaplin, Antony Sher. Lawrence Talbot returns to his ancestral home in England—and his estranged father—after his brother is brutally murdered by an unnamed creature. In his search for the killer he, too, is attacked and inflicted with the lycanthropic curse. Sober remake of the 1941 classic isn't bad but insists on expanding the story, to no good end. Del Toro's character is underwritten, while Hopkins (as his father) gets to chew the scenery. Still, Rick Heinrichs' production design is handsome, Rick Baker and Dave Elsey's Oscar-winning makeup is effective, and the scare scenes are well staged, so it's not a total loss. Alternate version runs 119m. [R] ▶

Wolverine SEE: **X-Men Origins: Wolverine**

Woman, a Gun and a Noodle Shop, A (2009-Chinese) **C-90m.** **½ D: Zhang Yimou. Sun Honglei, Xiao Shenyang, Yan Ni, Ni Dahong, Cheng Ye, Mao Mao, Zhao Benshan, Julien Gaudfroy. Jealous and abusive noodle shop owner hires a crooked lawman to kill his adulterous wife and her lover—but things do not go as planned. If the basic plot sounds familiar, it's because this is actually a period remake of BLOOD SIMPLE., transposing the setting from 1980s Texas to ancient China, and treating the material as broad farce rather than steamy noir. Curious, to say the least, but always dazzling to look at. HD Widescreen. [R] ▶

Woman Chaser, The (2000) **90m.** **½ D: Robinson Devor. Patrick Warburton, Emily Newman, Eugene Roche, Lynette Bennett, Joe Durrenberger, Pat Crowder. Film noir–ish takeoff set in early '60s L.A. A frustrated used-car salesman puts all his efforts into making a movie; when it blows up in his face he seeks revenge on those unlucky enough to get in his way. Debuting filmmaker Devor manages to make this look as if it could have been released on the bottom half of a 1960 double bill, right down to its nostalgic black-and-white look. Wry fun for film fans with a pitch-perfect lead performance by Warburton. [R]▼

Woman Hunt (1972-U.S.-Philippine) **C-81m.** BOMB D: Eddie Romero. John Ashley, Sid Haig, Laurie Rose, Lisa Todd, Eddie Garcia, Pat Woodell. Wretched knock-off of THE MOST DANGEROUS GAME, using kidnapped women as prey. Todd's dull performance as a black-leather-clad lesbian sadist wouldn't even amuse her *Hee Haw* fans. [R]▼

Woman in Berlin, A (2008-German) C-131m. *** D: Max Färberböck. Nina Hoss, Yevgeni Sidikhin, Irm Hermann, Rüdiger Vogler, Ulrike Krumbiegel, Rolf Kanies, Jördis Triebel, Roman Gribkov, Juliane Köhler, August Diehl. As WW2 comes to a close, the Russians are moving into Berlin and arbitrarily raping German women. One of them (Hoss) realizes that the only way she can control her fate is to find a protector—Russian major Sidikhin. Vivid, multilayered record of the horror of a time and place is based on a controversial, anonymously written diary published in 1959. ▶

Woman in Green, The (1945) 68m. *** D: Roy William Neill. Basil Rathbone, Nigel Bruce, Hillary Brooke, Henry Daniell, Paul Cavanagh, Matthew Boulton, Eve Amber. Blackmail, hypnotism, and murdered women with their right forefingers missing are the disparate elements in this solid *Sherlock Holmes* outing, with sleek Brooke and suave Daniell a formidable pair of foes for Holmes and Watson. Also shown in computer-colorized version.▼●▶

Woman in Question, The (1950-British) 89m. *** D: Anthony Asquith. Jean Kent, Dirk Bogarde, John McCallum, Susan Shaw, Hermione Baddeley, Charles Victor. As a cop investigates the slaying of a fortune teller, the various suspects' conflicting perceptions of the deceased emerge. Nifty whodunit, much of which is told in flashback; Kent is excellent as many different versions of the murder victim. Retitled: FIVE ANGLES ON MURDER. ▼

Woman in Red, The (1984) C-87m. *** D: Gene Wilder. Gene Wilder, Kelly LeBrock, Gilda Radner, Joseph Bologna, Charles Grodin, Judith Ivey. Broad remake of French farce PARDON MON AFFAIRE with happily married Wilder going ga-ga over beautiful LeBrock. Stevie Wonder score includes Oscar-winning "I Just Called to Say I Love You." [PG-13]▼●▶

Woman in the Dunes (1964-Japanese) 147m. ***½ D: Hiroshi Teshigahara. Eiji Okada, Kyoko Kishida, Koji Mitsui, Hiroko Ito, Sen Yano. Entomologist Okada becomes trapped in a sandpit and the prisoner of Kishida. Moving, memorable allegory, with striking direction and cinematography (by Hiroshi Segawa).▼▶

Woman in the Moon (1929-German) 156m. ** D: Fritz Lang. Klaus Pohl, Willy Fritsch, Gustav von Wangenheim, Gerda Maurus, Fritz Rasp. This lesser Lang effort, his last silent film, is about a spaceship and its trip to the moon. It's slow and way overlong, and it pales beside his brilliant METROPOLIS.▼

Woman in the Window, The (1944) 99m. ***½ D: Fritz Lang. Joan Bennett, Edward G. Robinson, Dan Duryea, Raymond Massey, Dorothy Peterson. High-grade melodrama about Robinson meeting subject of alluring painting (Bennett), becoming involved in murder and witnessing his own investigation. Surprise ending tops exciting film. Nunnally Johnson scripted. Look for *Our Gang* alumni Bobby Blake (as Robinson's son) and Spanky McFarland (as a scout in the newsreel). Also shown in computer-colored version. ▼●▶

Woman Is a Woman, A (1961-French) C-83m. **½ D: Jean-Luc Godard. Jean-Paul Belmondo, Jean-Claude Brialy, Anna Karina, Noel Pacquin. Pert stripper Karina wants a baby; boyfriend Brialy is not interested in fatherhood, so she approaches his best friend (Belmondo). Occasionally spirited, self-indulgent trifle. Franscope. ▼▶

Woman Next Door, The (1981-French) C-106m. *** D: François Truffaut. Gérard Depardieu, Fanny Ardant, Henri Garcin, Michele Baumgartner, Veronique Silver. Depardieu's new neighbor is ex-lover Ardant. Though now married, they revive their relationship. Somber, compassionate study of human nature and emotions, nicely acted by the two leads. [R]▼●▶

Woman Obsessed (1959) C-102m. **½ D: Henry Hathaway. Susan Hayward, Stephen Boyd, Barbara Nichols, Dennis Holmes, Theodore Bikel, Ken Scott. Energetic stars try hard in Canadian ranch-life soaper of widow Hayward who marries Boyd, with predictable clashing and making up. CinemaScope. ▶

Woman of Desire (1993) C-97m. ** D: Robert Ginty. Jeff Fahey, Bo Derek, Steven Bauer, Robert Mitchum. Wannabe erotic thriller with down-and-out Fahey being set up for the murder of playgirl Derek's wealthy boyfriend Bauer during a yacht trip—although sly lawyer Mitchum has his doubts in court. This went straight to video with an unrated 99m. version (more Bo nudity). [R]▼●▶

Woman of Distinction, A (1950) 85m. *** D: Edward Buzzell. Rosalind Russell, Ray Milland, Edmund Gwenn, Janis Carter, Mary Jane Saunders, Francis Lederer. Minor but very enjoyable slapstick, as visiting professor Milland causes scandal involving college dean Russell. Energetic cast puts this over. Lucille Ball appears uncredited as herself—as does future costar Gale Gordon, playing a train station clerk.▼●

Woman of Paris, A (1923) 91m. *** D: Charles Chaplin. Edna Purviance, Adolphe Menjou, Carl Miller, Lydia Knott, Charles French. French girl Purviance is set to marry her sweetheart (Miller), but a misunderstanding causes her to move to Paris, where she becomes the mistress of wealthy Menjou. Chaplin's one attempt to make a serious film (without himself as star) was quite sophisticated for its time, and remains interesting, even moving, today. It was a box-office flop in 1923; Chaplin reedited it, but waited until 1977 to reissue it, with his newly composed music score. Chaplin does a cameo as a railway porter, but he's virtually unrecognizable.▼◉❶

Woman of Straw (1964-British) **C-117m.** **½ D: Basil Dearden. Sean Connery, Gina Lollobrigida, Ralph Richardson, Johnny Sekka, Alexander Knox. Muddled suspenser of Connery and Lollobrigida plotting the "perfect murder" of old Richardson with ironic results.▼

Woman of the Rumor, The (1954-Japanese) **95m.** **½ D: Kenji Mizoguchi. Kinuyo Tanaka, Yoshiko Kuga, Tomoemon Otani, Eitaro Shindo. Melodramatic account of Geisha house operator Tanaka, whose lover really prefers her daughter. Minor Mizoguchi.

Woman of the Year (1942) **112m.** ***½ D: George Stevens. Spencer Tracy, Katharine Hepburn, Fay Bainter, Dan Tobin, Reginald Owen, Roscoe Karns, William Bendix. First teaming of Tracy and Hepburn is a joy; Kate's a world-famed political commentator brought down to earth by sports reporter Tracy, whom she later weds. Unforgettable scene of Hepburn trying to understand her first baseball game. Oscar-winning screenplay by Ring Lardner, Jr., and Michael Kanin; later a hit Broadway musical. Remade for TV in 1976. Also shown in computer-colored version.▼◉❶

Woman on Pier 13, The SEE: **I Married a Communist**

Woman on the Beach, The (1947) **71m.** *½ D: Jean Renoir. Robert Ryan, Joan Bennett, Charles Bickford, Nan Leslie, Walter Sande, Irene Ryan. Overheated melodrama wastes clever gimmick: Coast Guard officer isn't completely convinced his lover's husband is really blind. Loaded with laughable dialogue and sledgehammer music cues; easy to see why this was Renoir's American swan song.❶

Woman on Top (2000) **C-85m.** ** D: Fina Torres. Penélope Cruz, Murilo Benicio, Harold Perrineau, Jr., Mark Feuerstein, John de Lancie, Anne Ramsay, Ana Gasteyer. Brazilian woman who's a magnificent cook decides to come out from her restaurateur-husband's shadow. She moves to San Francisco and quickly becomes a sensation with a cooking show on TV. Strained fairy-tale romantic comedy exists solely as a vehicle for the charming Cruz. Panavision. [R]▼❶

Woman Rebels, A (1936) **88m.** *** D: Mark Sandrich. Katharine Hepburn, Herbert Marshall, Elizabeth Allan, Donald Crisp, Doris Dudley, David Manners, Lucile Watson, Van Heflin. Hepburn is marvelous as young girl whose experiences in Victorian England lead to her crusading for Women's Rights. Well-mounted soap opera remains surprisingly timely.❶

Woman's Face, A (1941) **105m.** *** D: George Cukor. Joan Crawford, Melvyn Douglas, Conrad Veidt, Osa Massen, Reginald Owen, Albert Bassermann, Marjorie Main, Donald Meek, Connie Gilchrist, Henry Daniell, Richard Nichols. Crawford has one of her most substantial roles in this exciting yarn of a scarred woman whose life changes when she undergoes plastic surgery. Taut climax spotlights villain Veidt. Originally filmed in 1938 in Sweden, as EN KVINNAS ANSIKTE, with Ingrid Bergman; script by Donald Ogden Stewart and Elliot Paul. Also shown in computer-colored version.▼◉❶

Woman's Secret, A (1949) **85m.** **½ D: Nicholas Ray. Maureen O'Hara, Melvyn Douglas, Gloria Grahame, Bill Williams, Victor Jory. Intriguing flashback drama of woman coming to hate singer she built up to success; good performances by two female stars. Just a bit too sloppy. Produced and scripted by Herman J. Mankiewicz, from a Vicki Baum novel. Director Ray married Grahame after film's completion. ▼

Woman's Tale, A (1991-Australian) **C-93m.** ***½ D: Paul Cox. Sheila Florance, Gosia Dobrowolska, Norman Kaye, Chris Haywood, Ernest Gray, Myrtle Woods, Bruce Myles. Seventy-eight-year-old woman dying of cancer is determined to live her final days with the same dignity she displayed her entire life. Simple tale—beautifully directed—is heartbreakingly real. Distinguished by the extraordinary and courageous performance of Sheila Florance, whose own illness while making the film paralleled that of her character. (She died two days after receiving Australia's Academy Award as Best Actress.) The kind of movie that, while painful to watch at times, can also illuminate our lives. [PG-13]▼◉

Woman's World (1954) **C-94m.** *** D: Jean Negulesco. Clifton Webb, June Allyson, Van Heflin, Arlene Dahl, Lauren Bacall, Fred MacMurray, Cornel Wilde, Elliott Reid. Slick look at diverse personalities in the world of big business as automobile mogul Webb decides to meet the wives of the men he's considering for a big promotion. CinemaScope.▼

Woman Thou Art Loosed (2004) **C-98m.** **½ D: Michael Schultz. Kimberly Elise, Loretta Divine, Debbi Morgan, Michael Boatman, Clifton Powell, Idalis De Leon, Bishop T. D. Jakes, Sean Blakemore, Jordan Moseley. Evangelical preacher Bishop T. D. Jakes portrays himself in this earnest adaptation of his self-help novel and play about the downward spiral and redemption of a young black woman who ends up on death row. Straightforward morality tale dealing with sexual abuse, drug addiction, and poverty sometimes comes off like a heavy-handed sermon, but is distinguished by Elise's poignant and impassioned performance. Alternate version runs 101m. [R] ▼▶

Woman Times Seven (1967) **C-99m.** ★★★ D: Vittorio De Sica. Shirley MacLaine, Peter Sellers, Rossano Brazzi, Vittorio Gassman, Lex Barker, Elsa Martinelli, Robert Morley, Patrick Wymark, Adrienne Corri, Alan Arkin, Michael Caine, Anita Ekberg, Philippe Noiret. A seven-episode film with MacLaine showing seven types of women; some funny moments, some perceptive comments, but with that cast and director, it should have been much better. ▼▶

Woman Under the Influence, A (1974) **C-147m.** ★★ D: John Cassavetes. Peter Falk, Gena Rowlands, Katherine Cassavetes, Lady Rowlands, Fred Draper. Typically overlong, overindulgent Cassavetes film, vaguely delineating relationship of woman who's cracking up and her hardhat husband, who can't handle it. Strong performances by Rowlands and Falk are chief virtue of this one. [R] ▼▶●

Wombling Free (1978-British) **C-96m.** ★½ D: Lionel Jeffries. David Tomlinson, Frances de la Tour, Bonnie Langford, Bernard Spear, Yasuko Nagazumi, John Junkin. Silly kiddie pic has the Wombles (actors in creature suits) cleaning up after man's litter and leading a protest against pollution. They're invisible to mankind except for a little girl (Langford) who believes. Objectionable use of stereotypes; best segment has big production-number tributes to Gene Kelly and Fred Astaire. Based on a BBC-TV series and later adapted as a U.S. series with Frank Gorshin. ▼

Women, The (1939) **132m.** ★★★½ D: George Cukor. Joan Crawford, Norma Shearer, Rosalind Russell, Mary Boland, Joan Fontaine, Paulette Goddard, Lucile Watson, Marjorie Main, Virginia Weidler, Phyllis Povah, Ruth Hussey, Mary Beth Hughes, Virginia Grey, Hedda Hopper, Butterfly McQueen. All-star (and all-female) cast shines in this hilarious adaptation of Clare Boothe play about divorce, cattiness, and competition in circle of "friends." Crawford has one of her best roles as bitchy homewrecker. Fashion show sequence is in color; script by Anita Loos and Jane Murfin. Remade in 1956 (as THE OPPOSITE SEX) and in 2008. ▼▶●

Women, The (2008) **C-114m.** ★★½ D: Diane English. Meg Ryan, Annette Bening, Eva Mendes, Debra Messing, Jada Pinkett Smith, Carrie Fisher, Cloris Leachman, Debi Mazar, Bette Midler, Candice Bergen, India Ennenga, Jill Flint, Ana Gasteyer, Joanna Gleason, Lynn Whitfield. Ryan has a seemingly perfect marriage, and a tight circle of female friends, but her world unravels when she learns that her husband is playing around with a perfume salesgirl from Saks. Update of Clare Boothe Luce's

play and the 1939 movie manages to retain the bones of the original, but has a tougher time creating a stylized modern reality for its backdrop. Uneven but entertaining, with plenty of sharp dialogue. Writer-director English does a creditable job, given the nearly impossible task of remaking a classic. [PG-13]▶

Women in Cages (1972-U.S.-Philippine) **C-78m.** BOMB D: Gerry De Leon. Judy Brown, Pam Grier, Roberta Collins. Lurid prison melodrama, with the emphasis on sadism, has the switcheroo of Grier cast as lesbian guard who tortures prisoners in her gothic chamber, known as "The Playpen." Video title: WOMEN'S PENITENTIARY III. [R]▼▶

Women in Limbo SEE: **Limbo** (1972)

Women in Love (1969-British) **C-129m.** ★★★½ D: Ken Russell. Alan Bates, Oliver Reed, Glenda Jackson, Eleanor Bron, Jennie Linden, Alan Webb. Fine adaptation of D. H. Lawrence novel about two interesting love affairs. Tends to bog down toward the end, but acting and direction are really impressive, as is memorable nude wrestling scene. Jackson won her first Oscar for this performance. Followed in 1989 by Russell's THE RAINBOW, a "prequel" in which Jackson plays the mother of her character in this film. [R]▼▶●

Women in Trouble (2009) **C-95m.** ★★★ D: Sebastian Gutierrez. Carla Gugino, Connie Britton, Adrianne Palicki, Emmanuelle Chriqui, Sarah Clarke, Simon Baker, Josh Brolin, Marley Shelton, Joseph Gordon-Levitt, Cameron Richardson, Garcelle Beauvais-Nilon, Elizabeth Berkley, Dolly Parton. Wild mix of high camp and grand passions, soap opera and soft-core sex, detailing the misadventures of colorful female characters during a long day in, around, and above L.A. Gugino is first among equals in a mostly terrific ensemble as a porn-movie superstar who discovers she is pregnant. Also figuring into the crazy-quilt plot: a therapist (Clarke) who rightly suspects her husband of adultery, a novice porno actress (Palicki), and a starstruck flight attendant (Shelton). Bawdy comedy in the style of Pedro Almodóvar, who has collaborated on other projects with writer-director Gutierrez. Followed by ELEKTRA LUXX. [R]▶

Women of the Prehistoric Planet (1966) **C-87m.** ★½ D: Arthur C. Pierce. Wendell Corey, Keith Larsen, John Agar, Irene Tsu, Merry Anders, Adam Roarke, Stuart Margolin. One of many studio-bound sci-fi pix from the '60s, a strange lot indeed. Spaceship crashes on mysterious planet full of prehistoric inhabitants. There's a twist ending, if you stick around for it. ▼

Women on the Verge of a Nervous Breakdown (1988-Spanish) **C-88m.** ★★★½ D: Pedro Almodóvar. Carmen Maura, Antonio Banderas, Julieta Serrano, Maria Barranco, Rossy De Palma. Witty, outrageous, and highly stylized comedy about charmingly off-kilter actress Maura and how she responds when suddenly abandoned by her longtime lover. A real audience-pleaser, with plenty of laughs; crammed with a colorful array of supporting characters (most memorably a taxi driver with a bleached-blond pompadour whose car is a combination drugstore/bar). [R]▼●▶

Women's Penitentiary I SEE: **Big Doll House, The**

Women's Penitentiary II SEE: **Big Bird Cage, The**

Women's Penitentiary III SEE: **Women in Cages**

Women's Prison (1955) **80m.** ** D: Lewis Seiler. Ida Lupino, Jan Sterling, Cleo Moore, Audrey Totter, Phyllis Thaxter, Howard Duff, Mae Clarke, Gertrude Michael, Juanita Moore. Campy 1950s programmer, with Lupino as a vicious prison superintendent riding herd over a cast that no B-movie lover could resist. ▶

Women Without Men SEE: **Blonde Bait**

Wonder Boys (2000) **C-112m.** *** D: Curtis Hanson. Michael Douglas, Tobey Maguire, Frances McDormand, Robert Downey, Jr., Katie Holmes, Richard Thomas, Rip Torn, Philip Bosco, Jane Adams. Intelligent, low-key comedy about the bond that develops between a college professor (Douglas), whose personal and professional life is floundering, and a strange but gifted student (Maguire), who adds to his chaos. A midlife coming-of-age story that benefits from its freshly observed academic milieu and a strong cast; Douglas is excellent in a change-of-pace role. Steve Kloves adapted Michael Chabon's novel. Bob Dylan's soundtrack song won an Oscar. Super 35. [R]▼▶

Wonderful Country, The (1959) **C-96m.** **½ D: Robert Parrish. Robert Mitchum, Julie London, Gary Merrill, Pedro Armendariz, Jack Oakie, Albert Dekker. Brooding Western involving Mitchum running guns along Mexico-Texas line, romancing London; script by Robert Ardrey.

Wonderful, Horrible Life of Leni Riefenstahl, The (1993-German-Belgian-British) **C/B&W-182m.** *** D: Ray Muller. Thorough, compelling portrait of Riefenstahl, infamous director of Nazi propaganda films TRIUMPH OF THE WILL and OLYMPIA, that serves as an investigation of her life (traced via film clips, and interviews made with the filmmaker in her early nineties). Was she a woman of evil—an opportunist and a collaborator in her dealings with Adolf Hitler and the Nazi Party? Or was she a feminist pioneer, an apolitical artist who became an innocent victim of circumstance? Ultimately, the film is most effective as a portrait of denial and an analysis of any filmmaker's respon-

sibility regarding the power of the moving image. ▼●▶

Wonderful Ice Cream Suit, The (1999) **C-77m.** **½ D: Stuart Gordon. Joe Mantegna, Esai Morales, Edward James Olmos, Clifton Gonzales Gonzales, Gregory Sierra, Liz Torres, Sid Caesar, Howard Morris, Lisa Vidal, Pedro Gonzales Gonzales. Well-meaning, upbeat adaptation of Ray Bradbury's short story and play about five L.A. Latinos who share the price of a beautiful white suit which, they believe, will help them realize their dreams. The flavor never seems genuine, and the treatment is heavy-handed, but there is still a magic to the story. Released direct to video. [PG] ▼●

Wonderful World (2010) **C-99m.** ** D: Josh Goldin. Matthew Broderick, Sanaa Lathan, Michael Kenneth Williams, Philip Baker Hall, Jesse Tyler Ferguson, Ally Walker, Jodelle Ferland. Cynical deadbeat dad, a failed children's folk singer, has his dark view of life slowly transformed when his ill roommate's sister comes to live in his apartment. Broderick is well cast as the loser and Lathan is a delightful presence, but this black comedy never really comes to life, though there is the germ of an interesting idea here. [R] ▶

Wonderful World of the Brothers Grimm, The (1962) **C-129m.** *** D: Henry Levin, George Pal. Laurence Harvey, Claire Bloom, Karl Boehm, Oscar Homolka, Martita Hunt, Jim Backus, Yvette Mimieux, Barbara Eden, Walter Slezak, Russ Tamblyn, Buddy Hackett, Beulah Bondi, Terry-Thomas. Fanciful adaptations of Grimm tales offset by OK look at famed brothers' lives. Best of all are Puppetoons sequences in toy shop, Hackett battling fire-breathing dragon. Colorful George Pal entertainment, with Oscar-winning costumes by Mary Wills, was originally shown in Cinerama. ▼●

Wonderland (1988) SEE: **Fruit Machine, The**

Wonderland (1999-British) **C-108m.** ** D: Michael Winterbottom. Shirley Henderson, Gina McKee, Molly Parker, Ian Hart, John Simm, Stuart Townsend, Kika Markham, Jack Shepherd. Dreary slice-of-life drama set in London over a long weekend, examining three unhappy generations of a single family. The mise-en-scène is impeccable, the situations completely believable, but the results are less than compelling. Super 35. ▼▶

Wonderland (2003) **C-104m.** BOMB D: James Cox. Val Kilmer, Kate Bosworth, Lisa Kudrow, Tim Blake Nelson, Dylan McDermott, Josh Lucas, Eric Bogosian, Christina Applegate, Natasha Gregson Wagner, Janeane Garofalo, Franky G., Carrie Fisher, Faizon Love, Ted Levine, Paris Hilton. Tedious look at events leading up to the grisly 1981 murders on L.A.'s Wonderland Avenue involving former porn film star John C. Holmes (Kilmer) and assorted other lowlifes. Sordid, violent, and filled with characters it's impossible to care about. [R] ▼◗

Wonder Man (1945) **C-98m.** *** D: H. Bruce Humberstone. Danny Kaye, Virginia Mayo, Vera-Ellen, Donald Woods, S. Z. Sakall, Allen Jenkins, Ed Brophy, Steve Cochran, Otto Kruger, Natalie Schafer. Kaye's fun as twins, the serious one forced to take the place of his brash entertainer brother when the latter is killed. Big, colorful production with Oscar-winning special effects. ▼◗

Won Ton Ton the Dog Who Saved Hollywood (1976) **C-92m.** ** D: Michael Winner. Bruce Dern, Madeline Kahn, Art Carney, Phil Silvers, Teri Garr, Ron Leibman. Fine cast struggles through inept spoof of 1920s Hollywood. Dog comes off better than dozens of veteran stars who make pointless cameo appearances (from Rhonda Fleming to the Ritz Brothers). [PG] ◗

Woo (1998) **C-83m.** BOMB D: Daisy V. S. Mayer. Jada Pinkett Smith, Tommy Davidson, Duane Martin, Dave Chappelle, Michael Ralph, LL Cool J, Foxy Brown, Aida Turturro, Billy Dee Williams. Misbegotten attempt at screwball comedy in which neurotic Manhattanite Pinkett Smith leads dorky law student Davidson on an all-night blind date from hell. Substitutes stupid slapstick and misogynist, homophobic potshots for wit and charm. Wants to be a '90s BRINGING UP BABY but ends up a sub-par HOUSE PARTY. [R] ▼◗

Wood, The (1999) **C-106m.** **½ D: Rick Famuyiwa. Omar Epps, Sean Nelson, Taye Diggs, Trent Cameron, Richard T. Jones, Duane Finley, Malinda Williams, Lisarae. So-so comedy about a reluctant, AWOL bridegroom (Diggs) whose two best pals (Epps, Jones) come to his rescue; in flashbacks we learn how they became friends in their formative years. The predictability of their story is partially offset by the film's charm and humor. [R] ▼◗

Wooden Horse, The (1950-British) **101m.** *** D: Jack Lee. Leo Genn, David Tomlinson, Anthony Steel, Peter Burton, David Greene, Anthony Dawson, Bryan Forbes, Peter Finch. Sturdy, exciting POW drama of men determined to tunnel their way out of Nazi prison camp using an exercise vaulting horse for cover. Based on Eric Williams' novel *The Tunnel Escape.* ▼

Woods, The (2006-U.S.-British) **C-91m.** BOMB D: Lucky McKee. Agnes Bruckner, Patricia Clarkson, Rachel Nichols, Lauren Birkell, Emma Campbell, Marcia Bennett, Gordon Currie, Jude Beny, Bruce Campbell. Alienated teen Bruckner, burdened with an unfeeling mother, is dispatched to a woodsy all-girls academy that has a mys-

terious history and a staff and student body who are all creepy or cruel. One-note horror film is thoroughly unpleasant, when it's not dull or idiotic. A real ordeal to sit through. Released direct to DVD in the U.S. [R]◗

Woodsman, The (2004) **C-87m.** *** D: Nicole Kassell. Kevin Bacon, Kyra Sedgwick, Eve, Mos Def, David Alan Grier, Benjamin Bratt, Michael Shannon, Hannah Pilkes, Carlos Leon. Just released from prison, child molester Bacon tries to acclimate to "normal" life (getting a job, having a relationship with a woman, trying to make peace with his family), but his biggest problem is battling his own demons. Provocative adult drama doesn't make its lead character sympathetic but does try to paint a three-dimensional portrait. Bacon and real-life spouse Sedgwick are exceptionally good; the climactic scene in a park is spine-tingling. Cowritten by first-time feature director Kassell and Steven Fechter from the latter's play. Bacon also coexecutive-produced. [R] ▼◗

Woodstock (1970) **C-184m.** **** D: Michael Wadleigh. Joan Baez, Richie Havens, Crosby, Stills and Nash, Jefferson Airplane, Joe Cocker, Sly and the Family Stone, Ten Years After, Santana, Country Joe and the Fish, John Sebastian, The Who, Jimi Hendrix, Arlo Guthrie. 1970 Oscar winner as Best Documentary brilliantly captures unique communal experience of outdoor rock festival, along with great performances which highlighted unusual weekend bash. Among highlights: Cocker, Sly Stone, Ten Years After, The Who. Makes exceptional use of multiscreen images and a "surround sound" mix. Martin Scorsese was one of the editors. Forty minutes of previously unseen footage were added in 1994, featuring Janis Joplin, Jimi Hendrix, Canned Heat, and Jefferson Airplane, among others. The video title is WOODSTOCK 3 DAYS OF PEACE & MUSIC (THE DIRECTOR'S CUT). Part Widescreen. [R] ▼◗

Woody Guthrie: Hard Travelin' (1984) **C/B&W-74m.** **** D: Jim Brown. Fascinating, beautifully made documentary about the wiry little drifter who is now recognized as one of the greatest American songwriters. Hosted by his son, Arlo, the film traces Woody's life from birth to his tragically lingering death. Interviewees include friends, like Pete Seeger, Herta Ware, and Ramblin' Jack Elliott, and those who were influenced by Woody, such as Joan Baez, Judy Collins, and Hoyt Axton. It leaves you singing, and wanting more. ▼

Wordplay (2006) **C-94m.** *** D: Patrick Creadon. Entertaining documentary about the *New York Times* crossword puzzle and Will Shortz, its longtime editor. Amusing and affectionate look at the gold standard of puzzles, its creators, and loyal fans (with on-screen graphics that cleverly simulate the process of puzzle solving), culminating in 2005's American Crossword Puzzle Tournament. Famous crossword devotees interviewed include Bill Clinton, Jon Stewart, Ken Burns, and Bob Dole. [PG]❒

Words and Music (1948) **C-119m.** **½ D: Norman Taurog. Mickey Rooney, Tom Drake, June Allyson, Ann Sothern, Judy Garland, Gene Kelly, Lena Horne, Vera-Ellen, Cyd Charisse, Allyn Ann McLerie, Mel Tormé, Betty Garrett, Perry Como, Janet Leigh. Sappy, Hollywoodized biography of songwriters Rodgers (Drake) and Hart (Rooney) is salvaged somewhat by their wonderful music, including Kelly and Vera-Ellen's dance to "Slaughter on Tenth Avenue." ▼O❒

Word Wars (2004) **C-76m.** *** D: Eric Chaikin, Julian Petrillo. Very enjoyable cinéma vérité–style documentary about professional Scrabble players. Follows four competitors—each one uniquely eccentric—as they work their way toward the one big-money tournament of the year. No screenwriter could invent better characters or a more unusual saga. Told with visual pizzazz and a clever music score by Thor Madsen. ❒

Working Class Goes to Heaven, The (1972-Italian) **C-126m.** *** D: Elio Petri. Gian Maria Volonté, Mariangela Melato, Salvo Randone, Gino Pernice, Luigi Diberti. A hardworking lathe operator is laid off after losing a finger on the assembly line, then becomes the leader of a strike that takes some very unexpected twists and turns. Superbly directed, thought-provoking critique of capitalism, with some surprisingly funny and sensuous touches. Music by Ennio Morricone. Originally released in the U.S. as LULU THE TOOL.

Working Girl (1988) **C-113m.** *** D: Mike Nichols. Harrison Ford, Sigourney Weaver, Melanie Griffith, Alec Baldwin, Joan Cusack, Philip Bosco, Nora Dunn, Oliver Platt, James Lally, Kevin Spacey, Robert Easton, Olympia Dukakis, Ricki Lake, David Duchovny. Cute comedy about a naive but ambitious secretary who tries to outfox her wily boss by closing a big deal—with the help of a man she just happens to fall in love with. Star-making showcase for Griffith also gives Ford an ideal opportunity to play light comedy and Weaver a sly supporting role as the villainess. Carly Simon's music was scored by Rob Mounsey; her song "Let the River Run" won an Oscar. Later a TV series. [R]▼O❒

Working Girls, The (1973) **C-81m.** **½ D: Stephanie Rothman. Sarah Kennedy, Laurie Rose, Lynne Guthrie, Solomon Sturges, Mary Beth Hughes, Cassandra Peterson. One of the better drive-in comedies, with three attractive girls struggling to make a success of themselves in a male-oriented world; Kennedy and Sturges (Preston's son) make an endearing couple.

A staple of cable-TV because of nifty striptease performed by Peterson (better known as TV's Elvira). [R]▼❒

Working Girls (1986) **C-90m.** ***½ D: Lizzie Borden. Louise Smith, Ellen McElduff, Amanda Goodwin, Marusia Zach, Janne Peters, Helen Nicholas. Beautifully realized, on-target account of a day in a N.Y.C. brothel; the sex is more humorous and businesslike than erotic, and the profession is depicted as an economic alternative to other traditional "women's" work. First-rate all the way. ▼❒

Work Is a 4-Letter Word (1967-British) **C-93m.** **½ D: Peter Hall. David Warner, Cilla Black, Elizabeth Spriggs, Zia Mohyeddin, Joe Gladwyn. Zany, but hit-and-miss comedy based on the play *Eh?* about young man who raises giant mushrooms that produce euphoria when eaten. Warner is well cast. [M/PG]

World According to Garp, The (1982) **C-136m.** **** D: George Roy Hill. Robin Williams, Mary Beth Hurt, Glenn Close, John Lithgow, Hume Cronyn, Jessica Tandy, Swoosie Kurtz, Amanda Plummer, Warren Berlinger, Brandon Maggart. Dazzling (if somewhat loose) adaptation of John Irving's novel, about an unusual young man's journey through life—an adventure shaped in large part by his unorthodox (and unmarried) mother. Absorbing, sure-footed odyssey through vignettes of social observation, absurdist humor, satire, and melodrama; beautifully acted by all, especially Close (in her feature debut) as Garp's mother and Lithgow as a transsexual. Script by Steve Tesich. Director Hill has cameo as pilot who crashes into Garp's house; novelist Irving plays wrestling match referee. [R]▼O❒

World Apart, A (1988) **C-112m.** **½ D: Chris Menges. Barbara Hershey, David Suchet, Jeroen Krabbé, Jodhi May, Rosalie Crutchley, Tim Roth, Adrian Dunbar, Paul Freeman. Personal story of South African apartheid as seen through the eyes of a teenage girl whose mother, a Communist activist, is jailed under the notorious 90-day detention act in 1963. Both a story of government abuse and a look at one mother's neglect of her family because of her involvement with a larger cause . . . but too diffuse to succeed completely on either count. Young May is remarkable as the girl, however. Autobiographical script by Shawn Slovo. Directorial debut for cinematographer Menges. [PG]▼O❒

World Gone Wild (1988) **C-95m.** ** D: Lee H. Katzin. Bruce Dern, Michael Paré, Catherine Mary Stewart, Adam Ant, Rick Podell, Anthony James. Post-apocalyptic science-fiction saga set in the 21st century, in the desolate village of Lost Wells, which is threatened by evil plunderers (led by Adam Ant). Who will come to the villagers' rescue? THE SEVEN SAMURAI meets

MAD MAX in this marginally successful, futuristic action yarn. [R]▼●

World in His Arms, The (1952) **C-104m.** *** D: Raoul Walsh. Gregory Peck, Ann Blyth, John McIntire, Anthony Quinn, Andrea King, Eugenie Leontovich, Sig Ruman. Unlikely but entertaining tale of skipper Peck romancing Russian Blyth, set in 1850s San Francisco and Alaska.▼▶

World Is Full of Married Men, The (1979-British) **C-107m.** ** D: Robert Young. Anthony Franciosa, Carroll Baker, Sherrie Cronn, Gareth Hunt, Georgina Hale, Anthony Steel. The sexual escapades—and downfall—of advertising executive Franciosa. Slick and sleazy exploitation melodrama that ultimately gives feminism a bad name, from a novel and screenplay by Jackie Collins. [R]▼

World Is Not Enough, The (1999) **C-125m.** **½ D: Michael Apted. Pierce Brosnan, Sophie Marceau, Robert Carlyle, Denise Richards, Robbie Coltrane, Judi Dench, Desmond Llewelyn, John Cleese, Maria Grazia Cucinotta, Samantha Bond, Goldie, Serena Scott Thomas. OK if typically overlong James Bond outing has 007 avenging the murder of an industrialist who was a close friend of M's. Brosnan is fine, as are the action set pieces, but film allows M (Dench) to look foolish, and absurdly casts Richards as a nuclear physicist (in shorts!) with lots of laughable dialogue. Carlyle is a good villain with an underwritten part; Marceau is delicious as Elektra. Llewelyn's final film as Q. Panavision. [PG-13]▼▶

World Moves On, The (1934) **104m.** **½ D: John Ford. Madeleine Carroll, Franchot Tone, Reginald Denny, Stepin Fetchit, Lumsden Hare, Raul Roulien, Louise Dresser, Sig Ruman. Long but interesting family saga covering 100 years as Louisiana family is split, three sons heading business operations in England, France, Germany, experiencing tremendous changes from peaceful 19th century through WW1.▶

World of Abbott and Costello, The (1965) **75m.** ** Narrated by Jack E. Leonard. Bud Abbott, Lou Costello, Marjorie Main, Bela Lugosi, Tom Ewell, others. Inept compilation of A&C footage, with curious selection of scenes, senseless narration. Still, there's "Who's on First?" and other fine routines.▼▶

World of Apu, The (1959-Indian) **103m.** ***½ D: Satyajit Ray. Soumitra Chatterjee, Sharmila Tagore, Alok Chakravarty, Swapan Mukherji. Sadly poetic tale of the shy Apu (Chatterjee) marrying and fathering a child. Magnificently acted; last of the director's "Apu" trilogy.▼▶

World of Henry Orient, The (1964) **C-106m.** ***½ D: George Roy Hill. Peter Sellers, Tippy Walker, Merrie Spaeth, Paula Prentiss, Angela Lansbury, Phyllis Thaxter,

Tom Bosley. Marvelous comedy of two teenage girls who idolize eccentric pianist (Sellers) and follow him around N.Y.C. Bosley and Lansbury are superb as Walker's parents, with Thaxter appealing as Spaeth's understanding mother. Screenplay by Nunnally and Nora Johnson, from her novel. Panavision.▼●▶

World of Suzie Wong, The (1960) **C-129m.** **½ D: Richard Quine. William Holden, Nancy Kwan, Sylvia Syms, Michael Wilding, Laurence Naismith. Holden's sluggish performance as American artist in love with prostitute Kwan doesn't help this soaper, lavishly filmed in Hong Kong. Script by John Patrick from Paul Osborn's Broadway play.▼●▶

World of Tomorrow, The (1984) **C/B&W-83m.** *** D: Lance Bird, Tom Johnson. Lovely documentary about 1939 New York World's Fair, a compilation of newsreels, home movies, promotional films, and various other period graphics . . . much of it in color! Occasionally teeters on the edge of pretentiousness, especially in narration spoken by Jason Robards. Cut to one hour for some showings.▼

World's Fastest Indian, The (2005-U.S.-New Zealand) **C-126m.** *** D: Roger Donaldson. Anthony Hopkins, Diane Ladd, Paul Rodriguez, Aaron Murphy, Annie Whittle, Chris Williams, Christopher Lawford, Jessica Cauffiel, Chris Bruno, Bruce Greenwood, William Lucking. Hopkins is marvelous as a spirited old man who's obsessed with his 1920 Indian Scout motorcycle and determined to take it from his little town in New Zealand to run on the Bonneville Salt Flats in Utah. It's the 1960s, and along the way he meets an assortment of characters, some of them almost as colorful as he. An openhearted film, not for cynics. Written by the director, who filmed a TV documentary about the real Burt Munro in 1972. Super 35. [PG-13]▶

World's Greatest Athlete, The (1973) **C-93m.** *** D: Robert Scheerer. John Amos, Jan-Michael Vincent, Tim Conway, Roscoe Lee Browne, Dayle Haddon, Howard Cosell. Hard-luck coach Amos returns to his roots in Africa and discovers superathlete Vincent; enjoyable Disney comedy with excellent special effects. Conway particularly funny in sequence in which he shrinks to Tom Thumb size. Cosell's classic line: "I've never seen anything like this in my entire illustrious career!" [G]▼▶

World's Greatest Dad (2009) **C-99m.** *** D: Bobcat Goldthwait. Robin Williams, Daryl Sabara, Alexie Gilmore, Geoff Pierson, Henry Simmons, Mitzi McCall, Tom Kenny, Toby Huss. Sharply etched black comedy/social satire about a hapless high school teacher (Williams) whose adolescent son is a foulmouthed misanthrope. Yet the boy's actions ultimately inspire his dad to build a bond with the people around him, in a most unexpected manner. Bold but never gratuitously "outrageous," this sardonic tale manages to ring true, thanks to writer-director Goldthwait's restraint and Williams' empathetic performance. [R] ❚

World's Greatest Lover, The (1977) **C-89m.** **½ D: Gene Wilder. Gene Wilder, Carol Kane, Dom DeLuise, Fritz Feld, Carl Ballantine, Michael Huddleston, Matt Collins, Ronny Graham, Danny DeVito. Sporadically funny comedy set in 1920s Hollywood, with Wilder screen-testing as new movie sheik and wife Kane deserting him for real-life Valentino. Wild slapstick combines unevenly with occasional vulgarities and moments of poignancy. Inspired by Fellini's THE WHITE SHEIK. [PG]▼❚

World's Greatest Sinner, The (1962) **76m.** **½ D: Timothy Carey. Timothy Carey, Gil Baretto, Betty Rowland, James Farley, Gail Griffen, Tyde Rule, Grace De Carolis; narrated by Paul Frees. The great, eccentric character actor Carey gives his creepiest, most over-the-top performance in this crazed vanity project, which he wrote, produced, and directed. A disillusioned insurance salesman declares himself to be God, becomes an Elvis-like rock 'n' roll evangelist, and is enticed to run for president by a shady power broker. Technically crude but weirdly fascinating as a prescient, primal scream of rage against cults, religious and political opportunism, and celebrity worship. A very young Frank Zappa (billed simply as "Zappa") composed the score and a hilarious title song.

World, the Flesh, and the Devil, The (1959) **95m.** **½ D: Ranald MacDougall. Harry Belafonte, Inger Stevens, Mel Ferrer. Belafonte and Stevens are only survivors of worldwide nuclear accident; their uneasy relationship is jarred by arrival of Ferrer. Intriguing film starts well, bogs down halfway through, and presents ridiculous conclusion. Best scenes are at beginning, when Belafonte is alone in an impressively deserted Manhattan. CinemaScope.▼●❚

World Trade Center (2006) **C-129m.** ***½ D: Oliver Stone. Nicolas Cage, Michael Peña, Maggie Gyllenhaal, Maria Bello, Stephen Dorff, Jay Hernandez, Michael Shannon, Frank Whaley, Donna Murphy, Patty D'Arbanville, Dorothy Lyman, Nicky Katt, Nicholas Turturro, Danny Nucci, William Mapother, Jude Ciccolella, Viola Davis. The tragedy of September 11, 2001, is vividly dramatized by following the actions of the Port Authority police squad that responded to the first tower attack. Bulk of the film is devoted to the plight of two such rescuers trapped in the rubble of the collapsed towers, while their families agonize over their fate. Superior storytelling from start to finish. Screenplay by Andrea Berloff,

based on the stories of John McLoughlin and Will Jimeno. Super 35. [PG-13]❚

World Traveler (2002-U.S.-Canadian) **C-104m.** ** D: Bart Freundlich. Billy Crudup, Julianne Moore, Cleavant Derricks, David Keith, James Le Gros, Karen Allen, Mary McCormack. A man walks out on his wife and son, takes to the road, and has a variety of encounters as he tries to sort out his life—and why he has become so completely alienated from it. Interesting in fits and starts, but unsatisfying; the ultimate revelation about its main character is both obvious and unconvincing. [R]▼❚

World Without End (1956) **C-80m.** **½ D: Edward Bernds. Hugh Marlowe, Nancy Gates, Nelson Leigh, Rod Taylor. Space flight headed for Mars breaks the time barrier and ends up on post-apocalyptic Earth in the 26th century. Pretty good sci-fi owes more than a little to H. G. Wells' *The Time Machine*. CinemaScope.▼❚

World Without Sun (1964) **C-93m.** **** D: Jacques Cousteau. Excellent, Oscar-winning documentary of Cousteau and his oceanauts, creating an underwater adventure that challenges any fiction.

Worth Winning (1989) **C-102m.** *½ D: Will Mackenzie. Mark Harmon, Madeleine Stowe, Lesley Ann Warren, Maria Holvöe, Mark Blum, Andrea Martin, David Brenner. Smug Harmon bets that he can hustle a trio of women into agreeing to marry him. Occasionally obnoxious (and predictable) comedy. [PG-13]▼●❚

Woyzeck (1978-German) **C-82m.** **½ D: Werner Herzog. Klaus Kinski, Eva Mattes, Wolfgang Reichmann, Willy Semmelrogge, Josef Bierbichler. Minor Herzog features the usual wide-eyed performance by Kinski as an ostensibly normal man who goes insane and becomes a murderer. Based on Georg Büchner's drama. Remade in 1994. ▼❚

Wraith, The (1986) **C-92m.** ** D: Mike Marvin. Charlie Sheen, Nick Cassavetes, Randy Quaid, Sherilyn Fenn, Griffin O'Neal, David Sherrill, Jamie Bozian, Clint Howard. A Dodge Turbo Interceptor—it's a car—strangely appears one day and takes on some auto thieves. For those who favor fast cars and lots of noise. [PG-13]▼●❚

Wrath of God, The (1972) **C-111m.** ** D: Ralph Nelson. Robert Mitchum, Rita Hayworth, Frank Langella, John Colicos, Victor Buono, Ken Hutchison, Paula Pritchett, Gregory Sierra. If you take this film—about a defrocked priest in a revolution-ridden country south of the border—seriously, it's an OK action yarn. Accept it as tongue-in-cheek, it may yield greater enjoyment. Hayworth's final film. Panavision. [PG]

Wrecked (2011-U.S.-Canadian) **C-90m.** ** D: Michael Greenspan. Adrien Brody, Caroline Dhavernas, Ryan Robbins. Bruised and battered man awakens in a forest ravine with no memory of how he's come to be injured and trapped inside a run-down car, mangled from—apparently—a forceful car crash. With little hope of being found, his survival instincts quickly kick in even as clues begin to surface indicating he may be a wanted man. That means if he's rescued, his life will still be in shambles. A mishmash of a psychodrama, almost made bearable by Brody. Tries to be engrossing—but isn't. [R] ◗

Wrecking Crew, The (1969) **C-105m.** *½ D: Phil Karlson. Dean Martin, Sharon Tate, Elke Sommer, Nancy Kwan, Tina Louise, Nigel Green. Fourth and final theatrical Matt Helm epic, while hardly a good film, is at least a step up from the last two, thanks to a return by the original director and the re-creation (in Tate) of an engaging klutz a la Stella Stevens in THE SILENCERS. Story has Helm after crime ring that's hijacked a train carrying a billion in gold. Chuck Norris has one line with Dino in a bar and Bruce Lee is credited as film's "karate advisor." A TVM and subsequent series (*Matt Helm*) followed in 1975. [M/PG] ▼◗

Wreck of the Mary Deare, The (1959-U.S.-British) **C-105m.** **½ D: Michael Anderson. Gary Cooper, Charlton Heston, Michael Redgrave, Emlyn Williams, Cecil Parker, Alexander Knox, Virginia McKenna, Richard Harris. Salvage boat skipper Heston boards an apparently abandoned freighter, finds hostile Captain Cooper aboard. What really happened to the *Mary Deare*? Stars outshine their material in Eric Ambler's adaptation of the novel by Hammond Innes. CinemaScope. ▼◗

Wrestler, The (2008-French-U.S.) **C-109m.** ***½ D: Darren Aronofsky. Mickey Rourke, Marisa Tomei, Evan Rachel Wood, Mark Margolis, Todd Barry, Wass Stevens, Judah Friedlander, Ernest Miller, Ajay Naidu. Professional wrestler who's past his prime is forced to take stock of his isolated existence and his estrangement from a teenage daughter. Robert Siegel's no-holds-barred script is dramatized in documentary-like fashion on a variety of N.J. locations and populated with actual denizens of the low-end wrestling world, including fighters and fans. Rourke's performance as the pumped-up pro who knows no other way of life is a tour de force; Tomei is every bit as good as a stripper who tries to separate her working "identity" from the rest of her life. Super 35. [R]◗

Wrestling Ernest Hemingway (1993) **C-122m.** **½ D: Randa Haines. Robert Duvall, Richard Harris, Shirley MacLaine, Sandra Bullock, Piper Laurie, Nicole Mercurio, Marty Belafsky. A great actor's showcase, if not a great movie, about two older men now living in Florida: a boozy Irish ex-sea captain (Harris) and a retired Cuban barber (Duvall).

They have practically nothing in common, but their need for companionship and interaction draws them together in this meandering but easy-to-take character study which was (incredibly) written by a 21-year-old, Steve Conrad. [PG-13] ▼◗

Wrestling with Angels: Playwright Tony Kushner (2006) **C-102m.** *** D: Freida Lee Mock. Engrossing documentary about playwright and social activist Kushner (*Angels in America*) follows him over three years' time, covering a broad canvas, from preparations for the opening of the Broadway musical *Caroline, or Change* to his marriage to life partner Mark Harris. Unabashedly positive portrait includes readings of Kushner's work (by the likes of Meryl Streep and Marcia Gay Harden) and a great deal of candid footage with family, friends, and coworkers.

Wristcutters: A Love Story (2007) **C-91m.** **½ D: Goran Dukic. Patrick Fugit, Shannyn Sossamon, Shea Whigham, Leslie Bibb, John Hawkes, Mikal P. Lazarev, Mark Boone Junior, Abraham Benrubi, Mary Pat Gleason, Azura Skye, Sarah Roemer, Jake Busey, Tom Waits, Will Arnett. After committing suicide, Fugit finds himself living in a peculiar purgatory that looks just like real life—only more desolate. When he learns that his ex-girlfriend is also "living" in this world, he sets out in search of her. Endearingly odd black comedy has a great premise but doesn't really go anywhere. [R]◗

Written on the Wind (1956) **C-99m.** *** D: Douglas Sirk. Rock Hudson, Lauren Bacall, Robert Stack, Dorothy Malone, Robert Keith, Grant Williams. Florid melodrama of playboy-millionaire Stack, his nymphomaniac sister Malone, and how they destroy themselves and others around them. Irresistible kitsch. Malone won Oscar for her performance. ▼◗

Wrong Arm of the Law, The (1963-British) **94m.** *** D: Cliff Owen. Peter Sellers, Lionel Jeffries, Bernard Cribbins, Davy Kaye, Nanette Newman, John Le Mesurier, Dennis Price, Michael Caine. Wacky comedy spoof has Australian trio being chased by police as well as crooks because they've been dressing as cops and confiscating loot from apprehended robbers. Some very funny moments. ▼◗

Wrong Bet SEE: **Lionheart** (1991)

Wrong Box, The (1966-British) **C-105m.** ***½ D: Bryan Forbes. John Mills, Ralph Richardson, Michael Caine, Peter Cook, Dudley Moore, Nanette Newman, Wilfred Lawson, Tony Hancock, Peter Sellers. Scramble for inheritance is basis for wacky black comedy set in Victorian England; aging Mills attempts to do in brother Richardson (with help from family cohorts) in order to be sole survivor. Sellers has hilarious cameo as oddball doctor. Based on a Robert Louis Stevenson story, scripted by Larry Gelbart and Burt Shevelove. ▼●▶

Wrongfully Accused (1998-U.S.-German) **C-85m.** ****** D: Pat Proft. Leslie Nielsen, Richard Crenna, Kelly LeBrock, Sandra Bernhard, Michael York, Melinda McGraw. Silly spoof of THE FUGITIVE is yet another vehicle for Nielsen's deadpan comic shtick. This time, he's on the run for a crime he didn't commit. Amidst the relentless barrage of gags are some that—while entirely obvious—are also pretty funny, if you like this sort of thing. [PG-13] ▼●▶

Wrong Guys, The (1988) **C-86m.** *½ D: Danny Bilson. Louie Anderson, Richard Lewis, Richard Belzer, Franklyn Ajaye, Tim Thomerson, Brion James, Biff Maynard, John Goodman, Ernie Hudson, Timothy Van Patten, Rita Rudner. Clumsy and unfunny comedy about a Cub Scout reunion campout that goes awry; cast of stand-up comics do battle with a stupid script. [PG] ▼●

Wrong Is Right (1982) **C-117m.** **½ D: Richard Brooks. Sean Connery, George Grizzard, Robert Conrad, Katharine Ross, G. D. Spradlin, John Saxon, Henry Silva, Leslie Nielsen, Robert Webber, Rosalind Cash, Hardy Kruger, Dean Stockwell, Ron Moody, Jennifer Jason Leigh. Broad, bizarre, free-swinging satire of our TV-dominated culture, keyed to superstar reporter Connery's involvement with a terrorist group, and the U.S. government's possible ties to it. Scattershot script manages to hit a few targets, and benefits from Brooks' breathless pace. [R] ▼●▶

Wrong Man, The (1957) **105m.** *** D: Alfred Hitchcock. Henry Fonda, Vera Miles, Anthony Quayle, Harold J. Stone, Nehemiah Persoff, Peggy Webber. Unusual Hitchcock film done as semidocumentary, using true story of N.Y.C. musician (Fonda) falsely accused of robbery. Miles is excellent as wife who cracks under strain; offbeat and compelling. Written by Maxwell Anderson and Angus MacPhail: Look for Tuesday Weld in giggly bit. ▼●▶

Wrong Move (1975-German) **C-103m.** **½ D: Wim Wenders. Rudiger Vogler, Hanna Schygulla, Ivan Desny, Marianne Hoppe, Peter Kern, Hans Christian Blech, Nastassja Kinski. Overly metaphorical (but occasionally worthwhile) tale of disgruntled Vogler attempting to understand himself—and his country's past—as he rambles through Germany with various companions. Scripted by Peter Handke, loosely based on Goethe's *Wilhelm Meister.* Kinski's film debut. The second (and least successful) in Wenders' "road movie" trilogy, after ALICE IN THE CITIES and followed by KINGS OF THE ROAD. Original English title: WRONG MOVEMENT. ▼▶

Wrong Rut, The SEE: **Not Wanted**

Wrong Turn (2003) **C-84m.** *½ D: Rob Schmidt. Eliza Dushku, Desmond Harrington, Emmanuelle Chriqui, Jeremy Sisto, Lindy Booth, Julian Richings, Kevin Zegers. Wrong is right, as a stereotyped group of young motorists become stranded in the backwoods of West Virginia and naturally find themselves stalked by cannibalistic, inbred hillbillies. Derivative gorefest for those who've never seen DELIVERANCE or THE TEXAS CHAIN SAW MASSACRE. Followed by three direct-to-DVD sequels. [R] ▼▶

WUSA (1970) **C-115m.** **½ D: Stuart Rosenberg. Paul Newman, Joanne Woodward, Anthony Perkins, Laurence Harvey, Pat Hingle, Cloris Leachman, Don Gordon, Leigh French, Moses Gunn, Bruce Cabot, Lou Gossett, Jr. Newman pet project casts him as cynical drifter who becomes a d.j. for an ultra-right-wing New Orleans radio station and struggles with his own apathy as he grows aware of WUSA's true (and sinister) intentions. Obvious sincerity undercut by simplistic, overwritten script; still, the acting is fine and there are some truly memorable scenes. Panavision. [M/PG]▶

Wuthering Heights (1939) **103m.** **** D: William Wyler. Merle Oberon, Laurence Olivier, David Niven, Flora Robson, Donald Crisp, Geraldine Fitzgerald, Leo G. Carroll, Cecil Kellaway, Miles Mander, Hugh Williams. Stirring adaptation of Emily Brontë's novel stops at chapter 17, but viewers shouldn't despair: sensitive direction and sweeping performances propel this magnificent story of doomed love in pre-Victorian England. Haunting, a must-see film. Gregg Toland's moody photography won an Oscar; script by Ben Hecht and Charles MacArthur. Remade in 1953, 1970, 1992, and in 2003 for cable TV. ▼●▶

Wuthering Heights (1953-Mexican) **90m.** **½ D: Luis Buñuel. Irasema Dilian, Jorge Mistral, Lilia Prado, Ernesto Alonso, Luis Aceves Castaneda. Strikingly directed but talky, overbaked, ultimately unsuccessful version of the Brontë classic: bitter, cold-hearted former servant Mistral, now rich, returns to disrupt the life of true love Dilian, now married to another.▼

Wuthering Heights (1970-British) **C-105m.** *** D: Robert Fuest. Anna Calder-Marshall, Timothy Dalton, Harry Andrews, Pamela Browne, Judy Cornwell, Ian Ogilvy, Hugh Griffith, Julian Glover. Good, realistic treatment of Brontë's novel with authentic locations and atmosphere, Dalton and Calder-Marshall believable looking as Heathcliff and Cathy, but film's point of view indistinct and pace too fast. [G] ▼●▶

Wuthering Heights (1992-U.S.-British) **C-106m.** *½ D: Peter Kosminsky. Juliette Binoche, Ralph Fiennes, Janet McTeer, Sophie Ward, Simon Shepherd, Jeremy

Northam. Excruciating remake of the classic Brontë novel of doomed love. Binoche plays both Cathy and her daughter exactly the same way, with a different hair color. Fiennes' torment is so intense, it's actually a relief when he dies. This was the first film produced by Paramount studio's European production wing but it made its U.S. debut several years after completion, on cable TV. Sinéad O'Connor appears unbilled as Emily Brontë. Title on-screen is EMILY BRONTË'S WUTHERING HEIGHTS. [PG]▼●◗

W.W. and the Dixie Dancekings (1975) C-91m. **½ D: John G. Avildsen. Burt Reynolds, Art Carney, Conny Van Dyke, Jerry Reed, James Hampton, Ned Beatty. Lightly likable film about a conman who hooks up with struggling country-western group and stops at nothing to promote their success; Carney has oddball role as religious lawman pursuing Burt. Script by Thomas Rickman. [PG]

Wyatt Earp (1994) C-190m. **½ D: Lawrence Kasdan. Kevin Costner, Dennis Quaid, Gene Hackman, Jeff Fahey, Mark Harmon, Michael Madsen, Catherine O'Hara, Bill Pullman, Isabella Rossellini, Tom Sizemore, JoBeth Williams, Mare Winningham, James Gammon, Annabeth Gish, Betty Buckley, Mackenzie Astin, Karen Grassle, Téa Leoni, Brett Cullen, John Doe, Martin Kove. Epic-length biography shows how fate and circumstance turned the fabled Earp into a hardened and heartless man who killed in the name of law and order. Good storytelling grows ponderous toward the end, as Earp is driven by revenge against his blood enemies from the O.K. Corral. Quaid makes a colorful Doc Holliday, though his equally flashy ladyfriend Big Nosed Kate (Rossellini) disappears just as we get to meet her! Special video edition runs 20m. longer! Panavision. [R]▼●◗

Wyoming Kid, The SEE: **Cheyenne**

Xanadu (1980) C-96m. *½ D: Robert Greenwald. Olivia Newton-John, Gene Kelly, Michael Beck, James Sloyan, Dimitra Arliss, Katie Hanley, Sandahl Bergman, Marilyn Tokuda, John "Fee" Waybill, voices of Wilfrid Hyde-White and Coral Browne. Flashy but empty-headed remake of DOWN TO EARTH, with Olivia as muse who pops in to inspire young roller-boogie artist. Designed as a showcase for the singer, whose screen charisma is nil. Kelly (using his character name from COVER GIRL) tries to perk things up; even a brief animated sequence by Don Bluth doesn't help. Newton-John's future husband, Matt Lattanzi, plays Kelly as a young man. Later a Broadway musical. [PG] ▼●◗

X-15 (1961) C-106m. ** D: Richard Donner. David McLean, Charles Bronson, Ralph Taeger, Brad Dexter, Mary Tyler Moore, Patricia Owens; narrated by Jimmy Stewart. Mild narrative of pilots testing the experimental space plane of the title, and their romantic and family lives. Unusual role for Bronson, even then. Panavision.◗

X Files, The (1998) C-120m. **½ D: Rob Bowman. David Duchovny, Gillian Anderson, Martin Landau, Armin Mueller-Stahl, Blythe Danner, William B. Davis, John Neville, Mitch Pileggi, Jeffrey DeMunn, Terry O'Quinn, Glenne Headly, Lucas Black. Feature version of popular TV series serves well enough as a conspiracy yarn for newcomers to the exploits of FBI agents Mulder and Scully. After surviving the bombing of a building in Texas, they defy orders and go in search of a new lead about aliens on Earth and the question of who's running what. Overlong by at least one climax, this large-scale thriller will have additional resonance for *X-Files* fans. Video version runs 122m. Followed by a sequel a decade later. Super 35. [PG-13]▼●◗

X Files: I Want to Believe, The (2008-U.S.-Canadian) C-104m. ** D: Chris Carter. David Duchovny, Gillian Anderson, Amanda Peet, Billy Connolly, Alvin 'Xzibit' Joiner, Mitch Pileggi, Callum Keith Rennie, Fagin Woodcock. When she's approached by the FBI to help investigate several abductions of women, Dana Scully (Anderson) turns for help to retired Fox Mulder (Duchovny). He believes a former priest (Connolly), jailed for pederasty, has real psychic powers; she doesn't. What follows is similar to an *X-Files* TV episode—but longer and less involving, centering on bizarre surgery. Devotees will likely enjoy this more than newcomers. Alternate version runs 108m. Super 35. [PG-13]◗

Xica (1978-Brazilian) C-107m. **½ D: Carlos Diegues. Zeze Motta, Walmor Chagas, Jose Wilker, Marcus Vinicius, Altair Lima. Saucy, if a bit overspiced, tale of strong-willed black slave Motta who seduces the new Royal Diamond Contractor (Chagas) in corrupt, repressive colonial Brazil. Nicely directed and acted—particularly by Motta—but curiously unmemorable. Filmed in 1976; released in the U.S. in 1982.▼

Xiu Xiu the Sent-down Girl (1999-Chinese-Hong Kong-U.S.) C-99m. **½ D: Joan Chen. Lu Lu, Lopsang, Gao Jie, Li Qianqian, Lu Yue. In 1980s China, a bright city girl (16-year-old Lu Lu) is sent to a remote rural area as part of a government cultural program, where she comes under the care of a kind Tibetan herder and horse trainer. Actress Chen's directorial debut is a well-made, richly detailed film with an intriguing story, but the resolution is unsatisfying. Banned in China for its critical stance. Chen also coscripted with Yan Geling, based on the latter's novella. [R]▼▶

X-Men (2000) C-104m. *** D: Bryan Singer. Hugh Jackman, Patrick Stewart, Ian McKellen, Famke Janssen, James Marsden, Halle Berry, Anna Paquin, Tyler Mane, Ray

Park, Rebecca Romijn-Stamos, Bruce Davison. Marvel Comics–inspired saga has two disparate misfits, Wolverine (Jackman) and Rogue (Paquin), linking up and finding a safe haven with Professor X (Stewart), who hopes to find ways to assimilate all mutants into human society. His brainy counterpart, Magneto (McKellen), however, sees humans as the enemy to be conquered. Long on razzle-dazzle, fun to watch, though some energy is sapped away by the climax. Based on characters created for Marvel by Stan Lee and Jack Kirby. Followed by two sequels and two prequels. Panavision. [PG-13] ▼▶

X2 (2003) **C-134m.** *** D: Bryan Singer. Patrick Stewart, Hugh Jackman, Ian McKellen, Halle Berry, Famke Janssen, James Marsden, Rebecca Romijn-Stamos, Brian Cox, Alan Cumming, Bruce Davison, Shawn Ashmore, Aaron Stanford, Kelly Hu, Anna Paquin. Action-packed sequel to X-MEN turns Stewart and McKellen into temporary allies in order to combat power-crazy Cox. That's just one plot thread in this breathless film, which doesn't have enough time to spend with all of its colorful characters, including Pyro, Colossus, and the colorful Nightcrawler (well played by Cumming). There's energy to spare in this entertaining yarn based on the Marvel comic book created by Stan Lee and Jack Kirby. Super 35. [PG-13] ▼▶

X-Men: The Last Stand (2006) **C-104m.** ** D: Brett Ratner. Hugh Jackman, Halle Berry, Ian McKellen, Patrick Stewart, Famke Janssen, Anna Paquin, Kelsey Grammer, James Marsden, Rebecca Romijn, Shawn Ashmore, Aaron Stanford, Vinnie Jones, Ben Foster, Michael Murphy, Shohreh Aghdashloo, Josef Sommer, Bill Duke, Cameron Bright, R. Lee Ermey, Ellen Page. Development of a "cure" for genetic mutations—like the X-Men—spurs the ultimate showdown between Magneto and Dr. Xavier. Third and weakest in the comic book series shortchanges character development in favor of explosions and special effects . . . so there's little emotion in spite of all the overheated goings-on. Was Foster's part (as Murphy's winged son) really meant to be so brief? Super 35. [PG-13] ▶

X-Men Origins: Wolverine (2009) **C-107m.** **½ D: Gavin Hood. Hugh Jackman, Liev Schreiber, Danny Huston, Will.i.am, Lynn Collins, Ryan Reynolds, Kevin Durand, Dominic Monaghan, Taylor Kitsch, Daniel Henney. Proposed backstory of the indestructible Wolverine character from Marvel's *X-Men* comics sets up the lifelong sibling relationship (and rivalry) with his bloodthirsty brother Sabretooth (Schreiber), and, less interestingly, shows how they and other mutants were exploited by a rogue U.S. military officer (Huston) bent on creating the ultimate humanoid weapon. Slick but heavy-handed and formulaic, this film lacks the sense of wonder and discovery that marks the first two X-MEN movies, and focuses instead on Wolverine and his adversaries beating the living daylights out of each other. Jackman gives it his best. Super 35. [PG-13] ▶

X-Men: First Class (2011) **C-132m.** **½ D: Matthew Vaughn. James McAvoy, Michael Fassbender, Rose Byrne, Jennifer Lawrence, Kevin Bacon, January Jones, Nicholas Hoult, Oliver Platt, Jason Flemyng, Lucas Till, Edi Gathegi, Caleb Landry Jones, Zoë Kravitz, Matt Craven, Rade Sherbedgia, Ray Wise, Michael Ironside. Origin story introduces the future Magneto (Fassbender) as a victim of Nazi torture during WW2, then jumps ahead to the early 1960s, when he and Oxford professor Charles Xavier (McAvoy) agree to help the CIA track down former Nazi—now would-be world conqueror—Bacon. They also recruit a new generation of mutants to train alongside them. Good story tries to cover too much ground and introduces an abundance of characters . . . but the appeal of Marvel's X-Men remains intact, especially in the solid performances of McAvoy and Fassbender. Newcomers Lawrence and Hoult score while Bacon seems miscast. A couple of amusing surprise cameos will please series fans. Panavision. [PG-13]

X: The Man with the X-Ray Eyes (1963) **C-80m.** **½ D: Roger Corman. Ray Milland, Diana Van Der Vlis, Harold J. Stone, John Hoyt, Don Rickles. Not-bad little film about scientist Milland developing serum that enables him to see through things. He lives to regret it. Title on-screen is simply X. ▼▶

X The Unknown (1956-British) **80m.** **½ D: Leslie Norman. Dean Jagger, Leo McKern, William Lucas, Edward Chapman, Anthony Newley. Well-thought-out sci-fi production set in Scotland. Radioactive mud from Earth's center grows and kills anything in its path. Effective chiller written by Jimmy Sangster. ▼▶

Xtro (1983-British) **C-82m.** *½ D: Harry Bromley Davenport. Philip Sayer, Bernice Stegers, Danny Brainin, Maryam d'Abo, Simon Nash. Father abducted by aliens returns to Earth three years later to claim his young son, but he's not the man he used to be. Crudely directed sci-fi/horror opus is guided by gruesomeness, not logic. Overwrought but dull, with lots of sexual elements. XTRO II and XTRO: WATCH THE SKIES are sequels in title only. [R] ▼▶

XXX (2002) **C-124m.** **½ D: Rob Cohen. Vin Diesel, Samuel L. Jackson, Asia Argento, Marton Csokas, Danny Trejo, Michael Roof, Tom Everett, Richy Müller, Thomas Ian Griffith, Eve. A hooligan/extreme-sports showoff/online entrepreneur is recruited by the NSA to go underground in Prague and get the goods on a renegade Russian. Check your brains at the door and you'll have a good time with this silly, high-energy action film, with some over-the-top stunt sequences and plenty of room for Diesel to strut his stuff. If only it didn't go on so long, and try to turn this antihero into a bona fide hero. One nice touch: a musical reference to THE THIRD MAN. Diesel coexecutive-produced. Unrated version runs 132m. Followed by a sequel. Panavision. [PG-13]▼◗

xXx: State of the Union (2005) C-100m. ** D: Lee Tamahori. Ice Cube, Samuel L. Jackson, Willem Dafoe, Scott Speedman, Peter Strauss, Xzibit, Michael Roof, Nona Gaye. In a pastoral Virginia horse-country setting where you half expect to run into Sam Shepard, a group of National Security Agency employees is slaughtered. To solve the crime, NSA honcho Jackson springs Cube from a maximum-security cooler (to replace Vin Diesel, from the original XXX film). Outlandish premise and execution are worth a few laughs, but when the Secretary of Defense is also a 4-star general played by Dafoe, you won't pull many muscles trying to determine who's behind a SEVEN DAYS IN MAY–type coup. Super 35. [PG-13]▼◗

xx/xy (2003) C-91m. *** D: Austin Chick. Mark Ruffalo, Kathleen Robertson, Maya Stange, Petra Wright, David Thornton, Kel O'Neill. Laid-back N.Y.C. artist hooks up with two college girls and indulges in a free-love, partying haze of sex and drugs. Story then fast-forwards as the three reconnect, years later, as "responsible" adults. Instead of just another romantic-triangle picture, this hearkens back to films of the 1960s and '70s in its examination of relationships. Good showcase for the talented Ruffalo, with strong performances from all the leads. Written by the director. [R]▼◗

X Y & Zee (1972-British) C-110m. ** D: Brian G. Hutton. Elizabeth Taylor, Michael Caine, Susannah York, Margaret Leighton, John Standing. Contrived, often perverse tale of a woman, her husband, another woman and the way the three are interchangeable in relationships. Original British title: ZEE AND COMPANY. [PG—edited from original R rating]▼◗

Yakuza, The (1975) C-112m. *** D: Sydney Pollack. Robert Mitchum, Takakura Ken, Brian Keith, Herb Edelman, Richard Jordan, Kishi Keiko. Mitchum tries to rescue pal Keith's kidnapped daughter by returning to Japan after several years; he gets more than he bargains for from title organization, a kind of Oriental Mafia. Mitchum and Ken are fine in suspenseful action pic, written by Paul Schrader and Robert Towne. Retitled: BROTHERHOOD OF THE YAKUZA. Originally shown at 123m. Panavision. [R]▼◗

Yank at Eton, A (1942) 88m. ** D: Norman Taurog. Mickey Rooney, Freddie Bartholomew, Tina Thayer, Ian Hunter, Edmund Gwenn, Alan Mowbray, Peter Lawford, Terry Kilburn. Rooney goes to school in England and it's a wonder he's not ejected immediately.

Yank at Oxford, A (1938-U.S.-British) 100m. *** D: Jack Conway. Robert Taylor, Lionel Barrymore, Maureen O'Sullivan, Vivien Leigh, Edmund Gwenn. Attractive cast, including young Leigh, in familiar story of cocky American trying to adjust to Oxford, and vice versa. Remade in 1984 as OXFORD BLUES.

Yankee Doodle Dandy (1942) 126m. **** D: Michael Curtiz. James Cagney, Joan Leslie, Walter Huston, Irene Manning, Rosemary DeCamp, Richard Whorf, Jeanne Cagney, S. Z. Sakall, Walter Catlett, Frances Langford, Eddie Foy, Jr., George Tobias. Cagney wraps up film in neat little package all his own with dynamic re-creation of George M. Cohan's life and times; he deservedly won Oscar for rare song-and-dance performance, as did music directors Ray Heindorf and Heinz Roemheld. Also shown in computer-colored version. ▼O◗

Yank in the RAF, A (1941) 98m. *** D: Henry King. Tyrone Power, Betty Grable, John Sutton, Reginald Gardiner, Donald Stuart, Richard Fraser. Power's only there so he can see London-based chorine Grable; they make a nice team. Songs: "Another Little Dream Won't Do Us Any Harm," "Hi-Ya Love."▼◗

Yank in Viet-Nam, A (1964) 80m. ** D: Marshall Thompson. Marshall Thompson, Enrique Magalona, Mario Barri, Urban Drew. Low-budget topical actioner set in Saigon, with Marine Thompson attempting to help the South Vietnamese. Retitled: YEAR OF THE TIGER.

Yanks (1979) C-139m. **½ D: John Schlesinger. Richard Gere, Lisa Eichhorn, Vanessa Redgrave, William Devane, Chick Vennera, Wendy Morgan, Rachel Roberts, Joan Hickson, John Ratzenberger, Antony Sher. Lavish production about WW2 romances between U.S. soldiers and British women doesn't deliver the goods, due to choppy structure and flabby direction. Gere's so-called star power seems to be a casualty of energy crisis cutbacks. [R]▼O◗

Yards, The (2000) C-115m. ** D: James Gray. Mark Wahlberg, Joaquin Phoenix, Charlize Theron, James Caan, Ellen Burstyn, Faye Dunaway, Andrew Davoli, Steve Lawrence, Tony Musante, Victor Argo, Tomas Milian. Somber N.Y.C. mood piece about an aimless young man (Wahlberg), just out of prison, who tries to go straight but winds up working with his friend (Phoenix) bending and breaking the law on behalf of his uncle, a city contractor (Caan). All the characters are doomed in this dark, operatic (but not always credible) tale of corruption . . . and fate. Panavision. [R]▼◗

Yearling, The (1946) C-128m. ***½ D: Clarence Brown. Gregory Peck, Jane Wyman, Claude Jarman, Jr., Chill Wills, Margaret Wycherly, Henry Travers, Jeff York, Forrest Tucker, June Lockhart. Marjorie Kinnan Rawling's sensitive tale of a boy attached to a young deer was exquisitely filmed in Technicolor on location in Florida, with memorable performances. Oscar winner for Cinematography and Art Direction, and a special Oscar for newcomer Jarman. Beware 94m. reissue print. Remade as a TV movie in 1994. ▼○▶

Year My Voice Broke, The (1987-Australian) **C-103m.** *** D: John Duigan. Noah Taylor, Loene Carmen, Ben Mendelsohn, Graeme Blundell, Lynette Curran, Malcolm Robertson, Judi Farr. Affecting story of a teenage boy's friendship and infatuation with a troubled girl; set in a small town in the early 1960s. A cut above the usual coming-of-age film, thanks to director Duigan's touching script and amazingly natural performances by his young actors. Followed by a sequel, FLIRTING. [PG-13] ▼○▶

Year of Getting to Know Us, The (2010) **C-97m.** ** D: Patrick Sisam. Jimmy Fallon, Sharon Stone, Tom Arnold, Chase Ellison, Tony Hale, Jordana Spiro, Bree Turner, Illeana Douglas, Lucy Liu. Emotionally damaged N.Y.C. writer (Fallon) is forced to deal with his issues when he returns to his childhood home in Florida after his estranged father (Arnold) suffers a stroke. Funnyman Fallon is fatally out of his depth in this standard indie mix of dysfunctional drama and quirky comedy. Released straight to DVD in 2010 following festival screenings in 2008. [R] ▶

Year of Living Dangerously, The (1983-Australian) **C-115m.** *** D: Peter Weir. Mel Gibson, Sigourney Weaver, Linda Hunt, Michael Murphy, Bill Kerr, Noel Ferrier. Fascinating political drama set in strife-ridden Indonesia just before Sukarno's fall in 1965 . . . much more successful as a mood-piece than as romance, however, with Weaver's flimsy character (and flimsier accent) a detriment. Diminutive Hunt—a woman playing a man—is mesmerizing and most deservedly won an Academy Award. Panavision. [PG] ▼○▶

Year of the Comet (1992) **C-89m.** ** D: Peter Yates. Penelope Ann Miller, Tim Daly, Louis Jourdan, Art Malik, Ian Richardson, Ian McNeice, Julia McCarthy. Listless, if not especially painful, variation on ROMANCING THE STONE: Wallflower Miller begins to bloom when her discovery of a priceless wine bottle lands her in the middle of some international intrigue. Agreeably performed, but a pretty slight non-event given William Goldman's first original script since BUTCH CASSIDY AND THE SUNDANCE KID. Panavision. [PG-13] ▼●

Year of the Dog (2007) **C-98m.** *** D: Mike White. Molly Shannon, Laura Dern, Regina King, Tom McCarthy, Peter Sars-

gaard, John C. Reilly, Josh Pais. A square peg (Shannon) who holds down a mundane office job is badly shaken when her beloved dog dies. This sets off a chain reaction of funny, sad, and shocking events. White's fondness for society's oddballs (see CHUCK & BUCK, THE GOOD GIRL) flowers in his directorial debut, a seriocomedy with Shannon capturing all the nuances of her character, a good-hearted woman who's never quite fit in. Evocative score by Christophe Beck. [PG-13] ▶

Year of the Dragon (1985) **C-136m.** **½ D: Michael Cimino. Mickey Rourke, John Lone, Ariane, Leonard Termo, Ray Barry, Caroline Kava, Eddie Jones. Highly charged, arresting melodrama scripted by Oliver Stone (from Robert Daley's book) about a Vietnam vet who's still fighting his own private war, as a N.Y.C. cop whose current target is corruption in Chinatown, and crime czar Lone in particular. Companion piece to Cimino's THE DEER HUNTER has same intensity but nearly drowns in a sea of excess and self-importance. Still worth watching. Incidentally, virtually all New York settings (including Mott Street) were re-created on location in North Carolina! J-D-C Scope. [R] ▼○▶

Year of the Gun (1991) **C-111m.** ** D: John Frankenheimer. Andrew McCarthy, Valeria Golino, Sharon Stone, John Pankow, Mattia Sbragia, George Murcell. Confused thriller about a young American novelist in Rome who stumbles onto the Red Brigade's plot to kidnap then-Premier Aldo Moro. Frankenheimer (who made such great political thrillers as SEVEN DAYS IN MAY and THE MANCHURIAN CANDIDATE) struggles to keep a wandering story in focus. McCarthy is somewhat blank in the lead role, but Stone is good as an aggressive photojournalist. [R] ▼○▶

Year of the Quiet Sun, A (1984-Polish-German) **C-106m.** *** D: Krzysztof Zanussi. Scott Wilson, Maja Komorowska, Hanna Skarzanka, Ewa Dalkowska, Vadim Glowna, Daniel Webb. Stark, haunting drama, set just after WW2, detailing the evolving relationship between two lost souls who don't even speak the same language: hard-luck Polish widow Komorowska and emotionally hungry American GI Wilson. A heartfelt film, loaded with raw emotion and deep feeling. [PG] ▼○▶

Year of the Tiger SEE: **Yank in Viet-Nam, A**

Year One (2009) **C-97m.** BOMB D: Harold Ramis. Jack Black, Michael Cera, Oliver Platt, David Cross, Christopher Mintz-Plasse, Vinnie Jones, Hank Azaria, Juno Temple, Olivia Wilde, Xander Berkeley, Gia Carides, Horatio Sanz, Bill Hader. Zed, the fat one, and Oh, the skinny one, are banished from their caveman tribe and somehow wind up in biblical times, encountering Cain and Abel and visiting Sodom, where they are determined to rescue their girlfriends. Nonsensical and moronic comedy relies on a series of jokes involving flatulence and bad eating habits. Where are Abbott and Costello when you need them most??? Paul Rudd appears unbilled. Unrated version runs 99m. [PG-13] ▐

Yella (2008-German) **C-86m.** *** D: Christian Petzold. Nina Hoss, Devid Striesow, Hinnerk Schönemann, Burghart Klaußner, Barbara Auer, Christian Redl. Cryptic account of the title character (Hoss), who has just ended her marriage. A desperate, violent act on the part of her ex leaves her drowned in a river—or does it? Remake of CARNIVAL OF SOULS is effective as a psychological study and an acute reflection of contemporary business practices. ▐

Yellowbeard (1983-British) **C-101m.** BOMB D: Mel Damski. Graham Chapman, Peter Boyle, Richard "Cheech" Marin, Tommy Chong, Peter Cook, Marty Feldman, Martin Hewitt, Michael Hordern, Eric Idle, Madeline Kahn, James Mason, John Cleese, Susannah York, Stacey Nelkin. Appalling waste of talent in a startlingly inept and unfunny pirate comedy. Written by costars Chapman and Cook with Bernard McKenna. They should have walked the plank for this one. This was Feldman's final film. [PG] ▼○▶

Yellow Earth (1984-Chinese) **C-87m.** *** D: Chen Kaige. Xue Bai, Wang Xueqi, Tan Tuo, Liu Qiang. One of the earliest films of the Chinese New Wave is an engrossing, poetic account of a wandering communist soldier who arrives in a rural farming village in 1939 to learn folk songs that he will teach to his regiment; he inspires a 14-year-old girl who is bound by tradition to a life of bitterness and hardship. Photographed by Zhang Yimou; it's interesting to contrast this film's "communism equals freedom" propaganda to the political content of Yimou and Kaige's later work. ▼

Yellow Handkerchief, The (2010-U.S.-Japanese) **C-102m.** *** D: Udayan Prasad. William Hurt, Maria Bello, Kristen Stewart, Eddie Redmayne, Emmanuel K. Cohn, Nurith Cohn, Veronica Russell. Three strangers—a man just released from prison, a girl running away from home, and a lovesick young drifter—take a road trip together through the backwaters of the Louisiana Bayou and find their lives are changed by the experience. Moody but worthwhile drama is a fine acting showcase, particularly for Hurt and Stewart, who manage to make this a journey worth taking. Cinematography by Chris Menges is stunning. Adapted from a story by Pete Hamill. Super 35. [PG-13]

Yellow Rolls-Royce, The (1964-British) **C-122m.** *** D: Anthony Asquith. Rex Harrison, Shirley MacLaine, Ingrid Bergman, Jeanne Moreau, Edmund Purdom, George C. Scott, Omar Sharif, Art Carney, Alain Delon, Roland Culver, Wally Cox. Slick Terence Rattigan drama involving trio of owners of title car, focusing on how romance plays a part in each of their lives; contrived but ever-so-smoothly handled. Panavision. ▼○▶

Yellow Sky (1948) **98m.** *** D: William A. Wellman. Gregory Peck, Anne Baxter, Richard Widmark, Robert Arthur, John Russell, Henry (Harry) Morgan, James Barton. Exciting Western with Peck heading a gang of thieves who come to a ghost town, where they confront tough, mysterious Baxter and her grandfather. Similar in atmosphere to Wellman's classic THE OX-BOW INCIDENT. Script by Lamar Trotti from a W. R. Burnett story. Remade as THE JACKALS. ▼▶

Yellow Submarine (1968-British) **C-85m.** **** D: George Dunning. Pure delight, a phantasmagorical animated feature with as much to hear as there is to see: Beatles' songs, puns, non sequitur jokes combined with surreal pop-art visions in story of Beatles trying to save Pepperland from the Blue Meanies. Unique, refreshing. Songs include "Lucy in the Sky With Diamonds," "When I'm Sixty-four," "All You Need Is Love." Alternate version runs 90m. and features "Hey Bulldog." [G] ▼○▶

Yentl (1983) **C-134m.** **½ D: Barbra Streisand. Barbra Streisand, Mandy Patinkin, Amy Irving, Nehemiah Persoff, Steven Hill. A young woman in Eastern Europe at the turn of the century disguises as a boy in order to fulfill her dream and get an education. Isaac Bashevis Singer's simple short story is handled with love and care by first-time director/producer/cowriter Streisand, but goes on far longer than necessary, with 12 (count 'em) soliloquy songs by Alan and Marilyn Bergman and Michel Legrand (who also earned Oscars for their score) and a finale uncomfortably reminiscent of FUNNY GIRL. A star vehicle if there ever was one; no wonder Streisand fans love it. Alternate DVD version runs 137m. [PG] ▼○▶

Yes (2005-U.S.-British) **C-100m.** ***½ D: Sally Potter. Joan Allen, Simon Abkarian, Sam Neill, Shirley Henderson, Sheila Hancock, Samantha Bond, Stephanie Leonidas. Challenging, artfully crafted tale (written in rhyming verse) about a woman whose marriage is strained, leaving her ripe for seduction. Enter a suave Lebanese man (Abkarian). Potter's scenario veers in many directions, with astute philosophical observations about the differences between East and West, relations between the classes, and the importance of seizing the moment. Talky but never boring, with Potter offering beautifully composed shots and stunning use of color. [R] ▐

Yes, Giorgio (1982) **C-110m.** *½ D: Franklin J. Schaffner. Luciano Pavarotti, Kathryn Harrold, Eddie Albert, Paola Borboni, James Hong, Beulah Quo. Opera superstar Pavarotti plays . . . an opera superstar, who pursues an independent-minded lady doctor during American tour. So-called romantic comedy gives the phrase "old fashioned" a bad name; missing ingredient is a parade of character actors like Mischa Auer and Herman Bing to make it palatable. Only saving grace: Pavarotti sings. [PG]▼●◗

Yes Man (2008) **C-104m.** **½ D: Peyton Reed. Jim Carrey, Zooey Deschanel, Bradley Cooper, John Michael Higgins, Rhys Darby, Danny Masterson, Fionnula Flanagan, Terence Stamp, Sasha Alexander, Molly Sims, Brent Briscoe. A working drone who's been miserable since his wife dumped him falls under the influence of a self-help guru who exhorts him to say nothing but yes for the next year—quite literally—and he finds that it does in fact open up all sorts of opportunities. Perfect role for Carrey, who makes the most of it, though the script loses its initial momentum . . . and the final gag falls flat. Based on a best-selling memoir by Danny Wallace. Luis Guzmán appears unbilled. Super 35. [PG-13]◗

Yes Men, The (2004) **C-83m.** *** D: Chris Smith, Sarah Price, Dan Ollman. Subversively hilarious documentary-satire in which a pair of merry pranksters pass themselves off as World Trade Organization hotshots. Their purpose: to infiltrate the culture of corporate executives and expose and lampoon their dubious intentions. Watching how far they carry their hoax proves again that Barnum was right. Michael Moore, sympathetic to The Yes Men's mission, appears briefly. Released in Canada in 2003. Followed by THE YES MEN FIX THE WORLD. [R]▼◗

Yesterday, Today and Tomorrow (1963-Italian) **C-119m.** **** D: Vittorio De Sica. Sophia Loren, Marcello Mastroianni, Tina Pica, Giovanni Ridolfi. Oscar winner for Best Foreign Film is impeccable trio of comic tales, with Loren playing three women who use sex in various ways to get what they want. Striptease for Marcello is among the most famous scenes in her career (and remains pretty steamy). Techniscope.▼◗

Yi Yi (A One and a Two) (2000-Taiwanese-Japanese) **C-173m.** ***½ D: Edward Yang. Nien-Jen Wu, Elaine Jin, Issey Ogata, Kelly Lee, Jonathan Chang, Hsi-Sheng Chen. Smart, spare slice-of-life about a middle-class Taiwanese family and their everyday problems: a husband-father must contend with business difficulties and the presence of an old girlfriend; his wife is deeply depressed by her mother's debilitating stroke; their adolescent daughter is attempting to define herself; their eight-year-old son has troubles at school. A knowing, beautifully textured portrait of birth and death, and the cycles of life in between. Written by the director.▼◗

Yogi Bear (2010) **C-80m.** ** D: Eric Brevig. Anna Faris, Tom Cavanagh, T. J. Miller, Nathan Corddry, Andrew Daly;

voices of Dan Aykroyd, Justin Timberlake. Live action/animation hybrid, based on the vintage Hanna-Barbera TV cartoon show, is formulaic family filmmaking at its worst. A greasy politician plans to sell off Jellystone Park unless Ranger Smith can prove its worth to the community. Aided by a pretty nature documentary filmmaker and two talking bears, Yogi (Aykroyd, trying to channel Daws Butler) and Boo-Boo (Timberlake doing Don Messick), they fumble their way through a variety of schemes to save the campgrounds. The CGI bruins are a grotesque hybrid of a real bear and the original cartoon characters. Younger viewers may enjoy the expected. 3-D. [PG]◗

Yojimbo (1961-Japanese) **110m.** **** D: Akira Kurosawa. Toshiro Mifune, Eijiro Tono, Seizaburo Kawazu, Isuzu Yamada, Hiroshi Tachikawa, Kyu Sazanka, Tatsuya Nakadai, Takashi Shimura. Superb tongue-in-cheek samurai picture, the plot of which resembles a Western; Mifune is perfection as samurai up for hire in town with two warring factions, both of whom he teaches a well-deserved lesson. Beautiful on all counts; the inspiration for FISTFUL OF DOLLARS and many other films. Later remade as LAST MAN STANDING. Sequel: SANJURO. Tohoscope.▼◗

Yol (1982-Turkish-Swiss) **C-111m.** *** D: Serif Goren. Tarik Akan, Serif Sezer, Halil Ergun, Meral Orhonsoy, Necmettin Cobanoglu. Incisive chronicle of the experiences of convicts who return home while on "leave" from jail. Screenplay by Yilmaz Guney, written while he was himself in prison. [PG]▼

Yolanda and the Thief (1945) **C-108m.** **½ D: Vincente Minnelli. Fred Astaire, Lucille Bremer, Frank Morgan, Leon Ames, Mildred Natwick, Mary Nash. Opulent musical fantasy about a con man (Astaire) who tries to convince rich convent-bred girl (Bremer) that he's her guardian angel. Unusual film that you'll either love or hate. Best musical number: "Coffee Time."▼●◗

Yoo-Hoo, Mrs. Goldberg (2009) **C/B&W-92m.** *** D: Aviva Kempner. Long-overdue appreciation of Gertrude Berg, pioneering, protofeminist radio and TV writer-producer-performer who created *The Goldbergs*, about a Jewish family from the Bronx, and became fixed in the public mind as its matriarch, Molly. The real-life Berg, we learn, couldn't have been more different from her alter ego, and had to fight many battles during her long career—notably against the blacklist of the 1950s. Kempner includes generous samples from the early TV series. Among the interviewees who recall the impression Molly made on them are comedy maestro Norman Lear and U.S. Supreme Court Justice Ruth Bader Ginsberg!◗

Yor, the Hunter from the Future (1983-

Italian) **C-88m.** BOMB D: Anthony M. Dawson (Antonio Margheriti). Reb Brown, Corinne Clery, John Steiner, Carole Andre, Alan Collins. Shamelessly idiotic muscleman movie with a nuclear-age twist. Humorously tacky at first, then just plain boring. [PG]▼●

You Again (2010) **C-105m.** ** D: Andy Fickman. Kristen Bell, Jamie Lee Curtis, Sigourney Weaver, Odette Yustman, Betty White, Victor Garber, Jimmy Wolk, Kristin Chenoweth, Kyle Bornheimer. Once upon a time, Bell was a high school nerd. A decade has passed, and she is none too happy to learn that her adored brother is about to wed the cheerleader who used to bully her. Barely funny, often silly comedy is formulaic to a fault. A number of familiar names and faces appear in cameos. HD Widescreen. [PG]▶

You and Me (1938) **90m.** **½ D: Fritz Lang. Sylvia Sidney, George Raft, Barton MacLane, Harry Carey, Roscoe Karns, George E. Stone, Warren Hymer, Robert Cummings. Genuinely odd but likable film about an ex-con (Raft) who falls in love with Sidney and marries her, unaware that she's a former jailbird herself. Unusual mix of gangsterism, sentiment, Damon Runyonesque comedy, and music (by Kurt Weill)—with even some rhythmic dialogue! Story by Norman Krasna, screenplay by Virginia Van Upp.▼

You Are What You Eat (1968) **C-75m.** ** D: Barry Feinstein. Tiny Tim, Peter Yarrow, Paul Butterfield, Barry McGuire, Father Malcom Boyd, The Electric Flag, Harper's Bizarre, Super Spade. Documentary of the mid-'60s does, by the mere appearance of some of the era's luminaries, carry one back; however, film is ill conceived, haphazardly put together.▼

You Belong to Me (1941) **94m.** ** D: Wesley Ruggles. Barbara Stanwyck, Henry Fonda, Edgar Buchanan, Roger Clark, Ruth Donnelly, Melville Cooper, Maude Eburne. Weak comedy of doctor Stanwyck and hubby Fonda who's wary of her male patients. Looks as though it was made in three days. Coscripted by Dalton Trumbo. Remade as EMERGENCY WEDDING.▶

You Better Watch Out (1980) **C-100m.** *** D: Lewis Jackson. Brandon Maggart, Dianne Hull, Scott McKay, Joe Jamrog, Peter Friedman, Ray Barry, Bobby Lesser, Sam Gray. Gripping, well-made little thriller about a killer disguised as Santa Claus, with Maggart excellent as the psychopathic Kris Kringle. A sleeper, with cult status possibilities. Video titles: CHRISTMAS EVIL and TERROR IN TOYLAND. [R]▼▶

You Can Count on Me (2000) **C-111m.** ***½ D: Kenneth Lonergan. Laura Linney, Mark Ruffalo, Matthew Broderick, Rory Culkin, Jon Tenney, Gaby Hoffmann, Amy Ryan. A woman raising an 8-year-old son on her own—in the house she grew up in—must simultaneously deal with a priggish new boss and the arrival of her much-loved but aimless brother who comes to stay for a while. Wonderful comedy-drama about the peccadilloes of sibling relationships, the workplace, and life in general, sparked by great performances and an unusually perceptive script. Directing debut for playwright/screenwriter Lonergan, who also appears as Linney's priest. [R]▼▶

You Can't Cheat an Honest Man (1939) **78m.** ***½ D: George Marshall. W. C. Fields, Edgar Bergen, Constance Moore, James Bush, Mary Forbes, Thurston Hall, Edward Brophy, Grady Sutton, Eddie "Rochester" Anderson. Fields (as Larson E. Whipsnade) runs circus with interference from Bergen and Charlie McCarthy in frantic comedy classic with loads of snappy one-liners and memorable ping-pong game. Most of Fields' scenes were directed by Eddie Cline.▼▶

You Can't Get Away With Murder (1939) **78m.** ** D: Lewis Seiler. Humphrey Bogart, Billy Halop, Gale Page, John Litel, Henry Travers, Harvey Stephens, Joe Sawyer, Eddie "Rochester" Anderson. Cocky punk Bogart takes angry, impressionable Halop under his wing, leading to plenty of complications. Overbaked melodramatics do this one in. Based on play *Chalked Out* by Jonathan Finn and Sing Sing warden Lewis E. Lawes.

You Can't Hurry Love (1988) **C-92m.** *½ D: Richard Martini. David Packer, Scott McGinnis, Bridget Fonda, David Leisure, Anthony Geary, Frank Bonner, Lu Leonard, Merete Van Kamp, Sally Kellerman, Charles Grodin, Kristy McNichol. Paper-thin, predictable fare about the adventures of young Packer, who's lost in the L.A. singles scene. [R]▼●▶

You Can't Steal Love SEE: **Live a Little, Steal a Lot**

You Can't Take It With You (1938) **127m.** ***½ D: Frank Capra. Jean Arthur, Lionel Barrymore, James Stewart, Edward Arnold, Mischa Auer, Ann Miller, Spring Byington, Eddie "Rochester" Anderson, Donald Meek, Halliwell Hobbes, Dub Taylor, Samuel S. Hinds, Harry Davenport, Charles Lane. George S. Kaufman– Moss Hart play about eccentric but blissfully happy household becomes prime Capracorn, not quite as compelling today as MR. DEEDS or MR. SMITH (due to Robert Riskin's extensive rewriting), but still highly entertaining. Oscar winner for Best Picture and Director. Followed a half-century later by a TV series.▼●▶

You Can't Win 'Em All (1970) **C-95m.** *½ D: Peter Collinson. Tony Curtis, Charles Bronson, Michele Mercier, Patrick Magee, Gregoire Aslan. Bronson and Curtis are friendly rivals caught in war-torn Turkey during the early 1920s. Bantering stars make the most of tired script by Leo Gordon (who also has supporting role). Filmed on location. Original title: THE DUBIOUS PATRIOTS. Video title: SOLDIERS OF FORTUNE. Panavision. [PG]▼

You Don't Mess With the Zohan (2008) C-113m. **½ D: Dennis Dugan. Adam Sandler, John Turturro, Emmanuelle Chriqui, Nick Swardson, Kevin Nealon, Lainie Kazan, Rob Schneider, Mariah Carey, Robert Smigel, Shelley Berman, Charlotte Rae, Chris Rock. Even by Sandler standards this plot defies description: super-Jew counterterrorist Zohan has a potential world of Palestinian behinds to kick, in and around home base in Israel, but what he really wants is to come to America and professionally ape the hair-care standards of Paul Mitchell (the more dated, the better). So, uh, he does. Predictably uneven and crude but ticklishly demented much of the time; above-average Sandler comedy supplies a romance (with Chriqui, as a New York–based Palestinian salon owner) and plenty of spirited cameos, including John McEnroe, who's become a Sandler regular. Unrated version runs 117m. [PG-13]▶

You Got Served (2004) C-94m. ** D: Chris Stokes. Marques Houston, Omari Grandberry, Jarell Houston, DeMario Thornton, Dreux Frederic, Jennifer Freeman, Lil' Kim, Steve Harvey, Michael "Bear" Taliferro, Meagan Good. Impressive street dancing and a likable cast can't save this predictable tale of local boys trying to make good, eventually becoming rivals. Simplistic plotting and often unintelligible street jargon make it laughable at times, although the leads (known for their work in such groups as B2K and IMX) do a decent job. Followed by two direct-to-DVD sequels. [PG-13]▼▶

You Gotta Stay Happy (1948) **100m.** **½ D: H. C. Potter. Joan Fontaine, James Stewart, Eddie Albert, Roland Young, Willard Parker, Percy Kilbride, Porter Hall. OK comedy about millionairess who runs off on wedding night to find new marriage. Could have been much better.▼▶

You Kill Me (2007) C-92m. ***½ D: John Dahl. Ben Kingsley, Téa Leoni, Luke Wilson, Philip Baker Hall, Dennis Farina, Bill Pullman, Marcus Thomas. Kingsley is superb as an alcoholic hit man who's banished by his Polish mob family in Buffalo, N.Y., and sent to San Francisco to dry out. He's set up with a job in a mortuary and in time he actually starts a new life, joins AA, and meets a smart woman who cares about him . . . but there's still some unfinished business to take care of back home. Smart, original, genuinely funny black comedy, written by Christopher Markus and Stephen McFeely. Super 35. [R]▶

You Light Up My Life (1977) C-90m. **½ D: Joseph Brooks. Didi Conn, Joe

Silver, Michael Zaslow, Stephen Nathan, Melanie Mayron. Oscar-winning title song may be best remembered thing about this film, but Conn and Silver are worth watching in loosely structured story of show-business-oriented girl trying to break loose and establish herself while putting her life in order. Produced, directed, written, and musically supervised by Brooks. [PG]▼▶

You'll Like My Mother (1972) C-92m. **½ D: Lamont Johnson. Patty Duke, Rosemary Murphy, Sian Barbara Allen, Richard Thomas, Dennis Rucker. Offbeat thriller with psychological undertones. Duke plays pregnant widow journeying to visit mother-in-law she's never met. Some good moments, but doesn't add up. [PG]▼

You'll Never Get Rich (1941) 88m. *** D: Sidney Lanfield. Fred Astaire, Rita Hayworth, John Hubbard, Robert Benchley, Osa Massen, Frieda Inescort, Guinn ("Big Boy") Williams, Cliff Nazarro. Broadway star Astaire is drafted, so producer Benchley brings the show to training camp, where Fred does his best to win over chorus girl Hayworth. Witty banter, a Cole Porter score (including "So Near and Yet So Far"), and terrific dancing by the two stars make this breezy fun.▼▶

You, Me and Dupree (2006) C-110m. **½ D: Anthony Russo, Joe Russo. Owen Wilson, Kate Hudson, Matt Dillon, Michael Douglas, Seth Rogen, Amanda Detmer, Bill Hader. Newlyweds Hudson and Dillon embark on married life with an unexpected glitch: his best friend (Wilson) is crashing on their living-room sofa. What's more, Dillon works for her father (Douglas), who enjoys throwing his weight around. Wilson elevates this fairly obvious comedy, as the character of Dupree turns out to be more human—and likable—than you might expect. Harry Dean Stanton appears unbilled. Wilson also coproduced. [PG-13]▶

You Must Be Joking! (1965-British) C-100m. *** D: Michael Winner. Michael Callan, Lionel Jeffries, Terry-Thomas, Denholm Elliott, Wilfrid Hyde-White, James Robertson Justice, Bernard Cribbins, Gabriella Licudi. Engaging poke at British army as zany psychologist (Jeffries) rounds up five weirdos to establish, via special testing, the "complete, quick thinking" exemplary British soldier.

Young Adam (2003-British-French) C-98m. ** D: David Mackenzie. Ewan McGregor, Tilda Swinton, Peter Mullan, Emily Mortimer. Murder and sex affect the dynamics on a barge where a young drifter (McGregor) has come to work for a simple man (Mullan) and his unhappy wife (Swinton). Dreary drama, set in the 1950s, benefits from McGregor's strong screen presence but sinks under its own weight. Even explicit sex scenes can't liven up this dour tale. Scripted by Mackenzie from the novel by Scottish Beat Generation writer Alexander Trocchi. Arriscope. [NC-17]▼●

Young Americans (1967) **C-104m.** ** D: Alex Grasshoff. Although this slick documentary about the "Young Americans" singing group won an Oscar (which it was forced to relinquish when it was discovered that it had played theatrically before the year of its contention), these kids sell America like those guys on TV sell machines that slice carrots 144 different ways.

Young and Innocent (1937-British) **80m.** *** D: Alfred Hitchcock. Nova Pilbeam, Derrick de Marney, Percy Marmont, Edward Rigby, Mary Clare, Basil Radford. A Hitchcock thriller with charm and humor; young girl helps runaway man accused of murder to find proof of his innocence. Pleasant echoes of THE 39 STEPS; nightclub revelation scene is especially memorable. Based on a novel by Josephine Tey.▼●

Young and the Damned, The SEE: **Los Olvidados**

Young and the Immoral, The SEE: **Sinister Urge, The**

Young at Heart (1954) **C-117m.** *** D: Gordon Douglas. Doris Day, Frank Sinatra, Gig Young, Ethel Barrymore, Dorothy Malone, Alan Hale, Jr. Musical remake of Fannie Hurst's FOUR DAUGHTERS with Sinatra romancing Day amid much tearshedding. Slickly done.▼●

Young@Heart (2008-U.S.-British) **C-110m.** *** D: Stephen Walker. Stirring documentary chronicling the musical journey of a group of senior citizens in Northampton, Massachusetts, as they prepare the latest performance of Young At Heart, a concert group originally formed in 1982 that features a revolving group of singers in their 70s, 80s and 90s performing the songs of Jimi Hendrix, The Clash, Sonic Youth, and James Brown, among others. Proving that age is all about attitude and a desire for "Stayin' Alive" (one of the highlighted tunes), this moving film captures moments of glory and sorrow as these lively subjects rehearse their remarkable show. [PG]●

Young Bess (1953) **C-112m.** *** D: George Sidney. Jean Simmons, Stewart Granger, Charles Laughton, Deborah Kerr, Cecil Kellaway, Leo G. Carroll, Kay Walsh. Splashy costumer with Simmons as Elizabeth I, Laughton repeating role of Henry VIII. Fine cast does quite well in historical setting. Simmons and Granger were then married in real life. ▼●

Young Billy Young (1969) **C-89m.** **½ D: Burt Kennedy. Robert Mitchum, Angie Dickinson, David Carradine, Robert Walker, Jack Kelly, John Anderson, Paul Fix. Sheriff Mitchum, seeking the killer of his son, takes young Walker under his wing as a surrogate. Peculiar Western, adapted by Kennedy from Will Henry's *Who Rides With*

Wyatt, is based on the alleged friendship between Wyatt Earp and Billy Clanton; interesting, but nothing special. [G]▼

Youngblood (1986) **C-109m.** *½ D: Peter Markle. Rob Lowe, Cynthia Gibb, Patrick Swayze, Ed Lauter, Eric Nesterenko, George Finn, Fionnula Flanagan. Boring, utterly predictable story of Lowe joining small-time Canadian hockey team, falling in love with the daughter of his no-nonsense coach. This movie has no energy, on the ice or off! Keanu Reeves' screen debut; that's him behind the mask, as the team's goalie. [R]▼●

Youngblood Hawke (1964) **137m.** **½ D: Delmer Daves. James Franciscus, Genevieve Page, Suzanne Pleshette, Eva Gabor, Mary Astor, Lee Bowman, Edward Andrews, Don Porter. Clichéd but somehow compelling trash from Herman Wouk's novel about a naive Southerner who writes a novel and becomes the toast of N.Y.C. literary society—with several women vying for his attention.

Young Cassidy (1965-British) **C-110m.** *** D: Jack Cardiff, John Ford. Rod Taylor, Julie Christie, Maggie Smith, Flora Robson, Michael Redgrave, Edith Evans, Jack MacGowran. Taylor's best role ever as the earthy intellectual Sean O'Casey, set in 1910 Dublin; filled with rich atmosphere and fine supporting players.

Young Doctors, The (1961) **100m.** *** D: Phil Karlson. Fredric March, Ben Gazzara, Dick Clark, Albert, Ina Balin, Aline MacMahon, Edward Andrews, Arthur Hill, George Segal, Rosemary Murphy, Barnard Hughes, Dick Button, Dolph Sweet; narrated by Ronald Reagan. Sturdy cast uplifts soaper set in large city hospital. Based on an Arthur Hailey novel. Segal's first film.

Young Doctors in Love (1982) **C-95m.** ** D: Garry Marshall. Michael McKean, Sean Young, Harry Dean Stanton, Patrick Macnee, Hector Elizondo, Dabney Coleman, Pamela Reed, Michael Richards, Taylor Negron, Saul Rubinek, Titos Vandis, Ted McGinley, Crystal Bernard. Hospital comedy has plenty of scattershot gags, but not enough laughs—and certainly not enough substance—to maintain a feature film. Many daytime soap opera stars appear in cameos (including Demi Moore and Janine Turner, both then on *General Hospital*). Feature directing debut of TV comedy writer-producer Marshall. [R]▼●

Young Dracula (1974-Italian-French) SEE: **Andy Warhol's Dracula**

Young Dracula (1974-British) SEE: **Son of Dracula**

Young Einstein (1988-Australian) **C-90m.** **½ D: Yahoo Serious. Yahoo Serious, Odile Le Clezio, John Howard, Pee Wee Wilson, Su Cruickshank. Nutty comedy from Down Under based on the premise that Albert Einstein not only developed the theory of relativity, but also invented rock 'n' roll! The silliness continues from there . . . though any movie with "cat pies" can't be all bad. Aptly named Yahoo (born Greg Pead) wrote, produced, directed, and stars in this slapstick epic. [PG]▼●◖

Younger & Younger (1993-German-French-Canadian) C-99m. **½ D: Percy Adlon. Donald Sutherland, Lolita Davidovich, Brendan Fraser, Sally Kellerman, Julie Delpy, Linda Hunt, Nicholas Gunn, Matt Damon. Likably offbeat modern-day fantasy about a self-styled gay blade and bon vivant who owns a self-storage facility in Glendale, California, and lives in a rarefied world of his own, until reality comes crashing down. This may be your only chance to hear Sutherland sing! Never released theatrically in the U.S. [R]▼

Younger Generation, The (1929) 88m. **½ D: Frank Capra. Jean Hersholt, Lina Basquette, Ricardo Cortez, Rosa Rosanova, Rex Lease. Ethnic heart-tugger by Fannie Hurst about a Jewish family that suffers because of one son's determination to abandon his roots and break into N.Y.C. society. (Cortez played a similar role in SYMPHONY OF SIX MILLION.) Director Capra pulls out all the stops in this silent film with talkie sequences.

Youngest Spy SEE: **Ivan's Childhood**

Young Frankenstein (1974) 105m. ***½ D: Mel Brooks. Gene Wilder, Peter Boyle, Marty Feldman, Teri Garr, Madeline Kahn, Cloris Leachman, Kenneth Mars, Richard Haydn. One of the funniest (and most quotable) movies of all time, a finely tuned parody of old FRANKENSTEIN pictures, scripted by Wilder and Brooks, with appropriate music (by John Morris), sets, laboratory equipment (some of it from the 1930s), and b&w camerawork by Gerald Hirschfeld). Plus vivid characterizations by mad doctor Wilder, monster Boyle, hunchback assistant Feldman, et al. Spoof of blind-man sequence from BRIDE OF FRANKENSTEIN with Gene Hackman is uproarious. Later a Broadway musical. [PG]▼●◖

Young Girls of Rochefort, The (1967-French) C-124m. ** D: Jacques Demy. Catherine Deneuve, Françoise Dorléac, Gene Kelly, George Chakiris, Danielle Darrieux, Grover Dale, Michel Piccoli. Director Demy's follow-up to THE UMBRELLAS OF CHERBOURG is a homage to the Hollywood musical, but what it has in style it lacks in substance; contrived story and repetitive Michel Legrand music score surely wear thin, and even Gene Kelly can't save it. Franscope. [G]▼◗

Young Guns (1988) C-107m. **½ D: Christopher Cain. Emilio Estevez, Kiefer Sutherland, Lou Diamond Phillips, Charlie Sheen, Dermot Mulroney, Casey Siemaszko, Terence Stamp, Jack Palance, Terry O'Quinn, Sharon Thomas, Brian Keith, Patrick Wayne. Six young punks, taken under the wing of a civilized British gentleman (Stamp), find it hard to retain their equilibrium when they're left on their own, and whipped into a frenzy of violence by their newest recruit—William Bonney, soon to be known as Billy the Kid (Estevez). Contemporary-minded Western adopts 1980s-style language and sensibilities, and has a plot with as many holes as some of Billy's victims. Still watchable, with several strong performances. Try to spot Tom Cruise, in disguise as a bad guy who gets shot. Followed by a sequel. [R]▼●◖

Young Guns II (1990) C-103m. **½ D: Geoff Murphy. Emilio Estevez, Kiefer Sutherland, Lou Diamond Phillips, Christian Slater, William Petersen, Alan Ruck, R.D. Call, James Coburn, Balthazar Getty, Jack Kehoe, Viggo Mortensen. Not-bad sequel finds Billy Bonney and his gang heading toward the safety of Old Mexico with a band of government men in hot pursuit. Slater is a standout on the trail. Great photography and a sweeping Alan Silvestri score almost make you forget the script ain't so hot. Panavision. [PG-13]▼●◖

Young Hearts SEE: **Promised Land**

Young Hellions SEE: **High School Confidential!**

Young in Heart, The (1938) 90m. ***½ D: Richard Wallace. Janet Gaynor, Douglas Fairbanks, Jr., Paulette Goddard, Roland Young, Billie Burke, Minnie Dupree, Richard Carlson. Refreshing comedy about wacky family of con artists going straight under influence of unsuspecting Dupree. Written by Paul Osborn and Charles Bennett from an I.A.R. Wylie novel. Also shown in computer-colored version.▼◗

Young Lions, The (1958) 167m. ***½ D: Edward Dmytryk. Marlon Brando, Montgomery Clift, Dean Martin, Hope Lange, Barbara Rush, Maximilian Schell, May Britt, Lee Van Cleef. One of the all-time best WW2 studies, adapted by Edward Anhalt from the Irwin Shaw novel. Martin and Clift play U.S. soldiers, Brando a confused Nazi officer; effectively photographed by Joe MacDonald, with Hugo Friedhofer's fine score. CinemaScope. ▼◗

Young Lovers, The (1950) SEE: **Never Fear**

Young Man With a Horn (1950) 112m. *** D: Michael Curtiz. Kirk Douglas, Lauren Bacall, Doris Day, Juano Hernandez, Hoagy Carmichael, Mary Beth Hughes. Effective drama of trumpet-player Douglas compulsively drawn to music, with Bacall the bad girl, Day the wholesome one. Carl Foreman–Edmund H. North script adapted from Dorothy Baker's book, and inspired by Bix Beiderbecke's life; Harry James dubbed Douglas' licks. ▼●◗

Young Mr. Lincoln (1939) 100m. ***½ D: John Ford. Henry Fonda, Alice Brady, Marjorie Weaver, Donald Meek, Richard Cromwell, Eddie Quillan, Milburn Stone, Ward Bond, Francis Ford. Series of vignettes present a portrait of Abraham Lincoln before he even thought of running for president, from his first courtship to an important courtroom showdown. Not so much a historical document as a slice of Americana, filtered through the sensibilities of director Ford and screenwriter Lamar Trotti. The early, episodic portion of the film, covering Abe Lincoln's formative years, includes some of Ford's most lyrical moments, luminously photographed by Bert Glennon. ▼●◗

Young Nurses, The (1973) C-77m. ** D: Clinton Kimbrough. Jean Manson, Ashley Porter, Angela Gibbs, Zack Taylor, Jack LaRue, Jr., Dick Miller, Sally Kirkland, Allan Arbus. Fourth of Roger Corman's "nurse" movies is OK, focusing on drug ring working out of the hospital. Neat appearance by director Samuel Fuller as a villain, and a rather sad one by aged Mantan Moreland (in his final film). Followed by CANDY STRIPE NURSES. [R] ▼◗

Young One, The (1961-Mexican) 96m. *½ D: Luis Buñuel. Zachary Scott, Bernie Hamilton, Key Meersman, Graham Denton, Claudio Brook. Racist Scott, who has violated Lolita-like Meersman on an isolated island, must contend with the presence of on-the-run black jazz musician Hamilton. Turgid, much-too-obvious melodrama is a disappointment from Buñuel. ▼◗

Young People (1940) 78m. ** D: Allan Dwan. Shirley Temple, Jack Oakie, Charlotte Greenwood, Arleen Whelan, George Montgomery, Kathleen Howard. Show-biz team Oakie and Greenwood raise orphaned Shirley and try to settle down in this weak musical, a later and lesser Temple vehicle. Good dance routine at the finish. Also shown in computer-colored version. ▼◗

Young Philadelphians, The (1959) 136m. *** D: Vincent Sherman. Paul Newman, Barbara Rush, Alexis Smith, Brian Keith, Diane Brewster, Billie Burke, John Williams, Robert Vaughn, Otto Kruger, Adam West. Newman and Rush have memorable roles as poor lawyer who schemes to the top and society girl he hopes to win; Vaughn is hard-drinking buddy Newman defends on murder charge, Smith quite good as frustrated wife of attorney Kruger. ▼◗

Young Poisoner's Handbook, The (1995-British-French-German) C-99m. *** D: Ben Ross. Hugh O'Conor, Antony Sher, Ruth Sheen, Roger Lloyd Pack, Charlotte Coleman. Gleefully gruesome British black comedy about a psychopathic teen

(O'Conor) who decides to become "the greatest poisoner the world has ever seen," using his clueless family as guinea pigs. Deliciously mean-spirited film (based on a true story!) is not for the squeamish. Flavored by a soundtrack of '60s pop oddities. ▼◗

Young Rebel (1967-French-Italian-Spanish) C-111m. ** D: Vincent Sherman. Horst Buchholz, Gina Lollobrigida, Jose Ferrer, Louis Jourdan, Francisco Rabal. Despite cast, historical claptrap about Buchholz being sent to Spain by Pope Pius V to obtain help in fighting the Moors. Also known as CERVANTES. Totalscope. [M/PG]

Young Runaways, The (1968) C-91m. ** D: Arthur Dreifuss. Brooke Bundy, Kevin Coughlin, Lloyd Bochner, Patty McCormack, Lynn Bari, Norman Fell. Silly B-picture about restless teenagers and how they are swept up into sordid lifestyles. Interesting mainly for early look at Richard Dreyfuss as cocky car thief. Panavision. [R]

Young Savages, The (1961) 103m. *** D: John Frankenheimer. Burt Lancaster, Dina Merrill, John Davis Chandler, Shelley Winters, Telly Savalas, Edward Andrews, Chris Robinson, Pilar Seurat, Milton Selzer. Lancaster is idealistic D.A. battling all odds to see justice done in street-gang slaying; at times brutal, too often pat. Adapted by Edward Anhalt and JP Miller from Evan Hunter's novel *A Matter of Conviction.* Savalas' film debut. ▼●◗

Young Sherlock Holmes (1985) C-109m. ** D: Barry Levinson. Nicholas Rowe, Alan Cox, Sophie Ward, Anthony Higgins, Susan Fleetwood, Freddie Jones, Nigel Stock, Michael Hordern. Promising film speculates about Conan Doyle's detective when he was a boy, introduces him to Watson, and involves him in his first great case. Knowing references to Holmes's later life, perfect Victorian atmosphere all give way to jarring 1980s special effects, inappropriate INDIANA JONES–type subplot, and action climax that doesn't make much sense. If you *do* watch it through, be sure to stay through the *very* end. Written by Chris Columbus. [PG-13] ▼●◗

Young Stranger, The (1957) 84m. *** D: John Frankenheimer. James MacArthur, James Daly, Kim Hunter, James Gregory, Marian Seldes, Whit Bissell. Excellent drama about a teenage boy's brush with delinquency and strained relationship with his wealthy, neglectful father. Surprisingly undated, sincere little film; MacArthur's impressive screen debut (and director Frankenheimer's, too). Frankenheimer also directed the TV play *Deal a Blow*, on which this was based. ●

Young Tom Edison (1940) 82m. *** D: Norman Taurog. Mickey Rooney, Fay Bainter, George Bancroft, Virginia Weidler, Eugene Pallette, Victor Kilian. Inventor's early life depicted with flair by effective

Rooney, who could tone down when he had to; followed by Spencer Tracy's EDISON, THE MAN.▼●▮

Young Victoria, The (2009) **C-104m.** ✱✱✱ D: Jean-Marc Vallée. Emily Blunt, Rupert Friend, Paul Bettany, Miranda Richardson, Jim Broadbent, Thomas Kretschmann, Mark Strong, Jesper Christensen, Harriet Walter, Julian Glover. Absorbing look at the intrigues surrounding the ascension of a teenaged Queen Victoria to the throne of England, and the complexities and strategies involved in her wooing by the future Prince Albert of Belgium. A rare costume picture in which the personalities and story twists aren't dwarfed by period detail—even though the film is impeccably handsome (Sandy Powell's costumes won an Academy Award). Intelligent, witty screenplay by Julian Fellowes. Super 35. [PG]▮

Young Warriors, The (1967) **C-93m.** ✱✱ D: John Peyser. James Drury, Steve Carlson, Jonathan Daly, Robert Pine, Michael Stanwood. Clichéd WW2 yarn loosely derived from Richard Matheson novel. Panavision.

Young Warriors (1983) **C-103m.** ✱½ D: Lawrence D. Foldes. Ernest Borgnine, Richard Roundtree, Lynda Day George, James Van Patten, Anne Lockhart, Mike Norris, Dick Shawn, Linnea Quigley. Self-righteous, violent exploitation film has students turning vigilantes to put local criminals out of business. Features several second-generation actors (Van Patten, Lockhart, Norris). Semi-sequel to MALIBU HIGH. [R]▼

Young Winston (1972-British) **C-145m.** ✱✱✱ D: Richard Attenborough. Simon Ward, Anne Bancroft, Robert Shaw, John Mills, Jack Hawkins, Patrick Magee, Ian Holm, Robert Flemyng, Jane Seymour, Edward Woodward, Anthony Hopkins, Laurence Naismith. Entertaining account of Churchill's early life, from school days, through journalistic experience in Africa, up to first election to Parliament. Handsome production, good performances, and rousing battle scenes. Scripted and produced by Carl Foreman. Panavision. [PG]▼

You Only Live Once (1937) **86m.** ✱✱✱ D: Fritz Lang. Sylvia Sidney, Henry Fonda, William Gargan, Barton MacLane, Jean Dixon, Jerome Cowan, Margaret Hamilton, Ward Bond, Guinn ("Big Boy") Williams. Beautifully crafted drama about ex-convict Fonda trying to go straight, finding that fate is against him. Loosely based on the Bonnie and Clyde legend, but impressive on its own.▼▮

You Only Live Twice (1967-British) **C-116m.** ✱✱½ D: Lewis Gilbert. Sean Connery, Akiko Wakabayashi, Tetsuro Tamba, Mie Hama, Karin Dor, Bernard Lee, Lois Maxwell, Desmond Llewelyn, Donald Pleasence. Big James Bond production with first look at arch-nemesis Blofeld (Pleasence), Japanese locales, but plot (SPECTRE out to cause major powers to declare war on each other) and lack of convincing, clever crisis situations are liabilities film can't shake off. Script by Roald Dahl (!), spectacular sets by Ken Adam. Panavision. [PG]▼●▮

Your Cheatin' Heart (1964) **99m.** ✱✱✱ D: Gene Nelson. George Hamilton, Susan Oliver, Red Buttons, Arthur O'Connell, Rex Ingram. One of Hamilton's best roles, as legendary country-western singer Hank Williams, who couldn't cope with fame on the ole opry circuit; songs dubbed by Hank Williams, Jr. Oliver most effective as Hank's wife. Also shown in computer-colored version. Panavision.▮

You're a Big Boy Now (1966) **C-96m.** ✱✱✱½ D: Francis Ford Coppola. Peter Kastner, Elizabeth Hartman, Geraldine Page, Julie Harris, Rip Torn, Michael Dunn, Tony Bill, Karen Black. Beguiling, wayout film of young man with overprotective parents learning about life from callous young actress Hartman. Will not appeal to everyone, but acting is marvelous, with Dolph Sweet hilarious as tough cop. Location filming in N.Y.C. adds to film, too. Written by Coppola, from the David Benedictus novel. Title song by The Lovin' Spoonful.▼●▮

You're in the Navy Now (1951) **93m.** ✱✱ D: Henry Hathaway. Gary Cooper, Jane Greer, Millard Mitchell, Eddie Albert, John McIntire, Ray Collins, Harry Von Zell, Jack Webb, Richard Erdman, Harvey Lembeck, Lee Marvin, Charles Buchinski (Bronson), Ed Begley, Jack Warden. Flat naval comedy, set during WW2, with Cooper commanding an unlikely crew on a ship outfitted with an experimental steam engine. Film debuts of Marvin and Bronson. Originally screened with the title U.S.S. TEAKETTLE.▮

You're Never Too Young (1955) **C-102m.** ✱✱✱ D: Norman Taurog. Dean Martin, Jerry Lewis, Diana Lynn, Raymond Burr, Nina Foch, Veda Ann Borg. Fast, funny remake of THE MAJOR AND THE MINOR (which also featured Lynn) with Jerry disguised as 12-year-old at a girls' school, involved in jewel robbery. Script by Sidney Sheldon. VistaVision.▮

You're Telling Me! (1934) **67m.** ✱✱✱½ D: Erle C. Kenton. W. C. Fields, Joan Marsh, Larry "Buster" Crabbe, Louise Carter, Kathleen Howard, Adrienne Ames. Hilarious remake of Fields' silent film SO'S YOUR OLD MAN, with thin storyline (about a friendly foreign princess giving lowly, browbeaten Fields respectability in his home town) a perfect excuse for some of his funniest routines—including classic golf game.▼▮

Your Friends & Neighbors (1998) **C-99m.** ✱✱ D: Neil LaBute. Amy Brenneman,

Jason Patric, Ben Stiller, Aaron Eckhart, Catherine Keener, Nastassja Kinski. Another somewhat smug "let's rip the lid off the hypocrisy of society" tract from writer-director LaBute about two socially and sexually dysfunctional couples and their friends. Some pungent, provocative dialogue, but as in LaBute's IN THE COMPANY OF MEN, it's not clear what the point of it all is. Patric (who also produced) has an especially potent role as a self-styled stud. Super 35. [R]▼◑

Your Highness (2011) **C-102m.** BOMB D: David Gordon Green. Danny McBride, James Franco, Natalie Portman, Zooey Deschanel, Justin Theroux, Toby Jones, Damian Lewis, Rasmus Hardiker, Charles Dance. Goofball prince whose older brother (Franco) will someday inherit the throne is goaded into making his first noble quest, to save Franco's virginal fiancée (Deschanel) from the clutches of an evil wizard (Theroux). Would-be parody of knightly adventure yarns is woefully unfunny from the get-go, resorting to puerile potty-mouth utterances and penis jokes. Franco and Portman play it straight (and give it their best shot) while McBride fumbles the "funny" role, which he cowrote. Ten times worse than you could possibly imagine. Unrated DVD version runs 106m. Panavision. [R]▶

Your Past Is Showing (1957-British) **92m.** *** D: Mario Zampi. Terry-Thomas, Peter Sellers, Peggy Mount, Shirley Eaton, Dennis Price, Georgina Cookson, Joan Sims, Miles Malleson. Scandal-sheet publisher Price is literally blackmailing celebrities to death by threatening to expose their past and present indiscretions. Several eventually band together and plot to rid themselves of their problem. Sellers (cast as a television star) is a special treat in this amusing satire. Original British title: THE NAKED TRUTH.▼▶

Yours, Mine and Ours (1968) **C-111m.** *** D: Melville Shavelson. Lucille Ball, Henry Fonda, Van Johnson, Tom Bosley, Tim Matheson. For once, a wholesome "family" picture with some intelligent scripting. Based on real situation of widowed mother of eight marrying widower with ten more children. Lucy's drunk scene is a delight in warm, well-made comedy. Among Fonda's brood: Suzanne Cupito (who grew up to be Morgan Brittany) and a very young Tracy Nelson. Remade in 2005. ▼◑

Yours, Mine & Ours (2005) **C-88m.** *½ D: Raja Gosnell. Dennis Quaid, Rene Russo, Rip Torn, Linda Hunt, Jerry O'Connell, David Koechner, Katija Pevec, Danielle Panabaker, Sean Faris. Bland, charmless update of the 1968 family comedy with Quaid and Russo replacing Henry Fonda and Lucille Ball. Here, a widowed, by-the-book Coast Guard admiral with eight offspring weds his old high school flame, a widowed, free-

spirited handbag designer with ten kids. Heavy on slapstick and short on originality. Super 35. [PG]▼▶

Your Three Minutes Are Up (1973) **C-92m.** ***½ D: Douglas N. Schwartz. Beau Bridges, Ron Leibman, Janet Margolin, Kathleen Freeman, David Ketchum, Stu Nisbet. Overlooked comedy with serious undertones vividly captures two American lifestyles in story of ultra-straight Bridges hanging out with swinging buddy Leibman, who's out to beat the system. Unpretentious film says more about our society than many more "important" movies; solid performances. Written by James Dixon. [R]

Your Ticket Is No Longer Valid (1979-Canadian) **C-91m.** BOMB D: George Kaczender. Richard Harris, George Peppard, Jeanne Moreau, Jennifer Dale, Alexandra Stewart, Winston Rekert. Trashy adaptation of a Romain Gary novel is an embarrassment for its cast: Harris is struggling to raise cash for his failed, inherited family business while suffering from impotency and recurring fantasies of a gypsy stud making love to his girlfriend Dale; Peppard is a foulmouthed banker who is also impotent; and Moreau is a Parisian madam who procures the gypsy boy for Harris' and Dale's eventual amusement. Lurid junk.▼

You So Crazy (1994) **C-85m.** *½ D: Thomas Schlamme. Martin Lawrence. Embarrassingly crude performance film full of off-color jokes, minus any of the wit or observational insights that made the Richard Pryor films classics of the standup genre. Hard to recall another instance in which a performer labored and sweated so hard for such a minimal payoff. [NC-17]▼◑

Youth in Revolt (2010) **C-90m.** **½ D: Miguel Arteta. Michael Cera, Portia Doubleday, Ari Graynor, Jean Smart, Steve Buscemi, Zach Galifianakis, Ray Liotta, Justin Long, Rooney Mara, Mary Kay Place, M. Emmet Walsh, Fred Willard, Christa B. Allen. Precocious, iconoclastic teenager Nick Twisp (Cera) despairs that he may never meet a girl; then he encounters Sheeni Saunders (Doubleday), who's smart and pretty, and likes him, too. He is hopelessly smitten but there are stumbling blocks in their path, which he determines to remove. Likable coming-of-age comedy/social satire is a perfect fit for Cera, but seems awfully lightweight given its source material, a well-regarded trilogy of books by C. D. Payne. [R]◑

Youth Without Youth (2007-U.S.-German-Italian-French-Romanian) **C-124m.** ** D: Francis Ford Coppola. Tim Roth, Alexandra Maria Lara, Bruno Ganz, André Hennicke, Marcel Iures, Adrian Pintea. A disastrous event thrusts a mild, elderly professor back into youth on a search for the mysteries of life, love, and aging. Self-described venture into experimental filmmaking finds Coppola adapting Romanian philosopher Mircea Eliade's novella set in the days preceding WW2. Talky, didactic script never lets the audience in emotionally; all that's left is a human puzzle few will want to bother solving. Matt Damon, unbilled, appears briefly. HD Widescreen. [R]🄳

You've Got Mail (1998) **C-119m.** ******* D: Nora Ephron. Tom Hanks, Meg Ryan, Parker Posey, Greg Kinnear, Jean Stapleton, Steve Zahn, Dave Chappelle, Dabney Coleman, John Randolph. Long but entertaining remake of THE SHOP AROUND THE CORNER, with Ryan as the proud proprietor of a neighborhood bookshop, Hanks as the head of a superstore chain poised to put her out of business. They should be mortal enemies, but they're already e-mail pen pals, without knowing each other's identity. Pleasant enough fluff with two irresistible stars. The use of old songs (which worked so well in Ephron's SLEEPLESS IN SEATTLE) is overbearing and unnecessary here. Jane Adams appears unbilled. [PG-13]▼●🄳

You've Got to Walk It Like You Talk It or You'll Lose That Beat (1971) **C-85m.** ****½** D: Peter Locke. Zalman King, Richard Pryor, Robert Downey, Sr., Liz Torres, Roz Kelly, Allen Garfield. Uneven, often crude satire focusing on the sorry escapades of a young loser, a product of the '60s. Filmed in 1968.

You Were Never Lovelier (1942) **97m.** *****½** D: William A. Seiter. Fred Astaire, Rita Hayworth, Adolphe Menjou, Leslie Brooks, Adele Mara, Xavier Cugat, Gus Schilling. Astaire pursuing Hayworth via matchmaking father Menjou becomes lilting musical with such lovely Jerome Kern–Johnny Mercer songs as title tune, "Dearly Beloved," "I'm Old-Fashioned." ▼●🄳

You Will Meet a Tall Dark Stranger (2010-U.S.-Spanish) **C-98m.** ******* D: Woody Allen. Naomi Watts, Josh Brolin, Anthony Hopkins, Antonio Banderas, Freida Pinto, Neil Jackson, Anna Friel, Ewen Bremner, Lucy Punch, Gemma Jones, Pauline Collins, Celia Imrie, Jim Piddock, Roger Ashton-Griffiths, Fenella Woolgar, Christian McKay, Alex MacQueen; narrated by Zak Orth. Abandoned by her husband after forty years, a flighty London woman (Jones) consults a medium (Collins) in whom she places great trust. Her daughter (Watts), who works for a high-end art dealer, and son-in-law (Brolin), a novelist whose career has stalled, put no stock in what she's doing, nor does her husband (Hopkins), but they each wander up blind alleys seeking happiness and satisfaction—which proves to be elusive. Allen's ironic fable may not add up to much but offers its stellar actors juicy roles and great scenes to play; if you're a Woodyphile that should be enough. [R]🄳

Y Tu Mamá También (2001-Mexican) **C-**105m. ******* D: Alfonso Cuarón. Maribel Verdú, Diego Luna, Gael García Bernal, Diana Bracho, Emilio Echevarria, Ana López Mercado, María Aura. Two oversexed Mexican teenage boys go on a joyride with an older woman—who is married to one of their cousins—and get a lot more than they bargained for. A road movie with a difference, alternately raucous and melancholy, with subtle (and not-so-subtle) ruminations on desire, fate, and politics, sexual and otherwise. ▼🄳

Yum-Yum Girls, The (1976) **C-93m.** ****** D: Barry Rosen. Judy Landers, Tanya Roberts, Michelle Dawn, Carey Poe, Stan Bernstein. Entertainingly trashy film, made before Landers' and Roberts' TV success, about young girls coming to N.Y.C. to become fashion models. OK cook's tour of the business, marred by unfunny script. [R]▼●

Z (1969-French) **C-127m.** ******* D: Costa-Gavras. Yves Montand, Irene Papas, Jean-Louis Trintignant, Charles Denner, Georges Geret, Jacques Perrin, Francois Perier, Marcel Bozzufi. Oscar winner for Best Foreign Film and Editing, based on true-life incident, concerns political assassination of Montand and chilling aftermath. Talky film praised more for its topicality than cinematics is nonetheless gripping; good acting. [M/PG]▼●🄳

Zabriskie Point (1970) **C-112m.** ****½** D: Michelangelo Antonioni. Mark Frechette, Daria Halprin, Rod Taylor, Paul Fix, Harrison Ford. Rambling study by a foreigner of the aggressive, materialistic, unflinching American lifestyle. Worth watching but difficult to stay with, though there's a real eye-opening finale. Sam Shepard was one of the scriptwriters. Panavision. [R] ▼●🄳

Zachariah (1971) **C-93m.** ****½** D: George Englund. John Rubinstein, Pat Quinn, Don Johnson, Country Joe and The Fish, Elvin Jones, New York Rock Ensemble, The James Gang, Dick Van Patten. Audacious rock Western with elements of a morality play and moments of sharp satire; coscripted by members of Firesign Theater. Certainly offbeat, but how much you like it is strictly personal taste. [PG]▼🄳

Zack and Miri Make a Porno (2008) **C-101m.** ******* D: Kevin Smith. Seth Rogen, Elizabeth Banks, Craig Robinson, Traci Lords, Katie Morgan, Ricky Mabe, Jeff Anderson, Jason Mewes, Brandon Routh, Tom Savini, Justin Long. Rogen and Banks, platonic pals and roommates, can't pay the rent so they decide to make a quick buck by shooting, marketing (and appearing in) a porn film. Despite its premise and the expected raunchiness, this is a sweet-natured and lightly likable farce. But isn't Smith getting a wee bit old for this sort of juvenilia? [R]🄳

Zandalee (1991) **C-100m.** *½ D: Sam Pillsbury. Nicolas Cage, Judge Reinhold, Erika Anderson, Joe Pantoliano, Viveca Lindfors, Aaron Neville, Ian Abercrombie, Marisa Tomei, Zach Galligan. In steamy New Orleans, thrill-seeking Zandalee (Anderson) falls for her now-staid husband's free-spirited friend; their affair leads to tragedy. Routine plot (with liberal doses of sex) gets sillier as it goes along; hampered, too, by unappealing characters. Released direct to video. [R]▼●]

Zandy's Bride (1974) **C-116m.** *½ D: Jan Troell. Gene Hackman, Liv Ullmann, Eileen Heckart, Harry Dean Stanton, Susan Tyrrell, Sam Bottoms, Joe Santos. Two frequently wasted stars in tepid romance of a mail-order bride and her pioneer husband; no one needs *these* scenes from a marriage. Aka FOR BETTER, FOR WORSE. Panavision. [PG]▼

Zapped! (1982) **C-96m.** *½ D: Robert J. Rosenthal. Scott Baio, Willie Aames, Felice Schachter, Heather Thomas, Robert Mandan, Greg Bradford, Scatman Crothers, Sue Ane Langdon. Attractive cast is wasted in this stupid spoof of CARRIE, in which Baio acquires telekinetic powers . . . which he's most anxious to use in undressing Thomas (or rather, her stand-in). Followed by a sequel. ▼●]

Zardoz (1974-British) **C-105m.** **½ D: John Boorman. Sean Connery, Charlotte Rampling, Sara Kestelman, Sally Anne Newton, John Alderton, Niall Buggy. Weird sci-fi entry, set in 2293, about technology góne wild in society run by group of eternally young intellectuals. Visually striking cult film will probably leave most viewers dissatisfied. Panavision. [R]▼●]

Zathura: A Space Adventure (2005) **C-101m.** *** D: Jon Favreau. Jonah Bobo, Josh Hutcherson, Dax Shepard, Kristen Stewart, Tim Robbins; voice of Frank Oz. Imaginative adaptation of Chris Van Allsburg's book (a cousin to JUMANJI) about two sparring brothers who, by playing a vintage mechanical board game, are magically transported into outer space, where every move on the game board brings new, often frightening, results. Smart, funny family film with a particularly believable relationship between the two brothers, and some cool special effects. Great opening title sequence by Kyle Cooper sets the tone for the film. [PG]▼]

Zatôichi, the Blind Swordsman (2003-Japanese) **C-116m.** *** D: Takeshi Kitano. Beat Takeshi (Takeshi Kitano), Tadanobu Asano, Michiyo Ogusu, Guadalcanal Taka, Daigoro Tachibana, Yuko Daike. Nineteenth-century blind nomad known as a gambler and masseur is also a lightning-fast master swordsman who stumbles into a town run by gangs and a powerful samurai. When he meets two geishas who are out to avenge their parents' murder, the fireworks begin. Based on the incredibly popular Japanese film series (and later TV program), which started in 1962 and ended in 1989 with the passing of its star, Shintaro Katsu. Actor-director Kitano ably fills his legendary shoes in this lively, nonstop martial arts fest. Great action set pieces make this a lot of fun. Aka THE BLIND SWORDSMAN: ZATÔICHI. [R] ▶

Zazie dans le Metro (1960-French) **C-88m.** **½ D: Louis Malle. Catherine Demongeot, Philippe Noiret, Vittorio Caprioli, Hubert Deschamps, Carla Marlier. Superficial comedy, coscripted by Malle, about a bright but impish 12-year-old (Demongeot), who visits her female-impersonator uncle (Noiret) in Paris, and is intent on riding in the city's subway.▼▶]

Zebra Force (1977) **C-100m.** ** D: Joe Tornatore. Mike Lane, Richard X. Slattery, Rockne Tarkington, Glenn Wilder, Anthony Caruso. A band of Vietnam vets uses military tactics against the Mob to fatten their own pockets and "rid society of scum." Straightforward low-budgeter suffers from Grade Z performances. Todd-AO 35. [PG] ▼▶

Zebrahead (1992) **C-100m.** *** D: Anthony Drazan. Michael Rapaport, DeShonn Castle, N'Bushe Wright, Ron Johnson, Ray Sharkey, Paul Butler, Candy Ann Brown, Helen Shaver, Luke Reilly, Martin Priest. Refreshing, straightforward drama about a white teen (Rapaport) who attends an integrated Detroit high school. His best friend (Castle) is black, and problems arise when he becomes romantically involved with his pal's cousin (Wright). Benefits from realistic dialogue, and a candid take on the characters' lives and feelings. Drazan also scripted; Oliver Stone was one of the executive producers. [R]▼●▲

Zed & Two Noughts, A (1985-British-Dutch) **C-115m.** *** D: Peter Greenaway. Andrea Ferreol, Brian Deacon, Eric Deacon, Frances Barber, Joss Ackland. Extremely provocative examination of birth, life, and death, focusing on Ferreol, who has lost a leg in a car crash, and two zoologist brothers (the Deacons) whose wives have been killed in the same accident and who become obsessed with decay. Difficult to watch but well worthwhile for those willing to be challenged. Not so much a film as a visual essay, exquisitely directed and photographed (by Sacha Vierny).▼▶

Želary (2003-Czech-Slovakian-Austrian) **C-148m.** *** D: Ondřej Trojan. Aňa Geislerová, György Cserhalmi, Ivan Trojan, Jan Hrušínský, Miroslav Donutil, Jaroslav Dušek, Iva Bittová, Jaroslava Adamová, Jan Tríska. A young Prague medical student, on the lam from the Gestapo during WW2, hides out in a provincial village and reluctantly agrees to marry her protector, a kindly older man. As they spend time together, much is revealed about the nature of good and evil. Has its slow spots but becomes more engrossing as their relationship deepens; at its best when contrasting the idyllic rural beauty against the constant threat of violence. [R] ▶

Zelig (1983) **C/B&W-79m.** *** D: Woody Allen. Woody Allen, Mia Farrow, Garrett Brown, Stephanie Farrow, Will Holt, Sol Lomita, Mary Louise Wilson, Michael Jeter. Pseudo-documentary using remarkable re-creations of old newsreels and recordings, about a chameleonlike man named Leonard Zelig (Allen), who became a celebrity in the fad-crazy '20s. A supremely well-executed joke, more clever than funny; it might have worked even better in a shorter format. Gordon Willis' cinematography and Dick Hyman's music are standouts. [PG] ▼●▶

Zelly and Me (1988) **C-87m.** **½ D: Tina Rathborne. Isabella Rossellini, Glynis Johns, Alexandra Johnes, Kaiulani Lee, David Lynch, Joe Morton. Uneven account of the trials and stresses in the life of wealthy, overprotected orphan Johnes. Occasionally insightful but far too introspective—with too much left unexplained. [PG] ▼●

Zentropa (1992-Danish-Swedish-French-German) **C/B&W-114m.** ***½ D: Lars von Trier. Barbara Sukowa, Jean-Marc Barr, Udo Kier, Ernst Hugo, Eddie Constantine; narrated by Max von Sydow. Sukowa plays a railroad magnate's daughter who may be in synch with postwar Nazi sympathizers called "werewolves." Audacious black-comic fantasy utilizes high-tech mixed media, creative use of rear projection, and dramatic shifts in pigment. Though it feels like a stunt, this is a rare contemporary movie that makes one feel privy to the reinvention of cinema. Panavision. ▼●

Zeppelin (1971-British) **C-101m.** *** D: Etienne Perier. Michael York, Elke Sommer, Peter Carsten, Marius Goring, Anton Diffring, Andrew Keir. Colorful cast and atmosphere (including interesting special effects) click in entertaining story of German-born British aviator emotionally torn by duty and homeland during WWI. Panavision. [G] ▼▶

Zero Effect (1998) **C-115m.** **½ D: Jake Kasdan. Bill Pullman, Ben Stiller, Ryan O'Neal, Kim Dickens, Angela Featherstone. Pullman is Daryl Zero, the world's greatest (and most eccentric) private detective, who never meets his clients, but sends emissary Stiller instead. O'Neal hires him to track down a blackmailer, but Pullman finds himself becoming emotionally involved with one of his suspects. Clever, original screenplay by first-time feature director Kasdan (son of Lawrence), but he shoots himself in the foot by deadening

the pace and stretching things out too long. Rate this a near miss. [R] ▼●▶

Zero for Conduct (1933-French) **44m.** **** D: Jean Vigo. Jean Daste, Robert le Flon, Louis Lefebvre, Constantin Kelber, Gerard de Bedarieux. Life in a French boarding school, where the authorities attempt to regiment the students—unsuccessfully. The kids are all wonderfully spontaneous; one of the best films ever about children among children. The inspiration for IF. . . . Written by the director. ▼▶

Zero Hour! (1957) **81m.** **½ D: Hall Bartlett. Dana Andrews, Linda Darnell, Sterling Hayden, Elroy "Crazylegs" Hirsch, Geoffrey Toone, Jerry Paris, Peggy King, John Ashley. Effective suspense story (based on Arthur Hailey teleplay) of potential airplane disaster when pilots are felled by ptomaine poisoning. Remade for TV in 1971 as TERROR IN THE SKY, and then spoofed in 1980 as AIRPLANE! ▶

Zero Kelvin (1995-Norwegian-Swedish) **C-113m.** *** D: Hans Petter Moland. Stellan Skarsgård, Gard B. Eidsvold, Bjørn Sundquist, Camilla Martens. Potent allegorical drama set in 1925 about an idealistic poet (Eidsvold) who leaves his beloved to work as a fur trapper in Greenland in the company of two very different coworkers; he promptly clashes with one of them (Skarsgård), a crude, embittered cynic. Quietly powerful tale mirrors the reality that to survive in a harsh and unforgiving world people must stick together. Breathtaking scenery contrasts with the graphic violence that comes with the killing of animals for survival. ▼▶

Zero to Sixty (1978) **C-100m.** *½ D: Don Weis. Darren McGavin, Sylvia Miles, Joan Collins, Denise Nickerson, The Hudson Brothers, Lorraine Gary. McGavin is improbably cast as a schnook who hooks up with a strident, street-smart 16-year-old girl who makes her living repossessing cars. Loud, stupid comedy with more car-chase thrills than humor. [PG] ▼

Zeus and Roxanne (1997) **C-98m.** ** D: George Miller. Steve Guttenberg, Kathleen Quinlan, Arnold Vosloo, Dawn McMillan, Miko Hughes, Jessica Howell. Kids' picture paralleling the up and down relationship between two single adults, as well as his dog and her dolphin (you read that right!). Lovely Bahamas locations and exceptional animal work lift this film only slightly above an uninspired script. [PG] ▼●▶

Ziegfeld Follies (1946) **C-110m.** *** D: Vincente Minnelli. William Powell, Judy Garland, Lucille Ball, Fred Astaire, Fanny Brice, Lena Horne, Red Skelton, Victor Moore, Virginia O'Brien, Cyd Charisse, Gene Kelly, Edward Arnold, Esther Williams. Variable all-star film introduced by Powell as Ziegfeld in heaven. Highlights are Brice-Hume Cronyn sketch, Astaire-

Kelly dance, Moore-Arnold comedy routine, Skelton's "Guzzler's Gin," Horne's solo, Garland's "The Interview." Various segments directed by George Sidney, Roy Del Ruth, Norman Taurog, Lemuel Ayers, Robert Lewis, Merrill Pye. Filmed mostly in 1944. ▼○▶

Ziegfeld Girl (1941) 131m. *** D: Robert Z. Leonard. James Stewart, Lana Turner, Judy Garland, Hedy Lamarr, Tony Martin, Jackie Cooper, Ian Hunter, Edward Everett Horton, Al Shean, Eve Arden, Dan Dailey, Philip Dorn, Charles Winninger. Large-scale musical drama opens brightly, bogs down into melodrama and preposterous subplots, as the lives of three girls (Turner, Garland, Lamarr) are changed by being recruited as Ziegfeld Follies girls. Busby Berkeley's "You Stepped Out of a Dream" is most famous number, but somewhat overshadowed by Judy's "I'm Always Chasing Rainbows," "Minnie from Trinidad." The MGM glitter has never been brighter. ▼○▶

Ziggy Stardust and The Spiders From Mars (1983) C-91m. *½ D: D. A. Pennebaker. David Bowie. Bowie in concert as Ziggy Stardust, his androgynous alter ego. Practically unwatchable, and unlistenable: cinema verité at its worst. Shot in 1973; of interest to Bowie fans only. [PG] ▼○▶

Zigzag (1970) 105m. **½ D: Richard A. Colla. George Kennedy, Anne Jackson, Eli Wallach, Steve Ihnat, William Marshall, Joe Maross. Dying insurance investigator (Kennedy) plans a complicated scheme to pin a murder on himself and be executed, so his family will collect a big insurance settlement, but his plans go awry. Good performances in moderately interesting drama. Panavision. [PG]

Zina (1985-British) C/B&W-90m. **½ D: Ken McMullen. Domiziana Giordano, Ian McKellen, Philip Madoc, Ron Anderson, Micha Bergese. Extremely (and deliberately) slow exploration of the problems and obsessions of Leon Trotsky's daughter while in psychoanalysis in prewar Berlin. Bryan Loftus' cinematography is exceptional. Not for all tastes.

Zita (1968-French) C-91m. *** D: Robert Enrico. Joanna Shimkus, Katina Paxinou, Suzanne Flon, Jose Marie Flotats, Paul Crauchet. Delicate story of young girl who learns about life as her beloved aunt is dying; love blossoms, as she breaks away from mother-figure to become an adult herself. Charming. [M]

Zodiac, The (2006) C-97m. *½ D: Alexander Bulkley. Justin Chambers, Robin Tunney, Rory Culkin, William Mapother, Rex Linn, Philip Baker Hall; voice of Brian Bloom. Earnest but flat examination of the infamous Northern California serial killer "The Zodiac" and the effect the murders have on a small-town detective and his fam-

ily. Well-defined feel of the late 1960s is undermined by a bland performance from Chambers as a cop struggling with a puzzling case, made more intense by a panicked community and the ensuing media pressure. Film is as unsatisfying as the real-life status of these crimes. Made in 2003. [R]▶

Zodiac (2007) C-156m. ***½ D: David Fincher. Mark Ruffalo, Jake Gyllenhaal, Robert Downey, Jr., Anthony Edwards, Brian Cox, Chloë Sevigny, Charles Fleischer, Zach Grenier, Philip Baker Hall, Elias Koteas, Donal Logue, John Carroll Lynch, Dermot Mulroney, John Getz, Adam Goldberg, Candy Clark, James Le Gros, Clea DuVall, Barry Livingston. Riveting drama based on the case of the so-called Zodiac killer who terrorized the San Francisco Bay area in the late 1960s (and partly inspired DIRTY HARRY). Focuses more on the manhunt than the crimes and shows how this frustrating case consumed the lives of reporters and detectives alike, especially *San Francisco Chronicle* cartoonist Robert Graysmith (Gyllenhaal), who spends decades trying to crack the case. Superbly made on every level, with meticulous re-creations of the 1970s, when most of the story takes place. Screenplay by James Vanderbilt, based on two best-selling books written by Graysmith. Ione Skye appears unbilled. Director's cut runs 162m. HD Widescreen. [R]▶

Zoltan, Hound of Dracula SEE: **Dracula's Dog**

Zombie (1979-Italian) C-91m. BOMB D: Lucio Fulci. Tisa Farrow, Ian McCulloch, Richard Johnson, Al Cliver, Annetta Gay. A zombie epidemic on a small Caribbean island. A poor imitation of George Romero's horror films, and pretty repellent. Techniscope. ▼○▶

Zombie High (1987) C-93m. ** D: Ron Link. Virginia Madsen, Richard Cox, James Wilder, Paul Feig, Kay Kuter, Sherilyn Fenn, Paul Williams. Slight, silly horror film is a junior version of THE STEPFORD WIVES. Madsen is newly enrolled at a private school whose preppie students are all suspiciously docile. Aka THE SCHOOL THAT ATE MY BRAIN. [R]▼

Zombie Island Massacre (1984) C-95m. BOMB D: John N. Carter. David Broadnax, Rita Jenrette, Tom Cantrell, Diane Clayre Holub. Ex-Abscam Congressional spouse (and *Playboy* subject) Jenrette has three gratuitous nude scenes in the opening 20 minutes—and then they have to ruin everything by going to the stupid island. The corpses keep a-comin' in this cheapo outing. Rita warbles title tune, "Di Reggae Picnic." [R]▼▶

Zombieland (2009) C-88m. **½ D: Ruben Fleischer. Woody Harrelson, Jesse Eisenberg, Emma Stone, Abigail Breslin, Amber Heard, Bill Murray, Derek Graf. The U.S. has been decimated by flesh-eating zombies, but a few "normal" humans remain, like young Eisenberg, who hooks up with a gun-toting zombie-eradicator named Tallahassee (Harrelson). Their road trip gets detoured when they encounter two savvy sisters (Stone, Breslin) heading for an amusement park in California. Murray is amusing in an off-kilter cameo as himself, but it's Harrelson's gung-ho performance that propels this likable if silly film. Mike White appears unbilled. HD Widescreen. [R] ◗

Zontar, the Thing from Venus (1968) **C-80m. BOMB** D: Larry Buchanan. John Agar, Anthony Houston, Susan Bjurman, Patricia De Laney, Warren Hammack. Title alien, resembling a bat, arrives to take over with INVASION OF THE BODY SNATCHERS-like methods; it's Agar to the rescue. Crude, Texas-filmed remake of IT CONQUERED THE WORLD.▼◗

Zoolander (2001) **C-89m. **½** D: Ben Stiller. Ben Stiller, Owen Wilson, Christine Taylor, pWill Ferrell, Milla Jovovich, Jerry Stiller, David Duchovny, Jon Voight, Judah Friedlander. Clever comedy about an empty-headed male model who searches for meaning in his life—while a nefarious designer (Ferrell) tries to brainwash him into carrying out the evil plans of an international fashion cartel. Funny gags, satiric ideas, eye-popping production design, and celebrity cameos (Cuba Gooding, Jr., Winona Ryder, David Bowie, to name just a few) make this fun for a while, but it can't sustain an entire film. Stiller cowrote, based on a skit he performed on a VH-1 award show; his father, Jerry, mother, Anne Meara, sister, Amy, and wife, Taylor, are featured in the cast. Super 35. [PG-13] ▼◗

Zoom (2006) **C-88m. *½** D: Peter Hewitt. Tim Allen, Courteney Cox, Chevy Chase, Spencer Breslin, Kevin Zegers, Kate Mara, Michael Cassidy, Ryan Newman, Rip Torn. Derivative (to put it kindly) sci-fi adventure about a former superhero who's called out of retirement to train a group of kids for a secret government project. Only problem: he's lost all his powers. Cheesy and awfully similar to SKY HIGH, although based on Jason Lethcoe's graphic novel. Allen seems to be phoning this one in; a sorry excuse for "family entertainment." [PG] ◗

Zoot Suit (1981) **C-103m. ***** D: Luis Valdez. Daniel Valdez, Edward James Olmos, Charles Aidman, Tyne Daly, John Anderson, Tony Plana. Fascinating, powerful, if too theatrical "stylized musical" based on railroading of Chicano gang members to San Quentin for murder in 1942 and efforts to obtain their release; adding commentary is the gang's leader (Valdez) and his zoot-suited alter ego (Olmos). Filmed on stage, with shots of an audience that is presumably watching the performance—a major distraction. Written by Luis Valdez, with music by Daniel Valdez. [R]▼◗

Zorba the Greek (1964) **146m. ***½** D: Michael Cacoyannis. Anthony Quinn, Alan Bates, Irene Papas, Lila Kedrova, George Foundas. Brooding, flavorful rendering of Nikos Kazantzakis novel. Quinn is zesty in title role of earthy peasant, Bates his intellectual British cohort. Kedrova won an Oscar as a dying prostitute, as did cinematographer Walter Lassally and the art direction–set decoration. Memorable Mikis Theodorakis score. Scripted by the director. Later a Broadway musical.▼◗

Zorro (1961-Spanish) **C-90m. **½** D: Joaquin Luis Romero Marchent. Frank Latimore, Mary Anderson, Ralph Marsch, Howard Vernon. Foreign-made Western with salty flavor of old California; Latimore is appropriately zealous as Zorro. SuperScope.▼

Zorro (1975-Italian-French) **C-100m. ***** D: Duccio Tessari. Alain Delon, Stanley Baker, Ottavia Piccolo, Moustache, Enzo Cerusico, Adriana Asti. Zesty retelling of saga of legendary masked rider and hero of the oppressed, not as distinctive as earlier versions (and set in South America rather than old California) but fun. [G] ▼◗

Zorro the Avenger SEE: **Shadow of Zorro, The**

Zorro, the Gay Blade (1981) **C-93m. **** D: Peter Medak. George Hamilton, Lauren Hutton, Brenda Vaccaro, Ron Leibman, Donovan Scott, James Booth. Hamilton is Don Diego Vega, foppish son of the legendary Zorro, and lookalike gay brother Bunny Wigglesworth. So-so, with Leibman overacting outrageously as the villain. Dedicated to Rouben Mamoulian! [PG]▼◗

Zotz! (1962) **87m. **** D: William Castle. Tom Poston, Julia Meade, Jim Backus, Fred Clark, Cecil Kellaway, Margaret Dumont. Goofy attempt at humorous chiller with Poston a teacher who finds strange coin that gives him mystical power over others.▼◗

Z.P.G. (1972-British) **C-95m. **** D: Michael Campus. Oliver Reed, Geraldine Chaplin, Don Gordon, Diane Cilento. Sci-fi tale with style but no class. Reproduction becomes crime punishable by death in the future, but some people try to defy the law. Title, of course, stands for Zero Population Growth. [PG]▼◗

Zulu (1964-British) **C-138m. ***** D: Cy Endfield. Stanley Baker, Jack Hawkins, Ulla Jacobsson, Michael Caine, Nigel Green, James Booth; narrated by Richard Burton. True story about undermanned British forces trying to defend their African mission from attack by hordes of Zulu warriors. Dramatic elements tend toward cliché, but virtually half the film is taken up by massive battle, which is truly spectacular and exciting. Followed 15 years later by prequel, ZULU DAWN. Technirama.▼◗

Zulu Dawn (1979-U.S.-Dutch) **C-121m. ***** D: Douglas Hickox. Burt Lancaster,

Peter O'Toole, Simon Ward, John Mills, Nigel Davenport, Michael Jayston, Denholm Elliott, Ronald Lacey, Freddie Jones, Christopher Cazenove, Anna Calder-Marshall, Bob Hoskins, Nicholas Clay. A prequel to 1964's ZULU (cowritten by that film's writer-director, Cy Endfield), showing the British command's bull-headed and ineffectual handling of the Zulu nation—first in diplomacy, then in battle. Solid war drama of the period, outstanding locations, though there's nothing new here. Released theatrically in U.S. at 98m. Panavision. [PG]▼●

Zu Warriors (2001-Hong Kong-Chinese) C-104m. ** D: Tsui Hark. Erik Cheng, Cecilia Cheung, Louis Koo, Patrick Tam, Kelly Lin, Wu Jing, Sammo Hung, Zhang Ziyi. Digital effects are the star of this visually sumptuous but dramatically muddled account of a band of flying superheroes in an ancient kingdom who unite to do battle against a ferocious demon. Beautiful to behold, but the plot is hopelessly confusing and the characters seem like automatons. Hark originally filmed this story in 1983 (as SUK SAN: SUN SUK SAN GEEN HAP). Aka THE LEGEND OF ZU. Released direct to DVD in the U.S. Super 35. [PG-13]❚

Index of Stars

Many older titles that no longer appear in this volume (or the index) can now be found in *Leonard Maltin's Classic Movie Guide*. That book also features a more extensive roster of actors whose main body of work was done before 1965.

This index includes *only the films that appear in this book*; therefore what follows doesn't feature a complete list of Ronald Colman's silent films, or John Wayne's B Westerns, or all the films of Gérard Depardieu.

The titles in each entry are in chronological order. Years are indicated in the reviews, and are included here to distinguish between two films of the same title, whether they are remakes (the two *Thomas Crown Affairs*, for example), or have nothing to do with each other (for instance, the two movies named *Where the Heart Is*).

When an actor directs but doesn't act in a movie, this is indicated by "(dir)" after the title; if the actor does appear, the designation is "(also dir)."

The prefix "co-" means a collaboration. "Cameo" indicates a well-known actor taking a small role, sometimes as a joke; their names almost never appear in the opening credits of a film, though in recent years, they are often listed in the end credits.

adapt	=	screenplay adaptation
app	=	appearance, not a performance (as in a documentary)
dir	=	director
mus	=	composer
narr	=	narrator
scr	=	screenplay
set dec	=	set decorator
sty	=	story
uncred	=	uncredited performance

Abbott and Costello: One Night in the Tropics; Buck Privates; In the Navy; Hold That Ghost; Keep 'Em Flying; Ride 'Em Cowboy; Rio Rita; Pardon My Sarong; Who Done It? (1942); It Ain't Hay; Hit the Ice; Lost in a Harem; In Society; Here Come the Co-Eds; The Naughty Nineties; Abbott and Costello in Hollywood; Little Giant; The Time of Their Lives; Buck Privates Come Home; The Wistful Widow of Wagon Gap; The Noose Hangs High; Abbott and Costello Meet Frankenstein; Mexican Hayride; Africa Screams; Abbott and Costello Meet the Killer Boris Karloff; Abbott and Costello in the Foreign Legion; Abbott and Costello Meet the Invisible Man; Comin' Round the Mountain; Jack and the Beanstalk; Lost in Alaska; Abbott and Costello Meet Captain Kidd; Abbott and Costello Go to Mars; Abbott and Costello Meet Dr. Jekyll and Mr. Hyde; Abbott and Costello Meet the Keystone Kops; Abbott and Costello Meet the Mummy; *Lou Costello alone:* The 30 Foot Bride of Candy Rock

Adams, Amy: Drop Dead Gorgeous; Psycho Beach Party; Pumpkin; Serving Sara; Catch Me If You Can; The Wedding Date; Junebug; Talladega Nights: The Ballad of Ricky Bobby; Tenacious D: The Pick of Destiny; The Ex; Underdog; Enchanted; Charlie Wilson's War; Sunshine Cleaning;

Miss Pettigrew Lives for a Day; Doubt; Night at the Museum: Battle of the Smithsonian; Julie & Julia; Leap Year; The Fighter

Affleck, Ben: The Dark End of the Street; School Ties; Buffy the Vampire Slayer (uncred); Dazed and Confused; Mallrats; Chasing Amy; Going All the Way; Good Will Hunting (also coscr); Phantoms; Armageddon; Shakespeare in Love; 200 Cigarettes; Forces of Nature; Dogma; Reindeer Games; Boiler Room; Bounce; Pearl Harbor; Jay and Silent Bob Strike Back; Daddy and Them; Changing Lanes; The Sum of All Fears; Daredevil; Gigli; Paycheck; Jersey Girl; Surviving Christmas; Clerks II; Hollywoodland; Smokin' Aces; Gone Baby Gone (dir, coadapt); He's Just Not That Into You; State of Play; Extract; The Town (also dir); The Company Men

Alda, Alan: Gone Are the Days!; Paper Lion; The Extraordinary Seaman; The Moonshine War; Jenny; The Mephisto Waltz; To Kill a Clown; California Suite; Same Time, Next Year; The Seduction of Joe Tynan (also scr); The Four Seasons (also dir, scr); Sweet Liberty (also dir, scr); A New Life (also dir, scr); Crimes and Misdemeanors; Betsy's Wedding (also dir, scr); Whispers in the Dark; Manhattan Murder Mystery; Canadian Bacon; Flirting With Disaster; Everyone Says I Love You; Murder at 1600; Mad City; The Object of My Affection; What Women Want; The Aviator (2004); Resurrecting the Champ; Diminished Capacity; Flash of Genius; Nothing But the Truth

Allen, Woody: What's New Pussycat (also scr); What's Up, Tiger Lily? (also dir, scr); Casino Royale (1967); Take the Money and Run (also dir, coscr); Bananas (also dir, coscr); Play It Again, Sam (also adapt); Everything You Always Wanted to Know About Sex (But Were Afraid to Ask) (also dir, scr); Sleeper (also dir, coscr); Love and Death (also dir, scr); The Front; Annie Hall (also dir, coscr); Interiors (dir, scr); Manhattan (also dir, coscr); Stardust Memories (also dir, scr); A Midsummer Night's Sex Comedy (also dir, scr); Zelig (also dir, scr); Broadway Danny Rose (also dir, scr); The Purple Rose of Cairo (dir, scr); Hannah and Her Sisters (also dir, scr); Radio Days (dir, scr, narr); September (dir, scr); King Lear (1987); Another Woman (dir, scr); New York Stories (seq dir); Crimes and Misdemeanors (also dir, scr); Alice (dir, scr); Scenes From a Mall; Shadows and Fog (also dir, scr); Husbands and Wives (also dir, scr); Manhattan Murder Mystery (also dir, coscr); Bullets Over Broadway (dir, coscr); Mighty Aphrodite (also dir, scr); Everyone Says I Love You (also dir, scr); Deconstructing Harry (also dir, scr); Wild Man Blues (app); The Impostors (cameo); Antz; Celebrity (dir, scr); Sweet and Lowdown (also dir, scr); Small Time Crooks (also dir, scr); Picking Up the Pieces; Company Man; The Curse of the Jade Scorpion (also dir, scr); Hollywood Ending (also dir, scr); Anything Else (also dir, scr); Melinda and Melinda (dir, scr); Match Point (dir, scr); Scoop (also dir, scr); Cassandra's Dream (dir, scr); Vicky Cristina Barcelona (dir, scr); Whatever Works (dir, scr); You Will Meet a Tall Dark Stranger (dir, scr); Midnight in Paris (dir, scr)

Andrews, Julie: Mary Poppins; The Americanization of Emily; The Sound of Music; Torn Curtain; Hawaii; Thoroughly Modern Millie; Star!; Darling Lili; The Tamarind Seed; 10; Little Miss Marker (1980); S.O.B.; Victor/Victoria; The Man Who Loved Women (1983); That's Life!; Duet for One; A Fine Romance; Relative Values; The Princess Diaries; Unconditional Love; Shrek 2; The Princess Diaries 2: Royal Engagement; Shrek the Third; Enchanted (narr); Tooth Fairy; Shrek Forever After; Despicable Me

Arthur, Jean: Seven Chances; The Whole Town's Talking; Mr. Deeds Goes to Town; The Ex-Mrs. Bradford; The Plainsman (1936); History Is Made at Night; Easy Living (1937); You Can't Take It With You; Only Angels Have Wings; Mr. Smith Goes to Washington; Too Many Husbands; Arizona; The Devil and Miss Jones; The Talk of the Town; The More the Merrier; A Lady Takes a Chance; A Foreign Affair; Shane

Astaire, Fred: Dancing Lady; Flying Down to Rio; The Gay Divorcee; Roberta; Top Hat; Follow the Fleet; Swing Time; Shall We Dance (1937); A Damsel in Distress; Carefree; The Story of Vernon & Irene Castle; Broadway Melody of 1940; Second Chorus; You'll Never Get Rich; Holiday Inn; You Were Never Lovelier; The Sky's the Limit; Yolanda and the Thief; Ziegfeld Follies; Blue Skies; Easter Parade; The Barkleys of Broadway; Three Little Words; Let's Dance; Royal Wedding; The Band Wagon; Daddy Long Legs (1955); Funny Face; Silk Stockings; On the Beach; The Pleasure of His Company; The Notorious Landlady; Finian's Rainbow; Midas Run; The Towering Inferno; That's Entertainment! (app); That's Entertainment, Part 2 (app); The Purple Taxi; The Amazing Dobermans; Ghost Story (1981); George Stevens: A Filmmaker's Journey (app)

Bacall, Lauren: To Have and Have Not; The Big Sleep (1946); Dark Passage; Key Largo; Young Man With a Horn; Bright Leaf; How to Marry a Millionaire; Woman's World; The Cobweb; Blood Alley; Written on the Wind; Designing Woman; The Gift of Love; Flame Over India; Shock Treatment (1964); Sex and the Single Girl; Harper; Murder on the Orient Express; The Shootist; Perfect Gentlemen; H.E.A.L.T.H.; The Fan (1981); Appointment With Death; Mr. North; Innocent Victim; Misery; All I Want for Christmas; Ready to Wear (Prêt-à-Porter); The Line King (app); The Mirror Has Two Faces (1996); My Fellow Americans; Diamonds (1999); Dogville; Birth; Howl's Moving Castle; Manderlay; The Walker (2007)

Baldwin, Alec: Forever, Lulu; She's Having a Baby; Beetle Juice; Married to the Mob; Talk Radio; Working Girl; Great Balls of Fire!; The Hunt for Red October; Miami Blues; Alice; The Marrying Man; Prelude to a Kiss; Glengarry Glen Ross; Malice; The Getaway (1994); The Shadow; Two Bits; The Juror; Heaven's Prisoners; Ghosts of Mississippi; Looking for Richard (app); The Edge; Mercury Rising; Notting Hill (cameo); Outside Providence; Thomas and the Magic Railroad; State and Main; Pearl Harbor; Cats & Dogs; Final Fantasy: The Spirits Within; The Royal Tenenbaums (narr); The Adventures of Pluto Nash; The Cooler; The Cat in the Hat; Along Came Polly; Broadway: The Golden Age (app); The Last Shot; The SpongeBob SquarePants Movie; The Aviator (2004); Elizabethtown; Fun With Dick and Jane (2005); Mini's First Time; The Departed; Running with Scissors; The Good Shepherd; Shortcut to Happiness (also dir); Brooklyn Rules; My Best Friend's Girl; Madagascar: Escape 2 Africa; Lymelife; My Sister's Keeper; It's Complicated

Bale, Christian: Empire of the Sun; Henry V (1989); Newsies; Swing Kids; Little Women (1994); Pocahontas; The Secret Agent (1996); The Portrait of a Lady; Metroland; Velvet Goldmine; A Midsummer Night's Dream (1999); American Psycho; Shaft (2000); Captain Corelli's Mandolin; Laurel Canyon; Reign of Fire; Equilibrium; The Machinist; Howl's Moving Castle; Batman Begins; Harsh Times; The New World; The Prestige; Rescue Dawn; 3:10 to Yuma (2007); I'm Not There; The Dark Knight; Terminator Salvation; Public Enemies; The Fighter

Bardem, Javier: High Heels; Jamón Jamón; Mouth to Mouth (1995); Live Flesh; Before Night Falls; The Dancer Upstairs; Mondays in the Sun; Collateral; The Sea Inside; Goya's Ghosts; No Country for Old Men; Love in the Time of Cholera; Vicky Cristina Barcelona; Eat Pray Love; Biutiful

Barrymore, Drew: Altered States; E.T. The Extra-Terrestrial; Firestarter; Irreconcilable Differences; Cat's Eye; Far from Home (1989); See You in the Morning; Doppelganger: The Evil Within; Guncrazy (1992); Poison Ivy (1992); Wayne's World 2; Bad Girls; Batman Forever; Boys on the Side; Mad Love (1995); Scream; Wishful Thinking; Everyone Says I Love You; The Wedding Singer; Ever After; Home Fries; Never Been Kissed; Titan A.E.; Charlie's Angels; Freddy Got Fingered; Skipped Parts; Donnie Darko; Riding in Cars With Boys; Confessions of a Dangerous Mind; Charlie's Angels: Full Throttle; Duplex;

50 First Dates; Fever Pitch (2005); Curious George; Music and Lyrics; Lucky You; Beverly Hills Chihuahua; He's Just Not That Into You; Whip It (also dir); Everybody's Fine (2009); Going the Distance

Beatty, Warren: Splendor in the Grass; The Roman Spring of Mrs. Stone; All Fall Down; Lilith; Mickey One; Promise Her Anything; Kaleidoscope; Bonnie and Clyde; The Only Game in Town; McCabe & Mrs. Miller; $ (Dollars); The Parallax View; The Fortune; Shampoo (also coscr); Heaven Can Wait (1978; also codir, coadapt); Reds (also dir, coscr); George Stevens: A Filmmaker's Journey (app); Ishtar; Dick Tracy (also dir); Truth or Dare (app); Bugsy; Love Affair (1994; also coadapt); Bulworth (also dir, coscr); Town & Country

Bening, Annette: The Great Outdoors; Valmont; Postcards From the Edge; The Grifters; Guilty by Suspicion; Regarding Henry; Bugsy; Love Affair (1994); The American President; Richard III (1995); Mars Attacks!; The Siege; In Dreams; American Beauty; What Planet Are You From?; Open Range; Being Julia; Running with Scissors; The Women (2008); Mother and Child; The Kids Are All Right

Bergman, Ingrid: Intermezzo; Rage in Heaven; Dr. Jekyll and Mr. Hyde (1941); Casablanca; For Whom the Bell Tolls; Gaslight (1944); The Bells of St. Mary's; Spellbound (1945); Saratoga Trunk; Notorious (1946); Arch of Triumph; Joan of Arc; Under Capricorn; Stromboli; The Greatest Love; Voyage in Italy; Elena and Her Men; Anastasia (1956); Indiscreet; The Inn of the Sixth Happiness; Goodbye Again; The Yellow Rolls-Royce; The Visit (1964); Cactus Flower; Walk in the Spring Rain; From the Mixed-Up Files of Mrs. Basil E. Frankweiler; Murder on the Orient Express; A Matter of Time; Autumn Sonata

Berry, Halle: Jungle Fever; Strictly Business; The Last Boy Scout; Boomerang (1992); Father Hood; The Program; The Flintstones; Losing Isaiah; Executive Decision; Race the Sun; The Rich Man's Wife; B*A*P*S; Bulworth; Why Do Fools Fall in Love; X-Men; Swordfish; Monster's Ball; Die Another Day; X2; Gothika; Catwoman; Robots; X-Men: The Last Stand; Perfect Stranger; Things We Lost in the Fire; Frankie & Alice

Black, Jack: Bob Roberts; Airborne; Demolition Man; Bye Bye Love; Waterworld; Dead Man Walking; Bio-Dome; The Cable Guy; The Fan (1996); Mars Attacks!; The Jackal; I Still Know What You Did Last Summer (uncred); Enemy of the State; Cradle Will Rock; The Love Letter (uncred); Jesus' Son; High Fidelity; Saving Silverman; Shallow Hal; Orange County; Ice Age; The School of Rock; Envy; Anchorman: The Legend of Ron Burgundy; Shark Tale; King Kong (2005); Nacho Libre; Tenacious D: The Pick of Destiny (also coscr); The Holiday (2006); Margot at the Wedding; Walk Hard: The Dewey Cox Story (uncred); Be Kind Rewind; Kung Fu Panda; Tropic Thunder; Year One; Gulliver's Travels (2010); Kung Fu Panda 2

Blanchett, Cate: Paradise Road; Oscar and Lucinda; Elizabeth; An Ideal Husband (1999); Pushing Tin; The Talented Mr. Ripley; The Man Who Cried; The Gift; Bandits (2001); The Lord of the Rings: The Fellowship of the Ring; Charlotte Gray; The Shipping News; Heaven (2002); The Lord of the Rings: The Two Towers; Veronica Guerin; Coffee and Cigarettes; The Missing; The Lord of the Rings: The Return of the King; The Life Aquatic with Steve Zissou; The Aviator (2004); Little Fish; Babel; The Good German; Notes on a Scandal; Hot Fuzz (cameo); Elizabeth: The Golden Age; I'm Not There; Indiana Jones and the Kingdom of the Crystal Skull; Ponyo; The Curious Case of Benjamin Button; Robin Hood (2010); Hanna

Bogart, Humphrey: Up the River; Three on a Match; The Petrified Forest; Bullets or Ballots; Isle of Fury; Black Legion; The Great O'Malley; Marked Woman; Kid Galahad (1937); San Quentin; Dead End; Stand-In; Crime School; Racket Busters; The Amazing Doctor Clitterhouse; Angels with Dirty Faces; King of the Underworld; The Oklahoma Kid; Dark Victory; You Can't Get Away With Murder; The Roaring Twenties; The Return of Dr. X; Invisible Stripes; Virginia City; It All Came True; Brother Orchid; They Drive By Night; High Sierra; The Wagons Roll at Night; The Maltese Falcon (1941); Across the Pacific; All Through the Night; The Big Shot; Casablanca; Action in the North Atlantic; Thank Your Lucky Stars (cameo); Sahara (1943); Passage to Marseille; To Have and Have Not; Conflict (1945); The Big Sleep (1946); Dead Reckoning; The Two Mrs. Carrolls; Dark Passage; The Treasure of the Sierra Madre; Key Largo; Knock on Any Door; Tokyo Joe; Chain Lightning; In a Lonely Place; The Enforcer (1951); Sirocco; The African Queen; Deadline U.S.A.; Battle Circus; Beat the Devil; The Caine Mutiny; Sabrina (1954); The Barefoot Contessa; We're No Angels (1955); The Left Hand of God; The Desperate Hours (1955); The Harder They Fall

Bonham Carter, Helena: A Room with a View; Lady Jane; Maurice (uncred); The Mask (1988); Francesco; Getting It Right; Hamlet (1990); Where Angels Fear to Tread; Howards End; Mary Shelley's Frankenstein; Mighty Aphrodite; Margaret's Museum; Twelfth Night; The Wings of the Dove; A Merry War; Sweet Revenge (1999); The Theory of Flight; Fight Club; Planet of the Apes (2001); Novocaine; The Heart of Me; Till Human Voices Wake Us;

Big Fish; Charlie and the Chocolate Factory; Wallace & Gromit in The Curse of the Were-Rabbit; Corpse Bride; Harry Potter and the Order of the Phoenix; Sweeney Todd: The Demon Barber of Fleet Street; Terminator Salvation; Harry Potter and the Half-Blood Prince; Alice in Wonderland (2010); The King's Speech; Harry Potter and the Deathly Hallows: Part 1

Boyer, Charles: Red-Headed Woman; Private Worlds; Break of Hearts; Mayerling (1936); The Garden of Allah; Tovarich; Conquest; History Is Made at Night; Algiers; Love Affair (1939); All This, and Heaven Too; Back Street (1941); Hold Back the Dawn; Tales of Manhattan; Gaslight (1944); Together Again; Cluny Brown; A Woman's Vengeance; Arch of Triumph; The First Legion; Thunder in the East; The 13th Letter; The Happy Time; The Earrings of Madame de . . .; The Cobweb; Around the World in Eighty Days (1956; cameo); La Parisienne; Lucky to Be a Woman; The Buccaneer (1958); Fanny (1961); Four Horsemen of the Apocalypse (1962); A Very Special Favor; Is Paris Burning?; How to Steal a Million; Casino Royale; Barefoot in the Park; The April Fools; The Madwoman of Chaillot; The Day the Hot Line Got Hot; Lost Horizon (1973); Stavisky . . .; A Matter of Time

Branagh, Kenneth: Coming Through; High Season; A Month in the Country; Henry V (1989; also dir, adapt); Dead Again (also dir); Peter's Friends (also dir); Swing Kids; Much Ado About Nothing (also dir, adapt); Mary Shelley's Frankenstein (also dir); Othello (1995); A Midwinter's Tale (also dir, scr); Anne Frank Remembered (narr); Looking for Richard (app); Hamlet (1996; also dir, adapt); The Gingerbread Man; The Proposition (1998); Celebrity; The Theory of Flight; Wild Wild West; The Road to El Dorado; Love's Labour's Lost (also dir, adapt); How to Kill Your Neighbor's Dog; Harry Potter and the Chamber of Secrets; Rabbit-Proof Fence; Sleuth (2007; dir); Valkyrie; Pirate Radio; Thor (dir)

Brando, Marlon: The Men; A Streetcar Named Desire; Viva Zapata!; Julius Caesar (1953); The Wild One; On the Waterfront; Desiree; Guys and Dolls; The Teahouse of the August Moon; Sayonara; The Young Lions; The Fugitive Kind; One-Eyed Jacks (also dir); Mutiny on the Bounty (1962); The Ugly American; Bedtime Story (1964); The Saboteur, Code Name Morituri; The Chase (1966); The Appaloosa; A Countess From Hong Kong; Reflections in a Golden Eye; Candy; The Night of the Following Day; Burn!; The Nightcomers; The Godfather; Last Tango in Paris; The Missouri Breaks; Superman; Superman II (Richard Donner cut); Apocalypse Now; The Formula; A Dry White Season; The Freshman (1990); Christopher Columbus: The

Discovery; Don Juan DeMarco; The Island of Dr. Moreau (1996); Free Money; The Score

Bridges, Jeff: The Company She Keeps; Halls of Anger; The Last Picture Show; Fat City; Bad Company (1972); The Last American Hero; The Iceman Cometh; Lolly Madonna XXX; Thunderbolt and Lightfoot; Rancho Deluxe; Hearts of the West; Stay Hungry; King Kong (1976); Somebody Killed Her Husband; Winter Kills; The American Success Company; Heaven's Gate; Cutter's Way; Kiss Me Goodbye; The Last Unicorn; Tron; Against All Odds (1984); Starman; Jagged Edge; 8 Million Ways to Die; The Morning After; Nadine; Tucker: The Man and His Dream; Cold Feet (1989; cameo); The Fabulous Baker Boys; See You in the Morning; Texasville; The Fisher King; The Vanishing (1993); American Heart; Fearless; Blown Away; Wild Bill; White Squall; The Mirror Has Two Faces (1996); The Big Lebowski; Arlington Road; The Muse; Simpatico; The Contender; K-PAX; Lost in La Mancha (narr); Seabiscuit; Masked and Anonymous; The Door in the Floor; Stick It; The Amateurs; Tideland; Surf's Up; Iron Man; How to Lose Friends & Alienate People; The Open Road; The Men Who Stare at Goats; Crazy Heart; True Grit (2010); Tron Legacy

Bronson, Charles (billed as Charles Buchinski or Buchinsky until Jubal): You're in the Navy Now; The People Against O'Hara; The Mob; The Marrying Kind (bit); Pat and Mike; Diplomatic Courier; Bloodhounds of Broadway (1952); House of Wax (1953); The Clown; Miss Sadie Thompson; Crime Wave; Apache; Vera Cruz; Jubal; Run of the Arrow; Machine-Gun Kelly; Ten North Frederick (bit); Never So Few; The Magnificent Seven; Master of the World; X-15; Kid Galahad (1962); The Great Escape; 4 for Texas; The Sandpiper; Battle of the Bulge; This Property Is Condemned; The Dirty Dozen; Guns for San Sebastian; Farewell, Friend; Villa Rides!; Once Upon a Time in the West; Lola (1969); Rider on the Rain; You Can't Win 'Em All; The Family (1970); Cold Sweat; Someone Behind the Door; Red Sun; The Mechanic (1972); The Valachi Papers; Chato's Land; The Stone Killer; Chino; Mr. Majestyk; Death Wish; Breakout (1975); Hard Times; From Noon Till Three; Breakheart Pass; St. Ives; Telefon; The White Buffalo; Love and Bullets; Caboblanco; Borderline (1980); Death Hunt; Death Wish II; Ten to Midnight; The Evil That Men Do; Death Wish 3; Murphy's Law; Assassination; Death Wish 4: The Crackdown; Messenger of Death; Kinjite: Forbidden Subjects; The Indian Runner; Death Wish V: The Face of Death

Brooks, Albert: Taxi Driver; Real Life (also dir, coscr); Private Benjamin; Modern Romance (also dir, coscr); Twilight Zone—The Movie; Unfaithfully Yours (1984); Lost in America (also dir, coscr); Broadcast News; Defending Your Life (also dir, scr); I'll Do Anything; The Scout (also coscr); Mother (1996; also dir, coscr); Critical Care; Out of Sight (1998); Doctor Dolittle (1998); The Muse (also dir, coscr); My First Mister; The In-Laws (2003); Finding Nemo; Looking for Comedy in the Muslim World (also dir, scr); The Simpsons Movie

Bullock, Sandra: A Fool and His Money; Who Shot Patakango?; Love Potion No. 9; When the Party's Over; The Vanishing (1993); Demolition Man; The Thing Called Love; Wrestling Ernest Hemingway; Speed (1994); While You Were Sleeping; The Net; Two If by Sea; Fire on the Amazon; A Time to Kill; In Love and War (1996); Speed 2: Cruise Control; Hope Floats; Practical Magic; The Prince of Egypt; Forces of Nature; Gun Shy; 28 Days; Miss Congeniality; Lisa Picard is Famous (cameo); Murder By Numbers; Divine Secrets of the Ya-Ya Sisterhood; Two Weeks Notice; Miss Congeniality 2: Armed and Fabulous; Crash (2005); Loverboy; The Lake House; Infamous; Premonition (2007); The Proposal; All About Steve; The Blind Side

Burton, Richard: My Cousin Rachel; The Desert Rats; The Robe; Demetrius and the Gladiators (cameo); Prince of Players; The Rains of Ranchipur; Alexander the Great; Bitter Victory; Look Back in Anger; The Bramble Bush; Ice Palace; The Longest Day; Cleopatra (1963); The V.I.P.s; Zulu (narr); Becket; The Night of the Iguana; The Spy Who Came In From the Cold; The Sandpiper; What's New Pussycat (cameo); Who's Afraid of Virginia Woolf?; The Taming of the Shrew; Doctor Faustus; The Comedians; Boom!; Candy; Where Eagles Dare; Anne of the Thousand Days; Staircase; Villain; Raid on Rommel; The Assassination of Trotsky; Hammersmith Is Out; Massacre in Rome; The Voyage; The Klansman; Exorcist II: The Heretic; Equus; The Medusa Touch; The Wild Geese; Lovespell; Breakthrough (1978); Circle of Two; Absolution; Wagner; Nineteen Eighty-Four (1984)

Caan, James: Irma la Douce; Lady in a Cage; Red Line 7000; El Dorado; Games; Countdown; Journey to Shiloh; Submarine X-1; The Rain People; Rabbit, Run; T.R. Baskin; The Godfather; Slither; Cinderella Liberty; The Gambler; Freebie and the Bean; The Godfather Part II (cameo); Funny Lady; Rollerball (1975); The Killer Elite; Harry and Walter Go to New York; Silent Movie (cameo); Another Man, Another Chance; A Bridge Too Far; Comes a Horseman; Chapter Two; Hide in Plain Sight (also dir); Thief; Bolero (1981); Kiss Me Goodbye; Gardens of Stone; Alien Nation; Dick Tracy (cameo); Misery; The Dark Backward (cameo); For the Boys; Honeymoon in Vegas; The Program; Flesh and Bone; Bottle Rocket; Eraser; Bulletproof (1996); This is my Father; Mickey Blue Eyes; The Way of the Gun; The Yards; Night at the Golden Eagle (cameo); City of Ghosts; Elf; Dogville; Get Smart; New York, I Love You; Cloudy With a Chance of Meatballs; Middle Men; Henry's Crime

Cage, Nicolas: Fast Times at Ridgemont High; Valley Girl; Rumble Fish; Racing With the Moon; The Cotton Club; Birdy; The Boy in Blue; Peggy Sue Got Married; Raising Arizona; Moonstruck; Vampire's Kiss; Fire Birds; Wild at Heart; Zandalee; Honeymoon in Vegas; Amos & Andrew; Red Rock West; Deadfall (1993); Guarding Tess; It Could Happen to You; Trapped in Paradise; Kiss of Death (1995); Leaving Las Vegas; The Rock; Con Air; Face/Off; City of Angels; Snake Eyes; 8MM; Bringing Out the Dead; Gone in Sixty Seconds (2000); The Family Man; Captain Corelli's Mandolin; Windtalkers; Adaptation.; Sonny (also dir, cameo); Matchstick Men; National Treasure; Lord of War; The Weather Man; The Ant Bully; World Trade Center; The Wicker Man (2006); Ghost Rider; Grindhouse (cameo); Next; National Treasure: Book of Secrets; Bangkok Dangerous; Knowing; G-Force; Astro Boy; The Bad Lieutenant: Port of Call: New Orleans; Kick-Ass; The Sorcerer's Apprentice; Season of the Witch; Drive Angry

Cagney, James: The Public Enemy; Blonde Crazy; Taxi! (1932); The Crowd Roars; Winner Take All; Hard to Handle; Lady Killer; Footlight Parade; Jimmy the Gent; Here Comes the Navy; Devil Dogs of the Air; "G" Men; Frisco Kid (1935); A Midsummer Night's Dream (1935); Ceiling Zero; Great Guy; Boy Meets Girl; Angels With Dirty Faces; The Oklahoma Kid; Each Dawn I Die; The Roaring Twenties; The Fighting 69th; Torrid Zone; City for Conquest; The Strawberry Blonde; The Bride Came C.O.D.; Captains of the Clouds; Yankee Doodle Dandy; Blood on the Sun; 13 Rue Madeleine; The Time of Your Life; White Heat; Kiss Tomorrow Goodbye; West Point Story; What Price Glory (1952); A Lion Is in the Streets; Run for Cover; The Seven Little Foys; Love Me or Leave Me; Mister Roberts; Tribute to a Bad Man; These Wilder Years; Man of a Thousand Faces; Shake Hands With the Devil; Never Steal Anything Small; The Gallant Hours; One, Two, Three; Arizona Bushwhackers (narr); Ragtime

Caine, Michael: The Key (1958); The Two-Headed Spy; Carve Her Name With Pride; The Day the Earth Caught Fire; The Wrong Arm of the Law; Zulu; The Ipcress File; Gambit; Alfie (1966); The Wrong Box; Funeral in Berlin; Hurry Sundown; Billion Dollar Brain; Woman Times Seven; Deadfall (1968); Play Dirty; The Magus;

The Italian Job (1969); Battle of Britain; Too Late the Hero; Get Carter (1970); The Last Valley; Kidnapped (1971); X, Y and Zee; Pulp; Sleuth (1972); The Destructors (1974); The Black Windmill; The Wilby Conspiracy; The Man Who Would Be King; The Romantic Englishwoman; Peeper; Harry and Walter Go to New York; The Eagle Has Landed; A Bridge Too Far; Silver Bears; The Swarm; California Suite; Ashanti; Beyond the Poseidon Adventure; The Island (1980); Dressed to Kill (1980); The Hand (1981); Victory (1981); Deathtrap; Educating Rita; Beyond the Limit; Blame It on Rio; The Jigsaw Man; Water; The Holcroft Covenant; Hannah and Her Sisters; Sweet Liberty; Mona Lisa; Half Moon Street; The Whistle Blower; Jaws the Revenge; The Fourth Protocol; Surrender (1987); Without a Clue; Dirty Rotten Scoundrels; Bullseye!; A Shock to the System; Mr. Destiny; Noises Off; Blue Ice; The Muppet Christmas Carol; On Deadly Ground; Blood and Wine; Curtain Call; Little Voice; The Cider House Rules; Get Carter (2000); Miss Congeniality; Quills; Last Orders; Shiner; Quicksand (2001); Austin Powers in Goldmember; The Quiet American (2002); Secondhand Lions; The Statement; Around the Bend; Batman Begins; Bewitched (2005); The Weather Man; The Prestige; Children of Men; Sleuth (2007); Flawless (2008); The Dark Knight; Is Anybody There?; Harry Brown; Inception; Gnomeo & Juliet; Cars 2

Carrey, Jim: Finders Keepers (1984); Once Bitten; Peggy Sue Got Married; The Dead Pool; High Strung (cameo); Earth Girls are Easy; Pink Cadillac; Ace Ventura, Pet Detective (also coscr); The Mask (1994); Dumb and Dumber; Batman Forever; Ace Ventura: When Nature Calls; The Cable Guy; Liar Liar; The Truman Show; Simon Birch; Man on the Moon; Me, Myself & Irene; How the Grinch Stole Christmas; The Majestic; Bruce Almighty; Eternal Sunshine of the Spotless Mind; Lemony Snicket's A Series of Unfortunate Events; Fun With Dick and Jane (2005); The Number 23; Horton Hears a Who!; Yes Man; Disney's A Christmas Carol; I Love You Phillip Morris; Mr. Popper's Penguins

Chan, Jackie: The Chinese Connection (bit); Enter the Dragon (bit); Drunken Master; The Big Brawl; The Cannonball Run; Project A (also dir, coscr); Cannonball Run II; The Protector; Police Story (also dir); Armour of God (also dir); Project A, Part II (also dir, coscr); Dragons Forever; Police Story Part 2 (also dir, coscr); Miracles (also dir, scr); Armour of God 2: Operation Condor (also dir, scr); Twin Dragons; Police Story III: Supercop; Drunken Master II; Rumble in the Bronx (also coscr); Jackie Chan's First Strike; Mr. Nice Guy; Jackie Chan's Who Am I? (also dir, coscr); Rush Hour; Shanghai Noon; Rush

Hour 2; The Tuxedo; Shanghai Knights; The Medallion; Around the World in 80 Days (2004); Rush Hour 3; The Forbidden Kingdom; Kung Fu Panda; The Spy Next Door; The Karate Kid (2010); Kung Fu Panda 2

Chaplin, Charles: (*features only*) Tillie's Punctured Romance; The Kid (also dir, scr); A Woman of Paris (dir, scr, cameo); The Gold Rush (also dir, scr); The Circus (also dir, scr); Show People (cameo); City Lights (also dir, scr); Modern Times (also dir, scr); The Great Dictator (also dir, scr); Monsieur Verdoux (also dir, scr, mus); Limelight (also dir, scr, mus); A King in New York (also dir, scr, mus); A Countess From Hong Kong (dir, scr, mus, cameo)

Cheadle, Don: Moving Violations; Hamburger Hill; Colors; Roadside Prophets; Meteor Man; Things to Do in Denver When You're Dead; Devil in a Blue Dress; Rosewood; Volcano; Boogie Nights; Bulworth; Out of Sight (1998); Mission to Mars; The Family Man; Traffic (2000); Manic; Swordfish; Rush Hour 2 (uncred); Ocean's Eleven (2001); The United States of Leland; The Assassination of Richard Nixon; Hotel Rwanda; After the Sunset; Ocean's Twelve; Crash (2005); Reign Over Me; Talk to Me; Ocean's Thirteen; Darfur Now (app); Traitor; Hotel for Dogs; Brooklyn's Finest; Iron Man 2

Cher: Alfie (1966; sings title song); Good Times; Chastity; Come Back to the 5 & Dime, Jimmy Dean, Jimmy Dean; Silkwood; Mask (1985); Moonstruck; Suspect; The Witches of Eastwick; Mermaids; The Player (cameo); Ready to Wear (Prêt-à-Porter); Faithful; Tea with Mussolini; Stuck on You; Burlesque

Clift, Montgomery: The Search; Red River; The Heiress; The Big Lift; A Place in the Sun; I Confess; From Here to Eternity; Indiscretion of an American Wife; Raintree County; The Young Lions; Lonelyhearts; Suddenly Last Summer (1959); Wild River; The Misfits; Judgment at Nuremberg; Freud; The Defector

Clooney, George: Return of the Killer Tomatoes!; Unbecoming Age; From Dusk Till Dawn; One Fine Day; The Peacemaker; Batman & Robin; Out of Sight (1998); The Thin Red Line (1998); South Park: Bigger, Longer & Uncut; Three Kings; The Perfect Storm; O Brother, Where Art Thou?; Spy Kids (cameo); Ocean's Eleven (2001); Welcome to Collinwood; Solaris (2002); Confessions of a Dangerous Mind (also dir); Spy Kids 3-D: Game Over (cameo); Intolerable Cruelty; Ocean's Twelve; Syriana; Good Night, And Good Luck. (also dir, coscr); The Good German; Ocean's Thirteen; Michael Clayton; Darfur Now (app); Leatherheads (also dir); Burn After Reading; The Men Who Stare at Goats; Up in the Air; Fantastic Mr. Fox; The American

Close, Glenn: The World According to Garp; The Big Chill; The Stone Boy; The Natural;

Greystoke: The Legend of Tarzan, Lord of the Apes; Maxie; Jagged Edge; Fatal Attraction (1987); Dangerous Liaisons; Light Years; Immediate Family; Reversal of Fortune; Hamlet (1990); Meeting Venus; Hook; The House of the Spirits; The Paper; Anne Frank Remembered (narr); Mary Reilly; Mars Attacks!; 101 Dalmatians (1996); Paradise Road; Air Force One; In & Out (cameo); Cookie's Fortune; Tarzan; 102 Dalmatians; Things You Can Tell Just by Looking at Her; Pinocchio (2002); The Safety of Objects; Le Divorce; The Stepford Wives (2004); Heights; Hoodwinked; Nine Lives; The Chumscrubber; Evening; Hoodwinked Too! Hood vs. Evil

Coburn, James: Ride Lonesome; The Magnificent Seven; Hell Is for Heroes; The Great Escape; Charade; The Americanization of Emily; Major Dundee; A High Wind in Jamaica; The Loved One (cameo); Our Man Flint; What Did You Do in the War, Daddy?; Dead Heat on a Merry-Go-Round; In Like Flint; Waterhole #3; The President's Analyst; Duffy; Candy; Hard Contract; Last of the Mobile Hot-Shots; Duck, You Sucker; The Honkers; The Carey Treatment; Pat Garrett & Billy the Kid; The Last of Sheila; Harry in Your Pocket; A Reason to Live, a Reason to Die; The Internecine Project; Hard Times; Bite the Bullet; Sky Riders; The Last Hard Men; Midway; Cross of Iron; California Suite (cameo); The Muppet Movie (cameo); Circle of Iron (costy); Goldengirl; Firepower; The Baltimore Bullet; Mr. Patman; Loving Couples; Looker; High Risk; Martin's Day; Death of a Soldier; Young Guns II; Hudson Hawk; The Player (cameo); Sister Act 2: Back in the Habit; Deadfall (1993); Maverick; Eraser; The Nutty Professor (1996); Keys to Tulsa; Affliction; Payback (uncred); Monsters, Inc.; Texas Rangers (2001; narr); Snow Dogs; The Man from Elysian Fields

Colbert, Claudette: The Smiling Lieutenant; The Sign of the Cross; It Happened One Night; Cleopatra (1934); Imitation of Life (1934); Under Two Flags; Tovarich; Bluebeard's Eighth Wife; Midnight (1939); Drums Along the Mohawk; It's a Wonderful World; Boom Town; Arise, My Love; Skylark (1941); The Palm Beach Story; So Proudly We Hail!; Since You Went Away; Tomorrow Is Forever; Without Reservations; The Egg and I; Three Came Home; Thunder on the Hill; Let's Make It Legal; Outpost in Malaya; Texas Lady; Parrish

Colman, Ronald: Bulldog Drummond; Arrowsmith; A Tale of Two Cities (1935); Under Two Flags; Lost Horizon (1937); The Prisoner of Zenda (1937); If I Were King; Lucky Partners; The Talk of the Town; Random Harvest; Kismet (1944); The Late George Apley; A Double Life; Champagne for Caesar; Around the World in Eighty Days (1956; cameo); The Story of Mankind

Connery, Sean: Let's Make Up; Hell Drivers; Another Time, Another Place; A Night to Remember; Darby O'Gill and the Little People; Tarzan's Greatest Adventure; The Frightened City; The Longest Day; Dr. No; From Russia With Love; Marnie; Woman of Straw; Goldfinger; The Hill; Thunderball; A Fine Madness; You Only Live Twice; Shalako; The Molly Maguires; The Red Tent; The Anderson Tapes; Diamonds Are Forever; The Offence; Zardoz; Murder on the Orient Express; The Terrorists; The Wind and the Lion; The Man Who Would Be King; Robin and Marian; The Next Man; A Bridge Too Far; The Great Train Robbery; Meteor; Cuba; Time Bandits; Outland; Wrong Is Right; Five Days One Summer; Never Say Never Again; Sword of the Valiant; Highlander; The Name of the Rose; The Untouchables; The Presidio; Memories of Me (cameo); Indiana Jones and the Last Crusade; Family Business (1989); The Hunt for Red October; The Russia House; Robin Hood: Prince of Thieves (cameo); Highlander II: The Quickening; Medicine Man; Rising Sun; A Good Man in Africa; Just Cause; First Knight; Dragonheart; The Rock; The Avengers; Playing by Heart; Entrapment; Finding Forrester; The League of Extraordinary Gentlemen

Cooper, Gary: Wings; It (1927); The Virginian (1929); Morocco; If I Had a Million; A Farewell to Arms (1932); Today We Live; Design for Living; The Wedding Night; The Lives of a Bengal Lancer; Mr. Deeds Goes to Town; The General Died at Dawn; The Plainsman (1936); Souls at Sea; Bluebeard's Eighth Wife; The Cowboy and the Lady; Beau Geste (1939); The Westerner; North West Mounted Police; Meet John Doe; Sergeant York; Ball of Fire; The Pride of the Yankees; For Whom the Bell Tolls; Casanova Brown; Saratoga Trunk; Cloak and Dagger; Variety Girl (cameo); Unconquered; Good Sam; The Fountainhead; It's a Great Feeling (cameo); Task Force; Bright Leaf; Dallas; You're in the Navy Now; It's a Big Country; Distant Drums; High Noon; Blowing Wild; Vera Cruz; Garden of Evil; The Court-Martial of Billy Mitchell; Friendly Persuasion; Love in the Afternoon; Ten North Frederick; Man of the West; The Hanging Tree; Alias Jesse James (cameo); They Came to Cordura; The Wreck of the Mary Deare; The Naked Edge

Costner, Kevin: Shadows Run Black; Night Shift; Chasing Dreams; Frances; Stacy's Knights; Table for Five; Testament; The Big Chill; The Gunrunner; American Flyers; Fandango; Silverado; Sizzle Beach; U.S.A.; The Untouchables; No Way Out (1987); Bull Durham; Field of Dreams; Revenge (1990); Dances With Wolves (also dir); Truth or Dare (app); Robin Hood: Prince of Thieves; JFK; The Bodyguard; A Perfect World; Wyatt Earp; The War; Waterworld; Tin Cup; The Postman (1997; also dir); Message in a Bottle; For Love of the Game; Play It to the

Bone (cameo); Thirteen Days; 3000 Miles to Graceland; Dragonfly (2002); Open Range (also dir); The Upside of Anger; Rumor has it . . .; The Guardian; Mr. Brooks; Swing Vote; The Company Men

Crawford, Joan: Hollywood Revue of 1929; Possessed (1931); Grand Hotel; Rain; Today We Live; Dancing Lady; Sadie McKee; Forsaking All Others; Chained; I Live My Life; The Bride Wore Red; Mannequin (1937); The Women (1939); Strange Cargo; Susan and God; A Woman's Face; They All Kissed the Bride; Reunion in France; Above Suspicion; Hollywood Canteen; Mildred Pierce; Humoresque; Possessed (1947); Daisy Kenyon; Flamingo Road; It's a Great Feeling (cameo); The Damned Don't Cry; Harriet Craig; Goodbye, My Fancy; This Woman Is Dangerous; Sudden Fear; Torch Song; Johnny Guitar; Female on the Beach; Queen Bee; Autumn Leaves; The Story of Esther Costello; The Best of Everything; What Ever Happened to Baby Jane?; The Caretakers; Strait-Jacket; I Saw What You Did; Berserk; Trog

Crosby, Bing: We're Not Dressing; Anything Goes (1936); Road to Singapore; If I Had My Way; Road to Zanzibar; My Favorite Blonde (cameo); Holiday Inn; Road to Morocco; Star Spangled Rhythm; Going My Way; Here Come the Waves; Road to Utopia; Duffy's Tavern; The Bells of St. Mary's; Blue Skies; Welcome Stranger; My Favorite Brunette (cameo); Road to Rio; Variety Girl (cameo); The Emperor Waltz; A Connecticut Yankee in King Arthur's Court; The Adventures of Ichabod and Mr. Toad (voice only); Top o' the Morning; Riding High; Mr. Music; Here Comes the Groom; Angels in the Outfield (1951; cameo); The Greatest Show on Earth (cameo); Son of Paleface (cameo); Just for You; Road to Bali; Little Boy Lost; Scared Stiff (1953; cameo); White Christmas; The Country Girl; Anything Goes (1956); High Society (1956); Man on Fire (1957); Alias Jesse James (cameo); Let's Make Love (cameo); High Time; Pepe (cameo); The Road to Hong Kong; Robin and the 7 Hoods; Stagecoach (1966); Cancel My Reservation (cameo); That's Entertainment!

Crowe, Russell: Prisoners of the Sun; Proof; Romper Stomper; Hammers Over the Anvil; The Sum of Us; The Quick and the Dead; Rough Magic; Virtuosity; Breaking Up; L.A. Confidential; The Insider; Mystery, Alaska; Gladiator (2000); Proof of Life; A Beautiful Mind; Master and Commander: The Far Side of the World; Cinderella Man; A Good Year; 3:10 to Yuma (2007); American Gangster; Body of Lies; State of Play; Tenderness; Robin Hood (2010); The Next Three Days

Cruise, Tom: Endless Love; Taps; All the Right Moves; Risky Business; Losin' It; The Outsiders; Legend; Top Gun (1986); The Color of Money; Cocktail; Young Guns (cameo); Rain Man; Born on the Fourth of

July; Days of Thunder (also costy); Far and Away; A Few Good Men; The Firm; Interview With the Vampire; Mission: Impossible; Jerry Maguire; Eyes Wide Shut; Magnolia; Mission: Impossible II; Vanilla Sky; Minority Report; Austin Powers in Goldmember (cameo); The Last Samurai; Collateral; War of the Worlds (2005); Mission: Impossible III; Lions for Lambs; Tropic Thunder; Valkyrie; Knight and Day

Cruz, Penélope: Jamón Jamón; Belle Epoque; Live Flesh; Open Your Eyes; Twice Upon a Yesterday; Talk of Angels; The Hi-Lo Country; All About My Mother; Woman on Top; All the Pretty Horses; Blow; Captain Corelli's Mandolin; Don't Tempt Me; Vanilla Sky; Waking Up in Reno; Masked and Anonymous (cameo); Gothika; Don't Move; Head in the Clouds; Noel; Sahara (2005); Bandidas; Volver; The Good Night; Elegy; Vicky Cristina Barcelona; Broken Embraces; G-Force; Nine; Sex and the City 2 (cameo); Pirates of the Caribbean: On Stranger Tides

Curtis, Tony: Criss Cross; City Across the River; The Lady Gambles; Winchester '73; Kansas Raiders; The Prince Who Was a Thief; Flesh and Fury; No Room for the Groom; Houdini; All American; Forbidden (1953); Beachhead; The Black Shield of Falworth; Six Bridges to Cross; Trapeze; Mister Cory; Sweet Smell of Success; The Vikings; Kings Go Forth; The Defiant Ones; The Perfect Furlough; Some Like It Hot (1959); Operation Petticoat; Pepe (cameo); Who Was That Lady?; The Rat Race (1960); Spartacus; The Great Impostor; The Outsider (1961); Taras Bulba; 40 Pounds of Trouble; The List of Adrian Messenger (cameo); Captain Newman, M.D.; Paris—When It Sizzles (cameo); Goodbye Charlie; Sex and the Single Girl; The Great Race; Boeing Boeing; Chamber of Horrors (cameo); Not With My Wife You Don't!; Arrivederci, Baby!; Don't Make Waves; On My Way to the Crusades I Met a Girl Who . . . ; Rosemary's Baby (voice only); The Boston Strangler; Those Daring Young Men in Their Jaunty Jalopies; You Can't Win 'Em All; Suppose They Gave a War and Nobody Came?; Lepke; The Last Tycoon; Casanova & Co.; The Manitou; Sextette; The Bad News Bears Go to Japan; Little Miss Marker (1980); The Mirror Crack'd; Brainwaves; Insignificance; Club Life; Midnight (1989); Center of the Web; Naked in New York; The Celluloid Closet (app); Play It to the Bone (cameo)

Cusack, John: Class; Grandview, U.S.A.; Sixteen Candles; Better Off Dead (1985); The Journey of Natty Gann; The Sure Thing; One Crazy Summer; Stand By Me; Hot Pursuit; Broadcast News (cameo); Eight Men Out; Tapeheads; Fat Man and Little Boy; Say Anything . . . ; The Grifters; True Colors; Shadows and Fog; The Player (cameo); Roadside Prophets (cameo); Bob Roberts (cameo); Map of the Human Heart; Money for Nothing;

The Road to Wellville; Bullets Over Broadway; Floundering; City Hall; Grosse Pointe Blank (also coscr); Con Air; Midnight in the Garden of Good and Evil; Anastasia (1997); The Thin Red Line (1998); Pushing Tin; This is my Father; Being John Malkovich; Cradle Will Rock; High Fidelity; America's Sweethearts; Serendipity; Adaptation. (cameo); Max; Identity; Runaway Jury; Must Love Dogs; The Ice Harvest; 1408; Martian Child; Joe Strummer: The Future Is Unwritten (app); The Contract (2006); Grace Is Gone; War, Inc. (also coscr); Igor; 2012; Hot Tub Time Machine

Cushing, Peter: The Man in the Iron Mask (1939; bit); A Chump at Oxford; Vigil in the Night; The Howards of Virginia (bit); Hamlet (1948); Moulin Rouge (1952); The End of the Affair (1955); Alexander the Great; Time Without Pity; Curse of Frankenstein; Horror of Dracula; Revenge of Frankenstein; Mania; The Hound of the Baskervilles (1959); John Paul Jones; The Mummy (1959); The Brides of Dracula; The Hellfire Club; The Naked Edge; The Evil of Frankenstein; The Gorgon; Dr. Terror's House of Horrors; She (1965); Dr. Who and the Daleks; The Skull; Island of Terror; Daleks—Invasion Earth 2150 A.D.; Frankenstein Created Woman; Island of the Burning Doomed; Torture Garden; Some May Live; Corruption; Frankenstein Must Be Destroyed; Scream and Scream Again (cameo); The Vampire Lovers; The House That Dripped Blood; One More Time (cameo); Bloodsuckers; I, Monster; Twins of Evil; Fear in the Night (1972); Asylum; Dr. Phibes Rises Again! (cameo); Dracula A.D. 1972; Nothing but the Night; Tales From the Crypt; Horror Express; The Creeping Flesh; Count Dracula and His Vampire Bride; And Now the Screaming Starts; From Beyond the Grave; Frankenstein and the Monster From Hell; The Beast Must Die; Legend of the Seven Golden Vampires; Madhouse (1974); Call Him Mr. Shatter; Legend of the Werewolf; The Ghoul; Shock Waves; Land of the Minotaur; At the Earth's Core; Dirty Knight's Work; The Uncanny; Star Wars; An Arabian Adventure; Monster Island; House of the Long Shadows; Top Secret!; Sword of The Valiant; Biggles: Adventures in Time

Damon, Matt: The Good Mother (extra); Mystic Pizza; Rising Son; School Ties; Geronimo: An American Legend; Younger and Younger; Courage Under Fire; Chasing Amy; The Rainmaker (1997); Good Will Hunting (also coscr); Rounders (1998); Saving Private Ryan; Dogma; The Talented Mr. Ripley; Titan A.E.; The Legend of Bagger Vance; Finding Forrester (uncred cameo); All the Pretty Horses; Jay and Silent Bob Strike Back; The Majestic (voice only); Ocean's Eleven (2001); Spirit: Stallion of the Cimarron; The Bourne Identity; Confessions of a Dangerous Mind (cameo); Gerry (also coscr); Stuck on You; Eurotrip; Jersey Girl; The Bourne Supremacy; Ocean's Twelve; The Brothers Grimm; Syriana; The Departed; The Good Shepherd; Ocean's Thirteen; The Bourne Ultimatum; Youth Without Youth (uncred cameo); Ponyo; Che (2008; cameo); The Informant!; Invictus; Green Zone; Hereafter; Inside Job (narr); True Grit (2010); The Adjustment Bureau

Davis, Bette: Waterloo Bridge (1931); Hell's House; The Cabin in the Cotton; Three on a Match; 20,000 Years in Sing Sing; Ex-Lady; Bureau of Missing Persons; Jimmy the Gent; Fog Over Frisco; Of Human Bondage (1934); Bordertown; Front Page Woman; Special Agent; Dangerous; The Petrified Forest; Satan Met a Lady; Kid Galahad (1937); Marked Woman; That Certain Woman; It's Love I'm After; Jezebel; The Sisters; The Private Lives of Elizabeth and Essex; Dark Victory; Juarez; The Old Maid; All This, and Heaven Too; The Letter; The Little Foxes; The Great Lie; Shining Victory (cameo); The Bride Came C.O.D.; The Man Who Came to Dinner; In This Our Life; Now, Voyager; Watch on the Rhine; Thank Your Lucky Stars; Old Acquaintance; Mr. Skeffington; Hollywood Canteen; The Corn Is Green (1945); Deception (1946); A Stolen Life; Winter Meeting; June Bride; Beyond the Forest; All About Eve; Another Man's Poison; Payment on Demand; Phone Call From a Stranger; The Star; The Virgin Queen; The Catered Affair; Storm Center; The Scapegoat; John Paul Jones; Pocketful of Miracles; What Ever Happened to Baby Jane?; The Empty Canvas; Dead Ringer; Hush . . . Hush, Sweet Charlotte; Where Love Has Gone; The Nanny; The Anniversary; Connecting Rooms; Bunny O'Hare; Burnt Offerings; Return From Witch Mountain; Death on the Nile; The Watcher in the Woods; The Whales of August; Wicked Stepmother

Day, Doris: Romance on the High Seas; My Dream Is Yours; It's a Great Feeling; Young Man With a Horn; West Point Story; Tea for Two; Storm Warning; Lullaby of Broadway; Starlift; On Moonlight Bay; I'll See You in My Dreams; The Winning Team; April in Paris; By the Light of the Silvery Moon; Calamity Jane; Lucky Me; Young at Heart; Love Me or Leave Me; Julie; The Man Who Knew Too Much (1956); The Pajama Game; Teacher's Pet (1958); The Tunnel of Love; It Happened to Jane; Pillow Talk; Midnight Lace; Please Don't Eat the Daisies; Lover Come Back (1961); That Touch of Mink; Billy Rose's Jumbo; The Thrill of It All; Move Over, Darling; Send Me No Flowers; Do Not Disturb; The Glass Bottom Boat; Caprice; The Ballad of Josie; Where Were You When the Lights Went Out?; With Six You Get Egg Roll

Day-Lewis, Daniel: Sunday, Bloody Sunday; Gandhi; The Bounty; The Insurance Man; My Beautiful Laundrette; A Room with a View; Stars and Bars; The Unbearable Lightness of Being; Eversmile, New Jersey; My Left Foot; The Last of the Mohicans (1992); The Age of Innocence (1993); In the Name of the Father; The Crucible (1996); The Boxer (1997); Gangs of New York; The Ballad of Jack and Rose; There Will Be Blood; Nine

Dean, James: Fixed Bayonets! (bit); Sailor Beware (bit); Deadline U.S.A. (bit); Has Anybody Seen My Gal? (bit); East of Eden; Rebel Without a Cause; Giant

de Havilland, Olivia: A Midsummer Night's Dream (1935); Captain Blood (1935); Anthony Adverse; The Charge of the Light Brigade (1936); It's Love I'm After; Gold Is Where You Find It; The Adventures of Robin Hood; Four's a Crowd; Dodge City; The Private Lives of Elizabeth and Essex; Gone With the Wind; Santa Fe Trail; The Strawberry Blonde; Hold Back the Dawn; They Died With Their Boots On; The Male Animal; In This Our Life; Thank Your Lucky Stars (cameo); Devotion; To Each His Own; The Snake Pit; The Heiress; My Cousin Rachel; That Lady; Not As a Stranger; The Ambassador's Daughter; The Proud Rebel; Libel; The Light in the Piazza; Lady in a Cage; Hush . . . Hush, Sweet Charlotte; The Adventurers (1970); Pope Joan; Airport '77; The Swarm; The Fifth Musketeer

Dench, Judi: The Third Secret; He Who Rides a Tiger; A Study in Terror; A Midsummer Night's Dream (1968); Luther (1973); Langrishe, Go Down; Dead Cert; A Room with a View; 84 Charing Cross Road; A Handful of Dust; Henry V (1989); Jack & Sarah; GoldenEye; Hamlet (1996); Mrs. Brown; Tomorrow Never Dies; Shakespeare in Love; Tea with Mussolini; The World Is Not Enough; Chocolat; Iris; The Shipping News; The Importance of Being Earnest (2002); Die Another Day; Home on the Range; The Chronicles of Riddick; Ladies in Lavender; Pride & Prejudice (2005); Mrs. Henderson Presents; Doogal; Casino Royale (2006); Notes on a Scandal; Quantum of Solace; Nine; Jane Eyre (2011); Pirates of the Caribbean: On Stranger Tides

Deneuve, Catherine: The Umbrellas of Cherbourg; Male Hunt; Repulsion; A Matter of Resistance; The Young Girls of Rochefort; Belle de Jour; Benjamin; Mayerling (1968); The April Fools; Mississippi Mermaid; Tristana; Donkey Skin; It Only Happens to Others; Dirty Money; La Grande Bourgeoise; Lovers Like Us; Hustle; March or Die; The Last Metro; Je Vous Aime; Choice of Arms; The Hunger; Fort Saganne; Let's Hope It's a Girl; Love Songs; Scene of the Crime (1986); Indochine; Ma Saison Préférée; One Hundred and One Nights; The Convent; Les Voleurs; Genealogies of a Crime; East-West; Place Vendôme; Pola X; Dancer in the Dark; Time Regained; The Musketeer; I'm Going Home; 8 Women; A Talking Picture; Changing Times; Persepolis; A Christmas Tale; The Girl on the Train

De Niro, Robert: Greetings; The Wedding Party; Sam's Song; Hi, Mom!; Bloody Mama; Jennifer on My Mind; Born to Win; The Gang That Couldn't Shoot Straight; Bang the Drum Slowly; Mean Streets; The Godfather Part II; The Last Tycoon; Taxi Driver; 1900; New York New York; The Deer Hunter; Raging Bull; True Confessions; The King of Comedy; Once Upon a Time in America; Falling in Love; Brazil; The Mission; Angel Heart; The Untouchables; Midnight Run; Jacknife; We're No Angels (1989); Stanley & Iris; GoodFellas; Awakenings; Guilty by Suspicion; Backdraft; Cape Fear (1991); Mistress; Night and the City (1992); Mad Dog and Glory; This Boy's Life; A Bronx Tale (also dir); Mary Shelley's Frankenstein; One Hundred and One Nights; Casino; Heat (1995); The Fan (1996); Sleepers; Marvin's Room; Cop Land; Jackie Brown; Wag the Dog; Great Expectations (1998); Ronin; Analyze This; Flawless (1999); The Adventures of Rocky and Bullwinkle; Meet the Parents; Men of Honor; 15 Minutes; The Score; Showtime; City by the Sea; Analyze That; Godsend (2004); Shark Tale; Meet the Fockers; The Bridge of San Luis Rey (2004); Hide and Seek; The Good Shepherd (also dir); Arthur and the Invisibles; Stardust (2007); What Just Happened; Righteous Kill; Everybody's Fine (2009); Stone; Little Fockers; Machete; Limitless

Depardieu, Gérard: Going Places (1974); Stavisky...; Vincent, François, Paul, and the Others; Maitresse; The Last Woman; 1900; The Left-Handed Woman; Get Out Your Handkerchiefs; Bye Bye Monkey; Buffet Froid; Loulou; Mon Oncle d'Amerique; The Last Metro; Je Vous Aime; Choice of Arms; The Woman Next Door; The Return of Martin Guerre; Danton; The Moon in the Gutter; Les Compères; Police; Fort Saganne; One Woman or Two; Ménage; Jean de Florette; I Hate Actors (cameo); Under Satan's Sun; Camille Claudel; Too Beautiful for You; I Want to Go Home; Cyrano de Bergerac (1990); Green Card; Uranus; Tous les Matins du Monde; 1492: Conquest of Paradise; Hélas Pour Moi; Germinal; My Father, the Hero; The Machine; Colonel Chabert; One Hundred and One Nights; A Pure Formality; Horseman on the Roof; Bogus; Unhook the Stars; The Secret Agent (1996); Hamlet (1996); The Man in the Iron Mask (1998); The Bridge (1999; also codir); Vatel; 102 Dalmatians; The Closet; CQ; Between Strangers; City of Ghosts; Crime Spree; Bon Voyage (2003); Nathalie...; Ruby & Quentin; Changing Times; Last Holiday (2006); Paris je t'aime (also seq codir); La Vie en Rose; Babylon A.D.; Mesrine: Part 1—Killer Instinct

Depp, Johnny: A Nightmare on Elm Street; Private Resort; Platoon; Edward Scissorhands; Cry-Baby; Freddy's Dead: The Final Nightmare (cameo); Benny & Joon; What's Eating Gilbert Grape; Arizona Dream; Ed Wood; Don Juan DeMarco; Nick of Time; Dead Man; Donnie Brasco; Fear and Loathing in Las Vegas; The Astronaut's Wife; The Ninth Gate; Sleepy Hollow; The Source (app); Before Night Falls; Chocolat; Blow; The Man Who Cried; From Hell; Lost in La Mancha; Pirates of the Caribbean: The Curse of the Black Pearl; Once Upon a Time in Mexico; Secret Window; Happily Ever After (2004); Finding Neverland; The Libertine; Charlie and the Chocolate Factory; Tim Burton's Corpse Bride; Pirates of the Caribbean: Dead Man's Chest; Pirates of the Caribbean: At World's End; Joe Strummer: The Future Is Unwritten (app); Sweeney Todd: The Demon Barber of Fleet Street (2007); Gonzo: The Life and Work of Dr. Hunter S. Thompson (narr); Public Enemies; The Imaginarium of Doctor Parnassus; Alice in Wonderland (2010); The Tourist; Rango; Pirates of the Caribbean: On Stranger Tides

Diaz, Cameron: The Mask (1994); The Last Supper; She's the One; Feeling Minnesota; Head Above Water; My Best Friend's Wedding; Keys to Tulsa; A Life Less Ordinary; Fear and Loathing in Las Vegas (cameo); There's Something About Mary; Very Bad Things; Being John Malkovich; Any Given Sunday; Charlie's Angels; The Invisible Circus; Things You Can Tell Just by Looking at Her; Shrek; Vanilla Sky; Slackers (cameo); The Sweetest Thing; Gangs of New York; Charlie's Angels: Full Throttle; Shrek 2; In Her Shoes; The Holiday (2006); Shrek the Third; What Happens in Vegas; My Sister's Keeper; The Box; Shrek Forever After; Knight and Day; The Green Hornet; Bad Teacher

DiCaprio, Leonardo: Poison Ivy (1992); What's Eating Gilbert Grape; This Boy's Life; Total Eclipse; The Quick and the Dead; One Hundred and One Nights; The Basketball Diaries; Romeo & Juliet (1996); Marvin's Room; Titanic (1997); The Man in the Iron Mask (1998); Celebrity; The Beach; Catch Me If You Can; Gangs of New York; The Aviator (2004); The Departed; Blood Diamond; The 11th Hour (narr); Body of Lies; Revolutionary Road; Shutter Island; Inception

Dietrich, Marlene: The Joyless Street (extra); The Blue Angel (1930); Morocco; Dishonored; Shanghai Express; Blonde Venus; Song of Songs; The Scarlet Empress; The Devil Is a Woman (1935); The Garden of Allah; Angel (1937); Destry Rides Again; Seven Sinners; The Flame of New Orleans; The Lady Is Willing; The Spoilers (1942);

Pittsburgh; Follow the Boys (1944); Kismet (1944); Golden Earrings; A Foreign Affair; Stage Fright; No Highway in the Sky; Rancho Notorious; Around the World in Eighty Days (1956; cameo); Witness for the Prosecution; Touch of Evil (cameo); Judgment at Nuremberg; Paris—When It Sizzles (cameo); Just a Gigolo; Marlene

Douglas, Kirk: The Strange Love of Martha Ivers; I Walk Alone; Out of the Past; Mourning Becomes Electra; A Letter to Three Wives; Champion; Young Man With a Horn; The Glass Menagerie (1950); Along the Great Divide; The Big Carnival; Detective Story; The Big Sky; The Big Trees; The Bad and the Beautiful; The Story of Three Loves; The Juggler; Act of Love; 20,000 Leagues Under the Sea; Ulysses (1955); The Racers; Man Without a Star; The Indian Fighter; Lust for Life; Top Secret Affair; Gunfight at the O.K. Corral; Paths of Glory; The Vikings; Last Train From Gun Hill; The Devil's Disciple; Strangers When We Meet; Spartacus; The Last Sunset; Town Without Pity; Lonely Are the Brave; Two Weeks in Another Town; The Hook (1963); The List of Adrian Messenger; For Love or Money (1963); Seven Days in May; In Harm's Way; The Heroes of Telemark; Cast a Giant Shadow; Is Paris Burning?; The Way West; The War Wagon; A Lovely Way to Die; The Brotherhood; The Arrangement; There Was a Crooked Man; The Light at the Edge of the World; A Gunfight; To Catch a Spy; The Master Touch; Scalawag (also dir); Jacqueline Susann's Once Is Not Enough; Posse (1975; also dir); The Chosen (1978); The Fury; The Villain; Home Movies; Saturn 3; The Final Countdown; The Man from Snowy River; Eddie Macon's Run; Tough Guys; Oscar (cameo); Greedy; Diamonds (1999); It Runs in the Family

Douglas, Michael: Hail, Hero!; Adam at 6 A.M.; Summertree; Napoleon and Samantha; Coma; The China Syndrome; Running; It's My Turn; The Star Chamber; Romancing the Stone; A Chorus Line; The Jewel of the Nile; Fatal Attraction; Wall Street; Black Rain (1989); The War of the Roses; Shining Through; Basic Instinct; Falling Down; Disclosure; The American President; The Ghost and the Darkness; The Game; A Perfect Murder; One Day in September (narr); Wonder Boys; Traffic (2000); One Night at McCool's; Don't Say a Word; It Runs in the Family; The In-Laws (2003); The Sentinel (2006); You, Me and Dupree; King of California; Ghosts of Girlfriends Past; Beyond a Reasonable Doubt (2009); Solitary Man; Wall Street: Money Never Sleeps

Downey, Robert Jr., or Downey Jr., Robert: Greaser's Palace (uncred); Up the Academy; Baby It's You; Firstborn; Tuff Turf; Weird Science; Back to School; America; The Pick-up Artist; Less Than Zero; Johnny Be Good; Rented Lips; 1969;

True Believer; Chances Are; Air America; Too Much Sun; Soapdish; Chaplin; Heart and Souls; The Last Party (app); Short Cuts; Hail Caesar; Natural Born Killers; Only You; Richard III (1995); Home for the Holidays; Restoration; One Night Stand; Two Girls and a Guy; Hugo Pool; The Gingerbread Man; U.S. Marshals; In Dreams; Friends and Lovers; Bowfinger; Black and White; Wonder Boys; The Singing Detective; Gothika; Eros; Game 6; Kiss Kiss, Bang Bang; Good Night, and Good Luck; A Guide to Recognizing Your Saints; The Shaggy Dog (2006); A Scanner Darkly; Fur: An Imaginary Portrait of Diane Arbus; Zodiac; Lucky You; Charlie Bartlett; Iron Man; The Incredible Hulk (cameo); Tropic Thunder; The Soloist; Sherlock Holmes (2009); Iron Man 2; Due Date

Dreyfuss, Richard: Valley of the Dolls; The Graduate (bit); The Young Runaways; Hello Down There; Dillinger (1973); American Graffiti; The Apprenticeship of Duddy Kravitz; The Second Coming of Suzanne; Jaws; Inserts; Close Encounters of the Third Kind; The Goodbye Girl; The Big Fix; The Competition; Whose Life Is It Anyway?; The Buddy System; Down and Out in Beverly Hills; Stand By Me; Tin Men; Stakeout; Nuts; Moon Over Parador; Let It Ride; Always (1989); Postcards From the Edge; Once Around; Rosencrantz and Guildenstern Are Dead; What About Bob?; Lost in Yonkers; Another Stakeout; Silent Fall; The American President; Mr. Holland's Opus; James and the Giant Peach; Mad Dog Time; Night Falls on Manhattan; Krippendorf's Tribe; The Crew; Who Is Cletis Tout?; Silver City (2004); Poseidon; W. (2008); My Life in Ruins; Leaves of Grass; Piranha (2010); Red (2010)

Dunaway, Faye: Hurry Sundown; The Happening (1967); Bonnie and Clyde; The Thomas Crown Affair (1968); The Extraordinary Seaman; A Place for Lovers; The Arrangement; Little Big Man; Puzzle of a Downfall Child; Doc; The Deadly Trap; Oklahoma Crude; The Three Musketeers (1974); Chinatown; The Towering Inferno; The Four Musketeers; Three Days of the Condor; Voyage of the Damned; Network; Eyes of Laura Mars; The Champ (1979); The First Deadly Sin; Mommie Dearest; The Wicked Lady (1983); Ordeal by Innocence; Supergirl; Barfly; Burning Secret; The Gamble; Midnight Crossing; Wait Until Spring, Bandini; The Handmaid's Tale; The Two Jakes; Double Edge; Arizona Dream; The Temp; Don Juan DeMarco; Dunston Checks In; The Chamber; Drunks; Albino Alligator; Twilight of the Golds; The Thomas Crown Affair (1999); The Messenger: The Story of Joan of Arc; The Yards; Festival in Cannes; The Rules of Attraction

Duvall, Robert: To Kill a Mockingbird; Captain Newman, M.D.; The Chase (1966);

Countdown; The Detective (1968); Bullitt; True Grit (1969); The Rain People; MASH; The Revolutionary; THX 1138; Lawman; The Godfather; Tomorrow; The Great Northfield, Minnesota Raid; Joe Kidd; Badge 373; Lady Ice; The Conversation; The Outfit; The Godfather Part II; Breakout (1975); The Killer Elite; Network; The Seven-Per-Cent Solution; The Eagle Has Landed; The Greatest (1977); The Betsy; Invasion of the Body Snatchers (1978; cameo); Apocalypse Now; The Great Santini; True Confessions; The Pursuit of D. B. Cooper; Angelo, My Love (dir, scr); Tender Mercies; Hotel Colonial; The Stone Boy; The Natural; Belizaire the Cajun; The Lightship; Let's Get Harry; Colors; The Handmaid's Tale; Days of Thunder; A Show of Force; Convicts; Rambling Rose; The Plague; Newsies; Falling Down; Geronimo: An American Legend; Wrestling Ernest Hemingway; The Paper; The Stars Fell on Henrietta; Something to Talk About; The Scarlet Letter (1995); A Family Thing; Phenomenon; Sling Blade; The Apostle (also dir, scr); The Gingerbread Man; Deep Impact; A Civil Action; Gone in Sixty Seconds (2000); The 6th Day; A Shot at Glory; John Q; Gods and Generals; Assassination Tango (also dir, scr); Open Range; Secondhand Lions; Kicking & Screaming (2005); Thank You for Smoking; Lucky You; We Own the Night; Four Christmases; The Road; Crazy Heart; Get Low

Eastwood, Clint: Revenge of the Creature; Lady Godiva; Tarantula; Away All Boats; Never Say Goodbye (1956); The First Traveling Saleslady; Escapade in Japan; Lafayette Escadrille; Fistful of Dollars; For a Few Dollars More; The Good, the Bad, and the Ugly; Hang 'Em High; Coogan's Bluff; Where Eagles Dare; Paint Your Wagon; Two Mules for Sister Sara; Kelly's Heroes; The Beguiled; Dirty Harry; Play Misty for Me (also dir); Joe Kidd; High Plains Drifter (also dir); Magnum Force; Breezy (dir); Thunderbolt and Lightfoot; The Eiger Sanction (also dir); The Outlaw—Josey Wales (also dir); The Enforcer (1976); The Gauntlet (also dir); Every Which Way But Loose; Escape From Alcatraz; Bronco Billy (also dir); Any Which Way You Can; Firefox (1982; also dir); Honkytonk Man (also dir); Sudden Impact (also dir); City Heat; Tightrope; Pale Rider (also dir); Heartbreak Ridge (also dir); Bird (dir); The Dead Pool; Pink Cadillac; White Hunter, Black Heart (also dir); The Rookie (1990; also dir); Unforgiven (1992; also dir); In the Line of Fire; A Perfect World (also dir); Casper (cameo); The Bridges of Madison County (also dir); Absolute Power (also dir); Midnight in the Garden of Good and Evil (dir); True Crime (also dir); Space Cowboys (also dir); Blood Work (also dir); Mystic River (dir, mus); Million Dollar Baby (also dir, mus); Flags of Our Fathers (dir, mus); Letters From Iwo Jima (dir); Grace Is Gone (mus); Changeling (2008; dir); Gran Torino (also dir); Invictus (dir); Hereafter (dir, mus)

Farrell, Colin: The War Zone; Ordinary Decent Criminal; Tigerland; American Outlaws; Hart's War; Minority Report; Phone Booth; The Recruit; Daredevil; Veronica Guerin; S.W.A.T.; Intermission; A Home at the End of the World; Alexander; The New World; Ask the Dust; Miami Vice; Cassandra's Dream; In Bruges; Pride and Glory; The Imaginarium of Doctor Parnassus; Crazy Heart; Triage; Ondine; The Way Back

Faye, Alice: Poor Little Rich Girl; Sing, Baby, Sing; Stowaway; On the Avenue; In Old Chicago; Alexander's Ragtime Band; Hollywood Cavalcade; Rose of Washington Square; Lillian Russell; Little Old New York; Tin Pan Alley; That Night in Rio; The Great American Broadcast; Weekend in Havana; Hello Frisco, Hello; The Gang's All Here; Four Jills in a Jeep; Fallen Angel (1945); State Fair (1962); Won Ton Ton, the Dog Who Saved Hollywood; The Magic of Lassie

Ferrell, Will: Austin Powers: International Man of Mystery; A Night at the Roxbury (also coscr); The Suburbans; Austin Powers: The Spy Who Shagged Me; Dick; Superstar; Drowning Mona; The Ladies Man (2000); Jay and Silent Bob Strike Back; Zoolander; Boat Trip; Old School; Elf; Starsky & Hutch (cameo); Anchorman: The Legend of Ron Burgundy (also coscr); Melinda and Melinda; Kicking & Screaming (2005); Bewitched (2005); Wedding Crashers (cameo); The Producers (2005); Curious George; Winter Passing; Talladega Nights: The Ballad of Ricky Bobby (also coscr); Stranger Than Fiction; Blades of Glory; The Wendell Baker Story (cameo); Semi-Pro; Step Brothers; Land of the Lost; The Goods: Live Hard, Sell Hard (cameo); Megamind; The Other Guys; Everything Must Go

Field, Sally: The Way West; Stay Hungry; Smokey and the Bandit; Heroes; Hooper; The End; Norma Rae; Beyond the Poseidon Adventure; Smokey and the Bandit II; Back Roads; Absence of Malice; Kiss Me Goodbye; Places in the Heart; Murphy's Romance; Surrender (1987); Punchline; Steel Magnolias; Not Without My Daughter; Soapdish; Homeward Bound: The Incredible Journey; Mrs. Doubtfire; Forrest Gump; Eye for an Eye; Homeward Bound II: Lost in San Francisco; Where the Heart Is (2000); Beautiful (dir); Say It Isn't So; Legally Blonde 2: Red, White and Blonde; Two Weeks

Fields, W. C.: If I Had a Million; Million Dollar Legs; International House; Tillie and Gus; Six of a Kind; You're Telling Me! (1934); The Old Fashioned Way (also sty, as Charles Bogle); It's a Gift (also sty, as

Charles Bogle); Mrs. Wiggs of the Cabbage Patch; David Copperfield (1935); The Man on the Flying Trapeze (also costy, as Charles Bogle); You Can't Cheat an Honest Man (also sty, as Charles Bogle); My Little Chickadee (also coscr); The Bank Dick (also scr, as Mahatma Kane Jeeves); Never Give a Sucker an Even Break (also sty, as Otis Criblecoblis); Tales of Manhattan; Follow the Boys (1944)

Finney, Albert: The Entertainer; Saturday Night and Sunday Morning; Tom Jones; The Victors; Night Must Fall (1964); Two for the Road; Charlie Bubbles (also dir); The Picasso Summer; Scrooge (1970); Gumshoe; Murder on the Orient Express; The Adventure of Sherlock Holmes' Smarter Brother (cameo); The Duellists; Loophole (1980); Looker; Wolfen; Shoot the Moon; Annie; The Dresser; Under the Volcano; Orphans; Miller's Crossing; The Playboys; Rich in Love; The Browning Version (1994); A Man of No Importance; The Run of the Country; Washington Square; Breakfast of Champions; Simpatico; Erin Brockovich; Traffic (2000); Big Fish; Ocean's Twelve (cameo); Tim Burton's Corpse Bride; A Good Year; Amazing Grace (2007); The Bourne Ultimatum; Before the Devil Knows You're Dead

Firth, Colin: Another Country; Nineteen Nineteen; A Month in the Country; Apartment Zero; Valmont; Femme Fatale (1991); The Advocate; Circle of Friends; The English Patient; Fever Pitch (1997); A Thousand Acres; Shakespeare in Love; My Life So Far; Relative Values; Bridget Jones's Diary; The Importance of Being Earnest (2002); What a Girl Wants; Hope Springs; Love Actually; Girl With a Pearl Earring; Bridget Jones: The Edge of Reason; Where the Truth Lies; Nanny McPhee; The Last Legion; When Did You Last See Your Father?; St. Trinian's; Then She Found Me; The Accidental Husband; Mamma Mia!; Easy Virtue (2008); Disney's A Christmas Carol; Dorian Gray (2009); A Single Man; A Summer in Genoa; The King's Speech

Flynn, Errol: Captain Blood (1935); The Charge of the Light Brigade (1936); The Green Light; The Prince and the Pauper (1937); Another Dawn; The Adventures of Robin Hood; The Sisters; Four's a Crowd; The Dawn Patrol (1938); Dodge City; The Private Lives of Elizabeth and Essex; Virginia City; The Sea Hawk (1940); Santa Fe Trail; Footsteps in the Dark; Dive Bomber; They Died With Their Boots On; Gentleman Jim; Edge of Darkness (1943); Thank Your Lucky Stars (cameo); Northern Pursuit; Uncertain Glory; Objective, Burma!; San Antonio; Cry Wolf; Escape Me Never; Silver River; Adventures of Don Juan; It's a Great Feeling (cameo); That Forsyte Woman; Kim; Against All Flags; The Master of Ballantrae; Crossed Swords (1954); The Warriors (1955); Istanbul (1957); The Sun Also Rises;

Too Much, Too Soon; The Roots of Heaven; Cuban Rebel Girls

Fonda, Henry: The Trail of the Lonesome Pine; That Certain Woman; You Only Live Once; Blockade; The Mad Miss Manton; Jezebel; Jesse James; The Story of Alexander Graham Bell; Drums Along the Mohawk; Young Mr. Lincoln; The Grapes of Wrath; The Return of Frank James; Lillian Russell; The Lady Eve; You Belong to Me; The Male Animal; The Big Street; Tales of Manhattan; The Ox-Bow Incident; My Darling Clementine; The Fugitive (1947); Daisy Kenyon; The Long Night; Fort Apache; On Our Merry Way; Mister Roberts; War and Peace (1956); The Wrong Man; 12 Angry Men; The Tin Star; Stage Struck; Warlock (1959); The Man Who Understood Women; Advise & Consent; The Longest Day; How the West Was Won; Spencer's Mountain; The Best Man; Fail-Safe; Sex and the Single Girl; The Rounders; In Harm's Way; Battle of the Bulge; A Big Hand for the Little Lady; Welcome to Hard Times; Firecreek; Madigan; Once Upon a Time in the West; Yours, Mine and Ours (1968); The Boston Strangler; Too Late the Hero; There Was a Crooked Man; The Cheyenne Social Club; Sometimes a Great Notion; Ash Wednesday (1973); Night Flight From Moscow; My Name Is Nobody; Midway; The Great Smokey Roadblock; Tentacles; Rollercoaster; The Great Battle; The Swarm; Fedora (cameo); Wanda Nevada (cameo); City on Fire; Meteor; On Golden Pond

Fonda, Jane: Tall Story; The Chapman Report; A Walk on the Wild Side; Period of Adjustment; In the Cool of the Day; Sunday in New York; Joy House; Circle of Love; Cat Ballou; The Chase (1966); The Game Is Over; Any Wednesday; Hurry Sundown; Barefoot in the Park; Spirits of the Dead; Barbarella; They Shoot Horses, Don't They?; Klute; Tout Va Bien; F.T.A.; Steelyard Blues; A Doll's House (Joseph Losey version); The Blue Bird (1976); Fun With Dick and Jane (1977); Julia (1977); Coming Home; Comes a Horseman; California Suite; The China Syndrome; The Electric Horseman; 9 to 5; No Nukes (app); On Golden Pond; Rollover; Agnes of God; The Morning After; Old Gringo; Stanley & Iris; Monster-in-Law; Georgia Rule

Fontaine, Joan: Quality Street; A Damsel in Distress; Gunga Din; The Women (1939); Rebecca; Suspicion; This Above All; Jane Eyre (1944); Frenchman's Creek; Letter From an Unknown Woman; Kiss the Blood Off My Hands; The Emperor Waltz; You Gotta Stay Happy; Born to Be Bad; Othello (1952; cameo); Something to Live For; Ivanhoe; The Bigamist; Casanova's Big Night; Beyond a Reasonable Doubt (1956); Island in the Sun; Until They Sail; A Certain Smile; Voyage to the Bottom of the Sea; Tender Is the Night; The Devil's Own (1966)

Ford, Glenn: Texas; Gilda; A Stolen Life; Framed (1947); The Loves of Carmen; The

Undercover Man; The Flying Missile; Follow the Sun; Affair in Trinidad; The Man From the Alamo; The Big Heat; Human Desire; The Americano; The Violent Men; Interrupted Melody; Blackboard Jungle; Trial; Ransom (1956); Jubal; The Fastest Gun Alive; The Teahouse of the August Moon; 3:10 to Yuma (1957); The Sheepman; Cowboy; Imitation General; It Started With a Kiss; The Gazebo; Cimarron (1960); Cry for Happy; Pocketful of Miracles; Four Horsemen of the Apocalypse (1962); Experiment in Terror; The Courtship of Eddie's Father; Advance to the Rear; Dear Heart; The Rounders; The Money Trap; Is Paris Burning?; Rage (1966); A Time for Killing; The Last Challenge; Day of the Evil Gun; Heaven With a Gun; Smith!; Santee; Midway; Superman; The Visitor (1979); Virus (1980); Happy Birthday to Me; Border Shootout

Ford, Harrison: Dead Heat on a Merry-Go-Round; Luv; A Time for Killing; Journey to Shiloh; Zabriskie Point; Getting Straight; American Graffiti; The Conversation; Star Wars; Heroes; Force 10 From Navarone; Hanover Street; Apocalypse Now (cameo); More American Graffiti (cameo); The Frisco Kid; The Empire Strikes Back; Raiders of the Lost Ark; Blade Runner; Return of the Jedi; Indiana Jones and the Temple of Doom; Witness; The Mosquito Coast; Frantic (1988); Working Girl; Indiana Jones and the Last Crusade; Presumed Innocent; Regarding Henry; Patriot Games; The Fugitive (1993); Jimmy Hollywood (cameo); Clear and Present Danger; One Hundred and One Nights; Sabrina (1995); The Devil's Own (1997); Air Force One; Six Days Seven Nights; Random Hearts; What Lies Beneath; K-19 The Widowmaker; Hollywood Homicide; Firewall; Indiana Jones and the Kingdom of the Crystal Skull; Crossing Over; Brüno (cameo); Extraordinary Measures; Morning Glory (2010)

Foster, Jodie: Napoleon and Samantha; Kansas City Bomber; Tom Sawyer (1973); One Little Indian; Alice Doesn't Live Here Anymore; Echoes of a Summer; Taxi Driver; Bugsy Malone; The Little Girl Who Lives Down the Lane; Freaky Friday (1977); Candleshoe; Carny; Foxes; O'Hara's Wife; The Hotel New Hampshire; Mesmerized; Siesta; Five Corners; Stealing Home; The Accused (1988); Backtrack (1989); The Silence of the Lambs; Little Man Tate (also dir); Shadows and Fog; Sommersby; Maverick; Nell; Home for the Holidays (dir); Contact; Anna and the King; Panic Room; The Dangerous Lives of Altar Boys; A Very Long Engagement; Flightplan; Inside Man; The Brave One (2007); Nim's Island; Motherhood (cameo); The Beaver (also dir)

Foxx, Jamie: Toys; The Truth About Cats & Dogs; The Great White Hype; Booty Call; The Players Club; Held Up; Any Given Sunday; Bait; Ali; Breakin' All the Rules; Collateral; Ray; Stealth; Jarhead; Miami Vice; Dreamgirls; The Kingdom; The Soloist; Law Abiding Citizen; Valentine's Day; I'm Still Here (app); Due Date; Rio

Franco, James: Never Been Kissed; Whatever It Takes; Spider-Man; Deuces Wild; Sonny; City by the Sea; The Company; Spider-Man 2; The Great Raid; Tristan + Isolde; Annapolis; The Wicker Man (2006); Flyboys; The Dead Girl; Spider-Man 3; Knocked Up; In the Valley of Elah; Camille (2007); Pineapple Express; Nights in Rodanthe (uncred); Milk; Howl; Date Night; Eat Pray Love; 127 Hours; The Green Hornet (uncred); Your Highness

Freeman, Morgan: Who Says I Can't Ride a Rainbow?; Blade (1973); Brubaker; Eyewitness (1981); Death of a Prophet; Harry and Son; Teachers; Marie; That Was Then, This Is Now; Resting Place; Street Smart; Clean and Sober; Lean on Me; Driving Miss Daisy; Glory (1989); Johnny Handsome; Bonfire of the Vanities; Robin Hood: Prince of Thieves; The Power of One; Unforgiven; Bopha! (dir); The Shawshank Redemption; Outbreak; Se7en; Moll Flanders; Chain Reaction (1996); Kiss the Girls; The Long Way Home (narr); Amistad; Hard Rain; Deep Impact; Nurse Betty; Under Suspicion (2000); Along Came a Spider; High Crimes; The Sum of All Fears; Levity; Dreamcatcher; Bruce Almighty; The Big Bounce (2004); Million Dollar Baby; Unleashed; Batman Begins; March of the Penguins (narr); War of the Worlds (2005; narr); An Unfinished Life; Edison Force; Lucky Number Slevin; 10 Items or Less; Feast of Love; Evan Almighty; The Contract (2006); Gone Baby Gone; The Bucket List; Wanted; The Dark Knight; The Code; The Maiden Heist; Invictus; Red (2010)

Gable, Clark: The Easiest Way; Night Nurse; Susan Lenox: Her Fall and Rise; Possessed (1931); Strange Interlude; Red Dust (1932); No Man of Her Own (1932); Hold Your Man; Dancing Lady; It Happened One Night; Manhattan Melodrama; Chained; Forsaking All Others; The Call of the Wild (1935); China Seas; Mutiny on the Bounty (1935); Wife vs. Secretary; San Francisco; Saratoga; Too Hot to Handle (1938); Test Pilot; Idiot's Delight; Gone With the Wind; Strange Cargo; Boom Town; Comrade X; They Met in Bombay; Honky Tonk; Somewhere I'll Find You; Adventure; The Hucksters; Command Decision; Homecoming; Any Number Can Play; Key to the City; To Please a Lady; Across the Wide Missouri; Callaway Went Thataway (cameo); Lone Star (1952); Never Let Me Go; Mogambo; Betrayed (1954); Soldier of Fortune; The Tall Men; The King and Four Queens; Band of Angels; Teacher's Pet (1958); Run Silent, Run Deep; But Not for Me; It Started in Naples; The Misfits

Garbo, Greta: Flesh and the Devil; Wild Orchids; Anna Christie; Susan Lenox: Her Fall and Rise; Inspiration; Mata Hari (1932);

Grand Hotel; As You Desire Me; Queen Christina; The Painted Veil (1934); Anna Karenina (1935); Camille (1937); Conquest; Ninotchka; Two-Faced Woman

Gardner, Ava: Shadow of the Thin Man (bit); H. M. Pulham, Esq. (bit); Babes on Broadway (bit); Kid Glove Killer; Reunion in France; Pilot #5; Hitler's Madman; Music for Millions; The Killers (1946); The Hucksters; One Touch of Venus; The Bribe; East Side, West Side; The Great Sinner; Pandora and the Flying Dutchman; Show Boat (1951); Lone Star (1952); The Snows of Kilimanjaro; The Band Wagon (cameo); Mogambo; Knights of the Round Table; The Barefoot Contessa; Bhowani Junction; The Little Hut; The Sun Also Rises; The Naked Maja; On the Beach; The Angel Wore Red; 55 Days at Peking; Seven Days in May; The Night of the Iguana; The Bible; Mayerling (1968); The Ballad of Tam Lin; The Life and Times of Judge Roy Bean; Earthquake; Permission to Kill; The Blue Bird (1976); The Cassandra Crossing; The Sentinel (1977); City on Fire; The Kidnapping of the President; Priest of Love

Garfield, John: Four Daughters; Juarez; They Made Me a Criminal; Dust Be My Destiny; Saturday's Children; The Sea Wolf (1941); Out of the Fog; Tortilla Flat; Air Force; Destination Tokyo; Thank Your Lucky Stars; The Fallen Sparrow; Hollywood Canteen; Pride of the Marines; The Postman Always Rings Twice (1946); Humoresque; Daisy Kenyon (cameo); Body and Soul (1947); Gentleman's Agreement; Force of Evil; We Were Strangers; Under My Skin; The Breaking Point; He Ran All the Way

Garland, Judy: Pigskin Parade; Thoroughbreds Don't Cry; Broadway Melody of 1938; Everybody Sing; Babes in Arms; The Wizard of Oz; Little Nellie Kelly; Strike Up the Band; Babes on Broadway; Ziegfeld Girl; For Me and My Gal; Girl Crazy; Thousands Cheer; Meet Me in St. Louis; The Clock; The Harvey Girls; Till the Clouds Roll By; Ziegfeld Follies; Easter Parade; The Pirate; Words and Music; In the Good Old Summertime; Summer Stock; A Star Is Born (1954); Pepe (cameo); Judgment at Nuremberg; Gay Purr-ee; A Child Is Waiting; I Could Go on Singing

Garner, James: Toward the Unknown; Sayonara; Darby's Rangers; Cash McCall; Up Periscope; The Children's Hour; Boys' Night Out; The Great Escape; Move Over, Darling; The Thrill of It All; The Wheeler Dealers; 36 Hours; The Americanization of Emily; The Art of Love; Mister Buddwing; Duel at Diablo; Grand Prix; A Man Could Get Killed; Hour of the Gun; How Sweet It Is!; The Pink Jungle; Marlowe; Support Your Local Sheriff!; A Man Called Sledge; Skin Game; Support Your Local Gunfighter; They Only Kill Their Masters; One Little Indian; The Castaway Cowboy;

H.E.A.L.T.H.; The Fan (1981); Victor/Victoria; Tank; Murphy's Romance; Sunset; The Distinguished Gentleman; Fire in the Sky; Maverick; My Fellow Americans; Twilight (1998); Space Cowboys; Atlantis: The Lost Empire; Divine Secrets of the Ya-Ya Sisterhood; The Notebook; The Ultimate Gift; Battle for Terra

Garson, Greer: Goodbye, Mr. Chips (1939); Pride and Prejudice (1940); Blossoms in the Dust; Mrs. Miniver; Random Harvest; Madame Curie; Mrs. Parkington; Adventure; The Valley of Decision; Desire Me; Julia Misbehaves; That Forsyte Woman; The Miniver Story; Julius Caesar (1953); Pepe (cameo); Sunrise at Campobello; The Singing Nun; The Happiest Millionaire

Gere, Richard: Report to the Commissioner; Baby Blue Marine; Looking for Mr. Goodbar; Bloodbrothers; Days of Heaven; Yanks; American Gigolo; An Officer and a Gentleman; Beyond the Limit; Breathless (1983); The Cotton Club; King David; No Mercy; Power; Miles From Home; Internal Affairs; Pretty Woman; Monster in a Box; Rhapsody in August; Final Analysis; Sommersby; Mr. Jones; Intersection; First Knight; Primal Fear; Red Corner; The Jackal; Runaway Bride; Autumn in New York; Dr. T & the Women; The Mothman Prophecies; Unfaithful; Chicago; Shall We Dance (2004); Bee Season; Hoax; The Hunting Party (2007); I'm Not There; Nights in Rodanthe; Hachi: A Dog's Tale; Amelia; Brooklyn's Finest

Giamatti, Paul: Past Midnight; Singles; Mighty Aphrodite; Sabrina (1995); Before and After (uncred); Breathing Room; Donnie Brasco; Private Parts (1997); My Best Friend's Wedding; Deconstructing Harry; The Break; The Truman Show; Doctor Dolittle (1998; uncred); Saving Private Ryan; The Negotiator; Safe Men; Cradle Will Rock; Man on the Moon; Big Momma's House; Duets; Storytelling; Planet of the Apes (2001); Big Fat Liar; American Splendor; Confidence (2003); Paycheck; Sideways; Robots; Cinderella Man; Lady in the Water; The Illusionist (2006); The Ant Bully; The Hawk Is Dying; Shoot 'Em Up; The Nanny Diaries; Fred Claus; Cold Souls; Duplicity; The Last Station; Barney's Version; Win Win; The Hangover Part II

Gibson, Mel: Summer City; Tim; Mad Max; Chain Reaction (1980); Attack Force Z; Gallipoli; The Road Warrior; The Year of Living Dangerously; The Bounty; Mrs. Soffel; The River (1984); Mad Max Beyond Thunderdome; Lethal Weapon; Tequila Sunrise; Lethal Weapon 2; Bird on a Wire; Air America; Hamlet (1990); Lethal Weapon 3; Forever Young; The Man Without a Face (also dir); Maverick; Casper (cameo); Braveheart (also dir); Pocahontas; Ransom (1996); Fathers' Day (cameo); Conspiracy Theory; Fairy Tale: A True Story (cameo); Lethal Weapon

4; Payback; Chicken Run; The Patriot; What Women Want; The Million Dollar Hotel; We Were Soldiers; Signs; The Singing Detective; The Passion of the Christ (dir, coscr); Paparazzi (cameo); Apocalypto (dir, coscr); Edge of Darkness (2010); The Beaver

Glover, Danny: Escape From Alcatraz; Chu Chu and the Philly Flash; Iceman; Places in the Heart; The Color Purple; Silverado; Witness; Lethal Weapon; Bat*21; Lethal Weapon 2; Predator 2; To Sleep With Anger; Flight of the Intruder; A Rage in Harlem; Pure Luck; Grand Canyon; Lethal Weapon 3; Bopha!; The Saint of Fort Washington; Maverick (cameo); Angels in the Outfield (1994); Operation Dumbo Drop; Switchback; Wild America (cameo); Gone Fishin'; The Rainmaker (1997; unbilled); Lethal Weapon 4; Antz; Beloved; The Prince of Egypt; Boesman & Lena; The Royal Tenenbaums; Saw; The Cookout; The Shaggy Dog (2006); Manderlay; Barnyard; Dreamgirls; Shooter; Honeydripper; Be Kind Rewind; Blindness; Saw V; Battle for Terra; 2012; Death at a Funeral (2010); I'm Still Here (app); Legendary; Alpha and Omega

Goldberg, Whoopi: The Color Purple; Jumpin' Jack Flash; Burglar; Fatal Beauty; The Telephone; Clara's Heart; Beverly Hills Brats (cameo); Ghost; Homer and Eddie; The Long Walk Home; House Party 2 (cameo); Soapdish; The Player; Sister Act; Sarafina!; Made in America; National Lampoon's Loaded Weapon I (cameo); Sister Act 2: Back in the Habit; Naked in New York; The Lion King; The Little Rascals (cameo); Corrina, Corrina; Star Trek: Generations; The Pagemaster; Boys on the Side; Moonlight and Valentino; The Celluloid Closet (app); Eddie; Theodore Rex; Bordello of Blood (cameo); Bogus; The Associate; Ghosts of Mississippi; In & Out (cameo); An Alan Smithee Film: Burn Hollywood Burn; How Stella Got Her Groove Back; Rudolph the Red-Nosed Reindeer: The Movie; The Deep End of the Ocean; Girl, Interrupted; Get Bruce! (app); The Adventures of Rocky and Bullwinkle (cameo); Monkey-Bone; Kingdom Come; Rat Race (2001); Star Trek: Nemesis (cameo); Superbabies: Baby Geniuses 2; Racing Stripes; Jiminy Glick in La La Wood (cameo); The Aristocrats (app); Doogal; Everyone's Hero; Toy Story 3; For Colored Girls

Grable, Betty: The Greeks Had a Word for Them (bit); Hold 'Em Jail; The Kid From Spain; Cavalcade; The Gay Divorcee; Pigskin Parade; Follow the Fleet; College Swing; Down Argentine Way; Tin Pan Alley; A Yank in the RAF; I Wake Up Screaming; Moon Over Miami; Footlight Serenade; Song of the Islands; Springtime in the Rockies; Coney Island; Sweet Rosie O'Grady; Diamond Horseshoe; The Dolly Sisters; Mother Wore Tights; That Lady in Ermine; The Beautiful Blonde From Bashful Bend; Wabash Avenue; My Blue Heaven (1950); Call Me Mister; The Farmer Takes a Wife (1953); How to Marry a Millionaire; Three for the Show; How to Be Very, Very Popular

Grant, Cary: Blonde Venus; She Done Him Wrong; The Eagle and the Hawk (1933); I'm No Angel; Sylvia Scarlett; Topper; The Toast of New York; The Awful Truth; Bringing Up Baby; Holiday (1938); Gunga Din; Only Angels Have Wings; In Name Only; His Girl Friday; My Favorite Wife; The Howards of Virginia; The Philadelphia Story; Penny Serenade; Suspicion; The Talk of the Town; Once Upon a Honeymoon; Mr. Lucky; Destination Tokyo; None But the Lonely Heart; Arsenic and Old Lace; Without Reservations (cameo); Night and Day; Notorious (1946); The Bachelor and the Bobby-Soxer; The Bishop's Wife; Mr. Blandings Builds His Dream House; Every Girl Should Be Married; I Was a Male War Bride; Crisis; People Will Talk (1951); Monkey Business (1952); Dream Wife; To Catch a Thief; The Pride and the Passion; An Affair to Remember; Kiss Them for Me; Indiscreet; Houseboat; North by Northwest; Operation Petticoat; The Grass Is Greener; That Touch of Mink; Charade; Father Goose; Walk, Don't Run; George Stevens: A Filmmaker's Journey (app)

Grant, Hugh: Maurice; White Mischief; The Lair of the White Worm; The Dawning; Crossing the Line; Impromptu; Bitter Moon; The Remains of the Day; Night Train to Venice; Sirens; Four Weddings and a Funeral; An Awfully Big Adventure; The Englishman Who Went Up a Hill but Came Down a Mountain; Sense and Sensibility; Nine Months; Restoration; Extreme Measures; Notting Hill; Mickey Blue Eyes; Small Time Crooks; Bridget Jones's Diary; About a Boy; Two Weeks Notice; Love Actually; Bridget Jones: The Edge of Reason; American Dreamz; Music and Lyrics; Did You Hear About the Morgans?

Guinness, Alec: Great Expectations (1946); Oliver Twist (1948); Kind Hearts and Coronets; Last Holiday (1950); The Mudlark; The Lavender Hill Mob; The Man in the White Suit; The Captain's Paradise; The Detective (1954); The Prisoner; The Ladykillers (1955); The Swan; The Bridge on the River Kwai; The Horse's Mouth (also adapt); The Scapegoat; Our Man in Havana; Tunes of Glory; A Majority of One; Damn the Defiant!; Lawrence of Arabia; The Fall of the Roman Empire; Doctor Zhivago; Hotel Paradiso; The Quiller Memorandum; The Comedians; Cromwell; Scrooge (1970); Brother Sun, Sister Moon; Hitler: The Last Ten Days; Murder by Death; Star Wars; The Empire Strikes Back; Raise the Titanic!; Lovesick; Return of the Jedi; A Passage to India; Monsignor Quixote; Little Dorrit; A Handful of Dust; Kafka; Mute Witness (cameo)

Gyllenhaal, Maggie: Waterland; A Dangerous Woman; Homegrown; Cecil B. Demented; Donnie Darko; Riding in Cars with Boys; Secretary (2002); 40 Days and 40 Nights; Adaptation.; Confessions of a Dangerous Mind; Casa de los Babys; Mona Lisa Smile; Criminal (2004); Happy Endings; The Great New Wonderful; Paris je t'aime; Monster House; Trust the Man; Sherry-Baby; World Trade Center; Stranger Than Fiction; The Dark Knight; Away We Go; Crazy Heart; Nanny McPhee Returns

Hackman, Gene: Lilith; Hawaii; Banning; First To Fight; Bonnie and Clyde; The Split; Riot; Downhill Racer; The Gypsy Moths; Marooned; I Never Sang for My Father; Doctors' Wives; The Hunting Party; The French Connection; Cisco Pike; Prime Cut; The Poseidon Adventure; Scarecrow; The Conversation; Zandy's Bride; Young Frankenstein (cameo); French Connection II; Bite the Bullet; Night Moves; Lucky Lady; The Domino Principle; March or Die; A Bridge Too Far; Superman; Superman II; All Night Long (1981); Reds; Eureka; Under Fire (1983); Uncommon Valor; Two of a Kind (1983); Misunderstood; Twice in a Lifetime; Target (1985); Power; Hoosiers; No Way Out (1987); Superman IV: The Quest for Peace; Another Woman; Bat*21; Full Moon in Blue Water; Split Decisions; Mississippi Burning; The Package; Loose Cannons; Narrow Margin; Postcards From the Edge; Class Action; Company Business; Unforgiven; The Firm; Geronimo: An American Legend; Wyatt Earp; The Quick and the Dead; Crimson Tide; Get Shorty; The birdcage; The Chamber; Extreme Measures; Absolute Power; Twilight (1998); Antz; Enemy of the State; Under Suspicion (2000); The Replacements; The Mexican (cameo); Heartbreakers (2001); Heist (2001); The Royal Tenenbaums; Behind Enemy Lines (2001); Runaway Jury; Welcome to Mooseport

Hanks, Tom: He Knows You're Alone; Bachelor Party; Splash; The Man With One Red Shoe; Volunteers; Every Time We Say Goodbye; The Money Pit; Nothing in Common; Dragnet (1987); Big; Punchline; The 'burbs; Turner and Hooch; Joe Versus the Volcano; Bonfire of the Vanities; Radio Flyer; A League of Their Own; Sleepless in Seattle; Philadelphia; Forrest Gump; Apollo 13; The Celluloid Closet (app); Toy Story; that thing you do! (also dir, scr); Saving Private Ryan; You've Got Mail; Toy Story 2; The Green Mile; Cast Away (2000); Road to Perdition; Catch Me If You Can; The Ladykillers (2004); The Terminal; The Polar Express; The Da Vinci Code; Cars (voice cameo); The Simpsons Movie (voice cameo); Charlie Wilson's War; The Great Buck Howard; Angels & Demons; Toy Story 3; Larry Crowne (also dir, coscr)

Harlow, Jean: The Love Parade (bit); Hell's Angels; City Lights (bit); The Public Enemy; Platinum Blonde; Red-Headed Woman; Red Dust (1932); Hold Your Man; Dinner at Eight; Bombshell; The Girl from Missouri; China Seas; Wife vs. Secretary; Libeled Lady; Saratoga

Harrelson, Woody: Wildcats; L.A. Story (uncred); Doc Hollywood; Ted & Venus; White Men Can't Jump; Indecent Proposal; I'll Do Anything; The Cowboy Way; Natural Born Killers; Money Train; The Sunchaser; Kingpin; The People Vs. Larry Flynt; Welcome to Sarajevo; Wag the Dog; Palmetto; The Thin Red Line (1998); The Hi-Lo Country; Ed TV; Play It to the Bone; Anger Management; She Hate Me; After the Sunset; The Prize Winner of Defiance, Ohio; North Country; The Big White; A Prairie Home Companion; A Scanner Darkly; The Walker (2007); No Country for Old Men; Semi-Pro; Sleepwalking; Transsiberian; Surfer, Dude; Battle in Seattle; Seven Pounds; Management; Zombieland; The Messenger; 2012; Defendor

Harris, Ed: Coma (bit); Borderline (1980); Knightriders; Creepshow; The Right Stuff; Under Fire; Swing Shift; Places in the Heart; A Flash of Green; Alamo Bay; Code Name: Emerald; Sweet Dreams; Walker; Jacknife; The Abyss; State of Grace; Paris Trout; Glengarry Glen Ross; Running Mates; The Firm; Needful Things; China Moon; Milk Money; Just Cause; Apollo 13; Nixon; Eye for an Eye; The Rock; Absolute Power; The Truman Show; Stepmom; The Third Miracle; Waking the Dead; The Prime Gig; Pollock (also dir); Enemy at the Gates; Buffalo Soldiers; A Beautiful Mind; The Hours; Masked and Anonymous (cameo); The Human Stain; Radio; A History of Violence; Winter Passing; Copying Beethoven; Gone Baby Gone; Cleaner; National Treasure: Book of Secrets; Appaloosa (2008; also dir, coadapt); Once Fallen; The Way Back

Hathaway, Anne: The Princess Diaries; The Other Side of Heaven; Nicholas Nickleby (2002); Ella Enchanted; The Princess Diaries 2: Royal Engagement; Hoodwinked; Havoc; Brokeback Mountain; The Devil Wears Prada; Becoming Jane; Get Smart; Rachel Getting Married; Passengers; Bride Wars; Valentine's Day; Alice in Wonderland (2010); Love and Other Drugs; Rio

Hawn, Goldie: The One and Only, Genuine, Original Family Band; Cactus Flower; There's a Girl in My Soup; $ (Dollars); Butterflies Are Free; The Sugarland Express; The Girl From Petrovka; Shampoo; The Duchess and the Dirtwater Fox; Foul Play; Lovers and Liars; Private Benjamin; Seems Like Old Times; Best Friends; Swing Shift; Protocol; Wildcats; Overboard; Bird on a Wire; Deceived; CrissCross; House Sitter; Death Becomes Her; The First Wives Club; Everyone Says I Love You; The Out-of-Towners (1999); Town & Country; The Banger Sisters

Hayek, Salma: Mi Vida Loca (My Crazy Life); Midaq Alley; Desperado; Four Rooms; Fair Game; From Dusk Till Dawn; Fled; Fools Rush In; Breaking Up; 54; The Velocity of Gary; The Faculty; Dogma; Wild Wild West; Timecode; Chain of Fools; Traffic (2000; uncred); Hotel (2002); Frida (2002); Spy Kids 3: Game Over; Once Upon a Time in Mexico; After the Sunset; Bandidas; Ask the Dust; Lonely Hearts (2007); Across the Universe (cameo); Cirque du Freak: The Vampire's Assistant; Grown Ups

Hayward, Susan: Hollywood Hotel (bit); The Sisters (bit); The Amazing Doctor Clitterhouse (bit); Beau Geste (1939); Reap the Wild Wind; I Married a Witch; Star Spangled Rhythm; The Fighting Seabees; Canyon Passage; Smash-up, the Story of a Woman; They Won't Believe Me; Tulsa; House of Strangers; I'd Climb the Highest Mountain; Rawhide; I Can Get It for You Wholesale; David and Bathsheba; With a Song in My Heart; The Snows of Kilimanjaro; The Lusty Men; White Witch Doctor; Demetrius and the Gladiators; Garden of Evil; Soldier of Fortune; I'll Cry Tomorrow; The Conqueror; Top Secret Affair; I Want to Live!; Woman Obsessed; Thunder in the Sun; Ada; Back Street (1961); The Stolen Hours; Where Love Has Gone; The Honey Pot; Valley of the Dolls; The Revengers

Hayworth, Rita: Only Angels Have Wings; Music in My Heart; Susan and God; Angels Over Broadway; The Strawberry Blonde; Blood and Sand (1941); You'll Never Get Rich; Tales of Manhattan; You Were Never Lovelier; Cover Girl; Tonight and Every Night; Gilda; Down to Earth (1947); The Lady From Shanghai; The Loves of Carmen; Affair in Trinidad; Salome; Miss Sadie Thompson; Fire Down Below (1957); Pal Joey; Separate Tables; They Came to Cordura; The Story on Page One; Circus World; The Money Trap; The Poppy Is Also a Flower; The Rover; The Road to Salina; The Wrath of God

Hepburn, Audrey: Laughter in Paradise (bit); The Lavender Hill Mob; Roman Holiday; Sabrina (1954); War and Peace (1956); Funny Face; Love in the Afternoon; Green Mansions; The Nun's Story; The Unforgiven (1960); Breakfast at Tiffany's; The Children's Hour; Charade; Paris—When It Sizzles; My Fair Lady; How to Steal a Million; Two for the Road; Wait Until Dark; Robin and Marian; Bloodline; They All Laughed; Always (1989)

Hepburn, Katharine: A Bill of Divorcement (1932); Christopher Strong; Morning Glory (1933); Little Women (1933); Spitfire (1934); The Little Minister; Break of Hearts; Alice Adams; Sylvia Scarlett; Mary of Scotland; A Woman Rebels; Quality Street; Stage Door; Bringing Up Baby; Holiday (1938); The Philadelphia Story; Woman of the Year; Keeper of the Flame; Stage Door Canteen; Dragon Seed; Without Love; Undercurrent; The Sea of Grass; Song of Love; State of the Union; Adam's Rib; The African Queen; Pat and Mike; Summertime; The Rainmaker (1956); The Iron Petticoat; Desk Set; Suddenly, Last Summer; Long Day's Journey Into Night; Guess Who's Coming to Dinner?; The Lion in Winter; The Madwoman of Chaillot; The Trojan Women; A Delicate Balance; Rooster Cogburn; Olly, Olly, Oxen Free; On Golden Pond; George Stevens: A Filmmaker's Journey (app); Grace Quigley; Love Affair (1994)

Heston, Charlton: The Greatest Show on Earth; Ruby Gentry; Pony Express; Arrowhead; Bad for Each Other; The Naked Jungle; The Far Horizons; Lucy Gallant; The Ten Commandments (1956); Three Violent People; Touch of Evil; The Big Country; The Buccaneer (1958); The Wreck of the Mary Deare; Ben Hur (1959); El Cid; Diamond Head; 55 Days at Peking; The Greatest Story Ever Told; Major Dundee; The Agony and the Ecstasy; The War Lord; Khartoum; Counterpoint; Planet of the Apes (1968); Will Penny; Number One; Julius Caesar (1970); Beneath the Planet of the Apes; King: A Filmed Record . . . Montgomery to Memphis (narr); The Hawaiians; The Omega Man; Call of the Wild (1972); Skyjacked; Antony and Cleopatra (also dir); Soylent Green; Airport 1975; The Three Musketeers (1974); Earthquake; The Four Musketeers; The Last Hard Men; Midway; Two Minute Warning; Crossed Swords (1978); Gray Lady Down; The Mountain Men; The Awakening; Mother Lode (also dir); Almost an Angel (cameo); Solar Crisis; Wayne's World 2 (cameo); Tombstone; True Lies (cameo); In the Mouth of Madness; Alaska; Hamlet (1996); Hercules (1997; narr); Armageddon (narr); Any Given Sunday; Town & Country; Cats & Dogs; Planet of the Apes (2001; uncred); Bowling for Columbine (app)

Hoffman, Dustin: The Tiger Makes Out; The Graduate; Madigan's Million; Midnight Cowboy; John and Mary; Little Big Man; Who Is Harry Kellerman and Why Is He Saying Those Terrible Things About Me?; Straw Dogs; Alfredo, Alfredo; Papillon; Lenny; All the President's Men; Marathon Man; Straight Time; Agatha; Kramer vs. Kramer; Tootsie; Ishtar; Rain Man; Family Business (1989); Common Threads: Stories From the Quilt (narr); Dick Tracy; Billy Bathgate; Hook (1991); Hero (1992); Outbreak; Sleepers; American Buffalo; Mad City; Wag the Dog; Sphere; The Messenger: The Story of Joan of Arc; The Kid Stays in the Picture (app); Moonlight Mile; Confidence; Runaway Jury; i ♥ Huckabees; Finding Neverland; Lemony Snicket's A Series of Unfortunate Events (cameo); Meet the Fockers; Racing Stripes; The Lost City; Perfume: The Story of a Murderer; Stranger Than Fiction; The

Holiday (2006; cameo); Mr. Magorium's Wonder Emporium; Kung Fu Panda; The Tale of Despereaux; Last Chance Harvey; Barney's Version; Little Fockers; Kung Fu Panda 2

Hoffman, Philip Seymour: My New Gun; Leap of Faith; Scent of a Woman; Joey Breaker; My Boyfriend's Back; Money for Nothing; The Getaway (1994); When a Man Loves a Woman; Nobody's Fool; Twister; Hard Eight; Boogie Nights; Next Stop Wonderland; The Big Lebowski; Happiness; Patch Adams; Flawless (1999); Magnolia; The Talented Mr. Ripley; State and Main; Almost Famous; Love Liza; Punch-Drunk Love; Red Dragon; 25th Hour (2002); Owning Mahowny; Cold Mountain; Along Came Polly; Capote; Mission: Impossible III; Strangers With Candy (cameo); The Savages (2007); Before the Devil Knows You're Dead; Charlie Wilson's War; Synecdoche, New York; Doubt; Pirate Radio; The Invention of Lying; Jack Goes Boating (also dir)

Holden, William: Golden Boy; Invisible Stripes; Our Town; Arizona; Texas; The Fleet's In; Variety Girl (cameo); Rachel and the Stranger; Born Yesterday (1950); Sunset Blvd.; Union Station; Force of Arms; The Turning Point (1952); The Moon Is Blue; Stalag 17; Forever Female; Escape From Fort Bravo; Executive Suite; The Bridges at Toko-Ri; Sabrina (1954); The Country Girl; Love Is a Many-Splendored Thing; Picnic; Toward the Unknown; The Proud and Profane; The Bridge on the River Kwai; The Key; The Horse Soldiers; The World of Suzie Wong; The Counterfeit Traitor; Satan Never Sleeps; The Lion; Paris—When It Sizzles; The 7th Dawn; Alvarez Kelly; Casino Royale (1967; cameo); The Devil's Brigade; The Christmas Tree; The Wild Bunch; Wild Rovers; The Revengers; Breezy; The Towering Inferno; Open Season (1974); Network; Damien—Omen II; Fedora; Escape to Athena; Ashanti; When Time Ran Out . . .; The Earthling; S.O.B.

Hope, Bob: Some Like It Hot (1939); The Cat and the Canary (1939); Road to Singapore; The Ghost Breakers; Road to Zanzibar; My Favorite Blonde; Road to Morocco; Star Spangled Rhythm; They Got Me Covered; Road to Utopia; Monsieur Beaucaire; My Favorite Brunette; Where There's Life; Variety Girl (cameo); Road to Rio; The Paleface; Sorrowful Jones; The Great Lover; Fancy Pants; The Lemon Drop Kid; My Favorite Spy (1951); The Greatest Show on Earth (cameo); Son of Paleface; Road to Bali; Scared Stiff (1953; cameo); Here Come the Girls; Casanova's Big Night; The Seven Little Foys; That Certain Feeling; The Iron Petticoat; Beau James; Paris Holiday; The Five Pennies (cameo); Alias Jesse James; The Facts of Life; Bachelor in Paradise; The Road to Hong Kong; Critic's Choice; Call Me Bwana; A Global

Affair; The Oscar (cameo); Not With My Wife You Don't! (cameo); Boy, Did I Get a Wrong Number!; Eight on the Lam; The Private Navy of Sgt. O'Farrell; How to Commit Marriage; Cancel My Reservation; The Muppet Movie (cameo); Spies Like Us (cameo)

Hopkins, Anthony: The Lion in Winter; Hamlet (1969); The Looking Glass War; When Eight Bells Toll; Young Winston; A Doll's House (Claire Bloom version); The Girl From Petrovka; Juggernaut; Audrey Rose; A Bridge Too Far; International Velvet; Magic; A Change of Seasons; The Elephant Man; The Bounty; The Good Father; 84 Charing Cross Road; The Dawning; A Chorus of Disapproval; Desperate Hours; The Silence of the Lambs; Freejack; Howards End; The Efficiency Expert; Bram Stoker's Dracula; Chaplin; The Innocent (1993); The Remains of the Day; Shadowlands (1993); The Road to Wellville; Legends of the Fall; Nixon; August (also dir, mus); Surviving Picasso; The Edge; Amistad; The Mask of Zorro; Meet Joe Black; Instinct; Titus; Mission: Impossible II; How the Grinch Stole Christmas (narr); Hannibal (2001); Hearts in Atlantis; Bad Company (2002); Red Dragon; The Human Stain; Alexander; Proof (2005); The World's Fastest Indian; All the King's Men (2006); Bobby; Fracture; Slipstream (2007; also dir, scr, mus); Shortcut to Happiness; Beowulf; The City of Your Final Destination; The Wolfman (2010); You Will Meet a Tall Dark Stranger; The Rite (2011); Thor

Hopper, Dennis: I Died a Thousand Times; Rebel Without a Cause; Giant; Gunfight at the O.K. Corral; The Story of Mankind; Night Tide; The Sons of Katie Elder; Planet of Blood; Cool Hand Luke; The Trip; The Glory Stompers; Panic in the City; Hang 'Em High; Easy Rider (also dir, coscr); True Grit (1969); The Last Movie (also dir); Kid Blue; Mad Dog Morgan; Tracks; The American Friend; Apocalypse Now; Out of the Blue (1980; also dir); King of the Mountain; Human Highway; The Osterman Weekend; Rumble Fish; My Science Project; Riders of the Storm; The Texas Chainsaw Massacre 2; Blue Velvet; Hoosiers; Black Widow (1986); River's Edge (1986); Straight to Hell; O.C. and Stiggs; The Pick-up Artist; Colors (1988; dir); Blood Red; Backtrack (1989; also dir); Flashback; Chattahoochee; The Hot Spot (dir); Superstar: The Life and Times of Andy Warhol; Paris Trout; The Indian Runner; Eye of the Storm; Nails; Boiling Point; Super Mario Bros.; Red Rock West; True Romance; Chasers (also dir); Speed; Search and Destroy (1995); Waterworld; Carried Away; Basquiat; The Last Days of Frankie the Fly; Meet the Deedles; Ed TV; Jesus' Son; The Source (app); Inside Deep Throat (narr); Land of the Dead; Sketches of Frank Gehry (app); Sleepwalking; Hell Ride; Elegy; Swing Vote; An American Carol; Alpha and Omega

Hudson, Rock: Winchester '73; Bright

Victory; Has Anybody Seen My Gal?; Bend of the River; Here Come the Nelsons; Horizons West; The Lawless Breed; Gun Fury; Seminole; The Golden Blade; Back to God's Country; Taza, Son of Cochise; Bengal Brigade; Magnificent Obsession (1954); Captain Lightfoot; All That Heaven Allows; Never Say Goodbye; Written on the Wind; Four Girls in Town (cameo); Giant; Battle Hymn; A Farewell to Arms (1957); Something of Value; The Tarnished Angels; Twilight for the Gods; This Earth Is Mine; Pillow Talk; The Last Sunset; Lover Come Back (1961); Come September; The Spiral Road; A Gathering of Eagles; Send Me No Flowers; Man's Favorite Sport?; Strange Bedfellows; A Very Special Favor; Blindfold; Seconds; Tobruk; Ice Station Zebra; A Fine Pair; The Undefeated; Darling Lili; Hornets' Nest; Pretty Maids All in a Row; Showdown (1973); Embryo; Avalanche (1978); The Mirror Crack'd; The Ambassador

Irons, Jeremy: Langrishe, Go Down; Nijinsky; The French Lieutenant's Woman; Moonlighting; Betrayal; The Wild Duck; Swann in Love; The Mission; Dead Ringers; A Chorus of Disapproval; Reversal of Fortune; Kafka; Damage; Waterland; M. Butterfly; The House of the Spirits; The Lion King; Die Hard With a Vengeance; Stealing Beauty; Chinese Box; Lolita (1997); The Man in the Iron Mask (1998); Dungeons & Dragons; The Time Machine (2002); And Now ... Ladies and Gentlemen . . .; Broadway: The Golden Age (app); Callas Forever; The Merchant of Venice; Being Julia; Kingdom of Heaven; Casanova (2005); Inland Empire; Eragon; Appaloosa (2008); Hamlet 2 (uncred narr); The Pink Panther 2

Jackman, Hugh: X-Men; Someone Like You; Swordfish; Kate & Leopold; X2; Van Helsing; X-Men: The Last Stand; Scoop; The Fountain; The Prestige; Flushed Away; Happy Feet; Deception (2008); Australia; X-Men Origins: Wolverine

Jackson, Samuel L. (formerly billed as Sam): Ragtime; Eddie Murphy Raw (bit); School Daze; Coming to America; Sea of Love; Do the Right Thing; A Shock to the System; The Return of Superfly (cameo); Mo' Better Blues; GoodFellas; The Exorcist III (bit); Def by Temptation; Betsy's Wedding (bit); Strictly Business; Jungle Fever; Johnny Suede; Jumpin at the Boneyard; Patriot Games; Juice; White Sands; National Lampoon's Loaded Weapon I; True Romance; The Meteor Man (cameo); Menace II Society; Jurassic Park; Amos & Andrew; Pulp Fiction; The New Age; Fresh; Losing Isaiah; Kiss of Death (1995); Die Hard With a Vengeance; Fluke; The Great White Hype; A Time to Kill; The Long Kiss Goodnight; The Search for One-Eyed Jimmy; Trees Lounge; Hard Eight; one eight seven; Eve's Bayou; Jackie Brown; Sphere; The Negotiator; Out of Sight (1998; cameo); Star Wars

Episode I: The Phantom Menace; The Red Violin; Deep Blue Sea; Rules of Engagement; Shaft (2000); Unbreakable; The Caveman's Valentine; Changing Lanes; Star Wars Episode II: Attack of the Clones; Formula 51; No Good Deed; XXX; Basic; S.W.A.T.; Twisted (2004); Kill Bill Vol. 2; The Incredibles; Coach Carter; In My Country; XXX: State of the Union; Star Wars Episode III: Revenge of the Sith; The Man (2005); Freedomland; Snakes on a Plane; Home of the Brave (2006); Black Snake Moan; Resurrecting the Champ; 1408; Cleaner; Jumper; Iron Man (cameo); Lakeview Terrace; The Clone Wars; Soul Men; The Spirit; Inglourious Basterds (narr); Astro Boy; Mother and Child; Unthinkable; Iron Man 2; The Other Guys; African Cats (narr); Thor (cameo)

Johansson, Scarlett: North; Just Cause; If Lucy Fell; Manny & Lo; Home Alone 3; The Horse Whisperer; The Man Who Wasn't There; Ghost World; An American Rhapsody; Eight Legged Freaks; Lost in Translation; Girl With a Pearl Earring; The Perfect Score; A Love Song for Bobby Long; A Good Woman; The SpongeBob SquarePants Movie; In Good Company; The Island (2005); Match Point; Scoop; The Black Dahlia; The Prestige; The Nanny Diaries; The Other Boleyn Girl; Vicky Cristina Barcelona; The Spirit; He's Just Not That Into You; Iron Man 2

Jolie, Angelina: Lookin' to Get Out; Hackers; Love Is All There Is; Foxfire (1996); Playing God; Playing by Heart; Pushing Tin; The Bone Collector; Girl, Interrupted; Gone in Sixty Seconds (2000); Lara Croft Tomb Raider; Original Sin; Life or Something Like It; Lara Croft Tomb Raider: The Cradle of Life; Beyond Borders; Taking Lives; Shark Tale; Sky Captain and the World of Tomorrow; Alexander; Mr. & Mrs. Smith (2005); The Good Shepherd; Beowulf; A Mighty Heart; Kung Fu Panda; Wanted; Changeling (2008); Salt; The Tourist; Kung Fu Panda 2

Jones, Tommy Lee: Love Story (1970); Jackson County Jail; Rolling Thunder; The Betsy; Eyes of Laura Mars; Coal Miner's Daughter; Back Roads; Nate and Hayes; The River Rat; Black Moon Rising; The Big Town; Stormy Monday; The Package; Fire Birds (1990); JFK; Under Siege; House of Cards (1993); The Fugitive (1993); Heaven & Earth; Blown Away; Natural Born Killers; The Client; Blue Sky; Cobb; Batman Forever; Volcano (1997); Men in Black; U.S. Marshals; Small Soldiers; Double Jeopardy; Rules of Engagement; Space Cowboys; Men in Black II; The Hunted (2003); The Missing (2003); Man of the House (2005); The Three Burials of Melquiades Estrada (also dir); A Prairie Home Companion; In the Valley of Elah; No Country for Old Men; In the Electric Mist; The Company Men

Karloff, Boris: The Criminal Code; Five Star Final; Frankenstein; Scarface (1932); The Old Dark House (1932); The Mask of Fu Manchu; The Mummy (1932); The Lost Patrol; The Black Cat (1934); Bride of Frankenstein; The Black Room; The Raven (1935); The Invisible Ray; Son of Frankenstein; The Man They Could Not Hang; Tower of London (1939); Black Friday; The Man With Nine Lives; The Boogie Man Will Get You; The Climax; House of Frankenstein (1944); The Body Snatcher; Isle of the Dead; Bedlam (1946); The Secret Life of Walter Mitty; Lured; Unconquered; Abbott and Costello Meet the Killer Boris Karloff; The Strange Door; The Black Castle; Abbott and Costello Meet Dr. Jekyll and Mr. Hyde; Voodoo Island; The Haunted Strangler; Frankenstein—1970; Corridors of Blood; The Raven (1963); The Terror; Black Sabbath; The Comedy of Terrors; Bikini Beach (cameo); Die, Monster, Die!; The Ghost in the Invisible Bikini; The Daydreamer; The Venetian Affair; The Sorcerers; Cauldron of Blood; Mad Monster Party?; Targets; Curse of the Crimson Altar; Snake People; The Fear Chamber; House of Evil; Sinister Invasion

Kaye, Danny: Up in Arms; Wonder Man; The Kid From Brooklyn; The Secret Life of Walter Mitty; A Song Is Born; It's a Great Feeling (cameo); The Inspector General; On the Riviera; Hans Christian Andersen; Knock on Wood; White Christmas; The Court Jester; Me and the Colonel; The Five Pennies; On the Double; The Man From the Diners' Club; The Madwoman of Chaillot

Keaton, Buster: Three Ages; Our Hospitality (also codir); Sherlock Jr.; The Navigator (also dir); Seven Chances; Battling Butler (also codir); The General (also codir); College; Steamboat Bill, Jr.; The Cameraman; The Hollywood Revue of 1929; Spite Marriage; Hollywood Cavalcade; Forever and a Day; In the Good Old Summertime; Sunset Blvd. (cameo); Limelight; Around the World in Eighty Days (1956; cameo); The Adventures of Huckleberry Finn; It's a Mad Mad Mad Mad World; Pajama Party; Beach Blanket Bingo; How to Stuff a Wild Bikini; War, Italian Style; A Funny Thing Happened on the Way to the Forum

Keaton, Diane: Lovers and Other Strangers; The Godfather; Play It Again, Sam; Sleeper; The Godfather Part II; Love and Death; I Will, I Will . . . for Now; Harry and Walter Go to New York; Looking for Mr. Goodbar; Annie Hall; Interiors; Manhattan; Reds; Shoot the Moon; The Little Drummer Girl; Mrs. Soffel; Crimes of the Heart; Radio Days; Heaven (1987; dir); Baby Boom; The Good Mother; The Lemon Sisters; The Godfather Part III; Father of the Bride (1991); Manhattan Murder Mystery; Look Who's Talking Now; Unstrung Heroes (dir); Father of the Bride Part II; The First Wives Club; Marvin's Room; The Only Thrill; The Other Sister; Hanging Up (also dir); Town & Country; Something's Gotta Give; The Family Stone; Because I Said So; Mama's Boy; Mad Money; Smother; Morning Glory (2010)

Kelly, Gene: For Me and My Gal; Pilot #5; DuBarry Was a Lady; Thousands Cheer; The Cross of Lorraine; Cover Girl; Christmas Holiday; Anchors Aweigh; Ziegfeld Follies; Living in a Big Way; The Pirate; The Three Musketeers (1948); Words and Music; Take Me Out to the Ball Game; On the Town (also codir); Black Hand; Summer Stock; An American in Paris; It's a Big Country; Love Is Better Than Ever (cameo); Singin' in the Rain (also codir); The Devil Makes Three; Brigadoon; Crest of the Wave; Deep in My Heart (cameo); It's Always Fair Weather (also codir); Invitation to the Dance (also dir); The Happy Road (also dir); Les Girls; The Tunnel of Love (dir); Marjorie Morningstar; Let's Make Love (cameo); Inherit the Wind; Gigot (dir); What a Way to Go!; The Young Girls of Rochefort; A Guide for the Married Man (dir); Hello, Dolly! (dir); The Cheyenne Social Club (dir, prod); 40 Carats; That's Entertainment!; That's Entertainment, Part 2; Viva Knievel!; Xanadu; That's Dancing!; That's Entertainment! III; Cats Don't Dance (choreography consultant)

Kelly, Grace: Fourteen Hours; High Noon; Mogambo; Dial M for Murder; Rear Window; The Country Girl; Green Fire; The Bridges at Toko-Ri; To Catch a Thief; The Swan; High Society (1956); The Children of Theatre Street

Kerr, Deborah: Major Barbara; The Life and Death of Colonel Blimp; Vacation From Marriage; Black Narcissus; The Hucksters; If Winter Comes; Edward, My Son; King Solomon's Mines (1950); Quo Vadis; The Prisoner of Zenda (1952); Thunder in the East; Young Bess; Julius Caesar (1953); Dream Wife; From Here to Eternity; The End of the Affair; The Proud and Profane; The King and I; Tea and Sympathy; Heaven Knows, Mr. Allison; An Affair to Remember; Bonjour Tristesse; Separate Tables; The Journey; Count Your Blessings; Beloved Infidel; The Sundowners (1960); The Grass Is Greener; The Naked Edge; The Innocents; The Chalk Garden; The Night of the Iguana; Marriage on the Rocks; Eye of the Devil; Casino Royale (1967); Prudence and the Pill; The Gypsy Moths; The Arrangement; The Assam Garden

Kidman, Nicole: Bush Christmas; BMX Bandits; Windrider; Watch the Shadows Dance; Dead Calm; Days of Thunder; Flirting; Billy Bathgate; Far and Away; My Life; Malice; To Die For (1995); Batman Forever; The Portrait of a Lady; The Peacemaker (1997); Practical Magic; Eyes Wide Shut; Moulin Rouge! (2001); The Others; Birthday Girl; Panic Room (voice cameo);

The Hours; The Human Stain; Cold Mountain; Dogville; The Stepford Wives (2004); Birth; The Interpreter; Bewitched (2005); Happy Feet; Fur: An Imaginary Portrait of Diane Arbus; God Grew Tired of Us (narr); The Invasion (2007); Margot at the Wedding; The Golden Compass; Australia; Nine; Rabbit Hole; Just Go With It

Kingsley, Ben: Fear Is the Key; Gandhi; Betrayal; Turtle Diary; Harem; Silas Marner; Maurice; Pascali's Island; Without a Clue; Testimony; Slipstream (1989); The Children; The Fifth Monkey; Bugsy; Freddie as F.R.O.7; Sneakers; Dave; Searching for Bobby Fischer; Schindler's List; Death and the Maiden; Species; Twelfth Night; The Assignment (1997); What Planet Are You From?; Rules of Engagement; Sexy Beast; AI Artificial Intelligence (narr); Triumph of Love; Tuck Everlasting (2002); House of Sand and Fog; Thunderbirds (2004); Suspect Zero; A Sound of Thunder; Oliver Twist (2005); Lucky Number Slevin; The Last Legion; You Kill Me; The Wackness; Transsiberian; Elegy; War, Inc.; The Love Guru; Shutter Island; Prince of Persia: The Sands of Time; Fifty Dead Men Walking

Kinnear, Greg: Blankman; Sabrina (1995); Dear God; Beavis and Butt-head Do America (uncred); A Smile Like Yours; As Good As It Gets; You've Got Mail; Mystery Men; What Planet Are You From?; Nurse Betty; Loser; The Gift (2000); Someone Like You; We Were Soldiers; Auto Focus; Stuck on You; Godsend (2004); The Matador; Robots; Bad News Bears (2005); Fast Food Nation; Little Miss Sunshine; Invincible (2006); Unknown (2006); Feast of Love; Baby Mama; Ghost Town (2008); Flash of Genius; Green Zone; The Last Song

Knightley, Keira: Star Wars: Episode I—The Phantom Menace; The Hole; Bend It Like Beckham; Pirates of the Caribbean: The Curse of the Black Pearl; Love Actually; King Arthur; The Jacket; Pride & Prejudice (2005); Domino; Pirates of the Caribbean: Dead Man's Chest; Pirates of the Caribbean: At World's End; Atonement; Silk; The Duchess; The Edge of Love; Never Let Me Go (2010); Last Night (2011)

Ladd, Alan: Pigskin Parade (bit); The Howards of Virginia (bit); Great Guns; Citizen Kane; The Black Cat (1941); This Gun for Hire; The Glass Key (1942); Star Spangled Rhythm (cameo); Duffy's Tavern (cameo); The Blue Dahlia; Two Years Before the Mast; Variety Girl (cameo); My Favorite Brunette (cameo); Beyond Glory; The Great Gatsby (1949); Branded; Thunder in the East; Shane; Botany Bay; Boy on a Dolphin; The Deep Six; The Proud Rebel; The Badlanders; The Carpetbaggers

Lancaster, Burt: The Killers (1946); Variety Girl (cameo); Brute Force; I Walk Alone; All My Sons; Sorry, Wrong Number; Kiss the Blood off My Hands; Criss Cross; Rope of Sand; The Flame and the Arrow; Mister 880; Vengeance Valley; Jim Thorpe—All American; Ten Tall Men; The Crimson Pirate; Come Back, Little Sheba; From Here to Eternity; His Majesty O'Keefe; Apache; Vera Cruz; The Kentuckian (also dir); The Rose Tattoo; Trapeze; The Rainmaker (1956); Gunfight at the O.K. Corral; Sweet Smell of Success; Run Silent, Run Deep; Separate Tables; The Devil's Disciple; The Unforgiven (1960); Elmer Gantry; The Young Savages; Judgment at Nuremberg; Birdman of Alcatraz; A Child Is Waiting; The List of Adrian Messenger (cameo); The Leopard; Seven Days in May; The Train; The Hallelujah Trail; The Professionals; The Scalphunters; The Swimmer; Castle Keep; The Gypsy Moths; King: A Filmed Record . . . Montgomery to Memphis (narr); Airport; Lawman; Valdez Is Coming; Ulzana's Raid; Scorpio; Executive Action; The Midnight Man; Conversation Piece; 1900; Buffalo Bill and the Indians, or Sitting Bull's History Lesson; The Cassandra Crossing; Twilight's Last Gleaming; The Island of Dr. Moreau (1977); Go Tell the Spartans; Zulu Dawn; Cattle Annie and Little Britches; Atlantic City (1980); La Pelle; Local Hero; The Osterman Weekend; Little Treasure; Tough Guys; Rocket Gibraltar; The Jeweller's Shop; Field of Dreams

Lange, Jessica: King Kong (1976); All That Jazz; How to Beat the High Co$t of Living; The Postman Always Rings Twice (1981); Tootsie; Frances; Country; Sweet Dreams; Crimes of the Heart; Everybody's All-American; Far North; Music Box; Men Don't Leave; Cape Fear (1991); Night and the City (1992); Blue Sky; Losing Isaiah; Rob Roy; A Thousand Acres; Hush; Cousin Bette; Titus; Masked and Anonymous; Big Fish; Prozac Nation; Broken Flowers; Neverwas; Don't Come Knocking; Bonneville

Lansbury, Angela: Gaslight (1944); National Velvet; The Picture of Dorian Gray; The Harvey Girls; The Hoodlum Saint; Till the Clouds Roll By; The Private Affairs of Bel Ami; If Winter Comes; Tenth Avenue Angel; State of the Union; The Three Musketeers (1948); The Red Danube; Samson and Delilah (1949); The Court Jester; The Long Hot Summer; The Reluctant Debutante; The Dark at the Top of the Stairs; A Breath of Scandal; Blue Hawaii; All Fall Down; The Manchurian Candidate (1962); In the Cool of the Day; The World of Henry Orient; Dear Heart; The Greatest Story Ever Told (cameo); The Amorous Adventures of Moll Flanders; Harlow (Carroll Baker version); Mister Buddwing; Something for Everyone; Bedknobs and Broomsticks; Death on the Nile; The Lady Vanishes (1979); The Mirror Crack'd; The Last Unicorn; The Pirates of Penzance; The Company of Wolves; Beauty and the Beast (1991); Anastasia (1997); Fantasia 2000; Broadway:

The Golden Age (app); Nanny McPhee; Mr. Popper's Penguins

Laughton, Charles: The Old Dark House (1932); The Sign of the Cross; If I Had a Million; Island of Lost Souls; The Private Life of Henry VIII; The Barretts of Wimpole Street (1934); Ruggles of Red Gap; Les Misérables (1935); Mutiny on the Bounty (1935); Rembrandt; Sidewalks of London; Jamaica Inn; The Hunchback of Notre Dame (1939); They Knew What They Wanted; Tales of Manhattan; Forever and a Day; This Land Is Mine; The Canterville Ghost; The Suspect; The Paradine Case; Arch of Triumph; The Big Clock; The Bribe; The Blue Veil; The Strange Door; O. Henry's Full House; Abbott and Costello Meet Captain Kidd; Salome; Young Bess; Hobson's Choice; The Night of the Hunter (dir); Witness for the Prosecution; Spartacus; Advise & Consent

Laurel & Hardy: The Hollywood Revue of 1929 (cameos); The Devil's Brother; Sons of the Desert; Hollywood Party (cameos); Babes in Toyland (1934); Bonnie Scotland; The Bohemian Girl; Our Relations; Way Out West; Swiss Miss; Block-Heads; The Flying Deuces; A Chump at Oxford; Great Guns; Utopia; *features with Oliver Hardy without Stan Laurel:* The Fighting Kentuckian; Riding High (1950)

Law, Jude: Shopping; Bent; Wilde; Gattaca; Midnight in the Garden of Good and Evil; eXistenZ; The Talented Mr. Ripley; Enemy at the Gates; AI Artificial Intelligence; Road to Perdition; Cold Mountain; i ♥ Huckabees; Sky Captain and the World of Tomorrow; Alfie (2004); Closer; The Aviator (2004); Lemony Snicket's A Series of Unfortunate Events (narr); All the King's Men (2006); The Holiday (2006); Breaking and Entering; Sleuth (2007); My Blueberry Nights; The Imaginarium of Doctor Parnassus; Sherlock Holmes (2009); Repo Men

Ledger, Heath: 10 Things I Hate About You; Two Hands; The Patriot (2000); A Knight's Tale; Monster's Ball; The Four Feathers (2002); Ned Kelly (2003); The Order; Lords of Dogtown; The Brothers Grimm; Brokeback Mountain; Casanova (2005); Candy (2006); I'm Not There; The Dark Knight; The Imaginarium of Doctor Parnassus

Lee, Bruce: The Wrecking Crew (karate advisor); Marlowe; Fists of Fury; The Chinese Connection; Enter the Dragon; Return of the Dragon (also dir); Game of Death; Circle of Iron (costy)

Lee, Christopher: Hamlet (1948; bit); Scott of the Antarctic; Captain Horatio Hornblower; Valley of the Eagles; The Crimson Pirate; Moulin Rouge (1952); That Lady; The Warriors (1955); Pursuit of the Graf Spee; The Curse of Frankenstein; Bitter Victory; A Tale of Two Cities (1958); Horror of Dracula; The Hound of the Baskervilles (1959); The Mummy (1959); Too Hot to Handle (1960); Wild for Kicks; The Two Faces of Dr. Jekyll; Horror Hotel (1960); The Hands of Orlac; The Puzzle of the Red Orchid; Hercules in the Haunted World; Corridors of Blood; The Whip and the Body; Horror Castle; The Gorgon; Dr. Terror's House of Horrors; She (1965); The Skull; The Face of Fu Manchu; Dracula—Prince of Darkness; Rasputin—the Mad Monk; The Brides of Fu Manchu; Psycho-Circus; Theatre of Death; The Torture Chamber of Dr. Sadism; The Vengeance of Fu Manchu; Five Golden Dragons; Island of the Burning Doomed; The Devil's Bride; Dracula Has Risen From The Grave; The Crimson Cult; The Blood of Fu Manchu; The Oblong Box; The Magic Christian (cameo); The Castle of Fu Manchu; Scream and Scream Again; Taste the Blood of Dracula; One More Time (cameo); Night of the Blood Monster; Julius Caesar (1970); The Private Life of Sherlock Holmes; Scars of Dracula; The House That Dripped Blood; Count Dracula; Hannie Caulder; I, Monster; Dracula A.D. 1972; Horror Express; Raw Meat (cameo); Nothing but the Night; The Wicker Man (1973); The Creeping Flesh; Count Dracula and His Vampire Bride; The Three Musketeers (1974); The Man With the Golden Gun; Dark Places; Diagnosis: Murder; Killer Force; The Four Musketeers; To the Devil a Daughter; Dracula and Son; Airport '77; End of the World; Starship Invasions; Return From Witch Mountain; Caravans; The Passage; Jaguar Lives!; An Arabian Adventure; Bear Island; 1941; Circle of Iron; Serial; The Salamander; An Eye for an Eye (1981); The Last Unicorn; The Return of Captain Invincible; House of the Long Shadows; The Rosebud Beach Hotel; Howling II: Your Sister Is a Werewolf; Jocks; The Return of the Musketeers; Gremlins 2 The New Batch; Honeymoon Academy; Curse III: Blood Sacrifice; The Rainbow Thief; Police Academy VII: Mission to Moscow; The Stupids; Jinnah; Sleepy Hollow; The Lord of the Rings: The Fellowship of the Ring; Star Wars Episode II: Attack of the Clones; The Lord of the Rings: The Two Towers; The Lord of the Rings: The Return of the King (extended version only); Star Wars Episode III: Revenge of the Sith; Charlie and the Chocolate Factory; Tim Burton's Corpse Bride; The Golden Compass; The Clone Wars; Boogie Woogie; Triage; Alice in Wonderland (2010); The Resident; Season of the Witch

Leigh, Janet: If Winter Comes; Hills of Home; Words and Music; Act of Violence; Little Women (1949); That Forsyte Woman; The Red Danube; Holiday Affair; Angels in the Outfield (1951); Scaramouche; The Naked Spur; Houdini; Prince Valiant; Living It Up; The Black Shield of Falworth; Pete Kelly's Blues; My Sister Eileen (1955); Jet Pilot; Touch of Evil; The Vikings; The Perfect Furlough; Who Was That Lady?; Psycho (1960); Pepe (cameo); The Manchurian Candidate (1962); Bye Bye Birdie; Wives and Lovers; Kid Rodelo; Harper; Three on a Couch; An American Dream; Grand Slam (1968); Hello Down There; One Is a Lonely Number; Night of the Lepus; Boardwalk; The Fog (1980); Halloween H2O: 20 Years Later

Leigh, Vivien: A Yank at Oxford; Sidewalks of London; Gone With the Wind; Waterloo Bridge (1940); That Hamilton Woman; Caesar and Cleopatra; Anna Karenina (1948); A Streetcar Named Desire; The Deep Blue Sea; The Roman Spring of Mrs. Stone; Ship of Fools

Lemmon, Jack: It Should Happen to You; Phffft!; Three for the Show; Mister Roberts; My Sister Eileen (1955); Fire Down Below; Operation Mad Ball; Cowboy; Bell, Book and Candle; Some Like It Hot (1959); It Happened to Jane; The Apartment; Pepe (cameo); The Wackiest Ship in the Army; The Notorious Landlady; Days of Wine and Roses; Irma la Douce; Under the Yum Yum Tree; Good Neighbor Sam; How to Murder Your Wife; The Great Race; The Fortune Cookie; Luv; The Odd Couple; The April Fools; The Out of Towners (1970); Kotch (dir, cameo); The War Between Men and Women; Avanti!; Save the Tiger; The Front Page (1974); The Prisoner of Second Avenue; Alex and the Gypsy; Airport '77; The China Syndrome; Tribute; Buddy Buddy; Missing; Mass Appeal; Macaroni; That's Life!; Dad; JFK; The Player (cameo); Glengarry Glen Ross; Short Cuts; Grumpy Old Men; Grumpier Old Men; Getting Away With Murder; The Grass Harp; My Fellow Americans; Hamlet (1996); Out to Sea; The Odd Couple II; The Legend of Bagger Vance (uncred)

Lewis, Jerry: My Friend Irma; At War With the Army; My Friend Irma Goes West; That's My Boy; Sailor Beware; Road to Bali (cameo); Jumping Jacks; The Stooge; Scared Stiff (1953); The Caddy; Money From Home; Living It Up; Three Ring Circus; You're Never Too Young; Artists and Models (1955); Pardners; Hollywood or Bust; The Delicate Delinquent; The Sad Sack; Rock-a-Bye Baby; The Geisha Boy; Lil'l Abner (1959; cameo); Don't Give Up the Ship; Visit to a Small Planet; The Bellboy (also dir, scr); Cinderfella; The Ladies Man (1961; also dir, scr); The Errand Boy (also dir, coscr); It's Only Money; It's a Mad Mad Mad Mad World (cameo); The Nutty Professor (1963; also dir, coscr); Who's Minding the Store?; The Patsy (also dir, coscr); The Disorderly Orderly; The Family Jewels (also dir, coscr); Boeing Boeing; Three on a Couch (also dir, coscr); Way . . . Way Out; The Big Mouth (also dir, coscr); Don't Raise the Bridge, Lower the River; Hook, Line, and Sinker; One More Time (dir); Which Way to the Front? (also dir); Hardly Working (also dir, coscr); The King

of Comedy; Cracking Up (also dir, coscr); Slapstick of Another Kind; Cookie; Mr. Saturday Night (cameo); Arizona Dream; Funny Bones

Linney, Laura: Lorenzo's Oil; Dave; Searching for Bobby Fischer; A Simple Twist of Fate; Congo; Primal Fear; Absolute Power; The Truman Show; You Can Count on Me; The House of Mirth; Maze (2000); The Mothman Prophecies; The Life of David Gale; Mystic River; Love Actually; Kinsey; p.s.; The Exorcism of Emily Rose; The Squid and the Whale; Driving Lessons; Man of the Year; Breach; Jindabyne; The Hottest State; The Nanny Diaries; The Savages (2007); The Other Man; The City of Your Final Destination; Sympathy for Delicious

Lloyd, Harold: Safety Last; Why Worry?; The Freshman (1925); For Heaven's Sake (1926); The Kid Brother; Movie Crazy; The Sin of Harold Diddlebock

Lombard, Carole: No Man of Her Own (1932); The Eagle and the Hawk (1933); We're Not Dressing; Twentieth Century; Hands Across the Table; My Man Godfrey (1936); Swing High, Swing Low; Nothing Sacred; Made For Each Other; In Name Only; Vigil in the Night; They Knew What They Wanted; Mr. & Mrs. Smith (1941); To Be or Not to Be (1942)

Lopez, Jennifer: My Little Girl; Lambada; My Family/Mi Familia; Money Train; Jack; Blood and Wine; Selena; Anaconda; U Turn; Out of Sight (1998); Antz; The Cell; The Wedding Planner; Angel Eyes (2001); Enough; Maid in Manhattan; Gigli; Jersey Girl; Shall We Dance (2004); Monster-in-Law; An Unfinished Life; Bordertown; El Cantante; Feel the Noise (cameo); The Back-up Plan

Loren, Sophia: Variety Lights (bit); Anna (1951; bit); Quo Vadis (extra); Gold of Naples; Boy on a Dolphin; The Pride and the Passion; Legend of the Lost; Desire Under the Elms; The Key (1958); Houseboat; The Black Orchid; That Kind of Woman; Heller in Pink Tights; It Started in Naples; A Breath of Scandal; The Millionairess; Two Women; El Cid; Boccaccio '70; The Condemned of Altona; Yesterday, Today and Tomorrow; The Fall of the Roman Empire; Marriage-Italian Style; Operation Crossbow; Lady L; Judith; Arabesque; A Countess From Hong Kong; More Than a Miracle; Ghosts—Italian Style; Sunflower; The Priest's Wife; Lady Liberty; Man of La Mancha; White Sister; The Voyage; Jury of One; The Cassandra Crossing; A Special Day; Brass Target; Blood Feud; Firepower; Angela (1984); Ready to Wear (Prêt-à-Porter); Grumpier Old Men; Between Strangers; Nine

Lorre, Peter: M (1931); The Man Who Knew Too Much (1934); Mad Love (1935); The Secret Agent (1936); Strange Cargo; Stranger on the Third Floor; The Face Behind the Mask; They Met in Bombay;

The Maltese Falcon (1941); All Through the Night; The Boogie Man Will Get You; Casablanca; Background to Danger; The Cross of Lorraine; Passage to Marseille; The Mask of Dimitrios; Arsenic and Old Lace; Hollywood Canteen (cameo); Three Strangers; The Verdict (1946); The Beast With Five Fingers; My Favorite Brunette; Casbah; Rope of Sand; Beat the Devil; 20,000 Leagues Under the Sea; Around the World in Eighty Days (1956; cameo); The Buster Keaton Story; Silk Stockings; The Story of Mankind (cameo); The Sad Sack; Big Circus; Voyage to the Bottom of the Sea; Tales of Terror; Five Weeks in a Balloon; The Raven (1963); The Comedy of Terrors; Muscle Beach Party (cameo); The Patsy

Loy, Myrna: Ben-Hur (1926; bit); The Jazz Singer (1927); Arrowsmith; Love Me Tonight; The Mask of Fu Manchu; Topaze; Manhattan Melodrama; The Thin Man; Broadway Bill; Wife vs. Secretary; The Great Ziegfeld; Libeled Lady; After the Thin Man; Double Wedding; Test Pilot; Too Hot to Handle (1938); The Rains Came; Another Thin Man; I Love You Again; Shadow of the Thin Man; The Thin Man Goes Home; The Best Years of Our Lives; The Bachelor and the Bobby-Soxer; Song of the Thin Man; Mr. Blandings Builds His Dream House; The Red Pony; Cheaper by the Dozen (1950); Belles on Their Toes; The Ambassador's Daughter; Lonelyhearts; From the Terrace; Midnight Lace; The April Fools; Airport 1975; The End; Just Tell Me What You Want

Lugosi, Bela: Dracula (1931); Murders in the Rue Morgue (1932); White Zombie; Island of Lost Souls; International House; The Black Cat (1934); Mark of the Vampire; The Raven (1935); The Invisible Ray; Son of Frankenstein; Ninotchka; Black Friday; The Black Cat (1941); The Wolf Man (1941); The Ghost of Frankenstein; Frankenstein Meets the Wolf Man; The Return of the Vampire; The Body Snatcher; Genius at Work; Abbott and Costello Meet Frankenstein; Bela Lugosi Meets a Brooklyn Gorilla; Glen or Glenda?; Bride of the Monster; The Black Sleep; Plan 9 From Outer Space

MacDonald, Jeanette: The Love Parade; Monte Carlo; One Hour With You; Love Me Tonight; The Merry Widow (1934); Naughty Marietta; Rose Marie (1936); San Francisco; Maytime; The Firefly; The Girl of the Golden West; Sweethearts; Broadway Serenade; New Moon; Bitter Sweet (1940); Smilin' Through (1941); I Married an Angel; Follow the Boys (1944; cameo); Three Daring Daughters

MacLaine, Shirley: The Trouble With Harry; Artists and Models (1955); Around the World in Eighty Days (1956); The Sheepman; The Matchmaker; Hot Spell; Some Came Running; Ask Any Girl; Career; Ocean's Eleven (1960; cameo);

Can-Can; The Apartment; All in a Night's Work; Two Loves; The Children's Hour; My Geisha; Two for the Seesaw; Irma la Douce; What a Way to Go!; The Yellow Rolls-Royce; John Goldfarb; Please Come Home; Gambit; Woman Times Seven; The Bliss of Mrs. Blossom; Sweet Charity; Two Mules for Sister Sara; Desperate Characters; The Possession of Joel Delaney; The Turning Point (1977); Being There; Loving Couples; A Change of Seasons; Terms of Endearment; Cannonball Run II; Madame Sousatzka; Steel Magnolias; Waiting for the Light; Postcards From the Edge; Defending Your Life (cameo); Used People; Wrestling Ernest Hemingway; Guarding Tess; The Celluloid Closet (app); Mrs. Winterbourne; The Evening Star; A Smile Like Yours (cameo); Get Bruce (app); Bruno (also dir); Carolina; Broadway: The Golden Age (app); Bewitched (2005); In Her Shoes; Rumor has it . . .; Valentine's Day

MacMurray, Fred: Alice Adams; Hands Across the Table; The Trail of the Lonesome Pine; Swing High, Swing Low; Cocoanut Grove; Remember the Night; Little Old New York; Too Many Husbands; Dive Bomber; The Lady Is Willing; Take a Letter, Darling; The Forest Rangers; Star Spangled Rhythm; Above Suspicion; Double Indemnity; Murder, He Says; Smoky (1946); The Egg and I; On Our Merry Way; The Miracle of the Bells; Callaway Went Thataway; The Moonlighter; The Caine Mutiny; Pushover; Woman's World; The Far Horizons; The Rains of Ranchipur; There's Always Tomorrow; The Shaggy Dog (1959); The Apartment; The Absent Minded Professor; Bon Voyage!; Son of Flubber; Kisses for My President; Follow Me, Boys!; The Happiest Millionaire; Charley and the Angel; The Swarm; George Stevens: A Filmmaker's Journey (app)

March, Fredric: The Wild Party (1929); Dr. Jekyll and Mr. Hyde (1932); The Sign of the Cross; The Eagle and the Hawk (1933); Design for Living; Death Takes a Holiday; The Barretts of Wimpole Street (1934); Les Miserables (1935); Anna Karenina (1935); Mary of Scotland; Anthony Adverse; A Star Is Born (1937); Nothing Sacred; The Buccaneer (1938); Susan and God; I Married a Witch; The Adventures of Mark Twain (1944); The Best Years of Our Lives; Another Part of the Forest; Christopher Columbus; Death of a Salesman; It's a Big Country; Man on a Tightrope; Executive Suite; The Bridges at Toko-Ri; The Desperate Hours (1955); Alexander the Great; The Man in the Gray Flannel Suit; Inherit the Wind; The Young Doctors; The Condemned of Altona; Seven Days in May; Hombre; . . . tick . . . tick . . . tick . . . ; The Iceman Cometh

Martin, Steve: Sgt. Pepper's Lonely Hearts Club Band; The Kids Are Alright; The Muppet Movie (cameo); The Jerk (also coscr); Pennies From Heaven; Dead Men Don't Wear Plaid (also coscr); The Man With Two Brains (also coscr); The Lonely Guy; All of Me (1984); Movers and Shakers; Little Shop of Horrors (1986); ¡Three Amigos! (also coscr); Roxanne (also adapt); Planes, Trains & Automobiles; Dirty Rotten Scoundrels; Parenthood; My Blue Heaven (1990); L.A. Story (also scr); Father of the Bride (1991); Grand Canyon; HouseSitter; Leap of Faith; A Simple Twist of Fate (also adapt); Mixed Nuts; Father of the Bride Part II; Sgt. Bilko; The Spanish Prisoner; The Prince of Egypt; The Out-of-Towners (1999); Bowfinger (also scr); Fantasia 2000 (app); Joe Gould's Secret; Novocaine; Bringing Down the House; Looney Tunes: Back in Action; Cheaper by the Dozen (2003); Jiminy Glick in La La Wood (cameo); Shopgirl (also adapt); Cheaper by the Dozen 2; The Pink Panther (2006; also coscr); Baby Mama; The Pink Panther 2 (also coscr); Traitor (costy); It's Complicated

Marvin, Lee: Teresa (bit); You're in the Navy Now; Hong Kong; We're Not Married; Diplomatic Courier; The Duel at Silver Creek; Seminole; The Big Heat; Gun Fury; The Wild One; Gorilla at Large; The Caine Mutiny; Bad Day at Black Rock; Violent Saturday; Not as a Stranger; Pete Kelly's Blues; I Died a Thousand Times; Shack Out on 101; Seven Men From Now; The Rack; Attack!; Raintree County; The Comancheros; The Man Who Shot Liberty Valance; Donovan's Reef; The Killers (1964); Cat Ballou; Ship of Fools; The Professionals; The Dirty Dozen; Point Blank; Sergeant Ryker; Hell in the Pacific; Paint Your Wagon; Monte Walsh; Pocket Money; Prime Cut; Emperor of the North; The Iceman Cometh; The Spikes Gang; The Klansman; Shout at the Devil; Great Scout and Cathouse Thursday; Avalanche Express; The Big Red One; Death Hunt; Gorky Park; Dog Day; The Delta Force

Marx Bros.: *all four:* The Cocoanuts; Animal Crackers; Monkey Business (1931); Horse Feathers; Duck Soup; *Groucho, Harpo; Chico only:* A Night at the Opera; A Day at the Races; Room Service; At the Circus; Go West (1940); The Big Store; A Night in Casablanca; Love Happy; The Story of Mankind; *Groucho only:* Copacabana; Mr. Music; Double Dynamite; A Girl in Every Port; Will Success Spoil Rock Hunter?; Skidoo

Mason, James: Hotel Reserve; The Seventh Veil; Odd Man Out; Caught (1949); Madame Bovary (1949); The Reckless Moment; East Side, West Side; The Desert Fox; Pandora and the Flying Dutchman; 5 Fingers; The Prisoner of Zenda (1952); The Story of Three Loves; The Desert Rats; Julius Caesar (1953); Botany Bay; Prince Valiant; A Star Is Born (1954); 20,000 Leagues Under the Sea; Forever, Darling; Bigger

Than Life; Island in the Sun; Cry Terror; North by Northwest; Journey to the Center of the Earth; The Trials of Oscar Wilde; Lolita; The Fall of the Roman Empire; The Pumpkin Eater; Lord Jim; Genghis Khan; The Blue Max; Georgy Girl; The Deadly Affair; Cop-Out; Duffy; The Sea Gull; Mayerling (1968); Age of Consent; Spring and Port Wine; Cold Sweat; Kill! Kill! Kill!; Bad Man's River; Child's Play (1972); The Last of Sheila; The Mackintosh Man; The Destructors (1974); 11 Harrowhouse; Inside Out (1975); The Flower in His Mouth; Autobiography of a Princess; Mandingo; Voyage of the Damned; Cross of Iron; Heaven Can Wait (1978); The Boys From Brazil; The Water Babies; The Passage; Murder by Decree; Bloodline; ffolkes; A Dangerous Summer; Evil Under the Sun; The Verdict (1982); Yellowbeard; The Shooting Party; The Assisi Underground

Mastroianni, Marcello: Les Misèrables (1947); White Nights (1957); Big Deal on Madonna Street; Where the Hot Wind Blows!; Bell'Antonio; La Dolce Vita; Divorce—Italian Style; La Notte; A Very Private Affair; 8½; The Organizer; Yesterday, Today and Tomorrow; Marriage-Italian Style; Casanova '70; The Tenth Victim; Shoot Loud, Louder . . . I Don't Understand; The Poppy Is Also a Flower; The Stranger (1967); Ghosts—Italian Style (cameo); A Place for Lovers; Diamonds for Breakfast; Sunflower; Leo the Last; The Priest's Wife; The Pizza Triangle; Fellini's Roma (cameo); It Only Happens to Others; What?; The Grande Bouffe; Massacre in Rome; Salut l'Artiste; We All Loved Each Other So Much (cameo); The Sunday Woman; A Special Day; Lunatics and Lovers; Wifemistress; Bye Bye Monkey; Stay As You Are; Blood Feud; The Divine Nymph; City of Women; La Pelle; La Nuit de Varennes; Beyond the Door (1982); Gabriela; The Story of Piera; Henry IV; Macaroni; Ginger and Fred; Dark Eyes; Intervista; Everybody's Fine; A Fine Romance; Used People; I Don't Want to Talk About It; Ready to Wear (Prêt-à-Porter); One Hundred and One Nights; Three Lives and Only One Death; Voyage to the Beginning of the World; Marcello Mastroianni: I Remember, Yes I Remember (app)

Matthau, Walter: The Kentuckian; The Indian Fighter; Bigger Than Life; A Face in the Crowd; King Creole; Gangster Story (also dir); Strangers When We Meet; Lonely Are the Brave; Who's Got the Action?; Charade; Ensign Pulver; Fail-Safe; Goodbye Charlie; Mirage; The Fortune Cookie; A Guide for the Married Man; The Odd Couple; The Secret Life of an American Wife; Candy; Hello, Dolly!; Cactus Flower; A New Leaf; Plaza Suite; Kotch; Pete 'n' Tillie; Charley Varrick; The Laughing Policeman; The Taking of Pelham One

[1625]

Two Three; Earthquake (cameo); The Front Page (1974); The Sunshine Boys; The Bad News Bears (1976); Casey's Shadow; House Calls; California Suite; Hopscotch; Little Miss Marker (1980); Buddy, Buddy; First Monday in October; I Ought to Be in Pictures; The Survivors; Movers and Shakers; Pirates; The Couch Trip; JFK (cameo); Dennis the Menace; Grumpy Old Men; I.Q.; Grumpier Old Men; The Grass Harp; I'm Not Rappaport; Out to Sea; The Odd Couple II; Hanging Up; The Life and Times of Hank Greenberg (app)

McCrea, Joel: The Lost Squadron; Bird of Paradise (1932); The Most Dangerous Game; Private Worlds; Barbary Coast; These Three; Come and Get It; Dead End; Union Pacific; Primrose Path; Foreign Correspondent; Sullivan's Travels; The Great Man's Lady; The Palm Beach Story; The More the Merrier; The Great Moment; The Virginian (1946); Four Faces West; South of St. Louis; Colorado Territory; Stars in My Crown; The Oklahoman; Ride the High Country; The Great American Cowboy; Mustang Country; George Stevens: A Filmmaker's Journey (app)

McGregor, Ewan: Being Human; Shallow Grave; Blue Juice; Trainspotting; The Pillow Book; Emma; Brassed Off; Nightwatch (1998); A Life Less Ordinary; Velvet Goldmine; Little Voice; Star Wars Episode I: The Phantom Menace; Eye of the Beholder; Moulin Rouge! (2001); Black Hawk Down; Star Wars Episode II: Attack of the Clones; Down With Love; Young Adam; Big Fish; Robots; Star Wars Episode III: Revenge of the Sith; The Island (2005); Valiant; Stay; Miss Potter; Alex Rider: Operation Stormbreaker; Cassandra's Dream; Deception (2008); Incendiary; Angels & Demons; The Men Who Stare at Goats; Amelia; The Ghost Writer; Nanny McPhee Returns; I Love You Phillip Morris; Beginners

McQueen, Steve: Somebody Up There Likes Me (bit); The Blob (1958); Never So Few; The Magnificent Seven; The Honeymoon Machine; Hell Is for Heroes; The War Lover; The Great Escape; Soldier in the Rain; Love With the Proper Stranger; Baby the Rain Must Fall; The Cincinnati Kid; Nevada Smith; The Sand Pebbles; The Thomas Crown Affair (1968); Bullitt; The Reivers; On Any Sunday (app); Le Mans; Junior Bonner; The Getaway (1972); Papillon; The Towering Inferno; An Enemy of the People (1979); Tom Horn; The Hunter

Midler, Bette: Hawaii (bit); The Rose; Divine Madness; Jinxed!; Down and Out in Beverly Hills; Ruthless People; Outrageous Fortune; Big Business; Oliver & Company; Beaches; Stella; Scenes From a Mall; For the Boys; Hocus Pocus; Get Shorty; The First Wives Club; That Old Feeling; Fantasia 2000 (app); Get Bruce (app); Isn't She Great; Drowning Mona; What Women Want

(uncred); The Stepford Wives (2004); Then She Found Me; The Women (2008); Cats & Dogs: The Revenge of Kitty Galore

Mifune, Toshiro: Stray Dog; Rashomon; The Idiot (1951); The Life of Oharu; Seven Samurai; Throne of Blood; The Lower Depths (1957); The Hidden Fortress; The Bad Sleep Well; Yojimbo; Sanjuro; Chushingura; High and Low; Red Beard; Grand Prix; Samurai Rebellion; Hell in the Pacific; Red Sun; Paper Tiger; Midway; Winter Kills; The Bushido Blade; 1941; Inchon!; The Challenge (1982); Shadow of the Wolf; Picture Bride

Minnelli, Liza: In the Good Old Summertime (as baby); Charlie Bubbles; The Sterile Cuckoo; Tell Me That You Love Me, Junie Moon; Cabaret; Journey Back to Oz; That's Entertainment! (app); Lucky Lady; A Matter of Time; Silent Movie; New York New York; Arthur (1981); The Muppets Take Manhattan (cameo); That's Dancing! (app); Rent-a-Cop; Arthur 2: On the Rocks; Stepping Out; The Oh in Ohio

Mirren, Helen: A Midsummer Night's Dream (1968); Age of Consent; Savage Messiah; O Lucky Man!; Caligula; Hussy; The Fiendish Plot of Dr. Fu Manchu; The Long Good Friday; Excalibur; Cal; 2010; The Gospel According to Vic; Coming Through; White Nights (1985); The Mosquito Coast; Pascali's Island; When the Whales Came; The Cook, The Thief, His Wife & Her Lover; Dr. Bethune; The Comfort of Strangers; Where Angels Fear to Tread; The Madness of King George; Some Mother's Son; Losing Chase; Critical Care; The Prince of Egypt; Teaching Mrs. Tingle; Greenfingers; The Pledge; No Such Thing; Last Orders; Gosford Park; Calendar Girls; The Clearing; Raising Helen; The Hitchhiker's Guide to the Galaxy; Shadowboxer; The Queen; National Treasure: Book of Secrets; Inkheart; State of Play; The Last Station; Love Ranch; Legend of the Guardians: The Owls of Ga'Hoole; Red (2010); The Tempest (2010); Arthur (2011)

Mitchum, Robert: The Human Comedy; Corvette K-225; Cry Havoc; Gung Ho!; Thirty Seconds Over Tokyo; The Story of G.I. Joe; Till the End of Time; Undercurrent; Pursued; Crossfire; Desire Me; Out of the Past; Rachel and the Stranger; Blood on the Moon; The Red Pony; The Big Steal; Holiday Affair; Where Danger Lives; His Kind of Woman; The Racket; Macao; The Lusty Men; Second Chance; Angel Face; White Witch Doctor; River of No Return; Track of the Cat; Not As a Stranger; Night of the Hunter; Bandido (1956); Heaven Knows, Mr. Allison; Fire Down Below (1957); The Enemy Below; Thunder Road; The Hunters; The Angry Hills; The Wonderful Country; Home From the Hill; The Sundowners (1960); The Grass Is Greener; Cape Fear (1962); The Longest Day; Two for the Seesaw; The List of Adrian Messenger; Rampage (1963); What a Way to Go!; Mister Moses; The Way West; El Dorado; Villa Rides; Anzio; 5 Card Stud; Secret Ceremony; Young Billy Young; The Good Guys and the Bad Guys; Ryan's Daughter; Going Home; The Wrath of God; The Friends of Eddie Coyle; The Yakuza; Farewell, My Lovely; Midway; The Last Tycoon; The Amsterdam Kill; Matilda (1978); The Big Sleep (1978); Breakthrough (1978); Nightkill; Agency; That Championship Season; Maria's Lovers; The Ambassador; Mr. North; Scrooged; Cape Fear (1991; cameo); Woman of Desire; Tombstone (narr); Backfire!; Dead Man

Monroe, Marilyn: Scudda Hoo! Scudda Hay!; Love Happy; A Ticket to Tomahawk; The Asphalt Jungle; All About Eve; Right Cross; As Young As You Feel; Love Nest; Let's Make It Legal; Clash by Night; We're Not Married; Don't Bother to Knock; Monkey Business (1952); O. Henry's Full House; Niagara; Gentlemen Prefer Blondes; How to Marry a Millionaire; River of No Return; There's No Business Like Show Business; The Seven Year Itch; Bus Stop; The Prince and the Showgirl; Some Like It Hot (1959); Let's Make Love; The Misfits

Moore, Demi: Choices; Parasite; Young Doctors in Love; Blame It on Rio; No Small Affair; St. Elmo's Fire; About Last Night . . . ; One Crazy Summer; Wisdom; The Seventh Sign; We're No Angels (1989); Ghost; Nothing but Trouble (1991); Mortal Thoughts; The Butcher's Wife; A Few Good Men; Indecent Proposal; Disclosure; Now and Then; The Scarlet Letter (1995); The Juror; Striptease; The Hunchback of Notre Dame (1996); Beavis and Butt-head Do America; G.I. Jane; Deconstructing Harry; Passion of Mind; Charlie's Angels: Full Throttle; Bobby; Mr. Brooks; Flawless (2008); Happy Tears; The Joneses

Moore, Julianne: Tales from the Darkside: The Movie; The Hand That Rocks the Cradle; The Gun in Betty Lou's Handbag; Body of Evidence; Benny & Joon; The Fugitive (1993); Short Cuts; Vanya on 42nd Street; Roommates; Safe; Nine Months; Assassins; Surviving Picasso; The Lost World: Jurassic Park; The Myth of Fingerprints; Boogie Nights; The Big Lebowski; Psycho (1998); Cookie's Fortune; An Ideal Husband; A Map of the World; The End of the Affair (1999); Magnolia; The Ladies Man (2000); Hannibal (2001); World Traveler; Evolution; The Shipping News; Far From Heaven; The Hours; Laws of Attraction; The Forgotten; The Prize Winner of Defiance, Ohio; Freedomland; Trust the Man; Children of Men; Next; I'm Not There; Savage Grace; Blindness; The Private Lives of Pippa Lee; A Single Man; Chloe; The Kids Are All Right; Elektra Luxx (cameo)

Mortensen, Viggo: Witness; Salvation!; Fresh Horses; Leatherface: Texas Chainsaw

Massacre III; The Reflecting Skin; Young Guns II; The Indian Runner; Boiling Point; Carlito's Way; Floundering; Crimson Tide; The Prophecy (1995); The Portrait of a Lady; Albino Alligator; Daylight; G.I. Jane; A Perfect Murder; Psycho (1998); A Walk on the Moon; 28 Days; The Lord of the Rings: The Fellowship of the Ring; The Lord of the Rings: The Two Towers; The Lord of the Rings: The Return of the King; Hidalgo; A History of Violence; Eastern Promises; Appaloosa (2008); Good; The Road

Muni, Paul: Scarface (1932); I Am a Fugitive From a Chain Gang; Bordertown; Black Fury; The Story of Louis Pasteur; The Good Earth; The Life of Emile Zola; Juarez; Stage Door Canteen; A Song to Remember; Angel on My Shoulder; The Last Angry Man

Murphy, Eddie: 48HRS.; Trading Places; Best Defense; Beverly Hills Cop; The Golden Child; Beverly Hills Cop II; Eddie Murphy Raw; Coming to America (also sty); Harlem Nights (also dir, scr); Another 48 HRS; Boomerang (1992); The Distinguished Gentleman; Beverly Hills Cop III; Vampire in Brooklyn; The Nutty Professor (1996); Metro; Mulan; Holy Man; Doctor Dolittle (1998); Life; Bowfinger; Nutty Professor II: The Klumps; Shrek; Dr. Dolittle 2; Showtime; The Adventures of Pluto Nash; I Spy; Daddy Day Care; The Haunted Mansion; Shrek 2; Dreamgirls; Norbit; Shrek the Third; Meet Dave; Imagine That; Shrek Forever After

Murray, Bill: Shame of the Jungle; Next Stop, Greenwich Village (bit); Meatballs; Caddyshack; Where the Buffalo Roam; Loose Shoes; Stripes; Tootsie (uncred); Ghostbusters; The Razor's Edge (1984; also coscr); Nothing Lasts Forever; Little Shop of Horrors; Scrooged; Ghostbusters II; Quick Change (also codir); What About Bob?; Groundhog Day; Mad Dog and Glory; Ed Wood; Kingpin; Space Jam (uncred); Larger Than Life; The Man Who Knew Too Little; Wild Things; Rushmore; With Friends Like These . . . ; Cradle Will Rock; Hamlet (2000); Charlie's Angels; Osmosis Jones; The Royal Tenenbaums; Lost in Translation; Coffee and Cigarettes; Garfield; The Life Aquatic with Steve Zissou; Broken Flowers; The Lost City; Garfield 2; The Darjeeling Limited (cameo); Get Smart (cameo); City of Ember; The Limits of Control; Zombieland (cameo); Fantastic Mr. Fox; Get Low; Passion Play

Myers, Mike: Wayne's World (also co-scr); So I Married an Axe Murderer; Wayne's World 2 (also coscr); Austin Powers: International Man of Mystery (also coscr); 54; Pete's Meteor; Mystery, Alaska; Austin Powers: The Spy Who Shagged Me (also coscr); Shrek; Austin Powers in Goldmember (also coscr); View from the Top; The Cat in the Hat; Shrek 2; Shrek the Third;

The Love Guru (also coscr); Inglourious Basterds; Shrek Forever After

Neeson, Liam: Excalibur; Krull; The Bounty; Lamb; The Innocent (1985); The Mission; Suspect (1987); A Prayer for the Dying; Duet for One; Satisfaction; The Dead Pool; The Good Mother; High Spirits; Next of Kin; Darkman; Crossing the Line; Under Suspicion; Shining Through; Leap of Faith; Husbands and Wives; Ethan Frome (1993); Deception (1993); Schindler's List; Nell; Rob Roy; Before and After; Michael Collins; Les Misérables (1998); Star Wars Episode I: The Phantom Menace; The Haunting (1999); Gun Shy; K-19 The Widowmaker; Gangs of New York; Love Actually; Kinsey; Kingdom of Heaven; Batman Begins; Breakfast on Pluto; The Chronicles of Narnia: The Lion, The Witch and The Wardrobe; Seraphim Falls; The Chronicles of Narnia: Prince Caspian; Taken; Ponyo; The Other Man; Five Minutes of Heaven; Chloe; Clash of the Titans (2010); After. Life (2010); The A-Team; The Chronicles of Narnia: The Voyage of the Dawn Treader; Unknown (2011); The Next Three Days

Newman, Paul: The Silver Chalice; Somebody Up There Likes Me; The Rack; The Helen Morgan Story; Until They Sail; The Long Hot Summer; The Left-Handed Gun; Cat on a Hot Tin Roof; Rally 'Round the Flag, Boys!; The Young Philadelphians; From the Terrace; Exodus; The Hustler; Paris Blues; Sweet Bird of Youth; Hemingway's Adventures of a Young Man; Hud; A New Kind of Love; The Prize; What a Way to Go!; The Outrage (1964); Lady L; Harper; Torn Curtain; Hombre; Cool Hand Luke; The Secret War of Harry Frigg; Rachel, Rachel (dir); Winning; Butch Cassidy and the Sundance Kid; King: A Filmed Record . . . Montgomery to Memphis (narr); WUSA; Sometimes a Great Notion (also dir); Pocket Money; The Effect of Gamma Rays on Man-in-the-Moon Marigolds (dir); The Life and Times of Judge Roy Bean; The Mackintosh Man; The Sting; The Towering Inferno; The Drowning Pool; Silent Movie (cameo); Buffalo Bill and the Indians, or Sitting Bull's History Lesson; Slap Shot; Quintet; When Time Ran Out . . . ; Fort Apache, The Bronx; Absence of Malice; The Verdict (1982); Harry and Son (also dir); The Color of Money; The Glass Menagerie (1987; dir); Fat Man and Little Boy; Blaze; Mr. & Mrs. Bridge; The Hudsucker Proxy; Nobody's Fool (1994); Twilight (1998); Message in a Bottle; Where the Money Is; Road to Perdition; Cars; The Price of Sugar (narr)

Nicholson, Jack: The Cry Baby Killer; The Wild Ride; Studs Lonigan; The Little Shop of Horrors (1960); The Raven (1963); The Terror; Thunder Island (also coscr); Ensign Pulver; Back Door to Hell; Ride in the Whirlwind (also scr); Flight to Fury (also scr); The Shooting; The St. Valentine's Day Massacre; Hell's Angels on Wheels; The Trip (scr); Psych-Out; Head (also coscr); Easy Rider; Rebel Rousers; On a Clear Day You Can See Forever; Five Easy Pieces; Carnal Knowledge; A Safe Place; Drive, He Said (dir, coscr); The King of Marvin Gardens; The Last Detail; Chinatown; Tommy; The Passenger; The Fortune; One Flew Over the Cuckoo's Nest; The Missouri Breaks; The Last Tycoon; Goin' South (also dir); The Shining; The Postman Always Rings Twice (1981); Reds; The Border; Terms of Endearment; Prizzi's Honor; Heartburn; The Witches of Eastwick; Broadcast News; Ironweed; Batman (1989); The Two Jakes (also dir); Man Trouble; A Few Good Men; Hoffa; Wolf; The Crossing Guard; Mars Attacks!; The Evening Star; Blood and Wine; As Good As It Gets; The Pledge; About Schmidt; Anger Management; Something's Gotta Give; The Departed; The Bucket List; I'm Still Here (app); How Do You Know

Nolte, Nick: Electra Glide in Blue; Return to Macon County; The Deep; Who'll Stop the Rain; North Dallas Forty; Heart Beat; 48HRS.; Cannery Row; Under Fire (1983); Teachers; Grace Quigley; Down and Out in Beverly Hills; Extreme Prejudice; Weeds; Three Fugitives; Farewell to the King; New York Stories; Q & A; Everybody Wins; Another 48 HRS; Cape Fear (1991); The Prince of Tides; The Player (cameo); Lorenzo's Oil; I'll Do Anything; Blue Chips; I Love Trouble (1994); Jefferson in Paris; Mulholland Falls; Mother Night; U Turn; Afterglow; Nightwatch; Affliction; The Thin Red Line (1998); Breakfast of Champions; Simpatico; Trixie; The Golden Bowl; The Good Thief; Northfork; Hulk; Hotel Rwanda; Neverwas; The Beautiful Country; Paris, je t'aime; Over the Hedge; Clean; Investigating Sex; Off the Black; The Spiderwick Chronicles; Chicago 10; Peaceful Warrior; Tropic Thunder; Cats & Dogs: The Revenge of Kitty Galore; Arthur (2011)

Norton, Edward: Primal Fear; Everyone Says I Love You; The People vs. Larry Flynt; Rounders (1998); American History X; Fight Club; Keeping the Faith (also dir); The Score; Death to Smoochy; Red Dragon; Frida (2002); 25th Hour (2002); The Italian Job (2003); Kingdom of Heaven; Down in the Valley; The Illusionist; The Painted Veil (2006); The Incredible Hulk; Pride and Glory; The Invention of Lying; Leaves of Grass; Stone

Novak, Kim: The French Line; Pushover; Phffft!; Son of Sinbad; 5 Against the House; The Man With the Golden Arm; Picnic; The Eddy Duchin Story; Jeanne Eagels; Pal Joey; Vertigo; Bell, Book and Candle; Strangers When We Meet; Pepe (cameo); Boys' Night Out; The Notorious Landlady; Of Human Bondage (1964); Kiss Me, Stupid; The Amorous Adventures of Moll Flanders; The

Legend of Lylah Clare; The Great Bank Robbery; Tales That Witness Madness; The White Buffalo; Just a Gigolo; The Mirror Crack'd; The Children (1990); Liebestraum

O'Hara, Maureen: Jamaica Inn; The Hunchback of Notre Dame (1939); A Bill of Divorcement (1940); How Green Was My Valley; The Black Swan; This Land Is Mine; The Fallen Sparrow; Sinbad the Sailor; Miracle on 34th Street (1947); The Foxes of Harrow; Sitting Pretty (1948); The Forbidden Street; A Woman's Secret; Rio Grande; At Sword's Point; The Quiet Man; Against All Flags; The Long Gray Line; The Magnificent Matador; Lady Godiva; The Wings of Eagles; Our Man in Havana; The Parent Trap (1961); The Deadly Companions; Mr. Hobbs Takes a Vacation; Spencer's Mountain; McLintock!; The Rare Breed; How Do I Love Thee?; Big Jake; Only the Lonely

Oldman, Gary: Meantime; Sid and Nancy; Prick Up Your Ears; We Think the World of You; Track 29; Criminal Law; State of Grace; Chattahoochee; Rosencrantz and Guildenstern Are Dead; JFK; Bram Stoker's Dracula; True Romance; Romeo Is Bleeding; The Professional; Immortal Beloved; Murder in the First; The Scarlet Letter (1995); Basquiat; The Fifth Element; Air Force One; Nil by Mouth (dir, scr); Lost in Space; Quest for Camelot; The Contender; Hannibal (2001); Harry Potter and the Prisoner of Azkaban; Batman Begins; Harry Potter and the Goblet of Fire; Harry Potter and the Order of the Phoenix; The Dark Knight; The Unborn (2009); Disney's A Christmas Carol; Planet 51; The Book of Eli; Harry Potter and the Deathly Hallows: Part 1; Red Riding Hood; Kung Fu Panda 2

Olivier, Laurence: As You Like It; Q Planes; Wuthering Heights (1939); Rebecca; Pride and Prejudice (1940); That Hamilton Woman; 49th Parallel; Henry V (1945; also dir, coadapt); Hamlet (1948; also dir); Carrie (1952); The Beggar's Opera; Richard III (1955; also dir); The Prince and the Showgirl (also dir); The Devil's Disciple; The Entertainer; Spartacus; Term of Trial; Bunny Lake Is Missing; Othello (1965); Khartoum; Romeo and Juliet (1968; narr); The Shoes of the Fisherman; Oh! What a Lovely War; Dance of Death (1969); Battle of Britain; Three Sisters (also dir); Nicholas and Alexandra; Sleuth (1972); Lady Caroline Lamb; Marathon Man; The Seven-Per-Cent Solution; A Bridge Too Far; The Betsy; The Boys From Brazil; A Little Romance; Dracula (1979); The Jazz Singer (1980); Clash of the Titans (1981); Inchon!; Wagner; The Jigsaw Man; The Bounty; Wild Geese II

O'Toole, Peter: The Savage Innocents; Kidnapped (1960); Lawrence of Arabia; Becket; Lord Jim; What's New Pussycat; The Sandpiper (voice only); How to Steal a Million; The Bible; Night of the Generals; Casino Royale (1967; cameo); The Lion in Winter; Great Catherine; Goodbye, Mr. Chips (1969); Brotherly Love; Murphy's War; Under Milk Wood; The Ruling Class; Man of La Mancha; Rosebud; Man Friday; Foxtrot; Power Play; Zulu Dawn; The Stunt Man; Caligula; My Favorite Year; Supergirl; Creator; Club Paradise; The Last Emperor; High Spirits; The Rainbow Thief; The Nutcracker Prince; King Ralph; The Seventh Coin; Fairy Tale: A True Story; Phantoms; Molokai: The Story of Father Damien; Rock My World; Bright Young Things; Troy; Lassie (2005); Venus; One Night With the King; Ratatouille; Stardust (2007)

Owen, Clive: Close My Eyes; Century; The Rich Man's Wife; Bent; Croupier; Greenfingers; Gosford Park; The Bourne Identity; I'll sleep when I'm dead; Beyond Borders; King Arthur; Closer; Sin City; Derailed; The Pink Panther (2006; cameo); Inside Man; Children of Men; Shoot 'Em Up; Elizabeth: The Golden Age; The International; Duplicity; The Boys Are Back; Trust (2011)

Pacino, Al: Me, Natalie; The Panic in Needle Park; The Godfather; Scarecrow; Serpico; The Godfather Part II; Dog Day Afternoon; Bobby Deerfield; . . . And Justice for All; Cruising; Author! Author!; Scarface (1983); Revolution (1985); Sea of Love; The Local Stigmatic; Dick Tracy; The Godfather Part III; Truth or Dare (app); Frankie and Johnny (1991); Glengarry Glen Ross; Scent of a Woman (1992); Carlito's Way; Two Bits; Heat (1995); City Hall; Looking for Richard (also dir, app); Donnie Brasco; The Devil's Advocate; The Insider; Any Given Sunday; Chinese Coffee (also dir); Insomnia (2002); S1MØNE; The Recruit; People I Know; Gigli; The Merchant of Venice; Two for the Money; Ocean's Thirteen; 88 Minutes; Righteous Kill

Paltrow, Gwyneth: Shout (1991); Hook (1991); Malice; Flesh and Bone; Mrs. Parker and the Vicious Circle; Jefferson in Paris; Moonlight and Valentino; Se7en; Hard Eight; The Pallbearer; Emma (1996); Great Expectations (1998); Hush; Sliding Doors; A Perfect Murder; Shakespeare in Love; The Talented Mr. Ripley; Duets; Bounce; The Anniversary Party; Pootie Tang (cameo); Shallow Hal; The Royal Tenenbaums; Possession (2002); Austin Powers in Goldmember (cameo); View from the Top; Sylvia (2003); Sky Captain and the World of Tomorrow; Proof (2005); Infamous (cameo); Running with Scissors; The Good Night; Iron Man; Two Lovers; Iron Man 2; Country Strong

Peck, Gregory: The Keys of the Kingdom; The Valley of Decision; Spellbound (1945); The Yearling; Duel in the Sun; The Macomber Affair; Gentleman's Agreement; The Paradine Case; Yellow Sky; The Great Sinner; Twelve O'Clock High; The Gunfighter; David and Bathsheba; Captain Horatio Hornblower; The Snows of Kilimanjaro; The World in His Arms; Roman Holiday; The Purple Plain; Night People; The Man in the Gray Flannel Suit; Moby Dick (1956); Designing Woman; The Bravados; The Big Country; Pork Chop Hill; Beloved Infidel; On the Beach; The Guns of Navarone; To Kill a Mockingbird; Cape Fear (1962); How the West Was Won; Captain Newman, M.D.; Behold a Pale Horse; John F. Kennedy: Years of Lightning, Day of Drums (narr); Mirage; Arabesque; The Stalking Moon; Mackenna's Gold; The Chairman; Marooned; I Walk the Line; Shoot Out; Billy Two Hats; The Omen (1976); MacArthur; The Boys From Brazil; The Sea Wolves; Amazing Grace and Chuck; Old Gringo; Other People's Money; Cape Fear (1991; cameo)

Penn, Sean: Taps; Fast Times at Ridgemont High; Bad Boys (1983); Crackers; Racing With the Moon; The Falcon and the Snowman; At Close Range; Shanghai Surprise; Colors; Judgment in Berlin; Casualties of War; We're No Angels (1989); State of Grace; The Indian Runner (dir, scr); The Last Party (app); Carlito's Way; The Crossing Guard (dir, scr); Dead Man Walking; The Game; She's So Lovely; U Turn; Hugo Pool; hurlyburly; The Thin Red Line (1998); Being John Malkovich (cameo); Sweet and Lowdown; Up at the Villa; Before Night Falls; The Pledge (dir); i am sam; The Weight of Water; Mystic River; 21 Grams; The Assassination of Richard Nixon; The Interpreter; All the King's Men (2006); Into the Wild (dir, adapt); Persepolis; Milk; What Just Happened; I'm Still Here (app); Fair Game (2010); The Tree of Life

Perkins, Anthony: The Actress; Friendly Persuasion (1956); Fear Strikes Out; The Tin Star; Desire Under the Elms; This Angry Age; The Matchmaker; Green Mansions; On the Beach; Tall Story; Psycho (1960); Goodbye Again; The Trial (1962); Is Paris Burning?; The Champagne Murders; Pretty Poison; Catch-22; WUSA; Someone Behind the Door; Ten Days Wonder; Play It As It Lays; The Life and Times of Judge Roy Bean; The Last of Sheila (coscr); Lovin' Molly; Murder on the Orient Express; Mahogany; Remember My Name; The Black Hole; Winter Kills; ffolkes; Double Negative; Psycho II; Crimes of Passion; Psycho III (also dir); Lucky Stiff (dir); Edge of Sanity

Pfeiffer, Michelle: Falling in Love Again; The Hollywood Knights; Charlie Chan and the Curse of the Dragon Queen; Grease 2; Scarface (1983); Into the Night; Ladyhawke; Sweet Liberty; The Witches of Eastwick; Amazon Women on the Moon; Married to the Mob; Tequila Sunrise; Dangerous Liaisons; The Fabulous Baker Boys; The Russia

House; Frankie and Johnny (1991); Batman Returns; Love Field; The Age of Innocence (1993); Wolf; Dangerous Minds; Up Close & Personal; To Gillian on Her 37th Birthday; One Fine Day; A Thousand Acres; The Prince of Egypt; The Deep End of the Ocean; A Midsummer Night's Dream (1999); The Story of Us; What Lies Beneath; i am sam; White Oleander; Sinbad: Legend of the Seven Seas; Hairspray (2007); Stardust (2007); I Could Never Be Your Woman; Chéri

Phoenix, Joaquin (billed as Leaf Phoenix until 1991): SpaceCamp; Russkies; Parenthood; To Die For (1995); Inventing the Abbotts; U Turn; Return to Paradise (1998); Clay Pigeons; 8MM; The Yards; Gladiator (2000); Quills; Buffalo Soldiers; Signs; Brother Bear; The Village; Hotel Rwanda; Ladder 49; Walk the Line; We Own the Night; Reservation Road; Two Lovers; I'm Still Here (app)

Pitt, Brad: Less Than Zero (bit); Cutting Class; Happy Together (1989); Across the Tracks; Thelma & Louise; Cool World; Johnny Suede; A River Runs Through It; True Romance; Kalifornia; The Favor; Interview With the Vampire: The Vampire Chronicles; Legends of the Fall; Se7en; Twelve Monkeys; Sleepers; The Devil's Own (1997); Seven Years in Tibet; The Dark Side of the Sun; Meet Joe Black; Fight Club; Being John Malkovich (uncred); Snatch; The Mexican; Spy Game; Ocean's Eleven (2001); Full Frontal (cameo); Confessions of a Dangerous Mind (cameo); Sinbad: Legend of the Seven Seas; Troy; Ocean's Twelve; Mr. & Mrs. Smith (2005); Babel; Ocean's Thirteen; The Assassination of Jesse James by the Coward Robert Ford; Burn After Reading; The Curious Case of Benjamin Button; Inglourious Basterds; Megamind; The Tree of Life

Poitier, Sidney: No Way Out (1950); Cry, the Beloved Country (1951); Red Ball Express; Go, Man, Go!; Blackboard Jungle; Good-bye, My Lady; Edge of the City; Something of Value; Band of Angels; The Mark of the Hawk; The Defiant Ones; Porgy and Bess; A Raisin in the Sun; Paris Blues; Lilies of the Field; The Long Ships; The Greatest Story Ever Told; The Bedford Incident; A Patch of Blue; The Slender Thread; Duel at Diablo; In the Heat of the Night; To Sir, With Love; Guess Who's Coming to Dinner; For Love of Ivy; The Lost Man; King: A Filmed Record . . . Montgomery to Memphis (narr); They Call Me MISTER Tibbs!; The Organization; Brother John; Buck and the Preacher (also dir); A Warm December (also dir); Uptown Saturday Night (also dir); Let's Do It Again (1975; also dir); The Wilby Conspiracy; A Piece of the Action (also dir); Stir Crazy (dir); Hanky Panky (dir); Fast Forward (dir); Shoot to Kill (1988); Little Nikita; Ghost Dad (dir); Sneakers; The Jackal

Portman, Natalie: The Professional; Heat (1995); Beautiful Girls; Everyone Says I Love You; Mars Attacks!; Star Wars Episode I: The Phantom Menace; Anywhere But Here; Where the Heart Is (2000); Star Wars Episode II: Attack of the Clones; Cold Mountain; Garden State; Closer; Star Wars Episode III: Revenge of the Sith; V for Vendetta; Paris je t'aime; Free Zone; The Darjeeling Limited (cameo); Mr. Magorium's Wonder Emporium; Goya's Ghosts; The Other Boleyn Girl; My Blueberry Nights; New York, I Love You (also seq dir); The Other Woman; Brothers (2009); I'm Still Here (app); Black Swan (2010); No Strings Attached; Your Highness; Thor; Hesher

Powell, Dick: Blessed Event; 42nd Street; Gold Diggers of 1933; Footlight Parade; Dames; Flirtation Walk; Gold Diggers of 1935; Thanks a Million; A Midsummer Night's Dream (1935); Gold Diggers of 1937; On the Avenue; Hollywood Hotel; The Cowboy From Brooklyn; Christmas in July; In the Navy; Star Spangled Rhythm; It Happened Tomorrow; Murder, My Sweet; Cornered; Johnny O'Clock; To the Ends of the Earth; Station West; Pitfall; The Tall Target; Cry Danger; Callaway Went Thataway (cameo); The Bad and the Beautiful; Susan Slept Here; The Conqueror (dir); The Enemy Below (dir); The Hunters (dir)

Powell, William: The Last Command (1928); One Way Passage; Manhattan Melodrama; The Thin Man; The Great Ziegfeld; The Ex-Mrs. Bradford; My Man Godfrey (1936); Libeled Lady; After the Thin Man; Double Wedding; Another Thin Man; I Love You Again; Shadow of the Thin Man; Crossroads (1942); The Thin Man Goes Home; Ziegfeld Follies; The Hoodlum Saint; Life With Father; Song of the Thin Man; Mr. Peabody and the Mermaid; It's a Big Country (cameo); The Girl Who Had Everything; How to Marry a Millionaire; Mister Roberts

Power, Tyrone: Flirtation Walk; Lloyd's of London; In Old Chicago; Alexander's Ragtime Band; Marie Antoinette (1938); Suez; Jesse James; The Rains Came; Brigham Young; The Mark of Zorro (1940); Blood and Sand (1941); A Yank in the RAF; Son of Fury; This Above All; The Black Swan (1942); Crash Dive, The Razor's Edge (1946); Nightmare Alley; Captain From Castile; Prince of Foxes; The Black Rose; Rawhide; Diplomatic Courier; King of the Khyber Rifles; The Long Gray Line; Untamed; The Eddy Duchin Story; Abandon Ship; The Rising of the Moon; The Sun Also Rises; Witness for the Prosecution

Presley, Elvis: Love Me Tender; Loving You; Jailhouse Rock; King Creole; G.I. Blues; Flaming Star; Wild in the Country; Blue Hawaii; Follow That Dream; Kid Galahad (1962); Girls! Girls! Girls!; It Happened at the World's Fair; Fun in Acapulco; Kissin' Cousins; Viva Las Vegas; Roustabout; Girl Happy; Tickle Me; Harum Scarum; Frankie and Johnny (1966); Paradise, Hawaiian Style; Spinout; Easy Come, Easy Go (1967); Double Trouble (1967); Clambake; Stay Away, Joe; Speedway; Live a Little, Love a Little; Charro!; The Trouble With Girls (and How to Get Into It); Change of Habit; Elvis: That's the Way It Is; Elvis on Tour; This Is Elvis

Preston, Robert: Union Pacific; Beau Geste (1939); Typhoon; North West Mounted Police; Reap the Wild Wind; This Gun for Hire; Wake Island; Star Spangled Rhythm; Variety Girl (cameo); The Macomber Affair; The Big City (1948); Blood on the Moon; Tulsa; The Lady Gambles; The Sundowners (1950); The Last Frontier (1956); The Dark at the Top of the Stairs; The Music Man; How the West Was Won; All the Way Home; Junior Bonner; Child's Play (1972); Mame; Semi-Tough; S.O.B.; Victor/Victoria; The Last Starfighter

Price, Vincent: The Private Lives of Elizabeth and Essex; Tower of London (1939); The Invisible Man Returns; The House of the Seven Gables; Brigham Young; The Song of Bernadette; Laura; The Keys of the Kingdom; A Royal Scandal; Leave Her to Heaven; Dragonwyck; The Long Night; Up in Central Park; Abbott and Costello Meet Frankenstein (cameo); The Three Musketeers (1948); The Bribe; Champagne for Caesar; The Baron of Arizona; His Kind of Woman; House of Wax (1953); Casanova's Big Night (cameo); The Mad Magician; Son of Sinbad; The Vagabond King; While the City Sleeps; The Ten Commandments (1956); The Story of Mankind; The Fly (1958); House on Haunted Hill (1959); Big Circus; The Bat; The Return of the Fly; The Tingler; House of Usher; Master of the World; Pit and the Pendulum; Convicts 4; Tales of Terror; Tower of London (1962); The Raven (1963); Beach Party (cameo); Twice-Told Tales; The Comedy of Terrors; The Haunted Palace; The Last Man on Earth; The Masque of the Red Death; The Tomb of Ligeia; Dr. Goldfoot and the Bikini Machine; Dr. Goldfoot and the Girl Bombs; House of 1,000 Dolls; The Jackals; Conqueror Worm; Spirits of the Dead; The Oblong Box; The Trouble With Girls (and How to Get Into It); Scream and Scream Again; Cry of the Banshee; The Abominable Dr. Phibes; Dr. Phibes Rises Again!; Theater of Blood; Madhouse (1974); It's Not the Size That Counts; Journey Into Fear (1975); Scavenger Hunt; The Monster Club; House of the Long Shadows; The Great Mouse Detective; The Offspring; The Whales of August; Dead Heat; Backtrack (1989); Edward Scissorhands; Arabian Knight

Pryor, Richard: The Busy Body; Wild in the Streets; The Phynx; You've Got to Walk It Like You Talk It or You'll Lose That Beat; Dynamite Chicken; Lady Sings the Blues; Wattstax; The Mack; Hit!; Some Call It

Loving; Blazing Saddles (coscr); Uptown Saturday Night; Adios Amigo; The Bingo Long Traveling All-Stars & Motor Kings; Car Wash; Silver Streak; Greased Lightning; Which Way Is Up?; Blue Collar; The Wiz; California Suite; Richard Pryor—Live in Concert; The Muppet Movie (cameo); Richard Pryor Is Back Live in Concert; In God We Tru$t; Wholly Moses; Stir Crazy; Bustin' Loose; Richard Pryor Live on the Sunset Strip; Some Kind of Hero; The Toy; Richard Pryor Here and Now; Superman III; Brewster's Millions; Jo Jo Dancer, Your Life Is Calling (also dir, coscr); Critical Condition; Moving; See No Evil, Hear No Evil; Harlem Nights; Another You; Mad Dog Time (cameo); Lost Highway

Quaid, Dennis: Crazy Mama (bit); I Never Promised You a Rose Garden; September 30, 1955; The Seniors; G.O.R.P.; Breaking Away; The Long Riders; All Night Long (1981); Caveman; The Night the Lights Went Out in Georgia; Tough Enough; Jaws 3-D; The Right Stuff; Dreamscape; Enemy Mine; The Big Easy; Innerspace; Suspect; D.O.A. (1988); Everybody's All-American; Great Balls of Fire!; Postcards From the Edge; Come See The Paradise; Undercover Blues; Wilder Napalm; Flesh and Bone; Wyatt Earp; Something to Talk About; Dragonheart; Switchback; Gang Related; The Savior; The Parent Trap (1998); Playing by Heart; Any Given Sunday; Frequency; Traffic (2000); The Rookie (2002); Far From Heaven; Cold Creek Manor; The Alamo (2004); The Day After Tomorrow; In Good Company; Flight of the Phoenix (2004); Yours, Mine & Ours (2005); American Dreamz; Vantage Point; Smart People; The Express; Battle for Terra; Horsemen (2009); G.I. Joe: The Rise of Cobra; Pandorum; Legion; Soul Surfer

Queen Latifah: Jungle Fever; House Party 2; Juice; My Life; Set It Off; Hoodlum; Sphere; Living Out Loud; The Bone Collector; Bringing Out the Dead (voice); The Country Bears; Brown Sugar; Pinocchio (2002); Chicago; Bringing Down the House; Scary Movie 3; Barbershop 2: Back in Business; The Cookout; Taxi (2004); Beauty Shop; Last Holiday (2006); Ice Age: The Meltdown; Stranger Than Fiction; Hairspray (2007); The Perfect Holiday; Mad Money; What Happens in Vegas; The Secret Life of Bees; Ice Age: Dawn of the Dinosaurs; Valentine's Day; Just Wright; The Dilemma

Quinn, Anthony: The Plainsman (1936); Swing High, Swing Low; Daughter of Shanghai; The Buccaneer (1938); Union Pacific; Road to Singapore; The Ghost Breakers; City for Conquest; Blood and Sand (1941); They Died With Their Boots On; Larceny, Inc.; Road to Morocco; The Black Swan; The Ox-Bow Incident; Guadalcanal Diary; Back to Bataan; Sinbad the Sailor; Tycoon; The Brave Bulls; Mask of the Avenger; Viva Zapata!; The World in His Arms; Against All Flags; Seminole; Blowing Wild; Ulysses (1954); La Strada; The Magnificent Matador; Lust for Life; The Hunchback of Notre Dame (1957); The River's Edge (1957); Wild Is the Wind; Hot Spell; The Buccaneer (1958; dir); The Black Orchid; Warlock (1959); Last Train From Gun Hill; The Savage Innocents; Heller in Pink Tights; Portrait in Black; The Guns of Navarone; Barabbas; Requiem for a Heavyweight; Lawrence of Arabia; The Visit (1964); Behold a Pale Horse; Zorba the Greek; A High Wind in Jamaica; Lost Command; The 25th Hour; The Happening (1967); The Rover; Guns for San Sebastian; The Shoes of the Fisherman; The Magus; The Secret of Santa Vittoria; A Dream of Kings; Walk in the Spring Rain; R.P.M.; Flap; Arruza; Across 110th Street; Deaf Smith and Johnny Ears; The Don Is Dead; The Destructors (1974); The Inheritance (1976); Target of an Assassin; Mohammad, Messenger of God; The Greek Tycoon; The Children of Sanchez; Caravans; The Passage; Lion of the Desert; High Risk; The Salamander; Ghosts Can't Do It; Revenge (1990); Only the Lonely; Jungle Fever; Mobsters; Last Action Hero; Somebody to Love; A Walk in the Clouds

Rathbone, Basil: David Copperfield (1935); Anna Karenina (1935); The Last Days of Pompeii (1935); A Tale of Two Cities (1935); Captain Blood (1935); Romeo and Juliet (1936); The Garden of Allah; Tovarich; The Adventures of Robin Hood; If I Were King; The Dawn Patrol (1938); Son of Frankenstein; The Hound of the Baskervilles (1939); The Adventures of Sherlock Holmes; Tower of London (1939); The Mark of Zorro (1940); The Black Cat (1941); Crossroads (1942); Sherlock Holmes and the Voice of Terror; Sherlock Holmes and the Secret Weapon; Sherlock Holmes in Washington; Above Suspicion; Sherlock Holmes Faces Death; The Spider Woman; The Scarlet Claw; Bathing Beauty; Frenchman's Creek; The House of Fear; The Woman in Green; Terror by Night; Dressed to Kill (1946); The Adventures of Ichabod and Mr. Toad; Casanova's Big Night; We're No Angels (1955); The Court Jester; The Black Sleep; The Last Hurrah; The Magic Sword; Tales of Terror; The Comedy of Terrors; Planet of Blood; The Ghost in the Invisible Bikini; Voyage to the Prehistoric Planet; Hillbillys in a Haunted House

Reagan, Ronald: Hollywood Hotel; Cowboy From Brooklyn; Boy Meets Girl; Brother Rat; Dark Victory; Hell's Kitchen; The Angels Wash Their Faces; Knute Rockne All American; Santa Fe Trail; Kings Row; This Is the Army; That Hagen Girl; The Voice of the Turtle; John Loves Mary; Night Unto Night; The Girl From Jones Beach; It's a Great Feeling (cameo); The Hasty Heart; Louisa; Storm Warning;

Bedtime for Bonzo; The Last Outpost; Hong Kong; The Winning Team; Tropic Zone; Law and Order (1953); Prisoner of War; Cattle Queen of Montana; Tennessee's Partner; Hellcats of the Navy; The Young Doctors (narr); The Killers (1964)

Redford, Robert: War Hunt; Inside Daisy Clover; The Chase (1966); This Property Is Condemned; Barefoot in the Park; Butch Cassidy and the Sundance Kid; Downhill Racer; Tell Them Willie Boy Is Here; Little Fauss and Big Halsy; The Hot Rock; The Candidate; Jeremiah Johnson; The Way We Were; The Sting; The Great Gatsby (1974); The Great Waldo Pepper; Three Days of the Condor; All the President's Men; A Bridge Too Far; The Electric Horseman; Brubaker; Ordinary People (dir); The Natural; Out of Africa; Legal Eagles; The Milagro Beanfield War (dir); Havana; Sneakers; A River Runs Through It (dir, narr); Indecent Proposal; Quiz Show (dir); Up Close & Personal; The Horse Whisperer (also dir); The Legend of Bagger Vance (dir); The Last Castle; Spy Game; The Clearing; An Unfinished Life; Charlotte's Web (2006); Lions for Lambs (also dir); The Conspirator (dir)

Redgrave, Vanessa: Morgan!; A Man for All Seasons (1966; cameo); Blowup; The Sailor From Gibraltar; Camelot; The Charge of the Light Brigade (1968); Isadora; The Sea Gull; Oh! What a Lovely War; The Devils; Mary, Queen of Scots; The Trojan Women; Murder on the Orient Express; Out of Season; The Seven-Per-Cent Solution; Julia (1977); Agatha; Yanks; Bear Island; Wagner; The Bostonians; Steaming; Wetherby; Prick Up Your Ears; Consuming Passions; The Ballad of the Sad Cafe; Howards End; Breath of Life; Shades of Fear; The House of the Spirits; Mother's Boys; Little Odessa; A Month by the Lake; Mission: Impossible; Looking for Richard (app); Smilla's Sense of Snow; Wilde; Déjà Vu (1998); Mrs. Dalloway; Deep Impact; Lulu on the Bridge; Cradle Will Rock; Girl, Interrupted; The Pledge; A Rumor of Angels; Merci Docteur Rey (cameo); Good Boy!; The Keeper: The Legend of Omar Khayyam; The White Countess; Venus; How About You . . .; Evening; Atonement; Letters to Juliet; Miral

Reeves, Keanu: Youngblood; River's Edge; Flying; Dangerous Liaisons (1988); The Prince of Pennsylvania; Permanent Record; The Night Before; Bill & Ted's Excellent Adventure; Parenthood; I Love You to Death; Tune in Tomorrow; Point Break; Bill & Ted's Bogus Journey; My Own Private Idaho; Bram Stoker's Dracula; Much Ado About Nothing; Freaked (cameo); Even Cowgirls Get the Blues; Little Buddha; Speed (1994); Johnny Mnemonic; A Walk in the Clouds; Chain Reaction (1996); Feeling Minnesota; The Last Time I Committed Suicide; The Devil's Advocate; The Matrix; The Replacements; The Watcher;

The Gift; Sweet November (2001); Hardball; The Matrix Reloaded; The Matrix Revolutions; Something's Gotta Give; Constantine; Thumbsucker; Ellie Parker; A Scanner Darkly; The Lake House; Street Kings; The Day the Earth Stood Still (2008); The Private Lives of Pippa Lee; Henry's Crime

Reynolds, Burt: Angel Baby (1961); Navajo Joe; Fade-In; Sam Whiskey; 100 Rifles; Shark!; Skullduggery; Fuzz; Deliverance; Everything You Always Wanted to Know About Sex (But Were Afraid to Ask); Shamus; The Man Who Loved Cat Dancing; White Lightning; The Longest Yard (1974); W.W. and the Dixie Dancekings; At Long Last Love; Lucky Lady; Hustle; Silent Movie (cameo); Gator (also dir); Nickelodeon; Smokey and the Bandit; Semi-Tough; The End (also dir); Hooper; Starting Over; Smokey and the Bandit II; Rough Cut; The Cannonball Run; Sharky's Machine (also dir); Paternity; The Best Little Whorehouse in Texas; Best Friends; The Man Who Loved Women (1983); Stroker Ace; Smokey and the Bandit 3 (cameo); Cannonball Run II; City Heat; Stick (also dir); Uphill All the Way (cameo); Heat (1987); Malone; Rent-a-Cop; Switching Channels; Physical Evidence; Breaking In; All Dogs Go to Heaven; Modern Love; The Player (cameo); Cop & ½; The Maddening; Striptease; Mad Dog Time; Citizen Ruth; Meet Wally Sparks; Bean; Boogie Nights; Mystery, Alaska; The Crew; Driven; Hotel (2002); Time of the Wolf; Without a Paddle; The Longest Yard (2005); The Dukes of Hazzard; Broken Bridges; In the Name of the King: A Dungeon Siege Tale; Deal (2008); Delgo

Reynolds, Debbie: June Bride; Three Little Words; Singin' in the Rain; Skirts Ahoy! (cameo); I Love Melvin; Give a Girl a Break; Susan Slept Here; Hit the Deck; The Tender Trap; The Catered Affair; Tammy and the Bachelor; This Happy Feeling; The Mating Game; It Started With a Kiss; The Gazebo; The Rat Race; Pepe (cameo); The Pleasure of His Company; How the West Was Won; The Unsinkable Molly Brown; Goodbye Charlie; The Singing Nun; Divorce American Style; How Sweet It Is!; What's the Matter with Helen?; Charlotte's Web (1973); That's Entertainment! (app); The Bodyguard (cameo); Heaven & Earth; That's Entertainment! III (app); Mother; Wedding Bell Blues; In & Out; Kiki's Delivery Service; Rudolph the Red-nosed Reindeer: The Movie; Rugrats in Paris: The Movie; Connie and Carla

Robbins, Tim: Toy Soldiers (1984); No Small Affair; The Sure Thing; Fraternity Vacation; Top Gun; Howard the Duck; Five Corners; Bull Durham; Tapeheads; Miss Firecracker; Erik the Viking; Cadillac Man; Twister; Jacob's Ladder; Jungle Fever; The Player; Bob Roberts (also dir, scr); Short Cuts; The Hudsucker Proxy; The

Shawshank Redemption; Ready to Wear (Prêt-à-Porter); I.Q.; Dead Man Walking (dir, scr); Nothing to Lose; Arlington Road; Cradle Will Rock (dir, scr, voice cameo); Austin Powers: The Spy Who Shagged Me (cameo); Mission to Mars; High Fidelity; Antitrust; Human Nature; The Truth About Charlie; Mystic River; Code 46; Anchorman: The Legend of Ron Burgundy (cameo); War of the Worlds (2005); Zathura: A Space Adventure; Tenacious D: The Pick of Destiny; Catch a Fire; The Secret Life of Words; Then She Found Me (cameo); Noise; The Lucky Ones; City of Ember; Green Lantern

Roberts, Julia: Blood Red; Satisfaction; Mystic Pizza; Steel Magnolias; Pretty Woman; Flatliners; Sleeping With the Enemy; Dying Young; Hook; The Player (cameo); The Pelican Brief; I Love Trouble (1994); Ready to Wear (Prêt-à-Porter); Something to Talk About; Mary Reilly; Michael Collins; Everyone Says I Love You; My Best Friend's Wedding; Conspiracy Theory; Stepmom; Notting Hill; Runaway Bride; Erin Brockovich; The Mexican; America's Sweethearts; Ocean's Eleven (2001); Full Frontal; Confessions of a Dangerous Mind; Mona Lisa Smile; Ocean's Twelve; Closer (2004); The Ant Bully; Charlotte's Web (2006); Charlie Wilson's War; Fuel (app); Duplicity; Valentine's Day; Eat Pray Love; Larry Crowne

Robinson, Edward G.: Little Caesar; Five Star Final; Tiger Shark; Dark Hazard; The Whole Town's Talking; Barbary Coast; Bullets or Ballots; Kid Galahad (1937); A Slight Case of Murder; The Amazing Doctor Clitterhouse; Confessions of a Nazi Spy; Blackmail (1939); Dr. Ehrlich's Magic Bullet; Brother Orchid; A Dispatch From Reuters; The Sea Wolf; Larceny, Inc.; Tales of Manhattan; Mr. Winkle Goes to War; Double Indemnity; The Woman in the Window; Our Vines Have Tender Grapes; Scarlet Street; The Stranger (1946); All My Sons; Key Largo; Night Has a Thousand Eyes; House of Strangers; It's a Great Feeling (cameo); Big Leaguer; Black Tuesday; The Violent Men; Tight Spot; Illegal; The Ten Commandments (1956); A Hole in the Head; Seven Thieves; Pepe (cameo); My Geisha; Two Weeks in Another Town; A Boy Ten Feet Tall; The Prize; Good Neighbor Sam; Robin and the 7 Hoods (cameo); The Outrage; Cheyenne Autumn; The Cincinnati Kid; Grand Slam (1967); Operation St. Peter's; The Biggest Bundle of Them All; Never a Dull Moment; Mackenna's Gold; Song of Norway; Soylent Green

Rogen, Seth: Donnie Darko; Anchorman: The Legend of Ron Burgundy; The 40 Year Old Virgin; You, Me and Dupree; Shrek the Third; Knocked Up; Superbad (also coscr); The Spiderwick Chronicles; Horton Hears a Who!; Drillbit Taylor (coscr); Kung Fu Panda; Step Brothers; Fanboys; Pineapple Express (also coscr); Zack and Miri Make a Porno; Monsters vs Aliens; Observe and Report; Funny People; Paper Heart; The Green Hornet (also coscr); Paul; Kung Fu Panda 2

Rogers, Ginger: 42nd Street; Gold Diggers of 1933; Flying Down to Rio; The Gay Divorcee; Roberta; Top Hat; Follow the Fleet; Swing Time; Shall We Dance (1937); Stage Door; Vivacious Lady; Carefree; The Story of Vernon & Irene Castle; Bachelor Mother; 5th Ave. Girl; Primrose Path; Lucky Partners; Kitty Foyle; Tom, Dick and Harry; Roxie Hart; Tales of Manhattan; The Major and the Minor; Once Upon a Honeymoon; Tender Comrade; Lady in the Dark; I'll Be Seeing You; Week-end at the Waldorf; The Barkleys of Broadway; Storm Warning; We're Not Married; Monkey Business (1952); Dreamboat; Forever Female; Black Widow (1954); Tight Spot; The First Traveling Saleslady; Teen-age Rebel; Oh, Men! Oh, Women!; Harlow (Carol Lynley version); Quick, Let's Get Married; George Stevens: A Filmmaker's Journey (app)

Rooney, Mickey: Manhattan Melodrama; Chained; A Midsummer Night's Dream (1935); Ah, Wilderness!; Little Lord Fauntleroy (1936); Captains Courageous; Thoroughbreds Don't Cry; Boys Town; Babes in Arms; Young Tom Edison; Strike Up the Band; Babes on Broadway; The Human Comedy; Thousands Cheer; Girl Crazy; National Velvet; Killer McCoy; Summer Holiday (1948); Words and Music; The Bridges at Toko-Ri; Operation Mad Ball; Baby Face Nelson; A Nice Little Bank That Should Be Robbed; The Big Operator; Platinum High School; King of the Roaring 20's—The Story of Arnold Rothstein; Breakfast at Tiffany's; Requiem for a Heavyweight; It's a Mad Mad Mad Mad World; How to Stuff a Wild Bikini; The Devil in Love; Skidoo; The Extraordinary Seaman; 80 Steps to Jonah; The Comic; Pulp; That's Entertainment! (app); Journey Back to Oz; Find the Lady; The Domino Principle; Pete's Dragon; The Magic of Lassie; The Black Stallion; An Arabian Adventure; Odyssey of the Pacific; The Fox and the Hound; The Care Bears Movie; Lightning; the White Stallion; Erik the Viking; Little Nemo: Adventures in Slumberland; My Heroes Have Always Been Cowboys; Silent Night, Deadly Night 5: The Toymaker; That's Entertainment! III (app); Babe: Pig in the City; Night at the Museum

Rourke, Mickey: 1941; Fade to Black; Heaven's Gate; Body Heat; Diner; Eureka; Rumble Fish; The Pope of Greenwich Village; Year of the Dragon; Nine ½ Weeks; Angel Heart; Barfly; A Prayer for the Dying; Homeboy; Francesco; Johnny Handsome; Wild Orchid; Desperate Hours (1990); Harley Davidson and the Marlboro Man; White Sands; Double Team; The Rainmaker (1997); Buffalo 66; Animal

Factory; Get Carter (2000); The Pledge; Spun; Masked and Anonymous (cameo); Once Upon a Time in Mexico; Man on Fire (2004); Sin City; Domino; Alex Rider: Operation Stormbreaker; The Wrestler; Killshot; The Informers (2009); Iron Man 2; The Expendables; Passion Play

Rush, Geoffrey: Starstruck; Shine; Children of the Revolution; Oscar and Lucinda; A Little Bit of Soul; Les Misérables (1998); Elizabeth (1998); Shakespeare in Love; Mystery Men; House on Haunted Hill (1999); Quills; The Tailor of Panama; Lantana; Frida; The Banger Sisters; Swimming Upstream; Ned Kelly (2003); Finding Nemo; Pirates of the Caribbean: The Curse of the Black Pearl; Intolerable Cruelty; Munich; Pirates of the Caribbean: Dead Man's Chest; Pirates of the Caribbean: At World's End; Elizabeth: The Golden Age; Bran Nue Dae; The King's Speech; Legend of the Guardians: The Owls of Ga'Hoole; The Warrior's Way; Pirates of the Caribbean: On Stranger Tides; Green Lantern

Russell, Rosalind: Forsaking All Others; China Seas; Under Two Flags; Craig's Wife; Night Must Fall (1937); Four's a Crowd; The Citadel; The Women (1939); His Girl Friday; No Time for Comedy; They Met in Bombay; Take a Letter, Darling; My Sister Eileen (1942); Sister Kenny; Mourning Becomes Electra; The Velvet Touch; Tell It to the Judge; A Woman of Distinction; Picnic; Auntie Mame; A Majority of One; Five Finger Exercise; Gypsy; The Trouble With Angels; Oh Dad, Poor Dad, Mama's Hung You in the Closet and I'm Feeling So Sad; Rosie!; Where Angels Go . . . Trouble Follows; Mrs. Pollifax—Spy

Ryan, Meg: Rich and Famous; Amityville 3-D; Top Gun (1986); Armed and Dangerous; Innerspace; Promised Land; D.O.A. (1988); The Presidio; When Harry Met Sally . . . ; Joe Versus the Volcano; The Doors; Prelude to a Kiss; Sleepless in Seattle; Flesh and Bone; When a Man Loves a Woman; I.Q.; French Kiss; Restoration; Courage Under Fire; Addicted to Love; Anastasia (1997); City of Angels; You've Got Mail; hurlyburly; Hanging Up; Proof of Life; Kate & Leopold; In the Cut; Against the Ropes; In the Land of Women; The Deal (2008); The Women (2008); My Mom's New Boyfriend; Serious Moonlight

Sandler, Adam: Going Overboard; Shakes the Clown; Coneheads; Airheads; Mixed Nuts; Billy Madison (also coscr); Happy Gilmore (also coscr); Bulletproof (1996); The Wedding Singer; Dirty Work (uncred); The Waterboy (also coscr); Big Daddy (also coscr); Little Nicky (also coscr); The Animal; Mr. Deeds; Punch-Drunk Love; Eight Crazy Nights (also coscr); The Hot Chick (cameo); Anger Management; 50 First Dates; Spanglish; The Longest Yard (2005); Deuce Biga-

low European Gigolo (cameo); Click; Reign Over Me; I Now Pronounce You Chuck and Larry; You Don't Mess with the Zohan (also coscr); Bedtime Stories; Funny People; Grown Ups (also coscr); Just Go With It

Sarandon, Susan: Joe; Lady Liberty; Lovin' Molly; The Front Page (1974); The Rocky Horror Picture Show; The Great Waldo Pepper; One Summer Love; Checkered Flag or Crash; The Other Side of Midnight; The Great Smokey Roadblock; Pretty Baby (1978); King of the Gypsies; Something Short of Paradise; Loving Couples; Atlantic City (1980); Tempest (1982); The Hunger; The Buddy System; Compromising Positions; The Witches of Eastwick; Bull Durham; Sweet Hearts Dance; The January Man; A Dry White Season; White Palace; Thelma & Louise; The Player (cameo); Bob Roberts (cameo); Light Sleeper; Lorenzo's Oil; The Client; Safe Passage; Little Women (1994); The Celluloid Closet (app); Dead Man Walking; James and the Giant Peach; Twilight (1998); Stepmom; Illuminata; Cradle Will Rock; Anywhere But Here; Joe Gould's Secret; Rugrats in Paris: The Movie; Cats & Dogs; The Banger Sisters; Igby Goes Down; Moonlight Mile; Noel; Shall We Dance (2004); Alfie (2004); Jiminy Glick in La La Wood (cameo); Elizabethtown; In the Valley of Elah; Mr. Woodcock; Romance & Cigarettes; Enchanted; Speed Racer; Emotional Arithmetic; The Lovely Bones; The Greatest (2010); Leaves of Grass; Peacock; Solitary Man; Wall Street: Money Never Sleeps

Schwarzenegger, Arnold: Hercules in New York (as Arnold Strong); The Long Goodbye (bit); Stay Hungry; Pumping Iron; The Villain; Scavenger Hunt; Conan the Barbarian; Conan the Destroyer; The Terminator; Red Sonja; Commando; Raw Deal (1986); Predator; The Running Man (1987); Red Heat; Twins; Total Recall; Kindergarten Cop; Terminator 2: Judgment Day; Dave (cameo); Last Action Hero; True Lies; Junior; Eraser; Jingle All the Way; Batman & Robin; End of Days; The 6th Day; Dr. Dolittle 2 (voice cameo); Collateral Damage; Terminator 3: Rise of the Machines; The Rundown (cameo); Around the World in 80 Days (2004); The Kid and I (cameo); The Expendables (cameo)

Scott, George C.: The Hanging Tree; Anatomy of a Murder; The Hustler; The List of Adrian Messenger; Dr. Strangelove or: How I Learned to Stop Worrying and Love the Bomb; The Yellow Rolls-Royce; The Bible: Not With My Wife You Don't!; The Flim Flam Man; Petulia; Patton; They Might Be Giants; The Last Run; The Hospital; The New Centurions; Rage (1972; also dir); Oklahoma Crude; The Day of the Dolphin; Bank Shot; The Savage Is Loose (also dir); The Hindenburg; Islands in the Stream; Crossed Swords (1978); Movie Movie; Hardcore; The Changeling (1979); The Formula; Taps; Firestarter; The Exorcist III; The Rescuers Down Under; Malice; Angus; Gloria (1999)

Sellers, Peter: Down Among the Z Men; The Ladykillers (1955); The Smallest Show on Earth; Your Past Is Showing; Up the Creek (1958); tom thumb; Man in a Cocked Hat; The Mouse That Roared; I'm All Right Jack; The Battle of the Sexes; Two Way Stretch; Never Let Go; The Millionairess; I Like Money (also dir); Waltz of the Toreadors; The Dock Brief; The Road to Hong Kong (cameo); Lolita (1962); The Wrong Arm of the Law; Heavens Above!; Dr. Strangelove or: How I Learned to Stop Worrying and Love the Bomb; The Pink Panther (1963); The World of Henry Orient; A Shot in the Dark; What's New Pussycat; The Wrong Box; After the Fox; Casino Royale (1967); Woman Times Seven; The Bobo; The Party; I Love You, Alice B. Toklas; The Magic Christian; Hoffman; There's a Girl in My Soup; Where Does It Hurt?; Alice's Adventures in Wonderland; The Optimists; The Blockhouse; Undercovers Hero; The Return of the Pink Panther; Murder by Death; The Pink Panther Strikes Again; Revenge of the Pink Panther; The Prisoner of Zenda (1979); Being There; The Fiendish Plot of Dr. Fu Manchu; Trail of the Pink Panther

Sinatra, Frank: Ship Ahoy (singer only); Higher and Higher; Step Lively; Anchors Aweigh; Till the Clouds Roll By; It Happened in Brooklyn; The Miracle of the Bells; The Kissing Bandit; Take Me Out to the Ball Game; On the Town; Double Dynamite; From Here to Eternity; Suddenly; Three Coins in the Fountain (sings title song); Young at Heart; Not as a Stranger; Guys and Dolls; The Tender Trap; The Man With the Golden Arm; High Society (1956); Johnny Concho; Around the World in Eighty Days (1956; cameo); Pal Joey; The Pride and the Passion; The Joker Is Wild; Kings Go Forth; Some Came Running; A Hole in the Head; Never So Few; Can-Can; Ocean's Eleven (1960); Pepe (cameo); The Devil at 4 O'Clock; Sergeants 3; The Road to Hong Kong (cameo); The Manchurian Candidate (1962); The List of Adrian Messenger (cameo); A New Kind of Love (sings title song); Come Blow Your Horn; 4 for Texas; Robin and the 7 Hoods; None But the Brave (also dir); Von Ryan's Express; Marriage on the Rocks; The Oscar (1966 cameo); Cast a Giant Shadow (cameo); Assault on a Queen; The Naked Runner; Tony Rome; The Detective (1968); Lady in Cement; Dirty Dingus Magee; That's Entertainment! (app); The First Deadly Sin; Cannonball Run II (cameo); Listen Up: The Lives of Quincy Jones (app)

Smith, Will: Where the Day Takes You; Six Degrees of Separation; Made in America; Bad Boys; Independence Day; Men in Black; Enemy of the State; Wild Wild West; The Legend of Bagger Vance; Ali; Men in Black II; Bad Boys II; Jersey Girl (cameo); I, Robot; Shark Tale; Hitch; The Pursuit of Happyness; I Am Legend; Hancock; Seven Pounds

Spacek, Sissy: Prime Cut; Ginger in the Morning; Badlands; Phantom of the Paradise (set dec); Carrie (1976); Welcome to L.A.; 3 Women; Heart Beat; Coal Miner's Daughter; Raggedy Man; Missing; The Man With Two Brains (voice); The River (1984); Marie; Violets Are Blue . . . ; 'Night, Mother; Crimes of the Heart; The Long Walk Home; Hard Promises; JFK; Trading Mom; The Grass Harp; Affliction; Blast from the Past; The Straight Story; In the Bedroom; Tuck Everlasting (2002); A Home at the End of the World; The Ring Two; Nine Lives; North Country; An American Haunting; Gray Matters; Hot Rod; Four Christmases; Get Low

Spacey, Kevin: Heartburn; Working Girl; Rocket Gibraltar; See No Evil, Hear No Evil; Dad; A Show of Force; Henry & June; Consenting Adults; Glengarry Glen Ross; The Ref; Iron Will; Swimming with Sharks; Outbreak; The Usual Suspects; Se7en; Looking for Richard (app); A Time to Kill (1996); L.A. Confidential; Albino Alligator (dir); Midnight in the Garden of Good and Evil; The Negotiator; hurlyburly; A Bug's Life; American Beauty; The Big Kahuna; Ordinary Decent Criminal; Pay It Forward; K-PAX; The Shipping News; Austin Powers in Goldmember (cameo); The Life of David Gale; The United States of Leland; Beyond the Sea (also dir, co-scr); Edison Force; Superman Returns; Fred Claus; 21; Moon (voice); Shrink; The Men Who Stare at Goats; Casino Jack

Stallone, Sylvester: Bananas (bit); Rebel; The Lord's of Flatbush (also coscr); The Prisoner of Second Avenue (bit); Capone; Death Race 2000; Farewell, My Lovely; Cannonball; Rocky (also scr); F.I.S.T. (also coscr); Paradise Alley (1978; also dir, scr); Rocky II (also dir, scr); Nighthawks; Victory (1981); First Blood (also coscr); Rocky III (also dir, scr); Staying Alive (dir, coscr, cameo); Rhinestone (also coscr); Rambo: First Blood Part II (also coscr); Rocky IV (also dir, scr); Cobra (also scr); Over the Top (also coscr); Rambo III (also coscr); Lock Up; Tango & Cash; Rocky V (also scr); Oscar (1991); Stop! or My Mom Will Shoot; Cliffhanger (also coscr); Demolition Man; The Specialist (1994); Judge Dredd; Assassins; Daylight; Cop Land; An Alan Smithee Film: Burn Hollywood, Burn; Antz; Get Carter (2002); Driven (also coscr); Eye See You; Spy Kids 3-D: Game Over; Rocky Balboa (also dir, scr); Rambo (also dir, coscr); The Expendables (also coscr, dir)

Stanwyck, Barbara: Ladies of Leisure; Night Nurse; The Miracle Woman; Forbidden (1932); The Purchase Price; So Big! (1932); The Bitter Tea of General Yen; Baby Face; Ever in My Heart; Annie Oakley; His

Brother's Wife; Banjo on My Knee; The Plough and the Stars; Stella Dallas; The Mad Miss Manton; Union Pacific; Golden Boy; Remember the Night; The Lady Eve; Meet John Doe; You Belong to Me; Ball of Fire; The Great Man's Lady; Lady of Burlesque; Double Indemnity; Hollywood Canteen; Christmas in Connecticut; The Bride Wore Boots; The Strange Love of Martha Ivers; The Two Mrs. Carrolls; Variety Girl (cameo); Cry Wolf; B. F.'s Daughter; Sorry, Wrong Number; The Lady Gambles; East Side, West Side; The File on Thelma Jordon; No Man of Her Own (1950); The Furies; To Please a Lady; Clash by Night; Jeopardy; Titanic (1953); All I Desire; The Moonlighter; Blowing Wild; Witness to Murder (1954); Executive Suite; Cattle Queen of Montana; The Violent Men; Escape to Burma; There's Always Tomorrow; The Maverick Queen; Forty Guns; Walk on the Wild Side; Roustabout; The Night Walker

Stewart, James: RoseMarie (1936); Wife Vs. Secretary; Born to Dance; After the Thin Man; Seventh Heaven; Navy Blue and Gold; Vivacious Lady; The Shopworn Angel; You Can't Take It With You; Made for Each Other (1939); It's a Wonderful World; Mr. Smith Goes to Washington; Destry Rides Again; The Shop Around the Corner; The Mortal Storm; No Time for Comedy; The Philadelphia Story; Ziegfeld Girl; It's a Wonderful Life; Magic Town; On Our Merry Way; Call Northside 777; Rope; You Gotta Stay Happy; The Stratton Story; Malaya; Winchester '73; Broken Arrow (1950); The Jackpot; Harvey; No Highway in the Sky; The Greatest Show on Earth; Bend of the River; Carbine Williams; The Naked Spur; Thunder Bay; The Glenn Miller Story; Rear Window; The Far Country; Strategic Air Command; The Man From Laramie; The Man Who Knew Too Much (1956); The Spirit of St. Louis; Night Passage; Vertigo; Bell, Book and Candle; Anatomy of a Murder; The FBI Story; The Mountain Road; X-15 (narr); Two Rode Together; The Man Who Shot Liberty Valance; Mr. Hobbs Takes a Vacation; How the West Was Won; Take Her, She's Mine; Cheyenne Autumn; Dear Brigitte; Shenandoah; The Flight of the Phoenix (1965); The Rare Breed; Firecreek; Bandolero!; The Cheyenne Social Club; Fools' Parade; That's Entertainment! (app); The Shootist; Airport '77; The Big Sleep (1978); The Magic of Lassie; Afurika Monogatari; An American Tail: Fievel Goes West

Stiller, Ben: Hot Pursuit; Empire of the Sun; Fresh Horses; Next of Kin; Stella; Highway to Hell; Reality Bites (also dir); Heavyweights; Happy Gilmore (uncred); If Lucy Fell; Flirting With Disaster; The Cable Guy (also dir); Zero Effect; There's Something About Mary; Your Friends & Neighbors; Permanent Midnight; The Suburbans; Mystery Men; Black and White; The Independent (cameo); Keeping the Faith; Meet the Parents; Zoolander (also dir, coscr); The Royal Tenenbaums; Orange County (uncred); Duplex; Along Came Polly; Starsky & Hutch; Envy; Dodgeball: A True Underdog Story; Anchorman: The Legend of Ron Burgundy (cameo); Meet the Fockers; Madagascar; Tenacious D: The Pick of Destiny; School for Scoundrels (2006); Night at the Museum; The Heartbreak Kid (2007); Tropic Thunder (also dir, coscr); Madagascar: Escape 2 Africa; Night at the Museum: Battle of the Smithsonian; The Marc Pease Experience; Greenberg; I'm Still Here (app); Megamind; Little Fockers; Submarine (cameo); The Trip (2011; cameo)

Streep, Meryl: Julia (1977); The Deer Hunter; Manhattan; The Seduction of Joe Tynan; Kramer vs. Kramer; The French Lieutenant's Woman; Sophie's Choice; Still of the Night; Silkwood; Falling in Love; Plenty; Out of Africa; Heartburn; Ironweed; A Cry in the Dark; She-Devil; Postcards From the Edge; Defending Your Life; Death Becomes Her; The House of the Spirits; The River Wild; The Bridges of Madison County; Before and After; Marvin's Room; Dancing at Lughnasa; One True Thing; Music of the Heart; AI Artificial Intelligence (voice cameo); Adaptation.; The Hours; Stuck on You (voice cameo); The Manchurian Candidate (2004); Lemony Snicket's A Series of Unfortunate Events; Prime; A Prairie Home Companion; The Devil Wears Prada; The Ant Bully; Wrestling with Angels: Playwright Tony Kushner (app); Evening; Rendition; Lions for Lambs; Dark Matter; Mamma Mia!; Doubt; Julie & Julia; Fantastic Mr. Fox; It's Complicated

Streisand, Barbra: Funny Girl; Hello, Dolly!; On a Clear Day You Can See Forever; The Owl and the Pussycat; What's Up, Doc?; Up the Sandbox; The Way We Were; For Pete's Sake; Funny Lady; A Star Is Born; The Main Event; All Night Long (1981); Yentl (also dir, coadapt); Nuts; Listen Up: The Lives of Quincy Jones (app); The Prince of Tides (also dir); The Mirror Has Two Faces (also dir); The King and I (1999); Meet the Fockers; Little Fockers

Sutherland, Donald: The Bedford Incident; Dr. Terror's House of Horrors; Die! Die! My Darling!; Promise Her Anything; The Dirty Dozen; Sebastian; Interlude (1968); Oedipus the King; The Split; Joanna; MASH; Start the Revolution Without Me; Kelly's Heroes; Alex in Wonderland; The Act of the Heart; Little Murders; Klute; Johnny Got His Gun; F.T.A.; Steelyard Blues; Lady Ice; Don't Look Now; Alien Thunder; S*P*Y*S; The Day of the Locust; End of the Game; Fellini's Casanova; 1900; The Eagle Has Landed; Bethune; The Kentucky Fried Movie (cameo); The Disappearance; Bethune; National Lampoon's Animal House; Invasion of the Body Snatchers (1978); Blood Relatives; The Great Train Robbery; Murder by Decree; A Man, a

Woman and a Bank; Bear Island; Nothing Personal; Ordinary People; Gas; Eye of the Needle; Threshold; Max Dugan Returns; Crackers; Ordeal by Innocence; Heaven Help Us; Revolution (1985); Wolf at the Door; The Rosary Murders; The Trouble With Spies; Apprentice to Murder; Lost Angels; Lock Up; A Dry White Season; Dr. Bethune; Backdraft; Eminent Domain; JFK; Buffy the Vampire Slayer; Shadow of the Wolf; Younger and Younger; Benefit of the Doubt; Six Degrees of Separation; The Puppet Masters; Disclosure; Outbreak; A Time to Kill; Shadow Conspiracy; The Assignment; Fallen; Without Limits; virus (1999); Free Money; Instinct; The Art of War; Panic; Space Cowboys; Final Fantasy: The Spirits Within; The Italian Job (2003); Cold Mountain; Fierce People; Pride & Prejudice (2005); American Gun; Lord of War; An American Haunting; Ask the Dust; Aurora Borealis; Beerfest (uncred); Reign Over Me; Fierce People; Fool's Gold; Astro Boy; The Eagle; The Mechanic (2011)

Swank, Hilary: Buffy the Vampire Slayer; The Next Karate Kid; Quiet Days in Hollywood; Boys Don't Cry; The Gift (2000); The Affair of the Necklace; Insomnia (2002); The Core; Red Dust (2004); Million Dollar Baby; 11:14; The Black Dahlia; Freedom Writers; The Reaping; P.S. I Love You; Amelia; Conviction; The Resident

Taylor, Elizabeth: There's One Born Every Minute; Lassie Come Home; Jane Eyre (1944); The White Cliffs of Dover; National Velvet; Courage of Lassie; Cynthia; Life With Father; A Date With Judy; Julia Misbehaves; Little Women (1949); The Big Hangover; Father of the Bride (1950); Quo Vadis (cameo); Father's Little Dividend; A Place in the Sun; Callaway Went Thataway (cameo); Love Is Better Than Ever; Ivanhoe; The Girl Who Had Everything; Rhapsody; Elephant Walk; Beau Brummell; The Last Time I Saw Paris; Giant; Raintree County; Cat on a Hot Tin Roof; Suddenly, Last Summer; Butterfield 8; Cleopatra (1963); The V.I.P.s; The Sandpiper; Who's Afraid of Virginia Woolf?; The Taming of the Shrew; Doctor Faustus; Reflections in a Golden Eye; The Comedians; Boom!; Secret Ceremony; The Only Game in Town; Under Milk Wood; X, Y and Zee; Hammersmith Is Out; Ash Wednesday (1973); The Driver's Seat; Night Watch; That's Entertainment! (app); The Blue Bird (1976); A Little Night Music; Winter Kills; The Mirror Crack'd; George Stevens: A Filmmaker's Journey (app); The Flintstones

Taylor, Robert: Broadway Melody of 1936; Magnificent Obsession (1935); His Brother's Wife; Camille (1937); Broadway Melody of 1938; A Yank at Oxford; Three Comrades; Waterloo Bridge (1940); Escape (1940); Flight Command; Billy the Kid (1941); Johnny Eager; Bataan; Undercurrent; The Bribe; Ambush; Devil's Doorway;

Quo Vadis; Westward the Women; Ivanhoe; Above and Beyond; I Love Melvin (cameo); All the Brothers Were Valiant; Knights of the Round Table; The Last Hunt; D-Day the Sixth of June; Tip on a Dead Jockey; Party Girl (1958); The Hangman; Miracle of the White Stallions; The Night Walker; Savage Pampas; Johnny Tiger; The Glass Sphinx; Where Angels Go . . . Trouble Follows; The Day the Hot Line Got Hot

Temple, Shirley: Stand Up and Cheer; Little Miss Marker (1934); Bright Eyes; The Little Colonel; The Littlest Rebel; Captain January; Poor Little Rich Girl; Dimples; Stowaway; Wee Willie Winkie; Heidi (1937); Rebecca of Sunnybrook Farm; Little Miss Broadway; Just Around the Corner; The Little Princess (1939); Susannah of the Mounties; The Blue Bird (1940); Young People; Since You Went Away; I'll Be Seeing You; Kiss and Tell (1945); Honeymoon (1947); The Bachelor and the Bobby-Soxer; That Hagen Girl; Fort Apache; The Story of Seabiscuit; A Kiss for Corliss

Theron, Charlize: 2 Days in the Valley; that thing you do!; Trial and Error; The Devil's Advocate; Mighty Joe Young (1998); Celebrity; The Astronaut's Wife; The Cider House Rules; Reindeer Games; The Yards; Men of Honor; The Legend of Bagger Vance; Sweet November (2001); 15 Minutes; The Curse of the Jade Scorpion; Trapped (2002); Waking Up in Reno; The Italian Job (2003); Monster (2003); Head in the Clouds; North Country; Æon Flux; In the Valley of Elah; Sleepwalking; Battle in Seattle; Hancock; The Burning Plain; Astro Boy; The Road

Thompson, Emma: Henry V (1989); The Tall Guy; Impromptu; Dead Again; Howards End; Peter's Friends; Much Ado About Nothing; The Remains of the Day; In the Name of the Father; My Father, the Hero (cameo); Junior; Carrington; Sense and Sensibility (also adapt); The Winter Guest; Primary Colors; Judas Kiss; Maybe Baby; Treasure Planet; Love Actually; Imagining Argentina; Harry Potter and the Prisoner of Azkaban; Nanny McPhee (also adapt); Stranger Than Fiction; Harry Potter and the Order of the Phoenix; I Am Legend (cameo); Last Chance Harvey; Brideshead Revisited; Pirate Radio; An Education; Nanny McPhee Returns (also scr)

Thornton, Billy Bob: Going Overboard; For the Boys; One False Move (also co-scr); Trouble Bound; Indecent Proposal; Bound by Honor; Tombstone; Floundering; On Deadly Ground; The Stars Fell on Henrietta; Dead Man; Sling Blade (also dirt, adapt); A Family Thing (coscr); The Winner; Princess Mononoke; An Alan Smithee Film: Burn Hollywood Burn; U Turn; The Apostle; Primary Colors; Homegrown; Armageddon; A Simple Plan; Pushing Tin; The Gift (2000; coscr); South of Heaven, West of Hell; All the Pretty Horses (dir); The Man Who

[1638]

Wasn't There; Bandits (2001); Monster's Ball; Daddy and Them (also dir, scr); Waking Up in Reno; Levity; Intolerable Cruelty; Love Actually; Bad Santa; Chrystal; The Alamo (2004); Friday Night Lights; Bad News Bears (2005); The Ice Harvest; School for Scoundrels (2006); The Astronaut Farmer; Mr. Woodcock; Eagle Eye; The Informers (2009); Faster

Thurman, Uma: Kiss Daddy Goodnight; Johnny Be Good; Dangerous Liaisons; The Adventures of Baron Munchausen; Where the Heart Is (1990); Henry & June; Jennifer Eight; Final Analysis; Mad Dog and Glory; Even Cowgirls Get the Blues; Pulp Fiction; A Month by the Lake; Beautiful Girls; The Truth About Cats & Dogs; Batman & Robin; Gattaca; Les Misérables (1998); The Avengers; Sweet and Lowdown; Vatel; The Golden Bowl; Tape; Chelsea Walls; Kill Bill Vol. 1; Paycheck; Kill Bill Vol. 2; Be Cool; Nausicaä and the Valley of the Wind; Prime; The Producers (2005); My Super Ex-Girlfriend; The Accidental Husband; The Life Before Her Eyes; Motherhood; Percy Jackson & the Olympians: The Lightning Thief; Ceremony (2011)

Tierney, Gene: The Return of Frank James; Tobacco Road; Belle Starr; The Shanghai Gesture; Son of Fury; China Girl (1942); Heaven Can Wait (1943); Laura; A Bell for Adano; Leave Her to Heaven; Dragonwyck; The Razor's Edge (1946); The Ghost and Mrs. Muir; The Iron Curtain; Whirlpool (1949); Night and the City (1950); Where the Sidewalk Ends; The Mating Season; On the Riviera; Plymouth Adventure; Never Let Me Go (1953); Black Widow (1954); The Egyptian; The Left Hand of God; Advise & Consent; Toys in the Attic; The Pleasure Seekers

Tracy, Spencer: Up the River; 20,000 Years in Sing Sing; The Power and the Glory; Man's Castle; Fury (1936); San Francisco; Libeled Lady; They Gave Him a Gun; Captains Courageous; The Big City (1937); Mannequin (1937); Test Pilot; Boys Town; Stanley and Livingstone; I Take This Woman; Northwest Passage (Book I—Roger's Rangers); Young Tom Edison (cameo); Edison, the Man; Boom Town; Dr. Jekyll and Mr. Hyde (1941); Woman of the Year; Tortilla Flat; Keeper of the Flame; A Guy Named Joe; The Seventh Cross; Thirty Seconds Over Tokyo; Without Love; The Sea of Grass; Cass Timberlane; State of the Union; Edward, My Son; Adam's Rib; Malaya; Father of the Bride (1950); Father's Little Dividend; The People Against O'Hara; Pat and Mike; Plymouth Adventure; The Actress; Broken Lance; Bad Day at Black Rock; The Mountain; Desk Set; The Old Man and the Sea; The Last Hurrah; Inherit the Wind; The Devil at 4 O'Clock; Judgment at Nuremberg; It's a Mad Mad Mad Mad World; Guess Who's Coming to Dinner

Travolta, John: The Devil's Rain; Carrie (1976); Saturday Night Fever; Grease; Moment by Moment; Urban Cowboy; Blow Out; Staying Alive; Two of a Kind (1983); Perfect; The Experts; Look Who's Talking; Look Who's Talking Too; Shout (1991); Chains of Gold; Boris and Natasha: The Movie (cameo); Look Who's Talking Now; Pulp Fiction; Eyes of an Angel; Get Shorty; White Man's Burden; Broken Arrow (1996); Phenomenon; Michael; Face/Off; She's So Lovely; Mad City; Primary Colors; A Civil Action; The Thin Red Line (1998); The General's Daughter; Battlefield Earth; Lucky Numbers; Swordfish; Domestic Disturbance; Austin Powers in Goldmember (cameo); Basic; The Punisher (2004); Ladder 49; A Love Song for Bobby Long; Be Cool; Wild Hogs; Lonely Hearts (2007); Hairspray (2007); Bolt; The Taking of Pelham 123 (2009); Old Dogs; From Paris With Love

Turner, Lana: A Star Is Born (1937; bit); They Won't Forget; Four's a Crowd; Ziegfeld Girl; Dr. Jekyll and Mr. Hyde (1941); Honky Tonk; Johnny Eager; Somewhere I'll Find You; Du Barry Was a Lady (cameo); Keep Your Powder Dry; Week-end at the Waldorf; The Postman Always Rings Twice (1946); Green Dolphin Street; Cass Timberlane; Homecoming; The Three Musketeers (1948); A Life of Her Own; The Merry Widow (1952); The Bad and the Beautiful; Latin Lovers (1953); Flame and the Flesh; Betrayed (1954); The Prodigal; The Sea Chase; The Rains of Ranchipur; Diane; Peyton Place; Another Time; Another Place; Imitation of Life (1959); Portrait in Black; By Love Possessed; Bachelor in Paradise; Who's Got the Action?; Love Has Many Faces; Madame X (1966); The Big Cube; Persecution; Bittersweet Love; Witches' Brew

Vaughn, Vince: For the Boys (bit); Rudy; Swingers; The Lost World: Jurassic Park; The Locusts; A Cool, Dry Place; Return to Paradise (1998); Clay Pigeons; Psycho (1998); South of Heaven, West of Hell; The Cell; The Prime Gig; Made; Zoolander; Domestic Disturbance; Old School; I Love Your Work; Starsky & Hutch; Dodgeball: A True Underdog Story; Anchorman: The Legend of Ron Burgundy (uncred); Thumbsucker; Be Cool; Mr. & Mrs. Smith (2005); Wedding Crashers; The Break-Up (also costy); Into the Wild; Fred Claus; Vince Vaughn's Wild West Comedy Show: 30 Days & 30 Nights—Hollywood to the Heartland; Four Christmases; Couples Retreat (also coscr); The Dilemma

Voight, Jon: Hour of the Gun; Fearless Frank; Out of It; Midnight Cowboy; Catch-22; The Revolutionary; Deliverance; The All-American Boy; Conrack; The Odessa File; End of the Game; Coming Home; The Champ (1979); Lookin' to Get Out; Table for Five; Runaway Train; Desert Bloom; Rainbow Warrior; Heat (1995); Mission:

Impossible; Rosewood; Anaconda; Most Wanted; U Turn; The Rainmaker (1997); Enemy of the State; The General (1998); Varsity Blues; A Dog of Flanders (1999); Pearl Harbor; Lara Croft Tomb Raider; Zoolander; Ali; Holes; The Manchurian Candidate (2004); Superbabies: Baby Geniuses 2; National Treasure; Glory Road; September Dawn; National Treasure: Book of Secrets; Transformers; Bratz; Tropic Thunder (cameo); Pride and Glory; An American Carol; Four Christmases

Wahlberg, Mark: Renaissance Man; The Basketball Diaries; Fear (1996); Traveller; Boogie Nights; The Big Hit; The Corruptor; Three Kings; The Yards; The Perfect Storm; Planet of the Apes (2001); Rock Star; The Truth About Charlie; The Italian Job (2003); i ♥ huckabees; Four Brothers; Invincible (2006); The Departed; Shooter; We Own the Night; The Happening (2008); Max Payne; The Lovely Bones; Date Night; The Other Guys; The Fighter

Washington, Denzel: Carbon Copy; A Soldier's Story; Power (1986); Cry Freedom; For Queen and Country; The Mighty Quinn; Glory (1989); Mo' Better Blues; Heart Condition; Ricochet; Mississippi Masala; Malcolm X (1992); Much Ado About Nothing; The Pelican Brief; Philadelphia; Crimson Tide; Devil in a Blue Dress; Virtuosity; Courage Under Fire; The Preacher's Wife; Fallen; He Got Game; The Siege; The Bone Collector; The Hurricane (1999); Remember the Titans; Training Day; John Q; Antwone Fisher (also dir); Out of Time; Man on Fire (2004); The Manchurian Candidate (2004); Inside Man; Deja Vu (2006); American Gangster; The Great Debaters (also dir); The Taking of Pelham 123 (2009); The Book of Eli; Unstoppable

Watts, Naomi: For Love Alone; Flirting; Matinee; Wide Sargasso Sea; Tank Girl; Dangerous Beauty; Babe: Pig in the City; Strange Planet; Mulholland Dr.; The Ring (2002); Undertaking Betty; Ned Kelly (2003); Le Divorce; 21 Grams; We Don't Live Here Anymore; The Assassination of Richard Nixon; I ♥ Huckabees; Ellie Parker; The Ring Two; Stay; King Kong (2005); Inland Empire; The Painted Veil (2006); Eastern Promises; Funny Games (2008); The International; Mother and Child; You Will Meet a Tall Dark Stranger; Fair Game

Wayne, John: The Big Trail; Baby Face; I Cover the War; Stagecoach (1939); Allegheny Uprising; Dark Command; Three Faces West; The Long Voyage Home; Seven Sinners; A Man Betrayed; Lady From Louisiana; Shepherd of the Hills; Lady for a Night; Reap the Wild Wind; The Spoilers (1942); In Old California; Flying Tigers; Reunion in France; Pittsburgh; A Lady Takes a Chance; In Old Oklahoma; The Fighting Seabees; Tall in the Saddle; Flame of the Barbary Coast; Back to Bataan; They Were Expendable; Dakota (1945); Without Reservations; Angel and the Badman; Tycoon; Fort Apache; Red River; 3 Godfathers; Wake of the Red Witch; The Fighting Kentuckian; She Wore a Yellow Ribbon; Sands of Iwo Jima; Rio Grande; Operation Pacific; Flying Leathernecks; The Quiet Man; Big Jim McLain; Trouble Along the Way; Island in the Sky; Hondo; The High and the Mighty; The Sea Chase; Blood Alley; The Conqueror; The Searchers; The Wings of Eagles; Jet Pilot; Legend of the Lost; The Barbarian and the Geisha; Rio Bravo; The Horse Soldiers; The Alamo (1960; also dir); North to Alaska; The Comancheros; The Man Who Shot Liberty Valance; Hatari!; The Longest Day; How the West Was Won; Donovan's Reef; McLintock!; Circus World; The Greatest Story Ever Told (cameo); In Harm's Way; The Sons of Katie Elder; Cast a Giant Shadow (cameo); The War Wagon; El Dorado; The Green Berets (also codir); Hellfighters; True Grit (1969); The Undefeated; Chisum; Rio Lobo; Big Jake; The Cowboys; Cancel My Reservation (cameo); The Train Robbers; Cahill—United States Marshal; McQ; Brannigan; Rooster Cogburn; The Shootist

Weaver, Sigourney: Annie Hall (bit); Madman; Alien; Eyewitness (1981); The Year of Living Dangerously; Deal of the Century; Ghostbusters; One Woman or Two; Aliens; Half Moon Street; Gorillas in the Mist; Working Girl; Ghostbusters II; Alien³; 1492: Conquest of Paradise; Dave; Death and the Maiden; Jeffrey; Copycat; The Ice Storm; Snow White: A Tale of Terror; Alien Resurrection; A Map of the World; Galaxy Quest; Get Bruce (app); Company Man; Heartbreakers (2001); Big Bad Love (voice); Tadpole; The Guys; Holes; The Village; Imaginary Heroes; Infamous; Happily N'Ever After; Snow Cake; The TV Set; Vantage Point; Be Kind Rewind; Baby Mama; Wall•E; The Tale of Despereaux; Avatar; Crazy on the Outside; You Again; Cedar Rapids; Paul

Welles, Orson: Swiss Family Robinson (1940; narr); Citizen Kane (also dir, coscr); The Magnificent Ambersons (also dir, narr, scr); Journey into Fear (1943; also uncred coscr); Jane Eyre (1944); Follow the Boys (1944); Tomorrow Is Forever; Duel in the Sun (narr); The Stranger (1946; also dir, uncred coscr); The Lady From Shanghai (also dir, scr); Macbeth (1948; also dir); Black Magic (1949); Prince of Foxes; The Third Man; The Black Rose; The Little World of Don Camillo (narr of English-language prints); Othello (1952; also dir, uncred adapt); Trouble in the Glen; Mr. Arkadin (also dir, scr); Three Cases of Murder; Moby Dick (1956); The Long Hot Summer; Touch of Evil (also dir, scr); The Vikings (narr); The Roots of Heaven; Compulsion; Ferry to Hong Kong; Crack in the Mirror; The Tar-

tars; King of Kings (narr); Lafayette; The
Trial (1962; also dir, scr); The V.I.P.s; The
Finest Hours (narr); A King's Story (narr);
Chimes at Midnight (1966; also dir, scr);
Is Paris Burning?; A Man for All Seasons
(1966); Casino Royale (1967); The Sailor
From Gibraltar; I'll Never Forget What's
'Isname; Oedipus the King; The Last Ro-
man; The Immortal Story (1968; also dir,
coscr); The Southern Star; House of Cards
(1969); The Thirteen Chairs; The Battle of
Neretva; Start the Revolution Without Me;
The Kremlin Letter; Catch-22; Waterloo;
A Safe Place; Ten Days Wonder; Treasure
Island (1972; also coscr as "O. W. Jeeves");
Get to Know Your Rabbit; Necromancy;
Bugs Bunny Superstar (narr); Ten Little
Indians (1975; voice); F for Fake (also dir,
scr); Voyage of the Damned; The Great
Battle; The Muppet Movie (cameo); The
Double McGuffin (voice); Butterfly; His-
tory of the World Part 1 (narr); Slapstick (Of
Another Kind) (voice); The Transformers;
Someone to Love; It's All True (app)

West, Mae: She Done Him Wrong (also
sty); I'm No Angel (also scr); Belle of the
Nineties (also scr); Goin' to Town (also
scr); Klondike Annie (also scr); Go West,
Young Man (also scr); Every Day's a Holiday (also scr); My Little Chickadee (also
coscr); Myra Breckinridge; Sextette

Whitaker, Forest: Tag; The Assassination
Game; Fast Times at Ridgemont High; Vi-
sion Quest; The Color of Money; Platoon;
Stakeout; Good Morning, Vietnam; Blood-
sport; Bird; Johnny Handsome; A Rage in
Harlem; Diary of a Hitman; Article 99; The
Crying Game; Consenting Adults; Body
Snatchers; Bank Robber; Blown Away; Ja-
son's Lyric; Ready to Wear (Pret-à-Porter);
Smoke; Species; Waiting to Exhale (dir);
Phenomenon; Body Count; Hope Floats
(dir); Ghost Dog: The Way of the Samurai;
Light It Up; Battlefield Earth; Panic Room;
Phone Booth; First Daughter (dir, narr);
American Gun; The Last King of Scotland;
Everyone's Hero; The Air I Breathe; The
Great Debaters; Vantage Point; Street Kings;
Where the Wild Things Are; Our Family
Wedding; Repo Men; The Experiment

Widmark, Richard: Kiss of Death (1947);
Road House (1948); Yellow Sky; Down to
the Sea in Ships (1949); Slattery's Hurricane; Night and the City (1950); Panic in
the Streets; No Way Out (1950); Halls of
Montezuma; The Frogmen; Don't Bother
to Knock; O. Henry's Full House; Destination Gobi; Pickup on South Street; Take the
High Ground!; Hell and High Water; Garden of Evil; Broken Lance; The Cobweb;
Backlash (1956); The Last Wagon; Saint
Joan; Time Limit; The Tunnel of Love; The
Trap (1959); Warlock (1959); The Alamo
(1960); Two Rode Together; Judgment
at Nuremberg; How the West Was Won;
The Long Ships; Cheyenne Autumn; The

Bedford Incident; Alvarez Kelly; The Way
West; Madigan; Death of a Gunfighter;
The Moonshine War; A Talent for Loving;
When the Legends Die; Murder on the Ori-
ent Express; To the Devil—A Daughter;
Twilight's Last Gleaming; The Domino
Principle; Rollercoaster; Coma; The Swarm;
Bear Island; National Lampoon Goes to the
Movies; Hanky Panky; The Final Option;
Against All Odds (1984); True Colors

Wilder, Gene: Bonnie and Clyde; The Producers; Start the Revolution Without Me;
Quackser Fortune Has a Cousin in the Bronx;
Willy Wonka and the Chocolate Factory;
Everything You Always Wanted to Know
About Sex (But Were Afraid to Ask); Blaz-
ing Saddles; Rhinoceros; Young Frankenstein
(also coscr); The Little Prince; The Adventure
of Sherlock Holmes' Smarter Brother (also
dir, scr); Silver Streak; The World's Great-
est Lover (also dir, scr); The Frisco Kid;
Stir Crazy; Sunday Lovers; Hanky Panky;
The Woman in Red (also dir, scr); Haunted
Honeymoon (1986; also dir, coscr); See No
Evil, Hear No Evil; Funny About Love; Another You

Williams, Robin: Can I Do It . . . Til I Need
Glasses?; Popeye; The World According to
Garp; The Survivors; Moscow on the Hudson;
The Best of Times; Club Paradise; Seize the
Day; Good Morning, Vietnam; The Adven-
tures of Baron Munchausen (cameo); Dead
Poets Society; Cadillac Man; Awakenings;
Dead Again; The Fisher King; Hook (1991);
FernGully . . . The Last Rainforest; Alad-
din; Toys; Mrs. Doubtfire; Being Human;
To Wong Foo, Thanks For Everything, Julie
Newmar (cameo); Nine Months; Jumanji;
The birdcage; Jack; The Secret Agent
(1996; cameo); Hamlet (1996); Fathers'
Day; Flubber; Deconstructing Harry; Good
Will Hunting; What Dreams May Come;
Patch Adams; Jakob the Liar; Bicentennial
Man; Get Bruce! (app); AI Artificial Intel-
ligence (voice cameo); Death to Smoochy;
Insomnia (2002); One Hour Photo; The Final
Cut; House of D; Noel (uncred); Robots; The
Aristocrats (app); The Big White; RV; The
Night Listener; Everyone's Hero; Man of
the Year; Happy Feet; Night at the Museum;
License to Wed; August Rush; Night at the
Museum: Battle of the Smithsonian; Shrink
(uncred); World's Greatest Dad; Old Dogs

Willis, Bruce: The First Deadly Sin (bit);
The Verdict (1982; bit); Blind Date (1987);
Sunset; Die Hard; Look Who's Talking; In
Country; Die Hard 2; Look Who's Talking
Too; The Bonfire of the Vanities; Mortal
Thoughts; Hudson Hawk (also sty); Billy
Bathgate; The Last Boy Scout; The Player
(cameo); Death Becomes Her; National
Lampoon's Loaded Weapon I (cameo);
Striking Distance; North; Color of Night;
Pulp Fiction; Nobody's Fool (1994); Die
Hard With a Vengeance; Four Rooms (un-
cred); Twelve Monkeys; Last Man Stand-

ing; Beavis and Butt-head Do America; The Fifth Element; The Jackal; Mercury Rising; Armageddon; The Siege; Breakfast of Champions; The Sixth Sense; The Story of Us; The Whole Nine Yards; Disney's The Kid; Unbreakable; Bandits; Hart's War; Tears of the Sun; Rugrats Go Wild; Charlie's Angels: Full Throttle (cameo); The Whole Ten Yards; Ocean's Twelve (cameo); Hostage (2005); Sin City; 16 Blocks; Lucky Number Slevin; Alpha Dog; Over the Hedge; Fast Food Nation; The Astronaut Farmer (uncred); Grindhouse (uncred); Perfect Stranger; Nancy Drew (cameo); Live Free or Die Hard; What Just Happened; Assassination of a High School President; Surrogates; Cop Out (2010); The Expendables (cameo); I'm Still Here (app); Red (2010)

Wilson, Owen: Bottle Rocket (also coscr); The Cable Guy; Anaconda; Armageddon; Permanent Midnight; Rushmore (also coscr); The Minus Man; Breakfast of Champions; The Haunting (1999); Shanghai Noon; Meet the Parents; Zoolander; The Royal Tenenbaums (also coscr); Behind Enemy Lines; I Spy; Shanghai Knights; The Big Bounce (2004); Starsky & Hutch; Around the World in 80 Days (2004; cameo); The Life Aquatic with Steve Zissou; Meet the Fockers (cameo); Wedding Crashers; Cars; You, Me and Dupree; Night at the Museum (uncred); The Wendell Baker Story; The Darjeeling Limited; Drillbit Taylor; Marley & Me; Night at the Museum: Battle of the Smithsonian; Fantastic Mr. Fox; Marmaduke; How Do You Know; Little Fockers; Hall Pass; Cars 2; Midnight in Paris

Winslet, Kate: Heavenly Creatures; A Kid in King Arthur's Court; Sense and Sensibility; Jude; Hamlet (1996); Titanic (1997); Hideous Kinky; Holy Smoke; Quills; Enigma (2001); Iris; The Life of David Gale; Eternal Sunshine of the Spotless Mind; Finding Neverland; All the King's Men (2006); Little Children; Flushed Away; The Holiday (2006); Romance & Cigarettes; The Reader; Revolutionary Road

Witherspoon, Reese: The Man in the Moon; A Far Off Place; Jack the Bear; S.F.W.; Freeway; Fear (1996); Twilight (1998); Overnight Delivery; Pleasantville; Cruel Intentions; Election; Best Laid Plans; American Psycho; Little Nicky; Legally Blonde; The Importance of Being Earnest (2002); Sweet Home Alabama; Legally Blonde 2: Red, White & Blonde; Vanity Fair; Walk the Line; Just Like Heaven; Rendition; Penelope (2008); Four Christmases; Monsters vs Aliens; How Do You Know; Water for Elephants

Wood, Natalie: Tomorrow Is Forever; The Bride Wore Boots; Miracle on 34th Street (1947); The Ghost and Mrs. Muir; The Jackpot; The Blue Veil; Just for You; The Star (1952); The Silver Chalice; Rebel Without a Cause; The Searchers; The Burning Hills; A Cry in the Night; Bombers B-52; Marjorie Morningstar; Kings Go Forth; Cash McCall; All the Fine Young Cannibals; Splendor in the Grass; West Side Story; Gypsy (1962); Love With the Proper Stranger; Sex and the Single Girl; The Great Race; Inside Daisy Clover; This Property Is Condemned; Penelope (1966); Bob & Carol & Ted & Alice; The Candidate (cameo); Peeper; Meteor; The Last Married Couple in America; Willie and Phil (cameo); Brainstorm (1983)

Woods, James: The Visitors (1972); Hickey & Boggs; The Way We Were; The Gambler; Distance; Night Moves; Alex and the Gypsy; The Choirboys; The Onion Field; The Black Marble (cameo); Eyewitness (1981); Fast-Walking; Split Image; Videodrome; Against All Odds (1984); Once Upon a Time in America; Cat's Eye; Joshua Then and Now; Salvador; Best Seller; Cop; The Boost; True Believer; Immediate Family; The Hard Way (1991); Straight Talk; Diggstown; Chaplin; The Getaway (1994); The Specialist (1994); Casino; Nixon; Killer: A Journal of Murder; Ghosts of Mississippi; Hercules (1997); Contact; Kicked in the Head; Vampires; Another Day in Paradise; True Crime; The General's Daughter; Any Given Sunday; Play It to the Bone (cameo); The Virgin Suicides; Recess: School's Out; Final Fantasy: The Spirits Within; Scary Movie 2; Riding in Cars With Boys; John Q; Stuart Little 2; Northfork; Be Cool (uncred); Pretty Persuasion; Surf's Up; An American Carol

Woodward, Joanne: Count Three and Pray; A Kiss Before Dying (1956); The Three Faces of Eve; No Down Payment; The Long Hot Summer; Rally 'Round the Flag, Boys!; The Sound and the Fury; The Fugitive Kind; From the Terrace; Paris Blues; The Stripper; A New Kind of Love; A Big Hand for the Little Lady; A Fine Madness; Rachel, Rachel; Winning; King: A Filmed Record . . . Montgomery to Memphis (narr); WUSA; They Might Be Giants; The Effect of Gamma Rays on Man-in-the-Moon Marigolds; Summer Wishes, Winter Dreams; The Drowning Pool; The End; Harry and Son; The Glass Menagerie (1987); Mr. & Mrs. Bridge; The Age of Innocence (1993; narr); Philadelphia

Wyman, Jane: The Kid From Spain (bit); Elmer the Great (bit); Anything Goes (1936; bit); Gold Diggers of 1937 (bit); My Man Godfrey (1936); Fools for Scandal (bit); Brother Rat; Larceny, Inc.; Footlight Serenade; The Doughgirls; Hollywood Canteen (cameo); The Lost Weekend; Night and Day; The Yearling; Cheyenne; Magic Town; Johnny Belinda; It's a Great Feeling (cameo); Stage Fright; The Glass Menagerie (1950); Here Comes the Groom; The Blue Veil; The Story of Will Rogers; Just for

You; So Big (1953); Magnificent Obsession (1954); Lucy Gallant; All That Heaven Allows; Miracle in the Rain; Holiday for Lovers; Pollyanna (1960); Bon Voyage! (1962); How to Commit Marriage

Young, Loretta: Platinum Blonde; Taxi! (1932); Heroes for Sale; Man's Castle; The Call of the Wild (1935); The Crusades; Four Men and a Prayer; Suez; The Story of Alexander Graham Bell; The Doctor Takes a Wife; Bedtime Story (1941); The Stranger (1946); The Farmer's Daughter (1947); The Bishop's Wife; Rachel and the Stranger; Come to the Stable; Key to the City; Cause for Alarm; Half Angel; Because of You

Zellweger, Renée: My Boyfriend's Back (uncred); Dazed and Confused; Reality Bites; Love and a .45; Texas Chainsaw Massacre: The Next Generation; Empire Records; The Whole Wide World; The Low Life; Jerry Maguire; Deceiver; A Price Above Rubies; One True Thing; The Bachelor (1999); Nurse Betty; Me, Myself & Irene; Bridget Jones's Diary; White Oleander; Chicago; Down With Love; Cold Mountain; Shark Tale; Bridget Jones: The Edge of Reason; Cinderella Man; Miss Potter; Bee Movie; Leatherheads; Appaloosa (2008); New in Town; Monsters vs Aliens; My One and Only; Case 39

Zeta-Jones, Catherine: Christopher Columbus: The Discovery; Splitting Heirs; Blue Juice; The Phantom; The Mask of Zorro; Entrapment; The Haunting (1999); High Fidelity; Traffic (2000); America's Sweethearts; Chicago; Sinbad: Legend of the Seven Seas; Intolerable Cruelty; The Terminal; Ocean's Twelve; The Legend of Zorro; No Reservations; Death Defying Acts